ç *ch* in German *ich*: a (j) sound as in *yes*, said without voice; similar to the first sound in *huge*.

β *b* in Spanish *Habana*: a voiced fricative sound similar to (v), but made by the two lips.

ʎ *ll* in Spanish *llamar*, *gl* in Italian *consiglio*: similar to the (lj) sequence in *million*, but with the tongue tip lowered and the sounds said simultaneously.

ɥ *u* in French *lui*: a short (y).

ɲ *gn* in French *vigne*, Italian *gnocchi*, *ñ* in Spanish *España*: similar to the (nj) sequence in *onion*, but with the tongue tip lowered and the two sounds said simultaneously.

ɣ *g* in Spanish *luego*: a weak (g) made with voiced friction.

Leng

The sy ... er with c ... are typica

Stres

Three grades of stress are shown ... crip-tions by the presence or absence of marks placed immediately *before* the affected syllable. Primary or strong stress is shown by ', while secondary or weak stress is shown by ˌ. Unstressed syllables are not marked. In *photographic* (ˌfəʊtə'græfɪk), for example, the first syllable carries secondary stress and the third primary stress, while the second and fourth are unstressed.

List of Abbreviations used in the Dictionary

abbrev. abbreviation
Abor. Aboriginal
adj adjective
adv adverb(ial)
Afrik. Afrikaans
Amerind American Indian
Anat. Anatomy
approx. approximate(ly)
Ar. Arabic
Arch. Archaic
Archaeol. Archaeology
Archit. Architecture
Astrol. Astrology
Astron. Astronomy
Austral. Australian

Biol. Biology
Bot. Botany
Brit. Britain; British

C century (e.g. **C14** = 14th century)
°C degrees Celsius
Canad. Canadian
cap. capital
cf. compare
Chem. Chemistry
comp. comparative
conj conjunction

Derog. Derogatory
dim. diminutive
Du. Dutch

E east(ern); (in etymologies) English
Econ. Economics
e.g. for example
esp. especially
est. estimate

F French
fem feminine
foll. followed
ft foot *or* feet

G German
Geog. Geography
Geol. Geology
Geom. Geometry
Gk Greek
Gmc Germanic

Heb. Hebrew

i.e. that is
imit. of imitative origin
in. inch(es)
Inf. Informal
infl. influence(d)
interj interjection
intr intransitive
It. Italian

km kilometre(s)

L Late; Latin
lit. literally
LL Late Latin

m metre(s)
M Middle
masc masculine
Maths Mathematics
Med. Medicine; (in etymologies) Medieval
MHG Middle High German
Mil. Military
Mod. Modern
Myth. Mythology

n noun
N north(ern)
Naut. Nautical
NE northeast(ern)
NL New Latin
no. number
NW northwest(ern)
NZ New Zealand

O Old
Obs. Obsolete
Offens. Offensive
OHG Old High German
ON Old Norse
orig. originally
ORIG origin

Photog. Photography
pl plural
pop. population
Port. Portuguese
p.p. past participle
prep preposition(al)
prob. probably
pron pronoun
Psychol. Psychology
pt. point
p.t. past tense

rel. related

S south(ern)
S. African South African
Sansk. Sanskrit
Scand. Scandinavian
Scot. Scottish; Scots
SE southeast(ern)
sing singular
Sl. slang
Sp. Spanish
sq. square
sup. superlative
SW southwest(ern)

Theol. Theology
tr transitive

ult. ultimately
US United States

var. variant
vb verb
vol. volume

W west(ern)
wt. weight

Zool. Zoology

? in etymologies indicates "query"

Dear Keith Feb 04
With love
Teresa
xx

Concise Dictionary

General Consultant

J M Sinclair

Formerly Professor, Department of English Language
and Literature
University of Birmingham

For Australian Edition

G A Wilkes

Challis Professor of English Literature
University of Sydney

W A Krebs

Associate Professor in Literature
and Communications
Bond University, Queensland

Concise Dictionary

An Imprint of HarperCollins*Publishers*

HarperCollins Publishers
PO Box, Glasgow G4 0NB

First Edition 1982
Second Edition 1988
Third Edition 1992
Revised Third Edition 1995
Fourth Edition 1999
Fifth Edition 2001
Reprinted 2001

2 3 4 5 6 7 8 9 10

Standard Edition	ISBN 0 00 710978 4
Thumb-indexed Edition	ISBN 0 00 710979 2
Australian Edition	ISBN 0 00 711634 9

The HarperCollins website address is
www.**fire**and**water**.com

A catalogue record for this book is
available from the British Library.

This edition prepared in conjunction with Market House Books Ltd, Aylesbury, England

Typeset by Market House Books Ltd, Aylesbury, England
Printed and bound in Great Britain by Omnia Books Limited, Glasgow

Collins concise dictionary.
5th ed.
ISBN 0 007 11634 9.
1 English language – Australia – Dictionaries. 2. English
language – Dictionaries.

423

Corpus Acknowledgments

We would like to thank those authors and publishers who kindly gave permission for copyright material to be used in the Bank of English. We would also like to thank Times Newspapers Ltd for providing valuable data.

Contents

General Consultant

J M Sinclair
Formerly Professor, Department of English Language and Literature
University of Birmingham

Special Consultants

AUSTRALIAN ENGLISH
G A Wilkes
Challis Professor of English Literature,
University of Sydney

W A Krebs
Associate Professor in Literature and Communications,
Bond University, Queensland

W S Ramson
Reader in English,
Australian National University

BRITISH REGIONAL ENGLISH, URBAN DIALECTS
Harold Orton
Professor Emeritus, Department of English,
University of Leeds

CANADIAN ENGLISH
R J Gregg
Formerly Professor, Department of Linguistics,
University of British Columbia

Patrick Drysdale
Editor, *A Dictionary of Canadianisms on Historical Principles*

Fraser Sutherland
Freelance lexicographer

James Arthurs
Professor, Department of Linguistics,
University of Victoria

CARIBBEAN ENGLISH
S R R Allsopp
Coordinator, Caribbean Lexicography Project,
University of the West Indies,
Barbados

EAST AFRICAN ENGLISH
J Kalema
Department of Linguistic Science,
University of Reading

INDIAN ENGLISH
R K Bansal
Professor, Department of Phonetics and Spoken English,
Central Institute of English and Foreign Languages, Hyderabad

IRISH ENGLISH
R J Gregg
Formerly Professor, Department of Linguistics,
University of British Columbia

T de Bhaldraithe
Professor, Department of Irish Dialectology,
University College, Dublin

Ian A Gordon
Professor Emeritus,
University of Wellington

Elizabeth Gordon
Associate Professor,
Department of Linguistics,
University of Canterbury

NEW ZEALAND ENGLISH
SCOTTISH ENGLISH
A J Aitken
Department of English Language,
University of Edinburgh,
Formerly Editor, *Dictionary of the Older Scottish Tongue*

SOUTH AFRICAN ENGLISH
L W Lanham
Professor, Department of Phonetics and General Linguistics,
University of the Witwatersrand

M V Aldridge
Professor, Department of Phonetics and General Linguistics,
University of the Witwatersrand

Geoffrey Hughes
Formerly Professor, Department of English,
University of the Witwatersrand

WEST AFRICAN ENGLISH
J Spencer
Director, Institute of Modern English Language Studies,
University of Leeds

PRONUNCIATION
A C Gimson
Formerly Professor, Department of Phonetics and Linguistics,
University College,
University of London

Specialist Contributors

AERONAUTICS
T C Wooldridge, Angus Boyd
Senior Lecturer in Aerodynamics,
The College of Aeronautics,
Cranfield

ARCHITECTURE; CIVIL ENGINEERING
Bruce Martin

AUSTRALIAN ENGLISH
Steve Higgs
Melbourne Grammar School

BIOGRAPHIES, PLACES
Market House Books
Aylesbury

BROADCASTING, FILM, ETC.
Patrick Leggatt
Chief Engineer,
External Relations,
British Broadcasting Corporation

BUSINESS
Alan Isaacs

CHEMISTRY
John Daintith

COMPUTERS
Richard Fryer
Department of Computer Science, University of Strathclyde

CONSTRUCTION
M J Walker
Construction Industry Research and Information Association

Specialist Contributors

EARTH SCIENCES
Peter J Smith
Reader in Earth Sciences, The Open University

ECONOMICS
P Donaldson
Ruskin College, Oxford

EDUCATION
Catherine Playford
Head Teacher of English, Priestnall School

ENGINEERING
J P Quayle
Editor, *Kempe's Engineering Year-Book*

INDUSTRIAL RELATIONS
Professor Angela M Bowey
Strathclyde Business School, University of Strathclyde
Alexander Purdie
Scottish College of Textiles, Galashiels

INFORMATION TECHNOLOGY
Professor Thomas Carbery
Andrew Doswell
Catherine M Young
Department of Information Science, University of Strathclyde

JUDAISM
Ephraim Borowski
Department of Philosophy, University of Glasgow

LANGUAGES & PEOPLES
David Kilby
Formerly, Department of Language and Linguistics, University of Essex

LAW
Richard Latham
Barrister-at-Law
Brian Russell Davis
Barrister-at-Law
Sandra Clarke

LIFE SCIENCES
Miranda Robertson
Life Sciences Editor, *Nature*
Dr W Gratzer
MRC Cell Biophysics Unit

LINGUISTICS
Professor Yorick Wilks
New Mexico State University

LINGUISTICS AND GRAMMAR
Lloyd Humberstone

LOGIC
Ephraim Borowski
Department of Philosophy, University of Glasgow

MALAYSIAN ENGLISH
U Yong-ee

MARKETING
Professor M Christopher
Department of Marketing and Logistics Systems, Cranfield School of Management

METALLURGY
Stanley White

MILITARY
Major S R Elliot
Colonel Andrew Duncan
The International Institute for Strategic Studies

MILITARY AND NAUTICAL TERMS
Cmdr I Johnston RN

PHILOSOPHY
Christopher Sion
Ephraim Borowski
Department of Philosophy, University of Glasgow

PHYSICAL SCIENCES
R Cutler

PHYSICS
J W Warren
Department of Physics, Brunel University

PIDGINS AND CREOLES
Loreto Todd
The School of English, University of Leeds

PLANTS
Sandra Holmes

POP MUSIC
Ingrid von Essen

PRINTING
C H Parsons
Laurence Chizlett

PSYCHOLOGY
Dr Eric Taylor
Professor Stuart Sutherland
Director, Centre for Research on Perception and Cognition, University of Sussex

RAILWAYS
James Barnes

RELIGION
The Rev D Lancashire
University of Essex

RELIGIOUS TERMS
David Bourke
Rev Canon D W Gundry
Chancellor of Leicester Cathedral

SOCIAL WELFARE
Bob Marsden
Harrow Social Services Department

SPORT
Stuart Bathgate
Freelance Journalist

STATISTICS
Ephraim Borowski
Department of Philosophy, University of Glasgow

TOOLS
N J Small
Associate of the Institute of Marine Engineers

Other Contributors

Jane Bartholomew ANIMALS
Jenny Baster COOKERY; CLOTHING AND FASHION; TEXTILES
Denise Bown PLACE NAMES
Ron Brown JAZZ
Daphne Butler CHEMISTRY
Christopher L Clarke HOROLOGY
Brian Dalgleish METALLURGY
Carolyn Eardley ANTIQUES; FURNITURE; TEXTILES
R J Edwards PSYCHOLOGY
Dennis Exton FILMS, TV, AND RADIO
Rosalind Fergusson BIOGRAPHIES
Ian Fuller PSYCHOLOGY
C Gallon PLANTS
Robert Hine BIOGRAPHIES
Amanda Isaacs BIOGRAPHIES
Cherry McDonald-Taylor EDUCATION; LIBRARY SCIENCE
David Martin PSYCHOLOGY
Mary Marshall CARDS; DANCING AND BALLET
Peter Miller SPORTS
Stewart Murray METALLURGY
Serena Penman ART
H G Procter PSYCHOLOGY
Mark Salad PLACE NAMES
David H Shaw ENGINEERING
Brian Street ANTHROPOLOGY
Andrew Treacher PSYCHOLOGY
Ralph Tyler FILMS, TV, AND RADIO; LITERATURE; MYTHOLOGY; THEATRE; BIOGRAPHIES
Jennifer Wearden ARCHAEOLOGY
Irene Wise BIOCHEMISTRY

This dictionary has been compiled by referring to the Bank of English, a unique database of the English language with examples of over 400 million words enabling Collins lexicographers to analyse how English is actually used today and how it is changing. This is the evidence on which the changes in this dictionary are based.

The Bank of English was set up as a joint initiative by HarperCollins Publishers and Birmingham University to be a resource for language research and lexicography. It contains a very wide range of material from books, newspapers, radio, TV, magazines, letters, and talks reflecting the whole spectrum of English today. Its size and range make it an unequalled resource and the purpose-built software for its analysis is unique to Collins Dictionaries.

This ensures that Collins Dictionaries accurately reflect English as it is used today in a way that is most helpful to the dictionary user as well as including the full range of rarer and historical words and meanings.

Foreword

The fifth edition of Collins Concise Dictionary offers, in its new extended length, an even more wide-ranging and up-to-date survey of the English language as it is used in Britain and around the world at the start of the new millennium. Continuing from the success of the last edition, it also includes entries for people and places; household names in all fields from arts to sport, both past and present; as well as essential facts about countries, cities, and towns the world over. This combination makes it an especially handy reference book for the home, college, or office, whether you are studying, writing, or just keeping up with the news.

Research shows that spelling is the most frequent reason for checking a dictionary and Collins Concise Dictionary is particularly helpful for this because it contains all the spelling forms you might want spelt out in full (no cryptic abbreviations) to give you aboslute confidence in your writing. Meanings are numbered and explained clearly and precisely with numerous examples. The modern core meaning is shown first and technical and specialist meanings are clearly labelled.

Deciding what is "correct English" can often pose problems, so Collins Concise Dictionary gives guidance on those knotty points of language by referring to current usage (as evidenced in the Bank of English) and pointing out where traditional preferences may differ. These helpful notes appear in boxes at the end of many entries, and have been completely rewritten for this edition.

As language use changes, so do the meanings and the very words we use. Collins Concise Dictionary covers a host of new words and meanings from all sorts of subjects like Computing, Marketing, Finance and Politics, and ranging in style from the most technical to the most informal. Collins lexicographers and Collins special subject and language consultants are constantly monitoring language change in Britain and around the world wherever English is spoken. This enables us to provide a truly international survey of English as a world language. In this Collins has the special advantage of the Bank of English which enables us to check an enormous number of examples of a word from an enormous range of sources. You will find more about this unique resource on page viii.

All this wealth of information is presented in an enhanced layout designed to make the Dictionary quick and easy to use as well as a pleasure to browse. The new edition of Collins Concise Dictionary provides essential, up-to-date reference for everyone whether reading, writing, or studying, and is an essential resource for all who love the English language.

Guide to the Text

Headword

Inflected forms

Grammatical information

Part of speech

Definition

Subject-field label

Sense number

Pronunciation

Cross-reference

Etymology

build (bɪld) *vb* **builds, building, built.** **1** to make, construct, or form by joining parts or materials: *to build a house.* **2** (*tr*) to order the building of: *the government builds most of our hospitals.* **3** (foll. by *on* or *upon*) to base; found: *his theory was not built on facts.* **4** (*tr*) to establish and develop: *it took ten years to build a business.* **5** (*tr*) to make in a particular way or for a particular purpose: *the car was not built for speed.* **6** (*intr*; often foll. by *up*) to increase in intensity. ◆ *n* **7** physical form, figure, or proportions: *a man with an athletic build.* ORIG OE *byldan*

builder ('bɪldə) *n* a person who builds, esp. one who contracts for and supervises the construction or repair of buildings.

building ('bɪldɪŋ) *n* **1** something built with a roof and walls. **2** the act, business, occupation, or art of building houses, boats, etc.

building society *n* a cooperative banking enterprise financed by deposits on which interest is paid and from which mortgage loans are advanced on homes and real property; many now offer a range of banking services.

build up *vb* (*adv*) **1** (*tr*) to construct gradually, systematically, and in stages. **2** to increase, accumulate, or strengthen, esp. by degrees: *the murmur built up to a roar.* **3** (*tr*) to improve the health or physique of (a person). **4** (*intr*) to prepare for or gradually approach a climax. ◆ *n* **build-up.** **5** progressive increase in number, size, etc.: *the build-up of industry.* **6** a gradual approach to a climax. **7** extravagant publicity or praise, esp. in the form of a campaign. **8** *Mil.* the process of attaining the required strength of forces and equipment.

built (bɪlt) *vb* the past tense and past participle of **build.**

built-in *adj* **1** made or incorporated as an integral part: *a built-in cupboard.* **2** essential; inherent. ◆ *n* **3** *Austral.* a built-in cupboard.

built-in obsolescence *n* See **planned obsolescence.**

built-up *adj* **1** having many buildings (esp. in **built-up area**). **2** increased by the addition of parts: *built-up heels.*

Buitenzorg ★ (*Dutch* 'bœitənzɔrx) *n* the former name of **Bogor.**

Bujumbura ★ (ˌbuːdʒəm'bʊərə) *n* the capital of Burundi, a port at the NE end of Lake Tanganyika. Pop.: 300 000 (1994 est.). Former name: **Usumbura.**

Bukavu ★ (buː'kɑːvuː) *n* a port in E Democratic Republic of Congo (formerly Zaïre), on Lake Kivu: commercial and industrial centre. Pop.: 201 569 (1994 est.). Former name (until 1966): **Costermansville.**

Bukhara *or* **Bokhara** ★ (bʊ'xɑːrə) *n* **1** a city in S Uzbekistan: capital of the former emirate of Bukhara. Pop.: 236 000 (1993 est.). **2** a former emirate of central Asia: a powerful kingdom and centre of Islam; became a territory of the Soviet Union (1920) and was divided between the former Uzbek, Tajik, and Turkmen SSRs.

Bukovina *or* **Bucovina** ★ (ˌbuːkə'viːnə) *n* a region of E central Europe, part of the NE Carpathians: the north was seized by the Soviet Union (1940) and later became part of Ukraine; the south remained Romanian.

Bulawayo ★ (ˌbʊlə'weɪəʊ) *n* a city in SW Zimbabwe founded (1893) on the site of the kraal of Lobengula, the last Matabele king; the country's main industrial centre. Pop.: 620 936 (1992).

bulb (bʌlb) *n* **1** a rounded organ of vegetative reproduction in plants such as the tulip and onion: a flattened stem bearing a central shoot surrounded by fleshy nutritive inner leaves and thin brown outer leaves. **2** a plant, such as a hyacinth or daffodil, that grows from a bulb. **3** See **light bulb.** **4** any bulb-shaped thing. ORIG C16: from L *bulbus*, from Gk *bolbos* onion
▸ **'bulbous** *adj*

bulbil ('bʌlbɪl) *n* **1** a small bulb produced from a parent bulb. **2** a bulblike reproductive organ in a leaf axil of certain plants. **3** any small bulblike structure in an animal. ORIG C19: from NL *bulbillus* BULB

bulbul ('bʊlbʊl) *n* a songbird of tropical Africa and Asia having brown plumage and, in many species, a distinct crest. ORIG C18: via Persian from Ar.

Bulg. *abbrev. for* Bulgaria(n).

Bulgakov ★ (*Russian* bul'gakəf) *n* **Mikhail Afanaseyev**

Guide to the Text

(mixa'il afa'nasjɪf). 1891–1940, Soviet writer; his novels include *The Master and Margarita* (1966–67).

Bulganin ★ (*Russian* bul'ganin) *n* **Nikolai Aleksandrovich** (nika'laj alɪk'sandrəvitʃ). 1895–1975, Soviet statesman and military leader.

People and Places

Bulgaria ★ (bʌl'gɛərɪə, bʊl-) *n* a republic in SE Europe, on the Balkan Peninsula on the Black Sea: under Turkish rule from 1395 until 1878; became an independent kingdom in 1908 and a Communist republic in 1946; in 1990 free elections ousted the Communist Party. Consists chiefly of the Danube valley in the north, the Balkan Mountains in the central part, separated from the Rhodope Mountains of the south by the valley of the Maritsa River. Language: Bulgarian. Religion: Christian (Bulgarian Orthodox) majority. Currency: lev. Capital: Sofia. Pop.: 8 206 000 (1999 est.). Area: 110 911 sq. km (42 823 sq. miles).
▸ **Bul'garian** *adj, n*

bulge (bʌldʒ) *n* **1** a swelling or an outward curve. **2** a sudden increase in number, esp. of population. ◆ *vb* **bulges, bulging, bulged. 3** to swell outwards. ORIG C13: from OF *bouge*, from L *bulga* bag, prob. of Gaulish origin
▸ **'bulging** *adj* ▸ **'bulgy** *adj*

Derived words

bulgur ('bʌlgə) *n* cracked wheat that has been hulled, steamed, and roasted so that it requires little or no cooking. Also called: **burghul.** ORIG C20: from Ar. *burghul*

bulimia (bju:'lɪmɪə) *n* **1** pathologically insatiable hunger. **2** Also called: **bulimia nervosa.** a disorder characterized by compulsive overeating followed by vomiting. ORIG C17: from NL, from Gk *bous* ox + *limos* hunger

Example

bulk (bʌlk) *n* **1** volume, size, or magnitude, esp. when great. **2** the main part: *the bulk of the work is repetitious.* **3** a large body, esp. of a person. **4** the part of food which passes unabsorbed through the digestive system. **5 in bulk. 5a** in large quantities. **5b** (of a cargo, etc.) unpackaged. ◆ *vb* **6** to cohere or cause to cohere in a mass. **7 bulk large.** to be or seem important or prominent. ORIG C15: from ON *bulki* cargo

> **USAGE NOTE** The use of a plural noun after *bulk* should be avoided, though it is occasionally encountered; most commonly, according to the Bank of English, when referring to *funds* and *profits*: *the bulk of our profits stem from the sale of beer.*

Usage note

bulk buying *n* the purchase of goods in large amounts, often at reduced prices.

bulkhead ('bʌlk,hɛd) *n* any upright wall-like partition in a ship, aircraft, etc. ORIG C15: prob. from *bulk* projecting framework from ON *bálkr* +HEAD

bulk modulus *n* a coefficient of elasticity of a substance equal to the ratio of the applied stress to the resulting fractional change in volume.

bulky ('bʌlkɪ) *adj* **bulkier, bulkiest.** very large and massive, esp. so as to be unwieldy.
▸ **'bulkily** *adv* ▸ **'bulkiness** *n*

Related adjective

Usage label

Idiom or phrase

bull[1] (bʊl) *n* **1** any male bovine animal, esp. one that is sexually mature. Related adj: **taurine. 2** the male of various other animals including the elephant and whale. **3** a very large, strong, or aggressive person. **4** *Stock Exchange.* **4a** a speculator who buys in anticipation of rising prices in order to make a profit on resale. **4b** (*as modifier*): *a bull market.* Cf. **bear**[2] (sense 5). **5** *Chiefly Brit.* short for **bull's-eye** (senses 1, 2). **6** *Sl.* short for **bullshit. 7 a bull in a china shop.** a clumsy person. **8 take the bull by the horns.** to face and tackle a difficulty without shirking. ◆ *adj* **9** male; masculine: *a bull elephant.* **10** large; strong. ORIG OE *bula*

bull[2] (bʊl) *n* a ludicrously self-contradictory or inconsistent statement. ORIG C17: from ?

bull[3] (bʊl) *n* a formal document issued by the pope. ORIG C13: from Med. L *bulla* seal attached to a bull, from L: round object

Bull[1] (bʊl) *n* **the.** the constellation Taurus, the second sign of the zodiac.

Bull[2] ★ (bʊl) *n* **1 John.** 1563–1628, English composer and organist. **2** See **John Bull.**

Editorial Staff

For the Fifth Edition

EDITORIAL DIRECTOR
Jeremy Butterfield

PUBLISHING MANAGER
Elaine Higgleton

EDITORIAL CONSULTANT
Alan Isaacs

MANAGING EDITOR
Sheila Ferguson

LEXICOGRAPHERS
Elspeth Summers (Senior Lexicographer)
Andrew Holmes **Lorna Gilmour**
Will Mackie **Carol Collins**
Ian Brookes **Mary O'Neill**

USAGE NOTES
Jeremy Butterfield

MARKET HOUSE EDITORS
John Daintith **Elizabeth Martin** **Fran Alexander**
Jonathan Law **Mark Salad**

COMPUTERS
Anne Stibbs

KEYBOARDERS
Sandra McQueen **Brenda Tomkins**

Guide to the Use of the Dictionary

Collins Concise Dictionary is designed to be easy to use so that you can go straight to the word you want. The Guide that follows sets out the main principles on which the Dictionary is arranged and enables you to make full use of the Dictionary by showing the range of information that it contains.

HEADWORD

All main entries, including place names, biographies, abbreviations, prefixes, and suffixes, are printed in large boldface type and are listed in strict alphabetical order. This applies even if the headword consists of more than one word.

Order of entries

Words that have the same spelling but are derived from different sources (homographs) are entered separately with superscript numbers after the headwords.

saw[1] (sɔː) *n* **1** any of various hand tools ...
saw[2] (sɔː) *vb* the past tense of **see**[1].
saw[3] (sɔː) *n* a wise saying, maxim, or proverb. ...

A word with a capital initial letter, if entered separately, follows the lower-case form. For example, **Arras** follows **arras.**

Place names

If a place has more than one name, its main entry is given at the name most often used in modern English, with a cross-reference at other names. Thus, the main entry for the capital of Bavaria is at **Munich**, with a cross-reference at **München.** If a place name has no current anglicized form, its main entry is at the form of the name used in the official language of the area. Thus, the main entry is at **Brno**, with a cross-reference at **Brünn.** Historical names of importance are also given, with dates where these can be ascertained.

Paris[1] ★ ('pærɪs; *French* pari) *n* ... Ancient name: **Lutetia.**

Volgograd ★ (*Russian* vəlga'grat; *English* 'vɒlgəˌgræd) *n* ...
Former names: **Tsaritsyn** (until 1925), **Stalingrad** (1925–61).

Statistical information about places has been obtained from the most up-to-date and reliable sources available. Population figures have been compiled from the most recent census available at the time of going to press. The date of the census is always given.

Biographical entries

Biographical entries are entered separately from and immediately following place names of the same spelling. They are entered at the surname of the subject or at his or her title if that is the name by which he or she is better known and are grouped under one headword when the spelling of the surname (or title) is identical.

Abbreviations, acronyms, and symbols

Abbreviations, acronyms, and symbols are entered as headwords in the main alphabetical list. In line with modern practice, full stops are generally not used but it can be assumed that nearly all abbreviations are equally acceptable with or without stops.

Prefixes, suffixes, and combining forms

Prefixes (e.g. **in-**, **pre-**, **sub-**), suffixes (e.g. **-able**, **-ation**, **-ity**), and combining forms (e.g. **psycho-**, **-iatry**) have been entered as headwords if they are still used freely to produce new words in English.

Variant spellings

Common acceptable variant spellings of English words are given as alternative forms of the headword.

capitalize *or* **capitalise** ('kæpɪtəˌlaɪz) *vb* ...

US spellings

Where it is different, the US spelling of a word is also recorded in the headword.

centre *or US* **center** ('sɛntə) *n*

PRONUNCIATION

Pronunciations of words in this Dictionary represent those that are common in educated British English speech. They are transcribed in the International Phonetic Alphabet (IPA). *A Key to the Pronunciation Symbols* is printed at the end of this Guide. The pronunciation is normally given in brackets immediately after the headword.

abase (ə'beɪs) *vb* **abases, abasing, abased.** (*tr*) **1** to humble ...

The stress pattern is marked by the symbols ' for primary stress and ˌ for secondary stress. The stress mark precedes the syllable to which it applies.

Variant pronunciations

When a headword has an acceptable variant pronunciation or stress pattern, the variant is given by repeating only the syllable or syllables that change.

Guide to the Use of the Dictionary

economic (ˌiːkəˈnɒmɪk, ˌɛkə-) *adj* **1** of or relating to ...

Pronunciations with different parts of speech

When two or more parts of speech of a word have different pronunciations, the pronunciations are shown in brackets before the relevant group of senses.

record *n* (ˈrɛkɔːd). **1** an account in permanent form, ... ◆ *vb* (rɪˈkɔːd). (*mainly tr*) **18** to set down in some permanent form ...

Pronunciation of individual senses

If one sense of a headword has a different pronunciation from that of the rest, the pronunciation is given in brackets after the sense number.

conjure (ˈkʌndʒə) *vb* **conjures, conjuring, conjured. 1** (*intr*) to practise conjuring. **2** (*intr*) to call upon supposed supernatural forces by spells and incantations. **3** (kənˈdʒʊə). (*tr*) to appeal earnestly to: *I conjure you to help me. ...*

INFLECTED FORMS

Inflected forms are shown for the following:

Nouns and verbs whose inflections involve a change in internal spelling.

goose[1] (guːs) *n, pl* **geese.** ...

drive (draɪv) *vb* **drives, driving, drove, driven.** ...

Nouns, verbs, and adjectives that end in a consonant plus *-y*, where *y* is changed to *i* before inflectional endings.

augury (ˈɔːgjʊrɪ) *n, pl* **auguries.** ...

Nouns having identical singular and plural forms.

sheep (ʃiːp) *n, pl* **sheep.** ...

Nouns that closely resemble others but form their plurals differently.

mongoose (ˈmɒŋˌguːs) *n, pl* **mongooses.** ...

Nouns that end in *-ful*, *-o*, and *-us*.

handful (ˈhændfʊl) *n, pl* **handfuls.** ...
tomato (təˈmɑːtəʊ) *n, pl* **tomatoes.** ...
prospectus (prəˈspɛktəs) *n, pl* **prospectuses.** ...

Nouns whose plurals are not regular English inflections.

basis (ˈbeɪsɪs) *n, pl* **bases** (-siːz) ...

Plural nouns whose singulars are not regular English forms.

bacteria (bækˈtɪərɪə) *pl n, sing* **bacterium.** ...

Nouns whose plurals have regular spellings but involve a change in pronunciation.

house *n* (haʊs), *pl* **houses** (ˈhaʊzɪz). ...

Multiword nouns when it is not obvious which word takes a plural inflection.

attorney-at-law *n, pl* **attorneys-at-law.** ...

Adjectives that change their roots to form comparatives and superlatives.

good (gʊd) *adj* **better, best.** ...

Adjectives and verbs that double their final consonant before adding endings.

fat (fæt) ... ◆ *adj* **fatter, fattest.** ...
control (kənˈtrəʊl) *vb* **controls, controlling, controlled.** ...

Verbs that are regular and do not (as might be expected) double their final consonant before adding endings.

rivet (ˈrɪvɪt) ... ◆ *vb* **rivets, riveting, riveted.** ...

Verbs and adjectives that end in a vowel plus *-e*.

canoe (kəˈnuː) ... ◆ *vb* **canoes, canoeing, canoed.** ...
free (friː) *adj* **freer, freest.** ... ◆ *vb* **frees, freeing, freed.** ...

Verbs that end in *-e*.

pace[1] (peɪs) ... ◆ *vb* **paces, pacing, paced.** ...

PARTS OF SPEECH

A part-of-speech label in italics precedes the sense or senses relating to that part of speech.

Standard parts of speech

The standard parts of speech, with the abbreviations used, are as follows:

adjective (*adj*), adverb (*adv*), conjunction (*conj*), interjection (*interj*), noun (*n*), preposition (*prep*), pronoun (*pron*), verb (*vb*).

Less traditional parts of speech

Certain other less traditional parts of speech have been used in this Dictionary.

determiner. This denotes such words as *the, a, some, any, that, this,* as well as the numerals, and possessives such as *my* and *your.* Many determiners can have a pronoun function without change of meaning:

some (sʌm; *unstressed* səm) *determiner* ... **2a** an unknown or unspecified quantity or amount of: *there's some rice on the table; he owns some horses.* **2b** (*as pron; functioning as sing or pl*): *we'll buy some.* ...

sentence connector. This description replaces the traditional classification of certain words, such as *therefore* and *however*, as adverbs or conjunctions. These words link sentences together rather in the manner of conjunctions; however, they are not confined to the first position in a clause as conjunctions are.

sentence substitute. Sentence substitutes are words such as *yes, no, perhaps, definitely*, and *maybe*. They can stand as meaningful utterances by themselves.

Words used as more than one part of speech

If a word can be used as more than one part of speech, the senses of one part of speech are separated from the others by a lozenge (◆).

lure (lʊə) *vb* **lures, luring, lured.** (*tr*) ... **2** *Falconry.* to entice (a hawk or falcon) from the air to the falconer by a lure. ◆ *n* **3** a person or thing that lures. ...

GRAMMATICAL INFORMATION

Grammatical information is provided in brackets and typically in italics to distinguish it from other types of information.

Adjectives and determiners

Some adjectives and determiners are restricted by usage to a particular position relative to the nouns they qualify. This is indicated by the following labels:

postpositive (used predicatively or after the noun, but not before the noun):

ablaze (əˈbleɪz) *adj* (*postpositive*), *adv* **1** on fire; burning. ...

immediately postpositive (always used immediately following the noun qualified and never used predicatively):

galore (gəˈlɔː) *determiner* (*immediately postpositive*) in great numbers or quantity: *there were daffodils galore in the park.* ...

prenominal (used before the noun, and never used predicatively):

chief (tʃiːf) ... ◆ *adj* **4** (*prenominal*) **4a** most important; principal. ...

Intensifiers

Adjectives and adverbs that perform an exclusively intensifying function, with no addition of meaning, are described as (intensifier) without further explanation.

blooming (ˈbluːmɪŋ) *adv, adj Brit. inf.* (intensifier): *a blooming genius; blooming painful.*

Conjunctions

Conjunctions are divided into two classes, marked by the following labels:

coordinating. Coordinating conjunctions connect words, phrases, or clauses that perform an identical function and are not dependent on each other. They include *and, but*, and *or*.

subordinating. Subordinating conjunctions introduce clauses that are dependent on a main clause in a complex sentence. They include *where, until*, and *if*.

Some conjunctions, such as *while* and *whereas*, can function as either coordinating or subordinating conjunctions.

Singular and plural labelling of nouns

Headwords and senses that are apparently plural in form but that take a singular verb, etc., are marked '*functioning as sing*'

physics (ˈfɪzɪks) *n* (*functioning as sing*) **1** the branch of science ...

Headwords and senses that appear to be singular, such as collective nouns, but that take a plural verb, etc., are marked '*functioning as pl*'

cattle (ˈkætᵊl) *n* (*functioning as pl*) **1** bovid mammals of the tribe *Bovini* ...

Headwords and senses that may take either a singular or a plural verb, etc., are marked '*functioning as sing or pl*'

bellows (ˈbɛləʊz) *n* (*functioning as sing or pl*) **1** Also: **pair of bellows.** an instrument consisting of an air chamber ...

Modifiers

A noun that is commonly used as if it were an adjective is labelled *modifier*. If the sense of the modifier can be understood from the sense of the noun, the modifier is shown without further explanation, with an example to illustrate its use. Otherwise its meaning and/or usage is explained separately.

key[1] (kiː) *n* ... **8** (*modifier*) of great importance: *a key issue.*

Verbs

The principal parts given are: 3rd person singular of the present tense; present participle; past tense; past participle if different from the past tense.

Intransitive and transitive verbs

When a sense of a verb (*vb*) is restricted to transitive use, it is labelled (*tr*); if it is intransitive only, it is labelled (*intr*). If all the senses of a verb are transitive or all are intransitive, the appropriate label appears before the first numbered sense and is not repeated.

Absence of a label is significant: it indicates that the sense may be used both transitively and intransitively.

If nearly all the senses of a verb are transitive, the label (*mainly tr*) appears immediately before the first numbered sense. This indicates that, unless otherwise labelled, any given sense of the verb is transitive. Similarly, all the senses of a verb may be labelled (*mainly intr*).

Copulas

A verb that takes a complement is labelled copula.

seem (siːm) *vb* (*may take an infinitive*) **1** (*copula*) to appear to the mind or eye; look: *the car seems to be running well. ...*

Phrasal verbs

Verbal constructions consisting of a verb and a prepositional or an adverbial particle are given headword status if the meaning of the phrasal verb cannot be deduced from the separate meanings of the verb and the particle.

Phrasal verbs are labelled to show four possible distinctions: a transitive verb with an adverbial particle (*tr, adv*); a transitive verb with a prepositional particle (*tr, prep*); an intransitive verb with an adverbial particle (*intr, adv*); an intransitive verb with a prepositional particle (*intr, prep*):

turn on ... **4** (*tr, adv*) *Inf.* to produce (charm, tears, etc.) suddenly or automatically.

take for *vb* (*tr, prep*) *Inf.* to consider or suppose to be, esp. mistakenly: *the fake coins were taken for genuine; who do you take me for?*

break off ... **3** (*intr, adv*) to stop abruptly: *he broke off in the middle of his speech.*

turn on ... **2** (*intr, prep*) to depend or hinge on: *the success of the party turns on you.*

The absence of a label is significant. If there is no label (*tr*) or (*intr*), the verb may be used either transitively or intransitively. If there is no label (*adv*) or (*prep*), the particle may be either adverbial or prepositional.

Any noun, adjective, or modifier formed from a phrasal verb is entered under the phrasal-verb headword. In some cases, where the noun or adjective is more common than the verb, the phrasal verb is entered after the noun or adjective form:

breakaway (ˈbreɪkəˌweɪ) *n* **1a** loss or withdrawal of a group of members from an association, club, etc. **1b** (*as modifier*): *a breakaway faction. ...* ◆ *vb* **break away.** (*intr, adv*) **3** (often foll. by *from*) to leave hastily or escape. **4** to withdraw or secede.

RESTRICTIVE LABELS

If a particular sense is restricted as to appropriateness, connotation, subject field, etc., an italic label is placed immediately before the relevant definition.

hang on *vb* (*intr*) ... **5** (*adv*) *Inf.* to wait: *hang on for a few minutes.*

If a label applies to all senses of one part of speech, it is placed immediately after the part-of-speech label.

assured (əˈʃʊəd) *adj* ... ◆ *n* **4** *Chiefly Brit.* **4a** the beneficiary under a life assurance policy. **4b** the person whose life is insured. ...

If a label applies to all senses of a headword, it is placed immediately after the pronunciation (or inflections).

con[1] (kɒn) *Inf.* ◆ *n* **1a** short for **confidence trick. 1b** (*as modifier*): *con man.* ◆ *vb* **cons, conning, conned. 2** (*tr*) to swindle ...

Usage labels

Sl. (*Slang*). Refers to words or senses that are informal and restricted in context, for example, to members of a particular social or cultural group. Slang words are inappropriate in formal speech or writing.

Inf. (*Informal*). Applies to words or senses that may be widely used, especially in conversation, letter-writing, etc., but that are not common in formal writing. Such words are subject to fewer contextual restrictions than slang words.

Taboo. Indicates words that are not acceptable in polite use.

Offens. (*Offensive*). Indicates that a word might be regarded as offensive by the person described or referred to, even if the speaker uses the word without any malicious intention.

Derog. (*Derogatory*). Implies that the connotations of a word are unpleasant with intent on the part of the speaker or writer.

Not standard. Indicates words or senses that are frequently encountered but widely regarded as incorrect.

Arch. (*Archaic*). Denotes a word or sense that is no longer in common use but that may be found in literary works or used to impart a historical colour to contemporary writing.

Obs. (*Obsolete*). Denotes a word or sense that is no longer in use. In specialist or technical fields the label often implies that the term has been superseded.

The word 'formerly' is placed in brackets before a sense when the practice, concept, etc., being described, rather than the word itself, is obsolete or out-of-date.

A number of other usage labels, such as *Ironic, Facetious*, and *Euphemistic*, are used where appropriate.

More extended help on usage is provided in usage notes after certain entries.

Subject-field labels

A number of italic labels are used to indicate that a word or sense is used in a particular specialist or technical field.

MEANING

The meaning of each headword in this Dictionary is explained in one or more definitions, together with information about context and typical use.

Order of senses

As a general rule, where a headword has more than one sense, the first sense given is the one most common in current usage.

> **complexion** (kəmˈplɛkʃən) *n* **1** the colour and general appearance of a person's skin, esp. of the face. **2** aspect or nature: *the general complexion of a nation's finances.* **3** *Obs.* temperament. ...

Where the lexicographers consider that a current sense is the 'core meaning' in that it illuminates the meaning of other senses, the core meaning may be placed first.

> **competition** (ˌkɒmpɪˈtɪʃən) *n* **1** the act of competing. **2** a contest in which a winner is selected from among two or more entrants. **3** a series of games, sports events, etc. **4** the opposition offered by competitors....

Subsequent senses are arranged so as to give a coherent account of the meaning of a headword. If a word is used as more than one part of speech, all the senses of each part of speech are grouped together in a single block. Within a part-of-speech block, closely related senses are grouped together; technical senses generally follow general senses; archaic and obsolete sense follow technical senses; idioms and fixed phrases are generally placed last.

Scientific and technical definitions

Units, physical quantities, formulas, etc. In accordance with the recommendations of the International Standards Organization, all scientific measurements are expressed in SI units (*Système International d'Unités*). Measurements and quantities in more traditional units are often given as well as SI units. The entries for chemical compounds give the systematic names as well as the more familiar popular names.

CROSS-REFERENCES

Cross-references introduced by the words 'See also' or 'Compare' refer the reader to additional information elsewhere in the Dictionary. If the cross-reference is preceded by a lozenge (◆), it applies to all senses of the headword that have gone before it, unless otherwise stated. If there is no lozenge, the cross-reference applies only to the sense immediately preceding it.

Variant spellings

Variant spellings (e.g. **foetus**...a variant spelling of **fetus**) are generally entered as cross-references if their place in the alphabetical list is more than ten entries distant from the main entry.

Alternative names

Alternative names or terms are printed in boldface type and introduced by the words 'Also' or 'Also called'. If the alternative name or term is preceded by a lozenge, it applies to the entire entry.

RELATED ADJECTIVES

Certain nouns, especially of Germanic origin, have related adjectives that are derived from Latin or French. For example, *mural* (from Latin) is an adjective related in meaning to *wall*. Such adjectives are shown in a number of cases after the sense (or part-of-speech block) to which they are related.

> **wall** (wɔːl) *n* **1a** a vertical construction made of stone, brick, wood, etc. ... Related adj: **mural**. ...

IDIOMS

Fixed noun phrases, such as **dark horse**, and certain other idioms are given full headword status. Other idioms are placed under the key word of the idiom, as a separate sense, generally at the end of the appropriate part-of-speech block.

> **ground**[1] (graʊnd) *n* ... **17 break new ground.** to do something that has not been done before. ...

ETYMOLOGIES

Etymologies are preceded by ORIG (origin) and appear after the definition. They are given for all headwords except those that are derivative forms (consisting of a base word and a suffix or prefix), compound words, inflected forms, and proper names.

Many headwords, such as **enlighten** and **prepossess**, consist of a prefix and a base word and are not accompanied by etymologies since the essential etymological information is shown for the component parts, all of which are entered in the Dictionary as headwords in their own right.

The purpose of the etymologies is to trace briefly the history of the word back from the present day, through its first recorded appearance in English, to its origin, often in some source language other than English. The etymologies show the history of the word both in English (wherever there has been significant change in form or sense) and in its pre-English source languages.

Words printed in SMALL CAPITALS refer to other headwords where relevant or additional information, either in the definition or in the etymology, may be found.

Dating

The etymology records the first known occurrence (a written citation) of a word in English. Words first appearing in the language during the Middle English period or later are dated by century, abbreviated **C**.

> **mantis** ('mæntɪs) ... [C17: NL, from Gk: prophet, alluding to its praying posture]

This indicates that there is a written citation for **mantis** in the seventeenth century. The absence of a New Latin or Greek form in the etymology means that the form of the word was the same in those languages as in English.

Old English

Native words from Old English are not dated, written records of Old English being scarce, but are simply identified as being of Old English origin.

DERIVED WORDS

Words derived from a base word by the addition of suffixes such as *-ly*, *-ness*, etc., are entered in boldface type immediately after the etymology or after the last definition if there is no etymology. They are preceded by an arrow head (▸). The meanings of such words may be deduced from the meanings of the suffix and the headword.

USAGE NOTES

A brief note introduced by the label **USAGE NOTE** has been added at the end of a number of entries in order to comment on matters of usage.

List of Abbreviations used in the Dictionary

abbrev. abbreviation
Abor. Aboriginal
adj adjective
adv adverb(ial)
Afrik. Afrikaans
Amerind American Indian
Anat. Anatomy
approx. approximate(ly)
Ar. Arabic
Arch. Archaic
Archaeol. Archaeology
Archit. Architecture
Astrol. Astrology
Astron. Astronomy
Austral. Australian

Biol. Biology
Bot. Botany
Brit. Britain; British

C century (e.g. **C14** = 14th century)
°**C** degrees Celsius
Canad. Canadian
cap. capital
cf. compare
Chem. Chemistry
comp. comparative
conj conjunction

Derog. Derogatory
dim. diminutive
Du. Dutch

E east(ern); (in etymologies) English
Econ. Economics
e.g. for example
esp. especially
est. estimate

F French
fem feminine
foll. followed
ft foot *or* feet

G German
Geog. Geography
Geol. Geology
Geom. Geometry
Gk Greek
Gmc Germanic

Heb. Hebrew

i.e. that is
imit. of imitative origin
in. inch(es)
Inf. Informal
infl. influence(d)
interj interjection
intr intransitive
It. Italian

km kilometre(s)

L Late; Latin
lit. literally
LL Late Latin

m metre(s)
M Middle
masc masculine
Maths Mathematics
Med. Medicine; (in etymologies) Medieval
MHG Middle High German
Mil. Military
Mod. Modern
Myth. Mythology

n noun
N north(ern)
Naut. Nautical
NE northeast(ern)
NL New Latin
no. number
NW northwest(ern)
NZ New Zealand

O Old
Obs. Obsolete
Offens. Offensive
OHG Old High German
ON Old Norse
orig. originally
ORIG origin

Photog. Photography
pl plural
pop. population
Port. Portuguese
p.p. past participle
prep preposition(al)
prob. probably
pron pronoun
Psychol. Psychology
pt. point
p.t. past tense

rel. related

S south(ern)
S. African South African
Sansk. Sanskrit
Scand. Scandinavian
Scot. Scottish; Scots
SE southeast(ern)
sing singular
Sl. slang
Sp. Spanish
sq. square
sup. superlative
SW southwest(ern)

Theol. Theology
tr transitive

ult. ultimately
US United States

var. variant
vb verb
vol. volume

W west(ern)
wt. weight

Zool. Zoology

? in etymologies indicates "query"

Pronunciation Key

The symbols used in the pronunciation transcriptions are those of the International Phonetic Alphabet. The following consonant symbols have their usual English values: *b, d, f, h, k, l, m, n, p, r, s, t, v, w, z*. The remaining symbols and their interpretations are listed below.

English Sounds

ɑ: as in *father* ('fɑ:ðə), *alms* (ɑ:mz), *clerk* (klɑ:k), *heart* (hɑ:t), *sergeant* ('sɑ:dʒənt)

æ as in *act* (ækt), *Caedmon* ('kædmən), *plait* (plæt)

aɪ as in *dive* (daɪv), *aisle* (aɪl), *guy* (gaɪ), *might* (maɪt), *rye* (raɪ)

aɪə as in *fire* ('faɪə), *buyer* ('baɪə), *liar* ('laɪə), *tyre* ('taɪə)

aʊ as in *out* (aʊt), *bough* (baʊ), *crowd* (kraʊd), *slouch* (slaʊtʃ)

aʊə as in *flour* ('flaʊə), *cower* ('kaʊə), *flower* ('flaʊə), *sour* ('saʊə)

ɛ as in *bet* (bɛt), *ate* (ɛt), *bury* ('bɛrɪ), *heifer* ('hɛfə), *said* (sɛd), *says* (sɛz)

eɪ as in *paid* (peɪd), *day* (deɪ), *deign* (deɪn), *gauge* (geɪdʒ), *grey* (greɪ), *neigh* (neɪ)

ɛə as in *bear* (bɛə), *dare* (dɛə), *prayer* (prɛə), *stairs* (stɛəz), *where* (wɛə)

g as in *get* (gɛt), *give* (gɪv), *ghoul* (gu:l), *guard* (gɑ:d), *examine* (ɪg'zæmɪn)

ɪ as in *pretty* ('prɪtɪ), *build* (bɪld), *busy* ('bɪzɪ), *nymph* (nɪmf), *pocket* ('pɒkɪt), *sieve* (sɪv), *women* ('wɪmɪn)

i: as in *see* (si:), *aesthete* ('i:sθi:t), *evil* ('i:vᵊl), *magazine* (ˌmægə'zi:n), *receive* (rɪ'si:v), *siege* (si:dʒ)

ɪə as in *fear* (fɪə), *beer* (bɪə), *mere* (mɪə), *tier* (tɪə)

j as in *yes* (jɛs), *onion* ('ʌnjən), *vignette* (vɪ'njɛt)

ɒ as in *pot* (pɒt), *botch* (bɒtʃ), *sorry* ('sɒrɪ)

əʊ as in *note* (nəʊt), *beau* (bəʊ), *dough* (dəʊ), *hoe* (həʊ), *slow* (sləʊ), *yeoman* ('jəʊmən)

ɔ: as in *thaw* (θɔ:), *broad* (brɔ:d), *drawer* ('drɔ:ə), *fault* (fɔ:lt), *halt* (hɔ:lt), *organ* ('ɔ:gən)

ɔɪ as in *void* (vɔɪd), *boy* (bɔɪ), *destroy* (dɪ'strɔɪ)

ʊ as in *pull* (pʊl), *good* (gʊd), *should* (ʃʊd), *woman* ('wʊmən)

u: as in *zoo* (zu:), *do* (du:), *queue* (kju:), *shoe* (ʃu:), *spew* (spju:), *true* (tru:), *you* (ju:)

ʊə as in *poor* (pʊə), *skewer* (skjʊə), *sure* (ʃʊə)

ə as in *potter* ('pɒtə), *alone* (ə'ləʊn), *furious* ('fjʊərɪəs), *nation* ('neɪʃən), *the* (ðə)

ɜ: as in *fern* (fɜ:n), *burn* (bɜ:n), *fir* (fɜ:), *learn* (lɜ:n), *term* (tɜ:m), *worm* (wɜ:m)

ʌ as in *cut* (kʌt), *flood* (flʌd), *rough* (rʌf), *son* (sʌn)

ʃ as in *ship* (ʃɪp), *election* (ɪ'lɛkʃən), *machine* (mə'ʃi:n), *mission* ('mɪʃən), *pressure* ('prɛʃə), *schedule* ('ʃɛdju:l), *sugar* ('ʃʊgə)

ʒ as in *treasure* ('trɛʒə), *azure* ('æʒə), *closure* ('kləʊʒə), *evasion* (ɪ'veɪʒən)

tʃ as in *chew* (tʃu:), *nature* ('neɪtʃə)

dʒ as in *jaw* (dʒɔ:), *adjective* ('ædʒɪktɪv), *lodge* (lɒdʒ), *soldier* ('səʊldʒə), *usage* ('ju:sɪdʒ)

θ as in *thin* (θɪn), *strength* (strɛŋθ), *three* (θri:)

ð as in *these* (ði:z), *bathe* (beɪð), *lather* ('lɑ:ðə)

ŋ as in *sing* (sɪŋ), *finger* ('fɪŋgə), *sling* (slɪŋ)

ᵊ indicates that the following consonant (*l or n*) is syllabic, as in *bundle* ('bʌndᵊl), *button* ('bʌtᵊn)

Foreign Sounds

The symbols above are also used to represent foreign sounds where these are similar to English sounds. However, certain common foreign sounds require symbols with markedly different values, as follows:

a *a* in French *ami*, German *Mann*, Italian *pasta*: a sound between English (æ) and (ɑ:), similar to the vowel in Northern English *cat* or London *cut*.

ɑ *a* in French *bas*: a sound made with the tongue position similar to that of English (ɑ:), but shorter.

e *é* in French *été*, *eh* in German *sehr*, *e* in Italian *che*: a sound similar to the first part of the English diphthong (eɪ) in *day* or to the Scottish vowel in *day*.

i *i* in French *il*, German *Idee*, Spanish *filo*, Italian *signor*: a sound made with a tongue position similar to that of English (i:), but shorter.

ɔ *o* in Italian *no*, French *bonne*, German *Sonne*: a vowel resembling English (ɒ), but with a higher tongue position and more rounding of the lips.

o *o* in French *rose*, German *so*, Italian *voce*: a sound between English (ɔ:) and (u:) with closely rounded lips, similar to the Scottish vowel in *so*.

u *ou* in French *genou*, *u* in German *kulant*,

Spanish *puna*: a sound made with a tongue position similar to that of English (u:), but shorter.

y *u* in French *tu*, *ü* in German *über* or *fünf*: a sound made with a tongue position similar to that of English (i:), but with closely rounded lips.

ø *eu* in French *deux*, *ö* in German *schön*: a sound made with the tongue position of (e), but with closely rounded lips.

œ *œu* in French *œuf*, *ö* in German *zwölf*: a sound made with a tongue position similar to that of English (ɛ), but with open rounded lips.

~ above a vowel indicates nasalization, as in French *un* (œ̃), *bon* (bɔ̃), *vin* (vɛ̃), *blanc* (blɑ̃).

χ *ch* in Scottish *loch*, German *Buch*, *j* in Spanish *Juan*.

ç *ch* in German *ich*: a (j) sound as in *yes*, said without voice; similar to the first sound in *huge*.

β *b* in Spanish *Habana*: a voiced fricative sound similar to (v), but made by the two lips.

ʎ *ll* in Spanish *llamar*, *gl* in Italian *consiglio*: similar to the (lj) sequence in *million*, but with the tongue tip lowered and the sounds said simultaneously.

ɥ *u* in French *lui*: a short (y).

ɲ *gn* in French *vigne*, Italian *gnocchi*, *ñ* in Spanish *España*: similar to the (nj) sequence in *onion*, but with the tongue tip lowered and the two sounds said simultaneously.

ɣ *g* in Spanish *luego*: a weak (g) made with voiced friction.

Length

The symbol : denotes length and is shown together with certain vowel symbols when the vowels are typically long.

Stress

Three grades of stress are shown in the transcriptions by the presence or absence of marks placed immediately *before* the affected syllable. Primary or strong stress is shown by ', while secondary or weak stress is shown by ˌ. Unstressed syllables are not marked. In *photographic* (ˌfəʊtə'græfɪk), for example, the first syllable carries secondary stress and the third primary stress, while the second and fourth are unstressed.

Notes

(i) Though words like *castle*, *path*, and *fast* are shown as pronounced with an /ɑ:/ sound, many speakers use an /æ/. Such variations are acceptable and are to be assumed by the reader.

(ii) The letter "r" in some positions is not sounded in the speech of Southern England and elsewhere. However, many speakers in other areas do sound the "r" in such positions with varying degrees of distinctness. Again such variations are to be assumed, and in such words as *fern*, *fear*, and *arm* the reader will sound or not sound the "r" according to his or her speech habits.

(iii) Though the widely received pronunciation of words like *which* and *why* is with a simple /w/ sound and is so shown in the dictionary, many speakers in Scotland and elsewhere preserve an aspirated sound: /hw/. Once again this variation is to be assumed.

A DICTIONARY OF THE ENGLISH LANGUAGE

Aa

a *or* **A** (eɪ) *n, pl* **a's, A's,** *or* **As. 1** the first letter and first vowel of the English alphabet. **2** any of several speech sounds represented by this letter, as in *take, bag,* or *calm.* **3** Also called: **alpha.** the first in a series, esp. the highest mark. **4** **from A to Z.** from start to finish.

a[1] (ə; *emphatic* eɪ) *determiner (indefinite article;* used before an initial consonant. Cf. **an**[1]) **1** used preceding a singular countable noun, not previously specified: *a dog; a great pity.* **2** used preceding a noun or determiner of quantity: *a dozen eggs; a great many; to read a lot.* **3** (preceded by *once, twice, several times,* etc.) each or every; per: *once a day.* **4** a certain; one: *a Mr Jones called.* **5** (preceded by *not*) any at all: *not a hope.* ◆ Cf. **the**[1].

> **USAGE NOTE** See at **an**[1].

a[2] *symbol for:* **1** acceleration. **2** are(s) (metric measure of area). **3** atto-.

A *symbol for:* **1** *Music.* **1a** the sixth note of the scale of C major. **1b** the major or minor key having this note as its tonic. **2** a human blood type of the ABO group, containing the A antigen. **3** (in Britain) a major arterial road. **4** ampere(s). **5** absolute (temperature). **6** area. **7** (*in combination*) atomic: *an A-bomb; an A-plant.* **8a** a person whose job is in top management, or who holds a senior administrative or professional position. **8b** (*as modifier*): *an A worker.* ◆ See also **occupation groupings.**

Å *symbol for* angstrom unit.

a. *abbrev. for:* **1** acre(s). **2** Also: **A.** alto.

A. *abbrev. for:* **1** acre(s). **2** America(n). **3** answer.

a-[1] *or before a vowel* **an-** *prefix* not; without; opposite to: *atonal; asocial.* ORIG from Gk *a-, an-* not, without

a-[2] *prefix* **1** on; in; towards: *aground; aback.* **2** in the state of: *afloat; asleep.*

A1, A-1, *or* **A-one** (ˈeɪˈwʌn) *adj* **1** physically fit. **2** *Inf.* first class; excellent. **3** (of a vessel) in first-class condition.

A4 *n* a standard paper size, 297 × 210 mm.

AA *abbrev. for:* **1** Alcoholics Anonymous. **2** anti-aircraft. **3** (in Britain) Automobile Association.

AAA *abbrev. for:* **1** (formerly) *Brit.* Amateur Athletic Association. **2** *US.* Automobile Association of America.

Aachen ★ (ˈɑːkən; *German* ˈaːxən) *n* a city and spa in W Germany, in North Rhine-Westphalia: the northern capital of Charlemagne's empire. Pop.: 247 923 (1996 est.). French name: **Aix-la-Chapelle.**

Aalborg *or* **Ålborg** ★ (*Danish* ˈɔlbɔr) *n* a city and port in Denmark, in N Jutland. Pop.: 159 980 (1996 est.).

Aalesund ★ (*Norwegian* ˈoːləsun) *n* a variant spelling of **Ålesund.**

Aalto ★ (*Finnish* ˈɑːltɔ) *n* **Alvar** (ˈalvar). 1898–1976, Finnish architect and furniture designer, noted particularly for his public and industrial buildings, in which wood is much used. He invented bent plywood furniture (1932).

A & E *abbrev. for* Accident and Emergency (in hospitals).

A & R *abbrev. for* artists and repertoire.

AAP *abbrev. for:* **1** Australian Associated Press. **2** (in the US) affirmative action programme.

Aarau ★ (*German* ˈaːrau) *n* a town in N Switzerland, capital of Aargau canton: capital of the Helvetic Republic from 1798 to 1803. Pop.: 15 881 (1990).

aardvark (ˈɑːdˌvɑːk) *n* a nocturnal burrowing African mammal that has long ears and snout and feeds on termites. Also called: **ant bear.** ORIG C19: from obs. Afrik., from *aarde* earth + *varken* pig

aardwolf (ˈɑːdˌwʊlf) *n, pl* **aardwolves.** a nocturnal mammal of the hyena family that inhabits the plains of southern Africa and feeds on termites and insect larvae. ORIG C19: from Afrik., from *aarde* earth + *wolf* wolf

Aargau ★ (*German* ˈaːrgau) *n* a canton in N Switzerland. Capital: Aarau. Pop.: 523 114 (1995 est.). Area: 1404 sq. km (542 sq. miles). French name: **Argovie.**

Aarhus *or* **Århus** ★ (*Danish* ˈɔrhuːs) *n* a city and port in Denmark, in E Jutland. Pop.: 279 759 (1996 est.).

Aaron ★ (ˈɛərən) *n Old Testament.* the first high priest of the Israelites, brother of Moses (Exodus 4:14).

Aaron's beard *n* another name for **rose of Sharon.**

Aaron's rod *n* a widespread Eurasian plant having tall erect spikes of yellow flowers.

A'asia *abbrev. for* Australasia.

AB *abbrev. for:* **1** Also: **a.b.** able-bodied seaman. **2** Alberta. **3** (in the US) Bachelor of Arts. ◆ **4** *symbol for* a human blood type of the ABO group, containing both the A antigen and the B antigen.

ab-[1] *prefix* away from; opposite to: *abnormal.* ORIG from L *ab* away from

ab-[2] *prefix* a cgs unit of measurement in the electromagnetic system: *abampere, abvolt.* ORIG from ABSOLUTE

aba (ˈæbə) *n* **1** a type of cloth from Syria, made of goat or camel hair. **2** a sleeveless outer garment of such cloth. ORIG from Ar.

abaca (ˈæbəkə) *n* **1** a Philippine plant, the source of Manila hemp. **2** another name for **Manila hemp.** ORIG via Sp. from Tagalog *abaká*

aback (əˈbæk) *adv* **taken aback. a** startled or disconcerted. **b** *Naut.* (of a vessel or sail) having the wind against the forward side so as to prevent forward motion. ORIG OE *on bæc* to the back

abacus (ˈæbəkəs) *n, pl* **abaci** (-ˌsaɪ) *or* **abacuses. 1** a counting device that consists of a frame holding rods on which a number of beads are free to move. **2** *Archit.* the flat upper part of the capital of a column. ORIG C16: from L, from Gk *abax* board covered with sand, from Heb. *ābhāq* dust

Abaddon ★ (əˈbædᵊn) *n* **1** the Devil (Revelation 9:11). **2** (in rabbinical literature) a part of Gehenna; Hell. ORIG Heb., lit.: destruction

abaft (əˈbɑːft) *Naut.* ◆ *adv, adj (postpositive)* **1** closer to the stern than to another place on a vessel. ◆ *prep* **2** behind; aft of. ORIG C13: *on baft; baft* from OE *beæftan,* from *be* by + *æftan* behind

Abakan ★ (*Russian* abaˈkan) *n* a city in S central Russia, capital of the Khakass Republic, at the confluence of the Yenisei and Abakan Rivers. Pop.: 161 000 (1995 est.).

abalone (ˌæbəˈləʊnɪ) *n* an edible marine mollusc having an ear-shaped shell perforated with a row of respiratory holes and lined with mother-of-pearl. Also called: **ear shell.** ORIG C19: from American Sp. *abulón*

abandon (əˈbændən) *vb (tr)* **1** to forsake completely; desert; leave behind. **2** to give up completely: *to abandon hope.* **3** to give up (something begun) before completion: *the game was abandoned.* **4** to surrender (oneself) to emotion without restraint. **5** to give (insured property that has suffered partial loss or damage) to the insurers in order that a claim for a total loss may be made. ◆ *n* **6** freedom from inhibitions, restraint, or worry: *she danced with abandon.* ORIG C14: *abandounen* (vb), from OF, from *a bandon* under one's control, from *a* at, to + *bandon* control

▸ **aˈbandonment** *n*

abandoned (əˈbændənd) *adj* **1** deserted: *an abandoned hut.* **2** forsaken: *an abandoned child.* **3** uninhibited.

abase (əˈbeɪs) *vb* **abases, abasing, abased.** *(tr)* **1** to humble or belittle (oneself, etc.). **2** to lower or reduce, as in rank. ORIG C15 *abessen,* from OF *abaissier* to make low. See BASE[2]

▸ **aˈbasement** *n*

★ people and places

abash (ə'bæʃ) *vb* (*tr; usually passive*) to cause to feel ill at ease, embarrassed, or confused. ORIG C14: from OF *esbair* to be astonished, from *es-* out + *bair* to gape
▸ **a'bashed** *adj*

abate (ə'beɪt) *vb* **abates, abating, abated.** **1** to make or become less in amount, intensity, degree, etc. **2** (*tr*) *Law.* **2a** to suppress or terminate (a nuisance). **2b** to suspend or extinguish (a claim or action). **2c** to annul (a writ). **3** (*intr*) *Law.* (of a writ, etc.) to become null and void. ORIG C14: from OF *abatre* to beat down
▸ **a'batement** *n*

abatis *or* **abattis** ('æbətɪs) *n* **1** a rampart of felled trees with their branches outwards. **2** a barbed-wire entanglement before a position. ORIG C18: from F, from *abattre* to fell

abattoir ('æbəˌtwɑː) *n* another name for **slaughterhouse.** ORIG C19: F, from *abattre* to fell

Abba ★ ('æbə) *n* **1** *New Testament.* father (used of God). **2** a title given to bishops and patriarchs in the Syrian, Coptic, and Ethiopian Churches. ORIG from Aramaic

abbacy ('æbəsɪ) *n, pl* **abbacies.** the office, term of office, or jurisdiction of an abbot or abbess. ORIG C15: from Church L *abbātia,* from *abbāt-* ABBOT

Abbado ★ (ə'bɑːdəʊ) *n* **Claudio.** born 1933, Italian conductor.

abbatial (ə'beɪʃəl) *adj* of an abbot, abbess, or abbey. ORIG C17: from Church L *abbātiālis,* from *abbāt-* ABBOT

Abbe ★ ('æbə; *German* 'abə) *n* **Ernst.** 1840–1905, German physicist, noted for his work in optics and the microscope condenser known as the **Abbe condenser.**

abbé ('æbeɪ) *n* **1** a French abbot. **2** a title used in addressing any other French cleric, such as a priest.

abbess ('æbɪs) *n* the female superior of a convent. ORIG C13: from OF, from Church L *abbātissa*

Abbevillian (æb'vɪlɪən) *Archaeol.* ◆ *n* **1** the period represented by Lower Palaeolithic European sites containing the earliest hand axes. ◆ *adj* **2** of this period. ORIG C20: after *Abbeville,* N France, where the stone tools were discovered

abbey ('æbɪ) *n* **1** a building inhabited by a community of monks or nuns. **2** a church built in conjunction with such a building. **3** a community of monks or nuns. ORIG C13: via OF *abeie* from Church L *abbātia* ABBACY

abbot ('æbət) *n* the superior of an abbey of monks. ORIG OE *abbod,* from Church L *abbāt-* (stem of *abbas*), ult. from Aramaic *abbā* father
▸ **'abbotship** *or* **'abbotcy** *n*

abbreviate (ə'briːvɪˌeɪt) *vb* **abbreviates, abbreviating, abbreviated.** (*tr*) **1** to shorten (a word or phrase) by contraction or omission of some letters or words. **2** to cut short; curtail. ORIG C15: from p.p. of LL *abbreviāre,* from L *brevis* brief

abbreviation (əˌbriːvɪ'eɪʃən) *n* **1** a shortened or contracted form of a word or phrase. **2** the process or result of abbreviating.

ABC[1] *n* **1** (*pl in US*) the rudiments of a subject. **2** an alphabetical guide. **3** (*often pl in US*) the alphabet.

ABC[2] *abbrev. for:* **1** American Broadcasting Company. **2** Australian Broadcasting Corporation.

Abdias ★ (æb'daɪəs) *n Bible.* the Douay form of **Obadiah.**

abdicate ('æbdɪˌkeɪt) *vb* **abdicates, abdicating, abdicated.** to renounce (a throne, rights, etc.), esp. formally. ORIG C16: from L *abdicāre* to disclaim
▸ **ˌabdi'cation** *n* ▸ **'abdiˌcator** *n*

abdomen ('æbdəmən) *n* **1** the region of the body of a vertebrate that contains the viscera other than the heart and lungs. **2** the front or surface of this region; belly. **3** (in arthropods) the posterior part of the body behind the thorax. ORIG C16: from L; from ?
▸ **abdominal** (æb'dɒmɪnᵊl) *adj*

abduct (æb'dʌkt) *vb* (*tr*) **1** to remove (a person) by force or cunning; kidnap. **2** (of certain muscles) to pull (a leg, arm, etc.) away from the median axis of the body. ORIG C19: from L *abdūcere* to lead away
▸ **ab'duction** *n* ▸ **ab'ductor** *n*

Abdul-Hamid II ★ (ˌæbdʊl'hæmɪd) *n* 1842–1918, sultan of Turkey (1876–1909), deposed by the Young Turks, noted for his brutal suppression of the Armenian revolt (1894–96).

abeam (ə'biːm) *adv, adj* (*postpositive*) at right angles to the length of a vessel or aircraft. ORIG C19: A-[2] + BEAM

abed (ə'bɛd) *adv Arch.* in bed.

Abednego ★ (ə'bɛdnɪˌgəʊ) *n Old Testament.* one of Daniel's three companions who, together with Shadrach and Meshach, was miraculously saved from destruction in Nebuchadnezzar's fiery furnace (Daniel 3:12–30).

Abel ★ ('eɪbᵊl) *n Old Testament.* the second son of Adam and Eve, a shepherd, murdered by his brother Cain (Genesis 4:1–8).

Abelard ★ ('æbəˌlɑːd) *n* **Peter.** French name *Pierre Abélard.* 1079–1142, French philosopher and theologian whose works include *Historia Calamitatum* and *Sic et Non* (1121). His love for Héloïse is recorded in their correspondence.

Abeokuta ★ (ˌæbɪəʊ'kuːtə) *n* a town in W Nigeria, capital of Ogun state. Pop.: 416 800 (1994 est.).

Aberdare ★ (ˌæbə'dɛə) *n* a town in South Wales, in Rhondda, Cynon, Taff county borough. Pop.: 29 040 (1991).

Aberdeen[1] (ˌæbə'diːn) **1** ★ *n* a city in NE Scotland: centre for processing North Sea oil and gas; university (1494). Pop.: 217 260 (1996 est.). **2 City of.** a council area in NE Scotland, established in 1996. Pop.: 219 100 (1995 est.). Area: 186 sq. km (72 sq. miles).
▸ **Aberdonian** (ˌæbə'dəʊnɪən) *n, adj*

Aberdeen[2] ★ (ˌæbə'diːn) *n* **George Hamilton-Gordon,** 4th Earl of. 1784–1860, British statesman. He was foreign secretary under Wellington (1828) and Peel (1841–46); became prime minister of a coalition ministry in 1852 but was compelled to resign after mismanagement of the Crimean War (1855).

Aberdeen Angus *n* a black hornless breed of beef cattle originating in Scotland.

Aberdeenshire ★ (ˌæbə'diːnˌʃɪə, -ʃə) *n* a council area and historic county of N Scotland: part of Grampian region (1975–96); restored as an independent unitary authority (with adjusted borders) in 1996. Administrative centre: Aberdeen. Pop.: 226 260 (1999 est.). Area 6318 sq. km (2439 sq. miles).

Aberfan ★ (ˌæbə'væn) *n* a village in S Wales, in Merthyr Tydfil county borough, formerly a coal-mining village: scene of a disaster in 1966 when a slag heap collapsed onto part of the village killing 144 people (including 116 children).

aberrant (æ'bɛrənt) *adj* **1** deviating from the normal or usual type. **2** behaving in an abnormal or untypical way. **3** deviating from morality. ORIG rare before C19: from L *aberrāre* to wander away
▸ **ab'errance** *or* **ab'errancy** *n*

aberration (ˌæbə'reɪʃən) *n* **1** deviation from what is normal, expected, or usual. **2** departure from truth, morality, etc. **3** a lapse in control of one's mental faculties. **4** *Optics.* a defect in a lens or mirror that causes either a distorted image or one with coloured fringes. **5** *Astron.* the apparent displacement of a celestial body due to the motion of the observer with the earth.

Aberystwyth ★ (ˌæbə'rɪstwɪθ) *n* a resort and university town in Wales, in Ceredigion on Cardigan Bay. Pop.: 11 154 (1991).

abet (ə'bɛt) *vb* **abets, abetting, abetted.** (*tr*) to assist or encourage, esp. in wrongdoing. ORIG C14: from OF *abeter* to lure on, from *beter* to bait
▸ **a'betment** *n* ▸ **a'better** *or* (*esp. Law*) **a'bettor** *n*

abeyance (ə'beɪəns) *n* **1** (usually preceded by *in* or *into*) a state of being suspended or put aside temporarily. **2** (usually preceded by *in*) *Law.* an indeterminate state of ownership. ORIG C16–17: from Anglo-F, from OF *abeance* expectation, lit. a gaping after

ABH *abbrev. for* actual bodily harm.

abhor (əb'hɔː) *vb* **abhors, abhorring, abhorred.** (*tr*) to detest vehemently; find repugnant. ORIG C15: from L *abhorrēre,* from *ab-* away from + *horrēre* to shudder
▸ **ab'horrer** *n*

abhorrence (əb'hɒrəns) *n* **1** a feeling of extreme loathing or aversion. **2** a person or thing that is loathsome.

abhorrent (əb'hɒrənt) *adj* **1** repugnant; loathsome. **2** (when *postpositive*, foll. by *of*) feeling extreme aversion (for): *abhorrent of vulgarity*. **3** (usually *postpositive* and foll. by *to*) conflicting (with): *abhorrent to common sense*.

Abia ★ (æb'iːə) *n* a state of SE Nigeria. Capital: Umuahia. Pop.: 2 569 362 (1995 est.). Area (including Imo state): 11 850 sq. km (4575 sq. miles).

abide (ə'baɪd) *vb* **abides, abiding, abode** *or* **abided. 1** (*tr*) to tolerate; put up with. **2** (*tr*) to accept or submit to. **3** (*intr*; foll. by *by*) **3a** to comply (with): *to abide by the decision*. **3b** to remain faithful (to): *to abide by your promise*. **4** (*intr*) to remain or continue. **5** (*intr*) *Arch.* to dwell. **6** (*tr*) *Arch.* to await in expectation. ORIG OE *ābīdan*, from *a-* (intensive) + *bīdan* to wait
▸ **a'bider** *n*

abiding (ə'baɪdɪŋ) *adj* permanent; enduring: *an abiding belief*.

Abidjan ★ (ˌæbɪ'dʒɑːn; *French* abidʒɑ̃) *n* a port in the Côte d'Ivoire, on the Gulf of Guinea: the legislative capital (Yamoussoukro became the administrative capital in 1983). Pop.: 2 797 000 (1995 est.).

Abigail ★ ('æbɪˌgeɪl) *n Old Testament*. the woman who brought provisions to David and his followers and subsequently became his wife (I Samuel 25:1–42).

ability (ə'bɪlɪtɪ) *n, pl* **abilities. 1** possession of necessary skill, competence, or power. **2** considerable proficiency; natural capability: *a man of ability*. **3** (*pl*) special talents. ORIG C14: from OF from L *habilitās* aptitude, from *habilis* ABLE

Abingdon ★ ('æbɪŋdən) *n* a market town in S England, in Oxfordshire. Pop.: 35 234 (1991).

ab initio *Latin*. (æb ɪ'nɪʃɪˌəʊ) from the start.

abiogenesis (ˌeɪbaɪəʊ'dʒɛnɪsɪs) *n* the hypothetical process by which living organisms arise from inanimate matter. Also called: **spontaneous generation**. ORIG C19: NL, from A-[1] + BIO- + GENESIS

abject ('æbdʒɛkt) *adj* **1** utterly wretched or hopeless. **2** forlorn; dejected. **3** submissive: *an abject apology*. **4** contemptible; despicable: *an abject liar*. ORIG C14 (in the sense: rejected, cast out): from L *abjectus* thrown away, from *abjicere*, from *ab-* away + *jacere* to throw
▸ **ab'jection** *n* ▸ **'abjectly** *adv* ▸ **'abjectness** *n*

abjure (əb'dʒʊə) *vb* **abjures, abjuring, abjured.** (*tr*) **1** to renounce or retract, esp. formally or under oath. **2** to abstain from. ORIG C15: from OF *abjurer* or L *abjurāre* to deny on oath
▸ **ˌabju'ration** *n* ▸ **ab'jurer** *n*

Abkhazia ★ (æb'kɑːzɪə) *n* an administrative division of NW Georgia, between the Black Sea and the Caucasus Mountains: a subtropical region, with narrow coastal lowlands and mountains rising over 3900 m (13 000 ft). Capital: Sukhumi. Pop.: 516 600 (1993 est.). Area: 8600 sq. km (3320 sq. miles). Also called: **Abkhaz Autonomous Republic** ('æbkæz).

ablation (æb'leɪʃən) *n* **1** the surgical removal of an organ, structure, or part. **2** the melting or wearing away of a part, such as the heat shield of a space re-entry vehicle on passing through the earth's atmosphere. **3** the wearing away of a rock or glacier. ORIG C15: from LL *ablatiōn-*, from L *auferre* to carry away
▸ **ablate** (æb'leɪt) *vb*

ablative ('æblətɪv) *Grammar*. ◆ *adj* **1** (in certain inflected languages such as Latin) denoting a case of nouns, pronouns, and adjectives indicating the agent, or the instrument, manner, or place of the action. ◆ *n* **2** the ablative case or a speech element in it.

ablaut ('æblaut) *n Linguistics*. vowel gradation, esp. in Indo-European languages. See **gradation** (sense 5). ORIG G, coined 1819 by Jakob Grimm from *ab* off + *Laut* sound

ablaze (ə'bleɪz) *adj* (*postpositive*), *adv* **1** on fire; burning. **2** brightly illuminated. **3** emotionally aroused.

able ('eɪbᵊl) *adj* **1** (*postpositive*) having the necessary power, resources, skill, opportunity, etc., to do something. **2** capable; talented. **3** *Law*. competent or authorized. ORIG C14: ult. from L *habilis* easy to hold, manageable, from *habēre* to have + *-ilis* -ILE

-able *suffix forming adjectives*. **1** capable of or deserving of (being acted upon as indicated): *enjoyable; washable*. **2** inclined to; able to; causing: *comfortable; variable*. ORIG via OF from L *-ābilis, -ībilis*, forms of *-bilis*, adjectival suffix
▸ **-ably** *suffix forming adverbs*. ▸ **-ability** *suffix forming nouns*.

able-bodied *adj* physically strong and healthy; robust.

able-bodied seaman *n* a seaman, esp. one in the merchant navy, who has been trained in certain skills. Also: **able seaman**. Abbrev.: **AB, a.b.**

abled ('eɪbᵊld) *adj* having a range of physical powers as specified (esp. in **less abled, differently abled**).

ableism ('eɪbᵊlˌɪzəm) *n* discrimination against disabled or handicapped people.

able rating *n* (esp. in the Royal Navy) a rating who is qualified to perform certain duties of seamanship.

abloom (ə'bluːm) *adj* (*postpositive*) in flower; blooming.

ablution (ə'bluːʃən) *n* **1** the ritual washing of a priest's hands or of sacred vessels. **2** (*often pl*) the act of washing: *perform one's ablutions*. **3** (*pl*) *Mil. inf.* a washing place. ORIG C14: ult. from L *ablūere* to wash away
▸ **ab'lutionary** *adj*

ably ('eɪblɪ) *adv* in a competent or skilful manner.

ABM *abbrev. for* antiballistic missile.

abnegate ('æbnɪˌgeɪt) *vb* **abnegates, abnegating, abnegated.** (*tr*) to deny to oneself; renounce. ORIG C17: from L *abnegāre* to deny
▸ **ˌabne'gation** *n* ▸ **'abneˌgator** *n*

abnormal (æb'nɔːməl) *adj* **1** not normal; deviating from the usual or typical. **2** concerned with abnormal behaviour: *abnormal psychology*. **3** *Inf.* odd; strange. ORIG C19: AB-[1] + NORMAL, replacing earlier *anormal* from Med. L *anormalus*, a blend of LL *anōmalus* ANOMALOUS + L *abnormis* departing from a rule
▸ **ab'normally** *adv*

abnormality (ˌæbnɔː'mælɪtɪ) *n, pl* **abnormalities. 1** an abnormal feature, event, etc. **2** a physical malformation. **3** deviation from the usual.

Abo ('æbəʊ) *n, pl* **Abos.** (*sometimes not cap.*) *Austral. inf., often derog.* short for **Aborigine** (sense 1).

Åbo ★ ('oːbuː) *n* the Swedish name for **Turku**.

aboard (ə'bɔːd) *adv, adj* (*postpositive*), *prep* **1** on, in, onto, or into (a ship, train, etc.). **2** *Naut.* alongside. **3 all aboard!** a warning to passengers to board a vehicle, ship, etc.

abode[1] (ə'bəʊd) *n* a place in which one lives; one's home. ORIG C17: n formed from ABIDE

abode[2] (ə'bəʊd) *vb* a past tense and past participle of **abide**.

abolish (ə'bɒlɪʃ) *vb* (*tr*) to do away with (laws, regulations, customs, etc.). ORIG C15: from OF, ult. from L *abolēre* to destroy
▸ **a'bolishable** *adj* ▸ **a'bolisher** *n* ▸ **a'bolishment** *n*

abolition (ˌæbə'lɪʃən) *n* **1** the act of abolishing or the state of being abolished; annulment. **2** (*often cap.*) (in British territories) the ending of the slave trade (1807) or of slavery (1833). **3** (*often cap.*) (in the US) the emancipation of slaves, by the Emancipation Proclamation (1863, ratified 1865). ORIG C16: from L *abolitio*, from *abolēre* to destroy
▸ **ˌabo'litionary** *adj* ▸ **ˌabo'litionism** *n* ▸ **ˌabo'litionist** *n, adj*

abomasum (ˌæbə'meɪsəm) *n* the fourth and last compartment of the stomach of ruminants. ORIG C18: NL, from AB-[1] + *omāsum* bullock's tripe

A-bomb *n* short for **atomic bomb**.

abominable (ə'bɒmɪnəbᵊl) *adj* **1** offensive; loathsome; detestable. **2** *Inf.* very bad or inferior: *abominable workmanship*. ORIG C14: from L, from *abōminārī* to ABOMINATE
▸ **a'bominably** *adv*

abominable snowman *n* a large manlike or apelike creature alleged to inhabit the Himalayas. Also called: **yeti**. ORIG translation of Tibetan *metohkangmi*, from *metoh* foul + *kangmi* snowman

abominate (ə'bɒmɪˌneɪt) *vb* **abominates, abominating,**

abominated. (*tr*) to dislike intensely; detest. ORIG C17: from L *abōminārī* to regard as an ill omen, from *ab-* away from + *ōmin-*, from OMEN
▸ **aˈbomiˌnator** *n*

abomination (əˌbɒmɪˈneɪʃən) *n* **1** a person or thing that is disgusting or loathsome. **2** an action that is vicious, vile, etc. **3** intense loathing or disgust.

aboriginal (ˌæbəˈrɪdʒɪnᵊl) *adj* existing in a place from the earliest known period; indigenous.
▸ **ˌaboˈriginally** *adv*

Aboriginal (ˌæbəˈrɪdʒɪnᵊl) *adj* **1** of, relating to, or characteristic of the native peoples of Australia. ◆ *n* **2** another word for **Aborigine** (sense 1).
▸ **ˌAboˌrigiˈnality** *n*

aborigine (ˌæbəˈrɪdʒɪnɪ) *n* an original inhabitant of a country or region. ORIG C16: back formation from *aborigines*, from L: inhabitants of Latium in pre-Roman times, associated in folk etymology with *ab origine* from the beginning

Aborigine (ˌæbəˈrɪdʒɪnɪ) *n* **1** Also called: **native Australian, Aboriginal.** a member of a dark-skinned hunting and gathering people who were living in Australia when European settlers arrived. **2** any of the languages of this people.

abort (əˈbɔːt) *vb* **1** to undergo or cause (a woman) to undergo the termination of pregnancy before the fetus is viable. **2** (*tr*) to cause (a fetus) to be expelled from the womb before it is viable. **3** (*intr*) to fail to come to completion. **4** (*tr*) to stop the development of; cause to be abandoned. **5** (*intr*) to give birth to a dead or nonviable fetus. **6** (of a space flight or other undertaking) to fail or terminate prematurely. **7** (*intr*) (of an organism or part of an organism) to fail to develop into the mature form. ◆ *n* **8** the premature termination or failure of (a space flight, etc.). ORIG C16: from L *abortāre*, from *aborīrī* to miscarry, from *ab-* wrongly + *orīrī* to be born

abortifacient (əˌbɔːtɪˈfeɪʃənt) *adj* **1** causing abortion. ◆ *n* **2** a drug or agent that causes abortion.

abortion (əˈbɔːʃən) *n* **1** an operation or other procedure to terminate pregnancy before the fetus is viable. **2** the premature termination of pregnancy by spontaneous or induced expulsion of a nonviable fetus from the uterus. **3** an aborted fetus. **4** a failure to develop to completion or maturity. **5** a person or thing that is deformed.

abortionist (əˈbɔːʃənɪst) *n* a person who performs abortions, esp. illegally.

abortion pill *n* a drug, such as mifepristone (Mifegyne), used to terminate a pregnancy in its earliest stage.

abortive (əˈbɔːtɪv) *adj* **1** failing to achieve a purpose; fruitless. **2** (of organisms) imperfectly developed. **3** causing abortion.

ABO system *n* a system for classifying human blood on the basis of the presence or absence of two antigens in the red cells: there are four such blood types (A, B, AB, and O).

Aboukir Bay *or* **Abukir Bay** ★ (ˌæbuːˈkɪə) *n* a bay on the N coast of Egypt, where the Nile enters the Mediterranean: site of the Battle of the Nile (1798), in which Nelson defeated the French fleet. Arabic name: **Abu Qîr** (abuˈkiːr).

aboulia (əˈbuːlɪə, -ˈbjuː-) *n* a variant spelling of **abulia.**

abound (əˈbaʊnd) *vb* (*intr*) **1** to exist or occur in abundance. **2** (foll. by *with* or *in*) to be plentifully supplied (with): *the fields abound in corn.* ORIG C14: via OF from L *abundāre* to overflow, from *undāre* to flow, from *unda* wave

about (əˈbaʊt) *prep* **1** relating to; concerning. **2** near or close to. **3** carried on: *I haven't any money about me.* **4** on every side of. **5** active in or engaged in. ◆ *adv* **6** near in number, time, degree, etc.: *about 50 years old.* **7** nearby. **8** here and there: *walk about to keep warm.* **9** all around; on every side. **10** in or to the opposite direction. **11** in rotation or revolution: *turn and turn about.* **12** used in informal phrases to indicate understatement: *it's about time you stopped.* **13** *Arch.* around. **14 about to. 14a** on the point of; intending to: *she was about to jump.* **14b** (*with a negative*) determined not to: *nobody is about to miss it.* ◆ *adj* **15** (*predicative*) active; astir after sleep: *up and about.* **16** (*predicative*) in existence, current, or in circulation: *there aren't many about nowadays.* ORIG OE *abūtan, onbūtan*, from ON + *būtan* outside

about turn *or US* **about face** *sentence substitute.* **1** a military command to a formation of men to reverse the direction in which they are facing. ◆ *n* **about-turn** *or US* **about-face. 2** a complete change of opinion, direction, etc. ◆ *vb* **about-turn** *or US* **about-face. 3** (*intr*) to perform an about-turn.

above (əˈbʌv) *prep* **1** on top of or higher than; over. **2** greater than in quantity or degree: *above average.* **3** superior to or prior to: *to place honour above wealth.* **4** too high-minded for: *above petty gossiping.* **5** too respected for; beyond: *above suspicion.* **6** too difficult to be understood by: *the talk was above me.* **7** louder or higher than (other noise). **8** in preference to. **9** north of. **10** upstream from. **11 above all.** most of all; especially. **12 above and beyond.** in addition to. ◆ *adv* **13** in or to a higher place: *the sky above.* **14a** in a previous place (in something written). **14b** (*in combination*): *the above-mentioned clause.* **15** higher in rank or position. **16** in or concerned with heaven. ◆ *n* **17 the above.** something previously mentioned. ◆ *adj* **18** appearing in a previous place (in something written). ORIG OE *abufan*, from *a-* on + *bufan* above

above board *adj* (**aboveboard** *when prenominal*), *adv* in the open; without dishonesty, concealment, or fraud.

abracadabra (ˌæbrəkəˈdæbrə) *interj* **1** a spoken formula, used esp. by conjurors. ◆ *n* **2** a word used in incantations, etc., considered to possess magic powers. **3** gibberish. ORIG C17: magical word used in certain Gnostic writings, ? rel. to Gk *Abraxas*, a Gnostic deity

abrade (əˈbreɪd) *vb* **abrades, abrading, abraded.** (*tr*) to scrape away or wear down by friction. ORIG C17: from L *abrādere*, from AB-[1] + *rādere* to scrape
▸ **aˈbrader** *n*

Abraham ★ (ˈeɪbrəˌhæm, -həm) *n* **1** *Old Testament.* the first of the patriarchs, the father of Isaac and the founder of the Hebrew people (Genesis 11–25). **2 Abraham's bosom.** the place where the just repose after death (Luke 16:22).

abranchiate (əˈbræŋkɪɪt, -ˌeɪt) *or* **abranchial** *adj Zool.* having no gills. ORIG C19: A-[1] + BRANCHIATE

abrasion (əˈbreɪʒən) *n* **1** the process of scraping or wearing down by friction. **2** a scraped area or spot; graze. **3** *Geog.* the effect of mechanical erosion of rock, esp. a river bed, by rock fragments scratching and scraping it. ORIG C17: from Med. L *abrāsiōn-*, from L *abrādere* to ABRADE

abrasive (əˈbreɪsɪv) *n* **1** a substance or material such as sandpaper, pumice, or emery, used for cleaning, smoothing, or polishing. ◆ *adj* **2** causing abrasion; rough. **3** irritating in manner or personality.

abreaction (ˌæbrɪˈækʃən) *n Psychoanal.* the release and expression of emotional tension associated with repressed ideas by bringing those ideas into consciousness.

abreast (əˈbrɛst) *adj* (*postpositive*) **1** alongside each other and facing in the same direction. **2** (foll. by *of* or *with*) up to date (with).

abridge (əˈbrɪdʒ) *vb* **abridges, abridging, abridged.** (*tr*) **1** to reduce the length of (a written work) by condensing. **2** to curtail. ORIG C14: via OF *abregier* from LL *abbreviāre* to shorten
▸ **aˈbridgable** *or* **aˈbridgeable** *adj* ▸ **aˈbridger** *n*

abridgment *or* **abridgement** (əˈbrɪdʒmənt) *n* **1** a shortened version of a written work. **2** the act of abridging or state of being abridged.

abroad (əˈbrɔːd) *adv, adj* (*postpositive*). **1** to or in a foreign country or countries. **2** (of rumours, etc.) in general circulation. **3** out in the open. **4** over a wide area. ORIG C13: from A-[2] + BROAD

abrogate (ˈæbrəʊˌgeɪt) *vb* **abrogates, abrogating, abrogated.** (*tr*) to cancel or revoke formally or officially. ORIG C16: from L *abrogātus* repealed, from AB-[1] + *rogāre* to propose (a law)
▸ **ˌabroˈgation** *n* ▸ **ˈabroˌgator** *n*

USAGE NOTE *Abrogate* is sometimes confused with *arrogate.* This pair of words have almost op-

★ people and places

posite meanings, *abrogate* meaning 'to get rid of' and *arrogate* meaning 'to acquire unjustifiably', as in *the State arrogated to itself more powers*. To use *abrogate* in this kind of context is incorrect, though it does occasionally happen. *Abrogate* is about four times more common in the Bank of English than *arrogate*, so the error may be due to people tending to associate this meaning mistakenly with the word they know better. The mistake does not seem to occur the other way round.

abrupt (ə'brʌpt) *adj* **1** sudden; unexpected. **2** brusque or brief in speech, manner, etc. **3** (of a style of writing or speaking) disconnected. **4** precipitous; steep. **5** *Bot.* truncate. **6** *Geol.* (of strata) cropping out suddenly. ORIG C16: from L *abruptus* broken off, from AB-[1] + *rumpere* to break
▸ **ab'ruptly** *adv* ▸ **ab'ruptness** *n*

Abruzzi ★ (*Italian* a'bruttsi) *n* a region of S central Italy, between the Apennines and the Adriatic: separated from the former administrative region **Abruzzi e Molise** in 1965. Capital: Aquila. Pop.: 1 270 591 (1996 est.). Area: 10 794 sq. km (4210 sq. miles).

Absalom ★ ('æbsələm) *n Old Testament.* the third son of David, who rebelled against his father and was eventually killed by Joab (II Samuel 15–18).

ABS brake *n* another name for **antilock brake.** ORIG from G *Antiblockiersystem*

abscess ('æbsɛs) *n* **1** a localized collection of pus formed as the product of inflammation. ◆ *vb* **2** (*intr*) to form such a collection of pus. ORIG C16: from L *abscessus,* from *abscēdere* to go away
▸ **'abscessed** *adj*

abscissa (æb'sɪsə) *n, pl* **abscissas** *or* **abscissae** (-'sɪsiː). the horizontal or *x*-coordinate of a point in a two-dimensional system of Cartesian coordinates. It is the distance from the *y*-axis measured parallel to the *x*-axis. Cf. **ordinate.** ORIG C17: NL, orig. *linea abscissa* a cut-off line

abscission (æb'sɪʒən) *n* **1** the separation of leaves, branches, flowers, and bark from plants. **2** the act of cutting off. ORIG C17: from L, from AB-[1] + *scissiō* a cleaving

abscond (əb'skɒnd) *vb* (*intr*) to run away secretly, esp. to avoid prosecution or punishment. ORIG C16: from L *abscondere,* from *abs-* AB-[1] + *condere* to stow
▸ **ab'sconder** *n*

abseil ('æbsaɪl) *Mountaineering.* ◆ *vb* (*intr*) **1** to descend a steep slope or vertical drop by a rope secured from above and coiled around one's body. ◆ *n* **2** an instance or the technique of abseiling. ORIG C20: from G *abseilen,* from *ab-* down + *Seil* rope

absence ('æbsəns) *n* **1** the state of being away. **2** the time during which a person or thing is away. **3** the fact of being without something; lack. ORIG C14: via OF from L *absentia,* from *absēns* a being away

absent *adj* ('æbsənt). **1** away or not present. **2** lacking. **3** inattentive. ◆ *vb* (æb'sɛnt). **4** (*tr*) to remove (oneself) or keep away. ORIG C14: from L *absent-,* from *abesse* to be away
▸ **ab'senter** *n*

absentee (ˌæbsən'tiː) *n* **a** a person who is absent. **b** (*as modifier*): *an absentee landlord.*

absenteeism (ˌæbsən'tiːɪzəm) *n* persistent absence from work, school, etc.

absent-minded *adj* preoccupied; forgetful.
▸ **ˌabsent-'mindedly** *adv* ▸ **ˌabsent-'mindedness** *n*

absinthe *or* **absinth** ('æbsɪnθ) *n* **1** a potent green alcoholic drink, originally having high wormwood content. **2** another name for **wormwood** (the plant). ORIG C15: via F and L from Gk *apsinthion* wormwood

absolute ('æbsəˌluːt) *adj* **1** complete; perfect. **2** free from limitations, restrictions, or exceptions. **3** despotic: *an absolute ruler.* **4** undoubted; certain: *the absolute truth.* **5** not dependent on, conditioned by, or relative to anything else; independent: *absolute humidity; absolute units.* **6** pure; unmixed: *absolute alcohol.* **7** (of a grammatical construction) syntactically independent of the main clause, as for example the construction *Joking apart* in the sentence *Joking apart, we'd better leave now.* **8** *Grammar.* (of a transitive verb) used without a direct object, as the verb *intimidate* in the sentence *His intentions are good, but his rough manner tends to intimidate.* **9** *Grammar.* (of an adjective) used as a noun, as for instance *young* and *aged* in the sentence *The young care little for the aged.* ◆ *n* **10** something that is absolute. ORIG C14: from L *absolūtus* unconditional, from *absolvere.* See ABSOLVE

Absolute ('æbsəˌluːt) *n* (*sometimes not cap.*) *Philosophy.* **1** the ultimate basis of reality. **2** that which is totally unconditioned, unrestricted, pure, perfect, or complete.

absolutely (ˌæbsə'luːtlɪ) *adv* **1** in an absolute manner, esp. completely or perfectly. ◆ *sentence substitute.* **2** yes; certainly.

absolute magnitude *n* the magnitude a given star would have if it were 10 parsecs (32.6 light years) from earth.

absolute majority *n* a number of votes totalling over 50 per cent, such as the total number of votes or seats obtained by a party that beats the combined opposition.

absolute pitch *n* **1** Also called: **perfect pitch.** the ability to identify the pitch of a note, or to sing a given note, without reference to one previously sounded. **2** the exact pitch of a note determined by vibration per second.

absolute temperature *n* another name for **thermodynamic temperature.**

absolute value *n* **1** the positive real number equal to a given real but disregarding its sign: written $|x|$. Where x is positive, $|x| = x = |-x|$. **2** Also called: **modulus.** a measure of the magnitude of a complex number.

absolute zero *n* the lowest temperature theoretically attainable, at which the particles constituting matter would be at rest: equivalent to –273.15°C or –459.67°F.

absolution (ˌæbsə'luːʃən) *n* **1** the act of absolving or the state of being absolved; release from guilt, obligation, or punishment. **2** *Christianity.* **2a** a formal remission of sin pronounced by a priest in the sacrament of penance. **2b** the form of words granting such a remission. ORIG C12: from L *absolūtiōn-* acquittal, from *absolvere* to ABSOLVE

absolutism ('æbsəluːˌtɪzəm) *n* the principle or practice of a political system in which unrestricted power is vested in a monarch, dictator, etc.; despotism.
▸ **abso'lutist** *n, adj*

absolve (əb'zɒlv) *vb* **absolves, absolving, absolved.** (*tr*) **1** (usually foll. by *from*) to release from blame, sin, obligation, or responsibility. **2** to pronounce not guilty. ORIG C15: from L *absolvere,* from AB-[1] + *solvere* to make loose
▸ **ab'solver** *n*

absorb (əb'sɔːb) *vb* (*tr*) **1** to soak or suck up (liquids). **2** to engage or occupy (the interest or time) of (someone). **3** to receive or take in (the energy of an impact). **4** *Physics.* to take in (all or part of incident radiated energy) and retain it. **5** to take in or assimilate; incorporate. **6** to pay for as part of a commercial transaction: *the distributor absorbed the cost of transport.* **7** *Chem.* to cause to undergo a process in which one substance permeates into or is dissolved by a liquid or solid: *porous solids absorb water.* ORIG C15: via OF from L *absorbēre,* from AB-[1] + *sorbēre* to suck
▸ **abˌsorba'bility** *n* ▸ **ab'sorbable** *adj*

absorbed (əb'sɔːbd) *adj* engrossed; deeply interested.

absorbed dose *n* the amount of energy transferred by radiation to a unit mass of absorbing material.

absorbent (əb'sɔːbənt) *adj* **1** able to absorb. ◆ *n* **2** a substance that absorbs.
▸ **ab'sorbency** *n*

absorbing (əb'sɔːbɪŋ) *adj* occupying one's interest or attention.
▸ **ab'sorbingly** *adv*

absorptance (əb'sɔːptəns) *or* **absorption factor** *n* *Physics.* the ability of an object to absorb radiation, measured as the ratio of absorbed flux to incident flux. ORIG C20: from ABSORPTION + -ANCE

absorption (əb'sɔːpʃən) *n* **1** the process of absorbing or

the state of being absorbed. **2** *Physiol.* **2a** normal assimilation by the tissues of the products of digestion. **2b** the process of taking up various fluids, drugs, etc., through the mucous membranes or skin. ORIG C16: from L *absorptiōn-*, from *absorbēre* to ABSORB
▸ **ab'sorptive** *adj*

absorption spectrum *n* the characteristic pattern of dark lines or bands that occurs when electromagnetic radiation is passed through an absorbing medium into a spectroscope. See also **emission spectrum.**

abstain (əb'steɪn) *vb* (*intr;* usually foll. by *from*) **1** to choose to refrain. **2** to refrain from voting, esp. in a committee, legislature, etc. ORIG C14: via OF from L *abstinēre*, from *abs-* AB-[1] + *tenēre* to hold
▸ **ab'stainer** *n*

abstemious (əb'sti:mɪəs) *adj* sparing, esp. in the consumption of alcohol or food. ORIG C17: from L *abstēmius*, from *abs-* AB-[1] + *tēm-*, from *tēmētum* intoxicating drink
▸ **ab'stemiously** *adv* ▸ **ab'stemiousness** *n*

abstention (əb'stɛnʃən) *n* **1** the act of refraining or abstaining. **2** the act of withholding one's vote. ORIG C16: from LL *abstentiōn;* see ABSTAIN

abstinence ('æbstɪnəns) *n* the act or practice of refraining from some action or from the use of something, esp. alcohol. ORIG C13: via OF from L *abstinentia*, from *abstinēre* to ABSTAIN
▸ **'abstinent** *adj*

abstract *adj* ('æbstrækt). **1** having no reference to material objects or specific examples. **2** not applied or practical; theoretical. **3** hard to understand. **4** denoting art characterized by geometric, formalized, or otherwise nonrepresentational qualities. ◆ *n* ('æbstrækt). **5** a condensed version of a piece of writing, speech, etc.; summary. **6** an abstract term or idea. **7** an abstract painting, sculpture, etc. **8 in the abstract.** without reference to specific circumstances. ◆ *vb* (æb'strækt). (*tr*) **9** to regard theoretically. **10** to form a general idea of (something) by abstraction. **11** ('æbstrækt). (*also intr*) to summarize. **12** to remove or extract. ORIG C14 (in the sense: extracted): from L *abstractus* drawn off, from *abs-* AB-[1] + *trahere* to draw

abstracted (æb'stræktɪd) *adj* **1** lost in thought; preoccupied. **2** taken out or separated.
▸ **ab'stractedly** *adv*

abstract expressionism *n* a school of painting in the 1940s that combined the spontaneity of expressionism with abstract forms in apparently random compositions.

abstraction (æb'strækʃən) *n* **1** preoccupation. **2** the process of formulating generalized concepts by extracting common qualities from specific examples. **3** a concept formulated in this way: *good and evil are abstractions.* **4** an abstract painting, sculpture, etc.
▸ **ab'stractive** *adj*

abstract noun *n* a noun that refers to an abstract concept, as for example *peace, joy,* etc.

abstract term *n* in traditional logic, the name of an attribute of many individuals: *humanity is an abstract term.*

abstruse (əb'stru:s) *adj* not easy to understand. ORIG C16: from L *abstrūsus*, from *abs-* AB-[1] + *trūdere* to thrust
▸ **ab'strusely** *adv* ▸ **ab'struseness** *n*

absurd (əb'sɜ:d) *adj* **1** at variance with reason; manifestly false. **2** ludicrous; ridiculous. ORIG C16: via F from L *absurdus*, from AB-[1] (intensive) + *surdus* dull-sounding
▸ **ab'surdity** *or* **ab'surdness** *n* ▸ **ab'surdly** *adv*

ABTA ('æbtə) *n acronym for* Association of British Travel Agents.

Abu Dhabi ★ ('æbu: 'dɑ:bɪ) *n* a sheikhdom (emirate) of SE Arabia, on the S coast of the Persian Gulf: the chief sheikhdom and capital of the United Arab Emirates, consisting principally of the port of Abu Dhabi and a desert hinterland; contains major oilfields. Pop.: 871 000 (1993). Area: 67 350 sq. km (25 998 sq. miles).

Abuja ★ (ə'bu:dʒə) *n* the federal capital of Nigeria: the seat of government since 1991. Pop.: 339 100 (1995 est.).

Abukir Bay ★ (ˌæbu:'kɪə) *n* a variant spelling of **Aboukir Bay.**

abulia *or* **aboulia** (ə'bu:lɪə, -'bju:-) *n Psychiatry.* a pathological inability to take decisions. ORIG C19: NL, from Gk *aboulia* lack of resolution, from A-[1] + *boulē* will

abundance (ə'bʌndəns) *n* **1** a copious supply; great amount. **2** fullness or benevolence: *from the abundance of my heart.* **3** degree of plentifulness: *the abundance of uranium-235 in natural uranium.* **4** Also: **abondance.** a call in solo whist undertaking to make nine tricks. **5** affluence. ORIG C14: via OF from L, from *abundāre* to ABOUND

abundant (ə'bʌndənt) *adj* **1** existing in plentiful supply. **2** (*postpositive;* foll. by *in*) having a plentiful supply (of). ORIG C14: from L *abundant-*, p.p. of *abundāre* to ABOUND
▸ **a'bundantly** *adv*

abuse *vb* (ə'bju:z), **abuses, abusing, abused.** (*tr*) **1** to use incorrectly or improperly; misuse. **2** to maltreat, esp. physically or sexually. **3** to speak insultingly or cruelly to. ◆ *n* (ə'bju:s). **4** improper, incorrect, or excessive use. **5** maltreatment of a person; injury. **6** insulting or coarse speech. **7** an evil, unjust, or corrupt practice. **8** See **child abuse. 9** *Arch.* a deception. ORIG C14 (vb): via OF from L *abūsus*, p.p. of *abūtī* to misuse, from AB-[1] + *ūtī* to USE
▸ **a'buser** *n*

Abu Simbel ★ (ˌæbu: 'sɪmbᵊl) *n* a former village in S Egypt: site of two temples of Rameses II, which were moved to higher ground (1966–67) before the area behind the Aswan High Dam was flooded. Also called: **Ipsambul.**

abusive (ə'bju:sɪv) *adj* **1** characterized by insulting or coarse language. **2** characterized by maltreatment. **3** incorrectly used.
▸ **a'busively** *adv* ▸ **a'busiveness** *n*

abut (ə'bʌt) *vb* **abuts, abutting, abutted.** (usually foll. by *on, upon,* or *against*) to adjoin, touch, or border on (something) at one end. ORIG C15: from OF *abouter* to join at the ends; infl. by *abuter* to touch at an end

abutment (ə'bʌtmənt) *or* **abuttal** *n* **1** the state or process of abutting. **2a** something that abuts. **2b** the thing on which something abuts. **2c** the point of junction between them. **3** a construction that supports the end of a bridge.

abutter (ə'bʌtə) *n Property law.* the owner of adjoining property.

abuzz (ə'bʌz) *adj* (*postpositive*) humming, as with conversation, activity, etc.; buzzing.

Abydos ★ (ə'baɪdəs) *n* **1** an ancient town in central Egypt: site of many temples and tombs. **2** an ancient Greek colony on the Asiatic side of the Dardanelles (Hellespont): scene of the legend of Hero and Leander.

abysm (ə'bɪzəm) *n* an archaic word for **abyss.** ORIG C13: via OF from Med. L *abysmus* ABYSS

abysmal (ə'bɪzməl) *adj* **1** immeasurable; very great. **2** *Inf.* extremely bad.
▸ **a'bysmally** *adv*

abyss (ə'bɪs) *n* **1** a very deep gorge or chasm. **2** anything that appears to be endless or immeasurably deep, such as time, despair, or shame. **3** hell. ORIG C16: via LL from Gk *abussos* bottomless, from A-[1] + *bussos* depth

abyssal (ə'bɪsəl) *adj* **1** of or relating to an abyss. **2** of or belonging to the ocean depths, esp. below 2000 metres (6500 ft): *abyssal zone.*

Abyssinia ★ (ˌæbɪ'sɪnɪə) *n* a former name for **Ethiopia.**
▸ **ˌAbys'sinian** *adj, n*

Ac *the chemical symbol for* actinium.

AC *abbrev. for:* **1** Air Corps. **2** alternating current. Cf. **DC. 3** ante Christum. ORIG L: before Christ **4** athletic club. **5** Companion of the Order of Australia.

a/c *Book-keeping. abbrev. for:* **1** account. **2** account current.

acacia (ə'keɪʃə) *n* **1** a tropical or subtropical shrub or tree, having small yellow or white flowers. In Australia, the term is applied esp. to the wattle. **2 false acacia.** another name for **locust** (senses 2, 3). **3 gum acacia.** another name for **gum arabic.** ORIG C16: from L, from Gk *akakia,* ? rel. to *akē* point

academe ('ækəˌdi:m) *n Literary.* any place of learning, such as a college or university. ORIG C16: first used by Shakespeare in *Love's Labour's Lost* (1594); see ACADEMY

academic (ˌækəˈdɛmɪk) *adj* **1** belonging or relating to a place of learning, esp. a college, university, or academy. **2** of purely theoretical or speculative interest. **3** (esp. of pupils) having an aptitude for study. **4** excessively concerned with intellectual matters. **5** conforming to set rules and traditions: *an academic painter.* **6** relating to studies such as languages and pure science rather than technical, applied, or professional studies. ◆ *n* **7** a member of a college or university.
▸ **ˌacaˈdemically** *adv*

academician (əˌkædəˈmɪʃən) *n* a member of an academy (senses 1, 2).

academy (əˈkædəmɪ) *n, pl* **academies. 1** an institution or society for the advancement of literature, art, or science. **2** a school for training in a particular skill or profession: *a military academy.* **3** a secondary school, esp. in Scotland: now only used as part of a name. ORIG C16: via L from Gk *akadēmeia* the grove where Plato taught, named after the legendary hero *Akadēmos*
▸ **ˌacaˈdemical** *adj*

Academy Award *n* the official name for an **Oscar.**

Acadia ★ (əˈkeɪdɪə) *n* **1a** the Atlantic Provinces of Canada. **1b** the French-speaking areas of these provinces. **2** (formerly) a French colony in the present-day Atlantic Provinces: ceded to Britain in 1713. ◆ French name: **Acadie** (akadi).
▸ **Aˈcadian** *adj, n*

acanthus (əˈkænθəs) *n, pl* **acanthuses** *or* **acanthi** (-θaɪ). **1** a shrub or herbaceous plant, native to the Mediterranean region but widely cultivated as an ornamental plant, having large spiny leaves and spikes of white or purplish flowers. **2** a carved ornament based on the leaves of the acanthus plant, esp. as used on the capital of a Corinthian column. ORIG C17: NL, from Gk *akanthos,* from *akantha* thorn, spine

a cappella (ɑː kəˈpɛlə) *adj, adv Music.* without instrumental accompaniment. ORIG It.: lit., according to (the style of the) chapel

Acapulco ★ (ˌækəˈpʊlkəʊ; *Spanish* akaˈpulko) *n* a port and resort in SW Mexico, in Guerrero state. Pop.: 515 374 (1990). Official name: **Acapulco de Juárez** (*Spanish* de ˈxwares).

acariasis (ˌækəˈraɪəsɪs) *n* infestation with mites or ticks. ORIG C19: NL: see ACARID, -IASIS

acarid (ˈækərɪd) *or* **acaridan** (əˈkærɪdᵊn) *n* any of an order of small arachnids that includes the ticks and mites. ORIG C19: from Gk *akari* a small thing, mite

acarpous (eɪˈkɑːpəs) *adj* (of plants) producing no fruit. ORIG from Gk *akarpos,* from A-[1] + *karpos* fruit

ACAS *or* **Acas** (ˈeɪkæs) *n* (in Britain) *acronym for* Advisory Conciliation and Arbitration Service.

acc. *abbrev. for:* **1** accompanied. **2** according. **3** *Bookkeeping.* account. **4** *Grammar.* accusative.

Accad ★ (ˈækæd) *n* a variant spelling of **Akkad.**

accede (ækˈsiːd) *vb* **accedes, acceding, acceded.** (*intr;* usually foll. by *to*) **1** to assent or give one's consent. **2** to enter upon or attain (to an office, right, etc.): *the prince acceded to the throne.* **3** *International law.* to become a party (to an agreement between nations, etc.). ORIG C15: from L *accēdere,* from *ad-* to + *cēdere* to yield
▸ **acˈcedence** *n*

accelerando (ækˌsɛləˈrændəʊ) *adj, adv Music.* (to be performed) with increasing speed. ORIG It.

accelerate (ækˈsɛləˌreɪt) *vb* **accelerates, accelerating, accelerated. 1** to go, occur, or cause to go or occur more quickly; speed up. **2** (*tr*) to cause to happen sooner than expected. **3** (*tr*) to increase the velocity of (a body, reaction, etc.). ORIG C16: from L *accelerātus,* from *accelerāre,* from *ad-* (intensive) + *celerāre* to hasten, from *celer* swift
▸ **acˈcelerative** *adj*

acceleration (ækˌsɛləˈreɪʃən) *n* **1** the act of accelerating or the state of being accelerated. **2** the rate of increase of speed or the rate of change of velocity. **3** the power to accelerate.

acceleration of free fall *n* the acceleration of a body falling freely in a vacuum in the earth's gravitational field. Symbol: *g* Also called: **acceleration due to gravity.**

accelerator (ækˈsɛləˌreɪtə) *n* **1** a device for increasing speed, esp. a pedal for controlling the fuel intake in a motor vehicle; throttle. **2** *Physics.* a machine for increasing the kinetic energy of subatomic particles or atomic nuclei. **3** Also: **accelerant.** *Chem.* a substance that increases the speed of a chemical reaction; catalyst.

accelerometer (ækˌsɛləˈrɒmɪtə) *n* an instrument for measuring acceleration, esp. of an aircraft or rocket.

accent *n* (ˈæksənt). **1** the characteristic mode of pronunciation of a person or group, esp. one that betrays social or geographical origin. **2** the relative prominence of a spoken or sung syllable, esp. with regard to stress or pitch. **3** a mark (such as ˈ , ˌ , ˊ, or ˋ) used in writing to indicate the stress or prominence of a syllable. **4** any of various marks or symbols conventionally used in writing certain languages to indicate the quality of a vowel. See **acute** (sense 8), **grave**[2] (sense 5), **circumflex. 5** rhythmic stress in verse or prose. **6** *Music.* **6a** stress placed on certain notes in a piece of music, indicated by a symbol printed over the note concerned. **6b** the rhythmic pulse of a piece or passage, usually represented as the stress on the first beat of each bar. **7** a distinctive characteristic of anything, such as taste, pattern, style, etc. **8** particular attention or emphasis: *an accent on learning.* **9** a strongly contrasting detail. ◆ *vb* (ækˈsɛnt). (*tr*) **10** to mark with an accent in writing, speech, music, etc. **11** to lay particular emphasis or stress on. ORIG C14: via OF from L *accentus,* from *ad-* to + *cantus* chant

accentor (ækˈsɛntə) *n* a small sparrow-like songbird, which inhabits mainly mountainous regions of Europe and Asia. See also **hedge sparrow.**

accentual (ækˈsɛntʃʊəl) *adj* **1** of, relating to, or having accents; rhythmic. **2** *Prosody.* of or relating to verse based on the number of stresses in a line.
▸ **acˈcentually** *adv*

accentuate (ækˈsɛntʃʊˌeɪt) *vb* **accentuates, accentuating, accentuated.** (*tr*) to stress or emphasize.
▸ **acˌcentuˈation** *n*

accept (əkˈsɛpt) *vb* (*mainly tr*) **1** to take or receive (something offered). **2** to give an affirmative reply to. **3** to take on the responsibilities, duties, etc., of: *he accepted office.* **4** to tolerate. **5** to consider as true or believe in (a philosophy, theory, etc.). **6** (*may take a clause as object*) to be willing to believe: *you must accept that he lied.* **7** to receive with approval or admit, as into a community, group, etc. **8** *Commerce.* to agree to pay (a bill, draft, etc.). **9** to receive as adequate or valid. ORIG C14: from L *acceptāre,* from *ad-* to + *capere* to take
▸ **acˈcepter** *n*

acceptable (əkˈsɛptəbᵊl) *adj* **1** satisfactory; adequate. **2** pleasing; welcome. **3** tolerable.
▸ **acˌceptaˈbility** *or* **acˈceptableness** *n* ▸ **acˈceptably** *adv*

acceptance (əkˈsɛptəns) *n* **1** the act of accepting or the state of being accepted or acceptable. **2** favourable reception. **3** (often foll. by *of*) belief (in) or assent (to). **4** *Commerce.* a formal agreement by a debtor to pay a draft, bill, etc. **5** (*pl*) *Austral. & NZ.* a list of horses accepted as starters in a race.

acceptation (ˌæksɛpˈteɪʃən) *n* the accepted meaning, as of a word, phrase, etc.

accepted (əkˈsɛptɪd) *adj* commonly approved or recognized; customary; established.

acceptor (əkˈsɛptə) *n* **1** *Commerce.* the person or organization on which a draft or bill of exchange is drawn. **2** *Electronics.* an impurity, such as gallium, added to a semiconductor material to increase its p-type semiconductivity.

access (ˈæksɛs) *n* **1** the act of approaching or entering. **2** the condition of allowing entry, esp. (of a building, etc.) entry by prams, wheelchairs, etc. **3** the right or privilege to approach, enter, or make use of something. **4** a way or means of approach or entry. **5** the opportunity or right to see or approach someone: *my ex-wife sabotages my access to the children.* **6** (*modifier*) designating programmes made by the general public: *access television.* **7** a sudden outburst or attack, as of rage or disease. ◆ *vb* (*tr*) **8** *Com-*

puting. **8a** to obtain or retrieve (information) from a storage device. **8b** to place (information) in a storage device. **9** to gain access to; make accessible or available. ORIG C14: from OF or from L *accessus,* from *accēdere* to ACCEDE

accessible (ək'sɛsəbᵊl) *adj* **1** easy to approach, enter, or use. **2 accessible to.** likely to be affected by. **3** obtainable; available.
▸ **ac,cessi'bility** *n*

accession (ək'sɛʃən) *n* **1** the act of attaining to an office, right, condition, etc. **2** an increase due to an addition. **3** an addition, as to a collection. **4** *Property law.* an addition to land or property by natural increase or improvement. **5** *International law.* the formal acceptance of a convention or treaty. **6** agreement. ◆ *vb* **7** (*tr*) to make a record of (additions to a collection).
▸ **ac'cessional** *adj*

accessory (ək'sɛsərɪ) *n, pl* **accessories. 1** a supplementary part or object, as of a car, appliance, etc. **2** (*often pl*) a small accompanying item of dress, esp. of women's dress. **3** (formerly) a person involved in a crime although absent during its commission. ◆ *adj* **4** supplementary; additional. **5** assisting in or having knowledge of an act, esp. a crime. ORIG C17: from LL *accessōrius*: see ACCESS
▸ **accessorial** (,æksɛ'sɔːrɪəl) *adj* ▸ **ac'cessorily** *adv*

access road *n* a road giving entry to a region or, esp., a motorway.

access time *n Computing.* the time required to retrieve a piece of stored information.

acciaccatura (ə,tʃækə'tʊərə) *n, pl* **acciaccaturas** *or* **acciaccature** (-reɪ). a small grace note melodically adjacent to a principal note and played simultaneously with or immediately before it. ORIG C18: It.: lit., a crushing sound

accidence ('æksɪdəns) *n* the part of grammar concerned with changes in the form of words for the expression of tense, person, case, number, etc. ORIG C15: from L *accidentia* accidental matters, from *accidere* to happen. See ACCIDENT

accident ('æksɪdənt) *n* **1** an unforeseen event or one without an apparent cause. **2** anything that occurs unintentionally or by chance: *I met him by accident.* **3** a misfortune or mishap, esp. one causing injury or death. **4** *Geol.* a surface irregularity in a natural formation. ORIG C14: via OF from L *accident-,* from the p.p. of *accidere* to happen, from *ad-* to + *cadere* to fall

accidental (,æksɪ'dɛntᵊl) *adj* **1** occurring by chance, unexpectedly, or unintentionally. **2** nonessential; incidental. **3** *Music.* denoting sharps, flats, or naturals that are not in the key signature of a piece. ◆ *n* **4** an incidental or supplementary circumstance, factor, or attribute. **5** *Music.* a symbol denoting a sharp, flat, or natural that is not a part of the key signature.
▸ **,acci'dentally** *adv*

accident-prone *adj* liable to become involved in accidents.

accidie ('æksɪdɪ) *or* **acedia** *n* spiritual sloth; apathy; indifference. ORIG in use C13 to C16 and revived C19: via LL from Gk *akēdia,* from A-[1] + *kēdos* care

accipiter (æk'sɪpɪtə) *n* any of a genus of hawks having short rounded wings and a long tail. ORIG C19: NL, from L: hawk
▸ **ac'cipitrine** *adj*

acclaim (ə'kleɪm) *vb* **1** (*tr*) to acknowledge publicly the excellence of (a person, act, etc.). **2** to applaud. **3** (*tr*) to acknowledge publicly: *they acclaimed him king.* ◆ *n* **4** an enthusiastic expression of approval, etc. ORIG C17: from L *acclāmāre,* from *ad-* to + *clamāre* to shout
▸ **ac'claimer** *n*

acclamation (,æklə'meɪʃən) *n* **1** an enthusiastic reception or exhibition of welcome, approval, etc. **2** an expression of approval with shouts or applause. **3** *Canad.* an instance of electing or being elected without opposition.
▸ **acclamatory** (ə'klæmətərɪ) *adj*

acclimatize *or* **acclimatise** (ə'klaɪmə,taɪz) *vb* **acclimatizes, acclimatizing, acclimatized** *or* **acclimatises, acclimatising, acclimatised.** to adapt or become accustomed to a new climate or environment.
▸ **ac'clima,tizable** *or* **ac'clima,tisable** *adj* ▸ **ac,climati'zation** *or* **ac,climati'sation** *n*

acclivity (ə'klɪvɪtɪ) *n, pl* **acclivities.** an upward slope, esp. of the ground. Cf. **declivity.** ORIG C17: from L, from *acclīvis* sloping up
▸ **ac'clivitous** *adj*

accolade ('ækə,leɪd) *n* **1** strong praise or approval. **2** an award or honour. **3** the ceremonial gesture used to confer knighthood, a touch on the shoulder with a sword. **4** a rare word for **brace** (sense 6). ORIG C17: via F & It. from Vulgar L *accollāre* (unattested) to hug; rel. to L *collum* neck

accommodate (ə'kɒmə,deɪt) *vb* **accommodates, accommodating, accommodated. 1** (*tr*) to supply or provide, esp. with lodging. **2** (*tr*) to oblige or do a favour for. **3** to adapt. **4** (*tr*) to bring into harmony. **5** (*tr*) to allow room for. **6** (*tr*) to lend money to. ORIG C16: from L *accommodāre,* from *ad-* to + *commodus* having the proper measure

accommodating (ə'kɒmə,deɪtɪŋ) *adj* willing to help; kind; obliging.

accommodation (ə,kɒmə'deɪʃən) *n* **1** lodging or board and lodging. **2** adjustment, as of differences or to new circumstances; settlement or reconciliation. **3** something fulfilling a need, want, etc. **4** *Physiol.* the automatic or voluntary adjustment of the thickness of the lens of the eye for far or near vision. **5** willingness to help or oblige. **6** *Commerce.* a loan.

accommodation address *n* an address on letters, etc., to a person or business that does not wish or is not able to receive post at a permanent or actual address.

accommodation ladder *n Naut.* a flight of stairs or a ladder for lowering over the side of a ship for access to and from a small boat, pier, etc.

accompaniment (ə'kʌmpənɪmənt) *n* **1** something that accompanies or is served or used with something else. **2** *Music.* a subordinate or supporting part for an instrument, voices, or an orchestra.

accompanist (ə'kʌmpənɪst) *n* a person who plays a musical accompaniment for another performer.

accompany (ə'kʌmpənɪ) *vb* **accompanies, accompanying, accompanied. 1** (*tr*) to go along with, so as to be in company with. **2** (*tr; foll. by with*) to supplement. **3** (*tr*) to occur or be associated with. **4** to provide a musical accompaniment for (a soloist, etc.). ORIG C15: from OF *accompaignier,* from *compaing* COMPANION[1]

accomplice (ə'kɒmplɪs, ə'kʌm-) *n* a person who has helped another in committing a crime. ORIG C15: from *a complice,* interpreted as one word, from OF, from LL *complex* partner, from L *complicāre* to COMPLICATE

accomplish (ə'kɒmplɪʃ, ə'kʌm-) *vb* (*tr*) **1** to manage to do; achieve. **2** to complete. ORIG C14: from OF *acomplir,* ult. from L *complēre* to fill up. See COMPLETE

accomplished (ə'kɒmplɪʃt, ə'kʌm-) *adj* **1** successfully completed; achieved. **2** expert; proficient.

accomplishment (ə'kɒmplɪʃmənt, ə'kʌm-) *n* **1** the act of achieving. **2** something successfully completed. **3** (*often pl*) skill or talent. **4** (*often pl*) social grace and poise.

accord (ə'kɔːd) *n* **1** agreement; accordance (esp. in **in accord with**). **2** concurrence of opinion. **3 with one accord.** unanimously. **4** pleasing relationship between sounds, colours, etc. **5 of one's own accord.** voluntarily. ◆ *vb* **6** to be or cause to be in harmony or agreement. **7** (*tr*) to grant; bestow. ORIG C12: via OF from L *ad-* to + *cord-,* stem of *cor* heart

accordance (ə'kɔːdəns) *n* conformity; agreement; accord (esp. in **in accordance with**).

according (ə'kɔːdɪŋ) *adj* **1** (foll. by *to*) in proportion. **2** (foll. by *to*) as stated (by). **3** (foll. by *to*) in conformity (with). **4** (foll. by *as*) depending (on whether).

accordingly (ə'kɔːdɪŋlɪ) *adv* **1** in an appropriate manner; suitably. ◆ *sentence connector.* **2** consequently.

accordion (ə'kɔːdɪən) *n* **1** a portable box-shaped instrument consisting of metallic reeds that are made to vibrate by air from a set of bellows controlled by the player's hands. Notes are produced by means of studlike

keys. **2** short for **piano accordion.** [ORIG] C19: from G, from *Akkord* harmony
▸ **ac'cordionist** *n*

accordion pleats *pl n* tiny knife pleats.

accost (ə'kɒst) *vb* (*tr*) to approach, stop, and speak to (a person), as to ask a question, solicit sexually, etc. [ORIG] C16: from LL *accostāre,* from L *costa* side, rib
▸ **ac'costable** *adj*

accouchement *French.* (akuʃmɑ̃) *n* childbirth or the period of confinement. [ORIG] C19: from *accoucher* to put to bed. See COUCH

account (ə'kaʊnt) *n* **1** a verbal or written report, description, or narration of some occurrence, event, etc. **2** an explanation of conduct, esp. one made to someone in authority. **3** basis; consideration: *on this account.* **4** importance, consequence, or value: *of little account.* **5** assessment; judgment. **6** profit or advantage: *to good account.* **7** part or behalf (only in **on one's** *or* **someone's account**). **8** *Finance.* **8a** a business relationship between a bank, department store, etc., and a depositor, customer, or client permitting the latter certain banking or credit services. **8b** the sum of money deposited at a bank. **8c** the amount of credit available to the holder of an account. **8d** a record of these. **9** a statement of monetary transactions with the resulting balance. **10** (formerly, on the London Stock Exchange) the period, ordinarily of a fortnight's duration, at the end of which settlements were made. **11a** a regular client or customer. **11b** an area of business assigned to another: *they transferred their publicity account to a new agent.* **12 call** (*or* **bring**) **to account. 12a** to insist on explanation. **12b** to reprimand. **12c** to hold responsible. **13 give a good** (**bad,** etc.) **account of oneself.** to perform well (badly, etc.). **14 on account. 14a** on credit. **14b** Also: **to account.** as partial payment. **15 on account of.** (*prep*) because of. **16 take account of** *or* **take into account.** to take into consideration; allow for. **17 settle** *or* **square accounts with. 17a** to pay or receive a balance due. **17b** to get revenge on (someone). **18** See **bank account.** ◆ *vb* **19** (*tr*) to consider or reckon: *he accounts himself poor.* [ORIG] C13: from OF *acont,* from *conter* to COUNT[1]

> **USAGE NOTE** The phrase *on account of* can provide a useful alternative to *because of* in writing. It occurs relatively infrequently in spoken language, where it is sometimes followed by a clause, as in *...on account of I don't do drugs.* This use is considered nonstandard.

accountable (ə'kaʊntəbᵊl) *adj* **1** responsible to someone or for some action. **2** able to be explained.
▸ **ac,counta'bility** *n* ▸ **ac'countably** *adv*

accountancy (ə'kaʊntənsɪ) *n* the profession or business of an accountant.

accountant (ə'kaʊntənt) *n* a person concerned with the maintenance and audit of business accounts.

account executive *n* an executive in an advertising agency or public relations firm who manages a client's account.

account for *vb* (*intr, prep*) **1** to give reasons for (an event, act, etc.). **2** to make or provide a reckoning of (expenditure, etc.). **3** to be responsible for destroying or putting (people, aircraft, etc.) out of action.

accounting (ə'kaʊntɪŋ) *n* **a** the skill or practice of maintaining and auditing accounts and preparing reports on the assets, liabilities, etc., of a business. **b** (*as modifier*): *an accounting period.*

accoutre *or US* **accouter** (ə'kuːtə) *vb* **accoutres, accoutring, accoutred** *or US* **accouters, accoutering, accoutered.** (*tr; usually passive*) to provide with equipment or dress, esp. military. [ORIG] C16: from OF *accoustrer,* ult. rel. to L *consuere* to sew together

accoutrement (ə'kuːtrəmənt, ə'kuːtə-) *or US* **accouterment** (ə'kuːtərmənt) *n* **1** equipment worn by soldiers in addition to their clothing and weapons. **2** (*usually pl*) clothing, equipment, etc.; trappings: *the correct accoutrements for any sport.*

Accra ★ (ə'krɑː) *n* the capital of Ghana, a port on the Gulf of Guinea: built on the site of three 17th-century trading fortresses founded by the English, Dutch, and Danish. Pop.: 949 113 (1988 est.).

accredit (ə'krɛdɪt) *vb* (*tr*) **1** to ascribe or attribute. **2** to give official recognition to. **3** to certify as meeting required standards. **4** (often foll. by *at* or *to*) **4a** to send (an envoy, etc.) with official credentials. **4b** to appoint (someone) as an envoy, etc. **5** to believe. [ORIG] C17: from F *accréditer,* from *mettre à crédit* to put to CREDIT
▸ **ac,credi'tation** *n*

accredited (ə'krɛdɪtɪd) *adj* **1** officially authorized; recognized. **2** (of milk, cattle, etc.) certified as free from disease; meeting certain standards.

accrete (ə'kriːt) *vb* **accretes, accreting, accreted. 1** to grow or cause to grow together. **2** to make or become bigger, as by addition. [ORIG] C18: back formation from ACCRETION

accretion (ə'kriːʃən) *n* **1** any gradual increase in size, as through growth or external addition. **2** something added, esp. extraneously, to cause growth or an increase in size. **3** the growing together of normally separate plant or animal parts. [ORIG] C17: from L *accretiō* increase, from *accrēscere.* See ACCRUE
▸ **ac'cretive** *adj*

accrual (ə'kruːəl) *n* **1** the act of accruing. **2** something that has accrued. **3** *Accounting* a charge incurred in one accounting period that has not been paid by the end of it.

accrue (ə'kruː) *vb* **accrues, accruing, accrued.** (*intr*) **1** to increase by growth or addition, esp. (of capital) to increase by periodic addition of interest. **2** (often foll. by *to*) to fall naturally (to). [ORIG] C15: from OF *accreue,* ult. from L *accrēscere,* from *ad-* to, in addition + *crēscere* to grow

acct *Book-keeping. abbrev. for* account.

acculturate (ə'kʌltʃə,reɪt) *vb* **acculturates, acculturating, acculturated.** (of a cultural or social group) to assimilate the cultural traits of another group. [ORIG] C20: from AD- + CULTURE + -ATE[1]
▸ **ac,cultur'ation** *n*

accumulate (ə'kjuːmjʊ,leɪt) *vb* **accumulates, accumulating, accumulated.** to gather or become gathered together in an increasing quantity; collect. [ORIG] C16: from L *accumulāre* to heap up, from *cumulus* a heap
▸ **ac'cumulable** *adj* ▸ **ac'cumulative** *adj*

accumulation (ə,kjuːmjʊ'leɪʃən) *n* **1** the act or process of collecting together or becoming collected. **2** something that has been collected, gathered, heaped, etc. **3** *Finance.* the continuous growth of capital by retention of interest or earnings.

accumulator (ə'kjuːmjʊ,leɪtə) *n* **1** Also called: **battery, storage battery.** a rechargeable device for storing electrical energy in the form of chemical energy. **2** *Horse racing, Brit.* a collective bet on successive races, with both stake and winnings being carried forward to accumulate progressively. **3** a register in a calculator or computer used for holding the results of a computation or data transfer.

accuracy ('ækjʊrəsɪ) *n, pl* **accuracies.** faithful measurement or representation of the truth; correctness; precision.

accurate ('ækjərɪt) *adj* **1** faithfully representing or describing the truth. **2** showing a negligible or permissible deviation from a standard: *an accurate ruler.* **3** without error; precise. **4** *Maths.* (of a number) correctly represented to a specified number of decimal places or significant figures. [ORIG] C16: from L *accūrāre* to perform with care, from *cūra* care
▸ **'accurately** *adv*

accursed (ə'kɜːsɪd, ə'kɜːst) *or* **accurst** (ə'kɜːst) *adj* **1** under or subject to a curse. **2** (*prenominal*) hateful; detestable. [ORIG] OE *ācursod,* p.p. of *ācursian* to put under a CURSE
▸ **accursedly** (ə'kɜːsɪdlɪ) *adv* ▸ **ac'cursedness** *n*

accusation (,ækjʊ'zeɪʃən) *n* **1** an allegation that a person is guilty of some fault or crime. **2** a formal charge brought against a person.

accusative (ə'kjuːzətɪv) *adj* **1** *Grammar.* denoting a case of nouns, pronouns, and adjectives in inflected languages that is used to identify the direct object of a finite verb, of certain prepositions, and for certain other pur-

poses. **2** another word for **accusatorial.** ◆ *n* **3** *Grammar.* the accusative case or a speech element in it. ORIG C15: from L; in grammar, from *cāsus accūsātīvus* accusative case, a mistaken translation of Gk *ptōsis aitiatikē* the case indicating causation. See ACCUSE
▸ **accusatival** (əˌkjuːzəˈtaɪvᵊl) *adj* ▸ **acˈcusatively** *adv*

accusatorial (əˌkjuːzəˈtɔːrɪəl) *or* **accusatory** (əˈkjuːzətərɪ) *adj* **1** containing or implying blame or strong criticism. **2** *Law.* denoting a legal system in which the defendant is prosecuted before a judge in public. Cf. **inquisitorial.**

accuse (əˈkjuːz) *vb* **accuses, accusing, accused.** to charge (a person or persons) with some fault, offence, crime, etc. ORIG C13: via OF from L *accūsāre* to call to account, from *ad-* to + *causa* lawsuit
▸ **acˈcuser** *n* ▸ **acˈcusing** *adj* ▸ **acˈcusingly** *adv*

accused (əˈkjuːzd) *n* (preceded by *the*) *Law.* the defendant or defendants on a criminal charge.

accustom (əˈkʌstəm) *vb* (*tr;* usually foll. by *to*) to make (oneself) familiar (with) or used (to), as by habit or experience. ORIG C15: from OF *acostumer,* from *costume* CUSTOM

accustomed (əˈkʌstəmd) *adj* **1** usual; customary. **2** (*postpositive;* foll. by *to*) used (to). **3** (*postpositive;* foll. by *to*) in the habit (of).

AC/DC *adj Inf.* (of a person) bisexual. ORIG C20: humorous reference to electrical apparatus that is adaptable for ALTERNATING CURRENT and DIRECT CURRENT

ace (eɪs) *n* **1** any die, domino, or any of four playing cards with one spot. **2** a single spot or pip on a playing card, die, etc. **3** *Tennis.* a winning serve that the opponent fails to reach. **4** a fighter pilot accredited with destroying several enemy aircraft. **5** *Inf.* an expert: *an ace at driving.* **6 an ace up one's sleeve.** a hidden and powerful advantage. ◆ *adj* **7** *Inf.* superb; excellent. ORIG C13: via OF from L *as* a unit

-acea *suffix forming plural proper nouns.* denoting animals belonging to a class or order: *Crustacea* (class); *Cetacea* (order). ORIG NL, from L, neuter pl of *-āceus* -ACEOUS

-aceae *suffix forming plural proper nouns.* denoting plants belonging to a family: *Liliaceae.* ORIG NL, from L, fem pl of *-āceus* -ACEOUS

acedia (əˈsiːdɪə) *n* another word for **accidie.**

ACE inhibitor *n* any one of a class of drugs, including captopril and enalpapril, that cause the arteries to widen by preventing the synthesis of angiotensin: used to treat high blood pressure and heart failure. ORIG C20: from *a(ngiotensin-)c(onverting) e(nzyme) inhibitor*

-aceous *suffix forming adjectives.* relating to, having the nature of, or resembling: *herbaceous.* ORIG NL, from L *-āceus* of a certain kind; rel. to *-āc, -āx,* adjectival suffix

acephalous (əˈsɛfələs) *adj* having no head or one that is reduced and indistinct, as certain insect larvae. ORIG C18: via Med. L from Gk *akephalos.* See A-[1], -CEPHALIC

acer (ˈeɪsə) *n* any tree or shrub of the genus *Acer,* often cultivated for their brightly coloured foliage. See also **maple.**

acerbate (ˈæsəˌbeɪt) *vb* **acerbates, acerbating, acerbated.** (*tr*) **1** to embitter or exasperate. **2** to make sour or bitter. ORIG C18: from L *acerbāre* to make sour

acerbic (əˈsɜːbɪk) *adj* harsh, bitter, or astringent; sour. ORIG C17: from L *acerbus* sour, bitter

acerbity (əˈsɜːbɪtɪ) *n, pl* **acerbities. 1** vitriolic or embittered speech, temper, etc. **2** sourness or bitterness of taste.

acetabulum (ˌæsɪˈtæbjʊləm) *n, pl* **acetabula** (-lə). the deep cuplike cavity on the side of the hipbone that receives the head of the thighbone. ORIG L: vinegar cup, hence a cuplike cavity, from *acētum* vinegar + *-abulum,* suffix denoting a container

acetal (ˈæsɪˌtæl) *n* **1** a type of organic compound formed by addition of an alcohol to an aldehyde or ketone. **2** a colourless pleasant-smelling volatile liquid used in perfumes. Formula: $CH_3CH(OC_2H_5)_2$. Systematic name: **diethoxyethane.** ORIG C19: from G *Azetal,* from ACETO- + ALCOHOL

acetaldehyde (ˌæsɪˈtældɪˌhaɪd) *n* a colourless volatile pungent liquid, used in the manufacture of organic compounds and as a solvent. Formula: CH_3CHO. Systematic name: **ethanal.**

acetanilide (ˌæsɪˈtænɪˌlaɪd) *n* a white crystalline powder used in the manufacture of dyes and as an analgesic in medicine. Formula: $C_6H_5NH(COCH_3)$. Systematic names: ***N*-phenylethanamide, phenylacetamide.** ORIG C19: from ACETO- + ANILINE + -IDE

acetate (ˈæsɪˌteɪt) *n* **1** any salt or ester of acetic acid. Systematic name: **ethanoate. 2** short for **acetate rayon** *or* **cellulose acetate. 3** an audio disc with an acetate lacquer coating: used for demonstration purposes, etc. ORIG C19: from ACETIC + -ATE[1]

acetate rayon *n* a synthetic textile fibre made from cellulose acetate.

acetic (əˈsiːtɪk) *adj* of, containing, producing, or derived from acetic acid or vinegar. ORIG C19: from L *acētum* vinegar

acetic acid *n* a colourless pungent liquid widely used in the manufacture of plastics, pharmaceuticals, dyes, etc. Formula: CH_3COOH. Systematic name: **ethanoic acid.** See also **vinegar.**

acetify (əˈsɛtɪˌfaɪ) *vb* **acetifies, acetifying, acetified.** to become or cause to become acetic acid or vinegar.
▸ **aˌcetifiˈcation** *n*

aceto- *or before a vowel* **acet-** *combining form.* containing an acetyl group or derived from acetic acid: *acetone.* ORIG from L *acētum* vinegar

acetone (ˈæsɪˌtəʊn) *n* a colourless volatile pungent liquid used in the manufacture of chemicals and as a solvent for paints, varnishes, and lacquers. Formula: CH_3COCH_3. Systematic name: **propanone.** ORIG C19: from G *Azeton,* from ACETO- + -ONE

acetous (ˈæsɪtəs) *or* **acetose** (ˈæsɪˌtəʊs) *adj* **1** producing or resembling acetic acid or vinegar. **2** tasting like vinegar. ORIG C18: from LL *acētōsus* vinegary, from *acētum* vinegar

acetyl (ˈæsɪˌtaɪl, əˈsiːtaɪl) *n* (*modifier*) of or containing the monovalent group CH_3CO-. ORIG C19: from ACET(IC) + -YL

acetylcholine (ˌæsɪtaɪlˈkəʊliːn, -lɪn) *n* a chemical substance secreted at the ends of many nerve fibres, responsible for the transmission of nervous impulses.

acetylene (əˈsɛtɪˌliːn) *n* **1** a colourless soluble flammable gas used in the manufacture of organic chemicals and in cutting and welding metals. Formula: C_2H_2. Systematic name: **ethyne. 2** another name for **alkyne.**

acetylene series *n* another name for **alkyne series.**

acetylsalicylic acid (ˌæsɪtaɪlˌsælɪˈsɪlɪk) *n* the chemical name for **aspirin.**

Achaea (əˈkiːə) *or* **Achaia** ★ (əˈkaɪə) *n* **1** a department of Greece, in the N Peloponnese. Capital: Patras. Pop.: 300 078 (1991). Area: 3209 sq. km (1239 sq. miles). Modern Greek name: **Akhaïa. 2** a province of ancient Greece, in the N Peloponnese on the Gulf of Corinth: enlarged as a Roman province in 27 B.C.

Achaean (əˈkiːən) *or* **Achaian** (əˈkaɪən) *n* **1** a member of a principal Greek tribe in the Mycenaean era. ◆ *adj* **2** of or relating to the Achaeans.

Achates ★ (əˈkeɪtiːz) *n* **1** *Classical myth.* Aeneas' faithful companion in Virgil's *Aeneid.* **2** a loyal friend.

ache (eɪk) *vb* **aches, aching, ached.** (*intr*) **1** to feel, suffer, or be the source of a continuous dull pain. **2** to suffer mental anguish. ◆ *n* **3** a continuous dull pain. ORIG OE *ācan* (vb), *æce* (n), ME *aken* (vb), *ache* (n)
▸ **ˈaching** *adj*

Achebe ★ (əˈtʃeɪbɪ) *n* **Chinua.** born 1930, Nigerian novelist. His works include *Things Fall Apart* (1958), *A Man of the People* (1966), and *Anthills of the Savannah* (1987).

Achelous ★ (ˌækɪˈləʊəs) *n Classical myth.* a river god who changed into a snake and a bull while fighting Hercules but was defeated when Hercules broke off one of his horns.

achene (əˈkiːn) *n* a dry one-seeded indehiscent fruit with the seed distinct from the fruit wall. ORIG C19: from NL *achaenium* that which does not open, from A-[1] + Gk *khainein* to yawn

Acheron ★ ('ækə,rɒn) *n Greek myth.* **1** one of the rivers in Hades over which the souls of the dead were ferried by Charon. Cf. **Styx. 2** the underworld or Hades.

Acheson ★ ('ætʃɪsᵊn) *n* **Dean (Gooderham).** 1893–1971, US lawyer and statesman: secretary of state (1949–53).

Acheulian *or* **Acheulean** (ə'ʃu:lɪən) *Archaeol.* ◆ *n* **1** (in Europe) the period in the Lower Palaeolithic following the Abbevillian, represented by the use of soft hammerstones in hand-axe production. **2** (in Africa) the period represented by every stage of hand-axe development. ◆ *adj* **3** of or relating to this period. ORIG C20: after *St Acheul,* town in N France

achieve (ə'tʃi:v) *vb* **achieves, achieving, achieved.** (*tr*) **1** to bring to a successful conclusion. **2** to gain as by hard work or effort: *to achieve success.* ORIG C14: from OF *achever* to bring to an end, from *a chef* to a head
▸ **a'chievable** *adj* ▸ **a'chiever** *n*

achievement (ə'tʃi:vmənt) *n* **1** something that has been accomplished, esp. by hard work, ability, or heroism. **2** successful completion; accomplishment.

achillea (,ækɪ'li:ə) *n* any of several cultivated varieties of yarrow. ORIG NL, from Gk *akhilleios* plant used medicinally by ACHILLES

Achilles ★ (ə'kɪli:z) *n Greek myth.* Greek hero, the son of Peleus and the sea goddess Thetis: in the *Iliad* the foremost of the Greek warriors at the siege of Troy. While he was a baby his mother plunged him into the river Styx making his body invulnerable except for the heel by which she held him. After slaying Hector, he was killed by Paris who wounded him in the heel.
▸ **Achillean** (,ækɪ'li:ən) *adj*

Achilles heel *n* a small but fatal weakness.

Achilles tendon *n* the fibrous cord that connects the muscles of the calf to the heelbone.

Achill Island ★ ('ækɪl) *n* an island in the Republic of Ireland, off the W coast of Co. Mayo. Pop.: 2853 (1991). Area: 148 sq. km (57 sq. miles).

Achitophel ★ (ə'kɪtə,fɛl) *n Bible.* the Douay spelling of **Ahithophel.**

achromat ('ækrə,mæt) *or* **achromatic lens** *n* a lens designed to reduce chromatic aberration.

achromatic (,ækrə'mætɪk) *adj* **1** without colour. **2** capable of reflecting or refracting light without chromatic aberration. **3** *Music.* involving no sharps or flats.
▸ **,achro'matically** *adv* ▸ **achromatism** (ə'krəʊmə,tɪzəm) *or* **achromaticity** (ə,krəʊmə'tɪsɪtɪ) *n*

acid ('æsɪd) *n* **1** any substance that dissociates in water to yield a sour corrosive solution containing hydrogen ions, and turning litmus red. **2** a sour-tasting substance. **3** a slang name for **LSD.** ◆ *adj* **4** *Chem.* **4a** of, derived from, or containing acid. **4b** being or having the properties of an acid. **5** sharp or sour in taste. **6** cutting, sharp, or hurtful in speech, manner, etc. ORIG C17: from F *acide* or L *acidus,* from *acēre* to be sour
▸ **'acidly** *adv* ▸ **'acidness** *n*

acid-fast *adj* (of bacteria and tissues) resistant to decolorization by mineral acids after staining.

Acid House *or* **Acid** *n* a dance music dominated by beat and bass line, created with synthesizers and digital sampling; popular in the late 1980s. ORIG C20: from ACID (LSD) + HOUSE (MUSIC)

acidic (ə'sɪdɪk) *adj* another word for **acid.**

acidify (ə'sɪdɪ,faɪ) *vb* **acidifies, acidifying, acidified.** to convert into or become acid.
▸ **a'cidi,fiable** *adj* ▸ **a,cidifi'cation** *n*

acidity (ə'sɪdɪtɪ) *n, pl* **acidities. 1** the quality or state of being acid. **2** the amount of acid present in a solution.

acidosis (,æsɪ'dəʊsɪs) *n* a condition characterized by an abnormal increase in the acidity of the blood.
▸ **acidotic** (,æsɪ'dɒtɪk) *adj*

acid rain *n* rain containing pollutants, chiefly sulphur dioxide and nitrogen oxide, released into the atmosphere by burning coal or oil.

acid rock *n* rock music characterized by bizarre amplified instrumental effects. ORIG C20: from ACID (LSD)

acid test *n* a rigorous and conclusive test to establish worth or value. ORIG C19: from the testing of gold with nitric acid

acidulate (ə'sɪdjʊ,leɪt) *vb* **acidulates, acidulating, acidulated.** (*tr*) to make slightly acid or sour. ORIG C18: ACIDULOUS + -ATE[1]
▸ **a,cidu'lation** *n*

acidulous (ə'sɪdjʊləs) *or* **acidulent** *adj* **1** rather sour. **2** sharp or sour in speech, manner, etc.; acid. ORIG C18: from L *acidulus* sourish, dim. of *acidus* sour

acinus ('æsɪnəs) *n, pl* **acini** (-,naɪ). **1** *Anat.* any of the terminal saclike portions of a compound gland. **2** *Bot.* any of the small drupes that make up the fruit of the raspberry, etc. **3** *Bot., obs.* a collection of berries, such as a bunch of grapes. ORIG C18: NL, from L: grape, berry

Acis ★ ('eɪsɪs) *n Greek myth.* a Sicilian shepherd and the lover of the nymph Galatea. In jealousy, Polyphemus crushed him with a huge rock, and his blood was turned by Galatea into a river.

ack-ack ('æk,æk) *n Mil.* **a** anti-aircraft fire. **b** (*as modifier*): *ack-ack guns.* ORIG C20: British Army World War I phonetic alphabet for AA, abbrev. of *anti-aircraft*

acknowledge (ək'nɒlɪdʒ) *vb* **acknowledges, acknowledging, acknowledged.** (*tr*) **1** (*may take a clause as object*) to recognize or admit the existence, truth, or reality of. **2** to indicate recognition or awareness of, as by a greeting, glance, etc. **3** to express appreciation or thanks for. **4** to make the receipt of known: *to acknowledge a letter.* **5** to recognize, esp. in legal form, the authority, rights, or claims of. ORIG C15: prob. from earlier *knowledge,* on the model of OE *oncnāwan,* ME *aknowen* to confess, recognize
▸ **ac'knowledgeable** *adj*

acknowledgment *or* **acknowledgement** (ək'nɒlɪdʒmənt) *n* **1** the act of acknowledging or state of being acknowledged. **2** something done or given as an expression of thanks. **3** (*pl*) an author's statement acknowledging his or her use of the works of other authors.

aclinic line (ə'klɪnɪk) *n* another name for **magnetic equator.** ORIG C19 *aclinic,* from Gk *aklinēs* not bending, from A-[1] + *klinein* to bend

acme ('ækmɪ) *n* the culminating point, as of achievement or excellence. ORIG C16: from Gk *akmē*

acne ('æknɪ) *n* a chronic skin disease common in adolescence, characterized by pustules on the face. ORIG C19: NL, from a misreading of Gk *akmē* eruption on the face. See ACME

acolyte ('ækə,laɪt) *n* **1** a follower or attendant. **2** *Christianity.* an officer who assists a priest. ORIG C16: via OF & Med. L from Gk *akolouthos* a follower

Aconcagua ★ (*Spanish* akon'kaɣwa) *n* a mountain in W Argentina: the highest peak in the Andes and in the W Hemisphere. Height: 6960 m (22 835 ft).

aconite ('ækə,naɪt) *n* **1** any of a genus of N temperate plants, such as monkshood and wolfsbane, many of which are poisonous. Cf. **winter aconite. 2** the dried poisonous root of many of these plants, sometimes used as a narcotic. ORIG C16: via OF or L from Gk *akoniton* aconite
▸ **aconitic** (,ækə'nɪtɪk) *adj*

Açôres ★ (ə'sorəʃ) *n* the Portuguese name for (the) **Azores.**

acorn ('eɪkɔ:n) *n* the fruit of the oak tree, consisting of a smooth thick-walled nut in a woody scaly cuplike base. ORIG C16: var. (infl. by *corn*) of OE *æcern* the fruit of a tree, acorn

acoustic (ə'ku:stɪk) *or* **acoustical** *adj* **1** of or related to sound, hearing, or acoustics. **2** designed to respond to or absorb sound: *an acoustic tile.* **3** (of a musical instrument or recording) without electronic amplification: *an acoustic guitar.* ORIG C17: from Gk *akoustikos,* from *akouein* to hear
▸ **a'coustically** *adv*

acoustics (ə'ku:stɪks) *n* **1** (*functioning as sing*) the scientific study of sound and sound waves. **2** (*functioning as pl*) the characteristics of a room, auditorium, etc., that determine the fidelity with which sound can be heard within it.

ACP *abbrev. for* African Caribbean Pacific: a group of 71 former European colonies.

acquaint (əˈkweɪnt) *vb* (*tr*) (foll. by *with* or *of*) to make (a person) familiar (with). ORIG C13: via OF & Med. L from L *accognitus,* from *accognōscere* to know perfectly, from *ad-* (intensive) + *cognōscere* to know

acquaintance (əˈkweɪntəns) *n* **1** a person whom one knows but who is not a close friend. **2** knowledge of a person or thing, esp. when slight. **3 make the acquaintance of.** to come into social contact with. **4** those persons collectively whom one knows.
▸ **acˈquaintanceship** *n*

acquainted (əˈkweɪntɪd) *adj* (*postpositive*) **1** (sometimes foll. by *with*) on terms of familiarity but not intimacy. **2** (foll. by *with*) familiar (with).

acquiesce (ˌækwɪˈɛs) *vb* **acquiesces, acquiescing, acquiesced.** (*intr;* often foll. by *in* or *to*) to comply (with); assent (to) without protest. ORIG C17: from L *acquiēscere,* from *ad-* at + *quiēscere* to rest, from *quiēs* QUIET
▸ **ˌacquiˈescence** *n* ▸ **ˌacquiˈescent** *adj*

acquire (əˈkwaɪə) *vb* **acquires, acquiring, acquired.** (*tr*) to get or gain (something, such as an object, trait, or ability). ORIG C15: via OF from L *acquīrere,* from *ad-* in addition + *quaerere* to get, seek
▸ **acˈquirable** *adj* ▸ **acˈquirement** *n*

acquired behaviour *n Psychol.* the behaviour of an organism resulting from the effects of the environment.

acquired characteristic *n* a characteristic of an organism resulting from the effects of the environment.

acquired immune deficiency syndrome *or* **acquired immunodeficiency syndrome** *n* the full name for **AIDS.**

acquired immunity *n* the immmunity produced by exposure of an organism to antigens, which stimulates the production of antibodies.

acquired taste *n* **1** a liking for something at first considered unpleasant. **2** the thing liked.

acquisition (ˌækwɪˈzɪʃən) *n* **1** the act of acquiring or gaining possession. **2** something acquired. **3** a person or thing of special merit added to a group. ORIG C14: from L *acquīsītiōn-,* from *acquīrere* to ACQUIRE

acquisitive (əˈkwɪzɪtɪv) *adj* inclined or eager to acquire things, esp. material possessions.
▸ **acˈquisitively** *adv* ▸ **acˈquisitiveness** *n*

acquit (əˈkwɪt) *vb* **acquits, acquitting, acquitted.** (*tr*) **1** (foll. by *of*) **1a** to free or release (from a charge of crime). **1b** to pronounce not guilty. **2** (foll. by *of*) to free or relieve (from an obligation, duty, etc.). **3** to repay or settle (a debt or obligation). **4** to conduct (oneself). ORIG C13: from OF *aquiter,* from *quiter* to release, QUIT
▸ **acˈquittal** *n* ▸ **acˈquitter** *n*

acquittance (əˈkwɪtəns) *n* **1** a release from or settlement of a debt, etc. **2** a record of this, such as a receipt.

acre (ˈeɪkə) *n* **1** a unit of area used in certain English-speaking countries, equal to 4840 square yards or 4046.86 square metres. **2** (*pl*) **2a** land, esp. a large area. **2b** *Inf.* a large amount. **3 farm the long acre.** *NZ.* to graze stock on the grass along a highway. ORIG OE *æcer* field, acre

Acre ★ *n* **1** (ˈɑːkrə). a state of W Brazil: mostly unexplored tropical forests; acquired from Bolivia in 1903. Capital: Rio Branco. Pop.: 483 593 (1996). Area: 152 589 sq. km (58 899 sq. miles). **2** (ˈeɪkə, ˈɑːkə). a city and port in N Israel, strategically situated on the **Bay of Acre** in the E Mediterranean: taken and retaken during the Crusades (1104, 1187, 1191, 1291), taken by the Turks (1517), by Egypt (1832), and by the Turks again (1839). Pop.: 40 500 (1989 est.). Old Testament name: **Accho** (ɑːˈkəʊ). Arabic name: **ʻAkka** (ɑːˈkɑː). Hebrew name: **ʻAkko** (ɑːˈkəʊ).

acreage (ˈeɪkərɪdʒ) *n* **1** land area in acres. ◆ *adj* **2** *Austral.* of or relating to a large residential block of land, esp. in a rural area.

acrid (ˈækrɪd) *adj* **1** unpleasantly pungent or sharp to the smell or taste. **2** sharp or caustic, esp. in speech or nature. ORIG C18: from L *ācer* sharp, sour; prob. infl. by ACID
▸ **acridity** (əˈkrɪdɪtɪ) *n* ▸ **ˈacridly** *adv*

acridine (ˈækrɪˌdiːn) *n* a colourless crystalline solid used in the manufacture of dyes.

acriflavine (ˌækrɪˈfleɪvɪn) *n* a brownish or orange-red powder used in medicine as an antiseptic. ORIG C20: from ACRIDINE + FLAVIN

acriflavine hydrochloride *n* a red crystalline substance obtained from acriflavine and used as an antiseptic.

Acrilan (ˈækrɪˌlæn) *n Trademark.* an acrylic fibre or fabric, characterized by strength and resistance to creasing and used for clothing, carpets, etc.

acrimony (ˈækrɪmənɪ) *n, pl* **acrimonies.** bitterness or sharpness of manner, speech, temper, etc. ORIG C16: from L *ācrimōnia,* from *ācer* sharp, sour
▸ **acrimonious** (ˌækrɪˈməʊnɪəs) *adj*

acro- *combining form.* **1** denoting something at a height, top, beginning, or end: *acropolis.* **2** denoting an extremity of the human body: *acromegaly.* ORIG from Gk *akros* extreme, topmost

acrobat (ˈækrəˌbæt) *n* **1** an entertainer who performs acts that require skill, agility, and coordination, such as swinging from a trapeze or walking a tightrope. **2** a person noted for his or her frequent and rapid changes of position or allegiance. ORIG C19: via F from Gk *akrobatēs,* one who walks on tiptoe, from ACRO- + *bat-,* from *bainein* to walk
▸ **ˌacroˈbatic** *adj* ▸ **ˌacroˈbatically** *adv*

acrobatics (ˌækrəˈbætɪks) *pl n* **1** the skills or feats of an acrobat. **2** any activity requiring agility and skill: *mental acrobatics.*

acrogen (ˈækrədʒən) *n* any flowerless plant, such as a fern or moss, in which growth occurs from the tip of the main stem.
▸ **acrogenous** (əˈkrɒdʒɪnəs) *adj*

acrolect (ˈækrəˌlɛkt) *n Linguistics.* the best level of spoken English developed in a Caribbean territory, considered to be the standard variety of English in that country. ORIG C20: from ACRO- + Gk *lektos* speech
▸ **acrolectal** *adj*

acromegaly (ˌækrəʊˈmɛɡəlɪ) *n* a chronic disease characterized by enlargement of the bones of the head, hands, and feet, and swelling and enlargement of soft tissue. It is caused by excessive secretion of growth hormone by the pituitary gland. ORIG C19: from F *acromégalie,* from ACRO- + Gk *megal-,* stem of *megas* big
▸ **acromegalic** (ˌækrəʊmɪˈɡælɪk) *adj, n*

acronym (ˈækrənɪm) *n* a pronounceable name made from a series of initial letters or parts of a group of words; for example, *UNESCO* for the *United Nations Educational, Scientific, and Cultural Organization.* ORIG C20: from ACRO- + -ONYM

acrophobia (ˌækrəˈfəʊbɪə) *n* abnormal fear or dread of being at a great height. ORIG C19: from ACRO- + -PHOBIA
▸ **ˌacroˈphobic** *adj, n*

acropolis (əˈkrɒpəlɪs) *n* the citadel of an ancient Greek city. ORIG C17: from Gk, from ACRO- + *polis* city

Acropolis ★ (əˈkrɒpəlɪs) *n* the citadel of Athens on which the Parthenon stands.

across (əˈkrɒs) *prep* **1** from one side to the other side of. **2** on or at the other side of. **3** so as to transcend the boundaries or barriers of: *across religious divisions.* ◆ *adv* **4** from one side to the other. **5** on or to the other side. ORIG C13 *on croice, acros,* from OF *a croix* crosswise

across-the-board *adj* (**across the board** *when postpositive*) (of salary increases, taxation cuts, etc.) affecting all levels or classes equally.

acrostic (əˈkrɒstɪk) *n* a number of lines of writing, such as a poem, certain letters of which form a word, proverb, etc. A **single acrostic** is formed by the initial letters of the lines, a **double acrostic** by the initial and final letters, and a **triple acrostic** by the initial, middle, and final letters. ORIG C16: via F from Gk, from ACRO- + *stikhos* line of verse

acrylic (əˈkrɪlɪk) *adj* **1** of, derived from, or concerned with acrylic acid. ◆ *n* **2** short for **acrylic fibre, acrylic resin.** ORIG C20: from L *ācer* sharp + *olēre* to smell + -IC

acrylic acid *n* a colourless corrosive pungent liquid, used in the manufacture of acrylic resins. Formula: CH_2:CHCOOH. Systematic name: **propenoic acid.**

acrylic fibre *n* a man-made fibre used in blankets, knitwear, etc.

acrylic resin *n* any of a group of polymers of acrylic

acid, its esters, or amides, used as synthetic rubbers, paints, and as plastics such as Perspex.

act (ækt) *n* **1** something done or performed. **2** the performance of some physical or mental process; action. **3** (*cap. when part of a name*) the formally codified result of deliberation by a legislative body. **4** (*often pl*) a formal written record of transactions, proceedings, etc., as of a society, committee, or legislative body. **5** a major division of a dramatic work. **6a** a short performance of skill, a comic sketch, dance, etc. **6b** those giving such a performance. **7** an assumed attitude or pose, esp. one intended to impress. **8 get in on the act.** *Inf.* to become involved in a profitable situation in order to share in the benefit. **9 get one's act together.** *Inf.* to organize oneself. ◆ *vb* **10** (*intr*) to do something. **11** (*intr*) to operate; react: *his mind acted quickly.* **12** to perform (a part or role) in a play, etc. **13** (*tr*) to present (a play, etc.) on stage. **14** (*intr;* usually foll. by *for* or *as*) to be a substitute (for). **15** (*intr;* foll. by *as*) to serve the function or purpose (of). **16** (*intr*) to conduct oneself or behave (as if one were): *she usually acts like a lady.* **17** (*intr*) to behave in an unnatural or affected way. **18** (*copula*) to play the part of: *to act the fool.* **19** (*copula*) to behave in a manner appropriate to: *to act one's age.* ◆ See also **act on, act up.** ORIG C14: from L *actus* a doing, & *actum* a thing done, from the p.p. of *agere* to do
▸ **'actable** *adj* ▸ **ˌacta'bility** *n*

ACT *abbrev. for:* **1** Australian Capital Territory. **2** advance corporation tax.

Actaeon ★ (æk'tiːən, 'æktɪən) *n Greek myth.* a hunter of Boeotia who, having accidentally seen Artemis bathing, was turned into a stag and torn apart by his own hounds.

ACTH *n* adrenocorticotrophic hormone; a hormone, secreted by the anterior lobe of the pituitary gland, that stimulates growth of the adrenal gland. It is used in treating rheumatoid arthritis, allergic and skin diseases, etc.

acting ('æktɪŋ) *adj* (*prenominal*) **1** taking on duties temporarily, esp. as a substitute for another. **2** performing the duties of though not yet holding the rank of: *acting lieutenant.* **3** operating or functioning. **4** intended for stage performance; provided with directions for actors: *an acting version of "Hedda Gabler".* ◆ *n* **5** the art or profession of an actor.

actinia (æk'tɪnɪə) *n, pl* **actiniae** (-'tɪnɪˌiː) *or* **actinias.** a sea anemone common in rock pools. ORIG C18: NL, lit.: things having a radial structure

actinic (æk'tɪnɪk) *adj* (of radiation) producing a photochemical effect. ORIG C19: from ACTINO- + -IC
▸ **ac'tinically** *adv* ▸ **'actinˌism** *n*

actinide series ('æktɪˌnaɪd) *n* a series of 15 radioactive elements with increasing atomic numbers from actinium to lawrencium.

actinium (æk'tɪnɪəm) *n* a radioactive element of the actinide series, occurring as a decay product of uranium. It is used in neutron production. Symbol: Ac; atomic no.: 89; half-life of most stable isotope, ^{227}Ac: 22 years. ORIG C19: NL, from ACTINO- + -IUM

actino- *or before a vowel* **actin-** *combining form.* **1** indicating a radial structure: *actinomorphic.* **2** indicating radioactivity or radiation: *actinometer.* ORIG from Gk, from *aktis* ray

actinobiology (ˌæktɪnəʊbaɪ'ɒlədʒɪ) *n* the branch of biology concerned with the effects of radiation on living organisms.

actinoid ('æktɪˌnɔɪd) *adj* having a radiate form, as a sea anemone or starfish.

actinometer (ˌæktɪ'nɒmɪtə) *n* an instrument for measuring the intensity of radiation, esp. of the sun's rays.

actinomycin (ˌæktɪnəʊ'maɪsɪn) *n* any of several toxic antibiotics obtained from soil bacteria, used in treating some cancers.

actinozoan (ˌæktɪnəʊ'zəʊən) *n, adj* another word for **anthozoan.**

action ('ækʃən) *n* **1** the state or process of doing something or being active. **2** something done, such as an act or deed. **3** movement or posture during some physical activity. **4** activity, force, or energy: *a man of action.* **5** (*usually pl*) conduct or behaviour. **6** *Law.* a legal proceeding brought by one party against another; lawsuit. **7** the operating mechanism, esp. in a piano, gun, watch, etc. **8** the force applied to a body. **9** the way in which something operates or works. **10 out of action.** not functioning. **11** the events that form the plot of a story, play, or other composition. **12** *Mil.* **12a** a minor engagement. **12b** fighting at sea or on land: *he saw action in the war.* **13** *Inf.* the profits of an enterprise or transaction (esp. in **a piece of the action**). **14** *Sl.* the main activity, esp. social activity. **15** short for **industrial action.** ◆ *vb* (*tr*) **16** to put into effect; take action concerning. ◆ *sentence substitute.* **17** a command given by a film director to indicate that filming is to begin. ORIG C14 *accioun,* ult. from L *āctiōn-,* from *agere* to do

actionable ('ækʃənəbᵊl) *adj Law.* affording grounds for legal action.
▸ **'actionably** *adv*

action committee *or* **group** *n* a committee or group formed to pursue an end, usually political, using petitions, marches, etc.

action painting *n* a development of abstract expressionism characterized by accidental effects of thrown, smeared, dripped, or spattered paint. Also called: **tachisme.**

action replay *n* the rerunning of a small section of a television film or tape of a match or other sporting contest, often in slow motion.

action stations *pl n* **1** *Mil.* the positions taken up by individuals in preparation for or during a battle. ◆ *sentence substitute.* **2** a command to take up such positions. **3** *Inf.* a warning to get ready for something.

Actium ★ ('æktɪəm) *n* a town of ancient Greece that overlooked the naval battle in 31 B.C. at which Octavian's fleet under Agrippa defeated that of Mark Antony and Cleopatra.

activate ('æktɪˌveɪt) *vb* **activates, activating, activated.** (*tr*) **1** to make active or capable of action. **2** *Physics.* to make radioactive. **3** *Chem.* to increase the rate of (a reaction). **4** to purify (sewage) by aeration. **5** *US mil.* to mobilize or organize (a unit).
▸ **ˌacti'vation** *n* ▸ **'actiˌvator** *n*

activated carbon *n* a highly adsorptive form of carbon used to remove colour or impurities from liquids and gases.

activated sludge *n* a mass of aerated precipitated sewage added to untreated sewage to bring about purification by hastening bacterial decomposition.

active ('æktɪv) *adj* **1** moving, working, or doing something. **2** busy or involved: *an active life.* **3** physically energetic. **4** effective: *an active ingredient.* **5** *Grammar.* denoting a voice of verbs used to indicate that the subject of a sentence is performing the action or causing the event or process described by the verb, as *kicked* in *The boy kicked the football.* **6** being fully engaged in military service. **7** (of a volcano) erupting periodically; not extinct. **8** *Astron.* (of the sun) exhibiting a large number of sunspots, solar flares, etc., and a marked variation in intensity and frequency of radio emission. ◆ *n* **9** *Grammar.* **9a** the active voice. **9b** an active verb. ORIG C14: from L *āctīvus.* See ACT, -IVE
▸ **'actively** *adv* ▸ **'activeness** *n*

active list *n Mil.* a list of officers available for full duty.

activism ('æktɪˌvɪzəm) *n* a policy of taking direct and often militant action to achieve an end, esp. a political or social one.
▸ **'activist** *n*

activity (æk'tɪvɪtɪ) *n, pl* **activities.** **1** the state or quality of being active. **2** lively action or movement. **3** any specific action, pursuit, etc.: *recreational activities.* **4** the number of disintegrations of a radioactive substance in a given unit of time. **5** *Chem.* a measure of the ability of a substance to take part in a chemical reaction.

act of God *n Law.* a sudden and inevitable occurrence caused by natural forces, such as a flood or earthquake.

act on *or* **upon** *vb* (*intr, prep*) **1** to regulate one's behaviour in accordance with (advice, information, etc.). **2** to have an effect on (illness, a part of the body, etc.).

actor (ˈæktə) *or* (*fem*) **actress** (ˈæktrɪs) *n* a person who acts in a play, film, broadcast, etc.

> **USAGE NOTE** The use of *actress* is now very much on the decline, and women who work in the profession invariably prefer to be referred to as *actors*.

actual (ˈæktʃʊəl) *adj* **1** existing in reality or as a matter of fact. **2** real or genuine. **3** existing at the present time; current. ◆ See also **actuals**. ORIG C14 *actuel* existing, from LL, from L *āctus* ACT

> **USAGE NOTE** In writing, it is best to avoid the excessive use of *actual* and *actually*, unless they really add something to the meaning of the sentence. In a sentence such as *he did actually go to the play but did not enjoy it*, the word *actually* is only necessary if there was any doubt about his going. An alternative here would be *in the end*.

actual bodily harm *n Criminal law.* injury caused by one person to another that is less serious than grievous bodily harm. Abbrev.: **ABH**.

actuality (ˌæktʃʊˈælɪtɪ) *n, pl* **actualities. 1** true existence; reality. **2** (*sometimes pl*) a fact or condition that is real.

actualize *or* **actualise** (ˈæktʃʊəˌlaɪz) *vb* **actualizes, actualizing, actualized** *or* **actualises, actualising, actualised.** (*tr*) **1** to make actual or real. **2** to represent realistically.
▸ **ˌactualiˈzation** *or* **ˌactualiˈsation** *n*

actually (ˈæktʃʊəlɪ) *adv* **1a** as an actual fact; really. **1b** (*as sentence modifier*): *actually, I haven't seen him.* **2** at present.

actuals (ˈæktʃʊəlz) *pl n Commerce.* commodities that can be purchased and used, as opposed to those bought and sold in a futures market. Also called: **physicals.**

actuary (ˈæktʃʊərɪ) *n, pl* **actuaries.** a person qualified to calculate commercial risks and probabilities involving uncertain future events, esp. in such contexts as life assurance. ORIG C16 (meaning: registrar): from L *āctuārius* one who keeps accounts, from *actum* public business, & *acta* documents
▸ **actuarial** (ˌæktʃʊˈɛərɪəl) *adj*

actuate (ˈæktʃʊˌeɪt) *vb* **actuates, actuating, actuated.** (*tr*) **1** to put into action or mechanical motion. **2** to motivate: *actuated by unworthy desires.* ORIG C16: from Med. L *actuātus*, from *actuāre* to incite to action, from L *āctus* ACT
▸ **ˌactuˈation** *n* ▸ **ˈactuˌator** *n*

act up *vb* (*intr, adv*) *Inf.* to behave in a troublesome way: *the engine began to act up.*

acuity (əˈkjuːɪtɪ) *n* keenness or acuteness, esp. in vision or thought. ORIG C15: from OF, from L *acūtus* ACUTE

aculeus (əˈkjuːlɪəs) *n* **1** a prickle, such as the thorn of a rose. **2** a sting. ORIG C19: from L, dim. of *acus* needle
▸ **aˈculeate** *adj*

acumen (ˈækjʊˌmɛn, əˈkjuːmən) *n* the ability to judge well; insight. ORIG C16: from L: sharpness, from *acuere* to sharpen
▸ **aˈcuminous** *adj*

acuminate *adj* (əˈkjuːmɪnɪt). **1** narrowing to a sharp point, as some types of leaf. ◆ *vb* (əˈkjuːmɪˌneɪt), **acuminates, acuminating, acuminated. 2** (*tr*) to make pointed or sharp. ORIG C17: from L *acūmināre* to sharpen
▸ **aˌcumiˈnation** *n*

acupoint (ˈækjʊˌpɔɪnt) *n* any of the specific points on the body into which a needle is inserted in acupuncture or onto which pressure is applied in shiatsu. ORIG C19: from ACU(PUNCTURE) + POINT

acupressure (ˈækjʊˌprɛʃə) *n* another name for **shiatsu.** ORIG C19: from ACU(PUNCTURE) + PRESSURE

acupuncture (ˈækjʊˌpʌŋktʃə) *n* the insertion of the tips of needles into the skin at specific points for the purpose of treating various disorders by stimulating nerve impulses. ORIG C17: from L *acus* needle + PUNCTURE
▸ **ˈacuˌpuncturist** *n*

acute (əˈkjuːt) *adj* **1** penetrating in perception or insight. **2** sensitive to details; keen. **3** of extreme importance; crucial. **4** sharp or severe; intense. **5** having a sharp end or point. **6** *Maths.* (of an angle) less than 90°. **7** (of a disease) **7a** arising suddenly and manifesting intense severity. **7b** of relatively short duration. **8** *Phonetics.* of or relating to an accent (´) placed over vowels, denoting that the vowel is pronounced with higher musical pitch (as in ancient Greek) or with certain special quality (as in French). **9** (of a hospital, hospital bed, or ward) intended to accommodate short-term patients. ◆ *n* **10** an acute accent. ORIG C14: from L *acūtus*, p.p. of *acuere* to sharpen, from *acus* needle
▸ **aˈcutely** *adv* ▸ **aˈcuteness** *n*

acute accent *n* the diacritical mark (´), used in some languages to indicate that the vowel over which it is placed has a special quality (as in French *été*) or that it receives the strongest stress in the word (as in Spanish *hablé*).

acute dose *n* a fatal dose of radiation.

ad (æd) *n Inf.* short for **advertisement.**

A.D. *or* **AD** (indicating years numbered from the supposed year of the birth of Christ) *abbrev. for* anno Domini: *70* A.D. ORIG L: in the year of the Lord

> **USAGE NOTE** In strict usage, A.D. should be only employed with specific years: *he died in 1621* A.D. In practice, it is often used with centuries, for clarity, and to mirror B.C. Formerly the practice was to write A.D. preceding the date (A.D. *1621*), and it is also strictly correct to omit *in* when A.D. is used, since this is already contained in the meaning of the Latin *anno Domini* (in the year of Our Lord), but nowadays this rule is not observed. Capitals without stops are often used in print these days for both AD and BC. B.C. is used with both specific dates and indications of the period: *Heraclitus was born about 540* B.C.; *the battle took place in the 4th century* B.C.

ad- *prefix* **1** to; towards: *adsorb.* **2** near; next to: *adrenal.* ORIG from L: towards. As a prefix in words of L origin, *ad-* became *ac-*, *af-*, *ag-*, *al-*, *an-*, *acq-*, *ar-*, *as-*, and *at-* before *c*, *f*, *g*, *l*, *n*, *q*, *r*, *s*, and *t*, and became *a-* before *gn*, *sc*, *sp*, *st*

adage (ˈædɪdʒ) *n* a traditional saying that is accepted by many as true; proverb. ORIG C16: via OF from L *adagium*; rel. to *āio* I say

adagio (əˈdɑːdʒɪˌəʊ) *Music.* ◆ *adj, adv* **1** (to be performed) slowly. ◆ *n, pl* **adagios. 2** a movement or piece to be performed slowly. ORIG C18: It., from *ad* at + *agio* ease

Adam[1] ★ (ˈædəm) *n* **1** *Bible.* the first man, created by God (Genesis 2–3). **2 not know (someone) from Adam.** to have no knowledge of or acquaintance with someone. **3 Adam's ale** *or* **wine.** water.

Adam[2] ★ (ˈædəm) *n* **1** (*French* adɑ̃). **Adolphe** (adɔlf). 1803–56, French composer, best known for his ballet *Giselle* (1841). **2 Robert.** 1728–92, Scottish neoclassical architect and furniture designer. Assisted by his brother, **James,** 1730–94. ◆ *adj* **3** in the neoclassical style made popular by Robert Adam.

adamant (ˈædəmənt) *adj* **1** unshakable in determination, purpose, etc.; inflexible. **2** unbreakable; impenetrable. ◆ *n* **3** any extremely hard substance. **4** a legendary stone said to be impenetrable. ORIG OE: from L *adamas*, from Gk, lit.: unconquerable, from A-[1] + *daman* to conquer
▸ **ˌadaˈmantine** *adj*

Adams[1] ★ (ˈædəmz) *n* a mountain in SW Washington, in the Cascade Range. Height: 3751 m (12 307 ft).

Adams[2] ★ (ˈædəmz) *n* **1 Ansel** (ˈænsᵊl). 1902–84, US photographer. **2 Gerard,** known as *Gerry.* born 1948, Irish politician; president of Sinn Féin from 1983. **3 Henry (Brooks).** 1838–1918, US historian and writer. His works include *Mont Saint Michel et Chartres* (1913) and his autobiography *The Education of Henry Adams* (1918). **4 John.** 1735–1826, second president of the US (1797–1801); US ambassador to Great Britain (1785–88). **5 John Couch.** 1819–92, British astronomer who deduced the existence and position of the planet Neptune. **6 John Quincy,** son of John Adams. 1767–1848, sixth president of the US (1825–29); secretary of state (1817–25). **7 Richard.** born 1920, British author, noted for his novels *Watership*

Down (1972), *The Plague Dogs* (1977), and *The Girl in a Swing* (1980). **8 Samuel.** 1722–1803, American revolutionary leader; one of the organizers of the Boston Tea Party; a signatory of the Declaration of Independence.

Adam's apple *n* the visible projection of the thyroid cartilage of the larynx at the front of the neck.

Adana ★ ('ædənə) *n* a city in S Turkey, capital of Adana province. Pop.: 1 047 300 (1994 est.). Also called: **Seyhan.**

adapt (ə'dæpt) *vb* **1** (often foll. by *to*) to adjust (someone or something) to different conditions. **2** (*tr*) to fit, change, or modify to suit a new or different purpose. ORIG C17: from L *adaptāre*, from *ad-* to + *aptāre* to fit
▸ **a'daptable** *adj* ▸ **a,dapta'bility** *n* ▸ **a'daptive** *adj*

adaptation (,ædəp'teɪʃən) *n* **1** the act or process of adapting or the state of being adapted. **2** something that is produced by adapting something else. **3** something that is changed or modified to suit new conditions. **4** *Biol.* a modification in organisms that makes them better suited to survive and reproduce in a particular environment.

adaptor *or* **adapter** (ə'dæptə) *n* **1** a person or thing that adapts. **2** any device for connecting two parts, esp. ones that are of different sizes. **3a** a plug used to connect an electrical device to a mains supply when they have different types of terminals. **3b** a device used to connect several electrical appliances to a single socket.

ADC *abbrev. for:* **1** aide-de-camp. **2** analogue-digital converter.

add (æd) *vb* **1** to combine (two or more numbers or quantities) by addition. **2** (*tr; foll. by to*) to increase (a number or quantity) by another number or quantity using addition. **3** (*tr; often foll. by to*) to join (something) to something else in order to increase the size, effect, or scope: *to add insult to injury*. **4** (*intr;* foll. by *to*) to have an extra and increased effect (on). **5** (*tr*) to say or write further. **6** (*tr;* foll. by *in*) to include. ◆ See also **add up.** ORIG C14: from L *addere*, from *ad-* to + *-dere*, *dare* to put

ADD *abbrev. for* attention deficit disorder.

Addams ★ ('ædəmz) *n* **Jane.** 1860–1935, US social reformer, feminist, and pacifist, who founded Hull House, a social settlement in Chicago: Nobel peace prize 1931.

addax ('ædæks) *n* a large light-coloured antelope having ribbed loosely spiralled horns and inhabiting desert regions in N Africa. ORIG C17: L, from an unidentified ancient N African language

addend ('ædɛnd) *n* any of a set of numbers that is to be added. ORIG C20: short for ADDENDUM

addendum (ə'dɛndəm) *n, pl* **addenda** (-də). **1** something added; an addition. **2** a supplement or appendix to a book, magazine, etc. ORIG C18: from L, gerundive of *addere* to ADD

adder ('ædə) *n* **1** Also called: **viper.** a common viper that is widely distributed in Europe, including Britain, and Asia and is dark grey with a black zigzag pattern along the back. **2** any of various similar venomous or nonvenomous snakes. ◆ See also **death adder, puff adder.** ORIG OE *nǣdre* snake; in ME *a naddre* was mistaken for *an addre*

adder's-tongue *n* any of several ferns that grow in the N hemisphere and have a narrow spore-bearing body that sticks out like a spike from the leaf.

addict *vb* (ə'dɪkt). **1** (*tr; usually passive;* often foll. by *to*) to cause (someone or oneself) to become dependent (on something, esp. a narcotic drug). ◆ *n* ('ædɪkt). **2** a person who is addicted, esp. to narcotic drugs. **3** *Inf.* a person devoted to something: *a jazz addict*. ORIG C16 (as adj and as vb; n use C20): from L *addictus* given over, from *addīcere*, from *ad-* to + *dīcere* to say
▸ **ad'diction** *n* ▸ **ad'dictive** *adj*

Addington ★ ('ædɪŋtən) *n* **Henry,** 1st Viscount Sidmouth. 1757–1844, British statesman; prime minister (1801–04) and Home Secretary (1812–21).

Addis Ababa ★ ('ædɪs 'æbəbə) *n* the capital of Ethiopia, on a central plateau 2400 m (8000 ft) above sea level: founded in 1887; became capital in 1896. Pop.: 2 316 400 (1994 est.).

Addison ★ ('ædɪsᵊn) *n* **Joseph.** 1672–1719, English essayist and poet who, with Richard Steele, founded *The Spectator* (1711–14) and contributed most of its essays, including the *de Coverley Papers*.

Addison's disease *n* a disease characterized by bronzing of the skin, anaemia, and extreme weakness, caused by underactivity of the adrenal glands. ORIG C19: after Thomas *Addison* (1793–1860), E physician who identified it

addition (ə'dɪʃən) *n* **1** the act, process, or result of adding. **2** a person or thing that is added or acquired. **3** a mathematical operation in which the sum of two numbers or quantities is calculated. Usually indicated by the symbol + **4** *Obs.* a title. **5 in addition.** (*adv*) also; as well. **6 in addition to.** (*prep*) besides; as well as. ORIG C15: from L *additiōn-*, from *addere* to ADD
▸ **ad'ditional** *adj*

additionality (ə,dɪʃə'nælɪtɪ) *n* **1** (in Britain) the principle that money raised by the National Lottery should be spent only on projects that would not otherwise be funded by government spending. **2** (in the European Union) the principle that the EU contributes to the funding of a project in a member country provided that the member country also contributes.

Additional Member System *n* a system of voting in which people vote separately for a candidate and a party. Parties are allocated extra seats if the number of constituencies they win does not reflect their overall share of the vote. See also **proportional representation.**

additive ('ædɪtɪv) *adj* **1** characterized or produced by addition. ◆ *n* **2** any substance added to something to improve it, prevent deterioration, etc. **3** short for **food additive.** ORIG C17: from LL *additīvus*, from *addere* to ADD

addle ('ædᵊl) *vb* **addles, addling, addled. 1** to make or become confused or muddled. **2** to make or become rotten. ◆ *adj* **3** (*in combination*) indicating a confused or muddled state: *addle-brained*. ORIG C18 (vb), back formation from *addled*, from C13 *addle* rotten, from OE *adela* filth

add-on *n* a feature that can be added to a standard model or package to give increased benefits.

address (ə'drɛs) *n* **1** the conventional form by which the location of a building is described. **2** the written form of this, as on a letter or parcel. **3** the place at which someone lives. **4** a speech or written communication, esp. one of a formal nature. **5** skilfulness or tact. **6** *Arch.* manner of speaking. **7** *Computing.* a number giving the location of a piece of stored information. **8** (*usually pl*) expressions of affection made by a man in courting a woman. ◆ *vb* (*tr*) **9** to mark (a letter, etc.) with an address. **10** to speak to, refer to in speaking, or deliver a speech to. **11** (used reflexively; foll. by *to*) **11a** to speak or write to. **11b** to apply oneself to: *he addressed himself to the task*. **12** to direct (a message, warning, etc.) to the attention of. **13** to adopt a position facing (the ball in golf, etc.). ORIG C14 (in the sense: to make right, adorn) and C15 (in the modern sense: to direct words): via OF from Vulgar L *addrictiāre* (unattested), from L *ad-* to + *dīrectus* DIRECT
▸ **ad'dresser** *or* **ad'dressor** *n*

addressee (,ædrɛ'siː) *n* a person or organization to whom a letter, etc., is addressed.

adduce (ə'djuːs) *vb* **adduces, adducing, adduced.** (*tr*) to cite (reasons, examples, etc.) as evidence or proof. ORIG C15: from L *addūcere* to lead to
▸ **ad'ducent** *adj* ▸ **ad'ducible** *adj* ▸ **adduction** (ə'dʌkʃən) *n*

adduct (ə'dʌkt) *vb* (*tr*) **1** (of a muscle) to draw or pull (a leg, arm, etc.) towards the median axis of the body. ◆ *n* **2** *Chem.* a compound formed by direct combination of two or more different compounds or elements. ORIG C19: from L *addūcere;* see ADDUCE
▸ **ad'duction** *n* ▸ **ad'ductor** *n*

add up *vb* (*adv*) **1** to find the sum (of). **2** (*intr*) to result in a correct total. **3** (*intr*) *Inf.* to make sense. **4** (*intr;* foll. by *to*) to amount to.

-ade *suffix forming nouns.* a sweetened drink made of various fruits: *lemonade*. ORIG from F, from L *-āta* made of, fem p.p. of verbs ending in *-āre*

Adelaide ★ ('ædɪ,leɪd) *n* the capital of South Australia: **Port Adelaide,** 11 km (7 miles) away on St Vincent Gulf, handles the bulk of exports. Pop.: 1 081 000 (1995 est.).

★ people and places

Aden ★ ('eɪdᵊn) *n* **1** the main port and commercial capital of Yemen, on the N coast of the **Gulf of Aden**, an arm of the Indian Ocean at the entrance to the Red Sea: capital of South Yemen until 1990: formerly an important port of call on shipping routes to the East. Pop.: 562 000 (1995 est.). **2** a former British colony and protectorate on the S coast of the Arabian Peninsula: became part of South Yemen in 1967, now part of Yemen. Area: 195 sq. km (75 sq. miles).

Adenauer ★ (*German* 'a:dənauər) *n* **Konrad** ('kɔnra:t). 1876–1967, German statesman; chancellor of West Germany (1949–63).

adenine ('ædənɪn) *n* a purine base present in animal and plant tissues as a constituent of the nucleic acids DNA and RNA.

adeno- *or before a vowel* **aden-** *combining form.* gland or glandular: *adenoid; adenology.* ORIG NL, from Gk *adēn* gland

adenoidal (,ædɪ'nɔɪdᵊl) *adj* **1** having the nasal tones or impaired breathing of one with enlarged adenoids. **2** of adenoids.

adenoids ('ædɪ,nɔɪdz) *pl n* a mass of lymphoid tissue at the back of the throat behind the uvula: when enlarged it often restricts nasal breathing, esp. in young children. ORIG C19 : from Gk *adenoeidēs.* See ADENO-, -OID

adenoma (,ædɪ'nəumə) *n, pl* **adenomas** *or* **adenomata** (-mətə). **1** a tumour occurring in glandular tissue. **2** a tumour having a glandlike structure.

adenopathy (,ædɪ'nɒpəθɪ) *n Pathol.* **1** enlargement of the lymph nodes. **2** enlargement of a gland.

adenosine (æ'dɛnə,si:n) *n Biochem.* a compound formed by the condensation of adenine and ribose. It is present in all living cells in a combined form. See also **ADP**[1], **AMP**, **ATP**. ORIG C20: a blend of ADENINE + RIBOSE

adept *adj* (ə'dɛpt). **1** proficient in something requiring skill or manual dexterity. **2** expert. ◆ *n* ('ædɛpt). **3** a person who is skilled or proficient in something. ORIG C17: from Med. L *adeptus,* from L *adipiscī,* from *ad-* to + *apiscī* to attain
▸ **a'deptness** *n*

adequate ('ædɪkwɪt) *adj* able to fulfil a need without being abundant, outstanding, etc. ORIG C17: from L *adaequāre,* from *ad-* to + *aequus* EQUAL
▸ **adequacy** ('ædɪkwəsɪ) *n* ▸ **'adequately** *adv*

à deux *French.* (a dø) *adj, adv* of or for two persons.

ADFA *abbrev. for* Australian Defence Force Academy.

ADH *abbrev. for* antidiuretic hormone. See **vasopressin**.

adhere (əd'hɪə) *vb* **adheres, adhering, adhered.** (*intr*) **1** (usually foll. by *to*) to stick or hold fast. **2** (foll. by *to*) to be devoted (to a political party, religion, etc.). **3** (foll. by *to*) to follow exactly. ORIG C16: via Med. L, from L *adhaerēre* to stick to

> **USAGE NOTE** See at **adhesion**.

adherent (əd'hɪərənt) *n* **1** (usually foll. by *of*) a supporter or follower. ◆ *adj* **2** sticking, holding fast, or attached.
▸ **ad'herence** *n*

adhesion (əd'hi:ʒən) *n* **1** the quality or condition of sticking together or holding fast. **2** ability to make firm contact without slipping. **3** attachment, as to a political party, cause, etc. **4** an attraction or repulsion between the molecules of unlike substances in contact. **5** *Pathol.* abnormal union of structures or parts. ORIG C17: from L *adhaesiōn-* a sticking. See ADHERE

> **USAGE NOTE** *Adhesion* is preferred when talking about sticking or holding fast in a physical sense. *Adherence* is preferred when talking about attachment to principles, rules, values, etc.

adhesive (əd'hi:sɪv) *adj* **1** able or designed to adhere: *adhesive tape.* **2** tenacious or clinging. ◆ *n* **3** a substance used for sticking, such as glue or paste.
▸ **ad'hesively** *adv* ▸ **ad'hesiveness** *n*

ad hoc (æd 'hɒk) *adj, adv* for a particular purpose only: *an ad hoc committee.* ORIG L, lit.: to this

ad hominem *Latin.* (æd 'hɒmɪ,nɛm) *adj, adv* directed against a person rather than his or her arguments. ORIG lit.: to the man

adiabatic (,ædɪə'bætɪk) *adj* **1** (of a thermodynamic process) taking place without loss or gain of heat. ◆ *n* **2** a curve on a graph representing the changes in a system undergoing an adiabatic process. ORIG C19: from Gk, from A-[1] + *diabatos* passable

adieu (ə'dju:) *sentence substitute, n, pl* **adieus** *or* **adieux** (ə'dju:z). goodbye. ORIG C14: from OF, from *a* to + *dieu* God

ad infinitum (æd ,ɪnfɪ'naɪtəm) *adv* without end; endlessly; to infinity. Abbrev.: **ad inf.** ORIG L

ad interim (æd 'ɪntərɪm) *adj, adv* for the meantime: *ad interim measures.* Abbrev.: **ad int.** ORIG L

adipocere (,ædɪpəu'sɪə) *n* a waxlike fatty substance sometimes formed during the decomposition of corpses. ORIG C19: from NL *adiposus* fat + F *cire* wax

adipose ('ædɪ,pəus) *adj* **1** of, resembling, or containing fat; fatty. ◆ *n* **2** animal fat. ORIG C18: from NL *adiposus,* from L *adeps* fat

Adirondack Mountains (,ædɪ'rɒndæk) *or* **Adirondacks** ★ *pl n* a mountain range in NE New York State. Highest peak: Mount Marcy, 1629 m (5344 ft).

adit ('ædɪt) *n* an almost horizontal shaft into a mine, for access or drainage. ORIG C17: from L *aditus,* from *adīre,* from *ad-* towards + *īre* to go

adj. *abbrev. for:* **1** adjective. **2** adjunct. **3** Also: **adjt.** adjutant.

adjacent (ə'dʒeɪsᵊnt) *adj* being near or close, esp. having a common boundary; contiguous. ORIG C15: from L *adjacēre,* from *ad-* near + *jacēre* to lie
▸ **ad'jacency** *n* ▸ **ad'jacently** *adv*

adjacent angles *pl n* two angles having the same vertex and a side in common.

adjective ('ædʒɪktɪv) *n* **1a** a word imputing a characteristic to a noun or pronoun. **1b** (*as modifier*): *an adjective phrase.* Abbrev.: **adj.** ◆ *adj* **2** additional or dependent. ORIG C14: from LL, from L from *adjicere,* from *ad-* to + *jacere* to throw
▸ **adjectival** (,ædʒɪk'taɪvᵊl) *adj*

adjoin (ə'dʒɔɪn) *vb* **1** to be next to (an area of land, etc.). **2** (*tr;* foll. by *to*) to join; attach. ORIG C14: via OF from L, from *ad-* to + *jungere* to join
▸ **ad'joining** *adj*

adjourn (ə'dʒɜ:n) *vb* **1** (*intr*) (of a court, etc.) to close at the end of a session. **2** to postpone or be postponed, esp. temporarily. **3** (*tr*) to put off (a problem, discussion, etc.) for later consideration. **4** (*intr*) *Inf.* to move elsewhere: *let's adjourn to the kitchen.* ORIG C14: from OF *ajourner* to defer to an arranged day, from *a-* to + *jour* day, from LL *diurnum,* from L *diēs* day
▸ **ad'journment** *n*

adjudge (ə'dʒʌdʒ) *vb* **adjudges, adjudging, adjudged.** (*tr; usually passive*) **1** to pronounce formally; declare. **2a** to judge. **2b** to decree: *he was adjudged bankrupt.* **2c** to award (costs, damages, etc.). **3** *Arch.* to condemn. ORIG C14: via OF from L *adjūdicāre.* See ADJUDICATE

adjudicate (ə'dʒu:dɪ,keɪt) *vb* **adjudicates, adjudicating, adjudicated.** **1** (when *intr,* usually foll. by *upon*) to give a decision (on), esp. a formal or binding one. **2** (*intr*) to serve as a judge or arbiter, as in a competition. ORIG C18: from L *adjūdicāre,* from *ad-* to + *jūdicāre* to judge, from *jūdex* judge
▸ **ad,judi'cation** *n* ▸ **ad'judi,cator** *n*

adjunct ('ædʒʌŋkt) *n* **1** something incidental or not essential that is added to something else. **2** a person who is subordinate to another. **3** *Grammar.* **3a** part of a sentence other than the subject or the predicate. **3b** a modifier. ◆ *adj* **4** added or connected in a secondary position. ORIG C16: from L *adjunctus,* p.p. of *adjungere* to ADJOIN
▸ **adjunctive** (ə'dʒʌŋktɪv) *adj* ▸ **'adjunctly** *adv*

adjure (ə'dʒuə) *vb* **adjures, adjuring, adjured.** (*tr*) **1** to command, often by exacting an oath. **2** to appeal earnestly

to. ORIG C14: from L *adjūrāre,* from *ad-* to + *jūrāre* to swear, from *jūs* oath
▸ **adjuration** (ˌædʒʊəˈreɪʃən) *n* ▸ **adˈjuratory** *adj* ▸ **adˈjurer** *or* **adˈjuror** *n*

adjust (əˈdʒʌst) *vb* **1** (*tr*) to alter slightly, esp. to achieve accuracy. **2** to adapt, as to a new environment, etc. **3** (*tr*) to put into order. **4** (*tr*) *Insurance.* to determine the amount payable in settlement of (a claim). ORIG C17: from OF *adjuster,* from *ad-* to + *juste* right, JUST
▸ **adˈjustable** *adj* ▸ **adˈjuster** *n*

adjustment (əˈdʒʌstmənt) *n* **1** the act of adjusting or state of being adjusted. **2** a control for regulating.

adjutant (ˈædʒətənt) *n* an officer who acts as administrative assistant to a superior officer. ORIG C17: from L *adjūtāre* to AID
▸ **ˈadjutancy** *n*

adjutant bird *or* **stork** *n* either of two large carrion-eating storks which are similar to the marabou and occur in S and SE Asia. ORIG so called for its supposedly military gait

adjutant general *n, pl* **adjutants general. 1** *Brit. Army.* a member of the Army Board responsible for personnel and administrative functions. **2** *US Army.* the adjutant of a military unit with general staff.

adjuvant (ˈædʒəvənt) *adj* **1** aiding or assisting. ◆ *n* **2** something that aids or assists; auxiliary. ORIG C17: from L *adjuvāre,* from *juvāre* to help

Adler ★ *n* **1** (*German* ˈa:dlər). **Alfred** (ˈalfre:t). 1870–1937, Austrian psychiatrist, noted for his descriptions of inferiority feelings. **2** (ˈædlə). **Larry,** full name *Lawrence Cecil Adler.* born 1914, US harmonica player.

Adlerian (ædˈlɪərɪən) *adj* of or relating to the work of Alfred Adler.

ad-lib (ædˈlɪb) *vb* **ad-libs, ad-libbing, ad-libbed. 1** to improvise and deliver spontaneously (a speech, etc.). ◆ *adj* (**ad lib** *when predicative*) **2** improvised. ◆ *adv* **ad lib. 3** spontaneously; freely. ◆ *n* **4** an improvised performance, often humorous. ORIG C18: short for L *ad libitum,* lit.: according to pleasure

ad libitum (ˌæd ˈlɪbɪtəm) *adv, adj Music.* at the performer's discretion. ORIG L.: see AD-LIB

Adm. *abbrev. for:* **1** Admiral. **2** Admiralty.

adman (ˈædˌmæn) *n, pl* **admen.** *Inf.* a man who works in advertising.

admass (ˈædmæs) *n* the section of the public that is susceptible to advertising, etc., and the processes involved in influencing them. ORIG C20: from AD + MASS

admeasure (ædˈmɛʒə) *vb* **admeasures, admeasuring, admeasured.** to measure out (land, etc.) as a share; apportion. ORIG C14 *amesuren,* from OF, from *mesurer* to MEASURE; the modern form derives from AD- + MEASURE

Admetus ★ (ædˈmi:təs) *n Greek myth.* a king of Thessaly, one of the Argonauts, who was married to Alcestis.

admin (ˈædmɪn) *n Inf.* short for **administration.**

administer (ədˈmɪnɪstə) *vb* (*mainly tr*) **1** (*also intr*) to direct or control (the affairs of a business, etc.). **2** to dispense: *administer justice.* **3** (when *intr,* foll. by *to*) to give or apply (medicine, etc.). **4** to supervise the taking of (an oath, etc.). **5** to manage (an estate, property, etc.). ORIG C14 *amynistre* via OF from L, from *ad-* to + *ministrāre* to MINISTER

administrate (ədˈmɪnɪˌstreɪt) *vb* **administrates, administrating, administrated.** to manage or direct (the affairs of a business, institution, etc.).

administration (ədˌmɪnɪˈstreɪʃən) *n* **1** management of the affairs of an organization, such as a business or institution. **2** the duties of an administrator. **3** the body of people who administer an organization. **4** the conduct of the affairs of government. **5** term of office: used of governments, etc. **6** the government as a whole. **7** (*often cap.*) *Chiefly US.* the political executive, esp. of the US. **8** *Property law.* **8a** the conduct or disposal of the estate of a deceased person. **8b** the management by a trustee of an estate. **9a** the administering of something, such as a sacrament or medical treatment. **9b** the thing that is administered.
▸ **adˈministrative** *adj* ▸ **adˈministratively** *adv*

administration order *n Law.* **1** an order by a court appointing a person to manage a company that is in financial difficulty. **2** an order by a court for the administration of the estate of a debtor who has been ordered by the court to pay money that he owes.

administrator (ədˈmɪnɪˌstreɪtə) *n* **1** a person who administers the affairs of an organization, official body, etc. **2** *Property law.* a person authorized to manage an estate.

admirable (ˈædmərəbᵊl) *adj* deserving or inspiring admiration; excellent.
▸ **ˈadmirably** *adv*

admiral (ˈædmərəl) *n* **1** the supreme commander of a fleet or navy. **2** Also called: **admiral of the fleet, fleet admiral.** a naval officer of the highest rank. **3** a senior naval officer entitled to fly his own flag. See also **rear admiral, vice admiral. 4** *Chiefly Brit.* the master of a fishing fleet. **5** any of various brightly coloured butterflies, esp. the red admiral or white admiral. ORIG C13 *amyral,* from OF *amiral* emir, & from Med. L *admīrālis* (spelling prob. infl. by *admīrābilis* admirable); both from Ar. *amīr* emir, commander, esp. in *amīr-al* commander of
▸ **ˈadmiralship** *n*

admiralty (ˈædmərəltɪ) *n, pl* **admiralties. 1** the office or jurisdiction of an admiral. **2** jurisdiction over naval affairs.

Admiralty Board *n* **the.** (formerly) a department of the British Ministry of Defence, responsible for the administration of the Royal Navy.

Admiralty House *n* the official residence of the Governor General of Australia, in Sydney.

Admiralty Islands ★ *pl n* a group of about 40 volcanic and coral islands in the SW Pacific, part of Papua New Guinea, in the Bismarck Archipelago: main island: Manus. Pop.: 35 200 (1995). Area: about 2000 sq. km (800 sq. miles). Also called: **Admiralties.**

Admiralty Range ★ *n* a mountain range in Antarctica, on the coast of Victoria Land, northwest of the Ross Sea.

admiration (ˌædməˈreɪʃən) *n* **1** pleasurable contemplation or surprise. **2** a person or thing that is admired.

admire (ədˈmaɪə) *vb* **admires, admiring, admired.** (*tr*) **1** to regard with esteem, approval, or pleased surprise. **2** *Arch.* to wonder at. ORIG C16: from L *admīrāri,* from *ad-* to, at + *mīrāri* to wonder
▸ **adˈmirer** *n* ▸ **adˈmiring** *adj* ▸ **adˈmiringly** *adv*

admissible (ədˈmɪsəbᵊl) *adj* **1** able or deserving to be considered or allowed. **2** deserving to be allowed to enter. **3** *Law.* (esp. of evidence) capable of being admitted in a court of law.
▸ **adˌmissiˈbility** *n*

admission (ədˈmɪʃən) *n* **1** permission to enter or the right to enter. **2** the price charged for entrance. **3** acceptance for a position, etc. **4** a confession, as of a crime, etc. **5** an acknowledgment of the truth of something. ORIG C15: from L *admissiōn-,* from *admittere* to ADMIT
▸ **adˈmissive** *adj*

admit (ədˈmɪt) *vb* **admits, admitting, admitted.** (*mainly tr*) **1** (*may take a clause as object*) to confess or acknowledge (a crime, mistake, etc.). **2** (*may take a clause as object*) to concede (the truth of something). **3** to allow to enter. **4** (foll. by *to*) to allow participation (in) or the right to be part (of). **5** (when *intr,* foll. by *of*) to allow (of). ORIG C14: from L *admittere,* from *ad-* to + *mittere* to send

admittance (ədˈmɪtᵊns) *n* **1** the right or authority to enter. **2** the act of giving entrance. **3** *Electricity.* the reciprocal of impedance.

admittedly (ədˈmɪtɪdlɪ) *adv* (*sentence modifier*) willingly conceded: *admittedly I am afraid.*

admix (ədˈmɪks) *vb* (*tr*) *Rare.* to mix or blend. ORIG C16: back formation from obs. *admixt,* from L *admīscēre* to mix with

admixture (ədˈmɪkstʃə) *n* **1** a less common word for **mixture. 2** an ingredient.

admonish (ədˈmɒnɪʃ) *vb* (*tr*) **1** to reprove firmly but not harshly. **2** to warn; caution. ORIG C14: via OF from Vulgar L *admonestāre* (unattested), from L *admonēre,* from *monēre* to advise

▸ **ad'monishment** *n* ▸ **admonition** (ˌædməˈnɪʃən) *n* ▸ **ad'monitory** *adj*

ad nauseam (æd ˈnɔːzɪˌæm) *adv* to a disgusting extent. ORIG L: to (the point of) nausea

> **USAGE NOTE** This phrase is quite often misspelt as *ad nauseum.*

ado (əˈduː) *n* bustling activity; fuss; bother; delay (esp. in **without more ado, with much ado**). ORIG C14: from *at do* a to-do, from ON *at* to (marking the infinitive) + DO[1]

adobe (əˈdəʊbɪ) *n* **1** a sun-dried brick used for building. **2** a building constructed of such bricks. **3** the clayey material from which such bricks are made. ORIG C19: from Sp.

adolescence (ˌædəˈlɛsəns) *n* the period in human development that occurs between the beginning of puberty and adulthood. ORIG C15: via OF from L, from *adolēscere* to grow up

adolescent (ˌædəˈlɛsᵊnt) *adj* **1** of or relating to adolescence. **2** *Inf.* behaving in an immature way. ◆ *n* **3** an adolescent person.

Adonai ★ (ˌædɒˈnaɪ, -ˈneɪaɪ) *n Judaism.* a name for God. ORIG C15: from Heb.: lord; cf. ADONIS

Adonis ★ (əˈdəʊnɪs) *n* **1** *Greek myth.* a handsome youth loved by Aphrodite. **2** a handsome young man. ORIG C16: from L via Gk from Phoenician *adōni* my lord; rel. to Heb. *Adonai* Lord

adopt (əˈdɒpt) *vb (tr)* **1** *Law.* to take (another's child) as one's own child. **2** to choose and follow (a plan, method, etc.). **3** to take over (an idea, etc.) as if it were one's own. **4** to assume: *to adopt a title.* **5** to accept (a report, etc.). ORIG C16: from L *adoptāre,* from *optāre* to choose
▸ ˌ**adop'tee** *n* ▸ **a'doption** *n*

adopted (əˈdɒptɪd) *adj* having been adopted.

adoptive (əˈdɒptɪv) *adj* **1** acquired or related by adoption: *an adoptive father.* Cf. **adopted. 2** of or relating to adoption.

adorable (əˈdɔːrəbᵊl) *adj* **1** very attractive; lovable. **2** *Becoming rare.* deserving adoration.
▸ **a'dorably** *adv*

adoration (ˌædəˈreɪʃən) *n* **1** deep love or esteem. **2** the act of worshipping.

adore (əˈdɔː) *vb* **adores, adoring, adored. 1** *(tr)* to love intensely or deeply. **2** to worship (a god) with religious rites. **3** *(tr) Inf.* to like very much. ORIG C15: via F from L *adōrāre,* from *ad-* to + *ōrāre* to pray
▸ **a'dorer** *n* ▸ **a'doring** *adj* ▸ **a'doringly** *adv*

adorn (əˈdɔːn) *vb (tr)* **1** to decorate. **2** to increase the beauty, distinction, etc., of. ORIG C14: via OF from L *adōrnāre,* from *ōrnāre* to furnish
▸ **a'dornment** *n*

Adowa ★ (ˈɑːdʊˌwɑː) *n* a variant spelling of **Aduwa.**

ADP *n Biochem.* adenosine diphosphate; a substance derived from ATP with the liberation of energy that is then used in the performance of muscular work.

Adrastus ★ (əˈdræstəs) *n Greek myth.* a king of Argos and leader of the Seven against Thebes of whom he was the sole survivor.

ad rem *Latin.* (æd ˈrɛm) *adj, adv* to the point; without digression.

adrenal (əˈdriːnᵊl) *adj* **1** on or near the kidneys. **2** of or relating to the adrenal glands or their secretions. ◆ *n* **3** an adrenal gland. ORIG C19: from AD- (near) + RENAL

adrenal gland *n* an endocrine gland at the anterior end of each kidney. It secretes adrenaline. Also called: **suprarenal gland.**

adrenaline *or* **adrenalin** (əˈdrɛnəlɪn) *n* a hormone that is secreted by the adrenal medulla in response to stress and increases heart rate, pulse rate, and blood pressure. It is extracted from animals or synthesized for medical use. US name: **epinephrine.**

Adrian IV ★ *n* original name *Nicholas Breakspear.* ?1100–59, the only English pope (1154–59).

Adrianople (ˌeɪdrɪəˈnəʊpᵊl) *or* **Adrianopolis** ★ (ˌeɪdrɪəˈnɒpəlɪs) *n* former names of **Edirne.**

Adriatic (ˌeɪdrɪˈætɪk) *adj* **1** of or relating to the Adriatic Sea, or to the inhabitants of its coast or islands. ◆ *n* **2 the.** short for the **Adriatic Sea.**

Adriatic Sea ★ *n* an arm of the Mediterranean between Italy and the Balkan Peninsula.

adrift (əˈdrɪft) *adj (postpositive), adv* **1** floating without steering or mooring; drifting. **2** without purpose; aimless. **3** *Inf.* off course.

adroit (əˈdrɔɪt) *adj* **1** skilful or dexterous. **2** quick in thought or reaction. ORIG C17: from F *à droit* rightly
▸ **a'droitly** *adv* ▸ **a'droitness** *n*

adsorb (ədˈsɔːb) *vb* to undergo or cause to undergo a process in which a substance, usually a gas, accumulates on the surface of a solid forming a thin film. ORIG C19: AD- + *-sorb* as in ABSORB
▸ **ad'sorbable** *adj* ▸ **ad'sorbent** *adj* ▸ **ad'sorption** *n*

adsorbate (ədˈsɔːbeɪt) *n* a substance that has been or is to be adsorbed.

ADT (in the US and Canada) *abbrev. for* Atlantic Daylight Time.

adulate (ˈædjʊˌleɪt) *vb* **adulates, adulating, adulated.** *(tr)* to flatter or praise obsequiously. ORIG C17: back formation from C15 *adulation,* from L *adūlārī* to flatter
▸ ˌ**adu'lation** *n* ▸ **'aduˌlator** *n* ▸ **adulatory** (ˌædjʊˈleɪtərɪ) *adj*

adult (ˈædʌlt, əˈdʌlt) *adj* **1** having reached maturity; fully developed. **2** of or intended for mature people: *adult education.* **3** suitable only for adults because of being pornographic. ◆ *n* **4** a person who has attained maturity. **5** a mature fully grown animal or plant. **6** *Law.* a person who has attained the age of legal majority. ORIG C16: from L *adultus,* from *adolēscere* to grow up
▸ **a'dulthood** *n*

adulterant (əˈdʌltərənt) *n* **1** a substance that adulterates. ◆ *adj* **2** adulterating.

adulterate *vb* (əˈdʌltəˌreɪt), **adulterates, adulterating, adulterated. 1** *(tr)* to debase by adding inferior material: *to adulterate milk with water.* ◆ *adj* (əˈdʌltərɪt). **2** debased or impure. ORIG C16: from L *adulterāre* to corrupt, commit adultery, prob. from *alter* another
▸ **aˌdulter'ation** *n* ▸ **a'dulterˌator** *n*

adulterer (əˈdʌltərə) *or (fem)* **adulteress** *n* a person who has committed adultery. ORIG C16: orig. also *adulter,* from L *adulter,* back formation from *adulterāre* to ADULTERATE

adulterous (əˈdʌltərəs) *adj* of, characterized by, or inclined to adultery.
▸ **a'dulterously** *adv*

adultery (əˈdʌltərɪ) *n, pl* **adulteries.** voluntary sexual intercourse between a married man or woman and a partner other than the legal spouse. ORIG C15 *adulterie,* altered from C14 *avoutrie,* via OF from L *adulterium,* from *adulter,* back formation from *adulterāre.* See ADULTERATE

adumbrate (ˈædʌmˌbreɪt) *vb* **adumbrates, adumbrating, adumbrated.** *(tr)* **1** to outline; give a faint indication of. **2** to foreshadow. **3** to obscure. ORIG C16: from L *adumbrāre* to cast a shadow on, from *umbra* shadow
▸ ˌ**adum'bration** *n* ▸ **adumbrative** (ædˈʌmbrətɪv) *adj*

Aduwa *or* **Adowa** ★ (ˈɑːdʊˌwɑː) *n* a town in N Ethiopia: Emperor Menelik II defeated the Italians here in 1896. Pop.: 17 476 (1989 est.). Italian name: **Adua** (ˈadua).

adv. *abbrev. for:* **1** adverb. **2** adverbial. **3** adversus. ORIG L: against **4** advertisement. **5** advocate.

ad valorem (æd vəˈlɔːrəm) *adj, adv* (of taxes) in proportion to the estimated value of the goods taxed. Abbrev.: **ad val., a.v., A/V.** ORIG from L

advance (ədˈvɑːns) *vb* **advances, advancing, advanced. 1** to go or bring forward in position. **2** (foll. by *on*) to move (towards) in a threatening manner. **3** *(tr)* to present for consideration. **4** to improve; further. **5** *(tr)* to cause (an event) to occur earlier. **6** *(tr)* to supply (money, goods, etc.) beforehand, either for a loan or as an initial payment. **7** to increase (a price, etc.) or (of a price, etc.) to be increased. **8** *(intr)* to be promoted. ◆ *n* **9** forward movement; progress in time or space. **10** improvement; prog-

ress in development. **11** *Commerce.* **11a** the supplying of commodities or funds before receipt of an agreed consideration. **11b** the commodities or funds supplied in this manner. **12** Also called: **advance payment.** a money payment made before it is legally due: *this is an advance on your salary.* **13** a loan of money. **14** an increase in price, etc. **15 in advance. 15a** beforehand: *payment in advance.* **15b** (foll. by *of*) ahead in time or development: *ideas in advance of the time.* **16** (*modifier*) forward in position or time: *advance booking.* ◆ See also **advances.** ORIG C15 *advauncen,* altered from C13 *avauncen,* via OF from L *abante,* from *ab-* away + *ante* before
▸ **ad'vancer** *n*

advance corporation tax *n* a British tax in which a company paying a dividend must deduct the basic rate of income tax from the grossed-up value of the dividend and pay it to the Inland Revenue. Abbrev.: **ACT.**

advanced (əd'vɑːnst) *adj* **1** being ahead in development, knowledge, progress, etc. **2** having reached a comparatively late stage: *a man of advanced age.* **3** ahead of the times.

advanced gas-cooled reactor *n* a nuclear reactor using carbon dioxide as the coolant, and ceramic uranium dioxide cased in stainless steel as the fuel. Abbrev.: **AGR.**

advance directive *n* another name for **living will.**

Advanced level *n* a formal name for **A level.**

advancement (əd'vɑːnsmənt) *n* **1** promotion in rank, status, etc. **2** a less common word for **advance** (senses 9, 10).

advances (əd'vɑːnsɪz) *pl n* (*sometimes sing;* often foll. by *to* or *towards*) overtures made in an attempt to become friendly, etc.

advantage (əd'vɑːntɪdʒ) *n* **1** (often foll. by *over* or *of*) a more favourable position; superiority. **2** benefit or profit (esp. in **to one's advantage**). **3** *Tennis.* the point scored after deuce. **4 take advantage of. 4a** to make good use of. **4b** to impose upon the weakness, good nature, etc., of. **4c** to seduce. **5 to advantage.** to good effect. ◆ *vb* **advantages, advantaging, advantaged. 6** (*tr*) to put in a better position; favour. ORIG C14 *avantage* (later altered to *advantage*), from OF *avant* before, from L *abante* from before. See ADVANCE

advantageous (ˌædvən'teɪdʒəs) *adj* producing advantage.
▸ **ˌadvan'tageously** *adv*

advection (əd'vɛkʃən) *n* the transference of heat energy in a horizontal stream of gas, esp. of air. ORIG C20: from L *advectiō,* from *advehere,* from *ad-* to + *vehere* to carry

advent ('ædvɛnt, -vənt) *n* an arrival or coming, esp. one which is awaited. ORIG C12: from L *adventus,* from *advenīre,* from *ad-* to + *venīre* to come

Advent ('ædvɛnt) *n* the season including the four Sundays preceding Christmas.

Advent calendar *n* a large card with small numbered doors for children to open on each of the days of Advent, revealing pictures beneath them.

Adventist ('ædvɛntɪst) *n* a member of a Christian group that holds that the Second Coming of Christ is imminent.

adventitious (ˌædvɛn'tɪʃəs) *adj* **1** added or appearing accidentally. **2** (of a plant or animal part) developing in an abnormal position. ORIG C17: from L *adventīcius* coming from outside, from *adventus* a coming
▸ **ˌadven'titiously** *adv*

adventure (əd'vɛntʃə) *n* **1** a risky undertaking of unknown outcome. **2** an exciting or unexpected event or course of events. **3** a hazardous financial operation. ◆ *vb* **adventures, adventuring, adventured. 4** to take a risk or put at risk. **5** (*intr;* foll. by *into, on,* or *upon*) to dare to enter (into a place, dangerous activity, etc.). **6** to dare to say (something): *he adventured his opinion.* ORIG C13 *aventure* (later altered to *adventure*), via OF ult. from L *advenīre* to happen to (someone), arrive

adventure playground *n Brit.* a playground for children that contains building materials, etc., used to build with, climb on, etc.

adventurer (əd'vɛntʃərə) *or* (*fem*) **adventuress** *n* **1** a person who seeks adventure, esp. one who seeks success or money through daring exploits. **2** a person who seeks money or power by unscrupulous means. **3** a speculator.

adventurism (əd'vɛntʃəˌrɪzəm) *n* recklessness, esp. in politics and finance.
▸ **ad'venturist** *n*

adventurous (əd'vɛntʃərəs) *adj* **1** Also: **adventuresome.** daring or enterprising. **2** dangerous; involving risk.

adverb ('ædˌvɜːb) *n* **a** a word or group of words that serves to modify a whole sentence, a verb, another adverb, or an adjective; for example, *easily, very,* and *happily* respectively in the sentence *They could easily envy the very happily married couple.* **b** (*as modifier*): *an adverb marker.* Abbrev.: **adv.** ORIG C15–C16: from L *adverbium* adverb, lit.: added word
▸ **ad'verbial** *adj*

adversarial (ˌædvɜː'sɛərɪəl) *adj* (of political parties) hostile to and opposing each other on party lines; antagonistic.

adversary ('ædvəsərɪ) *n, pl* **adversaries. 1** a person or group that is hostile to someone. **2** an opposing contestant in a sport. ORIG C14: from L *adversārius,* from *adversus* against

adversative (əd'vɜːsətɪv) *Grammar.* ◆ *adj* **1** (of a word, phrase, or clause) implying opposition. *But* and *although* are adversative conjunctions. ◆ *n* **2** an adversative word or speech element.

adverse ('ædvɜːs) *adj* **1** antagonistic; hostile: *adverse criticism.* **2** unfavourable to one's interests: *adverse circumstances.* **3** contrary or opposite: *adverse winds.* ORIG C14: from L *adversus,* from *advertere,* from *ad-* towards + *vertere* to turn
▸ **ad'versely** *adv* ▸ **ad'verseness** *n*

> **USAGE NOTE** The construction *adverse to* is sometimes mistakenly used instead of *averse to.* In the following example *averse* is correct, and *adverse* would be wrong: *...not averse to a little self-promotion.*

adversity (əd'vɜːsɪtɪ) *n, pl* **adversities. 1** distress; affliction; hardship. **2** an unfortunate event.

advert[1] (əd'vɜːt) *vb* (*intr;* foll. by *to*) to draw attention (to). ORIG C15: from L *advertere* to turn one's attention to

advert[2] ('ædvɜːt) *n Brit. inf.* short for **advertisement.**

advertise *or US* (*sometimes*) **advertize** ('ædvəˌtaɪz) *vb* **advertises, advertising, advertised** *or US* (*sometimes*) **advertizes, advertizing, advertized. 1** to present or praise (goods, a service, etc.) to the public, esp. in order to encourage sales. **2** to make (a vacancy, article for sale, etc.) publicly known: *to advertise a job.* **3** (*intr;* foll. by *for*) to make a public request (for): *she advertised for a cook.* ORIG C15: from OF *avertir,* ult. from L *advertere* to turn one's attention to. See ADVERSE
▸ **'adverˌtiser** *or US* (*sometimes*) **'adverˌtizer** *n*

advertisement *or US* (*sometimes*) **advertizement** (əd'vɜːtɪsmənt) *n* any public notice, as a printed display in a newspaper, short film on television, etc., designed to sell goods, publicize an event, etc.

advertising *or US* (*sometimes*) **advertizing** ('ædvəˌtaɪzɪŋ) *n* **1** the promotion of goods or services for sale through impersonal media such as television. **2** the business that specializes in creating such publicity. **3** advertisements collectively.

Advertising Standards Authority *n* (in Britain) an independent body set up by the advertising industry to ensure that all advertisements comply with the British Code of Advertising Practice. Abbrev.: **ASA.**

advertorial (ˌædvɜː'tɔːrɪəl) *n* **1** advertising presented under the guise of editorial material. ◆ *adj* **2** presented in such a manner. ORIG C20: from blend of ADVERT[2] + EDITORIAL

advice (əd'vaɪs) *n* **1** recommendation as to appropriate choice of action. **2** (*sometimes pl*) formal notification of facts. ORIG C13 *avis* (later *advise*), via OF from Vulgar L, from L *ad* to + *vīsum* view

advisable (əd'vaɪzəbᵊl) *adj* worthy of recommendation; prudent.
▸ **ad'visably** *adv* ▸ **ad,visa'bility** *or* **ad'visableness** *n*

advise (əd'vaɪz) *vb* **advises, advising, advised.** (*when tr, may take a clause as object or an infinitive*) **1** to offer advice (to a person or persons): *he advised caution.* **2** (*tr;* sometimes foll. by *of*) to inform or notify. **3** (*intr;* foll. by *with*) *Chiefly US, obs. in Britain.* to consult. ORIG C14: via OF from Vulgar L *advīsāre* (unattested), from L *ad-* to + *vidēre* to see

advised (əd'vaɪzd) *adj* resulting from deliberation. See also **ill-advised, well-advised.**
▸ **advisedly** (əd'vaɪzɪdlɪ) *adv*

adviser *or* **advisor** (əd'vaɪzə) *n* **1** a person who advises. **2** *Education.* a person responsible for advising students on career guidance, etc. **3** *Brit. education.* a subject specialist who advises on current teaching methods and facilities.

advisory (əd'vaɪzərɪ) *adj* **1** empowered to make recommendations: *an advisory body.* ◆ *n, pl* **advisories. 2** a statement issued to give advice, recommendations, or a warning: *a travel advisory.* **3** a person or organization with an advisory function: *the Prime Minister's media advisory.*

advocaat ('ædvəʊ,kɑː) *n* a liqueur having a raw egg base. ORIG C20: Du.

advocacy ('ædvəkəsɪ) *n, pl* **advocacies.** active support, esp. of a cause.

advocate *vb* ('ædvə,keɪt), **advocates, advocating, advocated. 1** (*tr; may take a clause as object*) to support or recommend publicly. ◆ *n* ('ædvəkɪt). **2** a person who upholds or defends a cause. **3** a person who intercedes on behalf of another. **4** a person who pleads his or her client's cause in a court of law. **5** *Scots Law.* the usual word for **barrister.** ORIG C14: via OF from L *advocātus* legal witness, from *advocāre,* from *vocāre* to call

advowson (əd'vaʊzᵊn) *n English ecclesiastical law.* the right of presentation to a vacant benefice. ORIG C13: via OF from L *advocātiōn-,* from *advocāre* to summon

advt *abbrev. for* advertisement.

Adygei Republic (,ɑːdɪ'geɪ) *or* **Adygea** ★ (,ɑːdɪ'geɪa; *Russian* adɪ'gɛja) *n* a constituent republic of SW Russia, bordering on the Caucasus Mountains: chiefly agricultural but with some mineral resources. Capital: Maikop. Pop.: 450 000 (1996 est.). Area: 7600 sq. km (2934 sq. miles).

adze *or US* **adz** (ædz) *n* a hand tool with a steel blade attached at right angles to a wooden handle, used for dressing timber. ORIG OE *adesa*

Adzhar Autonomous Republic (ə'dʒɑː) *or* **Adzharia** ★ (ə'dʒɑːrɪə) *n* an administrative division of SW Georgia, on the Black Sea: part of Turkey from the 17th century until 1878; mostly mountainous, reaching 2805 m (9350 ft), with a subtropical coastal strip. Capital: Batumi. Pop.: 386 700 (1993 est.). Area: 3000 sq. km (1160 sq. miles).

AEA (in Britain) *abbrev. for* Atomic Energy Authority.

AEC (in the US) *abbrev. for* Atomic Energy Commission.

aedes (eɪ'iːdiːz) *n* a mosquito of tropical and subtropical regions which transmits yellow fever. ORIG C20: NL, from Gk *aēdēs* unpleasant, from A-[1] + *ēdos* pleasant

aedile *or US* (*sometimes*) **edile** ('iːdaɪl) *n* a magistrate of ancient Rome in charge of public works, games, buildings, and roads. ORIG C16: from L *aedīlis,* from *aedēs* a building

Aeëtes ★ (iː'iːtiːz) *n Greek myth.* a king of Colchis, father of Medea and keeper of the Golden Fleece.

AEEU (in Britain) *abbrev. for* Amalgamated Engineering and Electrical Union.

Aegean (iː'dʒiːən) *adj* of or relating to the Aegean Sea or Islands.

Aegean Islands ★ *pl n* the islands of the Aegean Sea, including the Cyclades, Dodecanese, Euboea, and Sporades. The majority are under Greek administration.

Aegean Sea ★ *n* an arm of the Mediterranean between Greece and Turkey.

Aegeus ★ (iː'dʒiːuːs, 'iːdʒɪəs) *n Greek myth.* an Athenian king and father of Theseus.

Aegina ★ (iː'dʒaɪnə) *n* **1** an island in the Aegean Sea, in the Saronic Gulf. Area: 85 sq. km (33 sq. miles). **2** a town on the coast of this island: a city-state of ancient Greece. **3 Gulf of.** another name for the **Saronic Gulf.** ◆ Greek name: **Aiyina.**

Aegir ★ ('iːdʒɪə) *n Norse myth.* the god of the sea.

aegis *or US* (*sometimes*) **egis** ('iːdʒɪs) *n* **1** sponsorship or protection (esp. in **under the aegis of**). **2** *Greek myth.* the shield of Zeus. ORIG C18: from L, from Gk *aigis* shield of Zeus

Aegisthus ★ (iː'dʒɪsθəs) *n Greek myth.* a cousin to and the murderer of Agamemnon, whose wife Clytemnestra he had seduced. He usurped the kingship of Mycenae until Orestes, Agamemnon's son, returned home and killed him.

Aegospotami ★ (,iːgəs'pɒtə,maɪ) *n* a river of ancient Thrace that flowed into the Hellespont. At its mouth the Spartan fleet under Lysander defeated the Athenians in 405 B.C., ending the Peloponnesian War.

aegrotat ('aɪgrəʊ,tæt, 'iː-) *n* **1** (in British and certain other universities, and, sometimes, schools) a certificate allowing a candidate to pass an examination although he has missed all or part of it through illness. **2** a degree or other qualification obtained in such circumstances. ORIG C19: L, lit.: he is ill

Ælfric ★ ('ælfrɪk) *n* called *Grammaticus.* ?955–?1020, English abbot, writer, and grammarian.

-aemia, -haemia, *or US* **-emia, -hemia** *n combining form.* denoting blood, esp. a specified condition of the blood in diseases: *leukaemia.* ORIG NL, from Gk, from *haima* blood

Aeneas ★ (ɪ'niːəs) *n Classical myth.* a Trojan prince, the son of Anchises and Aphrodite, who escaped the sack of Troy and sailed to Italy via Carthage and Sicily. After seven years, he and his followers established themselves near the site of the future Rome.

Aeneid (ɪ'niːɪd) *n* an epic poem in Latin by Virgil relating the experiences of Aeneas after the fall of Troy.

aeolian harp (iː'əʊlɪən) *n* a stringed instrument that produces a musical sound when wind passes over the strings. Also called: **wind harp.** ORIG after AEOLUS

Aeolian Islands ★ *pl n* another name for the **Lipari Islands.**

Aeolis ('iːəlɪs) *or* **Aeolia** ★ (iː'əʊlɪə) *n* the ancient name for the coastal region of NW Asia Minor, including the island of Lesbos, settled by the Aeolian Greeks (about 1000 B.C.).

aeolotropic (,iːələʊ'trɒpɪk) *adj* a less common word for **anisotropic.** ORIG C19: from Gk *aiolos* fickle + -TROPIC
▸ **aeolotropy** (,iːə'lɒtrəpɪ) *n*

Aeolus ★ ('iːələs, iː'əʊləs) *n Greek myth.* **1** the god of the winds. **2** the founding king of the Aeolians in Thessaly.

aeon *or esp. US* **eon** ('iːən, 'iːɒn) *n* **1** an immeasurably long period of time. **2** *Astron.* a period of one thousand million years. ORIG C17: from Gk *aiōn* an infinitely long time

aerate ('ɛəreɪt) *vb* **aerates, aerating, aerated.** (*tr*) **1** to charge (a liquid) with a gas, as in the manufacture of effervescent drink. **2** to expose to the action or circulation of the air.
▸ **aer'ation** *n* ▸ **'aerator** *n*

aeri- *combining form.* a variant of **aero-.**

aerial ('ɛərɪəl) *adj* **1** of or resembling air. **2** existing, moving, or operating in the air: *aerial cable car.* **3** ethereal; light and delicate. **4** imaginary. **5** extending high into the air. **6** of or relating to aircraft: *aerial combat.* ◆ *n* **7** Also called: **antenna.** the part of a radio or television system by means of which radio waves are transmitted or received. ORIG C17: via L from Gk *aērios,* from *aēr* air

aerialist ('ɛərɪəlɪst) *n* a trapeze artist or tightrope walker.

aerie ('ɛərɪ) *n* a variant spelling (esp. US) of **eyrie.**

aeriform ('ɛərɪ,fɔːm) *adj* **1** having the form of air; gaseous. **2** unsubstantial.

aero ('ɛərəʊ) *n* (*modifier*) of or relating to aircraft or aeronautics: *an aero engine.*

aero-, aeri-, *or before a vowel* **aer-** *combining form.* **1** denoting air, atmosphere, or gas: *aerodynamics.* **2** denoting aircraft: *aeronautics.* ORIG ult. from Gk *aēr* air

aerobatics (ˌɛərəʊ'bætɪks) *n* (*functioning as sing or pl*) spectacular or dangerous manoeuvres, such as loops or rolls, performed in an aircraft or glider. ORIG C20: from AERO- + (ACRO)BATICS

aerobe ('ɛərəʊb) *or* **aerobium** (ɛə'rəʊbɪəm) *n, pl* **aerobes** *or* **aerobia** (-'əʊbɪə). an organism that requires free oxygen or air for respiration. ORIG C19: from AERO- + Gk *bios* life

aerobic (ɛə'rəʊbɪk) *adj* **1** (of an organism or process) depending on free oxygen or air. **2** of or relating to aerobes. **3** designed for or relating to aerobics: *aerobic shoes; aerobic dances.*

aerobics (ɛə'rəʊbɪks) *n* (*functioning as sing*) any system of exercises designed to increase the amount of oxygen in the blood.

aerodrome ('ɛərəˌdrəʊm) *n* a landing area that is smaller than an airport.

aerodynamic braking *n* **1** the use of aerodynamic drag to slow spacecraft re-entering the atmosphere. **2** the use of airbrakes to retard flying vehicles or objects. **3** the use of a parachute or reversed thrust to decelerate an aircraft before landing.

aerodynamics (ˌɛərəʊdaɪ'næmɪks) *n* (*functioning as sing*) the study of the dynamics of gases, esp. of the forces acting on a body passing through air.
▸ **ˌaerody'namic** *adj* ▸ **ˌaerody'namically** *adv* ▸ **ˌaerody'namicist** *n*

aeroembolism (ˌɛərəʊ'ɛmbəˌlɪzəm) *n* the presence in the blood of nitrogen bubbles, caused by an abrupt reduction in atmospheric pressure. See **decompression sickness.**

aero engine *n* an engine for powering an aircraft.

aerofoil ('ɛərəʊˌfɔɪl) *n* a cross section of a wing, rotor blade, etc.

aerogram *or* **aerogramme** ('ɛərəˌgræm) *n* an airmail letter written on a single sheet of lightweight paper that folds and is sealed to form an envelope. Also called: **air letter.**

aerolite ('ɛərəˌlaɪt) *n* a stony meteorite consisting of silicate minerals.

aerology (ɛə'rɒlədʒɪ) *n* the study of the atmosphere, including its upper layers.
▸ **aerological** (ˌɛərə'lɒdʒɪkᵊl) *adj* ▸ **aer'ologist** *n*

aeromechanics (ˌɛərəʊmɪ'kænɪks) *n* (*functioning as sing*) the mechanics of gases, esp. air.
▸ **ˌaerome'chanical** *adj*

aeronautics (ˌɛərə'nɔːtɪks) *n* (*functioning as sing*) the study or practice of all aspects of flight through the air.
▸ **ˌaero'nautical** *adj*

aeropause ('ɛərəˌpɔːz) *n* the region of the upper atmosphere above which aircraft cannot fly.

aeroplane ('ɛərəˌpleɪn) *or US* **airplane** ('ɛəˌpleɪn) *n* a heavier-than-air powered flying vehicle with fixed wings. ORIG C19: from F *aéroplane,* from AERO- + Gk *-planos* wandering

aerosol ('ɛərəˌsɒl) *n* **1** a colloidal dispersion of solid or liquid particles in a gas. **2** a substance, such as a paint or insecticide, dispensed from a small metal container by a propellant under pressure. **3** Also called: **air spray.** such a substance together with its container. ORIG C20: from AERO- + SOL(UTION)

aerospace ('ɛərəˌspeɪs) *n* **1** the atmosphere and space beyond. **2** (*modifier*) of rockets, missiles, space vehicles, etc.: *the aerospace industry.*

aerostat ('ɛərəˌstæt) *n* a lighter-than-air craft, such as a balloon. ORIG C18: from F *aérostat,* from AERO- + Gk *-statos* standing
▸ **ˌaero'static** *adj*

aerostatics (ˌɛərə'stætɪks) *n* (*functioning as sing*) **1** the study of gases in equilibrium and bodies held in equilibrium in gases. Cf. **aerodynamics.** **2** the study of lighter-than-air craft, such as balloons.

aerugo (ɪ'ruːgəʊ) *n* (esp. of old bronze) another name for **verdigris.** ORIG C18: from L, from *aes* copper, bronze
▸ **aeruginous** (ɪ'ruːdʒɪnəs) *adj*

aery ('ɛərɪ) *n, pl* **aeries.** a variant of **eyrie.**

Aeschylus ★ ('iːskələs) *n* ?525–?456 B.C., Greek dramatist, regarded as the father of Greek tragedy. His plays include *Seven Against Thebes, Prometheus Bound,* and the trilogy of the *Oresteia.*
▸ **Aeschylean** (ˌiːskə'liːən)*adj*

Aesculapius ★ (ˌiːskju'leɪpɪəs) *n* the Roman god of medicine or healing. Greek counterpart: **Asclepius.**
▸ **ˌAescu'lapian** *adj*

Aesir ★ ('eɪsɪə) *pl n* the chief gods of Norse mythology dwelling in Asgard. ORIG ON, lit.: gods

Aesop ★ ('iːsɒp) *n* ?620–564 B.C., Greek author of fables in which animals are given human characters and used to satirize human failings.
▸ **Ae'sopian** *or* **Ae'sopic** *adj*

aesthesia *or US* **esthesia** (iːs'θiːzɪə) *n* the normal ability to experience sensation. ORIG C20: back formation from ANAESTHESIA

aesthete *or US* **esthete** ('iːsθiːt) *n* a person who has or who affects a highly developed appreciation of beauty. ORIG C19: back formation from AESTHETICS

aesthetic (iːs'θɛtɪk, ɪs-) *or US* (*sometimes*) **esthetic** *adj also* **aesthetical** *or US* (*sometimes*) **esthetical.** **1** connected with aesthetics. **2a** relating to pure beauty rather than to other considerations. **2b** artistic: *an aesthetic consideration.* ◆ *n* **3** a principle of taste or style adopted by a particular person, group, or culture: *the Bauhaus aesthetic of functional modernity.* ORIG C19: from Gk *aisthētikos,* from *aisthanesthai* to perceive, feel
▸ **aes'thetically** *or US* (*sometimes*) **es'thetically** *adv* ▸ **aes'thetiˌcism** *or US* (*sometimes*) **es'thetiˌcism** *n*

aesthetics *or US* (*sometimes*) **esthetics** (iːs'θɛtɪks) *n* (*functioning as sing*) **1** the branch of philosophy concerned with the study of such concepts as beauty, taste, etc. **2** the study of the rules and principles of art.

aestival *or US* **estival** (iː'staɪvᵊl) *adj Rare.* of or occurring in summer. ORIG C14: from F, from LL *aestīvālis,* from L *aestās* summer

aestivate *or US* **estivate** ('iːstɪˌveɪt) *vb* **aestivates, aestivating, aestivated** *or US* **estivates, estivating, estivated.** (*intr*) **1** to pass the summer. **2** (of animals) to pass the summer or dry season in a dormant condition. ORIG C17: from L, from *aestīvāre,* from *aestās* summer
▸ **ˌaesti'vation** *or US* **ˌesti'vation** *n*

aet. *or* **aetat.** *abbrev. for* aetatis. ORIG L: at the age of

Æthelbert ★ ('æθəlˌbɜːt) *n* a variant of **Ethelbert.**

Æthelred ★ ('æθəlˌrɛd) *n* a variant of **Ethelred.**

aether ('iːθə) *n* a variant spelling of **ether** (senses 3, 4).

aetiology *or* **etiology** (ˌiːtɪ'ɒlədʒɪ) *n, pl* **aetiologies** *or* **etiologies.** **1** the philosophy or study of causation. **2** the study of the causes of diseases. **3** the cause of a disease. ORIG C16: from LL *aetologia,* from Gk *aitiologia,* from *aitia* cause
▸ **ˌaetio'logical** *or* **ˌetio'logical** *adj* ▸ **ˌaetio'logically** *or* **ˌetio'logically** *adv* ▸ **ˌaeti'ologist** *or* **ˌeti'ologist** *n*

Aetna ★ ('ɛtnə) *n* the Latin name for Mount **Etna.**

Aetolia ★ (iː'təʊlɪə) *n* a mountainous region forming (with the region of Acarnania) a department of W central Greece, north of the Gulf of Patras: a powerful federal state in the 3rd century B.C. Chief city: Missolonghi. Pop. (with Acarnania): 228 180 (1991). Area: 5461 sq. km (2108 sq. miles).

AEU (in Britain) *abbrev. for* Amalgamated Engineering Union.

Af. *abbrev. for* Africa(n).

a.f. *abbrev. for* audio frequency.

afar (ə'fɑː) *adv* **1** at, from, or to a great distance. ◆ *n* **2** a great distance (esp. in **from afar**). ORIG C14 *a fer,* altered from earlier *on fer* & *of fer;* see A-², FAR

Afars and the Issas ★ ('ɑːfɑːz; 'iːsɑːs) *n* **Territory of the.** a former name (1967–77) of **Djibouti.**

AFC *abbrev. for:* **1** Air Force Cross. **2** Association Football Club. **3** automatic frequency control.

★ people and places

afeard *or* **afeared** (əˈfɪəd) *adj* (*postpositive*) an archaic or dialect word for **afraid**. ORIG OE *āfǣred*, from *afǣran* to frighten

affable (ˈæfəbᵊl) *adj* **1** showing warmth and friendliness. **2** easy to converse with; approachable. ORIG C16: from L *affābilis*, from *affārī*, from *ad-* to + *fārī* to speak
▸ ˌ**affaˈbility** *n* ▸ ˈ**affably** *adv*

affair (əˈfɛə) *n* **1** a thing to be done or attended to; matter. **2** an event or happening: *a strange affair*. **3** (*qualified by an adjective or descriptive phrase*) something previously specified: *our house is a tumbledown affair*. **4** a sexual relationship between two people who are not married to each other. ORIG C13: from OF, from *à faire* to do

affairs (əˈfɛəz) *pl n* **1** personal or business interests. **2** matters of public interest: *current affairs*.

affect[1] *vb* (əˈfɛkt). (*tr*) **1** to act upon or influence, esp. in an adverse way. **2** to move or disturb emotionally or mentally. **3** (of pain, disease, etc.) to attack. ◆ *n* (ˈæfɛkt). **4** *Psychol.* the emotion associated with an idea or set of ideas. ORIG C17: from L *affectus*, p.p. of *afficere*, from *ad-* to + *facere* to do

USAGE NOTE See at **effect**.

affect[2] (əˈfɛkt) *vb* (*mainly tr*) **1** to put on an appearance or show of: *to affect ignorance*. **2** to imitate or assume, esp. pretentiously. **3** to have or use by preference. **4** to adopt the character, manner, etc., of. **5** to incline habitually towards. ORIG C15: from L *affectāre* to strive after; rel. to *afficere* to AFFECT[1]

affectation (ˌæfɛkˈteɪʃən) *n* **1** an assumed manner of speech, dress, or behaviour, esp. one that is intended to impress others. **2** (often foll. by *of*) deliberate pretence. ORIG C16: from L *affectātiōn-*, from *affectāre*; see AFFECT[2]

affected[1] (əˈfɛktɪd) *adj* (*usually postpositive*) **1** deeply moved, esp. by sorrow or grief. **2** changed, esp. detrimentally. ORIG C17: from AFFECT[1]

affected[2] (əˈfɛktɪd) *adj* **1** behaving, speaking, etc., in an assumed way, esp. in order to impress others. **2** feigned: *affected indifference*. ORIG C16: from AFFECT[2]
▸ **afˈfectedly** *adv*

affecting (əˈfɛktɪŋ) *adj* evoking feelings of pity; moving.
▸ **afˈfectingly** *adv*

affection (əˈfɛkʃən) *n* **1** a feeling of fondness or tenderness for a person or thing. **2** (*often pl*) emotion, feeling, or sentiment: *to play on a person's affections*. **3** *Pathol.* any disease or pathological condition. **4** the act of affecting or the state of being affected. ORIG C13: from L *affectiōn-*, from *afficere* to AFFECT[1]
▸ **afˈfectional** *adj*

affectionate (əˈfɛkʃənɪt) *adj* having or displaying tender feelings, affection, or warmth.
▸ **afˈfectionately** *adv*

affective (əˈfɛktɪv) *adj* concerned with the emotions or affection.
▸ **affectivity** (ˌæfɛkˈtɪvɪtɪ) *n*

affective disorder *n* any mental disorder, such as depression or mania, that is characterized by abnormal disturbances of mood.

affectless (ˈæfɛktˌlɪs, əˈfɛktlɪs) *adj* **a** showing no emotion or concern for others. **b** not giving rise to any emotion or feeling: *an affectless novel*. ORIG C20: from AFFECT[1] (sense 4) + -LESS

afferent (ˈæfərənt) *adj* bringing or directing inwards to a part or an organ of the body, esp. towards the brain or spinal cord. ORIG C19: from L *afferre*, from *ad-* to + *ferre* to carry

affiance (əˈfaɪəns) *vb* **affiances, affiancing, affianced.** (*tr*) to bind (a person or oneself) in a promise of marriage; betroth. ORIG C14: via OF from Med. L *affīdāre* to trust (oneself) to, from *fīdāre* to trust

affidavit (ˌæfɪˈdeɪvɪt) *n Law.* a declaration in writing made upon oath before a person authorized to administer oaths. ORIG C17: from Med. L, lit.: he declares on oath, from *affīdare*; see AFFIANCE

affiliate *vb* (əˈfɪlɪˌeɪt), **affiliates, affiliating, affiliated. 1** (*tr*; foll. by *to* or *with*) to receive into close connection or association (with a larger body, group, organization, etc.). **2** (foll. by *with*) to associate (oneself) or be associated, esp. as a subordinate or subsidiary. ◆ *n* (əˈfɪlɪɪt). **3a** a person or organization that is affiliated with another. **3b** (*as modifier*): *an affiliate member*. ORIG C18: from Med. L *affiliātus* adopted as a son, from *affīliāre*, from L *filius* son
▸ **afˌfiliˈation** *n*

affiliation order *n Law.* an order that a man adjudged to be the father of an illegitimate child shall contribute towards the child's maintenance.

affine (ˈæfaɪn) *adj Maths.* denoting transformations which preserve collinearity, esp. those of translation, rotation, and reflection. ORIG C16: from F: see AFFINITY

affinity (əˈfɪnɪtɪ) *n, pl* **affinities. 1** a natural liking, taste, or inclination for a person or thing. **2** the person or thing so liked. **3** a close similarity in appearance or quality. **4** relationship by marriage. **5** similarity in structure, form, etc., between different animals, plants, or languages. **6** *Chem.* chemical attraction. **7** *Immunol.* a measure of the degree of interaction between an antigen and an antibody. ORIG C14: via OF from L *affinitāt-*, from *affinis* bordering on, related
▸ **afˈfinitive** *adj*

affinity card *n* a credit card issued by a bank or credit-card company, which donates a small percentage of the money spent using the card to a specified charity.

affirm (əˈfɜːm) *vb* (*mainly tr*) **1** (*may take a clause as object*) to declare to be true. **2** to uphold, confirm, or ratify. **3** (*intr*) *Law.* to make an affirmation. ORIG C14: via OF from L *affirmāre*, from *ad-* to + *firmāre* to make FIRM[1]
▸ **afˈfirmer** *or* **afˈfirmant** *n*

affirmation (ˌæfəˈmeɪʃən) *n* **1** the act of affirming or the state of being affirmed. **2** a statement of the truth of something; assertion. **3** *Law.* a solemn declaration permitted on grounds of conscientious objection to taking an oath.

affirmative (əˈfɜːmətɪv) *adj* **1** confirming or asserting something as true or valid. **2** indicating agreement or assent. **3** *Logic.* (of a categorical proposition) affirming the satisfaction by the subject of the predicate, as in the proposition *some men are married*. ◆ *n* **4** a positive assertion. **5** a word or phrase stating agreement or assent, such as *yes*: *to answer in the affirmative*. ◆ *sentence substitute*. **6** *Mil., etc.* a signal codeword used to express assent or confirmation.
▸ **afˈfirmatively** *adv*

affix *vb* (əˈfɪks). (*tr*; usually foll. by *to* or *on*) **1** to attach, fasten, join, or stick. **2** to add or append: *to affix a signature to a document*. **3** to attach or attribute (guilt, blame, etc.). ◆ *n* (ˈæfɪks). **4** a linguistic element added to a word or root to produce a derived or inflected form, as *-ment* in *establishment*. See also **prefix, suffix, infix. 5** something fastened or attached. ORIG C15: from Med. L *affixāre*, from *ad-* to + *fixāre* to FIX
▸ **affixture** (əˈfɪkstʃə) *n*

afflatus (əˈfleɪtəs) *n* an impulse of creative power or inspiration considered to be of divine origin. ORIG C17: L, from *afflātus*, from *afflāre*, from *flāre* to blow

afflict (əˈflɪkt) *vb* (*tr*) to cause suffering or unhappiness to; distress greatly. ORIG C14: from L *afflictus*, p.p. of *afflīgere* to knock against, from *flīgere* to strike
▸ **afˈflictive** *adj*

affliction (əˈflɪkʃən) *n* **1** a condition of great distress or suffering. **2** something responsible for physical or mental suffering.

affluence (ˈæfluəns) *n* **1** an abundant supply of money, goods, or property; wealth. **2** *Rare.* abundance or profusion.

affluent (ˈæfluənt) *adj* **1** rich; wealthy. **2** abundant; copious. **3** flowing freely. ◆ *n* **4** a tributary stream. ORIG C15: from L *affluent-*, present participle of *affluere*, from *fluere* to flow

affluent society *n* a society in which the material benefits of prosperity are widely available.

afflux (ˈæflʌks) *n* a flowing towards a point: *an afflux of blood to the head*. ORIG C17: from L *affluxus*, from *fluxus* FLUX

afford (əˈfɔːd) *vb* **1** (preceded by *can, could*, etc.) to be able

to do or spare something, esp. without incurring financial difficulties or without risk of undesirable consequences. **2** to give, yield, or supply. ORIG OE *geforthian* to further, promote, from *forth* FORTH
▸ **af'fordable** *adj* ▸ **af,forda'bility** *n*

afforest (ə'fɒrɪst) *vb* (*tr*) to plant trees on. ORIG C15: from Med. L *afforestāre,* from *forestis* FOREST
▸ **af,forest'ation** *n*

affranchise (ə'fræntʃaɪz) *vb* **affranchises, affranchising, affranchised.** (*tr*) to release from servitude or an obligation. ORIG C15: from OF *afranchir*
▸ **af'franchisement** *n*

affray (ə'freɪ) *n* a fight, noisy quarrel, or disturbance between two or more persons in a public place. ORIG C14: via OF from Vulgar L *exfridāre* (unattested) to break the peace

affricate ('æfrɪkɪt) *n* a composite speech sound consisting of a stop and a fricative articulated at the same point, such as the sound written *ch,* as in *chair.* ORIG C19: from L *affricāre,* from *fricāre* to rub

affright (ə'fraɪt) *Arch. or poetic.* ◆ *vb* **1** (*tr*) to frighten. ◆ *n* **2** a sudden terror. ORIG OE *āfyrhtan,* from *a-* + *fyrhtan* to FRIGHT

affront (ə'frʌnt) *n* **1** a deliberate insult. ◆ *vb* (*tr*) **2** to insult, esp. openly. **3** to offend the pride or dignity of. ORIG C14: from OF *afronter* to strike in the face, from L *ad frontem* to the face

Afg. *or* **Afgh.** *abbrev. for* Afghanistan.

afghan ('æfgæn, -gən) *n* **1** a knitted or crocheted wool blanket or shawl, esp. one with a geometric pattern. **2** a sheepskin coat, often embroidered. ORIG from AFGHANISTAN

Afghan ('æfgæn) *or* **Afghani** (æf'gænɪ) *n* **1** a native, citizen, or inhabitant of Afghanistan. **2** another name for **Pashto** (the language). ◆ *adj* **3** denoting Afghanistan, its people, or their language.

Afghan hound *n* a tall graceful breed of hound with a long silky coat.

Afghanistan ★ (æf'gænɪ,stɑːn, -,stæn) *n* a republic in central Asia: became independent in 1919; occupied by Soviet troops 1979–89; Islamic fundamentalist factional fighting followed, the Taliban taking control in 1996; generally arid and mountainous, with the Hindu Kush range rising over 7500 m (25 000 ft) and fertile valleys of the Amu Darya, Helmand, and Kabul Rivers. Languages: Pashto, Dari (Persian), and Tajik. Religion: Muslim. Currency: afghani. Capital: Kabul. Pop.: 25 825 000 (1999 est.). Area: 657 500 sq. km (250 000 sq. miles).

aficionado (ə,fɪʃjə'nɑːdəʊ) *n, pl* **aficionados. 1** an ardent supporter or devotee: *a jazz aficionado.* **2** a devotee of bullfighting. ORIG Sp., from *aficionar,* from *afición* AFFECTION

afield (ə'fiːld) *adv, adj* (*postpositive*) **1** away from one's usual surroundings or home (esp. in **far afield**). **2** off the subject (esp. in **far afield**). **3** in or to the field.

afire (ə'faɪə) *adv, adj* (*postpositive*) **1** on fire. **2** intensely interested or passionate: *he was afire with enthusiasm for the new plan.*

aflame (ə'fleɪm) *adv, adj* (*postpositive*) **1** in flames. **2** deeply aroused, as with passion: *he was aflame with desire.*

aflatoxin (,æflə'tɒksɪn) *n* a toxin produced by a fungus growing on peanuts, maize, etc., causing liver disease (esp. cancer) in man. ORIG C20: from L name of fungus *A(spergillus) fla(vus)* + TOXIN

afloat (ə'fləʊt) *adj* (*postpositive*), *adv* **1** floating. **2** aboard ship; at sea. **3** covered with water. **4** aimlessly drifting. **5** in circulation: *nasty rumours were afloat.* **6** free of debt.

aflutter (ə'flʌtə) *adj* (*postpositive*), *adv* in or into a nervous or excited state.

AFM *abbrev. for* Air Force Medal.

afoot (ə'fʊt) *adj* (*postpositive*), *adv* **1** in operation; astir: *mischief was afoot.* **2** on or by foot.

afore (ə'fɔː) *adv, prep, conj* an archaic or dialect word for **before.**

aforementioned (ə'fɔː,mɛnʃənd) *adj* (*usually prenominal*) (chiefly in legal documents) stated or mentioned before.

aforesaid (ə'fɔː,sɛd) *adj* (*usually prenominal*) (chiefly in legal documents) spoken of or referred to previously.

aforethought (ə'fɔː,θɔːt) *adj* (*immediately postpositive*) premeditated (esp. in **malice aforethought**).

a fortiori ('eɪ ,fɔːtɪ'ɔːraɪ) *adv* for similar but more convincing reasons. ORIG L

afp *abbrev. for* alpha-fetoprotein.

Afr. *abbrev. for* Africa(n).

afraid (ə'freɪd) *adj* (*postpositive*) **1** (often foll. by *of*) feeling fear or apprehension. **2** reluctant (to do something), as through fear or timidity. **3** (often foll. by *that;* used to lessen the effect of an unpleasant statement) regretful: *I'm afraid that I shall have to tell you to go.* ORIG C14 *affraied,* p.p. of AFFRAY (*obs.*) to frighten

afreet *or* **afrit** ('æfriːt, ə'friːt) *n Arabian myth.* a powerful evil demon. ORIG C19: from Ar. *'ifrīt*

afresh (ə'frɛʃ) *adv* once more; again; anew.

Afric ('æfrɪkə) *adj* **1** of African descent and native to a place outside sub-Saharan Africa. ◆ *n* **2** an Afric person. ORIG C20: by analogy with INDIC

Africa ★ ('æfrɪkə) *n* the second largest of the continents, on the Mediterranean in the north, the Atlantic in the west, and the Red Sea, Gulf of Aden, and Indian Ocean in the east. The Sahara desert divides the continent unequally into North Africa (an early centre of civilization, in close contact with Europe and W Asia, now inhabited chiefly by Arabs) and Africa south of the Sahara (relatively isolated from the rest of the world until the 19th century and inhabited chiefly by Negroid peoples). It was colonized mainly in the 18th and 19th centuries by Europeans and now comprises independent nations. The largest lake is Lake Victoria and the chief rivers are the Nile, Niger, Congo, and Zambezi. Pop.: 720 363 000 (1996 est.). Area: about 30 300 000 sq. km (11 700 000 sq. miles).

African ('æfrɪkən) *adj* **1** denoting or relating to Africa or any of its peoples, languages, nations, etc. ◆ *n* **2** a native or inhabitant of any of the countries of Africa. **3** a member or descendant of any of the peoples of Africa, esp. a Black person.

Africana (,æfrɪ'kɑːnə) *n* objects of cultural or historical interest of southern African origin.

African-American *or* **Afro-American** *n* **1** an American of African descent. ◆ *adj* **2** of or relating to Americans of African descent.

Africander (,æfrɪ'kændə) *n* a breed of hump-backed beef cattle originally raised in southern Africa. ORIG C19: from South African Du., formed on the model of *Hollander*

African National Congress *n* (in South Africa) a political party, founded in 1912 in South Africa as an African nationalist movement and banned from 1960 until 1990 because of its opposition to apartheid. In 1994 the ANC won South Africa's first multiracial elections. Abbrev.: **ANC.**

African violet *n* a tropical African plant cultivated as a house plant, with violet, white, or pink flowers and hairy leaves.

Afrikaans (,æfrɪ'kɑːns, -'kɑːnz) *n* one of the official languages of the Republic of South Africa, closely related to Dutch. Sometimes called: **South African Dutch.** ORIG C20: from Du.: African

Afrikaner (,æfrɪ'kɑːnə) *n* a White native of the Republic of South Africa whose mother tongue is Afrikaans. See also **Boer.**

afrit ('æfriːt, ə'friːt) *n* a variant spelling of **afreet.**

Afro ('æfrəʊ) *n, pl* **Afros.** a hairstyle in which the hair is shaped into a wide frizzy bush. ORIG C20: independent use of AFRO-

Afro- *combining form.* indicating Africa or African: *Afro-Asiatic.*

Afro-American *n, adj* another word for **African-American.**

Afro-Caribbean *adj* **1** denoting or relating to Caribbean people of African descent or their culture. ◆ *n* **2** a Caribbean of African descent.

afrormosia (,æfrɔː'məʊzɪə) *n* a hard teaklike wood obtained from a genus of tropical African trees. ORIG C20: from AFRO- + *Ormosia* (genus name)

aft (ɑːft) *adv, adj Chiefly naut.* towards or at the stern or rear: *the aft deck.* ORIG C17: ? shortened from earlier ABAFT

after (ˈɑːftə) *prep* **1** following in time; in succession to: *after dinner.* **2** following; behind. **3** in pursuit or search of: *he's only after money.* **4** concerning: *to inquire after his health.* **5** considering: *after what you have done, you shouldn't complain.* **6** next in excellence or importance to. **7** in imitation of; in the manner of. **8** in accordance with or in conformity to: *a man after her own heart.* **9** with a name derived from. **10** *US.* past (the hour of): *twenty after three.* **11 after all. 11a** in spite of everything: *it's only a game after all.* **11b** in spite of expectations, efforts, etc. **12 after you.** please go, enter, etc., before me. ◆ *adv* **13** at a later time; afterwards. **14** coming afterwards. **15** *Naut.* further aft. ◆ *conj* **16** (*subordinating*) at a time later than that at which. ◆ *adj* **17** *Naut.* further aft: *the after cabin.* ORIG OE *æfter*

afterbirth (ˈɑːftəˌbɜːθ) *n* the placenta and fetal membranes expelled from the uterus after the birth of offspring.

afterburner (ˈɑːftəˌbɜːnə) *n* **1** a device in the exhaust system of an internal-combustion engine for removing dangerous exhaust gases. **2** a device in an aircraft jet engine to produce extra thrust by igniting additional fuel.

aftercare (ˈɑːftəˌkɛə) *n* **1** support services by a welfare agency for a person discharged from a hospital, prison, etc. **2** *Med.* the care of a patient after a serious illness or operation. **3** any system of maintenance or upkeep of an appliance or product: *contact-lens aftercare.*

afterdamp (ˈɑːftəˌdæmp) *n* a poisonous gas, consisting mainly of carbon monoxide, formed after the explosion of firedamp in coal mines.

aftereffect (ˈɑːftərɪˌfɛkt) *n* any result occurring some time after its cause.

afterglow (ˈɑːftəˌgləʊ) *n* **1** the glow left after a light has disappeared, such as that sometimes seen after sunset. **2** the glow of an incandescent metal after the source of heat has been removed.

afterimage (ˈɑːftərˌɪmɪdʒ) *n* a sustained or renewed sensation, esp. visual, after the original stimulus has ceased.

afterlife (ˈɑːftəˌlaɪf) *n* life after death or at a later time in a person's lifetime.

aftermath (ˈɑːftəˌmæθ) *n* **1** signs or results of an event or occurrence considered collectively: *the aftermath of war.* **2** *Agriculture.* a second crop of grass from land that has already yielded one crop earlier in the same year. ORIG C16: AFTER + *math* a mowing, from OE *mæth*

aftermost (ˈɑːftəˌməʊst) *adj* closer or closest to the rear or (in a vessel) the stern; last.

afternoon (ˌɑːftəˈnuːn) *n* **1a** the period between noon and evening. **1b** (*as modifier*): *afternoon tea.* **2** a later part: *the afternoon of life.*

afternoons (ˌɑːftəˈnuːnz) *adv Inf.* during the afternoon, esp. regularly.

afterpains (ˈɑːftəˌpeɪnz) *pl n* cramplike pains caused by contraction of the uterus after childbirth.

afters (ˈɑːftəz) *n* (*functioning as sing or pl*) *Brit. inf.* dessert; sweet.

aftershave lotion (ˈɑːftəˌʃeɪv) *n* a lotion, usually perfumed, for application to the face after shaving. Often shortened to **aftershave.**

aftertaste (ˈɑːftəˌteɪst) *n* **1** a taste that lingers on after eating or drinking. **2** a lingering impression or sensation.

afterthought (ˈɑːftəˌθɔːt) *n* **1** a comment, reply, etc., that occurs to one after the opportunity to deliver it has passed. **2** an addition to something already completed.

afterwards (ˈɑːftəwədz) *or* **afterward** *adv* after an earlier event or time. ORIG OE *æfterweard, æfteweard,* from AFT + WARD

Ag *the chemical symbol for* silver. ORIG from L *argentum*

AG *abbrev. for:* **1** Adjutant General. **2** Attorney General.

aga *or* **agha** (ˈɑːgə) *n* (in the Ottoman Empire) a title of respect, often used with the title of a senior position. ORIG C17: Turkish, lit.: lord

★ people and places

Agadir ★ (ˌægəˈdɪə) *n* a port in SW Morocco, which became the centre of an international crisis (1911), when a gunboat arrived to protect German interests. Britain issued a strong warning to Germany but the French negotiated and war was averted. In 1960 the town was virtually destroyed by an earthquake, about 10 000 people being killed. Pop.: 137 000 (1993 est.).

again (əˈgɛn, əˈgeɪn) *adv* **1** another or a second time: *he had to start again.* **2** once more in a previously experienced state or condition: *he is ill again.* **3** in addition to the original amount, quantity, etc. (esp. in **as much again; half as much again**). **4** (*sentence modifier*) on the other hand. **5** besides; also. **6** *Arch.* in reply; back: *he answered again.* **7 again and again.** continuously; repeatedly. ◆ *sentence connector.* **8** moreover; furthermore. ORIG OE *ongegn* opposite to, from A-[2] + *gegn* straight

against (əˈgɛnst, əˈgeɪnst) *prep* **1** opposed to; in conflict or disagreement with. **2** standing or leaning beside: *a ladder against the wall.* **3** coming in contact with. **4** in contrast to: *silhouettes are outlines against a light background.* **5** having an unfavourable effect on: *the system works against small companies.* **6** as a protection from: *a safeguard against contaminated water.* **7** in exchange for or in return for. **8** *Now rare.* in preparation for: *he gave them warm clothing against their journey.* **9 as against.** as opposed to or as compared with. ORIG C12 *ageines,* from *again, ageyn,* etc. AGAIN + *-es,* genitive ending

Aga Khan (ˈɑːgə ˈkɑːn) *n* the hereditary title of the head of the Ismaili Islamic sect.

Aga Khan IV ★ *n* Prince **Karim** (kəˈriːm). born 1936, spiritual leader of the Ismaili sect of Muslims from 1957.

Agamemnon ★ (ˌægəˈmɛmnɒn) *n Greek myth.* a king of Mycenae who led the Greeks at the siege of Troy. On his return home he was murdered by his wife Clytemnestra and her lover Aegisthus. See also **Menelaus.**

agamic (əˈgæmɪk) *adj* asexual; occurring or reproducing without fertilization. ORIG C19: from Gk *agamos* unmarried, from A-[1] + *gamos* marriage

agamogenesis (ˌægəməʊˈdʒɛnɪsɪs) *n* asexual reproduction, such as fission or parthenogenesis. ORIG C19: AGAMIC + GENESIS

Agaña ★ (əˈgɑːnjə) *n* the capital of the Pacific island of Guam, on its W coast. Pop.: 2000 (1995 est.).

agapanthus (ˌægəˈpænθəs) *n* a South African plant with blue funnel-shaped flowers, widely cultivated for ornament. ORIG C19: NL, from Gk *agape* love + *anthos* flower

agape (əˈgeɪp) *adj* (*postpositive*) **1** (esp. of the mouth) wide open. **2** very surprised, expectant, or eager. ORIG C17: A-[2] + GAPE

Agape (ˈægəpɪ) *n* **1** Christian love, esp. as contrasted with erotic love; charity. **2** a communal meal in the early Church in commemoration of the Last Supper. ORIG C17: Gk *agapē* love

agar (ˈeɪgə) *n* a gelatinous carbohydrate obtained from seaweeds, used as a culture medium for bacteria, as a laxative, a thickening agent (**E406**) in food, etc. Also called: **agar-agar.** ORIG C19: Malay

agaric (ˈægərɪk) *n* a fungus having gills on the underside of the cap. The group includes the edible mushrooms and poisonous forms such as the fly agaric. ORIG C16: via L from Gk *agarikon*

Agartala ★ (ˈʌgətəˌlɑː) *n* a city in NE India, capital of the state of Tripura. Pop.: 157 636 (1991).

Agassi (ˈægəsɪ) *n* **Andre** (ˈændreɪ). born 1970, US tennis player: won the Wimbledon men's singles in 1992 and the US Open in 1994 and 1999.

agate (ˈægɪt) *n* **1** an impure form of quartz consisting of a variegated, usually banded chalcedony, used as a gemstone and in making pestles and mortars. **2** a playing marble of this quartz or resembling it. ORIG C16: via F from L, from Gk *akhatēs*

agave (əˈgeɪvɪ) *n* a plant native to tropical America with tall flower stalks rising from thick fleshy leaves. Some species are the source of fibres such as sisal. ORIG C18: NL, from Gk *agauē,* fem. of *agauos* illustrious

age (eɪdʒ) *n* **1** the period of time that a person, animal, or plant has lived or is expected to live. **2** the period of existence of an object, material, group, etc.: *the age of this table is 200 years.* **3a** a period or state of human life: *he should know better at his age.* **3b** (*as modifier*): *age group.* **4** the latter part of life. **5a** a period of history marked by some feature or characteristic. **5b** (*cap. when part of a name*): *the Middle Ages.* **6** generation: *the Edwardian age.* **7** *Geol., palaeontol.* **7a** a period of the earth's history distinguished by special characteristics: *the age of reptiles.* **7b** a subdivision of an epoch. **8** (*often pl*) *Inf.* a relatively long time: *I've been waiting ages.* **9** *Psychol.* the level in years that a person has reached in any area of development, compared with the normal level for his chronological age. **10 of age.** adult and legally responsible for one's actions (usually at 18 years). ◆ *vb* **ages, ageing** *or* **aging, aged.** **11** to become or cause to become old or aged. **12** (*intr*) to begin to seem older: *to have aged a lot in the past year.* **13** *Brewing.* to mature or cause to mature. ORIG C13: via OF from Vulgar L, from L *aetās*

-age *suffix forming nouns.* **1** indicating a collection, set, or group: *baggage.* **2** indicating a process or action or the result of an action: *breakage.* **3** indicating a state or relationship: *bondage.* **4** indicating a house or place: *orphanage.* **5** indicating a charge or fee: *postage.* **6** indicating a rate: *dosage.* ORIG from OF, from LL *-āticum* belonging to

aged ('eɪdʒɪd) *adj* **1a** advanced in years; old. **1b** (*as collective n;* preceded by *the*): *the aged.* **2** of, connected with, or characteristic of old age. **3** (eɪdʒd). (*postpositive*) having the age of: *a woman aged twenty.*

Agee ★ ('eɪdʒiː) *n* **James.** 1909–55, US novelist, poet, and film critic. His works include the autobiographical novel *A Death in the Family* (1957).

ageing *or* **aging** ('eɪdʒɪŋ) *n* **1** the process of growing old or developing the appearance of old age. ◆ *adj* **2** becoming or appearing older: *an ageing car.* **3** giving the appearance of elderliness: *that dress is really ageing.*

ageism *or* **agism** ('eɪdʒɪzəm) *n* discrimination against people on the grounds of age.
▸ **'ageist** *or* **'agist** *adj*

ageless ('eɪdʒlɪs) *adj* **1** apparently never growing old. **2** timeless; eternal: *an ageless quality.*

agency ('eɪdʒənsɪ) *n, pl* **agencies.** **1** a business or other organization providing a specific service: *an employment agency.* **2** the place where an agent conducts business. **3** the business, duties, or functions of an agent. **4** action, power, or operation: *the agency of fate.* ORIG C17: from Med. L *agentia,* from L *agere* to do

agenda (ə'dʒɛndə) *n* **1** (*functioning as sing*) Also: **agendum.** a schedule or list of items to be attended to. **2** (*functioning as pl*) Also: **agendas, agendums.** matters to be attended to, as at a meeting. ORIG C17: L, lit.: things to be done, from *agere* to do

agent ('eɪdʒənt) *n* **1** a person who acts on behalf of another person, business, government, etc. **2** a person or thing that acts or has the power to act. **3** a substance or organism that exerts some force or effect: *a chemical agent.* **4** the means by which something occurs or is achieved. **5** a person representing a business concern, esp. a travelling salesman. ORIG C15: from L *agent-,* noun use of the present participle of *agere* to do
▸ **agential** (eɪ'dʒɛnʃəl) *adj*

agent-general *n, pl* **agents-general.** a representative in London of a Canadian province or an Australian state.

Agent Orange *n* a highly poisonous herbicide used as a spray for defoliation and crop destruction, esp. by US forces during the Vietnam War. ORIG C20: named after the identifying colour stripe on its container

agent provocateur *French.* (aʒɑ̃ prɔvɔkatœr) *n, pl* ***agents provocateurs*** (aʒɑ̃ prɔvɔkatœr). a secret agent employed to provoke suspected persons to commit illegal acts and so be discredited or liable to punishment.

age of consent *n* **1** the age at which a person, esp. a female, is considered legally competent to consent to marriage or sexual intercourse. **2** the age at which a person can enter into a legally binding contract.

Age of Reason *n* (usually preceded by *the*) the 18th century in W Europe. See also **Enlightenment.**

age-old *or* **age-long** *adj* very old or of long duration; ancient.

ageratum (ˌædʒə'reɪtəm) *n* a tropical American plant with thick clusters of purplish-blue flowers. ORIG C16: NL, via L from Gk *agēraton* that does not age, from A-[1] + *gērat-,* stem of *gēras* old age

agglomerate *vb* (ə'glɒməˌreɪt), **agglomerates, agglomerating, agglomerated.** **1** to form or be formed into a mass or cluster. ◆ *n* (ə'glɒmərɪt, -ˌreɪt). **2** a confused mass. **3** a volcanic rock consisting of angular fragments within a groundmass of lava. ◆ *adj* (ə'glɒmərɪt, -ˌreɪt). **4** formed into a mass. ORIG C17: from L *agglomerāre,* from *glomerāre* to wind into a ball
▸ **agˌglomer'ation** *n* ▸ **ag'glomerative** *adj*

agglutinate (ə'gluːtɪˌneɪt) *vb* **agglutinates, agglutinating, agglutinated.** **1** to adhere or cause to adhere, as with glue. **2** *Linguistics.* to combine or be combined by agglutination. **3** (*tr*) to cause (bacteria, red blood cells, etc.) to clump together. ORIG C16: from L *agglūtināre* to glue to, from *gluten* glue
▸ **ag'glutinable** *adj* ▸ **ag'glutinant** *adj*

agglutination (əˌgluːtɪ'neɪʃən) *n* **1** the act or process of agglutinating. **2** a united mass of parts. **3** *Chem.* the formation of clumps of particles in a suspension. **4** *Immunol.* the formation of a mass of particles, such as red blood cells, by the action of antibodies. **5** *Linguistics.* the building up of words from component morphemes in such a way that these undergo little or no change of form or meaning.

aggrandize *or* **aggrandise** (ə'grændaɪz) *vb* **aggrandizes, aggrandizing, aggrandized** *or* **aggrandises, aggrandising, aggrandised.** (*tr*) **1** to increase the power, wealth, prestige, scope, etc., of. **2** to cause (something) to seem greater. ORIG C17: from OF *aggrandiss-,* stem of *aggrandir,* from L *grandis* GRAND
▸ **aggrandizement** *or* **aggrandisement** (ə'grændɪzmənt) *n* ▸ **'aggranˌdizer** *or* **'aggranˌdiser** *n*

aggravate ('ægrəˌveɪt) *vb* **aggravates, aggravating, aggravated.** (*tr*) **1** to make (a disease, situation, problem, etc.) worse. **2** *Inf.* to annoy. ORIG C16: from L *aggravāre* to make heavier, from *gravis* heavy
▸ **'aggraˌvating** *adj* ▸ **ˌaggra'vation** *n*

aggregate *adj* ('ægrɪgɪt). **1** formed of separate units collected into a whole. **2** (of fruits and flowers) composed of a dense cluster of florets. ◆ *n* ('ægrɪgɪt, -ˌgeɪt). **3** a sum or assemblage of many separate units. **4** *Geol.* a rock, such as granite, consisting of a mixture of minerals. **5** the sand and stone mixed with cement and water to make concrete. **6 in the aggregate.** taken as a whole. ◆ *vb* ('ægrɪˌgeɪt). **7** to combine or be combined into a body, etc. **8** (*tr*) to amount to (a number). ORIG C16: from L *aggregāre* to add to a flock or herd, from *grex* flock
▸ **ˌaggre'gation** *n* ▸ **aggregative** ('ægrɪˌgeɪtɪv) *adj*

aggress (ə'grɛs) *vb* (*intr*) to attack first or begin a quarrel. ORIG C16: from Med. L *aggressāre,* from L *aggredī* to attack
▸ **aggressor** (ə'grɛsə) *n*

aggression (ə'grɛʃən) *n* **1** an attack or harmful action, esp. an unprovoked attack by one country against another. **2** any offensive activity, practice, etc. **3** *Psychol.* a hostile or destructive mental attitude. ORIG C17: from L *aggression-,* from *aggredī* to attack

aggressive (ə'grɛsɪv) *adj* **1** quarrelsome or belligerent. **2** assertive; vigorous.
▸ **ag'gressively** *adv* ▸ **ag'gressiveness** *n*

aggrieve (ə'griːv) *vb* **aggrieves, aggrieving, aggrieved.** (*tr*) **1** (*often impersonal or passive*) to grieve; distress; afflict. **2** to injure unjustly, esp. by infringing a person's legal rights. ORIG C14 *agreven,* via OF from L *aggravāre* to AGGRAVATE
▸ **ag'grieved** *adj* ▸ **aggrievedly** (ə'griːvɪdlɪ) *adv*

aggro ('ægrəʊ) *n Brit. sl.* aggressive behaviour. ORIG C20: from AGGRAVATION

aghast (ə'gɑːst) *adj* (*postpositive*) overcome with amazement or horror. ORIG C13 *agast,* from OE *gæstan* to frighten

agile ('ædʒaɪl) *adj* **1** quick in movement; nimble. **2** mentally quick or acute. ORIG C15: from L *agilis,* from *agere* to do, act
▸ **'agilely** *adv* ▸ **agility** (ə'dʒɪlɪtɪ) *n*

agin (əˈgɪn) *prep Inf. or dialect.* against. ORIG C19: from obs. *again* AGAINST

Agincourt (ˈædʒɪnˌkɔːt; *French* aʒɛ̃kur) *n* a battle fought in 1415 near the village of Azincourt, N France: a decisive victory for English longbowmen under Henry V over French forces vastly superior in number.

agio (ˈædʒɪəʊ) *n, pl* **agios. a** the difference between the nominal and actual values of a currency. **b** the charge payable for conversion of the less valuable currency. ORIG C17: from It., lit.: ease

agitate (ˈædʒɪˌteɪt) *vb* **agitates, agitating, agitated. 1** (*tr*) to excite, disturb, or trouble (a person, the mind or feelings). **2** (*tr*) to shake, stir, or disturb. **3** (*intr; often foll. by* *for* or *against*) to attempt to stir up public opinion for or against something. ORIG C16: from L *agitātus,* from *agitāre* to set into motion, from *agere* to act
▸ **ˈagiˌtated** *adj* ▸ **ˈagiˌtatedly** *adv* ▸ **ˌagiˈtation** *n*

agitato (ˌædʒɪˈtɑːtəʊ) *adj, adv Music.* (to be performed) in an agitated manner.

agitator (ˈædʒɪˌteɪtə) *n* **1** a person who agitates for or against a cause, etc. **2** a device for mixing or shaking.

agitprop (ˈædʒɪtˌprɒp) *n* **a** any promotion, as in the arts, of political propaganda, esp. of a Communist nature. **b** (*as modifier*): *agitprop theatre.* ORIG C20: short for Russian *Agitpropbyuro*

Aglaia ★ (əˈglaɪə) *n Greek myth.* one of the three Graces. ORIG Gk: splendour, from *aglaos* splendid

agleam (əˈgliːm) *adj* (*postpositive*) glowing; gleaming.

aglet (ˈæglɪt) *or* **aiglet** *n* **1** a metal sheath or tag at the end of a shoelace, ribbon, etc. **2** a variant spelling of **aiguillette.** ORIG C15: from OF *aiguillette* a small needle

agley (əˈgleɪ, əˈgliː, əˈglaɪ) *or* **aglee** (əˈgliː) *adv, adj Scot.* awry; askew. ORIG from *gley* squint

aglitter (əˈglɪtə) *adj* (*postpositive*) sparkling; glittering.

aglow (əˈgləʊ) *adj* (*postpositive*) glowing.

aglu *or* **agloo** (ˈægluː) *n Canad.* a breathing hole made in ice by a seal. ORIG C19: from Eskimo

AGM *abbrev. for* annual general meeting.

agnail (ˈægˌneɪl) *n* another name for **hangnail.**

agnate (ˈægneɪt) *adj* **1** related by descent from a common male ancestor. **2** related in any way. ◆ *n* **3** a male or female descendant by male links from a common male ancestor. ORIG C16: from L *agnātus* born in addition, from *agnāscī,* from *ad-* in addition + *gnāscī* to be born

Agnes ★ (ˈægnɪs) *n* **Saint.** ?292–?304 A.D., Christian child martyr under Diocletian. Feast day: Jan. 21.

Agnesi ★ (*Italian* aɲˈɲeːze) *n* **Maria** (**Gaetana**). 1718–99, Italian mathematician and philosopher, noted for her work on differential calculus.

Agnew ★ (ˈægnjuː) *n* **Spiro** (**Theodore**) (ˈspɪərəʊ). 1918–96, US Republican politician; vice president (1969–73).

Agni ★ (ˈʌgnɪ) *n Hinduism.* the god of fire, one of the three chief deities of the Vedas. ORIG Sansk.: fire

agnostic (ægˈnɒstɪk) *n* **1** a person who holds that knowledge of a Supreme Being, ultimate cause, etc., is impossible. Cf. **atheist, theist. 2** a person who claims, with respect to any particular question, that the answer cannot be known with certainty. ◆ *adj* **3** of or relating to agnostics. ORIG C19: coined 1869 by T. H. Huxley from A-[1] + GNOSTIC
▸ **agˈnostiˌcism** *n*

Agnus Dei (ˈægnʊs ˈdeɪɪ) *n* **1** the figure of a lamb bearing a cross or banner, emblematic of Christ. **2** a chant beginning with these words or a translation of them, forming part of the Roman Catholic Mass. ORIG L: Lamb of God

ago (əˈgəʊ) *adv* in the past: *five years ago; long ago.* ORIG C14 *ago,* from OE *āgān* to pass away

> **USAGE NOTE** The use of *ago* with *since,* as in *it's ten years ago since he wrote that novel,* is redundant. It should be replaced in writing by *it is ten years since he wrote that novel,* or *it is ten years ago that he wrote that novel.*

agog (əˈgɒg) *adj* (*postpositive*) eager or curious. ORIG C15: ?from OF *en gogues* in merriments

-agogue *or esp. US* **-agog** *n combining form.* indicating a person or thing that leads or incites to action: *demagogue.* ORIG via LL from Gk *agōgos,* from *agein* to lead
▸ **-agogic** *adj combining form.* ▸ **-agogy** *n combining form.*

agonic (əˈgɒnɪk) *adj* forming no angle. ORIG C19: from Gk *agōnos,* from A-[1] + *gōnia* angle

agonic line *n* an imaginary line on the surface of the earth connecting points of zero magnetic declination.

agonize *or* **agonise** (ˈægəˌnaɪz) *vb* **agonizes, agonizing, agonized** *or* **agonises, agonising, agonised. 1** to suffer or cause to suffer agony. **2** (*intr*) to struggle; strive. ORIG C16: via Med. L from Gk *agōnizesthai* to contend for a prize, from *agōn* contest
▸ **ˈagoˌnizingly** *or* **ˈagoˌnisingly** *adv*

agony (ˈægənɪ) *n, pl* **agonies. 1** acute physical or mental pain; anguish. **2** the suffering or struggle preceding death. ORIG C14: via LL from Gk *agōnia* struggle, from *agōn* contest

agony aunt *n* (*sometimes cap.*) a person who replies to readers' letters in an agony column.

agony column *n* **1** a newspaper or magazine feature offering sympathetic advice to readers on their personal problems. **2** *Inf.* a newspaper or magazine column devoted to advertisements relating esp. to personal problems.

agora (ˈægərə) *n, pl* **agorae** (-riː, -raɪ) *or* **agoras.** (*often cap.*) **a** the marketplace in Athens, used for popular meetings in ancient Greece. **b** the meeting itself. ORIG from Gk, from *agorein* to gather

agoraphobia (ˌægərəˈfəʊbɪə) *n* a pathological fear of being in public spaces.
▸ **ˌagoraˈphobic** *adj, n*

agouti (əˈguːtɪ) *n, pl* **agoutis** *or* **agouties.** a rodent of Central and South America and the Caribbean. Agoutis are agile and long-legged, with hooflike claws, and are valued for their meat. ORIG C18: via F & Sp. from Guarani

AGR *abbrev. for* advanced gas-cooled reactor.

Agra ★ (ˈɑːgrə) *n* a city in N India, in W Uttar Pradesh on the Jumna River: a capital of the Mogul empire until 1658; famous for its Mogul architecture, esp. the Taj Mahal. Pop.: 899 195 (1991).

Agram ★ (ˈaːgram) *n* the German name for **Zagreb.**

agrarian (əˈgrɛərɪən) *adj* **1** of or relating to land or its cultivation. **2** of or relating to rural or agricultural matters. ◆ *n* **3** a person who favours the redistribution of landed property. ORIG C16: from L *agrārius,* from *ager* field, land
▸ **aˈgrarianˌism** *n*

agree (əˈgriː) *vb* **agrees, agreeing, agreed.** (*mainly intr*) **1** (often foll. by *with*) to be of the same opinion. **2** (*also tr;* when *intr,* often foll. by *to;* when *tr, takes a clause as object or an infinitive*) to give assent; consent. **3** (*also tr;* when *intr,* foll. by *on* or *about;* when *tr, may take a clause as object*) to come to terms (about). **4** (foll. by *with*) to be similar or consistent; harmonize. **5** (foll. by *with*) to be agreeable or suitable (to one's health, etc.). **6** (*tr; takes a clause as object*) to concede: *they agreed that the price was too high.* **7** *Grammar.* to undergo agreement. ORIG C14: from OF *agreer,* from *a gre* at will or pleasure

agreeable (əˈgrɪəbᵊl) *adj* **1** pleasing; pleasant. **2** prepared to consent. **3** (foll. by *to* or *with*) in keeping. **4** (foll. by *to*) to one's liking.
▸ **aˈgreeableness** *n* ▸ **aˈgreeably** *adv*

agreed (əˈgriːd) *adj* **1** determined by common consent: *the agreed price.* ◆ *sentence substitute.* **2** an expression of consent or agreement.

agreement (əˈgriːmənt) *n* **1** the act of agreeing. **2** a settlement, esp. one that is legally enforceable. **3** a contract or document containing such a settlement. **4** the state of being of the same opinion. **5** the state of being similar or consistent. **6** *Grammar.* the determination of the inflectional form of one word by some grammatical feature, such as number or gender, of another word. ORIG C14: from OF

agribusiness (ˈægrɪˌbɪznɪs) *n* the various businesses that process and distribute farm products. ORIG C20: from AGRI(CULTURE) + BUSINESS

Agricola ★ (əˈgrɪkələ) *n* **Gnaeus Julius** (ˈniːəs ˈdʒuːlɪəs).

40–93 A.D., Roman general; governor of Britain who advanced Roman rule north to the Firth of Forth.

agriculture ('ægrɪˌkʌltʃə) *n* the science or occupation of cultivating land and rearing crops and livestock; farming. ORIG C17: from L *agricultūra,* from *ager* field, land + *cultūra* CULTURE

▸ ˌ**agri'cultural** *adj* ▸ ˌ**agri'culturist** *or* ˌ**agri'culturalist** *n*

Agrigento ★ (*Italian* agri'dʒɛnto) *n* a town in Italy, in SW Sicily: site of six Greek temples. Pop.: 56 372 (1990). Former name (until 1927): **Girgenti** (gɜː'gɛntɪ).

agrimony ('ægrɪmənɪ) *n* **1** any of various plants of the rose family, which have compound leaves, long spikes of small yellow flowers, and bristly burlike fruits. **2** any of several other plants, such as hemp agrimony. ORIG C15: via OF from L, from Gk *argemōnē* poppy

Agrippa ★ (ə'grɪpə) *n* **Marcus Vipsanius** ('mɑːkəs vɪp'seɪnɪəs). 63–12 B.C., Roman general: chief adviser and later son-in-law of Augustus.

Agrippina ★ (ˌægrɪ'piːnə) *n* **1** called *the Elder. c.* 14 B.C.–33 A.D., Roman matron: mother of Caligula and Agrippina the Younger. **2** called *the Younger.* 15–59 A.D., mother of Nero, who put her to death after he became emperor.

agro- *combining form.* denoting fields, soil, or agriculture: *agrobiology.* ORIG from Gk *agros* field

agrobiology (ˌægrəubaɪ'ɒlədʒɪ) *n* the science of plant growth and nutrition in relation to agriculture.

agroforestry (ˌægrəu'fɒrɪstrɪ) *n* a method of farming integrating herbaceous and tree crops.

agronomics (ˌægrə'nɒmɪks) *n* (*functioning as sing*) the branch of economics dealing with the distribution, management, and productivity of land.

▸ ˌ**agro'nomic** *adj*

agronomy (ə'grɒnəmɪ) *n* the science of cultivation of land, soil management, and crop production.

▸ **a'gronomist** *n*

agrostemma (ˌægrəu'stɛmə) *n* any cultivated variety of corncockle. ORIG NL, from Gk *agros* field + *stemma* wreath

aground (ə'graund) *adv, adj* (*postpositive*) on or onto the ground or bottom, as in shallow water.

agterskot ('axtəˌskɒt) *n* (in South Africa) the final payment to a farmer for crops. Cf. **voorskot.** ORIG C20: Afrikaans *agter* after + *skot* shot, payment

Aguascalientes ★ (*Spanish* ˌaɣwaska'ljentes) *n* **1** a state in central Mexico. Pop.: 888 444 (1997 est.). Area: 5471 sq. km (2112 sq. miles). **2** a city in central Mexico, capital of Aguascalientes state, about 1900 m (6200 ft) above sea level, with hot springs. Pop.: 440 425 (1990).

ague ('eɪgjuː) *n* **1** malarial fever with successive stages of fever and chills. **2** a fit of shivering. ORIG C14: from OF (*fievre*) *ague* acute fever; see ACUTE

▸ **'aguish** *adj*

ah (ɑː) *interj* an exclamation expressing pleasure, pain, sympathy, etc., according to the intonation of the speaker.

AH (indicating years in the Muslim system of dating, numbered from the Hegira (622 A.D.)) *abbrev. for* anno Hegirae. ORIG L

aha (ɑː'hɑː) *interj* an exclamation expressing triumph, surprise, etc., according to the intonation of the speaker.

Ahab ★ ('eɪhæb) *n Old Testament.* the king of Israel from approximately 869 to 850 B.C. and husband of Jezebel: rebuked by Elijah (I Kings 16:29–22:40).

Ahasuerus ★ (əˌhæzjuː'ɪərəs) *n Old Testament.* a king of ancient Persia and husband of Esther, generally identified with Xerxes.

ahead (ə'hɛd) *adj* **1** (*postpositive*) in front; in advance. ◆ *adv* **2** at or in the front; before. **3** forwards: *go straight ahead.* **4 ahead of. 4a** in front of; at a further advanced position than. **4b** *Stock Exchange.* in anticipation of: *the share price rose ahead of the annual figures.* **5 be ahead.** *Inf.* to have an advantage; be winning. **6 get ahead.** to attain success.

ahem (ə'hɛm) *interj* a clearing of the throat, used to attract attention, express doubt, etc.

Ahern ★ (ə'hɜːn) *n* **Bertie.** born 1951, Irish politician; prime minister of the Republic of Ireland from 1997.

ahimsa (ɑː'hɪmsɑː) *n* (in Hindu, Buddhist, and Jainist philosophy) the law of reverence for, and nonviolence to, every form of life. ORIG Sansk., from *a* without + *himsā* injury

Ahithophel (ə'hɪθəˌfɛl) *or* **Achitophel** ★ *n Old Testament.* a member of David's council, who became one of Absalom's advisers in his rebellion and hanged himself when his advice was overruled (II Samuel 15:12–17:23).

Ahmedabad *or* **Ahmadabad** ★ ('ɑːmədəˌbɑːd) *n* a city in W India, in Gujarat: famous for its mosque. Pop.: 2 872 865 (1991).

Ahmednagar *or* **Ahmadnagar** ★ (ˌɑːməd'nʌgə) *n* a city in W India, in Maharashtra: formerly one of the kingdoms of Deccan. Pop.: 181 015 (1991).

ahoy (ə'hɔɪ) *interj Naut.* a hail used to call a ship or to attract attention.

Ahriman ★ ('ɑːrɪmən) *n Zoroastrianism.* the supreme evil spirit and diabolical opponent of Ormazd.

Ahura Mazda ★ (ə'huərə 'mæzdə) *n Zoroastrianism.* another name for **Ormazd.**

Ahvenanmaa ★ ('ɑhvɛnɑmmɑː) *n* the Finnish name for the **Åland Islands.**

Ahwaz (ɑː'wɑːz) *or* **Ahvaz** ★ (ɑː'vɑːz) *n* a town in SW Iran, on the Karun River. Pop.: 828 380 (1994 est.).

ai ('ɑːɪ) *n, pl* **ais.** another name for **three-toed sloth** (see **sloth** (sense 1)). ORIG C17: from Port., from Tupi

AI *abbrev. for:* **1** Amnesty International. **2** artificial insemination. **3** artificial intelligence.

aid (eɪd) *vb* **1** to give support to (someone to do something); help or assist. **2** (*tr*) to assist financially. ◆ *n* **3** assistance; help; support. **4** a person, device, etc., that helps or assists. **5** *Mountaineering.* a device such as a piton when used as a direct help in the ascent. **6** (in medieval Europe) a feudal payment made to the king or any lord by his vassals on certain occasions such as the knighting of an eldest son. ORIG C15: via OF *aidier* from L *adjūtāre,* from *juvāre* to help

▸ **'aider** *n*

Aid *or* **-aid** *n combining form.* denoting a charitable organization or function that raises money for a cause: *Band Aid; Ferryaid.*

AID *abbrev. for:* **1** *US.* Agency for International Development. **2** artificial insemination (by) donor: former name for donor insemination (DI).

Aidan ★ ('eɪdᵊn) *n* **Saint.** died 651 A.D., Irish missionary in Northumbria, who founded the monastery at Lindisfarne (635). Feast day: Aug. 31.

aide (eɪd) *n* **1** an assistant. **2** short for **aide-de-camp.**

aide-de-camp *or* **aid-de-camp** ('eɪd də 'kɒŋ) *n, pl* **aides-de-camp** *or* **aids-de-camp.** a military officer serving as personal assistant to a senior. Abbrev.: **ADC.** ORIG C17: from F: camp assistant

aide-mémoire ('eɪdmɛm'wɑː) *n, pl* **aides-mémoire** ('eɪdzmɛm'wɑː). **1** a note serving as a reminder. **2** a summarized diplomatic communication. ORIG F, from *aider* to help + *mémoire* memory

Aidin ★ ('aɪdɪn) *n* a variant spelling of **Aydin.**

AIDS *or* **Aids** (eɪdz) *n acronym for* acquired immune (*or* immuno-) deficiency syndrome: a condition, caused by a virus, in which the body loses its ability to resist infection. AIDS is transmitted by sexual intercourse, through infected blood and blood products, and through the placenta.

AIDS-related complex *n* See **ARC.**

AIF (formerly) *abbrev. for* Australian Imperial Force.

aiglet ('eɪglɪt) *n* a variant of **aglet.**

aigrette *or* **aigret** ('eɪgrɛt) *n* **1** a long plume worn on hats or as a headdress, esp. one of long egret feathers. **2** an ornament in imitation of a plume of feathers. ORIG C17: from F; see EGRET

aiguille (eɪ'gwiːl) *n* **1** a rock mass or peak shaped like a needle. **2** an instrument for boring holes in rocks or masonry. ORIG C19: F, lit.: needle

aiguillette (ˌeɪgwɪˈlɛt) *n* **1** an ornamentation worn by certain military officers, consisting of cords with metal tips. **2** a variant of **aglet**. ORIG C19: F; see AGLET

AIH *abbrev. for* artificial insemination (by) husband.

aikido (aɪˈkiːdəʊ) *n* a Japanese system of self-defence employing similar principles to judo, but including blows from the hands and feet. ORIG from Japanese, from *ai* to join, receive + *ki* spirit, force + *do* way

ail (eɪl) *vb* **1** (*tr*) to trouble; afflict. **2** (*intr*) to feel unwell. ORIG OE *eglan*, from *egle* painful

ailanthus (eɪˈlænθəs) *n, pl* **ailanthuses.** an E Asian deciduous tree having pinnate leaves, small greenish flowers, and winged fruits. Also called: **tree of heaven.** ORIG C19: NL, from native name in the Moluccas in the Indian and Pacific Oceans

aileron (ˈeɪlərɒn) *n* a flap hinged to the trailing edge of an aircraft wing to provide lateral control. ORIG C20: from F, dim. of *aile* wing

ailing (ˈeɪlɪŋ) *adj* unwell or unsuccessful, esp. over a long period.

ailment (ˈeɪlmənt) *n* a slight but often persistent illness.

aim (eɪm) *vb* **1** to point (a weapon, missile, etc.) or direct (a blow) at a particular person or object. **2** (*tr*) to direct (satire, criticism, etc.) at a person, object, etc. **3** (*intr;* foll. by *at* or an infinitive) to propose or intend. **4** (*intr;* often foll. by *at* or *for*) to direct one's efforts or strive (towards). ◆ *n* **5** the action of directing something at an object. **6** the direction in which something is pointed: *to take aim.* **7** the object at which something is aimed. **8** intention; purpose. ORIG C14: via OF *aesmer* from L *aestimāre* to ESTIMATE

AIM *abbrev. for* Alternative Investment Market.

aimless (ˈeɪmlɪs) *adj* having no purpose or direction. ▸ **ˈaimlessly** *adv* ▸ **ˈaimlessness** *n*

Ain ★ (*French* ɛ̃) *n* **1** a department in E central France, in Rhône-Alpes region. Capital: Bourg. Pop.: 497 943 (1994 est.). Area: 5785 sq. km (2256 sq. miles). **2** a river in E France, rising in the Jura Mountains and flowing south to the Rhône. Length: 190 km (118 miles).

ain't (eɪnt) *Not standard. contraction of* am not, is not, are not, have not, *or* has not: *I ain't seen it.*

Aintree ★ (ˈeɪntrɪ) *n* a suburb of Liverpool, in Merseyside: site of the racecourse over which the Grand National steeplechase has been run since 1839.

Ainu (ˈaɪnuː) *n* **1** (*pl* **Ainus** *or* **Ainu**) a member of the aboriginal people of Japan. **2** the language of this people, sometimes tentatively associated with Altaic, still spoken in parts of Hokkaido. ORIG Ainu: man

air (ɛə) *n* **1** the mixture of gases that forms the earth's atmosphere. It consists chiefly of nitrogen, oxygen, argon, and carbon dioxide. **2** the space above and around the earth; sky. Related adj: **aerial. 3** breeze; slight wind. **4** public expression; utterance. **5** a distinctive quality: *an air of mystery.* **6** a person's distinctive appearance, manner, or bearing. **7** *Music.* a simple tune for either vocal or instrumental performance. **8** transportation in aircraft (esp. in **by air**). **9** an archaic word for **breath** (senses 1–3). **10 in the air. 10a** in circulation; current. **10b** unsettled. **11 into thin air.** leaving no trace behind. **12 on** (*or* **off**) **the air.** (not) in the act of broadcasting or (not) being broadcast on radio or television. **13 take the air.** to go out of doors, as for a short walk. **14 up in the air. 14a** uncertain. **14b** *Inf.* agitated or excited. **15** (*modifier*) *Astrol.* of or relating to a group of three signs of the zodiac, Gemini, Libra, and Aquarius. ◆ *vb* **16** to expose or be exposed to the air so as to cool or freshen. **17** to expose or be exposed to warm or heated air so as to dry: *to air linen.* **18** (*tr*) to make known publicly: *to air one's opinions.* **19** (*intr*) (of a television or radio programme) to be broadcast. ◆ See also **airs.** ORIG C13: via OF & L from Gk *aēr* the lower atmosphere

Aïr ★ (ˈɑːɪə) *n* a mountainous region of N central Niger, in the Sahara, rising to 1500 m (5000 ft): a former native kingdom. Area: about 77 700 sq. km (30 000 sq. miles). Also called: **Asben, Azbine.**

air bag *n* a safety device in a car, consisting of a bag that inflates automatically in an accident and prevents the passengers from being thrown forwards.

air base *n* a centre from which military aircraft operate.

air bladder *n* **1** an air-filled sac, lying above the alimentary canal in bony fishes, that regulates buoyancy at different depths by a variation in the pressure of the air. **2** any air-filled sac, such as one in seaweeds.

airborne (ˈɛəˌbɔːn) *adj* **1** conveyed by or through the air. **2** (of aircraft) flying; in the air.

air brake *n* **1** a brake operated by compressed air, esp. in heavy vehicles and trains. **2** an articulated flap or small parachute for reducing the speed of an aircraft.

airbrick (ˈɛəˌbrɪk) *n Chiefly Brit.* a brick with holes in it, put into the wall of a building for ventilation.

airbrush (ˈɛəˌbrʌʃ) *n* **1** an atomizer for spraying paint or varnish by means of compressed air. ◆ *vb* (*tr*) **2** to paint or varnish (something) by using an airbrush. **3** to improve the image of (a person or thing) by concealing defects beneath a bland exterior: *an airbrushed version of the government's record.*

air chief marshal *n* a senior officer of the Royal Air Force and certain other air forces, of equivalent rank to admiral in the Royal Navy.

air cleaner *n* a filter that prevents dust and other particles from entering the air intake of an internal-combustion engine. Also called: **air filter.**

air commodore *n* a senior officer of the Royal Air Force and certain other air forces, of equivalent rank to brigadier in the Army.

air conditioning *n* a system or process for controlling the temperature and sometimes the humidity of the air in a house, etc. ▸ **ˈair-conˌdition** *vb* (*tr*) ▸ **air conditioner** *n*

air-cool *vb* (*tr*) to cool (an engine) by a flow of air. Cf. **water-cool.**

aircraft (ˈɛəˌkrɑːft) *n, pl* **aircraft.** any machine capable of flying by means of buoyancy or aerodynamic forces, such as a glider, helicopter, or aeroplane.

aircraft carrier *n* a warship with an extensive flat deck for the launch of aircraft.

aircraftman (ˈɛəˌkrɑːftmən) *n, pl* **aircraftmen.** a serviceman of the most junior rank in the Royal Air Force. ▸ **ˈaircraftˌwoman** *fem n*

air curtain *n* an air stream across a doorway to exclude draughts, etc.

air cushion *n* **1** an inflatable cushion. **2** the pocket of air that supports a hovercraft.

Airdrie ★ (ˈɛədrɪ; *Scot.* ˈerdrɪ) *n* a town in W central Scotland in North Lanarkshire, E of Glasgow. Pop.: 36 998 (1991).

airdrop (ˈɛəˌdrɒp) *n* **1** a delivery of supplies, troops, etc., from an aircraft by parachute. ◆ *vb* **airdrops, airdropping, airdropped. 2** (*tr*) to deliver (supplies, etc.) by an airdrop.

Aire ★ (ɛə) *n* a river in N England rising in the Pennines and flowing southeast to the Ouse. Length: 112 km (70 miles).

Airedale (ˈɛəˌdeɪl) *n* a large rough-haired tan-coloured breed of terrier with a black saddle-shaped patch covering most of the back. Also called: **Airedale terrier.** ORIG C19: from district in Yorkshire

air engine *n* **1** an engine that uses the expansion of heated air to drive a piston. **2** a small engine that uses compressed air to drive a piston.

airfield (ˈɛəˌfiːld) *n* a landing and taking-off area for aircraft.

air filter *n* another name for **air cleaner.**

airfoil (ˈɛəˌfɔɪl) *n* the US and Canad. name for **aerofoil.**

air force *n* **a** the branch of a nation's armed services primarily responsible for air warfare. **b** (*as modifier*): *an air-force base.*

airframe (ˈɛəˌfreɪm) *n* the body of an aircraft, excluding its engines.

air guitar *n* an imaginary guitar played while miming to rock music.

air gun *n* a gun discharged by means of compressed air.

airhead (ˈɛəˌhɛd) *n Sl.* a stupid or simple-minded person; idiot. ORIG C20: from AIR + HEAD

air hole *n* **1** a hole that allows the passage of air, esp. for ventilation. **2** a section of open water in a frozen surface.

air hostess *n* a stewardess on an airliner.

airily (ˈɛərɪlɪ) *adv* **1** in a jaunty or high-spirited manner. **2** in a light or delicate manner.

airiness (ˈɛərɪnɪs) *n* **1** the quality or condition of being fresh, light, or breezy. **2** gaiety.

airing (ˈɛərɪŋ) *n* **1a** exposure to air or warmth, as for drying or ventilation. **1b** (*as modifier*): *airing cupboard.* **2** an excursion in the open air. **3** exposure to public debate.

airless (ˈɛəlɪs) *adj* **1** lacking fresh air; stuffy or sultry. **2** devoid of air.
▸ **ˈairlessness** *n*

air letter *n* another name for **aerogram.**

airlift (ˈɛəˌlɪft) *n* **1** the transportation by air of passengers, troops, cargo, etc., esp. when other routes are blocked. ◆ *vb* **2** (*tr*) to transport by an airlift.

airline (ˈɛəˌlaɪn) *n* **1a** a system or organization that provides scheduled flights for passengers or cargo. **1b** (*as modifier*): *an airline pilot.* **2** a hose or tube carrying air under pressure.

airliner (ˈɛəˌlaɪnə) *n* a large passenger aircraft.

airlock (ˈɛəˌlɒk) *n* **1** a bubble in a pipe causing an obstruction. **2** an airtight chamber with regulated air pressure used to gain access to a space that has air under pressure.

airmail (ˈɛəˌmeɪl) *n* **1** the system of conveying mail by aircraft. **2** mail conveyed by aircraft. ◆ *adj* **3** of or for airmail.

airman (ˈɛəmən) *n, pl* **airmen.** a man who serves in his country's air force.
▸ **ˈairˌwoman** *fem n*

air marshal *n* **1** a senior Royal Air Force officer of equivalent rank to a vice admiral in the Royal Navy. **2** a Royal Australian Air Force officer of the highest rank. **3** a Royal New Zealand Air Force officer of the highest rank when chief of defence forces.

air mass *n* a large body of air having characteristics of temperature, moisture, and pressure that are approximately uniform horizontally.

Air Miles *pl n* points awarded by certain companies to purchasers of flight tickets and some other products that may be used to pay for other flights.

air miss *n* a situation in which two aircraft pass very close to one another in the air; near miss.

airplane (ˈɛəˌpleɪn) *n* the US and Canad. name for **aeroplane.**

airplay (ˈɛəˌpleɪ) *n* (of recorded music) radio exposure.

air pocket *n* a localized region of low air density or a descending air current, causing an aircraft to suffer an abrupt decrease in height.

airport (ˈɛəˌpɔːt) *n* a landing and taking-off area for civil aircraft, usually with runways and aircraft maintenance and passenger facilities.

air power *n* the strength of a nation's air force.

air pump *n* a device for pumping air into or out of something.

air rage *n* aggressive behaviour by an airline passenger that endangers the safety of the crew or other passengers.

air raid *n* **a** an attack by hostile aircraft or missiles. **b** (*as modifier*): *an air-raid shelter.*

air-raid warden *n* a member of a civil defence organization responsible for enforcing regulations, etc., during an air attack.

air rifle *n* a rifle discharged by compressed air.

airs (ɛəz) *pl n* affected manners intended to impress others: *to give oneself airs; put on airs.*

air sac *n* any of the membranous air-filled extensions of the lungs of birds, which increase the efficiency of respiration.

airscrew (ˈɛəˌskruː) *n Brit.* an aircraft propeller.

air-sea rescue *n* an air rescue at sea.

air shaft *n* a shaft for ventilation, esp. in a mine or tunnel.

airship (ˈɛəˌʃɪp) *n* a lighter-than-air self-propelled craft. Also called: **dirigible.**

airshow (ˈɛəˌʃəʊ) *n* an occasion when an air base is open to the public and a flying display and, usually, static exhibitions are held.

airsick (ˈɛəˌsɪk) *adj* nauseated from travelling in an aircraft.

airside (ˈɛəˌsaɪd) *n* the part of an airport nearest the aircraft, the boundary of which is the security check, customs, passport control, etc. Cf. **landside** (sense 1).

airspace (ˈɛəˌspeɪs) *n* the atmosphere above the earth or part of the earth, esp. the atmosphere above a particular country.

airspeed (ˈɛəˌspiːd) *n* the speed of an aircraft relative to the air in which it moves.

airstrip (ˈɛəˌstrɪp) *n* a cleared area for the landing and taking-off of aircraft; runway. Also called: **landing strip.**

air terminal *n Brit.* a building in a city from which air passengers are taken to an airport.

airtight (ˈɛəˌtaɪt) *adj* **1** not permitting the passage of air. **2** having no weak points; rigid or unassailable.

air-to-air *adj* operating between aircraft in flight.

air-traffic control *n* an organization that determines the altitude, speed, and direction at which planes fly in a given area, giving instructions to pilots by radio.
▸ **air-traffic controller** *n*

air vice-marshal *n* **1** a senior Royal Air Force officer of equivalent rank to a rear admiral in the Royal Navy. **2** a Royal Australian Air Force officer of the second highest rank. **3** a Royal New Zealand Air Force officer of the highest rank.

airwaves (ˈɛəˌweɪvz) *pl n Inf.* radio waves used in radio and television broadcasting.

airway (ˈɛəˌweɪ) *n* **1** an air route, esp. one that is fully equipped with navigational aids, etc. **2** a passage for ventilation, esp. in a mine. **3** the passage of air from the nose or mouth to the lungs. **4** *Med.* a tubelike device inserted via the throat to keep open the airway of an unconscious patient.

air waybill *n* a document made out by the consigner of goods by air freight giving details of the goods and the name of the consignee.

airworthy (ˈɛəˌwɜːðɪ) *adj* (of an aircraft) safe to fly.

airy (ˈɛərɪ) *adj* **airier, airiest. 1** abounding in fresh air. **2** spacious or uncluttered. **3** nonchalant. **4** visionary; fanciful: *airy promises.* **5** of or relating to air. **6** weightless and insubstantial. **7** light and graceful in movement. **8** high up in the air.

Aisha *or* **Ayesha** ★ (ˈɑːiːˌʃɑː) *n* ?613–678 A.D., the favourite wife of Mohammed; daughter of Abu-Bekr.

aisle (aɪl) *n* **1** a passageway separating seating areas in a theatre, church, etc. **2** a lateral division in a church flanking the nave or chancel. ORIG C14 *ele* (later *aile, aisle,* through confusion with *isle*), via OF from L *āla* wing
▸ **aisled** *adj*

Aisne ★ (eɪn; *French* ɛn) *n* **1** a department of NE France, in Picardy region. Capital: Laon. Pop.: 539 097 (1994 est.). Area: 7428 sq. km (2897 sq. miles). **2** a river in N France, rising in the Argonne Forest and flowing northwest and west to the River Oise: scene of a major Allied offensive in 1918 which turned the tide finally against Germany in World War I. Length: 282 km (175 miles).

ait (eɪt) *or* **eyot** *n Dialect.* an islet, esp. in a river. ORIG OE *ȳgett* small island, from *ieg* ISLAND

aitch (eɪtʃ) *n* the letter *h* or the sound represented by it. ORIG C16: a phonetic spelling

aitchbone (ˈeɪtʃˌbəʊn) *n* **1** the rump bone in cattle. **2** a cut of beef from or including the rump bone. ORIG C15 *hach-boon,* altered from earlier *nache-bone* (*a nache* mistaken for *an ache, an aitch*); *nache* buttock, via OF from LL *natica,* from L *natis* buttock

Aitken ★ (ˈeɪtkən) *n* **1 Robert Grant.** 1864–1951, US as-

★ people and places

tronomer who discovered over three thousand double stars. **2 William Maxwell**. See **Beaverbrook**.

Aix-en-Provence ★ (*French* ɛksɑ̃prɔvɑ̃s) *n* a city and spa in SE France: the medieval capital of Provence. Pop.: 126 854 (1990). Also called: **Aix**.

Aix-la-Chapelle ★ (*French* ɛkslaʃapɛl) *n* the French name for **Aachen**.

Aix-les-Bains ★ (*French* ɛkslebɛ̃) *n* a town in E France: a resort with sulphurous springs. Pop.: 24 830 (1990).

Aíyina ★ ('ɛjina) *n* transliteration of the Modern Greek name for **Aegina**.

Ajaccio ★ (ə'dʒætsɪˌəʊ, -'dʒeɪ-) *n* the capital of Corsica, a port on the W coast. Pop.: 55 279 (1990).

ajar (ə'dʒɑː) *adj* (*postpositive*), *adv* (esp. of a door) slightly open. ORIG C18: altered form of obs. *on char*, lit.: on the turn; from OE *cierran* to turn

Ajax ★ ('eɪdʒæks) *n Greek myth*. **1** the son of Telamon; a Greek hero of the Trojan War who killed himself in vexation when Achilles' armour was given to Odysseus. **2** called *Ajax the Lesser*, a Locrian king, a swift-footed Greek hero of the Trojan War.

Ajmer ★ (ʌdʒ'mɪə) *n* a city in NW India, in Rajasthan: textile centre. Pop.: 402 700 (1991).

AK *abbrev. for* Alaska.

AK-47 *n Trademark*. a type of Kalashnikov.

a.k.a. *or* **AKA** *abbrev. for* also known as.

Akbar ★ ('ækbɑː) *n* called *Akbar the Great*. 1542–1605, Mogul emperor of India (1556–1605), who extended the Mogul empire to include N India.

akene (ə'kiːn) *n* a variant spelling of **achene**.

Akhaïa ★ (a'xaːja) *n* transliteration of the modern Greek name for **Achaea**.

Akhenaten *or* **Akhenaton** ★ (ˌækə'nɑːtᵊn) *n* original name *Amenhotep IV*. died ?1358 B.C., king of Egypt, of the 18th dynasty; he moved his capital from Thebes to Tell El Amarna and introduced the cult of Aten.

Akhmatova ★ (*Russian* ax'matəvə) *n* **Anna** ('annə). pseudonym of *Anna Gorenko*. 1889–1966, Russian poet.

Akihito ★ (ˌækɪ'hiːtəʊ) *n* born 1933, Emperor of Japan from 1989.

akimbo (ə'kɪmbəʊ) *adj, adv* (**with**) **arms akimbo**. with hands on hips and elbows out. ORIG C15 *in kenebowe*, lit.: in keen bow, that is, in a sharp curve

akin (ə'kɪn) *adj* (*postpositive*) **1** related by blood. **2** (often foll. by *to*) having similar characteristics, properties, etc.

Akkad *or* **Accad** ★ ('ækæd) *n* **1** a city on the Euphrates in N Babylonia, the centre of a major empire and civilization (2360–2180 B.C.). Ancient name: **Agade** (ə'gɑːdɪ, ə'geɪdɪ). **2** an ancient region lying north of Babylon, from which the Akkadian language and culture is named.

Akkadian *or* **Accadian** (ə'kædɪən) *n* **1** a member of an ancient Semitic people who lived in Mesopotamia in the third millennium B.C. **2** the extinct language of this people.

Akkerman ★ (*Russian* akɪr'man) *n* the former name (until 1946) of **Byelgorod-Dnestrovski**.

Akmola ★ (*Kazakh* ɑkmɔ'lɑ) *n* the former name (1994–98) of **Astana**.

Aktyubinsk ★ (*Russian* ak'tjubinsk) *n* the former name (until 1991) of **Aqtöbe**.

Akure ★ (ə'kuːre) *n* a city in SW Nigeria, capital of Ondo state: agricultural trade centre. Pop.: 158 200 (1995 est.).

Al *the chemical symbol for* aluminium.

AL *abbrev. for:* **1** Alabama. **2** Anglo-Latin.

-al[1] *suffix forming adjectives*. of; related to: *functional; sectional; tonal*. ORIG from L *-ālis*

-al[2] *suffix forming nouns*. the act or process of doing what is indicated by the verb stem: *renewal*. ORIG via OF *-aille*, *-ail*, from L *-ālia*, neuter pl used as substantive, from *-ālis* -AL[1]

-al[3] *suffix forming nouns*. **1** (*not used systematically*) indicating any aldehyde: *ethanal*. **2** indicating a pharmaceutical product: *phenobarbital*. ORIG shortened from ALDEHYDE

ala ('eɪlə) *n, pl* **alae** ('eɪliː). **1** *Zool*. a wing or flat winglike process or structure. **2** *Bot*. a winglike part, such as one of the wings of a sycamore seed. ORIG C18: from L *āla* a wing

à la (ɑː lɑː) *prep* **1** in the manner or style of. **2** as prepared in (a particular place) or by or for (a particular person). ORIG C17: from F, short for *à la mode de* in the style of

Ala. *abbrev. for* Alabama.

Alabama ★ (ˌælə'bæmə) *n* **1** a state of the southeastern US, on the Gulf of Mexico: consists of coastal and W lowlands crossed by the Tombigbee, Black Warrior, and Alabama Rivers, with parts of the Tennessee Valley and Cumberland Plateau in the north; noted for producing cotton and white marble. Capital: Montgomery. Pop.: 4 351 999 (1998 est.). Area: 131 333 sq. km (50 708 sq. miles). Abbrevs.: **Ala.** or (with zip code) **AL** **2** a river in Alabama, flowing southwest to the Mobile and Tensaw Rivers. Length: 507 km (315 miles).
▸ ˌ**Ala'bamian** *adj*

alabaster ('æləˌbɑːstə) *n* **1** a fine-grained usually white, opaque, or translucent variety of gypsum. **2** a variety of hard semitranslucent calcite. ◆ *adj* **3** of or resembling alabaster. ORIG C14: from OF *alabastre*, from L *alabaster*, from Gk *alabastros*
▸ ˌ**ala'bastrine** *adj*

à la carte (ɑː lɑː 'kɑːt) *adj, adv* (of a menu) having dishes listed separately and individually priced. Cf. **table d'hôte**. ORIG C19: from F, lit.: according to the card

alack (ə'læk) *or* **alackaday** (ə'lækəˌdeɪ) *interj* an archaic or poetic word for **alas**. ORIG C15: from *a* ah! + *lack* loss, LACK

alacrity (ə'lækrɪtɪ) *n* liveliness or briskness. ORIG C15: from L, from *alacer* lively

Ala Dağ *or* **Ala Dagh** ★ (*Turkish* ɑ'lɑ dɑː) *n* **1** the E part of the Taurus Mountains, in SE Turkey, rising over 3600 m (12 000 ft). **2** a mountain range in E Turkey, rising over 3300 m (11 000 ft). **3** a mountain range in NE Turkey, rising over 3000 m (10 000 ft).

Alagez *or* **Alagöz** ★ (ɑlɑ'gœz) *n* the Turkish name for (Mount) **Aragats**.

Alagoas ★ (*Portuguese* ala'goːaʃ) *n* a state in NE Brazil, on the Atlantic coast. Capital: Maceió. Pop.: 2 633 251 (1996). Area: 30 776 sq. km (11 031 sq. miles).

Alai ★ (ɑː'laɪ) *n* a mountain range in central Asia, in SW Kyrgyzstan running from the Tian Shan range in China into Tajikistan. Average height: 4800 m (16 000 ft), rising over 5850 m (19 500 ft).

Alain-Fournier ★ (*French* alɛ̃furnje) *n* real name *Henri-Alban Fournier*. 1886–1914, French novelist; author of *Le Grand Meaulnes* (1913; translated as *The Lost Domain*, 1959).

Alamein ★ ('æləˌmeɪn) *n* See **El Alamein**.

Alamo ★ ('æləˌməʊ) *n* **the**. a mission in San Antonio, Texas, the site of a siege and massacre in 1836 by Mexican forces under Santa Anna of a handful of American rebels fighting for Texan independence from Mexico.

à la mode (ɑː lɑː 'məʊd) *adj* **1** fashionable in style, design, etc. **2** (of meats) braised with vegetables in wine. ORIG C17: from F: according to the fashion

Alanbrooke ★ ('ælənˌbrʊk) *n* **Alan Francis Brooke**, 1st Viscount. 1883–1963, British field marshal; chief of Imperial General Staff (1941–46).

Åland Islands ★ ('ɑːlənd, 'ɔːlənd; *Swedish* 'oːland) *pl n* a group of over 6000 islands under Finnish administration, in the Gulf of Bothnia. Capital: Mariehamn. Pop.: 24 847 (1992). Finnish name: **Ahvenanmaa**.

Al-Anon ('æləˌnɒn) *n* an association for the families and friends of alcoholics to give mutual support.

alar ('eɪlə) *adj* relating to, resembling, or having wings or alae. ORIG C19: from L *āla* a wing

Alar ('eɪlɑː) *n* a chemical sprayed on cultivated apple trees in certain countries to increase fruit set; daminozide.

Alarcón ★ (*Spanish* alar'kon) *n* **Pedro Antonio de** ('peðro an'tonjo de). 1833–91, Spanish writer, noted for his *The Three-Cornered Hat* (1874).

Alaric ★ ('ælərɪk) *n* ?370–410 A.D., king of the Visigoths, who served under the Roman emperor Theodosius I but later invaded Greece and Italy, capturing Rome in 410.

alarm (əˈlɑːm) *vb (tr)* **1** to fill with apprehension, anxiety, or fear. **2** to warn about danger; alert. **3** to fit or activate a burglar alarm on (a house, car, etc.). ◆ *n* **4** fear or terror aroused by awareness of danger. **5** apprehension or uneasiness. **6** a noise, signal, etc., warning of danger. **7** any device that transmits such a warning: *a burglar alarm.* **8a** the device in an alarm clock that triggers off the bell or buzzer. **8b** short for **alarm clock. 9** *Arch.* a call to arms. ORIG C14: from OF *alarme,* from OIt. *all'arme* to arms; see ARM[2]
▸ **aˈlarming** *adj*

alarm clock *n* a clock with a mechanism that sounds at a set time: used esp. for waking a person up.

alarmist (əˈlɑːmɪst) *n* **1** a person who alarms or attempts to alarm others needlessly. **2** a person who is easily alarmed. ◆ *adj* **3** characteristic of an alarmist.

alarum (əˈlærəm, -ˈlɑːr-) *n* **1** *Arch.* an alarm, esp. a call to arms. **2** (used as a stage direction, esp. in Elizabethan drama) a loud disturbance or conflict (esp. in **alarums and excursions**). ORIG C15: var. of ALARM

alas (əˈlæs) *sentence connector.* **1** unfortunately; regrettably: *there were, alas, none left.* ◆ *interj* **2** *Arch.* an exclamation of grief or alarm. ORIG C13: from OF *ha las!* oh wretched!; *las* from L *lassus* weary

Alas. *abbrev. for* Alaska.

Alaska ★ (əˈlæskə) *n* **1** the largest state of the US, in the extreme northwest of North America: the aboriginal inhabitants are Eskimos; the earliest White settlements were made by the Russians; it was purchased by the US from Russia in 1867. It is mostly mountainous and volcanic, rising over 6000 m (20 000 ft), with the Yukon basin in the central region; large areas are covered by tundra; it has important mineral resources (chiefly coal, oil, and natural gas). Capital: Juneau. Pop.: 614 010 (1998 est.). Area: 1 530 694 sq. km (591 004 sq. miles). Abbrevs.: **Alas.** or (with zip code) **AK** **2 Gulf of.** the N part of the Pacific, between the Alaska Peninsula and the Alexander Archipelago.
▸ **Aˈlaskan** *adj, n*

Alaska Highway ★ *n* a road extending from Dawson Creek, British Columbia, to Fairbanks, Alaska: built by the US Army (1942). Length: 2452 km (1523 miles). Originally called: **Alcan Highway.**

Alaska Peninsula ★ *n* an extension of the mainland of SW Alaska between the Pacific and the Bering Sea, ending in the Aleutian Islands. Length: about 644 km (400 miles).

Alaska Range ★ *n* a mountain range in S central Alaska. Highest peak: Mount McKinley, 6194 m (20 320 ft).

alate (ˈeɪleɪt) *adj* having wings or winglike extensions. ORIG C17: from L, from *āla* wing

alb (ælb) *n Christianity.* a long white linen vestment with sleeves worn by priests and others. ORIG OE *albe,* from Med. L *alba (vestis)* white (clothing)

Alb. *abbrev. for* Albania(n).

Alba ★ (*Spanish* ˈalβa) *n* See (Duke of) **Alva.**

albacore (ˈælbəˌkɔː) *n* a tunny occurring mainly in warm regions of the Atlantic and Pacific. It has very long pectoral fins and is a valued food fish. ORIG C16: from Port., from Ar.

Alba Longa ★ (ˈælbə ˈlɒŋgə) *n* a city of ancient Latium, southeast of modern Rome: the legendary birthplace of Romulus and Remus.

Alban ★ (ˈɔːlbən) *n* **Saint.** 3rd century A.D., the first English martyr. He was beheaded by the Romans on the site on which St Alban's Abbey now stands, for admitting his conversion to Christianity. Feast day: June 17.

Albania ★ (ælˈbeɪnɪə) *n* a republic in SE Europe, on the Balkan Peninsula: became independent in 1912 after more than four centuries of Turkish rule; established as a republic (1946) under Communist rule. A noncommunist government was elected in 1992. It is generally mountainous, rising over 2700 m (9000 ft), with extensive forests. Language: Albanian. Religion: Muslim majority. Currency: lek. Capital: Tirana. Pop.: 3 365 000 (1999 est.). Area: 28 749 sq. km (11 100 sq. miles).

Albany ★ (ˈɔːlbənɪ) *n* **1** a city in E New York State, on the Hudson River: the state capital. Pop.: 104 828 (1994 est.). **2** a river in central Canada, flowing east and northeast to James Bay. Length: 982 km (610 miles).

albatross (ˈælbəˌtrɒs) *n* **1** a large bird of cool southern oceans, with long narrow wings and a powerful gliding flight. See also **wandering albatross. 2** a constant and inescapable burden or handicap. **3** *Golf.* a score of three strokes under par for a hole. ORIG C17: from Port. *alcatraz* pelican, from Ar., from *al* the + *ghattās* white-tailed sea eagle; infl. by L *albus* white: C20 in sense 2, from Coleridge's poem *The Rime of the Ancient Mariner* (1798)

albedo (ælˈbiːdəʊ) *n* the ratio of the intensity of light reflected from an object, such as a planet, to that of the light it receives from the sun. ORIG C19: from Church L: whiteness, from L *albus* white

Albee ★ (ˈɔːlbiː) *n* **Edward.** born 1928, US dramatist. His plays include *Who's Afraid of Virginia Woolf?* (1962), *Seascape* (1975), and *The Play about the Baby* (1998).

albeit (ɔːlˈbiːɪt) *conj* even though. ORIG C14 *al be it,* that is, although it be (that)

Albemarle Sound ★ (ˈælbəˌmɑːl) *n* an inlet of the Atlantic in NE North Carolina. Length: about 96 km (60 miles).

Alberich ★ (*German* ˈalbərɪç) *n* (in medieval German legend) the king of the dwarfs and guardian of the treasures of the Nibelungs.

Albers ★ (ˈælbəz) *n* **Josef.** 1888–1976, US painter and poet, born in Germany.

albert (ˈælbət) *n* a kind of watch chain usually attached to a waistcoat. ORIG C19: after Prince ALBERT, who was presented with one by the jewellers of Birmingham in 1845

Albert[1] ★ (ˈælbət) *n* **Lake.** a lake in E Africa, between the Democratic Republic of Congo and Uganda in the Great Rift Valley, 660 m (2200 ft) above sea level: a source of the Nile fed by the Victoria Nile, which leaves as the Albert Nile. Area: 5345 sq. km (2064 sq. miles). Former name (1970–97): **Lake Mobutu.**

Albert[2] ★ (ˈælbət) *n* **Prince.** full name *Albert Francis Charles Augustus Emmanuel of Saxe-Coburg-Gotha.* 1819–61, Prince Consort of Queen Victoria of Great Britain and Ireland.

Albert I ★ *n* **1** *c.* 1255–1308, king of Germany (1298–1308). **2** 1875–1934, king of the Belgians (1909–34). **3** called *Albert the Bear. c.* 1100–70, German military leader: first margrave of Brandenburg.

Albert II ★ *n* full name *Albert Felix Humbert Theodore Christian Eugene Marie.* born 1934, king of Belgium from 1993.

Alberta ★ (ælˈbɜːtə) *n* a province of W Canada: mostly prairie, with the Rocky Mountains in the southwest. Capital: Edmonton. Pop.: 2 968 992 (1999 est.). Area: 661 188 sq. km (255 285 sq. miles). Abbrevs.: **Alta, AB**
▸ **Alˈbertan** *adj, n*

Albert Edward ★ *n* a mountain in SE New Guinea, in the Owen Stanley Range. Height: 3993 m (13 100 ft).

Alberti ★ (*Italian* alˈbɛrti) *n* **1 Domenico** (doˈmeːniko). *c.* 1710–40, Italian composer of harpsichord sonatas. **2 Leon Battista** (leˈɔn batˈtista). 1404–72, Italian Renaissance architect and painter.

Albertus Magnus ★ (ælˈbɜːtəs ˈmægnəs) *n* **Saint.** original name *Albert, Count von Böllstadt.* ?1193–1280, German scholastic philosopher; teacher of Thomas Aquinas and commentator on Aristotle. Feast day: Nov. 15.

albescent (ælˈbɛsᵊnt) *adj* shading into or becoming white. ORIG C19: from L *albēscere,* from *albus* white
▸ **alˈbescence** *n*

Albi ★ (*French* albi) *n* a town in S France: connected with the Albigensian heresy and the crusade against it. Pop.: 48 700 (1990).

Albigenses (ˌælbɪˈdʒɛnsiːz) *pl n* members of a Manichean sect that flourished in S France from the 11th to the 13th century. ORIG from Med. L: inhabitants of ALBI
▸ **ˌAlbiˈgensian** *adj* ▸ **ˌAlbiˈgensianˌism** *n*

albino (æl'bi:nəʊ) *n, pl* **albinos.** **1** a person with congenital absence of pigmentation in the skin, eyes, and hair. **2** any animal or plant that is deficient in pigment. ORIG C18: via Port. & Sp. from L *albus* white
▸ **albinism** ('ælbɪˌnɪzəm) *n* ▸ **albinotic** (ˌælbɪ'nɒtɪk) *adj*

Albinoni ★ (*Italian* albi'no:ni) *n* **Tomaso** (to'ma:zo). 1671–1750, Italian composer.

Albinus ★ (æl'bi:nəs) *n* another name for **Alcuin.**

Albion ★ ('ælbɪən) *n Arch. or poetic.* Britain or England. ORIG C13: from L, of Celtic origin

albite ('ælbaɪt) *n* a white, bluish-green, or reddish-grey feldspar mineral used in the manufacture of glass and as a gemstone. ORIG C19: from L *albus* white

Ålborg ★ (*Danish* 'ɔlbɔr) *n* a variant spelling of **Aalborg.**

album ('ælbəm) *n* **1** a book or binder consisting of blank pages, for keeping photographs, stamps, autographs, etc. **2** one or more long-playing CDs, cassettes, or records released as a single item. **3** a booklike holder containing sleeves for gramophone records. **4** *Chiefly Brit.* an anthology. ORIG C17: from L: blank tablet, from *albus* white

albumen ('ælbjʊmɪn) *n* **1** the white of an egg; the nutritive substance that surrounds the yolk. **2** a variant spelling of **albumin.** ORIG C16: from L: white of an egg, from *albus* white

albumin *or* **albumen** ('ælbjʊmɪn) *n* any of a group of simple water-soluble proteins that are found in blood plasma, egg white, etc. ORIG C19: from ALBUMEN + -IN
▸ **al'buminous** *adj*

albuminoid (æl'bju:mɪˌnɔɪd) *adj* **1** resembling albumin. ◆ *n* **2** another name for **scleroprotein.**

albuminuria (ælˌbju:mɪ'njʊərɪə) *n* the presence of albumin in the urine. Also called: **proteinuria.**

Albuquerque[1] ★ ('ælbəˌkɜ:kɪ) *n* a city in central New Mexico, on the Rio Grande. Pop.: 366 750 (1986 est.).

Albuquerque[2] ★ ('ælbəˌkɜ:kɪ; *Portuguese* ɑlbu'kɛrkə) *n* **Afonso de** (ə'fõsu də). 1453–1515, Portuguese navigator who established Portuguese colonies in the East by conquering Goa, Ceylon, Malacca, and Ormuz.

alburnum (æl'bɜ:nəm) *n* a former name for **sapwood.** ORIG C17: from L: sapwood, from *albus* white

Albury-Wodonga ★ ('ɔ:lbərɪ, -brɪ ˌwʌ'dɒŋə) *n* a city in SE Australia, in S central New South Wales, on the Murray River: commercial centre of an agricultural region. Pop.: 63 610 (1991).

Alcaeus ★ (æl'sɪəs) *n* 7th century B.C., Greek lyric poet who wrote hymns, love songs, and political odes.

Alcaic (æl'keɪɪk) *adj* **1** of a metre used by Alcaeus, consisting of a strophe of four lines each with four feet. ◆ *n* **2** (*usually pl*) verse written in the Alcaic form. ORIG C17: from LL *Alcaicus* of ALCAEUS

alcalde (æl'kældɪ) *or* **alcade** (æl'keɪd) *n* (in Spain and Spanish America) the mayor or chief magistrate in a town. ORIG C17: from Sp., from Ar. *al-qāḍī* the judge

Alcan Highway ★ ('ælkæn) *n* original name of the **Alaska Highway.**

Alcatraz ★ ('ælkəˌtræz) *n* an island in W California, in San Francisco Bay: a federal prison until 1963.

alcazar (ˌælkə'zɑ:; *Spanish* al'kaθar) *n* any of various palaces or fortresses built in Spain by the Moors. ORIG C17: from Sp., from Ar. *al-qasr* the castle

Alcazar de San Juan ★ ('ælkəˌzɑ:; *Spanish* al'kaθar) *n* a town in S central Spain: associated with Cervantes and Don Quixote. Pop.: 25 679 (1991).

Alcestis ★ (æl'sɛstɪs) *n Greek myth.* the wife of king Admetus of Thessaly. To save his life, she died in his place, but was rescued from Hades by Hercules.

alchemist ('ælkəmɪst) *n* a person who practises alchemy.

alchemize *or* **alchemise** ('ælkəˌmaɪz) *vb* **alchemizes, alchemizing, alchemized** *or* **alchemises, alchemising, alchemised.** (*tr*) to alter (an element, metal, etc.) by alchemy.

alchemy ('ælkəmɪ) *n, pl* **alchemies.** **1** the pseudoscientific predecessor of chemistry that sought a method of transmuting base metals into gold, and an elixir to prolong life indefinitely. **2** a power like that of alchemy: *her beauty had a potent alchemy.* ORIG C14 *alkamye,* via OF from Med. L, from Ar., from *al* the + *kīmiyā'* transmutation, from LGk *khēmeia* the art of transmutation
▸ **alchemic** (æl'kɛmɪk) *or* **al'chemical** *adj*

alcheringa (ˌæltʃə'rɪŋgə) *n* another name for **Dreamtime.** ORIG from Abor., lit.: dream time

Alchevsk ★ (æl'tʃɛvsk) *n* a city in E Ukraine. Pop.: 124 000 (1996 est.). Former name (until 1992): **Kommunarsk.**

Alcibiades ★ (ˌælsɪ'baɪəˌdi:z) *n* 450–404 B.C., Athenian statesman and general in the Peloponnesian War: brilliant, courageous, and unstable, he defected to the Spartans in 415, but returned and led the Athenian victories at Abydos (411) and Cyzicus (410).
▸ **ˌAlciˌbia'dean** *adj*

Alcides ★ (æl'saɪdi:z) *n* another name for **Hercules** (sense 1).

Alcinoüs ★ (æl'sɪnəʊəs) *n* (in Homer's *Odyssey*) a Phaeacian king at whose court the shipwrecked Odysseus told of his wanderings. See also **Nausicaä.**

ALCM *abbrev. for* air-launched cruise missile: a type of cruise missile that can be launched from an aircraft.

Alcock ★ ('ɔ:lkɒk) *n* Sir **John William.** 1892–1919, English aviator who with A.W. Brown made the first nonstop flight across the Atlantic (1919).

alcohol ('ælkəˌhɒl) *n* **1** a colourless flammable liquid, the active principle of intoxicating drinks, produced by the fermentation of sugars. Formula: C_2H_5OH. Also called: **ethanol, ethyl alcohol.** **2** a drink or drinks containing this substance. **3** *Chem.* any one of a class of organic compounds that contain one or more hydroxyl groups bound to carbon atoms that are not part of an aromatic ring. Cf. **phenol** (sense 2). ORIG C16: via NL from Med. L, from Ar. *al-kuhl* powdered antimony

alcohol-free *adj* **1** (of beer or wine) containing only a trace of alcohol. Cf. **low-alcohol.** **2** (of a period of time) during which no alcoholic drink is consumed: *there should be one or two alcohol-free days per week.*

alcoholic (ˌælkə'hɒlɪk) *n* **1** a person affected by alcoholism. ◆ *adj* **2** of, relating to, containing, or resulting from alcohol.

Alcoholics Anonymous *n* an association of alcoholics who try, esp. by mutual assistance, to overcome alcoholism.

alcoholism ('ælkəhɒˌlɪzəm) *n* a condition in which dependence on alcohol harms a person's health, family life, etc.

alcoholize *or* **alcoholise** ('ælkəhɒˌlaɪz) *vb* **alcoholizes, alcoholizing, alcoholized** *or* **alcoholises, alcoholising, alcoholised.** (*tr*) to turn into alcoholic drink, as by fermenting or mixing with alcohol.
▸ **ˌalcoˌholi'zation** *or* **ˌalcoˌholi'sation** *n*

alcopop ('ælkəʊˌpɒp) *n Inf.* an alcoholic drink that tastes like a soft drink. ORIG C20: from ALCO(HOL) + POP[1] (sense 11)

Alcoran *or* **Alkoran** (ˌælkɒ'rɑ:n) *n* another name for the **Koran.**
▸ **ˌAlco'ranic** *or* **ˌAlko'ranic** *adj*

Alcott ★ ('ɔ:lkət) *n* **Louisa May.** 1832–88, US novelist, noted for her children's books, esp. *Little Women* (1869).

alcove ('ælkəʊv) *n* **1** a recess or niche in the wall of a room, as for a bed, books, etc. **2** any recessed usually vaulted area, as in a garden wall. **3** any covered or secluded spot. ORIG C17: from F, from Sp. *alcoba,* from Ar. *al-qubbah* the vault

Alcuin ('ælkwɪn) *or* **Albinus** ★ *n* 735–804 A.D., English scholar and theologian; friend and adviser of Charlemagne.

Aldabra ★ (æl'dæbrə) *n* an island group in the Indian Ocean: part of the British Indian Ocean Territory (1965–76); now administratively part of the Seychelles.

Aldan ★ (*Russian* al'dan) *n* a river in E Russia in SE Sakha Republic, rising in the **Aldan Mountains** and flowing north and west to the Lena River. Length: about 2700 km (1700 miles).

Aldeburgh ★ ('ɔ:lbərə) *n* a small resort in SE England, in Suffolk: site of an annual music festival established in 1948 by Benjamin Britten. Pop.: 2654 (1991).

aldehyde ('ældɪˌhaɪd) *n* **1** any organic compound containing the group -CHO. Aldehydes are oxidized to carboxylic acids. **2** (*modifier*) consisting of, containing, or concerned with the group -CHO. ORIG C19: from NL *al(cohol) dehyd(rogenātum)* dehydrogenated alcohol
▸ **aldehydic** (ˌældə'hɪdɪk) *adj*

al dente (ˌæl 'dɛntɪ) *adj* (of pasta) still firm after cooking. ORIG It., lit: to the tooth

alder ('ɔ:ldə) *n* **1** a shrub or tree of the birch family, having toothed leaves and conelike fruits. The wood is used for bridges, etc., because it resists underwater rot. **2** any of several similar trees or shrubs. ORIG OE *alor*

alderman ('ɔ:ldəmən) *n, pl* **aldermen. 1** (in England and Wales until 1974) one of the senior members of a local council, elected by other councillors. **2** (in the US, Canada, Australia, etc.) a member of the governing body of a municipality. **3** *History.* a variant spelling of **ealdorman.** ORIG OE *aldormann,* from *ealdor* chief (comp. of *eald* OLD) + *mann* MAN
▸ **aldermanic** (ˌɔ:ldə'mænɪk) *adj*

Aldermaston ★ ('ɔ:ldəˌmɑ:stən) *n* a village in S England, in Berkshire SW of Reading: site of the Atomic Weapons Research Establishment and starting point of the Aldermaston marches (1958–63), organized by the Campaign for Nuclear Disarmament. Pop.: 2200 (latest est.).

Alderney ★ ('ɔ:ldənɪ) *n* **1** one of the Channel Islands, in the English Channel: separated from the French coast by a dangerous tidal channel (the **Race of Alderney**). Pop.: 2375 (1994 est.). Area: 8 sq. km (3 sq. miles). French name: **Aurigny** (ɔriɲi). **2** any of a breed of dairy cattle originating from the island of Alderney.

Aldershot ★ ('ɔ:ldəˌʃɒt) *n* a town in S England, in Hampshire: site of a large military camp. Pop.: 51 356 (1991).

Aldington ★ ('ɔ:ldɪŋtən) *n* **Richard.** 1892–1962, English poet, novelist, and biographer. His novels include *Death of a Hero* (1929) and *The Colonel's Daughter* (1931), which reflect postwar disillusion following World War I.

Aldis lamp ('ɔ:ldɪs) *n* a portable signalling lamp. ORIG C20: after its inventor A.C.W. *Aldis*

Aldiss ★ ('ɔ:ldɪs) *n* **Brian W(ilson).** born 1925, British science fiction writer. His works include *Non-Stop* (1958), *Somewhere East of Life* (1994), and *The Detached Retina* (1995).

Aldridge-Brownhills ★ ('ɔ:ldrɪdʒ'braunˌhɪlz) *n* a town in central England, in Walsall unitary authority, West Midlands: formed by the amalgamation of neighbouring towns in 1966. Pop.: 37 444 (1991).

aldrin ('ɔ:ldrɪn) *n* a poisonous crystalline solid, mostly $C_{12}H_8Cl_6$, used as an insecticide. ORIG C20: after K. *Alder* (1902–58), G chemist

Aldrin ★ ('ɔ:ldrɪn) *n* **Edwin Eugene Jr.**, known as *Buzz.* born 1930, US astronaut; the second man to set foot on the moon.

Aldus Manutius ★ ('ɔ:ldəs mə'nju:ʃɪəs) *n* 1450–1515, Italian printer, noted for his fine editions of the classics. He introduced italic type.

ale (eɪl) *n* **1** a beer fermented in an open vessel using yeasts that rise to the top of the brew. Compare **beer, lager. 2** (formerly) an alcoholic drink made by fermenting a cereal, esp. barley, but differing from beer by being unflavoured by hops. **3** *Chiefly Brit.* another word for **beer.** ORIG OE *alu, ealu*

aleatory ('eɪlɪətərɪ) *or* **aleatoric** (ˌeɪlɪə'tɒrɪk) *adj* **1** dependent on chance. **2** (esp. of a musical composition) involving elements chosen at random by the performer. ORIG C17: from L, from *āleātor* gambler, from *ālea* game of chance

Alecto ★ (ə'lɛktəu) *n Greek myth.* one of the three Furies; the others are Megaera and Tisiphone.

alee (ə'li:) *adv, adj* (*postpositive*) *Naut.* on or towards the lee: *with the helm alee.*

alehouse ('eɪlˌhaus) *n* **1** *Arch.* a place where ale was sold; tavern. **2** *Inf.* a pub.

Aleichem ★ (ɑ:'leɪçɛm) *n* **Sholom** ('ʃɒləm), real name *Solomon Rabinowitz.* 1859–1916, US Jewish writer, born in Russia. His works include *Tevye the Milkman,* adapted for the musical *Fiddler on the Roof.*

Aleksandropol ★ (*Russian* alɪksan'drɔpəlj) *n* the former name (from 1837 until after the Revolution) of **Leninakan.**

Aleksandrovsk ★ (*Russian* alɪk'sandrəfsk) *n* the former name (until 1921) of **Zaporozhye.**

Alembert, d' ★ (*French* dalɑ̃bɛr) *n* **Jean Le Rond** (ʒɑ̃ lə rɔ̃). 1717–83, French mathematician, noted for his *Traité de dynamique* (1743).

alembic (ə'lɛmbɪk) *n* **1** an obsolete type of retort used for distillation. **2** anything that distils or purifies. ORIG C14: from Med. L, from Ar. *al-anbīq* the still, from Gk *ambix* cup

Alençon ★ (*French* alɑ̃sɔ̃) *n* a town in NW France: early lace-manufacturing centre. Pop.: 31 140 (1990).

aleph ('ɑ:lɪf; *Hebrew* 'alɛf) *n* the first letter in the Hebrew alphabet. ORIG Heb.: ox

aleph-null *or* **aleph-zero** *n* the smallest infinite cardinal number; the cardinal number of the set of positive integers.

Aleppo ★ (ə'lɛpəu) *n* an ancient city in NW Syria: industrial and commercial centre. Pop.: 1 591 400 (1994 est.). French name: **Alep** (alɛp). Arabic name: **Haleb** ('halɛp).

alert (ə'lɜ:t) *adj* (*usually postpositive*) **1** vigilantly attentive: *alert to the problems.* **2** brisk, nimble, or lively. ◆ *n* **3** an alarm or warning. **4** the period during which such a warning remains in effect. **5 on the alert. 5a** on guard against danger, attack, etc. **5b** watchful; ready. ◆ *vb* (*tr*) **6** to warn or signal (troops, police, etc.) to prepare for action. **7** to warn of danger, an attack, etc. ORIG C17: from It. *all'erta* on the watch, from *erta* lookout post
▸ **a'lertly** *adv* ▸ **a'lertness** *n*

Alessandria ★ (*Italian* ales'sandrja) *n* a town in NW Italy, in Piedmont. Pop.: 93 866 (1990).

Ålesund *or* **Aalesund** ★ (*Norwegian* 'o:ləsun) *n* a port and market town in W Norway, on an island between Bergen and Trondheim: fishing and sealing fleets. Pop.: 35 862 (1990).

aleurone (ə'luərən) *or* **aleuron** (ə'luərɒn) *n* a protein that occurs in the form of storage granules in plant cells, esp. in seeds such as maize. ORIG C19: from Gk *aleuron* flour

Aleut (æ'lu:t) *n* **1** a member of a people inhabiting the Aleutian Islands and SW Alaska, related to the Eskimos. **2** the language of this people, related to Eskimo. ORIG from Russian *aleút,* prob. of native origin
▸ **Aleutian** (ə'lu:ʃən) *n, adj*

Aleutian Islands ★ *n* a chain of over 150 volcanic islands, extending southwestwards from the Alaska Peninsula between the N Pacific and the Bering Sea.

A level *n Brit.* **1a** the advanced level of a subject taken for the General Certificate of Education. **1b** (*as modifier*): *A-level maths.* **2** a pass in a subject at A level: *he has two A levels.*

alewife ('eɪlˌwaɪf) *n, pl* **alewives.** a North American fish similar to the herring. ORIG C19: ?from F *alose* shad

Alexander ★ (ˌælɪg'zɑ:ndə) *n* **Harold** (**Rupert Leofric George**), Earl Alexander of Tunis. 1891–1969, British field marshal in World War II, who commanded in North Africa (1943) and Sicily and Italy (1944–45); governor general of Canada (1946–52); British minister of defence (1952–54).

Alexander I ★ *n* **1** *c.* 1080–1124, king of Scotland (1107–24), son of Malcolm III. **2** 1777–1825, tsar of Russia (1801–25), who helped defeat Napoleon and formed the Holy Alliance (1815).

Alexander II ★ *n* **1** 1198–1249, king of Scotland (1214–49), son of William I. **2** 1818–81, tsar of Russia (1855–81), son of Nicholas I; assassinated by the Nihilists.

Alexander III ★ *n* **1** 1241–86, king of Scotland (1249–86), son of Alexander II. **2** original name *Orlando*

Bandinelli. died 1181, pope (1159–81), who excommunicated Barbarossa. **3** 1845–94, tsar of Russia (1881–94), son of Alexander II.

Alexander VI ★ *n* original name *Rodrigo Borgia.* 1431–1503, pope (1492–1503): noted for his extravagance and patronage of the arts.

Alexander Archipelago ★ *n* a group of over 1000 islands along the coast of SE Alaska.

Alexander I Island ★ *n* an island of Antarctica, west of Palmer Land, in the Bellingshausen Sea. Length: about 378 km (235 miles).

Alexander Nevski ★ ('nɛvskɪ, 'nɛf-; *Russian* 'njɛfskij) *n* **Saint.** ?1220–63, Russian prince and military leader, who defeated the Swedes at the River Neva (1240) and the Teutonic knights at Lake Peipus (1242).

Alexander technique *n* a technique for developing awareness of one's posture and movement in order to improve it. ORIG C20: named after Frederick Matthias *Alexander* (d. 1955), Australian actor who originated it

Alexander the Great ★ *n* 356–323 B.C., king of Macedon, who conquered Greece (336), Egypt (331), and the Persian Empire (328), and founded Alexandria.

Alexandra ★ (ˌælɪg'zɑːndrə) *n* **1** 1844–1925, queen consort of Edward VII of Great Britain and Ireland. **2** 1872–1918, the wife of Nicholas II of Russia; her misrule while Nicholas was supreme commander of the Russian forces during World War I precipitated the Russian Revolution.

Alexandretta ★ (ˌælɪgzɑːn'drɛtə) *n* the former name of **Iskenderun.**

Alexandria ★ (ˌælɪg'zændrɪə, -'zɑːn-) *n* the chief port of Egypt, on the Nile Delta: cultural centre of ancient times, founded by Alexander the Great (332 B.C.). Pop.: 3 382 000 (1994 est.). Arabic name: **El Iskandariyah.**
▸ **ˌAlex'andrian** *adj, n*

Alexandrine (ˌælɪg'zændraɪn) *n* **1** a line of verse having six iambic feet, usually with a caesura after the third foot. ◆ *adj* **2** of or written in Alexandrines. ORIG C16: from F, from *Alexandre,* 15th-cent. poem in this metre

alexandrite (ˌælɪg'zændraɪt) *n* a green variety of chrysoberyl used as a gemstone. ORIG C19: after ALEXANDER I of Russia; see -ITE[1]

Alexandroúpolis ★ (*Greek* alɛksan'ðrupɔlis) *n* a port in NE Greece, in W Thrace. Pop.: 39 283 (1991 est.). Former name (until the end of World War I): **Dedéagach.**

alexia (ə'lɛksɪə) *n* a disorder of the central nervous system characterized by impaired ability to read. ORIG C19: from NL, from A-[1] + Gk *lexis* speech

Alexis Mikhailovich ★ (ə'lɛksɪs mɪ'kaɪləˌvɪtʃ) *n* 1629–76, tsar of Russia (1645–76); father of Peter the Great.

alfalfa (æl'fælfə) *n* a leguminous plant of Europe and Asia, widely cultivated for forage. Also called: **lucerne.** ORIG C19: from Sp., from Ar. *al-fasfasah*

Alfonso VI ★ (*Spanish* al'fonso) *n* died 1109, king of Léon (1065–1109) and of Castile (1072–1109). He appointed his vassal, the Spanish hero El Cid, ruler of Valencia.

Alfonso XIII ★ (*Spanish* al'fonso) *n* 1886–1941, king of Spain (1886–1931): abdicated on the establishment of the republic.

Alfred the Great ★ ('ælfrɪd) *n* 849–99, king of Wessex (871–99) and overlord of England, who defeated the Danes.

alfresco (æl'frɛskəʊ) *adj, adv* in the open air. ORIG C18: from It.: in the cool

Alfvén ★ (al'ven) *n* **Hannes Olaf Gösta** ('hannɛs 'uːlaf 'jøsta). 1908–95, Swedish physicist, noted for his research on magnetohydrodynamics; shared the Nobel prize for physics 1970.

alg. *abbrev. for* algebra *or* algebraic.

Alg. *abbrev. for* Algeria(n).

algae ('ældʒiː) *pl n, sing* **alga** ('ælgə). unicellular or multicellular organisms formerly classified as plants, occurring in water or moist ground, that have chlorophyll but lack true stems, roots, and leaves. ORIG C16: from L, pl of *alga* seaweed, from ?
▸ **algal** ('ælgəl) *or* **algoid** ('ælgɔɪd) *adj*

Algarve ★ (æl'gɑːv) *n* **the.** an area in the south of Portugal, on the Atlantic; it approximately corresponds to the administrative district of Faro: fishing and tourism important.

algebra ('ældʒɪbrə) *n* **1** a branch of mathematics in which arithmetical operations and relationships are generalized by using symbols to represent numbers. **2** any abstract calculus, a formal language in which functions and operations can be defined and their properties studied. ORIG C14: from Med. L, from Ar. *al-jabr* the bone-setting, mathematical reduction
▸ **algebraic** (ˌældʒɪ'breɪɪk) *or* **ˌalge'braical** *adj* ▸ **algebraist** (ˌældʒɪ'breɪɪst) *n*

Algeciras ★ (ˌældʒɪ'sɪərəs; *Spanish* alxe'θiras) *n* a port and resort in SW Spain, on the Strait of Gibraltar: scene of a conference of the Great Powers in 1906. Pop.: 103 787 (1994 est.).

Algeria ★ (æl'dʒɪərɪə) *n* a republic in NW Africa, on the Mediterranean: became independent in 1962, after more than a century of French rule; one-party constitution adopted in 1976; religious extremists began a campaign of violence in 1988; consists chiefly of the N Sahara, with the Atlas Mountains in the north, and contains rich deposits of oil and natural gas. Official language: Arabic; French and Berber also widely spoken. Religion: Muslim. Currency: dinar. Capital: Algiers. Pop.: 29 910 000 (1999 est.). Area: about 2 382 800 sq. km (920 000 sq. miles). French name: **Algérie** (alʒeri).
▸ **Al'gerian** *or* **Algerine** ('ældʒəˌriːn) *adj, n*

-algia *n combining form.* denoting pain in the part specified: *neuralgia; odontalgia.* ORIG from Gk *algos* pain
▸ **-algic** *adj combining form.*

algid ('ældʒɪd) *adj Med.* chilly or cold. ORIG C17: from L *algidus,* from *algēre* to be cold
▸ **al'gidity** *n*

Algiers ★ (æl'dʒɪəz) *n* the capital of Algeria, an ancient port on the Mediterranean; up to 1830 a centre of piracy. Pop.: 2 168 000 (1985 est.). Arabic name: **Al-Jezair** (ˌældʒɛ'zɑːɪə). French name: **Alger** (alʒe).

alginate ('ældʒɪˌneɪt) *n* a salt or ester of alginic acid.

alginic acid (æl'dʒɪnɪk) *n* a white or yellowish powdery substance having hydrophilic properties. Extracted from kelp, it is used mainly in the food and textile industries.

Algol ('ælgɒl) *n* a computer-programming language designed for mathematical and scientific purposes. ORIG C20: *alg(orithmic) o(riented) l(anguage)*

algolagnia (ˌælgə'lægnɪə) *n* sexual pleasure got from suffering or inflicting pain. ORIG ML, from Gk *algos* pain + *lagneiā* lust

Algonquian (æl'gɒŋkɪən, -kwɪ-) *or* **Algonkian** *n* **1** a widespread family of North American Indian languages. **2** (*pl* **Algonquians** *or* **Algonquian**) a member of any of the North American Indian peoples that speak any of these languages. ◆ *adj* **3** denoting or relating to this linguistic family or its speakers.

Algonquin (æl'gɒŋkɪn, -kwɪn) *or* **Algonkin** (æl'gɒŋkɪn) *n* **1** (*pl* **Algonquins, Algonquin** *or* **Algonkins, Algonkin**) a member of a North American Indian people formerly living along the St Lawrence and Ottawa Rivers in Canada. **2** the language of this people, a dialect of Ojibwa. ◆ *n, adj* **3** a variant of **Algonquian.** ORIG C17: from Canad. F., earlier written as *Algoumequin;* perhaps rel. to Micmac *algoomaking* at the fish-spearing place

algorism ('ælgəˌrɪzəm) *n* **1** the Arabic or decimal system of counting. **2** the skill of computation. **3** an algorithm. ORIG C13: from OF, from Med. L, from Ar., from the name of abu-Ja'far Mohammed ibn-Mūsa *al-Khuwārizmi,* 9th-cent. Persian mathematician

algorithm ('ælgəˌrɪðəm) *n* **1** a logical arithmetical or computational procedure that if correctly applied ensures the solution of a problem. **2** *Logic, maths.* a recursive procedure whereby an infinite sequence of terms can be generated. ◆ Also called: **algorism.** ORIG C17: changed from ALGORISM, infl. by Gk *arithmos* number
▸ **ˌalgo'rithmic** *adj*

Algren ★ ('ɔːlgrən) *n* **Nelson.** 1909–81, US novelist. His

★ people and places

novels, mostly set in Chicago, include *Never Come Morning* (1942) and *The Man with the Golden Arm* (1949).

Alhambra ★ (æl'hæmbrə) *n* a citadel and palace in Granada, Spain, built for the Moorish kings during the 13th and 14th centuries: noted for its rich ornamentation.
▸ **Alhambresque** (ˌælhæm'brɛsk) *adj*

Al Hijrah *or* **Al Hijra** (æl 'hɪdʒrə) *n* an annual Muslim festival marking the beginning of the Muslim year. It commemorates Mohammed's move from Mecca to Medina. See also **Hegira**. ORIG from Ar. *hijrah* emigration or flight

Al Hufuf *or* **Al Hofuf** ★ (æl hʊ'fu:f) *n* a town in E Saudi Arabia: a trading centre with nearby oilfields and oases. Pop.: 102 000 (latest est.).

Ali ★ ('ɑ:li:) *n* **1** ?600–661 A.D., fourth caliph of Islam (656–61 A.D.), considered the first caliph by the Shiites: cousin and son-in-law of Mohammed. **2 Mehemet.** See **Mehemet Ali. 3 Muhammad.** See **Muhammad Ali.**

alias ('eɪlɪəs) *adv* **1** at another time or place known as or named: *Dylan, alias Zimmerman.* ◆ *n, pl* **aliases. 2** an assumed name. ORIG C16: from L *aliās* (adv) otherwise, from *alius* other

aliasing ('eɪlɪəsɪŋ) *n Radio & TV.* the error in a vision or sound signal arising from limitations in the system that generates or processes the signal.

alibi ('ælɪˌbaɪ) *n, pl* **alibis. 1** *Law.* **1a** a defence by an accused person that he or she was elsewhere at the time the crime was committed. **1b** the evidence given to prove this. **2** *Inf.* an excuse. ◆ *vb* **alibis, alibiing, alibied. 3** (*tr*) to provide with an alibi. ORIG C18: from L *alibī* elsewhere, from *alius* other + *-bī* as in *ubī* where

Alicante ★ (ˌælɪ'kæntɪ) *n* a port in SE Spain: commercial centre. Pop.: 274 964 (1994 est.).

Alice ('ælɪs) *or* **the Alice** ★ *n Austral. sl.* short for **Alice Springs.**

Alice band *n* an ornamental band worn across the front of the hair to hold it back from the face.

Alice-in-Wonderland *adj* fantastic; irrational. ORIG C20: alluding to the absurdities of Wonderland in Lewis Carroll's book

Alice Springs ★ *n* a town in central Australia, in the Northern Territory, in the Macdonnell Ranges: capital of the former territory of Central Australia. Pop.: 24 852 (1994). Former name (until 1931): **Stuart.**

alicyclic (ˌælɪ'saɪklɪk, -'sɪk-) *adj* (of an organic compound) having essentially aliphatic properties, in spite of the presence of a ring of carbon atoms. ORIG C19: from ALI(PHATIC) + CYCLIC

alidade ('ælɪˌdeɪd) *or* **alidad** ('ælɪˌdæd) *n* **1** a surveying instrument used for drawing lines of sight on a distant object and taking angular measurements. **2** the upper rotatable part of a theodolite. ORIG C15: from F, from Med. L, from Ar. *al-'idāda* the revolving radius of a circle

alien ('eɪlɪən) *n* **1** a person owing allegiance to a country other than that in which he lives. **2** any being or thing foreign to its environment. **3** (in science fiction) a being from another world. ◆ *adj* **4** unnaturalized; foreign. **5** having foreign allegiance: *alien territory.* **6** unfamiliar: *an alien quality.* **7** (*postpositive;* foll. by *to*) repugnant or opposed (to): *war is alien to his philosophy.* **8** (in science fiction) of or from another world. ORIG C14: from L *aliēnus* foreign, from *alius* other

alienable ('eɪlɪənəbᵊl) *adj Law.* (of property) transferable to another owner.
▸ ˌ**aliena'bility** *n*

alienate ('eɪlɪəˌneɪt) *vb* **alienates, alienating, alienated.** (*tr*) **1** to cause (a friend, etc.) to become unfriendly or hostile. **2** to turn away: *to alienate the affections of a person.* **3** *Law.* to transfer the ownership of (property, etc.) to another person.
▸ ˌ**alien'ation** *n* ▸ '**alienˌator** *n*

alienee (ˌeɪlɪə'ni:) *n Law.* a person to whom a transfer of property is made.

alienist ('eɪlɪənɪst) *n US.* a psychiatrist who specializes in the legal aspects of mental illness.

alienor ('eɪlɪənə) *n Law.* a person who transfers property to another.

aliform ('ælɪˌfɔ:m) *adj* wing-shaped. ORIG C19: from NL *āliformis,* from L *āla* a wing

Aligarh ★ (ˌɑ:lɪ'gɜ:, ˌælɪ-) *n* a city in N India, in W Uttar Pradesh, with a famous Muslim university (1920). Pop.: 480 520 (1991).

alight[1] (ə'laɪt) *vb* **alights, alighting, alighted** *or* **alit.** (*intr*) **1** (usually foll. by *from*) to step out (of): *to alight from a taxi.* **2** to come to rest; land: *a thrush alighted on the wall.* ORIG OE *ālīhtan,* from A-[2] + *līhtan* to make less heavy

alight[2] (ə'laɪt) *adj* (*postpositive*), *adv* **1** burning; on fire. **2** illuminated. ORIG OE, from *ālīhtan* to light up

align (ə'laɪn) *vb* **1** to place or become placed in a line. **2** to bring (components or parts) into proper coordination or relation. **3** (*tr;* usually foll. by *with*) to bring (a person, country, etc.) into agreement with the policy, etc., of another. ORIG C17: from OF, from *à ligne* into line

alignment (ə'laɪnmənt) *n* **1** arrangement in a straight line. **2** the line or lines formed in this manner. **3** alliance with a party, cause, etc. **4** proper coordination or relation of components. **5** a ground plan of a railway, road, etc.

alike (ə'laɪk) *adj* (*postpositive*) **1** possessing the same or similar characteristics: *they all look alike.* ◆ *adv* **2** in the same or a similar manner or degree: *they walk alike.* ORIG OE *gelīc*

aliment ('ælɪmənt) *n* something that nourishes or sustains the body or mind. ORIG C15: from L *alimentum* food, from *alere* to nourish
▸ ˌ**ali'mental** *adj*

alimentary (ˌælɪ'mɛntərɪ) *adj* **1** of or relating to nutrition. **2** providing sustenance or nourishment.

alimentary canal *n* the tubular passage extending from the mouth to the anus, through which food is passed and digested.

alimentation (ˌælɪmɛn'teɪʃən) *n* **1** nourishment. **2** sustenance; support.

alimony ('ælɪmənɪ) *n Law.* (formerly) an allowance paid under a court order by one spouse to another when they are separated but not divorced. See also **maintenance.** ORIG C17: from L, from *alere* to nourish

A-line ('eɪˌlaɪn) *adj* (of garments) flaring out slightly from the waist or shoulders.

Ali Pasha ★ ('ɑ:li: 'pɑ:ʃə) *n* known as *the Lion of Janina.* 1741–1822, Turkish pasha and ruler of Albania (1787–1820), who was deposed and assassinated after intriguing against Turkey.

aliphatic (ˌælɪ'fætɪk) *adj* (of an organic compound) not aromatic, esp. having an open chain structure. ORIG C19: from Gk *aleiphat-, aleiphar* oil

aliquant ('ælɪkwənt) *adj Maths.* of or signifying a quantity or number that is not an exact divisor of a given quantity or number: *5 is an aliquant part of 12.* ORIG C17: from NL, from L *aliquantus* somewhat, a certain quantity of

aliquot ('ælɪˌkwɒt) *adj Maths.* of or signifying an exact divisor of a quantity or number: *3 is an aliquot part of 12.* ◆ *vb* to divide or be divided into aliquots. ORIG C16: from L: several, a few

A list *n* **a** the most socially desirable category. **b** (*as modifier*): *an A-list event.* ◆ Cf. **B list.**

alit (ə'lɪt) *vb* a rare past tense and past participle of **alight**[1].

aliterate (eɪ'lɪtərɪt) *n* **1** a person who is able to read but disinclined to do so. ◆ *adj* **2** of or relating to aliterates.

alive (ə'laɪv) *adj* (*postpositive*) **1** living; having life. **2** in existence; active: *they kept hope alive.* **3** (*immediately postpositive*) now living: *the happiest woman alive.* **4** full of life; lively. **5** (usually foll. by *with*) animated: *a face alive with emotion.* **6** (foll. by *to*) aware (of); sensitive (to). **7** (foll. by *with*) teeming (with): *the mattress was alive with fleas.* **8** *Electronics.* another word for **live**[2] (sense 11). ORIG OE *on līfe* in LIFE

alizarin (ə'lɪzərɪn) *n* a brownish-yellow powder or oraange-red crystalline solid used as a dye. ORIG C19:

prob. from F, from Ar. *al-'asārah* the juice, from *'asara* to squeeze

alkali ('ælkə,laɪ) *n, pl* **alkalis** *or* **alkalies. 1** *Chem.* a soluble base or a solution of a base. **2** a soluble mineral salt that occurs in arid soils. ORIG C14: from Med. L, from Ar. *al-qili* the ashes (of saltwort)

alkali metal *n* any of the monovalent metals lithium, sodium, potassium, rubidium, caesium, and francium.

alkaline ('ælkə,laɪn) *adj* having the properties of or containing an alkali.
▸ **alkalinity** (,ælkə'lɪnɪtɪ) *n*

alkaline earth *n* **1** Also called: **alkaline earth metal, alkaline earth element.** any of the divalent electropositive metals beryllium, magnesium, calcium, strontium, barium, and radium. **2** an oxide of one of the alkaline earth metals.

alkalize *or* **alkalise** ('ælkə,laɪz) *vb* **alkalizes, alkalizing, alkalized** *or* **alkalises, alkalising, alkalised.** (*tr*) to make alkaline.
▸ **'alka,lizable** *or* **'alka,lisable** *adj*

alkaloid ('ælkə,lɔɪd) *n* any of a group of nitrogenous compounds found in plants. Many are poisonous and some are used as drugs.

alkane ('ælkeɪn) *n* any saturated aliphatic hydrocarbon with the general formula C_nH_{2n+2}. Former name: **paraffin.**

alkane series *n* a homologous series of saturated hydrocarbons starting with methane and having the general formula C_nH_{2n+2}. Also called: **methane series.**

alkanet ('ælkə,nɛt) *n* **1** a European plant, the roots of which yield a red dye. **2** the dye obtained. ORIG C14: from Sp., from Med. L, from Ar. *al* the + *hinnā'* henna

alkene ('ælki:n) *n* any unsaturated aliphatic hydrocarbon with the general formula C_nH_{2n}. Former name: **olefine.**

alkene series *n* a homologous series of unsaturated hydrocarbons starting with ethylene (ethene) and having the general formula C_nH_{2n}. Also called: **ethylene series, ethene series.**

Alkmaar ★ (*Dutch* 'ɑlkma:r) *n* a city in the W Netherlands, in North Holland. Pop.: 92 962 (1994).

Alkoran *or* **Alcoran** (,ælkɒ'rɑ:n) *n* a less common name for the **Koran.**

alky *or* **alkie** ('ælkɪ) *n Sl.* a heavy drinker or alcoholic.

alkyd resin ('ælkɪd) *n* any of several synthetic resins made from a dicarboxylic acid, used in paints and adhesives.

alkyl ('ælkɪl) *n* (*modifier*) of or containing the monovalent group C_nH_{2n+1}: *alkyl radical.* ORIG C19: from G, from *Alk(ohol)* ALCOHOL + -YL

alkylating agent ('ælkɪ,leɪtɪŋ) *n* any cytotoxic drug containing alkyl groups that acts by damaging DNA; widely used in chemotherapy.

alkyne ('ælkaɪn) *n* any unsaturated aliphatic hydrocarbon with the general formula C_nH_{2n-2}.

alkyne series *n* a homologous series of unsaturated hydrocarbons starting with acetylene (ethyne) and having the general formula C_nH_{2n-2}. Also called: **acetylene series.**

all (ɔ:l) *determiner* **1a** the whole quantity or amount of; everyone of a class: *all the rice; all men are mortal.* **1b** (*as pronoun; functioning as sing or pl*): *all of it is nice; all are welcome.* **1c** (*in combination with a noun used as a modifier*): *an all-night sitting; an all-ticket match.* **2** the greatest possible: *in all earnestness.* **3** any whatever: *beyond all doubt.* **4 all along.** all the time. **5 all but.** nearly: *all but dead.* **6 all of.** no less or smaller than: *she's all of thirteen years.* **7 all over. 7a** finished. **7b** everywhere (in, on, etc.): *all over England.* **7c** *Inf.* typically (in **that's me** (**him,** etc.) **all over**). **7d** unduly effusive towards. **8 all in all. 8a** everything considered: *all in all, it was a great success.* **8b** the object of one's attention: *you are my all in all.* **9 all the.** (foll. by a comp. adj or adv) so much (more or less) than otherwise: *we must work all the faster now.* **10 all too.** definitely but regrettably: *it's all too true.* **11 at all. 11a** (*used with a negative or in a question*) in any way or to any degree: *I didn't know that at all.* **11b** anyway: *I'm surprised you came at all.* **12 be all for.** *Inf.* to be strongly in favour of. **13 for all. 13a** in so far as: *for all anyone knows, he was a baron.* **13b** notwithstanding: *for all my pushing, I still couldn't move it.* **14 for all that.** in spite of that: *he was a nice man for all that.* **15 in all.** altogether: *there were five in all.* ◆ *adv* **16** (in scores of games) apiece; each: *the score was three all.* ◆ *n* **17** (preceded by *my, his,* etc.) (one's) complete effort or interest: *to give your all.* **18** totality or whole. ORIG OE *eall*

all- *combining form.* a variant of **allo-** before a vowel.

alla breve ('ælə 'breɪvɪ) *Music.* ◆ *adj, adv* **1** with two beats to the bar instead of four, i.e. twice as fast as written. ◆ *n* **2** (formerly) a time of two or four minims to the bar. Symbol: ¢ ORIG C19: It., lit.: according to the breve

Allah ('ælə) *n* the name of God in Islam. ORIG C16: from Ar., from *al* the + *Ilāh* god

Allahabad ★ (,æləhə'bæd, -'bɑ:d) *n* a city in N India, in SE Uttar Pradesh at the confluence of the Ganges and Jumna Rivers: Hindu pilgrimage centre. Pop.: 792 858 (1991).

all-American *adj US.* **1** representative of the whole of the United States. **2** composed exclusively of American members. **3** (of a person) typically American.

allantois (,ælən'təʊɪs, ə'læntɔɪs) *n* a membranous sac growing out of the ventral surface of the hind gut of embryonic reptiles, birds, and mammals. ORIG C17: NL, from Gk *allantoeidēs* sausage-shaped
▸ **allantoic** (,ælən'təʊɪk) *adj*

allay (ə'leɪ) *vb* **1** to relieve (pain, grief, etc.) or be relieved. **2** (*tr*) to reduce (fear, anger, etc.). ORIG OE *ālecgan* to put down

All Blacks *pl n* **the.** the international Rugby Union football team of New Zealand. ORIG so named because of the players' black strip

all clear *n* **1** a signal indicating that some danger, such as an air raid, is over. **2** permission to proceed.

all-dayer (,ɔ:l'deɪə) *n* an entertainment, such as a pop concert or film screening, that lasts all day.

allegation (,ælɪ'geɪʃən) *n* **1** the act of alleging. **2** an unproved assertion, esp. an accusation.

allege (ə'lɛdʒ) *vb* **alleges, alleging, alleged.** (*tr; may take a clause as object*) **1** to state without or before proof: *he alleged malpractice.* **2** to put forward (an argument or plea) for or against an accusation, claim, etc. ORIG C14 *aleggen,* ult. from L *allēgāre* to dispatch on a mission, from *lēx* law

alleged (ə'lɛdʒd) *adj* (*prenominal*) **1** stated to be such: *the alleged murderer.* **2** dubious: *an alleged miracle.*
▸ **allegedly** (ə'lɛdʒɪdlɪ) *adv*

Allegheny Mountains (,ælɪ'geɪnɪ) *or* **Alleghenies** ★ *pl n* a mountain range in Pennsylvania, Maryland, Virginia, and West Virginia: part of the Appalachian system; rising from 600 m (2000 ft) to over 1440 m (4800 ft).

allegiance (ə'li:dʒəns) *n* **1** loyalty, as of a subject to his or her sovereign. **2** (in feudal society) the obligations of a vassal to his liege lord. ORIG C14: from OF, from *lige* LIEGE

allegorical (,ælɪ'gɒrɪk^əl) *or* **allegoric** *adj* used in, containing, or characteristic of allegory.

allegorize *or* **allegorise** ('ælɪgə,raɪz) *vb* **allegorizes, allegorizing, allegorized** *or* **allegorises, allegorising, allegorised. 1** to transform (a story, fable, etc.) into or compose in the form of allegory. **2** (*tr*) to interpret allegorically.
▸ **,allegori'zation** *or* **,allegori'sation** *n*

allegory ('ælɪgərɪ) *n, pl* **allegories. 1** a poem, play, picture, etc., in which the apparent meaning of the characters and events is used to symbolize a moral or spiritual meaning. **2** use of such symbolism. **3** anything used as a symbol. ORIG C14: from OF, from L, from Gk, from *allēgorein* to speak figuratively, from *allos* other + *agoreuein* to make a speech in public
▸ **'allegorist** *n*

allegretto (,ælɪ'grɛtəʊ) *Music.* ◆ *adj, adv* **1** (to be performed) fairly quickly or briskly. ◆ *n, pl* **allegrettos. 2** a piece or passage to be performed in this manner. ORIG C19: dim. of ALLEGRO

Allegri ★ (*Italian* al'le:gri) *n* **Gregorio** (gre'gɔrjo). 1582–1652, Italian composer and singer.

allegro (ə'leɪgrəʊ, -'lɛg-) *Music.* ◆ *adj, adv* **1** (to be performed) in a brisk lively manner. ◆ *n, pl* **allegros.** **2** a piece or passage to be performed in this manner. ORIG C17: from It.: cheerful, from L *alacer* brisk, lively

allele (əˈliːl) *n* any of two or more genes that are responsible for alternative characteristics, such as smooth or wrinkled seeds in peas. Also called: **allelomorph** (əˈliːləˌmɔːf). ORIG C20: from G *Allel,* from *Allelomorph,* from Gk *allēl-* one another + *morphē* form

alleluia (ˌælɪˈluːjə) *interj* praise the Lord! Used in liturgical contexts in place of *hallelujah.* ORIG C14: via Med. L from Heb. *hallelūyāh*

allemande (ˈælɪmænd) *n* **1** the first movement of the classical suite, composed in a moderate tempo. **2** any of several German dances. **3** a figure in country dancing or square dancing by which couples change position in the set. ORIG C17: from F *danse allemande* German dance

Allen[1] ★ (ˈælən) *n* **1 Bog of.** a region of peat bogs in central Ireland, west of Dublin. Area: over 10 sq. km (3.75 sq. miles). **2 Lough.** a lake in Ireland, in county Leitrim.

Allen[2] ★ (ˈælən) *n* **1 Ethan.** 1738–89, American soldier during the War of Independence who led the Green Mountain Boys of Vermont. **2 Woody.** real name *Allen Stewart Konigsberg.* born 1935, US film comedian, screenwriter, and director. His films as actor and director include *Annie Hall* (1977), *Manhattan* (1979), *Hannah and Her Sisters* (1986), and *Sweet and Lowdown* (1999).

Allenby ★ (ˈælənbɪ) *n* **Edmund Henry Hynman,** 1st Viscount Allenby. 1861–1936, British field marshal who captured Palestine and Syria from the Turks in 1918; high commissioner in Egypt (1919–25).

Allende ★ (*Spanish* aˈʎende) *n* **Salvador** (salβaˈðor). 1908–73, Chilean Marxist politician; president of Chile (1970–73): killed by army.

allergen (ˈæləˌdʒɛn) *n* any substance capable of inducing an allergy.
▸ **ˌallerˈgenic** *adj*

allergic (əˈlɜːdʒɪk) *adj* **1** of, having, or caused by an allergy. **2** (*postpositive;* foll. by *to*) *Inf.* having an aversion (to): *allergic to work.*

allergist (ˈælədʒɪst) *n* a physician skilled in the treatment of allergies.

allergy (ˈælədʒɪ) *n, pl* **allergies.** **1** a hypersensitivity to a substance that causes the body to react to any contact with it. Hay fever is an allergic reaction to pollen. **2** *Inf.* an aversion. ORIG C20: from G *Allergie* (indicating a changed reaction), from Gk *allos* other + *ergon* activity

alleviate (əˈliːvɪˌeɪt) *vb* **alleviates, alleviating, alleviated.** (*tr*) to make (pain, sorrow, etc.) easier to bear; lessen. ORIG C15: from LL, from L *levis* light
▸ **alˌleviˈation** *n* ▸ **alˈleviˌator** *n*

USAGE NOTE See at **ameliorate.**

alley[1] (ˈælɪ) *n* **1** a narrow passage, esp. one between or behind buildings. **2** See **bowling alley.** **3** *Tennis, chiefly US.* the space between the singles and doubles sidelines. **4** a walk in a garden, esp. one lined with trees. **5 up** (*or* **down**) **one's alley** *Sl.* suited to one's abilities or interests. ORIG C14: from OF, from *aler* to go, ult. from L *ambulāre* to walk

alley[2] (ˈælɪ) *n* a large playing marble. ORIG C18: shortened and changed from ALABASTER

alleyway (ˈælɪˌweɪ) *n* a narrow passage; alley.

All Fools' Day *n* another name for **April Fools' Day** (see **April fool**).

all found *adj* (of charges for accommodation) inclusive of meals, heating, etc.

all hail *sentence substitute.* an archaic greeting or salutation. ORIG C14, lit.: all health (to someone)

Allhallows (ˌɔːlˈhæləʊz) *n* a less common term for **All Saints' Day.**

alliaceous (ˌælɪˈeɪʃəs) *adj* **1** of or relating to a genus of plants that have a strong smell and often have bulbs. The genus occurs in the N hemisphere and includes onion and garlic. **2** tasting or smelling like garlic or onions. ORIG C18: from L *allium* garlic

alliance (əˈlaɪəns) *n* **1** the act of allying or state of being allied; union. **2** a formal agreement, esp. a military one, between two or more countries. **3** the countries involved. **4** a union between families through marriage. **5** affinity or correspondence in characteristics. **6** *Bot.* a taxonomic category consisting of a group of related families. ORIG C13: from OF, from *alier* to ALLY

allied (əˈlaɪd, ˈælaɪd) *adj* **1** joined, as by treaty or marriage; united. **2** of the same type or class.

Allied (ˈælaɪd) *adj* of or relating to the Allies.

Allier ★ (*French* alje) *n* **1** a department of central France, in Auvergne region. Capital: Moulins. Pop.: 352 970 (1994 est.). Area: 7382 sq. km (2879 sq. miles). **2** a river in S central France, rising in the Cévennes and flowing north to the Loire. Length: over 403 km (250 miles).

Allies (ˈælaɪz) *pl n* **1** (in World War I) the powers of the Triple Entente (France, Russia, and Britain) together with the nations allied with them. **2** (in World War II) the countries that fought against the Axis and Japan, esp. Britain and the Commonwealth countries, the US, the Soviet Union, China, Poland, and France.

alligator (ˈælɪˌgeɪtə) *n* **1** a large crocodilian of the southern US, having powerful jaws but differing from the crocodiles in having a shorter and broader snout. **2** a similar but smaller species occurring in China. **3** any of various tools or machines having adjustable toothed jaws. ORIG C17: from Sp. *el lagarto* the lizard, from L *lacerta*

alligator pear *n* another name for **avocado.**

all-important *adj* crucial; vital.

all in *adj* **1** (*postpositive*) *Inf.* completely exhausted. ◆ *adv, adj* (**all-in** *when prenominal*). **2** with all expenses included: *one hundred pounds a week all in.* **3** (of wrestling) in freestyle.

Allingham ★ (ˈælɪŋəm) *n* **Margery.** 1904–66, British author of detective stories, featuring Albert Campion. Her works include *Tiger in the Smoke* (1952) and *The Mind Readers* (1965).

alliterate (əˈlɪtəˌreɪt) *vb* **alliterates, alliterating, alliterated.** **1** to contain or cause to contain alliteration. **2** (*intr*) to speak or write using alliteration.

alliteration (əˌlɪtəˈreɪʃən) *n* the use of the same consonant (**consonantal alliteration**) or of a vowel (**vocalic alliteration**), at the beginning of each word or stressed syllable in a line of verse, as in *around the rock the ragged rascal ran.* ORIG C17: from L *litera* letter
▸ **alˈliterative** *adj*

allium (ˈælɪəm) *n* a genus of liliaceous plants that includes the onion, garlic, shallot, leek, and chive. ORIG C19: from L: garlic

all-nighter (ˌɔːlˈnaɪtə) *n* an entertainment, such as a pop concert or film screening, that lasts all night.

allo- *or before a vowel* **all-** *combining form.* indicating difference, variation, or opposition: *allopathy; allomorph.* ORIG from Gk *allos* other, different

Alloa ★ (ˈæləʊə) *n* a town in E central Scotland, the administrative centre of Clackmannanshire. Pop.: 18 842 (1991).

allocate (ˈæləˌkeɪt) *vb* **allocates, allocating, allocated.** (*tr*) **1** to assign for a particular purpose. **2** a less common word for **locate** (sense 2). ORIG C17: from Med. L, from L *locus* a place
▸ **ˈalloˌcatable** *adj* ▸ **ˌalloˈcation** *n*

allocution (ˌæləˈkjuːʃən) *n Rhetoric.* a formal or authoritative speech or address. ORIG C17: from LL *allocūtiō,* from L *alloquī* to address

allomerism (əˈlɒməˌrɪzəm) *n* similarity of crystalline structure in substances of different chemical composition.
▸ **allomeric** (ˌæləˈmɛrɪk) *or* **alˈlomerous** *adj*

allomorph (ˈæləˌmɔːf) *n* **1** *Linguistics.* any of the representations of a single morpheme. For example, the final (s) and (z) sounds of *bets* and *beds* are allomorphs. **2** any of the different crystalline forms of a chemical compound, such as a mineral.
▸ **ˌalloˈmorphic** *adj*

allopath (ˈæləˌpæθ) *or* **allopathist** (əˈlɒpəθɪst) *n* a person who practises or is skilled in allopathy.

allopathy (ə'lɒpəθɪ) *n* the usual method of treating disease, by inducing a condition different from the cause of the disease. Cf. **homeopathy.**
▸ **allopathic** (ˌælə'pæθɪk) *adj*

allophone ('æləˌfəʊn) *n* **1** any of several speech sounds regarded as variants of the same phoneme. In English the aspirated initial (p) in *pot* and the unaspirated (p) in *spot* are allophones of the phoneme /p/. **2** *Canad.* a Canadian whose native language is neither French nor English.
▸ **allophonic** (ˌælə'fɒnɪk) *adj*

All-Ordinaries Index *n* an index of share prices on the Australian Stock Exchange giving a weighted arithmetic average of 245 ordinary shares.

allot (ə'lɒt) *vb* **allots, allotting, allotted.** (*tr*) **1** to assign or distribute (shares, etc.). **2** to designate for a particular purpose; apportion: *we allotted two hours to the case.* ORIG C16: from OF, from *lot* portion

allotment (ə'lɒtmənt) *n* **1** the act of allotting. **2** a portion or amount allotted. **3** *Brit.* a small piece of land rented by an individual for cultivation.

allotrope ('æləˌtrəʊp) *n* any of two or more physical forms in which an element can exist.

allotropy (ə'lɒtrəpɪ) *or* **allotropism** *n* the existence of an element in two or more physical forms.
▸ **allotropic** (ˌælə'trɒpɪk) *adj*

all-out *Inf.* ◆ *adj* **1** using one's maximum powers: *an all-out effort.* ◆ *adv* **all out. 2** to one's maximum capacity: *he went all out.*

allow (ə'laʊ) *vb* **1** (*tr*) to permit (to do something). **2** (*tr*) to set aside: *five hours were allowed to do the job.* **3** (*tr*) to let enter or stay: *they don't allow dogs.* **4** (*tr*) to acknowledge (a point, claim, etc.). **5** (*tr*) to let have: *he was allowed few visitors.* **6** (*intr;* foll. by *for*) to take into account. **7** (*intr;* often foll. by *of*) to permit: *a question that allows of only one reply.* **8** (*tr; may take a clause as object*) *US dialect.* to assert; maintain. ORIG C14: from OF, from LL *allaudāre* to extol, infl. by Med. L *allocāre* to assign
▸ **al'lowable** *adj* ▸ **al'lowably** *adv*

allowance (ə'laʊəns) *n* **1** an amount of something, esp. money or food, given at regular intervals. **2** a discount, as in consideration for something given in part exchange; rebate. **3** (in Britain) an amount of a person's income that is not subject to income tax. **4** a portion set aside to cover special expenses. **5** admission; concession. **6** the act of allowing; toleration. **7 make allowances** (*or* **allowance**). (usually foll. by *for*) **7a** to take mitigating circumstances into account. **7b** to allow (for). ◆ *vb* **allowances, allowancing, allowanced.** (*tr*) **8** to supply (something) in limited amounts.

Alloway ★ ('æləˌweɪ) *n* a village in Scotland, in South Ayrshire, S of Ayr: birthplace of Robert Burns.

allowedly (ə'laʊɪdlɪ) *adv* (*sentence modifier*) by general admission or agreement; admittedly.

alloy *n* ('ælɔɪ, ə'lɔɪ). **1** a metallic material, such as steel, consisting of a mixture of two or more metals or of metallic with nonmetallic elements. **2** something that impairs the quality of the thing to which it is added. ◆ *vb* (ə'lɔɪ). (*tr*) **3** to add (one metal or element to another) to obtain a substance with a desired property. **4** to debase (a pure substance) by mixing with an inferior element. **5** to diminish or impair. ORIG C16: from OF *aloi* a mixture, from *aloier* to combine, from L *alligāre*

all-purpose *adj* useful for many things.

all right *adj* (*postpositive except in slang use*), *adv* **1** adequate; satisfactory. **2** unharmed; safe. **3 all-right.** *US sl.* acceptable; reliable. ◆ *sentence substitute.* **4** very well: used to express assent. ◆ *adv* **5** satisfactorily: *the car goes all right.* **6** without doubt. ◆ Also: **alright.**

> **USAGE NOTE** See at **alright.**

all-round *adj* **1** efficient in all respects, esp. in sport: *an all-round player.* **2** comprehensive; many-sided: *an all-round education.*

all-rounder *n* a versatile person, esp. in a sport.

All Saints' Day *n* a Christian festival celebrated on Nov. 1 to honour all the saints.

all-singing all-dancing *adj* having every desirable feature possible: *an all-singing all-dancing computer.*

All Souls' Day *n RC Church.* a day of prayer (Nov. 2) for the dead in purgatory.

allspice ('ɔːlˌspaɪs) *n* **1** a tropical American tree, having small white flowers and aromatic berries. **2** the seeds of this berry used as a spice, having a flavour said to resemble a mixture of cinnamon, cloves, and nutmeg. ◆ Also called: **pimento.**

all-star *adj* (*prenominal*) consisting of star performers.

all-time *adj* (*prenominal*) *Inf.* unsurpassed.

all told *adv* (*sentence modifier*) in all: *we were seven all told.*

allude (ə'luːd) *vb* **alludes, alluding, alluded.** (*intr;* foll. by *to*) **1** to refer indirectly. **2** (loosely) to mention. ORIG C16: from L *allūdere,* from *lūdere* to sport, from *lūdus* a game

> **USAGE NOTE** See at **elude.**

allure (ə'lʊə) *vb* **allures, alluring, allured. 1** (*tr*) to entice or tempt (someone); attract. ◆ *n* **2** attractiveness; appeal. ORIG C15: from OF *alurer,* from *lure* bait
▸ **al'lurement** *n* ▸ **al'luring** *adj*

allusion (ə'luːʒən) *n* **1** the act of alluding. **2** a passing reference. ORIG C16: from LL *allūsiō,* from L *allūdere* to sport with

allusive (ə'luːsɪv) *adj* containing or full of allusions.
▸ **al'lusiveness** *n*

alluvial (ə'luːvɪəl) *adj* **1** of or relating to alluvium. ◆ *n* **2** another name for **alluvium.**

alluvion (ə'luːvɪən) *n* **1a** the wash of the sea or a river. **1b** a flood. **1c** sediment; alluvium. **2** *Law.* the gradual formation of new land, as by the recession of the sea. ORIG C16: from L *alluviō* an overflowing, from *luere* to wash

alluvium (ə'luːvɪəm) *n, pl* **alluviums** *or* **alluvia** (-vɪə). a fine-grained fertile soil consisting of mud, silt, and sand deposited by flowing water. ORIG C17: from L; see ALLUVION

ally *vb* (ə'laɪ), **allies, allying, allied.** (usually foll. by *to* or *with*) **1** to unite or be united, esp. formally, as by treaty. **2** (*tr; usually passive*) to be related, as through being similar. ◆ *n* ('ælaɪ), *pl* **allies. 3** a country, person, or group allied with another. **4** a plant, animal, etc., closely related to another in characteristics or form. ORIG C14: from OF *alier* to join, from L *ligāre* to bind

allyl resin ('ælɪl) *n* any of several thermosetting synthetic resins, containing the CH_2:$CHCH_2$– group, used as adhesives. ORIG C19: from L *allium* garlic + -YL

Alma-Ata ★ (*Russian* al'maa'ta) *n* the Russian name for **Almaty.**

Almada ★ (*Portuguese* ɑl'mɑːdə) *n* a town in S central Portugal, on the S bank of the Tagus estuary opposite Lisbon: statue of Christ 110 m (360 ft) high, erected 1959. Pop.: 153 189 (1991).

Al Madinah ★ (ˌæl mæ'diːnə) *n* the Arabic name for **Medina.**

alma mater ('ælmə 'mɑːtə, 'meɪtə) *n* (*often caps.*) one's school, college, or university. ORIG C17: from L: bountiful mother

almanac ('ɔːlməˌnæk) *n* a yearly calendar giving statistical information, such as the phases of the moon, tides, anniversaries, etc. Also (archaic): **almanack.** ORIG C14: from Med. L *almanachus,* ?from LGk *almenikhiaka*

almandine ('ælməndɪn) *n* a deep violet-red garnet. ORIG C17: from F, from Med. L, from *Alabanda,* ancient city of Asia Minor where these stones were cut

Al Mansûrah ★ (ˌæl mæn'sʊərə) *n* a variant of **El Mansûra.**

Al Marj ★ (æl 'mɑːdʒ) *n* an ancient town in N Libya: founded in about 550 B.C. Pop.: 25 166 (latest est.). Italian name: **Barce.**

Alma-Tadema ★ ('ælmə'tædɪmə) *n* Sir **Lawrence.** 1836–1912, Dutch-English painter.

Almaty ★ (æl'mɑːtɪ) *n* a city in SE Kazakhstan, the capital until 1997; an important trading centre with many historic buildings. Pop.: 1 150 500 (1995 est.). Former name (until 1927): **Verny.** Russian name **Alma-Ata.**

almighty (ɔːlˈmaɪtɪ) *adj* **1** omnipotent. **2** *Inf.* (intensifier): *an almighty row.* ◆ *adv* **3** *Inf.* (intensifier): *an almighty loud bang.*

Almighty ★ (ɔːlˈmaɪtɪ) *n* **the.** another name for **God.**

almond (ˈɑːmənd) *n* **1** a small widely cultivated rosaceous tree that is native to W Asia and has pink flowers and an edible nutlike seed. **2** the seed, which has a yellowish-brown shell. **3** (*modifier*) made of or containing almonds: *almond cake.* ORIG C13: from OF *almande,* ult. from Gk *amugdalē*

almond-eyed *adj* having narrow oval eyes.

almoner (ˈɑːmənə) *n* **1** *Brit.* a former name for a trained hospital social worker. **2** (formerly) a person who distributes charity on behalf of a household or institution. ORIG C13: from OF, from *almosne* alms, ult. from LL *eleēmosyna*

almost (ˈɔːlməʊst) *adv* very nearly.

alms (ɑːmz) *pl n* charitable donations of money or goods to the poor or needy. ORIG OE *ælmysse,* from LL, from Gk *eleēmosunē* pity

almshouse (ˈɑːmzˌhaʊs) *n Brit. history.* a privately supported house offering accommodation to the aged or needy.

almucantar *or* **almacantar** (ˌælməˈkæntə) *n* **1** a circle on the celestial sphere parallel to the horizon. **2** an instrument for measuring altitudes. ORIG C14: from F, from Ar. *almukantarāt* sundial

aloe (ˈæləʊ) *n, pl* **aloes. 1** any plant of the genus *Aloe,* chiefly native to southern Africa, with fleshy spiny-toothed leaves. **2 American aloe.** Also called: **century plant.** a tropical American agave which blooms only once in 10 to 30 years. ORIG C14: from L *aloē,* from Gk

aloes (ˈæləʊz) *n* (*functioning as sing*) a bitter purgative drug made from the leaves of several species of aloe. Also called: **bitter aloes.**

aloe vera (ˈvɪərə) *n* **1** a plant of the species *Aloe vera,* the leaves of which yield a juice used as an emollient. **2** the juice of this plant, used in skin and hair preparations.

aloft (əˈlɒft) *adv, adj* (*postpositive*) **1** in or into a high or higher place. **2** *Naut.* in or into the rigging of a vessel. ORIG C12: from ON *ā lopt* in the air

alone (əˈləʊn) *adj* (*postpositive*), *adv* **1** apart from another or others. **2** without anyone or anything else: *one man alone could lift it.* **3** without equal: *he stands alone in the field of microbiology.* **4** to the exclusion of others: *she alone believed him.* **5 leave** *or* **let alone.** to refrain from annoying or interfering with. **6 leave well alone.** to refrain from interfering with something that is satisfactory. **7 let alone.** not to mention; much less: *he can't afford beer, let alone whisky.* ORIG OE *al one,* lit.: all (entirely) one

along (əˈlɒŋ) *prep* **1** over or for the length of: *along the road.* ◆ *adv* **2** continuing over the length of some specified thing. **3** together with some specified person or people: *he'd like to come along.* **4** forward: *the horse trotted along.* **5** to a more advanced state: *he got the work moving along.* **6 along with.** together with: *consider the advantages along with the disadvantages.* ORIG OE *andlang,* from *and-* against + *lang* LONG[1]

USAGE NOTE See at **plus.**

alongshore (əˌlɒŋˈʃɔː) *adv, adj* (*postpositive*) close to, by, or along a shore.

alongside (əˈlɒŋˌsaɪd) *prep* **1** (often foll. by *of*) close beside: *alongside the quay.* ◆ *adv* **2** near the side of something: *come alongside.*

aloof (əˈluːf) *adj* distant, unsympathetic, or supercilious in manner. ORIG C16: from A-[1] + *loof,* var. of LUFF
▸ **aˈloofly** *adv* ▸ **aˈloofness** *n*

alopecia (ˌæləˈpiːʃɪə) *n* baldness. ORIG C14: from L, from Gk *alōpekia,* orig.: mange in foxes

aloud (əˈlaʊd) *adv, adj* (*postpositive*) **1** in a normal voice. **2** in a spoken voice; not silently.

Aloysius ★ (ˌæləʊˈɪʃəs) *n* **Saint.** full name *Aloysius Luigi Gonzaga.* 1568–91, Italian Jesuit who died nursing plague victims; the patron saint of youth. Feast day: June 21.

alp (ælp) *n* **1** (in Switzerland) a mountain pasture. **2** a high mountain. **3 the Alps.** a high mountain range in S central Europe. ORIG C16: from L *Alpes*

ALP *abbrev. for* Australian Labor Party.

alpaca (ælˈpækə) *n* **1** a domesticated South American mammal related to the llama, with dark shaggy hair. **2** the cloth made from the wool of this animal. **3** a glossy fabric simulating this. ORIG C18: via Sp. from Aymara *allpaca*

alpenhorn (ˈælpənˌhɔːn) *n* another name for **alphorn.**

alpenstock (ˈælpənˌstɒk) *n* a stout stick with an iron tip used by hikers, mountain climbers, etc. ORIG C19: from G, from *Alpen* Alps + *Stock* STICK[1]

Alpes-de-Haute-Provence ★ (*French* alpdəotprɔvɑ̃s) *n* a department of SE France in Provence-Alpes-Côte-d'Azur region. Capital: Digne. Pop.: 137 903 (1994 est.). Area: 6988 sq. km (2725 sq. miles). Former name: **Basses-Alpes.**

Alpes Maritimes ★ (*French* alp maritim) *n* a department of the SE corner of France in Provence-Alpes-Côte-d'Azur region. Capital: Nice. Pop.: 1 010 196 (1994 est.). Area: 4298 sq. km (1676 sq. miles).

alpha (ˈælfə) *n* **1** the first letter in the Greek alphabet (Α, α). **2** *Brit.* the highest grade or mark, as in an examination. **3** (*modifier*) **3a** involving helium nuclei. **3b** denoting an isomeric or allotropic form of a substance. ORIG via L from Gk, of Phoenician origin

alpha and omega *n* the first and last, a phrase used in Revelation 1:8 to signify God's eternity.

alphabet (ˈælfəˌbɛt) *n* **1** a set of letters or other signs used in a writing system, each letter or sign being used to represent one or sometimes more than one phoneme in the language being transcribed. **2** any set of characters, esp. one representing sounds of speech. **3** basic principles or rudiments. ORIG C15: from LL, from the first two letters of the Gk alphabet; see ALPHA, BETA

alphabetical (ˌælfəˈbɛtɪkᵊl) *or* **alphabetic** *adj* **1** in the conventional order of the letters of an alphabet. **2** of or expressed by an alphabet.
▸ **ˌalphaˈbetically** *adv*

alphabetize *or* **alphabetise** (ˈælfəbəˌtaɪz) *vb* **alphabetizes, alphabetizing, alphabetized** *or* **alphabetises, alphabetising, alphabetised.** (*tr*) **1** to arrange in conventional alphabetical order. **2** to express by an alphabet.
▸ **ˌalphabetiˈzation** *or* **ˌalphabetiˈsation** *n*

alpha-blocker *n* any of a class of drugs that prevent the stimulation of alpha receptors, a type of receptor in the sympathetic nervous system, by adrenaline and that therefore cause widening of blood vessels: used in the treatment of high blood pressure.

alpha decay *n* the radioactive decay process resulting in emission of alpha particles.

alpha-fetoprotein (ˌælfəˌfiːtəʊˈprəʊtiːn) *n* a protein that forms in the liver of the human fetus; excessive quantities in the amniotic fluid may indicate spina bifida in the fetus; low levels may point to Down's syndrome. Abbrev.: **afp.**

alpha-hydroxy acid *n* a type of organic acid, commonly used in skin-care preparations, that has a hydroxyl group attached to the carbon atom next to the carbon atom carrying the carboxyl group.

alphanumeric (ˌælfənjuːˈmɛrɪk) *or* **alphameric** *adj* (of a character set or file of data) consisting of alphabetical and numerical symbols.

alpha particle *n* a helium nucleus, containing two neutrons and two protons, emitted during some radioactive transformations.

alpha ray *n* ionizing radiation consisting of a stream of alpha particles.

alpha rhythm *or* **wave** *n Physiol.* the normal bursts of electrical activity from the cerebral cortex of a person at rest. See also **brain wave.**

alpha stock *n* any of the most active securities on the

London stock exchange of which there are between 100 and 200.

Alpheus ★ (æl'fi:əs) *n Greek myth.* a river god, lover of the nymph Arethusa. She changed into a spring to evade him, but he changed into a river and mingled with her.

alphorn ('ælp,hɔ:n) *or* **alpenhorn** *n* a wind instrument used in the Swiss Alps, made from a very long tube of wood. ORIG C19: from G: Alps horn

alpine ('ælpaɪn) *adj* **1** of or relating to high mountains. **2** (of plants) growing on mountains above the limit for tree growth. **3** connected with mountaineering. **4** *Skiing.* of racing events on steep prepared slopes, such as the slalom and downhill. Cf. **nordic.** ◆ *n* **5** a plant grown in or native to high altitudes.

Alpine ('ælpaɪn) *adj* of or relating to the Alps or their inhabitants.

alpinist ('ælpɪnɪst) *n* a mountain climber.

Alps ★ (ælps) *pl n* **1** a mountain range in S central Europe, extending over 1000 km (650 miles) from the Mediterranean coast of France and NW Italy through Switzerland, N Italy, and Austria to NW Slovenia. Highest peak: Mont Blanc, 4807 m (15 771 ft). **2** a range of mountains in the NW quadrant of the moon, which is cut in two by a straight fracture, the **Alpine Valley.**

already (ɔ:l'rɛdɪ) *adv* **1** by or before a stated or implied time: *he is already here.* **2** at a time earlier than expected: *is it ten o'clock already?*

alright (ɔ:l'raɪt) *adv, sentence substitute, adj* a variant spelling of **all right.**

> **USAGE NOTE** The single-word form *alright* is still considered by many people to be wrong or less acceptable than *all right.* This is borne out by the data in the Bank of English, which suggests that the two-word form is about twenty times commoner than the alternative spelling.

Alsace ★ (æl'sæs; *French* alzas) *n* a region and former province of NE France, between the Vosges mountains and the Rhine: famous for its wines. Area: 8280 sq. km (3196 sq. miles). Ancient name: **Alsatia.** German name: **Elsass.**

Alsace-Lorraine ★ *n* an area of NE France, comprising the modern regions of Alsace and Lorraine: under German rule 1871–1919 and 1940–44. Area: 14 522 sq. km (5607 sq. miles). German name: **Elsass-Lothringen.**

Alsatia ★ (æl'seɪʃə) *n* **1** the ancient name for **Alsace. 2** an area around Whitefriars, London, in the 17th century, which was a sanctuary for criminals and debtors.

Alsatian (æl'seɪʃən) *n* **1** Also called: **German shepherd (dog).** a large wolflike breed of dog often used as a guard dog and by the police. **2** a native or inhabitant of Alsace. ◆ *adj* **3** of or relating to Alsace or its inhabitants.

also ('ɔ:lsəʊ) *adv* **1** (*sentence modifier*) in addition; as well; too. ◆ *sentence connector.* **2** besides; moreover. ORIG OE *alswā;* see ALL, SO[1]

also-ran *n* **1** a contestant, horse, etc., failing to finish among the first three. **2** a loser.

alstroemeria (,ælstrəʊ'mɪərɪə) *n* any of several plants with fleshy roots and brightly coloured flowers in summer, esp. the Peruvian lily. ORIG C18: NL, after Claude *Alstroemer* (1736–96), Swedish naturalist

alt. *abbrev. for:* **1** alternate. **2** altitude. **3** alto.

Alta. *abbrev. for* Alberta.

Altaic (æl'teɪɪk) *n* **1** a postulated family of languages of Asia and SE Europe, including the Turkic, Tungusic, and Mongolic subfamilies. See also **Ural-Altaic.** ◆ *adj* **2** denoting or relating to this linguistic family or its speakers.

Altai Mountains ★ (ɑ:l'taɪ) *pl n* a mountain system of central Asia, in W Mongolia, W China, and S Russia. Highest peak: Belukha, 4506 m (14 783 ft).

Altai Republic ★ *n* another name for **Gorno-Altai Republic.**

Altamira ★ (*Spanish* alta'mira) *n* a cave in N Spain, SW of Santander, noted for Old Stone Age wall drawings.

altar ('ɔ:ltə) *n* **1** a raised place or structure where sacrifices are offered and religious rites performed. **2** (in Christian churches) the communion table. **3** a step in the wall of a dry dock. ORIG OE, ult. from L *altus* high

altar boy *n RC Church, Church of England.* a boy serving as an acolyte.

altarpiece ('ɔ:ltə,pi:s) *n* a work of art set above and behind an altar; a reredos.

altazimuth (æl'tæzɪməθ) *n* an instrument for measuring the altitude and azimuth of a celestial body. ORIG C19: from ALT(ITUDE) + AZIMUTH

altazimuth mounting *n* a telescope mounting that allows motion of the telescope about a vertical axis (in altitude) and a horizontal axis (in azimuth).

Altdorf ★ (*German* 'altdɔrf) *n* a town in central Switzerland, capital of Uri canton: setting of the William Tell legend. Pop.: 8150 (1990).

alter ('ɔ:ltə) *vb* **1** to make or become different in some respect; change. **2** (*tr*) *Inf., chiefly US.* a euphemistic word for **castrate** or **spay.** ORIG C14: from OF, ult. from L *alter* other

▸ **'alterable** *adj*

alteration (,ɔ:ltə'reɪʃən) *n* **1** a change or modification. **2** the act of altering.

alterative ('ɔ:ltərətɪv) *adj* **1** likely or able to produce alteration. **2** (of a drug) able to restore health. ◆ *n* **3** such a drug.

altercate ('ɔ:ltə,keɪt) *vb* **altercates, altercating, altercated.** (*intr*) to argue, esp. heatedly; dispute. ORIG C16: from L *altercārī* to quarrel with another, from *alter* other

altercation (,ɔ:ltə'keɪʃən) *n* an angry or heated discussion or quarrel; argument.

alter ego ('æltər 'i:gəʊ, 'ɛgəʊ) *n* **1** a second self. **2** a very close friend. ORIG L: other self

alternate *vb* ('ɔ:ltə,neɪt), **alternates, alternating, alternated. 1** (often foll. by *with*) to occur or cause to occur by turns: *day and night alternate.* **2** (*intr;* often foll. by *between*) to swing repeatedly from one condition, action, etc., to another. **3** (*tr*) to interchange regularly or in succession. **4** (*intr*) (of an electric current, voltage, etc.) to reverse direction or sign at regular intervals. ◆ *adj* (ɔ:l'tɜ:nɪt). **5** occurring by turns: *alternate feelings of love and hate.* **6** every other or second one of a series: *he came on alternate days.* **7** being a second choice; alternative: *alternate director.* **8** *Bot.* (of leaves, flowers, etc.) arranged singly at different heights on either side of the stem. ◆ *n* ('ɔ:ltənɪt, ɔ:l'tɜ:nɪt). **9** *US & Canad.* a person who substitutes for another; stand-in. ORIG C16: from L *alternāre* to do one thing and then another, ult. from *alter* other

▸ **,alter'nation** *n*

alternate angles *pl n* two angles at opposite ends and on opposite sides of a transversal cutting two lines.

alternately (ɔ:l'tɜ:nɪtlɪ) *adv* in an alternating sequence or position.

alternating current *n* an electric current that periodically reverses direction. Abbrev.: **AC.**

alternation of generations *n* the occurrence in the life cycle of many plants and lower animals of alternating sexual and asexual reproductive forms.

alternative (ɔ:l'tɜ:nətɪv) *n* **1** a possibility of choice, esp. between two things. **2** either of such choices: *we took the alternative of walking.* ◆ *adj* **3** presenting a choice, esp. between two possibilities only. **4** (of two things) mutually exclusive. **5** denoting a lifestyle, culture, art form, etc., that is regarded as preferable to that of contemporary society because it is less conventional, materialistic, or institutionalized.

▸ **al'ternatively** *adv*

alternative curriculum *n Brit. education.* any course of study offered as an alternative to the National Curriculum.

alternative energy *n* a form of energy derived from a natural source, such as the sun, wind, tides, or waves. Also called: **renewable energy.**

Alternative Investment Market *n* a market on the London Stock Exchange for small companies that want to avoid the expenses of a main-market listing. Abbrev.: **AIM.**

alternative medicine *n* the treatment or alleviation of disease by techniques such as osteopathy and acupuncture, allied with attention to a person's general wellbeing. Also called: **complementary medicine.**

alternative society *n* a group of people who agree in rejecting the traditional values of the society around them.

Alternative Vote *n* (*modifier*) of or relating to a system of voting in which voters list the candidates in order of preference. If no candidate obtains more than 50% of first-preference votes, the votes for the bottom candidate are redistributed according to the voters' next preference. See **proportional representation.**

alternator ('ɔ:ltəˌneɪtə) *n* an electrical machine that generates an alternating current.

althaea *or US* **althea** (æl'θi:ə) *n* any Eurasian plant of the genus *Althaea,* such as the hollyhock, having tall spikes of showy flowers. ORIG C17: from L, from Gk *althaia* marsh mallow

althorn ('ælt,hɔ:n) *n* a valved brass musical instrument belonging to the saxhorn family.

Althorp House ★ ('ɔ:lθɔ:p, -θrʌp) *n* a mansion in Northamptonshire: seat of the Earls Spencer since 1508; Diana, Princess of Wales is buried on Round Oval Island in Althorp Park.

although (ɔ:l'ðəu) *conj* (*subordinating*) even though: *although she was ill, she worked hard.*

altimeter (æl'tɪmɪtə, 'æltɪˌmi:tə) *n* an instrument that indicates height above sea level, esp. one based on an aneroid barometer and fitted to an aircraft. ORIG C19: from L *altus* high + -METER

Altiplano ★ (*Spanish* alti'plano) *n* a plateau of the Andes, covering two thirds of Bolivia and extending into S Peru: contains Lake Titicaca. Height: 3000 m (10 000 ft) to 3900 m (13 000 ft).

altitude ('æltɪˌtju:d) *n* **1** the vertical height of an object, esp. above sea level. **2** *Geom.* the perpendicular distance from the vertex to the base of a geometrical figure or solid. **3** Also called: **elevation.** *Astron., navigation.* the angular distance of a celestial body from the horizon. **4** *Surveying.* the angle of elevation of a point above the horizontal plane of the observer. **5** (*often pl*) a high place or region. ORIG C14: from L *altus* high, deep

alto ('æltəu) *n, pl* **altos. 1** (in choral singing) short for **contralto. 2** the highest adult male voice; countertenor. **3** a singer with such a voice. **4** a flute, saxophone, etc., that is the third or fourth highest instrument in its group. ◆ *adj* **5** denoting such an instrument. ORIG C18: from It.: high, from L *altus*

alto clef *n* the clef that establishes middle C as being on the third line of the staff.

altocumulus (ˌæltəu'kju:mjuləs) *n, pl* **altocumuli** (-laɪ). a globular cloud at an intermediate height of about 2400 to 6000 m (8000 to 20 000 ft).

altogether (ˌɔ:ltə'geðə, 'ɔ:ltəˌgeðə) *adv* **1** with everything included: *altogether he owed me sixty pounds.* **2** completely; utterly: *altogether mad.* **3** on the whole: *altogether it was very good.* ◆ *n* **4 in the altogether.** *Inf.* naked.

> **USAGE NOTE** The single-word form *altogether* is frequently written by mistake instead of two separate words. As the examples in the entry show, *altogether* is an adverb, and should not be confused with *all together,* meaning 'everyone together'. Thus: *altogether there were six or seven families sharing the flat's facilities* means 'in total', as against *there were six or seven families all together in one flat,* meaning 'all crowded in together'.

altoist ('æltəuɪst) *n* a person who plays the alto saxophone.

altostratus (ˌæltəu'streɪtəs, -'strɑ:-) *n, pl* **altostrati** (-taɪ). a layer cloud at an intermediate height of about 2400 to 6000 m (8000 to 20 000 ft).

altricial (æl'trɪʃəl) *adj* **1** denoting birds whose young, after hatching, are naked, blind, and dependent on the parents for food. ◆ *n* **2** an altricial bird. ◆ Cf. **precocial.** ORIG C19: from NL, from L *altrix* a nurse

Altrincham ★ ('ɔ:ltrɪŋəm) *n* a residential town in NW England, in Trafford unitary authority, Greater Manchester. Pop.: 40 042 (1991).

altruism ('æltru:ˌɪzəm) *n* unselfish concern for the welfare of others. ORIG C19: from F, from It. *altrui* others, from L
▸ **'altruist** *n* ▸ **ˌaltru'istic** *adj* ▸ **ˌaltru'istically** *adv*

ALU *Computing. abbrev. for* arithmetical and logical unit.

alum ('æləm) *n* **1** a colourless soluble hydrated double sulphate of aluminium and potassium used in manufacturing and in medicine. Formula: $K_2SO_4.Al_2(SO_4)_3.24H_2O$. **2** any of a group of similar hydrated double sulphates of a monovalent metal or group and a trivalent metal. ORIG C14: from OF, from L *alūmen*

alumina (ə'lu:mɪnə) *n* another name for **aluminium oxide.** ORIG C18: from NL, pl of L *alūmen* ALUM

aluminium (ˌælju'mɪnɪəm) *or US & Canad.* **aluminum** (ə'lu:mɪnəm) *n* a light malleable silvery-white metallic element that resists corrosion; the third most abundant element in the earth's crust, occurring as a compound, principally in bauxite. Symbol: Al; atomic no.: 13; atomic wt.: 26.981.

aluminium oxide *n* a powder occurring naturally as corundum and used in the production of aluminium, abrasives, glass, and ceramics. Formula: Al_2O_3. Also called: **alumina.**

aluminize *or* **aluminise** (ə'lu:mɪˌnaɪz) *vb* **aluminizes, aluminizing, aluminized** *or* **aluminises, aluminising, aluminised.** (*tr*) to cover with aluminium or aluminium paint.

aluminous (ə'lu:mɪnəs) *adj* resembling aluminium.

alumnus (ə'lʌmnəs) *or* (*fem*) **alumna** (ə'lʌmnə) *n, pl* **alumni** (-naɪ) *or* **alumnae** (-ni:). *Chiefly US & Canad.* a graduate of a school, college, etc. ORIG C17: from L: nursling, pupil, from *alere* to nourish

Alva *or* **Alba** ★ ('ælvə; *Spanish* 'alβa) *n* **Duke of,** title of *Fernando Alvarez de Toledo.* 1508–82, Spanish general and statesman who suppressed the Protestant revolt in the Netherlands (1567–72) and conquered Portugal (1580).

Alvarez ★ ('ælvərɛz) *n* **Luis Walter.** 1911–88, US physicist. He measured the neutron's magnetic moment (1939). Nobel prize for physics 1968.

alveolar (æl'vɪələ, ˌælvɪ'əulə) *adj* **1** *Anat.* of an alveolus. **2** denoting the part of the jawbone containing the roots of the teeth. **3** (of a consonant) articulated with the tongue in contact with the part of the jawbone immediately behind the upper teeth. ◆ *n* **4** an alveolar consonant, such as *t, d,* and *s* in English.

alveolate (æl'vɪəlɪt, -ˌleɪt) *adj* having many small cavities. ORIG C19: from LL *alveolātus* hollowed, from L: ALVEOLUS
▸ **ˌalveo'lation** *n*

alveolus (æl'vɪələs) *n, pl* **alveoli** (-ˌlaɪ). any small pit, cavity, or saclike dilation, such as a honeycomb cell, a tooth socket, or the tiny air sacs in the lungs. ORIG C18: from L: a little hollow, dim. of *alveus*

always ('ɔ:lweɪz) *adv* **1** without exception; every time: *he always arrives on time.* **2** continually; repeatedly. **3** in any case: *you could always take a day off work.* ◆ Also (archaic): **alway.** ORIG C13 *alles weiss,* from OE *ealne weg,* lit.: all the way

Alwyn ★ ('ɔ:lwɪn) *n* **William.** 1905–85, British composer. His works include the oratorio *The Marriage of Heaven and Hell* (1936) and the *Suite of Scottish Dances* (1946).

alyssum ('ælɪsəm) *n* a widely cultivated herbaceous garden plant, having clusters of small yellow or white flowers. ORIG C16: from NL, from Gk *alusson,* from *alussos* (adj) curing rabies

Alzheimer's disease ('ælts,haɪməz) *n* a disorder of the brain resulting in progressive decline and eventual dementia. Often shortened to **Alzheimer's.** ORIG C20: after A. *Alzheimer* (1864–1915), G physician who first identified it

am (æm; *unstressed* əm) *vb* (used with *I*) a form of the present tense of **be**. ORIG OE *eam*

Am *the chemical symbol for* americium.

AM *abbrev. for:* **1** Also: **am.** amplitude modulation. **2** Assembly Member (of the National Assembly of Wales). **3** *US.* Master of Arts. **4** Member of the Order of Australia.

Am. *abbrev. for* America(n).

a.m., A.M., am, *or* **AM** (indicating the period from midnight to midday) *abbrev. for* ante meridiem. ORIG L: before noon

amabokoboko (ama'bɒkɒbɒkɒ) *pl n S. African.* an African name for the **Springbok** rugby team. ORIG C20: from Nguni *ama,* a plural prefix + *bokoboko,* from *bok* a diminutive of SPRINGBOK

amadoda (ama'dɔ:də) *pl n S. African.* grown men. ORIG from Nguni *ama,* a plural prefix + *doda* men

amadou ('æmə,du:) *n* a spongy substance got from some fungi, used (formerly) as tinder, a styptic, and by fishermen to dry flies. ORIG C18: from F, from Provençal: lover, from L *amāre* to love (because easily set alight)

amah ('ɑ:mə) *n* (in the East, esp. formerly) a nurse or maidservant. ORIG C19: from Port. *ama* nurse

amain (ə'meɪn) *adv Arch. or poetic.* with great strength or haste. ORIG C16: from A-[2] + MAIN[1]

Amalfi ★ (ə'mælfɪ) *n* a town in SW Italy: a major Mediterranean port from the 10th to the 18th century, now a resort.

amalgam (ə'mælgəm) *n* **1** an alloy of mercury with another metal, esp. silver: *dental amalgam.* **2** a blend or combination. ORIG C15: from Med. L *amalgama,* from ?

amalgamate (ə'mælgə,meɪt) *vb* **amalgamates, amalgamating, amalgamated. 1** to combine or cause to combine; unite. **2** to alloy (a metal) with mercury.

amalgamation (ə,mælgə'meɪʃən) *n* **1** the process of amalgamating. **2** the state of being amalgamated. **3** a method of extracting precious metals by treatment with mercury. **4** a merger.

amandla (a'mɑ:ndlə) *n S. African.* a political slogan calling for power to the Black population. ORIG C20: Nguni, lit.: power

amanuensis (ə,mænju'ɛnsɪs) *n, pl* **amanuenses** (-si:z). a person employed to take dictation or to copy manuscripts. ORIG C17: from L, from *servus ā manū* slave at hand (that is, handwriting)

Amanullah Khan ★ (,æmə'nʊlə 'kɑ:n) *n* 1892–1960, emir (1919–26) and king (1926–29) of Afghanistan; he obtained Afghan independence from Britain (1919).

Amapá ★ (*Portuguese* əma'pa) *n* a state of N Brazil, on the Amazon delta. Capital: Macapá. Pop.: 379 459 (1996). Area: 143 716 sq. km (55 489 sq. miles).

amaranth ('æmə,rænθ) *n* **1** *Poetic.* an imaginary flower that never fades. **2** any of numerous plants having tassel-like heads of small green, red, or purple flowers. **3** a synthetic red food colouring (**E123**), used in packet soups, cake mixes, etc. ORIG C17: from L *amarantus,* from Gk, from A-[1] + *marainein* to fade

amaretto (,æmə'rɛtəʊ) *n* an Italian liqueur with a flavour of almonds. ORIG C20: from It. *amaro* bitter

amaryllis (,æmə'rɪlɪs) *n* **1** a plant native to southern Africa having large lily-like reddish or white flowers. **2** any of several related plants. ORIG C18: from NL, from L: after *Amaryllis,* Gk conventional name for a shepherdess

amass (ə'mæs) *vb* **1** (*tr*) to accumulate or collect (esp. riches, etc.). **2** to gather in a heap. ORIG C15: from OF, from *masse* MASS

▸ **a'masser** *n*

amateur ('æmətə) *n* **1** a person who engages in an activity, esp. a sport, as a pastime rather than for gain. **2** a person unskilled in a subject or activity. **3** a person who is fond of or admires something. **4** (*modifier*) of or for amateurs: *an amateur event.* ◆ *adj* **5** not professional or expert: *an amateur approach.* ORIG C18: from F, from L *amātor* lover, from *amāre* to love

▸ **'amateurism** *n*

amateurish ('æmətərɪʃ) *adj* lacking professional skill or expertise.

▸ **'amateurishly** *adv*

Amati ★ *n* **1** (*Italian* a'ma:ti). a family of Italian violin makers, active in Cremona in the 16th and 17th centuries, esp. **Nicolò** (niko'lɔ), 1596–1684, who taught Guarneri and Stradivari. **2** (ə'mɑ:tɪ). (*pl* **Amatis**) a violin or other stringed instrument made by any member of this family.

amative ('æmətɪv) *adj* a rare word for **amorous.** ORIG C17: from Med. L, from L *amāre* to love

amatory ('æmətərɪ) *or* **amatorial** (,æmə'tɔ:rɪəl) *adj* of, relating to, or inciting sexual love or desire. ORIG C16: from L *amātōrius,* from *amāre* to love

amaurosis (,æmɔ:'rəʊsɪs) *n* blindness, esp. when occurring without observable damage to the eye. ORIG C17: via NL from Gk: darkening, from *amauroun* to dim

▸ **amaurotic** (,æmɔ:'rɒtɪk) *adj*

amaze (ə'meɪz) *vb* **amazes, amazing, amazed.** (*tr*) **1** to fill with incredulity or surprise; astonish. ◆ *n* **2** an archaic word for **amazement.** ORIG OE *āmasian*

▸ **a'mazing** *adj*

amazement (ə'meɪzmənt) *n* incredulity or great astonishment; complete wonder.

Amazon[1] ★ ('æməzᵊn) *n* **1** *Greek myth.* one of a race of women warriors of Scythia near the Black Sea. **2** (*often not cap.*) any tall, strong, or aggressive woman. ORIG C14: via L from Gk *Amazōn,* from ?

▸ **Amazonian** (,æmə'zəʊnɪən) *adj*

Amazon[2] ★ ('æməzᵊn) *n* a river in South America, rising in the Peruvian Andes and flowing east through N Brazil to the Atlantic: in volume, the largest river in the world; navigable for 3700 km (2300 miles). Length: over 6440 km (4000 miles). Area of basin: over 5 827 500 sq. km (2 250 000 sq. miles).

▸ **Amazonian** (,æmə'zəʊnɪən) *adj*

Amazonas ★ (,æmə'zəʊnəs) *n* a state of W Brazil, consisting of the central Amazon basin: vast areas of unexplored tropical rainforest. Capital: Manaus. Pop.: 2 389 279 (1996). Area: 1 542 277 sq. km (595 474 sq. miles).

Amazonia ★ (æmə'zəʊnɪə) *n* the land around the Amazon river.

Ambala ★ (əm'bɑ:lə) *n* a city in N India, in Haryana: site of archaeological remains of a prehistoric Indian civilization: grain, cotton, food processing. Pop.: 119 338 (1991).

ambassador (æm'bæsədə) *n* **1** a diplomat of the highest rank, accredited as permanent representative to another country. **2 ambassador extraordinary.** a diplomat of the highest rank sent on a special mission. **3 ambassador plenipotentiary.** a diplomat of the first rank with treaty-signing powers. **4 ambassador-at-large.** *US.* an ambassador with special duties who may be sent to more than one government. **5** an authorized representative or messenger. ORIG C14: from OF, from It., from OProvençal *ambaisador,* from *ambaisa* (unattested) mission, errand

▸ **am'bassadress** *fem n* ▸ **ambassadorial** (æm,bæsə'dɔ:rɪəl) *adj* ▸ **am'bassador,ship** *n*

amber ('æmbə) *n* **1** a yellow translucent fossil resin derived from extinct coniferous trees and often containing trapped insects. **2a** a brownish-yellow colour. **2b** (*as adj*): *an amber dress.* **3** an amber traffic light used as a warning between red and green. ORIG C14: from Med. L *ambar,* from Ar. *'anbar* ambergris

amber gambler *n Brit. inf.* a driver who races through traffic lights when they are at amber.

ambergris ('æmbə,gri:s, -grɪs) *n* a waxy substance secreted by the intestinal tract of the sperm whale and often found floating in the sea: used in the manufacture of some perfumes. ORIG C15: from OF *ambre gris* grey amber

amberjack ('æmbə,dʒæk) *n* any of several large fishes occurring in tropical and subtropical Atlantic waters. ORIG C19: from AMBER + JACK

ambi- *combining form.* indicating both: *ambidextrous; am-*

★ people and places

bivalence. ORIG from L: round, on both sides, both, from *ambo* both

ambidextrous (ˌæmbɪ'dɛkstrəs) *adj* **1** equally expert with each hand. **2** *Inf.* skilled or adept. **3** underhanded.
▸ **ambidexterity** (ˌæmbɪdɛk'stɛrɪtɪ) *or* ˌ**ambi'dextrousness** *n*

ambience *or* **ambiance** ('æmbɪəns) *n* the atmosphere of a place. ORIG C19: from F, from *ambiant* surrounding

ambient ('æmbɪənt) *adj* **1** surrounding. **2** creating a relaxing atmosphere: *ambient music.* ORIG C16: from L *ambiēns* going round, from AMBI- + *īre* to go

ambiguity (ˌæmbɪ'gju:ɪtɪ) *n, pl* **ambiguities. 1** the possibility of interpreting an expression in more than one way. **2** an instance or example of this, as in the sentence *they are cooking apples.* **3** vagueness or uncertainty of meaning.

ambiguous (æm'bɪgjʊəs) *adj* **1** having more than one possible interpretation. **2** difficult to understand; obscure. ORIG C16: from L *ambiguus* going here and there, uncertain, from *ambigere* to go around
▸ **am'biguously** *adv* ▸ **am'biguousness** *n*

ambisexual (ˌæmbɪ'sɛksjʊəl) *or* **ambosexual** *adj Biol.* relating to or affecting both the male and female sexes.

ambit ('æmbɪt) *n* **1** scope or extent. **2** limits or boundary. ORIG C16: from L *ambitus* a going round, from *ambīre* to go round

ambition (æm'bɪʃən) *n* **1** strong desire for success or distinction. **2** something so desired; goal. ORIG C14: from OF, from L *ambitiō* a going round (of candidates), from *ambīre* to go round

ambitious (æm'bɪʃəs) *adj* **1** having a strong desire for success or achievement. **2** necessitating extraordinary effort or ability: *an ambitious project.* **3** (often foll. by *of*) having a great desire (for something or to do something).
▸ **am'bitiousness** *n*

ambivalence (æm'bɪvələns) *or* **ambivalency** *n* the coexistence of two opposed and conflicting emotions, etc.
▸ **am'bivalent** *adj*

amble ('æmbᵊl) *vb* **ambles, ambling, ambled.** (*intr*) **1** to walk at a leisurely relaxed pace. **2** (of a horse) to move, lifting both legs on one side together. **3** to ride a horse at an amble. ◆ *n* **4** a leisurely motion in walking. **5** a leisurely walk. **6** the ambling gait of a horse. ORIG C14: from OF, from L *ambulāre* to walk

Ambler ★ ('æmblə) *n* **Eric.** 1909–98, British novelist. His thrillers include *The Mask of Dimitrios* (1939), *Journey into Fear* (1940), *A Kind of Anger* (1964), and *Doctor Frigo* (1974).

Ambleside ★ ('æmbᵊlˌsaɪd) *n* a town in NW England, in Cumbria: a tourist centre for the Lake District. Pop.: 2905 (1991).

amblyopia (ˌæmblɪ'əʊpɪə) *n* impaired vision with no discernible damage to the eye or optic nerve. ORIG C18: NL, from Gk *amblūōpia,* from *amblus* dull, dim + *ōps* eye
▸ **amblyopic** (ˌæmblɪ'ɒpɪk) *adj*

Amboina ★ (æm'bɔɪnə) *n* **1** an island in Indonesia, in the Moluccas. Capital: Amboina. Area: 1000 sq. km (386 sq. miles). **2** Also called: **Ambon** ('ɑ:mbɔ:n). a port in the Moluccas, the capital of Amboina island. Pop.: 313 100 (1995 est.).

Amboise ★ (*French* ɑ̃bwaz) *n* a town in NW central France, on the River Loire: famous castle, a former royal residence. Pop.: 11 415 (1982).

amboyna *or* **amboina** (æm'bɔɪnə) *n* the mottled curly-grained wood of an Indonesian tree, used in making furniture.

Ambrose ★ ('æmbrəʊz) *n* **Saint.** ?340–397 A.D., bishop of Milan; built up the secular power of the early Christian Church; also wrote music and Latin hymns. Feast day: Dec. 7 or April 4.
▸ **Am'brosian** *adj*

ambrosia (æm'brəʊzɪə) *n* **1** *Classical myth.* the food of the gods, said to bestow immortality. Cf. **nectar** (sense 2). **2** anything particularly delightful to taste or smell. **3** another name for **beebread.** ORIG C16: via L from Gk: immortality, from A-[1] + *brotos* mortal
▸ **am'brosial** *or* **am'brosian** *adj*

ambry ('æmbrɪ) *or* **aumbry** ('ɔ:mbrɪ) *n, pl* **ambries** *or* **aumbries. 1** a recessed cupboard in the wall of a church near the altar, used to store sacred vessels, etc. **2** *Obs.* a small cupboard. ORIG C14: from OF *almarie,* ult. from L *armārium* chest for storage, from *arma* arms

ambulance ('æmbjʊləns) *n* a motor vehicle designed to carry sick or injured people. ORIG C19: from F, based on (*hôpital*) *ambulant* mobile or field (hospital), from L *ambulāre* to walk

ambulance chaser *n US sl.* a lawyer who seeks to encourage and profit from the lawsuits of accident victims.
▸ **ambulance chasing** *n*

ambulance stocks *pl n* high-performance stocks and shares recommended by a broker to a dissatisfied client to improve their relationship.

ambulant ('æmbjʊlənt) *adj* **1** moving about from place to place. **2** *Med.* another word for **ambulatory** (sense 3).

ambulate ('æmbjʊˌleɪt) *vb* **ambulates, ambulating, ambulated.** (*intr*) to wander about or move from place to place. ORIG C17: from L *ambulāre* to walk
▸ ˌ**ambu'lation** *n*

ambulatory ('æmbjʊlətərɪ) *adj* **1** of or designed for walking. **2** changing position; not fixed. **3** Also: **ambulant.** able to walk. ◆ *n, pl* **ambulatories. 4** a place for walking, such as an aisle or a cloister.

ambuscade (ˌæmbə'skeɪd) *n* **1** an ambush. ◆ *vb* **ambuscades, ambuscading, ambuscaded. 2** to ambush or lie in ambush. ORIG C16: from F, from OIt. *imboscata,* prob. of Gmc origin; cf. AMBUSH

ambush ('æmbʊʃ) *n* **1** the act of waiting in a concealed position in order to launch a surprise attack. **2** a surprise attack from such a position. **3** the concealed position from which such an attack is launched. **4** the person or persons waiting to launch such an attack. ◆ *vb* **5** to lie in wait (for). **6** (*tr*) to attack suddenly from a concealed position. ORIG C14: from OF *embuschier* to position in ambush, from *em-* IM- + *-buschier,* from *busche* piece of firewood, prob. of Gmc origin

ameba (ə'mi:bə) *n, pl* **amebae** (-bi:) *or* **amebas.** the usual US spelling of **amoeba.**
▸ **a'mebic** *adj*

ameer (ə'mɪə) *n* a variant spelling of **emir.**

ameliorate (ə'mi:ljəˌreɪt) *vb* **ameliorates, ameliorating, ameliorated.** to make or become better. ORIG C18: from F *améliorer* to improve, from OF, from *meillor* better, from L *melior*
▸ **aˌmelio'ration** *n* ▸ **a'meliorative** *adj* ▸ **a'melioˌrator** *n*

> **USAGE NOTE** *Ameliorate* is sometimes confused with *alleviate. Ameliorate* comes ultimately from the Latin for 'better', and means 'to improve'. The nouns it typically goes with are *condition* and *situation. Alleviate* means 'to lessen', and frequently occurs with *poverty, suffering, pain, symptoms,* and *effects.* Occasionally *ameliorate* is used with *effects* and *poverty* where the other verb may be more appropriate.

amen (ˌeɪ'mɛn, ˌɑ:'mɛn) *sentence substitute.* **1** so be it!: a term used at the end of a prayer. ◆ *n* **2** the use of the word *amen.* ORIG C13: via LL via Gk from Heb. *āmēn* certainly

Amen ★ ('ɑ:mən) *n Egyptian myth.* a local Theban god, having a ram's head and symbolizing life and fertility, identified by the Egyptians with the national deity Amen-Ra.

amenable (ə'mi:nəbᵊl) *adj* **1** likely to listen, cooperate, etc. **2** accountable to some authority; answerable. **3** capable of being tested, judged, etc. ORIG C16: from Anglo-F, from OF, from L *mināre* to drive (cattle), from *minārī* to threaten
▸ **aˌmena'bility** *or* **a'menableness** *n* ▸ **a'menably** *adv*

amend (ə'mɛnd) *vb* (*tr*) **1** to improve; change for the better. **2** to correct. **3** to alter or revise (legislation, etc.)

by formal procedure. ORIG C13: from OF, from L *ēmendāre* to EMEND
▸ **a'mendable** *adj* ▸ **a'mender** *n*

amendment (ə'mɛndmənt) *n* **1** correction. **2** an addition or alteration to a document, etc.

amends (ə'mɛndz) *n* (*functioning as sing*) recompense or compensation for some injury, insult, etc.: *to make amends.* ORIG C13: from OF, from *amende* compensation, from *amender* to EMEND

Amenhotep III (ˌæmɛn'həutɛp) *or* **Amenhotpe III** ★ (ˌæmɛn'hɒtpɪ) *n* Greek name *Amenophis.* ?1411–?1375 B.C., Egyptian pharaoh who erected many buildings.

amenity (ə'miːnɪtɪ) *n, pl* **amenities. 1** (*often pl*) a useful or pleasant facility: *a swimming pool was one of the amenities.* **2** the fact or condition of being agreeable. **3** (*usually pl*) a social courtesy. ORIG C14: from L, from *amoenus* agreeable

amenorrhoea *or esp. US* **amenorrhea** (æˌmɛnə'rɪə, eɪ-) *n* abnormal absence of menstruation. ORIG C19: from A-[1] + MENO- + -RRHOEA

Amen-Ra ★ (ˌɑːmən'rɑː) *n Egyptian myth.* the sun-god; the principal deity during the period of Theban hegemony.

ament ('æmənt) *n* another name for **catkin.** Also called: **amentum** (ə'mɛntəm). ORIG C18: from L *āmentum* thong
▸ ˌ**amen'taceous** *adj*

amentia (ə'mɛnʃə) *n* severe mental deficiency, usually congenital. ORIG C14: from L: insanity, from *āmēns* mad, from *mēns* mind

Amer. *abbrev. for* America(n).

amerce (ə'mɜːs) *vb* **amerces, amercing, amerced.** (*tr*) *Obs.* **1** *Law.* to punish by a fine. **2** to punish with any arbitrary penalty. ORIG C14: from Anglo-F, from OF *à merci* at the mercy; see MERCY
▸ **a'mercement** *n*

America ★ (ə'mɛrɪkə) *n* **1** short for the **United States of America. 2** Also called: **the Americas.** the American continent, including North, South, and Central America. ORIG C16: from *Americus,* L form of *Amerigo;* see VESPUCCI

American (ə'mɛrɪkən) *adj* **1** of or relating to the United States of America, its inhabitants, or their form of English. **2** of or relating to the American continent. ◆ *n* **3** a native or citizen of the US. **4** a native or inhabitant of any country of North, Central, or South America. **5** the English language as spoken or written in the United States.

Americana (əˌmɛrɪ'kɑːnə) *pl n* objects, such as documents, relics, etc., relating to America.

American aloe *n* See **aloe** (sense 2).

American Civil War *n* see **Civil War** (sense 2).

American Dream *n* **the.** the notion that the American social, economic, and political system makes success possible for every individual.

American football *n* **1** a team game similar to rugby, with 11 players on each side. **2** the oval-shaped inflated ball used in this game.

American Indian *n* **1** Also called: **Indian, Amerindian, Native American.** a member of any of the indigenous peoples of America, typically having straight black hair and a yellow-to-brown skin. ◆ *adj* **2** Also called: **Amerindian.** of or relating to any of these peoples, their languages, or their cultures.

Americanism (ə'mɛrɪkəˌnɪzəm) *n* **1** a custom, linguistic usage, or other feature peculiar to or characteristic of the United States. **2** loyalty to the United States.

Americanize *or* **Americanise** (ə'mɛrɪkəˌnaɪz) *vb* **Americanizes, Americanizing, Americanized** *or* **Americanises, Americanising, Americanised.** to make or become American in outlook, attitudes, etc.
▸ **AˌmericaniˈzationAˌmericani'zation** *or* **Aˌmericani'sation** *n*

American Revolution *n* the usual US term for **War of American Independence.**

American Samoa ★ *n* the part of the Samoa Islands that is administered by the US. Capital: Pago Pago. Pop.: 52 860 (1993 est.). Area: 197 sq. km (76 sq. miles).

americium (ˌæmə'rɪsɪəm) *n* a white metallic transuranic element artificially produced from plutonium. It is used as an alpha-particle source. Symbol: Am; atomic no.: 95; half-life of most stable isotope, ^{243}Am: 7.4×10^3 years. ORIG C20: from AMERICA (where it was first produced) + -IUM

Amerigo Vespucci ★ (*Italian* ame'riːgo ves'puttʃi) *n* See **Vespucci.**

Amerindian (ˌæmə'rɪndɪən) *n also* **Amerind** ('æmərɪnd), *adj* another word for **American Indian.**
▸ ˌ**Amer'indic** *adj*

amethyst ('æmɪθɪst) *n* **1** a purple or violet variety of quartz used as a gemstone. **2** a purple variety of sapphire. **3a** the purple colour of amethyst. **3b** (*as adj*): *amethyst shadow.* ORIG C13: from OF, from L, from Gk *amethustos,* lit.: not drunken, from A-[1] + *methuein* to make drunk; from the belief that the stone could prevent intoxication
▸ **amethystine** (ˌæmɪ'θɪstaɪn) *adj*

Amex ('æmɛks) *n acronym for* **1** *Trademark.* American Express. **2** American Stock Exchange.

AMF *abbrev. for* Australian Military Forces.

Amhara ★ (æm'hɑːrə) *n* **1** a region of NW Ethiopia: formerly a kingdom. **2** an inhabitant of the former kingdom of Amhara.

Amharic (æm'hærɪk) *n* **1** the official language of Ethiopia. ◆ *adj* **2** denoting this language.

Amherst ★ ('æmhɜːst) *n* **Jeffrey,** 1st Baron Amherst. 1717–97, British general who defeated the French in Canada (1758–60): governor general of British North America (1761–63).

amiable ('eɪmɪəbᵊl) *adj* having or displaying a pleasant or agreeable nature; friendly. ORIG C14: from OF, from LL *amīcābilis* AMICABLE
▸ ˌ**amia'bility** *or* '**amiableness** *n* ▸ '**amiably** *adv*

amianthus (ˌæmɪ'ænθəs) *n* any of the fine silky varieties of asbestos. ORIG C17: from L *amiantus,* from Gk *amiantos* unsullied, from A-[1] + *miainein* to pollute

amicable ('æmɪkəbᵊl) *adj* characterized by friendliness: *an amicable agreement.* ORIG C15: from LL *amīcābilis,* from L *amīcus* friend
▸ ˌ**amica'bility** *or* '**amicableness** *n* ▸ '**amicably** *adv*

amice ('æmɪs) *n Christianity.* a rectangular piece of white linen worn by priests around the neck and shoulders under the alb or, formerly, on the head. ORIG C15: from OF, from L *amictus* cloak

amicus curiae (æ'miːkus 'kjuərɪˌiː) *n, pl* **amici curiae** (æ'miːkaɪ) *Law.* a person, not directly engaged in a case, who advises the court. ORIG L, lit.: friend of the court

amid (ə'mɪd) *or* **amidst** *prep* in the middle of; among. ORIG OE *on middan* in the middle

amide ('æmaɪd) *n* **1** any organic compound containing the group $-CONR_2$, where R denotes a hydrogen atom or a hydrocarbon group. **2** (*modifier*) containing the group $-CONR_2$: *amide group or radical.* **3** an inorganic compound containing the NH_2^- ion and having the general formula $M(NH_2)_x$, where M is a metal atom. ORIG C19: from AM(MONIA) + -IDE

amidships (ə'mɪdʃɪps) *adv, adj* (*postpositive*) *Naut.* at, near, or towards the centre of a vessel.

Amiens ★ ('æmɪənz; *French* amjɛ̃) *n* a city in N France: its Gothic cathedral is the largest church in France. Pop.: 136 234 (1990).

amigo (æ'miːgəu, ə-) *n, pl* **amigos.** a friend; comrade. ORIG Sp., from L *amicus*

Amin[1] ★ (æ'miːn, ɑː-) *n* **Lake.** a former official name for (Lake) **Edward.**

Amin[2] ★ (æ'miːn, ɑː-) *n* **Idi** ('iːdiː). born 1925, Ugandan dictator (1971–79). Notorious for his brutality; overthrown and exiled.

amine (ə'miːn, 'æmɪn) *n* an organic base formed by replacing one or more of the hydrogen atoms of ammonia by hydrocarbon groups. ORIG C19: from AM(MONIUM) + -INE[2]

amino (ə'miːnəu) *n* (*modifier*) of or containing the group of atoms $-NH_2$: *amino radical.*

amino acid *n* **1** any of a group of organic compounds containing one or more amino groups, $-NH_2$, and one or more carboxyl groups, -COOH. **2** any of a group of organic nitrogenous compounds that form the component molecules of proteins.

amino resin *n* a thermosetting synthetic resin used as an adhesive and coating for paper and textiles.

amir (əˈmɪə) *n* a variant spelling of **emir**. ORIG C19: from Ar., var. of EMIR
▸ **aˈmirate** *n*

Amis ★ (ˈeɪmɪs) *n* **1** Sir **Kingsley**. 1922–95, British writer, noted for his novels *Lucky Jim* (1954), *Stanley and the Women* (1984), and *The Folks that Live on the Hill* (1990). **2** his son, **Martin**. born 1949, British novelist. His works include *The Rachel Papers* (1974), *Time's Arrow* (1991), and *Night Train* (1997).

Amish (ˈæmɪʃ, ˈɑː-) *adj* of a US and Canadian Mennonite sect. ORIG C19: from G *Amisch,* after Jakob *Amman,* 17th-cent. Swiss Mennonite bishop

amiss (əˈmɪs) *adv* **1** in an incorrect or defective manner. **2 take (something) amiss.** to be annoyed or offended by (something). ◆ *adj* **3** (*postpositive*) wrong or faulty. ORIG C13 *a mis,* from *mis* wrong

amitosis (ˌæmɪˈtəʊsɪs) *n* a form of cell division in which the nucleus and cytoplasm divide without the formation of chromosomes. ORIG C20: from A-[1] + MITOSIS
▸ **amitotic** (ˌæmɪˈtɒtɪk) *adj*

amity (ˈæmɪtɪ) *n, pl* **amities.** friendship; cordiality. ORIG C15: from OF *amité,* ult. from L *amīcus* friend

Amman ★ (əˈmɑːn) *n* the capital of Jordan, northeast of the Dead Sea: ancient capital of the Ammonites, rebuilt by Ptolemy in the 3rd century B.C. Pop.: 963 490 (1994). Ancient names: **Rabbath Ammon, Philadelphia.**

ammeter (ˈæmˌmiːtə) *n* an instrument for measuring an electric current in amperes. ORIG C19: AM(PERE) + -METER

ammo (ˈæməʊ) *n Inf.* short for **ammunition.**

Ammon[1] ★ (ˈæmən) *n Old Testament.* the ancestor of the Ammonites.

Ammon[2] ★ (ˈæmən) *n Myth.* the classical name of the Egyptian god Amen, identified by the Greeks with Zeus and by the Romans with Jupiter.

ammonia (əˈməʊnɪə) *n* **1** a colourless pungent gas used in the manufacture of fertilizers and as a refrigerant and solvent. Formula: NH_3. **2** a solution of ammonia in water, containing ammonium hydroxide. ORIG C18: from NL, from L (*sal*) *ammōniacus* (sal) AMMONIAC

ammoniac (əˈməʊnɪˌæk) *n* a gum resin obtained from the stems of an Asian plant and formerly used as a stimulant, perfume, and in porcelain cement. Also called: **gum ammoniac.** ORIG C14: from L, from Gk *ammōniakos* belonging to Ammon (apparently the gum resin was extracted from plants found in Libya near the temple of Ammon)

ammoniacal (ˌæməˈnaɪəkəl) *adj* of, containing, or resembling ammonia.

ammoniate (əˈməʊnɪˌeɪt) *vb* **ammoniates, ammoniating, ammoniated.** to unite or treat with ammonia.
▸ **amˌmoniˈation** *n*

ammonify (əˈmɒnɪˌfaɪ) *vb* **ammonifies, ammonifying, ammonified.** to treat or impregnate with ammonia or a compound of ammonia.
▸ **amˌmonifiˈcation** *n*

ammonite (ˈæməˌnaɪt) *n* **1** any extinct marine cephalopod mollusc of the order *Ammonoidea,* which were common in Mesozoic times and had a coiled partitioned shell. **2** the shell of any of these animals, commonly occurring as a fossil. ORIG C18: from L *cornū Ammōnis,* lit.: horn of Ammon

ammonium (əˈməʊnɪəm) *n* (*modifier*) of or containing the monovalent group NH_4– or the ion NH_4^+: *ammonium compounds.*

ammonium chloride *n* a white soluble crystalline solid used as an electrolyte in dry batteries. Formula: NH_4Cl. Also called: **sal ammoniac.**

ammonium hydroxide *n* a compound existing in solution when ammonia is dissolved in water. Formula: NH_4OH.

ammonium sulphate *n* a white soluble crystalline solid used mainly as a fertilizer and in water purification. Formula: $(NH_4)_2SO_4$.

ammunition (ˌæmjʊˈnɪʃən) *n* **1** any projectiles, such as bullets, rockets, etc., that can be discharged from a weapon. **2** bombs, missiles, chemicals, etc., capable of use as weapons. **3** any means of defence or attack, as in an argument. ORIG C17: from obs. F *amunition,* by mistaken division from earlier *la munition;* see MUNITION

amnesia (æmˈniːzjə, -ʒjə, -zɪə) *n* a defect in memory, esp. one resulting from a pathological cause. ORIG C19: via NL from Gk: forgetfulness, prob. from *amnēstia* oblivion
▸ **amnesiac** (æmˈniːzɪˌæk) *or* **amnesic** (æmˈniːsɪk, -zɪk) *adj, n*

amnesty (ˈæmnɪstɪ) *n, pl* **amnesties. 1** a general pardon, esp. for offences against a government. **2** a period during which a law is suspended to allow offenders to admit their crime without fear of prosecution. ◆ *vb* **amnesties, amnestying, amnestied. 3** (*tr*) to overlook or forget (an offence). ORIG C16: from L *amnēstia,* from Gk: oblivion, from A-[1] + *-mnēstos,* from *mnasthai* to remember

Amnesty International *n* an international organization that works to secure the release of people imprisoned for their beliefs, to ban the use of torture, and to abolish the death penalty. Abbrev.: **AI.**

amniocentesis (ˌæmnɪəʊsɛnˈtiːsɪs) *n, pl* **amniocenteses** (-siːz). removal of amniotic fluid for diagnostic purposes by the insertion into the womb of a hollow needle. ORIG C20: from AMNION + *centesis* from Gk *kentēsis* from *kentein* to prick

amnion (ˈæmnɪən) *n, pl* **amnions** *or* **amnia** (-nɪə). the innermost of two membranes enclosing an embryonic reptile, bird, or mammal. ORIG C17: via NL from Gk: a little lamb, from *amnos* a lamb
▸ **amniotic** (ˌæmnɪˈɒtɪk) *adj*

amniotic fluid *n* the fluid surrounding the fetus in the womb.

amoeba *or US* **ameba** (əˈmiːbə) *n, pl* **amoebae** (-biː) *or* **amoebas** *or US* **amebae** (-biː) *or* **amebas.** any of a phylum of protozoans able to change shape because of the movements of cell processes. They live in fresh water or soil or as parasites in man and animals. ORIG C19: from NL, from Gk, from *ameibein* to change, exchange
▸ **aˈmoebic** *or US* **aˈmebic** *adj*

amok (əˈmʌk, əˈmɒk) *or* **amuck** (əˈmʌk) *n* **1** a state of murderous frenzy. ◆ *adv* **2 run amok.** to run about as with a frenzied desire to kill. ORIG C17: from Malay *amoq* furious assault

among (əˈmʌŋ) *or* **amongst** *prep* **1** in the midst of: *he lived among the Indians.* **2** to each of: *divide the reward among yourselves.* **3** in the group, class, or number of: *among the greatest writers.* **4** taken out of (a group): *he is one among many.* **5** with one another within a group: *decide it among yourselves.* **6** in the general opinion or practice of: *accepted among experts.* ORIG OE *amang,* contracted from *on gemang* in the group of, from ON + *gemang* crowd

> **USAGE NOTE** See at **between.**

amontillado (əˌmɒntɪˈlɑːdəʊ) *n* a medium-dry sherry. ORIG C19: from Sp. *vino amontillado* wine of *Montilla,* town in Spain

amoral (ˌeɪˈmɒrəl) *adj* **1** having no moral quality; nonmoral. **2** without moral standards or principles.
▸ **amorality** (ˌeɪmɒˈrælɪtɪ) *n*

> **USAGE NOTE** *Amoral* is sometimes confused with *immoral.* The *a-* at the beginning of the word means 'without' or 'lacking', so the word is properly used of people who have no moral code, or about places or situations where moral considerations do not apply: *the film was violent and amoral.* In contrast *immoral* should be used to talk about the breaking of moral rules, as in: *drug dealing is the most immoral and evil of all human activities.*

amorist ('æmərɪst) *n* a lover or a writer about love.

amoroso (ˌæmə'rəʊsəʊ) *adj, adv* **1** *Music.* (to be played) tenderly. ◆ *n* **2** a rich sweet sherry. ORIG from It. & Sp.: AMOROUS

amorous ('æmərəs) *adj* **1** inclined towards or displaying love or desire. **2** in love. **3** of or relating to love. ORIG C14: from OF, from Med. L, from L *amor* love
▸ **'amorously** *adv* ▸ **'amorousness** *n*

amorphous (ə'mɔːfəs) *adj* **1** lacking a definite shape. **2** of no recognizable character or type. **3** (of rocks, etc.) not having a crystalline structure. ORIG C18: from NL, from Gk, from A-[1] + *morphē* shape
▸ **a'morphism** *n* ▸ **a'morphousness** *n*

amortize *or* **amortise** (ə'mɔːtaɪz) *vb* **amortizes, amortizing, amortized** *or* **amortises, amortising, amortised.** (*tr*) **1** *Finance.* to liquidate (a debt, mortgage, etc.) by payments or by periodic transfers to a sinking fund. **2** to write off (a wasting asset) by transfers to a sinking fund. **3** *Property law.* (formerly) to transfer (lands, etc.) in mortmain. ORIG C14: from Med. L, from OF *amortir* to reduce to the point of death, ult. from L *ad* to + *mors* death
▸ **aˌmorti'zation** *or* **aˌmorti'sation** *n*

Amos ★ ('eɪmɒs) *n Old Testament.* **1** a Hebrew prophet of the 8th century B.C. **2** the book containing his oracles.

amount (ə'maʊnt) *n* **1** extent; quantity. **2** the total of two or more quantities. **3** the full value or significance of something. **4** a principal sum plus the interest on it, as in a loan. ◆ *vb* **5** (*intr;* usually foll. by *to*) to be equal or add up. ORIG C13: from OF *amonter* to go up, from *amont* upwards, from *a* to + *mont* mountain (from L *mōns*)

> **USAGE NOTE** The use of a plural noun after *amount of* (*the amount of people; the amount of goods*) should be avoided: *the number of people; the number of goods* is more appropriate.

amount of substance *n* a measure of the number of entities (atoms, molecules, ions, electrons, etc.) present in a substance, expressed in moles.

amour *French.* (amur) *n* a love affair, esp. a secret or illicit one. ORIG C13: from OF, from L *amor* love

amour-propre *French.* (amurprɔprə) *n* self-respect.

Amoy ★ (ə'mɔɪ) *n* **1** a port in SE China, in Fujian province on **Amoy Island,** at the mouth of the Jiu-long River opposite Taiwan: one of the first treaty ports opened to European trade (1842). Pop.: 368 786 (1990 est.). Modern Chinese name: **Xiamen. 2** the dialect of Chinese spoken in Amoy, Taiwan, and elsewhere: a Min dialect.

amp (æmp) *n* **1** an ampere. **2** *Inf.* an amplifier.

AMP *n Biochem.* adenosine monophosphate; a substance produced by hydrolysis of ATP with the liberation of energy. The cyclic form (**cyclic AMP**) acts as a messenger in many hormone-induced biochemical reactions.

ampelopsis (ˌæmpɪ'lɒpsɪs) *n* any of a genus of woody climbing plants of tropical and subtropical Asia and America. ORIG C19: from NL, from Gk *ampelos* grapevine

amperage ('æmpərɪdʒ) *n* the strength of an electric current measured in amperes.

ampere ('æmpɛə) *n* **1** the basic SI unit of electric current; the constant current that, when maintained in two parallel conductors of infinite length and negligible cross section placed 1 metre apart in free space, produces a force of 2×10^{-7} newton per metre between them. **2** a former unit of electric current (**international ampere**); the current that, when passed through a solution of silver nitrate, deposits silver at the rate of 0.001118 gram per second. ◆ Abbrev.: **amp.** Symbol: A ORIG C19: after A. M. AMPÈRE

Ampère ★ ('æmpɛə; *French* ɑ̃pɛr) *n* **André Marie** (ɑ̃dre mari). 1775–1836, French physicist who made major discoveries in magnetism and electricity.

ampere-turn *n* a unit of magnetomotive force; the magnetomotive force produced by a current of 1 ampere passing through one complete turn of a coil.

ampersand ('æmpəˌsænd) *n* the character (&), meaning *and: John Brown & Co.* ORIG C19: shortened from *and per se and,* that is, the symbol & by itself (represents) *and*

amphetamine (æm'fetəˌmiːn) *n* a synthetic colourless liquid used medicinally as the white crystalline sulphate, mainly for its stimulant action on the central nervous system. ORIG C20: from A(LPHA) + M(ETHYL) + PH(ENYL) + ET(HYL) + AMINE

amphi- *prefix* **1** on both sides; at both ends; of both kinds: *amphipod; amphibious.* **2** around: *amphibole.* ORIG from Gk

amphibian (æm'fɪbɪən) *n* **1** any cold-blooded vertebrate of the class *Amphibia,* typically living on land but breeding in water. The class includes newts, frogs, and toads. **2** an aircraft able to land and take off from both water and land. **3** any vehicle able to travel on both water and land. ◆ *adj* **4** another word for **amphibious. 5** of or belonging to the class *Amphibia.*

amphibious (æm'fɪbɪəs) *adj* **1** able to live both on land and in the water, as frogs, etc. **2** designed for operation on or from both water and land. **3** relating to military forces and operations launched from the sea against an enemy shore. **4** having a dual or mixed nature. ORIG C17: from Gk *amphibios,* lit.: having a double life, from AMPHI- + *bios* life
▸ **am'phibiousness** *n*

amphibole ('æmfɪˌbəʊl) *n* any of a large group of minerals consisting of the silicates of calcium, iron, magnesium, sodium, and aluminium, which are common constituents of igneous rocks. ORIG C17: from F, from Gk *amphibolos* uncertain; so called from the large number of varieties in the group

amphibology (ˌæmfɪ'bɒlədʒɪ) *or* **amphiboly** (æm'fɪbəlɪ) *n, pl* **amphibologies** *or* **amphibolies.** ambiguity of expression, esp. when due to a grammatical construction, as in *save rags and waste paper.* ORIG C14: from LL, ult. from Gk *amphibolos* ambiguous

amphimixis (ˌæmfɪ'mɪksɪs) *n, pl* **amphimixes** (-'mɪksiːz). true sexual reproduction, esp. the fusion of gametes from two organisms. ORIG C19: from AMPHI- + Gk *mixis* a blending
▸ **amphimictic** (ˌæmfɪ'mɪktɪk) *adj*

amphioxus (ˌæmfɪ'ɒksəs) *n, pl* **amphioxi** (-'ɒksaɪ) *or* **amphioxuses.** another name for the **lancelet.** ORIG C19: from NL, from AMPHI- + Gk *oxus* sharp

amphipod ('æmfɪˌpɒd) *n* **1** any marine or freshwater crustacean of the order *Amphipoda,* such as the sand hoppers, in which the body is laterally compressed. ◆ *adj* **2** of or belonging to the *Amphipoda.*

amphiprostyle (æm'fɪprəˌstaɪl) *adj* **1** (esp. of a classical temple) having a set of columns at both ends but not at the sides. ◆ *n* **2** a temple of this kind.

amphisbaena (æmfɪs'biːnə) *n, pl* **amphisbaenae** (-niː) *or* **amphisbaenas. 1** a genus of wormlike lizards of tropical America. **2** *Classical myth.* a fabulous serpent with a head at each end. ORIG C16: from L, from Gk *amphisbaina,* from *amphis* both ways + *bainein* to go

amphitheatre *or US* **amphitheater** ('æmfɪˌθɪətə) *n* **1** a building, usually circular or oval, in which tiers of seats rise from a central open arena. **2** a place where contests are held. **3** any level circular area of ground surrounded by higher ground. **4** a gallery in a theatre. **5** a lecture room in which seats are tiered away from a central area.

Amphitrite ★ (ˌæmfɪ'traɪtɪ) *n Greek myth.* a sea goddess, wife of Poseidon and mother of Triton.

amphora ('æmfərə) *n, pl* **amphorae** (-fəˌriː) *or* **amphoras.** a Greek or Roman two-handled narrow-necked jar for oil, etc. ORIG C17: from L, from Gk, from AMPHI- + *phoreus* bearer, from *pherein* to bear

amphoteric (ˌæmfə'terɪk) *adj Chem.* able to function as either a base or an acid. ORIG C19: from Gk *amphoteros* each of two (from *amphō* both) + -IC

ampicillin (ˌæmpɪ'sɪlɪn) *n* a form of penicillin used to treat various infections.

ample ('æmpᵊl) *adj* **1** more than sufficient: *an ample helping.* **2** large: *of ample proportions.* ORIG C15: from OF, from L *amplus* spacious
▸ **'ampleness** *n*

amplification (ˌæmplɪfɪ'keɪʃən) *n* **1** the act or result of amplifying. **2** material added to a statement, story, etc., to expand or clarify it. **3** a statement, story, etc., with such additional material. **4** *Electronics.* the increase in strength of an electrical signal by means of an amplifier.

amplifier ('æmplɪˌfaɪə) *n* **1** an electronic device used to increase the strength of the current fed into it, esp. one for the amplification of sound signals in a radio, record player, etc. **2** *Photog.* an additional lens for altering focal length. **3** a person or thing that amplifies.

amplify ('æmplɪˌfaɪ) *vb* **amplifies, amplifying, amplified.** **1** (*tr*) to increase in size, extent, effect, etc., as by the addition of extra material. **2** *Electronics.* to produce amplification of (electrical signals). **3** (*intr*) to expand a speech, narrative, etc. ORIG C15: from OF, ult. from L *amplificāre* to enlarge, from *amplus* spacious + *facere* to make

amplitude ('æmplɪˌtju:d) *n* **1** greatness of extent; magnitude. **2** abundance. **3** breadth or scope, as of the mind. **4** *Astron.* the angular distance along the horizon measured from true east or west to the point of intersection of the vertical circle passing through a celestial body. **5** *Physics.* the maximum displacement from the zero or mean position of a periodic motion. ORIG C16: from L, from *amplus* spacious

amplitude modulation *n* one of the principal methods of transmitting information using radio waves, the relevant signal being superimposed onto a radio-frequency carrier wave. The frequency of the carrier wave remains unchanged but its amplitude is varied in accordance with the amplitude of the input signal. Cf. **frequency modulation.**

amply ('æmplɪ) *adv* fully; generously.

ampoule ('æmpu:l, -pju:l) *or esp. US* **ampule** *n Med.* a small glass vessel in which liquids for injection are hermetically sealed. ORIG C19: from F, from L: see AMPULLA

ampulla (æm'pʊlə) *n, pl* **ampullae** (-'pʊli:). **1** *Anat.* the dilated end part of certain ducts or canals. **2** *Christianity.* **2a** a vessel for the wine and water used at the Eucharist. **2b** a small flask for consecrated oil. **3** a Roman two-handled bottle for oil, wine, or perfume. ORIG C16: from L, dim. of AMPHORA

amputate ('æmpjʊˌteɪt) *vb* **amputates, amputating, amputated.** *Surgery.* to remove (all or part of a limb). ORIG C17: from L, from *am-* around + *putāre* to trim, prune
▸ **ˌampu'tation** *n*

amputee (ˌæmpjʊ'ti:) *n* a person who has had a limb amputated.

Amritsar ★ (æm'rɪtsə) *n* a city in India, in NW Punjab: centre of the Sikh religion; site of a massacre in 1919 of unarmed supporters of Indian self-government by British troops; in 1984 the Golden Temple, fortified by Sikhs, was attacked by Indian troops with the loss of many Sikh lives. Pop.: 708 835 (1991).

Amsterdam ★ (ˌæmstə'dæm; *Dutch* ɑmstər'dɑm) *n* the commercial capital of the Netherlands, a major industrial centre and port on the IJsselmeer, connected with the North Sea by canal: built on about 100 islands within a network of canals. Pop.: 722 245 (1995 est.).

amu *abbrev. for* atomic mass unit.

amuck (ə'mʌk) *n, adv* a variant spelling of **amok.**

Amu Darya ★ (*Russian* a'mu darj'ja) *n* a river in central Asia, rising in the Pamirs and flowing northwest through the Hindu Kush and across Turkmenistan and Uzbekistan to its delta in the Aral Sea: forms much of the N border of Afghanistan. Length: 2400 km (1500 miles). Ancient name: **Oxus.**

amulet ('æmjʊlɪt) *n* a trinket or piece of jewellery worn as a protection against evil; charm. ORIG C17: from L *amulētum,* from ?

Amundsen ★ (*Norwegian* 'a:munsən) *n* **Roald** ('rɔald). 1872–1928, Norwegian explorer and navigator, who was the first man to reach the South Pole (1911).

Amundsen Sea ★ ('ɑ:mʊndsən) *n* a part of the South Pacific Ocean, in Antarctica off Byrd Land.

Amur ★ (ə'mʊə) *n* a river in NE Asia, rising in N Mongolia as the Argun and flowing southeast, then northeast to the Sea of Okhotsk: forms the boundary between Manchuria and Russia. Length: about 4350 km (2700 miles). Modern Chinese name: **Heilong Jiang.**

amuse (ə'mju:z) *vb* **amuses, amusing, amused.** (*tr*) **1** to entertain; divert. **2** to cause to laugh or smile. ORIG C15: from OF *amuser* to cause to be idle, from *muser* to MUSE[1]

amusement (ə'mju:zmənt) *n* **1** something that amuses, such as a game or pastime. **2** a mechanical device used for entertainment, as at a fair. **3** the act of amusing or the state or quality of being amused.

amusement arcade *n Brit.* a covered area having coin-operated game machines.

amusing (ə'mju:zɪŋ) *adj* entertaining; causing a smile or laugh.
▸ **a'musingly** *adv*

amygdalin (ə'mɪgdəlɪn) *n* a white soluble bitter-tasting glycoside extracted from bitter almonds. ORIG C17: from Gk: ALMOND + -IN

amyl ('æmɪl) *n* (*modifier*) (no longer in technical usage) of or containing any of eight isomeric forms of the monovalent group C_5H_{11}–: *amyl group or radical.* ORIG C19: from L: AMYLUM

amylaceous (ˌæmɪ'leɪʃəs) *adj* of or resembling starch.

amyl alcohol *n* **1** any of eight isomeric alcohols with the general formula $C_5H_{11}OH$. **2** a mixture of these alcohols, used in preparing amyl nitrite.

amylase ('æmɪˌleɪz) *n* any of several enzymes that hydrolyse starch and glycogen to simple sugars, such as glucose.

amyl nitrite *n* an ester of amyl alcohol and nitrous acid used as a vasodilator, esp. to treat angina.

amyloid ('æmɪˌlɔɪd) *n* **1** any substance resembling starch. ◆ *adj* **2** starchlike.

amylopsin (ˌæmɪ'lɒpsɪn) *n* an enzyme of the pancreatic juice that converts starch into sugar; pancreatic amylase. ORIG C19: from AMYL + (PE)PSIN

amylum ('æmɪləm) *n* another name for **starch** (senses 1,2). ORIG L, from Gk *amulon* fine meal, starch

amyotrophic lateral sclerosis (ˌæmɪəʊ'trəʊfɪk) *n* a form of motor neurone disease in which degeneration of motor tracts in the spinal cord causes progressive muscular paralysis starting in the limbs. Also called: **Lou Gehrig's disease.**

Amytal ('æmɪˌtæl) *n Trademark.* sodium amytal, used as a sedative and hypnotic.

an[1] (æn; *unstressed* ən) *determiner* (*indefinite article*) a form of **a**[1], used before an initial vowel sound: *an old car; an elf; an hour.* ORIG OE *ān* ONE

> **USAGE NOTE** *An* was formerly often used before words beginning with a pronounced *h* unstressed on the first syllable, as in *an hotel; an historic meeting.* Sometimes the initial *h* was not pronounced. This usage is neither more nor less correct than using *a,* and is now considerably less common even in written sources, though some newspapers recommend it as part of their house style. The Bank of English shows that *a* is hugely more common with *hotel,* and at least twice as common with *heroic, historian, historical,* and *horrendous. Habitual* and *horrific* are used almost as much with *an* as with *a,* while *historic* seems equally at home with either.

an[2] *or* **an'** (æn; *unstressed* ən) *conj* (*subordinating*) an obsolete or dialect word for **if.** See **and** (sense 8).

An ★ (ɑ:n) *n Myth.* the Sumerian sky god. Babylonian counterpart: **Anu.**

AN *abbrev. for* Anglo-Norman.

an. *abbrev. for* anno. ORIG L: in the year

an- *or before a consonant* **a-** *prefix* not; without: *anaphrodisiac.* ORIG from Gk

-an, -ean, *or* **-ian** *suffix.* **1** (*forming adjectives and nouns*) belonging to; coming from; typical of; adhering to: *European; Elizabethan; Christian.* **2** (*forming nouns*) a person who specializes or is expert in: *dietitian.* ORIG from L *-ānus,* suffix of adjectives

ana- *or before a vowel* **an-** *prefix* **1** up; upwards: *anadromous.* **2** again: *anagram.* **3** back; backwards: *anapaest.* ORIG from Gk *ana*

-ana *or* **-iana** *suffix forming nouns.* denoting a collection of objects or information relating to a particular individual, subject or place: *Victoriana, Americana.* ORIG NL, from L *-āna,* lit.: matters relating to, neuter pl of *-ānus;* see -AN

Anabaptist (ˌænəˈbæptɪst) *n* **1** a member of any of various Protestant movements, esp. of the 16th century, that rejected infant baptism, insisted that adults be rebaptized, and sought to establish Christian communism. ◆ *adj* **2** of these sects or their doctrines. ORIG C16: from Ecclesiastical L, from *anabaptīzāre* to baptize again, from LGk *anabaptizein*
▸ ˌ**Ana**ˈ**baptism** *n*

anabas (ˈænəˌbæs) *n* any of several freshwater fishes, esp. the climbing perch, that can travel on land. ORIG C19: from NL, from Gk *anabainein* to go up

anabasis (əˈnæbəsɪs) *n, pl* **anabases** (-ˌsiːz). **1** the march of Cyrus the Younger from Sardis to Cunaxa in Babylonia in 401 B.C., described by Xenophon in his *Anabasis.* **2** any military expedition, esp. one from the coast to the interior. ORIG C18: from Gk: a going up, from *anabainein* to go up

anabatic (ˌænəˈbætɪk) *adj Meteorol.* (of air currents) rising upwards. ORIG C19: from Gk *anabatikos* relating to ascents, from *anabainein* to go up

anabiosis (ˌænəbaɪˈəʊsɪs) *n* the ability to return to life after apparent death; suspended animation. ORIG C19: via NL from Gk, from *anabioein* to come back to life
▸ **anabiotic** (ˌænəbaɪˈɒtɪk) *adj*

anabolic steroid *n* any of a group of synthetic steroid hormones (androgens) used to stimulate muscle and bone growth for athletic or therapeutic purposes.

anabolism (əˈnæbəˌlɪzəm) *n* a metabolic process in which complex molecules are synthesized from simpler ones with the storage of energy; constructive metabolism. ORIG C19: from ANA- + (META)BOLISM
▸ **anabolic** (ˌænəˈbɒlɪk) *adj*

anachronism (əˈnækrəˌnɪzəm) *n* **1** the representation of an event, person, or thing in a historical context in which it could not have occurred or existed. **2** a person or thing that belongs or seems to belong to another time. ORIG C17: from L, from Gk *anakhronismos* a mistake in chronology, from ANA- + *khronos* time
▸ **a**ˌ**nachro**ˈ**nistic** *adj* ▸ **a**ˌ**nachro**ˈ**nistically** *adv*

anacoluthon (ˌænəkəˈluːθɒn) *n, pl* **anacolutha** (-θə). a construction that involves the change from one grammatical sequence to another within a single sentence. ORIG C18: from LL, from Gk, from *anakolouthos* not consistent, from AN- + *akolouthos* following

anaconda (ˌænəˈkɒndə) *n* a very large nonvenomous arboreal and semiaquatic snake of tropical South America, which kills its prey by constriction. ORIG C18: prob. changed from Sinhalese *henakandayā* whip snake; orig. referring to a snake of Sri Lanka

Anacreon ★ (əˈnækrɪˌɒn, -ən) *n* ?572–?488 B.C., Greek lyric poet.
▸ **A**ˌ**nacre**ˈ**ontic** *adj, n*

anacrusis (ˌænəˈkruːsɪs) *n, pl* **anacruses** (-siːz). **1** *Prosody.* one or more unstressed syllables at the beginning of a line of verse. **2** *Music.* an unstressed note or group of notes immediately preceding the strong first beat of the first bar. ORIG C19: from Gk, from *anakrouein* to strike up, from ANA- + *krouein* to strike

anadromous (əˈnædrəməs) *adj* (of fishes such as the salmon) migrating up rivers from the sea in order to breed. ORIG C18: from Gk *anadromos* running upwards

Anadyr ★ (*Russian* aˈnadirj) *n* **1** a town in Russia, in NE Siberia at the mouth of the Anadyr River. Pop.: 6586 (1993 est.). **2** a mountain range in Russia, in NE Siberia, rising over 1500 m (5000 ft). **3** a river in Russia, rising in mountains on the Arctic Circle, south of the Anadyr Range, and flowing east to the Gulf of Anadyr. Length: 725 km (450 miles). **4 Gulf of.** an inlet of the Bering Sea, off the coast of NE Russia.

anaemia *or US* **anemia** (əˈniːmɪə) *n* a deficiency in the number of red blood cells or in their haemoglobin content, resulting in pallor and lack of energy. ORIG C19: from NL, from Gk *anaimia* lack of blood, from AN- + *haima* blood

anaemic *or US* **anemic** (əˈniːmɪk) *adj* **1** relating to or suffering from anaemia. **2** pale and sickly looking; lacking vitality.

anaerobe (æˈnɛərəʊb, ˈænərəʊb) *or* **anaerobium** (ˌænɛəˈrəʊbɪəm) *n, pl* **anaerobes** *or* **anaerobia** (-ˈəʊbɪə). an organism that does not require, or requires the absence of, free oxygen or air.
▸ ˌ**anaer**ˈ**obic** *adj*

anaesthesia *or US* **anesthesia** (ˌænɪsˈθiːzɪə) *n* **1** loss of bodily sensation, esp. of touch, as the result of nerve damage or other abnormality. **2** loss of sensation, esp. of pain, induced by drugs: called **general anaesthesia** when consciousness is lost and **local anaesthesia** when only a specific area of the body is involved. ORIG C19: from NL, from Gk *anaisthēsia* absence of sensation

anaesthetic *or US* **anesthetic** (ˌænɪsˈθɛtɪk) *n* **1** a substance that causes anaesthesia. ◆ *adj* **2** causing or characterized by anaesthesia.

anaesthetics (ˌænɪsˈθɛtɪks) *n* (*functioning as sing*) the science of anaesthesia and its application. US name: **anesthesiology.**

anaesthetist (əˈniːsθətɪst) *n* **1** *Brit.* a doctor specializing in the administration of anaesthetics. US name: **anesthesiologist.** **2** *US.* See **anesthetist.**

anaesthetize, anaesthetise, *or US* **anesthetize** (əˈniːsθəˌtaɪz) *vb* **anaesthetizes, anaesthetizing, anaesthetized** *or* **anaesthetises, anaesthetising, anaesthetised** *or US* **anesthetizes, anesthetizing, anesthetized.** (*tr*) to render insensible to pain by administering an anaesthetic.
▸ **a**ˌ**naestheti**ˈ**zation, a**ˌ**naestheti**ˈ**sation,** *or US* **a**ˌ**nestheti**ˈ**zation** *n*

anaglyph (ˈænəˌɡlɪf) *n* **1** *Photog.* a stereoscopic picture consisting of two images of the same object, taken from slightly different angles, in two complementary colours. When viewed through coloured spectacles, the images merge to produce a stereoscopic sensation. **2** anything cut to stand in low relief, such as a cameo. ORIG C17: from Gk *anagluphē* carved in low relief, from ANA- + *gluphē* carving, from *gluphein* to carve
▸ ˌ**ana**ˈ**glyphic** *adj*

Anaglypta (ˌænəˈɡlɪptə) *n Trademark.* a type of thick embossed wallpaper designed to be painted. ORIG C19: from Gk *anagluptos;* see ANAGLYPH

anagram (ˈænəˌɡræm) *n* a word or phrase the letters of which can be rearranged into another word or phrase. ORIG C16: from NL, from Gk, from *anagrammatizein* to transpose letters, from ANA- + *gramma* a letter
▸ **anagrammatic** (ˌænəɡrəˈmætɪk) *or* ˌ**anagram**ˈ**matical** *adj*

anagrammatize *or* **anagrammatise** (ˌænəˈɡræməˌtaɪz) *vb* **anagrammatizes, anagrammatizing, anagrammatized** *or* **anagrammatises, anagrammatising, anagrammatised.** to arrange into an anagram.

anal (ˈeɪnᵊl) *adj* **1** of or near the anus. **2** *Psychoanal.* relating to a stage of psychosexual development during which the child's interest is concentrated on the anal region and excremental functions. ORIG C18: from NL *ānālis;* see ANUS
▸ ˈ**anally** *adv*

analects (ˈænəˌlɛkts) *or* **analecta** (ˌænəˈlɛktə) *pl n* selected literary passages from one or more works. ORIG C17: via L from Gk, from *analegein* to collect up, from *legein* to gather

analeptic (ˌænᵊˈlɛptɪk) *adj* **1** (of a drug, etc.) restorative or invigorating. ◆ *n* **2** a restorative remedy or drug. ORIG C17: from NL, from Gk *analēptikos* stimulating, from *analambanein* to take up

anal fin *n* an unpaired fin between the anus and tail fin in fishes that maintains equilibrium.

analgesia (ˌænᵊlˈdʒiːzɪə) *or* **analgia** (ænˈældʒɪə) *n* in-

★ people and places

ability to feel pain. ORIG C18: via NL from Gk: insensibility, from AN- + *algēsis* sense of pain

analgesic (ˌænᵊlˈdʒiːzɪk) *adj* **1** of or causing analgesia. ◆ *n* **2** a substance that produces analgesia.

analog (ˈænəˌlɒg) *n* a variant spelling of **analogue.**

> **USAGE NOTE** The spelling *analog* is a US variant of *analogue* in all its senses, and is also the generally preferred spelling in the computer industry.

analog computer *n* a computer that performs arithmetical operations using a variable physical quantity, such as mechanical movement or voltage, to represent numbers.

analogize *or* **analogise** (əˈnæləˌdʒaɪz) *vb* **analogizes, analogizing, analogized** *or* **analogises, analogising, analogised. 1** (*intr*) to make use of analogy, as in argument. **2** (*tr*) to make analogous or reveal analogy in.

analogous (əˈnæləgəs) *adj* **1** similar or corresponding in some respect. **2** *Biol.* (of organs and parts) having the same function but different evolutionary origin. **3** *Linguistics.* formed by analogy: *an analogous plural.* ORIG C17: from L, from Gk *analogos* proportionate, from ANA- + *logos* speech, ratio

> **USAGE NOTE** The use of *with* after *analogous*, though occasionally found, should be avoided: *swimming has no event that is analogous to* (not *with*) *the 100 metres in athletics.* In this word the *g* is pronounced as in *gate.*

analogue *or US* (*sometimes*) **analog** (ˈænᵊˌlɒg) *n* **1a** a physical object or quantity used to measure or represent another quantity. **1b** (*as modifier*): *analogue watch; analogue recording.* **2** something analogous to something else. **3** *Biol.* an analogous part or organ.

> **USAGE NOTE** See at **analog.**

analogue recording *n* a sound recording process in which an audio input is converted into an analogous electrical waveform.

analogy (əˈnælədʒɪ) *n, pl* **analogies. 1** agreement or similarity, esp. in a limited number of features. **2** a comparison made to show such a similarity: *an analogy between an atom and the solar system.* **3** *Biol.* the relationship between analogous organs or parts. **4** *Logic, maths, philosophy.* a form of reasoning in which a similarity between two or more things is inferred from a known similarity between them in other respects. **5** *Linguistics.* imitation of existing models or regular patterns in the formation of words, etc.: *a child may use "sheeps" as the plural of "sheep" by analogy with "cat," "cats," etc.* ORIG C16: from Gk *analogia* correspondence, from *analogos* ANALOGOUS
▸ **analogical** (ˌænəˈlɒdʒɪkᵊl) *adj*

anal retentive *Psychoanal.* ◆ *n* **1** a person who exhibits anal personality traits, such as orderliness, meanness, stubbornness, etc. ◆ *adj* **anal-retentive. 2** exhibiting anal personality traits, such as orderliness, meanness, stubbornness, etc.

analysand (əˈnælɪˌsænd) *n* any person who is undergoing psychoanalysis. ORIG C20: from ANALYSE + *-and,* on the model of *multiplicand*

analyse *or US* **analyze** (ˈænᵊˌlaɪz) *vb* **analyses, analysing, analysed** *or US* **analyzes, analyzing, analyzed.** (*tr*) **1** to examine in detail in order to discover meaning, essential features, etc. **2** to break down into components or essential features. **3** to make a mathematical, chemical, etc., analysis of. **4** another word for **psychoanalyse.** ORIG C17: back formation from ANALYSIS
▸ **ˈanaˌlyser** *or US* **ˈanaˌlyzer** *n*

analysis (əˈnælɪsɪs) *n, pl* **analyses** (-ˌsiːz). **1** the division of a physical or abstract whole into its constituent parts to examine or determine their relationship. **2** a statement of the results of this. **3** short for **psychoanalysis. 4** *Chem.* **4a** the decomposition of a substance in order to determine the kinds of constituents present (**qualitative analysis**) or the amount of each constituent (**quantitative analysis**). **4b** the result obtained by such a determination. **5** *Linguistics.* the use of word order together with word function to express syntactic relations in a language, as opposed to the use of inflections. **6** *Maths.* the branch of mathematics principally concerned with the properties of functions. **7 in the last, final,** *or* **ultimate analysis.** after everything has been given due consideration. ORIG C16: from NL, from Gk *analusis,* lit.: a dissolving, from ANA- + *luein* to loosen

analysis of variance *n Statistics.* a technique for analysing the total variation of a set of observations as measured by the variance of the observations multiplied by their number.

analyst (ˈænəlɪst) *n* **1** a person who analyses or is skilled in analysis. **2** short for **psychoanalyst.**

analytic (ˌænəˈlɪtɪk) *or* **analytical** *adj* **1** relating to analysis. **2** capable of or given to analysing: *an analytic mind.* **3** *Linguistics.* denoting languages characterized by analysis. **4** *Logic.* (of a proposition) true or false by virtue of the meanings of the words alone: *all spinsters are unmarried* is analytically true. ORIG C16: via LL from Gk *analutikos,* from *analuein* to dissolve, break down
▸ **ˌanaˈlytically** *adv* ▸ **analyticity** (ˌænəlɪˈtɪsɪtɪ) *n*

analytical geometry *n* the branch of geometry that uses algebraic notation to locate a point; coordinate geometry.

analytic philosophy *n* See **philosophical analysis.**

Anambra ★ (əˈnæmbrə) *n* a state of S Nigeria, formed in 1976 from part of East-Central State. Capital: Enugu. Pop.: 3 094 783 (1995 est.). Area: 4844 sq. km (1870 sq. miles).

Ananda ★ (əˈnændə) *n* 5th century B.C., the first cousin, favourite disciple, and personal attendant of the Buddha.

anandrous (ænˈændrəs) *adj* (of flowers) having no stamens. ORIG C19: from Gk *anandros* lacking males, from AN- + *anēr* man

Ananias ★ (ˌænəˈnaɪəs) *n* **1** *New Testament.* a Jewish Christian of Jerusalem who was struck dead for lying (Acts 5). **2** a liar.

anapaest *or* **anapest** (ˈænəpest, -piːst) *n Prosody.* a metrical foot of three syllables, the first two short, the last long (⏑⏑–). ORIG C17: via L from Gk *anapaistos* reversed, from *ana-* back + *paiein* to strike
▸ **ˌanaˈpaestic** *or* **ˌanaˈpestic** *adj*

anaphora (əˈnæfərə) *n* **1** *Grammar.* the use of a word such as a pronoun to avoid repetition, as for example *one* in *He offered me a drink but I didn't want one.* **2** *Rhetoric.* the repetition of a word or phrase at the beginning of successive clauses. ORIG C16: via L from Gk: repetition, from ANA- + *pherein* to bear

anaphrodisiac (ˌænæfrəˈdɪzɪˌæk) *adj* **1** tending to lessen sexual desire. ◆ *n* **2** an anaphrodisiac drug.

anaphylaxis (ˌænəfɪˈlæksɪs) *n* extreme sensitivity to an injected antigen following a previous injection. ORIG C20: from ANA- + (PRO)PHYLAXIS

anaplasmosis (ˌænəplæzˈməʊsɪs) *n* another name for **gallsickness.**

anaptyxis (ˌænæpˈtɪksɪs) *n, pl* **anaptyxes** (-ˈtɪksiːz). the insertion of a short vowel between consonants in order to make a word more easily pronounceable. ORIG C19: via NL from Gk *anaptuxis,* from *anaptussein* to unfold, from ANA- + *ptussein* to fold

Anapurna ★ (ˌænəˈpʊənə) *n* a variant spelling of **Annapurna.**

anarchism (ˈænəˌkɪzəm) *n* **1** *Political theory.* a doctrine advocating the abolition of government. **2** the principles or practice of anarchists.

anarchist (ˈænəkɪst) *n* **1** a person who advocates a society based on voluntary cooperation and the abolition of government. **2** a person who causes disorder or upheaval.

anarchy (ˈænəkɪ) *n* **1** general lawlessness and disorder, esp. when thought to result from an absence or failure of government. **2** the absence of government. **3** the ab-

sence of any guiding or uniting principle; chaos. **4** political anarchism. ORIG C16: from Med. L, from Gk, from *anarkhos* without a ruler, from AN- + *arkh-* leader, from *arkhein* to rule
▸ **anarchic** (æn'ɑːkɪk) *or* **an'archical** *adj*

Anastasia ★ (ˌænə'stɑːzɪə, -'steɪ-) *n* **Grand Duchess.** 1901–?18, daughter of Tsar Nicholas II, believed to have been executed by the Bolsheviks in 1918, although several women subsequently claimed to be her.

anastigmat (æ'næstɪgmæt, ˌænə'stɪgmæt) *n* a lens system designed to be free of astigmatism. ORIG C19: from AN- + ASTIGMATIC
▸ **ˌanastig'matic** *adj*

anastomose (ə'næstəˌməuz) *vb* **anastomoses, anastomosing, anastomosed.** to join (two parts of a blood vessel, etc.) by anastomosis.

anastomosis (əˌnæstə'məusɪs) *n, pl* **anastomoses** (-siːz). **1** a natural connection between two tubular structures, such as blood vessels. **2** the union of two hollow parts that are normally separate. ORIG C16: via NL from Gk: opening, from *anastomoun* to equip with a mouth, from *stoma* mouth

anastrophe (ə'næstrəfɪ) *n Rhetoric.* another term for **inversion** (sense 3). ORIG C16: from Gk, from *anastrephein* to invert

anathema (ə'næθəmə) *n, pl* **anathemas. 1** a detested person or thing: *he is anathema to me.* **2** a formal ecclesiastical excommunication, or denunciation of a doctrine. **3** the person or thing so cursed. **4** a strong curse. ORIG C16: via Church L from Gk: something accursed, from *anatithenai* to dedicate, from ANA- + *tithenai* to set

anathematize *or* **anathematise** (ə'næθɪməˌtaɪz) *vb* **anathematizes, anathematizing, anathematized** *or* **anathematises, anathematising, anathematised.** to pronounce an anathema (upon a person, etc.); curse.

Anatolia ★ (ˌænə'təulɪə) *n* the Asian part of Turkey, occupying the peninsula between the Black Sea, the Mediterranean, and the Aegean: consists of a plateau, largely mountainous, with salt lakes in the interior. Historical name: **Asia Minor.**
▸ **ˌAna'tolian** *adj, n*

anatomical (ˌænə'tɒmɪkᵊl) *adj* of anatomy.

anatomist (ə'nætəmɪst) *n* an expert in anatomy.

anatomize *or* **anatomise** (ə'nætəˌmaɪz) *vb* **anatomizes, anatomizing, anatomized** *or* **anatomises, anatomising, anatomised.** (*tr*) **1** to dissect (an animal or plant). **2** to examine in minute detail.

anatomy (ə'nætəmɪ) *n, pl* **anatomies. 1** the science concerned with the physical structure of animals and plants. **2** the physical structure of an animal or plant or any of its parts. **3** a book or treatise on this subject. **4** dissection of an animal or plant. **5** any detailed analysis: *the anatomy of a crime.* **6** *Inf.* the human body. ORIG C14: from L, from Gk *anatomē*, from ANA- + *temnein* to cut

anatto (ə'nætəu) *n, pl* **anattos.** a variant spelling of **annatto.**

Anaxagoras ★ (ˌænæk'sægərəs) *n* ?500–428 B.C., Greek philosopher who maintained that all things were composed of minute particles.

Anaximander ★ (əˌnæksɪ'mændə) *n* 611–547 B.C., Greek philosopher, astronomer, and mathematician.

ANC *abbrev. for* African National Congress.

-ance *or* **-ancy** *suffix forming nouns.* indicating an action, state or condition, or quality: *resemblance; tenancy.* ORIG via OF from L *-antia*

ancestor ('ænsɛstə) *n* **1** a person from whom another is directly descended; forefather. **2** an early animal or plant from which a later type has evolved. **3** a person or thing regarded as a forerunner: *the ancestor of the modern camera.* ORIG C13: from OF, from LL *antecēssor* one who goes before, from L *antecēdere*
▸ **'ancestress** *fem n*

ancestral (æn'sɛstrəl) *adj* of or inherited from ancestors.

ancestry ('ænsɛstrɪ) *n, pl* **ancestries. 1** lineage or descent, esp. when noble or distinguished. **2** ancestors collectively.

Anchises ★ (æn'kaɪsiːz) *n Classical myth.* a Trojan prince and father of Aeneas. In the *Aeneid,* he is rescued by his son at the fall of Troy and dies in Sicily.

anchor ('æŋkə) *n* **1** a device attached to a vessel by a cable and dropped overboard so as to grip the bottom and restrict movement. **2** an object used to hold something else firmly in place: *the rock provided an anchor for the rope.* **3** a source of stability or security. **4** short for **anchorman** *or* **anchorwoman. 5 cast, come to,** *or* **drop anchor.** to anchor a vessel. **6 ride at anchor.** to be anchored. ◆ *vb* **7** to use an anchor to hold (a vessel) in one place. **8** to fasten or be fastened securely; fix or become fixed firmly. ◆ See also **anchors.** ORIG OE *ancor,* from L, from Gk *ankura*

anchorage ('æŋkərɪdʒ) *n* **1** the act of anchoring. **2** any place where a vessel is anchored. **3** a place designated for vessels to anchor. **4** a fee imposed for anchoring. **5** anything used as an anchor. **6** a source of security or strength.

Anchorage ★ ('æŋkərɪdʒ) *n* the largest city in Alaska, a port in the south, at the head of Cook Inlet. Pop.: 253 649 (1994 est.).

anchorite ('æŋkəˌraɪt) *n* a person who lives in seclusion, esp. a religious recluse; hermit. ORIG C15: from Med. L, from LL, from Gk, from *anakhōrein* to retire, from *khōra* a space
▸ **'anchoress** *fem n*

anchorman ('æŋkəmæn) *n, fem* **anchorwoman** ('æŋkəwumən) pl **anchormen, anchorwomen. 1** *Sport.* the last person in a team to compete, esp. in a relay race. **2** (in broadcasting) a person in a central studio who links up and maintains contact with various outside camera units, reporters, etc.
▸ **'anchorˌwoman** *fem n*

anchors ('æŋkəz) *pl n Sl.* the brakes of a motor vehicle: *he rammed on the anchors.*

anchovy ('æntʃəvɪ) *n, pl* **anchovies** *or* **anchovy.** any of various small marine food fishes which have a salty taste and are often tinned or made into a paste or essence. ORIG C16: from Sp. *anchova,* ? ult. from Gk *aphuē* small fish

anchusa (æŋ'kjuːsə) *n* any of several Eurasian plants having rough hairy stems and leaves and blue flowers. ORIG C18: from L

anchylose ('æŋkɪˌləuz) *vb* a variant spelling of **ankylose.**

ancien régime *French.* (ɑ̃sjɛ̃ reʒim) *n, pl* ***anciens régimes*** (ɑ̃sjɛ̃ reʒim). the political and social system of France before the Revolution of 1789. ORIG lit.: old regime

ancient ('eɪnʃənt) *adj* **1** dating from very long ago: *ancient ruins.* **2** very old. **3** of the far past, esp. before the collapse of the Western Roman Empire (476 A.D.). ◆ *n* **4** (*often pl*) a member of a civilized nation in the ancient world, esp. a Greek or Roman. **5** (*often pl*) one of the classical authors of Greek or Roman antiquity. **6** *Arch.* an old man. ORIG C14: from OF *ancien,* from Vulgar L *anteanus* (unattested), from L *ante* before
▸ **'ancientness** *n*

ancient lights *n* (*usually functioning as sing*) the legal right to receive, by a particular window or windows, adequate and unobstructed daylight.

anciently ('eɪnʃəntlɪ) *adv* in ancient times.

Ancient of Days *n* a name for God, originating in the Authorized Version of the Old Testament (Daniel 7:9).

ancillary (æn'sɪlərɪ) *adj* **1** subsidiary. **2** auxiliary; supplementary: *ancillary services.* ◆ *n, pl* **ancillaries. 3** a subsidiary or auxiliary thing or person. ORIG C17: from L *ancillāris* concerning maidservants, ult. from *ancūla* female servant

Ancohuma ★ (ˌæŋkəu'uːmə) *n* one of the two peaks of (Mount) **Sorata.**

ancon ('æŋkɒn) *or* **ancone** ('æŋkəun) *n, pl* **ancones** (æŋ'kəuniːz). *Architect.* a projecting bracket or console supporting a cornice. ORIG C18: from Gk *ankōn* a bend

Ancona ★ (*Italian* aŋ'koːna) *n* a port in Central Italy, on the Adriatic, capital of the Marches: founded by Greeks from Syracuse in about 390 B.C. Pop.: 100 597 (1994 est.).

-ancy *suffix forming nouns.* a variant of **-ance,** indicating condition or quality: *poignancy.*

ancylostomiasis (ˌænsɪˌlɒstə'maɪəsɪs) *or* **ankylos-**

tomiasis (ˌæŋkɪˌlɒstəˈmaɪəsɪs) *n* infestation of the intestine with blood-sucking hookworms; hookworm disease. ORIG from NL, ult. from Gk *ankulos* hooked + *stoma* mouth

and (ænd; *unstressed* ənd, ən) *conj* (*coordinating*) **1** in addition to: *boys and girls.* **2** as a consequence: *he fell down and cut his knee.* **3** afterwards: *we pay and go through that door.* **4** plus: *two and two equals four.* **5** used to give emphasis or indicate repetition or continuity: *it rained and rained.* **6** used to express a contrast between instances of what is named: *there are jobs and jobs.* **7** *Inf.* used in place of *to* in infinitives after verbs such as *try, go,* and *come: try and see it my way.* **8** an obsolete word for **if**: *and it please you.* ORIG OE *and*

> **USAGE NOTE** The use of *and* instead of *to* after *try* and *wait* is typical of spoken language, but should be avoided in any writing which is not informal: *We must try to prevent* (not *try and prevent*) *this happening.*

-and *or* **-end** *suffix forming nouns.* indicating a person or thing that is to be dealt with in a specified way: *dividend; multiplicand.* ORIG from L gerundives ending in *-andus, -endus*

Andalusia ★ (ˌændəˈluːzɪə) *n* a region of S Spain, on the Mediterranean and the Atlantic, with the Sierra Morena in the north, the Sierra Nevada in the southeast, and the Guadalquivir River flowing over fertile lands between them; a centre of Moorish civilization; it became an autonomous region in 1981. Area: about 87 280 sq. km (33 700 sq. miles). Spanish name: **Andalucía** (andaluˈθia).

Andaman and Nicobar Islands ★ (ˈændəmən; ˈnɪkəʊˌbɑː) *pl n* a territory of India, in the E Bay of Bengal, consisting of two groups of over 200 islands. Capital: Port Blair. Pop.: 322 000 (1994 est.). Area: 8140 sq. km (3143 sq. miles).

Andaman Islands ★ *pl n* a group of islands in the E Bay of Bengal, part of the Indian territory of the Andaman and Nicobar Islands. Pop.: 240 089 (1991 est.). Area: 6408 sq. km (2474 sq. miles).

Andaman Sea ★ *n* part of the Bay of Bengal, between the Andaman and Nicobar Islands and the Malay Peninsula.

andante (ænˈdæntɪ) *Music.* ◆ *adj, adv* **1** (to be performed) at a moderately slow tempo. ◆ *n* **2** a passage or piece to be performed in this manner. ORIG C18: from It., from *andare* to walk, from L *ambulāre*

andantino (ˌændænˈtiːnəʊ) *Music.* ◆ *adj, adv* **1** (to be performed) slightly faster or slower than andante. ◆ *n, pl* **andantinos. 2** a passage or piece to be performed in this manner. ORIG C19: dim. of ANDANTE

AND circuit *or* **gate** (ænd) *n Computing.* a logic circuit that has a high-voltage output signal if and only if all input signals are at a high voltage simultaneously. Cf. **NAND circuit, NOR circuit, OR circuit.** ORIG C20: from similarity of operation of *and* in logical conjunctions

Andean (ænˈdiːən, ˈændɪən) *adj* of, relating to, or resembling the Andes.

Andersen ★ (ˈændəsᵊn) *n* **Hans Christian.** 1805–75, Danish author of fairy tales.

Andersen Nexø ★ (ˈanərsen) *n* See (Martin Andersen) **Nexø.**

Anderson[1] ★ (ˈændəsᵊn) *n* a river in N Canada, in the Northwest Territories, rising in lakes north of Great Bear Lake and flowing west and north to the Beaufort Sea. Length: about 580 km (360 miles).

Anderson[2] ★ (ˈændəsᵊn) *n* **1 Carl David.** 1905–91, US physicist, who discovered the positron in cosmic rays (1932): Nobel prize for physics 1936. **2 Elizabeth Garrett.** 1836–1917, British physician: campaigned for the admission of women to the professions. **3** Dame **Judith,** real name *Frances Margaret Anderson.* 1898–1992, Australian actress. **4 Lindsay (Gordon).** 1923–94, British film director: his films include *This Sporting Life* (1963) and *If* (1968). **5 Marian.** 1902–93, US contralto, the first Black permanent member of the Metropolitan Opera Company, New York. **6 Philip Warren.** 1923–96, US physicist, noted for his work on solid-state physics. Nobel prize for physics 1977. **7 Sherwood.** 1874–1941, US writer, best known for *Winesburg Ohio* (1919).

Andes ★ (ˈændiːz) *pl n* a major mountain system of South America, extending for about 7250 km (4500 miles) along the entire W coast, with several parallel ranges or cordilleras and many volcanic peaks: rich in minerals, including gold, silver, copper, iron ore, and nitrates. Average height: 3900 m (13 000 ft). Highest peak: Aconcagua, 6960 m (22 835 ft).

Andhra Pradesh ★ (ˈændrə prɑːˈdɛʃ) *n* a state of SE India, on the Bay of Bengal: formed in 1953 from parts of Madras and Hyderabad states. Capital: Hyderabad. Pop.: 71 800 000 (1994 est.). Area: 275 068 sq. km (106 204 sq. miles).

andiron (ˈændˌaɪən) *n* either of a pair of metal stands for supporting logs in a hearth; firedog. ORIG C14: from OF *andier,* from ?; infl. by IRON

Andong ★ (ænˈdʊŋ) *n* a port in E China, in Liaoning province at the mouth of the Yalu River. Pop.: 188 452 (1995). Also called: **Tan-tung.**

and/or *conj* (*coordinating*) used to join terms when either one or the other or both is indicated: *passports and/or other means of identification.*

> **USAGE NOTE** Many people think that *and/or* is only acceptable in legal and commercial contexts. In other contexts, it is better to use *or both*: *many drinkers lose their jobs or their driving licences or both* (not *their jobs and/or their driving licences*).

Andorra ★ (ænˈdɔːrə) *n* a mountainous principality in SW Europe, between France and Spain: according to tradition, given independence by Charlemagne in the 9th century for helping to fight the Moors; placed under the joint sovereignty of the Comte de Foix and the Spanish bishop of Urgel in 1278; under the joint overlordship of the French head of state and the bishop of Urgel from the 16th century. Languages: Catalan, French, and Spanish. Religion: Roman Catholic. Currency: French franc and Spanish peseta. Capital: Andorra la Vella. Pop.: 66 100 (1999 est.). Area: 464 sq. km (179 sq. miles). Official name: **Principat d'Andorra.**
▸ **Anˈdorran** *adj, n*

Andorra la Vella ★ (*Spanish* anˈdɔrra la ˈbeʎa) *n* the capital of Andorra, situated in the west of the principality. Pop.: 21 984 (1995 est.). French name: **Andorre la Vieille** (ɑ̃dɔr la vjɛj).

Andrássy ★ (ænˈdræsɪ; *Hungarian* ˈɔndraːʃi) *n* Count **Gyula** (ˈdjulɔ). 1823–90, Hungarian statesman; the first prime minister of Hungary under the Dual Monarchy of Austria-Hungary (1867).

Andrea del Sarto ★ (*Italian* anˈdrea del ˈsarto) *n* See **Sarto.**

Andreanof Islands ★ (ˌændrɪˈɑːnɒf) *pl n* a group of islands in the central Aleutian Islands, Alaska. Area: 3710 sq. km (1432 sq. miles).

Andrew ★ (ˈændruː) *n* **Saint.** *New Testament.* one of the twelve apostles of Jesus; the brother of Peter; patron saint of Scotland. Feast day: Nov. 30.

Andrewes ★ (ˈændruːz) *n* **Lancelot.** 1555–1626, English bishop and theologian.

Andrews ★ (ˈændruːz) *n* **Thomas.** 1813–85, Irish physical chemist, noted for his work on the liquefaction of gases.

Andrić ★ (*Serbo-Croat* ˈandritʃ) *n* **Ivo** (ˈiːvɔ). 1892–1975, Serbian novelist; author of *The Bridge on the Drina* (1945): Nobel prize for literature 1961.

andro- *or before a vowel* **andr-** *combining form.* **1** male; masculine: *androsterone.* **2** (in botany) stamen or anther: *androecium.* ORIG from Gk *anēr* (genitive *andros*) man

Androcles (ˈændrəˌkliːz) *or* **Androclus** ★ (ˈændrəkləs) *n* (in Roman legend) a slave whose life was spared in the arena by a lion from whose paw he had once extracted a thorn.

androecium (ænˈdriːsɪəm) *n, pl* **androecia** (-sɪə). the stamens of a flowering plant collectively. ORIG C19: from NL, from ANDRO- + Gk *oikion* a little house

androgen ('ændrədʒən) *n* any of several steroids that promote development of male sexual characteristics.
▸ **androgenic** (ˌændrə'dʒɛnɪk) *adj*

androgyne ('ændrəˌdʒaɪn) *n* another word for **hermaphrodite**. ORIG C17: from OF, via L from Gk *androgunos,* from *anēr* man + *gunē* woman

androgynous (æn'drɒdʒɪnəs) *adj* **1** *Bot.* having male and female flowers in the same inflorescence. **2** having male and female characteristics; hermaphrodite.
▸ **an'drogyny** *n*

android ('ændrɔɪd) *n* **1** (in science fiction) a robot resembling a human being. ◆ *adj* **2** resembling a human being. ORIG C18: from LGk *androeidēs* manlike; see ANDRO-, -OID

andrology (æn'drɒlədʒɪ) *n* the branch of medicine concerned with diseases in men, esp. of the reproductive organs. ORIG C20: from ANDRO- + -LOGY
▸ **an'drologist** *n*

Andromache ★ (æn'drɒməkɪ) *n Greek myth.* the wife of Hector.

Andromeda ★ (æn'drɒmɪdə) *n Greek myth.* the wife of Perseus, who saved her from a sea monster.

Andropov[1] ★ (æn'drɒpɒv; *Russian* ən'drɔːpəf) *n* a former name (1984–91) for **Rybinsk**.

Andropov[2] ★ (æn'drɒpɒv; *Russian* ən'drɔːpəf) *n* **Yuri Vladimirovich**. 1914–84, Soviet statesman; president of the Soviet Union (1983–84).

Andros ★ ('ændrəs) *n* **1** an island in the Aegean Sea, the northernmost of the Cyclades: long famous for wine. Capital: Andros. Pop.: 8155 (1990). Area: about 311 sq. km (120 sq. miles). **2** an island in the N Caribbean, the largest of the Bahamas. Pop.: 8177 (1990). Area: 4144 sq. km (1600 sq. miles).

androsterone (æn'drɒstəˌrəʊn) *n* an androgenic steroid hormone produced in the testes.

-androus *adj combining form.* (in botany) indicating number or type of stamens: *diandrous.* ORIG from NL, from Gk *-andros,* from *anēr* man

Andvari ★ (æn'dwɑːrɪ) *n Norse myth.* a dwarf who possessed a treasure hoard, which was robbed by Loki.

ane (eɪn) *determiner, pron, n* a Scottish word for **one**.

-ane *suffix forming nouns.* indicating a hydrocarbon of the alkane series: *hexane.* ORIG coined to replace *-ene, -ine,* and *-one*

anecdotage ('ænɪkˌdəʊtɪdʒ) *n Humorous.* garrulous old age. ORIG from ANECDOTE + -AGE, with play on *dotage*

anecdote ('ænɪkˌdəʊt) *n* a short usually amusing account of an incident. ORIG C17: from Med. L, from Gk *anekdotos* unpublished, from AN- + *ekdotos* published
▸ **ˌanec'dotal** *or* **ˌanec'dotic** *adj* ▸ **ˌanec'dotalist** *or* **'anecˌdotist** *n*

anechoic (ˌænɪ'kəʊɪk) *adj* having a low degree of reverberation: *an anechoic recording studio.*

Aneirin ★ (ə'naɪᵊrɪn) *n* 6th century A.D., Welsh poet. His *Y Gododdin,* preserved in *The Book of Aneirin* (?1250), is one of the earliest surviving Welsh poems.

anemia (ə'niːmɪə) *n* the usual US spelling of **anaemia**.
▸ **anemic** (ə'niːmɪk) *adj*

anemo- *combining form.* indicating wind: *anemometer; anemophilous.* ORIG from Gk *anemos* wind

anemograph (ə'nɛməʊˌgrɑːf) *n* a self-recording anemometer.

anemometer (ˌænɪ'mɒmɪtə) *n* an instrument for recording the speed and often the direction of winds. Also called: **wind gauge**.
▸ **ˌane'mometry** *n* ▸ **anemometric** (ˌænɪməʊ'mɛtrɪk) *adj*

anemone (ə'nɛmənɪ) *n* any woodland plant of the genus *Anemone* of N temperate regions, such as the white-flowered **wood anemone** or **windflower**. Some cultivated anemones have coloured flowers. ORIG C16: via L from Gk: windflower, from *anemos* wind

anemophilous (ˌænɪ'mɒfɪləs) *adj* (of flowering plants such as grasses) pollinated by the wind.
▸ **ˌane'mophily** *n*

★ people and places

anent (ə'nɛnt) *prep Arch. or Scot.* **1** lying against; alongside. **2** concerning; about. ORIG OE *on efen,* lit.: on even (ground)

aneroid barometer ('ænəˌrɔɪd) *n* a device for measuring atmospheric pressure without the use of fluids. It consists of a partially evacuated chamber, the lid of which is displaced by variations in air pressure. This displacement is magnified by levers and made to operate a pointer. ORIG C19 *aneroid,* from F, from AN- + Gk *nēros* wet + -OID

anesthesia (ˌænɪs'θiːzɪə) *n* the usual US spelling of **anaesthesia**.

anesthesiologist (ˌænɪsˌθiːzɪ'ɒlədʒɪst) *n* the US name for an **anaesthetist**.

anesthesiology (ˌænɪsˌθiːzɪ'ɒlədʒɪ) *n* the US name for **anaesthetics**.

anesthetic (ˌænɪs'θɛtɪk) *n, adj* the usual US spelling of **anaesthetic**.

anesthetist (ə'nɛsθətɪst) *n* (in the US) a person qualified to administer anaesthesia, often a nurse or someone other than a physician.

Aneto ★ (*Spanish* a'neto) *n* **Pico de** ('piko de). a mountain in N Spain, near the French border: the highest in the Pyrenees. Height: 3404 m (11 168 ft).

aneurysm *or* **aneurism** ('ænjəˌrɪzəm) *n* a sac formed by abnormal dilation of the weakened wall of a blood vessel. ORIG C15: from Gk *aneurusma,* from *aneurunein* to dilate

anew (ə'njuː) *adv* **1** once more. **2** in a different way; afresh. ORIG OE *of nīwe;* see OF, NEW

Anfinsen ★ ('ænfɪnsᵊn) *n* **Christian Boehmer** ('beɪmə). 1916–95, US biochemist, noted for his research on the structure of enzymes. Nobel prize for chemistry 1972.

Angara ★ (*Russian* anga'ra) *n* a river in S Russia, in Siberia, flowing from Lake Baikal north and west to the Yenisei River: important for hydroelectric power. Length: 1840 km (1150 miles).

angary ('æŋgərɪ) *n Law.* the right of a belligerent state to use the property of a neutral state or to destroy it subject to payment of compensation to the owners. ORIG C19: from F, from LL *angaria* enforced service, from Gk *angaros* courier

angel ('eɪndʒəl) *n* **1** one of a class of spiritual beings attendant upon God. In medieval angelology they are divided by rank into nine orders. **2** a divine messenger from God. **3** a guardian spirit. **4** a conventional representation of any of these beings, depicted in human form with wings. **5** *Inf.* a person who is kind, pure, or beautiful. **6** *Inf.* an investor, esp. in a theatrical production. **7** Also called: **angel-noble**. a former English gold coin with a representation of the archangel Michael on it. **8** *Inf.* an unexplained signal on a radar screen. ORIG OE, from LL *angelus,* from Gk *angelos* messenger

angel cake *or esp. US* **angel food cake** *n* a very light sponge cake made without egg yolks.

angel dust *n* a slang name for **PCP**.

Angel Falls ★ *n* a waterfall in SE Venezuela, on the Caroní River. Height (probably the highest in the world): 979 m (3211 ft).

angelfish ('eɪndʒəlˌfɪʃ) *n, pl* **angelfish** *or* **angelfishes**. **1** any of various small tropical marine fishes which have a deep flattened brightly coloured body. **2** a South American freshwater fish having a compressed body and large dorsal and anal fins: a popular aquarium fish. **3** a shark with flattened pectoral fins.

angelic (æn'dʒɛlɪk) *adj* **1** of or relating to angels. **2** Also: **angelical**. resembling an angel in beauty, etc.
▸ **an'gelically** *adv*

angelica (æn'dʒɛlɪkə) *n* **1** an umbelliferous plant, the aromatic seeds, leaves, and stems of which are used in medicine and cookery. **2** the candied stems of this plant, used for decorating and flavouring sweet dishes. ORIG C16: from Med. L (*herba*) *angelica* angelic (herb)

Angelico ★ (*Italian* an'dʒɛːliko) *n* **Fra** (fra), original name *Guido di Pietro;* monastic name *Fra Giovanni da Fiesole.* ?1400–55, Italian fresco painter and Dominican friar.

Angell ★ (ˈeɪndʒəl) *n* Sir **Norman,** real name *Ralph Norman Angell Lane.* 1874–1967, British writer and economist, noted for his work on the economic futility of war, *The Great Illusion* (1910): Nobel peace prize 1933.

Angel of the North *n* the UK's largest sculpture (wingspan 53 m), by Anthony Gormley, erected in 1997 on the outskirts of Gateshead.

Angelou ★ (ˈændʒəˌluː) *n* **Maya** (ˈmaɪə), real name *Marguerite Johnson.* born 1928, US Black writer. Her works include the novel *I Know Why the Caged Bird Sings* (1970) and its sequels and *Phenomenal Woman* (1995).

Angelus (ˈændʒɪləs) *n RC Church.* **1** a series of prayers recited in the morning, at midday, and in the evening. **2** the bell (**Angelus bell**) signalling the times of these prayers. ORIG C17: L, from *Angelus domini nuntiavit Mariae* the angel of the Lord brought tidings to Mary

anger (ˈæŋgə) *n* **1** a feeling of great annoyance or antagonism as the result of some real or supposed grievance; rage; wrath. ◆ *vb* (*tr*) **2** to make angry; enrage. ORIG C12: from ON *angr* grief

Angers ★ (*French* ɑ̃ʒe) *n* a city in W France, on the river Maine. Pop.: 146 163 (1990).

Angevin (ˈændʒɪvɪn) *n* **1** a native or inhabitant of Anjou. **2** *History.* a member of the Plantagenet royal line, esp. one of the kings of England from Henry II to John (1154–1216). ◆ *adj* **3** of Anjou or its inhabitants. **4** of the Plantagenet kings of England between 1154 and 1216.

angina (ænˈdʒaɪnə) *n* **1** any disease marked by painful attacks of spasmodic choking. **2** Also called: **angina pectoris** (ˈpɛktərɪs). a sudden intense pain in the chest, caused by momentary lack of adequate blood supply to the heart muscle. ORIG C16: from L: quinsy, from Gk *ankhonē* a strangling

angio- *or before a vowel* **angi-** *combining form.* indicating a blood or lymph vessel; seed vessel. ORIG from Gk *angeion* vessel

angioma (ˌændʒɪˈəʊmə) *n, pl* **angiomas** *or* **angiomata** (-mətə). a tumour consisting of a mass of blood vessels or a mass of lymphatic vessels.

angioplasty (ˈændʒɪəˌplæstɪ) *n* a surgical technique for restoring normal blood flow through an artery narrowed or blocked by atherosclerosis, either by inserting a balloon into it or by using a laser beam.

angiosperm (ˈændʒɪəˌspɜːm) *n* any seed-bearing plant in which the ovules are enclosed in an ovary which develops into the fruit after fertilization; any flowering plant. Cf. **gymnosperm.**
▸ **ˌangioˈspermous** *adj*

Angkor ★ (ˈæŋkɔː) *n* a large area of ruins in NW Cambodia, containing **Angkor Thom** (tɔːm), the capital of the former Khmer Empire, and **Angkor Wat** (wɒt), a three-storey temple, which were overgrown with dense jungle from the 14th to 19th centuries.

angle[1] (ˈæŋgᵊl) *n* **1** the space between two straight lines or two planes that extend from a common point. **2** the shape formed by two such lines or planes. **3** the extent to which one such line or plane diverges from the other, measured in degrees or radians. **4** a recess; corner. **5** point of view: *look at the question from another angle.* **6** See **angle iron.** ◆ *vb* **angles, angling, angled. 7** to move in or bend into angles or an angle. **8** (*tr*) to produce (an article, statement, etc.) with a particular point of view. **9** (*tr*) to present or place at an angle. **10** (*intr*) to turn in a different direction. ORIG C14: from F, from OL *angulus* corner

angle[2] (ˈæŋgᵊl) *vb* **angles, angling, angled.** (*intr*) **1** to fish with a hook and line. **2** (often foll. by *for*) to attempt to get: *he angled for a compliment.* ◆ *n* **3** *Obs.* a fish-hook. ORIG OE *angul* fish-hook

Angle (ˈæŋgᵊl) *n* a member of a people from N Germany who invaded and settled large parts of E and N England in the 5th and 6th centuries A.D. ORIG from L *Anglus,* of Gmc origin, an inhabitant of *Angul,* a district in Schleswig, a name identical with OE *angul* hook, ANGLE[2], referring to its shape
▸ **ˈAnglian** *adj, n*

angle iron *n* an iron or a steel structural bar that has an L-shaped cross section. Also called: **angle, angle bar.**

angle of incidence *n* **1** the angle that a line or beam of radiation makes with a line perpendicular to the surface at the point of incidence. **2** the angle between the chord line of an aircraft wing or tailplane and the aircraft's longitudinal axis.

angle of reflection *n* the angle that a beam of reflected radiation makes with the normal to a surface at the point of reflection.

angle of refraction *n* the angle that a refracted beam of radiation makes with the normal to the surface between two media at the point of refraction.

angle of repose *n* the maximum angle to the horizontal at which rock, soil, etc., will remain without sliding.

angler (ˈæŋglə) *n* **1** a person who fishes with a hook and line. **2** Also called: **anglerfish.** any of various spiny-finned fishes which live at the bottom of the sea and typically have a long movable dorsal fin with which they lure their prey.

Anglesey ★ (ˈæŋgᵊlsɪ) *n* an island and county of N Wales, formerly part of Gwynedd (1974–96), separated from the mainland by the Menai Strait. Administrative centre: Llangefni. Pop.: 68 400 (1994 est.). Area: 720 sq. km (278 sq. miles). Welsh name: **Ynys Môn.**

Anglia ★ (ˈæŋglɪə) *n* a Latin name for **England.**

Anglican (ˈæŋglɪkən) *adj* **1** denoting or relating to the Church of England or one of the churches in communion with it. ◆ *n* **2** a member of the Anglican Church. ORIG C17: from Med. L, from *Anglicus* English, from L *Anglī* the Angles
▸ **ˈAnglicanˌism** *n*

Anglicism (ˈæŋglɪˌsɪzəm) *n* **1** a word, or idiom peculiar to the English language, esp. as spoken in England. **2** an English mannerism, etc. **3** the fact of being English.

anglicize *or* **anglicise** (ˈæŋglɪˌsaɪz) *vb* **anglicizes, anglicizing, anglicized** *or* **anglicises, anglicising, anglicised.** (*sometimes cap.*) to make or become English in outlook, etc.

angling (ˈæŋglɪŋ) *n* the art or sport of catching fish with a baited hook or other lure, such as a fly; fishing.

Anglo (ˈæŋgləʊ) *n, pl* **Anglos. 1** *US.* a White inhabitant of the US who is not of Latin extraction. **2** *Canad.* an English-speaking Canadian, esp. one of Anglo-Celtic origin; an Anglo-Canadian.

Anglo- *combining form.* denoting English or England: *Anglo-Saxon.* ORIG from Med. L *Anglii*

Anglo-American *adj* **1** of relations between England and the United States. ◆ *n* **2** *Chiefly US.* an inhabitant of the United States who was or whose ancestors were born in England.

Anglo-Catholic *adj* **1** of or relating to a group within the Anglican Church that stresses the Catholic elements in its teaching and practice. ◆ *n* **2** a member of this group.
▸ **ˌAnglo-CaˈtholiˌCism** *n*

Anglo-Egyptian Sudan ★ *n* the former name (1899–1956) of the **Sudan.**

Anglo-French *adj* **1** of England and France. **2** of Anglo-French. ◆ *n* **3** the Norman-French language of medieval England.

Anglo-Indian *adj* **1** of England and India. **2** denoting or relating to Anglo-Indians. **3** (of a word) introduced into English from an Indian language. ◆ *n* **4** a person of mixed English and Indian descent. **5** an English person who lives or has lived for a long time in India.

Anglomania (ˌæŋgləʊˈmeɪnɪə) *n* excessive respect for English customs, etc.
▸ **ˌAngloˈmaniˌac** *n*

Anglo-Norman *adj* **1** relating to the Norman conquerors of England, their society, or their language. ◆ *n* **2** a Norman inhabitant of England after 1066. **3** the Anglo-French language.

Anglophile (ˈæŋgləʊfɪl, -ˌfaɪl) *or* **Anglophil** *n* a person having admiration for England or the English.

Anglophobe (ˈæŋgləʊˌfəʊb) *n* **1** a person who hates or fears England or its people. **2** *Canad.* a person who hates or fears Canadian Anglophones.

Anglophone (ˈæŋgləˌfəʊn) (*often not cap.*) ◆ *n* **1** a person who speaks English. ◆ *adj* **2** speaking English.

★ people and places

Anglo-Saxon *n* **1** a member of any of the West Germanic tribes that settled in Britain from the 5th century A.D. **2** the language of these tribes. See **Old English. 3** any White person whose native language is English. **4** *Inf.* plain blunt English. ◆ *adj* **5** forming part of the Germanic element in Modern English: *"forget" is an Anglo-Saxon word.* **6** of the Anglo-Saxons or the Old English language. **7** of the White Protestant culture of Britain, Australia, and the US.

Angola ★ (æŋ'gəʊlə) *n* a republic in SW Africa, on the Atlantic: includes the enclave of Cabinda, north of the River Congo; a Portuguese possession from 1575 until its independence in 1975; factional violence. It consists of a narrow coastal plain with a large fertile plateau in the east. Currency: kwanza. Religion: Christian majority. Capital: Luanda. Pop.: 11 178 000 (1999 est.). Area: 1 246 693 sq. km (481 351 sq. miles).
▸ **An'golan** *adj, n*

angora (æŋ'gɔːrə) *n* (*sometimes cap.*) **1** the long soft hair of the Angora goat or the fur of the Angora rabbit. **2** yarn, cloth, or clothing made from this hair or fur. **3** (*as modifier*): *an angora sweater.* ◆ See also **mohair.** ORIG from *Angora,* former name of Ankara, in Turkey

Angora goat (æŋ'gɔːrə) *n* a breed of domestic goat with long soft hair.

Angora rabbit *n* a breed of rabbit with long silky fur.

Angostura ★ (*Spanish* aŋgɔs'tura) *n* the former name (1764–1846) for **Ciudad Bolívar.**

angostura bark (ˌæŋgə'stjʊərə) *n* the bitter aromatic bark of certain South American trees, formerly used to reduce fever. ORIG C18: from ANGOSTURA

angostura bitters *pl n* (*often cap.*) *Trademark.* a bitter aromatic tonic, used as a flavouring in alcoholic drinks.

angry ('æŋgrɪ) *adj* **angrier, angriest. 1** feeling or expressing annoyance, animosity, or resentment. **2** suggestive of anger: *angry clouds.* **3** severely inflamed: *an angry sore.*
▸ **'angrily** *adv*

> **USAGE NOTE** It was formerly considered incorrect by some people to talk about being *angry at* a person. The evidence suggests that *with* is still more common, but *at* appears more often in American sources.

angst (æŋst) *n* an acute but nonspecific sense of anxiety or remorse. ORIG G

angstrom ('æŋstrəm) *n* a unit of length equal to 10^{-10} metre, used principally to express the wavelengths of electromagnetic radiations. Symbol: Å or A Also called: **angstrom unit.** ORIG C20: after Anders J. ÅNGSTRÖM

Ångström ★ ('æŋstrəm; *Swedish* 'ɔŋstrœm) *n* **Anders Jonas** ('andərs 'juːnas). 1814–74, Swedish physicist, noted for his work on spectroscopy, solar physics, and geomagnetism.

Anguilla ★ (æŋ'gwɪlə) *n* an island in the Caribbean, in the Leeward Islands, a United Kingdom overseas territory: part of the British associated state of St Kitts-Nevis-Anguilla from 1967 until 1980, when it reverted to the status of a British dependency. Pop.: 8960 (1992). Area: 90 sq. km (35 sq. miles).

anguine ('æŋgwɪn) *adj* of or similar to a snake. ORIG C17: from L *anguīnus,* from *anguis* snake

anguish ('æŋgwɪʃ) *n* **1** extreme pain or misery; mental or physical torture; agony. ◆ *vb* **2** to afflict or be afflicted with anguish. ORIG C13: from OF *angoisse* a strangling, from L, from *angustus* narrow
▸ **'anguished** *adj*

angular ('æŋgjʊlə) *adj* **1** lean or bony. **2** awkward or stiff. **3** having an angle or angles. **4** placed at an angle. **5** measured by an angle or by the rate at which an angle changes; *angular momentum; angular velocity.* ORIG C15: from L *angulāris,* from *angulus* ANGLE[1]

angularity (ˌæŋgjʊ'lærɪtɪ) *n, pl* **angularities. 1** the condition of being angular. **2** an angular shape.

Angus ★ ('æŋgəs) *n* a council area and historic county of E Scotland, on the North Sea: part of Tayside region (1975–96); restored as an independent unitary authority (with adjusted borders) in 1996. Administrative centre: Forfar. Pop.: 111 020 (1996 est.). Area: 2181 sq. km (842 sq. miles).

Angus Og ★ (əʊg) *n Irish myth.* the god of love and beauty.

Anhalt ★ (*German* 'anhalt) *n* a former duchy and state of central E Germany, now part of the state of Saxony-Anhalt: part of East Germany until 1990.

anhedral (æn'hiːdrəl) *n* the downward inclination of an aircraft wing in relation to the lateral axis.

Anhui *or* **Anhwei** ★ ('æn'weɪ) *n* a province of E China, crossed by the Yangtze River. Capital: Hefei. Pop.: 61 270 000 (1997 est.). Area: 139 860 sq. km (54 000 sq. miles).

anhydride (æn'haɪdraɪd) *n* **1** a compound that has been formed from another compound by dehydration. **2** a compound that forms an acid or base when added to water. ORIG C19: from ANHYDR(OUS) + -IDE

anhydrous (æn'haɪdrəs) *adj* containing no water, esp. no water of crystallization. ORIG C19: from Gk *anudros;* see AN-, HYDRO-

Aniakchak ★ (ˌænɪ'æktʃæk) *n* an active volcanic crater in SW Alaska, on the Alaska Peninsula: the largest explosion crater in the world. Height: 1347 m (4420 ft). Diameter: 9 km (6 miles).

anil ('ænɪl) *n* a leguminous West Indian shrub which is a source of indigo. Also called: **indigo.** ORIG C16: from Port., from Ar. *an-nīl,* the indigo

aniline ('ænɪlɪn, -ˌliːn) *n* a colourless oily poisonous liquid used in the manufacture of dyes, plastics, and explosives. Formula: $C_6H_5NH_2$.

aniline dye *n* any synthetic dye originally made from aniline, obtained from coal tar.

anima ('ænɪmə) *n* (in Jungian psychology) **a** the feminine principle as present in the male unconscious. **b** the inner personality. ORIG L: air, breath, spirit, fem of ANIMUS

animadversion (ˌænɪmæd'vɜːʃən) *n* criticism or censure.

animadvert (ˌænɪmæd'vɜːt) *vb* (*intr*) **1** (usually foll. by *on* or *upon*) to comment with strong criticism (upon); make censorious remarks (about). **2** to make an observation or comment. ORIG C16: from L *animadvertere* to notice, from *animus* mind + *advertere* to turn to

animal ('ænɪməl) *n* **1** *Zool.* any living organism characterized by voluntary movement, the possession of specialized sense organs enabling rapid response to stimuli, and the ingestion of complex organic substances. **2** any mammal, esp. except man. **3** a brutish person. **4** *Facetious.* a person or thing (esp. in **no such animal**). ◆ *adj* **5** of, relating to, or derived from animals. **6** of or relating to physical needs or desires; carnal; sensual. ORIG C14: from L, from *animālis* (adj) living, breathing; see ANIMA

animalcule (ˌænɪ'mælkjuːl) *n* a microscopic animal such as an amoeba or rotifer. ORIG C16: from NL *animalculum* a small animal
▸ **ˌani'malcular** *adj*

animal husbandry *n* the science of breeding, rearing, and caring for farm animals.

animalism ('ænɪməˌlɪzəm) *n* **1** preoccupation with physical matters; sensuality. **2** the doctrine that man lacks a spiritual nature. **3** a mode of behaviour typical of animals.

animality (ˌænɪ'mælɪtɪ) *n* **1** the animal side of man, as opposed to the intellectual or spiritual. **2** the characteristics of an animal.

animalize *or* **animalise** ('ænɪməˌlaɪz) *vb* **animalizes, animalizing, animalized** *or* **animalises, animalising, animalised.** (*tr*) to rouse to brutality or sensuality or make brutal or sensual.
▸ **ˌanimali'zation** *or* **ˌanimali'sation** *n*

animal magnetism *n* **1** the quality of being attractive, esp. to members of the opposite sex. **2** *Obs.* hypnotism.

animal rights *pl n* **a** the rights of animals to be protected from exploitation and abuse by humans. **b** (*as modifier*): *the animal-rights lobby.*

animal spirits *pl n* boisterous exuberance. ORIG from a vital force once supposed to be dispatched by the brain to all points of the body

animate *vb* ('ænɪˌmeɪt), **animates, animating, animated.** (*tr*) **1** to give life to or cause to come alive. **2** to make energetic or lively. **3** to encourage or inspire. **4** to impart motion to. **5** to record on film or video tape so as to give movement to. ◆ *adj* ('ænɪmɪt). **6** having life. **7** spirited or lively. ORIG C16: from L *animāre* to make alive, from *anima* breath, spirit
▸ **'aniˌmatedly** *adv*

animated cartoon *n* a film produced by photographing a series of gradually changing drawings, etc., which give the illusion of movement when the series is projected rapidly.

animation (ˌænɪ'meɪʃən) *n* **1** vivacity. **2** the condition of being alive. **3** the techniques used in the production of animated cartoons.

animato (ˌænɪ'mɑːtəʊ) *adj, adv Music.* lively; animated. ORIG It.

animatronics (ˌænɪmə'trɒnɪks) *n* (*functioning as sing*) a branch of film and theatre technology that combines traditional puppetry techniques with electronics to create lifelike animated effects. ORIG C20: from ANIMA(TION) + (ELEC)TRONICS

animé ('ænɪˌmeɪ, -mɪ) *n* any of various resins, esp. that obtained from a tropical American leguminous tree. ORIG F: from ?

animism ('ænɪˌmɪzəm) *n* **1** the belief that natural objects have desires and intentions. **2** (in the philosophies of Plato and Pythagoras) the hypothesis that there is an immaterial force that animates the universe. ORIG C19: from L *anima* vital breath, spirit
▸ **animistic** (ˌænɪ'mɪstɪk) *adj*

animosity (ˌænɪ'mɒsɪtɪ) *n, pl* **animosities.** a powerful and active dislike or hostility. ORIG C15: from LL *animōsitās,* from ANIMUS

animus ('ænɪməs) *n* **1** intense dislike; hatred; animosity. **2** motive or purpose. **3** (in Jungian psychology) the masculine principle present in the female unconscious. ORIG C19: from L: mind, spirit

anion ('ænˌaɪən) *n* a negatively charged ion; an ion that is attracted to the anode during electrolysis. Cf. **cation.** ORIG C19: from ANA- + ION
▸ **anionic** (ˌænaɪ'ɒnɪk) *adj*

anise ('ænɪs) *n* a Mediterranean umbelliferous plant having clusters of small yellowish-white flowers and liquorice-flavoured seeds. ORIG C13: from OF *anis,* via L from Gk *anison*

aniseed ('ænɪˌsiːd) *n* the liquorice-flavoured aromatic seeds of the anise plant, used medicinally for expelling intestinal gas and in cookery.

anisette (ˌænɪ'zɛt, -'sɛt) *n* a liquorice-flavoured liqueur made from aniseed. ORIG C19: from F

anisotropic (ænˌaɪsəʊ'trɒpɪk) *adj* **1** having different physical properties in different directions: *anisotropic crystals.* **2** (of a plant) responding unequally to an external stimulus in different parts.
▸ **anˌiso'tropically** *adv* ▸ **anisotropy** (ˌænaɪ'sɒtrəpɪ) *n*

Anjou ★ (*French* ɑ̃ʒu) *n* a former province of W France, in the Loire valley: a medieval countship from the 10th century, belonging to the English crown from 1154 until 1204; annexed by France in 1480.

Ankara ★ ('æŋkərə) *n* the capital of Turkey: an ancient city in the Anatolian highlands: first a capital in the 3rd century B.C., in the Celtic kingdom of Galatia. Pop.: 2 782 200 (1994 est.). Ancient name: **Ancyra.** Former name (until 1930): **Angora.**

ankh (æŋk) *n* a tau cross with a loop on the top, symbolizing eternal life: often appearing in Egyptian personal names, such as Tutankhamen. ORIG from Egyptian *'nh* life, soul

Anking ★ ('ɑːn'kɪŋ) *n* a variant transliteration of the Chinese name for **Anqing.**

ankle ('æŋkᵊl) *n* **1** the joint connecting the leg and the foot. **2** the part of the leg just above the foot. ORIG C14: from ON

ankle biter *n Austral. sl.* a child.

anklebone ('æŋkᵊlˌbəʊn) *n* the nontechnical name for **talus**[1].

anklet ('æŋklɪt) *n* an ornamental chain worn around the ankle.

ankylose *or* **anchylose** ('æŋkɪˌləʊz) *vb* **ankyloses, ankylosing, ankylosed** *or* **anchyloses, anchylosing, anchylosed.** (of bones in a joint, etc.) to fuse or stiffen by ankylosis.

ankylosis *or* **anchylosis** (ˌæŋkɪ'ləʊsɪs) *n* abnormal adhesion or immobility of the bones in a joint, as by a fibrous growth of tissues within the joint. ORIG C18: from NL, from Gk *ankuloun* to crook
▸ **ankylotic** *or* **anchylotic** (ˌæŋkɪ'lɒtɪk) *adj*

anna ('ænə) *n* a former Indian coin, worth one sixteenth of a rupee. ORIG C18: from Hindi *ānā*

Annaba ★ ('ænəbə) *n* a port in NE Algeria: site of the Roman city of Hippo Regius. Pop.: 222 518 (1987). Former name: **Bône.**

annals ('ænᵊlz) *pl n* **1** yearly records of events. **2** history in general. **3** regular reports of the work of a society, learned body, etc. ORIG C16: from L (*librī*) *annālēs* yearly (books), from *annus* year
▸ **'annalist** *n* ▸ **ˌannal'istic** *adj*

Annan ★ ('ænæn) *n* **Kofi** ('kəʊfɪ). born 1938, Ghanaian international civil servant; secretary-general of the United Nations from 1997.

Annapolis ★ (ə'næpəlɪs) *n* the capital of Maryland, near the mouth of the Severn River on Chesapeake Bay: site of the US Naval Academy. Pop.: 33 187 (1990).

Annapolis Royal ★ *n* a town in SE Canada in W Nova Scotia on an arm of the Bay of Fundy: the first settlement in Canada (1605). Pop.: 633 (1991). Former name (until 1710): **Port Royal.**

Annapurna *or* **Anapurna** ★ (ˌænə'pʊənə) *n* a massif of the Himalayas, in Nepal. Highest peak: 8078 m (26 502 ft).

Ann Arbor ★ (æn 'ɑːbə) *n* a city in SE Michigan: seat of the University of Michigan. Pop.: 108 817 (1994 est.).

annates ('æneɪts, -əts) *pl n RC Church.* the first year's revenue of a see, etc., paid to the pope. ORIG C16: from F, from Med. L *annāta,* from L *annus* year

annatto *or* **anatto** (ə'nætəʊ) *n, pl* **annattos** *or* **anattos. 1** a small tropical American tree having pulpy seeds that yield a dye. **2** the yellowish-red dye obtained from the seeds of this tree, used for colouring fabrics, butter, varnish, etc. ORIG from Carib

Anne ★ (æn) *n* **1 Princess,** the Princess Royal. born 1950, daughter of Elizabeth II of Great Britain and Northern Ireland; a noted horsewoman and president of the Save the Children Fund. **2 Queen.** 1665–1714, queen of Great Britain and Ireland (1702–14), daughter of James II. **3 Saint.** (in Christian tradition) the mother of the Virgin Mary. Feast day: July 26 or 25.

anneal (ə'niːl) *vb* **1** to temper or toughen (something) by heat treatment to remove internal stress, crystal defects, and dislocations. **2** (*tr*) to toughen or strengthen (the will, determination, etc.). ◆ *n* **3** an act of annealing. ORIG OE *onǣlan,* from ON + *ǣlan* to burn, from *āl* fire
▸ **an'nealer** *n*

Anne Boleyn ★ *n* See (Anne) **Boleyn.**

Annecy ★ (*French* ansi) *n* **1** a city and resort in E France, on Lake Annecy. Pop.: 51 143 (1990). **2 Lake.** a lake in E France, in the Alps.

annelid ('ænəlɪd) *n* **1** a worm in which the body is divided into segments both externally and internally, as the earthworms. ◆ *adj* **2** of such worms. ORIG C19: from NL *Annelida,* from OF, ult. from L *ānulus* ring
▸ **annelidan** (ə'nɛlɪdən) *n, adj*

Anne of Austria ★ *n* 1601–66, wife of Louis XIII of France and daughter of Philip III of Spain: regent of France (1643–61) for her son Louis XIV.

Anne of Cleves ★ (kliːvz) *n* 1515–57, the fourth wife of Henry VIII of England; their marriage (1540) was annulled.

annex *vb* (æ'nɛks). (*tr*) **1** to join or add, esp. to something larger. **2** to add (territory) by conquest or occupation. **3**

to add or append as a condition, etc. **4** to appropriate without permission. ◆ *n* ('ænɛks). **5** a variant spelling (esp. US) of **annexe.** ORIG C14: from Med. L, from L *annectere* to attach to, from *nectere* to join
▸ **an'nexable** *adj* ▸ **,annex'ation** *n*

annexe *or esp. US* **annex** ('ænɛks) *n* **1a** an extension to a main building. **1b** a building used as an addition to a main one nearby. **2** something added, esp. a supplement to a document.

Annigoni ★ (*Italian* anni'go:ni) *n* **Pietro** ('pjɛ:tro). 1910–88, Italian painter; noted esp. for his portraits.

annihilate (ə'naɪə,leɪt) *vb* **annihilates, annihilating, annihilated.** (*tr*) **1** to destroy completely; extinguish. **2** *Inf.* to defeat totally, as in argument. ORIG C16: from LL, from L *nihil* nothing
▸ **an,nihi'lation** *n* ▸ **an'nihi,lator** *n*

anniversary (,ænɪ'vɜ:sərɪ) *n, pl* **anniversaries. 1** the date on which an event occurred in some previous year: *a wedding anniversary.* **2** the celebration of this. ◆ *adj* **3** of or relating to an anniversary. ORIG C13: from L *anniversārius* returning every year, from *annus* year + *vertere* to turn

anno Domini ('ænəʊ 'dɒmɪ,naɪ, -,ni:) **1** the full form of **A.D.** ◆ *n* **2** *Inf.* advancing old age. ORIG L: in the year of our Lord

annotate ('ænəʊ,teɪt, 'ænə,teɪt) *vb* **annotates, annotating, annotated.** to supply (a written work) with critical or explanatory notes. ORIG C18: from L *annotāre,* from *nota* mark
▸ **'anno,tative** *adj* ▸ **'anno,tator** *n*

annotation (,ænəʊ'teɪʃən, ,ænə'teɪʃən) *n* **1** the act of annotating. **2** a note added in explanation, etc., esp. of some literary work.

announce (ə'naʊns) *vb* **announces, announcing, announced. 1** (*tr; may take a clause as object*) to make known publicly. **2** (*tr*) to declare the arrival of: *to announce a guest.* **3** (*tr; may take a clause as object*) to presage: *the dark clouds announced rain.* **4** (*intr*) to work as an announcer, as on radio or television. ORIG C15: from OF, from L *annuntiāre,* from *nuntius* messenger
▸ **an'nouncement** *n*

announcer (ə'naʊnsə) *n* a person who announces, esp. one who reads the news, etc., on radio or television.

annoy (ə'nɔɪ) *vb* **1** to irritate or displease. **2** to harass with repeated attacks. ORIG C13: from OF, from LL *inodiāre* to make hateful, from L *in odiō (esse)* (to be) hated, from *odium* hatred
▸ **an'noyer** *n* ▸ **an'noying** *adj* ▸ **an'noyingly** *adv*

annoyance (ə'nɔɪəns) *n* **1** the feeling of being annoyed. **2** the act of annoying. **3** a person or thing that annoys.

annual ('ænjʊəl) *adj* **1** occurring, done, etc., once a year or every year; yearly: *an annual income.* **2** lasting for a year: *an annual subscription.* ◆ *n* **3** a plant that completes its life cycle in one year. **4** a book, magazine, etc., published once every year. ORIG C14: from LL, from L *annuus* yearly, from *annus* year
▸ **'annually** *adv*

annual general meeting *n* the statutory meeting of the directors and shareholders of a company or of the members of a society, held once every financial year. Abbrev.: **AGM**.

annualize *or* **annualise** ('ænjʊə,laɪz) *vb* **annualizes, annualizing, annualized** *or* **annualises, annualising, annualised.** (*tr*) to convert (a rate of interest) to an annual rate when it is quoted for a period less than a year: *an annualized percentage rate.*

annual percentage rate *n* the annual equivalent of a rate of interest when the rate is quoted more frequently than annually, usually monthly. Abbrev.: **APR.**

annual ring *n* a ring indicating one year's growth, seen in the transverse section of stems and roots of woody plants. Also called: **tree ring.**

annuitant (ə'nju:ɪtənt) *n* a person in receipt of or entitled to an annuity.

annuity (ə'nju:ɪtɪ) *n, pl* **annuities.** a fixed sum payable at specified intervals over a period, such as the recipient's life, or in perpetuity, in return for a premium paid either in instalments or in a single payment. ORIG C15: from F, from Med. L *annuitās,* from L *annuus* ANNUAL

annul (ə'nʌl) *vb* **annuls, annulling, annulled.** (*tr*) to make (something, esp. a law or marriage) void; abolish. ORIG C14: from OF, from LL *adnullāre* to bring to nothing, from L *nullus* not any
▸ **an'nullable** *adj*

annular ('ænjʊlə) *adj* ring-shaped. ORIG C16: from L *annulāris,* from *annulus, ānulus* ring

annular eclipse *n* an eclipse of the sun in which the moon does not cover the entire disc of the sun, so that a ring of sunlight surrounds the shadow of the moon.

annular ligament *n Anat.* any of various ligaments that encircle a part, such as the wrist.

annulate ('ænjʊlɪt, -,leɪt) *adj* having, composed of, or marked with rings. ORIG C19: from L *ānulātus,* from *ānulus* a ring
▸ **,annu'lation** *n*

annulet ('ænjʊlɪt) *n* **1** *Archit.* a moulding in the form of a ring. **2** *Heraldry.* a ring-shaped device on a shield. **3** a little ring. ORIG C16: from L *ānulus* ring + -ET

annulment (ə'nʌlmənt) *n* **1** a formal invalidation, as of a marriage, judicial proceeding, etc. **2** the act of annulling.

annulus ('ænjʊləs) *n, pl* **annuli** (-,laɪ) *or* **annuluses. 1** the area between two concentric circles. **2** a ring-shaped part. ORIG C16: from L, var. of *ānulus* ring

annunciate (ə'nʌnsɪ,eɪt, -ʃɪ-) *vb* **annunciates, annunciating, annunciated.** (*tr*) a less common word for **announce.** ORIG C16: from Med L from L *annuntiāre;* see ANNOUNCE

Annunciation (ə,nʌnsɪ'eɪʃən) *n* **1 the.** the announcement of the Incarnation by the angel Gabriel to the Virgin Mary (Luke 1:26–38). **2** Also called: **Annunciation Day.** the festival commemorating this, on March 25 (Lady Day).

annunciator (ə'nʌnsɪ,eɪtə) *n* **1** a device that gives a visual indication as to which of a number of electric circuits has operated, such as an indicator showing in which room a bell has been rung. **2** a device giving an audible signal indicating the position of a train. **3** an announcer.

annus horribilis ('ænʊs hɒ'ri:bɪlɪs) *n* a terrible year. ORIG C20: from L, modelled on ANNUS MIRABILIS, first used by Elizabeth II of the year 1992

annus mirabilis ('ænʊs mɪ'ræbɪlɪs) *n, pl* **anni mirabiles** ('ænaɪ mɪ'ræbɪli:z). a year of wonders, catastrophes, or other notable events. ORIG L: wonderful year

anoa (ə'nəʊə) *n* the smallest of the cattle tribe, having small straight horns and inhabiting the island of Celebes in Indonesia. ORIG from a native name in Celebes

anode ('ænəʊd) *n* **1** the positive electrode in an electrolytic cell or in an electronic valve. **2** the negative terminal of a primary cell. Cf. **cathode.** ORIG C19: from Gk *anodos* a way up, from *hodos* a way; alluding to the movement of the current
▸ **anodal** (eɪ'nəʊdᵊl) *or* **anodic** (ə'nɒdɪk) *adj*

anodize *or* **anodise** ('ænə,daɪz) *vb* **anodizes, anodizing, anodized** *or* **anodises, anodising, anodised.** to coat (a metal, such as aluminium) with a protective oxide film by electrolysis.

anodyne ('ænə,daɪn) *n* **1** a drug that relieves pain. **2** anything that alleviates mental distress. ◆ *adj* **3** capable of relieving pain or distress. ORIG C16: from L, from Gk *anōdunos* painless, from AN- + *odunē* pain

anoint (ə'nɔɪnt) *vb* (*tr*) **1** to smear or rub over with oil. **2** to apply oil to as a sign of consecration or sanctification. ORIG C14: from OF, from L *inunguere,* from IN-[2] + *unguere* to smear with oil
▸ **a'nointer** *n* ▸ **a'nointment** *n*

anointing of the sick *n RC Church.* a sacrament in which a person who is seriously ill or dying is anointed by a priest with consecrated oil. Former name: **extreme unction.**

anomalistic (ə,nɒmə'lɪstɪk) *adj* **1** *Astron.* **1a** (of a month) measured between successive perigees of the moon. **1b**

(of a year) between successive perihelia of the earth. **2** anomalous.

anomalous (əˈnɒmələs) *adj* deviating from the normal or usual order, type, etc. ORIG C17: from LL, from Gk *anōmalos* uneven, inconsistent, from AN- + *homalos* even, from *homos* one and the same
▸ **aˈnomalousness** *n*

anomaly (əˈnɒməlɪ) *n, pl* **anomalies. 1** something anomalous. **2** deviation from the normal; irregularity. **3** *Astron.* the angle between a planet, the sun, and the previous perihelion of the planet.

anomie *or* **anomy** (ˈænəʊmɪ) *n Sociol.* lack of social or moral standards in an individual or society. ORIG from Gk *anomia* lawlessness, from A-[1] + *nomos* law
▸ **anomic** (əˈnɒmɪk) *adj*

anon (əˈnɒn) *adv Arch. or literary.* **1** soon. **2 ever and anon.** now and then. ORIG OE *on āne,* lit.: in one, that is, immediately

anon. *abbrev. for* anonymous.

anonym (ˈænənɪm) *n* **1** a less common word for **pseudonym. 2** an anonymous person or publication.

anonymize *or* **anonymise** (əˈnɒnɪˌmaɪz) *vb* **anonymizes, anonymizing, anonymized** *or* **anonymises, anonymising, anonymised.** (*tr*) to carry out or organize in such a way as to preserve anonymity: *anonymized AIDS screening.*

anonymous (əˈnɒnɪməs) *adj* **1** from or by a person, author, etc., whose name is unknown or withheld. **2** having no known name. **3** lacking individual characteristics. **4** (*often cap.*) denoting an organization which provides help to applicants who remain anonymous: *Alcoholics Anonymous.* ORIG C17: via LL from Gk *anōnumos,* from AN- + *onoma* name
▸ **anonymity** (ˌænəˈnɪmɪtɪ) *n*

anopheles (əˈnɒfɪˌliːz) *n, pl* **anopheles.** any of various mosquitoes constituting the genus *Anopheles,* some species of which transmit the malaria parasite to man. ORIG C19: via NL from Gk *anōphelēs* useless, from AN- + *ōphelein* to help

anorak (ˈænəˌræk) *n* **1** a warm waterproof hip-length jacket usually with a hood. **2** *Inf.* a boring or socially inept person. ORIG from Eskimo *ánorâq*

anorexia (ˌænɒˈrɛksɪə) *n* **1** loss of appetite. **2** Also called: **anorexia nervosa** (nɜːˈvəʊsə). a disorder characterized by fear of becoming fat and refusal of food, leading to debility and even death. ORIG C17: via NL from Gk, from AN- + *orexis* appetite
▸ **ˌanoˈrectic** *or* **ˌanoˈrexic** *adj, n*

anosmia (ænˈɒzmɪə, -ˈɒs-) *n* loss of the sense of smell. ORIG C19: from NL, from AN- + Gk *osmē* smell
▸ **anosmatic** (ˌænɒzˈmætɪk) *or* **anˈosmic** *adj*

another (əˈnʌðə) *determiner* **1a** one more: *another chance.* **1b** (*as pron*): *help yourself to another.* **2a** a different: *another era from ours.* **2b** (*as pron*): *to try one, then another.* **3a** a different example of the same sort. **3b** (*as pron*): *we got rid of one, but I think this is another.* ORIG C14: orig. *an other*

A.N. Other *n Brit.* an unnamed person: used in team lists, etc., to indicate a place that remains to be filled.

Anouilh ★ (*French* anuj) *n* **Jean** (ʒɑ̃). 1910–87, French dramatist, noted for his reinterpretations of Greek myths: his works include *Eurydice* (1942), *Antigone* (1944), and *Becket* (1959).

anoxia (ænˈɒksɪə) *n* lack or deficiency of oxygen. ORIG C20: from AN- + OX(YGEN) + -IA
▸ **anˈoxic** *adj*

Anqing (ˈɑːnˈtʃɪŋ) *or* **Anking** ★ *n* a city in E China, in SW Anhui province on the Yangtze River: famous seven-storeyed pagoda. Pop.: 250 718 (1990 est.).

Anschluss (ˈænʃlʊs) *n* a political or economic union, esp. the annexation of Austria by Nazi Germany (1938). ORIG G, from *anschliessen* to join

Anselm ★ (ˈænsɛlm) *n* **Saint.** 1033–1109, Italian Benedictine monk; archbishop of Canterbury (1093–1109): one of the founders of scholasticism; author of *Cur Deus Homo?* (*Why did God become Man?*). Feast day: Aug. 21.

anserine (ˈænsəˌraɪn) *adj* of or resembling a goose. ORIG C19: from L *anserīnus,* from *anser* goose

Ansermet ★ (*French* ɑ̃sɛrmɛ) *n* **Ernest** (ɛrnɛst). 1883–1969, Swiss orchestral conductor; principal conductor of Diaghilev's Ballet Russe.

answer (ˈɑːnsə) *n* **1** a reply, either spoken or written, as to a question, request, letter, or article. **2** a reaction or response: *drunkenness was his answer to disappointment.* **3** a solution, esp. of a mathematical problem. ◆ *vb* **4** (when *tr, may take a clause as object*) to reply or respond (to) by word or act: *to answer a question; to answer the door.* **5** (*tr*) to reply correctly to; solve: *I could answer only three questions.* **6** (*intr;* usually foll. by *to*) to respond or react: *the steering answers to the slightest touch.* **7a** (when *intr,* often foll. by *for*) to meet the requirements (of); be satisfactory (for): *this will answer his needs.* **7b** to be responsible (to a person or for a thing). **8** (when *intr,* foll. by *to*) to match or correspond (esp. in **answer** (*or* **answer to**) **the description**). **9** (*tr*) to give a defence or refutation of (a charge) or in (an argument). ORIG OE *andswaru* an answer; see SWEAR

answerable (ˈɑːnsərəbᵊl) *adj* **1** (*postpositive;* foll. by *for* or *to*) responsible or accountable: *answerable to one's boss.* **2** able to be answered.

answer back *vb* (*adv*) to reply rudely to (a person, esp. someone in authority) when one is expected to remain silent.

answering machine *n* a device by which a telephone call is answered automatically and the caller leaves a recorded message. In full: **telephone answering machine.** Also called: **answerphone.**

ant (ænt) *n* **1** a small social insect of a widely distributed hymenopterous family, typically living in highly organized colonies of winged males, wingless sterile females (workers), and fertile females (queens). Related adj: **formic. 2 white ant.** another name for a **termite.** ORIG OE *æmette*

-ant *suffix forming adjectives and nouns.* causing or performing an action or existing in a certain condition: *pleasant; deodorant; servant.* ORIG from L *-ant,* ending of present participles of the first conjugation

antacid (æntˈæsɪd) *n* **1** a substance used to treat acidity, esp. in the stomach. ◆ *adj* **2** having the properties of this substance.

Antaeus ★ (ænˈtiːəs) *n Greek myth.* an African giant who was invincible as long as he touched the ground, but was lifted into the air by Hercules and crushed to death.

antagonism (ænˈtægəˌnɪzəm) *n* **1** openly expressed and usually mutual opposition. **2** the inhibiting or nullifying action of one substance or organism on another.

antagonist (ænˈtægənɪst) *n* **1** an opponent or adversary. **2** any muscle that opposes the action of another. **3** a drug that counteracts the effects of another drug.
▸ **anˌtagoˈnistic** *adj* ▸ **anˌtagoˈnistically** *adv*

antagonize *or* **antagonise** (ænˈtægəˌnaɪz) *vb* **antagonizes, antagonizing, antagonized** *or* **antagonises, antagonising, antagonised.** (*tr*) **1** to make hostile; annoy or irritate. **2** to act in opposition to or counteract. ORIG C17: from Gk, from ANTI- + *agōnizesthai* to strive, from *agōn* contest
▸ **anˌtagoniˈzation** *or* **anˌtagoniˈsation** *n*

Antakiya ★ (ˌæntɑːˈkiːjə) *n* the Arabic name for **Antioch.**

Antakya ★ (ɑnˈtɑkjɑ) *n* the Turkish name for **Antioch.**

antalkali (æntˈælkəˌlaɪ) *n, pl* **antalkalis** *or* **antalkalies.** a substance that neutralizes alkalis.

Antananarivo ★ (ˌæntəˌnænəˈriːvəʊ) *n* the capital of Madagascar, on the central plateau: founded in the 17th century by a Hova chief; university (1961). Pop.: 1 052 835 (1993). Former name: **Tananarive.**

Antarctic ★ (æntˈɑːktɪk) *n* **1 the.** Also called: **Antarctic Zone.** Antarctica and the surrounding waters. ◆ *adj* **2** of or relating to the south polar regions. ORIG C14: via L from Gk *antarktikos;* see ANTI-, ARCTIC

Antarctica ★ (æntˈɑːktɪkə) *n* a continent around the South Pole: consists of an ice-covered plateau, 1800–3000 m (6000 ft to 10 000 ft) above sea level, and mountain ranges rising to 4500 m (15 000 ft) with some volcanic peaks; average temperatures all below freezing and human settlement is confined to research stations.

Antarctic Archipelago ★ *n* the former name of the **Palmer Archipelago.**

Antarctic Circle *n* the imaginary circle around the earth, parallel to the equator, at latitude 66° 32′ S.

Antarctic Ocean ★ *n* the sea surrounding Antarctica, consisting of the most southerly parts of the Pacific, Atlantic, and Indian Oceans. Also called: **Southern Ocean.**

Antarctic Peninsula ★ *n* the largest peninsula of Antarctica, between the Weddell Sea and the Pacific: consists of Graham Land in the north and the Palmer Peninsula in the south. Former name (until 1964): **Palmer Peninsula.**

ant bear *n* another name for **aardvark.**

ante (ˈæntɪ) *n* **1** the gaming stake put up before the deal in poker by the players. **2** *Inf.* a sum of money representing a person's share, as in a syndicate. **3 up the ante.** *Inf.* to increase the costs, risks, or considerations involved in taking an action or reaching a conclusion. ◆ *vb* **antes, anteing, anted** *or* **anteed. 4** to place (one's stake) in poker. **5** (usually foll. by *up*) *Inf.* to pay.

ante- *prefix* before in time or position: *antedate; antechamber.* ORIG from L

anteater (ˈæntˌiːtə) *n* any of several toothless mammals having a long tubular snout used for eating termites.

antebellum (ˌæntɪˈbɛləm) *adj* of or during the period before a war, esp. the American Civil War. ORIG L *ante bellum,* lit.: before the war

antecede (ˌæntɪˈsiːd) *vb* **antecedes, anteceding, anteceded.** (*tr*) to go before; precede. ORIG C17: from L *antecēdere,* from *cēdere* to go

antecedent (ˌæntɪˈsiːdᵊnt) *n* **1** an event, etc., that happens before another. **2** *Grammar.* a word or phrase to which a pronoun refers. In "People who live in glass houses shouldn't throw stones," *people* is the antecedent of *who.* **3** *Logic.* the first hypothetical clause in a conditional statement. ◆ *adj* **4** preceding in time or order; prior.
▸ ˌ**anteˈcedence** *n*

antecedents (ˌæntɪˈsiːdᵊnts) *pl n* **1** ancestry. **2** a person's past history.

antechamber (ˈæntɪˌtʃeɪmbə) *n* an anteroom. ORIG C17: from OF, from It. *anticamera;* see ANTE-, CHAMBER

antedate (ˈæntɪˌdeɪt) *vb* (*tr*) **1** to be or occur at an earlier date than. **2** to affix or assign a date to (a document, event, etc.) that is earlier than the actual date. **3** to cause to occur sooner. ◆ *n* **4** an earlier date.

antediluvian (ˌæntɪdɪˈluːvɪən) *adj* **1** of the ages before the biblical Flood. **2** old-fashioned. ◆ *n* **3** an antediluvian person or thing. ORIG C17: from ANTE- + L *dīluvium* flood

antelope (ˈæntɪˌləʊp) *n, pl* **antelopes** *or* **antelope.** any of a group of mammals of Africa and Asia. They are typically graceful, having long legs and horns, and include the gazelles, springbok, impala, and dik-diks. ORIG C15: from OF, from Med. L, from LGk *antholops* a legendary beast

antemeridian (ˌæntɪməˈrɪdɪən) *adj* before noon; in the morning. ORIG C17: from L

ante meridiem (ˈæntɪ məˈrɪdɪəm) the full form of **a.m.** ORIG L, from ANTE- + *merīdiēs* midday

antenatal (ˌæntɪˈneɪtᵊl) *adj* occurring or present before birth; during pregnancy.

antenna (ænˈtɛnə) *n* **1** (*pl* **antennae** (-niː)) one of a pair of mobile appendages on the heads of insects, crustaceans, etc., that often respond to touch and taste but may be specialized for swimming. **2** (*pl* **antennas**) an aerial. ORIG C17: from L: sail yard, from ?
▸ **anˈtennal** *or* **anˈtennary** *adj*

antenuptial contract (ˌæntɪˈnʌpʃəl) *n* (in South Africa) a marriage contract effected prior to the wedding giving each partner control over his or her property.

antependium (ˌæntɪˈpɛndɪəm) *n, pl* **antependia** (-dɪə). a covering hung over the front of an altar. ORIG C17: from Med. L, from L ANTE- + *pendēre* to hang

antepenult (ˌæntɪpɪˈnʌlt) *n* the third last syllable in a word. ORIG C16: shortened from L (*syllaba*) *antepaenultima;* see ANTE-, PENULT

antepenultimate (ˌæntɪpɪˈnʌltɪmɪt) *adj* **1** third from last. ◆ *n* **2** anything that is third from last.

ante-post *adj Brit.* (of a bet) placed before the runners in a race are confirmed.

anterior (ænˈtɪərɪə) *adj* **1** at or towards the front. **2** earlier. **3** *Zool.* of or near the head end. **4** *Bot.* (of part of a flower or leaf) farthest away from the main stem. ORIG C17: from L, comp. of *ante* before

anteroom (ˈæntɪˌruːm, -ˌrʊm) *n* a room giving entrance to a larger room, often used as a waiting room.

anthelion (ænˈθiːlɪən) *n, pl* **anthelia** (-lɪə). **1** a faint halo sometimes seen in high altitude regions around a shadow cast onto fog. **2** a white spot occasionally appearing at the same height as and opposite to the sun. ORIG C17: from LGk, from *anthēlios* opposite the sun, from ANTE- + *hēlios* sun

anthelmintic (ˌænθɛlˈmɪntɪk) *or* **anthelminthic** (ˌænθɛlˈmɪnθɪk) *n Med.* another name for **vermifuge.**

anthem (ˈænθəm) *n* **1** a song of loyalty: *a national anthem.* **2** a musical composition for a choir, usually set to words from the Bible. **3** a religious chant sung antiphonally. ORIG OE *antemne,* from LL *antiphōna* ANTIPHON

anthemis (ænˈθiːmɪs) *n* any of several cultivated varieties of camomile. ORIG NL, from L, from Gk *anthos* flower

anther (ˈænθə) *n* the terminal part of a stamen consisting of two lobes each containing two sacs in which the pollen matures. ORIG C18: from NL, from L, from Gk *anthēros* flowery, from *anthos* flower

antheridium (ˌænθəˈrɪdɪəm) *n, pl* **antheridia** (-ɪə). the male sex organ of algae, fungi, mosses, etc. ORIG C19: from NL, dim. of *anthēra* ANTHER

ant hill *n* a mound of soil, leaves, etc., near the entrance of an ants' or termites' nest, deposited there by the ants or termites while constructing the nest.

anthologize *or* **anthologise** (ænˈθɒləˌdʒaɪz) *vb* **anthologizes, anthologizing, anthologized** *or* **anthologises, anthologising, anthologised.** to compile or put into an anthology.

anthology (ænˈθɒlədʒɪ) *n, pl* **anthologies. 1** a collection of literary passages, esp. poems, by various authors. **2** any printed collection of literary pieces, songs, etc. ORIG C17: from Med. L, from Gk, lit.: a flower gathering, from *anthos* flower + *legein* to collect
▸ **anˈthologist** *n*

Anthony ★ (ˈæntənɪ) *n* **Saint.** ?251–?356 A.D., Egyptian hermit, commonly regarded as the founder of Christian monasticism. Feast day: Jan. 17.

Anthony of Padua ★ *n* **Saint.** 1195–1231, Franciscan friar, who preached in France and Italy. Feast day: June 13.

anthozoan (ˌænθəˈzəʊən) *n* **1** any of the sessile marine coelenterates of the class *Anthozoa,* including corals and sea anemones, in which the body is in the form of a polyp. ◆ *adj* also: **actinozoan. 2** of or relating to these.

anthracene (ˈænθrəˌsiːn) *n* a colourless crystalline solid, used in the manufacture of chemicals and as crystals in scintillation counters. ORIG C19: from ANTHRAX + -ENE

anthracite (ˈænθrəˌsaɪt) *n* a hard coal that burns slowly with a nonluminous flame giving out intense heat. Also called: **hard coal.** ORIG C19: from L, from Gk *anthrakitēs* coal-like, from *anthrax* coal
▸ **anthracitic** (ˌænθrəˈsɪtɪk) *adj*

anthracosis (ˌænθrəˈkəʊsɪs) *n* a lung disease due to inhalation of coal dust.

anthrax (ˈænθræks) *n, pl* **anthraces** (-θrəˌsiːz). **1** a highly infectious bacterial disease of animals, esp. cattle and sheep, which can be transmitted to man. **2** a pustule caused by this disease. ORIG C19: from LL, from Gk: carbuncle

anthropic principle *n Astron.* the cosmological theory that the presence of life in the universe limits the ways in which the very early universe could have evolved.

anthropo- *combining form.* indicating man or human: *anthropology.* ORIG from Gk *anthrōpos*

anthropocentric (ˌænθrəpəʊˈsɛntrɪk) *adj* regarding humans as the central factor in the universe.

anthropogenesis (ˌænθrəpəʊˈdʒɛnɪsɪs) *or* **anthropogeny** (ˌænθrəˈpɒdʒɪnɪ) *n* the study of the origins of humans.

anthropoid ('ænθrəˌpɔɪd) *adj* **1** resembling humans. **2** resembling an ape; apelike. ◆ *n* **3** any primate of the suborder *Anthropoidea,* including monkeys, apes, and humans.

anthropoid ape *n* any of a group of primates having no tail, elongated arms, and a highly developed brain, including gibbons, orang-utans, chimpanzees, and gorillas.

anthropology (ˌænθrə'pɒlədʒɪ) *n* the study of human beings, their origins, institutions, religious beliefs, social relationships, etc.
▸ **ˌanthropo'logical** *adj* ▸ **ˌanthro'pologist** *n*

anthropometry (ˌænθrə'pɒmɪtrɪ) *n* the comparative study of sizes and proportions of the human body.
▸ **ˌanthropo'metric** *or* **ˌanthropo'metrical** *adj*

anthropomorphic (ˌænθrəpə'mɔːfɪk) *adj* **1** of or relating to anthropomorphism. **2** resembling the human form.
▸ **'anthropoˌmorph** *n* ▸ **ˌanthropo'morphically** *adv*

anthropomorphism (ˌænθrəpə'mɔːfɪzəm) *n* the attribution of human form or behaviour to a deity, animal, etc.

anthropomorphous (ˌænθrəpə'mɔːfəs) *adj* **1** shaped like a human being. **2** another word for **anthropomorphic.**

anthropophagi (ˌænθrə'pɒfəˌgaɪ) *pl n, sing* **anthropophagus** (-gəs). cannibals. ORIG C16: from L, from Gk *anthrōpophagos;* see ANTHROPO-, -PHAGE

anthroposophy (ˌænθrə'pɒsəfɪ) *n* the spiritual and mystical teachings of Rudolph Steiner, based on the belief that creative activities are psychologically valuable, esp. for educational and therapeutic purposes.
▸ **ˌanthropo'sophic** *adj*

anti ('æntɪ) *Inf.* ◆ *adj* **1** opposed to a party, policy, attitude, etc. ◆ *n* **2** an opponent.

anti- *prefix* **1** against; opposing: *anticlerical.* **2** opposite to: *anticlimax.* **3** rival; false: *antipope.* **4** counteracting or neutralizing: *antifreeze; antihistamine.* **5** designating the antiparticle of the particle specified: *antineutron.* ORIG from Gk *anti*

anti-atom (ˌæntɪ'ætəm) *n* an atom composed of antiparticles, in which the nucleus contains antiprotons with orbiting positrons.

anti-aircraft (ˌæntɪ'ɛəkrɑːft) *n* (*modifier*) of or relating to defence against aircraft attack: *anti-aircraft batteries.*

anti-apartheid *adj* opposed to a policy of racial segregation.

antiar ('æntɪˌɑː) *n* another name for **upas** (senses 1, 2). ORIG from Javanese

antiballistic missile (ˌæntɪbə'lɪstɪk) *n* a ballistic missile designed to destroy another ballistic missile in flight.

Antibes ★ (*French* ɑ̃tib) *n* a port and resort in SE France, on the Mediterranean: an important Roman town. Pop.: 60 000 (latest est.).

antibiosis (ˌæntɪbaɪ'əʊsɪs) *n* an association between two organisms, esp. microorganisms, that is harmful to one of them.

antibiotic (ˌæntɪbaɪ'ɒtɪk) *n* **1** any of various chemical substances, such as penicillin, produced by microorganisms, esp. fungi, or made synthetically, and capable of destroying microorganisms, esp. bacteria. ◆ *adj* **2** of or relating to antibiotics.

antibody ('æntɪˌbɒdɪ) *n, pl* **antibodies.** any of various proteins produced in the blood in response to an antigen. By becoming attached to antigens on infectious organisms antibodies can render them harmless.

antic ('æntɪk) *Arch.* ◆ *n* **1** an actor in a ludicrous or grotesque part; clown. ◆ *adj* **2** fantastic; grotesque. ◆ See also **antics.** ORIG C16: from It. *antico* something grotesque (from its application to fantastic carvings found in ruins of ancient Rome)

anticathode (ˌæntɪ'kæθəʊd) *n* the target electrode for the stream of electrons in a vacuum tube, esp. an X-ray tube.

Antichrist ★ ('æntɪˌkraɪst) *n* **1** *Bible.* the antagonist of Christ, expected by early Christians to appear and reign over the world until overthrown at Christ's Second Coming. **2** (*sometimes not cap.*) an enemy of Christ or Christianity.

anticipant (æn'tɪsɪpənt) *adj* **1** operating in advance. ◆ *n* **2** a person who anticipates.

anticipate (æn'tɪsɪˌpeɪt) *vb* **anticipates, anticipating, anticipated.** (*mainly tr*) **1** (*may take a clause as object*) to foresee and act in advance of; forestall: *I anticipated his punch.* **2** (*also intr*) to mention (something) before its proper time: *don't anticipate the climax of the story.* **3** (*may take a clause as object*) to regard as likely; expect. **4** to make use of in advance of possession: *he anticipated his salary in buying a leather jacket.* ORIG C16: from L *anticipāre* to take before, from *anti-* ANTE- + *capere* to take
▸ **an'ticiˌpator** *n* ▸ **an'ticiˌpatory** *or* **an'ticipative** *adj*

> **USAGE NOTE** Some people consider that the use of *anticipate* to mean *expect* should be avoided. However, the Bank of English shows that this usage is well established. Moreover, the use of *anticipate* adds a suggestion of being prepared for the event referred to. The most common expressions associated with this use are clauses beginning with *that* and *problems.* This use is also markedly commoner in American sources than in British ones.

anticipation (ænˌtɪsɪ'peɪʃən) *n* **1** the act of anticipating; expectation, premonition, or foresight. **2** *Music.* an unstressed, usually short note introduced before a downbeat.

anticlerical (ˌæntɪ'klɛrɪkᵊl) *adj* **1** opposed to the power and influence of the clergy, esp. in politics. ◆ *n* **2** a supporter of an anticlerical party.
▸ **ˌanti'clericalism** *n*

anticlimax (ˌæntɪ'klaɪmæks) *n* **1** a disappointing or ineffective conclusion to a series of events, etc. **2** a sudden change from a serious subject to one that is disappointing or ludicrous.
▸ **anticlimactic** (ˌæntɪklaɪ'mæktɪk) *adj*

anticline ('æntɪˌklaɪn) *n* a formation of stratified rock raised up, by folding, into a broad arch so that the strata slope down on both sides from a common crest.
▸ **ˌanti'clinal** *adj*

anticlockwise (ˌæntɪ'klɒkˌwaɪz) *adv, adj* in the opposite direction to the rotation of the hands of a clock. US equivalent: **counterclockwise.**

anticoagulant (ˌæntɪkəʊ'ægjʊlənt) *adj* **1** acting to prevent or retard coagulation, esp. of blood. ◆ *n* **2** an agent that prevents or retards coagulation.

anti-Communist *adj* opposed to Communism or its principles.

anticonvulsant (ˌæntɪkən'vʌlsənt) *n* **1** any of a class of drugs used to relieve convulsions. ◆ *adj* **2** of or relating to such drugs

Anticosti ★ (ˌæntɪ'kɒstɪ) *n* an island of E Canada, in the Gulf of St Lawrence; part of Quebec. Area: 7881 sq. km (3043 sq. miles).

antics ('æntɪks) *pl n* absurd acts or postures.

anticyclone (ˌæntɪ'saɪkləʊn) *n Meteorol.* a body of moving air of higher pressure than the surrounding air, in which the pressure decreases away from the centre. Also called: **high.**
▸ **anticyclonic** (ˌæntɪsaɪ'klɒnɪk) *adj*

antidazzle mirror (ˌæntɪ'dæzᵊl) *n* a rear-view mirror for road vehicles that only partially reflects headlights behind.

antidepressant (ˌæntɪdɪ'prɛsᵊnt) *n* **1** any of a class of drugs used to alleviate depression. ◆ *adj* **2** of this class of drugs.

antidiuretic hormone (ˌæntɪˌdaɪjʊ'rɛtɪk) *n* another name for **vasopressin.** Abbrev.: **ADH.**

antidote ('æntɪˌdəʊt) *n* **1** *Med.* a drug or agent that counteracts or neutralizes the effects of a poison. **2** anything that counteracts or relieves a harmful condition. ORIG C15: from L, from Gk *antidoton* something given as a countermeasure, from ANTI- + *didonai* to give
▸ **ˌanti'dotal** *adj*

antiemetic (ˌæntɪɪˈmɛtɪk) *adj* **1** preventing vomiting. ◆ *n* **2** any antiemetic drug, such as promethazine.

antifreeze (ˈæntɪˌfriːz) *n* a liquid, usually ethylene glycol (ethanediol), added to water to lower its freezing point, esp. for use in an internal-combustion engine.

antifungal (ˌæntɪˈfʌŋgᵊl) *adj* **1** inhibiting the growth of fungi. **2** (of a drug) possessing antifungal activity and therefore used to treat fungal infections. ◆ Also: **antimycotic.**

antigen (ˈæntɪdʒən, -ˌdʒɛn) *n* a substance, usually a toxin produced by a bacterium, that stimulates the production of antibodies. ORIG C20: from ANTI(BODY) + -GEN

Antigone ★ (ænˈtɪgənɪ) *n Greek myth.* daughter of Oedipus and Jocasta, who was condemned to death for cremating the body of her brother Polynices in defiance of an edict of her uncle, King Creon of Thebes.

Antigua ★ (ænˈtiːgə) *n* an island in the Caribbean, one of the Leeward Islands: a British colony, with its dependency Barbuda, until 1967, when it became a British associated state; it became independent in 1981 as part of the state of Antigua and Barbuda. Area: 279 sq. km (108 sq. miles).
▸ **Anˈtiguan** *adj, n*

Antigua and Barbuda ★ *n* a state in the Caribbean, comprising the islands of Antigua, Barbuda, and Redonda: gained independence in 1981: a member of the Commonwealth. Official language: English. Religion: Christian majority. Currency: East Caribbean dollar. Capital: St John's. Pop.: 69 100 (1999 est.). Area: 442 sq. km (171 sq. miles).

antihero (ˈæntɪˌhɪərəʊ) *n, pl* **antiheroes.** a central character in a novel, play, etc., who lacks the traditional heroic virtues.

antihistamine (ˌæntɪˈhɪstəˌmiːn, -mɪn) *n* any drug that neutralizes the effects of histamine, used esp. in the treatment of allergies.

antihydrogen (ˌæntɪˈhaɪdrɪdʒən) *n* hydrogen in which the nucleus is an antiproton with an orbiting positron.

anti-inflammatory *adj* **1** reducing inflammation. ◆ *n, pl* **anti-inflammatories. 2** any anti-inflammatory drug, such as cortisone, aspirin, or ibuprofen.

anti-inflationary *adj* (of an economic policy) designed to reduce or counteract the effects of inflation.

antiknock (ˌæntɪˈnɒk) *n* a compound, such as lead tetraethyl, added to petrol to reduce knocking in the engine.

Anti-Lebanon ★ *n* a mountain range running north and south between Syria and Lebanon, east of the Lebanon Mountains. Highest peak: Mount Hermon, 2814 m (9232 ft).

Antilles ★ (ænˈtɪliːz) *pl n* **the.** a group of islands in the Caribbean consisting of the **Greater Antilles** and the **Lesser Antilles.**

antilock brake (ˈæntɪˌlɒk) *n* a brake fitted to some road vehicles that prevents skidding and improves control by sensing and compensating for overbraking. Also called: **ABS brake.**

antilogarithm (ˌæntɪˈlɒgəˌrɪðəm) *n* a number whose logarithm to a given base is a given number: *100 is the antilogarithm of 2 to base 10.* Often shortened to **antilog.**
▸ **ˌantiˌlogaˈrithmic** *adj*

antilogy (ænˈtɪlədʒɪ) *n, pl* **antilogies.** a contradiction in terms. ORIG C17: from Gk *antilogia*

antimacassar (ˌæntɪməˈkæsə) *n* a cloth covering the back and arms of chairs, etc., to prevent soiling. ORIG C19: from ANTI- + MACASSAR (OIL)

antimagnetic (ˌæntɪmægˈnɛtɪk) *adj* of a material that does not acquire permanent magnetism when exposed to a magnetic field.

antimalarial (ˌæntɪməˈlɛərɪəl) *adj* **1** effective in the treatment of malaria. ◆ *n* **2** an antimalarial drug or agent.

antimasque (ˈæntɪˌmɑːsk) *n* a comic dance, presented between the acts of a masque.

antimatter (ˈæntɪˌmætə) *n* a form of matter composed of antiparticles, such as antihydrogen, consisting of antiprotons and positrons.

antimetabolite (ˌæntɪmɪˈtæbəˌlaɪt) *n* any drug that acts by disrupting the normal growth of a cell. Antimetabolites are used in cancer treatment.

antimissile (ˌæntɪˈmɪsaɪl) *adj* **1** relating to defensive measures against missile attack: *an antimissile system.* ◆ *n* **2** Also called: **antimissile missile.** a defensive missile used to intercept and destroy attacking missiles.

antimony (ˈæntɪmənɪ) *n* a toxic metallic element that exists in two allotropic forms and is added to alloys to increase their strength and hardness. Symbol: Sb; atomic no.: 51; atomic wt.: 121.75. ORIG C15: from Med. L *antimōnium,* from ?
▸ **antimonial** (ˌæntɪˈməʊnɪəl) *adj*

antimuon (ˌæntɪˈmjuːɒn) *n* the antiparticle of a muon.

antimycotic (ˌæntɪmaɪˈkɒtɪk) *adj* another word for **antifungal.**

anti-Nazi *adj* opposed to Nazism or its principles.

antinoise (ˈæntɪˌnɔɪz) *n* sound generated so that it is out of phase with a noise, such as that made by an engine, in order to reduce the noise level by interference.

antinomian (ˌæntɪˈnəʊmɪən) *adj* **1** relating to the doctrine that by faith a Christian is released from the obligation of adhering to any moral law. ◆ *n* **2** a member of a Christian sect holding such a doctrine.
▸ **ˌantiˈnomianism** *n*

antinomy (ænˈtɪnəmɪ) *n, pl* **antinomies. 1** opposition of one law, principle, or rule to another. **2** *Philosophy.* contradiction existing between two apparently indubitable propositions. ORIG C16: from L, from Gk: conflict between laws, from ANTI- + *nomos* law
▸ **antinomic** (ˌæntɪˈnɒmɪk) *adj*

antinovel (ˈæntɪˌnɒvᵊl) *n* a type of prose fiction in which conventional or traditional novelistic elements are rejected.

antinuclear (ˌæntɪˈnjuːklɪə) *adj* opposed to nuclear weapons or nuclear power.

Antioch ★ (ˈæntɪˌɒk) *n* a city in S Turkey, on the Orontes River: ancient commercial centre and capital of Syria (300–64 B.C.); early centre of Christianity. Pop.: 137 200 (1994 est.). Arabic name: **Antakiya.** Turkish name: **Antakya.**

Antiochus III ★ (ænˈtaɪəkəs) *n* known as *Antiochus the Great.* 242–187 B.C., king of Syria (223–187), who was forced (190) to surrender most of Asia Minor to the Romans.

Antiochus IV ★ *n* ?215–164 B.C., Seleucid king of Syria (175–164), who attacked the Jews and provoked the revolt of the Maccabees.

antioxidant (ˌæntɪˈɒksɪdənt) *n* **1** any substance that retards deterioration by oxidation, esp. of fats, oils, foods, or rubber. **2** *Biol.* a substance, such as vitamin C, vitamin E, or beta carotene, that counteracts the damaging effects of oxidation in a living organism.

antiparticle (ˈæntɪˌpɑːtɪkᵊl) *n* any of a group of elementary particles that have the same mass as their corresponding particle but have a charge of equal magnitude but opposite sign. When a particle collides with its antiparticle mutual annihilation occurs.

antipasto (ˌæntɪˈpɑːstəʊ, -ˈpæs-) *n, pl* **antipastos.** a course of hors d'oeuvres in an Italian meal. ORIG It.: before food

antipathetic (ænˌtɪpəˈθɛtɪk, ˌæntɪpə-) *or* **antipathetical** *adj* (often foll. by *to*) having or arousing a strong aversion.

antipathy (ænˈtɪpəθɪ) *n, pl* **antipathies. 1** a feeling of dislike or hostility. **2** the object of such a feeling. ORIG C17: from L, from Gk, from ANTI- + *patheia* feeling

antipersonnel (ˌæntɪˌpɜːsəˈnɛl) *adj* (of weapons, etc.) designed to cause casualties to personnel rather than to destroy equipment.

antiperspirant (ˌæntɪˈpɜːspərənt) *n* **1** a substance applied to the skin to reduce or prevent perspiration. ◆ *adj* **2** reducing perspiration.

antiphlogistic (ˌæntɪfləˈdʒɪstɪk) *adj* **1** of or relating to the prevention or alleviation of inflammation. ◆ *n* **2** an antiphlogistic drug.

antiphon ('æntɪfən) *n* **1** a short passage, usually from the Bible, recited or sung as a response after certain parts of a liturgical service. **2** a psalm, hymn, etc., chanted or sung in alternate parts. **3** any response. ORIG C15: from LL *antiphōna* sung responses, from LGk, pl of *antiphōnon* (something) responsive, from ANTI- + *phōnē* sound
▸ **antiphonal** (æn'tɪfənəl) *adj*

antiphonary (æn'tɪfənərɪ) *n, pl* **antiphonaries.** a bound collection of antiphons.

antiphony (æn'tɪfənɪ) *n, pl* **antiphonies. 1** antiphonal singing. **2** any musical or other sound effect that answers or echoes another.

antipode ('æntɪpəʊd) *n* the exact or direct opposite.
▸ **antipodal** (æn'tɪpəd'l) *adj*

antipodes (æn'tɪpə,di:z) *pl n* **1** either or both of two places that are situated diametrically opposite one another on the earth's surface. **2** the people who live there. **3** (*often cap.*) **the.** Australia and New Zealand. ORIG C16: via LL from Gk, pl of *antipous* having the feet opposite, from ANTI- + *pous* foot
▸ **antipodean** (æn,tɪpə'di:ən) *adj*

Antipodes Islands ★ *pl n* **the.** a group of small uninhabited islands in the South Pacific, southeast of and belonging to New Zealand. Area: 62 sq. km (24 sq. miles).

antipope ('æntɪ,pəʊp) *n* a rival pope elected in opposition to one who has been canonically chosen.

anti-Protestant *adj* opposed to Protestantism.

antipsychotic (,æntɪsaɪ'kɒtɪk) *adj* **1** preventing or treating psychosis. ◆ *n* **2** any antipsychotic drug, such as chlorpromazine: used to treat such conditions as schizophrenia.

antipyretic (,æntɪpaɪ'rɛtɪk) *adj* **1** preventing or alleviating fever. ◆ *n* **2** an antipyretic remedy or drug.

antiquarian (,æntɪ'kwɛərɪən) *adj* **1** concerned with the study of antiquities or antiques. ◆ *n* **2** a less common name for **antiquary.**
▸ **,anti'quarianism** *n*

antiquark ('æntɪ,kwɑ:k) *n* the antiparticle of a quark.

antiquary ('æntɪkwərɪ) *n, pl* **antiquaries.** a person who collects, deals in, or studies antiques or ancient works of art. Also called: **antiquarian.**

antiquate ('æntɪ,kweɪt) *vb* **antiquates, antiquating, antiquated.** (*tr*) to make obsolete or old-fashioned. ORIG C15: from L *antīquāre* to make old, from *antīquus* ancient
▸ **'anti,quated** *adj*

antique (æn'ti:k) *n* **1a** a decorative object, piece of furniture, or other work of art created in an earlier period, that is valued for its beauty, workmanship, and age. **1b** (*as modifier*): *an antique shop.* **2** any object made in an earlier period. **3 the.** the style of ancient art, esp. Greek or Roman. ◆ *adj* **4** made in or in the style of an earlier period. **5** of or belonging to the distant past, esp. of ancient Greece or Rome. **6** *Inf.* old-fashioned. **7** *Arch.* aged or venerable. ◆ *vb* **antiques, antiquing, antiqued. 8** (*tr*) to give an antique appearance to. ORIG C16: from L *antīquus* ancient, from *ante* before

antiquities (æn'tɪkwɪtɪz) *pl n* remains or relics, such as statues, buildings, or coins, that date from ancient times.

antiquity (æn'tɪkwɪtɪ) *n, pl* **antiquities. 1** the quality of being ancient: *a vase of great antiquity.* **2** the far distant past, esp. preceding the Middle Ages. **3** the people of ancient times collectively.

antiracism (,æntɪ'reɪsɪzəm) *n* the policy of challenging racism and promoting racial tolerance.
▸ **,anti'racist** *n, adj*

anti-riot *adj* designed for or employed in controlling crowds: *anti-riot police.*

anti-roll bar *n* a crosswise rubber-mounted bar in the suspension of a motor vehicle, which counteracts the movement downwards on one side when cornering.

antirrhinum (,æntɪ'raɪnəm) *n* any plant of the genus *Antirrhinum,* esp. the snapdragon, which has two-lipped flowers of various colours. ORIG C16: via L from Gk *antirrhinon,* from ANTI- (imitating) + *rhis* nose

Antisana ★ (*Spanish* anti'sana) *n* a volcano in N central Ecuador, in the Andes. Height: 5756 m (18 885 ft).

antiscorbutic (,æntɪskɔ:'bju:tɪk) *adj* **1** preventing or curing scurvy. ◆ *n* **2** an antiscorbutic agent.

anti-Semite *n* a person who persecutes or discriminates against Jews.
▸ **,anti-Se'mitic** *adj* ▸ **,anti-'Semitism** *n*

antisepsis (,æntɪ'sɛpsɪs) *n* **1** destruction of undesirable microorganisms, such as those that cause disease or putrefaction. **2** the state of being free from such microorganisms.

antiseptic (,æntɪ'sɛptɪk) *adj* **1** of or producing antisepsis. **2** entirely free from contamination. **3** *Inf.* lacking spirit or excitement. ◆ *n* **4** an antiseptic agent.
▸ **,anti'septically** *adv*

antiserum (,æntɪ'sɪərəm) *n, pl* **antiserums** *or* **antisera** (-rə). blood serum containing antibodies against a specific antigen, used to treat or provide immunity to a disease.

antisocial (,æntɪ'səʊʃəl) *adj* **1** avoiding the company of other people; unsociable. **2** contrary or injurious to the interests of society in general.

antispasmodic (,æntɪspæz'mɒdɪk) *adj* **1** preventing or arresting spasms. ◆ *n* **2** an antispasmodic drug.

antistatic (,æntɪ'stætɪk) *adj* (of a substance, textile, etc.) retaining sufficient moisture to provide a conducting path, thus avoiding the effects of static electricity.

antistrophe (æn'tɪstrəfɪ) *n* (in ancient Greek drama) **a** the second of two movements made by a chorus during the performance of a choral ode. **b** the second part of a choral ode sung during this movement. ◆ See **strophe.** ORIG C17: via LL from Gk *antistrophē* an answering turn, from ANTI- + *strophē* a turning
▸ **antistrophically** (,æntɪ'strɒfɪkəlɪ) *adv*

antitank (,æntɪ'tæŋk) *adj* designed to immobilize or destroy armoured vehicles.

antithesis (æn'tɪθɪsɪs) *n, pl* **antitheses** (-,si:z). **1** the exact opposite. **2** contrast or opposition. **3** *Rhetoric.* the juxtaposition of contrasting ideas or words to produce an effect of balance, such as *my words fly up, my thoughts remain below.* ORIG C15: via L from Gk: a setting against, from ANTI- + *tithenai* to place
▸ **antithetical** (,æntɪ'θɛtɪk'l) *adj*

antitoxin (,æntɪ'tɒksɪn) *n* **1** an antibody that neutralizes a toxin. **2** blood serum that contains a specific antibody.
▸ **,anti'toxic** *adj*

antitrades ('æntɪ,treɪdz) *pl n* winds in the upper atmosphere blowing in the opposite direction from and above the trade winds.

antitrust (,æntɪ'trʌst) *n* (*modifier*) *Chiefly US.* regulating or opposing trusts, monopolies, cartels, or similar organizations.

antitussive (,æntɪ'tʌsɪv) *n* **1** any of a class of drugs used to suppress or alleviate coughing. ◆ *adj* **2** of or relating to such drugs. ORIG from ANTI- + L *tussis* a cough

antitype ('æntɪ,taɪp) *n* **1** a person or thing that is foreshadowed or represented by a type or symbol. **2** an opposite type.
▸ **antitypical** (,æntɪ'tɪpɪk'l) *adj*

antivenin (,æntɪ'vɛnɪn) *or* **antivenene** (,æntɪvɪ'ni:n) *n* an antitoxin that counteracts a specific venom, esp. snake venom. ORIG C19: from ANTI- + VEN(OM) + -IN

antiviral (,æntɪ'vaɪrəl) *adj* **1** inhibiting the growth of viruses. ◆ *n* **2** any antiviral drug.

antler ('æntlə) *n* one of a pair of bony outgrowths on the heads of male deer and some related species of either sex. ORIG C14: from OF *antoillier*
▸ **'antlered** *adj*

antlion ('ænt,laɪən) *n* **1** any of various insects which resemble dragonflies and are most common in tropical regions. **2** the larva of this insect, which buries itself in the sand to await its prey.

Antoinette ★ (*French* ɑ̃twanɛt) *n* See **Marie Antoinette.**

Antonello da Messina ★ (,æntə'nɛləʊ) *n* ?1430–?79, Italian painter, born in Sicily.

Antonescu ★ (,æntɒ'nɛskju:) *n* **Ion.** 1882–1946, Romanian general and statesman; appointed prime minister (1940) by King Carol II: executed for war crimes.

Antonine Wall ★ ('æntənaɪn) *n* a Roman frontier defence work across S Scotland, extending between the River Clyde and the Firth of Forth. It was built in 142 A.D. on the orders of Antoninus Pius.

Antoninus ★ (ˌæntəˈnaɪnəs) *n* See **Marcus Aurelius Antoninus.**

Antoninus Pius ★ *n* 86–161 A.D., emperor of Rome (138–161); adopted son and successor of Hadrian.

Antonioni ★ (ˌæntəʊnɪˈəʊnɪ) *n* **Michelangelo** (mike'landʒelo). born 1912, Italian film director; his films include *Blow-Up* (1966), *Zabriskie Point* (1970), and *Beyond the Clouds* (1995).

antonomasia (ˌæntənəˈmeɪzɪə) *n* **1** the substitution of a title or epithet for a proper name, such as *his highness.* **2** the use of a proper name for an idea: *he is a Daniel come to judgment.* ORIG C16: via L from Gk, from *antonomazein* to name differently, from *onoma* name

Antony ★ ('æntənɪ) *n* **Mark.** Latin name *Marcus Antonius.* ?83–30 B.C., Roman general who served under Julius Caesar and became a member of the second triumvirate (43). He defeated Brutus and Cassius at Philippi (42) but having repudiated his wife for Cleopatra, he was defeated by Octavian (Augustus) at Actium (31).

antonym ('æntənɪm) *n* a word that means the opposite of another. ORIG C19: from Gk, from ANTI- + *onoma* name
▸ **antonymous** (æn'tɒnɪməs) *adj*

Antrim ★ ('æntrɪm) *n* **1** a historic county of NE Northern Ireland, famous for the Giant's Causeway on the N coast: in 1973 it was replaced for administrative purposes by local government districts. Area: 3046 sq. km (1176 sq. miles). **2** a district in E Northern Ireland, bordering the NE shore of Lough Neagh: livestock, synthetic fibres. Administrative centre: Antrim. Pop.: 44 516 (1991). Area: 562 sq. km (217 sq. miles).

antrum ('æntrəm) *n, pl* **antra** (-trə). *Anat.* a natural cavity, hollow, or sinus, esp. in a bone. ORIG C14: from L: cave, from Gk *antron*
▸ **'antral** *adj*

Antung ★ ('æn'tuŋ) *n* a variant transliteration of the Chinese name for **Andong.**

Antwerp ★ ('æntwɜːp) *n* **1** a province of N Belgium. Pop.: 1 637 857 (1998 est.). Area: 2859 sq. km (1104 sq. miles). **2** a port in N Belgium, capital of Antwerp province, on the River Scheldt: a major European port. Pop.: 455 852 (1996 est.). Flemish name: **Antwerpen** ('ɑntwɛrpə). French name: **Anvers.**

Anu ★ ('ɑːnuː) *n Babylonian myth.* the sky god.

ANU *abbrev. for* Australian National University.

Anubis ★ (əˈnjuːbɪs) *n Egyptian myth.* a deity, a son of Osiris, who conducted the dead to judgment. He is represented as having a jackal's head and was identified by the Greeks with Hermes.

Anuradhapura ★ (əˈnʊərədəˌpʊərə, ˌʌnʊˈrɑːdə-) *n* a town in Sri Lanka: ancient capital of Ceylon; site of the sacred bo tree and place of pilgrimage for Buddhists. Pop.: 42 600 (1995 est.).

anuresis (ˌænjʊˈriːsɪs) *n* inability to urinate. ORIG C20: NL, from AN- + Gk *ouresis* urination

anus ('eɪnəs) *n* the excretory opening at the end of the alimentary canal. ORIG C16: from L

Anvers ★ (ɑ̃vɛr) *n* the French name for **Antwerp.**

anvil ('ænvɪl) *n* **1** a heavy iron or steel block on which metals are hammered during forging. **2** any part having a similar shape or function, such as the lower part of a telegraph key. **3** *Anat.* the nontechnical name for **incus.** ORIG OE *anfealt*

anxiety (æŋˈzaɪɪtɪ) *n, pl* **anxieties. 1** a state of uneasiness or tension caused by apprehension of possible misfortune, danger, etc. **2** intense desire; eagerness. **3** *Psychol.* a state of intense apprehension, common in mental illness or after a very distressing experience. ORIG C16: from L *anxietas*

anxiety disorder *n* any of various mental disorders characterized by extreme anxiety.

anxious ('æŋkʃəs, 'æŋʃəs) *adj* **1** worried and tense because of possible misfortune, danger, etc. **2** causing anxiety; worrying; distressing: *an anxious time.* **3** intensely desirous: *anxious for promotion.* ORIG C17: from L *anxius;* rel. to L *angere* to torment
▸ **'anxiously** *adv* ▸ **'anxiousness** *n*

any ('ɛnɪ) *determiner* **1a** one, some, or several, as specified, no matter how much, what kind, etc.: *you may take any clothes you like.* **1b** (*as pron; functioning as sing or pl*): *take any you like.* **2** (*usually used with a negative*) **2a** even the smallest amount or even one: *I can't stand any noise.* **2b** (*as pron; functioning as sing or pl*): *don't give her any.* **3** whatever or whichever: *any dictionary will do.* **4** an indefinite or unlimited (amount or number): *any number of friends.* ◆ *adv* **5** (*usually used with a negative*) (foll. by a comp. adj) to even the smallest extent: *it isn't any worse.* ORIG OE *ǣnig*

Anyang ★ ('ɑːnˈjɑːŋ) *n* a town in E China, in Henan province: archaeological site and capital of the Shang dynasty. Pop.: 590 996 (1995).

anybody ('ɛnɪˌbɒdɪ) *pron* **1** any person; anyone. **2** (*usually used with a negative or a question*) a person of any importance: *he isn't anybody.* ◆ *n, pl* **anybodies. 3** (often preceded by *just*) any person at random.

anyhow ('ɛnɪˌhaʊ) *adv* **1** in any case. **2** by any means whatever. **3** carelessly.

any more *or esp. US* **anymore** (ˌɛnɪˈmɔː) *adv* any longer; still; nowadays.

anyone ('ɛnɪˌwʌn) *pron* **1** any person; anybody. **2** (*used with a negative or a question*) a person of any importance: *is he anyone?* **3** (often preceded by *just*) any person at random.

anyplace ('ɛnɪˌpleɪs) *adv US & Canad. inf.* anywhere.

anything ('ɛnɪˌθɪŋ) *pron* **1** any object, event, action, etc., whatever: *anything might happen.* ◆ *n* **2** a thing of any kind: *have you anything to declare?* ◆ *adv* **3** in any way: *he wasn't anything like his father.* **4 anything but.** not in the least: *she was anything but happy.* **5 like anything.** (intensifier): *he ran like anything.*

anyway ('ɛnɪˌweɪ) *adv* **1** in any case; at any rate; nevertheless. **2** in a careless manner. **3** Usually **any way.** in any manner.

anywhere ('ɛnɪˌwɛə) *adv* **1** in, at, or to any place. **2 get anywhere.** to be successful.

anywise ('ɛnɪˌwaɪz) *adv Chiefly US.* in any way.

ANZAAS ('ænzəs, -zæs) *n acronym for* Australian and New Zealand Association for the Advancement of Science.

Anzac ('ænzæk) *n* **1** (in World War I) a soldier serving with the Australian and New Zealand Army Corps. **2** (now) any Australian or New Zealand soldier. **3** the Anzac landing at Gallipoli in 1915.

Anzac Day *n* April 25, a public holiday in Australia and New Zealand commemorating the Anzac landing at Gallipoli in 1915.

Anzio ★ ('ænzɪˌəʊ; *Italian* 'antsjo) *n* a port and resort on the W coast of Italy: site of Allied landings in World War II. Pop.: 32 383 (1991 est.).

ANZUS ('ænzəs) *n acronym for* Australia, New Zealand, and the United States, with reference to the security alliance between them.

AO *abbrev. for* Officer of the Order of Australia.

A/O *or* **a/o** (accounting, etc.) *abbrev. for* account of.

AOB *or* **a.o.b.** *abbrev. for* any other business.

AOC *abbrev. for* appellation d'origine contrôlée: the highest French wine classification; indicates that the wine meets strict requirements concerning area of production, strength, etc. Cf. **VDQS, vin de pays.**

AONB (in England and Wales) *abbrev. for* area of outstanding natural beauty: an area officially designated as requiring protection to conserve and enhance its natural beauty.

Aorangi-Mount Cook ★ (ˌeɪəʊˈræŋgɪ) *n* the official name for Mount **Cook.**

aorist ('eɪərɪst, 'ɛərɪst) *n Grammar.* a tense of the verb, esp. in classical Greek, indicating past action without reference to whether the action involved was momentary or continuous. ORIG C16: from Gk *aoristos* not limited, from A-[1] + *horistos,* from *horizein* to define

aorta (eɪ'ɔ:tə) *n, pl* **aortas** *or* **aortae** (-ti:). the main vessel in the arterial network, which conveys oxygen-rich blood from the heart. ORIG C16: from NL, from Gk *aortē,* lit.: something lifted, from *aeirein* to raise
▸ **a'ortic** *or* **a'ortal** *adj*

Aosta ★ (*Italian* a'ɔsta) *n* a town in NW Italy, capital of Valle d'Aosta region: Roman remains. Pop.: 36 339 (1990).

Aotearoa ★ ('æɒˌtɪəˌroːə) *n NZ.* the Maori name for New Zealand. ORIG Maori: the long white cloud

aoudad ('ɑ:uˌdæd) *n* a wild mountain sheep of N Africa. Also called: **Barbary sheep.** ORIG from F, from Berber *audad*

Aouita ★ (aʊ'i:tə) *n* **Saïd** (saɪ'i:d). born 1960, Moroccan middle-distance runner: world record holder in the 2000 m (1987–95), 5000 m (1987–94), and 1500 m events (1987–93).

ap (æp) son of: occurring as part of some surnames of Welsh origin: *ap Thomas.* ORIG from Welsh *mab* son

apace (ə'peɪs) *adv* quickly; rapidly. ORIG C14: prob. from OF *à pas,* at a (good) pace

apache (ə'pæʃ) *n* a Parisian gangster or ruffian. ORIG from F: APACHE

Apache (ə'pætʃɪ) *n* **1** (*pl* **Apaches** *or* **Apache**) a member of a North American Indian people inhabiting the southwestern US and N Mexico. **2** the language of this people. ORIG from Mexican Sp.

apanage ('æpənɪdʒ) *n* a variant spelling of **appanage.**

apart (ə'pɑ:t) *adj* (*postpositive*), *adv* **1** to or in pieces: *he had the television apart.* **2** placed or kept separately or for a particular purpose, etc.; aside (esp. in **set** *or* **put apart**). **3** separate in time, place, or position: *he stood apart from the group.* **4** not being taken into account: *these difficulties apart, the project ran smoothly.* **5** individual; distinct: *a race apart.* **6** separately or independently: *considered apart, his reasoning was faulty.* **7 apart from.** (*prep*) besides. ◆ See also **take apart, tell apart.** ORIG C14: from OF *a part* at (the) side

apartheid (ə'pɑ:thaɪt, -heɪt) *n* (formerly, in South Africa) the government policy of racial segregation; officially renounced in 1992. ORIG C20: Afrik., from *apart* APART + *-heid* -HOOD

apartment (ə'pɑ:tmənt) *n* **1** (*often pl*) any room in a building, usually one of several forming a suite, used as living accommodation, offices, etc. **2a** another name (esp. US and Canad.) for **flat**[2]. **2b** (*as modifier*): *apartment house.* ORIG C17: from F *appartement,* from It., from *appartare* to separate

apathetic (ˌæpə'θɛtɪk) *adj* having or showing little or no emotion or interest. ORIG C18: from APATHY + PATHETIC
▸ ˌ**apa'thetically** *adv*

apathy ('æpəθɪ) *n* **1** absence of interest in or enthusiasm for things generally considered interesting or moving. **2** absence of emotion. ORIG C17: from L, from Gk *apatheia,* from A-[1] + *pathos* feeling

apatite ('æpəˌtaɪt) *n* a common naturally occurring mineral consisting basically of calcium fluorophosphate. It is a source of phosphorus and is used in fertilizers. ORIG C19: from G *Apatit,* from Gk *apatē* deceit; from its misleading similarity to other minerals

ape (eɪp) *n* **1** any of various primates in which the tail is very short or absent. **2** (not in technical use) any monkey. **3** an imitator; mimic. ◆ *vb* **apes, aping, aped. 4** (*tr*) to imitate. ORIG OE *apa*
▸ '**apeˌlike** *adj*

APEC *Canad. abbrev. for* Atlantic Provinces Economic Council.

Apeldoorn ★ ('æpəlˌdɔ:n; *Dutch* 'a:pəldo:rn) *n* a town in the Netherlands, in Gelderland province: nearby is the summer residence of the Dutch royal family. Pop.: 149 904 (1995 est.).

Apelles ★ (ə'pɛli:z) *n* 4th century B.C., Greek painter of mythological subjects, none of whose work survives, his fame resting on the testimony of Pliny and other writers.

apeman ('eɪpˌmæn) *n, pl* **apemen.** any of various extinct apelike primates thought to have been the forerunners of modern man.

Apennines ★ ('æpəˌnaɪnz) *pl n* **1** a mountain range in Italy, extending over 1250 km (800 miles) from the northwest to the southernmost tip of the peninsula. Highest peak: Monte Corno, 2912 m (9554 ft). **2** a mountain range lying in the N quadrants of the moon, extending over 950 km along the SE border of the Mare Imbrium and rising to 6200 m.

aperçu *French.* (apɛrsy) *n* **1** an outline. **2** an insight. ORIG from *apercevoir* to PERCEIVE

aperient (ə'pɪərɪənt) *Med.* ◆ *adj* **1** laxative. ◆ *n* **2** a mild laxative. ORIG C17: from L *aperīre* to open

aperiodic (ˌeɪpɪərɪ'ɒdɪk) *adj* **1** not periodic; not occurring at regular intervals. **2** *Physics.* **2a** (of a system or instrument) being damped sufficiently to reach equilibrium without oscillation. **2b** (of an oscillation or vibration) not having a regular period. **2c** (of an electrical circuit) not having a measurable resonant frequency.
▸ **aperiodicity** (ˌeɪpɪərɪə'dɪsɪtɪ) *n*

apéritif (əˌperɪ'ti:f) *n* an alcoholic drink before a meal to whet the appetite. ORIG C19: from F, from Med. L, from L *aperīre* to open

aperture ('æpətʃə) *n* **1** a hole; opening. **2** *Physics.* a usually circular and often variable opening in an optical instrument or device that controls the quantity of radiation entering or leaving it. ORIG C15: from LL *apertūra* opening, from *aperīre* to open

apetalous (eɪ'pɛtələs) *adj* (of flowering plants such as the wood anemone) having no petals. ORIG C18: from NL; see A-[1], PETAL

apex ('eɪpɛks) *n, pl* **apexes** *or* **apices. 1** the highest point; vertex. **2** the pointed end or tip of something. **3** a high point, as of a career. ORIG C17: from L: point

APEX ('eɪpɛks) *n acronym for:* **1** Advance Purchase Excursion, a reduced airline or long-distance rail fare that must be paid a specified number of days in advance. **2** Association of Professional, Executive, Clerical, and Computer Staff.

Apex Club ('eɪpɛks) *n* (in Australia) an association of business and professional men to promote community welfare.
▸ **Apexian** (eɪ'pɛksɪən) *adj, n*

apgar score *or* **rating** ('æpgɑ:) *n* a system for determining the condition of an infant at birth by allotting a maximum of 2 points to each of the following: heart rate, breathing effort, muscle tone, response to stimulation, and colour. ORIG C20: after V. *Apgar* (1909–74), US anaesthetist

aphaeresis *or* **apheresis** (ə'fɪərɪsɪs) *n* the omission of a letter or syllable at the beginning of a word. ORIG C17: via LL from Gk, from *aphairein* to remove

aphasia (ə'feɪzɪə) *n* a disorder of the central nervous system characterized by loss of the ability to communicate, esp. in speech. ORIG C19: via NL from Gk, from A-[1] + *-phasia,* from *phanai* to speak

aphelion (æp'hi:lɪən, ə'fi:-) *n, pl* **aphelia** (-lɪə). the point in its orbit when a planet or comet is at its greatest distance from the sun. ORIG C17: from NL *aphēlium,* from AP(O)- + Gk *hēlios* sun

aphesis ('æfɪsɪs) *n* the gradual disappearance of an unstressed vowel at the beginning of a word, as in *squire* from *esquire.* ORIG C19: from Gk, from *aphienai* to set free
▸ **aphetic** (ə'fɛtɪk) *adj*

aphid ('eɪfɪd) *n* any of the small homopterous insects of the family Aphididae, which feed by sucking the juices from plants. ORIG C19: from *aphides,* pl. of APHIS

aphis ('eɪfɪs) *n, pl* **aphides** ('eɪfɪˌdi:z). any of a genus of aphids, such as the blackfly. ORIG C18: from NL (coined by Linnaeus for obscure reasons)

aphonia (ə'fəʊnɪə) *or* **aphony** ('æfənɪ) *n* loss of voice caused by damage to the vocal tract. ORIG C18: NL, from Gk, from A-[1] + *phōnē* sound

aphorism ('æfəˌrɪzəm) *n* a short pithy saying expressing

a general truth; maxim. ORIG C16: from LL, from Gk *aphorismos,* from *aphorizein* to define
▸ **'aphorist** *n* ▸ **,apho'ristic** *adj*

aphrodisiac (,æfrə'dɪzɪæk) *n* **1** a drug, food, etc., that excites sexual desire. ◆ *adj* **2** exciting sexual desire. ORIG C18: from Gk, from *aphrodisios* belonging to *Aphrodite,* goddess of love

Aphrodite ★ (,æfrə'daɪtɪ) *n Greek myth.* the goddess of love and beauty, daughter of Zeus. Roman counterpart: **Venus.** Also called: **Cytherea.**

aphyllous (ə'fɪləs) *adj* (of plants) having no leaves. ORIG C19: from NL, from Gk A-[1] + *phullon* leaf

apian ('eɪpɪən) *adj* of, relating to, or resembling bees. ORIG C19: from L *apiānus,* from *apis* bee

apiarist ('eɪpɪərɪst) *n* a person who studies or keeps bees.

apiary ('eɪpɪərɪ) *n, pl* **apiaries.** a place where bees are kept. ORIG C17: from L *apiārium,* from *apis* bee

apical ('æpɪkᵊl, 'eɪ-) *adj* of, at, or being the apex. ORIG C19: from NL *apicālis*
▸ **'apically** *adv*

apices ('æpɪ,siːz, 'eɪ-) *n* a plural of **apex.**

apiculture ('eɪpɪ,kʌltʃə) *n* the breeding and care of bees. ORIG C19: from L *apis* bee + CULTURE
▸ **,api'cultural** *adj* ▸ **,api'culturist** *n*

apiece (ə'piːs) *adv* (*postpositive*) for, to, or from each one: *they were given two apples apiece.*

Apis ★ ('ɑːpɪs) *n* (in ancient Egypt) a sacred bull worshipped at Memphis.

apish ('eɪpɪʃ) *adj* **1** stupid; foolish. **2** resembling an ape. **3** slavishly imitative.
▸ **'apishly** *adv* ▸ **'apishness** *n*

aplanatic (,æplə'nætɪk) *adj* (of a lens or mirror) free from spherical aberration. ORIG C18: from Gk *aplanetos* free from error, from A-[1] + *planaein* to wander

aplenty (ə'plɛntɪ) *adj* (*postpositive*), *adv* in plenty.

aplomb (ə'plɒm) *n* equanimity, self-confidence, or self-possession. ORIG C18: from F: uprightness, from *à plomb* according to the plumb line

apnoea *or US* **apnea** (æp'nɪə) *n* a temporary inability to breathe. ORIG C18: from NL, from Gk *apnoia,* from A-[1] + *pnein* to breathe

Apo ★ ('ɑːpəʊ) *n* the highest mountain in the Philippines, on SE Mindanao: active volcano with three peaks. Height: 2954 m (9690 ft).

apo- *or* **ap-** *prefix* **1** away from; off: *apogee.* **2** separation of: *apocarpous.* ORIG from Gk *apo* away, off

Apoc. *abbrev. for:* **1** Apocalypse. **2** Apocrypha *or* Apocryphal.

apocalypse (ə'pɒkəlɪps) *n* **1** a prophetic disclosure or revelation. **2** an event of great importance, violence, etc., like the events described in the Apocalypse. ORIG C13: from LL *apocalypsis,* from Gk, from APO- + *kaluptein* to hide
▸ **a,poca'lyptic** *adj*

Apocalypse (ə'pɒkəlɪps) *n Bible.* another name for the Book of Revelation.

apocarpous (,æpə'kɑːpəs) *adj* (of the ovaries of flowering plants) consisting of separate carpels. ORIG C19: from NL, from Gk APO- + *karpos* fruit

apochromat (,æpə'krəʊmæt) *or* **apochromatic lens** (,æpəkrə'mætɪk) *n* a lens system designed to bring trichromatic light to a single focus and reduce chromatic aberration.

apocope (ə'pɒkəpɪ) *n* omission of the final sound or sounds of a word. ORIG C16: via LL from Gk, from *apokoptein* to cut off

apocrine ('æpəkraɪn, -krɪn) *adj* losing cellular tissue in the process of secreting, as in mammary glands. Cf. **eccrine.** ORIG C20: from APO- + *-crine,* from Gk *krinein* to separate

Apocrypha (ə'pɒkrɪfə) *n* **the.** (*functioning as sing or pl*) the 14 books included as an appendix to the Old Testament in the Septuagint and the Vulgate but not in the Hebrew canon. ORIG C14: via LL *apocrypha* (*scripta*) hidden (writings), from Gk, from *apokruptein* to hide away

apocryphal (ə'pɒkrɪfəl) *adj* **1** of questionable authenticity. **2** (*sometimes cap.*) of or like the Apocrypha. **3** untrue; counterfeit.

apodal ('æpədᵊl) *or* **apodous** ('æpədəs) *adj* without feet; having no pelvic fins. ORIG C18: from Gk A-[1] + *pous* foot

apodosis (ə'pɒdəsɪs) *n, pl* **apodoses** (-,siːz). *Logic, grammar.* the consequent of a conditional statement, as *I won't go* in *if it rains I won't go.* ORIG C17: via LL from Gk, from *apodidonai* to give back

apogee ('æpə,dʒiː) *n* **1** the point in its orbit around the earth when the moon or an artificial satellite is at its greatest distance from the earth. **2** the highest point. ORIG C17: from NL, from Gk, from *apogaios* away from the earth
▸ **,apo'gean** *adj*

apolitical (,eɪpə'lɪtɪkᵊl) *adj* politically neutral; without political attitudes, content, or bias.

Apollinaire ★ (*French* apɔlinɛr) *n* **Guillaume** (gijom), real name *Wilhelm Apollinaris de Kostrowitzki.* 1880–1918, French poet, novelist, and dramatist, regarded as a precursor of surrealism; author of *Alcoöls* (1913) and *Calligrammes* (1918).

Apollo ★ (ə'pɒləʊ) *n Classical myth.* the god of light, poetry, music, healing, and prophecy: son of Zeus and Leto.

Apollyon (ə'pɒljən) *n* the destroyer, a name given to the Devil (Revelation 9:11). ORIG C14: via LL from Gk, from *apollunai* to destroy totally

apologetic (ə,pɒlə'dʒɛtɪk) *adj* **1** expressing or anxious to make apology; contrite. **2** defending in speech or writing.
▸ **a,polo'getically** *adv*

apologetics (ə,pɒlə'dʒɛtɪks) *n* (*functioning as sing*) **1** the branch of theology concerned with the rational justification of Christianity. **2** a defensive method of argument.

apologia (,æpə'ləʊdʒɪə) *n* a formal written defence of a cause or one's beliefs or conduct.

apologist (ə'pɒlədʒɪst) *n* a person who offers a defence by argument.

apologize *or* **apologise** (ə'pɒlə,dʒaɪz) *vb* **apologizes, apologizing, apologized** *or* **apologises, apologising, apologised.** (*intr*) **1** to express or make an apology; acknowledge faults. **2** to make a formal defence.

apologue ('æpə,lɒg) *n* an allegory or moral fable. ORIG C17: from L, from Gk *apologos*

apology (ə'pɒlədʒɪ) *n, pl* **apologies. 1** a verbal or written expression of regret or contrition for a fault or failing. **2** a poor substitute. **3** another word for **apologia.** ORIG C16: from OF, from LL, from Gk: a verbal defence, from APO- + *logos* speech

apophthegm *or* **apothegm** ('æpə,θɛm) *n* a short remark containing some general or generally accepted truth; maxim. ORIG C16: from Gk *apophthegma,* from *apophthengesthai* to speak frankly

apoplectic (,æpə'plɛktɪk) *adj* **1** of apoplexy. **2** *Inf.* furious.
▸ **,apo'plectically** *adv*

apoplexy ('æpə,plɛksɪ) *n* sudden loss of consciousness, often followed by paralysis, caused by rupture or occlusion of a blood vessel in the brain. ORIG C14: from OF *apoplexie,* from LL, from Gk, from *apoplēssein* to cripple by a stroke

aport (ə'pɔːt) *adv, adj* (*postpositive*) *Naut.* on or towards the port side: *with the helm aport.*

apostasy (ə'pɒstəsɪ) *n, pl* **apostasies.** abandonment of one's religious faith, party, a cause, etc. ORIG C14: from Church L *apostasia,* from Gk *apostasis* desertion

apostate (ə'pɒsteɪt, -tɪt) *n* **1** a person who abandons his or her religion, party, etc. ◆ *adj* **2** guilty of apostasy.
▸ **apostatical** (,æpə'stætɪkᵊl) *adj*

apostatize *or* **apostatise** (ə'pɒstə,taɪz) *vb* **apostatizes, apostatizing, apostatized** *or* **apostatises, apostatising, apostatised.** (*intr*) to abandon one's belief, faith, or allegiance.

a posteriori (eɪ pɒs,tɛrɪ'ɔːraɪ, -rɪ; ɑː) *adj Logic.* **1** relating to inductive reasoning from particular facts to a general principle. **2** derived from or requiring evidence for its validation; empirical. ORIG C18: from L, lit.: from the latter

apostle (əˈpɒsᵊl) *n* **1** (*often cap.*) one of the 12 disciples chosen by Christ to preach his gospel. **2** any prominent Christian missionary, esp. one who first converts a people. **3** an ardent early supporter of a cause, movement, etc. ORIG OE *apostol,* from Church L, from Gk *apostolos* a messenger

Apostles' Creed *n* a concise statement of Christian beliefs dating from about 500 A.D., traditionally ascribed to the Apostles.

apostolate (əˈpɒstəlɪt, -ˌleɪt) *n* the office, authority, or mission of an apostle.

apostolic (ˌæpəˈstɒlɪk) *adj* **1** of or relating to the Apostles or their teachings or practice. **2** of or relating to the pope as successor of the Apostles.
▸ **ˌaposˈtolical** *adj*

Apostolic See (ˌæpəˈstɒlɪk) *n* the see of the pope.

Apostolic succession *n* the doctrine that the authority of Christian bishops derives from the Apostles through an unbroken line of consecration.

apostrophe[1] (əˈpɒstrəfɪ) *n* the punctuation mark ' used to indicate the omission of a letter or number, such as *he's* for *he has* or *he is,* also used in English to form the possessive, as in *John's father.* ORIG C17: from LL, from Gk *apostrophos* mark of elision, from *apostrephein* to turn away

apostrophe[2] (əˈpɒstrəfɪ) *n Rhetoric.* a digression from a discourse, esp. an address to an imaginary or absent person or a personification. ORIG C16: from L *apostrophē,* from Gk: a turning away

apostrophize *or* **apostrophise** (əˈpɒstrəˌfaɪz) *vb* **apostrophizes, apostrophizing, apostrophized** *or* **apostrophises, apostrophising, apostrophised.** (*tr*) to address an apostrophe to.

apothecaries' measure *n* a system of liquid volume measure used in pharmacy in which 20 fluid ounces equal 1 pint.

apothecaries' weight *n* a system of weights formerly used in pharmacy based on the Troy ounce.

apothecary (əˈpɒθɪkərɪ) *n, pl* **apothecaries. 1** an archaic word for **chemist. 2** *Law.* a chemist licensed by the Society of Apothecaries of London to prescribe, prepare, and sell drugs. ORIG C14: from OF, from LL, from Gk *apothēkē* storehouse

apothegm (ˈæpəˌθɛm) *n* a variant spelling of **apophthegm.**

apothem (ˈæpəˌθɛm) *n* the perpendicular from the centre of a regular polygon to any of its sides. ORIG C20: from APO- + Gk *thema,* from *tithenai* to place

apotheosis (əˌpɒθɪˈəʊsɪs) *n, pl* **apotheoses** (-siːz). **1** elevation to the rank of a god; deification. **2** glorification of a person or thing. **3** a glorified ideal. ORIG C17: via LL from Gk: deification

apotheosize *or* **apotheosise** (əˈpɒθɪəˌsaɪz) *vb* **apotheosizes, apotheosizing, apotheosized** *or* **apotheosises, apotheosising, apotheosised.** (*tr*) **1** to deify. **2** to glorify or idealize.

app. *abbrev. for:* **1** apparatus. **2** appendix (of a book). **3** applied. **4** appointed. **5** apprentice. **6** approved. **7** approximate.

appal *or US* **appall** (əˈpɔːl) *vb* **appals, appalling, appalled** *or US* **appalls, appalling, appalled.** (*tr*) to fill with horror; shock or dismay. ORIG C14: from OF *appalir* to turn pale

Appalachia ★ (ˌæpəˈleɪtʃɪə) *n* a highland region of the eastern US, containing the Appalachian Mountains, extending from Pennsylvania to Alabama.
▸ **ˌAppaˈlachian** *adj*

Appalachian Mountains *or* **Appalachians** ★ *pl n* a mountain system of E North America, extending from Quebec province in Canada to central Alabama in the US: contains rich deposits of anthracite, bitumen, and iron ore. Highest peak: Mount Mitchell, 2038 m (6684 ft).

appalling (əˈpɔːlɪŋ) *adj* **1** causing dismay, horror, or revulsion. **2** *Inf.* very bad.
▸ **apˈpallingly** *adv*

Appaloosa (ˌæpəˈluːsə) *n* a breed of horse, originally from America, having a spotted rump. ORIG C19: ?from *Palouse,* river in Idaho

appanage *or* **apanage** (ˈæpənɪdʒ) *n* **1** land or other provision granted by a king for the support of esp. a younger son. **2** a customary accompaniment or perquisite, as to a job or position. ORIG C17: from OF, from Med. L, from *appānāre* to provide for, from L *pānis* bread

apparatchik (ˌæpəˈrɑːtʃɪk) *n* **1** a member of a Communist Party organization. **2** a bureaucrat in any organization. ORIG C20: from Russian, from *apparat* apparatus, instrument + *-ckik,* suffix denoting agent

apparatus (ˌæpəˈreɪtəs, -ˈrɑːtəs) *n, pl* **apparatus** *or* **apparatuses. 1** a collection of equipment used for a particular purpose. **2** a machine having a specific function: *breathing apparatus.* **3** the means by which something operates; organization. **4** *Anat.* any group of organs having a specific function. ORIG C17: from L, from *apparāre* to make ready

apparel (əˈpærəl) *n* **1** *Arch.* clothing. **2** *Naut.* a vessel's gear and equipment. ◆ *vb* **apparels, apparelling, apparelled** *or US* **apparels, appareling, appareled. 3** (*tr*) *Arch.* to clothe, adorn, etc. ORIG C13: from OF *apareillier* to make ready, from Vulgar L *appariculāre* (unattested), from L *parāre* to prepare

apparent (əˈpærənt) *adj* **1** readily seen or understood; obvious. **2** (*usually prenominal*) seeming, as opposed to real: *his apparent innocence.* **3** *Physics.* as observed but ignoring such factors as the motion of the observer, etc. ORIG C14: from L *appārēns,* from *appārēre* to APPEAR
▸ **apˈparently** *adv*

apparent magnitude *n* See **magnitude** (sense 4).

apparition (ˌæpəˈrɪʃən) *n* **1** an appearance, esp. of a ghost or ghostlike figure. **2** the figure so appearing; spectre. **3** the act of appearing. ORIG C15: from LL *appāritiō,* from L *appārēre* to APPEAR

appassionato (əˌpæsjəˈnɑːtəʊ) *adj, adv Music.* (to be performed) with passion. ORIG It.

appeal (əˈpiːl) *n* **1** a request for relief, aid, etc. **2** the power to attract, please, stimulate, or interest. **3** an application or resort to another authority, esp. a higher one, as for a decision. **4** *Law.* **4a** the judicial review by a superior court of the decision of a lower tribunal. **4b** a request for such review. **5** *Cricket.* a request to the umpire to declare a batsman out. ◆ *vb* **6** (*intr*) to make an earnest request. **7** (*intr*) to attract, please, stimulate, or interest. **8** *Law.* to apply to a superior court to review (a case or issue decided by a lower tribunal). **9** (*intr*) to resort (to), as for a decision. **10** (*intr*) *Cricket.* to ask the umpire to declare a batsman out. **11** (*intr*) to challenge the umpire's or referee's decision. ORIG C14: from OF *appeler,* from L *appellāre* to entreat, from *pellere* to drive
▸ **apˈpealable** *adj* ▸ **apˈpealer** *n* ▸ **apˈpealing** *adj* ▸ **apˈpealingly** *adv*

appear (əˈpɪə) *vb* (*intr*) **1** to come into sight. **2** (*copula; may take an infinitive*) to seem: *the evidence appears to support you.* **3** to be plain or clear, as after further evidence, etc.: *it appears you were correct after all.* **4** to develop; occur: *faults appeared during testing.* **5** to be published: *his biography appeared last month.* **6** to perform: *he has appeared in many London productions.* **7** to be present in court before a magistrate or judge: *he appeared on two charges of theft.* ORIG C13: from OF *aparoir,* from L *appārēre* to become visible, attend upon, from *pārēre* to appear

appearance (əˈpɪərəns) *n* **1** the act or an instance of appearing. **2** the outward aspect of a person or thing. **3** an outward show; pretence: *he gave an appearance of working hard.* **4 keep up appearances.** to maintain the public impression of wellbeing or normality. **5 put in** *or* **make an appearance.** to attend briefly, as out of politeness. **6 to all appearances.** apparently.

appearance money *n* money paid by a promoter of an event to a particular celebrity in order to ensure that the celebrity takes part in the event.

appease (əˈpiːz) *vb* **appeases, appeasing, appeased.** (*tr*) **1** to calm or pacify, esp. by acceding to the demands of. **2** to

satisfy or quell (a thirst, etc.). ORIG C16: from OF *apaisier,* from *pais* peace, from L *pax*
▸ **ap'peaser** *n*

appeasement (ə'piːzmənt) *n* **1** the policy of acceding to the demands of a potentially hostile nation in the hope of maintaining peace. **2** the act of appeasing.

Appel ★ (*Dutch* 'ɑpəl) *n* **Karel** ('kaːrəl). born 1921, Dutch abstract expressionist painter.

appellant (ə'pɛlənt) *n* **1** a person who appeals. **2** *Law.* the party who appeals to a higher court from the decision of a lower tribunal. ◆ *adj* **3** *Law.* another word for **appellate.** ORIG C14: from OF; see APPEAL

appellate (ə'pɛlɪt) *adj Law.* **1** of appeals. **2** (of a tribunal) having jurisdiction to review cases on appeal. ORIG C18: from L *appellātus* summoned, from *appellāre* to APPEAL

appellation (ˌæpɪ'leɪʃən) *n* **1** a name or title. **2** the act of naming.

appellative (ə'pɛlətɪv) *n* **1** a name or title. **2** *Grammar.* another word for **common noun.** ◆ *adj* **3** of or relating to a name. **4** (of a proper noun) used as a common noun.

append (ə'pɛnd) *vb* (*tr*) **1** to add as a supplement: *to append a footnote.* **2** to attach; hang on. ORIG C15: from LL *appendere* to hang (something) from, from L *pendere* to hang

appendage (ə'pɛndɪdʒ) *n* an ancillary or secondary part attached to a main part; adjunct, such as an organ that projects from the trunk of an animal.

appendant (ə'pɛndənt) *adj* **1** attached or added. **2** attendant or associated as an accompaniment or result. ◆ *n* **3** a person or thing attached or added.

appendicectomy (əˌpɛndɪ'sɛktəmɪ) *or esp. US & Canad.* **appendectomy** (ˌæpən'dɛktəmɪ) *n, pl* **appendicectomies** *or* **appendectomies.** surgical removal of any appendage, esp. the vermiform appendix.

appendicitis (əˌpɛndɪ'saɪtɪs) *n* inflammation of the vermiform appendix.

appendix (ə'pɛndɪks) *n, pl* **appendices** (-dɪˌsiːz) *or* **appendixes. 1** a body of separate additional material at the end of a book, etc. **2** any part that is dependent or supplementary. **3** *Anat.* See **vermiform appendix.** ORIG C16: from L: an appendage, from *appendere* to APPEND

Appenzell ★ (*German* apən'tsɛl, 'apəntsɛl) *n* **1** a canton of NE Switzerland, divided in 1597 into the Protestant demicanton of **Appenzell Outer Rhodes** and the Catholic demicanton of **Appenzell Inner Rhodes.** Capitals: Herisau and Appenzell. Pop.: 54 227 and 14 742 (1995 est.) respectively. Areas: 243 sq. km (94 sq. miles) and 171 sq. km (66 sq. miles) respectively. **2** a town in NE Switzerland, capital of Appenzell Inner Rhodes demicanton. Pop.: 5157 (1990).

apperceive (ˌæpə'siːv) *vb* **apperceives, apperceiving, apperceived.** (*tr*) **1** to be aware of perceiving. **2** *Psychol.* to comprehend by assimilating (a perception) to ideas already in the mind. ORIG C19: from OF, from L *percipere* to PERCEIVE

apperception (ˌæpə'sɛpʃən) *n* **1** *Psychol.* the attainment of full awareness of a sensation or idea. **2** the act of apperceiving.
▸ **ˌapper'ceptive** *adj*

appertain (ˌæpə'teɪn) *vb* (*intr;* usually foll. by *to*) to belong (to) as a part, function, right, etc.; relate (to) or be connected (with). ORIG C14: from OF *apertenir,* from LL, from L AD- + *pertinēre* to PERTAIN

appetence ('æpɪtəns) *or* **appetency** *n, pl* **appetences** *or* **appetencies. 1** a craving or desire. **2** an attraction or affinity. ORIG C17: from L *appetentia,* from *appetere* to crave

appetite ('æpɪˌtaɪt) *n* **1** a desire for food or drink. **2** a desire to satisfy a bodily craving, as for sexual pleasure. **3** (usually foll. by *for*) a liking or willingness: *a great appetite for work.* ORIG C14: from OF *apetit,* from L, from *appetere* to desire ardently
▸ **appetitive** (ə'pɛtɪtɪv) *adj*

appetizer *or* **appetiser** ('æpɪˌtaɪzə) *n* **1** a small amount of food or drink taken to stimulate the appetite. **2** any stimulating foretaste.

appetizing *or* **appetising** ('æpɪˌtaɪzɪŋ) *adj* pleasing or stimulating to the appetite; delicious; tasty.

Appian Way ★ ('æpɪən) *n* a Roman road in Italy, extending from Rome to Brindisi: begun in 312 B.C. by Appius Claudius Caecus. Length: about 560 km (350 miles).

applaud (ə'plɔːd) *vb* **1** to indicate approval of (a person, performance, etc.) by clapping the hands. **2** (*usually tr*) to express approval or praise of: *I applaud your decision.* ORIG C15: from L *applaudere,* from *plaudere* to beat, applaud

applause (ə'plɔːz) *n* appreciation or praise, esp. as shown by clapping the hands.

apple ('æpᵊl) *n* **1** a rosaceous tree, widely cultivated in temperate regions in many varieties. **2** the fruit of this tree, having red, yellow, or green skin and crisp whitish flesh. **3** the wood of this tree. **4** any of several unrelated trees that have fruit similar to the apple. **5 apple of one's eye.** a person or thing that is very much loved. ORIG OE *æppel*

apple green *n* **a** a bright light green. **b** (*as adj*): *an apple-green carpet.*

Apple Isle ★ *n* **the.** *Austral. inf.* Tasmania.
▸ **Apple Islander** *n*

apple-pie bed *n Brit.* a bed made with the sheets folded so as to prevent the person from entering it.

apple-pie order *n Inf.* perfect order or condition.

applet ('æplɪt) *n Computing.* a computer program that runs within a page on the World Wide Web. ORIG C20: from APP(LICATION) + -LET

Appleton ★ ('æpᵊltən) *n* Sir **Edward** (**Victor**). 1892–1965, English physicist, noted particularly for his research on the ionosphere: Nobel prize for physics 1947.

appliance (ə'plaɪəns) *n* **1** a machine or device, esp. an electrical one used domestically. **2** any piece of equipment having a specific function. **3** another name for a **fire engine.**

applicable ('æplɪkəbᵊl, ə'plɪkə-) *adj* being appropriate or relevant; able to be applied; fitting.
▸ **ˌapplica'bility** *n* ▸ **'applicably** *adv*

applicant ('æplɪkənt) *n* a person who applies, as for a job, grant, support, etc.; candidate. ORIG C15: from L *applicāns,* from *applicāre* to APPLY

application (ˌæplɪ'keɪʃən) *n* **1** the act of applying to a particular use. **2** relevance or value: *the practical applications of space technology.* **3** the act of asking for something. **4** a written request, as for a job, etc. **5** diligent effort: *a job requiring application.* **6** something, such as a lotion, that is applied, esp. to the skin.

applicator ('æplɪˌkeɪtə) *n* a device, such as a spatula or rod, for applying a medicine, glue, etc.

applicatory ('æplɪkətərɪ) *adj* suitable for application.

applied (ə'plaɪd) *adj* put to practical use: *applied mathematics.* Cf. **pure** (sense 5).

appliqué (æ'pliːkeɪ) *n* **1** a decoration of one material sewn or fixed onto another. **2** the practice of decorating in this way. ◆ *vb* **appliqués, appliquéing, appliquéd. 3** (*tr*) to sew or fix (a decoration) on as an appliqué. ORIG C18: from F, lit.: applied

apply (ə'plaɪ) *vb* **applies, applying, applied. 1** (*tr*) to put to practical use; employ. **2** (*intr*) to be relevant or appropriate. **3** (*tr*) to cause to come into contact with. **4** (*intr;* often foll. by *for*) to put in an application or request. **5** (*tr;* often foll. by *to*) to devote (oneself or one's efforts) with diligence. **6** (*tr*) to bring into use: *the police only applied the law to aliens.* ORIG C14: from OF *aplier,* from L *applicāre* to attach to
▸ **ap'plier** *n*

appoggiatura (əˌpɒdʒə'tʊərə) *n, pl* **appoggiaturas** *or* **appoggiature** (-reɪ). *Music.* an ornament consisting of a nonharmonic note preceding a harmonic one either before or on the stress. ORIG C18: from It., lit.: a propping

appoint (ə'pɔɪnt) *vb* (*mainly tr*) **1** (*also intr*) to assign officially, as to a position, responsibility, etc. **2** to establish by agreement or decree. **3** to prescribe: *laws appointed by tribunal.* **4** *Property law.* to nominate (a person) to take an interest in property. **5** to equip with usual features; furnish: *a well-appointed hotel.* ORIG C14: from OF *apointer* to put into a good state
▸ **appoin'tee** *n* ▸ **ap'pointer** *n*

appointive (əˈpɔɪntɪv) *adj Chiefly US.* filled by appointment: *an appointive position.*

appointment (əˈpɔɪntmənt) *n* **1** an arrangement to meet a person or be at a place at a certain time. **2** the act of placing in a job or position. **3** the person who receives such a job. **4** the job or position to which such a person is appointed. **5** (*usually pl*) a fixture or fitting.

apportion (əˈpɔːʃən) *vb* (*tr*) to divide, distribute, or assign shares of; allot proportionally.
▸ **apˈportionable** *adj* ▸ **apˈportionment** *n*

appose (əˈpəuz) *vb* **apposes, apposing, apposed.** (*tr*) **1** to place side by side. **2** (usually foll. by *to*) to place (something) near or against another thing. ORIG C16: from OF *apposer,* from *poser* to put, from L *pōnere*
▸ **apˈposable** *adj*

apposite (ˈæpəzɪt) *adj* appropriate; apt. ORIG C17: from L *appositus,* from *appōnere,* from *pōnere* to put
▸ **ˈappositely** *adv* ▸ **ˈappositeness** *n*

apposition (ˌæpəˈzɪʃən) *n* **1** a putting into juxtaposition. **2** a grammatical construction in which a word, esp. a noun, is placed after another to modify its meaning.
▸ **ˌappoˈsitional** *adj*

appositive (əˈpɒzɪtɪv) *Grammar.* ◆ *adj* **1** in, of, or relating to apposition. ◆ *n* **2** an appositive word or phrase.
▸ **apˈpositively** *adv*

appraisal (əˈpreɪzᵊl) *or* **appraisement** *n* **1** an assessment of the worth or quality of a person or thing. **2** a valuation.

appraise (əˈpreɪz) *vb* **appraises, appraising, appraised.** (*tr*) **1** to assess the worth, value, or quality of. **2** to make a valuation of, as for taxation. ORIG C15: from OF, from *prisier* to PRIZE[2]
▸ **apˈpraisable** *adj* ▸ **apˈpraiser** *n*

> **USAGE NOTE** *Appraise* is sometimes used where *apprise* is meant: *both patients had been fully apprised* (not *appraised*) *of the situation.* This may well be due to the fact that *appraise* is considerably more common, and that people therefore tend to associate this meaning mistakenly with a word they know better.

appreciable (əˈpriːʃəbᵊl) *adj* sufficient to be easily measured or noticed.
▸ **apˈpreciably** *adv*

appreciate (əˈpriːʃɪˌeɪt, -sɪ-) *vb* **appreciates, appreciating, appreciated.** (*mainly tr*) **1** to feel thankful or grateful for. **2** (*may take a clause as object*) to take sufficient account of: *to appreciate a problem.* **3** to value highly. **4** (*usually intr*) to increase in value. ORIG C17: from Med. L *appretiāre* to value, from L *pretium* PRICE
▸ **apˈpreciˌator** *n*

appreciation (əˌpriːʃɪˈeɪʃən, -sɪ-) *n* **1** thanks or gratitude. **2** assessment of the true worth of persons or things. **3** perceptive recognition of qualities, as in art. **4** an increase in value. **5** a review of a book, etc., esp. when favourable.

appreciative (əˈpriːʃɪətɪv) *or* **appreciatory** *adj* feeling or expressing appreciation.
▸ **apˈpreciatively** *adv* ▸ **apˈpreciativeness** *n*

apprehend (ˌæprɪˈhɛnd) *vb* **1** (*tr*) to arrest and escort into custody. **2** to grasp mentally; understand. **3** to await with fear or anxiety. ORIG C14: from L *apprehendere* to lay hold of

apprehensible (ˌæprɪˈhɛnsɪbᵊl) *adj* capable of being comprehended or grasped mentally.
▸ **ˌappreˌhensiˈbility** *n*

apprehension (ˌæprɪˈhɛnʃən) *n* **1** anxiety over what may happen. **2** the act of arresting. **3** understanding. **4** a notion or conception.

apprehensive (ˌæprɪˈhɛnsɪv) *adj* **1** fearful or anxious. **2** (*usually postpositive* and foll. by *of*) *Arch.* intelligent, perceptive.
▸ **ˌappreˈhensively** *adv* ▸ **ˌappreˈhensiveness** *n*

apprentice (əˈprɛntɪs) *n* **1** someone who works for a skilled or qualified person in order to learn a trade, esp. for a recognized period. **2** any beginner or novice. ◆ *vb* **apprentices, apprenticing, apprenticed. 3** (*tr*) to take, place, or bind as an apprentice. ORIG C14: from OF *aprentis,* from *aprendre* to learn, from L *apprehendere* to APPREHEND
▸ **apˈprenticeship** *n*

apprise *or* **apprize** (əˈpraɪz) *vb* **apprises, apprising, apprised** *or* **apprizes, apprizing, apprized.** (*tr;* often foll. by *of*) to make aware; inform. ORIG C17: from F *appris,* from *apprendre* to teach; learn

> **USAGE NOTE** See at **appraise.**

appro (ˈæprəu) *n* an informal shortening of **approval:** *on appro.*

approach (əˈprəutʃ) *vb* **1** to come nearer in position, time, quality, character, etc., to (someone or something). **2** (*tr*) to make a proposal or suggestion to. **3** (*tr*) to begin to deal with. ◆ *n* **4** the act of drawing close or closer. **5** a close approximation. **6** the way or means of entering or leaving. **7** (*often pl*) an overture to a person. **8** a means adopted in tackling a problem, job of work, etc. **9** Also called: **approach path.** the course followed by an aircraft preparing for landing. **10** Also called: **approach shot.** *Golf.* a shot made to or towards the green after a tee shot. ORIG C14: from OF *aprochier,* from LL *appropiāre* to draw near, from L *prope* near
▸ **apˈproachable** *adj* ▸ **apˌproachaˈbility** *n*

approbation (ˌæprəˈbeɪʃən) *n* **1** commendation; praise. **2** official recognition.
▸ **ˈapproˌbative** *or* **ˈapproˌbatory** *adj*

appropriate *adj* (əˈprəuprɪɪt). **1** right or suitable; fitting. ◆ *vb* (əˈprəuprɪˌeɪt), **appropriates, appropriating, appropriated.** (*tr*) **2** to take for one's own use, esp. illegally. **3** to put aside (funds, etc.) for a particular purpose or person. ORIG C15: from LL *appropriāre* to make one's own, from L *proprius* one's own
▸ **apˈpropriately** *adv* ▸ **apˈpropriateness** *n* ▸ **apˈpropriˌator** *n*

appropriation (əˌprəuprɪˈeɪʃən) *n* **1** the act of setting apart or taking for one's own use. **2** a sum of money set apart for a specific purpose.

approval (əˈpruːvᵊl) *n* **1** the act of approving. **2** formal agreement. **3** a favourable opinion. **4 on approval.** (of articles for sale) for examination with an option to buy or return.

approve (əˈpruːv) *vb* **approves, approving, approved. 1** (when *intr,* often foll. by *of*) to consider fair, good, or right. **2** (*tr*) to authorize or sanction. ORIG C14: from OF *aprover,* from L *approbāre* to approve, from *probāre* to test, PROVE

approved school *n* (in Britain) a former name for **community home.**

approx. *abbrev. for* approximate(ly).

approximate *adj* (əˈprɒksɪmɪt). **1** almost accurate or exact. **2** inexact; rough, loose. **3** much alike; almost the same. **4** near; close together. ◆ *vb* (əˈprɒksɪˌmeɪt), **approximates, approximating, approximated. 5** (usually foll. by *to*) to come or bring near or close; be almost the same (as). **6** *Maths.* to find an expression for (some quantity) accurate to a specified degree. ORIG C15: from LL *approximāre,* from L *proximus* nearest
▸ **apˈproximately** *adv*

approximation (əˌprɒksɪˈmeɪʃən) *n* **1** the process or result of making a rough calculation, estimate, or guess. **2** an imprecise or unreliable record or version. **3** *Maths.* an inexact number, relationship, or theory that is sufficiently accurate for a specific purpose.

appurtenance (əˈpɜːtɪnəns) *n* **1** a less significant thing or part. **2** (*pl*) accessories. **3** *Property law.* a minor right, interest, or privilege. ORIG C14: from Anglo-F *apurtenance,* from OF *apartenance,* from *apartenir* to APPERTAIN

APR *abbrev. for* annual percentage rate.

Apr. *abbrev. for* April.

apraxia (əˈpræksɪə) *n* a disorder of the central nervous system characterized by impaired ability to carry out certain purposeful muscular movements. ORIG C19: via NL from Gk: inactivity, from A-[1] + *praxis* action

après-ski (ˌæpreɪˈskiː) *n* **a** social activity following a day's skiing. **b** (*as modifier*): *an après-ski outfit.* ORIG F, lit.: after ski

apricot ('eɪprɪˌkɒt) *n* **1** a tree native to Africa and W Asia, but widely cultivated for its edible fruit. **2** the yellow juicy fruit of this tree, which resembles a small peach. ORIG C16: from Port., from Ar., from LGk, from L *praecox* early-ripening

April ('eɪprəl) *n* the fourth month of the year, consisting of 30 days. ORIG C14: from L *Aprīlis*

April fool *n* a victim of a practical joke performed on the first of April (**April Fools' Day** *or* **All Fools' Day**).

a priori (eɪ praɪ'ɔːraɪ, ɑː prɪ'ɔːrɪ) *adj* **1** *Logic.* relating to or involving deductive reasoning from a general principle to the expected facts or effects. **2** known to be true independently of experience of the subject matter. ORIG C18: from L, lit.: from the previous
▸ **apriority** (ˌeɪpraɪ'ɒrɪtɪ) *n*

apron ('eɪprən) *n* **1** a protective or sometimes decorative garment worn over the front of the body and tied around the waist. **2** the part of a stage extending in front of the curtain. **3** a hard-surfaced area in front of an aircraft hangar, terminal building, etc. **4** a continuous conveyor belt composed of metal slats. **5** a protective plate screening the operator of a machine, artillery piece, etc. **6** *Geol.* a sheet of sand, gravel, etc., deposited at the front of a moraine. **7** another name for **skirt** (sense 3). **8 tied to someone's apron strings.** dominated by someone, esp. a mother or wife. ◆ *vb* **9** (*tr*) to protect or provide with an apron. ORIG C16: mistaken division of *a napron,* from OF, from L *mappa* napkin

apron stage *n* a stage that projects into the auditorium so that the audience sits on three sides of it.

apropos (ˌæprə'pəʊ) *adj* **1** appropriate. ◆ *adv* **2** appropriately. **3** by the way; incidentally. **4 apropos of.** (*prep*) in respect of. ORIG C17: from F *à propos* to the purpose

apse (æps) *n* a domed or vaulted semicircular or polygonal recess, esp. at the east end of a church. Also called: **apsis.** ORIG C19: from L *apsis,* from Gk: a fitting together, from *haptein* to fasten
▸ **'apsidal** *adj*

apsis ('æpsɪs) *n, pl* **apsides** (æp'saɪdiːz). either of two points lying at the extremities of an eccentric orbit of a planet, satellite, etc. Also called: **apse.** ORIG C17: via L from Gk; see APSE
▸ **apsidal** ('æpsɪd°l) *adj*

apt (æpt) *adj* **1** suitable; appropriate. **2** (*postpositive;* foll. by an infinitive) having a tendency (to behave as specified). **3** having the ability to learn and understand easily. ORIG C14: from L *aptus* fitting, from *apere* to fasten
▸ **'aptly** *adv* ▸ **'aptness** *n*

APT *abbrev. for* Advanced Passenger Train.

apterous ('æptərəs) *adj* **1** (of insects) without wings, as silverfish. **2** without winglike expansions, as some seeds and fruits. ORIG C18: from Gk, from A-[1] + *pteron* wing
▸ **'apterˌism** *n*

apteryx ('æptərɪks) *n* another name for **kiwi** (the bird). ORIG C19: from NL; see APTEROUS

aptitude ('æptɪˌtjuːd) *n* **1** inherent or acquired ability. **2** ease in learning or understanding. **3** the quality of being apt. ORIG C15: via OF from LL, from L *aptus* APT

Apuleius ★ (ˌæpjʊ'liːəs) *n* **Lucius** ('luːsɪəs). 2nd century A.D., Roman writer, noted for his romance *The Golden Ass.*

Apulia ★ (ə'pjuːljə) *n* a region of SE Italy, on the Adriatic. Capital: Bari. Pop.: 4 082 953 (1996 est.). Area: 19 223 sq. km (7422 sq. miles). Italian name: **Puglia.**

Aqaba *or* **Akaba** ★ ('ækəbə) *n* the only port in Jordan, in the southwest, on the **Gulf of Aqaba.** Pop.: 46 090 (1990 est.).

Aqtöbe ★ (æk'tjuːbɪ; *Kazakh* ɑktø'be) *n* an industrial city in W Kazakhstan. Pop.: 258 900 (1995 est.). Former name (until 1991): **Aktyubinsk.**

aqua ('ækwə) *n, pl* **aquae** ('ækwiː) *or* **aquas. 1** water: used in compound names of certain liquid substances or solutions of substances in water. ◆ *n, adj* **2** short for **aquamarine** (the colour). ORIG L: water

aquaculture ('ækwəˌkʌltʃə) *or* **aquiculture** *n* the cultivation of freshwater and marine organisms for human consumption or use.

aquaerobics *or* **aquarobics** (ˌækwə'rəʊbɪks) *n* (*functioning as sing*) the practice of exercising to music in a swimming pool. ORIG C20: from L *aqua* water + AEROBICS

aqua fortis ('fɔːtɪs) *n* an obsolete name for **nitric acid.** ORIG C17: from L, lit.: strong water

aqualung ('ækwəˌlʌŋ) *n* breathing apparatus used by divers, etc., consisting of a mouthpiece attached to air cylinders strapped to the back.

aquamarine (ˌækwəmə'riːn) *n* **1** a pale greenish-blue transparent variety of beryl used as a gemstone. **2a** a pale blue to greenish-blue colour. **2b** (*as adj*): *an aquamarine dress.* ORIG C19: from NL, from L: sea water (referring to the gem's colour)

aquanaut ('ækwənɔːt) *n* a person who works, swims, or dives underwater. ORIG C20: from AQUA + *-naut,* as in ASTRONAUT

aquaplane ('ækwəˌpleɪn) *n* **1** a board on which a person stands and is towed by a motorboat. ◆ *vb* **aquaplanes, aquaplaning, aquaplaned.** (*intr*) **2** to ride on an aquaplane. **3** (of a motor vehicle travelling at high speeds on wet roads) to rise up onto a thin film of water so that contact with the road is lost.

aqua regia ('riːdʒɪə) *n* a mixture of nitric acid and hydrochloric acid. ORIG C17: from NL: royal water; referring to its use in dissolving gold, the royal metal

aquarist ('ækwərɪst) *n* **1** the curator of an aquarium. **2** a person who studies aquatic life.

aquarium (ə'kwɛərɪəm) *n, pl* **aquariums** *or* **aquaria** (-rɪə). **1** a tank, bowl, or pool in which aquatic animals and plants are kept for pleasure, study, or exhibition. **2** a building housing a collection of aquatic life, as for exhibition. ORIG C19: from L *aquārius* relating to water, on the model of VIVARIUM

Aquarius (ə'kwɛərɪəs) *n, Latin genitive* **Aquarii** (ə'kwɛərɪˌaɪ). **1** *Astron.* a S constellation. **2** *Astrol.* also called: the **Water Carrier.** the eleventh sign of the zodiac. The sun is in this sign between about Jan. 20 and Feb. 18. ORIG L

aquatic (ə'kwætɪk) *adj* **1** growing, living, or found in water. **2** *Sport.* performed in or on water. ◆ *n* **3** a marine animal or plant. ORIG C15: from L *aquāticus,* from *aqua* water

aquatics (ə'kwætɪks) *pl n* sports or pastimes performed in or on the water.

aquatint ('ækwəˌtɪnt) *n* **1** a technique of etching copper with acid to produce an effect resembling watercolour. **2** an etching made in this way. ◆ *vb* **3** (*tr*) to etch (a block, etc.) in aquatint. ORIG C18: from It. *acqua tinta* dyed water

aquavit ('ækwəˌvɪt) *n* a grain- or potato-based spirit flavoured with aromatic seeds. Also called: **akvavit.** ORIG of Scandinavian origin: see AQUA VITAE

aqua vitae ('viːtaɪ, 'vaɪtiː) *n* an archaic name for **brandy.** ORIG Med. L: water of life

aqueduct ('ækwɪˌdʌkt) *n* **1** a conduit used to convey water over a long distance. **2** a structure, often a bridge, that carries such a conduit or a canal across a valley or river. **3** a channel or conduit in the body. ORIG C16: from L *aquaeductus,* from *aqua* water + *dūcere* to convey

aqueous ('eɪkwɪəs) *adj* **1** of, like, or containing water. **2** dissolved in water: *aqueous ammonia.* **3** (of rocks, etc.) formed from material laid down in water. ORIG C17: from Med. L *aqueus,* from L *aqua* water

aqueous humour *n Physiol.* the watery fluid within the eyeball between the cornea and the lens.

aquiculture ('eɪkwɪˌkʌltʃə, 'ækwɪ-) *n* **1** another name for **hydroponics. 2** a variant of **aquaculture.**
▸ **'aquiˌculturist** *n* ▸ **'aquiˌcultural** *adj*

aquifer ('ækwɪfə) *n* a deposit or rock, such as a sandstone, containing water that can be used to supply wells.

Aquila ('ækwɪlə; *Italian* 'aːkwila) *or* **l'Aquila** ★ *n* a city in central Italy, capital of Abruzzi region. Pop.: 67 820 (1990). Official name: **Aquila degli Abruzzi** ('deʎʎi a'bruttsi).

aquilegia (ˌækwɪˈliːdʒɪə) *n* another name for **columbine.** ORIG C19: from Med. L, from ?

aquiline (ˈækwɪˌlaɪn) *adj* **1** (of a nose) having the curved shape of an eagle's beak. **2** of or like an eagle. ORIG C17: from L, from *aquila* eagle

Aquinas ★ (əˈkwaɪnəs) *n* **Saint Thomas.** 1225–74, Italian theologian, scholastic philosopher, and Dominican friar, whose works include *Summa contra Gentiles* (1259–64) and *Summa Theologiae* (1267–73). Feast day: Jan. 28. See also **Thomism.**

Aquino ★ (əˈkiːnəʊ) *n* **Corazón,** known as *Cory.* born 1933, Philippine stateswoman: president (1986–92).

Aquitaine ★ (ˌækwɪˈteɪn; *French* akitɛn) *n* a region of SW France, on the Bay of Biscay: a former Roman province and medieval duchy. It is generally flat in the west, rising to the slopes of the Massif Central in the northeast and the Pyrenees in the south; mainly agricultural. Ancient name: **Aquitania** (ˌækwɪˈteɪnɪə).

Ar *the chemical symbol for* argon.

ar. *abbrev. for:* **1** arrival. **2** arrive(s).

Ar. *abbrev. for:* **1** Arabia(n). **2** Also: **Ar** Arabic. **3** Aramaic.

a.r. *abbrev. for* anno regni. ORIG L: in the year of the reign

-ar *suffix forming adjectives.* of; belonging to; like: *linear; polar.* ORIG via OF *-er* from L *-āris*

ARA *abbrev. for:* **1** (in Britain) Associate of the Royal Academy. **2** (in New Zealand) Auckland Regional Authority.

Arab (ˈærəb) *n* **1** a member of a Semitic people originally inhabiting Arabia. **2** a small breed of horse, used for riding. **3** (*modifier*) of or relating to the Arabs. ORIG C14: from L, from Gk *Araps,* from Ar. *'Arab*

arabesque (ˌærəˈbɛsk) *n* **1** *Ballet.* a classical position in which the dancer has one leg raised behind. **2** *Music.* a piece or movement with a highly ornamented melody. **3** *Arts.* a type of curvilinear decoration in painting, metalwork, etc., with intricate intertwining designs. ORIG C18: from F, from It. *arabesco* in the Arabic style

Arabia ★ (əˈreɪbɪə) *n* a great peninsula of SW Asia, between the Red Sea and the Persian Gulf: consists chiefly of a desert plateau, with mountains rising over 3000 m (10 000 ft) in the west and scattered oases; includes the present-day countries of Saudi Arabia, Yemen, Oman, Bahrain, Qatar, Kuwait, and the United Arab Emirates. Area: about 2 600 000 sq. km (1 000 000 sq. miles).

Arabian (əˈreɪbɪən) *adj* **1** of or relating to Arabia or the Arabs. ◆ *n* **2** another word for **Arab.**

Arabian camel *n* a domesticated camel with one hump on its back, used as a beast of burden in the deserts of N Africa and SW Asia.

Arabian Desert ★ *n* **1** a desert in E Egypt, between the Nile, the Gulf of Suez, and the Red Sea: mountainous parts rise over 1800 m (6000 ft). Area: about 220 000 sq. km (85 000 sq. miles). **2** a desert, mainly in Saudi Arabia, that forms the desert area of the Arabian Peninsula, esp. in the north. Area: about 2 330 000 sq. km (900 000 sq. miles).

Arabian Sea ★ *n* the NW part of the Indian Ocean, between Arabia and India.

Arabic (ˈærəbɪk) *n* **1** the Semitic language of the Arabs, which has its own alphabet and is spoken in Algeria, Egypt, Iraq, Jordan, Saudi Arabia, Syria, Tunisia, etc. ◆ *adj* **2** denoting or relating to this language, any of the peoples that speak it, or the countries in which it is spoken.

arabica bean (əˈræbɪkə) *n* a high-quality coffee bean, obtained from the tree *Coffea arabica.*

Arabic numeral *n* one of the numbers 0, 1, 2, 3, 4, 5, 6, 7, 8, 9. Cf. **Roman numerals.**

arabis (ˈærəbɪs) *n* any of several trailing plants having pink or white flowers in spring. Also called: **rock cress.** ORIG C16: from Med. L, from Gk *arabis,* ult. from *Arābios* Arabian, prob. from growing in sandy or stony soil

Arabist (ˈærəbɪst) *n* a student of Arabic culture, language, history, etc.

arable (ˈærəbᵊl) *adj* **1** (of land) being or capable of being tilled for the production of crops. **2** of, relating to, or using such land. ORIG C15: from L *arābilis,* from *arāre* to plough

Araby ★ (ˈærəbɪ) *n* an archaic or poetic name for Arabia.

Aracajú ★ (*Portuguese* arakaˈʒu) *n* a port in E Brazil, capital of Sergipe state. Pop.: 401 676 (1991).

Arachne ★ (əˈræknɪ) *n Greek myth.* a maiden changed into a spider for having presumptuously challenged Athena to a weaving contest. ORIG from Gk *arakhnē* spider

arachnid (əˈræknɪd) *n* any of a class of arthropods characterized by simple eyes and four pairs of legs, including the spiders, scorpions, and ticks. ORIG C19: from NL *Arachnida,* from Gk *arakhnē* spider
▸ **aˈrachnidan** *adj, n*

arachnoid (əˈræknɔɪd) *n* **1** the middle one of three membranes that cover the brain and spinal cord. ◆ *adj* **2** of or relating to this membrane. **3** *Bot.* consisting of or covered with soft fine hairs or fibres.

arachnophobia (əˌræknəˈfəʊbɪə) *n* an abnormal fear of spiders. ORIG C20: from Gk *arakhnē* spider + -PHOBIA

Arafat ★ (ˈærəfæt) *n* **Yasser** (ˈjæsə). born 1929, Palestinian leader; cofounder of Al Fatah (1956); leader of the Palestine Liberation Organization from 1969 and chairman of the Palestine National Authority from 1994; shared Nobel peace prize 1994.

Arafura Sea ★ (ˌærəˈfʊərə) *n* a part of the W Pacific Ocean, between N Australia and SW New Guinea.

Aragats ★ (*Russian* ˌaraˈgats) *n* **Mount.** a volcanic mountain in NW Armenia. Height: 4090 m (13 419 ft). Turkish name: **Alagez.**

Aragon[1] ★ (ˈærəgən) *n* an autonomous region of NE Spain: independent kingdom from the 11th century until 1479, when it was united with Castile to form modern Spain. Pop.: 1 183 576 (1994 est.). Area: 47 609 sq. km (18 382 sq. miles).
▸ **Aragonese** (ˌærəgəˈniːz) *n, adj*

Aragon[2] ★ (*French* aragɔ̃) *n* **Louis** (lwi). 1897–1982, French writer. His works include the verse collections *Le Crève-Coeur* (1941) and *Les Yeux d'Elsa* (1942) and the series of novels *Le Monde réel* (1933–51).

Araguaia *or* **Araguaya** ★ (ˌɑːrəˈgwaɪə) *n* a river in central Brazil, rising in S Mato Grosso state and flowing north to the Tocantins River. Length: over 1771 km (1100 miles).

arak (ˈærək) *n* a variant spelling of **arrack.**

Arakan Yoma ★ (ˌɑːrɑːˈkɑːn ˈjəʊmɑː) *n* a mountain range in Myanmar, between the Irrawaddy River and the W coast: forms a barrier between Myanmar and India; teak forests.

Araks ★ (aˈraks) *n* the Russian name for the **Aras.**

Araldite (ˈærəldaɪt) *n Trademark.* an epoxy resin used as a glue for mending glass, plastic, and china.

Aral Sea ★ (ˈærəl) *n* a lake in Kazakhstan and Uzbekistan, east of the Caspian Sea, formerly the fourth largest lake in the world: shallow and saline, now badly polluted. Use of its source waters for irrigation led to a loss of 40% of its area between 1967 and 1987. Area: about 64 750 sq. km (25 000 sq. miles). Also called: **Lake Aral.**

Aram ★ (ˈɛəræm, -rəm) *n* the biblical name for ancient Syria.
▸ **Aramaean** *or* **Aramean** (ˌærəˈmiːən) *adj, n*

Aram. *abbrev. for* Aramaic.

Aramaic (ˌærəˈmeɪɪk) *n* **1** an ancient Semitic language of the Middle East, still spoken in parts of Syria and the Lebanon. ◆ *adj* **2** of, relating to, or using this language.

Aran (ˈærən) *adj* **1** of or relating to the Aran Islands. **2** made of thick natural wool: *an Aran sweater.*

Aran Islands ★ *pl n* a group of three islands in the Atlantic, off the W coast of the Republic of Ireland: Aranmore or Inishmore (the largest), Inishmaan, and Inisheer. Pop.: 1000 (latest est.). Area: 46 sq. km (18 sq. miles).

Ararat ★ (ˈærəˌræt) *n* an extinct volcanic mountain massif in E Turkey: two main peaks; **Great Ararat** 5155 m (16 916 ft), said to be the resting place of Noah's Ark after the Flood (Genesis 8:4), and **Little Ararat** 3914 m (12 843 ft).

Aras ★ (æ'ræs) *n* a river rising in Turkish Armenia and flowing east to the Caspian Sea: forms part of the E border of Turkey and the N border of Iran. Length: about 1100 km (660 miles). Ancient name: **Araxes**. Russian name: **Araks.**

Araucania ★ (ˌærɔː'keɪnɪə; *Spanish* arau'kanja) *n* a region of central Chile, inhabited by Araucanian Indians.
▸ **ˌArau'canian** *adj, n*

araucaria (ˌærɔː'kɛərɪə) *n* any of a group of coniferous trees of South America, Australia, and Polynesia, such as the monkey puzzle. ORIG C19: from NL (*arbor*) *Araucaria* (tree) from *Arauco,* a province in Chile

arbalest *or* **arbalist** ('ɑːbəlɪst) *n* a large medieval crossbow, usually cocked by mechanical means. ORIG C11: from OF, from LL *arcuballista,* from L *arcus* bow + BALLISTA

Arbela ★ (ɑː'biːlə) *n* an ancient city in Assyria, near which the **Battle of Arbela** took place (331 B.C.), in which Alexander the Great defeated the Persians. Modern name: **Erbil.**

Arber ★ ('ɑːbə) *n* **Werner** ('vɛːnə). born 1929, Swiss microbiologist, noted for his work on restriction enzymes. Nobel prize for physiology or medicine 1978.

Arbil ★ ('ɑːbɪl) *n* a variant spelling of **Erbil.**

arbiter ('ɑːbɪtə) *n* **1** a person empowered to judge in a dispute; referee. **2** a person having control of something. ORIG C15: from L, from ?
▸ **'arbitress** *fem n*

arbitrament (ɑː'bɪtrəmənt) *n* **1** the decision or award made by an arbitrator upon a disputed matter. **2** another word for **arbitration.**

arbitrary ('ɑːbɪtrərɪ) *adj* **1** founded on or subject to personal whims, prejudices, etc. **2** not absolute. **3** (of a government, ruler, etc.) despotic or dictatorial. **4** *Law.* (esp. of a penalty) within the court's discretion. ORIG C15: from L *arbitrārius* arranged through arbitration
▸ **'arbitrarily** *adv* ▸ **'arbitrariness** *n*

arbitrate ('ɑːbɪˌtreɪt) *vb* **arbitrates, arbitrating, arbitrated. 1** to achieve a settlement between parties. **2** to submit to or settle by arbitration. ORIG C16: from L *arbitrārī* to give judgment
▸ **'arbiˌtrator** *n*

arbitration (ˌɑːbɪ'treɪʃən) *n* the hearing and determination of a dispute, esp. an industrial one, by an impartial referee selected or agreed upon by the parties concerned.

Arblay, d' ★ ('dɑːbleɪ; *French* darblɛ) *n* **Madame.** the married name of (Fanny) **Burney.**

arbor[1] ('ɑːbə) *n* the US spelling of **arbour.**

arbor[2] ('ɑːbə) *n* **1** a rotating shaft in a machine on which a milling cutter or grinding wheel is fitted. **2** a rotating shaft. ORIG C17: from L: tree

arboraceous (ˌɑːbə'reɪʃəs) *adj Literary.* **1** resembling a tree. **2** wooded.

arboreal (ɑː'bɔːrɪəl) *adj* **1** of or resembling a tree. **2** living in or among trees.

arborescent (ˌɑːbə'rɛsᵊnt) *adj* having the shape or characteristics of a tree.
▸ **ˌarbo'rescence** *n*

arboretum (ˌɑːbə'riːtəm) *n, pl* **arboreta** (-tə) *or* **arboretums.** a place where trees or shrubs are cultivated. ORIG C19: from L, from *arbor* tree

arboriculture ('ɑːbərɪˌkʌltʃə) *n* the cultivation of trees or shrubs.
▸ **ˌarbori'culturist** *n*

arborio rice (ɑː'bɔːrɪəʊ) *n* a variety of round-grain rice used for making risotto. ORIG C20: after *Arborio* a town in N Italy

arbor vitae ('ɑːbɔː 'viːtaɪ, 'vaɪtiː) *n* any of several Asian and North American evergreen coniferous trees having tiny scalelike leaves and egglike cones. ORIG C17: from NL, lit.: tree of life

arbour ('ɑːbə) *n* a leafy glade or bower shaded by trees, vines, shrubs, etc. ORIG C14 *erber,* from OF, from L *herba* grass

Arbroath ★ (ɑː'brəʊθ) *n* a port and resort in E Scotland, in Angus council area: scene of the barons of Scotland's declaration of independence to Pope John XXII in 1320. Pop.: 23 474 (1991).

Arbus ★ ('ɑːbəs) *n* **Diane,** original name *Diane Nemerov.* 1923–71, US photographer.

Arbuthnot ★ (ɑː'bʌθnɒt) *n* **John.** 1667–1735, Scottish physician and satirist: author of *The History of John Bull* (1712) and, with others, of the *Memoirs of Martinus Scriblerus* (1741).

arbutus (ɑː'bjuːtəs) *n, pl* **arbutuses.** any of a genus of shrubs having clusters of white or pinkish flowers, broad evergreen leaves, and strawberry-like berries. ORIG C16: from L; rel. to *arbor* tree

arc (ɑːk) *n* **1** something curved in shape. **2** part of an unbroken curved line. **3** a luminous discharge that occurs when an electric current flows between two electrodes separated by a small gap. **4** *Maths.* a section of a curve, graph, or geometric figure. ◆ *vb* **arcs, arcing, arced** *or* **arcs, arcking, arcked. 5** (*intr*) to form an arc. ◆ *adj* **6** *Maths.* specifying an inverse trigonometric function: *arcsin, arccos, arctan.* ORIG C14: from OF, from L *arcus* bow, arch

ARC *abbrev. for* AIDS-related complex: a condition in which a person infected with the AIDS virus suffers from relatively mild symptoms, such as loss of weight, fever, etc.

arcade (ɑː'keɪd) *n* **1** a set of arches and their supporting columns. **2** a covered and sometimes arched passageway, usually with shops on one or both sides. ORIG C18: from F, from It. *arcata,* from L *arcus* bow, arch

Arcadia ★ (ɑː'keɪdɪə) *n* **1** a department of Greece, in the central Peloponnese. Capital: Tripolis. Pop.: 105 309 (1991). Area: 4367 sq. km (1686 sq. miles). **2** Also called (poetic): **Arcady** ('ɑːkədɪ). the traditional idealized rural setting of Greek and Roman bucolic poetry and later in the literature of the Renaissance.

Arcadian (ɑː'keɪdɪən) *adj* **1** of the idealized Arcadia of pastoral poetry. **2** rustic or bucolic. ◆ *n* **3** a person who leads a quiet simple rural life.
▸ **Ar'cadianism** *n*

arcane (ɑː'keɪn) *adj* requiring secret knowledge to be understood; esoteric. ORIG C16: from L *arcānus* secret, from *arcēre* to keep safe

arcanum (ɑː'keɪnəm) *n, pl* **arcana** (-nə). (*sometimes pl*) a secret or mystery. ORIG C16: from L; see ARCANE

Arc de Triomphe ★ ('ɑːk də 'triːəʊmf; *French* ark də trijɔ̃f) *n* the triumphal arch in Paris begun by Napoleon I to commemorate his victories of 1805–6 and completed in 1836.

arch[1] (ɑːtʃ) *n* **1** a curved structure that spans an opening. **2** Also called: **archway.** a structure in the form of an arch that serves as a gateway. **3** something curved like an arch. **4** any of various parts or structures of the body having a curved or archlike outline, such as the raised vault formed by the tarsal and metatarsal bones (**arch of the foot**). ◆ *vb* **5** (*tr*) to span (an opening) with an arch. **6** to form or cause to form an arch or a curve resembling that of an arch. **7** (*tr*) to span or extend over. ORIG C14: from OF *arche,* from L *arcus* bow, ARC

arch[2] (ɑːtʃ) *adj* **1** (*prenominal*) chief; principal; leading. **2** (*prenominal*) expert: *an arch criminal.* **3** knowing or superior; coyly playful: *an arch look.* ORIG C16: independent use of ARCH-
▸ **'archly** *adv* ▸ **'archness** *n*

arch. *abbrev. for:* **1** archaic. **2** archaism. **3** archipelago. **4** architect. **5** architectural. **6** architecture.

arch- *or* **archi-** *combining form.* **1** chief; principal: *archbishop.* **2** eminent above all others of the same kind: *archenemy.* ORIG ult. from Gk *arkhi-,* from *arkhein* to rule

-arch *n combining form.* leader; ruler; chief: *patriarch; monarch.* ORIG from Gk *-arkhēs,* from *arkhein* to rule

Archaean *or esp. US* **Archean** (ɑː'kiːən) *adj* of the metamorphosed rocks formed in the early Precambrian era.

archaeology *or* **archeology** (ˌɑːkɪ'ɒlədʒɪ) *n* the study of man's past by scientific analysis of the material remains of his cultures. ORIG C17: from LL, from Gk *arkhaiologia* study of what is ancient, from *arkhē* beginning

▸ **archaeological** *or* **archeological** (ˌɑːkɪəˈlɒdʒɪkᵊl) *adj* ▸ ˌ**archaeˈologist** *or* ˌ**archeˈologist** *n*

archaeopteryx (ˌɑːkɪˈɒptərɪks) *n* any of several extinct primitive birds which occurred in Jurassic times and had teeth, a long tail, and well-developed wings. ORIG C19: from Gk *arkhaios* ancient + *pterux* winged creature

archaic (ɑːˈkeɪɪk) *adj* **1** belonging to or characteristic of a much earlier period. **2** out of date; antiquated. **3** (of vocabulary, etc.) characteristic of an earlier period of a language. ORIG C19: from F, from Gk *arkhaïkos,* from *arkhaios* ancient, from *arkhē* beginning, from *arkhein* to begin
▸ **arˈchaically** *adv*

archaism (ˈɑːkeɪˌɪzəm) *n* **1** the adoption or imitation of archaic words or style. **2** an archaic word, style, etc. ORIG C17: from NL, from Gk, from *arkhaizein* to model one's style upon that of ancient writers; see ARCHAIC
▸ **ˈarchaist** *n* ▸ ˌ**archaˈistic** *adj*

archangel (ˈɑːkˌeɪndʒəl) *n* a principal angel.
▸ **archangelic** (ˌɑːkænˈdʒɛlɪk) *adj*

Archangel ★ (ˈɑːkˌeɪndʒəl) *n* a port in NW Russia, on the Dvina River: major centre for the timber trade and White Sea fisheries. Pop.: 374 000 (1995 est.). Russian name: **Arkhangelsk.**

archbishop (ˈɑːtʃˈbɪʃəp) *n* a bishop of the highest rank. Abbrev.: **abp, Abp, Arch., Archbp.**

archbishopric (ˈɑːtʃˈbɪʃəprɪk) *n* the rank, office, or jurisdiction of an archbishop.

archdeacon (ˈɑːtʃˈdiːkən) *n* **1** an Anglican clergyman ranking just below a bishop. **2** a clergyman of similar rank in other Churches.
▸ **ˈarchˈdeaconry** *n*

archdiocese (ˌɑːtʃˈdaɪəˌsiːs) *n* the diocese of an archbishop.
▸ **archdiocesan** (ˌɑːtʃdaɪˈɒsɪsᵊn) *adj*

archducal (ˈɑːtʃˈdjuːkᵊl) *adj* of or relating to an archduke, archduchess, or archduchy.

archduchess (ˈɑːtʃˈdʌtʃɪs) *n* **1** the wife or widow of an archduke. **2** (since 1453) a princess of the Austrian imperial family.

archduchy (ˈɑːtʃˈdʌtʃɪ) *n, pl* **archduchies.** the territory ruled by an archduke or archduchess.

archduke (ˈɑːtʃˈdjuːk) *n* a chief duke, esp. (since 1453) a prince of the Austrian imperial dynasty.

Archean (ɑːˈkiːən) *adj* a variant spelling (esp. US) of **Archaean.**

archegonium (ˌɑːkɪˈgəʊnɪəm) *n, pl* **archegonia** (-nɪə). a female sex organ, occurring in mosses, ferns, etc. ORIG C19: from NL, from Gk, from *arkhe-* chief, first + *gonos* seed, race

archenemy (ˈɑːtʃˈɛnɪmɪ) *n, pl* **archenemies. 1** a chief enemy. **2** (*often cap.; preceded by the*) the devil.

archeology (ˌɑːkɪˈɒlədʒɪ) *n* a variant of **archaeology.**

archer (ˈɑːtʃə) *n* a person skilled in the use of a bow and arrow. ORIG C13: from OF, from LL, from L *arcus* bow

Archer[1] (ˈɑːtʃə) *n* **the.** the constellation Sagittarius.

Archer[2] ★ (ˈɑːtʃə) *n* **1 Frederick Scott.** 1813–57, British inventor and sculptor. He developed (1851) the wet collodion photographic process, enabling multiple copies of pictures to be made. **2 Jeffrey (Howard),** Baron Archer of Weston-Super-Mare. born 1940, British novelist and Conservative politician; MP from 1969 until 1974. His works include *Kane and Abel* (1979) and *The Fourth Estate* (1996). **3 William.** 1856–1924, Scottish critic and dramatist: made the first English translations of Ibsen.

archerfish (ˈɑːtʃəˌfɪʃ) *n, pl* **archerfish** *or* **archerfishes.** a freshwater fish, related to the perch, of SE Asia and Australia, that catches insects by spitting water at them.

archery (ˈɑːtʃərɪ) *n* **1** the art or sport of shooting with bows and arrows. **2** archers or their weapons collectively.

archetype (ˈɑːkɪˌtaɪp) *n* **1** a perfect or typical specimen. **2** an original model; prototype. **3** *Psychoanal.* one of the inherited mental images postulated by Jung. **4** a recurring symbol or motif in literature, etc. ORIG C17: from L *archetypum* an original, from Gk, from *arkhetupos* first-moulded; see ARCH-, -TYPE
▸ ˌ**archeˈtypal** *adj*

archfiend (ˌɑːtʃˈfiːnd) *n* (*often cap.*) **the.** the devil; Satan.

archidiaconal (ˌɑːkɪdaɪˈækənᵊl) *adj* of or relating to an archdeacon or his or her office.
▸ ˌ**archidiˈaconate** *n*

archiepiscopal (ˌɑːkɪɪˈpɪskəpᵊl) *adj* of or associated with an archbishop.
▸ ˌ**archieˈpiscopate** *n*

archil (ˈɑːtʃɪl) *n* a variant of **orchil.**

archimandrite (ˌɑːkɪˈmændraɪt) *n Greek Orthodox Church.* the head of a monastery. ORIG C16: from LL, from LGk *arkhimandritēs,* from ARCHI- + *mandra* monastery

Archimedes ★ (ˌɑːkɪˈmiːdiːz) *n* ?287–212 B.C., Greek mathematician of Syracuse, noted for his work in geometry, hydrostatics, and mechanics.
▸ ˌ**Archiˈmedean** *adj*

Archimedes' principle *n* a law of physics stating that the apparent loss in weight of a body immersed in a fluid is equal to the weight of the displaced fluid.

Archimedes' screw *or* **Archimedean screw** *n* an ancient water-lifting device using a spiral passage in an inclined cylinder.

archipelago (ˌɑːkɪˈpɛləˌgəʊ) *n, pl* **archipelagos** *or* **archipelagoes. 1** a group of islands. **2** a sea studded with islands. ORIG C16 (meaning: the Aegean Sea): from It., from L *pelagus,* from Gk, from ARCH- + *pelagos* sea
▸ **archipelagic** (ˌɑːkɪpəˈlædʒɪk) *adj*

architect (ˈɑːkɪˌtɛkt) *n* **1** a person qualified to design buildings and to supervise their erection. **2** a person similarly qualified in another form of construction: *a naval architect.* **3** any planner or creator. ORIG C16: from F, from L, from Gk *arkhitektōn* director of works, from ARCHI- + *tektōn* workman; rel. to *tekhnē* art, skill

architectonic (ˌɑːkɪtɛkˈtɒnɪk) *adj* **1** denoting, relating to, or having architectural qualities. **2** *Metaphysics.* of the systematic classification of knowledge. ORIG C16: from LL *architectonicus* concerning architecture; see ARCHITECT

architectonics (ˌɑːkɪtɛkˈtɒnɪks) *n* (*functioning as sing*) **1** the science of architecture. **2** *Metaphysics.* the scientific classification of knowledge.

architecture (ˈɑːkɪˌtɛktʃə) *n* **1** the art and science of designing and superintending the erection of buildings, etc. **2** a style of building or structure. **3** buildings or structures collectively. **4** the structure or design of anything.
▸ ˌ**archiˈtectural** *adj*

architrave (ˈɑːkɪˌtreɪv) *n Archit.* **1** the lowest part of an entablature that bears on the columns. **2** a moulding around a doorway, window opening, etc. ORIG C16: via F from It., from ARCHI- + *trave* beam, from L *trabs*

archive (ˈɑːkaɪv) *n* (*often pl*) **1** a collection of records of an institution, family, etc. **2** a place where such records are kept. **3** *Computing.* data transferred to a tape or disk for long-term storage rather than frequent use. ◆ *vb* **4** (*tr*) to store (documents, data, etc.) in an archive or other repository. ORIG C17: from LL, from Gk *arkheion* repository of official records, from *arkhē* government
▸ **arˈchival** *adj*

archivist (ˈɑːkɪvɪst) *n* a person in charge of archives.

archon (ˈɑːkɒn) *n* (in ancient Athens) one of the nine chief magistrates. ORIG C17: from Gk *arkhōn* ruler, from *arkhein* to rule
▸ **ˈarchonˌship** *n*

archpriest (ˈɑːtʃˈpriːst) *n* **1** (formerly) a chief assistant to a bishop. **2** a senior priest.

archway (ˈɑːtʃˌweɪ) *n* a passageway or entrance under an arch or arches.

-archy *n combining form.* government; rule: *anarchy; monarchy.* ORIG from Gk *-arkhia;* see -ARCH

arc light *n* a light source in which an arc between two electrodes produces intense white illumination. Also called: **arc lamp.**

arctic (ˈɑːktɪk) *adj* **1** of or relating to the Arctic. **2** *Inf.* cold; freezing. ◆ *n* **3** (*modifier*) suitable for conditions of extreme cold: *arctic clothing.* ORIG C14: from L *arcticus,* from Gk *arktikos* northern, lit.: pertaining to (the constellation of) the Bear, from *arktos* bear

Arctic ★ ('ɑːktɪk) *n* **1 the.** Also called: **Arctic Zone.** the regions north of the Arctic Circle. ◆ *adj* **2** of or relating to the regions north of the Arctic Circle.

Arctic Circle *n* the imaginary circle round the earth, parallel to the equator, at latitude 66° 32′ N.

arctic hare *n* a large hare of the Canadian Arctic whose fur is white in winter.

Arctic Ocean ★ *n* the ocean surrounding the North Pole, north of the Arctic Circle. Area: about 14 100 000 sq. km (5 440 000 sq. miles).

arctic willow *n* a low-growing shrub of the Canadian tundra.

Arcturus (ɑːk'tjʊərəs) *n* the brightest star in the constellation Boötes: a red giant. ORIG C14: from L, from Gk *Arktouros,* from *arktos* bear + *ouros* guard, keeper

arcuate ('ɑːkjʊɪt) *adj* shaped or bent like an arc or bow. ORIG C17: from L *arcuāre,* from *arcus* ARC

arc welding *n* a technique in which metal is welded by heat generated by an electric arc.
▸ **arc welder** *n*

-ard *or* **-art** *suffix forming nouns.* indicating a person who does something, esp. to excess: *braggart; drunkard.* ORIG via OF, of Gmc origin

Ardèche ★ (*French* ardɛʃ) *n* a department of S France, in Rhône-Alpes region. Capital: Privas. Pop.: 282 432 (1994 est.). Area: 5556 sq. km (2167 sq. miles).

Arden[1] ★ ('ɑːdᵊn) *n* **Forest of.** a region of N Warwickshire, part of a former forest: scene of Shakespeare's *As You Like It.*

Arden[2] ★ ('ɑːdᵊn) *n* **John.** born 1930, British dramatist and novelist. His plays include *Serjeant Musgrave's Dance* (1959), *The Workhouse Donkey* (1963), and *A Suburban Suicide* (1994): often works with Margaretta D'Arcy.

Ardennes ★ (ɑː'dɛn; *French* ardɛn) *n* **1** a department of NE France, in Champagne-Ardenne region. Capital: Mézières. Pop.: 292 642 (1994 est.). Area: 5253 sq. km (2049 sq. miles). **2 the.** a wooded plateau in SE Belgium, Luxembourg, and NE France: scene of heavy fighting in both World Wars.

ardent ('ɑːdᵊnt) *adj* **1** expressive of or characterized by intense desire or emotion. **2** intensely enthusiastic; eager. **3** glowing or shining: *ardent eyes.* **4 ardent spirits.** alcoholic drinks. ORIG C14: from L *ārdēre* to burn
▸ **'ardency** *n* ▸ **'ardently** *adv*

ardour *or US* **ardor** ('ɑːdə) *n* **1** feelings of great intensity and warmth. **2** eagerness; zeal. ORIG C14: from OF, from L *ārdor,* from *ārdēre* to burn

Ards ★ (ɑːdz) *n* a district of E Northern Ireland, on the Irish Sea and Strangford Lough: agriculture. Administrative centre: Newtownards. Pop.: 64 764 (1991). Area: 361 sq. km (139 sq. miles).

arduous ('ɑːdjuːəs) *adj* **1** difficult to accomplish; strenuous. **2** hard to endure; harsh. **3** steep or difficult: *an arduous track.* ORIG C16: from L *arduus* steep, difficult
▸ **'arduously** *adv* ▸ **'arduousness** *n*

are[1] (ɑː; *unstressed* ə) *vb* the plural form of the present tense of **be** and the singular form used with *you.* ORIG OE *aron,* second person pl of *bēon* to BE

are[2] (ɑː) *n* a unit of area equal to 100 square metres. ORIG C19: from F, from L *ārea* piece of ground; see AREA

area ('ɛərɪə) *n* **1** any flat, curved, or irregular expanse of a surface. **2a** the extent of a two-dimensional surface: *the area of a triangle.* **2b** the two-dimensional extent of a plane or surface: *the area of a sphere.* **3** a section or part. **4** region; district. **5a** a geographical division of administrative responsibility. **5b** (*as modifier*): *area manager.* **6** a part or section, as of a building, town, etc., having some specified function: *reception area; commercial area.* **7** the range or scope of anything. **8** a subject field or field of study. **9** Also called: **areaway.** a sunken area, usually enclosed, giving light, air, and sometimes access to a cellar basement. ORIG C16: from L: level ground, threshing-floor; rel. to *ārēre* to be dry
▸ **'areal** *adj*

arena (ə'riːnə) *n* **1** an enclosure or platform, usually surrounded by seats, in which sports events, entertainments, etc., take place: *a boxing arena.* **2** the central area of an ancient Roman amphitheatre, in which gladiatorial contests were held. **3** a sphere of intense activity: *the political arena.* ORIG C17: from L *harēna* sand, place where sand was strewn for the combats

arenaceous (ˌærɪ'neɪʃəs) *adj* **1** (of sedimentary rocks) composed of sand. **2** (of plants) growing in a sandy soil. ORIG C17: from L *harēnāceus* sandy, from *harēna* sand

Arendt ★ ('ɛərənt) *n* **Hannah.** 1906–75, US political philosopher, born in Germany. Her publications include *The Origins of Totalitarianism* (1951) and *Eichmann in Jerusalem* (1961).

aren't (ɑːnt) **1** *contraction of* are not. **2** *Inf., chiefly Brit.* (used in interrogative sentences) *contraction of* am not.

areola (ə'rɪələ) *n, pl* **areolae** (-ˌliː) *or* **areolas.** *Anat.* any small circular area, such as the pigmented ring around the human nipple. ORIG C17: from L: dim. of AREA
▸ **a'reolar** *or* **areolate** (ə'rɪəlɪt, -ˌleɪt) *adj*

areole ('ærɪəʊl) *n* **1** *Biol.* a space outlined on a surface, such as an area between veins on a leaf. **2** a sunken area on a cactus from which spines, hairs, etc., arise.
▸ **'areoˌlate** *adj*

Areopagus ★ (ˌærɪ'ɒpəgəs) *n* **1a** the hill to the northwest of the Acropolis in Athens. **b** (in ancient Athens) the judicial council whose members (Areopagites) met on this hill. **2** *Literary.* any high court. ORIG via L from Gk *Areiopagus,* contracted from *Areios pagos,* hill of Ares
▸ **Areopagite** (ˌærɪ'ɒpəˌdʒaɪt) *n*

Arequipa ★ (ˌærɪ'kiːpə; *Spanish* are'kipa) *n* a city in S Peru, at an altitude of 2250 m (7500 ft): founded in 1540 on the site of an Inca city. Pop.: 725 838 (1995).

Ares ★ ('ɛəriːz) *n Greek myth.* the god of war, born of Zeus and Hera. Roman counterpart: **Mars.**

arête (ə'reɪt, ə'rɛt) *n* a sharp ridge that separates glacial valleys. ORIG C19: from F: fishbone, ridge, from L *arista* ear of corn, fishbone

Arethusa ★ (ˌærɪ'θjuːzə) *n Greek myth.* a nymph who was changed into a spring on the island of Ortygia to escape the amorous advances of the river god Alpheus.

Arezzo ★ (ə'rɛtsəʊ; *Italian* a'rettso) *n* a city in central Italy, in E Tuscany. Pop.: 91 527 (1990). Ancient Latin name: **Arretium.**

Arg. *abbrev. for* Argentina.

argal ('ɑːgəl) *n* another name for **argol.**

argali ('ɑːgəlɪ) *or* **argal** *n, pl* **argali** *or* **argals.** a wild sheep, with massive horns in the male, inhabiting semidesert regions in central Asia. ORIG C18: from Mongolian

argent ('ɑːdʒənt) *n* **a** an archaic or poetic word for **silver. b** (*as adj; often postpositive, esp. in heraldry*): *a bend argent.* ORIG C15: from OF, from L

Argenteuil ★ (*French* arʒɑ̃tœj) *n* a suburb of Paris, France, with a convent (656) that became famous when Héloïse was abbess (12th century). Pop.: 93 096 (1990).

argentiferous (ˌɑːdʒən'tɪfərəs) *adj* containing or bearing silver.

Argentina ★ (ˌɑːdʒən'tiːnə) *n* a republic in southern South America: colonized by the Spanish from 1516 onwards; gained independence in 1816 and became a republic in 1852; consists chiefly of subtropical plains and forests (the Chaco) in the north, temperate plains (the pampas) in the central parts, the Andes in the west, and an infertile plain extending to Tierra del Fuego in the south (Patagonia); an important meat producer. Language: Spanish. Religion: Roman Catholic. Currency: peso. Capital: Buenos Aires. Pop.: 36 578 000 (1999 est.). Area: 2 776 653 sq. km (1 072 067 sq. miles). Also called: **the Argentine.**

argentine ('ɑːdʒənˌtaɪn) *adj* **1** of or resembling silver. ◆ *n* **2** a small marine fish characterized by a long silvery body.

Argentine ★ ('ɑːdʒənˌtiːn, -ˌtaɪn) *n* **1 the.** another name for **Argentina. 2** a native or inhabitant of Argentina. ◆ *adj* **3** of or relating to Argentina. ◆ Also (for senses 2, 3): **Argentinian** (ˌɑːdʒən'tɪnɪən).

argillaceous (ˌɑːdʒɪ'leɪʃəs) *adj* (of sedimentary rocks) composed of very fine-grained material, such as clay. ORIG C18: from L *argilla* white clay, from Gk, from *argos* white

Argive ('ɑːdʒaɪv, -gaɪv) *adj* **1** of or relating to Argos. **2** a literary word for **Greek.** ◆ *n* **3** an ancient Greek, esp. one from Argos.

Argo ★ ('ɑːgəʊ) *n Greek myth.* the ship in which Jason sailed in search of the Golden Fleece.

argol ('ɑːgɒl) *or* **argal** ('ɑːgəl) *n* crude potassium hydrogentartrate. ORIG C14: from Anglo-F *argoil,* from ?

Argolis ★ ('ɑːgəlɪs) *n* **1** a department and ancient region of Greece, in the NE Peloponnese. Capital: Nauplion. Pop.: 97 636 (1991). Area: 2261 sq. km (873 sq. miles). **2 Gulf of.** an inlet of the Aegean Sea, in the E Peloponnese.

argon ('ɑːgɒn) *n* an unreactive colourless odourless element of the rare gas series that forms almost 1 per cent of the atmosphere. It is used in electric lights. Symbol: Ar; atomic no.: 18; atomic wt.: 39.95. ORIG C19: from Gk, from *argos* inactive, from A-[1] + *ergon* work

Argonaut ★ ('ɑːgəˌnɔːt) *n* **1** *Greek myth.* one of the heroes who sailed with Jason in quest of the Golden Fleece. **2** a person who took part in the Californian gold rush of 1849. **3** (*not cap.*) another name for the **paper nautilus.** ORIG C16: from Gk *Argonautēs,* from *Argō* the name of Jason's ship + *nautēs* sailor

▸ **ˌArgoˈnautic** *adj*

Argonne ★ ('ɑːgɒn; *French* argɔn) *n* **the.** a wooded region of NE France: scene of major battles in both World Wars.

Argos ★ ('ɑːgɒs, -gəs) *n* an ancient city in SE Greece, in the NE Peloponnese: one of the oldest Greek cities, it dominated the Peloponnese in the 7th century B.C. Pop.: 22 000 (1995 est.).

argosy ('ɑːgəsɪ) *n, pl* **argosies.** *Arch. or poetic.* a large abundantly laden merchant ship, or a fleet of such ships. ORIG C16: from It. *Ragusea* (*nave*) (ship) of Ragusa

argot ('ɑːgəʊ) *n* slang or jargon peculiar to a particular group, esp. (formerly) a group of thieves. ORIG C19: from F, from ?

Argovie ★ (argɔvi) *n* the French name for **Aargau.**

arguable ('ɑːgjʊəbᵊl) *adj* **1** capable of being disputed. **2** plausible; reasonable.

▸ **ˈarguably** *adv*

argue ('ɑːgjuː) *vb* **argues, arguing, argued. 1** (*intr*) to quarrel; wrangle. **2** (*intr; often foll. by* for *or* against) to present supporting or opposing reasons or cases in a dispute. **3** (*tr; may take a clause as object*) to try to prove by presenting reasons. **4** (*tr; often passive*) to debate or discuss. **5** (*tr*) to persuade. **6** (*tr*) to suggest: *her looks argue despair.* ORIG C14: from OF *arguer* to assert, from L *arguere* to make clear, accuse

▸ **ˈarguer** *n*

argufy ('ɑːgjʊˌfaɪ) *vb* **argufies, argufying, argufied.** *Facetious or dialect.* to argue or quarrel, esp. over something trivial.

argument ('ɑːgjʊmənt) *n* **1** a quarrel, altercation. **2** a discussion in which reasons are put forward; debate. **3** (*sometimes pl*) a point or series of reasons presented to support or oppose a proposition. **4** a summary of the plot or subject of a book, etc. **5** *Logic.* **5a** a process of reasoning in which the conclusion can be shown to be true or false. **5b** the middle term of a syllogism. **6** *Maths.* another name for **independent variable** of a function.

argumentation (ˌɑːgjʊmɛnˈteɪʃən) *n* **1** the process of reasoning methodically. **2** argument; debate.

argumentative (ˌɑːgjʊˈmɛntətɪv) *adj* **1** given to arguing. **2** characterized by argument; controversial.

Argus ★ ('ɑːgəs) *n* **1** *Greek myth.* a giant with a hundred eyes who was made guardian of the heifer Io. **2** a vigilant person.

Argus-eyed *adj* observant; vigilant.

argy-bargy *or* **argie-bargie** ('ɑːdʒɪ'bɑːdʒɪ) *n, pl* **argy-bargies.** *Brit. inf.* a wrangling argument or verbal dispute. ORIG C19: from Scot., from dialect *argle,* prob. from ARGUE

Argyll and Bute ★ (ɑː'gaɪl) *n* a council area in W Scotland on the Atlantic Ocean: in 1975 the historic counties of Argyllshire and Bute became part of Strathclyde region; in 1996 they were reinstated as a single unitary authority. Administrative centre: Lochgilphead. Pop.: 90 550 (1996 est.). Area: 6930 sq. km (2676 sq. miles).

Argyllshire ★ (ɑː'gaɪlˌʃɪə, -ʃə) *n* a historic county of W Scotland, part of Strathclyde region (1975–96), now part of Argyll and Bute.

Århus ★ (*Danish* 'ɔrhuːs) *n* a variant spelling of **Aarhus.**

aria ('ɑːrɪə) *n* an elaborate accompanied song for solo voice from a cantata, opera, or oratorio. ORIG C18: from It.: tune, AIR

Ariadne ★ (ˌærɪ'ædnɪ) *n Greek myth.* daughter of Minos and Pasiphaë: she gave Theseus the thread with which he found his way out of the Minotaur's labyrinth.

Arian ('ɛərɪən) *adj* **1** of or relating to Arius or to Arianism. ◆ *n* **2** an adherent of Arianism.

-arian *suffix forming nouns.* indicating a person or thing that advocates, believes, or is associated with something: *vegetarian; librarian.* ORIG from L *-ārius* -ARY + -AN

Arianism ('ɛərɪəˌnɪzəm) *n* the doctrine of Arius, declared heretical, which asserted that Christ was not of one substance with the Father.

Arias Sánchez ★ ('ærɪæs 'sæntʃɛz) *n* **Oscar.** born 1940, Costa Rican statesman; president (1986–90); Nobel peace prize 1987.

Arica ★ (ə'riːkə; *Spanish* a'rika) *n* a port in extreme N Chile: awarded to Chile in 1929 after the lengthy Tacna-Arica dispute with Peru; outlet for Bolivian and Peruvian trade. Pop.: 173 336 (1995 est.). See also **Tacna-Arica.**

arid ('ærɪd) *adj* **1** having little or no rain; dry. **2** devoid of interest. ORIG C17: from L *āridus,* from *ārēre* to be dry

▸ **aridity** (ə'rɪdɪtɪ) *or* **ˈaridness** *n*

arid zone *n* either of the zones of latitude 15–30° N and S, with low rainfall and desert or semidesert terrain.

Ariège ★ (*French* arjɛʒ) *n* a department of SW France, in Midi-Pyrénées region. Capital: Foix. Pop.: 136 667 (1994 est.). Area: 4903 sq. km (1912 sq. miles).

Aries ('ɛəriːz) *n, Latin genitive* **Arietis** (ə'raɪɪtɪs). **1** *Astron.* a N constellation. **2** *Astrol.* Also called: the **Ram.** the first sign of the zodiac. The sun is in this sign between about March 21 and April 19. ORIG C14: from L: ram

aright (ə'raɪt) *adv* correctly; rightly; properly.

aril ('ærɪl) *n* an additional covering formed on certain seeds, such as those of the yew and nutmeg, after fertilization. ORIG C18: from NL, from Med. L *arilli* raisins, pips of grapes

▸ **ˈarilˌlate** *adj*

Arimathea *or* **Arimathaea** ★ (ˌærɪmə'θiːə) *n* a town in ancient Palestine: location unknown.

Ariminum ★ (ə'rɪmɪnəm) *n* the ancient name of **Rimini.**

arioso (ˌɑːrɪ'əʊzəʊ) *n, pl* **ariosos** *or* **ariosi** (-siː). *Music.* a recitative with the lyrical quality of an aria. ORIG C18: from It., from ARIA

Ariosto ★ (*Italian* a'rjɔsto) *n* **Ludovico** (ludo'viːko). 1474–1533, Italian poet, famous for his romantic epic *Orlando Furioso* (1516).

arise (ə'raɪz) *vb* **arises, arising, arose, arisen** (ə'rɪzᵊn). (*intr*) **1** to come into being; originate. **2** (foll. by *from*) to proceed as a consequence. **3** to get or stand up, as from a sitting or lying position. **4** to come into notice. **5** to ascend. ORIG OE *ārīsan*

aristo ('ærɪstəʊ, ə'rɪstəʊ) *n, pl* **aristos.** *Inf.* short for **aristocrat.**

aristocracy (ˌærɪ'stɒkrəsɪ) *n, pl* **aristocracies. 1** a privileged class of people usually of high birth; the nobility. **2** such a class as the ruling body of a state. **3** government by such a class. **4** a state governed by such a class. **5** a class of people considered to be outstanding in a sphere of activity. ORIG C16: from LL, from Gk *aristokratia* rule by the best-born, from *aristos* best; see -CRACY

aristocrat ('ærɪstəˌkræt) *n* **1** a member of the aristocracy. **2** a person who has the manners or qualities of a member of a privileged class. **3** a supporter of aristocracy as a form of government.

aristocratic (ˌærɪstə'krætɪk) *adj* **1** relating to or characteristic of aristocracy or an aristocrat. **2** elegant or stylish in appearance and behaviour.

▸ **ˌaristoˈcratically** *adv*

Aristophanes ★ (ˌærɪˈstɒfəˌniːz) *n* ?448–?380 B.C., Greek comic dramatist, who satirized leading contemporary figures such as Socrates and Euripides. Eleven of his plays are extant, including *The Clouds, The Frogs, The Birds,* and *Lysistrata.*

Aristotelian (ˌærɪstəˈtiːlɪən) *adj* **1** of or relating to Aristotle or to his philosophy. ◆ *n* **2** a follower of Aristotle.

Aristotelian logic *n* **1** traditional logic, esp. relying on the theory of syllogism. **2** the logical method of Aristotle, esp. as developed in the Middle Ages.

Aristotle ★ (ˈærɪˌstɒtᵊl) *n* 384–322 B.C., Greek philosopher; pupil of Plato, tutor of Alexander the Great, and founder of the Peripatetic school at Athens; author of works on logic, ethics, politics, poetics, rhetoric, biology, zoology, and metaphysics. His works influenced Muslim philosophy and science and medieval scholastic philosophy.

arithmetic *n* (əˈrɪθmətɪk). **1** the branch of mathematics concerned with numerical calculations, such as addition, subtraction, multiplication, and division. **2** calculations involving numerical operations. **3** knowledge of or skill in using arithmetic. ◆ *adj* (ˌærɪθˈmɛtɪk) *also* **arithmetical. 4** of, relating to, or using arithmetic. ORIG C13: from L, from Gk *arithmētikē,* from *arithmein* to count, from *arithmos* number
▸ ˌ**arithˈmetically** *adv* ▸ **aˌrithmeˈtician** *n*

arithmetic mean *n* the average value of a set of terms or quantities, expressed as their sum divided by their number: *the arithmetic mean of 3, 4, and 8 is 5.* Also called: **average.**

arithmetic progression *n* a sequence, each term of which differs from the succeeding term by a constant amount, such as 3,6,9,12.

-arium *suffix forming nouns.* indicating a place for or associated with something: *aquarium; solarium.* ORIG from L *-ārium,* neuter of *-ārius* -ARY

Arius ★ (ˈɛərɪəs) *n* ?250–336 A.D., Greek Christian theologian, originator of the doctrine of Arianism.

Ariz. *abbrev. for* Arizona.

Arizona ★ (ˌærɪˈzəʊnə) *n* a state of the southwestern US: consists of the Colorado plateau in the northeast, including the Grand Canyon, divided from desert in the southwest by mountains rising over 3750 m (12 500 ft). Capital: Phoenix. Pop.: 4 668 631 (1998 est.). Area: 293 750 sq. km (113 417 sq. miles). Abbrevs.: **Ariz.** or (with zip code) **AZ**

Arjuna ★ (ˈɑːdʒʊnə) *n Hindu myth.* the most important of the five princes in the *Mahabharata.* Krishna served as his charioteer in the battle with the Kauravas.

ark (ɑːk) *n* **1** the vessel that Noah built which survived the Flood (Genesis 6–9). **2** a place or thing offering shelter or protection. **3** *Dialect.* a box. ORIG OE *arc,* from L *arca* box, chest

Ark (ɑːk) *n Judaism.* **1** Also called: **Holy Ark.** the cupboard in a synagogue in which the Torah scrolls are kept. **2** Also called: **Ark of the Covenant.** the most sacred symbol of God's presence among the Hebrew people, carried in their journey from Sinai to the Promised Land (Canaan).

Ark. *abbrev. for* Arkansas.

Arkansas ★ *n* **1** (ˈɑːkənˌsɔː). a state of the southern US: mountainous in the north and west, with the alluvial plain of the Mississippi in the east; has the only diamond mine in the US; the chief US producer of bauxite. Capital: Little Rock. Pop.: 2 538 303 (1998 est.). Area: 134 537 sq. km (51 945 sq. miles). Abbrevs.: **Ark.** or (with zip code) **AR** **2** (ɑːˈkænzəs). a river in the S central US, rising in central Colorado and flowing east and southeast to join the Mississippi in Arkansas. Length: 2335 km (1450 miles).
▸ **Arkansan** (ɑːˈkænzən) *n, adj*

Arkhangelsk ★ (arˈxangɪljsk) *n* the Russian name for **Archangel.**

Arkwright ★ (ˈɑːkraɪt) *n* Sir **Richard.** 1732–92, English cotton manufacturer: inventor of the spinning frame (1769) which produced cotton thread strong enough to be used as a warp.

Arles ★ (ɑːlz; *French* arl) *n* **1** a city in SE France, on the Rhône: Roman amphitheatre. Pop.: 52 590 (1990). **2** **Kingdom of.** a kingdom in SE France which had dissolved by 1378: known as the Kingdom of Burgundy until about 1200.

Arlington ★ (ˈɑːlɪŋtən) *n* a county of N Virginia: site of **Arlington National Cemetery.**

Arlon ★ (*French* arlɔ̃) *n* a town in SE Belgium, capital of Luxembourg province. Pop.: 17 000 (1991 est.).

arm[1] (ɑːm) *n* **1** (in man) either of the upper limbs from the shoulder to the wrist. Related adj: **brachial. 2** the part of either of the upper limbs from the elbow to the wrist; forearm. **3a** the corresponding limb of any other vertebrate. **3b** an armlike appendage of some invertebrates. **4** an object that covers or supports the human arm, esp. the sleeve of a garment or the side of a chair, etc. **5** anything considered to resemble an arm in appearance, function, etc.: *an arm of the sea; the arm of a record player.* **6** an administrative subdivision of an organization: *an arm of the government.* **7** power; authority: *the arm of the law.* **8** **arm in arm.** with arms linked. **9 at arm's length.** at a distance. **10 in the arms of Morpheus.** sleeping. **11 with open arms.** with great warmth and hospitality. ORIG OE

arm[2] (ɑːm) *vb* **1** to equip with weapons as a preparation for war. **2** (*tr*) to provide (a person or thing) with something that strengthens, protects, or increases efficiency. **3a** (*tr*) to activate (a fuse) so that it will explode at the required time. **3b** to prepare (an explosive device) for use by introducing a detonator, etc. ◆ *n* **4** (*usually pl*) a weapon, esp. a firearm. ORIG C14: from OF *armes,* from L *arma* arms, equipment

Arm. *abbrev. for:* **1** Armenia(n). **2** Armoric *or* Armorican.

armada (ɑːˈmɑːdə) *n* **1** a large number of ships or aircraft. **2** (*cap.*) **the.** Also called: **Spanish Armada.** the great fleet sent by Philip II of Spain against England in 1588. ORIG C16: from Sp., from Med. L *armāta* fleet, armed forces, from L *armāre* to provide with arms

armadillo (ˌɑːməˈdɪləʊ) *n, pl* **armadillos.** a burrowing mammal of Central and South America with a covering of strong horny plates over most of the body. ORIG C16: from Sp., dim. of *armado* armed (man), from L *armātus* armed; cf. ARMADA

Armageddon (ˌɑːməˈgɛdᵊn) *n* **1** *New Testament.* the final battle between good and evil at the end of the world. **2** a catastrophic and extremely destructive conflict. ORIG C19: from LL, from Gk, from Heb. *har megiddōn,* mountain district of *Megiddo* (in N Palestine)

Armagh ★ (ɑːˈmɑː) *n* **1** a historic county of S Northern Ireland: in 1973 its administrative functions were given to local government districts. Area: 1326 sq. km (512 sq. miles). **2** a district of SE Northern Ireland, bordering the Irish Republic: fruit growing, light industry. Administrative centre: Armagh. Area: 676 sq. km (261 sq. miles). Pop.: 51 817 (1991). **3** a city in S Northern Ireland, in the district of Armagh: seat of Roman Catholic and Protestant archbishops. Pop.: 14 640 (1991).

Armalite (ˈɑːməlaɪt) *n Trademark.* a lightweight high-velocity rifle of various calibres, capable of automatic and semiautomatic operation. ORIG C20: from *Armalite* Division, Fairchild Engine and Airplane Company, manufacturers

armament (ˈɑːməmənt) *n* **1** (*often pl*) the weapon equipment of a military vehicle, ship, or aircraft. **2** a military force raised and armed ready for war. **3** preparation for war. ORIG C17: from L *armāmenta* utensils, from *armāre* to equip

Armani ★ (ɑːˈmɑːnɪ; *Italian* arˈmaːni) *n* **Giorgio** (ˈdʒordʒo). born 1936, Italian fashion designer, noted for his restrained classical style.

armature (ˈɑːmətjʊə) *n* **1** a revolving structure in an electric motor or generator, wound with the coils that carry the current. **2** any part of an electric machine or device that moves under the influence of a magnetic field or within which an electromotive force is induced. **3** Also called: **keeper.** a soft iron or steel bar placed across the poles of a magnet to close the magnetic circuit. **4** *Sculpture.* a framework to support the clay or other material used in modelling. **5** the protective outer covering of an animal or plant. ORIG C15: from L *armātūra* armour, equipment, from *armāre* to furnish with equipment

armchair ('ɑːm,tʃɛə) *n* **1** a chair, esp. an upholstered one, that has side supports for the arms or elbows. **2** (*modifier*) taking or involving no active part: *an armchair strategist.*

armed[1] (ɑːmd) *adj* **1** equipped with or supported by arms, armour, etc. **2** prepared for conflict or any difficulty. **3** (of an explosive device) prepared for use. **4** (of plants) having the protection of thorns, spines, etc.

armed[2] (ɑːmd) *adj* **a** having an arm or arms. **b** (*in combination*): *long-armed; one-armed.*

armed forces *pl n* the military forces of a nation or nations, including the army, navy, air force, marines, etc.

Armenia ★ (ɑː'miːnɪə) *n* **1** a republic in W Asia: originally part of the Armenian kingdom; acquired by Russia in 1828: became the Armenian Soviet Socialist Republic in 1936; gained independence in 1991. It is mountainous, rising over 4000 m (13 000 ft). Language: Armenian. Religion: Christian majority. Currency: dram. Capital: Yerevan. Pop.: 3 773 000 (1997). Area: 29 800 sq km (11 490 sq. miles). **2** a former kingdom in W Asia, between the Black Sea and the Caspian Sea, south of Georgia. **3** a town in central Colombia: centre of a coffee-growing district. Pop.: 3 000 000 (1999 est.).
▸ **Ar'menian** *adj, n*

Armentières ★ ('ɑːmən,tɪəz; *French* armɑ̃tjɛr) *n* a town in N France: site of battles in both World Wars. Pop.: 26 240 (1990).

armful ('ɑːmfʊl) *n, pl* **armfuls.** the amount that can be held by one or both arms.

armhole ('ɑːm,həʊl) *n* the opening in an article of clothing through which the arm passes.

Armidale ★ ('ɑːmɪ,deɪl) *n* a town in Australia, in NE New South Wales: a centre for tourism. Pop.: 21 606 (1991 est.).

armillary sphere (ɑː'mɪlərɪ) *n* a model of the celestial sphere formerly used in fixing the positions of heavenly bodies.

Arminian (ɑː'mɪnɪən) *adj* denoting, relating to, or believing in the Protestant doctrines of Jacobus Arminius, which rejected absolute predestination and stressed free will in man.
▸ **Ar'minian,ism** *n*

armistice ('ɑːmɪstɪs) *n* an agreement between opposing armies to suspend hostilities; truce. ORIG C18: from NL, from L *arma* arms + *sistere* to stop

Armistice Day ('ɑːmɪstɪs) *n* the anniversary of the signing of the armistice that ended World War I, on Nov. 11, 1918. See also **Remembrance Sunday.**

armlet ('ɑːmlɪt) *n* **1** a small arm, as of a lake. **2** a band or bracelet worn round the arm.

armoire (ɑːm'wɑː) *n* a large cabinet, originally used for storing weapons. ORIG C16: from F, from OF *armaire,* from L *armārium* chest, closet; see AMBRY

armorial (ɑː'mɔːrɪəl) *adj* of or relating to heraldry or heraldic arms.

armour *or US* **armor** ('ɑːmə) *n* **1** any defensive covering, esp. that of metal, chain mail, etc., worn by medieval warriors. **2** the protective metal plates on a tank, warship, etc. **3** *Mil.* armoured fighting vehicles in general. **4** any protective covering, such as the shell of certain animals. **5** heraldic insignia; arms. ◆ *vb* **6** (*tr*) to equip or cover with armour. ORIG C13: from OF *armure,* from L *armātūra* armour, equipment

armoured *or US* **armored** ('ɑːməd) *adj* **1** having a protective covering. **2** comprising units making use of armoured vehicles: *an armoured brigade.*

armourer *or US* **armorer** ('ɑːmərə) *n* **1** a person who makes or mends arms and armour. **2** a person employed in the maintenance of small arms and weapons in a military unit.

armour plate *n* a tough heavy steel often hardened on the surface, used for protecting warships, tanks, etc.

armoury *or US* **armory** ('ɑːmərɪ) *n, pl* **armouries** *or* **armories. 1** a secure place for the storage of weapons. **2** armour generally; military supplies. **3** *Canad.* a building in which troops drill. **4** resources, such as arguments, on which to draw: *a few choice terms from her armoury of invective.*

armpit ('ɑːm,pɪt) *n* **1** the small depression beneath the arm where it joins the shoulder. Technical name: **axilla. 2** *Sl.* an extremely unpleasant place: *the armpit of the Middle West.*

armrest ('ɑːm,rɛst) *n* the part of a chair, sofa, etc., that supports the arm. Sometimes shortened to **arm.**

arms (ɑːmz) *pl n* **1** weapons collectively. See also **small arms. 2** military exploits: *prowess in arms.* **3** the official heraldic symbols of a family, state, etc. **4 bear arms. 4a** to carry weapons. **4b** to serve in the armed forces. **4c** to have a coat of arms. **5 in** *or* **under arms.** armed and prepared for war. **6 lay down one's arms.** to stop fighting; surrender. **7 take (up) arms.** to prepare to fight. **8 up in arms.** indignant; prepared to protest strongly. ORIG C13: from OF, from L *arma;* see ARM[2]

Armstrong ★ ('ɑːm,strɒŋ) *n* **1 Edwin Howard.** 1890–1954, US electrical engineer; invented the superheterodyne radio receiver and the FM radio. **2 Gillian,** born 1950, Australian film director; her films include *My Brilliant Career* (1978) and *Little Women* (1994). **3 (Daniel) Louis,** known as *Satchmo.* 1900–71, US jazz trumpeter and bandleader. **4 Neil (Alden).** born 1930, US astronaut; commanded Apollo 11 on the first manned lunar landing during which he became the first man to set foot on the moon on July 20, 1969.

arm wrestling *n* a contest of strength in which two people rest the elbow of one arm on a flat surface, grasp each other's hand, and try to force their opponent's forearm down flat.

army ('ɑːmɪ) *n, pl* **armies. 1** the military land forces of a nation. **2** a military unit usually consisting of two or more corps with supporting arms and services. **3** (*modifier*) of or characteristic of an army. **4** any large body of people united for some specific purpose. **5** a large number of people, animals, etc. ORIG C14: from OF, from Med. L *armāta* armed forces

army ant *n* any of various tropical American predatory ants which travel in vast hordes preying on other animals. Also called: **legionary ant.**

army worm *n* a type of caterpillar which travels in vast hordes and is a serious pest of cereal crops.

Arnaud ★ ('ɑːnəʊ; *French* arno) *n* **Yvonne.** 1892–1958, French actress, who was well known on the London stage and in British films. A theatre in Guildford is named after her.

Arne ★ (ɑːn) *n* **Thomas (Augustine).** 1710–78, English composer, noted for his setting of Shakespearean songs and for his song *Rule Britannia.*

Arnhem ★ ('ɑːnəm) *n* a city in the E Netherlands, capital of Gelderland province, on the Rhine: site of a World War II battle. Pop.: 134 499 (1995 est.).

Arnhem Land ★ *n* a region of N Australia, in the N Northern Territory, large areas of which are reserved for aboriginal Australians.

arnica ('ɑːnɪkə) *n* **1** any of a genus of N temperate or arctic plants having yellow flowers. **2** the tincture of the dried flower heads of any of these plants, used in treating bruises. ORIG C18: from NL, from ?

Arnim ★ (*German* 'arnɪm) *n* **Achim von** ('axɪm fɔn). 1781–1831, German romantic poet. He published, with Clemens Brentano, the collection of folk songs, *Des Knaben Wunderhorn* (1805–08).

Arno ★ ('ɑːnəʊ) *n* a river in central Italy, rising in the Apennines and flowing through Florence and Pisa to the Ligurian Sea. Length: about 240 km (150 miles).

Arnold[1] ★ ('ɑːnᵊld) *n* a town in N central England, in S Nottinghamshire. Pop.: 37 646 (1991).

Arnold[2] ★ ('ɑːnᵊld) *n* **1** Sir **Malcolm.** born 1921, English composer, esp. of orchestral works in a traditional idiom. **2 Matthew.** 1822–88, English poet, essayist, and literary critic, noted particularly for his poems *Sohrab and Rustum* (1853) and *Dover Beach* (1867), and for his *Essays in Criticism* (1865) and *Culture and Anarchy* (1869). **3** his father, **Thomas.** 1795–1842, English historian and educationalist, headmaster of Rugby School, noted for his reforms in public-school education.

aroha (ˈɑːrɒhə) *n NZ.* love, compassion, or affectionate regard. ORIG Maori

aroid (ˈærɔɪd, ˈɛər-) *adj* of or relating to a plant family that includes the arum, calla, and anthurium. ORIG C19: from ARUM + -OID

aroint thee *or* **ye** (əˈrɔɪnt) *sentence substitute. Arch.* away! begone! ORIG C17: from ?

aroma (əˈrəʊmə) *n* **1** a distinctive usually pleasant smell, esp. of spices, wines, and plants. **2** a subtle pervasive quality or atmosphere. ORIG C18: via L from Gk: spice

aromatherapy (əˌrəʊməˈθɛrəpɪ) *n* the use of fragrant essential oils as a treatment in alternative medicine to relieve tension and cure certain minor ailments.
▸ **aˌromaˈtherapist** *n*

aromatic (ˌærəˈmætɪk) *adj* **1** having a distinctive, usually fragrant smell. **2** (of an organic compound) having an unsaturated ring, esp. containing a benzene ring. Cf. **aliphatic.** ◆ *n* **3** something, such as a plant or drug, giving off a fragrant smell.
▸ **ˌaroˈmatically** *adv* ▸ **aˌromaˈticity** *n*

aromatize *or* **aromatise** (əˈrəʊməˌtaɪz) *vb* **aromatizes, aromatizing, aromatized** *or* **aromatises, aromatising, aromatised.** (*tr*) to make aromatic.
▸ **aˌromatiˈzation** *or* **aˌromatiˈsation** *n*

arose (əˈrəʊz) *vb* the past tense of **arise.**

around (əˈraʊnd) *prep* **1** situated at various points in: *a lot of shelves around the house.* **2** from place to place in: *driving around Ireland.* **3** somewhere in or near. **4** approximately in: *it happened around 1957.* ◆ *adv* **5** in all directions from a point of reference: *he owns the land for ten miles around.* **6** in the vicinity, esp. restlessly but idly: *to stand around.* **7** in no particular place or direction: *dotted around.* **8** *Inf.* (of people) active and prominent in a particular area or profession. **9** *Inf.* present in some place (the exact location being unknown or unspecified). **10** *Inf.* in circulation; available: *that type of phone has been around for some years now.* **11** *Inf.* to many places, so as to have gained considerable experience, often of a worldly or social nature: *I've been around.* ORIG C17 (rare earlier): from A-[2] + ROUND

> **USAGE NOTE** In American English, *around* is usually used instead of *round* in adverbial and prepositional senses, except in a few fixed phrases such as *all year round.* The use of *around* in adverbial senses is less common in British English.

arouse (əˈraʊz) *vb* **arouses, arousing, aroused.** **1** (*tr*) to evoke or elicit (a reaction, emotion, or response). **2** to awaken from sleep.
▸ **aˈrousal** *n* ▸ **aˈrouser** *n*

Arp ★ (*French* arp) *n* **Jean** (ʒɑ̃) *or* **Hans** (hans). 1887–1966, Alsatian sculptor, painter, and poet, cofounder of the Dada movement in Zürich, noted particularly for his abstract organic sculptures based on natural forms.

arpeggio (ɑːˈpɛdʒɪəʊ) *n, pl* **arpeggios.** a chord whose notes are played or sung in rapid succession rather than simultaneously. ORIG C18: from It., from *arpeggiare* to perform on the harp, from *arpa* HARP

arquebus (ˈɑːkwɪbəs) *or* **harquebus** *n* a portable long-barrelled gun dating from the 15th century. ORIG C16: via OF from MDu. *hakebusse,* lit.: hook gun, from the shape of the butt, from *hake* hook + *busse* box, gun, from LL *busis* box

arr. *abbrev. for:* **1** arranged (by). **2** arrival. **3** arrive(d).

arrack *or* **arak** (ˈærək) *n* a coarse spirit distilled in various Eastern countries from grain, rice, sugar cane, etc. ORIG C17: from Ar. *ʻaraq* sweat, sweet juice, liquor

arraign (əˈreɪn) *vb* (*tr*) **1** to bring (a prisoner) before a court to answer an indictment. **2** to call to account; accuse. ORIG C14: from OF, from Vulgar L *ratiōnāre* (unattested) to talk, argue, from L *ratiō* a reasoning
▸ **arˈraigner** *n* ▸ **arˈraignment** *n*

Arran ★ (ˈærən) *n* an island off the SW coast of Scotland, in the Firth of Clyde. Pop.: 4000 (latest est.). Area: 427 sq. km (165 sq. miles).

arrange (əˈreɪndʒ) *vb* **arranges, arranging, arranged.** **1** (*tr*) to put into a proper or systematic order. **2** (*tr; may take a clause as object or an infinitive*) to arrive at an agreement about. **3** (when *intr,* often foll. by *for;* when *tr, may take a clause as object or an infinitive*) to make plans or preparations in advance (for something): *we arranged for her to be met.* **4** (*tr*) to adapt (a musical composition) for performance in a different way, esp. on different instruments. **5** (*intr;* often foll. by *with*) to come to an agreement. ORIG C14: from OF *arangier,* from A-[2] + *rangier* to put in a row, RANGE
▸ **arˈrangeable** *adj* ▸ **arˈranger** *n*

arrangement (əˈreɪndʒmənt) *n* **1** the act of arranging or being arranged. **2** the form in which things are arranged. **3** a thing composed of various ordered parts: *a flower arrangement.* **4** (*often pl*) a preparation. **5** an understanding. **6** an adaptation of a piece of music for performance in a different way, esp. on different instruments.

arrant (ˈærənt) *adj* utter; out-and-out: *an arrant fool.* ORIG C14: var. of ERRANT (wandering, vagabond)
▸ **ˈarrantly** *adv*

arras (ˈærəs) *n* a wall hanging, esp. of tapestry.

Arras ★ (ˈærəs; *French* arɑs) *n* a town in N France: formerly famous for tapestry; severely damaged in both World Wars. Pop.: 42 715 (1990).

Arrau ★ (əˈraʊ) *n* **Claudio.** 1903–91, Chilean pianist.

array (əˈreɪ) *n* **1** an impressive display or collection. **2** an orderly arrangement, esp. of troops in battle order. **3** *Poetic.* rich clothing. **4** *Maths.* a set of numbers or symbols arranged in rows and columns, as in a determinant or matrix. **5** *Law.* a panel of jurors. **6** *Computing.* a regular data structure in which elements may be located by reference to index numbers. ◆ *vb* (*tr*) **7** to dress in rich attire. **8** to arrange in order (esp. troops for battle). **9** *Law.* to draw up (a panel of jurors). ORIG C13: from OF, from *arayer* to arrange, of Gmc origin
▸ **arˈrayal** *n*

arrears (əˈrɪəz) *n* (*sometimes sing*) **1** Also called: **arrearage.** something outstanding or owed. **2** **in arrears** *or* **arrear.** late in paying a debt or meeting an obligation. ORIG C18: from obs. *arrear* (adv) behindhand, from OF, from Med. L *adretrō,* from L *ad* to + *retrō* backwards

arrest (əˈrɛst) *vb* (*tr*) **1** to deprive (a person) of liberty by taking him or her into custody, esp. under lawful authority. **2** to seize (a ship) under lawful authority. **3** to slow or stop the development of (a disease, growth, etc.). **4** to catch and hold (one's attention, etc.). ◆ *n* **5** the act of taking a person into custody, esp. under lawful authority. **6** the act of seizing and holding a ship under lawful authority. **7** the state of being held: *under arrest.* **8** the slowing or stopping of something: *a cardiac arrest.* ORIG C14: from OF, from Vulgar L *arrestāre* (unattested), from L *ad* at, to + *restāre* to stand firm, stop

arresting (əˈrɛstɪŋ) *adj* attracting attention; striking.
▸ **arˈrestingly** *adv*

Arretium ★ (æˈriːtɪəm, -ˈrɛt-) *n* the ancient Latin name of **Arezzo.**
▸ **Arretine** (ˈærɪˌtaɪn) *adj*

arrhythmia (əˈrɪðmɪə) *n* any variation from the normal rhythm in the heartbeat. ORIG C19: NL, from Gk *arrhuthmia,* from A-[1] + *rhuthmos* RHYTHM

arrière-pensée *French.* (arjɛrpɑ̃se) *n* an unrevealed thought or intention. ORIG C19: lit.: behind thought

Ar Rimal ★ (ɑːr rɪˈmɑːl) *n* another name for **Rub' al Khali.**

arris (ˈærɪs) *n, pl* **arris** *or* **arrises.** a sharp edge at the meeting of two surfaces at an angle with one another. ORIG C17: from OF *areste* beard of grain, sharp ridge; see ARÊTE

arrival (əˈraɪvᵊl) *n* **1** the act or time of arriving. **2** a person or thing that arrives or has arrived.

arrive (əˈraɪv) *vb* **arrives, arriving, arrived.** (*intr*) **1** to come to a certain place during or after a journey. **2** to reach: *to arrive at a decision.* **3** to occur eventually: *the moment arrived when pretence was useless.* **4** *Inf.* (of a baby) to be born. **5** *Inf.* to attain success. ORIG C13: from OF, from Vulgar L *arrīpāre* (unattested) to land, reach the bank, from L *ad* to + *rīpa* river bank

arrivederci *Italian.* (arriveˈdertʃi) *sentence substitute.* goodbye.

arriviste (ˌæriːˈviːst) *n* a person who is unscrupulously ambitious. ORIG F: see ARRIVE, -IST

arrogant (ˈærəgənt) *adj* having or showing an exaggerated opinion of one's own importance, merit, ability, etc.: *an arrogant assumption.* ORIG C14: from L *arrogāre* to claim as one's own; see ARROGATE
▸ **ˈarrogance** *n* ▸ **ˈarrogantly** *adv*

arrogate (ˈærəˌgeɪt) *vb* **arrogates, arrogating, arrogated.** (*tr*) **1** to claim or appropriate for oneself without justification. **2** to attribute or assign to another without justification. ORIG C16: from L *arrogāre,* from *rogāre* to ask
▸ **ˌarroˈgation** *n* ▸ **arrogative** (əˈrɒgətɪv) *adj*

arrondissement (*French* arɔ̃dismɑ̃) *n* (in France) **1** the largest subdivision of a department. **2** a municipal district of large cities, esp. Paris. ORIG C19: from *arrondir* to make round

arrow (ˈærəʊ) *n* **1** a long slender pointed weapon, usually having feathers fastened at the end as a balance, that is shot from a bow. **2** any of various things that resemble an arrow in shape, function, or speed. ORIG OE *arwe*

arrowhead (ˈærəʊˌhɛd) *n* **1** the pointed tip of an arrow, often removable from the shaft. **2** something that resembles the head of an arrow in shape. **3** an aquatic herbaceous plant having arrow-shaped leaves.

arrowroot (ˈærəʊˌruːt) *n* **1** a white-flowered West Indian plant, whose rhizomes yield an easily digestible starch. **2** the starch obtained from this plant.

arroyo (əˈrɔɪəʊ) *n, pl* **arroyos.** *Chiefly southwestern US.* a steep-sided stream bed that is usually dry except after heavy rain. ORIG C19: from Sp.

Arru Islands ★ (ˈɑːruː) *pl n* a variant spelling of **Aru Islands.**

arse (ɑːs) *or US & Canad.* **ass** *n Taboo.* **1** the buttocks. **2** the anus. **3** a stupid person; fool. ◆ Also called (for senses 2, 3): **arsehole,** (US & Canad.) **asshole.** ORIG OE

arsenal (ˈɑːsənᵊl) *n* **1** a store for arms, ammunition, and other military items. **2** a workshop that produces munitions. **3** a store of anything regarded as weapons. ORIG C16: from It. *arsenale* dockyard, from Ar., from *dār* house + *sinā'ah* manufacture

arsenate (ˈɑːsəˌneɪt, -nɪt) *n* a salt or ester of arsenic acid.

arsenic *n* (ˈɑːsnɪk). **1** a toxic metalloid element used in transistors, lead-based alloys, and high-temperature brasses. Symbol: As; atomic no.: 33; atomic wt.: 74.92. **2** a nontechnical name for **arsenic trioxide** (As_2O_3), used as rat poison and an insecticide. ◆ *adj* (ɑːˈsɛnɪk). **3** of or containing arsenic, esp. in the pentavalent state; designating an arsenic(V) compound. ORIG C14: from L, from Gk *arsenikon* yellow arsenic ore, from Syriac *zarnīg* (infl. by Gk *arsenikos* virile)

arsenic acid *n* a white poisonous soluble crystalline solid used in the manufacture of insecticides.

arsenical (ɑːˈsɛnɪkᵊl) *adj* **1** of or containing arsenic. ◆ *n* **2** a drug or insecticide containing arsenic.

arsenious (ɑːˈsiːnɪəs) *or* **arsenous** (ˈɑːsɪnəs) *adj* of or containing arsenic in the trivalent state; designating an arsenic(III) compound.

arson (ˈɑːsᵊn) *n Criminal law.* the act of intentionally or recklessly setting fire to property for some improper reason. ORIG C17: from OF, from Med. L *ārsiō,* from L *ārdēre* to burn
▸ **ˈarsonist** *n*

art¹ (ɑːt) *n* **1a** the creation of works of beauty or other special significance. **1b** (*as modifier*): *an art movement.* **2** the exercise of human skill (as distinguished from *nature*). **3** imaginative skill as applied to representations of the natural world or figments of the imagination. **4a** works of art collectively, esp. of the visual arts. **4b** (*as modifier*): *an art gallery.* **5** any branch of the visual arts, esp. painting. **6a** any field using the techniques of art to display artistic qualities. **6b** (*as modifier*): *art film.* **7** method, facility, or knack: *the art of threading a needle.* **8** skill governing a particular human activity: *the art of government.* **9** cunning. **10 get something down to a fine art.** to become highly proficient at something through practice. ◆ See also **arts.** ORIG C13: from OF, from L *ars* craftsmanship

art² (ɑːt) *vb Arch.* (used with the pronoun *thou*) a singular form of the present tense of **be.** ORIG OE *eart,* part of *bēon* to BE

art. *abbrev. for:* **1** article. **2** artificial. **3** Also: **arty.** artillery.

-art *suffix forming nouns.* a variant of **-ard.**

Artaud ★ (*French* arto) *n* **Antonin** (ɑ̃tɔnɛ̃). 1896–1948, French stage director and dramatist, noted for his concept of the theatre of cruelty, esp. *Manifeste du théâtre de la cruauté* (1932).

Artaxerxes II ★ *n* died ?358 B.C., king of Persia (?404–?358). He defeated his brother Cyrus the Younger at Cunaxa (401).

Art Deco (ˈdɛkəʊ) *n* a style of interior decoration, architecture, etc., at its height in the 1930s and characterized by geometrical shapes. ORIG C20: from *art décoratif,* after the *Exposition des arts décoratifs* held in Paris in 1925

art director *n* a person responsible for the sets and costumes in a film.

artefact *or* **artifact** (ˈɑːtɪˌfækt) *n* **1** something made or given shape by man, such as a tool or a work of art, esp. an object of archaeological interest. **2** anything man-made, such as a spurious experimental result. **3** *Cytology.* a structure seen in dead tissue that is not normally present in the living tissue. ORIG C19: from L *arte factum,* from *ars* skill + *facere* to make

artel (ɑːˈtɛl) *n* (in the former Soviet Union) a cooperative union or organization, esp. of producers, such as peasants. ORIG from Russian *artel',* from It. *artieri* artisans, from *arte* work, from L *ars* ART¹

Artemis ★ (ˈɑːtɪmɪs) *n Greek myth.* the virgin goddess of the hunt and the moon: the twin sister of Apollo. Roman counterpart: **Diana.** Also called: **Cynthia.**

arterial (ɑːˈtɪərɪəl) *adj* **1** of or affecting an artery or arteries. **2** denoting or relating to the bright red reoxygenated blood that circulates in the arteries. **3** being a major route, esp. one with many minor branches.
▸ **arˈterially** *adv*

arterialize *or* **arterialise** (ɑːˈtɪərɪəˌlaɪz) *vb* **arterializes, arterializing, arterialized** *or* **arterialises, arterialising, arterialised.** (*tr*) **1** to change (venous blood) into arterial blood by replenishing the depleted oxygen. **2** to provide with arteries.
▸ **arˌterialiˈzation** *or* **arˌterialiˈsation** *n*

arteriole (ɑːˈtɪərɪˌəʊl) *n Anat.* any of the small subdivisions of an artery that form thin-walled vessels ending in capillaries. ORIG C19: from NL, from L *artēria* ARTERY

arteriosclerosis (ɑːˌtɪərɪəʊsklɪəˈrəʊsɪs) *n, pl* **arterioscleroses** (-siːz). a thickening and loss of elasticity of the walls of the arteries. Nontechnical name: **hardening of the arteries.**
▸ **arteriosclerotic** (ɑːˌtɪərɪəʊsklɪəˈrɒtɪk) *adj*

artery (ˈɑːtərɪ) *n, pl* **arteries. 1** any of the tubular thick-walled muscular vessels that convey oxygenated blood from the heart to various parts of the body. Cf. **pulmonary artery, vein. 2** a major road or means of communication. ORIG C14: from L *artēria,* rel. to Gk *aortē* the great artery, AORTA

artesian well (ɑːˈtiːzɪən) *n* a well sunk through impermeable strata into strata receiving water from an area at a higher altitude than that of the well, so the water is forced to flow upwards. ORIG C19: from F, from OF *Arteis* Artois, old province, where such wells were common

Artex (ˈɑːtɛks) *n Trademark.* a textured coating for walls and ceilings.

art form *n* **1** an accepted mode of artistic composition, such as the sonnet, symphony, etc. **2** a recognized medium of artistic expression.

artful (ˈɑːtfʊl) *adj* **1** cunning or tricky. **2** skilful in achieving a desired end.
▸ **ˈartfully** *adv* ▸ **ˈartfulness** *n*

art house *n* **1** a cinema that specializes in showing films that are not part of the commercial mainstream. ◆ *adj* **2** of or relating to such films or a cinema that specializes in showing them.

arthralgia (ɑːˈθrældʒə) *n Pathol.* pain in a joint.
▸ **arˈthralgic** *adj*

arthritis (ɑːˈθraɪtɪs) *n* inflammation of a joint or joints

characterized by pain and stiffness of the affected parts. ORIG C16: via L from Gk *arthron* joint + -ITIS
▸ **arthritic** (ɑːˈθrɪtɪk) *adj, n*

arthropod (ˈɑːθrəˌpɒd) *n* an invertebrate having jointed limbs, a segmented body, and an exoskeleton made of chitin, as the crustaceans, insects, arachnids, and centipedes. ORIG C19: from NL, from Gk *arthron* joint + *-podus* footed, from *pous* foot

Arthur ★ (ˈɑːθə) *n* **1** a legendary king of the Britons in the sixth century A.D., who led Celtic resistance against the Saxons: possibly based on a historical figure; represented as leader of the Knights of the Round Table at Camelot. **2** **Chester Alan.** 1830–86, 21st president of the US (1881–85).

Arthurian ★ (ɑːˈθjʊərɪən) *adj* of or relating to King Arthur and his Knights of the Round Table.

artic (ɑːˈtɪk) *n Inf.* short for **articulated lorry.**

artichoke (ˈɑːtɪˌtʃəʊk) *n* **1** Also called: **globe artichoke.** a thistle-like Eurasian plant, cultivated for its large edible flower head. **2** the unopened flower head of this plant, which can be cooked and eaten. **3** See **Jerusalem artichoke.** ORIG C16: from It., from OSp., from Ar. *al-kharshūf*

article (ˈɑːtɪkᵊl) *n* **1** one of a class of objects; item. **2** an unspecified or previously named thing, esp. a small object. **3** a written composition on a subject, often being one of several found in a magazine, newspaper, etc. **4** *Grammar.* a kind of determiner, occurring in many languages including English, that lacks independent meaning. See also **definite article, indefinite article. 5** a clause or section in a written document. **6** (*often cap.*) *Christianity.* See **Thirty-nine Articles.** ◆ *vb* **articles, articling, articled.** (*tr*) **7** to bind by a written contract, esp. one that governs a period of training: *an articled clerk.* ORIG C13: from OF, from L *articulus* small joint, from *artus* joint

articular (ɑːˈtɪkjʊlə) *adj* of or relating to joints or to the structural components in a joint. ORIG C15: from L *articulāris* concerning the joints, from *articulus* small joint

articulate *adj* (ɑːˈtɪkjʊlɪt). **1** able to express oneself fluently and coherently. **2** having the power of speech. **3** distinct, clear, or definite: *an articulate document.* **4** *Zool.* (of arthropods and higher vertebrates) possessing joints or jointed segments. ◆ *vb* (ɑːˈtɪkjʊˌleɪt), **articulates, articulating, articulated. 5** to speak or enunciate (words, syllables, etc.) clearly and distinctly. **6** (*tr*) to express coherently in words. **7** (*intr*) *Zool.* to be jointed or form a joint. ORIG C16: from L *articulāre* to divide into joints
▸ **arˈticulately** *adv* ▸ **arˈticulateness** *n* ▸ **arˈticuˌlator** *n*

articulated lorry *n* a large lorry made in two separate sections, a tractor and a trailer, connected by a pivoted bar.

articulation (ɑːˌtɪkjʊˈleɪʃən) *n* **1** the act or process of speaking or expressing in words. **2a** the process of articulating a speech sound. **2b** the sound so produced, esp. a consonant. **3** the act or the state of being jointed together. **4** *Zool.* **4a** a joint such as that between bones or arthropod segments. **4b** the way in which jointed parts are connected. **5** *Bot.* the part of a plant at which natural separation occurs.

artifact (ˈɑːtɪˌfækt) *n* a variant spelling of **artefact.**

artifice (ˈɑːtɪfɪs) *n* **1** a clever expedient. **2** crafty or subtle deception. **3** skill; cleverness. **4** a skilfully contrived device. ORIG C16: from OF, from L *artificium* skill, from *artifex* one possessed of a specific skill, from *ars* skill + -fex, from *facere* to make

artificer (ɑːˈtɪfɪsə) *n* **1** a skilled craftsman. **2** a clever or inventive designer. **3** a serviceman trained in mechanics.

artificial (ˌɑːtɪˈfɪʃəl) *adj* **1** produced by man; not occurring naturally. **2** made in imitation of a natural product: *artificial cream.* **3** pretended; insincere. **4** lacking in spontaneity; affected: *an artificial laugh.* ORIG C14: from L *artificiālis* belonging to art, from *artificium* skill, ARTIFICE
▸ **artificiality** (ˌɑːtɪˌfɪʃɪˈælɪtɪ) *n* ▸ ˌ**artiˈficially** *adv*

artificial daylight *n Physics.* artificial light having approximately the same spectral characteristics as natural daylight.

artificial disintegration *n Physics.* radioactive transformation of a substance by bombardment with high-energy particles, such as alpha particles or neutrons.

artificial insemination *n* introduction of spermatozoa into the vagina or uterus by means other than sexual union.

artificial intelligence *n* the ability of a machine, such as a computer, to imitate intelligent human behaviour.

artificial respiration *n* **1** any of various methods of restarting breathing after it has stopped. **2** any method of maintaining respiration, as by use of an iron lung.

artillery (ɑːˈtɪlərɪ) *n* **1** guns, cannon, mortars, etc., of calibre greater than 20mm. **2** troops or military units specializing in using such guns. **3** the science dealing with the use of guns. ORIG C14: from OF, from *artillier* to equip with weapons, from ?

artiodactyl (ˌɑːtɪəʊˈdæktɪl) *n* an ungulate with an even number of toes, as pigs, camels, deer, cattle, etc. ORIG C19: from Gk *artios* even-numbered + *daktulos* finger
▸ ˌ**artioˈdactylous** *adj*

artisan (ˈɑːtɪˌzæn, ˌɑːtɪˈzæn) *n* a skilled workman; craftsman. ORIG C16: from F, from OIt. *artigiano,* from *arte* ART[1]
▸ **artisanal** (ɑːˈtɪzənᵊl, ˈɑːtɪzənᵊl) *adj*

artist (ˈɑːtɪst) *n* **1** a person who practises or is skilled in an art, esp. painting, drawing, or sculpture. **2** a person who displays in his or her work qualities required in art, such as sensibility and imagination. **3** a person whose profession requires artistic expertise. **4** a person skilled in some task or occupation. **5** *Sl.* a person devoted to or proficient in something: *a con artist; a booze artist.*
▸ **arˈtistic** *adj* ▸ **arˈtistically** *adv*

artiste (ɑːˈtiːst) *n* **1** an entertainer, such as a singer or dancer. **2** a person who is highly skilled in some occupation: *a hair artiste.* ORIG F

artistry (ˈɑːtɪstrɪ) *n* **1** artistic workmanship, ability, or quality. **2** artistic pursuits. **3** great skill.

artless (ˈɑːtlɪs) *adj* **1** free from deceit; ingenuous: *an artless remark.* **2** natural; unpretentious. **3** without art or skill.
▸ **ˈartlessly** *adv*

Art Nouveau (ɑː nuːˈvəʊ; *French* ar nuvo) *n* a style of art and architecture of the 1890s, characterized by sinuous outlines and stylized natural forms. ORIG F, lit.: new art

art paper *n* a high-quality type of paper having a smooth coating of china clay or similar substance on it.

arts (ɑːts) *pl n* **1a the.** imaginative, creative, and nonscientific branches of knowledge considered collectively, esp. as studied academically. **1b** (*as modifier*): *an arts degree.* **2** See **fine art. 3** cunning actions or schemes.

Arts and Crafts *pl n* decorative handicraft and design, esp. that of the **Arts and Crafts movement**, in late nineteenth-century Britain, which sought to revive medieval craftsmanship.

art union *n Austral.* an officially approved lottery for prizes other than cash (formerly works of art).

arty (ˈɑːtɪ) *adj* **artier, artiest.** *Inf.* having an affected interest in artists or art.
▸ **ˈartiness** *n*

Aruba ★ (əˈruːbə; *Dutch* ɑˈryːbaː) *n* an island in the Caribbean, off the NW coast of Venezuela, a dependency of the Netherlands with special status; part of the Netherlands Antilles until 1986. Chief town: Oranjestad. Pop.: 68 897 (1991). Area: about 181 sq. km (70 sq. miles).

arugula (əˈruːgjʊlə) *n* a Mediterranean plant of the mustard family with yellowish-white flowers and pungent leaves that are used as a salad; rocket. See also **rocket**[2] (sense 1). ORIG C20: from N It. dialect

Aru Islands *or* **Arru Islands** ★ (ˈɑːruː) *pl n* a group of islands in Indonesia, in the SW Moluccas. Area: about 8500 sq. km (3300 sq. miles).

arum (ˈɛərəm) *n* **1** any of various aroid plants of Europe and the Mediterranean region, having arrow-shaped leaves and a typically white spathe, such as the cuckoopint. **2** **arum lily.** another name for **calla** (sense 1). ORIG C16: from L, var. of *aros* wake-robin, from Gk *aron*

Arunachal Pradesh ★ (ˌɑːrəˈnɑːkᵊl prəˈdɛʃ) *n* a state in

NE India, formed in 1986 from the former Union Territory. Capital: Itanagar. Pop.: 965 000 (1994 est.). Area: 83 743 sq. km (32 648 sq. miles). Former name (until 1972): **North East Frontier Agency**.

Arundel ★ ('ærəndəl) *n* a town in S England, in West Sussex: 11th-century castle. Pop.: 3033 (1991).

arvo ('ɑːvəʊ) *n Austral. inf.* afternoon.

-ary *suffix.* **1** (*forming adjectives*) of; related to; belonging to: *cautionary.* **2** (*forming nouns*) a person or thing connected with: *missionary; aviary.* ORIG from L *-ārius, -āria, -ārium*

Aryan ('ɛərɪən) *n* **1** (in Nazi ideology) a Caucasian of non-Jewish descent. **2** a member of any of the peoples supposedly descended from the Indo-Europeans. ◆ *adj* **3** of or characteristic of an Aryan or Aryans. ◆ *adj, n* **4** *Arch.* Indo-European. ORIG C19: from Sansk. *ārya* of noble birth

as[1] (æz; *unstressed* əz) *conj* (*subordinating*) **1** (often preceded by *just*) while; when: *he caught me as I was leaving.* **2** in the way that: *dancing as only she can.* **3** that which; what: *I did as I was told.* **4** (of) which fact, event, etc. (referring to the previous statement): *to become wise, as we all know, is not easy.* **5 as it were.** in a way; as if it were really so. **6** since; seeing that. **7** in the same way that: *he died of cancer, as his father had done.* **8** for instance: *capital cities, as London.* ◆ *adv, conj* **9a** used to indicate identity of extent, amount, etc.: *she is as heavy as her sister.* **9b** used with this sense after a noun phrase introduced by *the same: the same height as her sister.* ◆ *prep* **10** in the role of; being: *as his friend, I am probably biased.* **11 as for** *or* **to.** with reference to: *as for my past, I'm not telling you anything.* **12 as if** *or* **though.** as it would be if: *he talked as if he knew all about it.* **13 as (it) is.** in the existing state of affairs. **14 as was.** in a previous state. ORIG OE *alswā* likewise

USAGE NOTE See at **like.**

as[2] (æs) *n* **1** an ancient Roman unit of weight approximately equal to 1 pound troy (373 grams). **2** a copper coin of ancient Rome. ORIG C17: from L *ās* unity

As *symbol for:* **1** altostratus. **2** *Chem.* arsenic.

AS *abbrev. for:* **1** Also: **A.S.** Anglo-Saxon. **2** antisubmarine.

ASA *abbrev. for:* **1** (in Britain) Amateur Swimming Association. **2** (in Britain) Advertising Standards Authority. **3** (in the US) American Standards Association.

ASA/BS *abbrev.* an obsolete expression of the speed of a photographic film, replaced by the ISO rating. ORIG C20: from *American Standards Association/British Standard*

asafoetida *or* **asafetida** (ˌæsə'fɛtɪdə) *n* a bitter resin with an unpleasant onion-like smell, obtained from the roots of some umbelliferous plants: formerly used to treat flatulence, etc. ORIG C14: from Med. L, from *asa* gum (cf. Persian *azā* mastic) + L *foetidus* evil smelling

a.s.a.p. *abbrev. for* as soon as possible.

Asben ★ (æs'bɛn) *n* another name for **Aïr** (region of the Sahara).

asbestos (æs'bɛstɒs) *n* **a** any of the fibrous amphibole minerals that are incombustible and resistant to chemicals. It was formerly widely used in the form of fabric or board as a heat-resistant structural material. **b** (*as modifier*): *asbestos matting.* ORIG C14: via L from Gk: from *asbestos* inextinguishable, from A-[1] + *sbennunai* to extinguish

asbestosis (ˌæsbɛs'təʊsɪs) *n* inflammation of the lungs resulting from chronic inhalation of asbestos particles.

Ascanius ★ (æ'skeɪnɪəs) *n Roman myth.* the son of Aeneas and Creusa; founder of Alba Longa, mother city of Rome. Also called: **Iulus.**

ascarid ('æskərɪd) *n* a parasitic nematode worm such as the common roundworm of man and pigs. ORIG C14: from NL, from Gk *askarides,* pl. of *askaris*

ascend (ə'sɛnd) *vb* **1** to go or move up (a ladder, hill, slope, etc.). **2** (*intr*) to slope or incline upwards. **3** (*intr*) to rise to a higher point, level, etc. **4** to trace (a genealogy, etc.) back in time. **5** to sing or play (a scale, etc.) from the lower to higher notes. **6 ascend the throne.** to become king or queen. ORIG C14: from L *ascendere,* from *scandere*

ascendancy, ascendency (ə'sɛndənsɪ) *or* **ascendance, ascendence** *n* the condition of being dominant.

ascendant *or* **ascendent** (ə'sɛndənt) *adj* **1** proceeding upwards; rising. **2** dominant or influential. ◆ *n* **3** a position or condition of dominance. **4** *Astrol.* (*sometimes cap.*) **4a** a point on the ecliptic that rises on the eastern horizon at a particular moment. **4b** the sign of the zodiac containing this point. **5 in the ascendant.** increasing in influence, etc.

ascender (ə'sɛndə) *n* **1** *Printing.* the part of certain lowercase letters, such as *b* or *h,* that extends above the body of the letter. **2** a person or thing that ascends.

ascension (ə'sɛnʃən) *n* the act of ascending.
▸ **as'censional** *adj*

Ascension[1] (ə'sɛnʃən) *n Bible.* the passing of Jesus Christ from earth into heaven (Acts 1:9).

Ascension[2] ★ (ə'sɛnʃən) *n* an island in the S Atlantic, northwest of St Helena: uninhabited until claimed by Britain in 1815. Pop.: 1117 (1993). Area: 88 sq. km (34 sq. miles).

Ascension Day *n* the 40th day after Easter, when the Ascension of Christ into heaven is celebrated.

ascent (ə'sɛnt) *n* **1** the act of ascending; upward movement. **2** an upward slope. **3** movement back through time (esp. in **line of ascent**).

ascertain (ˌæsə'teɪn) *vb* (*tr*) **1** to determine definitely. **2** *Arch.* to make certain. ORIG C15: from OF *acertener* to make certain
▸ ˌ**ascer'tainable** *adj* ▸ ˌ**ascer'tainment** *n*

ascetic (ə'sɛtɪk) *n* **1** a person who practises great self-denial and abstains from worldly comforts and pleasures, esp. for religious reasons. ◆ *adj also* **ascetical. 2** rigidly abstinent or abstemious. **3** of or relating to ascetics or asceticism. ORIG C17: from Gk *askētikos,* from *askētēs,* from *askein* to exercise
▸ **as'cetically** *adv* ▸ **a'sceti**ˌ**cism** *n*

Asch ★ (æʃ) *n* **Sholem** ('ʃəʊləm). 1880–1957, US writer, born in Poland, who wrote in Yiddish.

Aschaffenburg ★ (*German* a'ʃafənburk) *n* a city in Germany, on the River Main in Bavaria: seat of the Imperial Diet (1447); ceded to Bavaria in 1814. Pop.: 62 050 (1989 est.).

Ascham ★ ('æskəm) *n* **Roger.** ?1515–68, English humanist writer and classical scholar: he was tutor to Queen Elizabeth I.

ascidian (ə'sɪdɪən) *n* any of a class of minute marine invertebrate animals, such as the sea squirt, the adults of which are degenerate and sedentary.

ascidium (ə'sɪdɪəm) *n, pl* **ascidia** (-'sɪdɪə). part of a plant that is shaped like a pitcher, such as the modified leaf of the pitcher plant. ORIG C18: from NL, from Gk *askidion* a little bag, from *askos* bag

Asclepius ★ (ə'skliːpɪəs) *n Greek myth.* a god of healing; son of Apollo. Roman counterpart: **Aesculapius** (ˌiːskju'leɪpɪəs).

ascomycete (ˌæskəmaɪ'siːt) *n* any of a phylum of fungi in which the spores (ascospores) are formed inside a club-shaped cell (ascus). The group includes yeast, penicillium, and certain mildews.
▸ ˌ**ascomy'cetous** *adj*

ascorbic acid (ə'skɔːbɪk) *n* a white crystalline vitamin present in plants, esp. citrus fruits, tomatoes, and green vegetables. A deficiency in the diet of man leads to scurvy. Also called: **vitamin C.**

Ascot ★ ('æskət) *n* a town in S England, in Berkshire: noted for its horse-race meetings, esp. **Royal Ascot,** a four-day meeting held in June. Pop.: 13 500 (latest est.).

ascribe (ə'skraɪb) *vb* **ascribes, ascribing, ascribed.** (*tr*) **1** to credit or assign, as to a particular origin or period. **2** to consider as belonging to: *to ascribe beauty to youth.* ORIG

C15: from L *ascrībere* to enrol, from *ad* in addition + *scrībere* to write
▸ **as'cribable** *adj*

USAGE NOTE *Ascribe* is sometimes used where *subscribe* is meant: *I do not subscribe* (not *ascribe*) *to this view of music.*

ascription (ə'skrɪpʃən) *n* **1** the act of ascribing. **2** a statement ascribing something to someone. ORIG C16: from L *ascrīptiō*, from *ascrībere* to ASCRIBE

asdic ('æzdɪk) *n* an early form of **sonar.** ORIG C20: from *A(nti-)S(ubmarine) D(etection) I(nvestigation) C(ommittee)*

-ase *suffix forming nouns.* indicating an enzyme: *oxidase.* ORIG from DIASTASE

ASEAN ('æsɪ,æn) *n acronym for* Association of South-East Asian Nations.

asepsis (ə'sɛpsɪs, eɪ-) *n* **1** the state of being free from living pathogenic organisms. **2** the methods of achieving a germ-free condition.
▸ **a'septic** *adj*

asexual (eɪ'sɛksjʊəl) *adj* **1** having no apparent sex or sex organs. **2** (of reproduction) not involving the fusion of male and female gametes. Cf.: **sexual** (sense 2).
▸ **,asexu'ality** *n* ▸ **a'sexually** *adv*

Asgard ('æsgɑːd) *or* **Asgarth** ★ ('æsgɑːθ) *n Norse myth.* the dwelling place of the principal gods, the Aesir.

ash[1] (æʃ) *n* **1** the residue formed when matter is burnt. **2** fine particles of lava thrown out by an erupting volcano. **3** a light silvery-grey colour. ◆ See also **ashes.** ORIG OE *æsce*

ash[2] (æʃ) *n* **1** a tree having compound leaves, clusters of small greenish flowers, and winged seeds. **2** the wood of this tree, used for tool handles, etc. **3** any of several trees resembling the ash, such as the mountain ash. **4** *Austral.* any of various eucalypts. ORIG OE *æsc*

ash[3] (æʃ) *n* the digraph æ, as in Old English, representing a vowel approximately like that of the *a* in Modern English *hat.*

ASH (æʃ) *n* (in Britain) *acronym for* Action on Smoking and Health.

ashamed (ə'ʃeɪmd) *adj* (*usually postpositive*) **1** overcome with shame or remorse. **2** (foll. by *of*) suffering from feelings of shame in relation to (a person or deed). **3** (foll. by *to*) unwilling through fear of humiliation, shame, etc. ORIG OE *āscamod*, p.p. of *āscamian* to shame, from *scamu* SHAME
▸ **ashamedly** (ə'ʃeɪmɪdlɪ) *adv*

Ashanti ★ (ə'ʃæntɪ) *n* **1** an administrative region of central Ghana: former native kingdom, suppressed by the British in 1900 after four wars. Capital: Kumasi. Pop.: 2 485 766 (1991 est.). Area: 24 390 sq. km (9417 sq. miles). **2** (*pl* **Ashanti** *or* **Ashantis**) a native or inhabitant of Ashanti.

A shares *pl n* ordinary shares in a company which carry restricted voting rights.

ash can *n* a US word for **dustbin.** Also called: **garbage can, ash bin, trash can.**

Ashcroft ★ ('æʃkrɒft) *n* Dame **Peggy.** 1907–91, English stage and film actress.

Ashdod ★ ('æʃdɒd) *n* a town in central Israel, on the Mediterranean coast: an important city in the Philistine Empire, with its artificial harbour (1961) it is now a major port. Pop.: 137 100 (1997 est.).

Ashdown ★ ('æʃdaʊn) *n* Sir **Paddy,** real name *Jeremy John Durham Ashdown.* born 1941, British politician; leader of the Liberal Democrats (1988–99).

Ashe ★ (æʃ) *n* **Arthur** (**Robert**). 1943–93, US tennis player: US champion 1968; Wimbledon champion 1975.

ashen[1] ('æʃən) *adj* **1** drained of colour. **2** consisting of or resembling ashes. **3** of a pale greyish colour.

ashen[2] ('æʃən) *adj* of, relating to, or made from the ash tree or its timber.

Asher ★ ('æʃə) *n* the son of Jacob and ancestor of one of the 12 tribes of Israel.

ashes ('æʃɪz) *pl n* **1** ruins or remains, as after burning. **2** the remains of a human body after cremation.

Ashes ('æʃɪz) *pl n* **the.** a cremated cricket stump constituting a trophy competed for by England and Australia in test cricket since 1882. ORIG from a mock obituary of English cricket after a great Australian victory

Ashford ★ ('æʃfəd) *n* a market town in SE England, in central Kent. Pop.: 52 002 (1991).

Ashkenazi (,æʃkə'nɑːzɪ) *n, pl* **Ashkenazim** (-zɪm). **1** (*modifier*) of or relating to the Jews of Germany and E Europe. **2** a Jew of German or E European descent. Cf. **Sephardi.** ORIG C19: LHeb., from Heb. *Ashkenaz,* the son of Gomer (Genesis 10:3; I Chronicles 1:6)

Ashkenazy ★ (,æʃkə'nɑːzɪ) *n* **Vladimir.** born 1937, Soviet-born pianist and conductor, living in Iceland.

Ashkhabad (*Russian* aʃxa'baict) *or* **Ashgabat** ★ ('ɑːʃgəbæt; *Turkmen* ɑʃgɑ'bɑt) *n* the capital of Turkmenistan. Pop.: 536 000 (1995 est.).

ashlar *or* **ashler** ('æʃlə) *n* **1** a square block of hewn stone for use in building. **2** a thin dressed stone with straight edges, used to face a wall. **3** masonry made of ashlar. ORIG C14: from OF *aisselier* crossbeam, from *ais* board, from L *axis* axletree

Ashley ★ ('æʃlɪ) *n* **Laura.** 1925–85, British fashion designer.

ashore (ə'ʃɔː) *adv* **1** towards or onto land from the water. ◆ *adj* (*postpositive*), *adv* **2** on land: *a day ashore before sailing.*

ashram ('æʃrəm) *n* a religious retreat or community where a Hindu holy man lives. ORIG from Sansk. *āśrama,* from *ā-* near + *śrama* religious exertion

Ashton ★ ('æʃtən) *n* Sir **Frederick.** 1906–88, British ballet dancer and choreographer. His ballets include *Façade* (1931) and *A Month in the Country* (1976).

Ashton-under-Lyne ★ (laɪn) *n* a town in NW England, in Tameside unitary authority, Greater Manchester. Pop.: 43 906 (1991).

Ashtoreth ★ ('æʃtə,rɛθ) *n Old Testament.* an ancient Semitic fertility goddess, identified with Astarte and Ishtar.

ashtray ('æʃ,treɪ) *n* a receptacle for tobacco ash, cigarette butts, etc.

Ashur ★ ('æʃʊə) *n* a variant spelling of **Assur.**

Ash Wednesday *n* the first day of Lent, named from the Christian custom of sprinkling ashes on penitents' heads.

ashy ('æʃɪ) *adj* **ashier, ashiest. 1** of a pale greyish colour; ashen. **2** consisting of, covered with, or resembling ash.

'Asi ★ ('æsɪ) *n* the Arabic name for the **Orontes.**

Asia ★ ('eɪʃə, 'eɪʒə) *n* the largest of the continents, bordering on the Arctic Ocean, the Pacific Ocean, the Indian Ocean, and the Mediterranean and Red Seas in the west. It includes the large peninsulas of Asia Minor, India, Arabia, and Indochina and the island groups of Japan, Indonesia, the Philippines, and Sri Lanka; contains the mountain ranges of the Hindu Kush, Himalayas, Pamirs, Tian Shan, Urals, and Caucasus, the great plateaus of India, Iran, and Tibet, vast plains and deserts, and the valleys of many large rivers including the Mekong, Irrawaddy, Indus, Ganges, Tigris, and Euphrates. Pop.: 3 499 626 (1996 est.). Area: 44 391 162 sq. km (17 139 445 sq. miles).

Asia Minor ★ *n* the historical name for **Anatolia.**

Asian ('eɪʃən, 'eɪʒən) *adj* **1** of or relating to Asia or to any of its peoples or languages. **2** *Brit.* of or relating to natives of the Indian subcontinent or their descendants, esp. when living in Britain. ◆ *n* **3** a native or inhabitant of Asia or a descendant of one. **4** *Brit.* a native of the Indian subcontinent or a descendant of one.

Asian flu *n* a type of influenza caused by a virus which apparently originated in China in 1957.

Asian pear *n* a variety of pear, apple-shaped with crisp juicy flesh.

Asiatic (,eɪʃɪ'ætɪk, -zɪ-) *n, adj* another word for **Asian.**

Asiatic cholera *n* another name for **cholera.**

aside (əˈsaɪd) *adv* **1** on or to one side. **2** out of hearing; in or into seclusion. **3** away from oneself: *he threw the book aside.* **4** out of mind or consideration: *he put aside all fears.* **5** in or into reserve: *to put aside money for old age.* ♦ *n* **6** something spoken by an actor, intended to be heard by the audience, but not by the others on stage. **7** any confidential statement spoken in undertones. **8** an incidental remark, note, etc.

A-side *n* the side of a gramophone record regarded as more important.

Asimov ★ (ˈæzɪmɒf) *n* **Isaac.** 1920–92, US writer and biochemist, born in Russia. His science-fiction works include *Foundation Trilogy* (1951–53; sequel 1982) and the collection of stories *I, Robot* (1950).

asinine (ˈæsɪˌnaɪn) *adj* **1** obstinate or stupid. **2** resembling an ass. ORIG C16: from L *asinīnus,* from *asinus* ASS[1]
▸ **ˈasiˌninely** *adv* ▸ **asininity** (ˌæsɪˈnɪnɪtɪ) *n*

ASIO *abbrev. for* Australian Security Intelligence Organization.

Asir ★ (æˈsɪə) *n* a region of SW Saudi Arabia, in the Southern Province on the Red Sea: under Turkish rule until 1933. Area: 81 000 sq. km (31 000 sq. miles).

ask (ɑːsk) *vb* **1** (often foll. by *about*) to put a question (to); request an answer (from). **2** (*tr*) to inquire about: *she asked the way.* **3** (*tr*) to direct or put (a question). **4** (*may take a clause as object or an infinitive;* often foll. by *for*) to make a request or demand: *they asked for a deposit.* **5** (*tr*) to demand or expect (esp. in **ask a lot of, ask too much of**). **6** (*tr*) Also: **ask out, ask over.** to request (a person) politely to come or go to a place: *he asked her to the party.* ORIG OE *āscian*
▸ **ˈasker** *n*

Ask ★ (ɑːsk) *n Norse myth.* the first man, created by the gods from an ash tree.

ask after *vb* (*prep*) to make inquiries about the health of (someone): *he asked after her mother.*

askance (əˈskæns) *or* **askant** (əˈskænt) *adv* **1** with an oblique glance. **2** with doubt or mistrust. ORIG C16: from ?

askew (əˈskjuː) *adv, adj* at an oblique angle; towards one side; awry.

Askey ★ (ˈæskɪ) *n* **Arthur.** 1900–82, British comedian.

ask for *vb* (*prep*) **1** to try to obtain by requesting. **2** (*intr*) *Inf.* to behave in a provocative manner that is regarded as inviting (trouble, etc.): *you're asking for it.*

asking price *n* the price suggested by a seller but usually considered to be subject to bargaining.

Askja ★ (ˈɑːskjə) *n* a volcano in E central Iceland: active in 1961; largest crater in Iceland. Height: 1510 m (4954 ft). Area of crater: 88 sq. km (34 sq. miles).

aslant (əˈslɑːnt) *adv* **1** at a slant. ♦ *prep* **2** at a slant across or athwart.

asleep (əˈsliːp) *adj* (*postpositive*) **1** in or into a state of sleep. **2** in or into a dormant or inactive state. **3** (of limbs) numb; lacking sensation. **4** *Euphemistic.* dead.

ASLEF (ˈæzlɛf) *n* (in Britain) *acronym for* Associated Society of Locomotive Engineers and Firemen.

AS level *n Brit.* **1a** an advanced level of a subject taken for the General Certificate of Education, with a smaller course content than an A level. **1b** (*as modifier*): *AS-level English.* **2** a pass in a subject at AS level: *I've got three AS levels.*

ASM *abbrev. for:* **1** air-to-surface missile. **2** *Theatre.* assistant stage manager.

Asmara ★ (æsˈmɑːrə) *n* the capital of Eritrea. Pop.: 431 000 (1995 est.).

Asnières ★ (*French* anjɛr) *n* a suburb of Paris, France, on the Seine. Pop.: 72 250 (1990).

Aso ★ (ˈɑːsəʊ) *n* a group of five volcanic cones in Japan on central Kyushu, one of which, Naka-dake, has the largest crater in the world, between 16 km (10 miles) and 24 km (15 miles) in diameter. Highest cone: 1592 m (5223 ft). Also called: **Asosan** (ˌɑːsəʊˈsɑːn).

asocial (eɪˈsəʊʃəl) *adj* **1** avoiding contact. **2** unconcerned about the welfare of others. **3** hostile to society.

asp (æsp) *n* **1** the venomous snake that caused the death of Cleopatra. **2** Also called: **asp viper.** a viper that occurs in S Europe and is very similar to but smaller than the adder. **3 horned asp.** another name for **horned viper.** ORIG C15: from L *aspis,* from Gk

asparagus (əˈspærəgəs) *n* **1** a plant of the lily family, having small scaly or needle-like leaves. **2** the succulent young shoots, which may be cooked and eaten. **3 asparagus fern.** a fernlike species of asparagus, native to southern Africa. ORIG C15: from L, from Gk *asparagos,* from ?

aspartame (əˈspɑːˌteɪm) *n* an artificial sweetener produced from a nonessential amino acid. ORIG C20: from *aspart(ic acid)* + (*phenyl*)*a*(*lanine*) *m*(*ethyl*) *e*(*ster*)

aspect (ˈæspɛkt) *n* **1** appearance to the eye; visual effect. **2** a distinct feature or element in a problem, situation, etc.; facet. **3** the way in which a problem, idea, etc., may be considered. **4** a facial expression: *a severe aspect.* **5** a position facing a particular direction: *the southern aspect of a house.* **6** a view in a certain direction. **7** *Astrol.* any of several specific angular distances between two planets. **8** *Grammar.* a category of verbal inflections that expresses such features as the continuity, repetition, or completedness of the action described. ORIG C14: from L *aspectus* a sight, from *ad-* to, at + *specere* to look

aspect ratio *n* **1** the ratio of width to height of a picture on a television or cinema screen. **2** *Aeronautics.* the ratio of the span of a wing to its mean chord.

aspen (ˈæspən) *n* a kind of poplar tree in which the leaves are attached to the stem by long flattened stalks so that they quiver in the wind. ORIG OE *æspe*

Asperger's syndrome (ˈæspəgəz) *n* a form of autism in which the sufferer has limited but obsessive interests and has difficulty relating to other people. ORIG C20: after Hans *Asperger* (20th century), Austrian physician who first described it

asperity (æˈspɛrɪtɪ) *n, pl* **asperities. 1** roughness or sharpness of temper. **2** roughness or harshness of a surface, sound, etc. **3** *Physics.* the elongated compressed region of contact between two surfaces caused by the normal force. ORIG C16: from L *asperitās,* from *asper* rough

asperse (əˈspɜːs) *vb* **asperses, aspersing, aspersed.** (*tr*) to spread false rumours about; defame. ORIG C15: from L *aspersus,* from *aspergere* to sprinkle
▸ **asˈperser** *n* ▸ **asˈpersive** *adj*

aspersion (əˈspɜːʃən) *n* **1** a disparaging or malicious remark (esp. in **cast aspersions (on)**). **2** the act of defaming.

asphalt (ˈæsfælt) *n* **1** any of several black semisolid substances composed of bitumen and inert mineral matter. They occur naturally and as a residue from petroleum distillation. **2** a mixture of this substance with gravel, used in road-surfacing and roofing materials. **3** (*modifier*) containing or surfaced with asphalt. ♦ *vb* **4** (*tr*) to cover with asphalt. ORIG C14: from LL *aspaltus,* from Gk *asphaltos,* prob. from A-[1] + *sphallein* to cause to fall; referring to its use as a binding agent
▸ **asˈphaltic** *adj*

asphodel (ˈæsfəˌdɛl) *n* **1** any of various S European plants of the lily family having clusters of white or yellow flowers. **2** an unidentified flower of Greek legend said to cover the Elysian fields. ORIG C16: from L *asphodelus,* from Gk *asphodelos,* from ?

asphyxia (æsˈfɪksɪə) *n* lack of oxygen in the blood due to restricted respiration; suffocation. ORIG C18: from NL, from Gk *asphuxia* a stopping of the pulse, from A-[1] + *sphuxis* pulse, from *sphuzein* to throb
▸ **asˈphyxial** *adj* ▸ **asˈphyxiant** *adj*

asphyxiate (æsˈfɪksɪˌeɪt) *vb* **asphyxiates, asphyxiating, asphyxiated.** to cause asphyxia in or undergo asphyxia; smother; suffocate.
▸ **asˌphyxiˈation** *n* ▸ **asˈphyxiˌator** *n*

aspic (ˈæspɪk) *n* a savoury jelly based on meat or fish stock, used as a relish or as a mould for meat, vegetables, etc. ORIG C18: from F: aspic (jelly), asp

aspidistra (ˌæspɪˈdɪstrə) *n* a popular house plant of the lily family with long tough evergreen leaves. ORIG C19: from NL, from Gk *aspis* shield, on the model of *Tupistra,* genus of liliaceous plants

aspirant (ˈæspɪrənt) *n* **1** a person who aspires, as to a high position. ♦ *adj* **2** aspiring.

aspirate *vb* ('æspɪˌreɪt), **aspirates, aspirating, aspirated.** (*tr*) **1** *Phonetics.* **1a** to articulate (a stop) with some force, so that breath escapes audibly. **1b** to pronounce (a word or syllable) with an initial *h.* **2** to remove by inhalation or suction, esp. to suck (air or fluid) from a body cavity. **3** to supply air to (an internal-combustion engine). ◆ *n* ('æspɪrɪt). **4** *Phonetics.* **4a** a stop pronounced with an audible release of breath. **4b** the glottal fricative represented in English and several other languages as *h.* ◆ *adj* ('æspɪrɪt). **5** *Phonetics.* (of a stop) pronounced with a forceful expulsion of breath.

aspiration (ˌæspɪ'reɪʃən) *n* **1** strong desire to achieve something, such as success. **2** the aim of such desire. **3** the act of breathing. **4** *Phonetics.* **4a** the pronunciation of an aspirated consonant. **4b** an aspirated consonant. **5** *Med.* **5a** the sucking of fluid or foreign matter into the air passages of the body. **5b** the removal of air or fluid from the body by suction.
▸ **ˌaspi'rational** *adj* ▸ **aspiratory** (ə'spaɪrətərɪ) *adj*

aspirator ('æspɪˌreɪtə) *n* a device employing suction, such as a jet pump or one for removing fluids from a body cavity.

aspire (ə'spaɪə) *vb* **aspires, aspiring, aspired.** (*intr*) **1** (usually foll. by *to* or *after*) to yearn (for), desire, or hope (to do or be something): *to aspire to be a great leader.* **2** to rise to a great height. ORIG C15: from L *aspīrāre* to breathe upon, from *spīrāre* to breathe
▸ **as'piring** *adj*

aspirin ('æsprɪn) *n, pl* **aspirin** *or* **aspirins. 1** a white crystalline compound widely used in the form of tablets to relieve pain, fever, and colds. Chemical name: **acetylsalicylic acid. 2** a tablet of aspirin. ORIG C19: from G, from *A(cetyl)* + *Spir(säure)* spiraeic acid (modern salicylic acid) + -IN

Aspirin ('æsprɪn) *n* (in Canada) a trademark for **aspirin.**

asquint (ə'skwɪnt) *adv, adj* (*postpositive*) with a glance from the corner of the eye, esp. a furtive one. ORIG C13: ?from Du. *schuinte* slant, from ?

Asquith ★ ('æskwɪθ) *n* **Herbert Henry,** 1st Earl of Oxford and Asquith. 1852–1928, British statesman; prime minister (1908–16); leader of the Liberal Party (1908–26).

ass[1] (æs) *n* **1** a mammal related to the horse. It is hardy and sure-footed, having longer ears than the horse. **2** (not in technical use) the donkey. **3** a foolish or ridiculously pompous person. ORIG OE *assa,* prob. from OIrish *asan,* from L *asinus;* rel. to Gk *onos* ass

ass[2] (æs) *n* the usual US and Canad. word for **arse.** ORIG OE *ærs*

Assad ★ ('asat) *n* **Hafezal** ('hafɛzal). 1928–2000, Syrian statesman and general; president of Syria (1971–2000).

assagai ('æsəˌgaɪ) *n, pl* **assagais.** a variant spelling of **assegai.**

assai (æ'saɪ) *adv Music.* (usually preceded by a musical direction) very: *allegro assai.* ORIG It.: enough

assail (ə'seɪl) *vb* (*tr*) **1** to attack violently; assault. **2** to criticize or ridicule vehemently. **3** to beset or disturb: *his mind was assailed by doubts.* **4** to encounter with the intention of mastering. ORIG C13: from OF *asalir,* from L *assilīre,* from *salīre* to leap
▸ **as'sailable** *adj* ▸ **as'sailer** *n*

assailant (ə'seɪlənt) *n* a person who attacks another, either physically or verbally.

Assam ★ (æ'sæm) *n* a state of NE India, situated in the central Brahmaputra valley: tropical forest, with the heaviest rainfall in the world; produces large quantities of tea. Capital: Dispur. Pop.: 24 200 000 (1994 est.). Area: 78 438 sq. km (30 285 sq. miles).
▸ **ˌAssa'mese** *adj, n*

assassin (ə'sæsɪn) *n* a murderer, esp. one who kills a prominent political figure. ORIG C16: from Med. L *assassīnus,* from Ar. *hashshāshīn,* pl. of *hashshāsh* one who eats HASHISH

assassinate (ə'sæsɪˌneɪt) *vb* **assassinates, assassinating, assassinated.** (*tr*) **1** to murder (a political figure). **2** to ruin or harm (a person's reputation, etc.) by slander.
▸ **asˌsassi'nation** *n*

assault (ə'sɔːlt) *n* **1** a violent attack, either physical or verbal. **2** *Law.* an act that threatens violence to another. **3a** the culmination of a military attack. **3b** (*as modifier*): *assault troops.* **4** rape or attempted rape. ◆ *vb* (*tr*) **5** to make an assault upon. **6** to rape or attempt to rape. ORIG C13: from OF *asaut,* from Vulgar L, from *assalīre* (unattested) to leap upon; see ASSAIL
▸ **as'saultive** *adj*

assault and battery *n Criminal law.* a threat of attack to another person followed by actual attack.

assault course *n* an obstacle course designed to give soldiers practice in negotiating hazards.

assay *vb* (ə'seɪ). **1** to subject (a substance, such as silver or gold) to chemical analysis, as in the determination of the amount of impurity. **2** (*tr*) to attempt (something or to do something). ◆ *n* (ə'seɪ, 'æseɪ). **3a** an analysis, esp. a determination of the amount of metal in an ore or the amounts of impurities in a precious metal. **3b** (*as modifier*): *an assay office.* **4** a substance undergoing an analysis. **5** a written report on the results of an analysis. **6** a test. ORIG C14: from OF *assai;* see ESSAY
▸ **as'sayer** *n*

assegai *or* **assagai** ('æsəˌgaɪ) *n, pl* **assegais** *or* **assagais. 1** a southern African tree, the wood of which is used for making spears. **2** a sharp light spear. ORIG C17: from Port. *azagaia,* from Ar. *az zaghāyah,* from *al* the + *zaghāyah* assegai, from Berber

assemblage (ə'sɛmblɪdʒ) *n* **1** a number of things or persons assembled together. **2** the act of assembling or the state of being assembled. **3** (ˌæsəm'blɑːʒ). a three-dimensional work of art that combines various objects.

assemble (ə'sɛmbᵊl) *vb* **assembles, assembling, assembled. 1** to come or bring together; collect or congregate. **2** to fit or join together (the parts of something, such as a machine). ORIG C13: from OF *assembler,* from Vulgar L *assimulāre* (unattested) to bring together, from L *simul* together

assembler (ə'sɛmblə) *n* **1** a person or thing that assembles. **2** a computer program that converts a program written in assembly language into machine code. Cf. **compiler. 3** another name for **assembly language.**

assembly (ə'sɛmblɪ) *n, pl* **assemblies. 1** a number of people gathered together, esp. for a formal meeting held at regular intervals. **2** the act of assembling or the state of being assembled. **3** the process of putting together a number of parts to make a machine. **4** *Mil.* a signal for personnel to assemble.

Assembly (ə'sɛmblɪ) *n, pl* **Assemblies.** the lower chamber in various state legislatures, esp. in Australia and America. See also **House of Assembly, legislative assembly.**

assembly language *n Computing.* a low-level programming language that allows a programmer complete control of the machine code to be generated.

assembly line *n* a sequence of machines, tools, operations, workers, etc., in a factory, arranged so that at each stage a further process is carried out.

Assen ★ (*Dutch* 'ɑsə) *n* a city in the N Netherlands, capital of Drenthe province. Pop.: 52 268 (1994).

assent (ə'sɛnt) *n* **1** agreement, as to a statement, proposal, etc. **2** compliance. ◆ *vb* (*intr;* usually foll. by *to*) **3** to agree or express agreement. ORIG C13: from OF *assenter,* from L *assentīrī,* from *sentīre* to think

assert (ə'sɜːt) *vb* (*tr*) **1** to insist upon (rights, etc.). **2** (*may take a clause as object*) to state to be true; declare. **3** to put (oneself) forward in an insistent manner. ORIG C17: from L *asserere* to join to oneself, from *serere* to join
▸ **as'serter** *or* **as'sertor** *n*

assertion (ə'sɜːʃən) *n* **1** a positive statement, usually made without evidence. **2** the act of asserting.

assertion sign *n* a sign ⊢ used in symbolic logic to introduce the conclusion of a valid argument: often read as "therefore."

assertive (ə'sɜːtɪv) *adj* **1** confident and direct in dealing with others. **2** given to making assertions; dogmatic or aggressive.
▸ **as'sertively** *adv* ▸ **as'sertiveness** *n*

assess (ə'sɛs) *vb* (*tr*) **1** to evaluate. **2** (foll. by *at*) to estimate the value of (income, property, etc.) for taxation

★ people and places

purposes. **3** to determine the amount of (a fine, tax, etc.). **4** to impose a tax, fine, etc., on (a person or property). ORIG C15: from OF *assesser,* from L *assidēre* to sit beside, from *sedēre* to sit
▸ **as'sessable** *adj*

assessment (ə'sɛsmənt) *n* **1** the act of assessing, esp. (in Britain) the evaluation of a student's achievement on a course. **2** an amount determined as payable. **3** a valuation set on taxable property, etc. **4** evaluation.

assessment tests *pl n Brit. education.* nationally standardized tests for pupil assessment based on attainment targets in the National Curriculum. Formal name: **standard assessment tasks, SATs.**

assessor (ə'sɛsə) *n* **1** a person who evaluates the merits of something. **2** a person who values property for taxation. **3** a person who estimates the value of damage to property for insurance purposes. **4** a person with technical expertise called in to advise a court.
▸ **assessorial** (ˌæsɛ'sɔːrɪəl) *adj*

asset ('æsɛt) *n* anything valuable or useful. ORIG C19: back formation from ASSETS

assets ('æsɛts) *pl n* **1** *Accounting.* the property and claims against debtors that are shown balanced against liabilities. **2** *Law.* the property available to an executor for settling a deceased person's estate. **3** any property owned by a person or firm. ORIG C16: from OF *asez* enough, from Vulgar L *ad satis* (unattested) from L *ad* up to + *satis* enough

asset-stripping *n Commerce.* the practice of taking over a failing company at a low price and then selling the assets piecemeal.
▸ **'asset-ˌstripper** *n*

asset value *n* the value of a share in a company calculated by dividing the difference between the total of its assets and its liabilities by the number of ordinary shares issued.

asseverate (ə'sɛvəˌreɪt) *vb* **asseverates, asseverating, asseverated.** (*tr*) to declare solemnly. ORIG C18: from L *asseverāre* to do (something) earnestly, from *sevērus* SEVERE
▸ **asˌsever'ation** *n*

Asshur ★ ('æʃʊə) *n* a variant spelling of **Assur.**

assibilate (ə'sɪbɪˌleɪt) *vb* **assibilates, assibilating, assibilated.** (*tr*) *Phonetics.* to pronounce (a speech sound) with or as a sibilant. ORIG C19: from LL *assībilāre* to hiss at, from *sībilāre* to hiss
▸ **asˌsibi'lation** *n*

assiduity (ˌæsɪ'djuːɪtɪ) *n, pl* **assiduities. 1** constant and close application. **2** (*often pl*) devoted attention.

assiduous (ə'sɪdjʊəs) *adj* **1** hard-working; persevering. **2** undertaken with perseverance and care. ORIG C16: from L, from *assidēre* to sit beside, from *sedēre* to sit
▸ **as'siduousness** *n*

assign (ə'saɪn) *vb* (*mainly tr*) **1** to select for and appoint to a post, etc. **2** to give out or allot (a task, problem, etc.). **3** to set apart (a place, person, time, etc.) for a particular function or event: *to assign a day for the meeting.* **4** to attribute to a specified cause, origin, or source. **5** to transfer (one's right, interest, or title to property) to someone else. ◆ *n* **6** *Law.* a person to whom property is assigned; assignee. ORIG C14: from OF, from L *assignāre,* from *signāre* to mark out
▸ **as'signable** *adj* ▸ **as'signer** *or* **ˌassign'or** *n*

assignation (ˌæsɪg'neɪʃən) *n* **1** a secret or forbidden arrangement to meet, esp. one between lovers. **2** the act of assigning; assignment. ORIG C14: from OF, from L *assignātiō* a marking out

assignee (ˌæsaɪ'niː) *n Law.* a person to whom some right, interest, or property is transferred.

assignment (ə'saɪnmənt) *n* **1** something that has been assigned, such as a mission or task. **2** a position or post to which a person is assigned. **3** the act of assigning or state of being assigned. **4** *Law.* **4a** the transfer to another of a right, interest, or title to property. **4b** the document effecting such a transfer.

assimilate (ə'sɪmɪˌleɪt) *vb* **assimilates, assimilating, assimilated. 1** (*tr*) to learn (information, etc.) and understand it thoroughly. **2** (*tr*) to absorb (food). **3** (*intr*) to become absorbed, incorporated, or learned and understood. **4** (usually foll. by *into* or *with*) to adjust or become adjusted: *the new immigrants assimilated easily.* **5** (usually foll. by *to* or *with*) to become or cause to become similar. **6** (usually foll. by *to*) *Phonetics.* to change (a consonant) or (of a consonant) to be changed into another under the influence of one adjacent to it. ORIG C15: from L *assimilāre* to make one thing like another, from *similis* like, SIMILAR
▸ **as'similable** *adj* ▸ **asˌsimi'lation** *n* ▸ **as'similative** *or* **as'similatory** *adj* ▸ **as'simiˌlator** *n*

Assiniboine ★ (ə'sɪnɪˌbɔɪn) *n* a river in W Canada, rising in E Saskatchewan and flowing southeast and east to the Red River at Winnipeg. Length: over 860 km (500 miles).

Assisi ★ (*Italian* as'siːzi) *n* a town in central Italy, in Umbria: birthplace of St Francis, who founded the Franciscan religious order here in 1208. Pop.: 24 790 (1990).

assist (ə'sɪst) *vb* **1** to give help or support to (a person, cause, etc.). **2** to work or act as an assistant or subordinate to (another). ◆ *n* **3** *US.* the act of helping. ORIG C15: from F, from L *assistere* to stand by, from *sistere* to cause to stand, from *stāre* to stand
▸ **as'sister** *n*

assistance (ə'sɪstəns) *n* **1** help; support. **2** the act of assisting. **3** *Brit. inf.* See **national assistance.**

assistant (ə'sɪstənt) *n* **1a** a person who assists, esp. in a subordinate position. **1b** (*as modifier*): *assistant manager.* **2** See **shop assistant.**

assistant referee *n Soccer.* the official name for **linesman** (sense 1).

assize (ə'saɪz) *n Scots Law.* **a** trial by a jury. **b** a jury. ORIG C13: from OF *assise* session, from *asseoir* to seat, from L *assidēre* to sit beside

assizes (ə'saɪzɪz) *pl n* (formerly in England and Wales) the sessions of the principal court in each county, exercising civil and criminal jurisdiction: replaced in 1971 by crown courts.

assoc. *abbrev. for:* **1** associate(d). **2** association.

associate *vb* (ə'səʊʃɪˌeɪt, -sɪ-). (usually foll. by *with*) **associates, associating, associated. 1** (*tr*) to link or connect in the mind or imagination. **2** (*intr*) to mix socially: *to associate with writers.* **3** (*intr*) to form or join an association, group, etc. **4** (*tr; usually passive*) to consider in conjunction: *rainfall is associated with humidity.* **5** (*tr*) to bring (a person, esp. oneself) into friendship, partnership, etc. **6** (*tr; often passive*) to express agreement (with): *Bertrand Russell was associated with the CND movement.* ◆ *n* (ə'səʊʃɪɪt, -sɪ-). **7** a person joined with another or others in an enterprise, business, etc. **8** a companion or friend. **9** something that usually accompanies another thing. **10** a person having a subordinate position in or admitted to only partial membership of an institution, association, etc. ◆ *adj* (ə'səʊʃɪɪt, -sɪ-). (*prenominal*) **11** joined with another or others in an enterprise, business, etc.: *an associate director.* **12** having partial rights or subordinate status: *an associate member.* **13** accompanying; concomitant. ORIG C14: from L *associāre* to ally with, from *sociāre* to join, from *socius* an ally
▸ **as'sociable** *adj* ▸ **as'sociˌator** *n* ▸ **as'sociateˌship** *n*

association (əˌsəʊsɪ'eɪʃən, -ʃɪ-) *n* **1** a group of people having a common purpose or interest; a society or club. **2** the act of associating or the state of being associated. **3** friendship or companionship: *their association will not last.* **4** a mental connection of ideas, feelings, or sensations. **5** *Chem.* the formation of groups of molecules and ions held together by weak chemical bonds. **6** *Ecology.* a group of similar plants that grow in a uniform environment.

association football *n* a more formal name for **soccer.**

associative (ə'səʊʃɪətɪv, -sɪ-) *adj* **1** of, relating to, or causing association or union. **2** *Maths, logic.* **2a** of an operation, such as multiplication or addition, in which the answer is the same regardless of the way in which the elements are grouped: $(2 \times 3) \times 4 = 2 \times (3 \times 4)$. **2b** referring to this property: *the associative laws of arithmetic.*

assonance ('æsənəns) *n* **1** the use of the same vowel sound with different consonants or the same consonant with different vowels, as in a line of verse. Examples are *time* and *light* or *mystery* and *mastery*. **2** partial correspondence. ORIG C18: from F, from L *assonāre* to sound, from *sonāre* to sound
▸ **'assonant** *adj, n*

assort (ə'sɔːt) *vb* **1** (*tr*) to arrange or distribute into groups of the same type; classify. **2** (*intr; usually foll. by with*) to fit or fall into a class or group. **3** (*tr*) to supply with an assortment of merchandise. **4** (*tr*) to put in the same category as others. ORIG C15: from OF *assorter*, from *sorte* SORT
▸ **as'sortative** *adj*

assorted (ə'sɔːtɪd) *adj* **1** consisting of various kinds mixed together. **2** classified: *assorted categories*. **3** matched (esp. in **well-assorted, ill-assorted**).

assortment (ə'sɔːtmənt) *n* **1** a collection or group of various things or sorts. **2** the act of assorting.

ASSR (formerly) *abbrev. for* Autonomous Soviet Socialist Republic.

asst *abbrev. for* assistant.

assuage (ə'sweɪdʒ) *vb* **assuages, assuaging, assuaged.** (*tr*) **1** to soothe, moderate, or relieve (grief, pain, etc.). **2** to give relief to (thirst, etc.). **3** to pacify; calm. ORIG C14: from OF, from Vulgar L *assuāviāre* (unattested) to sweeten, from L *suāvis* pleasant
▸ **as'suagement** *n* ▸ **as'suager** *n*

Assuan *or* **Assouan** ★ (ɑːs'wɑːn) *n* variant spellings of **Aswan.**

assume (ə'sjuːm) *vb* **assumes, assuming, assumed.** (*tr*) **1** (*may take a clause as object*) to take for granted; suppose. **2** to undertake or take on or over (a position, responsibility, etc.): *to assume office*. **3** to pretend to; feign: *he assumed indifference*. **4** to take or put on; adopt: *the problem assumed gigantic proportions*. **5** to appropriate or usurp (power, control, etc.). ORIG C15: from L *assūmere* to take up, from *sūmere* to take up, from SUB- + *emere* to take
▸ **as'sumable** *adj* ▸ **as'sumer** *n*

assumed (ə'sjuːmd) *adj* **1** false; fictitious: *an assumed name*. **2** taken for granted. **3** usurped.

assuming (ə'sjuːmɪŋ) *adj* **1** expecting too much; presumptuous. ◆ *conj* **2** (often foll. by *that*) if it is assumed or taken for granted.

assumption (ə'sʌmpʃən) *n* **1** the act of taking something for granted or something that is taken for granted. **2** an assuming of power or possession. **3** presumption. **4** *Logic*. a statement that is used as the premise of a particular argument but may not be otherwise accepted. ORIG C13: from L *assūmptiō* a taking up, from *assūmere* to ASSUME
▸ **as'sumptive** *adj*

Assumption (ə'sʌmpʃən) *n Christianity*. **1** the taking up of the Virgin Mary (body and soul) into heaven when her earthly life was ended. **2** the feast commemorating this.

Assur, Asur ('æsə), **Asshur,** *or* **Ashur** ★ ('æʃʊə) *n* **1** the supreme national god of the ancient Assyrians, chiefly a war god, whose symbol was an archer within a winged disc. **2** one of the chief cities of ancient Assyria, on the River Tigris about 100 km (60 miles) downstream from the present-day city of Mosul.

assurance (ə'ʃʊərəns) *n* **1** a statement, assertion, etc., intended to inspire confidence. **2** a promise or pledge of support. **3** freedom from doubt; certainty. **4** forwardness; impudence. **5** *Chiefly Brit*. insurance providing for certainties such as death as contrasted with fire.

assure (ə'ʃʊə) *vb* **assures, assuring, assured.** (*tr; may take a clause as object*) **1** to convince: *to assure a person of one's love*. **2** to promise; guarantee. **3** to state positively. **4** to make (an event) certain. **5** *Chiefly Brit*. to insure against loss, esp. of life. ORIG C14: from OF, from Med. L *assēcūrāre* to secure or make sure, from *sēcūrus* SECURE
▸ **as'surable** *adj* ▸ **as'surer** *n*

assured (ə'ʃʊəd) *adj* **1** sure; guaranteed. **2** self-assured. **3** *Chiefly Brit*. insured. ◆ *n* **4** *Chiefly Brit*. **4a** the beneficiary under a life assurance policy. **4b** the person whose life is insured.
▸ **assuredly** (ə'ʃʊərɪdlɪ) *adv*

asswipe ('æsˌwaɪp) *n US sl*. a despicable or stupid person. ORIG C20: orig.: toilet paper, from ASS[2] + WIPE

Assyria ★ (ə'sɪrɪə) *n* an ancient kingdom of N Mesopotamia: it established an empire that stretched from Egypt to the Persian Gulf, reaching its greatest extent between 721 and 633 B.C. Its chief cities were Assur and Nineveh.
▸ **A'ssyrian** *adj, n*

AST *abbrev. for* Atlantic Standard Time.

Astaire ★ (ə'steə) *n* **Fred**, real name *Frederick Austerlitz*. 1899–1987, US dancer and actor whose films include *Top Hat* (1935) and *The Band Wagon* (1953).

Astana ★ (æ'stænə) *n* the capital of Kazakhstan: an important railway junction. Pop.: 280 200 (1995 est.). Former names: **Akmolinsk** (until 1961), **Tselinograd** (1961–94), **Akmola** (1994–98).

Astarte ★ (æ'stɑːtɪ) *n* a fertility goddess worshipped by the Phoenicians: identified with Ashtoreth of the Hebrews and Ishtar of the Babylonians and Assyrians.

astatic (æ'stætɪk, eɪ-) *adj* **1** not static; unstable. **2** *Physics*. having no tendency to assume any particular position or orientation. ORIG C19: from Gk *astatos* unsteady
▸ **a'statically** *adv*

astatine ('æstəˌtiːn) *n* a radioactive element that occurs naturally in minute amounts and is artificially produced by bombarding bismuth with alpha particles. Symbol: At; atomic no.: 85; half-life of most stable isotope, ^{210}At: 8.1 hours. ORIG C20: from Gk *astatos* unstable

Astbury ★ ('æstbərɪ) *n* **John**. 1688–1743, English potter; earliest of the great Staffordshire potters.

aster ('æstə) *n* **1** a plant having white, blue, purple, or pink daisy-like flowers. **2** **China aster**. a related Chinese plant widely cultivated for its showy brightly coloured flowers. ORIG C18: from NL, from L *aster* star, from Gk

-aster *suffix forming nouns*. a person or thing that is inferior to what is specified: *poetaster*. ORIG from L

asterisk ('æstərɪsk) *n* **1** a star-shaped character (*) used in printing or writing to indicate a cross-reference to a footnote, an omission, etc. ◆ *vb* **2** (*tr*) to mark with an asterisk. ORIG C17: from LL *asteriscus* a small star, from Gk, from *astēr* star

asterism ('æstəˌrɪzəm) *n* **1** three asterisks arranged in a triangle (⁂ or ⁂), to draw attention to the text that follows. **2** a cluster of stars or a constellation. ORIG C16: from Gk *asterismos* arrangement of constellations, from *astēr* star

astern (ə'stɜːn) *adv, adj* (*postpositive*) *Naut*. **1** at or towards the stern. **2** with the stern first: *full speed astern!* **3** aft of the stern of a vessel.

asteroid ('æstəˌrɔɪd) *n* **1** Also called: **minor planet, planetoid**. any of numerous small celestial bodies that move around the sun mainly between the orbits of Mars and Jupiter. **2** a starfish. ◆ *adj also* **ˌaste'roidal**. **3** of a starfish. **4** shaped like a star. ORIG C19: from Gk *asteroeidēs* starlike, from *astēr* a star

asthenia (æs'θiːnɪə) *n Pathol*. an abnormal loss of strength; debility. ORIG C19: via NL from Gk *astheneia* weakness, from A-[1] + *sthenos* strength

asthenic (æs'θɛnɪk) *adj* **1** of or having asthenia; weak. **2** referring to a physique characterized by long limbs and a small trunk. ◆ *n* **3** a person with long limbs and a small trunk.

asthma ('æsmə) *n* a respiratory disorder, often of allergic origin, characterized by difficulty in breathing. ORIG C14: from Gk: laborious breathing, from *azein* to breathe hard

asthmatic (æs'mætɪk) *adj* **1** of or having asthma. ◆ *n* **2** a person who has asthma.
▸ **asth'matically** *adv*

Asti ★ ('æstɪ) *n* a town in NW Italy: famous for its sparkling wine, **Asti spumante** (spuː'mæntɪ). Pop.: 74 649 (1990).

astigmatic (ˌæstɪg'mætɪk) *adj* relating to or affected with astigmatism. ORIG C19: from A-[1] + Gk *stigmat-*, *stigma* spot, focus
▸ **ˌastig'matically** *adv*

astigmatism (ə'stɪgməˌtɪzəm) *or* **astigmia** (ə'stɪgmɪə) *n* **1** a defect of a lens resulting in the formation of distorted images, caused by light rays not meeting at a single focal point. **2** faulty vision resulting from defective curvature of the cornea or lens of the eye.

astilbe (əˈstɪlbɪ) *n* any perennial plant of the genus *Astilbe,* cultivated for its spikes of ornamental pink or white flowers. ORIG C19: NL, from Gk A-[1] + *stilbē,* from *stilbein* to glitter; referring to its inconspicuous individual flowers

astir (əˈstɜː) *adj* (*postpositive*) **1** awake and out of bed. **2** in motion; on the move.

Astolat ★ (ˈæstəʊˌlæt) *n* a town in Arthurian legend: location unknown.

Aston ★ (ˈæstən) *n* **Francis William.** 1877–1945, British physicist and chemist, who developed the first mass spectrograph: Nobel prize for chemistry 1922.

astonish (əˈstɒnɪʃ) *vb* (*tr*) to fill with amazement; surprise greatly. ORIG C15: from earlier *astonyen,* from OF, from Vulgar L *extonāre* (unattested) to strike with thunder, from L *tonāre* to thunder
▸ **aˈstonishing** *adj*

astonishment (əˈstɒnɪʃmənt) *n* **1** extreme surprise; amazement. **2** a cause of amazement.

Astor ★ (ˈæstə) *n* **1 John Jacob,** 1st Baron Astor of Hever. 1886–1971, British proprietor of *The Times* (1922–66). **2 Nancy** (**Witcher**), Viscountess, original name *Nancy Langhorne.* 1879–1964, British Conservative politician, born in the US; the first woman MP.

astound (əˈstaʊnd) *vb* (*tr*) to overwhelm with amazement; bewilder. ORIG C17: from *astoned* amazed, from OF, from *estoner* to ASTONISH
▸ **aˈstounding** *adj*

astraddle (əˈstrædᵊl) *adj* **1** (*postpositive*) with a leg on either side of something. ◆ *prep* **2** astride.

astragal (ˈæstrəgᵊl) *n* **1** *Archit.* Also called: **bead.** a small convex moulding, usually with a semicircular cross section. **2** *Anat.* the ankle or anklebone. ORIG C17: from L, from Gk *astragalos* anklebone, hence, small round moulding

astragalus (æˈstrægələs) *n, pl* **astragali** (-ˌlaɪ). *Anat.* another name for **talus**[1]. ORIG C16: via NL from L: ASTRAGAL

astrakhan (ˌæstrəˈkæn) *n* **1** a fur, usually black or grey, made of the closely curled wool of lambs from Astrakhan. **2** a cloth with curled pile resembling this. **3** (*modifier*) made of such fur or cloth.

Astrakhan ★ (ˌæstrəˈkæn, -ˈkɑːn; *Russian* ˈastrəxənj) *n* a city in SE Russia, on the delta of the Volga River, 21 m (70 ft) below sea level. Pop.: 486 000 (1995 est.).

astral (ˈæstrəl) *adj* **1** relating to or resembling the stars. **2** *Theosophy.* relating to a supposed supersensible substance taking the form of an aura discernible to certain gifted individuals. ORIG C17: from LL *astrālis,* from L *astrum* star, from Gk *astron*

astray (əˈstreɪ) *adj* (*postpositive*), *adv* **1** out of the correct path or direction. **2** out of the right or expected way. ORIG C13: from OF, from *estraier* to STRAY

astride (əˈstraɪd) *adj* (*postpositive*) **1** with a leg on either side. **2** with the legs far apart. ◆ *prep* **3** with a leg on either side of. **4** with a part on both sides of; spanning.

astringent (əˈstrɪndʒənt) *adj* **1** severe; harsh. **2** sharp or invigorating. **3** causing contraction of body tissues, checking blood flow; styptic. ◆ *n* **4** an astringent drug or lotion. ORIG C16: from L *astringēns* drawing together
▸ **asˈtringency** *n* ▸ **asˈtringently** *adv*

astro- *combining form.* indicating a star or star-shaped structure: *astrology.* ORIG from Gk, from *astron* star

astrobiology (ˌæstrəʊbaɪˈɒlədʒɪ) *n* the branch of biology that investigates the possibility of life on other planets.

astrochemistry (ˌæstrəʊˈkɛmɪstrɪ) *n* the study of the chemistry of celestial bodies and space.

astrodome (ˈæstrəˌdəʊm) *n* a transparent dome on the top of an aircraft, through which observations can be made.

astrol. *abbrev. for:* **1** astrologer. **2** astrological. **3** astrology.

astrolabe (ˈæstrəˌleɪb) *n* an instrument used by early astronomers to measure the altitude of stars and planets and also as a navigational aid. ORIG C13: via OF & Med. L from Gk, from *astrolabos,* from *astron* star + *lambanein* to take

astrology (əˈstrɒlədʒɪ) *n* **1** the study of the motions and relative positions of the planets, sun, and moon, interpreted in terms of human characteristics and activities. **2** primitive astronomy. ORIG C14: from OF, from L *astrologia,* from Gk, from *astrologos* (orig.: astronomer); see ASTRO-, -LOGY
▸ **asˈtrologer** *or* **asˈtrologist** *n* ▸ **astrological** (ˌæstrəˈlɒdʒɪkᵊl) *adj*

astron. *abbrev. for:* **1** astronomer. **2** astronomical. **3** astronomy.

astronaut (ˈæstrəˌnɔːt) *n* a person trained for travelling in space. See also **cosmonaut.** ORIG C20: from ASTRO- + *-naut,* from Gk *nautēs* sailor, on the model of *aeronaut*

astronautics (ˌæstrəˈnɔːtɪks) *n* (*functioning as sing*) the science and technology of space flight.
▸ ˌ**astroˈnautical** *adj*

Astronomer Royal *n* an honorary title awarded to an eminent British astronomer: until 1972, the Astronomer Royal was also director of the Royal Greenwich Observatory.

astronomical (ˌæstrəˈnɒmɪkᵊl) *or* **astronomic** *adj* **1** enormously large. **2** of or relating to astronomy.
▸ ˌ**astroˈnomically** *adv*

astronomical clock *n* **1** a complex clock showing astronomical phenomena, such as the phases of the moon. **2** any clock showing sidereal time used in observatories.

astronomical unit *n* a unit of distance used in astronomy equal to the mean distance between the earth and the sun. 1 astronomical unit is equivalent to 1.495×10^{11} metres.

astronomy (əˈstrɒnəmɪ) *n* the scientific study of the individual celestial bodies (excluding the earth) and of the universe as a whole. ORIG C13: from OF, from L *astronomia,* from Gk; see ASTRO-, -NOMY
▸ **asˈtronomer** *n*

astrophysics (ˌæstrəʊˈfɪzɪks) *n* (*functioning as sing*) the branch of physics concerned with the physical and chemical properties of the celestial bodies.
▸ ˌ**astroˈphysicist** *n*

Astroturf (ˈæstrəʊˌtɜːf) *n Trademark.* a type of grasslike artificial surface used for playing fields and lawns. ORIG C20: from *Astro*(*dome*) the baseball stadium in Texas where it was first used + *turf*

Asturias[1] ★ (æˈstʊərɪˌæs) *n* a region and former kingdom of NW Spain, consisting of a coastal plain and the Cantabrian Mountains: a Christian stronghold against the Moors (8th to 13th centuries); rich mineral resources.

Asturias[2] ★ (æˈstʊərɪˌæs) *n* **Miguel Ángel** 1899–1974, Guatemalan novelist and poet. His novels include *El Señor Presidente* (1946). Nobel prize for literature 1967.

astute (əˈstjuːt) *adj* having insight or acumen; perceptive; shrewd. ORIG C17: from L *astūtus* cunning, from *astus* (n) cleverness
▸ **asˈtutely** *adv* ▸ **asˈtuteness** *n*

Asunción ★ (*Spanish* asunˈsjon) *n* the capital and chief port of Paraguay, on the Paraguay River, 1530 km (950 miles) from the Atlantic. Pop.: 502 426 (1992).

asunder (əˈsʌndə) *adv, adj* (*postpositive*) in or into parts or pieces; apart: *to tear asunder.* ORIG OE *on sundran* apart

Asur ★ (ˈæsə) *n* a variant spelling of **Assur.**

Aswan, Assuan, *or* **Assouan ★** (ɑːsˈwɑːn) *n* an ancient town in SE Egypt, on the Nile, just below the First Cataract. Pop.: 220 000 (1992 est.). Ancient name: **Syene.**

Aswan High Dam ★ *n* a dam on the Nile forming a reservoir (Lake Nasser) extending 480 km (300 miles) from the First to the Third Cataracts: opened in 1971, it was built 6 km (4 miles) upstream from the old **Aswan Dam** (built in 1902 and twice raised). Height of dam: 109 m (365 ft).

asylum (əˈsaɪləm) *n* **1** shelter; refuge; sanctuary. **2** a safe or inviolable place of refuge, esp. as formerly offered by the Christian Church. **3** *International law.* refuge afforded to a person whose extradition is sought by a foreign government: *political asylum.* **4** an institution for the care or confinement of individuals, esp. (formerly) a mental hospital. ORIG C15: via L from Gk *asulon* refuge, from A-[1] + *sulon* right of seizure

asymmetric (ˌæsɪˈmɛtrɪk, ˌeɪ-) *or* **asymmetrical** *adj* **1** not symmetrical; lacking symmetry; misproportioned. **2** *Logic, maths.* (of a relation) never holding between a pair of values *x* and *y* when it holds between *y* and *x*, as in *John is the father of David.*
▸ ˌ**asymˈmetrically** *adv*

asymmetric bars *pl n Gymnastics.* **a** (*functioning as pl*) a pair of wooden or fibreglass bars placed parallel to each other but set at different heights, for various exercises. **b** (*functioning as sing*) an event in a gymnastic competition in which competitors exercise on such bars.

asymmetry (æˈsɪmɪtrɪ, eɪ-) *n* lack or absence of symmetry.

asymptomatic (ˌeɪsɪmptəˈmætɪk) *adj* not showing any symptoms of disease.

asymptote (ˈæsɪmˌtəʊt) *n* a straight line that is closely approached by a curve so that the distance between them decreases to zero as the distance from the origin increases to infinity. ORIG C17: from Gk *asumptōtos* not falling together, from A-[1] + SYN- + *ptōtos* inclined to fall, from *piptein* to fall
▸ **asymptotic** (ˌæsɪmˈtɒtɪk) *or* ˌ**asympˈtotical** *adj*

asystole (əˈsɪstəlɪ) *n Pathol.* the absence of heartbeat; cardiac arrest.
▸ **asystolic** (ˌæsɪsˈtɒlɪk) *adj*

at (æt) *prep* **1** used to indicate location or position: *are they at the table?* **2** towards; in the direction of: *looking at television.* **3** used to indicate position in time: *come at three o'clock.* **4** engaged in; in a state of (being): *children at play.* **5** (in expressions concerned with habitual activity) during the passing of: *he used to work at night.* **6** for; in exchange for: *it's selling at four pounds.* **7** used to indicate the object of an emotion: *shocked at his behaviour.* **8 where it's at.** *Sl.* the real place of action. ORIG OE *æt*

At *the chemical symbol for* astatine.

AT *Brit. education. abbrev. for* attainment target.

at. *abbrev. for:* **1** atmosphere (unit of pressure). **2** atomic.

Atacama Desert ★ (*Spanish* ataˈkama) *n* a desert region along the W coast of South America, mainly in N Chile: a major source of nitrates. Area: about 80 000 sq. km (31 000 sq. miles).

Atahualpa (ˌætəˈwɑːlpə) *or* **Atabalipa** ★ (ˌætəˈbɑːlɪpə) *n* ?1500–33, the last Inca emperor of Peru (1525–33), who was put to death by the Spanish under Pizarro.

Atalanta ★ (ˌætəˈlæntə) *n Greek myth.* a maiden who agreed to marry any man who could defeat her in a running race. She lost to Hippomenes when she paused to pick up three golden apples that he had deliberately dropped.

ataractic (ˌætəˈræktɪk) *or* **ataraxic** (ˌætəˈræksɪk) *adj* **1** able to calm or tranquillize. ◆ *n* **2** an ataractic drug.

ataraxia (ˌætəˈræksɪə) *or* **ataraxy** (ˈætəˌræksɪ) *n* calmness or peace of mind; emotional tranquillity. ORIG C17: from Gk: serenity, from A-[1] + *tarassein* to trouble

Atatürk ★ (ˈætəˌtɜːk) *n* **Kemal** (kɛˈmɑːl), real name *Mustafa Kemal.* 1881–1938, Turkish general and statesman; founder of the Turkish republic and president of Turkey (1923–38), who westernized and secularized the country.

atavism (ˈætəˌvɪzəm) *n* **1** the recurrence in a plant or animal of certain primitive characteristics that were present in an ancestor but have not occurred in intermediate generations. **2** reversion to a former type. ORIG C19: from F, from L *atavus* strictly: great-grandfather's grandfather, prob. from *atta* daddy + *avus* grandfather
▸ ˌ**ataˈvistic** *adj*

ataxia (əˈtæksɪə) *or* **ataxy** (əˈtæksɪ) *n Pathol.* lack of muscular coordination. ORIG C17: via NL from Gk: lack of coordination, from A-[1] + *-taxia,* from *tassein* to put in order
▸ **aˈtaxic** *adj*

ATB *abbrev. for* Advanced Technology Bomber.

Atbara ★ (ˈætbərə, ætˈbɑː-) *n* **1** a town in NE Sudan. Pop.: 73 000 (latest est.). **2** a river in NE Africa, rising in N Ethiopia and flowing through E Sudan to the Nile at Atbara. Length: over 800 km (500 miles).

ATC *abbrev. for:* **1** air-traffic control. **2** (in Britain) Air Training Corps.

ate (ɛt, eɪt) *vb* the past tense of **eat.**

Ate ★ (ˈeɪtɪ, ˈɑːtɪ) *n Greek myth.* a goddess who makes men blind so that they will blunder into guilty acts. ORIG C16: via L from Gk *atē* a rash impulse

-ate[1] *suffix.* **1** (*forming adjectives*) having the appearance or characteristics of: *fortunate.* **2** (*forming nouns*) a chemical compound, esp. a salt or ester of an acid: *carbonate.* **3** (*forming nouns*) the product of a process: *condensate.* **4** forming verbs from nouns and adjectives: *hyphenate.* ORIG from L *-ātus,* p.p. ending of verbs ending in *-āre*

-ate[2] *suffix forming nouns.* denoting office, rank, or a group having a certain function: *episcopate.* ORIG from L *-ātus,* suffix of collective nouns

atelier (ˈætəlˌjeɪ) *n* an artist's studio or workshop. ORIG C17: from OF, from *astele* chip of wood, from L *astula* splinter, from *assis* board

a tempo (ɑː ˈtɛmpəʊ) *Music.* ◆ *adj, adv* **1** to the original tempo. ◆ *n* **2** a passage thus marked. ◆ Also: **tempo primo.** ORIG It.: in (the original) time

Aten *or* **Aton** ★ (ˈɑːtᵊn) *n* (in ancient Egypt) the solar disc worshipped as the sole god in the reign of Akhenaten.

Atget ★ (*French* adʒe) *n* (**Jean**) **Eugène** (**Auguste**) (øʒɛn). 1856–1927, French photographer.

Athabaska *or* **Athabasca** ★ (ˌæθəˈbæskə) *n* **1 Lake.** a lake in W Canada, in NW Saskatchewan and NE Alberta. Area: about 7770 sq. km (3000 sq. miles). **2** a river in W Canada, rising in the Rocky Mountains and flowing northeast to Lake Athabaska. Length: 1230 km (765 miles).

Athanasian Creed (ˌæθəˈneɪʃən) *n Christianity.* a profession of faith widely used in the Western Church which, though formerly attributed to Athanasius, probably originated in Gaul between 381 and 428 A.D.

Athanasius ★ (ˌæθəˈneɪʃəs) *n* **Saint.** ?296–373 A.D., patriarch of Alexandria who championed Christian orthodoxy against Arianism. Feast day: May 2.
▸ ˌ**Athaˈnasian** *adj*

Athapascan, Athapaskan (ˌæθəˈpæskən) *or* **Athabascan, Athabaskan** (ˌæθəˈbæskən) *n* a group of North American Indian languages including Apache and Navaho. ORIG from Cree *athapaskaaw* scattered grass

atheism (ˈeɪθɪˌɪzəm) *n* rejection of belief in God or gods. ORIG C16: from F, from Gk *atheos* godless, from A-[1] + *theos* god
▸ ˈ**atheist** *n, adj* ▸ ˌ**atheˈistic** *adj*

Athelstan ★ (ˈæθəlstən) *n* ?895–939 A.D., king of Wessex and Mercia (924–939 A.D.), who extended his kingdom to include most of England.

athematic (ˌæθɪˈmætɪk) *adj* **1** *Music.* not based on themes. **2** *Linguistics.* (of verbs) having a suffix attached with no intervening vowel.

Athena (əˈθiːnə) *or* **Athene** ★ (əˈθiːnɪ) *n Greek myth.* a virgin goddess of wisdom, practical skills, and prudent warfare. She was born, fully armed, from the head of Zeus. Also called: **Pallas Athena, Pallas.** Roman counterpart: **Minerva.**

athenaeum *or US* **atheneum** (ˌæθɪˈniːəm) *n* **1** an institution for the promotion of learning. **2** a building containing a reading room or library. ORIG C18: from LL, from Gk *Athēnaion*temple of Athene, frequented by poets and teachers

Athenian (əˈθiːnɪən) *n* **1** a native or inhabitant of Athens. ◆ *adj* **2** of or relating to Athens.

Athens ★ (ˈæθɪnz) *n* the capital of Greece, in the southeast near the Saronic Gulf: became capital after independence in 1834; ancient city-state, most powerful in the 5th century B.C.; contains the hill citadel of the Acropolis. Pop.: 772 072 (1991). Greek name: **Athinai** (a'θinɛ).

atherosclerosis (ˌæθərəʊsklɪə'rəʊsɪs) *n, pl* **atheroscleroses** (-siːz). a degenerative disease of the arteries characterized by thickening of the arterial walls, caused by deposits of fatty material. ORIG C20: from NL, from Gk *athērōma* tumour full of grainy matter + SCLEROSIS
▸ **atherosclerotic** (ˌæθərəʊsklɪə'rɒtɪk) *adj*

athirst (ə'θɜːst) *adj* (*postpositive*) **1** (often foll. by *for*) having an eager desire; longing. **2** *Arch.* thirsty.

athlete ('æθliːt) *n* **1** a person trained to compete in sports or exercises. **2** a person who has a natural aptitude for physical activities. **3** *Chiefly Brit.* a competitor in track and field events. ORIG C18: from L via Gk, from *athlein* to compete for a prize, from *athlos* a contest

athlete's foot *n* a fungal infection of the skin of the foot, esp. between the toes and on the soles.

athletic (æθ'lɛtɪk) *adj* **1** physically fit or strong. **2** of, relating to, or suitable for an athlete or for athletics.
▸ **ath'letically** *adv* ▸ **ath'leticism** *n*

athletics (æθ'lɛtɪks) *n* (*functioning as sing or pl*) **1** *Chiefly Brit.* **1a** track and field events. **1b** (*as modifier*): *an athletics meeting.* **2** sports or exercises engaged in by athletes.

athletic support *n* a more formal term for **jockstrap**.

at-home *n* **1** a social gathering in a person's home. **2** another name for **open day**.

-athon *suffix forming nouns.* a variant of **-thon**.

Athos ★ ('æθɒs, 'eɪ-) *n* **Mount.** a mountain in NE Greece, in Macedonia Central region: site of the Monastic Republic of Mount Athos, autonomous since 1927; inhabited by Greek Orthodox Basilian monks in 20 monasteries founded in the 10th century. Pop.: 1557 (1991). Area: 336 sq. km (130 sq. miles).

athwart (ə'θwɔːt) *adv* **1** transversely; from one side to another. ◆ *prep* **2** across the path or line of (esp. a ship). **3** in opposition to; against. ORIG C15: from A-[2] + THWART

-atic *suffix forming adjectives.* of the nature of the thing specified: *problematic.* ORIG from F, from Gk *-atikos*

-ation *suffix forming nouns.* indicating an action, process, state, condition, or result: *arbitration; hibernation.* ORIG from L *-ātiōn-*, suffix of abstract nouns

-ative *suffix forming adjectives.* of, relating to, or tending to: *authoritative; informative.* ORIG from L *-ātīvus*

Atkinson ★ ('ætkɪnsᵊn) *n* Sir **Harry Albert.** 1831–92, New Zealand statesman, born in England: prime minister of New Zealand (1876–77; 1883–84; 1887–91).

Atlanta ★ (æt'læntə) *n* a city in N Georgia: the state capital. Pop.: 396 052 (1994 est.).

Atlantean (ˌætlæn'tiːən) *adj Literary.* of, relating to, or like Atlas; extremely strong.

Atlantic (ət'læntɪk) *n* **1 the.** short for the **Atlantic Ocean.** ◆ *adj* **2** of, relating to, or bordering the Atlantic Ocean. **3** of or relating to Atlas or the Atlas Mountains. ORIG C15: from L, from Gk (*pelagos*) *Atlantikos* (the sea) of Atlas (so called because it lay beyond the Atlas Mountains)

Atlantic City ★ *n* a resort in SE New Jersey on Absecon Beach, an island on the Atlantic coast. Pop.: 37 986 (1990).

Atlantic Intracoastal Waterway ★ *n* a system of inland and coastal waterways along the Atlantic coast of the US from Cape Cod to Florida Bay. Length: 2495 km (1550 miles).

Atlanticism (ət'læntɪˌsɪzəm) *n* advocacy of close cooperation in military, political, and economic matters between Western Europe, esp. the UK, and the US.
▸ **At'lanticist** *n*

Atlantic Ocean ★ *n* the world's second largest ocean, bounded in the north by the Arctic, in the south by the Antarctic, in the west by North and South America, and in the east by Europe and Africa. Greatest depth: 9220 m (30 246 ft). Area: about 81 585 000 sq. km (31 500 000 sq. miles).

Atlantic Provinces ★ *pl n* **the.** certain of the Canadian provinces with coasts facing the Gulf of St Lawrence or the Atlantic: New Brunswick, Nova Scotia, Prince Edward Island, and Newfoundland.

Atlantis ★ (ət'læntɪs) *n* (in ancient legend) a continent said to have sunk beneath the Atlantic west of Gibraltar.

atlas ('ætləs) *n* **1** a collection of maps, usually in book form. **2** a book of charts, graphs, etc.: *an anatomical atlas.* **3** *Anat.* the first cervical vertebra, supporting the skull in man. **4** (*pl* **atlantes**) *Archit.* another name for **telamon.** ORIG C16: via L from Gk; first applied to maps from depictions of Atlas supporting the heavens in 16th-cent. books of maps

Atlas ★ ('ætləs) *n Greek myth.* **1** a Titan compelled to support the sky on his shoulders as punishment for rebelling against Zeus. **2** a US intercontinental ballistic missile, also used in launching spacecraft.

Atlas Mountains ★ *pl n* a mountain system of N Africa, between the Mediterranean and the Sahara. Highest peak: Mount Toubkal, 4165 m (13 664 ft).

Atli ★ ('ɑːtlɪ) *n Norse legend.* a king of the Huns who married Gudrun for her inheritance and was slain by her after he killed her brothers.

ATM *abbrev. for* automated teller machine.

atm. *abbrev. for:* **1** atmosphere (unit of pressure). **2** atmospheric.

atman ('ɑːtmən) *n Hinduism.* **1** the personal soul or self. **2** Brahman considered as the Universal Soul. ORIG from Sansk. *ātman* breath

atmolysis (æt'mɒlɪsɪs) *n, pl* **atmolyses** (-ˌsiːz). the separation of gases by differential diffusion through a porous substance.

atmosphere ('ætməsˌfɪə) *n* **1** the gaseous envelope surrounding the earth or any other celestial body. **2** the air or climate in a particular place. **3** a general pervasive feeling or mood. **4** the prevailing tone or mood of a novel, symphony, painting, etc. **5** any local gaseous environment or medium: *an inert atmosphere.* **6** Abbrev: **at.**, **atm.** a unit of pressure; the pressure that will support a column of mercury 760 mm high at 0°C at sea level.
▸ **atmospheric** (ˌætməs'fɛrɪk) *adj* ▸ **ˌatmos'pherically** *adv*

atmospheric pressure *n* the pressure exerted by the atmosphere at the earth's surface. It has an average value of 1 atmosphere.

atmospherics (ˌætməs'fɛrɪks) *pl n* radio interference, heard as crackling or hissing in receivers, caused by electrical disturbance.

at. no. *abbrev. for* atomic number.

atoll ('ætɒl) *n* a circular coral reef or string of coral islands surrounding a lagoon. ORIG C17: from *atollon,* native name in the Maldive Islands

atom ('ætəm) *n* **1a** the smallest quantity of an element that can take part in a chemical reaction. **1b** this entity as a source of nuclear energy: *the power of the atom.* **2** the hypothetical indivisible particle of matter postulated by certain ancient philosophers. **3** a very small amount or quantity: *to smash something to atoms.* ORIG C16: via OF & L, from Gk, from *atomos* (adj) that cannot be divided, from A-[1] + *temnein* to cut

atomic (ə'tɒmɪk) *adj* **1** of, using, or characterized by atomic bombs or atomic energy: *atomic warfare.* **2** of or comprising atoms: *atomic hydrogen.*
▸ **a'tomically** *adv*

atomic bomb *or* **atom bomb** *n* a type of bomb in which the energy is provided by nuclear fission. Also called: **A-bomb, fission bomb.** Cf. **fusion bomb.**

atomic clock *n* an extremely accurate clock in which an electrical oscillator is controlled by the natural vibrations of an atomic or molecular system such as caesium or ammonia.

atomic energy *n* another name for **nuclear energy.**

atomicity (ˌætə'mɪsɪtɪ) *n* **1** the state of being made up of atoms. **2** the number of atoms in the molecules of an element. **3** a less common name for **valency.**

atomic mass unit *n* a unit of mass used to express atomic and molecular weights that is equal to one-twelfth of the mass of an atom of carbon-12. Abbrev.: **amu.**

atomic number *n* the number of protons in the nucleus of an atom of an element. Abbrev.: **at. no.**

atomic pile *n* the original name for a **nuclear reactor**.

atomic sentence *n Logic.* a sentence consisting of one predicate and a finite number of terms: *"it is raining" is an atomic sentence.*

atomic structure *n* the concept of an atom as a central positively charged nucleus consisting of protons and neutrons surrounded by a number of electrons. The number of electrons is equal to the number of protons: the whole entity is thus electrically neutral.

atomic theory *n* **1** any theory in which matter is regarded as consisting of atoms. **2** the current concept of the atom as an entity with a definite structure. See **atomic structure.**

atomic weight *n* the former name for **relative atomic mass.** Abbrev.: **at. wt.**

atomize *or* **atomise** ('ætəˌmaɪz) *vb* **atomizes, atomizing, atomized** *or* **atomises, atomising, atomised. 1** to separate or be separated into free atoms. **2** to reduce (a liquid or solid) to fine particles or spray or (of a liquid or solid) to be reduced in this way. **3** (*tr*) to destroy by weapons, esp. nuclear weapons.

atomizer *or* **atomiser** ('ætəˌmaɪzə) *n* a device for reducing a liquid to a fine spray, such as a bottle with a fine outlet used to spray perfumes.

atom smasher *n Physics.* the nontechnical name for **accelerator** (sense 2).

atomy ('ætəmɪ) *n, pl* **atomies.** *Arch.* a minute particle or creature. ORIG C16: from L *atomi* atoms, used as sing

Aton ★ ('ɑːtᵊn) *n* a variant spelling of **Aten.**

atonal (eɪ'təʊnᵊl) *adj Music.* having no established key.

atonality (ˌeɪtəʊ'nælɪtɪ) *n* **1** absence of or disregard for an established musical key in a composition. **2** the principles of composition embodying this.

atone (ə'təʊn) *vb* **atones, atoning, atoned.** (*intr;* foll. by *for*) to make amends or reparation (for a crime, sin, etc.). ORIG C16: back formation from ATONEMENT
▸ **a'toner** *n*

atonement (ə'təʊnmənt) *n* **1** satisfaction, reparation, or expiation given for an injury or wrong. **2** (*often cap.*) *Christian theology.* **2a** the reconciliation of man with God through the sacrificial death of Christ. **2b** the sufferings and death of Christ. ORIG C16: from ME *at onement* in harmony

atonic (eɪ'tɒnɪk, æ-) *adj* **1** (of a syllable, word, etc.) carrying no stress; unaccented. **2** lacking body or muscle tone. ◆ *n* **3** an unaccented or unstressed syllable, word, etc. ORIG C18: from L, from Gk *atonos* lacking tone

atop (ə'tɒp) *adv* **1** on top; at the top. ◆ *prep* **2** on top of; at the top of.

-ator *suffix forming nouns.* a person or thing that performs a certain action: *agitator; radiator.* ORIG from L *-ātor*

-atory *suffix forming adjectives.* of, relating to, characterized by, or serving to: *circulatory; explanatory.* ORIG from L *-ātōrius*

ATP *n* adenosine triphosphate; a substance found in all plant and animal cells. It is the major source of energy for cellular reactions.

atrabilious (ˌætrə'bɪlɪəs) *or* **atrabiliar** *adj Rare.* irritable or gloomy. ORIG C17: from L *ātra bīlis* black bile, from *āter* black + *bīlis* BILE[1]
▸ **ˌatra'biliousness** *n*

atrazine ('ætrəziːn) *n* a white crystalline compound widely used as a weedkiller. Formula: $C_8H_{14}N_5Cl$. ORIG C20: from A(MINO) *tr(i)azine*

Atreus ★ ('eɪtrɪˌuːs, 'eɪtrɪəs) *n Greek myth.* a king of Mycenae, son of Pelops, father of Agamemnon and Menelaus, and member of the family known as the **Atreids** ('eɪtrɪɪdz).

atrium ('eɪtrɪəm, 'ɑː-) *n, pl* **atria** ('eɪtrɪə, 'ɑː-). **1** the open main court of a Roman house. **2** a central often glass-roofed hall that extends through several storeys in a building, such as a shopping centre or hotel. **3** a court in front of an early Christian or medieval church. **4** *Anat.* a cavity or chamber in the body, esp. the upper chamber of each half of the heart. ORIG C17: from L; rel. to *āter* black
▸ **'atrial** *adj*

atrocious (ə'trəʊʃəs) *adj* **1** extremely cruel or wicked: *atrocious deeds.* **2** horrifying or shocking. **3** *Inf.* very bad: *atrocious writing.* ORIG C17: from L *ātrōx* dreadful, from *āter* black
▸ **a'trociousness** *n*

atrocity (ə'trɒsɪtɪ) *n, pl* **atrocities. 1** behaviour or an action that is wicked or ruthless. **2** the fact or quality of being atrocious. **3** (*usually pl*) acts of extreme cruelty.

atrophy ('ætrəfɪ) *n, pl* **atrophies. 1** a wasting away of an organ or part, or a failure to grow to normal size. **2** any degeneration or diminution. ◆ *vb* **atrophies, atrophying, atrophied. 3** to waste away or cause to waste away. ORIG C17: from LL, from Gk, from *atrophos* ill-fed, from A-[1] + *-trophos,* from *trephein* to feed
▸ **atrophic** (ə'trɒfɪk) *adj*

atropine ('ætrəˌpiːn) *n* a poisonous alkaloid obtained from the deadly nightshade, used to treat peptic ulcers, biliary and renal colic, etc. ORIG C19: from NL *atropa* deadly nightshade, from Gk *atropos* unchangeable, inflexible

Atropos ★ ('ætrəˌpɒs) *n Greek myth.* the one of the three Fates who severs the thread of life. ORIG Gk, from *atropos* that may not be turned, from A-[1] + *-tropos* from *trepein* to turn

attach (ə'tætʃ) *vb* (*mainly tr*) **1** to join, fasten, or connect. **2** (*reflexive or passive*) to become associated with or join. **3** (*intr;* foll. by *to*) to be connected (with): *responsibility attaches to the job.* **4** to attribute or ascribe. **5** to include or append: *a proviso is attached to the contract.* **6** (*usually passive*) *Mil.* to place on temporary duty with another unit. **7** to appoint officially. **8** *Law.* to arrest or take (a person, property, etc.) with lawful authority. ORIG C14: from OF *atachier* to fasten, changed from *estachier* to fasten with a stake
▸ **at'tachable** *adj* ▸ **at'tacher** *n*

attaché (ə'tæʃeɪ) *n* a specialist attached to a diplomatic mission: *military attaché.* ORIG C19: from F: someone attached (to a mission)

attaché case *n* a small flat rectangular briefcase used for carrying documents, papers, etc.

attached (ə'tætʃt) *adj* **1** (foll. by *to*) fond (of). **2** married, engaged, or associated in an exclusive sexual relationship.

attachment (ə'tætʃmənt) *n* **1** a fastening. **2** (often foll. by *to*) affection or regard (for). **3** an object to be attached: *an attachment for an electric drill.* **4** the act of attaching or the state of being attached. **5a** the lawful seizure of property and placing of it under control of a court. **5b** a writ authorizing such seizure.

attack (ə'tæk) *vb* **1** to launch a physical assault (against) with or without weapons. **2** (*intr*) to take the initiative in a game, sport, etc. **3** (*tr*) to criticize or abuse vehemently. **4** (*tr*) to turn one's mind or energies to (a job, problem, etc.). **5** (*tr*) to begin to injure or affect adversely: *rust attacked the metal.* ◆ *n* **6** the act or an instance of attacking. **7** strong criticism or abuse. **8** an offensive move in a game, sport, etc. **9 the attack.** *Ball games.* the players in a team whose main role is to attack the opponents. **10** commencement of a task, etc. **11** any sudden and usually severe manifestation of a disease or disorder: *a heart attack.* **12** *Music.* **12a** decisiveness in beginning a passage, movement, or piece. **12b** (in electronic instruments) the time between the start of a note and its maximum volume. ORIG C16: from F, from OIt. *attaccare* to attack, attach, from *estaccare* to attach
▸ **at'tacker** *n*

attain (ə'teɪn) *vb* **1** (*tr*) to achieve or accomplish (a task, aim, etc.). **2** (*tr*) to reach in space or time. **3** (*intr;* often foll. by *to*) to arrive (at) with effort or exertion. ORIG C14: from OF, from L *attingere* to reach, from *tangere* to touch
▸ **at'tainable** *adj* ▸ **atˌtaina'bility** *or* **at'tainableness** *n*

attainder (ə'teɪndə) *n* (formerly) the extinction of a person's civil rights resulting from a sentence of death or outlawry on conviction for treason or felony. ORIG C15:

from Anglo-F *attaindre* to convict, from OF *ateindre* to ATTAIN

attainment (ə'teɪnmənt) *n* an achievement or the act of achieving; accomplishment.

attainment target *n Brit. education.* a general defined level of ability that a pupil is expected to achieve in every subject at each key stage in the National Curriculum. Abbrev.: **AT.**

attaint (ə'teɪnt) *vb (tr) Arch.* **1** to pass judgment of death or outlawry upon (a person). **2** (of sickness) to affect or strike (somebody). ◆ *n* **3** a less common word for **attainder.** ORIG C14: from OF *ateint* convicted, from *ateindre* to ATTAIN

attar ('ætə), **otto** ('ɒtəʊ), *or* **ottar** ('ɒtə) *n* an essential oil from flowers, esp. the damask rose: *attar of roses.* ORIG C18: from Persian, from *'itr* perfume, from Ar.

attempt (ə'tɛmpt) *vb (tr)* **1** to make an effort (to do something) or to achieve (something); try. **2** to try to surmount (an obstacle). **3** to try to climb. ◆ *n* **4** an endeavour to achieve something; effort. **5** a result of an attempt or endeavour. **6** an attack, esp. with the intention to kill. ORIG C14: from OF, from L *attemptāre* to strive after, from *tentāre* to try
▸ **at'temptable** *adj*

Attenborough ★ ('æt^ə^nb^ə^rə) *n* **1** Sir **David.** born 1926, British naturalist and broadcaster. **2** his brother **Richard,** Baron Attenborough. born 1923, British film actor, director, and producer; noted for the films *Gandhi* (1982), *Cry Freedom* (1987), and *Shadowlands* (1993).

attend (ə'tɛnd) *vb* **1** to be present at (an event, etc.). **2** (when *intr,* foll. by *to*) to give care (to); minister (to). **3** (when *intr,* foll. by *to*) to pay attention. **4** (*tr; often passive*) to accompany or follow: *a high temperature attended by a severe cough.* **5** (*intr;* foll. by *on* or *upon*) to follow as a consequence (of). **6** (*intr;* foll. by *to*) to apply oneself: *to attend to the garden.* **7** (*tr*) to escort or accompany. **8** (*intr;* foll. by *on* or *upon*) to provide for the needs (of): *to attend on a guest.* ORIG C13: from OF, from L *attendere* to stretch towards, from *tendere* to extend

attendance (ə'tɛndəns) *n* **1** the act or state of attending. **2** the number of persons present.

attendant (ə'tɛndənt) *n* **1** a person who accompanies or waits upon another. **2** a person employed to assist, guide, or provide a service for others. **3** a person who is present. ◆ *adj* **4** being in attendance. **5** associated: *attendant problems.*

attendee (əˌtɛn'diː) *n* a person who is present at a specified event.

attention (ə'tɛnʃən) *n* **1** concentrated direction of the mind, esp. to a problem or task. **2** consideration, notice, or observation. **3** detailed care or special treatment: *to pay attention to one's appearance.* **4** (*usually pl*) an act of courtesy or gallantry indicating affection or love. **5** the motionless position of formal military alertness, an upright position with legs and heels together. ◆ *sentence substitute.* **6** the order to be alert or to adopt a position of formal military alertness. ORIG C14: from L, from *attendere* to apply the mind to

attention deficit disorder *n* a disorder, particularly of children, characterized by excessive activity and inability to concentrate on one task for any length of time. Abbrev.: **ADD.**

attentive (ə'tɛntɪv) *adj* **1** paying attention; listening carefully. **2** (*postpositive;* often foll. by *to*) careful to fulfil the needs or wants (of).
▸ **at'tentively** *adv* ▸ **at'tentiveness** *n*

attenuate *vb* (ə'tɛnjuˌeɪt) **attenuates, attenuating, attenuated. 1** to weaken or become weak. **2** to make or become thin or fine; extend. ◆ *adj* (ə'tɛnjuɪt, -ˌeɪt). **3** weakened or reduced. **4** *Bot.* tapering. ORIG C16: from L *attenuāre* to weaken, from *tenuis* thin
▸ **atˌtenu'ation** *n*

attest (ə'tɛst) *vb* **1** (*tr*) to affirm the correctness or truth of. **2** (when *intr,* usually foll. by *to*) to witness (an act, event, etc.) or bear witness (to an act, event, etc.). **3** (*tr*) to make evident; demonstrate. **4** (*tr*) to provide evidence for. ORIG C16: from L, from *testārī* to bear witness, from *testis* a witness
▸ **at'testable** *adj* ▸ **at'testant, at'tester** *or esp. in legal usage* **at'testor** *n* ▸ **attestation** (ˌætɛ'steɪʃən) *n*

attested (ə'tɛstɪd) *adj Brit.* (of cattle, etc.) certified to be free from a disease, esp. from tuberculosis.

attic ('ætɪk) *n* **1** a space or room within the roof of a house. **2** *Archit.* a storey or low wall above the cornice of a classical façade. ORIG C18: special use of ATTIC, from use of Attic-style pilasters on façade of top storey

Attic ('ætɪk) *adj* **1** of or relating to Attica, its inhabitants, or the dialect of Greek spoken there. **2** (*often not cap.*) classically elegant, simple, or pure. ◆ *n* **3** the dialect of Ancient Greek spoken and written in Athens.

Attica ★ ('ætɪkə) *n* a region and department of E central Greece: in ancient times the territory of Athens. Capital: Athens. Pop.: 3 523 407 (1991). Area: 14 157 sq. km (5466 sq. miles).

Atticism ('ætɪˌsɪzəm) *n* **1** the idiom or character of the Attic dialect of Ancient Greek. **2** an elegant, simple expression.

Attic salt *or* **wit** *n* refined incisive wit.

Attila ★ (ə'tɪlə) *n* ?406–453 A.D., king of the Huns, who devastated much of the Roman Empire, invaded Gaul in 451 A.D., but was defeated by the Romans and Visigoths at Châlons-sur-Marne.

attire (ə'taɪə) *vb* **attires, attiring, attired. 1** (*tr*) to dress, esp. in fine elegant clothes; array. ◆ *n* **2** clothes or garments, esp. if fine or decorative. ORIG C13: from OF *atirier* to put in order, from *tire* row

attitude ('ætɪˌtjuːd) *n* **1** the way a person views something or tends to behave towards it, often in an evaluative way. **2** a theatrical pose created for effect (esp. in **strike an attitude**). **3** a position of the body indicating mood or emotion. **4** *Inf.* a hostile manner: *don't give me attitude, my girl.* **5** the orientation of an aircraft's axes or a spacecraft in relation to some plane or the direction of motion. ORIG C17: from F, from It. *attitudine* disposition, from LL *aptitūdō* fitness, from L *aptus* APT
▸ **ˌatti'tudinal** *adj*

attitudinize *or* **attitudinise** (ˌætɪ'tjuːdɪˌnaɪz) *vb* **attitudinizes, attitudinizing, attitudinized** *or* **attitudinises, attitudinising, attitudinised.** (*intr*) to adopt a pose or opinion for effect; strike an attitude.

Attlee ★ ('ætlɪ) *n* **Clement Richard,** 1st Earl Attlee. 1883–1967, British statesman; prime minister (1945–51); leader of the Labour party (1935–55).

attn *abbrev. for* attention.

atto- *prefix* denoting 10^{-18}: *attotesla.* Symbol: a ORIG from Norwegian & Danish *atten* eighteen

attorney (ə'tɜːnɪ) *n* **1** a person legally appointed or empowered to act for another. **2** *US.* a lawyer qualified to represent clients in legal proceedings. ORIG C14: from OF, from *atourner* to direct to, from *tourner* to TURN
▸ **at'torneyˌship** *n*

attorney-at-law *n, pl* **attorneys-at-law.** *Law, now chiefly US.* a lawyer.

attorney general *n, pl* **attorneys general** *or* **attorney generals.** a chief law officer and senior legal adviser of some national, provincial, and state governments.

attract (ə'trækt) *vb* (*mainly tr*) **1** to draw (notice, a crowd of observers, etc.) to oneself (esp. in **attract attention**). **2** (*also intr*) to exert a force on (a body) that tends to oppose a separation: *the gravitational pull of the earth attracts objects to it.* **3** to possess some property that pulls or draws (something) towards itself. **4** (*also intr*) to exert a pleasing or fascinating influence (upon). ORIG C15: from L *attrahere* to draw towards, from *trahere* to pull
▸ **at'tractable** *adj* ▸ **at'tractor** *n*

attraction (ə'trækʃən) *n* **1** the act or quality of attracting. **2** a person or thing that attracts or is intended to attract. **3** a force by which one object attracts another: *magnetic attraction.*

attractive (ə'træktɪv) *adj* **1** appealing to the senses or mind through beauty, form, character, etc. **2** arousing interest: *an attractive opportunity.* **3** possessing the ability to draw or pull: *an attractive force.*
▸ **at'tractively** *adv*

attrib. *abbrev. for:* **1** attribute. **2** attributive.

attribute *vb* (ə'trɪbju:t). **attributes, attributing, attributed. 1** (*tr;* usually foll. by *to*) to regard as belonging (to), produced (by), or resulting (from): *to attribute a painting to Picasso.* ◆ *n* ('ætrɪˌbju:t). **2** a property, quality, or feature belonging to or representative of a person or thing. **3** an object accepted as belonging to a particular office or position. **4** *Grammar.* **4a** an adjective or adjectival phrase. **4b** an attributive adjective. **5** *Logic.* the property or feature that is affirmed or denied concerning the subject of a proposition. ORIG C15: from L *attribuere* to associate with, from *tribuere* to give
▸ **at'tributable** *adj* ▸ **attribution** (ˌætrɪ'bju:ʃən) *n*

attributive (ə'trɪbjʊtɪv) *adj* **1** relating to an attribute. **2** *Grammar.* (of an adjective or adjectival phrase) preceding the noun modified. Cf. **predicative. 3** *Philosophy.* relative to an understood domain, as *small* in *that elephant is small.*

attrition (ə'trɪʃən) *n* **1** the act of wearing away or the state of being worn away, as by friction. **2** constant wearing down to weaken or destroy (often in **war of attrition**). **3** *Geog.* the grinding down of rock particles by friction. **4** *Theol.* sorrow for sin arising from fear of damnation, esp. as contrasted with contrition. ORIG C14: from LL *attrītiō* a rubbing against something, from L *atterere* to weaken, from *terere* to rub

Attu ★ ('ætu:) *n* the westernmost of the Aleutian Islands, off the coast of SW Alaska: largest of the Near Islands.

attune (ə'tju:n) *vb* **attunes, attuning, attuned.** (*tr*) to adjust or accustom (a person or thing); acclimatize.

ATV *abbrev. for* all-terrain vehicle.

at. vol. *abbrev. for* atomic volume.

Atwood ★ ('ætˌwʊd) *n* **Margaret (Eleanor).** born 1939, Canadian writer. Her novels include *Lady Oracle* (1976), *The Handmaid's Tale* (1986), *Alias Grace* (1996), and *The Blind Assassin* (2000).

at. wt. *abbrev. for* atomic weight.

atypical (eɪ'tɪpɪkəl) *adj* not typical; deviating from or not conforming to type.
▸ **a'typically** *adv*

Au *the chemical symbol for* gold. ORIG from NL *aurum*

aubade (əʊ'bɑ:d) *n* a poem or short musical piece to greet the dawn. ORIG C19: F, from OProvençal *auba* dawn, ult. from L *albus* white

Aube ★ (*French* ob) *n* **1** a department of N central France, in Champagne-Ardenne region. Capital: Troyes. Pop.: 292 765 (1994 est.). Area: 6026 sq. km (2350 sq. miles). **2** a river in N central France, flowing northwest to the Seine. Length: about 225 km (140 miles).

aubergine ('əʊbəˌʒi:n) *n* **1** *Chiefly Brit.* a tropical Old World plant widely cultivated for its egg-shaped typically dark purple fruit. US, Canad., and Austral. name: **eggplant. 2** the fruit of this plant, which is cooked and eaten as a vegetable. **3a** a dark purple colour. **3b** (*as adj*): *an aubergine dress.* ORIG C18: from F, from Catalan *alberginia,* from Ar. *al-bādindjān,* ult. from Sansk. *vatinganah,* from ?

Aubrey ★ ('ɔ:brɪ) *n* **John.** 1626–97, English antiquary noted for his *Brief Lives* (edited 1898).

aubrietia, aubrieta, *or* **aubretia** (ɔ:'bri:ʃə) *n* a trailing purple-flowered plant native to European mountains but widely planted in rock gardens. ORIG C19: from NL, after Claude *Aubriet,* 18th-cent. F painter of flowers and animals

auburn ('ɔ:bən) *n* **a** a moderate reddish-brown colour. **b** (*as adj*): *auburn hair.* ORIG C15 (orig. meaning: blond): from OF *alborne* blond, from Med. L, from L *albus* white

Aubusson ★ (*French* obysɔ̃) *n* **1** a town in central France, in the Creuse department: a centre for flat-woven carpets and for tapestries since the 16th century. Pop.: 5000 (latest est.). ◆ *adj* **2** denoting or relating to these carpets or tapestries.

Auckland ★ ('ɔ:klənd) *n* the chief port of New Zealand, in the northern part of North Island: former capital of New Zealand (1840–65). Pop. (urban area): 353 670 (1996).

Auckland Islands ★ *pl n* a group of six uninhabited islands, south of New Zealand. Area: 611 sq. km (234 sq. miles).

au courant *French.* (o kurɑ̃) *adj* up-to-date, esp. in knowledge of current affairs. ORIG lit.: in the current

auction ('ɔ:kʃən) *n* **1** a public sale of goods or property in which prospective purchasers bid until the highest price is reached. **2** the competitive calls made in bridge before play begins. ◆ *vb* **3** (*tr;* often foll. by *off*) to sell by auction. ORIG C16: from L *auctiō* an increasing, from *augēre* to increase

auction bridge *n* a variety of bridge in which all the tricks made score towards game.

auctioneer (ˌɔ:kʃə'nɪə) *n* **1** a person who conducts an auction. ◆ *vb* **2** (*tr*) to sell by auction.

auctorial (ɔ:k'tɔ:rɪəl) *adj* of or relating to an author. ORIG C19: from L *auctor* AUTHOR

audacious (ɔ:'deɪʃəs) *adj* **1** recklessly bold or daring. **2** impudent or presumptuous. ORIG C16: from L *audāx* bold, from *audēre* to dare
▸ **au'daciousness** *or* **audacity** (ɔ:'dæsɪtɪ) *n*

Aude ★ (*French* od) *n* a department of S France on the Gulf of Lions, in Languedoc-Roussillon region. Capital: Carcassonne. Pop.: 304 707 (1994 est.). Area: 6342 sq. km (2473 sq. miles).

Auden ★ ('ɔ:dən) *n* **W(ystan) H(ugh).** 1907–73, US poet and dramatist, born in Britain.

audible ('ɔ:dɪbəl) *adj* perceptible to the hearing; loud enough to be heard. ORIG C16: from LL, from L *audīre* to hear
▸ ˌ**audi'bility** *or* '**audibleness** *n* ▸ '**audibly** *adv*

audience ('ɔ:dɪəns) *n* **1** a group of spectators or listeners, esp. at a concert or play. **2** the people reached by a book, film, or radio or television programme. **3** the devotees or followers of a public entertainer, etc. **4** a formal interview with a monarch or head of state. ORIG C14: from OF, from L *audientia* a hearing, from *audīre* to hear

audio ('ɔ:dɪəʊ) *n* (*modifier*) **1** of or relating to sound or hearing: *audio frequency.* **2** relating to or employed in the transmission or reproduction of sound. ORIG C20: from L *audīre* to hear

audio book *n* a reading of a book recorded on tape.

audio frequency *n* a frequency in the range 20 hertz to 20 000 hertz. A sound wave of this frequency would be audible to the human ear.

audiology (ˌɔ:dɪ'ɒlədʒɪ) *n* the scientific study of hearing, often including the treatment of persons with hearing defects.
▸ ˌ**audi'ologist** *n*

audiometer (ˌɔ:dɪ'ɒmɪtə) *n* an instrument for testing hearing.
▸ ˌ**audi'ometrist** *n* ▸ ˌ**audi'ometry** *n*

audiophile ('ɔ:dɪəʊˌfaɪl) *n* a person who has a great interest in high-fidelity sound reproduction.

audiotypist ('ɔ:dɪəʊˌtaɪpɪst) *n* a typist trained to type from a dictating machine.
▸ '**audioˌtyping** *n*

audiovisual (ˌɔ:dɪəʊ'vɪʒʊəl) *adj* (esp. of teaching aids) involving or directed at both hearing and sight.
▸ ˌ**audio'visually** *adv*

audit ('ɔ:dɪt) *n* **1a** an inspection, correction, and verification of business accounts, conducted by an independent qualified accountant. **1b** (*as modifier*): *audit report.* **2** *US.* an audited account. **3** any thoroughgoing examination or check. ◆ *vb* **audits, auditing, audited. 4** to inspect, correct, and certify (accounts, etc.). ORIG C15: from L *audītus* a hearing, from *audīre* to hear

audition (ɔ:'dɪʃən) *n* **1** a test at which a performer or musician is asked to demonstrate his ability for a particular role, etc. **2** the act or power of hearing. ◆ *vb* **3** to judge by means of or be tested in an audition. ORIG C16: from L *audītiō* a hearing, from *audīre* to hear

auditor ('ɔ:dɪtə) *n* **1** a person qualified to audit accounts. **2** a person who hears or listens. ORIG C14: from OF, from L *audītor* a hearer
▸ ˌ**audi'torial** *adj*

Auditor General *n* (in Canada) an officer appointed by

★ people and places

the Governor General to audit the accounts of the Federal Government and report to Parliament.

auditorium (ˌɔːdɪˈtɔːrɪəm) *n, pl* **auditoriums** *or* **auditoria** (-ˈtɔːrɪə). **1** the area of a concert hall, theatre, etc., in which the audience sits. **2** *US & Canad.* a building for public meetings. ORIG C17: from L: a judicial examination

auditory (ˈɔːdɪtərɪ) *adj* of or relating to hearing or the sense of hearing. ORIG C14: from L *audītōrius* relating to hearing, from *audīre* to hear

Audubon ★ (ˈɔːdəˌbɒn) *n* **John James.** 1785–1851, US naturalist and artist, noted for his paintings of birds.

Auerbach ★ (ˈaʊəˌbɑːk) *n* **Frank (Helmuth).** born 1931, British painter, born in Germany.

au fait *French.* (o fɛ) *adj* fully informed; in touch or expert. ORIG C18: lit.: to the point

au fond *French.* (o fɔ̃) *adv* fundamentally; essentially. ORIG lit.: at the bottom

auf Wiedersehen *German.* (auf ˈviːdərzeːən) *sentence substitute.* goodbye, until we see each other again.

Aug. *abbrev. for* August.

Augean (ɔːˈdʒiːən) *adj* extremely dirty or corrupt. ORIG C16: from *Augeas,* in Gk myth., king whose filthy stables Hercules cleaned in one day

augend (ˈɔːdʒɛnd, ɔːˈdʒɛnd) *n* a number to which another number, the addend, is added. ORIG from L *augendum,* from *augēre* to increase

auger (ˈɔːgə) *n* **1** a hand tool with a bit shaped like a corkscrew, for boring holes in wood. **2** a larger tool of the same kind for boring holes in the ground. ORIG C15: *an augur,* mistaken division of *a nauger,* from OE *nafugār* nave (of a wheel) spear, from *nafu* NAVE² + *gār* spear

aught *or* **ought** (ɔːt) (*used with a negative or in conditional or interrogative sentences or clauses*) *Arch. or literary.* ◆ *pron* **1** anything whatever (esp. in **for aught I know**). ◆ *adv* **2** *Dialect.* to any degree. ORIG OE *āwiht,* from *ā* ever, + *wiht* thing

augment (ɔːgˈmɛnt) *vb* to make or become greater in number, strength, etc. ORIG C15: from LL, from *augmentum* growth, from L *augēre* to increase
▸ **augˈmentable** *adj* ▸ **augˈmenter** *n*

augmentation (ˌɔːgmɛnˈteɪʃən) *n* **1** the act of augmenting or the state of being augmented. **2** the amount by which something is increased.

augmentative (ɔːgˈmɛntətɪv) *adj* **1** tending or able to augment. **2** *Grammar.* denoting an affix that may be added to a word to convey the meaning *large* or *great*: for example, the suffix *-ote* in Spanish, where *hombre* means man and *hombrote* big man.

augmented (ɔːgˈmɛntɪd) *adj* **1** *Music.* (of an interval) increased from being perfect or major by the raising of the higher note or the dropping of the lower note by one semitone: *C to G sharp is an augmented fifth.* **2** having been increased, esp. in number: *an augmented orchestra.*

au gratin (*French* o gratɛ̃) *adj* covered and cooked with browned breadcrumbs and sometimes cheese. ORIG F, lit.: with the grating

Augsburg ★ (*German* ˈauksburk) *n* a city in S Germany, in Bavaria: founded by the Romans in 14 B.C.; site of the diet that produced the **Peace of Augsburg** (1555), which ended the struggles between Lutherans and Catholics in the Holy Roman Empire and established the principle that each ruler should determine the form of worship in his lands. Pop.: 259 699 (1996 est.). Roman name: **Augusta Vindelicorum** (auˈguːstə vɪnˈdɛlɪˌkaurəm).

augur (ˈɔːgə) *n* **1** (in ancient Rome) a religious official who observed and interpreted omens and signs. **2** any prophet or soothsayer. ◆ *vb* **3** to predict (some future event), as from signs or omens. **4** (*tr; may take a clause as object*) to be an omen (of). **5** (*intr*) to foreshadow future events: *this augurs well for us.* ORIG C14: from L: a diviner, ?from *augēre* to increase
▸ **augural** (ˈɔːgjurəl) *adj*

augury (ˈɔːgjurɪ) *n, pl* **auguries. 1** the art of or a rite conducted by an augur. **2** a sign or portent; omen.

august (ɔːˈgʌst) *adj* **1** dignified or imposing. **2** of noble birth or high rank: *an august lineage.* ORIG C17: from L *augustus;* rel. to *augēre* to increase
▸ **auˈgustness** *n*

August (ˈɔːgəst) *n* the eighth month of the year, consisting of 31 days. ORIG OE, from L, after the emperor AUGUSTUS

Augusta ★ (ɔːˈgʌstə) *n* **1** a town in the US, in Georgia. Pop.: 44 639 (1990). **2** a port in S Italy, in E Sicily. Pop.: 38 900 (latest est.). **3** a city in the US, the state capital of Maine: founded (1628) as a trading post; timber industry. Pop.: 21 325 (1990).

Augustan (ɔːˈgʌstən) *adj* **1** characteristic of or relating to the Roman emperor Augustus Caesar, his period, or the poets writing during his reign. **2** of or characteristic of any literary period noted for refinement and classicism, esp. the 18th century in England. ◆ *n* **3** an author in an Augustan Age.

Augustine ★ (ɔːˈgʌstɪn) *n* **1 Saint.** 354–430 A.D., one of the Fathers of the Christian Church; bishop of Hippo in North Africa (396–430), noted for his *Confessions* and *De Civitate Dei.* Feast day: Aug. 28. **2 Saint.** died 604 A.D., Roman monk, sent to Britain (597 A.D.) to convert the Anglo-Saxons: first archbishop of Canterbury (601–604). Feast day: May 26 or 27. **3** a member of an Augustinian order.

Augustinian (ˌɔːgəˈstɪnɪən) *adj* **1** of Saint Augustine of Hippo, his doctrines, or the Christian religious orders founded on his doctrines. ◆ *n* **2** a member of any of several religious orders that are governed by the rule of Saint Augustine. **3** a person who follows the doctrines of Saint Augustine.

Augustus ★ (ɔːˈgʌstəs) *n* original name *Gaius Octavianus;* after his adoption by Julius Caesar (44 B.C.) known as *Gaius Julius Caesar Octavianus.* 63 B.C.–14 A.D., Roman statesman, a member of the second triumvirate (43 B.C.). After defeating Mark Antony at Actium (31 B.C.), he became first emperor of Rome, adopting the title Augustus (27 B.C.).

auk (ɔːk) *n* **1** a diving bird of northern oceans having a heavy body, short tail, narrow wings, and a black-and-white plumage. See also **great auk, razorbill. 2 little auk.** a small short-billed auk, abundant in Arctic regions. ORIG C17: from ON *ālka*

au lait (əu ˈleɪ) *adj* prepared or served with milk. ORIG F, lit.: with milk

auld (ɔːld) *adj* a Scottish word for **old.** ORIG OE *āld*

auld lang syne (ˈɔːld læŋ ˈsaɪn) *n* times past, esp. those remembered with nostalgia. ORIG Scot., lit.: old long since

Auld Reekie ★ (ˈriːkɪ) *n Scot.* a nickname for **Edinburgh**¹. ORIG lit.: Old Smoky

Aulis ★ (ˈɔːlɪs) *n* an ancient town in E central Greece, in Boeotia: traditionally the harbour from which the Greeks sailed at the beginning of the Trojan war.

aumbry (ˈɔːmbrɪ) *n, pl* **aumbries.** a variant of **ambry.**

au naturel *French.* (o natyrɛl) *adj, adv* **1** naked; nude. **2** uncooked or plainly cooked. ORIG lit.: in (a) natural (condition)

Aung San Suu Kyi ★ (ˈauŋ ˈsæn ˈsuː ˈkiː) *n* born 1945, Burmese politician; cofounder (1988) and general secretary (1988–91 and from 1995) of the National League for Democracy: Nobel peace prize 1991.

aunt (ɑːnt) *n* (*often cap., esp. as a term of address*) **1** a sister of one's father or mother. **2** the wife of one's uncle. **3** a term of address used by children for a female friend of the parents. **4 my (sainted) aunt!** an exclamation of surprise. ORIG C13: from OF, from L *amita* a father's sister

auntie *or* **aunty** (ˈɑːntɪ) *n, pl* **aunties.** a familiar or diminutive word for **aunt.**

Auntie (ˈɑːntɪ) *n Brit. inf.* the BBC.

Aunt Sally (ˈsælɪ) *n, pl* **Aunt Sallies.** *Brit.* **1** a figure of an old woman used in fairgrounds and fêtes as a target. **2** any person who is a target for insults or criticism.

au pair (əu ˈpɛə) *n* **a** a young foreigner, usually a girl, who undertakes housework in exchange for board and lodging, esp. in order to learn the language. **b** (*as modifier*): *an au pair girl.* ORIG C20: from F: on an equal footing

aura ('ɔːrə) *n, pl* **auras** *or* **aurae** ('ɔːriː). **1** a distinctive air or quality considered to be characteristic of a person or thing. **2** any invisible emanation, esp. surrounding a person or object. **3** *Pathol.* strange sensations, such as noises in the ears or flashes of light, that immediately precede an attack, esp. of epilepsy. ORIG C18: via L from Gk: breeze

aural ('ɔːrəl) *adj* of or relating to the sense or organs of hearing; auricular. ORIG C19: from L *auris* ear
▸ **'aurally** *adv*

USAGE NOTE *Aural* is sometimes mistakenly used for *oral*. Your *oral skills* are your proficiency in talking about events and situations; your *aural skills* relate to your ability to hear sounds and melodies.

aureate ('ɔːrɪɪt) *adj* **1** covered with gold; gilded. **2** (of a style of writing or speaking) excessively elaborate. ORIG C15: from LL, from L *aureus* golden, from *aurum* gold

Aurelian ★ (ɔː'riːlɪən) *n* Latin name *Lucius Domitius Aurelianus*. ?212–275 A.D., Roman emperor (270–275), who conquered Palmyra (273) and restored political unity to the Roman Empire.

Aurelius ★ (ɔː'riːlɪəs) *n* See **Marcus Aurelius Antoninus.**

aureole ('ɔːrɪˌəʊl) *or* **aureola** (ɔː'riːələ) *n* **1** a border of light or radiance enveloping the head of a figure represented as holy. **2** a less common word for **halo. 3** another name for **corona** (sense 2). ORIG C13: from OF, from Med. L (*corōna*) *aureola* golden (crown), from L, from *aurum* gold

au revoir *French.* (o rəvwar) *sentence substitute.* goodbye. ORIG lit.: to the seeing again

auric ('ɔːrɪk) *adj* of or containing gold, esp. in the trivalent state; designating a gold(III) compound. ORIG C19: from L *aurum* gold

Auric ★ (*French* ɔrik) *n* **Georges** (ʒɔrʒ). 1899–1983, French composer; one of *les Six*.

auricle ('ɔːrɪkᵊl) *n* **1** the upper chamber of the heart; atrium. **2** Also called: **pinna.** *Anat.* the external part of the ear. **3** *Biol.* an ear-shaped part or appendage. ORIG C17: from L *auricula* the external ear, from *auris* ear
▸ **'auricled** *adj*

auricula (ɔː'rɪkjʊlə) *n, pl* **auriculae** (-ˌliː) *or* **auriculas. 1** Also called: **bear's-ear.** a widely cultivated alpine primrose with leaves shaped like a bear's ear. **2** another word for **auricle** (sense 3). ORIG C17: from NL, from L; see AURICLE

auricular (ɔː'rɪkjʊlə) *adj* **1** of, relating to, or received by the sense or organs of hearing; aural. **2** shaped like an ear. **3** of or relating to an auricle of the heart.

auriferous (ɔː'rɪfərəs) *adj* (of rock) containing gold; gold-bearing. ORIG C18: from L, from *aurum* gold + *ferre* to bear

Aurignacian (ˌɔːrɪg'neɪʃən) *adj* of or produced during a flint culture of the Upper Palaeolithic type characterized by the use of bone and antler tools, and also by cave art. ORIG C20: after *Aurignac*, France, near the cave where remains were discovered

Auriol ★ (*French* ɔrjɔl) *n* **Vincent** (vɛ̃sɑ̃). 1884–1966, French statesman; president of the Fourth Republic (1947–54).

aurochs ('ɔːrɒks) *n, pl* **aurochs.** a recently extinct member of the cattle tribe that inhabited forests in N Africa, Europe, and SW Asia. Also called: **urus.** ORIG C18: from G, from OHG *ūrohso*, from *ūro* bison + *ohso* OX

aurora (ɔː'rɔːrə) *n, pl* **auroras** *or* **aurorae** (-riː). **1** an atmospheric phenomenon consisting of bands, curtains, or streamers of light, that move across the sky. **2** *Poetic.* the dawn. ORIG C14: from L: dawn
▸ **au'roral** *adj*

Aurora¹ ★ (ɔː'rɔːrə) *n* **1** the Roman goddess of the dawn. Greek counterpart: **Eos. 2** the dawn or rise of something.

Aurora² ★ (ɔː'rɔːrə) *n* another name for **Maewo.**

aurora australis (ɒ'streɪlɪs) *n* (*sometimes cap.*) the aurora seen around the South Pole. Also called: **southern lights.** ORIG NL: southern aurora

aurora borealis (ˌbɔːrɪ'eɪlɪs) *n* (*sometimes cap.*) the aurora seen around the North Pole. Also called: **northern lights.** ORIG C17: NL: northern aurora

aurous ('ɔːrəs) *adj* of or containing gold, esp. in the monovalent state; designating a gold(I) compound. ORIG C19: from F *aureux*, LL *aurōsus* gold-coloured, from L *aurum* gold

Aus. *abbrev. for:* **1** Australia(n). **2** Austria(n).

Auschwitz ★ (*German* 'auʃvɪts) *n* an industrial town in S Poland; site of a Nazi concentration camp during World War II. Pop.: 45 400 (1989 est.). Polish name: **Oświęcim.**

auscultation (ˌɔːskəl'teɪʃən) *n* **1** the diagnostic technique in medicine of listening to the various internal sounds made by the body, usually with the aid of a stethoscope. **2** the act of listening. ORIG C19: from L, from *auscultāre* to listen attentively; rel. to L *auris* ear
▸ **'auscul,tate** *vb* ▸ **auscultatory** (ɔː'skʌltətərɪ) *adj*

auspice ('ɔːspɪs) *n* **1** (*usually pl*) patronage (esp. in **under the auspices of**). **2** (*often pl*) an omen, esp. one that is favourable. ORIG C16: from L *auspicium* augury from birds

auspicious (ɔː'spɪʃəs) *adj* **1** favourable or propitious. **2** *Arch.* fortunate.
▸ **aus'piciously** *adv* ▸ **aus'piciousness** *n*

Aussie ('ɒzɪ) *n, adj Inf.* Australian.

Aust. *abbrev. for:* **1** Australia(n). **2** Austria(n).

Austen ★ ('ɒstɪn, 'ɔː-) *n* **Jane.** 1775–1817, English novelist, noted particularly for the insight and delicate irony of her portrayal of middle-class families. Her completed novels are *Sense and Sensibility* (1811), *Pride and Prejudice* (1813), *Mansfield Park* (1814), *Emma* (1816), *Northanger Abbey* (1818), and *Persuasion* (1818).

austere (ɒ'stɪə) *adj* **1** stern or severe in attitude or manner. **2** grave, sober, or serious. **3** self-disciplined, abstemious, or ascetic: *an austere life.* **4** severely simple or plain: *an austere design.* ORIG C14: from OF, from L *austērus* sour, from Gk *austēros* astringent; rel. to Gk *hauein* to dry
▸ **aus'terely** *adv*

austerity (ɒ'sterɪtɪ) *n, pl* **austerities. 1** the state or quality of being austere. **2** (*often pl*) an austere habit, practice, or act. **3a** reduced availability of luxuries and consumer goods. **3b** (*as modifier*): *an austerity budget.*

Austerlitz ★ ('ɔːstəlɪts) *n* a town in the Czech Republic, in Moravia: site of Napoleon's victory over the Russian and Austrian armies in 1805. Pop.: 4800 (latest est.). Czech name: **Slavkov.**

Austin¹ ★ ('ɒstɪn, 'ɔː-) *n* a city in central Texas, on the Colorado River: state capital since 1845. Pop.: 514 013 (1994 est.).

Austin² ★ ('ɒstɪn, 'ɔː-) *n* **1 Herbert**, 1st Baron. 1866–1941, British automobile engineer. **2 John.** 1790–1859, British jurist, noted for *The Province of Jurisprudence Determined* (1832). **3 J(ohn) L(angshaw).** 1911–60, British philosopher, noted for his posthumous *Sense and Sensibilia* (1962).

austral¹ ('ɔːstrəl) *adj* of or coming from the south: *austral winds.* ORIG C14: from L *austrālis*, from *auster* the south wind

austral² (aʊ'strɑːl) *n, pl* **australes** (-'strɑːles). a former monetary unit of Argentina. ORIG from Sp.; see AUSTRAL¹

Austral. *abbrev. for:* **1** Australasia. **2** Australia(n).

Australasia ★ (ˌɒstrə'leɪzɪə) *n* **1** Australia, New Zealand, and neighbouring islands in the S Pacific Ocean. **2** (loosely) the whole of Oceania.
▸ **ˌAustra'lasian** *adj*

Australia ★ (ɒ'streɪlɪə) *n* a country and the smallest continent, situated between the Indian Ocean and the Pacific: a former British colony, now an independent member of the Commonwealth, constitutional links with Britain formally abolished in 1986; consists chiefly of a low plateau, mostly arid in the west, with the basin of the Murray River and the Great Dividing Range in the east and the Great Barrier Reef off the NE coast. Language: English. Currency: dollar. Capital: Canberra. Pop.: 18 943 000 (1999 est.). Area: 7 682 300 sq. km (2 966 150 sq. miles).
▸ **Aus'tralian** *adj, n*

Australiana (ɒˌstreɪlɪˈɑːnə) *pl n* objects, books, documents, etc. relating to Australia and its history and culture.

Australian Alps ★ *pl n* a mountain range in SE Australia, in E Victoria and SE New South Wales. Highest peak: Mount Kosciusko, 2195 m (7316 ft).

Australian Antarctic Territory ★ *n* the area of Antarctica, other than Adélie Land, that is administered by Australia, lying south of latitude 60°S and between longitudes 45°E and 160°E.

Australian Capital Territory ★ *n* a territory of SE Australia, within New South Wales: consists of two exclaves, one containing Canberra, the capital of Australia, and one at Jervis Bay. Pop.: 299 243 (1996). Area: 2432 sq. km (939 sq. miles). Former name: **Federal Capital Territory.**

Australian Rules *n* (*functioning as sing*) a game resembling rugby, played in Australia between teams of 18 men each on an oval pitch, with a ball resembling a large rugby ball. Players attempt to kick the ball between posts (without crossbars) at either end of the pitch.

Austral Islands ★ (ˈɔːstrəl) *pl n* another name for the **Tubuai Islands.**

Australoid (ˈɒstrəˌlɔɪd) *adj* **1** denoting, relating to, or belonging to a racial group that includes the native Australians and certain other peoples of southern Asia and the Pacific islands. ◆ *n* **2** any member of this racial group.

australopithecine (ˌɒstrələʊˈpɪθɪˌsiːn) *n* any of various extinct apelike primates whose remains have been found in southern and E Africa. Some species are estimated to be over 4.5 million years old. ORIG C20: from NL, from L *austrālis* southern + Gk *pithēkos* ape

Australorp (ˈɒstrəˌlɔːp) *n* a heavy black breed of domestic fowl laying brown eggs. ORIG shortened from *Austral(ian Black) Orp(ington)*

Austrasia ★ (ɒˈstreɪʒə, -ʃə) *n* the eastern region of the kingdom of the Merovingian Franks that had its capital at Metz and lasted from 511 A.D. until 814 A.D. It covered the area now comprising NE France, Belgium, and western Germany.

Austria ★ (ˈɒstrɪə) *n* a republic in central Europe: ruled by the Hapsburgs from 1282 to 1918; formed a dual monarchy with Hungary in 1867 and became a republic in 1919; a member of the European Union; contains part of the Alps, the Danube basin in the east, and extensive forests. Language: German. Religion: chiefly Roman Catholic. Currency: schilling and euro. Capital: Vienna. Pop.: 8 080 000 (1999 est.). Area: 83 849 sq. km (32 374 sq. miles). German name: **Österreich.**
▸ ˈ**Austrian** *adj, n*

Austrian blind *n* a window blind consisting of rows of vertically gathered fabric that may be drawn up to form a series of ruches.

Austro-[1] (ˈɒstrəʊ) *combining form.* southern: *Austro-Asiatic.* ORIG from L *auster* the south wind

Austro-[2] (ˈɒstrəʊ) *combining form.* Austrian: *Austro-Hungarian.*

Austronesia ★ (ˌɒstrəʊˈniːʒə, -ʃə) *n* the islands of the central and S Pacific, including Indonesia, Melanesia, Micronesia, and Polynesia.
▸ ˌ**Austroˈnesian** *adj, n*

AUT (in Britain) *abbrev. for* Association of University Teachers.

autarchy (ˈɔːtɑːkɪ) *n, pl* **autarchies.** unlimited rule; autocracy. ORIG C17: from Gk *autarkhia,* from *autarkhos* autocratic
▸ **auˈtarchic** *or* **auˈtarchical** *adj*

autarky (ˈɔːtɑːkɪ) *n, pl* **autarkies.** (esp. of a political unit) a system or policy of economic self-sufficiency. ORIG C17: from Gk *autarkeia,* from *autarkēs* self-sufficient, from AUTO- + *arkein* to suffice
▸ **auˈtarkic** *adj* ▸ ˈ**autarkist** *n*

auteur (ɔːˈtɜː) *n* a director whose creative influence on a film is so great as to be considered its author. ORIG F: author
▸ **auˈteurism** *n* ▸ **auˈteurist** *n*

authentic (ɔːˈθɛntɪk) *adj* **1** of undisputed origin or authorship; genuine. **2** trustworthy; reliable: *an authentic account.* **3** (of a deed, etc.) duly executed. **4** *Music.* **4a** using period instruments and historically researched scores and playing techniques. **4b** (*in combination*): *an authentic-instrument performance.* **5** *Music.* commencing on the perfect and ending an octave higher. Cf. **plagal.** ORIG C14: from LL *authenticus* coming from the author, from Gk, from *authentēs* one who acts independently, from AUTO- + *hentēs* a doer
▸ **auˈthentically** *adv* ▸ **authenticity** (ˌɔːθɛnˈtɪsɪtɪ) *n*

authenticate (ɔːˈθɛntɪˌkeɪt) *vb* **authenticates, authenticating, authenticated.** (*tr*) **1** to establish as genuine or valid. **2** to give authority or legal validity to.
▸ **auˌthentiˈcation** *n* ▸ **auˈthentiˌcator** *n*

author (ˈɔːθə) *n* **1** a person who composes a book, article, or other written work. Related adj: **auctorial.** **2** a person who writes books as a profession; writer. **3** an originator or creator: *the author of this plan.* ◆ *vb* (*tr*) **4** to write or originate. ORIG C14: from OF, from L *auctor* author, from *augēre* to increase
▸ **authorial** (ɔːˈθɔːrɪəl) *adj*

authoring (ˈɔːθərɪŋ) *n Computing.* **a** the creation of documents, esp. multimedia documents. **b** (*as modifier*): *an authoring tool.*

authoritarian (ɔːˌθɒrɪˈtɛərɪən) *adj* **1** favouring or characterized by strict obedience to authority. **2** favouring or relating to government by a small elite. **3** dictatorial; domineering. ◆ *n* **4** a person who favours or practises authoritarian policies.

authoritative (ɔːˈθɒrɪtətɪv) *adj* **1** recognized or accepted as being true or reliable. **2** commanding: *an authoritative manner.* **3** possessing or supported by authority; official.
▸ **auˈthoritatively** *adv* ▸ **auˈthoritativeness** *n*

authority (ɔːˈθɒrɪtɪ) *n, pl* **authorities.** **1** the power or right to control, judge, or prohibit the actions of others. **2** (*often pl*) a person or group of people having this power, such as a government, police force, etc. **3** a position that commands such a power or right (often in **in authority**). **4** such a power or right delegated: *she has his authority.* **5** the ability to influence or control others. **6** an expert or an authoritative written work in a particular field. **7** evidence or testimony. **8** confidence resulting from great expertise. **9** (*cap. when part of a name*) a public board or corporation exercising governmental authority: *Advertising Standards Authority.* ORIG C14: from OF, from L, from *auctor* author

authorize *or* **authorise** (ˈɔːθəˌraɪz) *vb* **authorizes, authorizing, authorized** *or* **authorises, authorising, authorised.** (*tr*) **1** to confer authority upon (someone to do something). **2** to permit (someone to do or be something) with official sanction.
▸ ˌ**authoriˈzation** *or* ˌ**authoriˈsation** *n*

Authorized Version *n* **the.** an English translation of the Bible published in 1611 under James I. Also called: **King James Version.**

authorship (ˈɔːθəˌʃɪp) *n* **1** the origin or originator of a written work, plan, etc. **2** the profession of writing books.

autism (ˈɔːtɪzəm) *n Psychiatry.* abnormal self-absorption, usually affecting children, characterized by lack of response to people and limited ability to communicate. ORIG C20: from Gk *autos* self + -ISM
▸ **auˈtistic** *adj*

auto (ˈɔːtəʊ) *n, pl* **autos.** *US & Canad. inf.* **a** short for **automobile. b** (*as modifier*): *auto parts.*

auto. *abbrev. for:* **1** automatic. **2** automobile. **3** automotive.

auto- *or sometimes before a vowel* **aut-** *combining form.* **1** self; same; of or by the same one: *autobiography.* **2** self-caused: *autohypnosis.* **3** self-propelling: *automobile.* ORIG from Gk *autos* self

autobahn (ˈɔːtəˌbɑːn) *n* a motorway in German-speaking countries. ORIG C20: from G from *Auto* car + *Bahn* road, track

autobiography (ˌɔːtəʊbaɪˈɒgrəfɪ) *n, pl* **autobiographies.** an account of a person's life written or otherwise recorded by that person.

▸ ˌautobiˈographer *n* ▸ **autobiographical** (ˌɔːtəˌbaɪəˈgræfɪkᵊl) *adj*

autocephalous (ˌɔːtəʊˈsɛfələs) *adj* (of an Eastern Christian Church) governed by its own national synods and appointing its own patriarchs or prelates.

autochthon (ɔːˈtɒkθən) *n, pl* **autochthons** *or* **autochthones** (-θəˌniːz). **1** (*often pl*) one of the earliest known inhabitants of any country. **2** an animal or plant that is native to a particular region. ORIG C17: from Gk *autokhthōn* from the earth itself, from AUTO- + *khthōn* the earth
▸ **auˈtochthonous** *adj*

autoclave (ˈɔːtəˌkleɪv) *n* **1** a strong sealed vessel used for chemical reactions at high pressure. **2** an apparatus for sterilizing objects (esp. surgical instruments) by means of steam under pressure. ORIG C19: from F AUTO- + -*clave*, from L *clāvis* key

autocracy (ɔːˈtɒkrəsɪ) *n, pl* **autocracies. 1** government by an individual with unrestricted authority. **2** a country, society, etc., ruled by an autocrat.

autocrat (ˈɔːtəˌkræt) *n* **1** a ruler who possesses absolute and unrestricted authority. **2** a domineering or dictatorial person.
▸ ˌ**autoˈcratic** *adj* ▸ ˌ**autoˈcratically** *adv*

autocross (ˈɔːtəʊˌkrɒs) *n* a motor sport in which cars race over a half-mile circuit of rough grass.

Autocue (ˈɔːtəʊˌkjuː) *n Trademark.* an electronic television prompting device whereby a script, unseen by the audience, is displayed for the speaker.

auto-da-fé (ˌɔːtəʊdəˈfeɪ) *n, pl* **autos-da-fé. 1** *History.* a ceremony of the Spanish Inquisition including the pronouncement and execution of sentences passed on sinners or heretics. **2** the burning to death of people condemned as heretics by the Inquisition. ORIG C18: from Port., lit.: act of the faith

autoeroticism (ˌɔːtəʊɪˈrɒtɪˌsɪzəm) *or* **autoerotism** (ˌɔːtəʊˈɛrəˌtɪzəm) *n Psychol.* the arousal and use of one's own body as a sexual object.
▸ ˌ**autoeˈrotic** *adj*

autoexposure (ˌɔːtəʊɪkˈspəʊʒə) *n* another name for **automatic exposure.**

autofocus (ˈɔːtəʊˌfəʊkəs) *n* another name for **automatic focus.**

autogamy (ɔːˈtɒgəmɪ) *n* self-fertilization.
▸ **auˈtogamous** *adj*

autogenic training (ˌɔːtəʊˈdʒɛnɪk) *n* a technique for reducing stress through mental exercises. Also called: **autogenics.**

autogenous (ɔːˈtɒdʒɪnəs) *adj* **1** originating within the body. **2** self-produced. **3** denoting a weld in which the filler metal and the parent metal are of similar composition.
▸ **auˈtogenously** *adv*

autogiro *or* **autogyro** (ˌɔːtəʊˈdʒaɪrəʊ) *n, pl* **autogiros** *or* **autogyros.** a self-propelled aircraft supported in flight mainly by unpowered rotating horizontal blades. ORIG C20: orig. a trademark

autograph (ˈɔːtəˌgrɑːf) *n* **1a** a handwritten signature, esp. that of a famous person. **1b** (*as modifier*): *an autograph album.* **2** a person's handwriting. **3a** a book, document, etc., handwritten by its author. **3b** (*as modifier*): *an autograph letter.* ◆ *vb* (*tr*) **4** to write one's signature on or in; sign. **5** to write with one's own hand.
▸ **autographic** (ˌɔːtəˈgræfɪk) *adj* ▸ ˌ**autoˈgraphically** *adv*

autohypnosis (ˌɔːtəʊhɪpˈnəʊsɪs) *n Psychol.* the process or result of self-induced hypnosis.

autoimmune (ˌɔːtəʊɪˈmjuːn) *adj* (of a disease) caused by the action of antibodies produced against substances normally present in the body.
▸ ˌ**autoimˈmunity** *n*

autointoxication (ˌɔːtəʊɪnˌtɒksɪˈkeɪʃən) *n* self-poisoning caused by toxic products originating within the body.

autologous (ɔːˈtɒləgəs) *adj* (of a tissue graft, blood transfusion, etc.) originating from the recipient rather than from a donor.

Autolycus ★ (ɔːtɒlɪkəs) *n Greek myth.* a thief who stole cattle from his neighbour Sisyphus and prevented him from recognizing them by making them invisible.

autolysis (ɔːˈtɒlɪsɪs) *n* the destruction of cells and tissues of an organism by enzymes produced by the cells themselves.
▸ **autolytic** (ˌɔːtəˈlɪtɪk) *adj*

automat (ˈɔːtəˌmæt) *n* another name, esp. US, for **vending machine.**

automate (ˈɔːtəˌmeɪt) *vb* **automates, automating, automated.** to make (a manufacturing process, factory, etc.) automatic, or (of a manufacturing process, etc.) to be made automatic.

automated teller machine *n* a computerized cash dispenser. Abbrev.: **ATM.**

automatic (ˌɔːtəˈmætɪk) *adj* **1** performed from force of habit or without conscious thought: *an automatic smile.* **2a** (of a device, mechanism, etc.) able to activate, move, or regulate itself. **2b** (of an act or process) performed by such automatic equipment. **3** (of the action of a muscle, etc.) involuntary or reflex. **4** occurring as a necessary consequence: *promotion is automatic after a year.* **5** (of a firearm) utilizing some of the force of each explosion to eject the empty shell, replace it with a new one, and fire continuously until release of the trigger. ◆ *n* **6** an automatic firearm. **7** a motor vehicle having automatic transmission. **8** a machine that operates automatically. ORIG C18: from Gk *automatos* acting independently
▸ ˌ**autoˈmatically** *adv*

automatic door *n* a self-opening door.

automatic exposure *n* the automatic adjustment of the lens aperture and shutter speed of a camera by a control mechanism. Also called: **autoexposure.**

automatic focus *n* **a** a system in a camera that automatically adjusts the lens so that the object being photographed is in focus. **b** (*as modifier*): *automatic-focus lens.* Also called: **autofocus.**

automatic gain control *n* a control of a radio receiver which adjusts the magnitude of the input so that the output (or volume) remains approximately constant.

automatic pilot *n* **1** a device that automatically maintains an aircraft on a preset course. **2** *Inf.* a state of mind in which a person performs familiar tasks automatically: *I was on automatic pilot all day.* ◆ Also called: **autopilot.**

automatic transmission *n* a transmission system in a motor vehicle in which the gears change automatically.

automation (ˌɔːtəˈmeɪʃən) *n* **1** the use of methods for controlling industrial processes automatically, esp. by electronically controlled systems. **2** the extent to which a process is so controlled.

automatism (ɔːˈtɒməˌtɪzəm) *n* **1** the state or quality of being automatic; mechanical or involuntary action. **2** *Psychol.* the performance of actions, such as sleepwalking, without conscious knowledge or control.
▸ **auˈtomatist** *n*

automatize *or* **automatise** (ɔːˈtɒməˌtaɪz) *vb* **automatizes, automatizing, automatized** *or* **automatises, automatising, automatised.** to make (a process, etc.) automatic or (of a process, etc.) to be made automatic.
▸ **auˌtomatiˈzation** *or* **auˌtomatiˈsation** *n*

automaton (ɔːˈtɒmətᵊn) *n, pl* **automatons** *or* **automata. 1** a mechanical device operating under its own hidden power. **2** a person who acts mechanically. ORIG C17: from L, from Gk, from *automatos* spontaneous

automobile (ˈɔːtəməˌbiːl) *n* another word (esp. US) for **car** (sense 1).
▸ ˌ**automoˈbilist** *n*

automobilia (ˌɔːtəməˈbiːlɪə) *pl n* items connected with cars and motoring that are of interest to the collector.

automotive (ˌɔːtəˈməʊtɪv) *adj* **1** relating to motor vehicles. **2** self-propelling.

autonomic (ˌɔːtəˈnɒmɪk) *adj* **1** occurring spontaneously. **2** of or relating to the autonomic nervous system. **3** Also: **autonomous.** (of plant movements) occurring as a result of internal stimuli.
▸ ˌ**autoˈnomically** *adv*

★ people and places

autonomic nervous system *n* the section of the nervous system of vertebrates that controls the involuntary actions of the smooth muscles, heart, and glands.

autonomics (ˌɔːtəˈnɒmɪks) *n* (*functioning as sing*) *Electronics.* the study of self-regulating systems for process control.

autonomous (ɔːˈtɒnəməs) *adj* **1** (of a community, country, etc.) possessing a large degree of self-government. **2** of or relating to an autonomous community. **3** independent of others. **4** *Biol.* existing as an organism independent of other organisms or parts. ORIG C19: from Gk *autonomos* living under one's own laws, from AUTO- + *nomos* law
▸ **auˈtonomously** *adv*

autonomy (ɔːˈtɒnəmɪ) *n, pl* **autonomies. 1** the right or state of self-government, esp. when limited. **2** a state or individual possessing autonomy. **3** freedom to determine one's own actions, behaviour, etc. **4** *Philosophy.* the doctrine that the individual human will is, or ought to be, governed only by its own principles and laws. ORIG C17: from Gk *autonomia* freedom to live by one's own laws

autopilot (ˌɔːtəˈpaɪlət) *n* short for **automatic pilot.**

autopsy (ˈɔːtəpsɪ, ɔːˈtɒp-) *n, pl* **autopsies. 1** Also called: **postmortem examination.** dissection and examination of a dead body to determine the cause of death. **2** an eyewitness observation. **3** any critical analysis. ORIG C17: from NL, from Gk: seeing with one's own eyes, from AUTO- + *opsis* sight

autoroute (ˈɔːtəʊˌruːt) *n* a motorway in French-speaking countries. ORIG C20: from F from *auto* car + *route* road

autostrada (ˈɔːtəʊˌstrɑːdə) *n* a motorway in Italian-speaking countries. ORIG C20: from It. from *auto* car + *strada* road

autosuggestion (ˌɔːtəʊsəˈdʒɛstʃən) *n* a process of suggestion in which the person unconsciously supplies the means of influencing his own behaviour or beliefs.

autotelic (ˌɔːtəʊˈtɛlɪk) *adj* being or having an end or justification in itself. ORIG C20: from AUTO- + Gk *telos* end

autotomy (ɔːˈtɒtəmɪ) *n, pl* **autotomies.** the casting off by an animal of a part of its body, to facilitate escape when attacked.
▸ **autotomic** (ˌɔːtəˈtɒmɪk) *adj*

autotrophic (ˌɔːtəˈtrɒfɪk) *adj* (of organisms such as green plants) capable of manufacturing complex organic nutritive compounds from simple inorganic sources.
▸ **ˈautoˌtroph** *n*

autumn (ˈɔːtəm) *n* **1** (*sometimes cap.*) **1a** Also called (esp. US): **fall.** the season of the year between summer and winter, astronomically from the September equinox to the December solstice in the N hemisphere and from the March equinox to the June solstice in the S hemisphere. **1b** (*as modifier*): *autumn leaves.* **2** a period of late maturity, esp. one followed by a decline. ORIG C14: from L *autumnus*
▸ **autumnal** (ɔːˈtʌmnᵊl) *adj*

autumn crocus *n* a plant of the lily family having pink or purplish autumn flowers, found in Europe and N Africa.

Auvergne ★ (əʊˈvɛən, əʊˈvɜːn; *French* ovɛrɲ) *n* a region of S central France: largely mountainous, rising over 1800 m (6000 ft).

aux. *abbrev. for* auxiliary.

auxanometer (ˌɔːksəˈnɒmɪtə) *n* an instrument that measures the linear growth of plant shoots. ORIG C19: from Gk *auxanein* to increase + -METER

Aux Cayes ★ (əʊ ˈkeɪ; *French* o kaj) *n* the former name of **Les Cayes.**

Auxerre ★ (*French* osɛr) *n* a town in central France, capital of the Yonne department; Gothic cathedral. Pop.: 40 600 (1990).

auxiliaries (ɔːgˈzɪljərɪz, -ˈzɪlə-) *pl n* foreign troops serving another nation; mercenaries.

auxiliary (ɔːgˈzɪljərɪ, -ˈzɪlə-) *adj* **1** secondary or supplementary. **2** supporting. ◆ *n, pl* **auxiliaries. 3** a person or thing that supports or supplements. **4** *Naut.* **4a** a sailing vessel with an engine. **4b** the engine of such a vessel. ORIG C17: from L, from *auxilium* help, from *augēre* to increase, strengthen

auxiliary rotor *n* the tail rotor of a helicopter, used for directional and rotary control.

auxiliary verb *n* a verb used to indicate the tense, voice, or mood of another verb where this is not indicated by inflection, such as English *will* in *he will go.*

auxin (ˈɔːksɪn) *n* a plant hormone that promotes growth. ORIG C20: from Gk *auxein* to grow

AV *abbrev. for* Authorized Version (of the Bible).

av. *abbrev. for:* **1** average. **2** avoirdupois.

Av. *or* **av.** *abbrev. for* avenue.

a.v. *or* **A/V** *abbrev. for* ad valorem.

avadavat (ˌævədəˈvæt) *or* **amadavat** (ˌæmədəˈvæt) *n* either of two Asian weaverbirds having a red plumage: often kept as cagebirds. ORIG C18: from *Ahmadabad,* Indian city from which these birds were brought to Europe

avail (əˈveɪl) *vb* **1** to be of use, advantage, profit, or assistance (to). **2 avail oneself of.** to make use of to one's advantage. ◆ *n* **3** use or advantage (esp. in **of no avail, to little avail**). ORIG C13 *availen,* from OF *valoir,* from L *valēre* to be strong

available (əˈveɪləbᵊl) *adj* **1** obtainable or accessible; capable of being made use of. **2** *Arch.* advantageous.
▸ **aˌvailaˈbility** *or* **aˈvailableness** *n* ▸ **aˈvailably** *adv*

avalanche (ˈævəˌlɑːntʃ) *n* **1a** a fall of large masses of snow and ice down a mountain. **1b** a fall of rocks, sand, etc. **2** a sudden or overwhelming appearance of a large quantity of things. ◆ *vb* **avalanches, avalanching, avalanched. 3** to come down overwhelmingly (upon). ORIG C18: from F, by mistaken division from *la valanche,* from *valanche,* from dialect *lavantse*

Avalon ★ (ˈævəˌlɒn) *n Celtic myth.* an island paradise in the western seas: in Arthurian legend it is where King Arthur was taken after he was mortally wounded. ORIG from Med L *insula avallonis* island of Avalon, from O Welsh *aballon* apple

avant- (ˈævɒŋ) *prefix* of or belonging to the avant-garde of a specified field.

avant-garde (ˌævɒŋˈgɑːd) *n* **1** those artists, writers, musicians, etc., whose techniques and ideas are in advance of those generally accepted. ◆ *adj* **2** of such artists, etc., their ideas, or techniques. ORIG from F: VANGUARD

avarice (ˈævərɪs) *n* extreme greed for riches. ORIG C13: from OF, from L, from *avārus* covetous, from *avēre* to crave
▸ **avaricious** (ˌævəˈrɪʃəs) *adj*

avast (əˈvɑːst) *sentence substitute. Naut.* stop! cease! ORIG C17: ?from Du. *hou'vast* hold fast

avatar (ˈævəˌtɑː) *n* **1** *Hinduism.* the manifestation of a deity in human or animal form. **2** a visible manifestation of an abstract concept. ORIG C18: from Sansk. *avatāra* a going down, from *ava* down + *tarati* he passes over

avaunt (əˈvɔːnt) *sentence substitute. Arch.* go away! depart! ORIG C15: from OF *avant!* forward! from LL *ab ante* forward, from L *ab* from + *ante* before

avdp. *abbrev. for* avoirdupois.

ave (ˈɑːvɪ, ˈɑːveɪ) *sentence substitute.* welcome or farewell. ORIG L

Ave[1] (ˈɑːvɪ) *n RC Church.* short for **Ave Maria:** see **Hail Mary.** ORIG C13: from L: hail!

Ave[2] *or* **ave** *abbrev. for* avenue.

Avebury ★ (ˈeɪvbərɪ) *n* a village in Wiltshire, site of an extensive neolithic stone circle.

Aveiro ★ (*Portuguese* əˈveːiru) *n* a port in N central Portugal, on the **Aveiro lagoon:** ancient Roman town; linked by canal with the Atlantic Ocean. Pop.: 35 250 (1991). Ancient name: **Talabriga** (ˌtæləˈbriːgə).

Ave Maria (məˈriːə) *n* another name for **Hail Mary.** ORIG C14: from med L: hail, Mary!

avenge (əˈvɛndʒ) *vb* **avenges, avenging, avenged.** (*usually tr*) to inflict a punishment in retaliation for (harm, injury, etc.) done to (a person or persons): *to avenge a crime; to*

avenge a murdered friend. ORIG C14: from OF, from *vengier,* from L *vindicāre;* see VENGEANCE, VINDICATE
▸ **a'venger** *n*

> **USAGE NOTE** The use of *avenge* with *oneself* was formerly considered incorrect, but is now acceptable and relatively common: *one of those writers who avenged themselves on somebody in print.*

avens ('ævɪnz) *n, pl* **avens.** (*functioning as sing*) **1** any of a genus of plants, such as **water avens,** which has a purple calyx and orange-pink flowers. **2 mountain avens.** a trailing evergreen white-flowered shrub that grows on mountains in N temperate regions. ORIG C15: from OF, from Med. L *avencia* variety of clover

Aventine ★ ('ævən,taɪn, -tɪn) *n* one of the seven hills on which Rome was built.

aventurine (ə'vɛntjʊrɪn) *or* **avanturine** (ə'væntjʊrɪn) *n* **1** a dark-coloured glass, usually green or brown, spangled with fine particles of gold, copper, or some other metal. **2** a variety of quartz containing red or greenish particles of iron oxide or mica. ORIG C19: from F, from It., from *avventura* chance; so named because usually found by accident

avenue ('ævɪnju:) *n* **1a** a broad street, often lined with trees. **1b** (*cap. as part of a street name*) a road, esp. in a built-up area. **2** a main approach road, as to a country house. **3** a way bordered by two rows of trees. **4** a line of approach: *explore every avenue.* ORIG C17: from F, from *avenir* to come to, from L, from *venīre* to come

aver (ə'vɜ:) *vb* **avers, averring, averred.** (*tr*) **1** to state positively. **2** *Law.* to allege as a fact or prove to be true. ORIG C14: from OF, from Med. L *adverāre,* from L *vērus* true
▸ **a'verment** *n*

average ('ævərɪdʒ, 'ævrɪdʒ) *n* **1** the typical or normal amount, quality, degree, etc.: *above average in intelligence.* **2** Also called: **arithmetic mean.** the result obtained by adding the numbers or quantities in a set and dividing the total by the number of members in the set: *the average of 3, 4, and 8 is 5.* **3** a similar mean for continuously variable ratios, such as speed. **4** *Maritime law.* **4a** a loss incurred or damage suffered by a ship or its cargo at sea. **4b** the equitable apportionment of such loss among the interested parties. **5 on (the** *or* **an) average.** usually; typically. ◆ *adj* **6** usual or typical. **7** mediocre or inferior: *his performance was only average.* **8** constituting a numerical average: *an average speed.* **9** approximately typical of a range of values: *the average contents of a matchbox.* ◆ *vb* **averages, averaging, averaged. 10** (*tr*) to obtain or estimate a numerical average of. **11** (*tr*) to assess the general quality of. **12** (*tr*) to perform or receive a typical number of: *to average eight hours' work a day.* **13** (*tr*) to divide up proportionately. **14** to amount to or be on average: *the children averaged 15 years of age.* ORIG C15 *averay* loss arising from damage to ships, from OIt. *avaria,* ult. from Ar. *awār* damage, blemish
▸ **'averagely** *adv*

Averno ★ (*Italian* a'vɛrno) *n* a crater lake in Italy, near Naples: in ancient times regarded as an entrance to hell. Latin name: **Avernus** (ə'vɜ:nəs). ORIG from L, from Gk *aornos* without birds, from A-[1] + *ornis* bird; referring to the legend that the lake's sulphurous exhalations killed birds

Averroës ★ (ə'vɛrəʊ,i:z) *n* Arabic name *ibn-Rushd.* 1126–88, Arab philosopher and physician in Spain, noted particularly for his attempts to reconcile Aristotelian philosophy with Islamic religion, which profoundly influenced Christian scholasticism.

averse (ə'vɜ:s) *adj* (*postpositive;* usually foll. by *to*) opposed, disinclined, or loath. ORIG C16: from L, from *āvertere* to turn from, from *vertere* to turn
▸ **a'versely** *adv* ▸ **a'verseness** *n*

> **USAGE NOTE** See at **adverse.**

aversion (ə'vɜ:ʃən) *n* **1** (usually foll. by *to* or *for*) extreme dislike or disinclination. **2** a person or thing that arouses this: *he is my pet aversion.*

aversion therapy *n Psychiatry.* a way of suppressing an undesirable habit, such as smoking, by associating an unpleasant effect, such as an electric shock, with the habit.

avert (ə'vɜ:t) *vb* (*tr*) **1** to turn away or aside: *to avert one's gaze.* **2** to ward off: *to avert danger.* ORIG C15: from OF, from L *āvertere;* see AVERSE
▸ **a'vertible** *or* **a'vertable** *adj*

Avesta (ə'vɛstə) *n* a collection of sacred writings of Zoroastrianism, including the Songs of Zoroaster.

Avestan (ə'vɛstən) *n* **1** the earliest recorded form of the Iranian language, formerly called **Zend.** ◆ *adj* **2** of the Avesta or its language.

Aveyron ★ (*French* avɛrɔ̃) *n* a department of S France in Midi-Pyrénées region. Capital: Rodez. Pop.: 266 849 (1994 est.). Area: 8771 sq. km (3421 sq. miles).

avian ('eɪvɪən) *adj* of, relating to, or resembling a bird. ORIG C19: from L *avis* bird

aviary ('eɪvjərɪ) *n, pl* **aviaries.** a large enclosure in which birds are kept. ORIG C16: from L, from *aviārius* concerning birds, from *avis* bird

aviation (,eɪvɪ'eɪʃən) *n* **1** the art or science of flying aircraft. **2** the design, production, and maintenance of aircraft. ORIG C19: from F, from L *avis* bird

aviator ('eɪvɪ,eɪtə) *n Old-fashioned.* the pilot of an aeroplane or airship; flyer.
▸ **'avi,atrix** *or* **'avi,atress** *fem n*

Avicenna ★ (,ævɪ'sɛnə) *n* Arabic name *ibn-Sina.* 980–1037, Arab philosopher and physician whose philosophical writings, which combined Aristotelianism with neo-Platonist ideas, greatly influenced scholasticism, and whose medical work *Qanun* was the greatest single influence on medieval medicine.

avid ('ævɪd) *adj* **1** very keen; enthusiastic: *an avid reader.* **2** (*postpositive;* often foll. by *for* or *of*) eager (for): *avid for revenge.* ORIG C18: from L, from *avēre* to long for
▸ **avidity** (ə'vɪdɪtɪ) *n* ▸ **'avidly** *adv*

Aviemore ★ (,ævɪ'mɔ:) *n* a winter sports resort in Scotland, in Moray between the Monadhliath and Cairngorm Mountains. Pop.: 2214 (1991).

avifauna (,eɪvɪ'fɔ:nə) *n* all the birds in a particular region.
▸ **,avi'faunal** *adj*

Avignon ★ (*French* aviɲɔ̃) *n* a city in SE France, on the Rhône: seat of the papacy (1309–77); famous 12th-century bridge, now partly destroyed. Pop.: 181 136 (1990).

Ávila ★ (*Spanish* 'aβila) *n* a city in central Spain: 11th-century granite walls and Romanesque cathedral. Pop.: 45 092 (1988 est.).

avionics (,eɪvɪ'ɒnɪks) *n* **1** (*functioning as sing*) the science and technology of electronics applied to aeronautics. **2** (*functioning as pl*) the electronic circuits and devices of an aerospace vehicle. ORIG C20: from *avi(ation electr)onics*
▸ **,avi'onic** *adj*

avitaminosis (æ,vɪtəmɪn'əʊsɪs) *n, pl* **avitaminoses** (-si:z). any disease caused by a vitamin deficiency in the diet.

Avlona ★ (æv'ləʊnə) *n* the ancient name for **Vlorë.**

avocado (,ævə'kɑ:dəʊ) *n, pl* **avocados. 1** a pear-shaped fruit having a leathery green or blackish skin, a large stony seed, and a greenish-yellow edible pulp. **2** the tropical American tree that bears this fruit. **3a** a dull greenish colour. **3b** (*as adj*): *an avocado bathroom suite.* ◆ Also called (for senses 1 & 2): **avocado pear, alligator pear.** ORIG C17: from Sp. *aguacate,* from Nahuatl *ahuacatl* testicle, alluding to the shape of the fruit

avocation (,ævə'keɪʃən) *n* **1** *Formal.* a minor occupation undertaken as a diversion. **2** *Not standard.* a person's regular job. ORIG C17: from L, from *āvocāre* to distract, from *vocāre* to call

avocet ('ævə,sɛt) *n* a long-legged shore bird having black-and-white plumage and a long slender upward-curving bill. ORIG C18: from F, from It. *avocetta,* from ?

Avogadro ★ (,ævə'gɑ:drəʊ; *Italian* avo'ga:dro) *n* **Amedeo**

(ame'dɛ:o), *Conte di Quaregna.* 1776–1856, Italian physicist, noted for his work on gases.

Avogadro constant *or* **number** *n* the number of atoms or molecules in a mole of a substance, equal to 6.02252×10^{23} per mole.

Avogadro's law *or* **hypothesis** *n* the principle that equal volumes of all gases contain the same number of molecules at the same temperature and pressure.

avoid (ə'vɔɪd) *vb* (*tr*) **1** to keep out of the way of. **2** to refrain from doing. **3** to prevent from happening: *to avoid damage to machinery.* **4** *Law.* to invalidate; quash. ORIG C14: from Anglo-F, from OF *esvuidier,* from *vuidier* to empty
▸ **a'voidable** *adj* ▸ **a'voidably** *adv* ▸ **a'voidance** *n* ▸ **a'voider** *n*

avoirdupois *or* **avoirdupois weight** (ˌævədə'pɔɪz) *n* a system of weights used in many English-speaking countries. It is based on the pound, which contains 16 ounces or 7000 grains. ORIG C14: from OF *aver de peis* goods of weight

Avon[1] ★ ('eɪvᵊn) *n* **1** a former county of SW England, created in 1974 from parts of N Somerset and S Gloucestershire: replaced in 1996 by unitary authorities. **2** a river in central England, rising in Northamptonshire and flowing southwest through Stratford-on-Avon to the River Severn at Tewkesbury. Length: 154 km (96 miles). **3** a river in SW England, rising in Gloucestershire and flowing south and west through Bristol to the Severn estuary at **Avonmouth.** Length: 120 km (75 miles). **4** a river in S England, rising in Wiltshire and flowing south to the English Channel. Length: about 96 km (60 miles).

Avon[2] ★ ('eɪvᵊn) *n* **Earl of.** title of (Anthony) **Eden.**

avouch (ə'vautʃ) *vb* (*tr*) *Arch.* **1** to vouch for; guarantee. **2** to acknowledge. **3** to assert. ORIG C16: from OF *avochier* to summon, call on, from L *advocāre;* see ADVOCATE
▸ **a'vouchment** *n*

avow (ə'vaʊ) *vb* (*tr*) **1** to state or affirm. **2** to admit openly. ORIG C13: from OF *avouer* to confess, from L *advocāre* to appeal to, call upon
▸ **a'vowal** *n* ▸ **a'vowed** *adj* ▸ **avowedly** (ə'vaʊɪdlɪ) *adv* ▸ **a'vower** *n*

avuncular (ə'vʌŋkjʊlə) *adj* **1** of or concerned with an uncle. **2** resembling an uncle; friendly. ORIG C19: from L *avunculus* (maternal) uncle, dim. of *avus* grandfather

AWACS *or* **Awacs** ('eɪwæks) *n acronym for* Airborne Warning and Control System.

await (ə'weɪt) *vb* **1** (*tr*) to wait for. **2** (*tr*) to be in store for. **3** (*intr*) to wait, esp. with expectation.

awake (ə'weɪk) *vb* **awakes, awaking, awoke** *or* **awaked, awoken** *or* **awaked. 1** to emerge or rouse from sleep. **2** to become or cause to become alert. **3** (usually foll. by *to*) to become or make aware (of). **4** Also: **awaken.** (*tr*) to arouse (feelings, etc.) or cause to remember (memories, etc.). ◆ *adj* (*postpositive*) **5** not sleeping. **6** (sometimes foll. by *to*) lively or alert. ORIG OE *awacian, awacan*

USAGE NOTE See at **wake**[1].

award (ə'wɔ:d) *vb* (*tr*) **1** to give (something due), esp. as a reward for merit: *to award prizes.* **2** *Law.* to declare to be entitled, as by decision of a court or an arbitrator. ◆ *n* **3** something awarded, such as a prize or medal. **4** *Austral. & NZ.* the amount of an **award wage** (esp. in **above award**). **5** *Law.* **5a** the decision of an arbitrator. **5b** a grant made by a court of law. ORIG C14: from Anglo-F *awarder,* from OF *eswarder* to decide after investigation, from *es-* EX-[1] + *warder* to observe
▸ **a'warder** *n*

award wage *n* (in Australia and New Zealand) statutory minimum pay for a particular group of workers. Sometimes shortened to **award.**

aware (ə'wɛə) *adj* **1** (*postpositive;* foll. by *of*) having knowledge: *aware of his error.* **2** informed of current developments: *politically aware.* ORIG OE *gewær*
▸ **a'wareness** *n*

awash (ə'wɒʃ) *adv, adj* (*postpositive*) *Naut.* **1** level with the surface of the sea. **2** washed over by the waves.

away (ə'weɪ) *adv* **1** from a particular place: *to swim away.* **2** in or to another, a usual, or a proper place: *to put toys away.* **3** apart; at a distance: *to keep away from strangers.* **4** out of existence: *the music faded away.* **5** indicating motion, displacement, transfer, etc., from a normal or proper place: *to turn one's head away.* **6** indicating activity that is wasteful or designed to get rid of something: *to sleep away the hours.* **7** continuously: *laughing away.* **8 away with.** a command for a person to go or be removed: *away with him to prison!* ◆ *adj* (*usually postpositive*) **9** not present: *away from school.* **10** distant: *he is a good way away.* **11** having started; released: *he was away before sunrise.* **12** (*also prenominal*) *Sport.* played on an opponent's ground. ◆ *n* **13** *Sport.* a game played or won at an opponent's ground. ◆ *sentence substitute.* **14** an expression of dismissal. ORIG OE *on weg* on way

awayday (ə'weɪˌdeɪ) *n* a day trip taken for pleasure, relaxation, etc.; day excursion. ORIG C20: from *awayday ticket,* name applied to some special-rate railway day returns

awe (ɔ:) *n* **1** overwhelming wonder, respect, or dread. **2** *Arch.* power to inspire fear or reverence. ◆ *vb* **awes, awing, awed. 3** (*tr*) to inspire with reverence or dread. ORIG C13: from ON *agi*

aweigh (ə'weɪ) *adj* (*postpositive*) *Naut.* (of an anchor) no longer hooked into the bottom; hanging by its rope or chain.

awe-inspiring *adj* causing or worthy of admiration or respect; amazing or magnificent.

awesome ('ɔ:səm) *adj* **1** inspiring or displaying awe. **2** *Sl.* excellent or outstanding.
▸ **'awesomely** *adv* ▸ **'awesomeness** *n*

awestruck *or* **awe-stricken** *adj* overcome or filled with awe.

awful ('ɔ:fʊl) *adj* **1** very bad; unpleasant. **2** *Arch.* inspiring reverence or dread. **3** *Arch.* overcome with awe. ◆ *adv* **4** *Not standard.* (intensifier): *an awful cold day.* ORIG C13: see AWE, -FUL
▸ **'awfulness** *n*

awfully ('ɔ:fəlɪ) *adv* **1** in an unpleasant, bad, or reprehensible manner. **2** *Inf.* (intensifier): *I'm awfully keen to come.* **3** *Arch.* so as to express or inspire awe.

awhile (ə'waɪl) *adv* for a brief period.

USAGE NOTE *Awhile* written as a single word can only be used with a verb, and is most common after verbs such as *linger, rest,* and *pause.* It is quite commonly written by mistake where the meaning intended is 'for a period of time', and where *while* is being used as a noun: *I thought about that for a while* (not *awhile*).

awkward ('ɔ:kwəd) *adj* **1** lacking dexterity, proficiency, or skill; clumsy. **2** ungainly or inelegant in movements or posture. **3** unwieldy; difficult to use. **4** embarrassing: *an awkward moment.* **5** embarrassed: *he felt awkward about leaving.* **6** difficult to deal with; requiring tact: *an awkward customer.* **7** deliberately unhelpful. **8** dangerous or difficult. ORIG C14: *awk,* from ON *öfugr* turned the wrong way round + -WARD
▸ **'awkwardly** *adv* ▸ **'awkwardness** *n*

awl (ɔ:l) *n* a pointed hand tool with a fluted blade used for piercing wood, leather, etc. ORIG OE *ǣl*

awn (ɔ:n) *n* any of the bristles growing from the flowering parts of certain grasses and cereals. ORIG OE *agen* ear of grain
▸ **awned** *adj*

awning ('ɔ:nɪŋ) *n* a roof of canvas or other material supported by a frame to provide protection from the weather, esp. one placed over a doorway or part of a deck of a ship. ORIG C17: from ?

awoke (ə'wəʊk) *vb* a past tense and (now rare or dialectal) past participle of **awake.**

AWOL ('eɪwɒl) *or* **A.W.O.L.** *adj Mil.* absent without leave but without intending to desert.

awry (ə'raɪ) *adv, adj* (*postpositive*) **1** with a slant or twist to one side; askew. **2** away from the appropriate or right course; amiss. ORIG C14 *on wry;* see A-², WRY

AWS *abbrev. for* automatic warning system: a train safety system that gives audible warnings about the signals being passed, and can apply the brakes automatically if necessary.

axe *or US* **ax** (æks) *n, pl* **axes. 1** a hand tool with one side of its head forged and sharpened to a cutting edge, used for felling trees, splitting timber, etc. **2 an axe to grind. 2a** an ulterior motive. **2b** a grievance. **2c** a pet subject. **3 the axe.** *Inf.* **3a** dismissal, esp. from employment (esp. in **get the axe**). **3b** *Brit.* severe cutting down of expenditure, esp. in a public service. ◆ *vb* **axes, axing, axed.** (*tr*) **4** to chop or trim with an axe. **5** *Inf.* to dismiss (employees), restrict (expenditure or services), or terminate (a project, etc.). ORIG OE *æx*

axel ('æksəl) *n Skating.* a jump of one and a half, two and a half, or three and a half turns, taking off from the forward outside edge of one skate and landing on the backward outside edge of the other. ORIG C20: after *Axel* Paulsen (d. 1938), Norwegian skater

axeman ('æksmən) *n, pl* **axemen. 1** a man who wields an axe, esp. to cut down trees. **2** a person who makes cuts in expenditure or services, esp. on behalf of another: *the chancellor's axeman.*

axes¹ ('æksi:z) *n* the plural of **axis¹**.

axes² ('æksɪz) *n* the plural of **axe.**

axial ('æksɪəl) *adj* **1** forming or characteristic of an axis. **2** situated in, on, or along an axis.
► ˌ**axi'ality** *n* ► '**axially** *adv*

axil ('æksɪl) *n* the upper angle between a branch or leafstalk and the stem from which it grows. ORIG C18: from L *axilla* armpit

axilla (æk'sɪlə) *n, pl* **axillae** (-li:). **1** the technical name for the **armpit. 2** the area under a bird's wing corresponding to the armpit. ORIG C17: from L: armpit

axillary (æk'sɪlərɪ) *adj* **1** of, relating to, or near the armpit. **2** *Bot.* growing in or related to the axil. ◆ *n, pl* **axillaries. 3** (*usually pl*) Also called: **axillar** (æk'sɪlə). one of the feathers growing from the axilla of a bird's wing.

axiom ('æksɪəm) *n* **1** a generally accepted proposition or principle, sanctioned by experience. **2** a universally established principle or law that is not a necessary truth. **3** a self-evident statement. **4** *Logic, maths.* a statement that is stipulated to be true for the purpose of a chain of reasoning. ORIG C15: from L *axiōma* a principle, from Gk, from *axioun* to consider worthy, from *axios* worthy

axiomatic (ˌæksɪə'mætɪk) *adj* **1** self-evident. **2** containing maxims; aphoristic.
► ˌ**axio'matically** *adv*

axis¹ ('æksɪs) *n, pl* **axes. 1** a real or imaginary line about which a body, such as an aircraft, can rotate or about which an object, form, composition, or geometrical construction is symmetrical. **2** one of two or three reference lines used in coordinate geometry to locate a point in a plane or in space. **3** *Anat.* the second cervical vertebra. **4** *Bot.* the main central part of a plant, typically consisting of the stem and root. **5** an alliance between a number of states to coordinate their foreign policy. **6** Also called: **principal axis.** *Optics.* the line of symmetry of an optical system, such as the line passing through the centre of a lens. ORIG C14: from L: axletree, earth's axis; rel. to Gk *axōn* axis

axis² ('æksɪs) *n, pl* **axises.** a S Asian deer with a reddish-brown white-spotted coat and slender antlers. ORIG C18: from L: Indian wild animal, from ?

Axis ('æksɪs) *n* **a the.** the alliance (1936) of Nazi Germany and Fascist Italy, later joined by Japan and other countries, and lasting until their defeat in World War II. **b** (*as modifier*): *the Axis powers.*

axle ('æksəl) *n* a bar or shaft on which a wheel, pair of wheels, or other rotating member revolves. ORIG C17: from ON *öxull*

axletree ('æksəlˌtri:) *n* a bar fixed across the underpart of a wagon or carriage that has rounded ends on which the wheels revolve.

Axminster carpet ('æksˌmɪnstə) *n* a type of patterned carpet with a cut pile. Often shortened to **Axminster.** ORIG after *Axminster* in Devon

axolotl (ˌæksə'lɒtᵊl) *n* an aquatic salamander of N America, such as the **Mexican axolotl,** in which the larval form (including external gills) is retained throughout life under natural conditions. ORIG C18: from Nahuatl, from *atl* water + *xolotl* servant, doll

axon ('æksɒn) *n* the long threadlike extension of a nerve cell that conducts nerve impulses from the cell body. ORIG C19: via NL from Gk: axis, axle, vertebra

ay¹ *or* **aye** (eɪ) *adv Arch., poetic* always.

ay² (aɪ) *sentence substitute, n* a variant spelling of **aye.**

Ayacucho ★ (*Spanish* aja'kutʃo) *n* a city in SE Peru: nearby is the site of the battle (1824) that won independence for Peru. Pop.: 105 918 (1993).

ayah ('aɪə) *n* (in parts of the former British Empire) a native maidservant or nursemaid. ORIG C18: from Hindi *āyā,* from Port. *aia,* from L *avia* grandmother

ayatollah (ˌaɪə'tɒlə) *n* one of a class of Shiite religious leaders in Iran. ORIG via Persian from Ar., from *aya* creation + ALLAH

Ayckbourn ★ ('eɪkbɔ:n) *n* Sir **Alan.** born 1939, British dramatist. His plays include *Absurd Person Singular* (1973), the trilogy *The Norman Conquests* (1974), and *Comic Potential* (2000).

Aycliffe ★ ('eɪklɪf) *n* a town in Co. Durham: founded as a new town in 1947. Pop.: 40 000 (latest est.).

Aydin *or* **Aidin** ★ ('aɪdɪn) *n* a town in SW Turkey: an ancient city of Lydia. Pop.: 121 200 (1994 est.). Ancient name: **Tralles.**

aye *or* **ay** (aɪ) *sentence substitute.* **1** yes: archaic or dialectal except in voting by voice. ◆ *n* **2a** a person who votes in the affirmative. **2b** an affirmative vote. ◆ Cf. **nay.** ORIG C16: prob. from pron *I,* expressing assent

aye-aye ('aɪˌaɪ) *n* a rare nocturnal arboreal primate of Madagascar related to the lemurs. It has long bony fingers and rodent-like incisor teeth. ORIG C18: from F, from Malagasy *aiay,* prob. imit.

Ayer ★ (ɛə) *n* Sir **Alfred Jules.** 1910–89, British positivist philosopher, noted for *Language, Truth, and Logic* (1936).

Ayers Rock ★ (ɛəz) *n* the former name for **Uluru.**

Ayesha ★ ('ɑ:i:ˌʃɑ:) *n* a variant spelling of **Aisha.**

Aylesbury ★ ('eɪlzbərɪ, -brɪ) *n* a town in SE central England, administrative centre of Buckinghamshire. Pop.: 58 058 (1991).

Aylward ★ ('eɪlwəd) *n* **Gladys.** 1903–70, British missionary in China.

Aymara (ˌaɪmə'rɑ:) *n* **1** (*pl* **-ras** *or* **-ra**) a member of a S American Indian people of Bolivia and Peru. **2** the language of this people. ORIG from Sp. *aimará,* from Amerind

Ayodha ★ (aɪ'jəʊdjɑ:) *n* an ancient town in N India, in Uttar Pradesh state: sacred to Hindus and a Buddhist centre. Also called: **Awadh** (ə'wɒd), **Oudh** (aʊd).

Ayr ★ (ɛə) *n* a port in SW Scotland, in South Ayrshire. Pop.: 47 962 (1991).

Ayrshire ★ ('ɛəʃə) *n* **1** a historic county of SW Scotland: part of Strathclyde region (1975–96); in 1996 it was reorganized into three new council areas, East Ayrshire, North Ayrshire, and South Ayrshire. **2** any one of a hardy breed of brown-and-white dairy cattle.

Ayub Khan ★ (aɪ'ju:b 'kɑ:n) *n* **Mohammed.** 1907–74, Pakistani field marshal; president of Pakistan (1958–69).

Ayutthaya ★ (ɑ:'ju:təjə) *n* a city in S Thailand, on the Chao Phraya River: capital of the country until 1767; noted for its canals and ruins. Pop.: 61 185 (1990). Also called: **Ayudhya** (ɑ:'ju:djə), **Ayuthia** (ɑ:'ju:θɪə).

AZ *abbrev. for* Arizona.

azalea (ə'zeɪljə) *n* an ericaceous plant cultivated for its showy pink or purple flowers. ORIG C18: via NL from Gk, from *azaleos* dry; from its supposed preference for a dry situation

Azaña ★ (*Spanish* aˈθaɲa) *n* **Manuel** (maˈnwel). 1880–1940, Spanish statesman; president of the Spanish Republic (1936–39) until overthrown by Franco.

Azania ★ (əˈzɑːnɪə, əˈzɑːnjə) *n* another name (used esp. by many Black political activists) for **South Africa.** ORIG perhaps from Arabic *Adzan* East Africa
▸ **Aˈzanian** *n, adj*

Azbine ★ (æzˈbiːn) *n* another name for **Aïr.**

azeotrope (əˈziːəˌtrəʊp) *n* a mixture of liquids that boils at a constant temperature, at a given pressure, without change of composition. ORIG C20: from A-[1] + *zeo-*, from Gk *zein* to boil + -TROPE
▸ **azeotropic** (ˌeɪzɪəˈtrɒpɪk) *adj*

Azerbaijan ★ (ˌæzəbaɪˈdʒɑːn) *n* **1** a republic in NW Asia: the region was acquired by Russia from Persia in the early 19th century; became the Azerbaijan Soviet Socialist Republic in 1936; gained independence in 1991; consists of dry subtropical steppes around the Aras and Kura Rivers, surrounded by the Caucasus; contains the extensive Baku oilfields. Language: Azerbaijani. Currency: manat. Capital: Baku. Pop.: 7 617 000 (1997). Area: 86 600 sq. km (33 430 sq. miles). **2** a mountainous region of NW Iran, separated from the republic of Azerbaijan by the Aras River: divided administratively into **Eastern Azerbaijan** and **Western Azerbaijan.** Capitals: Tabriz and Rezaiyeh. Pop.: 7 993 000 (1999 est.).
▸ **ˌAzerbaiˈjani** *adj, n*

azerty *or* **AZERTY keyboard** (əˈzɜːtɪ) *n* a common European version of typewriter keyboard layout with the characters a, z, e, r, t, and y positioned at the top left of the keyboard.

azide (ˈeɪzaɪd) *n* **a** an acyl derivative or salt of hydrazoic acid, used as a coating to enhance electron emission. **b** *(as modifier): an azide group or radical.*

Azikiwe ★ (ˌɑːziːˈkiːweɪ) *n* **Nnamdi** (ᵊnˈnæmdɪ). 1904–96, Nigerian statesman; first president of Nigeria (1963–66).

Azilian (əˈzɪlɪən) *n* **1** a Palaeolithic culture of Spain and SW France that can be dated to the 10th millennium B.C., characterized by flat bone harpoons and schematically painted pebbles. ◆ *adj* **2** of or relating to this culture. ORIG C19: after Mas d'*Azil*, France, where artefacts were found

azimuth (ˈæzɪməθ) *n* **1** *Astron., navigation.* the angular distance usually measured clockwise from the south point of the horizon in astronomy or from the north point in navigation to the intersection with the horizon of the vertical circle passing through a celestial body. **2** *Surveying.* the horizontal angle of a bearing clockwise from north. ORIG C14: from OF *azimut*, from Ar. *as-sumūt*, pl. of *as-samt* the path, from L *semita* path
▸ **azimuthal** (ˌæzɪˈmʌθəl) *adj*

azine (ˈeɪziːn) *n* an organic compound having a six-membered ring with at least one nitrogen atom, the other atoms in the ring being carbon atoms.

azo (ˈeɪzəʊ, ˈæ-) *adj* of, consisting of, or containing the divalent group -N:N-: *an azo group or radical.* See also **diazo.** ORIG from F *azote* nitrogen, from Gk *azōos* lifeless

azoic (əˈzəʊɪk) *adj* without life; characteristic of the ages that have left no evidence of life in the form of organic remains. ORIG C19: from Gk *azōos* lifeless

Azores ★ (əˈzɔːz) *pl n* **the.** three groups of volcanic islands in the N Atlantic, since 1976 autonomous region of Portugal; includes the districts of Angra do Heroísmo, Horta, and Ponta Delgada. Capital: Ponta Delgada (on São Miguel). Pop.: 236 500 (1992 est.). Area: 2335 sq. km (901 sq. miles). Portuguese name: **Açôres.**

Azorín ★ (*Spanish* aθoˈrin) *n* real name *José Martínez Ruiz.* 1874–1967, Spanish writer.

Azov ★ (ˈɑːzɒv) *n* **Sea of.** a shallow arm of the Black Sea, to which it is connected by the Kerch Strait: almost entirely landlocked; fed chiefly by the River Don. Area: about 37 500 sq. km (14 500 sq. miles).

AZT *abbrev. for* azidothymidine: another name for **zidovudine.**

Aztec (ˈæztɛk) *n* **1** a member of a Mexican Indian people who established a great empire, centred on the valley of Mexico, that was overthrown by Cortés in the early 16th century. **2** the language of the Aztecs. See also **Nahuatl.** ◆ *adj also* **Aztecan. 3** of, relating to, or characteristic of the Aztecs, their civilization, or their language. ORIG C18: from Sp., from Nahuatl *Aztecatl*, from *Aztlan*, their traditional place of origin, lit.: near the cranes

azure (ˈæʒə, ˈeɪ-) *n* **1** a deep blue similar to the colour of a clear blue sky. **2** *Poetic.* a clear blue sky. ◆ *adj* **3** of the colour azure. **4** *(usually postpositive) Heraldry.* of the colour blue. ORIG C14: from OF, from OSp., from Ar. *lāzaward* lapis lazuli, from Persian *lāzhuward*

azurite (ˈæʒʊˌraɪt) *n* a deep blue mineral consisting of hydrated basic copper carbonate. It is used as an ore of copper and as a gemstone.

azygous (ˈæzɪgəs) *adj Biol.* developing or occurring singly. ORIG C17: via NL from Gk *azugos*, from A-[1] + *zugon* YOKE

Bb

b *or* **B** (biː) *n, pl* **b's, B's,** *or* **Bs. 1** the second letter of the English alphabet. **2** a speech sound represented by this letter. **3** Also: **beta.** the second in a series, class, or rank.

B *symbol for:* **1** *Music.* **1a** the seventh note of the scale of C major. **1b** the major or minor key having this note as its tonic. **2** the less important of two things. **3** a human blood type of the ABO group, containing the B antigen. **4** (in Britain) a secondary road. **5** *Chem.* boron. **6** magnetic flux density. **7** *Chess.* bishop. **8** (on Brit. pencils, signifying degree of softness of lead) black. **9** Also: **b** *Physics.* bel. **10** *Physics.* baryon number. **11a** a person whose job is in middle management, or who holds an intermediate administrative or professional position. **11b** (*as modifer*): *a B worker.* ◆ See also **occupation groupings.**

b. *abbrev. for:* **1** born. **2** *Cricket.* **2a** bowled. **2b** bye.

b. *or* **B.** *abbrev. for:* **1** *Music.* bass *or* basso. **2** billion. **3** book. **4** breadth.

B. *abbrev. for:* **1** (on maps, etc.) bay. **2** Bible.

B- (of US military aircraft) *abbrev. for* bomber.

B4 (bɪˈfɔː) before; an abbreviation used in text messages, e-mails, etc. ORIG C20

Ba[1] *the chemical symbol for* barium.

Ba[2] ★ (bɑː) *n Egyptian myth.* the soul, represented as a bird with a human head.

BA *abbrev. for:* **1** Bachelor of Arts. **2** British Academy. **3** British Airways. **4** British Association (for the Advancement of Science). **5** British Association screw thread.

baa (bɑː) *vb* **baas, baaing, baaed. 1** (*intr*) to make the cry of a sheep; bleat. ◆ *n* **2** the cry made by sheep.

BAA *abbrev. for* British Airports Authority.

Baader-Meinhof Gang (*German* ˈbaːdər ˈmainhoːf) *n* **the.** a group of West German guerrillas dedicated to the violent overthrow of capitalist society. Also called: **Red Army Faction.** ORIG C20: named after its leading members, Andreas *Baader* (1943–77) and Ulrike *Meinhof* (1934–76).

Baal ★ (bɑːl) *n* **1** any of several ancient Semitic fertility gods. **2** *Phoenician myth.* the sun god and supreme national deity. **3** (*sometimes not cap.*) any false god or idol. ORIG from Heb. *báʻal* lord, master

Baalbek ★ (ˈbɑːlbɛk) *n* a town in E Lebanon: an important city in Phoenician and Roman times; extensive ruins. Pop.: 15 600 (1995 est.). Ancient name: **Heliopolis.**

Baal Shem Tov *or* **Baal Shem Tob** ★ (bɑːl ˈʃɛm tɒv, ˈʃɑːm) *n* original name *Israel ben Eliezer.* ?1700–60, Jewish religious leader in Poland: founder of modern Chassidism.

baas (bɑːs) *n* a South African word for **boss**[1] (sense 1): used by Africans and Coloured people in addressing European managers or overseers. ORIG C17: from Afrik., from MDu. *baes* master

baaskap *or* **baasskap** (ˈbɑːsˌkap) *n* (*sometimes cap.*) (in South Africa) control by Whites of non-Whites. ORIG from Afrik., from BAAS + *-skap* -SHIP

Bab ★ (bɑːb) *n* **the.** title of *Mirza Ali Mohammed.* 1819–50, Persian religious leader: founded Babism; executed as a heretic of Islam. ORIG from Persian *bāb* gate, from Ar.

baba (ˈbɑːbɑː) *n* a small cake, usually soaked in rum (**rum baba**). ORIG C19: from F, from Polish, lit.: old woman

babalas (ˈbabalas) *n S. African.* a hangover. ORIG from Zulu *ibhabhalasi*

Babar ★ (ˈbɑːbə) *n* a variant spelling of **Baber.**

Babbage ★ (ˈbæbɪdʒ) *n* **Charles.** 1792–1871, British mathematician, who built a calculating machine.

babbitt (ˈbæbɪt) *vb* (*tr*) to line (a bearing) or face (a surface) with Babbitt metal.

Babbitt (ˈbæbɪt) *n US derog.* a narrow-minded and complacent member of the middle class. ORIG C20: after George *Babbitt,* central character in the novel *Babbitt* (1922) by Sinclair Lewis
▸ ˈ**Babbittry** *n*

Babbitt metal *n* any of a number of alloys originally based on tin, antimony, and copper but now often including lead: used esp. in bearings. ORIG C19: after Isaac *Babbitt* (1799–1862), US inventor

babble (ˈbæbᵊl) *vb* **babbles, babbling, babbled. 1** to utter (words, sounds, etc.) in an incoherent jumble. **2** (*intr*) to talk foolishly, incessantly, or irrelevantly. **3** (*tr*) to disclose (secrets, etc.) carelessly. **4** (*intr*) (of streams, birds, etc.) to make a low murmuring sound. ◆ *n* **5** incoherent or foolish speech. **6** a murmuring sound. ORIG C13: prob. imit.

babbler (ˈbæblə) *n* **1** a person or thing that babbles. **2** any of various birds of the Old World tropics and subtropics having an incessant song.

babe (beɪb) *n* **1** a baby. **2** *Inf.* a naive or gullible person. **3** *Sl.* a girl or young woman, esp. an attractive one.

Babel[1] (ˈbeɪbᵊl) *n* **1** *Old Testament.* Also called: **Tower of Babel.** a tower presumptuously intended to reach from earth to heaven, the building of which was frustrated when Jehovah confused the language of the builders (Genesis 11:1–10). **2** (*often not cap.*) **2a** a confusion of noises or voices. **2b** a scene of noise and confusion. ORIG from Heb. *Bābhél,* from Akkadian *Bāb-ilu,* lit.: gate of God

Babel[2] ★ (*Russian* ˈbabɪl) *n* **Isaak Emmanuilovich** (iˈsak imənuˈiləvitʃ). 1894–1941, Russian writer, whose works include *Red Cavalry* (1926).

Bab el Mandeb ★ (ˈbæb ɛl ˈmændɛb) *n* a strait between SW Arabia and E Africa, connecting the Red Sea with the Gulf of Aden.

Baber, Babar, *or* **Babur** ★ (ˈbɑːbə) *n* original name *Zahir ud-Din Mohammed.* 1483–1530, founder of the Mogul Empire: conquered India in 1526.

Babeuf ★ (*French* babœf) *n* **François Noël** (frɑ̃swa nɔɛl). 1760–97, French political agitator: plotted unsuccessfully to destroy the Directory and establish a communistic system.

Babington ★ (ˈbæbɪŋtən) *n* **Anthony.** 1561–86, English conspirator, executed for unsuccessful plot (1586) to assassinate Elizabeth I.

babirusa (ˌbɑːbɪˈruːsə) *n* a wild pig of Indonesia. It has an almost hairless wrinkled skin and enormous curved canine teeth. ORIG C17: from Malay, from *bābī* hog + *rūsa* deer

Babism (ˈbɑːbɪzəm) *n* a pantheistic Persian religious sect, founded in 1844, forbidding polygamy, concubinage, begging, trading in slaves, and indulgence in alcohol and drugs. ORIG C19: from the BAB

baboon (bəˈbuːn) *n* any of several medium-sized Old World monkeys. They have an elongated muzzle, large teeth, and a fairly long tail. ORIG C14 *babewyn* gargoyle, later, baboon, from OF

babu (ˈbɑːbuː) *n* (in India) **1** a form of address more or less equivalent to *Mr.* **2** (formerly) an Indian clerk who could write English. ORIG Hindi, lit.: father

Babur ★ (ˈbɑːbə) *n* a variant spelling of **Baber.**

babushka (bəˈbuːʃkə) *n* **1** a headscarf tied under the chin, worn by Russian peasant women. **2** (in Russia) an old woman. ORIG Russian: grandmother, from *baba* old woman

baby (ˈbeɪbɪ) *n, pl* **babies. 1a** a newborn child; infant. **1b** (*as modifier*): *baby food.* **2** an unborn child; fetus. **3** the youngest or smallest of a family or group. **4** a newborn or recently born animal. **5** *Usually derog.* an immature person. **6** *Sl.* a young woman or sweetheart. **7** a project of personal concern. **8 be left holding the baby.** to be left with the responsibility. ◆ *adj* **9** (*prenominal*) comparatively small of its type: *a baby car.* ◆ *vb* **babies, babying, babied. 10** (*tr*) to treat with love and attention. **11** to treat (some-

★ people and places

one) like a baby; pamper or overprotect. ORIG C14: prob. childish reduplication
▸ 'baby,hood *n* ▸ 'babyish *adj*

baby bonus *n Canad. inf.* Family Allowance.

baby boomer *n* a person born during a **baby boom,** a sharp increase in the birth rate, esp. (in Britain and the US) one born during the years 1945–55.

baby buggy *n* **1** *Brit. Trademark.* a child's pushchair. **2** *US & Canad. inf.* a small pram.

baby carriage *n* the US and Canad. name for **pram**[1].

Babylon ★ ('bæbɪlən) *n* **1** the chief city of ancient Mesopotamia: first settled around 3000 B.C. See also **Hanging Gardens of Babylon. 2** *Derog.* (in Protestant polemic) the Roman Catholic Church, regarded as the seat of luxury and corruption. **3** *Derog.* any society or group in a society considered as corrupt or as a place of exile by another society or group, esp. White Britain as viewed by some Rastafarians. ORIG via L and Gk from Heb. *Bābhel;* see BABEL[1]
▸ **Babylonian** (,bæbɪ'ləʊnɪən) *adj, n*

Babylonia ★ (,bæbɪ'ləʊnɪə) *n* the southern kingdom of ancient Mesopotamia: a great empire from about 2200–538 B.C., when it was conquered by the Persians.

baby-sit *vb* **baby-sits, baby-sitting, baby-sat.** (*intr*) to act or work as a baby-sitter.
▸ 'baby-,sitting *n, adj*

baby-sitter *n* a person who takes care of a child or children while the parents are out.

baby snatcher *n Inf.* **1** a person who steals a baby from its pram. **2** someone who marries or has an affair with a much younger person.

baby wipe *n* a disposable moistened medicated paper towel used for cleaning babies.

Bacău ★ (bə'kaʊ) *n* a city in E Romania on the River Bistrila: oil refining, textiles, paper. Pop.: 206 995 (1993 est.).

baccalaureate (,bækə'lɔːrɪɪt) *n* the university degree of Bachelor of Arts. ORIG C17: from Med. L *baccalaureātus,* from *baccalaureus* advanced student from *baccalārius* BACHELOR

baccarat ('bækə,rɑː, ,bækə'rɑː) *n* a card game in which two or more punters gamble against the banker. ORIG C19: from F *baccara* from ?

baccate ('bækeɪt) *adj Bot.* **1** like a berry. **2** bearing berries. ORIG C19: from L *bāca* berry

Bacchae ★ ('bækiː) *pl n* the priestesses or female devotees of Bacchus. ORIG L, from Gk *Bakkhai,* plural of *Bakkhē* priestess of BACCHUS

bacchanal ('bækən[ə]l) *n* **1** a follower of Bacchus. **2** a drunken and riotous celebration. **3** a participant in such a celebration. ◆ *adj* **4** of or relating to Bacchus. ORIG C16: from L *Bacchānālis*

bacchanalia (,bækə'neɪlɪə) *pl n* **1** (*often cap.*) orgiastic rites associated with Bacchus. **2** any drunken revelry.
▸ ,baccha'nalian *adj, n*

bacchant ('bækənt) *or* (*fem*) **bacchante** (bə'kæntɪ) *n, pl* **bacchants** *or* **bacchantes** (bə'kæntɪz). **1** a priest, priestess, or votary of Bacchus. **2** a drunken reveller. ORIG C17: from L *bacchāns,* from *bacchārī* to celebrate the BACCHANALIA

Bacchic ('bækɪk) *adj* **1** of or relating to Bacchus. **2** (*often not cap.*) riotously drunk.

Bacchus ★ ('bækəs) *n* (in ancient Greece and Rome) a god of wine and giver of ecstasy, identified with Dionysus. ORIG C15: from L, from Gk *Bakkhos;* related to L *bāca* small round fruit, berry

baccy ('bækɪ) *n* a Brit. informal name for **tobacco.**

bach (bætʃ) *NZ.* ◆ *n* **1** a seaside, bush, or country cottage. ◆ *vb* **2** a variant spelling of **batch**[2].

Bach ★ (*German* bax) *n* **1 Johann Christian** (jo'han 'krɪstjan), 11th son of J. S. Bach. 1735–82, German composer, called *the English Bach,* resident in London from 1762. **2 Johann Christoph** ('krɪstɔf). 1642–1703, German composer: wrote oratorios, cantatas, and motets, some of which were falsely attributed to J. S. Bach, of whom he was a distant relative. **3 Johann Sebastian** (ze'bastjan). 1685–1750, German composer: musical director for Prince Leopold of Köthen (1717–28); musical director for the city of Leipzig (1728–50). His works include cantatas and oratorios, settings of the *Passion according to St John* (1723) and *St Matthew* (1729), the six *Brandenburg Concertos* (1720–21), the 48 preludes and fugues, and the *Mass in B Minor* (1733–38). **4 Karl** (*or* **Carl**) **Philipp Emanuel** (karl 'fiːlɪp e'maːnuɛl), 3rd son of J. S. Bach. 1714–88, German composer, chiefly of symphonies, sonatas, and church music. **5 Wilhelm Friedemann** ('vɪlhɛlm 'friːdəman), eldest son of J. S. Bach. 1710–84, German composer, works include nine symphonies.

bachelor ('bætʃələ, 'bætʃlə) *n* **1a** an unmarried man. **1b** (*as modifier*): *a bachelor flat.* **2** a person who holds the degree of Bachelor of Arts, Bachelor of Education, Bachelor of Science, etc. **3** (in the Middle Ages) a young knight serving a great noble. **4 bachelor seal.** a young male seal that has not yet mated. ORIG C13: from OF *bacheler* youth, squire, from Vulgar L *baccalāris* (unattested) farm worker
▸ 'bachelor,hood *n*

bachelor girl *n* a young unmarried woman, esp. one who is self-supporting.

Bachelor of Arts *n* **1** a degree conferred on a person who has successfully completed undergraduate studies in the liberal arts or humanities. **2** a person who holds this degree.

Bachelor of Science *n* **1** a degree conferred on a person who has successfully completed undergraduate studies in a science. **2** a person who holds this degree.

bachelor's-buttons *n* (*functioning as sing or pl*) any of various plants with button-like flower heads, esp. a double-flowered buttercup.

Bach flower remedy (bɑːx) *n Trademark.* an alternative medicine consisting of a distillation from various flowers, supposed to counteract negative states of mind and restore emotional balance. ORIG C20: after Dr E. *Bach* (1886–1936), homeopath who developed this system

bacillary (bə'sɪlərɪ) *or* **bacillar** (bə'sɪlə) *adj* **1** of, relating to, or caused by bacilli. **2** Also: **bacilliform** (bə'sɪlɪ,fɔːm). shaped like a short rod.

bacillus (bə'sɪləs) *n, pl* **bacilli** (-'sɪlaɪ). **1** any rod-shaped bacterium. **2** any of various rodlike spore-producing bacteria constituting the family Bacillaceae. ORIG C19: from L, from *baculum* walking stick

back (bæk) *n* **1** the posterior part of the human body, from the neck to the pelvis. **2** the corresponding or upper part of an animal. **3** the spinal column. **4** the part or side of an object opposite the front. **5** the part or side of anything less often seen or used. **6** the part or side of anything that is furthest from the front or from a spectator: *the back of the stage.* **7** something that supports, covers, or strengthens the rear of an object. **8** *Ball games.* **8a** a mainly defensive player behind a forward. **8b** the position of such a player. **9** the part of a book to which the pages are glued or that joins the covers. **10 at the back of one's mind.** not in one's conscious thoughts. **11 back of Bourke.** *Austral.* a remote or backward place. **12 behind one's back.** secretly or deceitfully. **13 break one's back.** to overwork or work very hard. **14 break the back of.** to complete the greatest or hardest part of (a task). **15 get off someone's back.** *Inf.* to stop criticizing or pestering someone. **16 put one's back into.** to devote all one's strength to (a task). **17 put** (*or* **get**) **someone's back up.** to annoy someone. **18 the back of beyond.** a very remote place. **19 turn one's back on. 19a** to turn away from in anger or contempt. **19b** to refuse to help; abandon. ◆ *vb* (*mainly tr*) **20** (*also intr*) to move or cause to move backwards. **21 back water.** to reverse the direction of a boat, esp. to push the oars of a rowing boat. **22** to provide support, money, or encouragement for (a person, enterprise, etc.). **23** to bet on the success of: *to back a horse.* **24** to provide with a back, backing, or lining. **25** to provide with a musical accompaniment. **26** to countersign or endorse. **27** (*intr;* foll. by *on* or *onto*) to have the back facing (towards): *the house backs onto a river.* **28** (*intr*) (of the wind) to change direction anticlockwise. Cf. **veer** (sense 3). ◆ *adj* (*prenominal*) **29** situated behind: *a back lane.* **30** of the past: *back issues of a magazine.* **31** owing from an earlier date: *back rent.* **32** remote: *a back road.* **33** *Phonetics.* of or denoting a vowel articulated with the tongue retracted towards the soft palate, as for the vowels in English *hard, fall, hot, full, fool.* ◆ *adv* **34** at, to, or towards the rear; behind. **35** in, to, or towards the original starting point, place, or condition: *to go back home; put the book back.* **36** in or into the past: *to look back on one's childhood.* **37** in reply, repayment, or retaliation: *to hit someone back.* **38** in check: *the dam holds back the water.* **39** in concealment; in reserve: *to keep something back.* **40 back and forth.** to and fro. **41 back to front. 41a** in reverse. **41b** in disorder. ◆ See also **back down, back off, back out, back up.** ORIG OE *bæc*

backbencher ('bæk'bɛntʃə) *n Brit., Austral., NZ., etc.* a Member of Parliament who does not hold office in the government or opposition.

backbite ('bæk,baɪt) *vb* **backbites, backbiting, backbit; backbitten** *or* **backbit.** to talk spitefully about (an absent person).
▸ **'back,biter** *n*

backboard ('bæk,bɔːd) *n* **1** a board that is placed behind something to form or support its back. **2** a board worn to straighten or support the back, as after surgery. **3** (in basketball) a flat upright surface supported on a high frame, under which the basket is attached.

back boiler *n* a tank or series of pipes at the back of a fireplace for heating water.

backbone ('bæk,bəʊn) *n* **1** a nontechnical name for **spinal column. 2** something that resembles the spinal column in function, position, or appearance. **3** strength of character; courage.

backbreaking ('bæk,breɪkɪŋ) *adj* exhausting.

backburn ('bæk,bɜːn) *Austral. & NZ.* ◆ *vb* **1** (*tr*) to clear (an area of scrub, bush, etc.) by creating a new fire that burns in the opposite direction to the line of advancing fire. ◆ *n* **2** the act or result of backburning.

back-calculate *vb* **back-calculates, back-calculating, back-calculated.** to estimate (the probable amount of alcohol in a person's blood) at an earlier time than that at which the blood test was taken, based on an average rate at which alcohol leaves the bloodstream: used to determine whether a driver had more than the legal limit of alcohol at the time of an accident.
▸ **'back-,calcu'lation** *n*

back catalogue *n* the recordings that a musician has made in the past, as distinct from his or her current recording: *favourites from his back catalogue.*

backchat ('bæk,tʃæt) *n Inf.* the act of answering back, esp. impudently.

backcloth ('bæk,klɒθ) *n* a painted curtain at the back of a stage set. Also called: **backdrop.**

backcomb ('bæk,kəʊm) *vb* to comb the under layers of (the hair) towards the roots to give more bulk to a hairstyle. Also: **tease.**

back country *n Austral. & NZ.* land remote from settled areas.

backdate (,bæk'deɪt) *vb* **backdates, backdating, backdated.** (*tr*) to make effective from an earlier date.

back door *n* **1** a door at the rear or side of a building. **2** a means of entry to a job, etc., that is secret or obtained through influence.

back down *vb* **1** (*intr, adv*) to withdraw an earlier claim. ◆ *n* **backdown. 2** abandonment of an earlier claim.

backed (bækt) *adj* **a** having a back or backing. **b** (*in combination*): *high-backed; black-backed.*

backer ('bækə) *n* **1** a person who gives financial or other support. **2** a person who bets on a competitor or contestant.

backfield ('bæk,fiːld) *n American football.* **1** (usually preceded by *the*) the quarterback and running backs in a team. **2** the area behind the line of scrimmage from which the backfield begin each play.

backfill ('bæk,fɪl) *vb* (*tr*) to refill an excavated trench, esp. (in archaeology) at the end of an investigation.

backfire (,bæk'faɪə) *vb* **backfires, backfiring, backfired.** (*intr*) **1** (of an internal-combustion engine) to emit a loud noise as a result of an explosion in the exhaust system. **2** to fail to have the desired effect, and, instead, recoil upon the originator. **3** to start a controlled fire in order to halt an advancing forest or prairie fire by creating a barren area. ◆ *n* **4** (in an internal-combustion engine) an explosion of unburnt gases in the exhaust system. **5** a controlled fire started to create a barren area that will halt an advancing forest or prairie fire.

back formation *n* **1** the invention of a new word on the assumption that a familiar word is derived from it. The verbs *edit* and *burgle* in English were so created from *editor* and *burglar.* **2** a word formed by this process.

backgammon ('bæk,gæmən) *n* **1** a game for two people played on a board with pieces moved according to throws of the dice. **2** the most complete form of win in this game. ORIG C17: BACK + *gammon,* var. of GAME[1]

background ('bæk,graʊnd) *n* **1** the part of a scene furthest from the viewer. **2a** an inconspicuous or unobtrusive position (esp. in **in the background**). **2b** (*as modifier*): *a background influence.* **3** the plane or ground in a picture upon which all other planes or forms appear superimposed. **4** a person's social class, education, or experience. **5a** the circumstances that lead up to or help to explain something. **5b** (*as modifier*): *background information.* **6a** a low level of sound, lighting, etc., whose purpose is to be an unobtrusive accompaniment to something else. **6b** (*as modifier*): *background music.* **7** Also called: **background radiation.** *Physics.* low-intensity radiation from small amounts of radioisotopes in soil, air, etc. **8** *Electronics.* unwanted effects, such as noise, occurring in a measuring instrument, electronic device, etc.

backhand ('bæk,hænd) *n* **1** *Tennis, etc.* a stroke made across the body with the back of the hand facing the direction of the stroke. **2** the side on which backhand strokes are made. **3** handwriting slanting to the left. ◆ *adv* **4** with a backhand stroke.

backhanded (,bæk'hændɪd) *adj* **1** (of a blow, shot, etc.) performed with the arm moving across the body. **2** double-edged; equivocal: *a backhanded compliment.* **3** (of handwriting) slanting to the left. ◆ *adv* **4** in a backhanded manner.

backhander ('bæk,hændə) *n* **1** a backhanded stroke or blow. **2** *Inf.* an indirect attack. **3** *Sl.* a bribe.

backing ('bækɪŋ) *n* **1** support. **2** a body of supporters. **3** something that forms, protects, or strengthens the back of something. **4** musical accompaniment, esp. for a pop singer. **5** *Meteorol.* an anticlockwise change in wind direction.

backing dog *n NZ.* a dog that moves a flock of sheep in yards or trucks by jumping on their backs.

backlash ('bæk,læʃ) *n* **1** a sudden and adverse reaction. **2** a reaction or recoil between interacting worn or badly fitting parts in a mechanism. **3** the excessive play between such parts.

backlog ('bæk,lɒg) *n* an accumulation of uncompleted work, unsold stock, etc., to be dealt with.

back marker *n* a competitor who is at the back of a field in a race.

back matter *n* the parts of a book, such as the index and appendices, that follow the text.

backmost ('bæk,məʊst) *adj* furthest back.

back number *n* **1** an issue of a newspaper, magazine, etc., that appeared on a previous date. **2** *Inf.* a person or thing considered to be old-fashioned.

back off *vb* (*adv*) *Inf.* **1** (*intr*) to retreat. **2** (*tr*) to abandon (an intention, objective, etc.).

back out *vb* (*intr, adv;* often foll. by *of*) to withdraw (from an agreement, etc.).

backpack ('bæk,pæk) *n* **1** a rucksack. **2** a pack carried on the back of an astronaut, containing oxygen cylinders, etc. ◆ *vb* (*intr*) **3** to travel about with a backpack.

back passage *n* the rectum.

back-pedal *vb* **back-pedals, back-pedalling, back-pedalled** *or US* **back-pedals, back-pedaling, back-pedaled.** (*intr*) **1** to turn the pedals of a bicycle backwards. **2** to retract or modify a previous opinion, principle, etc.

back projection *n* a method of projecting pictures onto a translucent screen so that they are viewed from the opposite side, used esp. in films to create the illusion that the actors in the foreground are moving.

Back River ★ *n* a river in N Canada, rising in the Northwest Territories and flowing northeast to the Arctic Ocean. Length: about 966 km (600 miles).

back room *n* **a** a place where important and usually secret research or planning is done. **b** (*as modifier*): *backroom boys*.

Backs ★ (bæks) *pl n* **the.** the grounds between the River Cam and certain Cambridge colleges.

back seat *n* **1** a seat at the back, esp. of a vehicle. **2** *Inf.* a subordinate or inconspicuous position (esp. in **take a back seat**).

back-seat driver *n Inf.* **1** a passenger in a car who offers unwanted advice to the driver. **2** a person who offers advice on or tries to direct matters that are not his or her concern.

backsheesh ('bækʃiːʃ) *n* a variant spelling of **baksheesh**.

back shift *n Brit.* **1** a group of workers who work a shift from late afternoon to midnight in an industry or occupation where a day or a night shift is also worked. **2** the period worked. ◆ US and Canad. name: **swing shift**.

backside (ˌbæk'saɪd) *n Inf.* the buttocks.

backslide (ˌbæk'slaɪd) *vb* **backslides, backsliding, backslid.** (*intr*) to relapse into former bad habits.
▸ ˌ**back'slider** *n*

backspace ('bækˌspeɪs) *vb* **backspaces, backspacing, backspaced.** to move (a typewriter carriage, etc.) backwards.

backspin ('bækˌspɪn) *n Sport.* a backward spin imparted to a ball to reduce its speed at impact.

backstage (ˌbæk'steɪdʒ) *adv* **1** behind the part of the theatre in view of the audience. **2** towards the rear of the stage. ◆ *adj* **3** situated backstage. **4** *Inf.* away from public view.

backstairs (ˌbæk'stɛəz) *pl n* **1** a secondary staircase in a house, esp. one originally for the use of servants. ◆ *adj also* **backstair. 2** underhand: *backstairs gossip*.

backstay ('bækˌsteɪ) *n Naut.* a stay leading aft from the upper mast to the deck or stern.

backstreet ('bækˌstriːt) *n* **1** a street in a town remote from the main roads. **2** (*modifier*) denoting illicit activities regarded as likely to take place in such a street: *a backstreet abortion*.

backstroke ('bækˌstrəuk) *n Swimming.* a stroke performed on the back, using backward circular strokes of each arm and flipper movements of the feet. Also called: **back crawl**.

back-to-back *adj* (*usually postpositive*) **1** facing in opposite directions, often with the backs touching. **2** *Chiefly Brit.* (of urban houses) built so that their backs are joined or separated only by a narrow alley.

backtrack ('bækˌtræk) *vb* (*intr*) **1** to return by the same route by which one has come. **2** to retract or reverse one's opinion, policy, etc.

back up *vb* (*adv*) **1** (*tr*) to support. **2** (*intr*) *Cricket.* (of a nonstriking batsman) to move down the wicket in readiness for a run as a ball is bowled. **3** (of water) to accumulate. **4** (of traffic) to become jammed behind an accident or other obstruction. **5** *Computing.* to make a copy of (a data file), esp. as a security copy. **6** (*intr; usually foll. by on*) *Austral.* to repeat an action immediately. ◆ *n* **backup. 7** a support or reinforcement. **8a** a substitute. **8b** (*as modifier*): *a backup copy*. **9** the overflow from a blocked drain or pipe.

backward ('bækwəd) *adj* **1** (*usually prenominal*) directed towards the rear: *a backward glance*. **2** retarded in physical, material, or intellectual development. **3a** conservative or reactionary. **3b** (*in combination*): *backward-looking*. **4** reluctant or bashful: *a backward lover*. ◆ *adv* **5** a variant of **backwards**.
▸ '**backwardness** *n*

backwardation (ˌbækwə'deɪʃən) *n* **1** the difference between the spot price for a commodity, including rent and interest, and the forward price. **2** (formerly, on the Stock Exchange) postponement of delivery by a seller of securities until the next settlement period.

backwards ('bækwədz) *or* **backward** *adv* **1** towards the rear. **2** with the back foremost. **3** in the reverse of usual order or direction. **4** to or towards the past. **5** into a worse state. **6** towards the point of origin. **7 bend, lean,** *or* **fall over backwards.** *Inf.* to make a special effort, esp. in order to please.

backwash ('bækˌwɒʃ) *n* **1** water washed backwards by the motion of oars or other propelling devices. **2** the backward flow of air set up by aircraft engines. **3** a repercussion.

backwater ('bækˌwɔːtə) *n* **1** a body of stagnant water connected to a river. **2** an isolated or backward place or condition.

backwoods ('bækwudz) *pl n* **1** partially cleared, sparsely populated forests. **2** any remote sparsely populated place. **3** (*modifier*) of or like the backwoods. **4** (*modifier*) uncouth; rustic.
▸ '**back**ˌ**woodsman** *n*

backword ('bækˌwɜːd) *n Dialect.* a failure to keep a promise.

back yard *n* **1** a yard at the back of a house, etc. **2 in one's own back yard. 2a** close at hand. **2b** involving or implicating one.

baclava ('bɑːkləˌvɑː) *n* a variant spelling of **baklava**.

Bacolod ★ (bə'kɒləd) *n* a town in the Philippines, on the NW coast of Negros Island. Pop.: 343 048 (1994 est.).

bacon ('beɪkən) *n* **1** meat from the back and sides of a pig, dried, salted, and usually smoked. **2 bring home the bacon.** *Inf.* **2a** to achieve success. **2b** to provide material support. **3 save (someone's) bacon.** *Brit. inf.* to help (someone) to escape from danger. ORIG C12: from OF *bacon*, from OHG *bahho*

Bacon ★ ('beɪkən) *n* **1 Francis,** Baron Verulam, Viscount St Albans. 1561–1626, English philosopher and statesman; his works include *The Advancement of Learning* (1605) and *Novum Organum* (1620). **2 Francis.** 1909–92, Irish painter. **3 Roger.** ?1214–92, English Franciscan monk and scientist. His *Opus Majus* (1266) is a compendium of all the sciences of his age.

Baconian (beɪ'kəunɪən) *adj* **1** of or relating to Francis Bacon, the philosopher, or his inductive method of reasoning. ◆ *n* **2** a follower of Bacon's philosophy. **3** one who believes that plays attributed to Shakespeare were written by Bacon.

BACS (bæks) *n acronym for* Bankers Automated Clearing System; a method of making payments direct to a creditor's bank without using a cheque.

bacteria (bæk'tɪərɪə) *pl n, sing* **bacterium.** a large group of typically unicellular microorganisms, many of which cause disease. ORIG C19: NL, from Gk *baktērion*, from *baktron* rod, staff
▸ **bac'terial** *adj* ▸ **bac'terially** *adv*

> **USAGE NOTE** *Bacteria* is a plural noun, so the usage *a bacteria* is incorrect, though not uncommonly encountered, particularly in the media.

bactericide (bæk'tɪərɪˌsaɪd) *n* a substance able to destroy bacteria.
▸ **bac**ˌ**teri'cidal** *adj*

bacterio-, bacteri-, *or sometimes before a vowel* **bacter-** *combining form.* indicating bacteria or an action or condition relating to bacteria: *bacteriology; bactericide*.

bacteriology (bækˌtɪərɪ'ɒlədʒɪ) *n* the study of bacteria.
▸ **bacteriological** (bækˌtɪərɪə'lɒdʒɪkᵊl) *adj* ▸ **bac**ˌ**teri'ologist** *n*

bacteriophage (bæk'tɪərɪəˌfeɪdʒ) *n* a virus that is parasitic in a bacterium and destroys its host. Often shortened to **phage**.

bacterium (bæk'tɪərɪəm) *n* the singular of **bacteria**.

> **USAGE NOTE** See at **bacteria**.

Bactria ★ ('bæktrɪə) *n* an ancient country of SW Asia, between the Hindu Kush mountains and the Oxus River: forms the present Balkh region in N Afghanistan.
▸ '**Bactrian** *adj, n*

Bactrian camel *n* a two-humped camel, used in the cold deserts of central Asia.

bad[1] (bæd) *adj* **worse, worst. 1** not good; of poor quality; inadequate. **2** (often foll. by *at*) lacking skill or talent; incompetent. **3** (often foll. by *for*) harmful. **4** immoral; evil. **5** naughty; mischievous. **6** rotten; decayed: *a bad egg.* **7** severe; intense: *a bad headache.* **8** incorrect; faulty: *bad pronunciation.* **9** ill or in pain (esp. in **feel bad**). **10** sorry or upset (esp. in **feel bad about**). **11** unfavourable; distressing: *bad news.* **12** offensive; unpleasant: *bad language; bad temper.* **13** not valid or sound: *a bad cheque.* **14** not recoverable: *a bad debt.* **15** (**badder, baddest**) *Sl.* good; excellent. **16 go bad.** to putrefy; spoil. **17 in a bad way.** *Inf.* **17a** seriously ill. **17b** in trouble. **18 make the best of a bad job.** to manage as well as possible in unfavourable circumstances. **19 not bad** *or* **not so bad.** *Inf.* passable; fairly good. **20 too bad.** *Inf.* (often used dismissively) regrettable. ◆ *n* **21** unfortunate or unpleasant events (often in **take the bad with the good**). **22** an immoral or degenerate state (often in **go to the bad**). **23** the debit side of an account: *£200 to the bad.* **24 go from bad to worse.** to deteriorate even more. ◆ *adv* **25** *Not standard.* badly: *to want something bad.* ORIG C13: prob. from *bæd-*, as the first element of OE *bǣddel* hermaphrodite
▸ **'baddish** *adj* ▸ **'badness** *n*

bad[2] (bæd) *vb* a variant spelling of **bade.**

Badajoz ★ ('bædə,hɒz; *Spanish* ba'ðaxoθ) *n* a city in SW Spain: strategically positioned near the frontier with Portugal. Pop.: 130 153 (1994 est.).

Badalona ★ (*Spanish* baða'lona) *n* a port in NE Spain: an industrial suburb of Barcelona. Pop.: 219 340 (1994 est.).

bad blood *n* a feeling of intense hatred or hostility; enmity.

baddie *or* **baddy** ('bædɪ) *n, pl* **baddies.** *Inf.* a bad character in a film, etc., esp. an opponent of the hero.

bade (bæd, beɪd) *or* **bad** *vb past tense of* **bid.**

Baden ★ ('ba:dən) *n* a former state of SW Germany and West Germany, now part of Baden-Württemberg.

Baden-Baden ★ *n* a spa in SW Germany, in Baden-Württemberg. Pop.: 52 520 (1991).

Baden-Powell ★ ('beɪdᵊn'pəʊəl, -'paʊəl) *n* **Robert Stephenson Smyth** (smɪθ, smaɪθ), 1st Baron Baden-Powell. 1857–1941, British general, noted for his defence of Mafeking (1899–1900); founder of the Boy Scouts (1908) and (with his sister Agnes) the Girl Guides (1910).

Baden-Württemberg ★ *n* a state of SW Germany. Capital: Stuttgart. Pop.: 10 344 000 (1996 est.). Area: 35 742 sq. km (13 800 sq. miles).

Bader ★ ('bɑ:də) *n* Sir **Douglas.** 1910–82, British fighter pilot. Despite losing both legs, he became a national hero in World War II.

badge (bædʒ) *n* **1** a distinguishing emblem or mark worn to signify membership, employment, achievement, etc. **2** any revealing feature or mark. ORIG C14: from OF *bage*

badger ('bædʒə) *n* **1** any of various stocky omnivorous mammals occurring in Europe, Asia, and N America. They are large burrowing animals, with strong claws and a thick coat striped black and white on the head. ◆ *vb* **2** (*tr*) to pester or harass. ORIG C16: var. of *badgeard,* prob. from BADGE (from the white mark on its forehead) + -ARD

Bad Godesberg ★ (*German* ba:t 'go:dəsbɛrk) *n* the official name for **Godesberg.**

bad hair day *n Inf.* **1** a day on which one's hair is untidy and unmanageable. **2** a day of mishaps and general irritation.

badinage ('bædɪ,nɑ:ʒ) *n* playful or frivolous repartee or banter. ORIG C17: from F, from *badiner* to jest

badlands ('bæd,lændz) *pl n* any deeply eroded barren area.

Bad Lands ★ *pl n* a deeply eroded barren region of SW South Dakota and NW Nebraska.

badly ('bædlɪ) *adv* **worse, worst. 1** poorly; defectively; inadequately. **2** unfavourably; unsuccessfully: *our scheme worked out badly.* **3** severely; gravely: *badly hurt.* **4** incorrectly or inaccurately: *to speak German badly.* **5** improperly; wickedly: *to behave badly.* **6** cruelly: *to treat badly.* **7** very much (esp. in **need badly, want badly**). **8** regretfully: *he felt badly about it.* **9 badly off.** poor.

badminton ('bædmɪntən) *n* **1** a game played with rackets and a shuttlecock which is hit back and forth across a high net. **2** Also called: **badminton cup.** a long drink of claret with soda water and sugar. ORIG from *Badminton* House, Glos

Badminton ★ ('bædmɪntən) *n* a village in SW England, in Gloucestershire: site of Badminton House, seat of the Duke of Beaufort; annual horse trials.

bad-mouth *vb* (*tr*) *Sl., chiefly US & Canad.* to speak unfavourably about.

bad-tempered *adj* angry; irritable.

BAe *abbrev. for* British Aerospace.

Baedeker ('beɪdɪkə) *n* any of a series of travel guidebooks issued by the German publisher Karl Baedeker (1801–59) or his firm.

Baez ★ ('baɪez) *n* **Joan.** born 1941, US rock and folk singer.

BAF *abbrev. for* British Athletics Federation.

Baffin Bay ★ ('bæfɪn) *n* part of the Northwest Passage, situated between Baffin Island and Greenland. ORIG after William *Baffin,* 17th-century English navigator

Baffin Island ★ *n* the largest island of the Canadian Arctic, between Greenland and Hudson Bay. Area: 476 560 sq. km (184 000 sq. miles). ORIG see BAFFIN BAY

baffle ('bæfᵊl) *vb* **baffles, baffling, baffled.** (*tr*) **1** to perplex; bewilder; puzzle. **2** to frustrate (plans, efforts, etc.). **3** to check, restrain, or regulate (the flow of a fluid or the emission of sound or light). ◆ *n* **4** Also called: **baffle board, baffle plate.** a plate or mechanical device to restrain or regulate the flow of fluid, light, or sound, esp. in a loudspeaker or microphone. ORIG C16: ?from Scot. dialect *bachlen* to condemn publicly
▸ **'bafflement** *n* ▸ **'baffler** *n* ▸ **'baffling** *adj* ▸ **'bafflingly** *adv*

BAFTA ('bæftə) *n acronym for* British Academy of Film and Television Arts.

bag (bæg) *n* **1** a flexible container with an opening at one end. **2** Also: **bagful.** the contents of or amount contained in such a container. **3** a piece of portable luggage. **4** short for **handbag. 5** anything that sags, or is shaped like a bag, such as a loose fold of skin under the eyes. **6** any pouch or sac forming part of the body of an animal. **7** the quantity of quarry taken in a single hunting trip or by a single hunter. **8** *Derog. sl.* an ugly or bad-tempered woman or girl (often in **old bag**). **9 bag and baggage.** *Inf.* **9a** with all one's belongings. **9b** entirely. **10 bag of bones.** a lean creature. **11 in the bag.** *Sl.* almost assured of succeeding or being obtained. **12 rough as bags.** *Austral. sl.* **12a** uncouth. **12b** shoddy. ◆ *vb* **bags, bagging, bagged. 13** (*tr*) to put into a bag. **14** to bulge or cause to bulge. **15** (*tr*) to capture or kill, as in hunting. **16** (*tr*) to catch, seize, or steal. **17** (*intr*) to hang loosely; sag. **18** (*tr*) *Brit. & Austral. inf.* to secure the right to do or to have: *he bagged the best chair.* **19** (*tr*) to achieve or accomplish: *she bagged seven birdies.* ◆ See also **bags.** ORIG C13: prob. from ON *baggi*

bagasse (bə'gæs) *n* the dry pulp remaining after the extraction of juice from sugar cane or similar plants: used as fuel, for making fibreboard, etc. ORIG C19: from F, from Sp. *bagazo* dregs

bagatelle (,bægə'tɛl) *n* **1** something of little value. **2** a board game in which balls are struck into holes, with pins as obstacles. **3** a short light piece of music. ORIG C17: from F, from It. *bagattella,* from (dialect) *bagatta* a little possession

Bagdad ★ (bæg'dæd) *n* a variant spelling of **Baghdad.**

Bagehot ★ ('bædʒət) *n* **Walter.** 1826–77, British economist, author of *The English Constitution* (1867) and *Lombard Street* (1873).

bagel *or* **beigel** ('beɪgᵊl) *n* a hard ring-shaped bread roll. ORIG C20: from Yiddish *beygel*

baggage ('bægɪdʒ) *n* **1** suitcases, bags, etc., packed for a journey; luggage. **2** an army's portable equipment. **3** *Inf., old-fashioned.* **3a** a pert young woman. **3b** an immoral woman. **4** *Irish inf.* a cantankerous old woman. **5** *Inf.* previous knowledge and experience that a person may use

★ people and places

or be influenced by in new circumstances: *cultural baggage.* ORIG C15: from OF *bagage,* from *bague* a bundle

baggy ('bægɪ) *adj* **baggier, baggiest.** (of clothes) hanging loosely; puffed out.
▸ **'baggily** *adv* ▸ **'bagginess** *n*

Baghdad *or* **Bagdad** ★ (bæg'dæd) *n* the capital of Iraq, on the River Tigris: capital of the Abbasid Caliphate (762–1258). Pop.: 4 478 000 (1995 est.).

bag lady *n* a homeless woman who wanders city streets with all her possessions in shopping bags.

bagman ('bægmən) *n, pl* **bagmen. 1** *Brit. inf.* a travelling salesman. **2** *Sl., chiefly US.* a person who collects or distributes money for racketeers. **3** *Austral.* a tramp or swagman, esp. one on horseback. **4** *Inf., chiefly Canad.* a person who solicits money for a political party.

bagnio ('bɑːnjəʊ) *n, pl* **bagnios. 1** a brothel. **2** *Obs.* an oriental prison for slaves. **3** *Obs.* an Italian or Turkish bathhouse. ORIG C16: from It. *bagno,* from L *balneum* bath

Bagnold ★ ('bægnəʊld) *n* **Enid (Algerine).** 1889–1981, British writer; her works include the novel *National Velvet* (1935) and the play *The Chalk Garden* (1955).

bagpipes ('bæg,paɪps) *pl n* any of a family of musical wind instruments in which sounds are produced in reed pipes by air from a bag inflated either by the player's mouth or by arm-operated bellows.

bags (bægz) *pl n* **1** *Inf.* a lot. **2** *Brit. inf.* trousers. ◆ *interj* **3** Also: **bags I.** *Children's sl., Brit. & Austral.* an indication of the desire to do, be, or have something.

baguette *or* **baguet** (bæ'gɛt) *n* **1** a narrow French stick loaf. **2** a small gem cut as a long rectangle. **3** *Archit.* a small moulding having a semicircular cross section. ORIG C18: from F, from It. *bacchetta* a little stick, from *bacchio* rod

Baguio ★ ('bægɪ,əʊ) *n* a city in the N Philippines, on N Luzon: summer capital of the Republic. Pop.: 169 565 (1994 est.).

bah (bɑː, bæ) *interj* an expression of contempt or disgust.

Bahá'i (bə'hɑːɪ) *n* **1** an adherent of the Bahá'í Faith. ◆ *adj* **2** of or relating to the Bahá'í Faith. ORIG from Persian *bahā'ī,* lit.: of glory

Bahá'í Faith *or* **Bahí'í** *n* a religious system founded in 1863, based on Babism and emphasizing the value of all religions and the spiritual unity of mankind.

Bahá'ísm (bə'hɑː,ɪzəm) *n* another name, not in Bahá'í use, for the **Bahá'í Faith.**

Bahamas (bə'hɑːməz) *or* **Bahama Islands** ★ *pl n* **the.** a group of over 700 coral islands (about 20 of which are inhabited) in the Caribbean: a British colony (1783–1964); an independent nation within the Commonwealth from 1973. Language: English. Currency: Bahamian dollar. Capital: Nassau. Pop.: 297 000 (1999 est.). Area: 13 939 sq. km (5381 sq. miles).
▸ **Bahamian** (bə'heɪmɪən, -'hɑː-) *adj, n*

Bahawalpur ★ (,bæhə'wɒlpə) *n* an industrial city in Pakistan: cotton, soap. Pop.: 180 000 (latest est.).

Bahia ★ (bə'hiːə; *Portuguese* bə'iːə) *n* **1** a state of E Brazil, on the Atlantic coast. Capital: Salvador. Pop.: 12 541 675 (1996). Area: about 562 000 sq. km (217 000 sq. miles). **2** the former name of **San Salvador.**

Bahía Blanca ★ (*Spanish* ba'ia 'blanka) *n* a port in E Argentina. Pop.: 260 096 (1991).

Bahia de los Cochinos ★ (ba'ia de los ko'tʃinos) *n* the Spanish name for the **Bay of Pigs.**

Bahrain *or* **Bahrein** ★ (bɑː'reɪn) *n* an independent sheikhdom on the Persian Gulf, consisting of several islands: under British protection until the declaration of independence in 1971. It has large oil reserves. Language: Arabic. Religion: Muslim. Currency: dinar. Capital: Manama. Pop.: 646 000 (1999 est.). Area: 678 sq. km (262 sq. miles).
▸ **Bah'raini** *or* **Bah'reini** *adj, n*

Baikal ★ (baɪ'kɑːl, -'kæl) *n* **Lake.** a lake in Russia, in SE Siberia: the largest freshwater lake in Eurasia and the deepest in the world. Greatest depth: over 1500 m (5000 ft). Area: about 33 670 sq. km (13 000 sq. miles).

bail[1] (beɪl) *Law.* ◆ *n* **1** a sum of money by which a person is bound to take responsibility for the appearance in court of another person or himself, forfeited if the person fails to appear. **2** the person or persons so binding themselves; surety. **3** the system permitting release of a person from custody where such security has been taken: *he was released on bail.* **4 jump bail** *or* (*formal*) **forfeit bail.** to fail to appear in court to answer to a charge. **5 stand** *or* **go bail.** to act as surety (for someone). ◆ *vb* (*tr*) **6** (often foll. by *out*) to release or obtain the release of (a person) from custody, security having been made. ORIG C14: from OF: custody, from *baillier* to hand over, from L *bājulāre* to carry burdens

bail[2] *or* **bale** (beɪl) *vb* **bails, bailing, bailed** *or* **bales, baling, baled.** (often foll. by *out*) to remove (water) from (a boat). See also **bail out.** ORIG C13: from OF *baille* bucket, from L *bājulus* carrier
▸ **'bailer** *or* **'baler** *n*

bail[3] (beɪl) *n* **1** *Cricket.* either of two small wooden bars across the tops of the stumps. **2** a partition between stalls in a stable or barn. **3** *Austral. & NZ.* a framework in a cowshed used to secure the head of a cow during milking. **4** a movable bar on a typewriter that holds the paper against the platen. ◆ *vb* **5** See **bail up.** ORIG C18: from OF *baile* stake, fortification, prob. from L *baculum* stick

bail[4] *or* **bale** (beɪl) *n* the semicircular handle of a kettle, bucket, etc. ORIG C15: prob. of Scand. origin

bailey ('beɪlɪ) *n* the outermost wall or court of a castle. ORIG C13: from OF *baille* enclosed court, from *bailler* to enclose

Bailey ★ ('beɪlɪ) *n* **1 David.** born 1938, British photographer. **2 Nathan** *or* **Nathaniel.** died 1742, British lexicographer.

Bailey bridge ('beɪlɪ) *n* a temporary bridge made of prefabricated steel parts that can be rapidly assembled. ORIG C20: after Sir Donald Coleman *Bailey* (1901–85), its Brit. designer

bailie ('beɪlɪ) *n* (in Scotland) a municipal magistrate. ORIG C13: from OF *bailli,* from earlier *baillif* BAILIFF

bailiff ('beɪlɪf) *n* **1** *Brit.* the agent of a landlord or landowner. **2** a sheriff's officer who serves writs and summonses, makes arrests, and ensures that the sentences of the court are carried out. **3** *Chiefly Brit.* (formerly) a high official having judicial powers. **4** *Chiefly US.* an official having custody of prisoners appearing in court. ORIG C13: from OF *baillif,* from *bail* custody; see BAIL[1]

bailiwick ('beɪlɪwɪk) *n* **1** *Law.* the area over which a bailiff has jurisdiction. **2** a person's special field of interest. ORIG C15: from BAILIE + WICK[2]

bail out *or* **bale out** *vb* (*adv*) **1** (*intr*) to make an emergency parachute jump from an aircraft. **2** (*tr*) *Inf.* to help (a person, organization, etc.) out of a predicament.

bail up *vb* (*adv*) **1** *Austral. & NZ.* to confine (a cow) or (of a cow) to be confined by the head in a bail. See **bail**[3] (sense 3). **2** (*tr*) *Austral.* (of a bushranger) to hold under guard in order to rob. **3** (*intr*) *Austral.* to submit to robbery without offering resistance. **4** (*tr*) *Austral. inf.* to accost or detain, esp. in conversation.

Bainbridge ★ ('beɪn,brɪdʒ) *n* Dame **Beryl.** born 1934, British writer. Her novels include *The Dressmaker* (1973), *Injury Time* (1977), *Every Man for Himself* (1996), and *Master Georgie* (1998); plays include *It's a Lovely Day Tomorrow* (1977).

bain-marie *French.* (bɛ̃mari) *n, pl* ***bains-marie*** (bɛ̃mari). a vessel for holding hot water, in which sauces and other dishes are gently cooked or kept warm. ORIG C19: from F, from Med. L *balneum Mariae,* lit.: bath of Mary, inaccurate translation of Med. Gk *kaminos Marios,* lit.: furnace of *Miriam,* alleged author of a treatise on alchemy

Bairam (baɪ'ræm, 'baɪræm) *n* either of two Muslim festivals, one (**Lesser Bairam**) at the end of Ramadan, the other (**Greater Bairam**) at the end of the Islamic year. ORIG from Turkish *bayrām*

Baird ★ (bɛəd) *n* **John Logie** ('ləʊgɪ). 1888–1946, Scottish engineer: inventor of a television system, later replaced.

bairn (bɛən) *n Scot. & N English.* a child. ORIG OE *bearn*

bait[1] (beɪt) *n* **1** something edible fixed to a hook or in a trap to attract fish or animals. **2** an enticement; temptation. **3** a variant spelling of **bate**[3]. **4** *Arch.* a short stop for refreshment during a journey. ◆ *vb* **5** (*tr*) to put a piece of food on or in (a hook or trap). **6** (*tr*) to persecute or tease. **7** (*tr*) to entice; tempt. **8** (*tr*) to set dogs upon (a bear, etc.). **9** (*intr*) *Arch.* to stop for rest and refreshment during a journey. ORIG C13: from ON *beita* to hunt

> **USAGE NOTE** The phrase *with bated breath* is sometimes wrongly spelled *with baited breath.* The correct spelling may be more easily recalled if it is remembered that *bated* in this phrase is related to *abate.*

bait[2] (beɪt) *vb* a variant spelling of **bate**[2].

baize (beɪz) *n* a woollen fabric resembling felt, usually green, used mainly for the tops of billiard tables. ORIG C16: from OF *baies,* pl. of *baie* baize, from *bai* reddish brown, BAY[5]

Baja ('bæhə) **California Norte** ★ ('nɔː teɪ) *n* **1** a state of NW Mexico, in the N part of the Lower California peninsula. Capital: Mexicali. Pop.: 2 241 029 (1997 est.). Area: about 71 500 sq. km (27 600 sq. miles). **2** the Spanish name for **Lower California (North).**

Baja California Sur ★ *n* a state of NW Mexico, in the S part of the Lower California peninsula. Capital: La Paz. Pop.: 387 430 (1997 est.). Area: 73 475 sq. km (28 363 sq. miles).

bake (beɪk) *vb* **bakes, baking, baked. 1** (*tr*) to cook by dry heat as in an oven. **2** (*intr*) to cook bread, pastry, etc. **3** to make or become hardened by heat. **4** (*intr*) *Inf.* to be extremely hot. ◆ *n* **5** a batch of things baked at one time. **6** *Caribbean.* a small flat fried cake. ORIG OE *bacan*

bakeapple ('beɪkˌæpᵊl) *n Canad.* the fruit of the cloudberry.

baked Alaska (əˈlæskə) *n* a dessert made of cake and ice cream covered with meringue and cooked very quickly.

baked beans *pl n* haricot beans, baked and tinned in tomato sauce.

Bakelite ('beɪkəˌlaɪt) *n Trademark.* any one of a class of thermosetting resins used as electric insulators and for making plastic ware, etc. ORIG C20: after L. H. *Baekeland* (1863–1944), Belgian-born US inventor

baker ('beɪkə) *n* a person whose business or employment is to make or sell bread, cakes, etc.

Baker ★ ('beɪkə) *n* **1** Sir **Benjamin.** 1840–1907, British engineer who, with Sir John Fowler, designed much of the London underground railway and the first Aswan Dam. **2 James (Addison).** born 1930, US Republican politician; Secretary of State (1989–92). **3** Dame **Janet.** born 1933, British mezzo-soprano. **4** Sir **Samuel White.** 1821–93, British explorer: discovered Lake Albert (1864).

baker's dozen *n* thirteen. ORIG C16: from the bakers' former practice of giving thirteen rolls where twelve were requested, to protect themselves against accusations of giving light weight

bakery ('beɪkərɪ) *n, pl* **bakeries. 1** a room or building equipped for baking. **2** a shop in which bread, cakes, etc., are sold.

Bakewell ★ ('beɪkwel) *n* **Robert.** 1725–95, British agriculturist; radically improved livestock breeding.

Bakhtaran ★ (ˌbæktəˈrɑːn, -ˈræn) *n* a city in W Iran, in the valley of the Qareh Su: oil refinery. Pop.: 624 084 (1991). Former name (until 1987): **Kermanshah.**

baking powder *n* a powdered mixture that contains sodium bicarbonate and one or more acidic compounds, such as cream of tartar: used in baking as a raising agent.

bakkie ('bʌkiː) *n S. African.* a small truck with an open body and low sides. ORIG C20: from Afrik. *bak* container

baklava *or* **baclava** ('bɑːkləˌvɑː) *n* a rich cake consisting of thin layers of pastry filled with nuts and honey. ORIG from Turkish

baksheesh *or* **backsheesh** ('bækʃiːʃ) *n* (in some Eastern countries, esp. formerly) money given as a tip, a present, or alms. ORIG C17: from Persian *bakhshīsh,* from *bakhshīdan* to give

Bakst ★ (*Russian* bakst) *n* **Leon Nikolayevich** (lɪˈɔn nikaˈlajɪvitʃ). 1866–1924, Russian painter and stage designer, noted particularly for his richly coloured sets for Diaghilev's *Ballet Russe* (1909–21).

Baku ★ (*Russian* baˈku) *n* the capital of Azerbaijan, a port on the Caspian Sea: important for its extensive oilfields. Pop.: 1 739 900 (1995 est.).

Bakunin ★ (*Russian* baˈkunin) *n* **Mikhail** (mixaˈil). 1814–76, Russian anarchist and writer: a prominent member of the First International, expelled from it after conflicts with Marx.

bal. *Book-keeping. abbrev. for* balance.

Bala ★ ('bælə) *n* **Lake.** a narrow lake in Gwynedd: the largest natural lake in Wales. Length: 6 km (4 miles).

Balaam ★ ('beɪlæm) *n Old Testament.* a Mesopotamian diviner who, when summoned to curse the Israelites, prophesied future glories for them instead, after being reproached by his ass (Numbers 22–23).

Balaclava *or* **Balaclava helmet** (ˌbæləˈklɑːvə) *n* (*often not caps.*) a close-fitting woollen hood that covers the ears and neck, as originally worn by soldiers in the Crimean War. ORIG C19: from BALAKLAVA

Balakirev ★ (*Russian* baˈlakirɪf) *n* **Mily Alexeyevich** ('milij alɪkˈsjejɪvitʃ). 1837–1910, Russian composer, whose works include two symphonic poems and two symphonies.

Balaklava *or* **Balaclava** ★ (ˌbæləˈklɑːvə; *Russian* bəlaˈklavə) *n* a small port in Ukraine, in S Crimea: scene of an inconclusive battle (1854), which included the charge of the Light Brigade, during the Crimean War.

balalaika (ˌbæləˈlaɪkə) *n* a Russian plucked musical instrument, usually having a triangular body and three strings. ORIG C18: from Russian

balance ('bæləns) *n* **1** a weighing device, generally consisting of a horizontal beam pivoted at its centre, from the ends of which two pans are suspended. The substance to be weighed is placed in one pan and weights are placed in the other until the beam returns to the horizontal. **2** a state of equilibrium. **3** something that brings about such a state. **4** equilibrium of the body; steadiness: *to lose one's balance.* **5** emotional stability. **6** harmony in the parts of a whole. **7** the act of weighing factors, quantities, etc., against each other. **8** the power to influence or control: *the balance of power.* **9** something that remains: *the balance of what you owe.* **10** *Accounting.* **10a** equality of debit and credit totals in an account. **10b** a difference between such totals. **11 in the balance.** in an uncertain or undecided condition. **12 on balance.** after weighing up all the factors. **13 strike a balance.** to make a compromise. ◆ *vb* **balances, balancing, balanced. 14** (*tr*) to weigh in or as if in a balance. **15** (*intr*) to be or come into equilibrium. **16** (*tr*) to bring into or hold in equilibrium. **17** (*tr*) to compare the relative weight, importance, etc., of. **18** (*tr*) to be equal to. **19** (*tr*) to arrange so as to create a state of harmony. **20** (*tr*) *Accounting.* **20a** to compare the credit and debit totals of (an account). **20b** to equalize the credit and debit totals of (an account) by making certain entries. **20c** to settle or adjust (an account) by paying any money due. **21** (*intr*) (of a balance sheet, etc.) to have the debit and credit totals equal. ORIG C13: from OF, from Vulgar L *bilancia* (unattested), from LL *bilanx* having two scales, from BI- + *lanx* scale
▸ **'balanceable** *adj* ▸ **'balancer** *n*

Balance ('bæləns) *n* **the.** the constellation Libra, the seventh sign of the zodiac.

balance of payments *n* the difference over a given time between total payments to foreign nations and total receipts from foreign nations.

balance of power *n* the distribution of power among countries so that no one nation can seriously threaten another.

balance of trade *n* the difference in value between total exports and total imports of goods.

balance sheet *n* a statement that shows the financial position of a business by listing the asset balances and the claims on such assets.

balance wheel *n* a wheel oscillating against the hairspring of a timepiece, regulating its beat.

Balanchine ★ ('bælən,tʃi:n, ,bælən'tʃi:n) *n* **George.** 1904–83, US choreographer, born in Russia.

balata ('bælətə) *n* **1** a tropical American tree, yielding a latex-like sap. **2** a rubber-like gum obtained from this sap: a substitute for gutta-percha. ORIG from American Sp., of Carib origin

Balaton ★ (*Hungarian* 'bɔlɔton) *n* **Lake.** a large shallow lake in W Hungary. Area: 689 sq. km (266 sq. miles).

Balboa¹ ★ (bæl'bəʊə; *Spanish* bal'βoa) *n* **Vasco Núñez de** ('basko 'nuɲeθ de). ?1475–1519, Spanish explorer, who discovered the Pacific Ocean in 1513.

Balboa² ★ (bæl'bəʊə; *Spanish* bal'βoa) *n* a port in Panama at the Pacific end of the Panama Canal: the administrative centre of the former Canal Zone. Pop.: 2750 (1990).

Balcon ★ ('bɔ:lkən) *n* Sir **Michael.** 1896–1977, British film producer; his Ealing Studio films include *Kind Hearts and Coronets* (1949).

balcony ('bælkənɪ) *n, pl* **balconies. 1** a platform projecting from a building with a balustrade along its outer edge, often with access from a door or window. **2** a gallery in a theatre, above the dress circle. **3** *US & Canad.* any circle in a theatre. ORIG C17: from It. *balcone,* prob. from OHG *balko* beam
▸ **'balconied** *adj*

bald (bɔ:ld) *adj* **1** having no hair or fur, esp. (of a man) having no hair on the scalp. **2** lacking natural growth or covering. **3** plain or blunt: *a bald statement.* **4** bare or unadorned. **5** Also: **baldfaced.** (of birds and animals) having white markings on the head and face. **6** (of a tyre) having a worn tread. ORIG C14 *ballede* (lit.: having a white spot)
▸ **'baldish** *adj* ▸ **'baldly** *adv* ▸ **'baldness** *n*

baldachin *or* **baldaquin** ('bɔ:ldəkɪn) *n* **1** a richly ornamented brocade. **2** a canopy over an altar, shrine, or throne or carried in Christian religious processions over an object of veneration. ORIG OE *baldekin,* from It. *baldacchino,* lit.: stuff from Baghdad

bald eagle *n* a large eagle of North America, having a white head and tail. It is the US national bird.

Balder ★ ('bɔ:ldə) *n Norse myth.* a god, son of Odin and Frigg, noted for his beauty and sweet nature. He was killed by a bough of mistletoe thrown by the blind god Höd, misled by the malicious Loki.

balderdash ('bɔ:ldə,dæʃ) *n* stupid or illogical talk; senseless rubbish. ORIG C16: from ?

balding ('bɔ:ldɪŋ) *adj* somewhat bald or becoming bald.

baldric ('bɔ:ldrɪk) *n* a sash or belt worn over the right shoulder to the left hip for carrying a sword, etc. ORIG C13: from OF *baudrei,* of Frankish origin

Baldwin ★ ('bɔ:ldwɪn) *n* **1 James (Arthur).** 1924–87, US writer, whose works include the novel *Go Tell it on the Mountain* (1954). **2 Stanley,** 1st Earl Baldwin of Bewdley. 1867–1947, British Conservative statesman: prime minister (1923–24, 1924–29, 1935–37).

Baldwin I ★ *n* 1058–1118, crusader and first king of Jerusalem (1100–18), who captured Acre (1104), Beirut (1109), and Sidon (1110).

baldy ('bɔ:ldɪ) *Inf.* ◆ *adj* **1** bald. ◆ *n, pl* **baldies. 2** a bald person.

bale¹ (beɪl) *n* **1** a large bundle, package, or carton of goods bound by ropes, wires, etc., for storage or transportation. **2** *US.* 500 pounds of cotton. ◆ *vb* **bales, baling, baled. 3** to make (hay, etc.) or put (goods) into a bale or bales. ORIG C14: prob. from OF *bale,* from OHG *balla* BALL¹

bale² (beɪl) *n Arch.* **1** evil; injury. **2** woe; suffering; pain. ORIG OE *bealu*

bale³ (beɪl) *vb* a variant spelling of **bail²**.

bale⁴ (beɪl) *n* a variant spelling of **bail⁴**.

Bâle ★ (bɑl) *n* the French name for **Basel.**

Balearic Islands ★ (,bælɪ'ærɪk) *pl n* a group of islands in the W Mediterranean, consisting of Majorca, Minorca, Ibiza, Formentera, Cabrera, and 11 islets: a province of Spain. Capital: Palma, on Majorca. Pop.: 736 865 (1994 est.). Area: 5012 sq. km (1935 sq. miles). Spanish name: **Baleares** (bale'ares).

baleen (bə'li:n) *n* whalebone. ORIG C14: from L *bālaena* whale

baleen whale *n* another name for **whalebone whale.**

baleful ('beɪlfʊl) *adj* harmful, menacing, or vindictive.
▸ **'balefully** *adv* ▸ **'balefulness** *n*

Balenciaga ★ (*Spanish* balen'θjaɣa) *n* **Cristóbal** (kris'toβal). 1895–1972, Spanish couturier.

baler ('beɪlə) *n* a machine for making bales of hay, etc. Also called: **baling machine.**

Balfour ★ ('bælfɔ:, -fə, -fʊə) *n* **Arthur James,** 1st Earl of Balfour. 1848–1930, British Conservative statesman: prime minister (1902–05); foreign secretary (1916–19).

Bali ★ ('bɑ:lɪ) *n* an island in Indonesia, east of Java: mountainous, rising over 3000 m (10 000 ft). Capital: Denpasar. Pop.: 2 902 200 (1995 est.). Area: 5558 sq. km (2146 sq. miles).
▸ **,Bali'nese** *adj, n*

Balikpapan ★ (,bɑ:lɪk'pɑ:pɑ:n) *n* a city in Indonesia, on the SE coast of Borneo. Pop.: 416 200 (1995 est.).

Baliol *or* **Balliol** ★ ('beɪlɪəl) *n* **1 Edward.** ?1283–1364, king of Scotland (1332, 1333–56). **2 John.** 1249–1315, king of Scotland (1292–96): imprisoned by Edward I (1296).

balk *or* **baulk** (bɔ:k, bɔ:lk) *vb* **1** (*intr;* usually foll. by *at*) to stop short; jib: *the horse balked at the jump.* **2** (*intr;* foll. by *at*) to recoil: *he balked at the idea of murder.* **3** (*tr*) to thwart, check, or foil: *he was balked in his plans.* ◆ *n* **4** a roughly squared heavy timber beam. **5** a timber tie beam of a roof. **6** an unploughed ridge between furrows. **7** an obstacle; hindrance; disappointment. **8** *Baseball.* an illegal motion by a pitcher. ◆ See also **baulk.** ORIG OE *balca*

Balkan ('bɔ:lkən) *adj* of, denoting, or relating to the Balkan States or their inhabitants, the Balkan Peninsula, or the Balkan Mountains.

Balkan Mountains ★ *pl n* a mountain range extending across Bulgaria from the Black Sea to the western border. Highest peak: Mount Botev, 2376 m (7793 ft).

Balkan Peninsula ★ *n* a large peninsula in SE Europe, between the Adriatic and Aegean Seas.

Balkan States ★ *pl n* the countries of the Balkan Peninsula: the former Yugoslav Republic, Romania, Bulgaria, Albania, Greece, and the European part of Turkey. Also called: **the Balkans.**

Balkh ★ (bɑ:lk) *n* a region of N Afghanistan, corresponding to ancient Bactria. Chief town: Mazar-i-Sharif.

Balkhash ★ (*Russian* bal'xaʃ) *n* **Lake.** a salt lake in SE Kazakhstan. Area: about 18 000 sq. km (7000 sq. miles).

balky *or* **baulky** ('bɔ:kɪ, 'bɔ:lkɪ) *adj* **balkier, balkiest** *or* **baulkier, baulkiest.** inclined to stop abruptly and unexpectedly: *a balky horse.*

ball¹ (bɔ:l) *n* **1** a spherical or nearly spherical body or mass. **2** a round or roundish body, of a size and composition suitable for any of various games. **3** a ball propelled in a particular way: *a high ball.* **4** any rudimentary game with a ball: *to play ball.* **5** a single delivery of the ball in cricket and other games. **6a** a solid nonexplosive projectile for a firearm, cannon, etc. **6b** such projectiles collectively. **7** any more or less rounded part: *the ball of the foot.* **8 ball of muscle.** *Austral.* a very strong, fit person. **9 have the ball at one's feet.** to have the chance of doing something. **10 keep the ball rolling.** to maintain the progress of a project, plan, etc. **11 on the ball.** *Inf.* alert; informed. **12 play ball.** *Inf.* to cooperate. **13 set** *or* **start the ball rolling.** to initiate an action, discussion, etc. ◆ *vb* **14** to make, form, wind, gather, etc., into a ball or balls. ◆ See also **balls, balls-up.** ORIG C13: from ON *böllr*

ball² (bɔ:l) *n* **1** a social function for dancing, esp. one that is lavish or formal. **2** *Inf.* a very enjoyable time (esp. in **have a ball**). ORIG C17: from F *bal* (n), from OF *baller* (vb), from LL *ballāre* to dance

Ball ★ (bɔ:l) *n* **John.** died 1381, English priest: executed as one of the leaders of the Peasants' Revolt (1381).

ballad ('bæləd) *n* **1** a narrative song with a recurrent refrain. **2** a narrative poem in short stanzas of popular origin. **3** a slow sentimental song, esp. a pop song. ORIG C15: from OF *balade,* from OProvençal *balada* song accompanying a dance

ballade (bæ'lɑːd) *n* **1** *Prosody.* a verse form consisting of three stanzas and an envoy, all ending with the same line. **2** *Music.* an instrumental composition based on or intended to evoke a narrative.

balladeer (ˌbælə'dɪə) *n* a singer of ballads.

Ballance ★ ('bæləns) *n* **John.** 1839–93, New Zealand statesman, born in Northern Ireland: prime minister (1891–93).

ball-and-socket joint *n Anat.* a joint in which a rounded head fits into a rounded cavity, allowing a wide range of movement.

Ballarat ★ ('bæləˌræt, ˌbælə'ræt) *n* a town in SE Australia, in S central Victoria: originally a gold-mining region. Pop.: 64 980 (1991).

Ballard ★ ('bælɑːd) *n* **J(ames) G(raham).** born 1930, British novelist, born in China; his books include *Crash* (1973), *Empire of the Sun* (1984), and *Cocaine Nights* (1996).

ballast ('bæləst) *n* **1** any heavy material used to stabilize a vessel, esp. one that is not carrying cargo. **2** crushed rock, broken stone, etc., used for the foundation of a road or railway track or in making concrete. **3** anything that provides stability or weight. **4** *Electronics.* a device for maintaining the current in a circuit. ◆ *vb* (*tr*) **5** to give stability or weight to. ORIG C16: prob. from Low G

ball bearing *n* **1** a bearing consisting of steel balls rolling between a metal sleeve fitted over the rotating shaft and an outer sleeve held in the bearing housing, so reducing friction. **2** a metal ball, esp. one used in such a bearing.

ball boy *or* (*fem*) **ball girl** *n* (esp. in tennis) a person who retrieves balls that go out of play.

ballbreaker ('bɔːlˌbreɪkə) *n Sl.* someone, esp. a woman, whose behaviour may be regarded as threatening a man's sense of power. ORIG C20: from BALLS (in the sense: testicles) + BREAKER

ball cock *n* a device for regulating the flow of a liquid into a tank, cistern, etc., consisting of a floating ball mounted at one end of an arm and a valve on the other end that opens and closes as the ball falls and rises.

ballerina (ˌbælə'riːnə) *n* a female ballet dancer. ORIG C18: from It., fem of *ballerino* dancing master, from *ballare* to dance

Ballesteros ★ (ˌbælɛ'stɛrɒs; *Spanish* baʎes'terɔs) *n* **Severiano** (sevɛ'rjano). born 1957, Spanish professional golfer: won the British Open Championship (1979; 1984; 1988).

ballet ('bæleɪ, bæ'leɪ) *n* **1** a classical style of expressive dancing based on precise conventional steps. **2** a theatrical representation of a story or theme performed by ballet dancers. **3** a troupe of ballet dancers. **4** music written for a ballet. ORIG C17: from F, from It. *balletto,* lit.: a little dance, from *ballare* to dance
▸ **balletic** (bæ'lɛtɪk) *adj*

balletomane ('bælɪtəʊˌmeɪn) *n* a ballet enthusiast.

balletomania (ˌbælɪtəʊ'meɪnɪə) *n* passionate enthusiasm for ballet.

ball game *n* **1** any game played with a ball. **2** *US & Canad.* a game of baseball. **3** *Inf.* a situation; state of affairs (esp. in **a whole new ball game**).

Balliol ★ ('beɪlɪəl) *n* See **Baliol.**

ballista (bə'lɪstə) *n, pl* **ballistae** (-tiː). an ancient catapult for hurling stones, etc. ORIG C16: from L, ult. from Gk *ballein* to throw

ballistic (bə'lɪstɪk) *adj* **1** of or relating to ballistics. **2** denoting or relating to the flight of projectiles moving under their own momentum and the force of gravity. **3** (of a measurement or measuring instrument) depending on a brief impulse or current that causes a movement related to the quantity to be measured: *a ballistic pendulum.* **4 go ballistic.** *Inf.* to become enraged or frenziedly violent.
▸ **bal'listically** *adv*

ballistic missile *n* a missile that has no wings or fins and that follows a ballistic trajectory when its propulsive power is discontinued.

ballistics (bə'lɪstɪks) *n* (*functioning as sing*) **1** the study of the flight dynamics of projectiles. **2** the study of the effects of firing on firearms and their projectiles.

ball lightning *n Meteorol.* a luminous ball occasionally seen during electrical storms.

ballocks ('bɒləks) *pl n, interj* a variant spelling of **bollocks.**

ball of fire *n Inf.* a very lively person.

balloon (bə'luːn) *n* **1** an inflatable rubber bag used as a plaything or party decoration. **2** a large bag inflated with a lighter-than-air gas, designed to rise and float in the atmosphere. It may have a basket or gondola for carrying passengers, etc. **3** an outline containing the words or thoughts of a character in a cartoon. **4** a large rounded brandy glass. **5** *Commerce.* **5a** a large sum paid as an irregular instalment of a loan repayment. **5b** (*as modifier*): *a balloon loan.* **6** *Surgery.* **6a** an inflatable plastic tube used for dilating obstructed blood vessels or parts of the alimentary canal. **6b** (*as modifier*): *balloon angioplasty.* **7 go down like a lead balloon.** to prove unsuccessful or unpopular; fail: *the suggestion that the chairman should get a 77% pay rise went down like a lead balloon.* **8 when the balloon goes up.** *Inf.* when the action starts. ◆ *vb* **9** (*intr*) to go up or fly in a balloon. **10** to inflate or be inflated: *the wind ballooned the sails.* **11** (*intr*) to increase or expand significantly and rapidly: *losses ballooned to £278 million.* **12** (*tr*) *Brit.* to propel (a ball) high into the air. ORIG C16 (in the sense: ball, ball game): from It. dialect *ballone*
▸ **bal'loonist** *n* ▸ **bal'loon-ˌlike** *adj*

balloon loan *n* a loan in respect of which interest and capital are paid off in instalments at regular intervals.

ballot ('bælət) *n* **1** the practice of selecting a representative, course of action, etc., by submitting the options to a vote of all qualified persons. **2** an instance of voting, usually in secret. **3** a list of candidates standing for office. **4** the number of votes cast in an election. ◆ *vb* **ballots, balloting, balloted. 5** to vote or elicit a vote from: *we balloted the members on this issue.* **6** (*tr;* usually foll. by *for*) to vote for or decide on by lot or ballot. ORIG C16: from It. *ballotta,* lit.: a little ball

ballot box *n* a box into which ballot papers are dropped after voting.

ballotini (ˌbælə'tiːnɪ) *pl n* small glass beads used in reflective paints. ORIG C20: from Italian *ballotini* small balls

ballot paper *n* a paper used for voting.

ballpark ('bɔːlˌpɑːk) *n* **1** *US & Canad.* a stadium used for baseball games. **2** *Inf.* **2a** approximate range: *in the right ballpark.* **2b** (*as modifier*): *a ballpark figure.* **3** *Inf.* a situation; state of affairs: *it's a whole new ballpark.*

ball-peen hammer *n* a hammer with one end of the head rounded for beating metal.

ballpoint *or* **ballpoint pen** ('bɔːlˌpɔɪnt) *n* a pen having a small ball bearing as a writing point.

ballroom ('bɔːlˌruːm, -ˌrʊm) *n* a large hall for dancing.

ballroom dancing *n* social dancing, popular since the beginning of the 20th century, to dances in conventional rhythms (**ballroom dances**).

balls (bɔːlz) *Taboo sl.* ◆ *pl n* **1** the testicles. **2** nonsense; rubbish. **3** courage; determination. ◆ *interj* **4** an exclamation of disagreement, contempt, etc.

balls-up *Taboo sl.* ◆ *n* **1** something botched or muddled. ◆ *vb* **balls up. 2** (*tr, adv*) to muddle or botch.

ballsy ('bɔːlzɪ) *adj* **ballsier, ballsiest.** *Sl., chiefly US.* showing courage or determination; bold. ORIG C20: from BALLS (sense 3) + -Y[1]
▸ **'ballsiness** *n*

bally ('bælɪ) *adj, adv* (intensifier) *Brit. sl.* a euphemistic word for **bloody** (sense 5).

ballyhoo (ˌbælɪ'huː) *Inf.* ◆ *n* **1** a noisy, confused, or nonsensical situation. **2** sensational or blatant advertising or publicity. ◆ *vb* **ballyhoos, ballyhooing, ballyhooed. 3** (*tr*) *Chiefly US.* to advertise by sensational or blatant methods. ORIG C19: from ?

Ballymena ★ (ˌbælɪ'miːnə) *n* a district in central Northern Ireland: agriculture, textiles. Pop.: 56 641 (1991). Area: 634 sq. km (247 sq. miles).

Ballymoney ★ (ˌbælɪ'mʌnɪ) *n* a district of N Northern Ireland: agriculture. Pop.: 24 198 (1991). Area: 418 sq. km (161 sq. miles).

balm (bɑːm) *n* **1** any of various oily aromatic substances obtained from certain tropical trees and used for healing and soothing. See also **balsam** (sense 1). **2** any plant yielding such a substance, esp. the balm of Gilead. **3** something comforting or soothing. **4** Also called: **lemon balm.** an aromatic Eurasian plant, having clusters of small fragrant white flowers. **5** a pleasant odour. ORIG C13: from OF *basme,* from L *balsamum* BALSAM

Balmain ★ (*French* balmɛ̃) *n* **Pierre Alexandre** (pjer alɛksɑ̃drə). 1914–82, French couturier.

balm of Gilead (ˈgɪlɪˌæd) *n* **1** any of several trees of Africa and W Asia that yield a fragrant oily resin. **2** the resin exuded by these trees. **3** a North American poplar tree. **4** a fragrant resin obtained from the balsam fir.

Balmoral[1] (bælˈmɒrəl) *n* (*sometimes not cap.*) **1** a laced walking shoe. **2** a Scottish brimless hat usually with a cockade and plume. ORIG from BALMORAL Castle

Balmoral[2] ★ (bælˈmɒrəl) *n* a castle in NE Scotland, in SW Aberdeenshire: a private residence of the British sovereign.

balmy (ˈbɑːmɪ) *adj* **balmier, balmiest. 1** (of weather) mild and pleasant. **2** having the qualities of balm; fragrant or soothing. **3** a variant spelling of **barmy.**
▸ **ˈbalmily** *adv* ▸ **ˈbalminess** *n*

balneology (ˌbælnɪˈɒlədʒɪ) *n* the branch of medical science concerned with the therapeutic value of baths, esp. with natural mineral waters. ORIG C19: from L *balneum* bath
▸ **balneological** (ˌbælnɪəˈlɒdʒɪkᵊl) *adj* ▸ **ˌbalneˈologist** *n*

baloney *or* **boloney** (bəˈləʊnɪ) *n Inf.* foolish talk; nonsense. ORIG C20: from *Bologna* (sausage)

BALPA (ˈbælpə) *n acronym for* British Airline Pilots' Association.

balsa (ˈbɔːlsə) *n* **1** a tree of tropical America. **2** Also called: **balsawood.** the very light wood of this tree, used for making rafts, etc. **3** a light raft. ORIG C18: from Sp.: raft

balsam (ˈbɔːlsəm) *n* **1** any of various fragrant oleoresins, such as balm, obtained from any of several trees and shrubs and used as a base for medicines and perfumes. **2** any of various similar substances used as ointments. **3** any of certain aromatic resinous turpentines. See **Canada balsam. 4** any plant yielding balsam. **5** Also called: **busy Lizzie.** any of several plants of the genus *Impatiens.* **6** anything healing or soothing. ORIG C15: from L *balsamum,* from Gk *balsamon,* from Heb. *bāśām* spice
▸ **balsamic** (bɔːlˈsæmɪk) *adj*

balsam fir *n* a fir tree of NE North America, that yields Canada balsam.

Balthazar ★ (ˈbælθəˌzɑː, bælˈθæzə) *n* one of the Magi, the others being Caspar and Melchior.

Balthus ★ (*French* baltys) *n* real name *Balthasar Klossowski de Rola.* 1908–2001, French painter of Polish descent.

balti (ˈbɔːltɪ, ˈbæltɪ) *n* **a** a spicy Indian dish, stewed until most of the liquid has evaporated, and served in a woklike pot. **b** (*as modifier*): *a balti house.* ORIG C20: from ?

Baltic (ˈbɔːltɪk) *adj* **1** denoting or relating to the Baltic Sea or the Baltic states. **2** of or characteristic of Baltic as a group of languages. ◆ *n* **3** a branch of the Indo-European family of languages consisting of Lithuanian, Latvian, and Old Prussian. **4** Also called: **Baltic Exchange.** a commodity and freight-chartering market in the City of London.

Baltics ★ (ˈbɔːltɪks) *pl n* **the.** another name for the **Baltic States.**

Baltic Sea ★ *n* a sea in N Europe, connected with the North Sea by the Skaggerak, Kattegat, and Öresund; shallow, with low salinity and small tides.

Baltic Shield ★ *n* the wide area of ancient rock in Scandinavia. Also called: **Scandinavian Shield.** See **shield** (sense 6).

Baltic States ★ *pl n* the independent republics of Estonia, Latvia, and Lithuania; constituent republics of the Soviet Union (1940–91). Sometimes shortened to **Baltics.**

Baltimore[1] ★ (ˈbɔːltɪˌmɔː) *n* a port in N Maryland, on Chesapeake Bay. Pop.: 702 979 (1994 est.).

Baltimore[2] ★ (ˈbɔːltɪˌmɔː) *n* **1 David.** born 1938, US molecular biologist: shared the Nobel prize for physiology or medicine (1975) for his discovery of reverse transcriptase. **2 Lord.** See (Sir George) **Calvert.**

Baluchistan (bəˈluːtʃɪˌstɑːn, -ˌstæn) *or* **Balochistan** ★ (bəˈlɒtʃɪˌstɑːn, -ˌstæn) *n* **1** a mountainous region of SW Asia, in SW Pakistan and SE Iran. **2** a province of SW Pakistan: a former territory of British India (until 1947). Capital: Quetta. Pop.: 6 341 000 (1995 est.).

baluster (ˈbæləstə) *n* any of a set of posts supporting a rail or coping. ORIG C17: from F *balustre,* from It. *balaustro* pillar resembling a pomegranate flower, ult. from Gk *balaustion*

balustrade (ˈbæləˌstreɪd) *n* an ornamental rail or coping with its supporting set of balusters. ORIG C17: from F, from *balustre* BALUSTER

Balzac ★ (ˈbælzæk; *French* balzak) *n* **Honoré de** (ɔnɔre də). 1799–1850, French novelist: author of a collection of novels *La Comédie humaine.*

Bamako ★ (ˌbæməˈkəʊ) *n* the capital of Mali, in the south, on the River Niger. Pop.: 800 000 (1995 est.).

Bamberg ★ (ˈbæmbɜːg; *German* ˈbambɛrk) *n* a town in S Germany, in N Bavaria: seat of independent prince-bishops of the Holy Roman Empire (1007–1802). Pop.: 70 690 (1991).

bambino (bæmˈbiːnəʊ) *n, pl* **bambinos** *or* **bambini** (-niː). *Inf.* a young child, esp. Italian. ORIG C18: from It.

bamboo (bæmˈbuː) *n* **1** a tall treelike tropical or semi-tropical grass having hollow stems with ringed joints. **2** the stem, used for building, poles, and furniture. ORIG C16: prob. from Malay *bambu*

bamboozle (bæmˈbuːzᵊl) *vb* **bamboozles, bamboozling, bamboozled.** (*tr*) *Inf.* **1** to cheat; mislead. **2** to confuse. ORIG C18: from ?
▸ **bamˈboozlement** *n* ▸ **bamˈboozler** *n*

ban (bæn) *vb* **bans, banning, banned. 1** (*tr*) to prohibit, esp. officially, from action, display, entrance, sale, etc.; forbid. ◆ *n* **2** an official prohibition or interdiction. **3** a public proclamation, esp. of outlawry. **4** *Arch.* a curse; imprecation. ORIG OE *bannan* to proclaim

Banaba ★ (bəˈnɑːbə) *n* an island in the SW Pacific, in the Republic of Kiribati. Phosphates were mined by Britain (1900–79). Area: about 5 sq. km (2 sq. miles). Pop.: 284 (1990). Also called: **Ocean Island.**
▸ **Baˈnaban** *adj, n*

banal (bəˈnɑːl) *adj* lacking force or originality; trite; commonplace. ORIG C18: from OF: relating to compulsory feudal service, hence common to all, commonplace
▸ **banality** (bəˈnælɪtɪ) *n* ▸ **baˈnally** *adv*

banana (bəˈnɑːnə) *n* **1** any of several tropical and sub-tropical treelike plants, esp. a widely cultivated species having hanging clusters of edible fruit. **2** the crescent-shaped fruit of any of these plants. ORIG C16: from Sp. or Port., of African origin

banana republic *n Inf. & derog.* a small country, esp. in Central America, that is politically unstable and has an economy dominated by foreign interest, usually dependent on one export.

banana skin *n* **1** the soft outer covering of a banana. **2** *Inf.* something unforeseen that causes an obvious and embarrassing mistake. ORIG sense 2 from the common slapstick joke of slipping on a banana skin

Banaras ★ (bəˈnɑːrəz) *n* a variant spelling of **Benares.**

Banat ★ (ˈbænɪt, ˈbɑːnɪt) *n* a fertile plain extending through Hungary, Romania, and Yugoslavia.

Banbridge ★ (ˈbænbrɪdʒ) *n* a district of SE Northern Ireland: agriculture, linen, footwear. Administrative centre: Banbridge. Pop.: 33 800 (1992). Area: 445 sq. km (172 sq. miles).

Banbury ★ (ˈbænbərɪ) *n* a town in central England, in N Oxfordshire: telecommunications, financial services. Pop.: 39 906 (1991).

band[1] (bænd) *n* **1** a company of people having a common purpose; group: *a band of outlaws.* **2** a group of musicians playing either brass and percussion instruments only (**brass band**) or brass, woodwind, and percussion instruments (**concert band** or **military band**). **3** a group of musicians who play popular music, jazz, etc., often for dancing. **4** *Canad.* a formally recognized group of Indians on a reserve. ◆ *vb* **5** (usually foll. by *together*) to unite; assemble. ORIG C15: from F *bande,* prob. from OProvençal *banda,* of Gmc origin

band[2] (bænd) *n* **1** a thin flat strip of some material, used esp. to encircle objects and hold them together: *a rubber band.* **2a** a strip of fabric or other material used as an ornament or to reinforce clothing. **2b** (*in combination*): *waistband; hatband.* **3** a stripe of contrasting colour or texture. **4** a driving belt in machinery. **5** a range of values that are close or related in number, degree, or quality. **6** *Physics.* a range of frequencies or wavelengths between two limits. **7** short for **energy band.** **8** *Computing.* one or more tracks on a magnetic disk or drum. **9** *Anat.* any structure resembling a ribbon or cord that connects, encircles, or binds different parts. **10** *Archit.* a strip of flat panelling, such as a fascia, usually attached to a wall. **11** either of a pair of hanging extensions of the collar, forming part of academic, legal, or (formerly) clerical dress. ◆ *vb* (*tr*) **12** to fasten or mark with a band. ORIG C15: from OF *bende,* of Gmc origin

Banda ★ ('bændə) *n* **Hastings Kamuzu** (kæ'mu:zu:). 1906–97, Malawi statesman; first prime minister of Nyasaland (1963–64); president of Malawi (1966–94).

bandage ('bændɪdʒ) *n* **1** a piece of material used to dress a wound, bind a broken limb, etc. ◆ *vb* **bandages, bandaging, bandaged.** **2** to cover or bind with a bandage. ORIG C16: from F, from *bande* strip, BAND[2]

bandanna *or* **bandana** (bæn'dænə) *n* a large silk or cotton handkerchief or neckerchief. ORIG C18: from Hindi *bāndhnū* tie-dyeing

Bandaranaike ★ (ˌbændərə'naɪkə) *n* **1 Chandrika.** See Chandrika **Kumaratunga.** **2** Mrs **Sirimavo** (ˌsɪrɪ'mɑ:vəʊ). 1916–2000, prime minister of Sri Lanka, formerly Ceylon (1960–65; 1970–77; 1994–2000). **3** her husband, **Solomon.** 1899–1959, prime minister of Ceylon (1956–59); assassinated.

Bandar Seri Begawan ★ ('bɑ:ndɑ: 'sɛrɪ bə'gɑ:wən) *n* the capital of Brunei. Pop.: 21 484 (1991). Former name: **Brunei.**

Banda Sea ★ *n* a part of the Pacific in Indonesia, between Sulawesi and New Guinea.

B & B *abbrev. for* bed and breakfast.

bandbox ('bændˌbɒks) *n* a lightweight usually cylindrical box for small articles, esp. hats.

bandeau ('bændəʊ) *n, pl* **bandeaux** (-dəʊz). a narrow band of ribbon, velvet, etc., worn round the head. ORIG C18: from F, from OF *bandel* a little BAND[2]

banderole *or* **banderol** ('bændəˌrəʊl) *n* **1** a long narrow flag, usually with forked ends, esp. one attached to the mast of a ship. **2** a ribbon-like scroll or sculptured band bearing an inscription. ORIG C16: from OF, from It. *banderuola,* lit.: a little banner

bandicoot ('bændɪˌku:t) *n* **1** an agile terrestrial marsupial of Australia and New Guinea with a long pointed muzzle and a long tail. **2 bandicoot rat.** Also called: **mole rat.** any of three burrowing rats of S and SE Asia. ORIG C18: from Telugu *pandikokku*

banding ('bændɪŋ) *n Brit.* the practice of putting schoolchildren into ability groups to ensure a balanced intake to secondary school.

bandit ('bændɪt) *n, pl* **bandits** *or* **banditti** (bæn'dɪtɪ). a robber, esp. a member of an armed gang. ORIG C16: from It. *bandito,* from *bandire* to proscribe, from *bando* edict
▸ **'banditry** *n*

Bandjarmasin *or* **Bandjermasin** ★ (ˌbændʒə'mɑ:sɪn) *n* variant spellings of **Banjarmasin.**

bandmaster ('bændˌmɑ:stə) *n* the conductor of a band.

Band of Hope *n* a society devoted to abstinence from alcohol.

bandolier *or* **bandoleer** (ˌbændə'lɪə) *n* a soldier's broad shoulder belt having small pockets or loops for cartridges. ORIG C16: from OF *bandouliere*

band-pass filter *n* **1** *Electronics.* a filter that transmits only currents having frequencies within specified limits. **2** an optical device for transmitting waves of predetermined wavelengths.

band saw *n* a power-operated saw consisting of an endless toothed metal band running over and driven by two wheels.

bandsman ('bændzmən) *n, pl* **bandsmen.** a player in a musical band, esp. a brass or military band.

bandstand ('bændˌstænd) *n* a platform for a band, usually out of doors and roofed.

band theory *n* the theory that electrons in solids have a range of energies falling into allowed bands, between which are forbidden bands.

Bandung ★ ('bændʊŋ) *n* a city in Indonesia, in SW Java. Pop.: 2 368 200 (1995 est.).

bandwagon ('bændˌwægən) *n* **1** *US.* a wagon for the band in a parade. **2 jump, climb,** *or* **get on the bandwagon.** to join or support a party or movement that seems assured of success.

bandwidth ('bændˌwɪdθ) *n* the range of frequencies within a given waveband used for a particular radio transmission.

bandy ('bændɪ) *adj* **bandier, bandiest.** **1** Also: **bandy-legged.** having legs curved outwards at the knees. **2** (of legs) curved thus. ◆ *vb* **bandies, bandying, bandied.** (*tr*) **3** to exchange (words) in a heated or hostile manner. **4** to give and receive (blows). **5** (often foll. by *about*) to circulate (a name, rumour, etc.). ORIG C16: prob. from OF *bander* to hit the ball back and forth at tennis

bane (beɪn) *n* **1** a person or thing that causes misery or distress (esp. in **bane of one's life**). **2** something that causes death or destruction. **3a** a fatal poison. **3b** (*in combination*): *ratsbane.* **4** *Arch.* ruin or distress. ORIG OE *bana*
▸ **'baneful** *adj*

baneberry ('beɪnbərɪ) *n, pl* **baneberries.** **1** Also called: **herb Christopher** (Brit.). a plant which has small white flowers and red or white poisonous berries. **2** the berry.

Banff ★ (bæmf) *n* **1** a town in Canada, in SW Alberta, in the Rocky Mountains: surrounded by **Banff National Park.** Pop.: 5700 (1991). **2** a town in NE Scotland, in Aberdeenshire. Pop.: 6230 (1991).

Banffshire ★ ('bæmfˌʃɪə, -ʃə) *n* (until 1975) a county of NE Scotland, now part of Aberdeenshire.

bang[1] (bæŋ) *n* **1** a short loud explosive noise, as of the report of a gun. **2** a hard blow or knock, esp. a noisy one. **3** *Sl.* an injection of heroin or other narcotic. **4** *Taboo sl.* an act of sexual intercourse. **5 with a bang.** successfully: *the party went with a bang.* ◆ *vb* **6** to hit or knock, esp. with a loud noise. **7** to move noisily or clumsily: *to bang about the house.* **8** to close (a door, window, etc.) or (of a door, etc.) be closed noisily; slam. **9** (*tr*) to cause to move by hitting vigorously: *he banged the ball over the fence.* **10** to make or cause to make a loud noise, as of an explosion. **11** *Taboo sl.* to have sexual intercourse (with). **12** (*intr*) *Sl.* to inject heroin, etc. **13 bang one's head against a brick wall.** to try to achieve something impossible. ◆ *adv* **14** with a sudden impact or effect: *the car drove bang into a lamppost.* **15** precisely: *bang in the middle.* **16 go bang.** to burst, shut, etc., with a loud noise. ORIG C16: from ON *bang, banga* hammer

bang[2] (bæŋ) *n* **1** (*usually pl*) a section of hair cut straight across the forehead. ◆ *vb* (*tr*) **2** to cut (the hair) in such a style. **3** to dock (the tail of a horse, etc.). ORIG C19: prob. short for *bangtail* short tail

Bangalore ★ (ˌbæŋgə'lɔ:) *n* a city in S India, capital of Karnataka state: printing, textiles, pharmaceuticals. Pop.: 2 660 088 (1991).

banger ('bæŋə) *n Brit.* **1** *Sl.* a sausage. **2** *Inf.* an old decrepit car. **3** a firework that explodes loudly.

Bangka *or* **Banka** ★ ('bæŋkə) *n* an island in Indonesia, separated from Sumatra by the **Bangka Strait.** Chief town: Pangkalpinang. Area: about 11 914 sq. km (4600 sq. miles).

Bangkok ★ ('bæŋkɒk, bæŋ'kɒk) *n* the capital and chief port of Thailand, on the Chao Phraya River: became a royal city and the capital in 1782. Pop.: 5 584 228 (1993 est.). Thai name: **Krung Thep** ('krʊŋ 'teɪp).

Bangla ('bæŋglə) *n* another name for **Bengali** (sense 2).

Bangladesh ★ (ˌbɑːŋɡləˈdɛʃ, ˌbæŋ-) *n* a republic in S Asia: formerly the Eastern Province of Pakistan; became independent in 1971 after civil war and the defeat of Pakistan by India; consists of the plains and vast deltas of the Ganges and Brahmaputra Rivers; a member of the Commonwealth: economy based on jute and jute products (over 80 per cent of world production). Language: Bengali. Religion: Muslim. Currency: taka. Capital: Dhaka. Pop.: 127 118 000 (1999 est.). Area: 142 797 sq. km (55 126 sq. miles).
▸ **ˌBanglaˈdeshi** *adj, n*

bangle (ˈbæŋɡᵊl) *n* a bracelet, usually without a clasp, often worn round the arm or sometimes round the ankle. ORIG C19: from Hindi *bangrī*

bang on *adj, adv Brit. inf.* **1** with absolute accuracy. **2** excellent or excellently.

Bangor ★ (ˈbæŋɡɔː, -ɡə) *n* **1** a university town in NW Wales, in Gwynedd, on the Menai Strait. Pop.: 12 330 (1991). **2** a town in SE Northern Ireland, in Co. Down, on Belfast Lough. Pop.: 52 437 (1991).

bangtail (ˈbæŋˌteɪl) *n* **1** a horse's tail cut straight across but not through the bone. **2** a horse with a tail cut in this way. ORIG C19: from *bangtail* short tail

Bangui ★ (*French* bɑ̃ɡi) *n* the capital of the Central African Republic, in the south part, on the Ubangi River. Pop.: 552 000 (1995 est.).

Bangweulu ★ (ˌbæŋwɪˈuːluː) *n* **Lake.** a shallow lake in NE Zambia, discovered by David Livingstone, who died there in 1873. Area: about 9850 sq. km (3800 sq. miles), including swamps.

banian (ˈbænjən) *n* a variant spelling of **banyan.**

banish (ˈbænɪʃ) *vb (tr)* **1** to expel from a place, esp. by an official decree as a punishment. **2** to drive away: *to banish gloom.* ORIG C14: from OF *banir,* of Gmc origin
▸ **ˈbanishment** *n*

banisters *or* **bannisters** (ˈbænɪstəz) *pl n* the railing and supporting balusters on a staircase; balustrade. ORIG C17: altered from BALUSTER

Banja Luka ★ (*Serbo-Croat* ˈbaːnjaː ˌluːka) *n* a city in NW Bosnia-Herzegovina, on the Vrbas River: scene of battles between the Austrians and Turks in 1527, 1688, and 1737; besieged by Serb forces (1992–95). Pop.: 195 139 (1991).

Banjarmasin, Banjermasin, Bandjarmasin *or* **Bandjermasin** ★ (ˌbændʒəˈmɑːsɪn) *n* a port in Indonesia, in SW Borneo. Pop.: 534 600 (1995 est.).

banjo (ˈbændʒəʊ) *n, pl* **banjos** *or* **banjoes.** a stringed musical instrument with a long neck and a circular drumlike body overlaid with parchment, plucked with the fingers or a plectrum. ORIG C18: var. (US Southern pronunciation) of earlier *bandore,* ult. from Gk *pandora*
▸ **ˈbanjoist** *n*

Banjul ★ (bænˈdʒuːl) *n* the capital of The Gambia, a port at the mouth of the Gambia River. Pop.: 42 407 (1993). Former name (until 1973): **Bathurst.**

bank[1] (bæŋk) *n* **1** an institution offering certain financial services, such as the safekeeping of money and lending of money at interest. **2** the building used by such an institution. **3** a small container used at home for keeping money. **4** the funds held by a banker or dealer in some gambling games. **5** (in various games) **5a** the stock, as of money, etc., on which players may draw. **5b** the player holding this stock. **6** any supply, store, or reserve: *a data bank.* ◆ *vb* **7** *(tr)* to deposit (cash, cheques, etc.) in a bank. **8** *(intr)* to transact business with a bank. **9** *(intr)* to engage in banking. ◆ See also **bank on.** ORIG C15: prob. from It. *banca* bench, moneychanger's table, of Gmc origin

bank[2] (bæŋk) *n* **1** a long raised mass, esp. of earth; ridge. **2** a slope, as of a hill. **3** the sloping side of any hollow in the ground, esp. when bordering a river. **4** the ground beside a river or canal. **5a** an elevated section of the bed of a sea, lake, or river. **5b** *(in combination): sandbank.* **6** the face of a body of ore in a mine. **7** the lateral inclination of an aircraft about its longitudinal axis during a turn. **8** a bend on a road, athletics track, etc., having the outside built higher than the inside to reduce the effects of centrifugal force on vehicles, runners, etc., rounding it at speed. Also called: **camber, superelevation.** ◆ *vb* **9** (when *tr,* often foll. by *up*) to form into a bank or mound. **10** *(tr)* to border or enclose (a road, etc.) with a bank. **11** *(tr;* sometimes foll. by *up)* to cover (a fire) with ashes, fresh fuel, etc., so that it will burn slowly. **12** to cause (an aircraft) to tip laterally about its longitudinal axis or (of an aircraft) to tip in this way, esp. while turning. ORIG C12: of Scand. origin

bank[3] (bæŋk) *n* **1** an arrangement of similar objects in a row or in tiers: *a bank of dials.* **2** a tier of oars in a galley. ◆ *vb* **3** *(tr)* to arrange in a bank. ORIG C17: from OF *banc* bench, of Gmc origin

Banka ★ (ˈbæŋkə) *n* a variant spelling of **Bangka.**

bankable (ˈbæŋkəbᵊl) *adj* **1** appropriate for receipt by a bank. **2** dependable or reliable: *a bankable promise.* **3** (esp. of a star) likely to ensure the financial success of a film.
▸ **ˌbankaˈbility** *n*

bank account *n* **1** an account created by the deposit of money at a bank by a customer. **2** the amount credited to a depositor at a bank.

bank bill *n* **1** Also called: **bank draft.** a bill of exchange drawn by one bank on another. **2** *US.* a banknote.

bankbook (ˈbæŋkˌbʊk) *n* a book held by depositors at certain banks, in which the bank enters a record of deposits, withdrawals, and earned interest. Also called: **passbook.**

bank card *or* **banker's card** *n* any plastic card issued by a bank, such as a cash card or cheque card.

bank draft *n* a cheque drawn by a bank on itself, which is bought by a person to pay a supplier unwilling to accept a normal cheque. Also called: **banker's cheque.**

banker[1] (ˈbæŋkə) *n* **1** a person who owns or is an executive in a bank. **2** an official or player in charge of the bank in various games. **3** a result that has been forecast identically in a series of entries on a football pool coupon. **4** a person or thing that appears certain to win or be successful.

banker[2] (ˈbæŋkə) *n Austral. & NZ inf.* a stream almost overflowing its banks (esp. in **run a banker**).

banker's order *n* another name for **standing order** (sense 1).

Bankhead ★ (ˈbæŋkˌhɛd) *n* **Tallulah** (**Brockman**). 1902–68, US stage and film actress.

bank holiday *n* (in Britain) any of several weekdays on which banks are closed by law and which are observed as national holidays.

banking (ˈbæŋkɪŋ) *n* the business engaged in by a bank.

bank manager *n* a person who directs the business of a local branch of a bank.

banknote (ˈbæŋkˌnəʊt) *n* a promissory note, esp. one issued by a central bank, serving as money.

Bank of England *n* the central bank of the United Kingdom, which acts as banker to the government and the commercial banks.

bank on *vb (intr, prep)* to expect or rely with confidence on: *you can bank on him.*

bankroll (ˈbæŋkˌrəʊl) *Chiefly US & Canad.* ◆ *n* **1** a roll of currency notes. **2** the financial resources of a person, organization, etc. ◆ *vb* **3** *(tr) Sl.* to provide the capital for; finance.

bankrupt (ˈbæŋkrʌpt, -rəpt) *n* **1** a person adjudged insolvent by a court, his or her property being administered for the benefit of creditors. **2** any person unable to discharge all his or her debts. **3** a person whose resources in a certain field are exhausted: *a spiritual bankrupt.* ◆ *adj* **4** adjudged insolvent. **5** financially ruined. **6** depleted in resources: *spiritually bankrupt.* **7** (foll. by *of*) *Brit.* lacking: *bankrupt of intelligence.* ◆ *vb* **8** *(tr)* to make bankrupt. ORIG C16: from OF *banqueroute,* from OIt. *bancarotta,* from *banca* BANK[1] + *rotta* broken, from L *ruptus*
▸ **ˈbankruptcy** *n*

Banks ★ (bæŋks) *n* **1** **Iain** (**Menzies**). born 1954, Scottish novelist and science-fiction writer. His novels include *The Wasp Factory* (1984), *The Crow Road* (1992), and *A Song of Stone* (1997); science fiction (under the name Iain M. Banks) includes *Inversions* (1998). **2** Sir **Joseph.** 1743–1820, British botanist and explorer: circumnavigated the world with James Cook (1768–71).

banksia ('bæŋksɪə) *n* any shrub or tree of the Australian genus *Banksia,* having dense cylindrical heads of flowers that are often yellowish. ORIG C19: NL, after Sir Joseph BANKS

Banks Island ★ *n* **1** an island of N Canada, in the Northwest Territories: the westernmost island of the Arctic Archipelago. Area: about 67 340 sq. km (26 000 sq. miles). **2** an island of W Canada, off British Columbia. Length: about 72 km (45 miles).

bank statement *n* a statement of transactions in a bank account, esp. one of a series sent at regular intervals to the depositor.

banner ('bænə) *n* **1** a long strip of material displaying a slogan, advertisement, etc. **2** a placard carried in a procession or demonstration. **3** something that represents a belief or principle. **4** the flag of a nation, army, etc. **5** Also called: **banner headline.** a large headline in a newspaper, etc., extending across the page. ORIG C13: from OF *baniere,* of Gmc origin
▸ **'bannered** *adj*

Bannister ★ ('bænɪstə) *n* Sir **Roger** (**Gilbert**). born 1929, British athlete and doctor: first to run a four minute mile (1954).

bannisters ('bænɪstəz) *pl n* a variant spelling of **banisters.**

bannock ('bænək) *n* a round flat cake originating in Scotland, made from oatmeal or barley and baked on a griddle. ORIG OE *bannuc*

Bannockburn ★ ('bænək,bɜːn) *n* a village in central Scotland, south of Stirling: nearby is the site of a victory (1314) of the Scots, led by Robert the Bruce, over the English. Pop.: 2675 (1991).

banns *or* **bans** (bænz) *pl n* **1** the public declaration of an intended marriage, usually on three successive Sundays in the parish churches of the betrothed. **2 forbid the banns.** to raise an objection to a marriage announced in this way. ORIG C14: pl of *bann* proclamation

banquet ('bæŋkwɪt) *n* **1** a sumptuous meal; feast. **2** a ceremonial meal for many people. ◆ *vb* **banquets, banqueting, banqueted. 3** (*intr*) to hold or take part in a banquet. **4** (*tr*) to entertain (a person) with a banquet. ORIG C15: from OF, from It. *banchetto,* from *banco* a table, of Gmc origin
▸ **'banqueter** *n*

banquette (bæŋ'kɛt) *n* **1** an upholstered bench. **2** (formerly) a raised part behind a parapet. ORIG C17: from F, from Provençal *banqueta,* lit.: a little bench

banshee ('bænʃiː, bæn'ʃiː) *n* (in Irish folklore) a female spirit whose wailing warns of impending death. ORIG C18: from Irish Gaelic *bean sídhe,* lit.: woman of the fairy mound

Banstead ★ ('bæn,stɛd) *n* a town in S England, in NE Surrey: a dormitory town for London. Pop.: 37 245 (1991).

bantam ('bæntəm) *n* **1** any of various very small breeds of domestic fowl. **2** a small but aggressive person. **3** *Boxing.* short for **bantamweight.** ORIG C18: after *Bantam,* village in Java, said to be the original home of this fowl

bantamweight ('bæntəm,weɪt) *n* **1a** a professional boxer weighing 112–118 pounds (51–53.5 kg). **1b** an amateur boxer weighing 51–54 kg (112–119 pounds). **2** an amateur wrestler weighing usually 52–57 kg (115–126 pounds).

banter ('bæntə) *vb* **1** to speak or tease lightly or jokingly. ◆ *n* **2** teasing or joking language or repartee. ORIG C17: from ?
▸ **'banterer** *n*

Banting ★ ('bæntɪŋ) *n* Sir **Frederick Grant.** 1891–1941, Canadian physiologist: discovered the insulin treatment for diabetes with Best and Macleod (1922) and shared the Nobel prize for physiology or medicine (1923).

Bantock ★ ('bæntɒk) *n* Sir **Granville.** 1868–1946, British composer. His works include the *Hebridean Symphony* (1915), five ballets, and three operas.

Bantu ('bɑːntuː) *n* **1** a group of languages of Africa, including most of the principal languages spoken from the equator to the Cape of Good Hope. **2** (*pl* **Bantu** *or* **Bantus**) *Derog.* a Black speaker of a Bantu language. ◆ *adj* **3** of or relating to this group of peoples or their languages. ORIG C19: from Bantu *Ba-ntu* people

> **USAGE NOTE** This term is now generally avoided because of its use in the era of apartheid.

Bantustan ('bɑːntuː,stɑːn) *n Derog.* (formerly, in South Africa) an area reserved for occupation by a Black African people, with limited self-government; abolished in 1993. Official name: **homeland.** ORIG from BANTU + Hindi *-stan* country of

banyan *or* **banian** ('bænjən) *n* **1** an Indian tree with aerial roots that grow down into the soil forming additional trunks. **2** a member of the Hindu merchant caste of India. **3** a loose-fitting shirt, or robe, worn originally in India. ORIG C16: from Hindi *baniyā,* from Sansk. *vānija* merchant

banzai ('bɑːnzaɪ, bɑːn'zaɪ) *interj* a patriotic cheer, battle cry, or salutation. ORIG Japanese: lit.: (may you live for) ten thousand years

baobab ('beɪəʊ,bæb) *n* a tree native to Africa and N Australia that has a very thick trunk, angular branches, and a gourdlike fruit with an edible pulp. ORIG C17: prob. from a native African word

Baoding ('baʊ'dɪŋ), **Paoting,** *or* **Pao-ting** ★ *n* a city in NE China, in N Hebei province. Pop.: 483 155 (1990 est.). Former name: **Tsingyuan** *or* **Ch'ing-yüan.**

BAOR *abbrev. for* British Army of the Rhine.

Baotou ('baʊ'tuː) *or* **Paotow** ★ *n* an industrial city in N China, in the central Inner Mongolia AR on the Yellow River. Pop.: 1 200 000 (1991 est.).

bap (bæp) *n Brit.* a large soft bread roll. ORIG from ?

baptism ('bæp,tɪzəm) *n* a Christian religious rite consisting of immersion in or sprinkling with water as a sign that the subject is cleansed from sin and constituted as a member of the Church.
▸ **bap'tismal** *adj* ▸ **bap'tismally** *adv*

baptism of fire *n* **1** a soldier's first experience of battle. **2** any initiating ordeal.

Baptist ('bæptɪst) *n* **1** a member of any of various Christian sects that affirm the necessity of baptism (usually of adults and by immersion). **2 the Baptist.** John the Baptist, the cousin and forerunner of Jesus, whom he baptized. ◆ *adj* **3** denoting or characteristic of any Christian sect of Baptists.

baptistry *or* **baptistery** ('bæptɪstrɪ) *n, pl* **baptistries** *or* **baptisteries. 1** a part of a Christian church in which baptisms are carried out. **2** a tank in a Baptist church in which baptisms are carried out.

baptize *or* **baptise** (bæp'taɪz) *vb* **baptizes, baptizing, baptized** *or* **baptises, baptising, baptised. 1** *Christianity.* to immerse (a person) in water or sprinkle water on (a person) as part of the rite of baptism. **2** (*tr*) to give a name to; christen. ORIG C13: from LL *baptīzāre,* from Gk, from *baptein* to bathe, dip

bar[1] (bɑː) *n* **1** a rigid usually straight length of metal, wood, etc., used esp. as a barrier or as a structural part: *a bar of a gate.* **2** a solid usually rectangular block of any material: *a bar of soap.* **3** anything that obstructs or prevents. **4** an offshore ridge of sand, mud, or shingle across the mouth of a river, bay, or harbour. **5** a counter or room where alcoholic drinks are served. **6** a counter, room, or establishment where a particular range of goods, food, services, etc., are sold: *a coffee bar; a heel bar.* **7** a narrow band or stripe, as of colour or light. **8** a heating element in an electric fire. **9** See **Bar. 10** the place in a court of law where the accused stands during his or her trial. **11** a particular court of law. **12** *Brit.* (in Parliament) the boundary where nonmembers wishing to address either House appear and where persons are arraigned. **13** a plea showing that a plaintiff has no cause of action. **14** anything referred to as an authority or tribunal: *the bar of decency.* **15** *Music.* a group of beats that is repeated with a consistent rhythm throughout a piece of music. The number of beats in the bar is indicated by the time signature. Also called: **measure. 16a** *Brit.* insignia added to a decoration indicating a second award. **16b** *US.* a strip of metal worn with uniform, esp. to signify rank or as an award for service. **17** *Football, etc.* See **crossbar. 18** *Gymnastics.* See **horizontal bar. 19** *Heraldry.* a narrow horizontal line across a shield. **20 behind bars.** in prison. **21 won't have a bar of.** *Austral. & NZ inf.* cannot tolerate; dislikes. ◆ *vb* **bars, barring, barred.** (*tr*) **22** to secure with a bar: *to bar the door.* **23** to shut in or out with or as if with barriers: *to bar the entrances.* **24** to obstruct: *the fallen tree barred the road.* **25** (usually foll. by *from*) to prohibit; forbid: *to bar a couple from meeting.* **26** (usually foll. by *from*) to keep out; exclude: *to bar a person from membership.* **27** to mark with a bar or bars. **28** *Law.* to prevent or halt (an action) by showing that the plaintiff has no cause. ◆ *prep* **29** except for. **30 bar none.** without exception. ORIG C12: from OF *barre,* from Vulgar L *barra* (unattested) bar, rod, from ?

bar² (bɑː) *n* a cgs unit of pressure equal to 10^6 dynes per square centimetre. ORIG C20: from Gk *baros* weight

Bar (bɑː) *n* **the. 1** (in England and elsewhere) barristers collectively. **2** *US.* the legal profession collectively. **3 be called to the Bar.** *Brit.* to become a barrister. **4 be called within the Bar.** *Brit.* to be appointed as a Queen's Counsel.

bar. *abbrev. for:* **1** barometric. **2** barrel. **3** barrister.

Barabbas ★ (bəˈræbəs) *n New Testament.* a condemned robber who was released at the Passover instead of Jesus (Matthew 27:16).

Barak ★ (ˈbæræk) *n* **Ehud** (ɛˈhud). born 1942, Israeli politician and soldier; leader of the Labour Party from 1997; prime minister from 1999.

Baranof Island ★ (ˈbærənɔf) *n* an island off SE Alaska, in the western part of the Alexander Archipelago. Area: 4162 sq. km (1607 sq. miles).

barathea (ˌbærəˈθɪə) *n* a fabric made of silk and wool or cotton and rayon. ORIG C19: from ?

barb¹ (bɑːb) *n* **1** a point facing in the opposite direction to the main point of a fish-hook, harpoon, etc., intended to make extraction difficult. **2** any of various pointed parts. **3** a cutting remark. **4** any of the hairlike filaments that form the vane of a feather. **5** a beardlike growth, hair, or projection. ◆ *vb* **6** (*tr*) to provide with a barb or barbs. ORIG C14: from OF *barbe* beard, point, from L *barba* beard
▸ **barbed** *adj*

barb² (bɑːb) *n* a breed of horse of North African origin, similar to the Arab but less spirited. ORIG C17: from F *barbe,* from It. *barbero* a Barbary (horse)

Barbados ★ (bɑːˈbeɪdəʊs, -dəʊz, -dɒs) *n* an island in the Caribbean, in the E Lesser Antilles: a British colony from 1628 to 1966, now an independent state within the Commonwealth. Language: English. Currency: Barbados dollar. Capital: Bridgetown. Pop.: 266 000 (1999 est.). Area: 430 sq. km (166 sq. miles).
▸ **Barˈbadian** *adj, n*

barbarian (bɑːˈbɛərɪən) *n* **1** a member of a primitive or uncivilized people. **2** a coarse or uncultured person. **3** a vicious person. ◆ *adj* **4** of an uncivilized culture. **5** uncultured or brutal. ORIG C16: see BARBAROUS

barbaric (bɑːˈbærɪk) *adj* **1** of or characteristic of barbarians. **2** primitive; unrestrained. **3** brutal. ORIG C15: from L *barbaricus* outlandish; see BARBAROUS
▸ **barˈbarically** *adv*

barbarism (ˈbɑːbəˌrɪzəm) *n* **1** a brutal, coarse, or ignorant act. **2** the condition of being backward, coarse, or ignorant. **3** a substandard word or expression; solecism. **4** any act or object that offends against accepted taste. ORIG C16: from L *barbarismus* error of speech, from Gk *barbarismos,* from *barbaros* BARBAROUS

barbarity (bɑːˈbærɪtɪ) *n, pl* **barbarities. 1** the state of being barbaric or barbarous. **2** a vicious act.

barbarize *or* **barbarise** (ˈbɑːbəˌraɪz) *vb* **barbarizes, barbarizing, barbarized** *or* **barbarises, barbarising, barbarised. 1** to make or become barbarous. **2** to use barbarisms in (language).
▸ **ˌbarbariˈzation** *or* **ˌbarbariˈsation** *n*

Barbarossa ★ (ˌbɑːbəˈrɒsə) *n* **1** the nickname of the Holy Roman Emperor **Frederick I.** See **Frederick Barbarossa. 2** real name *Khair ed-Din. c.* 1465–1546, Turkish pirate and admiral: conquered Tunis for the Ottomans (1534).

barbarous (ˈbɑːbərəs) *adj* **1** uncivilized; primitive. **2** brutal or cruel. **3** lacking refinement. ORIG C15: via L from Gk *barbaros* barbarian, non-Greek, imit. of incomprehensible speech
▸ **ˈbarbarously** *adv* ▸ **ˈbarbarousness** *n*

Barbary ★ (ˈbɑːbərɪ) *n* a region of N Africa, extending from W Egypt to the Atlantic and including the former **Barbary States** of Tripolitania, Tunisia, Algeria, and Morocco.

Barbary ape *n* a tailless macaque that inhabits NW Africa and Gibraltar.

Barbary Coast ★ *n* **the.** the Mediterranean coast of North Africa: a centre of piracy against European shipping from the 16th to the 19th centuries.

barbate (ˈbɑːbeɪt) *adj Biol.* having tufts of long hairs; bearded. ORIG C19: from L *barba* a beard

barbecue (ˈbɑːbɪˌkjuː) *n* **1** a meal cooked out of doors over an open fire. **2** a grill or fireplace used in barbecuing. **3** the food so cooked. **4** a party or picnic at which barbecued food is served. ◆ *vb* **barbecues, barbecuing, barbecued.** (*tr*) **5** to cook (meat, fish, etc.) on a grill, usually over charcoal and often with a highly seasoned sauce. ORIG C17: from American Sp. *barbacoa:* frame made of sticks

barbed wire *n* strong wire with sharply pointed barbs at close intervals.

barbel (ˈbɑːbᵊl) *n* **1** any of several slender tactile spines or bristles that hang from the jaws of certain fishes, such as the carp. **2** any of several European cyprinid fishes that resemble the carp. ORIG C14: from OF, from LL from L *barba* beard

barbell (ˈbɑːˌbɛl) *n* a long metal rod to which heavy discs are attached at each end for weightlifting.

barber (ˈbɑːbə) *n* **1** a person whose business is cutting men's hair and shaving beards. ◆ *vb* (*tr*) **2** to cut the hair of. ORIG C13: from OF *barbeor,* from *barbe* beard, from L *barba*

Barber ★ (ˈbɑːbə) *n* **Samuel.** 1910–81, US composer: his works include an *Adagio for Strings* and the opera *Vanessa* (1958).

barberry (ˈbɑːbərɪ) *n, pl* **barberries.** any spiny Asian shrub of the genus *Berberis,* having clusters of yellow flowers and orange or red berries. ORIG C15: from OF *berberis,* from Ar. *barbāris*

barbershop (ˈbɑːbəˌʃɒp) *n* **1** *Now chiefly US.* the premises of a barber. **2** (*modifier*) denoting a type of close four-part harmony for male voices: *a barbershop quartet.*

barber's pole *n* a barber's sign consisting of a pole painted with red-and-white spiral stripes.

barbican (ˈbɑːbɪkən) *n* **1** a walled outwork to protect a gate or drawbridge of a fortification. **2** a watchtower projecting from a fortification. ORIG C13: from OF *barbacane,* from Med. L, from ?

Barbican ★ (ˈbɑːbɪkən) *n* **the.** a building complex in the City of London: includes residential developments and the Barbican Arts Centre (completed 1982) housing concert and exhibition halls, theatres, cinemas, etc.

barbicel (ˈbɑːbɪˌsɛl) *n Ornithol.* any of the minute hooks on the barbules of feathers that interlock with those of adjacent barbules. ORIG C19: from NL *barbicella,* lit.: a small beard

Barbirolli ★ (ˌbɑːbəˈrɒlɪ) *n* Sir **John.** 1899–1970, British conductor of the Hallé Orchestra (1943–68).

barbitone (ˈbɑːbɪˌtəʊn) *or US* **barbital** (ˈbɑːbɪˌtæl) *n* a long-acting barbiturate. ORIG C20: from BARBIT(URIC ACID) + -ONE

barbiturate (bɑːˈbɪtjʊrɪt, -ˌreɪt) *n* a derivative of barbituric acid, such as barbitone, used in medicine as a sedative or hypnotic.

barbituric acid (ˌbɑːbɪˈtjʊərɪk) *n* a white crystalline solid used in the preparation of barbiturate drugs. ORIG C19: partial translation of G *Barbitursäure*

Barbour jacket *or* **Barbour** (ˈbɑːbə) *n Trademark.* a hard-wearing waterproof waxed jacket.

Barbuda ★ (bɑːˈbuːdə) *n* a coral island in the E Caribbean, in the Leeward Islands: part of the independent state of Antigua and Barbuda. Area: 160 sq. km (62 sq. miles).

barbule ('bɑːbjuːl) *n Ornithol.* any of the minute hairs that project from a barb and in some feathers interlock. ORIG C19: from L *barbula* a little beard

Barbusse ★ (*French* barbys) *n* **Henri** (ɑ̃ri). 1873–1935, French novelist and poet. His novels include *L'Enfer* (1908) and *Le Feu* (1916).

barcarole *or* **barcarolle** ('bɑːkəˌrəʊl, -ˌrɒl; ˌbɑːkə'rəʊl) *n* **1** a Venetian boat song. **2** an instrumental composition resembling this. ORIG C18: from F, from It. *barcarola,* from *barcaruolo* boatman, from *barca* boat

Barce ('bartʃe) *or* **Barca** ★ ('barka) *n* the Italian name for **Al Marj**.

Barcelona ★ (ˌbɑːsɪ'ləʊnə) *n* the chief port of Spain, on the NE Mediterranean coast: seat of the Republican government during the Civil War (1936–39); the commercial capital of Spain. Pop.: 1 630 867 (1994 est.). Ancient name: **Barcino** (bɑː'siːnəʊ).

bar chart *n* another term for **bar graph**.

Barclay de Tolly ★ ('bɑːklɪ də 'tɒlɪ; *Russian* bar'klai də 'tɔlj) *n* Prince **Mikhail** (mixa'il). 1761–1818, Russian field marshal: commander in chief against Napoleon in 1812.

bar code *n Commerce.* a machine-readable arrangement of numbers and parallel lines printed on a package, which can be electronically scanned at a checkout to register the price of the goods and to activate computer stock checking and reordering.

Barcoo River ★ (bɑː'kuː) *n* a river in E Central Australia, in SW Queensland: joins with the Thomson River to form Cooper Creek.

bard[1] (bɑːd) *n* **1a** (formerly) one of an ancient Celtic order of poets. **1b** a poet who wins a verse competition at a Welsh eisteddfod. **2** *Arch. or literary.* any poet. ORIG C14: from Scot. Gaelic
▸ **'bardic** *adj*

bard[2] (bɑːd) *n* **1** a piece of bacon or pork fat placed on meat during roasting to prevent drying out. ◆ *vb* (*tr*) **2** to place a bard on. ORIG C15: from OF *barde,* from OIt. *barda,* from Ar. *barda'ah* packsaddle

Bard ★ (bɑːd) *n* **the.** an epithet of (William) **Shakespeare.**

Bardeen ★ (ˌbɑː'diːn) *n* **John.** 1908–91, US physicist and electrical engineer, noted for his research on electrical conduction in solids; shared the Nobel prize for physics 1956 for the invention of the transistor and shared Nobel prize for physics 1972 for work on superconductivity.

bardie ('bɑːdɪ) *n* **1** an edible white wood-boring grub of Australia. **2 starve the bardies!** *Austral.* an exclamation of surprise or protest. ORIG from Abor.

Bardot ★ (*French* bardo) *n* **Brigitte** (briʒit). born 1934, French film actress.

bare[1] (bɛə) *adj* **1** unclothed: used esp. of a part of the body. **2** without the natural, conventional, or usual covering. **3** lacking appropriate furnishings, etc. **4** unembellished; simple: *the bare facts.* **5** (*prenominal*) just sufficient: *the bare minimum.* **6 with one's bare hands.** without a weapon or tool. ◆ *vb* **bares, baring, bared. 7** (*tr*) to make bare; uncover. ORIG OE *bær*
▸ **'bareness** *n*

bare[2] (bɛə) *vb Arch.* a past tense of **bear**[1].

bareback ('bɛəˌbæk) *or* **barebacked** *adj, adv* (of horse-riding) without a saddle.

barefaced ('bɛəˌfeɪst) *adj* unconcealed or shameless: *a barefaced lie.*
▸ **barefacedly** ('bɛəˌfeɪsɪdlɪ) *adv* ▸ **'bareˌfacedness** *n*

barefoot ('bɛəˌfʊt) *or* **barefooted** *adj, adv* **1** with the feet uncovered. ◆ *adj* **2** denoting a worker with basic training sent to help people in remote rural areas, esp. of developing countries: *barefoot doctor.*

bareheaded (ˌbɛə'hɛdɪd) *adj, adv* with the head uncovered.

Bareilly ★ (bə'reɪlɪ) *n* a city in N India, in N central Uttar Pradesh. Pop.: 587 211 (1991).

bare-knuckle *adj* **1** without boxing gloves: *a bare-knuckle fighter.* **2** aggressive; without civilized restraint: *a bare-knuckle confrontation.*

barely ('bɛəlɪ) *adv* **1** only just: *barely enough.* **2** *Inf.* not quite: *barely old enough.* **3** scantily: *barely furnished.* **4** *Arch.* openly.

> **USAGE NOTE** See at **scarcely.**

Barenboim ★ ('bærənˌbɔɪm) *n* **Daniel.** born 1942, Israeli concert pianist and conductor, born in Argentina.

Barents Sea ★ ('bærənts) *n* a part of the Arctic Ocean, bounded by Norway, Russia, and the islands of Novaya Zemlya, Spitsbergen, and Franz Josef Land. ORIG after Willem *Barents* (1550–97), Dutch navigator and explorer who discovered it in 1596

barf (bɑːf) *vb* (*intr*) *Sl.* to vomit. ORIG C20: prob. imit.

bargain ('bɑːgɪn) *n* **1** an agreement establishing what each party will give, receive, or perform in a transaction. **2** something acquired or received in such an agreement. **3a** something bought or offered at a low price. **3b** (*as modifier*): *a bargain price.* **4 into the bargain.** in excess; besides. **5 make** *or* **strike a bargain.** to agree on terms. ◆ *vb* **6** (*intr*) to negotiate the terms of an agreement, transaction, etc. **7** (*tr*) to exchange, as in a bargain. **8** to arrive at (an agreement or settlement). ORIG C14: from OF *bargaigne,* from *bargaignier* to trade, of Gmc origin
▸ **'bargainer** *n*

bargain away *vb* (*tr, adv*) to lose (rights, etc.) in return for something valueless.

bargain for *vb* (*intr, prep*) to expect; anticipate: *he got more than he bargained for.*

bargain on *vb* (*intr, prep*) to rely or depend on (something): *he bargained on her support.*

barge (bɑːdʒ) *n* **1** a vessel, usually flat-bottomed and with or without its own power, used for transporting freight, esp. on canals. **2** a vessel, often decorated, used in pageants, etc. **3** *Navy.* a boat allocated to a flag officer, used esp. for ceremonial occasions. ◆ *vb* **barges, barging, barged. 4** (*intr;* foll. by *into*) *Inf.* to bump (into). **5** *Inf.* to push (someone or one's way) violently. **6** (*intr;* foll. by *into* or *in*) *Inf.* to interrupt rudely or clumsily: *to barge into a conversation.* ORIG C13: from OF, from Med. L *barga,* prob. from LL *barca* a small boat

bargeboard ('bɑːdʒˌbɔːd) *n* a board, often decorated, along the gable end of a roof.

bargee (bɑː'dʒiː) *n* a person employed on or in charge of a barge.

bargepole ('bɑːdʒˌpəʊl) *n* **1** a long pole used to propel a barge. **2 not touch with a bargepole.** *Inf.* to refuse to have anything to do with.

bar graph *n* a graph consisting of vertical or horizontal bars whose lengths are proportional to amounts or quantities.

Bari ★ ('bɑːrɪ; *Italian* 'baːri) *n* a port in SE Italy, capital of Apulia, on the Adriatic coast. Pop.: 336 560 (1996 est.).

bariatrics (ˌbærɪ'ætrɪks) *n* (*functioning as sing*) the branch of medicine concerned with the treatment of obese people. ORIG C20: from Gk *barōs* weight + -IATRICS

Baring ★ ('bɛərɪŋ) *n* **Evelyn,** 1st Earl of Cromer. 1841–1917, British administrator. As consul general he controlled the Egyptian government (1883–1907).

barite ('bɛəraɪt) *n* the usual US and Canad. name for **barytes.** ORIG C18: from BAR(IUM) + -ITE[1]

baritone ('bærɪˌtəʊn) *n* **1** the second lowest adult male voice. **2** a singer with such a voice. **3** the second lowest instrument in the families of the saxophone, horn, oboe, etc. ◆ *adj* **4** relating to or denoting a baritone. ORIG C17: from It., from Gk, from *barus* heavy, low + *tonos* TONE

barium ('bɛərɪəm) *n* a soft silvery-white metallic element of the alkaline earth group. Symbol: Ba; atomic no.: 56; atomic wt.: 137.34. ORIG C19: from BAR(YTA) + -IUM

barium meal *n* a preparation of barium sulphate, which is opaque to X-rays, swallowed by a patient before X-ray examination of the upper part of his or her alimentary canal.

bark[1] (bɑːk) *n* **1** the loud abrupt usually harsh cry of a dog or certain other animals. **2** a similar sound, such as one made by a person, gun, etc. **3 his** (*or* **her**) **bark is worse than his** (*or* **her**) **bite.** he (*or* she) is bad-tempered but harmless. ◆ *vb* **4** (*intr*) (of a dog, etc.) to make its typical cry. **5** (*intr*) (of a person, gun, etc.) to make a similar loud harsh sound. **6** to say or shout in a brusque or angry tone: *he barked an order.* **7 bark up the wrong tree.** *Inf.* to misdirect one's attention, efforts, etc.; be mistaken. ORIG OE *beorcan*

bark[2] (bɑːk) *n* **1** a protective layer of dead corky cells on the outside of the stems of woody plants. **2** any of several varieties of this, used in tanning, dyeing, or in medicine. ◆ *vb* (*tr*) **3** to scrape or rub off skin, as in an injury. **4** to remove the bark or a circle of bark from (a tree). **5** to tan (leather), principally by the tannins in barks. ORIG C13: from ON *börkr*

bark[3] (bɑːk) *n* a variant spelling of **barque.**

barkentine (ˈbɑːkənˌtiːn) *n* the usual US and Canad. spelling of **barquentine.**

barker (ˈbɑːkə) *n* **1** an animal or person that barks. **2** a person at a fair booth, etc., who loudly addresses passers-by to attract customers.

Barker ★ (ˈbɑːkə) *n* **1 George** (**Granville**). 1913–91, British poet: author of *Calamiterror* (1937). **2 Howard.** born 1946, British playwright: his plays include *The Castle* (1985) and *A Hard Heart* (1992).

barking (ˈbɑːkɪŋ) *Sl.* ◆ *adj* **1** mad; crazy. ◆ *adv* **2** (intensifier): *barking mad.*

Barking and Dagenham ★ (ˈbɑːkɪŋ, ˈdæɡənəm) *n* a borough of E Greater London. Pop.: 143 180 (1991). Area: 34 sq. km (13 sq. miles).

Bar Kochba *or* **Bar Kosba** ★ (bɑː ˈkɒxbə, ˈkɒs-) *n* **Simeon.** died 135 A.D., Jewish leader who led an unsuccessful revolt against the Romans in Palestine.

Barletta ★ (*Italian* barˈletta) *n* a port in SE Italy, in Apulia. Pop.: 88 750 (1990).

barley (ˈbɑːlɪ) *n* **1** any of various annual temperate grasses that have dense bristly flower spikes and are widely cultivated for grain and forage. **2** the grain of any of these grasses, used in making beer and whisky and for soups, puddings, etc. ORIG OE *bærlīc* (adj); rel. to *bere* barley

barleycorn (ˈbɑːlɪˌkɔːn) *n* **1** a grain of barley, or barley itself. **2** an obsolete unit of length equal to one third of an inch.

barley sugar *n* a brittle clear amber-coloured sweet.

barley water *n* a drink made from an infusion of barley.

barm (bɑːm) *n* **1** the yeasty froth on fermenting malt liquors. **2** an archaic or dialect word for **yeast.** ORIG OE *bearm*

barmaid (ˈbɑːˌmeɪd) *n* a woman who serves in a pub.

barman (ˈbɑːmən) *n, pl* **barmen.** a man who serves in a pub.

Barmecide (ˈbɑːmɪˌsaɪd) *adj* lavish in imagination only; illusory; sham: *a Barmecide feast.* ORIG C18: from a prince in the *Arabian Nights' Entertainment* who served empty plates to beggars, alleging that they held sumptuous food

Bar Mitzvah (bɑː ˈmɪtsvə) (*sometimes not caps.*) *Judaism.* ◆ *adj* **1** (of a Jewish boy) having assumed full religious obligations, being at least thirteen years old. ◆ *n* **2** the occasion or celebration of this. **3** the boy himself. ORIG Heb.: son of the law

barmy (ˈbɑːmɪ) *adj* **barmier, barmiest.** *Sl.* insane. ORIG C16: orig., full of BARM, hence frothing, excited

barn[1] (bɑːn) *n* **1** a large farm outbuilding, chiefly for storing grain, etc., but also for livestock. **2** *US & Canad.* a large shed for railroad cars, trucks, etc. **3** any large building, esp. an unattractive one. **4** (*modifier*) relating to a system of poultry farming in which birds are allowed to move freely within a barn: *barn eggs.* ORIG OE *beren,* from *bere* barley + *ærn* room

barn[2] (bɑːn) *n* a unit of nuclear cross section equal to 10^{-28} square metres. Symbol: b ORIG C20: from BARN[1]; so called because of the relatively large cross section

Barnabas ★ (ˈbɑːnəbəs) *n* **Saint.** *New Testament.* original name *Joseph.* a Cypriot Levite who supported Saint Paul in his apostolic work (Acts 4:36,37). Feast day: June 11.

barnacle (ˈbɑːnək°l) *n* **1** any of various marine crustaceans that, as adults, live attached to rocks, ship bottoms, etc. **2** a person or thing that is difficult to get rid of. ORIG C16: from earlier *bernak,* from OF *bernac,* from LL, from ?
▸ **ˈbarnacled** *adj*

barnacle goose *n* a N European goose that has a black-and-white head and body. ORIG C13 *bernekke:* it was formerly believed that the goose developed from a shellfish

Barnard ★ (ˈbɑːnɑːd) *n* **1 Christiaan** (**Neethling**). born 1923, South African surgeon, who performed the first human heart transplant (1967). **2 Edward Emerson.** 1857–1923, US astronomer: noted for his discovery of the fifth satellite of Jupiter.

Barnardo ★ (bəˈnɑːdəʊ, bɑː-) *n* Dr **Thomas John.** 1845–1905, British philanthropist, who founded homes for destitute children.

Barnaul ★ (*Russian* bərnaˈul) *n* a city in S Russia, on the River Ob. Pop.: 596 000 (1995 est.).

barn dance *n* **1** *Brit.* a progressive round country dance. **2** *Brit.* a disco or party held in a barn. **3** *US & Canad.* a party with hoedown music and square-dancing.

Barnet ★ (ˈbɑːnɪt) *n* a borough of N Greater London: scene of a Yorkist victory (1471) in the Wars of the Roses. Pop.: 292 783 (1991). Area: 89 sq. km (34 sq. miles).

barney (ˈbɑːnɪ) *Inf.* ◆ *n* **1** a noisy fight or argument. ◆ *vb* **2** (*intr*) *Chiefly Austral. & NZ.* to argue or quarrel. ORIG C19: from ?

barn owl *n* an owl with a pale brown and white plumage and a heart-shaped face.

Barnsley ★ (ˈbɑːnzlɪ) *n* **1** an industrial town in N England, in South Yorkshire. Pop.: 75 120 (1991). **2** a unitary authority in N England, in South Yorkshire. Pop.: 226 700 (1995 est.). Area: 329 sq. km (127 sq. miles).

Barnstaple ★ (ˈbɑːnstəp°l) *n* a town in SW England, in Devon, on the estuary of the River Taw: tourism, agriculture. Pop.: 27 691 (1991).

barnstorm (ˈbɑːnˌstɔːm) *vb* (*intr*) **1** to tour rural districts putting on shows. **2** *Chiefly US & Canad.* to tour rural districts making speeches in a political campaign.
▸ **ˈbarnˌstorming** *n, adj*

Barnum ★ (ˈbɑːnəm) *n* **P**(**hineas**) **T**(**aylor**). 1810–91, US showman, who with J. A. Bailey founded the Barnum and Bailey Circus (1881).

barnyard (ˈbɑːnˌjɑːd) *n* **1** a yard adjoining a barn. **2** (*modifier*) characteristic of a barnyard. **3** (*modifier*) crude or earthy.

baro- *combining form.* indicating weight or pressure: *barometer.* ORIG from Gk *baros* weight

baroceptor (ˈbærəʊˌsɛptə) *n* another name for **baroreceptor.**

Baroda ★ (bəˈrəʊdə) *n* **1** a former state of W India, part of Gujarat since 1960. **2** the former name (until 1976) of **Vadodara.**

barogram (ˈbærəˌɡræm) *n Meteorol.* the record of atmospheric pressure traced by a barograph or similar instrument.

barograph (ˈbærəˌɡrɑːf) *n Meteorol.* a self-recording aneroid barometer.
▸ **barographic** (ˌbærəˈɡræfɪk) *adj*

Baroja ★ (*Spanish* baˈroxa) *n* **Pio** (ˈpio). 1872–1956, Spanish Basque novelist, who wrote nearly 100 novels.

barometer (bəˈrɒmɪtə) *n* **1** an instrument for measuring atmospheric pressure, usually to determine altitude or weather changes. **2** anything that shows change.
▸ **barometric** (ˌbærəˈmɛtrɪk) *or* **ˌbaroˈmetrical** *adj* ▸ **baˈrometry** *n*

baron (ˈbærən) *n* **1** a member of a specific rank of nobility, esp. the lowest rank in the British Isles. **2** (in Europe from the Middle Ages) originally any tenant-in-chief of a king or other overlord. **3** a powerful businessman or financier: *a press baron.* ORIG C12: from OF, of Gmc origin

baronage (ˈbærənɪdʒ) *n* **1** barons collectively. **2** the rank or dignity of a baron.

Baron-Cohen ★ (ˌbærən ˈkəʊən) *n* **Sacha.** born 1970, British television comedian; best known for his spoof interviews of celebrities in the character of 'Ali G'.

baroness (ˈbærənɪs) *n* **1** the wife or widow of a baron. **2** a woman holding the rank of baron.

baronet (ˈbærənɪt, -ˌnɛt) *n* (in Britain) a commoner who holds the lowest hereditary title of honour, ranking below a baron. Abbrev.: **Bart, Bt.**
► ˈ**baronetage** *n* ► ˈ**baronetcy** *n*

baronial (bəˈrəʊnɪəl) *adj* of, relating to, or befitting a baron or barons.

baron of beef *n* a cut of beef consisting of a double sirloin joined at the backbone.

barony (ˈbærənɪ) *n, pl* **baronies. 1a** the domain of a baron. **1b** (in Ireland) a division of a county. **1c** (in Scotland) a large estate or manor. **2** the rank or dignity of a baron.

baroque (bəˈrɒk, bəˈrəʊk) *n* (*often cap.*) **1** a style of architecture and decorative art in Europe from the late 16th to the early 18th century, characterized by extensive ornamentation. **2** a 17th-century style of music characterized by extensive use of ornamentation. **3** any ornate or heavily ornamented style. ◆ *adj* **4** denoting, in, or relating to the baroque. **5** (of pearls) irregularly shaped. ORIG C18: from F, from Port. *barroco* a rough or imperfectly shaped pearl

baroreceptor (ˈbærəʊrɪˌsɛptə) *or* **baroceptor** *n* a collection of sensory nerve endings, principally in the carotid sinuses and the aortic arch, that monitor blood-pressure changes in the body.

baroscope (ˈbærəˌskəʊp) *n* any instrument for measuring atmospheric pressure.
► **baroscopic** (ˌbærəˈskɒpɪk) *adj*

barouche (bəˈruːʃ) *n* a four-wheeled horse-drawn carriage, popular in the 19th century, having a retractable hood over the rear half. ORIG C19: from G (dialect) *Barutsche*, from It. *baroccio*, from LL *birotus*, from BI- + *rota* wheel

Barozzi ★ (*Italian* baˈrottsi) *n* See (Giacomo Barozzi da) **Vignola.**

barperson (ˈbɑːˌpɜːsᵊn) *n, pl* **barpersons.** a person who serves in a pub: used esp. in advertisements.

barque (bɑːk) *n* **1** a sailing ship of three or more masts having the foremasts rigged square and the aftermast rigged fore-and-aft. **2** *Poetic.* any boat. ORIG C15: from OF, from OProvençal *barca*

barquentine *or* **barquantine** (ˈbɑːkənˌtiːn) *n* a sailing ship of three or more masts rigged square on the foremast and fore-and-aft on the others. ORIG C17: from BARQUE + (BRIG)ANTINE

Barquisimeto ★ (*Spanish* barkisiˈmeto) *n* a city in NW Venezuela. Pop.: 625 450 (1990).

Barra ★ (ˈbærə) *n* an island in NW Scotland, in the Outer Hebrides: fishing, crofting, tourism. Pop.: 1200 (latest est.).

barrack[1] (ˈbærək) *vb* to house (soldiers, etc.) in barracks.

barrack[2] (ˈbærək) *vb Brit., Austral., & NZ inf.* **1** to criticize loudly or shout against (a team, speaker, etc.); jeer. **2** (*intr;* foll. by *for*) to shout support (for). ORIG C19: from Irish: to boast

barrack-room lawyer *n* a person who freely offers opinions, esp. in legal matters, that he or she is unqualified to give.

barracks (ˈbærəks) *pl n* (*sometimes sing; when pl, sometimes functions as sing*) **1** a building or group of buildings used to accommodate military personnel. **2** any large building used for housing people, esp. temporarily. **3** a large and bleak building. ORIG C17: from F *baraque*, from OCatalan *barraca* hut, from ?

barracouta (ˌbærəˈkuːtə) *n* a large predatory Pacific fish. ORIG C17: var. of BARRACUDA

barracuda (ˌbærəˈkjuːdə) *n, pl* **barracuda** *or* **barracudas.** a predatory marine mostly tropical fish, which attacks man. ORIG C17: from American Sp., from ?

barrage (ˈbærɑːʒ) *n* **1** *Mil.* the firing of artillery to saturate an area, either to protect against an attack or to support an advance. **2** an overwhelming and continuous delivery of something, as questions. **3** a construction across a watercourse, esp. one to increase the depth. ORIG C19: from F, from *barrer* to obstruct; see BAR[1]

barrage balloon *n* one of a number of tethered balloons with cables or net suspended from them, used to deter low-flying air attack.

barramundi (ˌbærəˈmʌndɪ) *n, pl* **barramundis, barramundies,** *or* **barramundi.** a large edible Australian estuary fish of the perch family. ORIG from Abor.

Barranquilla ★ (*Spanish* barranˈkiʎa) *n* a port in N Colombia, on the Magdalena River. Pop.: 1 064 255 (1995 est.).

barratry *or* **barretry** (ˈbærətrɪ) *n* **1** *Criminal law.* (formerly) the vexatious stirring up of quarrels or bringing of lawsuits. **2** *Maritime law.* a fraudulent practice committed by the master or crew of a ship to the prejudice of the owner. **3** the purchase or sale of public or Church offices. ORIG C15: from OF *baraterie* deception, from *barater* to BARTER
► ˈ**barratrous** *or* ˈ**barretrous** *adj* ► ˈ**barrator** *n*

Barrault ★ (*French* baro) *n* **Jean-Louis** (ʒɑ̃lwi). 1910–94, French actor and director, noted as a mime.

barre *French.* (bar) *n* a rail at hip height used for ballet practice and leg exercises. ORIG lit.: bar

barrel (ˈbærəl) *n* **1** a cylindrical container usually bulging outwards in the middle and held together by metal hoops. **2** Also called: **barrelful.** the amount that a barrel can hold. **3** a unit of capacity of varying amount in different industries. **4** a thing shaped like a barrel, esp. a tubular part of a machine. **5** the tube through which the projectile of a firearm is discharged. **6** the trunk of a four-legged animal: *the barrel of a horse.* **7 over a barrel.** *Inf.* powerless. **8 scrape the barrel.** *Inf.* to be forced to use one's last and weakest resource. ◆ *vb* **barrels, barrelling, barrelled** *or US* **barrels, barreling, barreled. 9** (*tr*) to put into a barrel or barrels. ORIG C14: from OF *baril*, ?from *barre* BAR[1]

barrel-chested *adj* having a large rounded chest.

barrel organ *n* an instrument consisting of a cylinder turned by a handle and having pins on it that interrupt the air flow to certain pipes or pluck strings, thereby playing tunes.

barrel roll *n* a flight manoeuvre in which an aircraft rolls about its longitudinal axis while following a spiral course in line with the direction of flight.

barrel vault *n Archit.* a vault in the form of a half cylinder.

barren (ˈbærən) *adj* **1** incapable of producing offspring, seed, or fruit; sterile. **2** unable to support the growth of crops, etc. **3** lacking in stimulation; dull. **4** not producing worthwhile results; unprofitable: *a barren period.* **5** (foll. by *of*) devoid (of): *barren of wit.* **6** (of rock strata) having no fossils. ORIG C13: from OF *brahain*, from ?
► ˈ**barrenness** *n*

Barren Lands ★ *pl n* **the.** a sparsely inhabited region of tundras in N Canada, extending westwards from Hudson Bay. Also called: **Barren Grounds.**

barricade (ˌbærɪˈkeɪd, ˈbærɪˌkeɪd) *n* **1** a barrier for defence, esp. one erected hastily, as during street fighting. ◆ *vb* **barricades, barricading, barricaded.** (*tr*) **2** to erect a barricade across (an entrance, etc.) or at points of access to (a room, district, etc.). ORIG C17: from OF, from *barriquer* to barricade, from *barrique* a barrel, from Sp. *barrica*, from *barril* BARREL

Barrie ★ (ˈbærɪ) *n* Sir **James Matthew.** 1860–1937, Scottish writer, noted for his plays *The Admirable Crichton* (1902) and *Peter Pan* (1904).

barrier (ˈbærɪə) *n* **1** anything serving to obstruct passage or to maintain separation, such as a fence or gate. **2** anything that prevents progress. **3** anything that separates or hinders union: *a language barrier.* ORIG C14: from OF *barriere*, from *barre* BAR[1]

barrier cream *n* a cream used to protect the skin, esp. the hands.

barrier-nurse *vb* (*tr*) to tend (infectious patients) in isolation, to prevent the spread of infection.
► **barrier nursing** *n*

barrier reef *n* a long narrow coral reef near the shore, separated from it by deep water.

barring ('bɑːrɪŋ) *prep* unless (something) occurs; except for.

barrister ('bærɪstə) *n* **1** Also called: **barrister-at-law.** (in England) a lawyer who has been called to the bar and is qualified to plead in the higher courts. Cf. **solicitor. 2** (in Canada) a lawyer who pleads in court **3** *US.* a less common word for **lawyer.** ORIG C16: from BAR[1]

barrow[1] ('bærəʊ) *n* **1** See **wheelbarrow, handbarrow. 2** Also called: **barrowful.** the amount contained in or on a barrow. **3** *Chiefly Brit.* a handcart with a canvas roof, used esp. by street vendors. ORIG OE *bearwe*

barrow[2] ('bærəʊ) *n* a heap of earth placed over one or more prehistoric tombs, often surrounded by ditches. ORIG OE *beorg*

Barrow ★ ('bærəʊ) *n* **1** a river in SE Ireland, rising in the Slieve Bloom Mountains and flowing south to Waterford Harbour. Length: about 193 km (120 miles). **2** See **Barrow-in-Furness** and **Barrow Point.**

barrow boy *n Brit.* a man who sells his wares from a barrow; street vendor.

Barrow-in-Furness ★ *n* an industrial town in NW England, in S Cumbria. Pop.: 48 947 (1991).

Barrow Point ★ *n* the northernmost tip of Alaska, on the Arctic Ocean.

Barry[1] ★ ('bærɪ) *n* a port in SE Wales, on the Bristol Channel. Pop.: 49 887 (1991).

Barry[2] ('bærɪ) ★ *n* **1** Sir **Charles.** 1795–1860, British architect: designer, assisted by Pugin, of the Houses of Parliament in London. **2** (*French* bari). **Comtesse du.** See **du Barry.**

Barrymore ★ ('bærɪˌmɔː) *n* a US family of actors, esp. **Ethel** (1879–1959), **John** (1882–1942), and **Lionel** (1878–1954).

Barry Mountains ★ *pl n* a mountain range in SE Australia, in E Victoria: part of the Australian Alps.

bar sinister *n* **1** (not in heraldic usage) another name for **bend sinister. 2** the condition or stigma of being of illegitimate birth.

Bart ★ (bɑːt) *n* **Lionel.** 1930–99, British composer and playwright. His musicals include *Oliver* (1960).

Bart. *abbrev. for* Baronet.

bartender ('bɑːˌtɛndə) *n* another name (esp. US and Canad.) for **barman** or **barmaid.**

barter ('bɑːtə) *vb* **1** to trade (goods, services, etc.) in exchange for other goods, services, etc., rather than for money. **2** (*intr*) to haggle over such an exchange; bargain. ◆ *n* **3** trade by the exchange of goods. ORIG C15: from OF *barater* to cheat

Barth ★ *n* **1** (*German* bart). **Heinrich.** ('haɪnrɪç). 1821–65, German explorer: author of *Travels and Discoveries in North and Central Africa* (1857–58). **2** (bɑːθ). **John (Simmons).** born 1930, US novelist; his novels include *Giles Goat-Boy* (1966) and *Once Upon a Time* (1994). **3** (*German* bart). **Karl** (karl). 1886–1968, Swiss Protestant theologian.
▸ **Barthian** ('bɑːtɪən, -θɪən) *adj, n*

Barthes ★ (*French* bart) *n* **Roland** (rɔlɑ̃). 1915–80, French writer and critic, who applied structuralist theory to literature: his books include *Mythologies* (1957) and *Elements of Semiology* (1964).

Bartholdi ★ (*French* bartɔldi) *n* **Frédéric August** (frederik ogyst). 1834–1904, French sculptor and architect, who designed (1884) the Statue of Liberty.

Bartholomew ★ (bɑː'θɒləˌmjuː) *n* **Saint.** *New Testament.* one of the twelve apostles (Matthew 10:3). Feast day: Aug. 24 or June 11.

bartizan ('bɑːtɪzən, ˌbɑːtɪ'zæn) *n* a small turret projecting from a wall, parapet, or tower. ORIG C19: var. of *bertisene,* erroneously for *bretising,* from *bretasce* parapet; see BRATTICE
▸ **bartizaned** ('bɑːtɪzənd, ˌbɑːtɪ'zænd) *adj*

Bartók ★ ('bɑːtɒk; *Hungarian* 'bɔrtoːk) *n* **Béla** ('beːlɔ). 1881–1945, Hungarian composer and pianist. His works include six string quartets, three piano concertos, ballets (including *The Miraculous Mandarin,* 1919), and the opera *Bluebeard's Castle* (produced 1918).

Bartolommeo ★ (*Italian* bartolom'meo) *n* **Fra.** original name *Baccio della Porta.* 1472–1517, Italian painter.

Barton ★ ('bɑːtᵊn) *n* **1** Sir **Derek (Harold Richard).** 1918–98, British chemist: shared the Nobel prize for chemistry (1969) for his work on conformational analysis. **2** Sir **Edmund.** 1849–1920, Australian statesman; first prime minister of Australia (1901–03). **3 Elizabeth,** known as the *Maid of Kent.* ?1506–34, English nun; executed for criticizing Henry VIII's attempt to annul his first marriage.

Baruch ★ ('bɛərʊk, 'bɑː-) *n Bible.* **a** a disciple of Jeremiah (Jeremiah 32–36). **b** the book of the Apocrypha said to have been written by him.

baryon ('bærɪˌɒn) *n* any of a class of elementary particles that have a mass greater than or equal to that of the proton. Baryons are either nucleons or hyperons. The **baryon number** is the number of baryons in a system minus the number of antibaryons. ORIG C20: from Gk *barus* heavy + -ON
▸ ˌ**bary'onic** *adj*

baryta (bə'raɪtə) *n* another name for barium oxide or barium hydroxide. ORIG C19: NL, from Gk *barutēs* weight, from *barus* heavy

barytes (bə'raɪtiːz) *n* a colourless or white mineral occurring in sedimentary rocks and with sulphide ores: a source of barium. ORIG C18: from Gk *barus* heavy + *-itēs* -ITE[1]

basal ('beɪsᵊl) *adj* **1** at, of, or constituting a base. **2** of or constituting a basis; fundamental.

basal metabolism *n* the amount of energy required by an individual in the resting state, for such functions as breathing and blood circulation.

basalt ('bæsɔːlt) *n* **1** a dark basic igneous rock: the most common volcanic rock. **2** a form of black unglazed pottery resembling basalt. ORIG C18: from LL *basaltēs,* var. of *basanītēs,* from Gk *basanitēs* touchstone
▸ **ba'saltic** *adj*

bascule ('bæskjuːl) *n* **1** a bridge with a movable section hinged about a horizontal axis and counterbalanced by a weight. **2** a movable roadway forming part of such a bridge. ORIG C17: from F: seesaw, from *bas* low + *cul* rump

base[1] (beɪs) *n* **1** the bottom or supporting part of anything. **2** the fundamental principle or part. **3a** a centre of operations, organization, or supply. **3b** (*as modifier*): *base camp.* **4** starting point: *the new discovery became the base for further research.* **5** the main ingredient of a mixture: *to use rice as a base in cookery.* **6** a chemical compound that combines with an acid to form a salt and water. A solution of a base in water turns litmus paper blue and produces hydroxyl ions. **7** a medium such as oil or water in which the pigment is dispersed in paints, inks, etc. **8** *Biol.* the point of attachment of an organ or part. **9** the bottommost layer or part of anything. **10** *Archit.* the part of a column between the pedestal and the shaft. **11** the lower side or face of a geometric construction. **12** *Maths.* the number of units in a counting system that is equivalent to one in the next higher counting place: *10 is the base of the decimal system.* **13** *Maths.* the number that when raised to a certain power has a logarithm (based on that number) equal to that power: *the logarithm to the base 10 of 1000 is 3.* **14** *Linguistics.* a root or stem. **15** *Electronics.* the region in a transistor between the emitter and collector. **16** a starting or finishing point in any of various games. ◆ *vb* **bases, basing, based. 17** (*tr;* foll. by *on* or *upon*) to use as a basis (for); found (on). **18** (often foll. by *at* or *in*) to station, post, or place (a person or oneself). ORIG C14: from OF, from L *basis* pedestal; see BASIS

base[2] (beɪs) *adj* **1** devoid of honour or morality; contemptible. **2** of inferior quality or value. **3** debased; alloyed; counterfeit: *base currency.* **4** *English history.* (of land tenure) held by villein or other ignoble service. **5** *Arch.* born of humble parents. **6** *Arch.* illegitimate. ORIG C14: from OF *bas,* from LL *bassus* of low height
▸ '**baseness** *n*

baseball ('beɪsˌbɔːl) *n* **1** a team game with nine players on each side, played on a field with four bases connected to form a diamond. The object is to score runs by batting the ball and running round the bases. **2** the hard rawhide-covered ball used in this game.

baseball cap *n* a close-fitting thin cap with a deep peak.

baseborn ('beɪsˌbɔːn) *adj Arch.* **1** born of humble parents. **2** illegitimate.

base hospital *n Austral.* a hospital serving a large rural area.

Basel ('bɑːzᵊl) *or* **Basle** ★ (bɑːl) *n* **1** a canton of NW Switzerland, divided into the demicantons of **Basel-Land** and **Basel-Stadt**. Pops.: 251 229 and 197 054 (1995 est.). Areas: 427 sq. km (165 sq. miles) and 36 sq. km (14 sq. miles) respectively. **2** a city in NW Switzerland, capital of Basel canton, on the Rhine: oldest university in Switzerland. Pop.: 175 561 (1995 est.). French name: **Bâle**.

baseless ('beɪslɪs) *adj* not based on fact; unfounded.
▸ **'baselessness** *n*

baseline ('beɪsˌlaɪn) *n* **1** *Surveying.* a measured line through a survey area from which triangulations are made. **2** a line at each end of a tennis court that marks the limit of play.

basement ('beɪsmənt) *n* **1a** a partly or wholly underground storey of a building, esp. one used for habitation rather than storage. **1b** (*as modifier*): *a basement flat.* **2** the foundation of a wall or building.

base metal *n* any of certain common metals, such as copper and lead, as distinct from precious metals.

basenji (bə'sɛndʒɪ) *n* a small African breed of dog that is unable to bark. ORIG C20: from Bantu

base rate *n* **1** *Brit.* the rate of interest used by individual commercial banks as a basis for their lending rates. **2** *Brit. inf.* the rate at which the Bank of England lends to the discount houses, which effectively controls the interest rates charged throughout the banking system. **3** *Statistics.* the average number of times an event occurs divided by the average number of times on which it might occur.

bases[1] ('beɪsiːz) *n* the plural of **basis**.

bases[2] ('beɪsɪz) *n* the plural of **base**.

base unit *n Physics.* any of the fundamental units in a system of measurement. The base SI units are the metre, kilogram, second, ampere, kelvin, candela, and mole.

bash (bæʃ) *Inf.* ◆ *vb* **1** (*tr*) to strike violently or crushingly. **2** (*tr;* often foll. by *in, down,* etc.) to smash, break, etc., with a crashing blow. **3** (*intr;* foll. by *into*) to crash (into); collide (with). **4** to dent or be dented. ◆ *n* **5** a heavy blow. **6** a party. **7 have a bash.** *Inf.* to make an attempt. ORIG C17: from ?

bashful ('bæʃfʊl) *adj* **1** shy or modest; diffident. **2** indicating or characterized by shyness or modesty. ORIG C16: from *bash,* short for ABASH + -FUL
▸ **'bashfully** *adv* ▸ **'bashfulness** *n*

-bashing *n and adj combining form. Inf. or sl.* **a** indicating a malicious attack on members of a particular group: *union-bashing.* **b** indicating any of various other activities: *Bible-bashing.*
▸ **-basher** *n combining form.*

Bashkir Republic ★ (bæʃ'kɪə) *n* a constituent republic of E central Russia, in the S Urals: established as the first Soviet autonomous republic in 1919; rich mineral resources. Capital: Ufa. Pop.: 4 097 000 (1996 est.). Area: 143 600 sq. km (55 430 sq. miles). Also called: **Bashkiria** (bæʃ'kɪərɪə), **Bashkortostan** (bæʃ'kɔːtɔːˌstɑːn; *Russian* baʃkɔrtɔ'stɑːn).

basho ('bæʃəʊ) *n, pl* **basho.** a grand tournament in sumo wrestling. ORIG C20: from Japanese, lit.: place

Basho ★ (bɑː'ʃɔː) *n* full name **Matsuo Basho,** originally *Matsuo Munefusa.* 1644–94, Japanese poet and travel writer.

basic ('beɪsɪk) *adj* **1** of, relating to, or forming a base or basis; fundamental. **2** elementary or simple: *a few basic facts.* **3** excluding additions or extras: *basic pay.* **4** *Chem.* of, denoting, or containing a base; alkaline. **5** *Metallurgy.* of or made by a process in which the furnace or converter is made of a basic material, such as magnesium oxide. **6** (of such igneous rocks as basalt) containing between 52 and 45 per cent silica. ◆ *n* **7** (*usually pl*) a fundamental principle, fact, etc.
▸ **'basically** *adv*

BASIC *or* **Basic** ('beɪsɪk) *n* a computer programming language that uses common English terms. ORIG C20: *b(eginner's) a(ll-purpose) s(ymbolic) i(nstruction) c(ode)*

Basic Curriculum *n Brit. education.* the National Curriculum plus religious education.

basic English *n* a simplified form of English with a vocabulary of approximately 850 common words, intended as an international language.

basic industry *n* an industry which is highly important in a nation's economy.

basicity (beɪ'sɪsɪtɪ) *n Chem.* **a** the state of being a base. **b** the number of molecules of acid required to neutralize one molecule of a given base.

basic slag *n* a slag produced in steel-making, containing calcium phosphate.

basic wage *n* **1** a person's wage excluding overtime, bonuses, etc. **2** *Austral.* the statutory minimum wage for any worker.

basidiomycete (bæˌsɪdɪəʊmaɪ'siːt) *n* any of a class of fungi, including puffballs and rusts, which produce spores at the tips of slender projecting stalks. ORIG C19: see BASIS, -MYCETE
▸ **baˌsidiomy'cetous** *adj*

Basie ★ ('beɪsɪ) *n* **William,** known as *Count Basie.* 1904–84, US jazz pianist, bandleader, and composer.

basil ('bæzᵊl) *n* a Eurasian plant having spikes of small white flowers and aromatic leaves used as herbs for seasoning. Also called: **sweet basil.** ORIG C15: from OF *basile,* from LL, from Gk *basilikos* royal

Basil ★ ('bæzᵊl) *n* **Saint,** called *the Great.* ?329–379 A.D., Greek patriarch: one of the founders of monasticism. Feast day: Jan. 2, June 14, or Jan. 1.

Basilan ★ (bə'siːlɑːn, bæ'siːlæn) *n* **1** a group of islands in the Philippines, SW of Mindanao. **2** the main island of this group, separated from Mindanao by the **Basilan Strait.** Area: 1282 sq. km (495 sq. miles). **3** a city on Basilan Island. Pop.: 201 407 (1980).

basilar ('bæsɪlə) *adj Chiefly anat.* of or at a base. Also: **basilary** ('bæsɪlərɪ, -sɪlrɪ). ORIG C16: from NL *basilaris*

Basildon ★ ('bæzɪldən) *n* a town in SE England, in S Essex: designated a new town in 1955. Pop.: 100 924 (1991).

basilect ('beɪsɪˌlɛkt) *n Linguistics.* One level of spoken English developed from Creole speech in a Caribbean territory, considered to be of the lowest social status. ORIG C20: from Gk basi bottom + lektos speech
▸ˌ **basi'lectal** *adj*

basilica (bə'zɪlɪkə) *n* **1** a Roman building, used for public administration, having a large rectangular central nave with an aisle on each side and an apse at the end. **2** a Christian church of similar design. **3** a Roman Catholic church having special ceremonial rights. ORIG C16: from L, from Gk, from *basilikē oikia* the king's house
▸ **ba'silican** *or* **ba'silic** *adj*

Basilicata ★ (*Italian* bazili'kata) *n* a region of S Italy, between the Tyrrhenian Sea and the Gulf of Taranto. Capital: Potenza. Pop.: 611 155 (1994 est.). Area: 9985 sq. km (3855 sq. miles).

basilisk ('bæzɪˌlɪsk) *n* **1** (in classical legend) a serpent that could kill by its breath or glance. **2** a small semiaquatic lizard of tropical America. The males have an inflatable head crest, used in display. ORIG C14: from L *basiliscus,* from Gk *basiliskos* royal child

basin ('beɪsᵊn) *n* **1** a round container open and wide at the top with sides sloping inwards towards the bottom. **2** Also called: **basinful.** the amount a basin will hold. **3** a washbasin or sink. **4** any partially enclosed or sheltered area where vessels may be moored. **5** the catchment area of a particular river and its tributaries. **6** a depression in the earth's surface. **7** *Geol.* a part of the earth's surface consisting of rock strata that slope down to a common centre. ORIG C13: from OF *bacin,* from LL *bacchīnon*

Basingstoke ★ ('beɪzɪŋˌstəʊk) *n* a town in S England, in N Hampshire. Pop.: 77 837 (1991).

basis ('beɪsɪs) *n, pl* **bases** (-siːz). **1** something that underlies, supports, or is essential to something else, esp. an idea. **2** a principle on which something depends or from which something has issued. ORIG C14: via L from Gk: step

bask (bɑːsk) *vb* (*intr*; usually foll. by *in*) **1** to lie in or be exposed to pleasant warmth, esp. that of the sun. **2** to flourish or feel secure under some benevolent influence or favourable condition. ORIG C14: from ON *bathask* to BATHE

basket (ˈbɑːskɪt) *n* **1** a container made of interwoven strips of pliable materials, such as cane, and often carried by a handle. **2** Also called: **basketful**. the amount a basket will hold. **3** something resembling such a container, such as the structure suspended from a balloon. **4** *Basketball*. **4a** the hoop fixed to the backboard, through which a player must throw the ball to score points. **4b** a point or points scored in this way. **5** a group of similar or related things: *a basket of currencies*. **6** *Inf.* a euphemism for **bastard** (senses 1–3). ORIG C13: prob. from OF *baskot* (unattested), from L *bascauda* wickerwork holder

basketball (ˈbɑːskɪtˌbɔːl) *n* **1** a game played by two teams of five men (or six women), usually on an indoor court. Points are scored by throwing the ball through an elevated horizontal hoop. **2** the ball used in this game.

basket case *n Sl.* **1** *Chiefly US & Canad.* a person who has had both arms and both legs amputated. **2** a person who is suffering from extreme nervous strain; nervous wreck. **3a** someone or something that is incapable of functioning effectively. **3b** (*as modifier*): *a basket-case economy*.

basket chair *n* a chair made of wickerwork.

basketry (ˈbɑːskɪtrɪ) *n* **1** the art or practice of making baskets. **2** baskets collectively.

basket weave *n* a weave of yarns, resembling that of a basket.

basketwork (ˈbɑːskɪtˌwɜːk) *n* another word for **wickerwork**.

basking shark *n* a very large plankton-eating shark, often floating at the sea surface.

Basle ★ (bɑːl) *n* a variant spelling of **Basel**.

basmati rice (bəzˈmætɪ) *n* a variety of long-grain rice with slender aromatic grains, used for savoury dishes. ORIG from Hindi, lit.: aromatic

basophil (ˈbeɪsəfɪl) *or* **basophile** *adj also* **basophilic** (ˌbeɪsəˈfɪlɪk). **1** (of cells or cell contents) easily stained by basic dyes. ◆ *n* **2** a basophil cell, esp. a leucocyte. ORIG C19: from Gk; see BASIS, -PHILE

Basotho-Qwaqwa ★ (bəˈsuːtuːˈkwɑːkwə, -ˈsəʊtəʊ-) *n* (formerly) a Bantu homeland in South Africa; reintegrated into South Africa in 1994. Also called: **Qwaqwa**. Former name (until 1972): **Basotho-Ba-Borwa**.

basque (bæsk) *n* a type of tight-fitting bodice for women. ORIG from F, from BASQUE

Basque (bæsk, bɑːsk) *n* **1** a member of a people living around the W Pyrenees in France and Spain. **2** the language of this people, of no known relationship with any other language. ◆ *adj* **3** of or relating to this people or their language. ORIG C19: from F, from L *Vascō* a Basque

Basque Provinces ★ *n* an autonomous region of N Spain, comprising the provinces of Álava, Guipúzcoa, and Viscaya: inhabited mainly by Basques, who retained virtual autonomy from the 9th to the 19th century. Pop.: 2 075 561 (1994 est.). Area: about 7250 sq. km (2800 sq. miles).

Basra, Basrah (ˈbæzrə), **Busra,** *or* **Busrah** ★ (ˈbʌsrə) *n* a port in SE Iraq, on the Shatt-al-Arab. Pop.: 406 296 (1987).

bas-relief (ˌbɑːrɪˈliːf, ˈbæsrɪˌliːf) *n* sculpture in low relief, in which the forms project slightly from the background. ORIG C17: from F, from It. *basso rilievo* low relief

Bas-Rhin ★ (*French* barɛ̃) *n* a department of NE France in Alsace region. Capital: Strasbourg. Pop.: 990 724 (1994 est.). Area: 4793 sq. km (1869 sq. miles).

bass[1] (beɪs) *n* **1** the lowest adult male voice. **2** a singer with such a voice. **3 the bass**. the lowest part in a piece of harmony. **4** *Inf.* short for **bass guitar, double bass**. **5a** the low-frequency component of an electrical audio signal, esp. in a record player or tape recorder. **5b** the knob controlling this. ◆ *adj* **6** relating to or denoting the bass. ORIG C15 *bas* BASE[1]; modern spelling infl. by BASSO

bass[2] (bæs) *n* **1** any of various sea perches. **2** a European spiny-finned freshwater fish. **3** any of various predatory North American freshwater fishes. ORIG C15: from BASE[2], infl. by It. *basso* low

bass clef (beɪs) *n* the clef that establishes F a fifth below middle C on the fourth line of the staff.

bass drum (beɪs) *n* a large drum of low pitch.

Bassein ★ (bɑːˈseɪn) *n* a city in Myanmar, on the Irrawaddy delta: a port on the **Bassein River** (the westernmost distributary of the Irrawaddy). Pop.: 150 000 (latest est.).

Basse-Normandie ★ (*French* basnɔrmɑ̃di) *n* a region of NW France, on the English Channel: consists of the Cherbourg peninsula in the west rising to the Normandy hills in the east; mainly agricultural.

Bassenthwaite ★ (ˈbæsᵊnˌθweɪt) *n* a lake in NW England, in Cumbria near Keswick. Length: 6 km (4 miles).

Basses-Alpes ★ (*French* basalp) *n* the former name for **Alpes-de-Haute-Provence**.

Basses-Pyrénées ★ (*French* baspirene) *pl n* the former name for **Pyrénées (Atlantiques)**.

basset (ˈbæsɪt) *n* a smooth-haired breed of hound with short legs and long ears. Also: **basset hound**. ORIG C17: from F, from *basset* short, from *bas* low

Basseterre ★ (bæsˈtɛə; *French* bastɛr) *n* a port in St Kitts in the Leeward Islands: the capital of St Kitts-Nevis. Pop.: 12 605 (1994 est.).

Basse-Terre ★ (ˈbæsˈtɛə; *French* bastɛr) *n* **1** a mountainous island in the Caribbean, in the Leeward Islands, comprising part of Guadeloupe. Area: 848 sq. km (327 sq. miles). **2** a port in W Guadeloupe, on Basse-Terre Island: the capital of the French Overseas Department of Guadeloupe. Pop.: 29 522 (1994 est.).

basset horn *n* an obsolete woodwind instrument. ORIG C19: prob. from G *Bassetthorn*, from It. *bassetto*, dim. of BASSO + HORN

bass guitar (beɪs) *n* a guitar that has the same pitch and tuning as a double bass, usually electrically amplified.

bassinet (ˌbæsɪˈnɛt) *n* a wickerwork or wooden cradle or pram, usually hooded. ORIG C19: from F: little basin; associated in folk etymology with F *barcelonnette* a little cradle

bassist (ˈbeɪsɪst) *n* a player of a double bass or bass guitar.

basso (ˈbæsəʊ) *n, pl* **bassos** *or* **bassi** (-sɪ). (esp. in operatic or solo singing) a singer with a bass voice. ORIG C19: from It., from LL *bassus* low; see BASE[2]

bassoon (bəˈsuːn) *n* **1** a woodwind instrument, the tenor of the oboe family. **2** an orchestral musician who plays a bassoon. ORIG C18: from F *basson*, from It., from *basso* deep
▸ **basˈsoonist** *n*

basso rilievo (*Italian* ˈbasso riˈljeːvo) *n, pl* **basso rilievos**. Italian name for **bas-relief**.

Bass Strait ★ (bæs) *n* a channel between mainland Australia and Tasmania, linking the Indian Ocean and the Tasman Sea.

bass viol (beɪs) *n* **1** another name for **viola da gamba**. **2** *US.* a less common name for **double bass** (sense 1).

bast (bæst) *n* **1** *Bot.* another name for **phloem**. **2** fibrous material obtained from the phloem of jute, flax, etc., used for making rope, matting, etc. ORIG OE *bæst*

bastard (ˈbɑːstəd, ˈbæs-) *n* **1** *Inf., offens.* an obnoxious or despicable person. **2** *Inf.* a person, esp. a man: *lucky bastard*. **3** *Inf.* something extremely difficult or unpleasant. **4** *Arch. or offens.* a person born of parents not married to each other. **5** something irregular, abnormal, or inferior. **6** a hybrid, esp. an accidental or inferior one. ◆ *adj* (*prenominal*) **7** *Arch. or offens.* illegitimate by birth. **8** irregular, abnormal, or inferior. **9** resembling a specified thing, but not actually being such: *a bastard cedar*. **10** counterfeit; spurious. **11** hybrid. ORIG C13: from OF *bastart*, ?from *fils de bast* son of the packsaddle
▸ **ˈbastardy** *n*

bastardize *or* **bastardise** (ˈbɑːstəˌdaɪz, ˈbæs-) *vb* **bastardizes, bastardizing, bastardized** *or* **bastardises, bastardising, bastardised**. (*tr*) **1** to debase. **2** *Arch.* to declare illegitimate.

baste[1] (beɪst) *vb* **bastes, basting, basted.** (*tr*) to sew with loose temporary stitches. ORIG C14: from OF *bastir* to build, of Gmc origin
▸ **'basting** *n*

baste[2] (beɪst) *vb* **bastes, basting, basted.** (*tr*) to moisten (meat) during cooking with hot fat and the juices produced. ORIG C15: from ?

baste[3] (beɪst) *vb* **bastes, basting, basted.** (*tr*) to beat thoroughly; thrash. ORIG C16: prob. from ON *beysta*

Bastia ★ ('bɑːstjə) *n* a port in NE Corsica: the main commercial and industrial town of the island: capital of Haute-Corse department. Pop.: 38 728 (1990).

Bastille (bæ'stiːl) *n* a fortress in Paris: a prison until its destruction in 1789, at the beginning of the French Revolution. ORIG C14: from OF *bastile* fortress, from OProvençal *bastida,* from *bastir* to build

bastinado (ˌbæstɪ'neɪdəʊ) *n, pl* **bastinadoes. 1** punishment or torture in which the soles of the feet are beaten with a stick. ◆ *vb* **bastinadoes, bastinadoing, bastinadoed. 2** (*tr*) to beat (a person) thus. ORIG C16: from Sp. *bastonada,* from *baston* stick

bastion ('bæstɪən) *n* **1** a projecting part of a fortification, designed to permit fire to the flanks along the the face of the wall. **2** any fortified place. **3** a thing or person regarded as defending a principle, etc. ORIG C16: from F, from earlier *bastillon* bastion, from *bastille* BASTILLE

Bastogne ★ (bæ'stəʊn; *French* bastɔɲ) *n* a town in SE Belgium: of strategic importance to Allied defences during the Battle of the Bulge; besieged by the Germans during the winter of 1944–45. Pop.: 7000 (1991 est.).

Basutoland ★ (bə'suːtəʊˌlænd) *n* the former name (until 1966) of **Lesotho.**

bat[1] (bæt) *n* **1** any of various types of club with a handle, used to hit the ball in certain sports, such as cricket. **2** a flat round club with a short handle used by a man on the ground to guide the pilot of an aircraft when taxiing. **3** *Cricket.* short for **batsman. 4** *Inf.* a blow from a stick. **5** *Sl.* speed; pace: *they went at a fair bat.* **6 carry one's bat.** *Cricket.* (of an opening batsman) to reach the end of an innings without being dismissed. **7 off one's own bat. 7a** of one's own accord. **7b** by one's own unaided efforts. ◆ *vb* **bats, batting, batted. 8** (*tr*) to strike with or as if with a bat. **9** (*intr*) *Cricket, etc.* (of a player or a team) to take a turn at batting. ORIG OE *batt* club, prob. of Celtic origin

bat[2] (bæt) *n* **1** a nocturnal mouselike animal flying with a pair of membranous wings. **2** *Sl.* an irritating or eccentric woman. **3 blind as a bat.** having extremely poor eyesight. **4 have bats in the** (*or* **one's**) **belfry.** *Inf.* to be mad or eccentric. ORIG C14 *bakke,* prob. of Scand. origin

bat[3] (bæt) *vb* **bats, batting, batted.** (*tr*) **1** to wink or flutter (one's eyelids). **2 not bat an eye** (*or* **eyelid**). *Inf.* to show no surprise or concern. ORIG C17: prob. var. of BATE[2]

Bataan ★ (bə'tæn, -'tɑːn) *n* a peninsula in the Philippines, in W Luzon: scene of the surrender of US and Philippine forces to the Japanese during World War II, later retaken by American forces.

Batangas ★ (bə'tæŋgæs) *n* a port in the Philippines, in SW Luzon. Pop.: 190 627 (1994 est.).

Batan Islands ★ (bə'tɑːn) *pl n* a group of islands in the Philippines, north of Luzon. Capital: Basco. Pop.: 12 091 (1980). Area: 197 sq. km (76 sq. miles).

Batavia ★ (bə'teɪvɪə) *n* **1** an ancient district of the Netherlands, on an island at the mouth of the Rhine. **2** an archaic or literary name for **Holland**[1] (sense 1). **3** a former name for **Jakarta.**
▸ **Ba'tavian** *adj, n*

batch[1] (bætʃ) *n* **1** a group or set of usually similar objects or people, esp. if sent off, handled, or arriving at the same time. **2** the bread, cakes, etc., produced at one baking. **3** the amount of a material needed for an operation. ◆ *vb* **4** to group (items) for efficient processing. **5** to handle by batch processing. ORIG C15 *bache;* rel. to OE *bacan* to BAKE

batch[2] *or* **bach** (bætʃ) *vb* (*intr*) *Austral. & NZ inf.* (of a man) to do his own cooking and housekeeping.

batch processing *n* a system by which the computer programs of a number of individual users are submitted as a single batch.

bate[1] (beɪt) *vb* **bates, bating, bated. 1** another word for **abate. 2 with bated breath.** in suspense or fear.

bate[2] (beɪt) *vb* **bates, bating, bated.** (*intr*) (of a hawk) to jump violently from a perch or the falconer's fist, often hanging from the leash while struggling to escape. ORIG C13: from OF *batre* to beat

bate[3] (beɪt) *n Brit. Sl.* a bad temper or rage. ORIG C19: from BAIT[1], alluding to the mood of a person who is being baited

bateau (bæ'təʊ) *n, pl* **bateaux** (-'təʊz). a light flat-bottomed boat used on rivers in Canada and the northern US. ORIG C18: from F: boat

bateleur eagle ('bætəlɜː) *n* an African short-tailed bird of prey. ORIG C19: from F *bateleur* juggler

Bates ★ (beɪts) *n* **1 Alan (Arthur).** born 1934, British actor. **2 H(erbert) E(rnest).** 1905–74, British writer, noted for the novels *The Darling Buds of May* (1958) and *The Triple Echo* (1970).

bath (bɑːθ) *n, pl* **baths** (bɑːðz). **1** a large container used for washing the body. **2** the act or an instance of washing in such a container. **3** the amount of liquid contained in a bath. **4** (*usually pl*) a place having baths or a swimming pool for public use. **5a** a vessel in which something is immersed to maintain it at a constant temperature, to process it photographically, etc., or to lubricate it. **5b** the liquid used in such a vessel. ◆ *vb* **6** *Brit.* to wash in a bath. ORIG OE *bæth*

Bath ★ (bɑːθ) *n* a city in SW England, in Bath and North East Somerset unitary authority on the River Avon: famous for its hot springs; a fashionable spa in the 18th century; Roman remains, notably the baths; university 1966. Pop.: 85 202 (1991). Latin name: **Aquae Sulis** ('ækwiː-'suːlɪs).

Bath and North East Somerset ★ *n* a unitary authority in SW England; formerly (1974–96) part of the county of Avon. Pop.: 158 692 (1996). Area: 351 sq. km (136 sq. miles).

Bath bun (bɑːθ) *n Brit.* a sweet bun containing spices and dried fruit.

Bath chair *n* a wheelchair for invalids.

bath cube *n* a cube of soluble scented material for use in a bath.

bathe (beɪð) *vb* **bathes, bathing, bathed. 1** (*intr*) to swim in a body of open water, esp. for pleasure. **2** (*tr*) to apply liquid to (skin, a wound, etc.) in order to cleanse or soothe. **3** to immerse or be immersed in a liquid. **4** *Chiefly US & Canad.* to wash in a bath. **5** (*tr; often passive*) to suffuse. ◆ *n* **6** *Brit.* a swim in a body of open water. ORIG OE *bathian*
▸ **'bather** *n*

bathers ('beɪðəz) *pl n Austral.* a swimming costume.

bathhouse ('bɑːθˌhaʊs) *n* a building containing baths, esp. for public use.

bathing cap ('beɪðɪŋ) *n* a tight rubber cap worn by a swimmer to keep the hair dry.

bathing costume ('beɪðɪŋ) *n* another name for **swimming costume.**

bathing machine ('beɪðɪŋ) *n* a small hut, on wheels so that it could be pulled to the sea, used in the 18th and 19th centuries for bathers to change their clothes.

bathing suit ('beɪðɪŋ) *n* a garment worn for bathing, esp. an old-fashioned one that covers much of the body.

batho- *combining form.* a variant of **bathy-.**

batholith (ˌbæθəlɪθ) *or* **batholite** ('bæθəˌlaɪt) *n* a very large irregular-shaped mass of igneous rock, esp. granite, formed from an intrusion of magma at great depth, esp. one exposed after erosion of less resistant overlying rocks.
▸ **ˌbatho'lithic** *or* **batholitic** (ˌbæθə'lɪtɪk) *adj*

Bath Oliver ('ɒlɪvə) *n Brit.* a kind of unsweetened biscuit. ORIG C19: after William *Oliver* (1695–1764), a physician at Bath

bathometer (bə'θɒmɪtə) *n* an instrument for measuring the depth of water.
▸ **bathometric** (ˌbæθə'mɛtrɪk) *adj* ▸ **ba'thometry** *n*

★ people and places

bathos ('beɪθɒs) *n* **1** a sudden ludicrous descent from exalted to ordinary matters or style in speech or writing. **2** insincere or excessive pathos. ORIG C18: from Gk: depth
▸ **ba'thetic** *adj*

bathrobe ('bɑ:θˌrəʊb) *n* **1** a loose-fitting garment of towelling, for wear before or after a bath or swimming. **2** *US & Canad.* a dressing gown.

bathroom ('bɑ:θˌru:m, -ˌrʊm) *n* **1** a room containing a bath or shower and usually a washbasin and lavatory. **2** *US & Canad.* another name for **lavatory**.

bath salts *pl n* soluble scented salts for use in a bath.

Bathsheba ★ (bæθ'ʃi:bə, 'bæθʃɪbə) *n Old Testament.* the wife of Uriah, who committed adultery with David and later married him and became the mother of his son Solomon (II Samuel 11–12).

bathtub ('bɑ:θˌtʌb) *n* a bath, esp. one not permanently fixed.

Bathurst ★ ('bæθəst) *n* **1** a city in SE Australia, in E New South Wales: scene of a gold rush in 1851. Pop.: 24 682 (1991). **2** a port in E Canada, in NE New Brunswick: rich mineral resources discovered in 1953. Pop.: 15 890 (1991). **3** the former name (until 1973) of **Banjul**.

bathy- *or* **batho-** *combining form.* indicating depth: *bathysphere.* ORIG from Gk *bathus* deep

bathyscaph ('bæθɪˌskæf), **bathyscaphe** ('bæθɪˌskeɪf, -ˌskæf), *or* **bathyscape** ('bæθɪˌskæp) *n* a submersible vessel with an observation capsule underneath, capable of reaching ocean depths of over 10 000 metres. ORIG C20: from BATHY- + Gk *skaphē* light boat

bathysphere ('bæθɪˌsfɪə) *n* a strong steel deep-sea diving sphere, lowered by cable.

batik ('bætɪk) *n* **a** a process of printing fabric in which parts not to be dyed are covered by wax. **b** fabric printed in this way. ORIG C19: via Malay from Javanese: painted

Batista ★ (*Spanish* ba'tista) *n* **Fulgencio** (ful'xenθjo), full name *Batista y Zaldívar.* 1901–73, Cuban military leader and dictator: president of Cuba (1940–44, 1952–59); overthrown by Fidel Castro.

batiste (bæ'ti:st) *n* a fine plain-weave cotton. ORIG C17: from F, prob. after *Baptiste* of Cambrai, 13th-cent. F weaver, its reputed inventor

Batley ★ ('bætlɪ) *n* a town in N England, in Kirklees unitary authority, in West Yorkshire. Pop.: 48 030 (1991).

batman ('bætmən) *n, pl* **batmen.** an officer's servant in the armed forces. ORIG C18: from OF *bat, bast,* from Med. L *bastum* packsaddle

baton ('bætən) *n* **1** a thin stick used by the conductor of an orchestra, choir, etc. **2** *Athletics.* a short bar carried by a competitor in a relay race and transferred to the next runner at the end of each stage. **3** a long stick with a knob on one end, carried, twirled, and thrown up and down by a drum major or majorette, esp. at the head of a parade. **4** a police truncheon (esp. in **baton charge**). **5** a staff or club carried as a symbol of authority. ORIG C16: from F *bâton,* from LL *bastum* rod

Baton Rouge ★ ('bæt°n 'ru:ʒ) *n* the capital of Louisiana, in the SE part on the Mississippi River. Pop.: 227 482 (1994 est.).

baton round *n* the official name for **plastic bullet**.

batrachian (bə'treɪkɪən) *n* **1** any amphibian, esp. a frog or toad. ◆ *adj* **2** of or relating to the frogs and toads. ORIG C19: from NL *Batrachia,* from Gk *batrakhos* frog

bats (bæts) *adj Inf.* mad or eccentric.

batsman ('bætsmən) *n, pl* **batsmen. 1** *Cricket, etc.* **1a** a person who bats or whose turn it is to bat. **1b** a player who specializes in batting. **2** a person on the ground who uses bats to guide the pilot of an aircraft when taxiing.

battalion (bə'tæljən) *n* **1** a military unit comprised of three or more companies or formations of similar size. **2** (*usually pl*) any large array. ORIG C16: from F *bataillon,* from OIt., from *battaglia* company of soldiers, BATTLE

batten[1] ('bæt°n) *n* **1** a sawn strip of wood used in building to cover joints, support lathing, etc. **2** a long narrow board used for flooring. **3** a lath used for holding a tarpaulin along the side of a hatch on a ship. **4** *Theatre.* **4a** a row of lights. **4b** the bar supporting them. ◆ *vb* **5** (*tr*) to furnish or strengthen with battens. **6 batten down the hatches. 6a** to use battens in securing a tarpaulin over a hatch on a ship. **6b** to prepare for action, a crisis, etc. ORIG C15: from F *bâton* stick; see BATON

batten[2] ('bæt°n) *vb* (*intr*) (usually foll. by *on*) to thrive, esp. at the expense of someone else. ORIG C16: prob. from ON *batna* to improve

Batten ★ ('bæt°n) *n* **Jean.** 1909–82, New Zealand aviator: the first woman to fly from Australia to Britain (1935).

batter[1] ('bætə) *vb* **1** to hit (someone or something) repeatedly using heavy blows, as with a club. **2** (*tr; often passive*) to damage or injure, as by blows, heavy wear, etc. **3** (*tr*) to subject (a person, esp. a close relative) to repeated physical violence. ORIG C14: *bateren,* prob. from *batten* to BAT[1]
▸ **'batterer** *n* ▸ **'battering** *n*

batter[2] ('bætə) *n* a mixture of flour, eggs, and milk, used to make cakes, pancakes, etc., and to coat certain foods before frying. ORIG C15 *bater,* prob. from *bateren* to BATTER[1]

batter[3] ('bætə) *n Baseball, etc.* a player who bats.

batter[4] ('bætə) *n* **1** the slope of the face of a wall that recedes gradually backwards and upwards. ◆ *vb* **2** (*intr*) to have such a slope. ORIG C16 (vb: to incline): from ?

battered[1] ('bætəd) *adj* subjected to persistent physical violence, esp. by a close relative living in the house: *a battered baby.*

battered[2] ('bætəd) *adj* coated in batter: *battered cod.*

battering ram *n* (esp. formerly) a large beam used to break down fortifications.

Battersea ★ ('bætəsɪ) *n* a district in London, in Wandsworth: noted for its dogs' home, power station (being developed into a leisure centre), and park.

battery ('bætərɪ) *n, pl* **batteries. 1** two or more primary cells connected, usually in series, to provide a source of electric current. **2** another name for **accumulator** (sense 1). **3** a number of similar things occurring together: *a battery of questions.* **4** *Criminal law.* unlawful beating or wounding of a person or mere touching in a hostile or offensive manner. **5** a fortified structure on which artillery is mounted. **6** a group of guns, missile launchers, etc, operated as a single entity. **7** a small unit of artillery. **8** *Chiefly Brit.* **8a** a large group of cages for intensive rearing of poultry and other farm animals. **8b** (*as modifier*): *battery hens.* **9** *Baseball.* the pitcher and the catcher considered together. ORIG C16: from OF *batterie* beating, from *battre* to beat, from L *battuere*

batting ('bætɪŋ) *n* **1** cotton or woollen wadding used in quilts, etc. **2** the action of a person or team that hits with a bat.

battle ('bæt°l) *n* **1** a fight between large armed forces; military or naval engagement. **2** conflict; struggle. **3 do, give,** *or* **join battle.** to engage in conflict or competition. ◆ *vb* **battles, battling, battled. 4** (when *intr,* often foll. by *against, for,* or *with*) to fight in or as if in military combat; contend (with): *shop stewards battling to improve conditions at work.* **5** to struggle: *he battled through the crowd.* **6** (*intr*) *Austral.* to scrape a living. ORIG C13: from OF *bataile,* from LL *battālia* exercises performed by soldiers, from *battuere* to beat
▸ **'battler** *n*

Battle[1] ★ ('bæt°l) *n* a town in SE England, in East Sussex: site of the Battle of Hastings (1066); medieval abbey. Pop.: 5235 (1991).

Battle[2] ★ ('bæt°l) *n* **Kathleen.** born 1948, US opera singer.

battle-axe *n* **1** (formerly) a large broad-headed axe. **2** *Inf.* an argumentative domineering woman.

battle-axe block *n Austral.* a block of land behind another, with access from the street through a narrow drive.

battle cruiser *n* a high-speed warship of battleship size but with lighter armour.

battle cry *n* **1** a shout uttered by soldiers going into battle. **2** a slogan used to rally the supporters of a campaign, movement, etc.

battledore ('bæt°lˌdɔ:) *n* **1** Also called: **battledore and shuttlecock.** an ancient racket game. **2** a light racket used in this game. **3** (formerly) a wooden utensil used for beating clothes, in baking, etc. ORIG C15 *batyldoure,* ?from OProvençal *batedor* beater, from OF *battre* to beat

battledress ('bætᵊlˌdrɛs) *n* the ordinary uniform of a soldier.

battle fatigue *n Psychol.* mental disorder, characterized by anxiety and depression, caused by the stress of warfare. Also: **combat fatigue.**

battlefield ('bætᵊlˌfiːld) *or* **battleground** ('bætᵊlˌgraʊnd) *n* the place where a battle is fought.

battlement ('bætᵊlmənt) *n* a parapet or wall with indentations or embrasures, originally for shooting through. ORIG C14: from OF *batailles,* pl. of *bataille* BATTLE
▸ **'battlemented** *adj*

battle royal *n* **1** a fight, esp. with fists or cudgels, involving more than two combatants; melee. **2** a long violent argument.

battleship ('bætᵊlˌʃɪp) *n* a heavily armoured warship of the largest type.

batty ('bætɪ) *adj* **battier, battiest.** *Sl.* **1** insane; crazy. **2** odd; eccentric. ORIG C20: from BAT[2]

Batum (bɑː'tuːm) *or* **Batumi** ★ (bɑː'tuːmɪ) *n* a city in Georgia: capital of the Adzhar Autonomous Republic; a major Black Sea port. Pop.: 137 100 (1994 est.).

batwoman ('bætwʊmən) *n, pl* **batwomen.** a female servant in any of the armed forces.

bauble ('bɔːbᵊl) *n* **1** a trinket of little value. **2** (formerly) a mock staff of office carried by a jester. ORIG C14: from OF *baubel* plaything, from ?

Bauchi ★ ('baʊtʃɪ) *n* **1** a state of N Nigeria: formed in 1976 from part of North-Eastern State; tin mining. Capital: Bauchi. Pop.: 4 801 569 (1995 est.). Area: 64 605 sq. km (24 944 sq. miles). **2** a town in N central Nigeria, capital of Bauchi state. Pop.: 76 070 (1991 est.).

baud (bɔːd) *n* a unit used to measure the speed of electronic code transmissions. ORIG after J. M. E. *Baudot* (1845-1903), F inventor

Baudelaire ★ (*French* bodlɛr) *n* **Charles Pierre** (ʃarl pjɛr). 1821–67, French poet, noted for *Les fleurs du mal* (1857).

Baudouin I ★ (*French* bodwɛ̃) *n* 1930–93, king of Belgium (1951–93).

bauera ('baʊərə) *n* a small evergreen Australian shrub with pink or purple flowers. ORIG C19: after Franz & Ferdinand *Bauer,* 19th-cent. Austrian botanical artists

Bauhaus ('baʊˌhaʊs) *n* a German school of functionalist architecture and applied arts founded in 1919. ORIG G, lit.: building house

bauhinia (bɔː'hɪnɪə, bəʊ-) *n* a climbing leguminous plant of tropical and warm regions, cultivated for ornament. ORIG C18: NL, after Jean & Gaspard *Bauhin,* 16th-cent. F herbalists

baulk (bɔːk; *usually for sense 1* bɔːlk) *n* **1** Also: **balk.** *Billiards.* the space between the baulk line and the bottom cushion. **2** *Archaeol.* a strip of earth left between excavation trenches for the study of the complete stratigraphy of a site. ◆ *vb, n* **3** a variant spelling of **balk.**

baulk line *or* **balk line** *n Billiards.* a straight line across a billiard table behind which the cue balls are placed at the start of a game. Also: **string line.**

baulky ('bɔːkɪ, 'bɔːlkɪ) *adj* a variant of **balky.**

Bautzen ★ ('baʊtsən) *n* a city in E Germany, in Saxony: site of an indecisive battle in 1813 between Napoleon's army and an allied army of Russians and Prussians. Pop.: 52 390 (1989 est.).

bauxite ('bɔːksaɪt) *n* an amorphous claylike substance consisting of hydrated alumina with iron and other impurities: the chief source of alumina and aluminium and also used as an abrasive and catalyst. ORIG C19: from F, from (*Les*) *Baux* in southern France, where orig. found

Bav. *abbrev. for* Bavaria(n).

Bavaria ★ (bə'vɛərɪə) *n* a state of S Germany: a former duchy and kingdom; mainly wooded highland, with the Alps in the south. Capital: Munich. Pop.: 12 014 700 (1996 est.) Area: 70 531 sq. km (27 232 sq. miles). German name: **Bayern.**
▸ **Ba'varian** *adj, n*

bawd (bɔːd) *n Arch.* **1** a person who runs a brothel, esp. a woman. **2** a prostitute. ORIG C14: from OF *baude,* fem. of *baud* merry

bawdy ('bɔːdɪ) *adj* **bawdier, bawdiest. 1** (of language, plays, etc.) containing references to sex, esp. to be humorous. ◆ *n* **2** obscenity or eroticism, esp. in writing or drama.
▸ **'bawdily** *adv* ▸ **'bawdiness** *n* ▸ **bawdry** ('bɔːdrɪ) *n*

bawdyhouse ('bɔːdɪˌhaʊs) *n* an archaic word for **brothel.**

bawl (bɔːl) *vb* **1** (*intr*) to utter long loud cries, as from pain or frustration; wail. **2** to shout loudly, as in anger. ◆ *n* **3** a loud shout or cry. ORIG C15: imit.
▸ **'bawler** *n* ▸ **'bawling** *n*

bawl out *vb* (*tr, adv*) *Inf.* to scold loudly.

Bax ★ (bæks) *n* Sir **Arnold** (**Edward Trevor**). 1883–1953, British composer; his works include seven symphonies and the tone poem *Tintagel* (1917).

Baxter ★ ('bækstə) *n* **1 James** (**Keir**). 1926–72, New Zealand poet. His works include *The Fallen House* (1953). **2 Richard.** 1615–91, English Puritan devotional writer.

bay[1] (beɪ) *n* **1** a wide semicircular indentation of a shoreline, esp. between two headlands. **2** an extension of lowland into hills that partly surround it. ORIG C14: from OF *baie,* ?from OF *baer* to gape, from Med. L *batāre* to yawn

bay[2] (beɪ) *n* **1** an alcove or recess in a wall. **2** any partly enclosed compartment. **3** See **bay window. 4** an area off a road in which vehicles may park or unload. **5** a compartment in an aircraft: *the bomb bay.* **6** *Naut.* a compartment in the forward part of a ship between decks, often used as the ship's hospital. **7** *Brit.* a tracked recess in the platform of a railway station, esp. one forming the terminus of a branch line. ORIG C14: from OF *baee* gap, from *baer* to gape; see BAY[1]

bay[3] (beɪ) *n* **1** a deep howl, esp. of a hound on the scent. **2 at bay. 2a** forced to turn and face attackers: *the dogs held the deer at bay.* **2b** at a distance. **3 bring to bay.** to force into a position from which retreat is impossible. ◆ *vb* **4** (*intr*) to howl (at) in deep prolonged tones. **5** (*tr*) to utter in a loud prolonged tone. **6** (*tr*) to hold at bay. ORIG C13: from OF, imit.

bay[4] (beɪ) *n* **1** a Mediterranean laurel. See **laurel** (sense 1). **2** any of several magnolias. See **sweet bay. 3** any of certain other trees or shrubs, esp. bayberry. **4** (*pl*) a wreath of bay leaves. ORIG C14: from OF *baie* laurel berry, from L *bāca* berry

bay[5] (beɪ) *n, adj* **1** (of) a reddish-brown colour. ◆ *n* **2** an animal of this colour. ORIG C14: from OF *bai,* from L *badius*

Bayamón ★ (*Spanish* baja'mon) *n* a city in NE central Puerto Rico, south of San Juan. Pop.: 231 845 (1996 est.).

bayberry ('beɪbərɪ) *or* **bay** *n, pl* **bayberries. 1** any of several North American aromatic shrubs or small trees that bear grey waxy berries. **2** a tropical American tree that yields an oil used in making bay rum. **3** the fruit of any of these plants.

Bayern ★ ('baiərn) *n* the German name for **Bavaria.**

Bayeux ★ (*French* bajø) *n* a town in NW France, on the River Aure: its museum houses the Bayeux tapestry and there is a 13th-century cathedral: dairy foods, plastic. Pop.: 14 704 (1990).

bay leaf *n* a leaf, usually dried, of the Mediterranean laurel, used in cooking to flavour soups and stews.

Baylis ★ ('beɪlɪs) *n* **Lillian Mary.** 1874–1937, British theatre manager: founded the Old Vic (1912) and the Sadler's Wells company for opera and ballet (1931).

Bay of Pigs ★ *n* a bay on the SW coast of Cuba: scene of an unsuccessful invasion of Cuba by US-backed troops (April 17, 1961). Spanish name: **Bahia de los Cochinos.**

bayonet ('beɪənɪt) *n* **1** a blade for stabbing that can be attached to the muzzle of a firearm. **2** a type of fastening in which a cylindrical member is inserted into a socket against spring pressure and turned so that pins on its side engage in slots in the socket. ◆ *vb* **bayonets, bayoneting, bayoneted** *or* **bayonets, bayonetting, bayonetted. 3** (*tr*) to stab or kill with a bayonet. ORIG C17: from F *baïonnette,* from BAYONNE

★ people and places

Bayonne ★ (*French* bajɔn) *n* a port in SW France: a commercial centre for the Basque region. Pop.: 41 846 (1990).

bayou (ˈbaɪjuː) *n* (in the southern US) a sluggish marshy tributary of a lake or river. ORIG C18: from Louisiana F, from Amerind *bayuk*

Bayreuth ★ (*German* baɪˈrɔyt) *n* a city in E Germany, in NE Bavaria: home and burial place of Richard Wagner; annual festivals of his music. Pop.: 72 780 (1991).

bay rum *n* an aromatic liquid, used in medicines and cosmetics, originally obtained by distilling the leaves of the bayberry tree with rum: now also synthesized.

bay window *n* a window projecting from a wall and forming an alcove of a room.

bazaar *or* **bazar** (bəˈzɑː) *n* **1** (esp. in the Orient) a market area, esp. a street of small stalls. **2** a sale in aid of charity, esp. of second-hand or handmade articles. **3** a shop where a variety of goods is sold. ORIG C16: from Persian *bāzār*

bazooka (bəˈzuːkə) *n* a portable tubular rocket-launcher, used by infantrymen as a short-range antitank weapon. ORIG C20: after a comic pipe instrument

BB *abbrev. for:* **1** Boys' Brigade. **2** (on British pencils, signifying degrees of softness of lead) double black.

BBC *abbrev. for* British Broadcasting Corporation.

bbl. *abbrev. for* barrel (container or measure).

BBQ *abbrev. for* barbecue.

BC *abbrev. for* British Columbia.

B.C. *or* **BC** *abbrev. for* (indicating years numbered back from the supposed year of the birth of Christ) before Christ.

USAGE NOTE See at **A.D.**

BCE *abbrev. for:* **1** Before Common Era (used, esp. by non-Christians, in numbering years B.C.). **2** *Brit.* Board of Customs and Excise.

BCG *abbrev. for* Bacillus Calmette-Guérin (antituberculosis vaccine).

BCNZ *abbrev. for* Broadcasting Corporation of New Zealand.

B complex *n* short for **vitamin B complex**.

BD *abbrev. for* Bachelor of Divinity.

bdellium (ˈdɛlɪəm) *n* **1** any of several African or W Asian trees that yield a gum resin. **2** the aromatic gum resin produced by any of these trees. ORIG C16: from L, from Gk *bdellion*, ? from Heb. *bĕdhōlah*

BDS *abbrev. for* Bachelor of Dental Surgery.

be (biː; *unstressed* bɪ) *vb present sing 1st person* **am**; *2nd person* **are**; *3rd person* **is**. *present pl* **are**. *past sing 1st person* **was**; *2nd person* **were**; *3rd person* **was**. *past pl* **were**. *present participle* **being**. *past participle* **been**. (*intr*) **1** to have presence in perceived reality; exist; live: *I think, therefore I am.* **2** (*used in the perfect tenses only*) to pay a visit; go: *have you been to Spain?* **3** to take place: *my birthday was last Thursday.* **4** (*copula*) used as a linking verb between the subject of a sentence and its noun or adjective complement. In this case *be* expresses relationship of equivalence or identity (*John is a man; John is a musician*) or specifies an attribute (*honey is sweet; Susan is angry*). It is also used with an adverbial complement to indicate a relationship in space or time (*Bill is at the office; the party is on Saturday*). **5** (*takes a present participle*) forms the progressive present tense: *the man is running.* **6** (*takes a past participle*) forms the passive voice of all transitive verbs: *a good film is being shown on television tonight.* **7** (*takes an infinitive*) expresses intention, expectation, or obligation: *the president is to arrive at 9.30.* ORIG OE *bēon*

Be *the chemical symbol for* beryllium.

BE *abbrev. for:* **1** bill of exchange. **2** Bachelor of Education. **3** Bachelor of Engineering.

be- *prefix forming transitive verbs.* **1** (*from nouns*) to surround or cover: *befog.* **2** (*from nouns*) to affect completely: *bedazzle.* **3** (*from nouns*) to consider as or cause to be: *befriend.* **4** (*from nouns*) to provide or cover with: *bejewel.* **5** (*from verbs*) at, for, against, on, or over: *bewail; berate.* ORIG OE *be-, bi-*, unstressed var. of *bī* BY

beach (biːtʃ) *n* **1** an area of sand or shingle sloping down to a sea or lake, esp. the area between the high- and low-water marks on a seacoast. ◆ *vb* **2** to run or haul (a boat) onto a beach. ORIG C16: perhaps rel. to OE *bæce* river

beachcomber (ˈbiːtʃˌkəʊmə) *n* **1** a person who searches shore debris for anything of worth. **2** a long high wave rolling onto a beach.

beachhead (ˈbiːtʃˌhɛd) *n Mil.* an area on a beach that has been captured from the enemy and on which troops and equipment are landed.

Beachy Head ★ (ˈbiːtʃɪ) *n* a headland in East Sussex, on the English Channel, consisting of chalk cliffs 171 m (570 ft) high.

beacon (ˈbiːkən) *n* **1** a signal fire or light on a hill, tower, etc., esp. formerly as a warning of invasion. **2** a hill on which such fires were lit. **3** a lighthouse, signalling buoy, etc. **4** short for **radio beacon**. **5** a radio or other signal marking a flight course in air navigation. **6** short for **Belisha beacon**. **7** a person or thing that serves as a guide, inspiration, or warning. ORIG OE *beacen* sign

Beaconsfield[1] ★ (ˈbɛkənzˌfiːld, ˈbiːk-) *n* a town in SE England, in Buckinghamshire: a residential centre for London. Pop.: 12 292 (1991).

Beaconsfield[2] ★ (ˈbiːkənzˌfiːld, ˈbɛk-) *n* **1st Earl of**. title of (Benjamin) **Disraeli**.

bead (biːd) *n* **1** a small pierced usually spherical piece of glass, wood, plastic, etc., which may be strung with others to form a necklace, etc. **2 tell one's beads.** to pray with a rosary. **3** a small drop of moisture. **4** a small bubble in or on a liquid. **5** a small metallic knob acting as the sight of a firearm. **6 to draw** *or* **hold a bead on.** to aim a rifle or pistol at. **7** *Archit., furniture.* a small convex moulding having a semicircular cross section. ◆ *vb* **8** (*tr*) to decorate with beads. **9** to form into beads or drops. ORIG OE *bed* prayer
▸ **ˈbeaded** *adj*

beading (ˈbiːdɪŋ) *n* **1** another name for **bead** (sense 7). **2** Also called: **beadwork** (ˈbiːdˌwɜːk). a narrow strip of some material used for edging or ornamentation.

beadle (ˈbiːdᵊl) *n* **1** *Brit.* (formerly) a minor parish official who acted as an usher and kept order. **2** *Judaism.* a synagogue attendant. **3** *Scot.* a church official who attends the minister. **4** an official in certain British institutions. ORIG OE *bydel*
▸ **ˈbeadleship** *n*

beadsman *or* **bedesman** (ˈbiːdzmən) *n, pl* **beadsmen** *or* **bedesmen**. *Arch.* **1** a person who prays for another's soul, esp. one paid or fed for doing so. **2** a person kept in an almshouse.

beady (ˈbiːdɪ) *adj* **beadier, beadiest. 1** small, round, and glittering (esp. in **beady eyes**). **2** resembling or covered with beads.
▸ **ˈbeadiness** *n*

beagle (ˈbiːgᵊl) *n* **1** a small sturdy breed of hound. **2** *Arch.* a spy. ◆ *vb* **beagles, beagling, beagled. 3** (*intr*) to hunt with beagles. ORIG C15: from ?

Beaglehole ★ (ˈbiːgᵊlˌhəʊl) *n* **John**. 1901–71, New Zealand historian. His works include *The Journals of James Cook* (1955).

beak[1] (biːk) *n* **1** the projecting jaws of a bird, covered with a horny sheath. **2** any beaklike mouthpart in other animals. **3** *Sl.* a person's nose. **4** any projecting part, such as the pouring lip of a bucket. **5** *Naut.* another word for **ram** (sense 5). ORIG C13: from OF *bec*, from L *beccus*, of Gaulish origin
▸ **beaked** *adj* ▸ **ˈbeaky** *adj*

beak[2] (biːk) *n* a Brit. slang word for **judge, magistrate, headmaster**, or **schoolmaster**. ORIG C19: orig. thieves' jargon

beaker (ˈbiːkə) *n* **1** a cup usually having a wide mouth. **2** a cylindrical flat-bottomed container used in laboratories, usually made of glass and having a pouring lip. ORIG C14: from ON *bikarr*

Beaker folk (ˈbiːkə) *n* a prehistoric people inhabiting Europe and Britain during the second millennium B.C. ORIG after beakers found among their remains

Beale ★ (biːl) *n* **Dorothea**. 1831–1906, British champion of women's education and suffrage; principal of Cheltenham Ladies' College (1858–1906).

be-all and end-all *n Inf.* the ultimate aim or justification.

beam (biːm) *n* **1** a long thick piece of wood, metal, etc., esp. one used as a horizontal structural member. **2** the breadth of a ship or boat taken at its widest part. **3** a ray or column of light, as from a beacon. **4** a broad smile. **5** one of two cylindrical rollers on a loom, which hold the warp threads and the finished work. **6** the main stem of a deer's antler. **7** the central shaft of a plough to which all the main parts are attached. **8** a narrow unidirectional flow of electromagnetic radiation or particles: *an electron beam.* **9** the horizontal centrally pivoted bar in a balance. **10 beam in one's eye.** a fault or grave error greater in oneself than in another person. **11 broad in the beam.** *Inf.* having wide hips. **12 off (the) beam. 12a** not following a radio beam to maintain a course. **12b** *Inf.* mistaken or irrelevant. **13 on the beam. 13a** following a radio beam to maintain a course. **13b** *Inf.* correct, relevant, or appropriate. ◆ *vb* **14** to send out or radiate. **15** (*tr*) to divert or aim (a radio signal, light, etc.) in a certain direction: *to beam a programme to Tokyo.* **16** (*intr*) to smile broadly. ORIG OE
▸ **'beaming** *adj*

beam-ends *pl n* **1 on her beam-ends.** (of a vessel) heeled over through an angle of 90°. **2 on one's beam-ends.** out of resources; destitute.

bean (biːn) *n* **1** any of various leguminous plants producing edible seeds in pods. **2** any of various other plants whose seeds are produced in pods or podlike fruits. **3** the seed or pod of any of these plants. **4** any of various beanlike seeds, as coffee. **5** *US & Canad. sl.* another word for **head. 6 full of beans.** *Inf.* full of energy and vitality. **7 not have a bean.** *Sl.* to be without money. ORIG OE *bēan*

beanbag ('biːnˌbæg) *n* **1** a small cloth bag filled with dried beans and thrown in games. **2** a very large cushion filled with foam rubber or polystyrene granules and used as a seat.

bean counter *n Inf.* an accountant.

bean curd *n* another name for **tofu.**

beanfeast ('biːnˌfiːst) *n Brit. inf.* **1** an annual dinner given by employers to employees. **2** any festive or merry occasion.

beanie *or* **beany** ('biːnɪ) *n, pl* **beanies.** a close-fitting cap resembling a skullcap.

beano ('biːnəʊ) *n, pl* **beanos.** *Brit. sl.* a celebration, party, or other enjoyable time.

beanpole ('biːnˌpəʊl) *n* **1** a tall stick used to support bean plants. **2** *Sl.* a tall thin person.

bean sprout *n* the sprout of a newly germinated mung bean, eaten esp. in Chinese dishes.

beanstalk ('biːnˌstɔːk) *n* the stem of a bean plant.

bear[1] (bɛə) *vb* **bears, bearing, bore, borne.** (*mainly tr*) **1** to support or hold up. **2** to bring: *to bear gifts.* **3** to accept or assume the responsibility of: *to bear an expense.* **4** (**born** in passive use except when followed by *by*) to give birth to: *to bear children.* **5** (*also intr*) to produce as by natural growth: *to bear fruit.* **6** to tolerate or endure. **7** to admit of; sustain: *his story does not bear scrutiny.* **8** to hold in the mind: *to bear a grudge.* **9** to show or be marked with: *he still bears the scars.* **10** to render or supply (esp. in **bear witness**). **11** to conduct (oneself, the body, etc.). **12** to have, be, or stand in (relation or comparison): *his account bears no relation to the facts.* **13** (*intr*) to move or lie in a specified direction. **14 bear a hand.** to give assistance. **15 bring to bear.** to bring into operation or effect. ◆ See also **bear down, bear on,** etc. ORIG OE *beran*

bear[2] (bɛə) *n, pl* **bears** *or* **bear. 1** a plantigrade mammal typically having a large head, a long shaggy coat, and strong claws. **2** any of various bearlike animals, such as the koala. **3** a clumsy, churlish, or ill-mannered person. **4** a teddy bear. **5** *Stock Exchange.* **5a** a speculator who sells in anticipation of falling prices to make a profit on repurchase. **5b** (*as modifier*): *a bear market.* Cf. **bull**[1] (sense 4). ◆ *vb* **bears, bearing, beared. 6** (*tr*) to lower or attempt to lower the price or prices of (a stock market or a security) by speculative selling. ORIG OE *bera*

Bear (bɛə) *n* **the. 1** the English name for either Ursa Major (Great Bear) or Ursa Minor (Little Bear). **2** an informal name for **Russia.**

bearable ('bɛərəbᵊl) *adj* endurable; tolerable.

bear-baiting *n* (formerly) an entertainment in which dogs attacked a chained bear.

beard (bɪəd) *n* **1** the hair growing on the lower parts of a man's face. **2** any similar growth in animals. **3** a tuft of long hairs in plants such as barley; awn. **4** a barb, as on a fish-hook. ◆ *vb* (*tr*) **5** to oppose boldly or impertinently. ORIG OE *beard*
▸ **'bearded** *adj*

beardless ('bɪədlɪs) *adj* **1** without a beard. **2** too young to grow a beard; immature.

bear down *vb* (*intr, adv;* often foll. by *on* or *upon*) **1** to press or weigh down. **2** to approach in a determined or threatening manner.

Beardsley ★ ('bɪədzlɪ) *n* **Aubrey (Vincent).** 1872–98, British illustrator: noted for his stylized black-and-white illustrations.

bearer ('bɛərə) *n* **1** a person or thing that bears, presents, or upholds. **2** a person who presents a note or bill for payment. **3** (in Africa, India, etc., formerly) a native porter or servant. **4** (*modifier*) *Finance.* payable to the person in possession: *bearer bonds.*

bear garden *n* **1** (formerly) a place where bear-baiting took place. **2** a scene of tumult.

bear hug *n* **1** a wrestling hold in which the arms are locked tightly round an opponent's chest and arms. **2** any similar tight embrace. **3** *Commerce.* an approach to the board of one company by another to indicate that an offer is to be made for their shares.

bearing ('bɛərɪŋ) *n* **1** a support for a rotating or reciprocating mechanical part. **2** (foll. by *on* or *upon*) relevance (to): *it has no bearing on this problem.* **3** a person's general social conduct. **4** the act, period, or capability of producing fruit or young. **5** anything that carries weight or acts as a support. **6** the angular direction of a point or course measured from a known position. **7** (*usually pl*) the position, as of a ship, fixed with reference to two or more known points. **8** (*usually pl*) a sense of one's relative position; orientation (esp. in **lose, get,** *or* **take one's bearings**). **9** *Heraldry.* **9a** a device on a heraldic shield. **9b** another name for **coat of arms.**

bearing rein *n Chiefly Brit.* a rein from the bit to the saddle, designed to keep the horse's head in the desired position.

bearish ('bɛərɪʃ) *adj* **1** like a bear; rough; clumsy; churlish. **2** *Stock Exchange.* causing, expecting, or characterized by a fall in prices: *a bearish feel to the market.*
▸ **'bearishness** *n*

bear on *vb* (*intr, prep*) **1** to be relevant to; relate to. **2** to be burdensome to or afflict.

bear out *vb* (*tr, adv*) to show to be true or truthful; confirm: *the witness will bear me out.*

bear raid *n* an attempt to force down the price of a security or commodity by sustained selling.

bearskin ('bɛəˌskɪn) *n* **1** the pelt of a bear, esp. when used as a rug. **2** a tall helmet of black fur worn by certain British Army regiments.

bear up *vb* (*intr, adv*) to endure cheerfully.

bear with *vb* (*intr, prep*) to be patient with.

beast (biːst) *n* **1** any animal other than man, esp. a large wild quadruped. **2** savage nature or characteristics: *the beast in man.* **3** a brutal, uncivilized, or filthy person. ORIG C13: from OF *beste,* from L *bestia,* from ?

beastly ('biːstlɪ) *adj* **beastlier, beastliest. 1** *Inf.* unpleasant; disagreeable. **2** *Obs.* of or like a beast; bestial. ◆ *adv* **3** *Inf.* (intensifier): *the weather is so beastly hot.*
▸ **'beastliness** *n*

beast of burden *n* an animal, such as a donkey or ox, used for carrying loads.

beast of prey *n* any animal that hunts other animals for food.

beat (biːt) *vb* **beats, beating, beat; beaten** *or* **beat. 1** (when *intr,* often foll. by *against, on,* etc.) to strike with or as if with a series of violent blows. **2** (*tr*) to punish by striking; flog. **3**

to move up and down; flap: *the bird beat its wings heavily.* **4** (*intr*) to throb rhythmically; pulsate. **5** (*tr; sometimes* foll. by *up*) *Cookery.* to stir or whisk vigorously. **6** (*tr;* sometimes foll. by *out*) to shape, thin, or flatten (metal) by repeated blows. **7** (*tr*) *Music.* to indicate (time) by one's hand, baton, etc., or by a metronome. **8** (when *tr,* sometimes foll. by *out*) to produce (a sound or signal) by or as if by striking a drum. **9** to overcome; defeat. **10** (*tr*) to form (a path, track, etc.) by repeatedly walking or riding over it. **11** (*tr*) to arrive, achieve, or finish before (someone or something). **12** (*tr; often* foll. by *back, down, off,* etc.) to drive, push, or thrust. **13** to scour (woodlands or undergrowth) so as to rouse game for shooting. **14** (*tr*) *Sl.* to puzzle or baffle: *it beats me.* **15** (*intr*) *Naut.* to steer a sailing vessel as close as possible to the direction from which the wind is blowing. **16 beat a retreat.** to withdraw in haste. **17 beat it.** *Sl.* (*often imperative*) to go away. **18 beat the bounds.** *Brit.* (formerly) to define the boundaries of a parish by making a procession around them and hitting the ground with rods. **19 can you beat it** *or* **that?** *Sl.* an expression of surprise. ◆ *n* **20** a stroke or blow. **21** the sound made by a stroke or blow. **22** a regular throb. **23a** an assigned or habitual round or route, as of a policeman. **23b** (*as modifier*): *beat police officers.* **24** the basic rhythmic unit in a piece of music. **25a** pop or rock music characterized by a heavy rhythmic beat. **25b** (*as modifier*): *a beat group.* **26** *Physics.* one of the regular pulses produced by combining two sounds or electrical signals that have similar frequencies. **27** *Prosody.* the accent or stress in a metrical foot. **28** (*modifier*) (*often cap.*) of, characterized by, or relating to the Beat Generation. ◆ *adj* **29** (*postpositive*) *Sl.* totally exhausted. ◆ See also **beat down, beat up.** ORIG OE *bēatan*
▸ **'beatable** *adj*

beatbox ('bi:tˌbɒks) *n* another name for **drum machine.**

beat down *vb* (*adv*) **1** (*tr*) *Inf.* to force or persuade (a seller) to accept a lower price. **2** (*intr*) (of the sun) to shine intensely.

beaten ('bi:t^{ə}n) *adj* **1** defeated or baffled. **2** shaped or made thin by hammering: *beaten gold.* **3** much travelled; well trodden. **4 off the beaten track. 4a** in unfamiliar territory. **4b** out of the ordinary; unusual. **5** (of food) mixed by beating; whipped. **6** tired out; exhausted.

beater ('bi:tə) *n* **1** a person who beats or hammers: *a panel beater.* **2** a device used for beating: *a carpet beater.* **3** a person who rouses wild game.

Beat Generation *n* (*functioning as sing or pl*) **1** members of the generation that came to maturity in the 1950s, whose rejection of the social and political systems of the West was expressed through contempt for regular work, possessions, traditional dress, etc. **2** a group of US writers, notably Jack Kerouac, Allen Ginsberg, and William Burroughs, who emerged in the 1950s.

beatific (ˌbi:ə'tɪfɪk) *adj* **1** displaying great happiness, calmness, etc. **2** of or conferring a state of celestial happiness. ORIG C17: from LL *beātificus,* from L *beātus,* from *beāre* to bless + *facere* to make
▸ **ˌbea'tifically** *adv*

beatify (bɪ'ætɪˌfaɪ) *vb* **beatifies, beatifying, beatified.** (*tr*) **1** *RC Church.* (of the pope) to declare formally that (a deceased person) showed a heroic degree of holiness in life and is worthy of veneration: the first step towards canonization. **2** to make extremely happy. ORIG C16: from OF *beatifier;* see BEATIFIC
▸ **beatification** (bɪˌætɪfɪ'keɪʃən) *n*

beating ('bi:tɪŋ) *n* **1** a whipping or thrashing. **2** a defeat or setback. **3 take some** *or* **a lot of beating.** to be difficult to improve upon.

beatitude (bɪ'ætɪˌtju:d) *n* **1** supreme blessedness or happiness. **2** an honorific title of the Eastern Christian Church, applied to those of patriarchal rank. ORIG C15: from L *beātitūdō,* from *beātus* blessed; see BEATIFIC

Beatitude (bɪ'ætɪˌtju:d) *n Christianity.* any of eight sayings of Jesus in the Sermon on the Mount (Matthew 5:3 –11) in which he declares that the poor, the meek, etc., will, in various ways, receive the blessings of heaven.

Beatles ★ ('bi:t^{ə}lz) *pl n* **the.** British rock group (1961–70): comprised John Lennon, Paul McCartney, George Harrison (born 1943), and Ringo Starr (real name *Richard Starkey,* born 1940). See also (John Winston Ono) **Lennon,** (Paul) **McCartney.**

beatnik ('bi:tnɪk) *n* **1** a member of the Beat Generation (sense 1). **2** *Inf.* any person with long hair and shabby clothes. ORIG C20: from BEAT (n) + -NIK

Beaton ★ ('bi:t^{ə}n) *n* Sir **Cecil** (**Walter Hardy**). 1904–80, British photographer.

Beatrix ★ ('bi:ətrɪks) *n* full name *Beatrix Wilhelmina Armgard.* born 1938, queen of the Netherlands from 1980.

Beatty ★ ('bi:tɪ) *n* **David,** 1st Earl Beatty. 1871–1936, British admiral of the fleet in World War I.

beat up *Inf.* ◆ *vb* **1** (*tr, adv*) to strike or kick repeatedly, so as to inflict severe physical damage. ◆ *adj* **beat-up. 2** worn-out; dilapidated.

beau (bəʊ) *n, pl* **beaux** (bəʊ, bəʊz) *or* **beaus** (bəʊz). **1** a man who is greatly concerned with his clothes and appearance; dandy. **2** *Chiefly US.* a boyfriend; sweetheart. ORIG C17: from F, from OF *biau,* from L *bellus* handsome

Beaufort ★ ('bəʊfət) *n* **1 Henry.** ?1374–1447, English cardinal, half-brother of Henry IV; chancellor (1403–04, 1413–17, 1424–26). **2** Lady **Margaret,** Countess of Richmond and Derby. ?1443–1509, mother of Henry VII.

Beaufort scale *n Meteorol.* an international scale of wind velocities from 0 (calm) to 12 (hurricane) (0 to 17 in the US). ORIG C19: after Sir Francis *Beaufort* (1774–1857), Brit. admiral and hydrographer who devised it

Beaufort Sea ★ *n* part of the Arctic Ocean off the N coast of North America.

beau geste *French.* (bo ʒɛst) *n, pl* ***beaux gestes*** (bo ʒɛst). a noble or gracious gesture or act. ORIG lit.: beautiful gesture

Beauharnais ★ (*French* boarnɛ) *n* **1 Alexandre** (alɛksɑ̃dr), Vicomte de. 1760–94, French general; first husband of Empress Joséphine: guillotined. **2** his son, **Eugène de** (øʒɛn də). 1781–1824, viceroy of Italy (1805–14) for his stepfather Napoleon I. **3** (**Eugénie**) **Hortense de** (øʒeni ɔrtɑ̃s də). 1783–1837, queen of Holland (1806–10) as wife of Louis Bonaparte; daughter of Alexandre Beauharnais; mother of Napoleon III. **4 Joséphine de** (ʒozefin də). See (Empress) **Josephine.**

beaujolais ('bəʊʒəˌleɪ) *n* (*sometimes cap.*) a popular fresh-tasting red or white wine from southern Burgundy in France.

Beaulieu ★ ('bju:lɪ) *n* a village in S England, in Hampshire: site of Palace House, seat of Lord Montagu and once the gatehouse of the ruined 13th-century abbey; the National Motor Museum is in its grounds. Pop.: 1200 (latest est.).

Beaumarchais ★ (*French* bomarʃɛ) *n* **Pierre Augustin Caron de** (pjɛr ogystɛ̃ karɔ̃ də). 1732–99, French dramatist, noted for his comedies *The Barber of Seville* (1775) and *The Marriage of Figaro* (1784).

Beaumaris ★ (bəʊ'mærɪs) *n* a resort in N Wales, on the island of Anglesey: 13th-century castle. Pop.: 1561 (1991).

beau monde ('bəʊ 'mɒnd) *n* the world of fashion and society. ORIG C18: F, lit.: fine world

Beaumont[1] ★ ('bəʊmɒnt) *n* a city in SE Texas. Pop.: 115 022 (1994 est.).

Beaumont[2] ★ ('bəʊmɒnt) *n* **Francis.** 1584–1616, English dramatist, who collaborated with John Fletcher on plays including *The Maid's Tragedy* (1611).

Beaune ★ (bəʊn) *n* **1** a city in E France, near Dijon: an important trading centre for Burgundy wines. Pop.: 22 170 (1990). **2** a wine produced in this district.

beaut (bju:t) *Sl., chiefly Austral. & NZ.* ◆ *n* **1** an outstanding person or thing. ◆ *adj, interj* **2** excellent.

beauteous ('bju:tɪəs) *adj* a poetic word for **beautiful.**
▸ **'beauteousness** *n*

beautician (bju:'tɪʃən) *n* a person who works in or manages a beauty salon.

beautiful ('bju:tɪful) *adj* **1** possessing beauty; aesthetically pleasing. **2** highly enjoyable; very pleasant.
▸ **'beautifully** *adv*

beautify ('bjuːtɪˌfaɪ) *vb* **beautifies, beautifying, beautified.** to make or become beautiful.
▸ **beautification** (ˌbjuːtɪfɪ'keɪʃən) *n* ▸ **'beautiˌfier** *n*

beauty ('bjuːtɪ) *n, pl* **beauties. 1** the combination of all the qualities of a person or thing that delight the senses and mind. **2** a very attractive woman. **3** *Inf.* an outstanding example of its kind. **4** *Inf.* an advantageous feature: *one beauty of the job is the short hours.* ◆ *interj* **5** (*NZ* 'bjuːdɪ). *Austral. & NZ sl.* an expression of approval or agreement. ORIG C13: from OF *biauté,* from *biau* beautiful; see BEAU

beauty queen *n* an attractive young woman, esp. one who has won a beauty contest.

beauty salon *or* **parlour** *n* an establishment providing services such as hairdressing, facial treatment, and massage.

beauty sleep *n Inf.* sleep, esp. sleep before midnight.

beauty spot *n* **1** a place of outstanding beauty. **2** a mole or other similar natural mark on the skin. **3** (esp. in the 18th century) a small dark-coloured patch or spot worn on a lady's face as an adornment.

Beauvais ★ (*French* bovɛ) *n* a market town in N France, 64 km (40 miles) northwest of Paris. Pop.: 56 280 (1990).

Beauvoir ★ (*French* bovwar) *n* **Simone de** (simɔn də). 1908–86, French writer, whose works include *Le deuxième sexe* (1949), and *Les mandarins* (1954).

beaux (bəʊ, bəʊz) *n* a plural of **beau.**

beaux-arts (bəʊ'zɑː) *pl n* **1** another word for **fine art. 2** (*modifier*) relating to the classical decorative style, esp. that of the École des Beaux-Arts in Paris: *beaux-arts influences.* ORIG F

beaver[1] ('biːvə) *n* **1** a large amphibious rodent of Europe, Asia, and North America. It has soft brown fur, a broad flat hairless tail, and webbed hind feet, and constructs complex dams and houses (lodges) in rivers. **2** its fur. **3** a tall hat of beaver fur worn during the 19th century. **4** a woollen napped cloth resembling beaver fur. **5** *Obs.* a full beard. **6** a bearded man. **7** (*modifier*) made of beaver fur or similar material. ◆ *vb* **8** (*intr;* usually foll. by *away*) to work industriously or steadily. ORIG OE *beofor*

beaver[2] ('biːvə) *n* a movable piece on a medieval helmet used to protect the lower face. ORIG C15: from OF *baviere,* from *baver* to dribble

Beaverbrook ★ ('biːvəˌbrʊk) *n* **1st Baron,** title of *William Maxwell Aitken.* 1879–1964, British newspaper proprietor and Conservative politician, born in Canada. Minister of information (1918); minister of aircraft production (1940–41).

Bebington ★ ('bɛbɪŋtən) *n* a town in NW England, in Wirral unitary authority, Merseyside: docks and chemical works. Pop.: 60 148 (1991).

bebop ('biːbɒp) *n* the full name for **bop** (sense 1). ORIG C20: imit. of the rhythm
▸ **'bebopper** *n*

becalmed (bɪ'kɑːmd) *adj* (of a sailing boat or ship) motionless through lack of wind.

became (bɪ'keɪm) *vb* the past tense of **become.**

because (bɪ'kɒz, -'kəz) *conj* **1** (*subordinating*) on account of the fact that; since: *because it's so cold we'll go home.* **2** **because of.** (*prep*) on account of: *I lost my job because of her.* ORIG C14 *bi cause,* from *bi* BY + CAUSE

USAGE NOTE See at **account, reason.**

béchamel sauce (ˌbeɪʃə'mɛl) *n* a thick white sauce flavoured with onion and seasonings. ORIG C18: after the Marquis of *Béchamel,* its F inventor

Béchar ★ (*French* beʃar) *n* a city in NW Algeria: an oasis. Pop.: 107 311 (1987). Former name: **Colomb-Béchar.**

bêche-de-mer (ˌbɛʃdə'mɛə) *n, pl* **bêches-de-mer** (ˌbɛʃdə'mɛə) *or* **bêche-de-mer.** another name for **trepang.** ORIG C19: quasi-F, from earlier E *biche de mer,* from Port. *bicho do mar* worm of the sea

Bechet ★ ('beʃeɪ) *n* **Sidney (Joseph).** 1897–1959, US jazz soprano saxophonist and clarinettist.

Bechstein ★ (*German* 'bɛçʃtaɪn) *n* **Karl** (karl). 1826–1900, German piano maker; founder (1853) of the Bechstein company of piano manufacturers in Berlin.

Bechuana (bɛ'tʃwɑːnə; ˌbɛkjʊ'ɑːnə) *n, pl* **Bechuana** *or* **Bechuanas.** a former name for a Bantu of Botswana.

Bechuanaland ★ (bɛ'tʃwɑːnəˌlænd; ˌbɛtʃʊ'ɑːnəˌlænd, ˌbɛkjʊ-) *n* the former name (until 1966) of **Botswana.**

beck[1] (bɛk) *n* **1** a nod, wave, or other gesture. **2** **at (someone's) beck and call.** subject to (someone's) slightest whim. ORIG C14: short for *becnen* to BECKON

beck[2] (bɛk) *n* (in N England) a stream. ORIG OE *becc*

Beckenbauer ★ ('bɛkənˌbaʊə) *n* **Franz.** born 1945, German footballer: team captain when West Germany won the World Cup (1974): manager of West Germany (1984–90).

Becker ★ ('bɛkə) *n* **Boris** ('bɒrɪs). born 1967, German tennis player: Wimbledon champion 1985, 1986, and 1989.

Becket ★ ('bɛkɪt) *n* **Saint Thomas à.** 1118–70, English prelate; chancellor (1155–62) to Henry II; archbishop of Canterbury (1162–70): murdered. Feast day: Dec. 29 or July 7.

Beckett ★ ('bɛkɪt) *n* **1 Margaret (Mary).** born 1943, British Labour politician; leader of the House of Commons from 1998. **2 Samuel.** 1906–89, Irish dramatist and novelist writing in French and English, whose works include the plays *Waiting for Godot* (1952), *Endgame* (1957), and the novel *Malone Dies* (1951): Nobel prize for literature 1969.

Beckford ★ ('bɛkfəd) *n* **William.** 1759–1844, British writer; author of the oriental romance *Vathek* (1787).

Beckham ★ ('bɛkəm) *n* **1 David.** born 1975, British footballer; plays for Manchester United and England. **2** his wife **Victoria** (née *Adams,* known as *Posh Spice*). born 1974, British pop singer, a member of the Spice Girls.

Beckmann ★ (*German* 'bɛkman) *n* **1 Ernst Otto** (ɛrnst 'ɔto). 1853–1923, German chemist: devised the **Beckmann thermometer. 2 Max** (maks). 1884–1950, German expressionist painter.

beckon ('bɛkən) *vb* **1** to summon with a gesture of the hand or head. **2** to entice or lure. ◆ *n* **3** a summoning gesture. ORIG OE *bīecnan,* from *bēacen* sign
▸ **'beckoner** *n* ▸ **'beckoning** *adj, n*

becloud (bɪ'klaʊd) *vb* (*tr*) **1** to cover or obscure with a cloud. **2** to confuse or muddle.

become (bɪ'kʌm) *vb* **becomes, becoming, became, become.** (*mainly intr*) **1** (*copula*) to come to be; develop or grow into: *he became a monster.* **2** (foll. by *of; usually used in a question*) to happen (to): *what became of him?* **3** (*tr*) to suit: *that dress becomes you.* **4** (*tr*) to be appropriate; to befit: *it ill becomes you to complain.* ORIG OE *becuman* to happen

becoming (bɪ'kʌmɪŋ) *adj* suitable; appropriate.
▸ **be'comingly** *adv* ▸ **be'comingness** *n*

becquerel (ˌbɛkə'rɛl) *n* the SI unit of activity of a radioactive source. ORIG after A. H. BECQUEREL

Becquerel ★ (*French* bɛkrɛl) *n* **Antoine Henri** (ɑ̃twan ɑ̃ri). 1852–1908, French physicist, who instigated the study of radioactivity: Nobel prize for physics 1903.

bed (bɛd) *n* **1** a piece of furniture on which to sleep. **2** the mattress and bedclothes: *an unmade bed.* **3** sleep or rest: *time for bed.* **4** any place in which a person or animal sleeps or rests. **5** *Med.* a unit of potential occupancy in a hospital or residential institution. **6** *Inf.* sexual intercourse. **7** a plot of ground in which plants are grown. **8** the bottom of a river, lake, or sea. **9** a part of this used for cultivation of a plant or animal: *oyster beds.* **10** any underlying structure or part. **11** a layer of rock, esp. sedimentary rock. **12 go to bed. 12a** (often foll. by *with*) to have sexual intercourse (with). **12b** *Journalism, printing.* (of a newspaper, etc.) to go to press; start printing. **13 in bed with.** *Inf.* cooperating closely with (another person, organization, government, etc.), esp. covertly. **14 put to bed.** *Journalism.* to finalize work on (a newspaper, etc.) so that it is ready to go to press. **15 take to one's bed.** to remain in bed, esp. because of illness. ◆ *vb* **beds, bedding, bedded. 16** (usually foll. by *down*) to go to or put into a place to sleep or rest. **17** (*tr*) to have sexual intercourse with. **18** (*tr*) to place firmly into position; embed. **19** *Geol.* to form or be arranged in a distinct layer; stratify. **20** (*tr;* often foll. by *out*) to plant in a bed of soil. ORIG OE *bedd*

BEd *abbrev. for* Bachelor of Education.

bed and board *n* sleeping accommodation and meals.

bed and breakfast *n Chiefly Brit.* **1** (in a hotel, boarding house, etc.) overnight accommodation and breakfast. **2** the selling of shares after hours one evening on a stock exchange and buying them back the next morning, in order to establish a loss for capital-gains tax purposes.

bedaub (bɪˈdɔːb) *vb* (*tr*) **1** to smear all over with something thick, sticky, or dirty. **2** to ornament in a gaudy or vulgar fashion.

bedazzle (bɪˈdæzᵊl) *vb* **bedazzles, bedazzling, bedazzled.** (*tr*) to dazzle or confuse, as with brilliance.
▸ **beˈdazzlement** *n*

bed bath *n* another name for **blanket bath.**

bedbug (ˈbɛdˌbʌg) *n* any of several bloodsucking wingless insects of temperate regions, infesting dirty houses.

bedchamber (ˈbɛdˌtʃeɪmbə) *n* an archaic word for **bedroom.**

bedclothes (ˈbɛdˌkləʊðz) *pl n* sheets, blankets, and other coverings for a bed.

beddable (ˈbɛdəbᵊl) *adj* sexually attractive.

bedding (ˈbɛdɪŋ) *n* **1** bedclothes, sometimes considered with a mattress. **2** litter, such as straw, for animals. **3** a foundation, such as mortar under a brick. **4** the stratification of rocks.

bedding plant *n* an immature plant that may be planted out in a garden bed.

Beddoes ★ (ˈbɛdəʊz) *n* **Thomas Lovell.** 1803–49, British poet, noted for his macabre imagery, esp. in *Death's Jest-Book* (1850).

Bede ★ (biːd) *n* **Saint,** known as *the Venerable Bede.* ?673–735 A.D., English monk, scholar, historian, and theologian, noted for his Latin *Ecclesiastical History of the English People* (731). Feast day: May 27 or 25.

bedeck (bɪˈdɛk) *vb* (*tr*) to cover with decorations; adorn.

bedevil (bɪˈdɛvᵊl) *vb* **bedevils, bedevilling, bedevilled** *or US* **bedevils, bedeviling, bedeviled.** (*tr*) **1** to harass or torment. **2** to throw into confusion. **3** to possess, as with a devil.
▸ **beˈdevilment** *n*

bedew (bɪˈdjuː) *vb* (*tr*) to wet as with dew.

bedfellow (ˈbɛdˌfɛləʊ) *n* **1** a person with whom one shares a bed. **2** a temporary ally or associate.

Bedford[1] ★ (ˈbɛdfəd) *n* **1** a town in SE central England, administrative centre of Bedfordshire, on the River Ouse. Pop.: 73 917 (1991). **2** short for **Bedfordshire.**

Bedford[2] ★ (ˈbɛdfəd) *n* **1 David.** born 1937, British composer, influenced by rock music. **2 Duke of,** title of *John of Lancaster.* 1389–1435, son of Henry IV of England: protector of England and regent of France (1422–35).

Bedfordshire ★ (ˈbɛdfədˌʃɪə, -ʃə) *n* a county of S central England: mainly low-lying, with the Chiltern Hills in the south. Administrative centre: Bedford. Pop. (excluding Luton): 362 300 (1997 est.). Area (excluding Luton): 1192 sq. km (460 sq. miles). Abbrev.: **Beds.**

bedight (bɪˈdaɪt) *Arch.* ◆ *vb* **bedights, bedighting, bedight** *or* **bedighted. 1** (*tr*) to array or adorn. ◆ *adj* **2** (*p.p.*) adorned or bedecked. ORIG C14: from DIGHT

bedim (bɪˈdɪm) *vb* **bedims, bedimming, bedimmed.** (*tr*) to make dim or obscure.

Bedivere ★ (ˈbɛdɪˌvɪə) *n* **Sir.** (in Arthurian legend) a knight who took the dying King Arthur to the barge in which he was carried to Avalon.

bedizen (bɪˈdaɪzᵊn, -ˈdɪzᵊn) *vb* (*tr*) *Arch.* to dress or decorate gaudily or tastelessly. ORIG C17: from BE- + obs. *dizen* to dress up, from ?
▸ **beˈdizenment** *n*

bed jacket *n* a woman's short upper garment worn over a nightgown when sitting up in bed.

bedlam (ˈbɛdləm) *n* **1** a noisy confused situation. **2** *Arch.* a madhouse. ORIG C13 *bedlem, bethlem,* from Hospital of St Mary of *Bethlehem* in London

bed linen *n* sheets, pillowcases, etc., for a bed.

Bedloe's Island (ˈbɛdləʊz) *or* **Bedloe Island** ★ *n* the former name (until 1956) of **Liberty Island.**

Bedouin *or* **Beduin** (ˈbɛdʊɪn) *n* **1** (*pl* **Bedouins, Bedouin** *or* **Beduins, Beduin**) a nomadic Arab tribesman of the deserts of Arabia, Jordan, and Syria. **2** a wanderer. ◆ *adj* **3** of or relating to the Bedouins. **4** wandering. ORIG C14: from OF *beduin,* from Ar. *badāwi,* pl. of *badwi,* from *badw* desert

bedpan (ˈbɛdˌpæn) *n* a vessel used by a bedridden patient to collect faeces and urine.

bedraggle (bɪˈdrægᵊl) *vb* **bedraggles, bedraggling, bedraggled.** (*tr*) to make (hair, clothing, etc.) limp, untidy, or dirty, as with rain or mud.
▸ **beˈdraggled** *adj*

bedridden (ˈbɛdˌrɪdᵊn) *adj* confined to bed because of illness, esp. for a long or indefinite period. ORIG OE *bedreda*

bedrock (ˈbɛdˌrɒk) *n* **1** the solid rock beneath the surface soil, etc. **2** basic principles or facts. **3** the lowest point, level, or layer.

bedroll (ˈbɛdˌrəʊl) *n* a portable roll of bedding.

bedroom (ˈbɛdˌruːm, -ˌrʊm) *n* **1** a room used for sleeping. **2** (*modifier*) containing references to sex: *a bedroom comedy.*

Beds (bɛdz) *abbrev. for* Bedfordshire.

bedside (ˈbɛdˌsaɪd) *n* **a** the space beside a bed, esp. a sickbed. **b** (*as modifier*): *a bedside lamp.*

bedsit (ˈbɛdˌsɪt) *n* a furnished sitting room containing sleeping accommodation. Also called: **bedsitting room, bedsitter.**

bedsore (ˈbɛdˌsɔː) *n* a chronic ulcer on the skin of a bedridden person, caused by prolonged pressure.

bedspread (ˈbɛdˌsprɛd) *n* a top cover on a bed.

bedstead (ˈbɛdˌstɛd) *n* the framework of a bed.

bedstraw (ˈbɛdˌstrɔː) *n* any of numerous plants which have small white or yellow flowers and prickly or hairy fruits: formerly used as straw for beds.

bedtime (ˈbɛdˌtaɪm) *n* **a** the time when one usually goes to bed. **b** (*as modifier*): *a bedtime story.*

bed-wetting *n* the act of urinating in bed.

Bedworth ★ (ˈbɛdwəθ) *n* a town in central England, in N Warwickshire. Pop.: 31 932 (1991).

bee[1] (biː) *n* **1** any of various four-winged insects that collect nectar and pollen and make honey and wax. **2 busy bee.** a person who is industrious or has many things to do. **3 have a bee in one's bonnet.** to be obsessed with an idea. ORIG OE *bīo*

bee[2] (biː) *n Chiefly US.* a social gathering for a specific purpose, as to carry out a communal task: *quilting bee.* ORIG ?from dialect *bean* neighbourly help, from OE *bēn* boon

Beeb (biːb) *n* **the.** an informal name for the **BBC.**

beebread (ˈbiːˌbrɛd) *n* a mixture of pollen and nectar prepared by worker bees and fed to the larvae. Also called: **ambrosia.**

beech (biːtʃ) *n* **1** a European tree having smooth greyish bark. **2** a similar tree of temperate Australasia and South America. **3** the hard wood of either of these trees. **4** See **copper beech.** ORIG OE *bēce*
▸ **ˈbeechen** *or* **ˈbeechy** *adj*

Beecham ★ (ˈbiːtʃəm) *n* Sir **Thomas.** 1879–1961, British conductor.

Beecher Stowe ★ *n* See (Harriet Elizabeth Beecher) **Stowe.**

beechnut (ˈbiːtʃˌnʌt) *n* the small brown triangular edible nut of the beech tree, collectively often termed **beech mast.**

bee-eater *n* any of various insectivorous birds of the Old World tropics and subtropics.

beef (biːf) *n* **1** the flesh of various bovine animals, esp. the cow, when killed for eating. **2** (*pl* **beeves**) an adult ox, etc., reared for its meat. **3** *Inf.* human flesh, esp. when muscular. **4** (*pl* **beefs**) *Sl.* a complaint. ◆ *vb* **5** (*intr*) *Sl.* to complain, esp. repeatedly. **6** (*tr;* often foll. by *up*) *Inf.* to strengthen; reinforce. ORIG C13: from OF *boef,* from L *bōs* ox

beefburger (ˈbiːfˌbɜːgə) *n* a flat fried cake of minced beef; hamburger.

beefcake (ˈbiːfˌkeɪk) *n Sl.* men displayed for their muscular bodies, esp. in photographs.

★ people and places

beefeater ('bi:f,i:tə) *n* a nickname applied to the Yeomen of the Guard, and the Yeomen Warders at the Tower of London.

beef road *n Austral.* a road used for transporting cattle.

beefsteak ('bi:f,steɪk) *n* a lean piece of beef that can be grilled, fried, etc.

beef tomato *n* a very large fleshy variety of tomato. Also called: **beefsteak tomato.**

beef tea *n* a drink made by boiling pieces of lean beef.

beefy ('bi:fɪ) *adj* **beefier, beefiest. 1** like beef. **2** *Inf.* muscular; brawny.
▸ **'beefiness** *n*

beehive ('bi:,haɪv) *n* **1** a man-made receptacle used to house a swarm of bees. **2** a dome-shaped structure. **3** a place where busy people are assembled. **4 the Beehive.** the dome-shaped building which houses Parliament in Wellington, New Zealand.

beekeeper ('bi:,ki:pə) *n* a person who keeps bees for their honey.
▸ **'bee,keeping** *n*

beeline ('bi:,laɪn) *n* the most direct route between two places (esp. in **make a beeline for**).

Beelzebub (bɪ'ɛlzɪ,bʌb) *n* Satan or any devil. ORIG OE *Belzebub,* ult. from Heb. *bá'al zebūb,* lit.: lord of flies

bee moth *n* any of various moths whose larvae live in the nests of bees or wasps, feeding on nest materials and host larvae.

been (bi:n, bɪn) *vb* the past participle of **be.**

beep (bi:p) *n* **1** a short high-pitched sound, as made by a car horn or by electronic apparatus. ◆ *vb* **2** to make or cause to make such a noise. ORIG C20: imit.
▸ **'beeper** *n*

beer (bɪə) *n* **1** an alcoholic drink brewed from malt, sugar, hops, and water. **2** a slightly fermented drink made from the roots or leaves of certain plants: *ginger beer.* **3** (*modifier*) relating to beer: *beer glass.* **4** (*modifier*) in which beer is drunk, esp. (of licensed premises) having a licence to sell beer but not spirits: *beer house; beer garden.* ORIG OE *beor*

beer and skittles *n* (*functioning as sing*) *Inf.* enjoyment or pleasure.

Beerbohm ★ ('bɪəbəʊm) *n* Sir **(Henry) Max(imilian).** 1872–1956, British critic, and caricaturist, whose novels include *Zuleika Dobson* (1911).

beer parlour *n Canad.* a licensed place in which beer is sold to the public.

Beersheba ★ (bɪə'ʃi:bə) *n* a town in S Israel: commercial centre of the Negev. In biblical times it marked the southern limit of Palestine. Pop.: 152 600 (1996 est.).

beery ('bɪərɪ) *adj* **beerier, beeriest. 1** smelling or tasting of beer. **2** given to drinking beer.
▸ **'beerily** *adv* ▸ **'beeriness** *n*

bee's knees *n* **the** (*functioning as sing*) *Inf.* an excellent or ideally suitable person or thing.

beestings, biestings, *or US* **beastings** ('bi:stɪŋz) *n* (*functioning as sing*) the first milk secreted by a cow or similar animal after giving birth; colostrum. ORIG OE *bȳsting*

beeswax ('bi:z,wæks) *n* **1** a wax secreted by honeybees for constructing honeycombs. **2** this wax after refining, used in polishes, etc.

beeswing ('bi:z,wɪŋ) *n* a light filmy crust of tartar that forms in some wines after long keeping in the bottle.

beet (bi:t) *n* **1** a plant of a genus widely cultivated in such varieties as the sugar beet, mangelwurzel, and beetroot. **2** the leaves of any of several varieties of this plant, cooked and eaten as a vegetable. **3 red beet.** the US name for **beetroot.** ORIG OE *bēte,* from L *bēta*

Beethoven ★ ('beɪt,həʊvᵊn) *n* **Ludwig van** ('lu:tvɪç fan). 1770–1827, German composer. His works include nine symphonies, 32 piano sonatas, 16 string quartets, five piano concertos, a violin concerto, two masses, the opera *Fidelio* (1805), and choral music.

beetle[1] ('bi:tᵊl) *n* **1** an insect having biting mouthparts and forewings modified to form shell-like protective casings. **2** a game in which the players draw or assemble a beetle-shaped form. ◆ *vb* **beetles, beetling, beetled.** (*intr;* foll. by *along, off,* etc.) **3** *Inf.* to scuttle or scurry; hurry. ORIG OE *bitela*

beetle[2] ('bi:tᵊl) *n* **1** a heavy hand tool for pounding or beating. **2** a machine used to finish cloth by stamping it with wooden hammers. ORIG OE *bīetel,* from *bēatan* to BEAT

beetle[3] ('bi:tᵊl) *vb* **beetles, beetling, beetled. 1** (*intr*) to overhang; jut. ◆ *adj* **2** overhanging; prominent. ORIG C14: ? rel. to BEETLE[1]
▸ **'beetling** *adj*

beetle-browed *adj* having bushy or overhanging eyebrows.

Beeton ★ ('bi:tᵊn) *n* **Isabella Mary,** known as *Mrs Beeton.* 1836–65, British cookery writer, author of *The Book of Household Management* (1861).

beetroot ('bi:t,ru:t) *n* a variety of the beet plant that has a bulbous dark red root that may be eaten as a vegetable, in salads, or pickled.

beet sugar *n* the sucrose obtained from sugar beet, identical in composition to cane sugar.

beeves (bi:vz) *n* the plural of **beef** (sense 2).

BEF *abbrev. for* British Expeditionary Force, the British army that served in France 1939–40.

befall (bɪ'fɔ:l) *vb* **befalls, befalling, befell, befallen.** *Arch. or literary.* **1** (*intr*) to take place. **2** (*tr*) to happen to. **3** (*intr;* usually foll. by *to*) to be due, as by right. ORIG OE *befeallan;* see BE-, FALL

befit (bɪ'fɪt) *vb* **befits, befitting, befitted.** (*tr*) to be appropriate to or suitable for. ORIG C15: from BE- + FIT[1]
▸ **be'fitting** *adj* ▸ **be'fittingly** *adv*

befog (bɪ'fɒg) *vb* **befogs, befogging, befogged.** (*tr*) **1** to surround with fog. **2** to make confused.

before (bɪ'fɔ:) *conj* (*subordinating*) **1** earlier than the time when. **2** rather than: *he'll resign before he agrees to it.* ◆ *prep* **3** preceding in space or time; in front of; ahead of: *standing before the altar.* **4** in the presence of: *to be brought before a judge.* **5** in preference to: *to put friendship before money.* ◆ *adv* **6** at an earlier time; previously. **7** in front. ORIG OE *beforan*

beforehand (bɪ'fɔ:,hænd) *adj* (*postpositive*), *adv* early; in advance; in anticipation.

befoul (bɪ'faʊl) *vb* (*tr*) to make dirty or foul.

befriend (bɪ'frɛnd) *vb* (*tr*) to be a friend to; assist; favour.

befuddle (bɪ'fʌdᵊl) *vb* **befuddles, befuddling, befuddled.** (*tr*) **1** to confuse. **2** to make stupid with drink.
▸ **be'fuddlement** *n*

beg (bɛg) *vb* **begs, begging, begged. 1** (when *intr,* often foll. by *for*) to solicit (for money, food, etc.), esp. in the street. **2** to ask formally, humbly, or earnestly: *I beg forgiveness; I beg to differ.* **3** (*intr*) (of a dog) to sit up with forepaws raised expectantly. **4 beg the question. 4a** to evade the issue. **4b** to put forward an argument that assumes the very point it is supposed to establish or that depends on some other questionable assumption. **4c** to suggest that a question needs to be asked: *the firm's success begs the question: why aren't more companies doing the same?* **5 go begging.** to be unwanted or unused. ◆ See also **beg off.** ORIG C13: prob. from OE *bedecian*

> **USAGE NOTE** The use of *beg the question* to mean that a question needs to be asked is considered by some people to be incorrect.

began (bɪ'gæn) *vb* the past tense of **begin.**

beget (bɪ'gɛt) *vb* **begets, begetting, begot** *or* **begat; begotten** *or* **begot.** (*tr*) **1** to father. **2** to cause or create. ORIG OE *begietan;* see BE-, GET
▸ **be'getter** *n*

beggar ('bɛgə) *n* **1** a person who begs, esp. one who lives by begging. **2** a person who has no money or resources; pauper. **3** *Chiefly Brit.* a fellow: *lucky beggar!* ◆ *vb* (*tr*) **4** to be beyond the resources of (esp. in **beggar description**). **5** to impoverish.
▸ **'beggardom** *n*

beggarly ('bɛgəlɪ) *adj* meanly inadequate; very poor.
▸ **'beggarliness** *n*

★ people and places

beggar-my-neighbour *n* a card game in which one player tries to win all the cards of the other player.

beggary (ˈbɛgərɪ) *n* extreme poverty or need.

begin (bɪˈgɪn) *vb* **begins, beginning, began, begun. 1** to start or cause to start (something or to do something). **2** to bring or come into being; arise or originate. **3** to start to say or speak. **4** (*with a negative*) to have the least capacity (to do something): *he couldn't begin to compete.* **5 to begin with.** in the first place. ORIG OE *beginnan*

Begin ★ (ˈbɛgɪn) *n* **Menachem** (məˈnɑːkɪm). 1913–92, Israeli statesman, born in Poland. Prime minister of Israel (1977–83); Nobel peace prize jointly with Anwar Sadat of Egypt 1978, with whom he concluded the Camp David treaty.

beginner (bɪˈgɪnə) *n* a person who has just started to do or learn something; novice.

beginning (bɪˈgɪnɪŋ) *n* **1** a start; commencement. **2** (*often pl*) a first or early part or stage. **3** the place where or time when something starts. **4** an origin; source.

begird (bɪˈgɜːd) *vb* **begirds, begirding, begirt** *or* **begirded.** (*tr*) *Poetic.* **1** to surround; gird around. **2** to bind. ORIG OE *begierdan;* see BE-, GIRD[1]

beg off *vb* (*intr, adv*) to ask to be released from an engagement, obligation, etc.

begone (bɪˈgɒn) *sentence substitute.* go away! ORIG C14: from BE (imperative) + GONE

begonia (bɪˈgəʊnjə) *n* a plant of warm and tropical regions, having ornamental leaves and waxy flowers. ORIG C18: NL, after Michel *Bégon* (1638–1710), F patron of science

begorra (bɪˈgɔːrə) *interj* an emphatic exclamation, regarded as characteristic of Irishmen. ORIG C19: from *by God!*

begot (bɪˈgɒt) *vb* a past tense and past participle of **beget.**

begotten (bɪˈgɒt^{ə}n) *vb* a past participle of **beget.**

begrime (bɪˈgraɪm) *vb* **begrimes, begriming, begrimed.** (*tr*) to make dirty; soil.

begrudge (bɪˈgrʌdʒ) *vb* **begrudges, begrudging, begrudged.** (*tr*) **1** to give, admit, or allow unwillingly or with a bad grace. **2** to envy (someone) the possession of (something).
▸ **beˈgrudgingly** *adv*

beguile (bɪˈgaɪl) *vb* **beguiles, beguiling, beguiled.** (*tr*) **1** to charm; fascinate. **2** to delude; influence by slyness. **3** (often foll. by *of* or *out of*) to cheat (someone) of. **4** to pass pleasantly; while away.
▸ **beˈguilement** *n* ▸ **beˈguiler** *n* ▸ **beˈguiling** *adj* ▸ **beˈguilingly** *adv*

beguine (bɪˈgiːn) *n* **1** a dance of South American origin in bolero rhythm. **2** a piece of music in the rhythm of this dance. ORIG C20: from Louisiana F, from F *béguin* flirtation

begum (ˈbeɪgəm) *n* (in certain Muslim countries) a woman of high rank. ORIG C18: from Urdu *begam,* from Turkish *begim;* see BEY

begun (bɪˈgʌn) *vb* the past participle of **begin.**

behalf (bɪˈhɑːf) *n* interest, part, benefit, or respect (only in **on (someone's) behalf, on** *or US & Canad.* **in behalf of, in this** (*or* **that**) **behalf**). ORIG OE *be halfe,* from *be* by + *halfe* side

> **USAGE NOTE** *On behalf of* is sometimes wrongly used where *on the part of* is intended. The distinction is that *on behalf of someone* means 'for someone's benefit' or 'representing someone', while *on the part of someone* can be roughly paraphrased as 'by someone'. So, the following example is incorrect: *...another act of apparent negligence, this time not on behalf of the company itself, but on behalf of its banker,* when what is meant is that there was negligence by the company and its bankers.

Behan ★ (ˈbiːən) *n* **Brendan.** 1923–64, Irish writer, noted esp. for his plays *The Quare Fellow* (1954) and *The Hostage* (1958) and for *Borstal Boy* (1958).

behave (bɪˈheɪv) *vb* **behaves, behaving, behaved. 1** (*intr*) to act or function in a specified or usual way. **2** to conduct (oneself) in a specified way: *he behaved badly.* **3** to conduct (oneself) properly or as desired. ORIG C15: see BE-, HAVE

behaviour *or US* **behavior** (bɪˈheɪvjə) *n* **1** manner of behaving. **2 on one's best behaviour.** behaving with careful good manners. **3** *Psychol.* the response of an organism to a stimulus. **4** the reaction or functioning of a machine, etc., under normal or specified circumstances. ORIG C15: from BEHAVE; infl. by ME *havior,* from OF *havoir,* from L *habēre* to have
▸ **beˈhavioural** *or US* **beˈhavioral** *adj*

behavioural science *n* the scientific study of the behaviour of organisms.

behaviourism *or US* **behaviorism** (bɪˈheɪvjəˌrɪzəm) *n* a school of psychology that regards objective observation of the behaviour of organisms as the only valid subject for study.
▸ **beˈhaviourist** *or US* **beˈhaviorist** *adj, n* ▸ **beˌhaviourˈistic** *or US* **beˌhaviorˈistic** *adj*

behaviour therapy *n* any of various means of treating psychological disorders, such as aversion therapy, that depend on the patient systematically learning new behaviour.

behead (bɪˈhɛd) *vb* (*tr*) to remove the head from. ORIG OE *behēafdian,* from BE- + *heafod* HEAD

beheld (bɪˈhɛld) *vb* the past tense and past participle of **behold.**

behemoth (bɪˈhiːmɒθ) *n* **1** *Bible.* a gigantic beast described in Job 40:15. **2** a huge or monstrous person or thing. ORIG C14: from Heb. *bĕhēmōth,* pl. of *bĕhēmāh* beast

behest (bɪˈhɛst) *n* an order or earnest request. ORIG OE *behǣs,* from *behātan;* see BE-, HEST

behind (bɪˈhaɪnd) *prep* **1** in or to a position further back than. **2** in the past in relation to: *I've got the exams behind me now.* **3** late according to: *running behind schedule.* **4** concerning the circumstances surrounding: *the reasons behind his departure.* **5** supporting: *I'm right behind you in your application.* ◆ *adv* **6** in or to a position further back; following. **7** remaining after someone's departure: *he left his books behind.* **8** in debt; in arrears: *to fall behind with payments.* ◆ *adj* **9** (*postpositive*) in a position further back. ◆ *n* **10** *Inf.* the buttocks. **11** *Australian Rules football.* a score of one point made by kicking the ball over the **behind line** between a goalpost and one of the smaller outer posts (**behind posts**). ORIG OE *behindan*

behindhand (bɪˈhaɪndˌhænd) *adj* (*postpositive*), *adv* **1** remiss in fulfilling an obligation. **2** in arrears. **3** backward. **4** late.

Behistun (ˌbeɪhɪˈstuːn), **Bisitun,** *or* **Bisutun** ★ *n* a village in W Iran by the ancient road from Ecbatana to Babylon. On a nearby cliff is an inscription by Darius in Old Persian, Elamite, and Babylonian describing his enthronement.

Behn ★ (bɛn) *n* **Aphra** (ˈæfrə). 1640–89, English dramatist and novelist, best known for her play *The Rover* (1678) and her novel *Oroonoko* (1688).

behold (bɪˈhəʊld) *vb* **beholds, beholding, beheld.** (*often imperative*) *Arch. or literary.* to look (at); observe. ORIG OE *bihealdan;* see BE-, HOLD[1]
▸ **beˈholder** *n*

beholden (bɪˈhəʊld^{ə}n) *adj* indebted; obliged. ORIG OE *behealden,* p.p. of *behealdan* to BEHOLD

behoof (bɪˈhuːf) *n, pl* **behooves.** *Rare.* advantage or profit. ORIG OE *behōf;* see BEHOVE

behove (bɪˈhəʊv) *vb* **behoves, behoving, behoved.** (*tr; impersonal*) *Arch.* to be necessary or fitting for: *it behoves me to arrest you.* ORIG OE *behōfian*

> **USAGE NOTE** The mistaken form *behoven* is occasionally used where *beholden* is intended, especially in writing done in a rush, or in speech. *Behove* only ever really occurs in the structure 'it behoves somebody to...', with *ill* often modifying the verb.

Behrens ★ (ˈbɛərənz; *German* ˈbeːrəns) *n* **Peter.** 1868–1940, German architect.

Behring ★ *n* **1** (*German* ˈbeːrɪŋ), **Emil (Adolf) von** (ˈeːmiːl fɔn). 1854–1917, German bacteriologist, who discovered diphtheria and tetanus antitoxins: Nobel prize for physiology or medicine 1901. **2** (ˈbɛrɪŋ, ˈbɛər-). See (Vitus) **Bering.**

Beiderbecke ★ (ˈbaɪdəˌbɛk) *n* **Leon Bismarcke,** known as *Bix.* 1903–31, US jazz cornettist, composer, and pianist.

beige (beɪʒ) *n* **1a** a very light brown, sometimes with a yellowish tinge. **1b** (*as adj*): *beige gloves.* **2** a fabric made of undyed or unbleached wool. ORIG C19: from OF, from ?

Beijing ★ (ˈbeɪˈdʒɪŋ) *n* the capital of the People's Republic of China, in the northeast in central Hebei province: dates back to the 12th century B.C.; consists of two central walled cities, the Outer City (containing the commercial quarter) and the Inner City, which contains the Imperial City, within which is the Purple or Forbidden City; three universities. Pop.: 12 400 000 (1997 est.). Former English name: **Peking.**

being (ˈbiːɪŋ) *n* **1** the state or fact of existing; existence. **2** essential nature; self. **3** something that exists or is thought to exist: *a being from outer space.* **4** a person; human being.

Beira ★ (ˈbaɪərə) *n* a port in E Mozambique: terminus of a transcontinental railway from Lobito, Angola, through the Democratic Republic of Congo (formerly Zaïre), Zambia, and Zimbabwe. Pop.: 298 847 (1991 est.).

Beirut *or* **Beyrouth** ★ (ˌbeɪˈruːt) *n* the capital of Lebanon, a port on the Mediterranean: part of the Ottoman Empire from the 16th century until 1918; four universities (Lebanese, American, French, and Arab). Pop.: 1 100 000 (1991 est.).

bejabers (bɪˈdʒeɪbəz) *or* **bejabbers** (bɪˈdʒæbəz) *interj* an exclamation of surprise, emphasis, etc., regarded as characteristic of Irishmen. ORIG C19: from *by Jesus!*

bejewel (bɪˈdʒuːəl) *vb* **bejewels, bejewelling, bejewelled** *or US* **bejewels, bejeweling, bejeweled.** (*tr*) to decorate as with jewels.

Bekaa *or* **Beqaa** ★ (bɪˈkɑː) *n* a broad valley in central Lebanon, between the Lebanon and Anti-Lebanon Mountains. Ancient name: **Coelesyria** (ˌsiːliːˈsɪrɪə).

bel (bɛl) *n* a unit for comparing two power levels, equal to the logarithm to the base ten of the ratio of the two powers. ORIG C20: after A. G. BELL

Bel ★ (beɪl) *n* (in Babylonian and Assyrian mythology) the god of the earth.

belabour *or US* **belabor** (bɪˈleɪbə) *vb* (*tr*) **1** to beat severely; thrash. **2** to attack verbally.

Belarus ★ (ˈbɛləˌrʌs, -ˌrus) *n* a republic in E Europe; formerly a constituent republic of the Soviet Union (1919–91): mainly low-lying and forested. Languages: Belarussian, Russian. Religion: believers are mostly Christian. Currency: rouble. Capital: Minsk. Pop.: 10 164 000 (1999 est.). Area: 207 600 sq. km (80 134 sq. miles). Also called: **Belorussia, Byelorussia, Byelorussian Republic, Bielorussia.** Former name: **White Russia.**

Belarussian *or* **Belarusian** (ˌbɛləʊˈrʌʃən) *adj* **1** of, relating to, or characteristic of Belarus, its people, or their language. ◆ *n* **2** the official language of Belarus. **3** a native or inhabitant of Belarus. Also: **Belorussian, Byelorussian, Bielorussian.**

belated (bɪˈleɪtɪd) *adj* late or too late: *belated greetings.* ▸ **beˈlatedly** *adv* ▸ **beˈlatedness** *n*

Belau ★ (bəˈlaʊ) *n* **Republic of.** a republic comprising a group of islands in the W Pacific, in the W Caroline Islands; administratively part of the UN Trust Territory of the Pacific Islands 1947–94; entered into an agreement of free association with the US (1980); became autonomous in 1981 and independent in 1994. Chief island: Babelthuap. Currency: US dollar. Capital: Koror. Pop.: 18 500 (1999 est.). Area: 476 sq. km (184 sq. miles). Former names: **Pelew Islands,** (until 1981) **Palau Islands.**

belay *vb* (bɪˈleɪ) **belays, belaying, belayed. 1** *Naut.* to secure (a line) to a pin, cleat, or bitt. **2** (*usually imperative*) *Naut.* to stop. **3** (ˈbiːˌleɪ). *Mountaineering.* to secure (a climber) by means of a belay. ◆ *n* (ˈbiːlˌeɪ). **4** *Mountaineering.* the attachment of a climber to a mountain by securing a rope round a rock, piton, etc., to safeguard the party in the event of a fall. ORIG OE *belecgan*

belaying pin *n Naut.* a cylindrical metal or wooden pin used for belaying.

bel canto (ˈbɛl ˈkæntəʊ) *n Music.* a style of singing characterized by beauty of tone rather than dramatic power. ORIG It., lit.: beautiful singing

belch (bɛltʃ) *vb* **1** (*usually intr*) to expel wind from the stomach noisily through the mouth. **2** to expel or be expelled forcefully from inside: *smoke belching from factory chimneys.* ◆ *n* **3** an act of belching. ORIG OE *bialcan*

beldam *or* **beldame** (ˈbɛldəm) *n Arch.* an old woman. ORIG C15: from *bel-* grand (as in *grandmother*), from OF *bel* beautiful, + *dam* mother

beleaguer (bɪˈliːgə) *vb* (*tr*) **1** to lay siege to. **2** to harass. ORIG C16: from BE- + obs. *leaguer* a siege

Belém ★ (*Portuguese* bəˈlẽi) *n* a port in N Brazil, the capital of Pará state, on the Pará River: major trading centre for the Amazon basin. Pop.: 765 476 (1991).

belemnite (ˈbɛləmˌnaɪt) *n* **1** an extinct marine mollusc related to the cuttlefish. **2** its long pointed conical internal shell: a common fossil. ORIG C17: from Gk *belemnon* dart

Belfast ★ (ˈbɛlfɑːst, bɛlˈfɑːst) *n* the capital city and an administrative district of Northern Ireland; a port on Belfast Lough: became the centre of Irish Protestantism and of the linen industry in the 17th century. Pop.: 279 237 (1991). Area (district): 155 sq. km (44 sq. miles).

Belfort ★ (*French* bɛlfɔr) *n* **1 Territoire de** (tɛritwar də). a department of E France: the only part of Alsace remaining to France after 1871. Capital: Belfort. Pop.: 136 795 (1990). Area: 608 sq. km (237 sq. miles). **2** a fortress town in E France: strategically situated in the **Belfort Gap** between the Vosges and the Jura mountains. Pop.: 50 125 (1990).

belfry (ˈbɛlfrɪ) *n, pl* **belfries. 1** the part of a tower or steeple in which bells are hung. **2** a tower or steeple. ORIG C13: from OF *berfrei,* of Gmc origin

Belg. *or* **Bel.** *abbrev. for:* **1** Belgian. **2** Belgium.

Belgaum ★ (bɛlˈgaʊm) *n* a city in India, in Karnataka: cotton, furniture, leather. Pop.: 326 399 (1991).

Belgian (ˈbɛldʒən) *n* **1** a native or inhabitant of Belgium. ◆ *adj* **2** of or relating to Belgium, the Belgians, or their languages.

Belgian Congo ★ *n* a former name (1908–60) of the Democratic Republic of **Congo.**

Belgian hare *n* a large red domestic rabbit.

Belgium ★ (ˈbɛldʒəm) *n* a federal kingdom in NW Europe: at various times under the rulers of Burgundy, Spain, Austria, France, and the Netherlands before becoming an independent kingdom in 1830. It formed the Benelux customs union with the Netherlands and Luxembourg in 1947 and was a founder member of the EEC (now the EU). It consists chiefly of a low-lying region of sand, woods, and heath (the Campine) in the north and west, and a fertile undulating central plain rising to the Ardennes Mountains in the southeast. Languages: French, Flemish (Dutch), and German. Religion: chiefly Roman Catholic. Currency: franc and euro. Capital: Brussels. Pop.: 10 224 000 (1999 est.). Area: 30 513 sq. km (11 778 sq. miles).

Belgorod-Dnestrovski *or* **Byelgorod-Dnestrovski** ★ (*Russian* ˈbjɛlgərətdnjɪˈstrɔfskij) *n* a port in SW Ukraine: belonged to Romania (1918–40) and the Soviet Union (1944–91). Pop.: 56 800 (1991 est.). Romanian name: **Cetatea Albă.** Former name: (until 1946): **Akkerman.**

Belgrade ★ (bɛlˈgreɪd, ˈbɛlgreɪd) *n* the capital of Yugoslavia and of Serbia, in the E part at the confluence of the Danube and Sava Rivers: became the capital of Serbia in 1878 and of Yugoslavia in 1929. Pop.: 1 168 454 (1991). Serbo-Croat name: **Beograd.**

Belgravia ★ (bɛlˈgreɪvɪə) *n* a fashionable residential district of W central London, around Belgrave Square.

Belial (ˈbiːlɪəl) *n* the devil or Satan. ORIG C13: from Heb. *bəlīyya'al,* from *bəlīy* without + *ya'al* worth

belie (bɪˈlaɪ) *vb* **belies, belying, belied.** (*tr*) **1** to show to be untrue. **2** to misrepresent; disguise the nature of. **3** to fail to justify; disappoint. ORIG OE *belēogan;* see BE-, LIE[1]

belief (bɪˈliːf) *n* **1** a principle, etc., accepted as true, esp. without proof. **2** opinion; conviction. **3** religious faith. **4** trust or confidence, as in a person's abilities, etc.

believe (bɪˈliːv) *vb* **believes, believing, believed. 1** (*tr; may take a clause as object*) to accept (a statement or opinion) as true: *I believe God exists.* **2** (*tr*) to accept the statement or opinion of (a person) as true. **3** (*intr;* foll. by *in*) to be convinced of the truth or existence (of): *to believe in fairies.* **4** (*intr*) to have religious faith. **5** (when *tr, takes a clause as object*) to think, assume, or suppose. **6** (*tr*) to think that someone is able to do (a particular action): *I wouldn't have believed it of him.* ORIG OE *beliefan*
▸ **beˈlievable** *adj* ▸ **beˈliever** *n*

belike (bɪˈlaɪk) *adv Arch.* perhaps; maybe.

Belisarius ★ (ˌbɛlɪˈsɑːrɪəs) *n* ?505–565 A.D., Byzantine general under Justinian I. He recovered North Africa from the Vandals and Italy from the Ostrogoths and led forces against the Persians.

Belisha beacon (bəˈliːʃə) *n Brit.* a flashing orange globe on a post, indicating a pedestrian crossing on a road. ORIG C20: after L. Hore-*Belisha* (1893–1957), Brit. politician

belittle (bɪˈlɪtᵊl) *vb* **belittles, belittling, belittled.** (*tr*) **1** to consider or speak of (something) as less important than it really is. **2** to make small; dwarf.
▸ **beˈlittlement** *n* ▸ **beˈlittler** *n*

Belitung ★ (bɪˈliːtʊŋ) *n* another name for **Billiton.**

Belize ★ (bəˈliːz) *n* a state in Central America, on the Caribbean Sea: site of a Mayan civilization until the 9th century A.D.; colonized by the British from 1638; granted internal self-government in 1964; became an independent state within the Commonwealth in 1981. Official language: English; Carib and Spanish are also spoken. Currency: Belize dollar. Capital: Belmopan. Pop.: 250 000 (1999 est.). Area: 22 965 sq. km (8867 sq. miles). Former name (until 1973): **British Honduras.**
▸ **Beˈlizean** *adj, n*

Belize City ★ *n* a port in Belize: capital until 1973, when it was abandoned as hurricane-prone. Pop.: 48 655 (1994).

bell[1] (bɛl) *n* **1** a hollow, usually metal, cup-shaped instrument that emits a ringing sound when struck. **2** the sound made by such an instrument, as for marking the beginning or end of a period of time. **3** an electrical device that rings or buzzes as a signal. **4** something shaped like a bell, as the tube of certain musical wind instruments, or the corolla of certain flowers. **5** *Naut.* a signal rung on a ship's bell to count the number of half-hour intervals during each of six four-hour watches reckoned from midnight. **6** *Brit. sl.* a telephone call **7 bell, book, and candle. 7a** instruments used formerly in excommunications and other ecclesiastical rites. **7b** *Inf.* the solemn ritual ratification of such acts. **8 ring a bell.** to sound familiar; recall something previously experienced. **9 sound as a bell.** in perfect condition. ◆ *vb* **10** to be or cause to be shaped like a bell. **11** (*tr*) to attach a bell or bells to. ORIG OE *belle*

bell[2] (bɛl) *n* **1** a bellowing or baying cry, esp. that of a stag in rut. ◆ *vb* **2** to utter (such a cry). ORIG OE *bellan*

Bell ★ (bɛl) *n* **1 Acton, Currer** (ˈkʌrə), and **Ellis.** pen names of the sisters Anne, Charlotte, and Emily **Brontë. 2 Alexander Graham.** 1847–1922, US scientist, born in Scotland, who invented the telephone (1876). **3** Sir **Francis Henry Dillon.** 1851–1936, New Zealand statesman; prime minister (1925). **4 Gertrude (Margaret Lowthian).** 1868–1926, British writer and diplomat; secretary to the British High Commissioner in Baghdad (1917–26). **5 (Susan) Jocelyn,** married name *Jocelyn Bell Burnell,* born 1943, British radio astronomer, who discovered the first pulsar.

belladonna (ˌbɛləˈdɒnə) *n* **1** either of two alkaloid drugs obtained from the leaves and roots of the deadly nightshade. **2** another name for **deadly nightshade.** ORIG C16: from It., lit.: beautiful lady; supposed to refer to its use as a cosmetic

Bellarmine ★ (ˈbɛlɑːˌmiːn) *n* **Saint Robert.** 1542–1621, Italian Jesuit theologian and cardinal.

Bellay ★ (*French* bɛlɛ) *n* **Joachim du** (ʒɔaʃɛ̃ dy). 1522–60, French poet, a member of the Pléiade.

bellbird (ˈbɛlˌbɜːd) *n* **1** any of several tropical American birds having a bell-like call. **2** either of two other birds with a bell-like call: an Australian flycatcher (**crested bellbird**) or a New Zealand honeyeater.

bell-bottoms *pl n* trousers that flare from the knee.
▸ **ˈbell-ˌbottomed** *adj*

bellboy (ˈbɛlˌbɔɪ) *n Chiefly US & Canad.* a porter or page in a hotel, club, etc. Also called: **bellhop.**

bell buoy *n* a navigational buoy with a bell which strikes when the waves move the buoy.

belle (bɛl) *n* **1** a beautiful woman. **2** the most attractive woman at a function, etc. (esp. in **belle of the ball**). ORIG C17: from F, fem of BEAU

Belleau Wood ★ (ˈbɛləʊ; *French* bɛlo) *n* a forest in N France: site of a battle (1918) in which the US Marines halted a German advance on Paris.

belle époque *French.* (bɛl epɔk) *n* the period of comfortable well-established life before World War I. ORIG lit.: fine period

Belle Isle ★ *n* an island in the Atlantic, at the N entrance to the **Strait of Belle Isle,** between Labrador and Newfoundland. Area: about 39 sq. km (15 sq. miles).

Bellerophon ★ (bəˈlɛrəˌfɒn) *n Greek myth.* a hero of Corinth who performed many deeds with the help of the winged horse Pegasus, notably the killing of the monster Chimera.

belles-lettres (*French* bɛllɛtrə) *n* (*functioning as sing*) literary works, esp. essays and poetry, valued for their aesthetic content. ORIG C17: from F: fine letters
▸ **belˈletrist** *n*

bellflower (ˈbɛlˌflaʊə) *n* another name for **campanula.**

bellfounder (ˈbɛlˌfaʊndə) *n* a foundry worker who casts bells.

bellicose (ˈbɛlɪˌkəʊs, -ˌkəʊz) *adj* warlike; aggressive; ready to fight. ORIG C15: from L *bellicōsus,* from *bellum* war
▸ **bellicosity** (ˌbɛlɪˈkɒsɪtɪ) *n*

belligerence (bɪˈlɪdʒərəns) *n* the act or quality of being belligerent or warlike; aggressiveness.

belligerency (bɪˈlɪdʒərənsɪ) *n* the state of being at war.

belligerent (bɪˈlɪdʒərənt) *adj* **1** marked by readiness to fight or argue; aggressive. **2** relating to or engaged in a war. ◆ *n* **3** a person or country engaged in war. ORIG C16: from L *belliger,* from *bellum* war + *gerere* to wage

Bellingshausen Sea ★ (ˈbɛlɪŋzˌhaʊzᵊn) *n* an area of the S Pacific Ocean off the coast of Antarctica. ORIG named after Fabian Gottlieb *Bellingshausen* (1778–1852), Russian explorer

Bellini ★ (*Italian* belˈlini) *n* **1 Giovanni** (dʒoˈvanni). ?1430–1516, Italian painter of the Venetian school. His father **Jacopo** (?1400–70) and his brother **Gentile** (?1429–1507) were also painters. **2 Vincenzo** (vinˈtʃɛntso). 1801–35, Italian composer of operas, esp. *La Sonnambula* (1831) and *Norma* (1831).

Bellinzona ★ (*Italian* bellinˈtsona) *n* a town in SE central Switzerland, capital of Ticino canton. Pop.: 35 860 (1990).

bell jar *n* a bell-shaped glass cover to protect flower arrangements, etc., or to cover apparatus in experiments. Also called: **bell glass.**

bellman (ˈbɛlmən) *n, pl* **bellmen.** a man who rings a bell; (formerly) a town crier.

bell metal *n* an alloy of copper and tin, with some zinc and lead, used in casting bells.

Belloc ★ (ˈbɛlɒk) *n* **Hilaire** (ˈhɪlɛə, hɪˈlɛə). 1870–1953, British writer, born in France, noted for his verse *The Bad Child's Book of Beasts* (1896) and *Cautionary Tales* (1907).

bellow (ˈbɛləʊ) *vb* **1** (*intr*) to make a loud deep cry like that of a bull; roar. **2** to shout (something) unrestrainedly, as in anger or pain. ◆ *n* **3** the characteristic noise of a bull. **4** a loud deep sound, as of pain or anger. ORIG C14: prob. from OE *bylgan*

Bellow ★ ('bɛləʊ) *n* **Saul.** born 1915, US novelist, born in Canada. His works include *Dangling Man* (1944), *Herzog* (1964), *Humboldt's Gift* (1975), and *Ravelstein* (2000): Nobel prize for literature 1976.

bellows ('bɛləʊz) *n* (*functioning as sing or pl*) **1** Also: **pair of bellows.** an instrument consisting of an air chamber with flexible sides that is used to create a stream of air, as for producing a draught for a fire or for sounding organ pipes. **2** a flexible corrugated part, as that connecting the lens system of some cameras to the body. ORIG C16: from pl of OE *belig* BELLY

bell pull *n* a handle, rope, or cord pulled to operate a doorbell or servant's bell.

bell push *n* a button pressed to operate an electric bell.

bell-ringer *n* a person who rings church bells or musical handbells.
▸ **'bell-ˌringing** *n*

bells and whistles *pl n* additional features or accessories which are nonessential but very attractive. ORIG C20: from the bells and whistles which used to decorate fairground organs

bell tent *n* a cone-shaped tent having a single central supporting pole.

bellwether ('bɛlˌwɛðə) *n* **1** a sheep that leads the herd, often bearing a bell. **2** a leader, esp. one followed blindly.

belly ('bɛlɪ) *n, pl* **bellies. 1** the lower or front part of the body of a vertebrate, containing the intestines and other organs; abdomen. **2** the stomach, esp. when regarded as the seat of gluttony. **3** a part that bulges deeply: *the belly of a sail.* **4** the inside or interior cavity of something. **5** the front, lower, or inner part of something. **6** the surface of a stringed musical instrument over which the strings are stretched. **7** *Austral. & NZ.* the wool from a sheep's belly. **8** *Arch.* the womb. **9 go belly up.** *Inf.* to die, fail, or come to an end. ◆ *vb* **bellies, bellying, bellied. 10** to swell out or cause to swell out; bulge. ORIG OE *belig*

bellyache ('bɛlɪˌeɪk) *n* **1** an informal term for **stomachache.** ◆ *vb* **bellyaches, bellyaching, bellyached. 2** (*intr*) *Sl.* to complain repeatedly.
▸ **'bellyˌacher** *n*

bellyband ('bɛlɪˌbænd) *n* a strap around the belly of a draught animal, holding the shafts of a vehicle.

bellybutton ('bɛlɪˌbʌtᵊn) *n* an informal name for the **navel.** Also called: **tummy button.**

belly dance *n* **1** a sensuous dance of Middle Eastern origin, performed by women, with undulating movements of the abdomen. ◆ *vb* **belly-dance, belly-dances, belly-dancing, belly-danced. 2** (*intr*) to dance thus.
▸ **belly dancer** *n*

belly flop *n* **1** a dive into water in which the body lands horizontally. ◆ *vb* **belly-flop, belly-flops, belly-flopping, belly-flopped. 2** (*intr*) to perform a belly flop.

bellyful ('bɛlɪˌfʊl) *n* **1** as much as one wants or can eat. **2** *Sl.* more than one can tolerate.

belly landing *n* the landing of an aircraft on its fuselage without use of its landing gear.

belly laugh *n* a loud deep hearty laugh.

Belmopan ★ (ˌbɛlmə'pæn) *n* (since 1973) the capital of Belize, about 50 miles inland: founded in 1970. Pop.: 6490 (1996 est.).

Belo Horizonte ★ (*Portuguese* 'beːlori'zõːntə) *n* a city in SE Brazil, the capital of Minas Gerais state. Pop.: 1 529 566 (1991).

belong (bɪ'lɒŋ) *vb* (*intr*) **1** (foll. by *to*) to be the property or possession (of). **2** (foll. by *to*) to be bound (to) by ties of affection, allegiance, etc. **3** (foll. by *to, under, with,* etc.) to be classified (with): *this plant belongs to the daisy family.* **4** (foll. by *to*) to be a part or adjunct (of). **5** to have a proper or usual place. **6** *Inf.* to be acceptable, esp. socially. ORIG C14 *belongen,* from BE- (intensive) + *longen,* from OE *langian* to belong

belonging (bɪ'lɒŋɪŋ) *n* secure relationship; affinity (esp. in **a sense of belonging**).

belongings (bɪ'lɒŋɪŋz) *pl n* (*sometimes sing*) the things that a person owns or has with him or her.

Belorussia ★ (ˌbɛləʊ'rʌʃən) *n* a variant spelling of **Belarus.**
▸ **ˌBelo'russian** *n, adj*

Belostok ★ (bjɪla'stɔk) *n* transliteration of the Russian name for **Białystok.**

beloved (bɪ'lʌvɪd, -'lʌvd) *adj* **1** dearly loved. ◆ *n* **2** a person who is dearly loved.

Belovo ★ (*Russian* 'bjɛləvə) *n* a variant spelling of **Byelovo.**

below (bɪ'ləʊ) *prep* **1** at or to a position lower than; under. **2** less than. **3** south of. **4** downstream of. **5** unworthy of; beneath. ◆ *adv* **6** at or to a lower position. **7** at a later place (in something written). **8** *Arch.* on earth or in hell. ORIG C14 *bilooghe,* from *bi* BY + *looghe* LOW[1]

Bel Paese ('bɛl pɑː'eɪzɪ) *n* a mild creamy Italian cheese. ORIG from It., lit.: beautiful country

Belsen ★ ('bɛlsᵊn; *German* 'bɛlzən) *n* a village in NE Germany: with Bergen, the site of a Nazi concentration camp (1943–45).

Belshazzar ★ (bɛl'ʃæzə) *n* 6th century B.C., the son of Nabonidus, coregent of Babylon with his father for eight years: referred to as king and son of Nebuchadnezzar in the Old Testament (Daniel 5:1, 17; 8:1); described as having received a divine message of doom written on a wall at a banquet (**Belshazzar's Feast**).

belt (bɛlt) *n* **1** a band of cloth, leather, etc., worn, usually around the waist, to support clothing, carry weapons, etc., or as decoration. **2** a belt worn to show rank (as by a knight), to mark expertise (as in judo), or awarded as a prize (as in boxing). **3** a narrow band, circle, or stripe, as of colour. **4** an area where a specific thing is found; zone: *a belt of high pressure.* **5** See **seat belt. 6** a band of flexible material between rotating shafts or pulleys to transfer motion or transmit goods: *a fan belt; a conveyer belt.* **7** *Inf.* a sharp blow. **8 below the belt. 8a** *Boxing.* below the waist. **8b** *Inf.* in an unscrupulous or cowardly way. **9 tighten one's belt.** to take measures to reduce expenditure. **10 under one's belt. 10a** in one's stomach. **10b** as part of one's experience: *he had a degree under his belt.* ◆ *vb* **11** (*tr*) to fasten or attach with or as if with a belt. **12** (*tr*) to hit with a belt. **13** (*tr*) *Sl.* to give a sharp blow; punch. **14** (*intr;* often foll. by *along*) *Sl.* to move very fast, esp. in a car. **15** (*tr*) *Rare.* to encircle. ORIG OE, from L *balteus*
▸ **'belted** *adj*

belt-and-braces *adj* providing double security, in case one security measure should fail: *a belt-and-braces policy.*

Beltane ('bɛlteɪn, -tən) *n* an ancient Celtic festival with a sacrificial bonfire on May Day. ORIG C15: from Scot. Gaelic *bealltainn*

belter ('bɛltə) *n Sl.* **1** an event, person, quality, etc., that is admirable, outstanding, or thrilling: *a real belter of a match.* **2a** a rousing or spirited popular song that is sung loudly and enthusiastically. **2b** a person who sings popular songs in a loud and spirited manner.

belting ('bɛltɪŋ) *n* **1** material for belts. **2** belts collectively. **3** *Inf.* a beating.

belt man *n Austral. & NZ.* (formerly) the member of a beach life-saving team who swam out wearing a belt with a line attached.

belt out *vb* (*tr, adv*) *Inf.* to sing or emit sound loudly.

belt up *vb* (*adv*) **1** *Sl.* to stop talking: often imperative. **2** to fasten with a belt.

beluga (bɪ'luːgə) *n* **1** a large white sturgeon of the Black and Caspian Seas: a source of caviar and isinglass. **2** another name for **white whale.** ORIG C18: from Russian *byeluga,* from *byely* white

belvedere ('bɛlvɪˌdɪə, ˌbɛlvɪ'dɪə) *n* a building, such as a summerhouse, sited to command a fine view. ORIG C16: from It.: beautiful sight

Bembo ★ (*Italian* 'bembo) *n* **Pietro** ('pjɛːtro). 1470–1547, Italian scholar and cardinal (1539). Noted for his treatise *Prose della volgar lingua* (1525).

bemire (bɪ'maɪə) *vb* **bemires, bemiring, bemired.** (*tr*) **1** to soil as with mire. **2** (*usually passive*) to stick fast in mire.

bemoan (bɪ'məʊn) *vb* to mourn; lament (esp. in **bemoan one's fate**). ORIG OE *bemǣnan;* see BE-, MOAN

★ people and places

bemuse (bɪ'mju:z) *vb* **bemuses, bemusing, bemused.** (*tr*) to confuse; bewilder.

bemused (bɪ'mju:zd) *adj* preoccupied; lost in thought.

ben[1] (bɛn) *Scot.* ◆ *n* **1** an inner room in a cottage. ◆ *prep, adv* **2** in; within; inside. ◆ Cf. **but**[2]. ORIG OE *binnan,* from BE- + *innan* inside

ben[2] (bɛn) *n Scot., Irish.* a mountain peak: *Ben Lomond.* ORIG C18: from Gaelic *beinn,* from *beann*

Benares (bɪ'nɑ:rɪz) *or* **Banaras** ★ *n* the former name of **Varanasi.**

Ben Bella ★ (bɛn 'bɛlə) *n* **Mohammed Ahmed** ('ɑ:mɪd). born 1916, Algerian statesman: first prime minister (1962–65) and president (1963–65) of independent Algeria: overthrown and imprisoned (1965–80).

Benbow ★ ('bɛnbəʊ) *n* **John.** 1653–1702, English admiral killed during the War of the Spanish Succession.

bench (bɛntʃ) *n* **1** a long seat for more than one person, usually lacking a back. **2** a plain stout worktable. **3 the bench.** (*sometimes cap.*) **3a** a judge or magistrate sitting in court. **3b** judges or magistrates collectively. **4** a ledge in a mine or quarry from which work is carried out. **5** (in a gymnasium) a low table, which may be inclined, used for various exercises. **6** a platform on which dogs, etc., are exhibited at shows. **7** *NZ, old-fashioned.* a natural feature of terrain used by sheep for shelter. ◆ *vb* (*tr*) **8** to provide with benches. **9** to exhibit (a dog, etc.) at a show. **10** *US & Canad., Sports.* to take (a player) out of a game, often for disciplinary reasons. ORIG OE *benc*

bencher ('bɛntʃə) *n* (*often pl*) *Brit.* **1** a member of the governing body of one of the Inns of Court. **2** See **backbencher.**

benchmark ('bɛntʃˌmɑ:k) *n* **1** a mark on a stone post or other permanent feature, used as a reference point in surveying. **2** a criterion by which to measure something; reference point. ◆ *vb* **3** (*tr*) to measure or test against a benchmark: *the firm benchmarked its pay against that in industry.*

bench press *n* a weight-training exercise in which a person lies on a bench and pushes a barbell upwards with both hands from chest level until the arms are straight, then lowers it again.

bench test *n* the critical evaluation of a new or repaired component, device, apparatus, etc., prior to installation to ensure that it is in perfect condition.

bench warrant *n* a warrant issued by a judge or court directing that an offender be apprehended.

bend[1] (bɛnd) *vb* **bends, bending, bent. 1** to form or cause to form a curve. **2** to turn or cause to turn from a particular direction: *the road bends left.* **3** (*intr;* often foll. by *down,* etc.) to incline the body; stoop; bow. **4** to submit or cause to submit: *to bend before superior force.* **5** (*tr*) to turn or direct (one's eyes, steps, attention, etc.). **6** (*tr*) *Naut.* to attach or fasten, as a sail to a boom. **7 bend (someone's) ear.** to speak at length to an unwilling listener, esp. to voice one's troubles. **8 bend the rules.** *Inf.* to ignore rules or change them to suit one's own convenience. ◆ *n* **9** a curved part. **10** *Naut.* a knot in a line for joining it to another or to an object. **11** the act of bending. **12 round the bend.** *Brit. sl.* mad. ORIG OE *bendan*
▸ **'bendable** *adj* ▸ **'bendy** *adj*

bend[2] (bɛnd) *n Heraldry.* a diagonal line traversing a shield. ORIG OE *bend* BAND[2]

bender ('bɛndə) *n Inf.* **1** a drinking bout. **2** a makeshift shelter constructed by placing tarpaulin or plastic sheeting over bent saplings or woven branches.

Bendigo ★ ('bɛndɪˌgəʊ) *n* a city in SE Australia, in central Victoria: founded in 1851 after the discovery of gold. Pop.: 57 427 (1991).

bends (bɛndz) *pl n* (*functioning as sing or pl*) **the.** a nontechnical name for **decompression sickness.**

bend sinister *n Heraldry.* a diagonal line bisecting a shield from the top right to the bottom left, typically indicating a bastard line.

beneath (bɪ'ni:θ) *prep* **1** below, esp. if covered, protected, or obscured by. **2** not as great or good as would be demanded by: *beneath his dignity.* ◆ *adv* **3** below; underneath. ORIG OE *beneothan,* from BE- + *neothan* low

benedicite (ˌbɛnɪ'daɪsɪtɪ) *n* (esp. in Christian religious orders) a blessing or grace. ORIG C13: from L, from *benedīcere,* from *bene* well + *dīcere* to speak

Benedict ★ ('bɛnɪˌdɪkt) *n* **Saint.** ?480–?547 A.D., Italian monk: founded the Benedictine order at Monte Cassino in Italy in about 540 A.D. His *Regula Monachorum* became the basis of the rule of all Western Christian monastic orders. Feast day: July 11 or March 14.

Benedict XV ★ *n* original name *Giacomo della Chiesa.* 1854–1922, pope (1914–22); noted for his repeated attempts to end World War I and for his organization of war relief.

Benedictine *n* **1** (ˌbɛnɪ'dɪktɪn, -taɪn). a monk or nun who is a member of the order of Saint Benedict. **2** (ˌbɛnɪ'dɪkti:n). a greenish-yellow liqueur first made at the Benedictine monastery at Fécamp in France in about 1510. ◆ *adj* (ˌbɛnɪ'dɪktɪn, -taɪn). **3** of or relating to Saint Benedict or his order.

benediction (ˌbɛnɪ'dɪkʃən) *n* **1** an invocation of divine blessing. **2** a Roman Catholic service in which the congregation is blessed with the sacrament. **3** the state of being blessed. ORIG C15: from L *benedictio,* from *benedīcere* to bless; see BENEDICITE
▸ **ˌbene'dictory** *adj*

Benedictus (ˌbɛnɪ'dɪktəs) *n* (*sometimes not cap.*) *Christianity.* **1** a canticle beginning *Benedictus qui venit in nomine Domini* in Latin and *Blessed is he that cometh in the name of the Lord* in English. **2** a canticle beginning *Benedictus Dominus Deus Israel* in Latin and *Blessed be the Lord God of Israel* in English.

benefaction (ˌbɛnɪ'fækʃən) *n* **1** the act of doing good, esp. by giving a donation to charity. **2** the donation or help given. ORIG C17: from LL *benefactiō,* from L *bene* well + *facere* to do

benefactor ('bɛnɪˌfæktə, ˌbɛnɪ'fæk-) *n* a person who supports or helps a person, institution, etc., esp. by giving money.
▸ **'beneˌfactress** *fem n*

benefice ('bɛnɪfɪs) *n* **1** *Christianity.* an endowed Church office yielding an income to its holder; a Church living. **2** the property or revenue attached to such an office. ORIG C14: from OF, from L *beneficium* benefit, from *bene* well + *facere* to do
▸ **'beneficed** *adj*

beneficent (bɪ'nɛfɪsᵊnt) *adj* charitable; generous. ORIG C17: from L *beneficus;* see BENEFICE
▸ **be'neficence** *n*

beneficial (ˌbɛnɪ'fɪʃəl) *adj* **1** (sometimes foll. by *to*) advantageous. **2** *Law.* entitling a person to receive the profits or proceeds of property. ORIG C15: from LL *beneficiālis,* from L *beneficium* kindness

beneficiary (ˌbɛnɪ'fɪʃərɪ) *n, pl* **beneficiaries. 1** a person who gains or benefits. **2** *Law.* a person entitled to receive funds or other property under a trust, will, etc. **3** the holder of a benefice. **4** *NZ.* a person who receives government assistance: *social security beneficiary.* ◆ *adj* **5** of or relating to a benefice.

benefit ('bɛnɪfɪt) *n* **1** something that improves or promotes. **2** advantage or sake. **3** (*sometimes pl*) a payment or series of payments made by an institution or government to a person who is ill, unemployed, etc. **4** a theatrical performance, sports event, etc., to raise money for a charity. ◆ *vb* **benefits, benefiting, benefited** *or US* **benefits, benefitting, benefitted. 5** to do or receive good; profit. ORIG C14: from Anglo-F *benfet,* from L *benefactum,* from *bene facere* to do well

benefit in kind *n* a non-pecuniary benefit, such as a company car or medical insurance, given to an employee.

benefit of clergy *n Christianity.* **1** sanction by the church: *marriage without benefit of clergy.* **2** (in the Middle Ages) a privilege that placed the clergy outside the jurisdiction of secular courts.

benefit society *n* a US term for **friendly society.**

Benelux ★ ('bɛnɪˌlʌks) *n* **1** the customs union formed by Belgium, the Netherlands, and Luxembourg in 1948; became an economic union in 1960. **2** these countries collectively.

★ people and places

Beneš ★ (*Czech* 'bɛnɛʃ) *n* **Eduard** ('eːduart). 1884–1948, Czech statesman; president of Czechoslovakia (1935–38; 1946–48) and of its government in exile (1939–45).

Benevento ★ (ˌbɛnə'vɛntəʊ) *n* a city in S Italy, in N Campania: at various times under Samnite, Roman, Lombard, Saracen, Norman, and papal rule. Pop.: 64 690 (1990). Ancient name: **Beneventum** (ˌbɛnə'vɛntʊm).

benevolence (bɪ'nɛvələns) *n* **1** inclination to do good; charity. **2** an act of kindness.

benevolent (bɪ'nɛvələnt) *adj* **1** intending or showing goodwill; kindly; friendly. **2** doing good rather than making profit; charitable: *a benevolent organization.* ORIG C15: from L *benevolēns,* from *bene* well + *velle* to wish

Benfleet ★ ('bɛnˌfliːt) *n* a town in SE England, in S Essex on an inlet of the Thames estuary. Pop.: 49 701 (1991).

BEng *abbrev. for* Bachelor of Engineering.

Bengal ★ (bɛn'gɔːl, bɛŋ-) *n* **1** a former province of NE India, in the great deltas of the Ganges and Brahmaputra Rivers: in 1947 divided into West Bengal (belonging to India) and East Bengal (Bangladesh). **2 Bay of.** a wide arm of the Indian Ocean, between India and Myanmar.

Bengali (bɛn'gɔːlɪ, bɛŋ-) *n* **1** a member of a people living chiefly in Bangladesh and in West Bengal. **2** Also called: **Bangla.** their language. ◆ *adj* **3** of or relating to Bengal, the Bengalis, or their language.

Bengal light *n* a firework or flare that burns with a bright blue light, formerly used as a signal.

Bengbu ('bɛŋ'buː), **Pengpu** *or* **Pang-fou** ★ *n* a city in E China, in Anhui province. Pop.: 449 245 (1990 est.).

Benghazi *or* **Bengasi** ★ (bɛn'gɑːzɪ) *n* a port in N Libya, on the Gulf of Sidra: centre of Italian colonization (1911–42); scene of much fighting in World War II. Pop.: 446 250 (1988 est.). Ancient names: **Hesperides, Berenice** (bɛrə'naɪsɪ).

Benguela ★ (bɛŋ'gwɛlə) *n* a port in W Angola: founded in 1617; a terminus (with Lobito) of the railway that runs from Beira in Mozambique through the Copper Belt of Zambia and Zimbabwe. Pop.: 41 000 (latest est.).

Ben-Gurion ★ (bɛn'gʊərɪən) *n* **David,** original name *David Gruen.* 1886–1973, Israeli socialist statesman, born in Poland; first prime minister of Israel (1948–53, 1955–63).

Beni ★ (*Spanish* 'beni) *n* a river in N Bolivia, rising in the E Cordillera of the Andes and flowing north to the Marmoré River. Length: over 1600 km (1000 miles).

benighted (bɪ'naɪtɪd) *adj* **1** lacking cultural, moral, or intellectual enlightenment. **2** *Arch.* overtaken by night.
▸ **be'nightedness** *n*

benign (bɪ'naɪn) *adj* **1** showing kindliness; genial. **2** (of soil, climate, etc.) mild; gentle. **3** favourable; propitious. **4** *Pathol.* (of a tumour, etc.) not malignant. ORIG C14: from OF *benigne,* from L *benignus,* from *bene* well + *gignere* to produce
▸ **be'nignly** *adv*

benignant (bɪ'nɪgnənt) *adj* **1** kind; gracious. **2** a less common word for **benign** (senses 3, 4).
▸ **be'nignancy** *n*

benignity (bɪ'nɪgnɪtɪ) *n, pl* **benignities. 1** the quality of being benign. **2** a kind or gracious act.

Beni Hasan ★ ('bɛnɪ hæ'sɑːn) *n* a village in central Egypt, on the Nile, with cliff-cut tombs dating from 2000 B.C.

Benin ★ (bɛ'niːn) *n* **1** a republic in W Africa, on the **Bight of Benin,** a section of the Gulf of Guinea: in the early 19th century a powerful kingdom, famed for its women warriors; became a French colony in 1893, gaining independence in 1960. It consists chiefly of coastal lagoons and swamps in the south, a fertile plain and marshes in the centre, and the Atakora Mountains in the northwest. Official language: French. Religion: animist majority. Currency: franc. Capital: Porto Novo (the government sits in Cotonou). Pop.: 6 306 000 (1999 est.). Area: 112 622 sq. km (43 474 sq. miles). Former name (until 1975): **Dahomey. 2** a former kingdom of W Africa, powerful from the 14th to the 17th centuries: now a province of S Nigeria: noted for its bronzes.
▸ **Beˌni'nese** *or* **Beninois** (ˌbɛniː'nwɑː) *adj, n*

Benin City ★ *n* a city in S Nigeria: former capital of the kingdom of Benin. Pop.: 223 900 (1995 est.).

benison ('bɛnɪzᵊn, -sᵊn) *n Arch.* a blessing. ORIG C13: from OF *beneison,* from L *benedictiō* BENEDICTION

Benjamin[1] ★ ('bɛndʒəmɪn) *n* **1** *Old Testament.* **1a** the youngest and best-loved son of Jacob and Rachel (Genesis 35:16–18; 42:4). **1b** the tribe descended from this patriarch. **1c** the territory of this tribe, northwest of the Dead Sea. **2** *Arch.* a youngest and favourite son.

Benjamin[2] ★ *n* ('bɛndʒəmɪn). **Arthur.** 1893–1960, Australian composer. In addition to *Jamaican Rumba* (1938), he wrote five operas and a harmonica concerto (1953).

Ben Lomond ★ (bɛn 'ləʊmənd) *n* **1** a mountain in W central Scotland, on the E side of Loch Lomond. Height: 973 m (3192 ft). **2** a mountain in NE Tasmania. Height: 1527 m (5010 ft). **3** a mountain in SE Australia, in NE New South Wales. Height: 1520 m (4986 ft).

Benn ★ (bɛn) *n* **Antony (Neil) Wedgwood,** known as *Tony Benn.* born 1925, British left-wing Labour politician. He renounced (1963) the title of Viscount Stansgate.

Bennett ★ ('bɛnɪt) *n* **1 Alan.** born 1934, British actor and playwright. His plays include *Forty Years On* (1968), *The Madness of George III* (1991), and *The Lady in the Van* (1999). **2 (Enoch) Arnold.** 1867–1931, British novelist, noted for *The Old Wives' Tale* (1908) and *Clayhanger* (1910). **3 James Gordon.** 1837–1931, US newspaper editor, born in Scotland. He founded (1835) the *New York Herald.* **4 Richard Bedford,** 1st Viscount. 1870–1947, Canadian Conservative statesman; prime minister (1930–35). **5** Sir **Richard Rodney.** born 1936, British composer, noted for his operas *The Mines of Sulphur* (1965) and *Victory* (1970).

Ben Nevis ★ (bɛn 'nɛvɪs) *n* a mountain in W Scotland, in the Grampian mountains: highest peak in Great Britain. Height: 1343 m (4406 ft).

Bennington ★ ('bɛnɪŋtən) *n* a town in SW Vermont: the site of a British defeat (1777) in the War of American Independence. Pop.: 16 451 (1990).

Benny ★ ('bɛnɪ) *n* **Jack,** real name *Benjamin Kubelsky.* 1894–1974, US comedian.

Benoît de Sainte-Maure ★ (*French* bənwa də sɛ̃tmɔr) *n* 12th-century French trouvère: author of the *Roman de Troie,* which contains the episode of Troilus and Cressida.

Benoni ★ (bɪ'nəʊnɪ) *n* a city in NE South Africa: gold mines. Pop.: 113 501 (1991).

bent[1] (bɛnt) *adj* **1** not straight; curved. **2** (foll. by *on*) resolved (to); determined (to). **3** *Sl.* **3a** dishonest; corrupt. **3b** (of goods) stolen. **3c** crazy. **3d** sexually deviant. ◆ *n* **4** personal inclination or aptitude. **5** capacity of endurance (esp. in **to the top of one's bent**).

bent[2] (bɛnt) *n* **1** short for **bent grass. 2** *Arch.* any stiff grass or sedge. **3** *Arch. or dialect.* heath or moorland. ORIG OE *bionot*

bent grass *n* a perennial grass which has a spreading panicle of tiny flowers sometimes planted for hay or in lawns.

Bentham ★ ('bɛnθəm) *n* **Jeremy.** 1748–1832, British philosopher: a founder of utilitarianism. His works include *Introduction to the Principles of Morals and Legislation* (1789).

Benthamism ('bɛnθəmɪzəm) *n* the utilitarian philosophy of Jeremy Bentham, which holds that the ultimate goal of society should be to promote the greatest happiness of the greatest number.
▸ **'Benthamite** *n, adj*

benthos ('bɛnθɒs) *n* the animals and plants living at the bottom of a sea or lake. ORIG C19: from Gk: depth; rel. to *bathus* deep
▸ **'benthic** *adj*

Bentinck ★ ('bɛntɪŋk) *n* Lord **William Cavendish.** 1774–1839, British statesman, governor general of Bengal (1828–35).

Bentley ★ ('bɛntlɪ) *n* **Edmund Clerihew.** 1875–1956, British journalist, noted for his invention of the clerihew.

bento *or* **bento box** ('bɛntəʊ) *n, pl* **bentos.** a thin box, made of plastic or lacquered wood, divided into compartments, which contain small separate dishes comprising a Japanese meal, esp. lunch. ORIG from Japanese *bentō* box lunch

bentonite ('bɛntəˌnaɪt) *n* a clay that swells as it absorbs water: used as a filler in various industries. ORIG after Fort *Benton,* Montana, USA, where found

bentwood ('bɛntˌwʊd) *n* **a** wood bent in moulds after being heated by steaming, used mainly for furniture. **b** (*as modifier*): *a bentwood chair.*

Benue ★ ('bɛnʊˌeɪ) *n* **1** a state of SE Nigeria, formed in 1976 from part of Benue-Plateau state. Capital: Makurdi. Pop.: 3 108 754 (1995 est.). Area: 34 059 sq. km (13 150 sq. miles). **2** a river in W Africa, rising in N Cameroon and flowing west across Nigeria: chief tributary of the River Niger. Length: 1400 km (870 miles).

benumb (bɪ'nʌm) *vb* (*tr*) **1** to make numb or powerless; deaden, as by cold. **2** (*usually passive*) to stupefy (the mind, senses, will, etc.).

Benxi ('bɛn'ʃiː), **Penchi,** *or* **Penki** ★ *n* an industrial city in SE China, in S Liaoning province. Pop.: 768 778 (1990 est.).

Benz ★ (bɛnz; *German* bɛnts) *n* **Karl** (**Friedrich**) (karl). 1844–1929, German engineer; designed the first car driven by an internal-combustion engine (1885).

Benzedrine ('bɛnzɪˌdriːn, -drɪn) *n* a trademark for **amphetamine.**

benzene ('bɛnziːn) *n* a colourless flammable poisonous liquid used in the manufacture of styrene, phenol, etc., as a solvent for fats, resins, etc., and as an insecticide. Formula: C_6H_6.

benzene ring *n* the hexagonal ring of bonded carbon atoms in the benzene molecule.

benzine ('bɛnziːn, bɛn'ziːn) *or* **benzin** ('bɛnzɪn) *n* a volatile mixture of the lighter hydrocarbon constituents of petroleum.

benzo- *or* **benz-** *combining form.* **1** indicating a fused benzene ring. **2** indicating derivation from benzene or benzoic acid or the presence of phenyl groups. ORIG from BENZOIN

benzoate ('bɛnzəʊˌeɪt, -ɪt) *n* a salt or ester of benzoic acid.

benzocaine ('bɛnzəʊˌkeɪn) *n* a white crystalline ester used as a local anaesthetic.

benzodiazepine (ˌbɛnzəʊdaɪ'eɪzəˌpiːn) *n* any of a group of chemical compounds that are used as minor tranquillizers, such as diazepam (Valium) and chlordiazepoxide (Librium). ORIG C20: from BENZO- + DI-[1] + AZ(O)- + EP(OXY)- + -INE[2]

benzoic (bɛn'zəʊɪk) *adj* of, containing, or derived from benzoic acid or benzoin.

benzoic acid *n* a white crystalline solid occurring in many natural resins, used in plasticizers and dyes and as a food preservative (**E210**).

benzoin ('bɛnzɔɪn, -zəʊɪn) *n* a gum resin containing benzoic acid, obtained from various tropical Asian trees and used in ointments, perfume, etc. ORIG C16: from F *benjoin,* from OCatalan *benjui,* from Ar. *lubān jāwī,* lit.: frankincense of Java

benzol *or* **benzole** ('bɛnzɒl) *n* **1** a crude form of benzene obtained from coal tar or coal gas and used as a fuel. **2** an obsolete name for **benzene.**

Beograd ★ (bɛ'ɔgrad) *n* the Serbo-Croat name for **Belgrade.**

bequeath (bɪ'kwiːð, -'kwiːθ) *vb* (*tr*) **1** *Law.* to dispose of (property) by will. **2** to hand down; pass on. ORIG OE *becwethan*
▸ **be'queathal** *n*

bequest (bɪ'kwɛst) *n* **1** the act of bequeathing. **2** something that is bequeathed. ORIG C14: BE- + OE *-cwiss* degree

Berar ★ (bɛ'rɑː) *n* a region of W central India: part of Madhya Pradesh state since 1950; important for cotton growing.

berate (bɪ'reɪt) *vb* **berates, berating, berated.** (*tr*) to scold harshly.

Berber ('bɜːbə) *n* **1** a member of a Caucasoid Muslim people of N Africa. **2** the language of this people. ◆ *adj* **3** of or relating to this people or their language.

Berbera ★ ('bɜːbərə) *n* a port in N Somalia, on the Gulf of Aden. Pop.: 70 000 (latest est.).

berberis ('bɜːbərɪs) *n* any of a genus of mainly N temperate shrubs. See **barberry.** ORIG C19: from Med. L, from ?

berceuse (*French* bɛrsøz) *n* **1** a lullaby. **2** an instrumental piece suggestive of this. ORIG C19: from F: lullaby

Berchtesgaden ★ (*German* 'bɛrçtəsgaːdən) *n* a town in Germany, in SE Bavaria: site of the mountain retreat of Adolf Hitler. Pop.: 7865 (1992 est.).

bereave (bɪ'riːv) *vb* **bereaves, bereaving, bereaved.** (*tr*) (usually foll. by *of*) to deprive (of) something or someone valued, esp. through death. ORIG OE *bereafian*
▸ **be'reaved** *adj* ▸ **be'reavement** *n*

bereft (bɪ'rɛft) *adj* (usually foll. by *of*) deprived; parted (from): *bereft of hope.*

beret ('bɛreɪ) *n* a round close-fitting brimless cap. ORIG C19: from F *béret,* from OProvençal *berret*

Berezina ★ (*Russian* bɪrɪzi'na) *n* a river in Belarus, rising in the north and flowing south to the River Dnieper: linked with the River Dvina and the Baltic Sea by the **Berezina Canal.** Length: 563 km (350 miles).

Berezniki ★ (*Russian* bɪrɪzni'ki) *n* a city in E Russia: chemical industries. Pop.: 184 000 (1995 est.).

berg[1] (bɜːg) *n* short for **iceberg.**

berg[2] (bɜːg) *n* a South African word for **mountain.**

Berg ★ (bɜːg; *German* bɛrk) *n* **1 Alban** (**Maria Johannes**) ('albaːn). 1885–1935, Austrian composer. His works include the operas *Wozzeck* (1921) and *Lulu* (1935), chamber works, and songs. **2 Paul.** born 1926, US molecular biologist, the first to identify transfer RNA (1956). Nobel prize for chemistry 1980.

Bergamo ★ (*Italian* 'bɛrgamo) *n* a walled city in N Italy, in Lombardy. Pop.: 116 990 (1996 est.).

bergamot ('bɜːgəˌmɒt) *n* **1** a small Asian tree having sour pear-shaped fruit. **2 essence of bergamot.** a fragrant essential oil extracted from the fruit rind of this plant, used in perfumery. **3** a Mediterranean mint that yields a similar oil. ORIG C17: from F *bergamote,* from It. *bergamotta,* of Turkic origin

Bergen ★ *n* **1** (*Norwegian* 'bærgən) a port in SW Norway: chief city in medieval times. Pop.: 224 130 (1997 est.). **2** ('bɛrxən). the Flemish name for **Mons.**

Bergerac ★ (*French* bɛrʒərak) *n* See **Cyrano de Bergerac.**

bergie ('bɜːgiː) *n S. African inf.* a vagabond, esp. one living on the slopes of Table Mountain in SW South Africa. ORIG from Afrik. *berg* mountain

Bergius ★ (*German* 'bɛrgjʊs) *n* **Friedrich** (**Karl Rudolph**) ('friːdrɪç). 1884–1949, German chemist, who invented a process for producing oil from coal: Nobel prize for chemistry 1931.

Bergman ★ ('bɜːgmən) *n* **1** (**Ernst**) **Ingmar** ('ɪŋmɑː). born 1918, Swedish film director, whose films include *Wild Strawberries* (1957), *Autumn Sonata* (1978), and *Fanny and Alexander* (1982). **2 Ingrid.** 1915–82. Swedish actress, working in Hollywood 1938–48; noted for *Casablanca* (1942) and *The Inn of the Sixth Happiness* (1958).

bergschrund ('bɛrkʃrʊnt) *n* a crevasse at the head of a glacier. ORIG C19: G: mountain crack

Bergson ★ ('bɜːgsᵊn; *French* bɛrksɔn) *n* **Henri Louis** (ãri lwi). 1859–1941, French philosopher, who sought to bridge the gap between metaphysics and science. His main works are *Memory and Matter* (1896, trans. 1911) and *Creative Evolution* (1907, trans. 1911): Nobel prize for literature 1927.
▸ **Bergsonian** (bɜːg'səʊnɪən) *adj, n* ▸ **'Bergsonˌism** *n*

bergwind ('bɜːxvənt) *n* a hot dry wind in South Africa blowing from the plateau down to the coast.

Beria ★ ('bɛrɪə; *Russian* 'bjerijə) *n* **Lavrenti Pavlovich** (la'vrjentij 'pavləvitʃ). 1899–1953, Soviet chief of secret police; killed by his associates shortly after Stalin's death.

beriberi (ˌbɛrɪ'bɛrɪ) *n* a disease, endemic in E and S Asia, caused by dietary deficiency of thiamine (vitamin B_1). ORIG C19: from Sinhalese, by reduplication from *beri* weakness

Bering *or* **Behring** ★ ('bɛrɪŋ, 'bɛər-; *Danish* 'beːreŋ) *n* **Vitus** ('viːtʊs). 1681–1741, Danish navigator, who explored the N Pacific for the Russians and discovered Bering Island and the Bering Strait.

Bering Sea ★ *n* a part of the N Pacific Ocean, between NE Russia and Alaska. Area: about 2 275 000 sq. km (878 000 sq. miles).

Bering Strait ★ *n* a strait between Alaska and Russia, connecting the Bering Sea and the Arctic Ocean.

Beriosova ★ (bɛrɪ'əʊsəvə) *n* **Svetlana** (svɪt'lanə). 1932–98, British ballet dancer, born in Lithuania.

berk *or* **burk** (bɜːk) *n Brit. sl.* a stupid person; fool. ORIG C20: shortened from *Berkeley* or *Berkshire Hunt*, rhyming slang for *cunt*

Berkeley[1] ★ ('bɜːklɪ) *n* a city in W California, on San Francisco Bay: seat of the University of California. Pop.: 99 830 (1994 est.).

Berkeley[2] ★ *n* **1** ('bɜːklɪ). **Busby.** real name *William Berkeley Enos.* 1895–1976, US dance director. **2** ('bɑːklɪ). **George.** 1685–1753, Irish idealist philosopher and Anglican bishop, noted for *A Treatise concerning the Principles of Human Knowledge* (1710) and his *Essay towards a New Theory of Vision* (1709). **3** ('bɑːklɪ). Sir **Lennox (Randal Francis).** 1903–89, British composer; his works include four symphonies, four operas, and the *Serenade for Strings* (1939).

berkelium (bɜː'kiːlɪəm, 'bɜːklɪəm) *n* a radioactive transuranic element produced by bombardment of americium. Symbol: Bk; atomic no.: 97; half-life of most stable isotope, ^{247}Bk: 1400 years. ORIG C20: after BERKELEY[1], where it was discovered

Berks (bɑːks) *abbrev. for* Berkshire.

Berkshire ★ ('bɑːkʃɪə, -ʃə) *n* a historic county of S England: the River Thames marks the N boundary and the **Berkshire Downs** occupy central parts: for administrative purposes it was replaced by six unitary authorities in 1998. Abbrev.: **Berks.**

berley *or* **burley** ('bɜːlɪ) *Austral.* ◆ *n* **1** bait scattered on water to attract fish. **2** *Sl.* rubbish, nonsense. ◆ *vb (tr)* **3** to scatter (bait) on water. **4** to hurry (someone); urge on. ORIG from ?

berlin (bə'lɪn, 'bɜːlɪn) *n* **1** (*sometimes cap.*) Also called: **berlin wool.** a fine wool yarn used for tapestry work, etc. **2** a four-wheeled two-seated covered carriage, popular in the 18th century. ORIG after BERLIN[1]

Berlin[1] ★ (bɜː'lɪn; *German* bɛr'liːn) *n* the capital of Germany (1871–1945 and from 1990), formerly divided into the eastern sector, capital of East Germany, and the western sectors, which formed an exclave in East German territory closely affiliated politically and economically with West Germany: a wall dividing the sectors was built in 1961 by the East German authorities to stop the flow of refugees from east to west; demolition of the wall began in 1989 and the city was formally reunited in 1990: formerly (1618–1871) the capital of Brandenburg and Prussia. Pop.: 3 467 300 (1996 est.).
▸ **Ber'liner** *n*

Berlin[2] ★ (bɜː'lɪn) *n* **1 Irving.** original name *Israel Baline,* 1888–1989, US composer and writer of lyrics, born in Russia. **2** Sir **Isaiah.** 1909–97, British philosopher and diplomat, born in Latvia. His books include *Historical Inevitability* (1954) and *The Magus of the North* (1993).

Berlioz ★ ('bɛəlɪˌəʊz; *French* bɛrljoz) *n* **Hector (Louis)** (ɛktɔr). 1803–69, French composer. His works include the cantata *La Damnation de Faust* (1846), the opera *Les Troyens* (1856–59), the *Symphonie fantastique* (1830), and the oratorio *L'Enfance du Christ* (1854).

berm *or* **berme** (bɜːm) *n* **1** a narrow path or ledge as at the edge of a slope, road, or canal. **2** *Mil.* a man-made ridge of sand or earth, used as an obstacle to tanks. **3** *NZ.* the grass verge of a suburban street, usually kept mown. ORIG C18: from F *berme,* from Du. *berm*

Bermejo ★ (*Spanish* ber'mexo) *n* a river in Argentina, rising in the northwest and flowing southeast to the Paraguay River. Length: about 1600 km (1000 miles).

Bermuda ★ (bə'mjuːdə) *n* a United Kingdom overseas territory consisting of a group of over 150 coral islands (**the Bermudas**) in the NW Atlantic: discovered in about 1503, colonized by the British by 1612, acquired by the British crown in 1684. Capital: Hamilton. Pop.: 60 500 (1994). Area: 53 sq. km (20 sq. miles).
▸ **Ber'mudan** *or* **Ber'mudian** *n, adj*

Bermuda shorts *pl n* shorts that come down to the knees.

Bermuda Triangle ★ *n* an area in the Atlantic Ocean bounded by Bermuda, Puerto Rico, and Florida where ships and aeroplanes are alleged to have disappeared mysteriously.

Bern ★ (bɜːn; *German* bɛrn) *n* **1** the capital of Switzerland, in the W part, on the Aar River: entered the Swiss confederation in 1353 and became the capital in 1848. Pop.: 128 422 (1995 est.). **2** a canton of Switzerland, between the French frontier and the Bernese Alps. Capital: Bern. Pop.: 941 747 (1995 est.). Area: 6884 sq. km (2658 sq. miles). French name: **Berne** (bɛrn).

Bernadette of Lourdes ★ (ˌbɜːnə'dɛt) *n* **Saint.** original name *Marie Bernarde Soubirous.* 1844–79, French peasant girl born in Lourdes, whose visions of the Virgin Mary there made it a centre of pilgrimage. Feast day: Feb. 18.

Bernadotte ★ *n* **1** (*Swedish* 'bærnaˌdɔt). **Folke** ('fɔlkə), Count. 1895–1948, Swedish diplomat, noted for his work with the Red Cross during World War II and as United Nations mediator in Palestine (1948): assassinated by Jewish terrorists. **2** ('bɜːnəˌdɒt; *French* bɛrnadɔt). **Jean Baptiste Jules** (ʒɑ̃ batist ʒyl). 1764–1844, French marshal under Napoleon; king of Norway and Sweden (1818–44) as Charles XIV.

Bernard ★ *n* **1** (*French* bɛrnar). **Claude** (klod). 1813–78, French physiologist, noted for his research on the alimentary canal and the liver. **2** ('bɜːnəd). **Saint,** known as *Bernard of Menthon* and the *Apostle of the Alps.* 923–1008, French monk who founded hospices in the Alpine passes. Feast day: June 15.

Bernard of Clairvaux ('bɜːnəd; klɛə'vəʊ). ★ *n* **Saint.** ?1090–1153, French theologian, who founded the stricter branch of the Cistercians in 1115. Feast day: Aug. 20.

Bernese Alps *or* **Oberland** ★ ('bɜːniːz) *n* a mountain range in SW Switzerland, the N central part of the Alps. Highest peak: Finsteraarhorn, 4274 m (14 022 ft).

Bernhardt ★ ('bɜːnhɑːt; *French* bɛrnar) *n* **Sarah.** original name *Rosine Bernard.* 1844–1923, French actress.

Bernina ★ (bə'niːnə; *Italian* ber'niːna) *n* **Piz.** a mountain in SE Switzerland, the highest peak of the **Bernina Alps,** in the S Rhaetian Alps. Height: 4049 m (13 284 ft).

Bernina Pass ★ *n* a pass in the Alps between SE Switzerland and N Italy, east of Piz Bernina. Height: 2323 m (7622 ft).

Bernini ★ (*Italian* ber'niːni) *n* **Gian Lorenzo** (dʒan lo'rɛntso). 1598–1680, Italian painter, architect, and sculptor.

Bernoulli *or* **Bernouilli** ★ (*French* bɛrnuji; *German* bɛr'nʊli) *n* **1 Daniel** (danjɛl), son of Jean Bernoulli. 1700–82, Swiss mathematician and physicist, who developed an early form of the kinetic theory of gases and stated the principle of conservation of energy in fluid dynamics. **2 Jacques** (ʒɑk) *or* **Jakob** ('jaːkɔp). 1654–1705, Swiss mathematician, noted for his work on calculus and the theory of probability. **3** his brother, **Jean** (ʒɑ̃) *or* **Johann** (jo'han). 1667–1748, Swiss mathematician who developed the calculus of variations.

Bernstein ★ ('bɜːnstaɪn, -stiːn) *n* **Leonard.** 1918–90, US conductor and composer, whose works include the score of the musical *West Side Story* (1957), and *Mass* (1971).

berretta (bɪ'rɛtə) *n* a variant spelling of **biretta.**

berry ('bɛrɪ) *n, pl* **berries. 1** any of various small edible fruits such as the blackberry and strawberry. **2** *Bot.* a fruit with two or more seeds and a fleshy pericarp, such as the grape or gooseberry. **3** any of various seeds or dried kernels, such as a coffee bean. **4** the egg of a lobster, crayfish, or similar animal. ◆ *vb* **berries, berrying, berried.** *(intr)* **5** to bear or produce berries. **6** to gather or look for berries. ORIG OE *berie*

Berry ★ *n* **1** ('bɛrɪ). **Chuck,** full name *Charles Edward Berry.* born 1926, US rock-and-roll guitarist, singer, and songwriter. **2** (*French* bɛri). **Jean de France** (ʒɑ̃ də frɑ̃s), Duc de. 1340–1416, French prince, son of King John II; coregent (1380–88) for Charles VI.

berserk (bəˈzɜːk, -ˈsɜːk) *adj* **1** frenziedly violent or destructive (esp. in **go berserk**). ◆ *n* **2** Also called: **berserker.** one of a class of ancient Norse warriors who fought frenziedly. ORIG C19: Icelandic *berserkr, from björn* bear + *serkr* shirt

berth (bɜːθ) *n* **1** a bed or bunk in a vessel or train. **2** *Naut.* a place assigned to a ship at a mooring. **3** *Naut.* sufficient room for a ship to manoeuvre. **4 give a wide berth to.** to keep clear of. **5** *Inf.* a job, esp. as a member of a ship's crew. ◆ *vb* **6** (*tr*) *Naut.* to assign a berth to (a vessel). **7** *Naut.* to dock (a vessel). **8** (*tr*) to provide with a sleeping place. **9** (*intr*) *Naut.* to pick up a mooring in an anchorage. ORIG C17: prob. from BEAR[1] + -TH[1]

bertha (ˈbɜːθə) *n* a wide deep collar, often of lace, usually to cover a low neckline. ORIG C19: from F *berthe,* from *Berthe,* 8th-cent. Frankish queen

Bertolucci ★ (*Italian* bertoˈluttʃi) *n* **Bernardo** (berˈnardo). born 1940, Italian film director: his films include *The Spider's Stratagem* (1970), *The Last Emperor* (1987), and *Besieged* (1999).

Berwick ★ (ˈbɛrɪk) *n* **James Fitzjames,** Duke of Berwick. 1670–1734, marshal of France and illegitimate son of James II of England. He led French forces during the War of the Spanish Succession (1701–14).

Berwickshire ★ (ˈbɛrɪkˌʃɪə, -ʃə) *n* (until 1975) a county of SE Scotland, now part of Scottish Borders council area.

Berwick-upon-Tweed ★ (twiːd) *n* a town in N England, in N Northumberland at the mouth of the Tweed: much involved in border disputes between England and Scotland between the 12th and 16th centuries; neutral territory 1551–1885. Pop.: 13 544 (1991). Also called: **Berwick.**

beryl (ˈbɛrɪl) *n* a green, blue, yellow, pink, or white hard mineral consisting of beryllium aluminium silicate in hexagonal crystalline form. Emerald and aquamarine are transparent varieties. ORIG C13: from OF, from L, from Gk *bērullos*
▸ **ˈberyline** *adj*

beryllium (bɛˈrɪlɪəm) *n* a corrosion-resistant toxic silvery-white metallic element used mainly in X-ray windows and alloys. Symbol: Be; atomic no.: 4; atomic wt.: 9.012. ORIG C19: from L, from Gk *bērullos*

Berzelius ★ (bəˈziːlɪəs; *Swedish* bærˈseːlius) *n* Baron **Jöns Jakob** (ˈjœns ˈjɑːkɔp). 1779–1848, Swedish chemist, who invented the present system of chemical symbols and formulas, discovered several elements, and determined the atomic and molecular weight of many substances.

Besançon ★ (*French* bəzɑ̃sɔ̃) *n* a city in E France, on the Doubs River: university (1422). Pop.: 119 194 (1990).

Besant ★ (ˈbɛzᵊnt, bɪˈzænt) *n* **Annie,** *née* **Wood.** 1847–1933, British theosophist, writer, and political reformer in England and India.

beseech (bɪˈsiːtʃ) *vb* **beseeches, beseeching, besought** *or* **beseeched.** (*tr*) to ask (someone) earnestly (to do something or for something); beg. ORIG C12: see BE-, SEEK

beseem (bɪˈsiːm) *vb Arch.* to be suitable for or worthy of; befit.

beset (bɪˈsɛt) *vb* **besets, besetting, beset.** (*tr*) **1** (esp. of dangers or temptations) to trouble or harass constantly. **2** to surround or attack from all sides. **3** *Arch.* to cover with, esp. with jewels.

besetting (bɪˈsɛtɪŋ) *adj* tempting, harassing, or assailing (esp. in **besetting sin**).

beside (bɪˈsaɪd) *prep* **1** next to; at, by, or to the side of. **2** as compared with. **3** away from; wide of. **4** *Arch.* besides. **5 beside oneself.** (*postpositive;* often foll. by *with*) overwhelmed; overwrought: *beside oneself with grief.* ◆ *adv* **6** at, by, to, or along the side of something or someone. ORIG OE *be sīdan;* see BY, SIDE

USAGE NOTE There is occasional confusion between *beside* as a preposition, which can mean 'next to', and *besides,* which means 'in addition to'. The following sentence, taken from the Bank of English, illustrates the mistake: *beside all these considerations, trees are beautiful – or most of them are.* Conversely, the following is correct: *but that is beside* (not *besides*) *the point.*

besides (bɪˈsaɪdz) *prep* **1** apart from; even considering. ◆ *sentence connector.* **2** anyway; moreover. ◆ *adv* **3** as well.

besiege (bɪˈsiːdʒ) *vb* **besieges, besieging, besieged.** (*tr*) **1** to surround (a fortified area) with military forces to bring about its surrender. **2** to crowd round; hem in. **3** to overwhelm, as with requests.
▸ **beˈsieger** *n*

besmear (bɪˈsmɪə) *vb* (*tr*) **1** to smear over; daub. **2** to sully; defile (often in **besmear (a person's) reputation**).

besmirch (bɪˈsmɜːtʃ) *vb* (*tr*) **1** to make dirty; soil. **2** to reduce the brightness of. **3** to sully (often in **besmirch (a person's) name**).

besom[1] (ˈbiːzəm) *n* a broom, esp. one made of a bundle of twigs tied to a handle. ORIG OE *besma*

besom[2] (ˈbɪzəm) *n Scot. & N English dialect.* a derogatory term for a **woman.** ORIG ?from OE *bysen* example; rel. to ON *bysn* wonder

besotted (bɪˈsɒtɪd) *adj* **1** stupefied with drink. **2** infatuated; doting. **3** foolish; muddled.

besought (bɪˈsɔːt) *vb* a past tense and past participle of **beseech.**

bespangle (bɪˈspæŋgᵊl) *vb* **bespangles, bespangling, bespangled.** (*tr*) to cover or adorn with or as if with spangles.

bespatter (bɪˈspætə) *vb* (*tr*) **1** to splash, as with dirty water. **2** to defile; besmirch.

bespeak (bɪˈspiːk) *vb* **bespeaks, bespeaking, bespoke; bespoken** *or* **bespoke.** (*tr*) **1** to engage or ask for in advance. **2** to indicate or suggest: *this act bespeaks kindness.* **3** *Poetic.* to address.

bespectacled (bɪˈspɛktəkᵊld) *adj* wearing spectacles.

bespoke (bɪˈspəʊk) *adj Chiefly Brit.* **1** (esp. of a suit, jacket, etc.) made to the customer's specifications. **2** making or selling such suits, jackets, etc.: *a bespoke tailor.*

besprinkle (bɪˈsprɪŋkᵊl) *vb* **besprinkles, besprinkling, besprinkled.** (*tr*) to sprinkle all over with liquid, powder, etc.

Bessarabia ★ (ˌbɛsəˈreɪbɪə) *n* a region of E Europe, mostly in Moldova and Ukraine: long disputed by the Turks and Russians; a province of Romania from 1918 until 1940. Area: about 44 300 sq. km (17 100 sq. miles).

Bessel ★ (ˈbɛsᵊl) *n* **Friedrich Wilhelm** (ˈfriːdrɪç ˈvɪlhɛlm). 1784–1846, German astronomer and mathematician. He made the first measurement of a star's distance from the earth (1841) and devised mathematical Bessel functions, used in physics.

Bessemer process (ˈbɛsɪmə) *n* (formerly) a process for producing steel by blowing air through molten pig iron in a **Bessemer converter** (a refractory-lined furnace): impurities are removed and the carbon content is controlled. ORIG C19: after Sir Henry *Bessemer* (1813–98), E engineer

best (bɛst) *adj* **1** the superlative of **good. 2** most excellent of a particular group, category, etc. **3** most suitable, desirable, etc. **4 the best part of.** most of. ◆ *adv* **5** the superlative of **well**[1]. **6** in a manner surpassing all others; most excellently, attractively, etc. ◆ *n* **7 the best.** the most outstanding or excellent person, thing, or group in a category. **8** the utmost effort. **9** a winning majority. **10** Also: **all the best.** best wishes. **11** a person's smartest outfit of clothing. **12 at best. 12a** in the most favourable interpretation. **12b** under the most favourable conditions. **13 for the best. 13a** for an ultimately good outcome. **13b** with good intentions. **14 get** *or* **have the best of.** to defeat or outwit. **15 give (someone) the best.** to concede (someone's) superiority. **16 make the best of.** to cope as well as possible with. ◆ *vb* **17** (*tr*) to gain the advantage over or defeat. ORIG OE *betst*

Best ★ (bɛst) *n* **1 Charles Herbert.** 1899–1978, Canadian physiologist: associated with Banting and Macleod in their discovery of insulin in 1922. **2 George.** born 1946, Northern Ireland footballer.

bestead (bɪˈstɛd) *Arch.* ◆ *vb* **besteads, besteading, besteaded; besteaded** *or* **bestead. 1** (*tr*) to help; avail. ◆ *adj also* **bested. 2** placed; situated. ORIG C13: see BE-, STEAD

bestial (ˈbɛstɪəl) *adj* **1** brutal or savage. **2** sexually depraved. **3** lacking in refinement; brutish. **4** of or relating to a beast. ORIG C14: from LL *bestiālis,* from L *bestia* BEAST

bestiality (ˌbɛstɪˈælɪtɪ) *n, pl* **bestialities. 1** bestial behaviour. **2** sexual activity between a person and an animal.

bestialize *or* **bestialise** (ˈbɛstɪəˌlaɪz) *vb* **bestializes, bestializing, bestialized** *or* **bestialises, bestialising, bestialised.** (*tr*) to make bestial or brutal.

bestiary (ˈbɛstɪərɪ) *n, pl* **bestiaries.** a moralizing medieval collection of descriptions of real and mythical animals.

bestir (bɪˈstɜː) *vb* **bestirs, bestirring, bestirred.** (*tr*) to cause (oneself) to become active; rouse.

best man *n* the male attendant of the bridegroom at a wedding.

bestow (bɪˈstəʊ) *vb* (*tr*) **1** to present (a gift) or confer (an honour). **2** *Arch.* to apply (energy, resources, etc.). **3** *Arch.* to house (a person) or store (goods).
▸ **beˈstowal** *n*

bestrew (bɪˈstruː) *vb* **bestrews, bestrewing, bestrewed; bestrewn** *or* **bestrewed.** (*tr*) to scatter or lie scattered over (a surface).

bestride (bɪˈstraɪd) *vb* **bestrides, bestriding, bestrode** *or* (*Arch.*) **bestrid; bestridden** *or* (*Arch.*) **bestrid.** (*tr*) **1** to have or put a leg on either side of. **2** to extend across; span. **3** to stride over or across.

bestseller (ˌbɛstˈsɛlə) *n* **1** a book or other product that has sold in great numbers. **2** the author of one or more such books, etc.
▸ **ˌbestˈselling** *adj*

bet (bɛt) *n* **1** an agreement between two parties that a sum of money or other stake will be paid by the loser to the party who correctly predicts the outcome of an event. **2** the stake risked. **3** the predicted result in such an agreement. **4** a person, event, etc., considered as likely to succeed or occur. **5** a course of action (esp. in **one's best bet**). **6** *Inf.* an opinion: *my bet is that you've been up to no good.* ◆ *vb* **bets, betting, bet** *or* **betted. 7** (when *intr* foll. by *on* or *against*) to make or place a bet with (a person or persons). **8** (*tr*) to stake (money, etc.) in a bet. **9** (*tr; may take a clause as object*) *Inf.* to predict (a certain outcome). **10 you bet.** *Inf.* of course; naturally. ORIG C16: prob. short for ABET

beta (ˈbiːtə) *n* **1** the second letter in the Greek alphabet (Β or β). **2** the second in a group or series. ORIG from Gk *bēta,* from Heb.; see BETH

beta-blocker *n* any of a class of drugs, such as propranolol, that decrease the activity of the heart: used in the treatment of high blood pressure and angina.

betacarotene (ˌbiːtəˈkærəˌtiːn) *n* the most important form of the plant pigment carotene, which occurs in milk, vegetables, and other foods and, when eaten by man and animals, is converted in the body to vitamin A.

beta decay *n* the radioactive change in an atomic nucleus accompanying the emission of an electron.

betake (bɪˈteɪk) *vb* **betakes, betaking, betook, betaken.** (*tr*) **1 betake oneself.** to go; move. **2** *Arch.* to apply (oneself) to.

beta particle *n* a high-speed electron or positron emitted by a nucleus during radioactive decay or nuclear fission.

beta ray *n* a stream of beta particles.

beta rhythm *or* **wave** *n Physiol.* the normal electrical activity of the cerebral cortex.

beta stock *n* any of the second rank of active securities on the London stock exchange, of which there are about 500. Continuous display of prices by market makers is required but not immediate publication of transactions.

betatron (ˈbiːtəˌtrɒn) *n* a type of particle accelerator for producing high-energy beams of electrons by magnetic induction.

betel (ˈbiːtᵊl) *n* an Asian climbing plant, the leaves of which are chewed by the peoples of SE Asia. ORIG C16: from Port., from Malayalam *vettila*

betel nut *n* the seed of the betel palm, chewed with betel leaves and lime by people in S and SE Asia as a digestive stimulant and narcotic.

betel palm *n* a tropical Asian feather palm.

bête noire *French.* (bɛt nwar) *n, pl* ***bêtes noires*** (bɛt nwar). a person or thing that one particularly dislikes or dreads. ORIG lit.: black beast

beth (bɛt) *n* the second letter of the Hebrew alphabet. ORIG from Heb. *bēth-, bayith* house

Bethany ★ (ˈbɛθənɪ) *n* a village in the West Bank, near Jerusalem at the foot of the Mount of Olives: in the New Testament, the home of Lazarus and the lodging place of Jesus during Holy Week.

Bethe ★ (ˈbeɪtə) *n* **Hans Albrecht** (hans ˈalbrɛçt). born 1906, US physicist, born in Germany; noted for his work on nuclear physics: Nobel prize for physics 1967.

Bethel ★ (ˈbɛθəl) *n* **1** an ancient town in the West Bank, near Jerusalem: in the Old Testament, the place where the dream of Jacob occurred (Genesis 28:19). **2** a chapel of any of certain Nonconformist Christian sects. **3** a seamen's chapel. ORIG C17: from Heb. *bēth 'Ēl* house of God

Bethesda ★ (bəˈθɛzdə) *n* **1** *New Testament.* a pool in Jerusalem reputed to have healing powers, where a paralytic was healed by Jesus (John 5:2). **2** a chapel of any of certain Nonconformist Christian sects.

bethink (bɪˈθɪŋk) *vb* **bethinks, bethinking, bethought.** *Arch. or dialect.* **1** to cause (oneself) to consider or meditate. **2** (*tr; often foll. by of*) to remind (oneself).

Bethlehem ★ (ˈbɛθlɪˌhɛm, -lɪəm) *n* a town in the West Bank, near Jerusalem: birthplace of Jesus and early home of King David.

Bethmann Hollweg ★ (*German* ˈbeːtman ˈhɔlveːk) *n* **Theobald von** (ˈteːobalt fɔn). 1856–1921, chancellor of Germany (1909–17).

Bethsaida ★ (bɛθˈseɪdə) *n* a ruined town in N Israel, near the N shore of the Sea of Galilee.

betide (bɪˈtaɪd) *vb* **betides, betiding, betided.** to happen or happen to (often in **woe betide** (**someone**)). ORIG C13: from BE- + obs. *tide* to happen

betimes (bɪˈtaɪmz) *adv Arch.* **1** in good time; early. **2** soon. ORIG C14 *bitimes;* see BY, TIME

Betjeman ★ (ˈbɛtʃəmən) *n* Sir **John.** 1906–84, British poet, noted for his nostalgic verse. Poet laureate (1972–84).

betoken (bɪˈtəʊkən) *vb* (*tr*) **1** to indicate; signify. **2** to portend; augur.

betony (ˈbɛtənɪ) *n, pl* **betonies. 1** a Eurasian plant with a spike of reddish-purple flowers, formerly used in medicine and dyeing. **2** any of several related plants. ORIG C14: from OF, from L

betray (bɪˈtreɪ) *vb* (*tr*) **1** to hand over or expose (one's nation, friend, etc.) treacherously to an enemy. **2** to disclose (a secret, confidence, etc.) treacherously. **3** to break (a promise) or be disloyal to (a person's trust). **4** to show signs of; indicate. **5** to reveal unintentionally: *his grin betrayed his satisfaction.* ORIG C13: from BE- + *trayen,* from OF, from L *trādere* to hand over
▸ **beˈtrayal** *n* ▸ **beˈtrayer** *n*

betroth (bɪˈtrəʊð) *vb* (*tr*) *Arch.* to promise to marry or to give in marriage. ORIG C14 *betreuthen,* from BE- + *treuthe* TROTH, TRUTH

betrothal (bɪˈtrəʊðəl) *n* **1** engagement to be married. **2** a mutual promise to marry.

betrothed (bɪˈtrəʊðd) *adj* **1** engaged to be married: *he was betrothed to her.* ◆ *n* **2** the person to whom one is engaged; fiancé or fiancée.

better (ˈbɛtə) *adj* **1** the comparative of **good. 2** more excellent than others. **3** more suitable, advantageous, attractive, etc. **4** improved or fully recovered in health. **5 better off.** in more favourable circumstances, esp. financially. **6 the better part of.** a large part of. ◆ *adv* **7** the comparative of **well**[1]. **8** in a more excellent manner; more advantageously, attractively, etc. **9** in or to a greater degree or extent; more. **10 had better.** would be wise, sensible, etc., to: *I had better be off.* **11 think better of. 11a** to change one's mind about (a course of action, etc.) after reconsideration. **11b** to rate more highly. ◆ *n* **12 the better.** something that is the more excellent, useful, etc., of two such things. **13** (*usually pl*) a person who is superior, esp. in social standing or ability. **14 for the better.** by way of improvement. **15 get the better of.** to defeat, outwit, or surpass. ◆ *vb* **16** to make or become better. **17** (*tr*) to improve upon; surpass. ORIG OE *betera*

better half *n Humorous.* one's spouse.

betterment ('bɛtəmənt) *n* **1** a change for the better; improvement. **2** *Property law.* an improvement effected on real property that enhances the value of the property.

betting shop *n* (in Britain) a licensed bookmaker's premises not on a racecourse.

between (bɪ'twiːn) *prep* **1** at a point or in a region intermediate to two other points in space, times, degrees, etc. **2** in combination; together: *between them, they saved enough money to buy a car.* **3** confined or restricted to: *between you and me.* **4** indicating a reciprocal relation or comparison. **5** indicating two or more alternatives. ◆ *adv also* **in between. 6** between one specified thing and another. ORIG OE *betwēonum;* see TWO, TWAIN

> **USAGE NOTE** After *distribute* and words with a similar meaning, *among* should be used rather than *between: this enterprise issued shares which were distributed among its workers.*

betweentimes (bɪ'twiːnˌtaɪmz) *or* **betweenwhiles** *adv* between other activities; during intervals.

betwixt (bɪ'twɪkst) *prep, adv* **1** *Arch.* another word for **between. 2 betwixt and between.** in an intermediate or indecisive position. ORIG OE *betwix*

Betws-y-Coed ★ (ˌbɛtsɪ'kɔɪd) *n* a village in N Wales, in Conwy county borough on the River Conwy: noted for its scenery. Pop.: 2860 (1991).

Beulah ★ ('bjuːlə) *n Old Testament.* the land of Israel (Isaiah 62:4). ORIG Heb., lit.: married woman

Beuthen ★ ('bɔytən) *n* the German name for **Bytom.**

BeV (in the US) *abbrev. for* gigaelectronvolts (GeV). ORIG C20: from *b(illion) e(lectron) v(olts)*

Bevan ★ ('bɛvən) *n* **Aneurin** (ə'naɪ^ərɪn), known as *Nye.* 1897–1960, British Labour statesman: as minister of health (1945–51) he introduced the National Health Service (1948).
▸ **'Bevanˌite** *n, adj*

bevatron ('bɛvəˌtrɒn) *n* a synchrotron used to accelerate protons. ORIG C20: from BEV + -TRON

bevel ('bɛv^əl) *n* **1** Also called: **cant.** a surface that meets another at an angle other than a right angle. ◆ *vb* **bevels, bevelling, bevelled** *or US* **bevels, beveling, beveled. 2** (*intr*) to be inclined; slope. **3** (*tr*) to cut a bevel on (a piece of timber, etc.). ORIG C16: from OF, from *baer* to gape; see BAY[1]

bevel gear *n* a gear having teeth cut into a conical surface. Two such gears mesh together to transmit power between two shafts at an angle.

bevel square *n* a tool with an adjustable arm that can be set to mark out an angle.

beverage ('bɛvərɪdʒ, 'bɛvrɪdʒ) *n* any drink, usually other than water. ORIG C13: from OF *bevrage,* from *beivre* to drink, from L *bibere*

beverage room *n Canad.* another name for **beer parlour.**

Beveridge ★ ('bɛvərɪdʒ) *n* **William Henry,** 1st Baron Beveridge. 1879–1963, British economist, whose *Report on Social Insurance and Allied Services* (1942) formed the basis of the welfare state.

Beverley ★ ('bɛvəlɪ) *n* a market town in NE England; administrative centre of the East Riding of Yorkshire. Pop.: 23 632 (1991).

Beverly Hills ★ ('bɛvəlɪ) *n* a city in SW California, near Los Angeles: famous as the home of film stars. Pop.: 31 970 (1990).

Bevin ★ ('bɛvɪn) *n* **Ernest.** 1881–1951, British Labour statesman, who was largely responsible for the creation of the Transport and General Workers' Union (1922): minister of labour (1940–45); foreign secretary (1945–51).

bevvy ('bɛvɪ) *n, pl* **bevvies.** *Dialect.* **1** a drink, esp. an alcoholic one. **2** a session of drinking. ORIG prob. from OF *bevee, buvee* drinking

bevy ('bɛvɪ) *n, pl* **bevies. 1** a flock of quails. **2** a group, esp. of girls. ORIG C15: from ?

bewail (bɪ'weɪl) *vb* to express great sorrow over (a person or thing); lament.
▸ **be'wailer** *n*

beware (bɪ'wɛə) *vb* (*usually used in the imperative or infinitive;* often foll. by *of*) to be cautious or wary (of); be on one's guard (against). ORIG C13 *be war,* from BE (imperative) + *war* WARY

Bewick ★ ('bjuːɪk) *n* **Thomas.** 1753–1828, British wood engraver; his best-known works are *Aesop's Fables* (1818) and the *History of British Birds* (1797–1804).

bewilder (bɪ'wɪldə) *vb* (*tr*) to confuse utterly; puzzle. ORIG C17: see BE-, WILDER
▸ **be'wildering** *adj* ▸ **be'wilderingly** *adv* ▸ **be'wilderment** *n*

bewitch (bɪ'wɪtʃ) *vb* (*tr*) **1** to attract and fascinate. **2** to cast a spell over. ORIG C13 *bewicchen;* see BE-, WITCH[1]
▸ **be'witching** *adj*

bewray (bɪ'reɪ) *vb* (*tr*) an obsolete word for **betray.** ORIG C13: from BE- + OE *wrēgan* to accuse

Bexhill(-on-Sea) (ˌbɛks'hɪl) ★ *n* a resort in S England, in East Sussex on the English Channel. Pop.: 38 905 (1991).

Bexley ★ ('bɛkslɪ) *n* a borough of Greater London. Pop.: 210 257 (1991). Area: 61 sq. km (23 sq. miles).

bey (beɪ) *n* **1** (in the Ottoman Empire) a title given to provincial governors. **2** (in modern Turkey) a title of address, corresponding to *Mr.* ◆ Also called: **beg.** ORIG C16: Turkish: lord

Beyoğlu ★ ('beɪɔːluː) *n* a district of Istanbul, north of the Golden Horn: the European quarter. Former name: **Pera.**

beyond (bɪ'jɒnd) *prep* **1** at or to a point on the other side of; at or to the further side of: *beyond those hills.* **2** outside the limits or scope of. ◆ *adv* **3** at or to the other or far side of something. **4** outside the limits of something. ◆ *n* **5 the beyond.** the unknown, esp. life after death in certain religious beliefs. ORIG OE *begeondan;* see BY, YONDER

Beyrouth ★ (beɪ'ruːt, 'beɪruːt) *n* a variant spelling of **Beirut.**

Beza (*French* bəza) *or* **de Bèze** ★ (*French* də bɛz) *n* **Théodore** (teodɔr). 1519–1605, French Calvinist theologian and scholar, who lived in Switzerland. He succeeded Calvin as leader of the Swiss Protestants.

bezel ('bɛz^əl) *n* **1** the sloping face adjacent to the working edge of a cutting tool. **2** the upper oblique faces of a cut gem. **3** a grooved ring or part holding a gem, watch crystal, etc. **4** a retaining outer rim used in vehicle instruments such as tachometers and speedometers. **5** a small indicator light used in vehicle instrument panels. ORIG C17: prob. from F *biseau*

Béziers ★ (*French* bezje) *n* a city in S France: scene of a massacre (1209) during the Albigensian Crusade. It is a centre of the wine trade. Pop.: 70 996 (1990).

bezique (bɪ'ziːk) *n* **1** a card game for two or more players using two packs with nothing below a seven. **2** (in this game) the queen of spades and jack of diamonds declared together. ORIG C19: from F *bésigue,* from ?

Bezwada ★ ('beɪzˌwɑːdə) *n* the former name of **Vijayawada.**

B/F *or* **b/f** *Book-keeping. abbrev. for* brought forward.

BFPO *abbrev. for* British Forces Post Office.

Bhagalpur ★ ('bɑːgəlˌpʊə) *n* a city in India, in Bihar: agriculture, textiles, university (1960). Pop.: 253 225 (1991).

bhaji ('bɑːdʒɪ) *n, pl* **bhaji, bhajis,** *or* **bhajia** ('bɑːdʒɪə). an Indian savoury made of chopped vegetables mixed in a spiced batter and deep-fried. ORIG Hindi *bhājī* fried vegetables

bhang *or* **bang** (bæŋ) *n* a preparation of the leaves and flower tops of Indian hemp having psychoactive properties: much used in India. ORIG C16: from Hindi *bhāng*

bhangra ('bæŋgrə) *n* a type of Asian pop music that combines elements of traditional Punjabi music with Western pop. ORIG C20: from Hindi

bharal *or* **burhel** ('bʌrəl) *n* a wild Himalayan sheep with a bluish-grey coat. ORIG Hindi

Bharat ★ ('bʌrʌt) *n* transliteration of the Hindi name for **India.**

Bhatpara ★ (bɑːt'pɑːrə) *n* a city in NE India, in West Bengal on the Hooghly River: jute and cotton mills. Pop.: 304 952 (1991).

Bhavnagar ★ ('bɑːvnəgə) *n* a port in W India, in S Gujarat. Pop.: 402 338 (1991).

bhindi ('bɪndɪ) *n* the okra as used in Indian cooking. ORIG Hindi

Bhopal ★ (bəʊ'pɑːl) *n* a city in central India, the capital of Madhya Pradesh state: in 1984 2000 people were killed by poisonous gas, which leaked from a US-owned factory. Pop.: 1 062 771 (1991).

bhp *abbrev. for* brake horsepower.

BHP *Austral. abbrev. for* Broken Hill Proprietary.

Bhubaneswar ★ (ˌbʊbə'neɪʃwə) *n* an ancient city in E India, the capital of Orissa state: many temples built between the 7th and 16th centuries. Pop.: 411 542 (1991).

Bhutan ★ (buː'tɑːn) *n* a kingdom in central Asia: disputed by Tibet, China, India, and Britain since the 18th century, the conflict now being chiefly between China and India (which is responsible for Bhutan's external affairs); contains inaccessible stretches of the E Himalayas in the north. Official language: Dzongka; Nepali is also spoken. Official religion: Mahayana Buddhism. Currencies: ngultrum and Indian rupee. Capital: Thimbu. Pop.: 658 000 (1999 est.). Area: about 46 600 sq. km (18 000 sq. miles).
▸ ˌ**Bhutan'ese** *n, adj*

Bhutto ★ ('buːtəʊ) *n* **1 Benazir** ('bɛnəˌzɪə). born 1953, Pakistani stateswoman; prime minister (1988–90 and 1993–96). **2** her father, **Zulfikar Ali** ('zʊlfɪkɑː 'ɑːlɪ). 1928–79, Pakistani statesman; president (1971–73) and prime minister (1973–77): executed for the murder of a political rival.

Bi *the chemical symbol for* bismuth.

bi- *or sometimes before a vowel* **bin-** *combining form.* **1** two; having two: *bifocal.* **2** occurring every two; lasting for two: *biennial.* **3** on both sides, directions, etc.: *bilateral.* **4** occurring twice during: *biweekly.* **5a** denoting a compound containing two identical cyclic hydrocarbon systems: *biphenyl.* **5b** (rare in technical usage) indicating an acid salt of a dibasic acid: *sodium bicarbonate.* **5c** (not in technical usage) equivalent of **di-**[1] (sense 2). ORIG from L, from *bis* TWICE

Biafra ★ (bɪ'æfrə) *n* **1** a region of E Nigeria: seceded as an independent republic (1967–70) during the Civil War, but defeated by Nigerian government forces. **2 Bight of.** former name (until 1975) of (the Bight of) **Bonny.**
▸ **Bi'afran** *adj, n*

Biak ★ (biː'jɑːk) *n* an island in Indonesia, north of West Irian: the largest of the Schouten Islands. Area: 2455 sq. km (948 sq. miles).

Białystok ★ (*Polish* bja'wistɔk) *n* a city in E Poland: belonged to Prussia (1795–1807) and to Russia (1807–1919). Pop.: 277 100 (1995 est.). Russian name: **Belostock.**

biannual (baɪ'ænjʊəl) *adj* occurring twice a year. Cf. **biennial.**
▸ **bi'annually** *adv*

> **USAGE NOTE** An event which is *biannual* will occur four times as often as one which is *biennial.* In order to make your message simpler, it may be clearer to spell out exactly what you intend, by saying *six-monthly.*

Biarritz ★ ('bɪərɪts, bɪə'rɪts; *French* bjarits) *n* a town in SW France, on the Bay of Biscay: famous resort, patronized by Napoleon III and by Queen Victoria and Edward VII of Great Britain and Ireland. Pop.: 28 890 (1990).

bias ('baɪəs) *n* **1** mental tendency or inclination, esp. irrational preference or prejudice. **2** a diagonal line or cut across the weave of a fabric. **3** *Electronics.* the voltage applied to an electrode of a transistor or valve to establish suitable working conditions. **4** *Bowls.* **4a** a bulge or weight inside one side of a bowl. **4b** the curved course of such a bowl. **5** *Statistics.* a latent influence that disturbs an analysis. ◆ *adv* **6** obliquely; diagonally. ◆ *vb* **biases, biasing, biased** *or* **biasses, biassing, biassed. 7** (*tr; usually passive*) to cause to have a bias; prejudice; influence. ORIG C16: from OF *biais*
▸ **'biased** *or* **'biassed** *adj*

bias binding *n* a strip of material cut on the bias, used for binding hems or for decoration.

biathlon (baɪ'æθlən, -lɒn) *n Sport.* a contest in which skiers with rifles shoot at four targets along a 20-kilometre (12.5-mile) cross-country course.

biaxial (baɪ'æksɪəl) *adj* (esp. of a crystal) having two axes.

bib (bɪb) *n* **1** a piece of cloth or plastic worn, esp. by babies, to protect their clothes while eating. **2** the upper front part of some aprons, dungarees, etc. **3** Also called: **pout, whiting pout.** a light brown European marine gadoid food fish with a barbel on its lower jaw. **4 stick one's bib in.** *Austral. inf.* to interfere. ◆ *vb* **bibs, bibbing, bibbed. 5** *Arch.* to drink (something). ORIG C14 *bibben* to drink, prob. from L *bibere*

Bib. *abbrev. for:* **1** Bible. **2** Biblical.

bib and tucker *n Inf.* an outfit of clothes.

bibcock ('bɪbˌkɒk) *or* **bib** *n* a tap with a nozzle bent downwards fed from a horizontal pipe.

bibelot ('bɪbləʊ) *n* an attractive or curious trinket. ORIG C19: from F, from OF *beubelet*

bibl. *abbrev. for:* **1** bibliographical. **2** bibliography.

Bibl. *abbrev. for* Biblical.

Bible ('baɪbᵊl) *n* **1a the.** the sacred writings of the Christian religion, comprising the Old and New Testaments. **1b** (*as modifier*): *a Bible reading.* **2** (*often not cap.*) the sacred writings of a religion. **3** (*usually not cap.*) a book regarded as authoritative. ORIG C13: from OF, from Med. L *biblia* books, from Gk, dim. of *biblos* papyrus

Bible Belt *n* those states of the S US where Protestant fundamentalism is dominant.

Bible-thumper *n Sl.* an enthusiastic or aggressive exponent of the Bible. Also: **Bible-basher.**
▸ **'Bible-ˌthumping** *n, adj*

biblical ('bɪblɪkᵊl) *adj* **1** of or referring to the Bible. **2** resembling the Bible in written style.

Biblicist ('bɪblɪsɪst) *or* **Biblist** *n* **1** a biblical scholar. **2** a person who takes the Bible literally.

biblio- *combining form.* indicating book or books: *bibliography.* ORIG from Gk *biblion* book

bibliography (ˌbɪblɪ'ɒgrəfɪ) *n, pl* **bibliographies. 1** a list of books on a subject or by a particular author. **2** a list of sources used in a book, thesis, etc. **3a** the study of the history, classification, etc., of literary material. **3b** a work on this subject.
▸ ˌ**bibli'ographer** *n* ▸ **bibliographic** (ˌbɪblɪəʊ'græfɪk) *or* ˌ**biblio'graphical** *adj*

bibliomancy ('bɪblɪəʊˌmænsɪ) *n* prediction of the future by interpreting a passage chosen at random from a book, esp. the Bible.

bibliomania (ˌbɪblɪəʊ'meɪnɪə) *n* extreme fondness for books.
▸ ˌ**biblio'maniˌac** *n, adj*

bibliophile ('bɪblɪəˌfaɪl) *or* **bibliophil** ('bɪblɪəfɪl) *n* a person who collects or is fond of books.
▸ **bibliophilism** (ˌbɪblɪ'ɒfɪˌlɪzəm) *n* ▸ ˌ**bibli'ophily** *n*

bibliopole ('bɪblɪəʊˌpəʊl) *or* **bibliopolist** (ˌbɪblɪ'ɒpəlɪst) *n* a dealer in books, esp. rare or decorative ones. ORIG C18: from L, from Gk, from BIBLIO- + *pōlein* to sell
▸ ˌ**bibli'opoly** *n*

bibulous ('bɪbjʊləs) *adj* addicted to alcohol. ORIG C17: from L *bibulus,* from *bibere* to drink
▸ **'bibulously** *adv* ▸ **'bibulousness** *n*

bicameral (baɪ'kæmərəl) *adj* (of a legislature) consisting of two chambers. ORIG C19: from BI- + L *camera* CHAMBER
▸ **bi'cameralˌism** *n*

bicarb (ˈbaɪkɑːb) *n* short for **bicarbonate of soda.**

bicarbonate (baɪˈkɑːbənɪt, -ˌneɪt) *n* a salt of carbonic acid.

bicarbonate of soda *n* sodium bicarbonate, esp. as medicine or a raising agent in baking.

bice (baɪs) *n* **1** Also called: **bice blue.** medium blue. **2** Also called: **bice green.** a yellowish green. ORIG C14: from OF *bis* dark grey, from ?

bicentenary (ˌbaɪsɛnˈtiːnərɪ) *or US* **bicentennial** (ˌbaɪsɛnˈtɛnɪəl) *adj* **1** marking a 200th anniversary. **2** occurring every 200 years. **3** lasting 200 years. ◆ *n, pl* **bicentenaries. 4** a 200th anniversary.

bicephalous (baɪˈsɛfələs) *adj* **1** *Biol.* having two heads. **2** crescent-shaped.

biceps (ˈbaɪsɛps) *n, pl* **biceps.** *Anat.* any muscle having two heads or origins, esp. the muscle that flexes the forearm. ORIG C17: from L, from BI- + *caput* head

bichloride (baɪˈklɔːraɪd) *n* another name for **dichloride.**

bichloride of mercury *n* another name for **mercuric chloride.**

bichromate (baɪˈkrəʊˌmeɪt, -mɪt) *n* another name for **dichromate.**

bicker (ˈbɪkə) *vb* (*intr*) **1** to argue over petty matters; squabble. **2** *Poetic.* **2a** (esp. of a stream) to run quickly. **2b** to flicker; glitter. ◆ *n* **3** a squabble. ORIG C13: from ?
▸ ˈ**bickerer** *n*

bicolour (ˈbaɪˌkʌlə), **bicoloured** *or US* **bicolor, bicolored** *adj* two-coloured.

biconcave (baɪˈkɒnkeɪv, ˌbaɪkɒnˈkeɪv) *adj* (of a lens) having concave faces on both sides.

biconditional (ˌbaɪkənˈdɪʃənəl) *n* **1** *Logic, maths.* a relation, taken as meaning *if and only if,* between two propositions which are either both true or both false and such that each implies the other. **2** *Logic.* a logical connective between two propositions whose truth table is true only if both propositions are true or both false. ◆ Also called (esp. sense 1): **equivalence.**

biconvex (baɪˈkɒnvɛks, ˌbaɪkɒnˈvɛks) *adj* (of a lens) having convex faces on both sides.

bicuspid (baɪˈkʌspɪd) *or* **bicuspidate** (baɪˈkʌspɪˌdeɪt) *adj* **1** having two cusps or points. ◆ *n* **2** a bicuspid tooth; premolar.

bicycle (ˈbaɪsɪkəl) *n* **1** a vehicle with a tubular metal frame mounted on two spoked wheels, one behind the other. The rider sits on a saddle, propels the vehicle by means of pedals, and steers with handlebars on the front wheel. Often shortened to **bike** (inf.), **cycle.** ◆ *vb* **bicycles, bicycling, bicycled. 2** (*intr*) to ride a bicycle.
▸ ˈ**bicyclist** *or* ˈ**bicycler** *n*

bicycle clip *n* one of a pair of clips worn around the ankles by cyclists to keep the trousers tight and out of the chain.

bid (bɪd) *vb* **bids, bidding, bad, bade,** *or* (esp. for senses 1, 2, 5, 6) **bid, bidden** *or* (esp. for senses 1, 2, 5, 6) **bid. 1** (often foll. by *for* or *against*) to offer (an amount) in attempting to buy something. **2** *Commerce.* to respond to an offer by a seller stating (the more favourable terms) on which one is willing to make a purchase. **3** (*tr*) to say (a greeting, etc.): *to bid farewell.* **4** to order; command: *do as you are bid!* **5** (*intr;* usually foll. by *for*) to attempt to attain power, etc. **6** *Bridge, etc.* to declare before play how many tricks one expects to make. **7 bid defiance.** to resist boldly. **8 bid fair.** to seem probable. ◆ *n* **9a** an offer of a specified amount. **9b** the price offered. **10a** the quoting by a seller of a price. **10b** the price quoted. **11** *Commerce.* **11a** a statement by a buyer, in response to an offer by a seller, of the more favourable terms that would be acceptable. **11b** the price or other terms so stated. **12** an attempt, esp. to attain power. **13** *Bridge.* **13a** the number of tricks a player undertakes to make. **13b** a player's turn to make a bid. ◆ See also **bid up.** ORIG OE *biddan*
▸ ˈ**bidder** *n*

Bida (ˈbaɪdɑː) *or* **El Beda** ★ (ɛl ˈbeɪdɑː) *n* the former name of **Doha.**

biddable (ˈbɪdəbəl) *adj* **1** having sufficient value to be bid on, as a hand at bridge. **2** docile; obedient.
▸ ˈ**biddableness** *n*

bidding (ˈbɪdɪŋ) *n* **1** an order; command. **2** an invitation; summons. **3** bids or the act of making bids.

biddy[1] (ˈbɪdɪ) *n, pl* **biddies.** a dialect word for **chicken** or **hen.** ORIG C17: ? imit. of calling chickens

biddy[2] (ˈbɪdɪ) *n, pl* **biddies.** *Inf.* a woman, esp. an old gossipy one. ORIG C18: from pet form of *Bridget*

biddy-biddy (ˈbɪdɪˌbɪdɪ) *n, pl* **biddy-biddies. 1** a low-growing rosaceous plant of New Zealand, having prickly burs. **2** the burs of this plant. ◆ Also: **bidgee-widgee** (ˈbɪdʒɪˌwɪdʒɪ). ORIG from Maori *piripiri*

bide (baɪd) *vb* **bides, biding, bided** *or* **bode, bided. 1** (*intr*) *Arch. or dialect.* to continue in a certain place or state; stay. **2** (*tr*) *Arch. or dialect.* to tolerate; endure. **3 bide one's time.** to wait patiently for an opportunity. ORIG OE *bīdan*

bidentate (baɪˈdɛnˌteɪt) *adj* having two teeth or toothlike parts or processes.

bidet (ˈbiːdeɪ) *n* a small low basin for washing the genital area. ORIG C17: from F: small horse

bid up *vb* (*adv*) to increase the market price of (a commodity) by making artificial bids.

Biel ★ (biːl) *n* **1** a town in NW Switzerland, on Lake Biel. Pop.: 52 197 (1994). French name: **Bienne. 2 Lake.** a lake in NW Switzerland: remains of lake dwellings were discovered here in the 19th century. Area: 39 sq. km (15 sq. miles). German name: **Bielersee** (ˈbiːlərzeː).

Bielefeld ★ (*German* ˈbiːləfɛlt) *n* a city in Germany, in NE North Rhine-Westphalia. Pop.: 324 066 (1996 est.).

Bielsko-Biała ★ (*Polish* ˈbjɛlskɔˈbjawa) *n* a town in S Poland: created in 1951 by the union of Bielsko and Biala Krakowska; a leading textile centre since the 16th century. Pop.: 180 300 (1995 est.).

Bien Hoa ★ (ˈbjɛn ˈhəʊə) *n* a town in S Vietnam: a former capital of Cambodia. Pop.: 273 879 (1989).

Bienne ★ (bjɛn) *n* the French name for **Biel.**

biennial (baɪˈɛnɪəl) *adj* **1** occurring every two years. **2** lasting two years. Cf. **biannual.** ◆ *n* **3** a plant that completes its life cycle in two years. **4** an event that takes place every two years.
▸ **biˈennially** *adv*

bier (bɪə) *n* a platform or stand on which a corpse or a coffin containing a corpse rests before burial. ORIG OE *bǣr;* rel. to *beran* to BEAR[1]

Bierce ★ (bɪəs) *n* **Ambrose** (**Gwinett**). 1842–?1914, US journalist and author of *The Devil's Dictionary* (1906): he disappeared during a mission in Mexico (1913).

biestings (ˈbiːstɪŋz) *n* a variant spelling of **beestings.**

biff (bɪf) *Sl.* ◆ *n* **1** a blow with the fist. ◆ *vb* **2** (*tr*) to give (someone) such a blow. ORIG C20: prob. imit.

bifid (ˈbaɪfɪd) *adj* divided into two lobes by a median cleft. ORIG C17: from L, from BI- + *-fidus,* from *findere* to split
▸ **biˈfidity** *n* ▸ ˈ**bifidly** *adv*

bifocal (baɪˈfəʊkəl) *adj* **1** *Optics.* having two different focuses. **2** relating to a compound lens permitting near and distant vision.

bifocals (baɪˈfəʊkəlz) *pl n* a pair of spectacles with bifocal lenses.

BIFU (in Britain) *abbrev. for* Banking, Insurance and Finance Union.

bifurcate *vb* (ˈbaɪfəˌkeɪt), **bifurcates, bifurcating, bifurcated. 1** to fork or divide into two branches. ◆ *adj* (ˈbaɪfəˌkeɪt, -kɪt). **2** forked or divided into two branches. ORIG C17: from Med. L, from L, from BI- + *furca* fork
▸ ˌ**bifurˈcation** *n*

big (bɪg) *adj* **bigger, biggest. 1** of great or considerable size, height, weight, number, power, or capacity. **2** having great significance; important. **3** important through having power, influence, wealth, authority, etc. **4** *Inf.* considerable in extent or intensity (esp. in **in a big way**). **5a** elder: *my big brother.* **5b** grown-up. **6a** generous; magnanimous: *that's very big of you.* **6b** (*in combination*): *big-hearted.* **7** extravagant; boastful: *big talk.* **8 too big for one's boots** *or* **breeches.** conceited; unduly self-confident. **9** in an advanced stage of pregnancy (esp. in **big with child**). ◆ *adv Inf.* **10** boastfully; pretentiously (esp. in **talk big**). **11**

in an exceptional way; well: *his talk went over big*. **12** on a grand scale (esp. in **think big**). ◆ See also **big up**. ORIG C13: ?from ON
▸ ˈ**bigness** *n*

bigamy (ˈbɪgəmɪ) *n, pl* **bigamies**. the crime of marrying a person while still legally married to someone else. ORIG C13: via F from Med. L; see BI-, -GAMY
▸ ˈ**bigamist** *n* ▸ ˈ**bigamous** *adj*

Big Apple ★ *n* **the**. *Inf.* New York City. ORIG C20: prob. from US jazzmen's earlier use to mean any big, esp. northern, city; from ?

Big Bang *n* the reorganization of the London Stock Exchange that took effect in October 1986 when operations became fully computerized, fixed commissions were abolished, and the functions of jobbers and brokers were merged.

big-bang theory *n* a cosmological theory postulating that all the matter of the universe was hurled in all directions by a cataclysmic explosion and that the universe is still expanding. Cf. **steady-state theory**.

Big Brother *n* **1** a person, organization, etc., that exercises total dictatorial control. **2** a television gameshow format in which a small number of people living in accommodation sealed off from the outside world are constantly monitored by TV cameras. Viewers vote each week to expel a person from the group until there is only one person left, who wins a cash prize. ORIG C20: from George Orwell's novel *1984* (1949)

big business *n* large commercial organizations collectively, esp. when considered as exploitative or socially harmful.

Big C *n* **the**. a euphemism for **cancer** (senses 1 and 2).

big deal *interj Sl.* an exclamation of scorn, derision, etc., used esp. to belittle a claim or offer.

big dipper *n* (in amusement parks) a narrow railway with open carriages that run swiftly over a route of sharp curves and steep inclines.

big end *n Brit.* the larger end of a connecting rod in an internal-combustion engine.

big game *n* large animals that are hunted or fished for sport.

big gun *n Inf.* an important person.

bighead (ˈbɪg,hɛd) *n Inf.* a conceited person.
▸ ,**big**ˈ**headed** *adj* ▸ ,**big**ˈ**headedness** *n*

big hitter *n* **1** a sportsperson who is capable of hitting the ball long or hard. **2** an influential and important person: *one of the big hitters of the Government*.

bighorn (ˈbɪg,hɔːn) *n, pl* **bighorns** *or* **bighorn**. a large wild sheep inhabiting mountainous regions in North America.

bight (baɪt) *n* **1** a wide indentation of a shoreline, or the body of water bounded by such a curve. **2** the slack middle part or loop in a rope. ORIG OE *byht*; see BOW²

Bight ★ (baɪt) *n* **the**. the major indentation of the S coast of Australia. In full: **the Great Australian Bight**.

Big Mac (mæk) *n Trademark*. two hamburgers served with salad, dressing, and a pickle on a soft bread roll.

bigmouth (ˈbɪg,maʊθ) *n Sl.* a noisy, indiscreet, or boastful person.
▸ ˈ**big-**,**mouthed** *adj*

big name *n Inf.* **a** a famous person. **b** (*as modifier*): *a big-name performer*.

big noise *n Brit. inf.* an important person.

bignonia (bɪgˈnəʊnɪə) *n* a tropical American climbing shrub cultivated for its trumpet-shaped yellow or reddish flowers. ORIG C19: from NL, after the Abbé Jean-Paul *Bignon* (1662–1743)

big-note *vb* **big-notes, big-noting, big-noted**. (*tr*) *Austral. inf.* to boast about (oneself).

bigot (ˈbɪgət) *n* a person who is intolerant, esp. regarding religion, politics, or race. ORIG C16: from OF: name applied contemptuously to the Normans by the French, from ?
▸ ˈ**bigoted** *adj* ▸ ˈ**bigotry** *n*

big shot *n Inf.* an important person.

Big Smoke *n* **the**. *Inf.* a large city, esp. London.

big stick *n Inf.* force or the threat of force.

big time *n Inf.* **a the**. the highest level of a profession, esp. entertainment. **b** (*as modifier*): *a big-time comedian*.
▸ ˈ**big-**ˈ**timer** *n*

big top *n Inf.* **1** the main circus tent. **2** the circus itself.

big up *vb* **bigs, bigging, bigged**. (*tr, adv*) *Sl., chiefly Caribbean*. to make important, prominent, or famous: *we'll do our best to big you up*.

bigwig (ˈbɪg,wɪg) *n Inf.* an important person.

Bihar ★ (bɪˈhɑː) *n* a state of NE India: hilly in the south, with the Ganges plain in the north; important for rice and mineral resources. Capital: Patna. Pop.: 93 080 000 (1994 est.). Area: 174 038 sq. km (67 875 sq. miles).

Biisk ★ (*Russian* bijsk) *n* a variant spelling of **Biysk**.

Bijapur ★ (,bɪdʒəˈpʊə) *n* an ancient city in W India, in N Mysore: capital of a former kingdom, which fell at the end of the 17th century: cotton. Pop.: 186 939 (1991).

bijou (ˈbiːʒuː) *n, pl* **bijoux** (-ʒuːz). **1** something small and delicately worked. **2** (*modifier*) *Often ironic*. small but tasteful: *a bijou residence*. ORIG C19: from F, from Breton *bizou* finger ring, from *biz* finger

bijugate (ˈbaɪdʒʊ,geɪt, baɪˈdʒuːgeɪt) *or* **bijugous** *adj* (of compound leaves) having two pairs of leaflets.

Bikaner ★ (ˈbiːkə,nɪə) *n* a walled city in NW India, in Rajasthan: capital of the former state of Bikaner, on the edge of the Thar Desert. Pop.: 416 289 (1991).

bike (baɪk) *n* **1** *Inf.* short for **bicycle** or **motorcycle**. **2** *Sl.* a promiscuous woman. **3 get off one's bike**. *Austral. & NZ sl.* to lose one's self-control. ◆ *vb* **bikes, biking, biked**. **4** (*intr*) *Inf.* to ride a cycle.

biker (ˈbaɪkə) *n* a member of a motorcycle gang. Also called (Austral. and NZ): **bikie**.

biker jacket *n* a short, close-fitting leather jacket with zips and studs, often worn by motorcyclists.

bikini (bɪˈkiːnɪ) *n* a woman's very brief two-piece swimming costume. ORIG C20: after *Bikini* atoll, from a comparison between the powerful effect of the atom-bomb test and the effect (on men) of women wearing bikinis

Bikini ★ (bɪˈkiːnɪ) *n* an atoll in the N Pacific; one of the Marshall Islands: site of a US atom-bomb test in 1946.

Biko ★ (ˈbiːkəʊ) *n* **Steven Bantu**, known as *Steve*. 1946–77, Black South African civil rights leader: founder of the South African Students Organization. His death in police custody caused worldwide concern.

bilabial (baɪˈleɪbɪəl) *adj* **1** of or denoting a speech sound articulated using both lips: (*p*) *is a bilabial stop*. ◆ *n* **2** a bilabial speech sound.

bilabiate (baɪˈleɪbɪ,eɪt, -ɪt) *adj Bot.* divided into two lips: *the snapdragon has a bilabiate corolla*.

bilateral (baɪˈlætərəl) *adj* **1** having or involving two sides. **2** affecting or undertaken by two parties; mutual. **3** having identical sides or parts on each side of an axis.

bilateral symmetry *n* symmetry in one plane only. Cf. **radial symmetry**.

Bilbao ★ (bɪlˈbɑːəʊ; *Spanish* bilˈβau) *n* a port in N Spain, on the Bay of Biscay: famous since medieval times for the production of iron and steel goods, esp. swords; still contains the country's largest iron and steel works and exports iron ore. Pop.: 371 787 (1994 est.).

bilberry (ˈbɪlbərɪ) *n, pl* **bilberries**. **1** any of several shrubs, such as the whortleberry, having edible blue or blackish berries. **2** the fruit of any of these plants. ORIG C16: prob. of Scand. origin

bilboes (ˈbɪlbəʊz) *pl n* a long iron bar with sliding shackles, for the ankles of a prisoner. ORIG C16: ?from *Bilbao*, Spain

Bildungsroman *German*. (ˈbɪldʊŋsroma:n) *n* a novel about a person's formative years.

bile (baɪl) *n* **1** a bitter greenish to golden brown alkaline fluid secreted by the liver and stored in the gall bladder. It aids digestion of fats. **2** a health disorder due to faulty secretion of bile. **3** irritability or peevishness. ORIG C17: from F, from L *bīlis*

bilge (bɪldʒ) *n* **1** *Naut.* the parts of a vessel's hull where the sides curve inwards to form the bottom. **2** (*often pl*) the parts of a vessel between the lowermost floorboards and the bottom. **3** Also called: **bilge water.** the dirty water that collects in a vessel's bilge. **4** *Inf.* silly rubbish; nonsense. **5** the widest part of a cask. ◆ *vb* **bilges, bilging, bilged. 6** (*intr*) *Naut.* (of a vessel) to take in water at the bilge. **7** (*tr*) *Naut.* to damage (a vessel) in the bilge. ORIG C16: prob. var. of BULGE

bilharzia (bɪl'hɑːtsɪə) *n* **1** another name for a **schistosome. 2** another name for **schistosomiasis.** ORIG C19: NL, after Theodor *Bilharz* (1825–62), G parasitologist who discovered schistosomes

bilharziasis (ˌbɪlhɑː'tsaɪəsɪs) *or* **bilharziosis** (bɪlˌhɑːtsɪ'əʊsɪs) *n* another name for **schistosomiasis.**

biliary ('bɪlɪərɪ) *adj* of or relating to bile, to the ducts that convey bile, or to the gall bladder.

bilingual (baɪ'lɪŋgwəl) *adj* **1** able to speak two languages, esp. with fluency. **2** expressed in two languages. ◆ *n* **3** a bilingual person.
▸ **bi'lingualˌism** *n*

bilious ('bɪlɪəs) *adj* **1** of or relating to bile. **2** affected with or denoting any disorder related to secretion of bile. **3** *Inf.* bad-tempered; irritable. ORIG C16: from L *bīliōsus* full of BILE
▸ **'biliousness** *n*

bilk (bɪlk) *vb* (*tr*) **1** to balk; thwart. **2** (often foll. by *of*) to cheat or deceive, esp. to avoid making payment to. **3** to escape from; elude. ◆ *n* **4** a swindle or cheat. **5** a person who swindles or cheats. ORIG C17: ? var. of BALK
▸ **'bilker** *n*

bill[1] (bɪl) *n* **1** money owed for goods or services supplied. **2** a statement of money owed. **3** *Chiefly Brit.* such an account for food and drink in a restaurant, hotel, etc. **4** any list of items, events, etc., such as a theatre programme. **5** a statute in draft, before it becomes law. **6** a printed notice or advertisement. **7** *US & Canad.* a piece of paper money; note. **8** an obsolete name for **promissory note. 9** See **bill of exchange, bill of fare.** ◆ *vb* (*tr*) **10** to send or present an account for payment to (a person). **11** to enter (items, goods, etc.) on an account or statement. **12** to advertise by posters. **13** to schedule as a future programme. ORIG C14: from Anglo-L *billa,* alteration of LL *bulla* document, BULL[3]

bill[2] (bɪl) *n* **1** the projecting jaws of a bird, covered with a horny sheath; beak. **2** any beaklike mouthpart in other animals. **3** a narrow promontory. ◆ *vb* (*intr*) (esp. in **bill and coo**). **4** (of birds, esp. doves) to touch bills together. **5** (of lovers) to kiss and whisper amorously. ORIG OE *bile*

bill[3] (bɪl) *n* **1** a pike or halberd with a narrow hooked blade. **2** short for **billhook.** ORIG OE *bill* sword

billabong ('bɪləˌbɒŋ) *n Austral.* **1** a backwater channel that forms a lagoon or pool. **2** a branch of a river running to a dead end. ORIG C19: from Abor., from *billa* river + *bong* dead

billboard ('bɪlˌbɔːd) *n Chiefly US & Canad.* another name for **hoarding.** ORIG C19: from BILL[1] + BOARD

billet[1] ('bɪlɪt) *n* **1** accommodation, esp. for a soldier, in civilian lodgings. **2** the official requisition for such lodgings. **3** a space or berth in a ship. **4** *Inf.* a job. ◆ *vb* **5** (*tr*) to assign a lodging to (a soldier). **6** to lodge or be lodged. ORIG C15: from OF *billette,* from *bulle* a document; see BULL[3]

billet[2] ('bɪlɪt) *n* **1** a chunk of wood, esp. for fuel. **2** a small bar of iron or steel. ORIG C15: from OF *billette* a little log, from *bille* log

billet-doux (ˌbɪlɪ'duː) *n, pl* **billets-doux** (ˌbɪlɪ'duːz). *Old-fashioned or jocular.* a love letter. ORIG C17: from F, lit.: a sweet letter

billhook ('bɪlˌhʊk) *n* a tool with a curved blade terminating in a hook, used for pruning, chopping, etc. Also called: **bill.**

billiard ('bɪljəd) *n* (*modifier*) of or relating to billiards: *a billiard table; a billiard cue.*

billiards ('bɪljədz) *n* (*functioning as sing*) any of various games in which long cues are used to drive balls on a rectangular table covered with a smooth cloth and having raised cushioned edges. ORIG C16: from OF *billard* curved stick, from *bille* log; see BILLET[2]

billing ('bɪlɪŋ) *n* **1** *Theatre.* the relative importance of a performer or act as reflected in the prominence given in programmes, advertisements, etc. **2** *Chiefly US & Canad.* public notice or advertising.

billingsgate ('bɪlɪŋzˌgeɪt) *n* obscene or abusive language. ORIG C17: after BILLINGSGATE, notorious for such language

Billingsgate ★ ('bɪlɪŋzˌgeɪt) *n* the largest fish market in London, formerly on the N bank of the River Thames; moved to a new site on the Isle of Dogs in 1982.

Billings method ('bɪlɪŋz) *n* a natural method of birth control that involves examining the colour and viscosity of the cervical mucus to discover when ovulation is occurring. ORIG C20: after Drs John and Evelyn *Billings*

billion ('bɪljən) *n, pl* **billions** *or* **billion. 1** one thousand million: written as 1 000 000 000 or 10^9. **2** (formerly, in Britain) one million million: written as 1 000 000 000 000 or 10^{12}. US word: **trillion. 3** (*often pl*) any exceptionally large number. ◆ *determiner* **4** (preceded by *a* or a cardinal number) amounting to a billion. ORIG C17: from F, from BI- + *-llion* as in *million*
▸ **'billionth** *adj, n*

> **USAGE NOTE** The meaning of 'one thousand million' is now the established one in the UK as well as in the US, contrary to older British usage.

billionaire (ˌbɪljə'nɛə) *n* a person whose wealth exceeds a billion monetary units of his or her country.

Billiton ★ ('bɪlɪtɒn, bɪ'liːtɒn) *n* an island of Indonesia, in the Java Sea between Borneo and Sumatra. Chief town: Tandjungpandan. Area: 4833 sq. km (1866 sq. miles). Also called: **Belitung.**

bill of attainder *n* (formerly) a legislative act finding a person guilty without trial of treason or felony and declaring him or her attainted.

bill of exchange *n* (now chiefly in foreign transactions) a document, usually negotiable, instructing a third party to pay a stated sum at a designated future date or on demand.

bill of fare *n* another name for **menu.**

bill of health *n* **1** a certificate that attests to the health of a ship's company. **2 clean bill of health.** *Inf.* **2a** a good report of one's physical condition. **2b** a favourable account of a person's or a company's financial position.

bill of lading *n* (in foreign trade) a document containing full particulars of goods shipped.

bill of quantities *n* a document drawn up by a quantity surveyor providing details of the prices, dimensions, etc., of the materials required to build a large structure, such as a factory.

Bill of Rights *n* **1** an English statute of 1689 guaranteeing the rights and liberty of the individual subject. **2** the first ten amendments to the US Constitution which guarantee the liberty of the individual. **3** (*usually not caps.*) any charter of basic human rights.

bill of sale *n Law.* a deed transferring personal property.

billow ('bɪləʊ) *n* **1** a large sea wave. **2** a swelling or surging mass, as of smoke or sound. ◆ *vb* **3** to rise up, swell out, or cause to rise up or swell out. ORIG C16: from ON *bylgja*
▸ **'billowing** *adj, n* ▸ **'billowy** *adj* ▸ **'billowiness** *n*

billposter ('bɪlˌpəʊstə) *or* **billsticker** *n* a person who sticks advertising posters to walls, etc.
▸ **'billˌposting** *or* **'billˌsticking** *n*

billy ('bɪlɪ) *or* **billycan** ('bɪlɪˌkæn) *n, pl* **billies** *or* **billycans. 1** a metal can or pot for boiling water, etc., over a campfire. **2** *Austral. & NZ.* (*as modifier*): *billy-tea.* **3 boil the billy.** *Austral. & NZ. inf.* to make tea. ORIG C19: from Scot. *billypot* cooking vessel

billy goat *n* a male goat.

Billy the Kid ★ *n* nickname of *William H. Bonney.* 1859–81, US outlaw.

bilobate (baɪ'ləʊˌbeɪt) *or* **bilobed** ('baɪˌləʊbd) *adj* divided into or having two lobes.

biltong ('bɪlˌtɒŋ) *n S. African.* strips of meat dried and cured in the sun. ORIG C19: Afrik., from Du. *bil* buttock + *tong* TONGUE

BIM *abbrev. for* British Institute of Management.

bimanous ('bɪmənəs, baɪ'meɪ-) *adj* (of man and the higher primates) having two hands distinct in form and function from the feet. ORIG C19: from NL, from BI- + L *manus* hand

bimanual (ˌbaɪ'mænjʊəl) *adj* using both hands.

bimbo ('bɪmbəʊ) *n, pl* **bimbos.** *Derog. sl.* **1** an attractive but empty-headed young person, esp. a woman. **2** a fellow; a foolish or stupid person. ORIG C20: from It.: little child, perhaps via Polari

bimetallic (ˌbaɪmɪ'tælɪk) *adj* **1** consisting of two metals. **2** of or based on bimetallism.

bimetallic strip *n* strips of two metals that expand differently welded together for use in a thermostat.

bimetallism (baɪ'mɛtəˌlɪzəm) *n* the use of two metals, esp. gold and silver, in fixed relative values as the standard of value and currency.
▸ **bi'metallist** *n*

bimonthly (baɪ'mʌnθlɪ) *adj, adv* **1** every two months. **2** twice a month. ◆ *n, pl* **bimonthlies. 3** a periodical published every two months.

bimorph ('baɪmɔːf) *or* **bimorph cell** *n Electron.* two piezoelectric crystals cemented together so that their movement converts electrical signals into mechanical energy or vice versa: used in record-player pick-ups and loudspeakers.

bin (bɪn) *n* **1** a large container for storing something in bulk, such as coal, grain, or bottled wine. **2** Also called: **bread bin.** a small container for bread. **3** Also called: **dustbin, rubbish bin.** a container for rubbish, etc. ◆ *vb* **bins, binning, binned.** (*tr*) **4** to store in a bin. **5** to put in a wastepaper bin. ORIG OE *binne* basket

binary ('baɪnərɪ) *adj* **1** composed of or involving two; dual. **2** *Maths, computing.* of or expressed in binary notation or binary code. **3** (of a compound or molecule) containing atoms of two different elements. ◆ *n, pl* **binaries. 4** something composed of two parts. **5** *Astron.* See **binary star.** ORIG C16: from LL *bīnārius;* see BI-

binary code *n Computing.* the representation of each one of a set of numbers, letters, etc., as a unique group of bits.

binary notation *or* **system** *n* a number system having a base of two, numbers being expressed by sequences of the digits 0 and 1: used in computing, as 0 and 1 can be represented electrically as *off* and *on.*

binary number *n* a number expressed in binary notation.

binary star *n* a double star system containing two associated stars revolving around a common centre of gravity in different orbits.

binary weapon *n* a chemical weapon containing two substances separately that mix to produce a lethal agent when the projectile is fired.

binate ('baɪˌneɪt) *adj Bot.* occurring in two parts or in pairs: *binate leaves.* ORIG C19: from NL *bīnātus,* prob. from L *combīnātus* united
▸ **'biˌnately** *adv*

binaural (baɪ'nɔːrəl, bɪn'ɔːrəl) *adj* **1** relating to, having, or hearing with both ears. **2** employing two separate channels for recording or transmitting sound.

bind (baɪnd) *vb* **binds, binding, bound. 1** to make or become fast or secure with or as if with a tie or band. **2** (*tr; often* foll. by *up*) to encircle or enclose with a band: *to bind the hair.* **3** (*tr*) to place (someone) under obligation; oblige. **4** (*tr*) to impose legal obligations or duties upon (a person). **5** (*tr*) to make (a bargain, agreement, etc.) irrevocable; seal. **6** (*tr*) to restrain or confine with or as if with ties, as of responsibility or loyalty. **7** (*tr*) to place under certain constraints; govern. **8** (*tr;* often foll. by *up*) to bandage. **9** to cohere or cause to cohere: *egg binds fat and flour.* **10** to make or become compact, stiff, or hard: *frost binds the earth.* **11** (*tr*) to enclose and fasten (the pages of a book) between covers. **12** (*tr*) to provide (a garment, hem, etc.) with a border or edging. **13** (*tr;* sometimes foll. by *out* or *over*) to employ as an apprentice; indenture. **14** (*intr*) *Sl.* to complain. ◆ *n* **15** something that binds. **16** *Inf.* a difficult or annoying situation. **17** a situation in which freedom of action is restricted. ◆ See also **bind over.** ORIG OE *bindan*

binder ('baɪndə) *n* **1** a firm cover or folder for holding loose sheets of paper together. **2** a material used to bind separate particles together. **3** a person who binds books; bookbinder. **4** something used to fasten or tie, such as rope or twine. **5** Also called: **reaper binder.** *Obs.* a machine for cutting grain and binding it into sheaves. **6** an informal agreement giving insurance coverage pending formal issue of a policy.

bindery ('baɪndərɪ) *n, pl* **binderies.** a place in which books are bound.

bindi-eye ('bɪndɪˌaɪ) *n Austral.* **1** any of various small weedy Australian herbaceous plants with burlike fruits. **2** any bur or prickle. ORIG C20: ?from Abor.

binding ('baɪndɪŋ) *n* **1** anything that binds or fastens. **2** the covering within which the pages of a book are bound. **3** the tape used for binding hems, etc. ◆ *adj* **4** imposing an obligation or duty. **5** causing hindrance; restrictive.

bind over *vb* (*tr, adv*) to place (a person) under a legal obligation, such as one to keep the peace.

bindweed ('baɪndˌwiːd) *n* any of various plants that twine around a support. See also **convolvulus.**

bine (baɪn) *n* the climbing or twining stem of any of various plants, such as the woodbine. ORIG C19: var. of BIND

Binet-Simon scale ('biːneɪ'saɪmən) *n Psychol.* a test used to determine the mental age of subjects. Also called: **Binet scale** *or* **test.** ORIG C20: after Alfred *Binet* (1857–1911) + Théodore *Simon* (1873–1961), F psychologists

binge (bɪndʒ) *Inf.* ◆ *n* **1** a bout of excessive drinking or eating. **2** excessive indulgence in anything. ◆ *vb* **binges, bingeing** *or* **binging, binged. 3** (*intr*) to indulge in a binge. ORIG C19: prob. dial. *binge* to soak

Bingen ★ ('bɪŋən) *n* a town in W Germany on the Rhine: wine trade and tourist centre. Pop.: 23 141 (1989 est.).

bingo ('bɪŋgəʊ) *n, pl* **bingos.** a gambling game, usually played with several people, in which random numbers are called out and the players cover the numbers on their individual cards. The first to cover a given arrangement of numbers is the winner. ORIG C19: ?from *bing,* imit. of a bell ringing to mark the win

binman ('bɪnˌmæn, 'bɪnmən) *n, pl* **binmen.** *Inf.* another name for **dustman.**

binnacle ('bɪnək^{ə}l) *n* a housing for a ship's compass. ORIG C17: changed from C15 *bitakle,* from Port. from LL *habitāculum* dwelling-place, from L *habitāre* to inhabit

binocular (bɪ'nɒkjʊlə, baɪ-) *adj* involving, relating to, seeing with or intended for both eyes: *binocular vision.* ORIG C18: from BI- + L *oculus* eye

binoculars (bɪ'nɒkjʊləz, baɪ-) *pl n* an optical instrument for use with both eyes, consisting of two small telescopes joined together.

binomial (baɪ'nəʊmɪəl) *n* **1** a mathematical expression consisting of two terms, such as $3x + 2y$. **2** a two-part taxonomic name for an animal or plant indicating genus and species. ◆ *adj* **3** referring to two names or terms. ORIG C16: from Med. L, from BI- + L *nōmen* name
▸ **bi'nomially** *adv*

binomial distribution *n* a statistical distribution giving the probability of obtaining a specified number of independent trials of an experiment, with a constant probability of success in each.

binomial theorem *n* a general mathematical formula that expresses any power of a binomial without multiplying out, as in $(x+a)^n=x^n+nx^{n-1}a+[n(n-1)/2x^{n-2}a^2]\ldots+a^n$.

bint (bɪnt) *n Sl.* a derogatory term for **girl** or **woman.** ORIG C19: from Ar., lit.: daughter

binturong ('bɪntjʊˌrɒŋ, bɪn'tjʊərɒŋ) *n* a long-bodied short-legged arboreal SE Asian mammal having shaggy black hair. ORIG from Malay

Binyon ★ ('bɪnjən) *n* (**Robert**) **Laurence.** 1869–1943, British poet, noted for his war poems "For the Fallen" (1914) and "The Burning of the Leaves" (1944).

bio- *or before a vowel* **bi-** *combining form.* **1** indicating or involving life or living organisms: *biogenesis.* **2** indicating a human life or career: *biography.* ORIG from Gk *bios* life

bioassay (ˌbaɪəʊˈæseɪ) *n* **1** a method of determining the concentration or effect of a drug, etc., by comparing its effect on living organisms with that of a standard preparation. ◆ *vb (tr)* **2** to subject to a bioassay.

bioastronautics (ˌbaɪəʊˌæstrəˈnɔːtɪks) *n (functioning as sing)* the study of the effects of space flight on living organisms.

bioastronomy (ˌbaɪəʊəˈstrɒnəmɪ) *n* the branch of astronomy concerned with the search for life on other planets.

Bío-Bío ★ (*Spanish* ˈbiːoˈbiːo) *n* a river in central Chile, rising in the Andes and flowing northwest to the Pacific. Length: about 390 km (240 miles).

biochemical oxygen demand *n* a measure of the organic pollution of water; the number of milligrams of oxygen per litre of water absorbed in a given period. Abbrev.: **BOD**

biochemistry (ˌbaɪəʊˈkɛmɪstrɪ) *n* the study of the chemical compounds, reactions, etc., in living organisms.
▸ **biochemical** (ˌbaɪəʊˈkɛmɪkᵊl) *adj* ▸ ˌ**bioˈchemist** *n*

biochip (ˈbaɪəʊˌtʃɪp) *n* a small glass or silicon plate containing an array of biochemical molecules or structures, used as a biosensor or in gene sequencing.

biocide (ˈbaɪəˌsaɪd) *n* a chemical capable of killing living organisms.
▸ ˌ**bioˈcidal** *adj*

biocoenosis *or US* **biocenosis** (ˌbaɪəʊsɪˈnəʊsɪs) *n* the relationships between animals and plants subsisting together. ORIG C19: NL from BIO- + Gk *koinōsis* sharing

biodegradable (ˌbaɪəʊdɪˈgreɪdəbᵊl) *adj* (of sewage, packaging, etc.) capable of being decomposed by bacteria or other biological means.
▸ **biodegradability** (ˌbaɪəʊdɪˌgreɪdəˈbɪlɪtɪ) *n*

biodiesel (ˈbaɪəʊˌdiːzᵊl) *n* a biofuel intended for use in diesel engines.

biodiversity (ˌbaɪəʊdaɪˈvɜːsɪtɪ) *n* the existence of a wide variety of plant and animal species in their natural environments, the maintaining of which is the aim of conservationists concerned about the indiscriminate destruction of rainforests and other habitats.

bioengineering (ˌbaɪəʊˌɛndʒɪˈnɪərɪŋ) *n* **1** the design and manufacture of aids, such as artificial limbs, to rectify defective body functions. **2** the design, manufacture, and maintenance of engineering equipment used in biosynthetic processes.
▸ ˌ**bioˌengiˈneer** *n*

bioethics (ˌbaɪəʊˈɛθɪks) *n (functioning as sing)* the study of ethical problems arising from scientific advances, esp. in biology and medicine.

biofeedback (ˌbaɪəʊˈfiːdˌbæk) *n Physiol., psychol.* the technique of recording and presenting (usually visually) the activity of an autonomic function, such as the rate of heartbeat, in order to teach control of it.

biofuel (ˈbaɪəʊˌfjʊəl) *n* a substance of biological origin that is used as a fuel.

biog. *abbrev. for:* **1** biographical. **2** biography.

biogenesis (ˌbaɪəʊˈdʒɛnɪsɪs) *n* the principle that a living organism must originate from a parent organism similar to itself.
▸ ˌ**biogeˈnetic** *or* ˌ**biogeˈnetical** *adj*

biogenic (ˌbaɪəʊˈdʒɛnɪk) *adj* produced or originating from a living organism.

biography (baɪˈɒgrəfɪ) *n, pl* **biographies.** **1** an account of a person's life by another. **2** such accounts collectively.
▸ **biˈographer** *n* ▸ **biographical** (ˌbaɪəˈgræfɪkᵊl) *adj*

bioinformatics (ˌbaɪəʊˌɪnfəˈmætɪks) *n (functioning as sing)* the branch of information science concerned with large databases of biochemical or pharmaceutical information.

Bioko ★ (baɪˈəʊkəʊ) *n* an island in the Gulf of Guinea, off the coast of Cameroon: part of Equatorial Guinea. Capital: Malabo. Area: 2017 sq. km (786 sq. miles). Former names: **Fernando Po** (until 1973), **Macías Nguema** (1973–79).

biol. *abbrev. for:* **1** biological. **2** biology.

biological (ˌbaɪəˈlɒdʒɪkᵊl) *adj* **1** of or relating to biology. **2** (of a detergent) containing enzymes for removing stains of organic origin from items to be washed. ◆ *n* **3** (*usually pl*) a drug derived from a living organism.

biological clock *n* **1** an inherent periodicity in the physiological processes of living organisms that is independent of external periodicity. **2** the hypothetical mechanism responsible for this. ◆ See also **circadian.**

biological control *n* the control of destructive organisms by nonchemical means, such as introducing the natural enemy of a pest.

biological warfare *n* the use of living organisms or their toxic products to induce death or incapacity in humans.

biology (baɪˈɒlədʒɪ) *n* **1** the study of living organisms. **2** the animal and plant life of a particular region.
▸ **biˈologist** *n*

bioluminescence (ˌbaɪəʊˌluːmɪˈnɛsəns) *n* the production of light by living organisms, such as the firefly.
▸ ˌ**bioˌlumiˈnescent** *adj*

biomass (ˈbaɪəʊˌmæs) *n* the total number of living organisms in a given area, expressed in terms of living or dry weight per unit area.

biomathematics (ˌbaɪəʊˌmæθəˈmætɪks, -ˌmæθˈmæt-) *n (functioning as sing)* the study of the application of mathematics to biology.

biomechanics (ˌbaɪəʊmɪˈkænɪks) *n (functioning as sing)* the study of the mechanics of the movement of living organisms.

biomedicine (ˌbaɪəʊˈmɛdɪsɪn) *n* **1** the medical and biological study of the effects of unusual environmental stress, esp. in connection with space travel. **2** the study of herbal remedies.
▸ ˌ**bioˈmedical** *adj*

biometry (baɪˈɒmɪtrɪ) *or* **biometrics** (ˌbaɪəˈmɛtrɪks) *n (functioning as sing)* the study of biological data by means of statistical analysis.
▸ ˌ**bioˈmetric** *adj*

bionic (baɪˈɒnɪk) *adj* **1** of or relating to bionics. **2** (in science fiction) having physiological functions augmented by electronic equipment.

bionics (baɪˈɒnɪks) *n (functioning as sing)* **1** the study of certain biological functions that are applicable to the development of electronic equipment designed to operate similarly. **2** the replacement of limbs or body parts by artificial limbs or parts that are electronically or mechanically powered.

bionomics (ˌbaɪəˈnɒmɪks) *n (functioning as sing)* a less common name for **ecology.** ORIG C19: from BIO- + *nomics* on pattern of ECONOMICS
▸ ˌ**bioˈnomic** *adj* ▸ **bionomist** (baɪˈɒnəmɪst) *n*

biophysics (ˌbaɪəʊˈfɪzɪks) *n (functioning as sing)* the physics of biological processes and the application of the methods used in physics to biology.
▸ ˌ**bioˈphysical** *adj* ▸ ˌ**bioˈphysically** *adv* ▸ **biophysicist** (ˌbaɪəʊˈfɪzɪsɪst) *n*

biopic (ˈbaɪəʊˌpɪk) *n Inf.* a film based on the life of a famous person. ORIG C20: from *bio(graphical)* + *pic(ture)*

biopsy (ˈbaɪɒpsɪ) *n, pl* **biopsies.** examination, esp. under a microscope, of tissue from a living body to determine the cause or extent of a disease. ORIG C20: from BIO- + Gk *opsis* sight

biorhythm (ˈbaɪəʊˌrɪðəm) *n* a cyclically recurring pattern of physiological states, believed by some to affect a person's physical, emotional, and mental states and behaviour.

bioscope (ˈbaɪəˌskəʊp) *n* **1** a kind of early film projector. **2** a South African word for **cinema.**

bioscopy (baɪˈɒskəpɪ) *n, pl* **bioscopies.** examination of a body to determine whether it is alive.

biosensor (ˌbaɪəʊˈsɛnsə) *n* a device for detecting the presence of a specific chemical compound by its effect on enzymes, antibodies, or other biological substances.

★ people and places

-biosis *n combining form.* indicating a specified mode of life. ORIG NL, from Gk *biōsis;* see BIO-, -OSIS
▸ **-biotic** *adj combining form.*

biosphere ('baɪəˌsfɪə) *n* the part of the earth's surface and atmosphere inhabited by living things.

biosynthesis (ˌbaɪəʊ'sɪnθɪsɪs) *n* the formation of complex compounds from simple substances by living organisms.
▸ **biosynthetic** (ˌbaɪəʊsɪn'θɛtɪk) *adj* ▸ **ˌbiosyn'thetically** *adv*

biotech ('baɪəʊˌtɛk) *n Inf.* short for **biotechnology.**

biotechnology (ˌbaɪəʊtɛk'nɒlədʒɪ) *n* the use of micro-organisms for beneficial effect, as in the processing of waste matter or (using genetic engineering) to produce antibiotics, hormones, vaccines, etc.

biotic (baɪ'ɒtɪk) *adj* of or relating to living organisms. ORIG C17: from Gk *biotikos,* from *bios* life

biotin ('baɪətɪn) *n* a vitamin of the B complex, abundant in egg yolk and liver. ORIG C20: from Gk *biotē* life, way of life + -IN

bipartisan (ˌbaɪpɑːtɪ'zæn, baɪ'pɑːtɪˌzæn) *adj* consisting of or supported by two political parties.
▸ **ˌbiparti'sanship** *n*

bipartite (baɪ'pɑːtaɪt) *adj* **1** consisting of or having two parts. **2** affecting or made by two parties. **3** *Bot.* (esp. of some leaves) divided into two parts almost to the base.
▸ **bi'partitely** *adv* ▸ **bipartition** (ˌbaɪpɑː'tɪʃən) *n*

biped ('baɪpɛd) *n* **1** any animal with two feet. ◆ *adj also* **bipedal** (baɪ'piːdᵊl, -'pɛdᵊl). **2** having two feet.

bipinnate (baɪ'pɪneɪt) *adj* (of compound leaves) having both the leaflets and the stems bearing them arranged pinnately.
▸ **bi'pinnately** *adv*

biplane ('baɪˌpleɪn) *n* a type of aeroplane having two sets of wings, one above the other.

bipolar (baɪ'pəʊlə) *adj* **1** having two poles: *a bipolar dynamo.* **2** of or relating to the North and South Poles. **3** having or characterized by two opposed opinions, etc. **4** (of a transistor) utilizing both majority and minority charge carriers.
▸ **ˌbipo'larity** *n*

biprism ('baɪˌprɪzəm) *n Physics.* a prism that has a highly obtuse angle to facilitate beam splitting.

biquadratic (ˌbaɪkwɒ'drætɪk) *Maths.* ◆ *adj* **1** of or relating to the fourth power. ◆ *n* **2** a biquadratic equation, such as $x^4 + x + 6 = 0$.

biracial (baɪ'reɪʃəl) *adj* of or for members of two races.
▸ **bi'racialism** *n*

birch (bɜːtʃ) *n* **1** any catkin-bearing tree or shrub having thin peeling bark. See also **silver birch. 2** the hard close-grained wood of any of these trees. **3 the birch.** a bundle of birch twigs or a birch rod used, esp. formerly, for flogging offenders. ◆ *adj* **4** consisting or made of birch. ◆ *vb* **5** (*tr*) to flog with a birch. ORIG OE *bierce*
▸ **'birchen** *adj*

bird (bɜːd) *n* **1** any warm-blooded egg-laying vertebrate, characterized by a body covering of feathers and forelimbs modified as wings. **2** *Inf.* a person, as in **rare bird, odd bird, clever bird. 3** *Sl., chiefly Brit.* a girl or young woman. **4** *Sl.* prison or a term in prison (esp. in **do bird**). **5 a bird in the hand.** something definite or certain. **6 birds of a feather.** people with the same characteristics, ideas, interests, etc. **7 get the bird.** *Inf.* **7a** to be fired or dismissed. **7b** (esp. of a public performer) to be hissed at. **8 kill two birds with one stone.** to accomplish two things with one action. **9** (**strictly**) **for the birds.** *Inf.* deserving of disdain or contempt; not important. ORIG OE *bridd,* from ?

birdbath ('bɜːdˌbɑːθ) *n* a small basin or trough for birds to bathe in, usually in a garden.

bird-brained *adj Inf.* silly; stupid.

birdcage ('bɜːdˌkeɪdʒ) *n* **1** a wire or wicker cage for captive birds. **2** *Austral. & NZ.* an area on a racecourse where horses parade before a race. **3** *NZ inf.* a second-hand car dealer's yard.

bird call *n* **1** the characteristic call or song of a bird. **2** an imitation of this.

birdie ('bɜːdɪ) *n* **1** *Golf.* a score of one stroke under par for a hole. **2** *Inf.* a bird, esp. a small bird. ◆ *vb* **3** (*tr*) *Golf.* to play (a hole) in one stroke under par.

birdlime ('bɜːdˌlaɪm) *n* **1** a sticky substance smeared on twigs to catch small birds. ◆ *vb* **birdlimes, birdliming, birdlimed. 2** (*tr*) to smear (twigs) with birdlime to catch (small birds).

bird-nesting *or* **birds'-nesting** *n* searching for birds' nests as a hobby, often to steal the eggs.

bird of paradise *n* **1** any of various songbirds of New Guinea and neighbouring regions, the males having brilliantly coloured plumage. **2 bird-of-paradise flower.** any of various plants native to tropical southern Africa and South America that have purple bracts and large orange or yellow flowers resembling birds' heads.

bird of passage *n* **1** a bird that migrates seasonally. **2** a transient person.

bird of prey *n* a bird, such as a hawk or owl, that hunts other animals for food.

birdseed ('bɜːdˌsiːd) *n* a mixture of various kinds of seeds for feeding cagebirds.

bird's-eye *adj* **1a** seen or photographed from high above. **1b** summarizing (esp. in **bird's-eye view**). **2** having markings resembling birds' eyes.

bird's-foot *or* **bird-foot** *n, pl* **bird's-foots** *or* **bird-foots.** any of various plants whose flowers, leaves, or pods resemble a bird's foot or claw.

birdshot ('bɜːdˌʃɒt) *n* small pellets designed for shooting birds.

bird strike *n* a collision of an aircraft with a bird.

bird table *n* a table or platform in the open on which food for birds may be placed.

bird-watcher *n* a person who identifies and studies wild birds in their natural surroundings.
▸ **'bird-ˌwatching** *n*

birefringence (ˌbaɪrɪ'frɪndʒəns) *n* another name for **double refraction.**
▸ **ˌbire'fringent** *adj*

bireme ('baɪriːm) *n* an ancient galley having two banks of oars. ORIG C17: from L, from BI- + *-rēmus* oar

biretta *or* **berretta** (bɪ'rɛtə) *n RC Church.* a stiff square clerical cap. ORIG C16: from It. *berretta,* from OProvençal, from LL *birrus* hooded cape

Birgitta ★ (bɪə'gɪtə) *n* **Saint.** See (Saint) **Bridget** (sense 2).

Birkbeck ★ ('bɜːkˌbɛk) *n* **George.** 1776–1841, British educationalist; founder of the London Mechanics Institute (1824), which later became Birkbeck College.

Birkenhead[1] ★ (ˌbɜːkən'hɛd) *n* a port in NW England, in Wirral unitary authority: former shipbuilding centre. Pop.: 93 087 (1991).

Birkenhead[2] ★ ('bɜːkənˌhɛd) *n* **Frederick Edwin Smith,** 1st Earl of, known as *F. E. Smith.* 1872–1930, British Conservative statesman and lawyer.

birl (bɜːl) *vb* **1** *Scot.* to spin; twirl. **2** *US & Canad.* to cause (a floating log) to spin using the feet while standing on it, esp. as a sport among lumberjacks. ◆ *n* **3** a variant spelling of **burl[2]**. ORIG C18: prob. imit. & infl. by WHIRL & HURL

Birmingham ★ *n* **1** ('bɜːmɪŋəm) an industrial city in central England, in West Midlands: the second largest city in Great Britain; seat of Birmingham University (1900), Aston University (1966), and The University of Central England in Birmingham (1992). Pop.: 965 928 (1991). **2** a unitary authority in central England. Pop.: 1 017 500 (1995 est.). Area: 283 sq. km (109 sq. miles). **3** ('bɜːmɪŋˌhæm) an industrial city in N central Alabama: rich local deposits of coal, iron ore, and other minerals. Pop.: 264 527 (1994 est.).

Biro ('baɪrəʊ) *n, pl* **Biros.** *Trademark, Brit.* a kind of ballpoint. ORIG C20: after Laszlo *Bíró* (1900–85), its Hungarian inventor

Birobidzhan *or* **Birobijan** ★ (*Russian* birəbid'ʒan) *n* **1** a city in Russia, in SE Siberia: capital of the Jewish Autonomous Region. Pop.: 82 000 (1994). **2** another name for the **Jewish Autonomous Region.**

birth (bɜːθ) *n* **1** the process of bearing young; childbirth. **2** the act or fact of being born; nativity. **3** the coming into existence of something; origin. **4** ancestry; lineage: *of high birth.* **5** natural or inherited talent: *an artist by birth.* **6 give birth (to). 6a** to bear (offspring). **6b** to produce or originate (an idea, plan, etc.). ◆ *vb* **7** *(tr) Rare.* to bear or bring forth (a child). ORIG C12: from ON *byrth*

birth certificate *n* an official form giving details of the time and place of a person's birth.

birth control *n* limitation of child-bearing by means of contraception.

birthday ('bɜːθˌdeɪ) *n* **1a** an anniversary of the day of one's birth. **1b** *(as modifier): birthday present.* **2** the day on which a person was born.

birthing centre ('bɜːθɪŋ) *n NZ.* a private maternity hospital.

birthmark ('bɜːθˌmɑːk) *n* a blemish on the skin formed before birth; naevus.

birth mother *n* the woman who gives birth to a child, regardless of whether she is the genetic mother or subsequently brings up the child.

birthplace ('bɜːθˌpleɪs) *n* the place where someone was born or where something originated.

birth rate *n* the ratio of live births in a specified area, group, etc., to population, usually expressed per 1000 population per year.

birthright ('bɜːθˌraɪt) *n* **1** privileges or possessions that a person has or is believed to be entitled to as soon as he is born. **2** the privileges or possessions of a first-born son. **3** inheritance.

birthstone ('bɜːθˌstəʊn) *n* a precious or semiprecious stone associated with a month or sign of the zodiac and thought to bring luck if worn by a person born in that month or under that sign.

Birtwistle ★ ('bɜːtˌwɪsᵊl) *n* Sir **Harrison.** born 1934, British composer, whose works include the operas *Punch and Judy* (1967) and *Exody* (1998).

biryani *or* **biriani** (ˌbɪrɪ'ɑːnɪ) *n* an Indian dish made with rice, highly flavoured and coloured, mixed with meat or fish. ORIG from Urdu

Bisayas ★ (bi'sajas) *pl n* the Spanish name for the **Visayan Islands.**

Biscay ★ ('bɪskeɪ, -kɪ) *n* **Bay of.** a large bay of the Atlantic Ocean between W France and N Spain: notorious for storms.

biscuit ('bɪskɪt) *n* **1** *Brit.* a small flat dry sweet or plain cake of many varieties. US and Canad. word: **cookie. 2a** a pale brown or yellowish-grey colour. **2b** *(as adj): biscuit gloves.* **3** Also called: **bisque.** earthenware or porcelain that has been fired but not glazed. **4 take the biscuit.** *Brit.* to be regarded (by the speaker) as most surprising. ORIG C14: from OF, from *(pain) bescuit* twice-cooked (bread), from *bes* twice + *cuire* to cook

bise (biːz) *n* a cold dry northerly wind in Switzerland and parts of France and Italy. ORIG C14: from OF, of Gmc origin

bisect (baɪ'sɛkt) *vb* **1** *(tr) Maths.* to divide into two equal parts. **2** to cut or split into two. ORIG C17: BI- + *-sect,* from L *secāre* to cut
▸ **bisection** (baɪ'sɛkʃən) *n*

bisector (baɪ'sɛktə) *n Maths.* a straight line or plane that bisects an angle, etc.

bisexual (baɪ'sɛksjʊəl) *adj* **1** sexually attracted by both men and women. **2** showing characteristics of both sexes. **3** of or relating to both sexes. ◆ *n* **4** a bisexual organism; a hermaphrodite. **5** a bisexual person.
▸ **bisexuality** (ˌbaɪsɛksjʊ'ælɪtɪ) *n*

Bishkek ★ (bɪʃ'kɛk) *n* the capital of Kyrgyzstan. Pop.: 597 000 (1994 est.). Also called: **Pishpek.** Former name (1926–91): **Frunze.**

bishop ('bɪʃəp) *n* **1** a clergyman having spiritual and administrative powers over a diocese. See also **suffragan.** Related adj: **episcopal. 2** a chesspiece, capable of moving diagonally. **3** mulled wine, usually port, spiced with oranges, cloves, etc. ORIG OE *biscop,* from LL, from Gk *episkopos,* from EPI- + *skopos* watcher

Bishop Auckland ★ ('bɪʃəp) *n* a town in N England, in central Durham: seat of the bishops of Durham since the 12th century: light industries. Pop.: 23 154 (1991).

bishopric ('bɪʃəprɪk) *n* the see, diocese, or office of a bishop.

Bisitun ★ (ˌbiːsɪ'tuːn) *n* another name for **Behistun.**

Bisk ★ *(Russian* bijsk) *n* a variant spelling of **Biysk.**

Biskra ★ ('bɪskrɑː) *n* a town and oasis in NE Algeria, in the Sahara. Pop.: 128 280 (1987).

Bisley ★ ('bɪzlɪ) *n* a village in SE England, in Surrey: annual meetings of the National Rifle Association.

Bismarck[1] ★ ('bɪzmɑːk) *n* a city in North Dakota, on the Missouri River: the state capital. Pop.: 49 256 (1990).

Bismarck[2] ★ *(German* 'bɪsmark) *n* Prince **Otto (Eduard Leopold) von** ('ɔto fɔn), called *the Iron Chancellor.* 1815–98, German statesman; prime minister of Prussia (1862–90). Under his leadership Prussia defeated Austria and France, and Germany was united. In 1871 he became the first chancellor of the German Reich.

Bismarck Archipelago ★ *n* a group of over 200 islands in the SW Pacific, northeast of New Guinea: part of Papua New Guinea. Main islands: New Britain, New Ireland, Lavongai, and the Admiralty Islands. Chief town: Rabaul, on New Britain. Pop.: 424 000 (1995 est.). Area: 49 658 sq. km (19 173 sq. miles).

bismuth ('bɪzməθ) *n* a brittle pinkish-white crystalline metallic element. It is widely used in alloys; its compounds are used in medicines. Symbol: Bi; atomic no.: 83; atomic wt.: 208.98. ORIG C17: from NL *bisemūtum,* from G *Wismut,* from ?

bison ('baɪsᵊn) *n, pl* **bison. 1** Also called: **American bison, buffalo.** a member of the cattle tribe, formerly widely distributed over the prairies of W North America, with a massive head, shaggy forequarters, and a humped back. **2** Also called: **wisent, European bison.** a closely related and similar animal formerly widespread in Europe. ORIG C14: from L *bisōn,* of Gmc origin

bisque[1] (bɪsk) *n* a thick rich soup made from shellfish. ORIG C17: from F

bisque[2] (bɪsk) *n* **1a** a pink to yellowish tan colour. **1b** *(as adj): a bisque tablecloth.* **2** *Ceramics.* another name for **biscuit** (sense 3). ORIG C20: shortened from BISCUIT

bisque[3] (bɪsk) *n Tennis, golf, croquet.* an extra point, stroke, or turn allowed to an inferior player, usually taken when desired. ORIG C17: from F, from ?

Bissau (bɪ'saʊ) *or* **Bissão** ★ *(Portuguese* bi'sɐ̃u) *n* the capital of Guinea-Bissau, a port on the Atlantic: until 1974 the capital of Portuguese Guinea. Pop.: 233 000 (1995 est.).

bistable (ˌbaɪ'steɪbᵊl) *adj* **1** (of an electrical circuit switch, etc.) having two stable states. ◆ *n* **2** *Computing.* another name for **flip-flop** (sense 2).

bistort ('bɪstɔːt) *n* **1** Also called: **snakeweed.** a Eurasian plant having leaf stipules fused to form a tube around the stem and a spike of small pink flowers. **2** Also called: **snakeroot.** a related plant of W North America, with oval clusters of pink or white flowers. **3** any of several similar plants. ORIG C16: from F, from L *bis* twice + *tortus* from *torquēre* to twist

bistoury ('bɪstərɪ) *n, pl* **bistouries.** a long narrow-bladed surgical knife. ORIG C15: from OF *bistorie* dagger, from ?

bistre *or US* **bister** ('bɪstə) *n* **1** a transparent water-soluble brownish-yellow pigment made by boiling the soot of wood. **2a** a yellowish-brown to dark brown colour. **2b** *(as adj): bistre paint.* ORIG C18: from F, from ?

bistro ('biːstrəʊ) *n, pl* **bistros.** a small restaurant. ORIG F: ?from Russian *bistro* fast

bisulphate (baɪ'sʌlˌfeɪt) *n* a salt or ester of sulphuric acid containing the monovalent group $-HSO_4$ or the ion HSO_4^-. Systematic name: **hydrogensulphate.**

bisulphide (baɪ'sʌlfaɪd) *n* another name for **disulphide.**

Bisutun ★ (ˌbiːsʊ'tuːn) *n* another name for **Behistun.**

bit[1] (bɪt) *n* **1** a small piece, portion, or quantity. **2** a short time or distance. **3** *US & Canad. inf.* the value of an eighth of a dollar: spoken of only in units of two: *two bits.* **4** any small coin. **5** short for **bit part. 6 a bit.** rather; somewhat: *a bit dreary.* **7 a bit of. 7a** rather: *a bit of a dope.* **7b** a considerable amount: *it takes quite a bit of time.* **8 bit by bit.** gradually. **9 do one's bit.** to make one's expected contribution. ORIG OE *bite* action of biting; see BITE

bit[2] (bɪt) *n* **1** a metal mouthpiece on a bridle for controlling a horse. **2** anything that restrains or curbs. **3** a cutting or drilling tool, part, or head in a brace, drill, etc. **4** the part of a key that engages the levers of a lock. **5** the mouthpiece of a smoker's pipe. ◆ *vb* **bits, bitting, bitted.** (*tr*) **6** to put a bit in the mouth of (a horse). **7** to restrain; curb. ORIG OE *bita;* rel. to OE *bītan* to BITE

bit[3] (bɪt) *vb* the past tense of **bite.**

bit[4] (bɪt) *n Maths, computing.* **1** a single digit of binary notation, represented either by 0 or by 1. **2** the smallest unit of information, indicating the presence or absence of a single feature. ORIG C20: from B(INARY + DIG)IT

bitch (bɪtʃ) *n* **1** a female dog or other female canine animal, such as a wolf. **2** *Sl., derog.* a malicious, spiteful, or coarse woman. **3** *Inf.* a difficult situation or problem. ◆ *vb Inf.* **4** (*intr*) to complain; grumble. **5** to behave (towards) in a spiteful manner. **6** (*tr;* often foll. by *up*) to botch; bungle. ORIG OE *bicce*

bitchin' (ˈbɪtʃɪn) *or* **bitching** (ˈbɪtʃɪŋ) *US sl.* ◆ *adj* **1** wonderful or excellent. ◆ *adv* **2** extremely: *bitchin' good.*

bitchy (ˈbɪtʃɪ) *adj* **bitchier, bitchiest.** *Sl.* of or like a bitch; malicious; snide.
▸ ˈ**bitchiness** *n*

bite (baɪt) *vb* **bites, biting, bit, bitten. 1** to grip, cut off, or tear as with the teeth or jaws. **2** (of animals, insects, etc.) to injure by puncturing or tearing (the skin or flesh) with the teeth, fangs, etc. **3** (*tr*) to cut or penetrate, as with a knife. **4** (of corrosive material such as acid) to eat away or into. **5** to smart or cause to smart; sting. **6** (*intr*) *Angling.* (of a fish) to take or attempt to take the bait or lure. **7** to take firm hold (of) or act effectively (upon). **8** (*tr*) *Sl.* to annoy or worry: *what's biting her?* **9** (*tr;* often foll. by *for*) *Austral. & NZ sl.* to ask (for); scrounge from. **10 bite the dust. 10a** to fall down dead. **10b** to be rejected: *another good idea bites the dust.* ◆ *n* **11** the act of biting. **12** a thing or amount bitten off. **13** a wound, bruise, or sting inflicted by biting. **14** *Angling.* an attempt by a fish to take the bait or lure. **15** a light meal; snack. **16** a cutting, stinging, or smarting sensation. **17** *Dentistry.* the angle or manner of contact between the upper and lower teeth. **18 put the bite on.** *Sl.* to cadge or borrow from. ORIG OE *bītan*
▸ ˈ**biter** *n*

Bithynia ★ (bɪˈθɪnɪə) *n* an ancient country on the Black Sea in NW Asia Minor.

biting (ˈbaɪtɪŋ) *adj* **1** piercing; keen: *a biting wind.* **2** sarcastic; incisive.
▸ ˈ**bitingly** *adv*

bitmap (ˈbɪtˌmæp) *Computing.* ◆ *n* **1** a picture created on a visual display unit where each pixel corresponds to one or more bits in memory, the number of bits per pixel determining the number of available colours. ◆ *vb* **bitmaps, bitmapping, bitmapped. 2** (*tr*) to create a bitmap of.

Bitolj (*Serbo-Croat* ˈbitolj) *or* **Bitola** ★ (ˈbiːtəʊlə) *n* a city in SW Macedonia: under Turkish rule from 1382 until 1913. Pop.: 75 386 (1994).

bit part *n* a very small acting role with few lines to speak.

bitt (bɪt) *Naut.* ◆ *n* **1** one of a pair of strong posts on the deck of a ship for securing mooring and other lines. **2** another word for **bollard** (sense 1). ◆ *vb* **3** (*tr*) to secure (a line) by means of a bitt. ORIG C14: prob. from ON

bitten (ˈbɪtᵊn) *vb* the past participle of **bite.**

bitter (ˈbɪtə) *adj* **1** having or denoting an unpalatable harsh taste, as the peel of an orange. **2** showing or caused by strong unrelenting hostility or resentment. **3** difficult or unpleasant to accept or admit: *a bitter blow.* **4** cutting; sarcastic: *bitter words.* **5** bitingly cold: *a bitter night.* ◆ *adv* **6** very; extremely (esp. in **bitter cold**). ◆ *n* **7** a thing that is bitter. **8** *Brit.* beer with a slightly bitter taste. ORIG OE *biter;* rel. to *bītan* to BITE
▸ ˈ**bitterly** *adv* ▸ ˈ**bitterness** *n*

bitter end *n* **1** *Naut.* the end of a line, chain, or cable. **2 to the bitter end. 2a** until the finish of a task, etc., however unpleasant or difficult. **2b** until final defeat or death. ORIG C19: ?from BITT

★ people and places

Bitter Lakes ★ *pl n* two lakes, the **Great Bitter Lake** and **Little Bitter Lake,** in NE Egypt: part of the Suez Canal.

bittern (ˈbɪtən) *n* a wading bird related and similar to the herons but with shorter legs and neck and a booming call. ORIG C14: from OF *butor,* ?from L *būtiō* bittern + *taurus* bull

bitters (ˈbɪtəz) *pl n* **1** bitter-tasting spirits of varying alcoholic content flavoured with plant extracts. **2** a similar liquid containing a bitter-tasting substance, used as a tonic.

bittersweet (ˈbɪtəˌswiːt) *n* **1** any of several North American woody climbing plants having orange capsules that open to expose scarlet-coated seeds. **2** another name for **woody nightshade.** ◆ *adj* **3** tasting of or being a mixture of bitterness and sweetness. **4** pleasant but tinged with sadness.

bitty (ˈbɪtɪ) *adj* **bittier, bittiest. 1** lacking unity; disjointed. **2** containing bits, sediment, etc.
▸ ˈ**bittiness** *n*

bitumen (ˈbɪtjʊmɪn) *n* **1** any of various viscous or solid impure mixtures of hydrocarbons that occur naturally in asphalt, tar, mineral waxes, etc.: used as a road surfacing and roofing material. **2 the bitumen.** *Austral. & NZ inf.* any road with a bitumen surface. ORIG C15: from L *bitūmen*
▸ **bituminous** (bɪˈtjuːmɪnəs) *adj*

bituminize *or* **bituminise** (bɪˈtjuːmɪˌnaɪz) *vb* **bituminizes, bituminizing, bituminized** *or* **bituminises, bituminising, bituminised.** (*tr*) to treat with or convert into bitumen.

bituminous coal *n* a soft black coal that burns with a smoky yellow flame.

bivalent (baɪˈveɪlənt, ˈbɪvə-) *adj* **1** *Chem.* another word for **divalent. 2** (of homologous chromosomes) associated together in pairs.
▸ **biˈvalency** *n*

bivalve (ˈbaɪˌvælv) *n* **1** a marine or freshwater mollusc, having a laterally compressed body, a shell consisting of two hinged valves, and gills for respiration. The group includes clams, cockles, oysters, and mussels. ◆ *adj* **2** of or relating to these molluscs. ◆ Also: **lamellibranch.**

bivouac (ˈbɪvʊˌæk, ˈbɪvwæk) *n* **1** a temporary encampment, as used by soldiers, mountaineers, etc. ◆ *vb* **bivouacs, bivouacking, bivouacked. 2** (*intr*) to make such an encampment. ORIG C18: from F *bivuac,* prob. from Swiss G *Beiwacht,* lit.: BY + WATCH

biweekly (baɪˈwiːklɪ) *adj, adv* **1** every two weeks. **2** twice a week. See **bi-.** ◆ *n, pl* **biweeklies. 3** a periodical published every two weeks.

biyearly (baɪˈjɪəlɪ) *adj, adv* **1** every two years; biennial or biennially. **2** twice a year; biannual or biannually. See **bi-.**

Biysk, Biisk, *or* **Bisk** ★ (*Russian* bijsk) *n* a city in SW Russia, at the foot of the Altai Mountains. Pop: 228 000 (1995 est.).

biz (bɪz) *n Inf.* short for **business.**

bizarre (bɪˈzɑː) *adj* odd or unusual, esp. in an interesting or amusing way. ORIG C17: from F, from It. *bizzarro* capricious, from ?
▸ **biˈzarreness** *n*

Bizerte (bɪˈzɜːtə; *French* bizɛrt) *or* **Bizerta** ★ *n* a port in N Tunisia, on the Mediterranean at the canalized outlet of **Lake Bizerte.** Pop.: 98 900 (1994).

Bizet ★ (ˈbiːzeɪ; *French* bizɛ) *n* **Georges** (ʒɔrʒ). 1838–75, French composer, whose works include the opera *Carmen* (1875) and incidental music to Daudet's *L'Arlésienne* (1872).

bizzy (ˈbɪzɪ) *n, pl* **bizzies.** *Brit. sl., chiefly Liverpudlian.* a policeman. ORIG C20: from BUSY

Björneborg ★ (bjœrnəˈbɔrj) *n* the Swedish name for **Pori.**

bk *abbrev. for:* **1** bank. **2** book.

Bk *the chemical symbol for* berkelium.

bkg *abbrev. for* banking.

BL *abbrev. for:* **1** Bachelor of Law. **2** Bachelor of Letters. **3** Barrister-at-Law. **4** British Library.

B/L, b/l, *or* **b.l.** *pl* **Bs/L, bs/l,** *or* **bs.l.** *abbrev. for* bill of lading.

blab (blæb) *vb* **blabs, blabbing, blabbed. 1** to divulge (secrets, etc.) indiscreetly. **2** (*intr*) to chatter thoughtlessly; prattle. ◆ *n* **3** a less common word for **blabber**. ORIG C14: of Gmc origin

blabber ('blæbə) *n* **1** a person who blabs. **2** idle chatter. ◆ *vb* **3** (*intr*) to talk without thinking; chatter. ORIG C15 *blabberen*, prob. imit.

black (blæk) *adj* **1** of the colour of jet or carbon black, having no hue due to the absorption of all or nearly all incident light. **2** without light; completely dark. **3** without hope of alleviation; gloomy: *the future looked black*. **4** very dirty or soiled. **5** angry or resentful: *black looks*. **6** (of a play or other work) dealing with the unpleasant realities of life, esp. in a cynical or macabre manner: *black comedy*. **7** (of coffee or tea) without milk or cream. **8a** wicked or harmful: *a black lie*. **8b** (*in combination*): *black-hearted*. **9** *Brit.* (of goods, jobs, works, etc.) being subject to boycott by trade unionists. ◆ *n* **10** a black colour. **11** a dye or pigment of or producing this colour. **12** black clothing, worn esp. as a sign of mourning. **13** *Chess, draughts.* a black or dark-coloured piece or square. **14** complete darkness: *the black of the night*. **15 in the black.** in credit or without debt. ◆ *vb* **16** another word for **blacken**. **17** (*tr*) to polish (shoes, etc.) with blacking. **18** (*tr*) *Brit., Austral., & NZ.* (of trade unionists) to organize a boycott of (specified goods, jobs, work, etc.). ◆ See also **blackout**. ORIG OE *blæc*
▸ **'blackness** *n*

Black[1] (blæk) *n* **1** *Sometimes derog.* a member of a dark-skinned race, esp. someone of Negroid or Australoid origin. ◆ *adj* **2** of or relating to a Black person or Black people.

Black[2] ★ (blæk) *n* **1** Sir **James (Whyte)**. born 1924, British biochemist. He discovered beta-blockers and drugs for peptic ulcers: Nobel prize for physiology or medicine 1988. **2 Joseph.** 1728–99, Scottish physician and chemist, noted for his pioneering work on heat.

blackamoor ('blækəˌmʊə, -ˌmɔː) *n Arch.* a Black person or other person with dark skin. ORIG C16: see BLACK[1], MOOR

black-and-blue *adj* **1** (of the skin) discoloured, as from a bruise. **2** feeling pain or soreness, as from a beating.

Black and Tans *pl n* **the.** a specially recruited armed force sent to Ireland in 1921 by the British Government to combat Sinn Féin. ORIG named after the colour of their uniforms

black-and-white *n* **1a** a photograph, picture, sketch, etc., in black, white, and shades of grey rather than in colour. **1b** (*as modifier*): *black-and-white film*. **2 in black and white. 2a** in print or writing. **2b** in extremes: *he always saw things in black and white*.

black art *n* **the.** another name for **black magic**.

black-backed gull *n* either of two common black-and-white European coastal gulls, **lesser black-backed gull** and **great black-backed gull**.

blackball ('blækˌbɔːl) *n* **1** a negative vote or veto. **2** a black wooden ball used to indicate disapproval or to veto in a vote. ◆ *vb* (*tr*) **3** to vote against. **4** to exclude (someone) from a group, profession, etc.; ostracize. ORIG C18: from *black ball* used to veto

black bean *n* an Australian leguminous tree: used in furniture manufacture. Also called: **Moreton Bay chestnut**.

black bear *n* **1 American black bear.** a bear inhabiting forests of North America. It is smaller and less ferocious than the brown bear. **2 Asiatic black bear.** a bear of central and E Asia, black with a pale V-shaped mark on the chest.

black belt *n Judo, karate, etc.* **a** a black belt worn by an instructor or expert. **b** a person entitled to wear this.

blackberry ('blækbərɪ) *n, pl* **blackberries. 1** Also called: **bramble.** any of several woody rosaceous plants that have thorny stems and black or purple edible berry-like fruits. **2** the fruit of any of these plants. ◆ *vb* **blackberries, blackberrying, blackberried. 3** (*intr*) to gather blackberries.

blackbird ('blækˌbɜːd) *n* **1** a common European thrush in which the male has black plumage and a yellow bill. **2** any of various American orioles having dark plumage. **3** (formerly) a person, esp. a South Sea Islander, who was kidnapped and sold as a slave, esp. in Australia. ◆ *vb* **4** (*tr*) (formerly) to kidnap and sell into slavery.

blackboard ('blækˌbɔːd) *n* a hard or rigid surface made of a smooth usually dark substance, used for writing or drawing on with chalk, esp. in teaching.

black body *n Physics.* a hypothetical body capable of absorbing all the electromagnetic radiation falling on it. Also called: **full radiator**.

black book *n* **1** a book containing the names of people to be punished, blacklisted, etc. **2 in someone's black books.** *Inf.* out of favour with someone.

black box *n* **1** a self-contained unit in an electronic or computer system whose circuitry need not be known to understand its function. **2** an informal name for **flight recorder**.

blackboy ('blækˌbɔɪ) *n* another name for **grass tree** (sense 1).

blackbuck ('blækˌbʌk) *n* an Indian antelope, the male of which has a dark back.

Blackburn ★ ('blækbɜːn) *n* **1** a city in NW England, in central Lancashire: textile industries. Pop: 105 994 (1991). **2 Mount.** a mountain in SE Alaska, the highest peak in the Wrangell Mountains. Height: 5037 m (16 523 ft).

Blackburn with Darwen ★ ('dɑːwɛn) *n* a unitary authority in NW England, in Lancashire. Pop.: 139 500 (1996). Area: 137 sq. km (53 sq. miles).

blackbutt ('blækˌbʌt) *n* any of various Australian eucalyptus trees having rough fibrous bark and hard wood used as timber.

blackcap ('blækˌkæp) *n* a brownish-grey Old World warbler, the male of which has a black crown.

blackcock ('blækˌkɒk) *n* the male of the black grouse.

black coral *n* a dark coral with concentric rings, found deep in the sea, and, once polished, prized in the Caribbean as a semiprecious gem.

Black Country ★ *n* **the.** a formerly heavily industrialized region in the West Midlands of England.

blackcurrant (ˌblæk'kʌrənt) *n* **1** a N temperate shrub having red or white flowers and small edible black berries. **2** its fruit.

blackdamp ('blækˌdæmp) *n* air that is low in oxygen content and high in carbon dioxide as a result of an explosion in a mine. Also called: **chokedamp**.

Black Death *n* **the.** a form of bubonic plague pandemic in Europe and Asia during the 14th century. See **bubonic plague**.

black disc *n* a conventional black vinyl gramophone record as opposed to a compact disc.

black earth *n* another name for **chernozem**.

black economy *n* that portion of the income of a nation that remains illegally undeclared.

blacken ('blækən) *vb* **1** to make or become black or dirty. **2** (*tr*) to defame; slander (esp. in **blacken someone's name**).

Blackett ★ ('blækɪt) *n* **Patrick Maynard Stuart,** Baron. 1897–1974, British physicist, noted for his work on cosmic radiation; Nobel prize for physics 1948.

black eye *n* bruising round the eye.

black-eyed Susan ('suːzən) *n* any of several North American plants having flower heads of orange-yellow rays and brown-black centres.

blackface ('blækˌfeɪs) *n* **1** a variety of sheep with a black face. **2** the make-up used by a White performer imitating a Black person.

blackfish ('blækˌfɪʃ) *n, pl* **blackfish** *or* **blackfishes. 1** any of various dark fishes, esp. a common edible Australian estuary fish. **2** a female salmon that has recently spawned. Cf. **redfish** (sense 1).

black flag *n* another name for the **Jolly Roger**.

blackfly ('blækˌflaɪ) *n, pl* **blackflies.** a black aphid that infests beans, sugar beet, and other plants. Also called: **bean aphid**.

Black Forest ★ *n* **the.** a hilly wooded region of SW Germany, in Baden-Württemberg: a popular resort area. German name: **Schwarzwald**.

Black Friar *n* a Dominican friar.

black grouse *n* **1** a large N European grouse, the male of which has a bluish-black plumage. **2** a related and similar species of W Asia.

blackguard ('blægɑːd, -gəd) *n* **1** an unprincipled contemptible person; scoundrel. ♦ *vb* **2** (*tr*) to ridicule or denounce with abusive language. **3** (*intr*) to behave like a blackguard. ORIG C16: see BLACK, GUARD
▸ '**blackguardism** *n* ▸ '**blackguardly** *adj*

blackhead ('blæk,hɛd) *n* **1** a black-tipped plug of fatty matter clogging a pore of the skin. **2** any of various birds with black plumage on the head.

Blackheath ★ (,blæk'hiːθ) *n* a residential district in London, mainly in the borough of Lewisham and Greenwich: a large heath formerly notorious for highwaymen.

Black Hills ★ *pl n* a group of mountains in W South Dakota and NE Wyoming: famous for the gigantic sculptures of US presidents on the side of Mount Rushmore. Highest peak: Harney Peak, 2207 m (7242 ft).

black hole *n* **1a** *Astron.* a hypothetical region of space resulting from the gravitational collapse of a star and surrounded by a gravitational field so high that neither matter nor radiation could escape from it. **1b** a similar but much more massive region of space at the centre of a galaxy. **2** any place regarded as resembling a black hole in that items or information entering it cannot be retrieved.

black ice *n* a thin transparent layer of new ice on a road or similar surface.

blacking ('blækɪŋ) *n* any preparation for giving a black finish to shoes, metals, etc.

Black Isle ★ *n* **the.** a peninsula in NE Scotland, in Highland council area, between the Cromarty and Moray Firths. ORIG so called because until the late 18th century much of it was uncultivated black moor

blackjack[1] ('blæk,dʒæk) *Chiefly US & Canad.* ♦ *n* **1** a truncheon of leather-covered lead with a flexible shaft. ♦ *vb* (*tr*) **2** to hit as with a blackjack. **3** to compel (a person) by threats. ORIG C19: from BLACK + JACK (implement)

blackjack[2] ('blæk,dʒæk) *n* pontoon or any similar card game. ORIG C20: from BLACK + JACK (the knave)

black knight *n Commerce.* a person or firm that makes an unwelcome takeover bid for a company. Cf. **grey knight, white knight.**

black lead (lɛd) *n* another name for **graphite.**

blackleg ('blæklɛg) *n* **1** Also called **scab.** *Brit.* a person who acts against the interests of a trade union, as by continuing to work during a strike or taking over a striker's job. ♦ *vb* **blacklegs, blacklegging, blacklegged. 2** (*intr*) *Brit.* to act against the interests of a trade union, esp. by refusing to join a strike.

black light *n* the invisible electromagnetic radiation in the ultraviolet and infrared regions of the spectrum.

blacklist ('blæk,lɪst) *n* **1** a list of persons or organizations under suspicion, or considered untrustworthy, disloyal, etc. ♦ *vb* **2** (*tr*) to put on a blacklist.

black magic *n* magic used for evil purposes.

blackmail ('blæk,meɪl) *n* **1** the act of attempting to obtain money by intimidation, as by threats to disclose discreditable information. **2** the exertion of pressure, esp. unfairly, in an attempt to influence someone. ♦ *vb* (*tr*) **3** to exact or attempt to exact (money or anything of value) from (a person) by threats or intimidation; extort. **4** to attempt to influence (a person), esp. by unfair pressure. ORIG C16: from BLACK + OE *māl* terms
▸ '**black,mailer** *n*

Black Maria (mə'raɪə) *n* a police van for transporting prisoners.

black mark *n* an indication of disapproval, failure, etc.

black market *n* **1** any system in which goods or currencies are sold and bought illegally, esp. in violation of controls or rationing. **2** the place where such a system operates. ♦ *vb* **black-market. 3** to sell (goods) on the black market.
▸ **black marketeer** *n*

black mass *n* (*sometimes caps.*) a blasphemous travesty of the Christian Mass, performed by practitioners of black magic.

black money *n* **1** that part of a nation's income that relates to its black economy. **2** any money that a person or organization acquires illegally, as by a means that involves tax evasion. **3** *US.* money to fund a government project that is concealed in the cost of some other project.

Blackmore ★ ('blæk,mɔː) *n* **R(ichard) D(oddridge).** 1825–1900, British novelist; author of *Lorna Doone* (1869).

Black Mountain ★ *n* **the.** a mountain range in S Wales, in E Carmarthenshire and W Powys. Highest peak: Carmarthen Van, 802 m (2632 ft).

Black Mountains ★ *pl n* a mountain range in S Wales and SW Hereford and Worcester, England. Highest peak: Waun Fach, 811 m (2660 ft).

Black Muslim *n* (esp. in the US) a member of an Islamic political movement of Black people who seek to establish a new Black nation.

black nightshade *n* a common poisonous weed in cultivated land, having white flowers and black berry-like fruits.

blackout ('blækaʊt) *n* **1** the extinguishing or hiding of all artificial light, esp. in a city visible to an air attack. **2** a momentary loss of consciousness, vision, or memory. **3** a temporary electrical power failure or cut. **4** the suspension of broadcasting, as by a strike or for political reasons. ♦ *vb* **black out.** (*adv*) **5** (*tr*) to obliterate or extinguish (lights). **6** (*tr*) to create a blackout in (a city, etc.). **7** (*intr*) to lose vision, consciousness, or memory temporarily. **8** (*tr*) to stop (news, a television programme, etc.) from being broadcast.

black pepper *n* a pungent condiment made by grinding the dried unripe berries and husks of the pepper plant.

Blackpool ★ ('blæk,puːl) *n* **1** a resort town in NW England, in Lancashire on the Irish Sea: famous for its tower, 158 m (518 ft) high, and its illuminations. Pop.: 146 262 (1991). **2** a unitary authority in NW England, in Lancashire. Pop.: 151 200 (1997 est.). Area: 35 sq. km (13 sq. miles).

Black Power *n* a social, economic, and political movement of Black people, esp. in the US, to obtain equality with Whites.

Black Prince ★ *n* **the.** See **Edward**[2] (Prince of Wales).

black pudding *n* a kind of black sausage made from minced pork fat, pig's blood, and other ingredients. Also called: **blood pudding.**

Black Rod *n* (in Britain) an officer of the House of Lords and of the Order of the Garter, whose main duty is summoning the Commons at the opening and proroguing of Parliament.

Black Sea ★ *n* an inland sea between SE Europe and Asia: connected to the Aegean Sea by the Bosporus, the Sea of Marmara, and the Dardanelles, and to the Sea of Azov by the Kerch Strait. Area: about 415 000 sq. km (160 000 sq. miles). Also called: **Euxine Sea.** Ancient name: **Pontus Euxinus.**

black section *n* (in Britain) an unofficial group within the Labour Party in any constituency which represents the interests of local Black people.

black sheep *n* a person who is regarded as a disgrace or failure by his or her family or peer group.

Blackshirt ('blæk,ʃɜːt) *n* (in Europe) a member of a fascist organization, esp. the Italian Fascist party before and during World War II.

blacksmith ('blæk,smɪθ) *n* an artisan who works iron with a furnace, anvil, hammer, etc. ORIG C14: see BLACK, SMITH

black snake *n* **1** any of several Old World black venomous snakes, esp. the **Australian black snake. 2** any of various dark nonvenomous snakes.

black spot *n* **1** a place on a road where accidents frequently occur. **2** any dangerous or difficult place. **3** a disease of roses that causes black blotches on the leaves.

black stump *n* **the.** *Austral.* an imaginary marker of the extent of civilization (esp. in **beyond the black stump**).

black tea *n* tea made from fermented tea leaves.

blackthorn ('blæk,θɔ:n) *n* a thorny Eurasian shrub with black twigs, white flowers, and small sour plumlike fruits. Also called: **sloe.**

black tie *n* **1** a black bow tie worn with a dinner jacket. **2** (*modifier*) denoting an occasion when a dinner jacket should be worn.

blacktop ('blæk,tɒp) *n Chiefly US & Canad.* a bituminous mixture used for paving.

Black tracker *n Austral.* an Aboriginal tracker working for the police.

black velvet *n* a mixture of stout and champagne in equal proportions.

Black Volta ★ *n* a river in W Africa, rising in SW Burkina-Faso and flowing northeast, then south into Lake Volta: forms part of the border of Ghana with Burkina-Faso and with the Côte d'Ivoire. Length: about 800 km (500 miles).

Black Watch *n* **the.** the Royal Highland Regiment in the British Army.

blackwater fever ('blæk,wɔ:tə) *n* a rare and serious complication of malaria, characterized by massive destruction of red blood cells, producing dark red or blackish urine.

black widow *n* an American spider, the female of which is highly venomous, and commonly eats its mate.

Blackwood[1] ('blæk,wʊd) *n Bridge.* a conventional bidding sequence of four and five no-trumps, which are requests to the partner to show aces and kings respectively. ORIG C20: after E. F. *Blackwood,* its US inventor

Blackwood[2] ★ ('blæk,wʊd) *n* **Algernon** (**Henry**). 1869–1951, British novelist and short-story writer.

bladder ('blædə) *n* **1** *Anat.* a distensible membranous sac, usually containing liquid or gas, esp. the urinary bladder. **2** an inflatable part of something. **3** a hollow saclike part in certain plants, such as the bladderwrack. ORIG OE *blǣdre*
▸ **'bladdery** *adj*

bladderwort ('blædə,wɜ:t) *n* an aquatic plant some of whose leaves are modified as small bladders to trap minute aquatic animals.

bladderwrack ('blædə,ræk) *n* any of several seaweeds that grow in the intertidal regions of rocky shores and have branched brown fronds with air bladders.

blade (bleɪd) *n* **1** the part of a sharp weapon, tool, etc., that forms the cutting edge. **2** the thin flattish part of various tools, implements, etc., as of a propeller, turbine, etc. **3** the flattened expanded part of a leaf, sepal, or petal. **4** the long narrow leaf of a grass or related plant. **5** the striking surface of a bat, club, stick, or oar. **6** the metal runner on an ice skate. **7** the upper part of the tongue lying directly behind the tip. **8** *Arch.* a dashing or swaggering young man. **9** short for **shoulder blade. 10** a poetic word for a **sword** or **swordsman**. ORIG OE *blæd*
▸ **'bladed** *adj*

blaeberry ('bleɪbərɪ) *n, pl* **blaeberries.** *Brit.* another name for **whortleberry** (senses 1, 2). ORIG C15: from dialect *blae* bluish + BERRY

Blaenau Gwent ★ ('blaɪ,naʊ 'gwɛnt) *n* a county borough of SE Wales. Administrative centre: Ebbw Vale. Pop.: 73 300 (1996 est.). Area: 109 sq. km (42 sq. miles).

blag (blæg) *Sl.* ◆ *n* **1** a robbery, esp. with violence. ◆ *vb* **blags, blagging, blagged.** (*tr*) **2** to obtain by wheedling or cadging: *she blagged free tickets from her mate.* **3** to snatch (wages, someone's handbag, etc.); steal. **4** to rob (esp. a bank or post office). ORIG C19: from ?
▸ **'blagger** *n*

Blagoveshchensk ★ (*Russian* bləga'vjeʃtʃɪnsk) *n* a city in E Russia, on the Amur River. Pop.: 214 000 (1995 est.).

blah *or* **blah blah** (blɑ:) *n Sl.* worthless or silly talk. ORIG C20: imit.

blain (bleɪn) *n* a blister, blotch, or sore on the skin. ORIG OE *blegen*

Blair ★ (blɛə) *n* **Tony,** full name *Anthony Charles Lynton Blair.* born 1953, British politician; leader of the Labour Party from 1994; prime minister from 1997.

Blairite ('blɛəraɪt) *adj* **1** of or relating to the modernizing policies of Tony Blair. ◆ *n* **2** a supporter of the modernizing policies of Tony Blair.

Blake ★ (bleɪk) *n* **1 Peter.** born 1932, British pop-art painter, a co-founder of the Brotherhood of Ruralists (1969). **2 Robert.** 1599–1657, English admiral, who commanded Cromwell's fleet against the Royalists, the Dutch, and the Spanish. **3 William.** 1757–1827, British poet and engraver. His literary works include *Songs of Innocence* (1789) and *Songs of Experience* (1794), and *Jerusalem* (1820). His engravings include illustrations for *The Book of Job* (1826) and for Dante's poems.

blame (bleɪm) *n* **1** responsibility for something that is wrong; culpability. **2** an expression of condemnation. ◆ *vb* **blames, blaming, blamed.** (*tr*) **3** (usually foll. by *for*) to attribute responsibility to: *I blame him for the failure.* **4** (usually foll. by *on*) to ascribe responsibility for (something) to: *I blame the failure on him.* **5** to find fault with. **6** **be to blame.** to be at fault. ORIG C12: from OF *blasmer,* ult. from LL *blasphēmāre* to blaspheme
▸ **'blamable** *or* **'blameable** *adj* ▸ **'blamably** *or* **'blameably** *adv*

blameful ('bleɪmfʊl) *adj* deserving blame; guilty.
▸ **'blamefully** *adv* ▸ **'blamefulness** *n*

blameless ('bleɪmlɪs) *adj* free from blame; innocent.
▸ **'blamelessness** *n*

blameworthy ('bleɪm,wɜ:ðɪ) *adj* deserving censure.
▸ **'blame,worthiness** *n*

Blanc[1] ★ (*French* blɑ̃) *n* **1 Mont.** See **Mont Blanc. 2 Cape.** a headland in N Tunisia: the northernmost point of Africa. **3 Cape.** Also called: **Cape Blanco** ('blæŋkəʊ). a peninsula in Mauritania, on the Atlantic coast.

Blanc[2] ★ (*French* blɑ̃) *n* (**Jean Joseph Charles**) **Louis** (lwi). 1811–82, French socialist and historian: author of *L'Organisation du travail* (1840).

blanch (blɑ:ntʃ) *vb* (*mainly tr*) **1** to remove colour from; whiten. **2** (*usually intr*) to become or cause to become pale, as with sickness or fear. **3** to prepare (meat, green vegetables, nuts, etc.) by plunging them in boiling water. **4** to cause (celery, chicory, etc.) to grow free of chlorophyll by the exclusion of sunlight. ORIG C14: from OF *blanchir,* from *blanc* white; see BLANK

blancmange (blə'mɒnʒ) *n* a jelly-like dessert of milk, stiffened usually with cornflour. ORIG C14: from OF *blanc manger,* lit.: white food

bland (blænd) *adj* **1** devoid of distinctive or stimulating characteristics; uninteresting. **2** gentle and agreeable; suave. **3** mild and soothing. ORIG C15: from L *blandus* flattering
▸ **'blandly** *adv* ▸ **'blandness** *n*

blandish ('blændɪʃ) *vb* (*tr*) to seek to persuade or influence by mild flattery; coax. ORIG C14: from OF *blandir,* from L *blandīrī*

blandishments ('blændɪʃmənts) *pl n* (*rarely sing*) flattery intended to coax or cajole.

blank (blæŋk) *adj* **1** (of a writing surface) bearing no marks; not written on. **2** (of a form, etc.) with spaces left for details to be filled in. **3** without ornament or break. **4** not filled in; empty. **5** exhibiting no interest or expression: *a blank look.* **6** lacking understanding; confused: *he looked blank.* **7** absolute; complete: *blank rejection.* **8** devoid of ideas or inspiration: *his mind went blank.* ◆ *n* **9** an emptiness; void; blank space. **10** an empty space for writing in. **11** a printed form containing such empty spaces. **12** something characterized by incomprehension or confusion: *my mind went a complete blank.* **13** a mark, often a dash, in place of a word, esp. a taboo word. **14** short for **blank cartridge. 15** a piece of material prepared for stamping, punching, forging, or some other operation. **16 draw a blank.** to get no results from something. ◆ *vb* (*tr*) **17** (usually foll. by *out*) to cross out, blot, or obscure. ORIG C15: from OF *blanc* white, of Gmc origin
▸ **'blankness** *n*

blank cartridge *n* a cartridge containing powder but no bullet.

blank cheque *n* **1** a cheque that has been signed but on which the amount payable has not been specified. **2** complete freedom of action.

★ people and places

blanket ('blæŋkɪt) *n* **1** a large piece of thick cloth for use as a bed covering, animal covering, etc. **2** a concealing cover, as of smoke, leaves, or snow. **3** (*modifier*) applying to or covering a wide group or variety of people, conditions, situations, etc.: *blanket insurance against loss, injury, and theft.* **4** (**born**) **on the wrong side of the blanket.** *Inf.* illegitimate. **5 on the blanket.** *Irish.* (of an imprisoned terrorist) wearing only a blanket instead of prison uniform, as a protest against not being recognized as a political prisoner. ◆ *vb* (*tr*) **6** to cover as with a blanket; overlie. **7** to cover a wide area; give blanket coverage. **8** (usually foll. by *out*) to obscure or suppress. ORIG C13: from OF *blancquete,* from *blanc;* see BLANK

blanket bath *n* an all-over wash given to a person confined to bed.

blanket bog *n* a very acid peat bog, low in nutrients, extending widely over a flat terrain, found in cold wet climates.

blanket stitch *n* a strong reinforcing stitch for the edges of blankets and other thick material.

blankety ('blæŋkɪtɪ) *adj, adv* a euphemism for any taboo word. ORIG C20: from BLANK

blank verse *n Prosody.* unrhymed verse, esp. in iambic pentameters.

Blantyre-Limbe ★ (blæn'taɪə'lɪmbeɪ) *n* a city in S Malawi: largest city in the country; formed in 1956 from the adjoining towns of Blantyre and Limbe. Pop.: 446 800 (1994 est.).

blare (blɛə) *vb* **blares, blaring, blared. 1** to sound loudly and harshly. **2** to proclaim loudly and sensationally. ◆ *n* **3** a loud harsh noise. ORIG C14: from MDu. *bleren;* imit.

blarney ('blɑːnɪ) *n* **1** flattering talk. ◆ *vb* **2** to cajole with flattery; wheedle. ORIG C19: after the *Blarney* Stone in SW Ireland, said to endow whoever kisses it with skill in flattery

blasé ('blɑːzeɪ) *adj* **1** indifferent to something because of familiarity. **2** lacking enthusiasm; bored. ORIG C19: from F, p.p. of *blaser* to cloy

blaspheme (blæs'fiːm) *vb* **blasphemes, blaspheming, blasphemed. 1** (*tr*) to show contempt or disrespect for (God or sacred things), esp. in speech. **2** (*intr*) to utter profanities or curses. ORIG C14: from LL, from Gk, from *blasphēmos* BLASPHEMOUS
▸ **blas'phemer** *n*

blasphemous ('blæsfɪməs) *adj* involving impiousness or gross irreverence towards God or something sacred. ORIG C15: via LL, from Gk *blasphēmos* evil-speaking, from *blapsis* evil + *phēmē* speech

blasphemy ('blæsfɪmɪ) *n, pl* **blasphemies. 1** blasphemous behaviour or language. **2** Also called: **blasphemous libel.** *Law.* the crime committed if a person insults, offends, or vilifies the deity, Christ, or the Christian religion.

blast (blɑːst) *n* **1** an explosion, as of dynamite. **2** the rapid movement of air away from the centre of an explosion; shock wave. **3** the charge used in a single explosion. **4** a sudden strong gust of wind or air. **5** a sudden loud sound, as of a trumpet. **6** a violent verbal outburst, as of criticism. **7** a forcible jet of air, esp. one used to intensify the heating effect of a furnace. **8** any of several diseases of plants and animals. **9** *US sl.* a very enjoyable or thrilling experience: *the party was a blast.* **10** (**at**) **full blast.** at maximum speed, volume, etc. ◆ *interj* **11** *Sl.* an exclamation of annoyance. ◆ *vb* **12** (*tr*) to destroy or blow up with explosives, shells, etc. **13** to make or cause to make a loud harsh noise. **14** to wither or cause to wither; blight or be blighted. **15** (*tr*) to criticize severely. ORIG OE *blǣst*
▸ **'blaster** *n*

-blast *n combining form.* (in biology) indicating an embryonic cell or formative layer: *mesoblast.* ORIG from Gk *blastos* bud

blasted ('blɑːstɪd) *adj* **1** blighted or withered. ◆ *adj* (*prenominal*), *adv* **2** *Sl.* (intensifier): *a blasted idiot.*

blast furnace *n* a vertical cylindrical furnace for smelting into which a blast of preheated air is forced.

blasto- *combining form.* indicating an embryo or bud. ORIG see BLAST

blastoff ('blɑːstˌɒf) *n* **1** the launching of a rocket under its own power. **2** the time at which this occurs. ◆ *vb* **blast off. 3** (*adv; when tr, usually passive*) to be launched.

blastula ('blæstjʊlə) *n, pl* **blastulas** *or* **blastulae** (-liː). an early form of an animal embryo that develops a sphere of cells with a central cavity. Also called: **blastosphere.** ORIG C19: NL from Gk, from dim. of *blastos* bud
▸ **'blastular** *adj*

blat (blæt) *n Sl.* a newspaper. ORIG C20: from G *Blatt* leaf, sheet of paper

blatant ('bleɪtᵊnt) *adj* **1** glaringly conspicuous or obvious: *a blatant lie.* **2** offensively noticeable; obtrusive. **3** offensively noisy. ORIG C16: coined by Edmund Spenser; prob. infl. by L *blatīre* to babble
▸ **'blatancy** *n*

blather ('blæðə) *vb, n* a variant of **blether.**

blatherskite ('blæðəˌskaɪt) *n* **1** a talkative silly person. **2** foolish talk; nonsense. ORIG C17: from BLATHER + Scot. & N English dialect *skate* fellow

Blavatsky ★ (blə'vætskɪ) *n* **Helena Petrovna** (pɪ'trɒvnə), called *Madame Blavatsky.* 1831–91, Russian theosophist, cofounder (1875) of the Theosophical Society in New York; author of *The Secret Doctrine* (1888).

blaxploitation (ˌblæksplɔɪ'teɪʃən) *n* exploitative use of stereotypical images of Black people in films, books, etc. ORIG C20: from BLACK[1] + EXPLOITATION

Blaydon ★ ('bleɪdᵊn) *n* an industrial town in NE England, in Gateshead unitary authority. Pop: 15 510 (1991).

blaze[1] (bleɪz) *n* **1** a strong fire or flame. **2** a very bright light or glare. **3** an outburst (of passion, acclaim, patriotism, etc.). **4** brilliance; brightness. ◆ *vb* **blazes, blazing, blazed.** (*intr*) **5** to burn fiercely. **6** to shine brightly. **7** (often foll. by *up*) to become stirred, as with anger or excitement. **8** (usually foll. by *away*) to shoot continuously. ◆ See also **blazes.** ORIG OE *blæse*

blaze[2] (bleɪz) *n* **1** a mark, usually indicating a path, made on a tree. **2** a light-coloured marking on the face of a domestic animal. ◆ *vb* **blazes, blazing, blazed.** (*tr*) **3** to mark (a tree, path, etc.) with a blaze. **4 blaze a trail.** to explore new territories, areas of knowledge, etc., so that others can follow. ORIG C17: prob. from MLow G *bles* white marking

blaze[3] (bleɪz) *vb* **blazes, blazing, blazed.** (*tr;* often foll. by *abroad*) to make widely known; proclaim. ORIG C14: from MDu. *blāsen,* from OHG *blāsan*

blazer ('bleɪzə) *n* a fairly lightweight jacket, often in the colours of a sports club, school, etc.

blazes ('bleɪzɪz) *pl n* **1** *Sl.* a euphemistic word for **hell. 2** *Inf.* (intensifier): *to run like blazes.*

blazon ('bleɪzᵊn) *vb* (*tr*) **1** (often foll. by *abroad*) to proclaim publicly. **2** *Heraldry.* to describe (heraldic arms) in proper terms. **3** to draw and colour (heraldic arms) conventionally. ◆ *n* **4** *Heraldry.* a conventional description or depiction of heraldic arms. ORIG C13: from OF *blason* coat of arms
▸ **'blazoner** *n*

blazonry ('bleɪzənrɪ) *n, pl* **blazonries. 1** the art or process of describing heraldic arms in proper form. **2** heraldic arms collectively. **3** colourful or ostentatious display.

bldg *abbrev. for* building.

bleach (bliːtʃ) *vb* **1** to make or become white or colourless, as by exposure to sunlight, by the action of chemical agents, etc. ◆ *n* **2** a bleaching agent. **3** the act of bleaching. ORIG OE *blǣcan*
▸ **'bleacher** *n*

bleaching powder *n* a white powder consisting of chlorinated calcium hydroxide. Also called: **chloride of lime, chlorinated lime.**

bleak[1] (bliːk) *adj* **1** exposed and barren. **2** cold and raw. **3** offering little hope; dismal: *a bleak future.* ORIG OE *blāc* bright, pale
▸ **'bleakness** *n*

bleak[2] (bliːk) *n* any of various European cyprinid fishes occurring in slow-flowing rivers. ORIG C15: prob. from ON *bleikja* white colour

blear (blɪə) *Arch.* ◆ *vb* **1** (*tr*) to make (eyes or sight) dim as with tears; blur. ◆ *adj* **2** a less common word for **bleary.** ORIG C13: *blere* to make dim

bleary ('blɪərɪ) *adj* **blearier, bleariest. 1** (of eyes or vision) dimmed or blurred, as by tears or tiredness. **2** indistinct or unclear.
▸ **'bleariness** *n*

bleary-eyed *or* **blear-eyed** *adj* with eyes blurred, as with old age or after waking.

bleat (bli:t) *vb* **1** (*intr*) (of a sheep, goat, or calf) to utter its characteristic plaintive cry. **2** (*intr*) to speak with any similar sound. **3** to whine; whimper. ◆ *n* **4** the characteristic cry of sheep, goats, and calves. **5** any sound similar to this. **6** a weak complaint or whine. ORIG OE *blǣtan*
▸ **'bleater** *n* ▸ **'bleating** *n, adj*

bleb (blɛb) *n* **1** a fluid-filled blister on the skin. **2** a small air bubble. ORIG C17: var. of BLOB

bleed (bli:d) *vb* **bleeds, bleeding, bled** (blɛd). **1** (*intr*) to lose or emit blood. **2** (*tr*) to remove or draw blood from (a person or animal). **3** (*intr*) to be injured or die, as for a cause. **4** (of plants) to exude (sap or resin), esp. from a cut. **5** (*tr*) *Inf.* to obtain money, etc., from, esp. by extortion. **6** (*tr*) to draw liquid or gas from (a container or enclosed system): *to bleed the hydraulic brakes.* **7** (*intr*) (of dye or paint) to run or become mixed, as when wet. **8** to print or be printed so that text, illustrations, etc., run off the trimmed page. **9 one's heart bleeds.** used to express sympathetic grief, often ironically. ORIG OE *blēdan*

bleeder ('bli:də) *n* **1** *Sl.* **1a** *Derog.* a despicable person. **1b** any person. **2** *Pathol.* a nontechnical name for a **haemophiliac.**

bleeding ('bli:dɪŋ) *adj, adv Brit. sl.* (intensifier): *a bleeding fool.*

bleeding heart *n* **1** any of several plants, esp. a widely cultivated Japanese species which has heart-shaped nodding pink flowers. **2** *Inf.* **2a** an excessively softhearted person. **2b** (*as modifier*): *bleeding-heart liberals.*

bleep (bli:p) *n* **1** a single short high-pitched signal made by an electronic apparatus; beep. **2** another word for **bleeper.** ◆ *vb* **3** (*intr*) to make such a noise. **4** (*tr*) to call (somebody) by means of a bleeper. ORIG C20: imit.

bleeper ('bli:pə) *n* a small portable radio receiver, carried esp. by doctors, that sounds a coded bleeping signal to call the carrier. Also called: **bleep.**

blemish ('blɛmɪʃ) *n* **1** a defect; flaw; stain. ◆ *vb* **2** (*tr*) to flaw the perfection of; spoil; tarnish. ORIG C14: from OF *blemir* to make pale

blench (blɛntʃ) *vb* (*intr*) to shy away, as in fear; quail. ORIG OE *blencan* to deceive

blend (blɛnd) *vb* **1** to mix or mingle (components) together thoroughly. **2** (*tr*) to mix (different grades or varieties of tea, whisky, etc.). **3** (*intr*) to look good together; harmonize. **4** (*intr*) (esp. of colours) to shade imperceptibly into each other. ◆ *n* **5** a mixture or type produced by blending. **6** the act of blending. **7** Also called: **portmanteau word.** a word formed by joining together the beginning and the end of two other words: *"brunch" is a blend of "breakfast" and "lunch."* ORIG OE *blandan*

blende (blɛnd) *n* **1** another name for **sphalerite. 2** any of several sulphide ores. ORIG C17: G, from *blenden* to deceive, BLIND; so called because it is easily mistaken for galena

blender ('blɛndə) *n* **1** a person or thing that blends. **2** Also called: **liquidizer.** a kitchen appliance with blades used for puréeing vegetables, blending liquids, etc.

Blenheim ★ ('blɛnɪm) *n* a village in SW Germany, site of a victory of Anglo-Austrian forces under the Duke of Marlborough and Prince Eugène of Savoy that saved Vienna from the French and Bavarians (1704) during the War of the Spanish Succession. Modern name: **Blindheim.**

blenny ('blɛnɪ) *n, pl* **blennies.** any of various small fishes of coastal waters having a tapering scaleless body, a long dorsal fin, and long raylike pelvic fins. ORIG C18: from L, from Gk *blennos* slime

blent (blɛnt) *vb Arch. or literary.* a past participle of **blend.**

blepharitis (ˌblɛfə'raɪtɪs) *n* inflammation of the eyelids. ORIG C19: from Gk *blephar(on)* eyelid + -ITIS

Blériot ★ (*French* blerjo) *n* **Louis** (lwi). 1872–1936, French aviator: made the first flight across the English Channel (1909).

blesbok *or* **blesbuck** ('blɛsˌbʌk) *n, pl* **blesboks, blesbok** *or* **blesbucks, blesbuck.** an antelope of southern Africa. The coat is reddish brown with a white blaze between the eyes; the horns are lyre-shaped. ORIG C19: Afrik., from Du. *bles* BLAZE² + *bok* BUCK¹

bless (blɛs) *vb* **blesses, blessing, blessed** *or* **blest.** (*tr*) **1** to consecrate or render holy by means of a religious rite. **2** to give honour or glory to (a person or thing) as holy. **3** to call upon God to protect; give a benediction to. **4** to worship or adore (God). **5** (*often passive*) to grant happiness, health, or prosperity to. **6** (*usually passive*) to endow with a talent, beauty, etc. **7** *Rare.* to protect against evil or harm. **8 bless you!** (*interj*) **8a** a traditional phrase said to a person who has just sneezed. **8b** an exclamation of well-wishing or surprise. **9 bless me!** *or* **(God) bless my soul!** (*interj*) an exclamation of surprise. ORIG OE *blǣdsian* to sprinkle with sacrificial blood

blessed ('blɛsɪd, blɛst) *adj* **1** made holy; consecrated. **2** worthy of deep reverence or respect. **3** *RC Church.* (of a person) beatified by the pope. **4** characterized by happiness or good fortune. **5** bringing great happiness or good fortune. **6** a euphemistic word for **damned,** used in mild oaths: *I'm blessed if I know.*
▸ **'blessedly** *adv* ▸ **'blessedness** *n*

Blessed Sacrament *n Chiefly RC Church.* the consecrated elements of the Eucharist.

Blessed Virgin ★ *n Chiefly RC Church.* another name for **Mary** (sense 1a).

blessing ('blɛsɪŋ) *n* **1** the act of invoking divine protection or aid. **2** the words or ceremony used for this. **3** a short prayer before or after a meal; grace. **4** approval; good wishes. **5** the bestowal of a divine gift or favour. **6** a happy event.

blest (blɛst) *vb* a past tense and past participle of **bless.**

blether ('blɛðə) *Scot.* ◆ *vb* **1** (*intr*) to speak foolishly. ◆ *n* **2** foolish talk; nonsense. ORIG C16: from ON *blathr* nonsense

blew (blu:) *vb* the past tense of **blow**¹ and **blow**³.

Blida ★ ('bli:də) *n* a city in N Algeria, on the edge of the Mitidja Plain. Pop.: 127 284 (1987).

Bligh ★ (blaɪ) *n* **William.** 1754–1817, British admiral; Governor of New South Wales (1806–9); commander of *H.M.S. Bounty* when the crew mutinied in 1789.

blight (blaɪt) *n* **1** any plant disease characterized by withering and shrivelling without rotting. **2** any factor that causes the symptoms of blight in plants. **3** a person or thing that mars or prevents growth. **4** an ugly urban district. ◆ *vb* **5** to cause or suffer a blight. **6** (*tr*) to frustrate or disappoint. **7** (*tr*) to spoil; destroy. ORIG C17: ? rel. to OE *blǣce* rash

blighter ('blaɪtə) *n Brit. inf.* **1** a fellow. **2** a despicable or irritating person or thing.

Blighty ('blaɪtɪ) *n* (*sometimes not cap.*) *Brit. sl.* (used esp. by troops serving abroad) **1** England; home. **2** (*pl* **Blighties**) Also called: **a blighty one.** (esp. in World War I) a wound that causes the recipient to be sent home to England. ORIG C20: from Hindi *bilāyatī* foreign land, England, from Ar. *wilāyat* country

blimey ('blaɪmɪ) *interj Brit. sl.* an exclamation of surprise or annoyance. ORIG C19: short for *gorblimey* God blind me

blimp¹ (blɪmp) *n* **1** a small nonrigid airship. **2** *Films.* a soundproof cover fixed over a camera during shooting. ORIG C20: prob. from (*type*) *B-limp*

blimp² (blɪmp) *n* (*often cap.*) *Chiefly Brit.* a person, esp. a military officer, who is stupidly complacent and reactionary. Also called: **Colonel Blimp.** ORIG C20: from a character created by David Low
▸ **'blimpish** *adj*

blind (blaɪnd) *adj* **1a** unable to see; sightless. **1b** (*as collective n; preceded by the*): *the blind.* **2** (usually foll. by *to*) unable or unwilling to understand or discern. **3** not determined by reason: *blind hatred.* **4** acting or performed without control or preparation. **5** done without being able to see, relying on instruments for information. **6**

hidden from sight: *a blind corner.* **7** closed at one end: *a blind alley.* **8** completely lacking awareness or consciousness: *a blind stupor.* **9** *Inf.* very drunk. **10** having no openings or outlets: *a blind wall.* **11** (intensifier): *not a blind bit of notice.* ◆ *adv* **12** without being able to see ahead or using only instruments: *to drive blind; flying blind.* **13** without adequate knowledge or information; carelessly: *to buy a house blind.* **14 bake blind.** to bake (an empty pastry case) by half filling with dried peas, crusts, etc., to keep it in shape. ◆ *vb* (*mainly tr*) **15** to deprive of sight permanently or temporarily. **16** to deprive of good sense, reason, or judgment. **17** to darken; conceal. **18** (foll. by *with*) to overwhelm by showing detailed knowledge: *to blind somebody with science.* ◆ *n* **19** (*modifier*) for or intended to help the blind: *a blind school.* **20** a shade for a window, usually on a roller. **21** any obstruction or hindrance to sight, light, or air. **22** a person, action, or thing that serves to deceive or conceal the truth. **23** Also: **blinder.** *Brit. sl.* a drunken binge. ORIG OE *blind*
▸ **'blindly** *adv* ▸ **'blindness** *n*

USAGE NOTE See at **disabled.**

blind alley *n* **1** an alley open at one end only; cul-de-sac. **2** *Inf.* a situation in which no further progress can be made.

blind date *n Inf.* a prearranged social meeting between a man and a woman who have not met before.

blinder ('blaɪndə) *n* **1** an outstanding performance in sport. **2** *Brit. sl.* another name for **blind** (sense 23).

blinders ('blaɪndəz) *pl n* the usual US & Canad. word for **blinkers.**

blindfold ('blaɪnd,fəʊld) *vb* (*tr*) **1** to prevent (a person or animal) from seeing by covering (the eyes). ◆ *n* **2** a piece of cloth, bandage, etc., used to cover the eyes. ◆ *adj, adv* **3** having the eyes covered with a cloth or bandage. **4** rash; inconsiderate. ORIG changed (C16) through association with FOLD[1] from OE *blindfellian* to strike blind; see BLIND, FELL[2]

blinding ('blaɪndɪŋ) *n* **1** sand or grit spread over a road surface to fill up cracks. **2** the process of laying blinding. ◆ *adj* **3** making one blind or as if blind. **4** most noticeable; brilliant or dazzling.
▸ **blindingly** *adv*

blind man's buff *n* a game in which a blindfolded person tries to catch and identify the other players. ORIG C16: *buff,* ?from OF *buffe* a blow; see BUFFET[2]

blind register *n* (in Britain) a list of those who are blind and are therefore entitled to financial and other benefits.

blind side *n* **1** *Rugby.* the side of the field between the scrum or ruck and the nearer touchline. **2** the side on which a person's vision is obscured.

blindsight ('blaɪnd,saɪt) *n* the ability to respond to visual stimuli without having any conscious visual experience; it can occur after some forms of brain damage.

blind spot *n* **1** a small oval-shaped area of the retina, where the optic nerve enters, in which vision is not experienced. **2** a place or area where vision is obscured. **3** a subject about which a person is ignorant or prejudiced.

blind trust *n* a trust fund that manages the financial affairs of a person without informing him or her of any investments made, usually so that the beneficiary cannot be accused of using public office for private gain.

blindworm ('blaɪnd,wɜːm) *n* another name for **slowworm.**

blink (blɪŋk) *vb* **1** to close and immediately reopen (the eyes or an eye), usually involuntarily. **2** (*intr*) to look with the eyes partially closed. **3** to shine intermittently or unsteadily. **4** (*tr;* foll. by *away, from,* etc.) to clear the eyes of (dust, tears, etc.). **5** (when *tr,* usually foll. by *at*) to be surprised or amazed. **6** (when *intr,* foll. by *at*) to pretend not to know or see (a fault, injustice, etc.). ◆ *n* **7** the act or an instance of blinking. **8** a glance; glimpse. **9** short for **iceblink** (sense 1). **10 on the blink.** *Sl.* not working properly. ORIG C14: var. of BLENCH

blinker[1] ('blɪŋkə) *n* **1** a flashing light for sending messages, as a warning device, etc., such as a direction indicator on a road vehicle. **2** (*often pl*) a slang word for **eye[1]** (sense 1).

blinker[2] ('blɪŋkə) *vb* (*tr*) **1** to provide (a horse) with blinkers. **2** to obscure or be obscured with or as with blinkers.
▸ **'blinkered** *adj*

blinkers ('blɪŋkəz) *pl n* (*sometimes sing*) *Chiefly Brit.* leather sidepieces attached to a horse's bridle to prevent sideways vision.

blinking ('blɪŋkɪŋ) *adj, adv Inf.* (intensifier): *a blinking fool; a blinking good film.*

blip (blɪp) *n* **1** a repetitive sound, such as that produced by an electronic device. **2** Also called: **pip.** the spot of light on a radar screen indicating the position of an object. **3** a temporary irregularity recorded in the performance of something. ◆ *vb* **blips, blipping, blipped. 4** (*intr*) to produce a blip. ORIG C20: imit.

bliss (blɪs) *n* **1** perfect happiness; serene joy. **2** the ecstatic joy of heaven. ORIG OE *blīths;* rel. to *blīthe* BLITHE

Bliss ★ (blɪs) *n* Sir **Arthur.** 1891–1975, British composer; Master of the Queen's Musick (1953–75). His works include the *Colour Symphony* (1922), film and ballet music, and a piano concerto (1938).

blissful ('blɪsfʊl) *adj* **1** serenely joyful or glad. **2 blissful ignorance.** unawareness or inexperience of something unpleasant.
▸ **'blissfully** *adv* ▸ **'blissfulness** *n*

B list *n* **a** a category considered to be slightly below the most socially desirable. **b** (*as modifier*): *B-list celebrities.* ◆ Cf. **A list.**

blister ('blɪstə) *n* **1** a small bubble-like elevation of the skin filled with serum, produced as a reaction to a burn, mechanical irritation, etc. **2** a swelling containing air or liquid, as on a painted surface. **3** *NZ sl.* **3a** a rebuke. **3b** a summons to court. ◆ *vb* **4** to have or cause to have blisters. **5** (*tr*) to attack verbally with great scorn or sarcasm. ORIG C13: from OF *blestre*
▸ **'blistered** *adj*

blister pack *n* a type of pack for small goods, consisting of a transparent dome on a firm backing. Also called: **bubble pack.**

BLit *abbrev. for* Bachelor of Literature.

blithe (blaɪð) *adj* **1** very happy or cheerful; gay. **2** heedless; casual and indifferent. ORIG OE *blīthe*
▸ **'blithely** *adv* ▸ **'blitheness** *n*

blithering ('blɪðərɪŋ) *adj* **1** talking foolishly; jabbering. **2** *Inf.* stupid; foolish: *you blithering idiot.* ORIG C19: var. of BLETHER + -ING[2]

blithesome ('blaɪðsəm) *adj Literary.* cheery; merry.

BLitt *abbrev. for* Bachelor of Letters. ORIG L *Baccalaureus Litterarum*

blitz (blɪts) *n* **1** a violent and sustained attack, esp. with intensive aerial bombardment. **2** any sudden intensive attack or concerted effort. **3** *American football.* a defensive charge on the quarterback. ◆ *vb* **4** (*tr*) to attack suddenly and intensively. ORIG C20: shortened from G *Blitzkrieg* lightning war

Blitz (blɪts) *n* **the.** the systematic bombing of Britain in 1940–41 by the German Luftwaffe.

blitzkrieg ('blɪts,kriːg) *n* a swift intensive military attack designed to defeat the opposition quickly. ORIG C20: from G: lightning war

Blixen ★ ('blɪksən) *n* **Karen.** See (Isak) **Dinesen.**

blizzard ('blɪzəd) *n* a strong cold wind accompanied by widespread heavy snowfall. ORIG C19: from ?

bloat (bləʊt) *vb* **1** to swell or cause to swell, as with a liquid or air. **2** to become or cause to be puffed up, as with conceit. **3** (*tr*) to cure (fish, esp. herring) by half drying in smoke. ORIG C17: prob. rel. to ON *blautr* soaked
▸ **'bloated** *adj*

bloater ('bləʊtə) *n* a herring that has been salted in brine, smoked, and cured.

blob (blɒb) *n* **1** a soft mass or drop. **2** a spot, dab, or blotch of colour, ink, etc. **3** an indistinct or shapeless form or object. ORIG C15: ? imit.

bloc (blɒk) *n* a group of people or countries combined by a common interest. ORIG from F: BLOCK

Bloch ★ (blɒk) *n* **1 Ernest.** 1880–1959, US composer, born in Switzerland: his works include the symphonies *Israel* (1916) and *America* (1926). **2 Felix.** 1905–83, US physicist, born in Switzerland: Nobel prize for physics (1952) for his work on the magnetic moments of atomic particles. **3 Konrad Emil.** born 1912, US biochemist, born in Germany: shared the Nobel prize for physiology or medicine in 1964 for his work on fatty-acid metabolism. **4** (*French* blɔk). **Marc** (mark). 1886–1944, French historian and Resistance fighter; author of *Feudal Society* (1935) and *Strange Defeat* (1940): killed by the Nazis.

block (blɒk) *n* **1** a large solid piece of wood, stone, or other material usually having at least one face fairly flat. **2** such a piece on which particular tasks may be done, as chopping, cutting, or beheading. **3** Also called: **building block.** one of a set of wooden or plastic cubes as a child's toy. **4** a form on which things are shaped: *a wig block.* **5** *Sl.* a person's head. **6 do one's block.** *Austral. & NZ sl.* to become angry. **7** a dull, unemotional, or hardhearted person. **8** a large building of offices, flats, etc. **9a** a group of buildings in a city bounded by intersecting streets on each side. **9b** the area or distance between such intersecting streets. **10** *Austral. & NZ.* an area of land for a house, farm, etc. **11** *NZ.* an area of bush reserved by licence for a trapper or hunter. **12** a piece of wood, metal, or other material having a design in relief, used for printing. **13** *Austral. & NZ.* a log, usually of willow, fastened to a timber base and used in a wood-chopping competition. **14** a casing housing one or more freely rotating pulleys. See also **block and tackle. 15** an obstruction or hindrance. **16** *Pathol.* **16a** interference in the normal physiological functioning of an organ or part. **16b** See **heart block. 16c** See **nerve block. 17** *Psychol.* a short interruption of perceptual or thought processes. **18** obstruction of an opponent in a sport. **19a** a quantity handled or considered as a single unit. **19b** (*as modifier*): *a block booking.* **20** *Athletics.* short for **starting block.** ◆ *vb* (*mainly tr*) **21** (often foll. by *up*) to obstruct (a passage, channel, etc.) or prevent or impede the motion or flow of (something or someone) by introducing an obstacle: *to block the traffic; to block up a pipe.* **22** to impede, retard, or prevent (an action, procedure, etc.). **23** to stamp (a title, design, etc.) on (a book cover, etc.) esp. using gold leaf. **24** to shape by use of a block: *to block a hat.* **25** (*also intr*) *Sport.* to obstruct or impede movement by (an opponent). **26** to interrupt a physiological function, as by use of an anaesthetic. **27** (*also intr*) *Cricket.* to play (a ball) defensively. ◆ See also **block in, block out.** ORIG C14: from OF *bloc,* from Du. *blok*
▸ **ˈblocker** *n*

blockade (blɒˈkeɪd) *n* **1** *Mil.* the interdiction of a nation's sea lines of communications, esp. of an individual port by the use of sea power. **2** something that prevents access or progress. **3** *Med.* the inhibition of the effect of a hormone or the action of a nerve by a drug. ◆ *vb* **blockades, blockading, blockaded.** (*tr*) **4** to impose a blockade on. **5** to obstruct the way to. ORIG C17: from BLOCK + *-ade,* as in AMBUSCADE
▸ **blockˈader** *n*

blockage (ˈblɒkɪdʒ) *n* **1** the act of blocking or state of being blocked. **2** an object causing an obstruction.

block and tackle *n* a hoisting device in which a rope or chain is passed around a pair of blocks containing one or more pulleys.

blockboard (ˈblɒkˌbɔːd) *n* a bonded board in which strips of soft wood are sandwiched between two layers of veneer.

blockbuster (ˈblɒkˌbʌstə) *n Inf.* **1** a large bomb used to demolish extensive areas. **2** a very successful, effective, or forceful person, thing, etc. **3** a lavish film, show, novel, etc., that proves to be an outstanding popular success.

block diagram *n* **1** a diagram showing the interconnections between the parts of an industrial process. **2** *Computing.* a diagram showing the interconnections between electronic components or parts of a program.

blockhead (ˈblɒkˌhɛd) *n Derog.* a stupid person.
▸ **ˈblockˌheaded** *adj*

blockhouse (ˈblɒkˌhaʊs) *n* **1** (formerly) a wooden fortification with ports for defensive fire, observation, etc. **2** a concrete structure strengthened to give protection against enemy fire, with apertures to allow defensive gunfire. **3** a building constructed of logs or squared timber.

block in *vb* (*tr, adv*) to sketch or outline with little detail.

blockish (ˈblɒkɪʃ) *adj* lacking vivacity or imagination; stupid.
▸ **ˈblockishly** *adv*

block letter *n* **1** *Printing.* a less common name for **sans serif. 2** Also called: **block capital.** a plain capital letter.

block out *vb* (*tr, adv*) **1** to plan or describe (something) in a general fashion. **2** to prevent the entry or consideration of (something).

block release *n Brit.* the release of industrial trainees from work for study at a college for several weeks.

block vote *n Brit.* (at a trade-union conference) the system whereby each delegate's vote has a value in proportion to the number of people he represents.

Bloemfontein ★ (ˈbluːmfɒnˌteɪn) *n* a city in central South Africa: capital of Free State and judicial capital of South Africa. Pop.: 126 867 (1991).

Blois ★ (*French* blwa) *n* a city in N central France, on the Loire: 13th-century castle. Pop.: 51 550 (1990).

bloke (bləʊk) *n Brit. & Austral.* an informal word for **man.** ORIG C19: from Shelta

blokeish *or* **blokish** (ˈbləʊkɪʃ) *adj Brit. inf., sometimes derog.* denoting or exhibiting the characteristics believed typical of an ordinary man. Also: **blokey** (ˈbləʊkɪ).
▸ **ˈblokeishness** *or* **ˈblokishness** *n*

blonde *or* (*masc*) **blond** (blɒnd) *adj* **1** (of hair) of a light colour; fair. **2** (of people or a race) having fair hair, a light complexion, and, typically, blue or grey eyes. ◆ *n* **3** a person having light-coloured hair and skin. ORIG C15: from OF *blond* (fem *blonde*), prob. of Gmc origin
▸ **ˈblondeness** *or* **ˈblondness** *n*

Blondin ★ (*French* blɔ̃dɛ̃) *n* **Charles,** real name *Jean-François Gravelet.* 1824–97, French acrobat; best known for walking a tightrope across Niagara Falls (1859).

blood (blʌd) *n* **1** a reddish fluid in vertebrates that is pumped by the heart through the arteries and veins. **2** a similar fluid in invertebrates. **3** bloodshed, esp. when resulting in murder. **4** life itself; lifeblood. **5** relationship through being of the same family, race, or kind; kinship. **6 flesh and blood. 6a** near kindred or kinship, esp. that between a parent and child. **6b** human nature (esp. in **it's more than flesh and blood can stand**). **7 in one's blood.** as a natural or inherited characteristic or talent. **8 the blood.** royal or noble descent: *a prince of the blood.* **9** temperament; disposition; temper. **10a** good or pure breeding; pedigree. **10b** (*as modifier*): *blood horses.* **11** people viewed as members of a group, esp. as an invigorating force (**new blood, young blood**). **12** *Chiefly Brit., rare.* a dashing young man. **13 in cold blood.** showing no passion; deliberately; ruthlessly. **14 make one's blood boil.** to cause to be angry or indignant. **15 make one's blood run cold.** to fill with horror. ◆ *vb* (*tr*) **16** *Hunting.* to cause (young hounds) to taste the blood of a freshly killed quarry. **17** to initiate (a person) to war or hunting. ORIG OE *blōd*

blood-and-thunder *adj* denoting or relating to a melodramatic adventure story.

blood bank *n* a place where whole blood or blood plasma is stored until required in transfusion.

blood bath *n* indiscriminate slaughter; a massacre.

blood brother *n* **1** a brother by birth. **2** a man or boy who has sworn to treat another as his brother, often in a ceremony in which their blood is mingled.

blood count *n* determination of the number of red and white blood corpuscles in a specific sample of blood.

bloodcurdling (ˈblʌdˌkɜːdlɪŋ) *adj* terrifying; horrifying.
▸ **ˈbloodˌcurdlingly** *adv*

blood donor *n* a person who gives his or her blood to be used for transfusion.

blood doping *n* the illegal practice of removing a quantity of blood from an athlete long before a race and re-injecting it shortly before a race, so boosting oxygenation of the blood.

blooded ('blʌdɪd) *adj* **1** (of horses, cattle, etc.) of good breeding. **2** (*in combination*) having blood or temperament as specified: *hot-blooded, cold-blooded, warm-blooded, red-blooded.*

blood group *n* any one of the various groups into which human blood is classified on the basis of its specific agglutinating properties. Also called: **blood type.**

blood heat *n* the normal temperature of the human body, 98.4°F. or 37°C.

bloodhound ('blʌd,haʊnd) *n* a large breed of hound, formerly used in tracking and police work.

bloodless ('blʌdlɪs) *adj* **1** without blood. **2** conducted without violence (esp. in **bloodless revolution**). **3** anaemic-looking; pale. **4** lacking vitality; lifeless. **5** lacking in emotion; unfeeling.
▸ '**bloodlessly** *adv* ▸ '**bloodlessness** *n*

blood-letting ('blʌd,lɛtɪŋ) *n* **1** the therapeutic removal of blood. See also **phlebotomy. 2** bloodshed, esp. in a feud.

bloodline ('blʌd,laɪn) *n* all the members of a family group over generations, esp. regarding characteristics common to that group; pedigree.

blood money *n* **1** compensation paid to the relatives of a murdered person. **2** money paid to a hired murderer. **3** a reward for information about a criminal, esp. a murderer.

blood orange *n* a variety of orange all or part of the pulp of which is dark red when ripe.

blood poisoning *n* a nontechnical term for **septicaemia.**

blood pressure *n* the pressure exerted by the blood on the inner walls of the arteries, being relative to the elasticity and diameter of the vessels and the force of the heartbeat.

blood pudding *n* another name for **black pudding.**

blood relation *or* **relative** *n* a person related to another by birth, as distinct from one related by marriage.

bloodshed ('blʌd,ʃɛd) *n* slaughter; killing.

bloodshot ('blʌd,ʃɒt) *adj* (of an eye) inflamed.

blood sport *n* any sport involving the killing of an animal, esp. hunting.

bloodstain ('blʌd,steɪn) *n* a dark discoloration caused by blood, esp. dried blood.
▸ '**blood,stained** *adj*

bloodstock ('blʌd,stɒk) *n* thoroughbred horses.

bloodstone ('blʌd,stəʊn) *n* a dark green variety of chalcedony with red spots: used as a gemstone. Also called: **heliotrope.**

bloodstream ('blʌd,stri:m) *n* the flow of blood through the vessels of a living body.

blood substitute *n* a mixture of plasma, albumin, and dextran used to replace lost blood or increase the blood volume.

bloodsucker ('blʌd,sʌkə) *n* **1** an animal that sucks blood, esp. a leech or mosquito. **2** *Inf.* a person or thing that preys upon another person, esp. by extorting money.
▸ '**blood,sucking** *adj*

blood sugar *n Med.* the glucose circulating in the blood: the normal fasting level is between 3·9 and 5·6 millimoles per litre.

bloodthirsty ('blʌd,θɜ:stɪ) *adj* **bloodthirstier, bloodthirstiest. 1** murderous; cruel. **2** taking pleasure in bloodshed or violence. **3** describing or depicting killing and violence; gruesome.
▸ '**blood,thirstily** *adv* ▸ '**blood,thirstiness** *n*

blood type *n* another name for **blood group.**

blood vessel *n* an artery, capillary, or vein.

bloodwood ('blʌd,wʊd) *n* any of several species of Australian eucalyptus with red sap.

bloody ('blʌdɪ) *adj* **bloodier, bloodiest. 1** covered or stained with blood. **2** resembling or composed of blood. **3** marked by much killing and bloodshed: *a bloody war.* **4** cruel or murderous: *a bloody tyrant.* ◆ *adv, adj* **5** *Sl.* (intensifier): *a bloody fool.* ◆ *vb* **bloodies, bloodying, bloodied. 6** (*tr*) to stain with blood.
▸ '**bloodily** *adv* ▸ '**bloodiness** *n*

Bloody Mary *n* **1** nickname of **Mary I. 2** a drink consisting of tomato juice and vodka.

bloody-minded *adj Brit. inf.* deliberately obstructive and unhelpful.

bloom[1] (blu:m) *n* **1** a blossom on a flowering plant; a flower. **2** the state, time, or period when flowers open. **3** open flowers collectively. **4** a healthy, vigorous, or flourishing condition; prime. **5** youthful or healthy rosiness in the cheeks or face; glow. **6** a fine whitish coating on the surface of fruits, leaves, etc. **7** Also called: **chill.** a dull area on the surface of old gloss paint, lacquer, or varnish. **8** *Ecology.* a visible increase in the algal constituent of plankton, which may be due to excessive organic pollution. ◆ *vb* (*intr*) **9** (of flowers) to open; come into flower. **10** to bear flowers; blossom. **11** to flourish or grow. **12** to be in a healthy, glowing, or flourishing condition. ORIG C13: of Gmc origin; cf. ON *blōm* flower

bloom[2] (blu:m) *n* a rectangular mass of metal obtained by rolling or forging a cast ingot. ORIG OE *blōma* lump of metal

bloomer[1] ('blu:mə) *n* a plant that flowers, esp. in a specified way: *a night bloomer.*

bloomer[2] ('blu:mə) *n Brit. inf.* a stupid mistake; blunder. ORIG C20: from BLOOMING

bloomer[3] ('blu:mə) *n Brit.* a medium-sized loaf, glazed and notched on top. ORIG C20: from?

bloomers ('blu:məz) *pl n* **1** *Inf.* women's baggy knickers. **2** (formerly) loose trousers gathered at the knee worn by women for cycling, etc. **3** *History.* loose trousers gathered at the ankle and worn under a shorter skirt. ORIG after Amelia *Bloomer* (1818–94), US social reformer

Bloomfield ★ ('blu:m,fi:ld) *n* **Leonard.** 1887–1949, US linguist, influential for his strictly scientific and descriptive approach to comparative linguistics; author of *Language* (1933).

blooming ('blu:mɪŋ) *adv, adj Brit. inf.* (intensifier): *a blooming genius; blooming painful.* ORIG C19: euphemistic for BLOODY

Bloomington ★ ('blu:mɪŋtən) *n* a city in central Indiana: seat of the University of Indiana (1820). Pop.: 60 633 (1990).

Bloomsbury ★ ('blu:mzbərɪ, -brɪ) *n* a district of central London in the borough of Camden: contains the British Museum.

Bloomsbury Group *n* a group of writers, artists, and intellectuals living and working in and around Bloomsbury from about 1907 to 1930. They included Leonard and Virginia Woolf, Roger Fry, E. M. Forster, Lytton Strachey, and John Maynard Keynes.

blossom ('blɒsəm) *n* **1** the flower or flowers of a plant, esp. producing edible fruit. **2** the time or period of flowering. ◆ *vb* (*intr*) **3** (of plants) to come into flower. **4** to develop or come to a promising stage. ORIG OE *blōstm*
▸ '**blossomy** *adj*

blot (blɒt) *n* **1** a stain or spot of ink, paint, dirt, etc. **2** something that spoils. **3** a blemish or stain on one's character or reputation. **4** *Austral. sl.* the anus. ◆ *vb* **blots, blotting, blotted. 5** (of ink, dye, etc.) to form spots or blobs on (a material) or (of a person) to cause such spots or blobs to form on (a material). **6** (*intr*) to stain or become stained or spotted. **7** (*tr*) to cause a blemish in or on; disgrace. **8** to soak up (excess ink, etc.) by using blotting paper. **9** (of blotting paper) to absorb (excess ink, etc.). **10** (*tr;* often foll. by *out*) **10a** to darken or hide completely; obscure; obliterate. **10b** to destroy; annihilate. ORIG C14: prob. of Gmc origin

blotch (blɒtʃ) *n* **1** an irregular spot or discoloration, esp. a dark and relatively large one. ◆ *vb* **2** to become or cause to become marked by such discoloration. ORIG C17: prob. from BOTCH, infl. by BLOT
▸ '**blotchy** *adj*

blotter ('blɒtə) *n* something used to absorb excess ink, esp. a sheet of blotting paper.

blotting paper *n* a soft absorbent unsized paper, used esp. for soaking up surplus ink.

blotto ('blɒtəʊ) *adj Sl.* unconscious, esp. through drunkenness. ORIG C20: from BLOT (vb)

blouse (blaʊz) *n* **1** a woman's shirtlike garment. **2** a waist-length belted jacket worn by soldiers. ◆ *vb* **blouses, blousing, bloused. 3** to hang or make so as to hang in full loose folds. ORIG C19: from F, from ?

blouson ('blu:zɒn) *n* a tight-waisted jacket or top that blouses out. ORIG C20: from F

blow[1] (bləʊ) *vb* **blows, blowing, blew, blown. 1** (of a current of air, the wind, etc.) to be or cause to be in motion. **2** (*intr*) to move or be carried by or as if by wind. **3** to expel (air, cigarette smoke, etc.) through the mouth or nose. **4** to force or cause (air, dust, etc.) to move (into, in, over, etc.) by using an instrument or by expelling breath. **5** (*intr*) to breathe hard; pant. **6** (sometimes foll. by *up*) to inflate with air or the breath. **7** (*intr*) (of wind, a storm, etc.) to make a roaring sound. **8** to cause (a whistle, siren, etc.) to sound by forcing air into it or (of a whistle, etc.) to sound thus. **9** (*tr*) to force air from the lungs through (the nose) to clear out mucus. **10** (often foll. by *up, down, in,* etc.) to explode, break, or disintegrate completely. **11** *Electronics.* to burn out (a fuse, valve, etc.) because of excessive current or (of a fuse, valve, etc.) to burn out. **12** (*tr*) to wind (a horse) by making it run excessively. **13** to cause (a wind instrument) to sound by forcing one's breath into the mouthpiece or (of such an instrument) to sound in this way. **14** (*intr*) (of flies) to lay eggs (in). **15** to shape (glass, ornaments, etc.) by forcing air or gas through the material when molten. **16** (*tr*) *Sl.* to spend (money) freely. **17** (*tr*) *Sl.* to use (an opportunity) ineffectively. **18** *Sl.* to go suddenly away (from). **19** (*tr*) *Sl.* to expose or betray (a secret). **20** (p.p. **blowed**). *Inf.* another word for **damn. 21 blow hot and cold.** *Inf.* to vacillate. **22 blow one's top.** *Inf.* to lose one's temper. ◆ *n* **23** the act or an instance of blowing. **24** the sound produced by blowing. **25** a blast of air or wind. **26a** *Brit.* a slang name for **cannabis** (sense 2). **26b** *US* a slang name for **cocaine. 27** *Austral. sl.* a brief rest; a breather. ◆ See also **blow away, blow in,** etc. ORIG OE *blāwan*

blow[2] (bləʊ) *n* **1** a powerful or heavy stroke with the fist, a weapon, etc. **2 at one** *or* **a blow.** by or with only one action. **3** a sudden setback. **4 come to blows. 4a** to fight. **4b** to result in a fight. **5** an attacking action: *a blow for freedom.* **6** *Austral. & NZ.* a stroke of the shears in sheep-shearing. ORIG C15: prob. of Gmc origin

blow[3] (bləʊ) *vb* **blows, blowing, blew, blown. 1** (*intr*) (of a plant or flower) to blossom or open out. ◆ *n* **2** a mass of blossoms. **3** the state or period of blossoming. ORIG OE *blōwan*

blow away *vb* (*tr, adv*) *Sl., chiefly US.* **1** to kill (someone) by shooting. **2** to defeat decisively.

blow-by-blow *adj* (*prenominal*) explained in great detail: *a blow-by-blow account.*

blow-dry *vb* **blow-dries, blow-drying, blow-dried. 1** (*tr*) to style (the hair) while drying it with a hand-held hair dryer. ◆ *n* **2** this method of styling hair.

blower ('bləʊə) *n* **1** a mechanical device, such as a fan, that blows. **2** a low-pressure compressor, esp. in a furnace or internal-combustion engine. **3** an informal name for **telephone.**

blowfish ('bləʊˌfɪʃ) *n, pl* **blowfish** *or* **blowfishes.** a popular name for **puffer** (sense 2).

blowfly ('bləʊˌflaɪ) *n, pl* **blowflies.** any of various flies that lay their eggs in rotting meat, dung, carrion, and open wounds. Also called: **bluebottle.**

blowgun ('bləʊˌgʌn) *n* the US word for **blowpipe** (sense 1).

blowhard ('bləʊˌhɑ:d) *Inf.* ◆ *n* **1** a boastful person. ◆ *adj* **2** blustering or boastful.

blowhole ('bləʊˌhəʊl) *n* **1** the nostril of whales, situated far back on the skull. **2** a hole in ice through which whales, seals, etc., breathe. **3** *Geol.* a hole in a cliff top leading to a sea cave through which air is forced by the action of the sea. **4a** a vent for air or gas. **4b** *NZ.* a hole emitting gas or steam in a volcanic region.

blow in *Inf.* ◆ *vb* **1** (*intr, adv*) to arrive or enter suddenly. ◆ *n* **blow-in. 2** *Austral.* a newcomer.

blow job *Taboo.* a slang term for **fellatio.**

blowlamp ('bləʊˌlæmp) *n* another name for **blowtorch.**

blown (bləʊn) *vb* the past participle of **blow**[1] and **blow**[3].

blow out *vb* (*adv*) **1** to extinguish (a flame, candle, etc.) or (of a flame, etc.) to become extinguished. **2** (*intr*) (of a tyre) to puncture suddenly, esp. at high speed. **3** (*intr*) (of a fuse) to melt suddenly. **4** (*tr; often reflexive*) to diminish or use up the energy of: *the storm blew itself out.* **5** (*intr*) (of an oil or gas well) to lose oil or gas in an uncontrolled manner. ◆ *n* **blowout. 6** the sudden melting of an electrical fuse. **7** a sudden burst in a tyre. **8** the uncontrolled escape of oil or gas from an oil or gas well. **9** *Sl.* a large filling meal or lavish entertainment.

blow over *vb* (*intr, adv*) **1** to cease or be finished: *the storm blew over.* **2** to be forgotten.

blowpipe ('bləʊˌpaɪp) *n* **1** a long tube from which pellets, poisoned darts, etc., are shot by blowing. **2** Also called: **blow tube.** a tube for blowing air or oxygen into a flame to intensify its heat. **3** a long narrow iron pipe used to gather molten glass and blow it into shape.

blowsy *or* **blowzy** ('blaʊzɪ) *adj* **blowsier, blowsiest** *or* **blowzier, blowziest. 1** (esp. of a woman) untidy in appearance; slovenly or sluttish. **2** (of a woman) ruddy in complexion. ORIG C18: from dialect *blowze* beggar girl, from ?

blow through *vb* (*intr, adv*) *Austral. inf.* to leave; make off.

blowtorch ('bləʊˌtɔ:tʃ) *n* a small burner that produces a very hot flame, used to remove paint, melt soft metal, etc.

blow up *vb* (*adv*) **1** to explode or cause to explode. **2** (*tr*) to increase the importance of (something): *they blew the whole affair up.* **3** (*intr*) to arise: *we lived very quietly before this affair blew up.* **4** (*intr*) to come into existence with sudden force: *a storm had blown up.* **5** (*intr*) *Inf.* to lose one's temper (with a person). **6** (*tr*) *Inf.* to reprimand. **7** (*tr*) *Inf.* to enlarge the size of (a photograph). ◆ *n* **blow-up. 8** an explosion. **9** *Inf.* an enlarged photograph or part of a photograph. **10** *Inf.* a fit of temper.

blowy ('bləʊɪ) *adj* **blowier, blowiest.** another word for **windy** (sense 1).

blub (blʌb) *vb* **blubs, blubbing, blubbed.** *Brit.* a slang word for **blubber** (senses 1–3).

blubber ('blʌbə) *vb* **1** to sob without restraint. **2** to utter while sobbing. **3** (*tr*) to make (the face) wet and swollen by crying. ◆ *n* **4** the fatty tissue of aquatic mammals such as the whale. **5** *Inf.* flabby body fat. **6** the act or an instance of weeping without restraint. ◆ *adj* **7** (*often in combination*) swollen or fleshy: *blubber-faced.* ORIG C12: ?from Low G *blubbern* to BUBBLE, imit.
▸ **'blubberer** *n* ▸ **'blubbery** *adj*

Blücher ★ (*German* 'blʏçər) *n* **Gebhard Leberecht von** ('gɛphart 'le:bərɛçt fɔn). 1742–1819, Prussian field marshal, who commanded the Prussian army against Napoleon at Waterloo (1815).

bludge (blʌdʒ) *Austral. & NZ inf.* ◆ *vb* **bludges, bludging, bludged. 1** (often foll. by *on* or *off*) to scrounge from (someone). **2** (*intr*) to skive. ◆ *n* **3** a very easy task. ORIG C19: back formation from *bludger* pimp, from BLUDGEON

bludgeon ('blʌdʒən) *n* **1** a stout heavy club, typically thicker at one end. **2** a person, line of argument, etc., that is effective but unsubtle. ◆ *vb* (*tr*) **3** to hit as with a bludgeon. **4** (often foll. by *into*) to force; bully; coerce. ORIG C18: from ?

bludger ('blʌdʒə) *n Austral. & NZ inf.* **1** a person who scrounges. **2** a person who avoids work. **3** a person in authority regarded as ineffectual by those working under him or her.

blue (blu:) *n* **1** any of a group of colours, such as that of a clear unclouded sky or the deep sea. **2** a dye or pigment of any of these colours. **3** blue cloth or clothing: *dressed in blue.* **4** a sportsman who represents or has represented Oxford or Cambridge University and has the right to wear the university colour. **5** *Brit.* an informal name for **Tory. 6** any of numerous small blue-winged butterflies. **7**

a blue substance used in laundering. **8** *Austral. & NZ sl.* an argument or fight: *he had a blue with a taxi driver.* **9** Also: **bluey.** *Austral. & NZ sl.* a court summons. **10** *Austral. & NZ inf.* a mistake; error. **11 out of the blue.** apparently from nowhere; unexpectedly. ◆ *adj* **bluer, bluest. 12** of the colour blue. **13** (of the flesh) having a purple tinge, as from cold or contusion. **14** depressed, moody, or unhappy. **15** indecent, titillating, or pornographic: *blue films.* ◆ *vb* **blues, blueing** *or* **bluing, blued. 16** to make, dye, or become blue. **17** (*tr*) to treat (laundry) with blue. **18** (*tr*) *Sl.* to spend extravagantly or wastefully; squander. ◆ See also **blues.** ORIG C13: from OF *bleu,* of Gmc origin
▸ **'blueness** *n*

Blue (blu:) *or* **Bluey** ('blu:ɪ) *n Austral. inf.* a person with red hair.

blue baby *n* a baby born with a bluish tinge to the skin because of lack of oxygen in the blood.

Bluebeard ('blu:ˌbɪəd) *n* **1** a villain in European folk tales who marries several wives and murders them in turn. **2** a man who has had several wives.

bluebell ('blu:ˌbɛl) *n* **1** Also called: **wild** or **wood hyacinth.** a European woodland plant having a one-sided cluster of blue bell-shaped flowers. **2** a Scottish name for **harebell. 3** any of various other plants with blue bell-shaped flowers.

blueberry ('blu:bərɪ, -brɪ) *n, pl* **blueberries. 1** Also called: **huckleberry.** any of several North American ericaceous shrubs that have blue-black edible berries with tiny seeds. See also **bilberry. 2** the fruit of any of these plants.

bluebird ('blu:ˌbɜ:d) *n* **1** a North American songbird of the thrush family having a blue or partly blue plumage. **2** any of various other birds having a blue plumage.

blue blood *n* royal or aristocratic descent. ORIG C19: translation of Sp. *sangre azul*
▸ **ˌblue-'blooded** *adj*

blue book *n* **1** (in Britain) a government publication bound in a stiff blue paper cover: usually the report of a royal commission or a committee. **2** (in Canada) an annual statement of government accounts.

bluebottle ('blu:ˌbɒtᵊl) *n* **1** another name for the **blowfly. 2** any of various blue-flowered plants, esp. the cornflower. **3** *Brit.* an informal word for a **policeman. 4** *Austral. & NZ.* an informal name for **Portuguese man-of-war.**

blue button *n* a trainee market maker on the London stock exchange. ORIG C20: from the *blue button* badge worn in the lapel

blue cheese *n* cheese containing a blue mould, esp. Stilton, Roquefort, or Danish Blue.

blue chip *n* **1** a gambling chip with the highest value. **2** *Finance.* a stock considered reliable with respect to both dividend income and capital value. **3** (*modifier*) denoting something considered to be a valuable asset.

blue-collar *adj* of or designating manual industrial workers. Cf. **white-collar.**

blue-eyed boy *n Inf., chiefly Brit.* the favourite or darling of a person or group.

bluefish ('blu:ˌfɪʃ) *n, pl* **bluefish** *or* **bluefishes. 1** Also called: **snapper.** a bluish marine food and game fish, related to the horse mackerel. **2** any of various other bluish fishes.

Blue Flag *n* an award given to a seaside resort that meets EU standards of cleanliness of beaches and purity of water in bathing areas.

blue fox *n* **1** a variety of the arctic fox that has a pale grey winter coat. **2** the fur of this animal.

blue funk *n Sl.* a state of great terror.

bluegrass ('blu:ˌgrɑ:s) *n* **1** any of several North American bluish-green grasses, esp. **Kentucky bluegrass,** grown for forage. **2** a type of folk music originating in Kentucky.

blue-green algae *pl n* the former name for **cyanobacteria.**

blue ground *n Mineralogy.* another name for **kimberlite.**

blue gum *n* a tall fast-growing widely cultivated Australian eucalyptus, having bluish aromatic leaves containing a medicinal oil, bark that peels off in shreds, and hard timber.

blue heeler *n Austral.* a type of dog with dark speckled markings: used for herding cattle.

bluejacket ('blu:ˌdʒækɪt) *n* a sailor in the Navy.

blue jay *n* a common North American jay having bright blue plumage.

blue moon *n* **once in a blue moon.** *Inf.* very rarely; almost never.

blue mould *n* any fungus that forms a bluish mass on decaying food, leather, etc. Also called: **green mould.**

Blue Mountains ★ *pl n* **1** a mountain range in the US, in NE Oregon and SE Washington. Highest peak: Rock Creek Butte, 2773 m (9097 ft). **2** a mountain range in the Caribbean, in E Jamaica: Blue Mountain coffee is grown on its slopes. Highest peak: Blue Mountain Peak, 2256 m (7402 ft). **3** a plateau in SE Australia, in E New South Wales: part of the Great Dividing Range. Highest part: about 1134 m (3871 ft).

Blue Nile ★ *n* a river in E Africa, rising in central Ethiopia as the Abbai and flowing southeast, then northwest to join the White Nile. Length: about 1530 km (950 miles).

blue pencil *n* **1** deletion, alteration, or censorship of the contents of a book or other work. ◆ *vb* **blue-pencil, blue-pencils, blue-pencilling, blue-pencilled** *or US* **blue-pencils, blue-penciling, blue-penciled. 2** (*tr*) to alter or delete parts of (a book, film, etc.), esp. to censor.

blue peter *n* a signal flag of blue with a white square at the centre, displayed by a vessel about to leave port. ORIG C19: from the name *Peter*

blue pointer *n* a large shark of Australian coastal waters, having a blue back and pointed snout.

blueprint ('blu:ˌprɪnt) *n* **1** Also called: **cyanotype.** a photographic print of plans, technical drawings, etc., consisting of white lines on a blue background. **2** an original plan or prototype. ◆ *vb* **3** (*tr*) to make a blueprint of (a plan, etc.).

blue ribbon *n* **1** (in Britain) a badge of blue silk worn by members of the Order of the Garter. **2** a badge awarded as the first prize in a competition.

Blue Ridge Mountains ★ *pl n* a mountain range in the eastern US, extending from West Virginia into Georgia: part of the Appalachian mountains. Highest peak: Mount Mitchell, 2038 m (6684 ft).

blues (blu:z) *pl n* (*sometimes functioning as sing*) **the. 1** a feeling of depression or deep unhappiness. **2** a type of folk song devised by Black Americans, usually employing a basic 12-bar chorus and frequent minor intervals.

blue-sky *n* (*modifier*) of or denoting theoretical research without regard to any future application of its result: *a blue-sky project.*

bluestocking ('blu:ˌstɒkɪŋ) *n Usually disparaging.* a scholarly or intellectual woman. ORIG from the blue worsted stockings worn by members of an 18th-cent. literary society

bluestone ('blu:ˌstəʊn) *n* **1** a blue-grey sandstone containing much clay, used for building and paving. **2** the blue crystalline form of copper sulphate.

bluetit ('blu:ˌtɪt) *n* a common European tit having a blue crown, wings, and tail, yellow underparts, and a black-and-grey head.

blue whale *n* the largest mammal: a widely distributed bluish-grey whalebone whale, closely related and similar to the rorquals.

bluey ('blu:ɪ) *n Austral. inf.* **1** a blanket. **2** a swagman's bundle. **3 hump (one's) bluey.** to carry one's bundle; tramp. **4** a variant of **blue** (sense 9). **5** a cattle dog. ORIG (for senses 1, 2, 4) C19: from BLUE (on account of their colour) + -Y[2]

Bluey ('blu:ɪ) *n* a variant of **Blue.**

bluff[1] (blʌf) *vb* **1** to pretend to be confident about an uncertain issue in order to influence (someone). ◆ *n* **2** deliberate deception intended to create the impression of a stronger position than one actually has. **3 call someone's bluff.** to challenge someone to give proof of his or her claims. ORIG C19: orig. US poker-playing term, from Du. *bluffen* to boast
▸ **'bluffer** *n*

★ people and places

bluff² (blʌf) *n* **1** a steep promontory, bank, or cliff. **2** *Canad.* a clump of trees on the prairie; copse. ◆ *adj* **3** good-naturedly frank and hearty. **4** (of a bank, cliff, etc.) presenting a steep broad face. ORIG C17 (in the sense: nearly perpendicular): ?from MDu. *blaf* broad
▸ **'bluffly** *adv* ▸ **'bluffness** *n*

bluish *or* **blueish** ('bluːɪʃ) *adj* somewhat blue.

Blum ★ (bluːm) *n* **Léon** (leɔ̃). 1872–1950, French socialist statesman; premier of France (1936–37; 1938; 1946–47).

Blunden ★ ('blʌndən) *n* **Edmund (Charles)**. 1896–1974, British writer, noted for *Undertones of War* (1928).

blunder ('blʌndə) *n* **1** a stupid or clumsy mistake. **2** a foolish tactless remark. ◆ *vb* (*mainly intr*) **3** to make stupid or clumsy mistakes. **4** to make foolish tactless remarks. **5** (often foll. by *about, into,* etc.) to act clumsily; stumble. **6** (*tr*) to mismanage; botch. ORIG C14: of Scand. origin; cf. ON *blunda* to close one's eyes
▸ **'blunderer** *n* ▸ **'blundering** *n, adj*

blunderbuss ('blʌndəˌbʌs) *n* an obsolete short musket with large bore and flared muzzle. ORIG C17: changed (infl. by BLUNDER) from Du. *donderbus;* from *donder* THUNDER + obs. *bus* gun

blunge (blʌndʒ) *vb* **blunges, blunging, blunged.** (*tr*) to mix (clay or a similar substance) with water in order to form a suspension for use in ceramics. ORIG C19: prob. from BLEND + PLUNGE
▸ **'blunger** *n*

Blunkett ★ ('blʌŋkɪt) *n* **David.** born 1947, British Labour politician; secretary of state for education and employment from 1997.

blunt (blʌnt) *adj* **1** (esp. of a knife or blade) lacking sharpness or keenness; dull. **2** not having a sharp edge or point: *a blunt instrument.* **3** (of people, manner of speaking, etc.) straightforward and uncomplicated. ◆ *vb* (*tr*) **4** to make less sharp. **5** to diminish the sensitivity or perception of; make dull. ORIG C12: prob. of Scand. origin
▸ **'bluntly** *adv* ▸ **'bluntness** *n*

Blunt ★ (blʌnt) *n* **Anthony.** 1907–83, British art historian and Soviet spy.

blur (blɜː) *vb* **blurs, blurring, blurred. 1** to make or become vague or less distinct. **2** to smear or smudge. **3** (*tr*) to make (the judgment, memory, or perception) less clear; dim. ◆ *n* **4** something vague, hazy, or indistinct. **5** a smear or smudge. ORIG C16: ? var. of BLEAR
▸ **blurred** *adj* ▸ **'blurry** *adj*

blurb (blɜːb) *n* a promotional description, as on the jackets of books. ORIG C20: coined by G. Burgess (1866–1951), US humorist & illustrator

blurt (blɜːt) *vb* (*tr;* often foll. by *out*) to utter suddenly and involuntarily. ORIG C16: prob. imit.

blush (blʌʃ) *vb* **1** (*intr*) to become suddenly red in the face from embarrassment, shame, modesty, or guilt; redden. **2** to make or become reddish or rosy. ◆ *n* **3** a sudden reddening of the face from embarrassment, shame, modesty, or guilt. **4** a rosy glow. **5** a cloudy area on the surface of freshly applied gloss paint. **6** another word for **rosé. 7 at first blush.** when first seen; as a first impression. ORIG OE *blȳscan*

blusher ('blʌʃə) *n* a cosmetic applied to the cheeks to give a rosy colour.

bluster ('blʌstə) *vb* **1** to speak or say loudly or boastfully. **2** to act in a bullying way. **3** (*tr;* foll. by *into*) to force or attempt to force (a person) into doing something by behaving thus. **4** (*intr*) (of the wind) to be noisy or gusty. ◆ *n* **5** boisterous talk or action; swagger. **6** empty threats or protests. **7** a strong wind; gale. ORIG C15: prob. from MLow G *blüsteren* to storm, blow violently
▸ **'blusterer** *n* ▸ **'blustery** *adj*

Blvd *abbrev. for* Boulevard.

Blyth¹ ★ (blaɪð) *n* a port in N England, in SE Northumberland, on the North Sea. Pop.: 35 327 (1991).

Blyth² ★ (blaɪð) *n* Sir **Chay** (tʃeɪ). born 1940, British yachtsman, who sailed round the world alone (1970–71).

Blyton ★ ('blaɪtᵊn) *n* **Enid (Mary)**. 1897–1968, British writer of children's books.

BM *abbrev. for:* **1** Bachelor of Medicine. **2** *Surveying.* benchmark. **3** British Museum.

BMA *abbrev. for* British Medical Association.

BMC *abbrev. for* British Medical Council.

B-movie *n* a film originally made (esp. in the 1940s and 50s) as a supporting film, now often considered as a genre in its own right.

BMus *abbrev. for* Bachelor of Music.

BMX 1 *abbrev. for* bicycle motocross: stunt riding over an obstacle course on a bicycle. ◆ *n* **2** a bicycle designed for bicycle motocross.

Bn *abbrev. for:* **1** Baron. **2** Battalion.

BNFL *abbrev. for* British Nuclear Fuels Limited.

bo *or* **boh** (bəʊ) *interj* an exclamation to startle or surprise someone, esp. a child in a game.

BO *abbrev. for:* **1** *Inf.* body odour. **2** box office.

b.o. *abbrev. for:* **1** back order. **2** branch office. **3** broker's order. **4** buyer's option.

boa ('bəʊə) *n* **1** any of various large nonvenomous snakes of Central and South America and the Caribbean. They kill their prey by constriction. **2** a woman's long thin scarf, usually of feathers or fur. ORIG C19: from NL, from L

boa constrictor *n* a very large snake of tropical America and the Caribbean that kills its prey by constriction.

Boadicea ★ (ˌbəʊədɪ'siːə) *n* another name for **Boudicca.**

boar (bɔː) *n* **1** an uncastrated male pig. **2** See **wild boar.** ORIG OE *bār*

board (bɔːd) *n* **1** a long wide flat piece of sawn timber. **2a** a smaller flat piece of rigid material for a specific purpose: *ironing board.* **2b** (*in combination*): *breadboard.* **3** a person's meals, provided regularly for money. **4** *Arch.* a table, esp. when laden with food. **5a** (*sometimes functioning as pl*) a group of people who officially administer a company, trust, etc. **5b** (*as modifier*): *a board meeting.* **6** any other committee or council: *a board of interviewers.* **7** stiff cardboard or similar material, used for the outside covers of a book. **8** a flat thin rectangular sheet of composite material, such as plasterboard or chipboard. **9** *Chiefly US.* **9a** a list of stock-exchange prices. **9b** *Inf.* the stock exchange itself. **10** *Naut.* the side of a ship. **11** *Austral. & NZ.* the part of the floor of a sheep-shearing shed where the shearers work. **12** any of various portable surfaces specially designed for indoor games such as chess, backgammon, etc. **13 go by the board.** *Inf.* to be in disuse, neglected, or lost: *in these days courtesy goes by the board.* **14 on board.** on or in a ship, boat, aeroplane, or other vehicle. **15 the boards.** the stage. ◆ *vb* **16** to go aboard (a vessel, train, aircraft, or other vehicle). **17** to attack (a ship) by forcing one's way aboard. **18** (*tr;* often foll. by *up, in,* etc.) to cover or shut with boards. **19** (*intr*) to receive meals or meals and lodging in return for money. **20** (sometimes foll. by *out*) to arrange for (someone, esp. a child) to receive food and lodging away from home. **21** (in ice hockey and box lacrosse) to bodycheck an opponent against the boards. ◆ See also **boards.** ORIG OE *bord*

boarder ('bɔːdə) *n* **1** a pupil who lives at school during term time. **2** another word for **lodger. 3** a person who boards a ship, esp. in an attack.

boarding ('bɔːdɪŋ) *n* **1** a structure of boards. **2** timber boards collectively. **3a** the act of embarking on an aircraft, train, ship, etc. **3b** (*as modifier*): *a boarding pass.* **4** (in ice hockey and box lacrosse) an act of bodychecking an opponent against the boards.

boarding house *n* a private house in which accommodation and meals are provided for paying guests.

boarding school *n* a school providing living accommodation for some or all of its pupils.

Board of Trade *n* (in Britain) a part of the Department of Trade and Industry responsible for the supervision of commerce and the promotion of export trade.

boardroom ('bɔːdˌruːm, -ˌrʊm) *n* a room where the board of directors of a company meets.

boards (bɔːdz) *pl n* a wooden wall about one metre high forming the enclosure in which ice hockey or box lacrosse is played.

board school *n* (formerly) a school managed by a board of local ratepayers.

boardwalk ('bɔːdˌwɔːk) *n US & Canad.* a promenade, esp. along a beach, usually made of planks.

boast (bəʊst) *vb* **1** (*intr;* sometimes foll. by *of* or *about*) to speak in excessively proud terms of one's possessions, skills, or superior qualities; brag. **2** (*tr*) to possess (something to be proud of): *the city boasts a fine cathedral.* ◆ *n* **3** a bragging statement. **4** a possession, attribute, etc., that is or may be bragged about. ORIG C13: from ?
▸ **'boaster** *n* ▸ **'boasting** *n, adj*

boastful ('bəʊstfʊl) *adj* tending to boast; characterized by boasting.
▸ **'boastfully** *adv* ▸ **'boastfulness** *n*

boat (bəʊt) *n* **1** a small vessel propelled by oars, paddle, sails, or motor. **2** (not in technical use) another word for **ship. 3** a container for gravy, sauce, etc. **4 burn one's boats.** See **burn**[1] (sense 13). **5 in the same boat.** sharing the same problems. **6 miss the boat.** to lose an opportunity. **7 rock the boat.** *Inf.* to cause a disturbance in the existing situation. ◆ *vb* **8** (*intr*) to travel or go in a boat, esp. as a form of recreation. **9** (*tr*) to transport or carry in a boat. ORIG OE *bāt*

boater ('bəʊtə) *n* a stiff straw hat with a straight brim and flat crown.

boathook ('bəʊtˌhʊk) *n* a pole with a hook at one end, used aboard a vessel for fending off other vessels or for catching a mooring buoy.

boathouse ('bəʊtˌhaʊs) *n* a shelter by the edge of a river, lake, etc., for housing boats.

boatie ('bəʊtɪ) *n Austral. & NZ inf.* a boating enthusiast.

boating ('bəʊtɪŋ) *n* rowing, sailing, or cruising in boats as a form of recreation.

boatload ('bəʊtˌləʊd) *n* the amount of cargo or number of people held by a boat or ship.

boatman ('bəʊtmən) *n, pl* **boatmen.** a man who works on, hires out, or repairs a boat or boats.

boatswain, bosun, *or* **bo's'n** ('bəʊsᵊn) *n* a petty officer or a warrant officer who is responsible for the maintenance of a ship and its equipment. ORIG OE *bātswegen;* see BOAT, SWAIN

boat train *n* a train scheduled to take passengers to or from a particular ship.

Boa Vista ★ (*Portuguese* 'boːə 'viʃtə) *n* a town in N Brazil, capital of the federal territory of Roraima, on the Rio Branco. Pop.: 118 928 (1991).

Boaz ★ ('bəʊæz) *n Old Testament.* a kinsman of Naomi, who married her daughter-in-law Ruth (Ruth 2–4); one of David's ancestors.

bob[1] (bɒb) *vb* **bobs, bobbing, bobbed. 1** to move or cause to move up and down repeatedly, as while floating in water. **2** to move or cause to move with a short abrupt movement, as of the head. **3** (*intr;* usually foll. by *up*) to appear or emerge suddenly. **4** (*intr;* usually foll. by *for*) to attempt to get hold (of a floating or hanging object, esp. an apple) in the teeth as a game. ◆ *n* **5** a short abrupt movement, as of the head. ORIG C14: from ?

bob[2] (bɒb) *n* **1** a hairstyle for women and children in which the hair is cut short evenly all round the head. **2** a dangling or hanging object, such as the weight on a pendulum or on a plumb line. **3** short for **bobsleigh. 4** a docked tail, esp. of a horse. ◆ *vb* **bobs, bobbing, bobbed. 5** (*tr*) to cut (the hair) in a bob. **6** (*tr*) to cut short (something, esp. the tail of an animal); dock or crop. **7** (*intr*) to ride on a bobsleigh. ORIG C14 *bobbe* bunch of flowers

bob[3] (bɒb) *n, pl* **bob.** *Brit.* (formerly) an informal word for a **shilling.** ORIG C19: from ?

bobbejaan ('bɒbəˌjɑːn) *n S. African.* **1** a baboon. **2** a large black spider. **3** a monkey wrench. ORIG from Afrik., from MDu. *babiaen*

bobbin ('bɒbɪn) *n* a spool or reel on which thread or yarn is wound. ORIG C16: from OF *bobine,* from ?

bobble ('bɒbᵊl) *n* **1** a short jerky motion, as of a cork floating on disturbed water; bobbing movement. **2** a tufted ball, usually for ornament, as on a knitted hat. ◆ *vb* **3** (*intr*) *Sport.* (of a ball) to bounce with a rapid, erratic motion due to an uneven playing surface. ORIG C19: from BOB[1] (vb)

bobby ('bɒbɪ) *n, pl* **bobbies.** *Inf.* a British policeman. ORIG C19: from *Bobby,* after *Robert* PEEL, who set up the Metropolitan Police Force in 1828

bobby calf *n* an unweaned calf culled for slaughter.

bobby-dazzler *n Dialect.* anything outstanding, striking, or showy. ORIG C19: expanded from *dazzler* something striking or attractive

bobby pin *n US, Canad., Austral., & NZ.* a metal hairpin bent in order to hold the hair in place.

bobby socks *pl n* ankle-length socks worn by teenage girls, esp. in the US in the 1940s.

bobcat ('bɒbˌkæt) *n* a North American feline mammal, closely related to but smaller than the lynx, having reddish-brown fur with dark spots or stripes, tufted ears, and a short tail. Also called: **bay lynx.** ORIG C19: from BOB[2] + CAT[1]

Bobo-Dioulasso ★ ('bəʊbəʊdjuː'læsəʊ) *n* a city in W Burkina-Faso. Pop.: 300 000 (1993 est.).

bobolink ('bɒbəˌlɪŋk) *n* an American songbird, the male of which has a white back and black underparts. ORIG C18: imit.

bobotie (bʊ'bʊtɪ) *n* a South African dish consisting of curried mincemeat with a topping of beaten egg baked to a crust. ORIG C19: from Afrik., prob. from Malay

Bobruisk *or* **Bobruysk** ★ (*Russian* ba'brujsk) *n* a port in Belarus on the River Berezina: engineering, timber, tyre manufacturing. Pop.: 227 100 (1996 est.).

bobsleigh ('bɒbˌsleɪ) *n* **1** a racing sledge for two or more people, with a steering mechanism enabling the driver to direct it down a steeply banked ice-covered run. ◆ *vb* **2** (*intr*) to ride on a bobsleigh. ◆ Also called (esp. US and Canad.): **bobsled** ('bɒbˌslɛd). ORIG C19: BOB[2] + SLEIGH

bobstay ('bɒbˌsteɪ) *n* a strong stay between a bowsprit and the stem of a vessel for holding down the bowsprit. ORIG C18: ?from BOB[1] + STAY[3]

bobsy-die ('bɒbzɪˌdaɪ) *n NZ inf.* fuss; confusion (esp. in **kick up bobsy-die**). ORIG from C19 *Bob's a-dying*

bobtail ('bɒbˌteɪl) *n* **1** a docked or diminutive tail. **2** an animal with such a tail. ◆ *adj also* **bobtailed. 3** having the tail cut short. ◆ *vb* (*tr*) **4** to dock the tail of. **5** to cut short; curtail.

Boccaccio ★ (*Italian* bok'kattʃo) *n* **Giovanni** (dʒo'vani). 1313–75, Italian poet and writer, noted for his *Decameron* (1349–51), a collection of 100 short stories.

Boccherini ★ (*Italian* bokke'rini) *n* **Luigi** (lu'idʒi). 1743–1805, Italian composer and cellist.

Boche (bɒʃ) *n Derog. sl.* (esp. in World Wars I and II) **1** a German, esp. a German soldier. **2 the.** (*usually functioning as pl*) Germans collectively, esp. German soldiers regarded as the enemy. ORIG C20: from F, prob. shortened from *alboche* German, from *allemand* German + *caboche* pate

Bochum ★ (*German* 'boːxum) *n* an industrial city in NW Germany, in W North Rhine-Westphalia: university (1965). Pop.: 400 395 (1996 est.).

bockedy ('bɒkədɪ) *adj Irish.* (of a structure, piece of furniture, etc.) unsteady. ORIG from Irish Gaelic *bacaideach* limping

bod (bɒd) *n Inf.* **1** a fellow; chap: *he's a queer bod.* **2** another word for **body** (sense 1). ORIG C18: short for BODY

BOD *abbrev. for:* biochemical oxygen demand.

bodacious (bəʊ'deɪʃəs) *adj Sl., chiefly US.* impressive or remarkable; excellent. ORIG C19: from E dialect; blend of BOLD and AUDACIOUS

bode[1] (bəʊd) *vb* **bodes, boding, boded. 1** to be an omen of (good or ill, esp. of ill); portend; presage. **2** (*tr*) *Arch.* to predict; foretell. ORIG OE *bodian*
▸ **'bodement** *n*

bode[2] (bəʊd) *vb* a past tense of **bide.**

bodega (bəʊ'diːgə) *n* a shop selling wine and sometimes groceries, esp. in a Spanish-speaking country. ORIG C19: from Sp., ult. from Gk *apothēkē* storehouse

Bodensee ★ ('boːdənzeː) *n* the German name for (Lake) **Constance.**

★ people and places

bodge (bɒdʒ) *vb* **bodges, bodging, bodged.** *Inf.* to make a mess of; botch. ORIG C16: changed from BOTCH

bodgie ('bɒdʒɪ) *Austral. & NZ sl.* ◆ *n* **1** an unruly or uncouth young man, esp. in the 1950s. ◆ *adj* **2** false, fraudulent. ORIG C20: from BODGE

Bodh Gaya ★ ('bɒd gə'jɑː) *n* a variant spelling of **Buddh Gaya.**

Bodhidharma ★ (ˌbəʊdɪ'dɑːmə, ˌbɒd-) *n* 6th century A.D., Indian Buddhist monk, who taught in China (from 520): considered to be the founder of Zen Buddhism.

Bodhisattva (ˌbəʊdɪ'sætvə, -wə, ˌbɒd-) *n* (in Buddhism) a divine being worthy of nirvana who remains on the human plane to help men to salvation. ORIG Sansk., from *bodhi* enlightenment + *sattva* essence

bodice ('bɒdɪs) *n* **1** the upper part of a woman's dress, from the shoulder to the waist. **2** a tight-fitting corset worn laced over a blouse, or (formerly) as a woman's undergarment. ORIG C16: orig. Scot. *bodies,* pl. of BODY

bodice ripper *n Inf.* a romantic novel, usually on a historical theme, that involves some sex and violence.

-bodied *adj* (*in combination*) having a body or bodies as specified: *able-bodied; long-bodied.*

bodiless ('bɒdɪlɪs) *adj* having no body or substance.

bodily ('bɒdɪlɪ) *adj* **1** relating to or being a part of the human body. ◆ *adv* **2** by taking hold of the body: *he threw him bodily from the platform.* **3** in person; in the flesh.

bodkin ('bɒdkɪn) *n* **1** a blunt large-eyed needle. **2** *Arch.* a dagger. **3** *Arch.* a long ornamental hairpin. ORIG C14: prob. of Celtic origin

Bodmin ★ ('bɒdmɪn) *n* a market town in SW England, in Cornwall, near **Bodmin Moor,** a granite upland rising to 420 m (1375 ft). Pop.: 12 553 (1991).

body ('bɒdɪ) *n, pl* **bodies. 1a** the entire physical structure of an animal or human being. Related adj: **corporeal. 1b** (*as modifier*): *body odour.* **2** the trunk or torso. **3** a dead human or animal; corpse. **4** the flesh as opposed to the spirit. **5** the largest or main part of anything: *the body of a vehicle; the body of a plant.* **6** a separate or distinct mass of water or land. **7** a number of individuals regarded as a single entity; group. **8** fullness in the appearance of the hair. **9** the characteristic full quality of certain wines. **10** firmness, esp. of cloth. **11a** the pigment contained in or added to paint, dye, etc. **11b** the opacity of a paint. **11c** (*as modifier*): *body colour.* **12** an informal or dialect word for a **person. 13** another word for **bodysuit** (sense 1). **14 keep body and soul together.** to manage to keep alive; survive. ◆ *vb* **bodies, bodying, bodied.** (*tr*) **15** (usually foll. by *forth*) to give a body or shape to. ORIG OE *bodig*

body blow *n* **1** *Boxing.* a blow to an opponent's body. **2** a severe disappointment or setback.

body board *n Austral. & NZ.* a short surfboard made of polystyrene.

body building *n* the practice of exercises to make the muscles of the body conspicuous.

bodycheck ('bɒdɪˌtʃɛk) *Ice hockey, etc.* ◆ *n* **1** obstruction of another player. ◆ *vb* **2** (*tr*) to deliver a bodycheck to (an opponent).

body double *n Films.* a person who substitutes for a star for the filming of a scene that involves shots of the body rather than the face.

body dysmorphic disorder *n* a psychological disorder characterized by a strong feeling that one's appearance or health would be improved by the removal of a healthy body part.

bodyguard ('bɒdɪˌgɑːd) *n* a person or group of people who escort and protect someone.

body horror *n* a genre of horror film in which the main feature is the graphically depicted destruction or degeneration of a human body or bodies.

body language *n* the nonverbal imparting of information by means of conscious or subconscious bodily gestures, posture, etc.

body-line *adj Cricket.* denoting or relating to fast bowling aimed at the batsman's body.

body politic *n* **the.** the people of a nation or the nation itself considered as a political entity.

body search *n* **1** a form of search by police, customs officials, etc., that involves examination of a prisoner's or suspect's bodily orifices. ◆ *vb* **body-search. 2** (*tr*) to search (a prisoner or suspect) in this manner.

body shop *n* a repair yard for vehicle bodywork.

body snatcher *n* (formerly) a person who robbed graves and sold the corpses for dissection.

body stocking *n* a one-piece undergarment for women, usually of nylon, covering the torso.

bodysuit ('bɒdɪˌsuːt, -ˌsjuːt) *n* **1** a woman's close-fitting one-piece garment for the torso. Sometimes shortened to **body. 2** a one-piece undergarment for a baby.

body swerve *n* **1** *Sport.* (esp. in football games) the act or an instance of swerving past an opponent. **2** *Scot.* the act or an instance of avoiding (a situation considered unpleasant): *I think I'll give the meeting a body swerve.* ◆ *vb* **body-swerve, body-swerves, body-swerving, body-swerved. 3** *Sport.* (esp. in football games) to pass (an opponent) using a body swerve. **4** *Scot.* to avoid (a situation or person considered unpleasant).

body warmer *n* a sleeveless type of jerkin, usually quilted, worn as an outer garment.

bodywork ('bɒdɪˌwɜːk) *n* the external shell of a motor vehicle.

Boeotia ★ (bɪ'əʊʃɪə) *n* **1** a region of ancient Greece, northwest of Athens. It consisted of ten city-states, which formed the Boeotian League, led by Thebes: at its height in the 4th century B.C. **2** transliteration of the Modern Greek name for **Voiotia.**

Boeotian (bɪ'əʊʃɪən) *adj* **1** of Boeotia. **2** dull or stupid. ◆ *n* **3** a person from Boeotia. **4** a dull or stupid person.

Boer (bʊə) *n* **a** a descendant of any of the Dutch or Huguenot colonists who settled in South Africa. **b** (*as modifier*): *a Boer farmer.* ORIG C19: from Du. *Boer;* see BOOR

boerbul ('bʊəbəl) *n S. African.* a crossbred mastiff used esp. as a watchdog. ORIG from Afrik. *boerboel,* from *boel* large dog

boeremusiek ('bʊərəˌmœsɪk) *n S. African.* light music associated with the culture of the Afrikaners. ORIG from Afrik. *boere* country, folk + *musiek* music

boet (bʊt) *or* **boetie** *n S. African inf.* a friend. ORIG from Afrik.: brother

Boethius ★ (bəʊ'iːθɪəs) *n* **Anicius Manlius Severinus** (ə'nɪsɪəs 'mænlɪəs ˌsɛvə'raɪnəs). ?480–?524 A.D., Roman philosopher and statesman, noted for *De Consolatione Philosophiae*: executed by Theodoric for treason.

boffin ('bɒfɪn) *n Brit. inf.* **1** a scientist, esp. one carrying out military research. **2** a person who has extensive knowledge in a particular field. ORIG C20: from ?

boffo ('bɒfəʊ) *adj Sl.* very good; highly successful. ORIG C20: from ?

Bofors gun ('bəʊfəz) *n* an automatic 40 mm anti-aircraft gun, one or more of which are controlled by a radar-operated computer system mounted on a light-weight vehicle. ORIG C20: after the Swedish armament firm that developed it

bog (bɒg) *n* **1** wet spongy ground consisting of decomposing vegetation. **2** an area of such ground. **3** a slang word for **lavatory.** ORIG C13: from Gaelic *bogach* swamp, from *bog* soft
▸ **'boggy** *adj* ▸ **'bogginess** *n*

bogan[1] ('bəʊgən) *n Canad.* (esp. in the Maritime Provinces) a sluggish side stream. Also called: **logan, pokelogan.** ORIG of Algonquian origin

bogan[2] ('bəʊgən) *n Austral. & NZ inf.* a young person who behaves rebelliously. ORIG C20: from ?

Bogarde ★ ('bəʊgɑːd) *n* **Dirk,** real name *Derek Jules Gaspard Ulric Niven van den Bogaerde.* 1920–99, British film actor and writer: his films include *The Servant* (1963) and *Death in Venice* (1970). His writings include the autobiographical *A Postillion Struck by Lightning* (1977) and the novels *Jericho* (1992) and *A Period of Adjustment* (1994).

Bogart ★ ('bəʊgɑːt) *n* **Humphrey (DeForest).** nicknamed *Bogie.* 1899–1957, US film actor: his films include *High Sierra* (1941), *Casablanca* (1942), and *The Caine Mutiny* (1954).

Boğazköy ★ (*Turkish* bɔːˈɑzkœi) *n* a village in central Asia Minor: site of the ancient Hittite capital.

bogbean (ˈbɒɡˌbiːn) *n* another name for **buckbean.**

bog down *vb* **bogs, bogging, bogged.** (*adv; when tr, often passive*) to impede or be impeded physically or mentally.

bogey *or* **bogy** (ˈbəʊɡɪ) *n* **1** an evil or mischievous spirit. **2** something that worries or annoys. **3** *Golf.* **3a** a score of one stroke over par on a hole. Cf. **par** (sense 5). **3b** *Obs.* a standard score for a hole or course, regarded as one that a good player should make. **4** *Sl.* a piece of dried mucus discharged from the nose. ORIG C19: prob. rel. to obs. *bug* an evil spirit and BOGLE

bogeyman (ˈbəʊɡɪˌmæn) *n, pl* **bogeymen.** a person, real or imaginary, used as a threat, esp. to children.

boggle (ˈbɒɡᵊl) *vb* **boggles, boggling, boggled.** (*intr;* often foll. by *at*) **1** to be surprised, confused, or alarmed (esp. in **the mind boggles**). **2** to hesitate or be evasive when confronted with a problem. ORIG C16: prob. var. of BOGLE

bogie *or* **bogy** (ˈbəʊɡɪ) *n* **1** an assembly of four or six wheels forming a pivoted support at either end of a railway coach. **2** *Chiefly Brit.* a small railway truck of short wheelbase, used for conveying coal, ores, etc. ORIG C19: from ?

bogle (ˈbəʊɡᵊl, ˈbɒɡ-) *n* a dialect or archaic word for **bogey** (sense 1). ORIG C16: from Scot. *bogill*

bog myrtle *n* another name for **sweet gale.**

Bognor Regis ★ (ˈbɒɡnə ˈriːdʒɪs) *n* a resort in S England, in West Sussex on the English Channel: electronics industries. *Regis* was added to the name after King George V's convalescence there in 1929. Pop.: 56 744 (1991).

bog oak *n* oak found preserved in peat bogs.

bog off *Brit. sl.* ◆ *interj* **1** go away! ◆ *vb* **bogs, bogging, bogged. 2** (*intr, adv*) to go away.

bogong (ˈbəʊˌɡɒŋ) *or* **bugong** (ˈbuːˌɡɒŋ) *n* an edible dark-coloured Australian noctuid moth.

Bogor ★ (ˈbəʊɡɔː) *n* a city in Indonesia, in W Java: botanical gardens and research institutions. Pop.: 285 000 (1995 est.). Former name: **Buitenzorg.**

Bogotá ★ (ˌbəʊɡəˈtɑː; *Spanish* boɣoˈta) *n* the capital of Colombia, on a central plateau of the E Andes: originally the centre of Chibcha civilization; founded as a city in 1538 by the Spaniards. Pop.: 5 237 635 (1995 est.).

bog-standard *adj Brit. & Irish sl.* completely ordinary; run-of-the-mill.

bogtrotter (ˈbɒɡˌtrɒtə) *n* a derogatory term for an Irishman, esp. an Irish peasant.

bogus (ˈbəʊɡəs) *adj* spurious or counterfeit; not genuine. ORIG C19: from *bogus* apparatus for making counterfeit money
▸ **ˈbogusly** *adv* ▸ **ˈbogusness** *n*

bogy (ˈbəʊɡɪ) *n, pl* **bogies.** a variant spelling of **bogey** or **bogie.**

Bohai (ˈbɔːˈhaɪ) *or* **Pohai** ★ *n* a large inlet of the Yellow Sea on the coast of NE China. Also called: (Gulf of) **Chihli.**

bohea (bəʊˈhiː) *n* a black Chinese tea, once regarded as the choicest, but now as an inferior grade. ORIG C18: from Chinese *Wu-i Shan,* range of hills on which this tea was grown

Bohemia ★ (bəʊˈhiːmɪə) *n* **1** a former kingdom of central Europe, surrounded by mountains: independent from the 9th to the 13th century; belonged to the Hapsburgs from 1526 until 1918. **2** an area of the W Czech Republic, formerly a province (1918–49) of Czechoslovakia. From 1939 until 1945 it formed part of the German protectorate of **Bohemia-Moravia.** Czech name: **Čechy.** German name: **Böhmen** (ˈbøːmən). **3** a district frequented by unconventional people, esp. artists or writers.

Bohemian (bəʊˈhiːmɪən) *n* **1** a native or inhabitant of Bohemia; a Czech. **2** (*often not cap.*) a person, esp. an artist or writer, who lives an unconventional life. **3** the Czech language. ◆ *adj* **4** of, relating to, or characteristic of Bohemia, its people, or their language. **5** (*often not cap.*) unconventional in appearance, behaviour, etc.

Bohemian Forest ★ *n* a mountain range between the SW Czech Republic and SE Germany. Highest peak: Arber, 1457 m (4780 ft). Czech name: **Český Les** (ˈtʃɛskiː ˈlɛs). German name: **Böhmerwald** (ˈbøːmərˈvalt).

Bohemianism (bəʊˈhiːmɪəˌnɪzəm) *n* unconventional behaviour or appearance, esp. of an artist.

Böhm ★ (*German* bøːm) *n* **Karl** (karl). 1894–1981, Austrian orchestral conductor.

boho (ˈbəʊhəʊ) *n, pl* **bohos,** *adj* short for **Bohemian** (senses 2, 5).

Bohol ★ (bəʊˈhɔːl) *n* an island of the central Philippines. Chief town: Tagbilaran. Pop.: 948 000 (1990). Area: about 3900 sq. km (1500 sq. miles).

Bohr ★ (bɔː; *Danish* boːr) *n* **1 Aage Niels** (ˈɔːɣə neːls). born 1922, Danish physicist, noted for his work on nuclear structure: shared the Nobel prize for physics 1975. **2** his father, **Niels** (**Henrik David**) (neːls). 1885–1962, Danish physicist, who applied the quantum theory to Rutherford's model of the atom: Nobel prize for physics 1922.

bohrium (ˈbɔːrɪəm) *n* a transuranic element artificially produced in minute quantities by bombarding ^{204}Bi atoms with ^{54}Cr nuclei. Symbol: Bh; atomic no.: 107. Former names: **element 107, unnilheptium.** ORIG C20: after N. BOHR

boil¹ (bɔɪl) *vb* **1** to change or cause to change from a liquid to a vapour so rapidly that bubbles of vapour are formed in the liquid. **2** to reach or cause to reach boiling point. **3** to cook or be cooked by the process of boiling. **4** (*intr*) to bubble and be agitated like something boiling; seethe: *the ocean was boiling.* **5** (*intr*) to be extremely angry or indignant. ◆ *n* **6** the state or action of boiling. ◆ See also **boil away, boil down, boil over.** ORIG C13: from OF, from L, from *bulla* a bubble

boil² (bɔɪl) *n* a red painful swelling with a hard pus-filled core caused by bacterial infection of the skin. Technical name: **furuncle.** ORIG OE *bȳle*

boil away *vb* (*adv*) to cause (liquid) to evaporate completely by boiling or (of liquid) to evaporate completely.

boil down *vb* (*adv*) **1** to reduce or be reduced in quantity by boiling. **2 boil down to. 2a** (*intr*) to be the essential element in something. **2b** (*tr*) to summarize; reduce to essentials.

Boileau ★ (*French* bwalo) *n* **Nicolas** (nikɔlɑ). full name *Nicolas Boileau-Despréaux.* 1636–1711, French poet; author of *L'Art poétique* (1674).

boiled shirt *n Inf.* a dress shirt with a stiff front.

boiler (ˈbɔɪlə) *n* **1** a closed vessel in which water is heated to supply steam or provide heat. **2** a domestic device to provide hot water, esp. for central heating. **3** a large tub for boiling laundry.

boilermaker (ˈbɔɪləˌmeɪkə) *n* a person who works with metal in heavy industry; plater or welder.

boilerplate (ˈbɔɪləˌpleɪt) *n* **1** a form of mild-steel plate used in the production of boiler shells. **2** a copy made with the intention of making other copies from it. **3** a set of instructions incorporated in several places in a computer program or a standard form of words used repeatedly in drafting contracts, guarantees, etc. **4** a draft contract that can be modified to cover various types of transaction.

boiler suit *n Brit.* a one-piece overall work garment.

boiling point *n* **1** the temperature at which a liquid boils at sea level. **2** *Inf.* the condition of being angered or highly excited.

boiling-water reactor *n* a nuclear reactor using water as coolant and moderator, steam being produced in the reactor itself. Abbrev.: **BWR.**

boil over *vb* (*adv*) **1** to overflow or cause to overflow while boiling. **2** (*intr*) to burst out in anger or excitement.

Bois de Boulogne ★ (*French* bwa də bulɔɲ) *n* a large park in W Paris, formerly a forest: includes the racecourses of Auteuil and Longchamp.

Boise *or* **Boise City** ★ (ˈbɔɪzɪ, -sɪ) *n* a city in SW Idaho: the state capital. Pop.: 145 987 (1994 est.).

Bois-le-Duc ★ (bwa lə dyk) *n* the French name for **'s Hertogenbosch.**

boisterous ('bɔɪstərəs, -strəs) *adj* **1** noisy and lively; unruly. **2** (of the wind, sea, etc.) stormy. ORIG C13 *boistuous,* from ?
▸ **'boisterously** *adv* ▸ **'boisterousness** *n*

Boito ★ (*Italian* 'bɔːito) *n* **Arrigo** (ar'rigo). 1842–1918, Italian composer and librettist, whose works include the opera *Mefistofele* (1868) and the librettos for Verdi's *Otello* and *Falstaff.*

Bokassa I ★ (bə'kæsə) *n* original name *Jean Bedel Bokassa.* 1921–96, president of the Central African Republic (1972–76); emperor of the renamed Central African Empire from 1976 until overthrown in 1979.

bok choy ('bɒk 'tʃɔɪ) *n* a Chinese plant that is related to the cabbage and has edible stalks and leaves. Also called: **Chinese cabbage, Chinese leaf.** ORIG from Chinese dialect, lit.: white vegetable

Bokhara ★ (bʊ'xɑːrə) *n* a variant spelling of **Bukhara.**

Bol. *abbrev. for* Bolivia(n).

bola ('bəʊlə) *or* **bolas** ('bəʊləs) *n, pl* **bolas** *or* **bolases.** a missile used by gauchos and Indians of South America, consisting of heavy balls on a cord. It is hurled at a running quarry, so as to entangle its legs. ORIG Sp.: ball, from L *bulla* knob

Boland ★ ('bʊəlant) *n* an area of high altitude in SW South Africa.

Bolan Pass ★ (bəʊ'lɑːn) *n* a mountain pass in W central Pakistan through the Brahui Range, between Sibi and Quetta, rising to 1800 m (5900 ft).

bold (bəʊld) *adj* **1** courageous, confident, and fearless; ready to take risks. **2** showing or requiring courage: *a bold plan.* **3** immodest or impudent: *she gave him a bold look.* **4** standing out distinctly; conspicuous: *a figure carved in bold relief.* **5** very steep: *the bold face of the cliff.* **6** imaginative in thought or expression. ORIG OE *beald*
▸ **'boldly** *adv* ▸ **'boldness** *n*

bold face *Printing.* ◆ *n* **1** a weight of type characterized by thick heavy lines, as the entry words in this dictionary. ◆ *adj* **boldface. 2** (of type) having this weight.

Boldrewood ★ ('bəʊldəˌwʊd) *n* **Rolf,** real name *Thomas Alexander Browne.* 1826–1915, noted for his novels of the Australian outback, esp. *Robbery Under Arms* (1882–3).

bole (bəʊl) *n* the trunk of a tree. ORIG C14: from ON *bolr*

bolero (bə'lɛərəʊ) *n, pl* **boleros. 1** a Spanish dance, usually in triple time. **2** a piece of music for or in the rhythm of this dance. **3** (*also* 'bɒlərəʊ). a short open bodice-like jacket not reaching the waist. ORIG C18: from Sp.

Boleyn ★ (bə'lɪn, 'bʊlɪn) *n* **Anne.** 1507–36, second wife of Henry VIII of England; mother of Elizabeth I. She was executed on a charge of adultery.

Bolingbroke ★ ('bɒlɪŋˌbrʊk) *n* **1** the surname of **Henry IV** of England. **2 Henry St John,** 1st Viscount Bolingbroke. 1678–1751, English politician; fled to France in 1714 and acted as secretary of state to the Old Pretender; returned to England in 1723.

Bolivar ★ ('bɒlɪˌvɑː; *Spanish* bo'liβar) *n* **Simon** (si'mon). 1783–1830, South American soldier, who drove the Spaniards from Venezuela, Colombia, Ecuador, and Peru hoping to set up a republican confederation, but was prevented by separatist movements in Venezuela and Colombia (1829–30). Upper Peru became a separate state, called Bolivia in his honour.

Bolivia ★ (bə'lɪvɪə) *n* an inland republic in central S America: original Aymará Indian population conquered by the Incas in the 13th century; colonized by Spain from 1538; became a republic in 1825; consists of low plains in the east, with ranges of the Andes rising to over 6400 m (21 000 ft) and the Altiplano, a plateau averaging 3900 m (13 000 ft) in the west; contains some of the world's highest inhabited regions; important producer of tin and other minerals. Official languages: Spanish, Quechua, and Aymara. Religion: Roman Catholic. Currency: boliviano. Capital: La Paz (administrative); Sucre (judicial). Pop.: 8 137 000 (1999 est.). Area: 1 098 580 sq. km (424 260 sq. miles).
▸ **Bo'livian** *adj, n*

boliviano (bəˌlɪvɪ'ɑːnəʊ; *Spanish* boli'βjano) **bolivianos** (-nəʊz; *Spanish* -nos). (until 1963 and from 1987) the standard monetary unit of Bolivia, equal to 100 centavos.

boll (bəʊl) *n* the fruit of such plants as flax and cotton, consisting of a rounded capsule containing the seeds. ORIG C13: from Du. *bolle;* rel. to OE *bolla* BOWL[1]

bollard ('bɒlɑːd, 'bɒləd) *n* **1** a strong wooden or metal post on a wharf, quay, etc., used for securing mooring lines. **2** *Brit.* a small post placed on a kerb or traffic island to make it conspicuous to motorists. ORIG C14: ?from BOLE + -ARD

bollocking ('bɒləkɪŋ) *n Sl.* a severe telling-off. ORIG from *bollock* (vb) in the sense "to reprimand"

bollocks ('bɒləks) *or* **ballocks** *Taboo sl.* ◆ *pl n* **1** another word for **testicles. 2** nonsense; rubbish. ◆ *interj* **3** an exclamation of annoyance, disbelief, etc. ORIG OE *beallucas;* see BALL[1]

boll weevil *n* a greyish weevil of the southern US and Mexico, whose larvae live in and destroy cotton bolls.

Bollywood ('bɒlɪˌwʊd) *n Inf.* **a** the Indian film industry. **b** (*as modifier*): *a Bollywood star.* ORIG C20: from BO(MBAY) + (HO)LLYWOOD

Bologna[1] ★ (bə'ləʊnjə; *Italian* bo'loɲɲa) *n* a city in N Italy, at the foot of the Apennines: became a free city in the Middle Ages; university (1088). Pop.: 386 491 (1996 est.). Ancient name: **Bononia** (bə'nəʊnɪə).
▸ **Bolognese** (ˌbɒlə'niːz, -'neɪz) *adj, n*

Bologna[2] ★ (bə'ləʊnjə; *Italian* bo'loɲɲa) *n* **Giovanni da** (dʒo'vanni da). See **Giambologna.**

bologna sausage (bə'ləʊnjə) *n Chiefly US & Canad.* a large smoked sausage made of seasoned mixed meats. Also called: **baloney, boloney,** (esp. Brit.) **polony.**

bolometer (bəʊ'lɒmɪtə) *n* a sensitive instrument for measuring radiant energy. ORIG C19: from Gk *bolē* ray of light, from *ballein* to throw + -METER
▸ **bolometric** (ˌbəʊlə'mɛtrɪk) *adj*

boloney (bə'ləʊnɪ) *n* **1** a variant of **baloney. 2** another name for **bologna sausage.**

Bolshevik ('bɒlʃɪvɪk) *n, pl* **Bolsheviks** *or* **Bolsheviki** (ˌbɒlʃɪ'viːkɪ). **1** (formerly) a Russian Communist. Cf. **Menshevik. 2** any Communist. **3** (*often not cap.*) *Inf. & derog.* any political radical, esp. a revolutionary. ORIG C20: from Russian *Bol'shevik* majority, from *bol'shoi* great
▸ **'Bolsheˌvism** *n* ▸ **'Bolshevist** *adj, n*

bolshie *or* **bolshy** ('bɒlʃɪ) (*sometimes cap.*) *Brit. inf.* ◆ *adj* **1** difficult to manage; rebellious. **2** politically radical or left-wing. ◆ *n, pl* **bolshies. 3** *Derog.* any political radical. ORIG C20: shortened from BOLSHEVIK

bolster ('bəʊlstə) *vb* (*tr*) **1** (often foll. by *up*) to support or reinforce; strengthen: *to bolster morale.* **2** to prop up with a pillow or cushion. ◆ *n* **3** a long narrow pillow or cushion. **4** any pad or padded support. **5** a cold chisel used for cutting stone slabs, etc. ORIG OE *bolster*

bolt[1] (bəʊlt) *n* **1** a bar that can be slid into a socket to lock a door, gate, etc. **2** a bar or rod that forms part of a locking mechanism and is moved by a key or a knob. **3** a metal rod or pin that has a head and a screw thread to take a nut. **4** a sliding bar in a breech-loading firearm that ejects the empty cartridge, replaces it with a new one, and closes the breech. **5** a flash of lightning. **6** a sudden start or movement, esp. in order to escape. **7** a roll of something, such as cloth, wallpaper, etc. **8** an arrow, esp. for a crossbow. **9 a bolt from the blue.** a sudden, unexpected, and usually unwelcome event. **10 shoot one's bolt.** to exhaust one's efforts. ◆ *vb* **11** (*tr*) to secure or lock with or as with a bolt. **12** (*tr*) to eat hurriedly. **13** (*intr;* usually foll. by *from* or *out*) to move or jump suddenly: *he bolted from the chair.* **14** (*intr*) (esp. of a horse) to start hurriedly and run away without warning. **15** (*tr*) to roll (cloth, wallpaper, etc.) into bolts. **16** (*intr*) (of cultivated plants) to produce flowers and seeds prematurely. ◆ *adv* **17** stiffly, firmly, or rigidly (archaic except in **bolt upright**). ORIG OE *bolt* arrow
▸ **'bolter** *n*

bolt[2] *or* **boult** (bəʊlt) *vb* (*tr*) **1** to pass (a powder, etc.) through a sieve. **2** to examine and separate. ORIG C13: from OF *bulter,* prob. of Gmc origin
▸ **'bolter** *or* **'boulter** *n*

Bolt ★ (bəʊlt) *n* **Robert (Oxton)**. 1924–95, British playwright. His plays include *A Man for All Seasons* (1960) and he wrote a number of screenplays.

bolt hole *n* a place of escape from danger.

Bolton ★ ('bəʊltən) *n* **1** a town in NW England: centre of the woollen trade since the 14th century; later important for cotton. Pop.: 139 020 (1991). **2** a unitary authority in NW England, in Greater Manchester. Pop.: 258 584 (1999 est.). Area: 140 sq. km (54 sq. miles).

boltrope ('bəʊlt,rəʊp) *n Naut.* a rope sewn to the foot or luff of a sail to strengthen it.

Boltzmann ★ (*German* 'bɔltsman) *n* **Ludwig** ('lu:tvɪç). 1844–1906, Austrian physicist. He developed the kinetic theory of gases with J. C. Maxwell.

bolus ('bəʊləs) *n, pl* **boluses. 1** a small round soft mass, esp. of chewed food. **2** a large pill or tablet used in veterinary and clinical medicine. ORIG C17: from NL, from Gk *bōlos* clod, lump

Bolzano ★ (*Italian* bol'tsa:no) *n* a city in NE Italy, in Trentino-Alto Adige: belonged to Austria until 1919. Pop.: 100 380 (1990). German name: **Bozen.**

Boma ★ ('bəʊmə) *n* a port in the Democratic Republic of Congo (formerly Zaïre), capital (of the Belgian Congo) until 1926: forest products. Pop.: 135 284 (1994 est.).

bomb (bɒm) *n* **1a** a hollow projectile containing explosive, incendiary, or other destructive substance. **1b** (*as modifier*): *bomb disposal; a bomb bay.* **1c** (*in combination*): *bombproof.* **2** an object in which an explosive device has been planted: *a car bomb; a letter bomb.* **3** a round mass of volcanic rock, solidified from molten lava that has been thrown into the air. **4** *Med.* a container for radioactive material, applied therapeutically to any part of the body: *a cobalt bomb.* **5** *Brit. sl.* a large sum of money. **6** *US & Canad. sl.* a disastrous failure: *the new play was a total bomb.* **7** *Austral. & NZ sl.* an old or dilapidated motorcar. **8** *American football.* a very long high pass. **9** (in rugby union) another name for **up-and-under. 10 like a bomb.** *Brit. & NZ inf.* with great speed or success; very well. **11 the bomb.** a hydrogen or an atomic bomb considered as the ultimate destructive weapon. ◆ *vb* **12** to attack with or as if with a bomb or bombs; drop bombs (on). **13** (*intr; often foll. by off, along,* etc.) *Inf.* to move or drive very quickly. **14** (*intr*) *US sl.* to fail disastrously. ORIG C17: from F, from It., from L, from Gk *bombos,* imit.

bombard *vb* (bɒm'bɑ:d). (*tr*) **1** to attack with concentrated artillery fire or bombs. **2** to attack with vigour and persistence. **3** to attack verbally, esp. with questions. **4** *Physics.* to direct high-energy particles or photons against (atoms, nuclei, etc.). ◆ *n* ('bɒmbɑ:d). **5** an ancient type of cannon that threw stone balls. ORIG C15: from OF, from *bombarde* stone-throwing cannon, prob. from L *bombus* booming sound; see BOMB
▸ **bom'bardment** *n*

bombardier (,bɒmbə'dɪə) *n* **1** the member of a bomber aircrew responsible for aiming and releasing the bombs. **2** *Brit.* a noncommissioned rank, below the rank of sergeant, in the Royal Artillery. ORIG C16: from OF; see BOMBARD

Bombardier (,bɒmbə'dɪə) *n Canad. trademark.* a snow tractor, usually having caterpillar tracks at the rear and skis at the front. ORIG C20: after J. A. *Bombardier,* Canadian inventor and manufacturer

bombast ('bɒmbæst) *n* pompous and grandiloquent language. ORIG C16: from OF, from Med. L *bombāx* cotton
▸ **bom'bastic** *adj* ▸ **bom'bastically** *adv*

Bombay ★ (bɒm'beɪ) *n* a port in W India, capital of Maharashtra state, on the Arabian Sea: ceded by Portugal to England in 1661 and of major importance in British India; commercial and industrial centre, esp. for cotton. Pop.: 9 925 891 (1991). Official and Hindi name: **Mumbai.**

Bombay duck *n* a fish that is eaten dried with curry dishes as a savoury. Also called: **bummalo.** ORIG C19: changed from *bombil* through association with Bombay, from which it was exported

bombazine *or* **bombasine** (,bɒmbə'zi:n, 'bɒmbə,zi:n) *n* a twilled fabric, esp. one of silk and worsted, formerly worn dyed black for mourning. ORIG C16: from OF, from L, from *bombyx* silk

bomber ('bɒmə) *n* **1** a military aircraft designed to carry out bombing missions. **2** a person who plants bombs.

bomber jacket *n* a short jacket finishing at the waist with an elasticated band, usually having a zip front.

bombora (bɒm'bɔ:rə) *n Austral.* **1** a submerged reef. **2** a turbulent area of sea over such a reef. ORIG from Abor.

bombshell ('bɒm,ʃɛl) *n* **1** (esp. formerly) a bomb or artillery shell. **2** a shocking or unwelcome surprise.

bombsight ('bɒm,saɪt) *n* a mechanical or electronic device in an aircraft for aiming bombs.

Bomu ('bəʊmu:) *or* **Mbomu** ★ (ᵊm'bəʊmu:) *n* a river in central Africa, rising in the SE Central African Republic and flowing west into the Uele River, forming the Ubangi River. Length: about 800 km (500 miles).

Bon ★ (bɒn) *n* **Cape.** a peninsula of NE Tunisia.

Bona ★ ('bəʊnə) *n* **Mount.** a mountain in S Alaska, in the Wrangell Mountains. Height: 5005 m (16 420 ft).

bona fide ('bəʊnə 'faɪdɪ) *adj* **1** real or genuine: *a bona fide manuscript.* **2** undertaken in good faith: *a bona fide agreement.* ORIG C16: from L

bona fides ('bəʊnə 'faɪdi:z) *n Law.* good faith; honest intention. ORIG L

Bonaire ★ (bɒn'ɛə) *n* an island in the S Caribbean, in the E Netherlands Antilles: one of the Leeward Islands. Chief town: Kralendijk. Pop.: 12 533 (1994 est.). Area: about 288 sq. km (111 sq. miles).

bonanza (bə'nænzə) *n* **1** a source, usually sudden and unexpected, of luck or wealth. **2** *US & Canad.* a mine or vein rich in ore. ORIG C19: from Sp., lit.: calm sea, hence, good luck, from Med. L, from L *bonus* good + *malacia* calm, from Gk *malakia* softness

Bonaparte ★ ('bəʊnə,pɑ:t; *French* bɔnapart) *n* **1** See **Napoleon I. 2 Jérôme** (ʒerom), brother of Napoleon I. 1784–1860, king of Westphalia (1807–13). **3 Joseph** (ʒozɛf), brother of Napoleon I. 1768–1844, king of Naples (1806–08) and of Spain (1808–13). **4 Louis** (lwi), brother of Napoleon I. 1778–1846, king of Holland (1806–10). **5 Lucien** (lysjɛ̃), brother of Napoleon I. 1775–1840, prince of Canino.

Bonaventura (,bɒnəvɛn'tjʊərə) *or* **Bonaventure** ★ ('bɒnə,vɛntʃə) *n* **Saint,** called *the Seraphic Doctor.* 1221–74, Italian Franciscan monk, mystic, theologian, and philosopher. Feast day: July 14.

bonbon ('bɒnbɒn) *n* a sweet. ORIG C19: from F, orig. a children's word from *bon* good

bonce (bɒns) *n Brit. sl.* the head. ORIG C19 (orig.: a large playing marble): from ?

bond (bɒnd) *n* **1** something that binds, fastens, or holds together. **2** (*often pl*) something that brings or holds people together; tie: *a bond of friendship.* **3** (*pl*) something that restrains or imprisons; captivity or imprisonment. **4** a written or spoken agreement, esp. a promise. **5** *Finance.* a certificate of debt issued in order to raise funds. It is repayable with or without security at a specified future date. **6** *Law.* a written acknowledgment of an obligation to pay a sum or to perform a contract. **7** *S. African.* a mortgage. **8** any of various arrangements of bricks or stones in a wall in which they overlap so as to provide strength. **9 chemical bond.** a mutual attraction between two atoms resulting from a redistribution of their outer electrons, determining chemical properties; shown in some formulae by a dot (.) or score (—). **10** See **bond paper. 11 in bond.** *Commerce.* deposited in a bonded warehouse. ◆ *vb* (*mainly tr*) **12** (*also intr*) to hold or be held together, as by a rope or an adhesive; bind; connect. **13** (*intr*) to become emotionally attached. **14** to put or hold (goods) in bond. **15** *Law.* to place under bond. **16** *Finance.* to issue bonds on; mortgage. ORIG C13: from ON *band;* see BAND[2]

Bond ★ (bɒnd) *n* **Edward.** born 1934, British dramatist: his plays include *Saved* (1965), *Restoration* (1981), and *In the Company of Men* (1990).

bondage ('bɒndɪdʒ) *n* **1** slavery or serfdom; servitude. **2** subjection to some influence or duty. **3** a sexual practice in which one participant is physically bound.

bonded ('bɒndɪd) *adj* **1** *Finance.* consisting of, secured by, or operating under a bond or bonds. **2** *Commerce.* deposited in a bonded warehouse.

bonded warehouse *n* a warehouse in which goods are deposited until duty is paid.

bondholder ('bɒnd,həʊldə) *n* an owner of bonds issued by a company or other institution.

Bondi[1] ★ ('bɒndɪ) *n* Sir **Hermann.** born 1919, British mathematician, born in Austria; originator (with Sir Fred Hoyle and Thomas Gold) of the steady-state theory of the universe.

Bondi[2] ★ ('bɒndaɪ) *n* a beach in Sydney, Australia, popular with surfers.

bonding ('bɒndɪŋ) *n* the process by which individuals become emotionally attached to one another.

bondmaid ('bɒnd,meɪd) *n* an unmarried female serf or slave.

bond paper *n* a superior quality of strong white paper, used esp. for writing and typing.

bondservant ('bɒnd,sɜːvənt) *n* a serf or slave.

bondsman ('bɒndzmən) *n, pl* **bondsmen. 1** *Law.* a person bound by bond to act as surety for another. **2** another word for **bondservant.**

bond washing *n* a series of illegal deals in bonds made with the intention of avoiding taxation.

bone (bəʊn) *n* **1** any of the various structures that make up the skeleton in most vertebrates. **2** the porous rigid tissue of which these parts are made. **3** something consisting of bone or a bonelike substance. **4** (*pl*) the human skeleton or body. **5** a thin strip of whalebone, plastic, etc., used to stiffen corsets and brassieres. **6** (*pl*) the essentials (esp. in **the bare bones**). **7** (*pl*) dice. **8 close** *or* **near to the bone. 8a** risqué or indecent. **8b** in poverty; destitute. **9 feel in one's bones.** to have an intuition of. **10 have a bone to pick.** to have grounds for a quarrel. **11 make no bones about. 11a** to be direct and candid about. **11b** to have no scruples about. **12 point the bone.** (often foll. by *at*) *Austral.* **12a** to wish bad luck (on). **12b** to cast a spell (on) in order to kill. ◆ *vb* **bones, boning, boned.** (*mainly tr*) **13** to remove the bones from (meat for cooking, etc.). **14** to stiffen (a corset, etc.) by inserting bones. **15** *Brit.* a slang word for **steal.** ◆ See also **bone up.** ORIG OE *bān*
▸ **'boneless** *adj*

Bône ★ (*French* bon) *n* a former name of **Annaba.**

bone ash *n* ash obtained when bones are burnt in air, consisting mainly of calcium phosphate.

bone china *n* porcelain containing bone ash.

bone-dry *adj Inf.* **a** completely dry: *a bone-dry well.* **b** (*postpositive*): *the well was bone dry.*

bonehead ('bəʊn,hɛd) *n Sl.* a stupid or obstinate person.
▸ **'bone,headed** *adj*

bone idle *adj* very idle; extremely lazy.

bone marrow *n* See **marrow** (sense 1).

bone meal *n* dried and ground animal bones, used as a fertilizer or in stock feeds.

boner ('bəʊnə) *n Sl.* a blunder.

bonesetter ('bəʊn,sɛtə) *n* a person who sets broken or dislocated bones, esp. one who has no formal medical qualifications.

boneshaker ('bəʊn,ʃeɪkə) *n* **1** an early type of bicycle having solid tyres and no springs. **2** *Sl.* any decrepit or rickety vehicle.

bone up *vb* (*adv;* when *intr,* usually foll. by *on*) *Inf.* to study intensively.

bonfire ('bɒn,faɪə) *n* a large outdoor fire. ORIG C15: alteration (infl. by F *bon* good) of *bone-fire;* from the use of bones as fuel

bong (bɒŋ) *n* **1** a deep reverberating sound, as of a large bell. ◆ *vb* **2** to make a deep reverberating sound. ORIG C20: imit.

bongo[1] ('bɒŋgəʊ) *n, pl* **bongo** *or* **bongos.** a rare spiral-horned antelope inhabiting forests of central Africa. The coat is bright red-brown with narrow vertical stripes. ORIG of African origin

bongo[2] ('bɒŋgəʊ) *n, pl* **bongos** *or* **bongoes.** a small bucket-shaped drum, usually one of a pair, played by beating with the fingers. ORIG American Sp., prob. imit.

Bonhoeffer ★ (*German* 'boːnhœfər) *n* **Dietrich** ('diːtrɪç). 1906–45, German theologian: executed by the Nazis.

bonhomie ('bɒnəmiː) *n* exuberant friendliness. ORIG C18: from F, from *bon* good + *homme* man

Boniface ★ ('bɒnɪ,feɪs) *n* **Saint.** original name *Wynfrith.* ?680–?755 A.D. Anglo-Saxon missionary: archbishop of Mainz (746–755). Feast day: June 5.

Boniface VIII ★ *n* original name *Benedict Caetano.* ?1234–1303, pope (1294–1303).

Bonington ★ ('bɒnɪŋtən) *n* **1** Sir **Chris(tian John Storey).** born 1934, British mountaineer; led 1970 Annapurna I and 1975 Everest expeditions, reached summit in 1985. **2 Richard Parkes.** 1801–28, British painter.

Bonin Islands ★ ('bəʊnɪn) *pl n* a group of 27 volcanic islands in the W Pacific: occupied by the US after World War II; returned to Japan in 1968. Largest island: Chichijima. Area: 103 sq. km (40 sq. miles). Japanese name: **Ogasawara Gunto.**

bonito (bə'niːtəʊ) *n, pl* **bonitos.** any of various small tunny-like marine food fishes of warm Atlantic and Pacific waters. ORIG C16: from Sp., from L *bonus* good

bonk (bɒŋk) *vb Inf.* **1** (*tr*) to hit. **2** to have sexual intercourse (with). ORIG C20: prob. imit.
▸ **'bonking** *n*

bonkbuster ('bɒŋk,bʌstə) *n Inf.* a novel characterized by graphic descriptions of the heroine's frequent sexual encounters. ORIG C20: from BONK (sense 2) + (BLOCK)BUSTER

bonkers ('bɒŋkəz) *adj Sl., chiefly Brit.* mad; crazy. ORIG C20: from ?

bon mot (*French* bɔ̃ mo) *n, pl* **bons mots** (bɔ̃ mo). a clever and fitting remark. ORIG F, lit.: good word

Bonn ★ (bɒn; *German* bɔn) *n* a city in W Germany, in North Rhine-Westphalia on the Rhine: the capital (1949–90) of the former West Germany; university (1786). Pop.: 291 431 (1996 est.).

Bonnard ★ (*French* bɔnar) *n* **Pierre** (pjɛr). 1867–1947, French painter.

bonnet ('bɒnɪt) *n* **1** any of various hats worn, esp. formerly, by women and girls, and tied with ribbons under the chin. **2** (in Scotland) Also: **bunnet. 2a** a soft cloth cap. **2b** (formerly) a flat brimless cap worn by men. **3** the hinged metal part of a motor vehicle body that provides access to the engine. US name: **hood. 4** a cowl on a chimney. **5** *Naut.* a piece of sail laced to the foot of a foresail to give it greater area in light winds. **6** (in the US and Canada) a headdress of feathers worn by some tribes of American Indians. ORIG C14: from OF *bonet,* from ?

Bonnie Prince Charlie ★ ('bɒnɪ) *n* See (Charles Edward) **Stuart.**

bonny ('bɒnɪ) *adj* **bonnier, bonniest. 1** *Scot. & N English dialect.* beautiful or handsome: *a bonny lass.* **2** good or fine. **3** (esp. of babies) plump. ORIG C15: from OF *bon* good, from L *bonus*

Bonny ★ ('bɒnɪ) *n* **Bight of.** a wide bay at the E end of the Gulf of Guinea off the coasts of Nigeria and Cameroon. Former name (until 1975): **Bight of Biafra.**

bonsai ('bɒnsaɪ) *n, pl* **bonsai. 1** the art of growing dwarfed ornamental varieties of trees or shrubs in small shallow pots or trays by selective pruning, etc. **2** a tree or shrub grown by this method. ORIG C20: from Japanese, from *bon* bowl + *sai* to plant

bonsela (bɒn'sɛlə) *n S. African inf.* a present or gratuity. ORIG from Zulu *Ibanselo* a gift

bontebok ('bɒntɪ,bʌk) *n, pl* **bonteboks** *or* **bontebok.** an antelope of southern Africa, having a deep reddish-brown coat with a white blaze, tail, and rump patch. ORIG C18: Afrik. from *bont* pied + *bok* BUCK[1]

bonus ('bəʊnəs) *n* **1** something given, paid, or received above what is due or expected. **2** *Chiefly Brit.* an extra dividend allotted to shareholders out of profits. **3** *Insurance, Brit.* a dividend, esp. a percentage of net profits, distributed to policyholders. ORIG C18: from L *bonus* (adj) good

bonus issue *n Brit.* a free issue of shares distributed among shareholders pro rata with their holdings.

bon vivant *French.* (bɔ̃ vivɑ̃) *n, pl* **bons vivants** (bɔ̃ vivɑ̃). a person who enjoys luxuries, esp. good food and drink. Also called (but not in French): **bon viveur** (ˌbɒn viːˈvɜː). ORIG lit.: good-living (man)

bon voyage (*French* bɔ̃ vwajaʒ) *sentence substitute.* a phrase used to wish a traveller a pleasant journey. ORIG F, lit.: good journey

bony (ˈbəʊnɪ) *adj* **bonier, boniest. 1** resembling or consisting of bone. **2** having many bones. **3** having prominent bones. **4** thin or emaciated.

bony fish *n* any of a class of fishes, including most of the extant species, having a skeleton of bone rather than cartilage.

Bonynge ★ (ˈbɒnɪŋ) *n* **Richard.** born 1930, Australian conductor; married to the soprano Joan Sutherland.

bonze (bɒnz) *n* a Chinese or Japanese Buddhist priest or monk. ORIG C16: from F, from Port. *bonzo,* from Japanese *bonsō,* from Sanskrit *bon* + *sō* priest or monk

bonzer (ˈbɒnzə) *adj Austral & NZ sl., arch.* very good; excellent. ORIG C20: ?from BONANZA

boo (buː) *interj* **1** an exclamation uttered to startle or surprise someone, esp. a child. **2** a shout uttered to express disgust, dissatisfaction, or contempt. ◆ *vb* **boos, booing, booed. 3** to shout "boo" at (someone or something), esp. as an expression of disapproval.

boob (buːb) *Sl.* ◆ *n* **1** an ignorant or foolish person. **2** *Brit.* an embarrassing mistake; blunder. **3** a female breast. ◆ *vb* **4** (*intr*) *Brit.* to make a blunder. ORIG C20: back formation from BOOBY

boobialla (ˌbuːbɪˈælə) *n Austral.* **1** another name for **golden wattle** (sense 2). **2** any of various trees or shrubs of the genus *Myoporum.*

boo-boo *n, pl* **boo-boos.** an embarrassing mistake; blunder. ORIG C20: ?from nursery talk

boob tube *n Sl.* **1** a close-fitting strapless top, worn by women. **2** *Chiefly US & Canad.* a television receiver.

booby (ˈbuːbɪ) *n, pl* **boobies. 1** an ignorant or foolish person. **2** *Brit.* the losing player in a game. **3** any of several tropical marine birds related to the gannet. They have a straight stout bill and the plumage is white with darker markings. ORIG C17: from Sp. *bobo,* from L *balbus* stammering

booby prize *n* a mock prize given to the person having the lowest score.

booby trap *n* **1** a hidden explosive device primed in such a way as to be set off by an unsuspecting victim. **2** a trap for an unsuspecting person, esp. one intended as a practical joke. ◆ *vb* **booby-trap, booby-traps, booby-trapping, booby-trapped. 3** (*tr*) to set a booby trap in or on (a building or object) or for (a person).

boodle (ˈbuːdᵊl) *n Sl.* money or valuables, esp. when stolen, counterfeit, or used as a bribe. ORIG C19: from Du. *boedel* possessions

boogie (ˈbuːgɪ) *vb* **boogies, boogieing, boogied.** (*intr*) *Sl.* **1** to dance to pop music. **2** to make love. ORIG C20: orig. African-American slang, ?from Bantu *mbugi* devilishly good

boogie-woogie (ˈbʊgɪˈwʊgɪ, ˈbuːgɪˈwuːgɪ) *n* a style of piano jazz using a dotted bass pattern, usually with eight notes in a bar and the harmonies of the 12-bar blues. ORIG C20: ? imit.

boohai (buːˈhaɪ) *n* **up the boohai.** *NZ inf.* thoroughly lost. ORIG from the remote township of *Puhoi*

boohoo (ˌbuːˈhuː) *vb* **boohoos, boohooing, boohooed.** (*intr*) **1** to sob or pretend to sob noisily. ◆ *n, pl* **boohoos. 2** (*sometimes pl*) distressed or pretended sobbing. ORIG C20: nursery talk

book (bʊk) *n* **1** a number of printed or written pages bound together along one edge and usually protected by covers. **2a** a written work or composition, such as a novel, technical manual, or dictionary. **2b** (*as modifier*): *book reviews.* **2c** (*in combination*): *bookseller; bookshop; bookshelf.* **3** a number of blank or ruled sheets of paper bound together, used to record lessons, keep accounts, etc. **4** (*pl*) a record of the transactions of a business or society. **5** the libretto of an opera, musical, etc. **6** a major division of a written composition, as of a long novel or of the Bible. **7** a number of tickets, stamps, etc., fastened together along one edge. **8** a record of betting transactions. **9** (in card games) the number of tricks that must be taken by a side or player before any trick has a scoring value. **10** strict or rigid rules or standards (esp. in **by the book**). **11** a source of knowledge or authority: *the book of life.* **12 a closed book.** a person or subject that is unknown or beyond comprehension: *chemistry is a closed book to him.* **13 an open book.** a person or subject that is thoroughly understood. **14 bring to book.** to reprimand or require (someone) to give an explanation of his or her conduct. **15 close the books.** *Book-keeping.* to balance accounts in order to prepare a statement or report. **16 in someone's good** (*or* **bad**) **books.** regarded by someone with favour (*or* disfavour). **17 keep the books.** to keep written records of the finances of a business. **18 on the books. 18a** enrolled as a member. **18b** recorded. **19 the book.** (*sometimes cap.*) the Bible. **20 throw the book at. 20a** to charge with every relevant offence. **20b** to inflict the most severe punishment on. ◆ *vb* **21** to reserve (a place, passage, etc.) or engage the services of (a performer, driver, etc.) in advance. **22** (*tr*) to take the name and address of (a person guilty of a minor offence) with a view to bringing a prosecution. **23** (*tr*) (of a football referee) to take the name of (a player) who grossly infringes the rules. **24** (*tr*) *Arch.* to record in a book. ◆ See also **book in.** ORIG OE *bōc;* see BEECH (its bark was used as a writing surface)

bookbinder (ˈbʊkˌbaɪndə) *n* a person whose business is binding books.
▸ **ˈbookˌbinding** *n*

bookbindery (ˈbʊkˌbaɪndərɪ) *n, pl* **bookbinderies.** a place in which books are bound. Often shortened to **bindery.**

bookcase (ˈbʊkˌkeɪs) *n* a piece of furniture containing shelves for books.

book club *n* a club that sells books at low prices to members, usually by mail order.

book end *n* one of a pair of usually ornamental supports for holding a row of books upright.

Booker Prize (ˈbʊkə) *n* an annual prize for a work of British, Commonwealth, or Irish fiction of £20,000, awarded since 1969 by the Booker McConnell engineering company.

bookie (ˈbʊkɪ) *n Inf.* short for **bookmaker.**

book in *vb* (*adv*) **1** to reserve a room at a hotel. **2** *Chiefly Brit.* to register, esp. one's arrival at a hotel.

booking (ˈbʊkɪŋ) *n* **1** *Chiefly Brit.* a reservation, as of a table, room, or seat. **2** *Theatre.* an engagement of an actor or company.

bookish (ˈbʊkɪʃ) *adj* **1** fond of reading; studious. **2** consisting of or forming opinions through reading rather than experience; academic. **3** of or relating to books.
▸ **ˈbookishness** *n*

book-keeping *n* the skill or occupation of systematically recording business transactions.
▸ **ˈbook-ˌkeeper** *n*

book-learning *n* knowledge gained from books rather than from experience.

booklet (ˈbʊklɪt) *n* a thin book, esp. one having paper covers; pamphlet.

bookmaker (ˈbʊkˌmeɪkə) *n* a person who as an occupation accepts bets, esp. on horseraces, and pays out to winning betters.
▸ **ˈbookˌmaking** *n*

bookmark (ˈbʊkˌmɑːk) *n* **1** Also called: **bookmarker.** a strip of some material put between the pages of a book to mark a place. **2** *Computing.* an identifier put on a website that enables the user to return to it quickly and easily. ◆ *vb* **3** (*tr*) *Computing.* to identify and store (a website) so that one can return to it quickly and easily.

Book of Common Prayer *n* the official book of church services of the Church of England until 1980, when the Alternative Service Book was sanctioned.

bookplate (ˈbʊkˌpleɪt) *n* a label bearing the owner's name and a design, pasted into a book.

bookstall (ˈbʊkˌstɔːl) *n* a stall or stand where periodicals, newspapers, or books are sold.

book token *n Brit.* a gift token to be exchanged for books.

book value *n* **1** the value of an asset of a business according to its books. **2** the net capital value of an enterprise as shown by the excess of book assets over book liabilities.

bookworm ('bʊk,wɜːm) *n* **1** a person devoted to reading. **2** any of various small insects that feed on the binding paste of books.

Boole ★ (buːl) *n* **George.** 1815–64, English mathematician. He applied mathematical formulae to logic, creating **Boolean algebra**, which is used in computers to codify nonmathematical logical operations.

boom[1] (buːm) *vb* **1** to make a deep prolonged resonant sound. **2** to prosper or cause to prosper vigorously and rapidly: *business boomed.* ♦ *n* **3** a deep prolonged resonant sound. **4** a period of high economic growth. **5** any similar period of high activity. **6** the activity itself: *a baby boom.* ORIG C15: ?from Du. *bommen,* imit.

boom[2] (buːm) *n* **1** *Naut.* a spar to which a sail is fastened to control its position relative to the wind. **2** a pole carrying an overhead microphone and projected over a film or television set. **3** a barrier across a waterway, usually consisting of a chain of logs, to confine free-floating logs, protect a harbour from attack, etc. ORIG C16: from Du. *boom* tree, BEAM

boomer ('buːmə) *n* **1** *Austral.* a large male kangaroo. **2** *Austral. & NZ inf.* anything exceptionally large.

boomerang ('buːmə,ræŋ) *n* **1** a curved flat wooden missile of native Australians, which can be made to return to the thrower. **2** an action or statement that recoils on its originator. ♦ *vb* **3** (*intr*) (of a plan, etc.) to recoil or return unexpectedly, causing harm to its originator. ORIG C19: from Abor.

boomslang ('buːm,slæŋ) *n* a large greenish venomous arboreal snake of southern Africa. ORIG C18: from Afrik., from *boom* tree + *slang* snake

boon[1] (buːn) *n* **1** something extremely useful, helpful, or beneficial; a blessing or benefit. **2** *Arch.* a favour; request. ORIG C12: from ON *bōn* request

boon[2] (buːn) *adj* **1** close, special, or intimate (in **boon companion**). **2** *Arch.* jolly or convivial. ORIG C14: from OF *bon,* from L *bonus* good

boondocks ('buːn,dɒks) *pl n* **the.** *US & Canad. sl.* **1** wild, desolate, or uninhabitable country. **2** a remote rural or provincial area. ORIG C20: from Tagalog *bundok* mountain

boong (bʊŋ) *n Austral. offens.* a Black person. ORIG C20: from Abor.

boongary (buːn'geərɪ) *n, pl* **-ries.** a tree kangaroo of NE Queensland. ORIG from Abor.

boor (bʊə) *n* an ill-mannered, clumsy, or insensitive person. ORIG OE *gebūr* dweller, farmer; see NEIGHBOUR
▸ **'boorish** *adj* ▸ **'boorishly** *adv* ▸ **'boorishness** *n*

boost (buːst) *n* **1** encouragement, improvement, or help: *a boost to morale.* **2** an upward thrust or push. **3** an increase or rise. **4** the amount by which the induction pressure of a supercharged internal-combustion engine is increased. ♦ *vb* (*tr*) **5** to encourage, assist, or improve: *to boost morale.* **6** to lift by giving a push from below or behind. **7** to increase or raise: *to boost the voltage in an electrical circuit.* **8** to cause to rise; increase: *to boost sales.* **9** to advertise on a big scale. **10** to increase the induction pressure of (an internal-combustion engine); supercharge. ORIG C19: from ?

booster ('buːstə) *n* **1** a person or thing that supports, assists, or increases power. **2** Also called: **launch vehicle.** the first stage of a multistage rocket. **3** a radio-frequency amplifier to strengthen signals. **4** another name for **supercharger. 5** short for **booster shot.**

booster shot *n Inf.* a supplementary injection of a vaccine given to maintain the immunization provided by an earlier dose.

boot[1] (buːt) *n* **1** a strong outer covering for the foot; shoe that extends above the ankle, often to the knee. **2** *Brit.* an enclosed compartment of a car for holding luggage, etc., usually at the rear. US and Canad. name: **trunk. 3** an instrument of torture used to crush the foot and lower leg. **4** *Inf.* a kick: *he gave the door a boot.* **5 boots and all.** *Austral. & NZ inf.* making every effort. **6 die with one's boots on.** to die while still active. **7 lick the boots of.** to be servile towards. **8 put the boot in.** *Sl.* **8a** to kick a person, esp. when he or she is already down. **8b** to harass someone. **8c** to finish off (something) with unnecessary brutality. **9 the boot.** *Sl.* dismissal from employment; the sack. **10 the boot is on the other foot** *or* **leg.** the situation is or has now reversed. ♦ *vb* (*tr*) **11** to kick. **12** to equip with boots. **13** *Inf.* **13a** (often foll. by *out*) to eject forcibly. **13b** to dismiss from employment. **14** to bootstrap (a computer system). ORIG C14 *bote,* from OF, from ?

boot[2] (buːt) *vb* (*usually impersonal*) **1** *Arch.* to be of advantage or use to (a person): *what boots it to complain?* ♦ *n* **2** *Obs.* an advantage. **3 to boot.** as well; in addition. ORIG OE *bōt* compensation

bootblack ('buːt,blæk) *n* (esp. formerly) a person who shines boots and shoes.

boot camp *n* **1** *US sl.* a basic training camp for new recruits to the US Navy or Marine Corps. **2** a centre for juvenile offenders with a strict disciplinary regime, hard physical exercise, and community labour programmes.

boot-cut *adj* (of trousers) slightly flared at the bottom of the legs.

bootee ('buːtiː, buː'tiː) *n* **1** a soft shoe for a baby, esp. a knitted one. **2** a boot for women and children, esp. an ankle-length one.

Boötes (bəʊ'əʊtiːz) *n, Latin genitive* **Boötis** (bəʊ'əʊtɪs). a constellation in the N hemisphere containing the star Arcturus. ORIG C17: via L from Gk: ploughman

booth (buːð, buːθ) *n, pl* **booths** (buːðz). **1** a stall, esp. a temporary one at a fair or market. **2** a small partially enclosed cubicle, such as one for telephoning (**telephone booth**) or for voting (**polling booth**). **3** two high-backed benches with a table between, used esp. in bars and restaurants. **4** (formerly) a temporary structure for shelter, dwelling, storage, etc. ORIG C12: of Scand. origin

Booth ★ (buːð) *n* **1 Edwin Thomas,** son of Junius Brutus Booth. 1833–93, US actor. **2 John Wilkes,** son of Junius Brutus Booth. 1838–65, US actor; assassin of Abraham Lincoln. **3 Junius Brutus** ('dʒuːnɪəs 'bruːtəs). 1796–1852, US actor, born in England. **4 William.** 1829–1912, British religious leader; founder of the Salvation Army (1878).

Boothia Peninsula ★ ('buːθɪə) *n* a peninsula of N Canada: the northernmost part of the mainland of North America, lying west of the **Gulf of Boothia,** an arm of the Arctic Ocean.

bootjack ('buːt,dʒæk) *n* a device that grips the heel of a boot to enable the foot to be withdrawn easily.

Bootle ★ ('buːtᵊl) *n* a port in NW England, on the River Mersey adjoining Liverpool. Pop.: 65 454 (1991).

bootleg ('buːt,lɛg) *vb* **bootlegs, bootlegging, bootlegged. 1** to make, carry, or sell (illicit goods, esp. alcohol). ♦ *n* **2** something made or sold illicitly, such as alcohol. **3** an illegally made copy of a CD, tape, etc. ♦ *adj* **4** produced, distributed, or sold illicitly. ORIG C17: see BOOT[1], LEG; from smugglers carrying bottles of liquor concealed in their boots
▸ **'boot,legger** *n*

bootless ('buːtlɪs) *adj* of little or no use; vain; fruitless. ORIG OE *bōtlēas,* from *bōt* compensation

bootlicker ('buːt,lɪkə) *n Inf.* one who seeks favour by servile or ingratiating behaviour towards (someone, esp. in authority); toady.

bootstrap ('buːt,stræp) *n* **1** a loop on a boot for pulling it on. **2 by one's (own) bootstraps.** by one's own efforts; unaided. **3a** a technique for loading the first few program instructions into a computer main store to enable the rest of the program to be introduced from an input device. **3b** (*as modifier*): *a bootstrap loader.* **4** *Commerce.* an offer to purchase a controlling interest in a company, esp. with the intention of purchasing the remainder of the equity at a lower price. ♦ *vb* **bootstraps, bootstrapping, bootstrapped.** (*tr*) **5** to initiate (a computer system) by executing a bootstrap; boot.

booty ('buːtɪ) *n, pl* **booties.** any valuable article or articles, esp. when obtained as plunder. ORIG C15: from OF, from MLow G *buite* exchange

booze (buːz) *Inf.* ♦ *n* **1** alcoholic drink. **2** a drinking bout. ◆ *vb* **boozes, boozing, boozed. 3** (*usually intr*) to drink (alcohol), esp. in excess. ORIG C13: from MDu. *būsen*

boozer ('bu:zə) *n Inf.* **1** a person who is fond of drinking. **2** *Brit., Austral., & NZ.* a bar or pub.

booze-up *n Brit., Austral., & NZ sl.* a drinking spree.

boozy ('bu:zɪ) *adj* **boozier, booziest.** *Inf.* inclined to or involving excessive drinking of alcohol; drunken: *a boozy lecturer; a boozy party.*

bop (bɒp) *n* **1** a form of jazz originating in the 1940s, characterized by rhythmic and harmonic complexity and instrumental virtuosity. Originally called: **bebop.** ◆ *vb* **bops, bopping, bopped. 2** (*intr*) *Inf.* to dance to pop music. ORIG C20: shortened from BEBOP
▸ **'bopper** *n*

bo-peep (ˌbəʊ'pi:p) *n* a game for very young children, in which one hides (esp. hiding one's face in one's hands) and reappears suddenly.

Bophuthatswana ★ (ˌbəʊpu:tɑ:t'swɑ:nə) *n* (formerly) a Bantu homeland in N South Africa: reintegrated into South Africa in 1994.

bora[1] ('bɔ:rə) *n* (*sometimes cap.*) a violent cold north wind blowing from the Adriatic. ORIG C19: from It. dialect., from L *boreās* the north wind

bora[2] ('bɔ:rə) *n* an initiation ceremony of native Australians, introducing youths to manhood. ORIG from Abor.

Bora Bora ★ ('bɔ:rə 'bɔ:rə) *n* an island in the S Pacific, in French Polynesia, in the Society Islands: one of the Leeward Islands. Area: 39 sq. km (15 sq. miles).

boracic (bə'ræsɪk) *adj* another word for **boric.**

borage ('bɒrɪdʒ, 'bʌrɪdʒ) *n* a Mediterranean plant with star-shaped blue flowers. The young leaves are sometimes used in salads. ORIG C13: from OF, ?from Ar. *abū 'āraq,* lit.: father of sweat

Borås ★ (*Swedish* bu'ro:s) *n* a city in SW Sweden, chiefly producing textiles. Pop.: 96 123 (1994).

borate *n* ('bɔ:reɪt, -ɪt). **1** a salt or ester of boric acid. ◆ *vb* ('bɔ:reɪt), **borates, borating, borated. 2** (*tr*) to treat with borax, boric acid, or borate.

borax ('bɔ:ræks) *n, pl* **boraxes** *or* **boraces** (-rəˌsi:z). a soluble readily fusible white mineral in monoclinic crystalline form, occurring in alkaline soils and salt deposits. Formula: $Na_2B_4O_7.10H_2O$. ORIG C14: from OF, from Med. L, from Ar., from Persian *būrah*

borazon ('bɔ:rəˌzɒn) *n* an extremely hard form of boron nitride. ORIG C20: from BOR(ON) + AZO + -ON

borborygmus (ˌbɔ:bə'rɪgməs) *n, pl* **borborygmi** (-maɪ). rumbling of the stomach. ORIG C18: from Gk

Bordeaux ★ (bɔ:'dəʊ; *French* bɔrdo) *n* **1** a port in SW France, on the River Garonne: a major centre of the wine trade. Pop.: 213 274 (1990). **2** any of several red, white, or rosé wines produced around Bordeaux.

Bordeaux mixture *n Horticulture.* a fungicide consisting of a solution of equal quantities of copper sulphate and quicklime.

border ('bɔ:də) *n* **1** a band or margin around or along the edge of something. **2** the dividing line or frontier between political or geographic regions. **3** a region straddling such a boundary. **4** a design around the edge of something. **5** a long narrow strip of ground planted with flowers, shrubs, etc.: *a herbaceous border.* ◆ *vb* **6** (*tr*) to provide with a border. **7** (when *intr*, foll. by *on* or *upon*) **7a** to be adjacent (to); lie along the boundary (of). **7b** to be nearly the same (as); verge (on): *his stupidity borders on madness.* ORIG C14: from OF, from *bort* side of a ship, of Gmc origin

Border[1] ★ ('bɔ:də) *n* **the. 1** (*often pl*) the area straddling the border between England and Scotland. **2** the area straddling the border between Northern Ireland and the Republic of Ireland. **3** the region in S South Africa around East London.

Border[2] ★ ('bɔ:də) *n* **Allan (Robert).** born 1955, Australian cricketer; captain of Australia (1985–94).

borderer ('bɔ:dərə) *n* a person who lives in a border area.

borderland ('bɔ:dəˌlænd) *n* **1** land located on or near a frontier or boundary. **2** an indeterminate state or condition.

borderline ('bɔ:dəˌlaɪn) *n* **1** a border; dividing line. **2** an indeterminate position between two conditions: *the borderline between friendship and love.* ◆ *adj* **3** on the edge of one category and verging on another: *a borderline failure in the exam.*

Borders Region ★ *n* a former local government region in S Scotland; replaced in 1996 by Scottish Borders council area.

bore[1] (bɔ:) *vb* **bores, boring, bored. 1** to produce (a hole) in (a material) by use of a drill, auger, or rotary cutting tool. **2** to increase the diameter of (a hole), as by turning. **3** (*tr*) to produce (a hole in the ground, tunnel, mine shaft, etc.) by digging, drilling, etc. **4** (*intr*) *Inf.* (of a horse or athlete in a race) to push other competitors out of the way. ◆ *n* **5** a hole or tunnel in the ground, esp. one drilled in search of minerals, oil, etc. **6** *Austral.* an artesian well. **7a** the hollow part of a tube or cylinder, esp. of a gun barrel. **7b** the diameter of such a hollow part; calibre. ORIG OE *borian*

bore[2] (bɔ:) *vb* **bores, boring, bored. 1** (*tr*) to tire or make weary by being dull, repetitious, or uninteresting. ◆ *n* **2** a dull or repetitious person, activity, or state. ORIG C18: from ?
▸ **bored** *adj* ▸ **'boring** *adj*

bore[3] (bɔ:) *n* a high steep-fronted wave moving up a narrow estuary, caused by the tide. ORIG C17: from ON *bāra* wave, billow

bore[4] (bɔ:) *vb* the past tense of **bear**[1].

boreal ('bɔ:rɪəl) *adj* of or relating to the north or the north wind. ORIG C15: from L *boreās* the north wind

Boreal ('bɔ:rɪəl) *adj* of or denoting the coniferous forests in the north of the N hemisphere.

Boreas ★ ('bɔ:rɪəs) *n Greek myth.* the god personifying the north wind. ORIG C14: via L from Gk

boredom ('bɔ:dəm) *n* the state of being bored.

boree ('bɔ:ri:) *n Austral.* another name for **myall.** ORIG from Abor.

borer ('bɔ:rə) *n* **1** a tool for boring holes. **2** any of various insects, insect larvae, molluscs, or crustaceans, that bore into plant material, esp. wood.

Borg ★ (bɔ:g; *Swedish* bɔrj) *n* **Björn** (bjɔ:n; *Swedish* bjœrn). born 1956, Swedish tennis player: Wimbledon champion 1976–80.

Borgerhout ★ (*Flemish* bɔrxər'hɔut) *n* a city in N Belgium, near Antwerp. Pop.: 44 000 (latest est.).

Borges ★ (*Spanish* 'borxes) *n* **Jorge Luis** ('xorxe lwis). 1899–1986, Argentinian poet and scholar. His short stories include *Ficciones* (1944).

Borgia ★ (*Italian* 'bordʒa) *n* **1 Cesare** ('tʃezare), son of Rodrigo Borgia (Pope Alexander VI). 1475–1507, Italian cardinal, politician, and military leader; model for Machiavelli's *The Prince.* **2** his sister, **Lucrezia** (lu'krɛttsja), daughter of Rodrigo Borgia. 1480–1519, Italian noblewoman. After her third marriage (1501), to the Duke of Ferrara, she became a patron of the arts and science. **3 Rodrigo** (rod'rigo). See **Alexander VI.**

boric ('bɔ:rɪk) *adj* of or containing boron. Also: **boracic.**

boric acid *n* a white soluble weakly acid crystalline solid used in the manufacture of heat-resistant glass and porcelain enamels, as a fireproofing material, and as a mild antiseptic. Formula: H_3BO_3. Also called: **orthoboric acid.** Systematic name: **trioxoboric(III) acid.**

borlotti bean (bɔ:'lɒtɪ) *n* a variety of kidney bean with a pinkish-brown speckled skin that turns brown when cooked. ORIG from It., plural of *borlotto* kidney bean

Bormann ★ ('bɔ:mən; *German* 'bɔrman) *n* **Martin.** 1900–45, German Nazi politician; Hitler's adviser and private secretary (1942–45): committed suicide.

born (bɔ:n) *vb* **1** the past participle (in most passive uses) of **bear**[1] (sense 4). **2 not born yesterday.** not gullible or foolish. ◆ *adj* **3** possessing certain qualities from birth: *a born musician.* **4a** being at birth in a particular social status or other condition as specified: *ignobly born.* **4b** (*in* *combination): lowborn.* **5 in all one's born days.** *Inf.* so far in one's life.

> **USAGE NOTE** Care should be taken not to use *born* when *borne* is intended: *he had borne* (not *born*) *his ordeal with great courage; the following points should be borne in mind.*

Born ★ (bɔːn) *n* **Max.** 1882–1970, British nuclear physicist, born in Germany, noted for his fundamental contribution to quantum mechanics: Nobel prize for physics 1954.

born-again ('bɔːnəˌgɛn) *adj* **1** having experienced conversion, esp. to evangelical Christianity. **2** showing the enthusiasm of one newly converted to any cause: *a born-again monetarist.* ◆ *n* **3** a person who shows fervent enthusiasm for a new-found cause, belief, etc.

borne (bɔːn) *vb* **1** the past participle of **bear**[1] (for all active uses of the verb; also for all passive uses except sense 4 unless foll. by *by*). **2 be borne in on** *or* **upon.** (of a fact, etc.) to be realized by (someone).

> **USAGE NOTE** See at **born.**

Borneo ★ ('bɔːnɪˌəʊ) *n* an island in the W Pacific, between the Sulu and Java Seas, part of the Malay Archipelago: divided into Kalimantan (**Indonesian Borneo**), the Malaysian states of Sarawak and Sabah, and the British-protected sultanate of Brunei; mountainous and densely forested. Area: about 750 000 sq. km (290 000 sq. miles).
▸ **'Bornean** *adj, n*

Bornholm ★ (*Danish* bɔrn'hɔlm) *n* an island in the Baltic Sea, south of Sweden: administratively part of Denmark. Chief town: Rønne. Pop.: 46 100 (1990). Area: 588 sq. km (227 sq. miles).

Borno ★ ('bɔːnəʊ) *n* a state of NE Nigeria, on Lake Chad: the second largest state, formed in 1976 from part of North-Eastern State. Capital: Maiduguri. Pop.: 2 903 238 (1995 est.). Area: 70 898 sq. km (27 374 sq. miles).

Borodin ★ ('bɒrədɪn; *Russian* bəra'din) *n* **Aleksandr Porfirevich** (alɪk'sandr pərfi'rjevitʃ). 1834–87, Russian composer, whose works include the unfinished opera *Prince Igor,* symphonies, songs, and chamber music.

Borodino ★ (ˌbɒrə'diːnəʊ; *Russian* bərədi'nɔ) *n* a village in E central Russia, about 110 km (70 miles) west of Moscow: scene of a battle (1812) in which Napoleon defeated the Russians but irreparably weakened his army.

boron ('bɔːrɒn) *n* a very hard almost colourless crystalline metalloid element that in impure form exists as a brown amorphous powder. It occurs principally in borax and is used in hardening steel. Symbol: B; atomic no.: 5; atomic wt.: 10.81. ORIG C19: from BOR(AX) + (CARB)ON

boron carbide *n* a black extremely hard inert substance used as an abrasive and in control rods in nuclear reactors. Formula: B_4C.

boronia (bə'rəʊnɪə) *n* any aromatic shrub of the Australian genus *Boronia.*

boron nitride *n* a white inert crystalline solid, used as a refractory, high-temperature lubricant and insulator, and heat shield.

borosilicate glass (ˌbɔːrəʊ'sɪlɪkɪt, -ˌkeɪt) *n* any of a range of heat- and chemical-resistant glasses, such as Pyrex, prepared by fusing together oxides of boron and silicon and, usually, a metal oxide.

borough ('bʌrə) *n* **1** a town, esp. (in Britain) one that forms the constituency of an MP or that was originally incorporated by royal charter. See also **burgh. 2** any of the 32 constituent divisions of Greater London. **3** any of the five constituent divisions of New York City. **4** (in the US) a self-governing incorporated municipality. ORIG OE *burg*

Borromini ★ (*Italian* borro'miːni) *n* **Francesco** (fran'tʃesko), original name *Francesco Castelli.* 1599–1667, Italian baroque architect, working in Rome.

borrow ('bɒrəʊ) *vb* **1** to obtain or receive (something, such as money) on loan for temporary use, intending to give it, or something equivalent, back to the lender. **2** to adopt (ideas, words, etc.) from another source; appropriate. **3** *Not standard.* to lend. **4** (*intr*) *Golf.* to putt the ball uphill of the direct path to the hole: *make sure you borrow enough.* ORIG OE *borgian*
▸ **'borrower** *n*

> **USAGE NOTE** See at **off.**

Borrow ★ ('bɒrəʊ) *n* **George** (**Henry**). 1803–81, British writer. His works include the semiautobiographical *Lavengro* (1851) and its sequel *The Romany Rye* (1857).

Bors ★ (bɔːs) *n* **Sir.** (in Arthurian legend) **1** one the knights of the Round Table, nephew of Lancelot. **2** an illegitimate son of King Arthur.

borscht (bɔːʃt), **borsch** (bɔːʃ), *or* **borshch** (bɔːʃtʃ) *n* a Russian and Polish soup based on beetroot. ORIG from Russian *borshch*

borscht belt *n Inf., chiefly US.* a resort area of the Catskill Mountains in New York State, popular with Jewish holiday-makers; its hotels and nightclubs (the **borscht circuit**) are regarded as a training ground for entertainers.

borstal ('bɔːstəl) *n* **1** (formerly, in Britain) an establishment in which offenders aged 15 to 21 could be detained for corrective training. Since 1982 they have been replaced by **young offender institutions. 2** a similar establishment in Australia and New Zealand. ORIG C20: after *Borstal,* village in Kent where the first institution was founded

bort, boart (bɔːt), *or* **bortz** (bɔːts) *n* an inferior grade of diamond used for cutting and drilling or, in powdered form, as an industrial abrasive. ORIG OE *gebrot* fragment

borzoi ('bɔːzɔɪ) *n, pl* **borzois.** a tall fast-moving breed of dog with a long coat. Also called: **Russian wolfhound.** ORIG C19: Russian, lit.: swift

boscage *or* **boskage** ('bɒskɪdʒ) *n Literary.* a mass of trees and shrubs; thicket. ORIG C14: from OF *bosc,* prob. of Gmc origin; see BUSH[1], -AGE

Bosch ★ (bɒʃ) *n* **1 Carl.** 1874–1940, German chemist, who adapted the Haber process to produce ammonia. He shared the Nobel prize for chemistry 1931. **2 Hieronymus** (hɪ'rɒnɪməs), original name probably *Jerome van Aken* (or *Aeken*). ?1450–1516, Dutch painter, noted for his triptych *The Garden of Earthly Delights.*

Bose ★ (bəʊs) *n* **1** Sir **Jagadis Chandra** (dʒəgə'diːs 'tʃʌndrə). 1858–1937, Indian physicist and plant physiologist. **2 Satyendra Nath** (sə'tjɛndrə 'nɑːθ). 1894–1974, Indian physicist, who collaborated with Einstein in devising Bose-Einstein statistics. **3 Subhas Chandra** (sʊb'hɑːʃ 'tʃʌndrə), known as *Netaji.* 1897–1945, Indian nationalist leader; president of the Indian National Congress (1938–39); organized the Indian National Army, with Japanese support, in Singapore to free India from British Rule.

bosh (bɒʃ) *n Inf.* empty or meaningless talk or opinions; nonsense. ORIG C19: from Turkish *boş* empty

bosk (bɒsk) *n Literary.* a small wood of bushes and small trees. ORIG C13: var. of *busk* BUSH[1]

bosky ('bɒskɪ) *adj* **boskier, boskiest.** *Literary.* containing or consisting of bushes or thickets.

bo's'n ('bəʊsᵊn) *n Naut.* a variant spelling of **boatswain.**

Bosnia ★ ('bɒznɪə) *n* a region of Bosnia-Herzegovina: it has belonged to Turkey (1463–1878), to Austria-Hungary (1879–1918), and to Yugoslavia (1918–91).
▸ **'Bosnian** *adj*

Bosnia-Herzegovina, Bosnia-Hercegovina, *or esp. US* **Bosnia and Herzegovina** ★ *n* a country in SW Europe; a constituent republic of Yugoslavia until 1991; in a state of civil war also involving Serbian and Croatian forces (1992–95): mostly barren and mountainous, with forests in the east. Language: Serbo-Croat. Religion: Muslim, Serbian Orthodox, and Roman Catholic. Currency: dinar. Capital: Sarajevo. Pop.: 3 838 000 (1999 est.). Area: 51 129 sq. km (19 737 sq. miles).

bosom ('bʊzəm) *n* **1** the chest or breast of a person, esp. the female breasts. **2** the part of a woman's dress, coat, etc., that covers the chest. **3** a protective centre or part: *the bosom of the family.* **4** the breast considered as the seat of emotions. **5** (*modifier*) very dear; intimate: *a bosom friend.* ◆ *vb* (*tr*) **6** to embrace. **7** to conceal or carry in the bosom. ORIG OE *bōsm*

bosomy ('bʊzəmɪ) *adj* (of a woman) having large breasts.

boson ('bəʊzɒn) *n* any of a group of elementary particles, such as a photon or pion, that has zero or integral spin and does not obey the Pauli exclusion principle. Cf. **fermion.** ORIG C20: after S. N. BOSE; see -ON

Bosporus ('bɒspərəs) *or* **Bosphorus** ★ ('bɒsfərəs) *n* **the.** a strait between European and Asian Turkey, linking the Black Sea and the Sea of Marmara.

boss[1] (bɒs) *Inf.* ◆ *n* **1** a person in charge of or employing others. **2** *Chiefly US.* a professional politician who controls a political organization, often using devious or illegal methods. ◆ *vb* (*tr*) **3** to employ, supervise, or be in charge of. **4** (usually foll. by *around* or *about*) to be domineering or overbearing towards (others). ◆ *adj* **5** *Sl.* excellent; fine: *a boss hand at carpentry; that's boss!* ORIG C19: from Du. *baas* master

boss[2] (bɒs) *n* **1** a knob, stud, or other circular rounded protuberance, esp. an ornamental one on a vault, a ceiling, or a shield. **2** an area of increased thickness, usually cylindrical, that strengthens or provides room for a locating device on a shaft, hub of a wheel, etc. **3** a rounded mass of igneous rock. ◆ *vb* (*tr*) **4** to ornament with bosses; emboss. ORIG C13: from OF *boce*; rel. to It. *bozza* metal knob, swelling

bossa nova ('bɒsə 'nəʊvə) *n* **1** a dance similar to the samba, originating in Brazil. **2** a piece of music composed for or in the rhythm of this dance. ORIG C20: from Port., lit.: new voice

bosset ('bɒsɪt) *n* either of the rudimentary antlers found in young deer. ORIG C19: from F *bossette* a small protuberance, from *bosse* BOSS[2]

bossy ('bɒsɪ) *adj* **bossier, bossiest.** *Inf.* domineering, overbearing, or authoritarian.
▸ '**bossily** *adv* ▸ '**bossiness** *n*

Boston ★ ('bɒstən) *n* **1** a port in E Massachusetts, the state capital. Pop.: 547 725 (1994 est.). **2** a port in E England, in SE Lincolnshire. Pop.: 34 606 (1991).

bosun ('bəʊsᵊn) *n Naut.* a variant spelling of **boatswain.**

Boswell ★ ('bɒzwəl) *n* **James.** 1740–95, Scottish author and lawyer, noted for his *Life of Samuel Johnson* (1791).
▸ **Boswellian** (bɒz'wɛlɪən) *adj*

Bosworth Field ★ ('bɒzwɜːθ, -wəθ) *n English history.* the site, two miles south of Market Bosworth in Leicestershire, of the battle that ended the Wars of the Roses (August, 1485). Richard III was killed and Henry Tudor was crowned king as Henry VII.

bot[1] *or* **bott** (bɒt) *n* **1** the larva of a botfly, which typically develops inside the body of a horse, sheep, or man. **2** any similar larva. ORIG C15: prob. from Low G; rel. to Du. *bot,* from ?

bot[2] (bɒt) *Austral. inf.* ◆ *vb* **bots, botting, botted. 1** to scrounge or borrow. ◆ *n* **2** a scrounger. **3 on the bot** (**for**). wanting to scrounge. ORIG C20: ?from BOTFLY, alluding to its bite; see BITE (sense 9)

bot[3] (bɒt) *n Computing.* an autonomous computer program that performs time-consuming tasks, esp. on the Internet. ORIG C20: from (RO)BOT

bot. *abbrev. for:* **1** botanical. **2** botany. **3** bottle.

botanical (bə'tænɪkᵊl) *or* **botanic** *adj* **1** of or relating to botany or plants. ◆ *n* **2** any drug or pesticide that is made from parts of a plant. ORIG C17: from Med. L, from Gk *botanē* plant, pasture
▸ **bo'tanically** *adv*

botanize *or* **botanise** ('bɒtəˌnaɪz) *vb* **botanizes, botanizing, botanized** *or* **botanises, botanising, botanised. 1** (*intr*) to collect or study plants. **2** (*tr*) to explore and study the plants in (an area or region).

botany ('bɒtənɪ) *n, pl* **botanies. 1** the study of plants, including their classification, structure, physiology, ecology, and economic importance. **2** the plant life of a particular region or time. **3** the biological characteristics of a particular group of plants. ORIG C17: from BOTANICAL; cf. ASTRONOMY, ASTRONOMICAL
▸ '**botanist** *n*

★ people and places

Botany Bay ★ *n* **1** an inlet of the Tasman Sea, on the SE coast of Australia: surrounded by the suburbs of Sydney. **2** (in the 19th century) a British penal settlement that was in fact at Port Jackson, New South Wales.

Botany wool *n* a fine wool from the merino sheep. ORIG C19: from BOTANY BAY, where the wool came from originally

botch (bɒtʃ) *vb* (*tr;* often foll. by *up*) **1** to spoil through clumsiness or ineptitude. **2** to repair badly or clumsily. ◆ *n* **3** a badly done piece of work or repair (esp. in **make a botch of**). ORIG C14: from ?
▸ '**botcher** *n* ▸ '**botchy** *adj*

botfly ('bɒtˌflaɪ) *n, pl* **botflies.** any of various stout-bodied hairy dipterous flies, the larvae of which are parasites of man, sheep, and horses.

both (bəʊθ) *determiner* **1a** the two; two considered together: *both dogs were dirty.* **1b** (*as pron*): *both are to blame.* ◆ *conj* **2** (*coordinating*) used preceding words, phrases, or clauses joined by *and: both Ellen and Keith enjoyed the play; both new and exciting.* ORIG C12: from ON *bāthir*

Botha ★ ('bəʊtə) *n* **1 Louis.** 1862–1919, South African statesman and general; first prime minister of the Union of South Africa (1910–19). **2 P(ieter) W(illem)** born 1916, South African politician; defence minister (1965–78); prime minister (1978–84); state president (1984–89).

Botham ★ ('bəʊθəm) *n* **Ian (Terence).** born 1955, English cricketer: played for Somerset (1973–86), Worcestershire (1987–91), and Durham (1991–93); captained England (1980–81).

bother ('bɒðə) *vb* **1** (*tr*) to give annoyance, pain, or trouble to. **2** (*tr*) to trouble (a person) by repeatedly disturbing; pester. **3** (*intr*) to take the time or trouble; concern oneself: *don't bother to come with me.* **4** (*tr*) to make (a person) alarmed or confused. ◆ *n* **5** a state of worry, trouble, or confusion. **6** a person or thing that causes fuss, trouble, or annoyance. **7** *Inf.* a disturbance or fight; trouble (esp. in **a spot of bother**). ◆ *interj* **8** *Chiefly Brit.* an exclamation of slight annoyance. ORIG C18: ?from Irish Gaelic *bodhar* deaf, vexed

botheration (ˌbɒðə'reɪʃən) *n, interj Inf.* another word for **bother** (senses 5, 8).

bothersome ('bɒðəsəm) *adj* causing bother; troublesome.

Bothnia ★ ('bɒθnɪə) *n* **Gulf of.** an arm of the Baltic Sea, extending north between Sweden and Finland.

Bothwell ★ ('bɒθwəl, 'bɒð-) *n* **Earl of,** title of *James Hepburn.* 1535–78, Scottish nobleman; third husband of Mary Queen of Scots.

bothy ('bɒθɪ) *n, pl* **bothies.** *Chiefly Scot.* **1** a cottage or hut. **2** a farmworker's summer quarters. ORIG C18: ? rel. to BOOTH

bo tree (bəʊ) *n* another name for the **peepul.** ORIG C19: from Sinhalese, from Pali *bodhitaru* tree of wisdom

Botswana ★ (bʊ'tʃwɑːnə; bʊt'swɑːnə, bɒt-) *n* a republic in southern Africa: established as the British protectorate of Bechuanaland in 1885 as a defence against the Boers; became an independent state within the Commonwealth in 1966; consists mostly of a plateau averaging 1000 m (3300 ft), with the extensive Okavango swamps in the northwest and the Kalahari Desert in the southwest. Languages: English and Tswana. Religion: mostly animist. Currency: pula. Capital: Gaborone. Pop.: 1 464 000 (1999 est.). Area: about 570 000 sq. km (220 000 sq. miles).

bott (bɒt) *n* a variant spelling of **bot**[1].

Botticelli ★ (*Italian* botti'tʃɛlli) *n* **Sandro** ('sandro), original name *Alessandro di Mariano Filipepi.* 1444–1510, Italian (Florentine) painter.

bottle ('bɒtᵊl) *n* **1a** a vessel, often of glass and typically cylindrical with a narrow neck, for containing liquids. **1b** (*as modifier*): *a bottle rack.* **2** Also called: **bottleful.** the amount such a vessel will hold. **3** *Brit. sl.* courage; nerve; initiative. **4 the bottle.** *Inf.* drinking of alcohol, esp. to excess. ◆ *vb* **bottles, bottling, bottled.** (*tr*) **5** to put or place in a bottle or bottles. **6** to store (gas) in a portable container under pressure. ◆ See also **bottle out, bottle up.** ORIG C14:

from OF *botaille,* from Med. L *butticula,* from LL *buttis* cask

bottle bank *n* a large container into which the public may throw glass bottles for recycling.

bottlebrush ('bɒtᵊl,brʌʃ) *n* **1** a cylindrical brush on a thin shaft, used for cleaning bottles. **2** Also called: **callistemon.** any of various Australian shrubs or trees having dense spikes of large red flowers with protruding brush-like stamens.

bottled (*or* **bottle**) **gas** *n* butane or propane liquefied under pressure in portable metal containers for use in camping stoves, blowtorches, etc.

bottle-feed *vb* **bottle-feeds, bottle-feeding, bottle-fed.** to feed (a baby) with milk from a bottle.

bottle glass *n* glass used for making bottles, consisting of a silicate of sodium, calcium, and aluminium.

bottle green *n, adj* (of) a dark green colour.

bottle-jack *n NZ, old-fashioned.* a large jack used for heavy lifts.

bottleneck ('bɒtᵊl,nɛk) *n* **1a** a narrow stretch of road or a junction at which traffic is or may be held up. **1b** the hold-up. **2** something that holds up progress.

bottlenose dolphin ('bɒtᵊl,nəuz) *n* a type of dolphin with a bottle-shaped snout.

bottle out *vb* (*intr, adv*) *Brit. sl.* to lose one's nerve.

bottle party *n* a party to which guests bring drink.

bottler ('bɒtlə) *n Austral. & NZ inf.* an exceptional or outstanding person or thing.

bottle shop *n Austral. & NZ.* a shop selling alcohol in unopened containers for consumption elsewhere. Also called (Austral.): **bottle store.**

bottle tree *n* any of several Australian trees that have a bottle-shaped swollen trunk.

bottle up *vb* (*tr, adv*) **1** to restrain (powerful emotion). **2** to keep (an army or other force) contained or trapped.

bottom ('bɒtəm) *n* **1** the lowest, deepest, or farthest removed part of a thing: *the bottom of a hill.* **2** the least important or successful position: *the bottom of a class.* **3** the ground underneath a sea, lake, or river. **4** the inner depths of a person's true feelings (esp. in **from the bottom of one's heart**). **5** the underneath part of a thing. **6** *Naut.* the parts of a vessel's hull that are under water. **7** (in literary or commercial contexts) a boat or ship. **8** (*often pl*) *US & Canad.* the low land bordering a river. **9** (esp. of horses) staying power; stamina. **10** *Inf.* the buttocks. **11** importance, seriousness, or influence: *his views have weight and bottom.* **12 at bottom.** in reality; basically. **13 be at the bottom of.** to be the ultimate cause of. **14 get to the bottom of.** to discover the real truth about. ◆ *adj* (*prenominal*) **15** lowest or last. **16 bet** (*or* **put**) **one's bottom dollar on.** to be absolutely sure of. **17** of, relating to, or situated at the bottom. **18** fundamental; basic. ◆ *vb* **19** (*tr*) to provide (a chair, etc.) with a bottom or seat. **20** (*tr*) to discover the full facts or truth of; fathom. **21** (usually foll. by *on* or *upon*) to base or be founded (on an idea, etc.). ORIG OE *botm*

bottom drawer *n Brit.* a young woman's collection of linen, cutlery, etc., made in anticipation of marriage. US, Canad., and NZ equivalent: **hope chest.**

bottoming ('bɒtəmɪŋ) *n* the lowest level of foundation material for a road or other structure.

bottomless ('bɒtəmlɪs) *adj* **1** having no bottom. **2** unlimited; inexhaustible. **3** very deep.

bottom line *n* **1** the last line of a financial statement that shows the net profit or loss of a company or organization. **2** the conclusion or main point of a process, discussion, etc.

bottom out *vb* (*intr, adv*) to reach the lowest point and level out.

bottomry ('bɒtəmrɪ) *n, pl* **bottomries.** *Maritime law.* a contract whereby the owner of a ship borrows money to enable the vessel to complete the voyage and pledges the ship as security for the loan. ORIG C16: from Du. *bodemerij,* from *bodem* BOTTOM (hull of a ship) + *-erij* -RY

bottom-up processing *n* a processing technique, either in the brain or in a computer, in which incoming information is analysed in successive steps and later-stage processing does not affect processing in earlier stages.

Bottrop ★ (*German* 'bɔtrɔp) *n* an industrial city in W Germany, in North Rhine-Westphalia in the Ruhr. Pop.: 120 642 (1996 est.).

botulism ('bɒtjʊ,lɪzəm) *n* severe, often fatal, poisoning resulting from the potent bacterial toxin, **botulin,** produced in imperfectly preserved food, etc. ORIG C19: from G *Botulismus,* lit.: sausage poisoning, from L *botulus* sausage

Bouaké ★ (*French* bwake) *n* a market town in S central Côte d'Ivoire. Pop.: 330 000 (1995 est.).

Boucher ★ (*French* buʃe) *n* **François** (frɑ̃swa). 1703–70, French rococo artist.

Bouches-du-Rhône ★ (*French* buʃdyron) *n* a department of S central France, in Provence-Alpes-Côte d'Azur region. Capital: Marseille. Pop.: 1 793 876 (1994 est.). Area: 5284 sq. km (2047 sq. miles).

bouclé ('bu:kleɪ) *n* **1** a curled or looped yarn or fabric giving a thick knobbly effect. ◆ *adj* **2** of or designating such a yarn or fabric. ORIG C19: from F *bouclé* curly, from *boucle* a curl

Boudicca ★ (bəu'dɪkə) *n* died 62 A.D., a queen of the Iceni, who led a revolt against Roman rule in Britain; after being defeated she poisoned herself. Also called: **Boadicea.**

Boudin ★ (*French* budɛ̃) *n* **Eugène** (øʒɛn). 1824–98, French painter.

boudoir ('bu:dwɑ:, -dwɔ:) *n* a woman's bedroom or private sitting room. ORIG C18: from F, lit.: room for sulking in, from *bouder* to sulk

bouffant ('bu:fɔ:ŋ) *adj* **1** (of a hairstyle) having extra height and width through backcombing; puffed out. **2** (of sleeves, skirts, etc.) puffed out. ORIG C20: from F, from *bouffer* to puff up

Bougainville[1] ★ ('bu:gən,vɪl) *n* an island in the W Pacific, in Papua New Guinea: the largest of the Solomon Islands; unilaterally declared independence in 1990; occupied by government troops in 1992. Chief town: Kieta. Pop.: 159 500 (1990 est.). Area: 10 049 sq. km (3880 sq. miles).

Bougainville[2] ★ (*French* bugɛ̃vil) *n* **Louis Antoine de** (lwi ɑ̃twan də). 1729–1811, French navigator.

bougainvillea (,bu:gən'vɪlɪə) *n* a tropical woody climbing plant having inconspicuous flowers surrounded by showy red or purple bracts. ORIG C19: NL, after L. A. de BOUGAINVILLE

bough (bau) *n* any of the main branches of a tree. ORIG OE *bōg* arm, twig

bought (bɔ:t) *vb* the past tense and past participle of **buy.**

bougie ('bu:ʒi:, bu:'ʒi:) *n Med.* a slender semiflexible instrument for inserting into body passages such as the rectum or urethra to introduce medication, etc. ORIG C18: from F, orig. a wax candle from *Bougie* (Bujiya), Algeria

bouillabaisse (,bu:jə'bɛs) *n* a rich stew or soup of fish and vegetables. ORIG C19: from F, from Provençal *bouiabaisso,* lit.: boil down

bouillon ('bu:jɒn) *n* a plain unclarified broth or stock. ORIG C18: from F, from *bouillir* to BOIL[1]

Boulanger ★ (*French* bulɑ̃ʒe) *n* **1 Georges** (ʒɔrʒ). 1837–91, French general and minister of war (1886–87). Accused of attempting a coup d'état, he fled to Belgium, where he committed suicide. **2 Nadia** (**Juliette**) (nadja). 1887–1979, French teacher of musical composition.

boulder ('bəuldə) *n* a smooth rounded mass of rock that has been shaped by erosion. ORIG C13: prob. from ON; cf. OSwedish *bulder* rumbling + *sten* STONE

boulder clay *n* an unstratified glacial deposit consisting of fine clay, boulders, and pebbles.

Boulder Dam ★ *n* the former name (1933–47) of **Hoover Dam.**

boule ('bu:li:) *n* **1** the senate of an ancient Greek city-state. **2** the parliament in modern Greece. ORIG C19: from Gk *boulē* senate

boules *French.* (bul) *n* (*functioning as sing*) a game, popular in France, in which metal bowls are thrown to land as near as possible to a target ball. ORIG pl. of *boule* BALL[1]: see BOWL[2]

boulevard ('buːlvɑː, -vɑːd) *n* a wide usually tree-lined road in a city. ORIG C18: from F, from MDu. *bolwerc* BULWARK; so called because orig. often built on the ruins of an old rampart

Boulez ★ ('buːlɛz; *French* bulɛ) *n* **Pierre** (pjɛr). born 1925, French composer and conductor, whose works employ total serialism.

boulle, boule, *or* **buhl** (buːl) *adj* **1** denoting or relating to a type of marquetry of patterned inlays of brass and tortoiseshell, etc. ◆ *n* **2** something ornamented with such marquetry. ORIG C18: after A. C. *Boulle* (1642–1732), F cabinet-maker

Boulogne ★ (bu'lɔɪn; *French* bulɔɲ) *n* a port in N France, on the English Channel. Pop.: 44 244 (1990). Official name: **Boulogne-sur-Mer** (*French* bulɔɲsyrmɛr).

Boulogne-Billancourt ★ (*French* bulɔɲbijɑ̃kur) *n* an industrial suburb of SW Paris. Pop.: 101 971 (1990). Also called: **Boulogne-sur-Seine** (*French* bulɔɲsyrsɛn).

boult (bəʊlt) *vb* a variant spelling of **bolt**[2].

Boult ★ (bəʊlt) *n* Sir **Adrian** (**Cedric**). 1889–1983, British conductor.

Boulton ★ ('bəʊltᵊn) *n* **Matthew**. 1728–1809, British engineer and manufacturer, who financed Watt's steam engine and applied it to various industrial purposes.

Boumédienne ★ (buːˌmeɪdɪ'ɛn) *n* **Houari** ('haʊərɪ). 1927–78, Algerian statesman and soldier: prime minister of Algeria (1965–78) after overthrowing Ben Bella in a coup (1965).

bounce (baʊns) *vb* **bounces, bouncing, bounced. 1** (*intr*) (of a ball, etc.) to rebound from an impact. **2** (*tr*) to cause (a ball, etc.) to hit a solid surface and spring back. **3** to move or cause to move suddenly, excitedly, or violently; spring. **4** *Sl.* (of a bank) to send (a cheque) back or (of a cheque) to be sent back by a bank to a payee unredeemed because of lack of funds in the drawer's account. **5** (*tr*) *Sl.* to force (a person) to leave a place or job; throw out; eject. ◆ *n* **6** the action of rebounding from an impact. **7** a leap; jump; bound. **8** the quality of being able to rebound; springiness. **9** *Inf.* vitality; vigour; resilience. **10** *Brit.* swagger or impudence. ORIG C13: prob. imit.; cf. Low G *bunsen* to beat, Du. *bonken* to thump

bounce back *vb* (*intr, adv*) to recover one's health, good spirits, confidence, etc., easily.

bouncer ('baʊnsə) *n Sl.* a man employed at a club, disco, etc., to eject drunks or troublemakers.

bouncing ('baʊnsɪŋ) *adj* (when *postpositive,* foll. by *with*) vigorous and robust (esp. in **a bouncing baby**).

bouncy ('baʊnsɪ) *adj* **bouncier, bounciest. 1** lively, exuberant, or self-confident. **2** having the capability or quality of bouncing: *a bouncy ball.* **3** responsive to bouncing; springy: *a bouncy bed.*

Bouncy Castle *n Trademark.* a large inflatable model, usually of a castle, on which children may bounce at fairs, etc.

bound[1] (baʊnd) *vb* **1** the past tense and past participle of **bind.** ◆ *adj* **2** in bonds or chains; tied as with a rope. **3** (*in combination*) restricted; confined: *housebound.* **4** (*postpositive;* foll. by an infinitive) destined; sure; certain: *it's bound to happen.* **5** (*postpositive;* often foll. by *by*) compelled or obliged. **6** *Rare.* constipated. **7** (of a book) secured within a cover or binding. **8** *Logic.* (of a variable) occurring within the scope of a quantifier. Cf. **free** (sense 18). **9 bound up with.** closely or inextricably linked with.

bound[2] (baʊnd) *vb* **1** to move forwards by leaps or jumps. **2** to bounce; spring away from an impact. ◆ *n* **3** a jump upwards or forwards. **4** a bounce, as of a ball. ORIG C16: from OF *bond* a leap

bound[3] (baʊnd) *vb* **1** (*tr*) to place restrictions on; limit. **2** (when *intr,* foll. by *on*) to form a boundary of. ◆ *n* **3** See **bounds.** ORIG C13: from OF *bonde,* from Med. L *bodina*

bound[4] (baʊnd) *adj* **a** (*postpositive;* often foll. by *for*) going or intending to go towards: *bound for Jamaica; homeward bound.* **b** (*in combination*): *northbound traffic.* ORIG C13: from ON *buinn,* p.p. of *būa* to prepare

boundary ('baʊndərɪ, -drɪ) *n, pl* **boundaries. 1** something that indicates the farthest limit, as of an area; border. **2** *Cricket.* **2a** the marked limit of the playing area. **2b** a stroke that hits the ball beyond this limit. **2c** the four or six runs scored with such a stroke.

boundary rider *n Austral.* an employee on a sheep or cattle station whose job is to maintain fences.

bounden ('baʊndən) *adj* morally obligatory (arch. except in **bounden duty**). ORIG arch. p.p. of BIND

bounder ('baʊndə) *n Old-fashioned Brit. sl.* a morally reprehensible person; cad.

boundless ('baʊndlɪs) *adj* unlimited; vast: *boundless energy.*
▸ **'boundlessly** *adv*

bounds (baʊndz) *pl n* **1** (*sometimes sing*) a limit; boundary (esp. in **know no bounds**). **2** something that restrains or confines, esp. the standards of a society: *within the bounds of modesty.* ◆ See also **out of bounds.**

bounteous ('baʊntɪəs) *adj Literary.* **1** giving freely; generous. **2** plentiful; abundant.
▸ **'bounteously** *adv* ▸ **'bounteousness** *n*

bountiful ('baʊntɪfʊl) *adj* **1** plentiful; ample (esp. in **a bountiful supply**). **2** giving freely; generous.
▸ **'bountifully** *adv*

bounty ('baʊntɪ) *n, pl* **bounties. 1** generosity; liberality. **2** a generous gift. **3** a payment made by a government, as, formerly, to a sailor on enlisting or to a soldier after a campaign. **4** any reward or premium. ORIG C13 (in the sense: goodness): from OF, from L, from *bonus* good

bouquet (buː'keɪ) *n* **1** a bunch of flowers, esp. a large carefully arranged one. **2** the characteristic aroma or fragrance of a wine or liqueur. **3** a compliment or expression of praise. ORIG C18: from F: thicket, from OF *bosc* forest

bouquet garni ('buːkeɪ gɑː'niː) *n, pl* **bouquets garnis** ('buːkeɪz gɑː'niː). a bunch of herbs tied together and used for flavouring soups, stews, etc. ORIG C19: from F, lit.: garnished bouquet

bourbon ('bɜːbᵊn) *n* a whiskey distilled, chiefly in the US, from maize, esp. one containing at least 51 per cent maize. ORIG C19: after *Bourbon* county, Kentucky, where it was first made

Bourbon ★ ('bʊəbᵊn; *French* burbɔ̃) *n* **a** a member of the European royal line that ruled in France from 1589 to 1793 (when Louis XVI was executed by the revolutionaries) and was restored in 1815, continuing to rule in its Orleans branch from 1830 until 1848. Bourbon dynasties also ruled in Spain (1700–1808; 1813–1931) and Naples and Sicily (1734–1806; 1815–1860). **b** (*as modifier*): *the Bourbon kings.*

bourdon ('bʊədᵊn, 'bɔːdᵊn) *n* **1** a bass organ stop. **2** the drone of a bagpipe. ORIG C14: from OF: drone (of a musical instrument), imit.

bourgeois ('bʊəʒwɑː) *Often disparaging.* ◆ *n, pl* **bourgeois. 1** a member of the middle class, esp. one regarded as being conservative and materialistic or capitalistic. **2** a mediocre, unimaginative, or materialistic person. ◆ *adj* **3** characteristic of, relating to, or comprising the middle class. **4** conservative or materialistic in outlook. **5** (in Marxist thought) dominated by capitalists or capitalist interests. ORIG C16: from OF *borjois, burgeis* burgher, citizen; see BURGESS
▸ **bourgeoise** ('bʊəʒwɑːz, bʊə'ʒwɑːz) *fem n*

bourgeoisie (ˌbʊəʒwɑː'ziː) *n* **the. 1** the middle classes. **2** (in Marxist thought) the capitalist ruling class. The bourgeoisie owns the means of production, through which it exploits the working class.

bourgeon ('bɜːdʒən) *n, vb* a variant spelling of **burgeon.**

Bourges ★ (*French* burʒ) *n* a city in central France. Pop.: 75 609 (1990).

Bourgogne ★ (burgɔɲ) *n* the French name for **Burgundy.**

Bourguiba ★ (bʊə'giːbə) *n* **Habib ben Ali** (hæ'bɪb bɛn 'ɑːlɪ). 1903–2000, Tunisian statesman: president of Tunisia (1957–87).

bourn[1] *or* **bourne** (bɔːn) *n Arch.* **1** a destination; goal. **2** a boundary. ORIG C16: from OF *borne;* see BOUND[3]

bourn² (bɔːn) *n Chiefly southern Brit.* a stream. ORIG C16: from OF *bodne* limit; see BOUND³

Bournemouth ★ ('bɔːnməθ) *n* **1** a resort in S England, in SE Dorset, on the English Channel. Pop.: 155 488 (1991). **2** a unitary authority in S England, in E Dorset. Pop.: 160 700 (1999). Area: 46 sq. km (17 sq. miles).

bourrée ('bʊəreɪ) *n* **1** a traditional French dance in fast duple time. **2** a piece of music in the rhythm of this dance. ORIG C18: from F

Bourse (bʊəs) *n* a stock exchange of continental Europe, esp. Paris. ORIG C19: from F, lit.: purse, from Med. L *bursa,* ult. from Gk: leather

boustrophedon (ˌbaʊstrəˈfiːdᵊn) *adj* having alternate lines written from right to left and from left to right. ORIG C17: from Gk, lit.: turning as in ploughing with oxen, from *bous* ox + *strephein* to turn

bout (baʊt) *n* **1a** a period of time spent doing something, such as drinking. **1b** a period of illness. **2** a contest or fight, esp. a boxing or wrestling match. ORIG C16: var. of obs. *bought* turn

boutique (buːˈtiːk) *n* **1** a shop, esp. a small one selling fashionable clothes and other items. **2** (*modifier*) of or denoting a small specialized producer or business: *a boutique operation.* ORIG C18: from F, ult. from Gk *apothēkē* storehouse

boutonniere (ˌbuːtɒnɪˈɛə) *n* the US name for **buttonhole** (sense 2). ORIG C19: from F: buttonhole

bouzouki (buːˈzuːkɪ) *n* a Greek long-necked stringed musical instrument related to the mandolin. ORIG C20: from Mod. Gk, ?from Turkish *büjük* large

bovine ('bəʊvaɪn) *adj* **1** of or relating to cattle. **2** (of people) dull; sluggish; stolid. ORIG C19: from LL *bovīnus,* from L *bōs* ox, cow
▸ **ˈbovinely** *adv*

bovine somatotrophin *n* the full name for **BST** (sense 1).

bovine spongiform encephalopathy *n* the full name for **BSE.**

Bovril ('bɒvrɪl) *n Trademark.* a concentrated beef extract, used for flavouring, as a stock, etc.

bovver ('bɒvə) *n Brit. sl.* **a** rowdiness, esp. caused by gangs of teenage youths. **b** (*as modifier*): *a bovver boy.* ORIG C20: sl. pronunciation of BOTHER

bow¹ (baʊ) *vb* **1** to lower (one's head) or bend (one's knee or body) as a sign of respect, greeting, assent, or shame. **2** to bend or cause to bend. **3** (*intr;* usually foll. by *to* or *before*) to comply or accept: *bow to the inevitable.* **4** (*tr;* foll. by *in, out, to,* etc.) to usher (someone) in or out with bows and deference. **5** (*tr;* usually foll. by *down*) to bring (a person, nation, etc.) to a state of submission. **6 bow and scrape.** to behave in an excessively deferential or obsequious way. ◆ *n* **7** a lowering or inclination of the head or body as a mark of respect, greeting, or assent. **8 take a bow.** to acknowledge or receive applause or praise. ◆ See also **bow out.** ORIG OE *būgan*

bow² (bəʊ) *n* **1** a weapon for shooting arrows, consisting of an arch of flexible wood, plastic, etc., bent by a string fastened at each end. **2a** a long stick across which are stretched strands of horsehair, used for playing the strings of a violin, viola, cello, etc. **2b** a stroke with such a stick. **3a** a decorative interlacing of ribbon or other fabrics, usually having two loops and two loose ends. **3b** the knot forming such an interlacing. **4** something that is curved, bent, or arched. ◆ *vb* **5** to form or cause to form a curve or curves. **6** to make strokes of a bow across (violin strings). ORIG OE *boga* arch, bow

bow³ (baʊ) *n* **1** *Chiefly Naut.* **1a** (*often pl*) the forward end or part of a vessel. **1b** (*as modifier*): *the bow mooring line.* **2** *Rowing.* the oarsman at the bow. ORIG C15: prob. from Low G *boog*

bow compass (bəʊ) *n Geom.* a compass in which the legs are joined by a flexible metal bow-shaped spring rather than a hinge.

bowdlerize *or* **bowdlerise** ('baʊdləˌraɪz) *vb* **bowdlerizes, bowdlerizing, bowdlerized** *or* **bowdlerises, bowdlerising, bowdlerised.** (*tr*) to remove passages or words regarded as indecent from (a play, novel, etc.); expurgate. ORIG C19: after Thomas *Bowdler* (1754–1825), E editor who expurgated Shakespeare
▸ ˌ**bowdleriˈzation** *or* ˌ**bowdleriˈsation** *n* ▸ **ˈbowdlerism** *n*

bowel ('baʊəl) *n* **1** an intestine, esp. the large intestine in man. **2** (*pl*) innards; entrails. **3** (*pl*) the deep or innermost part (esp. in **the bowels of the earth**). ORIG C13: from OF *bouel,* from L *botellus* a little sausage

bowel movement *n* **1** the discharge of faeces; defecation. **2** the waste matter discharged; faeces.

Bowen ★ ('bəʊən) *n* **Elizabeth** (**Dorothea Cole**). 1899–1973, British writer, born in Ireland. Her novels include *The Death of the Heart* (1938) and *The Heat of the Day* (1949).

bower¹ ('baʊə) *n* **1** a shady leafy shelter or recess, as in a wood or garden; arbour. **2** *Literary.* a lady's bedroom or apartments; boudoir. ORIG OE *būr* dwelling

bower² ('baʊə) *n Naut.* a vessel's bow anchor. ORIG C18: from BOW³ + -ER¹

bowerbird ('baʊəˌbɜːd) *n* **1** any of various songbirds of Australia and New Guinea. The males build bower-like display grounds to attract the females. **2** *Inf., chiefly Austral.* a collector of unconsidered trifles.

Bowery ★ ('baʊərɪ) *n* **the.** a street in New York City noted for its cheap hotels and bars, frequented by vagrants and drunks. ORIG C17: from Du. *bouwerij,* from *bouwen* to farm + *erij* -ERY

bowfin ('bəʊˌfɪn) *n* a primitive North American freshwater bony fish with an elongated body and a very long dorsal fin.

bowhead ('bəʊˌhɛd) *n* a large-mouthed arctic right whale. Also called: **Greenland whale.**

Bowie ★ *n* **1** ('baʊɪ, 'bəʊɪ) **David,** real name *David Jones.* born 1947, British rock singer and film actor. His recordings include "Space Oddity" (1969), *Let's Dance* (1983), and *Earthling* (1997). **2** ('bəʊɪ). **James,** known as *Jim Bowie.* 1796–1836, US frontiersman. A hero of the Texas Revolution, he died at the Battle of Alamo.

bowie knife ('bəʊɪ) *n* a stout hunting knife with a short hilt and a guard for the hand. ORIG C19: named after Jim BOWIE, who popularized it

bowl¹ (bəʊl) *n* **1** a round container open at the top, used for holding liquid, serving food, etc. **2** Also: **bowlful.** the amount a bowl will hold. **3** the rounded or hollow part of an object, esp. of a spoon or tobacco pipe. **4** any container shaped like a bowl, such as a sink or lavatory. **5** a bowl-shaped building or other structure, such as an amphitheatre. **6** *Chiefly US.* a bowl-shaped depression of the land surface. **7** *Literary.* a drinking cup. ORIG OE *bolla*

bowl² (bəʊl) *n* **1** a wooden ball used in the game of bowls, having one flattened side in order to make it run on a curved course. **2** a large heavy ball with holes for gripping, used in tenpin bowling. ◆ *vb* **3** to roll smoothly or cause to roll smoothly along the ground. **4** (*intr;* usually foll. by *along*) to move easily and rapidly, as in a car. **5** *Cricket.* **5a** to send (a ball) from one's hand towards the batsman. **5b** Also: **bowl out.** to dismiss (the person batting) by delivering a ball that breaks the wicket. **6** (*intr*) to play bowls or tenpin bowling. ◆ See also **bowl over, bowls.** ORIG C15: from F *boule,* ult. from L *bulla* bubble

bow legs (bəʊ) *pl n* a condition in which the legs curve outwards like a bow between the ankle and the thigh. Also called: **bandy legs.**
▸ **bow-legged** (bəʊˈlɛgɪd, bəʊˈlɛgd) *adj*

bowler¹ ('bəʊlə) *n* **1** one who bowls in cricket. **2** a player at the game of bowls.

bowler² ('bəʊlə) *n* a stiff felt hat with a rounded crown and narrow curved brim. US and Canad. name: **derby.** ORIG C19: after John *Bowler,* 19th-cent. London hatter

Bowles ★ (bəʊlz) *n* **Paul.** 1910–99, US writer and composer, who lived in Tangiers. His novels include *The Sheltering Sky* (1949) and *The Spider's House* (1955).

bowline ('bəʊlɪn) *n Naut.* **1** a line for controlling the weather leech of a square sail when a vessel is close-hauled. **2** a knot used for securing a loop that will not slip at the end of a piece of rope. ORIG C14: prob. from MLow G *bōlīne,* equivalent to BOW³ + LINE¹

bowling ('bəʊlɪŋ) *n* **1** any of various games in which a heavy ball is rolled down a special alley at a group of wooden pins. **2** the game of bowls. **3** *Cricket.* the act of delivering the ball to the batsman.

bowling alley *n* **1a** a long narrow wooden lane down which the ball is rolled in tenpin bowling. **1b** a similar lane or alley for playing skittles. **2** a building having lanes for tenpin bowling.

bowling crease *n Cricket.* a line marked at the wicket, over which a bowler must not advance fully before delivering the ball.

bowling green *n* an area of closely mown turf on which the game of bowls is played.

bowl over *vb* (*tr, adv*) **1** *Inf.* to surprise (a person) greatly, esp. in a pleasant way; astound; amaze. **2** to knock down.

bowls (bəʊlz) *n* (*functioning as sing*) **1** a game played on a bowling green in which a small bowl (the jack) is pitched from a mark and two opponents take turns to roll biased wooden bowls as near the jack as possible. **2** skittles or tenpin bowling.

bowman ('bəʊmən) *n, pl* **bowmen.** *Arch.* an archer.

bow out (baʊ) *vb* (*adv; usually tr;* often foll. by *of*) to retire or withdraw gracefully.

bowser ('baʊzə) *n* **1** a tanker containing fuel for aircraft, military vehicles, etc. **2** *Austral. & NZ obs.* a petrol pump at a filling station. ORIG orig. a US proprietary name

bowshot ('bəʊˌʃɒt) *n* the distance an arrow travels from the bow.

bowsprit ('bəʊsprɪt) *n Naut.* a spar projecting from the bow of a vessel, esp. a sailing vessel. ORIG C13: from MLow G, from *bōch* BOW[3] + *sprēt* pole

bowstring ('bəʊˌstrɪŋ) *n* the string of an archer's bow.

bow tie (bəʊ) *n* a man's tie tied in a bow, now chiefly in plain black for formal evening wear.

bow window (bəʊ) *n* a bay window in the shape of a curve.

bow-wow ('baʊˌwaʊ, -'waʊ) *n* **1** a child's word for **dog. 2** an imitation of the bark of a dog. ◆ *vb* **3** (*intr*) to bark or imitate a dog's bark.

bowyangs ('bəʊjæŋz) *pl n Austral. & NZ sl.* a pair of strings or straps worn around the trouser leg below the knee, orig. esp. by agricultural workers. ORIG C19: from E dialect *bowy-yanks* leggings

box[1] (bɒks) *n* **1** a receptacle or container made of wood, cardboard, etc., usually rectangular and having a removable or hinged lid. **2** Also called: **boxful.** the contents of such a receptacle. **3** (*often in combination*) any of various small cubicles, kiosks, or shelters: *a telephone box; a signal box.* **4** a separate compartment in a public place for a small group of people, as in a theatre. **5** an enclosure within a courtroom: *witness box.* **6** a compartment for a horse in a stable or a vehicle. **7** *Brit.* a small country house occupied by sportsmen when following a field sport, esp. shooting. **8a** a protective housing for machinery or mechanical parts. **8b** (*in combination*): *a gearbox.* **9** a shaped device of light tough material worn by sportsmen to protect the genitals, esp. in cricket. **10** a section of printed matter on a page, enclosed by lines, a border, etc. **11** a central agency to which mail is addressed and from which it is collected or redistributed: *a post-office box; a box number in a newspaper advertisement.* **12** short for **penalty box. 13** the raised seat on which the driver sits in a horse-drawn coach. **14** *Austral. & NZ.* an accidental mixing of herds or flocks. **15** *Brit.* (esp. formerly) a present, esp. of money, given at Christmas to tradesmen, etc. **16** *Austral. taboo sl.* the female genitals. **17 out of the box.** *Austral. inf.* outstanding or excellent. **18 the box.** *Brit. inf.* television. ◆ *vb* **19** (*tr*) to put into a box. **20** (*tr;* usually foll. by *in* or *up*) to prevent from moving freely; confine. **21** (*tr;* foll. by *in*) *Printing.* to enclose (text) within a ruled frame. **22** *Austral. & NZ.* to mix (flocks or herds) or (of flocks) to become mixed accidentally. **23 box the compass.** *Naut.* to name the compass points in order. ORIG OE *box,* from L *buxus,* from Gk *puxos* BOX[3]
▸ **'boxˌlike** *adj*

box[2] (bɒks) *vb* **1** (*tr*) to fight (an opponent) in a boxing match. **2** (*intr*) to engage in boxing. **3** (*tr*) to hit (a person) with the fist. ◆ *n* **4** a punch with the fist, esp. on the ear. ORIG C14: from ?

box[3] (bɒks) *n* **1** a slow-growing evergreen tree or shrub with small shiny leaves: used for hedges. **2** the wood of this tree. **3** any of several trees the timber or foliage of which resembles this tree, esp. various eucalyptus trees with rough bark. ORIG OE, from L *buxus,* from Gk *puxus*

box camera *n* a simple box-shaped camera having an elementary lens, shutter, and viewfinder.

box chronometer *n Naut.* a ship's chronometer, supported on gimbals in a wooden box.

boxer ('bɒksə) *n* **1** a person who boxes; pugilist. **2** a medium-sized smooth-haired breed of dog with a short nose and a docked tail.

Boxer ('bɒksə) *n* a member of a nationalistic Chinese secret society that led an unsuccessful rebellion in 1900 against foreign interests in China. ORIG C18: rough translation of Chinese *I Ho Ch'üan,* lit.: virtuous harmonious fist

boxer shorts *pl n* men's underpants shaped like shorts but having a front opening. Also called: **boxers.**

box girder *n* a girder that is hollow and square or rectangular in shape.

boxing ('bɒksɪŋ) *n* **a** the act, art, or profession of fighting with the fists. **b** (*as modifier*): *a boxing enthusiast.*

Boxing Day *n Brit. & Canad.* the first day (traditionally and strictly, the first weekday) after Christmas, observed as a holiday. ORIG C19: from the custom of giving Christmas boxes to tradesmen and staff on this day

boxing glove *n* one of a pair of thickly padded mittens worn for boxing.

box junction *n* (in Britain) a road junction having yellow cross-hatching painted on the road surface. Vehicles may only enter the hatched area when their exit is clear.

box kite *n* a kite with a boxlike frame open at both ends.

box lacrosse *n Canad.* lacrosse played indoors. Also called: **boxla.**

box number *n* **1** the number of an individual pigeonhole at a newspaper to which replies to an advertisement may be addressed. **2** the number of an individual pigeonhole at a post office from which mail may be collected.

box office *n* **1** an office at a theatre, cinema, etc., where tickets are sold. **2a** the public appeal of an actor or production. **2b** (*as modifier*): *a box-office success.*

box pleat *n* a flat double pleat made by folding under the fabric on either side of it.

boxroom ('bɒksˌruːm, -ˌrʊm) *n* a small room or large cupboard in which boxes, cases, etc., may be stored.

box seat *n* **1** a seat in a theatre box. **2 in the box seat.** *Brit., Austral., & NZ.* in the best position.

box spanner *n* a spanner consisting of a steel cylinder with a hexagonal end that fits over a nut.

box spring *n* a coiled spring contained in a boxlike frame, used for mattresses, chairs, etc.

boxwood ('bɒksˌwʊd) *n* **1** the hard close-grained yellow wood of the box tree, used to make tool handles, etc. **2** the box tree.

boxy ('bɒksɪ) *adj* squarish or chunky in style or appearance: *a boxy square-cut jacket.*

boy (bɔɪ) *n* **1** a male child; lad; youth. **2** a man regarded as immature or inexperienced. **3 the boys.** *Inf.* a group of men, esp. a group of friends. **4** *S. African derog.* a Black male servant. **5 the boy.** *Irish inf.* the right tool for a particular task: *that's the boy to cut it.* ◆ *interj* **6** an exclamation of surprise, pleasure, contempt, etc. ORIG C13 (in the sense: male servant; C14: young male): ?from Anglo-F *abuié* fettered (unattested), from L *boia* fetter
▸ **'boyish** *adj*

Boyce ★ (bɔɪs) *n* **William.** ?1710–79, British composer, noted esp. for his church music and symphonies.

boycott ('bɔɪkɒt) *vb* **1** (*tr*) to refuse to have dealings with (a person, organization, etc.) or refuse to buy (a product) as a protest or means of coercion. ◆ *n* **2** an instance or the use of boycotting. ORIG C19: after Captain C. C. *Boycott* (1832–97), Irish land agent, a victim of such practices for refusing to reduce rents

Boycott ★ ('bɔɪkɒt) *n* **Geoff(rey).** born 1940, English cricketer: captained Yorkshire (1970–78); played for England (1964–74, 1977–82).

Boyd ★ (bɔɪd) *n* **1 Arthur.** 1920–99, Australian painter and sculptor. **2 Martin (A'Beckett).** 1893–1972, Australian novelist, best known for *The Montforts* (1928). **3 William (Andrew Murray).** born 1953, British writer born in Ghana. His novels include *An Ice-Cream War* (1982).

Boyer ★ (*French* bwaje) *n* **Charles** (ʃarl), known as *the Great Lover.* 1899–1978, French film actor.

boyfriend ('bɔɪˌfrɛnd) *n* a male friend with whom a person is romantically or sexually involved; sweetheart or lover.

boyhood ('bɔɪhʊd) *n* the state or time of being a boy.

Boyle ★ (bɔɪl) *n* **Robert.** 1627–91, Irish scientist who helped to dissociate chemistry from alchemy; author of *The Sceptical Chymist* (1661).

Boyle's law *n* the principle that the pressure of a gas varies inversely with its volume at constant temperature. ORIG C18: after Robert BOYLE

Boyne ★ (bɔɪn) *n* a river in the E Republic of Ireland, rising in the Bog of Allen and flowing northeast to the Irish Sea: William III of England defeated the deposed James II in a battle (**Battle of the Boyne**) on its banks in 1690, completing the overthrow of the Stuart cause in Ireland. Length: about 112 km (70 miles).

boyo ('bɔɪəʊ) *n Brit. inf.* a boy or young man: often used in direct address. ORIG from Irish and Welsh

Boyoma Falls ★ (bɔɪ'əʊmə) *pl n* a series of seven cataracts in the Democratic Republic of Congo (formerly Zaïre), on the upper River Congo: forms an unnavigable stretch of 90 km (56 miles), which falls 60 m (200 ft). Former name: **Stanley Falls.**

boy racer *n Derog. sl.* **a** a young man who drives a car irresponsibly and at high speeds. **b** (*as modifier*): *boy-racer accessories.*

Boys' Brigade *n* (in Britain) an organization for boys, founded in 1883, with the aim of promoting discipline and self-respect.

boy scout *n* See **Scout.**

boysenberry ('bɔɪzᵊnbərɪ) *n, pl* **boysenberries. 1** a type of bramble: a hybrid of the loganberry and various blackberries and raspberries. **2** the large red edible fruit of this plant. ORIG C20: after Rudolph *Boysen,* American botanist

Boz ★ (bɒz) *n* pen name of (Charles) **Dickens.**

Bozcaada ★ (ˌbɔzdʒaa'da) *n* the Turkish name for **Tenedos.**

Bozen ★ ('bo:tsən) *n* the German name for **Bolzano.**

bp *abbrev. for:* **1** (of alcoholic density) below proof. **2** boiling point. **3** bishop. **4** Also: **B/P.** bills payable.

BP *abbrev. for:* **1** blood pressure. **2** British Pharmacopoeia.

bp. *abbrev. for:* **1** baptized. **2** birthplace.

B/P *or* **bp** *abbrev. for* bills payable.

BPC *abbrev. for* British Pharmaceutical Codex.

BPhil *abbrev. for* Bachelor of Philosophy.

bpi *abbrev. for* bits per inch (used of a computer tape).

BPR *abbrev. for* business process re-engineering.

b.pt. *abbrev. for* boiling point.

Bq *Physics. symbol for* becquerel.

br *abbrev. for* brother.

Br 1 *abbrev. for* (in a religious order) Brother. ◆ **2** *the chemical symbol for* bromine.

BR *abbrev. for* British Rail (British Railways).

br. *abbrev. for:* **1** branch. **2** bronze.

Br. *abbrev. for:* **1** Breton. **2** Britain. **3** British.

bra (brɑ:) *n* a woman's undergarment for covering and supporting the breasts. ORIG C20: from BRASSIERE

braai (braɪ) *n* short for **braaivleis.**

braaivleis ('braɪˌfleɪs) *n S. African.* a barbecue. ORIG from Afrik. *braai* grill + *vleis* meat

Brabant ★ (brə'bænt) *n* **1** a former duchy of W Europe: divided when Belgium became independent (1830), the south forming the Belgian provinces of Antwerp and Brabant and the north forming the province of North Brabant in the Netherlands. **2** a former province of central Belgium; replaced in 1995 by the provinces of **Flemish Brabant** and **Walloon Brabant.**

Brabham ★ ('bræbəm) *n* Sir **John Arthur,** known as *Jack.* born 1926, Australian racing driver: world champion 1959, 1960, and 1966.

brace (breɪs) *n* **1** a hand tool for drilling holes, with a socket to hold the drill at one end and a cranked handle by which the tool can be turned. See also **brace and bit. 2** something that steadies, binds, or holds up another thing. **3** a structural member, such as a beam or prop, used to stiffen a framework. **4** a pair, esp. of game birds. **5** either of a pair of characters, { }, used for connecting lines of printing or writing. **6** Also called: **accolade.** a line or bracket connecting two or more staves of music. **7** (*often pl*) an appliance of metal bands and wires for correcting uneven alignment of teeth. **8** *Med.* any of various appliances for supporting the trunk or a limb. **9** See **braces.** ◆ *vb* **braces, bracing, braced.** (*mainly tr*) **10** to provide, strengthen, or fit with a brace. **11** to steady or prepare (oneself or something) as before an impact. **12** (*also intr*) to stimulate; freshen; invigorate: *sea air is bracing.* ORIG C14: from OF, from L *bracchia* arms

brace and bit *n* a hand tool for boring holes, consisting of a cranked handle into which a drilling bit is inserted.

bracelet ('breɪslɪt) *n* an ornamental chain worn around the arm or wrist. ORIG C15: from OF, from L *bracchium* arm

bracelets ('breɪslɪts) *pl n* a slang name for **handcuffs.**

bracer ('breɪsə) *n* **1** a person or thing that braces. **2** *Inf.* a tonic, esp. an alcoholic drink taken as a tonic.

braces ('breɪsɪz) *pl n Brit.* a pair of straps worn over the shoulders by men for holding up the trousers. US and Canad. word: **suspenders.**

brachial ('breɪkɪəl, 'bræk-) *adj* of or relating to the arm or to an armlike part or structure.

brachiate *adj* ('breɪkɪɪt, -ˌeɪt, 'bræk-). **1** *Bot.* having widely divergent paired branches. ◆ *vb* ('breɪkɪˌeɪt, 'bræk-), **brachiates, brachiating, brachiated. 2** (*intr*) (of some arboreal apes and monkeys) to swing by the arms from one hold to the next. ORIG C19: from L *bracchiātus* with armlike branches

▸ **ˌbrachi'ation** *n*

brachio- *or before a vowel* **brachi-** *combining form.* indicating a brachium: *brachiopod.*

brachiopod ('breɪkɪəˌpɒd, 'bræk-) *n* any marine invertebrate animal having a ciliated feeding organ and a shell consisting of dorsal and ventral valves. ORIG C19: from NL *Brachiopoda;* see BRACHIUM, -POD

brachiosaurus (ˌbreɪkɪə'sɔ:rəs, ˌbræk-) *n* a dinosaur up to 30 metres long: the largest land animal ever known.

brachium ('breɪkɪəm, 'bræk-) *n, pl* **brachia** (-kɪə). **1** *Anat.* the arm, esp. the upper part. **2** a corresponding part in an animal. **3** *Biol.* a branching or armlike part. ORIG C18: NL, from L *bracchium* arm

brachy- *combining form.* indicating something short: *brachycephalic.* ORIG from Gk *brakhus* short

brachycephalic (ˌbrækɪsɪ'fælɪk) *adj* having a head nearly as broad from side to side as from front to back. Also: **brachycephalous** (ˌbrækɪ'sɛfələs).

▸ **ˌbrachy'cephaly** *n*

bracing ('breɪsɪŋ) *adj* **1** refreshing; stimulating; invigorating. ◆ *n* **2** a system of braces used to strengthen or support.

bracken ('brækən) *n* **1** Also called: **brake.** any of various large coarse ferns having large fronds with spore cases along the undersides. **2** a clump of any of these ferns. ORIG C14: from ON

bracket ('brækɪt) *n* **1** an L-shaped or other support fixed to a wall to hold a shelf, etc. **2** one or more wall shelves carried on brackets. **3** *Archit.* a support projecting from the side of a wall or other structure. **4** Also called: **square bracket.** either of a pair of characters, [ ], used to enclose a section of writing or printing. **5** a general name for **parenthesis** (sense 2), **square bracket,** and **brace** (sense 5). **6** a group or category falling within certain defined limits:

the lower income bracket. **7** the distance between two preliminary shots of artillery fire in range-finding. ◆ *vb* **brackets, bracketing, bracketed.** (*tr*) **8** to fix or support by means of brackets. **9** to put (written or printed matter) in brackets. **10** to couple or join (two lines of text, etc.) with a brace. **11** (often foll. by *with*) to group or class together. **12** to adjust (artillery fire) until the target is hit. ORIG C16: from OF *braguette* codpiece, from OProvençal *braga*, from L *brāca* breeches

brackish ('brækɪʃ) *adj* (of water) slightly briny or salty. ORIG C16: from MDu. *brac* salty; see -ISH
▸ **'brackishness** *n*

Bracknell ★ ('bræknəl) *n* a town in SE England, designated a new town in 1949. Pop.: 60 895 (1991).

Bracknell Forest ★ *n* a unitary authority in SE England. Pop.: 110 100 (1999 est.). Area: 109 sq. km (42 sq. miles).

bract (brækt) *n* a specialized leaf with a single flower or inflorescence growing in its axil. ORIG C18: from L *bractea* thin metal plate, gold leaf, from ?
▸ **'bracteal** *adj* ▸ **bracteate** ('bræktɪɪt) *adj*

bracteole ('bræktɪˌəʊl) *n* a secondary or small bract. Also called: **bractlet.** ORIG C19: from NL *bracteola;* see BRACT

brad (bræd) *n* a small tapered nail with a small head. ORIG OE *brord* point, prick

bradawl ('brædˌɔːl) *n* an awl used to pierce wood, leather, etc.

Bradbury ★ ('brædbərɪ) *n* **1** Sir **Malcolm** (**Stanley**). 1932–2000, British novelist and critic. His novels include *The History Man* (1975) and *Doctor Criminale* (1992). **2 Ray.** born 1920, US science-fiction writer. His novels include *Fahrenheit 451* (1953), *Death is a Lonely Business* (1986), and *A Graveyard for Lunatics* (1990).

Bradford ★ ('brædfəd) *n* **1** an industrial city in N England, in West Yorkshire: a centre of the woollen industry from the 14th century and of the worsted trade from the 18th century; university (1966). Pop.: 289 376 (1991). **2** a unitary authority in West Yorkshire. Pop.: 457 344 (1999 est.). Area: 370 sq. km (143 sq. miles).

Bradley ★ ('brædlɪ) *n* **1 Andrew Cecil.** 1851–1935, British critic; author of *Shakespearian Tragedy* (1904). **2 F**(**rancis**) **H**(**erbert**). 1846–1924, British idealist philosopher and metaphysical thinker; author of *Ethical Studies* (1876), *Principles of Logic* (1883), and *Appearance and Reality* (1893). **3 Henry.** 1845–1923, British lexicographer; one of the editors of the *Oxford English Dictionary.* **4 James.** 1693–1762, English astronomer, who discovered the aberration of light and the nutation of the earth's axis.

Bradman ★ ('brædmən) *n* (Sir) **Don**(**ald George**). 1908–2001, Australian cricketer.

Bradshaw ('brædˌʃɔː) *n* a British railway timetable, published annually from 1839 to 1961. ORIG C19: after its original publisher, George *Bradshaw* (1801–53)

bradycardia (ˌbrædɪ'kɑːdɪə) *n Pathol.* an abnormally slow heartbeat. ORIG C19: from Gk *bradus* slow + *kardia* heart

brae (breɪ) *n Scot.* **1** a hill or hillside **2** (*pl*) an upland area. ORIG C14 *bra;* rel to ON *brā* eyelash

Braemar ★ (ˌbreɪ'mɑː) *n* a village in NE Scotland, in Aberdeenshire; Balmoral Castle is nearby: site of the Royal Braemar Gathering, an annual Highland Games meeting.

brag (bræg) *vb* **brags, bragging, bragged. 1** to speak arrogantly and boastfully. ◆ *n* **2** boastful talk or behaviour. **3** something boasted of. **4** a braggart; boaster. **5** a card game: an old form of poker. ORIG C13: from ?
▸ **'bragger** *n*

Braga ★ (*Portuguese* 'brɑːgə) *n* a city in N Portugal: capital of the Roman province of Lusitania; 12th-century cathedral, seat of the Primate of Portugal. Pop.: 90 535 (1991). Ancient name: **Bracara Augusta.**

Bragg ★ (bræg) *n* Sir **William Henry,** 1862–1942, and his son, Sir (**William**) **Lawrence,** 1890–1971, British physicists, who shared a Nobel prize for physics (1915) for their study of crystal structures by means of X-rays.

braggadocio (ˌbrægə'dəʊtʃɪˌəʊ) *n, pl* **braggadocios. 1** vain empty boasting. **2** a person who boasts; braggart. ORIG C16: from *Braggadocchio*, a boastful character in Spenser's *Faerie Queene;* prob. from BRAGGART + It. *-occhio* (augmentative suffix)

braggart ('brægət) *n* **1** a person who boasts loudly or exaggeratedly; bragger. ◆ *adj* **2** boastful. ORIG C16: see BRAG

Bragi ('brɑːgɪ) *or* **Brage** ★ ('brɑːgə) *n Norse myth.* the god of poetry and music, son of Odin.

Brahe ★ (brɑː, 'brɑːhɪ; *Danish* 'brɑːə) *n* **Tycho** ('tyːço). 1546–1601, Danish astronomer, who supported Copernicus and worked with Kepler.

Brahma ('brɑːmə) *n* a Hindu god, the Creator. ORIG from Sansk., from *brahman* praise

Brahman ('brɑːmən) *n, pl* **Brahmans. 1** (*sometimes not cap.*) Also (esp. formerly): **Brahmin.** a member of the highest or priestly caste in the Hindu caste system. **2** another name for **Brahma.** ORIG C14: from Sansk. *brahman* prayer
▸ **Brahmanic** (brɑː'mænɪk) *or* **Brah'manical** *adj*

Brahmanism ('brɑːməˌnɪzəm) *or* **Brahminism** *n* (*sometimes not cap.*) the religious and social system of orthodox Hinduism.
▸ **'Brahmanist** *or* **'Brahminist** *n*

Brahmaputra ★ (ˌbrɑːmə'puːtrə) *n* a river in S Asia, rising in SW Tibet as the Tsangpo and flowing through the Himalayas and NE India to join the Ganges at its delta in Bangladesh. Length: about 2900 km (1800 miles).

Brahmin ('brɑːmɪn) *n, pl* **Brahmin** *or* **Brahmins. 1** the older spelling of **Brahman** (a Hindu priest). **2** *US.* a highly intelligent or socially exclusive person.

Brahms ★ (brɑːmz) *n* **Johannes** (jo'hanəs). 1833–97, German composer. His works include four symphonies, four concertos, chamber music, and a requiem.

braid (breɪd) *vb* (*tr*) **1** to interweave (hair, thread, etc.); plait. **2** to decorate with an ornamental trim or border. ◆ *n* **3** a length of hair, fabric, etc., that has been braided; plait. **4** narrow ornamental tape of woven silk, wool, etc. ORIG OE *bregdan* to move suddenly, weave together
▸ **'braider** *n* ▸ **'braiding** *n*

Brăila ★ (*Romanian* brə'ila) *n* a port in E Romania: belonged to Turkey (1544–1828). Pop.: 236 344 (1993 est.).

Braille[1] (breɪl) *n* **1** a system of writing for the blind consisting of raised dots interpreted by touch. **2** any writing produced by this method. ◆ *vb* **Brailles, Brailling, Brailled. 3** (*tr*) to print or write using this method.

Braille[2] ★ (*French* braj) *n* **Louis** (lwi). 1809–52, French inventor, musician, and teacher of the blind; blind from the age of three, he devised the Braille system of writing.

brain (breɪn) *n* **1** the soft convoluted mass of nervous tissue within the skull of vertebrates that is the controlling and coordinating centre of the nervous system and the seat of thought, memory, and emotion. Related adj: **cerebral. 2** (*often pl*) *Inf.* intellectual ability: *he's got brains.* **3** *Inf.* shrewdness or cunning. **4** *Inf.* an intellectual or intelligent person. **5** (*usually pl; functioning as sing*) *Inf.* a person who plans and organizes. **6** an electronic device, such as a computer, that performs similar functions to those of the human brain. **7 on the brain.** *Inf.* constantly in mind: *I had that song on the brain.* ◆ *vb* (*tr*) **8** to smash the skull of. **9** *Sl.* to hit hard on the head. ORIG OE *brægen*

brainchild ('breɪnˌtʃaɪld) *n, pl* **brainchildren.** *Inf.* an idea or plan produced by creative thought.

braindead ('breɪnˌdɛd) *adj* **1** having suffered brain death. **2** *Inf.* not using or showing intelligence; stupid.

brain death *n* irreversible cessation of respiration due to irreparable brain damage: widely considered as the criterion of death.

brain drain *n Inf.* the emigration of scientists, technologists, academics, etc.

Braine ★ (breɪn) *n* **John** (**Gerard**). 1922–86, British novelist, whose works include *Room at the Top* (1957) and *Life at the Top* (1962).

brain fever *n* inflammation of the brain.

brainless ('breɪnlɪs) *adj* stupid or foolish.

brainpan ('breɪnˌpæn) *n Inf.* the skull.

brainstem ('breɪnˌstɛm) *n* the part of the brain that controls such reflex actions as breathing and is continuous with the spinal cord.

brainstorm ('breɪnˌstɔːm) *n* **1** a severe outburst of excitement, often as the result of a transitory disturbance of cerebral activity. **2** *Brit. inf.* a sudden mental aberration. **3** *US. & Canad. inf.* another word for **brainwave.**

brainstorming ('breɪnˌstɔːmɪŋ) *n* intensive discussion to solve problems or generate ideas.

brains trust *n* a group of knowledgeable people who discuss topics in public or on radio or television.

brain-teaser *or* **brain-twister** *n Inf.* a difficult problem.

brain up *vb* (*tr*) to make intellectually demanding or sophisticated: *we need to brain up the curriculum.*

brainwash ('breɪnˌwɒʃ) *vb* (*tr*) to effect a radical change in the ideas and beliefs of (a person), esp. by methods based on isolation, sleeplessness, etc.
▸ **'brainˌwashing** *n*

brainwave ('breɪnˌweɪv) *n Inf.* a sudden idea or inspiration.

brain wave *n* any of the fluctuations of electrical potential in the brain.

brainy ('breɪnɪ) *adj* **brainier, brainiest.** *Inf.* clever; intelligent.
▸ **'braininess** *n*

braise (breɪz) *vb* **braises, braising, braised.** to cook (meat, vegetables, etc.) by lightly browning in fat and then cooking slowly in a closed pan with a small amount of liquid. ORIG C18: from F *braiser,* from OF *brese* live coals

brak[1] (brak) *n S. African.* a crossbred dog; mongrel. ORIG from Du. *brak* setter

brak[2] (brak) *adj S. African.* (of water) brackish or salty. ORIG C19: Afrik.

brake[1] (breɪk) *n* **1** (*often pl*) a device for slowing or stopping a vehicle, wheel, shaft, etc., or for keeping it stationary, esp. by means of friction. **2** a machine or tool for crushing or breaking flax or hemp to separate the fibres. **3** Also called: **brake harrow.** a heavy harrow for breaking up clods. **4** short for **shooting brake.** ◆ *vb* **brakes, braking, braked. 5** to slow down or cause to slow down, by or as if by using a brake. **6** (*tr*) to crush or break up using a brake. ORIG C18: from MDu. *braeke;* rel. to *breken* to BREAK
▸ **'brakeless** *adj*

brake[2] (breɪk) *n* an area of dense undergrowth, shrubs, brushwood, etc.; thicket. ORIG OE *bracu*

brake[3] (breɪk) *n* another name for **bracken** (sense 1).

brake[4] (breɪk) *vb Arch., chiefly biblical.* a past tense of **break.**

brake-fade *n* a decrease in the efficiency of the braking system of a motor vehicle as a result of overheating of the brakes.

brake horsepower *n* the rate at which an engine does work, expressed in horsepower. It is measured by the resistance of an applied brake. Abbrev.: **bhp.**

brake light *n* a red light or lights at the rear of a motor vehicle that light up when the brakes are applied.

brake lining *n* a renewable strip of asbestos riveted to a brake shoe.

brake pad *n* the flat metal casting, together with the attached friction material, in a disc brake.

brake shoe *n* **1** the curved metal casting to which the brake lining is riveted in a drum brake. **2** the curved metal casting together with the attached brake lining. ◆ Sometimes shortened (for both senses) to **shoe.**

brakesman ('breɪksmən) *n, pl* **brakesmen. 1** a pithead winch operator. **2** a brake operator on railway rolling stock.

brake van *n Railways, Brit.* the coach or vehicle from which the guard applies the brakes; guard's van.

Brakpan ★ ('brækˌpæn) *n* a city in E South Africa: gold-mining centre. Pop.: 46 416 (1985).

Bramante ★ (*Italian* bra'mante) *n* **Donato** (do'nato). ?1444–1514, Italian Renaissance architect and artist.

bramble ('bræmbᵊl) *n* **1** any of various prickly rosaceous plants or shrubs, esp. the blackberry. **2** any of several similar and related shrubs, such as the dog rose. **3** *Scot. & N English.* a blackberry. ORIG OE *brǣmbel*
▸ **'brambly** *adj*

brambling ('bræmblɪŋ) *n* a Eurasian finch with a speckled head and back and, in the male, a reddish-brown breast.

bran (bræn) *n* **1** husks of cereal grain separated from the flour. **2** food prepared from these husks. ORIG C13: from OF, prob. of Gaulish origin

Branagh ★ ('brænə) *n* **Kenneth.** born 1961, British actor and director, born in Northern Ireland.

branch (brɑːntʃ) *n* **1** a secondary woody stem arising from the trunk or bough of a tree or the main stem of a shrub. **2** an offshoot or secondary part: *a branch of a deer's antlers.* **3a** a subdivision or subsidiary section of something larger or more complex: *branches of learning; branch of the family.* **3b** (*as modifier*): *a branch office.* **4** *US.* any small stream. ◆ *vb* **5** (*intr*) (of a tree or other plant) to produce or possess branches. **6** (*intr;* usually foll. by *from*) (of stems, roots, etc.) to grow and diverge (from another part). **7** to divide or be divided into subsidiaries or offshoots. **8** (*intr;* often foll. by *off*) to diverge from the main way, road, topic, etc. ORIG C13: from OF *branche,* from LL *branca* paw, foot
▸ **'branchˌlike** *adj*

branchia ('bræŋkɪə) *n, pl* **branchiae** (-kɪˌiː). a gill in aquatic animals.
▸ **'branchial** *or* **'branchiate** *adj*

branch out *vb* (*intr, adv;* often foll. by *into*) to expand or extend one's interests.

Brancusi ★ (bræŋ'kuːzɪ; *Romanian* briŋ'kuʃj) *n* **Constantin** (konstan'tin). 1876–1957, Romanian sculptor.

brand (brænd) *n* **1** a particular product or a characteristic that identifies a particular producer. **2** a particular kind or variety. **3** an identifying mark made, usually by burning, on the skin of animals or (formerly) slaves or criminals, esp. as a proof of ownership. **4** an iron heated and used for branding animals, etc. **5** a mark of disgrace or infamy; stigma. **6** a burning or burnt piece of wood, as in a fire. **7** *Arch. or poetic.* **7a** a flaming torch. **7b** a sword. **8** a fungal disease of garden plants characterized by brown spots on the leaves. ◆ *vb* (*tr*) **9** to label, burn, or mark with or as with a brand. **10** to place indelibly in the memory: *the scene was branded in their minds.* **11** to denounce; stigmatize: *they branded him a traitor.* ORIG OE *brand-;* see BURN[1]
▸ **'brander** *n* ▸ **'branding** *n*

Brandenburg ★ ('brændənˌbɜːg; *German* 'brandənburk) *n* **1** a state in NE Germany, part of East Germany until 1990. A former electorate, it expanded to become the kingdom of Prussia (1701). The district east of the Oder River became Polish in 1945. Capital: Potsdam. Pop.: 2 545 500 (1996 est.). Area: 29 481 sq. km (11 219 sq. miles). **2** a city in NE Germany: former capital of the Prussian province of Brandenburg. Pop.: 93 660 (1989 est.).

brandish ('brændɪʃ) *vb* **1** (*tr*) to wave or flourish (a weapon, etc.) in a triumphant, threatening, or ostentatious way. ◆ *n* **2** a threatening or defiant flourish. ORIG C14: from OF *brandir,* of Gmc origin
▸ **'brandisher** *n*

brand leader *n* the most widely sold brand of a particular product.

brandling ('brændlɪŋ) *n* a small red earthworm, found in manure and used as bait by anglers. ORIG C17: from BRAND (n) + -LING[1]

brand name *n* the name used for a particular make of a commodity.

brand-new *adj* absolutely new. ORIG C16: from BRAND (n) + NEW, likened to newly forged iron

Brando ★ ('brændəʊ) *n* **Marlon.** born 1924, US actor; his films include *On the Waterfront* (1954), *The Godfather* (1972), *Last Tango in Paris* (1972), and *The Island of Doctor Moreau* (1996).

Brandt ★ (brænt) *n* **1 Bill,** full name *William Brandt.* 1905–83, British photographer. His books include *The English at Home* (1936) and *Perspectives of Nudes* (1961). **2 Georg** (*Swedish* 'jeːɔrj). 1694–1768, Swedish chemist, who isolated cobalt (1742). **3** (*German* brant). **Willy** ('vɪli). 1913–92, German statesman; socialist chancellor of West Germany (1969–74); chairman of the Social Democratic party (1964–87). Nobel peace prize 1971.

brandy ('brændɪ) *n, pl* **brandies. 1** an alcoholic spirit distilled from grape wine. **2** a distillation of wines made from other fruits: *plum brandy.* ORIG C17: from earlier *brandewine,* from Du. *brandewijn* burnt (or distilled) wine

brandy butter *n* butter and sugar creamed together with brandy and served with Christmas pudding, etc. Also called: **hard sauce.**

brandy snap *n* a crisp sweet biscuit, rolled into a cylinder and filled with whipped cream.

Branson ★ ('brænsᵊn) *n* Sir **Richard.** born 1950, British entrepreneur. Founder of a number of companies, including Virgin record company, Virgin Atlantic Airways, and Virgin Rail Group. Made first Atlantic crossing by hot-air balloon (1987).

brant (brænt) *n, pl* **brants** *or* **brant.** another name (esp. US and Canad.) for **brent** (the goose).

Brantford ★ ('bræntfəd) *n* a city in central Canada, in SW Ontario. Pop.: 81 997 (1991).

bran tub *n Brit.* a tub containing bran in which small wrapped gifts are hidden.

Braque ★ (*French* brak) *n* **Georges** (ʒɔrʒ). 1882–1963, French cubist painter.

brash[1] (bræʃ) *adj* **1** tastelessly or offensively loud, showy, or bold. **2** hasty; rash. **3** impudent. ORIG C19: ? infl. by RASH[1]
▸ '**brashly** *adv* ▸ '**brashness** *n*

brash[2] (bræʃ) *n* loose rubbish, such as broken rock, hedge clippings, etc. ORIG C18: from ?
▸ '**brashy** *adj*

brasier ('breɪzɪə) *n* a less common spelling of **brazier.**

Brasil ★ (brə'zi:l) *n* the Portuguese spelling of **Brazil.**

Brasília ★ (brə'zɪljə; *Portuguese* brəzi'li:a) *n* the capital of Brazil (since 1960), on the central plateau: the former capital was Rio de Janeiro. Pop.: 1 778 000 (1995).

Braşov ★ (*Romanian* bra'ʃov) *n* an industrial city in central Romania: formerly a centre for expatriate Germans; ceded by Hungary to Romania in 1920. Pop.: 324 104 (1993 est.). Former name (1950–61): **Stalin.** German name: **Kronstadt.** Hungarian name: **Brassó.**

brass (brɑ:s) *n* **1** an alloy of copper and zinc containing more than 50 per cent of copper. Cf. **bronze** (sense 1). **2** an object, ornament, or utensil made of brass. **3a** the large family of wind instruments including the trumpet, trombone, French horn, etc., made of brass. **3b** (*sometimes functioning as pl*) instruments of this family forming a section in an orchestra. **4** (*functioning as pl*) *Inf.* important or high-ranking officials, esp. military officers: *the top brass.* See also **brass hat. 5** *N English dialect.* money. **6** *Brit.* an engraved brass memorial tablet or plaque in a church. **7** *Inf.* bold self-confidence; cheek; nerve. **8** (*modifier*) of, consisting of, or relating to brass or brass instruments: *a brass ornament; a brass band.* ORIG OE *bræs*

brassard ('bræsɑ:d) *or* **brassart** ('bræsət) *n* an identifying armband or badge. ORIG C19: from F, from *bras* arm

brass band *n* See **band**[1] (sense 2).

brasserie ('bræsərɪ) *n* **1** a bar in which drinks and often food are served. **2** a small and usually cheap restaurant. ORIG C19: from F, from *brasser* to stir

brass hat *n Brit. inf.* a top-ranking official, esp. a military officer. ORIG C20: from the gold decoration on the caps of officers of high rank

brassica ('bræsɪkə) *n* any plant of the genus *Brassica,* such as cabbage, rape, turnip, and mustard. ORIG C19: from L: cabbage

brassie *or* **brassy** ('bræsɪ, 'brɑ:-) *n, pl* **brassies.** *Golf.* a former name for a club, a No. 2 wood, originally having a brass-plated sole.

brassiere ('bræsɪə, 'bræz-) *n* the full name for **bra.** ORIG C20: from 17th-cent. F: bodice, from OF *braciere* a protector for the arm

Brassó ★ ('brɔʃʃo:) *n* the Hungarian name for **Braşov.**

brass rubbing *n* **1** the taking of an impression of an engraved brass tablet or plaque by rubbing a paper placed over it with heelball, chalk, etc. **2** an impression made in this way.

brass tacks *pl n Inf.* basic realities; hard facts (esp. in **get down to brass tacks**).

brassy ('brɑ:sɪ) *adj* **brassier, brassiest. 1** insolent; brazen. **2** flashy; showy. **3** (of sound) harsh and strident. **4** like brass, esp. in colour. **5** decorated with or made of brass.
▸ '**brassily** *adv* ▸ '**brassiness** *n*

brat (bræt) *n* a child, esp. one who is ill-mannered or unruly. ORIG C16: ?from earlier *brat* rag, from OE *bratt* cloak
▸ '**bratty** *adj*

Bratislava ★ (ˌbrætɪ'slɑ:və) *n* the capital of Slovakia, a port on the River Danube; capital of Hungary (1541–1784) and seat of the Hungarian parliament until 1848. Pop.: 452 053 (1996 est.). German name: **Pressburg.** Hungarian name: **Pozsony.**

bratpack ('bræt,pæk) *n* **1** a group of precocious and successful young actors, writers, etc. **2** a group of ill-mannered young people.
▸ '**brat,packer** *n*

Brattain ★ ('brætᵊn) *n* **Walter Houser.** 1902–87, US physicist, who shared the Nobel prize for physics (1956) for the invention of the transistor.

brattice ('brætɪs) *n* **1** a partition of wood or treated cloth used to control ventilation in a mine. **2** *Medieval fortifications.* a fixed wooden tower or parapet. ORIG C13: from OF *bretesche* wooden tower

Braun ★ (*German* braun) *n* **1 Eva** ('e:fa). 1910–45, Adolf Hitler's mistress, whom he married shortly before their suicides in 1945. **2 Karl Ferdinand** (karl 'fɛrdinənt). 1850–1918. German physicist, who invented crystal diodes and the oscilloscope. He shared the Nobel prize for physics (1909). **3** See (Wernher) **von Braun.**

Braunschweig ★ ('braunʃvaik) *n* the German name for **Brunswick.**

bravado (brə'vɑ:dəu) *n, pl* **bravadoes** *or* **bravados.** vaunted display of courage or self-confidence; swagger. ORIG C16: from Sp. *bravada;* see BRAVE

brave (breɪv) *adj* **1a** having or displaying courage, resolution, or daring; not cowardly or timid. **1b** (*as collective n; preceded by the*): *the brave.* **2** fine; splendid: *a brave sight.* ◆ *n* **3** a warrior of a North American Indian tribe. ◆ *vb* **braves, braving, braved.** (*tr*) **4** to dare or defy: *to brave the odds.* **5** to confront with resolution or courage: *to brave the storm.* ORIG C15: from F, from It. *bravo* courageous, wild, ? ult. from L *barbarus* BARBAROUS
▸ '**bravely** *adv* ▸ '**braveness** *n* ▸ '**bravery** *n*

bravo *interj* **1** (brɑ:'vəu). well done! ◆ *n* **2** (brɑ:'vəu) *pl* **bravos.** a cry of "bravo." **3** ('brɑ:vəu) *pl* **bravoes** *or* **bravos.** a hired killer or assassin. ORIG C18: from It.: splendid! see BRAVE

bravura (brə'vjuərə, -'vuərə) *n* **1** a display of boldness or daring. **2** *Music.* brilliance of execution. ORIG C18: from It.: spirit, courage; see BRAVE

braw (brɔ:, brɑ:) *adj Chiefly Scot.* fine or excellent, esp. in appearance or dress. ORIG C16: Scot. var. of BRAVE

brawl (brɔ:l) *n* **1** a loud disagreement or fight. **2** *US sl.* an uproarious party. ◆ *vb* (*intr*) **3** to quarrel or fight noisily; squabble. **4** (esp. of water) to flow noisily. ORIG C14: prob. rel. to Du. *brallen* to boast, behave aggressively
▸ '**brawler** *n*

brawn (brɔ:n) *n* **1** strong well-developed muscles. **2** physical strength, esp. as opposed to intelligence. **3** *Brit.* a seasoned jellied loaf made from the head of a pig or calf. ORIG C14: from OF *braon* slice of meat, of Gmc origin

brawny ('brɔ:nɪ) *adj* **brawnier, brawniest.** muscular and strong.
▸ '**brawniness** *n*

bray (breɪ) *vb* **1** (*intr*) (of a donkey) to utter its characteristic loud harsh sound; heehaw. **2** (*intr*) to make a similar sound, as in laughing. **3** (*tr*) to utter with a loud harsh sound. ◆ *n* **4** the loud harsh sound uttered by a donkey. **5** a similar loud cry or uproar. ORIG C13: from OF *braire,* prob. of Celtic origin

Braz. *abbrev. for* Brazil(ian).

braze[1] (breɪz) *vb* **brazes, brazing, brazed.** (*tr*) **1** to decorate with or make of brass. **2** to make like brass, as in hardness. ORIG OE *bræsen,* from *bræs* BRASS

braze[2] (breɪz) *vb* **brazes, brazing, brazed.** (*tr*) to make a joint between (two metal surfaces) by fusing a layer of brass or high-melting solder between them. ORIG C16: from OF: to burn, of Gmc origin; see BRAISE
▸ **'brazer** *n*

brazen ('breɪzᵊn) *adj* **1** shameless and bold. **2** made of or resembling brass. **3** having a ringing metallic sound. ◆ *vb* (*tr*) **4** (usually foll. by *out* or *through*) to face and overcome boldly or shamelessly. ORIG OE *bræsen,* from *bræs* BRASS
▸ **'brazenly** *adv* ▸ **'brazenness** *n*

brazier[1] *or* **brasier** ('breɪzɪə) *n* a person engaged in brass-working or brass-founding. ORIG C14: from OE *bræsian* to work in brass + -ER[1]
▸ **'braziery** *n*

brazier[2] *or* **brasier** ('breɪzɪə) *n* a portable metal receptacle for burning charcoal or coal. ORIG C17: from F *brasier,* from *braise* live coals; see BRAISE

brazil (brə'zɪl) *n* **1** Also called: **brazil wood.** the red wood obtained from various tropical trees of America: used for cabinetwork. **2** the red or purple dye extracted from these woods. **3** short for **brazil nut.** ORIG C14: from OSp., from *brasa* glowing coals, of Gmc origin; referring to the redness of the wood

Brazil ★ (brə'zɪl) *n* a republic in South America, comprising about half the area and half the population of South America: colonized by the Portuguese from 1500 onwards; became independent in 1822 and a republic in 1889; consists chiefly of the tropical Amazon basin in the north, semiarid scrub in the northeast, and a vast central tableland; an important producer of coffee and minerals, esp. iron ore. Official language: Portuguese. Religion: chiefly Roman Catholic. Currency: cruzeiro real. Capital: Brasília. Pop.: 163 947 000 (1999 est.). Area: 8 511 957 sq. km (3 286 470 sq. miles).
▸ **Bra'zilian** *adj, n*

brazil nut *n* **1** a tropical South American tree producing large globular capsules, each containing several closely packed triangular nuts. **2** the nut, having an edible oily kernel and a woody shell. ◆ Often shortened to **brazil.**

Brazzaville ★ (*French* brazavil) *n* the capital of Congo-Brazzaville in the south on the River Congo. Pop.: 937 579 (1995 est.). ORIG C19: named after Pierre de *Brazza* (1852–1905), F explorer

BRCS *abbrev. for* British Red Cross Society.

breach (bri:tʃ) *n* **1** a crack, break, or rupture. **2** a breaking, infringement, or violation of a promise, obligation, etc. **3** any severance or separation. ◆ *vb* (*tr*) **4** to break through or make an opening, hole, or incursion in. **5** to break a promise, law, etc. ORIG OE *bræc*

USAGE NOTE See at **breech.**

breach of promise *n Law.* (formerly) failure to carry out one's promise to marry.

breach of the peace *n Law.* an offence against public order causing an unnecessary disturbance of the peace.

bread (brɛd) *n* **1** a food made from a dough of flour or meal mixed with water or milk, usually raised with yeast or baking powder and then baked. **2** necessary food; nourishment. **3** *Sl.* money. **4 cast one's bread upon the waters.** to do good without expectation of advantage or return. **5 know which side one's bread is buttered.** to know what to do in order to keep one's advantages. **6 take the bread out of (someone's) mouth.** to deprive of a livelihood. ◆ *vb* **7** (*tr*) to cover with bread-crumbs before cooking. ORIG OE *brēad*

bread and butter *Inf.* ◆ *n* **1** a means of support or subsistence; livelihood. ◆ *modifier.* **bread-and-butter. 2a** providing a basic means of subsistence. **2b** expressing gratitude, as for hospitality (esp. in **bread-and-butter letter**).

breadbasket ('brɛd,bɑ:skɪt) *n* **1** a basket for carrying bread or rolls. **2** *Sl.* stomach.

breadboard ('brɛd,bɔ:d) *n* **1** a wooden board on which bread is sliced. **2** an experimental arrangement of electronic circuits.

breadfruit ('brɛd,fru:t) *n, pl* **breadfruits** *or* **breadfruit. 1** a tree of the Pacific Islands, having edible round, usually seedless, fruit. **2** the fruit, which is eaten baked or roasted and has a texture like bread.

breadline ('brɛd,laɪn) *n* **1** a queue of people waiting for free food. **2 on the breadline.** impoverished; living at subsistence level.

breadth (brɛdθ, brɛtθ) *n* **1** the linear extent or measurement of something from side to side; width. **2** a piece of fabric, etc., having a standard or definite width. **3** distance, extent, size, or dimension. **4** openness and lack of restriction, esp. of viewpoint or interest; liberality. ORIG C16: from obs. *brēde* (from OE *brǣdu,* from *brād* BROAD) + -TH[1]

breadthways ('brɛdθ,weɪz, 'brɛtθ-) *or esp. US* **breadthwise** ('brɛdθ,waɪz, 'brɛtθ-) *adv* from side to side.

breadwinner ('brɛd,wɪnə) *n* a person supporting a family with his or her earnings.

break (breɪk) *vb* **breaks, breaking, broke, broken. 1** to separate or become separated into two or more pieces. **2** to damage or become damaged so as to be inoperative: *my radio is broken.* **3** to crack or become cracked without separating. **4** to burst or cut the surface of (skin, etc.). **5** to discontinue or become discontinued: *to break a journey.* **6** to disperse or become dispersed: *the clouds broke.* **7** (*tr*) to fail to observe (an agreement, promise, law, etc.): *to break one's word.* **8** (foll. by *with*) to discontinue an association (with). **9** to disclose or be disclosed: *he broke the news gently.* **10** (*tr*) to fracture (a bone) in (a limb, etc.). **11** (*tr*) to divide (something complete or perfect): *to break a set of books.* **12** to bring or come to an end: *the summer weather broke at last.* **13** (*tr*) to bring to an end as by force: *to break a strike.* **14** (when *intr,* often foll. by *out*) to escape (from): *he broke out of jail.* **15** to weaken or overwhelm or be weakened or overwhelmed, as in spirit. **16** (*tr*) to cut through or penetrate: *a cry broke the silence.* **17** (*tr*) to improve on or surpass: *to break a record.* **18** (*tr;* often foll. by *in*) to accustom (a horse) to the bridle and saddle, to being ridden, etc. **19** (*tr;* often foll. by *of*) to cause (a person) to give up (a habit): *this cure will break you of smoking.* **20** (*tr*) to weaken the impact or force of: *this net will break his fall.* **21** (*tr*) to decipher: *to break a code.* **22** (*tr*) to lose the order of: *to break ranks.* **23** (*tr*) to reduce to poverty or the state of bankruptcy. **24** (when *intr,* foll. by *into*) to obtain, give, or receive smaller units in exchange for; change: *to break a pound note.* **25** (*tr*) *Chiefly mil.* to demote to a lower rank. **26** (*intr;* often foll. by *from* or *out of*) to proceed suddenly. **27** (*intr*) to come into being: *light broke over the mountains.* **28** (*intr;* foll. by *into* or *out into*) **28a** to burst into song, laughter, etc. **28b** to change to a faster pace. **29** (*tr*) to open with explosives: *to break a safe.* **30** (*intr*) (of waves) **30a** (often foll. by *against*) to strike violently. **30b** to collapse into foam or surf. **31** (*intr*) (of prices, esp. stock exchange quotations) to fall sharply. **32** (*intr*) to make a sudden effort, as in running, horse racing, etc. **33** (*intr*) *Cricket.* (of a ball) to change direction on bouncing. **34** (*intr*) *Snooker.* to scatter the balls at the start of a game. **35** (*intr*) *Boxing, wrestling.* (of two fighters) to separate from a clinch. **36** (*intr*) (of the male voice) to undergo a change in register, quality, and range at puberty. **37** (*tr*) to open the breech of (certain firearms) by snapping the barrel away from the butt on its hinge. **38** (*tr*) to interrupt the flow of current in (an electrical circuit). **39** *Inf., chiefly US.* to become successful. **40 break camp.** to pack up and leave a camp. **41 break service.** *Tennis.* to win a game in which an opponent is serving. **42 break the bank.** to ruin financially or deplete the resources of a bank (as in gambling). **43 break the mould.** to make a change that breaks an established habit, pattern, etc. ◆ *n* **44** the act or result of breaking; fracture. **45** a crack formed as the result of breaking. **46** a brief respite. **47** a sudden rush, esp. to escape: *to make a break for freedom.* **48** a breach in a relationship. **49** any sudden interruption in a continuous action. **50** *Brit.* a short period between classes at school. **51** *Inf.* a fortunate opportunity, esp. to prove oneself. **52** *Inf.* a piece of good or bad luck. **53** (esp. in a stock exchange) a sudden and substantial decline in prices. **54** *Billiards, snooker.* a series of successful shots during one turn. **55** *Billiards, snooker.* the opening shot that scatters the placed balls. **56** Also called: **service break, break of serve.** *Tennis.* the act or an instance of breaking an opponent's service. **57a** *Jazz.* a short usually improvised solo passage. **57b** an instrumental passage in a pop song. **58** a discontinuity in an electrical circuit. **59** access to a radio channel by a citizens' band radio operator. **60** **break of day.** the dawn. ◆ *interj* **61** *Boxing, wrestling.* a command by a referee for two opponents to separate. ◆ See also **breakaway, break down,** etc. ORIG OE *brecan*

breakable ('breɪkəbᵊl) *adj* **1** capable of being broken. ◆ *n* **2** (*usually pl*) a fragile easily broken article.

breakage ('breɪkɪdʒ) *n* **1** the act or result of breaking. **2** the quantity or amount broken. **3** compensation or allowance for goods damaged while in use, transit, etc.

breakaway ('breɪkəˌweɪ) *n* **1a** loss or withdrawal of a group of members from an association, club, etc. **1b** (*as modifier*): *a breakaway faction.* **2** *Austral.* a stampede of animals, esp. at the smell of water. ◆ *vb* **break away.** (*intr, adv*) **3** (often foll. by *from*) to leave hastily or escape. **4** to withdraw or secede.

break dance *n* **1** an acrobatic dance style of the 1980s. ◆ *vb* **break-dance, break-dances, break-dancing, break-danced.** (*intr*) **2** to perform a break dance.
▸ **break dancer** *n* ▸ **break dancing** *n*

break down *vb* (*adv*) **1** (*intr*) to cease to function; become ineffective. **2** to yield or cause to yield, esp. to strong emotion or tears. **3** (*tr*) to crush or destroy. **4** (*intr*) to have a nervous breakdown. **5** to analyse or be subjected to analysis. **6** to separate or cause to separate into simpler chemical elements; decompose. **7** **break it down.** *Austral. & NZ inf.* **7a** stop it. **7b** don't expect me to believe that; come off it. ◆ *n* **breakdown. 8** an act or instance of breaking down; collapse. **9** short for **nervous breakdown. 10** an analysis or classification of something into its component parts: *he prepared a breakdown of the report.* **11** a lively American country dance.

breaker ('breɪkə) *n* **1** a person or thing that breaks something, such as a person or firm that breaks up old cars, etc. **2** a large wave with a white crest on the open sea or one that breaks into foam on the shore. **3** a citizens' band radio operator.

break even *vb* **1** (*intr, adv*) to attain a level of activity, as in commerce, or a point of operation, as in gambling, at which there is neither profit nor loss. ◆ *n* **breakeven. 2** *Accounting.* the level of commercial activity at which the total cost and total revenue of a business enterprise are equal.

breakfast ('brɛkfəst) *n* **1** the first meal of the day. **2** the food at this meal. ◆ *vb* **3** to eat or supply with breakfast. ORIG C15: from BREAK + FAST[2]
▸ **'breakfaster** *n*

break in *vb* (*adv*) **1** (sometimes foll. by *on*) to interrupt. **2** (*intr*) to enter a house, etc., illegally, esp. by force. **3** (*tr*) to accustom (a person or animal) to normal duties or practice. **4** (*tr*) to use or wear (shoes, new equipment, etc.) until comfortable or running smoothly. **5** *Austral.* to bring new land under cultivation. ◆ *n* **break-in. 6** the illegal entering of a building, esp. by thieves.

breaking and entering *n* (formerly) the gaining of unauthorized access to a building with intent to commit a crime.

breaking point *n* the point at which something or someone gives way under strain.

breakneck ('breɪkˌnɛk) *adj* (*prenominal*) (of speed, pace, etc.) excessive and dangerous.

break off *vb* **1** to sever or detach or be severed or detached. **2** (*adv*) to end (a relationship, association, etc.) or (of a relationship, etc.) to be ended. **3** (*intr, adv*) to stop abruptly: *he broke off in the middle of his speech.*

break out *vb* (*intr, adv*) **1** to begin or arise suddenly. **2** to make an escape, esp. from prison. **3** (foll. by *in*) (of the skin) to erupt (in a rash, pimples, etc.). ◆ *n* **break-out. 4** an escape, esp. from prison or confinement.

break through *vb* **1** (*intr*) to penetrate. **2** (*intr, adv*) to achieve success, make a discovery, etc., esp. after lengthy efforts. ◆ *n* **breakthrough. 3** a significant development or discovery, esp. in science. **4** the penetration of an enemy's defensive position.

breakthrough bleeding ('breɪkˌθruː) *n* vaginal bleeding that occurs other than at a menstrual period while a woman is using a low-dose oral contraceptive.

break up *vb* (*adv*) **1** to separate or cause to separate. **2** to put an end to (a relationship) or (of a relationship) to come to an end. **3** to dissolve or cause to dissolve; disrupt or be disrupted: *the meeting broke up at noon.* **4** (*intr*) *Brit.* (of a school) to close for the holidays. **5** *Inf.* to lose or cause to lose control of the emotions. **6** *Sl.* to be or cause to be overcome with laughter. ◆ *n* **break-up. 7** a separation or disintegration. **8a** in the Canadian north, the breaking up of the ice on a body of water that marks the beginning of spring. **8b** this season.

break-up value *n Commerce.* **1** the value of an organization assuming that it will not continue to trade. **2** the value of a share in a company based only on the value of its assets.

breakwater ('breɪkˌwɔːtə) *n* **1** Also called: **mole.** a massive wall built out into the sea to protect a shore or harbour from the force of waves. **2** another name for **groyne.**

bream[1] (briːm; *Austral.* brɪm) *or Austral.* **brim** (brɪm) *n, pl* **bream** *or* **brim. 1** any of several Eurasian freshwater cyprinid fishes having a deep compressed body covered with silvery scales. **2** short for **sea bream. 3** *Austral.* any of various marine fishes. ORIG C14: from OF *bresme,* of Gmc origin

bream[2] (briːm) *vb Naut.* (formerly) to clean debris from (the bottom of a vessel) by heating to soften the pitch. ORIG C15: prob. from MDu. *bremme* broom; from burning broom as a source of heat

Bream ★ (briːm) *n* **Julian (Alexander).** born 1933, British guitarist and lutenist.

breast (brɛst) *n* **1** the front part of the body from the neck to the abdomen; chest. **2** either of the two soft fleshy milk-secreting glands on the chest in sexually mature human females. **3** a similar organ in certain other mammals. **4** anything that resembles a breast in shape or position: *the breast of the hill.* **5** a source of nourishment. **6** the source of human emotions. **7** the part of a garment that covers the breast. **8** a projection from the side of a wall, esp. that formed by a chimney. **9** **beat one's breast.** to display guilt and remorse publicly or ostentatiously. **10** **make a clean breast of.** to make a confession of. ◆ *vb* (*tr*) **11** to confront boldly; face: *breast the storm.* **12** to oppose with the breast or meet at breast level: *breasting the waves.* **13** to reach the summit of: *breasting the mountain top.* ORIG OE *brēost*

breastbone ('brɛstˌbəʊn) *n* the nontechnical name for **sternum.**

breast-feed *vb* **breast-feeds, breast-feeding, breast-fed.** to feed (a baby) with milk from the breast; suckle.

breastpin ('brɛstˌpɪn) *n* a brooch worn on the breast, esp. to close a garment.

breastplate ('brɛstˌpleɪt) *n* a piece of armour covering the chest.

breaststroke ('brɛstˌstrəʊk) *n* a swimming stroke in which the arms are extended in front of the head and swept back on either side while the legs are drawn up beneath the body and thrust back together.

breastwork ('brɛstˌwɜːk) *n Fortifications.* a temporary defensive work, usually breast-high.

breath (brɛθ) *n* **1** the intake and expulsion of air during respiration. **2** the air inhaled or exhaled during respiration. **3** a single respiration or inhalation of air, etc. **4** the vapour, heat, or odour of exhaled air. **5** a slight gust of air. **6** a short pause or rest. **7** a brief time. **8** a suggestion or slight evidence; suspicion: *a breath of scandal.* **9** a whisper or soft sound. **10** life, energy, or vitality: *the breath of new industry.* **11** *Phonetics.* the exhalation of air without vibration of the vocal cords, as in pronouncing fricatives such as (f) or (h) or stops such as (p) or (k). **12** **catch one's breath. 12a** to rest until breathing is normal, esp. after exertion. **12b** to stop breathing momentarily from excitement, fear, etc. **13** **in the same breath.** done or said at the same time. **14** **out of breath.** gasping for air after exertion. **15** **save one's breath.** to refrain from useless talk. **16** **take**

one's breath away. to overwhelm with surprise, etc. **17 under** *or* **below one's breath.** in a quiet voice or whisper. ORIG OE *brǣth*

breathable (ˈbriːðəbᵊl) *adj* **1** (of air) fit to be breathed. **2** (of a material) allowing air to pass through so that perspiration can evaporate.

Breathalyser *or* **Breathalyzer** (ˈbrɛθəˌlaɪzə) *n Trademark.* a device for estimating the amount of alcohol in the breath: used in testing people suspected of driving under the influence of alcohol. ORIG C20: BREATH + (AN)ALYSER
▸ **ˈbreathaˌlyse** *or* **ˈbreathaˌlyze** *vb*

breathe (briːð) *vb* **breathes, breathing, breathed. 1** to take in oxygen and give out carbon dioxide; respire. **2** (*intr*) to exist; be alive. **3** (*intr*) to rest to regain breath, composure, etc. **4** (*intr*) (esp. of air) to blow lightly. **5** (*intr*) *Machinery.* to take in air, esp. for combustion. **6** (*tr*) *Phonetics.* to articulate (a speech sound) without vibration of the vocal cords. **7** to exhale or emit: *the dragon breathed fire.* **8** (*tr*) to impart; instil: *to breathe confidence into the actors.* **9** (*tr*) to speak softly; whisper. **10** (*tr*) to permit to rest: *to breathe a horse.* **11** (*intr*) (of a material) to allow air to pass through so that perspiration can evaporate. **12 breathe again, freely,** *or* **easily.** to feel relief. **13 breathe one's last.** to die or be finished or defeated. ORIG C13: from BREATH

breather (ˈbriːðə) *n* **1** *Inf.* a short pause for rest. **2** a person who breathes in a specified way: *a deep breather.* **3** a vent in a container to equalize internal and external pressure.

breathing (ˈbriːðɪŋ) *n* **1** the passage of air into and out of the lungs to supply the body with oxygen. **2** a single breath: *a breathing between words.* **3** *Phonetics.* **3a** expulsion of breath (**rough breathing**) or absence of such expulsion (**smooth breathing**) preceding the pronunciation of an initial vowel or rho in ancient Greek. **3b** either of two symbols indicating this.

breathless (ˈbrɛθlɪs) *adj* **1** out of breath; gasping, etc. **2** holding one's breath or having it taken away by excitement, etc. **3** (esp. of the atmosphere) motionless and stifling. **4** *Rare.* lifeless; dead.
▸ **ˈbreathlessly** *adv* ▸ **ˈbreathlessness** *n*

breathtaking (ˈbrɛθˌteɪkɪŋ) *adj* causing awe or excitement.
▸ **ˈbreathˌtakingly** *adv*

breath test *n Brit.* a chemical test of a driver's breath to determine the amount of alcohol he has consumed.

breathy (ˈbrɛθɪ) *adj* **breathier, breathiest. 1** (of the speaking voice) accompanied by an audible emission of breath. **2** (of the singing voice) lacking resonance.
▸ **ˈbreathily** *adv* ▸ **ˈbreathiness** *n*

breccia (ˈbrɛtʃɪə) *n* a rock consisting of angular fragments embedded in a finer matrix. ORIG C18: from It.
▸ **ˈbrecciˌated** *adj*

Brecht ★ (*German* brɛçt) *n* **Bertolt** (ˈbɛrtɔlt). 1898–1956, German dramatist. His early works include *The Threepenny Opera* (1928) and *Rise and Fall of the City of Mahagonny* (1930) (both with music by Kurt Weill). His later plays include *Mother Courage and her Children* (1941) and *The Caucasian Chalk Circle* (1955).
▸ **Brechtian** (ˈbrɛktɪən) *adj, n*

Brecon (ˈbrɛkən) *or* **Brecknock** ★ (ˈbrɛknɒk) *n* **1** a town in SE Wales, in Powys: textile and leather industries. Pop.: 7523 (1991). **2** short for **Breconshire.**

Breconshire (ˈbrɛkənˌʃɪə, -ʃə) *or* **Brecknockshire** ★ (ˈbrɛknɒkˌʃɪə, -ʃə) *n* (until 1974) a county of SE Wales, now mainly in Powys: over half its area forms the **Brecon Beacons National Park.**

bred (brɛd) *vb* the past tense and past participle of **breed.**

Breda ★ (ˈbriːdə; *Dutch* breˈdaː) *n* a city in the S Netherlands, in North Brabant province: residence of Charles II of England during his exile. Pop.: 129 957 (1995 est.).

bredie (ˈbriːdɪ) *n S. African.* a meat and vegetable stew. ORIG C19: from Port. *bredo* ragout

breech *n* (briːtʃ). **1** the buttocks; rump. **2** the lower part or bottom of something. **3** the part of a firearm behind the barrel or bore. ◆ *vb* (briːtʃ, brɪtʃ). (*tr*) **4** to fit (a gun) with a breech. **5** *Arch.* to clothe in breeches or any other clothing. ORIG OE *brēc,* pl. of *brōc* leg covering

> **USAGE NOTE** *Breech* is sometimes wrongly used as a verb where *breach* is meant: *he admitted he breached* (not *breeched*) *the rules.*

breechblock (ˈbriːtʃˌblɒk) *n* a metal block in breech-loading firearms that is withdrawn to insert the cartridge and replaced before firing.

breech delivery *n* birth of a baby with the feet or buttocks appearing first.

breeches (ˈbrɪtʃɪz, ˈbriː-) *pl n* **1** trousers extending to the knee or just below, worn for riding, etc. **2** *Inf. or dialect.* any trousers or pants, esp. extending to the knee.

breeches buoy *n* a ring-shaped life buoy with a support in the form of a pair of short breeches, in which a person is suspended for safe transfer from a ship.

breeching (ˈbrɪtʃɪŋ, ˈbriː-) *n* the strap of a harness that passes behind a horse's haunches.

breech-loader (ˈbriːtʃˌləʊdə) *n* a firearm that is loaded at the breech.
▸ **ˈbreech-ˌloading** *adj*

breed (briːd) *vb* **breeds, breeding, bred. 1** to bear (offspring). **2** (*tr*) to bring up; raise. **3** to produce or cause to produce by mating; propagate. **4** to produce new or improved strains of (domestic animals and plants). **5** to produce or be produced; generate: *to breed trouble.* ◆ *n* **6** a group of organisms within a species, esp. domestic animals, having clearly defined characteristics. **7** a lineage or race. **8** a kind, sort, or group. ORIG OE *brēdan,* of Gmc origin; rel. to BROOD

breeder (ˈbriːdə) *n* **1** a person who breeds plants or animals. **2** something that reproduces. **3** an animal kept for breeding purposes. **4** a source or cause: *a breeder of discontent.* **5** short for **breeder reactor.**

breeder reactor *n* a type of nuclear reactor that produces more fissionable material than it consumes.

breeding (ˈbriːdɪŋ) *n* **1** the process of bearing offspring; reproduction. **2** the process of producing plants or animals by hybridization, inbreeding, or other methods of reproduction. **3** the result of good training, esp. the knowledge of correct social behaviour; refinement.

Breed's Hill ★ (briːdz) *n* a hill in E Massachusetts, adjoining Bunker Hill: site of the Battle of Bunker Hill (1775).

breeze[1] (briːz) *n* **1** a gentle or light wind. **2** *Meteorol.* a wind of force two to six (4–31 mph) inclusive on the Beaufort scale. **3** *US & Canad. inf.* an easy task or state of ease. **4** *Inf., chiefly Brit.* a disturbance, esp. a lively quarrel. ◆ *vb* **breezes, breezing, breezed.** (*intr*) **5** to move quickly or casually: *he breezed into the room.* ORIG C16: prob. from OSp. *briza* northeast wind

breeze[2] (briːz) *n* ashes of coal, coke, or charcoal used to make breeze blocks. ORIG C18: from F *braise* live coals; see BRAISE

breeze block *n* a light building brick made from the ashes of coal, coke, etc., bonded together by cement.

breezeway (ˈbriːzˌweɪ) *n* a roofed passageway connecting two buildings.

breezy (ˈbriːzɪ) *adj* **breezier, breeziest. 1** fresh; windy. **2** casual or carefree; lively; light-hearted.
▸ **ˈbreezily** *adv* ▸ **ˈbreeziness** *n*

Bregenz ★ (*German* ˈbreːgɛnts) *n* a resort in W Austria, the capital of Vorarlberg province. Pop.: 26 730 (1989).

Bremen ★ (ˈbreɪmən) *n* **1** a state of NW Germany, centred on the city of Bremen and its outport Bremerhaven; formerly in West Germany. Pop.: 678 700 (1996 est.). Area: 404 sq. km (156 sq. miles). **2** an industrial city and port in NW Germany, on the Weser estuary. Pop.: 549 357 (1996 est.).

Bremerhaven ★ (*German* breːmərˈhaːfən) *n* a port in NW Germany. Pop.: 130 400 (1996 est.). Former name (until 1947): **Wesermünde.**

bremsstrahlung (ˈbrɛmzˌʃtrɑːlʊŋ) *n* the x-radiation produced when an electrically charged particle, such as an electron, is slowed down by the electric field of an atomic nucleus. ORIG G: braking radiation

Brendel ★ (*German* 'brɛndəl) *n* **Alfred** ('alfre:t). born 1931, Austrian pianist and poet.

Bren gun (brɛn) *n* an air-cooled gas-operated light machine gun: used by the British in World War II. ORIG C20: after *Br*(*no*), now in the Czech Republic, where it was first made and *En*(*field*), England, where manufacture was continued

Brennan ★ ('brɛnən) *n* **Christopher John**. 1870–1932, Australian poet and classical scholar.

Brenner Pass ★ ('brɛnə) *n* a pass over the E Alps, between Austria and Italy. Highest point: 1372 m (4501 ft).

Brent ★ (brɛnt) *n* a borough of NW Greater London. Pop.: 244 500 (1994 est.). Area: 44 sq. km (17 sq. miles).

brent goose (brɛnt) *n* a small goose that has a dark grey plumage and short neck and occurs in most northern coastal regions. Also called: **brent**, (esp. US and Canad.) **brant**. ORIG C16: ? of Scand. origin

Brenton ★ ('brɛntᵊn) *n* **Howard**. born 1942, British dramatist, author of such controversial plays as *The Romans in Britain* (1980), *Ugly Rumours* (1998), and (with David Hare) *Pravda* (1985).

Brentwood ★ ('brɛnt͵wʊd) *n* a residential town in SE England, in SW Essex near London. Pop.: 49 463 (1991).

Brescia ★ (*Italian* 'breʃʃa) *n* a city in N Italy, in Lombardy: at its height in the 16th century. Pop.: 190 208 (1996 est.). Ancient name: **Brixia** ('brɪksɪə).

Breslau ★ ('brɛzlau) *n* the German name for **Wrocław**.

Brest ★ (brɛst) *n* **1** a port in NW France, in Brittany: chief naval station of the country, planned by Richelieu in 1631 and fortified by Vauban. Pop.: 153 099 (1990). **2** a city in SW Belarus: Polish until 1795 and from 1921 to 1945. Pop.: 293 000 (1996 est.). Former name (until 1921): **Brest Litovsk** (brest li'tɔfsk). Polish name: **Brześć nad Bugiem**.

Bretagne ★ (brətaɲ) *n* the French name for **Brittany**.

brethren ('brɛðrɪn) *pl n Arch. except when referring to fellow members of a religion, society, etc.* a plural of **brother**.

Breton[1] ('brɛtᵊn) *adj* **1** of, relating to, or characteristic of Brittany, its people, or their language. ◆ *n* **2** a native or inhabitant of Brittany. **3** the Celtic language of Brittany.

Breton[2] ★ (*French* brətɔ̃) *n* **André** (ɑ̃dre). 1896–1966, French poet and art critic: founder and chief theorist of surrealism, publishing the first surrealist manifesto in 1924.

Breuer ★ ('brɔɪə) *n* **1 Josef** (*German* 'jo:zɛf). 1842–1925, Austrian physician and hypnotist. **2 Marcel Lajos** (mɑ:'sɛl 'lɒjəʊʃ). 1902–81, US architect and furniture designer, born in Hungary. He developed tubular metal furniture.

Breughel ★ ('brɔɪgᵊl) *n* a variant spelling of **Brueghel**.

breve (bri:v) *n* **1** an accent, ˘, placed over a vowel to indicate that it is short or is pronounced in a specified way. **2** *Music*. a note, now rarely used, equivalent to two semibreves. **3** *RC Church*. a less common word for **brief** (papal letter). ORIG C13: from Med. L, from L *brevis* short

brevet ('brɛvɪt) *n* **1** a document entitling a commissioned officer to hold temporarily a higher military rank without the appropriate pay and allowances. ◆ *vb* **brevets, brevetting, brevetted** *or* **brevets, breveting, breveted**. **2** (*tr*) to promote by brevet. ORIG C14: from OF, from *brief* letter; see BRIEF
▸ **'brevetcy** *n*

breviary ('bri:vjərɪ) *n, pl* **breviaries**. *RC Church*. a book of psalms, hymns, prayers, etc., to be recited daily by clerics and certain members of religious orders as part of the divine office. ORIG C16: from L *breviārium* an abridged version, from *brevis* short

brevity ('brɛvɪtɪ) *n, pl* **brevities**. **1** conciseness of expression; lack of verbosity. **2** a short duration; brief time. ORIG C16: from L, from *brevis* BRIEF

brew (bru:) *vb* **1** to make (beer, ale, etc.) from malt and other ingredients by steeping, boiling, and fermentation. **2** to prepare (a drink, such as tea) by boiling or infusing. **3** (*tr*) to devise or plan: *to brew a plot*. **4** (*intr*) to be in the process of being brewed. **5** (*intr*) to be impending or forming: *there's a storm brewing*. ◆ *n* **6** a beverage produced by brewing, esp. tea or beer. **7** an instance or time of brewing: *last year's brew*. **8** a mixture. ORIG OE *brēowan*
▸ **'brewer** *n*

brewery ('brʊərɪ) *n, pl* **breweries**. a place where beer, ale, etc., is brewed.

brewing ('bru:ɪŋ) *n* a quantity of a beverage brewed at one time.

Brezhnev ★ ('brɛʒnɛf; *Russian* 'brjɛʒnɪf) *n* **Leonid Ilyich** (lɪa'nit 'ilitʃ). 1906–82, Soviet statesman; president of the Soviet Union (1977–82); general secretary of the Soviet Communist Party (1964–82).

Brian ★ ('braɪən) *n* **Havergal** ('hævəgəl). 1876–1972, British composer, who wrote 32 symphonies.

Brian Boru ★ (bə'ru:) *n* ?941–1014, king of Ireland (1002–14): killed during the defeat of the Danes at the battle of Clontarf.

Briand ★ (*French* briɑ̃) *n* **Aristide** (aristid). 1862–1932, French socialist statesman: prime minister of France 11 times. Nobel peace prize 1926.

briar[1] *or* **brier** ('braɪə) *n* **1** Also called: **tree heath**. a shrub of S Europe, having a hard woody root (briarroot). **2** a tobacco pipe made from the root of this plant. ORIG C19: from F *bruyère* heath
▸ **'briary** *or* **'briery** *adj*

briar[2] ('braɪə) *n* a variant spelling of **brier**[1].

Briareus ★ (braɪ'ɛərɪəs) *n Greek myth*. a giant with a hundred arms and fifty heads who aided Zeus and the Olympians against the Titans.
▸ **Bri'arean** *adj*

briarroot *or* **brierroot** ('braɪə͵ru:t) *n* the hard woody root of the briar, used for making tobacco pipes. Also called: **briarwood, brierwood**.

bribe (braɪb) *vb* **bribes, bribing, bribed**. **1** to promise, offer, or give something, often illegally, to (a person) to procure services or gain influence. ◆ *n* **2** a reward, such as money or favour, given or offered for this purpose. **3** any persuasion or lure. ORIG C14: from OF *briber* to beg, from ?
▸ **'bribery** *n*

bric-a-brac ('brɪkə͵bræk) *n* miscellaneous small objects, esp. furniture and curios, kept because they are ornamental or rare. ORIG C19: from F

brick (brɪk) *n* **1a** a rectangular block of clay mixed with sand and fired in a kiln or baked by the sun, used in building construction. **1b** (*as modifier*): *a brick house*. **2** the material used to make such blocks. **3** any rectangular block: *a brick of ice*. **4** bricks collectively. **5** *Inf*. a reliable, trustworthy, or helpful person. **6** *Brit*. a child's building block. **7 drop a brick**. *Brit. inf*. to make a tactless or indiscreet remark. **8 like a ton of bricks**. *Inf*. with great force; severely. ◆ *vb* **9** (*tr*; usually foll. by *in*, *up*, or *over*) to construct, line, pave, fill, or wall up with bricks: *to brick up a window*. ORIG C15: from OF *brique*, from MDu. *bricke*
▸ **'bricky** *adj*

brickbat ('brɪk͵bæt) *n* **1** a piece of brick or similar material, esp. one used as a weapon. **2** blunt criticism. ORIG C16: BRICK + BAT[1]

brickie ('brɪkɪ) *n Inf*. a bricklayer.

bricklayer ('brɪk͵leɪə) *n* a person trained or skilled in laying bricks.
▸ **'brick͵laying** *n*

brick red *n, adj* (of) a reddish-brown colour.

brickwork ('brɪk͵wɜ:k) *n* **1** a structure built of bricks. **2** construction using bricks.

brickyard ('brɪk͵jɑ:d) *n* a place in which bricks are made, stored, or sold.

bricolage ('brɪkə͵lɑ:ʒ; *French* brikəlaʒ) *n Archit*. a jumbled effect produced by the close proximity of buildings from different periods or in different styles. ORIG F: odd jobs, do-it-yourself

bridal ('braɪdᵊl) *adj* of or relating to a bride or a wedding; nuptial. ORIG OE *brȳdealu*, lit.: "bride ale", that is, wedding feast

bride (braɪd) *n* a woman who has just been or is about to be married. ORIG OE *brȳd*

Bride ★ (braɪd) *n* See (Saint) **Bridget**.

bridegroom ('braɪd͵gru:m, -͵grʊm) *n* a man who has just been or is about to be married. ORIG C14: changed

★ people and places

(through infl. of GROOM) from OE *brȳdguma,* from *brȳd* BRIDE + *guma* man

bride price *or* **wealth** *n* (in some societies) money, property, or services given by a bridegroom to the kinsmen of his bride.

bridesmaid ('braɪdz,meɪd) *n* a girl or young unmarried woman who attends a bride at her wedding.

bridge[1] (brɪdʒ) *n* **1** a structure that spans and provides a passage over a road, railway, river, or some other obstacle. **2** something that resembles this in shape or function. **3** the hard ridge at the upper part of the nose, formed by the underlying nasal bones. **4** the part of a pair of glasses that rests on the nose. **5** Also called: **bridgework.** a dental plate containing one or more artificial teeth that is secured to the surrounding natural teeth. **6** a platform from which a ship is piloted and navigated. **7** a piece of wood, usually fixed, supporting the strings of a violin, guitar, etc., and transmitting their vibrations to the sounding board. **8** Also called: **bridge passage.** a passage in a musical, literary, or dramatic work linking two or more important sections. **9** Also called: **bridge circuit.** *Electronics.* any of several networks across which a device is connected for measuring resistance, capacitance, etc. **10** *Computing.* a device that connects networks and sends packets between them. **11** *Billiards, snooker.* a support for a cue. **12 cross a bridge when (one) comes to it.** to deal with a problem only when it arises. ◆ *vb* **bridges, bridging, bridged.** (*tr*) **13** to build or provide a bridge over something; span: *to bridge a river.* **14** to connect or reduce the distance between: *let us bridge our differences.* ORIG OE *brycg*
▸ **'bridgeable** *adj*

bridge[2] (brɪdʒ) *n* a card game for four players, based on whist, in which one hand (the dummy) is exposed and the trump suit decided by bidding between the players. See also **contract bridge, auction bridge.** ORIG C19: from ?

Bridge ★ (brɪdʒ) *n* **Frank.** 1879–1941, British composer, esp. of chamber music.

bridgehead ('brɪdʒ,hɛd) *n* **1** *Mil.* an area of ground secured or to be taken on the enemy's side of an obstacle. **2** *Mil.* a fortified or defensive position at the end of a bridge nearest to the enemy. **3** an advantageous position gained for future expansion.

Bridgend ★ (,brɪdʒ'ɛnd) *n* a county borough in S Wales. Pop.: 130 874 (1996 est.). Area: 264 sq. km (102 sq. miles).

Bridge of Sighs ★ *n* a covered 16th-century bridge in Venice, between the Doge's Palace and the prisons, through which prisoners were formerly led to trial or execution.

Bridgeport ★ ('brɪdʒ,pɔːt) *n* a port in SW Connecticut, on Long Island Sound. Pop.: 132 919 (1994 est.).

bridge roll *n* a soft bread roll in a long thin shape. ORIG C20: from BRIDGE[2] or ? BRIDGE[1]

Bridges ★ ('brɪdʒɪz) *n* **Robert (Seymour).** 1844–1930, British poet: poet laureate (1913–30).

Bridget ★ ('brɪdʒɪt) *n* **Saint. 1** Also called: **Bride, Brigid.** 453–523 A.D., Irish abbess; a patron saint of Ireland. Feast day: Feb. 1. **2** Also called: **Birgitta.** ?1303-73, Swedish nun; patron saint of Sweden. Feast day: July 23.

Bridgetown ★ ('brɪdʒ,taʊn) *n* the capital of Barbados, a port on the SW coast. Pop.: 6070 (1990).

bridgework ('brɪdʒ,wɜːk) *n* a partial denture attached to the surrounding teeth.

bridging loan *n* a loan made to cover the period between two transactions, such as the buying of another house before the sale of the first is completed.

Bridgwater ★ ('brɪdʒ,wɔːtə) *n* a town in SW England, in central Somerset. Pop.: 34 610 (1991).

Bridie ★ ('braɪdɪ) *n* **James,** real name *Osborne Henry Mavor.* 1888–1951, Scottish physician and dramatist. His plays include *The Anatomist* (1930).

bridle ('braɪdᵊl) *n* **1** a headgear for a horse, etc., consisting of a series of buckled straps and a metal mouthpiece (bit) by which the animal is controlled through the reins. **2** something that curbs or restrains; check. **3** a Y-shaped cable, rope, or chain, used for holding, towing, etc. ◆ *vb* **bridles, bridling, bridled. 4** (*tr*) to put a bridle on (a horse, mule, etc.). **5** (*tr*) to restrain; curb: *he bridled his rage.* **6** (*intr;* often foll. by *at*) to show anger, scorn, or indignation. ORIG OE *brigdels*

bridle path *n* a path suitable for riding or leading horses.

Brie (briː) *n* **1** a soft creamy white cheese. **2** a mainly agricultural area in N France, between the Rivers Marne and Seine: noted esp. for its cheese.

brief (briːf) *adj* **1** short in duration. **2** short in length or extent; scanty: *a brief bikini.* **3** abrupt in manner; brusque: *the professor was brief with me.* **4** terse or concise. ◆ *n* **5** a condensed statement or written synopsis; abstract. **6** *Law.* a document containing all the facts and points of law of a case by which a solicitor instructs a barrister to represent a client. **7** *RC Church.* a letter issuing from the Roman court written in modern characters, as contrasted with a papal bull; papal brief. **8** Also called: **briefing.** instructions. **9 hold a brief for.** to argue for; champion. **10 in brief.** in short; to sum up. ◆ *vb* (*tr*) **11** to prepare or instruct by giving a summary of relevant facts. **12** to make a summary or synopsis of. **13** *English law.* **13a** to instruct (a barrister) by brief. **13b** to retain (a barrister) as counsel. ORIG C14: from OF *bref,* from L *brevis*
▸ **'briefly** *adv* ▸ **'briefness** *n*

briefcase ('briːf,keɪs) *n* a flat portable case, often of leather, for carrying papers, books, etc.

briefing ('briːfɪŋ) *n* **1** a meeting at which information and instructions are given. **2** the facts presented at such a meeting.

briefless ('briːflɪs) *adj* (said of a barrister) without clients.

briefs (briːfs) *pl n* men's underpants or women's pants without legs.

brier[1] *or* **briar** ('braɪə) *n* any of various thorny shrubs or other plants, such as the sweetbrier. ORIG OE *brēr, brǣr,* from ?
▸ **'briery** *or* **'briary** *adj*

brier[2] ('braɪə) *n* a variant spelling of **briar**[1].

brierroot ('braɪə,ruːt) *n* a variant spelling of **briarroot.** Also called: **brierwood.**

brig[1] (brɪg) *n* **1** *Naut.* a two-masted square-rigger. **2** *Chiefly US.* a prison, esp. in a navy ship. ORIG C18: shortened from BRIGANTINE

brig[2] (brɪg) *n* a Scot. and N English word for a **bridge**[1].

Brig. *abbrev. for* Brigadier.

brigade (brɪ'geɪd) *n* **1** a military formation smaller than a division and usually commanded by a brigadier. **2** a group of people organized for a certain task: *a rescue brigade.* ◆ *vb* **brigades, brigading, brigaded.** (*tr*) **3** to organize into a brigade. ORIG C17: from OF, from OIt., from *brigare* to fight; see BRIGAND

brigadier (,brɪgə'dɪə) *n* **1** an officer of the British Army or Royal Marines junior to a major general but senior to a colonel, usually commanding a brigade. **2** an equivalent rank in other armed forces. ORIG C17: from F, from BRIGADE

brigalow ('brɪgələʊ) *n Austral.* **a** any of various acacia trees, forming dense scrub. **b** (*as modifier*): *brigalow country.* ORIG C19: from Abor.

brigand ('brɪgənd) *n* a bandit, esp. a member of a gang operating in mountainous areas. ORIG C14: from OF, from OIt. *brigante* fighter, from *briga* strife
▸ **'brigandage** *or* **'brigandry** *n*

brigantine ('brɪgən,tiːn, -,taɪn) *n* a two-masted sailing ship, rigged square on the foremast and fore-and-aft on the mainmast. ORIG C16: from OIt. *brigantino* pirate ship, from *brigante* BRIGAND

Briggs ★ (brɪgz) *n* **Henry.** 1561–1631, English mathematician: introduced common logarithms.

Brighouse[1] ★ ('brɪg,haʊs) *n* a town in N England, in Calderdale unitary authority, in West Yorkshire: machine tools, textiles, engineering. Pop.: 32 198 (1991).

Brighouse[2] ★ ('brɪg,haʊs) *n* **Harold.** 1882–1958, British writer, noted for his play *Hobson's Choice* (1915).

bright (braɪt) *adj* **1** emitting or reflecting much light;

shining. **2** (of colours) intense or vivid. **3** full of promise: *a bright future.* **4** full of animation; cheerful: *a bright face.* **5** *Inf.* quick-witted or clever: *a bright child.* **6** magnificent; glorious. **7** polished; glistening. **8** (of a liquid) translucent and clear. **9 bright and early.** very early in the morning. ◆ *adv* **10** brightly: *the fire was burning bright.* ORIG OE *beorht*
▸ **'brightly** *adv* ▸ **'brightness** *n*

Bright ★ (braɪt) *n* **John.** 1811–89, British liberal statesman, economist: with Richard Cobden he led the Anti-Corn-Law League (1838–46).

brighten ('braɪtᵊn) *vb* **1** to make or become bright or brighter. **2** to make or become cheerful.

brightening agent *n* a compound applied to a textile to increase its brightness by the conversion of ultraviolet radiation to visible (blue) light, used in detergents.

Brighton ★ ('braɪtᵊn) *n* a resort in S England, in Brighton and Hove unitary authority, in East Sussex: patronized by the Prince Regent, who had the Royal Pavilion built (1782); seat of The University of Sussex (1961) and The University of Brighton (1992). Pop.: 124 851 (1991).

Brighton and Hove ★ (həʊv) *n* a city and unitary authority in S England, in East Sussex. Pop.: 248 100 (1995 est.). Area: 72 sq. km (28 sq. miles).

Bright's disease (braɪts) *n* chronic inflammation of the kidneys; chronic nephritis. ORIG C19: after Richard *Bright* (1789–1858), E physician

brightwork ('braɪtˌwɜːk) *n* shiny metal trimmings or fittings on ships, cars, etc.

Brigid ★ ('brɪdʒɪd) *n* See (Saint) **Bridget.**

brill[1] (brɪl) *n, pl* **brill** *or* **brills.** a European flatfish similar to the turbot. ORIG C15: prob. from Cornish *brȳthel* mackerel, from OCornish *brȳth* speckled

brill[2] (brɪl) *adj Brit sl.* excellent or wonderful. ORIG C20: shortened form of BRILLIANT

brilliance ('brɪljəns) *or* **brilliancy** *n* **1** great brightness; radiance. **2** excellence or distinction in physical or mental ability; exceptional talent. **3** splendour; magnificence.

brilliant ('brɪljənt) *adj* **1** shining with light; sparkling. **2** (of a colour) reflecting a considerable amount of light; vivid. **3** outstanding; exceptional: *a brilliant success.* **4** splendid; magnificent: *a brilliant show.* **5** of outstanding intelligence or intellect: *a brilliant mind.* ◆ *n* **6** Also called: **brilliant cut. 6a** a cut for diamonds and other gemstones in the form of two many-faceted pyramids joined at their bases. **6b** a diamond of this cut. ORIG C17: from F *brillant* shining, from It. *brillo* BERYL
▸ **'brilliantly** *adv*

brilliantine ('brɪljənˌtiːn) *n* a perfumed oil used to make the hair smooth and shiny. ORIG C19: from F, from *brillant* shining

brim (brɪm) *n* **1** the upper rim of a vessel: *the brim of a cup.* **2** a projecting rim or edge: *the brim of a hat.* **3** the brink or edge of something. ◆ *vb* **brims, brimming, brimmed. 4** to fill or be full to the brim: *eyes brimming with tears.* ORIG C13: from MHG *brem*
▸ **'brimless** *adj*

brimful *or* **brimfull** (ˌbrɪm'fʊl) *adj* (*postpositive;* foll. by *of*) filled up to the brim (with).

brimstone ('brɪmˌstəʊn) *n* **1** an obsolete name for **sulphur. 2** a common yellow butterfly of N temperate regions of the Old World. ORIG OE *brynstān;* see BURN[1], STONE

Brindisi ★ (*Italian* 'brindizi) *n* a port in SE Italy, in SE Apulia: important naval base in Roman times and a centre of the Crusades in the Middle Ages. Pop.: 93 290 (1991). Ancient name: **Brundisium.**

brindle ('brɪndᵊl) *n* **1** a brindled animal. **2** a brindled colouring. ORIG C17: back formation from BRINDLED

brindled ('brɪndᵊld) *adj* brown or grey streaked or patched with a darker colour: *a brindled dog.* ORIG C17: changed from C15 *brended,* lit.: branded

Brindley ★ ('brɪndlɪ) *n* **James.** 1716–72, British canal builder, who constructed (1759–61) the Bridgewater Canal, the first in England.

brine (braɪn) *n* **1** a strong solution of salt and water, used for salting and pickling meats, etc. **2** the sea or its water. ◆ *vb* **brines, brining, brined. 3** (*tr*) to soak in or treat with brine. ORIG OE *brīne*
▸ **'brinish** *adj*

bring (brɪŋ) *vb* **brings, bringing, brought.** (*tr*) **1** to carry, convey, or take (something or someone) to a designated place or person: *bring that book to me.* **2** to cause to happen or occur to (oneself or another): *to bring disrespect on oneself.* **3** to cause to happen as a consequence: *responsibility brings maturity.* **4** to cause to come to mind: *it brought back memories.* **5** to cause to be in a certain state, position, etc.: *the punch brought him to his knees.* **6** to force, persuade, or make (oneself): *I couldn't bring myself to do it.* **7** to sell for; fetch: *the painting brought 20 pounds.* **8** *Law.* **8a** to institute (proceedings, charges, etc.). **8b** to put (evidence, etc.) before a tribunal. **9 bring forth.** to give birth to. ◆ See also **bring about, bring down,** etc. ORIG OE *bringan*
▸ **'bringer** *n*

bring about *vb* (*tr, adv*) **1** to cause to happen. **2** to turn (a ship) around.

bring-and-buy sale *n Brit. & NZ.* an informal sale, often for charity, to which people bring items for sale and buy those that others have brought. Often shortened to **bring-and-buy.**

bring down *vb* (*tr, adv*) to cause to fall.

bring forward *vb* (*tr, adv*) **1** to present or introduce (a subject) for discussion. **2** *Book-keeping.* to transfer (a sum) to the top of the next page or column. 3 to move to an earlier time or date: *the kickoff has been brought forward to 2 p.m.*

bring in *vb* (*tr, adv*) **1** to yield (income, profit, or cash). **2** to produce or return (a verdict). **3** to introduce (a legislative bill, etc.).

bring off *vb* (*tr, adv*) to succeed in achieving (something), esp. with difficulty.

bring out *vb* (*tr, adv*) **1** to produce or publish or have published. **2** to expose, reveal, or cause to be seen: *she brought out the best in me.* **3** (foll. by *in*) to cause (a person) to become covered (with spots, a rash, etc.). **4** *Brit.* to introduce (a girl) formally into society as a debutante.

bring over *vb* (*tr, adv*) to cause (a person) to change allegiances.

bring round *or* **around** *vb* (*tr, adv*) **1** to restore (a person) to consciousness, esp. after a faint. **2** to convince (another person) of an opinion or point of view.

bring to *vb* (*tr, adv*) **1** to restore (a person) to consciousness. **2** to cause (a ship) to turn into the wind and reduce her headway.

bring up *vb* (*tr, adv*) **1** to care for and train (a child); rear. **2** to raise (a subject) for discussion; mention. **3** to vomit (food).

brinjal ('brɪndʒəl) *n* (in India and Africa) another name for the **aubergine.** ORIG C17: from Port. *berinjela,* from Ar.

brink (brɪŋk) *n* **1** the edge, border, or verge of a steep place. **2** the land at the edge of a body of water. **3** the verge of an event or state: *the brink of disaster.* ORIG C13: from MDu. *brinc,* of Gmc origin

brinkmanship ('brɪŋkmənˌʃɪp) *n* the art or practice of pressing a dangerous situation, esp. in international affairs, to the limit of safety and peace in order to win an advantage.

briny ('braɪnɪ) *adj* **brinier, briniest. 1** of or resembling brine; salty. ◆ *n* **2** (preceded by *the*) *Inf.* the sea.
▸ **'brininess** *n*

brio ('briːəʊ) *n* liveliness or vigour; spirit. See also **con brio.** ORIG C19: from It., of Celtic origin

brioche ('briːəʊʃ, -ɒʃ) *n* a soft roll made from a very light yeast dough. ORIG C19: from Norman dialect, from *brier* to knead, of Gmc origin

briquette *or* **briquet** (brɪ'kɛt) *n* a small brick made of compressed coal dust, sawdust, charcoal, etc., used for fuel. ORIG C19: from F: a little brick, from *brique* BRICK

Brisbane ★ ('brɪzbən) *n* a port in E Australia, the capital of Queensland: founded in 1824 as a penal settlement; vast agricultural hinterland. Pop.: 1 489 100 (1995 est.).

brisk (brɪsk) *adj* **1** lively and quick; vigorous: *a brisk walk.* **2** invigorating or sharp: *brisk weather.* ◆ *vb* **3** (often foll.

by *up*) to enliven; make or become brisk. ORIG C16: prob. var. of BRUSQUE
▸ **'briskly** *adv* ▸ **'briskness** *n*

brisket ('brɪskɪt) *n* **1** the breast of a four-legged animal. **2** the meat from this part, esp. of beef. ORIG C14: prob. from ON

brisling ('brɪslɪŋ) *n* another name for a **sprat**. ORIG C20: from Norwegian; rel. to obs. Danish *bretling*

bristle ('brɪsᵊl) *n* **1** any short stiff hair of an animal or plant, such as on a pig's back. **2** something resembling these hairs: *toothbrush bristle*. ◆ *vb* **bristles, bristling, bristled. 3** (when *intr*, often foll. by *up*) to stand up or cause to stand up like bristles. **4** (*intr;* sometimes foll. by *up*) to show anger, indignation, etc.: *she bristled at the suggestion*. **5** (*intr*) to be thickly covered or set: *the target bristled with arrows*. ORIG C13 *bristil, brustel*, from earlier *brust*, from OE *byrst*
▸ **'bristly** *adj*

Bristol ★ ('brɪstᵊl) *n* **1** a port and industrial city in SW England, mainly in Bristol unitary authority, on the River Avon seven miles from its mouth on the Bristol Channel: a major port, trading with America, in the 17th and 18th centuries; the modern port consists chiefly of docks at Avonmouth and Portishead; noted for the **Clifton Suspension Bridge** (designed by I. K. Brunel, 1834) over the Avon gorge; seat of Bristol University (1909) and the University of the West of England (1992). Pop.: 407 992 (1991). **2** a unitary authority in SW England created (1996) from part of Avon. Pop.: 374 300 (1996 est.). Area: 110 sq. km (42 sq. miles).

Bristol board *n* a heavy smooth cardboard of fine quality, used for drawing.

Bristol Channel ★ *n* an inlet of the Atlantic, between S Wales and SW England, merging into the Severn estuary. Length: about 137 km (85 miles).

Bristol fashion *adv, adj* (*postpositive*) in good order; efficiently arranged.

bristols ('brɪstᵊlz) *pl n Brit. sl.* a woman's breasts. ORIG C20: short for *Bristol Cities*, rhyming slang for *titties*

Brit (brɪt) *n Inf.* a British person.

Brit. *abbrev. for:* **1** Britain. **2** British.

Britain ★ ('brɪtᵊn) *n* another name for **Great Britain** or the **United Kingdom**.

Britannia (brɪ'tænɪə) *n* **1** a female warrior carrying a trident and wearing a helmet, personifying Great Britain or the British Empire. **2** (in the ancient Roman Empire) the S part of Great Britain. **3** short for **Britannia coin**.

Britannia coin *n* any of four British gold coins introduced in 1987 for investment purposes; their denominations are £100, £50, £25, and £10.

Britannia metal *n* an alloy of tin with antimony and copper: used for decorative purposes and for bearings.

Britannic (brɪ'tænɪk) *adj* of Britain; British (esp. in **His** *or* **Her Britannic Majesty**).

britches ('brɪtʃɪz) *pl n* a variant spelling of **breeches**.

Briticism ('brɪtɪˌsɪzəm) *n* a custom, linguistic usage, or other feature peculiar to Britain or its people. Also: **Britishism**.

British ('brɪtɪʃ) *adj* **1** of or denoting Britain. **2** relating to, denoting, or characteristic of the inhabitants of Britain. **3** relating to or denoting the English language as spoken and written in Britain. **4** of or relating to the Commonwealth: *British subjects*. ◆ *n* **5 the British.** (*functioning as pl*) the natives or inhabitants of Britain.
▸ **'Britishness** *n*

British Antarctic Territory ★ *n* a United Kingdom overseas territory in the S Atlantic: created in 1962 and consisting of the South Shetland Islands, the South Orkney Islands, and Graham Land; formerly part of the Falkland Islands Dependencies.

British Cameroons ★ *pl n* a former British trust territory of West Africa. See **Cameroon**.

British Columbia ★ *n* a province of W Canada, on the Pacific coast: largely mountainous with extensive forests, rich mineral resources, and important fisheries. Capital: Victoria. Pop.: 4 029 253 (1999 est.). Area: 930 532 sq. km (359 279 sq. miles). Abbrev.: **BC**.
▸ **British Columbian** *n, adj*

British Council *n* an organization founded (1934) to extend the influence of British culture and education throughout the world.

British East Africa ★ *n* the former British possessions of Uganda, Kenya, Tanganyika, and Zanzibar, before their independence in the 1960s.

British Empire ★ *n* (formerly) the United Kingdom and the territories under its control, which reached its greatest extent at the end of World War I when it embraced over a quarter of the world's population and more than a quarter of the world's land surface.

Britisher ('brɪtɪʃə) *n* (not used by the British) **1** a native or inhabitant of Great Britain. **2** any British subject.

British Guiana ★ *n* the former name (until 1966) of **Guyana**.

British Honduras ★ *n* the former name of **Belize**.

British India ★ *n* the 17 provinces of India formerly governed by the British under the British sovereign: ceased to exist in 1947 when the independent states of India and Pakistan were created.

British Indian Ocean Territory ★ *n* a United Kingdom overseas territory in the Indian Ocean: consists of the Chagos Archipelago (formerly a dependency of Mauritius) and formerly included (until 1976) Aldabra, Farquhar, and Des Roches, now administratively part of the Seychelles.

British Isles ★ *pl n* a group of islands in W Europe, consisting of Great Britain, Ireland, the Isle of Man, Orkney, the Shetland Islands, the Channel Islands belonging to Great Britain, and the islands adjacent to these.

Britishism ('brɪtɪˌʃɪzəm) *n* a variant of **Briticism**.

British Legion *n Brit.* an organization founded in 1921 to provide services and assistance for former members of the armed forces.

British North America ★ *n* (formerly) Canada or its constituent regions or provinces that formed part of the British Empire.

British Somaliland ★ *n* a former British protectorate (1884–1960) in E Africa, on the Gulf of Aden: united with Italian Somaliland in 1960 to form the Somali Republic.

British thermal unit *n* a unit of heat in the fps system equal to the quantity of heat required to raise the temperature of 1 pound of water by 1°F. 1 British thermal unit is equivalent to 1055.06 joules. Abbrev.: **btu, BThU**.

British Virgin Islands ★ *pl n* a United Kingdom overseas territory in the Caribbean, consisting of 36 islands in the E Virgin Islands: formerly part of the Federation of the Leeward Islands (1871–1956). Capital: Road Town, on Tortola. Pop.: 17 000 (1993 est.). Area: 153 sq. km (59 sq. miles).

British West Africa ★ *n* the former British possessions of Nigeria, The Gambia, Sierra Leone, and the Gold Coast, and the former trust territories of Togoland and Cameroons.

British West Indies ★ *pl n* the states in the Caribbean that are members of the Commonwealth: Antigua and Barbuda, the Bahamas, Barbados, Dominica, Grenada, Jamaica, Saint Kitts-Nevis, Saint Lucia, Saint Vincent and the Grenadines, and Trinidad and Tobago.

Briton ('brɪtᵊn) *n* **1** a native or inhabitant of Britain. **2** *History.* any of the early Celtic inhabitants of S Britain. ORIG C13: from OF *Breton*, of Celtic origin

Britpop ('brɪtˌpɒp) *n* the characteristic pop music performed by some British bands of the mid 1990s.

Brittany ★ ('brɪtənɪ) *n* a region of NW France, the peninsula between the English Channel and the Bay of Biscay: settled by Celtic refugees from Wales and Cornwall during the Anglo-Saxon invasions; disputed between England and France until 1364. Breton name: **Breiz** (braɪz). French name: **Bretagne**.

Britten ★ ('brɪtᵊn) *n* (**Edward**) **Benjamin**, Baron Britten. 1913–76, British composer. His works include the operas *Peter Grimes* (1945) and *Billy Budd* (1951), choral works, and orchestral pieces.

brittle (ˈbrɪtᵊl) *adj* **1** easily cracked, snapped, or broken; fragile. **2** curt or irritable. **3** hard or sharp in quality. ◆ *n* **4** a crunchy sweet made with treacle and nuts: *peanut brittle.* ORIG C14: ult. from OE *brēotan* to break
▸ ˈ**brittleness** *n*

brittle-star *n* an echinoderm occurring on the sea bottom and having long slender arms radiating from a small central disc.

Brno ★ (ˈbɜːnəʊ; *Czech* ˈbrnɔ) *n* a city in the Czech Republic, formerly the capital of Moravia: the country's second largest city. Pop.: 388 899 (1996 est.). German name: **Brünn.**

bro. *abbrev. for* brother.

broach (brəʊtʃ) *vb* (*tr*) **1** to initiate (a topic) for discussion. **2** to tap or pierce (a container) to draw off (a liquid): *to broach a cask.* **3** to open in order to begin to use. ◆ *n* **4** a long tapered toothed cutting tool for enlarging holes. **5** a spit for roasting meat, etc. ORIG C14: from OF *broche,* from L *brochus* projecting

USAGE NOTE *Broach* is occasionally wrongly used as the spelling for the item of jewellery (*brooch*).

broad (brɔːd) *adj* **1** having relatively great breadth or width. **2** of vast extent; spacious: *a broad plain.* **3** (*postpositive*) from one side to the other: *four miles broad.* **4** of great scope or potential: *that invention had broad applications.* **5** not detailed; general: *broad plans.* **6** clear and open; full (esp. in **broad daylight**). **7** obvious or plain: *broad hints.* **8** liberal; tolerant: *a broad political stance.* **9** widely spread; extensive: *broad support.* **10** vulgar; coarse; indecent: *a broad joke.* **11** (of a dialect or pronunciation) consisting of a large number of speech sounds characteristic of a particular geographic area: *a broad Yorkshire accent.* **12** *Finance.* denoting an assessment of liquidity as including notes and coin in circulation with the public, banks' till money and balances, most private-sector bank deposits, and sterling bank-deposit certificates: *broad money.* Cf. **narrow** (sense 7). **13** *Phonetics.* the long vowel in English words such as *father, half,* as represented in Received Pronunciation. ◆ *n* **14** the broad part of something. **15** *Sl., chiefly US & Canad.* **15a** a girl or woman. **15b** a prostitute. **16** See **Broads.** ORIG OE *brād*
▸ ˈ**broadly** *adv*

B-road *n* a secondary road in Britain.

broad arrow *n* **1** a mark shaped like a broad arrowhead designating British government property and formerly used on prison clothing. **2** an arrow with a broad head.

broadband (ˈbrɔːdˌbænd) n a transmission technique using a wide range of frequencies that enables messages to be telecommunicated simultaneously.

broad bean *n* **1** an erect annual Eurasian bean plant cultivated for its large edible flattened seeds. **2** the seed of this plant.

broadcast (ˈbrɔːdˌkɑːst) *vb* **broadcasts, broadcasting, broadcast** *or* **broadcasted. 1** to transmit (announcements or programmes) on radio or television. **2** (*intr*) to take part in a radio or television programme. **3** (*tr*) to make widely known throughout an area: *to broadcast news.* **4** (*tr*) to scatter (seed, etc.) over an area, esp. by hand. ◆ *n* **5a** a transmission or programme on radio or television. **5b** (*as modifier*): *a broadcast signal.* **6** the act of scattering seeds. ◆ *adj* **7** dispersed over a wide area. ◆ *adv* **8** far and wide.
▸ ˈ**broadˌcaster** *n* ▸ ˈ**broadˌcasting** *n*

Broad Church *n* **1** a party within the Church of England which favours a broad and liberal interpretation of Anglican doctrine. **2** (*usually not caps.*) a group which embraces a wide and varied number of views and opinions. ◆ *adj* **Broad-Church. 3** of or relating to this party in the Church of England.

broadcloth (ˈbrɔːdˌklɒθ) *n* **1** fabric woven on a wide loom. **2** a closely woven fabric of wool, worsted, cotton, or rayon with lustrous finish, used for clothing.

broaden (ˈbrɔːdᵊn) *vb* to make or become broader.

broad gauge *n* **1** a railway track with a greater distance between the lines than the standard gauge of 56½ inches (about 1·44 metres). ◆ *adj* **broad-gauge. 2** of or denoting a railway having this track.

broad-leaved *adj* denoting trees other than conifers; having broad rather than needle-shaped leaves.

broadloom (ˈbrɔːdˌluːm) *n* (*modifier*) of or designating carpets woven on a wide loom.

broad-minded *adj* **1** tolerant of opposing viewpoints; not prejudiced; liberal. **2** not easily shocked by permissive sexual habits, pornography, etc.
▸ ˌ**broad-ˈmindedly** *adv* ▸ ˌ**broad-ˈmindedness** *n*

Broads ★ (brɔːdz) *pl n* **the.** a group of shallow navigable lakes, connected by a network of rivers, in E England, in Norfolk and Suffolk.

broadsheet (ˈbrɔːdˌʃiːt) *n* **1** a newspaper having a large format, approximately 15 by 24 inches (38 by 61 centimetres). **2** another word for **broadside** (sense 4).

broadside (ˈbrɔːdˌsaɪd) *n* **1** *Naut.* the entire side of a vessel. **2** *Naval.* **2a** all the armament fired from one side of a warship. **2b** the simultaneous discharge of such armament. **3** a strong verbal or written attack. **4** Also called: **broadside ballad.** a ballad or popular song printed on one side of a sheet of paper, esp. in 16th-century England. ◆ *adv* **5** with a broader side facing an object; sideways.

broad-spectrum *n* (*modifier*) effective against a wide variety of diseases or microorganisms: *a broad-spectrum antibiotic.*

broadsword (ˈbrɔːdˌsɔːd) *n* a broad-bladed sword used for cutting rather than stabbing.

broadtail (ˈbrɔːdˌteɪl) *n* **1** the highly valued black wavy fur obtained from the skins of newly born karakul lambs; caracul. **2** another name for **karakul.**

Broadway ★ (ˈbrɔːdˌweɪ) *n* **1** a thoroughfare in New York City: the centre of the commercial theatre in the US. ◆ *adj* **2** of, relating to, or suitable for the commercial theatre, esp. on Broadway.

brocade (brəʊˈkeɪd) *n* **1** a rich fabric woven with a raised design, often using gold or silver threads. ◆ *vb* **brocades, brocading, brocaded. 2** (*tr*) to weave with such a design. ORIG C17: from Sp. *brocado,* from It. *broccato* embossed fabric, from L *brochus* projecting

broccoli (ˈbrɒkəlɪ) *n* **1** a cultivated variety of cabbage having branched greenish flower heads. **2** the flower head, eaten as a vegetable before the buds have opened. ORIG C17: from It., pl of *broccolo* a little sprout, from *brocco* sprout

broch (brɒk, brɒx) *n* (in Scotland) a prehistoric circular dry-stone tower large enough to serve as a fortified home. ORIG C17: from ON *borg;* rel. to OE *burh* settlement, burgh

brochette (brɒˈʃɛt) *n* a skewer or small spit, used for holding pieces of meat, etc., while roasting or grilling. ORIG C19: from OF *brochete* small pointed tool; see BROACH

brochure (ˈbrəʊʃjʊə, -ʃə) *n* a pamphlet or booklet, esp. one containing summarized or introductory information or advertising. ORIG C18: from F, from *brocher* to stitch (a book)

brock (brɒk) *n* a Brit. name for **badger** (sense 1). ORIG OE *broc,* of Celtic origin

Brocken ★ (*German* ˈbrɔkən) *n* a mountain in central Germany: the highest peak of the Harz Mountains; important in German folklore. Height: 1142 m (3747 ft). The **Brocken Bow** or **Brocken Spectre** is an atmospheric phenomenon in which an observer, when the sun is low, may see his enlarged shadow against the clouds, often surrounded by coloured lights.

brocket (ˈbrɒkɪt) *n* a small deer of tropical America, having small unbranched antlers. ORIG C15: from Anglo-F *broquet,* from *broque* horn

broderie anglaise (ˈbrəʊdəriː ɑːŋˈglɛz) *n* open embroidery on white cotton, fine linen, etc. ORIG C19: from F: English embroidery

Broederbond (ˈbrʊdəˌbɔːnt, ˈbruːdəˌbɒnt) *n* (in South Africa) a secret society of Afrikaner Nationalists. ORIG Afrik.: band of brothers

broekies (ˈbrʊkiːz) *pl n S. African inf.* underpants. ORIG C19: Afrik.

Broglie ★ (brɔj) *n* **1** Prince **Louis Victor de** (lwi viktɔr də). 1892–1987, French physicist, noted for his development of wave mechanics: Nobel prize for physics 1929. **2** his brother, **Maurice** (mɔris), Duc de Broglie. 1875–1960, French physicist, noted for his research into X-ray spectra.

brogue[1] (brəug) *n* a broad gentle-sounding dialectal accent, esp. that used by the Irish in speaking English. ORIG C18: from ?

brogue[2] (brəug) *n* **1** a sturdy walking shoe, often with ornamental perforations. **2** an untanned shoe worn formerly in Ireland and Scotland. ORIG C16: from Irish Gaelic *bróg* shoe

broil[1] (brɔɪl) *vb* **1** the usual US and Canad. word for **grill** (sense 1). **2** to become or cause to become extremely hot. **3** (*intr*) to be furious. ORIG C14: from OF *bruillir* to burn

broil[2] (brɔɪl) *Arch.* ◆ *n* **1** a loud quarrel or disturbance; brawl. ◆ *vb* **2** (*intr*) to brawl; quarrel. ORIG C16: from OF *brouiller* to mix

broiler (ˈbrɔɪlə) *n* **1** a young tender chicken suitable for roasting. **2** a pan, grate, etc., for broiling food. **3** a very hot day.

broke (brəuk) *vb* **1** the past tense of **break.** ◆ *adj* **2** *Inf.* having no money; bankrupt. **3 go for broke.** *Sl.* to risk everything in a gambling or other venture.

broken (ˈbrəukən) *vb* **1** the past participle of **break.** ◆ *adj* **2** fractured, smashed, or splintered: *a broken vase.* **3** interrupted; disturbed; disconnected: *broken sleep.* **4** intermittent or discontinuous: *broken sunshine.* **5** not functioning. **6** spoilt or ruined by divorce (esp. in **broken home, broken marriage**). **7** (of a trust, promise, contract, etc.) violated; infringed. **8** (of the speech of a foreigner) imperfect in grammar, vocabulary, and pronunciation: *broken English.* **9** Also: **broken-in.** made tame or disciplined by training. **10** exhausted or weakened, as through ill-health or misfortune. **11** irregular or rough; uneven: *broken ground.* **12** bankrupt. **13** (of colour) having a multicoloured decorative effect, as by stippling paint onto a surface.
▸ **ˈbrokenly** *adv*

broken chord *n* another term for **arpeggio.**

broken-down *adj* **1** worn out, as by age or long use; dilapidated. **2** not in working order.

brokenhearted (ˌbrəukənˈhɑːtɪd) *adj* overwhelmed by grief or disappointment.
▸ **ˌbrokenˈheartedly** *adv*

Broken Hill ★ *n* a city in SE Australia, in W New South Wales: mining centre for lead, silver, and zinc. Pop.: 24 500 (1988 est.).

broken wind (wɪnd) *n Vet. science.* another name for **heaves.**
▸ **ˌbrokenˈwinded** *adj*

broker (ˈbrəukə) *n* **1** an agent who, acting on behalf of a principal, buys or sells goods, securities, etc.: *insurance broker.* **2** short for **stockbroker. 3** a person who deals in second-hand goods. ORIG C14: from Anglo-F *brocour* broacher (of casks, hence, one who sells, agent), from OF *broquier* to tap a cask

brokerage (ˈbrəukərɪdʒ) *n* **1** commission charged by a broker. **2** a broker's business or office.

brolga (ˈbrɒlgə) *n* a large grey Australian crane having a red-and-green head and a trumpeting call. Also called: **native companion.** ORIG C19: from Abor.

brolly (ˈbrɒlɪ) *n, pl* **brollies.** an informal Brit. name for **umbrella** (sense 1).

Bromberg ★ (ˈbrɔmbɛrk) *n* the German name for **Bydgoszcz.**

bromeliad (brəuˈmiːlɪˌæd) *n* any of a family of tropical American plants, typically epiphytes with a rosette of fleshy leaves, such as the pineapple and Spanish moss. ORIG C19: from NL, after Olaf *Bromelius* (1639–1705), Swedish botanist

bromide (ˈbrəumaɪd) *n* **1** any salt of hydrobromic acid. **2** any compound containing a bromine atom. **3** a dose of sodium or potassium bromide given as a sedative. **4a** a platitude. **4b** a boring person.

bromide paper *n* a type of photographic paper coated with an emulsion of silver bromide.

bromine (ˈbrəumiːn, -mɪn) *n* a pungent dark red volatile liquid element that occurs in brine and is used in the production of chemicals. Symbol: Br; atomic no.: 35; atomic wt.: 79.91. ORIG C19: from F *brome* bromine, from Gk *brōmos* bad smell, from ?

Bromley ★ (ˈbrɒmlɪ) *n* a borough of SE Greater London. Pop.: 293 000 (1994 est.). Area: 153 sq. km (59 sq. miles).

Bromsgrove ★ (ˈbrɒmzˌgrəuv) *n* a town in W central England, in NE Hereford and Worcester. Pop.: 26 366 (1991).

bronchi (ˈbrɒŋkaɪ) *n* the plural of **bronchus.**

bronchial (ˈbrɒŋkɪəl) *adj* of or relating to the bronchi or the bronchial tubes.
▸ **ˈbronchially** *adv*

bronchial tubes *pl n* the bronchi or their smaller divisions.

bronchiectasis (ˌbrɒŋkɪˈɛktəsɪs) *n* chronic dilation and usually infection of the bronchi. ORIG C19: from BRONCHO- + Gk *ektasis* a stretching

bronchiole (ˈbrɒŋkɪˌəul) *n* any of the smallest bronchial tubes. ORIG C19: from NL; see BRONCHUS
▸ **ˌbronchiˈolar** *adj*

bronchitis (brɒŋˈkaɪtɪs) *n* inflammation of the bronchial tubes, characterized by coughing, difficulty in breathing, etc.
▸ **bronchitic** (brɒŋˈkɪtɪk) *adj, n*

broncho- *or before a vowel* **bronch-** *combining form.* indicating or relating to the bronchi: *bronchitis.* ORIG from Gk: BRONCHUS

bronchodilator (ˌbrɒŋkəudaɪˈleɪtə, -dɪ-) *n* any drug or other agent that causes dilation of the bronchial tubes by relaxing bronchial muscle: used, esp. in the form of aerosol sprays, for the relief of asthma and chronic bronchitis.

bronchopneumonia (ˌbrɒŋkəunjuːˈməunɪə) *n* inflammation of the lungs, starting in the bronchioles.

bronchoscope (ˈbrɒŋkəˌskəup) *n* an instrument for examining and providing access to the interior of the bronchial tubes.

bronchus (ˈbrɒŋkəs) *n, pl* **bronchi.** either of the two main branches of the trachea. ORIG C18: from NL, from Gk *bronkhos* windpipe

bronco *or* **broncho** (ˈbrɒŋkəu) *n, pl* **broncos** *or* **bronchos.** (in the US and Canada) a wild or partially tamed pony or mustang of the western plains. ORIG C19: from Mexican Sp., from Sp.: rough, wild

Brontë ★ (ˈbrɒntɪ) *n* **1 Anne,** pen name *Acton Bell.* 1820–49, British novelist; author of *The Tenant of Wildfell Hall* (1847). **2** her sister, **Charlotte,** pen name *Currer Bell.* 1816–55, British novelist, author of *Jane Eyre* (1847), *Villette* (1853), and *The Professor* (1857). **3** her sister, **Emily (Jane),** pen name *Ellis Bell.* 1818–48, British novelist and poet; author of *Wuthering Heights* (1847).

brontosaurus (ˌbrɒntəˈsɔːrəs) *or* **brontosaur** (ˈbrɒntəˌsɔː) *n* a very large herbivorous quadrupedal dinosaur, common in N America during late Jurassic times, having a long neck and long tail. ORIG C19: from NL, from Gk *brontē* thunder + *sauros* lizard

Bronx ★ (brɒŋks) *n* **the.** a borough of New York City, on the mainland, separated from Manhattan by the Harlem River. Pop.: 1 203 789 (1990).

Bronx cheer *n Chiefly US.* a loud spluttering noise made with the lips and tongue and expressing derision or contempt; raspberry.

bronze (brɒnz) *n* **1** any hard water-resistant alloy consisting of copper and smaller proportions of tin and sometimes zinc and lead. **2** a yellowish-brown colour or pigment. **3** a statue, medal, or other object made of bronze. Cf. **bronze** (sense 1). ◆ *adj* **4** made of or resembling bronze. **5** of a yellowish-brown colour. ◆ *vb* **bronzes, bronzing, bronzed. 6** (esp. of the skin) to make or become brown; tan. **7** (*tr*) to give the appearance of bronze to. ORIG C18: from F, from It. *bronzo*
▸ **ˈbronzy** *adj*

Bronze Age *n* **a** a technological stage between the Stone and Iron Ages, beginning in the Middle East about 4500 B.C. and lasting in Britain from about 2000 to 500

B.C., during which weapons and tools were made of bronze. **b** (*as modifier*): *a Bronze-Age tool.*

bronze medal *n* a medal awarded to a competitor who comes third in a contest or race.

bronzing ('brɒnzɪŋ) *n* **1** blue pigment producing a metallic lustre when ground into paint media at fairly high concentrations. **2** the application of a mixture of powdered metal or pigments of a metallic lustre to a surface.

Bronzino, Il ★ (*Italian* bron'dzi:no) *n* real name *Agnolo di Cosimo di Mariano.* 1503–72, Florentine mannerist painter.

brooch (brəʊtʃ) *n* an ornament with a hinged pin and catch, worn fastened to clothing. ORIG C13: from OF *broche;* see BROACH

USAGE NOTE See at **broach.**

brood (bru:d) *n* **1** a number of young animals, esp. birds, produced at one hatching. **2** all the offspring in one family: often used jokingly or contemptuously. **3** a group of a particular kind; breed. **4** (*modifier*) kept for breeding: *a brood mare.* ◆ *vb* **5** (of a bird) **5a** to sit on or hatch (eggs). **5b** (*tr*) to cover (young birds) protectively with the wings. **6** (when *intr,* often foll. by *on, over,* or *upon*) to ponder morbidly or persistently. ORIG OE *brōd*
▸ **'brooding** *n, adj*

brooder ('bru:də) *n* **1** a structure, usually heated, used for rearing young chickens or other fowl. **2** a person or thing that broods.

broody ('bru:dɪ) *adj* **broodier, broodiest. 1** moody; introspective. **2** (of poultry) wishing to sit on or hatch eggs. **3** *Inf.* (of a woman) wishing to have a baby.
▸ **'broodiness** *n*

brook[1] (brʊk) *n* a natural freshwater stream smaller than a river. ORIG OE *brōc*

brook[2] (brʊk) *vb* (*tr*) (*usually used with a negative*) to bear; tolerate. ORIG OE *brūcan*

Brooke ★ (brʊk) *n* **1 Alan Francis.** See (1st Viscount) **Alanbrooke. 2** Sir **James.** 1803–68, British soldier; first rajah of Sarawak (1841–63). **3 Rupert** (**Chawner**). 1887–1915, British poet, noted for his war poetry.

brooklet ('brʊklɪt) *n* a small brook.

brooklime ('brʊk,laɪm) *n* either of two blue-flowered trailing plants, *Veronica americana* of North America or *V. beccabunga* of Europe and Asia, growing in moist places. See also **speedwell.** ORIG C16: from BROOK[1] + *-lemk,* from OE *hleomoce*

Brooklyn ★ ('brʊklɪn) *n* a borough of New York City, on the SW end of Long Island. Pop.: 2 291 664 (1990).

Brookner ★ ('brʊknə) *n* **Anita.** born 1928, British writer. Her novels include *Hotel du Lac* (1984), which won the Booker Prize, *Brief Lives* (1990), and *Falling Slowly* (1998).

Brooks ★ (brʊks) *n* **Mel**, real name *Melvyn Kaminsky.* born 1926, US writer, actor, and film director. His films include *Blazing Saddles* (1974) and *Dracula: Dead and Loving It* (1996).

Brooks Range ★ (brʊks) *n* a mountain range in N Alaska. Highest peak: Mount Isto, 2761 m (9058 ft).

brook trout *n* a North American trout, valued as a food and game fish.

broom (bru:m, brʊm) *n* **1** an implement for sweeping consisting of a long handle to which is attached either a brush of straw or twigs, bound together, or a solid head into which are set tufts of bristles or fibres. **2** any of various yellow-flowered Eurasian leguminous shrubs. **3 new broom.** a newly appointed official, etc., eager to make changes. ◆ *vb* **4** (*tr*) to sweep with a broom. ORIG OE *brōm*

broomrape ('bru:m,reɪp, 'brʊm-) *n* any of a genus of leafless fleshy parasitic plants growing on the roots of other plants, esp. on broom. ORIG C16: adaptation & partial translation of Med. L *rāpum genistae* tuber (hence: root nodule) of Genista (a type of broom plant)

broomstick ('bru:m,stɪk, 'brʊm-) *n* the long handle of a broom.

bros. *or* **Bros.** *abbrev. for* brothers.

brose (brəʊz) *n Scot.* a porridge made by adding a boiling liquid to meal, esp. oatmeal. ORIG C13 *broys,* from OF *broez,* from *breu* broth, of Gmc origin

broth (brɒθ) *n* **1** a soup made by boiling meat, fish, vegetables, etc., in water. **2** another name for **stock** (sense 19). ORIG OE *broth*

brothel ('brɒθəl) *n* **1** a house where men pay to have sexual intercourse with prostitutes. **2** *Austral. inf.* any untidy place. ORIG C16: short for *brothel-house,* from C14 *brothel* useless person, from OE *brēothan* to deteriorate

brother ('brʌðə) *n* **1** a male person having the same parents as another person. **2a** a male person belonging to the same group, profession, nationality, trade union, etc., as another or others; fellow member. **2b** (*as modifier*): *brother workers.* **3** comrade; friend: used as a form of address. **4** *Christianity.* a member of a male religious order. ◆ Related adj: **fraternal.** ORIG OE *brōthor*

brotherhood ('brʌðə,hʊd) *n* **1** the state of being related as a brother or brothers. **2** an association or fellowship, such as a trade union. **3** all persons engaged in a particular profession, trade, etc. **4** the belief, feeling, or hope that all men should treat one another as brothers.

brother-in-law *n, pl* **brothers-in-law. 1** the brother of one's wife or husband. **2** the husband of one's sister. **3** the husband of the sister of one's husband or wife.

brotherly ('brʌðəlɪ) *adj* of, resembling, or suitable to a brother, esp. in showing loyalty and affection; fraternal.
▸ **'brotherliness** *n*

brougham ('bru:əm, bru:m) *n* **1** a four-wheeled horse-drawn closed carriage having a raised open driver's seat in front. **2** *Obs.* a large car with an open compartment at the front for the driver. **3** *Obs.* an early electric car. ORIG C19: after Lord *Brougham* (1778–1868)

brought (brɔ:t) *vb* the past tense and past participle of **bring.**

brouhaha ('bru:hɑ:hɑ:) *n* a loud confused noise; commotion; uproar. ORIG F, imit.

brow (braʊ) *n* **1** the part of the face from the eyes to the hairline; forehead. **2** short for **eyebrow. 3** the expression of the face; countenance: *a troubled brow.* **4** the jutting top of a hill, etc. ORIG OE *brū*

browbeat ('braʊ,bi:t) *vb* **browbeats, browbeating, browbeat, browbeaten.** (*tr*) to discourage or frighten with threats or a domineering manner; intimidate.

brown (braʊn) *n* **1** any of various dark colours, such as those of wood or earth. **2** a dye or pigment producing these colours. ◆ *adj* **3** of the colour brown. **4** (of bread) made from a flour that has not been bleached or bolted, such as wheatmeal or wholemeal flour. **5** deeply tanned or sunburnt. **6 in a brown study.** See **study** (sense 15). ◆ *vb* **7** to make (esp. food as a result of cooking) brown or (esp. of food) to become brown. ORIG OE *brūn*
▸ **'brownish** *or* **'browny** *adj* ▸ **'brownness** *n*

Brown ★ (braʊn) *n* **1** Sir **Arthur Whitten** ('wɪtᵊn). 1886–1948, British aviator who with J. W. Alcock made the first nonstop flight across the Atlantic (1919). **2 Ford Madox.** 1821–93, British Pre-Raphaelite painter. **3 George** (**Alfred**), Lord George-Brown. 1914–85, British Labour leader; deputy leader of the Labour party (1960–70); foreign secretary (1966–68). **4 George Mackay.** 1921–96, Scottish poet, novelist, and short-story writer. **5 Gordon.** born 1951, British Labour politician; chancellor of the exchequer from 1997. **6 Herbert Charles.** born 1912, US chemist, who worked on the compounds of boron. Nobel prize for chemistry, 1979. **7 James.** born 1928, US soul singer and songwriter. **8 John.** 1800–59, US abolitionist leader, hanged after leading an unsuccessful rebellion of slaves at Harper's Ferry, Virginia. **9 Lancelot,** called *Capability Brown.* 1716–83, British landscape gardener. **10 Michael** (**Stuart**). born 1941, US physician: shared Nobel prize for physiology or medicine (1985) for work on cholesterol. **11 Robert.** 1773–1858, Scottish botanist who was the first to observe the Brownian movement in fluids.

brown bear *n* a large ferocious brownish bear inhabiting temperate forests of North America, Europe, and Asia.

brown coal *n* another name for **lignite.**

brown dwarf *n* a type of celestial body midway in size between a large planet and a small star, thought to be one possible explanation of dark matter in the universe.

Browne ★ (braʊn) *n* **1 Coral (Edith)**. 1913–91, Australian actress. **2 Hablot Knight**. See **Phiz**. **3** Sir **Thomas**. 1605–82, English physician and author. His works include *Religio Medici* (1642).

browned-off *adj Inf.* thoroughly discouraged or disheartened; fed up.

brown fat *n* a dark form of adipose tissue that is readily converted into energy.

brownfield (ˈbraʊnˌfiːld) *n* (*modifier*) denoting or located in an urban area that has previously been built on: *Hampshire has many brownfield developments.*

Brownian movement (ˈbraʊnɪən) *n* random movement of microscopic particles suspended in a fluid, caused by bombardment of the particles by molecules of the fluid. ORIG C19: after Robert BROWN

brownie (ˈbraʊnɪ) *n* **1** (in folklore) an elf said to do helpful work at night, esp. household chores. **2** a small square nutty chocolate cake. ORIG C16: dim. of BROWN (that is, a small brown man)

Brownie Guide *or* **Brownie** (ˈbraʊnɪ) *n* a member of the junior branch of the Guides.

Brownie point *n* a notional mark to one's credit for being seen to do the right thing. ORIG C20: ?from the mistaken notion that Brownie Guides earn points for good deeds

browning (ˈbraʊnɪŋ) *n Brit.* a substance used to darken soups, gravies, etc.

Browning ★ (ˈbraʊnɪŋ) *n* **1 Elizabeth Barrett**. 1806–61, British poet and critic; author of the *Sonnets from the Portuguese* (1850). **2** her husband, **Robert**. 1812–89, British poet, noted for *The Ring and the Book* (1868–69).

brown paper *n* a kind of coarse unbleached paper used for wrapping.

brown rice *n* unpolished rice, in which the grains retain the outer yellowish-brown layer (bran).

Brown Shirt *n* **1** (in Nazi Germany) a storm trooper. **2** a member of any fascist party or group.

brownstone (ˈbraʊnˌstəʊn) *n US.* a reddish-brown iron-rich sandstone used for building.

brown sugar *n* sugar that is unrefined or only partially refined.

brown trout *n* a common brownish variety of the trout that occurs in the rivers of N Europe.

browse (braʊz) *vb* **browses, browsing, browsed. 1** to look through (a book, articles for sale in a shop, etc.) in a casual leisurely manner. **2** *Computing.* to read hypertext, esp. on the World Wide Web. **3** (of deer, goats, etc.) to feed upon (vegetation) by continual nibbling. ◆ *n* **4** the act or an instance of browsing. **5** the young twigs, shoots, leaves, etc., on which certain animals feed. ORIG C15: from F *broust, brost* bud, of Gmc origin

browser (ˈbraʊzə) *n* **1** a person or animal that browses. **2** *Computing.* a software package that enables a user to read hypertext, esp. on the World Wide Web.

Broz ★ (*Serbo-Croat* brɔːz) *n* **Josip** (ˈjɔsip). original name of (Marshal) **Tito**.

BRS *abbrev. for* British Road Services.

Brubeck ★ (ˈbruːbɛk) *n* **Dave.** born 1920, US modern jazz pianist and composer.

Bruce[1] ★ (bruːs) *n* **1 James.** 1730–94, British explorer, who discovered the source of the Blue Nile (1770). **2 Lenny.** 1925–66, US comedian. **3 Robert the.** See **Robert I. 4 Stanley Melbourne,** 1st Viscount Bruce of Melbourne. 1883–1967, Australian prime minister (1923–29).

Bruce[2] (bruːs) *n Brit.* a jocular name for an Australian man.

brucellosis (ˌbruːsɪˈləʊsɪs) *n* an infectious disease of cattle, goats, and pigs, caused by bacteria and transmittable to man. Also called: **undulant fever.** ORIG C20: from NL *Brucella*, after Sir David *Bruce* (1855–1931), Australian bacteriologist & physician

Bruch ★ (*German* brux) *n* **Max** (maks). 1838–1920, German composer, noted for his three violin concertos.

Bruckner ★ (*German* ˈbrʊknər) *n* **Anton** (ˈantoːn). 1824–96, Austrian composer. His works include nine symphonies, four masses, and a Te Deum.

Brudenell ★ (ˈbruːdənɛl) *n* **James Thomas.** See (7th Earl of) **Cardigan.**

Brueghel, Bruegel, *or* **Breughel** ★ (ˈbrɔɪgᵊl; *Flemish* ˈbrøːxəl) *n* **1 Jan** (jɑn). 1568–1625, Flemish painter. **2** his father, **Pieter** (ˈpiːtər), called *the Elder.* ?1525–69, Flemish painter. **3** his son, **Pieter,** called *the Younger.* ?1564–1637, Flemish painter.

Bruges ★ (bruːʒ; *French* bryʒ) *n* a city in NW Belgium, capital of West Flanders province: centre of the medieval European wool and cloth trade. Pop.: 115 815 (1996 est.). Flemish name: **Brugge** (ˈbryxə).

bruin (ˈbruːɪn) *n* a name for a bear, used in children's tales, etc. ORIG C17: from Du. *bruin* brown

bruise (bruːz) *vb* **bruises, bruising, bruised.** (*mainly tr*) **1** (*also intr*) to injure (tissues) without breaking the skin, usually with discoloration, or (of tissues) to be injured in this way. **2** to offend or injure (someone's feelings). **3** to damage the surface of (something). **4** to crush (food, etc.) by pounding. ◆ *n* **5** a bodily injury without a break in the skin, usually with discoloration; contusion. ORIG OE *brȳsan*

bruiser (ˈbruːzə) *n Inf.* a strong tough person, esp. a boxer or a bully.

bruit (bruːt) *vb* **1** (*tr; often passive;* usually foll. by *about*) to report; rumour. ◆ *n* **2** *Arch.* **2a** a rumour. **2b** a loud outcry; clamour. ORIG C15: via F from Med. L *brūgītus,* prob. from L *rugīre* to roar

brumby (ˈbrʌmbɪ) *n, pl* **brumbies.** *Austral.* **1** a wild horse, esp. one descended from runaway stock. **2** *Inf.* a wild or unruly person. ORIG C19: from ?

brume (bruːm) *n Poetic.* heavy mist or fog. ORIG C19: from F: mist, winter, from L *brūma,* contracted from *brevissima diēs* the shortest day

Brummagem ★ (ˈbrʌmədʒəm) *n* **1** an informal name for **Birmingham.** Often shortened to **Brum. 2** (*sometimes not cap.*) something that is cheap and flashy, esp. imitation jewellery. ◆ *adj* **3** (*sometimes not cap.*) cheap and gaudy; tawdry. ORIG C17: from earlier *Bromecham,* local variant of BIRMINGHAM

Brummell ★ (ˈbrʌməl) *n* **George Bryan,** called *Beau Brummell.* 1778–1840, British Regency dandy.

brunch (brʌntʃ) *n* a meal eaten late in the morning, combining breakfast with lunch. ORIG C20: from BR(EAKFAST) + (L)UNCH

Brundisium ★ (brʌnˈdɪzɪəm) *n* the ancient name for **Brindisi.**

Brundtland ★ (ˈbrʌntlənd) *n* **Gro Harlem** (grəʊ ˈhɑːləm). born 1939, Norwegian stateswoman: prime minister (1981 and from 1986).

Brunei ★ (bruːˈnaɪ, ˈbruːnaɪ) *n* **1** a sultanate in NW Borneo, consisting of two separate areas on the South China Sea, otherwise bounded by Sarawak: controlled all of Borneo and parts of the Philippines and the Sulu Islands in the 16th century; under British protection since 1888; internally self-governing since 1971; became independent in 1984 and is a member of the Commonwealth. The economy depends chiefly on oil and natural gas. Official language: Malay; English is also widely spoken. Religion: Muslim. Currency: Brunei dollar. Capital: Bandar Seri Begawan. Pop.: 323 000 (1999 est.). Area: 5765 sq. km (2226 sq. miles). **2** the former name of **Bandar Seri Begawan.**

Brunel ★ (bruːˈnɛl) *n* **1 Isambard Kingdom** (ˈɪzəmˌbɑːd). 1806–59, British engineer: designer of the Clifton Suspension Bridge (1828), railways, steamships, etc. **2** his father, Sir **Marc Isambard.** 1769–1849, French engineer in England.

Brunelleschi ★ (*Italian* brunelˈleski) *n* **Filippo** (fiˈlippo). 1377–1446, Italian Florentine architect.

brunette (bruːˈnɛt) *n* **1** a girl or woman with dark brown hair. ◆ *adj* **2** dark brown: *brunette hair.* ORIG C17: from F, fem of *brunet* dark, brownish, from *brun* brown

Brunhild (ˈbrʊnhɪld, -hɪlt) *or* **Brünnhilde** ★ (*German* brynˈhɪldə) *n* (in the *Nibelungenlied*) a legendary queen

★ people and places

won for King Gunther by the magic of Siegfried: corresponds to Brynhild in Norse mythology.

Brünn ★ (bryn) *n* the German name for **Brno**.

Brunswick ★ ('brʌnzwɪk) *n* **1** a former duchy (1635–1918) and state (1918–46) of central Germany: now part of Lower Saxony. **2** a city in central Germany: formerly capital of the duchy and state of Brunswick. Pop.: 252 544 (1996 est.). German name: **Braunschweig**.

brunt (brʌnt) *n* the main force or shock of a blow, attack, etc. (esp. in **bear the brunt of**). ORIG C14: from ?

Brusa ★ (*Turkish* 'bru:sɑ:) *n* the former name of **Bursa**.

brush[1] (brʌʃ) *n* **1** a device made of bristles, hairs, wires, etc., set into a firm back or handle: used to apply paint, clean or polish surfaces, groom the hair, etc. **2** the act or an instance of brushing. **3** a light stroke made in passing; graze. **4** a brief encounter or contact, esp. an unfriendly one; skirmish. **5** the bushy tail of a fox. **6** an electric conductor, esp. one made of carbon, that conveys current between stationary and rotating parts of a generator, motor, etc. ◆ *vb* **7** (*tr*) to clean, polish, scrub, paint, etc., with a brush. **8** (*tr*) to apply or remove with a brush or brushing movement. **9** (*tr*) to touch lightly and briefly. **10** (*intr*) to move so as to graze or touch something lightly. ◆ See also **brush aside, brush off, brush up**. ORIG C14: from OF *broisse*, ?from *broce* BRUSH[2]
▸ '**brusher** *n*

brush[2] (brʌʃ) *n* **1** a thick growth of shrubs and small trees; scrub. **2** land covered with scrub. **3** broken or cut branches or twigs; brushwood. **4** wooded sparsely populated country; backwoods. ORIG C16 (dense undergrowth), C14 (cuttings of trees): from OF *broce*, from Vulgar L *bruscia* (unattested) brushwood
▸ '**brushy** *adj*

brush aside *or* **away** *vb* (*tr, adv*) to dismiss without consideration; disregard.

brush discharge *n* a slightly luminous brushlike electrical discharge.

brushed (brʌʃt) *adj Textiles*. treated with a brushing process to raise the nap and give a softer and warmer finish: *brushed nylon*.

brushmark ('brʌʃ,mɑ:k) *n* the indented lines sometimes left by the bristles of a brush on a painted surface.

brush off *Sl*. ◆ *vb* (*tr, adv*) **1** to dismiss and ignore (a person), esp. curtly. ◆ *n* **brushoff. 2** an abrupt dismissal or rejection.

brush turkey *n* any of several gallinaceous flightless birds of New Guinea and Australia, having a black plumage.

brush up *vb* (*adv*) **1** (*tr*; often foll. by *on*) to refresh one's knowledge, skill, or memory of (a subject). **2** to make (a person or oneself) clean or neat as after a journey. ◆ *n* **brush-up. 3** *Brit*. the act or an instance of tidying one's appearance (esp. in **wash and brush-up**).

brushwood ('brʌʃ,wʊd) *n* **1** cut or broken-off tree branches, twigs, etc. **2** another word for **brush**[2] (sense 1).

brushwork ('brʌʃ,wɜ:k) *n* **1** a characteristic manner of applying paint with a brush: *Rembrandt's brushwork*. **2** work done with a brush.

brusque (bru:sk, brʊsk) *adj* blunt or curt in manner or speech. ORIG C17: from F, from It. *brusco* sour, rough, from Med. L *bruscus* butcher's broom
▸ '**brusquely** *adv* ▸ '**brusqueness** *n*

Brussels ★ ('brʌsᵊlz) *n* the capital of Belgium, in the central part: became capital of Belgium in 1830; seat of the European Commission. Pop.: 953 175 (1998 est.). Flemish name: **Brussel** ('brysəl). French name: **Bruxelles**.

Brussels carpet *n* a worsted carpet with a heavy pile formed by uncut loops of wool on a linen warp.

Brussels lace *n* a fine lace with a raised or appliqué design.

Brussels sprout *n* **1** a variety of cabbage, having a stout stem studded with budlike heads resembling tiny cabbages. **2** the head of this plant, eaten as a vegetable.

brut (bru:t) *adj* (of champagne or sparkling wine) very dry. ORIG F, lit.: dry

brutal ('bru:tᵊl) *adj* **1** cruel; vicious; savage. **2** extremely honest or coarse in speech or manner. **3** harsh; severe; extreme: *brutal cold*.
▸ **bru'tality** *n* ▸ '**brutally** *adv*

brutalism ('bru:tə,lɪzəm) *n* an austere style of architecture characterized by emphasis on such structural materials as undressed concrete and unconcealed service pipes. Also called: **new brutalism**.
▸ '**brutalist** *n, adj*

brutalize *or* **brutalise** ('bru:tə,laɪz) *vb* **brutalizes, brutalizing, brutalized** *or* **brutalises, brutalising, brutalised. 1** to make or become brutal. **2** (*tr*) to treat brutally.
▸ ,**brutali'zation** *or* ,**brutali'sation** *n*

brute (bru:t) *n* **1a** any animal except man; beast; lower animal. **1b** (*as modifier*): *brute nature*. **2** a brutal person. ◆ *adj* (*prenominal*) **3** wholly instinctive or physical (esp. in **brute strength, brute force**). **4** without reason or intelligence. **5** coarse and grossly sensual. ORIG C15: from L *brūtus* heavy, irrational

brutish ('bru:tɪʃ) *adj* **1** of, relating to, or resembling a brute; animal. **2** coarse; cruel; stupid.
▸ '**brutishly** *adv* ▸ '**brutishness** *n*

Bruton ★ ('bru:tᵊn) *n* **John Gerard**. born 1947, Irish politician: leader of the Fine Gael party from 1990; prime minister of the Republic of Ireland (1994–97).

Brutus ★ ('bru:təs) *n* **1 Lucius Junius** ('lu:ʃəs 'dʒu:nɪəs). late 6th century B.C., Roman statesman who ousted Tarquin (509) and helped found the Roman republic. **2 Marcus Junius** ('mɑ:kəs 'dʒu:nɪəs) ?85–42 B.C., Roman statesman who, with Cassius, led the conspiracy to assassinate Caesar (44): committed suicide after defeat at Philippi (42).

Bruxelles ★ (brysɛl) *n* the French name for **Brussels**.

Bryansk ★ (brɪ'ænsk; *Russian* brjansk) *n* a city in W Russia. Pop.: 462 000 (1995 est.).

Brynhild ★ ('brɪnhɪld) *n Norse myth*. a Valkyrie won as the wife of Gunnar by Sigurd who wakes her from an enchanted sleep: similar to Brunhild in the *Nibelungenlied*.

bryology (braɪ'ɒlədʒɪ) *n* the branch of botany concerned with the study of bryophytes.
▸ **bryological** (,braɪə'lɒdʒɪkᵊl) *adj* ▸ **bry'ologist** *n*

bryony *or* **briony** ('braɪənɪ) *n, pl* **bryonies** *or* **brionies**. any of several herbaceous climbing plants of Europe and N Africa. ORIG OE *bryōnia*, from L, from Gk *bruōnia*

bryophyte ('braɪə,faɪt) *n* any plant of the phylum *Bryophyta*, esp. mosses and liverworts. ORIG C19: from Gk *bruon* moss + -PHYTE
▸ **bryophytic** (,braɪə'fɪtɪk) *adj*

bryozoan (,braɪə'zəʊən) *n* any aquatic invertebrate animal forming colonies of polyps each having a ciliated feeding organ. Popular name: **sea mat**. ORIG C19: from Gk *bruon* moss + *zōion* animal

Brythonic (brɪ'θɒnɪk) *n* **1** the S group of Celtic languages, consisting of Welsh, Cornish, and Breton. ◆ *adj* **2** of or relating to this group of languages. ORIG C19: from Welsh; see BRITON

Brześć nad Bugiem ★ (bʒɛʃtʃ nad 'bugjɛm) *n* the Polish name for **Brest** (sense 2).

bs *abbrev. for:* **1** balance sheet. **2** bill of sale.

BS *abbrev. for* British Standard(s).

BSc *abbrev. for* Bachelor of Science.

BSE *abbrev. for* bovine spongiform encephalopathy: a fatal prion disease of cattle, affecting the nervous system. Informal name: **mad cow disease**.

BSI *abbrev. for* British Standards Institution.

B-side *n* the less important side of a gramophone record.

BST *abbrev. for:* **1** bovine somatotrophin: a growth hormone that can be used to increase milk production in dairy cattle. **2** British Summer Time.

Bt *abbrev. for* Baronet.

BT *abbrev. for* British Telecom. ORIG C20: shortened from TELECOMMUNICATIONS

btu *or* **BThU** *abbrev. for* British thermal unit. US abbrev.: **BTU**.

BTW *abbrev. for:* by the way; used esp. in e-mails, text messages, etc. ORIG C20

bu. *abbrev. for* bushel.

bubble (ˈbʌbᵊl) *n* **1** a thin film of liquid forming a hollow globule around air or a gas: *a soap bubble.* **2** a small globule of air or a gas in a liquid or a solid. **3** the sound made by a bubbling liquid. **4** something lacking substance, stability, or seriousness. **5** an unreliable scheme or enterprise. **6** a dome, esp. a transparent glass or plastic one. ◆ *vb* **bubbles, bubbling, bubbled. 7** to form or cause to form bubbles. **8** (*intr*) to move or flow with a gurgling sound. **9** (*intr;* often foll. by *over*) to overflow (with excitement, anger, etc.). ORIG C14: prob. from ON; imit.

bubble and squeak *n Brit. & Austral.* a dish of leftover boiled cabbage and potatoes fried together.

bubble bath *n* **1** a powder, liquid, or crystals used to scent, soften, and foam in bath water. **2** a bath to which such a substance has been added.

bubble car *n Brit.* (formerly) a small car with a transparent bubble-shaped top.

bubble chamber *n* a device that enables the tracks of ionizing particles to be photographed as a row of bubbles in a superheated liquid.

bubble gum *n* a type of chewing gum that can be blown into large bubbles.

bubble memory *n Computing.* a method of storing high volumes of data by using minute pockets of magnetism (bubbles) in a semiconducting material.

bubble point *n Chem.* the temperature at which bubbles just start to appear in a heated liquid mixture.

bubble wrap *n* a type of polythene wrapping containing many small air pockets, used as a protective covering when transporting breakable goods.

bubbly (ˈbʌblɪ) *adj* **bubblier, bubbliest. 1** full of or resembling bubbles. **2** lively; animated; excited. ◆ *n* **3** *Inf.* champagne.

Buber ★ (ˈbuːbə) *n* **Martin.** 1878–1965, Jewish theologian, existentialist philosopher, and scholar of Chassidism, born in Austria, whose works include *I and Thou* (1923).

bubo (ˈbjuːbəʊ) *n, pl* **buboes.** *Pathol.* inflammation and swelling of a lymph node, esp. in the armpit or groin. ORIG C14: from Med. L *bubō,* from Gk *boubōn* groin
▸ **bubonic** (bjuːˈbɒnɪk) *adj*

bubonic plague *n* an acute infectious febrile disease characterized by chills, prostration, delirium, and formation of buboes: caused by the bite of an infected rat flea.

Bucaramanga ★ (*Spanish* bukaraˈmanga) *n* a city in N central Colombia, in the Cordillera Oriental: centre of a district growing coffee, tobacco, and cotton. Pop.: 351 737 (1995 est.).

buccal (ˈbʌkᵊl) *adj* **1** of or relating to the cheek. **2** of or relating to the mouth; oral. ORIG C19: from L *bucca* cheek

buccaneer (ˌbʌkəˈnɪə) *n* **1** a pirate, esp. one who preyed on Spanish shipping in the Caribbean in the 17th and 18th centuries. ◆ *vb (intr)* **2** to be or act like a buccaneer. ORIG C17: from *boucan,* dried meat taken on long voyages, from F *boucaner* to smoke meat

buccinator (ˈbʌksɪˌneɪtə) *n* either of two flat cheek muscles used in chewing. ORIG C17: from L, from *buccina* a trumpet

Buchan ★ (ˈbʌkən) *n* **John,** 1st Baron Tweedsmuir. 1875–1940, Scottish statesman and writer of such adventure stories as *The Thirty-Nine Steps* (1915); governor general of Canada (1935–40).

Buchanan ★ (bjuːˈkænən) *n* **1 George.** 1506–82, Scottish historian, who was tutor to Mary, Queen of Scots and James VI; author of *History of Scotland* (1582). **2 James.** 1791–1868, 15th president of the US (1857–61).

Bucharest ★ (ˌbuːkəˈrɛst, ˌbjuː-) *n* the capital of Romania, in the southeast. Pop.: 2 343 824 (1993 est.). Romanian name: **Bucureşti.**

Buchenwald ★ (*German* ˈbuːxənvalt) *n* a village in E central Germany, near Weimar; formerly in East Germany: site of a Nazi concentration camp (1937–45).

Büchner ★ (*German* ˈbyːçnər) *n* **Georg** (ˈgeːɔrk). 1813–37, German dramatist; author of *Woyzeck* (1837).

buck[1] (bʌk) *n* **1a** the male of various animals including the goat, hare, kangaroo, rabbit, and reindeer. **1b** (*as modifier*): *a buck antelope.* **2** *S. African.* an antelope or deer of either sex. **3** *Arch.* a robust spirited young man. **4** the act of bucking. ◆ *vb* **5** (*intr*) (of a horse or other animal) to jump vertically, with legs stiff and back arched. **6** (*tr*) (of a horse, etc.) to throw (its rider) by bucking. **7** (when *intr,* often foll. by *against* or *at*) *Chiefly US, Canad., & Austral. inf.* to resist or oppose obstinately. **8** (*tr; usually passive*) *Inf.* to cheer or encourage: *I was very bucked at passing the exam.* ◆ See also **buck up.** ORIG OE *bucca* he-goat
▸ **ˈbucker** *n*

buck[2] (bʌk) *n Inf.* **1** *US, Canad., Austral., & S. African.* a dollar. **2** *S. African.* a rand. ORIG C19: from ?

buck[3] (bʌk) *n* **1** *Poker.* a marker in the jackpot to remind the winner of some obligation when his turn comes to deal. **2 pass the buck.** *Inf.* to shift blame or responsibility onto another. ORIG C19: prob. from *buckhorn knife,* placed before a player in poker to indicate that he was the next dealer

Buck ★ (bʌk) *n* **Pearl S(ydenstricker).** 1892–1973, US novelist, noted for her novel *The Good Earth* (1931): Nobel prize for literature 1938.

buckbean (ˈbʌkˌbiːn) *n* a marsh plant with white or pink flowers. Also called: **bogbean.**

buckboard (ˈbʌkˌbɔːd) *n US & Canad.* an open four-wheeled horse-drawn carriage with the seat attached to a flexible board between the front and rear axles.

bucket (ˈbʌkɪt) *n* **1** an open-topped roughly cylindrical container; pail. **2** Also called: **bucketful.** the amount a bucket will hold. **3** any of various bucket-like parts of a machine, such as the scoop on a mechanical shovel. **4** *Chiefly US.* a turbine rotor blade. **5** *Austral.* a small container for ice cream. **6 kick the bucket.** *Sl.* to die. ◆ *vb* **buckets, bucketing, bucketed. 7** (*tr*) to carry in or put into a bucket. **8** (*intr;* often foll. by *down*) (of rain) to fall very heavily. **9** (*intr;* often foll. by *along*) *Chiefly Brit.* to travel or drive fast. **10** (*tr*) *Austral. sl.* to criticize severely. ORIG C13: from Anglo-F *buket,* from OE *būc*

bucket seat *n* a seat in a car, etc., having curved sides.

bucket shop *n* **1** an unregistered firm of stockbrokers that engages in fraudulent speculation. **2** *Chiefly Brit.* a firm specializing in cheap airline tickets.

buckeye (ˈbʌkˌaɪ) *n* any of several North American trees of the horse chestnut family having erect clusters of white or red flowers and prickly fruits.

buckhorn (ˈbʌkˌhɔːn) *n* **a** horn from a buck, used for knife handles, etc. **b** (*as modifier*): *a buckhorn knife.*

Buckingham[1] ★ (ˈbʌkɪŋəm) *n* a town in S central England, in Buckinghamshire; university (1975). Pop.: 2786 (1991).

Buckingham[2] ★ (ˈbʌkɪŋəm) *n* **1 George Villiers, 1st Duke of.** 1592–1628, English courtier and statesman; favourite of James I and Charles I. **2** his son, **George Villiers, 2nd Duke of.** 1628–87, English courtier; chief minister of Charles II and member of the Cabal (1667–73).

Buckingham Palace ★ *n* the London residence of the British sovereign: built in 1703, rebuilt by John Nash in 1821–36 and partially redesigned in the early 20th century.

Buckinghamshire ★ (ˈbʌkɪŋəmˌʃɪə, -ʃə) *n* a county in SE central England, containing the Vale of Aylesbury and parts of the Chiltern Hills. Administrative centre: Aylesbury. Pop. (excluding Milton Keynes): 473 000 (1997 est.). Area (excluding Milton Keynes): 1568 sq. km (605 sq. miles). Abbrev.: **Bucks.**

buckjumper (ˈbʌkˌdʒʌmpə) *n Austral.* an untamed horse.

Buckland ★ (ˈbʌklənd) *n* **William.** 1784–1856, British geologist.

buckle (ˈbʌkᵊl) *n* **1** a clasp for fastening together two loose ends, esp. of a belt or strap, usually consisting of a frame with an attached movable prong. **2** an ornamental representation of a buckle, as on a shoe. **3** a kink, bulge, or other distortion. ◆ *vb* **buckles, buckling, buckled. 4** to fasten or be fastened with a buckle. **5** to bend or cause to bend out of shape. ORIG C14: from OF, from L *buccula* a little cheek, hence, cheek strap of a helmet

buckle down *vb (intr, adv) Inf.* to apply oneself with determination.

buckler ('bʌklə) *n* **1** a small round shield worn on the forearm. **2** a means of protection; defence. ORIG C13: from OF *bocler,* from *bocle* shield boss

Buckley's chance ('bʌklɪz) *n Austral. & NZ sl.* no chance at all. Often shortened to **Buckley's.** ORIG C19: from ?

buckminsterfullerene (ˌbʌkmɪnstə'fʊləˌriːn) *n* a form of carbon that contains molecules with 60 carbon atoms arranged in a structure resembling a geodesic dome. Often shortened to: **fullerene.** ORIG C20: after Buckminster FULLER

bucko ('bʌkəʊ) *n, pl* **buckoes.** *Irish.* a lively young fellow: often a term of address.

buckram ('bʌkrəm) *n* **a** cotton or linen cloth stiffened with size, etc., used in lining clothes, bookbinding, etc. **b** *(as modifier): a buckram cover.* ORIG C14: from OF *boquerant,* ult. from BUKHARA, once important for textiles

Bucks (bʌks) *abbrev. for* Buckinghamshire.

buckshee (ˌbʌk'ʃiː) *adj Brit. sl.* without charge; free. ORIG C20: from BAKSHEESH

buckshot ('bʌkˌʃɒt) *n* lead shot of large size used in shotgun shells, esp. for hunting game.

buckskin ('bʌkˌskɪn) *n* **1** the skin of a male deer. **2a** a strong greyish-yellow suede leather, originally made from deerskin but now usually made from sheepskin. **2b** *(as modifier): buckskin boots.* **3** a stiffly starched cotton cloth. **4** a strong and heavy satin-woven woollen fabric.

buckthorn ('bʌkˌθɔːn) *n* any of several thorny small-flowered shrubs whose berries were formerly used as a purgative. ORIG C16: from BUCK[1] (from the spiny branches resembling antlers) + THORN

bucktooth ('bʌkˌtuːθ) *n, pl* **buckteeth.** *Derog.* a projecting upper front tooth. ORIG C18: from BUCK[1] (deer) + TOOTH

buck up *vb (adv) Inf.* **1** to make or cause to make haste. **2** to make or become more cheerful, confident, etc.

buckwheat ('bʌkˌwiːt) *n* **1** a cereal plant with fragrant white flowers, cultivated, esp. in the US, for its seeds. **2** the edible seeds of this plant, ground into flour or used as animal fodder. **3** the flour obtained from these seeds. ORIG C16: from MDu. *boecweite,* from *boeke* BEECH + *weite* WHEAT, from the resemblance of the seeds to beechnuts

buckyball ('bʌkɪˌbɔːl) *n Inf.* a ball-like polyhedral carbon molecule, of the type found in buckminsterfullerene and other fullerenes.

buckytube ('bʌkɪˌtjuːb) *n* a tube of carbon atoms structurally similar to buckminsterfullerene.

bucolic (bjuː'kɒlɪk) *adj also* **bucolical. 1** of the countryside or country life; rustic. **2** of or relating to shepherds; pastoral. ◆ *n* **3** *(sometimes pl)* a pastoral poem. ORIG C16: from L, from Gk, from *boukolos* cowherd, from *bous* ox
▸ **bu'colically** *adv*

Bucovina ★ (ˌbuːkə'viːnə) *n* a variant spelling of **Bukovina.**

București ★ (buku'reʃtj) *n* the Romanian name for **Bucharest.**

bud (bʌd) *n* **1** a swelling on a plant stem consisting of overlapping immature leaves or petals. **2a** a partially opened flower. **2b** *(in combination): rosebud.* **3** any small budlike outgrowth: *taste buds.* **4** something small or immature. **5** an asexually produced outgrowth in simple organisms such as yeasts that develops into a new individual. **6 nip in the bud.** to put an end to (an idea, movement, etc.) in its initial stages. ◆ *vb* **buds, budding, budded. 7** *(intr)* (of plants and some animals) to produce buds. **8** *(intr)* to begin to develop or grow. **9** *(tr) Horticulture.* to graft (a bud) from one plant onto another. ORIG C14 *budde,* of Gmc origin

Budapest ★ (ˌbjuːdə'pɛst; *Hungarian* 'budɔpɛʃt) *n* the capital of Hungary, in the central part, on the River Danube: formed in 1873 from the towns of Buda and Pest. Traditionally Buda, the old Magyar capital, was the administrative and Pest the trade centre: suffered severely in the Russian siege of 1945 and in the unsuccessful revolt against the Communist regime (1956). Pop.: 1 909 000 (1996 est.).

Buddha ★ ('bʊdə) *n* **the.** ?563–483 B.C., a title applied to Gautama Siddhartha, a religious teacher of N India regarded by his followers as the most recent rediscoverer of the path to enlightenment: the founder of Buddhism.

Buddh Gaya ('bʊd gə'jɑː), **Buddha Gaya,** *or* **Bodh Gaya** ★ *n* a village in NE India, in Bihar: site of the sacred bo tree under which Gautama Siddhartha attained enlightenment and became the Buddha; pilgrimage centre. Pop.: 21 686 (1991 est.).

Buddhism ('bʊdɪzəm) *n* a religious teaching propagated by the Buddha and his followers, which declares that by destroying greed, hatred, and delusion, which are the causes of all suffering, man can attain perfect enlightenment.
▸ **'Buddhist** *n, adj*

buddleia ('bʌdlɪə) *n* an ornamental shrub which has long spikes of mauve flowers. Also called: **butterfly bush.** ORIG C19: after A. *Buddle* (died 1715), Brit. botanist

buddy ('bʌdɪ) *n, pl* **buddies. 1** Also (as a term of address): **bud.** *Chiefly US & Canad.* an informal word for **friend. 2** a volunteer who visits and gives help and support to a person suffering from AIDS. ◆ *vb* **buddies, buddying, buddied. 3** *(intr)* to act as a buddy to a person suffering from AIDS. ORIG C19: prob. baby-talk var. (US) of BROTHER

buddy-buddy *adj Inf., chiefly US.* on very friendly or intimate terms.

buddy movie *or* **film** *n* a genre of film dealing with the relationship and adventures of two friends.

budge (bʌdʒ) *vb* **budges, budging, budged.** *(usually used with a negative)* **1** to move, however slightly. **2** to change or cause to change opinions, etc. ORIG C16: from OF *bouger,* from L *bullīre* to boil

budgerigar ('bʌdʒərɪˌgɑː) *n* a small green Australian parrot: a popular cagebird bred in many different-coloured varieties. ORIG C19: from Abor., from *budgeri* good + *gar* cockatoo

budget ('bʌdʒɪt) *n* **1** an itemized summary of expected income and expenditure over a specified period. **2** *(modifier)* economical; inexpensive: *budget meals for a family.* **3** the total amount of money allocated for a specific purpose during a specified period. ◆ *vb* **budgets, budgeting, budgeted. 4** *(tr)* to enter or provide for in a budget. **5** to plan the expenditure of (money, time, etc.). **6** *(intr)* to make a budget. ORIG C15 (meaning: leather pouch, wallet): from OF *bougette,* dim. of *bouge,* from L *bulga*
▸ **'budgetary** *adj*

Budget ('bʌdʒɪt) *n* **the.** an estimate of British government expenditures and revenues and the financial plans for the ensuing fiscal year presented annually to the House of Commons by the Chancellor of the Exchequer.

budget account *n* **1** an account with a department store, etc., enabling a customer to make monthly payments to cover his past and future purchases. **2** a bank account that allows the holder credit to pay certain bills in return for regular deposits.

budget deficit *n* the amount by which government expenditure exceeds income from taxation, customs duties, etc., in any one fiscal year.

budgie ('bʌdʒɪ) *n Inf.* short for **budgerigar.**

Buenaventura ★ *(Spanish* bwenaβen'tura) *n* a major port in W Colombia, on the Pacific coast. Pop.: 174 397 (1985).

Buena Vista ★ *(Spanish* 'bwena 'vista) *n* a village in NE Mexico, near Saltillo: site of the defeat of the Mexicans by US forces (1847).

Buenos Aires ★ ('bweɪnɒs 'aɪrɪz; *Spanish* 'bwenos 'aires) *n* the capital of Argentina, a major port and industrial city on the Río de la Plata estuary: became capital in 1880; university (1821). Pop.: 2 988 006 (1995 est.).

buff[1] (bʌf) *n* **1a** a soft thick flexible undyed leather made chiefly from the skins of buffalo, oxen, and elk. **1b** *(as modifier): a buff coat.* **2a** a dull yellow or yellowish-brown colour. **2b** *(as adj): a buff envelope.* **3** Also called: **buffer. 3a** a cloth or pad of material used for polishing an object. **3b** a disc or wheel impregnated with a fine abrasive for polishing metals, etc. **4** *Inf.* one's bare skin (esp. in **in the buff**). ◆ *vb* **5** to clean or polish (a metal, floor, shoes, etc.) with a buff. **6** to remove the grain surface of (a leather).

ORIG C16: from OF, from OIt. *bufalo,* from LL *būfalus* BUFFALO

buff² (bʌf) *n Arch.* a blow or buffet (now only in **blind man's buff**). ORIG C15: back formation from BUFFET²

buff³ (bʌf) *n Inf.* an expert on or devotee of a given subject. ORIG C20: orig. US: an enthusiastic fire-watcher, from the buff-coloured uniforms worn by volunteer firemen in New York City

buffalo ('bʌfəˌləʊ) *n, pl* **buffaloes** *or* **buffalo. 1** a type of cattle, mostly found in game reserves in southern and eastern Africa and having upward-curving horns. **2** short for **water buffalo. 3** a US & Canad. name for **bison** (sense 1). ORIG C16: from It. *bufalo,* ult. from Gk *bous* ox

Buffalo ★ ('bʌfəˌləʊ) *n* a port in W New York State, at the E end of Lake Erie. Pop.: 312 965 (1994 est.).

Buffalo Bill ★ *n* nickname of *William Frederick Cody.* 1846–1917, US showman who toured Europe and the US with his *Wild West Show.*

buffalo grass *n* **1** a short grass growing on the dry plains of the central US. **2** *Austral.* a grass, *Stenotaphrum americanum,* introduced from North America.

buffel grass ('bʌfᵊl) *n* (in Australia) any of various grasses used for grazing or fodder, originally introduced from Africa.

buffer¹ ('bʌfə) *n* **1** one of a pair of spring-loaded steel pads attached at both ends of railway vehicles and at the end of a railway track to reduce shock due to contact. **2** a person or thing that lessens shock or protects from damaging impact, circumstances, etc. **3** *Chem.* **3a** an ionic compound added to a solution to resist changes in its acidity or alkalinity and thus stabilize its pH. **3b** Also called: **buffer solution.** a solution containing such a compound. **4** *Computing.* a memory device for temporarily storing data. ◆ *vb* (*tr*) **5** *Chem.* to add a buffer to (a solution). **6** to insulate against or protect from shock. ORIG C19: from BUFF²

buffer² ('bʌfə) *n* **1** any device used to shine, polish, etc.; buff. **2** a person who uses such a device.

buffer³ ('bʌfə) *n Brit. inf.* a stupid or bumbling man (esp. in **old buffer**). ORIG C18: ?from ME *buffer* stammerer

buffer state *n* a small and usually neutral state between two rival powers.

buffer stock *n Commerce.* a stock of a commodity built up by a government or trade organization with the object of using it to stabilize prices.

buffet¹ *n* **1** ('bʊfeɪ). a counter where light refreshments are served. **2** ('bʊfeɪ). **2a** a meal at which guests help themselves from a number of dishes. **2b** (*as modifier*): *a buffet lunch.* **3** ('bʌfɪt, 'bʊfeɪ). (formerly) a piece of furniture used for displaying plate, etc., and typically comprising cupboards and open shelves. ORIG C18: from F

buffet² ('bʌfɪt) *vb* **buffets, buffeting, buffeted. 1** (*tr*) to knock against or about; batter. **2** (*tr*) to hit, esp. with the fist; cuff. **3** to force (one's way), as through a crowd. **4** (*intr*) to struggle; battle. ◆ *n* **5** a blow, esp. with a fist or hand. **6** aerodynamic oscillation of an aircraft structure by separated flows. ORIG C13: from OF *buffet* a light blow

Buffet ★ (*French* byfɛ) *n* **Bernard** (bɛrnar). 1928–99, French painter.

buffet car ('bʊfeɪ) *n Brit.* a railway coach where light refreshments are served.

buffeting ('bʌfɪtɪŋ) *n* response of an aircraft structure to buffet, esp. an irregular oscillation of the tail.

bufflehead ('bʌfᵊlˌhɛd) *n* a small North American diving duck: the male has black-and-white plumage and a fluffy head. ORIG C17 *buffle,* from obs. *buffle* wild ox, referring to the duck's head

buffo ('bʊfəʊ) *n, pl* **buffi** (-fɪ) *or* **buffos. 1** (in Italian opera of the 18th century) a comic part, esp. one for a bass. **2** Also called: **buffo bass, basso buffo.** a bass singer who performs such a part. ORIG C18: from It. (adj): comic, from *buffo* (n) BUFFOON

buffoon (bə'fu:n) *n* **1** a person who amuses others by ridiculous or odd behaviour, jokes, etc. **2** a foolish person. ORIG C16: from F *bouffon,* from It. *buffone,* from Med. L *būfō,* from L: toad
▸ **buf'foonery** *n*

bug (bʌg) *n* **1** an insect having piercing and sucking mouthparts specialized as a beak. **2** *Chiefly US & Canad.* any insect. **3** *Inf.* **3a** a microorganism, esp. a bacterium, that produces disease. **3b** a disease, esp. a stomach infection, caused by a microorganism. **4** *Inf.* an obsessive idea, hobby, etc.; craze. **5** *Inf.* a person having such a craze. **6** (*often pl*) *Inf.* a fault, as in a machine. **7** *Inf.* a concealed microphone used for recording conversations, as in spying. ◆ *vb* **bugs, bugging, bugged.** *Inf.* **8** (*tr*) to irritate; bother. **9** (*tr*) to conceal a microphone in (a room, etc.). **10** (*intr*) *US.* (of eyes) to protrude. ORIG C16: from ?

Bug ★ (*Russian* buk) *n* **1** Also called: **Southern Bug.** a river in E Europe, rising in W Ukraine and flowing southeast to the Black Sea. Length: 853 km (530 miles). **2** Also called: **Western Bug.** a river in E Europe, rising in SW Ukraine and flowing northwest to the River Vistula in Poland, forming part of the border between Poland and Ukraine. Length: 724 km (450 miles).

bugaboo ('bʌgəˌbu:) *n, pl* **bugaboos.** an imaginary source of fear; bugbear; bogey. ORIG C18: prob. of Celtic origin; cf. Cornish *buccaboo* the devil

Buganda ★ (bʊ'gændə) *n* a region of Uganda: a powerful Bantu kingdom from the 17th century.

Bugatti ★ (*Italian* bu'gatti) *n* **Ettore** (**Arco Isidoro**) ('ɛttore). 1881–1947, Italian car manufacturer.

bugbear ('bʌgˌbɛə) *n* **1** a thing that causes obsessive anxiety. **2** (in English folklore) a goblin in the form of a bear. ORIG C16: from obs. *bug* an evil spirit+ BEAR²

bug-eyed *adj* having protruding eyes.

bugger ('bʌgə) *n* **1** a person who practises buggery. **2** *Taboo sl.* a person or thing considered to be contemptible, unpleasant, or difficult. **3** *Sl.* a humorous or affectionate term for a man or child: *a friendly little bugger.* **4** **bugger all.** *Sl.* nothing. ◆ *vb* **5** to practise buggery (with). **6** (*tr*) *Sl., chiefly Brit.* to ruin, complicate, or frustrate. **7** (*tr*) *Sl.* to tire; weary. ◆ *interj* **8** *Taboo sl.* an exclamation of annoyance or disappointment. ORIG C16: from OF *bougre,* from Med. L *Bulgarus* Bulgarian; from the condemnation of the Eastern Orthodox Bulgarians as heretics

bugger about *or* **around** *vb* (*adv*) *Sl.* **1** (*intr*) to fool about and waste time. **2** (*tr*) to create difficulties or complications for (a person).

bugger off *vb* (*intr, adv*) *Taboo sl.* to go away; depart.

buggery ('bʌgərɪ) *n* anal intercourse between a man and another man, a woman, or an animal.

buggy¹ ('bʌgɪ) *n, pl* **buggies. 1** a light horse-drawn carriage having either four wheels (esp. in the US and Canada) or two wheels (esp. in Britain and India). **2** any small light cart or vehicle, such as a baby buggy. ORIG C18: from ?

buggy² ('bʌgɪ) *adj* **buggier, buggiest.** infested with bugs.

bugle¹ ('bju:gᵊl) *n* **1** *Music.* a brass instrument similar to the cornet but usually without valves: used for military fanfares, signal calls, etc. ◆ *vb* **bugles, bugling, bugled. 2** (*intr*) to play or sound (on) a bugle. ORIG C14: short for *bugle horn* ox horn, from OF *bugle,* from L *būculus* young bullock, from *bōs* ox
▸ **'bugler** *n*

bugle² ('bju:gᵊl) *n* any of several Eurasian plants having small blue or white flowers. ORIG C13: from LL *bugula,* from ?

bugle³ ('bju:gᵊl) *n* a tubular glass or plastic bead sewn onto clothes for decoration. ORIG C16: from ?

bugloss ('bju:glɒs) *n* any of various hairy Eurasian plants having clusters of blue flowers. ORIG C15: from L, from Gk *buglōssos* ox-tongued

bugong ('bu:gɒŋ) *n* another name for **bogong.**

buhl (bu:l) *adj, n* a variant spelling of **boulle.**

build (bɪld) *vb* **builds, building, built. 1** to make, construct, or form by joining parts or materials: *to build a house.* **2** (*tr*) to order the building of: *the government builds most of our hospitals.* **3** (foll. by *on* or *upon*) to base; found: *his theory was not built on facts.* **4** (*tr*) to establish and develop: *it took ten years to build a business.* **5** (*tr*) to make in a particular way or for a particular purpose: *the car was not built for speed.* **6** (*intr;* often foll. by *up*) to increase in intensity.

◆ *n* **7** physical form, figure, or proportions: *a man with an athletic build.* ORIG OE *byldan*

builder ('bɪldə) *n* a person who builds, esp. one who contracts for and supervises the construction or repair of buildings.

building ('bɪldɪŋ) *n* **1** something built with a roof and walls. **2** the act, business, occupation, or art of building houses, boats, etc.

building society *n* a cooperative banking enterprise financed by deposits on which interest is paid and from which mortgage loans are advanced on homes and real property; many now offer a range of banking services.

build up *vb* (*adv*) **1** (*tr*) to construct gradually, systematically, and in stages. **2** to increase, accumulate, or strengthen, esp. by degrees: *the murmur built up to a roar.* **3** (*tr*) to improve the health or physique of (a person). **4** (*intr*) to prepare for or gradually approach a climax. ◆ *n* **build-up. 5** progressive increase in number, size, etc.: *the build-up of industry.* **6** a gradual approach to a climax. **7** extravagant publicity or praise, esp. in the form of a campaign. **8** *Mil.* the process of attaining the required strength of forces and equipment.

built (bɪlt) *vb* the past tense and past participle of **build**.

built-in *adj* **1** made or incorporated as an integral part: *a built-in cupboard.* **2** essential; inherent. ◆ *n* **3** *Austral.* a built-in cupboard.

built-in obsolescence *n* See **planned obsolescence**.

built-up *adj* **1** having many buildings (esp. in **built-up area**). **2** increased by the addition of parts: *built-up heels.*

Buitenzorg ★ (*Dutch* 'bœitənzɔrx) *n* the former name of **Bogor**.

Bujumbura ★ (ˌbuːdʒəm'bʊərə) *n* the capital of Burundi, a port at the NE end of Lake Tanganyika. Pop.: 300 000 (1994 est.). Former name: **Usumbura**.

Bukavu ★ (buː'kɑːvuː) *n* a port in E Democratic Republic of Congo (formerly Zaïre), on Lake Kivu: commercial and industrial centre. Pop.: 201 569 (1994 est.). Former name (until 1966): **Costermansville**.

Bukhara *or* **Bokhara** ★ (bʊ'xɑːrə) *n* **1** a city in S Uzbekistan: capital of the former emirate of Bukhara. Pop.: 236 000 (1993 est.). **2** a former emirate of central Asia: a powerful kingdom and centre of Islam; became a territory of the Soviet Union (1920) and was divided between the former Uzbek, Tajik, and Turkmen SSRs.

Bukovina *or* **Bucovina** ★ (ˌbuːkə'viːnə) *n* a region of E central Europe, part of the NE Carpathians: the north was seized by the Soviet Union (1940) and later became part of Ukraine; the south remained Romanian.

Bulawayo ★ (ˌbʊlə'weɪəʊ) *n* a city in SW Zimbabwe founded (1893) on the site of the kraal of Lobengula, the last Matabele king; the country's main industrial centre. Pop.: 620 936 (1992).

bulb (bʌlb) *n* **1** a rounded organ of vegetative reproduction in plants such as the tulip and onion: a flattened stem bearing a central shoot surrounded by fleshy nutritive inner leaves and thin brown outer leaves. **2** a plant, such as a hyacinth or daffodil, that grows from a bulb. **3** See **light bulb. 4** any bulb-shaped thing. ORIG C16: from L *bulbus,* from Gk *bolbos* onion
▸ **'bulbous** *adj*

bulbil ('bʌlbɪl) *n* **1** a small bulb produced from a parent bulb. **2** a bulblike reproductive organ in a leaf axil of certain plants. **3** any small bulblike structure in an animal. ORIG C19: from NL *bulbillus* BULB

bulbul ('bʊlbʊl) *n* a songbird of tropical Africa and Asia having brown plumage and, in many species, a distinct crest. ORIG C18: via Persian from Ar.

Bulg. *abbrev. for* Bulgaria(n).

Bulgakov ★ (*Russian* bul'gakəf) *n* **Mikhail Afanaseyev** (mixa'il afa'nasjɪf). 1891–1940, Soviet writer; his novels include *The Master and Margarita* (1966–67).

Bulganin ★ (*Russian* bul'ganin) *n* **Nikolai Aleksandrovich** (nika'laj alɪk'sandrəvitʃ). 1895–1975, Soviet statesman and military leader.

Bulgaria ★ (bʌl'gɛərɪə, bʊl-) *n* a republic in SE Europe, on the Balkan Peninsula on the Black Sea: under Turkish rule from 1395 until 1878; became an independent kingdom in 1908 and a Communist republic in 1946; in 1990 free elections ousted the Communist Party. Consists chiefly of the Danube valley in the north, the Balkan Mountains in the central part, separated from the Rhodope Mountains of the south by the valley of the Maritsa River. Language: Bulgarian. Religion: Christian (Bulgarian Orthodox) majority. Currency: lev. Capital: Sofia. Pop.: 8 206 000 (1999 est.). Area: 110 911 sq. km (42 823 sq. miles).
▸ **Bul'garian** *adj, n*

bulge (bʌldʒ) *n* **1** a swelling or an outward curve. **2** a sudden increase in number, esp. of population. ◆ *vb* **bulges, bulging, bulged. 3** to swell outwards. ORIG C13: from OF *bouge,* from L *bulga* bag, prob. of Gaulish origin
▸ **'bulging** *adj* ▸ **'bulgy** *adj*

bulgur ('bʌlgə) *n* cracked wheat that has been hulled, steamed, and roasted so that it requires little or no cooking. Also called: **burghul**. ORIG C20: from Ar. *burghul*

bulimia (bjuː'lɪmɪə) *n* **1** pathologically insatiable hunger. **2** Also called: **bulimia nervosa**. a disorder characterized by compulsive overeating followed by vomiting. ORIG C17: from NL, from Gk *bous* ox + *limos* hunger

bulk (bʌlk) *n* **1** volume, size, or magnitude, esp. when great. **2** the main part: *the bulk of the work is repetitious.* **3** a large body, esp. of a person. **4** the part of food which passes unabsorbed through the digestive system. **5 in bulk. 5a** in large quantities. **5b** (of a cargo, etc.) unpackaged. ◆ *vb* **6** to cohere or cause to cohere in a mass. **7 bulk large.** to be or seem important or prominent. ORIG C15: from ON *bulki* cargo

> **USAGE NOTE** The use of a plural noun after *bulk* should be avoided, though it is occasionally encountered; most commonly, according to the Bank of English, when referring to *funds* and *profits*: *the bulk of our profits stem from the sale of beer.*

bulk buying *n* the purchase of goods in large amounts, often at reduced prices.

bulkhead ('bʌlkˌhɛd) *n* any upright wall-like partition in a ship, aircraft, etc. ORIG C15: prob. from *bulk* projecting framework from ON *bálkr* +HEAD

bulk modulus *n* a coefficient of elasticity of a substance equal to the ratio of the applied stress to the resulting fractional change in volume.

bulky ('bʌlkɪ) *adj* **bulkier, bulkiest.** very large and massive, esp. so as to be unwieldy.
▸ **'bulkily** *adv* ▸ **'bulkiness** *n*

bull[1] (bʊl) *n* **1** any male bovine animal, esp. one that is sexually mature. Related adj: **taurine**. **2** the male of various other animals including the elephant and whale. **3** a very large, strong, or aggressive person. **4** *Stock Exchange.* **4a** a speculator who buys in anticipation of rising prices in order to make a profit on resale. **4b** (*as modifier*): *a bull market.* Cf. **bear**[2] (sense 5). **5** *Chiefly Brit.* short for **bull's-eye** (senses 1, 2). **6** *Sl.* short for **bullshit. 7 a bull in a china shop.** a clumsy person. **8 take the bull by the horns.** to face and tackle a difficulty without shirking. ◆ *adj* **9** male; masculine: *a bull elephant.* **10** large; strong. ORIG OE *bula*

bull[2] (bʊl) *n* a ludicrously self-contradictory or inconsistent statement. ORIG C17: from ?

bull[3] (bʊl) *n* a formal document issued by the pope. ORIG C13: from Med. L *bulla* seal attached to a bull, from L: round object

Bull[1] (bʊl) *n* **the.** the constellation Taurus, the second sign of the zodiac.

Bull[2] ★ (bʊl) *n* **1 John.** 1563–1628, English composer and organist. **2** See **John Bull**.

Bullamakanka (ˌbuːləmə'kæŋkə) *n Austral.* an imaginary very remote place.

bull bars *pl n* a large protective metal grille on the front of some vehicles, esp. four-wheel-drive vehicles.

bulldog ('bʊlˌdɒg) *n* a sturdy thickset breed of dog with an undershot jaw, broad head, and a muscular body.

bulldog clip *n* a clip for holding papers together, consisting of two T-shaped metal clamps held in place by a cylindrical spring.

bulldoze (ˈbʊlˌdəʊz) *vb* **bulldozes, bulldozing, bulldozed.** (*tr*) **1** to move, demolish, flatten, etc., with a bulldozer. **2** *Inf.* to force; push. **3** *Inf.* to intimidate or coerce. ORIG C19: prob. from BULL[1] + DOSE

bulldozer (ˈbʊlˌdəʊzə) *n* **1** a powerful tractor fitted with caterpillar tracks and a blade at the front, used for moving earth, rocks, etc. **2** *Inf.* a person who bulldozes.

bull dust *n Austral.* **1** fine dust, as on roads in outback Australia. **2** *Sl.* nonsense.

bullet (ˈbʊlɪt) *n* **1a** a small metallic missile enclosed in a cartridge, used as the projectile of a gun, rifle, etc. **1b** the entire cartridge. **2** something resembling a bullet, esp. in shape or effect. **3** *Stock Exchange.* a fixed interest security with a single maturity date. **4** *Commerce.* a security that offers a fixed interest and matures on a fixed date. **5** *Commerce.* **5a** the final repayment of a loan that repays the whole of the sum borrowed, as interim payments have been for interest only. **5b** (*as modifier*): *a bullet loan.* ORIG C16: from F *boulette,* dim. of *boule* ball; see BOWL[2]

bulletin (ˈbʊlɪtɪn) *n* **1** an official statement on a matter of public interest. **2** a broadcast summary of the news. **3** a periodical publication of an association, etc. ◆ *vb* **4** (*tr*) to make known by bulletin. ORIG C17: from F, from It., from *bulletta,* dim. of *bulla* papal edict, BULL[3]

bulletin board *n* **1** the US and Canad. name for **notice board. 2** *Computing.* a facility on a computer network allowing any user to leave messages that can be read by any other user, and to download software and information to the user's own computer.

bulletproof (ˈbʊlɪtˌpruːf) *adj* **1** not penetrable by bullets. ◆ *vb* **2** (*tr*) to make bulletproof.

bulletwood (ˈbʊlɪtˌwʊd) *n* the tough durable wood of a tropical American tree, widely used for construction.

bullfight (ˈbʊlˌfaɪt) *n* a traditional Spanish, Portuguese, and Latin American spectacle in which a matador baits and usually kills a bull in an arena.
▸ **ˈbullˌfighter** *n* ▸ **ˈbullˌfighting** *n*

bullfinch (ˈbʊlˌfɪntʃ) *n* **1** a common European finch: the male has a bright red throat and breast. **2** any of various similar finches. ORIG C14: see BULL[1], FINCH

bullfrog (ˈbʊlˌfrɒg) *n* any of various large frogs having a loud deep croak, esp. the **American bullfrog.**

bullhead (ˈbʊlˌhɛd) *n* any of various small northern mainly marine fishes that have a large head covered with bony plates and spines.

bull-headed *adj* blindly obstinate; stupid.
▸ **ˌbull-ˈheadedly** *adv* ▸ **ˌbull-ˈheadedness** *n*

bullhorn (ˈbʊlˌhɔːn) *n* the US and Canad. name for **loud-hailer.**

bullion (ˈbʊljən) *n* **1** gold or silver in mass. **2** gold or silver in the form of bars and ingots, suitable for further processing. ORIG C14: from Anglo-F: mint, prob. from OF *bouillir* to boil, from L *bullīre*

bullish (ˈbʊlɪʃ) *adj* **1** like a bull. **2** *Stock Exchange.* causing, expecting, or characterized by a rise in prices. **3** *Inf.* cheerful and optimistic.
▸ **ˈbullishness** *n*

bull-necked *adj* having a short thick neck.

bullock (ˈbʊlək) *n* **1** a gelded bull; steer. ◆ *vb* **2** (*intr*) *Austral. & NZ inf.* to work hard and long. ORIG OE *bulluc;* see BULL[1], -OCK

bullocky (ˈbʊləkɪ) *n, pl* **bullockies.** *Austral. & NZ.* a bullock driver; teamster.

bullring (ˈbʊlˌrɪŋ) *n* an arena for bullfighting.

bullroarer (ˈbʊlˌrɔːrə) *n* a wooden slat attached to a thong that makes a roaring sound when the thong is whirled: used esp. by native Australians in religious rites.

bull's-eye *n* **1** the small central disc of a target, usually the highest valued area. **2** a shot hitting this. **3** *Inf.* something that exactly achieves its aim. **4** a small circular or oval window or opening. **5** a thick disc of glass set into a ship's deck, etc., to admit light. **6** the glass boss at the centre of a sheet of blown glass. **7a** a small thick plano-convex lens used as a condenser. **7b** a lamp containing such a lens. **8** a peppermint-flavoured boiled sweet.

bullshit (ˈbʊlˌʃɪt) *Taboo sl.* ◆ *n* **1** exaggerated or foolish talk; nonsense. **2** deceitful or pretentious talk. **3** (in the British Army) exaggerated zeal, esp. for ceremonial drill, cleaning, etc. Usually shortened to **bull.** ◆ *vb* **bullshits, bullshitting, bullshitted** *or* **bullshit. 4** (*intr*) to talk in an exaggerated or foolish manner. **5** (*tr*) to talk bullshit to.

bullswool (ˈbʊlzˌwʊl) *n Austral. & NZ inf.* a euphemism for **bullshit** (sense 1).

bull terrier *n* a breed of terrier having a muscular body and thick neck, with a short smooth coat. See also **pit bull terrier, Staffordshire bull terrier.**

bully (ˈbʊlɪ) *n, pl* **bullies. 1** a person who hurts, persecutes, or intimidates weaker people. **2** a small New Zealand freshwater fish. ◆ *vb* **bullies, bullying, bullied. 3** (when *tr,* often foll. by *into*) to hurt, intimidate, or persecute (a weaker or smaller person), esp. to make him do something. ◆ *adj* **4** dashing; jolly: *my bully boy.* **5** *Inf.* very good; fine. ◆ *interj* **6** Also: **bully for you, him,** etc. *Inf.* well done! bravo! ORIG C16 (in the sense: sweetheart, hence fine fellow, hence swaggering coward): prob. from MDu. *boele* lover, from MHG *buole*

bully beef *n* canned corned beef. Often shortened to **bully.** ORIG C19 *bully,* anglicized version of F *bouilli,* from *boeuf bouilli* boiled beef

bully-off *Hockey.* ◆ *n* **1** the method by which a game is restarted after a stoppage. Two opposing players stand with the ball between them and alternately strike their sticks together and against the ground three times before trying to hit the ball. ◆ *vb* **bully off. 2** (*intr, adv*) to restart play with a bully-off. ◆ Often shortened to **bully.** ORIG C19: from ?

bullyrag (ˈbʊlɪˌræg) *vb* **bullyrags, bullyragging, bullyragged.** (*tr*) to bully, esp. by means of cruel practical jokes. Also: **ballyrag.** ORIG C18: from ?

Bülow ★ (*German* ˈbyːlo) *n* Prince **Bernhard von** (ˈbɛrnhart fɔn). 1849–1929, chancellor of Germany (1900–09).

bulrush (ˈbʊlˌrʌʃ) *n* **1** a popular name for **reed mace. 2** a grasslike marsh plant used for making mats, chair seats, etc. **3** a biblical word for **papyrus** (the plant). ORIG C15 *bulrish, bul-* ?from BULL[1] + *rish* RUSH[2]

bulwark (ˈbʊlwək) *n* **1** a wall or similar structure used as a fortification; rampart. **2** a person or thing acting as a defence. **3** (*often pl*) *Naut.* a solid vertical fencelike structure along the outward sides of a deck. **4** a breakwater or mole. ◆ *vb* **5** (*tr*) to defend or fortify with or as if with a bulwark. ORIG C15: via Du. from MHG *bolwerk,* from *bol* plank, BOLE + *werk* WORK

Bulwer-Lytton ★ (ˈbʊlwəˈlɪtᵊn) *n* See (1st Baron) **Lytton.**

bum[1] (bʌm) *n Brit. sl.* the buttocks or anus. ORIG C14: from ?

bum[2] (bʌm) *Inf.* ◆ *n* **1** a disreputable loafer or idler. **2** a tramp; hobo. ◆ *vb* **bums, bumming, bummed. 3** (*tr*) to get by begging; cadge: *to bum a lift.* **4** (*intr;* often foll. by *around*) to live by begging or as a vagrant or loafer. **5** (*intr;* usually foll. by *around*) to spend time to no good purpose; loaf; idle. **6 bum (someone) off.** *US & Canad. sl.* to disappoint, annoy, or upset (someone). ◆ *adj* **7** (*prenominal*) of poor quality; useless. ORIG C19: prob. shortened from earlier *bummer* a loafer, prob. from G *bummeln* to loaf

bum bag *n* a small bag worn on a belt, round the waist.

bumbailiff (ˌbʌmˈbeɪlɪf) *n Brit. derog.* (formerly) an officer employed to collect debts and arrest debtors. ORIG C17: from BUM[1] + *bailiff,* so called because he follows hard behind debtors

bumble (ˈbʌmbᵊl) *vb* **bumbles, bumbling, bumbled. 1** to speak or do in a clumsy, muddled, or inefficient way. **2** (*intr*) to proceed unsteadily. ORIG C16: ? a blend of BUNGLE + STUMBLE
▸ **ˈbumbler** *n* ▸ **ˈbumbling** *adj, n*

bumblebee (ˈbʌmbᵊlˌbiː) *or* **humblebee** *n* any large hairy social bee of temperate regions. ORIG C16: from *bumble* to buzz + BEE[1]

bumf *or* **bumph** (bʌmf) *n Brit.* **1** *Inf., derog.* official documents, forms, etc. **2** *Sl.* toilet paper. ORIG C19: short for earlier *bumfodder;* see BUM[1]

bummer (ˈbʌmə) *n Sl.* a disappointing or unpleasant experience.

bump (bʌmp) *vb* **1** (when *intr,* usually foll. by *against* or *into*) to knock or strike with a jolt. **2** (*intr;* often foll. by *along*) to travel or proceed in jerks and jolts. **3** (*tr*) to hurt by knocking. **4** *Cricket.* to bowl (a ball) so that it bounces high on pitching or (of a ball) to bounce high when bowled. **5** (*tr*) *Inf.* to exclude (a ticket-holding passenger) from a flight as a result of overbooking. ◆ *n* **6** an impact; knock; jolt; collision. **7** a dull thud or other noise from an impact or collision. **8** the shock of a blow or collision. **9** a lump on the body caused by a blow. **10** a protuberance, as on a road surface. **11** any of the natural protuberances of the human skull, said by phrenologists to indicate underlying faculties and character. ◆ See also **bump into, bump off, bump up.** ORIG C16: prob. imit.

bumper[1] ('bʌmpə) *n* **1** a horizontal usually metal bar attached to the front or rear end of a car, lorry, etc., to protect against damage from impact. **2** *Cricket.* a ball bowled so that it bounces high on pitching; bouncer.

bumper[2] ('bʌmpə) *n* **1** a glass, tankard, etc., filled to the brim, esp. as a toast. **2** an unusually large or fine example of something. ◆ *adj* **3** unusually large, fine, or abundant: *a bumper crop.* ORIG C17 (in the sense: a brimming glass): prob. from *bump* (obs. vb) to bulge; see BUMP

bumph (bʌmf) *n* a variant spelling of **bumf.**

bump into *vb* (*intr, prep*) *Inf.* to meet by chance; encounter unexpectedly.

bumpkin ('bʌmpkɪn) *n* an awkward simple rustic person (esp. in **country bumpkin**). ORIG C16: ?from Du. *boomken* small tree, or from MDu. *boomekijn* small barrel

bump off *vb* (*tr, adv*) *Sl.* to murder; kill.

bumptious ('bʌmpʃəs) *adj* offensively self-assertive or conceited. ORIG C19: ?from BUMP + FRACTIOUS
▸ **'bumptiously** *adv* ▸ **'bumptiousness** *n*

bump up *vb* (*tr, adv*) *Inf.* to raise or increase.

bumpy ('bʌmpɪ) *adj* **bumpier, bumpiest. 1** having an uneven surface. **2** full of jolts; rough.
▸ **'bumpily** *adv* ▸ **'bumpiness** *n*

bun (bʌn) *n* **1** a small roll, similar to bread but usually containing sweetening, currants, etc. **2** any of various small round cakes. **3** a hairstyle in which long hair is gathered into a bun shape at the back of the head. ORIG C14: from ?

bunch (bʌntʃ) *n* **1** a number of things growing, fastened, or grouped together: *a bunch of grapes; a bunch of keys.* **2** a collection; group: *a bunch of queries.* **3** *Inf.* a group or company: *a bunch of boys.* ◆ *vb* **4** (sometimes foll. by *up*) to group or be grouped into a bunch. ORIG C14: from ?

bunchy ('bʌntʃɪ) *adj* **bunchier, bunchiest. 1** composed of or resembling bunches. **2** bulging.

buncombe ('bʌŋkəm) *n* a variant spelling (esp. US) of **bunkum.**

Bundaberg ★ ('bʊndəˌbɜːg) *n* a city in E Australia, near the E coast of Queensland: centre of a sugar-growing area, with a nearby deep-water port. Pop.: 52 267 (1993).

Bundelkhand ★ (ˌbʌndᵊl'kʌnd, -'xʌnd) *n* a region of central India: formerly native states, now mainly part of Madhya Pradesh.

bundle ('bʌndᵊl) *n* **1** a number of things or a quantity of material gathered or loosely bound together: *a bundle of sticks.* Related adj: **fascicular. 2** something wrapped or tied for carrying; package. **3** *Sl.* a large sum of money. **4 go a bundle on.** *Sl.* to be extremely fond of. **5** *Biol.* a collection of strands of specialized tissue such as nerve fibres. **6** *Bot.* short for **vascular bundle. 7 drop one's bundle.** *Sl.* **7a** *Austral. & NZ.* to panic or give up hope. **7b** *NZ.* to give birth. ◆ *vb* **bundles, bundling, bundled. 8** (*tr;* often foll. by *up*) to make into a bundle. **9** (foll. by *out, off, into,* etc.) to go or cause to go, esp. roughly or unceremoniously. **10** (*tr;* usually foll. by *into*) to push or throw, esp. quickly and untidily. **11** (*tr*) to give away (a relatively cheap product) when selling an expensive one to attract business: *software is often bundled with computing.* **12** (*intr*) to sleep or lie in one's clothes on the same bed as one's betrothed: formerly a custom in New England, Wales, and elsewhere. ORIG C14: prob. from MDu. *bundel;* rel. to OE *bindele* bandage; see BIND, BOND
▸ **'bundler** *n*

bundle up *vb* (*adv*) **1** to dress (somebody) warmly and snugly. **2** (*tr*) to make (something) into a bundle or bundles, esp. by tying.

bun fight *n Brit. sl.* **1** a tea party. **2** *Ironic.* an official function.

bung[1] (bʌŋ) *n* **1** a stopper, esp. of cork or rubber, for a cask, etc. **2** short for **bunghole.** ◆ *vb* (*tr*) **3** (often foll. by *up*) *Inf.* to close or seal with or as with a bung. **4** *Brit. sl.* to throw; sling. **5 bung it on.** *Austral. sl.* to behave in a pretentious manner. ORIG C15: from MDu. *bonghe*

bung[2] (bʌŋ) *adj Austral. & NZ inf.* **1** useless. **2 go bung. 2a** to fail or collapse. **2b** to die. ORIG C19: from Abor.

bungalow ('bʌŋgəˌləʊ) *n* a one-storey house, sometimes with an attic. ORIG C17: from Hindi *banglā* (house) of the Bengal type

bungee jumping *or* **bungy jumping** ('bʌndʒɪ) *n* a sport in which a participant jumps from a high bridge, building, etc., secured only by a rubber cord attached to the ankles. ORIG C20: from *bungie,* slang for India rubber, of unknown origin

bunghole ('bʌŋˌhəʊl) *n* a hole in a cask, barrel, etc., through which liquid can be drained.

bungle ('bʌŋgᵊl) *vb* **bungles, bungling, bungled. 1** (*tr*) to spoil (an operation) through clumsiness, incompetence, etc. ◆ *n* **2** a clumsy or unsuccessful performance. ORIG C16: ? of Scand. origin
▸ **'bungler** *n* ▸ **'bungling** *adj, n*

bunion ('bʌnjən) *n* an inflamed swelling of the first joint of the big toe. ORIG C18: ?from obs. *bunny* a swelling, from ?

bunk[1] (bʌŋk) *n* **1** a narrow shelflike bed fixed along a wall. **2** short for **bunk bed. 3** *Inf.* any place where one sleeps. ◆ *vb* **4** (*intr;* often foll. by *down*) to prepare to sleep: *he bunked down on the floor.* **5** (*intr*) to occupy a bunk or bed. ORIG C19: prob. short for BUNKER

bunk[2] (bʌŋk) *n Inf.* short for **bunkum** (sense 1).

bunk[3] (bʌŋk) *n* **1** *Brit. sl.* a hurried departure, usually under suspicious circumstances (esp. in **do a bunk**). ◆ *vb* **2** (usually foll. by *off*) *Brit. & NZ sl.* to play truant from (school, work, etc.). ORIG C19: ?from BUNK[1] (in the sense: to occupy a bunk, hence a hurried departure)

bunk bed *n* one of a pair of beds constructed one above the other to save space.

bunker ('bʌŋkə) *n* **1** a large storage container or tank, as for coal. **2** Also called (esp. US and Canad.): **sand trap.** an obstacle on a golf course, usually a sand-filled hollow bordered by a ridge. **3** an underground shelter with a bank and embrasures for guns above ground. ◆ *vb* **4** (*tr*) *Golf.* **4a** to drive (the ball) into a bunker. **4b** (*passive*) to have one's ball trapped in a bunker. ORIG C16 (in the sense: chest, box): from Scot. *bonkar,* from ?

bunkhouse ('bʌŋkˌhaʊs) *n* (in the US and Canada) a building containing the sleeping quarters of workers on a ranch.

bunkum *or* **buncombe** ('bʌŋkəm) *n* **1** empty talk; nonsense. **2** *Chiefly US.* empty or insincere speechmaking by a politician. ORIG C19: after *Buncombe,* a county in North Carolina, alluded to in an inane speech by its Congressional representative Felix Walker (about 1820)

bunny ('bʌnɪ) *n, pl* **bunnies. 1** Also called: **bunny rabbit.** a child's word for **rabbit** (sense 1). **2** Also called: **bunny girl.** a night-club hostess whose costume includes rabbit-like tail and ears. **3** *Austral. sl.* a mug; dupe. ORIG C17: from Scot. Gaelic *bun* scut of a rabbit

Bunsen ★ ('bʌnsᵊn; *German* 'bʊnzən) *n* **Robert Wilhelm** ('roːbɛrt 'vɪlhɛlm). 1811–99, German chemist who with Kirchhoff developed spectrum analysis.

Bunsen burner *n* a gas burner consisting of a metal tube with an adjustable air valve at the base. ORIG C19: after R. W. BUNSEN

bunting[1] ('bʌntɪŋ) *n* **1** a coarse, loosely woven cotton fabric used for flags, etc. **2** decorative flags, pennants, and streamers. ORIG C18: from ?

bunting[2] ('bʌntɪŋ) *n* any of numerous seed-eating songbirds of the Old World and North America having short stout bills. ORIG C13: from ?

buntline ('bʌntlɪn, -ˌlaɪn) *n Naut.* one of several lines fastened to the foot of a square sail for hauling it up to the yard when furling. ORIG C17: from *bunt* centre of a sail + LINE[1] (sense 11)

Buñuel ★ (*Spanish* bu'ɲwel) *n* **Luis** (lwis). 1900–83, Spanish film director. He collaborated with Salvador Dali on the first surrealist film, *Un Chien Andalou* (1929). His later films include *The Discreet Charm of the Bourgeoisie* (1972).

bunya ('bʌnjə) *n* a tall dome-shaped Australian coniferous tree having edible cones (**bunya nuts**) and thickish flattened needles. Also called: **bunya-bunya.** ORIG C19: from Abor.

Bunyan ★ ('bʌnjən) *n* **John.** 1628–88, English preacher and writer, noted for *The Pilgrim's Progress* (1678).

bunyip ('bʌnjɪp) *n Austral.* a legendary monster said to inhabit swamps and lagoons. ORIG C19: from Abor.

Buonaparte ★ (bwona'parte) *n* the Italian spelling of **Bonaparte.**

Buonarroti ★ (*Italian* bwonar'roti) *n* See **Michelangelo.**

buoy (bɔɪ; *US* 'bu:ɪ) *n* **1** a distinctively shaped and coloured float, anchored to the bottom, for designating moorings, navigable channels, or obstructions in a body of water. See also **life buoy.** ◆ *vb* **2** (*tr;* usually foll. by *up*) to prevent from sinking: *the life belt buoyed him up.* **3** (*tr;* usually foll. by *up*) to raise the spirits of; hearten. **4** (*tr*) *Naut.* to mark (a channel or obstruction) with a buoy or buoys. **5** (*intr*) to rise to the surface; float. ORIG C13: prob. of Gmc origin

buoyancy ('bɔɪənsɪ) *n* **1** the ability to float in a liquid or to rise in liquid, air, or other gas. **2** the tendency of a fluid to keep a body afloat. **3** the ability to recover quickly after setbacks; resilience. **4** cheerfulness.

buoyant ('bɔɪənt) *adj* **1** able to float in or rise to the surface of a liquid. **2** (of a liquid or gas) able to keep a body afloat. **3** cheerful or resilient. ORIG C16: prob. from Sp. *boyante,* from *boyar* to float

BUPA ('bu:pə) *n acronym for* The British United Provident Association Limited: a company which provides private medical insurance.

bupivacaine (bju:'pɪvəˌkeɪn) *n* a local anaesthetic of long duration, used for nerve blocks. ORIG C20: ?from BU(TYL) + *pi(pecoloxylidide)* + *-vacaine,* from (NO)VOCAINE

bur (bɜ:) *n* **1** a seed vessel or flower head having hooks or prickles. **2** any plant that produces burs. **3** a person or thing that clings like a bur. **4** a small surgical or dental drill. ◆ *vb* **burs, burring, burred. 5** (*tr*) to remove burs from. ◆ Also: **burr.** ORIG C14: prob. from ON

Buraydah *or* **Buraida** ★ (bu'raɪdə) *n* a town and oasis in central Saudi Arabia. Pop.: 69 940 (latest est.).

Burbage ★ ('bɜ:bɪdʒ) *n* **1 James.** ?1530–97, English actor and theatre manager, who built (1576) the first public playhouse in England. **2** his son, **Richard.** ?1567–1619, English actor, closely associated with Shakespeare.

burble ('bɜ:bᵊl) *vb* **burbles, burbling, burbled. 1** to make or utter with a bubbling sound; gurgle. **2** (*intr;* often foll. by *away* or *on*) to talk quickly and excitedly. ◆ *n* **3** a bubbling or gurgling sound. **4** a flow of excited speech. ORIG C14: prob. imit.
▸ **'burbler** *n*

burbot ('bɜ:bət) *n, pl* **burbots** *or* **burbot.** a freshwater gadoid food fish that has barbels around its mouth and occurs in Europe, Asia, and North America. ORIG C14: from OF *bourbotte,* from *bourbeter* to wallow in mud, from *bourbe* mud

Burckhardt ★ (*German* 'burkhart) *n* **Jacob Christoph.** 1818–97, Swiss historian; author of *The Civilisation of the Renaissance in Italy* (1860).

burden[1] ('bɜ:dᵊn) *n* **1** something that is carried; load. **2** something that is exacting, oppressive, or difficult to bear. Related adj: **onerous. 3** *Naut.* **3a** the cargo capacity of a ship. **3b** the weight of a ship's cargo. ◆ *vb* (*tr*) **4** (sometimes foll. by *up*) to put or impose a burden on; load. **5** to weigh down; oppress. ORIG OE *byrthen*

burden[2] ('bɜ:dᵊn) *n* **1** a line of words recurring at the end of each verse of a song; chorus or refrain. **2** the theme of a speech, book, etc. **3** another word for **bourdon.** ORIG C16: from OF *bourdon* bass horn, droning sound, imit.

burden of proof *n Law.* the obligation to provide evidence that will convince the court or jury of the truth of one's contention.

burdensome ('bɜ:dᵊnsəm) *adj* hard to bear.

burdock ('bɜ:ˌdɒk) *n* a coarse weedy Eurasian plant having large heart-shaped leaves, tiny purple flowers surrounded by hooked bristles, and burlike fruits. ORIG C16: from BUR + DOCK[4]

bureau ('bjʊərəʊ) *n, pl* **bureaus** *or* **bureaux. 1** *Chiefly Brit.* a writing desk with pigeonholes, drawers, etc., against which the writing surface can be closed when not in use. **2** *US.* a chest of drawers. **3** an office or agency, esp. one providing services for the public. **4** a government department. ORIG C17: from F, orig.: type of cloth used for covering desks, from OF *burel*

bureaucracy (bjʊə'rɒkrəsɪ) *n, pl* **bureaucracies. 1** a system of administration based upon organization into bureaus, division of labour, a hierarchy of authority, etc. **2** government by such a system. **3** government or other officials collectively. **4** any administration in which action is impeded by unnecessary official procedures.

bureaucrat ('bjʊərəˌkræt) *n* **1** an official in a bureaucracy. **2** an official who adheres to bureaucracy, esp. rigidly.
▸ **ˌbureau'cratic** *adj* ▸ **ˌbureau'cratically** *adv*

bureaucratize *or* **bureaucratise** (bjʊə'rɒkrəˌtaɪz) *vb* **bureaucratizes, bureaucratizing, bureaucratized** *or* **bureaucratises, bureaucratising, bureaucratised.** (*tr*) to administer by or transform into a bureaucracy.
▸ **buˌreaucrati'zation** *or* **buˌreaucrati'sation** *n*

bureaux ('bjʊərəʊz) *n* a plural of **bureau.**

burette *or US* **buret** (bju'rɛt) *n* a graduated glass tube with a stopcock on one end for dispensing and transferring known volumes of fluids, esp. liquids. ORIG C15: from F, from OF *buire* ewer

burg (bɜ:g) *n* **1** *History.* a fortified town. **2** *US inf.* a town or city. ORIG C18 (in the sense: fortress): from OHG *burg*

burgage ('bɜ:gɪdʒ) *n History.* **1** (in England) tenure of land or tenement in a town or city, which originally involved a fixed money rent. **2** (in Scotland) the tenure of land direct from the crown in Scottish royal burghs in return for watching and warding. ORIG C14: from Med. L *burgāgium,* from OE *burg*

Burgas ★ (*Bulgarian* bur'gas) *n* a port in SE Bulgaria on an inlet of the Black Sea. Pop.: 199 470 (1996 est.).

Burgenland ★ (*German* 'burgənˌlant) *n* a state of E Austria. Capital: Eisenstadt. Pop.: 279 752 (1998 est.). Area: 3965 sq. km (1531 sq. miles).

burgeon *or* **bourgeon** ('bɜ:dʒən) *vb* **1** (often foll. by *forth* or *out*) (of a plant) to sprout (buds). **2** (*intr;* often foll. by *forth* or *out*) to develop or grow rapidly; flourish. ORIG C13: from OF *burjon*

burger ('bɜ:gə) *n Inf.* **a** a short for **hamburger. b** (*in combination*): *a cheeseburger.*

burgess ('bɜ:dʒɪs) *n* **1** (in England) a citizen, freeman, or inhabitant of a borough. **2** *English history.* a Member of Parliament from a borough, corporate town, or university. ORIG C13: from OF *burgeis;* see BOROUGH

Burgess ★ ('bɜ:dʒɪs) *n* **1 Anthony,** real name *John Burgess Wilson.* 1917–93, British writer, whose novels include *A Clockwork Orange* (1962), *Earthly Powers* (1980), and *A Dead Man in Deptford* (1993). **2 Guy.** 1911–63, British spy, who fled to the Soviet Union in 1951.

burgh ('bʌrə) *n* **1** (in Scotland until 1975) a town, esp. one incorporated by charter, that enjoyed a degree of self-government. **2** an archaic form of **borough.** ORIG C14: Scot. form of BOROUGH
▸ **burghal** ('bɜ:gᵊl) *adj*

burgher ('bɜ:gə) *n* **1** a member of the trading or mercantile class of a medieval city. **2** a respectable citizen; bourgeois. **3** *Arch.* a citizen or inhabitant of a corporate town, esp on the Continent. **4** *S. African history.* a citizen of the Cape Colony or of one of the Transvaal and Free State republics. ORIG C16: from G *Bürger* or Du. *burger* freeman of a BOROUGH

Burghley *or* **Burleigh** ★ ('bɜ:lɪ) *n* **William Cecil,** 1st Baron Burghley. 1520–98, English statesman: chief adviser to Elizabeth I; secretary of state (1558–72) and Lord High Treasurer (1572–98).

burghul (bɜːˈguːl) *n* another name for **bulgur**.

burglar (ˈbɜːglə) *n* a person who commits burglary; housebreaker. ORIG C15: from Anglo-F, from Med. L *burglātor,* prob. from *burgāre* to thieve

burglary (ˈbɜːglərɪ) *n, pl* **burglaries.** the crime of entering a building as a trespasser to commit theft or another offence.
▸ **burglarious** (bɜːˈglɛərɪəs) *adj*

burgle (ˈbɜːgᵊl) *vb* **burgles, burgling, burgled.** to commit burglary upon (a house, etc.).

burgomaster (ˈbɜːgəˌmɑːstə) *n* the chief magistrate of a town in Austria, Belgium, Germany, or the Netherlands; mayor. ORIG C16: partial translation of Du. *burgemeester;* see BOROUGH, MASTER

Burgos ★ (*Spanish* ˈburɣɔs) *n* a city in N Spain, in Old Castile: cathedral. Pop.: 166 251 (1994 est.).

Burgoyne ★ (bɜːˈgɔɪn) *n* **John.** 1722–92, British general in the War of American Independence, who was forced to surrender at Saratoga (1777).

Burgundy ★ (ˈbɜːgəndɪ) *n, pl* **Burgundies. 1** a region of E France famous for its wines, lying west of the Saône: formerly a semi-independent duchy; annexed to France in 1482. French name: **Bourgogne. 2 Free County of.** another name for **Franche-Comté. 3** a monarchy (1384–1477) of medieval Europe, at its height including the Low Countries, the duchy of Burgundy, and Franche-Comté. **4 Kingdom of.** a kingdom in E France, established in the early 6th century A.D., eventually including the later duchy of Burgundy, Franche-Comté, and the Kingdom of Provence: known as the Kingdom of Arles from the 13th century. **5a** any red or white wine produced in the region of Burgundy, around Dijon. **5b** any heavy red table wine. **6** (*often not cap.*) a blackish-purple to purplish-red colour.
▸ **Burgundian** (bɜːˈgʌndɪən) *adj, n*

burial (ˈbɛrɪəl) *n* the act of burying, esp. the interment of a dead body. ORIG OE *byrgels* burial place, tomb; see BURY, -AL²

burial ground *n* a graveyard or cemetery.

burin (ˈbjʊərɪn) *n* **1** a chisel of tempered steel used for engraving metal, wood, or marble. **2** *Archaeol.* a prehistoric flint tool. ORIG C17: from F, ?from It. *burino,* of Gmc origin

burk (bɜːk) *n* a variant spelling of **berk**.

Burke ★ (bɜːk) *n* **1 Edmund.** 1729–97, British Whig statesman, conservative political theorist, and orator, born in Ireland. **2 Robert O'Hara.** 1820–61, Irish explorer, who led the first expedition (1860–61) across Australia from south to north; died on return journey. **3 William.** 1792–1829, Irish murderer and body snatcher; associate of William Hare.

Burkina-Faso ★ (bɜːˈkiːnəˈfæsəʊ) *n* an inland republic in W Africa: dominated by Mossi kingdoms (10th–19th centuries); French protectorate established in 1896; became an independent republic in 1960; consists mainly of a flat savanna plateau. Official language: French; Mossi and other African languages also widely spoken. Religion: mostly animist, with a large Muslim minority. Currency: franc. Capital: Ouagadougou. Pop.: 11 576 000 (1999 est.). Area: 273 200 sq. km (105 900 sq. miles). Former name (until 1984): **Upper Volta.**

burl¹ (bɜːl) *n* **1** a small knot or lump in wool. **2** a roundish warty outgrowth from certain trees. ◆ *vb* **3** (*tr*) to remove the burls from (cloth). ORIG C15: from OF *burle* tuft of wool, prob. ult. from LL *burra* shaggy cloth

burl² *or* **birl** (bɜːl) *n Inf.* **1** *Scot., Austral., & NZ.* an attempt; try (esp. in **give it a burl**). **2** *Austral, & NZ.* a ride in a car. ORIG C20: ?from BIRL in Scots sense: to spin or turn

burlap (ˈbɜːlæp) *n* a coarse fabric woven from jute, hemp, or the like. ORIG C17: from *borel* coarse cloth, from OF *burel* (see BUREAU) + LAP¹

Burleigh ★ (ˈbɜːlɪ) *n* a variant spelling of **Burghley.**

burlesque (bɜːˈlɛsk) *n* **1** an artistic work, esp. literary or dramatic, satirizing a subject by caricaturing it. **2** a ludicrous imitation or caricature. **3** Also: **burlesk.** *US. & Canad. theatre.* a bawdy comedy show of the late 19th and early 20th centuries: the striptease eventually became one of its chief elements. ◆ *adj* **4** of, relating to, or characteristic of a burlesque. ◆ *vb* **burlesques, burlesquing, burlesqued. 5** to represent or imitate (a person or thing) in a ludicrous way; caricature. ORIG C17: from F, from It., from *burla* a jest, piece of nonsense
▸ **burˈlesquer** *n*

burley (ˈbɜːlɪ) *n* a variant spelling of **berley.**

Burlington ★ (ˈbɜːlɪŋtən) *n* **1** a city in S Canada on Lake Ontario, northeast of Hamilton. Pop.: 129 575 (1991). **2** a city in NW Vermont on Lake Champlain: largest city in the state; University of Vermont (1791). Pop.: 39 127 (1990).

burly (ˈbɜːlɪ) *adj* **burlier, burliest.** large and thick of build; sturdy. ORIG C13: of Gmc origin
▸ **ˈburliness** *n*

Burma ★ (ˈbɜːmə) *n* the former name (until 1984) of **Myanmar.**

Burma Road ★ *n* the route extending from Lashio in (Myanmar) to Chongqing in China, which was used by the Allies during World War II to supply military equipment to Chiang Kai-shek's forces in China.

Burmese (bɜːˈmiːz) *adj also* **Burman. 1** of or denoting Burma (Myanmar), or its inhabitants, their customs, etc. ◆ *n* **2** (*pl* **Burmese**) a native or inhabitant of Burma (Myanmar). **3** the language of the Burmese.

burn¹ (bɜːn) *vb* **burns, burning, burnt** *or* **burned. 1** to undergo or cause to undergo combustion. **2** to destroy or be destroyed by fire. **3** (*tr*) to damage, injure, or mark by heat: *he burnt his hand; she was burnt by the sun.* **4** to die or put to death by fire. **5** (*intr*) to be or feel hot: *my forehead burns.* **6** to smart or cause to smart: *brandy burns one's throat.* **7** (*intr*) to feel strong emotion, esp. anger or passion. **8** (*tr*) to use for the purposes of light, heat, or power: *to burn coal.* **9** (*tr*) to form by or as if by fire: *to burn a hole.* **10** to char or become charred: *the potatoes are burning.* **11** (*tr*) to brand or cauterize. **12** to produce by or subject to heat as part of a process: *to burn charcoal.* **13 burn one's bridges** *or* **boats.** to commit oneself to a particular course of action with no possibility of turning back. **14 burn one's fingers.** to suffer from having meddled or interfered. ◆ *n* **15** an injury caused by exposure to heat, electrical, chemical, or radioactive agents. **16** a mark, e.g. on wood, caused by burning. **17** a controlled use of rocket propellant, esp. for a course correction. **18** a hot painful sensation in a muscle, experienced during vigorous exercise. **19** *Sl.* tobacco or a cigarette. ◆ See also **burn out.** ORIG OE *beornan* (intr), *bærnan* (tr)

burn² (bɜːn) *n Scot. & N English.* a small stream; brook. ORIG OE *burna;* rel. to ON *brunnr* spring

Burne-Jones ★ (ˈbɜːnˈdʒəʊnz) *n* Sir **Edward.** 1833–98, British Pre-Raphaelite painter and designer.

burner (ˈbɜːnə) *n* **1** the part of a stove, lamp, etc., that produces flame or heat. **2** an apparatus for burning something, as fuel or refuse.

burnet (ˈbɜːnɪt) *n* **1** a plant of the rose family which has purple-tinged green flowers and leaves. **2 burnet rose.** a very prickly Eurasian rose with white flowers and purplish-black fruits. **3** a moth with red-spotted dark green wings and antennae with enlarged tips. ORIG C14: from OF *burnete,* var. of *brunete* BRUNETTE

Burnet ★ (bəˈnɛt, ˈbɜːnɪt) *n* Sir (**Frank**) **Macfarlane** (məkˈfɑːlən). 1899–1985, Australian physician and virologist, who shared a Nobel prize for physiology or medicine in 1960 for work in immunology.

Burnett ★ (bɜːˈnɛt) *n* **Frances Hodgson** (ˈhɒdʒsən). 1849–1924, US novelist, born in England; author of *Little Lord Fauntleroy* (1886) and *The Secret Garden* (1911).

Burney ★ (ˈbɜːnɪ) *n* **Frances.** known as *Fanny;* married name *Madame D'Arblay.* 1752–1840, British novelist and diarist: author of *Evelina* (1778).

burning (ˈbɜːnɪŋ) *adj* **1** intense; passionate. **2** urgent; crucial: *a burning problem.*

burning bush *n* **1** any of several shrubs or trees that have bright red fruits or seeds. **2** any of several plants with a bright red autumn foliage. **3** *Bible.* the bush that burned without being consumed, from which God spoke to Moses (Exodus 3:2–4).

burning glass *n* a convex lens for concentrating the sun's rays to produce fire.

burnish ('bɜːnɪʃ) *vb* **1** to make or become shiny or smooth by friction; polish. ◆ *n* **2** a shiny finish; lustre. ORIG C14 *burnischen*, from OF *brunir* to make brown, from *brun* BROWN
▸ **'burnisher** *n*

Burnley ★ ('bɜːnlɪ) *n* an industrial town in NW England, in E Lancashire. Pop.: 74 661 (1991).

burnoose, burnous, *or* **burnouse** (bɜː'nuːs, -'nuːz) *n* a long circular cloak with a hood attached, worn esp. by Arabs. ORIG C20: via F *burnous* from Ar. *burnus*, from Gk *birros* cloak

burn out *vb* (*adv*) **1** to become or cause to become inoperative as a result of heat or friction: *the clutch burnt out.* **2** (*intr*) (of a rocket, jet engine, etc.) to cease functioning as a result of exhaustion of the fuel supply. **3** (*tr; usually passive*) to destroy by fire. **4** to become or cause to become exhausted through overwork or dissipation.

Burns ★ (bɜːnz) *n* **Robert.** 1759–96, Scottish lyric poet. His verse, written mostly in dialect, includes love songs, nature poetry, and satires. *Auld Lang Syne* and *Tam o' Shanter* are among his best-known poems.

burnt (bɜːnt) *vb* **1** a past tense and past participle of **burn**[1]. ◆ *adj* **2** affected by or as if by burning; charred.

burnt offering *n* a sacrificial offering burnt, usually on an altar, to honour, propitiate, or supplicate a deity.

burnt sienna *n* **1** a reddish-brown pigment obtained by roasting raw sienna. ◆ *n, adj* **2** (of) a reddish-brown colour.

burnt umber *n* **1** a brown pigment obtained by heating umber. ◆ *n, adj* **2** (of) a dark brown colour.

burp (bɜːp) *n* **1** *Inf.* a belch. ◆ *vb* **2** (*intr*) *Inf.* to belch. **3** (*tr*) to cause (a baby) to burp. ORIG C20: imit.

burr[1] (bɜː) *n* **1** a small power-driven hand-operated rotary file, esp. for removing burrs or for machining recesses. **2** a rough edge left on a workpiece after cutting, drilling, etc. **3** a rough or irregular protuberance, such as a burl on a tree. **4** a variant spelling of **bur.** ORIG C14: var. of BUR

burr[2] (bɜː) *n* **1** an articulation of (r) characteristic of certain English dialects, esp. the uvular fricative trill of Northumberland or the retroflex *r* of the West of England. **2** a whirring sound. ◆ *vb* **3** to pronounce (words) with a burr. **4** (*intr*) to make a whirring sound. ORIG C18: either special use of BUR (in the sense: rough sound) or imit.

Burren ★ ('bʌrən) *n* **the.** a limestone area on the North Clare coast in the Irish Republic, famous for its wild flowers, caves, and dolmens.

burrito (bə'riːtəʊ) *n, pl* **burritos.** *Mexican cookery.* a tortilla folded over a filling of minced beef, chicken, cheese, or beans. ORIG C20: from Mexican Sp., from Sp.: literally, a young donkey

burro ('bʊrəʊ) *n, pl* **burros.** a donkey, esp. one used as a pack animal. ORIG C19: Sp., from Port., from *burrico*

Burroughs ★ ('bʌrəʊz) *n* **1 Edgar Rice.** 1875–1950, US novelist, author of the *Tarzan* stories. **2 William S(eward).** 1914–97, US novelist. His novels include *Junkie* (1953), *The Naked Lunch* (1959), and *Interzone* (1989).

burrow ('bʌrəʊ) *n* **1** a hole dug in the ground by a rabbit or other small animal. **2** a small snug place affording shelter or retreat. ◆ *vb* **3** to dig (a burrow) in, through, or under (ground). **4** (*intr; often foll. by through*) to move through by or as by digging. **5** (*intr*) to hide or live in a burrow. **6** (*intr*) to delve deeply: *he burrowed into his pockets.* **7** to hide (oneself). ORIG C13: prob. var. of BOROUGH
▸ **'burrower** *n*

burry ('bɜːrɪ) *adj* **burrier, burriest. 1** full of or covered in burs. **2** resembling burs; prickly.

bursa ('bɜːsə) *n, pl* **bursae** (-siː) *or* **bursas. 1** *Anat.* a small fluid-filled sac that reduces friction, esp. at joints. **2** *Zool.* any saclike cavity or structure. ORIG C19: from Med. L: bag, pouch, from Gk: skin, hide; see PURSE
▸ **'bursal** *adj*

Bursa ★ ('bɜːsə) *n* a city in NW Turkey: founded in the 2nd century B.C.; seat of Bithynian kings. Pop.: 996 600 (1994 est.). Former name: **Brusa.**

bursar ('bɜːsə) *n* **1** a treasurer of a school, college, or university. **2** *Chiefly Scot. & NZ.* a student holding a bursary. ORIG C13: from Med. L *bursārius* keeper of the purse, from *bursa* purse

bursary ('bɜːsərɪ) *n, pl* **bursaries. 1** Also called: **'bursar,ship.** a scholarship awarded esp. in Scottish and New Zealand schools and universities. **2** *Brit.* the treasury of a college, etc.
▸ **bursarial** (bɜː'sɛərɪəl) *adj*

bursitis (bɜː'saɪtɪs) *n* inflammation of a bursa.

burst (bɜːst) *vb* **bursts, bursting, burst. 1** to break or cause to break open or apart suddenly and noisily; explode. **2** (*intr*) to come, go, etc., suddenly and forcibly: *he burst into the room.* **3** (*intr*) to be full to the point of breaking open. **4** (*intr*) to give vent (to) suddenly or loudly: *to burst into song.* **5** (*tr*) to cause or suffer the rupture of: *to burst a blood vessel.* ◆ *n* **6** a sudden breaking open; explosion. **7** a break; breach; rupture. **8** a sudden display or increase of effort; spurt: *a burst of speed.* **9** a sudden and violent emission, occurrence, or outbreak: *a burst of applause.* **10** a volley of fire from a weapon. ORIG OE *berstan*

burthen ('bɜːðən) *n, vb* an archaic word for **burden**[1].
▸ **'burthensome** *adj*

burton ('bɜːtᵊn) *n* **go for a burton.** *Brit. sl.* **a** to be broken, useless, or lost. **b** to die. ORIG C20: from ?

Burton ★ ('bɜːtᵊn) *n* **1** Sir **Richard Francis.** 1821–90, English explorer, who discovered Lake Tanganyika (1858). **2 Richard,** real name *Richard Jenkins.* 1925–84, Welsh actor: films include *Who's Afraid of Virginia Woolf?* (1966) and *Equus* (1977). **3 Robert,** pen name *Democritus Junior.* 1577–1640, English clergyman, noted for his *Anatomy of Melancholy* (1621).

Burton-upon-Trent ★ *n* a town in W central England, in E Staffordshire: brewing. Pop.: 60 525 (1991).

Burundi ★ (bə'rʊndɪ) *n* a republic in E central Africa: inhabited chiefly by the Hutu, Tutsi, and Twa; made part of German East Africa in 1899; part of the Belgian territory of Ruanda-Urundi from 1923 until it became independent in 1962; ethnic violence has persisted; consists mainly of high plateaus along the main Nile-Congo dividing range, dropping rapidly to the Great Rift Valley in the west. Official languages: Kirundi and French. Religion: Christian majority. Currency: Burundi franc. Capital: Bujumbura. Pop.: 5 736 000 (1999 est.). Area: 27 731 sq. km (10 707 sq. miles). Former name (until 1962): **Urundi.**
▸ **Bu'rundian** *adj, n*

bury ('bɛrɪ) *vb* **buries, burying, buried.** (*tr*) **1** to place (a corpse) in a grave; inter. **2** to place in the earth and cover with soil. **3** to cover from sight; hide. **4** to embed; sink: *to bury a nail in plaster.* **5** to occupy (oneself) with deep concentration; engross: *to be buried in a book.* **6** to dismiss from the mind; abandon: *to bury old hatreds.* ORIG OE *byrgan*

Bury ★ ('bɛrɪ) *n* **1** a town in NW England, part of Greater Manchester: an early textile centre. Pop.: 62 633 (1991). **2** a unitary authority in NW England, in Greater Manchester. Pop.: 181 900 (1995 est.). Area: 99 sq. km (38 sq. miles).

Buryat Republic ★ (bʊə'jɑːt, ˌbʊərɪ'ɑːt) *n* a constituent republic of SE central Russia, on Lake Baikal: mountainous and forested. Capital: Ulan-Ude. Pop.: 1 053 000 (1996 est.). Area: 351 300 sq. km (135 608 sq. miles). Also called: **Buryatia** (bʊrɪ'jɑːtɪə; *Russian* bu'rjaːtija).

Bury St Edmunds ★ ('bɛrɪ sənt 'ɛdməndz) *n* a market town in E England, in Suffolk. Pop.: 31 237 (1991).

bus (bʌs) *n, pl* **buses** *or* **busses. 1** a large motor vehicle designed to carry passengers between stopping places along a regular route. More formal name: **omnibus. 2** (*modifier*) of or relating to a bus or buses: *a bus driver; a bus station.* **3** *Inf.* a car or aircraft, esp. one that is old and shaky. **4** *Electronics, computing.* short for **busbar. 5** *Astronautics.* a platform in a space vehicle used for various experiments and processes. **6 miss the bus.** to miss an opportunity. ◆ *vb* **buses, busing, bused** *or* **busses, bussing, bussed. 7** to travel or transport by bus. **8** *Chiefly US.* to transport (children) by bus from one area to another in order to create racially integrated schools. ORIG C19: short for OMNIBUS

bus. *abbrev. for* business.

busbar ('bʌzˌbɑː) *n* **1** an electrical conductor usually used to make a common connection between several circuits. **2** a group of such electrical conductors maintained at a low voltage, used for carrying data in binary form between the various parts of a computer or its peripherals.

busby ('bʌzbɪ) *n, pl* **busbies. 1** a tall fur helmet worn by hussars. **2** (not in official usage) another name for **bearskin** (the hat). ORIG C18: ?from a proper name

Busby ★ ('bʌzbɪ) *n* Sir **Matthew**, known as *Matt.* 1909–94, British footballer. He played for Manchester City (1929–36) and for Liverpool (1936–39); he was manager of Manchester United (1946–69).

bush[1] (bʊʃ) *n* **1** a dense woody plant, smaller than a tree, with many branches arising from the lower part of the stem; shrub. **2** a dense cluster of such shrubs; thicket. **3** something resembling a bush, esp. in density: *a bush of hair.* **4** (often preceded by *the*) an uncultivated or sparsely settled area, covered with trees or shrubs, which can vary from open, shrubby country to dense rainforest. **5** a forested area; woodland. **6** *Canad.* Also called: **bush lot, woodlot.** an area on a farm on which timber is grown and cut. **7** (often preceded by *the*) *Inf.* the countryside, as opposed to the city: *out in the bush.* **8** *Obs.* a bunch of ivy hung as a vintner's sign in front of a tavern. **9 beat about the bush.** to avoid the point at issue; prevaricate. ◆ *adj* **10** *Austral. & NZ inf.* rough-and-ready. **11** *US & Canad. inf.* unprofessional, unpolished, or second-rate. **12 go bush.** *Inf.* **12a** *Austral. & NZ.* to abandon city amenities and live rough. **12b** *Austral.* to go into hiding. ◆ *vb* **13** (*intr*) to grow thick and bushy. **14** (*tr*) to cover, decorate, support, etc., with bushes. **15 bush it.** *Austral.* to camp out in the bush. ORIG C13: of Gmc origin

bush[2] (bʊʃ) *n* **1** a thin metal sleeve or tubular lining serving as a bearing. ◆ *vb* **2** to fit a bush to (a bearing, etc.). ORIG C15: from MDu. *busse* box, bush; rel. to LL *buxis* BOX[1]

Bush ★ (bʊʃ) *n* **1 George.** born 1924, US Republican politician; vice president of the US (1981–93): 41st president of the US (1989–92). In 1993 he was awarded an honorary knighthood for his role in the Gulf War (1991). **2 George W(alker).** born 1946, US Republican politician, son of George Bush; governor of Texas (1994–2001); 43rd president of the US from 2001.

bushbaby ('bʊʃˌbeɪbɪ) *n, pl* **bushbabies.** an agile nocturnal arboreal primate occurring in Africa south of the Sahara. It has large eyes and ears and a long tail. Also called: **galago.**

bushbuck ('bʊʃˌbʌk) *or* **boschbok** ('bɒʃˌbʌk) *n, pl* **bushbucks, bushbuck** *or* **boschboks, boschbok.** a small nocturnal spiral-horned antelope of the bush and tropical forest of Africa.

bush carpenter *n Austral. & NZ sl.* a rough-and-ready unskilled workman.

bushed (bʊʃt) *adj Inf.* **1** (*postpositive*) extremely tired; exhausted. **2** *Canad.* mentally disturbed from living in isolation. **3** *Austral. & NZ.* lost or bewildered, as in the bush.

bushel ('bʊʃəl) *n* **1** a British unit of dry or liquid measure equal to 8 Imperial gallons. 1 Imperial bushel is equivalent to 0.036 37 cubic metres. **2** a US unit of dry measure equal to 64 US pints. 1 US bushel is equivalent to 0.035 24 cubic metres. **3** a container with a capacity equal to either of these quantities. **4** *US inf.* a large amount. **5 hide one's light under a bushel.** to conceal one's abilities or good qualities. ORIG C14: from OF *boissel*

bushfire ('bʊʃˌfaɪə) *n* an uncontrolled fire in the bush; a scrub or forest fire.

bushfly ('bʊʃˌflaɪ) *n pl* **bushflies.** any of various small black dipterous flies of Australia that breed in faeces and dung.

bush house *n Chiefly Austral.* a shed or hut in the bush or a garden.

Bushido (ˌbuːʃɪ'dəʊ) *n* (*sometimes not cap.*) the feudal code of the Japanese samurai. ORIG C19: from Japanese *bushi* warrior + *dō* way

bushie ('bʊʃɪ) *n* a variant spelling of **bushy**[2].

bushing ('bʊʃɪŋ) *n* **1** another word for **bush**[2]. **2** an adaptor used to connect pipes of different sizes. **3** a layer of electrical insulation enabling a live conductor to pass through an earthed wall, etc.

Bushire ★ (bjuː'ʃaɪə) *n* a port in SW Iran, on the Persian Gulf. Pop.: 133 000 (1991). Persian name: **Bushehr** (bu'ʃehr).

bush jacket *or* **shirt** *n* a casual jacket or shirt having four patch pockets and a belt.

bush lawyer *n Austral. & NZ.* **1** a trailing plant with sharp hooks. **2** *Inf.* a person who gives legal opinions but is not qualified to do so.

bush line *n* an airline operating in the bush country of Canada's northern regions.

bush lot *n Canad.* another name for **bush**[1] (sense 6).

bushman ('bʊʃmən) *n, pl* **bushmen.** *Austral. & NZ.* a person who lives or travels in the bush, esp. one versed in bush lore.

Bushman ('bʊʃmən) *n, pl* **Bushmen.** a member of a hunting and gathering people of southern Africa. ORIG C18: from Afrik. *boschjesman*

bushmaster ('bʊʃˌmɑːstə) *n* a large greyish-brown highly venomous snake of tropical America.

bush pilot *n Canad.* a pilot who operates in the bush country.

bushranger ('bʊʃˌreɪndʒə) *n* **1** *Austral.* (formerly) an outlaw living in the bush. **2** *US.* a person who lives away from civilization.

bush singlet *n NZ.* a black woollen singlet often worn by farm labourers.

bush tea *n* **1** a leguminous shrub of southern Africa. **2** a beverage prepared from the dried leaves of such a plant.

bush telegraph *n* a means of spreading rumour, gossip, etc.

Bushveld ★ ('bʊʃˌfɛlt, -ˌvɛlt) *n* **the.** an area of low altitude in NE South Africa, having scrub vegetation. Also called: **Lowveld.**

bushwhack ('bʊʃˌwæk) *vb* **1** (*tr*) *US, Canad., & Austral.* to ambush. **2** (*intr*) *US, Canad., & Austral.* to cut or beat one's way through thick woods. **3** (*intr*) *US, Canad., & Austral.* to range or move around in woods or the bush. **4** (*intr*) *NZ.* to work in the bush. **5** (*intr*) *US & Canad.* to fight as a guerrilla in wild regions.

bushwhacker ('bʊʃˌwækə) *n* **1** *US, Canad., & Austral.* a person who travels around or lives in thinly populated woodlands. **2** *Austral. sl.* an unsophisticated person. **3** *NZ.* a person who works in the bush. **4** a Confederate guerrilla in the American Civil War. **5** *US.* any guerrilla.

bushy[1] ('bʊʃɪ) *adj* **bushier, bushiest. 1** covered or overgrown with bushes. **2** thick and shaggy.
▸ **'bushily** *adv* ▸ **'bushiness** *n*

bushy[2] *or* **bushie** ('bʊʃɪ) *n, pl* **bushies.** *Austral. inf.* **1** a person who lives in the bush. **2** an unsophisticated uncouth person.

business ('bɪznɪs) *n* **1** a trade or profession. **2** the purchase and sale of goods and services. **3** a commercial or industrial establishment. **4** commercial activity; dealings (esp. in **do business**). **5** volume of commercial activity: *business is poor today.* **6** commercial policy: *overcharging is bad business.* **7** proper or rightful concern or responsibility (often in **mind one's own business**). **8** a special task; assignment. **9** an affair; matter. **10** serious work or activity: *get down to business.* **11** a difficult or complicated matter. **12** *Theatre.* an incidental action performed by an actor for dramatic effect. **13 mean business.** to be in earnest. ORIG OE *bisignis* solicitude, from *bisig* BUSY + *-nis* -NESS

business college *n* a college providing courses in secretarial studies, business management, accounting, commerce, etc.

businesslike ('bɪznɪsˌlaɪk) *adj* efficient and methodical.

businessman ('bɪznɪsˌmæn, -mən) *or* (*fem*) **businesswoman** *n, pl* **businessmen** *or* **businesswomen.** a person engaged in commercial or industrial business, esp. as an owner or executive.

business park *n* an area specially designated and landscaped to accommodate offices, warehouses, etc.

business plan *n* a detailed plan setting out the objectives of a business, the strategy and tactics planned to achieve them, and the expected profits.

business process re-engineering *n* restructuring an organization by means of a reassessment of its core processes and predominant competencies. Abbrev.: **BPR**.

business school *n* an institution that offers courses in aspects of business, such as marketing, finance, and law, designed to train managers in industry and commerce to do their jobs effectively.

busk (bʌsk) *vb (intr) Brit.* to make money singing, playing an instrument, performing, or dancing in public places. ORIG C20: ?from Sp. *buscar* to look for
▸ **'busker** *n*

buskin ('bʌskɪn) *n* **1** (formerly) a sandal-like covering for the foot and leg, reaching the calf. **2** a thick-soled laced half-boot worn esp. by actors of ancient Greece. **3** (usually preceded by *the*) *Chiefly literary.* tragic drama. ORIG C16: ?from Sp. *borzeguí;* rel. to OF *bouzequin*

busman's holiday ('bʌsmənz) *n Inf.* a holiday spent doing the same as one does at work. ORIG C20: from a bus driver having a driving holiday

Busra *or* **Busrah** ★ ('bʌsrə) *n* variant spellings of **Basra**.

buss (bʌs) *n, vb* an archaic or dialect word for **kiss**. ORIG C16: prob. imit.

Buss ★ (bʌs) *n* **Frances Mary.** 1827–94, British educationalist.

bust[1] (bʌst) *n* **1** the chest of a human being, esp. a woman's bosom. **2** a sculpture of the head, shoulders, and upper chest of a person. ORIG C17: from F, from It. *busto* a sculpture, from ?

bust[2] (bʌst) *Inf.* ◆ *vb* **busts, busting, busted** *or* **bust. 1** to burst or break. **2** to make or become bankrupt. **3** *(tr)* (of the police) to raid, search, or arrest. **4** *(tr) US & Canad.* to demote, esp. in military rank. ◆ *n* **5** a raid, search, or arrest by the police. **6** *Chiefly US.* a punch. **7** *US & Canad.* a failure, esp. bankruptcy. **8** a drunken party. ◆ *adj* **9** broken. **10** bankrupt. **11 go bust.** to become bankrupt. ORIG C19: from a dialect pronunciation of BURST

bustard ('bʌstəd) *n* a large terrestrial bird inhabiting open regions of the Old World. It has long strong legs, a heavy body, a long neck, and speckled plumage. ORIG C15: from OF *bistarde,* from L *avis tarda* slow bird

bustier ('bu:stɪeɪ) *n* a type of close-fitting usually strapless top worn by women.

bustle[1] ('bʌsᵊl) *vb* **bustles, bustling, bustled. 1** (when *intr,* often foll. by *about*) to hurry or cause to hurry with a great show of energy or activity. ◆ *n* **2** energetic and noisy activity. ORIG C16: prob. from obs. *buskle* to make energetic preparation
▸ **'bustling** *adj*

bustle[2] ('bʌsᵊl) *n* a cushion or framework worn by women in the late 19th century at the back in order to expand the skirt. ORIG C18: from ?

bust-up *Inf.* ◆ *n* **1** a quarrel, esp. a serious one ending a friendship, etc. **2** *Brit.* a disturbance or brawl. ◆ *vb* **bust up** *(adv)* **3** *(intr)* to quarrel and part. **4** *(tr)* to disrupt (a meeting), esp. violently.

busy ('bɪzɪ) *adj* **busier, busiest. 1** actively or fully engaged; occupied. **2** crowded with or characterized by activity. **3** *Chiefly US & Canad.* (of a room, telephone line, etc.) in use; engaged. **4** overcrowded with detail: *a busy painting.* **5** meddlesome; inquisitive. ◆ *vb* **busies, busying, busied. 6** *(tr)* to make or keep (someone, esp. oneself) busy. ORIG OE *bisig*
▸ **'busily** *adv* ▸ **'busyness** *n*

busybody ('bɪzɪˌbɒdɪ) *n, pl* **busybodies.** a meddlesome, prying, or officious person.

busy Lizzie ('lɪzɪ) *n* a flowering plant that has pink, red, or white flowers and is often grown as a pot plant.

but[1] (bʌt; *unstressed* bət) *conj (coordinating)* **1** contrary to expectation: *he cut his knee but didn't cry.* **2** in contrast; on the contrary: *I like opera but my husband doesn't.* **3** *(usually used after a negative)* other than: *we can't do anything but wait.* ◆ *conj (subordinating)* **4** *(usually used after a negative)* without it happening: *we never go out but it rains.* **5** (foll. by *that*) except that: *nothing is impossible but that we live forever.* **6** *Arch.* if not; unless. ◆ *prep* **7** except; save: *they saved all but one.* **8 but for.** were it not for: *but for you, we couldn't have managed.* ◆ *adv* **9** just; merely: *he was but a child.* **10** *Dialect & Austral.* though; however: *it's a rainy day; warm, but.* ◆ *n* **11** an objection (esp. in **ifs and buts**). ORIG OE *būtan* without, outside, except, from *be* BY + *ūtan* OUT

but[2] (bʌt) *n Scot.* the outer room of a two-roomed cottage. Cf. **ben**[1]. ORIG C18: from *but* (adv) outside; see BUT[1]

butadiene (ˌbju:tə'daɪi:n) *n* a colourless flammable gas used mainly in the manufacture of synthetic rubbers. Formula: CH_2:CHCH:CH_2. Systematic name: **buta-1,3-diene.** ORIG C20: from BUTA(NE) + DI-[1] + -ENE

butane ('bju:teɪn, bju:'teɪn) *n* a colourless flammable gaseous alkane used mainly in the manufacture of rubber and fuels. Formula: C_4H_{10}. ORIG C20: from BUT(YL) + -ANE

butanoic acid (ˌbju:tə'nəʊɪk) *n* a carboxylic acid that produces the smell in rancid butter. Formula: $CH_3(CH_2)_2COOH$. Also called: **butyric acid.** ORIG C20: from BUTAN(E) + -OIC

butanol ('bju:təˌnɒl) *n* a colourless substance existing in four isomeric forms. The three liquid isomers are used as solvents and in the manufacture of organic compounds. Formula: C_4H_9OH. Also called: **butyl alcohol.**

butanone ('bju:təˌnəʊn) *n* a colourless flammable liquid used as a resin solvent, and paint remover, and in lacquers, adhesives, etc. Formula: $CH_3COC_2H_5$.

butch (bʊtʃ) *Sl.* ◆ *adj* **1** (of a woman or man) markedly or aggressively masculine. ◆ *n* **2** a lesbian who is noticeably masculine. **3** a strong rugged man. ORIG C18: back formation from BUTCHER

butcher ('bʊtʃə) *n* **1** a retailer of meat. **2** a person who slaughters or dresses meat. **3** an indiscriminate or brutal murderer. ◆ *vb (tr)* **4** to slaughter or dress (animals) for meat. **5** to kill indiscriminately or brutally. **6** to make a mess of; botch. ORIG C13: from OF *bouchier,* from *bouc* he-goat

butcherbird ('bʊtʃəˌbɜ:d) *n* **1** a shrike, esp. of the genus *Lanius.* **2** any of several Australian magpies that impale their prey on thorns.

butcher's-broom *n* an evergreen shrub with stiff prickle-tipped flattened green stems, formerly used for making brooms.

butchery ('bʊtʃərɪ) *n, pl* **butcheries. 1** the business of a butcher. **2** wanton and indiscriminate slaughter. **3** a slaughterhouse.

Bute[1] ★ (bju:t) *n* an island off the coast of SW Scotland, in the Firth of Clyde, separated from the Cowal peninsula by the **Kyles of Bute**. Chief town: Rothesay. Pop.: 8000 (latest est.). Area: 121 sq. km (47 sq. miles).

Bute[2] ★ (bju:t) *n* **John Stuart,** 3rd Earl of Bute. 1713–92, British Tory statesman; prime minister (1762–63).

Butenandt ★ (*German* 'bu:tənant) *n* **Adolf Johann** ('a:dɔlf). 1903–95, German organic chemist. He shared the Nobel prize for chemistry (1939) for his work on hormones.

Buteshire ★ ('bju:tˌʃɪə, -ʃə) *n* (until 1975) a county of SW Scotland, now part of Argyll and Bute council area.

Buthelezi ★ (ˌbʊtə'leɪzɪ) *n* **Mangosouthu Gatsha** (ˌmæŋgəʊ'su:tu: 'gætʃə), known as *Chief Buthelezi.* born 1928, Zulu leader; founder of the Inkatha movement.

butler ('bʌtlə) *n* the male servant of a household in charge of the wines, table, etc.: usually the head servant. ORIG C13: from OF, from *bouteille* BOTTLE

Butler ★ ('bʌtlə) *n* **1 Joseph.** 1692–1752, English theologian and author. **2 Josephine (Elizabeth).** 1828–1906, British social reformer. **3 Reg,** full name *Reginald Cotterell Butler.* 1913–81, British metal sculptor. **4 R(ichard) A(usten),** Baron Butler of Saffron Walden, known as *Rab Butler.* 1902–82, British Conservative politician: Chancellor of the Exchequer (1951–55); Home Secretary (1957–62); Foreign Secretary (1963–64). **5 Samuel.** 1612–80, English poet; author of *Hudibras* (1663–78). **6 Samuel.** 1835–1902, British novelist, noted for *Erewhon* (1872) and *The Way of All Flesh* (1903).

butlery ('bʌtlərɪ) *n, pl* **butleries. 1** a butler's room. **2** another name for **buttery**[2].

butt[1] (bʌt) *n* **1** the thicker or blunt end of something, such as the end of the stock of a rifle. **2** the unused end of something, esp. of a cigarette; stub. **3** *Inf., chiefly US & Canad.* the buttocks. **4** *US.* a slang word for **cigarette. 5** *Building.* short for **butt joint.** ORIG C15 (in the sense: thick end of something, buttock): rel. to OE *buttuc* end, ridge

butt[2] (bʌt) *n* **1** a person or thing that is the target of ridicule, wit, etc. **2** *Shooting, archery.* **2a** a mound of earth behind the target that stops bullets or wide shots. **2b** the target itself. **2c** (*pl*) the target range. **3** a low barrier behind which sportsmen shoot game birds, esp. grouse. ◆ *vb* **4** (usually foll. by *on* or *against*) to lie or be placed end on to; abut. ORIG C14 (in the sense: mark for archery practice): from OF *but*

butt[3] (bʌt) *vb* **1** to strike or push (something) with the head or horns. **2** (*intr*) to project; jut. **3** (*intr;* foll. by *in* or *into*) to intrude, esp. into a conversation; interfere. ◆ *n* **4** a blow with the head or horns. ORIG C12: from OF *boter,* of Gmc origin

butt[4] (bʌt) *n* a large cask for storing wine or beer. ORIG C14: from OF *botte,* from LL *buttis* cask

butte (bju:t) *n US & Canad.* an isolated steep flat-topped hill. ORIG C19: F, from OF *bute* mound behind a target; see BUTT[2]

butter ('bʌtə) *n* **1** an edible fatty whitish-yellow solid made from cream by churning. **2** any substance with a butter-like consistency, such as peanut butter. **3 look as if butter wouldn't melt in one's mouth.** to look innocent, although probably not so. ◆ *vb* (*tr*) **4** to put butter on or in. **5** to flatter. ◆ See also **butter up.** ORIG OE *butere,* from L, from Gk *bouturon,* from *bous* cow + *turos* cheese

butter bean *n* a variety of lima bean that has large pale flat edible seeds.

butterbur ('bʌtəˌbɜː) *n* a plant of the composite family with fragrant whitish or purple flowers, and large leaves formerly used to wrap butter.

buttercup ('bʌtəˌkʌp) *n* any of various yellow-flowered plants of the genus *Ranunculus* of Europe, Asia, and North America.

butterfat ('bʌtəˌfæt) *n* the fatty substance of milk from which butter is made, consisting of a mixture of glycerides.

Butterfield ★ ('bʌtəˌfi:ld) *n* **William.** 1814–1900, British architect of the Gothic Revival: his buildings include Keble College, Oxford (1870).

butterfingers ('bʌtəˌfɪŋgəz) *n* (*functioning as sing*) *Inf.* a person who drops things inadvertently or fails to catch things.
▸ **'butterˌfingered** *adj*

butterfish ('bʌtəˌfɪʃ) *n, pl* **butterfish** *or* **butterfishes.** any of several species of fishes having a slippery skin.

butterflies ('bʌtəˌflaɪz) *pl n Inf.* tremors in the stomach region due to nervousness.

butterfly ('bʌtəˌflaɪ) *n, pl* **butterflies. 1** any diurnal insect that has a slender body with clubbed antennae and typically rests with the wings (often brightly coloured) closed over the back. **2** a person who never settles with one interest or occupation for long. **3** a swimming stroke in which the arms are plunged forward together in large circular movements. **4** *Commerce.* the simultaneous purchase and sale of traded call options, at different exercise prices or with different expiry dates, on a stock exchange or commodity market. ORIG OE *buttorflēoge*

butterfly collar *n* the Irish name for **wing collar.**

butterfly effect *n* the idea, used in chaos theory, that a very small difference in the initial state of a physical system can make a significant difference to the state at some later time. ORIG C20: from the theory that a butterfly flapping its wings in one part of the world might ultimately cause a hurricane in another part of the world

butterfly nut *n* another name for **wing nut.**

Buttermere ★ ('bʌtəˌmɪə) *n* a lake in NW England, in Cumbria, in the Lake District, southwest of Keswick. Length: 2 km (1.25 miles).

buttermilk ('bʌtəˌmɪlk) *n* the sourish liquid remaining after the butter has been separated from milk.

butter muslin *n* a fine loosely woven cotton material originally used for wrapping butter.

butternut ('bʌtəˌnʌt) *n* **1** *Austral. & NZ.* a type of small edible pumpkin. **2a** a walnut tree of North America. **2b** its oily edible nut.

butterscotch ('bʌtəˌskɒtʃ) *n* **1** a kind of hard brittle toffee made with butter, brown sugar, etc. **2** a flavouring made from these ingredients. ORIG C19: ? first made in Scotland

butter up *vb* (*tr, adv*) to flatter.

butterwort ('bʌtəˌwɜːt) *n* a plant that grows in wet places and has violet-blue spurred flowers and fleshy greasy glandular leaves on which insects are trapped and digested.

Butterworth ★ ('bʌtəwəθ) *n* **George.** 1885–1916, British composer, noted for his settings of Housman's poems.

buttery[1] ('bʌtərɪ) *adj* containing, like, or coated with butter.
▸ **'butteriness** *n*

buttery[2] ('bʌtərɪ) *n, pl* **butteries. 1** a room for storing foods or wines. **2** *Brit.* (in some universities) a room in which food and drink are supplied or sold to students. ORIG C14: from Anglo-F *boterie,* prob. from L *butta* cask, BUTT[4]

butt joint *n* a joint between two plates, planks, etc., fastened end to end without overlapping or interlocking. Sometimes shortened to **butt.**

buttock ('bʌtək) *n* **1** either of the two large fleshy masses of thick muscular tissue that form the human rump. See also **gluteus.** Related adj: **gluteal. 2** the analogous part in some mammals. ORIG C13: ?from OE *buttuc* round slope

button ('bʌtᵊn) *n* **1** a disc or knob of plastic, wood, etc., attached to a garment, etc., usually for fastening two surfaces together by passing it through a buttonhole or loop. **2** a small round object, such as any of various sweets, decorations, or badges. **3** a small disc that completes an electric circuit when pushed, as one that operates a machine. **4** *Biol.* any rounded knoblike part or organ, such as an unripe mushroom. **5** *Fencing.* the protective knob fixed to the point of a foil. **6** *Brit.* an object of no value (esp. in **not worth a button**). ◆ *vb* **7** to fasten with a button or buttons. **8** (*tr*) to provide with buttons. ORIG C14: from OF *boton,* from *boter* to thrust, butt; see BUTT[3]
▸ **'buttoner** *n* ▸ **'buttonless** *adj*

buttonhole ('bʌtᵊnˌhəʊl) *n* **1** a slit in a garment, etc., through which a button is passed to fasten two surfaces together. **2** a flower or small bunch of flowers worn pinned to the lapel or in the buttonhole, esp. at weddings. US name: **boutonniere.** ◆ *vb* **buttonholes, buttonholing, buttonholed.** (*tr*) **3** to detain (a person) in conversation. **4** to make buttonholes in.

buttonhook ('bʌtᵊnˌhʊk) *n* a thin tapering hooked instrument formerly used for pulling buttons through the buttonholes of shoes.

button up *vb* (*tr, adv*) **1** to fasten (a garment) with a button or buttons. **2** *Inf.* to conclude (business) satisfactorily. **3 button up one's lip** *or* **mouth.** *Sl.* to be silent.

buttress ('bʌtrɪs) *n* **1** Also called: **pier.** a construction, usually of brick or stone, built to support a wall. **2** any support or prop. **3** something shaped like a buttress, such as a projection from a mountainside. ◆ *vb* (*tr*) **4** to support (a wall) with a buttress. **5** to support or sustain. ORIG C13: from OF *bouterez,* from *bouter* to thrust, BUTT[3]

butty[1] ('bʌtɪ) *n, pl* **butties.** *Chiefly N English dialect.* a sandwich: *a jam butty.* ORIG C19: from *buttered* (bread)

butty[2] ('bʌtɪ) *n, pl* **butties.** *English dialect.* (esp. in mining parlance) a friend or workmate. ORIG C19: ?from obs. *booty* sharing, from BOOT[2]

Butung ★ ('bu:tʊŋ) *n* an island of Indonesia, southeast of Sulawesi: hilly and forested. Chief town: Baubau. Pop.: 317 124 (1980). Area: 4555 sq. km (1759 sq. miles).

butyl ('bju:ˌtaɪl, -tɪl) *n* (*modifier*) of or containing any of four isomeric forms of the group C_4H_9–: *butyl rubber.* ORIG C19: from BUT(YRIC ACID) + -YL

★ people and places

butyl alcohol *n* another name for **butanol.**

butyl rubber *n* a copolymer of isobutene and isoprene, used in tyres and as a waterproofing material.

butyric acid (bjuːˈtɪrɪk) *n* another name for **butanoic acid.** ORIG C19 *butyric,* from L *būtyrum* BUTTER

buxom (ˈbʌksəm) *adj* **1** (esp. of a woman) healthily plump, attractive, and vigorous. **2** (of a woman) full-bosomed. ORIG C12: *buhsum* compliant, pliant, from OE *būgan* to bend, BOW[1]
▸ **ˈbuxomness** *n*

Buxtehude ★ (*German* bʊkstəˈhuːdə) *n* **Dietrich** (ˈdiːtrɪç). 1637–1707, Danish composer, in Germany from 1668.

Buxton ★ (ˈbʌkstən) *n* a town in N England, in NW Derbyshire in the Peak District: thermal springs. Pop.: 19 854 (1991).

buy (baɪ) *vb* **buys, buying, bought.** (*mainly tr*) **1** to acquire by paying or promising to pay a sum of money; purchase. **2** to be capable of purchasing: *money can't buy love.* **3** to acquire by any exchange or sacrifice: *to buy time by equivocation.* **4** to bribe or corrupt; hire by or as by bribery. **5** *Sl.* to accept as true, practical, etc. **6** (*intr;* foll. by *into*) to purchase shares of (a company). ◆ *n* **7** a purchase (often in **good** or **bad buy**). ◆ See also **buy in, buy into,** etc. ORIG OE *bycgan*

USAGE NOTE See at **off.**

buy-back *n Commerce.* the repurchase by a company of some or all of its shares from an investor, who acquired them by putting venture capital into the company when it was formed.

buyer (ˈbaɪə) *n* **1** a person who buys; customer. **2** a person employed to buy merchandise, materials, etc., as for a shop or factory.

buy in *vb* (*adv*) **1** (*tr*) to buy back for the owner (an item in an auction) at or below the reserve price. **2** (*intr*) to purchase shares in a company. **3** (*tr*) Also: **buy into.** *US inf.* to pay money to secure a position or place for (someone, esp. oneself) in some organization, esp. a business or club. **4** to purchase (goods, etc.) in large quantities. ◆ *n* **buy-in. 5** the purchase of a company by a manager or group who does not work for that company.

buy into *vb* (*intr, prep*) **1** to agree with or accept as valid (an argument, theory, etc.). **2** *Austral. & NZ inf.* to get involved in (an argument, fight, etc.).

buy off *vb* (*tr, adv*) to pay (a person or group) to drop a charge, end opposition, etc.

buy out *vb* (*tr, adv*) **1** to purchase the ownership, controlling interest, shares, etc., of (a company, etc.). **2** to gain the release of (a person) from the armed forces by payment. **3** to pay (a person) to give up ownership of (property, etc.). ◆ *n* **buy-out. 4** the purchase of a company, esp. by its former management or staff. See also **leveraged buyout, management buyout.**

buy up *vb* (*tr, adv*) **1** to purchase all, or all that is available, of (something). **2** to purchase a controlling interest in (a company, etc.).

buzz (bʌz) *n* **1** a rapidly vibrating humming sound, as of a bee. **2** a low sound, as of many voices in conversation. **3** a rumour; report; gossip. **4** *Inf.* a telephone call. **5** *Inf.* **5a** a pleasant sensation. **5b** a sense of excitement; kick. **6** (*modifier*) fashionable, trendy. ◆ *vb* **7** (*intr*) to make a vibrating sound like that of a prolonged *z.* **8** (*intr*) to talk or gossip with an air of excitement: *the town buzzed with the news.* **9** (*tr*) to utter or spread (a rumour). **10** (*intr;* often foll. by *about*) to move around quickly and busily. **11** (*tr*) to signal or summon with a buzzer. **12** (*tr*) *Inf.* to call by telephone. **13** (*tr*) *Inf.* to fly an aircraft very low over (an object). **14** (*tr*) (esp. of insects) to make a buzzing sound with (wings, etc.). ORIG C16: imit.
▸ **ˈbuzzy** *adj*

buzzard (ˈbʌzəd) *n* a diurnal bird of prey of the hawk family, typically having broad wings and tail and a soaring flight. ORIG C13: from OF *buisard,* from L *būteō* hawk

buzzer (ˈbʌzə) *n* **1** a device that produces a buzzing sound, esp. one similar to an electric bell. **2** *NZ.* a wood-planing machine.

buzz off *vb* (*intr, adv; often imperative*) *Inf., chiefly Brit.* to go away; leave; depart.

buzz word *n Inf.* a word, originally from a particular jargon, which becomes a popular vogue word. ORIG C20: from ?

BVM *abbrev. for* Beata Virgo Maria. ORIG L: Blessed Virgin Mary

bwana (ˈbwɑːnə) *n* (in E Africa) a master, often used as a form of address corresponding to *sir.* ORIG Swahili, from Ar. *abūna* our father

by (baɪ) *prep* **1** used to indicate the agent after a passive verb: *seeds eaten by the birds.* **2** used to indicate the person responsible for a creative work: *this song is by Schubert.* **3** via; through: *enter by the back door.* **4** foll. by a gerund to indicate a means used: *he frightened her by hiding behind the door.* **5** beside; next to; near: *a tree by the house.* **6** passing the position of; past: *he drove by the old cottage.* **7** not later than; before: *return the books by Tuesday.* **8** used to indicate extent, after a comparative: *it is hotter by five degrees.* **9** (esp. in oaths) invoking the name of: *I swear by all the gods.* **10** multiplied by: *four by three equals twelve.* **11** during the passing of (esp. in **by day, by night**). **12** placed between measurements of the various dimensions of something: *a pane four inches by seven.* ◆ *adv* **13** near: *the house is close by.* **14** away; aside: *he put some money by each week.* **15** passing a point near something; past: *he drove by.* ◆ *n, pl* **byes. 16** a variant spelling of **bye**[1]. ORIG OE *bī*

by- *or* **bye-** *prefix* **1** near: *bystander.* **2** secondary or incidental: *by-election; by-product.* ORIG from BY

by and by *adv* presently or eventually.

by and large *adv* in general; on the whole. ORIG C17: orig. nautical: to the wind and off it

Byatt ★ (ˈbaɪət) *n* Dame **A**(**ntonia**) **S**(**usan**). born 1936, British writer. Her novels include *The Virgin in the Garden* (1978), *Possession* (1990), and *Babel Tower* (1996).

Bydgoszcz ★ (*Polish* ˈbidgɔʃtʃ) *n* an industrial city and port in N Poland: under Prussian rule from 1772 to 1919. Pop.: 385 700 (1995 est.). German name: **Bromberg.**

bye[1] (baɪ) *n* **1** *Sport.* the situation in which a player or team wins a preliminary round by virtue of having no opponent. **2** *Golf.* one or more holes that are left unplayed after the match has been decided. **3** *Cricket.* a run scored off a ball not struck by the batsman. **4** something incidental or secondary. **5 by the bye.** incidentally; by the way. ORIG C16: var. of BY

bye[2] *or* **bye-bye** *sentence substitute. Brit. inf.* goodbye.

bye-byes *n* (*functioning as sing*) an informal word for **sleep,** used esp. to children (as in **go to bye-byes**).

by-election *or* **bye-election** *n* (in Great Britain and other countries of the Commonwealth) an election held during the life of a parliament to fill a vacant seat.

Byelgorod-Dnestrovski ★ (*Russian* ˈbjelgərətdnjɪˈstrɔfskij) *n* a variant spelling of **Belgorod-Dnestrovski.**

Byelorussia ★ (ˌbjeləʊˈrʌʃə) *n* a variant spelling of **Belarus.**
▸ **Byelorussian** (ˌbjɛləʊˈrʌʃən) *adj, n*

Byelostok ★ (bjɪlaˈstɔk) *n* a Russian name for **Białystok.**

Byelovo *or* **Belovo** ★ (*Russian* ˈbjɛləvə) *n* a city in W central Russia. Pop.: 118 000 (1989).

bygone (ˈbaɪˌgɒn) *adj* **1** (*usually prenominal*) past; former. ◆ *n* **2** (*often pl*) a past occurrence. **3** an artefact, implement, etc., of former domestic or industrial use. **4 let bygones be bygones.** to agree to forget past quarrels.

bylaw *or* **bye-law** (ˈbaɪˌlɔː) *n* **1** a rule made by a local authority. **2** a regulation of a company, society, etc. ORIG C13: prob. of Scand. origin; cf. ON *bȳr* dwelling, town

by-line *n* **1** a line under the title of a newspaper or magazine article giving the author's name. **2** another word for **touchline.**

Byng ★ (bɪŋ) *n* **1 George,** Viscount Torrington. 1663–1733, British admiral: defeated fleet of James Edward Stuart, the Old Pretender, off Scotland (1708); defeated Spanish fleet off Messina (1717). **2** his son **John.** 1704–57, British admiral: executed after failing to relieve Minorca. **3 Julian Hedworth George,** 1st Viscount Byng of Vimy. 1862–1935, British general in World War I; governor general of Canada (1921–26).

BYO(G) *n Austral. & NZ.* an unlicensed restaurant at which diners may drink their own wine, etc. ORIG C20: from *bring your own (grog)*

bypass ('baɪˌpɑːs) *n* **1** a main road built to avoid a city or other congested area. **2** a means of redirecting the flow of a substance around an appliance through which it would otherwise pass. **3** *Surgery.* **3a** the redirection of blood flow, either to avoid a diseased blood vessel or in order to perform heart surgery. See **coronary bypass.** **3b** (*as modifier*): *bypass surgery.* **4** *Electronics.* an electrical circuit connected in parallel around one or more components, providing an alternative path for certain frequencies. ◆ *vb* (*tr*) **5** to go around or avoid (a city, obstruction, problem, etc.). **6** to cause (traffic, fluid, etc.) to go through a bypass. **7** to proceed without reference to (regulations, a superior, etc.); get round; avoid.

bypass engine *n* a gas turbine in which part of the compressor delivery bypasses the combustion zone, flowing directly into or around the exhaust to provide additional thrust.

bypath ('baɪˌpɑːθ) *n* a little-used path or track.

by-play *n* secondary action or talking carried on apart while the main action proceeds, esp. in a play.

by-product *n* **1** a secondary or incidental product of a manufacturing process. **2** a side effect.

Byrd ★ (bɜːd) *n* **1 Richard Evelyn.** 1888–1957, US rear admiral, aviator, and polar explorer. **2 William.** 1543–1623, English composer and organist.

Byrd Land ★ *n* a part of Antarctica, east of the Ross Ice Shelf and the Ross Sea: claimed for the US by Richard E. Byrd in 1929. Former name: **Marie Byrd Land.**

byre ('baɪə) *n Brit.* a shelter for cows. ORIG OE *bȳre;* rel. to *būr* hut, cottage

byroad ('baɪˌrəʊd) *n* a secondary or side road.

Byron ★ ('baɪərən) *n* **George Gordon,** 6th Baron. 1788–1824, British poet. His major works include *Childe Harold's Pilgrimage* (1812–18), and *Don Juan* (1819–24). ▸ **Byronic** (baɪ'rɒnɪk) *adj* ▸ **By'ronically** *adv* ▸ **'Byronˌism** *n*

byssinosis (ˌbɪsɪ'nəʊsɪs) *n* a lung disease caused by prolonged inhalation of fibre dust. ORIG C19: from NL, from Gk *bussinos* of linen + -OSIS

bystander ('baɪˌstændə) *n* a person present but not involved; onlooker; spectator.

byte (baɪt) *n Computing.* **1** a group of bits processed as one unit of data. **2** the storage space allocated to such a group of bits. **3** a subdivision of a word. ORIG C20: prob. a blend of BIT[4] + BITE

Bytom ★ (*Polish* 'bitɔm) *n* an industrial city in SW Poland, in Upper Silesia: under Prussian and German rule from 1742 to 1945. Pop.: 228 200 (1995 est.). German name: **Beuthen.**

byway ('baɪˌweɪ) *n* **1** a secondary or side road, esp. in the country. **2** an area, field of study, etc., that is very obscure or of secondary importance.

byword ('baɪˌwɜːd) *n* **1** a person or thing regarded as a perfect or proverbial example of something: *their name is a byword for good service.* **2** an object of scorn or derision. **3** a common saying; proverb. ORIG OE *bīwyrde;* see BY, WORD

Byzantine (bɪ'zænˌtaɪn, -ˌtiːn, baɪ-; 'bɪzənˌtiːn, -ˌtaɪn) *adj* **1** of, characteristic of, or relating to Byzantium or the Byzantine Empire. **2** of, relating to, or characterizing the Orthodox Church or its rites and liturgy. **3** of or relating to the highly coloured stylized form of religious art developed in the Byzantine Empire. **4** of or relating to the style of architecture developed in the Byzantine Empire, characterized by massive domes with square bases, rounded arches, spires and minarets, and the extensive use of mosaics. **5** denoting the Medieval Greek spoken in the Byzantine Empire. **6** (of attitudes, etc.) inflexible or complicated. ◆ *n* **7** an inhabitant of Byzantium. ▸ **Byzantinism** (bɪ'zæntaɪˌnɪzəm, -tiː, baɪ-; 'bɪzəntiːˌnɪzəm, -taɪ-) *n*

Byzantine Empire ★ *n* the continuation of the Roman Empire in the East, esp. after the deposition of the last emperor in Rome (476 A.D.). It was finally extinguished by the fall of Constantinople, its capital, in 1453.

Byzantium ★ (bɪ'zæntɪəm, baɪ-) *n* an ancient Greek city on the Bosphorus: founded about 660 B.C.; rebuilt by Constantine I in 330 A.D. and called Constantinople; present-day Istanbul.

Bz *or* **bz.** *abbrev. for* benzene.

Cc

c *or* **C** (si:) *n, pl* **c's, C's,** *or* **Cs. 1** the third letter of the English alphabet. **2** a speech sound represented by this letter, usually either as in *cigar* or as in *case.* **3** the third in a series, esp. the third highest grade in an examination. **4** something shaped like a C.

c *symbol for:* **1** centi-. **2** *Maths.* constant. **3** cubic. **4** cycle. **5** specific heat capacity. **6** the speed of light and other types of electromagnetic radiation in free space.

C *symbol for:* **1** *Music.* **1a** the first degree of a major scale containing no sharps or flats (**C major**). **1b** the major or minor key having this note as its tonic. **1c** a time signature denoting four crotchet beats to the bar. See also **alla breve** (sense 2), **common time. 2** *Chem.* carbon. **3** *Biochem.* cytosine. **4** capacitance. **5** heat capacity. **6** cold (water). **7** *Physics.* compliance. **8** Celsius. **9** centigrade. **10** century: *C20.* **11** coulomb. **12** *the Roman numeral for* 100. ◆ *n* **13** a type of high-level computer programming language.

c. *abbrev. for:* **1** carat. **2** carbon (paper). **3** *Cricket.* caught. **4** cent(s). **5** century *or* centuries. **6** (*pl* **cc.**) chapter. **7** (used esp. preceding a date) circa: *c. 1800.* ORIG L: about **8** colt. **9** contralto. **10** copyright. **11** coulomb.

C. *abbrev. for:* **1** (on maps as part of name) Cape. **2** Catholic. **3** Celtic. **4** Conservative. **5** Corps.

c/- (in Australia) *abbrev. for* care for.

C1 ('si:'wʌn) *n* **a** a person whose job is supervisory or clerical, or who works in junior management. **b** (*as adj*): *a C1 worker.* ◆ See also **occupation groupings.**

C2 ('si:'tu:) *n* **a** a skilled manual worker, or a manual worker with responsibility for other people. **b** (*as adj*): *a C2 worker.* ◆ See also **occupation groupings.**

Ca *the chemical symbol for* calcium.

CA *abbrev. for:* **1** California. **2** Central America. **3** chartered accountant. **4** Civil Aviation. **5** (in Britain) Consumers' Association.

ca. *abbrev. for* circa. ORIG L: about

CAA (in Britain) *abbrev. for* Civil Aviation Authority.

Caaba ('kɑ:bə) *n* a variant spelling of **Kaaba.**

cab (kæb) *n* **1a** a taxi. **1b** (*as modifier*): *a cab rank.* **2** the enclosed compartment of a lorry, crane, etc., from which it is driven. **3** (formerly) a horse-drawn vehicle used for public hire. ORIG C19: from CABRIOLET

cabal (kə'bæl) *n* **1** a small group of intriguers, esp. one formed for political purposes. **2** a secret plot; conspiracy. **3** a clique. ◆ *vb* **cabals, caballing, caballed. 4** (*intr*) to form a cabal; plot. ORIG C17: from F *cabale,* from Med. L *cabala*

cabala (kə'bɑ:lə) *n* a variant spelling of **cabbala.**

Caballé ★ (*Spanish* kaβa'ʎe) *n* **Montserrat** (monser'rat). born 1933, Spanish operatic soprano.

caballero (ˌkæbə'ljɛərəʊ) *n, pl* **caballeros** (-rəʊz). a Spanish gentleman. ORIG C19: from Sp.: gentleman, from LL *caballārius* rider, from *caballus* horse

cabana (kə'bɑ:nə) *n Chiefly US.* a tent used as a dressing room by the sea. ORIG from Sp. *cabaña:* CABIN

cabaret ('kæbəˌreɪ) *n* **1** a floor show of dancing, singing, etc., at a nightclub or restaurant. **2** *Chiefly US.* a nightclub or restaurant providing such entertainment. ORIG C17: from Norman F: tavern, prob. from LL *camera* an arched roof

cabbage ('kæbɪdʒ) *n* **1** Also called: **cole.** any of various cultivated varieties of a plant of the genus *Brassica* having a short thick stalk and a large head of green or reddish edible leaves. See also **brassica. 2a** the head of a cabbage. **2b** the edible leaf bud of the cabbage palm. **3** *Inf.* a dull or unimaginative person. **4** *Inf.* a person who has no mental faculties and is dependent on others. ORIG C14: from Norman F *caboche* head

cabbage palm *n* **1** a West Indian palm whose leaf buds are eaten like cabbage. **2** a similar Brazilian palm.

cabbage rose *n* a rose with a round compact full-petalled head.

cabbage tree *n* **1** a tall palmlike ornamental New Zealand tree. **2** a tall palm tree of Eastern Australia.

cabbage white *n* a large white butterfly, the larvae of which feed on the leaves of cabbages and related vegetables.

cabbala, cabala, kabbala, *or* **kabala** (kə'bɑ:lə) *n* **1** an ancient Jewish mystical tradition. **2** any secret or occult doctrine. ORIG C16: from Med. L, from Heb. *qabbālāh* tradition, from *qābal* to receive
▸ **cabbalism, cabalism, kabbalism,** *or* **kabalism** ('kæbəˌlɪzəm) *n* ▸ **'cabbalist, 'cabalist, 'kabbalist,** *or* **'kabalist** *n* ▸ **ˌcabba'listic, ˌcaba'listic, ˌkabba'listic,** *or* **ˌkaba'listic** *adj*

cabbie *or* **cabby** ('kæbɪ) *n, pl* **cabbies.** *Inf.* a cab driver.

caber ('keɪbə) *n Scot.* a heavy section of trimmed tree trunk thrown in competition at Highland games (**tossing the caber**). ORIG C16: from Gaelic *cabar* pole

Cabernet Sauvignon ('kæbəneɪ 'səʊvɪnjɒn; *French* kabɛrnɛ soviɲɔ̃) *n* (*sometimes not caps.*) **1** a black grape grown in the Bordeaux area of France, Australia, California, Bulgaria, and elsewhere, used for making wine. **2** any of various red wines made from this grape. ORIG F

cabin ('kæbɪn) *n* **1** a small simple dwelling; hut. **2** a simple house providing accommodation for travellers or holiday-makers. **3** a room used as an office or living quarters in a ship. **4** a covered compartment used for shelter in a small boat. **5** *Brit.* another name for **signal box. 6a** the enclosed part of a light aircraft in which the pilot and passengers sit. **6b** the part of an aircraft for passengers or cargo. ◆ *vb* **7** (*tr*) to confine in a small space. ORIG C14: from OF *cabane,* from OProvençal *cabana,* from LL *capanna* hut

cabin boy *n* a boy who waits on the officers and passengers of a ship.

cabin cruiser *n* a power boat fitted with a cabin for pleasure cruising or racing.

Cabinda ★ (kə'bi:ndə) *n* an exclave of Angola, separated from the rest of the country by part of the Democratic Republic of Congo (formerly Zaïre). Pop.: 174 000 (1993 est.). Area: 7270 sq. km (2807 sq. miles).

cabinet ('kæbɪnɪt) *n* **1** a piece of furniture containing shelves, cupboards, or drawers for storage or display. **2** the outer case of a television, radio, etc. **3a** (*often cap.*) the executive and policy-making body of a country, consisting of senior government ministers. **3b** (*sometimes cap.*) an advisory council to a president, governor, etc. **3c** (*as modifier*): *a cabinet reshuffle.* **4a** a standard size of paper, 6 × 4 inches (15 × 10 cm), for mounted photographs. **4b** (*as modifier*): *a cabinet photograph.* **5** *Arch.* a private room. ORIG C16: from OF, dim. of *cabine,* from ?

cabinet-maker *n* a craftsman specializing in making fine furniture.
▸ **'cabinet-ˌmaking** *n*

cabinetwork ('kæbɪnɪtˌwɜ:k) *n* **1** the making of furniture, esp. of fine quality. **2** an article made by a cabinet-maker.

cabin fever *n Canad.* acute depression resulting from being isolated or sharing cramped quarters in the wilderness.

cable ('keɪbᵊl) *n* **1** a strong thick rope, usually of twisted hemp or steel wire. **2** *Naut.* an anchor chain or rope. **3a** a unit of distance in navigation, equal to one tenth of a sea mile (about 600 ft). **3b** Also called: **cable length, cable's length.** a unit of length in nautical use that has various values, including 100 fathoms (600 ft). **4** a wire or bundle of wires that conducts electricity: *a submarine cable.* **5** Also called: **cablegram.** a telegram sent abroad by submarine cable, telephone line, etc. **6** Also called: **cable stitch.** a

★ people and places

knitting pattern resembling a twisted rope. ◆ *vb* **cables, cabling, cabled. 7** to send (a message) to (someone) by cable. **8** (*tr*) to fasten or provide with a cable or cables. **9** (*tr*) to supply (a place) with cable television. ORIG C13: from OF, from LL *capulum* halter

cable car *n* **1** a cabin suspended from and moved by an overhead cable in a mountain area. **2** the passenger car on a **cable railway**, drawn along by a strong cable operated by a motor.

cable television *n* a television service in which the subscriber's television is connected to the supplier by cable, enabling a much greater choice of channels to be provided.

cabochon ('kæbəˌʃɒn) *n* a smooth domed gem, polished but unfaceted. ORIG C16: from OF, from *caboche* head

caboodle (kə'buːdᵊl) *n Inf.* a lot, bunch, or group (esp. in **the whole caboodle**). ORIG C19: prob. contraction of KIT[1] & BOODLE

caboose (kə'buːs) *n* **1** *US inf.* short for **calaboose. 2** *Railways. US & Canad.* a guard's van. **3** *Naut.* **3a** a deckhouse for a galley aboard ship. **3b** *Chiefly Brit.* the galley itself. **4** *Canad.* **4a** a mobile bunkhouse used by lumbermen, etc. **4b** an insulated cabin on runners, equipped with a stove. ORIG C18: from Du. *cabūse,* from ?

Cabot ★ ('kæbət) *n* **1 John,** Italian name *Giovanni Caboto.* 1450–98, Italian explorer, who landed in North America in 1497, under patent from Henry VII of England. **2** his son, **Sebastian.** ?1476–1557, Italian navigator and cartographer who served the English and Spanish crowns: explored Brazil (1526–30).

cabotage ('kæbəˌtɑːʒ) *n* **1** *Naut.* coastal navigation or shipping. **2** reservation to a country's carriers of its internal traffic, esp. air traffic. ORIG C19: from F, from *caboter* to sail near the coast, apparently from Sp. *cabo* CAPE[2]

Cabral ★ (*Portuguese* kə'brɑl) *n* **Pedro Álvarez** ('pɛːdru 'ɑlvərəʃ). ?1460–?1526, Portuguese navigator: took possession of Brazil for Portugal in 1500.

cabriole ('kæbrɪˌəʊl) *n* a type of curved furniture leg, popular in the first half of the 18th century. Also called: **cabriole leg.** ORIG C18: from F, from *cabrioler* to caper; from its being based on the leg of a capering animal

cabriolet (ˌkæbrɪəʊ'leɪ) *n* **1** a small two-wheeled horse-drawn carriage with two seats and a folding hood. **2** a type of motorcar with a folding top. ORIG C18: from F, lit.: a little skip, from L, from *caper* goat; referring to the lightness of movement

cacao (kə'kɑːəʊ, -'keɪəʊ) *n* **1** a small tropical American evergreen tree having reddish-brown seed pods from which cocoa and chocolate are prepared. **2 cacao bean.** the seed pod; cocoa bean. **3 cacao butter.** another name for **cocoa butter.** ORIG C16: from Sp., from Nahuatl *cacauatl* cacao beans

cachalot ('kæʃəˌlɒt) *n* another name for **sperm whale.** ORIG C18: from F, from Port. *cachalote,* from ?

cache (kæʃ) *n* **1** a hidden store of provisions, weapons, treasure, etc. **2** the place where such a store is hidden. **3** *Computing.* a small high-speed memory that improves computer performance. ◆ *vb* **caches, caching, cached. 4** (*tr*) to store in a cache. ORIG C19: from F, from *cacher* to hide

cachepot ('kæʃˌpɒt, kæʃ'pəʊ) *n* an ornamental container for a flowerpot. ORIG F: pot-hider

cachet ('kæʃeɪ) *n* **1** an official seal on a document, letter, etc. **2** a distinguishing mark. **3** prestige; distinction. **4** *Philately.* a mark stamped by hand on mail for commemorative purposes. **5** a hollow wafer, formerly used for enclosing an unpleasant-tasting medicine. ORIG C17: from OF, from *cacher* to hide

cachexia (kə'kɛksɪə) *or* **cachexy** *n* a weakened condition of body or mind resulting from any debilitating disease. ORIG C16: from LL, from Gk, from *kakos* bad + *hexis* condition

cachinnate ('kækɪˌneɪt) *vb* **cachinnates, cachinnating, cachinnated.** (*intr*) to laugh loudly. ORIG C19: from L *cacchināre,* prob. imit.
▸ ˌ**cachin'nation** *n* ▸ ˌ**cachin'natory** *adj*

cachou ('kæʃuː, kæ'ʃuː) *n* **1** a lozenge eaten to sweeten the breath. **2** another name for **catechu.** ORIG C18: via F from Port., from Malay *kāchu*

cacique (kə'siːk) *or* **cazique** (kə'ziːk) *n* **1** an American Indian chief in a Spanish-speaking region. **2** (esp. in Spanish America) a local political boss. ORIG C16: from Sp., of Amerind origin

cack-handed (ˌkæk'hændɪd) *adj Inf.* **1** left-handed. **2** clumsy. ORIG from dialect *cack* excrement

cackle ('kækᵊl) *vb* **cackles, cackling, cackled. 1** (*intr*) (esp. of a hen) to squawk with shrill broken notes. **2** (*intr*) to laugh or chatter raucously. **3** (*tr*) to utter in a cackling manner. ◆ *n* **4** the noise or act of cackling. **5** noisy chatter. **6 cut the cackle.** *Inf.* to be quiet. ORIG C13: prob. from MLow G *kākelen,* imit.

caco- *combining form.* bad, unpleasant, or incorrect: *cacophony.* ORIG from Gk *kakos* bad

cacodyl ('kækəˌdaɪl) *n* an oily poisonous liquid with a strong garlic smell; tetramethyldiarsine. ORIG C19: from Gk, from *kakos* CACO- + *ozein* to smell + -YL

cacoethes (ˌkækəʊ'iːθiːz) *n* an uncontrollable urge or desire: *a cacoethes for smoking.* ORIG C16: from L *cacoēthes* malignant disease, from Gk, from *kakos* CACO- + *ēthos* character

cacography (kæ'kɒgrəfɪ) *n* **1** bad handwriting. **2** incorrect spelling.
▸ **cacographic** (ˌkækə'græfɪk) *adj*

cacophony (kə'kɒfənɪ) *n, pl* **cacophonies.** harsh discordant sound.
▸ **ca'cophonous** *adj*

cactus ('kæktəs) *n, pl* **cactuses** *or* **cacti** (-taɪ). **1** any of a family of spiny succulent plants of the arid regions of America with swollen tough stems and leaves reduced to spines. **2 cactus dahlia.** a double-flowered variety of dahlia. ORIG C17: from L: prickly plant, from Gk *kaktos* cardoon
▸ **cactaceous** (kæk'teɪʃəs) *adj*

> **USAGE NOTE** The plural *cacti* is the preferred form in all contexts, according to the Bank of English. It is about ten times commoner than the alternative plural, *cactuses.*

cacuminal (kæ'kjuːmɪnᵊl) *Phonetics.* ◆ *adj* **1** denoting a consonant articulated with the tip of the tongue turned back towards the hard palate. ◆ *n* **2** a consonant articulated in this manner. ORIG C19: from L *cacūmen* point

cad (kæd) *n Brit. inf. old-fashioned.* a man who does not behave in a gentlemanly manner towards others. ORIG C18: from CADDIE
▸ **'caddish** *adj*

CAD (kæd) *n acronym for* computer-aided design.

cadaver (kə'deɪvə, -'dɑːv-) *n Med.* a corpse. ORIG C16: from L, from *cadere* to fall
▸ **cadaveric** (kə'dævərɪk) *adj*

cadaverous (kə'dævərəs) *adj* **1** of or like a corpse, esp. in being deathly pale. **2** thin and haggard.
▸ **ca'daverousness** *n*

Cadbury ★ ('kædbərɪ) *n* **George.** 1839–1922, British Quaker industrialist and philanthropist. He established, with his brother **Richard Cadbury** (1835–99), the chocolate-making company Cadbury Brothers and the garden village Bournville, near Birmingham, for their workers.

CADCAM ('kædˌkæm) *n acronym for* computer-aided design and manufacture.

caddie *or* **caddy** ('kædɪ) *Golf.* ◆ *n, pl* **caddies. 1** an attendant who carries clubs, etc., for a player. ◆ *vb* **caddies, caddying, caddied. 2** (*intr*) to act as a caddie. ORIG C17 (C18 (Scot.): an errand-boy): from F CADET

caddis fly *n* a small mothlike insect having two pairs of hairy wings and aquatic larvae (caddis worms). ORIG C17: from ?

caddis worm *or* **caddis** ('kædɪs) *n* the aquatic larva of a caddis fly, which constructs a protective case around itself made of silk, sand, stones, etc. Also called: **caseworm, strawworm.**

★ people and places

caddy[1] ('kædɪ) *n, pl* **caddies.** *Chiefly Brit.* a small container, esp. for tea. ORIG C18: from Malay *kati*

caddy[2] ('kædɪ) *n, pl* **caddies,** *vb* **caddies, caddying, caddied.** a variant spelling of **caddie.**

Cade ★ (keɪd) *n* **Jack.** died 1450, English leader of the Kentish rebellion.

cadence ('keɪdᵊns) *or* **cadency** *n, pl* **cadences** *or* **cadencies. 1** the beat or measure of something rhythmic. **2** a fall in the pitch of the voice, as at the end of a sentence. **3** intonation. **4** rhythm in verse or prose. **5** the close of a musical phrase. ORIG C14: from OF, from OIt. *cadenza,* lit.: a falling, from L *cadere* to fall

cadenza (kə'dɛnzə) *n* **1** a virtuoso solo passage occurring near the end of a piece of music, formerly improvised by the soloist. **2** *S. African inf.* a fit or convulsion. ORIG C19: from It.; see CADENCE

cadet (kə'dɛt) *n* **1** a young person undergoing preliminary training, usually before full entry to the uniformed services, police, etc. **2** (in England and in France before 1789) a gentleman who entered the army to prepare for a commission. **3** a younger son. **4 cadet branch.** the family of a younger son. **5** (in New Zealand, formerly) a person learning sheep farming on a sheep station. ORIG C17: from F, from dialect *capdet* captain, ult. from L *caput* head
▸ **ca'detship** *n*

cadge (kædʒ) *vb* **cadges, cadging, cadged. 1** to get (food, money, etc.) by sponging or begging. ◆ *n* **2** *Brit.* a person who cadges. ORIG C17: from ?
▸ **'cadger** *n*

cadi *or* **kadi** ('kɑːdɪ, 'keɪdɪ) *n, pl* **cadis** *or* **kadis.** a judge in a Muslim community. ORIG C16: from Ar. *qādī* judge

Cádiz ★ (kə'dɪz; *Spanish* 'kaðiθ) *n* a port in SW Spain, on a narrow peninsula that forms the **Bay of Cádiz** at the E end of the **Gulf of Cádiz:** founded about 1100 B.C. as a Phoenician trading colony; centre of trade with America from the 16th to 18th centuries. Pop.: 155 438 (1994 est.).

Cadmean victory ('kædmɪən) *n* another name for **Pyrrhic victory.**

cadmium ('kædmɪəm) *n* a malleable bluish-white metallic element that occurs in association with zinc ores. It is used in electroplating and alloys. Symbol: Cd; atomic no.: 48; atomic wt.: 112.4. ORIG C19: from NL, from L *cadmīa* zinc ore, CALAMINE: both calamine and cadmium are found in the ore

cadmium yellow *n* an orange or yellow insoluble solid (cadmium sulphide) used as a pigment in paints, etc.

Cadmus ★ ('kædməs) *n Greek myth.* a Phoenician prince who killed a dragon and planted its teeth, from which sprang a multitude of warriors who fought among themselves until only five remained, who joined Cadmus to found Thebes.
▸ **'Cadmean** *adj*

cadre ('kɑːdə) *n* **1** the nucleus of trained professional servicemen forming the basis for military expansion. **2** a group of activists, esp. in the Communist Party. **3** a basic unit or structure; nucleus. **4** a member of a cadre. ORIG C19: from F, from It. *quadro,* from L *quadrum* square

caduceus (kə'djuːsɪəs) *n, pl* **caducei** (-sɪˌaɪ). **1** *Classical myth.* a winged staff entwined with two serpents carried by Hermes (Mercury) as messenger of the gods. **2** an insignia resembling this staff used as an emblem of the medical profession. ORIG C16: from L, from Doric Gk *karukeion,* from *karux* herald

caducous (kə'djuːkəs) *adj Biol.* (of parts of a plant or animal) shed during the life of the organism. ORIG C17: from L, from *cadere* to fall

Cadwalader ★ (kæd'wɒlədə) *n* 7th century A.D., legendary king of the Britons, probably a confusion of several historical figures.

caecilian (siː'sɪlɪən) *n* a tropical limbless cylindrical amphibian resembling the earthworm and inhabiting moist soil. ORIG C19: from L, from *caecus* blind

caecum *or US* **cecum** ('siːkəm) *n, pl* **caeca** *or US* **ceca** (-kə). *Anat.* any structure that ends in a blind sac or pouch, esp. that at the beginning of the large intestine. ORIG C18: short for L *intestinum caecum* blind intestine, translation of Gk *tuphlon enteron*
▸ **'caecal** *or US* **'cecal** *adj*

Cædmon ★ ('kædmən) *n* 7th century A.D., Anglo-Saxon poet and monk, the earliest English poet whose name survives.

Caelian ★ ('siːlɪən) *n* the southeasternmost of the Seven Hills of Rome.

Caen ★ (kɒŋ; *French* kɑ̃) *n* an industrial city in NW France. Pop.: 115 624 (1990).

Caenozoic (ˌsiːnə'zəʊɪk) *adj* a variant spelling of **Cenozoic.**

Caernarfon, Caernarvon, *or* **Carnarvon ★** (kɑː'nɑːvᵊn) *n* a port and resort in NW Wales, in Gwynedd on the Menai Strait: 13th-century castle. Pop.: 9695 (1991).

Caernarvonshire ★ (kɑː'nɑːvᵊnˌʃɪə, -ʃə) *n* (until 1974) a county of NW Wales, now part of Gwynedd.

Caerphilly ★ (kɛə'fɪlɪ) *n* **1** a market town in SE Wales, in SE Mid Glamorgan: site of the largest castle in Wales (13th–14th centuries). Pop.: 28 481 (1991). **2** a county borough in SE Wales, created in 1996 from parts of Mid Glamorgan and Gwent. Pop.: 170 000 (1996 est.). Area: 275 sq. km (106 sq. miles). **3** a creamy white mild-flavoured cheese.

Caesar ★ ('siːzə) *n* **1 Gaius Julius** ('gaɪəs 'dʒuːlɪəs). 100–44 B.C., Roman general and historian. He formed the first triumvirate with Pompey and Crassus (60), conquered Gaul (58–50), invaded Britain (55–54), mastered Italy (49), and defeated Pompey (46): assassinated by Marcus Brutus and Cassius Longinus. **2** any Roman emperor. **3** (*sometimes not cap.*) any emperor, autocrat, dictator, or other powerful ruler. **4** a title of the Roman emperors from Augustus to Hadrian. **5** (in the Roman Empire) **5a** a title borne by the imperial heir from the reign of Hadrian. **5b** the heir, deputy, and subordinate ruler to either of the two emperors under Diocletian's system of government.

Caesaraugusta ★ (ˌsiːzərɔː'gʌstə) *n* the Latin name for **Zaragoza.**

Caesarea ★ (ˌsiːzə'rɪə) *n* an ancient port in NW Israel, capital of Roman Palestine: founded by Herod the Great.

Caesarean, Caesarian, *or US* **Cesarean, Cesarian** (sɪ'zɛərɪən) *adj* **1** of or relating to any of the Caesars, esp. Julius Caesar. ◆ *n* **2** (*sometimes not cap.*) *Surgery.* **2a** a Caesarean section. **2b** (*as modifier*): *Caesarean operation.*

Caesarean section *n* surgical incision through the abdominal and uterine walls in order to deliver a baby. ORIG C17: from the belief that Julius Caesar was so delivered, the name allegedly being derived from *caedere* to cut

caesious *or US* **cesious** ('siːzɪəs) *adj Bot.* having a waxy bluish-grey coating. ORIG C19: from L *caesius* bluish grey

caesium *or US* **cesium** ('siːzɪəm) *n* a ductile silvery-white element of the alkali metal group. It is used in photocells and in an atomic clock (**caesium clock**) that uses the frequency of radiation from changing the spin of electrons. The radioisotope **caesium-137,** with a half-life of 30.2 years, is used in radiotherapy. Symbol: Cs; atomic no.: 55; atomic wt.: 132.905.

caesura (sɪ'zjʊərə) *n, pl* **caesuras** *or* **caesurae** (-riː). **1** (in modern prosody) a pause, esp. for sense, usually near the middle of a verse line. **2** (in classical prosody) a break between words within a metrical foot. ORIG C16: from L, lit.: a cutting, from *caedere* to cut
▸ **cae'sural** *adj*

Caetano ★ (kaɪ'tɑːnəʊ; *Portuguese* kɑi'tɐnu) *n* **Marcello** (mar'selu). 1906–80, Portuguese statesman; prime minister (1968–74).

café ('kæfeɪ, 'kæfɪ) *n* **1** a small or inexpensive restaurant serving light or easily prepared meals and refreshments. **2** *S. African.* a corner shop or grocer. ORIG C19: from F: COFFEE

café au lait *French.* (kafe o lɛ) *n* **1** coffee with milk. **2a** a light brown colour. **2b** (*as adj*): *café au lait brocade.*

café noir *French.* (kafe nwar) *n* black coffee.

cafeteria (ˌkæfɪˈtɪərɪə) *n* a self-service restaurant. ORIG C20: from American Sp.: coffee shop

caff (kæf) *n* a slang word for **café.**

caffeine *or* **caffein** (ˈkæfiːn) *n* a white crystalline bitter alkaloid responsible for the stimulant action of tea, coffee, and cocoa. ORIG C19: from G *Kaffein,* from *Kaffee* COFFEE

caftan (ˈkæfˌtæn, -ˌtɑːn) *n* a variant spelling of **kaftan.**

cage (keɪdʒ) *n* **1a** an enclosure, usually made with bars or wire, for keeping birds, monkeys, etc. **1b** (*in combination*): *cagebird.* **2** a thing or place that confines. **3** something resembling a cage in function or structure: *the rib cage.* **4** the enclosed platform of a lift, esp. as used in a mine. ◆ *vb* **cages, caging, caged. 5** (*tr*) to confine in or as in a cage. ORIG C13: from OF, from L *cavea* enclosure, from *cavus* hollow

Cage ★ (keɪdʒ) *n* **John.** 1912–92, US composer of such experimental works as *Imaginary Landscape* (1951) and *Apartment Building 1776* (1976).

cagey *or* **cagy** (ˈkeɪdʒɪ) *adj* **cagier, cagiest.** *Inf.* not frank; wary. ORIG C20: from ?
▸ **ˈcaginess** *n*

Cagliari ★ (kælˈjɑːrɪ; *Italian* ˈkaʎʎari) *n* a port in Italy, the capital of Sardinia, on the S coast. Pop.: 174 543 (1996 est.).

Cagney ★ (ˈkægnɪ) *n* **James.** 1899–1986, US actor, esp. in gangster roles; his films include *The Public Enemy* (1931) and *Yankee Doodle Dandy* (1942).

cagoule (kəˈguːl) *n* a lightweight usually knee-length type of anorak. ORIG C20: from F

Cahokia Mounds ★ (kəˈhəʊkɪə) *pl n* the largest group of prehistoric Indian earthworks in the US, located northeast of East St Louis.

cahoots (kəˈhuːts) *pl n* (*sometimes sing*) *Inf.* **1** *US.* partnership; league. **2 in cahoots.** in collusion. ORIG C19: from ?

Caiaphas ★ (ˈkaɪəˌfæs) *n New Testament.* the high priest at the beginning of John the Baptist's preaching and during the trial of Jesus (Luke 3:2; Matthew 26).

Caicos Islands ★ (ˈkeɪkəs) *pl n* a group of islands in the Caribbean: part of the British dependency of the **Turks and Caicos Islands.**

caiman (ˈkeɪmən) *n, pl* **caimans.** a variant spelling of **cayman.**

Cain ★ (keɪn) *n* **1** the first son of Adam and Eve, who killed his brother Abel (Genesis 4:1–16). **2 raise Cain. 2a** to cause a commotion. **2b** to react or protest heatedly.

Caine ★ (keɪn) *n* Sir **Michael.** real name *Maurice Micklewhite.* born 1933, British film actor. His films include *The Ipcress File* (1965) and *The Cider House Rules* (1999).

Cainozoic (ˌkaɪnəʊˈzəʊɪk, ˌkeɪ-) *adj* a variant spelling of **Cenozoic.**

caïque (kaɪˈiːk) *n* **1** a long rowing skiff used on the Bosporus. **2** a sailing vessel of the E Mediterranean with a square topsail. ORIG C17: from F, from It. *caicco,* from Turkish *kayik*

Caird Coast ★ (kɛəd) *n* a region of Antarctica: a part of Coats Land on the SE coast of the Weddell Sea; now included in the British Antarctic Territory.

cairn (kɛən) *n* **1** a mound of stones erected as a memorial or marker. **2** Also called: **cairn terrier.** a small rough-haired breed of terrier orig. from Scotland. ORIG C15: from Gaelic *carn*

cairngorm (ˌkɛənˈgɔːm) *n* a smoky yellow or brown variety of quartz, used as a gemstone. Also called: **smoky quartz.** ORIG C18: from *Cairn Gorm* (lit.: blue cairn), mountain in Scotland

Cairngorm Mountains ★ *pl n* a mountain range of NE Scotland: part of the Grampians. Highest peak: Ben Macdhui, 1309 m (4296 ft). Also called: **the Cairngorms.**

Cairo ★ (ˈkaɪrəʊ) *n* the capital of Egypt, on the Nile: the largest city in Africa and in the Middle East; industrial centre; site of the university and mosque of Al Azhar (founded in 972). Pop.: 6 849 000 (1994 est.). Arabic name: **El Qahira** (ɛl ˈkahiːrɔ).
▸ **ˈCairene** *n, adj*

★ people and places

caisson (kəˈsuːn, ˈkeɪsᵊn) *n* **1** a watertight chamber open at the bottom and containing air under pressure, used to carry out construction work under water. **2** a watertight float filled with air, used to raise sunken ships. **3** a watertight structure placed across the entrance of a dry dock, etc., to exclude water. **4a** a box containing explosives formerly used as a mine. **4b** an ammunition chest. ORIG C18: from F, assimilated to *caisse* CASE[2]

caisson disease *n* another name for **decompression sickness.**

Caithness ★ (keɪθˈnɛs, ˈkeɪθnɛs) *n* (until 1975) a county of NE Scotland, now part of Highland.

caitiff (ˈkeɪtɪf) *Arch. or poetic.* ◆ *n* **1** a cowardly or base person. ◆ *adj* **2** cowardly. ORIG C13: from OF, from L *captīvus* CAPTIVE

Caius ★ (ˈkaɪəs) *n* a variant of **Gaius.**

cajole (kəˈdʒəʊl) *vb* **cajoles, cajoling, cajoled.** to persuade (someone) by flattery to do what one wants; wheedle; coax. ORIG C17: from F *cajoler* to coax, from ?
▸ **caˈjolement** *n* ▸ **caˈjoler** *n* ▸ **caˈjolery** *n*

cake (keɪk) *n* **1** a baked food, usually in loaf or layer form, made from a mixture of flour, sugar, and eggs. **2** a flat thin mass of bread, esp. unleavened bread. **3** a shaped mass of dough or other food: *a fish cake.* **4** a mass, slab, or crust of a solidified substance, as of soap. **5 go** *or* **sell like hot cakes.** *Inf.* to be sold very quickly. **6 have one's cake and eat it.** to enjoy both of two desirable but incompatible alternatives. **7 piece of cake.** *Inf.* something that is easily achieved or obtained. **8 take the cake.** *Inf.* to surpass all others, esp. in stupidity, folly, etc. **9** *Inf.* the whole of something that is to be shared or divided: *a larger slice of the cake.* ◆ *vb* **cakes, caking, caked. 10** (*tr*) to encrust: *the hull was caked with salt.* **11** to form or be formed into a hardened mass. ORIG C13: from ON *kaka*

cakewalk (ˈkeɪkˌwɔːk) *n* **1** a dance based on a march with intricate steps, orig. performed by African-Americans for the prize of a cake. **2** a piece of music for this dance. **3** *Inf.* an easy task.

CAL (kæl) *acronym for* computer-aided (*or* -assisted) learning.

cal. *abbrev. for:* **1** calendar. **2** calibre. **3** calorie (small).

Cal. *abbrev. for* Calorie (large).

Calabar ★ (ˈkæləˌbɑː) *n* a port in SE Nigeria, capital of Cross River state. Pop.: 170 000 (1995 est.).

calabash (ˈkæləˌbæʃ) *n* **1** Also called: **calabash tree.** a tropical American evergreen tree that produces large round gourds. **2** the gourd. **3** the dried hollow shell of a gourd used as the bowl of a tobacco pipe, a bottle, etc. **4 calabash nutmeg.** a tropical African shrub whose seeds can be used as nutmegs. ORIG C17: from obs. F *calabasse,* from Sp., ?from Ar., from *qar'ah* gourd + *yābisah* dry

calaboose (ˈkæləˌbuːs) *n US inf.* a prison. ORIG C18: from Creole F, from Sp. *calabozo* dungeon, from ?

calabrese (ˌkæləˈbreɪzɪ) *n* a variety of green sprouting broccoli. ORIG C20: from It.: Calabrian

Calabria ★ (kəˈlæbrɪə) *n* **1** a region of SW Italy: mostly mountainous and subject to earthquakes. Chief town: Reggio di Calabria. Pop.: 2 075 842 (1996 est.). Area: 15 080 sq. km (5822 sq. miles). **2** an ancient region of extreme SE Italy (3rd century B.C. to about 668 A.D.); now part of Apulia.
▸ **Caˈlabrian** *adj, n*

Calais ★ (ˈkæleɪ, ˈkælɪ; *French* kalɛ) *n* a port in N France, on the Strait of Dover: the nearest French port to England; belonged to England 1347–1558. Pop.: 75 309 (1990).

calamander (ˈkæləˌmændə) *n* the hard black-and-brown striped wood of several trees of India and Sri Lanka, used in making furniture. See also **ebony** (sense 2). ORIG C19: metathetic var. of *coromandel* in COROMANDEL COAST

calamine (ˈkæləˌmaɪn) *n* a pink powder consisting of zinc oxide and iron(III) oxide, used medicinally in the form of soothing lotions or ointments. ORIG C17: from OF, from Med. L *calamīna,* from L *cadmīa;* see CADMIUM

calamint (ˈkæləmɪnt) *n* an aromatic Eurasian plant having clusters of purple or pink flowers. ORIG C14: from

OF *calament,* from Med. L *calamentum,* from Gk *kalaminthē*

calamitous (kəˈlæmɪtəs) *adj* causing, involving, or resulting in a calamity; disastrous.

calamity (kəˈlæmɪtɪ) *n, pl* **calamities. 1** a disaster or misfortune, esp. one causing distress or misery. **2** a state or feeling of deep distress or misery. ORIG C15: from F *calamité,* from L *calamitās*

Calamity Jane ★ *n* real name *Martha Canary.* ?1852–1903, US frontierswoman.

calamus (ˈkæləməs) *n, pl* **calami** (-ˌmaɪ). **1** any of a genus of tropical Asian palms, some of which are a source of rattan and canes. **2** another name for **sweet flag. 3** *Ornithol.* a quill. ORIG C14: from L, from Gk *kalamos* reed, stem

calandria (kəˈlændrɪə) *n* a cylindrical vessel through which vertical tubes pass, esp. one forming part of a heat exchanger or nuclear reactor. ORIG C20: arbitrarily named, from Sp., lit.: lark

calash (kəˈlæʃ) *or* **calèche** *n* **1** a horse-drawn carriage with low wheels and a folding top. **2** a woman's folding hooped hood worn in the 18th century. ORIG C17: from F, from G, from Czech *kolesa* wheels

calcaneus (kælˈkeɪnɪəs) *or* **calcaneum** *n, pl* **calcanei** (-nɪˌaɪ). the largest tarsal bone, forming the heel in man. Nontechnical name: **heel bone.** ORIG C19: from LL: heel, from L *calx* heel

calcareous (kælˈkɛərɪəs) *adj* of, containing, or resembling calcium carbonate; chalky. ORIG C17: from L *calcārius,* from *calx* lime

calceolaria (ˌkælsɪəˈlɛərɪə) *n* a tropical American plant cultivated for its speckled slipper-shaped flowers. Also called: **slipperwort.** ORIG C18: from L *calceolus* small shoe, from *calceus*

calces (ˈkælsiːz) *n* a plural of **calx.**

calci- *or before a vowel* **calc-** *combining form.* indicating lime or calcium: *calcify.* ORIG from L *calx, calc-* limestone

calciferol (kælˈsɪfərɒl) *n* a fat-soluble steroid, found esp. in fish-liver oils and used in the treatment of rickets. Also called: **vitamin D_2.** ORIG C20: from CALCIF(EROUS + ERGOST)EROL

calciferous (kælˈsɪfərəs) *adj* producing salts of calcium, esp. calcium carbonate.

calcify (ˈkælsɪˌfaɪ) *vb* **calcifies, calcifying, calcified. 1** to convert or be converted into lime. **2** to harden or become hardened by impregnation with calcium salts.
▸ **ˌcalcifiˈcation** *n*

calcine (ˈkælsaɪn, -sɪn) *vb* **calcines, calcining, calcined. 1** (*tr*) to heat (a substance) so that it is oxidized, is reduced, or loses water. **2** (*intr*) to oxidize as a result of heating. ORIG C14: from Med. L *calcināre* to heat, from L *calx* lime
▸ **calcination** (ˌkælsɪˈneɪʃən) *n*

calcite (ˈkælsaɪt) *n* a colourless or white mineral consisting of crystalline calcium carbonate: the transparent variety is Iceland spar. Formula: $CaCO_3$.

calcium (ˈkælsɪəm) *n* a malleable silvery-white metallic element of the alkaline earth group, occurring esp. as forms of calcium carbonate. It is an essential constituent of bones and teeth. Symbol: Ca; atomic no.: 20; atomic wt.: 40.08. ORIG C19: from NL, from L *calx* lime

calcium antagonist *or* **blocker** *n* any drug that prevents the influx of calcium ions into cardiac and smooth muscle: used to treat high blood pressure and angina.

calcium carbide *n* a grey salt of calcium used in the production of acetylene. Formula: CaC_2. Sometimes shortened to **carbide.**

calcium carbonate *n* a white crystalline salt occurring in limestone, chalk, and pearl: used in the production of lime. Formula: $CaCO_3$.

calcium chloride *n* a white deliquescent salt occurring naturally in seawater and used in the de-icing of roads. Formula: $CaCl_2$.

calcium hydroxide *n* a white crystalline slightly soluble alkali with many uses, esp. in cement, water softening, and the neutralization of acid soils. Formula: $Ca(OH)_2$. Also called: **lime, slaked lime, caustic lime.**

calcium oxide *n* a white crystalline base used in the production of calcium hydroxide and in the manufacture of glass and steel. Formula: CaO. Also called: **lime, quicklime, calx.**

calcium phosphate *n* an insoluble nonacid calcium salt that occurs in bones and is the main constituent of bone ash. Formula: $Ca_3(PO_4)_2$

calcspar (ˈkælkˌspɑː) *n* another name for **calcite.** ORIG C19: from Swedish *kalkspat,* from *kalk* lime (ult. from L *calx*) + *spat* SPAR[3]

calculable (ˈkælkjʊləbᵊl) *adj* **1** that may be computed or estimated. **2** predictable.
▸ **ˌcalculaˈbility** *n* ▸ **ˈcalculably** *adv*

calculate (ˈkælkjʊˌleɪt) *vb* **calculates, calculating, calculated. 1** to solve (one or more problems) by a mathematical procedure. **2** (*tr; may take a clause as object*) to determine beforehand by judgment, etc.; estimate. **3** (*tr; usually passive*) to aim: *the car was calculated to appeal to women.* **4** (*intr;* foll. by *on* or *upon*) to rely. **5** (*tr; may take a clause as object*) *US dialect.* to suppose. ORIG C16: from LL *calculāre,* from *calculus* pebble used as a counter
▸ **calculative** (ˈkælkjʊlətɪv) *adj*

calculated (ˈkælkjʊˌleɪtɪd) *adj* (*usually prenominal*) **1** undertaken after considering the likelihood of success or failure. **2** premeditated: *a calculated insult.*

calculating (ˈkælkjʊˌleɪtɪŋ) *adj* **1** selfishly scheming. **2** shrewd.
▸ **ˈcalcuˌlatingly** *adv*

calculation (ˌkælkjʊˈleɪʃən) *n* **1** the act, process, or result of calculating. **2** a forecast. **3** careful planning, esp. for selfish motives.

calculator (ˈkælkjʊˌleɪtə) *n* **1** a device for performing mathematical calculations, esp. an electronic device that can be held in the hand. **2** a person or thing that calculates. **3** a set of tables used as an aid to calculations.

calculous (ˈkælkjʊləs) *adj Pathol.* of or suffering from a calculus.

calculus (ˈkælkjʊləs) *n, pl* **calculuses. 1** a branch of mathematics, developed independently by Newton and Leibnitz. Both **differential calculus** and **integral calculus** are concerned with the effect on a function of an infinitesimal change in the independent variable. **2** any mathematical system of calculation involving the use of symbols. **3** (*pl* **calculi** (-ˌlaɪ)). *Pathol.* a stonelike concretion of minerals found in organs of the body. ORIG C17: from L: pebble, from *calx* small stone, counter

Calcutta ★ (kælˈkʌtə) *n* a port in E India, capital of West Bengal state, on the Hooghly River: former capital of the country (1833–1912); major commercial and industrial centre; three universities. Pop.: 4 399 819 (1991). Official name: **Kolkata.**

Calder ★ (ˈkɔːldə) *n* **Alexander.** 1898–1976, US sculptor, who originated mobiles.

caldera (kælˈdɛərə) *n* a large basin-shaped crater at the top of a volcano, formed by the collapse of the cone. ORIG C19: from Sp. *caldera,* lit.: CAULDRON

Calderdale ★ (ˈkɔːldəˌdeɪl) *n* a unitary authority in N England, in West Yorkshire. Pop.: 191 585 (1999). Area: 364 sq. km (140 sq. miles).

caldron (ˈkɔːldrən) *n* a variant spelling of **cauldron.**

Caldwell ★ (ˈkɔːldwɛl, -wəl) *n* **Erskine** (ˈɜːskɪn). 1903–87, US novelist whose works include *Tobacco Road* (1933).

calèche (*French* kalɛʃ) *n* a variant of **calash.**

Caledonia ★ (ˌkælɪˈdəʊnɪə) *n* the Roman name for **Scotland.**

Caledonian (ˌkælɪˈdəʊnɪən) *adj* **1** relating to Scotland. **2** of a period of mountain building in NW Europe in the Palaeozoic era. ◆ *n* **3** *Literary.* a native or inhabitant of Scotland.

Caledonian Canal ★ *n* a canal in N Scotland, linking the Atlantic with the North Sea through the Great Glen: built 1803–47; now little used.

calefacient (ˌkælɪˈfeɪʃənt) *adj* **1** causing warmth. ◆ *n* **2**

Med. an agent that warms, such as a mustard plaster. ORIG C17: from L, from *calefacere* to heat

calendar ('kælɪndə) *n* **1** a system for determining the beginning, length, and order of years and their divisions. **2** a table showing any such arrangement, esp. as applied to one or more successive years. **3** a list or schedule of pending court cases, appointments, etc. ◆ *vb* **calendars, calendaring, calendared. 4** (*tr*) to enter in a calendar; schedule. ORIG C13: via Norman F from Med. L *kalendārium* account book, from *Kalendae* the CALENDS
▸ **calendrical** (kæ'lɛndrɪkᵊl) *or* **ca'lendric** *adj*

calendar month *n* See **month** (sense 1).

calendar year *n* See **year** (sense 1).

calender ('kælɪndə) *n* **1** a machine in which paper or cloth is smoothed by passing between rollers. ◆ *vb* **2** (*tr*) to subject (material) to such a process. ORIG C17: from F *calandre,* from ?

calends *or* **kalends** ('kælɪndz) *pl n* the first day of each month in the ancient Roman calendar. ORIG C14: from L *kalendae*

calendula (kæ'lɛndjʊlə) *n* any of a genus of Eurasian plants, esp. the pot marigold, having orange-and-yellow rayed flowers. ORIG C19: from Med. L, from L *kalendae* CALENDS

calf[1] (kɑːf) *n, pl* **calves. 1** the young of cattle, esp. domestic cattle. **2** the young of certain other mammals, such as the buffalo and whale. **3** a large piece of ice detached from an iceberg, etc. **4 kill the fatted calf.** to celebrate lavishly, esp. as a welcome. ORIG OE *cealf*

calf[2] (kɑːf) *n, pl* **calves.** the thick fleshy part of the back of the leg between the ankle and the knee. ORIG C14: from ON *kalfi*

calf love *n* temporary infatuation of an adolescent for a member of the opposite sex.

calf's-foot jelly *n* a jelly made from the stock of boiled calves' feet and flavourings.

calfskin ('kɑːfˌskɪn) *n* **1** the skin or hide of a calf. **2** Also called: **calf. 2a** fine leather made from this skin. **2b** (*as modifier*): *calfskin boots.*

Calgary ★ ('kælgərɪ) *n* a city in Canada, in S Alberta: centre of a large agricultural region; oilfields. Pop.: 710 677 (1991).
▸ **Calgarian** (kæl'gɛərɪən) *adj, n*

Calgon ('kælgɒn) *n Trademark.* a chemical compound, sodium hexametaphosphate, with water-softening properties, used in detergents.

calibrate ('kælɪˌbreɪt) *vb* **calibrates, calibrating, calibrated.** (*tr*) **1** to measure the calibre of (a gun, etc.). **2** to mark (the scale of a measuring instrument) so that readings can be made in appropriate units. **3** to determine the accuracy of (a measuring instrument, etc.).
▸ ˌ**cali'bration** *n* ▸ '**caliˌbrator** *n*

calibre *or US* **caliber** ('kælɪbə) *n* **1** the diameter of a cylindrical body, esp. the internal diameter of a tube or the bore of a firearm. **2** the diameter of a shell or bullet. **3** ability; distinction. **4** personal character: *a man of high calibre.* ORIG C16: from OF, from It. *calibro,* from Ar. *qālib* shoemaker's last
▸ '**calibred** *or US* '**calibered** *adj*

calices ('kælɪˌsiːz) *n* the plural of **calix.**

calico ('kælɪˌkəʊ) *n, pl* **calicoes** *or* **calicos. 1** a white or unbleached cotton fabric. **2** *Chiefly US.* a coarse printed cotton fabric. ORIG C16: based on *Calicut,* town in India

calif ('keɪlɪf, 'kæl-) *n* a variant spelling of **caliph.**

Calif. *abbrev. for* California.

California ★ (ˌkælɪ'fɔːnɪə) *n* **1** a state on the W coast of the US: the third largest state in area and the largest in population; consists of a narrow, warm coastal plain rising to the Coast Range, deserts in the south, the fertile central valleys of the Sacramento and San Joaquin Rivers, and the mountains of the Sierra Nevada in the east; major industries include the growing of citrus fruits and grapes, fishing, oil production, computer technology, electronics, and films. Capital: Sacramento. Pop.: 32 666 550 (1998 est.). Area: 411 015 sq. km (158 693 sq. miles). Abbrevs.: **Cal., Calif.** or (with zip code) **CA 2 Gulf of.** an arm of the Pacific Ocean, between Sonora and Lower California.
▸ ˌ**Cali'fornian** *adj, n*

California poppy *n* a plant of the poppy family, native to the Pacific coast of North America, having yellow or orange flowers and finely dissected bluish-green leaves. Also called: **eschscholzia** *or* **eschscholtzia.**

californium (ˌkælɪ'fɔːnɪəm) *n* a transuranic element artificially produced from curium. Symbol: Cf; atomic no.: 98; half-life of most stable isotope, ^{251}Cf: 800 years (approx.). ORIG C20: NL; discovered at the University of *California*

Caligula ★ (kə'lɪgjʊlə) *n* original name *Gaius Caesar,* son of Germanicus. 12–41 A.D., Roman emperor (37–41), noted for his cruelty; assassinated.

calipash *or* **callipash** ('kælɪˌpæʃ) *n* the greenish glutinous edible part of the turtle found next to the upper shell. ORIG C17: ? changed from Sp. *carapacho* CARAPACE

calipee ('kælɪˌpiː) *n* the yellow glutinous edible part of the turtle found next to the lower shell. ORIG C17: ? a var. of CALIPASH

caliper ('kælɪpə) *n* the usual US spelling of **calliper.**

caliph, calif, *or* **khalif** ('keɪlɪf, 'kæl-) *n Islam.* the title of the successors of Mohammed as rulers of the Islamic world. ORIG C14: from OF, from Ar. *khalīfa* successor

caliphate, califate *or* **khalifate** ('keɪlɪˌfeɪt) *n* the office, jurisdiction, or reign of a caliph.

calisthenics (ˌkælɪs'θɛnɪks) *n* a variant spelling (esp. US) of **callisthenics.**

calix ('keɪlɪks, 'kæ-) *n, pl* **calices.** a cup; chalice. ORIG C18: from L: CHALICE

calk[1] (kɔːk) *vb* a variant spelling of **caulk.**

calk[2] (kɔːk) *or* **calkin** ('kɔːkɪn, 'kæl-) *n* **1** a metal projection on a horse's shoe to prevent slipping. ◆ *vb* (*tr*) **2** to provide with calks. ORIG C17: from L *calx* heel

call (kɔːl) *vb* **1** (often foll. by *out*) to speak or utter (words, sounds, etc.) loudly so as to attract attention: *he called out her name.* **2** (*tr*) to ask or order to come: *to call a policeman.* **3** (*intr;* sometimes foll. by *on*) to make a visit (to): *she called on him.* **4** (often foll. by *up*) to telephone (a person). **5** (*tr*) to summon to a specific office, profession, etc. **6** (of animals or birds) to utter (a characteristic sound or cry). **7** (*tr*) to summon (a bird or animal), as by imitating its cry. **8** (*tr*) to name or style: *they called the dog Rover.* **9** (*tr*) to designate: *they called him a coward.* **10** (*tr*) to regard in a specific way: *I call it a foolish waste of time.* **11** (*tr*) to attract (attention). **12** (*tr*) to read (a list, etc.) aloud to check for omissions or absentees. **13** (when *tr,* usually foll. by *for*) to give an order (for): *to call a strike.* **14** (*intr*) to try to predict the result of tossing a coin. **15** (*tr*) to awaken: *I was called early this morning.* **16** (*tr*) to cause to assemble. **17** (*tr*) *Sport.* (of an umpire, etc.) to pass judgment upon (a shot, etc.) with a call. **18** (*tr*) *Austral. & NZ.* to broadcast a commentary on (a horse race, etc.). **19** (*tr*) to demand repayment of (a loan, security, etc.). **20** (*tr*) *Brit.* to award (a student at an Inn of Court) the degree of barrister (esp. in **call to the bar**). **21** (*tr*) *Poker.* to demand that (a player) expose his or her hand, after equalling his or her bet. **22** (*intr*) *Bridge.* to make a bid. **23** (in square-dancing) to call out (instructions) to the dancers. **24** (*intr;* foll. by *for*) **24a** to require: *this problem calls for study.* **24b** to come or go (for) in order to fetch. **25** (*intr;* foll. by *on* or *upon*) to make an appeal or request (to): *they called upon him to reply.* **26** (*tr*) to predict the outcome of an event: *we don't know yet if the plan has succeeded because it's too soon to call.* **27 call into being.** to create. **28 call someone's bluff.** see **bluff**[1]. **29 call to mind.** to remember or cause to be remembered. ◆ *n* **30** a cry or shout. **31** the characteristic cry of a bird or animal. **32** a device, such as a whistle, intended to imitate the cry of a bird or animal. **33** a summons or invitation. **34** a summons or signal sounded on a horn, bugle, etc. **35** a short visit: *the doctor made six calls this morning.* **36** an inner urge to some task or profession; vocation. **37** allure or fascination, esp. of a place: *the call of the forest.* **38** need, demand, or occasion: *there is no call to shout.* **39** demand or claim (esp. in **the call of duty**). **40** *Theatre.* a notice to actors informing them of times of rehearsals. **41** a conversation or a request for a connection by telephone. **42** *Commerce.* **42a** a demand for repayment of a loan. **42b** (*as modifier*): *call money.* **43** *Finance.* a demand for redeemable bonds or shares to be presented for repayment. **44** *Poker.* a demand for a hand or hands to be exposed. **45** *Bridge.* a bid or a player's turn to bid. **46** *Sport.* a decision of an umpire or referee regarding a shot, pitch, etc. **47** *Austral.* a broadcast commentary on a horse race, etc. **48** Also called: **call option.** *Stock Exchange.* an option to buy a stated amount of securities at a specified price during a specified period. **49 on call. 49a** (of a loan, etc.) repayable on demand. **49b** available to be called for work outside normal working hours. **50 within call.** accessible. ◆ See also **call down, call forth,** etc. ORIG OE *ceallian*

calla ('kælə) *n* **1** Also called: **calla lily, arum lily.** a southern African plant which has a white funnel-shaped spathe enclosing a yellow spadix. **2** a plant that grows in wet places and has a white spathe and red berries. ORIG C19: from NL, prob. from Gk *kalleia* wattles on a cock, prob. from *kallos* beauty

Callaghan ★ ('kælə,hæn) *n* (**Leonard**) **James,** Baron Callaghan of Cardiff. born 1912, British Labour statesman; prime minister (1976–79).

Callanetics (,kælə'nɛtɪks) *n* (*functioning as sing*) *Trademark.* a system of exercise involving frequent repetition of small muscular movements and squeezes, designed to improve muscle tone. ORIG C20: after *Callan* Pinckney (born 1939), its US inventor

Callas ★ ('kæləs) *n* **Maria,** real name *Maria Anna Cecilia Kalageropoulos.* 1923–77, Greek soprano, born in the US.

call bird *n Marketing.* a cheap article displayed in a shop to attract custom, in the hope of selling expensive items.

call box *n* a soundproof enclosure for a public telephone. Also called: **telephone kiosk.**

callboy ('kɔːl,bɔɪ) *n* a person who notifies actors when it is time to go on stage.

call centre *n* an office where staff carry out an organization's telephone transactions.

call down *vb* (*tr, adv*) to request or invoke: *to call down God's anger.*

caller ('kɔːlə) *n* **1** a person or thing that calls, esp. a person who makes a brief visit. **2** *Austral.* a racing commentator.

call forth *vb* (*tr, adv*) to cause (something) to come into action or existence.

call girl *n* a prostitute with whom appointments are made by telephone.

Callicrates ★ (kə'lɪkrə,tiːz) *n* 5th century B.C., Greek architect: with Ictinus, designed the Parthenon.

calligraphy (kə'lɪgrəfɪ) *n* handwriting, esp. beautiful handwriting.
▸ **cal'ligrapher** *or* **cal'ligraphist** *n* ▸ **calligraphic** (,kælɪ'græfɪk) *adj*

Callimachus ★ (kə'lɪməkəs) *n* **1** late 5th century B.C., Greek sculptor, reputed to have invented the Corinthian capital. **2** ?305–?240 B.C., Greek poet of the Alexandrian School; author of hymns and epigrams.

call in *vb* (*adv*) **1** (*intr;* often foll. by *on*) to pay a visit, esp. a brief one: *call in if you are in the neighbourhood.* **2** (*tr*) to demand payment of: *to call in a loan.* **3** (*tr*) to take (something) out of circulation, because it is defective. **4** to summon to one's assistance: *to call in a specialist.*

calling ('kɔːlɪŋ) *n* **1** a strong inner urge to follow an occupation, etc.; vocation. **2** an occupation, profession, or trade.

calling card *n* the usual US and Canad. term for **visiting card.**

calliope (kə'laɪəpɪ) *n US & Canad.* a steam organ. ORIG after CALLIOPE (lit.: beautiful-voiced)

Calliope ★ (kə'laɪəpɪ) *n Greek myth.* the Muse of epic poetry.

calliper *or US* **caliper** ('kælɪpə) *n* **1** (*often pl*) Also called: **calliper compasses.** an instrument for measuring internal or external dimensions, consisting of two steel legs hinged together. **2** Also called: **calliper splint.** *Med.* a metal splint for supporting the leg. ◆ *vb* **3** (*tr*) to measure with callipers. ORIG C16: var. of CALIBRE

calliper rule *n* a measuring instrument having two parallel jaws, one fixed and the other sliding.

callistemon (kə'lɪstəmən) *n* another name for **bottlebrush** (sense 1).

callisthenics *or* **calisthenics** (,kælɪs'θɛnɪks) *n* **1** (*functioning as pl*) light exercises designed to promote general fitness. **2** (*functioning as sing*) the practice of callisthenic exercises. ORIG C19: from Gk *kalli-* beautiful + *sthenos* strength
▸ **,callis'thenic** *or* **,calis'thenic** *adj*

Callisto ★ (kə'lɪstəʊ) *n Greek myth.* a nymph who attracted the love of Zeus and was changed into a bear by Hera. Zeus then set her in the sky as the constellation Ursa Major.

call loan *n* a loan that is repayable on demand. Also called: **demand loan.**

call off *vb* (*tr, adv*) **1** to cancel or abandon: *the game was called off.* **2** to order (an animal or person) to desist: *the man called off his dog.* **3** to stop (something).

callose ('kæləʊz, -ləʊs) *n* a carbohydrate, a polymer of glucose, found in plants.

callosity (kə'lɒsɪtɪ) *n, pl* **callosities. 1** hard-heartedness. **2** a callus.

callous ('kæləs) *adj* **1** insensitive. **2** (of skin) hardened and thickened. ◆ *vb* **3** *Pathol.* to make or become callous. ORIG C16: from L *callōsus;* see CALLUS
▸ **'callously** *adv* ▸ **'callousness** *n*

call out *vb* (*adv*) **1** to utter aloud, esp. loudly. **2** (*tr*) to summon: *call out the troops.* **3** (*tr*) to order (workers) to strike. **4** (*tr*) to challenge to a duel.

callow ('kæləʊ) *adj* lacking experience of life; immature. ORIG OE *calu*
▸ **'callowness** *n*

call sign *n* a group of letters and numbers identifying a radio transmitting station.

call up *vb* (*tr, adv*) **1** to summon to report for active military service, as in time of war. **2** to recall (something); evoke. **3** to bring or summon (people, etc.) into action. **4** to telephone. ◆ *n* **call-up. 5a** a general order to report for military service. **5b** the number of men so summoned.

callus ('kæləs) *n, pl* **calluses. 1** Also called: **callosity.** an area of skin that is hard or thick, esp. on the sole of the foot. **2** an area of bony tissue formed during the healing of a fractured bone. **3** *Bot.* a mass of hard protective tissue produced in woody plants at the site of an injury. ORIG C16: from L, var. of *callum* hardened skin

calm (kɑːm) *adj* **1** still: *a calm sea.* **2** *Meteorol.* without wind, or with wind of less than 1 mph. **3** not disturbed, agitated, or excited. **4** tranquil; serene: *a calm voice.* ◆ *n* **5** an absence of disturbance or rough motion. **6** absence of wind. **7** tranquillity. ◆ *vb* **8** (often foll. by *down*) to make or become calm. ORIG C14: from OF *calme,* from OIt., from LL *cauma* heat, hence a rest during the heat of the day, from Gk, from *kaiein* to burn
▸ **'calmly** *adv* ▸ **'calmness** *n*

calmative ('kælmətɪv, 'kɑːmə-) *adj* (of a remedy or agent) sedative.

caló (kə'ləʊ; *Spanish* ka'lo) *n* a form of Mexican Spanish incorporating many slang terms and English words: spoken esp. by Mexican Americans in the SW US.

calomel ('kælə,mɛl, -məl) *n* a colourless tasteless powder consisting chiefly of mercurous chloride, used medicinally, esp. as a cathartic. ORIG C17: ?from NL *calomelas* (unattested), lit.: beautiful black, from Gk *kalos* beautiful + *melas* black

Calor Gas ('kælə) *n Trademark.* butane gas liquefied under pressure in portable containers for domestic use.

caloric (kə'lɒrɪk) *adj* **1** of or concerned with heat or calories. ◆ *n* **2** *Obs.* a hypothetical elastic fluid, the embodiment of heat.

calorie *or* **calory** ('kælərɪ) *n, pl* **calories.** a unit of heat, equal to 4.1868 joules (**International Table calorie**): formerly defined as the quantity of heat required to raise the temperature of 1 gram of water by 1°C. Abbrev.: **cal.** Also called: **small calorie.** ORIG C19: from F, from L *calor* heat

Calorie ('kælərɪ) *n* **1** Also called: **kilogram calorie, large cal-**

orie. a unit of heat, equal to one thousand calories. Abbrev.: **Cal. 2** the amount of a specific food capable of producing one thousand calories of energy.

calorific (ˌkælə'rɪfɪk) *adj* of, concerning, or generating heat.
▸ **ˌcalo'rifically** *adv*

calorific value *n* the quantity of heat produced by the complete combustion of a given mass of a fuel.

calorimeter (ˌkælə'rɪmɪtə) *n* an apparatus for measuring amounts of heat, esp. to find calorific values, etc.
▸ **calorimetric** (ˌkælərɪ'mɛtrɪk) *adj* ▸ **ˌcalo'rimetry** *n*

calorize *or* **calorise** ('kæləˌraɪz) *vb* **calorizes, calorizing, calorized** *or* **calorises, calorising, calorised.** (*tr*) to coat (a ferrous metal) by spraying with aluminium powder and then heating.

Calpe ★ ('kælpɪ) *n* the ancient name for the (Rock of) **Gibraltar.**

calque (kælk) *n* another word for **loan translation.** ORIG C20: from F: a tracing, from L *calcāre* to tread

calumet ('kæljuˌmɛt) *n* the peace pipe. ORIG C18: from Canad. F, from F: straw, from LL *calamellus* a little reed, from L: CALAMUS

calumniate (kə'lʌmnɪˌeɪt) *vb* **calumniates, calumniating, calumniated.** (*tr*) to slander.
▸ **caˌlumni'ation** *n* ▸ **ca'lumniˌator** *n*

calumny ('kæləmnɪ) *n, pl* **calumnies. 1** the malicious utterance of false charges or misrepresentation. **2** such a false charge or misrepresentation. ORIG C15: from L *calumnia* deception, slander
▸ **calumnious** (kə'lʌmnɪəs) *or* **ca'lumniatory** *adj*

Calvados ★ ('kælvəˌdɒs) *n* **1** a department of N France in the Basse-Normandie region. Capital: Caen. Pop.: 632 462 (1994 est.). Area: 5693 sq. km (2198 sq. miles). **2** an apple brandy distilled from cider in this region.

Calvary ★ ('kælvərɪ) *n* the place just outside the walls of Jerusalem where Jesus was crucified. Also called: **Golgotha.** ORIG from LL *Calvāria,* translation of Gk *kranion* skull, translation of Aramaic *gulgulta* Golgotha

calve (kɑːv) *vb* **calves, calving, calved. 1** to give birth to (a calf). **2** (of a glacier or iceberg) to release (masses of ice) in breaking up.

Calvert ★ ('kælvət) *n* **1** Sir **George,** 1st Baron Baltimore. ?1580–1632, English statesman; founder of the colony of Maryland. **2** his son, **Leonard.** 1606–47, English statesman; first colonial governor of Maryland (1634–47).

calves (kɑːvz) *n* the plural of **calf**[1] and **calf**[2].

Calvin ★ ('kælvɪn) *n* **1 John,** original name *Jean Cauvin, Caulvin,* or *Chauvin.* 1509–64, French theologian: a leader of the Protestant Reformation, who established the first presbyterian government in Geneva; author of *Institutes of the Christian Religion* (1536). **2 Melvin.** 1911–97, US chemist, noted for his research on photosynthesis: Nobel prize for chemistry 1961.

Calvin cycle *n Bot.* a series of reactions, occurring during photosynthesis, in which glucose is synthesized from carbon dioxide. ORIG C20: named after M. CALVIN, who elucidated it

Calvinism ('kælvɪˌnɪzəm) *n* the theological system of John Calvin and his followers, characterized by emphasis on predestination and justification by faith.
▸ **'Calvinist** *n, adj* ▸ **ˌCalvin'istic** *or* **ˌCalvin'istical** *adj*

Calvino ★ (*Italian* kal'viːno) *n* **Italo** ('iːtalo). 1923–85, Italian writer. His works include *Our Ancestors* (1960) and *Invisible Cities* (1972).

calx (kælks) *n, pl* **calxes** *or* **calces. 1** the powdery metallic oxide formed when an ore or mineral is roasted. **2** calcium oxide. **3** *Anat.* the heel. ORIG C15: from L: lime, from Gk *khalix* pebble

calypso (kə'lɪpsəʊ) *n, pl* **calypsos.** a popular type of satirical West Indian ballad, esp. from Trinidad, usually extemporized to a syncopated accompaniment. ORIG C20: prob. from CALYPSO

Calypso ★ (kə'lɪpsəʊ) *n Greek myth.* (in Homer's *Odyssey*) a sea nymph who detained Odysseus on the island of Ogygia for seven years.

calyx ('keɪlɪks, 'kælɪks) *n, pl* **calyxes** *or* **calyces** ('kælɪˌsiːz, 'keɪlɪ-). **1** the sepals of a flower collectively that protect the developing flower bud. **2** any cup-shaped cavity or structure. ORIG C17: from L, from Gk *kalux* shell, from *kaluptein* to cover

calzone (kæl'tsəʊnɪ) *n* a dish of Italian origin consisting of pizza dough folded over a filling of cheese and tomatoes, herbs, ham, etc. ORIG C20: It., lit.: trouser leg, from *calzoni* trousers

cam (kæm) *n* a slider or roller attached to a moving shaft to give a particular type of motion to a part in contact with it. ORIG C16: from Du. *kam* comb

Cam ★ (kæm) *n* a river in E England, in Cambridgeshire, flowing through Cambridge to the River Ouse. Length: about 64 km (40 miles).

CAM (kæm) *acronym for* computer-aided manufacture.

-cam *n combining form.* a camera: *webcam.*

Camagüey ★ ('kæməˌgweɪ; *Spanish* kama'ɣwej) *n* a city in E central Cuba. Pop.: 293 961 (1994 est.).

camaraderie (ˌkæmə'rɑːdərɪ) *n* a spirit of familiarity and trust existing between friends. ORIG C19: from F, from *camarade* COMRADE

Camargue ★ (kæ'mɑːg) *n* **la** (la). a delta region in S France, between the channels of the Grand and Petit Rhône: cattle, esp. bulls for the Spanish bullrings, and horses are reared.

camarilla (ˌkæmə'rɪlə) *n* a group of confidential advisers, esp. formerly, to the Spanish kings. ORIG C19: from Sp., lit.: a little room

Cambay ★ (kæm'beɪ) *n* **Gulf of.** an inlet of the Arabian Sea on the W coast of India, SE of the Kathiawar Peninsula.

camber ('kæmbə) *n* **1** a slight upward curve to the centre of the surface of a road, ship's deck, etc. **2** another name for **bank**[2] (sense 8). **3** an outward inclination of the front wheels of a road vehicle so that they are slightly closer together at the bottom. **4** aerofoil curvature expressed by the ratio of the maximum height of the aerofoil mean line to its chord. ◆ *vb* **5** to form or be formed with a surface that curves upwards to its centre. ORIG C17: from OF *cambre* curved, from L *camurus*

cambium ('kæmbɪəm) *n, pl* **cambiums** *or* **cambia** (-bɪə). *Bot.* a layer of cells that increases the girth of stems and roots. ORIG C17: from Med. L: exchange, from LL *cambiāre* to exchange
▸ **'cambial** *adj*

Cambodia ★ (kæm'bəʊdɪə) *n* a country in SE Asia: became part of French Indochina in 1887; achieved self-government in 1949 and independence in 1953; civil war (1970–74) ended in victory for the Khmer Rouge, who renamed the country Kampuchea (1975); Vietnamese forces ousted the Khmer Rouge in 1979 and set up a pro-Vietnamese government who reverted (1981) to the name of Cambodia; in 1982 exiled factions formed the Coalition Government of Democratic Kampuchea (CGDK), which is recognized by the UN; after the Vietnamese withdrawal in 1989 CGDK guerrillas continued to engage government forces; in 1993 Sihanouk was restored to the throne: contains the central plains of the Mekong River and the Cardamom Mountains in the SW. Official language: Khmer; French is also widely spoken. Currency: riel. Capital: Phnom Penh. Pop.: 10 981 000 (1999 est.). Area: 181 000 sq. km (69 895 sq. miles). See also **Kampuchea.**
▸ **Cam'bodian** *adj, n*

Cambrai ★ (*French* kɑ̃brɛ) *n* a town in NE France: textile industry: scene of a battle in which massed tanks were first used and broke through the German line (November, 1917). Pop.: 34 210 (1990).

Cambria ★ ('kæmbrɪə) *n* the Medieval Latin name for **Wales.**

Cambrian ('kæmbrɪən) *adj* **1** of or formed in the first 100 million years of the Palaeozoic era. **2** of or relating to Wales. ◆ *n* **3 the.** the Cambrian period or rock system. **4** a Welshman.

Cambrian Mountains ★ *pl n* a mountain range in Wales, extending from Carmarthenshire in the S to

Denbighshire in the N. Highest peak: Aran Fawddwy 891 m (2970 ft).

cambric ('keɪmbrɪk) *n* a fine white linen fabric. ORIG C16: from Flemish *Kamerijk* CAMBRAI

Cambridge ★ ('keɪmbrɪdʒ) *n* **1** a city in E England, administrative centre of Cambridgeshire, on the River Cam: centred around the university, founded in the 12th century. Pop.: 113 800 (1994 est.). Medieval Latin name: **Cantabrigia. 2** short for **Cambridgeshire. 3** a city in the US, in E Massachusetts: educational centre, with Harvard University (1636) and the Massachusetts Institute of Technology. Pop.: 99 890 (1994 est.).

Cambridgeshire ★ ('keɪmbrɪdʒˌʃɪə, -ʃə) *n* a county of E England, in East Anglia: includes the former counties of the Isle of Ely and Huntingdon and lies largely in the Fens; Peterborough became an independent unitary authority in 1968. Administrative centre: Cambridge. Pop. (excluding Peterborough): 544 600 (1996 est.). Area (excluding Peterborough): 3068 sq. km (1184 sq. miles).

Cambs *abbrev. for* Cambridgeshire.

Cambyses ★ (kæm'baɪsiːz) *n* died ?522 B.C., king of Persia (529–522 B.C.), who conquered Egypt (525); son of Cyrus the Great.

camcorder ('kæmˌkɔːdə) *n* a video camera and recorder combined in a portable unit.

Camden[1] ★ ('kæmdən) *n* a borough of N Greater London. Pop.: 182 500 (1994 est.). Area: 21 sq. km (8 sq. miles).

Camden[2] ★ ('kæmdən) *n* **William.** 1551–1623, English antiquary; author of *Britannia* (1586).

came (keɪm) *vb* the past tense of **come.**

camel ('kæməl) *n* **1** either of two cud-chewing, humped mammals (see **Arabian camel, Bactrian camel**) that are adapted for surviving long periods without food or water in desert regions. **2** a float attached to a vessel to increase its buoyancy. **3a** a fawn colour. **3b** (*as adj*): *a camel coat.* ORIG OE, from L, from Gk *kamēlos,* of Semitic origin

cameleer (ˌkæmɪ'lɪə) *n* a camel driver.

camel hair *or* **camel's hair** *n* **1** the hair of the camel, used in rugs, etc. **2a** soft cloth made of or containing this hair or a substitute, usually tan in colour. **2b** (*as modifier*): *a camelhair coat.* **3a** the hair of the squirrel's tail, used for paintbrushes. **3b** (*as modifier*): *a camelhair brush.*

camellia (kə'miːlɪə) *n* any of a genus of ornamental shrubs having glossy evergreen leaves and showy white, pink, or red flowers. Also called: **japonica.** ORIG C18: NL, after Georg Josef *Kamel* (1661–1706), Moravian Jesuit missionary

camelopard ('kæmɪləˌpɑːd, kə'mɛl-) *n* an obsolete word for **giraffe.** ORIG C14: from Med. L, from Gk, from *kamēlos* CAMEL + *pardalis* LEOPARD, because the giraffe was thought to have a head like a camel's and spots like a leopard's

Camelot ★ ('kæmɪˌlɒt) *n* (in Arthurian legend) the English town where King Arthur's palace and court were situated.

Camembert ('kæməmˌbɛə) *n* a soft creamy cheese. ORIG F, from *Camembert,* a village in Normandy

cameo ('kæmɪˌəʊ) *n, pl* **cameos. 1** a medallion, as on a brooch or ring, with a profile head carved in relief. **2** an engraving upon a gem or other stone so that the background is of a different colour from the raised design. **3** a stone with such an engraving. **4a** a brief dramatic scene played by a well-known actor or actress in a film or television play. **4b** (*as modifier*): *a cameo performance.* **5** a short literary work. ORIG C15: from It. *cammeo,* from ?

camera ('kæmərə) *n* **1** an optical device consisting of a lens system set in a light-proof construction inside which a light-sensitive film or plate can be positioned. **2** *Television.* the equipment used to convert the optical image of a scene into the corresponding electrical signals. **3** (*pl* **camerae** (-əˌriː)). a judge's private room. **4 in camera. 4a** *Law.* relating to a hearing from which members of the public are excluded. **4b** in private. ORIG C18: from L: vault, from Gk *kamara*

cameraman ('kæmərəˌmæn) *n, pl* **cameramen.** a person who operates a film or television camera.

camera obscura (ɒb'skjʊərə) *n* a darkened chamber with an aperture, in which images of outside objects are projected onto a flat surface. ORIG NL: dark chamber

Cameron ★ ('kæmərən) *n* **1** (**Mark**) **James** (**Walter**). 1911–85, British journalist. His books include *Witness in Vietnam* (1966). **2 Julia Margaret.** 1815–79, British photographer, born in India.

Cameroon ★ (ˌkæmə'ruːn, 'kæməˌruːn) *n* **1** a republic in West Africa, on the Gulf of Guinea: became a German colony in 1884; divided in 1919 into the **Cameroons** (administered by Britain) and **Cameroun** (administered by France); Cameroun and the S part of the Cameroons formed a republic in 1961 (the N part joined Nigeria); joined the Commonwealth in 1995. Official languages: French and English. Religions: Christian, Muslim, and animist. Currency: franc. Capital: Yaoundé. Pop.: 15 456 000 (1999 est.). Area: 475 500 sq. km (183 591 sq. miles). French name: **Cameroun.** German name: **Kamerun. 2** an active volcano in W Cameroon: the highest peak on the West African coast. Height: 4070 m (13 352 ft).

Cameroun ★ (kamrun) *n* the French name for **Cameroon.**

camiknickers ('kæmɪˌnɪkəz) *pl n* women's knickers attached to a camisole top.

camisole ('kæmɪˌsəʊl) *n* **1** a woman's underbodice with shoulder straps, originally designed as a cover for a corset. **2** a woman's short negligee. ORIG C19: from F, from Provençal *camisola,* from *camisa* shirt, from LL *camīsia*

camomile *or* **chamomile** ('kæməˌmaɪl) *n* **1** any of a genus of aromatic plants whose finely dissected leaves and daisy-like flowers are used medicinally. **2** any plant of a related genus as **German** or **wild camomile. 3 camomile tea.** a herbal beverage made from the fragrant leaves and flowers of any of these plants. ORIG C14: from OF, from Med. L, from Gk *khamaimēlon* lit., earth-apple (referring to the scent of the flowers)

camouflage ('kæməˌflɑːʒ) *n* **1** the exploitation of natural surroundings or artificial aids to conceal or disguise the presence of military units, etc. **2** (*modifier*) (of fabric or clothing) having a design of irregular patches, in dull colours (such as browns and greens), as used in military camouflage. **3** the means by which animals escape the notice of predators. **4** a device or expedient designed to conceal or deceive. ◆ *vb* **camouflages, camouflaging, camouflaged. 5** (*tr*) to conceal by camouflage. ORIG C20: from F, from *camoufler,* from It. *camuffare* to disguise, from ?

camp[1] (kæmp) *n* **1** a place where tents, cabins, etc., are erected for the use of military troops, etc. **2** tents, cabins, etc., used as temporary lodgings by holiday-makers, Scouts, Gypsies, etc. **3** the group of people living in such lodgings. **4** a group supporting a given doctrine: *the socialist camp.* **5** (*modifier*) suitable for use in temporary quarters, on holiday, etc.: *a camp bed; a camp chair.* **6** *S. African.* a field or pasture. **7** *Austral.* a place where sheep or cattle gather to rest. ◆ *vb* (*intr*) **8** (often foll. by *down*) to establish or set up a camp. **9** (often foll. by *out*) to live temporarily in or as if in a tent. ORIG C16: from OF, ult. from L *campus* field
▸ **'camping** *n*

camp[2] (kæmp) *Inf.* ◆ *adj* **1** effeminate; affected. **2** homosexual. **3** consciously artificial, vulgar, or mannered. ◆ *vb* **4** (*tr*) to perform or invest with a camp quality. **5 camp it up. 5a** to overact. **5b** to flaunt one's homosexuality. ORIG C20: from ?
▸ **'campness** *n* ▸ **'campy** *adj*

Campagna ★ (kæm'pɑːnjə) *n* a low-lying plain surrounding Rome, Italy: once fertile, it deteriorated to malarial marshes; recently reclaimed. Area: about 2000 sq. km (800 sq. miles). Also called: **Campagna di Roma** (dɪ 'rəʊmə).

campaign (kæm'peɪn) *n* **1** a series of coordinated activities, such as public speaking, designed to achieve a social, political, or commercial goal: *a presidential campaign.* **2** *Mil.* a number of operations aimed at achieving a single objective. ◆ *vb* **3** (*intr;* often foll. by *for*) to conduct, serve in, or go on a campaign. ORIG C17: from

F *campagne* open country, from It., from LL, from L *campus* field
▸ **cam'paigner** *n*

Campanella ★ (*Italian* kampa'nɛlla) *n* **Tommaso** (tom'ma:zo). 1568–1639, Italian philosopher and Dominican friar, who wrote *La città del sole* (1599–1626), while imprisoned in Spain.

Campania ★ (kæm'peɪnɪə; *Italian* kam'paɲɲa) *n* a region of SW Italy: includes the islands of Capri and Ischia. Chief town: Naples. Pop.: 5 762 518 (1996 est.). Area: 13 595 sq. km (5248 sq. miles).

campanile (ˌkæmpə'ni:lɪ) *n* (esp. in Italy) a bell tower, not usually attached to another building. ORIG C17: from It., from *campana* bell

campanology (ˌkæmpə'nɒlədʒɪ) *n* the art or skill of ringing bells. ORIG C19: from NL, from LL *campāna* bell
▸ **campanological** (ˌkæmpənə'lɒdʒɪkᵊl) *adj* ▸ **ˌcampa'nologist** *or* **ˌcampa'nologer** *n*

campanula (kæm'pænjʊlə) *n* any of a genus of N temperate plants having blue or white bell-shaped flowers. Also called: **bellflower**. ORIG C17: from NL: a little bell, from LL *campāna* bell

Campbell ★ ('kæmbᵊl) *n* **1** Sir **Colin**, Baron Clyde. 1792–1863, British field marshal who relieved Lucknow for the second time (1857). **2 Donald**. 1921–67, British water speed record-holder. **3** his father, Sir **Malcolm**. 1885–1948, British racing driver and land speed record-holder. **4** Mrs **Patrick**, original name *Beatrice Stella Tanner*. 1865–1940, British actress. **5 Roy**. 1901–57, South African poet. His poetry includes *The Flaming Terrapin* (1924). **6 Thomas**. 1777–1844, British poet, noted for his war poems *Ye Mariners of England*.

Campbell-Bannerman ★ ('kæmbᵊl'bænəmən) *n* Sir **Henry**. 1836–1908, British statesman and leader of the Liberal Party (1899–1908); prime minister (1905–08).

Camp David ★ *n* the US president's retreat in the Appalachian Mountains, Maryland: scene of the **Camp David Agreement** (Sept., 1978) between Anwar Sadat of Egypt and Menachem Begin of Israel, mediated by Jimmy Carter, outlining a framework for peace in the Middle East.

camp drafting *n Austral.* a competitive test of horsemen's skill in drafting cattle.

Campeche ★ (*Spanish* kam'petʃe) *n* **1** a state of SE Mexico, on the SW of the Yucatán peninsula: forestry and fishing. Capital: Campeche. Pop.: 668 715 (1997 est.). Area: 56 114 sq. km (21 666 sq. miles). **2** a port in SE Mexico, capital of Campeche state. Pop.: 150 518 (1990). **3 Bay of.** Also called: **Gulf of Campeche**. the SW part of the Gulf of Mexico.

camper ('kæmpə) *n* **1** a person who lives or temporarily stays in a tent, cabin, etc. **2** *US & Canad.* a vehicle equipped for camping out.

Campese ★ (kæm'peɪzɪ) *n* **David**. born 1962, Australian rugby union player.

camp follower *n* **1** any civilian, esp. a prostitute, who unofficially provides services to military personnel. **2** a nonmember who is sympathetic to a particular group, theory, etc.

camphor ('kæmfə) *n* a whitish crystalline aromatic ketone obtained from the wood of an Asian or Australian laurel (**camphor tree**): used in medicine as a liniment. ORIG C15: from OF *camphre*, from Med. L *camphora*, from Ar. *kāfūr*, from Malay *kāpūr* chalk
▸ **camphoric** (kæm'fɒrɪk) *adj*

camphorate ('kæmfəˌreɪt) *vb* **camphorates, camphorating, camphorated.** (*tr*) to apply, treat with, or impregnate with camphor.

camphor ball *n* another name for **mothball** (sense 1).

camphor ice *n* an ointment consisting of camphor, white wax, spermaceti, and castor oil, used to treat skin ailments, esp. chapped skin.

camphor wood *n Austral.* a popular name for any of several trees with pungent smelling wood.

Campin ★ ('kæmpɪn) *n* **Robert**. 1379–1444, Flemish painter, noted esp. for his altarpieces: usually identified with the so-called Master of Flémalle.

campion ('kæmpɪən) *n* any of various plants related to the pink, having red, pink, or white flowers. ORIG C16: prob. from *campion*, obs. var. of CHAMPION

Campion ★ ('kæmpɪən) *n* **1 Saint Edmund.** 1540–81, English martyr. He joined the Jesuits in 1573 and returned to England (1580) as a missionary: charged with treason and hanged. **2 Jane.** born 1954, New Zealand film director and screenwriter. Her films include *Sweetie* (1987), *The Piano* (1993), and *Holy Smoke* (2000). **3 Thomas.** 1567–1620, English poet and musician, noted for his songs.

Campobello ★ (ˌkæmpə'bɛləʊ) *n* an island in the Bay of Fundy, off the coast of SE Canada: part of New Brunswick province. Area: about 52 sq. km (20 sq. miles). Pop.: 1317 (1991).

Campo Formio ★ (*Italian* 'kampo 'fɔrmjo) *n* a village in NE Italy, in Friuli-Venezia Giulia: scene of the signing of a treaty in 1797 that ended the war between revolutionary France and Austria. Modern name: **Campoformido** (kampo'fɔrmido).

Campo Grande ★ (*Portuguese* 'kɐ:mpu 'grɐ:ndə) *n* a city in SW Brazil, capital of Mato Grosso do Sul state on the São Paulo-Corumbá railway: market centre. Pop.: 516 403 (1991).

camp oven *n Austral. & NZ.* a heavy metal pot or box with a lid, used for baking over an open fire.

camp pie *n Austral.* tinned meat.

camp site *n* an area on which holiday-makers may pitch a tent, etc. Also called: **camping site**.

campus ('kæmpəs) *n, pl* **campuses. 1** the grounds and buildings of a university. **2** *Chiefly US.* the outside area of a college, etc. ORIG C18: from L: field

campylobacter ('kæmpɪləʊˌbæktə) *n* a rod-shaped bacterium that causes infections in animals and man; a common cause of gastroenteritis. ORIG from Gk *kampulos* bent + BACTER(IUM)

Cam Ranh ★ ('kæm 'ræn) *n* a port in SE Vietnam: large natural harbour, in recent years used as a naval base by French, Japanese, US, and Russian forces successively. Pop.: 114 041 (1989).

camshaft ('kæmˌʃɑ:ft) *n* a shaft having one or more cams attached to it.

Camus ★ (*French* kamy) *n* **Albert** (albɛr). 1913–60, French writer, noted for the novels *L'Étranger* (1942) and *La Peste* (1947), the play *Caligula* (1946), and the essay *L'Homme révolté* (1951): Nobel prize for literature 1957.

can[1] (kæn; *unstressed* kən) *vb, past* **could.** (takes an infinitive without *to* or an implied infinitive) used as an auxiliary: **1** to indicate ability, skill, or fitness to perform a task: *I can run.* **2** to indicate permission or the right to something: *can I have a drink?* **3** to indicate knowledge of how to do something: *he can speak three languages.* **4** to indicate the possibility, opportunity, or likelihood: *my trainer says I can win the race.* ORIG OE *cunnan*

can[2] (kæn) *n* **1** a container, esp. for liquids, usually of thin metal: *a petrol can.* **2** a tin (metal container): *a beer can.* **3** Also: **canful.** the contents of a can or the amount a can will hold. **4** a slang word for **prison. 5** *US & Canad.* a slang word for **toilet. 6** a shallow cylindrical metal container used for storing and handling film. **7 can of worms.** *Inf.* a complicated problem. **8 in the can. 8a** (of a film, piece of music, etc.) having been recorded, edited, etc. **8b** *Inf.* agreed: *the contract is in the can.* ◆ *vb* **cans, canning, canned. 9** to put (food, etc.) into a can or cans. ORIG OE *canne*
▸ **'canner** *n*

Can. *abbrev. for:* **1** Canada. **2** Canadian.

Cana ★ ('keɪnə) *n New Testament.* the town in Galilee, north of Nazareth, where Jesus performed his first miracle by changing water into wine (John 2:1, 11).

Canaan ★ ('keɪnən) *n* an ancient region between the River Jordan and the Mediterranean: the Promised Land of the Israelites.

Canaanite ('keɪnəˌnaɪt) *n* a member of an ancient Semitic people who occupied the land of Canaan before the Israelite conquest.

Canada ★ ('kænədə) *n* a country in North America: the second largest country in the world; first permanent settlements made by the French from 1605; ceded to Britain in 1763 after a series of colonial wars; established as the Dominion of Canada in 1867; a member of the Commonwealth. It consists generally of sparsely inhabited tundra regions, rich in natural resources, in the north, the Rocky Mountains in the west, the Canadian Shield in the east, and vast central prairies; the bulk of the population is concentrated along the US border and the Great Lakes in the south. Languages: English and French. Religion: Christian majority. Currency: Canadian dollar. Capital: Ottawa. Pop.: 30 626 000 (1999 est.). Area: 9 976 185 sq. km (3 851 809 sq. miles).

Canada balsam *n* **1** a yellow transparent resin obtained from the balsam fir. Because its refractive index is similar to that of glass, it is used as a mounting medium for microscope specimens. **2** another name for **balsam fir.**

Canada Day *n* (in Canada) July 1, the anniversary of the day in 1867 when Canada received dominion status: a public holiday.

Canada goose *n* a large common greyish-brown North American goose with a black neck and head and a white throat patch.

Canada jay *n* a grey crestless jay, notorious in northern parts of N America for its stealing. Also called: **camp robber, whisky-jack.**

Canadian (kəˈneɪdɪən) *adj* **1** of or relating to Canada or its people. ◆ *n* **2** a native, citizen, or inhabitant of Canada.

Canadiana (kəˌneɪdɪˈɑːnə; *Canad.* -ˈænə) *n* objects, such as books, furniture, and antiques, relating to Canadian history and culture.

Canadian football *n* a game like American football played on a grass pitch between teams of 12 players.

Canadianism (kəˈneɪdɪəˌnɪzəm) *n* **1** the Canadian national character or spirit. **2** a linguistic usage, custom, or other feature peculiar to Canada, its people, or their culture.

Canadianize *or* **Canadianise** (kəˈneɪdɪəˌnaɪz) *vb* **Canadianizes, Canadianizing, Canadianized** *or* **Canadianises, Canadianising, Canadianised.** to make or become Canadian by changing customs, ownership, character, content, etc.
▸ **CaˌnadianiˈzationorCaˌnadianiˈsation** *n*

Canadian River ★ *n* a river in the southern US, rising in NE New Mexico and flowing east to the Arkansas River in E Oklahoma. Length: 1458 km (906 miles).

Canadian Shield *n* the wide area of Precambrian rock extending over most of E and central Canada: rich in minerals. Also called: **Laurentian Shield.**

Canadien (*French* kanadjɛ̃; *English* kəˌnædɪˈɛn) *or* (*fem*) **Canadienne** (*French* kanadjɛn; *English* kəˌnædɪˈɛn) *n* a French Canadian.

canaille *French.* (kanɑj) *n* the masses; mob; rabble. ORIG C17: from F, from It. *canaglia* pack of dogs

canakin (ˈkænɪkɪn) *n* a variant spelling of **cannikin.**

canal (kəˈnæl) *n* **1** an artificial waterway constructed for navigation, irrigation, etc. **2** any of various passages or ducts: *the alimentary canal.* **3** any of various intercellular spaces in plants. **4** *Astron.* any of the indistinct surface features of Mars orig. thought to be a network of channels. ◆ *vb* **canals, canalling, canalled** *or US* **canals, canaling, canaled.** (*tr*) **5** to dig a canal through. **6** to provide with a canal or canals. ORIG C15 (in the sense: pipe, tube): from L *canālis* channel, from *canna* reed

canal boat *n* a long narrow boat used on canals, esp. for carrying freight.

Canaletto ★ (*Italian* kanaˈlɛtto) *n* original name *Giovanni Antonio Canale.* 1697–1768, Venetian painter, noted also for his London views.

canaliculus (ˌkænəˈlɪkjʊləs) *n, pl* **canaliculi** (-ˌlaɪ). a small channel or groove, as in some bones. ORIG C16: from L: a little channel, from *canālis* CANAL
▸ **ˌcanaˈlicular** *or* **ˌcanaˈliculate** *adj*

canalize *or* **canalise** (ˈkænəˌlaɪz) *vb* **canalizes, canalizing, canalized** *or* **canalises, canalising, canalised.** (*tr*) **1** to provide with or convert into a canal or canals. **2** to give a particular direction to or provide an outlet for.
▸ **ˌcanaliˈzation** *or* **ˌcanaliˈsation** *n*

canal ray *n Physics.* a stream of positive ions produced in a discharge tube by allowing them to pass through holes in the cathode.

Canal Zone ★ *n* a former administrative region of the US, on the Isthmus of Panama around the Panama Canal: bordered on each side by the Republic of Panama, into which it was incorporated in 1979. Also called: **Panama Canal Zone.**

canapé (ˈkænəpɪ, -ˌpeɪ) *n* a small piece of bread, toast, etc., spread with a savoury topping. ORIG C19: from F: sofa

Canara ★ (kəˈnɑːrə) *n* a variant spelling of **Kanara.**

canard (kæˈnɑːd) *n* **1** a false report; rumour or hoax. **2** an aircraft in which the tailplane is mounted in front of the wing. ORIG C19: from F: a duck, from OF *caner* to quack, imit.

canary (kəˈnɛərɪ) *n, pl* **canaries. 1** a small finch of the Canary Islands and Azores: a popular cagebird noted for its singing. **2 canary yellow. 2a** a light yellow. **2b** (*as adj*): *a canary-yellow car.* **3** a sweet wine similar to Madeira. **4** *Arch.* a sweet wine from the Canary Islands. ORIG C16: from OSp. *canario* of or from the Canary Islands

Canary Islands *or* **Canaries** ★ *pl n* a group of mountainous islands in the Atlantic off the NW coast of Africa, forming an Autonomous Community of Spain. Pop.: 1 522 380 (1988 est.).

canasta (kəˈnæstə) *n* **1** a card game for two to six players who seek to amass points by declaring sets of cards. **2** Also called: **meld.** a declared set in this game, containing seven or more like cards. ORIG C20: from Sp.: basket (because two packs of cards are required), from L *canistrum;* see CANISTER

canaster (ˈkænəstə) *n* coarsely broken dried tobacco leaves. ORIG C19: (meaning: basket in which tobacco was packed): from Sp.; see CANISTER

Canaveral ★ (kəˈnævərəl) *n* **Cape.** a cape on the E coast of Florida: site of the US Air Force Missile Test Centre, from which the majority of US space missions have been launched. Former name (1963–73): Cape **Kennedy.**

Canberra ★ (ˈkænbərə, -brə) *n* the capital of Australia, in Australian Capital Territory: founded in 1913 as a planned capital. Pop.: 303 700 (1995 est.).

cancan (ˈkænˌkæn) *n* a high-kicking dance performed by a female chorus, originating in the music halls of 19th-century Paris. ORIG C19: from F, from ?

cancel (ˈkænsᵊl) *vb* **cancels, cancelling, cancelled** *or US* **cancels, canceling, canceled.** (*mainly tr*) **1** to order (something already arranged, such as a meeting or event) to be postponed indefinitely; call off. **2** to revoke or annul: *the order was cancelled.* **3** to delete (writing, numbers, etc.); cross out. **4** to mark (a cheque, stamp, etc.) with an official stamp to prevent further use. **5** (*also intr;* usually foll. by *out*) to counterbalance: *his generosity cancelled out his past unkindness.* **6** *Maths.* to eliminate (numbers or terms) as common factors from both the numerator and denominator of a fraction or as equal terms from opposite sides of an equation. ◆ *n* **7** a new leaf or section of a book replacing one containing errors, or one that has been omitted. **8** a cancellation. **9** *Music.* a US word for **natural** (sense 16). ORIG C14: from OF *canceller,* from Med. L, from LL: to make like a lattice, from L *cancellī* lattice
▸ **ˈcanceller** *or US* **ˈcanceler** *n*

cancellate (ˈkænsɪˌleɪt) *or* **cancellated** *adj* **1** *Anat.* having a spongy internal structure: *cancellate bones.* **2** *Bot.* forming a network. ORIG C17: from L *cancellāre* to make like a lattice

cancellation (ˌkænsɪˈleɪʃən) *n* **1** the fact or an instance of cancelling. **2** something that has been cancelled, such as a theatre ticket: *we have a cancellation in the stalls.* **3** the marks made by cancelling.

cancer (ˈkænsə) *n* **1** any type of malignant growth or tumour, caused by abnormal and uncontrolled cell division. **2** the condition resulting from this. **3** an evil influence that spreads dangerously. ORIG C14: from L: crab, a creeping tumour
▸ **ˈcancerous** *adj*

Cancer (ˈkænsə) *n, Latin genitive* **Cancri** (ˈkæŋkriː). **1**

Astron. Also called: the **Crab.** a small N constellation. **2** *Astrol.* the fourth sign of the zodiac. The sun is in this sign between about June 21 and July 22. **3 tropic of Cancer.** See **tropic** (sense 1).

cancerophobia (ˌkænsərəʊˈfəʊbɪə) *n* a morbid dread of being afflicted by cancer.

cancroid (ˈkæŋkrɔɪd) *adj* **1** resembling a cancerous growth. **2** resembling a crab. ◆ *n* **3** a skin cancer.

candela (kænˈdiːlə, -ˈdeɪlə) *n* the basic SI unit of luminous intensity; the intensity, in a perpendicular direction, of a surface of 1/600 000 square metre of a black body at the temperature of freezing platinum under a pressure of 101 325 newtons per square metre. Symbol: cd ORIG C20: from L: CANDLE

Candela ★ (kænˈdiːlə) *n* **Felix.** born 1910, Mexican architect.

candelabrum (ˌkændɪˈlɑːbrəm) *or* **candelabra** *n, pl* **candelabra** (-brə), **candelabrums,** *or* **candelabras.** a large branched candleholder or holder for overhead lights. ORIG C19: from L, from *candēla* CANDLE

candescent (kænˈdɛsᵊnt) *adj Rare.* glowing or starting to glow with heat. ORIG C19: from L, from *candēre* to be white, shine
▸ **canˈdescence** *n*

c & f *abbrev. for* cost and freight.

C & G *abbrev. for* City and Guilds.

Candia ★ (ˈkandja) *n* the Italian name for **Iráklion.**

candid (ˈkændɪd) *adj* **1** frank and outspoken. **2** without partiality; unbiased. **3** unposed or informal: *a candid photograph.* ORIG C17: from L, from *candēre* to be white
▸ **ˈcandidly** *adv* ▸ **ˈcandidness** *n*

candida (ˈkændɪdə) *n* any of a genus of yeastlike parasitic fungi, esp. one that causes thrush (**candidiasis**).

candidate (ˈkændɪˌdeɪt) *n* **1** a person seeking or nominated for election to a position of authority or selection for a job, etc. **2** a person taking an examination or test. **3** a person or thing regarded as suitable or likely for a particular fate or position. ORIG C17: from L *candidātus* clothed in white (because the candidate wore a white toga), from *candidus* white
▸ **candidacy** (ˈkændɪdəsɪ) *or* **candidature** (ˈkændɪdətʃə) *n*

candid camera *n* a small camera that may be used to take informal photographs of people.

candied (ˈkændɪd) *adj* impregnated or encrusted with or as if with sugar: *candied peel.*

candle (ˈkændᵊl) *n* **1** a cylindrical piece of wax, tallow, or other fatty substance surrounding a wick, which is burned to produce light. **2** *Physics.* another name for **candela.** **3 burn the candle at both ends.** to exhaust oneself by doing too much, esp. by being up late and getting up early to work. **4 not hold a candle to.** *Inf.* to be inferior or contemptible in comparison with. **5 not worth the candle.** *Inf.* not worth the price or trouble entailed. ◆ *vb* **candles, candling, candled.** **6** (*tr*) to examine (eggs) for freshness or the likelihood of being hatched by viewing them against a bright light. ORIG OE *candel,* from L *candēla,* from *candēre* to glitter
▸ **ˈcandler** *n*

candleberry (ˈkændᵊlbərɪ) *n, pl* **candleberries.** another name for **wax myrtle.**

candlelight (ˈkændᵊlˌlaɪt) *n* **1a** the light from a candle or candles. **1b** (*as modifier*): *a candlelight dinner.* **2** dusk; evening.

Candlemas (ˈkændᵊlməs) *n Christianity.* Feb. 2, the Feast of the Purification of the Virgin Mary and the presentation of Christ in the Temple.

candlenut (ˈkændᵊlˌnʌt) *n* **1** a tree of tropical Asia and Polynesia. **2** the nut of this tree, which yields an oil used in paints. In their native regions the nuts are burned as candles.

candlepower (ˈkændᵊlˌpaʊə) *n* the luminous intensity of a source of light in a given direction: now expressed in candelas.

candlestick (ˈkændᵊlˌstɪk) *or* **candleholder** (ˈkændᵊlˌhəʊldə) *n* a holder, usually ornamental, with a spike or socket for a candle.

candlewick (ˈkændᵊlˌwɪk) *n* **1** unbleached cotton or muslin into which loops of yarn are hooked and then cut to give a tufted pattern. **2** (*modifier*) being or made of candlewick fabric.

C & M *abbrev. for* care and maintenance.

can-do *adj* confident and resourceful in the face of challenges: *a can-do attitude.*

Candolle ★ (*French* kɑ̃dɔl) *n* **Augustin Pyrame de** (ogystɛ̃ piram də). 1778–1841, Swiss botanist; his *Théorie élémentaire de la botanique* (1813) introduced a new system of plant classification.

candour *or US* **candor** (ˈkændə) *n* **1** the quality of being open and honest; frankness. **2** fairness; impartiality. ORIG C17: from L *candor,* from *candēre* to be white

C & W *abbrev. for* country and western.

candy (ˈkændɪ) *n, pl* **candies.** **1** *Chiefly US. & Canad.* sweets, chocolate, etc. ◆ *vb* **candies, candying, candied.** **2** to cause (sugar, etc.) to become crystalline or (of sugar) to become crystalline. **3** (*tr*) to preserve (fruit peel, ginger, etc.) by boiling in sugar. **4** (*tr*) to cover with any crystalline substance, such as ice or sugar. ORIG C18: from OF *sucre candi* candied sugar, from Ar. *qandi* candied, from *qand* cane sugar

candyfloss (ˈkændɪˌflɒs) *n Brit.* a very light fluffy confection made from coloured spun sugar, usually held on a stick. US and Canad. name: **cotton candy.** Austral. name: **fairyfloss.**

candy-striped *adj* (esp. of clothing fabric) having narrow coloured stripes on a white background.
▸ **candy stripe** *n*

candytuft (ˈkændɪˌtʌft) *n* either of two species of *Iberis* having clusters of white, red, or purplish flowers. ORIG C17: *Candy,* obs. var. of CANDIA (town in Crete) + TUFT

cane (keɪn) *n* **1a** the long jointed pithy or hollow flexible stem of the bamboo, rattan, or any similar plant. **1b** any plant having such a stem. **2a** strips of such stems, woven or interlaced to make wickerwork, etc. **2b** (*as modifier*): *a cane chair.* **3** the woody stem of a reed, blackberry, or loganberry. **4** a flexible rod with which to administer a beating. **5** a slender rod used as a walking stick. **6** See **sugar cane.** ◆ *vb* **canes, caning, caned.** (*tr*) **7** to whip or beat with or as if with a cane. **8** to make or repair with cane. **9** *Inf.* to defeat: *we got well caned in the match.* ORIG C14: from OF, from L *canna,* from Gk *kanna,* of Semitic origin
▸ **ˈcaner** *n*

Canea ★ (kæˈnɪə) *n* the capital and chief port of Crete, on the NW coast. Pop.: 50 000 (latest est.). Also called: **Chania** (ˈhɑːnɪə). Greek name: **Khaniá.**

canebrake (ˈkeɪnˌbreɪk) *n US.* a thicket of canes.

cane sugar *n* **1** the sucrose obtained from sugar cane. **2** another name for **sucrose.**

Canetti ★ (kəˈnɛtɪ) *n* **Elias.** 1905–94, British writer, born in Bulgaria; wrote chiefly in German. His works include the novel *Auto da Fé* (1935). Nobel prize for literature 1981.

cangue *or* **cang** (kæŋ) *n* (formerly in China) a large wooden collar worn by petty criminals as a punishment. ORIG C18: from F, from Port. *canga* yoke

canikin (ˈkænɪkɪn) *n* a variant spelling of **cannikin.**

canine (ˈkeɪnaɪn, ˈkæn-) *adj* **1** of or resembling a dog. **2** of or belonging to the Canidae, a family of mammals, including dogs, wolves, and foxes, typically having a bushy tail, erect ears, and a long muzzle. **3** of or relating to any of the four teeth, two in each jaw, situated between the incisors and the premolars. ◆ *n* **4** any animal of the family Canidae. **5** a canine tooth. ORIG C17: from L *canīnus,* from *canis* dog

caning (ˈkeɪnɪŋ) *n Inf.* a severe defeat or punishment.

Canis Major (ˈkeɪnɪs) *n, Latin genitive* **Canis Majoris** (məˈdʒɔːrɪs). a S constellation containing Sirius, the brightest star in the sky. Also called: the **Great Dog.** ORIG L: the greater dog

Canis Minor *n, Latin genitive* **Canis Minoris** (maɪˈnɔːrɪs). a small N constellation. Also called: the **Little Dog.** ORIG L: the lesser dog

canister (ˈkænɪstə) *n* **1** a container, usually made of metal, in which dry food, such as tea or coffee, is stored.

★ people and places

2 (formerly) **2a** a type of shrapnel shell for firing from a cannon. **2b** Also called: **canister shot.** the shot or shrapnel packed inside this. ORIG C17: from L *canistrum* basket woven from reeds, from Gk, from *kanna* reed

canker ('kæŋkə) *n* **1** an ulceration, esp. of the lips. **2** *Vet. science.* **2a** a disease of horses in which the horn of the hoofs becomes spongy. **2b** an ulcerative disease of the lining of the external ear, esp. in dogs and cats. **2c** ulceration or abscess of the mouth, eyelids, ears, or cloaca of birds. **3** an open wound in the stem of a tree or shrub. **4** something evil that spreads and corrupts. ◆ *vb* **5** to infect or become infected with or as if with canker. ORIG OE *cancer,* from L *cancer* cancerous sore
▸ **'cankerous** *adj*

cankerworm ('kæŋkə,wɜːm) *n* the larva of either of two moths, which feed on and destroy fruit and shade trees in North America.

canna ('kænə) *n* any of a genus of tropical plants having broad leaves and red or yellow showy flowers. ORIG C17: from NL CANE

cannabis ('kænəbɪs) *n* **1** another name for **hemp** (the plant), esp. Indian hemp. **2** the drug obtained from the dried leaves and flowers of the hemp plant, which is smoked or chewed for its psychoactive properties. See also **hashish, marijuana. 3 cannabis resin.** a poisonous resin obtained from the hemp plant. ORIG C18: from L, from Gk *kannabis*

Cannae ★ ('kæniː) *n* an ancient city in SE Italy: scene of a victory by Hannibal over the Romans (216 B.C.).

canned (kænd) *adj* **1** preserved and stored in airtight cans or tins. **2** *Inf.* prepared or recorded in advance: *canned music.* **3** *Sl.* drunk.

cannel coal *or* **cannel** ('kænᵊl) *n* a dull coal burning with a smoky luminous flame. ORIG C16: from N English dialect *cannel* candle

cannelloni *or* **canneloni** (,kænɪ'ləʊnɪ) *pl n* tubular pieces of pasta filled with meat or cheese. ORIG It., pl of *cannellone,* from *cannello* stalk

cannery ('kænərɪ) *n, pl* **canneries.** a place where foods are canned.

Cannes ★ (kæn, kænz; *French* kan) *n* a port and resort in SE France: developed in the 19th century from a fishing village; annual film festival. Pop.: 335 647 (1990).

cannibal ('kænɪbᵊl) *n* **1** a person who eats the flesh of other human beings. **2** an animal that feeds on the flesh of others of its kind. ORIG C16: from Sp. *Canibales,* the name used by Columbus to designate the Caribs of Cuba and Haiti
▸ **'canniba,lism** *n*

cannibalize *or* **cannibalise** ('kænɪbə,laɪz) *vb* **cannibalizes, cannibalizing, cannibalized** *or* **cannibalises, cannibalising, cannibalised.** (*tr*) to use (serviceable parts from one machine or vehicle) to repair another.
▸ **,cannibali'zation** *or* **,cannibali'sation** *n*

cannikin, canakin, *or* **canikin** ('kænɪkɪn) *n* a small can, esp. one used as a drinking vessel. ORIG C16: from MDu. *kanneken;* see CAN², -KIN

canning ('kænɪŋ) *n* the process or business of sealing food in cans or tins to preserve it.

Canning ★ ('kænɪŋ) *n* **1 Charles John,** 1st Earl Canning. 1812–62, British statesman; governor general of India (1856–58) and first viceroy (1858–62). **2** his father, **George.** 1770–1827, British Tory statesman; foreign secretary (1822–27) and prime minister (1827).

Cannock ★ ('kænək) *n* a town in W central England, in S Staffordshire: **Cannock Chase** (a public area of heathland, once a royal preserve) is just to the E. Pop.: 60 106 (1991).

cannon ('kænən) *n, pl* **cannons** *or* **cannon. 1** an automatic aircraft gun. **2** *History.* a heavy artillery piece consisting of a metal tube mounted on a carriage. **3** a heavy tube or drum, esp. one that can rotate freely. **4** See **cannon bone. 5** *Billiards.* a shot in which the cue ball is caused to contact one object ball after another. Usual US and Canad. word: **carom.** ◆ *vb* **6** (*intr*) to rebound; collide (*with* into). **7** (*intr*) *Billiards.* to make a cannon. ORIG C16: from OF *canon,* from It. *cannone* cannon, from *canna* tube

cannonade (,kænə'neɪd) *n* **1** an intense and continuous artillery bombardment. ◆ *vb* **cannonades, cannonading, cannonaded. 2** to attack (a target) with cannon.

cannonball ('kænən,bɔːl) *n* **1** a projectile fired from a cannon: usually a solid round metal shot. ◆ *vb* (*intr*) **2** (often foll. by *along,* etc.) to rush along. ◆ *adj* **3** very fast or powerful.

cannon bone *n* a bone in the legs of horses and other hoofed animals consisting of greatly elongated fused metatarsals or metacarpals.

cannoneer (,kænə'nɪə) *n* (formerly) a soldier who served and fired a cannon; artilleryman.

cannon fodder *n* men regarded as expendable in war because they are part of a huge army.

cannot ('kænɒt, kæ'nɒt) an auxiliary verb expressing incapacity, inability, withholding permission, etc.; can not.

cannula *or* **canula** ('kænjʊlə) *n, pl* **cannulas, cannulae** (-,liː), *or* **canulas, canulae** (-,liː). *Surgery.* a narrow tube for draining fluid from or introducing medication into the body. ORIG C17: from L: a small reed, from *canna* a reed

canny ('kænɪ) *adj* **cannier, canniest. 1** shrewd, esp. in business. **2** *Scot. & NE English dialect.* good or nice: used as a general term of approval. **3** *Scot.* lucky or fortunate. ORIG C16: from CAN¹ (in the sense: to know how) + -Y¹
▸ **'cannily** *adv* ▸ **'canniness** *n*

canoe (kə'nuː) *n* **1** a light narrow open boat, propelled by one or more paddles. ◆ *vb* **canoes, canoeing, canoed. 2** to go in or transport by canoe. ORIG C16: from Sp. *canoa,* of Carib origin
▸ **ca'noeist** *n*

canon¹ ('kænən) *n* **1** *Christianity.* a Church decree enacted to regulate morals or religious practices. **2** (*often pl*) a general rule or standard, as of judgment, morals, etc. **3** (*often pl*) a principle or criterion applied in a branch of learning or art. **4** *RC Church.* the list of the canonized saints. **5** *RC Church.* Also called: **Eucharistic Prayer.** the prayer in the Mass in which the Host is consecrated. **6** a list of writings, esp. sacred writings, recognized as genuine. **7** a piece of music in which an extended melody in one part is imitated successively in one or more other parts. **8** a list of the works of an author that are accepted as authentic. ORIG OE, from L, from Gk *kanōn* rule, rod for measuring

canon² ('kænən) *n* **1** one of several priests on the permanent staff of a cathedral, who are responsible for organizing services, maintaining the fabric, etc. **2** *RC Church.* Also called: **canon regular.** a member of either of two religious orders living communally as monks but performing clerical duties.. ORIG C13: from Anglo-F, from LL *canonicus* one living under a rule, from CANON¹

canonical (kə'nɒnɪkᵊl) *or* **canonic** *adj* **1** included in a canon of sacred or other officially recognized writings. **2** in conformity with canon law. **3** accepted; authoritative. **4** *Music.* in the form of a canon. **5** of or relating to a cathedral chapter. **6** of a canon (clergyman).
▸ **ca'nonically** *adv*

canonical hour *n* **1** *RC Church.* one of the seven prayer times appointed for each day by canon law. **2** *Church of England.* any time at which marriages may lawfully be celebrated.

canonicals (kə'nɒnɪkᵊlz) *pl n* the vestments worn by clergy when officiating.

canonicity (,kænə'nɪsɪtɪ) *n* the fact or quality of being canonical.

canonist ('kænənɪst) *n* a specialist in canon law.

canonize *or* **canonise** ('kænə,naɪz) *vb* **canonizes, canonizing, canonized** *or* **canonises, canonising, canonised.** (*tr*) **1** *RC Church.* to declare (a person) to be a saint. **2** to regard as a saint. **3** to sanction by canon law.
▸ **,canoni'zation** *or* **,canoni'sation** *n*

canon law *n* the codified body of laws enacted by the supreme authorities of a Christian Church.

canonry ('kænənrɪ) *n, pl* **canonries. 1** the office, benefice, or status of a canon. **2** canons collectively. ORIG C15: from CANON² + -RY

canoodle (kə'nuːdᵊl) *vb* **canoodles, canoodling, canoodled.**

(*intr;* often by *with*) *Sl.* to kiss and cuddle. ORIG C19: from ?

Canopic jar, urn, *or* **vase** (kəˈnəʊpɪk) *n* (in ancient Egypt) one of four containers for holding the entrails of a mummy.

Canopus ★ (kəˈnəʊpəs) *n* a port in ancient Egypt east of Alexandria where granite monuments have been found inscribed with the name of Rameses II and written in languages similar to those of the Rosetta stone.
▸ **Caˈnopic** *adj*

canopy (ˈkænəpɪ) *n, pl* **canopies. 1** an ornamental awning above a throne, bed, person, etc. **2** a rooflike covering over an altar, niche, etc. **3** a roofed structure serving as a sheltered passageway. **4** a large or wide covering: *the sky was a grey canopy.* **5** the hemisphere that forms the supporting surface of a parachute. **6** the transparent cover of an aircraft cockpit. **7** the highest level of foliage in a forest, formed by the crowns of the trees. ◆ *vb* **canopies, canopying, canopied. 8** (*tr*) to cover with or as with a canopy. ORIG C14: from Med. L *canōpeum* mosquito net, from L, from Gk *kōnōpeion* bed with protective net

canst (kænst) *vb Arch.* the form of **can**[1] used with the pronoun *thou* or its relative form.

cant[1] (kænt) *n* **1** insincere talk, esp. concerning religion or morals. **2** phrases that have become meaningless through repetition. **3** specialized vocabulary of a particular group, such as thieves, journalists, or lawyers. ◆ *vb* **4** (*intr*) to speak in or use cant. ORIG C16: prob. via Norman F *canter* to sing, from L *cantāre;* used disparagingly, from the 12th cent., of chanting in religious services
▸ **ˈcantingly** *adv*

cant[2] (kænt) *n* **1** inclination from a vertical or horizontal plane. **2** a sudden movement that tilts or turns something. **3** the angle or tilt thus caused. **4** a corner or outer angle. **5** an oblique or slanting surface, edge, or line. ◆ *vb* (*tr*) **6** to tip, tilt, or overturn. **7** to set in an oblique position. **8** another word for **bevel** (sense 1). ◆ *adj* **9** oblique; slanting. **10** having flat surfaces. ORIG C14 (in the sense: edge): ?from L *canthus* iron hoop round a wheel, from ?

Cant. *abbrev. for:* **1** Canterbury. **2** *Bible.* Canticles.

can't (kɑːnt) *contraction of* cannot.

Cantab. (kænˈtæb) *abbrev. for* Cantabrigiensis. ORIG L: of Cambridge

cantabile (kænˈtɑːbɪlɪ) *Music.* ◆ *adj, adv* **1** (to be performed) flowingly and melodiously. ◆ *n* **2** a piece or passage performed in this way. ORIG It., from LL, from L *cantāre* to sing

Cantabrian Mountains ★ (kænˈteɪbrɪən) *pl n* a mountain chain along the N coast of Spain, consisting of a series of high ridges that rise over 2400 m (8000 ft): rich in minerals (esp. coal and iron).

Cantabrigian (ˌkæntəˈbrɪdʒɪən) *adj* **1** of or characteristic of Cambridge or Cambridge University. ◆ *n* **2** a member or graduate of Cambridge University. **3** an inhabitant or native of Cambridge. ORIG C17: from Med. L *Cantabrigia*

Cantal ★ (*French* kɑ̃tal) *n* **1** a department of S central France, in the Auvergne region. Capital: Aurillac. Pop.: 155 587 (1994 est.). Area: 5779 sq. km (2254 sq. miles). **2** a hard strong cheese made in this area.

cantaloupe *or* **cantaloup** (ˈkæntəˌluːp) *n* **1** a cultivated variety of muskmelon with ribbed warty rind and orange flesh. **2** any of several other muskmelons. ORIG C18: from F, from *Cantaluppi,* near Rome, where first cultivated in Europe

cantankerous (kænˈtæŋkərəs) *adj* quarrelsome; irascible. ORIG C18: ?from C14 (obs.) *conteckour* a contentious person, from Anglo-F *contek* strife, from ?
▸ **canˈtankerously** *adv* ▸ **canˈtankerousness** *n*

cantata (kænˈtɑːtə) *n* a musical setting of a text, esp. a religious text, consisting of arias, duets, and choruses. ORIG C18: from It., from *cantare* to sing, from L

canteen (kænˈtiːn) *n* **1** a restaurant attached to a factory, school, etc., providing meals for large numbers. **2a** a small shop that provides a limited range of items to a military unit. **2b** a recreation centre for military personnel. **3** a temporary or mobile stand at which food is provided. **4a** a box in which a set of cutlery is laid out. **4b** the cutlery itself. **5** a flask for carrying water or other liquids. ORIG C18: from F, from It. *cantina* wine cellar, from *canto* corner, from L *canthus* iron hoop encircling chariot wheel

Canteloube ★ (ˈkæntəˌluːb; *French* kɑ̃tlub) *n* (**Marie**) **Joseph** (*French* ʒozɛf). 1879–1957, French composer, best known for his *Chants d'Auvergne* (1923–30).

canter (ˈkæntə) *n* **1** a gait of horses, etc., between a trot and a gallop in speed. **2 at a canter.** easily; without effort. ◆ *vb* **3** to move or cause to move at a canter. ORIG C18: short for *Canterbury trot,* the supposed pace at which pilgrims rode to Canterbury

Canterbury ★ (ˈkæntəbərɪ, -brɪ) *n* **1** a city in SE England, in E Kent: starting point for St Augustine's mission to England (597 A.D.); cathedral where St Thomas à Becket was martyred (1170); seat of the archbishop and primate of England; seat of the University of Kent at Canterbury (1965). Pop.: 36 464 (1991). Latin name: **Durovernum** (ˌduːrəʊˈvɜːnəm, ˌdjʊə-). **2** a regional council of New Zealand, on E central South Island on **Canterbury Bight**: mountainous with coastal lowlands; agricultural. Chief town: Christchurch. Pop.: 477 667 (1996). Area: 43 371 sq. km (16 742 sq. miles).

Canterbury bell *n* a biennial European plant related to the campanula and widely cultivated for its blue, violet, or white flowers.

cantharides (kænˈθærɪˌdiːz) *pl n, sing* **cantharis** (ˈkænθərɪs). a diuretic and urogenital stimulant prepared from the dried bodies of Spanish fly. Also called: **Spanish fly.** ORIG C15: from L, pl of *cantharis,* from Gk *kantharis* Spanish fly

cant hook *or* **dog** *n Forestry.* a wooden pole with a blunt steel tip and an adjustable hook at one end, used for handling logs.

canthus (ˈkænθəs) *n, pl* **canthi** (-ˌθaɪ). the inner or outer corner of the eye, formed by the natural junction of the eyelids. ORIG C17: from NL, from L: iron tyre

canticle (ˈkæntɪkᵊl) *n* a nonmetrical hymn, derived from the Bible and used in the liturgy of certain Christian churches. ORIG C13: from L *canticulum,* dim. of *canticus* a song, from *canere* to sing

cantilena (ˌkæntɪˈleɪnə) *n* a smooth flowing style in the writing of vocal music. ORIG C18: It.

cantilever (ˈkæntɪˌliːvə) *n* **1** a beam, girder, or structural framework that is fixed at one end only. **2** a part of a beam or a structure projecting outwards beyond its support. ORIG C17: ?from CANT[2] + LEVER

cantilever bridge *n* a bridge having spans that are constructed as cantilevers.

cantillate (ˈkæntɪˌleɪt) *vb* **cantillates, cantillating, cantillated. 1** to chant (passages of the Hebrew Scriptures) according to the traditional Jewish melody. **2** to intone or chant. ORIG C19: from LL *cantillāre* to sing softly, from L *cantāre* to sing
▸ **ˌcantilˈlation** *n*

cantle (ˈkæntᵊl) *n* **1** the back part of a saddle that slopes upwards. **2** a broken-off piece. ORIG C14: from OF *cantel,* from *cant* corner

canto (ˈkæntəʊ) *n, pl* **cantos.** a main division of a long poem. ORIG C16: from It.: song, from L, from *canere* to sing

canto fermo (ˈkæntəʊ ˈfɜːməʊ) *or* **cantus firmus** (ˈkæntəs ˈfɜːməs) *n* **1** a melody that is the basis to which other parts are added in polyphonic music. **2** the traditional Church plainchant as prescribed by use and regulation. ORIG It., from Med L: fixed song

canton *n* **1** (ˈkæntɒn, kænˈtɒn). a political division of Switzerland. **2** (ˈkæntən). *Heraldry.* a small square charge on a shield, usually in the top left corner. ◆ *vb* **3** (kænˈtɒn). (*tr*) to divide into cantons. **4** (kənˈtuːn). (esp. formerly) to allocate accommodation to (military personnel, etc.). ORIG C16: from OF: corner, from It., from *canto* corner, from L *canthus* iron rim
▸ **ˈcantonal** *adj*

Canton ★ *n* **1** (kænˈtɒn). a port in SE China, capital of

★ people and places

Guangdong province, on the Zhu Jiang (Pearl River): the first Chinese port open to European trade. Pop.: 3 580 000 (1991 est.). Chinese names: **Guangzhou, Kwangchow.** **2** ('kæntən). a city in the US, in NE Ohio. Pop.: 84 188 (1994 est.).

Cantonese (ˌkæntəˈniːz) *n* **1** the Chinese language spoken in the city of Canton, Guangdong and Guanxi provinces, Hong Kong, and elsewhere inside and outside China. **2** (*pl* **Cantonese**) a native or inhabitant of Canton city or Guangdong province. ◆ *adj* **3** of or relating to Canton or Guangdong or the Chinese language spoken there.

cantonment (kənˈtuːnmənt) *n Mil.* (esp. formerly) **1** a large training camp. **2** the winter quarters of a campaigning army. **3** *History.* a permanent military camp in British India.

Canton River ★ (kænˈtɒn) *n* another name for the **Zhu Jiang.**

cantor (ˈkæntɔː) *n* **1** *Judaism.* a man employed to lead synagogue services. **2** *Christianity.* the leader of the singing in a church choir. ORIG C16: from L: singer, from *canere* to sing

cantorial (kænˈtɔːrɪəl) *adj* **1** of a precentor. **2** (of part of a choir) on the same side of a cathedral, etc., as the precentor.

cantoris (kænˈtɔːrɪs) *adj* (in antiphonal music) to be sung by the cantorial side of a choir. Cf. **decani.** ORIG L: genitive of *cantor* precentor

Cantuar. (ˈkæntjʊˌɑː) *abbrev. for* Cantuariensis. ORIG L: (Archbishop) of Canterbury

Canuck (kəˈnʌk) *n, adj US & Canad. inf.* Canadian. ORIG C19: from ?

Canute, Cnut, *or* **Knut** ★ (kəˈnjuːt) *n* died 1035, Danish king of England (1016–35), Denmark (1018–35), and Norway (1028–35). He defeated Edmund II of England (1016), but divided the kingdom with him until Edmund's death. He invaded Scotland (1027) and drove Olaf II from Norway (1028).

canvas (ˈkænvəs) *n* **1a** a heavy cloth made of cotton, hemp, or jute, used for sails, tents, etc. **1b** (*as modifier*): *a canvas bag.* **2a** a piece of canvas, etc., on which a painting is done, usually in oils. **2b** an oil painting. **3** a tent or tents collectively. **4** *Naut.* the sails of a vessel collectively. **5** any coarse loosely woven cloth on which tapestry, etc., is done. **6** (preceded by *the*) the floor of a boxing or wrestling ring. **7** *Rowing.* the covered part at either end of a racing boat: *to win by a canvas.* **8 under canvas. 8a** in tents. **8b** *Naut.* with sails unfurled. ORIG C14: from Norman F *canevas,* ult. from L *cannabis* hemp

canvasback (ˈkænvəsˌbæk) *n, pl* **canvasbacks** *or* **canvasback.** a North American diving duck, the male of which has a reddish-brown head.

canvass (ˈkænvəs) *vb* **1** to solicit votes, orders, etc., (from). **2** to determine the opinions of (voters before an election, etc.), esp. by conducting a survey. **3** to investigate (something) thoroughly, esp. by discussion. **4** *Chiefly US.* to inspect (votes) to determine their validity. ◆ *n* **5** a solicitation of opinions, votes, etc. ORIG C16: prob. from obs. sense of CANVAS (to toss someone in a canvas sheet, hence, to criticize)
▸ **ˈcanvasser** *n*

canyon *or* **cañon** (ˈkænjən) *n* a gorge or ravine, esp. in North America, usually formed by a river. ORIG C19: from Sp., from *caña* tube, from L *canna* cane

canzonetta (ˌkænzəˈnɛtə) *or* **canzonet** (ˌkænzəˈnɛt) *n* a short, lively song, typically of the 16th to 18th centuries. ORIG C16: It.: dim. of *canzone,* from L *canere* to sing

caoutchouc (ˈkaʊtʃʊk) *n* another name for **rubber**[1] (sense 1). ORIG C18: from F, from obs. Sp., from Quechua

cap (kæp) *n* **1** a covering for the head, esp. a small close-fitting one. **2** such a covering serving to identify the wearer's rank, occupation, etc.: *a nurse's cap.* **3** something that protects or covers: *lens cap.* **4** an uppermost surface or part: *the cap of a wave.* **5a** See **percussion cap. 5b** a small amount of explosive enclosed in paper and used in a toy gun. **6** *Sport, chiefly Brit.* **6a** an emblematic hat or beret given to someone chosen for a representative team. **6b** a player chosen for such a team. **7** any part like a cap in shape. **8** *Bot.* the pileus of a mushroom or toadstool. **9** *Hunting.* money contributed to the funds of a hunt by a follower who is neither a subscriber nor a farmer, in return for a day's hunting. **10** *Anat.* **10a** the natural enamel covering a tooth. **10b** an artificial protective covering for a tooth. **11** Also: **Dutch cap, diaphragm.** a contraceptive membrane placed over the mouth of the cervix. **12** an upper financial limit. **13** a mortarboard worn at an academic ceremony (esp. in **cap and gown**). **14** *Meteorol.* **14a** the cloud covering the peak of a mountain. **14b** the transient top of detached clouds above an increasing cumulus. **15 set one's cap at.** (of a woman) to be determined to win as a husband or lover. **16 cap in hand.** humbly, as when asking a favour. ◆ *vb* **caps, capping, capped.** (*tr*) **17** to cover, as with a cap: *snow capped the mountain tops.* **18** *Inf.* to outdo; excel. **19 cap it all.** to provide the finishing touch. **20** *Sport, Brit.* to select (a player) for a representative team. **21** to seal off (an oil or gas well). **22** to impose an upper limit on the level of increase of (a tax): *charge-cap.* **23** *Chiefly Scot. & NZ.* to award a degree to. ORIG OE *cæppe,* from LL *cappa* hood, ?from L *caput* head

CAP *abbrev. for:* Common Agricultural Policy: (in the EU) the system for supporting farm incomes by maintaining agricultural prices at agreed levels.

cap. *abbrev. for:* **1** capacity. **2** capital. **3** capitalize. **4** capital letter.

Capa ★ (ˈkæpə) *n* **Robert,** real name *André Friedmann.* 1913–54, Hungarian photographer.

capability (ˌkeɪpəˈbɪlɪtɪ) *n, pl* **capabilities. 1** the quality of being capable; ability. **2** the quality of being susceptible to the use or treatment indicated: *the capability of a metal to be fused.* **3** (*usually pl*) potential aptitude.

Capablanca ★ (*Spanish* kapaˈβlaŋka) *n* **José Raúl** (xoˈse raˈul), called *Capa* or *the Chess Machine.* 1888–1942, Cuban chess player; world champion 1921–27.

capable (ˈkeɪpəbᵊl) *adj* **1** having ability; competent. **2** (*postpositive;* foll. by *of*) able or having the skill (to do something): *she is capable of hard work.* **3** (*postpositive;* foll. by *of*) having the temperament or inclination (to do something): *he seemed capable of murder.* ORIG C16: from F, from LL *capābilis* able to take in, from L *capere* to take
▸ **ˈcapableness** *n* ▸ **ˈcapably** *adv*

capacious (kəˈpeɪʃəs) *adj* capable of holding much; roomy. ORIG C17: from L, from *capere* to take
▸ **caˈpaciously** *adv* ▸ **caˈpaciousness** *n*

capacitance (kəˈpæsɪtəns) *n* **1** the property of a system that enables it to store electric charge. **2** a measure of this, equal to the charge that must be added to such a system to raise its electrical potential by one unit. Former name: **capacity.** ORIG C20: from CAPACIT(Y) + -ANCE
▸ **caˈpacitive** *adj*

capacitor (kəˈpæsɪtə) *n* a device for accumulating electric charge, usually consisting of two conducting surfaces separated by a dielectric. Former name: **condenser.**

capacity (kəˈpæsɪtɪ) *n, pl* **capacities. 1** the ability or power to contain, absorb, or hold. **2** the amount that can be contained: *a capacity of six gallons.* **3a** the maximum amount something can contain or absorb (esp. in **filled to capacity**). **3b** (*as modifier*): *a capacity crowd.* **4** the ability to understand or learn: *he has a great capacity for Greek.* **5** the ability to do or produce: *the factory's output was not at capacity.* **6** a specified position or function. **7** a measure of the electrical output of a piece of apparatus such as a generator or accumulator. **8** *Electronics.* a former name for **capacitance. 9** *Computing.* **9a** the number of words or characters that can be stored in a storage device. **9b** the range of numbers that can be processed in a register. **10** legal competence: *the capacity to make a will.* ORIG C15: from OF *capacite,* from L, from *capāx* spacious, from *capere* to take

cap and bells *n* the traditional garb of a court jester, including a cap with bells.

cap-a-pie (ˌkæpəˈpiː) *adv* (dressed, armed, etc.) from head to foot. ORIG C16: from OF

caparison (kəˈpærɪsᵊn) *n* **1** a decorated covering for a horse. **2** rich or elaborate clothing and ornaments. ◆ *vb*

3 (*tr*) to put a caparison on. ORIG C16: via obs. F from OSp. *caparazón* saddlecloth, prob. from *capa* CAPE[1]

cape[1] (keɪp) *n* a sleeveless garment like a cloak but usually shorter. ORIG C16: from F, from Provençal *capa,* from LL *cappa;* see CAP

cape[2] (keɪp) *n* a headland or promontory. ORIG C14: from OF *cap,* from OProvençal, from L *caput* head

Cape ★ (keɪp) *n* **the. 1** the SW region of South Africa, in Western Cape province. **2** See **Cape of Good Hope.**

Cape Breton Island ★ *n* an island off SE Canada, in NE Nova Scotia, separated from the mainland by the Strait of Canso: its easternmost point is **Cape Breton.** Pop.: 120 098 (1991). Area: 10 280 sq. km (3970 sq. miles).

Cape Cod ★ *n* a long sandy peninsula in SE Massachusetts, between **Cape Cod Bay** and the Atlantic.

Cape Colony ★ *n* the name from 1652 until 1910 of the former **Cape Province** of South Africa.

Cape Coloured *n* (in South Africa) another name for a **Coloured** (sense 2).

Cape doctor *n S. African inf.* a strong fresh SE wind blowing in the vicinity of Cape Town, esp. in the summer.

Cape Dutch *n* **1** (in South Africa) a distinctive style in furniture or buildings. **2** an obsolete name for **Afrikaans.**

Cape Flats ★ *pl n* the strip of low-lying land in South Africa joining the Cape Peninsula proper to the African mainland.

Cape gooseberry *n* another name for **strawberry tomato.**

Cape Horn ★ *n* a rocky headland on an island at the extreme S tip of South America, belonging to Chile. It is notorious for gales and heavy seas; until the building of the Panama Canal it lay on the sea route between the Atlantic and the Pacific. Also called: **the Horn.**

Čapek ★ (*Czech* 'tʃapɛk) *n* **Karel** ('karel). 1890–1938, Czech writer; author of *R.U.R.* (1921), which introduced the word "robot", and *The Insect Play* (1921).

capelin ('kæpəlɪn) *or* **caplin** ('kæplɪn) *n* a small marine food fish of northern and Arctic seas. ORIG C17: from F *capelan,* from OProvençal, lit.: chaplain

capellmeister *or* **kapellmeister** (kæ'pɛlˌmaɪstə) *n* a person in charge of an orchestra, esp. in an 18th-century princely household. ORIG from G, from *Kapelle* chapel + *Meister* MASTER

Cape of Good Hope ★ *n* a cape in SW South Africa south of Cape Town.

Cape Peninsula ★ *n* (in South Africa) the peninsula and the part of the mainland on which Cape Town and most of its suburbs are located.

Cape pigeon *n* a kind of petrel common in S Africa.

Cape Province ★ *n* a former province of S South Africa: replaced in 1994 by the new provinces of Northern Cape, Western Cape, Eastern Cape, and part of North-West. Official name: **Cape of Good Hope Province.** Former name (1652–1910): **Cape Colony.**

caper[1] ('keɪpə) *n* **1** a playful skip or leap. **2** a high-spirited escapade. **3 cut a caper** *or* **capers.** to skip, leap, or frolic. **4** *US & Canad. sl.* a crime. ◆ *vb* **5** (*intr*) to leap or dance about in a light-hearted manner. ORIG C16: prob. from CAPRIOLE

caper[2] ('keɪpə) *n* **1** a spiny trailing Mediterranean shrub with edible flower buds. **2** its pickled flower buds, used in sauces. ORIG C15: from earlier *capers, capres* (assumed to be pl), from L, from Gk *kapparis*

capercaillie *or* **capercailzie** (ˌkæpə'keɪljɪ) *n* a large European woodland grouse having a black plumage. ORIG C16: from Scot. Gaelic *capull coille* horse of the woods

Capernaum ★ (kə'pɜːnɪəm) *n* a ruined town in N Israel, on the NW shore of the Sea of Galilee: closely associated with Jesus Christ during his ministry.

Cape sparrow *n* a sparrow very common in southern Africa. Also called (esp. S. African): **mossie.**

Capet ★ ('kæpɪt, kæ'pɛt; *French* kapɛ) *n* **Hugh** *or* **Hugues** (yg). ?938–996 A.D., king of France (987–96); founder of the Capetian dynasty.
▸ **Capetian** (kə'piːʃən) *adj, n*

Cape Town ★ *n* the legislative capital of South Africa, situated in the southwest on Table Bay: founded in 1652, the first White settlement in southern Africa; important port. Pop.: 854 616 (1991).

Cape Verde ★ (vɜːd) *n* a republic in the Atlantic off the coast of West Africa, consisting of a group of ten islands and five islets: an overseas territory of Portugal until 1975, when the islands became independent. Official language: Portuguese. Religions: Roman Catholic and animist. Currency: Cape Verdean escudo. Capital: Praia. Pop.: 406 000 (1999 est.). Area: 4033 sq. km (1557 sq. miles).
▸ **Cape Verdean** ('vɜːdɪən) *adj, n*

Cape York ★ *n* the northernmost point of the Australian mainland, in N Queensland on the Torres Strait at the tip of **Cape York Peninsula** (a peninsula between the Coral Sea and the Gulf of Carpentaria).

Cap-Haitien ★ (*French* kapaisjɛ̃, -tjɛ̃) *n* a port in N Haiti: capital during the French colonial period. Pop.: 100 638 (1995 est.). Also called: **le Cap** (lə kap).

capias ('keɪpɪˌæs, 'kæp-) *n Law.* a writ directing a sheriff or other officer to arrest a named person. ORIG C15: from L, lit.: you must take, from *capere*

capillarity (ˌkæpɪ'lærɪtɪ) *n* a phenomenon caused by surface tension and resulting in the elevation or depression of the surface of a liquid in contact with a solid. Also called: **capillary action.**

capillary (kə'pɪlərɪ) *adj* **1** resembling a hair; slender. **2** (of tubes) having a fine bore. **3** *Anat.* of the delicate thin-walled blood vessels that interconnect between the arterioles and the venules. **4** *Physics.* of or relating to capillarity. ◆ *n, pl* **capillaries. 5** *Anat.* any of the capillary blood vessels. ORIG C17: from L *capillāris,* from *capillus* hair

capital[1] ('kæpɪt[ə]l) *n* **1a** the seat of government of a country. **1b** (*as modifier*): *a capital city.* **2** material wealth owned by an individual or business enterprise. **3** wealth available for or capable of use in the production of further wealth, as by industrial investment. **4 make capital (out) of.** to get advantage from. **5** (*sometimes cap.*) the capitalist class or their interests: *capital versus labour.* **6** *Accounting.* **6a** the ownership interests of a business as represented by the excess of assets over liabilities. **6b** the nominal value of the issued shares. **7** any assets or resources. **8a** a capital letter. Abbrev.: **cap. 8b** (*as modifier*): *capital B.* ◆ *adj* **9** (*prenominal*) *Law.* involving or punishable by death: *a capital offence.* **10** very serious: *a capital error.* **11** primary, chief, or principal: *our capital concern.* **12** of, relating to, or designating the large letter used chiefly as the initial letter in personal names and place names and often for abbreviations and acronyms. See also **upper case. 13** *Chiefly Brit.* excellent; first-rate: *a capital idea.* ORIG C13: from L *capitālis* (adj) concerning the head, from *caput* head

capital[2] ('kæpɪt[ə]l) *n* the upper part of a column or pier that supports the entablature. ORIG C14: from OF, from LL *capitellum,* dim. of *caput* head

capital account *n* **1** *Econ.* that part of a balance of payments composed of movements of capital. **2** *Accounting.* a financial statement showing the net value of a company at a specified date.

capital expenditure *n* expenditure to increase fixed assets.

capital gain *n* the amount by which the selling price of a financial asset exceeds its cost.

capital gains tax *n* a tax on the profit made from sale of an asset.

capital goods *pl n Econ.* goods that are themselves utilized in the production of other goods.

capitalism ('kæpɪtəˌlɪzəm) *n* an economic system based on the private ownership of the means of production, distribution, and exchange. Also called: **free enterprise, private enterprise.** Cf. **socialism** (sense 1).

capitalist ('kæpɪtəlɪst) *n* **1** a person who owns capital, esp. capital invested in a business. **2** *Politics.* a supporter of capitalism. ◆ *adj* **3** relating to capital, capitalists, or capitalism.
▸ **ˌcapital'istic** *adj*

★ people and places

capitalization *or* **capitalisation** (ˌkæpɪtəlaɪˈzeɪʃən) *n* **1a** the act of capitalizing. **1b** the sum so derived. **2** *Accounting.* the par value of the total share capital issued by a company. **3** the act of estimating the present value of future payments, etc.

capitalize *or* **capitalise** (ˈkæpɪtəˌlaɪz) *vb* **capitalizes, capitalizing, capitalized** *or* **capitalises, capitalising, capitalised.** (*mainly tr*) **1** (*intr;* foll. by *on*) to take advantage (of). **2** to write or print (text) in capital letters. **3** to convert (debt or earnings) into capital stock. **4** to authorize (a business enterprise) to issue a specified amount of capital stock. **5** to provide with capital. **6** *Accounting.* to treat (expenditures) as assets. **7a** to estimate the present value of (a periodical income). **7b** to compute the present value of (a business) from actual or potential earnings.

capitally (ˈkæpɪtəlɪ) *adv Chiefly Brit.* in an excellent manner; admirably.

capital punishment *n* the punishment of death for a crime; death penalty.

capital ship *n* one of the largest and most heavily armed ships in a naval fleet.

capital stock *n* **1** the par value of the total share capital that a company is authorized to issue. **2** the total physical capital existing in an economy at any moment of time.

capital transfer tax *n* (in Britain) a tax payable from 1974 to 1986 on the cumulative total of gifts of money or property made during the donor's lifetime or after his death. It was replaced by inheritance tax.

capitation (ˌkæpɪˈteɪʃən) *n* **1** a tax levied on the basis of a fixed amount per head. **2 capitation grant.** a grant of money given to every person who qualifies under certain conditions. ORIG C17: from LL, from L *caput* head

Capitol ★ (ˈkæpɪtᵊl) *n* **1a** another name for the **Capitoline. 1b** the temple on the Capitoline. **2 the.** the main building of the US Congress. **3** (*sometimes not cap.*) Also called: **statehouse.** (in the US) the building housing any state legislature. ORIG C14: from Latin *Capitōlium,* from *caput* head

Capitoline ★ (ˈkæpɪtᵊˌlaɪn, kəˈpɪtəʊ-) *n* **1 the.** the most important of the Seven Hills of Rome. The temple of Jupiter was on the southern summit and the ancient citadel on the northern summit. ◆ *adj* **2** of or relating to the Capitoline or the temple of Jupiter.

capitulate (kəˈpɪtjʊˌleɪt) *vb* **capitulates, capitulating, capitulated.** (*intr*) to surrender, esp. under agreed conditions. ORIG C16 (meaning: to draw up in order): from Med. L *capitulare* to draw up under heads, from *capitulum* CHAPTER

▸ **caˈpituˌlator** *n*

capitulation (kəˌpɪtjʊˈleɪʃən) *n* **1** the act of capitulating. **2** a document containing terms of surrender. **3** a statement summarizing the main divisions of a subject.

▸ **caˈpitulatory** *adj*

capitulum (kəˈpɪtjʊləm) *n, pl* **capitula** (-lə). an inflorescence in the form of a disc, the youngest at the centre. It occurs in the daisy and related plants. ORIG C18: from L, lit.: a little head, from *caput* head

capo (ˈkæpəʊ) *n, pl* **capos.** a device fitted across all the strings of a guitar, lute, etc., so as to raise the pitch of each string simultaneously. Also called: **capo tasto** (ˈtæstəʊ). ORIG from It. *capo tasto* head stop

capon (ˈkeɪpən) *n* a castrated cock fowl fattened for eating. ORIG OE *capun,* from L *cāpō* capon

▸ **ˈcaponˌize** *or* **ˈcaponˌise** *vb*

Capone ★ (kəˈpəʊn) *n* **Alphonse,** called *Al.* 1899–1947, US gangster in Chicago during Prohibition.

Caporetto ★ (kapoˈretto) *n* the Italian name for **Kobarid.**

capote (kəˈpəʊt) *n* a long cloak or soldier's coat, usually with a hood. ORIG C19: from F: cloak, from *cape*

Capote ★ (kəˈpəʊtɪ) *n* **Truman.** 1924–84, US writer; his novels include *Other Voices, Other Rooms* (1948) and *In Cold Blood* (1964).

Capp ★ (kæp) *n* **Al,** full name *Alfred Caplin.* 1909–79, US cartoonist, noted for his comic strip *Li'l Abner.*

Cappadocia ★ (ˌkæpəˈdəʊsɪə) *n* an ancient region of E Asia Minor famous for its horses.

▸ **ˌCappaˈdocian** *adj, n*

capping (ˈkæpɪŋ) *n Scot. & NZ.* **a** the act of conferring an academic degree. **b** (*as modifier*): *Capping Day.*

cappuccino (ˌkæpʊˈtʃiːnəʊ) *n, pl* **cappuccinos.** coffee with steamed milk, usually sprinkled with powdered chocolate. ORIG It.: CAPUCHIN

Capra ★ (ˈkæprə) *n* **Frank.** 1896–1991, US film director born in Italy. His films include *It Happened One Night* (1934) and *It's a Wonderful Life* (1946).

Capri ★ (kəˈpriː; *Italian* ˈkapri) *n* an island off W Italy, in the Bay of Naples: resort since Roman times. Pop.: 8000 (latest est.). Area: about 13 sq. km (5 sq. miles).

capriccio (kəˈprɪtʃɪˌəʊ) *or* **caprice** *n, pl* **capriccios, capricci** (-ˈpriːtʃɪ), *or* **caprices.** *Music.* a lively piece of irregular musical form. ORIG C17: from It.: CAPRICE

capriccioso (kəˌprɪtʃɪˈəʊzəʊ) *adv Music.* to be played in a free and lively style. ORIG It.: from *capriccio* CAPRICE

caprice (kəˈpriːs) *n* **1** a sudden change of attitude, behaviour, etc. **2** a tendency to such changes. **3** another word for **capriccio.** ORIG C17: from F, from It. *capriccio* a shiver, caprice, from *capo* head + *riccio* lit.: hedgehog

capricious (kəˈprɪʃəs) *adj* characterized by or liable to sudden unpredictable changes in attitude or behaviour.

▸ **caˈpriciously** *adv*

Capricorn (ˈkæprɪˌkɔːn) *n* **1** *Astrol.* Also called: the **Goat, Capricornus.** the tenth sign of the zodiac. The sun is in this sign between about Dec. 22 and Jan. 19. **2** *Astron.* a S constellation. **3 tropic of Capricorn.** See **tropic** (sense 1). ORIG C14: from L *Capricornus,* from *caper* goat + *cornū* horn

Capricornia ★ (ˌkæprɪˈkɔːnɪə) *n* the regions of Australia in the tropic of Capricorn.

caprine (ˈkæpraɪn) *adj* of or resembling a goat. ORIG C17: from L *caprīnus,* from *caper* goat

capriole (ˈkæprɪˌəʊl) *n* **1** *Dressage.* a high upward but not forward leap made by a horse with all four feet off the ground. ◆ *vb* **caprioles, caprioling, caprioled. 2** (*intr*) to perform a capriole. ORIG C16: from F, from OIt., from *capriolo* roebuck, from L *capreolus, caper* goat

caps. *abbrev. for:* **1** capital letters. **2** capsule.

capsicum (ˈkæpsɪkəm) *n* **1** any of a genus of tropical American plants related to the potato, having mild or pungent seeds enclosed in a bell-shaped fruit. **2** the fruit of any of these plants, used as a vegetable or ground to produce a condiment. ◆ See also **pepper** (sense 4). ORIG C18: from NL, from L *capsa* box

capsid[1] (ˈkæpsɪd) *n* a bug related to the water bug that feeds on plant tissues, causing damage to crops. ORIG C19: from NL *Capsus* (genus)

capsid[2] (ˈkæpsɪd) *n* the outer protein coat of a mature virus. ORIG C20: from F *capside,* from L *capsa* box

capsize (kæpˈsaɪz) *vb* **capsizes, capsizing, capsized.** to overturn accidentally; upset. ORIG C18: from ?

▸ **capˈsizal** *n*

capstan (ˈkæpstən) *n* **1** a machine with a drum equipped with a ratchet, used for hauling in heavy ropes, etc. **2** the rotating shaft in a tape recorder that pulls the tape past the head. ORIG C14: from OProvençal *cabestan,* from L *capistrum* a halter, from *capere* to seize

capstan lathe *n* a lathe for repetitive work, having a rotatable turret to hold tools for successive operations. Also called: **turret lathe.**

capstone (ˈkæpˌstəʊn) *n* another word for **copestone** (sense 2).

capsule (ˈkæpsjuːl) *n* **1** a soluble case of gelatine enclosing a dose of medicine. **2** a thin metal cap, seal, or cover. **3** *Bot.* **3a** a dry fruit that liberates its seeds by splitting, as in the violet, or through pores, as in the poppy. **3b** the spore-producing organ of mosses and liverworts. **4** *Anat.* a membranous envelope surrounding any of certain organs or parts. **5** See **space capsule. 6** an aeroplane cockpit that can be ejected in a flight emergency, complete with crew, instruments, etc. **7** (*modifier*) in a highly concise form: *a capsule summary.* ORIG C17: from F, from L *capsula,* dim. of *capsa* box

▸ **ˈcapsuˌlate** *adj*

capsulize *or* **capsulise** ('kæpsjʊˌlaɪz) *vb* **capsulizes, capsulizing, capsulized** *or* **capsulises, capsulising, capsulised.** (*tr*) **1** to state (information, etc.) in a highly condensed form. **2** to enclose in a capsule.

Capt. *abbrev. for* Captain.

captain ('kæptɪn) *n* **1** the person in charge of a vessel. **2** an officer of the navy who holds a rank junior to a rear admiral. **3** an officer of the army, certain air forces, and the marines who holds a rank junior to a major. **4** the officer in command of a civil aircraft. **5** the leader of a team in games. **6** a person in command over a group, organization, etc.: *a captain of industry*. **7** *US.* a policeman in charge of a precinct. **8** *US & Canad.* (formerly) a head waiter. ♦ *vb* **9** (*tr*) to be captain of. ORIG C14: from OF, from LL *capitāneus* chief, from L *caput* head
▸ **'captaincy** *or* **'captainship** *n*

Captain Cooker ('kʊkə) *n NZ.* a wild pig. ORIG from Captain James COOK, who first released pigs in the New Zealand bush

caption ('kæpʃən) *n* **1** a title, brief explanation, or comment accompanying an illustration. **2** a heading or title of a chapter, article, etc. **3** graphic material used in television presentation. **4** another name for **subtitle** (sense 2). **5** the formal heading of a legal document. ♦ *vb* **6** to provide with a caption or captions. ORIG C14 (meaning: seizure): from L *captiō* a seizing, from *capere* to take

captious ('kæpʃəs) *adj* apt to make trivial criticisms. ORIG C14 (meaning: catching in error): from L *captiōsus*, from *captiō* a seizing
▸ **'captiously** *adv* ▸ **'captiousness** *n*

captivate ('kæptɪˌveɪt) *vb* **captivates, captivating, captivated.** (*tr*) to hold the attention of by fascinating; enchant. ORIG C16: from LL *captivāre*, from *captīvus* CAPTIVE
▸ **'captiˌvating** *adj* ▸ **ˌcapti'vation** *n*

captive ('kæptɪv) *n* **1** a person or animal that is confined or restrained. **2** a person whose behaviour is dominated by some emotion: *a captive of love*. ♦ *adj* **3** held as prisoner. **4** held under restriction or control; confined. **5** captivated. **6** unable to avoid speeches, advertisements, etc.: *a captive audience*. ORIG C14: from L *captīvus*, from *capere* to take

captivity (kæp'tɪvɪtɪ) *n, pl* **captivities. 1** imprisonment. **2** the period of imprisonment.

captor ('kæptə) *n* a person or animal that holds another captive. ORIG C17: from L, from *capere* to take

capture ('kæptʃə) *vb* **captures, capturing, captured.** (*tr*) **1** to take prisoner or gain control over: *to capture a town*. **2** (in a game) to win possession of: *to capture a pawn in chess*. **3** to succeed in representing (something elusive): *the artist captured her likeness*. **4** *Physics.* (of an atom, etc.) to acquire (an additional particle). **5** to insert or transfer (data) into a computer. ♦ *n* **6** the act of taking by force. **7** the person or thing captured. **8** *Physics.* a process by which an atom, etc., acquires an additional particle. **9** *Geog.* the process by which the headwaters of one river are diverted into another. **10** *Computing.* the collection of data for processing. ORIG C16: from L *captūra* a catching, that which is caught, from *capere* to take
▸ **'capturer** *n*

Capua ★ ('kæːpjʊə; *Italian* 'kaːpwa) *n* a town in S Italy, in NW Campania: strategically important in ancient times, situated on the Appian Way. Pop.: 19 520 (1990).

Capuana ★ (*Italian* ka'pwaːna) *n* **Luigi** ('lwiːʒi). 1839–1915, Italian realist novelist, dramatist, and critic. His works include the novel *Giacinta* (1879) and the play *Malia* (1895).

capuchin ('kæpjʊtʃɪn, -jʊʃɪn) *n* **1** an agile intelligent S American monkey having a cowl of thick hair on the top of the head. **2** a woman's hooded cloak. **3** (*sometimes cap.*) a variety of domestic fancy pigeon. ORIG C16: from F, from It., from *cappuccio* hood

Capuchin ('kæpjʊtʃɪn, -jʊʃɪn) *n* **1** a friar belonging to a branch of the Franciscan Order founded in 1525. ♦ *adj* **2** of or relating to this order. ORIG C16: from F, from It. *cappuccio* hood

capybara (ˌkæpɪ'bɑːrə) *n* the largest rodent, resembling a guinea pig and native to Central and South America. ORIG C18: from Port. *capibara*, from Tupi

Caquetá ★ (*Spanish* kake'ta) *n* the Japurá River from its source in Colombia to the border with Brazil.

car (kɑː) *n* **1a** Also called: **motorcar, automobile.** a self-propelled road vehicle designed to carry passengers, that is powered by an internal-combustion engine. **1b** (*as modifier*): *car coat*. **2** a conveyance for passengers, freight, etc., such as a cable car or the carrier of an airship or balloon. **3** *Brit.* a railway vehicle for passengers only. **4** *Chiefly US. & Canad.* a railway carriage or van. **5** a poetic word for **chariot.** ORIG C14: from Anglo-F *carre*, ult. rel. to L *carra, carrum* two-wheeled wagon, prob. of Celtic origin

CAR *abbrev. for* compound annual return.

carabineer *or* **carabinier** (ˌkærəbɪ'nɪə) *n* variants of **carbineer.**

carabiner (ˌkærə'biːnə) *n* a variant of **karabiner.**

caracal ('kærəˌkæl) *n* **1** a lynxlike feline mammal inhabiting deserts of N Africa and S Asia, having a smooth coat of reddish fur. **2** this fur. ORIG C18: from F, from Turkish *kara kūlāk*, lit.: black ear

Caracalla ★ (ˌkærə'kælə) *n* real name *Marcus Aurelius Antoninus*, original name *Bassianus*. 188–217 A.D., Roman emperor (211–17): ruled with cruelty and extravagance; assassinated.

caracara (ˌkɑːrə'kɑːrə) *n* a large carrion-eating bird of prey of Central and South America, having long legs. ORIG C19: from Sp. or Port., from Tupi; imit.

Caracas ★ (kə'rækəs, -'rɑː-; *Spanish* ka'rakas) *n* the capital of Venezuela, in the north: founded in 1567; major industrial and commercial centre, notably for oil companies. Pop.: 1 822 465 (1990).

caracole ('kærəˌkəʊl) *or* **caracol** ('kærəˌkɒl) *Dressage.* ♦ *n* **1** a half turn to the right or left. ♦ *vb* **caracoles, caracoling, caracoled** *or* **caracols, caracoling, caracoled.** (*intr*) **2** to execute a half turn. ORIG C17: from F, from Sp. *caracol* snail, spiral staircase

Caractacus ★ (kə'ræktəkəs) *n* a variant of **Caratacus.**

caracul ('kærəˌkʌl) *n* **1** Also called: **Persian lamb.** the black loosely curled fur obtained from the skins of newly born lambs of the karakul sheep. **2** a variant spelling of **karakul.**

carafe (kə'ræf, -'rɑːf) *n* an open-topped glass container for serving water or wine at table ORIG C18: from F, from It., from Sp., from Ar. *gharrāfah* vessel

carageen ('kærəˌgiːn) *n* a variant spelling of **carrageen.**

carambola (ˌkærəm'bəʊlə) *n* the yellow edible star-shaped fruit of a Brazilian tree, cultivated in the tropics, esp. SE Asia. Also called: **star fruit.** ORIG Sp., from Port.

caramel ('kærəməl) *n* **1** burnt sugar, used for colouring and flavouring food. **2** a chewy sweet made from sugar, milk, etc. ORIG C18: from F, from Sp. *caramelo*, from ?

caramelize *or* **caramelise** ('kærəməˌlaɪz) *vb* **caramelizes, caramelizing, caramelized** *or* **caramelises, caramelising, caramelised.** to convert or be converted into caramel.

carapace ('kærəˌpeɪs) *n* the thick hard shield that covers part of the body of crabs, tortoises, etc. ORIG C19: from F, from Sp. *carapacho*, from ?

carat ('kærət) *n* **1** a measure of the weight of precious stones, esp. diamonds, now standardized as 0.20 grams. **2** Usual US and Canad. spelling: **karat.** a measure of the gold in an alloy, expressed as the number of parts of gold in 24 parts of the alloy. ORIG C16: from OF, from Med. L, from Ar. *qīrāt* weight of four grains, from Gk, from *keras* horn

Caratacus (kə'rætəkəs), **Caractacus,** or **Caradoc** ★ (kə'rædək) *n* died ?54 A.D., British chieftain: led an unsuccessful resistance against the Romans (43–50).

Caravaggio ★ (*Italian* kara'vaddʒo) *n* **Michelangelo Merisi da** (mike'landʒelo me'riːzi da). 1571–1610, Italian painter.

caravan ('kærəˌvæn) *n* **1a** a large enclosed vehicle capable of being pulled by a car and equipped to be lived in. US and Canad. name: **trailer. 1b** (*as modifier*): *a caravan* *site.* **2** (esp. in some parts of Asia and Africa) a company of traders or other travellers journeying together. **3** a large covered vehicle, esp. a gaily coloured one used by Gypsies, circuses, etc. ◆ *vb* **caravans, caravanning, caravanned. 4** (*intr*) *Brit.* to travel or have a holiday in a caravan. ORIG C16: from It. *caravana,* from Persian *kārwān*

caravanserai (ˌkærəˈvænsəˌraɪ) *or* **caravansary** (ˌkærəˈvænsərɪ) *n, pl* **caravanserais** *or* **caravansaries.** (in some Eastern countries) a large inn enclosing a courtyard, providing accommodation for caravans. ORIG C16: from Persian *kārwānsarāī* caravan inn

caravel (ˈkærəˌvɛl) *or* **carvel** *n* a two- or three-masted sailing ship used by the Spanish and Portuguese in the 15th and 16th centuries. ORIG C16: from Port. *caravela,* dim. of *caravo* ship, ult. from Gk *karabos* crab

caraway (ˈkærəˌweɪ) *n* **1** an umbelliferous Eurasian plant having finely divided leaves and clusters of small whitish flowers. **2 caraway seed.** the pungent aromatic fruit of this plant, used in cooking. ORIG C14: prob. from Med. L *carvi,* from Ar. *karawyā,* from Gk *karon*

carb (kɑːb) *n Inf.* short for **carburettor.**

carbaryl (ˈkɑːbərɪl) *n* an organic compound of the carbamate group: used as an insecticide, esp. to treat head lice.

carbide (ˈkɑːbaɪd) *n* **1** a binary compound of carbon with a metal. **2** See **calcium carbide.**

carbine (ˈkɑːbaɪn) *n* **1** a light automatic or semiautomatic rifle. **2** a light short-barrelled rifle formerly used by cavalry. ORIG C17: from F *carabine,* from OF *carabin* carabineer

carbineer (ˌkɑːbɪˈnɪə), **carabineer,** *or* **carabinier** (ˌkærəbɪˈnɪə) *n* (formerly) a soldier equipped with a carbine.

carbo- *or before a vowel* **carb-** *combining form.* carbon: *carbohydrate; carbonate.*

carbocyclic (ˌkɑːbəʊˈsaɪklɪk) *adj* (of a chemical compound) containing a closed ring of carbon atoms.

carbohydrate (ˌkɑːbəʊˈhaɪdreɪt) *n* any of a large group of organic compounds, including sugars and starch, that contain carbon, hydrogen, and oxygen, with the general formula $C_m(H_2O)_n$: a source of food and energy for animals.

carbolic acid (kɑːˈbɒlɪk) *n* another name for **phenol,** esp. when used as a disinfectant. ORIG C19: from CARBO- + -OL[1] + -IC

carbon (ˈkɑːbᵊn) *n* **1a** a nonmetallic element existing in three crystalline forms: graphite, diamond, and buckminsterfullerene: occurring in all organic compounds. The isotope **carbon-12** is the standard for atomic wt.; **carbon-14** is used in radiocarbon dating and as a tracer. Symbol: C; atomic no.: 6; atomic wt.: 12.011 15. **1b** (*as modifier*): *a carbon compound.* **2** short for **carbon paper** or **carbon copy. 3** a carbon electrode used in a carbon-arc light. **4** a rod or plate, made of carbon, used in some types of battery. ORIG C18: from F, from L *carbō* charcoal

carbon-14 dating *n* another name for **carbon dating.**

carbonaceous (ˌkɑːbəˈneɪʃəs) *adj* of, resembling, or containing carbon.

carbonade (ˌkɑːbəˈneɪd, -ˈnɑːd) *n* beef and onions stewed in beer. ORIG C20: F

carbonado (ˌkɑːbəˈneɪdəʊ) *n, pl* **carbonados** *or* **carbonadoes.** an inferior variety of diamond used in industry. Also called: **black diamond.** ORIG Port., lit.: carbonated

carbon arc *n* an electric arc between two carbon electrodes or between a carbon electrode and materials to be welded.

carbonate *n* (ˈkɑːbəˌneɪt, -nɪt). **1** a salt or ester of carbonic acid. ◆ *vb* (ˈkɑːbəˌneɪt), **carbonates, carbonating, carbonated. 2** to turn into a carbonate. **3** (*tr*) to treat with carbon dioxide, as in the manufacture of soft drinks. ORIG C18: from F, from *carbone* CARBON

carbon black *n* a finely divided form of carbon produced by incomplete combustion of natural gas or petroleum: used in pigments and ink.

carbon brush *n* a small spring-loaded block of carbon used to convey current between the stationary and moving parts of an electric generator, motor, etc.

carbon copy *n* **1** a duplicate copy of writing, typewriting, or drawing obtained by using carbon paper. **2** *Inf.* a person or thing that is identical to another.

carbon credit *n* a certificate showing that a government or company has paid to have a certain amount of carbon dioxide removed from the environment.

carbon dating *n* a technique for determining the age of organic materials, such as wood, based on their content of the radioisotope ^{14}C acquired from the atmosphere when they formed part of a living plant.

carbon dioxide *n* a colourless odourless incombustible gas present in the atmosphere and formed during respiration, etc.: used in fire extinguishers, and as dry ice for refrigeration. Formula: CO_2. Also called: **carbonic-acid gas.**

carbonette (ˌkɑːbəˈnɛt) *n NZ.* a ball of compressed coal dust used as fuel.

carbon fibre *n* a thread of pure carbon used because of its lightness and strength at high temperatures for reinforcing resins, ceramics, and metals, and for fishing rods.

carbonic (kɑːˈbɒnɪk) *adj* (of a compound) containing carbon, esp. tetravalent carbon.

carbonic acid *n* a weak acid formed when carbon dioxide combines with water. Formula: H_2CO_3.

carboniferous (ˌkɑːbəˈnɪfərəs) *adj* yielding coal or carbon.

Carboniferous (ˌkɑːbəˈnɪfərəs) *adj* **1** of, denoting, or formed in the fifth period of the Palaeozoic era during which coal measures were formed. ◆ *n* **2 the.** the Carboniferous period or rock system divided into the **Upper Carboniferous** period and the **Lower Carboniferous** period.

carbonize *or* **carbonise** (ˈkɑːbəˌnaɪz) *vb* **carbonizes, carbonizing, carbonized** *or* **carbonises, carbonising, carbonised. 1** to turn or be turned into carbon as a result of heating, fossilization, chemical treatment, etc. **2** (*tr*) to coat (a substance) with carbon.
▸ **ˌcarboniˈzation** *or* **ˌcarboniˈsation** *n*

carbon monoxide *n* a colourless odourless poisonous gas formed when carbon compounds burn in insufficient air. Formula: CO.

carbon paper *n* a thin sheet of paper coated on one side with a dark waxy pigment, often containing carbon, that is transferred by pressure onto the copying surface below.

carbon sequestration *n* the prevention of greenhouse gas build-up in the earth's atmosphere by methods such as planting trees to absorb carbon dioxide or pumping carbon dioxide into underground reservoirs.

carbon tax *n* a tax on the emissions caused by the burning of coal, gas, and oil, aimed at reducing the production of greenhouse gases.

carbon tetrachloride *n* a colourless volatile nonflammable liquid made from chlorine and used as a solvent, cleaning fluid, and insecticide. Formula: CCl_4. Systematic name: **tetrachloromethane.**

car-boot sale *n* a sale of goods from car boots in a site hired for the occasion.

Carborundum (ˌkɑːbəˈrʌndəm) *n Trademark.* any of various abrasive materials, esp. one consisting of silicon carbide.

carboxyl group *or* **radical** (kɑːˈbɒksaɪl) *n* the monovalent group -COOH: the functional group in organic acids. ORIG C19 *carboxyl,* from CARBO- + OXY-[2] + -YL

carboxylic acid (ˌkɑːbɒkˈsɪlɪk) *n* any of a class of organic acids containing the carboxyl group. See also **fatty acid.**

carboy (ˈkɑːˌbɔɪ) *n* a large bottle, usually protected by a basket or box, used for containing corrosive liquids. ORIG C18: from Persian *qarāba*

carbuncle (ˈkɑːˌbʌŋkᵊl) *n* **1** an extensive skin eruption, similar to a boil, with several openings. **2** a rounded gemstone, esp. a garnet cut without facets. ORIG C13: from L *carbunculus,* dim. of *carbō* coal
▸ **carbuncular** (kɑːˈbʌŋkjʊlə) *adj*

carburation (ˌkɑːbjʊˈreɪʃən) *n* the process of mixing a hydrocarbon fuel with air to make an explosive mixture for an internal-combustion engine.

carburet ('kɑːbjʊˌrɛt, ˌkɑːbjʊ'rɛt) *vb* **carburets, carburetting, carburetted** *or US* **carburets, carbureting, carbureted.** (*tr*) to combine or mix (a gas, etc.) with carbon or carbon compounds. ORIG C18: from CARB(ON) + -URET

carburettor, carburetter (ˌkɑːbə'rɛtə, 'kɑːbəˌrɛtə), *or US & Canad.* **carburetor** ('kɑːbəˌreɪtə) *n* a device used in some petrol engines for mixing atomized petrol with air, and regulating the intake of the mixture into the engine.

carcajou ('kɑːkəˌdʒuː, -kəˌʒuː) *n* a North American name for **wolverine.** ORIG C18: from Canad. F, from Algonquian *karkajou*

carcass *or* **carcase** ('kɑːkəs) *n* **1** the dead body of an animal, esp. one that has been slaughtered for food. **2** *Inf., usually facetious or derog.* a person's body. **3** the skeleton or framework of a structure. **4** the remains of anything when its life or vitality is gone. ORIG C14: from OF *carcasse,* from ?

Carcassonne ★ (*French* karkasɔn) *n* a city in SW France: extensive remains of medieval fortifications. Pop.: 44 990 (1990).

carcinogen (kɑː'sɪnədʒən) *n Pathol.* any substance that produces cancer. ORIG C20: from Gk *karkinos* CANCER + -GEN
▸ ˌ**carcino'genic** *adj*

carcinogenesis (ˌkɑːsɪnəʊ'dʒɛnɪsɪs) *n Pathol.* the development of cancerous cells from normal ones.

carcinoma (ˌkɑːsɪ'nəʊmə) *n, pl* **carcinomas** *or* **carcinomata** (-mətə). *Pathol.* any malignant tumour derived from epithelial tissue. ORIG C18: from L, from Gk, from *karkinos* CANCER

card[1] (kɑːd) *n* **1** a piece of stiff paper or thin cardboard, usually rectangular, with varied uses, as for bearing a written notice for display, etc. **2** such a card used for identification, reference, proof of membership, etc.: *identity card.* **3** such a card used for sending greetings, messages, or invitations: *birthday card.* **4a** one of a set of small pieces of cardboard, marked with figures, symbols, etc., used for playing games or for fortune-telling. See also **playing card. 4b** (*as modifier*): *a card game.* **5** short for **cheque card** or **credit card. 6** *Inf.* a witty or eccentric person. **7** See **compass card. 8** Also called: **racecard.** *Horse racing.* a daily programme of all the races at a meeting. **9 a card up one's sleeve.** a thing or action used in order to gain an advantage, esp. one kept in reserve until needed. ◆ See also **cards.** ORIG C15: from OF *carte,* from L *charta* leaf of papyrus, from Gk *khartēs,* prob. of Egyptian origin

card[2] (kɑːd) *vb* **1** (*tr*) to comb out and clean (fibres of wool or cotton) before spinning. ◆ *n* **2** (formerly) a machine or comblike tool for carding fabrics or for raising the nap on cloth. ORIG C15: from OF *carde* card, teasel, from L *carduus* thistle
▸ '**carder** *n* ▸ '**carding** *n*

cardamom ('kɑːdəməm) *or* **cardamon** ('kɑːdəmən) *n* **1** a tropical Asian plant that has large hairy leaves. **2** the seeds of this plant, used esp. as a spice or condiment. ORIG C15: from L, from Gk, from *kardamon* cress + *amōmon* an Indian spice

cardboard ('kɑːdˌbɔːd) *n* **1a** a thin stiff board made from paper pulp. **1b** (*as modifier*): *cardboard boxes.* ◆ *adj* **2** (*prenominal*) without substance.

cardboard city *n Inf.* an area of a city in which homeless people sleep rough, often in cardboard boxes.

card-carrying *adj* being an official member of an organization: *a card-carrying Communist.*

Cardenal ★ (*Spanish* karðe'nal) *n* **Ernesto** ('ɜːnɛsˌtəʊ). born 1925, Nicaraguan poet, revolutionary, and Roman Catholic priest.

cardiac ('kɑːdɪˌæk) *adj* **1** of or relating to the heart. **2** of or relating to the portion of the stomach connected to the oesophagus. ◆ *n* **3** a person with a heart disorder. ORIG C17: from L *cardiacus,* from Gk, from *kardia* heart

cardiac arrest *n* failure of the pumping action of the heart, resulting in loss of consciousness and absence of pulse and breathing: a medical emergency requiring immediate resuscitative treatment.

cardie *or* **cardy** ('kɑːdɪ) *n, pl* **cardies.** *Inf.* short for **cardigan.**

Cardiff ★ ('kɑːdɪf) *n* **1** the capital of Wales, situated in the southeast: an important port; home to the Welsh Assembly (1999); University College Cardiff (1883). Pop.: 272 129 (1991). **2** a county borough in SE Wales. Pop.: 306 500 (1996 est.). Area: 139 sq. km (54 sq. miles).

cardigan ('kɑːdɪgən) *n* a knitted jacket or sweater with buttons up the front. ORIG C19: after 7th Earl of CARDIGAN

Cardigan ★ ('kɑːdɪgən) *n* **7th Earl of,** title of *James Thomas Brudenell.* 1797–1868, British cavalry officer. He led the charge of the Light Brigade at Balaklava (1854).

Cardigan Bay ★ *n* an inlet of St George's Channel, on the W coast of Wales.

Cardiganshire ★ ('kɑːdɪgənˌʃɪə, -ʃə) *n* See **Ceredigion.**

Cardin ★ (*French* kardɛ̃) *n* **Pierre** (pjɛr). born 1922, French couturier, noted esp. for his collections for men.

cardinal ('kɑːdɪnᵊl) *n* **1** *RC Church.* any of the members of the Sacred College who elect the pope and act as his chief counsellors. **2** Also called: **cardinal red.** a deep red colour. **3** See **cardinal number. 4** Also called (US): **redbird.** a crested North American bunting, the male of which has a bright red plumage. **5** a woman's hooded shoulder cape worn in the 17th and 18th centuries. ◆ *adj* **6** (*usually prenominal*) fundamentally important; principal. **7** of a deep red. ORIG C13: from L *cardinālis,* lit.: relating to a hinge, from *cardō* hinge
▸ '**cardinally** *adv*

cardinalate ('kɑːdɪnᵊˌleɪt) *or* **cardinalship** *n* **1** the rank, office, or term of office of a cardinal. **2** the cardinals collectively.

cardinal flower *n* a lobelia of E North America that has brilliant scarlet flowers.

cardinal number *or* **numeral** *n* a number denoting quantity but not order in a group. Sometimes shortened to **cardinal.** Cf. **ordinal number.**

cardinal points *pl n* the four main points of the compass: north, south, east, and west.

cardinal virtues *pl n* the most important moral qualities, traditionally justice, prudence, temperance, and fortitude.

cardinal vowels *pl n* a set of theoretical vowel sounds, based on the shape of the mouth needed to articulate them, that can be used to classify the vowel sounds of any speaker in any language.

card index *or* **file** *n* **1** an index in which each item is separately listed on systematically arranged cards. ◆ *vb* **card-index** *or* **card-file, card-indexes, card-indexing, card-indexed** *or* **card-files, card-filing, card-filed.** (*tr*) **2** to make such an index of (a book, etc.).

cardio- *or before a vowel* **cardi-** *combining form.* heart: *cardiogram.* ORIG from Gk *kardia* heart

cardiocentesis (ˌkɑːdɪəʊsɛn'tiːsɪs) *n Med.* surgical puncture of the heart.

cardiogram ('kɑːdɪəʊˌgræm) *n* short for **electrocardiogram.** See **electrocardiograph.**

cardiograph ('kɑːdɪəʊˌgrɑːf) *n* **1** an instrument for recording heart movements. **2** short for **electrocardiograph.**
▸ **cardiographer** (ˌkɑːdɪ'ɒgrəfə) *n* ▸ ˌ**cardi'ography** *n*

cardiology (ˌkɑːdɪ'ɒlədʒɪ) *n* the branch of medical science concerned with the heart and its diseases.
▸ ˌ**cardi'ologist** *n*

cardioplegia (ˌkɑːdɪəʊ'pliːdʒə) *n Med.* deliberate arrest of the action of the heart, as by hypothermia or the injection of chemicals, to enable complex heart surgery to be carried out.

cardiopulmonary resuscitation (ˌkɑːdɪəʊ'pʌlmənərɪ, -'pʊl-) *n* an emergency measure to revive a patient whose heart has stopped beating, in which compressions applied with the hands to the patient's chest are alternated with mouth-to-mouth respiration. Abbrev.: **CPR.**

cardiovascular (ˌkɑːdɪəʊ'væskjʊlə) *adj* of or relating to the heart and the blood vessels.

cardoon (kɑː'duːn) *n* a thistle-like relative of the artichoke with an edible leafstalk. ORIG C17: from F, from L *carduus* thistle, artichoke

cardphone ('kɑ:dfəʊn) *n* a public telephone operated by the insertion of a phonecard instead of coins.

card punch *n* a device, no longer widely used, controlled by a computer, for transferring information from the central processing unit onto punched cards which can then be read by a **card reader**.

card reader *n* a device, no longer widely used, for reading information on a punched card and transferring it to a computer or storage device.

cards (kɑ:dz) *n* **1** (*usually functioning as sing*) **1a** any game played with cards, esp. playing cards. **1b** the playing of such a game. **2** an employee's tax and national insurance documents or information held by the employer. **3 ask for** *or* **get one's cards.** to ask *or* be told to terminate one's employment. **4 on the cards.** possible. **5 play one's cards (right).** to manoeuvre (cleverly). **6 put** *or* **lay one's cards on the table.** to declare one's intentions, etc.

cardsharp ('kɑ:d,ʃɑ:p) *or* **cardsharper** *n* a professional card player who cheats.

Cardus ★ ('kɑ:dəs) *n* Sir **Neville.** 1889–1975, British music critic and cricket writer.

card vote *n Brit.* a vote by delegates, esp. at a trade-union conference, in which each delegate's vote counts as a vote by all his constituents.

care (kɛə) *vb* **cares, caring, cared. 1** (when *tr, may take a clause as object*) to be troubled or concerned: *he is dying, and she doesn't care.* **2** (*intr;* foll. by *for* or *about*) to have regard or consideration (for): *he cares more for his hobby than his job.* **3** (*intr;* foll. by *for*) to have a desire or taste (for): *would you care for tea?* **4** (*intr;* foll. by *for*) to provide physical needs, help, or comfort (for). **5** (*tr*) to agree or like (to do something): *would you care to sit down?* **6 for all I care** *or* **I couldn't care less.** I am completely indifferent. ◆ *n* **7** careful or serious attention: *he does his work with care.* **8** protective or supervisory control: *in the care of a doctor.* **9** (*often pl*) trouble; worry. **10** an object of or cause for concern. **11** caution: *handle with care.* **12 care of.** at the address of: written on envelopes. Usual abbrev.: **c/o. 13 in** (*or* **into**) **care.** *Brit.* made the legal responsibility of a local authority by order of a court. ORIG OE *cearu* (n), *cearian* (vb), of Gmc origin
▸ **'carer** *n*

CARE (kɛə) *n acronym for:* **1** Cooperative for American Relief Everywhere. **2** communicated authenticity, regard, empathy: the three qualities believed to be essential in the therapist practising client-centred therapy.

care and maintenance *n Commerce.* the state of a building, ship, machinery, etc., that is not in current use although it is kept in good condition to enable it to be brought into service quickly if there is a demand for it. Abbrev.: **C & M.**

careen (kə'ri:n) *vb* **1** to sway or cause to sway over to one side. **2** (*tr*) *Naut.* to cause (a vessel) to keel over to one side, esp. in order to clean its bottom. **3** (*intr*) *Naut.* (of a vessel) to keel over to one side. ORIG C17: from F, from It., from L *carīna* keel
▸ **ca'reenage** *n*

career (kə'rɪə) *n* **1** a path through life or history. **2a** a profession or occupation chosen as one's life's work. **2b** (*as modifier*): *a career diplomat.* **3** a course or path, esp. a headlong one. ◆ *vb* **4** (*intr*) to rush in an uncontrolled way. ORIG C16: from F, from LL *carrāria* carriage road, from L *carrus* two-wheeled wagon

career girl *or* **woman** *n* a woman, often unmarried, who follows a profession.

careerist (kə'rɪərɪst) *n* a person who seeks to advance his or her career by any possible means.

carefree ('kɛə,fri:) *adj* without worry or responsibility.
▸ **'care,freeness** *n*

careful ('kɛəfʊl) *adj* **1** cautious in attitude or action. **2** painstaking in one's work; exact and thorough. **3** (*usually postpositive;* foll. by *of, in,* or *about*) solicitous; protective. **4** *Brit.* mean or miserly.
▸ **'carefully** *adv* ▸ **'carefulness** *n*

careless ('kɛəlɪs) *adj* **1** done with or acting with insufficient attention. **2** (often foll. by *in, of,* or *about*) unconcerned in attitude or action. **3** (*usually prenominal*) carefree. **4** (*usually prenominal*) unstudied: *careless elegance.*
▸ **'carelessly** *adv* ▸ **'carelessness** *n*

Carême ★ (*French* karɛm) *n* **Marie Antonin** (mari ɑ̃tɔnɛ̃). 1784–1833, French chef, regarded as the founder of *haute cuisine.*

caress (kə'rɛs) *n* **1** a gentle touch or embrace, esp. one given to show affection. ◆ *vb* **2** (*tr*) to touch or stroke gently with or as with affection. ORIG C17: from F, from It., from L *cārus* dear

caret ('kærɪt) *n* a symbol (‸) used to indicate the place in written or printed matter at which something is to be inserted. ORIG C17: from L, lit.: there is missing, from *carēre* to lack

caretaker ('kɛə,teɪkə) *n* **1** a person who looks after a place or thing, esp. in the owner's absence. **2** (*modifier*) interim: *a caretaker government.*

Carew ★ (kə'ru:) *n* **Thomas.** ?1595–?1639, English Cavalier poet.

careworn ('kɛə,wɔ:n) *adj* showing signs of care, stress, worry, etc.: *a careworn face.*

Carey ★ ('kɛərɪ) *n* **1 George (Leonard).** born 1935, British cleric, Archbishop of Canterbury from 1991. **2 William.** 1761–1834, British orientalist and pioneer Baptist missionary in India.

Carey Street ★ *n* **1** (formerly) the street in which the London bankruptcy court was situated. **2** the state of bankruptcy.

cargo ('kɑ:gəʊ) *n, pl* **cargoes** *or esp. US* **cargos. 1a** goods carried by a ship, aircraft, or other vehicle; freight. **1b** (*as modifier*): *a cargo vessel.* **2** any load: *a cargo of new arrivals.* ORIG C17: from Sp.: from *cargar* to load, from LL, from L *carrus* CAR

cargo trousers *or* **pants** *pl n* loose trousers with a large external pocket on the side of each leg.

Carib ('kærɪb) *n* **1** (*pl* **Caribs** *or* **Carib**) a member of a group of American Indian peoples of NE South America and the Lesser Antilles. **2** the family of languages spoken by these peoples. ORIG C16: from Sp. *Caribe,* from Amerind

Caribbean (,kærɪ'bɪən; *US* kə'rɪbɪən) *adj* **1** of or relating to the Caribbean Sea and its islands. **2** of or relating to the Carib or any of their languages. ◆ *n* **3 the.** short for the **Caribbean Sea. 4 the.** the states and islands of the Caribbean, esp. when considered as a geopolitical region. **5** a member of any of the peoples inhabiting the islands of the Caribbean Sea, such as a West Indian or a Carib.

USAGE NOTE This word is stressed on the third syllable in the UK, and on the second in the US and in the Caribbean itself.

Caribbean Sea ★ *n* an almost landlocked sea, part of the Atlantic Ocean, bounded by the Caribbean islands, Central America, and the N coast of South America. Area: 2 718 200 sq. km (1 049 500 sq. miles).

Caribbees ★ ('kærɪ,bi:z) *pl n* **the.** another name for the **Lesser Antilles.**

Cariboo ★ ('kærɪ,bu:) *n* **the.** *Canad.* a region in the W foothills of the Cariboo Mountains, scene of a gold rush beginning in 1860.

Cariboo Mountains ★ *pl n* a mountain range in SW Canada, in SE British Columbia. Highest peak: Mount Sir Wilfrid Laurier, 3582 m (11 750 ft).

caribou ('kærɪ,bu:) *n, pl* **caribou** *or* **caribous.** a large North American reindeer. ORIG C18: from Canad. F, of Algonquian origin

caricature ('kærɪkə,tjʊə) *n* **1** a pictorial, written, or acted representation of a person, which exaggerates his characteristic traits for comic effect. **2** an inadequate or inaccurate imitation. ◆ *vb* **caricatures, caricaturing, caricatured. 3** (*tr*) to represent in caricature or produce a caricature of. ORIG C18: from It. *caricatura* a distortion, from *caricare* to load, exaggerate
▸ **'carica,turist** *n*

CARICOM ('kærɪ,kɒm) *n acronym for* Caribbean Community and Common Market.

caries ('kɛəri:z) *n, pl* **caries.** progressive decay of a bone or a tooth. ORIG C17: from L: decay

carillon (kə'rɪljən) *n Music.* **1** a set of bells usually hung in a tower. **2** a tune played on such bells. **3** a mixture stop on an organ giving the effect of a bell. ORIG C18: from F: set of bells, from OF *quarregnon,* ult. from L *quattuor* four

carina (kə'ri:nə, -'raɪ-) *n, pl* **carinae** (-ni:) *or* **carinas.** a keel-like part or ridge, as in the breastbone of birds or the fused lower petals of a leguminous flower. ORIG C18: from L: keel

carinate ('kærɪˌneɪt) *or* **carinated** *adj Biol.* having a keel or ridge. ORIG C17: from L *carīnāre,* from *carīna* keel

caring (kɛərɪŋ) *adj* **1** showing care and compassion: *a caring attitude.* **2** of or relating to professional social or medical care: *nursing is a caring job.* ◆ *n* **3** the practice of providing care.

Carinthia ★ (kə'rɪnθɪə) *n* a state of S Austria: an independent duchy from 976 to 1276; mainly mountainous, with many lakes and resorts. Capital: Klagenfurt. Pop.: 564 431 (1998 est.). Area: 9533 sq. km (3681 sq. miles). German name: **Kärnten.**

carioca (ˌkærɪ'əʊkə) *n* **1** a Brazilian dance similar to the samba. **2** a piece of music for this dance. ORIG C19: from Brazilian Port.

cariogenic (ˌkɛərɪəʊ'dʒɛnɪk) *adj* (of a substance) producing caries of the teeth.

cariole *or* **carriole** ('kærɪˌəʊl) *n* **1** a small open two-wheeled horse-drawn vehicle. **2** a covered cart. ORIG C19: from F, ult. from L *carrus;* see CAR

carious ('kɛərɪəs) *or* **cariose** ('kɛərɪˌəʊz) *adj* (of teeth or bone) affected with caries; decayed.

carjack ('kɑ:ˌdʒæk) *vb (tr)* to attack (a driver in a car) in order to rob the driver or to steal the car for another crime. ORIG C20: CAR + (HI)JACK

cark (kɑ:k) *vb (intr) Austral. & NZ sl.* to die (esp. in **cark it**). ORIG ?from the cry of a crow, as a carrion-feeding bird

carl *or* **carle** (kɑ:l) *n Arch. or Scot.* another word for **churl.** ORIG OE, from ON *karl*

Carl XVI Gustaf ★ (*Swedish* kɑ:rl 'gʊstav) *n* born 1946, king of Sweden from 1973.

Carlisle ★ (kɑ:'laɪl, 'kɑ:laɪl) *n* a city in NW England, administrative centre of Cumbria: industrial centre. Pop.: 72 439 (1991). Latin name: **Luguvallum** (ˌlu:gu:'væləm).

Carlos ★ ('kɑ:lɒs) *n* **Don.** full name *Carlos María Isidro de Borbón.* 1788–1855, second son of Charles IV: pretender to the Spanish throne and leader of the Carlists.

Carlota ★ (*Spanish* kar'lota) *n* original name *Marie Charlotte Amélie Augustine Victoire Clémentine Léopoldine.* 1840–1927, wife of Maximilian; empress of Mexico (1864–67).

Carlovingian (ˌkɑ:ləʊ'vɪndʒɪən) *adj, n History.* a variant of **Carolingian.**

Carlow ★ ('kɑ:ləʊ) *n* **1** a county of SE Republic of Ireland, in Leinster: mostly flat, with barren mountains in the southeast. County town: Carlow. Pop.: 42 000 (1996). Area: 896 sq. km (346 sq. miles). **2** a town in SE Republic of Ireland, county town of Co. Carlow. Pop.: 11 275 (1991).

Carlyle ★ (kɑ:'laɪl) *n* **Thomas.** 1795–1881, Scottish historian. His works include *Sartor Resartus* (1833–34), *The French Revolution* (1837), and lectures *On Heroes, Hero-Worship, and the Heroic in History* (1841).

carmagnole (ˌkɑ:mən'jəʊl) *n* **1** a dance and song popular during the French Revolution. **2** the costume worn by many French Revolutionaries. ORIG C18: from F, prob. after *Carmagnola,* Italy

Carmarthen ★ (kɑ:'mɑ:ðən) *n* a market town in S Wales, the administrative centre of Carmarthenshire: Norman castle. Pop.: 13 524 (1991).

Carmarthenshire ★ (kɑ:'mɑ:ðənˌʃɪə, -ʃə) *n* a county of S Wales, formerly part of Dyfed (1974–96). Administrative centre: Carmarthen. Pop.: 169 000 (1996 est.). Area: 2398 sq. km (926 sq. miles).

Carmel ★ ('kɑ:məl) *n* **Mount.** a mountain ridge in NW Israel, extending from the Samarian Hills to the Mediterranean. Highest point: about 540 m (1800 ft).

Carmelite ('kɑ:məˌlaɪt) *n RC Church.* **1** a member of an order of mendicant friars founded about 1154. **2** a member of a corresponding order of nuns founded in 1452, noted for its austere rule. ◆ *adj* **3** of or relating to either of these orders. ORIG C14: from F, after Mount CARMEL, where the order was founded

Carmichael ★ (kɑ:'maɪkᵊl) *n* **Hoaglund Howard** ('həʊglənd), known as *Hoagy.* 1899–1981, US pianist and composer of such songs as "Star Dust" (1929).

carminative ('kɑ:mɪnətɪv) *adj* **1** able to relieve flatulence. ◆ *n* **2** a carminative drug. ORIG C15: from F, from L *carmināre* to card wool

carmine ('kɑ:maɪn) *n* **1a** a vivid red colour. **1b** *(as adj): carmine paint.* **2** a pigment of this colour obtained from cochineal. ORIG C18: from Med. L *carmīnus,* from Ar. *qirmiz* KERMES

Carnac ★ ('kɑ:næk) *n* a village in NW France: noted for its many megalithic monuments, including alignments of stone menhirs.

carnage ('kɑ:nɪdʒ) *n* extensive slaughter. ORIG C16: from F, from It., from Med. L, from L *carō* flesh

carnal ('kɑ:nᵊl) *adj* relating to the appetites and passions of the body. ORIG C15: from LL, from L *carō* flesh
▸ **car'nality** *n* ▸ **'carnally** *adv*

carnal knowledge *n Chiefly law.* sexual intercourse.

Carnap ★ ('kɑ:næp) *n* **Rudolf.** 1891–1970, US logical positivist philosopher, born in Germany.

Carnarvon ★ (kɑ:'nɑ:vᵊn) *n* a variant spelling of **Caernarfon.**

carnation (kɑ:'neɪʃən) *n* **1** Also called: **clove pink.** a Eurasian plant cultivated in many varieties for its white, pink, or red flowers, which have a fragrant scent of cloves. **2** the flower of this plant. **3a** a pink or reddish-pink colour. **3b** *(as adj): a carnation dress.* ORIG C16: from F: flesh colour, from LL, from L *carō* flesh

carnauba (kɑ:'naʊbə) *n* **1** Also called: **wax palm.** a Brazilian fan palm. **2** Also called: **carnauba wax.** the wax obtained from the young leaves of this tree. ORIG from Brazilian Port., prob. of Tupi origin

Carné ★ ('kɑ:neɪ; *French* karne) *n* **Marcel** (marsɛl). 1906–96, French film director. His films include *Le Jour se lève* (1939) and *Les Portes de la nuit* (1946).

Carnegie ★ ('kɑ:nəgɪ, kɑ:'neɪ-) *n* **Andrew.** 1835–1919, US steel manufacturer and philanthropist, born in Scotland.

Carnegie Hall ★ ('kɑ:nəgɪ) *n* a famous concert hall in New York (opened 1891); endowed by Andrew Carnegie.

carnelian (kɑ:'ni:ljən) *n* a reddish-yellow translucent variety of chalcedony, used as a gemstone. ORIG C17: var. of *cornelian,* from OF, from ?

carnet ('kɑ:neɪ) *n* **1** a customs licence authorizing the temporary importation of a motor vehicle. **2** an official document permitting motorists to cross certain frontiers. ORIG F: notebook, from OF, ult. from L *quaternī* four at a time

Carniola ★ (ˌkɑ:nɪ'əʊlə) *n* a region of N Slovenia: a former duchy and crownland of Austria (1335–1919); divided between Yugoslavia and Italy in 1919; part of Yugoslavia (1947–92). German name: **Krain** (krain). Slovene name: **Kranj.**

carnival ('kɑ:nɪvᵊl) *n* **1a** a festive period marked by merrymaking, etc.: esp. in some Roman Catholic countries, the period just before Lent. **1b** *(as modifier): a carnival atmosphere.* **2** a travelling fair having sideshows, rides, etc. **3** a show or display arranged as an amusement. **4** *Austral.* a sports meeting. ORIG C16: from It., from OIt. *carnelevare* a removing of meat (referring to the Lenten fast)

carnivore ('kɑ:nɪˌvɔ:) *n* **1** any of an order of mammals having large pointed canine teeth specialized for eating flesh. The order includes cats, dogs, bears, and weasels. **2** any other animal or any plant that feeds on animals. **3** *Inf.* an aggressively ambitious person. ORIG C19: prob. back formation from CARNIVOROUS

carnivorous (kɑ:'nɪvərəs) *adj* **1** (esp. of animals) feeding on flesh. **2** (of plants such as the pitcher plant and sundew) able to trap and digest insects. **3** of or relating

to the carnivores. **4** *Inf.* aggressively ambitious or reactionary. ORIG C17: from L, from *carō* flesh + *vorāre* to consume
▸ **car'nivorousness** *n*

Carnot ★ ('kɑːnəʊ; *French* karno) *n* **1 Lazare (Nicolas Marguerite)** (laʒar), known as *the Organizer of Victory*. 1753–1823, French military engineer: organized the French Revolutionary army (1793–95). **2 Nicolas Léonard Sadi** (nikɔla leɔnar sadi). 1796–1832, French physicist, noted for his work on thermodynamics.

Caro ★ *n* **1** ('kærəʊ). Sir **Antony.** born 1924, British abstract sculptor. **2** ('kɑːrəʊ). **Joseph (ben Ephraim).** 1488–1575, Jewish legal scholar, born in Spain; compiler of the *Shulhan Arukh* (1564–65).

carob ('kærəb) *n* **1** an evergreen Mediterranean tree with compound leaves and edible pods. **2** the long blackish sugary pod of this tree, used for animal fodder and sometimes for human food. ORIG C16: from OF, from Med. L *carrūbium,* from Ar. *al kharrūbah*

carol ('kærəl) *n* **1** a joyful hymn or religious song, esp. one (a **Christmas carol**) celebrating the birth of Christ. ◆ *vb* **carols, carolling, carolled** *or US* **carols, caroling, caroled. 2** (*intr*) to sing carols at Christmas. **3** to sing (something) in a joyful manner. ORIG C13: from OF, from ?

Carol II ★ ('kærəl) *n* 1893–1953, king of Romania (1930–40), who was deposed by the Iron Guard.

Carolina ★ (ˌkærə'laɪnə) *n* a former English colony on the E coast of North America, first established in 1663: divided in 1729 into North and South Carolina, which are often referred to as **the Carolinas.**

Caroline ('kærəˌlaɪn) *or* **Carolean** (ˌkærə'liːən) *adj* characteristic of or relating to Charles I or Charles II (kings of England, Scotland, and Ireland), the society over which they ruled, or their government. Also called: **Carolinian.**

Caroline Islands ★ *pl n* an archipelago of over 500 islands and islets in the W Pacific Ocean east of the Philippines, all are now part of the Federated States of Micronesia except for the Belau group: formerly part of the US Trust Territory of the Pacific Islands; centre of a typhoon zone.

Carolingian (ˌkærə'lɪndʒɪən) *adj* **1** of or relating to the Frankish dynasty founded by Pepin the Short which ruled in France from 751–987 A.D. and in Germany until 911 A.D. ◆ *n* **2** a member of the dynasty of the Carolingian Franks. ◆ Also: **Carlovingian, Carolinian.**

Carolinian (ˌkærə'lɪnɪən) *adj, n* a variant of **Caroline** or **Carolingian.**

carom ('kærəm) *n Billiards.* another word (esp. US & Canad.) for **cannon** (sense 5). ORIG C18: from earlier *carambole* (taken as *carom ball*), from Sp. *carambola* a CARAMBOLA

carotene ('kærəˌtiːn) *or* **carotin** ('kærətɪn) *n* any of four orange-red isomers of a hydrocarbon present in many plants and converted to vitamin A in the liver. ORIG C19 *carotin,* from L *carōta* CARROT

carotenoid *or* **carotinoid** (kə'rɒtɪˌnɔɪd) *n* any of a group of red or yellow pigments, including carotenes, found in plants and certain animal tissues.

carotid (kə'rɒtɪd) *n* **1** either of the two principal arteries that supply blood to the head and neck. ◆ *adj* **2** of either of these arteries. ORIG C17: from F, from Gk, from *karoun* to stupefy; so named because pressure on them produced unconsciousness

carousal (kə'raʊzᵊl) *n* a merry drinking party.

carouse (kə'raʊz) *vb* **carouses, carousing, caroused. 1** (*intr*) to have a merry drinking spree. ◆ *n* **2** another word for **carousal.** ORIG C16: via F *carrousser* from G (*trinken*) *gar aus* (to drink) right out
▸ **ca'rouser** *n*

carousel (ˌkærə'sɛl, -'zɛl) *n* **1** a circular tray in which slides for a projector are held in slots from which they can be released in turn. **2** a revolving luggage conveyor, as at an airport. **3** *US and Canad.* a merry-go-round. **4** *History.* a tournament in which horsemen took part in races. ORIG C17: from F, from It. *carosello,* from ?

carp[1] (kɑːp) *n, pl* **carp** *or* **carps. 1** a freshwater food fish having one long dorsal fin, and two barbels on each side of the mouth. **2** a cyprinid. ORIG C14: from OF *carpe,* of Gmc origin

carp[2] (kɑːp) *vb* (*intr;* often foll. by *at*) to complain or find fault. ORIG C13: from ON *karpa* to boast
▸ **'carper** *n* ▸ **'carping** *adj, n*

-carp *n combining form.* (in botany) fruit or a reproductive structure that develops into a particular part of the fruit: *epicarp.* ORIG from NL *-carpium,* from Gk *-karpion,* from *karpos* fruit

Carpaccio ★ (ˌkɑː'pætʃɪəʊ, -tʃəʊ; *Italian* kar'pattʃo) *n* **Vittore** (vit'toːre). ?1460–?1525, Venetian painter.

carpal ('kɑːpᵊl) *n* **a** any bone of the wrist. **b** (*as modifier*): *carpal bones.* ORIG C18: from NL *carpālis,* from Gk *karpos* wrist

car park *n* an area or building reserved for parking cars. Usual US and Canad. term: **parking lot.**

Carpathian Mountains (kɑː'peɪθɪən) *or* **Carpathians** ★ *pl n* a mountain system of central and E Europe, extending from Slovakia to central Romania: mainly forested, with rich iron ore resources. Highest peak: Gerlachovka, 2663 m (8788 ft).

Carpatho-Ukraine ★ (kɑː'peɪθəʊjuː'kreɪn) *n* another name for **Ruthenia.**

carpe diem *Latin.* ('kɑːpɪ 'diːɛm) *sentence substitute.* enjoy the pleasures of the moment, without concern for the future. ORIG lit.: seize the day!

carpel ('kɑːpᵊl) *n* the female reproductive organ of flowering plants, consisting of an ovary, style, and stigma. ORIG C19: from NL *carpellum,* from Gk *karpos* fruit
▸ **'carpellary** *adj*

Carpentaria ★ (ˌkɑːpən'tɛərɪə) *n* **Gulf of.** a shallow inlet of the Arafura Sea, in N Australia between Arnhem Land and Cape York Peninsula.

carpenter ('kɑːpɪntə) *n* **1** a person skilled in woodwork, esp. in buildings, ships, etc. ◆ *vb* **2** (*intr*) to do the work of a carpenter. **3** (*tr*) to make or fit together by or as if by carpentry. ORIG C14: from Anglo-F, from L, from *carpentum* wagon

Carpenter ★ ('kɑːpɪntə) *n* **John Alden.** 1876–1951, US composer: his works include the ballet *Skyscrapers* (1926) and the suite *Adventures in a Perambulator* (1915).

Carpentier ★ (*French* karpɑ̃tje) *n* **Georges** (ʒɔrʒ), known as *Gorgeous Georges.* 1894–1975, French boxer: world light-heavyweight champion (1920–22).

carpentry ('kɑːpɪntrɪ) *n* **1** the art or technique of working wood. **2** the work produced by a carpenter; woodwork.

carpet ('kɑːpɪt) *n* **1** a heavy fabric for covering floors. **2** a covering like a carpet: *a carpet of leaves.* **3 on the carpet.** *Inf.* **3a** before authority to be reproved. **3b** under consideration. ◆ *vb* **carpets, carpeting, carpeted.** (*tr*) **4** to cover with or as if with a carpet. **5** *Inf.* to reprimand. ORIG C14: from OF, from OIt., from LL *carpeta,* from L *carpere* to pluck, card

carpetbag ('kɑːpɪtˌbæg) *n* a travelling bag originally made of carpeting.

carpetbagger ('kɑːpɪtˌbægə) *n* **1** a politician who seeks public office in a locality where he or she has no real connections. **2** *Brit.* a person who makes a short-term investment in a mutual savings or life-assurance organization in order to benefit from free shares issued following the organization's conversion to a public limited company.

carpet beetle *or US* **carpet bug** *n* any of various beetles, the larvae of which feed on carpets, furnishing fabrics, etc.

carpet bombing *n* systematic intensive bombing of an area.

carpeting ('kɑːpɪtɪŋ) *n* carpet material or carpets in general.

carpet slipper *n* one of a pair of slippers, originally one made with woollen uppers resembling carpeting.

carpet snake *or* **python** *n* a large nonvenomous Australian snake having a carpet-like pattern on its back.

carpet-sweeper *n* a household device with a revolving brush for sweeping carpets.

car phone *n* a telephone that operates by cellular radio for use in a car.

carpo- *combining form.* (in botany) indicating fruit or a seed. ORIG from Gk *karpos* fruit

carport ('kɑːˌpɔːt) *n* a shelter for a car usually consisting of a roof built out from the side of a building and supported by posts.

-carpous *or* **-carpic** *adj combining form.* (in botany) indicating a certain kind or number of fruit: *apocarpous.* ORIG from NL, from Gk *karpos* fruit

carpus ('kɑːpəs) *n, pl* **carpi** (-paɪ). **1** the technical name for **wrist. 2** the eight small bones of the human wrist. ORIG C17: NL, from Gk *karpos*

Carracci ★ (kə'rɑːtʃɪ; *Italian* kar'rattʃi) *n* a family of Italian painters, born in Bologna: **Agostino** (agos'tiːno) (1557–1602); his brother, **Annibale** (an'niːbale) (1560–1609), noted for his frescoes, and their cousin, **Ludovico** (ludo'viːko) (1555–1619). They founded a teaching academy (1582) in Bologna.

carrack ('kærək) *n* a galleon sailed in the Mediterranean as a merchantman in the 15th and 16th centuries. ORIG C14: from OF *caraque,* from OSp. *carraca,* from Ar. *qarāqīr* merchant ships

carrageen, carragheen, *or* **carageen** ('kærəˌgiːn) *n* an edible red seaweed of North America and N Europe. Also called: **Irish moss.** ORIG C19: from *Carragheen,* near Waterford, Ireland

carrageenan, carragheenan, *or* **carageenan** (ˌkærə'giːnən) *n* a carbohydrate extracted from carrageen, used to make a beverage, medicine, and jelly, and as an emulsifying and gelling agent (**E407**) in various processed desserts and drinks.

Carrara ★ (kə'rɑːrə; *Italian* kar'raːra) *n* a town in NW Italy, in NW Tuscany: famous for its marble. Pop.: 68 480 (1990).

carrel *or* **carrell** ('kærəl) *n* a small individual study room or private desk, often in a library. ORIG C20: from obs. *carrel* study area, var. of CAROL

Carrel ★ (kə'rɛl, 'kærəl; *French* karɛl) *n* **Alexis** (ə'lɛksɪs; *French* alɛksi). 1873–1944, French surgeon, active in the US (1905–39): developed a method of suturing blood vessels. Nobel prize for physiology or medicine 1912.

Carreras ★ (kə'rɛərəs) *n* **José** (həʊ'zeɪ). born 1947, Spanish tenor.

Carrey ★ ('kɛərɪ) *n* **Jim.** Canadian film actor. His films include *The Mask* (1994) and *The Truman Show* (1998).

carriage ('kærɪdʒ) *n* **1** *Brit.* a railway coach for passengers. **2** the manner in which a person holds and moves his or her head and body. **3** a four-wheeled horse-drawn vehicle for persons. **4** the moving part of a machine that bears another part: *a typewriter carriage.* **5** ('kærɪdʒ, 'kærɪɪdʒ). **5a** the act of conveying. **5b** the charge made for conveying (esp. in **carriage forward,** when the charge is to be paid by the receiver, and **carriage paid**). ORIG C14: from OF *cariage,* from *carier* to CARRY

carriage clock *n* a portable clock, usually in a rectangular case, originally used by travellers.

carriage trade *n* trade from the wealthy part of society.

carriageway ('kærɪdʒˌweɪ) *n Brit.* the part of a road along which traffic passes in a single line moving in one direction only: *a dual carriageway.*

Carrickfergus ★ (ˌkærɪk'fɜːgəs) *n* **1** a town in NE Northern Ireland, on Belfast Lough; historic settlement of Scottish Protestants; Norman castle. Pop.: 22 885 (1991). **2** a district of E Northern Ireland, on Belfast Lough N of Belfast: tourism. Administrative centre: Carrickfergus. Pop.: 32 750 (1991). Area: 77 sq. km (30 sq. miles).

carrier ('kærɪə) *n* **1** a person, thing, or organization employed to carry goods, etc. **2** a mechanism by which something is carried or moved, such as a device for transmitting rotation from the faceplate of a lathe to the workpiece. **3** *Pathol.* another name for **vector** (sense 3). **4** *Pathol.* a person or animal that, without having any symptoms of a disease, is capable of transmitting it to others. **5** Also called: **charge carrier.** *Physics.* an electron or hole that carries the charge in a conductor or semiconductor. **6** short for **carrier wave. 7** *Chem.* **7a** an inert substance used to absorb a dyestuff, transport a sample through a gas chromatography column, contain a radioisotope for radioactive tracing, etc. **7b** a substance used to support a catalyst. **8** See **aircraft carrier.**

carrier bag *n Brit.* a large paper or plastic bag for carrying shopping, etc.

carrier pigeon *n* any homing pigeon, esp. one used for carrying messages.

carrier wave *n Radio.* a wave modulated in amplitude, frequency, or phase in order to carry a signal in radio transmission, etc.

Carrington ★ ('kærɪŋtən) *n* **1 Dora,** known as *Carrington.* 1893–1932, British painter; a member of the Bloomsbury Group. **2 Peter (Alexander Rupert),** 6th Baron. born 1919, British Conservative politician: secretary of state for defence (1970–74); foreign secretary (1979–82); secretary general of NATO (1984–88).

carriole ('kærɪˌəʊl) *n* a variant spelling of **cariole.**

carrion ('kærɪən) *n* **1** dead and rotting flesh. **2** (*modifier*) eating carrion. **3** something rotten. ORIG C13: from Anglo-F *caroine,* ult. from L *carō* flesh

carrion crow *n* a common predatory and scavenging European crow similar to the rook but having a pure black bill.

Carroll ★ ('kærəl) *n* **Lewis.** real name *Charles Lutwidge Dodgson.* 1832–98, British writer; an Oxford mathematics don, he wrote *Alice's Adventures in Wonderland* (1865) and *Through the Looking-Glass* (1872).

carrot ('kærət) *n* **1** an umbelliferous plant with finely divided leaves. **2** the long tapering orange root of this plant, eaten as a vegetable. **3a** something offered as a lure or incentive. **3b carrot and stick.** reward and punishment as methods of persuasion. ORIG C16: from OF *carotte,* from LL *carōta,* from Gk *karōton*

carroty ('kærətɪ) *adj* **1** of a reddish or yellowish-orange colour. **2** having red hair.

carrousel (ˌkærə'sɛl, -'zɛl) *n* a variant spelling of **carousel.**

carry ('kærɪ) *vb* **carries, carrying, carried.** (*mainly tr*) **1** (*also intr*) to take or bear (something) from one place to another. **2** to transfer for consideration: *he carried his complaints to her superior.* **3** to have on one's person: *he carries a watch.* **4** (*also intr*) to be transmitted or serve as a medium for transmitting: *sound carries over water.* **5** to bear or be able to bear the weight, pressure, or responsibility of: *her efforts carry the whole production.* **6** to have as an attribute or result: *this crime carries a heavy penalty.* **7** to bring or communicate: *to carry news.* **8** (*also intr*) to be pregnant with (young). **9** to bear (the head, body, etc.) in a specified manner: *she carried her head high.* **10** to conduct or bear (oneself) in a specified manner: *she carried herself well.* **11** to continue or extend: *the war was carried into enemy territory.* **12** to cause to move or go: *desire for riches carried him to the city.* **13** to influence, esp. by emotional appeal: *his words carried the crowd.* **14** to secure the passage of (a bill, motion, etc.). **15** to win (an election). **16** to obtain victory for (a candidate). **17** *Chiefly US.* to win a majority of votes in (a district, etc.): *the candidate carried 40 states.* **18** to capture: *our troops carried the town.* **19** (of communications media) to include as the content: *this newspaper carries no book reviews.* **20** Also (esp. US): **carry over.** *Book-keeping.* to transfer (an item) to another account, esp. to transfer to the following year's account: *to carry a loss.* **21** *Maths.* to transfer (a number) from one column of figures to the next. **22** (of a shop, trader, etc.) to keep in stock: *to carry confectionery.* **23** to support (a musical part or melody) against the other parts. **24** (*intr*) (of a ball, projectile, etc.) to travel through the air or reach a specified point: *his first drive carried to the green.* **25** *Inf.* to imbibe (alcoholic drink) without showing ill effects. **26** (*intr*) *Sl.* to have drugs on one's person. **27 carry all before (one).** to win unanimous support or approval for (oneself). **28 carry the can (for).** *Inf.* to take responsibility for some misdemeanour, etc. (on behalf of). **29 carry the day.** to be successful. ◆ *n, pl* **carries. 30** the act of carrying. **31** *US & Canad.* a portion of land over which a boat must be portaged. **32** the range of a firearm or its projectile. **33** *Golf.* the distance from where the ball is struck to where it first touches the ground. ◆ See also **carry away, carry forward,** etc. ORIG C14 *carien,* from OF *carier* to move by vehicle, from *car,* from L *carrum* transport wagon

carryall ('kærɪˌɔːl) *n* the usual US and Canad. name for a **holdall.**

carry away *vb* (*tr, adv*) **1** to remove forcefully. **2** (*usually passive*) to cause (a person) to lose self-control. **3** (*usually passive*) to delight: *he was carried away by your gift.*

carrycot ('kærɪˌkɒt) *n* a light cot with handles, similar to but smaller than the body of a pram.

carry forward *vb* (*tr, adv*) **1** *Book-keeping.* to transfer (a balance) to the next column, etc. **2** *Tax accounting.* to apply (a legally permitted credit, esp. an operating loss) to the taxable income of following years. ◆ Also: **carry over.**

carrying-on *n, pl* **carryings-on.** *Inf.* **1** unconventional behaviour. **2** excited or flirtatious behaviour.

carry off *vb* (*tr, adv*) **1** to remove forcefully. **2** to win. **3** to handle (a situation) successfully: *he carried off the introductions well.* **4** to cause to die: *he was carried off by pneumonia.*

carry on *vb* (*adv*) **1** (*intr*) to continue or persevere. **2** (*tr*) to conduct: *to carry on a business.* **3** (*intr;* often foll. by *with*) *Inf.* to have an affair. **4** (*intr*) *Inf.* to cause a fuss or commotion. ◆ *n* **carry-on. 5** *Inf., chiefly Brit.* a fuss.

carry out *vb* (*tr, adv*) **1** to perform or cause to be implemented: *I wish he could afford to carry out his plan.* **2** to accomplish. ◆ *n* **carry-out.** *Chiefly Scot.* **3** alcohol bought at an off-licence, etc., for consumption elsewhere. **4a** a shop which sells hot cooked food for consumption away from the premises. **4b** (*as modifier*): *a carry-out shop.*

carry over *vb* (*tr, adv*) **1** to postpone or defer. **2** *Book-keeping, tax accounting.* another term for **carry forward.** ◆ *n* **carry-over. 3** something left over for future use, esp. goods to be sold. **4** *Book-keeping.* a sum or balance carried forward.

carry through *vb* (*tr, adv*) **1** to bring to completion. **2** to enable to endure (hardship, trouble, etc.); support.

carse (kɑːs) *n Scot.* a riverside area of flat fertile alluvium. ORIG C14: from ?

carsick ('kɑːˌsɪk) *adj* nauseated from riding in a car or other vehicle.
▸ **'carˌsickness** *n*

Carson ★ ('kɑːsᵊn) *n* **1 Christopher,** known as *Kit Carson.* 1809–68, US frontiersman, trapper, scout, and Indian agent. **2 Edward Henry,** Baron. 1854–1935, Irish politician and lawyer; led northern Irish resistance to the British government's home rule for Ireland. **3 Rachel (Louise).** 1907–64, US marine biologist and science writer; author of *Silent Spring* (1962).

Carson City ★ *n* a city in W Nevada, capital of the state. Pop.: 46 770 (1995 est.).

Carstensz ★ ('kɑːstənz) *n* **Mount.** a former name of (Mount) **Jaya.**

cart (kɑːt) *n* **1** a heavy open vehicle, usually having two wheels and drawn by horses. **2** a light open horse-drawn vehicle for business or pleasure. **3** any small vehicle drawn or pushed by hand, such as a trolley. **4 in the cart. 4a** in an awkward situation. **4b** in the lurch. **5 put the cart before the horse.** to reverse the usual order of things. ◆ *vb* **6** (*usually tr*) to use or draw a cart to convey (goods, etc.). **7** (*tr*) to carry with effort: *to cart wood home.* ORIG C13: from ON *kartr*
▸ **'carter** *n*

cartage ('kɑːtɪdʒ) *n* the process or cost of carting.

Cartagena ★ (ˌkɑːtə'dʒiːnə; *Spanish* karta'xena) *n* **1** a port in NW Colombia, on the Caribbean: centre for the Inquisition and the slave trade in the 16th century; chief oil port of Colombia. Pop.: 745 689 (1995 est.). **2** a port in SE Spain, on the Mediterranean: important since Carthaginian and Roman times for its minerals. Pop.: 179 659 (1994 est.).

carte blanche ('kɑːt 'blɑːntʃ) *n, pl* **cartes blanches** ('kɑːts 'blɑːntʃ). complete discretion or authority: *the government gave their negotiator carte blanche.* ORIG C18: from F: blank paper

cartel (kɑː'tɛl) *n* **1** Also called: **trust.** a collusive association of independent enterprises formed to monopolize production and distribution of a product or service. **2** *Politics.* an alliance of parties to further common aims. ORIG C20: from G *Kartell,* from F, from It. *cartello* public notice, dim. of *carta* CARD[1]

Carter ★ ('kɑːtə) *n* **1 Angela.** 1940–92, British writer; her novels include *The Magic Toyshop* (1967) and *Nights at the Circus* (1984). **2 Elliot (Cook).** born 1908, US composer. His works include the *Piano Sonata* (1945–46), four string quartets, and orchestral pieces. **3 Howard.** 1873–1939, British Egyptologist: excavated the tomb of Tutankhamen. **4 James Earl,** known as *Jimmy.* born 1924, US Democratic statesman; 39th president of the US (1977–81).

Carteret ★ ('kɑːtərɪt) *n* **John,** 1st Earl Granville. 1690–1763, British statesman, who led the opposition to Walpole (1730–42), after whose fall he became secretary of state (1742–44).

Cartesian (kɑː'tiːzɪən) *adj* **1** of or relating to the works of Descartes. **2** of or used in Descartes' mathematical system.
▸ **Car'tesianˌism** *n*

Cartesian coordinates *pl n* a system of coordinates that defines the location of a point in space in terms of its perpendicular distance from each of a set of mutually perpendicular axes.

Carthage ★ ('kɑːθɪdʒ) *n* an ancient city state, on the N African coast near present-day Tunis. Founded about 800 B.C. by Phoenician traders, it grew into an empire dominating N Africa and the Mediterranean. Destroyed and then rebuilt by Rome, it was finally razed by the Arabs in 697 A.D.
▸ **Carthaginian** (ˌkɑːθə'dʒɪnɪən) *adj, n*

carthorse ('kɑːtˌhɔːs) *n* a large heavily built horse kept for pulling carts or carriages.

Carthusian (kɑː'θjuːzɪən) *RC Church.* ◆ *n* **1** a member of a monastic order founded by Saint Bruno in 1084 near Grenoble, France. ◆ *adj* **2** of or relating to this order: *a Carthusian monastery.* ORIG C14: from Med. L, from L *Carthusia* Chartreuse, near Grenoble

Cartier ★ (*French* kartje) *n* **Jacques** (ʒɑk). 1491–1557, French navigator and explorer in Canada.

Cartier-Bresson ★ (*French* kartjebrɛsɔ̃) *n* **Henri** (ɑ̃ri). born 1908, French photographer.

cartilage ('kɑːtɪlɪdʒ) *n* a tough elastic tissue composing most of the embryonic skeleton of vertebrates. In the adults of higher vertebrates it is mostly converted into bone. Nontechnical name: **gristle.** ORIG C16: from L *cartilāgō*
▸ **cartilaginous** (ˌkɑːtɪ'lædʒɪnəs) *adj*

cartilaginous fish *n* any of a class of fish including the sharks and rays, having a skeleton composed entirely of cartilage.

Cartland ★ ('kɑːtlənd) *n* Dame **Barbara (Hamilton).** 1901–2000, British writer of popular fiction.

cartload ('kɑːtˌləʊd) *n* the amount a cart can hold.

cart off, away, *or* **out** *vb* (*tr, adv*) *Inf.* to carry or remove brusquely or by force.

cartogram ('kɑːtəˌgræm) *n* a map showing statistical information in diagrammatic form. ORIG C20: from F *cartogramme,* from *carte* map, CHART

cartography (kɑː'tɒgrəfɪ) *n* the art, technique, or practice of compiling or drawing maps or charts. ORIG C19: from F *cartographie,* from *carte* map, CHART
▸ **car'tographer** *n* ▸ **cartographic** (ˌkɑːtə'græfɪk) *or* **ˌcarto'graphical** *adj*

carton ('kɑːtᵊn) *n* **1** a cardboard box for containing goods. **2** a container of waxed paper in which liquids, such as milk, are sold. ORIG C19: from F, from It. *cartone* pasteboard, from *carta* CARD[1]

cartoon (kɑː'tuːn) *n* **1** a humorous or satirical drawing, esp. one in a newspaper or magazine. **2** Also called: **comic strip.** a sequence of drawings in a newspaper, magazine, etc. **3** See **animated cartoon. 4** a full-size preparatory sketch

for a fresco, tapestry, mosaic, etc. ORIG C17: from It. *cartone* pasteboard
▸ **car'toonist** *n*

cartouche *or* **cartouch** (kɑː'tuːʃ) *n* **1** a carved or cast ornamental tablet or panel in the form of a scroll. **2** an oblong figure enclosing characters expressing royal or divine names in Egyptian hieroglyphics. ORIG C17: from F: scroll, cartridge, from It., from *carta* paper

cartridge ('kɑːtrɪdʒ) *n* **1** a metal casing containing an explosive charge and often a bullet, for a rifle or other small arms. **2** a stylus unit of a record player, either containing a piezoelectric crystal (**crystal cartridge**) or an induction coil that moves in the field of a permanent magnet (**magnetic cartridge**). **3** an enclosed container of magnetic tape, photographic film, ink, etc., for insertion into a tape deck, camera, pen, etc. **4** *Computing.* a removable unit in a computer, such as an integrated circuit, containing software. ORIG C16: from earlier *cartage,* var. of CARTOUCHE (cartridge)

cartridge belt *n* a belt with pockets for cartridge clips or loops for cartridges.

cartridge clip *n* a metallic container holding cartridges for an automatic firearm.

cartridge paper *n* **1** an uncoated type of drawing or printing paper. **2** a heavy paper used in making cartridges or as drawing or printing paper.

cartwheel ('kɑːtˌwiːl) *n* **1** the wheel of a cart, usually having wooden spokes. **2** an acrobatic movement in which the body makes a revolution supported on the hands with legs outstretched.

Cartwright ★ ('kɑːtˌraɪt) *n* **Edmund.** 1743–1823, British clergyman, who invented the power loom.

caruncle ('kærəŋkᵊl, kə'rʌŋ-) *n* **1** a fleshy outgrowth on the heads of certain birds, such as a cock's comb. **2** an outgrowth near the hilum on the seeds of some plants. ORIG C17: from obs. F *caruncule,* from L *caruncula* a small piece of flesh, from *carō* flesh
▸ **caruncular** (kə'rʌŋkjʊlə) *or* **ca'runculous** *adj*

Caruso ★ (*Italian* ka'ruːso) *n* **Enrico** (en'riːko). 1873–1921, Italian tenor; one of the first to make records.

carve (kɑːv) *vb* **carves, carving, carved. 1** (*tr*) to cut or chip in order to form something: *to carve wood.* **2** to form (something) by cutting or chipping: *to carve statues.* **3** to slice (meat) into pieces. ◆ See also **carve out, carve up.** ORIG OE *ceorfan*

carvel ('kɑːvᵊl) *n* another word for **caravel.**

carvel-built *adj* (of a vessel) having a hull with planks made flush at the seams. Cf. **clinker-built.**

carven ('kɑːvᵊn) *vb* an archaic or literary past participle of **carve.**

carve out *vb* (*tr, adv*) *Inf.* to make or create (a career): *he carved out his own future.*

carver ('kɑːvə) *n* **1** a carving knife. **2** (*pl*) a large matched knife and fork for carving meat. **3** *Brit.* a chair having arms that forms part of a set of dining chairs.

carvery ('kɑːvərɪ) *n, pl* **carveries.** an eating establishment at which customers pay a set price for unrestricted helpings from a variety of meats, salads, etc.

carve up *vb* (*tr, adv*) **1** to cut (something) into pieces. **2** to divide (land, etc.). ◆ *n* **carve-up. 3** *Inf.* an act or instance of dishonestly prearranging the result of a competition. **4** *Sl.* the distribution of something.

carving ('kɑːvɪŋ) *n* a figure or design produced by carving stone, wood, etc.

carving knife *n* a long-bladed knife for carving cooked meat for serving.

Cary ★ ('kɛərɪ, 'kærɪ) *n* (**Arthur**) **Joyce** (**Lunel**). 1888–1957, British novelist; author of *Mister Johnson* (1939) and *The Horse's Mouth* (1944).

caryatid (ˌkærɪ'ætɪd) *n, pl* **caryatids** *or* **caryatides** (-ɪˌdiːz). a column, used to support an entablature, in the form of a draped female figure. ORIG C16: from L, from Gk *Karuatides* priestesses of Artemis at *Karuai* (Caryae), in Laconia

Casablanca ★ (ˌkæsə'blæŋkə) *n* a port in NW Morocco, on the Atlantic: largest city in the country; industrial centre. Pop.: 2 943 000 (1993 est.).

Casals ★ (*Spanish* ka'sals) *n* **Pablo** ('paβlo). 1876–1973, Spanish cellist and composer.

Casanova ★ (ˌkæsə'nəʊvə) *n* **1 Giovanni Jacopo** (dʒo'vanni 'jaːkopo). 1725–98, Italian adventurer noted for his *Mémoires,* a vivid account of his sexual adventures. **2** any man noted for his amorous adventures; a rake.

casbah ('kæzbɑː) *n* (*sometimes cap.*) a variant spelling of **kasbah.**

cascade (kæs'keɪd) *n* **1** a waterfall or series of waterfalls over rocks. **2** something resembling this, such as folds of lace. **3** a consecutive sequence of chemical or physical processes. **4** a series of stages or devices in which each operates the next in turn. ◆ *vb* **cascades, cascading, cascaded. 5** (*intr*) to flow or fall in or like a cascade. ORIG C17: from F, from It., ult. from L *cadere* to fall

Cascade Range ★ *n* a chain of mountains in the US and Canada: a continuation of the Sierra Nevada range from N California through Oregon and Washington to British Columbia. Highest peak: Mount Rainier, 4392 m (14 408 ft).

cascara (kæs'kɑːrə) *n* **1** Also called: **cascara sagrada.** the dried bark of the cascara buckthorn, used as a laxative and stimulant. **2** Also called: **cascara buckthorn.** a shrub or small tree of NW North America. ORIG C19: from Sp.: bark

case[1] (keɪs) *n* **1** a single instance or example of something. **2** an instance of disease, injury, etc. **3** a question or matter for discussion. **4** a specific condition or state of affairs; situation. **5** a set of arguments supporting a particular action, cause, etc. **6a** a person attended or served by a doctor, social worker, solicitor, etc. **6b** (*as modifier*): *a case study.* **7a** an action or suit at law: *he has a good case.* **7b** the evidence offered in court to support a claim. **8** *Grammar.* **8a** a set of grammatical categories of nouns, pronouns, and adjectives indicating the relation of the noun, adjective, or pronoun to other words in the sentence. **8b** any one of these categories: *the dative case.* **9** *Inf.* an eccentric. **10 in any case.** (*adv*) no matter what. **11 in case.** (*adv*) **11a** in order to allow for eventualities. **11b** (*conj*) in order to allow for the possibility that: *take your coat in case it rains.* **12 in case of.** (*prep*) in the event of. **13 in no case.** (*adv*) under no circumstances. ORIG OE *casus* (grammatical) case, associated also with OF *cas* a happening; both from L *cāsus,* a befalling, from *cadere* to fall

case[2] (keɪs) *n* **1a** a container, such as a box or chest. **1b** (*in combination*): *suitcase.* **2** an outer cover, esp. for a watch. **3** a receptacle and its contents: *a case of ammunition.* **4** *Archit.* another word for **casing** (sense 3). **5** a cover ready to be fastened to a book to form its binding. **6** *Printing.* a tray in which a compositor keeps individual metal types of a particular size and style. Cases were originally used in pairs, one (the **upper case**) for capitals, the other (the **lower case**) for small letters. ◆ *vb* **cases, casing, cased.** (*tr*) **7** to put into or cover with a case. **8** *Sl.* to inspect carefully (esp. a place to be robbed). ORIG C13: from OF *casse,* from L, from *capere* to take, hold

casebook ('keɪsˌbʊk) *n* a book in which records of legal or medical cases are kept.

case-harden *vb* (*tr*) **1** *Metallurgy.* to form a hard surface layer of high carbon content on (a steel component). **2** to make callous: *experience case-hardened the judge.*

case history *n* a record of a person's background, medical history, etc.

casein ('keɪsɪɪn, -siːn) *n* a protein, precipitated from milk by the action of rennin, forming the basis of cheese. ORIG C19: from L *cāseus* cheese + -IN

case law *n* law established by following judicial decisions given in earlier cases. Cf. **statute law.**

caseload ('keɪsˌləʊd) *n* the number of cases constituting the work of a doctor, solicitor, social worker, etc., over a specified period.

casemate ('keɪsˌmeɪt) *n* an armoured compartment in a ship or fortification in which guns are mounted. ORIG C16: from F, from It. *casamatta,* ?from Gk *khasmata* apertures

casement ('keɪsmənt) *n* **1** a window frame that is

hinged on one side. **2** a window containing frames hinged at the side. **3** a poetic word for **window**. ORIG C15: prob. from OF *encassement* frame, from *encasser* to encase, from *casse* framework

Casement ★ ('keɪsmənt) *n* Sir **Roger (David)**. 1864–1916, British diplomat and Irish nationalist: hanged by the British for seeking German support for Irish independence.

caseous ('keɪsɪəs) *adj* of or like cheese. ORIG C17: from L *cāseus* CHEESE

casern *or* **caserne** (kə'zɜːn) *n* (formerly) a billet or accommodation for soldiers in a town. ORIG C17: from F *caserne,* from OProvençal *cazerna* group of four men, ult. from L *quattuor* four

Caserta ★ (*Italian* ka'zɛrta) *n* a town in S Italy, in Campania: centre of Garibaldi's campaigns for the unification of Italy (1860); Allied headquarters in World War II. Pop.: 69 350 (1990).

casework ('keɪsˌwɜːk) *n* social work based on close study of the personal histories and circumstances of individuals and families.
▸ **'caseˌworker** *n*

cash[1] (kæʃ) *n* **1** banknotes and coins, esp. when readily available. **2** immediate payment for goods or services (esp. in **cash down**). **3** (*modifier*) of, for, or paid by cash: *a cash transaction.* ◆ *vb* **4** (*tr*) to obtain or pay ready money for. ◆ See also **cash in, cash up.** ORIG C16: from OIt. *cassa* money box, from L *capsa* CASE[2]
▸ **'cashable** *adj*

cash[2] (kæʃ) *n, pl* **cash.** any of various Chinese or Indian coins of low value. ORIG C16: from Port. *caixa,* from Tamil *kāsu,* from Sansk. *karsa* weight of gold

Cash ★ (kæʃ) *n* **1 Johnny.** born 1932, US country-and-western singer and songwriter. His records include "A Boy named Sue" (1969). **2 Pat.** born 1965, Australian tennis player: Wimbledon champion 1987.

cash-and-carry *adj, adv* **1** sold or operated on a basis of cash payment for merchandise that is not delivered but removed by the purchaser. ◆ *n, pl* **cash-and-carries. 2** a wholesale store, esp. for groceries, that operates on this basis. **3** an operation on a commodities futures market in which spot goods are purchased for cash and sold at a profit on a futures contract, after paying interest and storage charges.

cashback ('kæʃˌbæk) *n* **1a** a discount offered in return for immediate payment. **1b** (*as modifier*): *cashback price £519.99 – save £30!* **2a** a service provided by some supermarkets in which customers paying by debit card can draw cash. **2b** the cash so drawn.

cash-book *n Book-keeping.* a journal in which all receipts and disbursements are recorded.

cash card *n* a plastic card issued by a bank or building society enabling the holder to obtain cash from a cash dispenser.

cash cow *n* a product, acquisition, etc., that produces a steady flow of cash, esp. one with a well-known brand name commanding a high market share.

cash crop *n* a crop grown for sale rather than for subsistence.

cash desk *n* a counter or till in a shop where purchases are paid for.

cash discount *n* a discount granted to a purchaser who pays before a stipulated date.

cash dispenser *n* a computerized device outside a bank that supplies cash when the user inserts his or her cash card and keys in his or her identification number. Also called: **automated teller machine.**

cashew ('kæʃuː, kæ'ʃuː) *n* **1** a tropical American evergreen tree, bearing kidney-shaped nuts. **2** Also called: **cashew nut.** the edible nut of this tree. ORIG C18: from Port. *cajú,* from Tupi *acajú*

cash flow *n* **1** the movement of money into and out of a business. **2** a document that records or predicts this movement.

cashier[1] (kæ'ʃɪə) *n* **1** a person responsible for receiving payments for goods, services, etc., as in a shop. **2** an employee of a bank responsible for receiving deposits, cashing cheques, etc.: bank clerk. **3** any person responsible for handling cash in a business. ORIG C16: from Du. or F, from *casse* money chest

cashier[2] (kæ'ʃɪə) *vb* (*tr*) to dismiss with dishonour, esp. from the armed forces. ORIG C16: from MDu., from OF, from L *quassāre* to QUASH

cash in *vb* (*adv*) **1** (*tr*) to give (something) in exchange. **2** (*intr; often foll. by on*) *Inf.* **2a** to profit (from). **2b** to take advantage (of).

cashmere *or* **kashmir** ('kæʃmɪə) *n* **1** a fine soft wool from goats of the Kashmir area. **2a** cloth or knitted material made from this or similar wool. **2b** (*as modifier*): *a cashmere sweater.*

Cashmere ★ (kæʃ'mɪə) *n* a variant spelling of **Kashmir.**

cash on delivery *n* a service entailing cash payment to the carrier on delivery of merchandise. Abbrev.: **COD.**

cash point *n* **1** any retail outlet at which goods are bought for cash. **2** a cash dispenser.

cash register *n* a till with a keyboard that operates a mechanism for displaying and adding the amounts of cash received in individual sales.

cash up *vb* (*intr, adv*) *Brit.* (of cashiers, shopkeepers, etc.) to add up the money taken, esp. at the end of a working day.

casing ('keɪsɪŋ) *n* **1** a protective case or cover. **2** material for a case or cover. **3** Also called: **case.** a frame containing a door or window.

casino (kə'siːnəʊ) *n, pl* **casinos. 1** a public building or room in which gaming takes place. **2** a variant spelling of **cassino.** ORIG C18: from It., dim. of *casa* house, from L

cask (kɑːsk) *n* **1** a strong wooden barrel used mainly to hold alcoholic drink: *a wine cask.* **2** any barrel. **3** the quantity contained in a cask. **4** *Austral.* a lightweight cardboard container used to hold and serve wine. ORIG C15: from Sp. *casco* helmet

casket ('kɑːskɪt) *n* **1** a small box or chest for valuables, esp. jewels. **2** *Chiefly US.* another word for **coffin** (sense 1). ORIG C15: prob. from OF *cassette* little box

Caspar ('kæspə, 'kæspɑː) *or* **Gaspar** ★ *n* (in Christian tradition) one of the Magi, the other two being Melchior and Balthazar.

Caspian Sea ★ ('kæspɪən) *n* a salt lake between SE Europe and Asia: the largest inland sea in the world; fed mainly by the River Volga. Area: 394 299 sq. km (152 239 sq. miles).

casque (kæsk) *n Zool.* a helmet or a helmet-like structure, as on the bill of most hornbills. ORIG C17: from F, from Sp. *casco*
▸ **casqued** *adj*

Cassandra ★ (kə'sændrə) *n* **1** *Greek myth.* a daughter of Priam and Hecuba, endowed with the gift of prophecy but fated never to be believed. **2** anyone whose prophecies of doom are unheeded.

Cassatt ★ (kə'sæt) *n* **Mary.** 1845–1926, US impressionist painter, who lived in France.

cassava (kə'sɑːvə) *n* **1** Also called: **manioc.** any of various tropical plants, esp. the widely cultivated American species (**bitter cassava, sweet cassava**). **2** a starch derived from the root of this plant: a source of tapioca. ORIG C16: from Sp. *cazabe* cassava bread, from Taino *caçábi*

Cassel ★ (*German* 'kasəl) *n* a variant spelling of **Kassel.**

casserole ('kæsəˌrəʊl) *n* **1** a covered dish of earthenware, glass, etc., in which food is cooked and served. **2** any food cooked and served in such a dish: *chicken casserole.* ◆ *vb* **casseroles, casseroling, casseroled. 3** to cook or be cooked in a casserole. ORIG C18: from F, from OF *casse* ladle, from OProvençal, from LL *cattia* dipper, from Gk *kuathion,* dim. of *kuathos* cup

cassette (kæ'sɛt) *n* **1a** a plastic container for magnetic tape, inserted into a tape deck to be played or used. **1b** (*as modifier*): *a cassette recorder.* **2** *Photog.* another term for **cartridge** (sense 3). **3** the injection of genes from one species into the fertilized egg of another species. ORIG C18: from F: little box

cassia ('kæsɪə) *n* **1** any of a genus of tropical plants whose pods yield **cassia pulp,** a mild laxative. See also

senna. 2 a lauraceous tree of tropical Asia. **3 cassia bark.** the cinnamon-like bark of this tree, used as a spice. ORIG OE, from L *casia,* from Gk *kasia,* of Semitic origin

Cassini ★ (*French* kasini) *n* **Giovanni Domenico** (ʒovani dɔmeniko). 1625–1712, French astronomer, born in Italy. He discovered (1675) **Cassini's division**, the gap that divides Saturn's rings into two parts.

cassino *or* **casino** (kəˈsiːnəʊ) *n* a card game for two to four players in which players pair cards with those exposed on the table.

Cassiodorus ★ (ˌkæsɪəʊˈdɔːrəs) *n* **Flavius Magnus Aurelius** (ˈfleɪvɪəs ˈmægnəs ɔːˈriːlɪəs). ?490–?585 A.D., Roman statesman and monk; author of *Variae.*

Cassiopeia[1] ★ (ˌkæsɪəˈpiːə) *n Greek myth.* the wife of Cepheus and mother of Andromeda.

Cassiopeia[2] (ˌkæsɪəˈpiːə) *n, Latin genitive* **Cassiopeiae** (ˌkæsɪəˈpiːiː). a very conspicuous W-shaped constellation near the Pole Star.

Cassirer ★ (*German* kaˈsiːrər) *n* **Ernst** (ɛrnst). 1874–1945, German neo-Kantian philosopher, noted for *The Philosophy of Symbolic Forms* (1923–29).

cassis (kɑːˈsiːs) *n* a blackcurrant cordial. ORIG C19: from F

cassiterite (kəˈsɪtəˌraɪt) *n* a hard heavy brownish-black mineral, the chief ore of tin. Formula: SnO_2. Also called: **tinstone.** ORIG C19: from Gk *kassiteros* tin

Cassius Longinus ★ (ˈkæsɪəs lɒnˈdʒaɪnəs) *n* **Gaius** (ˈgaɪəs). died 42 B.C., Roman general: led the conspiracy against Julius Caesar (44); defeated at Philippi by Mark Antony (42).

Cassivelaunus ★ (ˌkæsɪvəˈlɔːnəs) *n* 1st century B.C., British chieftain, king of the Catuvellauni tribe, who organized resistance to Caesar's invasion of Britain (54 B.C.).

cassock (ˈkæsək) *n* an ankle-length garment, usually black, worn by Christian priests. ORIG C16: from OF, from It. *casacca* a long coat, from ?

Casson ★ (ˈkæsᵊn) *n* Sir **Hugh** (**Maxwell**). 1910–99, British architect; president of the Royal Academy (1976–84).

cassowary (ˈkæsəˌwɛərɪ) *n, pl* **cassowaries.** a large flightless bird inhabiting forests in NE Australia, New Guinea, and adjacent islands, having a horny head crest, black plumage, and brightly coloured neck. ORIG C17: from Malay *kĕsuari*

cast (kɑːst) *vb* **casts, casting, cast.** (*mainly tr*) **1** to throw or expel with force. **2** to throw off or away: *she cast her clothes to the ground.* **3** to reject: *he cast the idea from his mind.* **4** to shed or drop: *the horse cast a shoe.* **5** to cause to appear: *to cast a shadow.* **6** to express (doubts, etc.) or cause (them) to be felt. **7** to direct (a glance, etc.): *cast your eye over this.* **8** to place, esp. violently: *he was cast into prison.* **9** (*also intr*) *Angling.* to throw (a line) into the water. **10** to draw or choose (lots). **11** to give or deposit (a vote). **12** to select (actors) to play parts in (a play, etc.). **13a** to shape (molten metal, glass, etc.) by pouring into a mould. **13b** to make (an object) by such a process. **14** (*also intr; often foll. by up*) to compute (figures or a total). **15** *Astrol.* to draw on (a horoscope) details concerning the positions of the planets in the signs of the zodiac at a particular time for interpretation. **16** to contrive (esp. in **cast a spell**). **17** to formulate: *he cast his work in the form of a chart.* **18** (*also intr*) to twist or cause to twist. **19** (*intr*) (of birds of prey) to eject from the crop and bill a pellet consisting of the indigestible parts of birds or animals previously eaten. **20** *Printing.* to stereotype or electrotype. **21 be cast.** *NZ.* (of sheep) to have fallen and been unable to rise. ◆ *n* **22** the act of casting or throwing. **23a** Also called: **casting.** something that is shed, dropped, or egested, such as the coil of earth left by an earthworm. **23b** another name for **pellet** (sense 4). **24** the distance an object is or may be thrown. **25a** a throw at dice. **25b** the resulting number shown. **26** *Angling.* the act or an instance of casting a line. **27** the wide sweep made by a sheepdog to get behind a flock of sheep or by a hunting dog in search of a scent. **28a** the actors in a play collectively. **28b** (*as modifier*): *a cast list.* **29a** an object made of metal, glass, etc., that has been shaped in a molten state by being poured or pressed into a mould. **29b** the mould used to shape such an object. **30** form or appearance. **31** a sort, kind, or style. **32** a fixed twist or defect, esp. in the eye. **33** a distortion of shape. **34** *Surgery.* a rigid encircling casing, often made of plaster of Paris (**plaster cast**), for immobilizing broken bones while they heal. **35** a slight tinge or trace, as of colour. **36** fortune or stroke of fate. ◆ See also **cast about, castaway,** etc. ORIG C13: from ON *kasta*

cast about *or* **around** *vb* (*intr, adv*) to make a mental or visual search: *to cast about for a plot.*

Castalia ★ (kæˈsteɪlɪə) *n* a spring on Mount Parnassus: in ancient Greece sacred to Apollo and the Muses and believed to be a source of inspiration.
▸ **Casˈtalian** *adj*

castanets (ˌkæstəˈnɛts) *pl n* curved pieces of hollow wood, usually held between the fingers and thumb and made to click together: used esp. by Spanish dancers. ORIG C17 *castanet,* from Sp. *castañeta,* dim. of *castaña* CHESTNUT

castaway (ˈkɑːstəˌweɪ) *n* **1** a person who has been shipwrecked. ◆ *adj* (*prenominal*) **2** shipwrecked. **3** thrown away or rejected. ◆ *vb* **cast away. 4** (*tr, adv; often passive*) to cause (a ship, person, etc.) to be shipwrecked.

cast back *vb* (*adv*) to turn (the mind) to the past.

cast down *vb* (*tr, adv*) to make (a person) discouraged or dejected.

caste (kɑːst) *n* **1a** any of the four major hereditary classes, namely the **Brahman, Kshatriya, Vaisya,** and **Sudra,** into which Hindu society is divided. **1b** Also called: **caste system.** the system or basis of such classes. **2** any social class or system based on such distinctions as heredity, rank, wealth, etc. **3** the position conferred by such a system. **4 lose caste.** *Inf.* to lose one's social position. **5** *Entomol.* any of various types of individual, such as the worker, in social insects. ORIG C16: from Port. *casta* race, from *casto* pure, chaste, from L *castus*

Castellammare di Stabia ★ (*Italian* kastɛllamˈmaːre di ˈstabja) *n* a port and resort in SW Italy, in Campania on the Bay of Naples: site of the Roman resort of Stabiae, which was destroyed by the eruption of Vesuvius in 79 A.D. Pop.: 67 974 (1993 est.).

castellan (ˈkæstɪlən) *n Rare.* a keeper or governor of a castle. Also called: **chatelain.** ORIG C14: from L *castellānus,* from *castellum* CASTLE

castellated (ˈkæstɪˌleɪtɪd) *adj* **1** having turrets and battlements, like a castle. **2** having indentations similar to battlements: *a castellated nut.* ORIG C17: from Med. L *castellātus,* from *castellāre* to fortify as a CASTLE
▸ **ˌcastelˈlation** *n*

caster (ˈkɑːstə) *n* **1** a person or thing that casts. **2** a bottle with a perforated top for sprinkling sugar, etc. **3** a small swivelled wheel fixed to a piece of furniture to enable it to be moved easily in any direction. ◆ Also (for senses 2, 3): **castor.**

caster sugar (ˈkɑːstə) *n* finely ground white sugar.

castigate (ˈkæstɪˌgeɪt) *vb* **castigates, castigating, castigated.** (*tr*) to rebuke or criticize in a severe manner. ORIG C17: from L *castīgāre* to correct, from *castum* pure + *agere* to compel (to be)
▸ **ˌcastiˈgation** *n* ▸ **ˈcastiˌgator** *n*

Castiglione ★ (ˌkæstɪlˈjəʊnɪ) *n* Count **Baldassare** (baldasˈsaːre). 1478–1529, Italian diplomat and writer, noted for *Il Libro del Cortegiano* (The Courtier) (1528).

Castile (kæˈstiːl) *or* **Castilla** ★ (*Spanish* kasˈtiʎa) *n* a former kingdom comprising most of modern Spain: originally part of León, it became an independent kingdom in the 10th century and united with Aragon (1469), the first step in the formation of the Spanish state.

Castile soap *n* a hard soap made from olive oil and sodium hydroxide.

Castilian (kæˈstɪljən) *n* **1** the Spanish dialect of Castile; the standard form of European Spanish. **2** a native or inhabitant of Castile. ◆ *adj* **3** denoting or of Castile, its inhabitants, or the standard form of European Spanish.

Castilla la Vieja ★ (kasˈtiʎa la ˈbjexa) *n* the Spanish name for **Old Castile.**

casting (ˈkɑːstɪŋ) *n* **1** an object that has been cast, esp. in metal from a mould. **2** the process of transferring molten steel to a mould. **3** the choosing of actors for a production. **4** *Zool.* another word for **cast** (sense 23) or **pellet** (sense 4).

casting couch *n Inf.* a couch on which a casting director is said to seduce girls seeking a part in a film or play.

casting vote *n* the deciding vote used by the presiding officer of an assembly when votes cast on both sides are equal in number.

cast iron *n* **1** iron containing so much carbon that it cannot be wrought and must be cast into shape. ◆ *adj* **cast-iron. 2** made of cast iron. **3** rigid or unyielding: *a cast-iron decision.*

castle ('kɑːsᵊl) *n* **1** a fortified building or set of buildings as in medieval Europe. **2** any fortified place or structure. **3** a large magnificent house, esp. when the present or former home of a nobleman or prince. **4** *Chess.* another name for **rook**[2]. ◆ *vb* **castles, castling, castled. 5** *Chess.* to move (the king) two squares laterally on the first rank and place the nearest rook on the square passed over by the king. ORIG C11: from L *castellum,* dim. of *castrum* fort

Castlebar ★ (ˌkɑːsᵊl'bɑː) *n* the county town of Co. Mayo, Republic of Ireland; site of the battle (1798) between the French and British known as Castlebar Races: bacon-curing. Pop.: 6070 (1991).

castle in the air *or* **in Spain** *n* a hope or desire unlikely to be realized; daydream.

Castlereagh[1] ★ ('kɑːsᵊlˌreɪ) *n* a district of E Northern Ireland, SE of Belfast: a residential area for Belfast, whence it is administered. Pop.: 60 799 (1991). Area: 84 sq. km (33 sq. miles).

Castlereagh[2] ★ ('kɑːsᵊlˌreɪ) *n* **Viscount.** title of *Robert Stewart,* Marquis of Londonderry. 1769–1822, British statesman: as foreign secretary (1812–22) led the Grand Alliance against Napoleon and attended the Congress of Vienna (1815).

Castner ★ ('kæstnə) *n* **Hamilton Young.** 1858–98, US chemist, who devised the **Castner process** for extracting sodium from sodium hydroxide.

cast-off *adj* **1** (*prenominal*) abandoned: *cast-off shoes.* ◆ *n* **castoff. 2** a person or thing that has been discarded or abandoned. **3** *Printing.* an estimate of the amount of space that a piece of copy will occupy. ◆ *vb* **cast off.** (*adv*) **4** to remove (mooring lines) that hold (a vessel) to a dock. **5** to knot (a row of stitches, esp. the final row) in finishing off knitted or woven material. **6** *Printing.* to estimate the amount of space that will be taken up by (a book, piece of copy, etc.).

cast on *vb* (*adv*) to form (the first row of stitches) in knitting and weaving.

castor[1] ('kɑːstə) *n* **1** the aromatic secretion of a beaver, used in perfumery and medicine. **2** the fur of the beaver. **3** a hat made of beaver or similar fur. ORIG C14: from L, from Gk *kastōr* beaver

castor[2] ('kɑːstə) *n* a variant spelling of **caster** (senses 2, 3).

Castor and Pollux ★ *n Classical myth.* the twin sons of Leda: Pollux was fathered by Zeus, Castor by the mortal Tyndareus. After Castor's death, Pollux spent half his days with his half-brother in Hades and half with the gods in Olympus.

castor oil *n* an oil obtained from the seeds of the castor-oil plant and used as a lubricant and cathartic.

castor-oil plant *n* a tall Indian plant cultivated for its poisonous seeds, from which castor oil is extracted.

castrate (kæ'streɪt) *vb* **castrates, castrating, castrated.** (*tr*) **1** to remove the testicles of. **2** to deprive of vigour, masculinity, etc. **3** to remove the ovaries of; spay. ORIG C17: from L *castrāre* to emasculate, geld
▸ **cas'tration** *n*

castrato (kæ'strɑːtəʊ) *n, pl* **castrati** (-tɪ) *or* **castratos.** (in 17th- and 18th-century opera, etc.) a male singer whose testicles were removed before puberty, allowing the retention of a soprano or alto voice. ORIG C18: from It., from L *castrātus* castrated

Castries ★ (kæs'triːs) *n* the capital and chief port of St Lucia. Pop.: 13 615 (1992 est.).

Castro ★ ('kæstrəʊ; *Spanish* 'kastro) *n* **Fidel** (fi'del; *Spanish* fi'ðel). full name *Fidel Castro Ruz.* born 1927, Cuban statesman: communist prime minister from 1959 and president from 1976.

cast steel *n* steel containing varying amounts of carbon, manganese, etc., that is cast into shape rather than wrought.

cast stone *n Building trades.* a building component, such as a block or lintel, made from cast concrete with a facing that resembles natural stone.

casual ('kæʒjʊəl) *adj* **1** happening by accident or chance. **2** offhand: *a casual remark.* **3** shallow or superficial: *a casual affair.* **4** being or seeming unconcerned or apathetic: *he assumed a casual attitude.* **5** (esp. of dress) for informal wear: *a casual coat.* **6** occasional or irregular: *a casual labourer.* ◆ *n* **7** (*usually pl*) an informal article of clothing or footwear. **8** an occasional worker. **9** (*usually pl*) a young man dressed in expensive casual clothes who goes to football matches in order to start fights. ORIG C14: from LL *cāsuālis* happening by chance, from L *cāsus* event, from *cadere* to fall
▸ **'casually** *adv* ▸ **'casualness** *n*

casualization *or* **casualisation** (ˌkæʒjʊəlaɪ'zeɪʃən) *n* the altering of working practices so that regular workers are re-employed on a casual or short-term basis.

casualty ('kæʒjʊəltɪ) *n, pl* **casualties. 1** a serviceman who is killed, wounded, captured, or missing as a result of enemy action. **2** a person who is injured or killed in an accident. **3** the hospital department treating victims of accidents. **4** anything that is lost, damaged, or destroyed as the result of an accident, etc.

casuarina (ˌkæzjʊə'riːnə) *n* any of a genus of trees of Australia and the East Indies, having jointed leafless branchlets. ORIG C19: from NL, from Malay *kěsuari* CASSOWARY, referring to the resemblance of the branches to the feathers of the cassowary

casuist ('kæzjʊɪst) *n* **1** a person, esp. a theologian, who attempts to resolve moral dilemmas by the application of general rules and the careful distinction of special cases. **2** a sophist. ORIG C17: from F, from Sp. *casuista,* from L *cāsus* CASE[1]
▸ **ˌcasu'istic** *or* **ˌcasu'istical** *adj*

casuistry ('kæzjʊɪstrɪ) *n, pl* **casuistries. 1** *Philosophy.* the resolution of particular moral dilemmas, esp. those arising from conflicting general moral rules, by the careful distinction of the cases to which these rules apply. **2** reasoning that is specious or oversubtle.

cat[1] (kæt) *n* **1** Also called: **domestic cat.** a small domesticated feline mammal having thick soft fur and occurring in many breeds in which the colour of the fur varies greatly: kept as a pet or to catch rats and mice. **2** Also called: **big cat.** any of the larger felines, such as a lion or tiger. **3** any wild feline mammal such as the lynx or serval, resembling the domestic cat. **4** *Inf.* a woman who gossips maliciously. **5** *Sl.* a man. **6** *Naut.* a heavy tackle for hoisting an anchor to the cathead. **7** *Austral. sl.* a coward. **8** short for **catboat. 9** *Inf.* short for **caterpillar** (the vehicle). **10** short for **cat-o'-nine-tails. 11 a bag of cats.** *Irish inf.* a bad-tempered person: *she's a real bag of cats this morning.* **12 fight like Kilkenny cats.** to fight until both parties are destroyed. **13 let the cat out of the bag.** to disclose a secret, often by mistake. **14 like a cat on a hot tin roof** *or* **on hot bricks.** in an uneasy or agitated state. **15 put, set,** etc., **the cat among the pigeons.** to introduce some violently disturbing new element. **16 rain cats and dogs.** to rain very heavily. ◆ *vb* **cats, catting, catted. 17** (*tr*) *Naut.* to hoist (an anchor) to the cathead. **18** (*intr*) *Sl.* to vomit. ORIG OE *catte,* from L *cattus*
▸ **'catˌlike** *adj* ▸ **'cattish** *adj*

cat[2] (kæt) *adj* short for **catalytic:** *a cat cracker.*

CAT *abbrev. for* computer-assisted trading.

cat. *abbrev. for:* **1** catalogue. **2** catamaran.

cata-, kata-, *before an aspirate* **cath-,** *or before a vowel* **cat-** *prefix* **1** down; downwards; lower in position: *catadromous.* **2** indicating reversal, opposition, degeneration, etc.: *catatonia.* ORIG from Gk *kata-,* from *kata.* In compound words borrowed from Gk *kata-* means: down, away, off, against, according to, and thoroughly

catabolism *or* **katabolism** (kə'tæbəˌlɪzəm) *n* a meta-

bolic process in which complex molecules are broken down into simple ones with the release of energy; destructive metabolism. ORIG C19: from Gk *katabolē* a throwing down, from *kata-* down + *ballein* to throw
▸ **catabolic** *or* **katabolic** (ˌkætəˈbɒlɪk) *adj*

catachresis (ˌkætəˈkriːsɪs) *n* the incorrect use of words, as *luxuriant* for *luxurious.* ORIG C16: from L, from Gk *katakhrēsis* a misusing, from *khrēsthai* to use
▸ **catachrestic** (ˌkætəˈkrɛstɪk) *adj*

cataclysm (ˈkætəˌklɪzəm) *n* **1** a violent upheaval, esp. of a political, military, or social nature. **2** a disastrous flood. ORIG C17: via F from L, from Gk, from *katakluzein* to flood, from *kluzein* to wash
▸ **ˌcataˈclysmic** *or* **ˌcataˈclysmal** *adj* ▸ **ˌcataˈclysmically** *adv*

catacomb (ˈkætəˌkəʊm) *n* **1** (*usually pl*) an underground burial place, esp. in Rome, consisting of tunnels with niches leading off them for tombs. **2** a series of underground tunnels or caves. ORIG OE *catacumbe,* from LL *catacumbas* (sing), name of the cemetery under the Basilica of St Sebastian, near Rome; from ?

catadioptric (ˌkætədaɪˈɒptrɪk) *adj* involving a combination of reflecting and refracting components: *a catadioptric telescope.* ORIG C18: from CATA- + DIOPTRIC(S)

catadromous (kəˈtædrəməs) *adj* (of fishes such as the eel) migrating down rivers to the sea in order to breed. Cf. **anadromous.** ORIG C19: from Gk, from *kata-* down + *dromos,* from *dremein* to run

catafalque (ˈkætəˌfælk) *n* a temporary raised platform on which a body lies in state before or during a funeral. ORIG C17: from F, from It. *catafalco,* from ?

Catalan (ˈkætəˌlæn) *n* **1** a language of Catalonia, closely related to Spanish and Provençal. **2** a native or inhabitant of Catalonia. ◆ *adj* **3** denoting or characteristic of Catalonia, its inhabitants, or their language.

catalepsy (ˈkætəˌlɛpsɪ) *n* a state of prolonged rigid posture, occurring for example in schizophrenia. ORIG C16: from LL *catalēpsis,* from Gk *katalēpsis,* lit.: a seizing, from *kata-* down + *lambanein* to grasp
▸ **ˌcataˈleptic** *adj*

catalogue *or US* **catalog** (ˈkætəˌlɒg) *n* **1** a complete, usually alphabetical, list of items. **2** a book, usually illustrated, containing details of items for sale. **3** a list of all the books of a library. **4** *US and Canad.* a publication issued by a university, college, etc., listing courses offered, regulations, services, etc. ◆ *vb* **catalogues, cataloguing, catalogued** *or US* **catalogs, cataloging, cataloged. 5** to compile a catalogue of (a library, etc.). **6** to add (books, items, etc.) to an existing catalogue. ORIG C15: from LL *catalogus,* from Gk, from *katalegein* to list, from *kata-* completely + *legein* to collect
▸ **ˈcataˌloguer** *n*

Catalonia ★ (ˌkætəˈləʊnɪə) *n* a region of NE Spain, with a strong separatist tradition: became an autonomous region with its own parliament in 1979; an important agricultural and industrial region, with many resorts. Pop.: 6 090 107 (1994 est.). Area: 31 929 sq. km (12 328 sq. miles). Catalan name: **Catalunya** (ˌkatəˈluːnɪə). Spanish name: **Cataluña** (kataˈluɲa).

catalpa (kəˈtælpə) *n* any of a genus of trees of North America and Asia, having large leaves, bell-shaped whitish flowers, and long slender pods. ORIG C18: NL, from Carolina Creek *kutuhlpa,* lit.: winged head

catalyse *or US* **catalyze** (ˈkætəˌlaɪz) *vb* **catalyses, catalysing, catalysed** *or US* **catalyzes, catalyzing, catalyzed.** (*tr*) to influence (a chemical reaction) by catalysis.

catalysis (kəˈtælɪsɪs) *n, pl* **catalyses** (-ˌsiːz). acceleration of a chemical reaction by the action of a catalyst. ORIG C17: from NL, from Gk, from *kataluein* to dissolve
▸ **catalytic** (ˌkætəˈlɪtɪk) *adj*

catalyst (ˈkætəlɪst) *n* **1** a substance that increases the rate of a chemical reaction without itself suffering any permanent chemical change. **2** a person or thing that causes a change.

catalytic converter *n* a device using three-way catalysts to reduce the poisonous products of combustion (mainly oxides of nitrogen, carbon monoxide, and unburnt hydrocarbons) from the exhaust of motor vehicles.

catalytic cracker *n* a unit in an oil refinery in which mineral oils with high boiling points are converted to fuels with lower boiling points by a catalytic process.

catamaran (ˌkætəməˈræn) *n* **1** a vessel, usually a sailing vessel, with twin hulls held parallel by a rigid framework. **2** a primitive raft made of logs lashed together. **3** *Inf.* a quarrelsome woman. ORIG C17: from Tamil *kattumaram* tied timber

catamite (ˈkætəˌmaɪt) *n* a boy kept for homosexual purposes. ORIG C16: from L *Catamītus,* var. of *Ganymēdēs* GANYMEDE

catamount (ˈkætəˌmaʊnt) *or* **catamountain** *n* any of various felines, such as the puma or lynx. ORIG C17: short for *cat of the mountain*

catananche (kætənˈæŋkɪ) *n* any herb of the genus *Catananche,* having blue or yellow flowers. ORIG C18: NL, from L, from Gk *kata* down + *anagkē* compulsion (from its use by ancient Greeks as a philtre)

Catania ★ (*Italian* kaˈtaːnja) *n* a port in E Sicily, near Mount Etna. Pop.: 341 623 (1996 est.).

cataplexy (ˈkætəˌplɛksɪ) *n* **1** sudden temporary paralysis, brought on by severe shock. **2** a state assumed by animals while shamming death. ORIG C19: from Gk *kataplēxis* amazement, from *kataplēssein,* from *kata-* down + *plēssein* to strike
▸ **ˌcataˈplectic** *adj*

catapult (ˈkætəˌpʌlt) *n* **1** a Y-shaped implement with a loop of elastic fastened to the ends of the prongs, used mainly by children for shooting stones, etc. US and Canad. name: **slingshot. 2** a war engine used formerly for hurling stones, etc. **3** a device installed in warships to launch aircraft. ◆ *vb* **4** (*tr*) to shoot forth from or as if from a catapult. **5** (foll. by *over, into,* etc.) to move precipitately. ORIG C16: from L, from Gk *katapeltēs,* from *kata-* down + *pallein* to hurl

cataract (ˈkætəˌrækt) *n* **1** a large waterfall or rapids. **2** a downpour. **3** *Pathol.* **3a** partial or total opacity of the lens of the eye. **3b** the opaque area. ORIG C15: from L, from Gk, from *katarassein* to dash down, from *arassein* to strike

catarrh (kəˈtɑː) *n* inflammation of a mucous membrane with increased production of mucus, esp. affecting the nose and throat. ORIG C16: via F from LL, from Gk, from *katarrhein* to flow down, from *kata-* down + *rhein* to flow
▸ **caˈtarrhal** *adj*

catarrhine (ˈkætəˌraɪn) *adj* **1** (of apes and Old World monkeys) having the nostrils set close together and opening to the front of the face. ◆ *n* **2** an animal with this characteristic. ORIG C19: ult. from Gk *katarrhin* having a hooked nose, from *kata-* down + *rhis* nose

catastrophe (kəˈtæstrəfɪ) *n* **1** a sudden, extensive disaster or misfortune. **2** the denouement of a play. **3** a final decisive event, usually causing a disastrous end. ORIG C16: from Gk, from *katastrephein* to overturn, from *strephein* to turn
▸ **catastrophic** (ˌkætəˈstrɒfɪk) *adj* ▸ **ˌcataˈstrophically** *adv*

catastrophism (kəˈtæstrəˌfɪzəm) *n* **1** a former doctrine that the earth was formed by sudden divine acts rather than by evolutionary processes. **2** a modern doctrine that the evolutionary processes shaping the earth have in the past been supplemented by the effects of huge natural catastrophes.

catatonia (ˌkætəˈtəʊnɪə) *n* a form of schizophrenia characterized by stupor, with outbreaks of excitement. ORIG C20: NL, from G *Katatonie,* from CATA- + Gk *tonos* tension
▸ **catatonic** (ˌkætəˈtɒnɪk) *adj, n*

catbird (ˈkætˌbɜːd) *n* **1** any of several North American songbirds whose call resembles the mewing of a cat. **2** any of several Australian bowerbirds having a catlike call.

catboat (ˈkætˌbəʊt) *n* a sailing vessel with a single mast, set well forward, and a large sail. Shortened form: **cat.**

cat burglar *n* a burglar who enters buildings by climbing through upper windows, etc.

catcall (ˈkætˌkɔːl) *n* **1** a shrill whistle or cry expressing disapproval, as at a public meeting, etc. ◆ *vb* **2** to utter such a call (at).

catch (kætʃ) *vb* **catches, catching, caught. 1** (*tr*) to take hold of so as to retain or restrain. **2** (*tr*) to take or capture, esp. after pursuit. **3** (*tr*) to ensnare or deceive. **4** (*tr*) to surprise or detect in an act: *he caught the dog rifling the larder.* **5** (*tr*) to reach with a blow: *the stone caught him on the side of the head.* **6** (*tr*) to overtake or reach in time to board. **7** (*tr*) to see or hear; attend. **8** (*tr*) to be infected with: *to catch a cold.* **9** to hook or entangle or become hooked or entangled. **10** to fasten or be fastened with or as if with a latch or other device. **11** (*tr*) to attract: *she tried to catch his eye.* **12** (*tr*) to comprehend: *I didn't catch his meaning.* **13** (*tr*) to hear accurately: *I didn't catch what you said.* **14** (*tr*) to captivate or charm. **15** (*tr*) to reproduce accurately: *the painter managed to catch his model's beauty.* **16** (*tr*) to hold back or restrain: *he caught his breath in surprise.* **17** (*intr*) to become alight: *the fire won't catch.* **18** (*tr*) *Cricket.* to dismiss (the person batting) by intercepting and holding a ball struck by him or her before it touches the ground. **19** (*intr;* often foll. by *at*) **19a** to grasp or attempt to grasp. **19b** to take advantage (of): *he caught at the chance.* **20** **catch it.** *Inf.* to be scolded or reprimanded. ◆ *n* **21** the act of catching or grasping. **22** a device that catches and fastens, such as a latch. **23** anything that is caught. **24** the amount or number caught. **25** *Inf.* an eligible matrimonial prospect. **26** a check or break in the voice. **27** *Inf.* **27a** a concealed, unexpected, or unforeseen drawback. **27b** (*as modifier*): *a catch question.* **28** *Cricket.* the catching of a ball struck by a batsman before it touches the ground, resulting in him being out. **29** *Music.* a type of round having a humorous text that is often indecent or bawdy and hard to articulate. ◆ See also **catch on, catch out, catch up.** ORIG C13 *cacchen* to pursue, from OF *cachier,* from L *captāre* to snatch, from *capere* to seize
▸ **'catchable** *adj*

catch-22 *n* a situation in which a person is frustrated by a set of circumstances that preclude any attempt to escape from them. ORIG C20: from the title of a novel (1961) by J. Heller

catch-as-catch-can *n* a style of wrestling in which trips, holds below the waist, etc., are allowed.

catchfly ('kætʃˌflaɪ) *n, pl* **catchflies.** any of various plants that have sticky calyxes and stems on which insects are sometimes trapped.

catching ('kætʃɪŋ) *adj* **1** infectious. **2** attractive; captivating.

catching pen *n Austral. & NZ.* a pen adjacent to a shearer's stand containing the sheep ready for shearing.

catchment ('kætʃmənt) *n* **1** the act of catching or collecting water. **2** a structure in which water is collected. **3** the water so collected. **4** *Brit.* the intake of a school from one catchment area.

catchment area *n* **1** the area of land bounded by watersheds draining into a river, basin, or reservoir. **2** the area from which people are allocated to a particular school, hospital, etc.

catch on *vb* (*intr, adv*) *Inf.* **1** to become popular or fashionable. **2** to understand.

catch out *vb* (*tr, adv*) *Inf., chiefly Brit.* to trap (a person), esp. in an error.

catchpenny ('kætʃˌpɛnɪ) *adj* (*prenominal*) designed to have instant appeal, esp. in order to sell quickly: *catchpenny ornaments.*

catch phrase *n* a well-known frequently used phrase, esp. one associated with a particular group, etc.

catch up *vb* (*adv*) **1** (*tr*) to seize and take up (something) quickly. **2** (when *intr,* often foll. by *with*) to reach or pass (someone or something): *he caught him up.* **3** (*intr;* usually foll. by *on* or *with*) to make up for lost ground or deal with a backlog. **4** (*tr; often passive*) to absorb or involve: *she was caught up in her reading.* **5** (*tr*) to raise by or as if by fastening.

catchweight ('kætʃˌweɪt) *adj Wrestling.* of or relating to a contest in which normal weight categories have been waived by agreement.

catchword ('kætʃˌwɜːd) *n* **1** a word or phrase made temporarily popular; slogan. **2** a word printed as a running head in a book. **3** *Theatre.* an actor's cue to speak or enter. **4** the first word of a page repeated at the bottom of the page preceding.

catchy ('kætʃɪ) *adj* **catchier, catchiest. 1** (of a tune, etc.) pleasant and easily remembered. **2** deceptive: *a catchy question.* **3** irregular: *a catchy breeze.*

cat cracker *n* an informal name for **catalytic cracker.**

catechetical (ˌkætɪ'kɛtɪk^{ə}l) *or* **catechetic** *adj* of or relating to teaching by question and answer.
▸ **ˌcate'chetically** *adv*

catechism ('kætɪˌkɪzəm) *n* instruction by a series of questions and answers, esp. a book containing such instruction on the religious doctrine of a Christian Church. ORIG C16: from LL, ult. from Gk *katēkhizein* to CATECHIZE
▸ **ˌcate'chismal** *adj*

catechize *or* **catechise** ('kætɪˌkaɪz) *vb* **catechizes, catechizing, catechized** *or* **catechises, catechising, catechised.** (*tr*) **1** to teach or examine by means of questions and answers. **2** to give oral instruction in Christianity, esp. by using a catechism. **3** to put questions to (someone). ORIG C15: from LL, from Gk *katēkhizein,* from *katēkhein* to instruct orally, from *kata-* down + *ēkhein* to sound
▸ **'catechist, 'cateˌchizer** *or* **'cateˌchiser** *n*

catechu ('kætɪˌtʃuː) *or* **cachou** *n* an astringent resinous substance obtained from certain tropical plants, and used in medicine, tanning, and dyeing. ORIG C17: prob. from Malay *kachu*

catechumen (ˌkætɪ'kjuːmɛn) *n Christianity.* a person, esp. in the early Church, undergoing instruction prior to baptism. ORIG C15: via OF, from LL, from Gk *katēkhoumenos* one being instructed verbally

categorial (ˌkætɪ'gɔːrɪəl) *adj* **1** of or relating to a category. **2** *Logic.* (of a statement) consisting of a subject, S, and a predicate, P, each of which denote a class, as in: *all S are P.*

categorical (ˌkætɪ'gɒrɪk^{ə}l) *or* **categoric** *adj* **1** unqualified; unconditional: *a categorical statement.* **2** relating to or included in a category. **3** another word for **categorial** (sense 2).
▸ **ˌcate'gorically** *adv*

categorize *or* **categorise** ('kætɪgəˌraɪz) *vb* **categorizes, categorizing, categorized** *or* **categorises, categorising, categorised.** (*tr*) to place in a category.
▸ **ˌcategori'zation** *or* **ˌcategori'sation** *n*

category ('kætɪgərɪ) *n, pl* **categories. 1** a class or group of things, people, etc., possessing some quality or qualities in common. **2** *Metaphysics.* one of the most basic classes into which objects and concepts can be analysed. **3a** (in the philosophy of Aristotle) any one of ten most fundamental modes of being, such as quantity, quality, and substance. **3b** (in the philosophy of Kant) one of twelve concepts required by human beings to interpret the empirical world. ORIG C15: from LL, from Gk *katēgoria,* from *kategorein* to accuse, assert

catena (kə'tiːnə) *n, pl* **catenae** (-niː). a connected series, esp. of patristic comments on the Bible. ORIG C17: from L: chain

catenaccio (*Italian* kate'nattʃo) *n Soccer.* an extremely defensive style of play. ORIG C20: from L *catena* chain

catenary (kə'tiːnərɪ) *n, pl* **catenaries. 1** the curve formed by a heavy uniform flexible cord hanging freely from two points. **2** the hanging cable between pylons along a railway track, from which the trolley wire is suspended. ◆ *adj* **3** of, resembling, relating to, or constructed using a catenary or suspended chain. ORIG C18: from L *catēnārius* relating to a chain

catenate ('kætɪˌneɪt) *vb* **catenates, catenating, catenated.** *Biol.* to arrange or be arranged in a series of chains or rings. ORIG C17: from L *catēnāre* to bind with chains
▸ **ˌcate'nation** *n*

cater ('keɪtə) *vb* **1** (*intr;* foll. by *for* or *to*) to provide what is required or desired (for). **2** (when *intr,* foll. by *for*) to provide food, services, etc. (for): *we cater for parties.* ORIG C16: from earlier *catour* purchaser, var. of *acatour,* from Anglo-Norman *acater* to buy
▸ **'catering** *n*

cater-cornered (ˈkætəˌkɔːnəd) *adj, adv US & Canad. inf.* diagonal. Also: **catty-cornered, kitty-cornered.** ORIG C16: from dialect *cater* (adv) diagonally, from obs. *cater* (n) four-spot of dice, from OF *quatre* four, from L *quattuor*

caterer (ˈkeɪtərə) *n* one who as a profession provides food for large social events, etc.

caterpillar (ˈkætəˌpɪlə) *n* **1** the wormlike larva of butterflies and moths, having numerous pairs of legs and powerful biting jaws. **2** *Trademark.* an endless track, driven by sprockets or wheels, used to propel a heavy vehicle. **3** *Trademark.* a vehicle, such as a tractor, tank, etc., driven by such tracks. ORIG C15 *catyrpel,* prob. from OF *catepelose,* lit.: hairy cat

caterwaul (ˈkætəˌwɔːl) *vb* (*intr*) **1** to make a yowling noise, as a cat on heat. ◆ *n* **2** a yell made by or sounding like a cat on heat. ORIG C14: imit.

Catesby ★ (ˈkeɪtzbɪ) *n* **Robert.** 1573–1605, English leader of the Gunpowder Plot (1605): killed resisting arrest.

catfish (ˈkætˌfɪʃ) *n, pl* **catfish** *or* **catfishes. 1** any of numerous mainly freshwater fishes having whisker-like barbels around the mouth. **2** another name for **wolffish.**

cat flap *or* **door** *n* a small flap or door in a larger door through which a cat can pass.

catgut (ˈkætˌgʌt) *n* a strong cord made from the dried intestines of sheep and other animals that is used for stringing certain musical instruments and sports rackets.

Cath. *abbrev. for:* **1** Cathedral. **2** Catholic.

cath- *prefix* a variant of **cata-** before an aspirate: *cathode.*

Cathar (ˈkæθə) *or* **Catharist** (ˈkæθərɪst) *n, pl* **Cathars, Cathari** (-ərɪ) *or* **Catharists.** a member of a Christian sect in Provence in the 12th and 13th centuries who believed the material world was evil and only the spiritual was good. ORIG from Med. L, from Gk *katharoi* the pure
▸ **ˈCatharˌism** *n*

catharsis (kəˈθɑːsɪs) *n, pl* **catharses** (-siːz). **1** the purging or purification of the emotions through the evocation of pity and fear, as in tragedy. **2** *Psychoanal.* the bringing of repressed ideas or experiences into consciousness, thus relieving tensions. **3** purgation, esp. of the bowels. ORIG C19: NL, from Gk *katharsis,* from *kathairein* to purge, purify

cathartic (kəˈθɑːtɪk) *adj* **1** purgative. **2** effecting catharsis. ◆ *n* **3** a purgative drug or agent.
▸ **caˈthartically** *adv*

Cathay ★ (kæˈθeɪ) *n* a literary or archaic name for **China.** ORIG C14: from Med. L *Cataya*

cathead (ˈkætˌhɛd) *n* a fitting at the bow of a vessel for securing the anchor when raised.

cathedral (kəˈθiːdrəl) *n* **a** the principal church of a diocese, containing the bishop's official throne. **b** (*as modifier*): *a cathedral city.* ORIG C13: from LL (*ecclesia*) *cathedrālis* cathedral (church), from Gk *kathedra* seat

Cather ★ (ˈkæðə) *n* **Willa (Sibert).** 1873–1947, US novelist, whose works include *O Pioneers!* (1913) and *My Ántonia* (1918).

Catherine ★ (ˈkæθrɪn) *n* **Saint.** died 307 A.D., legendary Christian martyr of Alexandria, who was tortured on a spiked wheel and beheaded.

Catherine I ★ *n* ?1684–1727, second wife of Peter the Great, whom she succeeded as empress of Russia (1725–27).

Catherine II ★ *n* known as *Catherine the Great.* 1729–96, empress of Russia (1762–96).

Catherine de' Medici *or* **de Médicis** ★ *n* 1519–89, queen of Henry II of France; mother of Francis II, Charles IX, and Henry III of France; regent of France (1560–74).

Catherine of Aragon ★ *n* 1485–1536, first wife of Henry VIII of England and mother of Mary I. The annulment of Henry's marriage to her (1533) marked an initial stage in the English Reformation.

Catherine of Braganza ★ *n* 1638–1705, wife of Charles II of England, daughter of John IV of Portugal.

Catherine of Siena ★ *n* **Saint.** 1347–80, Italian mystic; patron saint of the Dominican order. Feast day: April 29.

Catherine wheel *n* **1** a firework which rotates, producing coloured flame. **2** a circular window having ribs radiating from the centre. ORIG C16: after St CATHERINE of Alexandria

catheter (ˈkæθɪtə) *n Med.* a long slender flexible tube for inserting into a bodily cavity for introducing or withdrawing fluid. ORIG C17: from LL, from Gk *kathetēr,* from *kathienai* to insert

catheterize *or* **catheterise** (ˈkæθɪtəˌraɪz) *vb* **catheterizes, catheterizing, catheterized** *or* **catheterises, catheterising, catheterised.** (*tr*) to insert a catheter into.

cathexis (kəˈθɛksɪs) *n, pl* **cathexes** (-ˈθɛksiːz). *Psychoanal.* concentration of psychic energy on a single goal. ORIG C20: from NL, from Gk *kathexis,* from *katekhein* to hold fast

cathode (ˈkæθəʊd) *n* **1** the negative electrode in an electrolytic cell. **2** the negatively charged electron source in an electronic valve. **3** the positive terminal of a primary cell. ◆ Cf. **anode.** ORIG C19: from Gk *kathodos* a descent, from *kata-* down + *hodos* way
▸ **cathodal** (kæˈθəʊdᵊl) *or* **cathodic** (kæˈθɒdɪk, -ˈθəʊ-) *adj*

cathode rays *pl n* a stream of electrons emitted from the surface of a cathode in a vacuum tube.

cathode-ray tube *n* a vacuum tube in which a beam of electrons is focused onto a fluorescent screen to give a visible spot of light. The device is used in television receivers, visual display units, etc.

catholic (ˈkæθəlɪk, ˈkæθlɪk) *adj* **1** universal; relating to all men. **2** broad-minded; liberal. ORIG C14: from L, from Gk *katholikos* universal, from *kata-* according to + *holos* whole
▸ **catholically** *or* **catholicly** (kəˈθɒlɪklɪ) *adv*

Catholic (ˈkæθəlɪk, ˈkæθlɪk) *Christianity.* ◆ *adj* **1** denoting or relating to the entire body of Christians, esp. to the Church before separation into the Eastern and Western Churches. **2** denoting or relating to the Latin or Western Church after this separation. **3** denoting or relating to the Roman Catholic Church. ◆ *n* **4** a member of the Roman Catholic Church.

Catholicism (kəˈθɒlɪˌsɪzəm) *n* **1** short for **Roman Catholicism. 2** the beliefs, practices, etc., of any Catholic Church.

catholicity (ˌkæθəˈlɪsɪtɪ) *n* **1** a wide range of interests, tastes, etc. **2** comprehensiveness.

catholicize *or* **catholicise** (kəˈθɒlɪˌsaɪz) *vb* **catholicizes, catholicizing, catholicized** *or* **catholicises, catholicising, catholicised. 1** to make or become catholic. **2** (*often cap.*) to convert to or become converted to Catholicism.

Catiline ★ (ˈkætɪˌlaɪn) *n* Latin name *Lucius Sergius Catilina.* ?108–62 B.C., Roman politician: organized an unsuccessful conspiracy against Cicero (63–62).
▸ **Catilinarian** (ˌkætɪlɪˈnɛərɪən) *adj*

cation (ˈkætaɪən) *n* a positively charged ion; an ion that is attracted to the cathode during electrolysis. Cf. **anion.** ORIG C19: from CATA- + ION
▸ **cationic** (ˌkætaɪˈɒnɪk) *adj*

catkin (ˈkætkɪn) *n* an inflorescence consisting of a hanging spike of much reduced flowers of either sex: occurs in birch, hazel, etc. ORIG C16: from obs. Du. *katteken* kitten

cat litter *n* absorbent material used to line a receptacle in which a domestic cat can urinate and defecate.

catmint (ˈkætˌmɪnt) *n* a Eurasian plant having spikes of purple-spotted white flowers and scented leaves of which cats are fond. Also called: **catnip.**

catnap (ˈkætˌnæp) *n* **1** a short sleep or doze. ◆ *vb* **catnaps, catnapping, catnapped. 2** (*intr*) to sleep or doze for a short time or intermittently.

Cato ★ (ˈkeɪtəʊ) *n* **1 Marcus Porcius** (ˈmɑːkəs ˈpɔːʃɪəs), known as *Cato the Elder* or *the Censor.* 234–149 B.C., Roman statesman, noted for his opposition to Carthage. **2** his great-grandson, **Marcus Porcius,** known as *Cato the Younger* or *Uticensis.* 95–46 B.C., Roman statesman and Stoic philosopher; opponent of Catiline and Caesar.

cat-o'-nine-tails *n, pl* **cat-o'-nine-tails.** a rope whip consisting of nine knotted thongs, used formerly to flog prisoners. Often shortened to **cat.**

CATS (kæts) *n acronym for* credit accumulation transfer scheme: a scheme enabling school-leavers and others to acquire transferable certificates for relevant work experience and study towards a recognized qualification.

CAT scanner (kæt) *n* former name for **CT scanner.** ORIG C20: from *C*omputerized *A*xial *T*omography

cat's cradle *n* a game played by making patterns with a loop of string between the fingers.

cat's-eye *n* any of a group of gemstones that reflect a streak of light when cut in a rounded unfaceted shape.

Catseye ('kætsaɪ) *n Trademark, Brit.* a glass reflector set into a small fixture, placed at intervals along roads to indicate traffic lanes at night.

Catskill Mountains ★ ('kætskɪl) *pl n* a mountain range in SE New York State: resort. Highest peak: Slide Mountain, 1261 m (4204 ft). Also called: **Catskills.**

cat's-paw *n* **1** a person used by another as a tool; dupe. **2** a pattern of ripples on the surface of water caused by a light wind. ORIG (sense 1) C18: so called from the tale of the monkey who used a cat's paw to draw chestnuts out of a fire

catsup ('kætsəp) *n* a variant spelling (esp. US) of **ketchup.**

cat's whisker *n* a pointed wire formerly used to make contact with the crystal in a crystal radio receiver.

cat's whiskers *or* **cat's pyjamas** *n* **the.** *Sl.* a person or thing that is excellent or superior.

Cattegat ★ ('kætɪˌgæt) *n* a variant spelling of **Kattegat.**

cattery ('kætərɪ) *n, pl* **catteries.** a place where cats are bred or looked after.

cattle ('kætᵊl) *n* (*functioning as pl*) **1** bovid mammals of the tribe *Bovini* (bovines). **2** Also called: **domestic cattle.** any domesticated bovine mammals. ORIG C13: from OF *chatel* CHATTEL

cattle-cake *n* concentrated food for cattle in the form of cakes.

cattle-grid *n* a grid of metal bars covering a hole dug in a roadway intended to prevent the passage of livestock while allowing vehicles, etc., to pass unhindered.

cattleman ('kætᵊlmən) *n, pl* **cattlemen. 1** a person who breeds, rears, or tends cattle. **2** *Chiefly US & Canad.* a person who rears cattle on a large scale.

cattle market *n* **1** a place in which cattle are bought and sold. **2** *Brit. sl.* a situation or place in which women are on display and judged solely by their appearance.

cattle-stop *n* the New Zealand name for a **cattle-grid.**

catty ('kætɪ) *or* **cattish** *adj* **cattier, cattiest. 1** *Inf.* spiteful: *a catty remark.* **2** of or resembling a cat.
▸ **'cattily** *or* **'cattishly** *adv* ▸ **'cattiness** *or* **'cattishness** *n*

Catullus ★ (kə'tʌləs) *n* **Gaius Valerius** ('gaɪəs və'lɪərɪəs). ?84–?54 B.C., Roman lyric poet.
▸ **Catullan** (kə'tʌlən) *adj*

CATV *abbrev. for* community antenna television.

catwalk ('kætˌwɔːk) *n* **1** a narrow ramp extending from the stage into the audience in a theatre etc., esp. as used by models in a fashion show. **2** a narrow pathway over the stage of a theatre, along a bridge, etc.

Cauca ★ (*Spanish* 'kauka) *n* a river in W Colombia, rising in the northwest and flowing north to the Magdalena River. Length: about 1350 km (840 miles).

Caucasia ★ (kɔː'keɪzɪə, -ʒə) *n* a region of SW Russia, Georgia, Armenia, and Azerbaijan, between the Caspian Sea and the Black Sea: contains the Caucasus Mountains, dividing it into Ciscaucasia in the north and Transcaucasia in the south; one of the most complex ethnic areas in the world, with over 50 different peoples. Also called: the **Caucasus.**

Caucasian (kɔː'keɪzɪən) *adj* **1** another word for **Caucasoid. 2** of or relating to Caucasia or the Caucasus. ◆ *n* **3** a member of the Caucasoid race; a White person. **4** a native or inhabitant of Caucasia or the Caucasus.

Caucasoid ('kɔːkəˌzɔɪd) *adj* **1** denoting or belonging to the light-complexioned racial group of mankind, which includes the peoples indigenous to Europe, N Africa, SW Asia, and the Indian subcontinent. ◆ *n* **2** a member of this racial group.

Caucasus ★ ('kɔːkəsəs) *n* **the. 1** Also called: **Caucasus Mountains.** a mountain range in SW Russia, in Caucasia between the Black Sea and the Caspian Sea: mostly over 2700 m (9000 ft). Highest peak: Mount Elbrus, 5642 m (18 510 ft). **2** another name for **Caucasia.**

Cauchy ★ ('kəʊʃɪ; *French* koʃi) *n* **Augustin Louis** (ogystɛ̃ lwi), Baron Cauchy. 1789–1857, French mathematician, noted for his theory of functions.

caucus ('kɔːkəs) *n, pl* **caucuses. 1** *Chiefly US & Canad.* a closed meeting of the members of one party in a legislative chamber, etc., to coordinate policy, choose candidates, etc. **2** *Chiefly US.* a local meeting of party members. **3** *Brit.* a group or faction within a larger group, esp. a political party, who discuss tactics, choose candidates, etc. **4** *NZ.* a formal meeting of all MPs of one party. **5** *Austral.* a group of MPs from one party who meet to discuss tactics, etc. ◆ *vb* **6** (*intr*) to hold a caucus. ORIG C18: prob. of Algonquian origin

caudal ('kɔːdᵊl) *adj* **1** *Anat.* of the posterior part of the body. **2** *Zool.* resembling or in the position of the tail. ORIG C17: from NL, from L *cauda* tail
▸ **'caudally** *adv*

caudal fin *n* the tail fin of fishes and some other aquatic vertebrates, used for propulsion.

caudate ('kɔːdeɪt) *or* **caudated** *adj* having a tail or a tail-like appendage. ORIG C17: from NL *caudātus,* from L *cauda* tail
▸ **cau'dation** *n*

caudillo (kɔː'diːljəʊ) *n, pl* **caudillos** (-ljəʊz). (in Spanish-speaking countries) a military or political leader. ORIG Sp., from LL *capitellum,* dim. of L *caput* head

caudle ('kɔːdᵊl) *n* a hot spiced wine drink made with gruel, formerly used medicinally. ORIG C13: from OF *caudel,* from Med. L, from L *calidus* warm

caught (kɔːt) *vb* the past tense and past participle of **catch.**

caul (kɔːl) *n Anat.* a portion of the amniotic sac sometimes covering a child's head at birth. ORIG C13: from OF *cale,* back formation from *calotte* close-fitting cap, of Gmc origin

cauldron *or* **caldron** ('kɔːldrən) *n* a large pot used for boiling, esp. one with handles. ORIG C13: from Anglo-F, from L *caldārium* hot bath, from *calidus* warm

cauliflower ('kɒlɪˌflaʊə) *n* **1** a variety of cabbage having a large edible head of crowded white flowers on a very short thick stem. **2** the flower head of this plant, used as a vegetable. ORIG C16: from It. *caoli fiori,* lit.: cabbage flowers

cauliflower ear *n* permanent swelling and distortion of the external ear as the result of ruptures of the blood vessels: usually caused by blows received in boxing.

caulk *or* **calk** (kɔːk) *vb* **1** to stop up (cracks, crevices, etc.) with a filler. **2** *Naut.* to pack (the seams) between the planks of the bottom of (a vessel) with waterproof material to prevent leakage. ORIG C15: from OF *cauquer* to press down, from L *calcāre* to trample, from *calx* heel

causal ('kɔːzᵊl) *adj* **1** acting as or being a cause. **2** stating, involving, or implying a cause: *the causal part of the argument.*
▸ **'causally** *adv*

causality (kɔː'zælɪtɪ) *n, pl* **causalities. 1a** the relationship of cause and effect. **1b** the principle that nothing can happen without being caused. **2** causal agency or quality.

causation (kɔː'zeɪʃən) *n* **1** the production of an effect by a cause. **2** the relationship of cause and effect.
▸ **cau'sational** *adj*

causative ('kɔːzətɪv) *adj* **1** *Grammar.* relating to a form or class of verbs, such as *persuade,* that express causation. **2** (*often postpositive* and foll. by *of*) producing an effect. ◆ *n* **3** the causative form or class of verbs.
▸ **'causatively** *adv*

cause (kɔːz) *n* **1** a person, thing, event, state, or action that produces an effect. **2** grounds for action; justifica-

tion: *she had good cause to shout like that.* **3** the ideals, etc., of a group or movement: *the Palestinian cause.* **4** the welfare or interests of a person or group in a dispute: *they fought for the miners' cause.* **5a** a ground for legal action; matter giving rise to a lawsuit. **5b** the lawsuit itself. **6** *Arch.* a subject of debate or discussion. **7 make common cause with.** to join with (a person, group, etc.) for a common objective. ◆ *vb* **causes, causing, caused. 8** (*tr*) to be the cause of; bring about. ORIG C13: from L *causa* cause, reason, motive
▸ **'causeless** *adj*

cause célèbre ('kɔːz sə'lɛbrə) *n, pl* **causes célèbres** ('kɔːz sə'lɛbrəz). a famous lawsuit, trial, or controversy. ORIG C19: from F: famous case

causerie ('kəʊzərɪ) *n* an informal talk or conversational piece of writing. ORIG C19: from F, from *causer* to chat

causeway ('kɔːzˌweɪ) *n* **1** a raised path or road crossing water, marshland, etc. **2** a paved footpath. ORIG C15 *cauciwey* (from *cauci* + WAY); *cauci* paved road, from Med. L, from L *calx* limestone

caustic ('kɔːstɪk) *adj* **1** capable of burning or corroding by chemical action: *caustic soda.* **2** sarcastic; cutting: *a caustic reply.* ◆ *n* **3** Also called: **caustic surface.** a surface that envelops the light rays reflected or refracted by a curved surface. **4** Also called: **caustic curve.** a curve formed by the intersection of a caustic surface with a plane. **5** *Chem.* a caustic substance, esp. an alkali. ORIG C14: from L, from Gk *kaustikos,* from *kaiein* to burn
▸ **'caustically** *adv* ▸ **causticity** (kɔː'stɪsɪtɪ) *n*

caustic potash *n* another name for **potassium hydroxide.**

caustic soda *n* another name for **sodium hydroxide.**

cauterize *or* **cauterise** ('kɔːtəˌraɪz) *vb* **cauterizes, cauterizing, cauterized** *or* **cauterises, cauterising, cauterised.** (*tr*) (esp. in the treatment of a wound) to burn or sear (body tissue) with a hot iron or caustic agent. ORIG C14: from OF, from LL, from *cautērium* branding iron, from Gk *kautērion,* from *kaiein* to burn
▸ **ˌcauteri'zation** *or* **ˌcauteri'sation** *n*

cautery ('kɔːtərɪ) *n, pl* **cauteries. 1** the coagulation of blood or destruction of body tissue by cauterizing. **2** an instrument or agent for cauterizing. ORIG C14: from OF *cautère,* from L *cautērium*

caution ('kɔːʃən) *n* **1** care, forethought, or prudence, esp. in the face of danger. **2** something intended or serving as a warning. **3** *Law, chiefly Brit.* a formal warning given to a person suspected of an offence that his words will be taken down and may be used in evidence. **4** *Inf.* an amusing or surprising person or thing. ◆ *vb* **5** (*tr*) to warn (a person) to be careful. **6** (*tr*) *Law, chiefly Brit.* to give a caution to (a person). **7** (*intr*) to warn, urge, or advise: *he cautioned against optimism.* ORIG C13: from OF, from L *cautiō,* from *cavēre* to beware

cautionary ('kɔːʃənərɪ) *adj* serving as a warning; intended to warn: *a cautionary tale.*

cautious ('kɔːʃəs) *adj* showing or having caution.
▸ **'cautiously** *adv* ▸ **'cautiousness** *n*

Cavaco Silva ★ ('kavaku 'silvə) *n* **Aníbal** (a'nibal). born 1939, Portuguese statesman; prime minister (1985–95).

Cavafy ★ (kə'vɑːfɪ) *n* **Constantine.** Greek name *Kavafis.* 1863–1933, Greek poet of Alexandria in Egypt.

cavalcade (ˌkævəl'keɪd) *n* **1** a procession of people on horseback, in cars, etc. **2** any procession. ORIG C16: from F, from It., from *cavalcare* to ride on horseback, from LL, from *caballus* horse

Cavalcanti ★ (*Italian* kaval'kanti) *n* **Guido** ('gwiːdo). ?1255–1300, Italian poet.

cavalier (ˌkævə'lɪə) *adj* **1** supercilious; offhand. ◆ *n* **2** a courtly gentleman, esp. one acting as a lady's escort. **3** *Arch.* a horseman, esp. one who is armed. ORIG C16: from It., from OProvençal, from LL *caballārius* rider, from *caballus* horse, from ?
▸ **ˌcava'lierly** *adv*

Cavalier (ˌkævə'lɪə) *n* a supporter of Charles I during the English Civil War.

Cavallini ★ (*Italian* kaval'liːni) *n* **Pietro** ('pjɜːtro). ?1250–?1330, Italian fresco painter and mosaicist.

cavalry ('kævəlrɪ) *n, pl* **cavalries. 1** (esp. formerly) the part of an army composed of mounted troops. **2** the armoured element of a modern army. **3** (*as modifier*): *a cavalry unit.* ORIG C16: from F *cavallerie,* from It., from *cavaliere* horseman
▸ **'cavalryman** *n*

Cavan ★ ('kævᵊn) *n* **1** a county of north Republic of Ireland: hilly, with lakes and bogs. County town: Cavan. Pop.: 53 000 (1996). Area: 1890 sq. km (730 sq. miles). **2** a market town in north Republic of Ireland, county town of Co. Cavan. Pop.: 5000 (latest est.).

cavatina (ˌkævə'tiːnə) *n, pl* **cavatine** (-nɪ). **1** a simple solo song. **2** an instrumental composition reminiscent of this. ORIG C19: from It.

cave[1] (keɪv) *n* **1** an underground hollow with access from the ground surface or from the sea. **2** *Brit. history.* a secession or a group seceding from a political party on some issue. **3** (*modifier*) living in caves. ◆ *vb* **caves, caving, caved. 4** (*tr*) to hollow out. ORIG C13: from OF, from L *cava,* pl. of *cavum* cavity, from *cavus* hollow

cave[2] ('keɪvɪ) *Brit. school sl.* ◆ *n* **1** lookout: *keep cave.* ◆ *sentence substitute.* **2** watch out! ORIG from L *cavē* beware!

caveat ('keɪvɪˌæt, 'kæv-) *n* **1** *Law.* a formal notice requesting the court not to take a certain action without warning the person lodging the caveat. **2** a caution. ORIG C16: from L, lit.: let him beware

caveat emptor ('ɛmptɔː) *n* the principle that the buyer must bear the risk for the quality of goods purchased. ORIG L: let the buyer beware

cave in *vb* (*intr, adv*) **1** to collapse; subside. **2** *Inf.* to yield completely, esp. under pressure. ◆ *n* **cave-in. 3** the sudden collapse of a roof, piece of ground, etc. **4** the site of such a collapse, as at a mine or tunnel.

cavel ('keɪvᵊl) *n NZ.* a drawing of lots among miners for an easy and profitable place at the coalface. ORIG C19: from E dialect *cavel* to cast lots, apportion

Cavell ★ ('kævᵊl) *n* **Edith Louisa.** 1865–1915, British nurse: executed by the Germans in World War I for helping Allied prisoners to escape.

caveman ('keɪvˌmæn) *n, pl* **cavemen. 1** a man of the Palaeolithic age; cave dweller. **2** *Inf.* a man who is primitive or brutal in behaviour, etc.

cavendish ('kævəndɪʃ) *n* tobacco that has been sweetened and pressed into moulds to form bars. ORIG C19: ?from the name of the first maker

Cavendish ★ ('kævəndɪʃ) *n* **Henry.** 1731–1810, British physicist: recognized hydrogen and calculated the density of the earth.

cavern ('kævᵊn) *n* **1** a cave, esp. when large. ◆ *vb* (*tr*) **2** to shut in or as if in a cavern. **3** to hollow out. ORIG C14: from OF *caverne,* from L *caverna,* from *cavus* hollow

cavernous ('kævənəs) *adj* **1** suggestive of a cavern in vastness, etc.: *cavernous eyes.* **2** filled with small cavities. **3** (of rocks) containing caverns.

caviar *or* **caviare** ('kævɪˌɑː, ˌkævɪ'ɑː) *n* the salted roe of sturgeon, usually served as an hors d'oeuvre. ORIG C16: from earlier *cavery,* from OIt. *caviari,* pl. of *caviaro* caviar, from Turkish *havyār*

cavil ('kævɪl) *vb* **cavils, cavilling, cavilled** *or US* **cavils, caviling, caviled. 1** (*intr;* foll. by *at* or *about*) to raise annoying petty objections. ◆ *n* **2** a trifling objection. ORIG C16: from OF, from L *cavillārī* to jeer, from *cavilla* raillery
▸ **'caviller** *n*

caving ('keɪvɪŋ) *n* the sport of climbing in and exploring caves.
▸ **'caver** *n*

cavity ('kævɪtɪ) *n, pl* **cavities. 1** a hollow space. **2** *Dentistry.* a decayed area on a tooth. **3** any empty or hollow space within the body. ORIG C16: from F, from LL *cavitās,* from L *cavus* hollow

cavity wall *n* a wall that consists of two separate walls with an airspace between them.

cavort (kə'vɔːt) *vb* (*intr*) to prance; caper. ORIG C19: ?from CURVET
▸ **ca'vorter** *n*

Cavour ★ (*Italian* ka'vur) *n* Conte **Camillo Benso di** (ka'millo 'bɛnzo di). 1810–61, Italian statesman and premier of Piedmont-Sardinia (1852–59; 1860–61): a leader of the movement for the unification of Italy.

cavy ('keɪvɪ) *n, pl* **cavies.** a small South American rodent having a thickset body and very small tail. See also **guinea pig.** ORIG C18: from NL *Cavia,* from Carib *cabiai*

caw (kɔː) *n* **1** the cry of a crow, rook, or raven. ◆ *vb* **2** (*intr*) to make this cry. ORIG C16: imit.

Cawley ★ ('kɔːlɪ) *n* **Evonne** (née *Goolagong*). born 1951, Australian tennis player: Wimbledon champion 1971 and 1980; Australian champion 1974–76.

Cawnpore (ˌkɔːn'pɔː) *or* **Cawnpur** ★ (ˌkɔːn'pʊə) *n* the former name of **Kanpur.**

Caxton ★ ('kækstən) *n* **William.** ?1422–91, English printer; published, in Bruges, the first book printed in English (1475) and established the first press in England (1477).

cay (keɪ, kiː) *n* a small low island or bank composed of sand and coral fragments. ORIG C18: from Sp. *cayo,* prob. from OF *quai* QUAY

Cayenne ★ (keɪ'ɛn) *n* the capital of French Guiana, on an island at the mouth of the Cayenne River: French penal settlement from 1854 to 1938. Pop.: 41 659 (1990).

cayenne pepper (keɪ'ɛn) *n* a very hot red condiment made from the dried seeds of various capsicums. Often shortened to **cayenne.** Also called: **red pepper.** ORIG C18: ult. from Tupi *quiynha*

Cayes ★ (keɪ; *French* kaj) *n* short for **Les Cayes.**

Cayley ★ ('keɪlɪ) *n* **1 Arthur.** 1821–93, British mathematician, who invented matrices. **2** Sir **George.** 1773–1857, British engineer and pioneer of aerial navigation.

cayman *or* **caiman** ('keɪmən) *n, pl* **caymans** *or* **caimans.** a tropical American crocodilian similar to alligators but with a more heavily armoured belly. ORIG C16: from Sp. *caimán,* from Carib *cayman*

Cayman Islands ★ ('keɪmən) *pl n* three coral islands in the Caribbean Sea northwest of Jamaica: a dependency of Jamaica until 1962, now a United Kingdom Overseas Territory. Capital: George Town. Pop.: 31 930 (1994). Area: about 260 sq. km (100 sq. miles).

CB *abbrev. for:* **1** Citizens' Band. **2** Companion of the (Order of the) Bath (a Brit. title). **3** County Borough.

CBC *abbrev. for* Canadian Broadcasting Corporation.

CBE *abbrev. for* Commander of the (Order of the) British Empire.

CBI *abbrev. for:* **1** *US.* Central Bureau of Investigation. **2** Confederation of British Industry.

CBT *abbrev. for* computer-based training.

cc *or* **c.c.** *abbrev. for:* **1** carbon copy *or* copies. **2** cubic centimetre(s).

CC *abbrev. for:* **1** City Council. **2** (in Britain) Competition Commission. **3** County Council. **4** Cricket Club.

cc. *abbrev. for* chapters.

c.c.c. *abbrev. for* cwmni cyfyngedig cyhoeddus; a public limited company in Wales.

C clef *n Music.* a symbol (𝄡), placed at the beginning of the staff, establishing the position of middle C: see **alto clef, soprano clef, tenor clef.**

CCTV *abbrev. for* closed-circuit television.

CCW *abbrev. for* Curriculum Council for Wales.

cd *symbol for* candela.

Cd *the chemical symbol for* cadmium.

CD *abbrev. for:* **1** compact disc. **2** Civil Defence (Corps). **3** Corps Diplomatique (Diplomatic Corps). **4** Conference on Disarmament: a United Nations standing conference, held in Geneva, to negotiate a global ban on chemical weapons.

CDE *abbrev. for:* compact disc erasable: a compact disc that can be used to record and rerecord. Cf. **CDR.**

CDI *abbrev. for* compact disc interactive.

Cdn *abbrev. for* Canadian.

cDNA *abbrev. for* complementary DNA.

CD player *n* a device for playing compact discs. In full: **compact-disc player.**

Cdr *Mil. abbrev. for* Commander.

CDR *abbrev. for* compact disc recordable: a compact disc that can be used to record only once. Cf. **CDE.**

CD-ROM (ˌsiːdiː'rɒm) *abbrev. for* compact disc read only memory; a compact disc used for storing written information to be displayed on a visual-display unit.

CDT *abbrev. for:* **1** *US & Canad.* Central Daylight Time. **2** Craft, Design, and Technology: a subject on the GCSE syllabus, related to the National Curriculum.

CDV *abbrev. for* compact disc video.

CD-video *n* a compact-disc player that, when connected to a television and hi-fi, produces high-quality stereo sound and synchronized pictures from a disc resembling a compact audio disc. In full **compact-disc video.**

Ce *the chemical symbol for* cerium.

CE *abbrev. for:* **1** Church of England. **2** civil engineer. **3** Common Era.

Ceará ★ (*Portuguese* sja'ra) *n* **1** a state of NE Brazil: sandy coastal plain, rising to a high plateau. Capital: Fortaleza. Pop.: 6 809 290 (1996). Area: 150 630 sq. km (58 746 sq. miles). **2** another name for **Fortaleza.**

cease (siːs) *vb* **ceases, ceasing, ceased. 1** (when *tr,* may take a gerund or an infinitive as object) to bring or come to an end. ◆ *n* **2 without cease.** without stopping. ORIG C14: from OF, from L *cessāre,* frequentative of *cēdere* to yield

ceasefire ('siːsˌfaɪə) *Chiefly mil.* ◆ *n* **1** a period of truce, esp. one that is temporary. ◆ *sentence substitute, n* **2** the order to stop firing.

ceaseless ('siːslɪs) *adj* without stop or pause; incessant.
▸ **'ceaselessly** *adv*

Ceauşescu ★ (tʃaʊ'ʃɛskuː) *n* **Nicolae** (ˌnɪkɒ'laɪ). 1918–89, Romanian statesman; chairman of the state council (1967–89) and president (1974–89): deposed and executed.

Cebú ★ (sɪ'buː) *n* **1** an island in the central Philippines. Pop.: 2 091 602 (1980). Area: 4422 sq. km (1707 sq. miles). **2** a port in the Philippines, on E Cebú island. Pop.: 688 196 (1994 est.).

Čechy ★ ('tʃɛxi) *n* the Czech name for **Bohemia.**

Cecil ★ ('sɛsᵊl, 'sɪs-) *n* **1** Lord **David.** 1902–86, British biographer. **2 Robert.** See (3rd Marquess of) **Salisbury. 3 William.** See (William Cecil) **Burghley.**

Cecilia ★ (sɪ'siːljə) *n* **Saint.** died ?230 A.D., Roman martyr; patron saint of music. Feast day: Nov. 22.

cecum ('siːkəm) *n, pl* **ceca** (-kə). *US.* a variant spelling of **caecum.**
▸ **'cecal** *adj*

cedar ('siːdə) *n* **1** any of a genus of Old World coniferous trees having needle-like evergreen leaves, and erect barrel-shaped cones. See also **cedar of Lebanon, deodar. 2** any of various other conifers, such as the red cedars and white cedars. **3** the wood of any of these trees. ◆ *adj* **4** made of the wood of a cedar tree. ORIG C13: from OF, from L *cedrus,* from Gk *kedros*

cedar of Lebanon ('lɛbənən) *n* a cedar of SW Asia with level spreading branches and fragrant wood.

cede (siːd) *vb* **cedes, ceding, ceded. 1** (when *intr,* often foll. by *to*) to transfer, make over, or surrender (something, esp. territory or legal rights). **2** (*tr*) to allow or concede (a point in an argument, etc.). ORIG C17: from L *cēdere* to yield
▸ **'ceder** *n*

cedilla (sɪ'dɪlə) *n* a character (¸) placed underneath a *c* before *a, o,* or *u,* esp. in French, Portuguese, or Catalan, denoting that it is to be pronounced (s), not (k). ORIG C16: from Sp.: little *z,* from *ceda* zed, from LL *zeta*

Ceefax ('siːfæks) *n Trademark.* the BBC Teletext service. See **Teletext.**

CEGB (in Britain) *abbrev. for* Central Electricity Generating Board.

ceil (siːl) *vb* (*tr*) **1** to line (a ceiling) with plaster, etc. **2** to provide with a ceiling. ORIG C15 *celen,* ? back formation from CEILING

ceilidh ('keɪlɪ) *n* (esp. in Scotland and Ireland) an informal social gathering with singing, dancing, and storytelling. ORIG C19: from Gaelic

ceiling ('si:lɪŋ) *n* **1** the inner upper surface of a room. **2** an upper limit, such as one set by regulation on prices or wages. **3** the upper altitude to which an aircraft can climb measured under specified conditions. **4** *Meteorol.* the highest level in the atmosphere from which the earth's surface is visible at a particular time, usually the base of a cloud layer. ORIG C14: from ?

Cela ★ (*Spanish* 'θela) *n* **Camilo José** (ka'milo xo'se). born 1916, Spanish novelist and essayist. His works include *The Family of Pascual Duarte* (1942), *La Colmena* (1951), and *Reloj de Sangre* (1989). Nobel prize for literature 1989.

celadon ('sɛlə,dɒn) *n* **1** a type of porcelain having a greyish-green glaze: mainly Chinese. **2a** a pale greyish-green colour. **2b** (*as adj*): *a celadon jar.* ORIG C18: from F, from the name of the shepherd hero of *L'Astrée* (1610), a romance by Honoré d'Urfé

Celan ★ ('sɛlæn) *n* **Paul**, real name *Paul Antschel.* 1920–70, Romanian Jewish poet, writing in German.

celandine ('sɛlən,daɪn) *n* either of two unrelated plants, **greater celandine** or **lesser celandine,** with yellow flowers. ORIG C13: earlier *celydon,* from L, from Gk *khelidōn* swallow; the plant's season was believed to parallel the migration of swallows

-cele *n combining form.* tumour or hernia: *hydrocele.* ORIG from Gk *kēlē* tumour

celeb (sɪ'lɛb) *n Inf.* a celebrity.

Celebes ★ ('sɛlɪbi:z, sɛ'li:bɪz) *n* the English name for **Sulawesi.**

Celebes Sea ★ *n* the part of the Pacific Ocean between Sulawesi, Borneo, and Mindanao.

celebrant ('sɛlɪbrənt) *n* a person participating in a religious ceremony, esp. at the Eucharist.

celebrate ('sɛlɪ,breɪt) *vb* **celebrates, celebrating, celebrated. 1** to rejoice in or have special festivities to mark (a happy day, event, etc.). **2** (*tr*) to observe (a birthday, anniversary, etc.). **3** (*tr*) to perform (a solemn or religious ceremony), esp. to officiate at (Mass). **4** (*tr*) to praise publicly; proclaim. ORIG C15: from L, from *celeber* numerous, renowned
▸ **,cele'bration** *n* ▸ **'cele,brator** *n* ▸ **'cele,bratory** *adj*

celebrated ('sɛlɪ,breɪtɪd) *adj* (*usually prenominal*) famous: *a celebrated pianist.*

celebrity (sɪ'lɛbrɪtɪ) *n, pl* **celebrities. 1** a famous person. **2** fame or notoriety.

celeriac (sɪ'lɛrɪ,æk) *n* a variety of celery with a large turnip-like root, used as a vegetable. ORIG C18: from CELERY + *-ac,* from ?

celerity (sɪ'lɛrɪtɪ) *n* rapidity; swiftness; speed. ORIG C15: from OF *celerite,* from L *celeritās,* from *celer* swift

celery ('sɛlərɪ) *n* **1** an umbelliferous Eurasian plant whose blanched leafstalks are used in salads or cooked as a vegetable. **2 wild celery.** a related and similar plant. ORIG C17: from F *céleri,* from It. (Lombardy) dialect *selleri* (pl), from Gk *selinon* parsley

celesta (sɪ'lɛstə) *or* **celeste** (sɪ'lɛst) *n Music.* a keyboard percussion instrument consisting of a set of steel plates of graduated length that are struck with key-operated hammers. ORIG C19: from F, Latinized var. of *céleste* heavenly

celestial (sɪ'lɛstɪəl) *adj* **1** heavenly; divine: *celestial peace.* **2** of or relating to the sky: *celestial bodies.* **3** of or connected with the celestial sphere: *celestial pole.* ORIG C14: from Med. L, from L *caelestis,* from *caelum* heaven
▸ **ce'lestially** *adv*

Celestial Empire ★ *n* an archaic or literary name for the **Chinese Empire.**

celestial equator *n* the great circle lying on the celestial sphere the plane of which is perpendicular to the line joining the north and south celestial poles. Also called: **equinoctial, equinoctial circle.**

celestial mechanics *n* the study of the motion of celestial bodies under the influence of gravitational fields.

celestial sphere *n* an imaginary sphere of infinitely large radius enclosing the universe so that all celestial bodies appear to be projected onto its surface.

celiac ('si:lɪ,æk) *adj Anat.* the usual US spelling of **coeliac.**

celibate ('sɛlɪbɪt) *n* **1** a person who is unmarried, esp. one who has taken a religious vow of chastity. ◆ *adj* **2** abstaining from sexual intercourse. **3** unmarried. ORIG C17: from L, from *caelebs* unmarried, from ?
▸ **'celibacy** *n*

Céline ★ (*French* selin) *n* **Louis-Ferdinand** (lwifɛrdinɑ̃), real name *Louis-Ferdinand Destouches.* 1894–1961, French novelist and physician; noted for his novel *Journey to the End of the Night* (1932).

cell (sɛl) *n* **1** a small simple room, as in a prison, convent, etc. **2** any small compartment: *the cells of a honeycomb.* **3** *Biol.* the smallest unit of an organism that is able to function independently. It consists of a nucleus, containing the genetic material, surrounded by the cytoplasm. **4** *Biol.* any small cavity, such as the cavity containing pollen in an anther. **5** a device for converting chemical energy into electrical energy, usually consisting of a container with two electrodes immersed in an electrolyte. See also **dry cell, fuel cell. 6** In full: **electrolytic cell.** a device in which electrolysis occurs. **7** a small religious house dependent upon a larger one. **8** a small group of persons operating as a nucleus of a larger organization: *Communist cell.* **9** the geographical area served by an individual transmitter in a cellular-radio network. ORIG C12: from Med. L *cella* monk's cell, from L: room, storeroom

cellar ('sɛlə) *n* **1** an underground room, or storey of a building, usually used for storage. **2** a place where wine is stored. **3** a stock of bottled wines. ◆ *vb* **4** (*tr*) to store in a cellar. ORIG C13: from Anglo-F, from L *cellārium* foodstore, from *cella* cell

cellarage ('sɛlərɪdʒ) *n* **1** an area of a cellar. **2** a charge for storing goods in a cellar, etc.

cellarer ('sɛlərə) *n* a monastic official responsible for food, drink, etc.

cellaret (,sɛlə'rɛt) *n* a cabinet or sideboard with compartments for holding wine bottles.

Cellini ★ (tʃɪ'li:nɪ; *Italian* tʃel'li:ni) *n* **Benvenuto** (benve'nu:to). 1500–71, Italian sculptor, goldsmith, and engraver, noted also for his autobiography.

cell line *n Biol.* a cell culture derived from a single cell and thus of invariable genetic make-up.

Cellnet ('sɛl,nɛt) *n Trademark.* a British Telecom mobile phone.

cello ('tʃɛləʊ) *n, pl* **cellos.** *Music.* a bowed stringed instrument of the violin family. It has four strings, is held between the knees, and has a metal spike at the lower end, which acts as a support. Full name: **violoncello.**
▸ **'cellist** *n*

Cellophane ('sɛlə,feɪn) *n Trademark.* a flexible thin transparent sheeting made from wood pulp and used as a moisture-proof wrapping. ORIG C20: from CELLULOSE + -PHANE

cellphone ('sɛl,fəʊn) *n* a portable telephone operated by cellular radio. In full: **cellular telephone.**

cellular ('sɛljʊlə) *adj* **1** of, relating to, or composed of a cell or cells. **2** having cells or small cavities; porous. **3** divided into a network of cells. **4** *Textiles.* woven with an open texture: *a cellular blanket.* **5** designed for or involving cellular radio.

cellular radio *n* radio communication based on a network of transmitters each serving a small area known as a cell: used esp. in car phones in which the receiver switches frequencies automatically as it passes from one cell to another.

cellule ('sɛlju:l) *n* a very small cell. ORIG C17: from L *cellula,* dim. of *cella* CELL

cellulite ('sɛljʊ,laɪt) *n* subcutaneous fat alleged to resist dieting.

cellulitis (,sɛljʊ'laɪtɪs) *n* inflammation of body tissue, with fever, pain, and swelling. ORIG C19: from L *cellula* CELLULE + -ITIS

celluloid ('sɛljʊ,lɔɪd) *n* **1** a flammable material consisting of cellulose nitrate and camphor: used in sheets, rods, etc. **2a** a cellulose derivative used for coating film. **2b** cinema film.

cellulose ('sɛlju,ləuz, -,ləus) *n* a substance which is the main constituent of plant cell walls and used in making paper, rayon, and film. ORIG C18: from F *cellule* cell (see CELLULE) + -OSE[2]

cellulose acetate *n* nonflammable material used in the manufacture of film, dopes, lacquers, and artificial fibres.

cellulose nitrate *n* cellulose treated with nitric and sulphuric acids, used in plastics, lacquers, and explosives. See also **guncotton.**

Celsius ('sɛlsɪəs) *adj* denoting a measurement on the Celsius scale. Symbol: C ORIG C18: after Anders *Celsius* (1701–44), Swedish astronomer who invented it

Celsius scale *n* a scale of temperature in which 0° represents the melting point of ice and 100° represents the boiling point of water. See also **centigrade.** Cf. **Fahrenheit scale.**

celt (sɛlt) *n Archaeol.* a stone or metal axelike instrument. ORIG C18: from LL *celtes* chisel, from ?

Celt (kɛlt, sɛlt) *or* **Kelt** *n* **1** a person who speaks a Celtic language. **2** a member of an Indo-European people who in pre-Roman times inhabited Britain, Gaul, and Spain.

Celtic ('kɛltɪk, 'sɛl-) *or* **Keltic** *n* **1** a branch of the Indo-European family of languages that includes Gaelic, Welsh, and Breton. Modern Celtic is divided into the Brythonic (southern) and Goidelic (northern) groups. ◆ *adj* **2** of, relating to, or characteristic of the Celts or the Celtic languages.
▸ **Celticism** ('kɛltɪ,sɪzəm, 'sɛl-) *or* **'Kelti,cism** *n*

Celtic cross *n* a Latin cross with a broad ring surrounding the point of intersection.

cembalo ('tʃɛmbələu) *n, pl* **cembali** (-lɪ) *or* **cembalos.** another word for **harpsichord.** ORIG C19: from It. *clavicembalo* from Med. L *clāvis* key + *cymbalum* CYMBAL

cement (sɪ'mɛnt) *n* **1** a fine grey powder made of a mixture of limestone and clay, used with water and sand to make mortar, or with water, sand, and aggregate, to make concrete. **2** a binder, glue, or adhesive. **3** something that unites or joins. **4** *Dentistry.* any of various materials used in filling teeth. **5** another word for **cementum.** ◆ *vb* (*tr*) **6** to join, bind, or glue together with or as if with cement. **7** to coat or cover with cement. ORIG C13: from OF, from L *caementum* stone from the quarry, from *caedere* to hew

cementum (sɪ'mɛntəm) *n* a thin bonelike tissue that covers the dentine in the root of a tooth. ORIG C19: NL, from L: CEMENT

cemetery ('sɛmɪtrɪ) *n, pl* **cemeteries.** a place where the dead are buried, esp. one not attached to a church. ORIG C14: from LL, from Gk *koimētērion,* from *koiman* to put to sleep

-cene *n and adj combining form.* denoting a recent geological period. ORIG from Gk *kainos* new

Cenis ★ (*French* səni) *n* **Mont.** a pass over the Graian Alps in SE France, between Lanslebourg (France) and Susa (Italy): nearby tunnel, opened in 1871. Highest point: 2082 m (6831 ft). Italian name: **Monte Cenisio** ('monte tʃe'ni:zjo).

cenobite ('si:nəu,baɪt) *n* a variant spelling of **coenobite.**

cenotaph ('sɛnə,tɑ:f) *n* a monument honouring a dead person or persons buried elsewhere. ORIG C17: from L, from Gk, from *kenos* empty + *taphos* tomb

Cenotaph ★ ('sɛnə,tɑ:f) *n* **the.** the monument in Whitehall, London, honouring the dead of both World Wars: designed by Sir Edwin Lutyens: erected in 1920.

Cenozoic, Caenozoic (,si:nəu'zəuɪk), *or* **Cainozoic** *adj* **1** of, denoting, or relating to the most recent geological era characterized by the development and increase of the mammals. ◆ *n* **2 the.** the Cenozoic era. ORIG C19: from Gk *kainos* recent + *zōikos,* from *zōion* animal

censer ('sɛnsə) *n* a container for burning incense. Also called: **thurible.**

censor ('sɛnsə) *n* **1** a person authorized to examine publications, films, letters, etc., in order to suppress in whole or part those considered obscene, politically unacceptable, etc. **2** any person who controls or suppresses the behaviour of others, usually on moral grounds. **3** (in republican Rome) either of two senior magistrates elected to keep the list of citizens up to date, and supervise public morals. **4** *Psychoanal.* the postulated factor responsible for regulating the translation of ideas and desires from the unconscious to the conscious mind. ◆ *vb* (*tr*) **5** to ban or cut portions of (a film, letter, etc.). **6** to act as a censor of (behaviour, etc.). ORIG C16: from L, from *cēnsēre* to consider
▸ **censorial** (sɛn'sɔ:rɪəl) *adj*

censorious (sɛn'sɔ:rɪəs) *adj* harshly critical; fault-finding.
▸ **cen'soriously** *adv*

censorship ('sɛnsə,ʃɪp) *n* **1** a policy or programme of censoring. **2** the act or system of censoring.

censure ('sɛnʃə) *n* **1** severe disapproval. ◆ *vb* **censures, censuring, censured. 2** to criticize (someone or something) severely. ORIG C14: from L *censūra,* from *cēnsēre:* see CENSOR
▸ **'censurable** *adj*

census ('sɛnsəs) *n, pl* **censuses. 1** an official periodic count of a population including such information as sex, age, occupation, etc. **2** any official count: *a traffic census.* **3** (in ancient Rome) a registration of the population and a property evaluation for taxation. ORIG C17: from L, from *cēnsēre* to assess

cent (sɛnt) *n* a monetary unit of Australia, Barbados, Canada, Cyprus, Dominica, Estonia, Ethiopia, the countries of the European Union that have adopted European Monetary Union, Fiji, Grenada, Guyana, Jamaica, Kenya, Malaysia, New Zealand, Singapore, South Africa, Tanzania, Trinidad and Tobago, Uganda, the United States, etc. It is worth one hundredth of their respective standard units. ORIG C16: from L *centēsimus* hundredth, from *centum* hundred

cent. *abbrev. for:* **1** centigrade. **2** central. **3** century.

centaur ('sɛntɔ:) *n Greek myth.* one of a race of creatures with the head, arms, and torso of a man, and the lower body and legs of a horse. ORIG C14: from L, from Gk *kentauros,* from ?

centaurea (sɛntɔ:'rɪə, sɛn'tɔ:rɪə) *n* any plant of the genus *Centaurea* which includes the cornflower and knapweed. ORIG C19: ult. from Gk *Kentauros* the Centaur; see CENTAURY

centaury ('sɛntɔ:rɪ) *n, pl* **centauries. 1** any of a genus of Eurasian plants having purplish-pink flowers and formerly believed to have medicinal properties. **2** another name for **centaurea.** ORIG C14: ult. from Gk *Kentauros* the Centaur; from the legend that Chiron the Centaur divulged its healing properties

centavo (sɛn'tɑ:vəu) *n, pl* **centavos.** a monetary unit of Argentina, Brazil, Colombia, Ecuador, El Salvador, Mexico, Nicaragua, the Philippines, Portugal, etc. It is worth one hundredth of their respective standard units. ORIG Sp.: one hundredth part

centenarian (,sɛntɪ'nɛərɪən) *n* **1** a person who is at least 100 years old. ◆ *adj* **2** being at least 100 years old. **3** of or relating to a centenarian.

centenary (sɛn'ti:nərɪ) *adj* **1** of or relating to a period of 100 years. **2** occurring once every 100 years. ◆ *n, pl* **centenaries. 3** a 100th anniversary or its celebration. ORIG C17: from L, from *centēnī* a hundred each, from *centum* hundred

centennial (sɛn'tɛnɪəl) *adj* **1** relating to or completing a period of 100 years. **2** occurring every 100 years. ◆ *n* **3** *US & Canad.* another name for **centenary.** ORIG C18: from L *centum* hundred, on the model of BIENNIAL

center ('sɛntə) *n, vb* the US spelling of **centre.**

centesimal (sɛn'tɛsɪməl) *n* **1** hundredth. ◆ *adj* **2** relating to division into hundredths. ORIG C17: from L, from *centum* hundred
▸ **cen'tesimally** *adv*

centesimo (sɛn'tɛsɪ,məu) *n, pl* **centesimos** *or* **centesimi.** a monetary unit of Italy, Panama, Uruguay, etc. It is worth one hundredth of their respective standard units. ORIG C19: from Sp. & It., from L, from *centum* hundred

centi- *or before a vowel* **cent-** *prefix* **1** denoting one hundredth: *centimetre*. Symbol: c **2** *Rare*. denoting a hundred: *centipede*. ORIG from F, from L *centum* hundred

centiare ('sɛntɪˌɛə) *or* **centare** ('sɛntɛə) *n* a unit of area equal to one square metre. ORIG F, from CENTI- + *are* from L *ārea*

centigrade ('sɛntɪˌgreɪd) *adj* **1** a former name for **Celsius**. ◆ *n* **2** a unit of angle equal to one hundredth of a grade.

centigram *or* **centigramme** ('sɛntɪˌgræm) *n* one hundredth of a gram.

centilitre *or US* **centiliter** ('sɛntɪˌliːtə) *n* one hundredth of a litre.

centime ('sɒnˌtiːm; *French* sɑ̃tim) *n* a monetary unit of Algeria, Belgium, the Central African Republic, France, Guinea, Haiti, Liechtenstein, Luxembourg, Mali, Switzerland, Togo, etc. It is worth one hundredth of their respective standard units. ORIG C18: from F, from OF, from L, from *centum* hundred

centimetre *or US* **centimeter** ('sɛntɪˌmiːtə) *n* one hundredth of a metre.

centimetre-gram-second *n* See **cgs units**.

céntimo ('sɛntɪˌməʊ) *n, pl* **céntimos**. a monetary unit of Costa Rica, Peru, Spain, Venezuela, etc. It is worth one hundredth of their respective standard currency units. ORIG from Sp.; see CENTIME

centipede ('sɛntɪˌpiːd) *n* a carnivorous arthropod having a body of between 15 and 190 segments, each bearing one pair of legs.

cento ('sɛntəʊ) *n, pl* **centos**. a piece of writing, esp. a poem, composed of quotations from other authors. ORIG C17: from L, lit.: patchwork garment

CENTO ('sɛntəʊ) *n acronym for* Central Treaty Organization; an organization for military and economic cooperation formed in 1959 by the UK, Iran, Pakistan, and Turkey: disbanded 1979.

central ('sɛntrəl) *adj* **1** in, at, of, from, containing, or forming the centre of something: *the central street in a city*. **2** main, principal, or chief: *the central cause of a problem*.
▸ **centrality** (sɛn'trælɪtɪ) *n* ▸ **'centrally** *adv*

Central African Federation ★ *n* another name for the **Federation of Rhodesia and Nyasaland**.

Central African Republic ★ *n* a landlocked country of central Africa: joined with Chad as a territory of French Equatorial Africa in 1910; became an independent republic in 1960; a parliamentary monarchy (1976–79); consists of a huge plateau, mostly savanna, with dense forests in the south; drained chiefly by the Shari and Ubangi Rivers. Languages: French and Sangho. Religion: Christian and animist. Currency: franc. Capital: Bangui. Pop.: 3 445 000 (1999 est.). Area: 622 577 sq. km (240 376 sq. miles). Former names: (until 1958) **Ubangi-Shari**; (1976-79) **Central African Empire**. French name: **République Centrafricaine** (repyblik sɑ̃trafrikɛn).

Central America ★ *n* an isthmus joining the continents of North and South America, extending from the S border of Mexico to the NW border of Colombia and consisting of Belize, Guatemala, Honduras, El Salvador, Nicaragua, Costa Rica, and Panama. Area: about 518 000 sq. km (200 000 sq. miles).
▸ **Central American** *adj*

central bank *n* a national bank that does business mainly with a government and with other banks: it regulates the volume of credit.

central heating *n* a system for heating the rooms of a building by means of radiators or air vents connected to a central source of heat.

Central India Agency ★ *n* a former group of 89 states in India, under the supervision of a British political agent until 1947: most important were Indore, Bhopal, and Rewa.

centralism ('sɛntrəˌlɪzəm) *n* the principle or act of bringing something under central control.
▸ **'centralist** *n, adj*

centralize *or* **centralise** ('sɛntrəˌlaɪz) *vb* **centralizes, centralizing, centralized** *or* **centralises, centralising, centralised**. **1** to draw or move (something) to or towards a centre. **2** to bring or come under central, esp. governmental, control.
▸ **ˌcentraliˈzation** *or* **ˌcentraliˈsation** *n*

Central Karoo ★ (kə'ruː) *n* an arid plateau of S central South Africa, separated from the Little Karoo to the southwest by the Swartberg range. Average height: 750 m (2500 ft).

central limit theorem *n Statistics*. the fundamental result that the sum of independent identically distributed random variables with finite variance approaches a normally distributed random variable as their number increases.

central locking *n* a system by which all the doors of a motor vehicle can be locked simultaneously.

central nervous system *n* the mass of nerve tissue that controls and coordinates the activities of an animal. In vertebrates it consists of the brain and spinal cord.

central processing unit *n* the part of a computer that performs logical and arithmetical operations on the data. Abbrev.: **CPU**.

Central Region ★ *n* a former local government region in central Scotland, replaced in 1996 by the council areas of Stirling, Falkirk, and Clackmannanshire.

central reserve *or* **reservation** *n Brit. & Austral*. the strip, often covered with grass, that separates the two sides of a motorway or dual carriageway.

central tendency *n Statistics*. the tendency of the values of a random variable to cluster around the mean, median, and mode.

centre *or US* **center** ('sɛntə) *n* **1** *Geom*. **1a** the midpoint of any line or figure, esp. the point within a circle or sphere that is equidistant from any point on the circumference or surface. **1b** the point within a body through which a specified force may be considered to act, such as the centre of gravity. **2** the point, axis, or pivot about which a body rotates. **3** a point, area, or part that is approximately in the middle of a larger area or volume. **4** a place at which some specified activity is concentrated: *a shopping centre*. **5** a person or thing that is a focus of interest. **6** a place of activity or influence: *a centre of power*. **7** a person, group, or thing in the middle. **8** (*usually cap.*) *Politics*. a political party or group favouring moderation. **9** a bar with a conical point upon which a workpiece or part may be turned or ground. **10** *Football, hockey, etc*. **10a** a player who plays in the middle of the forward line. **10b** an instance of passing the ball from a wing to the middle of the field, etc. ◆ *vb* **centres, centring, centred** *or US* **centers, centering, centered**. **11** to move towards, mark, put, or be at a centre. **12** (*tr*) to focus or bring together: *to centre one's thoughts*. **13** (*intr*; often foll. by *on*) to have as a main theme: *the novel centred on crime*. **14** (*intr*; foll. by *on* or *round*) to have as a centre. **15** (*tr*) *Football, hockey, etc*. to pass (the ball) into the middle of the field or court. ORIG C14: from L *centrum* the stationary point of a compass, from Gk *kentron* needle, from *kentein* to prick

Centre ★ ('sɛntə) *n* **the**. the sparsely inhabited central region of Australia. Also called: **the Red Centre**.

centre bit *n* a drilling bit with a central point and two side cutters.

centreboard ('sɛntəˌbɔːd) *n* a supplementary keel for a sailing vessel.

centrefold *or US* **centerfold** ('sɛntəˌfəʊld) *n* **1** a large coloured illustration folded so that it forms the central spread of a magazine. **2a** a photograph of a nude or nearly nude woman (or man) in a magazine on such a spread. **2b** the subject of such a photograph.

centre forward *n Soccer, hockey, etc*. the central forward in the attack.

centre half *or* **centre back** *n Soccer*. a defender who plays in the middle of the defence.

centre of gravity *n* the point through which the resultant of the gravitational forces on a body always acts.

centre pass *n Hockey*. a push or hit made in any direction to start the game or restart the game after a goal has been scored.

centrepiece ('sɛntəˌpiːs) *n* an object used as the centre of something, esp. for decoration.

centre spread *n* **1** the pair of two facing pages in the middle of a magazine, newspaper, etc. **2a** a photograph of a nude or nearly nude woman (or man) in a magazine on such pages. **2b** the subject of such a photograph.

centri- *combining form.* a variant of **centro-**.

centric ('sɛntrɪk) *or* **centrical** *adj* **1** being central or having a centre. **2** relating to a nerve centre.
▸ **centricity** (sɛn'trɪsɪtɪ) *n*

-centric *suffix forming adjectives.* having a centre as specified: *heliocentric.* ORIG abstracted from ECCENTRIC, CONCENTRIC, etc.

centrifugal (sɛn'trɪfjʊgᵊl, 'sɛntrɪˌfjuːgᵊl) *adj* **1** acting, moving, or tending to move away from a centre. Cf. **centripetal. 2** of, concerned with, or operated by centrifugal force: *centrifugal pump.* ORIG C18: from NL, from CENTRI- + L *fugere* to flee
▸ **cen'trifugally** *adv*

centrifugal force *n* a fictitious force that can be thought of as acting outwards on any body that rotates or moves along a curved path.

centrifuge ('sɛntrɪˌfjuːdʒ) *n* **1** any of various rotating machines that separate liquids from solids or other liquids by the action of centrifugal force. **2** any of various rotating devices for subjecting human beings or animals to varying accelerations. ◆ *vb* **centrifuges, centrifuging, centrifuged. 3** (*tr*) to subject to the action of a centrifuge.
▸ **centrifugation** (ˌsɛntrɪfjʊ'geɪʃən) *n*

centring ('sɛntrɪŋ) *or US* **centering** ('sɛntərɪŋ) *n* a temporary structure, esp. one made of timber, used to support an arch during construction.

centripetal (sɛn'trɪpɪtᵊl, 'sɛntrɪˌpiːtᵊl) *adj* **1** acting, moving, or tending to move towards a centre. Cf. **centrifugal. 2** of, concerned with, or operated by centripetal force. ORIG C17: from NL *centripetus* seeking the centre
▸ **cen'tripetally** *adv*

centripetal force *n* a force that acts inwards on any body that rotates or moves along a curved path.

centrist ('sɛntrɪst) *n* a person holding moderate political views.
▸ **'centrism** *n*

centro-, centri-, *or before a vowel* **centr-** *combining form.* denoting a centre: *centrosome; centrist.* ORIG from Gk *kentron* CENTRE

centrosome ('sɛntrəˌsəʊm) *n* a small protoplasmic body found near the cell nucleus.

centuplicate *vb* (sɛn'tjuːplɪˌkeɪt), **centuplicates, centuplicating, centuplicated. 1** (*tr*) to increase 100 times. ◆ *adj* (sɛn'tjuːplɪkɪt). **2** increased a hundredfold. ◆ *n* (sɛn'tjuːplɪkɪt). **3** one hundredfold. ◆ Also **centuple** ('sɛntjʊpᵊl). ORIG C17: from LL, from *centuplex* hundredfold, from L *centum* hundred + *-plex* -fold

centurion (sɛn'tjʊərɪən) *n* the officer commanding a Roman century. ORIG C14: from L *centuriō*, from *centuria* CENTURY

century ('sɛntʃərɪ) *n, pl* **centuries. 1** a period of 100 years. **2** one of the successive periods of 100 years dated before or after an epoch or event, esp. the birth of Christ. **3** a score or grouping of 100: *to score a century in cricket.* **4** (in ancient Rome) a unit of foot soldiers, originally consisting of 100 men. **5** (in ancient Rome) a division of the people for purposes of voting. ORIG C16: from L *centuria*, from *centum* hundred

cep (sɛp) *n* an edible woodland fungus with a brown shining cap and a rich nutty flavour. ORIG C19: from F, from Gascon dialect *cep*, from L *cippus* stake

cephalic (sɪ'fælɪk) *adj* **1** of or relating to the head. **2** situated in, on, or near the head.

-cephalic *or* **-cephalous** *adj combining form.* indicating skull or head; -headed: *brachycephalic.* ORIG from Gk *-kephalos*
▸ **-cephaly** *or* **-cephalism** *n combining form*

cephalic index *n* the ratio of the greatest width of the human head to its greatest length, multiplied by 100.

cephalo- *or before a vowel* **cephal-** *combining form.* indicating the head: *cephalopod.* ORIG via L from Gk, from *kephalē* head

Cephalonia ★ (ˌsɛfə'ləʊnɪə) *n* a mountainous island in the Ionian Sea, the largest of the Ionian Islands, off the W coast of Greece. Pop.: 32 474 (1991). Area: 935 sq. km (365 sq. miles). Modern Greek name: **Kephallinía.**

cephalopod ('sɛfələˌpɒd) *n* any of various marine molluscs, characterized by well-developed head and eyes and a ring of sucker-bearing tentacles, including the octopuses, squids, and cuttlefish.
▸ **ˌcepha'lopodan** *adj, n*

cephalothorax (ˌsɛfələʊ'θɔːræks) *n, pl* **cephalothoraxes** *or* **cephalothoraces** (-rəˌsiːz). the anterior part of many crustaceans and some other arthropods consisting of a united head and thorax.

-cephalus *n combining form.* denoting a cephalic abnormality: *hydrocephalus.* ORIG NL *-cephalus*; see -CEPHALIC

Cepheid variable ('siːfɪɪd) *n Astron.* any of a class of variable stars with regular cycles of variations in luminosity, which are used for measuring distances.

Cepheus ★ ('siːfjuːs) *n Greek myth.* a king of Ethiopia, father of Andromeda and husband of Cassiopeia.

Ceram ★ (sɪ'ræm) *n* a variant spelling of **Seram.**

ceramic (sɪ'ræmɪk) *n* **1** a hard brittle material made by firing clay and similar substances. **2** an object made from such a material. ◆ *adj* **3** of or made from a ceramic. **4** of or relating to ceramics: *ceramic arts.* ORIG C19: from Gk, from *keramos* potter's clay

ceramic hob *n* (on an electric cooker) a flat ceramic cooking surface having heating elements fitted on the underside.

ceramic oxide *n* a compound of oxygen with nonorganic material: recently discovered to act as a high-temperature superconductor.

ceramics (sɪ'ræmɪks) *n* (*functioning as sing*) the art and techniques of producing articles of clay, porcelain, etc.
▸ **ceramist** ('sɛrəmɪst) *n*

ceramide ('sɛrəˌmaɪd) *n* any of a class of biologically important compounds used as moisturizers in skin-care preparations.

Cerberus ★ ('sɜːbərəs) *n* **1** *Greek myth.* a dog, usually represented as having three heads, that guarded the entrance to Hades. **2 a sop to Cerberus.** a bribe or something given to propitiate a potential source of danger or problems.
▸ **Cerberean** (sə'bɪərɪən) *adj*

cere (sɪə) *n* a soft waxy swelling, containing the nostrils, at the base of the upper beak, as in the parrot. ORIG C15: from OF *cire* wax, from L *cēra*

cereal ('sɪərɪəl) *n* **1** any grass that produces an edible grain, such as oat, wheat, rice, maize, and millet. **2** the grain produced by such a plant. **3** any food made from this grain, esp. breakfast food. **4** (*modifier*) of or relating to any of these plants or their products. ORIG C19: from L *cereālis* concerning agriculture

cerebellum (ˌsɛrɪ'bɛləm) *n, pl* **cerebellums** *or* **cerebella** (-lə). one of the major divisions of the vertebrate brain whose function is coordination of voluntary movements. ORIG C16: from L, dim. of CEREBRUM
▸ **ˌcere'bellar** *adj*

cerebral ('sɛrɪbrəl; *US also* sə'riːbrəl) *adj* **1** of or relating to the cerebrum or to the entire brain. **2** involving intelligence rather than emotions or instinct. **3** *Phonetics.* another word for **cacuminal.**
▸ **'cerebrally** *adv*

cerebral haemorrhage *n* bleeding from an artery in the brain, which in severe cases causes a stroke.

cerebral palsy *n* a nonprogressive impairment of muscular function and weakness of the limbs, caused by lack of oxygen to the brain immediately after birth, brain injury during birth, or viral infection.

cerebrate ('sɛrɪˌbreɪt) *vb* **cerebrates, cerebrating, cerebrated.** (*intr*) *Usually facetious.* to use the mind; think; ponder; consider.
▸ **ˌcere'bration** *n*

cerebro- *or before a vowel* **cerebr-** *combining form.* indicating the brain: *cerebrospinal.* ORIG from CEREBRUM

cerebrospinal (ˌsɛrɪbrəʊˈspaɪnᵊl) *adj* of or relating to the brain and spinal cord: *cerebrospinal fluid.*

cerebrovascular (ˌsɛrɪbrəʊˈvæskjʊlə) *adj* of or relating to the blood vessels and the blood supply of the brain.

cerebrum (ˈsɛrɪbrəm) *n, pl* **cerebrums** *or* **cerebra** (-brə). **1** the anterior portion of the brain of vertebrates, consisting of two lateral hemispheres: the dominant part of the brain in man, associated with intellectual function, emotion, and personality. **2** the brain considered as a whole. ORIG C17: from L: the brain
► ˈ**cerebric** *adj*

cerecloth (ˈsɪəˌklɒθ) *n* waxed waterproof cloth of a kind formerly used as a shroud. ORIG C15: from earlier *cered cloth,* from L *cērāre* to wax

Ceredigion ★ (ˌkɛrəˈdɪgjᵊn) *n* a county of W Wales, created in 1996: corresponds to the historic county of Cardiganshire, which ceased to have an administrative function in 1974. Administrative centre: Aberaeron. Pop.: 63 700 (1996 est.). Area: 1793 sq. km (692 sq. miles).

cerement (ˈsɪəmənt) *n* **1** cerecloth. **2** any burial clothes. ORIG C17: from F, from *cirer* to wax

ceremonial (ˌsɛrɪˈməʊnɪəl) *adj* **1** involving or relating to ceremony or ritual. ◆ *n* **2** the observance of formality, esp. in etiquette. **3** a plan for formal observances; ritual. **4** *Christianity.* **4a** the prescribed order of rites and ceremonies. **4b** a book containing this.
► ˌ**cereˈmonialism** *n* ► ˌ**cereˈmonialist** *n* ► ˌ**cereˈmonially** *adv*

ceremonious (ˌsɛrɪˈməʊnɪəs) *adj* **1** especially or excessively polite or formal. **2** involving formalities.
► ˌ**cereˈmoniously** *adv*

ceremony (ˈsɛrɪmənɪ) *n, pl* **ceremonies. 1** a formal act or ritual, often set by custom or tradition, performed in observation of an event or anniversary. **2** a religious rite or series of rites. **3** a courteous gesture or act: *the ceremony of toasting the Queen.* **4** ceremonial observances or gestures collectively. **5 stand on ceremony.** to insist on or act with excessive formality. ORIG C14: from Med. L, from L *caerimōnia* what is sacred

Cerenkov ★ (*Russian* tʃɪˈrjenkəf) *n* See (Pavel Alekseyevich) **Cherenkov.**

Ceres ★ (ˈsɪəriːz) *n* the Roman goddess of agriculture. Greek counterpart: **Demeter.**

cerise (səˈriːz, -ˈriːs) *n, adj* (of) a moderate to dark red colour. ORIG C19: from F: CHERRY

cerium (ˈsɪərɪəm) *n* a malleable ductile steel-grey element of the lanthanide series of metals, used in lighter flints. Symbol: Ce; atomic no.: 58; atomic wt.: 140.12. ORIG C19: NL, from *Ceres* (the asteroid) + -IUM

CERN (sɜːn) *n acronym for* Conseil Européen pour la Recherche Nucléaire; an organization of European states with a centre in Geneva, for research in high-energy particle physics, now called the European Laboratory for Particle Physics.

Cernăuţi ★ (tʃernəˈutsj) *n* the Romanian name for **Chernovtsy.**

Cernuda ★ (*Spanish* θɛrˈnuða) *n* **Luis** (lwiʃ). 1902–63, Spanish poet, noted for his *Reality and Desire* (1936–64).

cerography (sɪəˈrɒgrəfɪ) *n* the art of engraving on a waxed plate on which a printing surface is created by electrotyping.

ceroplastic (ˌsɪərəʊˈplæstɪk) *adj* **1** relating to wax modelling. **2** modelled in wax.

Cerro de Pasco ★ (*Spanish* ˈθɛrrɔ ðe ˈpasko) *n* a town in central Peru, in the Andes: one of the highest towns in the world, 4400 m (14 436 ft) above sea level; mining centre. Pop.: 62 749 (1993).

cert (sɜːt) *n Inf.* something that is a certainty, esp. a horse that is certain to win a race.

cert. *abbrev. for:* **1** certificate. **2** certification. **3** certified.

certain (ˈsɜːtᵊn) *adj* **1** (*postpositive*) positive and confident about the truth of something; convinced: *I am certain that he wrote a book.* **2** (*usually postpositive*) definitely known: *it is certain that they were on the bus.* **3** (*usually postpositive*) sure; bound: *he was certain to fail.* **4** fixed: *the date is already certain for the invasion.* **5** reliable: *his judgment is certain.* **6** moderate or minimum: *to a certain extent.* **7 for certain.** without a doubt. ◆ *determiner* **8a** known but not specified or named: *certain people.* **8b** (*as pron; functioning as pl*): *certain of the members have not paid.* **9** named but not known: *he had written to a certain Mrs Smith.* ORIG C13: from OF, from L *certus* sure, from *cernere* to decide

certainly (ˈsɜːtᵊnlɪ) *adv* **1** without doubt: *he certainly rides very well.* ◆ *sentence substitute.* **2** by all means; definitely.

certainty (ˈsɜːtᵊntɪ) *n, pl* **certainties. 1** the condition of being certain. **2** something established as inevitable. **3 for a certainty.** without doubt.

CertEd (in Britain) *abbrev. for* Certificate in Education.

certes (ˈsɜːtɪz) *adv Arch.* with certainty; truly. ORIG C13: from OF, ult. from L *certus* CERTAIN

certificate *n* (səˈtɪfɪkɪt). **1** an official document attesting the truth of the facts stated, as of birth, death, completion of an academic course, ownership of shares, etc. ◆ *vb* (səˈtɪfɪˌkeɪt), **certificates, certificating, certificated. 2** (*tr*) to authorize by or present with an official document. ORIG C15: from OF, from *certifier* to CERTIFY
► **cerˈtificatory** *adj*

Certificate of Secondary Education *n* the full name for **CSE.**

certification (ˌsɜːtɪfɪˈkeɪʃən) *n* **1** the act of certifying or state of being certified. **2** *Law.* a document attesting the truth of a fact or statement.

certified (ˈsɜːtɪˌfaɪd) *adj* **1** holding or guaranteed by a certificate. **2** endorsed or guaranteed: *a certified cheque.* **3** (of a person) declared legally insane.

certified accountant *n* (in Britain) a member of the Chartered Association of Certified Accountants, who is authorized to audit company accounts. Cf. **chartered accountant.**

certify (ˈsɜːtɪˌfaɪ) *vb* **certifies, certifying, certified. 1** to confirm or attest (to), usually in writing. **2** (*tr*) to endorse or guarantee that certain required standards have been met. **3** to give reliable information or assurances: *he certified that it was Walter's handwriting.* **4** (*tr*) to declare legally insane. ORIG C14: from OF, from Med. L, from L *certus* CERTAIN + *facere* to make
► ˈ**certiˌfiable** *adj*

certiorari (ˌsɜːtɪɔːˈreəraɪ) *n Law.* an order of a superior court directing that a record of proceedings in a lower court be sent up for review. ORIG C15: from legal L: to be informed

certitude (ˈsɜːtɪˌtjuːd) *n* confidence; certainty. ORIG C15: from Church L *certitūdō,* from L *certus* CERTAIN

cerulean (sɪˈruːlɪən) *n, adj* (of) a deep blue colour. ORIG C17: from L *caeruleus,* prob. from *caelum* sky

cerumen (sɪˈruːmɛn) *n* the soft brownish-yellow wax secreted by glands in the external ear. Nontechnical name: **earwax.** ORIG C18: from NL, from L *cēra* wax + ALBUMEN
► **ceˈruminous** *adj*

Cervantes ★ (səˈvæntiːz; *Spanish* θɛrˈβantes) *n* **Miguel de** (miˈɣel ðe), full surname *Cervantes Saavedra.* 1547–1616, Spanish poet and writer, noted for his romance *Don Quixote* (1605).

cervelat (ˈsɜːvəˌlæt, -ˌlɑː) *n* a smoked sausage made from pork and beef. ORIG C17: via obs. F from It. *cervellata*

cervical (səˈvaɪkᵊl, ˈsɜːvɪkᵊl) *adj* of or relating to the neck or cervix. ORIG C17: from NL, from L *cervīx* neck

cervical smear *n Med.* a smear taken from the neck (cervix) of the uterus for detection of cancer. See also **Pap test** *or* **smear.**

Cervin ★ (sɛrvɛ̃) *n* **Mont.** the French name for the **Matterhorn.**

cervine (ˈsɜːvaɪn) *adj* resembling or relating to a deer. ORIG C19: from L *cervīnus,* from *cervus* a deer

cervix (ˈsɜːvɪks) *n, pl* **cervixes** *or* **cervices** (səˈvaɪsiːz). **1** the technical name for **neck. 2** any necklike part, esp. the lower part of the uterus that extends into the vagina. ORIG C18: from L

cesium ('siːzɪəm) *n* the usual US spelling of **caesium.**

Československo ★ ('tʃɛskɔslɔvɛnskɔ) *n* the Czech name for **Czechoslovakia.**

cess[1] (sɛs) *n Brit.* any of several special taxes, such as a land tax in Scotland. ORIG C16: short for ASSESSMENT

cess[2] (sɛs) *n* an Irish slang word for **luck** (esp. in **bad cess to you!**). ORIG C19: prob. from CESS[1]

cessation (sɛ'seɪʃən) *n* a ceasing or stopping; pause: *temporary cessation of hostilities.* ORIG C14: from L, from *cessāre* to be idle, from *cēdere* to yield

cession ('sɛʃən) *n* **1** the act of ceding. **2** something that is ceded, esp. land or territory. ORIG C14: from L *cessiō,* from *cēdere* to yield

cessionary ('sɛʃənərɪ) *n, pl* **cessionaries.** *Law.* a person to whom something is transferred.

cesspool ('sɛsˌpuːl) *or* **cesspit** ('sɛsˌpɪt) *n* **1** Also called: **sink, sump.** a covered cistern, etc., for collecting and storing sewage or waste water. **2** a filthy or corrupt place: *a cesspool of iniquity.* ORIG C17: ? changed from earlier *cesperalle,* from OF *souspirail* vent, air, from *soupirer* to sigh

cestoid ('sɛstɔɪd) *adj* (esp. of tapeworms and similar animals) ribbon-like in form.

cesura (sɪ'zjʊərə) *n, pl* **cesuras** *or* **cesurae** (-riː). *Prosody.* a variant spelling of **caesura.**

cetacean (sɪ'teɪʃən) *adj also* **cetaceous. 1** of or belonging to an order of aquatic placental mammals having no hind limbs and a blowhole for breathing: includes toothed whales (dolphins, porpoises, etc.) and whalebone whales (rorquals, etc.). ◆ *n* **2** a whale. ORIG C19: from NL, ult. from L *cētus* whale, from Gk *kētos*

cetane ('siːteɪn) *n* a colourless insoluble liquid hydrocarbon used in the determination of the cetane number of diesel fuel. Also called: **hexadecane.** ORIG C19: from L *cētus* whale + -ANE

cetane number *n* a measure of the quality of a diesel fuel expressed as the percentage of cetane. Also called: **cetane rating.** Cf. **octane number.**

Cetatea Albă ★ (tʃe'tatea 'albə) *n* the Romanian name for **Byelgorod-Dnestrovski.**

Cetinje ★ (*Serbo-Croat* 'tsɛtinjɛ) *n* a city in S Yugoslavia, in SW Montenegro: former capital of Montenegro (until 1945); palace and fortified monastery, residences of Montenegrin prince-bishops. Pop.: 15 924 (1991).

cetrimide ('sɛtrɪˌmaɪd) *n* an ammonium compound used as a detergent and, having powerful antiseptic properties, for sterilizing surgical instruments, cleaning wounds, etc.

Cetshwayo *or* **Cetewayo** ★ (*Zulu* kɛ'tʃwɑːjɒ) *n* ?1826–84, king of the Zulus (1873–79): defeated the British at Isandhlwana (1879) but was overwhelmed at Ulundi (1879); and reinstated as ruler of part of Zululand (1883).

Ceuta ★ (*Spanish* 'θeuta) *n* an enclave in Morocco on the Strait of Gibraltar, consisting of a port and military station: held by Spain since 1580. Pop.: 68 867 (1994 est.).

Cévennes ★ (*French* sevɛn) *n* a mountain range in S central France, on the SE edge of the Massif Central. Highest peak: 1754 m (5755 ft).

Ceylon ★ (sɪ'lɒn) *n* **1** the former name (until 1972) of **Sri Lanka. 2** an island in the Indian Ocean, off the SE coast of India: consists politically of the republic of Sri Lanka. Area: 64 644 sq. km (24 959 sq. miles).
▸ **Ceylonese** (ˌsɛlə'niːz, ˌsiːlə-) *adj*

Cézanne ★ (*French* sezan) *n* **Paul** (pɔl). 1839–1906, French postimpressionist painter, who was a major influence on modern art, esp. cubism, in stressing the structural elements latent in nature, such as the sphere and the cone.

Cf *the chemical symbol for* californium.

CF *abbrev. for* Canadian Forces.

cf. *abbrev. for:* **1** (in bookbinding, etc.) calfskin. **2** compare. ORIG L: *confer*

CFB *abbrev. for* Canadian Forces Base.

CFC *abbrev. for* chlorofluorocarbon.

CFL *abbrev. for* Canadian Football League.

CFS *abbrev. for* chronic fatigue syndrome.

cg *abbrev. for* centigram.

CGBR *abbrev. for* Central Government Borrowing Requirement.

cgs units *pl n* a metric system of units based on the centimetre, gram, and second. For scientific and technical purposes these units have been replaced by SI units.

CGT *abbrev. for* Capital Gains Tax.

CH 1 *abbrev. for* Companion of Honour (a Brit. title). **2** *international car registration for* Switzerland. ORIG from F *Confédération Helvétique*

ch. *abbrev. for:* **1** chain (unit of measure). **2** chapter. **3** *Chess.* check. **4** chief. **5** church.

Chablis ('ʃæblɪ) *n* (*sometimes not cap.*) a dry white wine made around Chablis, France.

Chabrier ★ ('ʃæbrɪeɪ, *French* ʃabrie) *n* (**Alexis**) **Emmanuel** (emanɥɛl). 1841–94, French composer; noted for the orchestral rhapsody *España* (1883).

Chabrol ★ (*French* ʃabrɔl) *n* **Claude** (klod). born 1930, French film director, whose films include *Les Biches* (1968) and *Au couleur du mensonge* (1999).

cha-cha-cha (ˌtʃɑːtʃɑː'tʃɑː) *or* **cha-cha** *n* **1** a modern ballroom dance from Latin America with small steps and swaying hip movements. **2** a piece of music composed for this dance. ◆ *vb* (*intr*) **3** to perform this dance. ORIG C20: from American (Cuban) Sp.

Chaco ★ (*Spanish* 'tʃako) *n* See **Gran Chaco.**

chaconne (ʃə'kɒn) *n* **1** a musical form consisting of a set of continuous variations upon a ground bass. **2** *Arch.* a dance in slow triple time probably originating in Spain. ORIG C17: from F, from Sp. *chacona*

Chad ★ (tʃæd) *n* **1** a republic in N central Africa: made a territory of French Equatorial Africa in 1910; became independent in 1960; contains much desert and the Tibesti Mountains, with Lake Chad in the west; produces chiefly cotton and livestock; has suffered intermittent civil war from 1963 and prolonged drought. Official languages: French and Arabic. Religion: chiefly Muslim, also animist and Christian. Currency: franc. Capital: Ndjamena. Pop.: 7 557 000 (1999 est.). Area: 1 284 000 sq. km (495 750 sq. miles). French name: **Tchad. 2 Lake.** a lake in N central Africa: fed chiefly by the Shari River, it has no apparent outlet. Area: 10 000 to 26 000 sq. km (4000 to 10 000 sq. miles), varying seasonally.

Chadwick ★ ('tʃædwɪk) *n* **1** Sir **Edwin.** 1800–90, British social reformer. **2** Sir **James.** 1891–1974, British physicist: discovered the neutron (1932): Nobel prize for physics 1935. **3 Lynn** (**Russell**). born 1914, British sculptor in metal.

chafe (tʃeɪf) *vb* **chafes, chafing, chafed. 1** to make or become sore or worn by rubbing. **2** (*tr*) to warm (the hands, etc.) by rubbing. **3** to irritate or be irritated or impatient. **4** (*intr;* often foll. by *on, against,* etc.) to rub. ◆ *n* **5** a soreness or irritation caused by friction. ORIG C14: from OF *chaufer* to warm, ult. from L, from *calēre* to be warm + *facere* to make

chafer ('tʃeɪfə) *n* any of various beetles, such as the cockchafer. ORIG OE *ceafor*

chaff[1] (tʃɑːf) *n* **1** the mass of husks, etc., separated from the seeds during threshing. **2** finely cut straw and hay used to feed cattle. **3** something of little worth; rubbish: *to separate the wheat from the chaff.* **4** thin strips of metallic foil released into the earth's atmosphere to deflect radar signals and prevent detection. ORIG OE *ceaf*
▸ **'chaffy** *adj*

chaff[2] (tʃɑːf) *n* **1** light-hearted teasing or joking; banter. ◆ *vb* **2** to tease good-naturedly. ORIG C19: prob. slang var. of CHAFE
▸ **'chaffer** *n*

chaffer ('tʃæfə) *vb* **1** (*intr*) to haggle or bargain. **2** to chatter, talk, or say idly. ◆ *n* **3** haggling or bargaining. ORIG C13 *chaffare,* from *chep* bargain + *fare* journey
▸ **'chafferer** *n*

chaffinch ('tʃæfɪntʃ) *n* a European finch with black-and-white wings and, in the male, a reddish body and blue-grey head. ORIG OE *ceaffinc,* from *ceaf* CHAFF[1] + *finc* FINCH

chafing dish *n* a vessel with a heating apparatus beneath it, for cooking or keeping food warm at the table.

Chagall ★ (*French* ʃagal) *n* **Marc** (mark). 1887–1985, French painter, born in Russia: his work includes the decorations for the ceiling of the Paris Opera House (1964).

chagrin (ˈʃæɡrɪn) *n* **1** a feeling of annoyance or mortification. ◆ *vb* **2** to embarrass and annoy. ORIG C17: from F *chagrin, chagriner,* from ?

chain (tʃeɪn) *n* **1** a flexible length of metal links, used for confining, connecting, etc., or in jewellery. **2** (*usually pl*) anything that confines or restrains: *the chains of poverty.* **3** (*usually pl*) a set of metal links that fit over the tyre of a motor vehicle to reduce skidding on an icy surface. **4** a series of related or connected facts, events, etc. **5a** a number of establishments such as hotels, shops, etc., having the same owner or management. **5b** (*as modifier*): *a chain store.* **6** Also called: **Gunter's chain.** a unit of length equal to 22 yards. **7** Also called: **engineer's chain.** a unit of length equal to 100 feet. **8** Also called: **nautical chain.** a unit of length equal to 15 feet. **9** *Chem.* two or more atoms or groups bonded together so that the resulting molecule, ion, or radical resembles a chain. **10** *Geog.* a series of natural features, esp. mountain ranges. ◆ *vb* **11** (*tr;* often foll. by *up*) to confine, tie, or make fast with or as if with a chain. ORIG C13: from OF, ult. from L; see CATENA

Chain ★ (tʃeɪn) *n* Sir **Ernst Boris.** 1906–79, British biochemist, born in Germany: purified penicillin for clinical use; shared the Nobel prize for physiology or medicine 1945.

chain gang *n US.* a group of convicted prisoners chained together.

chain letter *n* a letter, often with a request for and promise of money, that is sent to many people who add to or recopy it and send it on.

chain mail *n* **a** another term for **mail**[2] (sense 1). **b** (*as modifier*): *a chain-mail hood.*

chain printer *n* a line printer in which the type is on a continuous chain.

chain reaction *n* **1** a process in which a neutron colliding with an atomic nucleus causes fission and the ejection of one or more other neutrons. **2** a chemical reaction in which the product of one step is a reactant in the following step. **3** a series of events, each of which precipitates the next.
▸ **ˌchain-reˈact** *vb* (*intr*)

chain saw *n* a motor-driven saw in which the cutting teeth form links in a continuous chain.

chain-smoke *vb* **chain-smokes, chain-smoking, chain-smoked.** to smoke (cigarettes, etc.) continually, esp. lighting one from the preceding one.
▸ **chain smoker** *n*

chain stitch *n* **1** a looped embroidery stitch resembling the links of a chain. ◆ *vb* **chain-stitch. 2** to sew (something) with this stitch.

chainwheel (ˈtʃeɪnˌwiːl) *n* (esp. on a bicycle) a toothed wheel that transmits drive via the chain.

chair (tʃɛə) *n* **1** a seat with a back on which one person sits, typically having four legs and often having arms. **2** an official position of authority. **3** the chairman of a debate or meeting: *the speaker addressed the chair.* **4** a professorship. **5** *Railways.* an iron or steel cradle bolted to a sleeper in which the rail is locked. **6** short for **sedan chair. 7 take the chair.** to preside as chairman for a meeting, etc. **8 the chair.** *Inf.* the electric chair. ◆ *vb* (*tr*) **9** to preside over (a meeting). **10** *Brit.* to carry aloft in a sitting position after a triumph. **11** to provide with a chair of office. **12** to install in a chair. ORIG C13: from OF, from L *cathedra,* from Gk *kathedra,* from *kata-* down + *hedra* seat

chairlift (ˈtʃɛəˌlɪft) *n* a series of chairs suspended from a power-driven cable for conveying people, esp. skiers, up a mountain.

chairman (ˈtʃɛəmən) *n, pl* **chairmen.** a person who presides over a company's board of directors, a committee, a debate, etc. Also: **chair, chairperson,** *or* (*fem*) **chairwoman.**

> **USAGE NOTE** The general trend of nonsexist language is to find a term which can apply to both sexes equally, as in the use of *actor* to refer to both men and women. Since *chairman* can seem inappropriate when applied to a woman, while *chairwoman* specifies gender, the terms *chair* and *chairperson* are generally preferred.

chaise (ʃeɪz) *n* **1** a light open horse-drawn carriage, esp. one with two wheels. **2** short for **post chaise** and **chaise longue.** ORIG C18: from F, var. of OF *chaiere* CHAIR

chaise longue (ˈʃeɪz ˈlɒŋ) *n, pl* **chaise longues** *or* **chaises longues** (ˈʃeɪz ˈlɒŋ). a long low chair with a back and single armrest. ORIG C19: from F: long chair

Chaka ★ (ˈʃaka) *n* a variant spelling of **Shaka.**

chakra (ˈtʃækrə, ˈtʃʌkrə) *n* (in yoga) any of the seven major energy centres in the human body. ORIG C19: from Sansk. *cakra* wheel, circle

chalaza (kəˈleɪzə) *n, pl* **chalazas** *or* **chalazae** (-ziː). one of a pair of spiral threads holding the yolk of a bird's egg in position. ORIG C18: NL, from Gk: hailstone

chalcedony (kælˈsɛdənɪ) *n, pl* **chalcedonies.** a form of quartz with crystals arranged in parallel fibres: a gemstone. ORIG C15: from LL, from Gk *khalkēdōn* a precious stone, ? after *Khalkēdōn* Chalcedon, town in Asia Minor
▸ **chalcedonic** (ˌkælsɪˈdɒnɪk) *adj*

Chalcidice ★ (kælˈsɪdɪsɪ) *n* a peninsula of N central Greece, in Macedonia Central, ending in the three promontories of Kassandra, Sithonia, and Akti. Area: 2945 sq. km (1149 sq. miles). Modern Greek name: **Khalkidíki.**

Chalcis ★ (ˈkælsɪs) *n* a city in SE Greece, at the narrowest point of the Euripus strait: important since the 7th century B.C., founding many colonies in ancient times. Pop.: 47 600 (1995 est.). Modern Greek name: **Khalkís.** Medieval English name: **Negropont.**

chalcogen (ˈkælkəˌdʒɛn) *n* any of the elements oxygen, sulphur, selenium, tellurium, or polonium, of group 6A of the periodic table. ORIG C20: from CHALCO(PYRITE) + -GEN

chalcolithic (ˌkælkəˈlɪθɪk) *adj Archaeol.* of or relating to the period in which both stone and bronze tools were used. ORIG C19: from Gk *khalkos* copper + *lithos* stone

chalcopyrite (ˌkælkəˈpaɪraɪt) *n* a common ore of copper, a crystalline sulphide of copper and iron. Formula: $CuFeS_2$. Also called: **copper pyrites.**

Chaldea *or* **Chaldaea** ★ (kælˈdiːə) *n* **1** an ancient region of Babylonia; the land lying between the Euphrates delta, the Persian Gulf, and the Arabian desert. **2** another name for **Babylonia.**

chaldron (ˈtʃɔːldrən) *n* a unit of capacity equal to 36 bushels. ORIG C17: from OF *chauderon* CAULDRON

chalet (ˈʃæleɪ) *n* **1** a type of wooden house of Swiss origin, with wide projecting eaves. **2** a similar house used as a ski lodge, etc. ORIG C19: from F (Swiss dialect)

Chaliapin ★ (*Russian* ʃaˈljapin) *n* **Fyodor Ivanovich** (ˈfjɔdər iˈvanəvitʃ). 1873–1938, Russian operatic bass.

chalice (ˈtʃælɪs) *n* **1** *Poetic.* a drinking cup; goblet. **2** *Christianity.* a gold or silver cup containing the wine at Mass. **3** a cup-shaped flower. ORIG C13: from OF, from L *calix* cup

chalk (tʃɔːk) *n* **1** a soft fine-grained white sedimentary rock consisting of nearly pure calcium carbonate, containing minute fossil fragments of marine organisms. **2** a piece of chalk, or substance like chalk, often coloured, used for writing and drawing on blackboards. **3 as alike** (*or* **different**) **as chalk and cheese.** *Inf.* totally different in essentials. **4 by a long chalk.** *Brit. inf.* by far. **5 not by a long chalk.** *Brit. inf.* by no means. **6** (*modifier*) made of chalk. ◆ *vb* **7** to draw or mark (something) with chalk. **8** (*tr*) to mark, rub, or whiten with or as with chalk. ORIG OE *cealc,* from L *calx* limestone, from Gk *khalix* pebble
▸ **ˈchalkˌlike** *adj* ▸ **ˈchalky** *adj* ▸ **ˈchalkiness** *n*

chalk out *vb* (*tr, adv*) to outline (a plan, scheme, etc.); sketch.

chalkpit (ˈtʃɔːkˌpɪt) *n* a quarry for chalk.

chalk up *vb (tr, adv) Inf.* **1** to score or register (something). **2** to credit (money) to an account, etc. (esp. in **chalk it up**).

challenge ('tʃælɪndʒ) *vb* **challenges, challenging, challenged.** *(mainly tr)* **1** to invite or summon (someone to do something, esp. to take part in a contest). **2** *(also intr)* to call (something) into question. **3** to make demands on; stimulate: *the job challenges his ingenuity.* **4** to order (a person) to halt and be identified. **5** *Law.* to make formal objection to (a juror or jury). **6** to lay claim to (attention, etc.). **7** to inject (an experimental animal immunized with a test substance) with disease microorganisms to test for immunity to the disease. ◆ *n* **8** a call to engage in a fight, argument, or contest. **9** a questioning of a statement or fact. **10** a demanding or stimulating situation, career, etc. **11** a demand by a sentry, etc., for identification or a password. **12** *Law.* a formal objection to a person selected to serve on a jury or to the whole body of jurors. ORIG C13: from OF *chalenge,* from L *calumnia* CALUMNY
▸ **'challengeable** *adj* ▸ **'challenger** *n* ▸ **'challenging** *adj*

challis ('ʃælɪ, -lɪs) *or* **challie** ('ʃælɪ) *n* a lightweight fabric of wool, cotton, etc., usually with a printed design. ORIG C19: prob. from a surname

Châlons-sur-Marne ★ *(French* ʃalɔ̃syrmarn) *n* a city in NE France, on the River Marne: scene of Attila's defeat by the Romans (451 A.D.). Pop.: 51 530 (1990). Shortened form: **Châlons.**

Chalon-sur-Saône ★ *(French* ʃalɔ̃syrson) *n* an industrial city in E central France, on the Saône River. Pop.: 54 575 (1990). Shortened form: **Chalon.**

chalybeate (kə'lɪbɪɪt) *adj* containing or impregnated with iron salts. ORIG C17: from NL *chalybēātus,* ult. from Gk *khalups* iron

chamber ('tʃeɪmbə) *n* **1** a meeting hall, esp. one used for a legislative or judicial assembly. **2** a reception room in an official residence, palace, etc. **3** *Arch. or poetic.* a room in a private house, esp. a bedroom. **4a** a legislative, judicial, or administrative assembly. **4b** any of the houses of a legislature. **5** an enclosed space; compartment; cavity. **6** an enclosure for a cartridge in the cylinder of a revolver or for a shell in the breech of a cannon. **7** short for **chamber pot. 8** *(modifier)* of, relating to, or suitable for chamber music: *a chamber concert.* **9** *(modifier)* on a small, quasi-domestic scale. ◆ See also **chambers.** ORIG C13: from OF, from LL *camera* room, L: vault, from Gk *kamara*

chamberlain ('tʃeɪmbəlɪn) *n* **1** an officer who manages the household of a king. **2** the steward of a nobleman or landowner. **3** the treasurer of a municipal corporation. ORIG C13: from OF *chamberlayn,* of Frankish origin

Chamberlain ★ ('tʃeɪmbəlɪn) *n* **1** Sir **(Joseph) Austen.** 1863–1937, British Conservative statesman; foreign secretary (1924–29); Nobel peace prize for his negotiation of the Locarno Pact (1925). **2** his father, **Joseph.** 1836–1914, British statesman; originally a Liberal, he resigned in 1886 over Home Rule for Ireland and became leader of the Liberal Unionists. **3** his son, **(Arthur) Neville.** 1869–1940, British Conservative statesman; prime minister (1937–40): the failure of his policy of appeasement towards Germany led to World War II. **4 Owen.** born 1920, US physicist, who discovered the antiproton; shared Nobel prize for physics 1959.

chambermaid ('tʃeɪmbəˌmeɪd) *n* a woman employed to clean bedrooms, esp. in hotels.

chamber music *n* music for performance by a small group of instrumentalists.

chamber of commerce *n (sometimes cap.)* an organization composed mainly of local businessmen to promote, regulate, and protect their interests.

chamber orchestra *n* a small orchestra of about 25 players, used for the authentic performance of baroque and early classical music as well as modern music.

chamber pot *n* a vessel for urine, used in bedrooms.

chambers ('tʃeɪmbəz) *pl n* **1** a judge's room for hearing private cases not taken in open court. **2** (in England) the set of rooms occupied by barristers where clients are interviewed.

Chambéry ★ *(French* ʃɑ̃beri) *n* a city in SE France, in the Alps: skiing centre; former capital of the duchy of Savoy. Pop.: 54 120 (1990).

chambray ('ʃæmbreɪ) *n* a smooth light fabric of cotton, linen, etc., with white weft and a coloured warp. ORIG C19: after CAMBRAI

chameleon (kə'miːlɪən) *n* **1** a lizard of Africa and Madagascar, having long slender legs, a prehensile tail and tongue, and the ability to change colour. **2** a changeable or fickle person. ORIG C14: from L, from Gk *khamaileōn,* from *khamai* on the ground + *leōn* LION
▸ **chameleonic** (kəˌmiːlɪ'ɒnɪk) *adj*

chamfer ('tʃæmfə) *n* **1** a narrow flat surface at the corner of a beam, post, etc. ◆ *vb (tr)* **2** to cut such a surface on (a beam, etc.). ORIG C16: back formation from *chamfering,* from OF, from *chant* edge (see CANT[2]) + *fraindre* to break, from L *frangere*

chamois ('ʃæmɪ; *for senses 1 and 4* 'ʃæmwɑː) *n, pl* **chamois. 1** a sure-footed goat antelope of Europe and SW Asia, having vertical horns with backward-pointing tips. **2** a soft suede leather formerly made from this animal, now obtained from the skins of sheep and goats. **3** Also called: **chamois leather, shammy (leather), chammy (leather).** a piece of such leather or similar material used for polishing, etc. **4a** a greyish-yellow colour. **4b** *(as adj): a chamois stamp.* ◆ *vb (tr)* **5** to dress (leather or skin) like chamois. **6** to polish with a chamois. ORIG C16: from OF, from LL *camox,* from ?

chamomile ('kæməˌmaɪl) *n* a variant spelling of **camomile.**

Chamonix ★ ('ʃæmənɪ; *French* ʃamɔni) *n* a town in SE France, in the Alps at the foot of Mont Blanc: skiing and tourist centre. Pop.: 9255 (latest est.).

champ[1] (tʃæmp) *vb* **1** to munch (food) noisily like a horse. **2** (when *intr,* often foll. by *on, at,* etc.) to bite (something) nervously or impatiently. **3 champ** (*or* **chafe**) **at the bit.** *Inf.* to be impatient to start work, a journey, etc. ◆ *n* **4** the act or noise of champing. ORIG C16: prob. imit.

champ[2] (tʃæmp) *n Inf.* short for **champion.**

champagne (ʃæm'peɪn) *n* **1** *(sometimes cap.)* a white sparkling wine produced around Reims and Épernay, France. **2** (loosely) any effervescent white wine. **3a** a pale tawny colour. **3b** *(as adj): champagne tights.* **4** *(modifier)* denoting a luxurious lifestyle: *a champagne capitalist.* ORIG from *Champagne,* a region of NE France

Champagne-Ardenne ★ (ʃæm'peɪnɑː'dɛn; *French* ʃɑ̃paɲardɛn) *n* a region of NE France: a countship and commercial centre in medieval times; it consists of a great plain, with sheep and dairy farms and many vineyards.

champagne socialist *n* a professed socialist who enjoys an extravagant lifestyle.

Champaigne ★ (ʃæm'peɪn; *French* ʃɑ̃pɛɲ) *n* **Philippe de** (filip də). 1602–74, French painter, born in Brussels.

champers ('ʃæmpəz) *n (functioning as sing) Sl.* champagne.

champerty ('tʃæmpətɪ) *n, pl* **champerties.** *Law.* (formerly) an illegal bargain between a party to litigation and an outsider whereby the latter agrees to pay for the action and thereby share in any proceeds recovered. ORIG C14: from Anglo-F *champartie,* from OF *champart* share of produce, from *champ* field + *part* share

Champigny-sur-Marne ★ *(French* ʃɑ̃piɲisyrmarn) *n* a suburb of Paris, on the River Marne. Pop.: 80 290 (latest est.).

champion ('tʃæmpɪən) *n* **1a** a person, plant, or animal that has defeated all others in a competition: *a chess champion.* **1b** *(as modifier): a champion team; a champion marrow.* **2** a person who defends a person or cause: *champion of the underprivileged.* **3** (formerly) a knight who did battle for another, esp. a king or queen. ◆ *adj* **4** *N English dialect.* excellent. ◆ *adv* **5** *N English dialect.* very well. ◆ *vb (tr)* **6** to support: *we champion the cause of liberty.* ORIG C13: from OF, from LL *campiō,* from L *campus* field

championship ('tʃæmpɪənˌʃɪp) *n* **1** *(sometimes pl)* any of various contests held to determine a champion. **2** the title of being a champion. **3** support for a cause, person, etc.

Champlain[1] ★ (ʃæm'pleɪn) *n* **Lake.** a lake in the northeastern US, between the Green Mountains and the Adirondack Mountains: linked by the **Champlain Canal** to the Hudson River and by the Richelieu River to the St Lawrence; a major communications route in colonial times.

Champlain[2] ★ (ʃæm'pleɪn; *French* ʃɑ̃plɛ̃) *n* **Samuel de** (samɥɛl də). ?1567–1635, French explorer; founder of Quebec (1608) and governor of New France (1633–35).

champlevé *French.* (ʃɑ̃lve) *adj* **1** of a process of enamelling by which grooves are cut into a metal base and filled with enamel colours. ◆ *n* **2** an object enamelled by this process. ORIG C19: from *champ* field (level surface) + *levé* raised

Champollion ★ (*French* ʃɑ̃pɔljɔ̃) *n* **Jean François** (ʒɑ̃ frɑ̃swa). 1790–1832, French Egyptologist, who deciphered the hieroglyphics on the Rosetta stone.

Champs Elysées ★ (ʃɒnz eɪ'liːzeɪ; *French* ʃɑ̃z elize) *n* a major boulevard in Paris, leading from the Arc de Triomphe: site of the Elysées Palace and government offices.

Chanc. *abbrev. for:* **1** Chancellor. **2** Chancery.

chance (tʃɑːns) *n* **1a** the unknown and unpredictable element that causes an event to result in a certain way rather than another, spoken of as a real force. **1b** (*as modifier*): *a chance meeting.* Related adj: **fortuitous. 2** fortune; luck; fate. **3** an opportunity or occasion. **4** a risk; gamble. **5** the extent to which an event is likely to occur; probability. **6** an unpredicted event, esp. a fortunate one. **7 by chance.** accidentally: *he slipped by chance.* **8 on the (off) chance.** acting on the (remote) possibility. ◆ *vb* **chances, chancing, chanced. 9** (*tr*) to risk; hazard. **10** (*intr*) to happen by chance: *I chanced to catch sight of her.* **11 chance on** (*or* **upon**). to come upon by accident. **12 chance one's arm.** to attempt to do something although the chance of success may be slight. ORIG C13: from OF, from *cheoir* to occur, from L *cadere*
▸ **'chanceful** *adj*

chancel ('tʃɑːnsəl) *n* the part of a church containing the altar, sanctuary, and choir. ORIG C14: from OF, from L *cancellī* (pl) lattice

chancellery *or* **chancellory** ('tʃɑːnsələrɪ) *n, pl* **chancelleries** *or* **chancellories. 1** the building or room occupied by a chancellor's office. **2** the position or office of a chancellor. **3** *US.* the office of an embassy or legation. ORIG C14: from Anglo-F *chancellerie*, from OF *chancelier* CHANCELLOR

chancellor ('tʃɑːnsələ) *n* **1** the head of the government in several European countries. **2** *US.* the president of a university. **3** *Brit. & Canad.* the honorary head of a university. Cf. **vice chancellor. 4** *Christianity.* a clergyman acting as the law officer of a bishop. ORIG C11: from Anglo-F *chanceler*, from LL *cancellārius* porter, from L *cancellī* lattice
▸ **'chancellor,ship** *n*

Chancellor of the Exchequer *n Brit.* the cabinet minister responsible for finance.

chance-medley *n Law.* a sudden quarrel in which one party kills another. ORIG C15: from Anglo-F *chance medlee* mixed chance

chancer ('tʃɑːnsə) *n Sl.* an unscrupulous or dishonest opportunist. ORIG C19: from CHANCE + -ER[1]

chancery ('tʃɑːnsərɪ) *n, pl* **chanceries.** (*usually cap.*) **1** Also called: **Chancery Division.** (in England) the Lord Chancellor's court, now a division of the High Court of Justice. **2** Also called: **court of chancery.** (in the US) a court of equity. **3** *Brit.* the political section or offices of an embassy or legation. **4** another name for **chancellery. 5** a court of public records. **6** *Christianity.* a diocesan office under the supervision of a bishop's chancellor. **7 in chancery. 7a** *Law.* (of a suit) pending in a court of equity. **7b** in an awkward situation. ORIG C14: shortened from CHANCELLERY

chancre ('ʃæŋkə) *n Pathol.* a small hard growth, which is the first sign of syphilis. ORIG C16: from F, from L: CANCER
▸ **'chancrous** *adj*

chancroid ('ʃæŋkrɔɪd) *n* **1** a soft venereal ulcer, esp. of the male genitals. ◆ *adj* **2** relating to or resembling a chancroid or chancre.

chancy *or* **chancey** ('tʃɑːnsɪ) *adj* **chancier, chanciest.** *Inf.* uncertain; risky.

chandelier (ˌʃændɪ'lɪə) *n* an ornamental hanging light with branches and holders for several candles or bulbs. ORIG C17: from F: candleholder, from L CANDELABRUM

Chandernagore ★ (ˌtʃʌndənə'gɔː) *n* a port in E India, in S West Bengal on the Hooghly River: a former French settlement (1686–1950). Pop.: 120 378 (1991).

Chandigarh ★ (ˌtʃʌndɪ'gɑː) *n* a city and Union Territory of N India, joint capital of the Punjab and Haryana: modern city planned in the 1950s by Le Corbusier. Pop. (of city): 504 094 (1991); (of union territory): 642 015 (1991). Area (of union territory): 114 sq. km (44 sq. miles).

chandler ('tʃɑːndlə) *n* **1** a dealer in a specified trade or merchandise: *ship's chandler.* **2** a person who makes or sells candles. ORIG C14: from OF *chandelier* one who makes or deals in candles, from *chandelle* CANDLE
▸ **'chandlery** *n*

Chandler ★ ('tʃɑːndlə) *n* **Raymond (Thornton).** 1888–1959, US writer: created Philip Marlowe, an early detective hero.

Chandragupta ★ (ˌtʃʌndrə'guptə) *n* Greek name *Sandracottos.* died ?297 B.C., ruler of N India, who founded the Maurya dynasty (325) and defeated Seleucus (?305).

Chandrasekhar ★ (ˌtʃændrə'siːkə) *n* **Subrahmanyan** (ˌsubrə'mænjən). 1910–95, US astronomer born in Lahore, India (now Pakistan): shared Nobel prize for physics 1983.

Chandrasekhar limit *n Astron.* the upper limit to the mass of a white dwarf, equal to 1.44 solar masses. A star with greater mass will continue to collapse to form a neutron star. ORIG C20: named after S. CHANDRASEKHAR

Chanel ★ (*French* ʃanɛl) *n* **Gabrielle** (gabriɛl), known as *Coco Chanel.* 1883–1971, French couturière and perfumer, who created "the little black dress" and the perfume Chanel No. 5.

Chang ★ (tʃæŋ) *n* another name for the **Yangtze.**

Changan ★ ('tʃæŋ'ɑːn) *n* a former name of **Xi An.**

Changchiakow *or* **Changchiak'ou** ★ ('tʃæŋ'tʃjɑː'kaʊ) *n* a variant transliteration of the Chinese name for **Zhangjiakou.**

Changchow *or* **Ch'ang-chou** ★ ('tʃæŋ'tʃaʊ) *n* a variant transliteration of the Chinese name for **Zhangzhou.**

Changchun *or* **Ch'ang Ch'un** ★ ('tʃæŋ'tʃʊn) *n* a city in NE China, capital of Jilin province: as **Hsinking,** capital of the Japanese state of Manchukuo (1932–45). Pop.: 2 110 000 (1991 est.).

Changde ('tʃæŋ'deɪ), **Changteh,** *or* **Ch'ang-te** ★ *n* a port in SE central China, in N Hunan province, near the mouth of the Yuan River: severely damaged by the Japanese in World War II. Pop.: 301 276 (1990 est.).

change (tʃeɪndʒ) *vb* **changes, changing, changed. 1** to make or become different; alter. **2** (*tr*) to replace with or exchange for another: *to change one's name.* **3** (sometimes foll. by *to* or *into*) to transform or convert or be transformed or converted. **4** to give and receive (something) in return: *to change places.* **5** (*tr*) to give or receive (money) in exchange for the equivalent sum in a smaller denomination or different currency. **6** (*tr*) to remove or replace the coverings of: *to change a baby.* **7** (when *intr*, may be foll. by *into* or *out of*) to put on other clothes. **8** to operate (the gear lever of a motor vehicle): *to change gear.* **9** to alight from (one bus, train, etc.) and board another. ◆ *n* **10** the act or fact of changing or being changed. **11** a variation or modification. **12** the substitution of one thing for another. **13** anything that is or may be substituted for something else. **14** variety or novelty (esp. in **for a change**). **15** a different set, esp. of clothes. **16** money given or received in return for its equivalent in a larger denomination or in a different currency. **17** the balance of money when the amount tendered is larger than the amount due. **18** coins of a small denomination. **19** (*often cap.*) *Arch.* a place where merchants meet to transact business. **20** the act of passing from one state or phase to

another. **21** the transition from one phase of the moon to the next. **22** the order in which a peal of bells may be rung. **23 get no change out of (someone)**. *Sl.* not to be successful in attempts to exploit (someone). **24 ring the changes.** to vary the manner or performance of an action that is often repeated. ◆ See also **change down, changeover, change up.** ORIG C13: from OF, from L *cambīre* to exchange, barter
▸ **'changeful** *adj* ▸ **'changeless** *adj* ▸ **'changer** *n*

changeable ('tʃeɪndʒəbᵊl) *adj* **1** able to change or be changed: *changeable weather.* **2** varying in colour as when viewed from different angles.
▸ **ˌchangea'bility** *n* ▸ **'changeably** *adv*

change down *vb* (*intr, adv*) to select a lower gear when driving.

changeling ('tʃeɪndʒlɪŋ) *n* a child believed to have been exchanged by fairies for the parents' true child.

change of life *n* a nontechnical name for **menopause.**

changeover ('tʃeɪndʒˌəʊvə) *n* **1** an alteration or complete reversal from one method, system, or product to another. **2** a reversal of a situation, attitude, etc. **3** *Sport.* the act of transferring to or being relieved by a teammate in a relay race, as by handing over a baton, etc. ◆ *vb* **change over.** (*adv*) **4** to adopt (a different position or attitude): *the driver and navigator changed over.*

change-ringing *n* the art of bell-ringing in which a set of bells is rung in an established order which is then changed.

change up *vb* (*intr, adv*) to select a higher gear when driving.

Changsha *or* **Ch'ang-sha** ★ ('tʃæŋ'ʃɑː) *n* a port in SE China, capital of Hunan province, on the Xiang River. Pop.: 1 330 000 (1991 est.).

Changteh *or* **Ch'ang-te** ★ ('tʃæŋ'teɪ) *n* a variant transliteration of the Chinese name for **Changde.**

Chania ★ ('hɑːnɪə) *n* a variant spelling of **Canea.**

channel ('tʃænᵊl) *n* **1** a broad strait connecting two areas of sea. **2** the bed or course of a river, stream, or canal. **3** a navigable course through a body of water. **4** (*often pl*) a means or agency of access, communication, etc.: *through official channels.* **5** a course into which something can be directed or moved. **6** *Electronics.* **6a** a band of radio frequencies assigned for a particular purpose, esp. the broadcasting of a television signal. **6b** a path for an electrical signal: *a stereo set has two channels.* **7** a tubular passage for fluids. **8** a groove, as in the shaft of a column. **9** *Computing.* **9a** a path along which data can be transmitted. **9b** one of the lines along the length of a paper tape on which information can be stored in the form of punched holes. ◆ *vb* **channels, channelling, channelled** *or US* **channels, channeling, channeled. 10** to make or cut channels in (something). **11** (*tr*) to guide into or convey through a channel or channels: *information was channelled through to them.* **12** to serve as a medium through whom the spirit of (a person of a former age) allegedly communicates with the living. **13** (*tr*) to form a groove or flute in (a column, etc.). ORIG C13: from OF, from L *canālis* pipe, groove, conduit

Channel ★ ('tʃænᵊl) *n* **the.** short for **English Channel.**

Channel Country ★ *n* **the.** an area of E central Australia, in SW Queensland: crossed by intermittent rivers and subject to both flooding and long periods of drought.

channel-hop *vb* **channel-hops, channel-hopping, channel-hopped.** (*intr*) to change television channels repeatedly using a remote control device.

Channel Islands ★ *pl n* a group of islands in the English Channel, off the NW coast of France, consisting of Jersey, Guernsey, Alderney, Brechou, Great Sark, Little Sark, Herm, Jethou, and Lihou (British crown dependencies), and the Roches Douvres and the Îles Chausey (which belong to France): the only part of the duchy of Normandy remaining to Britain. Pop.: 142 949 (1991). Area: 194 sq. km (75 sq. miles).

Channel Tunnel ★ *n* the Anglo-French railway tunnel that runs beneath the English Channel, between Folkestone and Coquelles, near Calais, opened in 1994. Also called: **Chunnel, Eurotunnel.**

chanson de geste *French.* (ʃɑ̃sɔ̃ də ʒɛst) *n* one of a genre of Old French epic poems, the most famous of which is the *Chanson de Roland.* ORIG lit.: song of exploits

chant (tʃɑːnt) *n* **1** a simple song. **2** a short simple melody in which several words or syllables are assigned to one note. **3** a psalm or canticle performed by using such a melody. **4** a rhythmic or repetitious slogan, usually spoken or sung, as by sports supporters, etc. ◆ *vb* **5** to sing or recite (a psalm, etc.) as a chant. **6** to intone (a slogan). ORIG C14: from OF *chanter* to sing, from L *cantāre,* frequentative of *canere* to sing
▸ **'chanting** *n, adj*

chanter ('tʃɑːntə) *n* the pipe on a set of bagpipes on which the melody is played.

chanterelle (ˌtʃæntə'rɛl) *n* any of a genus of fungi having an edible yellow funnel-shaped mushroom. ORIG C18: from F, from L *cantharus* drinking vessel, from Gk *kantharos*

chanteuse (*French* ʃɑ̃tøz) *n* a female singer, esp. in a nightclub or cabaret. ORIG F: singer

chanticleer (ˌtʃæntɪ'klɪə) *n* a name for a cock, used esp. in fables. ORIG C13: from OF, from *chanter cler* to sing clearly

Chantilly ★ (ʃæn'tɪlɪ; *French* ʃɑ̃tiji) *n* **1** a town in N France, near the **Forest of Chantilly:** formerly famous for lace and porcelain. Pop.: 11 341 (1990). ◆ *adj* **2** (of cream) lightly sweetened and whipped.

chantry ('tʃɑːntrɪ) *n, pl* **chantries.** *Christianity.* **1** an endowment for the singing of Masses for the soul of the founder. **2** a chapel or altar so endowed. ORIG C14: from OF, from *chanter* to sing; see CHANT

chanty ('ʃæntɪ, 'tʃæn-) *n, pl* **chanties.** a variant of **shanty**².

Chanukah *or* **Hanukkah** ('hɑːnəkə, -nʊˌkɑː) *n* the eight-day Jewish festival of lights commemorating the rededication of the temple by Judas Maccabaeus in 165 B.C. Also called: **Feast of Dedication, Feast of Lights.** ORIG from Heb., lit.: a dedication

Chaoan ★ ('tʃaʊ'ɑːn) *n* a city in SE China, in E Guangdong province, on the Han River: river port. Pop.: 313 469 (1990). Also called: **Chaochow.**

Chaochow ★ ('tʃaʊ'tʃəʊ) *n* another name for **Chaoan.**

chaology (keɪ'ɒlədʒɪ) *n* the study of chaos theory.
▸ **cha'ologist** *n*

chaos ('keɪɒs) *n* **1** (*usually cap.*) the disordered formless matter supposed to have existed before the ordered universe. **2** complete disorder; utter confusion. ORIG C15: from L, from Gk *khaos*
▸ **chaotic** (keɪ'ɒtɪk) *adj* ▸ **cha'otically** *adv*

chaos theory *n* a theory, applied in various branches of science, that apparently random phenomena have underlying order.

chap¹ (tʃæp) *vb* **chaps, chapping, chapped. 1** (of the skin) to make or become raw and cracked, esp. by exposure to cold. ◆ *n* **2** (*usually pl*) a cracked patch on the skin. ORIG C14: prob. of Gmc origin

chap² (tʃæp) *n Inf.* a man or boy; fellow. ORIG C16 (in the sense: buyer): shortened from CHAPMAN

chap³ (tʃɒp, tʃæp) *n* a less common word for **chop**³.

chaparejos *or* **chaparajos** (ˌʃæpə'reɪəʊs) *pl n* another name for **chaps.** ORIG from Mexican Sp.

chaparral (ˌtʃæpə'ræl, ˌʃæp-) *n* (in the southwestern US) a dense growth of shrubs and trees. ORIG C19: from Sp., from *chaparra* evergreen oak

chapati *or* **chapatti** (tʃə'pætɪ, -'pɑːtɪ) *n, pl* **chapati, chapatis, chapaties** *or* **chapatti, chapattis, chapatties.** (in Indian cookery) a flat unleavened bread resembling a pancake. ORIG from Hindi

chapbook ('tʃæpˌbʊk) *n* a book of popular ballads, stories, etc., formerly sold by chapmen.

chapel ('tʃæpᵊl) *n* **1** a place of Christian worship, esp. with a separate altar, in a church or cathedral. **2** a similar place of worship in a large house or institution, such as a college. **3** a church subordinate to a parish church. **4** (in Britain) **4a** a Nonconformist place of worship. **4b** Nonconformist religious practices or doctrine. **5a** the members of a trade union in a newspaper office, printing

★ people and places

house, etc. **5b** a meeting of these members. ORIG C13: from OF, from LL *cappella,* dim. of *cappa* cloak (see CAP); orig. the sanctuary where the cloak of St Martin was kept

chaperon *or* **chaperone** ('ʃæpəˌrəʊn) *n* **1** (esp. formerly) an older or married woman who accompanies or supervises a young unmarried woman on social occasions. ◆ *vb* **chaperons, chaperoning, chaperoned** *or* **chaperones, chaperoning, chaperoned. 2** to act as a chaperon to. ORIG C14: from OF, from *chape* hood; see CAP
▸ **'chaperˌonage** *n*

chapfallen ('tʃæpˌfɔːlən) *or* **chopfallen** *adj* dejected; downhearted. ORIG C16: from CHOPS + FALLEN

chaplain ('tʃæplɪn) *n* a Christian clergyman attached to a chapel of an institution or ministering to a military body, etc. ORIG C12: from OF, from LL, from *cappella* CHAPEL
▸ **'chaplaincy** *n*

chaplet ('tʃæplɪt) *n* **1** an ornamental wreath of flowers worn on the head. **2** a string of beads. **3** *RC Church.* **3a** a string of prayer beads constituting one third of the rosary. **3b** the prayers counted on this string. **4** a narrow moulding in the form of a string of beads; astragal. ORIG C14: from OF, from *chapel* hat
▸ **'chapleted** *adj*

Chaplin ★ ('tʃæplɪn) *n* Sir **Charles Spencer,** known as *Charlie Chaplin.* 1889–1977, British comedian, film actor, and director. His films, mostly made in Hollywood, include *The Gold Rush* (1924), *Modern Times* (1936), and *The Great Dictator* (1940).
▸ **ˌChaplin'esque** *adj*

chapman ('tʃæpmən) *n, pl* **chapmen.** *Arch.* a trader, esp. an itinerant pedlar. ORIG OE *cēapman,* from *cēap* buying and selling

Chapman ★ ('tʃæpmən) *n* **George.** 1559–1634, English dramatist and poet, noted for his translation of Homer.

Chappell ★ ('tʃæpᵊl) *n* **Greg**(**ory Stephen**). born 1948, Australian cricketer.

chappie ('tʃæpɪ) *n Inf.* another word for **chap**[2].

chaps (tʃæps, ʃæps) *pl n* leather overleggings without a seat, worn by cowboys. Also called: **chaparajos, chaparejos.** ORIG C19: shortened from CHAPAREJOS

chapter ('tʃæptə) *n* **1** a division of a written work. **2** a sequence of events: *a chapter of disasters.* **3** a period in a life, history, etc. **4** a numbered reference to that part of a Parliamentary session which relates to a specified Act of Parliament. **5** a branch of some societies, clubs, etc. **6** the collective body or a meeting of the canons of a cathedral or of the members of a monastic or knightly order. **7 chapter and verse.** exact authority for an action or statement. ◆ *vb* **8** (*tr*) to divide into chapters. ORIG C13: from OF *chapitre,* from L *capitulum,* lit.: little head, hence, section of writing, from *caput* head

chapterhouse ('tʃæptəˌhaʊs) *n* **1** the building in which a chapter meets. See **chapter** (sense 6). **2** *US.* the meeting place of a college fraternity or sorority.

char[1] (tʃɑː) *vb* **chars, charring, charred. 1** to burn or be burned partially; scorch. **2** (*tr*) to reduce (wood) to charcoal by partial combustion. ORIG C17: short for CHARCOAL

char[2] *or* **charr** (tʃɑː) *n, pl* **char, chars** *or* **charr, charrs.** any of various troutlike fishes occurring in cold lakes and northern seas. ORIG C17: from ?

char[3] (tʃɑː) *n* **1** *Inf.* short for **charwoman.** ◆ *vb* **chars, charring, charred. 2** (*intr*) *Brit. inf.* to do cleaning as a job. ORIG C18: from OE *cęrran*

char[4] (tʃɑː) *n Brit.* a slang word for **tea.** ORIG from Chinese *ch'a*

charabanc ('ʃærəˌbæŋ) *n Brit.* a coach, esp. for sightseeing. ORIG C19: from F: wagon with seats

character ('kærɪktə) *n* **1** the combination of traits and qualities distinguishing the individual nature of a person or thing. **2** one such distinguishing quality; characteristic. **3** moral force: *a man of character.* **4a** reputation, esp. a good reputation. **4b** (*as modifier*): *character assassination.* **5** a person represented in a play, film, story, etc.; role. **6** an outstanding person: *one of the great characters of the century.* **7** *Inf.* an odd, eccentric, or unusual person: *he's quite a character.* **8** an informal word for **person:** *a shady character.* **9** a symbol used in a writing system, such as a letter of the alphabet. **10** Also called: **sort.** *Printing.* any single letter, numeral, etc., cast as a type. **11** *Computing.* any letter, numeral, etc., which can be represented uniquely by a binary pattern. **12** a style of writing or printing. **13** *Genetics.* any structure, function, attribute, etc., in an organism that is determined by a gene or group of genes. **14** a short prose sketch of a distinctive type of person. **15 in** (*or* **out of**) **character.** typical (*or* not typical) of the apparent character of a person. ORIG C14: from L: distinguishing mark, from Gk *kharaktēr* engraver's tool
▸ **'characterful** *adj* ▸ **'characterless** *adj*

character actor *n* an actor who specializes in playing odd or eccentric characters.

character assassination *n* the act of deliberately attempting to destroy a person's reputation by defamatory remarks.

characteristic (ˌkærɪktə'rɪstɪk) *n* **1** a distinguishing quality, attribute, or trait. **2** *Maths.* **2a** the integral part of a common logarithm: *the characteristic of 2.4771 is 2.* **2b** another name for **exponent** (sense 4). ◆ *adj* **3** indicative of a distinctive quality, etc.; typical.
▸ **ˌcharacter'istically** *adv*

characterize *or* **characterise** ('kærɪktəˌraɪz) *vb* **characterizes, characterizing, characterized** *or* **characterises, characterising, characterised.** (*tr*) **1** to be a characteristic of. **2** to distinguish or mark as a characteristic. **3** to describe or portray the character of.
▸ **ˌcharacteri'zation** *or* **ˌcharacteri'sation** *n*

charade (ʃə'rɑːd) *n* **1** an act in the game of charades. **2** *Chiefly Brit.* an absurd act; travesty.

charades (ʃə'rɑːdz) *n* (*functioning as sing*) a parlour game in which one team acts out each syllable of a word, the other team having to guess the word. ORIG C18: from F, from Provençal *charrado* chat, from *charra* chatter

charcoal ('tʃɑːˌkəʊl) *n* **1** a black amorphous form of carbon made by heating wood or other organic matter in the absence of air. **2** a stick of this for drawing. **3** a drawing done in charcoal. **4** Also: **charcoal grey. 4a** a dark grey colour. **4b** (*as adj*): *a charcoal suit.* ◆ *vb* **5** (*tr*) to write, draw, or blacken with charcoal. ORIG C14: from *char* (from ?) + COAL

Charcot ★ (*French* ʃarko) *n* **Jean Martin** (ʒɑ̃ martɛ̃). 1825–93, French neurologist, noted for his work on hysteria, which influenced Freud.

charcuterie (ʃɑː'kuːtərɪː) *n* **1** cooked cold meats. **2** a shop selling cooked cold meats. ORIG F

chard (tʃɑːd) *n* a variety of beet with large succulent leaves and thick stalks, used as a vegetable. Also called: **Swiss chard.** ORIG C17: prob. from F *carde,* ult. from L *carduus* thistle

Chardin ★ (*French* ʃardɛ̃) *n* **Jean-Baptiste Siméon** (ʒɑ̃batist simeɔ̃). 1699–1779, French genre painter.

Chardonnay ('ʃɑːdəˌneɪ) *n* (*sometimes not cap.*) **1** a white grape grown in the Burgundy region of France, Australia, California, New Zealand and elsewhere, used for making wine. **2** any of various white wines made from this grape. ORIG F

Chardonnet ★ (*French* ʃardɔnɛ) *n* (**Louis Marie**) **Hilaire Bernigaud** (ilɛr bɛrnigo), Comte de. 1839–1924, French chemist and industrialist who produced rayon.

Charente ★ (*French* ʃarɑ̃t) *n* **1** a department of W central France, in Poitou-Charentes region. Capital: Angoulême. Pop.: 341 383 (1994 est.). Area: 5972 sq. km (2329 sq. miles). **2** a river in W France, flowing west to the Bay of Biscay. Length: 362 km (225 miles).

Charente-Maritime ★ (*French* ʃarɑ̃tmaritim) *n* a department of W France, in Poitou-Charentes region. Capital: La Rochelle. Pop.: 539 134 (1994 est.). Area: 7232 sq. km (2820 sq. miles).

charge (tʃɑːdʒ) *vb* **charges, charging, charged. 1** to set or demand (a price). **2** (*tr*) to enter a debit against a person or his account. **3** (*tr*) to accuse or impute a fault to (a person, etc.), as formally in a court of law. **4** (*tr*) to command; place a burden upon or assign responsibility to: *I was charged to take the message to headquarters.* **5** to make a rush at or sudden attack upon (a person or thing). **6** (*tr*) to fill (a receptacle) with the proper quantity. **7** (often foll. by *up*) to cause (an accumulator, capacitor, etc.) to take or store electricity or (of an accumulator) to have electricity fed into it. **8** to fill or be filled with matter by dispersion, solution, or absorption: *to charge water with carbon dioxide.* **9** (*tr*) to fill or suffuse with feeling, emotion, etc.: *the atmosphere was charged with excitement.* **10** (*tr*) *Law.* (of a judge) to address (a jury) authoritatively. **11** (*tr*) to load (a firearm). **12** (*tr*) *Heraldry.* to paint (a shield, banner, etc.) with a charge. ◆ *n* **13** a price charged for some article or service; cost. **14** a financial liability, such as a tax. **15** a debt or a book entry recording it. **16** an accusation or allegation, such as a formal accusation of a crime in law. **17a** an onrush, attack, or assault. **17b** the call to such an attack in battle. **18** custody or guardianship. **19** a person or thing committed to someone's care. **20a** a cartridge or shell. **20b** the explosive required to discharge a firearm. **20c** an amount of explosive to be detonated at any one time. **21** the quantity of anything that a receptacle is intended to hold. **22** *Physics.* **22a** the attribute of matter responsible for all electrical phenomena, existing in two forms: *negative charge; positive charge.* **22b** an excess or deficiency of electrons in a system. **22c** a quantity of electricity determined by the product of an electric current and the time for which it flows, measured in coulombs. **22d** the total amount of electricity stored in a capacitor or an accumulator. **23** a load or burden. **24** a duty or responsibility; control. **25** a command, injunction, or order. **26** *Heraldry.* a design depicted on heraldic arms. **27 in charge.** in command. **28 in charge of. 28a** having responsibility for. **28b** *US.* under the care of. ORIG C13: from OF *chargier* to load, from LL *carricāre;* see CARRY

chargeable ('tʃɑːdʒəbᵊl) *adj* **1** liable to be charged. **2** liable to result in a legal charge.

chargeable asset *n* any asset that can give rise to assessment for capital gains tax on its disposal. Exempt assets include principal private residences, cars, investments held in a personal equity plan, and government securities.

charge account *n* another term for **credit account.**

charge-cap ('tʃɑːdʒˌkæp) *vb* **charge-caps, charge-capping, charge-capped.** (*tr*) (in Britain) to impose on (a local authority) an upper limit on the community charge it may levy.
▸ **'charge-ˌcapping** *n*

charge card *n* a card issued by a chain store, shop, or organization, that enables customers to obtain goods and services for which they pay at a later date.

charge carrier *n* an electron, hole, or ion that transports the electric charge in an electric current.

chargé d'affaires ('ʃɑːʒeɪ dæ'fɛə) *n, pl* **chargés d'affaires** ('ʃɑːʒeɪ, -ʒeɪz). **1** the temporary head of a diplomatic mission in the absence of the ambassador or minister. **2** the head of a diplomatic mission of the lowest level. ORIG C18: from F: (one) charged with affairs

charge hand *n Brit.* a workman whose grade of responsibility is just below that of a foreman.

charge nurse *n Brit.* a nurse in charge of a ward in a hospital. Male equivalent of **sister.**

charger[1] ('tʃɑːdʒə) *n* **1** a person or thing that charges. **2** a horse formerly ridden into battle. **3** a device for charging an accumulator.

charger[2] ('tʃɑːdʒə) *n Antiques.* a large dish. ORIG C14 *chargeour,* from *chargen* to CHARGE

charge sheet *n Brit.* a document on which a police officer enters details of the charge against a prisoner and the court in which he will appear.

char-grilled *adj* (of food) grilled over charcoal.

Chari ('tʃɑːrɪ) *or* **Shari** ★ *n* a river in N central Africa, rising in the N Central African Republic and flowing north to Lake Chad. Length: about 2250 km (1400 miles).

charily ('tʃɛərɪlɪ) *adv* **1** cautiously; carefully. **2** sparingly.

chariness ('tʃɛərɪnɪs) *n* the state of being chary.

Charing Cross ★ ('tʃærɪŋ) *n* a district of London, in the city of Westminster: the modern cross (1863) in front of Charing Cross railway station replaces the one erected by Edward I (1290), the last of twelve marking the route of the funeral procession of his queen, Eleanor.

chariot ('tʃærɪət) *n* **1** a two-wheeled horse-drawn vehicle used in ancient wars, races, etc. **2** a light four-wheeled horse-drawn ceremonial carriage. **3** *Poetic.* any stately vehicle. ORIG C14: from OF, augmentative of *char* CAR

charioteer (ˌtʃærɪə'tɪə) *n* the driver of a chariot.

charisma (kə'rɪzmə) *or* **charism** ('kærɪzəm) *n* **1** a special personal quality or power making an individual capable of influencing or inspiring people. **2** a quality inherent in a thing, such as a particular type of car, which inspires great enthusiasm and devotion. **3** *Christianity.* a divinely bestowed power or talent. ORIG C17: from Church L, from Gk *kharisma,* from *kharis* grace, favour
▸ **charismatic** (ˌkærɪz'mætɪk) *adj*

charismatic movement *n Christianity.* any of various groups, within existing denominations, emphasizing the charismatic gifts of speaking in tongues, healing, etc.

charitable ('tʃærɪtəbᵊl) *adj* **1** generous in giving to the needy. **2** kind or lenient in one's attitude towards others. **3** of or for charity.
▸ **'charitableness** *n* ▸ **'charitably** *adv*

charitable trust *n* a trust set up for the benefit of a charity that complies with the regulations of the Charity Commissioners to enable it to be exempt from paying income tax.

charity ('tʃærɪtɪ) *n, pl* **charities. 1a** the giving of help, money, food, etc., to those in need. **1b** (*as modifier*): *a charity show.* **2** an institution or organization set up to provide help, money, etc., to those in need. **3** the help, money, etc., given to the needy; alms. **4** a kindly attitude towards people. **5** love of one's fellow men. ORIG C13: from OF, from L *cāritās* affection, from *cārus* dear

charivari (ˌʃɑːrɪ'vɑːrɪ), **shivaree,** *or esp. US.* **chivaree** *n* **1** a discordant mock serenade to newlyweds, made with pans, kettles, etc. **2** a confused noise; din. ORIG C17: from F, from LL, from Gk *karēbaria,* from *karē* head + *barus* heavy

charlady ('tʃɑːˌleɪdɪ) *n, pl* **charladies.** another name for **charwoman.**

charlatan ('ʃɑːlətᵊn) *n* someone who professes expertise, esp. in medicine, that he does not have; quack. ORIG C17: from F, from It., from *ciarlare* to chatter
▸ **'charlatanˌism** *or* **'charlatanry** *n*

Charlemagne ★ ('ʃɑːləˌmeɪn) *n* ?742–814 A.D., king of the Franks (768–814) and, as Charles I, Holy Roman Emperor (800–814). He conquered the Lombards (774), the Saxons (772–804), and the Avars (791–799).

Charles ★ (tʃɑːlz) *n* **1** *Prince of Wales.* born 1948, son of Elizabeth II; heir apparent to the throne of Great Britain and Northern Ireland. He married (1981) Lady Diana Spencer; they divorced in 1996. **2 Ray,** real name *Ray Charles Robinson.* born 1930, US singer and songwriter, whose work spans jazz, blues, gospel, pop, and country music.

Charles I ★ *n* **1** title as Holy Roman Emperor of **Charlemagne. 2** title as king of France of **Charles II** (Holy Roman Emperor). **3** title as king of Spain of **Charles V** (Holy Roman Emperor). **4** title of **Charles Stuart.** 1600–49, king of England, Scotland, and Ireland (1625–49); son of James I. He ruled for 11 years (1629–40) without parliament until rebellion broke out in Scotland. Conflict with the Long Parliament led to the Civil War and his defeat at Naseby (1645): executed by the English army under Cromwell (1647). **5** 1887–1922, emperor of Austria, and, as Charles IV, king of Hungary (1916–18). The last ruler of the Austro-Hungarian monarchy; abdicated at the end of World War I.

Charles II ★ *n* **1** known as *Charles the Bald.* 823–877 A.D., Holy Roman Emperor (875–877) and, as Charles I, king of France (843–877). **2** the title as king of France of **Charles III** (Holy Roman Emperor). **3** 1630–85, king of England, Scotland, and Ireland (1660–85) following the Restoration (1660); son of Charles I. **4** 1661–1700, the last Hapsburg king of Spain: his reign saw the end of Spanish power in Europe.

Charles III ★ *n* **1** known as *Charles the Fat.* 839–888 A.D., Holy Roman Emperor (881–887) and, as Charles II, king of France (884–887). He briefly reunited the empire of Charlemagne. **2** 1716–88, king of Spain (1759–88), who curbed the power of the Church and tried to modernize his country.

Charles IV ★ *n* **1** known as *Charles the Fair.* 1294–1328, king of France (1322–28). **2** 1316–78, king of Bohemia (1346–78) and Holy Roman Emperor (1355–78). **3** 1748–1819, king of Spain (1788–1808), whose reign saw the domination of Spain by Napoleonic France: abdicated. **4** title as king of Hungary of **Charles I** (sense 5).

Charles V ★ *n* **1** known as *Charles the Wise.* 1337–80, king of France (1364–80) during the Hundred Years' War. **2** 1500–58, Holy Roman Emperor (1519–56), king of Burgundy and the Netherlands (1506–55), and, as Charles I, king of Spain (1516–56): his reign saw the empire threatened by Francis I of France, the Turks, and the spread of Protestantism; abdicated.

Charles VI ★ *n* **1** known as *Charles the Mad* or *Charles the Well-Beloved.* 1368–1422, king of France (1380–1422): defeated by Henry V of England at Agincourt (1415), he was forced by the Treaty of Troyes (1420) to recognize Henry as his successor. **2** 1685–1740, Holy Roman Emperor (1711–40). His claim to the Spanish throne (1700) led to the War of Spanish Succession.

Charles VII ★ *n* **1** 1403–61, king of France (1422–61), son of Charles VI. He was excluded from the French throne by the Treaty of Troyes, but following Joan of Arc's victory over the English at Orléans (1429), was crowned. **2** 1697–1745, Holy Roman Emperor (1742–45) during the War of Austrian Succession.

Charles IX ★ *n* 1550–74, king of France (1560–74), son of Catherine de' Medici and Henry II: his reign was marked by war between Huguenots and Catholics.

Charles X ★ *n* **1** title of *Charles Gustavus.* 1622–60, king of Sweden. **2** 1757–1836, king of France (1824–30): his attempt to restore absolutism led to his enforced exile.

Charles XIV ★ *n* the title as king of Sweden and Norway of (Jean Baptiste Jules) **Bernadotte.**

Charles Edward Stuart ★ *n* See (Charles Edward) **Stuart.**

Charles Martel ★ (mɑːˈtɛl) *n* grandfather of Charlemagne. ?688–741 A.D., Frankish ruler of Austrasia (715–41), who checked the Muslim invasion of Europe by defeating the Moors at Poitiers (732).

Charles's Wain (weɪn) *n* another name for the **Plough.** ORIG OE *Carles wægn,* from *Carl* CHARLEMAGNE + *wægn* WAIN

Charles the Great ★ *n* another name for **Charlemagne.**

charleston (ˈtʃɑːlstən) *n* a fast rhythmic dance of the 1920s, characterized by kicking and by twisting of the legs from the knee down. ORIG named after *Charleston,* South Carolina

Charleston ★ (ˈtʃɑːlstən) *n* **1** a city in central West Virginia: the state capital. Pop.: 59 371 (1985 est.). **2** a port in SE South Carolina, on the Atlantic: scene of the first action in the Civil War. Pop.: 76 854 (1994 est.).

Charleville-Mézières ★ (*French* ʃarləvilmezjɛr) *n* twin towns on opposite sides of the River Meuse in NE France. Pop.: 59 440 (1990). See **Mézières.**

charley horse (ˈtʃɑːlɪ) *n US & Canad. inf.* cramp following strenuous athletic exercise. ORIG C19: from ?

charlie (ˈtʃɑːlɪ) *n Brit. inf.* a silly person; fool.

charlock (ˈtʃɑːlɒk) *n* a weedy Eurasian plant with hairy stems and foliage and yellow flowers. Also called: **wild mustard.** ORIG OE *cerlic,* from ?

charlotte (ˈʃɑːlət) *n* **1** a dessert made with fruit and layers or a casing of bread or cake crumbs, sponge cake, etc.: *apple charlotte.* **2** short for **charlotte russe.** ORIG C19: from F, from the name *Charlotte*

Charlotte ★ (ˈʃɑːlət) *n* a city in S North Carolina: the largest city in the state. Pop.: 437 797 (1994 est.).

Charlotte Amalie ★ (ˈʃɑːlət əˈmɑːlɪə) *n* the capital of the Virgin Islands of the United States, a port on St Thomas Island. Pop.: 12 331 (1990). Former name (1921–37): **Saint Thomas.**

Charlottenburg ★ (*German* ʃarˈlɔtənburk) *n* a district of Berlin (West Berlin until 1990), formerly an independent city. Pop.: 145 564 (1986 est.).

charlotte russe (ruːs) *n* a cold dessert made with sponge fingers enclosing a mixture of cream, custard, etc. ORIG F.: Russian charlotte

Charlottetown ★ (ˈʃɑːlətˌtaʊn) *n* a port in SE Canada, capital of the province of Prince Edward Island. Pop.: 15 396 (1991).

Charlton ★ (ˈtʃɑːltᵊn) *n* **1** **Bobby,** full name *Sir Robert Charlton.* born 1937, English footballer; played for Manchester United and England. **2** his brother, **Jack,** full name *John Charlton.* born 1935, English footballer; played for Leeds United (1952–73) and England; manager of the Republic of Ireland soccer team (1986–95).

charm (tʃɑːm) *n* **1** the quality of pleasing, fascinating, or attracting people. **2** a pleasing or attractive feature. **3** a small object worn for supposed magical powers; amulet. **4** a trinket worn on a bracelet. **5** a magic spell. **6** a formula used in casting such a spell. **7** *Physics.* a property of certain elementary particles, used to explain some scattering experiments. **8** **like a charm.** perfectly; successfully. ◆ *vb* **9** to attract or fascinate; delight greatly. **10** to cast a magic spell on. **11** to protect, influence, or heal, supposedly by magic. **12** (*tr*) to influence or obtain by personal charm. ORIG C13: from OF, from L *carmen* song
▸ **ˈcharmer** *n*

charming (ˈtʃɑːmɪŋ) *adj* delightful; pleasant; attractive.
▸ **ˈcharmingly** *adv*

charm offensive *n* a concentrated attempt to gain favour or respectability by conspicuously cooperative and obliging behaviour.

charnel (ˈtʃɑːnᵊl) *n* **1** short for **charnel house.** ◆ *adj* **2** ghastly; sepulchral; deathly. ORIG C14: from OF: burial place, from L *carnālis* fleshly, CARNAL

charnel house *n* (esp. formerly) a building or vault where corpses or bones are deposited.

Charnley ★ (ˈtʃɑːnlɪ) *n* Sir **John.** 1911–82, British surgeon noted for his hip-replacement surgery.

Charon (ˈkɛərən) *n Greek myth.* the ferryman who brought the dead across the rivers Styx or Acheron to Hades.

Charpentier ★ (*French* ʃarpɑ̃tje) *n* **1** **Gustave** (gystav). 1860–1956, French composer, noted for his opera *Louise* (1900). **2** **Marc-Antoine** (markɑ̃twan). ?1645–1704, French composer, noted for his sacred music, esp. his *Te Deum.*

chart (tʃɑːt) *n* **1** a map designed to aid navigation by sea or air. **2** an outline map, esp. one on which weather information is plotted. **3** a sheet giving graphical, tabular, or diagrammatical information. **4** **the charts.** *Inf.* the lists produced weekly of the bestselling pop singles and albums or the most popular videos. ◆ *vb* **5** (*tr*) to make a chart of. **6** (*tr*) to plot or outline the course of. **7** (*intr*) (of a record) to appear in the charts. ORIG C16: from L, from Gk *khartēs* papyrus
▸ **ˈchartless** *adj*

charter (ˈtʃɑːtə) *n* **1** a formal document from the sovereign or state incorporating a city, bank, college, etc., and specifying its purposes and rights. **2** (*sometimes cap.*) a formal document granting or demanding certain rights or liberties. **3** a document issued by a society or an organization authorizing the establishment of a local branch or chapter. **4** a special privilege or exemption. **5** (*often cap.*) the fundamental principles of an organization; constitution. **6a** the hire or lease of transportation. **6b** (*as modifier*): *a charter flight.* **7** a law, policy, or decision containing a loophole that allows a specified group to engage more easily in an activity considered undesirable: *a beggars' charter.* ◆ *vb* (*tr*) **8** to lease or hire by charter. **9** to hire (a vehicle, etc.). **10** to grant a charter to (a group or person). ORIG C13: from OF, from L *chartula,* dim. of *charta* leaf of papyrus; see CHART
▸ **ˈcharterer** *n*

chartered accountant *n* (in Britain) an accountant who has passed the examinations of the Institute of Chartered Accountants.

chartered bank *n Canad.* a privately owned bank that

has been incorporated by Parliament to operate in the commercial banking system.

chartered librarian *n* (in Britain) a librarian who has obtained a qualification from the Library Association in addition to a degree or diploma in librarianship.

chartered surveyor *n* (in Britain) a member of the Royal Institution of Chartered Surveyors.

Charteris ★ ('tʃɑːtərɪs) *n* **Leslie**, original name *Leslie Charles Bowyer Yin*. 1907–93, British novelist, born in Singapore: created the character Simon Templar, known as The Saint.

Chartism ('tʃɑːtɪzəm) *n English history*. a movement (1838-48) to achieve certain political reforms, demand for which was embodied in charters presented to Parliament.
▸ '**Chartist** *n, adj*

Chartres ★ ('ʃɑːtrə, ʃɑːt; *French* ʃartrə) *n* a city in NW France: Gothic cathedral; market town. Pop.: 41 850 (1990).

chartreuse (ʃɑː'trɜːz; *French* ʃartrøz) *n* **1** either of two liqueurs, green or yellow, made from herbs. **2a** a yellowish-green colour. **2b** (*as adj*): *a chartreuse dress*. ORIG C19: from F, after *La Grande Chartreuse*, monastery near Grenoble, where the liqueur is produced

charwoman ('tʃɑːˌwʊmən) *n, pl* **charwomen**. *Brit.* a woman who is hired to clean a house.

chary ('tʃɛərɪ) *adj* **charier, chariest. 1** wary; careful. **2** choosy; finicky. **3** shy. **4** sparing; mean. ORIG OE *cearig;* rel. to *caru* CARE

Charybdis (kə'rɪbdɪs) *n* a ship-devouring monster in classical mythology, identified with a whirlpool off the coast of Sicily. Cf. **Scylla.**

chase[1] (tʃeɪs) *vb* **chases, chasing, chased. 1** to follow or run after (a person, animal, or goal) persistently or quickly. **2** (*tr;* often foll. by *out, away,* or *off*) to force to run (away); drive (out). **3** (*tr*) *Inf.* to court (a member of the opposite sex) in an unsubtle manner. **4** (*tr;* often foll. by *up*) *Inf.* to pursue persistently and energetically in order to obtain results, information, etc. **5** (*intr*) *Inf.* to hurry; rush. ◆ *n* **6** the act of chasing; pursuit. **7** any quarry that is pursued. **8** *Brit.* an unenclosed area of land where wild animals are preserved to be hunted. **9** *Brit.* the right to hunt a particular quarry over the land of others. **10 the chase.** the act or sport of hunting. **11** short for **steeplechase. 12 give chase.** to pursue (a person, animal, or thing) actively. ORIG C13: from OF *chacier,* from Vulgar L *captiāre* (unattested), from L, from *capere* to take; see CATCH

chase[2] (tʃeɪs) *n* **1** *Letterpress printing*. a rectangular steel frame into which metal type and blocks are locked for printing. **2** the part of a gun barrel from the trunnions to the muzzle. **3** a groove or channel, esp. to take a pipe, cable, etc. ◆ *vb* **chases, chasing, chased.** (*tr*) **4** Also: **chamfer.** to cut a groove, furrow, or flute in (a surface, column, etc.). ORIG C17: prob. from F *châsse* frame, from OF *chas* enclosure, from LL *capsus* pen for animals; both from L *capsa* CASE[2]

chase[3] (tʃeɪs) *vb* **chases, chasing, chased.** (*tr*) to ornament (metal) by engraving or embossing. Also: **enchase.** ORIG C14: from OF *enchasser* ENCHASE

chaser ('tʃeɪsə) *n* **1** a person or thing that chases. **2** a drink drunk after another of a different kind, as beer after spirits.

chasm ('kæzəm) *n* **1** a deep cleft in the ground; abyss. **2** a break in continuity; gap. **3** a wide difference in interests, feelings, etc. ORIG C17: from L, from Gk *khasma;* rel. to *khainein* to gape
▸ **chasmal** ('kæzməl) *or* '**chasmic** *adj*

chasseur (ʃæ'sɜː) *n* **1** *French Army*. a member of a unit specially trained for swift deployment. **2** a uniformed attendant. ◆ *adj* **3** (*often postpositive*) designating or cooked in a sauce consisting of white wine and mushrooms. ORIG C18: from F: huntsman

Chassid *or* **Hassid** ('hæsɪd) *n pl* **Chassidim** *or* **Hassidim** ('hæsɪˌdiːm, -dɪm). **1** a sect of Jewish mystics founded in Poland about 1750, characterized by religious zeal and a spirit of prayer, joy, and charity. **2** a Jewish sect of the 2nd century B.C., formed to combat Hellenistic influences.
▸ **Chassidic** *or* **Hassidic** (hə'sɪdɪk) *adj*

chassis ('ʃæsɪ) *n, pl* **chassis** (-sɪz). **1** the steel frame, wheels, and mechanical parts of a motor vehicle. **2** *Electronics*. a mounting for the circuit components of an electrical or electronic device, such as a radio or television. **3** the landing gear of an aircraft. **4** the frame on which a cannon carriage moves. ORIG C17 (meaning: window frame): from F *châssis,* from Vulgar L *capsicum* (unattested), ult. from L *capsa* CASE[2]

chaste (tʃeɪst) *adj* **1** not having experienced sexual intercourse; virginal. **2** abstaining from unlawful sexual intercourse. **3** abstaining from all sexual intercourse. **4** (of conduct, speech, etc.) pure; decent; modest. **5** (of style) simple; restrained. ORIG C13: from OF, from L *castus* pure
▸ '**chastely** *adv* ▸ '**chasteness** *n*

chasten ('tʃeɪsᵊn) *vb* (*tr*) **1** to bring to submission; subdue. **2** to discipline or correct by punishment. **3** to moderate; restrain. ORIG C16: from OF, from L *castigāre;* see CASTIGATE
▸ '**chastener** *n*

chastise (tʃæs'taɪz) *vb* **chastises, chastising, chastised.** (*tr*) **1** to punish, esp. by beating. **2** to scold severely. ORIG C14 *chastisen,* irregularly from *chastien* to CHASTEN
▸ **chastisement** ('tʃæstɪzmənt, tʃæs'taɪz-) *n* ▸ **chas'tiser** *n*

chastity ('tʃæstɪtɪ) *n* **1** the state of being chaste; purity. **2** abstention from sexual intercourse; virginity or celibacy. ORIG C13: from OF, from L, from *castus* CHASTE

chasuble ('tʃæzjʊbᵊl) *n Christianity*. a long sleeveless outer vestment worn by a priest when celebrating Mass. ORIG C13: from F, from LL *casubla* garment with a hood

chat (tʃæt) *n* **1** informal conversation or talk in an easy familiar manner. **2** the exchange of messages in an Internet or other network chatroom. **3** an Old World songbird of the thrush family, having a harsh chattering cry. **4** any of various North American warblers. **5** any of various Australian wrens. ◆ *vb* **chats, chatting, chatted. 6** (*intr*) to talk in an easy familiar way. **7** (*intr*) to exchange messages in a chatroom. ◆ See also **chat up.** ORIG C16: short for CHATTER

chateau *or* **château** ('ʃætəʊ) *n, pl* **chateaux** (-təʊ, -təʊz), **chateaus** *or* **châteaux, châteaus. 1** a country house or castle, esp. in France. **2** (in the name of a wine) estate or vineyard. ORIG C18: from F, from OF, from L *castellum* CASTLE

Chateaubriand ★ (*French* ʃatobrijɑ̃) *n* **1 François René** (frɑ̃swa rəne), Vicomte de Chateaubriand. 1768–1848, French writer and statesman: his works include *Le Génie du Christianisme* (1802) and *Mémoires d'outre-tombe* (1849–50). **2** a thick steak cut from the fillet of beef.

Châteauroux ★ (*French* ʃatoru) *n* a city in central France: tenth-century castle (**Château-Raoul**). Pop.: 52 950 (1990).

Château-Thierry ★ ('ʃætəʊ'tɪərɪ; *French* ʃatotjɛri) *n* a town in N central France, on the River Marne: scene of the second battle of the Marne (1918) during World War I. Pop.: 15 830 (1990).

chatelaine ('ʃætəˌleɪn) *n* **1** (esp. formerly) the mistress of a castle or large household. **2** a chain or clasp worn at the waist by women in the 16th to the 19th centuries, with handkerchief, keys, etc., attached. ORIG from F, from OF, ult. from L *castellum* CASTLE

Chatham[1] ★ ('tʃætəm) *n* **1** a town in SE England, in N Kent on the River Medway: formerly royal naval dockyard. Pop.: 71 691 (1991). **2** a city in SE Canada, in SE Ontario on the Thames River. Pop.: 43 557 (1991).

Chatham[2] ★ ('tʃætəm) *n* **1st Earl of.** title of the elder (William) **Pitt.**

Chatham Island ★ *n* another name for **San Cristóbal** (sense 1).

Chatham Islands ★ *pl n* a group of islands in the S Pacific Ocean, forming a county of South Island, New Zealand: consists of the main islands of Chatham, Pitt, and several rocky islets. Chief settlement: Waitangi. Pop.: 769 (1991). Area: 963 sq. km (372 sq. miles).

chatline ('tʃætˌlaɪn) *n* a telephone service enabling callers to join in general conversation with each other.

chatroom ('tʃætˌruːm) *n* a site on the Internet, or another computer network, where users have group discussions in real time, typically about one subject.

chat show *n Brit.* a television or radio show in which guests are interviewed informally.

Chattanooga ★ (ˌtʃætᵊˈnuːgə) *n* a city in SE Tennessee, on the Tennessee River: scene of two battles during the Civil War, in which the North defeated the Confederates, cleared Tennessee, and opened the way to Georgia (1863). Pop.: 152 259 (1994 est.).

chattel (ˈtʃætᵊl) *n* **1** (*often pl*) *Property law.* **1a chattel personal.** an item of movable personal property, such as furniture, etc. **1b chattel real.** an interest in land less than a freehold. **2 goods and chattels.** personal property. ORIG C13: from OF *chatel* personal property, from Med. L *capitāle* wealth

chatter (ˈtʃætə) *vb* **1** to speak (about unimportant matters) rapidly and incessantly. **2** (*intr*) (of birds, monkeys, etc.) to make rapid repetitive high-pitched noises. **3** (*intr*) (of the teeth) to click together rapidly through cold or fear. **4** (*intr*) to make rapid intermittent contact with a component, as in machining. ◆ *n* **5** idle or foolish talk; gossip. **6** the high-pitched repetitive noise made by a bird, monkey, etc. **7** the rattling of objects, such as parts of a machine. ORIG C13: imit.
▸ **ˈchatterer** *n*

chatterbox (ˈtʃætəˌbɒks) *n Inf.* a person who talks constantly, esp. about trivial matters.

chattering classes *n Inf., often derog.* (usually preceded by *the*) those members of the educated sections of society who enjoy talking about politics, society, culture, etc.

Chatterton ★ (ˈtʃætətən) *n* **Thomas.** 1752–70, British poet; author of spurious medieval verse: he committed suicide at the age of 17.

chatty (ˈtʃætɪ) *adj* **chattier, chattiest. 1** full of trivial conversation; talkative. **2** informal and friendly; gossipy.
▸ **ˈchattily** *adv* ▸ **ˈchattiness** *n*

chat up *vb* (*tr, adv*) *Brit. inf.* **1** to talk flirtatiously to (someone) with a view to starting a romantic or sexual relationship. **2** to talk persuasively to (a person), esp. with an ulterior motive.

Chaucer ★ (ˈtʃɔːsə) *n* **Geoffrey.** ?1340–1400, English poet, noted for *The Canterbury Tales.* His other works include *Troilus and Criseyde, The Legende of Good Women,* and *The Parlement of Foules.*

chauffeur (ˈʃəufə, ʃəuˈfɜː) *n* **1** a person employed to drive a car. ◆ *vb* **2** to act as driver for (a person, etc.): *he chauffeured me to the stadium.* ORIG C20: from F, lit.: stoker, from *chauffer* to heat
▸ **chauffeuse** (ʃəuˈfɜːz) *fem n*

chaunt (tʃɔːnt) *n* a less common variant of **chant.**
▸ **ˈchaunter** *n*

chauvinism (ˈʃəuvɪˌnɪzəm) *n* **1** aggressive or fanatical patriotism; jingoism. **2** enthusiastic devotion to a cause. **3** smug irrational belief in the superiority of one's own race, party, sex, etc.: *male chauvinism.* ORIG C19: from F, after Nicolas *Chauvin,* F soldier under Napoleon, noted for his unthinking patriotism
▸ **ˈchauvinist** *n, adj* ▸ **ˌchauvinˈistic** *adj* ▸ **ˌchauvinˈistically** *adv*

cheap (tʃiːp) *adj* **1** costing relatively little; inexpensive; of good value. **2** charging low prices: *a cheap hairdresser.* **3** of poor quality; shoddy: *cheap furniture.* **4** worth relatively little: *promises are cheap.* **5** not worthy of respect; vulgar. **6** ashamed; embarrassed: *to feel cheap.* **7** stingy; miserly. **8** *Inf.* mean; despicable: *a cheap liar.* ◆ *n* **9 on the cheap.** *Brit. inf.* at a low cost. ◆ *adv* **10** at very little cost. ORIG OE *ceap* barter, bargain, price, property
▸ **ˈcheaply** *adv* ▸ **ˈcheapness** *n*

cheapen (ˈtʃiːpᵊn) *vb* **1** to make or become lower in reputation, quality, etc. **2** to make or become cheap or cheaper.
▸ **ˈcheapener** *n*

cheap-jack *Inf.* ◆ *n* **1** a person who sells cheap and shoddy goods. ◆ *adj* **2** shoddy or inferior. ORIG C19: from CHEAP + JACK

cheapo (ˈtʃiːpəu) *adj Inf.* very cheap and possibly shoddy.

★ people and places

cheapskate (ˈtʃiːpˌskeɪt) *n Inf.* a miserly person.

cheat (tʃiːt) *vb* **1** to deceive or practise deceit, esp. for one's own gain; trick or swindle (someone). **2** (*intr*) to obtain unfair advantage by trickery, as in a game of cards. **3** (*tr*) to escape or avoid (something unpleasant) by luck or cunning: *to cheat death.* **4** (when *intr,* usually foll. by *on*) *Inf.* to be sexually unfaithful to (one's wife, husband, or lover). ◆ *n* **5** a person who cheats. **6** a deliberately dishonest transaction, esp. for gain; fraud. **7** *Inf.* sham. **8** *Law.* the obtaining of another's property by fraudulent means. ORIG C14: short for ESCHEAT
▸ **ˈcheater** *n*

Cheb ★ (*Czech* xɛp) *n* a town in the W Czech Republic, in W Bohemia on the Ohře River: 12th-century castle where Wallenstein was murdered (1634); a centre of the Sudeten-German movement after World War I. Pop.: 31 847 (1991). German name: **Eger.**

Cheboksary ★ (*Russian* tʃɪbakˈsari) *n* a port in W central Russia, on the River Volga: capital of the Chuvash Republic. Pop.: 450 000 (1995 est.).

Chechenia (tʃɪˈtʃɛnɪə) *or* **Chechnya** ★ (ˈtʃɛtʃnjɑː) *n* a constituent republic of S Russia, on the N slopes of the Caucasus Mountains: part of the former Checheno-Ingush Autonomous Republic, which was split into Chechenia and Ingushetia in 1992; oil, gas, and mineral resources. Chechenia declared itself independent of Russia following the break-up of the Soviet Union in 1991; Russian troops fought separatists from 1994 to 1996. Capital: Grozny. Pop. (including Ingushetia): 1 234 000 (1995 est.). Area (including Ingushetia): 19 300 sq. km (7450 sq. miles).

check (tʃɛk) *vb* **1** to pause or cause to pause, esp. abruptly. **2** (*tr*) to restrain or control: *to check one's tears.* **3** (*tr*) to slow the growth or progress of; retard. **4** (*tr*) to rebuke or rebuff. **5** (when *intr,* often foll. by *on* or *up on*) to examine, investigate, or make an inquiry into (facts, a product, etc.) for accuracy, quality, or progress. **6** (*tr*) *Chiefly US & Canad.* to mark off so as to indicate approval, correctness, or preference. **7** (*intr;* often foll. by *with*) *Chiefly US & Canad.* to correspond or agree: *this report checks with the other.* **8** (*tr*) *Chiefly US, Canad., & NZ.* to leave in or accept (property) for temporary custody. **9** *Chess.* to place (an opponent's king) in check. **10** (*tr*) to mark with a pattern of squares or crossed lines. **11** to crack or cause to crack. **12** (*tr*) *Ice hockey.* to impede (an opponent). **13** (*intr*) *Hunting.* (of hounds) to pause while relocating a lost scent. ◆ *n* **14** a break in progress; stoppage. **15** a restraint or rebuff. **16** a person or thing that restrains, halts, etc. **17** a control, esp. a rapid or informal one, to ensure accuracy, progress, etc. **18** a means or standard to ensure against fraud or error. **19** the US word for **tick**[1] (senses 3, 6). **20** the US spelling of **cheque. 21** *US & Canad.* the bill in a restaurant. **22** *Chiefly US & Canad.* a tag used to identify property deposited for custody. **23** a pattern of squares or crossed lines. **24** a single square in such a pattern. **25** fabric with a pattern of squares or crossed lines. **26** *Chess.* the state or position of a king under direct attack. **27** a small crack, as one that occurs in timber during drying. **28** a chip or counter used in some card and gambling games. **29** *Hunting.* a pause by the hounds owing to loss of the scent. **30** *Ice hockey.* the act of impeding an opponent with one's body or stick. **31 in check.** under control or restraint. ◆ *sentence substitute.* **32** *Chess.* a call made to an opponent indicating that his or her king is in check. **33** *Chiefly US & Canad.* an expression of agreement. ◆ See also **check in, check out, checkup.** ORIG C14: from OF *eschec* a check at chess, via Ar. from Persian *shāh* the king
▸ **ˈcheckable** *adj*

checked (tʃɛkt) *adj* having a pattern of squares.

checker[1] (ˈtʃɛkə) *n, vb* **1** the usual US spelling of **chequer.** ◆ *n* **2** *Textiles.* the US spelling of **chequer** (sense 2). **3** the US and Canad. name for **draughtsman** (sense 3).

checker[2] (ˈtʃɛkə) *n Chiefly US.* **1** a cashier, esp. in a supermarket. **2** an attendant in a cloakroom, left-luggage office, etc.

checkerboard (ˈtʃɛkəˌbɔːd) *n* the US and Canad. name for a **draughtboard.**

checkers ('tʃɛkəz) *n* (*functioning as sing*) the US and Canad. name for **draughts.**

check in *vb* (*adv*) **1** (*intr*) to record one's arrival, as at a hotel or for work; sign in or report. **2** (*tr*) to register the arrival of (passengers, etc.). ◆ *n* **check-in. 3** the formal registration of arrival, as at an airport or a hotel. **4** the place where one registers arrival at an airport, etc.

check list *n* a list of items, names, etc., to be referred to for identification or verification.

checkmate ('tʃɛk,meɪt) *n* **1** *Chess.* **1a** the winning position in which an opponent's king is under attack and unable to escape. **1b** the move by which this position is achieved. **2** utter defeat. ◆ *vb* **checkmates, checkmating, checkmated.** (*tr*) **3** *Chess.* to place (an opponent's king) in checkmate. **4** to thwart or render powerless. ◆ *sentence substitute.* **5** *Chess.* a call made when placing an opponent's king in checkmate. ORIG C14: from OF, from Ar. *shāh māt* the king is dead; see CHECK

check out *vb* (*adv*) **1** (*intr*) to pay the bill and depart, esp. from a hotel. **2** (*intr*) to depart from a place; record one's departure from work. **3** (*tr*) to investigate or prove to be in order after investigation: *the police checked out all the statements.* **4** (*tr*) *Inf.* to have a look at; inspect: *check out the wally in the pink shirt.* ◆ *n* **checkout. 5** the latest time for vacating a room in a hotel, etc. **6** a counter, esp. in a supermarket, where customers pay.

checkpoint ('tʃɛk,pɔɪnt) *n* a place, as at a frontier, where vehicles or travellers are stopped for official identification, inspection, etc.

checkup ('tʃɛk,ʌp) *n* **1** an examination to see if something is in order. **2** *Med.* a medical examination, esp. one taken at regular intervals. ◆ *vb* **check up. 3** (*intr, adv;* sometimes foll. by *on*) to investigate or make an inquiry into (a person's character, evidence, etc.).

Cheddar ★ ('tʃɛdə) *n* **1** (*sometimes not cap.*) any of several types of smooth hard yellow or whitish cheese. **2** a village in SW England, in N Somerset: situated near **Cheddar Gorge,** a pass through the Mendip Hills renowned for its stalactitic caverns and rare limestone flora. Pop.: 4484 (1991).

cheek (tʃi:k) *n* **1** either side of the face, esp. that part below the eye. **2** *Inf.* impudence; effrontery. **3** (*often pl*) *Inf.* either side of the buttocks. **4** (*often pl*) a side of a door jamb. **5** one of the jaws of a vice. **6 cheek by jowl.** close together; intimately linked. **7 turn the other cheek.** to be submissive and refuse to retaliate. ◆ *vb* **8** (*tr*) *Inf.* to speak or behave disrespectfully to. ORIG OE *ceace*

cheekbone ('tʃi:k,bəʊn) *n* the nontechnical name for **zygomatic bone.**

cheeky ('tʃi:kɪ) *adj* **cheekier, cheekiest.** disrespectful in speech or behaviour; impudent.
▸ **'cheekily** *adv* ▸ **'cheekiness** *n*

cheep (tʃi:p) *n* **1** the short weak high-pitched cry of a young bird; chirp. ◆ *vb* **2** (*intr*) (of young birds) to utter such sounds.
▸ **'cheeper** *n*

cheer (tʃɪə) *vb* **1** (usually foll. by *up*) to make or become happy or hopeful; comfort or be comforted. **2** to applaud with shouts. **3** (when *tr,* sometimes foll. by *on*) to encourage (a team, etc.) with shouts. ◆ *n* **4** a shout or cry of approval, encouragement, etc., often using **hurrah! 5 three cheers.** three shouts of hurrah given in unison to honour someone or celebrate something. **6** happiness; good spirits. **7** state of mind; spirits (archaic, except in **be of good cheer, with good cheer**). **8** *Arch.* provisions for a feast; fare. ORIG C13 (in the sense: face, welcoming aspect): from OF *chere,* from LL *cara* face, from Gk *kara* head

cheerful ('tʃɪəfʊl) *adj* **1** having a happy disposition; in good spirits. **2** pleasantly bright: *a cheerful room.* **3** ungrudging: *cheerful help.*
▸ **'cheerfully** *adv* ▸ **'cheerfulness** *n*

cheerio (,tʃɪərɪ'əʊ) *Inf.* ◆ *sentence substitute. Chiefly Brit.* **1** a farewell greeting. **2** a drinking toast. ◆ *n, pl* **cheerios. 3** *NZ.* a type of small sausage.

cheerleader ('tʃɪə,li:də) *n US & Canad.* a person who leads a crowd in cheers, esp. at sports events.

cheerless ('tʃɪəlɪs) *adj* dreary or gloomy.
▸ **'cheerlessly** *adv* ▸ **'cheerlessness** *n*

cheers (tʃɪəz) *sentence substitute. Inf., chiefly Brit.* **1** a drinking toast. **2** goodbye! cheerio! **3** thanks!

cheery ('tʃɪərɪ) *adj* **cheerier, cheeriest.** showing or inspiring cheerfulness.
▸ **'cheerily** *adv* ▸ **'cheeriness** *n*

cheese (tʃi:z) *n* **1** the curd of milk separated from the whey and variously prepared as a food. **2** a mass or cake of this substance. **3** any of various substances of similar consistency, etc.: *lemon cheese.* **4** *Sl.* an important person (esp. in **big cheese**). ORIG OE *cēse,* from L *cāseus* cheese

cheeseburger ('tʃi:z,bɜ:gə) *n* a hamburger cooked with a slice of cheese on top of it.

cheesecake ('tʃi:z,keɪk) *n* **1** a rich tart filled with cheese, esp. cream cheese, cream, sugar, etc. **2** *Sl.* women displayed for their sex appeal, as in photographs in magazines or films.

cheesecloth ('tʃi:z,klɒθ) *n* a loosely woven cotton cloth formerly used for wrapping cheese.

cheesed off *adj* (*usually postpositive*) *Brit. sl.* bored, disgusted, or angry. ORIG C20: from ?

cheeseparing ('tʃi:z,pɛərɪŋ) *adj* **1** penny-pinching. ◆ *n* **2a** a paring of cheese rind. **2b** anything similarly worthless. **3** stinginess.

cheesy ('tʃi:zɪ) *adj* **cheesier, cheesiest. 1** like cheese in flavour, smell, or consistency. **2** *Inf.* (of a smile) broad but possibly insincere: *a big cheesy grin.* **3** *Inf.* banal or trite; in poor taste.
▸ **'cheesiness** *n*

cheetah *or* **chetah** ('tʃi:tə) *n* a large feline of Africa and SW Asia: the swiftest mammal, having very long legs, and a black-spotted coat. ORIG C18: from Hindi *cītā,* from Sansk. *citra* speckled

Cheever ★ ('tʃi:və) *n* **John.** 1912–82, US writer. His novels include *The Wapshot Chronicle* (1957) and *Bullet Park* (1969).

chef (ʃɛf) *n* a cook, esp. the principal cook in a restaurant. ORIG C19: from F, from OF *chief* head, CHIEF

chef-d'œuvre *French.* (ʃɛdœvrə) *n, pl* ***chefs-d'œuvre*** (ʃɛdœvrə). a masterpiece.

Chefoo ★ ('tʃi:'fu:) *n* another name for **Yantai.**

Che Guevara ★ (tʃeɪ gə'vɑ:rə; *Spanish* tʃe ge'βara) *n* See **Guevara.**

Cheiron ★ ('kaɪrɒn, -rən) *n* a variant spelling of **Chiron.**

Cheju ★ ('tʃɛ'dʒu:) *n* a volcanic island in the N East China Sea, southwest of Korea: constitutes the province of Cheju-do in South Korea. Capital: Cheju. Pop.: 258 509 (1995). Area: 1792 sq. km (692 sq. miles). Also called: **Quelpart.**

Chekhov *or* **Chekov** ★ ('tʃɛkɒf; *Russian* 'tʃɛxəf) *n* **Anton Pavlovich** (an'tɔn 'pavləvitʃ). 1860–1904, Russian writer. His plays include *The Seagull* (1896), *Uncle Vanya* (1900), *The Three Sisters* (1901), and *The Cherry Orchard* (1904).
▸ **Chekhovian** *or* **Chekovian** (tʃɛ'kəʊvɪən) *adj*

Chekiang ★ ('tʃɛ'kjæŋ, -kaɪ'æŋ) *n* a variant transliteration of the Chinese name for **Zhejiang.**

chela[1] ('ki:lə) *n, pl* **chelae** (-li:). a large pincer-like claw of such arthropods as the crab and scorpion. ORIG C17: NL, from Gk *khēlē* claw

chela[2] ('tʃeɪlə) *n Hinduism.* a disciple of a religious teacher. ORIG C19: from Hindi *celā,* from Sansk. *ceta* servant, slave

chelate ('ki:leɪt) *n* **1** *Chem.* a chemical compound whose molecules contain a closed ring of atoms of which one is a metal atom. ◆ *adj* **2** *Zool.* of or possessing chelae. **3** *Chem.* of a chelate. ◆ *vb* **chelates, chelating, chelated. 4** (*intr*) *Chem.* to form a chelate. ORIG C20: from CHELA[1]
▸ **che'lation** *n*

chelicera (kɪ'lɪsərə) *n, pl* **chelicerae** (-ə,ri:). one of a pair of appendages on the head of spiders and other arachnids: often modified as food-catching claws. ORIG C19: from NL, from Gk *khēle* claw+ *keras* horn

Chelmsford ★ ('tʃɛlmzfəd) *n* a town in SE England, administrative centre of Essex: market town; seat of Anglia Polytechnic University (1992). Pop.: 197 451 (1991).

cheloid ('ki:lɔɪd) *n Pathol.* a variant spelling of **keloid.**
▸ **che'loidal** *adj*

chelonian (kɪ'ləʊnɪən) *n* **1** any reptile of the order *Chelonia,* including the tortoises and turtles, in which most of the body is enclosed in a bony capsule. ◆ *adj* **2** of or belonging to the *Chelonia.* ORIG C19: from NL, from Gk *khelōnē* tortoise

Chelsea ★ ('tʃɛlsɪ) *n* a residential district of SW London, in the Royal Borough of Kensington and Chelsea: site of the Chelsea Royal Hospital for old and invalid soldiers (**Chelsea Pensioners**).

Cheltenham ★ ('tʃɛltᵊnəm) *n* **1** a town in W England, in central Gloucestershire: famous for its schools, racecourse, and saline springs (discovered in 1716). Pop.: 91 301 (1991). **2** a style of type.

Chelyabinsk ★ (*Russian* tʃɪ'ljabinsk) *n* a city in SW Russia: a major industrial centre. Pop.: 1 086 000 (1995 est.).

Chelyuskin ★ (*Russian* tʃɪ'ljuskin) *n* **Cape.** a cape in N central Russia, in N Siberia at the end of the Taimyr Peninsula: the northernmost point of Asia.

chem. *abbrev. for:* **1** chemical. **2** chemist. **3** chemistry.

chem- *combining form.* a variant of **chemo-** before a vowel.

chemical ('kɛmɪkᵊl) *n* **1** any substance used in or resulting from a reaction involving changes to atoms or molecules. **2** a compound that has been produced artificially. ◆ *adj* **3** of or used in chemistry. **4** of, made from, or using chemicals: *chemical fertilizer.*
▸ **'chemically** *adv*

chemical engineering *n* the branch of engineering concerned with the design and manufacture of the plant used in industrial chemical processes.
▸ **chemical engineer** *n*

chemical warfare *n* warfare using asphyxiating or nerve gases, poisons, defoliants, etc.

chemiluminescence (ˌkɛmɪˌluːmɪ'nɛsəns) *n* the phenomenon in which a chemical reaction leads to the emission of light without incandescence.
▸ **ˌchemiˌlumi'nescent** *adj*

chemin de fer (ʃə'mæn də 'fɛə) *n* a gambling game, a variation of baccarat. ORIG F: railway, referring to the fast tempo of the game

chemise (ʃə'miːz) *n* **1** an unwaisted loose-fitting dress hanging straight from the shoulders. **2** a loose shirtlike undergarment. ◆ Also called: **shift.** ORIG C14: from OF: shirt, from LL *camisa*

chemist ('kɛmɪst) *n* **1** *Brit.* a shop selling medicines, cosmetics, etc. **2** *Brit.* a qualified dispenser of prescribed medicines. **3** a person studying, trained in, or engaged in chemistry. ORIG C16: from earlier *chimist,* from NL, shortened from Med. L *alchimista* ALCHEMIST

chemistry ('kɛmɪstrɪ) *n, pl* **chemistries. 1** the branch of physical science concerned with the composition, properties, and reactions of substances. **2** the composition, properties, and reactions of a particular substance. **3** the nature and effects of any complex phenomenon: *the chemistry of humour.* ORIG C17: from earlier *chimistrie,* from *chimist* CHEMIST

Chemnitz ★ (*German* 'kɛmnɪts) *n* a city in E Germany, in Saxony at the foot of the Erzgebirge: textiles, engineering. Pop.: 266 737 (1996 est.). Also called (1953–90): **Karl-Marx-Stadt.**

chemo ('kiːməʊ) *n Inf.* short for **chemotherapy.**

chemo-, chemi-, *or before a vowel* **chem-** *combining form.* indicating that chemicals or chemical reactions are involved: *chemotherapy.* ORIG NL, from LGk *khēmeia;* see ALCHEMY

chemoreceptor (ˌkiːməʊrɪ'sɛptə) *or* **chemoceptor** *n* a sensory receptor in a biological cell membrane to which an external molecule binds to generate a smell or taste sensation.

chemosynthesis (ˌkiːməʊ'sɪnθɪsɪs) *n* the formation of organic material by some bacteria using energy from simple chemical reactions.

chemotherapy (ˌkiːməʊ'θɛrəpɪ) *n* treatment of disease, esp. cancer, by means of chemical agents. Cf. **radiotherapy.**
▸ **ˌchemo'therapist** *n*

Chemulpo ★ (ˌtʃɛmʊl'pəʊ) *n* a former name of **Inchon.**

chemurgy ('kɛmɜːdʒɪ) *n* the branch of chemistry concerned with the industrial use of organic raw materials, esp. of agricultural origin.
▸ **chem'urgic** *or* **chem'urgical** *adj*

Chenab ★ (tʃɪ'næb) *n* a river rising in the Himalayas and flowing southwest to the Sutlej River in Pakistan. Length: 1087 km (675 miles).

Cheney ★ ('tʃeɪnɪ) *n* **Richard B(ruce),** known as *Dick.* born 1941, US Republican politician; secretary of defense (1989–93); vice president of the US from 2001.

Cheng-chiang ★ ('tʃɛŋ'tʃæŋ) *n* a variant transliteration of the Chinese name for **Jinjiang.**

Chengchow *or* **Cheng-chou** ★ ('tʃɛŋ'tʃaʊ) *n* a variant transliteration of the Chinese name for **Zhengzhou.**

Chengde, Chengteh, *or* **Ch'eng-te** ★ ('tʃɛŋ'teɪ) *n* a city in NE China, in Hebei on the Luan River: summer residence of the Manchu emperors. Pop.: 246 799 (1990 est.).

Chengdu, Chengtu, *or* **Ch'eng-tu** ★ ('tʃɛŋ'tuː) *n* a city in S central China, capital of Sichuan province. Pop.: 2 810 000 (1991 est.).

Chénier ★ (*French* ʃenje) *n* **1 André** (**Marie de**) (ɑ̃dre). 1762–94, French poet; guillotined during the French Revolution. **2** his brother, **Marie-Joseph** (**Blaise de**) (mariʒozɛf). 1764–1811, French dramatist and politician.

chenille (ʃə'niːl) *n* **1** a thick soft tufty silk or worsted velvet cord or yarn used in embroidery and for trimmings, etc. **2** a fabric of such yarn. **3** a carpet of such fabric. ORIG C18: from F, lit.: hairy caterpillar, from L *canicula,* dim. of *canis* dog

Chennai ★ (tʃɪ'naɪ) *n* the official name for **Madras.**

cheongsam ('tʃɒŋ'sæm) *n* a straight dress with a stand-up collar and a slit in one side of the skirt, worn by Chinese women. ORIG from Chinese *ch'ang shan* long jacket

Cheops ★ ('kiːɒps) *n* original name *Khufu.* Egyptian king of the fourth dynasty (?2613–?2494 B.C.), who built the largest pyramid at El Gîza.

Chepstow ★ ('tʃɛpstəʊ) *n* a town in S Wales, in Monmouthshire on the River Wye: tourism, light industry. Pop.: 9461 (1991).

cheque *or US* **check** (tʃɛk) *n* **1** a bill of exchange drawn on a bank by the holder of a current account. **2** *Austral. & NZ.* the total sum of money received for contract work or a crop. **3** *Austral. & NZ.* wages. ORIG C18: from CHECK, in the sense: means of verification

cheque account *n* an account at a bank or a building society upon which cheques can be drawn.

chequebook *or US* **checkbook** ('tʃɛkˌbʊk) *n* a book of detachable blank cheques issued by a bank or building society to holders of cheque accounts.

chequebook journalism *n* the practice of securing exclusive rights to material for newspaper stories by paying a high price, regardless of any moral implications.

cheque card *n* a card issued by a bank or building society, guaranteeing payment of a customer's cheques up to a stated value.

chequer *or US* **checker** ('tʃɛkə) *n* **1** any of the marbles, pegs, or other pieces used in the game of Chinese chequers. **2a** a pattern of squares. **2b** one of the squares in such a pattern. ◆ *vb* (*tr*) **3** to make irregular in colour or character; variegate. **4** to mark off with alternating squares of colour. ◆ See also **chequers.** ORIG C13: chessboard, from Anglo-F *escheker,* from *eschec* CHECK

chequered *or esp. US* **checkered** ('tʃɛkəd) *adj* marked by fluctuations of fortune (esp. in **a chequered career**).

chequers ('tʃɛkəz) *n* (*functioning as sing*) another name for **draughts.**

Chequers ★ ('tʃɛkəz) *n* an estate and country house in S England, in central Buckinghamshire: the official country residence of the British prime minister.

Cher ★ (*French* ʃɛr) *n* **1** a department of central France, in E Centre region. Capital: Bourges. Pop.: 320 174 (1982). Area: 7304 sq. km (2849 sq. miles). **2** a river in central

France, rising in the Massif Central and flowing northwest to the Loire. Length: 354 km (220 miles).

Cherbourg ★ ('ʃɛəbʊəg; *French* ʃɛrbur) *n* a port in NW France, on the English Channel. Pop.: 28 773 (1990).

Cherenkov *or* **Cerenkov** ★ (tʃɪ'rɛŋkɒf; *Russian* tʃɪ'rjenkəf) *n* **Pavel Alekseyevich** ('pavɪl alɪk'sjejɪvitʃ). 1904–90, Soviet physicist: noted for his work on the effects produced by high-energy particles: shared Nobel prize for physics 1958.

Cheribon ★ ('tʃɪərə,bɒn) *n* a variant spelling of **Tjirebon.**

cherish ('tʃɛrɪʃ) *vb* (*tr*) **1** to feel or show great tenderness or care for. **2** to cling fondly to (a hope, idea, etc.); nurse: *to cherish ambitions.* ORIG C14: from OF, from *cher* dear, from L *cārus*

Chernenko ★ (tʃɜː'njɛŋkəʊ; *Russian* tʃɪr'ɲɪnkə) *n* **Konstantin** (**Ustinovich**) (kənstan'tin). 1911–85, Soviet statesman; general secretary of the Soviet Communist Party (1984–85).

Chernobyl ★ (tʃɜː'nəʊbᵊl, -'nɒbᵊl) *n* a town in N Ukraine; site of a nuclear power station accident in 1986.

Chernovtsy ★ (*Russian* tʃɪrnaf'tsi) *n* a city in Ukraine on the Prut River: formerly under Polish, Austro-Hungarian, and Romanian rule; part of the Soviet Union (1947–91). Pop.: 261 000 (1996 est.). German name: **Czernowitz.** Romanian name: **Cernăuţi.**

chernozem ('tʃɜːnəʊ,zɛm) *n* a rich black soil found in temperate semiarid regions, such as the grasslands of Russia. ORIG from Russian *chernaya zemlya* black earth

Cherokee ('tʃɛrə,kiː) *n* **1** (*pl* **Cherokees** *or* **Cherokee**) a member of a North American Indian people formerly living in the Appalachian Mountains. **2** the Iroquois language of this people.

cheroot (ʃə'ruːt) *n* a cigar with both ends cut off squarely. ORIG C17: from Tamil *curuttu* curl, roll

cherry ('tʃɛrɪ) *n, pl* **cherries. 1** any of several trees of the genus *Prunus,* having a small fleshy rounded fruit containing a hard stone. **2** the fruit or wood of any of these trees. **3** any of various unrelated plants, such as the ground cherry and Jerusalem cherry. **4a** a bright red colour; cerise. **4b** (*as adj*): *a cherry coat.* **5** *Taboo sl.* virginity or the hymen as its symbol. ORIG C14: back formation from OE *ciris* (mistakenly thought to be pl), ult. from LL *ceresia,* ?from L *cerasus* cherry tree, from Gk *kerasios*

cherry tomato *n* a miniature tomato not much bigger than a cherry.

chert (tʃɜːt) *n* an impure black or grey microcrystalline variety of quartz that resembles flint. ORIG C17: from ?
▸ '**cherty** *adj*

Chertsey ★ ('tʃɜːtsɪ) *n* a town in S England, in N Surrey on the River Thames. Pop.: 11 786 (1991).

cherub ('tʃɛrəb) *n, pl* **cherubs** *or* (*for sense 1*) **cherubim** ('tʃɛrəbɪm, -ʊbɪm). **1** a member of the second order of angels, often represented as a winged child. **2** an innocent or sweet child. ORIG OE, from Heb. *kĕrūbh*
▸ **cherubic** (tʃə'ruːbɪk) *or* **che'rubical** *adj* ▸ **che'rubically** *adv*

Cherubini ★ (,kɛru'biːnɪ) *n* (**Maria**) **Luigi** (**Carlo Zenobio Salvatore**) ('lwiːdʒi). 1760–1842, Italian composer, noted for his church music and his operas.

chervil ('tʃɜːvɪl) *n* an aromatic umbelliferous Eurasian plant with small white flowers and aniseed-flavoured leaves used as herbs in soups and salads. ORIG OE *cerfelle,* from L, from Gk, from *khairein* to enjoy + *phullon* leaf

Cherwell ★ ('tʃɜːwəl) *n* **Frederick Alexander Lindemann** ('lɪndəmən), Baron. 1886–1957, British physicist, born in Germany. He was scientific adviser to Winston Churchill during World War II.

Ches. *abbrev. for* Cheshire.

Chesapeake Bay ★ ('tʃɛsə,piːk) *n* the largest inlet of the Atlantic in the coast of the US: bordered by Maryland and Virginia.

Cheshire[1] ★ ('tʃɛʃə, 'tʃɛʃɪə) *n* a county of NW England: low-lying and undulating, bordering on the Pennines in the east; Warrington and Halton became independent unitary authorities in 1998; mainly agricultural. Administrative centre: Chester. Pop. (excluding unitary authorities): 668 000 (1996 est.). Area (excluding unitary authorities): 2077 sq. km (802 sq. miles). Abbrev.: **Ches.**

Cheshire[2] ★ ('tʃɛʃə) *n* (**Geoffrey**) **Leonard,** Baron. 1917–92, British philanthropist: awarded the Victoria Cross in World War II; founded the Leonard Cheshire Foundation Homes for the Disabled: married to Sue, Baroness Ryder.

Cheshire cheese *n* a mild-flavoured cheese with a crumbly texture, originally made in Cheshire.

chess (tʃɛs) *n* a game of skill for two players using a chessboard on which chessmen are moved. The object is to checkmate the opponent's king. ORIG C13: from OF *esches,* pl. of *eschec* CHECK

chessboard ('tʃɛs,bɔːd) *n* a square board divided into 64 squares of two alternating colours, used for playing chess or draughts.

chessman ('tʃɛs,mæn, -mən) *n, pl* **chessmen.** any of the pieces and pawns used in a game of chess. ORIG C17: from *chessmen,* from ME *chessemeyne* chess company

chest (tʃɛst) *n* **1a** the front part of the trunk from the neck to the belly. Related adj: **pectoral. 1b** (*as modifier*)*: a chest cold.* **2 get** (**something**) **off one's chest.** *Inf.* to unburden oneself of troubles, worries, etc., by talking about them. **3** a box used for storage or shipping: *a tea chest.* ORIG OE *cest,* from L, from Gk *kistē* box
▸ '**chested** *adj*

Chester ★ ('tʃɛstə) *n* a city in NW England, administrative centre of Cheshire, on the River Dee: intact surrounding walls; 16th- and 17th-century double-tier shops. Pop.: 80 110 (1991). Latin name: **Deva.**

chesterfield ('tʃɛstə,fiːld) *n* **1** a man's overcoat, usually with a velvet collar. **2** a large tightly stuffed sofa, with straight upholstered arms of the same height as the back. ORIG C19: after a 19th-cent. Earl of *Chesterfield*

Chesterfield[1] ★ ('tʃɛstə,fiːld) *n* an industrial town in N central England, in Derbyshire: famous 14th-century church with twisted spire. Pop.: 71 945 (1991).

Chesterfield[2] ★ ('tʃɛstə,fiːld) *n* **Philip Dormer Stanhope,** 4th Earl of Chesterfield. 1694–1773, British statesman and writer; author of *Letters to His Son* (1774).

Chesterton ★ ('tʃɛstətᵊn) *n* **G**(**ilbert**) **K**(**eith**). 1874–1936, British writer, noted for his Father Brown detective stories and his novels including *The Napoleon of Notting Hill* (1904).

chestnut ('tʃɛs,nʌt) *n* **1** a N temperate tree such as the **sweet** or **Spanish chestnut,** which produces flowers in long catkins and nuts in a prickly bur. Cf. **horse chestnut. 2** the edible nut of any of these trees. **3** the hard wood of any of these trees, used in making furniture, etc. **4a** a reddish-brown colour. **4b** (*as adj*)*: chestnut hair.* **5** a horse of a golden-brown colour. **6** *Inf.* an old or stale joke. ORIG C16: from earlier *chesten nut: chesten,* from OF, from L, from Gk *kastanea*

chest of drawers *n* a piece of furniture consisting of a set of drawers in a frame.

chesty ('tʃɛstɪ) *adj* **chestier, chestiest.** *Inf.* **1** *Brit.* suffering from or symptomatic of chest disease: *a chesty cough.* **2** having a large well-developed chest or bosom.
▸ '**chestiness** *n*

cheval glass (ʃə'væl) *n* a full-length mirror mounted so as to swivel within a frame. ORIG C19: from F *cheval* support (lit.: horse)

chevalier (,ʃɛ'vælɪə) *n* **1** a member of certain orders of merit, such as the French Legion of Honour. **2** the lowest title of rank in the old French nobility. **3** an archaic word for **knight. 4** a chivalrous man; gallant. ORIG C14: from OF, from Med. L *caballārius* horseman, CAVALIER

Chevalier ★ *n* **1** (,ʃɛvə'lɪə). **Albert.** 1861–1923, British music-hall entertainer, remembered for his cockney songs. **2** (,ʃɛ'vælɪə; *French* ʃəvalje). **Maurice** (mɔris). 1888–1972, French singer and film actor.

Cheviot ('tʃiːvɪət, 'tʃɛv-) *n* **1** a large British breed of sheep reared for its wool. **2** (*often not cap.*) a rough twill-weave woollen suiting fabric.

Cheviot Hills ★ *pl n* a range of hills on the border between England and Scotland, mainly in Northumberland.

chèvre (ˈʃɛvrə) *n* any cheese made from goats' milk. ORIG C20: from F, lit.: goat

chevron (ˈʃɛvrən) *n* **1** *Mil.* a badge or insignia consisting of one or more V-shaped stripes to indicate a noncommissioned rank or length of service. **2** *Heraldry.* an inverted V-shaped charge on a shield. **3** (*usually pl*) a pattern of horizontal black and white V-shapes on a road sign indicating a sharp bend. **4** any V-shaped pattern or device. ORIG C14: from OF, ult. from L *caper* goat; cf. L *capreoli* pair of rafters (lit.: little goats)

chevrotain (ˈʃɛvrəˌteɪn, -tɪn) *n* a small timid ruminant mammal of S and SE Asia. Also called: **mouse deer.** ORIG C18: from F, from OF *chevrot* kid, from *chèvre* goat, ult. from L *caper* goat

chevy (ˈtʃɛvɪ) *n, vb* a variant spelling of **chivy.**

chew (tʃuː) *vb* **1** to work the jaws and teeth in order to grind (food); masticate. **2** to bite repeatedly: *she chewed her nails anxiously.* **3** (*intr*) to use chewing tobacco. **4 chew the fat** *or* **rag.** *Sl.* **4a** to argue over a point. **4b** to talk idly; gossip. ◆ *n* **5** the act of chewing. **6** something that is chewed. ORIG OE *ceowan*
▸ **ˈchewable** *adj* ▸ **ˈchewer** *n*

chewing gum *n* a preparation for chewing, usually made of flavoured and sweetened chicle or such substitutes as polyvinyl acetate.

chew over *vb* (*tr, adv*) to consider carefully.

chewy (ˈtʃuːɪ) *adj* **chewier, chewiest.** of a consistency requiring chewing.

Cheyenne ★ (ʃaɪˈæn, -ˈɛn) *n* a city in SE Wyoming, capital of the state. Pop.: 50 008 (1990).

chez *French.* (ʃe) *prep* **1** at the home of. **2** with, among, or in the manner of.

chi[1] (kaɪ) *n* the 22nd letter of the Greek alphabet (Χ, χ).

chi[2] *or* **ch'i** *or* **qi** (tʃiː) *n* (*sometimes cap.*) (in Oriental medicine, martial arts, etc.) vital energy believed to circulate round the body in currents. ORIG Chinese, lit.: energy

chiack *or* **chyack** (ˈtʃaɪæk) *Austral inf.* ◆ *vb* (*tr*) **1** to tease or banter. ◆ *n* **2** good-humoured banter. ORIG C19: from *chi-hike,* a shout of greeting

Chiang Ch'ing ★ (ˈtʃæŋ ˈtʃɪŋ) *n* a variant transliteration of the Chinese name for **Jiang Qing.**

Chiang Ching-kuo (ˈtʃæŋ tʃɪŋˈkwəʊ) *or* **Jiang Jing Guo** ★ *n* 1910–88, Chinese statesman; the son of Chiang Kai-shek. He was prime minister of Taiwan (1971–78); president (1978–88).

Chiang Kai-shek (ˈtʃæŋ kaɪˈʃɛk) *or* **Jiang Jie Shi** ★ *n* original name *Chiang Chung-cheng,* 1887–1975, Chinese general: president of China (1928–31; 1943–49) and of the Republic of China (Taiwan) (1950–75). As chairman of the Kuomintang, he allied with the Communists against the Japanese (1937–45), but in the Civil War that followed was forced to withdraw to Taiwan.

chianti (kɪˈæntɪ) *n* (*sometimes cap.*) a dry red wine produced in Tuscany, Italy.

Chiapas ★ (*Spanish* ˈtʃjapas) *n* a state of S Mexico: mountainous and forested; Maya ruins in the northeast; rich mineral resources. Capital: Tuxtla Gutiérrez. Pop.: 3 637 142 (1997 est.). Area: 73 887 sq. km (28 816 sq. miles).

chiaroscuro (kɪˌɑːrəˈskʊərəʊ) *n, pl* **chiaroscuros. 1** the artistic distribution of light and dark masses in a picture. **2** monochrome painting using light and dark only. ORIG C17: from It., from *chiaro* CLEAR + *oscuro* OBSCURE

chiasma (kaɪˈæzmə) *n, pl* **chiasmas, chiasmata** (-mətə) **1** *Cytology.* the cross-shaped connection produced by the crossing over of pairing chromosomes during meiosis. **2** *Anat.* the crossing over of two parts or structures. ORIG C19: from Gk *khiasma,* from *khi* CHI[1]

chiasmus (kaɪˈæzməs) *n, pl* **chiasmi** (-maɪ). *Rhetoric.* reversal of word order in the second of two parallel phrases: *he came in triumph and in defeat departs.* ORIG NL from Gk: see CHIASMA
▸ **chiastic** (kaɪˈæstɪk) *adj*

★ people and places

Chiba ★ (ˈtʃiːbə) *n* an industrial city in central Japan, in SE Honshu on Tokyo Bay. Pop.: 856 882 (1995).

chic (ʃiːk, ʃɪk) *adj* **1** (esp. of fashionable clothes, women, etc.) stylish or elegant. ◆ *n* **2** stylishness, esp. in dress; modishness; fashionable good taste. ORIG C19: from F, from ?
▸ **ˈchicly** *adv*

Chicago ★ (ʃɪˈkɑːgəʊ) *n* a port in NE Illinois, on Lake Michigan: the third largest city in the US; it is a major railway and air traffic centre. Pop.: 2 731 743 (1994 est.).

chicane (ʃɪˈkeɪn) *n* **1** a bridge or whist hand without trumps. **2** *Motor racing.* a short section of sharp narrow bends formed by barriers placed on a motor-racing circuit. **3** a less common word for **chicanery.** ◆ *vb* **chicanes, chicaning, chicaned. 4** (*tr*) to deceive or trick by chicanery. **5** (*intr*) to use tricks or chicanery. ORIG C17: from F *chicaner* to quibble, from ?
▸ **chiˈcaner** *n*

chicanery (ʃɪˈkeɪnərɪ) *n, pl* **chicaneries. 1** verbal deception or trickery, dishonest or sharp practice. **2** a trick, deception, or quibble.

chicano (tʃɪˈkɑːnəʊ) *n, pl* **chicanos.** *US.* an American citizen of Mexican origin. ORIG C20: from Sp. *mejicano* Mexican

Chichagof Island ★ (ˈtʃɪtʃəˌgɔːf) *n* an island of Alaska, in the Alexander Archipelago. Area: 5439 sq. km (2100 sq. miles).

Chichen Itzá ★ (*Spanish* tʃiˈtʃen itˈsa) *n* a village in Yucatán state in Mexico: site of important Mayan ruins.

Chichester[1] ★ (ˈtʃɪtʃɪstə) *n* a city in S England, administrative centre of West Sussex: Roman ruins; 11th-century cathedral; Festival Theatre. Pop.: 26 572 (1991).

Chichester[2] ★ (ˈtʃɪtʃɪstə) *n* Sir **Francis.** 1901–72, British yachtsman, who sailed alone round the world (1966–67).

chichi (ˈʃiːˌʃiː) *adj* **1** affectedly pretty or stylish. ◆ *n* **2** the quality of being affectedly pretty or stylish. ORIG C20: from F

Chichihaerh *or* **Ch'i-ch'i-haerh** ★ (ˈtʃiːˌtʃiːˈhɑː) *n* a variant transliteration of the Chinese name for **Qiqihar.**

chick (tʃɪk) *n* **1** the young of a bird, esp. of a domestic fowl. **2** *Sl.* a girl or young woman, esp. an attractive one. **3** a young child: used as a term of endearment. ORIG C14: short for CHICKEN

chickadee (ˈtʃɪkəˌdiː) *n* any of various small North American songbirds, typically having grey-and-black plumage. ORIG C19: imit.

chicken (ˈtʃɪkɪn) *n* **1** a domestic fowl bred for its flesh or eggs. **2** the flesh of such a bird used for food. **3** any of various similar birds, such as a prairie chicken. **4** *Sl.* a cowardly person. **5** *Sl.* a young inexperienced person. **6** *Inf.* any of various, often dangerous, games or challenges in which the object is to make one's opponent lose his nerve. **7 count one's chickens before they are hatched.** to be over-optimistic in acting on expectations which are not yet fulfilled. ◆ *adj* **8** *Sl.* easily scared; cowardly; timid. ORIG OE *ciecen*

chicken feed *n Sl.* a trifling amount of money.

chicken-hearted *or* **chicken-livered** *adj* easily frightened; cowardly.

chicken out *vb* (*intr, adv*) *Inf.* to fail to do something through fear or lack of conviction.

chickenpox (ˈtʃɪkɪnˌpɒks) *n* a highly communicable viral disease most commonly affecting children, characterized by slight fever and the eruption of a rash.

chicken wire *n* wire netting with a hexagonal mesh.

chick flick *n Inf., derog.* a film aimed at or appealing to women. ORIG C20: from CHICK (sense 2) + FLICK[2]

chickpea (ˈtʃɪkˌpiː) *n* **1** a bushy leguminous plant, cultivated for its edible pealike seeds. **2** the seed of this plant. ORIG C16 *ciche peasen,* from *ciche* (from F, from L *cicer* chickpea) + *peasen;* see PEA

chickweed (ˈtʃɪkˌwiːd) *n* any of various plants of the pink family, esp. a common garden weed with small white flowers.

Chiclayo ★ (*Spanish* tʃiˈklajo) *n* a city in NW Peru. Pop.: 668 066 (1995).

chicle (ˈtʃɪkᵊl) *n* a gumlike substance obtained from the sapodilla; the main ingredient of chewing gum. ORIG from Sp., from Nahuatl *chictli*

chicory (ˈtʃɪkərɪ) *n, pl* **chicories. 1** a blue-flowered plant, cultivated for its leaves, which are used in salads, and for its roots. **2** the root of this plant, roasted, dried, and used as a coffee substitute. ◆ Cf. **endive.** ORIG C15: from OF, from L *cichorium,* from Gk *kikhōrion*

chide (tʃaɪd) *vb* **chides, chiding, chided** *or* **chid** (tʃɪd); **chided, chid** *or* **chidden** (ˈtʃɪdᵊn). **1** to rebuke or scold. **2** (*tr*) to goad into action. ORIG OE *cīdan*
▸ **ˈchider** *n* ▸ **ˈchidingly** *adv*

chief (tʃiːf) *n* **1** the head or leader of a group or body of people. **2** *Heraldry.* the upper third of a shield. **3 in chief.** primarily; especially. ◆ *adj* **4** (*prenominal*) **4a** most important; principal. **4b** highest in rank or authority. ◆ *adv* **5** *Arch.* principally. ORIG C13: from OF, from L *caput* head

chief executive *n* the person with overall responsibility for the efficient running of a company, organization, etc.

chief justice *n* **1** (in any of several Commonwealth countries) the judge presiding over a supreme court. **2** (in the US) the presiding judge of a court composed of a number of members. ◆ See also **Lord Chief Justice.**

chiefly (ˈtʃiːflɪ) *adv* **1** especially or essentially; above all. **2** in general; mainly; mostly. ◆ *adj* **3** of or relating to a chief or chieftain.

Chief of Staff *n* **1** the senior staff officer under the commander of a major military formation or organization. **2** the senior officer of each service of the armed forces.

chief petty officer *n* the senior naval rank for personnel without commissioned or warrant rank.

chieftain (ˈtʃiːftən, -tɪn) *n* the head or leader of a tribe or clan. ORIG C14: from OF, from LL *capitāneus* commander; see CAPTAIN
▸ **ˈchieftaincy** *or* **ˈchieftainˌship** *n*

chief technician *n* a noncommissioned officer in the Royal Air Force, junior to a flight sergeant.

chiffchaff (ˈtʃɪfˌtʃæf) *n* a common European warbler with a yellowish-brown plumage. ORIG C18: imit.

chiffon (ʃɪˈfɒn, ˈʃɪfɒn) *n* **1** a fine almost transparent fabric of silk, nylon, etc. **2** (*often pl*) *Now rare.* feminine finery. ◆ *adj* **3** made of chiffon. **4** (of soufflés, pies, cakes, etc.) having a very light fluffy texture. ORIG C18: from F, from *chiffe* rag

chiffonier *or* **chiffonnier** (ˌʃɪfəˈnɪə) *n* **1** a tall, elegant chest of drawers. **2** a wide low open-fronted cabinet. ORIG C19: from F, from *chiffon* rag

Chifley ★ (ˈtʃɪflɪ) *n* **Joseph Benedict.** 1885–1951, Australian statesman; prime minister (1945–49).

chigetai (ˌtʃɪgɪˈtaɪ) *n* a variety of the Asiatic wild ass of Mongolia. Also spelled: **dziggetai.** ORIG from Mongolian *tchikhitei* long-eared, from *tchikhi* ear

chigger (ˈtʃɪgə) *n* **1** *US & Canad.* the parasitic larva of a mite, which causes intense itching. **2** another name for **chigoe.**

chignon (ˈʃiːnjɒn) *n* an arrangement of long hair in a roll or knot at the back of the head. ORIG C18: from F, from OF *chaignon* link, from *chaine* CHAIN; infl. also by OF *tignon* coil of hair

chigoe (ˈtʃɪgəʊ) *n* **1** a tropical flea, the female of which burrows into the skin of its host, which includes man. **2** another name for **chigger.** ORIG C17: from Carib *chigo*

Chigwell ★ (ˈtʃɪgwəl) *n* a town in S England, in W Essex. Pop.: 10 332 (1991).

Chihli ★ (ˈtʃiːliː) *n* **Gulf of.** another name for the **Bohai.**

Chihuahua ★ (tʃɪˈwɑːwɑː, -wə) *n* **1** a state of N Mexico: mostly high plateau; important mineral resources, with many silver mines. Capital: Chihuahua. Pop.: 2 895 672 (1997 est.). Area: 247 087 sq. km (153 194 sq. miles). **2** a city in N Mexico, capital of Chihuahua state. Pop.: 516 153 (1990). **3** a breed of tiny dog originally from Mexico, having short smooth hair, large erect ears, and protruding eyes.

chilblain (ˈtʃɪlˌbleɪn) *n* (*usually pl*) an inflammation of the fingers or toes, caused by exposure to cold. ORIG C16: from CHILL (n) + BLAIN
▸ **ˈchilˌblained** *adj*

child (tʃaɪld) *n, pl* **children. 1a** a boy or girl between birth and puberty. **1b** (*as modifier*): *child labour.* **2** a baby or infant. **3** an unborn baby. **4 with child.** an old-fashioned term for **pregnant. 5** a human offspring; a son or daughter. Related adj: **filial. 6** a childish or immature person. **7** a member of a family or tribe; descendant: *a child of Israel.* **8** a person or thing regarded as the product of an influence or environment: *a child of nature.* ORIG OE *cild*
▸ **ˈchildless** *adj* ▸ **ˈchildlessness** *n*

child abuse *n* physical, sexual, or emotional ill-treatment of a child by its parents or other adults responsible for its welfare.

child-bearing *n* **a** the act or process of carrying and giving birth to a child. **b** (*as modifier*): *of child-bearing age.*

childbed (ˈtʃaɪldˌbɛd) *n* (often preceded by *in*) the condition of giving birth to a child.

child benefit *n* (in Britain and New Zealand) a regular government payment to parents of children up to a certain age.

childbirth (ˈtʃaɪldˌbɜːθ) *n* the act of giving birth to a child.

childcare (ˈtʃaɪldˌkɛə) *n Brit.* **1** care provided for children without homes (or with a seriously disturbed home life) by a local authority. **2** care and supervision of children whose parents are working, provided by a childminder or local authority.

child endowment *n* (in Australia) a social security payment for dependent children.

Childers ★ (ˈtʃɪldəz) *n* (**Robert**) **Erskine.** 1870–1922, Irish politician, executed by the Irish Free State for his IRA activities: author of *The Riddle of the Sands* (1903).

childhood (ˈtʃaɪldhʊd) *n* the condition of being a child; the period of life before puberty.

childish (ˈtʃaɪldɪʃ) *adj* **1** in the manner of or suitable to a child. **2** foolish or petty: *childish fears.*
▸ **ˈchildishly** *adv* ▸ **ˈchildishness** *n*

childlike (ˈtʃaɪldˌlaɪk) *adj* like or befitting a child, as in being innocent, trustful, etc.

childminder (ˈtʃaɪldˌmaɪndə) *n* a person who looks after children, esp. those whose parents are working.

children (ˈtʃɪldrən) *n* the plural of **child.**

Children of Israel *pl n* the Jewish people or nation.

child-resistant *adj* (of packaging etc., esp. of drugs) designed to be difficult for children to open or tamper with. Also: **child-proof.**

child's play *n Inf.* something easy to do.

chile (ˈtʃɪlɪ) *n* a variant spelling of **chilli.**

Chile ★ (ˈtʃɪlɪ) *n* a republic in South America, on the Pacific, with a total length of about 4090 km (2650 miles) and an average width of only 177 km (110 miles): gained independence from Spain in 1818; the government of President Allende (elected 1970) attempted the implementation of Marxist policies within a democratic system until overthrown by a military coup (1973); democracy restored 1988. Chile consists chiefly of the Andes in the east, the Atacama Desert in the north, a central fertile region, and a huge S region of almost uninhabitable mountains, glaciers, fjords, and islands; an important producer of copper, iron ore, nitrates, etc. Language: Spanish. Religion: Roman Catholic. Currency: peso. Capital: Santiago. Pop.: 15 018 000 (1999 est.). Area: 756 945 sq. km (292 256 sq. miles).
▸ **ˈChilean** *adj, n*

Chile pine *n* another name for the **monkey puzzle.**

Chile saltpetre *or* **nitre** *n* a naturally occurring form of sodium nitrate.

chiliad (ˈkɪlɪˌæd) *n* **1** a group of one thousand. **2** one thousand years. ORIG C16: from Gk, from *khilioi* a thousand

chill (tʃɪl) *n* **1** a moderate coldness. **2** a sensation of coldness resulting from a cold or damp environment, or from a sudden emotional reaction. **3** a feverish cold. **4** a check on enthusiasm or joy. ◆ *adj* **5** another word for

chilly. ◆ *vb* **6** to make or become cold. **7** (*tr*) to cool or freeze (food, drinks, etc.). **8** (*tr*) **8a** to depress (enthusiasm, etc.). **8b** to discourage. **9** (*intr*) *Sl., chiefly US.* to relax; calm oneself. ◆ See also **chill out.** ORIG OE *ciele*
▸ **'chilling** *adj* ▸ **'chillingly** *adv* ▸ **'chillness** *n*

chiller ('tʃɪlə) *n* **1** short for **spine-chiller. 2** *NZ.* a refrigerated storage area for meat.

chilli *or* **chili** ('tʃɪlɪ) *n, pl* **chillies** *or* **chilies.** the small red hot-tasting pod of a type of capsicum used for flavouring sauces, etc. ORIG C17: from Sp., from Nahuatl *chilli*

chilli con carne ('tʃɪlɪ kɒn 'kɑːnɪ) *n* a highly seasoned Mexican dish of meat, onions, beans, and chilli powder. ORIG from Sp.: chilli with meat

chilli dog *n US.* a frankfurter garnished with chilli con carne, served in a roll.

chilli powder *n* ground chilli blended with other spices.

chilli sauce *n* a highly seasoned sauce made of tomatoes cooked with chilli and other spices.

chill out *Inf.* ◆ *vb* **1** (*intr, adv*) to relax, esp. after energetic dancing at a rave. ◆ *adj* **chill-out. 2** suitable for relaxation after energetic dancing: *a chill-out area; chill-out music.*

chilly ('tʃɪlɪ) *adj* **chillier, chilliest. 1** causing or feeling cool or moderately cold. **2** without warmth; unfriendly. **3** (of people) sensitive to cold.
▸ **'chilliness** *n*

chilly bin *n NZ inf.* a portable insulated container with provision for packing food and drink in ice.

Chiloé Island ★ (,tʃɪləʊ'eɪ) *n* an island administered by Chile, off the W coast of South America in the Pacific Ocean: timber. Pop.: 116 000 (1984 est.). Area: 8394 sq. km (3240 sq. miles).

Chilpancingo ★ (*Spanish* tʃilpan'θiŋgo) *n* a town in S Mexico, capital of Guerrero state, in the Sierra Madre del Sur. Pop.: 136 243 (1990).

Chiltern Hills ★ ('tʃɪltən) *pl n* a range of low chalk hills in SE England extending northwards from the Thames valley. Highest point: 260 m (852 ft).

Chiltern Hundreds ('tʃɪltən) *pl n* (in Britain) short for **Stewardship of the Chiltern Hundreds;** a nominal office that an MP applies for in order to resign his seat.

Chilung *or* **Chi-lung** ★ ('tʃiː'lʊŋ) *n* a port in N Taiwan: fishing and industrial centre. Pop.: 370 049 (1996 est.). Also called: **Keelung, Kilung.**

Chimborazo ★ (,tʃɪmbə'rɑːzəʊ, -'reɪ-; *Spanish* tʃimbo'raθo) *n* an extinct volcano in central Ecuador, in the Andes: the highest peak in Ecuador. Height: 6267 m (20 561 ft).

Chimbote ★ (*Spanish* tʃim'bote) *n* a port in N central Peru: contains Peru's first steelworks (1958), using hydroelectric power from the Santa River. Pop.: 268 979 (1993).

chime[1] (tʃaɪm) *n* **1** an individual bell or the sound it makes when struck. **2** (*often pl*) the machinery employed to sound a bell in this way. **3** Also called: **bell.** a percussion instrument consisting of a set of vertical metal tubes of graduated length, suspended in a frame and struck with a hammer. **4** agreement; concord. ◆ *vb* **chimes, chiming, chimed. 5a** to sound (a bell) or (of a bell) to be sounded by a clapper or hammer. **5b** to produce (music or sounds) by chiming. **6** (*tr*) to indicate or show (time or the hours) by chiming. **7** (*intr;* foll. by *with*) to agree or harmonize. ORIG C13: prob. shortened from earlier *chymbe bell,* ult. from L *cymbalum* CYMBAL
▸ **'chimer** *n*

chime[2]**, chimb** (tʃaɪm), *or* **chine** *n* the projecting rim of a cask or barrel. ORIG OE *cimb-*

chime in *vb* (*intr, adv*) *Inf.* **1** to join in or interrupt (a conversation), esp. repeatedly and unwelcomely. **2** to voice agreement.

chimera *or* **chimaera** (kaɪ'mɪərə, kɪ-) *n* **1** a wild and unrealistic dream or notion. **2** (*often cap.*) *Greek myth.* a fire-breathing monster with the head of a lion, body of a goat, and tail of a serpent. **3** a fabulous beast made up of parts taken from various animals. **4** *Biol.* an organism consisting of at least two genetically different kinds of tissue as a result of mutation, grafting, etc. ORIG C16: from L, from Gk *khimaira* she-goat

chimerical (kaɪ'merɪk°l, kɪ-) *or* **chimeric** *adj* **1** wildly fanciful; imaginary. **2** given to or indulging in fantasies.
▸ **chi'merically** *adv*

Chimkent ★ (tʃɪm'kɛnt) *n* a city in S Kazakhstan: a major railway junction. Pop.: 397 600 (1995 est.).

chimney ('tʃɪmnɪ) *n* **1** a vertical structure of brick, masonry, or steel that carries smoke or steam away from a fire, engine, etc. **2** another name for **flue** (sense 1). **3** short for **chimney stack. 4** an open-ended glass tube fitting around the flame of an oil or gas lamp in order to exclude draughts. **5** *Brit.* a fireplace, esp. an old and large one. **6** the vent of a volcano. **7** *Mountaineering.* a vertical fissure large enough for a person's body to enter. ORIG C14: from OF *cheminée,* from LL *camīnāta,* from L *camīnus* furnace, from Gk *kaminos* oven

chimney breast *n* the wall or walls that surround the base of a chimney or fireplace.

chimneypot ('tʃɪmnɪ,pɒt) *n* a short pipe on the top of a chimney.

chimney stack *n* the part of a chimney that rises above the roof of a building.

chimney sweep *or* **sweeper** *n* a person who cleans soot from chimneys.

chimp (tʃɪmp) *n Inf.* short for **chimpanzee.**

chimpanzee (,tʃɪmpæn'ziː) *n* a gregarious and intelligent anthropoid ape, inhabiting forests in central W Africa. ORIG C18: from Central African dialect

chin (tʃɪn) *n* **1** the protruding part of the lower jaw. **2** the front part of the face below the lips. **3 keep one's chin up.** *Inf.* to keep cheerful under difficult circumstances. **4 take it on the chin.** *Inf.* to face squarely up to a defeat, adversity, etc. ◆ *vb* **chins, chinning, chinned. 5** *Gymnastics.* to raise one's chin to (a horizontal bar, etc.) when hanging by the arms. ORIG OE *cinn*

Chin. *abbrev. for:* **1** China. **2** Chinese.

china[1] ('tʃaɪnə) *n* **1** ceramic ware of a type originally from China. **2** any porcelain or similar ware. **3** cups, saucers, etc., collectively. **4** (*modifier*) made of china. ORIG C16 *chiny,* from Persian *chīnī*

china[2] ('tʃaɪnə) *n Brit. & S. African inf.* a friend or companion. ORIG C19: orig. Cockney rhyming sl.: *china plate, mate*

China ★ ('tʃaɪnə) *n* **1 People's Republic of.** Also called: **Communist China, Red China.** a republic in E Asia: the third largest and the most populous country in the world; the oldest continuing civilization (beginning over 2000 years B.C.); republic established in 1911 after the overthrow of the Manchu dynasty by Sun Yat-sen; People's Republic formed in 1949; pro-democracy demonstrations violently suppressed in 1989: contains vast deserts, steppes, great mountain ranges (Himalayas, Kunlun, Tian Shan, and Nan Shan), a central rugged plateau, and intensively cultivated E plains. Language: Chinese in various dialects, the chief of which is Mandarin. Religion: nonreligious majority. Currency: yuan. Capital: Beijing. Pop.: 1 251 238 000 (1999 est.). Area: 9 560 990 sq. km (3 691 502 sq. miles). **2 Republic of.** Also called: **Nationalist China, Taiwan.** a republic (recognized as an independent nation by 28 countries) in E Asia occupying the island of Taiwan, 13 nearby islands, and 64 islands of the Penghu (Pescadores) group: established in 1949 by the Nationalist government of China under Chiang Kai-shek after its expulsion by the Communists from the mainland; under US protection 1954–79; lost its seat at the UN to the People's Republic of China in 1971; state of war with the People's Republic of China formally ended in 1991. Language: Mandarin Chinese. Religion: predominantly Buddhist and Taoist. Currency: New Taiwan dollar. Capital: Taipei. Pop.: 22 024 000 (1999 est.). Area: 35 981 sq. km (13 892 sq. miles). Former name: **Formosa.** ◆ Related adj: **Sinitic.**

china clay *n* another name for **kaolin.**

Chinagraph ('tʃaɪnə,grɑːf) *n Trademark.* a coloured pencil used for writing on china, glass, etc.

Chinaman ('tʃaɪnəmən) *n, pl* **Chinamen. 1** *Arch. or derog.* a native or inhabitant of China. **2** (*often not cap.*) *Cricket.* a ball bowled by a left-handed bowler to a right-handed batsman that spins from off to leg.

Chinan *or* **Chi-nan** ★ ('tʃiː'næn) *n* a variant transliteration of the Chinese name for **Jinan**.

China Sea ★ *n* part of the Pacific Ocean off the coast of China: divided by Taiwan into the East China Sea in the north and the South China Sea in the south.

china stone *n* **1** a type of kaolinized granitic rock containing unaltered plagioclase. **2** any of certain limestones having a very fine grain and smooth texture.

Chinatown ('tʃaɪnəˌtaʊn) *n* a quarter of any city or town outside China with a predominantly Chinese population.

chinaware ('tʃaɪnəˌwɛə) *n* articles made of china, esp. those made for domestic use.

chincherinchee (ˌtʃɪntʃərɪn'tʃiː, -'rɪntʃɪ) *n* a bulbous South African liliaceous plant having long spikes of white or yellow long-lasting flowers. ORIG from ?

chinchilla (tʃɪn'tʃɪlə) *n* **1** a small gregarious rodent inhabiting mountainous regions of South America. It is bred in captivity for its soft silvery grey fur. **2** the highly valued fur of this animal. **3** a thick napped woollen cloth used for coats. ORIG C17: from Sp., ?from Aymara

chin-chin *sentence substitute. Inf.* a greeting or toast. ORIG C18: from Chinese (Peking) *ch'ing-ch'ing,* please-please

Chin-Chou *or* **Chin-chow** ★ ('tʃɪn'tʃaʊ) *n* a variant transliteration of the Chinese name for **Jinzhou**.

Chindit ('tʃɪndɪt) *n* a member of the Allied forces fighting behind the Japanese lines in Burma (1943–45). ORIG C20: from Burmese *chinthé* a fabulous lion

Chindwin ★ ('tʃɪn'dwɪn) *n* a river in N Myanmar, rising in the Kumôn Range and flowing northwest then south to the Irrawaddy, of which it is the main tributary. Length: about 966 km (600 miles).

chine[1] (tʃaɪn) *n* **1** the backbone. **2** the backbone of an animal with adjoining meat, cut for cooking. **3** a ridge or crest of land. ◆ *vb* **chines, chining, chined. 4** (*tr*) to cut (meat) along or across the backbone. ORIG C14: from OF *eschine,* of Gmc origin; see SHIN

chine[2] (tʃaɪn) *n S English dialect.* a deep fissure in the wall of a cliff. ORIG OE *cīnan* to crack

Chinese (tʃaɪ'niːz) *adj* **1** of, relating to, or characteristic of China, its people, or their languages. ◆ *n* **2** (*pl* **Chinese**) a native or inhabitant of China or a descendant of one. **3** any of the languages of China.

Chinese cabbage *n* **1** a Chinese plant that is related to the cabbage and has crisp edible leaves growing in a loose cylindrical head. **2** another name for **bok choy**.

Chinese chequers *n* (*functioning as sing*) a board game played with marbles or pegs.

Chinese Empire ★ *n* China as ruled by the emperors until the establishment of the republic in 1911–12.

Chinese gooseberry *n* another name for **kiwi fruit**.

Chinese lantern *n* **1** a collapsible lantern made of thin coloured paper. **2** an Asian plant, cultivated for its attractive orange-red inflated calyx.

Chinese leaf *n* another name for **bok choy**.

Chinese puzzle *n* **1** an intricate puzzle, esp. one consisting of boxes within boxes. **2** a complicated problem.

Chinese Turkestan ★ *n* the E part of the central Asian region of Turkestan: corresponds generally to the present-day Xinjiang Uygur Autonomous Region of China.

Chinese wall *n* (esp. in financial institutions) a notional barrier between departments in the same company in order to avoid conflicts of interest between them.

Chinghai *or* **Ch'ing-hai** ★ ('tʃɪŋ'haɪ) *n* a variant transliteration of the Chinese name for **Qinghai**.

Chingtao *or* **Ch'ing-tao** ★ ('tʃɪŋ'taʊ) *n* a variant transliteration of the Chinese name for **Qingdao**.

Ch'ing-yüan ★ ('tʃɪŋ'juːɑːn) *n* a former name of **Baoding**.

Chin-Hsien ★ ('tʃɪn'ʃjɛn) *n* the former name (1913–47) of **Jinzhou**.

chink[1] (tʃɪŋk) *n* **1** a small narrow opening, such as a fissure or crack. **2 chink in one's armour.** a small but fatal weakness. ORIG C16: ? var. of earlier *chine,* from OE *cine* crack

chink[2] (tʃɪŋk) *vb* **1** to make or cause to make a light ringing sound, as by the striking of glasses or coins. ◆ *n* **2** such a sound. ORIG C16: imit.

Chinkiang ★ ('tʃɪn'kjæŋ, -kaɪ'æŋ) *n* a variant transliteration of the Chinese name for **Jinjiang**.

chinless wonder ('tʃɪnlɪs) *n Brit. inf.* a person, esp. upper-class, lacking strength of character.

chinoiserie (ʃiːnˌwɑːzə'riː, -'wɑːzərɪ) *n* **1** a style of decorative or fine art based on imitations of Chinese motifs. **2** an object or objects in this style. ORIG F, from *chinois* CHINESE; see -ERY

chinook (tʃɪ'nuːk, -'nʊk) *n* **1** a warm dry southwesterly wind blowing down the eastern slopes of the Rocky Mountains. **2** a warm moist wind blowing onto the Washington and Oregon coasts from the sea. ORIG C19: from Amerind

Chinook (tʃɪ'nuːk, -'nʊk) *n* **1** (*pl* **Chinook** *or* **Chinooks**) a North American Indian people of the Pacific coast near the Columbia River. **2** the language of this people.

Chinook Jargon *n* a pidgin language containing elements of North American Indian languages, English, and French: formerly used among fur traders and Indians on the NW coast of North America.

Chinook salmon *n* a Pacific salmon valued as a food fish.

chinos ('tʃiːnəʊz) *pl n* trousers made of a durable cotton twill cloth. ORIG C20: from *chino,* the cloth, from ?

chintz (tʃɪnts) *n* a printed, patterned cotton fabric, with glazed finish. ORIG C17: from Hindi *chīnt,* from Sansk. *citra* gaily-coloured

chintzy ('tʃɪntsɪ) *adj* **chintzier, chintziest. 1** of, resembling, or covered with chintz. **2** *Brit. inf.* typical of the décor associated with the use of chintz soft furnishings.

chinwag ('tʃɪnˌwæg) *n Brit. inf.* a chat.

Chios ★ ('kaɪɒs, -əʊs, 'kiː-) *n* **1** an island in the Aegean Sea, off the coast of Turkey: belongs to Greece. Capital: Chios. Pop.: 52 184 (1991). Area: 904 sq. km (353 sq. miles). **2** a port on the island of Chios: in ancient times, one of the 12 Ionian city-states. Pop.: 54 000 (1995 est.). Modern Greek name: **Khíos**.

chip (tʃɪp) *n* **1** a small piece removed by chopping, cutting, or breaking. **2** a mark left after a small piece has been broken off something. **3** (in some games) a counter used to represent money. **4** a thin strip of potato fried in deep fat. **5** the US, Canad., Austral., and NZ name for **crisp** (sense 10). **6** *Sport.* a shot, kick, etc., lofted into the air, and travelling only a short distance. **7** *Electronics.* Also called: **microchip.** a tiny wafer of semiconductor material, such as silicon, processed to form a type of integrated circuit or component such as a transistor. **8** a thin strip of wood or straw used for making woven hats, baskets, etc. **9** *NZ.* a container for soft fruit, made of thin sheets of wood; punnet. **10 chip off the old block.** *Inf.* a person who resembles one of his or her parents in behaviour. **11 have a chip on one's shoulder.** *Inf.* to be aggressive or bear a grudge. **12 have had one's chips.** *Brit. inf.* to be defeated, condemned to die, killed, etc. **13 when the chips are down.** *Inf.* at a time of crisis. ◆ *vb* **chips, chipping, chipped. 14** to break small pieces from or become broken off in small pieces: *will the paint chip?* **15** (*tr*) to break or cut into small pieces: *to chip ice.* **16** (*tr*) to shape by chipping. **17** *Austral.* to dig or weed (a crop) with a hoe. **18** *Sport.* to strike or kick (a ball) in a high arc. ORIG OE *cipp* (n), *cippian* (vb), from ?

chip-based *adj* using or incorporating microchips in electronic equipment.

chipboard ('tʃɪpˌbɔːd) *n* a thin rigid sheet made of compressed wood chips.

chip heater *n Austral. & NZ.* a domestic water heater that burns chips of wood.

chip in *vb* (*adv*) *Inf.* **1** to contribute (money, time, etc.) to a cause or fund. **2** (*intr*) to interpose a remark or interrupt with a remark.

chipmunk ('tʃɪpˌmʌŋk) *n* a burrowing rodent of North

America and Asia, typically having black-striped yellowish fur and cheek pouches for storing food. ORIG C19: of Algonquian origin

chipolata (ˌtʃɪpəˈlɑːtə) *n Chiefly Brit.* a small sausage. ORIG via F from It., from *cipolla* onion

Chippendale ★ (ˈtʃɪpᵊnˌdeɪl) *n* **1 Thomas.** ?1718–79, English cabinet-maker and furniture designer. ◆ *adj* **2** (of furniture) designed by, made by, or in the style of Thomas Chippendale, characterized by the use of Chinese and Gothic motifs, cabriole legs, and massive carving.

chipper (ˈtʃɪpə) *adj Inf.* **1** cheerful; lively. **2** smartly dressed.

chippy[1] (ˈtʃɪpɪ) *n, pl* **chippies. 1** *Brit. inf.* a fish-and-chip shop. **2** Also: **chippie.** *NZ.* a potato crisp.

chippy[2] (ˈtʃɪpɪ) *adj* **chippier, chippiest.** *Inf.* resentful or oversensitive about being perceived as inferior: *a chippy miner's son.* ORIG C20: from CHIP (sense 11)
▸ **ˈchippiness** *n*

chip shot *n Golf.* a short approach shot to the green, esp. one that is lofted.

Chirac ★ (*French* ʃirak) *n* **Jacques (René)** (ʒɑk). born 1932, French Gaullist politician: president of France from 1995; prime minister (1974–76 and 1986–88).

chiral (ˈkaɪrəl) *adj* relating to chirality. ORIG C20: from CHIRO- + -AL[1]

chirality (kaɪˈrælɪtɪ) *n* right- or left-handedness in an asymmetric molecule.

Chirico ★ (*Italian* ˈkiːriko) *n* **Giorgio de** (ˈdʒordʒo de). 1888–1978, Italian artist born in Greece.

chiro- *or* **cheiro-** *combining form.* of or by means of the hand: *chiromancy; chiropractic.* ORIG via L from Gk *kheir* hand

chirography (kaɪˈrɒgrəfɪ) *n* another name for **calligraphy.**
▸ **chiˈrographer** *n* ▸ **chirographic** (ˌkaɪrəˈgræfɪk) *or* ˌ**chiroˈgraphical** *adj*

chiromancy (ˈkaɪrəˌmænsɪ) *n* another word for **palmistry.**
▸ **ˈchiroˌmancer** *n*

Chiron *or* **Cheiron** ★ (ˈkaɪrɒn, -rən) *n* **1** *Greek myth.* a wise and kind centaur who taught many great heroes in their youth, including Achilles, Actaeon, and Jason. **2** a minor planet, discovered by Charles Kowal in 1977, revolving round the sun between the orbits of Saturn and Uranus.

chiropody (kɪˈrɒpədɪ) *n* the treatment of the feet, esp. corns, verrucas, etc.
▸ **chiˈropodist** *n*

chiropractic (ˌkaɪrəˈpræktɪk) *n* a system of treating bodily disorders by manipulation of the spine and other parts. ORIG C20: from CHIRO- + Gk *praktikos* PRACTICAL
▸ **ˈchiroˌpractor** *n*

chirp (tʃɜːp) *vb* (*intr*) **1** (esp. of some birds and insects) to make a short high-pitched sound. **2** to speak in a lively fashion. ◆ *n* **3** a chirping sound. ORIG C15 (as *chirpinge,* gerund): imit.
▸ **ˈchirper** *n*

chirpy (ˈtʃɜːpɪ) *adj* **chirpier, chirpiest.** *Inf.* cheerful; lively.
▸ **ˈchirpily** *adv* ▸ **ˈchirpiness** *n*

chirr *or* **churr** (tʃɜː) *vb* **1** (*intr*) (esp. of certain insects, such as crickets) to make a shrill trilled sound. ◆ *n* **2** such a sound. ORIG C17: imit.

chirrup (ˈtʃɪrəp) *vb* (*intr*) **1** (esp. of some birds) to chirp repeatedly. **2** to make clucking sounds with the lips. ◆ *n* **3** such a sound. ORIG C16: var. of CHIRP
▸ **ˈchirruper** *n* ▸ **ˈchirrupy** *adj*

chisel (ˈtʃɪzᵊl) *n* **1a** a hand tool for working wood, consisting of a flat steel blade with a handle. **1b** a similar tool without a handle for working stone or metal. ◆ *vb* **chisels, chiselling, chiselled** *or US* **chisels, chiseling, chiseled. 2** to carve (wood, stone, metal, etc.) or form (an engraving, statue, etc.) with or as with a chisel. **3** *Sl.* to cheat or obtain by cheating. ORIG C14: via OF, from Vulgar L *cīsellus* (unattested), from L *caesus* cut

chiseller (ˈtʃɪzᵊlə) *n* **1** a person who uses a chisel. **2** *Inf.* a cheat. **3** *Dublin sl.* a child.

Chishima ★ (ˌtʃiːʃiːˈma) *n* the Japanese name for the **Kuril Islands.**

Chisimaio ★ (ˌkiːzɪˈmɑːjəʊ) *n* a port in S Somalia, on the Indian Ocean. Pop.: 200 000 (1987 est.). Also called: **Kismayu.**

Chişinău ★ (kiʃiˈnəu) *n* the Romanian name for **Kishinev.**

chi-square distribution *n Statistics.* a continuous single-parameter distribution used esp. to measure goodness of fit and to test hypotheses.

chi-square test *n Statistics.* a test derived from the chi-square distribution to compare the goodness of fit of theoretical and observed frequency distributions.

chit[1] (tʃɪt) *n* **1** a voucher for a sum of money owed, esp. for food or drink. **2** Also called: **chitty.** *Chiefly Brit.* **2a** a note or memorandum. **2b** a requisition or receipt. ORIG C18: from earlier *chitty,* from Hindi *cittha* note, from Sansk. *citra* marked

chit[2] (tʃɪt) *n Facetious or derog.* a pert, impudent, or self-confident girl or child. ORIG C14 (in the sense: young of an animal, kitten): from ?

Chita ★ (*Russian* tʃiˈta) *n* a city in SE Russia, on the Trans-Siberian railway: a major industrial centre. Pop.: 322 000 (1995 est.).

chital (ˈtʃiːtᵊl) *n* another name for **axis**[2] (the deer). ORIG from Hindi

chitchat (ˈtʃɪtˌtʃæt) *n* **1** gossip. ◆ *vb* **chitchats, chitchatting, chitchatted. 2** (*intr*) to gossip.

chitin (ˈkaɪtɪn) *n* a polysaccharide that is the principal component of the exoskeletons of arthropods and of the bodies of fungi. ORIG C19: from F, from Gk *khitōn* CHITON + -IN
▸ **ˈchitinous** *adj*

chiton (ˈkaɪtᵊn, -tɒn) *n* **1** (in ancient Greece) a loose woollen tunic worn by men and women. **2** any small primitive marine mollusc having an elongated body covered with eight overlapping shell plates. ORIG C19: from Gk *khitōn* coat of mail

Chittagong ★ (ˈtʃɪtəˌgɒŋ) *n* a port in E Bangladesh, on the Bay of Bengal: industrial centre. Pop.: 1 599 000 (1991).

chitterlings (ˈtʃɪtəlɪŋz) *or* **chitlings** (ˈtʃɪtlɪŋz) *pl n* (*sometimes sing*) the intestines of a pig or other animal prepared as a dish. ORIG C13: from ?

chiv (tʃɪv, ʃɪv) *or* **shiv** (ʃɪv) *Sl.* ◆ *n* **1** a knife. ◆ *vb* **chivs, chivving, chivved** *or* **shivs, shivving, shivved. 2** to stab (someone). ORIG C17: ?from Romany *chiv* blade

chivalrous (ˈʃɪvəlrəs) *adj* **1** gallant; courteous. **2** involving chivalry. ORIG C14: from OF, from CHEVALIER
▸ **ˈchivalrously** *adv* ▸ **ˈchivalrousness** *n*

chivalry (ˈʃɪvəlrɪ) *n, pl* **chivalries. 1** the combination of qualities expected of an ideal knight, esp. courage, honour, justice, and a readiness to help the weak. **2** courteous behaviour, esp. towards women. **3** the medieval system and principles of knighthood. **4** knights, noblemen, etc., collectively. ORIG C13: from OF *chevalerie,* from CHEVALIER
▸ **ˈchivalric** *adj*

chive (tʃaɪv) *n* a small Eurasian purple-flowered alliaceous plant, whose long slender hollow leaves are used in cooking. Also called: **chives.** ORIG C14: from OF *cive,* ult. from L *caepa* onion

chivy, chivvy (ˈtʃɪvɪ), *or* **chevy** *Brit.* ◆ *vb* **chivies, chivying, chivied, chivvies, chivvying, chivvied,** *or* **chevies, chevying, chevied. 1** (*tr*) to harass or nag. **2** (*tr*) to hunt. **3** (*intr*) to run about. ◆ *n, pl* **chivies, chivvies,** *or* **chevies. 4** a hunt. **5** *Obs.* a hunting cry. ORIG C19: var. of *chevy,* prob. from *Chevy Chase,* title of a Scottish border ballad

Chkalov ★ (*Russian* ˈtʃkaləf) *n* the former name (1938–57) of **Orenburg.**

chlamydia (kləˈmɪdɪə) *n* any of a genus of virus-like bacteria responsible for such diseases as trachoma, psittacosis, and some sexually transmitted diseases. ORIG C20: NL, from Gk *khlamus* mantle + -IA

chloral ('klɔːrəl) *n* **1** a colourless oily liquid with a pungent odour, made from chlorine and acetaldehyde and used in preparing chloral hydrate and DDT. Formula: CCl_3CHO. **2** short for **chloral hydrate.**

chloral hydrate *n* a colourless crystalline soluble solid produced by the reaction of chloral with water and used as a sedative and hypnotic. Formula: $CCl_3C(OH)_3$.

chloramphenicol (ˌklɔːræm'fɛnɪˌkɒl) *n* a broad-spectrum antibiotic used esp. in treating typhoid fever and rickettsial infections. ORIG C20: from CHLORO- + AM(IDE)- + PHE(NO)- + NI(TRO)- + (GLY)COL

chlorate ('klɔːreɪt, -rɪt) *n* any salt of chloric acid, containing the monovalent ion ClO_3^-.

chlordane ('klɔːdeɪn) *or* **chlordan** *n* a white insoluble toxic solid used as an insecticide. ORIG C20: from CHLORO- + (IN)D(OLE + -ENE) + -ANE

chlorhexidine (klɔː'hɛksɪdiːn) *n* an antiseptic compound used in skin cleansers, mouthwashes, etc. ORIG C20: from CHLOR(O)- + HEX(ANE) + -I(DE) + (AM)INE

chloric ('klɔːrɪk) *adj* of or containing chlorine in the pentavalent state.

chloric acid *n* a strong acid with a pungent smell, known only in solution and in the form of chlorate salts. Formula: $HClO_3$.

chloride ('klɔːraɪd) *n* **1** any salt of hydrochloric acid, containing the chloride ion Cl^-. **2** any compound containing a chlorine atom, such as methyl chloride (chloromethane), CH_3Cl.

chloride of lime *or* **chlorinated lime** *n* another name for **bleaching powder.**

chlorinate ('klɔːrɪˌneɪt) *vb* **chlorinates, chlorinating, chlorinated.** (*tr*) **1** to combine or treat (a substance) with chlorine. **2** to disinfect (water) with chlorine.
▸ **ˌchlorin'ation** *n* ▸ **'chlorinˌator** *n*

chlorine ('klɔːriːn) *or* **chlorin** ('klɔːrɪn) *n* a toxic pungent greenish-yellow gas of the halogen group; occurring only in the combined state, mainly in common salt: used in the manufacture of many organic chemicals, in water purification, and as a disinfectant and bleaching agent. Symbol: Cl; atomic no.: 17; atomic wt.: 35.453. ORIG C19 (coined by Sir Humphrey Davy): from CHLORO- + -INE[2], referring to its colour

chlorite[1] ('klɔːraɪt) *n* any of a group of green soft secondary minerals consisting of the hydrated silicates of aluminium, iron, and magnesium. ORIG C18: from L, from Gk, from *khlōros* greenish yellow
▸ **chloritic** (klɔː'rɪtɪk) *adj*

chlorite[2] ('klɔːraɪt) *n* any salt of chlorous acid.

chloro- *or before a vowel* **chlor-** *combining form.* **1** indicating the colour green: *chlorophyll.* **2** chlorine: *chloroform.*

chlorofluorocarbon (ˌklɔːrəˌfluərəʊ'kɑːbən) *n Chem.* any of various gaseous compounds of carbon, hydrogen, chlorine, and fluorine, used as refrigerants, aerosol propellants, solvents, and in foam: some cause a breakdown of ozone in the earth's atmosphere.

chloroform ('klɔːrəˌfɔːm) *n* a heavy volatile liquid with a sweet taste and odour, used as a solvent and cleansing agent and in refrigerants: formerly used as an inhalation anaesthetic. Formula: $CHCl_3$. Systematic name: **trichloromethane.** ORIG C19: from CHLORO- + *formyl* from FORMIC

Chloromycetin (ˌklɔːrəʊmaɪ'siːtɪn) *n Trademark.* a brand of **chloramphenicol.**

chlorophyll *or US* **chlorophyl** ('klɔːrəfɪl) *n* the green pigment of plants, occurring in chloroplasts, that traps the energy of sunlight for photosynthesis: used as a colouring agent (**E140**) in medicines and food.
▸ **'chloroˌphylloid** *adj* ▸ **ˌchloro'phyllous** *adj*

chloroplast ('klɔːrəʊˌplæst) *n* a plastid containing chlorophyll and other pigments, occurring in plants that carry out photosynthesis.

chlorosis (klɔː'rəʊsɪs) *n* **1** Also called: **greensickness.** *Pathol.* a once-common iron-deficiency disease of adolescent girls, characterized by greenish-yellow skin colour, weakness, and palpitation. **2** *Bot.* a deficiency of chlorophyll in green plants caused by mineral deficiency, lack of light, disease, etc., the leaves appearing uncharacteristically pale. ORIG C17: from CHLORO- + -OSIS
▸ **chlorotic** (klɔː'rɒtɪk) *adj*

chlorous ('klɔːrəs) *adj* **1** of or containing chlorine in the trivalent state. **2** of or containing chlorous acid.

chlorous acid *n* an unstable acid that is a strong oxidizing agent. Formula: $HClO_2$.

chlorpromazine (klɔː'prɒməˌziːn) *n* a drug used as a sedative and tranquillizer. ORIG C20: from CHLORO- + PRO(PYL + A)M(INE) + AZINE

chlortetracycline (klɔːˌtɛtrə'saɪkliːn) *n* an antibiotic used in treating many bacterial and rickettsial infections and some viral infections.

chock (tʃɒk) *n* **1** a block or wedge of wood used to prevent the sliding or rolling of a heavy object. **2** *Naut.* **2a** a ringlike device with an opening at the top through which a rope is placed. **2b** a cradle-like support for a boat, barrel, etc. ◆ *vb* (*tr*) **3** (usually foll. by *up*) *Brit.* to cram full. **4** to fit with or secure by a chock. **5** to support (a boat, barrel, etc.) on chocks. ◆ *adv* **6** as closely or tightly as possible: *chock against the wall.* ORIG C17: from ?; ? rel. to OF *çoche* log

chock-a-block *adj, adv* **1** filled to capacity; in a crammed state. **2** *Naut.* with the blocks brought close together, as when a tackle is pulled as tight as possible.

chocker ('tʃɒkə) *adj* **1** *Austral. & NZ inf.* full up; packed. **2** *Brit. sl.* irritated; fed up. ORIG C20: from CHOCK-A-BLOCK

chock-full *or* **choke-full** *adj* (*postpositive*) completely full. ORIG C17 *choke-full;* see CHOKE, FULL[1]

choco *or* **chocko** ('tʃɒkəʊ) *n, pl* **chocos** *or* **chockos.** *Austral. sl.* a conscript or militiaman. ORIG from *chocolate soldier*

chocolate ('tʃɒkəlɪt, 'tʃɒklɪt, -lət) *n* **1** a food preparation made from roasted ground cacao seeds, usually sweetened and flavoured. **2** a drink or sweetmeat made from this. **3a** a deep brown colour. **3b** (*as adj*): *a chocolate carpet.* ORIG C17: from Sp., from Aztec *xocolatl,* from *xococ* sour + *atl* water
▸ **'chocolaty** *adj*

chocolate-box *n* (*modifier*) *Inf.* sentimentally pretty or appealing.

Choctaw ('tʃɒktɔː) *n* **1** (*pl* **-taws** *or* **-taw**) a member of a N American people originally of Alabama. **2** their language. ORIG C18: from Choctaw *Chahta*

choice (tʃɔɪs) *n* **1** the act or an instance of choosing or selecting. **2** the opportunity or power of choosing. **3** a person or thing chosen or that may be chosen: *he was a possible choice.* **4** an alternative action or possibility: *what choice did I have?* **5** a supply from which to select. ◆ *adj* **6** of superior quality; excellent: *choice wine.* **7** carefully chosen, appropriate: *a few choice words will do the trick.* **8** vulgar or rude: *choice language.* **9 of choice.** preferred; favourite. ORIG C13: from OF, from *choisir* to CHOOSE
▸ **'choicely** *adv* ▸ **'choiceness** *n*

choir ('kwaɪə) *n* **1** an organized group of singers, esp. for singing in church services. **2** the part of a cathedral, abbey, or church in front of the altar and used by the choir and clergy. **3** a number of instruments of the same family playing together: *a brass choir.* **4** Also called: **choir organ.** one of the manuals on an organ controlling a set of soft sweet-toned pipes. ORIG C13 *quer,* from OF *cuer,* from L CHORUS

choirboy ('kwaɪəˌbɔɪ) *n* a young boy who sings the treble part in a church choir.

choir school *n* (in Britain) a school attached to a cathedral, college, etc., offering general education to boys whose singing ability is good.

Choiseul ★ (*French* ʃwazœl) *n* an island in the SW Pacific Ocean, in the Solomon Islands: hilly and densely forested. Area: 3885 sq. km (1500 sq. miles).

choke (tʃəʊk) *vb* **chokes, choking, choked.** **1** (*tr*) to hinder or stop the breathing of (a person or animal), esp. by constricting the windpipe or by asphyxiation. **2** (*intr*) to have trouble or fail in breathing, swallowing, or speaking. **3** (*tr*) to block or clog up (a passage, pipe, street, etc.). **4** (*tr*) to retard the growth or action of: *the weeds are choking my plants.* **5** (*tr*) to enrich the petrol-air mixture by re-

ducing the air supply to (a carburettor, petrol engine, etc.). ◆ *n* **6** the act or sound of choking. **7** a device in the carburettor of a petrol engine that enriches the petrol-air mixture by reducing the air supply. **8** any mechanism for reducing the flow of a fluid in a pipe, tube, etc. **9** Also called: **choke coil.** *Electronics.* an inductor having a relatively high impedance, used to prevent the passage of high frequencies or to smooth the output of a rectifier. ORIG OE *ācēocian*
▸ '**choky** *or* '**chokey** *adj*

choke back *or* **down** *vb* (*tr, adv*) to suppress (anger, tears, etc.).

choke chain *n* a collar and lead for a dog so designed that if the dog drags on the lead the collar tightens round its neck.

choked (tʃəʊkt) *adj Brit. inf.* annoyed or disappointed.

choker ('tʃəʊkə) *n* **1** a woman's high collar. **2** any neckband or necklace worn tightly around the throat. **3** a high clerical collar; stock. **4** a person who chokes. **5** something that causes a person to choke.

choke up *vb* (*tr, adv*) **1** to block (a drain, pipe, etc.) completely. **2** *Inf.* (*usually passive*) to overcome (a person) with emotion.

chokey *or* **choky** ('tʃəʊkɪ) *n Brit. sl.* prison. ORIG C17: from Anglo-Indian, from Hindi *caukī* a lockup

choko ('tʃəʊkəʊ) *n, pl* **chokos.** *Austral. & NZ.* the cucumber-like fruit of a tropical American vine: eaten as a vegetable in the Caribbean, Australia, and New Zealand. ORIG C18: from Brazilian Indian

cholangiography (kəˌlændʒɪ'ɒgrəfɪ) *n* radiographic examination of the bile ducts after the introduction into them of a contrast medium.

chole- *or before a vowel* **chol-** *combining form.* bile or gall: *cholesterol.* ORIG from Gk *kholē*

choler ('kɒlə) *n* **1** anger or ill humour. **2** *Arch.* one of the four bodily humours; yellow bile. ORIG C14: from OF, from Med. L, from L: jaundice, CHOLERA

cholera ('kɒlərə) *n* an acute intestinal infection characterized by severe diarrhoea, cramp, etc.: caused by ingestion of water or food contaminated with the bacterium *Vibrio comma.* ORIG C14: from L, from Gk *kholera* jaundice, from *kholē* bile
▸ **choleraic** (ˌkɒlə'reɪɪk) *adj*

choleric ('kɒlərɪk) *adj* **1** bad-tempered. **2** *Obs.* bilious or causing biliousness.
▸ '**cholerically** *adv*

cholesterol (kə'lɛstəˌrɒl) *or* **cholesterin** (kə'lɛstərɪn) *n* a sterol found in all animal tissues, blood, bile, and animal fats. A high level of cholesterol is implicated in some cases of atherosclerosis. ORIG C19: from CHOLE- + Gk *stereos* solid

choline ('kəʊliːn, -ɪn, 'kɒl-) *n* a colourless viscous soluble alkaline substance present in animal tissues, esp. as a constituent of lecithin. ORIG C19: from CHOLE- + -INE[2]

Cholula ★ (*Spanish* tʃo'lula) *n* a town in S Mexico, in Puebla state: ancient ruins, notably a pyramid, 53 m (177 ft) high. Pop.: 37 791 (1990).

chomp (tʃɒmp) *or* **chump** *vb* **1** to chew (food) noisily; champ. ◆ *n* **2** the act or sound of chewing in this manner. ORIG var. of CHAMP[1]

Chomsky ★ ('tʃɒmskɪ) *n* (**Avram**) **Noam** ('nəʊəm). born 1928, US linguist, noted for his *Syntactic Structures* (1957) on transformational grammar and his opposition to the Vietnam War.
▸ '**Chomskyan** *or* '**Chomskyˌite** *n, adj*

Chondokyo (ˌtʃɒndəʊ'kjəʊ) *n* an indigenous religion of Korea, incorporating elements of Buddhism, Confucianism, Christianity, and shamanism. Former name: **Tongchak.** ORIG C20: from Korean: Religion of the Heavenly Way

chondrite ('kɒndraɪt) *n* a stony meteorite consisting mainly of silicate minerals in small spherical masses.

Chongqing ('tʃʊŋ'tʃɪŋ), **Chungking,** *or* **Ch'ung-ch'ing** ★ *n* a port in SW China, in Sichuan province at the confluence of the Yangtze and Jialing rivers: site of a city since the 3rd millennium B.C.; wartime capital of China (1938–45); major trade centre for W China. Pop.: 2 980 000 (1991 est.). Also called: **Pahsien.**

choof off (tʃʊf) *vb* (*intr, adv*) *Austral. sl.* to go away; make off.

chook (tʃʊk) *n Inf., chiefly Austral. & NZ.* a hen or chicken. Also called: **chookie.**

choose (tʃuːz) *vb* **chooses, choosing, chose, chosen. 1** to select (a person, thing, course of action, etc.) from a number of alternatives. **2** (*tr; takes a clause as object or an infinitive*) to consider it desirable or proper: *I don't choose to read that book.* **3** (*intr*) to like; please: *you may stand if you choose.* ORIG OE *ceosan*
▸ '**chooser** *n*

choosy ('tʃuːzɪ) *adj* **choosier, choosiest.** *Inf.* particular in making a choice; difficult to please.

chop[1] (tʃɒp) *vb* **chops, chopping, chopped. 1** (often foll. by *down* or *off*) to cut (something) with a blow from an axe or other sharp tool. **2** (*tr;* often foll. by *up*) to cut into pieces. **3** (*tr*) *Brit. inf.* to dispense with or reduce. **4** (*intr*) to move quickly or violently. **5** *Tennis, cricket, etc.* to hit (a ball) sharply downwards. **6** *Boxing, karate, etc.* to punch or strike (an opponent) with a short sharp blow. ◆ *n* **7** a cutting blow. **8** the act or an instance of chopping. **9** a piece chopped off. **10** a slice of mutton, lamb, or pork, generally including a rib. **11** *Austral. & NZ sl.* a share (esp. in **get** *or* **hop in for one's chop**). **12** *Austral. & NZ.* a competition of skill and speed in chopping logs. **13** *Sport.* a sharp downward blow or stroke. **14 not much chop.** *Austral. & NZ inf.* not much good; poor. **15 the chop.** *Brit. & Austral. sl.* dismissal from employment. ORIG C16: var. of CHAP[1]

chop[2] (tʃɒp) *vb* **chops, chopping, chopped. 1** (*intr*) to change direction suddenly; vacillate (esp. in **chop and change**). **2 chop logic.** use excessively subtle or involved argument. ORIG OE *ceapian* to barter

chop[3] (tʃɒp) *n* a design stamped on goods as a trademark, esp. in the Far East. ORIG C17: from Hindi *chhāp*

chop chop *adv* pidgin English for **quickly.** ORIG C19: from Chinese dialect

chophouse ('tʃɒpˌhaʊs) *n* a restaurant specializing in steaks, grills, chops, etc.

Chopin ★ ('ʃɒpæn; *French* ʃɔpɛ̃) *n* **Frédéric** (**François**) (frederik). 1810–49, Polish composer and pianist active in France: noted for his piano music.

chopper ('tʃɒpə) *n* **1** *Chiefly Brit.* a small hand axe. **2** a butcher's cleaver. **3** a person or thing that cuts or chops. **4** an informal name for a **helicopter. 5** a device for periodically interrupting an electric current or beam of radiation to produce a pulsed current or beam. **6** a type of bicycle or motorcycle with very high handlebars. **7** *Sl., chiefly US.* a sub-machine-gun.

choppy ('tʃɒpɪ) *adj* **choppier, choppiest.** (of the sea, weather, etc.) fairly rough.
▸ '**choppily** *adv* ▸ '**choppiness** *n*

chops (tʃɒps) *pl n* **1** the jaws or cheeks; jowls. **2** the mouth. **3 lick one's chops.** *Inf.* to anticipate with pleasure. ORIG C16: from ?

chopsticks ('tʃɒpstɪks) *pl n* a pair of thin sticks, of ivory, wood, etc., used for eating Chinese or other East Asian food. ORIG C17: from pidgin E, from *chop* quick, from Chinese dialect + STICK[1]

chop suey ('suːɪ) *n* a Chinese-style dish originating in the US, consisting of meat, bean sprouts, etc., served with rice. ORIG C19: from Chinese *tsap sui* odds and ends

choral ('kɔːrəl) *adj* relating to, sung by, or designed for a chorus or choir.
▸ '**chorally** *adv*

chorale *or* **choral** (kɒ'rɑːl) *n* **1** a slow stately hymn tune. **2** *Chiefly US.* a choir or chorus. ORIG C19: from G *Choralgesang,* translation of L *cantus chorālis* choral song

chord[1] (kɔːd) *n* **1** *Maths.* a straight line connecting two points on a curve or curved surface. **2** *Engineering.* one of the principal members of a truss, esp. one that lies along the top or the bottom. **3** *Anat.* a variant spelling of **cord. 4** an emotional response, esp. one of sympathy: *the story struck the right chord.* ORIG C16: from L, from Gk *khordē* gut, string; see CORD

chord[2] (kɔːd) *n* **1** the simultaneous sounding of a group of musical notes, usually three or more in number. ◆ *vb* **2** (*tr*) to provide (a melodic line) with chords. ORIG C15: short for ACCORD; spelling infl. by CHORD[1]
▸ ˈ**chordal** *adj*

chordate (ˈkɔːdeɪt) *n* **1** an animal with a backbone or notochord. ◆ *adj* **2** of or relating to the chordates. ORIG C19: from Med. L *chordata:* see CHORD[1] & -ATE[1]

chore (tʃɔː) *n* **1** a routine task, esp. a domestic one. **2** a boring task. ORIG C19: from ME *chare,* from OE *cierr* a job

-chore *n combining form.* (in botany) indicating a plant that is distributed by a certain means: *anemochore.* ORIG from Gk *khōrein* to move
▸ **-chorous** *or* **-choric** *adj combining form.*

chorea (kɒˈrɪə) *n* a disorder of the central nervous system characterized by uncontrollable irregular jerky movements. See **Huntington's disease, Sydenham's chorea.** ORIG C19: from NL, from L: dance, from Gk *khoreia;* see CHORUS

choreograph (ˈkɒrɪəˌgrɑːf) *vb* (*tr*) to compose the steps and dances for (a ballet, etc.)

choreography (ˌkɒrɪˈɒgrəfɪ) *or* **choregraphy** (kɒˈrɛgrəfɪ) *n* **1** the composition of dance steps and sequences for ballet and stage and film dancing. **2** the steps and sequences of a ballet or dance. **3** the notation representing such steps. **4** the art of dancing. ORIG C18: from Gk *khoreia* dance + -GRAPHY
▸ ˌ**choreˈographer** *or* **choˈregrapher** *n* ▸ **choreographic** (ˌkɒrɪəˈgræfɪk) *or* **choregraphic** (ˌkɒrəˈgræfɪk) *adj* ▸ ˌ**choreoˈgraphically** *or* ˌ**choreˈgraphically** *adv*

choric (ˈkɒrɪk) *adj* of, like, or for a chorus, esp. of singing, dancing, or the speaking of verse.

chorion (ˈkɔːrɪən) *n* the outer membrane surrounding an embryo. ORIG C16: from Gk *khorion* afterbirth
▸ **chorionic** (ˌkɔːrɪˈɒnɪk) *adj*

chorionic gonadotrophin *n* a hormone, secreted by the placenta in mammals, that promotes the secretion of progesterone. See **HCG.**

chorionic villus sampling *n* a method of diagnosing genetic disorders early in pregnancy by the removal by catheter through the cervix of a tiny sample of tissue from the chorionic villi. Abbrev.: **CVS.**

chorister (ˈkɒrɪstə) *n* a singer in a choir, esp. a choirboy. ORIG C14: from Med. L *chorista*

Chorley ★ (ˈtʃɔːlɪ) *n* a town in NW England, in S Lancashire: cotton textiles. Pop.: 33 536 (1991).

choroid (ˈkɔːrɔɪd) *or* **chorioid** (ˈkɔːrɪˌɔɪd) *adj* **1** resembling the chorion, esp. in being vascular. ◆ *n* **2** the vascular membrane of the eyeball between the sclera and the retina. ORIG C18: from Gk *khoroeidēs,* erroneously for *khorioeidēs,* from CHORION

choropleth (ˈkɔrəˌplɛθ) *n* **a** a symbol or marked area on a map denoting the distribution of some property. **b** (*as modifier*): *a choropleth map.* ORIG C20: from Gk *khōra* place + *plēthos* multitude

chortle (ˈtʃɔːtᵊl) *vb* **chortles, chortling, chortled. 1** (*intr*) to chuckle gleefully. ◆ *n* **2** a gleeful chuckle. ORIG C19: coined (1871) by Lewis Carroll; prob. a blend of CHUCKLE + SNORT
▸ ˈ**chortler** *n*

chorus (ˈkɔːrəs) *n, pl* **choruses. 1** a large choir of singers or a piece of music composed for such a choir. **2** a body of singers or dancers who perform together. **3** a section of a song in which a soloist is joined by a group of singers, esp. in a recurring refrain. **4** an intermediate section of a pop song, blues, etc., as distinct from the verse. **5** *Jazz.* any of a series of variations on a theme. **6** (in ancient Greece) **6a** a lyric poem sung by a group of dancers, originally as a religious rite. **6b** an ode or series of odes sung by a group of actors. **6c** the actors who sang the chorus and commented on the action of the play. **7a** (esp. in Elizabethan drama) the actor who spoke the prologue, etc. **7b** the part spoken by this actor. **8** a group of people or animals producing words or sounds simultaneously. **9** any speech, song, or utterance produced by a group of people or animals simultaneously: *the dawn chorus.* **10 in chorus.** in unison. ◆ *vb* **11** to speak, sing, or utter (words, sounds, etc.) in unison. ORIG C16: from L, from Gk *khoros*

chorus girl *n* a girl who dances or sings in the chorus of a musical comedy, revue, etc.

Chorzów ★ (*Polish* ˈxɔʒuf) *n* an industrial city in SW Poland: under German administration from 1794 to 1921. Pop.: 126 500 (1995 est.). German name: **Königshütte.**

chose (tʃəuz) *vb* the past tense of **choose.**

chosen (ˈtʃəuzᵊn) *vb* **1** the past participle of **choose.** ◆ *adj* **2** selected, esp. for some special quality.

Chosen ★ (ˈtʃəuˈsɛn) *n* the official name for **Korea** as a Japanese province (1910–45).

Chosŏn ★ (ˈtʃəuˈsɒn) *n* the Korean name for **North Korea.**

Chota Nagpur ★ (ˈtʃəutə ˈnɑːgpuə) *n* a plateau in E India, in Bihar state: forested, with rich mineral resources and much heavy industry; produces chiefly lac (world's leading supplier), coal (half India's total output), and mica.

Chou En-lai (ɛnˈlaɪ) *or* **Zhou En Lai** ★ *n* 1898–1976, Chinese Communist statesman; foreign minister of the People's Republic of China (1949–58) and premier (1949–76).

chough (tʃʌf) *n* a large black passerine bird of parts of Europe, Asia, and Africa, with a long downward-curving red bill: family Corvidae (crows). ORIG C14: from ?

choux pastry (ʃuː) *n* a very light pastry made with eggs, used for éclairs, etc. ORIG partial translation of F *pâte choux* cabbage dough

chow (tʃau) *n* **1** *Inf.* food. **2** short for **chow-chow** (sense 1).

chow-chow *n* **1** a thick-coated breed of dog with a curled tail, originally from China. Often shortened to **chow. 2** a Chinese preserve of ginger, orange peel, etc., in syrup. **3** a mixed vegetable pickle. ORIG C19: from pidgin E, prob. based on Chinese *cha* miscellaneous

chowder (ˈtʃaudə) *n Chiefly US & Canad.* a thick soup or stew containing clams or fish. ORIG C18: from F *chaudière* kettle, from LL *caldāria;* see CAULDRON

chow mein (meɪn) *n* a Chinese-American dish, consisting of mushrooms, meat, shrimps, etc., served with fried noodles. ORIG from Chinese *ch'ao mien* fried noodles

Chr. *abbrev. for:* **1** Christ. **2** Christian.

Chrétien ★ (*French* kretjɛ̃) *n* (**Joseph Jacques**) Jean (ʒɑ̃). born 1934, Canadian Liberal politician; prime minister of Canada from 1993.

Chrétien de Troyes ★ (*French* də trwa) *n* 12th century, French poet, who wrote five Arthurian romances (?1155–?1190).

chrism *or* **chrisom** (ˈkrɪzəm) *n* a mixture of olive oil and balsam used for sacramental anointing in the Greek Orthodox and Roman Catholic Churches. ORIG OE, from Med. L, from Gk, from *khriein* to anoint
▸ **chrismal** (ˈkrɪzməl) *adj*

Christ ★ (kraɪst) *n* **1** Jesus of Nazareth (Jesus Christ), regarded by Christians as fulfilling Old Testament prophecies of the Messiah. **2** the Messiah or anointed one of God as the subject of Old Testament prophecies. **3** an image or picture of Christ. ◆ *interj* **4** *Taboo sl.* an oath expressing anger, etc. ◆ See also **Jesus.** ORIG OE *Crīst,* from L *Chrīstus,* from Gk *khristos* anointed one (from *khriein* to anoint), translating Heb. *māshīah* MESSIAH
▸ ˈ**Christly** *adj*

Christadelphian (ˌkrɪstəˈdɛlfɪən) *n* **1** a member of a Christian millenarian sect founded in the US about 1848, holding that only the just will enter eternal life, and that the ignorant and unconverted will not be raised from the dead. ◆ *adj* **2** of or relating to this body or its beliefs and practices. ORIG C19: from LGk *khristadelphos, khristos* CHRIST + *adelpos* brother

Christchurch ★ (ˈkraɪstˌtʃɜːtʃ) *n* **1** a city in New Zealand, on E South Island: manufacturing centre of a rich agricultural region. Pop. (urban area): 313 969 (1996). **2** a town and resort in S England, in SE Dorset. Pop.: 36 379 (1991).

christen (ˈkrɪsᵊn) *vb* (*tr*) **1** to give a Christian name to in baptism as a sign of incorporation into a Christian Church. **2** another word for **baptize. 3** to give a name to anything, esp. with some ceremony. **4** *Inf.* to use for the first time. ORIG OE *cristnian,* from *Crīst* CHRIST
▸ ˈ**christening** *n*

Christendom ('krɪsᵊndəm) *n* the collective body of Christians throughout the world.

Christian[1] ('krɪstʃən) *n* **1a** a person who believes in and follows Jesus Christ. **1b** a member of a Christian Church or denomination. **2** *Inf.* a person who possesses Christian virtues. ♦ *adj* **3** of, relating to, or derived from Jesus Christ, his teachings, example, or followers. **4** (*sometimes not cap.*) exhibiting kindness or goodness.
▸ **'christianly** *adj, adv*

Christian[2] ★ ('krɪstʃən) *n* **Charlie.** 1919–42, US modern-jazz guitarist.

Christian IV ★ *n* 1577–1648, king of Denmark and Norway (1588–1648).

Christian X ★ ('krɪstʃən; *Danish* 'kresdjan) *n* 1890–1947, king of Denmark (1912–47) and Iceland (1918–44).

Christian Democrat *n* a member or supporter of any of various right-of-centre political parties in Europe and Latin America that combine moderate conservatism with historical links to the Christian Church.
▸ **Christian Democracy** *n* ▸ **Christian Democratic** *adj*

Christian Era *n* the period beginning with the year of Christ's birth.

Christiania ★ (ˌkrɪstɪ'ɑːnɪə) *n* a former name (1624–1877) of **Oslo.**

Christianity (ˌkrɪstɪ'ænɪtɪ) *n* **1** the Christian religion. **2** Christian beliefs or practices. **3** a less common word for **Christendom.**

Christianize *or* **Christianise** ('krɪstʃəˌnaɪz) *vb* **Christianizes, Christianizing, Christianized** *or* **Christianises, Christianising, Christianised.** (*tr*) **1** to make Christian or convert to Christianity. **2** to imbue with Christian principles, spirit, or outlook.
▸ **ˌChristianiˈzation** *or* **ˌChristianiˈsation** *n* ▸ **'Christianˌizer** *or* **'Christianˌiser** *n*

Christian name *n* a personal name formally given to Christians at christening: loosely used to mean any person's first name.

> **USAGE NOTE** There are more multicultural alternatives for this term, such as *first name* and *forename.* In US usage, *given name* is also often used.

Christiansand ★ ('krɪstʃənˌsænd; *Norwegian* kristian-'san) *n* a variant spelling of **Kristiansand.**

Christian Science *n* the religious system of the Church of Christ, Scientist, founded by Mary Baker Eddy (1879), emphasizing spiritual regeneration and healing through prayer alone.
▸ **Christian Scientist** *n*

Christie ★ ('krɪstɪ) *n* **1** Dame **Agatha** (**Mary Clarissa**). 1890–1976, British author of detective stories, many featuring Hercule Poirot, and several plays, including *The Mousetrap* (1952). **2 John** (**Reginald Halliday**). 1898–1953, British murderer: hanged. Suspected of murdering the baby of Timothy Evans, for which Evans had already been hanged. **3 Linford** ('lɪnfəd). born 1960, British athlete: Commonwealth (1990) and Olympic (1992), 100 metres gold medallist.

Christina ★ (krɪ'stiːnə) *n* 1626–89, queen of Sweden (1632–54), daughter of Gustavus Adolphus.

Christine de Pisan ★ (*French* krɪstin də pizɑ̃) *n* ?1364–?1430, French writer, born in Venice. Her works include ballads, rondeaux, lays, and a biography of Charles V of France.

Christingle (ˌkrɪs'tɪŋgl) *n* (in Britain) a Christian service for children held shortly before Christmas, in which each child is given a decorated fruit with a lighted candle in it. ORIG C20: from CHRIST(MAS) + INGLE

Christlike ('kraɪstˌlaɪk) *adj* resembling the spirit of Jesus Christ.
▸ **'Christˌlikeness** *n*

Christmas ('krɪsməs) *n* **1a** the annual commemoration by Christians of the birth of Jesus Christ, on Dec. 25. **1b** Also called: **Christmas Day.** Dec. 25, observed as a day of secular celebrations when gifts and greetings are exchanged. **1c** (*as modifier*): *Christmas celebrations.* **2** Also called: **Christmastide.** the season of Christmas extending from Dec. 24 (Christmas Eve) to Jan. 6 (the festival of the Epiphany or Twelfth Night). ORIG OE *Crīstes mæsse* MASS of CHRIST
▸ **'Christmassy** *adj*

Christmas box *n* a tip or present given at Christmas, esp. to postmen, tradesmen, etc.

Christmas Eve *n* the evening or the whole day before Christmas Day.

Christmas Island ★ *n* **1** the former name (until 1981) of **Kiritimati. 2** an island in the Indian Ocean, south of Java: administered by Singapore (1900–58), now by Australia; phosphate mining. Pop.: 2500 (1994 est.). Area: 135 sq. km (52 sq. miles).

Christmas pudding *n Brit.* a rich steamed pudding containing suet, dried fruit, spices, etc. Also called: **plum pudding.**

Christmas rose *n* an evergreen plant of S Europe and W Asia with white or pinkish winter-blooming flowers. Also called: **hellebore, winter rose.**

Christmastide ('krɪsməsˌtaɪd) *n* another name for **Christmas** (sense 2).

Christmas tree *n* **1** an evergreen tree or an imitation of one, decorated as part of Christmas celebrations. **2** Also called: **Christmas bush.** *Austral.* any of various trees or shrubs flowering at Christmas and used for decoration. **3** *NZ.* another name for the **pohutukawa.**

Christoff ★ ('krɪstɒf) *n* **Boris.** 1919–93, Bulgarian bass-baritone.

Christopher ★ ('krɪstəfə) *n* **Saint.** 3rd century A.D., Christian martyr; patron saint of travellers.

Christy *or* **Christie** ('krɪstɪ) *n, pl* **Christies.** (*sometimes not cap.*) *Skiing.* a turn in which the body is swung sharply round with the skis parallel: used for stopping or changing direction quickly. ORIG C20: from CHRISTIANIA

chroma ('krəʊmə) *n* the attribute of a colour that enables an observer to judge how much chromatic colour it contains. See also **saturation** (sense 4). ORIG C19: from Gk *khrōma* colour

chromate ('krəʊmeɪt) *n* any salt or ester of chromic acid.

chromatic (krə'mætɪk) *adj* **1** of, relating to, or characterized by a colour or colours. **2** *Music.* **2a** involving the sharpening or flattening of notes or the use of such notes in chords and harmonic progressions. **2b** of or relating to the chromatic scale or an instrument capable of producing it. ORIG C17: from Gk, from *khrōma* colour
▸ **chroˈmatically** *adv* ▸ **chroˈmaticism** *n* ▸ **chromaticity** (ˌkrəʊmə'tɪsɪtɪ) *n*

chromatic aberration *n* a defect in a lens system in which different wavelengths of light are focused at different distances because they are refracted through different angles. It produces a blurred image with coloured fringes.

chromatics (krəʊ'mætɪks) *n* (*functioning as sing*) the science of colour.

chromatic scale *n* a twelve-note scale including all the semitones of the octave.

chromatin ('krəʊmətɪn) *n* the part of the nucleus that consists of DNA, RNA, and proteins, forms the chromosomes, and stains with basic dyes.

chromato- *or before a vowel* **chromat-** *combining form.* **1** indicating colour or coloured: *chromatophore.* **2** indicating chromatin: *chromatolysis.* ORIG from Gk *khrōma, khrōmat-* colour

chromatography (ˌkrəʊmə'tɒgrəfɪ) *n* the technique of separating and analysing the components of a mixture of liquids or gases by selective adsorption.

chrome (krəʊm) *n* **1a** another word for **chromium,** esp. when present in a pigment or dye. **1b** (*as modifier*): *a chrome dye.* **2** anything plated with chromium. **3** a pigment or dye that contains chromium. ♦ *vb* **chromes, chroming, chromed. 4** to plate or be plated with chromium. **5** to treat or be treated with a chromium compound, as in dyeing or tanning. ORIG C19: via F from Gk *khrōma* colour

-chrome *n and adj combining form.* colour, coloured, or pigment: *monochrome.* ORIG from Gk *khrōma* colour

chrome dioxide *n* another name for **chromium dioxide.**

chromel ('krəumɛl) *n* a nickel-based alloy containing about 10 per cent chromium, used in heating elements. ORIG C20: from CHRO(MIUM) + ME(TA)L

chrome steel *n* any of various hard rust-resistant steels containing chromium.

chrome yellow *n* any yellow pigment consisting of lead chromate.

chromic ('krəumɪk) *adj* **1** of or containing chromium in the trivalent state. **2** of or derived from chromic acid.

chromic acid *n* an unstable dibasic oxidizing acid known only in solution and as chromate salts. Formula: H_2CrO_4.

chromite ('krəumaɪt) *n* a brownish-black mineral consisting of a ferrous chromic oxide in crystalline form: the only commercial source of chromium. Formula: $FeCr_2O_4$.

chromium ('krəumɪəm) *n* a hard grey metallic element, used in steel alloys and electroplating to increase hardness and corrosion-resistance. Symbol: Cr; atomic no.: 24; atomic wt.: 51.996. ORIG C19: from NL, from F: CHROME

chromium dioxide *n* a chemical compound used as a magnetic coating on cassette tapes; chromium(IV) oxide. Formula: CrO_2. Also called (*not in technical usage*): **chrome dioxide.**

chromium steel *n* another name for **chrome steel.**

chromo ('krəuməu) *n, pl* **chromos.** short for **chromolithograph.**

chromo- *or before a vowel* **chrom-** *combining form.* **1** indicating colour, coloured, or pigment: *chromogen.* **2** indicating chromium: *chromyl.* ORIG from Gk *khrōma* colour

chromolithograph (ˌkrəuməu'lɪθəˌgrɑːf) *n* a picture produced by chromolithography.

chromolithography (ˌkrəuməulɪ'θɒgrəfɪ) *n* the process of making coloured prints by lithography.
▸ **ˌchromoli'thographer** *n* ▸ **chromolithographic** (ˌkrəuməulɪθə'græfɪk) *adj*

chromosome ('krəuməˌsəum) *n* any of the microscopic rod-shaped structures that appear in a cell nucleus during cell division, consisting of nucleoprotein arranged into units (genes) that are responsible for the transmission of hereditary characteristics.
▸ **ˌchromo'somal** *adj*

chromosome map *n* a graphic representation of the positions of genes on chromosomes, obtained by observation of stained chromosomes or by determining the degree of linkage between genes. See also **genetic map.**
▸ **chromosome mapping** *n*

chromosphere ('krəuməˌsfɪə) *n* a gaseous layer of the sun's atmosphere extending from the photosphere to the corona.
▸ **chromospheric** (ˌkrəumə'sfɛrɪk) *adj*

chromous ('krəuməs) *adj* of or containing chromium in the divalent state.

chron. *or* **chronol.** *abbrev. for:* **1** chronological. **2** chronology.

Chron. *Bible. abbrev. for* Chronicles.

chronic ('krɒnɪk) *adj* **1** continuing for a long time; constantly recurring. **2** (of a disease) developing slowly, or of long duration. Cf. **acute** (sense 7). **3** inveterate; habitual: *a chronic smoker.* **4** *Inf.* **4a** very bad: *the play was chronic.* **4b** very serious: *he left her in a chronic condition.* ORIG C15: from L, from Gk, from *khronos* time
▸ **'chronically** *adv* ▸ **chronicity** (krɒ'nɪsɪtɪ) *n*

chronic fatigue syndrome *n* a condition characterized by painful muscles and general weakness, sometimes persisting long after a viral illness. Also called: **myalgic encephalomyelitis, postviral syndrome.** Abbrev.: **CFS.**

chronicle ('krɒnɪk^əl) *n* **1** a record or register of events in chronological order. ◆ *vb* **chronicles, chronicling, chronicled.** **2** (*tr*) to record in or as if in a chronicle. ORIG C14: from Anglo-F, via L *chronica* (pl), from Gk *khronika* annals; see CHRONIC
▸ **'chronicler** *n*

chrono- *or before a vowel* **chron-** *combining form.* time: *chronology.* ORIG from Gk *khronos* time

chronograph ('krɒnəˌgrɑːf, 'krəunə-) *n* **1** an accurate instrument for recording small intervals of time. **2** any timepiece, esp. a wristwatch designed for maximum accuracy.
▸ **chronographic** (ˌkrɒnə'græfɪk) *adj*

chronological (ˌkrɒnə'lɒdʒɪk^əl, ˌkrəu-) *or* **chronologic** *adj* **1** (esp. of a sequence of events) arranged in order of occurrence. **2** relating to or in accordance with chronology.
▸ **ˌchrono'logically** *adv*

chronology (krə'nɒlədʒɪ) *n, pl* **chronologies.** **1** the determination of the proper sequence of past events. **2** the arrangement of dates, events, etc., in order of occurrence. **3** a table of events arranged in order of occurrence.
▸ **chro'nologist** *n*

chronometer (krə'nɒmɪtə) *n* a timepiece designed to be accurate in all conditions of temperature, pressure, etc., used esp. at sea.
▸ **chronometric** (ˌkrɒnə'mɛtrɪk) *or* **ˌchrono'metrical** *adj*
▸ **ˌchrono'metrically** *adv*

chronometry (krə'nɒmɪtrɪ) *n* the science of measuring time with extreme accuracy.

chronon ('krəunɒn) *n* a unit of time equal to the time that a photon would take to traverse the diameter of an electron: about 10^{-24} seconds.

chrysalid ('krɪsəlɪd) *n* **1** another name for **chrysalis.** ◆ *adj* **2** of or relating to a chrysalis.

chrysalis ('krɪsəlɪs) *n, pl* **chrysalises** *or* **chrysalides** (krɪ'sælɪˌdiːz). **1** the pupa of a moth or butterfly, in a case or cocoon. **2** anything in the process of developing. ORIG C17: from L, from Gk *khrusallis,* from *khrusos* gold

chrysanthemum (krɪ'sænθəməm) *n* **1** any of various widely cultivated plants of the composite family, having brightly coloured showy flower heads in autumn. **2** any other plant of the genus *Chrysanthemum,* such as the oxeye daisy. ORIG C16: from L: marigold, from Gk, from *khrusos* gold + *anthemon* flower

chryselephantine (ˌkrɪsɛlɪ'fæntɪn) *adj* (of ancient Greek statues, etc.) made of or overlaid with gold and ivory. ORIG C19: from Gk, from *khrusos* gold + *elephas* ivory

chrysoberyl ('krɪsəˌbɛrɪl) *n* a rare very hard greenish-yellow mineral consisting of beryllium aluminate: used as a gemstone. Formula: $BeAl_2O_4$. ORIG C17: from L, from Gk, from *khrusos* gold + *bērullos* beryl

chrysolite ('krɪsəˌlaɪt) *n* a brown or yellowish-green olivine: used as a gemstone. ORIG C14 *crisolite,* from OF, from L, from Gk, from *khrusos* gold + *lithos* stone

chrysoprase ('krɪsəˌpreɪz) *n* an apple-green variety of chalcedony: used as a gemstone. ORIG C13 *crisopace,* from OF, from L, from Gk, from *khrusos* gold + *prason* leek

Chrysostom ★ ('krɪsəstəm) *n* Saint **John.** ?345–407 A.D., Greek patriarch; archbishop of Constantinople (398–404). Feast day: Sept. 13 or Nov. 13.

chthonian ('θəunɪən) *or* **chthonic** ('θɒnɪk) *adj* of or relating to the underworld. ORIG C19: from Gk *khthonios* in or under the earth, from *khthōn* earth

chub (tʃʌb) *n, pl* **chub** *or* **chubs.** **1** a common European freshwater cyprinid game fish, having a cylindrical dark greenish body. **2** any of various North American fishes, esp. certain whitefishes and minnows. ORIG C15: from ?

chubby ('tʃʌbɪ) *adj* **chubbier, chubbiest.** (esp. of the human form) plump. ORIG C17: ?from CHUB
▸ **'chubbiness** *n*

Chu Chiang ★ ('tʃuː 'kjæŋ, kaɪ'æŋ) *n* a variant transliteration of the Chinese name for the **Zhu Jiang.**

chuck[1] (tʃʌk) *vb* (*mainly tr*) **1** *Inf.* to throw. **2** to pat affectionately, esp. under the chin. **3** *Inf.* (sometimes foll. by *in* or *up*) to give up; reject: *he chucked up his job.* **4** *US, Austral. & NZ sl.* to vomit. ◆ *n* **5** a throw or toss. **6** a pat under the chin. **7 the chuck.** *Inf.* dismissal. ◆ See also **chuck in, chuck off, chuck out.** ORIG C16: from ?

chuck[2] (tʃʌk) *n* **1** Also called: **chuck steak.** a cut of beef from the neck to the shoulder blade. **2** a device that holds a workpiece in a lathe or tool in a drill. ORIG C17: var. of CHOCK

chuck[3] (tʃʌk) *n W Canad.* **1** a large body of water. **2** In full: **saltchuck.** the sea. ORIG C19: from Chinook Jargon, of Amerind origin, from *chauk*

chuck in *vb (adv)* **1** *(tr) Brit inf.* to abandon or give up: *to chuck in a hopeless attempt.* **2** *(intr) Austral. inf.* to contribute to the cost of something.

chuckle ('tʃʌkᵊl) *vb* **chuckles, chuckling, chuckled.** *(intr)* **1** to laugh softly or to oneself. **2** (of animals, esp. hens) to make a clucking sound. ◆ *n* **3** a partly suppressed laugh. ORIG C16: prob. from *chuck* cluck + *le*

chucklehead ('tʃʌkᵊlˌhɛd) *n Inf.* a stupid person; dolt.

chuck off *vb (intr, adv;* often foll. by *at) Austral. & NZ inf.* to abuse or make fun of.

chuck out *vb (tr, adv;* often foll. by *of) Inf.* to eject forcibly (from); throw out (of).

chuddy ('tʃʌdɪ) *n Austral. & NZ.* an informal name for **chewing gum.**

Chudskoye Ozero ★ *(Russian* 'tʃutskəjɪ 'ɔzɪrə) *n* the Russian name for Lake **Peipus.**

chuff[1] (tʃʌf) *n* **1** a puffing sound as of a steam engine. ◆ *vb* **2** *(intr)* to move while emitting such sounds. ORIG C20: imit.

chuff[2] (tʃʌf) *vb (tr; usually passive) Brit. sl.* to please or delight: *he was chuffed by his pay rise.* ORIG prob. from *chuff* (adj) pleased, happy

chug (tʃʌg) *n* **1** a short dull sound, such as that made by an engine. ◆ *vb* **chugs, chugging, chugged. 2** *(intr)* (of an engine, etc.) to operate while making such sounds. ORIG C19: imit.

chukar (tʃʌ'kɑː) *n* a common Indian partridge having a red bill and black-barred sandy plumage. ORIG from Hindi *cakor,* from Sansk. *cakora,* prob. imit.

Chu Kiang ★ ('tʃuː 'kjæŋ, kaɪ'æŋ) *n* a variant transliteration of the Chinese name for the **Zhu Jiang.**

chukka *or US* **chukker** ('tʃʌkə) *n Polo.* a period of continuous play, generally lasting 7½ minutes. ORIG C20: from Hindi *cakkar,* from Sansk. *cakra* wheel

chukka boot ('tʃʌkə) *or* **chukka** *n* an ankle-high boot worn for playing polo. ORIG C19: from CHUKKA

chum (tʃʌm) *n* **1** *Inf.* a close friend. ◆ *vb* **chums, chumming, chummed. 2** *(intr;* usually foll. by *up with)* to be or become an intimate friend (of). ORIG C17 (meaning: a person sharing rooms with another): prob. shortened from *chamber fellow*

chummy ('tʃʌmɪ) *adj* **chummier, chummiest.** *Inf.* friendly.
▸ **'chummily** *adv* ▸ **'chumminess** *n*

chump (tʃʌmp) *n* **1** *Inf.* a stupid person. **2** a thick heavy block of wood. **3** the thick blunt end of anything, esp. of a piece of meat. **4** *Brit. sl.* the head (esp. in **off one's chump**). ORIG C18: ? a blend of CHUNK + LUMP[1]

chunder ('tʃʌndə) *Sl., chiefly Austral.* ◆ *vb (intr)* **1** to vomit. ◆ *n* **2** vomit. ORIG C20: from ?

Chungking ('tʃuŋ'kɪŋ, 'tʃʌŋ-) *or* **Ch'ung-ch'ing** ★ ('tʃuŋ'tʃɪŋ, 'tʃʌŋ-) *n* a variant transliteration of the Chinese name for **Chongqing.**

chunk (tʃʌŋk) *n* **1** a thick solid piece, as of meat, wood, etc. **2** a considerable amount. ORIG C17: var. of CHUCK[2]

chunky ('tʃʌŋkɪ) *adj* **chunkier, chunkiest. 1** thick and short. **2** containing thick pieces. **3** *Chiefly Brit.* (of clothes, esp. knitwear) made of thick bulky material.
▸ **'chunkiness** *n*

Chunnel ('tʃʌnᵊl) *n* an informal name for **Channel Tunnel.** ORIG C20: from CH(ANNEL) + T(UNNEL)

chunter ('tʃʌntə) *vb (intr;* often foll. by *on) Brit. inf.* to mutter or grumble incessantly in a meaningless fashion. ORIG C16: prob. imit.

Chuquisaca ★ *(Spanish* tʃuki'saka) *n* the former name (until 1839) of **Sucre**[1].

Chur ★ *(German* kuːr) *n* a city in E Switzerland, capital of Grisons canton. Pop.: 30 236 (1990). Ancient name: **Curia Rhaetorum** ('kuːrɪə riː'təurəm, 'kjuː-). French name: **Coire.**

church (tʃɜːtʃ) *n* **1** a building for public worship, esp. Christian worship. **2** an occasion of public worship. **3** the clergy as distinguished from the laity. **4** *(usually cap.)* institutionalized forms of religion as a political or social force: *conflict between Church and State.* **5** *(usually cap.)* the collective body of all Christians. **6** *(often cap.)* a particular Christian denomination or group. **7** *(often cap.)* the Christian religion. ◆ Related adj: **ecclesiastical.** ◆ *vb (tr)* **8** *Church of England.* to bring (someone, esp. a woman after childbirth) to church for special ceremonies. ORIG OE *cirice,* from LGk, from Gk *kuriakon* (*dōma*) the Lord's (house), from *kurios* master, from *kuros* power

Church Army *n* a voluntary Anglican organization founded to assist the parish clergy.

Church Commissioners *pl n Brit.* a group of representatives of Church and State that administers the property of the Church of England.

churchgoer ('tʃɜːtʃˌgəuə) *n* a person who attends church regularly.
▸ **'churchˌgoing** *adj, n*

Churchill[1] ★ ('tʃɜːtʃɪl) *n* **1** a river in E Canada, rising in SE Labrador and flowing north and southeast over Churchill Falls, then east to the Atlantic. Length: about 1000 km (600 miles). Former name: **Hamilton River. 2** a river in central Canada, rising in NW Saskatchewan and flowing east through several lakes to Hudson Bay. Length: about 1600 km (1000 miles).

Churchill[2] ★ ('tʃɜːtʃɪl) *n* **1 Charles.** 1731–64, British poet, noted for *The Rosciad* (1761) and *The Prophecy of Famine* (1763). **2 John.** See (1st Duke of) **Marlborough. 3** Lord **Randolph.** 1849–95, British Conservative politician: secretary of state for India (1885–86) and chancellor of the Exchequer (1886). **4** his son, Sir **Winston** (**Leonard Spencer**). 1874–1965, British Conservative statesman and writer, noted for his leadership during World War II. 1st Lord of the Admiralty (1911–15); prime minister (1940–45; 1951–55). His writings include *Marlborough* (1933–38), *The Second World War* (1948–54), and *History of the English-Speaking Peoples* (1956–58): Nobel prize for literature 1953.

Churchill Falls ★ *pl n* a waterfall in E Canada, in SW Labrador on the Churchill River: site of one of the largest hydroelectric power projects in the world. Height: 75 m (245 ft). Former name: **Grand Falls.**

churchly ('tʃɜːtʃlɪ) *adj* appropriate to or associated with the church.
▸ **'churchliness** *n*

churchman ('tʃɜːtʃmən) *n, pl* **churchmen. 1** a clergyman. **2** a male member of a church.

Church of Christ, Scientist *n* See **Christian Science.**

Church of England *n* the reformed established state Church in England, with the Sovereign as its temporal head.

Church of Jesus Christ of Latter-Day Saints *n* See **Mormon** (sense 1).

churchwarden (ˌtʃɜːtʃ'wɔːdᵊn) *n* **1** *Church of England, Episcopal Church.* one of two assistants of a parish priest who administer the secular affairs of the church. **2** a long-stemmed tobacco pipe made of clay.

churchwoman ('tʃɜːtʃˌwumən) *n, pl* **churchwomen.** a female member of a church.

churchyard ('tʃɜːtʃˌjɑːd) *n* the grounds round a church, used as a graveyard.

churinga (tʃə'rɪŋgə) *n, pl* **churinga** *or* **churingas.** a sacred amulet of the native Australians. ORIG from Abor.

churl (tʃɜːl) *n* **1** a surly ill-bred person. **2** *Arch.* a farm labourer. **3** *Arch.* a miserly person. ORIG OE *ceorl*
▸ **'churlish** *adj*

churn (tʃɜːn) *n* **1** *Brit.* a large container for milk. **2** a vessel or machine in which cream or whole milk is vigorously agitated to produce butter. **3** the number of customers who switch from one supplier to another. ◆ *vb* **4a** to agitate (milk or cream) to make butter. **4b** to make (butter) by this process. **5** (sometimes foll. by *up*) to move or cause to move with agitation. **6** (of a bank, broker, etc.) to encourage an investor or policyholder to change investments, endowment policies, etc., to increase commissions at the client's expense. **7** (of a government) to

pay benefits to a wide category of people and claw it back by taxation from the well off. **8** to promote the turnover of existing subscribers leasing, and new subscribers joining, a cable television system or mobile phone company. ORIG OE *ciern*
▸ **'churner** *n*

churn out *vb (tr, adv) Inf.* **1** to produce (something) at a rapid rate: *to churn out ideas.* **2** to perform (something) mechanically: *to churn out a song.*

churr (tʃɜː) *vb, n* a variant spelling of **chirr.**

chute[1] (ʃuːt) *n* **1** an inclined channel or vertical passage down which water, parcels, coal, etc., may be dropped. **2** a steep slope, used as a slide as for toboggans. **3** a slide into a swimming pool. **4** a rapid or waterfall. ORIG C19: from OF *cheoite,* fem. p.p. of *cheoir* to fall, from L *cadere;* in some senses, var. spelling of SHOOT

chute[2] (ʃuːt) *n, vb* **chutes, chuting, chuted.** *Inf.* short for **parachute.**
▸ **'chutist** *n*

Chu Teh ('tʃuː 'teɪ) *or* **Zhu De** ★ *n* 1886–1976, Chinese military leader and politician; commander in chief of the Red Army (1931) and was chairman of the Standing Committee of the National People's Congress of the People's Republic of China (1959–76).

chutney ('tʃʌtnɪ) *n* a pickle of Indian origin, made from fruit, vinegar, spices, sugar, etc.: *mango chutney.* ORIG C19: from Hindi *catni,* from ?

chutzpah ('xʊtspə) *n US & Canad. inf.* shameless audacity; impudence. ORIG C20: from Yiddish

Chuvash Republic ★ (tʃu'vɑːʃ) *n* a constituent republic of W central Russia, in the middle Volga valley: generally low and undulating, with large areas of forest. Capital: Cheboksary. Pop.: 1 361 000 (1996 est.). Area: 18 300 sq. km (7064 sq. miles). Also called: **Chuvashia** (tʃuː'vɑːʃɪə).

chyack ('tʃaɪæk) *vb, n* a variant spelling of **chiack.**

chyle (kaɪl) *n* a milky fluid composed of lymph and emulsified fat globules, formed in the small intestine during digestion. ORIG C17: from LL, from Gk *khulos* juice
▸ **chylaceous** (kaɪ'leɪʃəs) *or* **'chylous** *adj*

chyme (kaɪm) *n* the thick fluid mass of partially digested food that leaves the stomach. ORIG C17: from LL, from Gk *khumos* juice
▸ **'chymous** *adj*

chypre *French.* (ʃiprə) *n* a perfume made from sandalwood. ORIG lit.: Cyprus, ? where it originated

Ci *symbol for* curie.

CI *abbrev. for* Channel Islands.

CIA *abbrev. for* Central Intelligence Agency; a federal US bureau created in 1947 to coordinate and conduct espionage and intelligence activities.

ciabatta (tʃə'bætə) *n* a type of open-textured bread made with olive oil. ORIG C20: from It., lit.: slipper

Ciano ★ (*Italian* tʃaːno) *n* **Galeazzo** (gale'attso), full name *Conte Galeazzo Ciano di Cortellazzo.* 1903–44, Italian fascist politician; minister of foreign affairs (1936–43) and son-in-law of Mussolini: executed.

CIB *abbrev. for* Criminal Investigation Branch (of the New Zealand and Australian police).

Cibber ★ ('sɪbə) *n* **Colley** ('kɒlɪ). 1671–1757, English actor and dramatist; poet laureate (1730–57).

ciborium (sɪ'bɔːrɪəm) *n, pl* **ciboria** (-rɪə). *Christianity.* **1** a goblet-shaped lidded vessel used to hold consecrated wafers in Holy Communion. **2** a canopy fixed over an altar. ORIG C17: from Med. L, from L, from Gk *kibōrion* cup-shaped seed vessel of the Egyptian lotus

cicada (sɪ'kɑːdə) *or* **cicala** *n, pl* **cicadas, cicadae** (-diː) *or* **cicale** (-leɪ). any large broad insect, most common in warm regions, having membranous wings: the males produce a high-pitched drone by vibration of a pair of drumlike abdominal organs. ORIG C19: from L

cicatrix ('sɪkətrɪks) *n, pl* **cicatrices** (ˌsɪkə'traɪsiːz). **1** the tissue that forms in a wound during healing; scar. **2** a scar on a plant indicating the former point of attachment of a part, esp. a leaf. ORIG C17: from L: scar, from ?
▸ **cicatricial** (ˌsɪkə'trɪʃəl) *adj*

cicatrize *or* **cicatrise** ('sɪkəˌtraɪz) *vb* **cicatrizes, cicatrizing, cicatrized** *or* **cicatrises, cicatrising, cicatrised.** (of a wound or defect in tissue) to be closed by scar formation; heal.
▸ **ˌcicatri'zation** *or* **ˌcicatri'sation** *n*

cicely ('sɪsəlɪ) *n, pl* **cicelies.** short for **sweet cicely.** ORIG C16: from L *seselis,* from Gk, from ?

Cicero ★ ('sɪsəˌrəʊ) *n* **Marcus Tullius** ('mɑːkəs 'tʌlɪəs). 106–43 B.C., Roman consul and writer. He foiled Catiline's conspiracy (63) and was killed by Mark Antony's agents. Formerly known in English as **Tully.**

cicerone (ˌsɪsə'rəʊnɪ, ˌtʃɪtʃ-) *n, pl* **cicerones** *or* **ciceroni** (-nɪ). a person who conducts and informs sightseers. ORIG C18: from It.: antiquarian scholar, guide, after CICERO

Cid ★ (sɪd; *Spanish* θið) *n* **El** *or* **the.** original name *Rodrigo Diaz de Vivar.* ?1043–99, Spanish soldier and hero of the wars against the Moors.

CID (in Britain) *abbrev. for* Criminal Investigation Department; the detective division of a police force.

-cide *n combining form.* **1** indicating a person or thing that kills: *insecticide.* **2** indicating a killing; murder: *homicide.* ORIG from L *-cīda* (agent), *-cīdium* (act), from *caedere* to kill
▸ **-cidal** *adj combining form.*

cider *or* **cyder** ('saɪdə) *n* **1** an alcoholic drink made from the fermented juice of apples. **2** Also called: **sweet cider.** *US & Canad.* an unfermented drink made from apple juice. ORIG C14: from OF, via Med. L, from LGk *sikera* strong drink, from Heb. *shēkhār*

c.i.f. *or* **CIF** *abbrev. for* cost, insurance, and freight (included in the price quoted).

c.i.f.c.i. *abbrev. for* cost, insurance, freight, commission, and interest (included in the price quoted).

cig (sɪg) *or* **ciggy** ('sɪgɪ) *n, pl* **cigs** *or* **ciggies.** *Inf.* a cigarette.

cigar (sɪ'gɑː) *n* a cylindrical roll of cured tobacco leaves, for smoking. ORIG C18: from Sp. *cigarro*

cigarette *or US (sometimes)* **cigaret** (ˌsɪgə'rɛt) *n* a short tightly rolled cylinder of tobacco, wrapped in thin paper for smoking. ORIG C19: from F, lit.: a little CIGAR

cigarette card *n* a small picture card, formerly given away with cigarettes, now collected as a hobby.

cigarillo (ˌsɪgə'rɪləʊ) *n, pl* **cigarillos.** a small cigar, often only slightly larger than a cigarette.

cilantro (sɪ'læntrəʊ) *n* the US and Canad. name for **coriander.** ORIG C20: Sp.

ciliary ('sɪlɪərɪ) *adj* of or relating to cilia.

ciliary body *n* the part of the eye that joins the choroid to the iris.

Cilician Gates ★ (sɪ'lɪʃɪən) *pl n* a pass in S Turkey, over the Taurus Mountains. Turkish name: **Gülek Bogaz.**

cilium ('sɪlɪəm) *n, pl* **cilia** ('sɪlɪə). **1** any of the short threads projecting from the surface of a cell, organism, etc., whose rhythmic beating causes movement. **2** the technical name for **eyelash.** ORIG C18: NL, from L: (lower) eyelid, eyelash
▸ **ciliate** ('sɪlɪɪt, -eɪt) *or* **'ciliˌated** *adj*

Çiller ★ (ʃɪlə) *n* **Tansu** ('tænzuː). born 1945, Turkish politician; prime minister (1993–96).

Cimarosa ★ (*Italian* tʃima'roza) *n* **Domenico** (do'meːniko). 1749–1801, Italian composer, noted for his opera buffa *The Secret Marriage* (1792).

C in C *or* **C.-in-C.** *Mil. abbrev. for* Commander in Chief.

cinch (sɪntʃ) *n* **1** *Sl.* an easy task. **2** *Sl.* a certainty. **3** a US and Canad. name for **girth** (sense 2). **4** *US inf.* a firm grip. ♦ *vb* **5** (often foll. by *up*) *US & Canad.* to fasten a girth around (a horse). **6** *(tr) Inf.* to make sure of. **7** *(tr) Inf., chiefly US.* to get a firm grip on. ORIG C19: from Sp., from L, from *cingere* to encircle

cinchona (sɪŋ'kəʊnə) *n* **1** any tree or shrub of the South American genus *Cinchona,* having medicinal bark. **2** the dried bark of any of these trees, which yields quinine. **3** any of the drugs derived from cinchona bark. ORIG C18: NL, after the Countess of *Chinchón* (1576–1639), vicereine of Peru
▸ **cinchonic** (sɪŋ'kɒnɪk) *adj*

Cincinnati ★ (ˌsɪnsɪ'nætɪ) *n* a city in SW Ohio, on the Ohio River. Pop.: 358 170 (1994 est.).

Cincinnatus ★ (ˌsɪnsɪˈnɑːtəs) *n* **Lucius Quinctius** (ˈluːsɪəs ˈkwɪŋktɪəs). ?519–438 B.C., Roman general; dictator of Rome during two crises (458; 439).

cincture (ˈsɪŋktʃə) *n* something that encircles, esp. a belt or girdle. ORIG C16: from L, from *cingere* to gird

cinder (ˈsɪndə) *n* **1** a piece of incombustible material left after the combustion of coal, coke, etc.; clinker. **2** a piece of charred material that burns without flames; ember. **3** any solid waste from smelting or refining. **4** (*pl*) fragments of volcanic lava; scoriae. ORIG OE *sinder*
▸ ˈ**cindery** *adj*

Cinderella (ˌsɪndəˈrɛlə) *n* **1** a girl who achieves fame after being obscure. **2** a poor, neglected, or unsuccessful person or thing. ORIG C19: after *Cinderella,* the heroine of a fairy tale

cine- *combining form.* indicating motion picture or cinema: *cine camera; cinephotography.*

cineaste (ˈsɪnɪˌæst) *n* an enthusiast for films. ORIG C20: F

cinema (ˈsɪnɪmə) *n* **1** *Chiefly Brit.* a place designed for the exhibition of films. **2 the cinema. 2a** the art or business of making films. **2b** films collectively. ORIG C19 (earlier spelling: *kinema*): shortened from CINEMATOGRAPH
▸ **cinematic** (ˌsɪnɪˈmætɪk) *adj* ▸ ˌ**cineˈmatically** *adv*

cinematograph (ˌsɪnɪˈmætəˌgrɑːf) *Chiefly Brit.* ◆ *n* **1** a combined camera, printer, and projector. ◆ *vb* **2** to take (pictures) with a film camera. ORIG C19 (earlier spelling: *kinematograph*): from Gk *kinēma* motion + -GRAPH
▸ **cinematographer** (ˌsɪnɪməˈtɒgrəfə) *n* ▸ **cinematographic** (ˌsɪnɪˌmætəˈgræfɪk) *adj* ▸ ˌ**cineˌmatoˈgraphically** *adv* ▸ ˌ**cinemaˈtography** *n*

cinéma vérité (*French* sinema verite) *n* films characterized by subjects, actions, etc., that have the appearance of real life. ORIG F, lit.: truth cinema

cineraria (ˌsɪnəˈrɛərɪə) *n* a plant of the Canary Islands, widely cultivated for its blue, purple, red, or variegated daisy-like flowers. ORIG C16: from NL, from L, from *cinis* ashes; from its downy leaves

cinerarium (ˌsɪnəˈrɛərɪəm) *n, pl* **cineraria** (-ˈrɛərɪə). a place for keeping the ashes of the dead after cremation. ORIG C19: from L, from *cinerārius* relating to ashes
▸ **cinerary** (ˈsɪnərərɪ) *adj*

cinerator (ˈsɪnəˌreɪtə) *n Chiefly US.* a furnace for cremating corpses.
▸ ˌ**cineˈration** *n*

cinnabar (ˈsɪnəˌbɑː) *n* **1** a heavy red mineral consisting of mercury(II) sulphide: the chief ore of mercury. Formula: HgS. **2** the red form of mercury(II) sulphide, esp. when used as a pigment. **3a** a bright red; vermilion. **3b** (*as adj*): *a cinnabar tint.* **4** a large red-and-black European moth. ORIG C15: from OF, from L, from Gk *kinnabari,* of Oriental origin

cinnamon (ˈsɪnəmən) *n* **1** a tropical Asian tree, having aromatic yellowish-brown bark. **2** the spice obtained from the bark of this tree, used for flavouring food and drink. **3a** a light yellowish brown. **3b** (*as adj*): *a cinnamon coat.* ORIG C15: from OF, via L & Gk, from Heb. *qinnamown*

cinque (sɪŋk) *n* the number five in cards, dice, etc. ORIG C14: from OF *cinq* five

cinquecento (ˌtʃɪŋkwɪˈtʃɛntəʊ) *n* the 16th century, esp. in reference to Italian art, architecture, or literature. ORIG C18: It., shortened from *milcinquecento* 1500

cinquefoil (ˈsɪŋkˌfɔɪl) *n* **1** any plant of the N temperate rosaceous genus *Potentilla,* typically having five-lobed compound leaves. **2** an ornamental carving in the form of five arcs arranged in a circle and separated by cusps. ORIG C13 *sink foil,* from OF, from L *quinquefolium* plant with five leaves

Cinque Ports (sɪŋk) *pl n* an association of ports on the SE coast of England, which from late Anglo-Saxon times until 1685 provided ships for the king's service in return for the profits of justice in their courts.

Cintra ★ (ˈsɪntrə) *n* the former name for **Sintra**.

cipher *or* **cypher** (ˈsaɪfə) *n* **1** a method of secret writing using substitution of letters according to a key. **2** a secret message. **3** the key to a secret message. **4** an obsolete name for **zero** (sense 1). **5** any of the Arabic numerals or the Arabic system of numbering. **6** a person or thing of no importance; nonentity. **7** a design consisting of interwoven letters; monogram. ◆ *vb* **8** to put (a message) into secret writing. **9** *Rare.* to perform (a calculation) arithmetically. ORIG C14: from OF *cifre* zero, from Med. L, from Ar. *sifr* zero

circa (ˈsɜːkə) *prep* (used with a date) at the approximate time of: *circa 1182* B.C. Abbrev.: **c, ca.** ORIG L: about

circadian (sɜːˈkeɪdɪən) *adj* of or relating to biological processes that occur regularly at 24-hour intervals. See also **biological clock.** ORIG C20: from L *circa* about + *diēs* day

Circassia ★ (sɜːˈkæsɪə) *n* a region of S Russia, on the Black Sea north of the Caucasus Mountains.

Circe ★ (ˈsɜːsɪ) *n Greek myth.* an enchantress who detained Odysseus on her island and turned his men into swine.
▸ **Circean** (sɜːˈsɪən) *adj*

circle (ˈsɜːkᵊl) *n* **1** a closed plane curve every point of which is equidistant from a given fixed point, the centre. **2** the figure enclosed by such a curve. **3** *Theatre.* the section of seats above the main level of the auditorium, usually comprising the dress circle and the upper circle. **4** something formed or arranged in the shape of a circle. **5** a group of people sharing an interest, activity, upbringing, etc.; set: *golf circles; a family circle.* **6** a domain or area of activity, interest, or influence. **7** a circuit. **8** a process or chain of events or parts that forms a connected whole; cycle. **9** a parallel of latitude. See also **great circle, small circle. 10** one of a number of Neolithic or Bronze Age rings of standing stones, such as Stonehenge. **11 come full circle.** to arrive back at one's starting point. See also **vicious circle.** ◆ *vb* **circles, circling, circled. 12** to move in a circle (around). **13** (*tr*) to enclose in a circle; encircle. ORIG C14: from L *circulus,* from *circus* ring, circle
▸ ˈ**circler** *n*

circlet (ˈsɜːklɪt) *n* a small circle or ring, esp. a circular ornament worn on the head. ORIG C15: from OF *cerclet* a little CIRCLE

circuit (ˈsɜːkɪt) *n* **1a** a complete route or course, esp. one that is curved or circular or that lies around an object. **1b** the area enclosed within such a route. **2** the act of following such a route: *we made three circuits of the course.* **3a** a complete path through which an electric current can flow. **3b** (*as modifier*): *a circuit diagram.* **4a** a periodical journey around an area, as made by judges, salesmen, etc. **4b** the places visited on such a journey. **4c** the persons making such a journey. **5** an administrative division of the Methodist Church comprising a number of neighbouring churches. **6** a number of theatres, cinemas, etc., under one management. **7** *Sport.* **7a** a series of tournaments in which the same players regularly take part: *the international tennis circuit.* **7b** (usually preceded by *the*) the contestants who take part in such a series. **8** *Chiefly Brit.* a motor-racing track, usually of irregular shape. ◆ *vb* **9** to make or travel in a circuit around (something). ORIG C14: from L *circuitus,* from *circum* around + *īre* to go
▸ ˈ**circuital** *adj*

circuit breaker *n* a device that under abnormal conditions, such as a short circuit, stops the flow of current in an electrical circuit.

circuitous (səˈkjuːɪtəs) *adj* indirect and lengthy; roundabout: *a circuitous route.*
▸ **cirˈcuitously** *adv* ▸ **cirˈcuitousness** *n*

circuitry (ˈsɜːkɪtrɪ) *n* **1** the design of an electrical circuit. **2** the system of circuits used in an electronic device.

circuity (səˈkjuːɪtɪ) *n, pl* **circuities.** (of speech, reasoning, etc.) a roundabout or devious quality.

circular (ˈsɜːkjʊlə) *adj* **1** of, involving, resembling, or shaped like a circle. **2** circuitous. **3** (of arguments) futile because the truth of the premises cannot be established independently of the conclusion. **4** travelling or occurring in a cycle. **5** (of letters, announcements, etc.) intended for general distribution. ◆ *n* **6** a printed advertisement or notice for mass distribution.
▸ **circularity** (ˌsɜːkjʊˈlærɪtɪ) *n* ▸ ˈ**circularly** *adv*

★ people and places

circular breathing *n* a technique for sustaining a phrase on a wind instrument, using the cheeks to force air out of the mouth while breathing in through the nose.

circularize *or* **circularise** ('sɜːkjʊləˌraɪz) *vb* **circularizes, circularizing, circularized** *or* **circularises, circularising, circularised.** (*tr*) **1** to distribute circulars to. **2** to canvass or petition (people), as for support, votes, etc., by distributing letters, etc. **3** to make circular.
▸ **ˌcirculariˈzation** *or* **ˌcirculariˈsation** *n*

circular saw *n* a power-driven saw in which a circular disc with a toothed edge is rotated at high speed.

circulate ('sɜːkjʊˌleɪt) *vb* **circulates, circulating, circulated. 1** to send, go, or pass from place to place or person to person: *don't circulate the news.* **2** to distribute or be distributed over a wide area. **3** to move or cause to move through a circuit, system, etc., returning to the starting point: *blood circulates through the body.* **4** to move in a circle. ORIG C15: from L *circulārī*, from *circulus* CIRCLE
▸ **ˈcirculative** *adj* ▸ **ˈcircuˌlator** *n* ▸ **ˈcirculatory** *adj*

circulating library *n* **1** another word (esp. US) for **lending library. 2** a small library circulated in turn to a group of institutions.

circulation (ˌsɜːkjʊˈleɪʃən) *n* **1** the transport of oxygenated blood through the arteries, and the return of oxygen-depleted blood through the veins to the heart, where the cycle is renewed. **2** the flow of sap through a plant. **3** any movement through a closed circuit. **4** the spreading or transmission of something to a wider group of people or area. **5** (of air and water) free movement within an area or volume. **6a** the distribution of newspapers, magazines, etc. **6b** the number of copies of an issue that are distributed. **7 in circulation. 7a** (of currency) serving as a medium of exchange. **7b** (of people) active in a social or business context.

circulatory system *n Anat., zool.* the system concerned with the transport of blood and lymph, consisting of the heart, blood vessels, lymph vessels, etc.

circum- *prefix* around; surrounding; on all sides: *circumlocution; circumpolar.* ORIG from L *circum* around, from *circus* circle

circumambient (ˌsɜːkəmˈæmbɪənt) *adj* surrounding. ORIG C17: from LL, from L CIRCUM- + *ambīre* to go round
▸ **ˌcircumˈambience** *or* **ˌcircumˈambiency** *n*

circumambulate (ˌsɜːkəmˈæmbjʊˌleɪt) *vb* **circumambulates, circumambulating, circumambulated. 1** to walk around (something). **2** (*intr*) to avoid the point. ORIG C17: from LL, from L CIRCUM- + *ambulāre* to walk
▸ **ˌcircumˌambuˈlation** *n*

circumcise ('sɜːkəmˌsaɪz) *vb* **circumcises, circumcising, circumcised.** (*tr*) **1** to remove the foreskin of (a male). **2** to incise surgically the skin over the clitoris of (a female). **3** to remove the clitoris of (a female). **4** to perform such an operation as a religious rite on (someone). ORIG C13: from L from CIRCUM- + *caedere* to cut
▸ **circumcision** (ˌsɜːkəmˈsɪʒən) *n*

circumference (səˈkʌmfərəns) *n* **1** the boundary of a specific area or figure, esp. of a circle. **2** the length of a closed geometric curve, esp. of a circle. ORIG C14: from OF, from L from CIRCUM- + *ferre* to bear
▸ **circumferential** (səˌkʌmfəˈrɛnʃəl) *adj* ▸ **cirˌcumferˈentially** *adv*

circumflex ('sɜːkəmˌflɛks) *n* **1** a mark (ˆ) placed over a vowel to show that it is pronounced with rising and falling pitch, as in ancient Greek, or as a long vowel, as in French. ◆ *adj* **2** (of nerves, arteries, etc.) bending or curving around. ORIG C16: from L, from CIRCUM- + *flectere* to bend
▸ **ˌcircumˈflexion** *n*

circumfuse (ˌsɜːkəmˈfjuːz) *vb* **circumfuses, circumfusing, circumfused.** (*tr*) **1** to pour or spread (a liquid, powder, etc.) around. **2** to surround with a substance, such as a liquid. ORIG C16: from L *circumfūsus*, from CIRCUM- + *fundere* to pour
▸ **circumfusion** (ˌsɜːkəmˈfjuːʒən) *n*

circumlocution (ˌsɜːkəmləˈkjuːʃən) *n* **1** an indirect way of expressing something. **2** an indirect expression.
▸ **circumlocutory** (ˌsɜːkəmˈlɒkjətərɪ, -trɪ) *adj*

circumnavigate (ˌsɜːkəmˈnævɪˌgeɪt) *vb* **circumnavigates, circumnavigating, circumnavigated.** (*tr*) to sail or fly completely around.
▸ **ˌcircumˌnaviˈgation** *n* ▸ **ˌcircumˈnaviˌgator** *n*

circumscribe (ˌsɜːkəmˈskraɪb, ˈsɜːkəmˌskraɪb) *vb* **circumscribes, circumscribing, circumscribed.** (*tr*) **1** to restrict within limits. **2** to mark or set the bounds of. **3** to draw a geometric construction around (another construction) so that the two are in contact but do not intersect. **4** to draw a line round. ORIG C15: from L from CIRCUM- + *scrībere* to write
▸ **ˌcircumˈscribable** *adj* ▸ **ˌcircumˈscriber** *n* ▸ **circumscription** (ˌsɜːkəmˈskrɪpʃən) *n*

circumspect ('sɜːkəmˌspɛkt) *adj* cautious, prudent, or discreet. ORIG C15: from L, from CIRCUM- + *specere* to look
▸ **ˌcircumˈspection** *n* ▸ **ˈcircumˌspectly** *adv*

circumstance ('sɜːkəmstəns) *n* **1** (*usually pl*) a condition of time, place, etc., that accompanies or influences an event or condition. **2** an incident or occurrence, esp. a chance one. **3** accessory information or detail. **4** formal display or ceremony (archaic except in **pomp and circumstance**). **5 under** *or* **in no circumstances.** in no case; never. **6 under the circumstances.** because of conditions; this being the case. ◆ *vb* **circumstances, circumstancing, circumstanced.** (*tr*) **7** to place in a particular condition or situation. ORIG C13: from OF, from L *circumstantia*, from CIRCUM- + *stāre* to stand

circumstantial (ˌsɜːkəmˈstænʃəl) *adj* **1** of or dependent on circumstances. **2** fully detailed. **3** incidental.
▸ **ˌcircumˌstantiˈality** *n* ▸ **ˌcircumˈstantially** *adv*

circumstantial evidence *n* indirect evidence that tends to establish a conclusion by inference.

circumstantiate (ˌsɜːkəmˈstænʃɪˌeɪt) *vb* **circumstantiates, circumstantiating, circumstantiated.** (*tr*) to support by giving particulars.
▸ **ˌcircumˌstantiˈation** *n*

circumvallate (ˌsɜːkəmˈvæleɪt) *vb* **circumvallates, circumvallating, circumvallated.** (*tr*) to surround with a defensive fortification. ORIG C19: from L, from CIRCUM- + *vallum* rampart
▸ **ˌcircumvalˈlation** *n*

circumvent (ˌsɜːkəmˈvɛnt) *vb* (*tr*) **1** to evade or go around. **2** to outwit. **3** to encircle (an enemy) so as to intercept or capture. ORIG C15: from L, from CIRCUM- + *venīre* to come
▸ **ˌcircumˈvention** *n*

circus ('sɜːkəs) *n, pl* **circuses. 1** a travelling company of entertainers such as acrobats, clowns, trapeze artists, and trained animals. **2** a public performance given by such a company. **3** an arena, usually tented, in which such a performance is held. **4** a travelling group of professional sportsmen: *a cricket circus.* **5** (in ancient Rome) **5a** an open-air stadium, usually oval or oblong, for chariot races or public games. **5b** the games themselves. **6** *Brit.* **6a** an open place, usually circular, where several streets converge. **6b** (*cap. when part of a name*): *Piccadilly Circus.* **7** *Inf.* noisy or rowdy behaviour. **8** *Inf.* a group of people travelling together and putting on a display. ORIG C16: from L, from Gk *kirkos* ring

ciré ('sɪəreɪ) *adj* **1** (of fabric) treated with a heat or wax process to make it smooth. ◆ *n* **2** such a surface on a fabric. **3** a fabric having such a surface. ORIG C20: F, from L *cēra* wax

Cirencester ★ ('saɪrənˌsɛstə) *n* a market town in S England, in Gloucestershire: Roman amphitheatre. Pop.: 15 221 (1991). Latin name: **Corinium.**

cirque (sɜːk) *n* a steep-sided semicircular or crescent-shaped depression found in mountainous regions. ORIG C17: from F, from L *circus* ring

cirrhosis (sɪˈrəʊsɪs) *n* any of various chronic progressive diseases of the liver, characterized by death of liver cells, irreversible fibrosis, etc. ORIG C19: NL, from Gk *kirrhos* orange-coloured + -OSIS; referring to the appearance of the diseased liver
▸ **cirrhotic** (sɪˈrɒtɪk) *adj*

cirripede ('sɪrɪˌpiːd) *or* **cirriped** ('sɪrɪˌpɛd) *n* **1** any marine crustacean of the subclass *Cirripedia*, including the barnacles. ◆ *adj* **2** of, relating to, or belonging to the *Cirripedia.*

cirrocumulus (ˌsɪrəʊˈkjuːmjʊləs) *n, pl* **cirrocumuli** (-ˌlaɪ). a high cloud of ice crystals grouped into small separate globular masses.

cirrostratus (ˌsɪrəʊˈstrɑːtəs) *n, pl* **cirrostrati** (-taɪ). a uniform layer of cloud above about 6000 metres.

cirrus (ˈsɪrəs) *n, pl* **cirri** (-raɪ). **1** a thin wispy fibrous cloud at high altitudes, composed of ice particles. **2** a plant tendril or similar part. **3a** a slender tentacle or filament in barnacles and other marine invertebrates. **3b** any of various hairlike structures in other animals. ORIG C18: from L: curl

CIS *abbrev. for* Commonwealth of Independent States.

cis- *prefix* on this side of, as in **cismontane** on this side of the mountains. Often retains the original Latin sense of 'side nearest Rome', as in **cispadane** on this (the southern) side of the Po. ORIG from L

cisalpine (sɪsˈælpaɪn) *adj* on this (the southern) side of the Alps, as viewed from Rome.

Cisalpine Gaul ★ *n* (in the ancient world) that part of Gaul between the Alps and the Apennines.

Ciscaucasia ★ (ˌsɪskɔːˈkeɪzɪə, -ʒə) *n* the part of Caucasia north of the Caucasus Mountains.

cisco (ˈsɪskəʊ) *n, pl* **ciscoes** *or* **ciscos.** any of various whitefish, esp. the lake herring of cold deep lakes of North America. ORIG C19: short for Canad. F *ciscoette,* of Algonquian origin

Ciskei ★ (ˈsɪskaɪ) *n* (formerly) a Bantu homeland in SE South Africa; reintegrated into South Africa in 1994.

cislunar (sɪsˈluːnə) *adj* of or relating to the space between the earth and the moon.

cisplatin (sɪsˈplætɪn) *n* a cytotoxic drug that acts by preventing DNA replication and hence cell divisions, used in the treatment of tumours of the ovary and testis. ORIG C20: from CIS- + PLATIN(UM)

cissing (ˈsɪsɪŋ) *n Building trades.* the appearance of pinholes, craters, etc., in paintwork due to poor adhesion of the paint to the surface.

cissy (ˈsɪsɪ) *n, pl* **-sies.** a variant spelling of **sissy.**

cist[1] (sɪst) *n* a wooden box for holding ritual objects used in ancient Rome and Greece. ORIG C19: from L *cista* box, from Gk *kistē*

cist[2] (sɪst) *or* **kist** *n* a box-shaped burial chamber made from stone slabs or a hollowed tree trunk. ORIG C19: from Welsh: chest, from L; see CIST[1]

Cistercian (sɪˈstɜːʃən) *n* **1** Also called: **White Monk.** a member of a Christian order of monks and nuns founded in 1098, which follows an especially strict form of the Benedictine rule. ◆ *adj* **2** of or relating to this order ORIG C17: from F, from Med. L, from *Cistercium* (modern *Cîteaux*), original home of the order

cistern (ˈsɪstən) *n* **1** a tank for the storage of water, esp. on or within the roof of a house or connected to a WC. **2** an underground reservoir for the storage of a liquid, esp. rainwater. **3** Also called: **cisterna.** *Anat.* a sac or partially enclosed space containing body fluid. ORIG C13: from OF, from L *cisterna* underground tank, from *cista* box

cistus (ˈsɪstəs) *n* any plant of the genus *Cistus.* See **rockrose.** ORIG C16: NL, from Gk *kistos*

citadel (ˈsɪtədᵊl, -ˌdɛl) *n* **1** a stronghold within or close to a city. **2** any strongly fortified building or place of safety; refuge. ORIG C16: from OF, from OIt. *cittadella* a little city, from L *cīvitās*

citation (saɪˈteɪʃən) *n* **1** the quoting of a book or author. **2** a passage or source cited. **3a** an official commendation or award, esp. for bravery or outstanding service. **3b** a formal public statement of this. **4** *Law.* **4a** an official summons to appear in court. **4b** the document containing such a summons.
▸ **citatory** (ˈsaɪtətərɪ) *adj*

cite (saɪt) *vb* **cites, citing, cited.** (*tr*) **1** to quote or refer to (a passage, book, or author). **2** to mention or commend (a soldier, etc.) for outstanding bravery or meritorious action. **3** to summon to appear before a court of law. **4** to enumerate: *he cited the king's virtues.* ORIG C15: from OF *citer* to summon, ult. from L *ciēre* to excite
▸ **ˈcitable** *or* **ˈciteable** *adj*

cithara (ˈsɪθərə) *or* **kithara** (ˈkɪθərə) *n* a stringed musical instrument of ancient Greece, similar to the lyre. ORIG C18: from Gk *kithara*

cither (ˈsɪθə) *or* **cithern** (ˈsɪθən) *n* a variant spelling of **cittern.** ORIG C17: from L, from Gk *kithara*

citified *or* **cityfied** (ˈsɪtɪˌfaɪd) *adj Often derog.* having the customs, manners, or dress of city people.

citizen (ˈsɪtɪzᵊn) *n* **1** a native registered or naturalized member of a state, nation, or other political community. **2** an inhabitant of a city or town. **3** a civilian, as opposed to a soldier, public official, etc. ORIG C14: from Anglo-F *citesein,* from OF *citeien,* from *cité* CITY

citizenry (ˈsɪtɪzənrɪ) *n, pl* **citizenries.** citizens collectively.

Citizens' Band *n* a range of radio frequencies assigned officially for use by the public for private communication. Abbrev.: **CB**

Citizens' Charter *n* (in Britain) a government document setting out standards of service for various public and private sector companies.

citizenship (ˈsɪtɪzənʃɪp) *n* **1** the condition or status of a citizen, with its rights and duties. **2** a person's conduct as a citizen.

Citlaltépetl ★ (ˌsiːtlɑːlˈteɪpɛtᵊl) *n* a volcano in SE Mexico, in central Veracruz state: the highest peak in the country. Height: 5699 m (18 698 ft). Spanish name: **Pico de Orizaba** (piko de oriˈsaba).

citrate (ˈsɪtreɪt, -rɪt; ˈsaɪtreɪt) *n* any salt or ester of citric acid. ORIG C18: from CITR(US) + -ATE[1]

citric (ˈsɪtrɪk) *adj* of or derived from citrus fruits or citric acid.

citric acid *n* a water-soluble weak tribasic acid found in many fruits, esp. citrus fruits, and used in pharmaceuticals and as a flavouring (**E330**). Formula: $CH_2(COOH)C(OH)(COOH)CH_2COOH$.

citrine (ˈsɪtrɪn) *n* **1** a brownish-yellow variety of quartz: a gemstone; false topaz. **2a** the yellow colour of a lemon. **2b** (*as adj*): *citrine hair.*

citron (ˈsɪtrən) *n* **1** a small Asian tree, having lemon-like fruit with a thick aromatic rind. **2** the fruit of this tree. **3** the rind of this fruit candied and used for decoration and flavouring of foods. ORIG C16: from OF, from L *citrus* citrus tree

citronella (ˌsɪtrəˈnɛlə) *n* **1** a tropical Asian grass with bluish-green lemon-scented leaves. **2** Also called: **citronella oil.** the yellow aromatic oil obtained from this grass, used in insect repellents, soaps, perfumes, etc. ORIG C19: NL, from F, from *citron* lemon

citrus (ˈsɪtrəs) *n, pl* **citruses. 1** any tree or shrub of the tropical and subtropical genus *Citrus,* which includes the orange, lemon, and lime. ◆ *adj also* **citrous. 2** of or relating to the genus *Citrus* or to the fruits of plants of this genus. ORIG C19: from L: citrus tree

Città del Vaticano ★ (tʃitˈta del vatiˈkaːno) *n* the Italian name for **Vatican City.**

cittern (ˈsɪtɜːn), **cither,** *or* **cithern** *n* a medieval stringed instrument resembling a lute but having wire strings and a flat back. ORIG C16: ? a blend of CITHER + GITTERN

city (ˈsɪtɪ) *n, pl* **cities. 1** any large town or populous place. **2** (in Britain) a town that has received this title from the Crown: usually the seat of a bishop. **3** (in the US) an incorporated urban centre with its own government and administration established by state charter. **4** (in Canada) a similar urban municipality incorporated by the provincial government **5** the people of a city collectively. **6** (*modifier*) in or characteristic of a city: *city habits.*
◆ Related adjs.: **civic, urban, municipal.** ORIG C13: from OF *cité,* from L *cīvitās* state, from *cīvis* citizen

City ★ (ˈsɪtɪ) *n* **the. 1** short for **City of London**: the original settlement of London on the N bank of the Thames; a municipality governed by the Lord Mayor and Corporation. Resident pop.: 5893 (1981). **2** the area in central London in which the United Kingdom's major financial business is transacted. **3** the various financial institutions located in this area.

City and Guilds Institute *n* (in Britain) an examining body for technical and craft skills.

city chambers *n* (*functioning as sing*) (in Scotland) the municipal buildings of a city; town hall.

City Code *n* (in Britain) short for **City Code on Takeovers and Mergers**: a code laid down in 1968 (later modified) to control takeovers and mergers.

city desk *n* the editorial section of a newspaper dealing in Britain with financial news, in the US and Canada with local news.

city editor *n* (on a newspaper) **1** *Brit.* the editor in charge of financial and commercial news. **2** *US & Canad.* the editor in charge of local news.

city father *n* a person who is active or prominent in the public affairs of a city.

cityscape ('sɪtɪˌskeɪp) *n* an urban landscape; view of a city.

city-state *n Ancient history.* a state consisting of a sovereign city and its dependencies.

city technology college *n* (in Britain) a type of senior secondary school specializing in technological subjects, set up in inner-city areas with funding from industry as well as the government.

Ciudad Bolívar ★ (*Spanish* θiu'ðað bo'liβar) *n* a port in E Venezuela, on the Orinoco River: accessible to ocean-going vessels. Pop.: 225 340 (1990). Former name (1764–1846): **Angostura.**

Ciudad Guayana ★ (*Spanish* θiu'ðað gwa'jana) *n* an industrial conurbation in E Venezuela, on the River Orinoco: iron and steel processing, gold mining. Pop.: 453 047 (1990). Former name: **Santo Tomé de Guayana.**

Ciudad Juárez ★ (*Spanish* θiu'ðað 'xwarɛθ) *n* a city in N Mexico, in Chihuahua state on the Río Grande, opposite El Paso, Texas. Pop.: 789 522 (1990). Former name (until 1888): **El Paso del Norte** (ɛl 'paso del 'nɔrte).

Ciudad Trujillo ★ (*Spanish* θiu'ðað tru'xiʎo) *n* the former name (1936–61) of **Santo Domingo.**

Ciudad Victoria ★ (*Spanish* θiu'ðað bik'torja) *n* a city in E central Mexico, capital of Tamaulipas state. Pop.: 194 996 (1990).

civet ('sɪvɪt) *n* **1** a catlike mammal of Africa and S Asia, typically having spotted fur and secreting a powerfully smelling fluid from anal glands. **2** the yellowish fatty secretion of such an animal, used as a fixative in the manufacture of perfumes. **3** the fur of such an animal. ORIG C16: from OF, from It., from Ar. *zabād* civet perfume

civic ('sɪvɪk) *adj* of or relating to a city, citizens, or citizenship. ORIG C16: from L, from *cīvis* citizen
▸ **'civically** *adv*

civic centre *n Brit.* the public buildings of a town, including recreational facilities and offices of local administration.

civics ('sɪvɪks) *n* (*functioning as sing*) the study of the rights and responsibilities of citizenship.

civies ('sɪvɪz) *pl n Inf.* a variant spelling of **civvies.** See **civvy** (sense 2).

civil ('sɪvᵊl) *adj* **1** of the ordinary life of citizens as distinguished from military, legal, or ecclesiastical affairs. **2** of or relating to the citizen as an individual: *civil rights.* **3** of or occurring within the state or between citizens: *civil strife.* **4** polite or courteous: *a civil manner.* **5** of or in accordance with Roman law. ORIG C14: from OF, from L *cīvīlis,* from *cīvis* citizen
▸ **'civilly** *adv*

civil defence *n* the organizing of civilians to deal with enemy attacks.

civil disobedience *n* a refusal to obey laws, pay taxes, etc.: a nonviolent means of protesting.

civil engineer *n* a person qualified to design and construct public works, such as roads, bridges, harbours, etc.
▸ **civil engineering** *n*

civilian (sɪ'vɪljən) *n* **a** a person whose occupation is civil or nonmilitary. **b** (*as modifier*): *civilian life.* ORIG C14 (orig.: a practitioner of civil law): from *civile* (from L *jūs cīvīle* civil law) + -IAN

civility (sɪ'vɪlɪtɪ) *n, pl* **civilities. 1** politeness or courtesy. **2** (*often pl*) an act of politeness.

civilization *or* **civilisation** (ˌsɪvɪlaɪ'zeɪʃən) *n* **1** a human society that has a complex cultural, political, and legal organization; an advanced state in social development. **2** the peoples or nations collectively who have achieved such a state. **3** the total culture and way of life of a particular people, nation, region, or period. **4** the process of bringing or achieving civilization. **5** intellectual, cultural, and moral refinement. **6** cities or populated areas, as contrasted with sparsely inhabited areas, deserts, etc.

civilize *or* **civilise** ('sɪvɪˌlaɪz) *vb* **civilizes, civilizing, civilized** *or* **civilises, civilising, civilised.** (*tr*) **1** to bring out of savagery or barbarism into a state characteristic of civilization. **2** to refine, educate, or enlighten.
▸ **'civiˌlizable** *or* **'civiˌlisable** *adj* ▸ **'civiˌlized** *or* **'civiˌlised** *adj*

civil law *n* **1** the law of a state relating to private and civilian affairs. **2** the body of law in ancient Rome, esp. as applicable to private citizens. **3** law based on the Roman system as distinguished from common law and canon law.

civil liberty *n* the right of an individual to certain freedoms of speech and action.

civil list *n* (in Britain) the annuities voted by Parliament for the support of the royal household and the royal family.

civil marriage *n Law.* a marriage performed by an official other than a clergyman.

civil rights *pl n* **1** the personal rights of the individual citizen. **2** (*modifier*) of, relating to, or promoting equality in social, economic, and political rights.

civil servant *n* a member of the civil service.

civil service *n* **1** the service responsible for the public administration of the government of a country. It excludes the legislative, judicial, and military branches. **2** the members of the civil service collectively.

civil war *n* war between parties or factions within the same nation.

Civil War *n* **1** *English history.* the conflict between Charles I and the Parliamentarians resulting from disputes over their respective prerogatives. Parliament gained decisive victories at Marston Moor in 1644 and Naseby in 1645, and Charles was executed in 1649. **2** *US history.* the war fought from 1861 to 1865 between the North and the South, sparked off by Lincoln's election as president but with deep-rooted political and economic causes, exacerbated by the slavery issue. The advantages of the North in terms of population, finance, and communications brought about the South's eventual surrender at Appomattox.

civvy ('sɪvɪ) *n, pl* **civvies.** *Sl.* **1** a civilian. **2** (*pl*) Also: **civies.** civilian dress as opposed to uniform. **3 civvy street.** civilian life.

CJ *abbrev. for* Chief Justice.

CJA (in Britain) *abbrev. for* Criminal Justice Act.

CJD *abbrev. for* Creutzfeldt-Jakob disease.

Cl *the chemical symbol for* chlorine.

clachan (*Gaelic* 'klaxən; *English* 'klæ-) *n Scot. & Irish dialect.* a small village; hamlet. ORIG C15: from Scot. Gaelic: prob. from *clach* stone

clack (klæk) *vb* **1** to make or cause to make a sound like that of two pieces of wood hitting each other. **2** (*intr*) to jabber. ◆ *n* **3** a short sharp sound. **4** chatter. **5** Also called: **clack valve.** a simple nonreturn valve using a hinged flap or a ball. ORIG C13: prob. from ON *klaka* to twitter, imit.
▸ **'clacker** *n*

Clackmannanshire ★ (klæk'mænənˌʃɪə, -ʃə) *n* a historic county and council area of central Scotland; part of Central region (1975–96). Administrative centre: Alloa. Pop.: 47 900 (1996 est.). Area: 142 sq. km (55 sq. miles).

Clacton *or* **Clacton-on-Sea** ★ ('klæktən) *n* a town and resort in SE England, in E Essex. Pop.: 43 571 (1981).

clad[1] (klæd) *vb* a past tense and past participle of **clothe**. ORIG OE *clāthode* clothed, from *clāthian* to CLOTHE

clad[2] (klæd) *vb* **clads, cladding, clad.** (*tr*) to bond a metal to (another metal), esp. to form a protective coating. ORIG C14: special use of CLAD[1]

cladding ('klædɪŋ) *n* **1** the process of protecting one metal by bonding a second metal to its surface. **2** the protective coating so bonded to metal. **3** the material used for the outside facing of a building, etc.

clade (kleɪd) *n Biol.* a group of organisms considered as having evolved from a common ancestor. ORIG C20: from Gk *klados* branch, shoot

cladistics (klə'dɪstɪks) *n* (*functioning as sing*) a method of grouping animals by measurable likenesses or homologues. ORIG C20: NL from Gk *klados* branch, shoot
▸ **cladism** ('klædɪzəm) *n* ▸ **cladist** ('klædɪst) *n*

claim (kleɪm) *vb* (*mainly tr*) **1** to demand as being due or as one's property; assert one's right to. **2** (*takes a clause as object or an infinitive*) to assert as a fact; maintain against denial: *he claimed to be telling the truth.* **3** to call for or need; deserve: *this problem claims our attention.* **4** to take: *the accident claimed four lives.* ◆ *n* **5** an assertion of a right; a demand for something as due. **6** an assertion of something as true, real, or factual. **7** a right or just title to something; basis for demand: *a claim to fame.* **8** anything that is claimed, such as a piece of land staked out by a miner. **9a** a demand for payment in connection with an insurance policy, etc. **9b** the sum of money demanded. ORIG C13: from OF *claimer* to call, from L *clāmāre* to shout
▸ **'claimable** *adj* ▸ **'claimant** *or* **'claimer** *n*

Clair ★ (*French* klɛr) *n* **René** (rəne), real name *René Chomette*. 1898–1981, French film director; noted for his comedies including *An Italian Straw Hat* (1928); later films include *Les Belles de nuit* (1952).

clairvoyance (klɛə'vɔɪəns) *n* **1** the alleged power of perceiving things beyond the natural range of the senses. **2** keen intuitive understanding. ORIG C19: from F: clear-seeing, from *clair* clear + *voyance,* from *voir* to see

clairvoyant (klɛə'vɔɪənt) *adj* **1** of or possessing clairvoyance. **2** having great insight. ◆ *n* **3** a person claiming to have the power to foretell future events.
▸ **clair'voyantly** *adv*

clam (klæm) *n* **1** any of various burrowing bivalve molluscs. **2** the edible flesh of such a mollusc. **3** *Inf.* a reticent person. ◆ *vb* **clams, clamming, clammed. 4** (*intr*) *Chiefly US.* to gather clams. ◆ See also **clam up.** ORIG C16: from earlier *clamshell,* that is, shell that clamps

clamant ('kleɪmənt) *adj* **1** noisy. **2** calling urgently. ORIG C17: from L, from *clāmāre* to shout

clamber ('klæmbə) *vb* **1** (usually foll. by *up, over,* etc.) to climb (something) awkwardly, esp. by using both hands and feet. ◆ *n* **2** a climb performed in this manner. ORIG C15: prob. var. of CLIMB
▸ **'clamberer** *n*

clammy ('klæmɪ) *adj* **clammier, clammiest. 1** unpleasantly sticky; moist. **2** (of the weather) close; humid. ORIG C14: from OE *clǣman* to smear
▸ **'clammily** *adv* ▸ **'clamminess** *n*

clamour *or US* **clamor** ('klæmə) *n* **1** a loud persistent outcry. **2** a vehement expression of collective feeling or outrage. **3** a loud and persistent noise. ◆ *vb* **4** (*intr; often* foll. by *for* or *against*) to make a loud noise or outcry; make a public demand. **5** (*tr*) to move or force by outcry. ORIG C14: from OF, from L, from *clāmāre* to cry out
▸ **'clamorous** *adj* ▸ **'clamorously** *adv* ▸ **'clamorousness** *n*

clamp[1] (klæmp) *n* **1** a mechanical device with movable jaws with which an object can be secured to a bench or with which two objects may be secured together. **2** See **wheel clamp.** ◆ *vb* (*tr*) **3** to fix or fasten with or as if with a clamp **4** to immobilize (a car) by means of a wheel clamp. **5** to inflict or impose forcefully: *they clamped a curfew on the town.* ORIG C14: from Du. or Low G *klamp*

clamp[2] (klæmp) *n* **1** a mound of a harvested root crop, covered with straw and earth to protect it from winter weather. ◆ *vb* **2** (*tr*) to enclose (a harvested root crop) in a mound. ORIG C16: from MDu. *klamp* heap

clamp down *vb* (*intr, adv; often* foll. by *on*) **1** to behave repressively; attempt to suppress something regarded as undesirable. ◆ *n* **clampdown. 2** a sudden restrictive measure.

clam up *vb* (*intr, adv*) *Inf.* to keep or become silent or withhold information.

clan (klæn) *n* **1** a group of people interrelated by ancestry or marriage. **2** a group of families with a common surname and a common ancestor, esp. among the Scots and the Irish. **3** a group of people united by common characteristics, aims, or interests. ORIG C14: from Scot. Gaelic *clann* family, descendants, from L *planta* sprout

Clancy ★ ('klænsɪ) *n* **Tom.** born 1947, US novelist; his thrillers, many of which have been filmed, include *The Hunt for Red October* (1984), *Clear and Present Danger* (1989), and *Carrier* (1999).

clandestine (klæn'dɛstɪn) *adj* secret and concealed, often for illicit reasons. ORIG C16: from L, from *clam* secretly
▸ **clan'destinely** *adv*

clang (klæŋ) *vb* **1** to make or cause to make a loud resounding noise, as metal when struck. **2** (*intr*) to move or operate making such a sound. ◆ *n* **3** a resounding metallic noise. **4** the harsh cry of certain birds. ORIG C16: from L *clangere*

clanger ('klæŋə) *n* **1** *Inf.* a conspicuous mistake (esp. in **drop a clanger**). **2** something that clangs or causes a clang. ORIG C20: from CLANG

clangour *or US* **clangor** ('klæŋgə, 'klæŋə) *n* **1** a loud resonant often-repeated noise. **2** an uproar. ◆ *vb* **3** (*intr*) to make or produce a loud resonant noise.
▸ **'clangorous** *adj* ▸ **'clangorously** *adv*

clank (klæŋk) *n* **1** an abrupt harsh metallic sound. ◆ *vb* **2** to make or cause to make such a sound. **3** (*intr*) to move or operate making such a sound. ORIG C17: imit.
▸ **'clankingly** *adv*

clannish ('klænɪʃ) *adj* **1** of or characteristic of a clan. **2** tending to associate closely within a group to the exclusion of outsiders; cliquish.
▸ **'clannishly** *adv* ▸ **'clannishness** *n*

clansman ('klænzmən) *or* (*fem*) **clanswoman** *n, pl* **clansmen** *or* **clanswomen.** a person belonging to a clan.

clap[1] (klæp) *vb* **claps, clapping, clapped. 1** to make or cause to make a sharp abrupt sound, as of two nonmetallic objects struck together. **2** to applaud (someone or something) by striking the palms of the hands together sharply. **3** (*tr*) to strike (a person) lightly with an open hand, in greeting, etc. **4** (*tr*) to place or put quickly or forcibly: *they clapped him into jail.* **5** (of certain birds) to flap (the wings) noisily. **6** (*intr;* foll. by *up* or *together*) to contrive or put together hastily. **7 clap eyes on.** *Inf.* to catch sight of. **8 clap hold of.** *Inf.* to grasp suddenly or forcibly. ◆ *n* **9** the sharp abrupt sound produced by striking the hands together. **10** the act of clapping, esp. in applause. **11** a sudden sharp sound, esp. of thunder. **12** a light blow. **13** *Arch.* a sudden action or mishap. ORIG OE *clæppan;* imit.

clap[2] (klæp) *n* (usually preceded by *the*) a slang word for **gonorrhoea.** ORIG C16: from OF *clapoir* venereal sore, from *clapier* brothel, from ?

clapboard ('klæp,bɔːd, 'klæbəd) *n* **1** a long thin timber board, used esp. in the US and Canada in wood-frame construction by lapping each board over the one below. ◆ *vb* **2** (*tr*) to cover with such boards. ORIG C16: partial translation of Low G *klappholt,* from *klappen* to crack + *holt* wood

clapped out *adj* (**clapped-out** *when prenominal*). *Inf.* **1** *Brit., Austral. & NZ.* worn out; dilapidated. **2** *Austral. & NZ.* extremely tired; exhausted.

clapper ('klæpə) *n* **1** a person or thing that claps. **2** Also called: **tongue.** a small piece of metal within a bell that sounds when made to strike against its side. **3 go (run, move) like the clappers.** *Brit. inf.* to move extremely fast.

clapperboard ('klæpə,bɔːd) *n* a pair of hinged boards clapped together during film shooting to aid in synchronizing sound and picture prints.

Clapton ★ ('klæptən) *n* **Eric.** born 1945, British rock guitarist, noted for his virtuoso style, his work with the Yardbirds (1963–65), Cream (1966–68), and, with Derek and the Dominos, the album *Layla* (1970).

claptrap ('klæpˌtræp) *n Inf.* **1** contrived but foolish talk. **2** insincere and pretentious talk: *politicians' claptrap.* ORIG C18: from CLAP[1] + TRAP[1]

claque (klæk) *n* **1** a group of people hired to applaud. **2** a group of fawning admirers. ORIG C19: from F, from *claquer* to clap, imit.

Clare[1] ★ (klɛə) *n* a county of W Republic of Ireland, in Munster between Galway Bay and the Shannon estuary. County town: Ennis. Pop.: 94 000 (1996). Area: 3188 sq. km (1231 sq. miles).

Clare[2] ★ (klɛə) *n* **John.** 1793–1864, British poet, noted for *The Shepherd's Calendar* (1827) and *The Rural Muse* (1835). He was confined in a lunatic asylum from 1837.

Clarendon[1] ★ ('klærəndən) *n* a village near Salisbury in S England: site of a council held by Henry II in 1164 that produced a code of laws (the **Constitutions of Clarendon**) defining relations between church and state.

Clarendon[2] ★ ('klærəndən) *n* **1st Earl of,** title of *Edward Hyde.* 1609–74, English statesman and historian; chief adviser to Charles II (1660–67); author of *History of the Rebellion and Civil Wars in England* (1704–07).

Clare of Assisi ★ *n* **Saint.** 1194–1253, Italian nun; founder of the Franciscan Order of Poor Clares. Feast day: Aug. 11.

claret ('klærət) *n* **1** a red wine, esp. one from the Bordeaux district of France. **2a** a purplish-red colour. **2b** (*as adj*): *a claret football strip.* ORIG C14: from OF (*vin*) *claret* clear (wine), from Med. L *clārātum,* from L *clārus* clear

clarify ('klærɪˌfaɪ) *vb* **clarifies, clarifying, clarified. 1** to make or become clear or easy to understand. **2** to make or become free of impurities. **3** to make (fat, butter, etc.) clear by heating, etc., or (of fat, etc.) to become clear as a result of such a process. ORIG C14: from OF, from LL, from L *clārus* clear + *facere* to make
▸ **ˌclarifiˈcation** *n* ▸ **ˈclariˌfier** *n*

clarinet (ˌklærɪˈnɛt) *n Music.* **1** a keyed woodwind instrument with a cylindrical bore and a single reed. **2** an orchestral musician who plays the clarinet. ORIG C18: from F, prob. from It., from *clarino* trumpet
▸ **ˌclariˈnettist** *or US sometimes* **ˌclariˈnetist** *n*

clarion ('klærɪən) *n* **1** a stop of trumpet quality on an organ. **2** an obsolete, high-pitched, small-bore trumpet. **3** the sound of such an instrument or any similar sound. ◆ *adj* **4** (*prenominal*) clear and ringing; inspiring: *a clarion call to action.* ◆ *vb* **5** to proclaim loudly. ORIG C14: from Med. L *clāriō* trumpet, from L *clārus* clear

clarity ('klærɪtɪ) *n* **1** clearness, as of expression. **2** clearness, as of water. ORIG C16: from L *clāritās,* from *clārus* clear

Clark ★ (klɑːk) *n* **1 James,** known as *Jim.* 1936–68, Scottish racing driver; World Champion (1963, 1965). **2** (**Charles**) **Joseph,** known as *Joe.* born 1939, Canadian politician; prime minister (1979–80). **3 Kenneth,** Baron Clark of Saltwood. 1903–83, British art historian: his books include *Civilization* (1969). **4 William.** 1770–1838, US explorer and frontiersman: noted for his expedition to the Pacific Northwest (1804–06).

Clarke ★ (klɑːk) *n* **1** Sir **Arthur C**(**harles**). born 1917, British science-fiction writer. **2 Austin.** 1896–1974, Irish poet and verse dramatist. His work includes the poem *The Vengeance of Fionn* (1917) and the play *The Son of Learning* (1927). **3 Jeremiah.** ?1673–1707, English composer, noted for his *Trumpet Voluntary.* **4 Kenneth** (**Harry**). born 1940, British Conservative politician; home secretary (1992–93); chancellor of the exchequer (1993–97). **5 Marcus** (**Andrew Hislop**). 1846–81, Australian novelist born in England, noted for his novel *For the Term of His Natural Life* (1870–72) and *Old Tales of a Young Country* (1871).

clarkia ('klɑːkɪə) *n* any North American plant of the genus *Clarkia:* cultivated for their red, purple, or pink flowers. ORIG C19: NL, after William CLARK

Clarkson ★ ('klɑːksən) *n* **Thomas.** 1760–1846, British campaigner for the abolition of slavery.

clary ('klɛərɪ) *n, pl* **claries.** any of several European plants having aromatic leaves and blue flowers. ORIG C14: from earlier *sclarreye,* from Med. L *sclareia,* from ?

-clase *n combining form.* (in mineralogy) indicating a particular type of cleavage: *plagioclase.* ORIG via F from Gk *klasis* a breaking

clash (klæʃ) *vb* **1** to make or cause to make a loud harsh sound, esp. by striking together. **2** (*intr*) to be incompatible. **3** (*intr*) to engage together in conflict. **4** (*intr*) (of dates or events) to coincide. **5** (*intr*) (of colours) to look inharmonious together. ◆ *n* **6** a loud harsh noise. **7** a collision or conflict. ORIG C16: imit.
▸ **ˈclasher** *n*

clasp (klɑːsp) *n* **1** a fastening, such as a catch or hook, for holding things together. **2** a firm grasp or embrace. **3** *Mil.* a bar on a medal ribbon, to indicate either a second award or the battle, campaign, or reason for its award. ◆ *vb* (*tr*) **4** to hold in a firm grasp. **5** to grasp firmly with the hand. **6** to fasten together with or as if with a clasp. ORIG C14: from ?
▸ **ˈclasper** *n*

claspers ('klɑːspəz) *pl n Zool.* **1** a paired organ of male insects, used to clasp the female during copulation. **2** a paired organ of male sharks and related fish, used to assist the transfer of spermatozoa into the body of the female during copulation.

clasp knife *n* a large knife with one or more blades or other devices folding into the handle.

class (klɑːs) *n* **1** a collection or division of people or things sharing a common characteristic. **2** a group of persons sharing a similar social and economic position. **3a** the pattern of divisions that exist within a society on the basis of rank, economic status, etc. **3b** (*as modifier*): *the class struggle; class distinctions.* **4a** a group of pupils or students who are taught together. **4b** a meeting of a group of students for tuition. **5** *US.* a group of students who graduated in a specified year: *the class of '53.* **6** (*in combination and as modifier*) *Brit.* a grade of attainment in a university honours degree: *second-class honours.* **7** one of several standards of accommodation in public transport. **8** *Inf.* excellence or elegance, esp. in dress, design, or behaviour. **9** *Biol.* any of the taxonomic groups into which a phylum is divided and which contains one or more orders. **10** *Maths.* another name for **set**[2] (sense 3). **11 in a class of its own** *or* **in a class by oneself.** unequalled; unparalleled. ◆ *vb* **12** to have or assign a place within a group, grade, or class. ORIG C17: from L *classis* class, rank, fleet

class. *abbrev. for:* **1** classic(al). **2** classification. **3** classified.

class-conscious *adj* aware of belonging to a particular social rank.
▸ **ˌclass-ˈconsciousness** *n*

classic ('klæsɪk) *adj* **1** of the highest class, esp. in art or literature. **2** serving as a standard or model of its kind. **3** adhering to an established set of principles in the arts or sciences: *a classic proof.* **4** characterized by simplicity, balance, regularity, and purity of form; classical. **5** of lasting interest or significance. **6** continuously in fashion because of its simple style: *a classic dress.* ◆ *n* **7** an author, artist, or work of art of the highest excellence. **8** a creation or work considered as definitive. **9** *Horse racing.* any of the five principal races for three-year-old horses in Britain, namely the One Thousand Guineas, Two Thousand Guineas, Derby, Oaks, and Saint Leger. ORIG C17: from L *classicus* of the first rank, from *classis* division, rank, class

classical ('klæsɪk[ə]l) *adj* **1** of, relating to, or characteristic of the ancient Greeks and Romans or their civilization. **2** designating, following, or influenced by the art or culture of ancient Greece or Rome: *classical architecture.* **3** *Music.* **3a** of, relating to, or denoting any music or its period of composition marked by stability of form, intellectualism, and restraint. Cf. **romantic** (sense 5). **3b** accepted as a standard: *the classical suite.* **3c** denoting serious art music in general. Cf. **pop**[2]. **4** denoting or relating to a style in any of the arts characterized by emotional restraint and conservatism: *a classical style of painting.* **5** (of an education) based on the humanities and the study of Latin and Greek. **6** *Physics.* not involving the quantum theory or the theory of relativity: *classical mechanics.*
▸ **ˌclassiˈcality** *or* **ˈclassicalness** *n* ▸ **ˈclassically** *adv*

Classical school *n* economic theory based on the

works of Adam Smith and David Ricardo, which explains the creation of wealth and advocates free trade.

classic car *n Chiefly Brit.* a car that is more than twenty five years old. Cf. **veteran car, vintage car.**

classicism ('klæsɪˌsɪzəm) *or* **classicalism** ('klæsɪkəˌlɪzəm) *n* **1** a style based on the study of Greek and Roman models, characterized by emotional restraint and regularity of form; the antithesis of romanticism. **2** knowledge of the culture of ancient Greece and Rome. **3a** a Greek or Latin expression. **3b** an expression in a modern language that is modelled on a Greek or Latin form.
▸ **'classicist** *n*

classicize *or* **classicise** ('klæsɪˌsaɪz) *vb* **classicizes, classicizing, classicized** *or* **classicises, classicising, classicised. 1** (*tr*) to make classic. **2** (*intr*) to imitate classical style.

classics ('klæsɪks) *n* **1 the.** a body of literature regarded as great or lasting, esp. that of ancient Greece or Rome. **2 the.** the ancient Greek and Latin languages. **3** (*functioning as sing*) ancient Greek and Roman culture as a subject for academic study.

classification (ˌklæsɪfɪ'keɪʃən) *n* **1** systematic placement in categories. **2** one of the divisions in a system of classifying. **3** *Biol.* **3a** the placing of animals and plants in a series of increasingly specialized groups because of similarities in structure, origin, etc., that indicate a common relationship. **3b** the study of the principles and practice of this process; taxonomy. ORIG C18: from F; see CLASS, -IFY, -ATION
▸ **'classificatory** *adj*

classified ('klæsɪˌfaɪd) *adj* **1** arranged according to some system of classification. **2** *Government.* (of information) not available to people outside a restricted group, esp. for reasons of national security. **3** *US & Canad. inf.* (of information) closely concealed or secret. **4** (of advertisements in newspapers, etc.) arranged according to type. **5** *Brit.* (of newspapers) containing sports results. **6** (of British roads) having a number in the national road system.

classify ('klæsɪˌfaɪ) *vb* **classifies, classifying, classified.** (*tr*) **1** to arrange or order by classes; categorize. **2** *Government.* to declare (information, documents, etc.) of possible aid to an enemy and therefore not available to people outside a restricted group. ORIG C18: back formation from CLASSIFICATION
▸ **'classiˌfiable** *adj* ▸ **'classiˌfier** *n*

class interval *n Statistics.* one of the intervals into which the range of a variable of a distribution is divided, esp. one of the divisions of the base line of a bar chart or histogram.

classless ('klɑːslɪs) *adj* **1** not belonging to a class. **2** characterized by the absence of economic and social distinctions.
▸ **'classlessness** *n*

class list *n* (in Britain) a list categorizing students according to the class of honours they have obtained in their degree examination.

classmate ('klɑːsˌmeɪt) *n* a friend or contemporary of the same class in a school.

classroom ('klɑːsˌruːm, -ˌrʊm) *n* a room in which classes are conducted, esp. in a school.

class struggle *n* **the.** *Marxism.* the continual conflict between the capitalist and working classes for economic and political power.

classy ('klɑːsɪ) *adj* **classier, classiest.** *Sl.* elegant; stylish.
▸ **'classiness** *n*

clatter ('klætə) *vb* **1** to make or cause to make a rattling noise, esp. as a result of movement. **2** (*intr*) to chatter. ◆ *n* **3** a rattling sound or noise. **4** a noisy commotion, such as loud chatter. ORIG OE *clatrung* clattering (gerund)
▸ **'clatterer** *n* ▸ **'clatteringly** *adv*

Claude Lorrain ★ (*French* klod lɔrɛ̃) *n* real name *Claude Gelée.* 1600–82, French painter.

Claudius ★ ('klɔːdɪəs) *n* full name *Tiberius Claudius Drusus Nero Germanicus.* 10 B.C.–54 A.D., Roman emperor (41–54); invaded Britain (43); poisoned by his fourth wife, Agrippina.

Claudius II ★ *n* full name *Marcus Aurelius Claudius,* called *Gothicus.* 214–270 A.D., Roman emperor (268–270).

clause (klɔːz) *n* **1** *Grammar.* a group of words, consisting of a subject and a predicate including a finite verb, that does not necessarily constitute a sentence. Cf. **phrase.** See also **main clause, subordinate clause. 2** a section of a legal document such as a contract, will, or draft statute. ORIG C13: from OF, from Med. L *clausa* a closing (of a rhetorical period), from L, from *claudere* to close
▸ **'clausal** *adj*

Clausewitz ★ (*German* 'klauzəvɪts) *n* **Karl von** (karl fɔn). 1780–1831, Prussian general, noted for his works on military strategy, esp. *Vom Kriege* (1833).

Clausius ★ (*German* 'klauziʊs) *n* **Rudolf Julius** ('ruːdɔlf 'juːliʊs). 1822–88, German physicist. He enunciated the second law of thermodynamics (1850) and developed the kinetic theory of gases.

claustrophobia (ˌklɔːstrə'fəʊbɪə, ˌklɒs-) *n* an abnormal fear of being in a confined space. ORIG C19: NL from L *claustrum* CLOISTER + -PHOBIA
▸ **'claustroˌphobe** *n* ▸ **ˌclaustro'phobic** *adj*

clavate ('kleɪveɪt, -vɪt) *or* **claviform** ('klævɪˌfɔːm) *adj Biol.* shaped like a club. ORIG C19: from L *clāva* club
▸ **'clavately** *adv*

clave[1] (kleɪv, klɑːv) *n Music.* one of a pair of hardwood sticks struck together to make a hollow sound, esp. to mark the beat in Latin-American dance music. ORIG C20: from American Sp., from L *clavis* key

clave[2] (kleɪv) *vb Arch.* a past tense of **cleave.**

clavichord ('klævɪˌkɔːd) *n* a keyboard instrument consisting of a number of thin wire strings struck from below by brass tangents. ORIG C15: from Med. L, from L *clāvis* key + *chorda* CHORD[1]

clavicle ('klævɪkᵊl) *n* **1** either of the two bones connecting the shoulder blades with the upper part of the breastbone. Nontechnical name: **collarbone. 2** the corresponding structure in other vertebrates. ORIG C17: from Med. L *clāvicula,* from L *clāvis* key
▸ **clavicular** (klə'vɪkjʊlə) *adj*

clavier (klə'vɪə, 'klævɪə) *n* **a** any keyboard instrument. **b** the keyboard itself. ORIG C18: from F: keyboard, from L *clāvis* key

claw (klɔː) *n* **1** a curved pointed horny process on the end of each digit in birds, some reptiles, and certain mammals. **2** a corresponding structure in some invertebrates, such as the pincer of a crab. **3** a part or member like a claw in function or appearance. ◆ *vb* **4** to scrape, tear, or dig (something or someone) with claws, etc. **5** (*tr*) to create by scratching as with claws: *to claw an opening.* ORIG OE *clawu*
▸ **'clawer** *n*

claw back *vb* (*tr, adv*) **1** to get back (something) with difficulty. **2** to recover (a sum of money), esp. by taxation or a penalty. ◆ *n* **clawback. 3** the recovery of a sum of money, esp. by taxation or a penalty. **4** the sum so recovered.

claw hammer *n* a hammer with a cleft at one end of the head for extracting nails.

clay (kleɪ) *n* **1** a very fine-grained material that occurs as sedimentary rocks, soils, and other deposits. It becomes plastic when moist but hardens on heating and is used in the manufacture of bricks, ceramics, etc. **2** earth or mud. **3** *Poetic.* the material of the human body. ORIG OE *clǣg*
▸ **'clayey, 'clayish,** *or* **'clayˌlike** *adj*

Clay ★ (kleɪ) *n* **1 Cassius.** See **Muhammad Ali. 2 Henry.** 1777–1852, US statesman; secretary of state (1825–29).

claymore ('kleɪˌmɔː) *n* a large two-edged broadsword used formerly by Scottish Highlanders. ORIG C18: from Gaelic *claidheamh mōr* great sword

clay pigeon *n* a disc of baked clay hurled into the air from a machine as a target to be shot at.

CLC *abbrev. for* Canadian Labour Congress.

-cle *suffix forming nouns.* indicating smallness: *cubicle; particle.* ORIG via OF from L *-culus.* See -CULE

clean (kli:n) *adj* **1** without dirt or other impurities; unsoiled. **2** without anything in it or on it: *a clean page.* **3** recently washed; fresh. **4** without extraneous or foreign materials. **5** without defect, difficulties, or problems. **6** (of a nuclear weapon) producing little or no radioactive fallout or contamination. **7** (of a wound, etc.) having no pus or other sign of infection. **8** pure; morally sound. **9** without objectionable language or obscenity. **10** thorough or complete: *a clean break.* **11** dexterous or adroit: *a clean throw.* **12** *Sport.* played fairly and without fouls. **13** simple in design: *a ship's clean lines.* **14** *Aeronautics.* causing little turbulence; streamlined. **15** honourable or respectable. **16** habitually neat. **17** (esp. of a driving licence) showing or having no record of offences. **18** *Sl.* **18a** innocent; not guilty. **18b** not carrying illegal drugs, weapons, etc. ◆ *vb* **19** to make or become free of dirt, filth, etc.: *the stove cleans easily.* **20** (*tr*) to remove in making clean: *to clean marks off the wall.* **21** (*tr*) to prepare (fish, poultry, etc.) for cooking: *to clean a chicken.* ◆ *adv* **22** in a clean way; cleanly. **23** *Not standard.* (intensifier): *clean forgotten.* **24 come clean.** *Inf.* to make a revelation or confession. ◆ *n* **25** the act or an instance of cleaning: *he gave his shoes a clean.* **26 clean sweep.** See **sweep** (sense 28). ◆ See also **clean out, clean up.** ORIG OE *clǣne*
▸ '**cleanable** *adj* ▸ '**cleanness** *n*

clean-cut *adj* **1** clearly outlined; neat: *clean-cut lines of a ship.* **2** definite.

cleaner ('kli:nə) *n* **1** a person, device, chemical agent, etc., that removes dirt, as from clothes or carpets. **2** (*usually pl*) a shop, etc., that provides a dry-cleaning service. **3 take (a person) to the cleaners.** *Inf.* to rob or defraud (a person).

cleanly *adv* ('kli:nlɪ). **1** in a fair manner. **2** easily or smoothly. ◆ *adj* ('klɛnlɪ), **cleanlier, cleanliest. 3** habitually clean or neat.
▸ **cleanlily** ('klɛnlɪlɪ) *adv* ▸ **cleanliness** ('klɛnlɪnɪs) *n*

clean out *vb* (*tr, adv*) **1** (foll. by *of* or *from*) to remove (something) (from or away from). **2** *Sl.* to leave (someone) with no money. **3** *Inf.* to exhaust (stocks, goods, etc.) completely.

cleanse (klɛnz) *vb* **cleanses, cleansing, cleansed.** (*tr*) **1** to remove dirt, filth, etc., from. **2** to remove guilt from. **3** to remove a group of people from (an area) by means of ethnic cleansing. **4** *Arch.* to cure. ORIG OE *clǣnsian;* see CLEAN

cleanser ('klɛnzə) *n* a cleansing agent.

clean-shaven *adj* (of men) having the facial hair shaved off.

clean sheet *n Sport.* an instance of conceding no goals or points in a match or competition (esp. in **keep a clean sheet**).

clean up *vb* (*adv*) **1** to rid (something) of dirt, filth, or other impurities. **2** to make (someone or something) orderly or presentable. **3** (*tr*) to rid (a place) of undesirable people or conditions. **4** *Inf., chiefly US & Canad.* to make (a great profit). ◆ *n* **cleanup. 5** the process of cleaning up. **6** *Inf., chiefly US.* a great profit.

clear (klɪə) *adj* **1** free from darkness or obscurity; bright. **2** (of weather) free from dullness or clouds. **3** transparent. **4** even and pure in tone or colour. **5** without blemish: *a clear skin.* **6** easy to see or hear; distinct. **7** free from doubt or confusion. **8** (*postpositive*) certain in the mind; sure: *are you clear?* **9** (*in combination*) perceptive, alert: *clear-headed.* **10** evident or obvious: *it is clear that he won't come now.* **11** (of sounds or the voice) not harsh or hoarse. **12** serene; calm. **13** without qualification; complete: *a clear victory.* **14** free of suspicion, guilt, or blame: *a clear conscience.* **15** free of obstruction; open: *a clear passage.* **16** free from debt or obligation. **17** (of money, profits, etc.) without deduction; net. **18** emptied of freight or cargo. **19** *Showjumping.* (of a round) ridden without any points being lost. ◆ *adv* **20** in a clear or distinct manner. **21** completely or utterly. **22** (*postpositive;* often foll. by *of*) not in contact (with); free: *stand clear of the gates.* ◆ *n* **23** a clear space. **24 in the clear. 24a** free of suspicion, guilt, or blame. **24b** *Sport.* able to receive a pass without being tackled. ◆ *vb* **25** to make or become free from darkness, obscurity, etc. **26** (*intr*) **26a** (of the weather) to become free from dullness, fog, rain, etc. **26b** (of mist, fog, etc.) to disappear. **27** (*tr*) to free from impurity or blemish. **28** (*tr*) to free from doubt or confusion. **29** (*tr*) to rid of objects, obstructions, etc. **30** (*tr*) to make or form (a path, way, etc.) by removing obstructions. **31** (*tr*) to free or remove (a person or thing) from something, as of suspicion, blame, or guilt. **32** (*tr*) to move or pass by or over without contact: *he cleared the wall easily.* **33** (*tr*) to rid (the throat) of phlegm. **34** (*tr*) to make or gain (money) as profit. **35** (*tr;* often foll. by *off*) to discharge or settle (a debt). **36** (*tr*) to free (a debtor) from obligation. **37** (*intr*) (of a cheque) to pass through one's bank and be charged against one's account. **38** *Banking.* to settle accounts by exchanging (commercial documents) in a clearing house. **39** to permit (ships, aircraft, cargo, passengers, etc.) to unload, disembark, depart, etc., or (of ships, etc.) to be permitted to unload, etc. **40** to obtain or give (clearance). **41** (*tr*) to obtain clearance from. **42** (*tr*) to permit (a person, company, etc.) to see or handle classified information. **43** (*tr*) *Mil., etc.* to decode (a message, etc.). **44** (*tr*) *Computing.* to remove data from a storage device and revert to zero. **45 clear the air.** to dispel tension, confusion, etc., by settling misunderstandings, etc. ◆ See also **clear away, clear off,** etc. ORIG C13: *clere,* from OF *cler,* from L *clārus* clear
▸ '**clearer** *n* ▸ '**clearly** *adv* ▸ '**clearness** *n*

clearance ('klɪərəns) *n* **1a** the process or an instance of clearing: *slum clearance.* **1b** (*as modifier*): *a clearance order.* **2** space between two parts in motion or in relative motion. **3** permission for an aircraft, ship, passengers, etc., to proceed. **4** official permission to have access to secret information, projects, areas, etc. **5** *Banking.* the exchange of commercial documents drawn on the members of a clearing house. **6a** the disposal of merchandise at reduced prices. **6b** (*as modifier*): *a clearance sale.* **7** the act of clearing an area of land by mass eviction: *the Highland Clearances.*

clear away *vb* (*adv*) to remove (objects) from (the table) after a meal.

clear-cut *adj* (**clear cut** *when postpositive*). **1** definite; not vague: *a clear-cut proposal.* **2** clearly outlined.

clearing ('klɪərɪŋ) *n* an area with few or no trees or shrubs in wooded or overgrown land.

clearing bank *n* (in Britain) any bank that makes use of the central clearing house in London.

clearing house *n* **1** *Banking.* an institution where cheques and other commercial papers drawn on member banks are cancelled against each other so that only net balances are payable. **2** a central agency for the collection and distribution of information or materials.

clear off *vb* (*intr, adv*) *Inf.* to go away: often used imperatively.

clear out *vb* (*adv*) **1** (*intr*) *Inf.* to go away: often used imperatively. **2** (*tr*) to remove and sort the contents of (a room, etc.). **3** (*tr*) *Sl.* to leave (someone) with no money. **4** (*tr*) *Sl.* to exhaust (stocks, goods, etc.) completely.

clearstory ('klɪəˌstɔ:rɪ) *n* a variant of **clerestory.**

clear up *vb* (*adv*) **1** (*tr*) to explain or solve (a mystery, misunderstanding, etc.). **2** to put (a place or thing that is disordered) in order. **3** (*intr*) (of the weather) to become brighter.

clearway ('klɪəˌweɪ) *n* **1** *Brit.* a stretch of road on which motorists may stop only in an emergency. **2** an area at the end of a runway over which an aircraft taking off makes its initial climb.

cleat (kli:t) *n* **1** a wedge-shaped block attached to a structure to act as a support. **2** a device consisting of two hornlike prongs projecting horizontally in opposite directions from a central base, used for securing lines on vessels, wharves, etc. ◆ *vb* (*tr*) **3** to supply or support with a cleat or cleats. **4** to secure (a line) on a cleat. ORIG C14: of Gmc origin

cleavage ('kli:vɪdʒ) *n* **1** *Inf.* the separation between a woman's breasts, esp. as revealed by a low-cut dress. **2** a division or split. **3** (of crystals) the act of splitting or the tendency to split along definite planes so as to yield smooth surfaces. **4** Also called: **segmentation.** (in animals) the repeated division of a fertilized ovum into a solid ball of cells. **5** the breaking of a chemical bond in a molecule to give smaller molecules or radicals. **6** *Geol.* the natural splitting of certain rocks, such as slates, into thin plates.

cleave[1] (kliːv) *vb* **cleaves, cleaving; cleft, cleaved,** *or* **clove; cleft, cleaved,** *or* **cloven. 1** to split or cause to split, esp. along a natural weakness. **2** (*tr*) to make by or as if by cutting: *to cleave a path.* **3** (when *intr,* foll. by *through*) to penetrate or traverse. ORIG OE *clēofan*
▸ **ˈcleavable** *adj*

cleave[2] (kliːv) *vb* **cleaves, cleaving, cleaved.** (*intr;* foll. by *to*) to cling or adhere. ORIG OE *cleofian*

cleaver (ˈkliːvə) *n* a heavy knife or long-bladed hatchet, esp. one used by butchers.

cleavers (ˈkliːvəz) *n* (*functioning as sing*) a Eurasian plant, having small white flowers and prickly stems and fruits. Also called: **goosegrass, hairif.** ORIG OE *clīfe;* see CLEAVE[2]

Cleese ★ (kliːz) *n* **John** (**Marwood**). born 1939, British writer and actor, noted for the TV series *Monty Python's Flying Circus* (1969–74) and *Fawlty Towers* (1975, 1978); films include *Fierce Creatures* (1997).

Cleethorpes ★ (ˈkliːθɔːps) *n* a resort in E England, in NE Lincolnshire. Pop.: 32 719 (1991).

clef (klɛf) *n* one of several symbols placed on the left-hand side beginning of each stave indicating the pitch of the music written after it. ORIG C16: from F: key, clef, from L *clāvis*

cleft (klɛft) *vb* **1** a past tense and past participle of **cleave**[1]. ◆ *n* **2** a fissure or crevice. **3** an indentation or split in something, such as the chin, palate, etc. ◆ *adj* **4** split; divided. ORIG OE *geclyft* (n); see CLEAVE[1]

cleft palate *n* a congenital crack or fissure in the midline of the hard palate, often associated with a harelip.

cleg (klɛg) *n* another name for a **horsefly.** ORIG C15: from ON *kleggi*

Cleland ★ (ˈklɛlənd) *n* **John.** 1709–89, British writer, noted for his bawdy novel *Fanny Hill* (1748–49).

clematis (ˈklɛmətɪs, kləˈmeɪtɪs) *n* any N temperate climbing plant of the genus *Clematis.* Many species are cultivated for their large colourful flowers. ORIG C16: from L, from Gk, from *klēma* vine twig

Clemenceau ★ (*French* klemɑ̃so) *n* **Georges Eugène Benjamin** (ʒɔrʒ œʒɛn bɛ̃ʒamɛ̃). 1841–1929, French statesman; prime minister of France (1906–09; 1917–20); negotiated the Treaty of Versailles (1919).

clemency (ˈklɛmənsɪ) *n, pl* **clemencies. 1** mercy or leniency. **2** mildness, esp. of the weather. ORIG C15: from L, from *clēmēns* gentle

Clemens ★ (ˈklɛmənz) *n* **Samuel Langhorne.** See (Mark) **Twain.**

clement (ˈklɛmənt) *adj* **1** merciful. **2** (of the weather) mild. ORIG C15: from L *clēmēns* mild

Clement I ★ (ˈklɛmənt) *n* **Saint,** called *Clement of Rome.* pope (?88–?97 A.D.). Feast day: Nov. 23.

Clement V ★ *n* original name *Bertrand de Got.* ?1264–1314, pope (1305–14): removed the papal seat from Rome to Avignon in France (1309).

Clement VII ★ *n* original name *Giulio de' Medici.* 1478–1534, pope (1523–34): refused to authorize the annulment of the marriage of Henry VIII of England to Catherine of Aragon (1533).

clementine (ˈklɛmən͵tiːn, -͵taɪn) *n* a citrus fruit thought to be either a variety of tangerine or a hybrid between a tangerine and sweet orange. ORIG C20: from F *clémentine*

Clement of Alexandria ★ *n* **Saint.** original name *Titus Flavius Clemens.* ?150–?215 A.D., Greek Christian theologian: head of the catechetical school at Alexandria; teacher of Origen. Feast day: Dec. 5.

clench (klɛntʃ) *vb* (*tr*) **1** to close or squeeze together (the teeth, a fist, etc.) tightly. **2** to grasp or grip firmly. ◆ *n* **3** a firm grasp or grip. **4** a device that grasps or grips. ◆ *n, vb* **5** another word for **clinch.** ORIG OE *beclencan*

Cleon ★ (ˈkliːɒn) *n* died 422 B.C., Athenian demagogue and military leader.

Cleopatra ★ (͵kliːəˈpætrə, -ˈpɑː-) *n* ?69–30 B.C., queen of Egypt (51–30): the mistress of Julius Caesar and later of Mark Antony. She killed herself with an asp to avoid capture by Octavian (Augustus).

Cleopatra's Needle *n* either of two Egyptian obelisks, originally set up at Heliopolis about 1500 B.C.: one was moved to the Thames Embankment, London, in 1878, the other to Central Park, New York, in 1880.

clepsydra (ˈklɛpsɪdrə) *n, pl* **clepsydras** *or* **clepsydrae** (-͵driː). an ancient device for measuring time by the flow of water or mercury through a small aperture. Also called: **water clock.** ORIG C17: from L, from Gk, from *kleptein* to steal + *hudōr* water

cleptomania (͵klɛptəʊˈmeɪnɪə) *n* a variant spelling of **kleptomania.**

clerestory *or* **clearstory** (ˈklɪə͵stɔːrɪ) *n, pl* **clerestories** *or* **clearstories. 1** a row of windows in the upper part of the wall of a church that divides the nave from the aisle. **2** the part of the wall in which these windows are set. ORIG C15: from CLEAR + STOREY
▸ **ˈclere͵storied** *or* **ˈclear͵storied** *adj*

clergy (ˈklɜːdʒɪ) *n, pl* **clergies.** the collective body of men and women ordained as religious ministers, esp. of the Christian Church. ORIG C13: from OF; see CLERK

clergyman (ˈklɜːdʒɪmən) *n, pl* **clergymen.** a member of the clergy.

cleric (ˈklɛrɪk) *n* a member of the clergy. ORIG C17: from Church L *clēricus* priest, CLERK

clerical (ˈklɛrɪkᵊl) *adj* **1** relating to or associated with the clergy: *clerical dress.* **2** of or relating to office clerks or their work: *a clerical error.* **3** supporting or advocating clericalism.
▸ **ˈclerically** *adv*

clerical collar *n* a stiff white collar with no opening at the front that buttons at the back of the neck; the distinctive mark of the clergy in certain Churches. Informal name: **dog collar.**

clericalism (ˈklɛrɪkᵊ͵lɪzəm) *n* **1** a policy of upholding the power of the clergy. **2** the power of the clergy.
▸ **ˈclericalist** *n*

clericals (ˈklɛrɪkᵊlz) *pl n* the distinctive dress of a clergyman.

clerihew (ˈklɛrɪ͵hjuː) *n* a form of comic or satiric verse, consisting of two couplets of metrically irregular lines, containing the name of a well-known person. ORIG C20: after E. *Clerihew* BENTLEY, its inventor

clerk (klɑːk; *US & Canad.* klɜːrk) *n* **1** a worker, esp. in an office, who keeps records, files, etc. **2** an employee of a court, legislature, board, corporation, etc., who keeps records and accounts, etc.: *a town clerk.* **3** Also called: **clerk in holy orders.** a cleric. **4** *US & Canad.* short for **salesclerk. 5** Also called: **desk clerk.** *US & Canad.* a hotel receptionist. **6** *Arch.* a scholar. ◆ *vb* **7** (*intr*) to serve as a clerk. ORIG OE *clerc,* from Church L *clēricus,* from Gk *klērikos* cleric, from *klēros* heritage
▸ **ˈclerkess** *fem n* (*chiefly Scot.*) ▸ **ˈclerkish** *adj* ▸ **ˈclerkship** *n*

clerk of works *n* an employee who supervises building work in progress.

Clermont-Ferrand ★ (*French* klɛrmɔ̃fɛrɑ̃) *n* a city in S central France: capital of Puy-de-Dôme department; industrial centre. Pop.: 140 167 (1990).

Cleveland[1] ★ (ˈkliːvlənd) *n* **1** a former county of NE England formed in 1974 from parts of E Durham and N Yorkshire; replaced in 1996 by four unitary authorities. **2** a port in NE Ohio, on Lake Erie: major heavy industries. Pop.: 492 901 (1994 est.). **3** a hilly region of NE England, extending from the **Cleveland Hills** to the River Tees.

Cleveland[2] ★ (ˈkliːvlənd) *n* **Stephen Grover.** 1837–1908, US Democratic politician; the 22nd and 24th president of the US (1885–89; 1893–97).

clever (ˈklɛvə) *adj* **1** displaying sharp intelligence or mental alertness. **2** adroit or dexterous, esp. with the hands. **3** smart in a superficial way. **4** *Brit. inf.* sly; cunning. ORIG C13 *cliver* (in the sense: quick to seize, adroit), from ?
▸ **ˈcleverly** *adv* ▸ **ˈcleverness** *n*

clevis (ˈklɛvɪs) *n* the U-shaped component of a shackle. ORIG C16: rel. to CLEAVE[1]

clew (klu:) *n* **1** a ball of thread, yarn, or twine. **2** *Naut.* either of the lower corners of a square sail or the after lower corner of a fore-and-aft sail. ◆ *vb* **3** (*tr*) to coil into a ball. ORIG OE *cliewen* (vb)

clianthus (klɪ'ænθəs) *n* a leguminous plant of Australia and New Zealand with ornamental clusters of slender flowers. ORIG C19: NL, prob. from Gk *klei-, kleos* glory + *anthos* flower

cliché ('kli:ʃeɪ) *n* **1** a word or expression that has lost much of its force through overexposure. **2** an idea, action, or habit that has become trite from overuse. **3** *Printing, chiefly Brit.* a stereotype or electrotype plate. ORIG C19: from F, from *clicher* to stereotype; imit.
▸ **'clichéd** *or* **'cliché'd** *adj*

click (klɪk) *n* **1** a short light often metallic sound. **2** the locking member of a ratchet mechanism, such as a pawl or detent. **3** *Phonetics.* any of various stop consonants that are produced by the suction of air into the mouth. ◆ *vb* **4** to make or cause to make a clicking sound: *to click one's heels.* **5** (usually foll. by *on*) *Computing.* to press and release (a button on a mouse) or to select (a particular function) by pressing and releasing a button on a mouse. **6** (*intr*) *Sl.* to be a great success: *that idea really clicked.* **7** (*intr*) *Inf.* to become suddenly clear: *it finally clicked.* **8** (*intr*) *Sl.* to get on well: *they clicked from their first meeting.* ORIG C17: imit.
▸ **'clicker** *n*

client ('klaɪənt) *n* **1** a person, company, etc., that seeks the advice of a professional man or woman. **2** a customer. **3** a person for whom a social worker, etc., is responsible. **4** *Computing.* a program or work station that requests data or information from a server. ORIG C14: from L *cliēns* retainer, dependent
▸ **cliental** (klaɪ'ɛntᵊl) *adj*

clientele (ˌkli:ɒn'tel) *or* **clientage** ('klaɪəntɪdʒ) *n* customers or clients collectively. ORIG C16: from L, from *cliēns* CLIENT

cliff (klɪf) *n* a steep high rock face, esp. one that runs along the seashore. ORIG OE *clif*
▸ **'cliffy** *adj*

cliffhanger ('klɪfˌhæŋə) *n* **1a** a situation of imminent disaster usually occurring at the end of each episode of a serialized film. **1b** the serialized film itself. **2** a situation that is dramatic or uncertain.
▸ **'cliffˌhanging** *adj*

climacteric (klaɪ'mæktərɪk, ˌklaɪmæk'terɪk) *n* **1** a critical event or period. **2** another name for **menopause. 3** the period in the life of a man corresponding to the menopause, chiefly characterized by diminished sexual activity. ◆ *adj also* **climacterical** (ˌklaɪmæk'terɪkᵊl). **4** involving a crucial event or period. ORIG C16: from L, from Gk, from *klimakter* rung of a ladder from *klimax* ladder

climactic (klaɪ'mæktɪk) *or* **climactical** *adj* consisting of, involving, or causing a climax.
▸ **cli'mactically** *adv*

> **USAGE NOTE** See at **climate.**

climate ('klaɪmɪt) *n* **1** the long-term prevalent weather conditions of an area, determined by latitude, altitude, etc. **2** an area having a particular kind of climate. **3** a prevailing trend: *the political climate.* ORIG C14: from LL, from Gk *klima* inclination, region
▸ **climatic** (klaɪ'mætɪk), **cli'matical,** *or* **'climatal** *adj* ▸ **cli'matically** *adv*

> **USAGE NOTE** *Climatic* is sometimes wrongly used where *climactic* is meant. *Climatic* should be used to talk about things relating to climate; *climactic* is used to describe something which forms a climax: *...the climactic moment of the Revolution.*

climatic zone *n* any of the eight principal zones, roughly demarcated by lines of latitude, into which the earth can be divided on the basis of climate.

climatology (ˌklaɪmə'tɒlədʒɪ) *n* the study of climates.
▸ **climatologic** (ˌklaɪmətə'lɒdʒɪk) *or* **ˌclimato'logical** *adj*
▸ **ˌclima'tologist** *n*

climax ('klaɪmæks) *n* **1** the most intense or highest point of an experience or of a series of events: *the party was the climax of the week.* **2** a decisive moment in a dramatic or other work. **3** a rhetorical device by which a series of sentences, clauses, or phrases are arranged in order of increasing intensity. **4** *Ecology.* the stage in the development of a community during which it remains stable under the prevailing environmental conditions. **5** another word for **orgasm.** ◆ *vb* **6** to reach or bring to a climax. ORIG C16: from LL, from Gk *klimax* ladder

climb (klaɪm) *vb* (*mainly intr*) **1** (*also tr;* often foll. by *up*) to go up or ascend (stairs, a mountain, etc.). **2** (often foll. by *along*) to progress with difficulty: *to climb along a ledge.* **3** to rise to a higher point or intensity: *the temperature climbed.* **4** to incline or slope upwards: *the road began to climb.* **5** to ascend in social position. **6** (of plants) to grow upwards by twining, using tendrils or suckers, etc. **7** *Inf.* (foll. by *into*) to put (on) or get (into). **8** to be a climber or mountaineer. ◆ *n* **9** the act or an instance of climbing. **10** a place or thing to be climbed, esp. a route in mountaineering. ORIG OE *climban*
▸ **'climbable** *adj*

climb down *vb* (*intr, adv*) **1** to descend. **2** (often foll. by *from*) to retreat (from an opinion, position, etc.). ◆ *n* **climb-down. 3** a retreat from an opinion, etc.

climber ('klaɪmə) *n* **1** a person or thing that climbs, esp. a mountaineer. **2** a plant that grows upwards by twining or clinging with tendrils and suckers. **3** *Chiefly Brit.* short for **social climber.**

clime (klaɪm) *n Poetic.* a region or its climate. ORIG C16: from LL *clima;* see CLIMATE

clinch (klɪntʃ) *vb* **1** (*tr*) to secure (a driven nail), by bending the protruding point over. **2** (*tr*) to hold together in such a manner. **3** (*tr*) to settle (something, such as an argument, bargain, etc.) in a definite way. **4** (*tr*) *Naut.* to fasten by means of a clinch. **5** (*intr*) to engage in a clinch, as in boxing or wrestling. ◆ *n* **6** the act of clinching. **7a** a nail with its point bent over. **7b** the part of such a nail, etc., that has been bent over. **8** *Boxing, wrestling, etc.* an act or an instance in which one or both competitors hold on to the other to avoid punches, regain wind, etc. **9** *Sl.* a lovers' embrace. **10** *Naut.* a loop or eye formed in a line. ◆ Also (for senses 1, 2, 4, 7, 8, 10): **clench.** ORIG C16: var. of CLENCH

clincher ('klɪntʃə) *n* **1** *Inf.* something decisive, such as fact, score, etc. **2** a person or thing that clinches.

cline (klaɪn) *n* the range of variation of form within a species. ORIG C20: from Gk *klinein* to lean
▸ **'clinal** *adj*

-cline *n combining form.* indicating a slope: *anticline.* ORIG back formation from INCLINE
▸ **-clinal** *adj combining form.*

cling (klɪŋ) *vb* **clings, clinging, clung.** (*intr*) **1** (often foll. by *to*) to hold fast or adhere closely (to something), as by gripping or sticking. **2** (foll. by *together*) to remain in contact (with each other). **3** to be or remain physically or emotionally close. ◆ *n* **4** short for **clingstone.** ORIG OE *clingan*
▸ **'clinging** *adj* ▸ **'clingingly** *adv* ▸ **'clingy** *adj*
▸ **'clinginess** *or* **'clingingness** *n*

clingfilm ('klɪŋˌfɪlm) *n* a thin polythene material having the power to adhere closely: used for wrapping food.

clingstone ('klɪŋˌstəʊn) *n* **a** a fruit, such as certain peaches, in which the flesh adheres to the stone. **b** (*as modifier*): *a clingstone peach.*

clinic ('klɪnɪk) *n* **1** a place in which outpatients are given medical treatment or advice. **2** a similar place staffed by specialist physicians or surgeons: *eye clinic.* **3** *Brit.* a private hospital or nursing home. **4** the teaching of medicine to students at the bedside. **5** *Chiefly US & Canad.* a group or centre that offers advice or instruction. ORIG C17: from L *clīnicus* one on a sickbed, from Gk, from *klinē* bed

clinical ('klɪnɪkᵊl) *adj* **1** of or relating to a clinic. **2** of or relating to the observation and treatment of patients directly: *clinical medicine.* **3** scientifically detached; strictly

objective: *a clinical attitude to life.* **4** plain, simple, and usually unattractive.
▸ **'clinically** *adv*

clinical thermometer *n* a thermometer for determining the temperature of the body.

clinician (klɪ'nɪʃən) *n* a physician, psychiatrist, etc., who specializes in clinical work as opposed to one engaged in experimental studies.

clink[1] (klɪŋk) *vb* **1** to make or cause to make a light and sharply ringing sound. ◆ *n* **2** such a sound. ORIG C14: ?from MDu. *klinken*

clink[2] (klɪŋk) *n* a slang word for **prison.** ORIG C16: after *Clink,* a prison in Southwark, London

clinker ('klɪŋkə) *n* **1** the ash and partially fused residues from a coal-fired furnace or fire. **2** a partially vitrified brick or mass of brick. **3** *Sl., chiefly US.* something of poor quality, such as a film. ◆ *vb* **4** (*intr*) to form clinker. ORIG C17: from Du. *klinker* a type of brick, from *klinken* to CLINK[1]

clinker-built *or* **clincher-built** *adj* (of a boat or ship) having a hull constructed with each plank overlapping that below. ORIG C18 *clinker* a nailing together, prob. from CLINCH

clinometer (klaɪ'nɒmɪtə) *n* an instrument used in surveying for measuring an angle of inclination.
▸ **clinometric** (ˌklaɪnə'mɛtrɪk) *or* ˌ**clino'metrical** *adj* ▸ **cli'nometry** *n*

Clinton ★ ('klɪntən) *n* **1 Hillary (Rodham).** born 1947, US Democrat politician, wife of Bill Clinton; senator for New York from 2000. **2 William Jefferson,** known as *Bill.* born 1946, US Democrat politician; 42nd president of the US (1993–2001).

Clio ★ ('klaɪəʊ) *n Greek myth.* the Muse of history. ORIG C19: from L, from Gk *Kleiō,* from *kleein* to celebrate

clip[1] (klɪp) *vb* **clips, clipping, clipped.** (*mainly tr*) **1** (*also intr*) to cut or trim with scissors or shears, esp. in order to shorten or remove a part. **2** *Brit.* to punch (a hole) in something, esp. a ticket. **3** to curtail. **4** to move a short section from (a film, etc.). **5** to shorten (a word). **6** *Inf.* to strike with a sharp, often slanting, blow. **7** *Sl.* to obtain (money) by deception or cheating. ◆ *n* **8** the act or process of clipping. **9** something clipped off. **10** a short extract from a film, etc. **11** *Inf.* a sharp, often slanting, blow. **12** *Inf.* speed: *a rapid clip.* **13** *Austral. & NZ.* the total quantity of wool shorn, as in one season, etc. **14** another word for **clipped form.** ORIG C12: from ON *klippa* to cut

clip[2] (klɪp) *n* **1** any of various small implements used to hold loose articles together or to attach one article to another. **2** an article of jewellery that can be clipped onto a dress, hat, etc. **3** short for **paperclip** or **cartridge clip.** ◆ *vb* **clips, clipping, clipped.** (*tr*) **4** to hold together tightly, as with a clip. ORIG OE *clyppan* to embrace

clipboard ('klɪpˌbɔːd) *n* **1** a portable writing board with a clip at the top for holding paper. **2** *Computing.* a temporary storage area in desktop publishing and other programs where text or graphics are held when cut or copied.

clip joint *n Sl.* a place, such as a nightclub or restaurant, in which customers are overcharged.

clipped (klɪpt) *adj* (of speech or tone of voice) abrupt, terse, and distinct.

clipped form *n* a shortened form of a word.

clipper ('klɪpə) *n* **1** any fast sailing ship. **2** a person or thing that cuts or clips.

clippers ('klɪpəz) *or* **clips** *pl n* **1** a hand tool for clipping fingernails, veneers, etc. **2** a hairdresser's tool for cutting short hair.

clippie ('klɪpɪ) *n Brit. inf.* a bus conductress.

clipping ('klɪpɪŋ) *n* **1** something cut out, esp. an article from a newspaper; cutting. **2** the distortion of an audio or visual signal in which the tops of peaks with a high amplitude are cut off, caused by, for example, overloading of amplifier circuits.

clique (kliːk, klɪk) *n* a small exclusive group of friends or associates. ORIG C18: from F, ?from OF: latch, from *cliquer* to click
▸ **'cliquey** *or* **'cliquy** *adj* ▸ **'cliquish** *adj* ▸ **'cliquishly** *adv* ▸ **'cliquishness** *n*

clitoridectomy (ˌklɪtərɪ'dɛktəmɪ) *n* surgical removal of the clitoris: a form of female circumcision, esp. practised as a religious or ethnic rite.

clitoris ('klɪtərɪs, 'klaɪ-) *n* a part of the female genitalia consisting of a small elongated highly sensitive erectile organ at the front of the vulva. ORIG C17: from NL, from Gk *kleitoris*
▸ **'clitoral** *adj*

Clive ★ (klaɪv) *n* **Robert,** Baron Clive of Plassey. 1725–74, British general and statesman, whose victory at Plassey (1757) strengthened British control in India.

Cllr *abbrev. for* Councillor.

cloaca (kləʊ'eɪkə) *n, pl* **cloacae** (-kiː). **1** a cavity in most vertebrates, except higher mammals, and certain invertebrates, into which the alimentary canal and the genital and urinary ducts open. **2** a sewer. ORIG C18: from L: sewer
▸ **clo'acal** *adj*

cloak (kləʊk) *n* **1** a wraplike outer garment fastened at the throat and falling straight from the shoulders. **2** something that covers or conceals. ◆ *vb* (*tr*) **3** to cover with or as if with a cloak. **4** to hide or disguise. ORIG C13: from OF *cloque,* from Med. L *clocca* cloak, bell

cloak-and-dagger *n* (*modifier*) characteristic of or concerned with intrigue and espionage.

cloakroom ('kləʊkˌruːm, -rʊm) *n* **1** a room in which hats, coats, etc., may be temporarily deposited. **2** *Brit.* a euphemistic word for **toilet.**

clobber[1] ('klɒbə) *vb* (*tr*) *Sl.* **1** to batter. **2** to defeat utterly. **3** to criticize severely. ORIG C20: from ?

clobber[2] ('klɒbə) *n Brit. sl.* personal belongings, such as clothes. ORIG C19: from ?

clobbering machine *n NZ inf.* pressure to conform with accepted standards.

cloche (klɒʃ) *n* **1** a bell-shaped cover used to protect young plants. **2** a woman's close-fitting hat. ORIG C19: from F: bell, from Med. L *clocca*

clock[1] (klɒk) *n* **1** a timepiece having mechanically or electrically driven pointers that move constantly over a dial showing the numbers of the hours. Cf. **watch** (sense 7). **2** any clocklike device for recording or measuring, such as a taximeter or pressure gauge. **3** the downy head of a dandelion that has gone to seed. **4** short for **time clock. 5** (usually preceded by *the*) an informal word for **speedometer** or **mileometer. 6** *Brit.* a slang word for **face. 7 around** *or* **round the clock.** all day and all night. ◆ *vb* (*tr*) **8** *Brit., Austral., & NZ sl.* to strike, esp. on the face or head. **9** to record time as with a stopwatch, esp. in the calculation of speed. **10** *Inf.* to turn back the mileometer on (a car) illegally so that its mileage appears less. ORIG C14: from MDu. *clocke* clock, from Med. L *clocca* bell, ult. of Celtic origin

clock[2] (klɒk) *n* an ornamental design on the side of a stocking. ORIG C16: see CLOCK[1]

clock off *or* **out** *vb* (*intr, adv*) to depart from work, esp. when it involves registering the time of departure on a card.

clock on *or* **in** *vb* (*intr, adv*) to arrive at work, esp. when it involves registering the time of arrival on a card.

clock up *vb* (*tr, adv*) to record or register: *this car has clocked up 80 000 miles.*

clock-watcher *n* an employee who frequently checks the time in anticipation of a break or of the end of the working day.

clockwise ('klɒkˌwaɪz) *adv, adj* in the direction that the hands of a clock rotate; from top to bottom towards the right when seen from the front.

clockwork ('klɒkˌwɜːk) *n* **1** the mechanism of a clock. **2** any similar mechanism, as in a wind-up toy. **3 like clockwork.** with complete regularity and precision; smoothly.

clod (klɒd) *n* **1** a lump of earth or clay. **2** earth, esp. when heavy or in hard lumps. **3** Also called: **clod poll, clodpate.** a dull or stupid person. ORIG OE *clod-* (occurring in compound words) lump

► **'cloddy** *adj* ► **'cloddish** *adj* ► **'cloddishly** *adv* ► **'cloddishness** *n*

clodhopper ('klɒdˌhɒpə) *n Inf.* **1** a clumsy person; lout. **2** (*usually pl*) a large heavy shoe.

clog (klɒg) *vb* **clogs, clogging, clogged. 1** to obstruct or become obstructed with thick or sticky matter. **2** (*tr*) to encumber; hinder; impede. **3** (*intr*) to adhere or stick in a mass. ◆ *n* **4a** any of various wooden or wooden-soled shoes. **4b** (*as modifier*): *clog dance.* **5** a heavy block, esp. of wood, fastened to the leg of a person or animal to impede motion. **6** something that impedes motion or action. ORIG C14 (in the sense: block of wood): from ?
► **'cloggy** *adj*

cloisonné (klwɑː'zɒneɪ) *n* **1a** a design made by filling in with coloured enamel an outline of flattened wire. **1b** the method of doing this. ◆ *adj* **2** of or made by cloisonné. ORIG C19: from F, from *cloisonner* to divide into compartments, ult. from L *claudere* to close

cloister ('klɔɪstə) *n* **1** a covered walk, usually around a quadrangle in a religious institution, having an open colonnade on the inside. **2** (*sometimes pl*) a place of religious seclusion, such as a monastery. **3** life in a monastery or convent. ◆ *vb* **4** (*tr*) to confine or seclude in or as if in a monastery. ORIG C13: from OF *cloistre,* from Med. L *claustrum* monastic cell, from L *claudere* to close
► **'cloistered** *adj* ► **'cloistral** *adj*

clomb (kləʊm) *vb Arch.* a past tense and past participle of **climb.**

clomp (klɒmp) *n, vb* a less common word for **clump** (senses 2, 7).

clone (kləʊn) *n* **1** a group of organisms or cells of the same genetic constitution that are descended from a common ancestor by asexual reproduction, as by cuttings, grafting, etc., or by transplantation of parent nuclei into donor egg cells whose nuclei have been removed. **2** Also called: **gene clone.** a segment of DNA that has been isolated and replicated by laboratory manipulation. **3** *Inf.* a person or thing that closely resembles another. **4** *Sl.* **4a** a mobile phone that has been given the electronic identity of an existing mobile phone, so that calls made on either phone are charged to the same account. **4b** any similar object, such as a credit card, that has been given the electronic identity of another device, usually in order to commit theft. **5** a microcomputer designed to simulate the operating characteristics of another type of microcomputer. ◆ *vb* **clones, cloning, cloned. 6** to produce or cause to produce a clone. **7** *Inf.* to produce near copies of (a person or thing). **8** (*tr*) to give (a phone or other device) the same electronic identity as an existing device. ORIG C20: from Gk *klōn* twig, shoot
► **'cloning** *n*

clonk (klɒŋk) *vb* **1** (*intr*) to make a loud dull thud. **2** (*tr*) *Inf.* to hit. ◆ *n* **3** a loud thud. ORIG C20: imit.

Clonmel ★ (klɒn'mɛl) *n* the county town of Co. Tipperary, Republic of Ireland; birthplace of Laurence Sterne; meat processing and enamelware. Pop.: 14 500 (1991).

clonus ('kləʊnəs) *n* a type of convulsion characterized by rapid contraction and relaxation of a muscle. ORIG C19: from NL, from Gk *klonos* turmoil
► **clonic** ('klɒnɪk) *adj* ► **clonicity** (klɒ'nɪsɪtɪ) *n*

Clooney ★ ('kluːnɪ) *n* **George.** born 1961, US film actor; he starred in the television series *ER* (1994–99) and the films *Batman and Robin* (1997), and *The Perfect Storm* (2000).

clop (klɒp) *vb* **clops, clopping, clopped. 1** (*intr*) to make or move along with a sound as of a horse's hooves striking the ground. ◆ *n* **2** a sound of this nature. ORIG C20: imit.

close[1] (kləʊs) *adj* **1** near in space or time; in proximity. **2** having the parts near together; dense: *a close formation.* **3** near to the surface; short: *a close haircut.* **4** near in relationship: *a close relative.* **5** intimate: *a close friend.* **6** almost equal: *a close contest.* **7** not deviating or varying greatly from a model or standard: *a close resemblance; a close translation.* **8** careful, strict, or searching: *a close study.* **9** confined or enclosed. **10** shut or shut tight. **11** oppressive, heavy, or airless: *a close atmosphere.* **12** strictly guarded: *a close prisoner.* **13** neat or tight in fit. **14** secretive or reticent. **15** miserly; not generous, esp. with money. **16** (of money or credit) hard to obtain. **17** restricted as to public admission or membership. **18** hidden or secluded. **19** Also: **closed.** restricted or prohibited as to the type of game or fish able to be taken. ◆ *adv* **20** closely; tightly. **21** near or in proximity. **22 close to the wind.** *Naut.* sailing as nearly as possible towards the direction from which the wind is blowing. See also **wind**[1] (sense 23). ORIG C13: from OF *clos,* from L *clausus,* from *claudere* to close
► **'closely** *adv* ► **'closeness** *n*

close[2] (kləʊz) *vb* **closes, closing, closed. 1** to put or be put in such a position as to cover an opening; shut: *the door closed behind him.* **2** (*tr*) to bar, obstruct, or fill up (an entrance, a hole, etc.): *to close a road.* **3** to bring the parts or edges of (a wound, etc.) together or (of a wound, etc.) to be brought together. **4** (*intr;* foll. by *on, over,* etc.) to take hold: *his hand closed over the money.* **5** to bring or be brought to an end; terminate. **6** (of agreements, deals, etc.) to complete or be completed successfully. **7** to cease or cause to cease to render service: *the shop closed at six.* **8** (*intr*) *Stock Exchange.* to have a value at the end of a day's trading, as specified: *steels closed two points down.* **9** (*tr*) *Arch.* to enclose or shut in. ◆ *n* **10** the act of closing. **11** the end or conclusion: *the close of the day.* **12** (kləʊs). *Brit.* a courtyard or quadrangle enclosed by buildings or an entry leading to such a courtyard. **13** (kləʊs). *Brit.* (*cap. when part of a street name*) a small quiet residential road: *Hillside Close.* **14** (kləʊs). the precincts of a cathedral or similar building. **15** (kləʊs). *Scot.* the entry from the street to a tenement building. ◆ See also **close down, close in,** etc. ORIG C13: from OF *clos,* from L *clausus,* from *claudere* to close
► **'closer** *n*

close company *n* a company that is controlled by its directors or by five or fewer participants.

closed (kləʊzd) *adj* **1** blocked against entry; shut. **2** restricted; exclusive. **3** not open to question or debate. **4** (of a hunting season, etc.) close. **5** *Maths.* **5a** (of a curve or surface) completely enclosing an area or volume. **5b** (of a set) having members that can be produced by a specific operation on other members of the same set. **6** *Phonetics.* denoting a syllable that ends in a consonant. **7** not open to public entry or membership: *a closed society.*

closed chain *n Chem.* another name for **ring**[1] (sense 17).

closed circuit *n* a complete electrical circuit through which current can flow.

closed-circuit television *n* a television system in which signals are transmitted from the television camera to the receivers by cables or telephone links.

close down (kləʊz) *vb* (*adv*) **1** to cease or cause to cease operations. **2** (*tr*) *Soccer.* to deny (an opposing player) space to run with the ball or to make or receive a pass. ◆ *n* **close-down. 3** a closure or stoppage, esp. in a factory. **4** *Brit. radio, television.* the end of a period of broadcasting, esp. late at night.

closed shop *n* (formerly) an industrial establishment in which there exists a contract between a trade union and the employer permitting the employment of the union's members only.

close-fisted (ˌkləʊs'fɪstɪd) *adj* very careful with money.
► ˌ**close-'fistedness** *n*

close harmony (kləʊs) *n* a type of singing in which all the parts except the bass lie close together.

close-hauled (ˌkləʊs'hɔːld) *adj Naut.* with the sails flat, so as to sail as close to the wind as possible.

close in (kləʊz) *vb* (*intr, adv*) **1** (of days) to become shorter with the approach of winter. **2** (foll. by *on* or *upon*) to advance (on) so as to encircle or surround.

close out (kləʊz) *vb* (*adv*) to terminate (a client's or other account) usually by sale of securities to realize cash.

close punctuation (kləʊs) *n* punctuation which uses many commas, full stops, etc.. Cf. **open punctuation.**

close quarters (kləʊs) *pl n* **1** a narrow cramped space or position. **2 at close quarters. 2a** engaged in hand-to-hand combat. **2b** in close proximity; very near together.

close season (kləʊs) *or* **closed season** *n* **1** the period of the year when it is prohibited to kill certain game or fish. **2** *Sport.* the period of the year when there is no domestic competition.

close shave (kləʊs) *n Inf.* a narrow escape.

closet ('klɒzɪt) *n* **1** a small cupboard or recess. **2** a small private room. **3** short for **water closet**. **4** (*modifier*) private or secret. ◆ *vb* **closets, closeting, closeted. 5** (*tr*) to shut up or confine in a small private room, esp. for conference or meditation. ORIG C14: from OF, from *clos* enclosure; see CLOSE[1]

close-up ('kləʊsˌʌp) *n* **1** a photograph or film or television shot taken at close range. **2** a detailed or intimate view or examination. ◆ *vb* **close up** (kləʊz). (*adv*) **3** to shut entirely. **4** (*intr*) to draw together: *the ranks closed up.* **5** (*intr*) (of wounds) to heal completely.

close with (kləʊz) *vb* (*intr, prep*) to engage in battle with (an enemy).

closure ('kləʊʒə) *n* **1** the act of closing or the state of being closed. **2** an end or conclusion. **3** something that closes or shuts, such as a cap or seal for a container. **4** Also called: **gag.** (in a deliberative body) a procedure by which debate may be halted and an immediate vote taken. **5** *Chiefly US.* **a** the resolution of a significant event or relationship in a person's life. **b** the sense of contentment experienced after such a resolution. ◆ *vb* **closures, closuring, closured. 6** (*tr*) (in a deliberative body) to end (debate) by closure. ORIG C14: from OF, from LL, from L *claudere* to close

clot (klɒt) *n* **1** a soft thick lump or mass. **2** *Brit. inf.* a stupid person; fool. ◆ *vb* **clots, clotting, clotted. 3** to form or cause to form into a soft thick lump or lumps. ORIG OE *clott*, of Gmc origin

cloth (klɒθ) *n, pl* **cloths** (klɒθs, klɒðz). **1a** a fabric formed by weaving, felting or knitting wool, cotton, etc. **1b** (*as modifier*): *a cloth bag.* **2** a piece of such fabric used for a particular purpose, as for a dishcloth. **3** (usually preceded by *the*) the clergy. ORIG OE *clāth*

clothe (kləʊð) *vb* **clothes, clothing, clothed** *or* **clad.** (*tr*) **1** to dress or attire (a person). **2** to provide with clothing. **3** to conceal or disguise. **4** to endow or invest. ORIG OE *clāthian*, from *clāth* cloth

clothes (kləʊðz) *pl n* **1** articles of dress. **2** *Chiefly Brit.* short for **bedclothes**. ORIG OE *clāthas*, pl. of *clāth* cloth

clotheshorse ('kləʊðzˌhɔːs) *n* **1** a frame on which to hang laundry for drying or airing. **2** *Inf.* an excessively fashionable person.

clothesline ('kləʊðzˌlaɪn) *n* a piece of rope or wire on which clean washing is hung to dry.

clothes peg *n* a small wooden or plastic clip for attaching washing to a clothesline.

clothes pole *n* a post to which a clothesline is attached. Also called: **clothes post.**

clothes-press *n* a piece of furniture for storing clothes, usually containing wide drawers.

clothes prop *n* a long wooden pole with a forked end used to raise a line of washing to enable it to catch the breeze.

clothier ('kləʊðɪə) *n* a person who makes, sells, or deals in clothes or cloth.

clothing ('kləʊðɪŋ) *n* **1** garments collectively. **2** something that covers or clothes.

Clotho ★ ('kləʊθəʊ) *n Greek myth.* one of the three Fates, spinner of the thread of life. ORIG L, from Gk *Klōtho*, one who spins, from *klōthein* to spin

cloth of gold *n* cloth woven from silk threads interspersed with gold.

clotted cream *n Brit.* a thick cream made from scalded milk, esp. in SW England.

clotting factor *n* any one of a group of substances, including factor VIII, the presence of which in the blood is essential for blood clotting to occur. Also called: **coagulation factor.**

cloture ('kləʊtʃə) *n* **1** closure in the US Senate. ◆ *vb* **clotures, cloturing, clotured. 2** (*tr*) to end (debate) by cloture. ORIG C19: from F *clôture*, from OF CLOSURE

cloud (klaʊd) *n* **1** a mass of water or ice particles visible in the sky. **2** any collection of particles visible in the air, esp. of smoke or dust. **3** a large number of insects or other small animals in flight. **4** something that darkens, threatens, or carries gloom. **5** *Jewellery.* a cloudlike blemish in a transparent stone. **6 in the clouds.** not in contact with reality. **7 on cloud nine.** *Inf.* elated; very happy. **8 under a cloud. 8a** under reproach or suspicion. **8b** in a state of gloom or bad temper. ◆ *vb* **9** (when *intr*, often foll. by *over* or *up*) to make or become cloudy, overcast, or indistinct. **10** (*tr*) to make obscure; darken. **11** to make or become gloomy or depressed. **12** (*tr*) to place under or render liable to suspicion or disgrace. **13** to render (liquids) milky or dull or (of liquids) to become milky or dull. ORIG C13 (in the sense: a mass of vapour): from OE *clūd* rock, hill
▸ **'cloudless** *adj* ▸ **'cloudlessly** *adv* ▸ **'cloudlessness** *n*

cloudberry ('klaʊdbərɪ, brɪ) *n, pl* **cloudberries.** a creeping Eurasian herbaceous rosaceous plant with white flowers and orange berry-like fruits.

cloudburst ('klaʊdˌbɜːst) *n* a heavy downpour.

cloud chamber *n Physics.* an apparatus for detecting high-energy particles by observing their tracks through a chamber containing a supersaturated vapour.

cloud-cuckoo-land *n* a realm of fantasy, dreams, or impractical notions.

cloudy ('klaʊdɪ) *adj* **cloudier, cloudiest. 1** covered with cloud or clouds. **2** of or like clouds. **3** streaked or mottled like a cloud. **4** opaque or muddy. **5** obscure or unclear. **6** troubled or gloomy.
▸ **'cloudily** *adv* ▸ **'cloudiness** *n*

clough (klʌf) *n Dialect.* a ravine. ORIG OE *clōh*

Clough ★ (klʌf) *n* **1 Arthur Hugh.** 1819–61, British poet, author of *Amours de Voyage* (1858) and *Dipsychus* (1865). **2 Brian.** born 1935, British footballer and manager.

clout (klaʊt) *n* **1** *Inf.* a blow with the hand or a hard object. **2** power or influence, esp. political. **3** Also called: **clout nail.** a short, flat-headed nail. **4** *Dialect.* **4a** a piece of cloth: *a dish clout.* **4b** a garment. ◆ *vb* (*tr*) **5** *Inf.* to give a hard blow to, esp. with the hand. ORIG OE *clūt* piece of metal or cloth, *clūtian* to patch (C14: to strike with the hand)

clove[1] (kləʊv) *n* **1** a tropical evergreen tree of the myrtle family. **2** the dried unopened flower buds of this tree, used as a pungent fragrant spice. ORIG C14: from OF, lit.: nail of clove, *clou* from L *clāvus* nail + *girofle* clove tree

clove[2] (kləʊv) *n* any of the segments of a compound bulb that arise from the axils of the scales of a large bulb. ORIG OE *clufu* bulb; see CLEAVE[1]

clove[3] (kləʊv) *vb* a past tense of **cleave**[1].

clove hitch *n* a knot or hitch used for securing a rope to a spar, post, or larger rope.

Clovelly ★ (kləˈvɛlɪ) *n* a village in SW England, in Devon on the Bristol Channel: famous for its steep cobbled streets: tourism, fishing. Pop.: 500 (1989).

cloven ('kləʊvᵊn) *vb* **1** a past participle of **cleave**[1]. ◆ *adj* **2** split; cleft; divided.

cloven hoof *or* **foot** *n* **1** the divided hoof of a pig, goat, cow, deer, or related animal. **2** the mark or symbol of Satan.
▸ **ˌcloven-'hoofed** *or* **ˌcloven-'footed** *adj*

clove oil *n* a volatile pale-yellow aromatic oil obtained from clove flowers, formerly much used in confectionery, dentistry, and microscopy. Also called: **oil of cloves.**

clover ('kləʊvə) *n* **1** a leguminous fodder plant having trifoliate leaves and dense flower heads. **2** any of various similar or related plants. **3 in clover.** *Inf.* in a state of ease or luxury. ORIG OE *clāfre*

cloverleaf ('kləʊvəˌliːf) *n, pl* **cloverleaves. 1** an arrangement of connecting roads, resembling a four-leaf clover in form, that joins two intersecting main roads. **2** (*modifier*) in the shape or pattern of a leaf of clover.

Clovis I ★ ('kləʊvɪs) *n* German name *Chlodwig.* ?466–511 A.D., king of the Franks (481–511).

clown (klaʊn) *n* **1** a comic entertainer, usually grotesquely costumed and made up, appearing in the circus. **2** a person who acts in a comic or buffoon-like manner. **3** a clumsy rude person; boor. **4** *Arch.* a countryman or rustic. ◆ *vb* (*intr*) **5** to perform as a clown. **6** to play jokes or tricks. **7** to act foolishly. ORIG C16: ?from Low G
▸ **'clownery** *n* ▸ **'clownish** *adj* ▸ **'clownishly** *adv*
▸ **'clownishness** *n*

cloy (klɔɪ) *vb* to make weary or cause weariness through an excess of something initially pleasurable or sweet. ORIG C14 (orig.: to nail, hence, to obstruct): from earlier *acloyen,* from OF, from Med. L *inclavāre,* from L, from *clāvus* a nail
▸ **'cloying** *adj* ▸ **'cloyingly** *adv*

cloze test (kləʊz) *n* a test of the ability to comprehend text in which the reader has to supply the missing words that have been removed from the text. ORIG altered from *close* to complete a pattern (in Gestalt theory)

club (klʌb) *n* **1** a stout stick, usually with one end thicker than the other, esp. one used as a weapon. **2** a stick or bat used to strike the ball in various sports, esp. golf. See **golf club. 3** short for **Indian club. 4** a group or association of people with common aims or interests. **5** the room, building, or facilities used by such a group. **6** a building in which elected, fee-paying members go to meet, dine, read, etc. **7** a commercial establishment in which people can drink and dance; disco. See also **nightclub. 8** *Chiefly Brit.* an organization, esp. in a shop, set up as a means of saving. **9** *Brit.* an informal word for **friendly society. 10a** the black trefoil symbol on a playing card. **10b** a card with one or more of these symbols or (*when pl*) the suit of cards so marked. **11 in the club.** *Brit. sl.* pregnant. ◆ *vb* **clubs, clubbing, clubbed. 12** (*tr*) to beat with or as if with a club. **13** (often foll. by *together*) to gather or become gathered into a group. **14** (often foll. by *together*) to unite or combine (resources, efforts, etc.) for a common purpose. ORIG C13: from ON *klubba,* rel. to CLUMP
▸ **'clubbing** *n*

clubbed (klʌbd) *adj* having a thickened end, like a club.

clubber ('klʌbə) *n* a person who regularly frequents nightclubs and similar establishments.

club class *n* **1** a class of air travel that is less luxurious than first class but more luxurious than economy class. ◆ *adj* **club-class. 2** of or relating to this class of travel.

club foot *n* **1** a congenital deformity of the foot, esp. one in which the foot is twisted so that most of the weight rests on the heel. Technical name: **talipes. 2** a foot so deformed.
▸ **ˌclub-'footed** *adj*

clubhouse ('klʌbˌhaʊs) *n* the premises of a sports or other club, esp. a golf club.

clubman ('klʌbmən) *or* (*fem*) **clubwoman** *n, pl* **clubmen** *or* **clubwomen.** a person who is an enthusiastic member of a club or clubs.

club root *n* a fungal disease of cabbages and related plants, in which the roots become thickened and distorted.

cluck (klʌk) *n* **1** the low clicking sound made by a hen or any similar sound. ◆ *vb* **2** (*intr*) (of a hen) to make a clicking sound. **3** (*tr*) to call or express (a feeling) by making a similar sound. ORIG C17: imit.

clucky ('klʌkɪ) *adj Austral. inf.* **1** wanting to have a baby. **2** excessively protective towards children.

clue (kluː) *n* **1** something that helps to solve a problem or unravel a mystery. **2 not have a clue. 2a** to be completely baffled. **2b** to be ignorant or incompetent. ◆ *vb* **clues, cluing, clued. 3** (*tr;* usually foll. by *in* or *up*) to provide with helpful information. ORIG C15: var. of CLEW

clued-up *adj Inf.* shrewd; well-informed.

clueless ('kluːlɪs) *adj Sl.* helpless; stupid.

Cluj ★ (kluʃ, kluːʒ) *n* an industrial city in NW Romania, on the Someşul-Mic River: former capital of Transylvania. Pop.: 321 850 (1993 est.). German name: **Klausenburg.** Hungarian name: **Kolozsvár.**

clump (klʌmp) *n* **1** a cluster, as of trees or plants. **2** a dull heavy tread or any similar sound. **3** an irregular mass. **4** an inactive mass of microorganisms, esp. a mass of bacteria produced as a result of agglutination. **5** an extra sole on a shoe. **6** *Sl.* a blow. ◆ *vb* **7** (*intr*) to walk or tread heavily. **8** to gather or be gathered into clumps, clusters, clots, etc. **9** to cause (bacteria, blood cells, etc.) to collect together or (of bacteria, etc.) to collect together. **10** (*tr*) *Sl.* to punch (someone). ORIG OE *clympe*
▸ **'clumpy** *adj*

clumsy ('klʌmzɪ) *adj* **clumsier, clumsiest. 1** lacking in skill or physical coordination. **2** awkwardly constructed or contrived. ORIG C16 (in obs. sense: benumbed with cold; hence, awkward): ?from C13 dialect *clumse* to benumb, prob. of Scand. origin
▸ **'clumsily** *adv* ▸ **'clumsiness** *n*

clung (klʌŋ) *vb* the past tense and past participle of **cling.**

clunk (klʌŋk) *n* **1** a blow or the sound of a blow. **2** a dull metallic sound. ◆ *vb* **3** to make or cause to make such a sound. ORIG C19: imit.

clunker ('klʌŋkə) *n Inf.* **1** *Chiefly US.* a dilapidated old car or other machine **2** something that fails: *the novel's last line is a clunker.*

clunky ('klʌŋkɪ) *adj* **clunkier, clunkiest. 1** making a clunking noise. **2** clumsy or inelegant: *clunky ankle-strap shoes.* **3** awkward or unsophisticated: *then you guffaw at clunky dialogue.*

Cluny ★ ('kluːnɪ; *French* klyni) *n* a town in E central France: reformed Benedictine order founded here in 910; important religious and cultural centre in the Middle Ages. Pop.: 4724 (1990).
▸ **'Cluniac** *adj*

cluster ('klʌstə) *n* **1** a number of things growing, fastened, or occurring close together. **2** a number of persons or things grouped together. ◆ *vb* **3** to gather or be gathered in clusters. ORIG OE *clyster*
▸ **'clustered** *adj* ▸ **'clustery** *adj*

clutch[1] (klʌtʃ) *vb* **1** (*tr*) to seize with or as if with hands or claws. **2** (*tr*) to grasp or hold firmly. **3** (*intr;* usually foll. by *at*) to attempt to get hold or possession (of). ◆ *n* **4** a device that enables two revolving shafts to be joined or disconnected, esp. one that transmits the drive from the engine to the gearbox in a vehicle. **5** a device for holding fast. **6** a firm grasp. **7** a hand, claw, or talon in the act of clutching: *in the clutches of a bear.* **8** (*often pl*) power or control: *in the clutches of the Mafia.* ORIG OE *clyccan*

clutch[2] (klʌtʃ) *n* **1** a hatch of eggs laid by a particular bird or laid in a single nest. **2** a brood of chickens. **3** *Inf.* a group or cluster. ◆ *vb* **4** (*tr*) to hatch (chickens). ORIG C17 (N English dialect) *cletch,* from ON *klekja* to hatch

Clutha ★ ('kluːθə) *n* a river in New Zealand, the longest river in the South Island; rising in the Southern Alps it flows southeast to the Pacific. Length: 338 km (210 miles).

clutter ('klʌtə) *vb* **1** (*usually tr;* often foll. by *up*) to strew or amass (objects) in a disorderly manner. **2** (*intr*) to move about in a bustling manner. ◆ *n* **3** a disordered heap or mass of objects. **4** a state of disorder. **5** unwanted echoes that confuse the observation of signals on a radar screen. ORIG C15 *clotter,* from *clotteren* to CLOT

Clwyd ★ ('kluːɪd) *n* a former county in NE Wales, formed in 1974 from Flintshire, most of Denbighshire, and part of Merionethshire; replaced in 1996 as part of local government reorganization.

Clyde ★ (klaɪd) *n* **1 Firth of.** an inlet of the Atlantic in SW Scotland. Length: 103 km (64 miles). **2** a river in S Scotland, rising in South Lanarkshire and flowing northwest to the Firth of Clyde: formerly extensive shipyards. Length: 170 km (106 miles).

Clydebank ★ (ˌklaɪd'bæŋk, 'klaɪdˌbæŋk) *n* a town in W Scotland, on the north bank of the River Clyde. Pop.: 29 171 (1991).

Clydesdale ('klaɪdzˌdeɪl) *n* a heavy powerful breed of carthorse, originally from Scotland.

clypeus ('klɪpɪəs) *n, pl* **clypei** ('klɪpɪˌaɪ). a cuticular plate on the head of some insects. ORIG C19: from NL, from L *clipeus* round shield
▸ **'clypeal** *adj* ▸ **clypeate** ('klɪpɪˌeɪt) *adj*

Clytemnestra *or* **Clytaemnestra** ★ (ˌklaɪtɪm'nɛstrə) *n Greek myth.* the wife of Agamemnon, whom she killed on his return from the Trojan War.

cm *symbol for* centimetre.

Cm *the chemical symbol for* curium.

Cmdr *Mil. abbrev. for* Commander.

CMEA *abbrev. for* Council for Mutual Economic Assistance. See **Comecon.**

CMG *abbrev. for* Companion of St Michael and St George (a Brit. title).

CMOS ('si:mɒs) *adj Computing. acronym for* complementary metal oxide silicon: *CMOS memory.*

CMV *abbrev. for* cytomegalovirus.

CNAA *abbrev. for* Council for National Academic Awards.

CNAR *abbrev. for* compound net annual rate.

CND *Chiefly Brit. abbrev. for* Campaign for Nuclear Disarmament.

CNG *abbrev. for* compressed natural gas.

Cnossus ★ ('nɒsəs, 'knɒs-) *n* a variant spelling of **Knossos.**

Cnut ★ (kə'nju:t) *n* a variant spelling of **Canute.**

Co *the chemical symbol for* cobalt.

CO *abbrev. for:* **1** Commanding Officer. **2** conscientious objector.

Co. *or* **co.** *abbrev. for:* **1** (esp. in names of business organizations) Company. **2 and co.** (kəu) *Inf.* and the rest of them: *Harold and co.*

Co. *abbrev. for* County.

co- *prefix* **1** together; joint or jointly; mutual or mutually: *coproduction.* **2** indicating partnership or equality: *cofounder; copilot.* **3** to the same or a similar degree: *coextend.* **4** (in mathematics and astronomy) of the complement of an angle: *cosecant.* ORIG from L, reduced form of COM-

c/o *abbrev. for:* **1** care of. **2** *Book-keeping.* carried over.

coach (kəutʃ) *n* **1** a large vehicle for several passengers, used for transport over long distances, sightseeing, etc. **2** a large four-wheeled enclosed carriage, usually horse-drawn. **3** a railway carriage. **4** a trainer or instructor: *a drama coach.* **5** a tutor who prepares students for examinations. ◆ *vb* **6** to give tuition or instruction to (a pupil). **7** (*tr*) to transport in a bus or coach. ORIG C16: from F *coche,* from Hungarian *kocsi szekér* wagon of Kocs, village in Hungary where coaches were first made
▸ **'coacher** *n*

coach-built *adj* (of a vehicle) having specially built bodywork.
▸ **'coach-ˌbuilder** *n*

coachman ('kəutʃmən) *n, pl* **coachmen.** the driver of a coach or carriage.

coachwork ('kəutʃˌwɜ:k) *n* **1** the design and manufacture of car bodies. **2** the body of a car.

coadjutor (kəu'ædʒutə) *n* **1** a bishop appointed as assistant to a diocesan bishop. **2** *Rare.* an assistant. ORIG C15: via OF from L *co-* together + *adjūtor* helper, from *adjūtāre* to assist

coagulate *vb* (kəu'ægjuˌleɪt), **coagulates, coagulating, coagulated. 1** to cause (a fluid, such as blood) to change into a soft semisolid mass or (of such a fluid) to change into such a mass; clot; curdle. ◆ *n* (kəu'ægjulɪt, -ˌleɪt). **2** the solid or semisolid substance produced by coagulation. ORIG C16: from L *coāgulāre,* from *coāgulum* rennet, from *cōgere* to drive together
▸ **co'agulant** *or* **co'aguˌlator** *n* ▸ **coˌagu'lation** *n*
▸ **coagulative** (kəu'ægjulətɪv) *adj*

coagulation factor *n Med.* another name for **clotting factor.**

Coahuila ★ (*Spanish* koa'wila) *n* a state of N Mexico: mainly plateau, crossed by several mountain ranges that contain rich mineral resources. Capital: Saltillo. Pop.: 2 227 305 (1997 est.). Area: 151 571 sq. km (59 112 sq. miles).

coal (kəul) *n* **1a** a compact black or dark brown carbonaceous rock consisting of layers of partially decomposed vegetation deposited in the Carboniferous period: a fuel and a source of coke, coal gas, and coal tar. **1b** (*as modifier*): *coal cellar; coal mine; coal dust.* **2** one or more lumps of coal. **3** short for **charcoal. 4 coals to Newcastle.** something supplied where it is already plentiful. ◆ *vb* **5** to take in, provide with, or turn into coal. ORIG OE *col*
▸ **'coaly** *adj*

coaler ('kəulə) *n* a ship, train, etc., used to carry or supply coal.

coalesce (ˌkəuə'lɛs) *vb* **coalesces, coalescing, coalesced.** (*intr*) to unite or come together in one body or mass; merge; fuse; blend. ORIG C16: from L CO- + *alēscere* to increase, from *alere* to nourish
▸ **ˌcoa'lescence** *n* ▸ **ˌcoa'lescent** *adj*

coalface ('kəulˌfeɪs) *n* the exposed seam of coal in a mine.

coalfield ('kəulˌfi:ld) *n* an area rich in deposits of coal.

coalfish ('kəulˌfɪʃ) *n, pl* **coalfish** *or* **coalfishes.** a dark-coloured gadoid food fish occurring in northern seas. Also called (Brit.): **saithe, coley.**

coal gas *n* a mixture of gases produced by the distillation of bituminous coal and used for heating and lighting.

coalition (ˌkəuə'lɪʃən) *n* **1a** an alliance between groups or parties, esp. for some temporary and specific reason. **1b** (*as modifier*): *a coalition government.* **2** a fusion or merging into one body or mass. ORIG C17: from Med. L *coalitiō,* from L *coalēscere* to COALESCE
▸ **ˌcoa'litionist** *n*

Coal Measures *pl n* **the.** a series of coal-bearing rocks formed in the upper Carboniferous period.

coal miner's lung *n* an informal name for **anthracosis.**

coal scuttle *n* a container to supply coal to a domestic fire.

coal tar *n* a black tar, produced by the distillation of bituminous coal, that can be further distilled to yield benzene, toluene, etc.

coal tit *n* a small European songbird having a black head with a white patch on the nape.

coaming ('kəumɪŋ) *n* a raised frame round a ship's hatchway for keeping out water. ORIG C17: from ?

coarse (kɔ:s) *adj* **1** rough in texture, structure, etc.; not fine: *coarse sand.* **2** lacking refinement or taste; indelicate; vulgar: *coarse jokes.* **3** of inferior quality. **4** (of a metal) not refined. ORIG C14: from ?
▸ **'coarsely** *adv* ▸ **'coarseness** *n*

coarse fish *n* a freshwater fish that is not of the salmon family.
▸ **coarse fishing** *n*

coarsen ('kɔ:sᵊn) *vb* to make or become coarse.

coast (kəust) *n* **1** the line or zone where the land meets the sea. Related adj: **littoral. 2** *Brit.* the seaside. **3** *US.* **3a** a slope down which a sledge may slide. **3b** the act or an instance of sliding down a slope. **4 the coast is clear.** *Inf.* the obstacles or dangers are gone. ◆ *vb* **5** to move or cause to move by momentum or force of gravity. **6** (*intr*) to proceed without great effort: *to coast to victory.* **7** to sail along (a coast). ORIG C13: from OF *coste,* from L *costa* side, rib
▸ **'coastal** *adj*

coaster ('kəustə) *n* **1** *Brit.* a vessel engaged in coastal commerce. **2** a small tray for holding a decanter, wine bottle, etc. **3** a person or thing that coasts. **4** a protective mat for glasses. **5** *US.* short for **roller coaster.**

Coaster ('kəustə) *n NZ.* a person from the West Coast of the South Island, New Zealand.

coastguard ('kəustˌgɑ:d) *n* **1** a maritime force which aids shipping, saves lives at sea, prevents smuggling, etc. **2** Also called: **coastguardsman.** a member of such a force.

coastline ('kəustˌlaɪn) *n* the outline of a coast.

Coast Mountains ★ *pl n* a mountain range in Canada, on the Pacific coast of British Columbia. Highest peak: Mount Waddington, 4043 m (13 266 ft).

coat (kəut) *n* **1** an outdoor garment with sleeves, covering the body from the shoulders to waist, knees, or feet. **2** any similar garment, esp. one forming the top to a suit. **3** a layer that covers or conceals a surface: *a coat of dust.* **4** the hair, wool, or fur of an animal. ◆ *vb* (*tr*) **5** (often foll. by *with*) to cover (with) a layer or covering. **6** to provide with a coat. ORIG C16: from OF *cote,* of Gmc origin

Coates ★ (kəuts) *n* **Joseph Gordon.** 1878–1943, New Zealand statesman; prime minister (1925–28).

coat hanger *n* a curved piece of wood, wire, etc., with a hook, used to hang up clothes.

coati (kəu'ɑ:tɪ), **coati-mondi,** *or* **coati-mundi** (kəuˌɑ:tɪ'mʌndɪ) *n, pl* **coatis, coati-mondis,** *or* **coati-mundis.** an omnivorous mammal of Central and South America, related to but larger than the raccoons, having a long flexible snout and a brindled coat. ORIG C17: from Port., from Tupi, lit.: belt-nosed, from *cua* belt + *tim* nose

coating ('kəʊtɪŋ) *n* **1** a layer or film spread over a surface. **2** fabric suitable for coats.

coat of arms *n* the heraldic bearings of a person, family, or corporation.

coat of mail *n* a protective garment made of linked metal rings or overlapping metal plates.

coat-tail *n* the long tapering tails at the back of a man's tailed coat.

coauthor (kəʊ'ɔ:θə) *n* **1** a person who shares the writing of a book, etc., with another. ♦ *vb* **2** (*tr*) to be the joint author of (a book, etc.).

coax (kəʊks) *vb* **1** to seek to manipulate or persuade (someone) by tenderness, flattery, pleading, etc. **2** (*tr*) to obtain by persistent coaxing. **3** (*tr*) to work on (something) carefully and patiently so as to make it function as desired: *he coaxed the engine into starting.* ORIG C16: verb formed from obs. noun *cokes* fool, from ?
▸ **'coaxer** *n* ▸ **'coaxingly** *adv*

coaxial (kəʊ'æksɪəl) *or* **coaxal** (kəʊ'æksᵊl) *adj* **1** having or mounted on a common axis. **2** *Geom.* (of a set of circles) having the same radical axis. **3** *Electronics.* formed from, using, or connected to a coaxial cable.

coaxial cable *n* a cable consisting of an inner insulated core of stranded or solid wire surrounded by an outer insulated flexible wire braid, used esp. as a transmission line for radio-frequency signals. Often shortened to **coax** ('kəʊæks).

cob (kɒb) *n* **1** a male swan. **2** a thickset type of riding and draught horse. **3** short for **corncob** or **cobnut. 4** *Brit.* another name for **hazel** (sense 1). **5** a small rounded lump or heap of coal, ore, etc. **6** *Brit. & NZ.* a building material consisting of a mixture of clay and chopped straw. **7** *Brit.* a round loaf of bread. ORIG C15: from ?

cobalt ('kəʊbɔ:lt) *n* a brittle hard silvery-white element that is a ferromagnetic metal: used in alloys. The radioisotope **cobalt-60** is used in radiotherapy and as a tracer. Symbol: Co; atomic no.: 27; atomic wt.: 58.933. ORIG C17: G *Kobalt,* from MHG *kobolt* goblin; from the miners' belief that goblins placed it in the silver ore

cobalt blue *n* **1** any greenish-blue pigment containing cobalt aluminate. **2a** a deep blue colour. **2b** (*as adj*): *a cobalt-blue car.*

cobalt bomb *n* **1** a cobalt-60 device used in radiotherapy. **2** a nuclear weapon consisting of a hydrogen bomb encased in cobalt, which releases large quantities of radioactive cobalt-60 into the atmosphere.

cobber ('kɒbə) *n Austral. arch. & NZ.* a friend; mate: used as a term of address to males. ORIG C19: from E dialect *cob* to take a liking to someone

Cobbett ★ ('kɒbɪt) *n* **William.** 1763–1835, British journalist and social reformer; founded *The Political Register* (1802); author of *Rural Rides* (1830).

cobble[1] ('kɒbᵊl) *n* **1** short for **cobblestone.** ♦ *vb* **cobbles, cobbling, cobbled. 2** (*tr*) to pave (a road, etc.) with cobblestones. ORIG C15 (in *cobblestone*): from COB

cobble[2] ('kɒbᵊl) *vb* **cobbles, cobbling, cobbled.** (*tr*) **1** to make or mend (shoes). **2** to put together clumsily. ORIG C15: back formation from COBBLER[1]

cobbler[1] ('kɒblə) *n* a person who makes or mends shoes. ORIG C13 (as surname): from ?

cobbler[2] ('kɒblə) *n* **1** a sweetened iced drink, usually made from fruit and wine. **2** *Chiefly US.* a hot dessert made of fruit covered with a rich cakelike crust. ORIG C19: (for sense 1) ? shortened from *cobbler's punch*

cobblers ('kɒbləz) *pl n Brit. taboo sl.* **1** another word for **testicles. 2** (**a load of old**) **cobblers.** rubbish; nonsense. ORIG C20: from rhyming sl. *cobblers' awls* balls

cobblestone ('kɒbᵊl,stəʊn) *n* a rounded stone used for paving. Sometimes shortened to **cobble.**

Cobden ★ ('kɒbdən) *n* **Richard.** 1804–65, British economist and statesman: a leader of the campaign to abolish the Corn Laws (1846).

cobelligerent (,kəʊbɪ'lɪdʒərənt) *n* a country fighting in a war on the side of another country.

Cobham ★ ('kɒbəm) *n* **Lord,** title of (Sir John) **Oldcastle.**

Coblenz ★ (*German* 'ko:blɛnts) *n* a variant spelling of **Koblenz.**

cobnut ('kɒb,nʌt) *or* **cob** *n* other names for a **hazelnut.** ORIG C16: from earlier *cobylle nut*

COBOL *or* **Cobol** ('kəʊ,bɒl) *n* a high-level computer programming language designed for general commercial use. ORIG C20: *co(mmon) b(usiness) o(riented) l(anguage)*

cobra ('kəʊbrə) *n* any of several highly venomous snakes of tropical Africa and Asia. When alarmed they spread the skin of the neck region into a hood. ORIG C19: from Port. *cobra (de capello)* snake (with a hood), from L *colubra* snake

Coburg ★ ('kəʊbɜ:g; *German* 'ko:bʊrk) *n* a city in E Germany, in N Bavaria. Pop.: 44 690 (1991).

cobweb ('kɒb,wɛb) *n* **1** a web spun by certain spiders. **2** a single thread of such a web. **3** something like a cobweb, as in its flimsiness or ability to trap. ORIG C14: *cob,* from OE *(ātor)coppe* spider
▸ **'cob,webbed** *adj* ▸ **'cob,webby** *adj*

cobwebs ('kɒb,wɛbz) *pl n* **1** mustiness, confusion, or obscurity. **2** *Inf.* stickiness of the eyelids experienced upon first awakening.

coca ('kəʊkə) *n* either of two shrubs, native to the Andes, the dried leaves of which contain cocaine and are chewed for their stimulating effects. ORIG C17: from Sp., from Quechuan *kúka*

Coca-Cola (,kəʊkə'kəʊlə) *n* **1** *Trademark.* a carbonated soft drink flavoured with coca leaves, cola nuts, caramel, etc. **2** (*modifier*) denoting the spread of American culture and values to other parts of the world: *Coca-Cola generation.*

cocaine *or* **cocain** (kə'keɪn) *n* an addictive narcotic drug derived from coca leaves or synthesized, used medicinally as a topical anaesthetic. ORIG C19: from COCA + -INE[1]

coccus ('kɒkəs) *n, pl* **cocci** (-kaɪ, -ki:). any spherical or nearly spherical bacterium, such as a staphylococcus. ORIG C18: from NL, from Gk *kokkos* berry, grain
▸ **'coccoid** *or* **'coccal** *adj*

coccyx ('kɒksɪks) *n, pl* **coccyges** (kɒk'saɪdʒi:z). a small triangular bone at the end of the spinal column in man and some apes. ORIG C17: from NL, from Gk *kokkux* cuckoo, imit.; from its likeness to a cuckoo's beak
▸ **coccygeal** (kɒk'sɪdʒɪəl) *adj*

Cochin ★ ('kəʊtʃɪn, 'kɒtʃ-) *n* **1** a region and former state of SW India: part of Kerala state since 1956. **2** a port in SW India, on the Malabar Coast: the first European settlement in India, founded by Vasco da Gama in 1502. Pop.: 564 589 (1991).

Cochin China ★ *n* a former French colony of Indochina (1862–1948): now the part of Vietnam that lies south of Phan Thiet.

cochineal (,kɒtʃɪ'ni:l, 'kɒtʃɪ,ni:l) *n* **1** a Mexican insect that feeds on cacti. **2** a crimson substance obtained from the crushed bodies of these insects, used for colouring food and for dyeing. **3** the colour of this dye. ORIG C16: from OSp. *cochinilla,* from L *coccineus* scarlet-coloured, from Gk *kokkos* kermes berry

cochlea ('kɒklɪə) *n, pl* **cochleae** (-lɪ,i:). the spiral tube that forms part of the internal ear, converting sound vibrations into nerve impulses. ORIG C16: from L: snail, spiral, from Gk *kokhlias*
▸ **'cochlear** *adj*

cochlear implant ('kɒklɪə) *n* a device that stimulates the acoustic nerve in the inner ear in order to produce some form of hearing in people who are deaf from inner ear disease.

cochleate ('kɒklɪ,eɪt, -lɪɪt) *or* **cochleated** *adj Biol.* shaped like a snail's shell.

cock[1] (kɒk) *n* **1** the male of the domestic fowl. **2a** any other male bird. **2b** the male of certain other animals, such as the lobster. **2c** (*as modifier*): *a cock sparrow.* **3** short for **stopcock** or **weathercock. 4** a taboo slang word for **penis. 5a** the hammer of a firearm. **5b** its position when the firearm is ready to be discharged. **6** *Brit. inf.* a friend, mate, or fellow. **7** a jaunty or significant tilting upwards: *a cock of the head.* ◆ *vb* **8** (*tr*) to set the firing pin, hammer, or breech block of (a firearm) so that a pull on the trigger will release it and thus fire the weapon. **9** (*tr; sometimes foll. by up*) to raise in an alert or jaunty manner. **10** (*intr*) to stick or stand up conspicuously. ◆ See also **cockup**. ORIG OE *cocc,* ult. imit.

cock[2] (kɒk) *n* **1** a small, cone-shaped heap of hay, straw, etc. ◆ *vb* **2** (*tr*) to stack (hay, etc.) in such heaps. ORIG C14: ? of Scand. origin

cockabully (ˌkɒkəˈbʊlɪ) *n, pl* **cockabullies.** any of several small freshwater fish of New Zealand. ORIG Maori *kokopu*

cockade (kɒˈkeɪd) *n* a feather or ribbon worn on military headwear. ORIG C18: changed from earlier *cockard,* from F, from *coq* COCK[1]
▸ **cockˈaded** *adj*

cock-a-doodle-doo (ˌkɒkəˌduːdᵊlˈduː) *interj* an imitation or representation of a cock crowing.

cock-a-hoop *adj* (*usually postpositive*) **1** in very high spirits. **2** boastful. **3** askew; confused. ORIG C16: ?from *set the cock a hoop*: to put a cock on a *hoop,* a full measure of grain

cockalorum (ˌkɒkəˈlɔːrəm) *n* **1** a self-important little man. **2** bragging talk. ORIG C18: from COCK[1] + *-alorum,* var. of L genitive pl ending; ? intended to suggest: the cock of all cocks

cockamamie (ˌkɒkəˈmeɪmɪ) *adj Sl., chiefly US.* ridiculous or nonsensical: *a cockamamie story.* ORIG C20: in an earlier sense: a paper transfer, prob. from DECALCOMANIA

cock-and-bull story *n Inf.* an obviously improbable story, esp. one used as an excuse.

cockatoo (ˌkɒkəˈtuː, ˈkɒkəˌtuː) *n, pl* **cockatoos. 1** any of a genus of parrots having an erectile crest and light-coloured plumage. **2** *Austral. & NZ obs.* a small farmer or settler. **3** *Austral. inf.* a lookout during some illegal activity. ORIG C17: from Du., from Malay *kakatua*

cockatrice (ˈkɒkətrɪs, -ˌtraɪs) *n* **1** a legendary monster, part snake and part cock, that could kill with a glance. **2** another name for **basilisk** (sense 1). ORIG C14: from OF, ult. from L *calcāre* to tread, from *calx* heel

cockboat (ˈkɒkˌbəʊt) *or* **cockleboat** *n* a ship's small boat. ORIG C15 *cokbote,* ? ult. from LL *caudica* dugout canoe, from L *caudex* tree trunk

cockchafer (ˈkɒkˌtʃeɪfə) *n* any of various Old World beetles, whose larvae feed on crops and grasses. Also called: **May beetle, May bug.** ORIG C18: from COCK[1] + CHAFER

Cockcroft ★ (ˈkɒkˌkrɒft) *n* Sir **John Douglas.** 1897–1967, British nuclear physicist. Shared the Nobel prize for physics 1951, for his artificial transmutation of a nucleus.

cockcrow (ˈkɒkˌkrəʊ) *n* daybreak.

cocked hat *n* **1** a hat with brims turned up and caught together in order to give two points (bicorn) or three points (tricorn). **2 knock into a cocked hat.** *Sl.* to outdo or defeat.

Cocker ★ (ˈkɒkə) *n* **1 Edward.** 1631–75, English arithmetician. **2 according to Cocker.** reliable or reliably; correct or correctly.

cockerel (ˈkɒkərəl, ˈkɒkrəl) *n* a young domestic cock, less than a year old. ORIG C15: dim. of COCK[1]

Cockerell ★ (ˈkɒkərəl) *n* Sir **Christopher Sydney.** 1910–99, British engineer who invented the hovercraft.

cocker spaniel (ˈkɒkə) *n* a small compact breed of spaniel. ORIG C19: from *cocking* hunting woodcocks

cockeyed (ˈkɒkˌaɪd) *adj Inf.* **1** afflicted with strabismus or squint. **2** physically or logically abnormal, absurd, etc.; crooked; askew: *cockeyed ideas.* **3** drunk.

cockfight (ˈkɒkˌfaɪt) *n* a fight between two gamecocks fitted with sharp metal spurs.
▸ **ˈcockˌfighting** *n*

cockhorse (ˌkɒkˈhɔːs) *n* another name for **rocking horse** or **hobbyhorse.**

cockieleekie, cockyleeky, *or* **cock-a-leekie** (ˈkɒkəˈliːkɪ) *n Scot.* a soup made from a fowl boiled with leeks.

cockle[1] (ˈkɒkᵊl) *n* **1** any edible sand-burrowing bivalve mollusc of Europe, typically having a rounded shell with radiating ribs. **2** any of certain similar or related molluscs. **3** short for **cockleshell** (sense 1). **4** a wrinkle or puckering. **5** one's deepest feelings (esp. in **warm the cockles of one's heart**). ◆ *vb* **cockles, cockling, cockled. 6** to contract or cause to contract into wrinkles. ORIG C14: from OF *coquille* shell, from L *conchȳlium* shellfish, from Gk *konkhule* mussel; see CONCH

cockle[2] (ˈkɒkᵊl) *n* any of several plants, esp. the corn cockle, that grow as weeds in cornfields.

cockleshell (ˈkɒkᵊlˌʃɛl) *n* **1** the shell of the cockle. **2** any of the shells of certain other molluscs. **3** any small light boat.

cockney (ˈkɒknɪ) (*often cap.*) ◆ *n* **1** a native of London, esp. of the East End, speaking a characteristic dialect of English. Traditionally defined as someone born within the sound of the bells of St Mary-le-Bow church. **2** the urban dialect of London or its East End. ◆ *adj* **3** characteristic of cockneys or their dialect of English. ORIG C14: from *cokeney,* lit.: cock's egg, later applied contemptuously to townsmen, from *cokene,* genitive pl of *cok* COCK[1] + *ey* EGG[1]
▸ **ˈcockneyish** *adj* ▸ **ˈcockneyˌism** *n*

cock of the walk *n Inf.* a person who asserts himself in a strutting pompous way.

cockpit (ˈkɒkˌpɪt) *n* **1** the compartment in a small aircraft in which the pilot, crew, and sometimes the passengers sit. Cf. **flight deck** (sense 1). **2** the driver's compartment in a racing car. **3** *Naut.* an enclosed or recessed area towards the stern of a small vessel from which it is steered. **4** the site of numerous battles or campaigns. **5** an enclosure used for cockfights.

cockroach (ˈkɒkˌrəʊtʃ) *n* an insect having an oval flattened body with long antennae and biting mouthparts: a household pest. ORIG C17: from Sp. *cucaracha,* from ?

cockscomb *or* **coxcomb** (ˈkɒksˌkəʊm) *n* **1** the comb of a domestic cock. **2** a garden plant with yellow, crimson, or purple feathery plumelike flowers in a broad spike resembling the comb of a cock. **3** *Inf.* a conceited dandy.

cockshy (ˈkɒkˌʃaɪ) *n, pl* **cockshies.** *Brit.* **1** a target aimed at in throwing games. **2** the throw itself. ◆ Often shortened to **shy.** ORIG C18: from shying at a cock, the prize for the person who hit it

cocksure (ˌkɒkˈʃʊə, -ˈʃɔː) *adj* overconfident; arrogant. ORIG C16: from ?
▸ **ˌcockˈsureness** *n*

cocktail (ˈkɒkˌteɪl) *n* **1a** any mixed drink with a spirit base. **1b** (*as modifier*): *the cocktail hour.* **2** an appetizer of seafood, mixed fruits, etc. **3** any combination of diverse elements, esp. one considered potent. **4** (*modifier*) appropriate for formal occasions: *a cocktail dress.* ORIG C19: from ?

cockup (ˈkɒkˌʌp) *n* **1** *Brit. sl.* something done badly. ◆ *vb* **cock up.** (*tr, adv*) **2** (of an animal) to raise (its ears etc.), esp. in an alert manner. **3** *Brit. sl.* to botch.

cocky[1] (ˈkɒkɪ) *adj* **cockier, cockiest.** excessively proud of oneself.
▸ **ˈcockily** *adv* ▸ **ˈcockiness** *n*

cocky[2] (ˈkɒkɪ) *n, pl* **cockies.** *Austral. & NZ inf.* short for **cockatoo** (sense 2).

coco (ˈkəʊkəʊ) *n, pl* **cocos.** short for **coconut** or **coconut palm.** ORIG C16: from Port. *coco* grimace; from the likeness of the three holes of the nut to a face

cocoa (ˈkəʊkəʊ) *or* **cacao** *n* **1** a powder made from cocoa beans after they have been roasted and ground. **2** a hot or cold drink made from cocoa and milk or water. **3a** a light to moderate brown colour. **3b** (*as adj*): *cocoa paint.* ORIG C18: altered from CACAO

cocoa bean *n* the seed of the cacao.

cocoa butter *n* a yellowish-white waxy solid that is obtained from cocoa beans and used for confectionery, soap, etc.

coconut *or* **cocoanut** (ˈkəʊkəˌnʌt) *n* **1** the fruit of the coconut palm, consisting of a thick fibrous oval husk inside which is a thin hard shell enclosing edible white meat. The hollow centre is filled with a milky fluid (**coconut milk**). **2** the meat of the coconut, often shredded and used in cakes, curries, etc. ORIG C18: see COCO

coconut matting *n* a form of coarse matting made from the fibrous husk of the coconut.

coconut oil *n* the oil obtained from the meat of the coconut and used for making soap, etc.

coconut palm *n* a tall palm tree, widely planted throughout the tropics, having coconuts as fruits. Also called: **coco palm, coconut tree.**

cocoon (kə'ku:n) *n* **1** a silky protective envelope secreted by silkworms and certain other insect larvae, in which the pupae develop. **2** a protective spray covering used as a seal on machinery. **3** a cosy warm covering. ◆ *vb* **4** (*tr*) to wrap in a cocoon. ORIG C17: from F, from Provençal *coucoun* eggshell, from *coco* shell

cocopan ('kəukəu,pæn) *n* (in South Africa) a small wagon running on narrow-gauge railway lines used in mines. Also called: **hopper.** ORIG C20: from Zulu *'ngkumbana* short truck

Cocos Islands ★ ('kəukɒs, 'kəukəs) *pl n* a group of 27 coral islands in the Indian Ocean, southwest of Java: a Territory of Australia since 1955. Pop.: 593 (1993). Area: 13 sq. km (5 sq. miles). Also called: **Keeling Islands.**

cocotte (kəu'kɒt, kə-) *n* **1** a small fireproof dish in which individual portions of food are cooked and served. **2** a prostitute or promiscuous woman. ORIG C19: from F, from fem of *coq* COCK[1]

Cocteau ★ (*French* kɔkto) *n* **Jean** (ʒɑ̃). 1889–1963, French dramatist, novelist, poet, critic, designer, and film director. His works include the novel *Les Enfants terribles* (1929) and the play *La Machine infernale* (1934).

cod[1] (kɒd) *n, pl* **cod** *or* **cods. 1** any of the gadoid food fishes which occur in the North Atlantic and have a long body with three rounded dorsal fins. **2** any of various Australian fishes of fresh or salt water, such as the Murray cod or the red cod. ORIG C13: prob. of Gmc origin

cod[2] (kɒd) *n* **1** *Brit. & US dialect.* a pod or husk. **2** *Taboo.* an obsolete word for **scrotum.** ORIG OE *codd* husk, bag

cod[3] (kɒd) *Brit. sl.* ◆ *vb* **cods, codding, codded.** (*tr*) **1** to make fun of; tease. **2** to play a trick on; befool. ◆ *n* **3** a hoax or trick. ORIG C19: ?from earlier *cod* a fool

Cod ★ *n* **Cape.** See **Cape Cod.**

COD *abbrev. for:* **1** cash on delivery. **2** (in the US) collect on delivery.

coda ('kəudə) *n* **1** *Music.* the final passage of a musical structure. **2** a concluding part of a literary work that rounds off the main work but is independent of it. ORIG C18: from It.: tail, from L *cauda*

cod-act *vb* (*intr*) *Irish inf.* to play tricks; fool. ORIG from COD[3] + ACT

coddle ('kɒd'l) *vb* **coddles, coddling, coddled.** (*tr*) **1** to treat with indulgence. **2** to cook (something, esp. eggs) in water just below the boiling point. ORIG C16: from ?; ? rel. to CAUDLE
▸ **'coddler** *n*

code (kəud) *n* **1** a system of letters or symbols, by which information can be communicated secretly, briefly, etc.: *binary code; Morse code.* See also **genetic code. 2** a message in code. **3** a symbol used in a code. **4** a conventionalized set of principles or rules: *a code of behaviour.* **5** a system of letters or digits used for identification purposes. ◆ *vb* **codes, coding, coded.** (*tr*) **6** to translate or arrange into a code. ORIG C14: from F, from L *cōdex* book, CODEX
▸ **'coder** *n*

codeine ('kəudi:n) *n* a white crystalline alkaloid prepared mainly from morphine. It is used as an analgesic, a sedative, and to relieve coughing. ORIG C19: from Gk *kōdeia* head of a poppy, from *kōos* hollow place + -INE[2]

Co. Derry *abbrev. for* County Londonderry.

codex ('kəudɛks) *n, pl* **codices** ('kəudɪ,si:z, 'kɒdɪ-). **1** a volume of manuscripts of an ancient text. **2** *Obs.* a legal code. ORIG C16: from L: tree trunk, wooden block, book

codfish ('kɒd,fɪʃ) *n, pl* **codfish** *or* **codfishes.** a cod.

codger ('kɒdʒə) *n Inf.* a man, esp. an old or eccentric one: often in **old codger.** ORIG C18: prob. var. of CADGER

codicil ('kɒdɪsɪl) *n* **1** *Law.* a supplement modifying a will or revoking some provision of it. **2** an additional provision; appendix. ORIG C15: from LL dim. of CODEX
▸ **,codi'cillary** *adj*

codify ('kəudɪ,faɪ, 'kɒ-) *vb* **codifies, codifying, codified.** (*tr*) to organize or collect together (laws, rules, procedures, etc.) into a system or code.
▸ **'codi,fier** *n* ▸ **,codifi'cation** *n*

codling[1] ('kɒdlɪŋ) *or* **codlin** ('kɒdlɪn) *n* **1** any of several varieties of long tapering apples. **2** any unripe apple. ORIG C15 *querdlyng,* from ?

codling[2] ('kɒdlɪŋ) *n* a codfish, esp. a young one.

cod-liver oil *n* an oil extracted from the livers of cod and related fish, rich in vitamins A and D.

codology (kɒd'ɒlədʒɪ) *n Irish inf.* the art or practice of bluffing or deception.

codpiece ('kɒd,pi:s) *n* a bag covering the male genitals, attached to breeches: worn in the 15th and 16th centuries. ORIG C15: from COD[2] + PIECE

codswallop ('kɒdz,wɒləp) *n Brit. sl.* nonsense. ORIG C20: from ?

Co. Durham *abbrev. for* County Durham.

Cody ★ ('kəudɪ) *n* **William Frederick.** the real name of **Buffalo Bill.**

Coe ★ (kəu) *n* **Sebastian,** Baron Coe of Ranmore. born 1956, British middle-distance runner and Conservative politician: winner of the 1500m in the 1980 and 1984 Olympic Games; held records at 800m, 1000m, 1500m, and a mile: member of parliament (1992–97).

co-ed (,kəu'ɛd) *adj* **1** coeducational. ◆ *n* **2** *US.* a female student in a coeducational college or university. **3** *Brit.* a school or college providing coeducation.

coeducation (,kəuɛdju'keɪʃən) *n* instruction in schools, colleges, etc., attended by both sexes.
▸ **,coedu'cational** *adj* ▸ **,coedu'cationally** *adv*

coefficient (,kəuɪ'fɪʃənt) *n* **1** *Maths.* a numerical or constant factor in an algebraic term: *the coefficient of the term 3xyz is 3.* **2** *Physics.* a number that is the value of a given substance under specified conditions. ORIG C17: from NL, from L *co-* together + *efficere* to EFFECT

coefficient of variation *n Statistics.* a measure of the relative variation of distributions independent of the units of measurement; the standard deviation divided by the mean, sometimes expressed as a percentage.

coel- *prefix* indicating a cavity within a body or a hollow organ or part: *coelacanth; coelenterate.* ORIG NL, from Gk *koilos* hollow

coelacanth ('si:lə,kænθ) *n* a primitive marine bony fish, having fleshy limblike pectoral fins: thought to be extinct until a living specimen was discovered in 1938. ORIG C19: from NL, from COEL- + Gk *akanthos* spine

coelenterate (sɪ'lɛntə,reɪt, -rɪt) *n* any of various invertebrates having a saclike body with a single opening (mouth), such as jellyfishes, sea anemones, and corals. ORIG C19: from NL *Coelenterata,* hollow-intestined (creatures)

coeliac *or US* **celiac** ('si:lɪ,æk) *adj* of the abdomen. ORIG C17: from L, from Gk, from *koilia* belly

coeliac disease *n* an illness, esp. of children, in which the lining of the small intestine is sensitive to gluten in the diet, causing an impairment of food absorption.

coelom *or esp. US* **celom** ('si:ləum, -ləm) *n* the body cavity of many multicellular animals, containing the digestive tract and other visceral organs. ORIG C19: from Gk, from *koilos* hollow
▸ **coelomic** *or esp. US* **celomic** (sɪ'lɒmɪk) *adj*

coeno- *or before a vowel* **coen-** *combining form.* common: *coenobite.* ORIG NL, from Gk *koinos*

coenobite *or* **cenobite** ('si:nəu,baɪt) *n* a member of a religious order following a communal rule of life. ORIG C17: from OF or ecclesiastical L, from Gk *koinobion* convent, from *koinos* common + *bios* life
▸ **coenobitic** (,si:nəu'bɪtɪk), **,coeno'bitical** *or* **,ceno'bitic, ,ceno'bitical** *adj*

coenzyme (kəʊ'ɛnzaɪm) *n Biochem.* a nonprotein organic molecule that forms a complex with certain enzymes and is essential for their activity.

coequal (kəʊ'i:kwəl) *adj* **1** of the same size, rank, etc. ◆ *n* **2** a person or thing equal with another.
▸ **coequality** (ˌkəʊɪ'kwɒlɪtɪ) *n*

coerce (kəʊ'ɜ:s) *vb* **coerces, coercing, coerced.** (*tr*) to compel or restrain by force or authority without regard to individual wishes or desires. ORIG C17: from L, from *co-* together + *arcēre* to enclose
▸ **co'ercer** *n* ▸ **co'ercible** *adj*

coercion (kəʊ'ɜ:ʃən) *n* **1** the act or power of coercing. **2** government by force.
▸ **coercive** (kəʊ'ɜ:sɪv) *adj* ▸ **co'ercively** *adv*

Coetzee ★ ('kɜ:tzɪ) *n* **J(ohn) M(ichael).** born 1940, South African novelist. His books include *In the Heart of the Country* (1977), *The Life and Times of Michael K* (1983), and *Disgrace* (1999).

Coeur ★ (kɜ:; *French* kœr) *n* **Jacques.** ?1395–1456, French merchant; councillor and court banker to Charles VII of France.

coeval (kəʊ'i:vᵊl) *adj* **1** of or belonging to the same age or generation. ◆ *n* **2** a contemporary. ORIG C17: from LL, from L *co-* + *aevum* age
▸ **coevality** (ˌkəʊɪ'vælɪtɪ) *n* ▸ **co'evally** *adv*

coexecutor (ˌkəʊɪg'zɛkjʊtə) *n Law.* a person acting jointly with another or others as executor.

coexist (ˌkəʊɪg'zɪst) *vb* (*intr*) **1** to exist together at the same time or in the same place. **2** to exist together in peace.
▸ **ˌcoex'istence** *n* ▸ **ˌcoex'istent** *adj*

coextend (ˌkəʊɪk'stɛnd) *vb* to extend or cause to extend equally in space or time.
▸ **ˌcoex'tension** *n* ▸ **ˌcoex'tensive** *adj*

C of C *abbrev. for* Chamber of Commerce.

C of E *abbrev. for* Church of England.

coffee ('kɒfɪ) *n* **1a** a drink consisting of an infusion of the roasted and ground seeds of the coffee tree. **1b** (*as modifier*): *coffee grounds.* **2** Also called: **coffee beans.** the beanlike seeds of the coffee tree, used to make this beverage. **3** the tree yielding these seeds. **4a** a light brown colour. **4b** (*as adj*): *a coffee carpet.* ORIG C16: from It. *caffè,* from Turkish *kahve,* from Ar. *qahwah* coffee, wine

coffee bar *n* a café; snack bar.

coffee cup *n* a small cup for serving coffee.

coffee house *n* a place where coffee is served, esp. one that was a fashionable meeting place in 18th-century London.

coffee mill *n* a machine for grinding roasted coffee beans.

coffeepot ('kɒfɪˌpɒt) *n* a pot in which coffee is brewed or served.

coffee shop *n* a shop where coffee is sold or drunk.

coffee table *n* a low table on which coffee may be served.

coffee-table book *n* a book, usually glossily illustrated, designed chiefly to be looked at, rather than read.

coffer ('kɒfə) *n* **1** a chest, esp. for storing valuables. **2** (*usually pl*) a store of money. **3** an ornamental sunken panel in a ceiling, dome, etc. **4** a watertight box or chamber. **5** short for **cofferdam.** ◆ *vb* (*tr*) **6** to store, as in a coffer. **7** to decorate (a ceiling, dome, etc.) with coffers. ORIG C13: from OF *coffre,* from L, from Gk *kophinos* basket

cofferdam ('kɒfəˌdæm) *n* **1** a watertight structure that encloses an area under water, pumped dry to enable construction work to be carried out. **2** (on a ship) a compartment separating two bulkheads, as for insulation or to serve as a barrier against the escape of gas, etc. ◆ Often shortened to **coffer.**

coffin ('kɒfɪn) *n* **1** a box in which a corpse is buried or cremated. **2** the bony part of a horse's foot. ◆ *vb* **3** (*tr*) to place in or as in a coffin. ORIG C14: from OF *cofin,* from L *cophinus* basket

coffin nail *n* a slang term for **cigarette.**

coffle ('kɒfᵊl) *n* a line of slaves, beasts, etc., fastened together. ORIG C18: from Ar. *qāfilah* caravan

C of S *abbrev. for* Church of Scotland.

cog[1] (kɒg) *n* **1** any of the teeth or projections on the rim of a gearwheel. **2** a gearwheel, esp. a small one. **3** a person or thing playing a small part in a large organization or process. ORIG C13: of Scand. origin

cog[2] (kɒg) *n* **1** a tenon that projects from the end of a timber beam for fitting into a mortise. ◆ *vb* **cogs, cogging, cogged.** **2** (*tr*) to join (pieces of wood) with cogs. ORIG C19: from ?

cogent ('kəʊdʒənt) *adj* compelling belief or assent; forcefully convincing. ORIG C17: from L *cōgent-, cōgēns,* from *co-* together + *agere* to drive
▸ **'cogency** *n* ▸ **'cogently** *adv*

cogitate ('kɒdʒɪˌteɪt) *vb* **cogitates, cogitating, cogitated.** to think deeply about (a problem, possibility, etc.); ponder. ORIG C16: from L, from *co-* (intensive) + *agitāre* to turn over
▸ **ˌcogi'tation** *n* ▸ **'cogitative** *adj* ▸ **'cogiˌtator** *n*

Cognac ★ ('kɒnjæk; *French* kɔɲak) *n* **1** a town in SW France: centre of the district famed for its brandy. Pop.: 21 000 (latest est.). **2** (*sometimes not cap.*) a high-quality grape brandy.

cognate ('kɒgneɪt) *adj* **1** akin; related: *cognate languages.* **2** related by blood or descended from a common maternal ancestor. ◆ *n* **3** something that is cognate with something else. ORIG C17: from L, from *co-* same + *gnātus* born, var. of *nātus,* p.p. of *nāscī* to be born
▸ **'cognately** *adv* ▸ **'cognateness** *n* ▸ **cog'nation** *n*

cognition (kɒg'nɪʃən) *n* **1** the mental act or process by which knowledge is acquired, including perception, intuition, and reasoning. **2** the knowledge that results from such an act or process. ORIG C15: from L, from *co-* (intensive) + *nōscere* to learn
▸ **cog'nitional** *adj* ▸ **'cognitive** *adj*

cognitive therapy *n Psychol.* a form of psychotherapy in which the patient is encouraged to change the way he sees the world and himself: used particularly to treat depression.

cognizable *or* **cognisable** ('kɒgnɪzəbᵊl, 'kɒnɪ-) *adj* **1** perceptible. **2** *Law.* susceptible to the jurisdiction of a court.

cognizance *or* **cognisance** ('kɒgnɪzəns, 'kɒnɪ-) *n* **1** knowledge; acknowledgment. **2 take cognizance of.** to take notice of; acknowledge, esp. officially. **3** the range or scope of knowledge or perception. **4** *Law.* the right of a court to hear and determine a cause or matter. **5** *Heraldry.* a distinguishing badge or bearing. ORIG C14: from OF, from L *cognōscere* to learn; see COGNITION

cognizant *or* **cognisant** ('kɒgnɪzənt, 'kɒnɪ-) *adj* (usually foll. by *of*) aware; having knowledge.

cognomen (kɒg'nəʊmɛn) *n, pl* **cognomens** *or* **cognomina** (-'nɒmɪnə, -'nəʊ-). (originally) an ancient Roman's third name or nickname, which later became his family name. ORIG C19: from L: additional name, from *co-* together + *nōmen* name
▸ **cognominal** (kɒg'nɒmɪnᵊl, -'nəʊ-) *adj*

cognoscenti (ˌkɒnjəʊ'ʃɛntɪ, ˌkɒgnəʊ-) *or* **conoscenti** (ˌkɒnəʊ'ʃɛntɪ) *pl n, sing* **cognoscente** *or* **conoscente** (-ti:). (*sometimes sing*) people with informed appreciation of a particular field, esp. in the fine arts; connoisseurs. ORIG C18: from obs. It., from L *cognōscere* to learn

cogwheel ('kɒgˌwi:l) *n* another name for **gearwheel.**

cohab ('kəʊˌhæb) *n* a sexual partner with whom one lives but to whom one is not married. ORIG C20: a shortened form of *cohabitee;* see COHABIT

cohabit (kəʊ'hæbɪt) *vb* (*intr*) to live together as husband and wife, esp. without being married. ORIG C16: from L *co-* together + *habitāre* to live
▸ **ˌcohabi'tee, co'habitant,** *or* **co'habiter** *n*

cohabitation (kəʊˌhæbɪ'teɪʃən) *n* **1** the state or condition of living together as husband and wife without being married. **2** (of political parties) the state or condition of cooperating for specific purposes without forming a coalition.

coheir (kəʊ'ɛə) *n* a person who inherits jointly with others.
▸ **co'heiress** *fem n*

Cohen ★ ('kəʊən) *n* **1 Leonard.** born 1934, Canadian singer and songwriter. **2 Stanley.** born 1922, US biochemist: shared the Nobel prize for physiology or medicine 1986.

cohere (kəʊ'hɪə) *vb* **coheres, cohering, cohered.** (*intr*) **1** to hold or stick firmly together. **2** to be connected logically; be consistent. **3** *Physics.* to be held together by the action of molecular forces. ORIG C16: from L *co-* together + *haerēre* to cling

coherence (kəʊ'hɪərəns) *or* **coherency** *n* **1** logical or natural connection or consistency. **2** another word for **cohesion** (sense 1).

coherent (kəʊ'hɪərənt) *adj* **1** capable of intelligible speech. **2** logical; consistent and orderly. **3** cohering or sticking together. **4** *Physics.* (of two or more waves) having the same phase or a fixed phase difference: *coherent light.*
▸ **co'herently** *adv*

cohesion (kəʊ'hiːʒən) *n* **1** the act or state of cohering; tendency to unite. **2** *Physics.* the force that holds together the atoms or molecules in a solid or liquid, as distinguished from adhesion. **3** *Bot.* the fusion in some plants of flower parts, such as petals, that are usually separate. ORIG C17: from L *cohaesus,* p.p. of *cohaerēre* to COHERE
▸ **co'hesive** *adj*

coho ('kəʊhəʊ) *n, pl* **coho** *or* **cohos.** a Pacific salmon. Also called: **silver salmon.** ORIG from ?

cohort ('kəʊhɔːt) *n* **1** one of the ten units of an ancient Roman Legion. **2** any band of warriors or associates: *the cohorts of Satan.* **3** *Chiefly US.* an associate or follower. ORIG C15: from L *cohors* yard, company of soldiers

COHSE ('kəʊzɪ) *n* (formerly, in Britain) *acronym for* Confederation of Health Service Employees.

COI (in Britain) *abbrev. for* Central Office of Information.

coif (kɔɪf) *n* **1** a close-fitting cap worn under a veil in the Middle Ages. **2** a leather cap worn under a chain-mail hood. **3** (kwɑːf). a less common word for **coiffure** (sense 1). ◆ *vb* **coifs, coiffing, coiffed.** (*tr*) **4** to cover with or as if with a coif. **5** (kwɑːf). to arrange (the hair). ORIG C14: from OF *coiffe,* from LL *cofea* helmet, cap, from ?

coiffeur (kwɑː'fɜː) *n* a hairdresser.
▸ **coiffeuse** (kwɑː'fɜːz) *fem n*

coiffure (kwɑː'fjʊə) *n* **1** a hairstyle. **2** an obsolete word for **headdress.** ◆ *vb* **coiffures, coiffuring, coiffured. 3** (*tr*) to dress or arrange (the hair).

coign of vantage (kɔɪn) *n* an advantageous position for observation or action.

coil[1] (kɔɪl) *vb* **1** to wind or gather (ropes, hair, etc.) into loops or (of ropes, hair, etc.) to be formed in such loops. **2** (*intr*) to move in a winding course. ◆ *n* **3** something wound in a connected series of loops. **4** a single loop of such a series. **5** an arrangement of pipes in a spiral or loop, as in a condenser. **6** an electrical conductor wound into the form of a spiral, to provide inductance or a magnetic field. **7** an intrauterine contraceptive device in the shape of a coil. **8** the transformer in a petrol engine that supplies the high voltage to the sparking plugs. ORIG C16: from OF *coillir* to collect together; see CULL

coil[2] (kɔɪl) *n* the troubles of the world (in Shakespeare's phrase **this mortal coil**). ORIG C16: from ?

Coimbra ★ (*Portuguese* 'kuimbrə) *n* a city in central Portugal: capital of Portugal from 1190 to 1260; seat of the country's oldest university. Pop.: 96 140 (1991).

coin (kɔɪn) *n* **1** a metal disc or piece used as money. **2** metal currency, as opposed to paper currency, etc. **3** *Archit.* a variant spelling of **quoin. 4 pay (a person) back in (his** *or* **her) own coin.** to treat (a person) in the way that he or she has treated others. ◆ *vb* (*tr*) **5** to make or stamp (coins). **6** to make into a coin. **7** to fabricate or invent (words, etc.). **8** *Inf.* to make (money) rapidly (esp. in **coin it in**). ORIG C14: from OF: stamping die, from L *cuneus* wedge

coinage ('kɔɪnɪdʒ) *n* **1** coins collectively. **2** the act of striking coins. **3** the currency of a country. **4** the act of inventing something, esp. a word or phrase. **5** a newly invented word, phrase, usage, etc.

coincide (ˌkəʊɪn'saɪd) *vb* **coincides, coinciding, coincided.** (*intr*) **1** to occur or exist simultaneously. **2** to be identical in nature, character, etc. **3** to agree. ORIG C18: from Med. L, from L *co-* together + *incidere* to occur, befall, from *cadere* to fall

coincidence (kəʊ'ɪnsɪdəns) *n* **1** a chance occurrence of events remarkable either for being simultaneous or for apparently being connected. **2** the fact, condition, or state of coinciding. **3** (*modifier*) *Electronics.* of or relating to a circuit that produces an output pulse only when both its input terminals receive pulses within a specified interval: *coincidence gate.*

coincident (kəʊ'ɪnsɪdənt) *adj* **1** having the same position in space or time. **2** (usually *postpositive* and foll. by *with*) in exact agreement.

coincidental (kəʊˌɪnsɪ'dɛntᵊl) *adj* of or happening by a coincidence; fortuitous.
▸ **coˌinci'dentally** *adv*

coin-op ('kɔɪnˌɒp) *n* a launderette or other installation in which the machines are operated by the insertion of coins.
▸ **'coin-ˌoperˌated** *adj*

Cointreau ('kwɑːntrəʊ) *n Trademark.* a colourless liqueur with orange flavouring.

coir ('kɔɪə) *n* the fibre from the husk of the coconut, used in making rope and matting. ORIG C16: from Malayalam *kāyar* rope, from *kāyaru* to be twisted

Coire ★ (kwar) *n* the French name for **Chur.**

coitus ('kəʊɪtəs) *or* **coition** (kəʊ'ɪʃən) *n* a technical term for **sexual intercourse.** ORIG C18: from L, from *coīre* to meet, from *īre* to go
▸ **'coital** *adj*

coke[1] (kəʊk) *n* **1** a solid-fuel product produced by distillation of coal to drive off its volatile constituents: used as a fuel. **2** the layer formed in the cylinders of a car engine by incomplete combustion of the fuel. ◆ *vb* **cokes, coking, coked. 3** to become or convert into coke. ORIG C17: prob. var. of C14 N English dialect *colk* core, from ?

coke[2] (kəʊk) *n Sl.* short for **cocaine.**

Coke[1] (kəʊk) *n Trademark.* short for **Coca-Cola.**

Coke[2] ★ *n* **1** (kʊk, kəʊk). Sir **Edward.** 1552–1634, English jurist: the Petition of Right (1628) was largely his work. **2** (kʊk). **Thomas William,** 1st Earl of Leicester, known as *Coke of Holkham.* 1752–1842, British agriculturist.

col (kɒl) *n* **1** Also called: **saddle.** the lowest point of a ridge connecting two mountain peaks. **2** *Meteorol.* a low-pressure region between two anticyclones. ORIG C19: from F: neck, col, from L *collum* neck

Col. *abbrev. for:* **1** Colombia(n). **2** Colonel. **3** *Bible.* Colossians.

col- *prefix* a variant of **com-** before *l: collateral.*

cola *or* **kola** ('kəʊlə) *n* **1** either of two trees widely cultivated in tropical regions for their seeds (see **cola nut**). **2** a sweet carbonated drink flavoured with cola nuts. ORIG C18: from *kola,* prob. var. of W African *kolo* nut

colander ('kɒləndə, 'kʌl-) *or* **cullender** *n* a pan with a perforated bottom for straining or rinsing foods. ORIG C14 *colyndore,* prob. from OProvençal *colador,* from LL, from L *cōlum* sieve

cola nut *n* any of the seeds of the cola tree, which contain caffeine and theobromine and are used medicinally and in soft drinks.

Colbert ★ (*French* kɔlbɛr) *n* **1 Claudette** (klɔː'dɛt). real name *Lily Claudette Chauchoin.* 1903–96, US film actress, born in France. Her comedies include *It Happened One Night* (1934). **2 Jean Baptiste** (ʒɑ̃ batist). 1619–83, French statesman; chief minister to Louis XIV.

Colchester ★ ('kəʊltʃɪstə) *n* a town in E England, in NE Essex: seat of The University of Essex (1964). Pop.: 96 063 (1991). Latin name: **Camulodunum** (ˌkæmjʊləʊ'djuːnəm, ˌkæmʊləʊ'duːnəm).

colchicine ('kɒltʃɪˌsiːn, -sɪn, 'kɒlkɪ-) *n* a pale yellow crystalline alkaloid extracted from seeds or corms of the autumn crocus and used in the treatment of gout. ORIG C19: from COLCHICUM + -INE[2]

colchicum ('kɒltʃɪkəm, 'kɒlkɪ-) *n* **1** any Eurasian plant of the lily family, such as the autumn crocus. **2** the dried seeds or corms of the autumn crocus. ORIG C16: from L, from Gk, from *kolkhikos* of COLCHIS

Colchis ★ ('kɒlkɪs) *n* an ancient country on the Black Sea south of the Caucasus; the land of Medea and the Golden Fleece in Greek mythology.

cold (kəʊld) *adj* **1** having relatively little warmth; of a rather low temperature: *cold weather; cold hands.* **2** without proper warmth: *this meal is cold.* **3** lacking in affection or enthusiasm: *a cold manner.* **4** not affected by emotion: *cold logic.* **5** dead. **6** sexually unresponsive or frigid. **7** lacking in freshness: *a cold scent; cold news.* **8** chilling to the spirit; depressing. **9** (of a colour) having violet, blue, or green predominating; giving no sensation of warmth. **10** *Sl.* unconscious. **11** *Inf.* (of a seeker) far from the object of a search. **12** denoting the contacting of potential customers, voters, etc., without previously approaching them in order to establish their interest: *cold mailing.* **13 cold comfort.** little or no comfort. **14 leave (someone) cold.** *Inf.* to fail to excite: *the performance left me cold.* **15 throw cold water on.** *Inf.* to be unenthusiastic about or discourage. ◆ *n* **16** the absence of heat regarded as a positive force: *the cold took away our breath.* **17** the sensation caused by loss or lack of heat. **18 (out) in the cold.** *Inf.* neglected; ignored. **19** an acute viral infection of the upper respiratory passages characterized by discharge of watery mucus from the nose, sneezing, etc. **20 catch a cold.** *Inf.* to make a financial loss. ◆ *adv* **21** *Inf.* without preparation: *he played his part cold.* ORIG OE *ceald*
▸ **'coldish** *adj* ▸ **'coldly** *adv* ▸ **'coldness** *n*

cold-blooded *adj* **1** having or showing a lack of feeling or pity. **2** *Inf.* particularly sensitive to cold. **3** (of all animals except birds and mammals) having a body temperature that varies with that of the surroundings. Technical name: **poikilothermic.**
▸ **,cold-'bloodedly** *adv* ▸ **,cold-'bloodedness** *n*

cold cathode *n Electronics.* a cathode from which electrons are emitted at an ambient temperature.

cold chisel *n* a toughened steel chisel.

cold cream *n* an emulsion of water and fat used for softening and cleansing the skin.

cold cuts *pl n* cooked meats sliced and served cold.

cold feet *n Inf.* loss or lack of confidence.

cold frame *n* an unheated wooden frame with a glass top, used to protect young plants.

cold front *n Meteorol.* the boundary line between a warm air mass and the cold air pushing it from beneath and behind as it moves.

cold-hearted *adj* lacking in feeling or warmth; unkind.
▸ **,cold-'heartedly** *adv* ▸ **,cold-'heartedness** *n*

Colditz ★ ('kəʊldɪts) *n* a town in E Germany, on the River Mulde: during World War II its castle was used as a top-security camp for Allied prisoners of war; many daring escape attempts, some successful, were made.

cold-rolled *adj* (of metal sheets, etc.) having been rolled without heating, producing a smooth surface finish.

cold shoulder *Inf.* ◆ *n* **1** (often preceded by *the*) a show of indifference; a slight. ◆ *vb* **cold-shoulder.** *(tr)* **2** to treat with indifference.

cold sore *n* a cluster of blisters at the margin of the lips: a form of herpes simplex.

cold start *n Computing.* the reloading of a program or operating system.

cold storage *n* **1** the storage of things in an artificially cooled place for preservation. **2** *Inf.* a state of temporary suspension: *to put an idea into cold storage.*

Coldstream ★ ('kəʊld,striːm) *n* a town in SE Scotland, on the English border: the Coldstream Guards were formed here (1660). Pop.: 1746 (1991).

cold sweat *n Inf.* a bodily reaction to fear or nervousness, characterized by chill and moist skin.

cold turkey *n Sl.* **1** a method of curing drug addiction by abrupt withdrawal of all doses. **2** the withdrawal symptoms, esp. nausea and shivering, brought on by this method.

cold war *n* a state of political hostility and military tension between two countries or power blocs, involving propaganda, threats, etc., esp. that between the American and Soviet blocs after World War II (the **Cold War**).

cold wave *n* **1** *Meteorol.* a sudden spell of low temperatures over a wide area. **2** *Hairdressing.* a permanent wave made by chemical agents applied at normal temperatures.

cole (kəʊl) *n* any of various plants such as the cabbage and rape. Also called: **colewort.** ORIG OE *cāl,* from L *caulis* cabbage

Cole ★ (kəʊl) *n* **Nat 'King',** real name *Nathaniel Adams Cole.* 1917–65, US popular singer and jazz pianist.

Coleman ★ ('kəʊlmən) *n* **Ornette** (ɔː'nɛt). born 1930, US avant-garde jazz saxophonist.

coleopter (,kɒlɪ'ɒptə) *n Aeronautics.* an aircraft that has an annular wing with the fuselage and engine on the centre line.

coleopteran (,kɒlɪ'ɒptərən) *n also* **coleopteron. 1** any of the order of insects in which the forewings are modified to form shell-like protective elytra. It includes the beetles and weevils. ◆ *adj also* **coleopterous. 2** of, relating to, or belonging to this order. ORIG C18: from NL, from Gk, from *koleon* sheath + *pteron* wing

Coleraine ★ (kəʊl'reɪn) *n* **1** a town in N Northern Ireland, in Co. Antrim, on the River Bann: light industries; site of the New University of Ulster (1965). Pop.: 20 721 (1991). **2** a district of N Northern Ireland, on the Atlantic Ocean: agriculture, tourism. Administrative centre: Coleraine. Area: 490 sq. km (189 sq. miles). Pop.: 50 438 (1991).

Coleridge ★ ('kəʊlərɪdʒ) *n* **Samuel Taylor.** 1772–1834, British poet, noted for *The Rime of the Ancient Mariner* (1798), *Kubla Khan* (1816), and *Christabel* (1816).

Coleridge-Taylor ★ (,kəʊlərɪdʒ'teɪlə) *n* **Samuel.** 1875–1912, British composer, best known for his oratorios *Song of Hiawatha* (1898–1900).

coleslaw ('kəʊl,slɔː) *n* a salad of shredded cabbage, mayonnaise, carrots, onions, etc. ORIG C19: from Du. *koolsla,* from *koolsalade,* lit.: cabbage salad

colestipol (kə'lɛstɪ,pɒl) *n* a drug that reduces the level of cholesterol in the blood: used to prevent atherosclerosis.

Colet ★ ('kɒlɪt) *n* **John.** ?1467–1519, English humanist and theologian; founder of St Paul's School, London (1509).

coletit ('kəʊltɪt) *n* another name for **coal tit.**

Colette ★ (kɒ'lɛt) *n* full name *Sidonie Gabrielle Claudine Colette.* 1873–1954, French novelist; her works include *Chéri* (1920), *Gigi* (1944), and the series of *Claudine* books.

coleus ('kəʊlɪəs) *n, pl* **coleuses.** any plant of the Old World genus *Coleus:* cultivated for their variegated leaves. ORIG C19: from NL, from Gk, var. of *koleon* sheath

coley ('kəʊlɪ, 'kɒlɪ) *n Brit.* any of various edible fishes, esp. the coalfish.

colic ('kɒlɪk) *n* a condition characterized by acute spasmodic abdominal pain, esp. that caused by inflammation, distention, etc., of the gastrointestinal tract. ORIG C15: from OF, from LL, from Gk *kōlon,* var. of *kolon* COLON[2]
▸ **'colicky** *adj*

coliform bacteria ('kɒlɪfɔːm) *pl n* a large group of bacteria that inhabit the intestinal tract of man.

Coligny *or* **Coligni** ★ (*French* kɔliɲi) *n* **Gaspard de** (gaspar də), Seigneur de Châtillon. 1519–72, French Huguenot leader.

Colima ★ (*Spanish* ko'lima) *n* **1** a state of SW Mexico, on the Pacific coast: mainly a coastal plain, rising to the foothills of the Sierra Madre, with important mineral resources. Capital: Colima. Pop.: 515 313 (1997 est.). Area: 5455 sq. km (2106 sq. miles). **2** a city in SW Mexico, capital of Colima state, on the Colima River. Pop.: 106 967 (1990). **3 Nevado de.** a volcano in SW Mexico, in Jalisco state. Height: 4339 m (14 235 ft).

coliseum (,kɒlɪ'sɪəm) *or* **colosseum** (,kɒlə'sɪəm) *n* a large building, such as a stadium, used for entertainments, sports, etc. ORIG C18: from Med. L, var. of COLOSSEUM

colitis (kɒˈlaɪtɪs) *n* inflammation of the colon.

collaborate (kəˈlæbəˌreɪt) *vb* **collaborates, collaborating, collaborated.** (*intr*) **1** (often foll. by *on, with,* etc.) to work with another or others on a joint project. **2** to cooperate as a traitor, esp. with an enemy occupying one's own country. ORIG C19: from LL, from L *com-* together + *labōrāre* to work
▸ **colˌlaboˈration** *n* ▸ **colˈlaborative** *adj* ▸ **colˈlaboˌrator** *n*

collage (kəˈlɑːʒ, kɒ-) *n* **1** an art form in which compositions are made out of pieces of paper, cloth, photographs, etc., pasted on a dry ground. **2** a composition made in this way. **3** any work, such as a piece of music, created by combining unrelated styles. ORIG C20: F, from *colle* glue, from Gk *kolla*
▸ **colˈlagist** *n*

collagen (ˈkɒlədʒən) *n* a fibrous protein of connective tissue and bones that yields gelatine on boiling. ORIG C19: from Gk *kolla* glue + -GEN

collapsar (kɒˈlæpsɑː) *n Astron.* another name for **black hole.**

collapse (kəˈlæps) *vb* **collapses, collapsing, collapsed. 1** (*intr*) to fall down or cave in suddenly: *the whole building collapsed.* **2** (*intr*) to fail completely. **3** (*intr*) to break down or fall down from lack of strength. **4** to fold (furniture, etc.) compactly or (of furniture, etc.) to be designed to fold compactly. ◆ *n* **5** the act or instance of suddenly falling down, caving in, or crumbling. **6** a sudden failure or breakdown. ORIG C18: from L, from *collābī* to fall in ruins, from *lābī* to fall
▸ **colˈlapsible** *or* **colˈlapsable** *adj* ▸ **colˌlapsiˈbility** *n*

collar (ˈkɒlə) *n* **1** the part of a garment around the neck and shoulders, often detachable or folded over. **2** any band, necklace, garland, etc., encircling the neck. **3** a band or chain of leather, rope, or metal placed around an animal's neck. **4** *Biol.* a marking resembling a collar, such as that found around the necks of some birds. **5** a section of a shaft or rod having a locally increased diameter to provide a bearing seat or a locating ring. **6** a cut of meat, esp. bacon, taken from around the neck of an animal. ◆ *vb* (*tr*) **7** to put a collar on; furnish with a collar. **8** to seize by the collar. **9** *Inf.* to seize; arrest; detain. ORIG C13: from L *collāre* neckband, from *collum* neck

collarbone (ˈkɒləˌbəʊn) *n* the nontechnical name for **clavicle.**

collard (ˈkɒləd) *n* a variety of the cabbage, having a crown of edible leaves. See also **kale.** ORIG C18: var. of *colewort,* from COLE + WORT

collate (kɒˈleɪt, kə-) *vb* **collates, collating, collated.** (*tr*) **1** to examine and compare (texts, statements, etc.) in order to note points of agreement and disagreement. **2** to check the number and order of (the pages of a book). **3** *Bookbinding.* **3a** to check the sequence of (the sections of a book) after gathering. **3b** a nontechnical word for **gather** (sense 8). **4** (often foll. by *to*) *Christianity.* to appoint (an incumbent) to a benefice. ORIG C16: from L, from *com-* together + *lātus,* p.p. of *ferre* to bring
▸ **colˈlator** *n*

collateral (kɒˈlætərəl, kə-) *n* **1a** security pledged for the repayment of a loan. **1b** (*as modifier*): *a collateral loan.* **2** a person, animal, or plant descended from the same ancestor as another but through a different line. ◆ *adj* **3** situated or running side by side. **4** descended from a common ancestor but through different lines. **5** serving to support or corroborate. ORIG C14: from Med. L, from L *com-* together + *laterālis* of the side, from *latus* side
▸ **colˈlaterally** *adv*

collateral damage *n Mil.* unintentional damage to civil property and civilian casualties, caused by military operations.

collation (kɒˈleɪʃən, kə-) *n* **1** the act or process of collating. **2** a description of the technical features of a book. **3** *RC Church.* a light meal permitted on fast days. **4** any light informal meal.

colleague (ˈkɒliːg) *n* a fellow worker or member of a staff, department, profession, etc. ORIG C16: from F, from L *collēga,* from *com-* together + *lēgāre* to choose

collect[1] (kəˈlɛkt) *vb* **1** to gather together or be gathered together. **2** to accumulate (stamps, books, etc.) as a hobby or for study. **3** (*tr*) to call for or receive payment of (taxes, dues, etc.). **4** (*tr*) to regain control of (oneself, one's emotions, etc.) as after a shock or surprise: *he collected his wits.* **5** (*tr*) to fetch: *collect your own post.* **6** (*intr;* sometimes foll. by *on*) *Sl.* to receive large sums of money. **7** (*tr*) *Austral. & NZ inf.* to collide with; be hit by. ◆ *adv, adj* **8** *US.* (of telephone calls, etc.) on a reverse-charge basis. ORIG C16: from L, from *com-* together + *legere* to gather

collect[2] (ˈkɒlɛkt) *n Christianity.* a short Church prayer in Communion and other services. ORIG C13: from Med. L *collecta* (from *ōrātiō ad collēctam* prayer at the assembly), from L *colligere* to COLLECT[1]

collectable *or* **collectible** (kəˈlɛktəbᵊl) *adj* **1** (of antiques) of interest to a collector. ◆ *n* **2** (*often pl*) any object regarded as being of interest to a collector.

collected (kəˈlɛktɪd) *adj* **1** in full control of one's faculties; composed. **2** assembled in totality or brought together into one volume or a set of volumes: *the collected works of Dickens.*
▸ **colˈlectedly** *adv* ▸ **colˈlectedness** *n*

collection (kəˈlɛkʃən) *n* **1** the act or process of collecting. **2** a number of things collected or assembled together. **3** something gathered into a mass or pile; accumulation: *a collection of rubbish.* **4** a sum of money collected or solicited, as in church. **5** removal, esp. regular removal of letters from a postbox. **6** (*often pl*) (at Oxford University) a college examination or an oral report by a tutor.

collective (kəˈlɛktɪv) *adj* **1** formed or assembled by collection. **2** forming a whole or aggregate. **3** of, done by, or characteristic of individuals acting in cooperation. ◆ *n* **4a** a cooperative enterprise or unit, such as a collective farm. **4b** the members of such a cooperative. **5** short for **collective noun.**
▸ **colˈlectively** *adv* ▸ **colˈlectiveness** *n* ▸ **ˌcollecˈtivity** *n*

collective bargaining *n* negotiation between a trade union and an employer or an employers' organization on the incomes and working conditions of the employees.

collective noun *n* a noun that is singular in form but that refers to a group of people or things.

> **USAGE NOTE** Collective nouns are often used with singular verbs: *the family is on holiday; General Motors is mounting a big sales campaign.* In British usage, however, plural verbs are often employed in this context, especially where reference is being made to a collection of individual objects or people rather than to the group as a unit: *the family are all on holiday.* Care should be taken that the same collective noun is not treated as both singular and plural in the same sentence: *the family is well and sends its best wishes* or *the family are all well and send their best wishes,* but not *the family is well and send their best wishes.*

collective ownership *n* ownership by a group for the benefit of members of that group.

collective unconscious *n* (in Jungian psychological theory) a part of the unconscious mind incorporating patterns of memories, instincts, and experiences common to all mankind.

collectivism (kəˈlɛktɪˌvɪzəm) *n* the principle of ownership of the means of production by the state or the people.
▸ **colˈlectivist** *n* ▸ **colˌlectivˈistic** *adj*

collectivize *or* **collectivise** (kəˈlɛktɪˌvaɪz) *vb* **collectivizes, collectivizing, collectivized** *or* **collectivises, collectivising, collectivised.** (*tr*) to organize according to the principles of collectivism.
▸ **colˌlectiviˈzation** *or* **colˌlectiviˈsation** *n*

collector (kəˈlɛktə) *n* **1** a person or thing that collects. **2** a person employed to collect debts, rents, etc. **3** a person who collects objects as a hobby. **4** (in India, formerly) the head of a district administration. **5** *Electronics.* the region in a transistor into which charge carriers flow from the base.

colleen ('kɒli:n, kɒ'li:n) *n* an Irish word for **girl**. ORIG C19: from Irish Gaelic *cailín*

college ('kɒlɪdʒ) *n* **1** an institution of higher education; part of a university. **2** a school or an institution providing specialized courses: *a college of music.* **3** the buildings in which a college is housed. **4** the staff and students of a college. **5** an organized body of persons with specific rights and duties: *an electoral college.* **6** a body organized within a particular profession, concerned with regulating standards. **7** *Brit.* a name given to some secondary schools. ORIG C14: from L, from *collēga;* see COLLEAGUE

College of Cardinals *n RC Church.* the collective body of cardinals having the function of electing and advising the pope.

college of education *n Brit.* a professional training college for teachers.

collegian (kə'li:dʒɪən) *n* a member of a college.

collegiate (kə'li:dʒɪɪt) *adj* **1** Also: **col'legial.** of or relating to a college or college students. **2** (of a university) composed of various colleges of equal standing.

collegiate church *n* **1** *RC Church, Church of England.* a church that has an endowed chapter of canons and prebendaries attached to it but that is not a cathedral. **2** *US Protestantism.* one of a group of churches presided over by a body of pastors. **3** *Scot. Protestantism.* a church served by two or more ministers.

collegiate institute *n Canad.* (in certain provinces) a large secondary school meeting set requirements in terms of courses, facilities, and specialist staff.

col legno ('kɒl 'lɛgnəʊ, 'leɪnjəʊ) *adv Music.* to be played (on a stringed instrument) with the back of the bow. ORIG It.: with the wood

Colles' fracture ('kɒlɪs) *n* a fracture of the radius just above the wrist with backward and outward displacement of the hand. ORIG C19: after Abraham *Colles* (d. 1843), Irish surgeon

collet ('kɒlɪt) *n* **1** (in a jewellery setting) a band or coronet-shaped claw that holds an individual stone. **2** *Mechanical engineering.* an externally tapered sleeve made in two or more segments and used to grip a shaft passed through its centre. **3** *Horology.* a small metal collar that supports the inner end of the hairspring. ORIG C16: from OF: a little collar, from *col,* from L *collum* neck

collide (kə'laɪd) *vb* **collides, colliding, collided.** (*intr*) **1** to crash together with a violent impact. **2** to conflict; clash; disagree. ORIG C17: from L, from *com-* together + *laedere* to strike

collider (kə'laɪdə) *n Physics.* a particle accelerator in which beams of particles are made to collide.

collie ('kɒlɪ) *n* any of several silky-coated breeds of dog developed for herding sheep and cattle. ORIG C17: Scot., prob. from earlier *colie* black from *cole* coal

collier ('kɒlɪə) *n Chiefly Brit.* **1** a coal miner. **2a** a ship designed to transport coal. **2b** a member of its crew. ORIG C14: from COAL + -IER

colliery ('kɒljərɪ) *n, pl* **collieries.** *Chiefly Brit.* a coal mine.

collimate ('kɒlɪˌmeɪt) *vb* **collimates, collimating, collimated.** (*tr*) **1** to adjust the line of sight of (an optical instrument). **2** to use a collimator on (a beam of radiation). **3** to make parallel or bring into line. ORIG C17: from NL *collimāre,* erroneously for L *collīneāre* to aim, from *com-* (intensive) + *līneāre,* from *līnea* line
► ˌ**colli'mation** *n*

collimator ('kɒlɪˌmeɪtə) *n* **1** a small telescope attached to a larger optical instrument as an aid in fixing its line of sight. **2** an optical system of lenses and slits producing a nondivergent beam of light. **3** any device for limiting the size and angle of spread of a beam of radiation or particles.

collinear (kɒ'lɪnɪə) *adj* lying on the same straight line.
► **collinearity** (ˌkɒlɪnɪ'ærɪtɪ) *n*

collins ('kɒlɪnz) *n* (*functioning as sing*) an iced drink made with gin, vodka, rum, etc., mixed with fruit juice, soda water, and sugar. ORIG C20: prob. from the name *Collins*

Collins ★ ('kɒlɪnz) *n* **1 Michael.** 1890–1922, Irish republican revolutionary: a leader of Sinn Féin. **2** (**William**) **Wilkie.** 1824–89, British author, noted particularly for his suspense novel *The Moonstone* (1868). **3 William.** 1721–59, British poet.

collision (kə'lɪʒən) *n* **1** a violent impact of moving objects; crash. **2** the conflict of opposed ideas, wishes, attitudes, etc. ORIG C15: from LL, from L *collīdere* to COLLIDE

collocate ('kɒləˌkeɪt) *vb* **collocates, collocating, collocated.** (*tr*) to group or place together in some system or order. ORIG C16: from L, from *com-* together + *locāre* to place
► ˌ**collo'cation** *n*

collocutor ('kɒləˌkju:tə) *n* a person who talks or engages in conversation with another.

collodion (kə'ləʊdɪən) *or* **collodium** (kə'ləʊdɪəm) *n* a syrupy liquid that consists of a solution of pyroxylin in ether and alcohol: used in medicine and in the manufacture of photographic plates, lacquers, etc. ORIG C19: from NL, from Gk *kollōdēs* glutinous, from *kolla* glue

collogue (kɒ'ləʊg) *vb* **collogues, colloguing, collogued.** (*intr;* usually foll. by *with*) to confer confidentially; conspire. ORIG C16: ?from obs. *colleague* (vb) to conspire, infl. by L *colloquī* to talk with

colloid ('kɒlɔɪd) *n* **1** a mixture having particles of one component suspended in a continuous phase of another component. The mixture has properties between those of a solution and a fine suspension. **2** *Physiol.* a gelatinous substance of the thyroid follicles that holds the hormonal secretions of the thyroid gland. ORIG C19: from Gk *kolla* glue + -OID
► **col'loidal** *adj*

collop ('kɒləp) *n Dialect.* **1** a slice of meat. **2** a small piece of anything. ORIG C14: of Scand. origin

colloq. *abbrev. for* colloquial(ly).

colloquial (kə'ləʊkwɪəl) *adj* **1** of or relating to conversation. **2** denoting or characterized by informal or conversational idiom or vocabulary.
► **col'loquially** *adv* ► **col'loquialness** *n*

colloquialism (kə'ləʊkwɪəˌlɪzəm) *n* **1** a word or phrase appropriate to conversation and other informal situations. **2** the use of colloquial words and phrases.

colloquium (kə'ləʊkwɪəm) *n, pl* **colloquiums** *or* **colloquia** (-kwɪə). **1** a gathering for discussion. **2** an academic seminar. ORIG C17: from L: COLLOQUY

colloquy ('kɒləkwɪ) *n, pl* **colloquies. 1** a formal conversation or conference. **2** an informal conference on religious or theological matters. ORIG C16: from L *colloquium,* from *com-* together + *loquī* to speak
► **'colloquist** *n*

collotype ('kɒləʊˌtaɪp) *n* **1** a method of lithographic printing (usually of high-quality reproductions) from a plate of hardened gelatine. **2** a print so made.

collude (kə'lu:d) *vb* **colludes, colluding, colluded.** (*intr*) to conspire together, esp. in planning a fraud. ORIG C16: from L, from *com-* together + *lūdere* to play
► **col'luder** *n*

collusion (kə'lu:ʒən) *n* **1** secret agreement for a fraudulent purpose; conspiracy. **2** a secret agreement between opponents at law for some improper purpose. ORIG C14: from L, from *collūdere* to COLLUDE
► **col'lusive** *adj*

collywobbles ('kɒlɪˌwɒbᵊlz) *pl n* (usually preceded by *the*) *Sl.* **1** an upset stomach. **2** an intense feeling of nervousness. ORIG C19: prob. from NL *cholera morbus,* infl. through folk etymology by COLIC and WOBBLE

Colmar ★ (*French* kɔlmar) *n* a city in NE France: annexed to Germany 1871–1919 and 1940–45; textile industry. Pop.: 63 498 (1990). German name: **Kolmar.**

Colo. *abbrev. for* Colorado.

colobus ('kɒləbəs) *n* any leaf-eating arboreal Old World monkey of W and central Africa, having long silky fur and reduced or absent thumbs. ORIG C19: NL, from Gk *kolobos* cut short; referring to its thumb

cologarithm (kəʊ'lɒgəˌrɪðəm) *n* the logarithm of the reciprocal of a number; the negative value of the logarithm: *the cologarithm of 4 is log ¼.* Abbrev.: **colog.**

cologne (kə'ləʊn) *n* a perfumed liquid or solid made of fragrant essential oils and alcohol. Also called: **Cologne**

water, eau de cologne. ORIG C18: *Cologne water* from COLOGNE, where it was first manufactured (1709)

Cologne ★ (kə'ləʊn) *n* an industrial city and river port in W Germany, in North Rhine-Westphalia on the Rhine: important commercially since ancient times; university (1388). Pop.: 965 697 (1996 est.). German name: **Köln.**

Colomb-Béchar ★ (*French* kɔlɔ̃beʃar) *n* the former name of **Béchar.**

Colombes ★ (*French* kɔlɔ̃b) *n* an industrial and residential suburb of NW Paris, in France. Pop.: 79 060 (1990).

Colombia ★ (kə'lɒmbɪə) *n* a republic in NW South America: inhabited by Chibchas and other Indians before Spanish colonization in the 16th century; independence won by Bolívar in 1819; became the Republic of Colombia in 1886. It consists chiefly of a hot swampy coastal plain, separated by ranges of the Andes from the pampas and the equatorial forests of the Amazon basin in the east. Language: Spanish. Religion: Roman Catholic majority. Currency: peso. Capital: Bogotá. Pop.: 38 297 000 (1999 est.). Area: 1 138 908 sq. km (439 735 sq. miles).
▸ **Co'lombian** *adj, n*

Colombo ★ (kə'lʌmbəʊ) *n* the capital and chief port of Sri Lanka, on the W coast, with one of the largest artificial harbours in the world. Pop.: 615 000 (1990 est.).

colon[1] ('kəʊlən) *n, pl* **colons. 1** the punctuation mark :, usually preceding an explanation or an example, a list, or an extended quotation. **2** this mark used for certain other purposes, such as when a ratio is given in figures, as in *5:3*. ORIG C16: from L, from Gk *kōlon* limb, clause

colon[2] ('kəʊlən) *n, pl* **colons** *or* **cola** (-lə). the part of the large intestine between the caecum and the rectum. ORIG C16: from L: large intestine, from Gk *kolon*
▸ **colonic** (kə'lɒnɪk) *adj*

colón (kəʊ'ləʊn; *Spanish* ko'lon) *n, pl* **colons** *or* **colones** (*Spanish* -'lones). **1** the standard monetary unit of Costa Rica, divided into 100 céntimos. **2** the standard monetary unit of El Salvador, divided into 100 centavos. ORIG C19: American Sp., from Sp., after Cristóbal *Colón* Christopher Columbus

Colón ★ (kɒ'lɒn; *Spanish* ko'lɔn) *n* **1** a port in Panama, at the Caribbean entrance to the Panama Canal. Chief Caribbean port. Pop.: 137 825 (1992 est.). **2 Archipiélago de** (ˌartʃi'pjelaɣo ðe). the official name of the **Galápagos Islands.**

colonel ('kɜːnᵊl) *n* an officer of land or air forces junior to a brigadier but senior to a lieutenant colonel. ORIG C16: via OF, from OIt. *colonnello* column of soldiers, from *colonna* COLUMN
▸ **'colonelcy** *or* **'colonelship** *n*

colonial (kə'ləʊnɪəl) *adj* **1** of, characteristic of, relating to, possessing, or inhabiting a colony or colonies. **2** (*often cap.*) characteristic of or relating to the 13 British colonies that became the United States of America (1776). **3** (*often cap.*) of or relating to the colonies of the British Empire. **4** denoting or having the style of Neoclassical architecture used in the British colonies in America in the 17th and 18th centuries. **5** of or relating to the period of Australian history before federation (1901). **6** (of animals and plants) having become established in a community in a new environment. ◆ *n* **7** a native of a colony.
▸ **co'lonially** *adv*

colonial goose *n NZ.* an old-fashioned name for stuffed roast mutton.

colonialism (kə'ləʊnɪəˌlɪzəm) *n* the policy and practice of a power in extending control over weaker peoples or areas. Also called: **imperialism.**
▸ **co'lonialist** *n, adj*

Colonies ('kɒlənɪz) *pl n* **the. 1** *Brit.* the subject territories formerly in the British Empire. **2** *US history.* the 13 states forming the original United States of America when they declared their independence (1776).

colonist ('kɒlənɪst) *n* **1** a person who settles or colonizes an area. **2** an inhabitant of a colony.

colonize *or* **colonise** ('kɒləˌnaɪz) *vb* **colonizes, colonizing, colonized** *or* **colonises, colonising, colonised. 1** to send colonists to or establish a colony in (an area). **2** to settle in (an area) as colonists. **3** (*tr*) to transform (a community, etc.) into a colony. **4** (of plants and animals) to become established in (a new environment).
▸ **ˌcoloni'zation** *or* **ˌcoloni'sation** *n* ▸ **'coloˌnizer** *or* **'coloˌniser** *n*

colonnade (ˌkɒlə'neɪd) *n* **1** a set of evenly spaced columns. **2** a row of regularly spaced trees. ORIG C18: from F, from *colonne* COLUMN; on the model of It. *colonnato*
▸ **ˌcolon'naded** *adj*

Colonsay ★ ('kɒlənseɪ, -zeɪ) *n* an island in W Scotland, in the Inner Hebrides. Area: about 41 sq. km (16 sq. miles).

colony ('kɒlənɪ) *n, pl* **colonies. 1** a body of people who settle in a country distant from their homeland but maintain ties with it. **2** the community formed by such settlers. **3** a subject territory occupied by a settlement from the ruling state. **4a** a community of people who form a national, racial, or cultural minority concentrated in a particular place: *an artists' colony*. **4b** the area itself. **5** *Zool.* a group of the same type of animal or plant living or growing together. **6** *Bacteriol.* a group of bacteria, fungi, etc., derived from one or a few spores, esp. when grown on a culture medium. ORIG C16: from L, from *colere* to cultivate, inhabit

colony-stimulating factor *n Immunol.* any of a number of substances, secreted by the bone marrow, that stimulate the formation of blood cells. Synthetic forms are being tested for their ability to reduce the toxic effects of chemotherapy. Abbrev.: **CSF.**

colophon ('kɒləˌfɒn, -fən) *n* **1** a publisher's emblem on a book. **2** (formerly) an inscription at the end of a book showing the title, printer, date, etc. ORIG C17: via LL, from Gk *kolophōn* a finishing stroke

colophony (kɒ'lɒfənɪ) *n* another name for **rosin** (sense 1). ORIG C14: from L: resin from Colophon, town in Lydia

color ('kʌlə) *n, vb* the US spelling of **colour.**

Colorado ★ (ˌkɒlə'rɑːdəʊ) *n* **1** a state of the central US: consists of the Great Plains in the east and the Rockies in the west; drained chiefly by the Colorado, Arkansas, South Platte, and Rio Grande Rivers. Capital: Denver. Pop.: 3 970 971 (1998 est.). Area: 269 998 sq. km (104 247 sq. miles). Abbrevs.: **Colo.** or (with zip code) **CO 2** a river in SW North America, rising in the Rocky Mountains and flowing southwest to the Gulf of California: famous for the 1600 km (1000 miles) of canyons along its course. Length: about 2320 km (1440 miles). **3** a river in central Texas, flowing southeast to the Gulf of Mexico. Length: about 1450 km (900 miles). **4** a river in central Argentina, flowing southeast to the Atlantic. Length: about 850 km (530 miles). ORIG Sp., lit.: red, from L *colōrātus* coloured, tinted red; see COLOUR

Colorado beetle *n* a black-and-yellow beetle that is a serious pest of potatoes, feeding on the leaves.

Colorado Desert ★ *n* an arid region of SE California and NW Mexico, West of the Colorado River. Area: over 5000 sq. km (2000 sq. miles).

Colorado Springs ★ *n* a city and resort in central Colorado. Pop.: 316 480 (1994 est.).

colorant ('kʌlərənt) *n* any substance that imparts colour, such as a pigment, dye, or ink.

coloration *or* **colouration** (ˌkʌlə'reɪʃən) *n* **1** arrangement of colour; colouring. **2** the colouring or markings of insects, birds, etc.

coloratura (ˌkɒlərə'tʊərə) *n Music.* **1** (in 18th- and 19th-century arias) a florid virtuoso passage. **2** Also called: **coloratura soprano.** a soprano who specializes in such music. ORIG C19: from obs. It., lit.: colouring.

colorific (ˌkʌlə'rɪfɪk) *adj* producing, imparting, or relating to colour.

colorimeter (ˌkʌlə'rɪmɪtə) *n* apparatus for measuring the quality of a colour by comparison with standard colours or combinations of colours.
▸ **colorimetric** (ˌkʌlərɪ'mɛtrɪk) *adj* ▸ **ˌcolor'imetry** *n*

colossal (kə'lɒsᵊl) *adj* **1** of immense size; huge; gigantic. **2** (in figure sculpture) approximately twice life-size. **3**

Archit. of the order of columns that extend more than one storey in a façade.
▸ **co'lossally** *adv*

Colosseum ★ (ˌkɒlə'sɪəm) *n* an amphitheatre in Rome built about 75–80 A.D.

colossus (kə'lɒsəs) *n, pl* **colossi** (-saɪ) *or* **colossuses.** something very large, esp. a statue. ORIG C14: from L, from Gk *kolossos*

Colossus of Rhodes *n* a giant bronze statue of Apollo built on Rhodes in about 292–280 B.C.; destroyed by an earthquake in 225 B.C.; one of the Seven Wonders of the World.

colostomy (kə'lɒstəmɪ) *n, pl* **colostomies.** the surgical formation of an opening from the colon onto the surface of the body, which functions as an anus.

colostrum (kə'lɒstrəm) *n* the thin milky secretion from the nipples that precedes and follows true lactation. ORIG C16: from L, from ?

colotomy (kə'lɒtəmɪ) *n, pl* **colotomies.** a colonic incision. ORIG C19: COLON[2] + -TOMY

colour *or US* **color** ('kʌlə) *n* **1a** an attribute of things that results from the light they reflect or emit in so far as this causes a visual sensation that depends on its wavelengths. **1b** the aspect of visual perception by which an observer recognizes this attribute. **1c** the quality of the light producing this visual perception. **2** Also called: **chromatic colour. 2a** a colour, such as red or green, that possesses hue, as opposed to achromatic colours such as white or black. **2b** (*as modifier*): *colour television.* **3** a substance, such as a dye or paint, that imparts colour. **4a** the skin complexion of a person, esp. as determined by race. **4b** (*as modifier*): *colour prejudice.* **5** the use of all the hues in painting as distinct from composition, form, and light and shade. **6** the quantity and quality of ink used in a printing process. **7** the distinctive tone of a musical sound. **8** vividness or authenticity: *period colour.* **9** semblance or pretext: *under colour of.* **10** *Physics.* one of three characteristics of quarks, designated red, blue, or green, but having only a remote formal relationship with the physical sensation. ◆ *vb* **11** (*tr*) to apply colour to (something). **12** (*tr*) to give a convincing appearance to: *to colour an alibi.* **13** (*tr*) to influence or distort: *anger coloured her judgment.* **14** (*intr;* often foll. by *up*) to become red in the face, esp. when embarrassed or annoyed. ◆ See also **colours.** ORIG C13 from OF *colour* from L *color* tint, hue

colourable ('kʌlərəbᵊl) *adj* **1** capable of being coloured. **2** appearing to be true; plausible. **3** pretended; feigned.

colour bar *n* discrimination against people of a different race, esp. as practised by Whites against Blacks.

colour-blind *adj* of or relating to any defect in the normal ability to distinguish certain colours.
▸ **colour blindness** *n*

colour code *n* a system of easily distinguishable colours, as for the identification of electrical wires or resistors.

coloured ('kʌləd) *adj* **1** possessing colour. **2** having a strong element of fiction or fantasy; distorted (esp. in **highly coloured**).

Coloured ('kʌləd) *n* **1** an individual who is not a White person, esp. a Black person. **2** Also called: **Cape Coloured.** (in South Africa) a person of racially mixed parentage or descent. ◆ *adj* **3a** (in South Africa) designating or relating to a person or people of racially mixed descent. **3b** designating or relating to a person or people who are not White.

> **USAGE NOTE** The use of *Coloured* to refer to people is now generally considered to be offensive.

colourfast ('kʌləˌfɑːst) *adj* (of a fabric) having a colour that does not run or change when washed or worn.
▸ **'colourˌfastness** *n*

colourful ('kʌləfʊl) *adj* **1** having intense colour or richly varied colours. **2** vivid, rich, or distinctive in character.
▸ **'colourfully** *adv*

colour guard *n* a military guard in a parade, ceremony, etc., that carries and escorts the flag.

colouring ('kʌlərɪŋ) *n* **1** the process or art of applying colour. **2** anything used to give colour, such as paint. **3** appearance with regard to shade and colour. **4** arrangements of colours, as in the markings of birds. **5** the colour of a person's complexion. **6** a false or misleading appearance.

colourist ('kʌlərɪst) *n* a person who uses colour, esp. an artist.

colourize, colourise, *or US* **colorize** ('kʌləˌraɪz) *vb* **colourizes, colourizing, colourized** *or* **colourises, colourising, colourised** *or US* **colorizes, colorizing, colorized.** (*tr*) to add colour electronically to (an old black-and-white film).
▸ **ˌcolouri'zation, ˌcolouri'sation** *or US* **ˌcolori'zation** *n*

colourless ('kʌləlɪs) *adj* **1** without colour. **2** lacking in interest: *a colourless individual.* **3** grey or pallid in tone or hue. **4** without prejudice; neutral.
▸ **'colourlessly** *adv*

colours ('kʌləz) *pl n* **1a** the flag that indicates nationality. **1b** *Mil.* the ceremony of hoisting or lowering the colours. **2** a pair of silk flags borne by a military unit and showing its crest and battle honours. **3** true nature or character (esp. in **show one's colours**). **4** a distinguishing badge or flag. **5** *Sport, Brit.* a badge or other symbol denoting membership of a team, esp. at a school or college. **6 nail one's colours to the mast. 6a** to commit oneself publicly and irrevocably to some party, course of action, etc. **6b** to refuse to admit defeat.

colour sergeant *n* a sergeant who carries the regimental, battalion, or national colours.

colour supplement *n Brit.* an illustrated magazine accompanying a newspaper.

colourway ('kʌləˌweɪ) *n* one of several different combinations of colours in which a given pattern is printed on fabrics or wallpapers, etc.

colposcope ('kɒlpəˌskəʊp) *n* an instrument for examining the cervix. ORIG C20: from Gk *kolpos* womb + -SCOPE
▸ **colposcopy** (kɒl'pɒskəpɪ) *n*

colt (kəʊlt) *n* **1** a male horse or pony under the age of four. **2** *Sport.* **2a** a young and inexperienced player. **2b** a member of a junior team. ORIG OE *colt* young ass

colter ('kəʊltə) *n* a variant spelling (esp. US) of **coulter.**

coltish ('kəʊltɪʃ) *adj* **1** inexperienced; unruly. **2** playful and lively.
▸ **'coltishness** *n*

Coltrane ★ (kɒl'treɪn) *n* **John (William).** 1926–67, US jazz saxophonist and composer.

coltsfoot ('kəʊltsˌfʊt) *n, pl* **coltsfoots.** a European plant with yellow daisy-like flowers and heart-shaped leaves: a common weed.

colubrine ('kɒljʊˌbraɪn) *adj* **1** of or resembling a snake. **2** of or belonging to the Colubrinae, a subfamily of harmless snakes. ORIG C16: from L *colubrīnus,* from *coluber* snake

Colum ★ ('kɒləm) *n* **Padraic** ('pɑːdrɪk). 1881–1972, Irish lyric poet, resident in the US (1914–72).

Columba ★ (kə'lʌmbə) *n* **Saint.** ?521–597 A.D., Irish missionary: founded the monastery at Iona (563) from which the Picts were converted to Christianity. Feast day: June 9.

Columbia ★ (kə'lʌmbɪə) *n* **1** a river in NW North America, rising in the Rocky Mountains and flowing through British Columbia, then west to the Pacific. Length: about 1930 km (1200 miles). **2** a city in central South Carolina, on the Congaree River: the state capital. Pop.: 104 101 (1994 est.).

columbine ('kɒləmˌbaɪn) *n* any plant of the genus *Aquilegia,* having flowers with five spurred petals. Also called: **aquilegia.** ORIG C13: from Med. L *columbīna herba* dovelike plant

Columbine ('kɒləmˌbaɪn) *n* the sweetheart of Harlequin in English pantomime.

Columbus[1] ★ (kə'lʌmbəs) *n* **1** a city in central Ohio: the state capital. Pop.: 635 913 (1994 est.). **2** a city in W Georgia, on the Chattahoochee River. Pop.: 186 470 (1994 est.).

Columbus[2] ★ (kə'lʌmbəs) *n* **Christopher.** Spanish name *Cristóbal Colón,* Italian name *Cristoforo Colombo.* 1451–

1506, Italian navigator in the service of Spain, who discovered the New World (1492).

column ('kɒləm) *n* **1** an upright pillar usually having a cylindrical shaft, a base, and a capital. **2a** a form or structure in the shape of a column: *a column of air.* **2b** a monument. **3** a line, as of people in a queue. **4** *Mil.* a narrow formation in which individuals or units follow one behind the other. **5** *Journalism.* **5a** any of two or more vertical sections of type on a printed page, esp. on a newspaper page. **5b** a regular feature in a paper: *the fashion column.* **6** a vertical array of numbers. ORIG C15: from L *columna,* from *columen* top, peak
▸ **columnar** (kə'lʌmnə) *adj* ▸ **'columned** *adj*

column inch *n* a unit of measurement for advertising space, one inch deep and one column wide.

columnist ('kɒləmnɪst, -əmɪst) *n* a journalist who writes a regular feature in a newspaper.

colure (kə'lʊə, 'kəulʊə) *n* either of two great circles on the celestial sphere, one passing through the poles and the equinoxes, the other through the poles and the solstices. ORIG C16: from LL, from Gk *kolourai,* dock-tailed, from *kolos* docked + *oura* tail (because the lower portion is not visible)

Colwyn Bay ★ ('kɒlwɪn) *n* a town and resort in N Wales, in Conwy county borough. Pop.: 29 883 (1991).

colza ('kɒlzə) *n* another name for **rape**[2]. ORIG C18: via F (Walloon) from Du., from *kool* cabbage, COLE + *zaad* SEED

COM (kɒm) *n* direct conversion of computer output to microfiche or film. ORIG C20: *C(omputer) O(utput on) M(icrofilm)*

Com. *abbrev. for:* **1** Commander. **2** Committee. **3** Commodore. **4** Communist.

com- *or* **con-** *prefix* together; with; jointly: *commingle.* ORIG from L *com-;* rel. to *cum* with. In compound words of L origin, *com-* becomes *col-* and *cor-* before *l* and *r, co-* before *gn, h,* and most vowels, and *con-* before consonants other than *b, p,* and *m*

coma[1] ('kəumə) *n, pl* **comas.** a state of unconsciousness from which a person cannot be aroused, caused by injury, narcotics, poisons, etc. ORIG C17: from medical L, from Gk *kōma* heavy sleep

coma[2] ('kəumə) *n, pl* **comae** (-mi:). **1** *Astron.* the luminous cloud surrounding the nucleus in the head of a comet. **2** *Bot.* **2a** a tuft of hairs attached to the seed coat of some seeds. **2b** the terminal crown of leaves of palms and moss stems. ORIG C17: from L: hair of the head, from Gk *komē*

comanche (kə'mæntʃɪ) *n* **1** (*pl* **comanches** *or* **comanche**) a member of a North American Indian people formerly inhabiting the W plains of the US. **2** the language of this people.

Comaneci ★ (ˌkɒmə'netʃɪ) *n* **Nadia.** born 1961, Romanian gymnast; gold medal winner in the 1976 Olympic Games: defected to the US in 1989.

comatose ('kəuməˌtəus) *adj* **1** in a state of coma. **2** torpid; lethargic.

comb (kəum) *n* **1** a toothed device for disentangling or arranging hair. **2** a tool or machine that cleans and straightens wool, cotton, etc. **3** *Austral. & NZ.* the fixed cutter on a sheep-shearing machine. **4** anything resembling a comb in form or function. **5** the fleshy serrated outgrowth on the heads of certain birds, esp. the domestic fowl. **6** a honeycomb. ◆ *vb* **7** (*tr*) to use a comb on. **8** (when *tr,* often foll. by *through*) to search with great care: *the police combed the woods.* ◆ **See also comb out.** ORIG OE *camb*

combat *n* ('kɒmbæt, -bət, 'kʌm-). **1** a fight, conflict, or struggle. **2a** an action fought between two military forces. **2b** (*as modifier*): *a combat jacket.* **3 single combat.** a duel. ◆ *vb* (kəm'bæt; 'kɒmbæt, 'kʌm-). **-bats, -bating, -bated. 4** (*tr*) to fight. **5** (*intr;* often foll. by *with* or *against*) to struggle or strive (against): *to combat against disease.* ORIG C16: from F, from OF *combattre,* from Vulgar L *combattere* (unattested), from L *com-* with + *battuere* to beat

combatant ('kɒmbətᵊnt, 'kʌm-) *n* **1** a person or group engaged in or prepared for a fight. ◆ *adj* **2** engaged in or ready for combat.

combat fatigue *n* another term for **battle fatigue.**

combative ('kɒmbətɪv, 'kʌm-) *adj* eager or ready to fight, argue, etc.
▸ **'combativeness** *n*

combe *or* **comb** (ku:m) *n* variant spellings of **coomb.**

comber ('kəumə) *n* **1** a person, tool, or machine that combs wool, flax, etc. **2** a long curling wave; roller.

combination (ˌkɒmbɪ'neɪʃən) *n* **1** the act of combining or state of being combined. **2** a union of separate parts, qualities, etc. **3** an alliance of people or parties. **4** the set of numbers that opens a combination lock. **5** *Brit.* a motorcycle with a sidecar attached. **6** *Maths.* an arrangement of the numbers, terms, etc., of a set into specified groups without regard to order in the group. **7** the chemical reaction of two or more compounds, usually to form one other compound. **8** *Chess.* a tactical manoeuvre involving a sequence of moves and more than one piece.
▸ **ˌcombi'national** *adj*

combination lock *n* a type of lock that can only be opened when a set of dials is turned to show a specific sequence of numbers.

combinations (ˌkɒmbɪ'neɪʃənz) *pl n Brit.* a one-piece undergarment with long sleeves and legs. Often shortened to **combs** or **coms.**

combine *vb* (kəm'baɪn), **combines, combining, combined. 1** to join together. **2** to unite or cause to unite to form a chemical compound. ◆ *n* ('kɒmbaɪn). **3** short for **combine harvester. 4** an association of enterprises, esp. in order to gain a monopoly of a market. **5** an association of related bodies, such as business corporations or sports clubs, for a common purpose. ORIG C15: from LL *combīnāre,* from L *com-* together + *bīnī* two by two
▸ **com'binable** *adj* ▸ **comˌbina'bility** *n* ▸ **combinative** ('kɒmbɪˌneɪtɪv) *or* **combinatory** ('kɒmbɪˌneɪtərɪ) *adj*

combine harvester ('kɒmbaɪn) *n* a machine that simultaneously cuts, threshes, and cleans a standing crop of grain.

combings ('kəumɪŋz) *pl n* **1** the loose hair removed by combing. **2** the unwanted fibres removed in combing cotton, etc.

combining form *n* a linguistic element that occurs only as part of a compound word, such as *anthropo-* in *anthropology* and *anthropomorph.*

combo ('kɒmbəu) *n, pl* **combos. 1** a small group of jazz musicians. **2** *Inf.* any combination.

comb out *vb* (*tr, adv*) **1** to remove (tangles) from (the hair) with a comb. **2** to remove for a purpose. **3** to examine systematically.

combustible (kəm'bʌstɪbᵊl) *adj* **1** capable of igniting and burning. **2** easily annoyed; excitable. ◆ *n* **3** a combustible substance.
▸ **comˌbusti'bility** *or* **com'bustibleness** *n*

combustion (kəm'bʌstʃən) *n* **1** the process of burning. **2** any process in which a substance reacts to produce a significant rise in temperature and the emission of light. **3** a process in which a compound reacts slowly with oxygen to produce little heat and no light. ORIG C15: from OF, from L *combūrere* to burn up
▸ **com'bustive** *n, adj*

combustion chamber *n* an enclosed space in which combustion takes place, such as the space above the piston in the cylinder head of an internal-combustion engine.

combustor (kəm'bʌstə) *n* the combustion system of a jet engine or ramjet.

Comdr *Mil. abbrev. for* Commander.

Comdt *Mil. abbrev. for* Commandant.

come (kʌm) *vb* **comes, coming, came, come.** (*mainly intr*) **1** to move towards a specified person or place. **2** to arrive by movement or by making progress. **3** to become perceptible: *light came into the sky.* **4** to occur: *Christmas comes but once a year.* **5** to happen as a result: *no good will come of this.* **6** to be derived: *good may come of evil.* **7** to occur to the mind: *the truth suddenly came to me.* **8** to reach: *she comes up to my shoulder.* **9** to be produced: *that dress comes in red.* **10** to arrive at or be brought into a particular state: *you will soon come to grief.* **11** (foll. by *from*) to be or have been a resident or native (of): *I come from London.* **12** to become: *your wishes will come true.* **13** (*tr; takes an infinitive*) to be given awareness: *I came to realize its value.* **14** *Taboo sl.* to have an orgasm. **15** (*tr*) *Brit. inf.* to play the part of: *don't come the fine gentleman with me.* **16** (*tr*) *Brit. inf.* to cause or produce: *don't come that nonsense.* **17** (*subjunctive use*): *come next August, he will be fifty years old:* when next August arrives. **18 as ... as they come.** the most characteristic example of a type. **19 come again?** *Inf.* what did you say? **20 come good.** to recover and perform well after a setback or poor start. **21 come to light.** to be revealed. **22 come to light with.** *Austral. & NZ inf.* to find or produce. ◆ *interj* **23** an exclamation expressing annoyance, etc.: *come now!* ◆ See also **come about, come across,** etc. ORIG OE *cuman*

come about *vb* (*intr, adv*) **1** to take place; happen. **2** *Naut.* to change tacks.

come across *vb* (*intr*) **1** (*prep*) to meet or find by accident. **2** (*adv*) to communicate the intended meaning or impression. **3** (often foll. by *with*) to provide what is expected.

come at *vb* (*intr, prep*) **1** to discover (facts, the truth, etc.). **2** to attack: *he came at me with an axe.* **3** (*usually used with a negative*) *Austral. sl.* to agree to do (something).

comeback ('kʌmˌbæk) *n Inf.* **1** a return to a former position, status, etc. **2** a response, esp. recriminatory. **3** a quick retort. ◆ *vb* **come back.** (*intr, adv*) **4** to return, esp. to the memory. **5** to become fashionable again. **6 come back to (someone).** (of something forgotten) to return to (someone's) memory.

come between *vb* (*intr, prep*) to cause the estrangement or separation of (two people).

come by *vb* (*intr, prep*) to find or obtain, esp. accidentally: *do you ever come by any old books?*

Comecon ('kɒmɪˌkɒn) *n* (formerly) an association of Soviet-oriented Communist nations, founded in 1949 to coordinate economic development, etc.: disbanded in 1991. ORIG C20: *Co(uncil for) M(utual) Econ(omic Aid)*

comedian (kə'mi:dɪən) *n* **1** an entertainer who specializes in jokes, comic skits, etc. **2** an actor in comedy. **3** an amusing person: sometimes used ironically.

comedienne (kəˌmi:dɪ'ɛn) *n* a female comedian.

comedo ('kɒmɪˌdəʊ) *n, pl* **comedos** *or* **comedones** (ˌkɒmɪ'dəʊni:z). *Pathol.* the technical name for **blackhead**. ORIG C19: from NL, from L: glutton

comedown ('kʌmˌdaʊn) *n* **1** a decline in status or prosperity. **2** *Inf.* a disappointment. ◆ *vb* **come down.** (*intr, adv*) **3** to come to a place regarded as lower. **4** to lose status, etc. (esp. in **come down in the world**). **5** (of prices) to become lower. **6** to reach a decision: *the report came down in favour of a pay increase.* **7** (often foll. by *to*) to be handed down by tradition or inheritance. **8** *Brit.* to leave university. **9** (foll. by *with*) to succumb (to illness). **10** (foll. by *on*) to rebuke harshly. **11** (foll. by *to*) to amount in essence (to): *it comes down to two choices.*

comedy ('kɒmɪdɪ) *n, pl* **comedies. 1** a dramatic or other work of light and amusing character. **2** the genre of drama represented by works of this type. **3** (in classical literature) a play in which the main characters triumph over adversity. **4** the humorous aspect of life or of events. **5** an amusing event or sequence of events. **6** humour: *the comedy of Chaplin.* ORIG C14: from OF, from L, from Gk *kōmōidia,* from *kōmos* village festival + *aeidein* to sing

▸ **comedic** (kə'mi:dɪk) *adj*

comedy of manners *n* a comedy dealing with the way of life and foibles of a social group.

come forward *vb* (*intr, adv*) **1** to offer one's services; volunteer. **2** to present oneself.

come-hither *adj* (*usually prenominal*) *Inf.* alluring; seductive: *a come-hither look.*

come in *vb* (*intr, mainly adv*) **1** to enter. **2** to prove to be: *it came in useful.* **3** to become fashionable or seasonable. **4** *Cricket.* to begin an innings. **5** to finish a race (in a certain position). **6** to be received: *news is coming in of a big fire in Glasgow.* **7** (of money) to be received as income. **8** to play a role: *where do I come in?* **9** (foll. by *for*) to be the object of: *the Chancellor came in for a lot of criticism.*

come into *vb* (*intr, prep*) **1** to enter. **2** to inherit.

comely ('kʌmlɪ) *adj* **comelier, comeliest. 1** good-looking; attractive. **2** *Arch.* suitable; fitting. ORIG OE *cȳmlīc* beautiful

▸ **'comeliness** *n*

come of *vb* (*intr, prep*) **1** to be descended from. **2** to result from: *nothing came of it.*

come off *vb* (*intr, mainly adv*) **1** (*also prep*) to fall (from). **2** to become detached. **3** (*prep*) to be removed from (a price, tax, etc.): *will anything come off income tax in the budget?* **4** (*copula*) to emerge from or as if from a contest: *he came off the winner.* **5** *Inf.* to happen. **6** *Inf.* to have the intended effect: *his jokes did not come off.* **7** *Taboo sl.* to have an orgasm.

come on *vb* (*intr, mainly adv*) **1** (of power, water, etc.) to start running or functioning. **2** to progress: *my plants are coming on nicely.* **3** to advance, esp. in battle. **4** to begin: *she felt a cold coming on.* **5** to make an entrance on stage. **6 come on! 6a** hurry up! **6b** cheer up! pull yourself together! **6c** make an effort! **6d** don't exaggerate! stick to the facts! **7** to attempt to give a specified impression: *he came on like a hard man.* **8 come on strong.** to make a forceful or exaggerated impression. **9 come on to.** *Inf.* to make sexual advances to. ◆ *n* **come-on. 10** anything that serves as a lure or enticement.

come out *vb* (*intr, adv*) **1** to be made public or revealed: *the news of her death came out last week.* **2** to make a debut in society. **3** Also: **come out of the closet. 3a** to declare openly that one is a homosexual. **3b** to reveal or declare any practice or habit formerly concealed. **4** *Chiefly Brit.* to go on strike. **5** to declare oneself: *the government came out in favour of scrapping the project.* **6** to be shown clearly: *you came out very well in the photos.* **7** to yield a satisfactory solution: *these sums just won't come out.* **8** to be published: *the paper comes out on Fridays.* **9** (foll. by *in*) to become covered (with). **10** (foll. by *with*) to declare openly: *you can rely on him to come out with the facts.*

come over *vb* (*intr, adv*) **1** to communicate the intended meaning or impression: *he came over very well.* **2** to change allegiances. **3** *Inf.* to feel a particular sensation: *I came over funny.*

comer ('kʌmə) *n* **1** (*in combination*) a person who comes: *all-comers; newcomers.* **2** *Inf.* a potential success.

come round *vb* (*intr, adv*) **1** to be restored to consciousness. **2** to modify one's opinion.

comestible (kə'mɛstɪbᵊl) *n* (*usually pl*) food. ORIG C15: from LL *comestibilis,* from *comedere* to eat up

comet ('kɒmɪt) *n* a celestial body that travels around the sun, usually in a highly elliptical orbit: thought to consist of a frozen nucleus, part of which vaporizes on approaching the sun to form a long luminous tail. ORIG C13: from OF, from L, from Gk *komētēs* long-haired

▸ **'cometary** *or* **cometic** (kɒ'mɛtɪk) *adj*

come through *vb* (*intr*) **1** (*adv*) to emerge successfully. **2** (*prep*) to survive (an illness, etc.).

come to *vb* (*intr*) **1** (*adv* or *prep and reflexive*) to regain consciousness. **2** (*adv*) *Naut.* to slow a vessel or bring her to a stop. **3** (*prep*) to amount to (a sum of money). **4** (*prep*) to arrive at: *what is the world coming to?*

come up *vb* (*intr, adv*) **1** to come to a place regarded as higher. **2** (of the sun) to rise. **3** to present itself: *that question will come up again.* **4** *Brit.* to begin a term at a university. **5** to appear from out of the ground: *my beans have come up early.* **6** *Inf.* to win: *have your premium bonds ever come up?* **7 come up against.** to come into conflict with. **8 come up to.** to meet a standard. **9 come up with.** to produce.

come upon *vb* (*intr, prep*) to meet or encounter unexpectedly.

comeuppance (ˌkʌm'ʌpəns) *n Inf.* just retribution. ORIG C19: from *come up* (in the sense): to appear before a court

comfit ('kʌmfɪt, 'kɒm-) *n* a sugar-coated sweet containing a nut or seed. ORIG C15: from OF, from L *confectum* something prepared

comfort ('kʌmfət) *n* **1** a state of ease or well-being. **2** relief from affliction, grief, etc. **3** a person, thing, or event that brings solace or ease. **4** (*usually pl*) something that

affords physical ease and relaxation. ◆ *vb (tr)* **5** to soothe; cheer. **6** to bring physical ease to. ORIG C13: from OF *confort,* from LL *confortāre* to strengthen, from L *con-* (intensive) + *fortis* strong
▸ **'comforting** *adj* ▸ **'comfortless** *adj*

comfortable ('kʌmftəbᵊl) *adj* **1** giving comfort. **2** at ease. **3** free from affliction or pain. **4** (of a person or situation) relaxing. **5** *Inf.* having adequate income. **6** *Inf.* (of income, etc.) adequate to provide comfort.
▸ **'comfortably** *adv*

comforter ('kʌmfətə) *n* **1** a person or thing that comforts. **2** *Chiefly Brit.* a woollen scarf. **3** a baby's dummy. **4** *US.* a quilted bed covering.

Comforter ('kʌmfətə) *n Christianity.* an epithet of the Holy Spirit. ORIG C14: translation of L *consolātor,* representing Gk *paraklētos* advocate

comfrey ('kʌmfrɪ) *n* a hairy Eurasian plant having blue, purplish-pink, or white flowers. ORIG C15: from OF *cunfirie,* from L *conferva* water plant

comfy ('kʌmfɪ) *adj* **comfier, comfiest.** *Inf.* short for **comfortable.**

comic ('kɒmɪk) *adj* **1** of, characterized by, or characteristic of comedy. **2** *(prenominal)* acting in or composing comedy: *a comic writer.* **3** humorous; funny. ◆ *n* **4** a person who is comic; comedian. **5** a book or magazine containing comic strips. ORIG C16: from L *cōmicus,* from Gk *kōmikos*

comical ('kɒmɪkᵊl) *adj* **1** causing laughter. **2** ludicrous; laughable.
▸ **'comically** *adv*

comic opera *n* a play largely set to music, employing comic effects or situations.

comic strip *n* a sequence of drawings in a newspaper, magazine, etc., relating a humorous story or an adventure.

coming ('kʌmɪŋ) *adj* **1** *(prenominal)* (of time, events, etc.) approaching or next. **2** promising (esp. in **up and coming**). **3** of future importance: *this is the coming thing.* **4 have it coming to one.** *Inf.* to deserve what one is about to suffer. ◆ *n* **5** arrival or approach.

Comintern *or* **Komintern** ('kɒmɪn,tɜːn) *n* short for **Communist International;** an international Communist organization founded by Lenin in 1919 and dissolved in 1943; it degenerated under Stalin into an instrument of Soviet politics. Also called: **Third International.**

comity ('kɒmɪtɪ) *n, pl* **comities. 1** mutual civility; courtesy. **2** short for **comity of nations.** ORIG C16: from L *cōmitās,* from *cōmis* affable

comity of nations *n* the friendly recognition accorded by one nation to the laws and usages of another.

comm. *abbrev. for:* **1** commerce. **2** commercial. **3** committee. **4** commonwealth.

comma ('kɒmə) *n* **1** the punctuation mark , indicating a slight pause and used where there is a listing of items or to separate a nonrestrictive clause from a main clause. **2** *Music.* a minute difference in pitch. ORIG C16: from L, from Gk *komma* clause, from *koptein* to cut

comma bacillus *n* a comma-shaped bacterium that causes cholera in man.

command (kə'mɑːnd) *vb* **1** (when *tr,* may take a clause as object or an infinitive) to order or compel. **2** to have or be in control or authority over. **3** *(tr)* to receive as due: *his nature commands respect.* **4** to dominate (a view, etc.) as from a height. ◆ *n* **5** an order. **6** the act of commanding. **7** the right to command. **8** the exercise of the power to command. **9** knowledge; control: *a command of French.* **10** *Chiefly mil.* the jurisdiction of a commander. **11** a military unit or units commanding a specific function, as in the RAF. **12** *Brit.* **12a** an invitation from the monarch. **12b** *(as modifier): a command performance.* **13** *Computing.* a word or phrase that can be selected from a menu or typed after a prompt in order to carry out an action. ORIG C13: from OF *commander,* from L *com-* (intensive) + *mandāre* to enjoin

commandant ('kɒmən,dænt, -,dɑːnt) *n* an officer commanding a group or establishment.

command economy *n* an economy in which business activities and the allocation of resources are determined by government order rather than market forces. Also called: **planned economy.**

commandeer (,kɒmən'dɪə) *vb (tr)* **1** to seize for public or military use. **2** to seize arbitrarily. ORIG C19: from Afrik. *kommandeer,* from F *commander* to COMMAND

commander (kə'mɑːndə) *n* **1** an officer in command of a military formation or operation. **2** a naval commissioned rank junior to captain but senior to lieutenant commander. **3** the second in command of larger British warships. **4** someone who holds authority. **5** a high-ranking member of some knightly orders. **6** an officer responsible for a district of the Metropolitan Police in London.
▸ **com'mander,ship** *n*

commander in chief *n, pl* **commanders in chief.** the officer holding supreme command of the forces in an area or operation.

commanding (kə'mɑːndɪŋ) *adj (usually prenominal)* **1** being in command. **2** having the air of authority: *a commanding voice.* **3** (of a situation) exerting control. **4** (of a viewpoint, etc.) overlooking; advantageous.
▸ **com'mandingly** *adv*

commanding officer *n* an officer in command of a military unit.

command language *n Computing.* the language used to access a computer system.

commandment (kə'mɑːndmənt) *n* **1** a divine command, esp. one of the Ten Commandments of the Old Testament. **2** *Literary.* any command.

command module *n* the module used as the living quarters in an Apollo spacecraft and functioning as the splashdown vehicle.

commando (kə'mɑːndəʊ) *n, pl* **commandos** *or* **commandoes. 1a** an amphibious military unit trained for raiding. **1b** a member of such a unit. **2** the basic unit of the Royal Marine Corps. **3** (originally) an armed force raised by Boers during the Boer War. **4** *(modifier)* denoting or relating to commandos: *a commando unit.* ORIG C19: from Afrik. *kommando,* from Du. *commando* command

command paper *n* (in Britain) a government document that is presented to Parliament, in theory by royal command.

command post *n Mil.* the position from which a commander exercises command.

commedia dell'arte *(Italian* kom'meːdia del'larte) *n* a form of popular improvised comedy in Italy during the 16th to 18th centuries, with stock characters such as Punchinello, Harlequin, and Columbine. ORIG It., lit.: comedy of art

comme il faut *French.* (kɔm il fo) correct or correctly.

commemorate (kə'mɛmə,reɪt) *vb* **commemorates, commemorating, commemorated.** *(tr)* to honour or keep alive the memory of. ORIG C16: from L *commemorāre,* from *com-* (intensive) + *memorāre* to remind
▸ **com,memo'ration** *n* ▸ **com'memorative** *adj* ▸ **com'memo,rator** *n*

commence (kə'mɛns) *vb* **commences, commencing, commenced.** to begin; come or cause to come into being, operation, etc. ORIG C14: from OF *comencer,* from Vulgar L *cominitiāre* (unattested), from L *com-* (intensive) + *initiāre* to begin

commencement (kə'mɛnsmənt) *n* **1** the beginning; start. **2** *US.* a ceremony for the conferment of academic degrees. **3** *US & Canad.* a ceremony for the presentation of awards at secondary schools.

commend (kə'mɛnd) *vb (tr)* **1** to represent as being worthy of regard, confidence, etc.; recommend. **2** to give in charge; entrust. **3** to praise. **4** to give the regards of: *commend me to your aunt.* ORIG C14: from L *commendāre,* from *com-* (intensive) + *mandāre* to entrust
▸ **com'mendable** *adj* ▸ **com'mendably** *adv* ▸ **com'mendatory** *adj*

commendation (,kɒmɛn'deɪʃən) *n* **1** the act of commending; praise. **2** *US.* an award.

commensal (kə'mɛnsəl) *adj* **1** (of two different species of plant or animal) living in close association without

being interdependent. See also **inquiline** (sense 1). **2** *Rare.* of or relating to eating together, esp. at the same table. ◆ *n* **3** a commensal plant or animal. **4** *Rare.* a companion at table. ORIG C14: from Med. L *commensālis,* from L *com-* together + *mensa* table
▸ **com'mensalism** *n* ▸ **commensality** (ˌkɒmɛn'sælɪtɪ) *n*

commensurable (kə'mɛnsərəbəl, -ʃə-) *adj* **1** *Maths.* **1a** having a common factor. **1b** having units of the same dimensions and being related by whole numbers. **2** proportionate.
▸ **comˌmensura'bility** *n* ▸ **com'mensurably** *adv*

commensurate (kə'mɛnsərɪt, -ʃə-) *adj* **1** having the same extent or duration. **2** corresponding in degree, amount, or size; proportionate. **3** commensurable. ORIG C17: from LL *commēnsūrātus,* from L *com-* same + *mēnsurāre* to MEASURE
▸ **com'mensurately** *adv*

comment ('kɒmɛnt) *n* **1** a remark, criticism, or observation. **2** talk or gossip. **3** a note explaining or criticizing a passage in a text. **4** explanatory or critical matter added to a text. ◆ *vb* **5** (when *intr,* often foll. by *on;* when *tr,* takes a clause as object) to remark or express an opinion. **6** (*intr*) to write notes explaining or criticizing a text. ORIG C15: from L *commentum* invention, from *comminiscī* to contrive
▸ **'commenter** *n*

commentary ('kɒməntərɪ) *n, pl* **commentaries. 1** an explanatory series of notes. **2** a spoken accompaniment to a broadcast, film, etc. **3** an explanatory treatise on a text. **4** (*usually pl*) a personal record of events: *the commentaries of Caesar.*

commentate ('kɒmənˌteɪt) *vb* **commentates, commentating, commentated. 1** (*intr*) to serve as a commentator. **2** (*tr*) *US.* to make a commentary on.

commentator ('kɒmənˌteɪtə) *n* **1** a person who provides a spoken commentary for a broadcast, film, etc., esp. of a sporting event. **2** a person who writes notes on a text, etc.

commerce ('kɒmɜːs) *n* **1** the activity embracing all forms of the purchase and sale of goods and services. **2** social relations. **3** *Arch.* sexual intercourse. ORIG C16: from L *commercium,* from *commercārī,* from *mercārī* to trade, from *merx* merchandise

commercial (kə'mɜːʃəl) *adj* **1** of or engaged in commerce. **2** sponsored or paid for by an advertiser: *commercial television.* **3** having profit as the main aim: *commercial music.* **4** (of chemicals, etc.) unrefined and produced in bulk for use in industry. ◆ *n* **5** a commercially sponsored advertisement on radio or television.
▸ **commerciality** (kəˌmɜːʃɪ'ælɪtɪ) *n* ▸ **com'mercially** *adv*

commercial art *n* graphic art for commercial uses such as advertising, packaging, etc.

commercial bank *n* a bank primarily engaged in making short-term loans from funds deposited in current accounts.

commercial break *n* an interruption in a radio or television programme for the broadcasting of advertisements.

commercialism (kə'mɜːʃəˌlɪzəm) *n* **1** the spirit, principles, or procedure of commerce. **2** exclusive or inappropriate emphasis on profit.

commercialize *or* **commercialise** (kə'mɜːʃəˌlaɪz) *vb* **commercializes, commercializing, commercialized** *or* **commercialises, commercialising, commercialised.** (*tr*) **1** to make commercial. **2** to exploit for profit, esp. at the expense of quality.
▸ **comˌmerciali'zation** *or* **comˌmerciali'sation** *n*

commercial paper *n* a short-term negotiable document, such as a bill of exchange, calling for the transference of a specified sum of money at a designated date.

commercial traveller *n* another name for a **travelling salesman.**

commercial vehicle *n* a vehicle for carrying goods or (less commonly) passengers.

commie *or* **commy** ('kɒmɪ) *n, pl* **commies,** *adj Inf. & derog.* short for **communist.**

commination (ˌkɒmɪ'neɪʃən) *n* **1** the act of threatening punishment or vengeance. **2** *Church of England.* a recital of prayers, including a list of God's judgments against sinners, in the office for Ash Wednesday. ORIG C15: from L *comminātiō,* from *com-* (intensive) + *minārī* to threaten
▸ **comminatory** ('kɒmɪnətərɪ) *adj*

commingle (kɒ'mɪŋg^əl) *vb* **commingles, commingling, commingled.** to mix or be mixed.

comminute ('kɒmɪˌnjuːt) *vb* **comminutes, comminuting, comminuted. 1** to break (a bone) into small fragments. **2** to divide (property) into small lots. ORIG C17: from L *comminuere,* from *com-* (intensive) + *minuere* to reduce
▸ **ˌcommi'nution** *n*

commis ('kɒmɪs, 'kɒmɪ) *n, pl* **commis. 1** an agent or deputy. ◆ *adj* **2** (of a waiter or chef) apprentice. ORIG C16 (meaning: deputy): from F, from *commettre* to employ

commiserate (kə'mɪzəˌreɪt) *vb* **commiserates, commiserating, commiserated.** (when *intr,* usually foll. by *with*) to feel or express sympathy or compassion (for). ORIG C17: from L *commiserārī,* from *com-* together + *miserārī* to bewail
▸ **comˌmiser'ation** *n* ▸ **com'miserˌator** *n*

commissar ('kɒmɪˌsɑː, ˌkɒmɪ'sɑː) *n* (in the former Soviet Union) **1** an official of the Communist Party responsible for political education. **2** (before 1946) the head of a government department. ORIG C20: from Russian *kommissar*

commissariat (ˌkɒmɪ'sɛərɪət) *n* **1** (in the former Soviet Union) a government department before 1946. **2** a military department in charge of food supplies, etc. ORIG C17: from NL *commissāriātus,* from Med. L *commissārius* COMMISSARY

commissary ('kɒmɪsərɪ) *n, pl* **commissaries. 1** *US.* a shop supplying food or equipment, as in a military camp. **2** *US army.* an officer responsible for supplies. **3** *US.* a restaurant in a film studio. **4** a representative or deputy, esp. of a bishop. ORIG C14: from Med. L *commissārius* official in charge, from L *committere* to COMMIT
▸ **commissarial** (ˌkɒmɪ'sɛərɪəl) *adj*

commission (kə'mɪʃən) *n* **1** a duty committed to a person or group to perform. **2** authority to perform certain duties. **3** a document granting such authority. **4** *Mil.* **4a** a document conferring a rank on an officer. **4b** the rank granted. **5** a group charged with certain duties: *a commission of inquiry.* **6** a government board empowered to exercise administrative, judicial, or legislative authority. See also **Royal Commission. 7a** the authority given to a person or organization to act as an agent to a principal in commercial transactions. **7b** the fee allotted to an agent for services rendered. **8** the state of being charged with specific responsibilities. **9** the act of committing a sin, crime, etc. **10** good working condition or (esp. of a ship) active service (esp. in **in commission, out of commission**). ◆ *vb* (*mainly tr*) **11** to grant authority to. **12** *Mil.* to confer a rank on. **13** to equip and test (a ship) for active service. **14** to place an order for (something): *to commission a portrait.* **15** to make or become operative or operable: *the plant is due to commission next year.* ORIG C14: from OF, from L *commissiō* a bringing together, from *committere* to COMMIT

commissionaire (kəˌmɪʃə'nɛə) *n Chiefly Brit.* a uniformed doorman at a hotel, theatre, etc. ORIG C18: from F, from COMMISSION

commissioned officer *n* a military officer holding a commission, such as Second Lieutenant in the British Army, Acting Sub-Lieutenant in the Royal Navy, Pilot Officer in the Royal Air Force, and officers of all ranks senior to these.

commissioner (kə'mɪʃənə) *n* **1** a person endowed with certain powers. **2** any of several types of civil servant. **3** a member of a commission.
▸ **com'missionerˌship** *n*

commissioner for oaths *n* a solicitor authorized to authenticate oaths on sworn statements.

commit (kə'mɪt) *vb* **commits, committing, committed.** (*tr*) **1** to hand over, as for safekeeping; entrust. **2 commit to memory.** to memorize. **3** to take into custody: *to commit someone to prison.* **4** (*usually passive*) to pledge or align (oneself), as to

a particular cause: *a committed radical.* **5** to order (forces) into action. **6** to perform (a crime, error, etc.). **7** to surrender, esp. for destruction: *she committed the letter to the fire.* **8** to refer (a bill, etc.) to a committee. ORIG C14: from L *committere* to join, from *com-* together + *mittere* to send
▸ **com'mittable** *adj* ▸ **com'mitter** *n*

commitment (kə'mɪtmənt) *n* **1** the act of committing or pledging. **2** the state of being committed or pledged. **3** an obligation, promise, etc., that restricts freedom of action. **4** Also called (esp. formerly): **mittimus.** *Law.* a written order of a court directing that a person be imprisoned. **5** a future financial obligation or contingent liability. ◆ Also called (esp. for sense 4): **committal** (kə'mɪtᵊl).

committee *n* **1** (kə'mɪtɪ). a group of people appointed to perform a specified service or function. **2** (ˌkɒmɪ'tiː). (formerly) a person to whom the care of a mentally incompetent person or his or her property was entrusted by a court. ORIG C15: from *committen* to entrust + -EE

committeeman (kə'mɪtɪmən, -ˌmæn) *n, pl* **committeemen.** *Chiefly US.* a member of one or more committees.
▸ **com'mittee,woman** *fem n*

Committee of the Whole House *n* (in Britain) an informal sitting of the House of Commons to discuss and amend a bill.

commode (kə'məʊd) *n* **1** a piece of furniture, usually highly ornamented, containing drawers or shelves. **2** a bedside table with a cabinet for a chamber pot or washbasin. **3** a chair with a hinged flap concealing a chamber pot. ORIG C17: from F, from L *commodus* COMMODIOUS

commodious (kə'məʊdɪəs) *adj* **1** roomy; spacious. **2** *Arch.* convenient. ORIG C15: from Med. L, from L *commodus* convenient, from *com-* with + *modus* measure
▸ **com'modiousness** *n*

commodity (kə'mɒdɪtɪ) *n, pl* **commodities. 1** an article of commerce. **2** something of use or profit. **3** *Econ.* an exchangeable unit of economic wealth, such as a primary product. ORIG C14: from OF *commodité,* from L *commoditās* suitability; see COMMODIOUS

commodo (kə'məʊdəʊ) *adv* a variant spelling of **comodo.**

commodore ('kɒməˌdɔː) *n* **1** *Brit.* a naval rank junior to rear admiral and senior to captain. **2** the captain of a shipping line. **3** the officer in command of a merchant convoy. **4** the titular head of a yacht club. ORIG C17: prob. from Du. *commandeur,* from F, from OF *commander* to COMMAND

Commodus ★ (kə'məʊdəs, 'kɒmədəs) *n* **Lucius Aelius Aurelius** ('luːsɪəs 'iːlɪəs ɔː'riːlɪəs), son of Marcus Aurelius. 161–192 A.D., Roman emperor (180–192), noted for his tyrannical reign.

common ('kɒmən) *adj* **1** belonging to two or more people: *common property.* **2** belonging to members of one or more communities; public: *a common culture.* **3** of ordinary standard; average. **4** prevailing; widespread: *common opinion.* **5** frequently encountered; ordinary: *a common brand of soap.* **6** notorious: *a common nuisance.* **7** *Derog.* considered by the speaker to be low-class, vulgar, or coarse. **8** (*prenominal*) having no special distinction: *the common man.* **9** *Maths.* having a specified relationship with a group of numbers or quantities: *common denominator.* **10** *Prosody.* (of a syllable) able to be long or short. **11** *Grammar.* (in certain languages) denoting or belonging to a gender of nouns that includes both masculine and feminine referents. **12 common or garden.** *Inf.* ordinary; unexceptional. ◆ *n* **13** a tract of open public land. **14** *Law.* the right to go onto someone else's property and remove natural products, as by pasturing cattle (esp. in **right of common**). **15** *Christianity.* **15a** a form of the proper of the Mass used on festivals that have no special proper of their own. **15b** the ordinary of the Mass. **16 in common.** mutually held or used. ◆ See also **commons.** ORIG C13: from OF *commun,* from L *commūnis* general
▸ **'commonly** *adv* ▸ **'commonness** *n*

commonage ('kɒmənɪdʒ) *n* **1** *Chiefly law.* **1a** the use of something, esp. a pasture, in common with others. **1b** the right to such use. **2** the state of being held in common. **3** another word for **commonalty** (sense 1).

commonality (ˌkɒmə'nælɪtɪ) *n, pl* **commonalities. 1** the fact of being common. **2** another word for **commonalty** (sense 1).

commonalty ('kɒmənəltɪ) *n, pl* **commonalties. 1** the ordinary people as distinct from those with rank or title. **2** the members of an incorporated society. ORIG C13: from OF *comunalte,* from *comunal* communal

common carrier *n* a person or firm engaged in the business of transporting goods or passengers.

common chord *n Music.* a chord consisting of the keynote, a major or minor third, and a perfect fifth.

common cold *n* a mild viral infection of the upper respiratory tract, characterized by sneezing, coughing, etc.

commoner ('kɒmənə) *n* **1** a person who does not belong to the nobility. **2** a person who has a right in or over common land. **3** *Brit.* a student at a university who is not on a scholarship.

common fraction *n* another name for **simple fraction.**

common knowledge *n* something widely or generally known.

common law *n* **1** the body of law based on judicial decisions and custom, as distinct from statute law. **2** (*modifier*) of or denoting a marriage that is deemed to exist after a man and a woman have cohabited for a number of years: *common-law marriage; common-law wife; common-law husband.*

Common Market *n* **the.** an informal name for the European Economic Community (now the **European Union**) and its policies of greater economic cooperation between member states. See also **European Community.**

common noun *n Grammar.* a noun that refers to each member of a whole class sharing the features connoted by the noun, as for example *orange* and *drum.* Cf. **proper noun.**

commonplace ('kɒmənˌpleɪs) *adj* **1** ordinary; everyday. **2** dull; trite: *commonplace prose.* ◆ *n* **3** a platitude; truism. **4** a passage in a book marked for inclusion in a commonplace book, etc. **5** an ordinary thing. ORIG C16: translation of L *locus commūnis* argument of wide application
▸ **'common,placeness** *n*

commonplace book *n* a notebook in which quotations, poems, etc., that catch the owner's attention are entered.

common room *n Chiefly Brit.* a sitting room in schools, colleges, etc.

commons ('kɒmənz) *n* **1** (*functioning as pl*) the lower classes as contrasted with the ruling or noble classes of society. **2** (*functioning as sing*) *Brit.* a hall for dining, recreation, etc., usually attached to a college, etc. **3** (*usually functioning as pl*) *Brit.* food or rations (esp. in **short commons**).

Commons ('kɒmənz) *n* **the.** See **House of Commons.**

common sense *n* **1** sound practical sense. ◆ *adj* **common-sense;** *also* **common-sensical. 2** inspired by or displaying this.

common time *n Music.* a time signature indicating four crotchet beats to the bar; four-four time. Symbol: **C**

commonweal ('kɒmənˌwiːl) *n Arch.* **1** the public good. **2** another name for **commonwealth.**

commonwealth ('kɒmənˌwɛlθ) *n* **1** the people of a state or nation viewed politically; body politic. **2** a state in which the people possess sovereignty; republic. **3** a group of persons united by some common interest.

Commonwealth ('kɒmənˌwɛlθ) *n* **the. 1** Official name: **the Commonwealth of Nations.** an association of sovereign states, most of which are or at some time were ruled by Britain. **2** the republic that existed in Britain from 1649 to 1660. **3** the official designation of Australia, four states of the US, and Puerto Rico.

Commonwealth Day *n* the anniversary of Queen Victoria's birth, May 24, celebrated (now on the second Monday in March) in many parts of the Commonwealth. Former name: **Empire Day.**

Commonwealth of Independent States *n* a loose organization of former Soviet republics, excluding the Baltic States, formed in 1991. Abbrev.: **CIS.**

commotion (kə'məʊʃən) *n* **1** violent disturbance; upheaval. **2** political insurrection. **3** a confused noise; din. ORIG C15: from L *commōtiō,* from *commovēre,* from *com-* (intensive) + *movēre* to MOVE

communal ('kɒmjʊnᵊl) *adj* **1** belonging to a community as a whole. **2** of a commune or a religious community. ▸ **communality** (ˌkɒmjʊ'nælɪtɪ) *n* ▸ **'communally** *adv*

communalism ('kɒmjʊnəˌlɪzəm) *n* **1** a system or theory of government in which the state is seen as a loose federation of self-governing communities. **2** the practice or advocacy of communal living or ownership. ▸ **'communalist** *n* ▸ **ˌcommunal'istic** *adj*

communalize *or* **communalise** ('kɒmjʊnəˌlaɪz) *vb* **communalizes, communalizing, communalized** *or* **communalises, communalising, communalised.** (*tr*) to render (something) the property of a commune or community. ▸ **ˌcommunali'zation** *or* **ˌcommunali'sation** *n*

communautaire *French.* (kɔmynotɛr) *adj* supporting the principles of the European Union. ORIG lit.: community (as modifier)

commune¹ *vb* (kə'mjuːn), **communes, communing, communed.** (*intr;* usually foll. by *with*) **1** to talk intimately. **2** to experience strong emotion (for): *to commune with nature.* ◆ *n* ('kɒmjuːn). **3** intimate conversation; communion. ORIG C13: from OF *comuner* to hold in common, from *comun* COMMON

commune² ('kɒmjuːn) *n* **1** a group of families or individuals living together and sharing possessions and responsibilities. **2** any small group of people having common interests or responsibilities. **3** the smallest administrative unit in Belgium, France, Italy, and Switzerland. **4** a medieval town enjoying a large degree of autonomy. ORIG C18: from F, from Med. L *commūnia,* from L: things held in common

Commune ('kɒmjuːn) *n French history.* **1** See **Paris Commune. 2** a committee that governed Paris during the French Revolution: suppressed 1794.

communicable (kə'mjuːnɪkəbᵊl) *adj* **1** capable of being communicated. **2** (of a disease) capable of being passed on readily. ▸ **comˌmunica'bility** *n* ▸ **com'municably** *adv*

communicant (kə'mjuːnɪkənt) *n* **1** *Christianity.* a person who receives Communion. **2** a person who communicates or informs.

communicate (kə'mjuːnɪˌkeɪt) *vb* **communicates, communicating, communicated. 1** to impart (knowledge) or exchange (thoughts) by speech, writing, gestures, etc. **2** (*tr;* usually foll. by *to*) to transmit (to): *the dog communicated his fear to the other animals.* **3** (*intr*) to have a sympathetic mutual understanding. **4** (*intr;* usually foll. by *with*) to make or have a connecting passage: *the kitchen communicates with the dining room.* **5** (*tr*) to transmit (a disease). **6** (*intr*) *Christianity.* to receive Communion. ORIG C16: from L *commūnicāre* to share, from *commūnis* COMMON ▸ **com'muniˌcator** *n* ▸ **com'municatory** *adj*

communication (kəˌmjuːnɪ'keɪʃən) *n* **1** the imparting or exchange of information, ideas, or feelings. **2** something communicated, such as a message. **3** (*usually pl; sometimes functioning as sing*) the study of ways in which human beings communicate. **4** a connecting route or link. **5** (*pl*) *Mil.* the system of routes by which forces, supplies, etc., are moved within an area of operations.

communication cord *n Brit.* a cord or chain in a train which may be pulled by a passenger to stop the train in an emergency.

communications satellite *n* an artificial satellite used to relay radio, television, and telephone signals around the earth's surface, usually in geostationary orbit.

communicative (kə'mjuːnɪkətɪv) *adj* **1** inclined or able to communicate readily; talkative. **2** of or relating to communication.

communion (kə'mjuːnjən) *n* **1** an exchange of thoughts, emotions, etc. **2** sharing in common; participation. **3** (foll. by *with*) strong feelings (for): *communion with nature.* **4** a religious group or denomination having common beliefs and practices. **5** spiritual union. ORIG C14: from L *commūniō,* from *commūnis* COMMON

Communion (kə'mjuːnjən) *n Christianity.* **1** the act of participating in the Eucharist. **2** the celebration of the Eucharist. **3** the consecrated elements of the Eucharist. ◆ Also called: **Holy Communion.**

communiqué (kə'mjuːnɪˌkeɪ) *n* an official communication or announcement, esp. to the press or public. ORIG C19: from F

communism ('kɒmjʊˌnɪzəm) *n* **1** advocacy of a classless society in which private ownership has been abolished and the means of production belong to the community. **2** any movement or doctrine aimed at achieving such a society. **3** (*usually cap.*) a political movement based upon the writings of Marx that considers history in terms of class conflict and revolutionary struggle. **4** (*usually cap.*) a system of government established by a ruling Communist Party, esp. in the former Soviet Union. **5** communal living. ORIG C19: from F *communisme,* from *commun* COMMON

communist ('kɒmjʊnɪst) *n* **1** a supporter of communism. **2** (*often cap.*) a supporter of a Communist movement or state. **3** (*often cap.*) a member of a Communist party. **4** (*often cap.*) *Chiefly US.* any person holding left-wing views, esp. when considered subversive. **5** a person who practises communal living. ◆ *adj* **6** of, favouring, or relating to communism. ▸ **ˌcommu'nistic** *adj*

Communist China ★ *n* another name for (the People's Republic of) **China.**

community (kə'mjuːnɪtɪ) *n, pl* **communities. 1a** the people living in one locality. **1b** the locality in which they live. **1c** (*as modifier*): *community spirit.* **2** a group of people having cultural, religious, or other characteristics in common: *the Protestant community.* **3** a group of nations having certain interests in common. **4** the public; society. **5** common ownership. **6** similarity or agreement: *community of interests.* **7** (in Wales and Scotland) the smallest unit of local government. **8** *Ecology.* a group of interdependent plants and animals inhabiting the same region. ORIG C14: from L *commūnitās,* from *commūnis* COMMON

community centre *n* a building used by a community for social gatherings, etc.

community charge *n* (formerly in Britain) a flat-rate charge paid by each adult in a community to their local authority in place of rates. Also called: **poll tax.**

community chest *n US.* a fund raised by voluntary contribution for local welfare activities.

community council *n* (in Scotland and Wales) an independent voluntary local body set up to attend to local interests and organize community activities.

community education *n* the provision of a wide range of educational and special-interest courses and activities by a local authority.

community home *n* (in Britain) **1** a home provided by a local authority for children who cannot remain with their parents. **2** a boarding school for young offenders.

community medicine *n* the branch of medicine concerned with evaluating and providing for the health needs of populations, esp. through monitoring and preventive measures.

community policing *n* the assigning of the same one or two policemen to a particular area so that they become familiar with the residents and they with them, as a way of reducing crime.

community service *n* work undertaken for the community by an offender without pay, by the order of a court.

communize *or* **communise** ('kɒmjʊˌnaɪz) *vb* **communizes, communizing, communized** *or* **communises, communising, communised.** (*tr*) (*sometimes cap.*) **1** to make (property) public; nationalize. **2** to make (a person or country) communist. ▸ **ˌcommuni'zation** *or* **ˌcommuni'sation** *n*

commutate ('kɒmjʊˌteɪt) *vb* **commutates, commutating, commutated.** (*tr*) **1** to reverse the direction of (an electric current). **2** to convert (an alternating current) into a direct current.

commutation (ˌkɒmjʊ'teɪʃən) *n* **1** a substitution or exchange. **2** the replacement of one method of payment by another. **3** the reduction in severity of a penalty imposed by law. **4** the process of commutating an electric current.

commutative (kəˈmjuːtətɪv, ˈkɒmjʊˌteɪtɪv) *adj* **1** relating to or involving substitution. **2** *Maths, logic.* **2a** giving the same result irrespective of the order of the arguments; thus addition is commutative but subtraction is not. **2b** relating to this property: *the commutative law of addition.*

commutator (ˈkɒmjʊˌteɪtə) *n* **1** a device used to reverse the direction of flow of an electric current. **2** the segmented metal cylinder or disc of an electric motor, generator, etc., used to make electrical contact with the rotating coils.

commute (kəˈmjuːt) *vb* **commutes, commuting, commuted. 1** (*intr*) to travel some distance regularly between one's home and one's place of work. **2** (*tr*) to substitute. **3** (*tr*) *Law.* to reduce (a sentence) to one less severe. **4** to pay (an annuity, etc.) at one time, instead of in instalments. **5** to change: *to commute base metal into gold.* ORIG C17: from L *commūtāre,* from *com-* mutually + *mūtāre* to change
▸ **comˈmutable** *adj* ▸ **comˌmutaˈbility** *n*

commuter (kəˈmjuːtə) *n* a person who travels to work over an appreciable distance, usually from the suburbs to the centre of a city.

Como ★ (ˈkəʊməʊ; *Italian* ˈkɔːmo) *n* a city in N Italy, in Lombardy at the SW end of **Lake Como**: tourist centre. Pop.: 96 900 (1995 est.). Latin name: **Comum** (ˈkəʊmʊm).

comodo *or* **commodo** (kəˈməʊdəʊ) *adv Music.* in a convenient tempo. ORIG It.: comfortable, from L *commodus* convenient: see COMMODIOUS

Comoros ★ (ˈkɒməˌrəʊz, kəˈmɔːrəʊz) *pl n* a republic consisting of three volcanic islands in the Indian Ocean, off the NW coast of Madagascar; a French territory from 1947; became independent in 1976 except for Mayotte, the fourth island in the group, which chose to remain French. Official languages: Comorian, French, and Arabic. Religion: Islam. Currency: franc. Capital: Moroni. Pop.: 563 000 (1999 est.). Area: 1862 sq. km (719 sq. miles). Official name: **Federal Islamic Republic of the Comoros.**

comose (ˈkəʊməʊs, kəʊˈməʊs) *adj Bot.* having tufts of hair; hairy. Also: **comate.** ORIG C18: from L *comōsus* hairy

comp (kɒmp) *Inf.* ◆ *n* **1** a compositor. **2** an accompaniment. **3** a competition. ◆ *vb* **4** (*intr*) to work as a compositor in the printing industry. **5** to play an accompaniment (to).

comp. *abbrev. for:* **1** companion. **2** comparative. **3** compare. **4** compiled. **5** composer. **6** composition. **7** compositor. **8** compound. **9** comprehensive. **10** comprising.

compact[1] *adj* (kəmˈpækt). **1** closely packed together. **2** neatly fitted into a restricted space. **3** concise; brief. **4** well constructed; solid, firm. **5** (foll. by *of*) composed (of). ◆ *vb* (kəmˈpækt). (*tr*) **6** to pack closely together; compress. **7** (foll. by *of*) to form by pressing together: *sediment compacted of three types of clay.* **8** *Metallurgy.* to compress (a metal powder) to form a stable product suitable for sintering. ◆ *n* (ˈkɒmpækt). **9** a small flat case containing a mirror, face powder, and powder puff, designed to be carried in a woman's handbag. **10** *US & Canad.* a small and economical car. ORIG C16: from L *compactus,* from *compingere,* from *com-* together + *pangere* to fasten
▸ **comˈpactly** *adv* ▸ **comˈpactness** *n*

compact[2] (ˈkɒmpækt) *n* an official contract or agreement. ORIG C16: from L *compactum,* from *compacīscī,* from *com-* together + *pacīscī* to contract

compact disc (ˈkɒmpækt) *n* a small digital audio disc on which sound is recorded as a series of metallic pits enclosed in PVC and read by an optical laser system. Also called: **compact audio disc.** Abbrev.: **CD, CAD.**

compact video disc *n* a compact laser disc that plays both pictures and sound.

compages (kəmˈpeɪdʒiːz) *n* (*functioning as sing*) a structure or framework. ORIG C17: from L: from *com-* together + *pangēre* to fasten

companion[1] (kəmˈpænjən) *n* **1** a person who is an associate of another or others; comrade. **2** (esp. formerly) an employee, usually a woman, who provides company for an employer. **3a** one of a pair. **3b** (*as modifier*): *a companion volume.* **4** a guidebook or handbook. **5** a member of the lowest rank of certain orders of knighthood. **6** *Astron.* the fainter of the two components of a double star. ◆ *vb* **7** (*tr*) to accompany. ORIG C13: from LL *compāniō,* lit.: one who eats bread with another, from L *com-* with + *pānis* bread
▸ **comˈpanionˌship** *n*

companion[2] (kəmˈpænjən) *n Naut.* a raised frame on an upper deck with windows to give light to the deck below. ORIG C18: from Du. *kompanje* quarterdeck, from OF *compagne,* from OIt. *compagna* pantry, ? ult. from L *pānis* bread

companionable (kəmˈpænjənəbᵊl) *adj* sociable.
▸ **comˈpanionableness** *n* ▸ **comˈpanionably** *adv*

companionate (kəmˈpænjənɪt) *adj* **1** resembling, appropriate to, or acting as a companion. **2** harmoniously suited.

companionway (kəmˈpænjənˌweɪ) *n* a ladder from one deck to another in a ship.

company (ˈkʌmpənɪ) *n, pl* **companies. 1** a number of people gathered together; assembly. **2** the fact of being with someone; companionship: *I enjoy her company.* **3** a guest or guests. **4** a business enterprise. **5** the members of an enterprise not specifically mentioned in the enterprise's title. Abbrev.: **Co., co. 6** a group of actors. **7** a small unit of troops. **8** the officers and crew of a ship. **9** a unit of Guides. **10** *English history.* a medieval guild. **11 keep company. 11a** to accompany (someone). **11b** (esp. of lovers) to spend time together. ◆ *vb* **companies, companying, companied. 12** *Arch.* to associate (with someone). ORIG C13: from OF *compaignie,* from LL *compāniō;* see COMPANION[1]

company doctor *n* **1** a businessman or accountant who specializes in turning ailing companies into profitable enterprises. **2** a physician employed by a company to look after its staff and to advise on health matters.

company sergeant major *n Mil.* the senior noncommissioned officer in a company.

company town *n US & Canad.* a town built by a company for its employees.

compar. *abbrev. for* comparative.

comparable (ˈkɒmpərəbᵊl) *adj* **1** worthy of comparison. **2** able to be compared (with).
▸ **ˌcomparaˈbility** *or* **ˈcomparableness** *n*

comparative (kəmˈpærətɪv) *adj* **1** denoting or involving comparison: *comparative literature.* **2** relative: *a comparative loss of prestige.* **3** *Grammar.* denoting the form of an adjective that indicates that the quality denoted is possessed to a greater extent. In English the comparative is marked by the suffix *-er* or the word *more.* ◆ *n* **4** the comparative form of an adjective.
▸ **comˈparatively** *adv* ▸ **comˈparativeness** *n*

comparative advertising *n* the usual US term for **knocking copy.**

compare (kəmˈpɛə) *vb* **compares, comparing, compared. 1** (*tr;* foll. by *to*) to regard as similar; liken: *the general has been compared to Napoleon.* **2** (*tr*) to examine in order to observe resemblances or differences: *to compare rum and gin.* **3** (*intr;* usually foll. by *with*) to be the same or similar: *gin compares with rum in alcoholic content.* **4** (*intr*) to bear a specified relation when examined: *this car compares badly with the other.* **5** (*tr*) *Grammar.* to give the positive, comparative, and superlative forms of (an adjective). **6 compare notes.** to exchange opinions. ◆ *n* **7** comparison (esp. in **beyond compare**). ORIG C15: from OF, from L *comparāre,* from *compar,* from *com-* together + *par* equal

comparison (kəmˈpærɪsᵊn) *n* **1** the act of comparing. **2** the state of being compared. **3** likeness: *there was no comparison between them.* **4** a rhetorical device involving comparison, such as a simile. **5** Also called: **degrees of comparison.** *Grammar.* the listing of the positive, comparative, and superlative forms of an adjective or adverb. **6 bear** *or* **stand comparison (with).** to be sufficiently similar to be compared with (something else), esp. favourably.

compartment (kəmˈpɑːtmənt) *n* **1** one of the sections

into which an area, esp. an enclosed space, is partitioned. **2** any separate section: *a compartment of the mind.* **3** a small storage space. ORIG C16: from F *compartiment,* ult. from LL *compartīrī* to share
▸ **compartmental** (ˌkɒmpɑːt'mɛntᵊl) *adj* ▸ **ˌcompart'mentally** *adv*

compartmentalize *or* **compartmentalise** (ˌkɒmpɑːt'mɛntᵊˌlaɪz) *vb* **compartmentalizes, compartmentalizing, compartmentalized** *or* **compartmentalises, compartmentalising, compartmentalised.** (*usually tr*) to put into categories, etc., esp. to an excessive degree.
▸ **ˌcompartˌmentali'zation** *or* **ˌcompartˌmentali'sation** *n*

compass ('kʌmpəs) *n* **1** Also called: **magnetic compass.** an instrument for finding direction, having a magnetized needle which points to magnetic north. **2** (*often pl*) Also called: **pair of compasses.** an instrument used for drawing circles, measuring distances, etc., that consists of two arms, joined at one end. **3** limits or range: *within the compass of education.* **4** *Music.* the interval between the lowest and highest note attainable. ◆ *vb* (*tr*) **5** to surround; hem in. **6** to grasp mentally. **7** to achieve; accomplish. **8** *Obs.* to plot. ORIG C13: from OF *compas,* from Vulgar L *compassāre* (unattested) to pace out, ult. from L *passus* step
▸ **'compassable** *adj*

compass card *n* a compass in the form of a card that rotates so that "0°" or "North" points to magnetic north.

compassion (kəm'pæʃən) *n* a feeling of distress and pity for the suffering or misfortune of another. ORIG C14: from OF, from LL *compassiō,* from L *com-* with + *patī* to suffer

compassionate (kəm'pæʃənɪt) *adj* showing or having compassion.
▸ **com'passionately** *adv*

compassionate leave *n* leave granted on the grounds of bereavement, family illness, etc.

compassion fatigue *n* the inability to react sympathetically to a crisis, disaster, etc., because of overexposure to previous crises, disasters, etc.

compass rose *n* a circle or decorative device printed on a map or chart showing the points of the compass.

compass saw *n* a hand saw with a narrow tapered blade for making a curved cut.

compatible (kəm'pætɪbᵊl) *adj* **1** (usually foll. by *with*) able to exist together harmoniously. **2** (usually foll. by *with*) consistent: *her deeds were not compatible with her ideology.* **3** (of pieces of machinery, etc.) capable of being used together without modification or adaptation. ORIG C15: from Med. L *compatibilis,* from LL *compatī;* see COMPASSION
▸ **comˌpati'bility** *n* ▸ **com'patibly** *adv*

compatriot (kəm'pætrɪət) *n* a fellow countryman. ORIG C17: from F *compatriote,* from LL; see PATRIOT
▸ **comˌpatri'otic** *adj*

compeer ('kɒmpɪə) *n* **1** a person of equal rank, status, or ability. **2** a comrade. ORIG C13: from OF *comper,* from Med. L *compater* godfather

compel (kəm'pɛl) *vb* **compels, compelling, compelled.** (*tr*) **1** to cause (someone) by force (to be or do something). **2** to obtain by force; exact: *to compel obedience.* ORIG C14: from L *compellere,* from *com-* together + *pellere* to drive
▸ **com'pellable** *adj*

compelling (kəm'pɛlɪŋ) *adj* **1** arousing or denoting strong interest, esp. admiring interest. **2** (of an argument, evidence, etc.) convincing.

compendious (kəm'pɛndɪəs) *adj* stating the essentials of a subject in a concise form.
▸ **com'pendiously** *adv* ▸ **com'pendiousness** *n*

compendium (kəm'pɛndɪəm) *n, pl* **compendiums** *or* **compendia** (-dɪə). **1** *Brit.* a book containing a collection of useful hints. **2** *Brit.* a selection, esp. of different games in one container. **3** a summary. ORIG C16: from L: a saving, lit.: something weighed

compensate ('kɒmpɛnˌseɪt) *vb* **compensates, compensating, compensated. 1** to make amends to (someone), esp. for loss or injury. **2** (*tr*) to serve as compensation or damages for (injury, loss, etc.). **3** to counterbalance the effects of (a force, weight, etc.) so as to produce equilibrium. **4** (*intr*) to attempt to conceal one's shortcomings by the exaggerated exhibition of qualities regarded as desirable. ORIG C17: from L *compēnsāre,* from *pendere* to weigh
▸ **compensatory** ('kɒmpɛnˌseɪtərɪ, kəm'pɛnsətərɪ) *or* **compensative** ('kɒmpɛnˌseɪtɪv, kəm'pɛnsə-) *adj*

compensation (ˌkɒmpɛn'seɪʃən) *n* **1** the act of making amends for something. **2** something given as reparation for loss, injury, etc. **3** the attempt to conceal one's shortcomings by the exaggerated exhibition of qualities regarded as desirable.
▸ **ˌcompen'sational** *adj*

comper ('kɒmpə) *n Inf.* a person who regularly enters competitions in newspapers, magazines, etc., esp. competitions offering consumer goods as prizes. ORIG C20: COMP(ETITION) + -ER[1]
▸ **'comping** *n*

compere ('kɒmpɛə) *Brit.* ◆ *n* **1** a master of ceremonies who introduces cabaret, television acts, etc. ◆ *vb* **comperes, compering, compered. 2** to act as a compere (for). ORIG C20: from F, lit.: godfather

compete (kəm'piːt) *vb* **competes, competing, competed.** (*intr;* often foll. by *with*) to contend (against) for profit, an award, etc. ORIG C17: from LL *competere,* from L, from *com-* together + *petere* to seek

competence ('kɒmpɪtəns) *or* **competency** *n* **1** the condition of being capable; ability. **2** a sufficient income to live on. **3** the state of being legally competent or qualified.

competent ('kɒmpɪtənt) *adj* **1** having sufficient skill, knowledge, etc.; capable. **2** suitable or sufficient for the purpose: *a competent answer.* **3** *Law.* (of a witness, etc.) qualified to testify, etc. ORIG C14: from L *competēns,* from *competere;* see COMPETE
▸ **'competently** *adv*

competition (ˌkɒmpɪ'tɪʃən) *n* **1** the act of competing. **2** a contest in which a winner is selected from among two or more entrants. **3** a series of games, sports events, etc. **4** the opposition offered by competitors. **5** competitors offering opposition.

competitive (kəm'pɛtɪtɪv) *adj* **1** involving rivalry: *competitive sports.* **2** sufficiently low in price or high in quality to be successful against commercial rivals. **3** characterized by an urge to compete: *a competitive personality.*
▸ **com'petitiveness** *n*

competitor (kəm'pɛtɪtə) *n* a person, group, team, firm, etc., that vies or competes; rival.

Compiègne ★ (*French* kɔ̃pjɛɲ) *n* a city in N France, on the Oise River: scene of the armistice at the end of World War I (1918) and of the Franco-German armistice of 1940. Pop.: 44 703 (1990).

compile (kəm'paɪl) *vb* **compiles, compiling, compiled.** (*tr*) **1** to make or compose from other sources: *to compile a list of names.* **2** to collect for a book, hobby, etc. **3** *Computing.* to create (a set of machine instructions) from a high-level programming language, using a compiler. ORIG C14: from L *compīlāre,* from *com-* together + *pīlāre* to thrust down, pack
▸ **compilation** (ˌkɒmpɪ'leɪʃən) *n*

compiler (kəm'paɪlə) *n* **1** a person who compiles something. **2** a computer program by which a high-level programming language is converted into machine language that can be acted upon by a computer. Cf. **assembler.**

complacency (kəm'pleɪsənsɪ) *or* **complacence** *n* extreme self-satisfaction; smugness.

complacent (kəm'pleɪsᵊnt) *adj* extremely self-satisfied. ORIG C17: from L *complacēns* very pleasing, from *complacēre,* from *com-* (intensive) + *placēre* to please
▸ **com'placently** *adv*

complain (kəm'pleɪn) *vb* (*intr*) **1** to express resentment, displeasure, etc.; grumble. **2** (foll. by *of*) to state the presence of pain, illness, etc.: *she complained of a headache.* ORIG C14: from OF *complaindre,* from Vulgar L *complangere* (unattested), from L *com-* (intensive) + *plangere* to bewail
▸ **com'plainer** *n* ▸ **com'plainingly** *adv*

complainant (kəm'pleɪnənt) *n Law.* a plaintiff.

complaint (kəm'pleɪnt) *n* **1** the act of complaining. **2** a cause for complaining; grievance. **3** a mild ailment.

complaisant (kəm'pleɪzᵊnt) *adj* showing a desire to comply or oblige; polite. ORIG C17: from F *complaire,* from L *complacēre* to please greatly; cf. COMPLACENT
▸ **com'plaisance** *n*

complement *n* ('kɒmplɪmənt). **1** a person or thing that completes something. **2** a complete amount, number, etc. (often in **full complement**). **3** the officers and crew needed to man a ship. **4** *Grammar.* a word, phrase, or clause that completes the meaning of the predicate, as *an idiot* in *He is an idiot* or *that he would be early* in *I hoped that he would be early.* **5** *Maths.* the angle that when added to a specified angle produces a right angle. **6** *Logic.* the class of all the things that are not members of a given class. **7** *Immunol.* a group of proteins in the blood serum that, when activated by antibodies, destroys alien cells, such as bacteria. ◆ *vb* ('kɒmplɪˌmɛnt). **8** (*tr*) to complete or form a complement to. ORIG C14: from L *complēmentum,* from *complēre,* from *com-* (intensive) + *plēre* to fill
▸ **ˌcomplemen'tation** *n*

> **USAGE NOTE** This is sometimes confused with **compliment.**

complementary (ˌkɒmplɪ'mɛntərɪ) *adj* **1** forming a complement. **2** forming a satisfactory or balanced whole. **3** involving or using the treatments and techniques of alternative (complementary) medicine.
▸ **ˌcomple'mentarily** *adv* ▸ **ˌcomple'mentariness** *n*

complementary angle *n* either of two angles whose sum is 90°. Cf. **supplementary angle.**

complementary colour *n* one of any pair of colours, such as yellow and blue, that give white or grey when mixed in the correct proportions.

complementary DNA *n* a form of DNA artificially synthesized from a messenger RNA template and used in genetic engineering to produce gene clones. Abbrev.: **cDNA.**

complementary medicine *n* another name for **alternative medicine.**

complete (kəm'pliːt) *adj* **1** having every necessary part; entire. **2** finished. **3** (*prenominal*) thorough: *he is a complete rogue.* **4** perfect in quality or kind: *he is a complete scholar.* **5** (of a logical system) constituted such that a contradiction or inconsistency arises on the addition of an axiom that cannot be deduced from the axioms of the system. **6** *Arch.* skilled; accomplished. ◆ *vb* **completes, completing, completed.** (*tr*) **7** to make perfect. **8** to finish. **9** (in land law) to pay any outstanding balance on a contract for the conveyance of land in exchange for the title deeds, so that the ownership of the land changes hands. **10** *American football.* (of a quarterback) to make a forward pass successfully. ORIG C14: from L *complētus,* p.p. of *complēre* to fill up; see COMPLEMENT
▸ **com'pletely** *adv* ▸ **com'pleteness** *n* ▸ **com'pletion** *n*

completist (kəm'pliːtɪst) *n* a person who collects objects or memorabilia obsessively.

complex ('kɒmplɛks) *adj* **1** made up of interconnected parts. **2** (of thoughts, writing, etc.) intricate. **3** *Maths.* **3a** of or involving complex numbers. **3b** consisting of a real and an imaginary part, either of which can be zero. ◆ *n* **4** a whole made up of related parts: *a building complex.* **5** *Psychoanal.* a group of emotional impulses that have been banished from the conscious mind but continue to influence a person's behaviour. **6** *Inf.* an obsession: *he's got a complex about cats.* **7** any chemical compound in which one molecule is linked to another by a coordinate bond. ORIG C17: from L *complexus,* from *complectī,* from *com-* together + *plectere* to braid
▸ **'complexness** *n*

> **USAGE NOTE** *Complex* is sometimes used where *complicated* is meant. *Complex* should be used to say only that something consists of several parts rather than that it is difficult to understand, analyse, or deal with, which is what *complicated* inherently means. In the following real example a clear distinction is made between the two words: *the British benefits system is phenomenally complex and is administered by a complicated range of agen-*

complex fraction *n Maths.* a fraction in which the numerator or denominator or both contain fractions. Also called: **compound fraction.**

complexion (kəm'plɛkʃən) *n* **1** the colour and general appearance of a person's skin, esp. of the face. **2** aspect or nature: *the general complexion of a nation's finances.* **3** *Obs.* temperament. ORIG C14: from L *complexiō* a combination, from *complectī* to embrace; see COMPLEX
▸ **com'plexional** *adj*

complexioned (kəm'plɛkʃənd) *adj* of a specified complexion: *light-complexioned.*

complexity (kəm'plɛksɪtɪ) *n, pl* **complexities. 1** the state or quality of being intricate or complex. **2** something intricate or complex; complication.

complex number *n* any number of the form $a + bi$, where a and b are real numbers and $i = \sqrt{-1}$.

complex sentence *n Grammar.* a sentence containing at least one main clause and one subordinate clause.

compliance (kəm'plaɪəns) *or* **compliancy** *n* **1** acquiescence. **2** a disposition to yield to others. **3** a measure of the ability of a mechanical system to respond to an applied vibrating force.

compliance officer *or* **lawyer** *n* a specialist, usually a lawyer, employed by a financial group operating in a variety of fields and for multiple clients to ensure that no conflict of interest arises and that all obligations and regulations are complied with.

compliant (kəm'plaɪənt) *adj* complying, obliging, or yielding.
▸ **com'pliantly** *adv*

complicate *vb* ('kɒmplɪˌkeɪt), **complicates, complicating, complicated. 1** to make or become complex, etc. ◆ *adj* ('kɒmplɪkɪt). **2** *Biol.* folded on itself: *a complicate leaf.* ORIG C17: from L *complicāre* to fold together

complicated ('kɒmplɪˌkeɪtɪd) *adj* made up of intricate parts or aspects that are difficult to understand or analyse.
▸ **'compliˌcatedly** *adv*

> **USAGE NOTE** See at **complex.**

complication (ˌkɒmplɪ'keɪʃən) *n* **1** a condition, event, etc., that is complex or confused. **2** the act of complicating. **3** an event or condition that complicates or frustrates: *her coming was a serious complication.* **4** a disease arising as a consequence of another.

complicity (kəm'plɪsɪtɪ) *n, pl* **complicities. 1** the fact of being an accomplice, esp. in a criminal act. **2** a less common word for **complexity.**

compliment *n* ('kɒmplɪmənt). **1** a remark or act expressing respect, admiration, etc. **2** (*usually pl*) a greeting of respect or regard. ◆ *vb* ('kɒmplɪˌmɛnt). (*tr*) **3** to express admiration for; congratulate. **4** to express or show regard for, esp. by a gift. ORIG C17: from F, from It. *complimento,* from Sp. *cumplimiento,* from *cumplir* to complete

> **USAGE NOTE** This is sometimes confused with **complement.**

complimentary (ˌkɒmplɪ'mɛntərɪ) *adj* **1** conveying a compliment. **2** flattering. **3** given free, esp. as a courtesy or for publicity purposes.
▸ **ˌcompli'mentarily** *adv*

compline ('kɒmplɪn, -plaɪn) *or* **complin** ('kɒmplɪn) *n RC Church.* the last of the seven canonical hours of the divine office. ORIG C13: from OF *complie,* from Med. L *hōra complēta,* lit.: the completed hour

comply (kəm'plaɪ) *vb* **complies, complying, complied.** (*intr*) (usually foll. by *with*) to act in accordance with rules, wishes, etc.; be obedient (to). ORIG C17: from It. *complire,* from Sp. *cumplir* to complete

compo ('kɒmpəʊ) *n, pl* **compos. 1** a mixture of materials, such as mortar, plaster, etc. **2** *Austral. & NZ inf.* compensation, esp. for injury or loss of work. ◆ *adj* **3** *Mil.* intended to last for several days: *a compo pack.* ORIG short for *composition, compensation, composite*

component (kəm'pəʊnənt) *n* **1** a constituent part or aspect of something more complex. **2** any electrical device that has distinct electrical characteristics and may be connected to other devices to form a circuit. **3** *Maths.* one of a set of two or more vectors whose resultant is a given vector. **4** See **phase rule.** ◆ *adj* **5** forming or functioning as a part or aspect; constituent. ORIG C17: from L *compōnere* to put together
▸ **componential** (ˌkɒmpə'nɛnʃəl) *adj*

comport (kəm'pɔːt) *vb* **1** (*tr*) to conduct or bear (oneself) in a specified way. **2** (*intr;* foll. by *with*) to agree (with). ORIG C16: from L *comportāre* collect, from *com-* together + *portāre* to carry
▸ **com'portment** *n*

compose (kəm'pəʊz) *vb* **composes, composing, composed.** (*mainly tr*) **1** to put together or make up. **2** to be the component elements of. **3** to create (a musical or literary work). **4** (*intr*) to write music. **5** to calm (someone, esp. oneself); make quiet. **6** to adjust or settle (a quarrel, etc.). **7** to order the elements of (a painting, sculpture, etc.); design. **8** *Printing.* to set up (type). ORIG C15: from OF *composer,* from L *compōnere* to put in place

composed (kəm'pəʊzd) *adj* (of people) calm; tranquil.
▸ **composedly** (kəm'pəʊzɪdlɪ) *adv*

composer (kəm'pəʊzə) *n* **1** a person who composes music. **2** a person or machine that composes anything, esp. type for printing.

composite *adj* ('kɒmpəzɪt). **1** composed of separate parts; compound. **2** of or belonging to the plant family Compositae. **3** *Maths.* capable of being factorized: *a composite function.* **4** (*sometimes cap.*) denoting one of the five classical orders of architecture: characterized by a combination of the Ionic and Corinthian styles. ◆ *n* ('kɒmpəzɪt). **5** something composed of separate parts; compound. **6** any plant of the family Compositae, having flower heads composed of many small flowers (e.g. dandelion, daisy). **7** a material, such as reinforced concrete, made of two or more distinct materials. **8** a proposal that has been composited. ◆ *vb* ('kɒmpəˌzaɪt), **composites, compositing, composited.** (*tr*) **9** to merge related motions from local branches (of a political party, trade union, etc.) so as to produce a manageable number of proposals for discussion at national level. ORIG C16: from L *compositus* well arranged, from *compōnere* to arrange
▸ **'compositely** *adv* ▸ **'compositeness** *n*

composite school *n E. Canad.* a secondary school offering both academic and nonacademic courses.

composition (ˌkɒmpə'zɪʃən) *n* **1** the act of putting together or making up by combining parts. **2** something formed in this manner; a mixture. **3** the parts of which something is composed; constitution. **4** a work of music, art, or literature. **5** the harmonious arrangement of the parts of a work of art in relation to each other. **6** a piece of writing undertaken as an academic exercise; an essay. **7** *Printing.* the act or technique of setting up type. **8** a settlement by mutual consent, esp. a legal agreement whereby the creditors agree to accept partial payment of a debt in full settlement. ORIG C14: from OF, from L *compositus;* see COMPOSITE, -ION

compositor (kəm'pɒzɪtə) *n Printing.* a person who sets and corrects type.

compos mentis *Latin.* ('kɒmpəs 'mɛntɪs) *adj* (*postpositive*) of sound mind; sane.

compost ('kɒmpɒst) *n* **1** a mixture of organic residues such as decomposed vegetation, manure, etc., used as a fertilizer. **2** a mixture, as of sand, peat, and charcoal, in which plants are grown, esp. in pots. **3** *Rare.* a mixture. ◆ *vb* (*tr*) **4** to make (vegetable matter) into compost. **5** to fertilize with compost. ORIG C14: from OF *compost,* from L *compositus* put together

Compostela ★ (*Spanish* kɔmpɔs'tela) *n* See **Santiago de Compostela.**

composure (kəm'pəʊʒə) *n* calmness, esp. of the mind; tranquillity; serenity.

compote ('kɒmpəʊt) *n* a dish of fruit stewed with sugar or in a syrup. ORIG C17: from F *composte,* from L *compositus* put in place

compound[1] *n* ('kɒmpaʊnd). **1** a substance that contains atoms of two or more chemical elements held together by chemical bonds. **2** any combination of two or more parts, aspects, etc. **3** a word formed from two existing words or combining forms. ◆ *vb* (kəm'paʊnd). (*mainly tr*) **4** to combine so as to create a compound. **5** to make by combining parts, aspects, etc.: *to compound a new plastic.* **6** to intensify by an added element: *his anxiety was compounded by her crying.* **7** (*also intr*) to come to an agreement in (a dispute, etc.) or to settle (a debt, etc.) for less than what is owed; compromise. **8** *Law.* to agree not to prosecute in return for a consideration: *to compound a crime.* ◆ *adj* ('kɒmpaʊnd). **9** composed of two or more parts, elements, etc. **10** (of a word) consisting of elements that are also words or combining forms. **11** *Grammar.* (of tense, mood, etc.) formed by using an auxiliary verb in addition to the main verb. **12** *Music.* **12a** denoting a time in which the number of beats per bar is a multiple of three: *six-four is an example of compound time.* **12b** (of an interval) greater than an octave. **13** (of a steam engine, etc.) having multiple stages in which the steam or working fluid from one stage is used in a subsequent stage. **14** (of a piston engine) having a supercharger powered by a turbine in the exhaust stream. ORIG C14: from earlier *compounen,* from OF *compondre* to set in order, from L *compōnere*
▸ **com'poundable** *adj*

compound[2] ('kɒmpaʊnd) *n* **1** (esp. formerly in South Africa) an enclosure, esp. on the mines, containing the living quarters for Black workers. **2** any similar enclosure, such as a camp for prisoners of war. ORIG C17: from Malay *kampong* village

compound eye *n* the convex eye of insects and some crustaceans, consisting of numerous separate light-sensitive units (ommatidia).

compound fraction *n* another name for **complex fraction.**

compound fracture *n* a fracture in which the broken bone pierces the skin.

compound interest *n* interest calculated on both the principal and its accrued interest.

compound leaf *n* a leaf consisting of two or more leaflets borne on the same leafstalk.

compound number *n* a quantity expressed in two or more different but related units: *3 hours 10 seconds is a compound number.*

compound sentence *n* a sentence containing at least two coordinate clauses.

compound time *n* See **compound**[1] (sense 12).

comprehend (ˌkɒmprɪ'hɛnd) *vb* **1** to understand. **2** (*tr*) to comprise; include. ORIG C14: from L *comprehendere,* from *prehendere* to seize

comprehensible (ˌkɒmprɪ'hɛnsəbᵊl) *adj* capable of being comprehended.
▸ **ˌcompreˌhensi'bility** *n* ▸ **ˌcompre'hensibly** *adv*

comprehension (ˌkɒmprɪ'hɛnʃən) *n* **1** the act or capacity of understanding. **2** the state of including; comprehensiveness.

comprehensive (ˌkɒmprɪ'hɛnsɪv) *adj* **1** of broad scope or content. **2** (of a car insurance policy) providing protection against most risks, including third-party liability, fire, theft, and damage. **3** of or being a comprehensive school. ◆ *n* **4** short for **comprehensive school.**
▸ **ˌcompre'hensively** *adv* ▸ **ˌcompre'hensiveness** *n*

comprehensive school *n Chiefly Brit.* a secondary school for children of all abilities from the same district.

compress *vb* (kəm'prɛs). **1** (*tr*) to squeeze together; condense. ♦ *n* ('kɒmprɛs). **2** a cloth or gauze pad applied firmly to some part of the body to relieve discomfort, reduce fever, etc. ORIG C14: from LL *compressāre*, from L *comprimere*, from *premere* to press
▸ **com'pressible** *adj* ▸ **com'pressive** *adj*

compressed air *n* air at a higher pressure than atmospheric pressure: used esp. as a source of power for machines.

compressibility (kəm,prɛsɪ'bɪlɪtɪ) *n* **1** the ability to be compressed. **2** *Physics.* the reciprocal of the bulk modulus; the ratio of volume strain to stress at constant temperature. Symbol: *k*

compression (kəm'prɛʃən) *n* **1** the act of compressing or the condition of being compressed. **2** an increase in pressure of the charge in an engine or compressor obtained by reducing its volume.

compressor (kəm'prɛsə) *n* **1** any device that compresses a gas. **2** the part of a gas turbine that compresses the air before it enters the combustion chambers. **3** any muscle that causes compression. **4** an electronic device for reducing the variation in signal amplitude in a transmission system.

comprise (kəm'praɪz) *vb* **comprises, comprising, comprised.** (*tr*) **1** to be made up of. **2** to constitute the whole of; consist of: *her singing comprised the entertainment.* ORIG C15: from F *compris* included, from *comprendre* to COMPREHEND
▸ **com'prisable** *adj*

USAGE NOTE The use of *of* after *comprise* should be avoided: *the library comprises* (not *comprises of*) *500,000 books and manuscripts.*

compromise ('kɒmprə,maɪz) *n* **1** settlement of a dispute by concessions on both or all sides. **2** the terms of such a settlement. **3** something midway between different things. ♦ *vb* **compromises, compromising, compromised. 4** to settle (a dispute) by making concessions. **5** (*tr*) to expose (oneself or another) to disrepute. ORIG C15: from OF *compromis*, from L, from *comprōmittere*, from *prōmittere* to promise
▸ **'compro,miser** *n* ▸ **'compro,misingly** *adv*

compte rendu *French.* (kɔ̃t rɑ̃dy) *n, pl* ***comptes rendus*** (kɔ̃t rɑ̃dy). **1** a review or notice. **2** an account. ORIG lit.: account rendered

Compton ★ *n* **1** ('kɒmptən). **Arthur Holly.** 1892–1962, US physicist, noted for his research on X-rays, gamma rays, and nuclear energy: Nobel prize for physics 1927. **2** ('kʌmptən). **Denis.** 1918–97, English cricketer, who played for Middlesex and England (1937–57).

Compton-Burnett ★ ('kɒmptənbɜː'nɛt, -'bɜːnɪt) *n* Dame **Ivy.** 1884–1969, British novelist. Her novels include *Men and Wives* (1931) and *Mother and Son* (1955).

comptroller (kən'trəʊlə) *n* a variant spelling of **controller** (sense 2), esp. as a title of any of various financial executives.

compulsion (kəm'pʌlʃən) *n* **1** the act of compelling or the state of being compelled. **2** something that compels. **3** *Psychiatry.* an inner drive that causes a person to perform actions, often repetitive, against his or her will. See also **obsession.** ORIG C15: from OF, from L *compellere* to COMPEL

compulsive (kəm'pʌlsɪv) *adj* relating to or involving compulsion.
▸ **com'pulsively** *adv*

compulsory (kəm'pʌlsərɪ) *adj* **1** required by regulations or laws; obligatory. **2** involving or employing compulsion; compelling; essential.
▸ **com'pulsorily** *adv* ▸ **com'pulsoriness** *n*

compulsory purchase *n* purchase of a property by a local authority or government department for public use or development, regardless of whether or not the owner wishes to sell.

compunction (kəm'pʌŋkʃən) *n* a feeling of remorse, guilt, or regret. ORIG C14: from Church L *compunctiō*, from L *compungere* to sting
▸ **com'punctious** *adj* ▸ **com'punctiously** *adv*

computation (,kɒmpjʊ'teɪʃən) *n* a calculation involving numbers or quantities.
▸ **,compu'tational** *adj*

compute (kəm'pjuːt) *vb* **computes, computing, computed.** to calculate (an answer, result, etc.), often with the aid of a computer. ORIG C17: from L *computāre*, from *putāre* to think
▸ **com'putable** *adj* ▸ **com,puta'bility** *n*

computed tomography *n Med.* another name (esp. US) for **computerized tomography.**

computer (kəm'pjuːtə) *n* **1a** a device, usually electronic, that processes data according to a set of instructions. The **digital computer** stores data in discrete units and performs operations at very high speed. The **analog computer** has no memory and is slower than the digital computer but has a continuous rather than a discrete input. **1b** (*as modifier*): *computer technology.* **2** a person who computes or calculates.

computer-aided design *n* the use of computer techniques in designing products, esp. involving the use of computer graphics. Abbrev.: **CAD.**

computer-aided engineering *n* the use of computers to automate manufacturing processes. Abbrev.: **CAE.**

computer architecture *n* the structure, behaviour, and design of computing.

computerate (kəm'pjuːtərɪt) *adj* able to use computing. ORIG C20: COMPUTER + -ATE[1], by analogy with *literate*

computer dating *n* the use of computers by dating agencies to match their clients.

computer game *n* any of various games, recorded on cassette or disc for use in a home computer, that are played by manipulating a mouse, joystick or the keys on the keyboard of a computer in response to the graphics on the screen.

computer graphics *n* (*functioning as sing*) the use of a computer to produce and manipulate pictorial images on a video screen, as in animation techniques or the production of audiovisual aids.

computerize *or* **computerise** (kəm'pjuːtə,raɪz) *vb* **computerizes, computerizing, computerized** *or* **computerises, computerising, computerised. 1** (*tr*) to cause (certain operations) to be performed by a computer, esp. as a replacement for human labour. **2** (*intr*) to install a computer. **3** (*tr*) to control or perform (operations) by means of a computer. **4** (*tr*) to process or store (information) by or in a computer.
▸ **com,puteri'zation** *or* **com,puteri'sation** *n*

computerized tomography *n Med.* a radiological technique that produces images of cross sections through a patient's body. Also called (esp. US): **computed tomography.** Abbrev.: **CT.** See also **CT scanner.**

computer language *n* another term for **programming language.**

computer science *n* the study of computers and their application.

comrade ('kɒmreɪd, -rɪd) *n* **1** a companion. **2** a fellow member of a political party, esp. a fellow Communist. ORIG C16: from F *camarade*, from Sp. *camarada* group of soldiers sharing a billet, from *cámara* room, from L
▸ **'comradely** *adj* ▸ **'comrade,ship** *n*

Comsat ('kɒmsæt) *n Trademark.* short for **communications satellite.**

Comte ★ (*French* kɔ̃t) *n* (**Isidore**) **Auguste** (**Marie François**) (ogyst). 1798–1857, French mathematician and philosopher; the founder of positivism.
▸ **Comtism** ('kɔːn,tɪzəm) *n* ▸ **'Comtist** *or* **'Comtian** *adj, n*

Comus ★ ('kəʊməs) *n* (in late Roman mythology) a god of revelry. ORIG C17: from L, from Gk *kōmos* a revel

con[1] (kɒn) *Inf.* ♦ *n* **1a** short for **confidence trick. 1b** (*as modifier*): *con man.* ♦ *vb* **cons, conning, conned. 2** (*tr*) to swindle or defraud. ORIG C19: from CONFIDENCE

con[2] (kɒn) *n* (*usually pl*) an argument or vote against a proposal, motion, etc. See also **pros and cons.** ORIG from L *contrā* against

★ people and places

con[3] *or esp. US* **conn** (kɒn) *vb* **cons** *or esp. US* **conns, conning, conned.** (*tr*) *Naut.* to direct the steering of (a vessel). ORIG C17 *cun,* from earlier *condien* to guide, from OF *conduire,* from L *condūcere;* see CONDUCT

con[4] (kɒn) *vb* **cons, conning, conned.** (*tr*) *Arch.* to study attentively or learn. ORIG C15: var. of CAN[1] in the sense: to come to know

con[5] (kɒn) *prep Music.* with. ORIG It.

con. *abbrev. for:* **1** concerto. **2** conclusion. **3** connection. **4** consolidated. **5** continued.

con- *prefix* a variant of **com-**.

Conakry *or* **Konakri** ★ (*French* kɔnakri) *n* the capital of Guinea, a port on the island of Tombo. Pop.: 1 508 000 (1995 est.).

con amore (kɒn æ'mɔːrɪ) *adj, adv Music.* (to be performed) lovingly. ORIG C19: from It.: with love

Conan Doyle ★ ('kəʊnən 'dɔɪl, 'kɒnən) *n* Sir **Arthur.** 1859–1930, British author of detective stories and creator of *Sherlock Holmes.*

con brio (kɒn 'briːəʊ) *adj, adv Music.* (to be performed) with liveliness or spirit. ORIG It.: with energy

concatenate (kɒn'kætɪˌneɪt) *vb* **concatenates, concatenating, concatenated.** (*tr*) to link or join together, esp. in a chain or series. ORIG C16: from LL *concatēnāre,* from L *com-* together + *catēna* CHAIN
▸ ˌ**concate'nation** *n*

concave ('kɒnkeɪv, kɒn'keɪv) *adj* **1** curving inwards; having the shape of a section of the interior of a sphere, paraboloid, etc.: *a concave lens.* ◆ *vb* **2** (*tr*) to make concave. ORIG C15: from L *concavus* arched, from *cavus* hollow
▸ '**concavely** *adv* ▸ '**concaveness** *n*

concavity (kɒn'kævɪtɪ) *n, pl* **concavities. 1** the state of being concave. **2** a concave surface or thing.

concavo-concave (kɒnˌkeɪvəʊkɒn'keɪv) *adj* (esp. of a lens) having both sides concave.

concavo-convex *adj* **1** having one side concave and the other side convex. **2** (of a lens) having a concave face with greater curvature than the convex face.

conceal (kən'siːl) *vb* (*tr*) **1** to keep from discovery; hide. **2** to keep secret. ORIG C14: from OF *conceler,* from L *concēlāre,* from *com-* (intensive) + *cēlāre* to hide
▸ **con'cealer** *n* ▸ **con'cealment** *n*

concede (kən'siːd) *vb* **concedes, conceding, conceded. 1** (when *tr, may take a clause as object*) to admit or acknowledge (something) as true or correct. **2** to yield or allow (something, such as a right). **3** (*tr*) to admit as certain in outcome: *to concede an election.* ORIG C17: from L *concēdere,* from *cēdere* to give way
▸ **con'ceder** *n*

conceit (kən'siːt) *n* **1** a high, often exaggerated, opinion of oneself or one's accomplishments. **2** *Literary.* an elaborate image or far-fetched comparison. **3** *Arch.* **3a** a witty expression. **3b** fancy; imagination. **3c** an idea. ◆ *vb* (*tr*) **4** *Obs.* to think. ORIG C14: from CONCEIVE

conceited (kən'siːtɪd) *adj* having an exaggerated opinion of oneself or one's accomplishments.
▸ **con'ceitedly** *adv* ▸ **con'ceitedness** *n*

conceivable (kən'siːvəbᵊl) *adj* capable of being understood, believed, or imagined; possible.
▸ **conˌceiva'bility** *n* ▸ **con'ceivably** *adv*

conceive (kən'siːv) *vb* **conceives, conceiving, conceived. 1** (when *intr,* foll. by *of;* when *tr, often takes a clause as object*) to have an idea (of); imagine; think. **2** (*tr; takes a clause as object or an infinitive*) to believe. **3** (*tr*) to develop: *she conceived a passion for music.* **4** to become pregnant with (a child). **5** (*tr*) *Rare.* to express in words. ORIG C13: from OF *conceivre,* from L *concipere* to take in, from *capere* to take

concelebrate (kən'sɛlɪˌbreɪt) *vb* **concelebrates, concelebrating, concelebrated.** *Christianity.* to celebrate (the Eucharist or Mass) jointly with one or more other priests. ORIG C16: from L *concelebrāre*
▸ **conˌcele'bration** *n*

concentrate ('kɒnsənˌtreɪt) *vb* **concentrates, concentrating, concentrated. 1** to come or cause to come to a single purpose or aim: *to concentrate one's hopes on winning.* **2** to make or become denser or purer by the removal of certain elements. **3** (*intr;* often foll. by *on*) to think intensely (about). ◆ *n* **4** a concentrated material or solution. ORIG C17: back formation from CONCENTRATION, ult. from L *com-* same + *centrum* CENTRE
▸ '**concenˌtrative** *adj* ▸ '**concenˌtrator** *n*

concentration (ˌkɒnsən'treɪʃən) *n* **1** intense mental application. **2** the act of concentrating. **3** something that is concentrated. **4** the strength of a solution, esp. the amount of dissolved substance in a given volume of solvent. **5** *Mil.* **5a** the act of bringing together military forces. **5b** the application of fire from a number of weapons against a target.

concentration camp *n* a guarded prison camp for nonmilitary prisoners, esp. one in Nazi Germany.

concentre *or US* **concenter** (kən'sɛntə) *vb* **concentres, concentring, concentred** *or US* **concenters, concentering, concentered.** to converge or cause to converge on a common centre; concentrate. ORIG C16: from F *concentrer*

concentric (kən'sɛntrɪk) *adj* having a common centre: *concentric circles.* ORIG C14: from Med. L *concentricus,* from L *com-* same + *centrum* CENTRE
▸ **con'centrically** *adv*

Concepción ★ (*Spanish* kɔnθɛp'θjɔn) *n* an industrial city in S central Chile. Pop.: 350 268 (1995 est.).

concept ('kɒnsɛpt) *n* **1** an idea, esp. an abstract idea: *the concepts of biology.* **2** *Philosophy.* a general idea that corresponds to some class of entities and consists of the essential features of the class. **3** a new idea; invention. **4** (*modifier*) (of a product, esp. a car) created to demonstrate the technical skills and imagination of the designers, and not for mass production or sale. ORIG C16: from L *conceptum,* from *concipere* to CONCEIVE

conception (kən'sɛpʃən) *n* **1** something conceived; notion, idea, or plan. **2** the description under which someone considers something: *a strange conception of freedom.* **3** the fertilization of an ovum by a sperm in the Fallopian tube followed by implantation in the womb. **4** origin or beginning. ORIG C13: from L *conceptiō,* from *concipere* to CONCEIVE
▸ **con'ceptional** *or* **con'ceptive** *adj*

conceptual (kən'sɛptjʊəl) *adj* of or characterized by concepts.
▸ **con'ceptually** *adv*

conceptualize *or* **conceptualise** (kən'sɛptjʊəˌlaɪz) *vb* **conceptualizes, conceptualizing, conceptualized** *or* **conceptualises, conceptualising, conceptualised.** to form (a concept or concepts) out of observations, experience, data, etc.
▸ **conˌceptuali'zation** *or* **conˌceptuali'sation** *n*

concern (kən'sɜːn) *vb* (*tr*) **1** to relate to; affect. **2** (usually foll. by *with* or *in*) to involve or interest (oneself): *he concerns himself with other people's affairs.* ◆ *n* **3** something that affects a person; affair; business. **4** regard or interest: *he felt a strong concern for her.* **5** anxiety or solicitude. **6** important relation: *his news has great concern for us.* **7** a commercial company. **8** *Inf.* a material thing, esp. one of which one has a low opinion. ORIG C15: from LL *concernere,* from L *com-* together + *cernere* to sift

concerned (kən'sɜːnd) *adj* **1** (*postpositive*) interested, guilty, or involved: *I shall find the boy concerned and punish him.* **2** worried or solicitous.
▸ **concernedly** (kən'sɜːnɪdlɪ) *adv*

concerning (kən'sɜːnɪŋ) *prep* **1** about; regarding. ◆ *adj* **2** worrying or troublesome.

concernment (kən'sɜːnmənt) *n Rare.* affair or business; concern.

concert *n* ('kɒnsɜːt). **1a** a performance of music by players or singers that does not involve theatrical staging. **1b** (*as modifier*): *a concert version of an opera.* **2** agreement in design, plan, or action. **3** **in concert. 3a** acting with a common purpose. **3b** (of musicians, etc.) performing live. ◆ *vb* (kən'sɜːt). **4** to arrange or contrive (a plan) by mutual agreement. ORIG C16: from F *concerter* to bring into agreement, from It., from LL *concertāre* to work together, from L *certāre* to contend

concertante (ˌkɒntʃə'tæntɪ) *adj Music.* characterized by contrasting alternating tutti and solo passages. ORIG It.: from *concertare* to perform a CONCERT

concerted (kən'sɜːtɪd) *adj* **1** mutually contrived,

planned, or arranged; combined: *a concerted effort.* **2** *Music.* arranged in parts for a group of singers or players.

Concertgebouw ★ (*Dutch* kɔn'sɛrtxəbɔu) *n* a concert hall in Amsterdam, inaugurated in 1888: the **Concertgebouw Orchestra,** established in 1888, has been independent of the hall since World War II.

concert grand *n* a grand piano of the largest size.

concertina (ˌkɒnsə'tiːnə) *n* **1** a hexagonal musical instrument similar to the accordion, in which metallic reeds are vibrated by air from a set of bellows operated by the player's hands. ◆ *vb* **concertinas, concertinaing, concertinaed. 2** (*intr*) to collapse or fold up like the bellows of a concertina. ORIG C19: CONCERT + *-ina*
▸ ˌ**concer'tinist** *n*

concertino (ˌkɒntʃə'tiːnəʊ) *n, pl* **concertini** (-nɪ). *Music.* **1** the solo group in a concerto grosso. **2** a short concerto. ORIG It.: a little CONCERTO

concertmaster ('kɒnsətˌmɑːstə) *n* a US and Canad. word for **leader** (of an orchestra).

concerto (kən'tʃɛətəʊ) *n, pl* **concertos** *or* **concerti** (-tɪ). a composition for an orchestra and one or more soloists. ORIG C18: from It.: CONCERT

concerto grosso ('grɒsəʊ) *n, pl* **concerti grossi** ('grɒsɪ) *or* **concerto grossos.** a composition for an orchestra and a group of soloists. ORIG It., lit.: big concerto

concert party *n* **1** a musical entertainment popular in the early 20th century, esp. one at a British seaside resort. **2** *Stock Exchange inf.* a group of individuals or companies who secretly agree together to purchase shares separately in a particular company which they plan to amalgamate later into a single holding: a malpractice which is illegal in some countries.

concert pitch *n* **1** the frequency of 440 hertz assigned to the A above middle C. **2** *Inf.* a state of extreme readiness.

concession (kən'sɛʃən) *n* **1** the act of yielding or conceding. **2** something conceded. **3** *Brit.* a reduction in the usual price of a ticket granted to a special group of customers: *a student concession.* **4** any grant of rights, land, or property by a government, local authority, corporation, or individual. **5** the right, esp. an exclusive right, to market a particular product in a given area. **6** *Canad.* **6a** a land subdivision in a township survey. **6b** another name for a **concession road.** ORIG C16: from L *concēssiō,* from *concēdere* to CONCEDE
▸ **con'cessible** *adj* ▸ **con'cessive** *adj*

concessionaire (kənˌsɛʃə'nɛə), **concessioner** (kən'sɛʃənə), *or* **concessionary** *n* someone who holds or operates a concession.

concessionary (kən'sɛʃənərɪ) *adj* **1** of, granted, or obtained by a concession. ◆ *n, pl* **concessionaries. 2** another word for **concessionaire.**

concession road *n Canad.* one of a series of roads separating concessions in a township.

conch (kɒŋk, kɒntʃ) *n, pl* **conchs** (kɒŋks) *or* **conches** ('kɒntʃɪz). **1** any of various tropical marine gastropod molluscs characterized by a large brightly coloured spiral shell. **2** the shell of such a mollusc, used as a trumpet. ORIG C16: from L *concha,* from Gk *konkhē* shellfish

conchie *or* **conchy** ('kɒntʃɪ) *n, pl* **conchies.** *Inf.* short for **conscientious objector.**

Conchobar ★ ('kɒŋkəuwə, 'kɒnʊə) *n* (in Irish legend) a king of Ulster at about the beginning of the Christian era. See also **Deirdre.**

conchology (kɒŋ'kɒlədʒɪ) *n* the study of mollusc shells.
▸ **con'chologist** *n*

concierge (ˌkɒnsɪ'ɛəʒ) *n* (esp. in France) a caretaker of a block of flats, hotel, etc., esp. one who lives on the premises. ORIG C17: from F, ult. from L *conservus,* from *servus* slave

conciliar (kən'sɪlɪə) *adj* of, from, or by means of a council, esp. an ecclesiastical one.

conciliate (kən'sɪlɪˌeɪt) *vb* **conciliates, conciliating, conciliated.** (*tr*) **1** to overcome the hostility of; win over. **2** to gain (favour, regard, etc.), esp. by making friendly overtures. ORIG C16: from L *conciliāre* to bring together, from *concilium* COUNCIL
▸ **con'ciliable** *adj* ▸ **con'ciliˌator** *n*

conciliation (kənˌsɪlɪ'eɪʃən) *n* **1** the act or process of conciliating. **2** a method of helping the parties in a dispute to reach agreement, esp. divorcing or separating couples to part amicably.

conciliatory (kən'sɪljətərɪ) *or* **conciliative** (kən'sɪljətɪv) *adj* intended to placate or reconcile.
▸ **con'ciliatorily** *adv*

concise (kən'saɪs) *adj* brief and to the point. ORIG C16: from L *concīsus* cut short, from *concīdere,* from *caedere* to cut, strike down
▸ **con'cisely** *adv* ▸ **con'ciseness** *or* **concision** (kən'sɪʒən) *n*

conclave ('kɒnkleɪv) *n* **1** a secret meeting. **2** *RC Church.* **2a** the closed apartments where the college of cardinals elects a new pope. **2b** a meeting of the college of cardinals for this purpose. ORIG C14: from Med. L *conclāve,* from L: place that may be locked, from *clāvis* key

conclude (kən'kluːd) *vb* **concludes, concluding, concluded.** (*mainly tr*) **1** (*also intr*) to come or cause to come to an end. **2** (*takes a clause as object*) to decide by reasoning; deduce: *the judge concluded that the witness had told the truth.* **3** to settle: *to conclude a treaty.* **4** *Obs.* to confine. ORIG C14: from L *conclūdere,* from *claudere* to close

conclusion (kən'kluːʒən) *n* **1** end or termination. **2** the last main division of a speech, essay, etc. **3** outcome or result (esp. in **a foregone conclusion**). **4** a final decision or judgment (esp. in **come to a conclusion**). **5** *Logic.* **5a** a statement that purports to follow from another or others (the **premises**) by means of an argument. **5b** a statement that does validly follow from given premises. **6** *Law.* **6a** an admission or statement binding on the party making it; estoppel. **6b** the close of a pleading or of a conveyance. **7 in conclusion.** lastly; to sum up. **8 jump to conclusions.** to come to a conclusion prematurely, without sufficient thought or on incomplete evidence. ORIG C14: via OF from L; see CONCLUDE, -ION

conclusive (kən'kluːsɪv) *adj* **1** putting an end to doubt; decisive; final. **2** approaching or involving an end.
▸ **con'clusively** *adv*

concoct (kən'kɒkt) *vb* (*tr*) **1** to make by combining different ingredients. **2** to invent; make up; contrive. ORIG C16: from L *concoctus* cooked together, from *coquere* to cook
▸ **con'cocter** *or* **con'coctor** *n* ▸ **con'coction** *n*

concomitance (kən'kɒmɪtəns) *n* **1** existence together. **2** *Christianity.* the doctrine that the body and blood of Christ are present in the Eucharist.

concomitant (kən'kɒmɪtənt) *adj* **1** existing or occurring together. ◆ *n* **2** a concomitant act, person, etc. ORIG C17: from LL *concomitārī* to accompany, from *com-* with + *comes* companion

concord ('kɒnkɔːd) *n* **1** agreement or harmony. **2** a treaty establishing peaceful relations between nations. **3** *Music.* a combination of musical notes, esp. one containing a series of consonant intervals. **4** *Grammar.* another word for **agreement** (sense 6). ORIG C13: from OF *concorde,* from L *concordia,* from *com-* same + *cor* heart

Concord ★ ('kɒŋkəd) *n* **1** a town in NE Massachusetts: scene of one of the opening military actions (1775) of the War of American Independence. Pop.: 17 080 (1990). **2** a city in New Hampshire, the state capital: printing, publishing. Pop.: 36 364 (1992).

concordance (kən'kɔːdᵊns) *n* **1** a state of harmony. **2** a book that indexes the principal words in a literary work, often with the immediate context and an account of the meaning. **3** an index produced by computer or machine.

concordant (kən'kɔːdᵊnt) *adj* being in agreement; harmonious.
▸ **con'cordantly** *adv*

concordat (kɒn'kɔːdæt) *n* a pact or treaty, esp. one between the Vatican and another state concerning the interests of religion in that state. ORIG C17: via F, from Med. L *concordātum,* from L: something agreed; see CONCORD

concourse ('kɒnkɔːs) *n* **1** a crowd; throng. **2** a coming together; confluence. **3** a large open space for the gathering of people in a public place. ORIG C14: from OF *concours,* ult. from L *concurrere* to run together

concrete ('kɒnkriːt) *n* **1** a construction material made of cement, sand, stone and water that hardens to a stonelike mass. ◆ *adj* **2** relating to a particular instance; specific as opposed to general. **3** relating to things capable of being perceived by the senses, as opposed to abstractions. **4** formed by the coalescence of particles; condensed; solid. ◆ *vb* **concretes, concreting, concreted. 5** (*tr*) to construct in or cover with concrete. **6** (kən'kriːt). to become or cause to become solid; coalesce. ORIG C14: from L *concrētus,* from *concrēscere* to grow together
▸ **'concretely** *adv* ▸ **'concreteness** *n*

concrete music *n* music consisting of an electronically modified montage of tape-recorded sounds.

concrete noun *n* a noun that refers to a material object.

concrete poetry *n* poetry in which the visual form of the poem is used to convey meaning.

concretion (kən'kriːʃən) *n* **1** the act of growing together; coalescence. **2** a solidified mass. **3** something made real, tangible, or specific. **4** a rounded or irregular mineral mass different in composition from the sedimentary rock that surrounds it. **5** *Pathol.* another word for **calculus.**
▸ **con'cretionary** *adj*

concretize *or* **concretise** ('kɒnkrɪˌtaɪz) *vb* **concretizes, concretizing, concretized** *or* **concretises, concretising, concretised.** (*tr*) to render concrete; make real or specific.

concubine ('kɒŋkjʊˌbaɪn, 'kɒn-) *n* **1** (in polygamous societies) a secondary wife. **2** a woman who cohabits with a man, esp. (formerly) the mistress of a king, nobleman, etc. ORIG C13: from OF, from L *concubīna,* from *concumbere* to lie together
▸ **concubinage** (kɒn'kjuːbɪnɪdʒ) *n* ▸ **con'cubinary** *adj*

concupiscence (kən'kjuːpɪsəns) *n* strong desire, esp. sexual desire. ORIG C14: from Church L *concupiscentia,* from L *concupiscere* to covet
▸ **con'cupiscent** *adj*

concur (kən'kɜː) *vb* **concurs, concurring, concurred.** (*intr*) **1** to agree; be in accord. **2** to combine or cooperate. **3** to occur simultaneously; coincide. ORIG C15: from L *concurrere* to run together

concurrence (kən'kʌrəns) *n* **1** the act of concurring. **2** agreement; accord. **3** cooperation or combination. **4** simultaneous occurrence.

concurrent (kən'kʌrənt) *adj* **1** taking place at the same time or in the same location. **2** cooperating. **3** meeting at, approaching, or having a common point: *concurrent lines.* **4** in agreement; harmonious.
▸ **con'currently** *adv*

concurrent engineering *n* a method of designing and marketing new products in which development stages are run in parallel rather than in series, to reduce lead times and costs. Also called: **interactive engineering.**

concuss (kən'kʌs) *vb* (*tr*) **1** to injure (the brain) by a violent blow, fall, etc. **2** to shake violently. ORIG C16: from L *concussus,* from *concutere* to disturb greatly, from *quatere* to shake

concussion (kən'kʌʃən) *n* **1** a jarring of the brain, caused by a blow or a fall, usually resulting in loss of consciousness. **2** any violent shaking.

Condé ★ (*French* kɔ̃de) *n* **Prince de** (prɛ̃s də), title of *Louis II de Bourbon, Duc d'Enghien,* called *the Great Condé.* 1621–86, French general, who led Louis XIV's armies against the Fronde (1649) but joined the Fronde in a new revolt (1650–52).

condemn (kən'dɛm) *vb* (*tr*) **1** to express strong disapproval of. **2** to pronounce judicial sentence on. **3** to demonstrate the guilt of: *his secretive behaviour condemned him.* **4** to judge or pronounce unfit for use. **5** to force into a particular state: *his disposition condemned him to boredom.* ORIG C13: from OF *condempner,* from L *condemnāre,* from *damnāre* to condemn
▸ **condemnable** (kən'dɛmnəbᵊl) *adj* ▸ **ˌcondem'nation** *n*
▸ **condemnatory** (kən'dɛmnətərɪ) *adj*

condensate (kən'dɛnseɪt) *n* a substance formed by condensation.

condensation (ˌkɒndɛn'seɪʃən) *n* **1** the act or process of condensing, or the state of being condensed. **2** anything that has condensed from a vapour, esp. on a window. **3** *Chem.* a type of reaction in which two organic molecules combine to form a larger molecule as well as a simple molecule such as water, etc. **4** an abridged version of a book.
▸ **ˌconden'sational** *adj*

condensation trail *n* another name for **vapour trail.**

condense (kən'dɛns) *vb* **condenses, condensing, condensed. 1** (*tr*) to increase the density of; compress. **2** to reduce or be reduced in volume or size. **3** to change or cause to change from a gaseous to a liquid or solid state. **4** *Chem.* to undergo or cause to undergo condensation. ORIG C15: from L *condēnsāre,* from *dēnsāre* to make thick, from *dēnsus* DENSE
▸ **con'densable** *or* **con'densible** *adj*

condensed matter *n Physics.* **a** crystalline and amorphous solids and liquids, including liquid crystals, glasses, polymers, and gels. **b** (*as modifier*): *condensed-matter physics.*

condensed milk *n* milk reduced by evaporation to a thick concentration, with sugar added.

condenser (kən'dɛnsə) *n* **1a** an apparatus for reducing gases to their liquid or solid form by the abstraction of heat. **1b** a device for abstracting heat, as in a refrigeration unit. **2** a lens that concentrates light. **3** another name for **capacitor. 4** a person or device that condenses.

condescend (ˌkɒndɪ'sɛnd) *vb* (*intr*) **1** to act graciously towards another or others regarded as being on a lower level; behave patronizingly. **2** to do something that one regards as below one's dignity. ORIG C14: from Church L *condēscendere,* from L *dēscendere* to DESCEND
▸ **ˌconde'scending** *adj* ▸ **ˌconde'scendingly** *adv* ▸ **ˌconde'scension** *n*

condign (kən'daɪn) *adj* (esp. of a punishment) fitting; deserved. ORIG C15: from OF *condigne,* from L *condignus,* from *dignus* worthy
▸ **con'dignly** *adv*

condiment ('kɒndɪmənt) *n* any spice or sauce such as salt, pepper, mustard, etc. ORIG C15: from L *condīmentum* seasoning, from *condīre* to pickle

condition (kən'dɪʃən) *n* **1** a particular state of being or existence: *the human condition.* **2** something that limits or restricts; a qualification. **3** (*pl*) circumstances: *conditions were right for a takeover.* **4** state of physical fitness, esp. good health: *out of condition.* **5** an ailment: *a heart condition.* **6** something indispensable: *your happiness is a condition of mine.* **7** something required as part of an agreement; term: *the conditions of the lease are set out.* **8** *Law.* **8a** a provision in a will, contract, etc., that makes some right or liability contingent upon the happening of some event. **8b** the event itself. **9** *Logic.* a statement whose truth is either required for the truth of a given statement (a **necessary condition**) or sufficient to guarantee the truth of the given statement (a **sufficient condition**). **10** rank, status, or position. **11 on condition that.** (*conj*) provided that. ◆ *vb* (*mainly tr*) **12** *Psychol.* **12a** to alter the response of (a person or animal) to a particular stimulus or situation. **12b** to establish a conditioned response in. **13** to put into a fit condition. **14** to improve the condition of (one's hair) by use of special cosmetics. **15** to accustom or inure. **16** to subject to a condition. ORIG C14: from L *conditiō,* from *condīcere* to discuss, from *con-* together + *dīcere* to say
▸ **con'ditioner** *n* ▸ **con'ditioning** *n, adj*

conditional (kən'dɪʃənᵊl) *adj* **1** depending on other factors. **2** *Grammar.* expressing a condition on which something else is contingent: *"If he comes" is a conditional clause in the sentence "If he comes I shall go".* **3** *Logic.* Also called: **hypothetical.** (of a proposition) consisting of two component propositions associated by the words *if...then* so that the proposition is false only when the antecedent is true and the consequent false. ◆ *n* **4** a conditional verb form, clause, sentence, etc.
▸ **conˌdition'ality** *n* ▸ **con'ditionally** *adv*

conditional access *n* the distortion of television

★ people and places

programme transmissions so that only authorized subscribers with suitable decoding apparatus may have access to them.

conditioned response *n Psychol.* a response that is transferred from the second to the first of a pair of stimuli. A well-known Pavlovian example is salivation by a dog when it hears a bell ring, because food has always been presented when the bell has been rung previously. Also called (esp. formerly): **conditioned reflex.**

condo ('kɒndəʊ) *n, pl* **condos.** *US & Canad. inf.* a condominium building or apartment.

condole (kən'dəʊl) *vb* **condoles, condoling, condoled.** (*intr;* foll. by *with*) to express sympathy with someone in grief, pain, etc. ORIG C16: from Church L *condolēre,* from L *com-* together + *dolēre* to grieve
▸ **con'dolence** *n*

condom ('kɒndɒm, 'kɒndəm) *n* a rubber sheath worn on the penis or in the vagina during sexual intercourse to prevent conception or infection. ORIG C18: from ?

condominium (ˌkɒndə'mɪnɪəm) *n, pl* **condominiums. 1** joint rule or sovereignty. **2** a country ruled by two or more foreign powers. **3** *US & Canad.* **3a** an apartment building in which each apartment is individually owned and the common areas are jointly owned. **3b** an apartment in such a building. Sometimes shortened to **condo.** ORIG C18: from NL, from L *com-* together + *dominium* ownership

condone (kən'dəʊn) *vb* **condones, condoning, condoned.** (*tr*) **1** to overlook or forgive (an offence, etc.). **2** *Law.* (esp. of a spouse) to pardon or overlook (an offence, usually adultery). ORIG C19: from L *condōnāre,* from *com-* (intensive) + *dōnāre* to donate
▸ **condonation** (ˌkɒndəʊ'neɪʃən) *n* ▸ **con'doner** *n*

condor ('kɒndɔː) *n* either of two very large rare New World vultures, the **Andean condor,** which has black plumage with white around the neck, and the **California condor,** which is nearly extinct. ORIG C17: from Sp. *cóndor,* from Quechuan *kuntur*

condottiere (ˌkɒndɒ'tjɛərɪ) *n, pl* **condottieri** (-riː). a commander or soldier in a professional mercenary company in Europe from the 13th to the 16th centuries. ORIG C18: from It., from *condotto* leadership, from *condurre* to lead, from L *condūcere*

conduce (kən'djuːs) *vb* **conduces, conducing, conduced.** (*intr;* foll. by *to*) to lead or contribute (to a result). ORIG C15: from L *condūcere,* from *com-* together + *dūcere* to lead

conducive (kən'djuːsɪv) *adj* (when *postpositive,* foll. by *to*) contributing, leading, or tending.

conduct *n* ('kɒndʌkt). **1** behaviour. **2** the way of managing a business, affair, etc.; handling. **3** *Rare.* the act of leading. ◆ *vb* (kən'dʌkt). **4** (*tr*) to accompany and guide (people, a party, etc.) (esp. in **conducted tour**). **5** (*tr*) to direct (affairs, business, etc.); control. **6** (*tr*) to carry out; organize: *conduct a survey.* **7** (*tr*) to behave (oneself). **8** to control (an orchestra, etc.) by the movements of the hands or a baton. **9** to transmit (heat, electricity, etc.). ORIG C15: from Med. L *conductus* escorted, from L, from *condūcere* to CONDUCE
▸ **con'ductible** *adj* ▸ **conˌducti'bility** *n*

conductance (kən'dʌktəns) *n* the ability of a system to conduct electricity, measured by the ratio of the current flowing through the system to the potential difference across it. Symbol: G

conducting tissue *n Bot.* another name for **vascular tissue.**

conduction (kən'dʌkʃən) *n* **1** the transfer of energy by a medium without bulk movement of the medium itself. Cf. **convection** (sense 1). **2** the transmission of an impulse along a nerve fibre. **3** the act of conveying or conducting, as through a pipe. **4** *Physics.* another name for **conductivity** (sense 1).
▸ **con'ductional** *adj*

conductive (kən'dʌktɪv) *adj* of, denoting, or having the property of conduction.

conductive education *n* an educational system, developed in Hungary, in which teachers (**conductors**) teach children and adults with motor disorders to function independently, by guiding them to attain their own goals in their own way.

conductivity (ˌkɒndʌk'tɪvɪtɪ) *n, pl* **conductivities. 1** the property of transmitting heat, electricity, or sound. **2** a measure of the ability of a substance to conduct electricity. Symbol: κ

conductivity water *n* water that has a conductivity of less than 0.043×10^{-6} S cm^{-1}.

conductor (kən'dʌktə) *n* **1** an official on a bus who collects fares. **2** a person who conducts an orchestra, choir, etc. **3** a person who leads or guides. **4** *US & Canad.* a railway official in charge of a train. **5** a substance, body, or system that conducts electricity, heat, etc. **6** See **lightning conductor.**
▸ **con'ductorship** *n* ▸ **conductress** (kən'dʌktrɪs) *fem n*

conduit ('kɒndɪt, -djʊɪt) *n* **1** a pipe or channel for carrying a fluid. **2** a rigid tube for carrying electrical cables. **3** an agency or means of access, communication, etc. ORIG C14: from OF, from Med. L *conductus* channel, from L *condūcere* to lead

condyle ('kɒndɪl) *n* the rounded projection on the articulating end of a bone. ORIG C17: from L *condylus,* from Gk *kondulos*
▸ **'condylar** *adj*

cone (kəʊn) *n* **1** a geometric solid consisting of a plane base bounded by a closed curve, usually a circle or an ellipse, every point of which is joined to a fixed point lying outside the plane of the base. **2** anything that tapers from a circular section to a point, such as a wafer shell used to contain ice cream. **3a** the reproductive body of conifers and related plants, made up of overlapping scales. **3b** a similar structure in horsetails, club mosses, etc. **4** a small cone used as a temporary traffic marker on roads. **5** any one of the cone-shaped cells in the retina of the eye, sensitive to colour and bright light. ◆ *vb* **cones, coning, coned. 6** (*tr*) to shape like a cone. ORIG C16: from L *cōnus,* from Gk *kōnus* pine cone, geometrical cone

cone off *vb* (*tr, adv*) *Brit.* to close (one carriageway of a motorway) by placing warning cones across it.

coney ('kəʊnɪ) *n* a variant spelling of **cony.**

Coney Island ★ ('kəʊnɪ) *n* an island off the S shore of Long Island, New York: site of a large amusement park.

confab ('kɒnfæb) *Inf.* ◆ *n* **1** a conversation. ◆ *vb* **confabs, confabbing, confabbed. 2** (*intr*) to converse.

confabulate (kən'fæbjʊˌleɪt) *vb* **confabulates, confabulating, confabulated.** (*intr*) **1** to talk together; chat. **2** *Psychiatry.* to replace the gaps left by a disorder of the memory with imaginary remembered experiences consistently believed to be true. ORIG C17: from L *confābulārī,* from *fābulārī* to talk, from *fābula* a story
▸ **conˌfabu'lation** *n*

confect (kən'fɛkt) *vb* (*tr*) **1** to prepare by combining ingredients. **2** to make; construct. ORIG C16: from L *confectus* prepared, from *conficere,* from *com-* (intensive) + *facere* to make

confection (kən'fɛkʃən) *n* **1** the act of compounding or mixing. **2** any sweet preparation, such as a preserve or a sweet. **3** *Old-fashioned.* an elaborate article of clothing, esp. for women. ORIG C14: from OF, from L *confectiō* a preparing, from *conficere;* see CONFECT

confectioner (kən'fɛkʃənə) *n* a person who makes or sells sweets or confections.

confectionery (kən'fɛkʃənərɪ) *n, pl* **confectioneries. 1** sweets and other confections collectively. **2** the art or business of a confectioner.

confederacy (kən'fɛdərəsɪ) *n, pl* **confederacies. 1** a union of states, etc.; alliance; league. **2** a combination of groups or individuals for unlawful purposes. ORIG C14: from OF *confederacie,* from LL *confoederātiō* agreement
▸ **con'federal** *adj*

Confederacy ★ (kən'fɛdərəsɪ, -'fɛdrəsɪ) *n* **the.** another name for the **Confederate States of America.**

confederate *n* (kən'fɛdərɪt). **1** a nation, state, or individual that is part of a confederacy. **2** someone who is part of a conspiracy. ◆ *adj* (kən'fɛdərɪt). **3** united; allied. ◆ *vb* (kən'fɛdəˌreɪt), **confederates, confederating, confeder-**

ated. 4 to form into or become part of a confederacy. ORIG C14: from LL *confoederātus,* from *confoederāre* to unite by a league

Confederate (kən'fɛdərɪt) *adj* **1** of or supporting the Confederate States of America. ◆ *n* **2** a supporter of the Confederate States.

Confederate States of America ★ *pl n US history.* the 11 Southern states (Alabama, Arkansas, Florida, Georgia, North Carolina, South Carolina, Texas, Virginia, Tennessee, Louisiana, and Mississippi) that seceded from the Union in 1861, precipitating a civil war with the North. The Confederacy was defeated in 1865 and the South reincorporated into the US.

confederation (kən,fɛdə'reɪʃən) *n* **1** the act of confederating or the state of being confederated. **2** a loose alliance of political units. **3** (esp. in Canada) another name for a **federation.**
▸ **con,feder'ationist** *n*

Confederation ★ (kən,fɛdə'reɪʃən) *n* **1 the.** *US history.* the original 13 states of the United States of America constituted under the Articles of Confederation and superseded by the more formal union established in 1789. **2** the federation of Canada, formed with four original provinces in 1867 and since joined by eight more.

confer (kən'fɜː) *vb* **confers, conferring, conferred. 1** (*tr;* foll. by *on* or *upon*) to grant or bestow (an honour, gift, etc.). **2** (*intr*) to consult together. ORIG C16: from L *conferre,* from *com-* together + *ferre* to bring
▸ **con'ferment** *or* **con'ferral** *n* ▸ **con'ferrable** *adj*

conferee *or* **conferree** (,kɒnfɜː'riː) *n* **1** a person who takes part in a conference. **2** a person on whom an honour or gift is conferred.

conference ('kɒnfərəns) *n* **1** a meeting for consultation or discussion, esp. one with a formal agenda. **2** an assembly of the clergy or of clergy and laity of any of certain Protestant Churches acting as representatives of their denomination. **3** *Sport.* a league or division of clubs or teams. ORIG C16: from Med. L *conferentia,* from L *conferre* to bring together
▸ **conferential** (,kɒnfə'rɛnʃəl) *adj*

conference call *n* a special telephone facility by which three or more people using conventional or cellular phones can be linked up to speak to one another.

conferencing ('kɒnfərənsɪŋ) *n* the practice of holding a conference, esp. by means of a telephone service. See **conference call.**

confess (kən'fɛs) *vb* (when *tr, may take a clause as object*) **1** (when *intr,* often foll. by *to*) to make an admission (of faults, crimes, etc.). **2** (*tr*) to admit to be true; concede. **3** *Christianity.* to declare (one's sins) to God or to a priest as his representative, so as to obtain pardon and absolution. ORIG C14: from OF *confesser,* from LL, from L *confessus* confessed, from *confitērī* to admit

confessedly (kən'fɛsɪdlɪ) *adv* (*sentence modifier*) by admission or confession; avowedly.

confession (kən'fɛʃən) *n* **1** the act of confessing. **2** something confessed. **3** an acknowledgment, esp. of one's faults or crimes. **4** *Christianity.* the act of a penitent accusing himself of his sins. **5 confession of faith.** a formal public avowal of religious beliefs. **6** a religious sect united by common beliefs.
▸ **con'fessionary** *adj*

confessional (kən'fɛʃənᵊl) *adj* **1** of or suited to a confession. ◆ *n* **2** *Christianity.* a small stall where a priest hears confessions.

confessor (kən'fɛsə) *n* **1** *Christianity.* a priest who hears confessions and sometimes acts as a spiritual counsellor. **2** *History.* a person who bears witness to the Christian religious faith by the holiness of his or her life, but does not suffer martyrdom. **3** a person who makes a confession.

confetti (kən'fɛtɪ) *n* small pieces of coloured paper thrown on festive occasions, esp. at weddings. ORIG C19: from It., pl of *confetto,* orig., a bonbon

confidant *or* (*fem*) **confidante** (,kɒnfɪ'dænt, 'kɒnfɪ,dænt) *n* a person to whom private matters are confided. ORIG C17: from F *confident,* from It. *confidente,* n. use of adj: trustworthy

confide (kən'faɪd) *vb* **confides, confiding, confided. 1** (usually foll. by *in;* when *tr, may take a clause as object*) to disclose (secret or personal matters) in confidence (to). **2** (*intr;* foll. by *in*) to have complete trust. **3** (*tr*) to entrust into another's keeping. ORIG C15: from L *confīdere,* from *fīdere* to trust
▸ **con'fider** *n*

confidence ('kɒnfɪdəns) *n* **1** trust in a person or thing. **2** belief in one's own abilities; self-assurance. **3** trust or a trustful relationship: *take me into your confidence.* **4** something confided; secret. **5 in confidence.** as a secret.

confidence trick *or US & Canad.* **confidence game** *n* a swindle involving money in which the victim's trust is won by the swindler.

confident ('kɒnfɪdənt) *adj* **1** (*postpositive;* foll. by *of*) having or showing certainty; sure: *confident of success.* **2** sure of oneself. **3** presumptuous. ORIG C16: from L *confīdens,* from *confīdere* to have complete trust in
▸ **'confidently** *adv*

confidential (,kɒnfɪ'dɛnʃəl) *adj* **1** spoken or given in confidence; private. **2** entrusted with another's secret affairs: *a confidential secretary.* **3** suggestive of intimacy: *a confidential approach.*
▸ **,confi,denti'ality** *n* ▸ **,confi'dentially** *adv*

confiding (kən'faɪdɪŋ) *adj* unsuspicious; trustful.
▸ **con'fidingly** *adv* ▸ **con'fidingness** *n*

configuration (kən,fɪgjʊ'reɪʃən) *n* **1** the arrangement of the parts of something. **2** the external form or outline achieved by such an arrangement. **3** *Psychol.* the unit or pattern in perception studied by Gestalt psychologists. ORIG C16: from LL *configūrātiō,* from *configūrāre* to model on something, from *figūrāre* to shape, fashion
▸ **con,figu'rational** *or* **con'figurative** *adj*

confine *vb* (kən'faɪn), **confines, confining, confined.** (*tr*) **1** to keep within bounds; limit; restrict. **2** to restrict the free movement of: *arthritis confined him to bed.* ◆ *n* ('kɒnfaɪn). **3** (*often pl*) a limit; boundary. ORIG C16: from Med. L *confīnāre,* from L *confīnis* adjacent, from *fīnis* boundary
▸ **con'finer** *n*

confined (kən'faɪnd) *adj* **1** enclosed; limited. **2** in childbed; undergoing childbirth.

confinement (kən'faɪnmənt) *n* **1** the act of confining or the state of being confined. **2** the period of the birth of a child.

confirm (kən'fɜːm) *vb* (*tr*) **1** (*may take a clause as object*) to prove to be true or valid; corroborate. **2** (*may take a clause as object*) to assert for a further time, so as to make more definite: *he confirmed that he would appear in court.* **3** to strengthen: *his story confirmed my doubts.* **4** to make valid by a formal act; ratify. **5** to administer the rite of confirmation to. ORIG C13: from OF *confermer,* from L *confirmāre,* from *firmus* FIRM[1]
▸ **con'firmatory** *or* **con'firmative** *adj*

confirmation (,kɒnfə'meɪʃən) *n* **1** the act of confirming. **2** something that confirms. **3** a rite in several Christian churches that confirms a baptized person in his faith and admits him to full participation in the church.

confirmed (kən'fɜːmd) *adj* **1** (*prenominal*) long-established in a habit, way of life, etc. **2** having received the rite of confirmation.

confiscate ('kɒnfɪ,skeɪt) *vb* **confiscates, confiscating, confiscated.** (*tr*) **1** to seize (property), esp. for public use and esp. by way of a penalty. ◆ *adj* **2** confiscated; forfeit. ORIG C16: from L *confiscāre* to seize for the public treasury, from *fiscus* treasury
▸ **,confis'cation** *n* ▸ **'confis,cator** *n* ▸ **confiscatory** (kən'fɪskətərɪ) *adj*

Confiteor (kən'fɪtɪ,ɔː) *n RC Church.* a prayer consisting of a general confession of sinfulness and an entreaty for forgiveness. ORIG C13: from L: I confess

conflagration (,kɒnflə'greɪʃən) *n* a large destructive fire. ORIG C16: from L *conflagrātiō,* from *conflagrāre,* from *com-* (intensive) + *flagrāre* to burn

conflate (kən'fleɪt) *vb* **conflates, conflating, conflated.** (*tr*) to combine or blend (two things, esp. two versions of a text) so as to form a whole. ORIG C16: from L *conflāre* to blow together, from *flāre* to blow
▸ **con'flation** *n*

conflict *n* (ˈkɒnflɪkt). **1** a struggle between opposing forces; battle. **2** opposition between ideas, interests, etc.; controversy. **3** *Psychol.* opposition between two simultaneous but incompatible wishes or drives, sometimes leading to emotional tension. ◆ *vb* (kənˈflɪkt). (*intr*) **4** to come into opposition; clash. **5** to fight. ORIG C15: from L *conflictus,* from *conflīgere* to combat, from *flīgere* to strike
▸ **conˈflicting** *adj* ▸ **conˈflictingly** *adv* ▸ **conˈfliction** *n*

confluence (ˈkɒnfluəns) *or* **conflux** (ˈkɒnflʌks) *n* **1** a flowing together, esp. of rivers. **2** a gathering.
▸ **ˈconfluent** *adj*

conform (kənˈfɔːm) *vb* **1** (*intr;* usually foll. by *to*) to comply in actions, behaviour, etc., with accepted standards. **2** (*intr;* usually foll. by *with*) to be in accordance: *he conforms with my idea of a teacher.* **3** to make or become similar. **4** (*intr*) to comply with the practices of an established church, esp. the Church of England. ORIG C14: from OF *conformer,* from L *confirmāre* to strengthen, from *firmāre* to make firm
▸ **conˈformer** *n* ▸ **conˈformist** *n, adj*

conformable (kənˈfɔːməbᵊl) *adj* **1** corresponding in character; similar. **2** obedient; submissive. **3** (foll. by *to*) consistent (with). **4** (of rock strata) lying in a parallel arrangement so that their original relative positions have remained undisturbed.
▸ **conˌformaˈbility** *n* ▸ **conˈformably** *adv*

conformal (kənˈfɔːməl) *adj* (of a map projection) maintaining true shape over a small area and scale in every direction. ORIG C17: from LL *conformālis,* from L *com-* same + *forma* shape

conformation (ˌkɒnfɔːˈmeɪʃən) *n* **1** the general shape of an object; configuration. **2** the arrangement of the parts of an object. **3** *Chem.* the three-dimensional arrangement of the atoms in a molecule.

conformity (kənˈfɔːmɪtɪ) *or* **conformance** *n, pl* **conformities** *or* **conformances. 1** compliance in actions, behaviour, etc., with certain accepted standards. **2** likeness; congruity; agreement. **3** compliance with the practices of an established church.

confound (kənˈfaʊnd) *vb* (*tr*) **1** to astound; bewilder. **2** to confuse. **3** to treat mistakenly as similar to or identical with. **4** (kɒnˈfaʊnd). to curse (usually in **confound it!**). **5** to contradict or refute (an argument, etc.). **6** to rout or defeat (an enemy). ORIG C13: from OF *confondre,* from L *confundere* to mingle, pour together
▸ **conˈfounder** *n*

confounded (kənˈfaʊndɪd) *adj* **1** bewildered; confused. **2** (*prenominal*) *Inf.* execrable; damned.
▸ **conˈfoundedly** *adv*

confraternity (ˌkɒnfrəˈtɜːnɪtɪ) *n, pl* **confraternities.** a group of men united for some particular purpose, esp. Christian laymen organized for religious or charitable service; brotherhood. ORIG C15: from Med. L *confrāternitās,* ult. from L *frāter* brother

confrère (ˈkɒnfrɛə) *n* a fellow member of a profession, etc. ORIG C15: from OF, from Med. L *confrāter*

confront (kənˈfrʌnt) *vb* (*tr*) **1** (usually foll. by *with*) to present (with something), esp. in order to accuse or criticize. **2** to face boldly; oppose in hostility. **3** to be face to face with. ORIG C16: from Med. L *confrontārī,* from *frons* forehead
▸ **confrontation** (ˌkɒnfrʌnˈteɪʃən) *n* ▸ **ˌconfronˈtational** *adj*

Confucian (kənˈfjuːʃən) *adj* **1** of or relating to the doctrines of Confucius. ◆ *n* **2** a follower of Confucius.

Confucianism (kənˈfjuːʃəˌnɪzəm) *n* the ethical system of Confucius, emphasizing moral order, the virtue of China's ancient rules, and gentlemanly education.
▸ **Conˈfucianist** *n*

Confucius ★ (kənˈfjuːʃəs) *n* Chinese name *Kong Zi* or *K'ung Fu-tse.* 551–479 B.C., Chinese philosopher and teacher (see **Confucianism**). His doctrines were compiled after his death as *The Analects of Confucius.*

confuse (kənˈfjuːz) *vb* **confuses, confusing, confused.** (*tr*) **1** to bewilder; perplex. **2** to mix up (things, ideas, etc.). **3** to make unclear: *he confused his talk with irrelevant details.* **4** to mistake (one thing) for another. **5** to disconcert; embarrass. **6** to cause to become disordered: *the enemy ranks were confused by gas.* ORIG C18: back formation from *confused,* from L *confūsus,* from *confundere* to pour together
▸ **conˈfusable** *adj* ▸ **confusedly** (kənˈfjuːzɪdlɪ, -ˈfjuːzd-) *adv* ▸ **conˈfusing** *adj* ▸ **conˈfusingly** *adv*

confusion (kənˈfjuːʒən) *n* **1** the act of confusing or the state of being confused. **2** disorder. **3** bewilderment; perplexity. **4** lack of clarity. **5** embarrassment; abashment.

confute (kənˈfjuːt) *vb* **confutes, confuting, confuted.** (*tr*) to prove (a person or thing) wrong, invalid, or mistaken; disprove. ORIG C16: from L *confūtāre* to check, silence
▸ **conˈfutable** *adj* ▸ **confutation** (ˌkɒnfjuˈteɪʃən) *n*

conga (ˈkɒŋgə) *n* **1** a Latin American dance of three steps and a kick to each bar, performed by a number of people in single file. **2** Also called: **conga drum.** a large tubular bass drum played with the hands. ◆ *vb* **congas, congaing, congaed. 3** (*intr*) to perform this dance. ORIG C20: from American Sp., fem of *congo* belonging to the *Congo*

congé (ˈkɒnʒeɪ) *n* **1** permission to depart or dismissal, esp. when formal. **2** a farewell. ORIG C16: from OF *congié,* from L *commeātus* leave of absence, from *meāre* to go

congeal (kənˈdʒiːl) *vb* **1** to change or cause to change from a soft or fluid state to a firm state. **2** to form or cause to form into a coagulated mass; jell. ORIG C14: from OF *congeler,* from L *congelāre,* from *com-* together + *gelāre* to freeze
▸ **conˈgealable** *adj* ▸ **conˈgealment** *n*

congelation (ˌkɒndʒɪˈleɪʃən) *n* **1** the process of congealing. **2** something formed by this process.

congener (kənˈdʒiːnə, ˈkɒndʒɪnə) *n* a member of a class, group, or other category, esp. any animal of a specified genus. ORIG C18: from L, from *com-* same + *genus* kind

congenial (kənˈdʒiːnjəl) *adj* **1** friendly, pleasant, or agreeable: *a congenial atmosphere to work in.* **2** having a similar disposition, tastes, etc.; compatible. ORIG C17: from CON- (same) + GENIAL[1]
▸ **congeniality** (kənˌdʒiːnɪˈælɪtɪ) *n*

congenital (kənˈdʒɛnɪtᵊl) *adj* **1** denoting any nonhereditary condition, esp. an abnormal condition, existing at birth: *congenital blindness.* **2** *Inf.* complete, as if from birth: *a congenital idiot.* ORIG C18: from L *congenitus,* from *genitus* born, from *gignere* to bear
▸ **conˈgenitally** *adv*

conger (ˈkɒŋgə) *n* a large marine eel occurring in temperate and tropical coastal waters. ORIG C14: from OF *congre,* from L *conger,* from Gk *gongros*

congeries (kɒnˈdʒɪəriːz) *n* (*functioning as sing or pl*) a collection; mass; heap. ORIG C17: from L, from *congerere* to pile up, from *gerere* to carry

congest (kənˈdʒɛst) *vb* **1** to crowd or become crowded to excess; overfill. **2** to clog (an organ) with blood or (of an organ) to become clogged with blood. **3** (*tr; usually passive*) to block (the nose) with mucus. ORIG C16: from L *congestus,* from *congerere;* see CONGERIES
▸ **conˈgestion** *n*

conglomerate *n* (kənˈglɒmərɪt). **1** a thing composed of heterogeneous elements. **2** any coarse-grained sedimentary rock consisting of rounded fragments of rock embedded in a finer matrix. **3** a large corporation consisting of a group of companies dealing in widely diversified goods, services, etc. ◆ *vb* (kənˈglɒməˌreɪt), **conglomerates, conglomerating, conglomerated. 4** to form into a mass. ◆ *adj* (kənˈglɒmərɪt). **5** made up of heterogeneous elements. **6** (of sedimentary rocks) consisting of rounded fragments within a finer matrix. ORIG C16: from L *conglomerāre* to roll up, from *glomerāre* to wind into a ball, from *glomus* ball of thread
▸ **conˌglomerˈation** *n*

Congo ★ (ˈkɒŋgəʊ) *n* **1 Democratic Republic of.** a republic in S central Africa, with a narrow strip of land along the Congo estuary leading to the Atlantic in the west: Congo Free State established in 1885, with Leopold II of Belgium as absolute monarch; became the Belgian Congo colony in 1908; gained independence in 1960, followed by civil war and the secession of Katanga (until 1963); under Mobutu renamed Zaïre in 1971 and declared a one-party state in 1978; Mobutu's overthrow by rebels in 1997 was followed by civil war involving neighbouring countries. The country consists chiefly of

the Congo basin, with large areas of dense tropical forest and marshes, and the Mitumba highlands reaching over 5000 m (16 000 ft) in the east. Official language: French. Religion: Christian majority, animist minority. Currency: Congolese franc. Capital: Kinshasa. Pop.: 50 481 000 (1999 est.). Area: 2 344 116 sq. km (905 063 sq. miles). Former names: **Congo Free State** (1885–1908), **Belgian Congo** (1908–60), **Congo-Kinshasa** (1960–71), **Zaïre** (1971–97). **2 Republic of.** a former name (1960–99) for **Congo-Brazzaville. 3** the second longest river in Africa, rising as the Lualaba on the Katanga plateau in the Democratic Republic of Congo and flowing in a wide northerly curve to the Atlantic: forms the border between Congo-Brazzaville and the Democratic Republic of Congo. Length: about 4800 km (3000 miles). Area of basin: about 3 000 000 sq. km (1 425 000 sq. miles). Former (Zaïrese) name (1971–97): **Zaïre**.
► **Congolese** (ˌkɒŋgəˈliːz) *adj, n*

Congo-Brazzaville ★ (ˈkɒŋgəʊˈbræzəvɪl) *n* a republic in W Central Africa: formerly the French colony of Middle Congo, part of French Equatorial Africa, it became independent in 1960; consists mostly of equatorial forest, with savanna and extensive swamps; drained chiefly by the Rivers Congo and Ubangi. Official language: French. Religion: animist and Christian. Currency: franc. Capital: Brazzaville. Pop.: 2 717 000 (1999 est). Area: 342 000 sq. km (132 018 sq. miles). Former names: **Middle Congo** (until 1958), **Republic of Congo** (1960–99).

Congo Free State ★ *n* a former name (1885–1908) of the Democratic Republic of **Congo** (sense 1).

congrats (kənˈgræts) *pl n, sentence substitute.* informal shortened form of **congratulations.**

congratulate (kənˈgrætjʊˌleɪt) *vb* **congratulates, congratulating, congratulated.** (*tr*) **1** (usually foll. by *on*) to communicate pleasure, approval, or praise to; compliment. **2** (often foll. by *on*) to consider (oneself) clever or fortunate (as a result of): *she congratulated herself on her tact.* **3** *Obs.* to greet; salute. ORIG C16: from L *congrātulārī*, from *grātulārī* to rejoice, from *grātus* pleasing
► **conˌgratuˈlation** *n* ► **conˈgratulatory** *or* **conˈgratulative** *adj*

congratulations (kənˌgrætjʊˈleɪʃənz) *pl n, sentence substitute.* expressions of pleasure or joy on another's success, good fortune, etc.

congregate (ˈkɒŋgrɪˌgeɪt) *vb* **congregates, congregating, congregated.** to collect together in a body or crowd; assemble. ORIG C15: from L *congregāre* to collect into a flock, from *grex* flock

congregation (ˌkɒŋgrɪˈgeɪʃən) *n* **1** a group of persons gathered for worship, prayer, etc., esp. in a church. **2** the act of congregating together. **3** a group collected together; assemblage. **4** the group of persons habitually attending a given church, chapel, etc. **5** *RC Church.* **5a** a society of persons who follow a common rule of life but who are bound only by simple vows. **5b** an administrative subdivision of the papal curia. **6** *Chiefly Brit.* an assembly of senior members of a university.

congregational (ˌkɒŋgrɪˈgeɪʃənᵊl) *adj* **1** of or relating to a congregation. **2** (*usually cap.*) of or denoting Congregationalism.

Congregationalism (ˌkɒŋgrɪˈgeɪʃənəˌlɪzəm) *n* a system of Christian doctrines and ecclesiastical government in which each congregation is self-governing.
► ˌ**Congreˈgationalist** *adj, n*

congress (ˈkɒŋgrɛs) *n* **1** a meeting or conference, esp. of representatives of sovereign states. **2** a national legislative assembly. **3** a society or association. ORIG C16: from L *congressus*, from *congredī*, from *com-* together + *gradī* to walk

Congress (ˈkɒŋgrɛs) *n* **1** the bicameral federal legislature of the US, consisting of the House of Representatives and the Senate. **2** Also called: **Congress Party.** (in India) a major political party.
► **Conˈgressional** *adj*

congressional (kənˈgrɛʃənᵊl) *adj* of or relating to a congress.
► **conˈgressionalist** *n*

Congressman (ˈkɒŋgrɛsmən) *or* (*fem*) **Congresswoman** *n, pl* **Congressmen** *or* **Congresswomen.** (in the US) a member of Congress, esp. of the House of Representatives.

Congreve ★ (ˈkɒŋgriːv) *n* **William.** 1670–1729, English Restoration dramatist, author of *Love for Love* (1695) and *The Way of the World* (1700).

congruence (ˈkɒŋgrʊəns) *or* **congruency** *n* **1** the quality or state of corresponding, agreeing, or being congruent. **2** *Maths.* the relationship between two integers, *x* and *y*, such that their difference, with respect to another integer called the modulus, *n*, is a multiple of the modulus.

congruent (ˈkɒŋgrʊənt) *adj* **1** agreeing; corresponding. **2** having identical shapes so that all parts correspond: *congruent triangles.* **3** of or concerning two integers related by a congruence. ORIG C15: from L *congruere* to agree

congruous (ˈkɒŋgrʊəs) *adj* **1** corresponding or agreeing. **2** appropriate. ORIG C16: from L *congruus*; see CONGRUENT
► **congruity** (kənˈgruːɪtɪ) *n*

conic (ˈkɒnɪk) *adj also* **conical. 1a** having the shape of a cone. **1b** of a cone. ◆ *n* **2** another name for **conic section.**
► ˈ**conically** *adv*

conics (ˈkɒnɪks) *n* (*functioning as sing*) the geometry of the parabola, ellipse, and hyperbola.

conic section *n* one of a group of curves formed by the intersection of a plane and a right circular cone. It is either a circle, ellipse, parabola, or hyperbola.

conidium (kəʊˈnɪdɪəm) *n, pl* **conidia** (-ˈnɪdɪə). an asexual spore formed at the tip of a specialized hypha in fungi such as *Penicillium.* ORIG C19: from NL, from Gk *konis* dust + -IUM

conifer (ˈkəʊnɪfə, ˈkɒn-) *n* any tree or shrub of the phylum *Coniferophyta*, typically bearing cones and evergreen leaves. The group includes the pines, spruces, firs, larches, etc. ORIG C19: from L, from *cōnus* CONE + *ferre* to bear
► **coˈniferous** *adj*

Coniston Water ★ (ˈkɒnɪstən) *n* a lake in NW England, in Cumbria: scene of the establishment of world water speed records by Sir Malcolm Campbell (1939) and his son Donald Campbell (1959). Length: 8 km (5 miles).

conj. *abbrev. for:* **1** conjugation. **2** conjunction.

conjectural (kənˈdʒɛktʃərəl) *adj* involving or inclined to conjecture.
► **conˈjecturally** *adv*

conjecture (kənˈdʒɛktʃə) *n* **1** the formation of conclusions from incomplete evidence; guess. **2** the conclusion so formed. ◆ *vb* **conjectures, conjecturing, conjectured. 3** to infer or arrive at (an opinion, conclusion, etc.) from incomplete evidence. ORIG C14: from L *conjectūra*, from *conjicere* to throw together, from *jacere* to throw
► **conˈjecturable** *adj*

conjoin (kənˈdʒɔɪn) *vb* to join or become joined. ORIG C14: from OF *conjoindre*, from L *conjungere*, from *jungere* to JOIN
► **conˈjoiner** *n*

conjoined twins *pl n* twin babies born joined together at some point, such as at the hips. Also called (not in technical usage): **Siamese twins.**

conjoint (kənˈdʒɔɪnt) *adj* united, joint, or associated.
► **conˈjointly** *adv*

conjugal (ˈkɒndʒʊgᵊl) *adj* of or relating to marriage or the relationship between husband and wife: *conjugal rights.* ORIG C16: from L *conjugālis*, from *conjunx* wife or husband
► **conjugality** (ˌkɒndʒʊˈgælɪtɪ) *n* ► ˈ**conjugally** *adv*

conjugate *vb* (ˈkɒndʒʊˌgeɪt), **conjugates, conjugating, conjugated. 1** (*tr*) *Grammar.* to state or set out the conjugation of (a verb). **2** (*intr*) (of a verb) to undergo inflection according to a specific set of rules. **3** (*intr*) *Biol.* to undergo conjugation. **4** (*tr*) *Obs.* to join together, esp. in marriage. ◆ *adj* (ˈkɒndʒʊgɪt, -ˌgeɪt). **5** joined together in pairs. **6** *Maths.* **6a** (of two angles) having a sum of 360°. **6b** (of two complex numbers) differing only in the sign of the imaginary part as 4 + 3i and 4 – 3i. **7** *Chem.* of the state of equilibrium in which two liquids can exist as separate phases that are both solutions. **8** *Chem.* (of acids and

bases) related by loss or gain of a proton. **9** (of a compound leaf) having one pair of leaflets. **10** (of words) cognate; related in origin. ♦ *n* ('kɒndʒʊgɪt). **11** one of a pair or set of conjugate substances, values, quantities, words, etc. ORIG C15: from L *conjugāre,* from *com-* together + *jugāre* to connect, from *jugum* a yoke
▸ **'conju,gative** *adj* ▸ **'conju,gator** *n*

conjugation (,kɒndʒʊ'geɪʃən) *n* **1** *Grammar.* **1a** inflection of a verb for person, number, tense, voice, mood, etc. **1b** the complete set of the inflections of a given verb. **2** a joining. **3** a type of sexual reproduction in ciliate protozoans involving the temporary union of two individuals and the subsequent migration and fusion of the gametic nuclei. **4** the union of gametes, as in some fungi. **5** the pairing of chromosomes in the early phase of a meiotic division. **6** *Chem.* the existence of alternating double or triple bonds in a chemical compound, with consequent electron delocalization over part of the molecule.
▸ **,conju'gational** *adj*

conjunct ('kɒndʒʌŋkt, kən'dʒʌŋkt) *n Logic.* one of the propositions or formulas in a conjunction.

conjunction (kən'dʒʌŋkʃən) *n* **1** the act of joining together; union. **2** simultaneous occurrence of events; coincidence. **3** any word or group of words, other than a relative pronoun, that connects words, phrases, or clauses; for example *and* and *while.* **4** *Astron.* **4a** the position of a planet when it is in line with the sun as seen from the earth. **4b** the apparent proximity or coincidence of two celestial bodies on the celestial sphere. **5** *Logic.* **5a** the operator that forms a compound sentence from two given sentences, and corresponds to the English *and.* **5b** a sentence so formed: it is true only when both the component sentences are true. **5c** the relation between such sentences.
▸ **con'junctional** *adj*

conjunctiva (,kɒndʒʌŋk'taɪvə) *n, pl* **conjunctivas** *or* **conjunctivae** (-viː). the delicate mucous membrane that covers the eyeball and the under surface of the eyelid. ORIG C16: from NL *membrāna conjunctīva* the conjunctive membrane
▸ **,conjunc'tival** *adj*

conjunctive (kən'dʒʌŋktɪv) *adj* **1** joining; connective. **2** joined. **3** of or relating to conjunctions. ♦ *n* **4** a less common word for **conjunction** (sense 3). ORIG C15: from LL *conjunctīvus,* from L *conjungere* to CONJOIN

conjunctivitis (kən,dʒʌŋktɪ'vaɪtɪs) *n* inflammation of the conjunctiva.

conjuncture (kən'dʒʌŋktʃə) *n* a combination of events, esp. a critical one.

conjuration (,kɒndʒʊ'reɪʃən) *n* **1** a magic spell; incantation. **2** a less common word for **conjuring. 3** *Arch.* supplication; entreaty.

conjure ('kʌndʒə) *vb* **conjures, conjuring, conjured. 1** (*intr*) to practise conjuring. **2** (*intr*) to call upon supposed supernatural forces by spells and incantations. **3** (kən'dʒʊə). (*tr*) to appeal earnestly to: *I conjure you to help me.* **4 a name to conjure with. 4a** a person thought to have great power or influence. **4b** any name that excites the imagination. ORIG C13: from OF *conjurer* to plot, from L *conjūrāre* to swear together

conjure up *vb* (*tr, adv*) **1** to present to the mind; evoke or imagine: *he conjured up a picture of his childhood.* **2** to call up or command (a spirit or devil) by an incantation.

conjuring ('kʌndʒərɪŋ) *n* **1** the performance of tricks that appear to defy natural laws. ♦ *adj* **2** denoting or of such tricks or entertainment.

conjuror *or* **conjurer** ('kʌndʒərə) *n* **1** a person who practises conjuring, esp. for people's entertainment. **2** a sorcerer.

conk (kɒŋk) *Sl.* ♦ *vb* **1** to strike (someone) a blow, esp. on the head or nose. ♦ *n* **2** a punch or blow, esp. on the head or nose. **3** the head or nose. ORIG C19: prob. changed from CONCH

conker ('kɒŋkə) *n* an informal name for the **horse chestnut** (sense 2).

conkers ('kɒŋkəz) *n* (*functioning as sing*) *Brit.* a game in which a player swings a horse chestnut (conker), threaded onto a string, against that of another player to try to break it. ORIG C19: from dialect *conker* snail shell, orig. used in the game

conk out *vb* (*intr, adv*) *Inf.* **1** (of machines, cars, etc.) to fail suddenly. **2** to tire suddenly or collapse. ORIG C20: from ?

con man *n Inf.* a person who swindles another by means of a confidence trick. More formal term: **confidence man.**

con moto (kɒn 'məʊtəʊ) *adj, adv Music.* (to be performed) in a brisk or lively manner. ORIG It., lit.: with movement

conn (kɒn) *vb, n* a variant spelling (esp. US) of **con**[3].

Conn ★ (kɒn) *n* 2nd century A.D., king of Leinster and high king of Ireland.

Conn. *abbrev. for* Connecticut.

Connacht ★ ('kɒnət) *n* a province and ancient kingdom of NW Republic of Ireland: consists of the counties of Galway, Leitrim, Mayo, Roscommon, and Sligo. Pop.: 433 000 (1996). Area: 17 122 sq. km (6611 sq. miles). Former name: **Connaught.**

connate ('kɒneɪt) *adj* **1** existing from birth; congenital or innate. **2** allied in nature or origin. **3** *Biol.* (of similar parts or organs) closely joined or united by growth. **4** *Geol.* (of fluids) produced at the same time as the rocks surrounding them; *connate water.* ORIG C17: from LL *connātus* born at the same time

connect (kə'nɛkt) *vb* **1** to link or be linked. **2** (*tr*) to associate: *I connect him with my childhood.* **3** (*tr*) to establish telephone communications with or between. **4** (*intr*) to be meaningful or meaningfully related. **5** (*intr*) (of two public vehicles, such as trains or buses) to have the arrival of one timed to occur just before the departure of the other, for the convenient transfer of passengers. **6** (*intr*) *Inf.* to hit, punch, kick, etc., solidly. ORIG C17: from L *connectere* to bind together, from *nectere* to tie
▸ **con'nectible** *or* **con'nectable** *adj* ▸ **con'nector** *or* **con'necter** *n*

Connecticut ★ (kə'nɛtɪkət) *n* **1** a state of the northeastern US, in New England. Capital: Hartford. Pop.: 3 274 069 (1998 est.). Area: 12 973 sq. km (5009 sq. miles). Abbrevs.: **Conn.** or (with zip code) **CT 2** a river in the northeastern US, rising in N New Hampshire and flowing south to Long Island Sound. Length: 651 km (407 miles).

connecting rod *n* **1** a rod or bar for transmitting motion, esp. one that connects a rotating part to a reciprocating part. **2** such a rod that connects the piston to the crankshaft in an internal-combustion engine.

connection *or* **connexion** (kə'nɛkʃən) *n* **1** the act of connecting; union. **2** something that connects or relates; link or bond. **3** a relationship or association. **4** logical sequence in thought or expression; coherence. **5** the relation of a word or phrase to its context: *in this connection the word has no political significance.* **6** (*often pl*) an acquaintance, esp. one who is influential. **7** a relative, esp. if distant and related by marriage. **8a** an opportunity to transfer from one train, bus, etc., to another. **8b** the vehicle scheduled to provide such an opportunity. **9** a link, usually a wire or metallic strip, between two components in an electric circuit. **10** a communications link, esp. by telephone. **11** *Sl.* a supplier of illegal drugs, such as heroin. **12** *Rare.* sexual intercourse.
▸ **con'nectional** *or* **con'nexional** *adj*

connective (kə'nɛktɪv) *adj* **1** connecting. ♦ *n* **2** a thing that connects. **3** *Grammar, logic.* **3a** any word that connects phrases, clauses, or individual words. **3b** a symbol used in a formal language in the construction of compound sentences, corresponding to terms such as *or, and,* etc., in ordinary speech. **4** *Bot.* the tissue of a stamen that connects the two lobes of the anther.

connective tissue *n* an animal tissue that supports organs, fills the spaces between them, and forms tendons and ligaments.

Connemara ★ (,kɒnɪ'mɑːrə) *n* a barren coastal region of W Republic of Ireland, in Co. Galway: consists of quartzite mountains, peat bogs, and many lakes.

Connery ★ ('kɒnərɪ) *n* Sir **Sean**, real name *Thomas Connery.* born 1929, Scottish film actor; his films include

Goldfinger (1964), *The Name of the Rose* (1986), and *Playing by Heart* (1999).

conning tower ('kɒnɪŋ) *n* **1** a superstructure of a submarine, used as the bridge when the vessel is on the surface. **2** the armoured pilot house of a warship. ORIG C19: see CON[3]

connivance (kə'naɪvəns) *n* **1** the act or fact of conniving. **2** *Law.* the tacit encouragement of or assent to another's wrongdoing.

connive (kə'naɪv) *vb* **connives, conniving, connived.** (*intr*) **1** to plot together; conspire. **2** (foll. by *at*) *Law.* to give assent or encouragement (to the commission of a wrong). ORIG C17: from F *conniver,* from L *connīvēre* to blink, hence, leave uncensured
▸ **con'niver** *n*

connoisseur (ˌkɒnɪ'sɜː) *n* a person with special knowledge or appreciation of a field, esp. in the arts. ORIG C18: from F, from OF *conoiseor,* from *connoistre* to know, from L *cognōscere*
▸ ˌ**connois'seurship** *n*

Connolly ★ ('kɒnəlɪ) *n* **1 Cyril (Vernon).** 1903–74, British writer, founder of *Horizon* (1939–50): his books include *Enemies of Promise* (1938). **2 James.** 1868–1916, Irish labour leader: executed by the British for his part in the Easter Rising (1916).

Connors ★ ('kɒnəz) *n* **Jimmy.** born 1952, US tennis player: Wimbledon champion 1974 and 1982; US champion 1974, 1976, 1978, 1982, and 1983.

connotation (ˌkɒnə'teɪʃən) *n* **1** an association or idea suggested by a word or phrase. **2** the act of connoting. **3** *Logic.* the characteristic or set of characteristics that determines to which object the common name properly applies. In traditional logic synonymous with **intension.**
▸ **connotative** ('kɒnəˌteɪtɪv, kə'nəutə-) *or* **con'notive** *adj*

connote (kɒ'nəut) *vb* **connotes, connoting, connoted.** (*tr; often takes a clause as object*) **1** (of a word, phrase, etc.) to imply or suggest (associations or ideas) other than the literal meaning: *the word "maiden" connotes modesty.* **2** to involve as a consequence or condition. ORIG C17: from Med. L *connotāre,* from L *notāre* to mark, note, from *nota* sign, note

connubial (kə'njuːbɪəl) *adj* of or relating to marriage: *connubial bliss.* ORIG C17: from L *cōnūbiālis,* from *cōnūbium* marriage
▸ **conˌnubi'ality** *n*

conoid ('kəunɔɪd) *n* **1** a cone-shaped object. ◆ *adj also* **conoidal** (kəu'nɔɪdᵊl). **2** cone-shaped. ORIG C17: from Gk *kōnoeidēs,* from *kōnos* CONE
▸ **co'noidally** *adv*

conquer ('kɒŋkə) *vb* **1** to overcome (an enemy, army, etc.); defeat. **2** to overcome (an obstacle, desire, etc.); surmount. **3** (*tr*) to gain possession or control of as by force or war; win. ORIG C13: from OF *conquerre,* from Vulgar L *conquērere* (unattested) to obtain, from L *conquīrere* to search for, from *quaerere* to seek
▸ **'conquerable** *adj* ▸ **'conquering** *adj* ▸ **'conqueror** *n*

Conqueror ★ ('kɒŋkərə) *n* **William the.** See **William I.**

conquest ('kɒnkwɛst) *n* **1** the act of conquering or the state of having been conquered; victory. **2** a person, thing, etc., that has been conquered. **3** a person, whose compliance, love, etc., has been won. ORIG C13: from OF *conqueste,* from Vulgar L *conquēsta* (unattested), from L *conquīsīta,* fem. p.p. of *conquīrere;* see CONQUER

Conquest ('kɒnkwɛst) *n* **the.** See **Norman Conquest.**

conquistador (kɒn'kwɪstəˌdɔː) *n, pl* **conquistadors** *or* **conquistadores** (kɒnˌkwɪstə'dɔːrɛs). an adventurer or conqueror, esp. one of the Spanish conquerors of the New World in the 16th century. ORIG C19: from Sp., from *conquistar* to conquer

Conrad ★ ('kɒnræd) *n* **Joseph.** real name *Teodor Josef Konrad Korzeniowski.* 1857–1924, British novelist born in Poland, noted for sea stories such as *Lord Jim* (1900) and novels such as *Nostromo* (1904).

cons. *abbrev. for:* **1** consecrated. **2** consigned. **3** consignment. **4** consolidated. **5** consonant. **6** constitutional. **7** construction.

Cons. *abbrev. for* Conservative.

consanguinity (ˌkɒnsæŋ'gwɪnɪtɪ) *n* **1** relationship by blood; kinship. **2** close affinity or connection. ORIG C14: see CON-, SANGUINE
▸ ˌ**consan'guineous** *or* **con'sanguine** *adj*

conscience ('kɒnʃəns) *n* **1** the sense of right and wrong that governs a person's thoughts and actions. **2** conscientiousness; diligence. **3** a feeling of guilt or anxiety: *he has a conscience about his unkind action.* **4 in (all) conscience. 4a** with regard to truth and justice. **4b** certainly. **5 on one's conscience.** causing feelings of guilt or remorse. ORIG C13: from OF, from L *conscientia* knowledge, from *conscīre* to know; see CONSCIOUS

conscience clause *n* a clause in a law or contract exempting persons with moral scruples.

conscience money *n* money paid voluntarily to compensate for dishonesty, esp. for taxes formerly evaded.

conscience-stricken *adj* feeling anxious or guilty. Also: **conscience-smitten.**

conscientious (ˌkɒnʃɪ'ɛnʃəs) *adj* **1** involving or taking great care; painstaking. **2** governed by or done according to conscience.
▸ ˌ**consci'entiously** *adv* ▸ ˌ**consci'entiousness** *n*

conscientious objector *n* a person who refuses to serve in the armed forces on the grounds of conscience.

conscious ('kɒnʃəs) *adj* **1** alert and awake. **2** aware of one's surroundings, one's own motivations and thoughts, etc. **3a** aware (of) and giving value and emphasis (to a particular fact): *I am conscious of your great kindness to me.* **3b** (*in combination*): *clothes-conscious.* **4** deliberate or intended: *a conscious effort; conscious rudeness.* **5a** denoting a part of the human mind that is aware of a person's self, environment, and mental activity and that to a certain extent determines his choices of action. **5b** (*as n*): *the conscious is only a small part of the mind.* ORIG C17: from L *conscius* sharing knowledge, from *com-* with + *scīre* to know
▸ **'consciously** *adv* ▸ **'consciousness** *n*

consciousness raising *n* **a** the process of developing awareness in a person or group of a situation regarded as wrong or unjust, with the aim of producing active participation in changing it. **b** (*as modifier*): *a consciousness-raising group.*

conscript *n* ('kɒnskrɪpt). **1a** a person who is enrolled for compulsory military service. **1b** (*as modifier*): *a conscript army.* ◆ *vb* (kən'skrɪpt). **2** (*tr*) to enrol (youths, civilians, etc.) for compulsory military service. ORIG C15: from L *conscrīptus,* p.p. of *conscrībere* to enrol, from *scrībere* to write

conscription (kən'skrɪpʃən) *n* compulsory military service.

consecrate ('kɒnsɪˌkreɪt) *vb* **consecrates, consecrating, consecrated.** (*tr*) **1** to make or declare sacred or holy. **2** to dedicate (one's life, time, etc.) to a specific purpose. **3** *Christianity.* to sanctify (bread and wine) for the Eucharist to be received as the body and blood of Christ. **4** to cause to be respected or revered: *time has consecrated this custom.* ORIG C15: from L *consecrāre,* from *com-* (intensive) + *sacrāre* to devote, from *sacer* sacred
▸ ˌ**conse'cration** *n* ▸ **'conseˌcrator** *n* ▸ **'conseˌcratory** *adj*

Consecration (ˌkɒnsɪ'kreɪʃən) *n RC Church.* the part of the Mass after the sermon during which the bread and wine are believed to change into the Body and Blood of Christ.

consecutive (kən'sɛkjutɪv) *adj* **1** (of a narrative, account, etc.) following chronological sequence. **2** following one another without interruption; successive. **3** characterized by logical sequence. **4** *Grammar.* expressing consequence or result: *consecutive clauses.* **5** *Music.* another word for **parallel** (sense 3). ORIG C17: from F *consécutif,* from L *consecūtus,* from *consequī* to pursue
▸ **con'secutively** *adv* ▸ **con'secutiveness** *n*

consensual (kən'sɛnsjuəl) *adj* **1** *Law.* (of a contract, etc.) existing by consent. **2** (of reflex actions of the body) responding to stimulation of another part.
▸ **con'sensually** *adv*

consensus (kən'sɛnsəs) *n* general or widespread agree-

★ people and places

ment (esp. in **consensus of opinion**). ORIG C19: from L, from *consentīre*; see CONSENT

> **USAGE NOTE** Given the word's original meaning, namely referring to a collective opinion, some purists would argue that the phrase *consensus of opinion* is tautological and should therefore be avoided. Nevertheless, it is an extremely common use of the word, and is unlikely to jar with the majority of speakers.

consent (kən'sɛnt) *vb* **1** to give assent or permission; agree. ◆ *n* **2** acquiescence to or acceptance of something done or planned by another. **3** harmony in opinion; agreement (esp. in **with one consent**). ORIG C13: from OF *consentir*, from L *consentīre* to agree, from *sentīre* to feel
▸ **con'senting** *adj*

consequence ('kɒnsɪkwəns) *n* **1** a result or effect. **2** an unpleasant result (esp. in **take the consequences**). **3** an inference reached by reasoning; conclusion. **4** significance or importance: *it's of no consequence; a man of consequence.* **5 in consequence.** as a result.

consequent ('kɒnsɪkwənt) *adj* **1** following as an effect. **2** following as a logical conclusion. **3** (of a river) flowing in the direction of the original slope of the land. ◆ *n* **4** something that follows something else, esp. as a result. **5** *Logic.* the resultant clause in a conditional sentence. ORIG C15: from L *consequēns* following closely, from *consequī* to pursue

consequential (ˌkɒnsɪ'kwɛnʃəl) *adj* **1** important or significant. **2** self-important. **3** following as a consequence, esp. indirectly: *consequential loss.*
▸ **ˌconseˌquenti'ality** *n* ▸ **ˌconse'quentially** *adv*

consequently ('kɒnsɪkwəntlɪ) *adv, sentence connector.* as a result or effect; therefore; hence.

conservancy (kən'sɜːvənsɪ) *n, pl* **conservancies. 1** (in Britain) a court or commission with jurisdiction over a river, port, area of countryside, etc. **2** another word for **conservation** (sense 2).

conservation (ˌkɒnsə'veɪʃən) *n* **1** the act of conserving or keeping from change, loss, injury, etc. **2a** protection, preservation, and careful management of natural resources. **2b** (*as modifier*): *a conservation area.* **3** *Physics, etc.* the preservation of a specified aspect or value of a system, as in **conservation of charge, conservation of momentum, conservation of parity.**
▸ **ˌconser'vational** *adj* ▸ **ˌconser'vationist** *n*

conservation of energy *n* the principle that the total energy of any isolated system is constant and independent of any changes occurring within the system.

conservation of mass *n* the principle that the total mass of any isolated system is constant and is independent of any chemical and physical changes taking place within the system.

conservatism (kən'sɜːvəˌtɪzəm) *n* **1** opposition to change and innovation. **2** a political philosophy advocating the preservation of the best of the established order in society.

conservative (kən'sɜːvətɪv) *adj* **1** favouring the preservation of established customs, values, etc., and opposing innovation. **2** of conservatism. **3** moderate or cautious: *a conservative estimate.* **4** conventional in style: *a conservative suit.* **5** *Med.* (of treatment) designed to alleviate symptoms. Cf. **radical** (sense 4). ◆ *n* **6** a person who is reluctant to change or consider new ideas; conformist. **7** a supporter of conservatism.
▸ **con'servatively** *adv* ▸ **con'servativeness** *n*

Conservative (kən'sɜːvətɪv) ◆ *adj* **1** (in Britain and elsewhere) of, supporting, or relating to a Conservative Party. **2** (in Canada) of, supporting, or relating to the Progressive Conservative Party. **3** of, relating to, or characterizing Conservative Judaism. ◆ *n* **4** a supporter or member of a Conservative Party, or, (in Canada) of the Progressive Conservative Party.

Conservative Judaism *n* a movement rejecting extreme change and advocating moderate relaxations of traditional Jewish law.

Conservative Party *n* **1** (in Britain) the major right-wing party, which developed from the Tories in the 1830s. It encourages property owning and free enterprise. **2** (in Canada) short for Progressive Conservative Party. **3** (in other countries) any of various political parties generally opposing change.

conservatoire (kən'sɜːvəˌtwɑː) *n* an institution or school for instruction in music. Also called: **conservatory.** ORIG C18: from F: CONSERVATORY

conservator ('kɒnsəˌveɪtə, kən'sɜːvə-) *n* a custodian, guardian, or protector.

conservatorium (kənˌsɜːvə'tɔːrɪəm) *n Austral.* the usual term for **conservatoire.**

conservatory (kən'sɜːvətrɪ) *n, pl* **conservatories. 1** a greenhouse, esp. one attached to a house. **2** another word for **conservatoire.**

conserve *vb* (kən'sɜːv), **conserves, conserving, conserved.** (*tr*) **1** to keep or protect from harm, decay, loss, etc. **2** to preserve (a foodstuff, esp. fruit) with sugar. ◆ *n* ('kɒnsɜːv, kən'sɜːv). **3** a preparation similar to jam but usually containing whole pieces of fruit. ORIG (vb) C14: from L *conservāre* to keep safe, from *servāre* to save; (n) C14: from Med. L *conserva*, from L *conservāre*

consider (kən'sɪdə) *vb* (*mainly tr*) **1** (*also intr*) to think carefully about (a problem, decision, etc.). **2** (*may take a clause as object*) to judge; deem: *I consider him a fool.* **3** to have regard for: *consider your mother's feelings.* **4** to look at: *he considered her face.* **5** (*may take a clause as object*) to bear in mind: *when buying a car consider this make.* **6** to describe or discuss. ORIG C14: from L *consīderāre* to inspect closely

considerable (kən'sɪdərəbᵊl) *adj* **1** large enough to reckon with: *a considerable quantity.* **2** a lot of; much: *he had considerable courage.* **3** worthy of respect: *a considerable man in the scientific world.*
▸ **con'siderably** *adv*

considerate (kən'sɪdərɪt) *adj* **1** thoughtful towards other people; kind. **2** *Rare.* carefully thought out; considered.
▸ **con'siderately** *adv*

consideration (kənˌsɪdə'reɪʃən) *n* **1** deliberation; contemplation. **2 take into consideration.** to bear in mind; consider. **3 under consideration.** being currently discussed. **4** a fact to be taken into account when making a judgment or decision. **5** thoughtfulness for other people; kindness. **6** payment for a service. **7** thought resulting from deliberation; opinion. **8** *Law.* the promise, object, etc., given by one party to persuade another to enter into a contract. **9** esteem. **10 in consideration of. 10a** because of. **10b** in return for.

considered (kən'sɪdəd) *adj* **1** presented or thought out with care: *a considered opinion.* **2** (*qualified by a preceding adverb*) esteemed: *highly considered.*

considering (kən'sɪdərɪŋ) *prep* **1** in view of. ◆ *adv* **2** *Inf.* all in all, taking into account the circumstances: *it's not bad considering.* ◆ *conj* **3** (*subordinating*) in view of the fact that.

consign (kən'saɪn) *vb* (*mainly tr*) **1** to give into the care or charge of; entrust. **2** to commit irrevocably: *he consigned the papers to the flames.* **3** to commit: *to consign someone to jail.* **4** to address or deliver (goods): *it was consigned to his London address.* ORIG C15: from OF *consigner*, from L *consignāre* to put one's seal to, sign, from *signum* mark
▸ **con'signable** *adj* ▸ **ˌconsign'ee** *n* ▸ **con'signor** *or* **con'signer** *n*

consignment (kən'saɪnmənt) *n* **1** the act of consigning; commitment. **2** a shipment of goods consigned. **3 on consignment.** for payment by the consignee after sale.

consist (kən'sɪst) *vb* (*intr*) **1** (foll. by *of* or *in*) to be composed (of). **2** (foll. by *in* or *of*) to have its existence (in): *his religion consists only in going to church.* **3** to be consistent; accord. ORIG C16: from L *consistere* to stand firm, from *sistere* to stand

consistency (kən'sɪstənsɪ) *or* **consistence** *n, pl* **consistencies** *or* **consistences. 1** agreement or accordance. **2** degree of viscosity or firmness. **3** the state or quality of holding or sticking together and retaining shape. **4** conformity with previous attitudes, behaviour, practice, etc.

consistent (kən'sɪstənt) *adj* **1** (usually foll. by *with*) showing consistency or harmony. **2** steady; even: *consistent growth.* **3** *Logic.* (of a logical system) constituted so that the propositions deduced from different axioms of the system do not contradict each other.
▸ **con'sistently** *adv*

consistory (kən'sɪstərɪ) *n, pl* **consistories. 1** *Church of England.* the court of a diocese (other than Canterbury) administering ecclesiastical law. **2** *RC Church.* an assembly of the cardinals and the pope. **3** (in certain Reformed Churches) the governing body of a local congregation. **4** *Arch.* a council. ORIG C14: from OF, from Med. L *consistōrium* ecclesiastical tribunal, ult. from L *consistere* to stand still
▸ **consistorial** (ˌkɒnsɪ'stɔːrɪəl) *adj*

consolation (ˌkɒnsə'leɪʃən) *n* **1** the act of consoling or state of being consoled. **2** a person or thing that is a comfort in a time of grief, disappointment, etc.
▸ **consolatory** (kən'sɒlətərɪ) *adj*

consolation prize *n* a prize given to console a loser of a game.

console[1] (kən'səʊl) *vb* **consoles, consoling, consoled.** to serve as a comfort to (someone) in disappointment, sadness, etc. ORIG C17: from L *consōlārī*, from *sōlārī* to comfort
▸ **con'solable** *adj* ▸ **con'soler** *n* ▸ **con'solingly** *adv*

console[2] ('kɒnsəʊl) *n* **1** an ornamental bracket used to support a wall fixture, etc. **2** the part of an organ comprising the manuals, pedals, stops, etc. **3** a unit on which the controls of an electronic system are mounted. **4** a cabinet for a television, etc., designed to stand on the floor. **5** See **console table.** ORIG C18: from F, from OF *consolateur* one that provides support; see CONSOLE[1]

console table *n* a table with one or more curved legs of bracket-like construction, designed to stand against a wall.

consolidate (kən'sɒlɪˌdeɪt) *vb* **consolidates, consolidating, consolidated. 1** to form or cause to form into a whole. **2** to make or become stronger or more stable. **3** *Mil.* to strengthen one's control over (a situation, area, etc.). ORIG C16: from L *consolidāre* to make firm, from *solidus* strong
▸ **conˌsoli'dation** *n* ▸ **con'soliˌdator** *n*

consolidated fund *n Brit.* a fund maintained from tax revenue to meet standing charges, esp. national debt interest.

consols ('kɒnsɒlz, kən'sɒlz) *pl n* irredeemable British government securities carrying annual interest. ORIG short for *consolidated stock*

consommé (kən'sɒmeɪ) *n* a clear soup made from meat stock. ORIG C19: from F, from *consommer* to use up

consonance ('kɒnsənəns) *n* **1** agreement, harmony, or accord. **2** *Prosody.* similarity between consonants, but not between vowels, as between the *s* and *t* sounds in *sweet silent thought.* **3** *Music.* a combination of notes which can sound together without harshness.

consonant ('kɒnsənənt) *n* **1** a speech sound or letter of the alphabet other than a vowel. ◆ *adj* **2** (*postpositive;* foll. by *with* or *to*) consistent; in agreement. **3** harmonious. **4** *Music.* characterized by the presence of a consonance. ORIG C14: from L *consonāns*, from *consonāre* to sound at the same time, from *sonāre* to sound
▸ **'consonantly** *adv*

consonantal (ˌkɒnsə'næntᵊl) *adj* relating to, functioning as, or characterized by consonants.

consort *vb* (kən'sɔːt). (*intr*) **1** (usually foll. by *with*) to keep company (with undesirable people); associate. **2** to harmonize. ◆ *n* ('kɒnsɔːt). **3** (esp. formerly) a small group of instruments, either of the same type (**a whole consort**) or of different types (**a broken consort**). **4** the husband or wife of a reigning monarch. **5** a husband or wife. **6** a ship that escorts another. ORIG C15: from OF, from L *consors* partner, from *sors* lot, portion

consortium (kən'sɔːtɪəm) *n, pl* **consortia** (-tɪə). **1** an association of financiers, companies, etc., esp. for a particular purpose. **2** *Law.* the right of husband or wife to the company and affection of the other. ORIG C19: from L: partnership; see CONSORT

conspectus (kən'spɛktəs) *n* **1** an overall view; survey. **2** a summary; résumé. ORIG C19: from L: a viewing, from *conspicere*, from *specere* to look

conspicuous (kən'spɪkjʊəs) *adj* **1** clearly visible. **2** attracting attention because of a striking feature: *conspicuous stupidity.* ORIG C16: from L *conspicuus*, from *conspicere* to perceive; see CONSPECTUS
▸ **con'spicuously** *adv* ▸ **con'spicuousness** *n*

conspiracy (kən'spɪrəsɪ) *n, pl* **conspiracies. 1** a secret plan to carry out an illegal or harmful act, esp. with political motivation; plot. **2** the act of making such plans in secret.
▸ **con'spirator** *n* ▸ **conˌspira'torial** *adj*

conspiracy theory *n* the belief that the government or a covert organization is responsible for an unusual or unexplained event.

conspire (kən'spaɪə) *vb* **conspires, conspiring, conspired.** (when *intr*, sometimes foll. by *against*) **1** to plan (a crime) together in secret. **2** (*intr*) to act together as if by design: *the elements conspired to spoil our picnic.* ORIG C14: from OF, from L *conspīrāre* to plot together, lit.: to breathe together, from *spīrāre* to breathe

con spirito (kɒn 'spɪrɪtəʊ) *adj, adv Music.* (to be performed) in a spirited or lively manner. ORIG It.: with spirit

constable ('kʌnstəbᵊl, 'kɒn-) *n* **1** (in Britain, Australia, New Zealand, Canada, etc.) a police officer of the lowest rank. **2** any of various officers of the peace, esp. one who arrests offenders, serves writs, etc. **3** the keeper of a royal castle. **4** (in medieval Europe) the chief military officer and functionary of a royal household. **5** an officer of a hundred in medieval England. ORIG C13: from OF, from LL *comes stabulī* officer in charge of the stable
▸ **'constableˌship** *n*

Constable ★ ('kʌnstəbᵊl) *n* **John.** 1776–1837, British landscape painter.

constabulary (kən'stæbjʊlərɪ) *Chiefly Brit.* ◆ *n, pl* **constabularies. 1** the police force of a town or district. ◆ *adj* **2** of or relating to constables.

Constance ★ ('kɒnstəns) *n* **1** a city in S Germany, in Baden-Württemberg on Lake Constance: tourist centre. Pop.: 72 860 (1989 est.). German name: **Konstanz. 2 Lake.** a lake in W Europe, bounded by S Germany, W Austria, and N Switzerland, through which the Rhine flows. Area: 536 sq. km. (207 sq. miles). German name: **Bodensee.**

constant ('kɒnstənt) *adj* **1** unchanging. **2** incessant: *constant interruptions.* **3** resolute; loyal. ◆ *n* **4** something that is unchanging. **5** a specific quantity that is invariable: *the velocity of light is a constant.* **6a** *Maths.* a symbol representing an unspecified number that remains invariable throughout a particular series of operations. **6b** *Physics.* a quantity or property that is considered invariable throughout a particular series of experiments. ORIG C14: from OF, from L *constāns*, from *constāre* to be steadfast, from *stāre* to stand
▸ **'constancy** *n* ▸ **'constantly** *adv*

Constanţa ★ (*Romanian* kon'stantsa) *n* a port and resort in SE Romania, on the Black Sea: founded by the Greeks in the 6th century B.C. and rebuilt by Constantine the Great (4th century); exports petroleum. Pop.: 348 985 (1993 est.).

Constantia ★ (kɒn'stænʃə) *n S. African.* **1** a region of the Cape Peninsula. **2** any of several red or white wines produced around Constantia.

Constantine ★ ('kɒnstənˌtaɪn; *French* kɔ̃stɑ̃tin) *n* a walled city in NE Algeria: built on an isolated rock; military and trading centre. Pop.: 440 842 (1987).

Constantine I ★ ('kɒnstənˌtaɪn, -ˌtiːn) *n* **1** known as *Constantine the Great.* Latin name *Flavius Valerius Aurelius Constantinus.* ?280–337 A.D., first Christian Roman emperor (306–337): moved his capital to Byzantium, which he renamed Constantinople (330). **2** 1868–1923, king of Greece (1913–17; 1920–22): deposed (1917), recalled by a plebiscite (1920), but forced to abdicate again (1922) after defeat by the Turks.

Constantine II ★ *n* official title *Constantine XIII.* born

★ people and places

1940, king of Greece (1964–73): exiled in 1967 and deposed in 1973 when Greece became a republic.

Constantine VII ★ *n* known as *Porphyrogenitus.* 905–59 A.D., Byzantine emperor (913–59) and scholar.

Constantine XI ★ *n* 1404–53, last Byzantine emperor (1448–53): killed when Constantinople was captured by the Turks.

Constantinople ★ (ˌkɒnstæntɪ'nəʊpᵊl) *n* the former name (330–1926) of **Istanbul.**

constellate ('kɒnstɪˌleɪt) *vb* **constellates, constellating, constellated.** to form into clusters in or as if in constellations.

constellation (ˌkɒnstɪ'leɪʃən) *n* **1** any of the 88 groups of stars as seen from the earth, many of which were named by the ancient Greeks after animals, objects, or mythological persons. **2** a gathering of brilliant people or things. **3** *Psychoanalysis.* a group of ideas felt to be related. ORIG C14: from LL *constellātiō,* from L *com-* together + *stella* star
▸ **constellatory** (kən'stɛlətərɪ) *adj*

consternate ('kɒnstəˌneɪt) *vb* **consternates, consternating, consternated.** (*tr; usually passive*) to fill with anxiety, dismay, dread, or confusion. ORIG C17: from L *consternāre,* from *sternere* to lay low

consternation (ˌkɒnstə'neɪʃən) *n* a feeling of anxiety, dismay, dread, or confusion.

constipate ('kɒnstɪˌpeɪt) *vb* **constipates, constipating, constipated.** (*tr*) to cause constipation in. ORIG C16: from L *constīpāre* to press closely together
▸ **'constiˌpated** *adj*

constipation (ˌkɒnstɪ'peɪʃən) *n* infrequent or difficult evacuation of the bowels.

constituency (kən'stɪtjʊənsɪ) *n, pl* **constituencies. 1** the whole body of voters who elect one representative to a legislature or all the residents represented by one deputy. **2** a district that sends one representative to a legislature.

constituent (kən'stɪtjʊənt) *adj* (*prenominal*) **1** forming part of a whole; component. **2** having the power to frame a constitution or to constitute a government: *constituent assembly.* ◆ *n* **3** a component part; ingredient. **4** a resident of a constituency, esp. one entitled to vote. **5** *Chiefly law.* a person who appoints another to act on his or her behalf. ORIG C17: from L *constituēns,* from *constituere* to establish, CONSTITUTE
▸ **con'stituently** *adv*

constitute ('kɒnstɪˌtjuːt) *vb* **constitutes, constituting, constituted.** (*tr*) **1** to form; compose: *the people who constitute a jury.* **2** to appoint to an office: *a legally constituted officer.* **3** to set up (an institution) formally; found. **4** *Law.* to give legal form to (a court, assembly, etc.). ORIG C15: from L *constituere,* from *com-* (intensive) + *statuere* to place
▸ **'constiˌtutor** *n*

constitution (ˌkɒnstɪ'tjuːʃən) *n* **1** the act of constituting or state of being constituted. **2** physical make-up; structure. **3** the fundamental principles on which a state is governed, esp. when considered as embodying the rights of the subjects. **4** (*often cap.*) (in certain countries, esp. the US and Australia) a statute embodying such principles. **5** a person's state of health. **6** a person's temperament.

constitutional (ˌkɒnstɪ'tjuːʃənᵊl) *adj* **1** of a constitution. **2** authorized by or subject to a constitution: *constitutional monarchy.* **3** inherent in the nature of a person or thing: *a constitutional weakness.* **4** beneficial to one's physical wellbeing. ◆ *n* **5** a regular walk taken for the benefit of one's health.
▸ **ˌconstiˌtution'ality** *n* ▸ **ˌconsti'tutionally** *adv*

constitutionalism (ˌkɒnstɪ'tjuːʃənəˌlɪzəm) *n* **1** the principles or system of government in accord with a constitution. **2** adherence to or advocacy of such a system.
▸ **ˌconsti'tutionalist** *n*

constitutive ('kɒnstɪˌtjuːtɪv) *adj* **1** having power to enact or establish. **2** another word for **constituent** (sense 1).
▸ **'constiˌtutively** *adv*

constrain (kən'streɪn) *vb* (*tr*) **1** to compel, esp. by circumstances, etc. **2** to restrain as by force. ORIG C14: from OF, from L *constringere* to bind together
▸ **con'strainer** *n*

constrained (kən'streɪnd) *adj* embarrassed, unnatural, or forced: *a constrained smile.*

constraint (kən'streɪnt) *n* **1** compulsion or restraint. **2** repression of natural feelings. **3** a forced unnatural manner. **4** something that serves to constrain; restrictive condition.

constrict (kən'strɪkt) *vb* (*tr*) **1** to make smaller or narrower, esp. by contracting at one place. **2** to hold in or inhibit; limit. ORIG C18: from L *constrictus,* from *constringere* to tie up together

constriction (kən'strɪkʃən) *n* **1** a feeling of tightness in some part of the body, such as the chest. **2** the act of constricting or condition of being constricted. **3** something that is constricted.
▸ **con'strictive** *adj*

constrictor (kən'strɪktə) *n* **1** any of various nonvenomous snakes, such as the boas, that coil around and squeeze their prey to kill it. **2** any muscle that constricts; sphincter.

construct *vb* (kən'strʌkt). (*tr*) **1** to put together substances or parts systematically; build; assemble. **2** to frame mentally (an argument, sentence, etc.). **3** *Geom.* to draw (a line, angle, or figure) so that certain requirements are satisfied. ◆ *n* ('kɒnstrʌkt). **4** something formulated or built systematically. **5** a complex idea resulting from a synthesis of simpler ideas. ORIG C17: from L *constructus,* from *construere* to build, from *struere* to arrange, erect
▸ **con'structor** *or* **con'structer** *n*

construction (kən'strʌkʃən) *n* **1** the act of constructing or manner in which a thing is constructed. **2** a structure. **3a** the business or work of building dwellings, offices, etc. **3b** (*as modifier*): *a construction site.* **4** an interpretation: *they put a sympathetic construction on her behaviour.* **5** *Grammar.* a group of words that make up one of the constituents into which a sentence may be analysed; a phrase or clause. **6** an abstract work of art in three dimensions.
▸ **con'structional** *adj* ▸ **con'structionally** *adv*

constructive (kən'strʌktɪv) *adj* **1** serving to improve; positive: *constructive criticism.* **2** *Law.* deduced by inference; not expressed. **3** another word for **structural.**
▸ **con'structively** *adv*

constructivism (kən'strʌktɪˌvɪzəm) *n* a movement in abstract art evolved after World War I, which explored the use of movement and machine-age materials in sculpture.
▸ **con'structivist** *adj, n*

construe (kən'struː) *vb* **construes, construing, construed.** (*mainly tr*) **1** to interpret the meaning of (something): *you can construe that in different ways.* **2** (*may take a clause as object*) to infer; deduce. **3** to analyse the grammatical structure of; parse (esp. a Latin or Greek text as a preliminary to translation). **4** to combine words syntactically. **5** (*also intr*) *Old-fashioned.* to translate literally, esp. aloud. ORIG C14: from L *construere*; see CONSTRUCT
▸ **con'struable** *adj*

consubstantial (ˌkɒnsəb'stænʃəl) *adj Christian theol.* (esp. of the three persons of the Trinity) regarded as identical in essence though different in aspect. ORIG C15: from Church L, from L *com-* COM- + *substantia* SUBSTANCE
▸ **ˌconsubˌstanti'ality** *n*

consubstantiation (ˌkɒnsəbˌstænʃɪ'eɪʃən) *n Christian theol.* (in the Lutheran branch of Protestantism) the doctrine that after the consecration of the Eucharist the substance of the body and blood of Christ coexists within the substance of the consecrated bread and wine. Cf. **transubstantiation.**

consuetude ('kɒnswɪˌtjuːd) *n* an established custom or usage, esp. one having legal force. ORIG C14: from L *consuētūdō,* from *consuēscere,* from CON- + *suēscere* to be wont

consul ('kɒnsᵊl) *n* **1** an official appointed by a sovereign

state to protect its commercial interests and aid its citizens in a foreign city. **2** (in ancient Rome) either of two annually elected magistrates who jointly exercised the highest authority in the republic. **3** (in France from 1799 to 1804) any of the three chief magistrates of the First Republic. ORIG C14: from L, from *consulere* to CONSULT
▸ **consular** ('kɒnsjulə) *adj* ▸ **'consul,ship** *n*

consulate ('kɒnsjulɪt) *n* **1** the premises of a consul. **2** government by consuls. **3** the office or period of office of a consul. **4** (*often cap.*) **4a** the government of France by the three consuls from 1799 to 1804. **4b** this period. **5** (*often cap.*) the consular government of the Roman republic.

consul general *n, pl* **consuls general.** a consul of the highest grade, usually stationed in a city of considerable commercial importance.

consult (kən'sʌlt) *vb* **1** (when *intr,* often foll. by *with*) to ask advice from (someone). **2** (*tr*) to refer to for information: *to consult a map.* **3** (*tr*) to have regard for (a person's feelings, interests, etc.); consider. ORIG C17: from F, from L *consultāre,* from *consulere* to consult

consultant (kən'sʌltᵊnt) *n* **1a** a specialist physician who is asked to confirm a diagnosis. **1b** a physician or surgeon holding the highest appointment in a particular branch of medicine or surgery in a hospital. **2** a specialist who gives expert advice or information. **3** a person who asks advice in a consultation.
▸ **con'sultancy** *n*

consultant nurse *n* (in Britain) another name for **supernurse.**

consultation (,kɒnsᵊl'teɪʃən) *n* **1** the act of consulting. **2** a conference for discussion or the seeking of advice.
▸ **consultative** (kən'sʌltətɪv) *adj*

consulting (kən'sʌltɪŋ) *adj* (*prenominal*) acting in an advisory capacity on professional matters: *a consulting engineer.*

consulting room *n* a room in which a doctor sees patients.

consume (kən'sju:m) *vb* **consumes, consuming, consumed. 1** (*tr*) to eat or drink. **2** (*tr; often passive*) to obsess. **3** (*tr*) to use up; expend. **4** to destroy or be destroyed by: *fire consumed the forest.* **5** (*tr*) to waste. **6** (*passive*) to waste away. ORIG C14: from L *consūmere,* from *com-* (intensive) + *sūmere* to take up
▸ **con'sumable** *adj* ▸ **con'suming** *adj*

consumedly (kən'sju:mɪdlɪ) *adv Old-fashioned.* (intensifier): *consumedly fascinating.*

consumer (kən'sju:mə) *n* **1** a person who purchases goods and services for his own personal needs. Cf. **producer** (sense 6). **2** a person or thing that consumes.

consumer durable *n* a manufactured product that has a relatively long useful life, such as a car or a television.

consumer goods *pl n* goods that satisfy personal needs rather than those required for the production of other goods or services.

consumerism (kən'sju:mə,rɪzəm) *n* **1** protection of the interests of consumers. **2** advocacy of a high rate of consumption as a basis for a sound economy.
▸ **con'sumerist** *n, adj*

consumer terrorism *n* the practice of introducing dangerous substances to foodstuffs or other consumer products, esp. to extort money from the manufacturers.

consummate *vb* ('kɒnsə,meɪt), **consummates, consummating, consummated.** (*tr*) **1** to bring to completion; fulfil. **2** to complete (a marriage) legally by sexual intercourse. ◆ *adj* (kən'sʌmɪt, 'kɒnsəmɪt). **3** supremely skilled: *a consummate artist.* **4** (*prenominal*) (intensifier): *a consummate fool.* ORIG C15: from L *consummāre* to complete, from *summus* utmost
▸ **con'summately** *adv* ▸ **,consum'mation** *n*

consumption (kən'sʌmpʃən) *n* **1** the act of consuming or the state of being consumed, esp. by eating, burning, etc. **2** *Econ.* expenditure on goods and services for final personal use. **3** the quantity consumed. **4** a wasting away of the tissues of the body, esp. in tuberculosis of the lungs. ORIG C14: from L *consumptiō,* from *consūmere* to CONSUME

consumptive (kən'sʌmptɪv) *adj* **1** causing consumption; wasteful; destructive. **2** relating to or affected with tuberculosis of the lungs. ◆ *n* **3** *Pathol.* a person who suffers from consumption.
▸ **con'sumptively** *adv* ▸ **con'sumptiveness** *n*

cont. *abbrev. for:* **1** contents. **2** continued.

contact *n* ('kɒntækt). **1** the act or state of touching. **2** the state or fact of communication (esp. in **in contact, make contact**). **3a** a junction of electrical conductors. **3b** the part of the conductors that makes the junction. **3c** the part of an electrical device to which such connections are made. **4** an acquaintance, esp. one who might be useful in business, etc. **5** any person who has been exposed to a contagious disease. **6** (*modifier*) caused by touching the causative agent: *contact dermatitis.* **7** (*modifier*) denoting a herbicide or insecticide that kills on contact. **8** (*modifier*) of or maintaining contact. **9** (*modifier*) requiring or involving (physical) contact: *a contact sport.* ◆ *vb* ('kɒntækt, kən'tækt). **10** (when *intr,* often foll. by *with*) to put, come, or be in association, touch, or communication. ORIG C17: from L *contactus,* from *contingere* to touch on all sides, from *tangere* to touch
▸ **contactual** (kɒn'tæktjuəl) *adj*

contact lens *n* a thin convex lens, usually of plastic, which floats on the layer of tears in front of the cornea to correct defects of vision.

contact print *n* a photographic print made by exposing the printing paper through a negative placed directly on to it.

contagion (kən'teɪdʒən) *n* **1** the transmission of disease from one person to another by contact. **2** a contagious disease. **3** a corrupting influence that tends to spread. **4** the spreading of an emotional or mental state among a number of people: *the contagion of mirth.* ORIG C14: from L *contāgiō* infection, from *contingere;* see CONTACT

contagious (kən'teɪdʒəs) *adj* **1** (of a disease) capable of being passed on by direct contact with a diseased individual or by handling his clothing, etc. **2** (of an organism) harbouring the causative agent of a transmissible disease. **3** causing or likely to cause the same reaction in several people: *her laughter was contagious.*

contain (kən'teɪn) *vb* (*tr*) **1** to hold or be capable of holding: *this contains five pints.* **2** to restrain (feelings, behaviour, etc.). **3** to consist of: *the book contains three sections.* **4** *Mil.* to prevent (enemy forces) from operating beyond a certain area. **5** to be a multiple of, leaving no remainder: *6 contains 2 and 3.* ORIG C13: from OF, from L *continēre,* from *com-* together + *tenēre* to hold
▸ **con'tainable** *adj*

container (kən'teɪnə) *n* **1** an object used for or capable of holding, esp. for transport or storage. **2a** a large cargo-carrying standard-sized container that can be loaded from one mode of transport to another. **2b** (*as modifier*): *a container ship.*

containerize *or* **containerise** (kən'teɪnə,raɪz) *vb* **containerizes, containerizing, containerized** *or* **containerises, containerising, containerised.** (*tr*) **1** to convey (cargo) in standard-sized containers. **2** to adapt (a port or transportation system) to the use of standard-sized containers.
▸ **con,taineri'zation** *or* **con,taineri'sation** *n*

containment (kən'teɪnmənt) *n* the act of containing, esp. of restraining the power of a hostile country or the operations of a hostile military force.

contaminate (kən'tæmɪ,neɪt) *vb* **contaminates, contaminating, contaminated.** (*tr*) **1** to make impure; pollute. **2** to make radioactive by the addition of radioactive material. ORIG C15: from L *contamināre* to defile
▸ **con'taminable** *adj* ▸ **con'taminant** *n* ▸ **con,tami'nation** *n*
▸ **con'tami,nator** *n*

contango (kən'tæŋgəʊ) *n, pl* **contangos. 1** (formerly, on the London Stock Exchange) postponement of payment for and delivery of stock from one account day to the next. **2** the fee paid for such a postponement. ◆ Also called: **carry-over, continuation.** Cf. **backwardation.** ORIG C19: apparently an arbitrary coinage

conte *French.* (kɔ̃t) *n* a tale or short story.

contemn (kən'tɛm) *vb* (*tr*) *Formal.* to regard with con-

tempt; scorn. ORIG C15: from L *contemnere,* from *temnere* to slight
▸ **contemner** (kən'tɛmnə, -'tɛmə) *n*

contemplate ('kɒntɛm,pleɪt) *vb* **contemplates, contemplating, contemplated.** (*mainly tr*) **1** to think about intently and at length. **2** (*intr*) to think intently and at length, esp. for spiritual reasons; meditate. **3** to look at thoughtfully. **4** to have in mind as a possibility. ORIG C16: from L *contemplāre,* from *templum* TEMPLE[1]
▸ **,contem'plation** *n* ▸ **'contem,plator** *n*

contemplative ('kɒntɛm,pleɪtɪv, -təm-; kən'tɛmplə-) *adj* **1** denoting, concerned with, or inclined to contemplation; meditative. ◆ *n* **2** a person dedicated to religious contemplation.

contemporaneous (kən,tɛmpə'reɪnɪəs) *adj* existing, beginning, or occurring in the same period of time.
▸ **contemporaneity** (kən,tɛmpərə'niːɪtɪ) *or* **con,tempo'raneousness** *n*

contemporary (kən'tɛmprərɪ) *adj* **1** living or occurring in the same period. **2** existing or occurring at the present time. **3** conforming to modern ideas in style, fashion, etc. **4** having approximately the same age as one another. ◆ *n, pl* **contemporaries. 5** a person living at the same time or of approximately the same age as another. **6** something that is contemporary. ORIG C17: from Med. L *contemporārius,* from L *com-* together + *temporārius* relating to time, from *tempus* time
▸ **con'temporarily** *adv* ▸ **con'temporariness** *n*

USAGE NOTE Since *contemporary* can mean either of the same period or of the present period, it is best to avoid it where ambiguity might arise, as in *...a production of* Othello *in contemporary dress.* Specifying either *modern dress* or *Elizabethan dress,* according to whichever was intended, would avoid any possible confusion in this particular example.

contemporize *or* **contemporise** (kən'tɛmpə,raɪz) *vb* **contemporizes, contemporizing, contemporized** *or* **contemporises, contemporising, contemporised.** to be or make contemporary.

contempt (kən'tɛmpt) *n* **1** the feeling of a person towards a person or thing that he considers despicable; scorn. **2** the state of being scorned; disgrace (esp. in **hold in contempt**). **3** wilful disregard of the authority of a court of law or legislative body: *contempt of court.* ORIG C14: from L *contemptus,* from *contemnere* to CONTEMN

contemptible (kən'tɛmptɪb°l) *adj* deserving or worthy of contempt.
▸ **con,tempti'bility** *or* **con'temptibleness** *n* ▸ **con'temptibly** *adv*

contemptuous (kən'tɛmptjʊəs) *adj* (when *predicative,* often foll. by *of*) showing or feeling contempt; disdainful.
▸ **con'temptuously** *adv*

contend (kən'tɛnd) *vb* **1** (*intr;* often foll. by *with*) to struggle in rivalry, battle, etc.; vie. **2** to argue earnestly. **3** (*tr; may take a clause as object*) to assert. ORIG C15: from L *contendere* to strive, from *com-* with + *tendere* to stretch
▸ **con'tender** *n*

content[1] ('kɒntɛnt) *n* **1** (*often pl*) everything inside a container. **2** (*usually pl*) **2a** the chapters or divisions of a book. **2b** a list of these printed at the front of a book. **3** the meaning or significance of a work of art, as distinguished from its style or form. **4** all that is contained or dealt with in a piece of writing, etc.; substance. **5** the capacity or size of a thing. **6** the proportion of a substance contained in an alloy, mixture, etc.: *the lead content of petrol.* ORIG C15: from L *contentus* contained, from *continēre* to CONTAIN

content[2] (kən'tɛnt) *adj* (*postpositive*) **1** satisfied with things as they are. **2** assenting to or willing to accept circumstances, a proposed course of action, etc. ◆ *vb* **3** (*tr*) to make (oneself or another person) satisfied. ◆ *n* **4** peace of mind. ORIG C14: from OF, from L *contentus* contented, having restrained desires, from *continēre* to restrain
▸ **con'tentment** *n*

contented (kən'tɛntɪd) *adj* accepting one's situation or life with equanimity and satisfaction.
▸ **con'tentedly** *adv* ▸ **con'tentedness** *n*

contention (kən'tɛnʃən) *n* **1** a struggling between opponents; competition. **2** a point of dispute (esp. in **bone of contention**). **3** a point asserted in argument. ORIG C14: from L *contentiō,* from *contendere* to CONTEND

contentious (kən'tɛnʃəs) *adj* **1** tending to quarrel. **2** causing or characterized by dispute; controversial.
▸ **con'tentiousness** *n*

conterminous (kən'tɜːmɪnəs) *or* **coterminous** (kəʊ'tɜːmɪnəs) *adj* **1** enclosed within a common boundary. **2** without a break or interruption. ORIG C17: from L *conterminus,* from CON- + *terminus* boundary

contest *n* ('kɒntɛst). **1** a formal game or match in which people, teams, etc., compete. **2** a struggle for victory between opposing forces. ◆ *vb* (kən'tɛst). **3** (*tr*) to try to disprove; call in question. **4** (when *intr,* foll. by *with* or *against*) to dispute or contend (with): *to contest an election.* ORIG C16: from L *contestārī* to introduce a lawsuit, from *testis* witness
▸ **con'testable** *adj* ▸ **con'tester** *n*

contestant (kən'tɛstənt) *n* a person who takes part in a contest; competitor.

context ('kɒntɛkst) *n* **1** the parts of a piece of writing, speech, etc., that precede and follow a word or passage and contribute to its full meaning: *it is unfair to quote out of context.* **2** the circumstances that are relevant to an event, fact, etc. ORIG C15: from L *contextus* a putting together, from *contexere,* from *com-* together + *texere* to weave
▸ **con'textual** *adj*

contiguous (kən'tɪgjʊəs) *adj* **1** touching along the side or boundary; in contact. **2** neighbouring. **3** preceding or following in time. ORIG C17: from L *contiguus,* from *contingere* to touch; see CONTACT
▸ **con'tiguously** *adv*

continent[1] ('kɒntɪnənt) *n* **1** one of the earth's large land masses (Asia, Australia, Africa, Europe, North and South America, and Antarctica). **2** *Obs.* **2a** mainland. **2b** a continuous extent of land. ORIG C16: from the L phrase *terra continens* continuous land
▸ **continental** (,kɒntɪ'nɛnt°l) *adj* ▸ **,conti'nentally** *adv*

continent[2] ('kɒntɪnənt) *adj* **1** able to control urination and defecation. **2** exercising self-restraint, esp. from sexual activity; chaste. ORIG C14: from L *continēre;* see CONTAIN
▸ **'continence** *n*

Continent ★ ('kɒntɪnənt) *n* **the.** the mainland of Europe as distinguished from the British Isles.

Continental (,kɒntɪ'nɛnt°l) *adj* **1** of or characteristic of Europe, excluding the British Isles. **2** of or relating to the 13 original British North American colonies during the War of American Independence. ◆ *n* **3** (*sometimes not cap.*) an inhabitant of Europe, excluding the British Isles. **4** a regular soldier of the rebel army during the War of American Independence.

continental breakfast *n* a light breakfast of coffee and rolls.

continental climate *n* a climate characterized by hot summers, cold winters, and little rainfall, typical of the interior of a continent.

continental drift *n Geol.* the theory that the earth's continents move gradually over the surface of the planet on a substratum of magma.

continental quilt *n Brit.* a quilt, stuffed with down or a synthetic material, used as a bed cover in place of the top sheet and blankets. Also called: **duvet,** (Austral.) **doona.**

continental shelf *n* the sea bed surrounding a continent at depths of up to about 200 metres (100 fathoms), at the edge of which the **continental slope** drops steeply.

contingency (kən'tɪndʒənsɪ) *or* **contingence** (kən'tɪndʒəns) *n, pl* **contingencies** *or* **contingences. 1a** a possible but not very likely future event or condition. **1b** (*as modifier*): *a contingency plan.* **2** something dependent on a possible future event. **3** a fact, event, etc., incidental to something else. **4** *Logic.* the state of being contingent. **5** uncertainty. **6** *Statistics.* **6a** the degree of association between theoretical and observed common frequencies of two graded or classified variables. **6b** (*as modifier*): *a contingency table.*

contingent (kən'tɪndʒənt) *adj* **1** (when *postpositive,* often foll. by *on* or *upon*) dependent on events, conditions, etc., not yet known; conditional. **2** *Logic.* (of a proposition) true under certain conditions, false under others; not logically necessary. **3** happening by chance; accidental. **4** uncertain. ◆ *n* **5** a part of a military force, parade, etc. **6** a group distinguished by common interests, etc., that is part of a larger group. **7** a chance occurrence. ORIG C14: from L *contingere* to touch, befall

continual (kən'tɪnjuəl) *adj* **1** recurring frequently, esp. at regular intervals. **2** occurring without interruption; continuous in time. ORIG C14: from OF *continuel,* from L *continuus* uninterrupted, from *continēre* to CONTAIN
▸ **con'tinually** *adv*

continuance (kən'tɪnjuəns) *n* **1** the act of continuing. **2** the duration of an action, etc. **3** *US.* the adjournment of a legal proceeding.

continuant (kən'tɪnjuənt) *Phonetics.* ◆ *n* **1** a speech sound, such as (l), (r), (f), or (s), in which the closure of the vocal tract is incomplete, allowing the continuous passage of the breath. ◆ *adj* **2** relating to or denoting a continuant.

continuation (kən,tɪnju'eɪʃən) *n* **1** a part or thing added, esp. to a book or play; sequel. **2** a renewal of an interrupted action, process, etc.; resumption. **3** the act of continuing; prolongation. **4** another word for **contango.**

continue (kən'tɪnju:) *vb* **continues, continuing, continued. 1** (when *tr,* may take an infinitive) to remain or cause to remain in a particular condition or place. **2** (when *tr,* may take an infinitive) to carry on uninterruptedly (a course of action): *he continued running.* **3** (when *tr,* may take an infinitive) to resume after an interruption: *we'll continue after lunch.* **4** to prolong or be prolonged: *continue the chord until it meets the tangent.* **5** (*tr*) *Law, chiefly Scots.* to adjourn (legal proceedings). ORIG C14: from OF *continuer,* from L *continuāre* to join together

continuity (,kɒntɪ'nju:ɪtɪ) *n, pl* **continuities. 1** logical sequence. **2** a continuous or connected whole. **3** the comprehensive script or scenario of detail in a film or broadcast. **4** the continuous projection of a film.

continuity girl *or* **man** *n* a woman or man whose job is to ensure continuity and consistency in successive shots of a film.

continuo (kən'tɪnjuəʊ) *n, pl* **continuos. 1** *Music.* **1a** a shortened form of **basso continuo** (see **thorough bass**). **1b** (*as modifier*): *a continuo accompaniment.* **2** the thorough-bass part as played on a keyboard instrument. ORIG It., lit.: continuous

continuous (kən'tɪnjuəs) *adj* **1** unceasing: *a continuous noise.* **2** in an unbroken series or pattern. **3** *Statistics.* (of a variable) having a continuum of possible values so that its distribution requires integration rather than summation to determine its cumulative probability. **4** *Grammar.* another word for **progressive** (sense 7). ORIG C17: from L *continuus,* from *continēre* to CONTAIN
▸ **con'tinuously** *adv*

continuous assessment *n* the assessment of a pupil's progress throughout a course of study rather than exclusively by examination at the end of it.

continuous creation *n* the theory that matter is created continuously in the universe. See **steady-state theory.**

continuum (kən'tɪnjuəm) *n, pl* **continua** (-'tɪnjuə) *or* **continuums.** a continuous series or whole, no part of which is perceptibly different from the adjacent parts. ORIG C17: from L, neuter of *continuus* CONTINUOUS

contort (kən'tɔ:t) *vb* to twist or bend out of place or shape. ORIG C15: from L *contortus* intricate, from *contorquēre* to whirl around, from *torquēre* to twist
▸ **con'tortion** *n* ▸ **con'tortive** *adj*

contortionist (kən'tɔ:ʃənɪst) *n* **1** a performer who contorts his or her body for the entertainment of others. **2** a person who twists or warps meaning.

contour ('kɒntʊə) *n* **1** the outline of a mass of land, figure, or body; a defining line. **2a** See **contour line. 2b** (*as modifier*): *a contour map.* **3** (*often pl*) the shape of a curving form: *the contours of her body were full and round.* ◆ *vb* (*tr*) **4** to shape so as to form the contour of something. **5** to mark contour lines on. **6** to construct (a road, railway, etc.) to follow the outline of the land. ORIG C17: from F, from It. *contorno,* from *contornare* to sketch, from *tornare* to TURN

contour line *n* a line on a map or chart joining points of equal height or depth.

contour ploughing *n* ploughing along the contours of the land to minimize erosion.

Contra ('kɒntrə) *n* a member of a US-backed guerrilla army, founded in 1979, whose aim was to overthrow the Sandinista government in Nicaragua.

contra- *prefix* **1** against; contrary; opposing; contrasting: *contraceptive.* **2** (in music) pitched below: *contrabass.* ORIG from L, from *contrā* against

contraband ('kɒntrə,bænd) *n* **1a** goods that are prohibited by law from being exported or imported. **1b** illegally imported or exported goods. **2** illegal traffic in such goods; smuggling. **3** Also called: **contraband of war.** goods that a neutral country may not supply to a belligerent. ◆ *adj* **4** (of goods) **4a** forbidden by law from being imported or exported. **4b** illegally imported or exported. ORIG C16: from Sp. *contrabanda,* from It., from Med. L, from CONTRA- + *bannum* ban
▸ **'contra,bandist** *n*

contrabass (,kɒntrə'beɪs) *n* **1** another name for **double bass.** ◆ *adj* **2** denoting the instrument of a family that is lower than the bass.

contrabassoon (,kɒntrəbə'su:n) *n* the largest instrument in the oboe family, pitched an octave below the bassoon; double bassoon.

contraception (,kɒntrə'sɛpʃən) *n* the intentional prevention of conception by artificial or natural means. ORIG C19: from CONTRA- + CONCEPTION
▸ **,contra'ceptive** *adj, n*

contract *vb* (kən'trækt). **1** to make or become smaller, narrower, shorter, etc. **2** ('kɒntrækt). (when *intr,* sometimes foll. by *for;* when *tr,* may take an infinitive) to enter into an agreement with (a person, company, etc.) to deliver (goods or services) or to do (something) on mutually agreed terms. **3** to draw or be drawn together. **4** (*tr*) to incur or become affected by (a disease, debt, etc.). **5** (*tr*) to shorten (a word or phrase) by the omission of letters or syllables, usually indicated in writing by an apostrophe. **6** (*tr*) to wrinkle (the brow or a muscle). **7** (*tr*) to arrange (a marriage) for; betroth. ◆ *n* ('kɒntrækt). **8** a formal agreement between two or more parties. **9** a document that states the terms of such an agreement. **10** the branch of law treating of contracts. **11** marriage considered as a formal agreement. **12** See **contract bridge. 13** *Bridge.* **13a** the highest bid, which determines trumps and the number of tricks one side must make. **13b** the number and suit of these tricks. **14** *Sl.* **14a** a criminal agreement to kill a particular person in return for an agreed sum of money. **14b** (*as modifier*): *a contract killing.* ORIG C16: from L *contractus* agreement, from *contrahere* to draw together, from *trahere* to draw
▸ **con'tractible** *adj*

contract bridge ('kɒntrækt) *n* the most common variety of bridge, in which the declarer receives points counting towards game and rubber only for tricks he bids as well as makes. Cf. **auction bridge.**

contractile (kən'træktaɪl) *adj* having the power to contract or to cause contraction.

contraction (kən'trækʃən) *n* **1** an instance of contracting or the state of being contracted. **2** a shortening of a word or group of words, often marked by an apostrophe: *I've come* for *I have come.*
▸ **con'tractive** *adj*

contractor (kən'træktə) *n* **1** a person or firm that contracts to supply materials or labour, esp. for building. **2** something that contracts.

contract out ('kɒntrækt) *vb* (*intr, adv*) *Brit.* to agree not to participate in something, esp. the state pension scheme.

contractual (kən'træktjʊəl) *adj* of the nature of or assured by a contract.

contradict (ˌkɒntrə'dɪkt) *vb* **1** (*tr*) to affirm the opposite of (a statement, etc.). **2** (*tr*) to declare (a statement, etc.) to be false or incorrect; deny. **3** (*tr*) to be inconsistent with: *the facts contradicted his theory.* **4** (*intr*) to be at variance; be in contradiction. ORIG C16: from L *contrādīcere,* from CONTRA- + *dīcere* to speak
▸ **ˌcontra'dictable** *adj* ▸ **ˌcontra'dictor** *n*

contradiction (ˌkɒntrə'dɪkʃən) *n* **1** opposition; denial. **2** a declaration of the opposite. **3** a statement that is at variance with itself (often in **a contradiction in terms**). **4** conflict or inconsistency, as between events, qualities, etc. **5** a person or thing containing conflicting qualities. **6** *Logic.* a statement that is false under all circumstances; necessary falsehood.

contradictory (ˌkɒntrə'dɪktərɪ) *adj* **1** inconsistent; incompatible. **2** given to argument and contention: *a contradictory person.* **3** *Logic.* (of a pair of statements) unable both to be true or both to be false under the same circumstances.
▸ **ˌcontra'dictorily** *adv* ▸ **ˌcontra'dictoriness** *n*

contradistinction (ˌkɒntrədɪ'stɪŋkʃən) *n* a distinction made by contrasting different qualities.
▸ **ˌcontradis'tinctive** *adj*

contraflow ('kɒntrəˌfləʊ) *n Brit.* two-way traffic on one carriageway of a motorway.

contrail ('kɒntreɪl) *n* another name for **vapour trail.** ORIG C20: from CON(DENSATION) + TRAIL

contralto (kən'træltəʊ) *n, pl* **contraltos** *or* **contralti** (-tɪ). **1** the lowest female voice: in the context of a choir often shortened to **alto. 2** a singer with such a voice. ◆ *adj* **3** of or denoting a contralto: *the contralto part.* ORIG C18: from It.; see CONTRA-, ALTO

contraposition (ˌkɒntrəpə'zɪʃən) *n* **1** the act of placing opposite or against. **2** *Logic.* the conclusion drawn from a subject-predicate proposition by negating its terms and changing their order.

contraption (kən'træpʃən) *n Inf., often facetious or derog.* a device or contrivance, esp. one considered strange, unnecessarily intricate, or improvised. ORIG C19: ?from CON(TRIVANCE) + TRAP[1] + (INVEN)TION

contrapuntal (ˌkɒntrə'pʌntᵊl) *adj Music.* characterized by counterpoint. ORIG C19: from It. *contrappunto*
▸ **ˌcontra'puntally** *adv* ▸ **ˌcontra'puntist** *or* **ˌcontra'puntalist** *n*

contrariety (ˌkɒntrə'raɪətɪ) *n, pl* **contrarieties. 1** opposition between one thing and another; disagreement. **2** an instance of such opposition; inconsistency; discrepancy.

contrariwise ('kɒntrərɪˌwaɪz) *adv* **1** from a contrasting point of view. **2** in the reverse way. **3** (kən'trɛərɪˌwaɪz). in a contrary manner.

contrary ('kɒntrərɪ) *adj* **1** opposed in nature, position, etc.: *contrary ideas.* **2** (kən'trɛərɪ). perverse; obstinate. **3** (esp. of wind) adverse; unfavourable. **4** (of plant parts) situated at right angles to each other. **5** *Logic.* (of a pair of propositions) related so they cannot both be true, although they may both be false. ◆ *n, pl* **contraries. 6** the exact opposite (esp. in **to the contrary**). **7 on the contrary.** quite the reverse. **8** either of two exactly opposite objects, facts, or qualities. ◆ *adv* (usually foll. by *to*) **9** in an opposite or unexpected way: *contrary to usual belief.* **10** in conflict (with): *contrary to nature.* ORIG C14: from L *contrārius* opposite, from *contrā* against
▸ **con'trarily** *adv* ▸ **con'trariness** *n*

contrast *vb* (kən'trɑːst). **1** (often foll. by *with*) to distinguish or be distinguished by comparison of unlike or opposite qualities. ◆ *n* ('kɒntrɑːst). **2** distinction by comparison of opposite or dissimilar things, qualities, etc. (esp. in **by contrast, in contrast to** *or* **with**). **3** a person or thing showing differences when compared with another. **4** the effect of the juxtaposition of different colours, tones, etc. **5** the extent to which adjacent areas of an optical image, esp. on a television screen or in a photograph, differ in brightness. ORIG C16: (n): via F from It., from *contrastare* (vb), from L *contra-* against + *stare* to stand
▸ **con'trasting** *adj* ▸ **con'trastive** *adj*

contrast medium *n Med.* a radiopaque substance, such as barium sulphate, used to increase the contrast of an image in radiography.

contravene (ˌkɒntrə'viːn) *vb* **contravenes, contravening, contravened.** (*tr*) **1** to come into conflict with or infringe (rules, laws, etc.). **2** to dispute or contradict (a statement, proposition, etc.). ORIG C16: from LL *contrāvenīre,* from L CONTRA- + *venīre* to come
▸ **ˌcontra'vener** *n* ▸ **contravention** (ˌkɒntrə'vɛnʃən) *n*

contretemps ('kɒntrəˌtɑːn) *n, pl* **contretemps. 1** an awkward or difficult situation or mishap. **2** a small disagreement that is rather embarrassing. ORIG C17: from F, from *contre* against + *temps* time

contribute (kən'trɪbjuːt) *vb* **contributes, contributing, contributed.** (often foll. by *to*) **1** to give (support, money, etc.) for a common purpose or fund. **2** to supply (ideas, opinions, etc.). **3** (*intr*) to be partly responsible (for): *drink contributed to the accident.* **4** to write (articles, etc.) for a publication. ORIG C16: from L *contribuere* to collect, from *tribuere* to grant
▸ **con'tributable** *adj* ▸ **con'tributive** *adj* ▸ **con'tributor** *n*

contribution (ˌkɒntrɪ'bjuːʃən) *n* **1** the act of contributing. **2** something contributed, such as money. **3** an article, etc., contributed to a newspaper or other publication. **4** *Arch.* a levy.

contributory (kən'trɪbjʊtərɪ, -trɪ) *adj* **1** (often foll. by *to*) being partly responsible: *a contributory factor.* **2** giving to a common purpose or fund. **3** of or designating an insurance or pension scheme in which the premiums are paid partly by the employer and partly by the employees who benefit from it. ◆ *n, pl* **contributories. 4** a person or thing that contributes. **5** *Company law.* a member or former member of a company liable to contribute to the assets on the winding-up of the company.

contrite (kən'traɪt, 'kɒntraɪt) *adj* **1** full of guilt or regret; remorseful. **2** arising from a sense of shame or guilt: *contrite promises.* ORIG C14: from L *contrītus* worn out, from *conterere* to bruise, from *terere* to grind
▸ **con'tritely** *adv* ▸ **con'triteness** *or* **contrition** (kən'trɪʃən) *n*

contrivance (kən'traɪvəns) *n* **1** something contrived, esp. an ingenious device; contraption. **2** inventive skill or ability. **3** an artificial rather than natural arrangement of details, parts, etc. **4** an elaborate or deceitful plan; stratagem.

contrive (kən'traɪv) *vb* **contrives, contriving, contrived. 1** (*tr*) to manage (something or to do something), esp. by a trick: *he contrived to make them meet.* **2** (*tr*) to think up or adapt ingeniously: *he contrived a new mast for the boat.* **3** to plot or scheme. ORIG C14: from OF *controver,* from LL *contropāre* to represent by figures of speech, compare
▸ **con'triver** *n*

contrived (kən'traɪvd) *adj* obviously planned; artificial; forced; unnatural.

control (kən'trəʊl) *vb* **controls, controlling, controlled.** (*tr*) **1** to command, direct, or rule. **2** to check, limit, or restrain: *to control one's emotions.* **3** to regulate or operate (a machine). **4** to verify (a scientific experiment) by conducting a parallel experiment in which the variable being investigated is held constant or is compared with a standard. **5a** to regulate (financial affairs). **5b** to examine (financial accounts). **6** to restrict or regulate the authorized supply of (certain substances, such as drugs). ◆ *n* **7** power to direct: *under control.* **8** a curb; check: *a frontier control.* **9** (*often pl*) a mechanism for operating a car, aircraft, etc. **10a** a standard of comparison used in a statistical analysis, etc. **10b** (*as modifier*): *a control group.* **11a** a device that regulates the operation of a machine. **11b** (*as modifier*): *control room.* ORIG C15: from OF *conteroller* to regulate, from *contrerolle* duplicate register, from *contre-* COUNTER- + *rolle* ROLL
▸ **con'trollable** *adj* ▸ **conˌtrolla'bility** *n* ▸ **con'trollably** *adv*

control experiment *n* an experiment designed to check or correct the results of another experiment by removing the variable or variables operating in that other experiment.

control freak *n Inf.* a person who is obsessed with gaining and exercising control.

controller (kən'trəʊlə) *n* **1** a person who directs. **2** Also called: **comptroller.** a business executive or government officer responsible for financial planning, control, etc. **3** the equipment concerned with controlling the operation of an electrical device.
▸ **con'troller,ship** *n*

controlling interest *n* a quantity of shares in a business that is sufficient to ensure control over its direction.

control tower *n* a tower at an airport from which air traffic is controlled.

controversy ('kɒntrə,vɜːsɪ, kən'trɒvəsɪ) *n, pl* **controversies.** dispute, argument, or debate, esp. one concerning a matter about which there is strong disagreement and esp. one carried on in public or in the press. ORIG C14: from L *contrōversia,* from *contrōversus,* from CONTRA- + *vertere* to turn
▸ **controversial** (,kɒntrə'vɜːʃəl) *adj* ▸ **,contro'versial,ism** *n* ▸ **,contro'versialist** *n*

controvert ('kɒntrə,vɜːt, ,kɒntrə'vɜːt) *vb* (*tr*) **1** to deny, refute, or oppose (argument or opinion). **2** to argue about. ORIG C17: from L *contrōversus;* see CONTROVERSY
▸ **,contro'vertible** *adj*

contumacious (,kɒntjʊ'meɪʃəs) *adj* stubbornly resistant to authority.
▸ **,contu'maciously** *adv*

contumacy ('kɒntjʊməsɪ) *n, pl* **contumacies.** obstinate and wilful resistance to authority, esp. refusal to comply with a court order. ORIG C14: from L *contumācia,* from *contumāx* obstinate

contumely ('kɒntjʊmɪlɪ) *n, pl* **contumelies. 1** scornful or insulting language or behaviour. **2** a humiliating insult. ORIG C14: from L *contumēlia,* from *tumēre* to swell, as with wrath
▸ **contumelious** (,kɒntjʊ'miːlɪəs) *adj* ▸ **,contu'meliously** *adv*

contuse (kən'tjuːz) *vb* **contuses, contusing, contused.** (*tr*) to injure (the body) without breaking the skin; bruise. ORIG C15: from L *contūsus* bruised, from *contundere* to grind, from *tundere* to beat
▸ **con'tusion** *n*

conundrum (kə'nʌndrəm) *n* **1** a riddle, esp. one whose answer makes a play on words. **2** a puzzling question or problem. ORIG C16: from ?

conurbation (,kɒnɜː'beɪʃən) *n* a large densely populated urban sprawl formed by the growth and coalescence of individual towns or cities. ORIG C20: from CON- + *-urbation,* from L *urbs* city

convalesce (,kɒnvə'lɛs) *vb* **convalesces, convalescing, convalesced.** (*intr*) to recover from illness, injury, or the aftereffects of a surgical operation. ORIG C15: from L *convalēscere,* from *com-* (intensive) + *valēscere* to grow strong

convalescence (,kɒnvə'lɛsəns) *n* **1** gradual return to health after illness, injury, or an operation. **2** the period during which such recovery occurs.
▸ **,conva'lescent** *n, adj*

convection (kən'vɛkʃən) *n* **1** a process of heat transfer through a gas or liquid by bulk motion of hotter material into a cooler region. Cf. **conduction** (sense 1). **2** *Meteorol.* the process by which masses of relatively warm air are raised into the atmosphere, often cooling and forming clouds, with compensatory downward movements of cooler air. ORIG C19: from LL *convectiō,* from L *convehere* to bring together, from *vehere* to carry
▸ **con'vectional** *adj* ▸ **con'vective** *adj*

convector (kən'vɛktə) *n* a space-heating device from which heat is transferred to the surrounding air by convection.

convene (kən'viːn) *vb* **convenes, convening, convened. 1** to gather, call together or summon, esp. for a formal meeting. **2** (*tr*) to order to appear before a court of law, judge, tribunal, etc. ORIG C15: from L *convenīre* to assemble, from *venīre* to come
▸ **con'venable** *adj*

convener *or* **convenor** (kən'viːnə) *n* **1** a person who convenes or chairs a meeting, committee, etc., esp. one who is specifically elected to do so: *a convener of shop stewards.* **2** the chairman and civic head of certain Scottish councils. Cf. **provost** (sense 2).
▸ **con'venership** *or* **con'venorship** *n*

convenience (kən'viːnɪəns) *n* **1** the quality of being suitable or opportune. **2** a convenient time or situation. **3 at your convenience.** at a time suitable to you. **4** usefulness, comfort, or facility. **5** an object that is useful, esp. a labour-saving device. **6** *Euphemistic, chiefly Brit.* a lavatory, esp. a public one. **7 make a convenience of.** to take advantage of; impose upon.

convenience food *n* food that needs little preparation, especially food that has been pre-prepared and preserved for long-term storage.

convenience store *n* a shop that has long opening hours, caters to local tastes, and is conveniently situated.

convenient (kən'viːnɪənt) *adj* **1** suitable; opportune. **2** easy to use. **3** close by; handy. ORIG C14: from L *conveniēns,* from *convenīre* to be in accord with, from *venīre* to come
▸ **con'veniently** *adv*

convent ('kɒnvənt) *n* **1** a building inhabited by a religious community, usually of nuns. **2** the religious community inhabiting such a building. **3** Also called: **convent school.** a school in which the teachers are nuns. ORIG C13: from OF, from L *conventus* meeting, from *convenīre;* see CONVENE

conventicle (kən'vɛntɪk^{ə}l) *n* **1** a secret or unauthorized assembly for worship. **2** a small meeting house or chapel, esp. of Dissenters. ORIG C14: from L *conventiculum,* from *conventus;* see CONVENT

convention (kən'vɛnʃən) *n* **1** a large formal assembly of a group with common interests, such as a trade union. **2** *US politics.* an assembly of delegates of one party to select candidates for office. **3** an international agreement second only to a treaty in formality. **4** any agreement or contract. **5** the established view of what is thought to be proper behaviour, good taste, etc. **6** an accepted rule, usage, etc.: *a convention used by printers.* **7** *Bridge.* a bid or play not to be taken at its face value, which one's partner can interpret according to a prearranged bidding system. ORIG C15: from L *conventiō* an assembling

conventional (kən'vɛnʃən^{ə}l) *adj* **1** following the accepted customs and proprieties, esp. in a way that lacks originality. **2** established by accepted usage or general agreement. **3** of a convention or assembly. **4** *Visual arts.* conventionalized. **5** (of weapons, warfare, etc.) not nuclear.
▸ **con'ventionalism** *n* ▸ **con'ventionally** *adv*

conventionality (kən,vɛnʃə'nælɪtɪ) *n, pl* **conventionalities. 1** the quality of being conventional. **2** (*often pl*) something conventional.

conventionalize *or* **conventionalise** (kən'vɛnʃənə,laɪz) *vb* **conventionalizes, conventionalizing, conventionalized** *or* **conventionalises, conventionalising, conventionalised.** (*tr*) **1** to make conventional. **2** to simplify or stylize (a design, decorative device, etc.).
▸ **con,ventionali'zation** *or* **con,ventionali'sation** *n*

conventual (kən'vɛntjʊəl) *adj* **1** of, belonging to, or characteristic of a convent. ◆ *n* **2** a member of a convent.
▸ **con'ventually** *adv*

converge (kən'vɜːdʒ) *vb* **converges, converging, converged. 1** to move or cause to move towards the same point. **2** to meet or join. **3** (*intr*) (of opinions, effects, etc.) to tend towards a common conclusion or result. **4** (*intr*) *Maths.* (of an infinite series) to approach a finite limit as the number of terms increases. **5** (*intr*) (of animals and plants) to undergo convergence. ORIG C17: from LL *convergere,* from L *com-* together + *vergere* to incline
▸ **con'vergent** *adj*

convergence (kən'vɜːdʒəns) *n* **1** Also: **convergency.** the act, degree, or a point of converging. **2** Also called: **convergent evolution.** the evolutionary development of a superficial resemblance between unrelated animals that occupy a similar environment, as in the evolution of wings in birds and bats.

convergent thinking *n Psychol.* analytical, usually deductive, thinking in which ideas are examined for their logical validity or in which a set of rules is followed, for example in arithmetic.

conversable (kən'vɜːsəbᵊl) *adj* **1** easy or pleasant to talk to. **2** able or inclined to talk.

conversant (kən'vɜːsᵊnt) *adj* (*usually postpositive* and foll. by *with*) experienced (in), familiar (with), or acquainted (with).
▸ **con'versance** *or* **con'versancy** *n* ▸ **con'versantly** *adv*

conversation (ˌkɒnvə'seɪʃən) *n* the interchange through speech of information, ideas, etc.; spoken communication.

conversational (ˌkɒnvə'seɪʃənᵊl) *adj* **1** of, using, or in the manner of conversation. **2** inclined to conversation; conversable.
▸ **ˌconver'sationalist** *n* ▸ **ˌconver'sationally** *adv*

conversation piece *n* **1** something, esp. an unusual object, that provokes conversation. **2** (esp. in 18th-century Britain) a group portrait in a landscape or domestic setting.

converse[1] *vb* (kən'vɜːs), **converses, conversing, conversed.** (*intr*; often foll. by *with*) **1** to engage in conversation (with). **2** to commune spiritually (with). ◆ *n* ('kɒnvɜːs). **3** conversation (often in **hold converse with**). ORIG C16: from OF *converser*, from L *conversārī* to keep company with, from *conversāre* to turn constantly, from *vertere* to turn
▸ **con'verser** *n*

converse[2] ('kɒnvɜːs) *adj* **1** (*prenominal*) reversed; opposite; contrary. ◆ *n* **2** something that is opposite or contrary. **3** *Logic.* a categorial proposition obtained from another by the transposition of the subject and predicate, as *no bad man is bald* from *no bald man is bad*. ORIG C16: from L *conversus* turned around; see CONVERSE[1]
▸ **con'versely** *adv*

conversion (kən'vɜːʃən) *n* **1a** a change or adaptation in form, character, or function. **1b** something changed in one of these respects. **2** a change to another belief, as in a change of religion. **3** alteration to the structure or fittings of a building undergoing a change in function or legal status. **4** *Maths.* a change in the units or form of a number or expression: *the conversion of miles to kilometres.* **5** *Rugby.* a score made after a try by kicking the ball over the crossbar from a place kick. **6** *Physics.* a change of fertile material to fissile material in a reactor. **7** an alteration to a car engine to improve its performance. ORIG C14: from L *conversiō* a turning around; see CONVERT

conversion disorder *n* a psychological disorder in which severe physical symptoms like blindness or paralysis appear with no apparent physical cause.

convert *vb* (kən'vɜːt). (*mainly tr*) **1** to change or adapt the form, character, or function of. **2** to cause (someone) to change in opinion, belief, etc. **3** (*intr*) to admit of being changed (into): *the table converts into a tray.* **4** (*also intr*) to change or be changed into another state: *to convert water into ice.* **5** *Law.* to assume unlawful proprietary rights over (personal property). **6** (*also intr*) *Rugby.* to make a conversion after (a try). **7** *Logic.* to transpose the subject and predicate of (a proposition). **8** to change (a value or measurement) from one system of units to another. **9** to exchange (a security or bond) for something of equivalent value. ◆ *n* ('kɒnvɜːt). **10** a person who has been converted to another belief, religion, etc. ORIG C13: from OF, from L *convertere* to turn around, alter, from *vertere* to turn

converter *or* **convertor** (kən'vɜːtə) *n* **1** a person or thing that converts. **2** *Physics.* **2a** a device for converting alternating current to direct current or vice versa. **2b** a device for converting a signal from one frequency to another. **3** a vessel in which molten metal is refined, using a blast of air or oxygen. **4** *Computing.* a device for converting one form of coded information to another, such as an analogue-to-digital converter.

converter reactor *n* a nuclear reactor for converting one fuel into another, esp. fertile material into fissionable material.

convertible (kən'vɜːtɪbᵊl) *adj* **1** capable of being converted. **2** (of a car) having a folding or removable roof. **3** *Finance.* **3a** (of a currency) freely exchangeable into other currencies. **3b** (of a paper currency) exchangeable on demand for precious metal to an equivalent value. **3c** (of a bond, debenture, etc.) able to be exchanged for a share on a specified date at a specified price. ◆ *n* **4** a car with a folding or removable roof. **5** any convertible document or currency.
▸ **conˌverti'bility** *n* ▸ **con'vertibly** *adv*

convex ('kɒnvɛks, kɒn'vɛks) *adj* **1** curving outwards. **2** having one or two surfaces curved or ground in the shape of a section of the exterior of a sphere, ellipsoid, etc.: *a convex lens.* ORIG C16: from L *convexus* vaulted, rounded
▸ **con'vexity** *n* ▸ **'convexly** *adv*

convexo-concave (kənˌvɛksəʊkɒn'keɪv) *adj* **1** having one side convex and the other side concave. **2** (of a lens) having a convex face with greater curvature than the concave face.

convexo-convex *adj* (esp. of a lens) having both sides convex; biconvex.

convey (kən'veɪ) *vb* (*tr*) **1** to take, carry, or transport from one place to another. **2** to communicate (a message, information, etc.). **3** (of a channel, path, etc.) to conduct or transfer. **4** *Law.* to transfer (the title to property). ORIG C13: from OF *conveier*, from Med. L *conviāre* to escort, from L *com-* with + *via* way
▸ **con'veyable** *adj*

conveyance (kən'veɪəns) *n* **1** the act of conveying. **2** a means of transport. **3** *Law.* **3a** a transfer of the legal title to property. **3b** the document effecting such a transfer.
▸ **con'veyancer** *n* ▸ **con'veyancing** *n*

conveyor *or* **conveyer** (kən'veɪə) *n* **1** a person or thing that conveys. **2** short for **conveyor belt.**

conveyor belt *n* a flexible endless strip of fabric or linked plates driven by rollers and used to transport objects, esp. in a factory.

convict *vb* (kən'vɪkt). (*tr*) **1** to pronounce (someone) guilty of an offence. ◆ *n* ('kɒnvɪkt). **2** a person found guilty of an offence against the law. **3** a person serving a prison sentence. ORIG C14: from L *convictus* convicted, from *convincere* to prove guilty, CONVINCE

conviction (kən'vɪkʃən) *n* **1** the state of being convinced. **2** a firmly held belief, opinion, etc. **3** the act of convincing. **4** the act of convicting or the state of being convicted. **5 carry conviction.** to be convincing.
▸ **con'victional** *adj* ▸ **con'victive** *adj*

convince (kən'vɪns) *vb* **convinces, convincing, convinced.** (*tr*) (*may take a clause as object*) to make (someone) agree, understand, or realize the truth or validity of something; persuade. ORIG C16: from L *convincere* to demonstrate incontrovertibly, from *com-* (intensive) + *vincere* to overcome
▸ **con'vincer** *n* ▸ **con'vincible** *adj* ▸ **con'vincing** *adj*
▸ **con'vincingly** *adv*

> **USAGE NOTE** The use of *convince* to talk about persuading someone to do something is considered by many British speakers to be wrong or unacceptable.

convivial (kən'vɪvɪəl) *adj* sociable; jovial or festive: *a convivial atmosphere.* ORIG C17: from LL *convīviālis*, from L *convīvium*, a living together, banquet, from *vīvere* to live
▸ **conˌvivi'ality** *n*

convocation (ˌkɒnvə'keɪʃən) *n* **1** a large formal assembly. **2** the act of convoking or state of being convoked. **3** *Church of England.* either of the synods of the provinces of Canterbury or York. **4** *Episcopal Church.* an assembly of the clergy and part of the laity of a diocese. **5** (*sometimes cap.*) (in some British universities) a legislative assembly. **6** (in Australia and New Zealand) the graduate membership of a university.
▸ **ˌconvo'cational** *adj*

convoke (kən'vəuk) *vb* **convokes, convoking, convoked.** (*tr*) to call (a meeting, assembly, etc.) together; summon. ORIG C16: from L *convocāre*, from *vocāre* to call
▸ **con'voker** *n*

convolute ('kɒnvəˌlu:t) *vb* **convolutes, convoluting, convoluted.** (*tr*) **1** to form into a twisted, coiled, or rolled shape. ◆ *adj* **2** *Bot.* rolled longitudinally upon itself: *a convolute petal.* ORIG C18: from L *convolūtus*, from *convolvere* to roll together, from *volvere* to turn

convoluted ('kɒnvəˌlu:tɪd) *adj* **1** (esp. of meaning, style, etc.) difficult to comprehend; involved. **2** coiled.
▸ **'convoˌlutedly** *adv*

convolution (ˌkɒnvə'lu:ʃən) *n* **1** a turn, twist, or coil. **2** an intricate or confused matter or condition. **3** any of the numerous convex folds of the surface of the brain.
▸ **ˌconvo'lutional** *or* **ˌconvo'lutionary** *adj*

convolve (kən'vɒlv) *vb* **convolves, convolving, convolved.** to wind or roll together; coil; twist. ORIG C16: from L *convolvere*; see CONVOLUTE

convolvulus (kən'vɒlvjuləs) *n, pl* **convolvuluses** *or* **convolvuli** (-ˌlaɪ). a twining herbaceous plant having funnel-shaped flowers and triangular leaves. ORIG C16: from L: bindweed; see CONVOLUTE

convoy ('kɒnvɔɪ) *n* **1** a group of merchant ships with an escort of warships. **2** a group of land vehicles assembled to travel together. **3** the act of travelling or escorting by convoy (esp. in **in convoy**). ◆ *vb* **4** (*tr*) to escort while in transit. ORIG C14: from OF *convoier* to CONVEY

convulse (kən'vʌls) *vb* **convulses, convulsing, convulsed. 1** (*tr*) to shake or agitate violently. **2** (*tr*) to cause (muscles) to undergo violent spasms or contractions. **3** (*intr; often* foll. by *with*) *Inf.* to shake or be overcome (with violent emotion, esp. laughter). **4** (*tr*) to disrupt the normal running of (a country, etc.): *student riots have convulsed India.* ORIG C17: from L *convulsus*, from *convellere*, from *vellere* to pluck, pull
▸ **con'vulsive** *adj* ▸ **con'vulsively** *adv*

convulsion (kən'vʌlʃən) *n* **1** a violent involuntary muscular contraction. **2** a violent upheaval, esp. a social one. **3** (*usually pl*) *Inf.* uncontrollable laughter: *I was in convulsions.*

Conwy ★ ('kɒnwɪ) *n* **1** a market town and resort in N Wales, in Gwynnedd on the estuary of the River Conwy: medieval town walls, 13th-century castle. Pop.: 3627 (1991). Former name: **Conway. 2** a county borough in N Wales. Pop.: 70 200 (1996 est.). Area: 1130 sq. km (436 sq. miles).

cony *or* **coney** ('kəunɪ) *n, pl* **conies** *or* **coneys. 1** a rabbit or fur made from the skin of a rabbit. **2** (in the Bible) another name for the **hyrax.** ORIG C13: back formation from *conies*, from OF *conis*, pl. of *conil*, from L *cunīculus* rabbit

Conybeare ★ ('kɒnɪˌbɪə, 'kʌn-) *n* **William David.** 1787–1857, British geologist, noted for his *Outlines of the Geology of England and Wales* (1822).

coo (ku:) *vb* **coos, cooing, cooed. 1** (*intr*) (of doves, pigeons, etc.) to make a characteristic soft throaty call. **2** (*tr*) to speak in a soft murmur. **3** (*intr*) to murmur lovingly (esp. in **bill and coo**). ◆ *n* **4** the sound of cooing. ◆ *interj* **5** *Brit. sl.* an exclamation of surprise, awe, etc.
▸ **'cooing** *adj, n* ▸ **'cooingly** *adv*

Cooch Behar *or* **Kuch Bihar** ★ (ku:tʃ bɪ'hɑ:) *n* **1** a former state of NE India: part of West Bengal since 1950. **2** a city in India, in NE West Bengal: capital of the former state of Cooch Behar. Pop.: 62 500 (latest est.).

cooee *or* **cooey** ('ku:i:) *interj* **1** a call used to attract attention, esp. a long loud high-pitched call on two notes. ◆ *vb* **cooees, cooeeing, cooeed** *or* **cooeys, cooeying, cooeyed. 2** (*intr*) to utter this call. ◆ *n* **3** *Austral. & NZ inf.* calling distance (esp. in **within (a) cooee (of)**). ORIG C19: from Abor.

cook (kuk) *vb* **1** to prepare (food) by the action of heat, or (of food) to become ready for eating through such a process. Related adj: **culinary. 2** to subject or be subjected to intense heat: *the town cooked in the sun.* **3** (*tr*) *Sl.* to alter or falsify (figures, accounts, etc.): *to cook the books.* **4** (*tr*) *Sl.* to spoil (something). **5** (*intr*) *Sl.* to happen (esp. in **what's cooking?**). ◆ *n* **6** a person who prepares food for eating. ◆ See also **cook up.** ORIG OE *cōc* (n), from L *coquus* a cook, from *coquere* to cook
▸ **'cookable** *adj*

Cook[1] ★ (kuk) *n* **Mount. 1** Official name: **Aorangi-Mount Cook.** a mountain in New Zealand, in the South Island, in the Southern Alps: the highest peak in New Zealand. Height: 3764 m (12 349 ft). **2** a mountain in SE Alaska, in the St Elias Mountains. Height: 4194 m (13 760 ft).

Cook[2] ★ (kuk) *n* **1** Captain **James.** 1728–79, British navigator and explorer: claimed the E coast of Australia for Britain, circumnavigated New Zealand, and discovered several Pacific and Atlantic islands (1768–79). **2** Sir **Joseph.** 1860–1947, Australian statesman, born in England: prime minister (1913–14). **3 Peter (Edward).** 1937–95, British actor and writer, noted esp. for his partnership (1960–73) with Dudley Moore. **4 Robin,** full name *Robert Finlayson Cook.* born 1946, British Labour politician; foreign secretary from 1997. **5 Thomas.** 1808–92, British travel agent; innovator of conducted excursions and founder of Thomas Cook and Son.

cook-chill *n* a method of food preparation used by caterers, in which cooked dishes are chilled rapidly and reheated as required.

cooker ('kukə) *n* **1** an apparatus heated by gas, electricity, oil, or solid fuel, for cooking food. **2** *Brit.* another name for **cooking apple.**

cookery ('kukərɪ) *n* **1** the art, study, or practice of cooking. **2** *US.* a place for cooking.

cookery book *or* **cookbook** ('kukˌbuk) *n* a book containing recipes.

cook-general *n, pl* **cooks-general.** *Brit.* (formerly, esp. in the 1920s and 30s) a domestic servant who did cooking and housework.

cookie *or* **cooky** ('kukɪ) *n, pl* **cookies. 1** the US and Canad. word for **biscuit. 2** *Inf.* a person: *smart cookie.* **3** *Computing.* A small file placed on a user's computer by a website, containing information about the user's preferences for future use in visits to the site. **4 that's the way the cookie crumbles.** *Inf.* matters are inevitably so. ORIG C18: from Du. *koekje*, dim. of *koek* cake

cooking apple *n* any large sour apple used in cooking.

Cook Islands ★ *pl n* a group of islands in the SW Pacific, an overseas territory of New Zealand: consists of the **Lower Cooks** and the **Northern Cooks.** Capital: Avarua, on Rarotonga. Pop.: 18 500 (1994). Area: 234 sq. km (90 sq. miles).

cook shop *n* **1** *Brit.* a shop that sells cookery equipment. **2** *US.* a restaurant.

Cookson ★ ('kuksᵊn) *n* Dame **Catherine.** 1906–98, British novelist, known for her popular novels.

Cook's tour (kuks) *n Inf.* a rapid but extensive tour or survey of anything. ORIG C19: after Thomas COOK

Cookstown ★ ('kukstaun) *n* a district of central Northern Ireland, bordering the E shore of Lough Neagh: agriculture. Administrative centre: Cookstown. Pop.: 31 082 (1991). Area: 623 sq. km (240 sq. miles).

Cook Strait ★ *n* the strait between North and South Islands, New Zealand. Width: 26 km (16 miles).

cook up *vb* (*tr, adv*) **1** *Inf.* to concoct or invent (a story, alibi, etc.). **2** to prepare (a meal), esp. quickly. **3** *Sl.* to prepare (a drug) for use by heating, as by melting heroin.

cool (ku:l) *adj* **1** moderately cold: *a cool day.* **2** comfortably free of heat: *a cool room.* **3** calm: *a cool head.* **4** lacking in enthusiasm, cordiality, etc.: *a cool welcome.* **5** calmly impudent. **6** *Inf.* (of sums of money, etc.) without exaggeration; actual: *a cool ten thousand.* **7** (of a colour) having violet, blue, or green predominating; cold. **8** (of jazz) economical and rhythmically relaxed. **9** *Inf.* sophisticated or elegant; unruffled. **10** *Inf., chiefly US & Canad.* marvellous. ◆ *n* **11** coolness: *the cool of the evening.* **12** *Sl.* calmness; composure (esp. in **keep** *or* **lose one's cool**). **13** *Sl.* unruffled elegance or sophistication. ◆ *vb* **14** (usually foll. by *down* or *off*) to make or become cooler. **15** (usually foll. by *down* or *off*) to lessen the intensity of (anger or excitement) or (of anger or excitement) to become less intense; calm down. **16 cool it.** (*usually imperative*) *Sl.* to calm down. ORIG OE *cōl*
▸ **'coolly** *adv* ▸ **'coolness** *n*

coolant ('kuːlənt) *n* **1** a fluid used to cool a system or to transfer heat from one part of it to another. **2** a liquid used to lubricate and cool the workpiece and cutting tool during machining.

cool bag *or* **box** *n* an insulated container for keeping food cool.

cool-down *n* another name for **warm-down.**

cool drink *n S. African.* a soft drink.

cooler ('kuːlə) *n* **1** a container, vessel, or apparatus for cooling, such as a heat exchanger. **2** a slang word for **prison. 3** a drink consisting of wine, fruit juice, and carbonated water.

coolibah *or* **coolabah** ('kuːləˌbɑː) *n* an Australian eucalyptus that grows along rivers and has smooth bark and long narrow leaves. ORIG from Abor.

Coolidge ★ ('kuːlɪdʒ) *n* **(John) Calvin.** 1872–1933, 30th president of the US (1923–29).

coolie *or* **cooly** ('kuːlɪ) *n, pl* **coolies.** an unskilled Oriental labourer. ORIG C17: from Hindi *kulī*

cooling-off period *n* **1** a period during which the contending sides to a dispute reconsider their options before taking further action. **2** *Brit.* a period, often 14 days, that begins when a sale contract or life-assurance policy is received by a member of the public, during which the contract or policy can be cancelled without loss.

cooling tower *n* a tall, hollow structure, designed to permit free passage of air, inside which hot water trickles down, becoming cool as it does so: the water is normally reused as part of an industrial process.

Coomaraswamy ★ (kuːˌmɑːrə'swɑːmɪ) *n* **Ananda (Kentish).** 1877–1947, Ceylonese art historian and interpreter of Indian culture to the West.

coomb, combe, coombe, *or* **comb** (kuːm) *n* **1** *Chiefly southern English.* a short valley or deep hollow. **2** *Chiefly northern English.* another name for a **cirque.** ORIG OE *cumb*

coon (kuːn) *n* **1** *Inf.* short for **raccoon. 2** *Offens. sl.* a Black or a native Australian. **3** *S. African offens.* a person of mixed race.

coonskin ('kuːnˌskɪn) *n* **1** the pelt of a raccoon. **2** a raccoon cap with the tail hanging at the back. **3** *US.* an overcoat made of raccoon.

coop[1] (kuːp) *n* **1** a cage or small enclosure for poultry or small animals. **2** a small narrow place of confinement, esp. a prison cell. **3** a wicker basket for catching fish. ◆ *vb* **4** (*tr;* often foll. by *up* or *in*) to confine in a restricted area. ORIG C15: prob. from MLow G *kūpe* basket

coop[2] *or* **co-op** ('kəʊˌɒp) *n* a cooperative society or a shop run by a cooperative society.

cooper ('kuːpə) *n* **1** a person skilled in making and repairing barrels, casks, etc. ◆ *vb* **2** (*tr*) to make or mend (barrels, casks, etc.). ORIG C13: from MDu. *cūper* or MLow G *kūper;* see COOP[1]

Cooper ★ ('kuːpə) *n* **1 Anthony Ashley.** See (Earl of) **Shaftesbury. 2 Gary,** real name *Frank James Cooper.* 1901–61, US film actor; his films include *Sergeant York* (1941) and *High Noon* (1952). **3** Sir **Henry.** born 1934, British boxer; European heavyweight champion (1964; 1968–71). **4 James Fenimore.** 1789–1851, US novelist, noted for *The Last of the Mohicans* (1826). **5 Leon Neil.** born 1930, US physicist, noted for his work on superconductivity. He shared the Nobel prize for physics 1972. **6 Samuel.** 1609–72, English miniaturist.

cooperage ('kuːpərɪdʒ) *n* **1** Also called: **coopery.** the craft, place of work, or products of a cooper. **2** the labour fee charged by a cooper.

cooperate *or* **co-operate** (kəʊ'ɒpəˌreɪt) *vb* **cooperates, cooperating, cooperated** *or* **co-operates, co-operating, co-operated.** (*intr*) **1** to work or act together. **2** to be of assistance or be willing to assist. **3** *Econ.* to engage in economic cooperation. ORIG C17: from LL *cooperārī* to combine, from L *operārī* to work
▸ **co'operˌator** *or* **co-'operˌator** *n*

cooperation *or* **co-operation** (kəʊˌɒpə'reɪʃən) *n* **1** joint operation or action. **2** assistance or willingness to assist. **3** *Econ.* the combination of consumers, workers, etc., in activities usually embracing production, distribution, or trade.
▸ **coˌoper'ationist** *or* **co-ˌoper'ationist** *n*

cooperative *or* **co-operative** (kəʊ'ɒpərətɪv, -'ɒprə-) *adj* **1** willing to cooperate; helpful. **2** acting in conjunction with others; cooperating. **3a** (of an enterprise, farm, etc.) owned collectively and managed for joint economic benefit. **3b** (of an economy) based on collective ownership and cooperative use of the means of production and distribution. ◆ *n* **4** a cooperative organization, such as a farm.

cooperative society *n* a commercial enterprise owned and managed by and for the benefit of customers or workers.

Cooper Creek ★ *n* an intermittent river in E central Australia, in the Channel Country: rises in central Queensland and flows generally southwest, reaching Lake Eyre only during wet-year floods; scene of the death of the explorers Burke and Wills in 1861; the surrounding basin provides cattle pastures after the floods subside. Total length: 1420 km (880 miles). Former name: **Cooper's Creek.**

coopt *or* **co-opt** (kəʊ'ɒpt) *vb* (*tr*) to add (someone) to a committee, board, etc., by the agreement of the existing members. ORIG C17: from L *cooptāre,* from *optāre* to choose
▸ **co'option, co-'option** *or* **ˌcoop'tation, ˌco-op'tation** *n*

coordinate *or* **co-ordinate** *vb* (kəʊ'ɔːdɪˌneɪt), **coordinates, coordinating, coordinated** *or* **co-ordinates, co-ordinating, co-ordinated. 1** (*tr*) to integrate (diverse elements) in a harmonious operation. **2** to place (things) in the same class, or (of things) to be placed in the same class, etc. **3** (*intr*) to work together harmoniously. **4** (*intr*) to take or be in the form of a harmonious order. ◆ *n* (kəʊ'ɔːdɪnɪt). **5** *Maths.* any of a set of numbers that defines the location of a point with reference to a system of axes. **6** a person or thing equal in rank, type, etc. ◆ *adj* (kəʊ'ɔːdɪnɪt). **7** of or involving coordination. **8** of the same rank, type, etc. **9** of or involving the use of coordinates: *coordinate geometry.* **10** *Chem.* denoting a type of covalent bond in which both the shared electrons are provided by one of the atoms.
▸ **co'ordinative** *or* **co-'ordinative** *adj* ▸ **co'ordiˌnator** *or* **co-'ordiˌnator** *n*

coordinate clause *n* one of two or more clauses in a sentence having the same status and introduced by coordinating conjunctions.

coordinates (kəʊ'ɔːdɪnɪts) *pl n* clothes of matching or harmonious colours and design, suitable for wearing together.

coordinating conjunction *n* a conjunction that introduces coordinate clauses, such as *and, but,* and *or.*

coordination *or* **co-ordination** (kəʊˌɔːdɪ'neɪʃən) *n* balanced and effective interaction of movement, actions, etc. ORIG C17: from LL *coordinātiō,* from L *ordinātiō* an arranging

coot (kuːt) *n* **1** an aquatic bird of Europe and Asia, having dark plumage, and a white bill with a frontal shield: family Rallidae (rails, etc.). **2** a foolish person, esp. an old man. ORIG C14: prob. from Low G

cootie ('kuːtɪ) *n US & NZ.* a slang name for the body louse. ORIG C20: from Maori & ? (for US) Malay *kutu* louse

cop[1] (kɒp) *Sl.* ◆ *n* **1** another name for **policeman. 2** *Brit.* an arrest (esp. in **a fair cop**). ◆ *vb* **cops, copping, copped.** (*tr*) **3** to catch. **4** to steal. **5** to suffer (a punishment): *you'll cop a clout if you do that!* **6 cop it sweet.** *Austral. sl.* **6a** to accept a punishment without complaint. **6b** to have good fortune. **7 cop this!** just look at this! ◆ See also **cop out.** ORIG C18: (vb) ?from obs. *cap* to arrest, from OF *caper* to seize

cop[2] (kɒp) *n* **1** a conical roll of thread wound on a spindle. **2** *Now chiefly dialect.* the top or crest, as of a hill. ORIG OE *cop, copp* top, summit

cop[3] (kɒp) *n Brit. sl.* (*usually used with a negative*) value: *not much cop.* ORIG C19: n use of COP[1]

copal ('kəʊpᵊl, -pæl) *n* a hard aromatic resin obtained from various tropical trees and used in making varnishes and lacquers. ORIG C16: from Sp., from Nahuatl *copalli*

copartner (kəʊ'pɑːtnə) *n* a partner or associate, esp. an equal partner in business.
▸ **co'partnership** *n*

★ people and places

cope[1] (kəʊp) *vb* **copes, coping, coped.** (*intr*) **1** (foll. by *with*) to contend (against). **2** to deal successfully (with); manage: *she coped well with the problem.* ORIG C14: from OF *coper* to strike, cut, from *coup* blow

cope[2] (kəʊp) *n* **1** a large ceremonial cloak worn at liturgical functions by priests of certain Christian sects. **2** any covering shaped like a cope. ◆ *vb* **copes, coping, coped. 3** (*tr*) to dress (someone) in a cope. ORIG OE *cāp,* from Med. L *cāpa,* from LL *cappa* hooded cloak

cope[3] (kəʊp) *vb* **copes, coping, coped.** (*tr*) **1** to provide (a wall, etc.) with a coping. ◆ *n* **2** another name for **coping.** ORIG C17: prob. from F *couper* to cut

copeck ('kəʊpɛk) *n* a variant spelling of **kopeck.**

Copenhagen ★ (ˌkəʊpən'heɪgən, -'hɑː-; 'kəʊpənˌheɪ-, -ˌhɑː-) *n* the capital of Denmark, a port on Zealand and Amager Islands on a site inhabited for some 6000 years: exports chiefly agricultural products; iron and steel works; university (1479). Pop. (urban area): 1 362 264 (1996 est.). Danish name: **København.**

Copenhagen interpretation *n* an interpretation of quantum mechanics developed by Niels Bohr (1885–1962) and his colleagues at the University of Copenhagen, based on the concept of wave–particle duality and the idea that the observation influences the result of an experiment.

copepod ('kəʊpɪˌpɒd) *n* a minute marine or freshwater crustacean, an important constituent of plankton. ORIG C19: from NL *copepoda,* from Gk *kōpē* oar + *pous* foot

coper ('kəʊpə) *n* a horse dealer. ORIG C17 (a dealer): from dialect *cope* to buy, barter, from Low G

Copernican system *n* the theory published in 1543 by Copernicus which stated that the earth and the planets rotated round the sun.

Copernicus ★ (kə'pɜːnɪkəs) *n* **Nicolaus** (ˌnɪkə'leɪəs). Polish name *Mikolaj Kopernik.* 1473–1543, Polish astronomer, whose theory of the solar system (the **Copernican system**) was published in 1543.
► **Co'pernican** *adj*

copestone ('kəʊpˌstəʊn) *n* **1** Also called: **coping stone.** a stone used to form a coping. **2** the stone at the top of a building, wall, etc.

copier ('kɒpɪə) *n* a person or device that copies.

copilot ('kəʊˌpaɪlət) *n* a second or relief pilot of an aircraft.

coping ('kəʊpɪŋ) *n* the sloping top course of a wall, usually made of masonry or brick.

coping saw *n* a handsaw with a U-shaped frame used for cutting curves in a material too thick for a fret saw.

copious ('kəʊpɪəs) *adj* **1** abundant; extensive. **2** having an abundant supply. **3** full of words, ideas, etc.; profuse. ORIG C14: from L *cōpiōsus,* from *cōpia* abundance
► **'copiously** *adv* ► **'copiousness** *n*

coplanar (kəʊ'pleɪnə) *adj* lying in the same plane: *coplanar lines.*
► **ˌcopla'narity** *n*

Copland ★ ('kəʊplənd) *n* **Aaron.** 1900–90, US composer of orchestral and chamber music, ballets, and film music.

cop off *vb* (*intr, adv*) **cop off with.** *Brit. inf.* to establish an amorous or sexual relationship with.

copolymer (kəʊ'pɒlɪmə) *n* a chemical compound of high molecular weight formed by uniting the molecules of two or more different compounds (monomers).

cop out *Sl.* ◆ *vb* **1** (*intr, adv*) to fail to assume responsibility or fail to perform. ◆ *n* **cop-out. 2** a way or an instance of avoiding responsibility or commitment. ORIG C20: prob. from COP[1]

copper[1] ('kɒpə) *n* **1** a malleable reddish metallic element occurring as the free metal, copper glance, and copper pyrites: used in such alloys as brass and bronze. Symbol: Cu; atomic no.: 29; atomic wt.: 63.54. Related adjs.: **cupric, cuprous. 2a** the reddish-brown colour of copper. **2b** (*as adj*): *copper hair.* **3** *Inf.* any copper or bronze coin. **4** *Chiefly Brit.* a large vessel, formerly of copper, used for boiling or washing. **5** any of various small widely distributed butterflies having reddish-brown wings. ◆ *vb* **6** (*tr*) to coat or cover with copper. ORIG OE *coper,* from L *Cyprium aes* Cyprian metal, from Gk *Kupris* Cyprus

copper[2] ('kɒpə) *n* a slang word for **policeman.** Often shortened to **cop.** ORIG C19: from COP[1] (vb)

copperas ('kɒpərəs) *n* a less common name for **ferrous sulphate.** ORIG C14 *coperose,* via OF from Med. L *cuperosa,* ? orig. in *aqua cuprosa* copper water

copper beech *n* a cultivated variety of European beech that has reddish leaves.

Copper Belt ★ *n* a region of Central Africa, along the border between Zambia and the Democratic Republic of Congo: rich in deposits of copper.

copper-bottomed *adj* reliable, esp. financially reliable. ORIG from the practice of coating bottom of ships with copper to prevent the timbers rotting

copper-fasten *vb* (*tr*) *Irish.* to make (a bargain or agreement) binding.

copperhead ('kɒpəˌhɛd) *n* **1** a venomous pit viper of the US, with a reddish-brown head. **2** a venomous marsh snake of Australia, with a reddish band behind the head.

copperplate ('kɒpəˌpleɪt) *n* **1** a polished copper plate on which a design has been etched or engraved. **2** a print taken from such a plate. **3** a fine handwriting based upon that used on copperplate engravings.

copper pyrites ('paɪraɪts) *n* (*functioning as sing*) another name for **chalcopyrite.**

coppersmith ('kɒpəˌsmɪθ) *n* a person who works in copper.

copper sulphate *n* a copper salt found naturally and made by the action of sulphuric acid on copper oxide: used as a mordant, in electroplating, and in plant sprays. Formula: $CuSO_4$.

coppice ('kɒpɪs) *n* **1** a dense growth of small trees or bushes, esp. one regularly trimmed back so that a continual supply of small poles and firewood is obtained. ◆ *vb* **coppices, coppicing, coppiced. 2** (*tr*) to trim back (trees or bushes) to form a coppice. ORIG C14: from OF *copeiz*
► **'coppiced** *adj*

Coppola ★ ('kɒpələ) *n* **Francis Ford.** born 1939, US film director. His films include *The Godfather* (1972) and *Tucker* (1988).

copra ('kɒprə) *n* the dried, oil-yielding kernel of the coconut. ORIG C16: from Port., from Malayalam *koppara* coconut

copro- *or before a vowel* **copr-** *combining form.* indicating dung or obscenity, as in **cop'rology** *n* preoccupation with excrement, **cop'rophagous** *adj* feeding on dung. ORIG from Gk *kopros* dung

copse (kɒps) *n* another word for **coppice** (sense 1). ORIG C16: from COPPICE

Copt (kɒpt) *n* **1** a member of the Coptic Church. **2** an Egyptian descended from the ancient Egyptians. ORIG C17: from Ar., from Coptic *kyptios* Egyptian, from Gk *Aiguptios,* from *Aiguptos* Egypt

Coptic ('kɒptɪk) *n* **1** an Afro-Asiatic language, written in the Greek alphabet but descended from ancient Egyptian. Extinct as a spoken language, it survives in the Coptic Church. ◆ *adj* **2** of this language. **3** of the Copts.

Coptic Church *n* the ancient Christian Church of Egypt.

copula ('kɒpjʊlə) *n, pl* **copulas** *or* **copulae** (-ˌliː). **1** a verb, such as *be, seem,* or *taste,* that is used to identify or link the subject with the complement of a sentence, as in *he became king, sugar tastes sweet.* **2** anything that serves as a link. ORIG C17: from L: bond, from *co-* together + *apere* to fasten
► **'copular** *adj*

copulate ('kɒpjʊˌleɪt) *vb* **copulates, copulating, copulated.** (*intr*) to perform sexual intercourse. ORIG C17: from L *copulāre* to join together; see COPULA
► **ˌcopu'lation** *n* ► **'copulatory** *adj*

copulative ('kɒpjʊlətɪv) *adj* **1** serving to join or unite. **2** of copulation. **3** *Grammar.* (of a verb) having the nature of a copula.

copy ('kɒpɪ) *n, pl* **copies. 1** an imitation or reproduction of an original. **2** a single specimen of something that occurs in a multiple edition, such as a book. **3a** matter to be reproduced in print. **3b** written matter or text as distinct from graphic material in books, etc. **4** the words used to present a promotional message in an advertisement. **5** *Journalism, inf.* suitable material for an article: *disasters are always good copy.* **6** *Arch.* a model to be copied, esp. an example of penmanship. ◆ *vb* **copies, copying, copied. 7** (when *tr,* often foll. by *out*) to make a copy (of). **8** (*tr*) to imitate as a model. **9** to imitate unfairly. ORIG C14: from Med. L *cōpia* an imitation, from L: abundance

copybook ('kɒpɪ,bʊk) *n* **1** a book of specimens, esp. of penmanship, for imitation. **2** *Chiefly US.* a book for or containing documents. **3 blot one's copybook.** *Inf.* to spoil one's reputation by a mistake or indiscretion. **4** (*modifier*) trite or unoriginal.

copycat ('kɒpɪ,kæt) *n Inf.* **a** a person, esp. a child, who imitates or copies another. **b** (*as modifier*): *copycat murders.*

copyhold ('kɒpɪ,həʊld) *n Law.* (formerly) a tenure less than freehold of land in England evidenced by a copy of the Court roll.

copyist ('kɒpɪɪst) *n* **1** a person who makes written copies. **2** a person who imitates.

copyreader ('kɒpɪ,riːdə) *n US.* a person who edits and prepares newspaper copy for publication; subeditor.

copyright ('kɒpɪ,raɪt) *n* **1** the exclusive right to produce copies and to control an original literary, musical, or artistic work, granted by law for a specified number of years. ◆ *adj* **2** (of a work, etc.) subject to copyright. ◆ *vb* **3** (*tr*) to take out a copyright on.

copy typist *n* a typist whose job is to type from written or typed drafts rather than dictation.

copywriter ('kɒpɪ,raɪtə) *n* a person employed to write advertising copy.
▸ **'copy,writing** *n*

coquet (kəʊ'kɛt, kɒ-) *vb* **coquets, coquetting, coquetted.** (*intr*) **1** to behave flirtatiously. **2** to dally or trifle. ORIG C17: from F: a gallant, lit.: a little cock, from *coq* cock
▸ **'coquetry** *n*

coquette (kəʊ'kɛt, kɒ-) *n* **1** a woman who flirts. **2** any hummingbird of the genus *Lophornis.* ORIG C17: from F, fem of COQUET
▸ **co'quettish** *adj* ▸ **co'quettishness** *n*

Cor. *Bible. abbrev. for* Corinthians.

coracle ('kɒrək³l) *n* a small roundish boat made of waterproofed hides stretched over a wicker frame. ORIG C16: from Welsh *corwgl*

coracoid ('kɒrə,kɔɪd) *n* a paired ventral bone of the pectoral girdle in vertebrates. In mammals it is reduced to a peg (the **coracoid process**) on the scapula. ORIG C18: from NL *coracoīdēs,* from Gk *korakoeidēs* like a raven, from *korax* raven

coral ('kɒrəl) *n* **1** any of a class of marine colonial coelenterates having a calcareous, horny, or soft skeleton. **2a** the calcareous or horny material forming the skeleton of certain of these animals. **2b** (*as modifier*): *a coral reef.* **3** a rocklike aggregation of certain of these animals or their skeletons, forming an island or reef. **4a** something made of coral. **4b** (*as modifier*): *a coral necklace.* **5a** a yellowish-pink colour. **5b** (*as adj*): *coral lipstick.* **6** the roe of a lobster or crab, which becomes pink when cooked. ORIG C14: from OF, from L *corāllium,* from Gk *korallion,* prob. of Semitic origin

coral reef *n* a marine reef consisting of coral consolidated into limestone.

coralroot ('kɒrəl,ruːt) *n* a N temperate leafless orchid with branched roots resembling coral.

Coral Sea ★ *n* the SW arm of the Pacific, between Australia, New Guinea, and Vanuatu.

coral snake *n* **1** a venomous snake of tropical and subtropical America, marked with red, black, yellow, and white transverse bands. **2** any of various other brightly coloured snakes of Africa and SE Asia.

cor anglais ('kɔːr 'ɑːŋgleɪ) *n, pl* **cors anglais** ('kɔːz 'ɑːŋgleɪ). *Music.* a woodwind instrument, the alto of the oboe family. Also called: **English horn.** ORIG C19: from F: English horn

corbel ('kɔːb³l) *Archit.* ◆ *n* **1** a bracket, usually of stone or brick. ◆ *vb* **corbels, corbelling, corbelled** *or US* **corbels, corbeling, corbeled. 2** (*tr*) to lay (a stone) so that it forms a corbel. ORIG C15: from OF, lit.: a little raven, from Med. L *corvellus,* from L *corvus* raven

corbie ('kɔːbɪ) *n* a Scot. name for **raven**[1] (sense 1) or **crow**[1] (sense 1). ORIG C15: from OF *corbin,* from L *corvīnus* CORVINE

corbie-step *or* **corbel step** *n Archit.* any of a set of steps on the top of a gable. Also called: **crow step.**

Corbusier ★ (*French* kɔrbyzje) *n* **Le.** See **Le Corbusier.**

Corcovado ★ *n* **1** (*Spanish* korko'βaðo). a volcano in S Chile, in the Andes. Height: 2300 m (7546 ft). **2** (*Portuguese* korku'vaːdu). a mountain in SE Brazil, in SW Rio de Janeiro city. Height: 704 m (2310 ft).

Corcyra ★ (kɔː'saɪərə) *n* the ancient name for **Corfu.**

cord (kɔːd) *n* **1** string or thin rope made of twisted strands. **2** a length of woven or twisted strands of silk, etc., used as a belt, etc. **3** a ribbed fabric, esp. corduroy. **4** the US and Canad. name for **flex** (sense 1). **5** *Anat.* any part resembling a rope: *the spinal cord.* **6** a unit for measuring cut wood, equal to 128 cubic feet. ◆ *vb* (*tr*) **7** to bind or furnish with a cord or cords. ◆ See also **cords.** ORIG C13: from OF *corde,* from L *chorda,* from Gk *khordē*
▸ **'cord,like** *adj*

cordage ('kɔːdɪdʒ) *n* **1** *Naut.* the lines and rigging of a vessel. **2** an amount of wood measured in cords.

cordate ('kɔːdeɪt) *adj* heart-shaped.

Corday ★ (*French* kɔrdɛ) *n* **Charlotte** (ʃarlɔt), full name *Marie Anne Charlotte Corday d'Armont.* 1768–93, French Girondist revolutionary, who assassinated Marat.

corded ('kɔːdɪd) *adj* **1** bound or fastened with cord. **2** (of a fabric) ribbed. **3** (of muscles) standing out like cords.

cordial ('kɔːdɪəl) *adj* **1** warm and friendly: *a cordial greeting.* **2** stimulating. ◆ *n* **3** a drink with a fruit base: *lime cordial.* **4** another word for **liqueur.** ORIG C14: from Med. L *cordiālis,* from L *cor* heart
▸ **'cordially** *adv*

cordiality (,kɔːdɪ'ælɪtɪ) *n, pl* **cordialities.** warmth of feeling.

cordillera (,kɔːdɪl'jɛərə) *n* a series of parallel ranges of mountains, esp. in the northwestern US. ORIG C18: from Sp., from *cordilla,* lit.: a little cord

Cordilleras ★ (,kɔːdɪl'jɛərəz; *Spanish* korði'ʎeras) *pl n* **the.** the complex of mountain ranges on the W side of the Americas, extending from Alaska to Cape Horn and including the Andes and the Rocky Mountains.

cordite ('kɔːdaɪt) *n* any of various explosive materials containing cellulose nitrate, sometimes mixed with nitroglycerine. ORIG C19: from CORD + -ITE[1], from its stringy appearance

cordless ('kɔːdlɪs) *adj* (of an electrical device) operated by an internal battery so that no connection to mains supply is needed.

cordless telephone *n* a portable battery-powered telephone with a short-range radio link to a fixed base unit.

Córdoba[1] ★ (*Spanish* 'kɔrðoβa) *n* **1** a city in central Argentina: university (1613). Pop.: 1 208 713 (1991). **2** a city in S Spain, on the Guadalquivir River: centre of Moorish Spain (711–1236). Pop.: 315 948 (1994 est.). English name: **Cordova.**

Córdoba[2] *or* **Córdova** ★ (*Spanish* 'kɔrðoβa) *n* **Francisco Fernández de** (fran'θisko fɛr'nandɛθ de). died 1518, Spanish soldier and explorer, who discovered Yucatán.

cordon ('kɔːd³n) *n* **1** a chain of police, soldiers, ships, etc., stationed around an area. **2** a ribbon worn as insignia of honour. **3** a cord or ribbon worn as an ornament. **4** *Archit.* another name for **string course. 5** *Horticulture.* a fruit tree consisting of a single stem bearing fruiting spurs, produced by cutting back all lateral branches. ◆ *vb* **6** (*tr;* often foll. by *off*) to put or form a cordon (around); close (off). ORIG C16: from OF, lit.: a little cord, from *corde* CORD

★ people and places

cordon bleu (*French* kɔrdɔ̃ blø) *n* **1** *French history.* the sky-blue ribbon worn by members of the highest order of knighthood under the Bourbon monarchy. **2** any very high distinction. ◆ *adj* **3** of or denoting food prepared to a very high standard. ORIG F, lit.: blue ribbon

cordon sanitaire *French.* (kɔrdɔ̃ sanitɛr) *n* **1** a guarded line isolating an infected area. **2** a line of buffer states shielding a country. ORIG C19: lit.: sanitary line

Cordova ★ ('kɔːdəvə) *n* the English name for **Córdoba**[1] (sense 2).

cordovan ('kɔːdəvᵊn) *n* a fine leather now made mainly from horsehide. ORIG C16: from Sp. *cordobán* of CÓRDOBA[1]

cords (kɔːdz) *pl n* trousers made of corduroy.

corduroy ('kɔːdəˌrɔɪ, ˌkɔːdə'rɔɪ) *n* a heavy cotton pile fabric with lengthways ribs. ORIG C18: ?from the proper name *Corderoy*

corduroys (ˌkɔːdə'rɔɪz, 'kɔːdəˌrɔɪz) *pl n* trousers or breeches of corduroy.

cordwainer ('kɔːdˌweɪnə) *n Arch.* a shoemaker or worker in leather. ORIG C12: *cordwaner,* from OF, from OSp. *cordován* CORDOVAN

cordwood ('kɔːdˌwʊd) *n* wood that has been cut into lengths of four feet so that it can be stacked in cords.

core (kɔː) *n* **1** the central part of certain fleshy fruits, such as the apple, consisting of the seeds. **2** the central or essential part of something: *the core of the argument.* **3** a piece of magnetic material, such as soft iron, inside an electromagnet or transformer. **4** *Geol.* the central part of the earth. **5** a cylindrical sample of rock, soil, etc., obtained by the use of a hollow drill. **6** *Physics.* the region of a nuclear reactor in which the reaction takes place. **7** *Computing.* **7a** a ferrite ring formerly used in a computer memory to store one bit of information. **7b** (*as modifier*): *core memory.* **8** *Archaeol.* a stone or flint from which flakes have been removed. **9** *Physics.* the nucleus together with all complete electron shells of an atom. ◆ *vb* **cores, coring, cored. 10** (*tr*) to remove the core from (fruit). ORIG C14: from ?

coreligionist (ˌkəʊrɪ'lɪdʒənɪst) *n* an adherent of the same religion as another.

Corelli ★ *n* **1** (*Italian* ko'rɛlli). **Arcangelo** (ar'kandʒelo). 1653–1713, Italian violinist and composer of sonatas and concerti grossi. **2** (kɒ'rɛlɪ). **Marie,** real name *Mary Mackay.* 1854–1924, British novelist. Her works include *The Murder of Delicia* (1896).

coreopsis (ˌkɒrɪ'ɒpsɪs) *n* a plant of America and Africa, with yellow, brown, or yellow-and-red daisy-like flowers. ORIG C18: from NL, from Gk *koris* bedbug + -OPSIS; so called from the appearance of the seed

co-respondent (ˌkəʊrɪ'spɒndənt) *n Law.* a person cited in divorce proceedings, alleged to have committed adultery with the respondent.

core subjects *pl n Brit. education.* three foundation subjects (English, mathematics, and science) that are compulsory throughout each key stage in the National Curriculum.

core time *n* See **flexitime.**

corf (kɔːf) *n, pl* **corves.** *Brit.* a wagon or basket used formerly in mines. ORIG C14: from MDu. *corf* or MLow G *korf,* prob. from L *corbis* basket

Corfu ★ (kɔː'fuː) *n* **1** an island in the Ionian Sea, in the Ionian Islands: forms, with neighbouring islands, a department of Greece. Pop.: 107 592 (1991). Area: 641 sq. km (247 sq. miles). **2** a port on E Corfu island. Pop.: 105 000 (1995 est.). Modern Greek name: **Kérkyra.** ◆ Ancient name: **Corcyra.**

corgi ('kɔːgɪ) *n* either of two short-legged sturdy breeds of dog, the Cardigan and the Pembroke. ORIG C20: from Welsh, from *cor* dwarf + *ci* dog

coriander (ˌkɒrɪ'ændə) *n* a European umbelliferous plant, cultivated for its aromatic seeds and leaves, used in flavouring foods. US and Canad. name: **cilantro.** ORIG C14: from OF *coriandre,* from L *coriandrum,* from Gk *koriannon,* from ?

Corinth ★ ('kɒrɪnθ) *n* **1** a port in S Greece, in the NE Peloponnese: the modern town is near the site of the ancient city, the largest and richest of the city-states after Athens. Pop.: 29 600 (1995 est.). Modern Greek name: **Kórinthos. 2** a region of ancient Greece, occupying most of the Isthmus of Corinth and part of the NE Peloponnese. **3 Gulf of.** Also called: Gulf of **Lepanto.** an inlet of the Ionian Sea between the Peloponnese and central Greece. **4 Isthmus of.** a narrow strip of land between the Gulf of Corinth and the Saronic Gulf: crossed by the **Corinth Canal,** making navigation possible between the gulfs.

Corinthian (kə'rɪnθɪən) *adj* **1** of Corinth. **2** denoting one of the five classical orders of architecture: characterized by a bell-shaped capital having carved ornaments based on acanthus leaves. **3** *Obs.* given to luxury; dissolute. ◆ *n* **4** a native or inhabitant of Corinth.

Coriolanus ★ (ˌkɒrɪə'leɪnəs) *n* **Gaius Marcius** ('gaɪəs 'mɑːsɪəs). 5th century B.C., a legendary Roman general, who allegedly led an army against Rome but was dissuaded from conquering it by his mother and wife.

Coriolis force (ˌkɒrɪ'əʊlɪs) *n* a hypothetical force postulated to explain a deflection in the path of a body moving relative to the earth: it is due to the earth's rotation and is to the left in the S hemisphere and to the right in the N hemisphere. ORIG C19: after Gaspard G. *Coriolis* (1792–1843), F civil engineer

corium ('kɔːrɪəm) *n, pl* **coria** (-rɪə). the deep inner layer of the skin, beneath the epidermis, containing connective tissue, blood vessels, and fat. Also called: **derma, dermis.** ORIG C19: from L: rind, skin

cork (kɔːk) *n* **1** the thick light porous outer bark of the cork oak. **2** a piece of cork used as a stopper. **3** an angling float. **4** Also called: **phellem.** *Bot.* a protective layer of dead impermeable cells on the outside of the stems and roots of woody plants. ◆ *adj* **5** made of cork. Related adj: **suberose.** ◆ *vb* (*tr*) **6** to stop up (a bottle, etc.) with or as with a cork. **7** (often foll. by *up*) to restrain. **8** to black (the face, hands, etc.) with burnt cork. ORIG C14: prob. from Ar. *qurq,* from L *cortex* bark
▸ **'corkˌlike** *adj*

Cork ★ (kɔːk) *n* **1** a county of SW Republic of Ireland, in Munster province: crossed by ridges of low mountains; scenic coastline. County town: Cork. Pop.: 420 000 (1996). Area: 7459 sq. km (2880 sq. miles). **2** a port in S Republic of Ireland, county town of Co. Cork, at the mouth of the River Lee: seat of the University College of Cork (1849). Pop.: 127 092 (1996). Gaelic name: **Corcaigh.**

corkage ('kɔːkɪdʒ) *n* a charge made at a restaurant for serving wine, etc., bought off the premises.

corked (kɔːkt) *adj* tainted through having a cork containing excess tannin.

corker ('kɔːkə) *n Old-fashioned sl.* **1** something or somebody striking or outstanding. **2** an irrefutable remark that puts an end to discussion.

cork oak *n* an evergreen Mediterranean oak whose porous bark yields cork.

corkscrew ('kɔːkˌskruː) *n* **1** a device for drawing corks from bottles, typically consisting of a pointed metal spiral attached to a handle or screw mechanism. **2** (*modifier*) resembling a corkscrew in shape. ◆ *vb* **3** to move or cause to move in a spiral or zigzag course.

corm (kɔːm) *n* an organ of vegetative reproduction in plants such as the crocus, consisting of a globular stem base swollen with food and surrounded by papery scale leaves. ORIG C19: from NL *cormus,* from Gk *kormos* tree trunk from which the branches have been lopped

cormorant ('kɔːmərənt) *n* an aquatic bird having a dark plumage, a long neck and body, and a slender hooked beak. ORIG C13: from OF *cormareng,* from *corp* raven + *-mareng* of the sea

corn[1] (kɔːn) *n* **1** *Brit.* **1a** any of various cereal plants, esp. the predominant crop of a region, such as wheat in England and oats in Scotland. **1b** the seeds of such plants, esp. after harvesting. **1c** a single seed of such plants; a grain. **2** the usual US, Canad., Austral., and NZ name for **maize. 3** *Sl.* an idea, song, etc., regarded as banal or sentimental. ◆ *vb* (*tr*) **4a** to preserve in brine. **4b** to salt. ORIG OE *corn*

corn[2] (kɔːn) *n* **1** a hardening of the skin, esp. of the toes, caused by pressure. **2 tread on (someone's) corns.** *Brit. inf.* to offend or hurt (someone) by touching on a sensitive subject. ORIG C15: from OF *corne* horn, from L *cornū*

corn borer *n* the larva of a moth native to Europe: in E North America a serious pest of maize.

corn bread *n Chiefly US.* bread made from maize meal. Also called: **Indian bread.**

corn bunting *n* a heavily built European songbird with a streaked brown plumage.

corncob ('kɔːnˌkɒb) *n* the core of an ear of maize, to which kernels are attached.

corncob pipe *n* a pipe with a bowl made from a dried corncob.

corncockle ('kɔːnˌkɒkᵊl) *n* a European plant that has reddish-purple flowers and grows in cornfields and by roadsides.

corncrake ('kɔːnˌkreɪk) *n* a common Eurasian rail with a buff speckled plumage and reddish wings.

corn dolly *n* a decorative figure made by plaiting straw.

cornea ('kɔːnɪə) *n, pl* **corneas** *or* **corneae** (-nɪˌiː). the convex transparent membrane that forms the anterior covering of the eyeball. ORIG C14: from Med. L *cornea tēla* horny web, from L *cornū* HORN
▸ **'corneal** *adj*

corned (kɔːnd) *adj* (esp. of beef) cooked and then preserved or pickled in salt or brine.

Corneille ★ (*French* kɔrnɛj) *n* **Pierre** (pjɛr). 1606–84, French dramatist, whose plays include *Médée* (1635), *Le Cid* (1636), and *Polyeucte* (1642).

cornel ('kɔːnᵊl) *n* any shrub of the genus *Cornus,* such as the dogwood. ORIG C16: prob. from MLow G *kornelle,* ult. from L *cornus*

cornelian (kɔː'niːlɪən) *n* a variant spelling of **carnelian.**

corner ('kɔːnə) *n* **1** the place or angle formed by the meeting of two converging lines or surfaces. **2** a projecting angle of a solid object. **3** the place where two streets meet. **4** any small, secluded, or private place. **5** a dangerous position from which escape is difficult: *a tight corner.* **6** any region, esp. a remote place. **7** something used to protect or mark a corner, as of the hard cover of a book. **8** *Commerce.* a monopoly over the supply of a commodity so that its market price can be controlled. **9** *Soccer, hockey, etc.* a free kick or shot from the corner of the field, taken against a defending team when the ball goes out of play over their goal line after last touching one of their players. **10** either of two opposite angles of a boxing ring in which the opponents take their rests. **11 cut corners.** to take the shortest or easiest way, esp. at the expense of high standards. **12 turn the corner.** to pass the critical point (in an illness, etc.). **13** (*modifier*) on a corner: *a corner shop.* ◆ *vb* **14** (*tr*) to manoeuvre (a person or animal) into a position from which escape is difficult or impossible. **15** (*tr*) **15a** to acquire enough of (a commodity) to attain control of the market. **15b** Also: **engross.** to attain control of (a market) in such a manner. **16** (*intr*) (of vehicles, etc.) to turn a corner. **17** (*intr*) (in soccer, etc.) to take a corner. ORIG C13: from OF *corniere,* from L *cornū* point, HORN

Corner ★ *n* **the.** *Inf.* an area in central Australia, at the junction of the borders of Queensland and South Australia.

cornerback ('kɔːnəˌbæk) *n American football.* a defensive back.

cornerstone ('kɔːnəˌstəʊn) *n* **1** a stone at the corner of a wall, uniting two intersecting walls. **2** a stone placed at the corner of a building during a ceremony to mark the start of construction. **3** a person or thing of prime importance: *the cornerstone of the whole argument.*

cornerwise ('kɔːnəˌwaɪz) *or* **cornerways** ('kɔːnəˌweɪz) *adv, adj* with a corner in front; diagonally.

cornet ('kɔːnɪt) *n* **1** a three-valved brass instrument of the trumpet family. **2** a person who plays the cornet. **3** a cone-shaped paper container for sweets, etc. **4** *Brit.* a cone-shaped wafer container for ice cream. **5** (formerly) the lowest rank of commissioned cavalry officer in the British Army. **6** the large white headdress of some nuns. ORIG C14: from OF, from L *cornū* HORN
▸ **cor'netist** *or* **cor'nettist** *n*

corn exchange *n* a building where corn is bought and sold.

cornfield ('kɔːnˌfiːld) *n* a field planted with cereal crops.

cornflakes ('kɔːnˌfleɪks) *pl n* a breakfast cereal made from toasted maize.

cornflour ('kɔːnˌflaʊə) *n* a fine maize flour, used for thickening sauces. US and Canad. name: **cornstarch.**

cornflower ('kɔːnˌflaʊə) *n* a herbaceous plant, with blue, purple, pink, or white flowers, formerly a common weed in cornfields.

Cornforth ★ ('kɔːnˌfɔːθ) *n* Sir **John Warcup.** born 1917, Australian chemist, who shared the 1975 Nobel prize for chemistry for his work on stereochemistry.

cornice ('kɔːnɪs) *n* **1** *Archit.* **1a** the top projecting mouldings of an entablature. **1b** a continuous horizontal projecting course or moulding at the top of a wall, building, etc. **2** an overhanging ledge of snow. ORIG C16: from OF, from It., ?from L *cornix* crow, but infl. also by L *corōnis* decorative flourish

corniche ('kɔːnɪʃ) *n* a coastal road, esp. one built into the face of a cliff. ORIG C19: from *corniche road;* see CORNICE

Cornish ('kɔːnɪʃ) *adj* **1** of Cornwall or its inhabitants. ◆ *n* **2** a former language of Cornwall: extinct by 1800. **3 the.** (*functioning as pl*) the natives or inhabitants of Cornwall.
▸ **'Cornishman** *n*

Cornish pasty ('pæstɪ) *n Cookery.* a pastry case with a filling of meat and vegetables.

corn meal *n* meal made from maize. Also called: **Indian meal.**

Corno ★ (*Italian* 'kɔrno) *n* **Monte** ('monte). a mountain in central Italy: the highest peak in the Apennines. Height: 2912 m (9554 ft).

corn salad *n* a plant which often grows in cornfields and whose leaves are sometimes used in salads. Also called: **lamb's lettuce.**

cornstarch ('kɔːnˌstɑːtʃ) *n* the US and Canad. name for **cornflour.**

cornucopia (ˌkɔːnjʊ'kəʊpɪə) *n* **1** a representation of a horn in painting, sculpture, etc., overflowing with fruit, vegetables, etc.; horn of plenty. **2** a great abundance. **3** a horn-shaped container. ORIG C16: from LL, from L *cornū cōpiae* horn of plenty
▸ **ˌcornu'copian** *adj*

Cornwall ★ ('kɔːnˌwɔːl, -wəl) *n* a county of SW England: hilly, with a deeply indented coastline. Administrative centre: Truro. Pop.: 483 300 (1996 est.). Area: 3564 sq. km (1376 sq. miles).

Cornwallis ★ (kɔːn'wɒlɪs) *n* **Charles,** 1st Marquis Cornwallis. 1738–1805, British general in the War of American Independence: governor general of Bengal (1786–93, 1805).

corn whisky *n* whisky made from maize.

corny ('kɔːnɪ) *adj* **cornier, corniest.** *Sl.* **1** trite or banal. **2** sentimental or mawkish. **3** abounding in corn. ORIG C16 (C20 in the sense banal): from CORN[1] + -Y[1]

corolla (kə'rɒlə) *n* the petals of a flower collectively, forming an inner floral envelope. ORIG C17: dim. of L *corōna* crown

corollary (kə'rɒlərɪ) *n, pl* **corollaries. 1** a proposition that follows directly from the proof of another proposition. **2** an obvious deduction. **3** a natural consequence. ORIG C14: from L *corollārium* money paid for a garland, from L *corolla* garland

Coromandel Coast ★ (ˌkɒrə'mændᵊl) *n* the SE coast of India, along the Bay of Bengal, extending from Point Calimere to the mouth of the Krishna River.

corona (kə'rəʊnə) *n, pl* **coronas** *or* **coronae** (-niː). **1** a circle of light around a luminous body, usually the moon. **2** Also called: **aureole.** the outermost region of the sun's atmosphere, visible as a faint halo during a solar eclipse. **3** *Archit.* the flat vertical face of a cornice. **4** a circular chandelier. **5** *Bot.* **5a** the trumpet-shaped part of the corolla of

★ people and places

daffodils and similar plants. **5b** a crown of leafy outgrowths from inside the petals of some flowers. **6** *Anat.* a crownlike structure. **7** a long cigar with blunt ends. **8** *Physics.* an electrical discharge appearing around the surface of a charged conductor. ORIG C16: from L: crown

coronach ('kɒrənəx) *n Scot. & Irish.* a dirge or lamentation for the dead. ORIG C16: from Scot. Gaelic *corranach*

coronary ('kɒrənərɪ) *adj* **1** *Anat.* designating blood vessels, nerves, ligaments, etc., that encircle a part or structure. ◆ *n, pl* **coronaries. 2** short for **coronary thrombosis.** ORIG C17: from L *corōnārius* belonging to a wreath or crown

coronary artery *n* either of the two arteries branching from the aorta and supplying blood to the heart.

coronary bypass *n* the surgical bypass of a narrowed or blocked coronary artery by grafting a section of a healthy blood vessel taken from another part of the patient's body.

coronary heart disease *n* any heart disorder caused by disease of the coronary arteries.

coronary thrombosis *n* a condition of interrupted blood flow to the heart due to a blood clot in a coronary artery.

coronation (ˌkɒrə'neɪʃən) *n* the act or ceremony of crowning a monarch. ORIG C14: from OF, from *coroner* to crown, from L *corōnāre*

coroner ('kɒrənə) *n* a public official responsible for the investigation of violent, sudden, or suspicious deaths. ORIG C14: from Anglo-F *corouner,* from OF *corone* CROWN
▸ **'coronerˌship** *n*

coronet ('kɒrənɪt) *n* **1** any small crown, esp. one worn by princes or peers. **2** a woman's jewelled circlet for the head. **3** the margin between the skin of a horse's pastern and the horn of the hoof. **4** the knob at the base of a deer's antler. ORIG C15: from OF *coronete*

Corot ★ (*French* kɔro) *n* **Jean Baptiste Camille** (ʒɑ̃ batist kamij). 1796–1875, French landscape and portrait painter.

coroutine ('kəuruːˌtiːn) *n Computing.* a section of a computer program similar to but differing from a subroutine in that it can be left and re-entered at any point.

corp. *abbrev. for:* **1** corporation. **2** corporal.

corporal[1] ('kɔːpərəl, 'kɔːprəl) *adj* of or relating to the body. ORIG C14: from L *corporālis,* from *corpus* body
▸ **ˌcorpo'rality** *n* ▸ **'corporally** *adv*

corporal[2] ('kɔːpərəl) *n* **1** a noncommissioned officer junior to a sergeant in the army, air force, or marines. **2** (in the Royal Navy) a petty officer who assists the master-at-arms. ORIG C16: from OF, via It., from L *caput* head; ? also infl. in OF by *corps* body (of men)

corporal[3] ('kɔːpərəl) *or* **corporale** (ˌkɔːpə'reɪlɪ) *n* a white linen cloth on which the bread and wine are placed during the Eucharist. ORIG C14: from Med. L *corporāle pallium* eucharistic altar cloth, from L *corporālis,* from *corpus* body (of Christ)

Corporal of Horse *n* a noncommissioned rank in the British Army, above that of sergeant and below that of staff sergeant.

corporal punishment *n* punishment of a physical nature, such as caning.

corporate ('kɔːpərɪt) *adj* **1** forming a corporation; incorporated. **2** of a corporation or corporations: *corporate finance.* **3** of or belonging to a united group; joint. ORIG C15: from L *corporātus,* from *corpus* body
▸ **'corporatism** *n*

corporate advertising *n* advertising designed to publicize or create a favourable image of a company rather than a particular product.

corporate anorexia *n* a malaise of a business organization resulting from making too many creative people redundant in a cost-cutting exercise.

corporate culture *n* the distinctive ethos of an organization that influences the level of formality, loyalty, and general behaviour of its employees.

corporate identity *or* **image** *n* the way an organization is presented to or perceived by its members and the public.

corporate raider *n Finance.* a person or organization that acquires a substantial holding of the shares of a company in order to take it over or to force its management to act in a desired way.

corporate venturing *n Finance.* the provision of venture capital by one company for another in order to obtain information about the company requiring capital or as a step towards acquiring it.

corporation (ˌkɔːpə'reɪʃən) *n* **1** a group of people authorized by law to act as an individual and having its own powers, duties, and liabilities. **2** Also called: **municipal corporation.** the municipal authorities of a city or town. **3** a group of people acting as one body. **4** See **public corporation. 5** *Inf.* a large paunch.
▸ **'corporative** *adj*

corporation tax *n* a British tax on the profits of a company or other incorporated body.

corporeal (kɔː'pɔːrɪəl) *adj* **1** of the nature of the physical body; not spiritual. **2** of a material nature; physical. ORIG C17: from L *corporeus,* from *corpus* body
▸ **corˌpore'ality** *or* **corporeity** (ˌkɒːpə'riːɪtɪ) *n* ▸ **cor'poreally** *adv*

corps (kɔː) *n, pl* **corps** (kɔːz). **1** a military formation that comprises two or more divisions. **2** a military body with a specific function: *medical corps.* **3** a body of people associated together: *the diplomatic corps.* ORIG C18: from F, from L *corpus* body

corps de ballet ('kɔː də 'bæleɪ) *n* the members of a ballet company who dance together in a group.

corps diplomatique (ˌdɪpləumæ'tiːk) *n* another name for **diplomatic corps.**

corpse (kɔːps) *n* a dead body, esp. of a human being. ORIG C14: from OF *corps,* from L *corpus*

corpulent ('kɔːpjulənt) *adj* physically bulky; fat. ORIG C14: from L *corpulentus*
▸ **'corpulence** *n*

cor pulmonale (ˌkɔː ˌpʌlmə'nɑːlɪ) *n* pulmonary heart disease: a serious heart condition in which there is enlargement and failure of the right ventricle resulting from lung disease. ORIG NL

corpus ('kɔːpəs) *n, pl* **corpora** (-pərə). **1** a body of writings, esp. by a single author or on a specific topic: *the corpus of Dickens' works.* **2** the main body or substance of something. **3** *Anat.* **3a** any distinct mass or body. **3b** the main part of an organ or structure. **4** *Obs.* a corpse. ORIG C14: from L: body

Corpus Christi[1] ('krɪstɪ) *n Chiefly RC Church.* a festival in honour of the Eucharist, observed on the Thursday after Trinity Sunday. ORIG C14: from L: body of Christ

Corpus Christi[2] ★ ('krɪstɪ) *n* a port in S Texas, on **Corpus Christi Bay,** an inlet of the Gulf of Mexico. Pop.: 275 419 (1994 est.).

corpuscle ('kɔːpʌsᵊl) *n* **1** any cell or similar minute body that is suspended in a fluid, esp. any of the **red blood corpuscles** (see **erythrocyte**) or **white blood corpuscles** (see **leucocyte**). **2** Also: **corpuscule** (kɔː'pʌskjuːl). any minute particle. ORIG C17: from L *corpusculum* a little body, from *corpus* body
▸ **corpuscular** (kɔː'pʌskjulə) *adj*

corpuscular theory *n* the theory, originally proposed by Newton, that light consists of a stream of particles. Cf. **wave theory.**

corpus delicti (dɪ'lɪktaɪ) *n Law.* the body of facts that constitute an offence. ORIG NL, lit.: the body of the crime

corpus juris ('dʒuərɪs) *n* a body of law, esp. of a nation or state. ORIG from LL, lit.: a body of law

corpus luteum ('luːtɪəm) *n, pl* **corpora lutea** ('luːtɪə). a mass of tissue that forms in a Graafian follicle following release of an ovum. ORIG NL, lit.: yellow body

corral (kɒ'rɑːl) *n* **1** *Chiefly US & Canad.* an enclosure for cattle or horses. **2** *Chiefly US.* (formerly) a defensive enclosure formed by a ring of covered wagons. ◆ *vb* **corrals, corralling, corralled.** (*tr*) *US & Canad.* **3** to drive into a corral. **4** *Inf.* to capture. ORIG C16: from Sp., ult. from L *currere* to run

corrasion (kəˈreɪʒən) *n* erosion of a rock surface by rock fragments transported over it by water, wind, or ice. ORIG C17: from L *corrādere* to scrape together

correa (ˈkɒrɪə, kəˈriːə) *n* an Australian evergreen shrub with large showy tubular flowers. ORIG C19: after Jose Francesco *Correa* da Serra (1750-1823), Portuguese botanist

correct (kəˈrɛkt) *vb (tr)* **1** to make free from errors. **2** to indicate the errors in. **3** to rebuke or punish in order to improve: *to stand corrected.* **4** to rectify (a malfunction, ailment, etc.). **5** to adjust or make conform, esp. to a standard. ◆ *adj* **6** true; accurate: *the correct version.* **7** in conformity with accepted standards: *correct behaviour.* ORIG C14: from L *corrigere* to make straight, from *com-* (intensive) + *regere* to rule
▸ **corˈrectly** *adv* ▸ **corˈrectness** *n*

correction (kəˈrɛkʃən) *n* **1** the act of correcting. **2** something substituted for an error; an improvement. **3** a reproof. **4** a quantity added to or subtracted from a scientific calculation or observation to increase its accuracy.
▸ **corˈrectional** *adj*

corrective (kəˈrɛktɪv) *adj* **1** tending or intended to correct. ◆ *n* **2** something that tends or is intended to correct.

Correggio ★ (*Italian* korˈreddʒo) *n* **Antonio Allegri da** (anˈtɔːnjo alˈleːgri da). 1494–1534, Italian painter.

Corregidor ★ (kəˈrɛgɪˌdɔː) *n* an island at the entrance to Manila Bay, in the Philippines: site of the defeat of American forces by the Japanese (1942) in World War II.

correlate (ˈkɒrɪˌleɪt) *vb* **correlates, correlating, correlated. 1** to place or be placed in a complementary or reciprocal relationship. **2** *(tr)* to establish or show a correlation between. ◆ *n* **3** either of two things mutually related.

correlation (ˌkɒrɪˈleɪʃən) *n* **1** a mutual relationship between two or more things. **2** the act of correlating or the state of being correlated. **3** *Statistics.* the extent of correspondence between the ordering of two variables. ORIG C16: from Med. L *correlātiō,* from *com-* together + *relātiō* RELATION
▸ **ˌcorreˈlational** *adj*

correlation coefficient *n Statistics.* a statistic measuring the degree of correlation between two variables.

correlative (kɒˈrɛlətɪv) *adj* **1** in complementary or reciprocal relationship; corresponding. **2** denoting words, usually conjunctions, occurring together though not adjacently in certain grammatical constructions, as *neither* and *nor.* ◆ *n* **3** either of two things that are correlative. **4** a correlative word.
▸ **corˈrelatively** *adv* ▸ **corˌrelaˈtivity** *n*

correspond (ˌkɒrɪˈspɒnd) *vb (intr)* **1** (usually foll. by *with* or *to*) to be consistent or compatible (with); tally (with). **2** (usually foll. by *to*) to be similar in character or function. **3** (usually foll. by *with*) to communicate by letter. ORIG C16: from Med. L *correspondēre,* from L *rēspondēre* to RESPOND
▸ **ˌcorreˈsponding** *adj* ▸ **ˌcorreˈspondingly** *adv*

correspondence (ˌkɒrɪˈspɒndəns) *n* **1** the condition of agreeing or corresponding. **2** similarity. **3** agreement or conformity. **4a** communication by letters. **4b** the letters so exchanged.

correspondence school *n* an educational institution that offers tuition (**correspondence courses**) by post.

correspondent (ˌkɒrɪˈspɒndənt) *n* **1** a person who communicates by letter. **2** a person employed by a newspaper, etc., to report on a special subject or from a foreign country. **3** a person or firm that has regular business relations with another, esp. one abroad. ◆ *adj* **4** similar or analogous.

corrida (koˈrriða) *n* the Spanish word for **bullfight.** ORIG Sp., from *corrida de toros,* lit.: a running of bulls

corridor (ˈkɒrɪˌdɔː) *n* **1** a passage connecting parts of a building. **2** a strip of land or airspace that affords access, either from a landlocked country to the sea or from a state to an exclave. **3** a passageway connecting the compartments of a railway coach. **4** a flight path that affords safe access for intruding aircraft. **5** the path that a spacecraft must follow when re-entering the atmosphere, above which lift is insufficient and below which heating effects are excessive. **6 corridors of power.** the higher echelons of government, the Civil Service, etc., considered as the location of power and influence. ORIG C16: from OF, from OIt. *corridore,* lit.: place for running

corrie (ˈkɒrɪ) *n* **1** (in Scotland) a circular hollow on a hillside. **2** *Geol.* another name for **cirque.** ORIG C18: from Gaelic *coire* cauldron

corrigendum (ˌkɒrɪˈdʒɛndəm) *n, pl* **corrigenda** (-də). **1** an error to be corrected. **2** *(sometimes pl)* Also called: **erratum.** a slip of paper inserted into a book after printing, listing corrections. ORIG C19: from L: that which is to be corrected

corrigible (ˈkɒrɪdʒɪbᵊl) *adj* **1** capable of being corrected. **2** submissive. ORIG C15: from OF, from Med. L *corrigibilis,* from L *corrigere* to CORRECT

corroborate (kəˈrɒbəˌreɪt) *vb* **corroborates, corroborating, corroborated.** *(tr)* to confirm or support (facts, opinions, etc.), esp. by providing fresh evidence. ORIG C16: from L *corrōborāre,* from *rōborāre* to make strong, from *rōbur* strength
▸ **corˌroboˈration** *n* ▸ **corroborative** (kəˈrɒbərətɪv) *or* **corˈroboratory** *adj* ▸ **corˈroboˌrator** *n*

corroboree (kəˈrɒbərɪ) *n Austral.* **1** a native assembly of sacred, festive, or warlike character. **2** *Inf.* any noisy gathering. ORIG C19: from Abor.

corrode (kəˈrəud) *vb* **corrodes, corroding, corroded. 1** to eat away or be eaten away, esp. as in the oxidation or rusting of a metal. **2** *(tr)* to destroy gradually: *his jealousy corroded his happiness.* ORIG C14: from L *corrōdere* to gnaw to pieces, from *rōdere* to gnaw
▸ **corˈrodible** *adj*

corrosion (kəˈrəuʒən) *n* **1** a process in which a solid, esp. a metal, is eaten away and changed by a chemical action, as in the oxidation of iron. **2** slow deterioration by being eaten or worn away. **3** the product of corrosion.

corrosive (kəˈrəusɪv) *adj* **1** tending to eat away or consume. ◆ *n* **2** a corrosive substance, such as a strong acid.
▸ **corˈrosively** *adv* ▸ **corˈrosiveness** *n*

corrosive sublimate *n* another name for **mercuric chloride.**

corrugate (ˈkɒruˌgeɪt) *vb* **corrugates, corrugating, corrugated.** *(usually tr)* to fold or be folded into alternate furrows and ridges. ORIG C18: from L *corrūgāre,* from *rūga* a wrinkle
▸ **ˈcorruˌgated** *adj* ▸ **ˌcorruˈgation** *n*

corrugated iron *n* a thin sheet of iron or steel, formed with alternating ridges and troughs.

corrupt (kəˈrʌpt) *adj* **1** open to or involving bribery or other dishonest practices: *a corrupt official; corrupt practices.* **2** morally depraved. **3** putrid or rotten. **4** (of a text or manuscript) made meaningless or different in meaning by scribal errors or alterations. **5** (of computer programs or data) containing errors. ◆ *vb* **6** to become or cause to become dishonest or disloyal. **7** *(tr)* to deprave. **8** *(tr)* to infect or contaminate. **9** *(tr)* to cause to become rotten. **10** *(tr)* to alter (a text, etc.) from the original. **11** *(tr) Computing.* to introduce errors into (data or a program). ORIG C14: from L *corruptus* spoiled, from *corrumpere* to ruin, from *rumpere* to break
▸ **corˈrupter** *or* **corˈruptor** *n* ▸ **corˈruptly** *adv* ▸ **corˈruptness** *n*

corruptible (kəˈrʌptɪbᵊl) *adj* capable of being corrupted.
▸ **corˈruptibly** *adv*

corruption (kəˈrʌpʃən) *n* **1** the act of corrupting or state of being corrupt. **2** depravity. **3** dishonesty, esp. bribery. **4** decay. **5** alteration, as of a manuscript. **6** an altered form of a word.

corsage (kɔːˈsɑːʒ) *n* **1** a small bunch of flowers worn pinned to the lapel, bosom, etc. **2** the bodice of a dress. ORIG C15: from OF, from *cors* body, from L *corpus*

corsair (ˈkɔːsɛə) *n* **1** a pirate. **2** a privateer, esp. of the Barbary Coast. ORIG C15: from OF *corsaire,* from Med. L *cursārius,* from L *cursus* a running

corse (kɔːs) *n* an archaic word for **corpse**.

corselet (ˈkɔːslɪt) *n* **1** Also spelt: **corslet**. a piece of armour for the top part of the body. **2** a one-piece foundation garment. ORIG C15: from OF, from *cors* bodice, from L *corpus* body

corset (ˈkɔːsɪt) *n* **1a** a stiffened, elasticated, or laced foundation garment, worn esp. by women. **1b** a similar garment worn because of injury, weakness, etc., by either sex. **2** *Inf.* a restriction or limitation, esp. government control of bank lending. ◆ *vb* **3** (*tr*) to dress or enclose in, or as in, a corset. ORIG C14: from OF, lit.: a little bodice
▸ **corsetière** (ˌkɔːsɛtɪˈɛə) *n* ▸ **ˈcorsetry** *n*

Corsica ★ (ˈkɔːsɪkə) *n* an island in the Mediterranean, west of N Italy: forms, with 43 islets, a region of France; mountainous; settled by Greeks in about 560 B.C.; sold by Genoa to France in 1768. Capital: Ajaccio. Pop.: 258 879 (1994 est.). Area: 8682 sq. km (3367 sq. miles). French name: **Corse**.
▸ **ˈCorsican** *adj, n*

cortege *or* **cortège** (kɔːˈteɪʒ) *n* **1** a formal procession, esp. a funeral procession. **2** a train of attendants; retinue. ORIG C17: from F, from It. *corteggio,* from *corteggiare* to attend

Cortés (ˈkɔːtɛz; *Spanish* korˈtes) *or* **Cortez** ★ (kɔːˈtɛz) *n* **Hernando** (ɛrˈnando) *or* **Hernán** (ɛrˈnan). 1485–1547, Spanish conquistador: defeated the Aztecs and conquered Mexico (1523).

cortex (ˈkɔːtɛks) *n, pl* **cortices** (-tɪˌsiːz). **1** *Anat.* the outer layer of any organ or part, such as the grey matter in the brain that covers the cerebrum (**cerebral cortex**). **2** *Bot.* **2a** the tissue in plant stems and roots between the vascular bundles and the epidermis. **2b** the outer layer of a part such as the bark of a stem. ORIG C17: from L: bark, outer layer
▸ **cortical** (ˈkɔːtɪkᵊl) *adj*

corticate (ˈkɔːtɪkɪt, -ˌkeɪt) *or* **corticated** *adj* (of plants, seeds, etc.) having a bark, husk, or rind. ORIG C19: from L *corticātus*

cortisone (ˈkɔːtɪˌzəʊn) *n* a steroid hormone, the synthetic form of which has been used in treating rheumatoid arthritis, allergic and skin diseases, leukaemia, etc. ORIG C20: from *corticosterone,* a hormone

Cortona ★ (kɔːˈtəʊnə; *Italian* korˈtoːna) *n* a town in Italy, in Tuscany: Roman and Etruscan remains, 15th-century cathedral. Pop.: 22 700 (1987 est.).

Cortot ★ (*French* kɔrto) *n* **Alfred** (alfrɛd). 1877–1962, French pianist, born in Switzerland.

corundum (kəˈrʌndəm) *n* a hard mineral consisting of aluminium oxide: used as an abrasive. Precious varieties include ruby and white sapphire. Formula: Al_2O_3. ORIG C18: from Tamil *kuruntam;* rel. to Sansk. *kuruvinda* ruby

Corunna ★ (kəˈrʌnə) *n* the English name for **La Coruña**.

coruscate (ˈkɒrəˌskeɪt) *vb* **coruscates, coruscating, coruscated.** (*intr*) to emit flashes of light; sparkle. ORIG C18: from L *coruscāre* to flash
▸ **ˌcorusˈcation** *n*

corvée (ˈkɔːveɪ) *n* **1** *European history.* a day's unpaid labour owed by a feudal vassal to his lord. **2** the practice or an instance of forced labour. ORIG C14: from OF, from LL *corrogāta* contribution, from L *corrogāre* to collect, from *rogāre* to ask

corvette (kɔːˈvɛt) *n* a lightly armed escort warship. ORIG C17: from OF, ?from MDu. *corf*

corvine (ˈkɔːvaɪn) *adj* **1** of or resembling a crow. **2** of the passerine bird family Corvidae, which includes the crows, ravens, rooks, jackdaws, magpies, and jays. ORIG C17: from L *corvīnus,* from *corvus* a raven

Corvo ★ (ˈkɔːvəʊ) *n* **Baron.** See (Frederick William) **Rolfe**.

Corybant (ˈkɒrɪˌbænt) *n, pl* **Corybants** *or* **Corybantes** (ˌkɒrɪˈbæntiːz). *Classical myth.* a wild attendant of the goddess Cybele. ORIG C14: from L *Corybās,* from Gk *Korubas*
▸ **ˌCoryˈbantic** *adj*

corymb (ˈkɒrɪmb, -rɪm) *n* an inflorescence in the form of a flat-topped flower cluster with the oldest flowers at the periphery. ORIG C18: from L *corymbus,* from Gk *korumbos* cluster

coryza (kəˈraɪzə) *n* acute inflammation of the mucous membrane of the nose, with discharge of mucus; a head cold. ORIG C17: from LL: catarrh, from Gk *koruza*

cos[1] *or* **cos lettuce** (kɒs) *n* a variety of lettuce with a long slender head and crisp leaves. Usual US and Canad. name: **romaine**. ORIG C17: after *Kos,* the Aegean island of its origin

cos[2] (kɒz) *abbrev. for* cosine.

Cos ★ (kɒs) *n* a variant spelling of **Kos**.

Cosa Nostra (ˈkəʊzə ˈnɒstrə) *n* the branch of the Mafia that operates in the US. ORIG It.: our thing

cosec (ˈkəʊsɛk) *abbrev. for* cosecant.

cosecant (kəʊˈsiːkənt) *n* (of an angle) a trigonometric function that in a right-angled triangle is the ratio of the length of the hypotenuse to that of the opposite side.

coset (ˈkəʊˌsɛt) *n Maths.* a set that produces a specified larger set when added to another set.

Cosgrave ★ (ˈkɒzˌgreɪv) *n* **1 Liam** (ˈliːəm). born 1920, Irish politician; prime minister of the Republic of Ireland (1973–77). **2** his father, **W**(**illiam**) **T**(**homas**). 1880–1965, Irish statesman; first president of the Irish Free State (1922–32).

cosh[1] (kɒʃ) *Brit.* ◆ *n* **1** a blunt weapon, often made of hard rubber; bludgeon. **2** an attack with such a weapon. ◆ *vb* **3** to hit with such a weapon, esp. on the head. ORIG C19: from Romany *kosh*

cosh[2] (kɒʃ, kɒsˈeɪtʃ) *n* hyperbolic cosine. ORIG C19: from COS(INE) + H(YPERBOLIC)

cosignatory (kəʊˈsɪgnətərɪ, -trɪ) *n, pl* **cosignatories**. **1** a person, country, etc., that signs a document jointly with others. ◆ *adj* **2** signing jointly.

Cosimo I ★ (*Italian* ˈkɔːzimo) *n* See (Cosimo I) **Medici**.

cosine (ˈkəʊˌsaɪn) *n* (of an angle) a trigonometric function that in a right-angled triangle is the ratio of the length of the adjacent side to that of the hypotenuse. ORIG C17: from NL *cosinus;* see CO-, SINE[1]

cosmetic (kɒzˈmɛtɪk) *n* **1** any preparation applied to the body, esp. the face, with the intention of beautifying it. ◆ *adj* **2** serving or designed to beautify the body, esp. the face. **3** having no other function than to beautify: *cosmetic illustrations in a book.* ORIG C17: from Gk *kosmētikos,* from *kosmein* to arrange, from *kosmos* order
▸ **cosˈmetically** *adv*

cosmic (ˈkɒzmɪk) *adj* **1** of or relating to the whole universe: *cosmic laws.* **2** occurring or originating in outer space, esp. as opposed to the vicinity of the earth: *cosmic rays.* **3** immeasurably extended; vast.
▸ **ˈcosmically** *adv*

cosmic dust *n* fine particles of solid matter occurring throughout interstellar space and often collecting into clouds of extremely low density.

cosmic rays *pl n* radiation consisting of atomic nuclei, esp. protons, of very high energy, that reach the earth from outer space. Also called: **cosmic radiation**.

cosmic string *n* any of a number of linear defects in space-time postulated in certain theories of cosmology to exist in the universe as a consequence of the big bang.

cosmo- *or before a vowel* **cosm-** *combining form.* indicating the world or universe: *cosmology; cosmonaut.* ORIG from Gk: COSMOS

cosmogony (kɒzˈmɒgənɪ) *n, pl* **cosmogonies**. the study of the origin and development of the universe or of a particular system in the universe, such as the solar system. ORIG C17: from Gk *kosmogonia,* from COSMO- + *gonos* creation
▸ **cosmogonic** (ˌkɒzməˈgɒnɪk) *or* **ˌcosmoˈgonical** *adj*
▸ **cosˈmogonist** *n*

cosmography (kɒzˈmɒgrəfɪ) *n* **1** a representation of the world or the universe. **2** the science dealing with the whole order of nature.
▸ **cosˈmographer** *n* ▸ **cosmographic** (ˌkɒzməˈgræfɪk) *or* **ˌcosmoˈgraphical** *adj*

cosmological principle *n Astron.* the theory that the

universe is uniform, homogenous, and isotropic, and therefore appears the same from any position.

cosmology (kɒz'mɒlədʒɪ) *n* **1** the study of the origin and nature of the universe. **2** a particular account of the origin or structure of the universe.
▸ **cosmological** (ˌkɒzmə'lɒdʒɪkᵊl) *or* **ˌcosmo'logic** *adj*
▸ **cos'mologist** *n*

cosmonaut ('kɒzməˌnɔːt) *n* an astronaut, esp. in the former Soviet Union. ORIG C20: from Russian *kosmonavt*, from COSMO- + Gk *nautēs* sailor

cosmopolitan (ˌkɒzmə'pɒlɪtᵊn) *n* **1** a person who has lived and travelled in many countries, esp. one who is free of national prejudices. ◆ *adj* **2** familiar with many parts of the world. **3** sophisticated or urbane. **4** composed of people or elements from all parts of the world or from many different spheres. ORIG C17: from F, ult. from Gk *kosmopolitēs*, from *kosmo-* COSMO- + *politēs* citizen
▸ **ˌcosmo'politanism** *n*

cosmopolite (kɒz'mɒpəˌlaɪt) *n* **1** a less common word for **cosmopolitan** (sense 1). **2** an animal or plant that occurs in most parts of the world.
▸ **cos'mopolitˌism** *n*

cosmos ('kɒzmɒs) *n* **1** the universe considered as an ordered system. **2** any ordered system. **3** (*pl* **cosmos** *or* **cosmoses**) any tropical American plant of the genus *Cosmos* cultivated as garden plants for their brightly coloured flowers. ORIG C17: from Gk *kosmos* order

Cosmos ('kɒzmɒs) *n Astronautics*. any of various types of Soviet satellite, including Cosmos 1 (launched 1962) and nearly 2000 subsequent satellites.

Cossack ('kɒsæk) *n* **1** (formerly) any of the free warrior-peasants of chiefly East Slavonic descent who served as cavalry under the tsars. ◆ *adj* **2** of, relating to, or characteristic of the Cossacks: *a Cossack dance*. ORIG C16: from Russian *kazak* vagabond, of Turkic origin

cosset ('kɒsɪt) *vb* **cossets, cosseting, cosseted. 1** (*tr*) to pamper; pet. ◆ *n* **2** any pet animal, esp. a lamb. ORIG C16: from ?

cost (kɒst) *n* **1** the price paid or required for acquiring, producing, or maintaining something, measured in money, time, or energy; outlay. **2** suffering or sacrifice: *I know to my cost*. **3a** the amount paid for a commodity by its seller: *to sell at cost*. **3b** (*as modifier*): *the cost price*. **4** (*pl*) *Law*. the expenses of judicial proceedings. **5 at all costs.** regardless of sacrifice involved. **6 at the cost of.** at the expense of losing. ◆ *vb* **costs, costing, cost. 7** (*tr*) to be obtained or obtainable in exchange for: *the ride cost one pound*. **8** to cause or require the loss or sacrifice (of): *the accident cost him dearly*. **9** (*p.t. & p.p.* **costed**) to estimate the cost of (a product, process, etc.) for the purposes of pricing, budgeting, control, etc. ORIG C13: from OF (n), from *coster* to cost, from L *constāre* to stand at, cost, from *stāre* to stand

costa ('kɒstə) *n, pl* **costae** (-tiː). **1** the technical name for rib[1] (sense 1). **2** a riblike part. ORIG C19: from L: rib, side
▸ **'costal** *adj*

Costa Brava ★ ('kɒstə 'brɑːvə) *n* a coastal region of NE Spain along the Mediterranean, extending from Barcelona to the French border: many resorts.

cost accounting *n* the recording and controlling of all the expenditures of an enterprise in order to facilitate control of separate activities. Also called: **management accounting.**
▸ **cost accountant** *n*

Costa Rica ★ ('kɒstə 'riːkə) *n* a republic in Central America: gained independence from Spain in 1821; mostly mountainous and volcanic, with extensive forests. Official language: Spanish. Official religion: Roman Catholic. Currency: colón. Capital: San José. Pop.: 3 594 000 (1999 est.). Area: 50 900 sq. km (19 652 sq. miles).
▸ **Costa Rican** *adj, n*

cost-benefit *adj* denoting or relating to a method of assessing a project that takes into account its costs and its benefits to society as well as the revenue it generates: *a cost-benefit analysis; the project was assessed on a cost-benefit basis*.

cost-effective *adj* providing adequate financial return in relation to outlay.
▸ **ˌcost-ef'fectiveness** *n*

costermonger ('kɒstəˌmʌŋgə) *or* **coster** *n Brit., rare*. a person who sells fruit, vegetables, etc., from a barrow. ORIG C16: from *costard* a kind of apple + MONGER

costive ('kɒstɪv) *adj* **1** constipated. **2** niggardly. ORIG C14: from OF *costivé*, from L *constipātus*; see CONSTIPATE
▸ **'costiveness** *n*

costly ('kɒstlɪ) *adj* **costlier, costliest. 1** expensive. **2** entailing great loss or sacrifice: *a costly victory*. **3** splendid; lavish.
▸ **'costliness** *n*

cost of living *n* **a** the basic cost of the food, clothing, shelter, and fuel necessary to maintain life, esp. at a standard of living regarded as basic. **b** (*as modifier*): *the cost-of-living index*.

cost-plus *n* a method of establishing a selling price in which an agreed percentage is added to the cost price to cover profit.

costume ('kɒstjuːm) *n* **1** a style of dressing, including all the clothes, accessories, etc., worn at one time, as in a particular country or period. **2** *Old-fashioned*. a woman's suit. **3** a set of clothes, esp. unusual or period clothes: *a jester's costume*. **4** short for **swimming costume.** ◆ *vb* **costumes, costuming, costumed.** (*tr*) **5** to furnish the costumes for (a show, film, etc.). **6** to dress (someone) in a costume. ORIG C18: from F, from It.: dress, habit, CUSTOM

costumier (kɒ'stjuːmɪə) *or* **costumer** *n* a person or firm that makes or supplies theatrical or fancy costumes.

cosy *or US* **cozy** ('kəʊzɪ) *adj* **cosier, cosiest** *or US* **cozier, coziest. 1** warm and snug. **2** intimate; friendly. ◆ *n, pl* **cosies** *or US* **cozies. 3** a cover for keeping things warm: *egg cosy*. ORIG C18: from Scot., from ?
▸ **'cosily** *or US* **'cozily** *adv* ▸ **'cosiness** *or US* **'coziness** *n*

cot[1] (kɒt) *n* **1** a child's boxlike bed, usually incorporating vertical bars. **2** a portable bed. **3** a light bedstead. **4** *Naut*. a hammock-like bed. ORIG C17: from Hindi *khāt* bedstead

cot[2] (kɒt) *n* **1** *Literary or arch*. a small cottage. **2** Also called: **cote. 2a** a small shelter, esp. one for pigeons, sheep, etc. **2b** (*in combination*): *dovecot*. ORIG OE *cot*

cot[3] (kɒt) *abbrev. for* cotangent.

cotangent (kəʊ'tændʒənt) *n* (of an angle) a trigonometric function that in a right-angled triangle is the ratio of the length of the adjacent side to that of the opposite side.

COTC *abbrev. for* Canadian Officers Training Corps.

cot death *n* the unexplained sudden death of an infant during sleep. Technical name: **sudden infant death syndrome.**

cote (kəʊt) *or* **cot** *n* **1** a small shelter for pigeons, sheep, etc. **2** (*in combination*): *dovecote*. ORIG OE *cote*

Côte d'Azur ★ (*French* kot dazyr) *n* the Mediterranean coast of France, including the French Riviera: forms an administrative region with Provence.

Côte d'Ivoire ★ (*French* kot divwar) *n* a republic in West Africa, on the Gulf of Guinea: Portuguese trading for ivory and slaves began in the 16th century; made a French protectorate in 1842 and became independent in 1960; major producer of coffee and cocoa. Official language: French. Religion: Muslim majority, with animist, atheist, and Roman Catholic minorities. Currency: franc. Capital: Yamoussoukro (administrative); Abidjan (legislative). Pop.: 15 818 000 (1999 est.). Area: 319 820 sq. km (123 483 sq. miles). Former name (until 1986): **the Ivory Coast.**

Côte-d'Or ★ (*French* kotdɔr) *n* a department of E central France, in NE Burgundy. Capital: Dijon. Pop.: 505 896 (1994 est.). Area: 8787 sq. km (3427 sq. miles).

coterie ('kəʊtərɪ) *n* a small exclusive group of people with common interests; clique. ORIG C18: from F, from OF: association of tenants, from *cotier* (unattested) cottager

coterminous (kəʊ'tɜːmɪnəs) *or* **conterminous** *adj* **1** having a common boundary. **2** coextensive or coincident in range, time, etc.

Côtes-d'Armor ★ (*French* kotdɑːmɔr) *n* a department of W France, on the N coast of Brittany. Capital: St Brieuc. Pop.: 536 320 (1994 est.). Area: 6878 sq. km (2656 sq. miles). Former name: **Côtes-du-Nord.**

coth (kɒθ, ˈkɒtˈeɪtʃ) *n* hyperbolic cotangent. ORIG C20: from COT(ANGENT) + H(YPERBOLIC)

cotillion *or* **cotillon** (kəˈtɪljən, kəʊ-) *n* **1** a French formation dance of the 18th century. **2** *US.* a quadrille. **3** *US.* a formal ball. ORIG C18: from F *cotillon* dance, from OF: petticoat

cotinga (kəˈtɪŋɡə) *n* a tropical American passerine bird having a broad slightly hooked bill.

cotoneaster (kəˌtəʊnɪˈæstə) *n* any Old World shrub of the rosaceous genus *Cotoneaster:* cultivated for their ornamental flowers and red or black berries. ORIG C18: from NL, from L *cotōneum* QUINCE

Cotonou ★ (ˌkəʊtəˈnuː) *n* the official capital of Benin, a port on the Bight of Benin. Pop.: 750 000 (1994 est.).

Cotopaxi ★ (*Spanish* kotoˈpaksi) *n* a volcano in central Ecuador, in the Andes: the world's highest active volcano. Height: 5896 m (19 344 ft).

Cotswolds ★ (ˈkɒtsˌwəʊldz, -wəldz) *pl n* a range of low hills in SW England, mainly in Gloucestershire: formerly a centre of the wool industry.

cotta (ˈkɒtə) *n RC Church.* a short form of surplice. ORIG C19: from It.: tunic

cottage (ˈkɒtɪdʒ) *n* a small simple house, esp. in a rural area. ORIG C14: from COT[2]

cottage cheese *n* a mild loose soft white cheese made from skimmed milk curds.

cottage hospital *n Brit.* a small rural hospital.

cottage industry *n* an industry in which employees work in their own homes, often using their own equipment.

cottage pie *n Brit.* another term for **shepherd's pie.**

cottager (ˈkɒtɪdʒə) *n* **1** a person who lives in a cottage. **2** a rural labourer.

cottaging (ˈkɒtɪdʒɪŋ) *n Brit. sl.* homosexual activity between men in a public lavatory.

cotter[1] (ˈkɒtə) *n Machinery.* **1** any part, such as a pin, wedge, key, etc., that is used to secure two other parts so that relative motion between them is prevented. **2** short for **cotter pin.** ORIG C14: shortened from *cotterel,* from ?

cotter[2] (ˈkɒtə) *n* **1** *English history.* a villein in late Anglo-Saxon and early Norman times occupying a cottage and land in return for labour. **2** Also called: **cottar.** a peasant occupying a cottage and land in the Scottish Highlands. ORIG C14: from Med. L *cotārius,* from ME *cote* COT[2]

cotter pin *n Machinery.* a split pin secured, after passing through holes in the parts to be attached, by spreading the ends.

Cottian Alps ★ (ˈkɒtɪən) *pl n* a mountain range in SW Europe, between NW Italy and SE France: part of the Alps. Highest peak: Monte Viso, 3841 m (12 600 ft).

cotton (ˈkɒtᵊn) *n* **1** any of various herbaceous plants and shrubs cultivated in warm climates for the fibre surrounding the seeds and the oil within the seeds. **2** the soft white downy fibre of these plants, used to manufacture textiles. **3** cotton plants collectively, as a cultivated crop. **4** a cloth or thread made from cotton fibres. ORIG C14: from OF *coton,* from Ar. *qutn*
▸ **ˈcottony** *adj*

Cotton ★ (ˈkɒtᵊn) *n* **Henry.** 1907–87, British professional golfer: won the British Open championship (1934; 1937; 1948).

cotton bud *n* a small stick with a cotton-wool tip used for cleaning the ears, applying make-up, etc.

cotton grass *n* any of various N temperate and arctic grasslike bog plants whose clusters of long silky hairs resemble cotton tufts.

cotton on *vb* (*intr, adv;* often foll. by *to*) *Inf.* to perceive the meaning (of).

cotton-picking *adj US & Canad. sl.* (intensifier qualifying something undesirable): *you cotton-picking layabout!*

cottonseed (ˈkɒtᵊnˌsiːd) *n, pl* **cottonseeds** *or* **cottonseed.** the seed of the cotton plant: a source of oil and fodder.

cotton wool *n* **1** *Chiefly Brit.* bleached and sterilized cotton from which the impurities, such as the seeds, have been removed. Usual US term: **absorbent cotton. 2** cotton in the natural state. **3** *Brit. inf.* a state of pampered comfort and protection.

cotyledon (ˌkɒtɪˈliːdᵊn) *n* a simple embryonic leaf in seed-bearing plants, which, in some species, forms the first green leaf after germination. ORIG C16: from L: a plant, navelwort, from Gk *kotulēdōn,* from *kotulē* cup, hollow
▸ **ˌcotyˈledonous** *adj* ▸ **ˌcotyˈledonal** *adj*

coucal (ˈkuːkæl) *n* any ground-living bird of the genus *Centropus* of Africa, S Asia, and Australia. ORIG C19: from F, ?from *couc(ou)* cuckoo + *al(ouette)* lark

couch (kaʊtʃ) *n* **1** a piece of upholstered furniture, usually having a back and armrests, for seating more than one person. **2** a bed, esp. one used in the daytime by the patients of a doctor or a psychoanalyst. ◆ *vb* **3** (*tr*) to express in a particular style of language: *couched in an archaic style.* **4** (when *tr, usually reflexive or passive*) to lie down or cause to lie down for or as for sleep. **5** (*intr*) *Arch.* to crouch. **6** (*intr*) *Arch.* to lie in ambush; lurk. **7** (*tr*) *Surgery.* to remove (a cataract) by downward displacement of the lens of the eye. **8** (*tr*) *Arch.* to lower (a lance) into a horizontal position. ORIG C14: from OF *couche* a bed, lair, from *coucher* to lay down, from L *collocāre* to arrange, from *locāre* to place

couchant (ˈkaʊtʃənt) *adj* (*usually postpositive*) *Heraldry.* in a lying position: *a lion couchant.* ORIG C15: from F: lying

couchette (kuːˈʃɛt) *n* a bed or berth in a railway carriage, esp. one converted from seats. ORIG C20: from F, dim. of *couche* bed

couch grass (kaʊtʃ, kuːtʃ) *n* a grass with a yellowish-white creeping underground stem by which it spreads quickly: a troublesome weed. Also called: **twitch grass, quitch grass.**

couch potato *n Sl., chiefly US.* a lazy person whose recreation consists chiefly of watching television.

Coué ★ (*French* kue) *n* **Émile** (emil). 1857–1926, French psychologist: advocated psychotherapy by autosuggestion.
▸ **Couéism** (ˈkuːeɪˌɪzəm) *n*

cougar (ˈkuːɡə) *n* another name for **puma.** ORIG C18: from F *couguar,* from Port., from Tupi

cough (kɒf) *vb* **1** (*intr*) to expel air abruptly and explosively through the partially closed vocal chords. **2** (*intr*) to make a sound similar to this. **3** (*tr*) to utter or express with a cough or coughs. ◆ *n* **4** an act or sound of coughing. **5** a condition of the lungs or throat which causes frequent coughing. ORIG OE *cohhetten*
▸ **ˈcougher** *n*

cough drop *n* a lozenge to relieve a cough.

cough mixture *n* any medicine that relieves coughing.

cough up *vb* (*adv*) **1** *Inf.* to surrender (money, information, etc.), esp. reluctantly. **2** (*tr*) to bring into the mouth or eject (phlegm, food, etc.) by coughing.

could (kʊd) *vb* (takes an infinitive without *to* or an implied infinitive) used as an auxiliary: **1** to make the past tense of **can**[1]. **2** to make the subjunctive mood of **can**[1], esp. used in polite requests or in conditional sentences: *could I see you tonight?* **3** to indicate suggestion of a course of action: *you could take the car if it's raining.* **4** (often foll. by *well*) to indicate a possibility: *he could well be a spy.* ORIG OE *cūthe*

couldn't (ˈkʊdᵊnt) *contraction of* could not.

couldst (kʊdst) *vb Arch.* the form of **could** used with the pronoun *thou* or its relative form.

coulee (ˈkuːleɪ, -lɪ) *n* **1a** a flow of molten lava. **1b** such lava when solidified. **2** *Western US & Canad.* a steep-sided ravine. ORIG C19: from Canad. F *coulée* a flow, from F, from *couler* to flow, from L *cōlāre* to sift

coulis (ˈkuːliː) *n* a thin purée of vegetables, fruit, etc., usually served as a sauce. ORIG C20: F, lit.: purée

coulomb (ˈkuːlɒm) *n* the derived SI unit of electric charge; the quantity of electricity transported in one second by a current of 1 ampere. Symbol: C ORIG C19: after C.A. de COULOMB

Coulomb ★ ('ku:lɒm; *French* kulɔ̃) *n* **Charles Augustin de** (ʃarl ogystɛ̃ də). 1736–1806, French physicist: made many discoveries in the field of electricity and magnetism.

coulter ('kəʊltə) *n* a blade or sharp-edged disc attached to a plough so that it cuts through the soil vertically in advance of the ploughshare. Also (esp. US): **colter.** ORIG OE *culter,* from L: ploughshare, knife

coumarin *or* **cumarin** ('ku:mərɪn) *n* a white vanilla-scented crystalline ester, used in perfumes and flavouring. ORIG C19: from F, from *coumarou* tonka-bean tree, from Sp., from Tupi

council ('kaʊnsəl) *n* **1** an assembly of people meeting for discussion, consultation, etc. **2a** a body of people elected or appointed to serve in an administrative, legislative, or advisory capacity: *a student council.* **2b** short for **legislative council. 3** (*sometimes cap.;* often preceded by *the*) *Brit.* the local governing authority of a town, county, etc. **4** *Austral.* an administrative or legislative assembly, esp. the upper house of a state parliament in Australia. **5** a meeting of a council. **6** (*modifier*) of, provided for, or used by a local council: *a council chamber; council offices.* **7** (*modifier*) *Brit.* provided by a local council, esp. (of housing) at a subsidized rent: *a council house; a council estate; a council school.* **8** *Christianity.* an assembly of bishops, etc., convened for regulating matters of doctrine or discipline. ORIG C12: from OF *concile,* from L *concilium* assembly, from *com-* together + *calāre* to call

> **USAGE NOTE** This word is sometimes confused with **counsel.**

council area *n* any of the 32 unitary authorities into which Scotland was divided for administrative purposes in 1996.

councillor *or US* **councilor** ('kaʊnsələ) *n* a member of a council.

> **USAGE NOTE** This word is sometimes confused with **counsellor.**

councilman ('kaʊnsəlmən) *n, pl* **councilmen.** *Chiefly US.* a councillor.

council tax *n* (in Britain) a tax based on the relative value of property levied to fund local council services.

counsel ('kaʊnsəl) *n* **1** advice or guidance on conduct, behaviour, etc. **2** discussion; consultation: *to take counsel with a friend.* **3** a person whose advice is sought. **4** a barrister or group of barristers engaged in conducting cases in court and advising on legal matters. **5** *Christianity.* any of the **counsels of perfection,** namely poverty, chastity, and obedience. **6 counsel of perfection.** excellent but unrealizable advice. **7** private opinions (esp. in **keep one's own counsel**). **8** *Arch.* wisdom; prudence. ◆ *vb* **counsels, counselling, counselled** *or US* **counsels, counseling, counseled. 9** (*tr*) to give advice or guidance to. **10** (*tr; often takes a clause as object*) to recommend; urge. **11** (*intr*) *Arch.* to take counsel; consult. ORIG C13: from OF *counseil,* from L *consilium* deliberating body; rel. to CONSULT

> **USAGE NOTE** This word is sometimes confused with **council.**

counselling *or US* **counseling** ('kaʊnsəlɪŋ) *n* systematic guidance offered by social workers, doctors, etc., in which a person's problems are discussed and advice is given.

counsellor *or US* **counselor** ('kaʊnsələ) *n* **1** a person who gives counsel; adviser. **2** Also called: **counselor-at-law.** *US.* a lawyer, esp. one who conducts cases in court. **3** a senior diplomatic officer.

> **USAGE NOTE** This word is sometimes confused with **councillor.**

count[1] (kaʊnt) *vb* **1** to add up or check (each unit in a collection) in order to ascertain the sum: *count your change.* **2** (*tr*) to recite numbers in ascending order up to and including. **3** (*tr;* often foll. by *in*) to take into account or include: *we must count him in.* **4 not counting.** excluding. **5** (*tr*) to consider; deem: *count yourself lucky.* **6** (*intr*) to have importance: *this picture counts as a rarity.* **7** (*intr*) *Music.* to keep time by counting beats. ◆ *n* **8** the act of counting. **9** the number reached by counting; sum: *a blood count.* **10** *Law.* a paragraph in an indictment containing a separate charge. **11 keep** *or* **lose count.** to keep or fail to keep an accurate record of items, events, etc. **12** *Boxing, wrestling.* the act of telling off a number of seconds by the referee, as when a boxer has been knocked down by his opponent. **13 out for the count.** *Boxing.* knocked out and unable to continue after a count of ten by the referee. ◆ See also **count against, countdown,** etc. ORIG C14: from Anglo-F *counter,* from OF *conter,* from L *computāre* to calculate
▸ '**countable** *adj*

count[2] (kaʊnt) *n* **1** a nobleman in any of various European countries having a rank corresponding to that of a British earl. **2** any of various officials in the late Roman Empire and in the early Middle Ages. ORIG C16: from OF *conte,* from L *comes* associate, from COM- with + *īre* to go

count against *vb* (*intr, prep*) to have influence to the disadvantage of.

countdown ('kaʊnt,daʊn) *n* **1** the act of counting backwards to time a critical operation exactly, such as the launching of a rocket. ◆ *vb* **count down.** (*intr, adv*) **2** to count thus.

countenance ('kaʊntɪnəns) *n* **1** the face, esp. when considered as expressing a person's character or mood. **2** support or encouragement; sanction. **3** composure; self-control (esp. in **keep** *or* **lose one's countenance**). ◆ *vb* **countenances, countenancing, countenanced.** (*tr*) **4** to support or encourage; sanction. **5** to tolerate; endure. ORIG C13: from OF *contenance* mien, behaviour, from L *continentia* restraint, control; see CONTAIN

counter[1] ('kaʊntə) *n* **1** a horizontal surface, as in a shop or bank, over which business is transacted. **2** (in some cafeterias) a long table on which food is served. **3a** a small flat disc of wood, metal, or plastic, used in various board games. **3b** a similar disc or token used as an imitation coin. **4** a person or thing that may be used or manipulated. **5 under the counter.** (**under-the-counter** *when prenominal*) (of the sale of goods) clandestine or illegal. **6 over the counter.** (**over-the-counter** *when prenominal*) (of security transactions) through a broker rather than on a stock exchange. ORIG C14: from OF *comptouer,* ult. from L *computāre* to COMPUTE

counter[2] ('kaʊntə) *n* **1** a person who counts. **2** an apparatus that records the number of occurrences of events. ORIG C14: from OF *conteor,* from L *computātor;* see COUNT[1]

counter[3] ('kaʊntə) *adv* **1** in a contrary direction or manner. **2** in a wrong or reverse direction. **3 run counter to.** to have a contrary effect or action to. ◆ *adj* **4** opposing; opposite; contrary. ◆ *n* **5** something that is contrary or opposite to some other thing. **6** an act, effect, or force that opposes another. **7** a return attack, such as a blow in boxing. **8** *Fencing.* a parry in which the foils move in a circular fashion. **9** the portion of the stern of a boat or ship that overhangs the water aft of the rudder. **10** a piece of leather forming the back of a shoe. ◆ *vb* **11** to say or do (something) in retaliation or response. **12** (*tr*) to move, act, or perform in a manner or direction opposite to (a person or thing). **13** to return the attack of (an opponent). ORIG C15: from OF *contre,* from L *contrā* against

counter- *prefix* **1** against; opposite; contrary: *counterattack.* **2** complementary; corresponding: *counterfoil.* **3** duplicate or substitute: *counterfeit.* ORIG via OF from L *contrā* against, opposite; see CONTRA-

counteract (,kaʊntər'ækt) *vb* (*tr*) to oppose or neutralize by contrary action; check.
▸ ,**counter'action** *n* ▸ ,**counter'active** *adj*

counterattack ('kaʊntərə,tæk) *n* **1** an attack in response to an attack. ◆ *vb* **2** to make a counterattack (against).

counterbalance *n* ('kaʊntə,bæləns). **1** a weight or force that balances or offsets another. ◆ *vb* (ˌkauntəˈbæləns), **counterbalances, counterbalancing, counterbalanced.** (*tr*) **2** Also: **counterweigh.** to act as a counterbalance to. ◆ Also: **counterpoise.**

counterblast (ˈkauntəˌblɑːst) *n* an aggressive response to a verbal attack.

countercheck *n* (ˈkauntəˌtʃɛk). **1** a check or restraint, esp. one that acts in opposition to another. **2** a double check, as for accuracy. ◆ *vb* (ˌkauntəˈtʃɛk). (*tr*) **3** to oppose by counteraction. **4** to double-check.

counterclaim (ˈkauntəˌkleɪm) *Chiefly law.* ◆ *n* **1** a claim set up in opposition to another. ◆ *vb* **2** to set up (a claim) in opposition to another claim.
▸ **ˌcounterˈclaimant** *n*

counterclockwise (ˌkauntəˈklɒkˌwaɪz) *adv, adj* the US and Canad. equivalent of **anticlockwise.**

counterculture (ˈkauntəˌkʌltʃə) *n* an alternative culture, deliberately at variance with the social norm.

counterespionage (ˌkauntərˈɛspɪəˌnɑːʒ) *n* activities to counteract enemy espionage.

counterfeit (ˈkauntəfɪt) *adj* **1** made in imitation of something genuine with the intent to deceive or defraud; forged. **2** simulated; sham: *counterfeit affection.* ◆ *n* **3** an imitation designed to deceive or defraud. ◆ *vb* **4** (*tr*) to make a fraudulent imitation of. **5** (*intr*) to make counterfeits. **6** to feign; simulate. ORIG C13: from OF *contrefait,* from *contrefaire* to copy, from *contre-* COUNTER- + *faire* to make
▸ **ˈcounterfeiter** *n*

counterfoil (ˈkauntəˌfɔɪl) *n Brit.* the part of a cheque, receipt, etc., retained as a record. Also called (esp. in the US and Canada): **stub.**

counterforce (ˈkauntəˌfɔːs) *n* (*modifier*) denoting military strategy based on retaliation against attacking forces.

counterinsurgency (ˌkauntərɪnˈsɜːdʒənsɪ) *n* action taken by a government against rebels, guerrillas, etc.

counterintelligence (ˌkauntərɪnˈtɛlɪdʒəns) *n* activities designed to frustrate enemy espionage.

counterintuitive *adj Chiefly US.* (of an idea, proposal, etc.) seemingly contrary to common sense.

counterirritant (ˌkauntərˈɪrɪtᵊnt) *n* **1** an agent that causes a superficial irritation of the skin and thereby relieves inflammation of deep structures. ◆ *adj* **2** producing a counterirritation.
▸ **ˌcounterˌirriˈtation** *n*

countermand *vb* (ˌkauntəˈmɑːnd). (*tr*) **1** to revoke or cancel (a command, order, etc.). **2** to order (forces, etc.) to retreat; recall. ◆ *n* (ˈkauntəˌmɑːnd). **3** a command revoking another. ORIG C15: from OF *contremander,* from *contre-* COUNTER- + *mander* to command, from L *mandāre*

countermarch (ˈkauntəˌmɑːtʃ) *Chiefly mil.* ◆ *vb* **1** to march or cause to march back or in the opposite direction. ◆ *n* **2** the act or an instance of countermarching.

countermeasure (ˈkauntəˌmɛʒə) *n* action taken to oppose, neutralize, or retaliate against some other action.

countermove (ˈkauntəˌmuːv) *n* **1** an opposing move. ◆ *vb* **countermoves, countermoving, countermoved. 2** to make or do (something) as an opposing move.
▸ **ˈcounterˌmovement** *n*

counteroffensive (ˈkauntərəˌfɛnsɪv) *n* a series of attacks by a defending force against an attacking enemy.

counteroffer (ˈkauntərˌɒfə) *n* a response to a bid in which a seller amends his or her original offer, making it more favourable to the buyer.

counterpane (ˈkauntəˌpeɪn) *n* another word for **bedspread.** ORIG C17: from obs. *counterpoint* (infl. by *pane* coverlet), changed from OF *coutepointe* quilt, from Med. L *culcita puncta* quilted mattress

counterpart (ˈkauntəˌpɑːt) *n* **1** a person or thing identical to or closely resembling another. **2** one of two parts that complement or correspond to each other. **3** a duplicate, esp. of a legal document; copy.

counterparty (ˈkauntəˌpɑːtɪ) *n* a person who is a party to a contract.

counterplot (ˈkauntəˌplɒt) *n* **1** a plot designed to frustrate another plot. ◆ *vb* **counterplots, counterplotting, counterplotted. 2** (*tr*) to oppose with a counterplot.

counterpoint (ˈkauntəˌpɔɪnt) *n* **1** the technique involving the simultaneous sounding of two or more parts or melodies. **2** a melody or part combined with another melody or part. **3** the musical texture resulting from the simultaneous sounding of two or more melodies or parts. ◆ *vb* **4** (*tr*) to set in contrast. ◆ Related adj: **contrapuntal.** ORIG C15: from OF *contrepoint,* from *contre-* COUNTER- + *point* dot, note in musical notation, i.e. an accompaniment set against the notes of a melody

counterpoise (ˈkauntəˌpɔɪz) *n* **1** a force, influence, etc., that counterbalances another. **2** a state of balance; equilibrium. **3** a weight that balances another. ◆ *vb* **counterpoises, counterpoising, counterpoised.** (*tr*) **4** to oppose with something of equal effect, weight, or force; offset. **5** to bring into equilibrium.

counterproductive (ˌkauntəprəˈdʌktɪv) *adj* tending to hinder the achievement of an aim; having effects contrary to those intended.

counterproposal (ˈkauntəprəˌpəuzᵊl) *n* a proposal offered as an alternative to a previous proposal.

Counter-Reformation (ˌkauntəˌrɛfəˈmeɪʃən) *n* the reform movement of the Roman Catholic Church in the 16th and early 17th centuries considered as a reaction to the Reformation.

counter-revolution (ˌkauntəˌrɛvəˈluːʃən) *n* a revolution opposed to a previous revolution.
▸ **ˌcounter-ˌrevoˈlutionist** *n* ▸ **counter-ˌrevoˈlutionary** *n, adj*

countershaft (ˈkauntəˌʃɑːft) *n* an intermediate shaft driven by a main shaft, esp. in a gear train.

countersign *vb* (ˈkauntəˌsaɪn, ˌkauntəˈsaɪn). **1** (*tr*) to sign (a document already signed by another). ◆ *n* (ˈkauntəˌsaɪn). **2** Also called: **countersignature.** the signature so written. **3** a secret sign given in response to another sign. **4** *Chiefly mil.* a password.

countersink (ˈkauntəˌsɪŋk) *vb* **countersinks, countersinking, countersank, countersunk.** (*tr*) **1** to enlarge the upper part of (a hole) in timber, metal, etc., so that the head of a bolt or screw can be sunk below the surface. **2** to drive (a screw) or sink (a bolt) into such a hole. ◆ *n* **3** Also called: **countersink bit.** a tool for countersinking. **4** a countersunk hole.

countertenor (ˌkauntəˈtɛnə) *n* **1** an adult male voice with an alto range. **2** a singer with such a voice.

countervail (ˌkauntəˈveɪl, ˈkauntəˌveɪl) *vb* **1** (when *intr,* usually foll. by *against*) to act or act against with equal power or force. **2** (*tr*) to make up for; compensate; offset. ORIG C14: from OF *contrevaloir,* from L *contrā valēre,* from *contrā* against + *valēre* to be strong

countervailing duty *n* an extra import duty imposed by a country on certain imports, esp. to prevent dumping or to counteract subsidies in the exporting country.

counterweigh (ˌkauntəˈweɪ) *vb* another word for **counterbalance** (sense 2).

counterweight (ˈkauntəˌweɪt) *n* a counterbalancing weight, influence, or force.

countess (ˈkauntɪs) *n* **1** the wife or widow of a count or earl. **2** a woman of the rank of count or earl.

counting house *n Rare, chiefly Brit.* a room or building used by the accountants of a business.

countless (ˈkauntlɪs) *adj* innumerable; myriad.

count noun *n* a noun that can be qualified by the indefinite article and may be used in the plural, as *telephone* and *thing* but not *airs and graces* or *bravery.* Cf. **mass noun.**

count on *vb* (*intr, prep*) to rely or depend on.

count out *vb* (*tr, adv*) **1** *Inf.* to leave out; exclude. **2** (of a boxing referee) to judge (a floored boxer) to have failed to recover within the specified time.

count palatine *n, pl* **counts palatine.** *History.* **1** (in the Holy Roman Empire) a count who exercised royal authority in his own domain. **2** (in England and Ireland) the lord of a county palatine.

countrified *or* **countryfied** (ˈkʌntrɪˌfaɪd) *adj* in the style, manners, etc., of the country; rural.

country ('kʌntrɪ) *n, pl* **countries. 1** a territory distinguished by its people, culture, geography, etc. **2** an area of land distinguished by its political autonomy; state. **3** the people of a territory or state. **4a** the part of the land that is away from cities or industrial areas; rural districts. **4b** (*as modifier*): *country cottage.* Related adjs.: **pastoral, rural. 5** short for **country music. 6 across country.** not keeping to roads, etc. **7 go** *or* **appeal to the country.** *Chiefly Brit.* to dissolve Parliament and hold an election. **8 up country.** away from the coast or the capital. **9** one's native land or nation of citizenship. ORIG C13: from OF *contrée,* from Med. L *contrāta,* lit.: that which lies opposite, from L *contrā* opposite

country and western *n* another name for **country music.**

country club *n* a club in the country, having sporting and social facilities.

country dance *n* a type of folk dance in which couples face one another in a line.

country house *n* a large house in the country, esp. belonging to a wealthy family.

countryman ('kʌntrɪmən) *n, pl* **countrymen. 1** a person who lives in the country. **2** a person from a particular country or from one's own country.
▸ **'country,woman** *fem n*

country music *n* a type of 20th-century popular music based on White folk music of the southeastern US.

country park *n Brit.* an area of countryside set aside for public recreation.

country seat *n* a large estate or property in the country.

countryside ('kʌntrɪ,saɪd) *n* a rural area or its population.

county ('kaʊntɪ) *n, pl* **counties. 1a** any of various administrative, political, judicial, or geographic subdivisions of certain English-speaking countries or states. **1b** (*as modifier*): *county cricket.* ◆ *adj* **2** *Brit. inf.* upper class; of or like the landed gentry. ORIG C14: from OF *conté* land belonging to a count, from LL *comes* COUNT[2]

county borough *n* **1** (in England from 1888 to 1974 and in Wales from 1888 to 1974 and from 1996) a borough administered independently of any higher tier of local government. **2** (in the Republic of Ireland) a borough governed by an elected council that constitutes an all-purpose authority.

county palatine *n, pl* **counties palatine. 1** the lands of a count palatine. **2** (in England and Ireland) a county in which the earl (or other lord) exercised many royal powers, esp. judicial authority.

county town *n* the town in which a county's affairs are or were administered.

coup (kuː) *n* **1** a brilliant and successful stroke or action. **2** short for **coup d'état.** ORIG C18: from F: blow, from L *colaphus* blow with the fist, from Gk *kolaphos*

coup de grâce *French.* (ku də grɑs) *n, pl* ***coups de grâce*** (ku də grɑs). **1** a mortal or finishing blow, esp. one delivered as an act of mercy to a sufferer. **2** a final or decisive stroke. ORIG lit.: blow of mercy

coup d'état ('kuː deɪ'tɑː) *n, pl* **coups d'état** ('kuːz deɪ'tɑː). a sudden violent or illegal seizure of government. ORIG F, lit.: stroke of state

coupe (kuːp) *n* **1** a dessert of fruit and ice cream. **2** a dish or stemmed glass bowl designed for this dessert. ORIG C19: from F: goblet, CUP

coupé ('kuːpeɪ) *n* **1** a four-seater car with a sloping back, and usually two doors. **2** a four-wheeled horse-drawn carriage with two seats inside and one outside for the driver. ORIG C19: from F *carrosse coupé,* lit.: cut-off carriage

Couperin ★ (*French* kuprɛ̃) *n* **François** (frɑ̃swa). 1668–1733, French composer, noted for his harpsichord suites and organ music.

couple ('kʌpᵊl) *n* **1** two people who regularly associate with each other or live together: *an engaged couple.* **2** (*functioning as sing or pl*) two people considered as a pair, for or as if for dancing, games, etc. **3** a pair of equal and opposite parallel forces that have a tendency to produce rotation. **4** a connector or link between two members, such as a tie connecting a pair of rafters in a roof. **5 a couple of.** (*functioning as sing or pl*) **5a** a combination of two; a pair of: *a couple of men.* **5b** *Inf.* a small number of; a few: *a couple of days.* ◆ *pron* **6** (usually preceded by *a; functioning as sing or pl*) two; a pair: *give him a couple.* ◆ *vb* **couples, coupling, coupled. 7** (*tr*) to connect (two things) together or to connect (one thing) to (another): *to couple railway carriages.* **8** to form or be formed into a pair or pairs. **9** to associate, put, or connect together. **10** (*intr*) to have sexual intercourse. ORIG C13: from OF: a pair, from L *cōpula* a bond; see COPULA

coupledom ('kʌpᵊldəm) *n* the state of living as a couple.

coupler ('kʌplə) *n Music.* a device on an organ or harpsichord connecting two keys, two manuals, etc., so that both may be played at once.

couplet ('kʌplɪt) *n* two successive lines of verse, usually rhymed and of the same metre. ORIG C16: from F, lit.: a little pair; see COUPLE

coupling ('kʌplɪŋ) *n* **1** a mechanical device that connects two things. **2** a device for connecting railway cars or trucks together.

coupon ('kuːpɒn) *n* **1a** a detachable part of a ticket or advertisement entitling the holder to a discount, free gift, etc. **1b** a detachable slip usable as a commercial order form. **1c** a voucher given away with certain goods, a certain number of which are exchangeable for goods offered by the manufacturers. **2** one of a number of detachable certificates attached to a bond, the surrender of which entitles the bearer to receive interest payments. **3** *Brit.* a detachable entry form for any of certain competitions, esp. football pools. ORIG C19: from F, from OF *colpon* piece cut off, from *colper* to cut, var. of *couper*

courage ('kʌrɪdʒ) *n* **1** the power or quality of dealing with or facing danger, fear, pain, etc. **2 the courage of one's convictions.** the confidence to act in accordance with one's beliefs. ORIG C13: from OF *corage,* from *cuer* heart, from L *cor*

courageous (kə'reɪdʒəs) *adj* possessing or expressing courage.
▸ **cou'rageously** *adv* ▸ **cou'rageousness** *n*

courante (kʊ'rɑːnt) *n Music.* **1** an old dance in quick triple time. **2** a movement of a (mostly) 16th- to 18th-century suite based on this. ORIG C16: from F, lit.: running, from *courir* to run, from L *currere*

Courantyne ★ ('kɜːrən,taɪn) *n* a river in N South America, rising in S Guyana and flowing north to the Atlantic, forming the boundary between Guyana and Surinam. Length: 765 km (475 miles). Dutch name: **Corantijn.**

courbaril ('kʊəbərɪl) *n* a tropical American leguminous tree: its wood is a useful timber and its gum is a source of copal. Also called: **West Indian locust.** ORIG C18: from Amerind

Courbet ★ (*French* kurbɛ) *n* **Gustave** (gystav). 1819–77, French painter, a leader of the realist movement; noted for his depiction of contemporary life.

coureur de bois (*French* kurœr də bwa) *n, pl* **coureurs de bois** (kurœr də bwa). *Canad. history.* a French Canadian woodsman or Métis who traded with Indians for furs. ORIG Canad. F: trapper (lit.: wood-runner)

courgette (kʊə'ʒɛt) *n* a small variety of vegetable marrow. US, Canad., and Austral. name: **zucchini.** ORIG from F, dim. of *courge* marrow, gourd

courier ('kʊərɪə) *n* **1** a special messenger, esp. one carrying diplomatic correspondence. **2** a person employed to collect and deliver parcels, packages, etc. **3** a person who makes arrangements for or accompanies a group of travellers on a journey or tour. ◆ *vb* **4** (*tr*) to send (a parcel, letter, etc.) by courier. ORIG C16: from OF *courrier,* from OIt. *correre* to run, from L *currere*

Cournand ★ ('kʊənənd, -nænd; *French* kurnɑ̃) *n* **André (Frederic).** 1895–1988, US physician, born in France: shared the 1956 Nobel prize for physiology or medicine for his work on heart catheterization.

Courrèges ★ (*French* kurɛʒ) *n* **André** (ɑ̃dre). born 1923, French couturier.

course (kɔːs) *n* **1** a continuous progression in time or space; onward movement. **2** a route or direction followed. **3** the path or channel along which something moves: *the course of a river.* **4** an area or stretch of land or water on which a sport is played or a race is run: *a golf course.* **5** a period of time; duration: *in the course of the next hour.* **6** the usual order of and time required for a sequence of events; regular procedure: *the illness ran its course.* **7** a mode of conduct or action: *if you follow that course, you will fail.* **8** a connected series of events, actions, etc. **9a** a prescribed number of lessons, lectures, etc., in an educational curriculum. **9b** the material covered in such a curriculum. **10** a regimen prescribed for a specific period of time: *a course of treatment.* **11** a part of a meal served at one time. **12** a continuous, usually horizontal, layer of building material, such as a row of bricks, tiles, etc. **13 as a matter of course.** as a natural or normal consequence, mode of action, or event. **14 in course of.** in the process of. **15 in due course.** at some future time, esp. the natural or appropriate time. **16 of course. 16a** (*adv*) as expected; naturally. **16b** (*sentence substitute*) certainly; definitely. **17 the course of nature.** the ordinary course of events. ◆ *vb* **courses, coursing, coursed. 18** (*intr*) to run, race, or flow. **19** to cause (hounds) to hunt by sight rather than scent or (of hounds) to hunt (a quarry) thus. ORIG C13: from OF *cours,* from L *cursus* a running, from *currere* to run

courser[1] (ˈkɔːsə) *n* **1** a person who courses hounds or dogs, esp. greyhounds. **2** a hound or dog trained for coursing.

courser[2] (ˈkɔːsə) *n Literary.* a swift horse; steed. ORIG C13: from OF *coursier,* from *cours* COURSE

coursework (ˈkɔːsˌwɜːk) *n* written or oral work completed by a student within a given period, which is assessed as part of an educational course.

coursing (ˈkɔːsɪŋ) *n* **1** hunting with hounds or dogs that follow their quarry by sight. **2** a sport in which hounds are matched against one another in pairs for the hunting of hares by sight.

court (kɔːt) *n* **1** an area of ground wholly or partly surrounded by walls or buildings. **2** *Brit.* **2a** a block of flats. **2b** a mansion or country house. **2c** a short street, sometimes closed at one end. **3a** the residence, retinues, or household of a sovereign or nobleman. **3b** (*as modifier*)*: a court ball.* **4** a sovereign or prince and his retinue, advisers, etc. **5** any formal assembly held by a sovereign or nobleman. **6** homage, flattering attention, or amorous approaches (esp. in **pay court to someone**). **7** *Law.* **7a** a tribunal having power to adjudicate in civil, criminal, military, or ecclesiastical matters. **7b** the regular sitting of such a judicial tribunal. **7c** the room or building in which such a tribunal sits. **8a** a marked outdoor or enclosed area used for any of various ball games, such as tennis, squash, etc. **8b** a marked section of such an area. **9 go to court.** to take legal action. **10 hold court.** to preside over admirers, attendants, etc. **11 out of court.** without a trial or legal case. **12 the ball is in your court.** you are obliged to make the next move. ◆ *vb* **13** to attempt to gain the love of; woo. **14** (*tr*) to pay attention to (someone) in order to gain favour. **15** (*tr*) to try to obtain (fame, honour, etc.). **16** (*tr*) to invite, usually foolishly, as by taking risks. ORIG C12: from OF, from L *cohors* COHORT

Court ★ (kɔːt) *n* **Margaret** (née *Smith*). born 1942, Australian tennis player: Wimbledon champion 1963, 1965, and 1970.

court-bouillon (ˈkuətˈbuːjɒn) *n* a stock made from root vegetables, water, and wine or vinegar, used primarily for poaching fish. ORIG from F, from *court* short, + *bouillon* broth, from *bouillir* to BOIL[1]

court card *n* (in a pack of playing cards) a king, queen, or jack of any suit. ORIG C17: altered from earlier *coat-card,* from the decorative coats worn by the figures depicted

court circular *n* a daily report of the activities, engagements, etc., of the sovereign, published in a national newspaper.

Courtelle (kɔːˈtɛl) *n Trademark.* a synthetic acrylic fibre resembling wool.

courteous (ˈkɜːtɪəs) *adj* polite and considerate in manner. ORIG C13 *corteis,* lit.: with courtly manners, from OF; see COURT
▸ **ˈcourteously** *adv* ▸ **ˈcourteousness** *n*

courtesan *or* **courtezan** (ˌkɔːtɪˈzæn) *n* (esp. formerly) a prostitute, or the mistress of a man of rank. ORIG C16: from OF *courtisane,* from It. *cortigiana* female courtier, from *corte* COURT

courtesy (ˈkɜːtɪsɪ) *n, pl* **courtesies. 1** politeness; good manners. **2** a courteous gesture or remark. **3** favour or consent (esp. in (**by**) **courtesy of**). **4** common consent as opposed to right (esp. in **by courtesy**). ORIG C13 *curteisie,* from OF, from *corteis* COURTEOUS

courtesy light *n* the interior light in a motor vehicle.

courtesy title *n* any of several titles having no legal significance, such as those borne by the children of peers.

courthouse (ˈkɔːtˌhaʊs) *n* a public building in which courts of law are held.

courtier (ˈkɔːtɪə) *n* **1** an attendant at a court. **2** a person who seeks favour in an ingratiating manner. ORIG C13: from Anglo-F *courteour* (unattested), from OF *corteier* to attend at court

courtly (ˈkɔːtlɪ) *adj* **courtlier, courtliest. 1** of or suitable for a royal court. **2** refined in manner. **3** ingratiating.
▸ **ˈcourtliness** *n*

court martial *n, pl* **court martials** *or* **courts martial. 1** a military court that tries persons subject to military law. ◆ *vb* **court-martial, court-martials, court-martialling, court-martialled** *or US* **court-martials, court-martialing, court-martialed. 2** (*tr*) to try by court martial.

Court of Appeal *n* a court that hears appeals from the High Court and from the county and crown courts.

Court of St James's *n* the official name of the royal court of Britain.

court plaster *n* a plaster, composed of isinglass on silk, formerly used to cover superficial wounds. ORIG C18: so called because formerly used by court ladies for beauty spots

courtroom (ˈkɔːtˌruːm, -ˌrʊm) *n* a room in which the sittings of a law court are held.

courtship (ˈkɔːtʃɪp) *n* **1** the act, period, or art of seeking the love of someone with intent to marry. **2** the seeking or soliciting of favours.

court shoe *n* a low-cut shoe for women, without any laces or straps.

courtyard (ˈkɔːtˌjɑːd) *n* an open area of ground surrounded by walls or buildings; court.

couscous (ˈkuːskuːs) *n* a spicy dish, originating in North Africa, consisting of steamed semolina served with a meat stew. ORIG C17: via F from Ar. *kouskous,* from *kaskasa* to pound until fine

cousin (ˈkʌzᵊn) *n* **1** Also called: **first cousin, cousin-german, full cousin.** the child of one's aunt or uncle. **2** a relative descended from one of one's common ancestors. **3** a title used by a sovereign when addressing another sovereign or a nobleman. ORIG C13: from OF *cosin,* from L *consōbrīnus,* from *sōbrīnus* cousin on the mother's side
▸ **ˈcousinˌhood** *or* **ˈcousinˌship** *n* ▸ **ˈcousinly** *adj, adv*

Cousin ★ (*French* kuzɛ̃) *n* **Victor** (viktɔr). 1792–1867, French philosopher and educational reformer.

Cousteau ★ (*French* kusto) *n* **Jacques Yves** (ʒɑk iv). 1910–97, French underwater explorer.

couture (kuːˈtʊə) *n* **a** high-fashion designing and dressmaking. **b** (*as modifier*): *couture clothes.* ORIG from F: sewing, from OF *cousture* seam, from L *consuere* to stitch together

couturier (kuːˈtʊərɪˌeɪ) *n* a person who designs, makes, and sells fashion clothes for women. ORIG from F: dressmaker; see COUTURE
▸ **couturière** (kuːˌtuːrɪˈɛə) *fem n*

couvade (kuːˈvɑːd) *n Anthropol.* the custom in certain cultures of treating the husband of a woman giving birth as if he were bearing the child. ORIG C19: from F, from *couver* to hatch, from L *cubāre* to lie down

covalency (kəʊˈveɪlənsɪ) *or US* **covalence** *n* **1** the formation and nature of covalent bonds, that is, chemical bonds involving the sharing of electrons between atoms in a molecule. **2** the number of covalent bonds that a

particular atom can make with other atoms in forming a molecule.
▸ **co'valent** *adj* ▸ **co'valently** *adv*

cove[1] (kəʊv) *n* **1** a small bay or inlet. **2** a narrow cavern in the side of a cliff, mountain, etc. **3** Also called: **coving.** *Archit.* a concave curved surface between the wall and ceiling of a room. ORIG OE *cofa*

cove[2] (kəʊv) *n Sl., Brit. old-fashioned & Austral.* a fellow; chap. ORIG C16: prob. from Romany *kova* thing, person

coven ('kʌvᵊn) *n* a meeting of witches. ORIG C16: prob. from OF *covin* group, ult. from L *convenīre* to come together

covenant ('kʌvənənt) *n* **1** a binding agreement; contract. **2** *Law.* an agreement in writing under seal, as to pay a stated annual sum to a charity. **3** *Bible.* God's promise to the Israelites and their commitment to worship him alone. ◆ *vb* **4** to agree to a covenant (concerning). ORIG C13: from OF, from *covenir* to agree, from L *convenīre* to come together, make an agreement; see CONVENE
▸ **covenantal** (ˌkʌvə'næntᵊl) *adj* ▸ **'covenantor** *or* **'covenanter** *n*

Covenanter ('kʌvənəntə, ˌkʌvə'næntə) *n Scot. history.* a person upholding either of two 17th-century covenants to establish and defend Presbyterianism.

Covent Garden ★ ('kʌvənt, 'kɒv-) *n* **1** a district of central London: famous for its former fruit, vegetable, and flower market, now a shopping precinct. **2** the Royal Opera House (built 1858) in Covent Garden.

Coventry ★ ('kɒvəntrɪ) *n* **1** a city in central England, in the West Midlands: devastated in World War II; modern cathedral (1954–62); industrial centre, esp. for motor vehicles; seat of The University of Warwick (1965) and Coventry University (1992). Pop.: 299 316 (1991). **2** a unitary authority in central England. Pop.: 306 500 (1996 est.). Area: 97 sq. km (37 sq. miles). **3 send to Coventry.** to ostracize or ignore.

cover ('kʌvə) *vb* (*mainly tr*) **1** to place or spread something over so as to protect or conceal. **2** to provide with a covering; clothe. **3** to put a garment, esp. a hat, on (the body or head). **4** to extend over or lie thickly on the surface of: *snow covered the fields.* **5** to bring upon (oneself); invest (oneself) as if with a covering: *covered with shame.* **6** (sometimes foll. by *up*) to act as a screen or concealment for; hide from view. **7** *Mil.* to protect (an individual, formation, or place) by taking up a position from which fire may be returned if those being protected are fired upon. **8** (*also intr,* sometimes foll. by *for*) to assume responsibility for (a person or thing). **9** (*intr;* foll. by *for* or *up for*) to provide an alibi (for). **10** to have as one's territory: *this salesman covers your area.* **11** to travel over. **12** to have or place in the aim and within the range of (a firearm). **13** to include or deal with. **14** (of an asset or income) to be sufficient to meet (a liability or expense). **15a** to insure against loss, risk, etc. **15b** to provide for (loss, risk, etc.) by insurance. **16** to deposit (an equivalent stake) in a bet. **17** to act as reporter or photographer on (a news event, etc.) for a newspaper or magazine: *to cover sports events.* **18** *Music.* to record a cover version of. **19** *Sport.* to guard or protect (an opponent, team-mate, or area). **20** (of a male animal, esp. a horse) to copulate with (a female animal). ◆ *n* **21** anything that covers, spreads over, protects, or conceals. **22a** a blanket used on a bed for warmth. **22b** another word for **bedspread. 23** a pretext, disguise, or false identity: *the thief sold brushes as a cover.* **24** an envelope or package for sending through the post: *under plain cover.* **25a** an individual table setting, esp. in a restaurant. **25b** (*as modifier*): *a cover charge.* **26** Also called: **cover version.** a version by a different artist of a previously recorded musical item. **27** *Cricket.* **27a** (*often pl*) the area more or less at right angles to the pitch on the off side and usually about halfway to the boundary. **27b** (*as modifier*): *a cover drive.* **28** *Philately.* an entire envelope that has been postmarked. **29 break cover.** to come out from a shelter or hiding place. **30 take cover.** to make for a place of safety or shelter. **31 under cover.** protected, concealed, or in secret. ◆ See also **cover-up.** ORIG C13: from OF *covrir,* from L *cooperīre* to cover completely, from *operīre* to cover over
▸ **'coverable** *adj* ▸ **'coverer** *n*

coverage ('kʌvərɪdʒ) *n* **1** the amount or extent to which something is covered. **2** *Journalism.* the amount and quality of reporting or analysis given to a particular subject or event. **3** the extent of the protection provided by insurance.

cover crop *n* a crop planted between main crops to prevent leaching or soil erosion or to provide green manure.

Coverdale ★ ('kʌvəˌdeɪl) *n* **Miles.** 1488–1568, the first translator of the complete Bible into English (1535).

covered wagon *n US & Canad.* a large horse-drawn wagon with an arched canvas top, used formerly for prairie travel.

cover girl *n* a glamorous girl whose picture appears on the cover of a magazine.

covering letter *n* an accompanying letter sent as an explanation, introduction, or record.

coverlet ('kʌvəlɪt) *n* another word for **bedspread.**

cover note *n Brit.* a certificate issued by an insurance company stating that a policy is operative: used as a temporary measure between the commencement of cover and the issue of the policy.

cover point *n Cricket.* **a** a fielding position in the covers. **b** a fielder in this position.

cover slip *n* a very thin piece of glass placed over a specimen on a glass slide that is to be examined under a microscope.

covert ('kʌvət) *adj* **1** concealed or secret. ◆ *n* **2** a shelter or disguise. **3** a thicket or woodland providing shelter for game. **4** short for **covert cloth. 5** *Ornithol.* Also called: **tectrix.** any of the small feathers on the wings and tail of a bird that surround the bases of the larger feathers. ORIG C14: from OF: covered, from *covrir* to COVER
▸ **'covertly** *adv*

covert cloth *n* a twill-weave cotton or worsted suiting fabric.

coverture ('kʌvətʃə) *n Rare.* shelter, concealment, or disguise. ORIG C13: from OF, from *covert* covered; see COVERT

cover-up *n* **1** concealment or attempted concealment of a mistake, crime, etc. ◆ *vb* **cover up.** (*adv*) **2** (*tr*) to cover completely. **3** (when *intr,* often foll. by *for*) to attempt to conceal (a mistake or crime).

cover version *n* another name for **cover** (sense 26).

covet ('kʌvɪt) *vb* **covets, coveting, coveted.** (*tr*) to wish, long, or crave for (something, esp. the property of another person). ORIG C13: from OF *coveitier,* from *coveitié* eager desire, ult. from L *cupiditās* CUPIDITY
▸ **'covetable** *adj*

covetous ('kʌvɪtəs) *adj* (*usually postpositive* and foll. by *of*) jealously eager for the possession of something (esp. the property of another person).
▸ **'covetously** *adv* ▸ **'covetousness** *n*

covey ('kʌvɪ) *n* **1** a small flock of grouse or partridge. **2** a small group, as of people. ORIG C14: from OF *covee,* from *cover* to sit on, hatch

cow[1] (kaʊ) *n* **1** the mature female of any species of cattle, esp. domesticated cattle. **2** the mature female of various other mammals, such as the elephant, whale, and seal. **3** (not in technical use) any domestic species of cattle. **4** *Inf.* a disagreeable woman. **5** *Austral. & NZ sl.* something objectionable (esp. in **a fair cow**). ORIG OE *cū*

cow[2] (kaʊ) *vb* (*tr*) to frighten or overawe, as with threats. ORIG C17: from ON *kūga* to oppress

coward ('kaʊəd) *n* a person who shrinks from or avoids danger, pain, or difficulty. ORIG C13: from OF *cuard,* from *coue* tail, from L *cauda;* ? suggestive of a frightened animal with its tail between its legs

Coward ★ ('kaʊəd) *n* Sir **Noël** (**Pierce**). 1899–1973, British dramatist and actor, noted for his comedies, which include *Private Lives* (1930) and *Blithe Spirit* (1941).

cowardice ('kaʊədɪs) *n* lack of courage in facing danger, pain, or difficulty.

cowardly ('kaʊədlɪ) *adj* of or characteristic of a coward; lacking courage.
▸ **'cowardliness** *n*

cowbell ('kau,bɛl) *n* a bell hung around a cow's neck so that the cow can be easily located.

cowberry ('kaubərɪ, -brɪ) *n, pl* **cowberries. 1** a creeping evergreen shrub of N temperate and arctic regions, with pink or red flowers and edible slightly acid berries. **2** the berry of this plant.

cowbird ('kau,bɜːd) *n* any of various American orioles, having dark plumage and a short bill.

cowboy ('kau,bɔɪ) *n* **1** Also called: **cowhand.** a hired man who herds and tends cattle, usually on horseback, esp. in the western US. **2** a conventional character of Wild West folklore, films, etc., esp. one involved in fighting Indians. **3** *Inf.* an irresponsible or unscrupulous operator in business, etc.
▸ **'cow,girl** *fem n*

cowcatcher ('kau,kætʃə) *n* a metal frame on the front of a locomotive to clear the track of animals or other obstructions.

cow-cocky *n, pl* **cow-cockies.** *Austral. & NZ.* a one-man dairy farmer.

Cowdrey ★ ('kaudrɪ) *n* (**Michael**) **Colin**, Baron. 1932–2000, English cricketer. He played for Kent and captained England 27 times.

cower ('kauə) *vb* (*intr*) to crouch or cringe, as in fear. ORIG C13: from MLow G *kūren* to lie in wait; rel. to Swedish *kura*

Cowes ★ (kauz) *n* a town in S England, on the Isle of Wight: famous for its annual regatta. Pop.: 16 335 (1991).

cowherd ('kau,hɜːd) *n* a person employed to tend cattle.

cowhide ('kau,haɪd) *n* **1** the hide of a cow. **2** the leather made from such a hide.

cowl (kaul) *n* **1** a hood, esp. a loose one. **2** the hooded habit of a monk. **3** a cover fitted to a chimney to increase ventilation and prevent draughts. **4** the part of a car body that supports the windscreen and the bonnet. ◆ *vb* (*tr*) **5** to cover or provide with a cowl. ORIG OE *cugele,* from LL *cuculla* cowl, from L *cucullus* hood

cowlick ('kau,lɪk) *n* a tuft of hair over the forehead.

cowling ('kaulɪŋ) *n* a streamlined metal covering, esp. around an aircraft engine.

cowman ('kaumən) *n, pl* **cowmen. 1** *Brit.* another name for **cowherd. 2** *US & Canad.* a man who owns cattle; rancher.

co-worker *n* a fellow worker; associate.

cow parsley *n* a common Eurasian umbelliferous hedgerow plant having umbrella-shaped clusters of white flowers.

cowpat ('kau,pæt) *n* a single dropping of cow dung.

cowpea ('kau,piː) *n* **1** a leguminous tropical climbing plant producing pods containing edible pealike seeds. **2** the seed of this plant.

Cowper ★ ('kuːpə, 'kau-) *n* **William.** 1731–1800, British poet, noted for *The Task* (1785) and his hymns.

cowpox ('kau,pɒks) *n* a contagious viral disease of cows characterized by vesicles, esp. on the teats and udder. Inoculation of humans with this virus provides temporary immunity to smallpox.

cowpuncher ('kau,pʌntʃə) *or* **cowpoke** ('kau,pəuk) *n US & Canad.* an informal word for **cowboy.**

cowrie *or* **cowry** ('kaurɪ) *n, pl* **cowries. 1** any marine gastropod mollusc of a mostly tropical family having a glossy brightly marked shell. **2** the shell of any of these molluscs, esp. the money cowrie, used as money in parts of Africa and S Asia. ORIG C17: from Hindi *kaurī,* from Sansk. *kaparda*

cowslip ('kau,slɪp) *n* **1** a primrose native to temperate regions of the Old World, having yellow flowers. **2** *US & Canad.* another name for **marsh marigold.** ORIG OE *cūslyppe;* see COW[1], SLIP[3]

cox (kɒks) *n* **1** a coxswain. ◆ *vb* **2** to act as coxswain of (a boat).
▸ **'coxless** *adj*

coxa ('kɒksə) *n, pl* **coxae** ('kɒksiː). **1** a technical name for the hipbone or hip joint. **2** the basal segment of the leg of an insect. ORIG C18: from L: hip
▸ **'coxal** *adj*

coxalgia (kɒk'sældʒɪə) *n* **1** pain in the hip joint. **2** disease of the hip joint causing pain. ORIG C19: from COXA + -ALGIA
▸ **cox'algic** *adj*

coxcomb ('kɒks,kəum) *n* **1** a variant spelling of **cockscomb. 2** *Obs.* the cap, resembling a cock's comb, worn by a jester.
▸ **'cox,combry** *n*

coxswain ('kɒksən, -,sweɪn) *n* **1** (usually shortened to **cox** in competitive rowing) the helmsman of a lifeboat, racing shell, etc. **2** the senior petty officer on a small naval craft. ◆ Also called: **cockswain.** ORIG C15: from *cock* a ship's boat + SWAIN

coy (kɔɪ) *adj* **1** affectedly demure, esp. in a playful or provocative manner. **2** shy; modest. **3** evasive, esp. in an annoying way. ORIG C14: from OF *coi* reserved, from L *quiētus* QUIET
▸ **'coyly** *adv* ▸ **'coyness** *n*

Coy. *Mil. abbrev. for* company.

coyote ('kɔɪəut, kɔɪ'əutɪ; *esp. US.* 'kaɪəut, kaɪ'əutɪ) *n, pl* **coyotes** *or* **coyote.** a predatory canine mammal of the deserts and prairies of North America. Also called: **prairie wolf.** ORIG C19: from Mexican Sp., from Nahuatl *coyotl*

coypu ('kɔɪpuː) *n, pl* **coypus** *or* **coypu. 1** an aquatic South American rodent, naturalized in Europe. It resembles a small beaver and is bred for its fur. **2** the fur of this animal. ◆ Also called: **nutria.** ORIG C18: from American Sp. *coipú,* from Amerind *kóypu*

coz (kʌz) *n* an archaic word for **cousin.**

cozen ('kʌzᵊn) *vb* to cheat or trick (someone). ORIG C16: cant term ? rel. to COUSIN
▸ **'cozenage** *n*

cozy ('kəuzɪ) *adj, n* the usual US spelling of **cosy.**

CP *abbrev. for:* **1** Canadian Pacific. **2** Common Prayer. **3** Communist Party.

cp. *abbrev. for* compare.

CPAG *abbrev. for* Child Poverty Action Group.

cpd *abbrev. for* compound.

cpi *abbrev. for* characters per inch.

Cpl *abbrev. for* Corporal.

CPO *abbrev. for* Chief Petty Officer.

CPR *abbrev. for* cardiopulmonary resuscitation.

cps *abbrev. for:* **1** *Physics.* cycles per second. **2** *Computing.* characters per second.

CPS (in England and Wales) *abbrev. for* Crown Prosecution Service.

CPSA *abbrev. for* Civil and Public Services Association.

CPVE (in Britain) *abbrev. for* Certificate of Pre-vocational Education: a certificate awarded for completion of a broad-based course of study offered as a less advanced alternative to traditional school-leaving qualifications.

CQ a symbol transmitted by an amateur radio operator requesting communication with any other amateur radio operator.

Cr 1 *abbrev. for* Councillor. **2** *the chemical symbol for* chromium.

cr. *abbrev. for:* **1** credit. **2** creditor.

crab[1] (kræb) *n* **1** any chiefly marine decapod crustacean having a broad flattened carapace covering the cephalothorax, beneath which is folded the abdomen. The first pair of limbs are pincers. **2** any of various similar or related arthropods. **3** short for **crab louse. 4** a mechanical lifting device, esp. the travelling hoist of a gantry crane. **5 catch a crab.** *Rowing.* to make a stroke in which the oar either misses the water or digs too deeply, causing the rower to fall backwards. ◆ *vb* **crabs, crabbing, crabbed. 6** (*intr*) to hunt or catch crabs. ORIG OE *crabba*

crab[2] (kræb) *Inf.* ◆ *vb* **crabs, crabbing, crabbed. 1** (*intr*) to find fault; grumble. ◆ *n* **2** an irritable person. ORIG C16: prob. back formation from CRABBED

crab[3] (kræb) *n* short for **crab apple.** ORIG C15: ? of Scand. origin; cf. Swedish *skrabbe* crab apple

Crab (kræb) *n* **the.** the constellation Cancer, the fourth sign of the zodiac.

crab apple *n* **1** any of several rosaceous trees that have white, pink, or red flowers and small sour apple-like fruits. **2** the fruit of any of these trees, used to make jam.

Crabbe ★ (kræb) *n* **George.** 1754–1832, British poet, noted for *The Village* (1783) and *The Borough* (1810).

crabbed ('kræbɪd) *adj* **1** surly; irritable; perverse. **2** (esp. of handwriting) cramped and hard to decipher. **3** *Rare.* abstruse. ORIG C13: prob. from CRAB[1] (from its wayward gait), infl. by CRAB (APPLE) (from its tartness)
▸ **'crabbedly** *adv* ▸ **'crabbedness** *n*

crabby ('kræbɪ) *adj* **crabbier, crabbiest.** bad-tempered.

crab louse *n* a parasitic louse that infests the pubic region in man.

crabwise ('kræb,waɪz) *adj, adv* (of motion) sideways; like a crab.

crack (kræk) *vb* **1** to break or cause to break without complete separation of the parts. **2** to break or cause to break with a sudden sharp sound; snap. **3** to make or cause to make a sudden sharp sound: *to crack a whip.* **4** to cause (the voice) to change tone or become harsh or (of the voice) to change tone, esp. to a higher register; break. **5** *Inf.* to fail or cause to fail. **6** to yield or cause to yield. **7** (*tr*) to hit with a forceful or resounding blow. **8** (*tr*) to break into or force open: *to crack a safe.* **9** (*tr*) to solve or decipher (a code, problem, etc.). **10** (*tr*) *Inf.* to tell (a joke, etc.). **11** (*tr*) to break (a molecule) into smaller molecules or radicals by the action of heat, as in the distillation of petroleum. **12** (*tr*) to open (a bottle) for drinking. **13** (*intr*) *Scot. & N English dialect.* to chat; gossip. **14** (*tr*) *Inf.* to achieve (esp. in **crack it**). **15 crack a smile.** *Inf.* to break into a smile. **16 crack hardy** *or* **hearty.** *Austral. & NZ inf.* to disguise one's discomfort, etc.; put on a bold front. ◆ *n* **17** a sudden sharp noise. **18** a break or fracture without complete separation of the two parts. **19** a narrow opening or fissure. **20** *Inf.* a resounding blow. **21** a physical or mental defect; flaw. **22** a moment or specific instant: *the crack of day.* **23** a broken or cracked tone of voice, as a boy's during puberty. **24** (often foll. by *at*) *Inf.* an attempt; opportunity to try. **25** *Sl.* a gibe; wisecrack; joke. **26** *Sl.* a person that excels. **27** *Scot. & N English dialect.* a talk; chat. **28** *Sl.* a concentrated highly addictive form of cocaine made into pellets or powder and smoked. **29** Also: **craic.** *Inf., chiefly Irish.* fun; informal entertainment: *the crack was great in here last night.* **30 a fair crack of the whip.** *Inf.* a fair chance or opportunity. **31 crack of doom.** doomsday; the end of the world; the Day of Judgment. ◆ *adj* **32** (*prenominal*) *Sl.* first-class; excellent: *a crack shot.* ◆ See also **crack down, crack up.** ORIG OE *cracian*

crackbrained ('kræk,breɪnd) *adj* insane, idiotic, or crazy.

crack down *vb* (*intr, adv;* often foll. by *on*) **1** to take severe measures (against); become stricter (with). ◆ *n* **crackdown. 2** severe or repressive measures.

cracked (krækt) *adj* **1** damaged by cracking. **2** *Inf.* crazy.

cracked wheat *n* whole wheat cracked between rollers so that it will cook more quickly.

cracker ('krækə) *n* **1** a decorated cardboard tube that emits a bang when pulled apart, releasing a toy, a joke, or a paper hat. **2** short for **firecracker. 3** a thin crisp biscuit, usually unsweetened. **4** a person or thing that cracks. **5** *Brit., Austral., & NZ sl.* a thing or person of notable qualities or abilities. **6** See **catalytic cracker.**

crackerjack ('krækə,dʒæk) *Inf.* ◆ *adj* **1** excellent. ◆ *n* **2** a person or thing of exceptional quality or ability. ORIG C20: changed from CRACK (first-class) + JACK (man)

crackers ('krækəz) *adj* (*postpositive*) *Brit.* a slang word for **insane.**

crackhead ('kræk,hɛd) *n Sl.* a person addicted to the drug crack.

cracking ('krækɪŋ) *adj* **1** (*prenominal*) *Inf.* fast; vigorous (esp. in **a cracking pace**). **2 get cracking.** *Inf.* to start doing something quickly or with increased speed. ◆ *adv, adj* **3** *Brit. inf.* first-class; excellent. ◆ *n* **4** the process in which molecules are cracked, esp. the oil-refining process in which heavy oils are broken down into hydrocarbons of lower molecular weight by heat or catalysis.

crackjaw ('kræk,dʒɔː) *Inf.* ◆ *adj* **1** difficult to pronounce. ◆ *n* **2** a word or phrase that is difficult to pronounce.

crackle ('kræk[ə]l) *vb* **crackles, crackling, crackled. 1** to make or cause to make a series of slight sharp noises, as of paper being crushed. **2** (*tr*) to decorate (porcelain or pottery) by causing fine cracks to appear in the glaze. **3** (*intr*) to abound in vivacity or energy. ◆ *n* **4** the act or sound of crackling. **5** intentional crazing in the glaze of porcelain or pottery. **6** Also called: **crackleware.** porcelain or pottery so decorated.
▸ **'crackly** *adj*

crackling ('kræklɪŋ) *n* the crisp browned skin of roast pork.

crackpot ('kræk,pɒt) *Inf.* ◆ *n* **1** an eccentric person; crank. ◆ *adj* **2** eccentric; crazy.

crack up *vb* (*adv*) **1** (*intr*) to break into pieces. **2** (*intr*) *Inf.* to undergo a physical or mental breakdown. **3** (*tr*) *Inf.* to present or report, esp. in glowing terms: *it's not all it's cracked up to be.* **4** *Inf., chiefly US & Canad.* to laugh or cause to laugh uncontrollably. ◆ *n* **crackup. 5** *Inf.* a physical or mental breakdown.

Cracow ★ ('krækaʊ, -əʊ, -ɒf) *n* an industrial city in S Poland, on the River Vistula: former capital of the country (1320–1609); university (1364). Pop.: 746 000 (1995 est.). Polish name: **Kraków.** German name: **Krakau.**

-cracy *n combining form.* indicating a type of government or rule: *plutocracy; mobocracy.* See also **-crat.** ORIG from Gk *-kratia,* from *kratos* power

cradle ('kreɪd[ə]l) *n* **1** a baby's bed, often with rockers. **2** a place where something originates. **3** a frame, rest, or trolley made to support a piece of equipment, aircraft, ship, etc. **4** a platform or trolley in which workmen are suspended on the side of a building or ship. **5** *Agriculture.* **5a** a framework of several wooden fingers attached to a scythe to gather the grain into bunches as it is cut. **5b** a scythe with such a cradle. **6** Also called: **rocker.** a boxlike apparatus for washing rocks, sand, etc., containing gold or gemstones. **7 rob the cradle.** *Inf.* to take for a lover, husband, or wife a person much younger than oneself. ◆ *vb* **cradles, cradling, cradled.** (*tr*) **8** to rock or place in or as if in a cradle; hold tenderly. **9** to nurture in or bring up from infancy. **10** to wash (soil bearing gold, etc.) in a cradle. ORIG OE *cradol*

cradle snatcher *n Inf.* another name for **baby snatcher** (sense 2).

cradlesong ('kreɪd[ə]l,sɒŋ) *n* a lullaby.

craft (krɑːft) *n* **1** skill or ability. **2** skill in deception and trickery. **3** an occupation or trade requiring special skill, esp. manual dexterity. **4a** the members of such a trade, regarded collectively. **4b** (*as modifier*): *a craft union.* **5** a single vessel, aircraft, or spacecraft. **6** (*functioning as pl*) ships, boats, aircraft, or spacecraft collectively. ◆ *vb* **7** (*tr*) to make or fashion with skill, esp. by hand. ORIG OE *cræft* skill, strength

craftsman ('krɑːftsmən) *n, pl* **craftsmen. 1** a member of a skilled trade; someone who practises a craft; artisan. **2** an artist skilled in an art or craft.
▸ **'craftsman,ship** *n*

crafty ('krɑːftɪ) *adj* **craftier, craftiest. 1** skilled in deception; shrewd; cunning. **2** *Arch.* skilful.
▸ **'craftily** *adv* ▸ **'craftiness** *n*

crag (kræg) *n* a steep rugged rock or peak. ORIG C13: of Celtic origin

craggy ('krægɪ) *or US* **cragged** ('krægɪd) *adj* **craggier, craggiest. 1** having many crags. **2** (of the face) rugged; rocklike.
▸ **'cragginess** *n*

craic (kræk) *n* an Irish spelling of **crack** (sense 29).

Craig ★ (kreɪg) *n* **Edward Gordon.** 1872–1966, English theatrical designer, actor, and director. His nonrealistic scenic design greatly influenced theatre in Europe and the US.

Craigavon ★ (kreɪg'eɪvən) *n* a district of S central Northern Ireland, bordering the S shore of Lough Neagh: light industries, agriculture, fruit growing. Administrative centre: Portadown. Pop.: 77 359 (1994). Area: 388 sq. km (150 sq. miles).

Craigie ★ ('kreɪgɪ) *n* Sir **William A(lexander).** 1867–1957, Scottish lexicographer; joint editor of the *Oxford English Dictionary* (1901–33).

crake (kreɪk) *n Zool.* any of several rails of the Old World, such as the corncrake. ORIG C14: from ON *krāka* crow or *krākr* raven, imit.

cram (kræm) *vb* **crams, cramming, crammed. 1** (*tr*) to force more (people, material, etc.) into (a room, container, etc.) than it can hold; stuff. **2** to eat or cause to eat more than necessary. **3** *Inf.* to study or cause to study (facts, etc.), esp. for an examination, by hastily memorizing. ◆ *n* **4** the act or condition of cramming. **5** a crush. ORIG OE *crammian*

crambo ('kræmbəʊ) *n* a word game in which one team says a rhyme or rhyming line for a word or line given by the other team. ORIG C17: from earlier *crambe*, prob. from L *crambē repetīta* cabbage repeated, hence an old story

crammer ('kræmə) *n* a person or school that prepares pupils for an examination.

cramp[1] (kræmp) *n* **1** a painful involuntary contraction of a muscle, typically caused by overexertion, heat, or chill. **2** temporary partial paralysis of a muscle group: *writer's cramp*. **3** (*usually pl in the US and Canada*) severe abdominal pain. ◆ *vb* **4** (*tr*) to affect with or as if with a cramp. ORIG C14: from OF *crampe*, of Gmc origin

cramp[2] (kræmp) *n* **1** Also called: **cramp iron.** a strip of metal with its ends bent at right angles, used to bind masonry. **2** a device for holding pieces of wood while they are glued; clamp. **3** something that confines or restricts. ◆ *vb* (*tr*) **4** to hold with a cramp. **5** to confine or restrict. **6 cramp (someone's) style.** *Inf.* to prevent (a person) from using his or her abilities or from acting freely and confidently. ORIG C15: from MDu. *crampe* cramp, hook, of Gmc origin

cramped (kræmpt) *adj* **1** closed in; restricted. **2** (esp. of handwriting) small and irregular.

crampon ('kræmpən) *or* **crampoon** (kræm'pu:n) *n* **1** one of a pair of pivoted steel levers used to lift heavy objects; grappling iron. **2** (*often pl*) one of a pair of frames each with 10 or 12 metal spikes, strapped to boots for climbing or walking on ice or snow. ORIG C15: from F, from MDu. *crampe* hook; see CRAMP[2]

cran (kræn) *n* a unit of capacity used for fresh herring, equal to 37.5 gallons. ORIG C18: from ?

Cranach ★ (*German* 'kra:nax) *n* **Lucas** ('lu:kas), known as *the Elder*, real name *Lucas Müller*. 1472–1553, German painter.

cranberry ('krænbərɪ, -brɪ) *n, pl* **cranberries. 1** any of several trailing shrubs that bear sour edible red berries. **2** the berry of this plant. ORIG C17: from Low G *kraanbere*, from *kraan* CRANE + *bere* BERRY

crane (kreɪn) *n* **1** a large long-necked long-legged wading bird inhabiting marshes and plains in most parts of the world. **2** (not in ornithological use) any similar bird, such as a heron. **3** a device for lifting and moving heavy objects, typically consisting of a pivoted boom rotating about a vertical axis with lifting gear suspended from the end of the boom. ◆ *vb* **cranes, craning, craned. 4** (*tr*) to lift or move (an object) by or as if by a crane. **5** to stretch out (esp. the neck), as to see over other people's heads. ORIG OE *cran*

Crane ★ (kreɪn) *n* **1** **(Harold) Hart.** 1899–1932, US poet; author of *The Bridge* (1930). **2** **Stephen.** 1871–1900, US writer, noted for his novel *The Red Badge of Courage* (1895). **3 Walter.** 1845–1915, British painter.

crane fly *n* a dipterous fly having long legs, slender wings, and a narrow body. Also called (Brit.): **daddy-longlegs.**

cranesbill ('kreɪnz,bɪl) *n* any of various plants of the genus *Geranium*, having pink or purple flowers and long slender beaked fruits.

cranial ('kreɪnɪəl) *adj* of or relating to the skull.
▸ **'cranially** *adv*

cranial index *n* the ratio of the greatest length to the greatest width of the cranium, multiplied by 100.

cranial nerve *n* any of the 12 paired nerves that have their origin in the brain.

craniate ('kreɪnɪɪt, -,eɪt) *adj* **1** having a skull or cranium. ◆ *adj, n* **2** another word for **vertebrate.**

cranio- *or before a vowel* **crani-** *combining form.* indicating the cranium or cranial.

craniology (,kreɪnɪ'ɒlədʒɪ) *n* the branch of science concerned with the shape and size of the human skull.
▸ **craniological** (,kreɪnɪə'lɒdʒɪkᵊl) *adj* ▸ **,cranio'logically** *adv* ▸ **,crani'ologist** *n*

craniometry (,kreɪnɪ'ɒmɪtrɪ) *n* the study and measurement of skulls.
▸ **craniometric** (,kreɪnɪə'mɛtrɪk) *or* **,cranio'metrical** *adj* ▸ **,cranio'metrically** *adv* ▸ **,crani'ometrist** *n*

craniotomy (,kreɪnɪ'ɒtəmɪ) *n, pl* **craniotomies. 1** surgical incision into the skull. **2** surgical crushing of a fetal skull to extract a dead fetus.

cranium ('kreɪnɪəm) *n, pl* **craniums** *or* **crania** (-nɪə). **1** the skull of a vertebrate. **2** the part of the skull that encloses the brain. ORIG C16: from Med. L *crānium* skull, from Gk *kranion*

crank (kræŋk) *n* **1** a device for communicating or converting motion, consisting of an arm projecting from a shaft, often with a second member attached to it parallel to the shaft. **2** Also called: **crank handle, starting handle.** a handle incorporating a crank, used to start an engine or motor. **3** *Inf.* **3a** an eccentric or odd person. **3b** *US, Canad., Austral., & Irish.* a bad-tempered person. ◆ *vb* (*tr*) **4** to rotate (a shaft) by means of a crank. **5** to start (an engine, motor, etc.) by means of a crank handle. ORIG OE *cranc*

crankcase ('kræŋk,keɪs) *n* the metal housing that encloses the crankshaft, connecting rods, etc., in an internal-combustion engine.

Cranko ★ ('kræŋkəʊ) *n* **John.** 1927–73, British choreographer, born in South Africa.

crankpin ('kræŋk,pɪn) *n* a short cylindrical surface fitted between two arms of a crank parallel to the main shaft of the crankshaft.

crankshaft ('kræŋk,ʃɑ:ft) *n* a shaft having one or more cranks, to which the connecting rods are attached.

crank up *vb* (*adv*) *Sl.* **1** (*tr*) to increase (loudness, output, etc.): *he cranked up his pace*. **2** (*tr*) to set in motion or invigorate: *news editors have to crank up tired reporters*. **3** (*intr*) to inject a narcotic drug.

cranky ('kræŋkɪ) *adj* **crankier, crankiest. 1** *Inf.* eccentric. **2** *Inf.* fussy and bad-tempered. **3** shaky; out of order.
▸ **'crankily** *adv* ▸ **'crankiness** *n*

Cranmer ★ ('krænmə) *n* **Thomas.** 1489–1556, the first Protestant archbishop of Canterbury (1533–56) and principal author of the Book of Common Prayer: burnt as a heretic by Mary I.

crannog ('krænəg) *n* an ancient Celtic lake or bog dwelling. ORIG C19: from Irish Gaelic *crannóg*, from OIrish *crann* tree

cranny ('krænɪ) *n, pl* **crannies.** a narrow opening, as in a wall or rock face; chink; crevice (esp. in **every nook and cranny**). ORIG C15: from OF *cran* notch, fissure; cf. CRENEL
▸ **'crannied** *adj*

Cranwell ★ ('krænwəl) *n* a village in E England, in Lincolnshire: Royal Air Force College (1920).

crap[1] (kræp) *n* **1** a losing throw in the game of craps. **2** another name for **craps.** ORIG C20: back formation from CRAPS

crap[2] (kræp) *Sl.* ◆ *n* **1** nonsense. **2** rubbish. **3** a taboo word for **faeces.** ◆ *vb* **craps, crapping, crapped. 4** (*intr*) a taboo word for **defecate.** ORIG C15 *crappe* chaff, from MDu., prob. from *crappen* to break off

crape (kreɪp) *n* **1** a variant spelling of **crepe. 2** crepe, esp. when used for mourning clothes. **3** a band of black crepe worn in mourning.

crap out *vb* (*intr, adv*) *Sl.* **1** *US.* to make a losing throw in craps. **2** *US.* to fail; withdraw. **3** to fail to attempt something through fear.

craps (kræps) *n* (*usually functioning as sing*) **1** a gambling game using two dice. **2 shoot craps.** to play this game.

★ people and places

ORIG C19: prob. from *crabs* lowest throw at dice, pl of CRAB[1]
▸ **'crap,shooter** *n*

crapulent ('kræpjʊlənt) *or* **crapulous** ('kræpjʊləs) *adj* **1** given to or resulting from intemperance. **2** suffering from intemperance; drunken. ORIG C18: from LL *crāpulentus* drunk, from L *crāpula,* from Gk *kraipalē* drunkenness, headache resulting therefrom
▸ **'crapulence** *n*

crash[1] (kræʃ) *vb* **1** to make or cause to make a loud noise as of solid objects smashing or clattering. **2** to fall or cause to fall with force, breaking in pieces with a loud noise. **3** (*intr*) to break or smash in pieces with a loud noise. **4** (*intr*) to collapse or fail suddenly. **5** to cause (an aircraft) to land violently resulting in severe damage or (of an aircraft) to land in this way. **6** to cause (a car, etc.) to collide with another car or other object or (of two or more cars) to be involved in a collision. **7** to move or cause to move violently or noisily. **8** (*intr*) (of a computer system or program) to fail suddenly because of a malfunction. **9** *Brit. inf.* short for **gate-crash.** ◆ *n* **10** an act or instance of breaking and falling to pieces. **11** a sudden loud noise. **12** a collision, as between vehicles. **13** a sudden descent of an aircraft as a result of which it hits land or water. **14** the sudden collapse of a business, stock exchange, etc. **15** (*modifier*) requiring or using intensive effort and all possible resources in order to accomplish something quickly: *a crash course.* ORIG C14: prob. from *crasen* to smash, shatter + *dasshen* to strike violently, DASH[1]; see CRAZE

crash[2] (kræʃ) *n* a coarse cotton or linen cloth. ORIG C19: from Russian *krashenina* coloured linen

Crashaw ★ ('kræʃɔː) *n* **Richard.** 1613–49, English religious poet, noted for the *Steps to the Temple* (1646).

crash barrier *n* a barrier erected along the centre of a motorway, around a racetrack, etc., for safety purposes.

crash dive *n* **1** a sudden steep dive from the surface by a submarine. ◆ *vb* **crash-dive, crash-dives, crash-diving, crash-dived. 2** (*intr*) (usually of an aircraft) to descend steeply and rapidly, before hitting the ground. **3** to perform or cause to perform a crash dive.

crash helmet *n* a padded helmet worn for motorcycling, flying, etc., to protect the head.

crashing ('kræʃɪŋ) *adj* (*prenominal*) *Inf.* (intensifier) (esp. in **a crashing bore**).

crash-land *vb* to land (an aircraft) causing some damage to it or (of an aircraft) to land in this way.
▸ **'crash-,landing** *n*

crash team *n* a medical team with special equipment able to be mobilized quickly to treat cardiac arrest.

crass (kræs) *adj* **1** stupid; gross. **2** *Rare.* thick or coarse. ORIG C16: from L *crassus* thick, dense, gross
▸ **'crassly** *adv* ▸ **'crassness** *or* **'crassi,tude** *n*

Crassus ★ ('kræsəs) *n* **Marcus Licinius** ('mɑːkəs lɪ'sɪnɪəs). ?115–53 B.C., Roman general; member of the first triumvirate with Caesar and Pompey.

-crat *n combining form.* indicating a person who takes part in or is a member of a form of government or class. ORIG from Gk *-kratēs,* from *-kratia* -CRACY
▸ **-cratic** *or* **-cratical** *adj combining form.*

crate (kreɪt) *n* **1** a fairly large container, usually made of wooden slats or wickerwork, used for packing, storing, or transporting goods. **2** *Sl.* an old car, aeroplane, etc. ◆ *vb* **crates, crating, crated. 3** (*tr*) to pack or place in a crate. ORIG C16: from L *crātis* wickerwork, hurdle
▸ **'crater** *n* ▸ **'crateful** *n*

crater ('kreɪtə) *n* **1** the bowl-shaped opening in a volcano or a geyser. **2** a similar depression formed by the impact of a meteorite or exploding bomb. **3** any of the roughly circular or polygonal walled formations on the moon and some planets. **4** a large open bowl with two handles, used for mixing wines, esp. in ancient Greece. ◆ *vb* **5** to make or form craters in (a surface, such as the ground). ORIG C17: from L: mixing bowl, crater, from Gk *kratēr,* from *kerannunai* to mix
▸ **'crater-,like** *adj* ▸ **'craterous** *adj*

cravat (krə'væt) *n* a scarf worn round the neck instead of a tie, esp. by men. ORIG C17: from F *cravate,* from Serbo-Croat *Hrvat* Croat; so called because worn by Croats in the French army during the Thirty Years' War

crave (kreɪv) *vb* **craves, craving, craved. 1** (when *intr,* foll. by *for* or *after*) to desire intensely; long (for). **2** (*tr*) to need greatly or urgently. **3** (*tr*) to beg or plead for. ORIG OE *crafian*
▸ **'craver** *n* ▸ **'craving** *n*

craven ('kreɪvᵊn) *adj* **1** cowardly. ◆ *n* **2** a coward. ORIG C13 *cravant,* prob. from OF *crevant* bursting, from *crever* to burst, die, from L *crepāre* to burst, crack
▸ **'cravenly** *adv* ▸ **'cravenness** *n*

craw (krɔː) *n* **1** a less common word for **crop** (sense 6). **2** the stomach of an animal. **3 stick in one's craw.** *Inf.* to be difficult, or against one's conscience, for one to accept, utter, etc. ORIG C14: rel. to MHG *krage,* MDu. *crāghe* neck, Icelandic *kragi* collar

crawfish ('krɔː,fɪʃ) *n, pl* **crawfish** *or* **crawfishes.** a variant of **crayfish** (esp. sense 2).

Crawford ★ ('krɔːfəd) *n* **Joan,** real name *Lucille le Sueur.* 1908–77, US film actress.

crawl[1] (krɔːl) *vb* (*intr*) **1** to move slowly, either by dragging the body along the ground or on the hands and knees. **2** to proceed very slowly or laboriously. **3** to act in a servile manner; fawn. **4** to be or feel as if overrun by something unpleasant, esp. crawling creatures: *the pile of refuse crawled with insects.* **5** (of insects, worms, snakes, etc.) to move with the body close to the ground. **6** to swim the crawl. ◆ *n* **7** a slow creeping pace or motion. **8** *Swimming.* a stroke in which the feet are kicked like paddles while each arm in turn reaches forward and pulls back through the water. ORIG C14: prob. from ON *krafla* to creep
▸ **'crawlingly** *adv*

crawl[2] (krɔːl) *n* an enclosure in shallow, coastal water for fish, lobsters, etc. ORIG C17: from Du. KRAAL

crawler ('krɔːlə) *n* **1** *Sl.* a servile flatterer. **2** a person or animal that crawls. **3** *US.* an informal name for **earthworm. 4** (*pl*) a baby's overalls; rompers. **5** a computer program that is capable of performing recursive searches on the World Wide Web. Also called: **spider.**

crawler lane *n* a lane on an uphill section of a motorway reserved for slow vehicles.

Crawley ★ ('krɔːlɪ) *n* a town in S England, in NE West Sussex: designated a new town in 1956. Pop.: 88 203 (1991).

crawling ('krɔːlɪŋ) *n* a defect in freshly applied paint or varnish characterized by bare patches and ridging.

crawly ('krɔːlɪ) *adj* **crawlier, crawliest.** *Inf.* feeling or causing a sensation like creatures crawling on one's skin.

Craxi ★ ('kræksɪ) *n* **Bettino** (be'tiːno). 1934–2000, Italian socialist statesman; prime minister (1983–87).

crayfish ('kreɪ,fɪʃ) *or esp. US* **crawfish** *n, pl* **crayfish** *or* **crayfishes. 1** a freshwater decapod crustacean resembling a small lobster. **2** any of various similar crustaceans, esp. the spiny lobster. ORIG C14: *cray,* by folk etymology, from OF *crevice* crab, from OHG *krebiz* + fish

crayon ('kreɪən, -ɒn) *n* **1** a small stick or pencil of charcoal, wax, clay, or chalk mixed with coloured pigment. **2** a drawing made with crayons. ◆ *vb* **3** to draw or colour with crayons. ORIG C17: from F, from *craie,* from L *crēta* chalk
▸ **'crayonist** *n*

craze (kreɪz) *n* **1** a short-lived fashion. **2** a wild or exaggerated enthusiasm. ◆ *vb* **crazes, crazing, crazed. 3** to make or become mad. **4** *Ceramics, metallurgy.* to develop or cause to develop fine cracks. ORIG C14 (in the sense: to break, shatter): prob. from ON

crazy ('kreɪzɪ) *adj* **crazier, craziest. 1** *Inf.* insane. **2** fantastic; strange; ridiculous. **3** (*postpositive;* foll. by *about* or *over*) *Inf.* extremely fond (of).
▸ **'crazily** *adv* ▸ **'craziness** *n*

Crazy Horse ★ *n* Indian name *Ta-Sunko-Witko.* ?1849–77, Sioux Indian chief, remembered for his attempts to resist White settlement in Sioux territory.

crazy paving *n Brit.* a form of paving, as for a path, made of irregular slabs of stone.

creak (kriːk) *vb* **1** to make or cause to make a harsh

squeaking sound. **2** (*intr*) to make such sounds while moving: *the old car creaked along.* ◆ *n* **3** a harsh squeaking sound. ORIG C14: var. of CROAK, imit.
▸ **'creaky** *adj* ▸ **'creakily** *adv* ▸ **'creakiness** *n* ▸ **'creakingly** *adv*

cream (kriːm) *n* **1a** the fatty part of milk, which rises to the top. **1b** (*as modifier*): *cream buns.* **2** anything resembling cream in consistency. **3** the best one or most essential part of something; pick. **4** a soup containing cream or milk: *cream of chicken soup.* **5** any of various foods resembling or containing cream. **6a** a yellowish-white colour. **6b** (*as adj*): *cream wallpaper.* ◆ *vb* (*tr*) **7** to skim or otherwise separate the cream from (milk). **8** to beat (foodstuffs) to a light creamy consistency. **9** to add or apply cream or any creamlike substance to. **10** (sometimes foll. by *off*) to take away the best part of. **11** to prepare or cook (vegetables, chicken, etc.) with cream or milk. ORIG C14: from OF *cresme,* from LL *crāmum* cream, of Celtic origin; infl. by Church L *chrisma* unction, CHRISM
▸ **'cream,like** *adj*

cream cheese *n* a smooth soft white cheese made from soured cream or milk.

cream cracker *n Brit.* a crisp unsweetened biscuit, often eaten with cheese.

creamer ('kriːmə) *n* **1** a vessel or device for separating cream from milk. **2** a powdered substitute for cream, used in coffee. **3** *Now chiefly US & Canad.* a small jug or pitcher for serving cream.

creamery ('kriːmərɪ) *n, pl* **creameries. 1** an establishment where milk and cream are made into butter and cheese. **2** a place where dairy products are sold.

cream of tartar *n* potassium hydrogen tartrate, esp. when used in baking powders.

cream puff *n* a shell of light pastry with a custard or cream filling.

cream soda *n* a soft drink flavoured with vanilla.

cream tea *n* afternoon tea including bread or scones served with clotted cream and jam.

creamy ('kriːmɪ) *adj* **creamier, creamiest. 1** resembling cream in colour, taste, or consistency. **2** containing cream.
▸ **'creaminess** *n*

crease (kriːs) *n* **1** a line or mark produced by folding, pressing, or wrinkling. **2** a wrinkle or furrow, esp. on the face. **3** *Cricket.* any of four lines near each wicket marking positions for the bowler or batsman. See also **bowling crease, popping crease, return crease.** ◆ *vb* **creases, creasing, creased. 4** to make or become wrinkled or furrowed. **5** (*tr*) to graze with a bullet. ORIG C15: from earlier *crēst;* prob. rel. to OF *cresté* wrinkled
▸ **'creaser** *n* ▸ **'creasy** *adj*

create (kriː'eɪt) *vb* **creates, creating, created. 1** (*tr*) to cause to come into existence. **2** (*tr*) to invest with a new honour, office, or title; appoint. **3** (*tr*) to be the cause of. **4** (*tr*) to act (a role) in the first production of a play. **5** (*intr*) *Brit. sl.* to make a fuss or uproar. ORIG C14 *creat* created, from L *creātus,* from *creāre* to produce, make

creatine ('kriːəˌtiːn, -tɪn) *n* an important compound involved in many biochemical reactions and present in many types of living cells. ORIG C19: from Gk *kreas* flesh + -INE[2]

creation (kriː'eɪʃən) *n* **1** the act or process of creating. **2** the fact of being created or produced. **3** something brought into existence or created. **4** the whole universe.

Creation (kriː'eɪʃən) *n Christianity.* **1** (often preceded by *the*) God's act of bringing the universe into being. **2** the universe as thus brought into being by God.

creative (kriː'eɪtɪv) *adj* **1** having the ability to create. **2** characterized by originality of thought; having or showing imagination. **3** designed to or tending to stimulate the imagination. **4** characterized by sophisticated bending of the rules or conventions: *creative accounting.* ◆ *n* **5** a creative person, esp. one who devises advertising campaigns.
▸ **cre'atively** *adv* ▸ **cre'ativeness** *n* ▸ **ˌcrea'tivity** *n*

creator (kriː'eɪtə) *n* a person or thing that creates; originator.
▸ **cre'atorship** *n*

Creator (kriː'eɪtə) *n* (usually preceded by *the*) an epithet of God.

creature ('kriːtʃə) *n* **1** a living being, esp. an animal. **2** something that has been created, whether animate or inanimate. **3** a human being; person: used as a term of scorn, pity, or endearment. **4** a person who is dependent upon another; tool. ORIG C13: from Church L *creātūra,* from L *creāre* to create
▸ **'creatural** *or* **'creaturely** *adj*

crèche (krɛʃ, kreɪʃ) *n* **1** *Chiefly Brit.* **1a** a day nursery for very young children. **1b** a supervised play area provided for young children for short periods. **2** a tableau of Christ's Nativity. ORIG C19: from OF: manger, crib, ult. of Gmc origin

Crécy ★ ('krɛsɪ; *French* kresi) *n* a village in N France: scene of the first decisive battle of the Hundred Years' War when the English defeated the French (1346). Official name: **Crécy-en-Ponthieu** (-ɑ̃pɔ̃tjø). English name: **Cressy.**

cred (krɛd) *n Sl.* short for **credibility** (esp. in **street cred**).

credence ('kriːdᵊns) *n* **1** acceptance or belief, esp. with regard to the evidence of others. **2** something supporting a claim to belief; credential (esp. in **letters of credence**). **3** short for **credence table.** ORIG C14: from Med. L *crēdentia* trust, credit, from L *crēdere* to believe

credence table *n Christianity.* a small table on which the Eucharistic bread and wine are placed.

credential (krɪ'dɛnʃəl) *n* **1** something that entitles a person to confidence, authority, etc. **2** (*pl*) a letter or certificate giving evidence of the bearer's identity or competence. ORIG C16: from Med. L *crēdentia* credit, trust; see CREDENCE

credenza (krɪ'dɛnzə) *n* another name for **credence table.** ORIG It.: see CREDENCE

credibility gap *n* a disparity between claims or statements made and the evident facts of the situation or circumstances to which they relate.

credible ('krɛdɪbᵊl) *adj* **1** capable of being believed. **2** trustworthy or reliable: *the latest claim is the only one to involve a credible witness.* ORIG C14: from L *crēdibilis,* from L *crēdere* to believe
▸ **'credibleness** *or* **ˌcredi'bility** *n* ▸ **'credibly** *adv*

credit ('krɛdɪt) *n* **1** commendation or approval, as for an act or quality. **2** a person or thing serving as a source of good influence, repute, etc. **3** influence or reputation coming from the good opinion of others. **4** belief in the truth, reliability, quality, etc., of someone or something. **5** a sum of money or equivalent purchasing power, available for a person's use. **6a** the positive balance in a person's bank account. **6b** the sum of money that a bank makes available to a client in excess of any deposit. **7a** the practice of permitting a buyer to receive goods or services before payment. **7b** the time permitted for paying for such goods or services. **8** reputation for solvency and probity, inducing confidence among creditors. **9** *Accounting.* **9a** acknowledgment of an income, liability, or capital item by entry on the right-hand side of an account. **9b** the right-hand side of an account. **9c** an entry on this side. **9d** the total of such entries. **9e** (*as modifier*): *credit entries.* **10** *Education.* **10a** a distinction awarded to an examination candidate obtaining good marks. **10b** a section of an examination syllabus satisfactorily completed. **11 on credit.** with payment to be made at a future date. ◆ *vb* **credits, crediting, credited.** (*tr*) **12** (foll. by *with*) to ascribe (to); give credit (for). **13** to accept as true; believe. **14** to do credit to. **15** *Accounting.* **15a** to enter (an item) as a credit in an account. **15b** to acknowledge (a payer) by making such an entry. ◆ See also **credits.** ORIG C16: from OF *crédit,* from It. *credito,* from L *crēditum* loan, from *crēdere* to believe

creditable ('krɛdɪtəbᵊl) *adj* deserving credit, honour, etc.; praiseworthy.
▸ **'creditableness** *or* **ˌcredita'bility** *n* ▸ **'creditably** *adv*

credit account *n Brit.* a credit system by means of

★ people and places

which customers may obtain goods and services before payment.

credit card *n* a card issued by banks, businesses, etc., enabling the holder to obtain goods and services on credit.

creditor (ˈkrɛdɪtə) *n* a person or commercial enterprise to whom money is owed.

credit rating *n* an evaluation of the creditworthiness of an individual or business.

credits (ˈkrɛdɪts) *pl n* a list of those responsible for the production of a film or a television programme.

credit transfer *n* a method of settling a debt by transferring money through a bank or post office, esp. for those who do not have cheque accounts.

creditworthy (ˈkrɛdɪtˌwɜːðɪ) *adj* (of an individual or business) adjudged as meriting credit on the basis of earning power, previous record of debt repayment, etc. ▸ **ˈcreditˌworthiness** *n*

credo (ˈkriːdəʊ, ˈkreɪ-) *n, pl* **credos.** any formal statement of beliefs, principles, or opinions.

Credo (ˈkriːdəʊ, ˈkreɪ-) *n, pl* **Credos. 1** the Apostles' or Nicene Creed. **2** a musical setting of the Creed. ORIG C12: from L, lit.: I believe; first word of the Apostles' and Nicene Creeds

credulity (krɪˈdjuːlɪtɪ) *n* disposition to believe something on little evidence; gullibility.

credulous (ˈkrɛdjʊləs) *adj* **1** tending to believe something on little evidence. **2** arising from or characterized by credulity: *credulous beliefs.* ORIG C16: from L *crēdulus,* from *crēdere* to believe ▸ **ˈcredulously** *adv* ▸ **ˈcredulousness** *n*

Cree (kriː) *n* **1** (*pl* **Cree** *or* **Crees**) a member of a N American Indian people living in Ontario, Saskatchewan, and Manitoba. **2** the language of this people.

creed (kriːd) *n* **1** a concise, formal statement of the essential articles of Christian belief, such as the Apostles' Creed or the Nicene Creed. **2** any statement or system of beliefs or principles. ORIG OE *crēda,* from L *crēdo* I believe ▸ **ˈcreedal** *or* **ˈcredal** *adj*

creek (kriːk) *n* **1** *Chiefly Brit.* a narrow inlet or bay, esp. of the sea. **2** *US, Canad., Austral., & NZ.* a small stream or tributary. **3 up the creek.** *Sl.* in trouble; in a difficult position. ORIG C13: from ON *kriki* nook; rel. to MDu. *krēke* creek, inlet

Creek (kriːk) *n* **1** (*pl* **Creek** *or* **Creeks**) a member of a confederacy of N American Indian tribes formerly living in Georgia and Alabama. **2** any of their languages.

creel (kriːl) *n* **1** a wickerwork basket, esp. one used to hold fish. **2** a wickerwork trap for catching lobsters, etc. ORIG C15: from Scot., from ?

creep (kriːp) *vb* **creeps, creeping, crept.** (*intr*) **1** to crawl with the body near to or touching the ground. **2** to move slowly, quietly, or cautiously. **3** to act in a servile way; fawn; cringe. **4** to move or slip out of place, as from pressure or wear. **5** (of plants) to grow along the ground or over rocks. **6** to develop gradually: *creeping unrest.* **7** to have the sensation of something crawling over the skin. ◆ *n* **8** the act of creeping or a creeping movement. **9** *Sl.* a person considered to be obnoxious or servile. **10** *Geol.* the gradual downward movement of loose rock material, soil, etc., on a slope. ORIG OE *crēopan*

creeper (ˈkriːpə) *n* **1** a person or animal that creeps. **2** a plant, such as the ivy, that grows by creeping. **3** the US and Canad. name for the **tree creeper. 4** a hooked instrument for dragging deep water. **5** *Inf.* a shoe with a soft sole.

creeps (kriːps) *pl n* (preceded by *the*) *Inf.* a feeling of fear, repulsion, disgust, etc.

creepy (ˈkriːpɪ) *adj* **creepiest. 1** *Inf.* having or causing a sensation of repulsion or fear, as of creatures crawling on the skin. **2** creeping; slow-moving. ▸ **ˈcreepily** *adv* ▸ **ˈcreepiness** *n*

creepy-crawly *Brit. inf.* ◆ *n, pl* **creepy-crawlies. 1** a small crawling creature. ◆ *adj* **2** feeling or causing a sensation as of creatures crawling on one's skin.

cremate (krɪˈmeɪt) *vb* **cremates, cremating, cremated.** (*tr*) to burn up (something, esp. a corpse) and reduce to ash. ORIG C19: from L *cremāre* ▸ **creˈmation** *n* ▸ **creˈmator** *n* ▸ **crematory** (ˈkrɛmətərɪ, -trɪ) *adj*

crematorium (ˌkrɛməˈtɔːrɪəm) *n, pl* **crematoriums** *or* **crematoria** (-rɪə). a building in which corpses are cremated. Also called (esp. US): **crematory.**

crème (krɛm, kriːm, kreɪm; *French* krɛm) *n* **1** cream. **2** any of various sweet liqueurs: *crème de moka.* ◆ *adj* **3** (of a liqueur) rich and sweet.

crème de la crème *French.* (krɛm də la krɛm) *n* the very best. ORIG lit.: cream of the cream

crème de menthe (ˈkrɛm də ˈmɛnθ, ˈmɪnt; ˈkriːm, ˈkreɪm) *n* a liqueur flavoured with peppermint. ORIG F, lit.: cream of mint

crème fraîche (ˈkrɛm ˈfrɛʃ) *n* thickened and slightly fermented cream. ORIG F, lit.: fresh cream

Cremona ★ (*Italian* kreˈmoːna) *n* a city in N Italy, in Lombardy on the River Po: noted for the manufacture of fine violins in the 16th–18th centuries. Pop.: 75 160 (1990).

crenate (ˈkriːneɪt) *or* **crenated** *adj* having a scalloped margin, as certain leaves. ORIG C18: from NL *crēnātus,* from Med. L, prob. from LL *crēna* a notch ▸ **ˈcrenately** *adv* ▸ **crenation** (krɪˈneɪʃən) *n*

crenel (ˈkrɛnᵊl) *or* **crenelle** (krɪˈnɛl) *n* any of a set of openings formed in the top of a wall or parapet and having slanting sides, as in a battlement. ORIG C15: from OF, lit.: a little notch, from *cren* notch, from LL *crēna*

crenellate *or US* **crenelate** (ˈkrɛnɪˌleɪt) *vb* **crenellates, crenellating, crenellated** *or US* **crenelates, crenelating, crenelated.** (*tr*) to supply with battlements. ORIG C19: from OF *creneler,* from CRENEL ▸ **ˈcrenelˌlated** *or US* **ˈcrenelˌated** *adj* ▸ **ˌcrenelˈlation** *or US* **ˌcrenelˈation** *n*

creole (ˈkriːəʊl) *n* **1** a language that has its origin in extended contact between two language communities, one of which is European. ◆ *adj* **2** of or relating to creole. **3** (of a sauce or dish) containing or cooked with tomatoes, green peppers, onions, etc. ORIG C17: via F & Sp., prob. from Port. *crioulo* slave born in one's household, prob. from *criar* to bring up, from L *creāre* to CREATE

Creole (ˈkriːəʊl) *n* **1** (*sometimes not cap.*) (in the Caribbean and Latin America) **1a** a native-born person of European ancestry. **1b** a native-born person of mixed European and African ancestry who speaks a creole. **2** (in Louisiana and other Gulf States of the US) a native-born person of French ancestry. **3** the French Creole spoken in Louisiana. ◆ *adj* **4** of or relating to any of these peoples.

Creon ★ (ˈkriːɒn) *n Greek myth.* the successor to Oedipus as king of Thebes; the brother of Jocasta. See also **Antigone.**

creosol (ˈkriːəˌsɒl) *n* a colourless or pale yellow insoluble oily liquid with a smoky odour and a burning taste. ORIG C19: from CREOS(OTE) + -OL[1]

creosote (ˈkrɪəˌsəʊt) *n* **1** a colourless or pale yellow liquid with a burning taste and penetrating odour distilled from wood tar. It is used as an antiseptic. **2** a thick dark liquid mixture prepared from coal tar: used as a preservative for wood. ◆ *vb* **creosotes, creosoting, creosoted. 3** to treat (wood) with creosote. ORIG C19: from Gk *kreas* flesh + *sōtēr* preserver, from *sōzein* to keep safe ▸ **creosotic** (ˌkrɪəˈsɒtɪk) *adj*

crepe *or* **crape** (kreɪp) *n* **1a** a light cotton, silk, or other fabric with a fine ridged or crinkled surface. **1b** (*as modifier*): *a crepe dress.* **2** a black armband originally made of this, worn as a sign of mourning. **3** a very thin pancake, often folded around a filling. **4** short for **crepe paper** or **crepe rubber.** ORIG C19: from F *crêpe,* from L *crispus* curled, uneven, wrinkled

crepe de Chine (kreɪp də ʃiːn) *n* a very thin crepe of silk or a similar light fabric. ORIG C19: from F: Chinese crepe

crepe paper *n* thin crinkled coloured paper, resembling crepe and used for decorations.

creperie (ˈkrɛpərɪ, ˈkreɪp-) *n* an eating establishment that specializes in pancakes.

crepe rubber *n* a type of rubber in the form of colourless or pale yellow crinkled sheets: used for the soles of shoes.

crêpe suzette (kreɪp suːˈzɛt) *n, pl* **crêpes suzettes.** (*sometimes pl*) an orange-flavoured pancake flambéed in a liqueur or brandy.

crepitate (ˈkrɛpɪˌteɪt) *vb* **crepitates, crepitating, crepitated.** (*intr*) to make a rattling or crackling sound. ORIG C17: from L *crepitāre*
▸ **ˈcrepitant** *adj* ▸ **ˌcrepiˈtation** *n*

crepitus (ˈkrɛpɪtəs) *n* **1** a crackling chest sound heard in pneumonia, etc. **2** the grating sound of two ends of a broken bone rubbing together. ◆ Also called: **crepitation.** ORIG C19: from L, from *crepāre* to crack, creak

crept (krɛpt) *vb* the past tense and past participle of **creep.**

crepuscular (krɪˈpʌskjʊlə) *adj* **1** of or like twilight; dim. **2** (of certain creatures) active at twilight or just before dawn. ORIG C17: from L *crepusculum* dusk, from *creper* dark

crepy *or* **crepey** (ˈkreɪpɪ) *adj* **crepier, crepiest.** (esp. of the skin) having a dry wrinkled appearance.

Cres. *abbrev. for* Crescent.

crescendo (krɪˈʃɛndəʊ) *n, pl* **crescendos** *or* **crescendi** (-dɪ). **1** *Music.* **1a** a gradual increase in loudness or the musical direction or symbol indicating this. Abbrev.: **cresc.** Symbol: < **1b** (*as modifier*): *a crescendo passage.* **2** any similar gradual increase in loudness. **3** a peak of noise or intensity: *the cheers reached a crescendo.* ◆ *vb* **crescendos, crescendoing, crescendoed. 4** (*intr*) to increase in loudness or force. ◆ *adv* **5** with a crescendo. ORIG C18: from It., lit.: increasing, from *crescere* to grow, from L

crescent (ˈkrɛsᵊnt, -zᵊnt) *n* **1** the curved shape of the moon in its first or last quarter. **2** any shape or object resembling this. **3** *Chiefly Brit.* a crescent-shaped street. **4** (*often cap.* and preceded by *the*) **4a** the emblem of Islam or Turkey. **4b** Islamic or Turkish power. ◆ *adj* **5** *Arch. or poetic.* increasing or growing. ORIG C14: from L *crescēns* increasing, from *crescere* to grow

cresol (ˈkriːsɒl) *n* an aromatic compound found in coal tar and creosote and used in making synthetic resins and as an antiseptic and disinfectant. Formula: $C_6H_4(CH_3)OH$. Systematic name: **methylphenol.**

cress (krɛs) *n* any of various plants having pungent-tasting leaves often used as a garnish. ORIG OE *cressa*

cresset (ˈkrɛsɪt) *n History.* a metal basket mounted on a pole in which oil or pitch was burned for illumination. ORIG C14: from OF *craisset,* from *craisse* GREASE

Cressida (ˈkrɛsɪdə), **Criseyde,** *or* **Cressid** ★ *n* (in medieval adaptations of the story of Troy) a lady who deserts her Trojan lover Troilus for the Greek Diomedes.

Cressy ★ (ˈkrɛsɪ) *n Rare.* the English name for **Crécy.**

crest (krɛst) *n* **1** a tuft or growth of feathers, fur, or skin along the top of the heads of some birds, reptiles, etc. **2** something resembling or suggesting this. **3** the top, highest point, or highest stage of something. **4** an ornamental piece, such as a plume, on top of a helmet. **5** *Heraldry.* a symbol of a family or office, borne in addition to a coat of arms and used in medieval times to decorate the helmet. ◆ *vb* **6** (*intr*) to come or rise to a high point. **7** (*tr*) to lie at the top of; cap. **8** (*tr*) to reach the top of (a hill, wave, etc.). ORIG C14: from OF *creste,* from L *crista*
▸ **ˈcrested** *adj* ▸ **ˈcrestless** *adj*

crestfallen (ˈkrɛstˌfɔːlən) *adj* dejected or disheartened.
▸ **ˈcrestˌfallenly** *adv*

cretaceous (krɪˈteɪʃəs) *adj* consisting of or resembling chalk. ORIG C17: from L *crētāceus,* from *crēta,* lit.: Cretan earth, that is, chalk

Cretaceous (krɪˈteɪʃəs) *adj* **1** of, denoting, or formed in the last period of the Mesozoic era, during which chalk deposits were formed. ◆ *n* **2 the.** the Cretaceous period or rock system.

Crete ★ (kriːt) *n* a mountainous island in the E Mediterranean, the largest island of Greece: of archaeological importance for the ruins of Minoan civilization. Capital: Canea (Khaniá). Pop.: 540 054 (1991). Area: 8331 sq. km (3216 sq. miles). Modern Greek name: **Kríti.**
▸ **ˈCretan** *adj, n*

cretin (ˈkrɛtɪn) *n* **1** a person afflicted with cretinism. **2** a person considered to be extremely stupid. ORIG C18: from F *crétin,* from Swiss F *crestin,* from L *Chrīstiānus* Christian, alluding to the humanity of such people, despite their handicaps
▸ **ˈcretinous** *adj*

cretinism (ˈkrɛtɪˌnɪzəm) *n* a condition arising from a deficiency of thyroid hormone, present from birth, characterized by dwarfism and mental retardation. See also **myxoedema.**

cretonne (krɛˈtɒn, ˈkrɛtɒn) *n* a heavy cotton or linen fabric with a printed design, used for furnishing. ORIG C19: from F, from *Creton* Norman village where it originated

Creutzfeldt-Jakob disease (ˈkrɔɪtsfɛlt ˈjɑːkɒp) *n* a fatal slow-developing disease that affects the central nervous system, characterized by mental deterioration and loss of coordination of the limbs. It is thought to be caused by an abnormal prion protein in the brain. Abbrev.: **CJD.** ORIG C20: after Hans G. *Creutzfeldt* (1885–1964) and Alfons *Jakob* (1884–1931), German physicians

crevasse (krɪˈvæs) *n* **1** a deep crack or fissure, esp. in the ice of a glacier. **2** *US.* a break in a river embankment. ◆ *vb* **crevasses, crevassing, crevassed. 3** (*tr*) *US.* to make a break or fissure in (a dyke, wall, etc.). ORIG C19: from F: CREVICE

crevice (ˈkrɛvɪs) *n* a narrow fissure or crack; split; cleft. ORIG C14: from OF *crevace,* from *crever* to burst, from L *crepāre* to crack

crew¹ (kruː) *n* (*sometimes functioning as pl*) **1** the men who man a ship, boat, aircraft, etc. **2** *Naut.* a group of people assigned to a particular job or type of work. **3** *Inf.* a gang, company, or crowd. ◆ *vb* **4** to serve on (a ship) as a member of the crew. ORIG C15 *crue* (military) reinforcement, from OF *creue* augmentation, from OF *creistre* to increase, from L *crescere*

crew² (kruː) *vb Arch.* a past tense of **crow².**

crew cut *n* a closely cropped haircut for men. ORIG C20: from the style of haircut worn by the boat crews at Harvard and Yale Universities

Crewe ★ (kruː) *n* a town in NW England, in Cheshire: major railway junction. Pop.: 63 351 (1991).

crewel (ˈkruːɪl) *n* a loosely twisted worsted yarn, used in fancy work and embroidery. ORIG C15: from ?
▸ **ˈcrewelist** *n* ▸ **ˈcrewelˌwork** *n*

crew neck *n* a plain round neckline in sweaters.
▸ **ˈcrew-ˌneck** *or* **ˈcrew-ˌnecked** *adj*

crib (krɪb) *n* **1** a child's bed with slatted wooden sides; cot. **2** a cattle stall or pen. **3** a fodder rack or manger. **4** a small crude cottage or room. **5** *NZ.* a weekend cottage: term is South Island usage only. **6** any small confined space. **7** a representation of the manger in which the infant Jesus was laid at birth. **8** *Inf.* a theft, esp. of another's writing or thoughts. **9** *Inf., chiefly Brit.* a translation of a foreign text or a list of answers used by students, often illicitly, as an aid in lessons, examinations, etc. **10** short for **cribbage. 11** *Cribbage.* the discard pile. **12** Also called: **cribwork.** a framework of heavy timbers used in the construction of foundations, mines, etc. ◆ *vb* **cribs, cribbing, cribbed. 13** (*tr*) to put or enclose in or as if in a crib; furnish with a crib. **14** (*tr*) *Inf.* to steal (another's writings or thoughts). **15** (*intr*) *Inf.* to copy either from a crib or from someone else during a lesson or examination. **16** (*intr*) *Inf.* to grumble. ORIG OE *cribb*
▸ **ˈcribber** *n*

cribbage (ˈkrɪbɪdʒ) *n* a game of cards for two to four, in which players try to win a set number of points before their opponents. ORIG C17: from ?

cribbage board *n* a board, with pegs and holes, used for scoring at cribbage.

crib-biting *n* a harmful habit of horses in which the animal leans on the manger or seizes it with the teeth and swallows a gulp of air.

Crichton ★ (ˈkraɪtᵊn) *n* (**John**) **Michael.** born 1942, US novelist, screenwriter, and film director; his thrillers, many of which have been filmed, include *The Andromeda Strain* (1969), *Jurassic Park* (1990), and *Disclosure* (1994).

crick (krɪk) *Inf.* ◆ *n* **1** a painful muscle spasm or cramp, esp. in the neck or back. ◆ *vb* **2** (*tr*) to cause a crick in. ORIG C15: from ?

Crick ★ (krɪk) *n* **Francis Harry Compton.** born 1916, British molecular biologist: helped to discover the structure of DNA; shared the Nobel prize for physiology or medicine 1962.

cricket[1] ('krɪkɪt) *n* an insect having long antennae and, in the males, the ability to produce a chirping sound by rubbing together the leathery forewings. ORIG C14: from OF *criquet,* from *criquer* to creak, imit.

cricket[2] ('krɪkɪt) *n* **1a** a game played by two teams of eleven players on a field with a wicket at either end of a 22-yard pitch, the object being for one side to score runs by hitting a hard leather-covered ball with a bat while the other side tries to dismiss them by bowling, catching, running them out, etc. **1b** (*as modifier*): *a cricket bat.* **2** **not cricket.** *Inf.* not fair play. ◆ *vb* (*intr*) **3** to play cricket. ORIG C16: from OF *criquet* goalpost, wicket, from ?
▸ **'cricketer** *n*

cricoid ('kraɪkɔɪd) *adj* **1** of or relating to the ring-shaped lowermost cartilage of the larynx. ◆ *n* **2** this cartilage. ORIG C18: from NL *cricoīdes,* from Gk *krikoeidēs* ring-shaped, from *krikos* ring

cri de coeur (kri: də kɜ:) *n, pl* **cris de coeur.** (kri: də kɜ:). a heartfelt or impassioned appeal. ORIG C20: altered from F *cri du coeur*

crier ('kraɪə) *n* **1** a person or animal that cries. **2** (formerly) an official who made public announcements, esp. in a town or court.

crime (kraɪm) *n* **1** an act or omission prohibited and punished by law. **2** unlawful acts in general. **3** an evil act. **4** *Inf.* something to be regretted. ORIG C14: from OF, from L *crīmen* verdict, accusation, crime

Crimea ★ (kraɪ'mɪə) *n* a peninsula and Autonomous Region of S Ukraine, between the Black Sea and the Sea of Azov: an autonomous republic of the Soviet Union (1921–45). Russian name: **Krym.**
▸ **Cri'mean** *adj, n*

crimen injuria ('krɪmɛn ɪn'dʒu:rɪə) *n S. African law.* the crime of injuring the dignity of a person by using racist or foul language, obscene gestures, etc. ORIG L, lit.: crime of insult

criminal ('krɪmɪn°l) *n* **1** a person charged with and convicted of crime. **2** a person who commits crimes for a living. ◆ *adj* **3** of, involving, or guilty of crime. **4** (*prenominal*) of or relating to crime or its punishment. **5** *Inf.* senseless or deplorable. ORIG C15: from LL *crīminālis;* see CRIME, -AL[1]
▸ **'criminally** *adv* ▸ **,crimi'nality** *n*

criminal conversation *n* another term for **adultery.**

criminalize *or* **criminalise** ('krɪmɪnə,laɪz) *vb* **criminalizes, criminalizing, criminalized** *or* **criminalises, criminalising, criminalised.** (*tr*) **1** to make (an action or activity) criminal. **2** to treat (a person) as a criminal.
▸ **,criminali'zation** *or* **,criminali'sation** *n*

criminal law *n* the body of law dealing with offences and offenders.

criminology (,krɪmɪ'nɒlədʒɪ) *n* the scientific study of crime. ORIG C19: from L *crimin-* CRIME, + -LOGY
▸ **criminological** (,krɪmɪnə'lɒdʒɪk°l) *or* **,crimino'logic** *adj*
▸ **,crimino'logically** *adv* ▸ **,crimi'nologist** *n*

crimp (krɪmp) *vb* (*tr*) **1** to fold or press into ridges. **2** to fold and pinch together (something, such as two pieces of metal). **3** to curl or wave (the hair) tightly, esp. with curling tongs. **4** *Inf., chiefly US.* to hinder. ◆ *n* **5** the act or result of folding or pressing together or into ridges. **6** a tight wave or curl in the hair. ORIG OE *crympan;* rel. to *crump* bent; see CRAMP
▸ **'crimper** *n* ▸ **'crimpy** *adj*

Crimplene ('krɪmpli:n) *n Trademark.* a synthetic material similar to Terylene, characterized by its crease-resistance.

crimson ('krɪmzən) *n* **1a** a deep or vivid red colour. **1b** (*as adj*): *a crimson rose.* ◆ *vb* **2** to make or become crimson. **3** (*intr*) to blush. ORIG C14: from OSp. *cremesin,* from Ar. *qirmizi* red of the kermes, from *qirmiz* KERMES
▸ **'crimsonness** *n*

cringe (krɪndʒ) *vb* **cringes, cringing, cringed.** (*intr*) **1** to shrink or flinch, esp. in fear or servility. **2** to behave in a servile or timid way. **3** *Inf.* to experience a sudden feeling of embarrassment or distaste. ◆ *n* **4** the act of cringing. **5** **the cultural cringe.** *Austral.* subservience to overseas cultural standards. ORIG OE *cringan* to yield in battle
▸ **'cringer** *n*

cringle ('krɪŋg°l) *n* an eyelet at the edge of a sail. ORIG C17: from Low G *Kringel* small ring

crinkle ('krɪŋk°l) *vb* **crinkles, crinkling, crinkled. 1** to form or cause to form wrinkles, twists, or folds. **2** to make or cause to make a rustling noise. ◆ *n* **3** a wrinkle, twist, or fold. **4** a rustling noise. ORIG OE *crincan* to bend, give way

crinkly ('krɪŋklɪ) *adj* **1** wrinkled; crinkled. ◆ *n, pl* **crinklies. 2** *Sl.* an old person.

crinoid ('kraɪnɔɪd, 'krɪn-) *n* **1** a primitive echinoderm having delicate feathery arms radiating from a central disc. ◆ *adj* **2** of, relating to, or belonging to the *Crinoidea.* **3** shaped like a lily. ORIG C19: from Gk *krinoeidēs* lily-like
▸ **cri'noidal** *adj*

crinoline ('krɪn°lɪn) *n* **1** a stiff fabric, originally of horsehair and linen used in lining garments. **2** a petticoat stiffened with this, worn to distend skirts, esp. in the mid-19th century. **3** a framework of steel hoops worn for the same purpose. ORIG C19: from F, from It. *crinolino,* from *crino* horsehair, from L *crīnis* hair + *lino* flax, from L *līnum*

Crippen ★ ('krɪp°n) *n* **Hawley Harvey,** known as *Doctor Crippen.* 1862–1910, US doctor living in England: executed for poisoning his wife.

cripple ('krɪp°l) *n* **1** a person who is lame. **2** a person who is or seems disabled or deficient in some way: *a mental cripple.* ◆ *vb* **cripples, crippling, crippled. 3** (*tr*) to make a cripple of; disable. ORIG OE *crypel;* rel. to *crēopan* to creep
▸ **'crippler** *n*

Cripple Creek ★ *n* a village in central Colorado: gold-mining centre since 1891, once the richest in the world.

Cripps ★ (krɪps) *n* Sir (**Richard**) **Stafford.** 1889–1952, British Labour statesman; Chancellor of the Exchequer (1947–50).

Criseyde ★ (krɪ'seɪdə) *n* a variant of **Cressida.**

crisis ('kraɪsɪs) *n, pl* **crises** (-si:z). **1** a crucial stage or turning point, esp. in a sequence of events or a disease. **2** an unstable period, esp. one of extreme trouble or danger. **3** *Pathol.* a sudden change in the course of a disease. ORIG C15: from L: decision, from Gk *krisis,* from *krinein* to decide

crisp (krɪsp) *adj* **1** dry and brittle. **2** fresh and firm. **3** invigorating or bracing: *a crisp breeze.* **4** clear; sharp: *crisp reasoning.* **5** lively or stimulating. **6** clean and orderly. **7** concise and pithy. **8** wrinkled or curly: *crisp hair.* ◆ *vb* **9** to make or become crisp. ◆ *n* **10** *Brit.* a very thin slice of potato fried and eaten cold as a snack. **11** something that is crisp. ORIG OE, from L *crispus* curled, uneven, wrinkled
▸ **'crisply** *adv* ▸ **'crispness** *n*

crispbread ('krɪsp,brɛd) *n* a thin dry biscuit made of wheat or rye.

crisper ('krɪspə) *n* a compartment in a refrigerator for storing salads, vegetables, etc., in order to keep them fresh.

Crispin ★ ('krɪspɪn) *n* **Saint,** 3rd century A.D., legendary Roman Christian martyr, with his brother **Crispinian** (krɪ'spɪnɪən): they are the patron saints of shoemakers. Feast day: Oct. 25.

crispy ('krɪspɪ) *adj* **crispier, crispiest. 1** crisp. **2** having waves or curls.
▸ **'crispiness** *n*

crisscross ('krɪs,krɒs) *vb* **1** to move or cause to move in a crosswise pattern. **2** to mark with or consist of a pattern of crossing lines. ◆ *adj* **3** (esp. of lines) crossing one another in different directions. ◆ *n* **4** a pattern made of crossing lines. ◆ *adv* **5** in a crosswise manner or pattern.

crit. *abbrev. for:* **1** *Med.* critical. **2** criticism.

criterion (kraɪ'tɪərɪən) *n, pl* **criteria** (-rɪə) *or* **criterions.** a standard by which something can be judged or decided.

ORIG C17: from Gk *kritērion,* from *kritēs* judge, from *krinein* to decide

> **USAGE NOTE** *Criteria,* the plural of *criterion,* is occasionally mistakenly used as a singular noun: *this criterion is not valid; these criteria are not valid.*

critic (ˈkrɪtɪk) *n* **1** a person who judges something. **2** a professional judge of art, music, literature, etc. **3** a person who often finds fault and criticizes. ORIG C16: from L *criticus,* from Gk *kritikos* capable of judging, from *kritēs* judge; see CRITERION

critical (ˈkrɪtɪkᵊl) *adj* **1** containing or making severe or negative judgments. **2** containing analytical evaluations. **3** of a critic or criticism. **4** of or forming a crisis; crucial. **5** urgently needed. **6** *Inf.* so seriously injured or ill as to be in danger of dying. **7** *Physics.* of, denoting, or concerned with a state in which the properties of a system undergo an abrupt change. **8 go critical.** (of a nuclear power station or reactor) to reach a state in which a nuclear-fission chain reaction becomes self-sustaining.
▸ **ˌcritiˈcality** *n* ▸ **ˈcritically** *adv* ▸ **ˈcriticalness** *n*

critical mass *n* the minimum mass of fissionable material that can sustain a nuclear chain reaction.

critical path analysis *n* a technique for planning projects with reference to the critical path, which is the sequence of stages requiring the longest time.

critical temperature *n* the temperature of a substance in its critical state. A gas can only be liquefied at temperatures below this.

criticism (ˈkrɪtɪˌsɪzəm) *n* **1** the act or an instance of making an unfavourable or severe judgment, comment, etc. **2** the analysis or evaluation of a work of art, literature, etc. **3** the occupation of a critic. **4** a work that sets out to evaluate or analyse.

criticize *or* **criticise** (ˈkrɪtɪˌsaɪz) *vb* **criticizes, criticizing, criticized** *or* **criticises, criticising, criticised. 1** to judge (something) with disapproval; censure. **2** to evaluate or analyse (something).
▸ **ˈcritiˌcizable** *or* **ˈcritiˌcisable** *adj* ▸ **ˈcritiˌcizer** *or* **ˈcritiˌciser** *n*

critique (krɪˈtiːk) *n* **1** a critical essay or commentary. **2** the act or art of criticizing. ORIG C17: from F, from Gk *kritikē,* from *kritikos* able to discern

croak (krəʊk) *vb* **1** (*intr*) (of frogs, crows, etc.) to make a low, hoarse cry. **2** to utter (something) in this manner. **3** (*intr*) to grumble or be pessimistic. **4** *Sl.* **4a** (*intr*) to die. **4b** (*tr*) to kill. ◆ *n* **5** a low hoarse utterance or sound. ORIG OE *crācettan*
▸ **ˈcroaky** *adj* ▸ **ˈcroakiness** *n*

croaker (ˈkrəʊkə) *n* **1** an animal, bird, etc., that croaks. **2** a grumbling person.

Croat (ˈkrəʊæt) *n* **1a** a native or inhabitant of Croatia. **1b** a speaker of Croatian. ◆ *n, adj* **2** another word for **Croatian.**

Croatia ★ (krəʊˈeɪʃə) *n* a republic in SE Europe: settled by Croats in the 7th century; belonged successively to Hungary, Turkey, Austria, and Yugoslavia (1918–91); independence was gained (1991) following armed conflict with Serbia; involved in the civil war in Bosnia-Herzegovina (1991–95). Official language: Croatian. Religion: Roman Catholic majority. Currency: kuna. Capital: Zagreb. Pop.: 4 677 000 (1999 est.). Area: 55 322 sq. km (21 359 sq. miles). Croatian name: **Hrvatska.**

Croatian (krəʊˈeɪʃən) *adj* **1** of or relating to Croatia, its people, or their language. ◆ *n* **2** the official language of Croatia, a dialect of Serbo-Croat. **3a** a native or inhabitant of Croatia. **3b** a speaker of Croatian.

croc (krɒk) *n* short for **crocodile** (senses 1 and 2).

Croce ★ (*Italian* ˈkroːtʃe) *n* **Benedetto** (beneˈdetto). 1866–1952, Italian philosopher: an opponent of Fascism, he helped re-establish liberalism in postwar Italy.

crochet (ˈkrəʊʃeɪ, -ʃɪ) *vb* **crochets, crocheting** (-ʃeɪɪŋ, -ʃɪɪŋ), **crocheted** (-ʃeɪd, -ʃɪd). **1** to make (a piece of needlework, a garment, etc.) by looping and intertwining thread with a hooked needle (**crochet hook**). ◆ *n* **2** work made by crocheting. ORIG C19: from F *crochet,* dim. of *croc* hook, prob. of Scand. origin
▸ **ˈcrocheter** *n*

crock¹ (krɒk) *n* **1** an earthen pot, jar, etc. **2** a piece of broken earthenware. ORIG OE *crocc* pot

crock² (krɒk) *Sl., chiefly Brit.* ◆ *n* **1** a person or thing that is old or decrepit (esp. in **old crock**). ◆ *vb* **2** to become or cause to become weak or disabled. ORIG C15: orig. Scot.; rel. to Norwegian *krake* unhealthy animal, Du. *kraak* decrepit person or animal

crockery (ˈkrɒkərɪ) *n* china dishes, earthen vessels, etc., collectively.

crocket (ˈkrɒkɪt) *n* a carved ornament in the form of a curled leaf or cusp, used in Gothic architecture. ORIG C17: from Anglo-F *croket* a little hook, from *croc* hook, of Scand. origin

Crockett ★ (ˈkrɒkɪt) *n* **David,** known as *Davy Crockett.* 1786–1836, US frontiersman and soldier.

crocodile (ˈkrɒkəˌdaɪl) *n* **1** a large tropical reptile having a broad head, tapering snout, massive jaws, and a thick outer covering of bony plates. **2a** leather made from the skin of any of these animals. **2b** (*as modifier*): *crocodile shoes.* **3** *Brit. inf.* a line of people, esp. schoolchildren, walking two by two. ORIG C13: via OF, from L *crocodīlus,* from Gk *krokodeilos* lizard, ult. from *krokē* pebble + *drilos* worm; referring to its basking on shingle

crocodile clip *n* a clasp with serrated interlocking edges used for making electrical connections, etc.

Crocodile River ★ *n* **1** a river in N South Africa; a tributary of the Limpopo. **2** a river that rises in NE South Africa and flows southeasterly into Mozambique.

crocodile tears *pl n* an insincere show of grief; false tears. ORIG from the belief that crocodiles wept over their prey to allure further victims

crocodilian (ˌkrɒkəˈdɪlɪən) *n* **1** any large predatory reptile of the order *Crocodilia,* which includes the crocodiles, alligators, and caymans. ◆ *adj* **2** of, relating to, or belonging to the *Crocodilia.* **3** of, relating to, or resembling a crocodile.

crocus (ˈkrəʊkəs) *n, pl* **crocuses.** any plant of the iridaceous genus *Crocus,* having white, yellow, or purple flowers. ORIG C17: from NL, from L *crocus,* from Gk *krokos* saffron

Croesus ★ (ˈkriːsəs) *n* **1** died ?546 B.C., the last king of Lydia (560–546), noted for his great wealth. **2** any very rich man.

croft (krɒft) *n Brit.* a small enclosed plot of land, adjoining a house, worked by the occupier and his family, esp. in Scotland. ORIG OE *croft*
▸ **ˈcrofter** *n* ▸ **ˈcrofting** *adj, n*

croissant (ˈkrwʌsɒŋ) *n* a flaky crescent-shaped bread roll. ORIG F, lit.: crescent

Croix de Guerre *French.* (krwa də gɛr) *n* a French military decoration awarded for gallantry in battle: established 1915. ORIG lit.: cross of war

Cro-Magnon man (ˈkrəʊˈmænjɒn, -ˈmægnɒn) *n* an early type of modern man, *Homo sapiens,* who lived in Europe during late Palaeolithic times. ORIG C19: after the cave (Cro-Magnon), Dordogne, France, where the remains were first found

Cromer ★ (ˈkrəʊmə) *n* **1st Earl of,** title of (Evelyn) **Baring.**

cromlech (ˈkrɒmlɛk) *n* **1** a circle of prehistoric standing stones. **2** (no longer in technical usage) a megalithic chamber tomb or dolmen. ORIG C17: from Welsh, from *crom,* fem. of *crwm* bent, arched + *llech* flat stone

Crompton ★ (ˈkrɒmptən) *n* **1 Richmal,** full name *Richmal Crompton Lamburn.* 1890–1969, British children's author, best known for her *Just William* stories. **2 Samuel.** 1753–1827, British inventor of the spinning mule (1779).

Cromwell ★ (ˈkrɒmwəl, -wɛl) *n* **1 Oliver.** 1599–1658, English general and statesman. A Puritan, he was a leader of the parliamentary army in the Civil War. After the execution of Charles I he quelled the Royalists in Scotland and Ireland, and became Lord Protector of the Commonwealth (1653–58). **2** his son, **Richard.** 1626–1712, Lord Protector of the Commonwealth (1658–59).

3 Thomas, Earl of Essex. ?1485–1540, English statesman. He was secretary to Cardinal Wolsey (1514), and later chief adviser to Henry VIII: executed.
▸ **Cromwellian** (krɒmˈwɛlɪən) *adj, n*

crone (krəʊn) *n* a witchlike old woman. ORIG C14: from OF *carogne* carrion, ult. from L *caro* flesh

Cronenberg ★ (ˈkrəʊnənˌbɜːg) *n* **David.** born 1943, Canadian film director. His films include *Videodrome* (1983) and *Crash* (1996).

Cronin ★ (ˈkrəʊnɪn) *n* **1 A(rchibald) J(oseph).** 1896–1981, British novelist and physician. His works include *Hatter's Castle* (1931), *The Judas Tree* (1961), and *Dr Finlay's Casebook*, a TV series based on his medical experiences. **2 James Watson.** born 1931, US physicist; shared Nobel prize for physics (1980) for his work on parity conservation.

cronk (krɒŋk) *adj Austral. sl.* **1** unfit; unsound. **2** dishonest. ORIG C19: ?from G *krank* ill

Cronus (ˈkrəʊnəs), **Cronos,** *or* **Kronos** ★ (ˈkrəʊnɒs) *n Greek myth.* a Titan, son of Uranus (sky) and Gaea (earth), who ruled the world until his son Zeus dethroned him. Roman counterpart: **Saturn.**

crony (ˈkrəʊnɪ) *n, pl* **cronies.** a friend or companion. ORIG C17: student sl. (Cambridge), from Gk *khronios* of long duration, from *khronos* time

cronyism (ˈkrəʊnɪˌɪzəm) *n* the practice of appointing friends to high-level posts, esp. political posts, regardless of their suitability.

crook (krʊk) *n* **1** a curved or hooked thing. **2** a staff with a hooked end, such as a bishop's crosier or shepherd's staff. **3** a turn or curve; bend. **4** *Inf.* a dishonest person, esp. a swindler or thief. ◆ *vb* **5** to bend or curve or cause to bend or curve. ◆ *adj* **6** *Austral. & NZ sl.* **6a** ill. **6b** of poor quality. **6c** unpleasant; bad. **7 go (off) crook.** *Austral. & NZ sl.* to lose one's temper. **8 go crook at** *or* **on.** *Austral. & NZ sl.* to rebuke or upbraid. ORIG C12: from ON *krokr* hook

crooked (ˈkrʊkɪd) *adj* **1** bent, angled or winding. **2** set at an angle; not straight. **3** deformed or contorted. **4** *Inf.* dishonest or illegal. **5 crooked on.** (*also* krʊkt) *Austral. inf.* hostile or averse to.
▸ ˈ**crookedly** *adv* ▸ ˈ**crookedness** *n*

Crookes ★ (krʊks) *n* Sir **William.** 1832–1919, British chemist: he investigated cathode rays and invented a type of radiometer and the lens named after him.

croon (kruːn) *vb* **1** to sing or speak in a soft low tone. ◆ *n* **2** a soft low singing or humming. ORIG C14: via MDu. *crōnen* to groan
▸ ˈ**crooner** *n*

crop (krɒp) *n* **1** the produce of cultivated plants, esp. cereals, vegetables, and fruit. **2a** the amount of such produce in any particular season. **2b** the yield of some other farm produce: *the lamb crop.* **3** a group of products, thoughts, people, etc., appearing at one time or in one season. **4** the stock of a thonged whip. **5** short for **riding crop. 6** a pouchlike part of the oesophagus of birds, in which food is stored or partially digested before passing on to the gizzard. **7** a short cropped hairstyle. **8** a notch in or a piece cut out of the ear of an animal. **9** the act of cropping. ◆ *vb* **crops, cropping, cropped.** (*mainly tr*) **10** to cut (hair, grass, etc.) very short. **11** to cut and collect (mature produce) from the land or plant on which it has been grown. **12** to clip part of (the ear or ears) of (an animal), esp. as a means of identification. **13** (of herbivorous animals) to graze on (grass or similar vegetation). ◆ See also **crop out, crop up.** ORIG OE *cropp*

crop-dusting *n* the spreading of fungicide, etc., on crops in the form of dust, often from an aircraft.

crop-eared *adj* having the ears or hair cut short.

crop out *vb* (*intr, adv*) (of a formation of rock strata) to appear or be exposed at the surface.

cropper (ˈkrɒpə) *n* **1** a person who cultivates or harvests a crop. **2 come a cropper.** *Inf.* **2a** to fall heavily. **2b** to fail completely.

crop rotation *n* the system of growing a sequence of different crops on the same ground so as to maintain or increase its fertility.

crop up *vb* (*intr, adv*) *Inf.* to occur or appear, esp. unexpectedly.

croquet (ˈkrəʊkeɪ, -kɪ) *n* a game for two to four players who hit a wooden ball through iron hoops with mallets in order to hit a peg. ORIG C19: ?from F dialect, var. of CROCHET (little hook)

croquette (krəʊˈkɛt, krɒ-) *n* a savoury cake of minced meat, fish, etc., fried in breadcrumbs. ORIG C18: from F, from *croquer* to crunch, imit.

Crosby ★ (ˈkrɒzbɪ) *n* **Bing,** real name *Harry Lillis Crosby.* 1904–77, US singer and film actor; noted for the song "White Christmas" from the film *Holiday Inn* (1942).

crosier *or* **crozier** (ˈkrəʊʒə) *n* a staff surmounted by a crook or cross, carried by bishops as a symbol of pastoral office. ORIG C14: from OF *crossier* staff bearer, from *crosse* pastoral staff

cross (krɒs) *n* **1** a structure or symbol consisting of two intersecting lines or pieces at right angles to one another. **2** a wooden structure used as a means of execution, consisting of an upright post with a transverse piece to which people were nailed or tied. **3** a representation of the Cross used as an emblem of Christianity or as a reminder of Christ's death. **4** any mark or shape consisting of two intersecting lines, esp. such a symbol (×) used as a signature, error mark, etc. **5** a sign representing the Cross made either by tracing a figure in the air or by touching the forehead, breast, and either shoulder in turn. **6** any variation of the Christian symbol, such as a Maltese or Greek cross. **7** a cruciform emblem awarded to indicate membership of an order or as a decoration for distinguished service. **8** (*sometimes cap.*) Christianity or Christendom, esp. as contrasted with non-Christian religions. **9** the place in a town or village where a cross has been set up. **10** *Biol.* **10a** the process of crossing; hybridization. **10b** an individual produced as a result of this process. **11** a mixture of two qualities or types. **12** an opposition, hindrance, or misfortune; affliction (esp. in **bear one's cross**). **13** *Boxing.* a straight punch delivered from the side, esp. with the right hand. **14** *Football.* the act or an instance of passing the ball from a wing to the middle of the field. ◆ *vb* **15** (sometimes foll. by *over*) to move or go across (something); traverse or intersect. **16a** to meet and pass. **16b** (of each of two letters in the post) to be dispatched before receipt of the other. **17** (*tr;* usually foll. by *out, off,* or *through*) to cancel with a cross or with lines; delete. **18** (*tr*) to place or put in a form resembling a cross: *to cross one's legs.* **19** (*tr*) to mark with a cross or crosses. **20** (*tr*) *Brit.* to draw two parallel lines across the face of (a cheque) and so make it payable only into a bank account. **21** (*tr*) **21a** to trace the form of the Cross upon (someone or something) in token of blessing. **21b** to make the sign of the Cross upon (oneself). **22** (*intr*) (of telephone lines) to interfere with each other so that several callers are connected together at one time. **23** to cause fertilization between (plants or animals of different breeds, races, varieties, etc.). **24** (*tr*) to oppose the wishes or plans of; thwart. **25** *Football.* to pass (the ball) from a wing to the middle of the field. **26 cross one's fingers.** to fold one finger across another in the hope of bringing good luck. **27 cross one's heart.** to promise or pledge, esp. by making the sign of a cross over one's heart. **28 cross one's mind.** to occur to one briefly or suddenly. **29 cross the path (of).** to meet or thwart (someone). **30 cross swords.** to argue or fight. ◆ *adj* **31** angry; ill-humoured; vexed. **32** lying or placed across; transverse: *a cross timber.* **33** involving interchange; reciprocal. **34** contrary or unfavourable. **35** another word for **crossbred.** ORIG OE *cros,* from OIrish *cross* (unattested), from L *crux;* see CRUX
▸ ˈ**crossly** *adv* ▸ ˈ**crossness** *n*

Cross[1] (krɒs) *n* **the. 1** the cross on which Jesus Christ was crucified. **2** the Crucifixion of Jesus.

Cross[2] ★ (krɒs) *n* **Richard Assheton,** 1st Viscount. 1823–1914, British Conservative statesman, home secretary (1874–80).

cross- *combining form.* **1** indicating action from one individual, group, etc., to another: *cross-cultural; cross-fertilize; cross-refer.* **2** indicating movement, position, etc., across something: *crosscurrent; crosstalk.* **3** indicating a crosslike figure or intersection: *crossbones.* ORIG from CROSS (in various senses)

crossbar ('krɒsˌbɑː) *n* **1** a horizontal bar, line, stripe, etc. **2** a horizontal beam across a pair of goalposts. **3** the horizontal bar on a man's bicycle.

crossbeam ('krɒsˌbiːm) *n* a beam that spans from one support to another.

cross-bench *n* (*usually pl*) *Brit.* a seat in Parliament occupied by a neutral or independent member.
▸ **'cross-ˌbencher** *n*

crossbill ('krɒsˌbɪl) *n* any of various widely distributed finches that occur in coniferous woods and have a bill with crossed tips.

crossbones ('krɒsˌbəʊnz) *pl n* See **skull and crossbones.**

crossbow ('krɒsˌbəʊ) *n* a type of medieval bow fixed transversely on a stock grooved to direct a square-headed arrow.
▸ **'crossˌbowman** *n*

crossbred ('krɒsˌbrɛd) *adj* **1** (of plants or animals) produced as a result of crossbreeding. ◆ *n* **2** a crossbred plant or animal.

crossbreed ('krɒsˌbriːd) *vb* **crossbreeds, crossbreeding, crossbred. 1** Also: **interbreed.** to breed (animals or plants) using parents of different races, varieties, breeds, etc. ◆ *n* **2** the offspring produced by such a breeding.

crosscheck (ˌkrɒs'tʃɛk) *vb* **1** to verify (a fact, report, etc.) by considering conflicting opinions or consulting other sources. ◆ *n* **2** the act or an instance of crosschecking.

cross-country *adj, adv* **1** by way of fields, etc., as opposed to roads. **2** across a country. ◆ *n* **3** a long race held over open ground.

crosscurrent ('krɒsˌkʌrənt) *n* **1** a current flowing across another current. **2** a conflicting tendency moving counter to the usual trend.

cross-curricular *adj Brit. education.* denoting or relating to an approach to a topic that includes contributions from several different disciplines and viewpoints.

crosscut ('krɒsˌkʌt) *adj* **1** cut at right angles or obliquely to the major axis. ◆ *n* **2** a transverse cut or course. **3** *Mining.* a tunnel through a vein of ore or from the shaft to a vein. ◆ *vb* **crosscuts, crosscutting, crosscut. 4** to cut across.

crosscut saw *n* a saw for cutting timber across the grain.

crosse (krɒs) *n* a light staff with a triangular frame to which a network is attached, used in playing lacrosse. ORIG F, from OF *croce* CROSIER

cross-examine *vb* **cross-examines, cross-examining, cross-examined.** (*tr*) **1** *Law.* to examine (a witness for the opposing side), as in attempting to discredit his testimony. **2** to examine closely or relentlessly.
▸ **'cross-exˌami'nation** *n* ▸ **ˌcross-ex'aminer** *n*

cross-eye *n* a turning inwards towards the nose of one or both eyes, caused by abnormal alignment.
▸ **'cross-ˌeyed** *adj*

cross-fertilize *vb* **cross-fertilizes, cross-fertilizing, cross-fertilized. 1** to fertilize by fusion of male and female gametes from different individuals of the same species. **2** a non-technical term for **cross-pollinate.**
▸ **'cross-ˌfertili'zation** *n*

crossfire ('krɒsˌfaɪə) *n* **1** *Mil., etc.* converging fire from one or more positions. **2** a lively exchange of ideas, opinions, etc.

cross-grained *adj* **1** (of timber) having the fibres arranged irregularly or across the axis of the piece. **2** perverse, cantankerous, or stubborn.

cross hairs *pl n* two fine mutually perpendicular lines or wires that cross in the focal plane of a theodolite, gunsight, or other optical instrument and are used to define the line of sight. Also called: **cross wires.**

crosshatch ('krɒsˌhætʃ) *vb Drawing.* to shade or hatch with two or more sets of parallel lines that cross one another.

crossing ('krɒsɪŋ) *n* **1** the place where one thing crosses another. **2** a place where a street, railway, etc., may be crossed. **3** the act or an instance of travelling across something, esp. the sea. **4** the act or process of crossbreeding.

crossing over *n Genetics.* the interchange of sections between pairing chromosomes during meiosis that produces variations in inherited characteristics by rearranging genes.

cross-legged ('krɒs'lɛgɪd, -'lɛgd) *adj* standing or sitting with one leg crossed over the other.

Crossman ★ ('krɒsmən) *n* **Richard** (**Howard Stafford**). 1907–74, British Labour politician, noted for his posthumous *Crossman Papers* (1975).

cross-match *vb Immunol.* to test the compatibility of (a donor's and recipient's blood) by checking that the red cells of each do not agglutinate in the other's serum.

crossover ('krɒsˌəʊvə) *n* **1** a place at which a crossing is made. **2** *Railways.* a point of transfer between two main lines. **3** short for **crossover network. 4** *Genetics.* another term for **crossing over. 5** a recording, book, or other product that becomes popular in a genre other than its own. ◆ *adj* **6** (of music, fashion, art, etc.) combining two distinct styles. **7** (of a performer, writer, recording, book, etc.) having become popular in more than one genre.

crossover network *n Electronics.* an arrangement in a loudspeaker system that separates the signal into two or more frequency bands for feeding into different speakers.

crosspatch ('krɒsˌpætʃ) *n Inf.* a bad-tempered person. ORIG C18: from CROSS + obs. *patch* fool

crosspiece ('krɒsˌpiːs) *n* a transverse beam, joist, etc.

cross-ply *adj* (of a motor tyre) having the fabric cords in the outer casing running diagonally to stiffen the sidewalls.

cross-pollinate *vb* **cross-pollinates, cross-pollinating, cross-pollinated.** to transfer pollen from the anthers of one flower to the stigma of another.
▸ **ˌcross-polli'nation** *n*

cross-purpose *n* **1** a contrary aim or purpose. **2 at cross-purposes.** conflicting; opposed; disagreeing.

cross-question *vb* **1** to cross-examine. ◆ *n* **2** a question asked in cross-examination.

cross-refer *vb* to refer from one part of something, esp. a book, to another.

cross-reference *n* **1** a reference within a text to another part of the text. ◆ *vb* **cross-references, cross-referencing, cross-referenced. 2** to cross-refer.

crossroad ('krɒsˌrəʊd) *n US & Canad.* **1** a road that crosses another road. **2** Also called: **crossway.** a road that crosses from one main road to another.

crossroads ('krɒsˌrəʊdz) *n* (*functioning as sing*) **1** the point at which two or more roads cross each other. **2** the point at which an important choice has to be made (esp. in **at the crossroads**).

crossruff ('krɒsˌrʌf) *Bridge, whist.* ◆ *n* **1** the alternate trumping of each other's leads by two partners, or by declarer and dummy. ◆ *vb* **2** (*intr*) to trump alternately in this way.

cross section *n* **1** *Maths.* a plane surface formed by cutting across a solid, esp. perpendicular to its longest axis. **2** a section cut off in this way. **3** the act of cutting anything in this way. **4** a random sample, esp. one regarded as representative.
▸ **ˌcross-'sectional** *adj*

cross-stitch *n* **1** an embroidery stitch made by two stitches forming a cross. **2** embroidery worked with this stitch. ◆ *vb* **3** to embroider (a piece of needlework) with cross-stitch.

crosstalk ('krɒsˌtɔːk) *n* **1** unwanted signals in one channel of a communications system as a result of a transfer of energy from other channels. **2** *Brit.* rapid or witty talk.

cross training *n* training in two or more sports to improve performance, esp. in one's main sport.

crosstree ('krɒsˌtriː) *n Naut.* either of a pair of wooden or metal braces on the head of a mast to support the topmast, etc.

crosswise ('krɒsˌwaɪz) *or* **crossways** ('krɒsˌweɪz) *adj, adv* **1** across; transversely. **2** in the shape of a cross.

crossword puzzle ('krɒsˌwɜːd) *n* a puzzle in which the solver guesses words suggested by numbered clues and writes them into a grid to form a vertical and horizontal pattern.

crotch (krɒtʃ) *n* **1** Also called (Brit.): **crutch. 1a** the angle formed by the legs where they join the human trunk. **1b** the human genital area. **1c** the corresponding part of a pair of trousers, pants, etc. **2** a forked region formed by the junction of two members. **3** a forked pole or stick. ORIG C16: prob. var. of CRUTCH
▸ **crotched** *adj*

crotchet ('krɒtʃɪt) *n* **1** *Music.* Also called (US and Canad.): **quarter note.** a note having the time value of a quarter of a semibreve. **2** a perverse notion. ORIG C14: from OF *crochet,* lit.: little hook, from *croche* hook; see CROCKET

crotchety ('krɒtʃɪtɪ) *adj* **1** *Inf.* irritable; contrary. **2** full of crotchets.
▸ **'crotchetiness** *n*

croton ('krəutᵊn) *n* **1** any shrub or tree of the chiefly tropical genus *Croton,* esp. *C. tiglium,* the seeds of which yield croton oil, formerly used as a purgative. **2** any of various tropical plants of the related genus *Codiaeum.* ORIG C18: from NL, from Gk *krotōn* tick, castor-oil plant (whose berries resemble ticks)

crouch (krautʃ) *vb* (*intr*) **1** to bend low with the limbs pulled up close together, esp. (of an animal) in readiness to pounce. **2** to cringe, as in humility or fear. ◆ *n* **3** the act of stooping or bending. ORIG C14: ?from OF *crochir* to become bent like a hook, from *croche* hook

croup[1] (kruːp) *n* a throat condition, occurring usually in children, characterized by a hoarse cough and laboured breathing, resulting from inflammation of the larynx. ORIG C16 *croup* to cry hoarsely, prob. imit.
▸ **'croupous** *or* **'croupy** *adj*

croup[2] (kruːp) *n* the hindquarters, esp. of a horse. ORIG C13: from OF *croupe;* rel. to G *Kruppe*

croupier ('kruːpɪə) *n* a person who deals cards, collects bets, etc., at a gaming table. ORIG C18: lit.: one who rides behind another, from F *croupe* CROUP[2]

crouton ('kruːtɒn) *n* a small piece of fried or toasted bread, usually served in soup. ORIG F: dim. of *croûte* CRUST

crow[1] (krəu) *n* **1** any large gregarious songbird of the genus *Corvus* of Europe and Asia, such as the raven, rook, and jackdaw. All have a heavy bill, glossy black plumage, and rounded wings. **2** any of various similar birds. **3** *Sl.* an old or ugly woman. **4 as the crow flies.** as directly as possible. **5 eat crow.** *US & Canad. inf.* to be forced to do something humiliating. **6 stone the crows.** (*interj*) *Brit. & Austral. sl.* an expression of surprise, dismay, etc. ORIG OE *crāwa*

crow[2] (krəu) *vb* (*intr*) **1** (p.t. **crowed** *or* **crew**) to utter a shrill squawking sound, as a cock. **2** (often foll. by *over*) to boast one's superiority. **3** (esp. of babies) to utter cries of pleasure. ◆ *n* **4** an act or instance of crowing. ORIG OE *crāwan;* rel. to OHG *krāen,* Du. *kraaien*
▸ **'crowingly** *adv*

crowbar ('krəuˌbɑː) *n* a heavy iron lever with one end forged into a wedge shape.

crowd (kraud) *n* **1** a large number of things or people gathered or considered together. **2** a particular group of people, esp. considered as a set: *the crowd from the office.* **3** (preceded by *the*) the common people; the masses. ◆ *vb* **4** (*intr*) to gather together in large numbers; throng. **5** (*tr*) to press together into a confined space. **6** (*tr*) to fill to excess; fill by pushing into. **7** (*tr*) *Inf.* to urge or harass by urging. ORIG OE *crūdan*
▸ **'crowded** *adj* ▸ **'crowdedness** *n*

crowfoot ('krəuˌfut) *n, pl* **crowfoots.** any of several plants that have yellow or white flowers and divided leaves resembling the foot of a crow.

crown (kraun) *n* **1** an ornamental headdress denoting sovereignty, usually made of gold embedded with precious stones. **2** a wreath or garland for the head, awarded as a sign of victory, success, honour, etc. **3** (*sometimes cap.*) monarchy or kingship. **4** an award, distinction, or title, given as an honour to reward merit, victory, etc. **5** anything resembling or symbolizing a crown. **6a** a coin worth five shillings (25 pence). **6b** a coin worth £5. **6c** any of several continental coins, such as the krona or krone, with a name meaning *crown.* **7** the top or summit of something: *crown of a hill.* **8** the centre part of a road, esp. when it is cambered. **9** the outstanding quality, achievement, state, etc.: *the crown of his achievements.* **10a** the enamel-covered part of a tooth above the gum. **10b artificial crown.** a substitute crown, usually of gold, porcelain, or acrylic resin, fitted over a decayed or broken tooth. **11** the part of an anchor where the arms are joined to the shank. ◆ *vb* (*tr*) **12** to put a crown on the head of, symbolically vesting with royal title, powers, etc. **13** to place a crown, wreath, garland, etc., on the head of. **14** to place something on or over the head or top of. **15** to confer a title, dignity, or reward upon. **16** to form the summit or topmost part of. **17** to cap or put the finishing touch to (a series of events): *to crown it all it rained, too.* **18** *Draughts.* to promote (a draught) to a king by placing another draught on top of it. **19** to attach a crown to (a tooth). **20** *Sl.* to hit over the head. ORIG C12: from OF *corone,* from L *corōna* wreath, crown, from Gk *korōnē* crown, something curved

Crown (kraun) *n* (*sometimes not cap.;* usually preceded by *the*) **1** the sovereignty or realm of a monarch. **2a** the government of a monarchy. **2b** (*as modifier*): *Crown property.*

crown colony *n* a British colony whose administration is controlled by the Crown.

crown court *n English law.* a court of criminal jurisdiction holding sessions in towns throughout England and Wales.

Crown Derby *n* **1** a type of porcelain manufactured at Derby from 1784–1848. **2** *Trademark.* shortened form of Royal Crown Derby.

crown glass *n* **1** another name for **optical crown. 2** an old form of window glass made by blowing a globe and spinning it until it forms a flat disc.

crown green *n* a type of bowling green in which the sides are lower than the middle.

crowning ('kraunɪŋ) *n Obstetrics.* the stage of labour at which the infant's head is passing through the vaginal opening.

crown jewels *pl n* the jewellery, including the regalia, used by a sovereign on a state occasion.

Crown Office *n* (in Britain) an administrative office of the Queen's Bench Division of the High Court, where actions are entered for trial.

crown prince *n* the male heir to a sovereign throne.

crown princess *n* **1** the wife of a crown prince. **2** the female heir to a sovereign throne.

Crown Prosecution Service *n* (in England and Wales) an independent prosecuting body, established in 1986, that decides whether cases brought by the police should go to the courts: headed by the Director of Public Prosecutions. Cf. **procurator fiscal.** Abbrev.: **CPS.**

crown wheel *n* **1** *Horology.* a wheel that has one set of teeth at right angles to another. **2** the larger of two wheels in a bevel gear.

crow's-foot *n, pl* **crow's-feet.** (*often pl*) a wrinkle at the outer corner of the eye.

crow's-nest *n* a lookout platform high up on a ship's mast.

crow step *n* another term for **corbie-step.**

Croydon ★ ('krɔɪdᵊn) *n* a borough in S Greater London (since 1965): formerly important for its airport (1915–59). Pop.: 326 800 (1994 est.). Area: 87 sq. km (33 sq. miles).

crozier ('krəuʒə) *n* a variant spelling of **crosier.**

CRT *abbrev. for:* **1** cathode-ray tube. **2** (in Britain) composite rate tax: a system of paying interest to savers by which a rate of tax for a period is determined in advance and interest is paid net of tax which is deducted at source.

crucial ('kruːʃəl) *adj* **1** involving a final or supremely important decision or event; decisive; critical. **2** *Inf.* very important. **3** *Sl.* very good. ORIG C18: from F, from L *crux* CROSS
▸ **'crucially** *adv*

crucible (ˈkruːsɪbᵊl) *n* **1** a vessel in which substances are heated to high temperatures. **2** the hearth at the bottom of a metallurgical furnace in which the metal collects. **3** a severe trial or test. ORIG C15 *corusible,* from Med. L *crūcibulum* night lamp, crucible, from ?

crucifix (ˈkruːsɪfɪks) *n* a cross or image of a cross with a figure of Christ upon it. ORIG C13: from Church L *crucifixus* the crucified Christ, from *crucifigere* to CRUCIFY

crucifixion (ˌkruːsɪˈfɪkʃən) *n* a method of putting to death by nailing or binding to a cross, normally by the hands and feet.

Crucifixion (ˌkruːsɪˈfɪkʃən) *n* **1** (usually preceded by *the*) the crucifying of Christ. **2** a picture or representation of this.

cruciform (ˈkruːsɪˌfɔːm) *adj* shaped like a cross. ORIG C17: from L *crux* cross + -FORM
▸ **ˈcruciˌformly** *adv*

crucify (ˈkruːsɪˌfaɪ) *vb* **crucifies, crucifying, crucified.** (*tr*) **1** to put to death by crucifixion. **2** *Sl.* to defeat, ridicule, etc., totally. **3** to treat very cruelly; torment. ORIG C13: from OF *crucifier,* from LL *crucifigere* to crucify, to fasten to a cross, from L *crux* cross + *figere* to fasten
▸ **ˈcruciˌfier** *n*

crud (krʌd) *n* **1** *Sl.* a sticky substance, esp. when dirty and encrusted. **2** *Sl.* something or someone that is worthless, disgusting, or contemptible. **3** an undesirable residue, esp. one inside a nuclear reactor. ORIG C14: earlier form of CURD
▸ **ˈcruddy** *adj*

crude (kruːd) *adj* **1** lacking taste, tact, or refinement; vulgar. **2** in a natural or unrefined state. **3** lacking care, knowledge, or skill. **4** (*prenominal*) stark; blunt. ◆ *n* **5** short for **crude oil.** ORIG C14: from L *crūdus* bloody, raw; rel. to L *cruor* blood
▸ **ˈcrudely** *adv* ▸ **ˈcrudity** *or* **ˈcrudeness** *n*

Cruden ★ (ˈkruːdᵊn) *n* **Alexander.** 1701–70, Scottish bookseller and compiler of a biblical concordance (1737).

crude oil *n* unrefined petroleum.

crudités (ˌkruːdɪˈteɪ) *pl n* a selection of raw vegetables, served as an hors d'oeuvre. ORIG C20: from F, pl of *crudité,* lit.: rawness

cruel (ˈkruːəl) *adj* **1** causing or inflicting pain without pity. **2** causing pain or suffering. ◆ *vb* **cruels, cruelling, cruelled** *or US* **cruels, crueling, crueled.** (*tr*) **3 cruel someone's pitch.** *Austral. sl.* to ruin someone's chances. ORIG C13: from OF, from L *crūdēlis,* from *crūdus* raw, bloody
▸ **ˈcruelly** *adv* ▸ **ˈcruelness** *n*

cruelty (ˈkruːəltɪ) *n, pl* **cruelties. 1** deliberate infliction of pain or suffering. **2** the quality or characteristic of being cruel. **3** a cruel action. **4** *Law.* conduct that causes danger to life or limb or a threat to bodily or mental health.

cruelty-free *adj* (of a cosmetic or other product) developed without being tested on animals.

cruet (ˈkruːɪt) *n* **1** a small container for holding pepper, salt, vinegar, oil, etc., at table. **2** a set of such containers, esp. on a stand. ORIG C13: from Anglo-F, dim. of OF *crue* flask, of Gmc origin

Cruft ★ (krʌft) *n* **Charles.** 1852–1938, British dog breeder, who organized the first (1886) of the annual dog shows known as Cruft's.

Cruikshank ★ (ˈkrʊkˌʃæŋk) *n* **George.** 1792–1878, British illustrator and caricaturist.

cruise (kruːz) *vb* **cruises, cruising, cruised. 1** (*intr*) to make a trip by sea for pleasure, usually calling at a number of ports. **2** to sail or travel over (a body of water) for pleasure. **3** (*intr*) to search for enemy vessels in a warship. **4** (*intr*) (of a vehicle, aircraft, or vessel) to travel at a moderate and efficient speed. ◆ *n* **5** an act or instance of cruising, esp. a trip by sea. ORIG C17: from Du. *kruisen* to cross, from *cruis* CROSS

Cruise ★ (kruːz) *n* **Tom,** real name *Thomas Cruise Malpother IV.* born 1962, US film actor. His films include *Top Gun* (1985) and *Eyes Wide Shut* (1997).

cruise control *n* a system in a road vehicle that automatically maintains a selected speed until cancelled.

cruise missile *n* a low-flying subsonic missile that is guided throughout its flight.

cruiser (ˈkruːzə) *n* **1** a high-speed, long-range warship armed with medium-calibre weapons. **2** Also called: **cabin cruiser.** a pleasure boat, esp. one that is power-driven and has a cabin. **3** any person or thing that cruises.

cruiserweight (ˈkruːzəˌweɪt) *n Boxing.* another term (esp. Brit.) for **light heavyweight.**

crumb (krʌm) *n* **1** a small fragment of bread, cake, or other baked foods. **2** a small piece or bit. **3** the soft inner part of bread. **4** *Sl.* a contemptible person. ◆ *vb* **5** (*tr*) to prepare or cover (food) with breadcrumbs. **6** to break into small fragments. ORIG OE *cruma*

crumble (ˈkrʌmbᵊl) *vb* **crumbles, crumbling, crumbled. 1** to break or be broken into crumbs or fragments. **2** (*intr*) to fall apart or away. ◆ *n* **3** *Brit., Austral., & NZ.* a baked pudding consisting of a crumbly mixture of flour, fat, and sugar over stewed fruit: *apple crumble.* ORIG C16: var. of *crimble,* of Gmc origin

crumbly (ˈkrʌmblɪ) *adj* **crumblier, crumbliest. 1** easily crumbled or crumbling. ◆ *n, pl* **crumblies. 2** *Brit. sl.* an older person.
▸ **ˈcrumbliness** *n*

crumby (ˈkrʌmɪ) *adj* **crumbier, crumbiest. 1** full of or littered with crumbs. **2** soft, like the inside of bread. **3** a variant spelling of **crummy.**

crummy (ˈkrʌmɪ) *adj* **crummier, crummiest.** *Sl.* **1** of little value; contemptible. **2** unwell or depressed: *to feel crummy.* ORIG C19: var. spelling of CRUMBY

crumpet (ˈkrʌmpɪt) *n Chiefly Brit.* **1** a light soft yeast cake, eaten toasted and buttered. **2** *Sl.* women collectively. ORIG C17: from ?

crumple (ˈkrʌmpᵊl) *vb* **crumples, crumpling, crumpled. 1** (when *intr,* often foll. by *up*) to collapse or cause to collapse. **2** (when *tr,* often foll. by *up*) to crush or cause to be crushed so as to form wrinkles or creases. ◆ *n* **3** a loose crease or wrinkle. ORIG C16: from obs. *crump* to bend
▸ **ˈcrumply** *adj*

crumple zones *pl n* parts of a motor vehicle, at the front and the rear, that are designed to crumple in a collision, thereby absorbing part of the energy of the impact.

crunch (krʌntʃ) *vb* **1** to bite or chew with a crushing or crackling sound. **2** to make or cause to make a crisp or brittle sound. ◆ *n* **3** the sound or act of crunching. **4 the crunch.** *Inf.* the critical moment or situation. ◆ *adj* **5** *Inf.* critical; decisive: *crunch time.* ORIG C19: changed (through infl. of MUNCH) from earlier *craunch,* imit.
▸ **ˈcrunchy** *adj* ▸ **ˈcrunchily** *adv* ▸ **ˈcrunchiness** *n*

crupper (ˈkrʌpə) *n* **1** a strap from the back of a saddle that passes under a horse's tail. **2** the horse's rump. ORIG C13: from OF *crupiere,* from *crupe* CROUP[2]

crusade (kruːˈseɪd) *n* **1** (*often cap.*) any of the military expeditions undertaken in the 11th, 12th, and 13th centuries by the Christian powers of Europe to recapture the Holy Land from the Muslims. **2** (formerly) any holy war. **3** a vigorous and dedicated action or movement in favour of a cause. ◆ *vb* **crusades, crusading, crusaded.** (*intr*) **4** to campaign vigorously for something. **5** to go on a crusade. ORIG C16: from earlier *croisade,* from OF *crois* cross, from L *crux;* infl. also by Sp. *cruzada,* from *cruzar* to take up the cross
▸ **cruˈsader** *n*

cruse (kruːz) *n* a small earthenware container used, esp. formerly, for liquids. ORIG OE *crūse*

crush (krʌʃ) *vb* (*mainly tr*) **1** to press, mash, or squeeze so as to injure, break, crease, etc. **2** to break or grind into small particles. **3** to put down or subdue, esp. by force. **4** to extract (juice, water, etc.) by pressing. **5** to oppress harshly. **6** to hug or clasp tightly. **7** to defeat or humiliate utterly, as in argument or by a cruel remark. **8** (*intr*) to crowd; throng. **9** (*intr*) to become injured, broken, or distorted by pressure. ◆ *n* **10** a dense crowd, esp. at a social occasion. **11** the act of crushing; pressure. **12** a drink or pulp prepared by or as if by crushing fruit: *orange crush.* **13** *Inf.* **13a** an infatuation: *she had a crush on him.* **13b** the

person with whom one is infatuated. ORIG C14: from OF *croissir,* of Gmc origin
▸ **'crushable** *adj* ▸ **'crusher** *n*

crush barrier *n* a barrier erected to separate sections of large crowds.

Crusoe ★ ('kru:səʊ, -zəʊ) *n* **Robinson.** See **Robinson Crusoe.**

crust (krʌst) *n* **1a** the hard outer part of bread. **1b** a piece of bread consisting mainly of this. **2** the baked shell of a pie, tart, etc. **3** any hard or stiff outer covering or surface: *a crust of ice.* **4** the solid outer shell of the earth. **5** the dry covering of a skin sore or lesion; scab. **6** *Sl.* impertinence. **7** *Brit., Austral., & NZ sl.* a living (esp. in **earn a crust**). ◆ *vb* **8** to cover with or acquire a crust. **9** to form or be formed into a crust. ORIG C14: from L *crūsta* hard surface, rind, shell

crustacean (krʌ'steɪʃən) *n* **1** any arthropod of the mainly aquatic class *Crustacea,* typically having a carapace and including the lobsters, crabs, woodlice, and water fleas. ◆ *adj also* **crustaceous. 2** of, relating to, or belonging to the *Crustacea.* ORIG C19: from NL *crūstāceus* hard-shelled, from L *crūsta* shell

crustal ('krʌstᵊl) *adj* of or relating to the earth's crust.

crusty ('krʌstɪ) *adj* **crustier, crustiest. 1** having or characterized by a crust. **2** having a rude or harsh character or exterior.
▸ **'crustily** *adv* ▸ **'crustiness** *n*

crutch (krʌtʃ) *n* **1** a long staff having a rest for the armpit, for supporting the weight of the body. **2** something that supports, helps, or sustains. **3** *Brit.* another word for **crotch** (sense 1). ◆ *vb* **4** (*tr*) to support or sustain (a person or thing) as with a crutch. **5** *Austral. & NZ.* to clip (wool) from the hindquarters of a sheep. ORIG OE *cryc*

crutchings ('krʌtʃɪŋz) *pl n Austral. & NZ.* wool clipped from a sheep's hindquarters.

crux (krʌks) *n, pl* **cruxes** *or* **cruces** ('kru:si:z). **1** a vital or decisive stage, point, etc. (often in **the crux of the matter**). **2** a baffling problem or difficulty. ORIG C18: from L: cross

Cruyff ★ (krɔɪf; *Dutch* krœjf) *n* **Johan** (jo:'hɑn). born 1947, Dutch footballer: captained the Dutch team in the 1974 World Cup.

cruzado (kru:'zeɪdəʊ) *n, pl* **cruzadoes** *or* **cruzados** (-dəʊz). a former standard monetary unit of Brazil. ORIG C16: lit., marked with a cross, from *cruzar* to bear a cross; see CRUSADE

cruzeiro (kru:'zɛərəʊ) *n, pl* **cruzeiros** (-rəʊz). a former standard monetary unit of Brazil. ORIG Port.: from *cruz* CROSS

cry (kraɪ) *vb* **cries, crying, cried. 1** (*intr*) to utter inarticulate sounds, esp. when weeping; sob. **2** (*intr*) to shed tears; weep. **3** (*intr; usually foll. by out*) to scream or shout in pain, terror, etc. **4** (*tr; often foll. by out*) to utter or shout (words of appeal, exclamation, fear, etc.). **5** (*intr; often foll. by out*) (of animals, birds, etc.) to utter loud characteristic sounds. **6** (*tr*) to hawk or sell by public announcement: *to cry newspapers.* **7** to announce (something) publicly or in the streets. **8** (*intr; foll. by for*) to clamour or beg. **9 cry for the moon.** to desire the unattainable. **10 cry one's eyes** *or* **heart out.** to weep bitterly. ◆ *n, pl* **cries. 11** the act or sound of crying; a shout, scream, or wail. **12** the characteristic utterance of an animal or bird. **13** a fit of weeping. **14** *Hunting.* the baying of a pack of hounds hunting their quarry by scent. **15 a far cry. 15a** a long way. **15b** something very different. **16 in full cry.** (esp. of a pack of hounds) in hot pursuit of a quarry. ◆ See also **cry down, cry off,** etc. ORIG C13: from OF *crier,* from L *quirītāre* to call for help

crybaby ('kraɪˌbeɪbɪ) *n, pl* **crybabies.** a person, esp. a child, given to frequent crying or complaint.

cry down *vb* (*tr, adv*) to belittle; disparage.

crying ('kraɪɪŋ) *adj* (*prenominal*) notorious; lamentable (esp. in **crying shame**).

cryo- *combining form.* cold or freezing: *cryogenics.* ORIG from Gk *kruos* icy cold, frost

cryobiology (ˌkraɪəʊbaɪ'ɒlədʒɪ) *n* the biology of the effects of very low temperatures on organisms.
▸ **ˌcryobi'ologist** *n*

cry off *vb* (*intr*) *Inf.* to withdraw from or cancel (an agreement or arrangement).

cryogen ('kraɪədʒən) *n* a substance used to produce low temperatures; a freezing mixture.

cryogenics (ˌkraɪə'dʒɛnɪks) *n* (*functioning as sing*) the branch of physics concerned with very low temperatures and the phenomena occurring at these temperatures.
▸ **ˌcryo'genic** *adj*

cryolite ('kraɪəˌlaɪt) *n* a white or colourless fluoride of sodium and aluminium: used in the production of aluminium, glass, and enamel. Formula: Na_3AlF_6.

cryonics (kraɪ'ɒnɪks) *n* (*functioning as sing*) the practice of freezing a human corpse in the hope of restoring it to life later.

cryoprecipitate (ˌkraɪəʊprɪ'sɪpɪtɪt) *n* a precipitate obtained by controlled thawing of a previously frozen substance. Factor VIII, for treating haemophilia, is often obtained as a cryoprecipitate from frozen blood.

cryostat ('kraɪəˌstæt) *n* an apparatus for maintaining a constant low temperature.

cryosurgery (ˌkraɪəʊ'sɜ:dʒərɪ) *n* surgery involving quick freezing for therapeutic benefit.

cry out *vb* (*intr, adv*) **1** to scream or shout aloud, esp. in pain, terror, etc. **2** (often foll. by *for*) *Inf.* to demand in an obvious manner.

crypt (krɪpt) *n* a vault or underground chamber, esp. beneath a church, often used as a chapel, burial place, etc. ORIG C18: from L *crypta,* from Gk *kruptē* vault, secret place, ult. from *kruptein* to hide

cryptanalysis (ˌkrɪptə'nælɪsɪs) *n* the study of codes and ciphers; cryptography. ORIG C20: from CRYPTO- + ANALYSIS
▸ **cryptanalytic** (ˌkrɪptænə'lɪtɪk) *adj* ▸ **crypt'analyst** *n*

cryptic ('krɪptɪk) *adj* **1** hidden; secret. **2** esoteric or obscure in meaning. **3** (of coloration) effecting camouflage or concealment. ORIG C17: from LL *crypticus,* from Gk *kruptikos,* from *kruptos* concealed; see CRYPT
▸ **'cryptically** *adv*

crypto- *or before a vowel* **crypt-** *combining form.* secret, hidden, or concealed. ORIG NL, from Gk *kruptos* hidden, from *kruptein* to hide

cryptocrystalline (ˌkrɪptəʊ'krɪstəlaɪn) *adj* (of rocks) composed of crystals visible only under a polarizing microscope.

cryptogam ('krɪptəʊˌgæm) *n* (in former plant classification schemes) any organism that does not produce seeds, including algae, fungi, mosses, and ferns. ORIG C19: from NL *Cryptogamia,* from CRYPTO- + Gk *gamos* marriage
▸ **ˌcrypto'gamic** *or* **cryptogamous** (krɪp'tɒgəməs) *adj*

cryptograph ('krɪptəʊˌgrɑ:f) *n* **1** something written in code or cipher. **2** a code using secret symbols (**cryptograms**).

cryptography (krɪp'tɒgrəfɪ) *n* the science or study of analysing and deciphering codes, ciphers, etc. Also called: **cryptanalysis.**
▸ **cryp'tographer** *or* **cryp'tographist** *n* ▸ **cryptographic** (ˌkrɪptə'græfɪk) *or* **ˌcrypto'graphical** *adj* ▸ **ˌcrypto'graphically** *adv*

crystal ('krɪstᵊl) *n* **1** a solid, such as quartz, with a regular shape in which plane faces intersect at definite angles. **2** a single grain of a crystalline substance. **3** anything resembling a crystal, such as a piece of cut glass. **4a** a highly transparent and brilliant type of glass. **4b** (*as modifier*): *a crystal chandelier.* **5** something made of or resembling crystal. **6** crystal glass articles collectively. **7** *Electronics.* **7a** a crystalline element used in certain electronic devices as a detector, oscillator, etc. **7b** (*as modifier*): *crystal pick-up.* **8** a transparent cover for the face of a watch. **9** (*modifier*) of or relating to a crystal or the regular atomic arrangement of crystals: *crystal structure.* ◆ *adj* **10** resembling crystal; transparent: *crystal water.* ORIG OE *cristalla,* from L *crystallum,* from Gk *krustallos* ice, crystal, from *krustainein* to freeze

crystal ball *n* the glass globe used in crystal gazing.

crystal class *n Crystallography.* any of 32 possible types of crystals, classified according to their rotational symmetry about axes through a point. Also called: **point group.**

crystal detector *n Electronics.* a demodulator, used esp. in early radio receivers, incorporating a semiconductor crystal.

crystal gazing *n* **1** the act of staring into a crystal ball supposedly in order to arouse visual perceptions of the future, etc. **2** the act of trying to foresee or predict.
▸ **crystal gazer** *n*

crystal healing *n* (in alternative therapy) the use of the supposed power of crystals to affect the human energy field.

crystal lattice *n* the regular array of points about which the atoms, ions, or molecules composing a crystal are centred.

crystalline (ˈkrɪstəˌlaɪn) *adj* **1** having the characteristics or structure of crystals. **2** consisting of or containing crystals. **3** made of or like crystal; transparent; clear.

crystalline lens *n* a biconvex transparent elastic lens in the eye.

crystallize *or* **crystallise** (ˈkrɪstəˌlaɪz) *vb* **crystallizes, crystallizing, crystallized** *or* **crystallises, crystallising, crystallised. 1** to form or cause to form crystals; assume or cause to assume a crystalline form or structure. **2** to coat or become coated with sugar. **3** to give a definite form or expression to (an idea, argument, etc.) or (of an idea, argument, etc.) to assume a definite form.
▸ **ˈcrystalˌlizable** *or* **ˈcrystalˌlisable** *adj* ▸ **ˌcrystalliˈzation** *or* **ˌcrystalliˈsation** *n*

crystallo- *or before a vowel* **crystall-** *combining form.* crystal: *crystallography.*

crystallography (ˌkrɪstəˈlɒgrəfɪ) *n* the science of crystal structure.
▸ **ˌcrystalˈlographer** *n* ▸ **crystallographic** (ˌkrɪstələʊˈgræfɪk) *adj*

crystalloid (ˈkrɪstəˌlɔɪd) *adj* **1** resembling or having the properties of a crystal. ◆ *n* **2** a substance that in solution can pass through a semipermeable membrane.

Crystal Palace ★ *n* a building of glass and iron designed by Joseph Paxton to house the Great Exhibition of 1851. Erected in Hyde Park, London, it was moved to Sydenham (1852–53): destroyed by fire in 1936.

crystal set *n* an early form of radio receiver having a crystal detector.

cry up *vb* (*tr, adv*) to praise highly; extol.

Cs *the chemical symbol for* caesium.

CS *abbrev. for:* **1** Also: **cs.** capital stock. **2** chartered surveyor. **3** Christian Science. **4** Civil Service. **5** Also: **cs.** Court of Session.

CSA (in Britain) *abbrev. for* Child Support Agency.

csc *abbrev. for* cosecant.

CSC *abbrev. for* Civil Service Commission.

CSE (in Britain) *abbrev. for* Certificate of Secondary Education; a former examination the first grade pass of which was an equivalent to a GCE O level.

CSEU *abbrev. for* Confederation of Shipbuilding and Engineering Unions.

CSF *abbrev. for:* **1** cerebrospinal fluid. **2** *Immunol.* colony-stimulating factor.

CS gas *n* a gas causing tears, salivation, and painful breathing, used in civil disturbances. ORIG C20: from the surname initials of its US inventors, Ben Carson and Roger Staughton

CSIRO (in Australia) *abbrev. for* Commonwealth Scientific and Industrial Research Organization.

CSM (in Britain) *abbrev. for* Company Sergeant-Major.

C-spanner *n* a sickle-shaped spanner having a projection at the end of the curve, used for turning large narrow nuts that have an indentation into which the projection on the spanner fits.

CST (in the US and Canada) *abbrev. for* Central Standard Time.

CSU *abbrev. for* Civil Service Union.

ct *abbrev. for:* **1** carat. **2** cent. **3** court.

CTC (in Britain) *abbrev. for* city technology college.

ctenophore (ˈtɛnəˌfɔː, ˈtiːnə-) *n* any marine invertebrate of the phylum *Ctenophora,* whose body bears eight rows of fused cilia, for locomotion. ORIG C19: from NL *ctenophorus,* from Gk *kteno-, kteis* comb + -PHORE

ctn *abbrev. for* cotangent.

CT scanner *n* computerized tomography scanner: an X-ray machine that can produce multiple cross-sectional images of the soft tissues (**CT scans**). Former name: **CAT scanner.**

CTT *abbrev. for* Capital Transfer Tax.

CTV *abbrev. for* Canadian Television (Network Limited).

Cu *the chemical symbol for* copper. ORIG from LL *cuprum*

cu. *abbrev. for* cubic.

cub (kʌb) *n* **1** the young of certain animals, such as the lion, bear, etc. **2** a young or inexperienced person. ◆ *vb* **cubs, cubbing, cubbed. 3** to give birth to (cubs). ORIG C16: ?from ON *kubbi* young seal
▸ **ˈcubbish** *adj*

Cub (kʌb) *n* short for **Cub Scout.**

Cuba ★ (ˈkjuːbə) *n* a republic and the largest island in the Caribbean, at the entrance to the Gulf of Mexico: became a Spanish colony after its discovery by Columbus in 1492; gained independence after the Spanish-American War of 1898 but remained subject to US influence until declared a people's republic under Castro in 1960; subject of an international crisis in 1962, when the US blockaded the island in order to compel the Soviet Union to dismantle its nuclear missile base. Sugar comprises about 80 per cent of total exports, but the economy was devastated by loss of trade following the collapse of the Soviet Union. Language: Spanish. Religion: nonreligious majority. Currency: peso. Capital: Havana. Pop.: 11 143 000 (1999 est.). Area: 110 922 sq. km (42 827 sq. miles).
▸ **ˈCuban** *adj, n*

cubby (ˈkʌbɪ) *n, pl* **cubbies.** *Austral.* a small room or enclosed area, esp. one used as a child's play area. Also: **cubbyhole, cubby-house.**

cubbyhole (ˈkʌbɪˌhəʊl) *n* a small enclosed space or room. ORIG C19: from dialect *cub* cattle pen

cube (kjuːb) *n* **1** a solid having six plane square faces in which the angle between two adjacent sides is a right angle. **2** the product of three equal factors. **3** something in the form of a cube. ◆ *vb* **cubes, cubing, cubed. 4** to raise (a number or quantity) to the third power. **5** (*tr*) to make, shape, or cut (something) into cubes. ORIG C16: from L *cubus* die, cube, from Gk *kubos*
▸ **ˈcuber** *n*

cubeb (ˈkjuːbɛb) *n* **1** a SE Asian treelike climbing plant. **2** its spicy fruit, dried and used as a stimulant and diuretic and sometimes smoked in cigarettes. ORIG C14: from OF *cubebe,* from Med. L *cubēba,* from Ar. *kubābah*

cube root *n* the number or quantity whose cube is a given number or quantity: 2 is the cube root of 8 (usually written $\sqrt[3]{8}$ or $8^{1/3}$).

cubic (ˈkjuːbɪk) *adj* **1** having the shape of a cube. **2a** having three dimensions. **2b** denoting or relating to a linear measure that is raised to the third power: *a cubic metre.* **3** *Maths.* of, relating to, or containing a variable to the third power or a term in which the sum of the exponents of the variables is three.
▸ **ˈcubical** *adj*

cubicle (ˈkjuːbɪkᵊl) *n* an enclosed compartment, screened for privacy, as in a dormitory, shower, etc. ORIG C15: from L *cubiculum,* from *cubāre* to lie down

cubic measure *n* a system of units for the measurement of volumes.

cubiform (ˈkjuːbɪˌfɔːm) *adj* having the shape of a cube.

cubism (ˈkjuːbɪzəm) *n* (*often cap.*) a French school of art, initiated in 1907 by Picasso and Braque, which amalgamated viewpoints of natural forms into a multifaceted surface of geometrical planes.
▸ **ˈcubist** *adj, n* ▸ **cuˈbistic** *adj*

cubit (ˈkjuːbɪt) *n* an ancient measure of length based on the length of the forearm. ORIG C14: from L *cubitum* elbow, cubit

cuboid (ˈkjuːbɔɪd) *adj also* **cuboidal** (kjuːˈbɔɪdᵊl). **1** shaped like a cube; cubic. **2** of or denoting the cuboid bone. ◆ *n*

3 the cubelike bone of the foot. 4 *Maths.* a geometric solid whose six faces are rectangles.

Cub Scout *or* **Cub** *n* a member of the junior branch of the Scout Association.

Cuchulain, Cuchulainn, *or* **Cuchullain** ★ (kuːˈkʌlɪn, kʊˈxʊlɪn) *n Celtic myth.* a legendary hero of Ulster.

cucking stool (ˈkʌkɪŋ) *n History.* a stool to which suspected witches, scolds, etc., were tied and pelted or ducked into water. ORIG C13 *cucking stol,* lit.: defecating chair, from *cukken* to defecate

cuckold (ˈkʌkəld) *n* **1** a man whose wife has committed adultery. ◆ *vb* **2** (*tr*) to make a cuckold of. ORIG C13 *cukeweld,* from OF *cucuault,* from *cucu* CUCKOO; ? an allusion to cuckoos that lay eggs in the nests of other birds ▸ **ˈcuckoldry** *n*

cuckoo (ˈkʊkuː) *n, pl* **cuckoos. 1** any bird of the family Cuculidae, having pointed wings and a long tail. Many species, including the **European cuckoo,** lay their eggs in the nests of other birds and have a two-note call. **2** *Inf.* an insane or foolish person. ◆ *adj* **3** *Inf.* insane or foolish. ◆ *interj* **4** an imitation or representation of the call of a cuckoo. ◆ *vb* **cuckoos, cuckooing, cuckooed. 5** (*intr*) to make the sound imitated by the word *cuckoo.* ORIG C13: from OF *cucu,* imit.

cuckoo clock *n* a clock in which a mechanical cuckoo pops out with a sound like a cuckoo's call when the clock strikes.

cuckoopint (ˈkʊkuːˌpaɪnt, -ˌpɪnt) *n* a European plant with arrow-shaped leaves, a spathe marked with purple, a pale purple spadix, and scarlet berries. Also called: **lords-and-ladies.**

cuckoo spit *n* a white frothy mass on the stems and leaves of many plants, produced by froghopper larvae.

cucumber (ˈkjuːˌkʌmbə) *n* **1** a creeping plant cultivated in many forms for its edible fruit. **2** the cylindrical fruit of this plant, which has hard thin green rind and white crisp flesh. ORIG C14: from L *cucumis,* from ?

cucurbit (kjuːˈkɜːbɪt) *n* any of a family of creeping flowering plants that includes the pumpkin, cucumber, and gourds. ORIG C14: from OF, from L *cucurbita* gourd, cup ▸ **cuˌcurbiˈtaceous** *adj*

cud (kʌd) *n* **1** partially digested food regurgitated from the first stomach of ruminants to the mouth for a second chewing. **2 chew the cud.** to reflect or think over something. ORIG OE *cudu,* from *cwidu* what has been chewed

cuddle (ˈkʌdᵊl) *vb* **cuddles, cuddling, cuddled. 1** to hold close or (of two people, etc.) to hold each other close, as for affection or warmth; hug. **2** (*intr;* foll. by *up*) to curl or snuggle up into a comfortable or warm position. ◆ *n* **3** a close embrace, esp. when prolonged. ORIG C18: from ? ▸ **ˈcuddlesome** *adj* ▸ **ˈcuddly** *adj*

cuddy (ˈkʌdɪ) *n, pl* **cuddies.** a small cabin in a boat. ORIG C17: ?from Du. *kajute*

cudgel (ˈkʌdʒəl) *n* **1** a short stout stick used as a weapon. **2 take up the cudgels.** (often foll. by *for* or *on behalf of*) to join in a dispute, esp. to defend oneself or another. ◆ *vb* **cudgels, cudgelling, cudgelled** *or US* **cudgels, cudgeling, cudgeled. 3** (*tr*) to strike with a cudgel. **4 cudgel one's brains.** to think hard. ORIG OE *cycgel*

cudgerie (ˈkʌdʒərɪ) *n Austral.* any of various large rainforest trees, such as the pink poplar or blush cudgerie, with pink wood. ORIG from Abor.

Cudlipp ★ (ˈkʌdlɪp) *n* **Hugh,** Baron. 1913–98, British newspaper editor, a pioneer of tabloid journalism.

cudweed (ˈkʌdˌwiːd) *n* any of various temperate woolly plants having clusters of whitish or yellow button-like flowers.

cue¹ (kjuː) *n* **1a** (in the theatre, films, music, etc.) anything that serves as a signal to an actor, musician, etc., to follow with specific lines or action. **1b on cue.** at the right moment. **2** a signal or reminder to do something. ◆ *vb* **cues, cueing, cued. 3** (*tr*) to give a cue or cues to (an actor). **4** (usually foll. by *in* or *into*) to signal (to something or somebody) at a specific moment in a musical or dramatic performance. ORIG C16: prob. from name of the letter *q,* used in an actor's script to represent L *quando* when

cue² (kjuː) *n* **1** *Billiards, etc.* a long tapered shaft used to drive the balls. **2** hair caught at the back forming a tail or braid. ◆ *vb* **cues, cueing, cued. 3** to drive (a ball) with a cue. ORIG C18: var. of QUEUE

cue ball *n Billiards, etc.* the ball struck by the cue, as distinguished from the object balls.

Cuernavaca ★ (*Spanish* kwɛrnaˈβaka) *n* a city in S central Mexico, capital of Morelos state: resort with nearby Cacahuamilpa Caverns. Pop.: 279 187 (1990).

cuesta (ˈkwɛstə) *n* a long low ridge with a steep scarp slope and a gentle back slope. ORIG Sp.: shoulder, from L *costa* side, rib

cuff¹ (kʌf) *n* **1** the end of a sleeve, sometimes turned back. **2** the part of a glove that extends past the wrist. **3** the US, Canad., and Austral. name for **turn-up** (sense 4). **4 off the cuff.** *Inf.* improvised; extemporary. ORIG C14 *cuffe* glove, from ?

cuff² (kʌf) *vb* **1** (*tr*) to strike with an open hand. ◆ *n* **2** a blow of this kind. ORIG C16: from ?

cuff link *n* one of a pair of linked buttons, used to join the buttonholes on the cuffs of a shirt.

Cuiabá *or* **Cuyabá** ★ (*Portuguese* kuiaˈba) *n* **1** a port in W Brazil, capital of Mato Grosso state, on the Cuibá River. Pop.: 167 894 (1980). **2** a river in SW Brazil, rising on the Mato Grosso plateau and flowing southwest into the São Lourenço River. Length: 483 km (300 miles).

cui bono *Latin.* (kwiː ˈbəʊnəʊ) for whose benefit? for what purpose?

cuirass (kwɪˈræs) *n* **1** a piece of armour covering the chest and back. ◆ *vb* **2** (*tr*) to equip with a cuirass. ORIG C15: from F *cuirasse,* from LL *coriacea,* from *coriaceus* made of leather

cuirassier (ˌkwɪərəˈsɪə) *n* a mounted soldier, esp. of the 16th century, who wore a cuirass.

Cuisenaire rod (ˌkwɪzəˈnɛə) *n Trademark.* one of a set of rods of various colours and lengths representing different numbers, used to teach arithmetic to young children. ORIG C20: after Emil-Georges *Cuisenaire* (?1891–1976), Belgian educationalist

cuisine (kwɪˈziːn) *n* **1** a style or manner of cooking: *French cuisine.* **2** the food prepared by a restaurant, household, etc. ORIG C18: from F, lit.: kitchen, from LL *coquīna,* from L *coquere* to cook

cuisse (kwɪs) *or* **cuish** (kwɪʃ) *n* a piece of armour for the thigh. ORIG C15: back formation from *cuisses* (pl), from OF *cuisseaux,* from *cuisse* thigh

Culbertson ★ (ˈkʌlbətsᵊn) *n* **Ely** (ˈiːlaɪ). 1891–1955, US authority on contract bridge.

cul-de-sac (ˈkʌldəˌsæk, ˈkʊl-) *n, pl* **culs-de-sac** *or* **cul-de-sacs. 1** a road with one end blocked off; dead end. **2** an inescapable position. ORIG C18: from F, lit.: bottom of the bag

-cule *suffix forming nouns.* indicating smallness. ORIG from L *-culus,* dim. suffix

Culebra Cut ★ (kuːˈlɛbrə) *n* the former name of the **Gaillard Cut.**

culex (ˈkjuːlɛks) *n, pl* **culices** (-lɪˌsiːz). any mosquito of the genus *Culex,* such as *C. pipiens,* the common mosquito. ORIG C15: from L: midge, gnat

Culham ★ (ˈkʌləm) *n* a village in S central England, in Oxfordshire: site of the UK centre for thermonuclear reactor research and of the Joint European Torus (JET).

Culiacán ★ (*Spanish* kuljaˈkan) *n* a city in NW Mexico, capital of Sinaloa state. Pop.: 415 046 (1990).

culinary (ˈkʌlɪnərɪ) *adj* of, relating to, or used in the kitchen or in cookery. ORIG C17: from L *culīnārius,* from *culīna* kitchen ▸ **ˈculinarily** *adv*

cull (kʌl) *vb* (*tr*) **1** to choose or gather the best or required examples of. **2** to take out (an animal, esp. an inferior one) from a herd or group. **3** to reduce the size of (a herd, etc.) by killing a proportion of its members. **4** to gather (flowers, fruit, etc.). ◆ *n* **5** the act or product of culling. **6** an inferior animal taken from a herd or group.

ORIG C15: from OF *coillir* to pick, from L *colligere;* see COLLECT[1]
▸ **'culler** *n*

Culloden ★ (kə'lɒdᵊn) *n* a moor near Inverness in N Scotland: site of a battle in 1746 in which government troops under the Duke of Cumberland defeated the Jacobites under Prince Charles Edward Stuart.

culm[1] (kʌlm) *n Mining.* **1** coal-mine waste. **2** inferior anthracite. ORIG C14: prob. rel. to COAL

culm[2] (kʌlm) *n* the hollow jointed stem of a grass or sedge. ORIG C17: from L *culmus* stalk; see HAULM

culminate ('kʌlmɪˌneɪt) *vb* **culminates, culminating, culminated. 1** (when *intr,* usually foll. by *in*) to reach or bring to a final or climactic stage. **2** (*intr*) (of a celestial body) to cross the meridian. ORIG C17: from LL *culmināre* to reach the highest point, from L *culmen* top
▸ **'culminant** *adj*

culmination (ˌkʌlmɪ'neɪʃən) *n* **1** the final or highest point. **2** the act of culminating. **3** *Astron.* the highest or lowest altitude attained by a heavenly body as it crosses the meridian.

culottes (kjuː'lɒts) *pl n* women's flared trousers cut to look like a skirt. ORIG C20: from F, lit.: breeches, from *cul* bottom

culpable ('kʌlpəbᵊl) *adj* deserving censure; blameworthy. ORIG C14: from OF *coupable,* from L *culpābilis,* from *culpāre* to blame, from *culpa* fault
▸ **ˌculpa'bility** *n* ▸ **'culpably** *adv*

culpable homicide *n Scots Law.* manslaughter.

Culpeper ★ ('kʌlˌpɛpə) *n* **Nicholas.** 1616–54, English herbalist and astrologer.

culprit ('kʌlprɪt) *n* **1** *Law.* a person awaiting trial. **2** the person responsible for a particular offence, misdeed, etc. ORIG C17: from Anglo-F *cul-,* short for *culpable* guilty + *prit* ready, indicating that the prosecution was ready to prove the guilt of the one charged

cult (kʌlt) *n* **1** a specific system of religious worship. **2** a sect devoted to such a system. **3** a quasi-religious organization using devious psychological techniques to gain and control adherents. **4** intense interest in and devotion to a person, idea, or activity. **5** the person, idea, etc., arousing such devotion. **6** something regarded as fashionable or significant by a particular group; craze. **7** (*modifier*) of, relating to, or characteristic of a cult or cults: *a cult figure; a cult show.* ORIG C17: from L *cultus* cultivation, refinement, from *colere* to till
▸ **'cultism** *n* ▸ **'cultist** *n*

cultic ('kʌltɪk) *adj* of or relating to a religious cult.

cultish ('kʌltɪʃ) *or* **culty** ('kʌltɪ) *adj* intended to appeal to a small group of fashionable people.

cultivable ('kʌltɪvəbᵊl) *or* **cultivatable** ('kʌltɪˌveɪtəbᵊl) *adj* (of land) capable of being cultivated. ORIG C17: from F, from OF *cultiver* to CULTIVATE
▸ **ˌcultiva'bility** *n*

cultivar ('kʌltɪˌvɑː) *n* a variety of a plant produced from a natural species and maintained by cultivation. ORIG C20: from CULTI(VATED) + VAR(IETY)

cultivate ('kʌltɪˌveɪt) *vb* **cultivates, cultivating, cultivated.** (*tr*) **1** to prepare (land or soil) for the growth of crops. **2** to plant, tend, harvest, or improve (plants). **3** to break up (land or soil) with a cultivator or hoe. **4** to improve (the mind, body, etc.) as by study, education, or labour. **5** to give special attention to: *to cultivate a friendship.* ORIG C17: from Med. L *cultivāre* to till, from *cultīvus* cultivable, from L *cultus* cultivated, from *colere* to till, toil over
▸ **'cultiˌvated** *adj*

cultivation (ˌkʌltɪ'veɪʃən) *n* **1** *Agriculture.* **1a** the cultivating of crops or plants. **1b** the preparation of ground to promote their growth. **2** development, esp. through education, training, etc. **3** culture or sophistication.

cultivator ('kʌltɪˌveɪtə) *n* **1** a farm implement used to break up soil and remove weeds. **2** a person or thing that cultivates.

cultural ('kʌltʃərəl) *adj* **1** of or relating to artistic or social pursuits or events considered valuable or enlightened. **2** of or relating to a culture. **3** obtained by specialized breeding.

culture ('kʌltʃə) *n* **1** the total of the inherited ideas, beliefs, values, and knowledge, which constitute the shared bases of social action. **2** the total range of activities and ideas of a people. **3** a particular civilization at a particular period. **4** the artistic and social pursuits, expression, and tastes valued by a society or class. **5** the enlightenment or refinement resulting from these pursuits. **6** the attitudes and general behaviour of a particular social group, profession, etc. **7** the cultivation of plants to improve stock or to produce new ones. **8** the rearing and breeding of animals, esp. with a view to improving the strain. **9** the act or practice of tilling or cultivating the soil. **10** *Biol.* **10a** the experimental growth of microorganisms in a nutrient substance. **10b** a group of microorganisms grown in this way. ◆ *vb* **cultures, culturing, cultured.** (*tr*) **11** to cultivate (plants or animals). **12** to grow (microorganisms) in a culture medium. ORIG C15: from OF, from L *cultūra* a cultivating, from *colere* to till; see CULT
▸ **'culturist** *n*

cultured ('kʌltʃəd) *adj* **1** showing or having good taste, manners, and education. **2** artificially grown or synthesized: *cultured pearls.* **3** treated by a culture of microorganisms.

cultured pearl *n* a pearl induced to grow in the shell of an oyster or clam, by the insertion of a small object.

culture shock *n Sociol.* the feelings of isolation, rejection, etc., experienced when one culture is brought into sudden contact with another.

culture vulture *n Inf.* a person considered to be excessively, and often pretentiously, interested in the arts.

cultus ('kʌltəs) *n, pl* **cultuses** *or* **culti** (-taɪ). another word for **cult** (sense 1). ORIG C17: from L: a toiling over something, refinement, CULT

culverin ('kʌlvərɪn) *n* **1** a medium-to-heavy cannon used during the 15th, 16th, and 17th centuries. **2** a medieval musket. ORIG C15: from OF *coulevrine,* from *couleuvre,* from L *coluber* serpent

culvert ('kʌlvət) *n* **1** a drain or covered channel that crosses under a road, railway, etc. **2** a channel for an electric cable. ORIG C18: from ?

cum (kʌm) *prep* used between nouns to designate a combined nature: *a kitchen-cum-dining room.* ORIG L: with, together with

Cumae ★ ('kjuːmiː) *n* the oldest Greek colony in Italy, founded about 750 B.C. near Naples.
▸ **Cu'maean** *adj*

cumber ('kʌmbə) *vb* (*tr*) **1** to obstruct or hinder. **2** *Obs.* to inconvenience. ORIG C13: prob. from OF *combrer* to impede, prevent, from *combre* barrier; see ENCUMBER

Cumberland[1] ★ ('kʌmbələnd) *n* (until 1974) a county of NW England, now part of Cumbria.

Cumberland[2] ★ ('kʌmbələnd) *n* **William Augustus,** Duke of Cumberland, known as *Butcher Cumberland.* 1721–65, British soldier, younger son of George II, noted for his defeat of Charles Edward Stuart at Culloden (1746) and his subsequent ruthless destruction of Jacobite rebels.

cumbersome ('kʌmbəsəm) *or* **cumbrous** ('kʌmbrəs) *adj* **1** awkward because of size, weight, or shape. **2** difficult because of extent or complexity: *cumbersome accounts.* ORIG C14: *cumber,* short for ENCUMBER + -SOME[1]
▸ **'cumbersomeness** *or* **'cumbrousness** *n*

Cumbria ★ ('kʌmbrɪə) *n* (since 1974) a county of NW England comprising the former counties of Westmorland and Cumberland together with N Lancashire: includes the Lake District mountain area and surrounding coastal lowlands with the Pennine uplands in the extreme east. Administrative centre: Carlisle. Pop.: 490 600 (1996 est.). Area: 6810 sq. km (2629 sq. miles).
▸ **'Cumbrian** *adj, n*

Cumbrian Mountains ★ ('kʌmbrɪən) *pl n* a mountain range in NW England, in Cumbria. Highest peak: Scafell Pike, 978 m (3210 ft).

cumin *or* **cummin** ('kʌmɪn) *n* **1** an umbelliferous Mediterranean plant with small white or pink flowers. **2** the aromatic seeds (collectively) of this plant, used as a condiment and a flavouring. ORIG C12: from OF, from L *cumīnum,* from Gk *kuminon,* of Semitic origin

cummerbund ('kʌmə,bʌnd) *n* a wide sash worn round the waist, esp. with a dinner jacket. ORIG C17: from Hindi *kamarband,* from Persian, from *kamar* loins, waist + *band* band

Cummings ★ ('kʌmɪŋz) *n* **Edward Estlin** ('ɛstlɪn), preferred typographical representation of name **e e cummings.** 1894–1962, US poet.

cum new *adv, adj* (of shares, etc.) with the right to take up any scrip issue or rights issue. Cf. **ex new.**

cumquat ('kʌmkwɒt) *n* a variant spelling of **kumquat.**

cumulate *vb* ('kju:mjʊ,leɪt), **cumulates, cumulating, cumulated. 1** to accumulate. **2** (*tr*) to combine (two or more sequences) into one. ◆ *adj* ('kju:mjʊlɪt). **3** heaped up. ORIG C16: from L *cumulāre* from *cumulus* heap
▸ **,cumu'lation** *n*

cumulative ('kju:mjʊlətɪv) *adj* **1** growing in quantity, strength, or effect by successive additions. **2** (of dividends or interest) intended to be accumulated. **3** *Statistics.* **3a** (of a frequency) including all values of a variable either below or above a specified value. **3b** (of error) tending to increase as the sample size is increased.
▸ **'cumulatively** *adv* ▸ **'cumulativeness** *n*

cumulonimbus (,kju:mjʊləʊ'nɪmbəs) *n, pl* **cumulonimbi** (-baɪ) *or* **cumulonimbuses.** *Meteorol.* a cumulus cloud of great vertical extent, the bottom being dark-coloured, indicating rain or hail.

cumulus ('kju:mjʊləs) *n, pl* **cumuli** (-,laɪ). a bulbous or billowing white or dark grey cloud. ORIG C17: from L: mass
▸ **'cumulous** *adj*

Cunaxa ★ (kju:'næksə) *n* the site near the lower Euphrates where Artaxerxes II defeated Cyrus the Younger in 401 B.C.

cuneate ('kju:nɪɪt, -,eɪt) *adj* wedge-shaped. ORIG C19: from L *cuneāre* to make wedge-shaped, from *cuneus* a wedge
▸ **'cuneately** *adv* ▸ **'cuneal** *adj*

cuneiform ('kju:nɪ,fɔ:m) *adj* **1** Also: **cuneal.** wedge-shaped. **2** of, relating to, or denoting the wedge-shaped characters in several ancient languages of Mesopotamia and Persia. **3** of or relating to a tablet in which this script is employed. ◆ *n* **4** cuneiform characters. ORIG C17: prob. from OF *cunéiforme,* from L *cuneus* wedge

cunjevoi ('kʌndʒɪ,vɔɪ) *n Austral.* **1** an arum of tropical Asia and Australia, cultivated for its edible rhizome. **2** a sea squirt. Often shortened to **cunjie, cunjy.** ORIG C19: from Abor.

cunnilingus (,kʌnɪ'lɪŋgəs) *or* **cunnilinctus** (,kʌnɪ'lɪŋktəs) *n* a sexual activity in which the female genitalia are stimulated by the partner's lips and tongue. Cf. **fellatio.** ORIG C19: from NL, from L *cunnus* vulva + *lingere* to lick

cunning ('kʌnɪŋ) *adj* **1** crafty and shrewd, esp. in deception. **2** made with or showing skill; ingenious. ◆ *n* **3** craftiness, esp. in deceiving. **4** skill or ingenuity. ORIG OE *cunnende;* rel. to *cunnan* to know (see CAN[1])
▸ **'cunningly** *adv* ▸ **'cunningness** *n*

Cunningham ★ ('kʌnɪŋhæm) *n* **Merce** (mɜ:s). born 1919, US dancer and choreographer. His experimental ballets include *Suit for Five* (1956) and *Travelogue* (1977).

Cunninghame Graham ★ ('kʌnɪŋhəm 'greɪəm) *n* **R(obert) B(ontine).** 1852–1936, Scottish writer and politician: first president (1928) of the Scottish Nationalist Party.

Cunobelinus ★ (,kju:nəʊbə'laɪnəs) *n* died ?42 A.D., British ruler of the Catuvellauni tribe (?10–?42); founder of Colchester (?10). Also called: **Cymbeline.**

cunt (kʌnt) *n Taboo.* **1** the female genitals. **2** *Offens. sl.* a woman considered sexually. **3** *Offens. sl.* a mean or obnoxious person. ORIG C13: of Gmc origin; rel. to ON *kunta,* MLow G *kunte*

cup (kʌp) *n* **1** a small open container, usually having one handle, used for drinking from. **2** the contents of such a container. **3** Also called: **teacup, cupful.** a unit of capacity used in cooking. **4** something resembling a cup. **5** either of two cup-shaped parts of a brassiere. **6** a cup-shaped trophy awarded as a prize. **7** *Brit.* **7a** a sporting contest in which a cup is awarded to the winner. **7b** (*as modifier*): *a cup competition.* **8** a mixed drink with one ingredient as a base: *claret cup.* **9** *Golf.* the hole or metal container in the hole on a green. **10** the chalice or the consecrated wine used in the Eucharist. **11** one's lot in life. **12 in one's cups.** drunk. **13 one's cup of tea.** *Inf.* one's chosen or preferred thing, task, company, etc. ◆ *vb* **cups, cupping, cupped.** (*tr*) **14** to form (something, such as the hands) into the shape of a cup. **15** to put into or as if into a cup. **16** to draw blood to the surface of the body of (a person) by cupping. ORIG OE *cuppe,* from LL *cuppa* cup, alteration of L *cūpa* cask

cupbearer ('kʌp,bɛərə) *n* an attendant who fills and serves wine cups, as in a royal household.

cupboard ('kʌbəd) *n* a piece of furniture or a recessed area of a room, with a door concealing storage space.

cupboard love *n* a show of love inspired only by some selfish or greedy motive.

cupcake ('kʌp,keɪk) *n* a small cake baked in a cup-shaped foil or paper case.

cupel ('kju:pᵊl, kju'pɛl) *n* **1** a refractory pot in which gold or silver is refined. **2** a small bowl in which gold and silver are recovered during assaying. ◆ *vb* **cupels, cupelling, cupelled** *or US* **cupels, cupeling, cupeled. 3** (*tr*) to refine (gold or silver) using a cupel. ORIG C17: from F *coupelle,* dim. of *coupe* CUP
▸ **,cupel'lation** *n*

Cup Final *n* **1** (often preceded by *the*) the annual final of the FA or Scottish Cup soccer competition. **2** (*often not cap.*) the final of any cup competition.

Cupid ★ ('kju:pɪd) *n* **1** the Roman god of love, represented as a winged boy with a bow and arrow. Greek counterpart: **Eros. 2** (*not cap.*) any similar figure. ORIG C14: from L *Cupīdō,* from *cupīdō* desire, from *cupidus* desirous; see CUPIDITY

cupidity (kju:'pɪdɪtɪ) *n* strong desire, esp. for wealth; greed. ORIG C15: from L *cupiditās,* from *cupidus* eagerly desiring, from *cupere* to long for

cupola ('kju:pələ) *n* **1** a roof or ceiling in the form of a dome. **2** a small structure, usually domed, on the top of a roof or dome. **3** a protective dome for a gun on a warship. **4** a furnace in which iron is remelted. ORIG C16: from It., from LL *cūpula* a small cask, from L *cūpa* tub
▸ **'cupo,lated** *adj*

cuppa *or* **cupper** ('kʌpə) *n Brit. inf.* a cup of tea.

cupping ('kʌpɪŋ) *n Med.* formerly, the use of an evacuated glass cup to draw blood to the surface of the skin for blood-letting.

cupreous ('kju:prɪəs) *adj* **1** of, containing, or resembling copper. **2** of the colour of copper. ORIG C17: from LL *cupreus,* from *cuprum* COPPER[1]

cupressus (kə'prɛsəs) *n* any evergreen tree of the genus *Cupressus.*

cupric ('kju:prɪk) *adj* of or containing copper in the divalent state. ORIG C18: from LL *cuprum* copper

cupriferous (kju:'prɪfərəs) *adj* (of a substance such as an ore) containing or yielding copper.

cupro-, cupri-, *or before a vowel* **cupr-** *combining form.* indicating copper. ORIG from L *cuprum*

cupronickel (,kju:prəʊ'nɪkᵊl) *n* any copper alloy containing up to 40 per cent nickel: used in coins, condenser tubes, etc.

cuprous ('kju:prəs) *adj* of or containing copper in the monovalent state.

cup tie *n Sport.* an eliminating match or round between two teams in a cup competition.

cupule ('kju:pju:l) *n Biol.* a cup-shaped part or structure. ORIG C19: from LL *cūpula;* see CUPOLA

cur (kɜ:) *n* **1** any vicious dog, esp. a mongrel. **2** a despicable or cowardly person. ORIG C13: from *kurdogge;* prob. rel. to ON *kurra* to growl

curable ('kjʊərəbᵊl) *adj* capable of being cured.
▸ **,cura'bility** *or* **'curableness** *n*

Curaçao ★ (,kjʊərə'səʊ) *n* **1** an island in the Caribbean, the largest in the Netherlands Antilles. Capital:

Willemstad. Pop.: 149 376 (1994 est.). Area: 444 sq. km (171 sq. miles). **2** an orange-flavoured liqueur originally made there.

curacy ('kjʊərəsɪ) *n, pl* **curacies.** the office or position of a curate.

curare *or* **curari** (kjʊ'rɑːrɪ) *n* **1** black resin obtained from certain tropical South American trees, which causes muscular paralysis: used medicinally as a muscle relaxant and by South American Indians as an arrow poison. **2** any of various trees from which this resin is obtained. ORIG C18: from Port. & Sp., from Carib *kurari*

curassow ('kjʊərəˌsəʊ) *n* any of various ground-nesting birds of S North, Central, and South America, having long legs and tail and a crest of curled feathers. ORIG C17: anglicized from CURAÇAO (island)

curate ('kjʊərɪt) *n* **1** a clergyman appointed to assist a parish priest. **2** *Irish.* an assistant barman. ORIG C14: from Med. L *cūrātus,* from *cūra* spiritual oversight, CURE

curate's egg *n* something that has good and bad parts. ORIG C20: derived from a cartoon in *Punch* (Nov., 1895) in which a timid curate, who has been served a bad egg while breakfasting with his bishop, says that parts of the egg are excellent

curative ('kjʊərətɪv) *adj* **1** able or tending to cure. ◆ *n* **2** anything able to heal or cure.
▸ '**curatively** *adv* ▸ '**curativeness** *n*

curator (kjʊə'reɪtə) *n* the administrative head of a museum, art gallery, etc. ORIG C14: from L: one who cares, from *cūrāre* to care for, from *cūra* care
▸ **curatorial** (ˌkjʊərə'tɔːrɪəl) *adj* ▸ **cu'rator,ship** *n*

curb (kɜːb) *n* **1** something that restrains or holds back. **2** any enclosing framework, such as a wall around the top of a well. **3** Also called: **curb bit.** a horse's bit with an attached chain or strap, which checks the horse. ◆ *vb* (*tr*) **4** to control with or as if with a curb; restrain. ◆ See also **kerb.** ORIG C15: from OF *courbe* curved piece of wood or metal, from L *curvus* curved

curcuma ('kɜːkjʊmə) *n* any tropical Asian tuberous plant of the genus *Curcuma,* such as *C. longa,* which is the source of turmeric. ORIG C17: from NL, from Ar. *kurkum* turmeric

curd (kɜːd) *n* **1** (*often pl*) a substance formed from the coagulation of milk, used in making cheese or eaten as a food. **2** something similar in consistency. ◆ *vb* **3** to turn into or become curd. ORIG C15: from earlier *crud,* from ?
▸ '**curdy** *adj*

curdle ('kɜːdᵊl) *vb* **curdles, curdling, curdled. 1** to turn or cause to turn into curd. **2 curdle someone's blood.** to fill someone with fear. ORIG C16 (*crudled,* p.p.): from CURD

cure (kjʊə) *vb* **cures, curing, cured. 1** (*tr*) to get rid of (an ailment or problem); heal. **2** (*tr*) to restore to health or good condition. **3** (*intr*) to bring about a cure. **4** (*tr*) to preserve (meat, fish, etc.) by salting, smoking, etc. **5** (*tr*) **5a** to treat or finish (a substance) by chemical or physical means. **5b** to vulcanize (rubber). **6** (*tr*) to assist the hardening of (concrete, mortar, etc.) by keeping it moist. ◆ *n* **7** a return to health. **8** any course of medical therapy, esp. one proved effective. **9** a means of restoring health or improving a situation, etc. **10** the spiritual and pastoral charge of a parish. **11** a process or method of preserving meat, fish, etc. ORIG (n) C13: from OF, from L *cūra* care; in ecclesiastical sense, from Med. L *cūra* spiritual charge; (vb) C14: from OF *curer,* from L *cūrāre* to attend to, heal, from *cūra* care
▸ '**cureless** *adj* ▸ '**curer** *n*

curé ('kjʊəreɪ) *n* a parish priest in France. ORIG F, from Med. L *cūrātus;* see CURATE

cure-all *n* something reputed to cure all ailments.

curettage (ˌkjʊərɪ'tɑːʒ, kjʊə'rɛtɪdʒ) *or* **curettement** (kjʊə'rɛtmənt) *n* the process of using a curette. See also **D and C.**

curette *or* **curet** (kjʊə'rɛt) *n* **1** a surgical instrument for removing dead tissue, growths, etc., from the walls of body cavities. ◆ *vb* **curettes** *or* **curets, curetting, curetted. 2** (*tr*) to scrape or clean with such an instrument. ORIG C18: from F *curette,* from *curer* to heal, make clean; see CURE

curfew ('kɜːfjuː) *n* **1** an official regulation setting restrictions on movement, esp. after a specific time at night. **2** the time set as a deadline by such a regulation. **3** (in medieval Europe) **3a** the ringing of a bell to prompt people to extinguish fires and lights. **3b** the time at which the curfew bell was rung. **3c** the bell itself. ORIG C13: from OF *cuevrefeu,* lit.: cover the fire

curia ('kjʊərɪə) *n, pl* **curiae** (-rɪˌiː). **1** (*sometimes cap.*) the papal court and government of the Roman Catholic Church. **2** (in the Middle Ages) a court held in the king's name. ORIG C16: from L, from OL *coviria* (unattested), from CO- + *vir* man
▸ '**curial** *adj*

curie ('kjʊərɪ, -riː) *n* a unit of radioactivity equal to 3.7×10^{10} disintegrations per second. ORIG C20: after Pierre CURIE

Curie ★ ('kjʊərɪ, -riː; *French* kyri) *n* **1 Marie** (mari). 1867–1934, French physicist, born in Poland: discovered and isolated radium and polonium. She shared a Nobel prize for physics (1903) with her husband and Henri Becquerel, and was awarded a Nobel prize for chemistry (1911). **2** her husband, **Pierre** (pjɛr). 1859–1906, French physicist.

curio ('kjʊərɪˌəʊ) *n, pl* **curios.** a small article valued as a collector's item, esp. something unusual. ORIG C19: shortened from CURIOSITY

curiosity (ˌkjʊərɪ'ɒsɪtɪ) *n, pl* **curiosities. 1** an eager desire to know; inquisitiveness. **2** the quality of being curious; strangeness. **3** something strange or fascinating.

curious ('kjʊərɪəs) *adj* **1** eager to learn; inquisitive. **2** overinquisitive; prying. **3** interesting because of oddness or novelty. ORIG C14: from L *cūriōsus* taking pains over something, from *cūra* care
▸ '**curiously** *adv* ▸ '**curiousness** *n*

Curitiba ★ (ˌkʊərɪ'tiːbə) *n* a city in SE Brazil, capital of Paraná state: seat of the University of Paraná (1946). Pop.: 841 882 (1991).

curium ('kjʊərɪəm) *n* a silvery-white metallic transuranic element artificially produced from plutonium. Symbol: Cm; at. no.: 96; half-life of most stable isotope, ^{247}Cm: 1.6×10^7 years. ORIG C20: NL, after Pierre and Marie CURIE

curl (kɜːl) *vb* **1** (*intr*) (esp. of hair) to grow into curves or ringlets. **2** (*tr; sometimes foll. by up*) to twist or roll (esp. hair) into coils or ringlets. **3** (often foll. by *up*) to become or cause to become spiral-shaped or curved. **4** (*intr*) to move in a curving or twisting manner. **5** (*intr*) to play the game of curling. **6 curl one's lip.** to show contempt, as by raising a corner of the lip. ◆ *n* **7** a curve or coil of hair. **8** a curved or spiral shape or mark. **9** the act of curling or state of being curled. ◆ See also **curl up.** ORIG C14: prob. from MDu. *crullen* to curl

curler ('kɜːlə) *n* **1** any of various pins, clasps, or rollers used to curl or wave hair. **2** a person or thing that curls. **3** a person who plays curling.

curlew ('kɜːljuː) *n* any of certain large shore birds of Europe and Asia. They have a long downward-curving bill and occur in northern and arctic regions. ORIG C14: from OF *corlieu,* ? imit.

curlicue ('kɜːlɪˌkjuː) *n* an intricate ornamental curl or twist. ORIG C19: from CURLY + CUE²

curling ('kɜːlɪŋ) *n* a game played on ice, esp. in Scotland, in which heavy stones with handles (**curling stones**) are slid towards a target (**tee**).

curling tongs *pl n* a metal scissor-like device that is heated, so that strands of hair may be twined around it in order to form curls. Also called: **curling iron, curling irons, curling pins.**

curl up *vb* (*adv*) **1** (*intr*) to adopt a reclining position with the legs close to the body and the back rounded. **2** to become or cause to become spiral-shaped or curved. **3** (*intr*) to retire to a quiet cosy setting: *to curl up with a good novel.* **4** *Brit. inf.* to be or cause to be embarrassed or disgusted (esp. in **curl up and die**).

curly ('kɜːlɪ) *adj* **curlier, curliest. 1** tending to curl; curling. **2** having curls. **3** (of timber) having waves in the grain.
▸ '**curliness** *n*

curmudgeon (kɜːˈmʌdʒən) *n* a surly or miserly person. ORIG C16: from ?
▸ **curˈmudgeonly** *adj*

Curnow ★ (kɜːnaʊ) *n* **T.A.M.** born 1911, New Zealand poet and anthologist.

currach *or* **curragh** *Gaelic.* (ˈkʌrəx, ˈkʌrə) *n* a Scottish or Irish name for **coracle.** ORIG C15: from Irish Gaelic *currach;* Cf. CORACLE

currajong (ˈkʌrəˌdʒɒŋ) *n* a variant spelling of **kurrajong.**

currant (ˈkʌrənt) *n* **1** a small dried seedless grape of the Mediterranean region. **2** any of several mainly N temperate shrubs, esp. redcurrant and blackcurrant. **3** the small acid fruit of any of these plants. ORIG C16: shortened from *rayson of Corannte* raisin of Corinth

currawong (ˈkʌrəˌwɒŋ) *n* any Australian crowlike songbird of the genus *Strepera,* having black, grey, and white plumage. Also called: **bell-magpie.** ORIG from Abor.

currency (ˈkʌrənsɪ) *n, pl* **currencies. 1** a metal or paper medium of exchange in current use in a particular country. **2** general acceptance or circulation; prevalence. **3** the period of time during which something is valid, accepted, or in force. ◆ *adj* **4** *Austral. inf.* native-born as distinct from immigrant: *a currency lad.* ORIG C17: from Med. L *currentia,* lit.: a flowing, from L *currere* to run, flow

current (ˈkʌrənt) *adj* **1** of the immediate present; in progress. **2** most recent; up-to-date. **3** commonly known, practised, or accepted. **4** circulating and valid at present: *current coins.* ◆ *n* **5** (esp. of water or air) a steady, usually natural, flow. **6** a mass of air, body of water, etc., that has a steady flow in a particular direction. **7** the rate of flow of such a mass. **8** *Physics.* **8a** a flow of electric charge through a conductor. **8b** the rate of flow of this charge. **9** a general trend or drift: *currents of opinion.* ORIG C13: from OF *corant,* lit.: running, from *corre* to run, from L *currere*
▸ **ˈcurrently** *adv* ▸ **ˈcurrentness** *n*

current account *n* an account at a bank or building society against which cheques may be drawn at any time.

current-cost accounting *n* a method of accounting that values assets at their current replacement cost rather than their original cost. It is often used in times of high inflation. Cf. **historical-cost accounting.**

curricle (ˈkʌrɪkᵊl) *n* a two-wheeled open carriage drawn by two horses side by side. ORIG C18: from L *curriculum* from *currus* chariot, from *currere* to run

curriculum (kəˈrɪkjʊləm) *n, pl* **curricula** (-lə) *or* **curriculums. 1** a course of study in one subject at a school or college. **2** a list of all the courses of study offered by a school or college. **3** any programme or plan of activities. ORIG C19: from L: course, from *currere* to run
▸ **curˈricular** *adj*

curriculum vitae (kəˈrɪkjʊləm ˈviːtaɪ, ˈvaɪtiː) *n, pl* **curricula vitae** (kəˈrɪkjʊlə). an outline of a person's educational and professional history, usually prepared for job applications. ORIG L, lit.: the course of one's life

currish (ˈkɜːrɪʃ) *adj* of or like a cur; rude or bad-tempered.
▸ **ˈcurrishly** *adv* ▸ **ˈcurrishness** *n*

curry¹ (ˈkʌrɪ) *n, pl* **curries. 1** a spicy dish of oriental, esp. Indian, origin that usually consists of meat or fish prepared in a hot piquant sauce. **2** curry seasoning or sauce. **3 give someone curry.** *Austral. sl.* to assault (a person) verbally or physically. ◆ *vb* **curries, currying, curried. 4** *(tr)* to prepare (food) with curry powder or sauce. ORIG C16: from Tamil *kari* sauce, relish

curry² (ˈkʌrɪ) *vb* **curries, currying, curried. 1** to beat vigorously, as in order to clean. **2** to dress and finish (leather) after it has been tanned. **3** to groom (a horse). **4 curry favour.** to ingratiate oneself, esp. with superiors. ORIG C13: from OF *correer* to make ready

currycomb (ˈkʌrɪˌkəʊm) *n* a square comb used for grooming horses.

curry powder *n* a mixture of finely ground pungent spices, such as turmeric, cumin, coriander, ginger, etc., used in making curries.

curse (kɜːs) *n* **1** a profane or obscene expression of anger, disgust, surprise, etc.; oath. **2** an appeal to a supernatural power for harm to come to a specific person, group, etc. **3** harm resulting from an appeal to a supernatural power. **4** something that brings or causes great trouble or harm. **5** (preceded by *the*) *Inf.* menstruation or a menstrual period. ◆ *vb* **curses, cursing, cursed** *or* (*Arch.*) **curst. 6** *(intr)* to utter obscenities or oaths. **7** *(tr)* to abuse (someone) with obscenities or oaths. **8** *(tr)* to invoke supernatural powers to bring harm to (someone or something). **9** *(tr)* to bring harm upon. ORIG OE *cursian* to curse, from *curs* a curse
▸ **ˈcurser** *n*

cursed (ˈkɜːsɪd, kɜːst) *or* **curst** *adj* **1** under a curse. **2** deserving to be cursed; detestable; hateful.
▸ **ˈcursedly** *adv* ▸ **ˈcursedness** *n*

cursive (ˈkɜːsɪv) *adj* **1** of or relating to handwriting in which letters are joined in a flowing style. **2** *Printing.* of or relating to typefaces that resemble handwriting. ◆ *n* **3** a cursive letter or printing type. ORIG C18: from Med. L *cursīvus* running, ult. from L *currere* to run
▸ **ˈcursively** *adv*

cursor (ˈkɜːsə) *n* **1** the sliding part of a measuring instrument, esp. on a slide rule. **2** any of various means, typically a flashing bar or underline, of identifying a particular position on a computer screen.

cursorial (kɜːˈsɔːrɪəl) *adj Zool.* adapted for running: *a cursorial skeleton; cursorial birds.*

cursory (ˈkɜːsərɪ) *adj* hasty and usually superficial; quick. ORIG C17: from LL *cursōrius* of running, from L *cursus* a course, from *currere* to run
▸ **ˈcursorily** *adv* ▸ **ˈcursoriness** *n*

curst (kɜːst) *vb* **1** *Arch.* a past tense and past participle of **curse.** ◆ *adj* **2** a variant of **cursed.**

curt (kɜːt) *adj* **1** rudely blunt and brief. **2** short or concise. ORIG C17: from L *curtus* cut short, mutilated
▸ **ˈcurtly** *adv* ▸ **ˈcurtness** *n*

curtail (kɜːˈteɪl) *vb (tr)* to cut short; abridge. ORIG C16: changed (through infl. of TAIL[1]) from obs. *curtal* to dock
▸ **curˈtailer** *n* ▸ **curˈtailment** *n*

curtain (ˈkɜːtᵊn) *n* **1** a piece of material that can be drawn across an opening or window, to shut out light or to provide privacy. **2** a barrier to vision, access, or communication. **3** a hanging cloth or similar barrier for concealing all or part of a theatre stage from the audience. **4** (often preceded by *the*) the end of a scene of a play, opera, etc., marked by the fall or closing of the curtain. **5** the rise or opening of the curtain at the start of a performance. ◆ *vb* **6** *(tr;* sometimes foll. by *off)* to shut off or conceal as with a curtain. **7** *(tr)* to provide (a window, etc.) with curtains. ORIG C13: from OF *courtine,* from LL *cortīna* enclosed place, curtain, prob. from L *cohors* courtyard

curtain call *n* the appearance of performers at the end of a theatrical performance to acknowledge applause.

curtain lecture *n* a scolding or rebuke given in private, esp. by a wife to her husband. ORIG alluding to the curtained beds where such rebukes were once given

curtain raiser *n* **1** *Theatre.* a short dramatic piece presented before the main play. **2** any preliminary event.

curtains (ˈkɜːtᵊnz) *pl n Inf.* death or ruin: the end.

curtain wall *n* a non-load-bearing external wall attached to a framed structure.

Curtin ★ (ˈkɜːtɪn) *n* **John Joseph.** 1885–1945, Australian statesman; prime minister (1941–45).

curtsy *or* **curtsey** (ˈkɜːtsɪ) *n, pl* **curtsies** *or* **curtseys. 1** a formal gesture of greeting and respect made by women, in which the knees are bent and the head slightly bowed. ◆ *vb* **curtsies, curtsying, curtsied** *or* **curtseys, curtseying, curtseyed. 2** *(intr)* to make a curtsy. ORIG C16: var. of COURTESY

curvaceous (kɜːˈveɪʃəs) *adj Inf.* (of a woman) having a well-rounded body.

curvature (ˈkɜːvətʃə) *n* **1** something curved or a curved part of a thing. **2** any curving of a bodily part. **3** the act of curving or the state or degree of being curved or bent.

curve (kɜːv) *n* **1** a continuously bending line that has no straight parts. **2** something that curves or is curved. **3** the act or extent of curving; curvature. **4** *Maths.* a system of points whose coordinates satisfy a given equation. **5** a line representing data on a graph. ◆ *vb* **curves, curving, curved. 6** to take or cause to take the shape or path of a

curve; bend. ORIG C15: from L *curvāre* to bend, from *curvus* crooked
▸ **'curvedness** *n* ▸ **'curvy** *adj*

curvet (kɜːˈvɛt) *n* **1** *Dressage.* a low leap with all four feet off the ground. ◆ *vb* **curvets, curvetting, curvetted** *or* **curvets, curveting, curveted. 2** *Dressage.* to make or cause to make such a leap. **3** (*intr*) to prance or frisk about. ORIG C16: from OIt. *corvetta,* from OF *courbette,* from *courber* to bend, from L *curvāre*

curvilinear (ˌkɜːvɪˈlɪnɪə) *or* **curvilineal** *adj* consisting of, bounded by, or characterized by a curved line.

Curzon ★ (ˈkɜːzᵊn) *n* **1** Sir **Clifford.** 1907–82, British pianist. **2 George Nathaniel,** 1st Marquis Curzon of Kedleston. 1859–1925, British Conservative statesman; viceroy of India (1898–1905).

Cusack ★ (ˈkjuːsæk) *n* **Cyril (James).** 1910–93, Irish actor.

Cusanus ★ (kjuːˈseɪnəs) *n* **Nicholas.** See **Nicholas of Cusa.**

Cusco ★ (*Spanish* ˈkusko) *n* a variant of **Cuzco.**

cuscus (ˈkʌskʌs) *n, pl* **cuscuses.** any of several large nocturnal phalangers of N Australia, New Guinea, and adjacent islands, having dense fur, prehensile tails, large eyes, and a yellow nose. ORIG C17: NL, prob. from a native name in New Guinea

cusec (ˈkjuːsɛk) *n* a unit of flow equal to 1 cubic foot per second. ORIG C20: from *cu(bic foot per) sec(ond)*

Cush *or* **Kush** ★ (kʌʃ, kʊʃ) *n Old Testament.* **1** the son of Ham and brother of Canaan (Genesis 10:6). **2** the country of the supposed descendants of Cush (ancient Ethiopia), comprising approximately Nubia and the modern Sudan, and the territory of southern (or Upper) Egypt.

cushat (ˈkʌʃət) *n* another name for **wood pigeon.** ORIG OE *cūscote;* ? rel. to *sceōtan* to shoot

Cushing ★ (ˈkʊʃɪŋ) *n* **Harvey Williams.** 1869–1939, US neurosurgeon: identified a pituitary tumour as a cause of the disease named after him.

cushion (ˈkʊʃən) *n* **1** a bag filled with a yielding substance, used for sitting on, leaning against, etc. **2** something resembling a cushion in function or appearance, esp. one to support or pad or to absorb shock. **3** the resilient felt-covered rim of a billiard table. ◆ *vb* (*tr*) **4** to place on or as on a cushion. **5** to provide with cushions. **6** to protect. **7** to lessen or suppress the effects of. **8** to provide with a means of absorbing shock. ORIG C14: from OF *coussin,* from L *culcita* mattress
▸ **'cushiony** *adj*

cushion plant *n* a type of low-growing plant having many closely spaced short upright shoots, typical of alpine and arctic habitats.

Cushitic (kʊˈʃɪtɪk) *n* **1** a group of languages of Somalia, Ethiopia, and adjacent regions. ◆ *adj* **2** of or relating to this group of languages.

cushy (ˈkʊʃɪ) *adj* **cushier, cushiest.** *Inf.* easy; comfortable. ORIG C20: from Hindi *khush* pleasant, from Persian *khōsh*

cusp (kʌsp) *n* **1** any of the small elevations on the grinding or chewing surface of a tooth. **2** any of the triangular flaps of a heart valve. **3** a point or pointed end. **4** *Geom.* a point at which two arcs of a curve intersect and at which the two tangents are coincident. **5** *Archit.* a carving at the meeting place of two arcs. **6** *Astron.* either of the points of a crescent moon. **7** *Astrol.* any division between houses or signs of the zodiac. ORIG C16: from L *cuspis* point, pointed end
▸ **'cuspate** *adj*

cuspid (ˈkʌspɪd) *n* a tooth having one point; canine tooth.

cuspidate (ˈkʌspɪˌdeɪt), **cuspidated,** *or* **cuspidal** (ˈkʌspɪdᵊl) *adj* **1** having a cusp or cusps. **2** (esp. of leaves) narrowing to a point. ORIG C17: from L *cuspidāre* to make pointed, from *cuspis* a point

cuspidor (ˈkʌspɪˌdɔː) *n* another name (esp. US) for **spittoon.** ORIG C18: from Port., from *cuspir* to spit, from L *conspuere,* from *spuere* to spit

cuss (kʌs) *Inf.* ◆ *n* **1** a curse; an oath. **2** a person or animal, esp. an annoying one. ◆ *vb* **3** another word for **curse** (senses 6, 7).

cussed (ˈkʌsɪd) *adj Inf.* **1** another word for **cursed. 2** obstinate. **3** annoying: *a cussed nuisance.*
▸ **'cussedly** *adv* ▸ **'cussedness** *n*

custard (ˈkʌstəd) *n* **1** a baked sweetened mixture of eggs and milk. **2** a sauce made of milk and sugar and thickened with cornflour. ORIG C15: alteration of ME *crustade* kind of pie

custard apple *n* **1** a West Indian tree. **2** its large heart-shaped fruit, which has a fleshy edible pulp.

custard pie *n* **a** a flat, open pie filled with real or artificial custard, as thrown in slapstick comedy. **b** (*as modifier*): *custard-pie humour.*

Custer ★ (ˈkʌstə) *n* **George Armstrong.** 1839–76, US cavalry general: Civil War hero, killed fighting the Sioux Indians at Little Bighorn, Montana.

custodian (kʌˈstəʊdɪən) *n* **1** a person who has custody, as of a prisoner, ward, etc. **2** a keeper of an art collection, etc.
▸ **cus'todian,ship** *n*

custody (ˈkʌstədɪ) *n, pl* **custodies. 1** the act of keeping safe or guarding. **2** the state of being held by the police; arrest. ORIG C15: from L *custōdia,* from *custōs* guard, defender
▸ **custodial** (kʌˈstəʊdɪəl) *adj*

custom (ˈkʌstəm) *n* **1** a usual or habitual practice; typical mode of behaviour. **2** the long-established habits or traditions of a society collectively; convention. **3a** a practice which by long-established usage has come to have the force of law. **3b** such practices collectively (esp. in **custom and practice**). **4** habitual patronage, esp. of a shop or business. **5** the customers of a shop or business collectively. ◆ *adj* **6** made to the specifications of an individual customer. ◆ See also **customs.** ORIG C12: from OF *costume,* from L *consuētūdō,* from *consuēscere* to grow accustomed to

customary (ˈkʌstəmərɪ, -təmrɪ) *adj* **1** in accordance with custom or habitual practice; usual. **2** *Law.* **2a** founded upon long-continued practices and usage. **2b** (of land) held by custom. ◆ *n, pl* **customaries. 3** a statement in writing of customary laws and practices.
▸ **'customarily** *adv* ▸ **'customariness** *n*

custom-built *adj* (of cars, houses, etc.) made according to the specifications of an individual buyer.

customer (ˈkʌstəmə) *n* **1** a person who buys. **2** *Inf.* a person with whom one has dealings.

custom house *n* a government office, esp. at a port, where customs are collected and ships cleared for entry.

customize *or* **customise** (ˈkʌstəˌmaɪz) *vb* **customizes, customizing, customized** *or* **customises, customising, customised.** (*tr*) to make (something) according to a customer's individual requirements.

custom-made *adj* (of suits, dresses, etc.) made according to the specifications of an individual buyer.

customs (ˈkʌstəmz) *n* (*functioning as sing or pl*) **1** duty on imports or exports. **2** the government department responsible for the collection of these duties. **3** the part of a port, airport, etc., where baggage and freight are examined for dutiable goods and contraband.

cut (kʌt) *vb* **cuts, cutting, cut. 1** to open up or incise (a person or thing) with a sharp edge or instrument. **2** (of a sharp instrument) to penetrate or incise (a person or thing). **3** to divide or be divided with or as if with a sharp instrument. **4** (*intr*) to use an instrument that cuts. **5** (*tr*) to trim or prune by or as if by clipping. **6** (*tr*) to reap or mow (a crop, grass, etc.). **7** (*tr;* sometimes foll. by *out*) to make, form, or shape by cutting. **8** (*tr*) to hollow or dig out; excavate. **9** to strike (an object) sharply. **10** *Cricket.* to hit (the ball) to the off side with a roughly horizontal bat. **11** to hurt the feelings of (a person). **12** (*tr*) *Inf.* to refuse to recognize; snub. **13** (*tr*) *Inf.* to absent oneself from, esp. without permission or in haste: *to cut a class.* **14** (*tr*) to abridge or shorten. **15** (*tr;* often foll. by *down*) to lower, reduce, or curtail. **16** (*tr*) to dilute or weaken: *to cut whisky with water.* **17** (*tr*) to dissolve or break up: *to cut fat.* **18** (when *intr,* foll. by *across* or *through*) to cross or traverse. **19** (*intr*) to make a sharp or sudden change in direction; veer. **20** to grow (teeth) through the gums or (of teeth) to appear through the gums. **21** (*intr*) *Films.* **21a** to call a halt to a shooting sequence. **21b** (foll. by *to*) to move quickly to another scene. **22** *Films.* to edit (film). **23** to switch off (a light, car engine, etc.). **24** (*tr*) to make (a record or tape of a song, performance, etc.). **25** *Cards.* **25a** to divide (the pack) at random into two parts after shuffling. **25b** (*intr*) to pick cards from a spread pack to decide dealer, partners, etc. **26** (*tr*) (of a tool) to bite into (an object). **27 cut a dash.** to make a stylish impression. **28 cut (a person) dead.** *Inf.* to ignore (a person) completely. **29 cut a (good, poor,** etc.) **figure.** to appear or behave in a specified manner. **30 cut and run.** *Inf.* to make a rapid escape. **31 cut both ways. 31a** to have both good and bad effects. **31b** to affect both sides, as two parties in an argument, etc. **32 cut it.** *Sl.* to be successful in doing something. **33 cut it fine.** *Inf.* to allow little margin of time, space etc. **34 cut loose.** to free or become freed from restraint, custody, anchorage, etc. **35 cut no ice.** *Inf.* to fail to make an impression. **36 cut one's teeth on.** *Inf.* **36a** to use at an early age or stage. **36b** to practise on. ◆ *adj* **37** detached, divided, or separated by cutting. **38** made, shaped, or fashioned by cutting. **39** reduced or diminished as by cutting: *cut prices.* **40** weakened or diluted. **41** *Brit.* a slang word for **drunk:** *half cut.* **42 cut and dried.** *Inf.* settled or arranged in advance. ◆ *n* **43** the act of cutting. **44** a stroke or incision made by cutting; gash. **45** a piece or part cut off: *a cut of meat.* **46** the edge of anything cut or sliced. **47** a passage, channel, path, etc., cut or hollowed out. **48** an omission or deletion, esp. in a text, film, or play. **49** a reduction in price, salary, etc. **50** a decrease in government finance in a particular department or area. **51** *Inf.* a portion or share. **52** *Inf.* a straw, slip of paper, etc., used in drawing lots. **53** the manner or style in which a thing, esp. a garment, is cut. **54a** *Irish inf.* a person's general appearance: *I didn't like the cut of him.* **54b** *Irish derog.* a dirty or untidy condition: *look at the cut of your shoes.* **55** a direct route; short cut. **56** the US name for **block** (sense 13). **57** *Cricket.* a stroke made with the bat in a roughly horizontal position. **58** *Films.* an immediate transition from one shot to the next. **59** words or an action that hurt another person's feelings. **60** a refusal to recognize an acquaintance; snub. **61** *Brit.* a stretch of water, esp. a canal. **62 a cut above.** *Inf.* superior to; better than. ◆ See also **cut across, cutback,** etc. ORIG C13: prob. from ON

cut across *vb* (*intr, prep*) **1** to be contrary to ordinary procedure or limitations. **2** to cross or traverse, making a shorter route.

cut and paste *n* a technique used in word processing by which a section of text can be moved within a document.

cutaneous (kju:ˈteɪnɪəs) *adj* of or relating to the skin. ORIG C16: from NL *cutāneus,* from L *cutis* skin

cutaway (ˈkʌtəˌweɪ) *n* **1** a man's coat cut diagonally from the front waist to the back of the knees. **2a** a drawing or model of a machine, engine, etc., in which part of the casing is omitted to reveal the workings. **2b** (*as modifier*): *a cutaway model.* **3** *Films, television.* a shot separate from the main action of a scene.

cutback (ˈkʌtˌbæk) *n* **1** a decrease or reduction. ◆ *vb* **cut back** (*adv*) **2** (*tr*) to shorten by cutting off the end. **3** (when *intr,* foll. by *on*) to reduce or make a reduction (in).

Cutch ★ (kʌtʃ) *n* a variant spelling of **Kutch.**

cut down *vb* (*adv*) **1** (*tr*) to fell. **2** (when *intr,* often foll. by *on*) to reduce or make a reduction (in). **3** (*tr*) to remake (an old garment) in order to make a smaller one. **4** (*tr*) to kill. **5 cut (a person) down to size.** to reduce in importance or decrease the conceit of (a person).

cute (kju:t) *adj* **1** appealing or attractive, esp. in a pretty way. **2** *Inf.* affecting cleverness or prettiness. **3** clever; shrewd. ORIG C18 (in the sense: clever): shortened from ACUTE
▸ **ˈcutely** *adv* ▸ **ˈcuteness** *n*

cut glass *n* **1a** glass, esp. bowls, vases, etc., decorated by facet-cutting or grinding. **1b** (*as modifier*): *a cut-glass vase.* **2** (*modifier*) (of an accent) upper-class; refined.

Cuthbert ★ (ˈkʌθbət) *n* **Saint.** ?635–87A.D., English monk; bishop of Lindisfarne. Feast day: March 20.

cuticle (ˈkju:tɪkᵊl) *n* **1** dead skin, esp. round the base of a fingernail or toenail. **2** another name for **epidermis. 3** the protective layer that covers the epidermis of higher plants. **4** the protective layer covering the epidermis of many invertebrates. ORIG C17: from L *cutīcula* dim. of *cutis* skin
▸ **cuticular** (kju:ˈtɪkjʊlə) *adj*

cut in *vb* (*adv*) **1** (*intr;* often foll. by *on*) Also: **cut into.** to break in or interrupt. **2** (*intr*) to interrupt a dancing couple to dance with one of them. **3** (*intr*) (of a driver, motor vehicle, etc.) to draw in front of another vehicle leaving too little space. **4** (*tr*) *Inf.* to allow to have a share. **5** (*intr*) to take the place of a person in a card game.

cutis (ˈkju:tɪs) *n, pl* **cutes** (-ti:z) *or* **cutises.** *Anat.* a technical name for the **skin.** ORIG C17: from L: skin

cutlass (ˈkʌtləs) *n* a curved, one-edged sword formerly used by sailors. ORIG C16: from F *coutelas,* from *coutel* knife, ult. from L *culter* knife

cutler (ˈkʌtlə) *n* a person who makes or sells cutlery. ORIG C14: from F *coutelier,* ult. from L *culter* knife

cutlery (ˈkʌtlərɪ) *n* **1** implements used for eating, such as knives, forks, and spoons. **2** instruments used for cutting. **3** the art or business of a cutler.

cutlet (ˈkʌtlɪt) *n* **1** a piece of meat taken esp. from the best end of neck of lamb, pork, etc. **2** a flat croquette of minced chicken, lobster, etc. ORIG C18: from OF *costelette,* lit.: a little rib, from *coste* rib, from L *costa*

cut off *vb* (*tr, adv*) **1** to remove by cutting. **2** to intercept or interrupt something, esp. a telephone conversation. **3** to discontinue the supply of. **4** to bring to an end. **5** to deprive of rights; disinherit: *cut off without a penny.* **6** to sever or separate. **7** to occupy a position so as to prevent or obstruct (a retreat or escape). ◆ *n* **cutoff. 8a** the act of cutting off; limit or termination. **8b** (*as modifier*): *the cut-off point.* **9** *Chiefly US.* a short cut. **10** a device to terminate the flow of a fluid in a pipe or duct.

cut out *vb* (*adv*) **1** (*tr*) to delete or remove. **2** (*tr*) to shape or form by cutting. **3** (*tr; usually passive*) to suit or equip for: *you're not cut out for this job.* **4** (*intr*) (of an engine, etc.) to cease to operate suddenly. **5** (*intr*) (of an electrical device) to switch off, usually automatically. **6** (*tr*) *Inf.* to oust and supplant (a rival). **7** (*intr*) (of a person) to be excluded from a card game. **8** (*tr*) *Inf.* to cease doing something, esp. something undesirable (esp. in **cut it out**). **9** (*tr*) *Soccer.* to intercept (a pass). **10** (*tr*) to separate (cattle) from a herd. **11** (*intr*) *Austral.* to end or finish: *the road cuts out at the creek.* **12 have one's work cut out.** to have as much work as one can manage. ◆ *n* **cutout. 13** something that has been or is intended to be cut out from something else. **14** a device that switches off or interrupts an electric circuit, esp. as a safety device. **15** *Austral. sl.* the end of shearing.

cut-price *or esp. US* **cut-rate** *adj* **1** available at prices or rates below the standard price or rate. **2** (*prenominal*) offering goods or services at prices below the standard price.

cutpurse (ˈkʌtˌpɜ:s) *n* an archaic word for **pickpocket.**

cutter (ˈkʌtə) *n* **1** a person or thing that cuts, esp. a person who cuts cloth for clothing. **2** a sailing boat with its mast stepped further aft than that of a sloop. **3** a ship's boat, powered by oars or sail, for carrying passengers or light cargo. **4** a small lightly armed boat, as used in the enforcement of customs regulations.

cut-throat (ˈkʌtˌθrəʊt) *n* **1** a person who cuts throats; murderer. **2** Also called: **cut-throat razor, straight razor.** *Brit.* a razor with a long blade that usually folds into the handle. ◆ *adj* **3** bloodthirsty or murderous; cruel. **4** fierce or relentless in competition: *cut-throat prices.* **5** (of some games) played by three people: *cut-throat poker.*

cutting (ˈkʌtɪŋ) *n* **1** a piece cut off from something. **2** *Horticulture.* **2a** a method of propagation in which a part of a plant is induced to form its own roots. **2b** a part separated for this purpose. **3** Also called (esp. US and Canad.): **clipping.** an article, photograph, etc., cut from a publication. **4** the editing process of a film. **5** an excavation in a piece of high land for a road, railway, etc. **6** *Irish inf.* sharp-wittedness: *there is no cutting in him.* ◆ *adj* **7** designed for or adapted to cutting; sharp. **8** keen; piercing. **9** tending to hurt the feelings: *a cutting remark.*
▸ **ˈcuttingly** *adv*

cutting compound *n Engineering.* a mixture, such as

oil, water, and soap, used for cooling drills and other cutting tools.

cutting edge *n* the leading position in any field; forefront: *on the cutting edge of space technology.*

cuttlebone ('kʌtᵊl,bəʊn) *n* the internal calcareous shell of the cuttlefish, used as a mineral supplement to the diet of cagebirds and as a polishing agent. ORIG C16: OE *cudele* + BONE

cuttlefish ('kʌtᵊl,fɪʃ) *n, pl* **cuttlefish** *or* **cuttlefishes.** a cephalopod mollusc which occurs near the bottom of inshore waters and has a broad flattened body. Sometimes shortened to **cuttle.**

cut up *vb (tr, adv)* **1** to cut into pieces. **2** to inflict injuries on. **3** *(usually passive) Inf.* to affect the feelings of deeply. **4** *Inf.* to subject to severe criticism. **5** *Inf.* (of a driver) to overtake or pull in front of (another driver) in a dangerous manner. **6 cut up rough.** *Brit. inf.* to become angry or bad-tempered. ◆ *n* **cut-up. 7** *Inf., chiefly US.* a joker or prankster.

cutwater ('kʌt,wɔːtə) *n* the forward part of the stem of a vessel, which cuts through the water.

cutworm ('kʌt,wɜːm) *n* the caterpillar of various noctuid moths, which is a pest of young crop plants in North America.

cuvée (kuː'veɪ) *n* an individual batch or blend of wine. ORIG C19: from F, lit.: put in a cask, from *cuve* cask

Cuxhaven ★ ('kʊks,hɑːvᵊn; *German* kʊks'haːfən) *n* a port in NW Germany, at the mouth of the River Elbe. Pop.: 55 250 (1989 est.).

Cuyabá ★ *(Portuguese* kuja'ba) *n* a variant spelling of **Cuiabá.**

Cuyp *or* **Kuyp** ★ (kaɪp; *Dutch* kœip) *n* **Aelbert** ('aːlbert). 1620–91, Dutch painter of landscapes and animals.

cuz (kʌz) *n Inf.* **1** Also: **cuzzie.** *NZ.* a term used by a Maori to refer to or address a family member. **2** *Austral.* a term used by an Aboriginal person to refer to or address a family member. ORIG shortened from COUSIN

Cuzco *(Spanish* 'kuθko) *or* **Cusco** ★ *n* a city in S central Peru: former capital of the Inca Empire, with extensive Inca remains; university (1692). Pop.: 255 568 (1993).

CV *abbrev. for* curriculum vitae.

CVS *abbrev. for* chorionic villus sampling.

Cwlth *abbrev. for* Commonwealth.

cwm (kuːm) *n* **1** (in Wales) a valley. **2** *Geol.* another name for **cirque.**

c.w.o. *or* **CWO** *abbrev. for* cash with order.

CWS *abbrev. for* Cooperative Wholesale Society.

cwt *abbrev. for* hundredweight. ORIG *c,* from the L numeral *C* one hundred *(centum)*

CWU (in Britain) *abbrev. for* Communication Workers Union.

-cy *suffix.* **1** indicating state, quality, or condition: *plutocracy; lunacy.* **2** rank or office: *captaincy.* ORIG via OF from L *-cia, -tia,* Gk *-kia, -tia,* abstract noun suffixes

CYA ('siːjɑː) see ya; an abbreviation used as a farewell in text messages, e-mails, etc.

cyan ('saɪæn, 'saɪən) *n* **1** a green-blue colour. ◆ *adj* **2** of this colour. ORIG C19: from Gk *kuanos* dark blue

cyanate ('saɪə,neɪt) *n* any salt or ester of cyanic acid.

cyanic (saɪ'ænɪk) *adj* **1** of or containing cyanogen. **2** blue.

cyanic acid *n* a colourless poisonous volatile liquid acid. Formula: HOCN.

cyanide ('saɪə,naɪd) *or* **cyanid** ('saɪənɪd) *n* any salt of hydrocyanic acid. Cyanides are extremely poisonous.
▸ **,cyani'dation** *n*

cyanite ('saɪə,naɪt) *n* a grey, green, or blue mineral consisting of aluminium silicate in crystalline form.
▸ **cyanitic** (,saɪə'nɪtɪk) *adj*

cyano- *or before a vowel* **cyan-** *combining form.* **1** blue or dark blue. **2** indicating cyanogen. **3** indicating cyanide. ORIG from Gk *kuanos* (adj) dark blue, (n) dark blue enamel, lapis lazuli

cyanobacteria (,saɪənəʊbæk'tɪərɪə) *pl n, sing* **cyanobacterium** (-rɪəm). a group of bacteria (phylum *Cyanobacteria)* containing a blue photosynthetic pigment and formerly regarded as algae. Former name: **blue-green algae.**

cyanocobalamin (,saɪənəʊkəʊ'bæləmɪn) *n* vitamin B_{12}, a complex crystalline compound of cobalt and cyanide, lack of which leads to pernicious anaemia. ORIG C20: from CYANO- + COBAL(T) + (VIT)AMIN

cyanogen (saɪ'ænədʒɪn) *n* an extremely poisonous colourless flammable gas. Formula: $(CN)_2$. ORIG C19: from F *cyanogène;* see CYANO-, -GEN; so named because it is one of the constituents of Prussian blue

cyanosis (,saɪə'nəʊsɪs) *n Pathol.* a bluish-purple discoloration of skin and mucous membranes usually resulting from a deficiency of oxygen in the blood.
▸ **cyanotic** (,saɪə'nɒtɪk) *adj*

Cybele ★ ('sɪbɪlɪ) *n Classical myth.* the Phrygian goddess of nature, mother of all living things and consort of Attis; identified with the Greek Rhea or Demeter.

cyber- *combining form.* indicating computers: *cyberphobia.* ORIG C20: back formation from CYBERNETICS

cybercafé ('saɪbə,kæfɪ, -,kæfeɪ) *n* a café with computer equipment that gives public access to the Internet.

cybernate ('saɪbə,neɪt) *vb* **cybernates, cybernating, cybernated.** to control with a servomechanism or to be controlled by a servomechanism. ORIG C20: from CYBER(NETICS) + -ATE[1]
▸ **,cyber'nation** *n*

cybernetics (,saɪbə'nɛtɪks) *n (functioning as sing)* the branch of science concerned with control systems and comparisons between man-made and biological systems. ORIG C20: from Gk *kubernētēs* steersman, from *kubernan* to steer
▸ **,cyber'netic** *adj* ▸ **,cyber'neticist** *n*

cyberpet ('saɪbə,pɛt) *n* an electronic toy that simulates the activities of a pet, requiring the owner to feed, discipline, and entertain it.

cyberphobia (,saɪbə'fəʊbɪə) *n* an irrational fear of computing.
▸ **,cyber'phobic** *adj*

cyberpunk ('saɪbə,pʌŋk) *n* **1** a genre of science fiction that features rebellious computer hackers and is set in a society integrated by computer networks. **2** a writer of cyberpunk.

cybersex ('saɪbə,sɛks) *n* the exchange of sexual messages or information via the Internet.

cyberspace ('saɪbə,speɪs) *n* all of the data stored in a large computer or network represented as a three-dimensional model through which a virtual-reality user can move.

cybersquatting ('saɪbə,skwɒtɪŋ) *n* the practice of registering an Internet domain name that is likely to be wanted by a person, business, or organization in the hope that it can be sold to them for a profit.
▸ **'cyber,squatter** *n*

cycad ('saɪkæd) *n* a tropical or subtropical plant, having an unbranched stem with fernlike leaves crowded at the top. ORIG C19: from NL *Cycas* name of genus, from Gk *kukas,* scribe's error for *koïkas,* from *koïx* a kind of palm
▸ **,cyca'daceous** *adj*

Cyclades ★ ('sɪklə,diːz) *pl n* a group of over 200 islands in the S Aegean Sea, forming a department of Greece. Capital: Hermoupolis (Siros). Pop.: 94 005 (1991). Area: 2572 sq. km (993 sq. miles). Modern Greek name: **Kikládhes.**
▸ **Cycladic** (sɪ'klædɪk) *adj*

cyclamate ('saɪklə,meɪt, 'sɪkləmeɪt) *n* any of certain compounds formerly used as food additives and sugar substitutes. ORIG C20: *cycl(ohexyl-sulph)amate*

cyclamen ('sɪkləmən, -,mɛn) *n* **1** any Old World plant of the genus *Cyclamen,* having white, pink, or red flowers, with reflexed petals. ◆ *adj* **2** of a dark reddish-purple colour. ORIG C16: from Med. L, from L *cyclamīnos,* from Gk *kuklaminos,* prob. from *kuklos* circle, referring to the bulblike roots

cycle ('saɪkᵊl) *n* **1** a recurring period of time in which certain events or phenomena occur and reach completion. **2** a completed series of events that follows or is followed by another series of similar events occurring in the same

★ people and places

sequence. **3** the time taken or needed for one such series. **4** a vast period of time; age; aeon. **5** a group of poems or prose narratives about a central figure or event: *the Arthurian cycle*. **6** short for **bicycle, motorcycle,** etc. **7** a recurrent series of events or processes in plants and animals: *a life cycle*. **8** one of a series of repeated changes in the magnitude of a periodically varying quantity, such as current or voltage. ◆ *vb* **cycles, cycling, cycled. 9** (*tr*) to process through a cycle or system. **10** (*intr*) to move in or pass through cycles. **11** to travel by or ride a bicycle or tricycle. ORIG C14: from LL *cyclus*, from Gk *kuklos* cycle, circle, ring, wheel

cyclic (ˈsaɪklɪk, ˈsɪklɪk) *or* **cyclical** *adj* **1** recurring or revolving in cycles. **2** (of an organic compound) containing a closed saturated or unsaturated ring of atoms. **3** *Bot.* **3a** arranged in whorls: *cyclic petals*. **3b** having parts arranged in this way: *cyclic flowers*.
▸ **ˈcyclically** *adv*

cycling shorts *pl n* tight-fitting shorts reaching partway to the knee for cycling, sport, etc.

cyclist (ˈsaɪklɪst) *or US* **cycler** *n* a person who rides or travels by bicycle, motorcycle, etc.

cyclo- *or before a vowel* **cycl-** *combining form.* **1** indicating a circle or ring: *cyclotron*. **2** denoting a cyclic compound: *cyclopropane*. ORIG from Gk *kuklos* CYCLE

cyclogiro (ˈsaɪkləʊˌdʒaɪrəʊ) *n, pl* **cyclogiros.** *Aeronautics.* an aircraft lifted and propelled by pivoted blades rotating parallel to roughly horizontal transverse axes.

cyclohexanone (ˌsaɪkləʊˈhɛksəˌnəʊn) *n* a colourless liquid used as a solvent for cellulose lacquers. Formula: $C_6H_{10}O$.

cycloid (ˈsaɪklɔɪd) *adj* **1** resembling a circle. ◆ *n* **2** *Geom.* the curve described by a point on the circumference of a circle as the circle rolls along a straight line.
▸ **cyˈcloidal** *adj*

cyclometer (saɪˈklɒmɪtə) *n* a device that records the number of revolutions made by a wheel and hence the distance travelled.

cyclone (ˈsaɪkləʊn) *n* **1** another name for **depression** (sense 6). **2** a violent tropical storm; hurricane. ◆ *adj* **3** *Austral. & NZ trademark.* (of fencing) made of interlaced wire and metal. ORIG C19: from Gk *kuklōn* a turning around, from *kuklos* wheel
▸ **cyclonic** (saɪˈklɒnɪk) *adj* ▸ **cyˈclonically** *adv*

Cyclopean (ˌsaɪkləʊˈpiːən, saɪˈkləʊpɪən) *adj* **1** of, relating to, or resembling the Cyclops. **2** denoting or having the kind of masonry used in preclassical Greek architecture, characterized by large undressed blocks of stone.

cyclopedia *or* **cyclopaedia** (ˌsaɪkləʊˈpiːdɪə) *n* a less common word for **encyclopedia.**

cyclopentadiene (ˌsaɪkləʊˌpɛntəˈdaɪiːn) *n* a colourless liquid unsaturated cyclic hydrocarbon obtained in the cracking of petroleum hydrocarbons and the distillation of coal tar: used in the manufacture of plastics and insecticides. Formula: C_5H_6.

cyclophosphamide (ˌsaɪkləʊˈfɒsfəˌmaɪd) *n* a cytotoxic drug used in the treatment of leukaemia and lymphoma. ORIG C20: from CYCLO- + PHOSPH(ORUS) + AMIDE

cyclopropane (ˌsaɪkləʊˈprəʊpeɪn) *n* a colourless gaseous hydrocarbon, used as an anaesthetic. Formula: C_3H_6.

Cyclops (ˈsaɪklɒps) *n, pl* **Cyclopes** (saɪˈkləʊpiːz) *or* **Cyclopses.** *Classical myth.* one of a race of giants having a single eye in the middle of the forehead. ORIG C15: from L *Cyclōps*, from Gk *Kuklōps*, lit.: round eye, from *kuklos* circle + *ōps* eye

cyclorama (ˌsaɪkləʊˈrɑːmə) *n* **1** a large picture on the interior wall of a cylindrical room, designed to appear in natural perspective to a spectator. **2** *Theatre.* a curtain or wall curving along the back of a stage, usually painted to represent the sky. ORIG C19: CYCLO- + Gk *horama* view, sight, on the model of *panorama*
▸ **cycloramic** (ˌsaɪkləʊˈræmɪk) *adj*

cyclosporin-A (ˌsaɪkləʊˈspɔːrɪn-) *n* a drug extracted from a fungus and used in transplant surgery to suppress the body's immune mechanisms, and so prevent rejection of an organ.

cyclostome (ˈsaɪkləˌstəʊm, ˈsɪk-) *n* any primitive aquatic jawless vertebrate, such as the lamprey, having a round sucking mouth.
▸ **cyclostomate** (saɪˈklɒstəmɪt, -ˌmeɪt) *or* **cyclostomatous** (ˌsaɪkləʊˈstɒmətəs, -ˈstəʊmə-, ˌsɪk-) *adj*

cyclostyle (ˈsaɪkləˌstaɪl) *n* **1** a kind of pen with a small toothed wheel, used for cutting holes in a specially prepared stencil. **2** an office duplicator using such a stencil. ◆ *vb* **cyclostyles, cyclostyling, cyclostyled. 3** (*tr*) to print using such a stencil.
▸ **ˈcycloˌstyled** *adj*

cyclothymia (ˌsaɪkləʊˈθaɪmɪə) *n Psychiatry.* a condition characterized by alternating periods of excitement and depression. ORIG from CYCLO- + Gk *thumos*, cast of mind + -IA
▸ **ˌcycloˈthymic** *adj*

cyclotron (ˈsaɪkləˌtrɒn) *n* a type of particle accelerator in which the particles spiral under the effect of a strong vertical magnetic field.

cyder (ˈsaɪdə) *n* a variant spelling of **cider.**

cygnet (ˈsɪgnɪt) *n* a young swan. ORIG C15 *sygnett*, from OF *cygne* swan, from L *cygnus*, from Gk *kuknos*

cylinder (ˈsɪlɪndə) *n* **1** a solid consisting of two parallel planes bounded by identical closed curves, usually circles, that are interconnected at every point by a set of parallel lines, usually perpendicular to the planes. **2** a surface formed by a line moving round a closed plane curve at a fixed angle to it. **3** any object shaped like a cylinder. **4** the chamber in a reciprocating internal-combustion engine, pump, or compressor within which the piston moves. The cylinders are housed in the metal **cylinder block,** which is topped by the **cylinder head. 5** the rotating mechanism of a revolver, containing cartridge chambers. **6** *Printing.* any of the rotating drums on a printing press. **7** Also called: **cylinder seal.** an ancient cylindrical seal found in the Middle East and Balkans. ORIG C16: from L *cylindrus*, from Gk *kulindros* a roller, from *kulindein* to roll
▸ **ˈcylinder-ˌlike** *adj*

cylindrical (sɪˈlɪndrɪkəl) *or* **cylindric** *adj* of, shaped like, or characteristic of a cylinder.
▸ **cyˌlindriˈcality** *n* ▸ **cyˈlindrically** *adv*

cymbal (ˈsɪmbəl) *n* a percussion instrument consisting of a thin circular piece of brass, which vibrates when clashed together with another cymbal or struck with a stick. ORIG OE *cymbala*, from L *cymbalum*, from Gk *kumbalon*, from *kumbē* something hollow
▸ **ˈcymbalist** *n*

Cymbeline ★ (ˈsɪmbəˌliːn) *n* See **Cunobelinus.**

cyme (saɪm) *n* an inflorescence in which the first flower is the terminal bud of the main stem and subsequent flowers develop as terminal buds of lateral stems. ORIG C18: from L *cȳma* cabbage sprout, from Gk *kuma* anything swollen
▸ **cymiferous** (saɪˈmɪfərəs) *adj* ▸ **cymose** (ˈsaɪməʊs, -məʊz, saɪˈməʊs) *adj*

Cymric *or* **Kymric** (ˈkɪmrɪk) *n* **1** the Welsh language. **2** the Brythonic group of Celtic languages. ◆ *adj* **3** of or relating to the Cymry, any of their languages, Wales, or the Welsh.

Cymru ★ (*Welsh* kumˈri) *n* the Welsh name for **Wales.**

Cymry *or* **Kymry** (ˈkɪmrɪ) *n* **the.** (*functioning as pl*) **1** the Brythonic Celts, comprising the present-day Welsh, Cornish, and Bretons. **2** the Welsh people. ORIG Welsh: the Welsh

Cynewulf, Kynewulf (ˈkɪnɪˌwʊlf), *or* **Cynwulf** ★ (ˈkɪnˌwʊlf) *n* ?8th century A.D., Anglo-Saxon poet; author of *Juliana, The Ascension*, and *The Fates of the Apostles*.

cynic (ˈsɪnɪk) *n* **1** a person who believes the worst about people or the outcome of events. ◆ *adj* **2** a less common word for **cynical.** ORIG C16: via L from Gk *Kunikos*, from *kuōn* dog

Cynic (ˈsɪnɪk) *n* a member of an ancient Greek sect that scorned worldly things.

cynical (ˈsɪnɪkəl) *adj* **1** believing the worst of others, esp. that all acts are selfish. **2** sarcastic; mocking. **3** showing

contempt for accepted standards, esp. of honesty or morality.
▸ **'cynically** *adv* ▸ **'cynicalness** *n*

cynicism ('sɪnɪˌsɪzəm) *n* **1** the attitude or beliefs of a cynic. **2** a cynical action, idea, etc.

Cynicism ('sɪnɪˌsɪzəm) *n* the doctrines of the Cynics.

cynosure ('sɪnəˌzjʊə, -ʃʊə) *n* **1** a person or thing that attracts notice. **2** something that serves as a guide. ORIG C16: from L *Cynosūra* the constellation of Ursa Minor, from Gk *Kunosoura,* from *kuōn* dog + *oura* tail

Cynthia ★ ('sɪnθɪə) *n* another name for **Artemis** (Diana).

cypher ('saɪfə) *n, vb* a variant spelling of **cipher**.

cypress ('saɪprəs) *n* **1** any coniferous tree of a N temperate genus having dark green scalelike leaves and rounded cones. **2** any of several similar and related trees. **3** the wood of any of these trees. **4** cypress branches used as a symbol of mourning. ORIG OE *cypresse,* from L *cyparissus,* from Gk *kuparissos;* rel. to L *cupressus*

cypress pine *n* any coniferous tree of an Australian genus yielding valuable timber.

Cyprian ★ ('sɪprɪən) *n* **Saint.** ?200–258 A.D., bishop of Carthage and martyr. Feast day: Sept. 26 or 16.

cyprinid (sɪ'praɪnɪd, 'sɪprɪnɪd) *n* **1** any teleost fish of the mainly freshwater family Cyprinidae, typically having toothless jaws and including the carp, tench, and dace. ◆ *adj* **2** of, relating to, or belonging to the Cyprinidae. **3** resembling a carp; cyprinoid. ORIG C19: from NL *Cyprīnidae,* from L *cyprīnus* carp, from Gk *kuprinos*

cyprinoid ('sɪprɪˌnɔɪd, sɪ'praɪnɔɪd) *adj* **1** of or relating to the Cyprinoidea, a large suborder of teleost fishes including the cyprinids, electric eels, and loaches. **2** of, relating to, or resembling the carp. ◆ *n* **3** any fish belonging to the Cyprinoidea. ORIG C19: from L *cyprīnus* carp

Cypriot ('sɪprɪət) *or* **Cypriote** ('sɪprɪˌəʊt) *n* **1** a native or inhabitant of Cyprus. **2** the dialect of Greek spoken in Cyprus. ◆ *adj* **3** denoting or relating to Cyprus, its inhabitants, or dialects.

cypripedium (ˌsɪprɪ'piːdɪəm) *n* any orchid of a genus having large flowers with an inflated pouchlike lip. See also **lady's-slipper.** ORIG C18: from NL, from L *Cypria* the Cyprian, that is, Venus + *pēs* foot (that is, Venus' slipper)

Cyprus ★ ('saɪprəs) *n* an island in the E Mediterranean: ceded to Britain by Turkey in 1878 and made a colony in 1925; became an independent republic and member of the Commonwealth in 1960; invaded by Turkey in 1974 following a Greek-supported military coup, leading to the virtual partition of the island. In 1983 the Turkish-controlled northern sector declared itself to be an independent state as the Turkish Republic of Northern Cyprus but failed to receive international recognition. Attempts by the UN to negotiate a reunification agreement have failed. Languages: Greek and Turkish. Religions: Greek Orthodox and Muslim. Currency: pound and Turkish lira. Capital: Nicosia. Pop. (Greek): 662 000 (1997); (Turkish): 198 000 (1997). Area: 9251 sq. km (3571 sq. miles).

Cyrano de Bergerac ★ (*French* sirano də bɛrʒərak) *n* **Savinien** (savinjɛ̃). 1619–55, French writer and soldier, famous as a duellist and for his large nose.

Cyrenaic (ˌsaɪrə'neɪɪk, ˌsɪrə-) *adj* **1** of or relating to the ancient Greek city of Cyrene. **2** of or relating to the philosophical school founded by Aristippus in Cyrene that held pleasure to be the highest good. ◆ *n* **3** a follower of the Cyrenaica school of philosophy.

Cyrene ★ (saɪ'riːnɪ) *n* an ancient Greek city of N Africa: famous for its medical school.

Cyril ★ ('sɪrəl) *n* **Saint.** ?827–869 A.D., Greek Christian theologian, missionary to the Moravians and said to be the inventor of the Cyrillic alphabet; he and his brother Saint Methodius were called *the Apostles of the Slavs.* Feast day: Feb. 14 or May 11.

Cyrillic (sɪ'rɪlɪk) *adj* **1** denoting or relating to the alphabet said to have been devised by Saint Cyril, for Slavonic languages: now used primarily for Russian and Bulgarian. ◆ *n* **2** this alphabet.

Cyril of Alexandria ★ *n* **Saint.** ?375–444 A.D., Christian theologian and patriarch of Alexandria. Feast day: June 27 or June 9.

Cyrus ★ ('saɪrəs) *n* **1** known as *Cyrus the Great* or *Cyrus the Elder.* died ?529 B.C., king of Persia and founder of the Persian empire. **2** called *the Younger.* died 401 B.C., Persian satrap of Lydia: revolted against his brother Artaxerxes II, but was killed at the battle of Cunaxa. See also **anabasis.**

cyst (sɪst) *n* **1** *Pathol.* any abnormal membranous sac or blister-like pouch containing fluid or semisolid material. **2** *Anat.* any normal sac in the body. **3** a protective membrane enclosing a cell, larva, or organism. ORIG C18: from NL *cystis,* from Gk *kustis* pouch, bag, bladder

-cyst *n combining form.* indicating a bladder or sac: *otocyst.* ORIG from Gk *kustis* bladder

cystectomy (sɪ'stɛktəmɪ) *n, pl* **cystectomies. 1** surgical removal of the gall bladder or part of the urinary bladder. **2** surgical removal of a cyst.

cystic ('sɪstɪk) *adj* **1** of, relating to, or resembling a cyst. **2** having or enclosed within a cyst; encysted. **3** relating to the gall bladder or urinary bladder.

cysticercus (ˌsɪstɪ'sɜːkəs) *n, pl* **cysticerci** (-saɪ). an encysted larval form of many tapeworms, consisting of a head inverted in a fluid-filled bladder. ORIG C19: from NL, from Gk *kustis* pouch, bladder + *kerkos* tail

cystic fibrosis *n* an inheritable disease of the exocrine glands, controlled by a recessive gene: affected children inherit defective alleles from both parents. It is characterized by chronic infection of the respiratory tract and by pancreatic insufficiency.

cystitis (sɪ'staɪtɪs) *n* inflammation of the urinary bladder.

cysto- *or before a vowel* **cyst-** *combining form.* indicating a cyst or bladder: *cystoscope.*

cystoid ('sɪstɔɪd) *adj* **1** resembling a cyst or bladder. ◆ *n* **2** a tissue mass that resembles a cyst but lacks an outer membrane.

cystoscope ('sɪstəˌskəʊp) *n* a slender tubular medical instrument for examining the interior of the urethra and urinary bladder.
▸ **cystoscopic** (ˌsɪstə'skɒpɪk) *adj* ▸ **cystoscopy** (sɪs'tɒskəpɪ) *n*

-cyte *n combining form.* indicating a cell. ORIG from NL *-cyta,* from Gk *kutos* vessel

Cythera ★ (sɪ'θɪərə) *n* **1** a Greek island off the SE coast of the Peloponnese: in ancient times a centre of the worship of Aphrodite. Pop.: 3500 (latest est.). Area: about 285 sq. km (110 sq. miles). **2** the chief town of this island, on the S coast. Pop.: 300 (latest est.). ◆ Modern Greek name: **Kíthira.**

Cytherea ★ (ˌsɪθə'riːə) *n* another name for **Aphrodite** (Venus).
▸ **ˌCyther'ean** *adj*

cyto- *combining form.* indicating a cell: *cytoplasm.* ORIG from Gk *kutos* vessel

cytogenetics (ˌsaɪtəʊdʒɪ'nɛtɪks) *n* (*functioning as sing*) the branch of genetics that correlates the structure of chromosomes with heredity and variation.
▸ **ˌcytoge'netic** *adj*

cytokine ('saɪtəʊˌkaɪn) *n* any of various proteins, secreted by cells, that carry signals to neighbouring cells. Cytokines include interferon.

cytokinin (ˌsaɪtəʊ'kaɪnɪn) *n* any of a group of plant hormones that promote cell division and retard ageing. Also called: **kinin.**

cytology (saɪ'tɒlədʒɪ) *n* **1** the study of plant and animal cells. **2** the detailed structure of a tissue as revealed by microscopic examination.
▸ **cytological** (ˌsaɪtə'lɒdʒɪkᵊl) *adj* ▸ **ˌcyto'logically** *adv* ▸ **cy'tologist** *n*

cytomegalovirus (ˌsaɪtəʊˌmɛgələʊ'vaɪrəs) *n* a virus that may cause serious disease in patients whose immune systems are compromised and the birth of handicapped children to pregnant women infected with it. Abbrev.: **CMV.**

cytoplasm ('saɪtəʊˌplæzəm) *n* the protoplasm of a cell excluding the nucleus.
▸ **ˌcyto'plasmic** *adj*

cytosine (ˈsaɪtəsɪn) *n* a white crystalline base occurring in nucleic acids. ORIG C19: from CYTO- + -OSE[2] + -INE[2]

cytotoxic (ˌsaɪtəʊˈtɒksɪk) *adj* destructive to cells, esp. to cancer cells: *cytotoxic drugs.*
▸ **cytotoxicity** (ˌsaɪtəʊtɒkˈsɪsɪtɪ) *n*

cytotoxin (ˌsaɪtəʊˈtɒksɪn) *n* any substance that is poisonous to living cells.

Cyzicus ★ (ˈsɪzɪkəs) *n* an ancient Greek colony in NW Asia Minor on the S shore of the Sea of Marmara: site of Alcibiades' victory over the Peloponnesians (410 B.C.).

czar (zɑː) *n* a variant spelling (esp. US) of **tsar.**
▸ **ˈczardom** *n* ▸ **ˈCzarevitch, czaˈrevna, czaˈrina, ˈczarism, ˈczarist:** see **ts-** spellings.

czardas (ˈtʃɑːdæʃ) *n* **1** a Hungarian national dance of alternating slow and fast sections. **2** music for this dance. ORIG from Hungarian *csárdás*

Czech (tʃɛk) *adj* **1a** of, relating to, or characteristic of the Czech Republic, its people, or their language. **1b** of, relating to, or characteristic of Bohemia and Moravia, their people, or their language. **1c** (loosely) of, relating to, or characteristic of the former Czechoslovakia or its people. ♦ *n* **2** the official languages of the Czech Republic, belonging to the West Slavonic branch of the Indo-European family. Czech is closely related to Slovak; they are mutually intelligible. **3a** a native or inhabitant of the Czech Republic. **3b** a native or inhabitant of Bohemia or Moravia. **3c** (loosely) a native, inhabitant, or citizen of the former Czechoslovakia. ORIG C19: from Polish, from Czech *Čech*

Czechoslovak (ˌtʃɛkəʊˈsləʊvæk) *or* **Czechoslovakian** (ˌtʃɛkəʊsləʊˈvækɪən) *adj* **1** of or relating to the former Czechoslovakia, its peoples, or languages. ♦ *n* **2** (loosely) either of the two languages of the former Czechoslovakia: Czech or Slovak.

Czechoslovakia ★ (ˌtʃɛkəʊsləʊˈvækɪə) *n* a former republic in central Europe: formed after the defeat of Austria-Hungary (1918) as a nation of Czechs in Bohemia and Moravia and Slovaks in Slovakia; occupied by Germany from 1939 until its liberation by the Soviet Union in 1945; became a people's republic under the Communists in 1948; invaded by Warsaw Pact troops in 1968, ending Dubček's attempt to liberalize communism; in 1989 popular unrest led to the resignation of the Politburo and the formation of a non-Communist government. It consisted of two federal republics, the **Czech Republic** and the **Slovak Republic**, which became independent countries in 1993. Czech name: **Československo.**
▸ **ˌCzechosloˈvakian** *adj, n*

Czech Republic ★ *n* a country in central Europe; formed part of Czechoslovakia until 1993; mostly wooded, with lowlands surrounding the River Morava, rising to the Bohemian plateau in the W and to highlands in the N. Language: Czech. Religion: Christian majority Currency: koruna. Capital: Prague. Pop.: 10 290 000 (1999 est.). Area: 78 864 sq. km (30 450 sq. miles).

Czernowitz ★ (ˈtʃɛrnovɪts) *n* the German name for **Chernovtsy.**

Czerny ★ (*German* ˈtʃɛrni) *n* **Karl** (karl). 1791–1857, Austrian pianist, composer, and teacher, noted for his studies.

Częstochowa ★ (*Polish* tʃɛ̃stɔˈxɔva) *n* an industrial city in S Poland, on the River Warta: pilgrimage centre. Pop.: 259 800 (1995 est.).

Dd

d *or* **D** (diː) *n, pl* **d's, D's,** *or* **Ds. 1** the fourth letter of the modern English alphabet. **2** a speech sound represented by this letter.

d *symbol for Physics.* density.

D *symbol for:* **1** *Music.* **1a** the second note of the scale of C major. **1b** the major or minor key having this note as its tonic. **2** *Chem.* deuterium. **3a** a semiskilled or unskilled manual worker, or a trainee or apprentice to a skilled worker. **3b** (*as modifier*): *D worker.* ◆ See also **occupation groupings.** ◆ **4** *the Roman numeral for* 500.

2,4-D *n* a synthetic auxin widely used as a weedkiller; 2,4-dichlorophenoxyacetic acid.

d. *abbrev. for:* **1** date. **2** daughter. **3** degree. **4** delete. **5** *Brit. currency before decimalization.* penny *or* pennies. ORIG L *denarius* or *denarii* **6** depart(s). **7** diameter. **8** died. **9** dose.

D. *abbrev. for:* **1** *US.* Democrat(ic). **2** Department. **3** Deus. ORIG L: God **4** *Optics.* dioptre. **5** Director. **6** Dominus. ORIG L: Lord **7** Dutch.

'd *contraction for* would *or* had: *I'd; you'd.*

DA *abbrev. for:* **1** (in the US) District Attorney. **2** Diploma of Art. **3** duck's arse (hairstyle). **4** drug addict.

dab[1] (dæb) *vb* **dabs, dabbing, dabbed. 1** to touch or pat lightly and quickly. **2** (*tr*) to daub with short tapping strokes: *to dab the wall with paint.* **3** (*tr*) to apply (paint, cream, etc.) with short tapping strokes. ◆ *n* **4** a small amount, esp. of something soft or moist. **5** a light stroke or tap, as with the hand. **6** (*often pl*) *Chiefly Brit.* a slang word for **fingerprint.** ORIG C14: imit.
▸ **'dabber** *n*

dab[2] (dæb) *n* **1** a small common European flatfish covered with rough toothed scales. **2** any of various other small flatfish. ORIG C15: from Anglo-F *dabbe,* from ?

DAB *abbrev. for* digital audio broadcasting.

dabble ('dæbᵊl) *vb* **dabbles, dabbling, dabbled. 1** to dip, move, or splash (the fingers, feet, etc.) in a liquid. **2** (*intr;* usually foll. by *in, with,* or *at*) to deal (with) or work (at) frivolously or superficially. **3** (*tr*) to splash or smear. ORIG C16: prob. from Du. *dabbelen*
▸ **'dabbler** *n*

dabchick ('dæbˌtʃɪk) *n* any of several small grebes. ORIG C16: prob. from OE *dop* to dive + CHICK

dab hand *n Brit. inf.* a person who is particularly skilled at something: *a dab hand at chess.* ORIG ?from DAB[1]

da capo (dɑː 'kɑːpəʊ) *adj, adv Music.* to be repeated from the beginning. ORIG C18: from It., lit.: from the head

Dacca ★ ('dækə) *n* the former name (until 1982) of **Dhaka.**

dace (deɪs) *n, pl* **dace** *or* **daces. 1** a European freshwater fish of the carp family. **2** any of various similar fishes. ORIG C15: from OF *dars* DART

dacha *or* **datcha** ('dætʃə) *n* a country house or cottage in Russia. ORIG from Russian: a giving, gift

Dachau ★ (*German* 'daxau) *n* a town in S Germany, in Bavaria: site of a Nazi concentration camp. Pop.: 34 183 (1989 est.).

dachshund ('dæksˌhʊnd, 'dæʃənd) *n* a long-bodied short-legged breed of dog. ORIG C19: from G, from *Dachs* badger + *Hund* dog

Dacia ★ ('deɪsɪə) *n* an ancient region bounded by the Carpathians, the Tisza, and the Danube, roughly corresponding to modern Romania. United under kings from about 60 B.C., it later contained the Roman province of the same name (about 105 to 270 A.D.).
▸ **'Dacian** *adj, n*

dacoit (də'kɔɪt) *n* (in India and Myanmar) a member of a gang of armed robbers. ORIG C19: from Hindi *dakait,* from *dākā* robbery

Dacron ('deɪkrɒn, 'dæk-) *n* the US name (trademark) for **Terylene.**

dactyl ('dæktɪl) *n Prosody.* a metrical foot of three syllables, one long followed by two short (–⏑⏑) ORIG C14: via L from Gk *daktulos* finger, comparing the finger's three joints to the three syllables

dactylic (dæk'tɪlɪk) *adj* **1** of, relating to, or having a dactyl: *dactylic verse.* ◆ *n* **2** a variant of **dactyl.**
▸ **dac'tylically** *adv*

dad (dæd) *n* an informal word for **father.** ORIG C16: childish word

Dada ('dɑːdɑː) *or* **Dadaism** ('dɑːdɑːˌɪzəm) *n* a nihilistic artistic movement of the early 20th century, founded on principles of irrationality, incongruity, and irreverence towards accepted aesthetic criteria. ORIG C20: from F, from children's word for hobbyhorse
▸ **'Dadaist** *n, adj* ▸ **ˌDada'istic** *adj*

daddy ('dædɪ) *n, pl* **daddies. 1** an informal word for **father. 2 the daddy.** *Sl., chiefly US, Canad., & Austral.* the supreme or finest example.

daddy-longlegs *n* **1** *Brit., Austral., & NZ.* an informal name for **crane fly. 2** *US, Canad., Austral., & NZ.* an informal name for **harvestman** (sense 2).

dado ('deɪdəʊ) *n, pl* **dadoes** *or* **dados. 1** the lower part of an interior wall that is decorated differently from the upper part. **2** *Archit.* the part of a pedestal between the base and the cornice. ◆ *vb* **3** (*tr*) to provide with a dado. ORIG C17: from It.: die, die-shaped pedestal

Dadra and Nagar Haveli ★ (də'drɑː; 'nʌgə ə'vɛlɪ) *n* a union territory of W India, on the Gulf of Cambay: until 1961 administratively part of Portuguese Damão. Capital: Silvassa. Pop.: 153 000 (1994 est.). Area: 489 sq. km (191 sq. miles).

Daedalus ★ ('diːdələs) *n Greek myth.* an Athenian architect and inventor who built the labyrinth for Minos on Crete and fashioned wings for himself and his son Icarus to flee their imprisonment on the island.
▸ **Daedalian, Daedalean** (dɪ'deɪlɪən), *or* **Daedalic** (dɪ'dælɪk) *adj*

daemon ('diːmən) *or* **daimon** *n* **1** a demigod. **2** the guardian spirit of a place or person. **3** a variant spelling of **demon** (sense 3).
▸ **daemonic** (diː'mɒnɪk) *adj*

daff (dæf) *n Inf.* short for **daffodil.**

daffodil ('dæfədɪl) *n* **1** Also called: **Lent lily.** a widely cultivated Eurasian plant, *Narcissus pseudonarcissus,* having spring-blooming yellow nodding flowers. **2** any other plant of the genus *Narcissus.* **3a** a brilliant yellow colour. **3b** (*as adj*): *daffodil paint.* **4** a daffodil as a national emblem of Wales. ORIG C14: from Med. L *affodillus,* var. of L *asphodelus* ASPHODEL

daffy ('dæfɪ) *adj* **daffier, daffiest.** *Inf.* another word for **daft** (senses 1, 2). ORIG C19: from obs. *daff* fool

daft (dɑːft) *adj Chiefly Brit.* **1** *Inf.* foolish, simple, or stupid. **2** a slang word for **insane. 3** (*postpositive;* foll. by *about*) *Inf.* extremely fond (of). **4** *Sl.* frivolous; giddy. ORIG OE *gedæfte* gentle, foolish
▸ **'daftness** *n*

daftie ('dɑːftɪ) *n Inf.* a daft person.

Dafydd ap Gruffudd ★ (*Welsh* 'davɪð æp 'grɪfɪθ) *n* died 1283, Welsh leader. Claiming the title Prince of Wales (1282), he led an unsuccessful revolt against Edward I: executed.

Dafydd ap Gwilym ★ (*Welsh* 'gwɪlɪm) *n* ?1320–?1380, Welsh poet.

dag[1] (dæg) *n* **1** short for **daglock.** ◆ *vb* **dags, dagging, dagged. 2** to cut the daglock away from (a sheep). ORIG C18: from ?
▸ **'dagger** *n*

dag[2] (dæg) *n Austral. & NZ inf.* **1** a character; eccentric. **2** a person who is untidily dressed. **3** a person with a good sense of humour.4 **rattle one's dags.** to hurry up. ORIG back formation from DAGGY

★ people and places

Da Gama ★ (də 'gɑːmə) *n* See (Vasco da) **Gama.**

Dagan ★ ('dɑːgən) *n* an earth god of the Babylonians and Assyrians.

Dagenham ★ ('dægənəm) *n* part of the Greater London borough of Barking and Dagenham: motor-vehicle manufacturing.

Dagestan Republic ★ (ˌdɑːgɪ'stɑːn) *n* a constituent republic of S Russia, on the Caspian Sea: annexed from Persia in 1813; rich mineral resources. Capital: Makhachkala. Pop.: 2 098 000 (1996 est.). Area: 50 278 sq. km (19 416 sq. miles). Also called: **Dagestan** or **Daghestan.**

dagga ('daxə, 'dɑːgə) *n S. African inf.* a local name for marijuana. ORIG C19: from Afrik., from Khoikhoi *dagab*

dagger ('dægə) *n* **1** a short stabbing weapon with a pointed blade. **2** Also called: **obelisk.** a character (†) used in printing to indicate a cross reference. **3 at daggers drawn.** in a state of open hostility. **4 look daggers.** to glare with hostility; scowl. ORIG C14: from ?

daggy ('dægɪ) *adj* **daggier, daggiest.** *Inf.* **1** *Austral.* untidy; dishevelled. **2** *NZ.* amusing; comical. ORIG from DAG[1]

daglock ('dægˌlɒk) *n* a dung-caked lock of wool around the hindquarters of a sheep. ORIG C17: see DAG[1], LOCK[2]

dago ('deɪgəʊ) *n, pl* **dagos** *or* **dagoes.** *Derog.* a foreigner, esp. a Spaniard or Portuguese. ORIG C19: from *Diego,* a common Sp. name

Dagon ★ ('deɪgɒn) *n Bible.* a god worshipped by the Philistines, represented as half man and half fish. ORIG C14: via L and Gk from Heb. *Dāgōn,* lit.: little fish

Daguerre ★ (*French* dagɛr) *n* **Louis Jacques Mandé** (lwi ʒak mɑ̃de). 1789–1851, French inventor, who devised one of the first practical photographic processes (1838).

daguerreotype (də'gɛrəʊˌtaɪp) *n* **1** one of the earliest photographic processes, in which the image was produced on iodine-sensitized silver and developed in mercury vapour. **2** a photograph formed by this process.
▸ **da'guerreoˌtypy** *n*

Dahl ★ (dɑːl) *n* **Roald** ('rəʊəld). 1916–90, British writer with Norwegian parents, noted for such children's books as *Charlie and the Chocolate Factory* (1964).

dahlia ('deɪljə) *n* **1** any herbaceous perennial plant of the Mexican genus *Dahlia,* having showy flowers and tuberous roots. **2** the flower or root of any of these plants. ORIG C19: after Anders *Dahl,* 18th-cent. Swedish botanist

Dahna ★ ('dɑːxnɑː) *n* another name for **Rub' al Khali.**

Dahomey ★ (də'həʊmɪ) *n* the former name (until 1975) of **Benin.**

Dáil Éireann ('dɑːl 'eːrɪn) *or* **Dáil** *n* (in the Republic of Ireland) the lower chamber of parliament. ORIG from Irish *dáil* assembly + *Éireann* of Eire

daily ('deɪlɪ) *adj* **1** of or occurring every day or every weekday. ◆ *n, pl* **dailies. 2** a daily newspaper. **3** *Brit.* a charwoman. ◆ *adv* **4** every day. **5** constantly; often. ORIG OE *dæglīc*

Daimler ★ ('deɪmlə) *n* **Gottlieb** (**Wilhelm**) (*German* 'gɔtliːp). 1834–1900, German engineer and car manufacturer, who collaborated with Nikolaus Otto in inventing the first internal-combustion engine (1876).

daimon ('daɪmɒn) *n* a variant spelling of **daemon** or **demon** (sense 3).
▸ **dai'monic** *adj*

daimyo bond ('daɪmjəʊ) *n* a bearer bond issued in Japan and the eurobond market by the World Bank. ORIG from Japanese, from Ancient Chinese

dainty ('deɪntɪ) *adj* **daintier, daintiest. 1** delicate or elegant. **2** choice; delicious: *a dainty morsel.* **3** excessively genteel; fastidious. ◆ *n, pl* **dainties. 4** a choice piece of food; delicacy. ORIG C13: from OF *deintié,* from L *dignitās* DIGNITY
▸ **'daintily** *adv*

daiquiri ('daɪkɪrɪ, 'dæk-) *n, pl* **daiquiris.** an iced drink containing rum, lime juice, and sugar. ORIG C20: after *Daiquiri,* town in Cuba

dairy ('dɛərɪ) *n, pl* **dairies. 1** a company that supplies milk and milk products. **2** a room or building where milk and cream are stored or made into butter and cheese. **3a** (*modifier*) of, relating to, or containing milk and milk products. **3b** (*in combination*): *a dairymaid.* **4a** a general shop, selling provisions, esp. milk and milk products. **4b** *NZ.* a shop selling milk and groceries that remains open outside normal trading hours. ORIG C13 *daierie,* from OE *dǣge* servant girl, one who kneads bread

dairying ('dɛərɪɪŋ) *n* the business of producing, processing, and selling dairy products.

dairyman ('dɛərɪmən) *n, pl* **dairymen.** a man who works in a dairy.

dais ('deɪɪs, deɪs) *n* a raised platform, usually at one end of a hall, used by speakers, etc. ORIG C13: from OF *deis,* from L *discus* DISCUS

daisy ('deɪzɪ) *n, pl* **daisies. 1** a small low-growing European plant having flower heads with a yellow centre and pinkish-white outer rays. **2** any of various other composite plants having conspicuous ray flowers. **3** *Sl.* an excellent person or thing. **4 pushing up the daisies.** dead and buried. ORIG OE *dægesēge* day's eye
▸ **'daisied** *adj*

daisy chain *n* a garland made, esp. by children, by threading daisies together.

daisycutter ('deɪzɪˌkʌtə) *n Sport.* a ball bowled so that it rolls along the ground.

daisywheel ('deɪzɪˌwiːl) *n Computing.* a component of a computer printer shaped like a wheel with many spokes that prints using a disk with characters around the circumference. Also called: **printwheel.**

Dak. *abbrev. for* Dakota.

Dakar ★ ('dækə) *n* the capital and chief port of Senegal, on the SE side of Cape Verde peninsula. Pop.: 1 500 000 (1995 est.).

Dakota ★ (də'kəʊtə) *n* a former territory of the US: divided into the states of North Dakota and South Dakota in 1889.
▸ **Da'kotan** *adj, n*

daks (dæks) *pl n Austral. inf.* trousers. ORIG C20: from trade name *Daks*

dal (dɑːl) *n* **1** split grain, a common foodstuff in India; pulse. **2** a variant spelling of **dhal.**

Daladier ★ (*French* daladje) *n* **Édouard** (edwar). 1884–1970, French socialist statesman; premier (1933; 1934; 1938–40).

Dalai Lama ★ ('dælaɪ 'lɑːmə) *n* **1** (until 1959) the chief lama and ruler of Tibet. **2** born 1935, the 14th holder of this office (from 1940), who fled to India (1959); Nobel peace prize 1989. ORIG from Mongolian *dalai* ocean; see LAMA

dale (deɪl) *n* an open valley. ORIG OE *dæl*

Dale ★ (deɪl) *n* Sir **Henry Hallet.** 1875–1968, British physiologist: shared a Nobel prize for physiology or medicine in 1936 for work on the transmission of nerve impulses.

Dalek ('dɑːlɛk) *n* a fictional robot-like creation that is aggressive, mobile, and produces rasping staccato speech. ORIG C20: from a children's television series, *Dr Who*

d'Alembert ★ (*French* dalɑ̃bɛr) *n* See (Jean le Rond d') **Alembert.**

Dales ★ (deɪlz) *pl n* (*sometimes not cap.*) **the.** short for the **Yorkshire Dales.**

dalesman ('deɪlzmən) *n, pl* **dalesmen.** a person living in a dale, esp. in the Yorkshire Dales.

Dalglish ★ (dæl'gliːʃ, dəl-) *n* **Kenny,** born 1951, Scottish footballer: Scotland's most-capped footballer.

Dalhousie ★ (dæl'haʊzɪ) *n* **1 9th Earl of,** title of *George Ramsay.* 1770–1838, British general; governor of British Canada (1819–28). **2** his son, **1st Marquis and 10th Earl of,** title of *James Andrew Broun Ramsay.* 1812–60, British statesman: governor general of India (1848–56).

Dali ★ ('dɑːlɪ; *Spanish* da'liː) *n* **Salvador** ('sælvədɔː). 1904–89, Spanish surrealist painter.

Dalian (dɑːl'jɛn) *or* **Talien** ★ (tɑːl'jɛn) *n* a city in NE China; with the adjoining city of Lü-shun comprises the port complex of Lüda. Pop.: 2 330 000 (1993). Former name: **Dairen.**

Dallapiccola ★ (*Italian* dalla'pikkola) *n* **Luigi** (lu'iːdʒi). 1904–75, Italian composer; his works include the opera *Il Prigioniero* (1944–48) and the ballet *Marsia* (1948).

Dallas ★ (ˈdæləs) *n* a city in NE Texas, on the Trinity River: scene of the assassination of President John F. Kennedy (1963). Pop.: 1 053 292 (1996 est.).

dalles (ˈdæləs, dælz) *pl n Canad.* a stretch of river between high rock walls, with rapids and dangerous currents. ORIG from Canad. F.: sink; see DALE

dalliance (ˈdælɪəns) *n* waste of time in frivolous action or in dawdling.

dally (ˈdælɪ) *vb* **dallies, dallying, dallied.** (*intr*) **1** to waste time idly; dawdle. **2** (usually foll. by *with*) to deal frivolously; trifle: *to dally with someone's affections.* ORIG C14: from Anglo-F *dalier* to gossip, from ?

Dalmatia ★ (dælˈmeɪʃə) *n* a region of W Croatia along the Adriatic: mountainous, with many offshore islands; formerly part of Yugoslavia (1947–91).

Dalmatian (dælˈmeɪʃən) *n* **1** a large breed of dog having a short smooth white coat with black or brown spots. **2** a native or inhabitant of Dalmatia. ♦ *adj* **3** of Dalmatia or its inhabitants.

dalmatic (dælˈmætɪk) *n* a wide-sleeved tunic-like vestment open at the sides, worn by deacons and bishops, and by a king at his coronation. ORIG C15: from LL *dalmatica* (*vestis*) Dalmatian (robe) (orig. made of Dalmatian wool)

dal segno (ˈdæl ˈsɛnjəʊ) *adj, adv Music.* to be repeated from the point marked with a sign to the word *fine.* ORIG It., lit.: from the sign

dalton (ˈdɔːltən) *n* another name for **atomic mass unit.** ORIG C20: after J. DALTON

Dalton ★ (ˈdɔːltən) *n* **John.** 1766–1844, British chemist, who formulated the modern form of the atomic theory and the law of partial pressures for gases.

daltonism (ˈdɔːltəˌnɪzəm) *n* colour blindness, esp. the confusion of red and green. ORIG C19: from F *daltonisme,* after J. DALTON

Dalton's atomic theory *n Chem.* the theory that matter consists of indivisible particles called atoms and that atoms of a given element are all identical and can neither be created nor destroyed. ORIG C19: after J. DALTON

dam[1] (dæm) *n* **1** a barrier of concrete, earth, etc., built across a river to create a body of water. **2** a reservoir of water created by such a barrier. **3** something that resembles or functions as a dam. ♦ *vb* **dams, damming, dammed. 4** (*tr;* often foll. by *up*) to restrict by a dam. ORIG C12: prob. from MLow G

dam[2] (dæm) *n* the female parent of an animal, esp. of domestic livestock. ORIG C13: var. of DAME

damage (ˈdæmɪdʒ) *n* **1** injury or harm impairing the function or condition of a person or thing. **2** loss of something desirable. **3** *Inf.* cost; expense. ♦ *vb* **damages, damaging, damaged. 4** (*tr*) to cause damage to. **5** (*intr*) to suffer damage. ORIG C14: from OF, from L *damnum* injury, loss
▸ ˈ**damaging** *adj*

damages (ˈdæmɪdʒɪz) *pl n Law.* money to be paid as compensation for injury, loss, etc.

Daman ★ (dɑːˈmɑːn) *n* the chief town of Daman and Diu, on the coast. Pop.: 26 895 (1991 est.). Portuguese name: **Damão.**

Daman and Diu ★ (ˈdiːuː) *n* a Union Territory in W India: formerly part of Portuguese India (1559–1961) then part of the Union Territory of Goa, Daman, and Diu (1961–87). Area: 112 sq. km (43 sq. miles). Pop.: 111 000 (1994 est.).

damascene (ˈdæməˌsiːn) *vb* **damascenes, damascening, damascened. 1** (*tr*) to ornament (metal, esp. steel) by etching or by inlaying other metals, usually gold or silver. ♦ *n* **2** a design or article produced by this process. ♦ *adj* **3** of or relating to this process. ORIG C14: from L *damascēnus* of Damascus

Damascene (ˈdæməˌsiːn) *adj* **1** of Damascus. ♦ *n* **2** a native or inhabitant of Damascus.

Damascus ★ (dəˈmɑːskəs, -ˈmæs-) *n* the capital of Syria, in the southwest: reputedly the oldest city in the world, having been inhabited continuously since before 2000 B.C. Pop.: 1 549 932 (1994 est.). Arabic names: **Dimashq, Esh Sham** (ɛʃ ʃæm).

Damascus steel *or* **damask steel** *n History.* a hard flexible steel with wavy markings, used for sword blades.

damask (ˈdæməsk) *n* **1a** a reversible fabric, usually silk or linen, with a pattern woven into it. It is used for table linen, curtains, etc. **1b** table linen made from this. **1c** (*as modifier*): *a damask tablecloth.* **2** short for **Damascus steel. 3** the wavy markings on such steel. **4a** the greyish-pink colour of the damask rose. **4b** (*as adj*): *damask wallpaper.* ♦ *vb* **5** (*tr*) another word for **damascene.** ORIG C14: from Med. L *damascus,* from Damascus, where fabric orig. made

damask rose *n* a rose with fragrant flowers, which are used to make the perfume attar. ORIG C16: from Med. L *rosa damascēna* rose of Damascus

dame (deɪm) *n* **1** (formerly) a woman of rank or dignity; lady. **2** *Arch., chiefly Brit.* an elderly woman. **3** *Sl., chiefly US & Canad.* a woman. **4** *Brit.* the role of a comic old woman in a pantomime, usually played by a man. ORIG C13: from OF, from L *domina* lady, mistress of household

Dame (deɪm) *n* (in Britain) **1** the title of a woman who has been awarded the Order of the British Empire or any of certain other orders of chivalry. **2** the title of the wife of a knight or baronet.

dame school *n* (formerly) a small school, offering basic education, usually run by an elderly woman in her own home.

Damien ★ (*French* damjɛ̃) *n* **Joseph** (ʒozɛf), known as *Father Damien.* 1840–89, Belgian Roman Catholic missionary to the leper colony at Molokai, Hawaii.

damn (dæm) *interj* **1** *Sl.* an exclamation of annoyance. **2** *Inf.* an exclamation of surprise or pleasure. ♦ *adj* **3** (*prenominal*) *Sl.* deserving damnation. ♦ *adv, adj* (*prenominal*) **4** *Sl.* (intensifier): *a damn good pianist.* ♦ *adv* **5 damn all.** *Sl.* absolutely nothing. ♦ *vb* (*mainly tr*) **6** to condemn as bad, worthless, etc. **7** to curse. **8** to condemn to eternal damnation. **9** (*often passive*) to doom to ruin. **10** (*also intr*) to prove (someone) guilty: *damning evidence.* **11 damn with faint praise.** to praise so unenthusiastically that the effect is condemnation. ♦ *n* **12** *Sl.* something of negligible value (esp. in **not worth a damn**). **13 not give a damn.** *Inf.* not care. ORIG C13: from OF *dampner,* from L *damnāre,* from *damnum* loss, injury

damnable (ˈdæmnəbᵊl) *adj* **1** execrable; detestable. **2** liable to or deserving damnation.
▸ ˈ**damnableness** *or* ˌ**damnaˈbility** *n*

damnably (ˈdæmnəblɪ) *adv* **1** in a detestable manner. **2** (intensifier): *it was damnably unfair.*

damnation (dæmˈneɪʃən) *n* **1** the act of damning or state of being damned. ♦ *interj* **2** an exclamation of anger, disappointment, etc.

damnatory (ˈdæmnətərɪ) *adj* threatening or occasioning condemnation.

damned (dæmd) *adj* **1a** condemned to hell. **1b** (*as collective n;* preceded by *the*): *the damned.* ♦ *adv, adj Sl.* **2** (intensifier): *a damned good try.* **3** used to indicate amazement, disavowal, or refusal (as in **damned if I care**).

damnedest (ˈdæmdɪst) *n Inf.* utmost; best (esp. in the phrases **do** or **try one's damnedest**).

damnify (ˈdæmnɪˌfaɪ) *vb* **damnifies, damnifying, damnified.** (*tr*) *Law.* to cause loss or damage to (a person); injure. ORIG C16: from OF *damnifier,* ult. from L *damnum* harm, + *facere* to make
▸ ˌ**damnifiˈcation** *n*

Damocles ★ (ˈdæməˌkliːz) *n Classical legend.* a sycophant forced by Dionysius, tyrant of Syracuse, to sit under a sword suspended by a hair to demonstrate that being a king was not the happy state Damocles had said it was. See also **Sword of Damocles.**
▸ ˌ**Damoˈclean** *adj*

Damodar ★ (ˈdæməˌdɑː) *n* a river in NE India, rising in Bihar and flowing east through West Bengal to the Hooghly River: the **Damodar Valley** is an important centre of heavy industry.

damoiselle, damosel, *or* **damozel** (ˌdæməˈzɛl) *n* archaic variants of **damsel.**

damp (dæmp) *adj* **1** slightly wet. ◆ *n* **2** slight wetness; moisture. **3** rank air or poisonous gas, esp. in a mine. **4** a discouragement; damper. ◆ *vb* (*tr*) **5** to make slightly wet. **6** (often foll. by *down*) to stifle or deaden: *to damp one's ardour.* **7** (often foll. by *down*) to reduce the flow of air to (a fire) to make it burn more slowly. **8** *Physics.* to reduce the amplitude of (an oscillation or wave). **9** *Music.* to muffle (the sound of an instrument). ORIG C14: from MLow G *damp* steam
▸ **'dampness** *n*

dampcourse ('dæmp,kɔ:s) *n* a layer of impervious material in a wall, to stop moisture rising. Also called: **damp-proof course.**

dampen ('dæmpən) *vb* **1** to make or become damp. **2** (*tr*) to stifle; deaden.
▸ **'dampener** *n*

damper ('dæmpə) *n* **1** a person, event, or circumstance that depresses or discourages. **2 put a damper on.** to produce a depressing or stultifying effect on. **3** a movable plate to regulate the draught in a stove or furnace flue. **4** a device to reduce electronic, mechanical, acoustic, or aerodynamic oscillations in a system. **5** the pad in a piano or harpsichord that deadens the vibration of each string as its key is released. **6** *Chiefly Austral. & NZ.* any of various unleavened loaves and scones, typically cooked on an open fire.

damping off *n* any of various diseases of plants caused by fungi in conditions of excessive moisture.

damp-proof *Building trades.* ◆ *vb* **1** to protect against the incursion of damp by adding a dampcourse or by coating with a moisture-resistant preparation. ◆ *adj* **2** protected against damp or causing protection against damp: *a damp-proof course.*

damsel ('dæmzᵊl) *n Arch. or poetic.* a young unmarried woman; maiden. ORIG C13: from OF *damoisele,* from Vulgar L *domnicella* (unattested) young lady, from L *domina* mistress

damselfly ('dæmzᵊl,flaɪ) *n, pl* **damselflies.** any of various insects similar to dragonflies but usually resting with the wings closed over the back.

damson ('dæmzən) *n* **1** a small tree cultivated for its blue-black edible plumlike fruit. **2** the fruit of this tree. ORIG C14: from L *prūnum damascēnum* Damascus plum

dan (dæn) *n Judo, karate, etc.* **1** any one of the 10 black-belt grades of proficiency. **2** a competitor entitled to dan grading. ORIG Japanese

Dan ★ (dæn) *n Old Testament.* **1a** the fourth son of Jacob (Genesis 30:1–6). **1b** the tribe descended from him. **2** a city in the northern territory of Canaan.

Dan. *abbrev. for:* **1** *Bible.* Daniel. **2** Danish.

Dana ★ ('deɪnə) *n* **James Dwight** (dwaɪt). 1813–95, US geologist; noted for *The System of Mineralogy* (1837).

Danaë ★ ('dæneɪ,i:) *n Greek myth.* the mother of Perseus by Zeus, who came to her in prison as a shower of gold.

Danaides ★ (də'neɪɪ,di:z) *pl n, sing* **Danaid.** *Greek myth.* the fifty daughters of Danaüs. All but Hypermnestra murdered their bridegrooms and were punished in Hades by having to pour water perpetually into a jar with a hole in the bottom.
▸ **Danaidean** (,dænɪ'ɪdɪən, ,dænɪə'di:ən) *adj*

Da Nang ★ (dɑ: 'næŋ) *n* a port in central Vietnam, on the South China Sea. Pop.: 382 674 (1992 est.). Former name: **Tourane.**

Danaüs ★ ('dænɪəs) *n Greek myth.* a king of Argos who told his fifty daughters, the Danaides, to kill their bridegrooms on their wedding night.

dance (dɑ:ns) *vb* **dances, dancing, danced.** **1** (*intr*) to move the feet and body rhythmically, esp. in time to music. **2** (*tr*) to perform (a particular dance). **3** (*intr*) to skip or leap. **4** to move or cause to move in a rhythmic way. **5 dance attendance on (someone).** to attend (someone) solicitously or obsequiously. ◆ *n* **6** a series of rhythmic steps and movements, usually in time to music. **7** an act of dancing. **8a** a social meeting arranged for dancing. **8b** (*as modifier*): *a dance hall.* **9** a piece of music in the rhythm of a particular dance form. **10** dancelike movements. **11 lead (someone) a dance.** *Brit. inf.* to cause (someone) continued worry and exasperation. ORIG C13: from OF *dancier*
▸ **'danceable** *adj* ▸ **'dancer** *n* ▸ **'dancing** *n, adj*

dance floor *n* **a** an area of floor in a disco, etc., where patrons may dance. **b** (*as modifier*): *dancefloor music.*

dancehall ('dɑ:ns,hɔ:l) *n* **1** a style of dance-oriented reggae, originating in the late 1980s. **2** a style of dancing associated with this music, involving close body contact with one's partner or partners.

dance of death *n* a medieval representation of a dance in which people are led off to their graves, by a personification of death. Also called (French): **danse macabre.**

D and C *n Med.* dilation (of the cervix) and curettage (of the uterus).

dandelion ('dændɪ,laɪən) *n* **1** a plant native to Europe and Asia and naturalized as a weed in North America, having yellow rayed flowers and deeply notched leaves. **2** any of several similar plants. ORIG C15: from OF *dent de lion,* lit.: tooth of a lion, referring to its leaves

dander ('dændə) *n* **1** small particles of hair or feathers. **2 get one's** (*or* **someone's**) **dander up.** *Inf.* to become (*or* cause to become) annoyed or angry. ORIG C19: from DANDRUFF

dandify ('dændɪ,faɪ) *vb* **dandifies, dandifying, dandified.** (*tr*) to dress like or cause to resemble a dandy.

dandle ('dændᵊl) *vb* **dandles, dandling, dandled.** (*tr*) **1** to move (a young child) up and down (on the knee or in the arms). **2** to pet; fondle. ORIG C16: from ?
▸ **'dandler** *n*

dandruff ('dændrəf) *n* loose scales of dry dead skin shed from the scalp. ORIG C16: *dand-* from ? + *-ruff,* prob. from ME *roufe* scab, from ON *hrūfa*

dandy ('dændɪ) *n, pl* **dandies.** **1** a man greatly concerned with smartness of dress. ◆ *adj* **dandier, dandiest.** **2** *Inf.* good or fine. ORIG C18: ? short for *jack-a-dandy*
▸ **'dandyish** *adj*

dandy-brush *n* a stiff brush used for grooming a horse.

dandy roll *or* **roller** *n* a roller used in the manufacture of paper to produce watermarks.

Dane (deɪn) *n* **1** a native, citizen, or inhabitant of Denmark. **2** any of the Vikings who invaded England from the late 8th to the 11th century A.D.

Danegeld ('deɪn,gɛld) *or* **Danegelt** ('deɪn,gɛlt) *n* the tax levied in Anglo-Saxon England to provide protection money for or to finance forces to oppose Viking invaders. ORIG C11: from *Dan* Dane + *geld* tribute; see YIELD

Danelaw ('deɪn,lɔ:) *n* the parts of Anglo-Saxon England in which Danish law and custom were observed. ORIG OE *Dena lagu* Danes' law

danger ('deɪndʒə) *n* **1** the state of being vulnerable to injury, loss, or evil; risk. **2** a person or thing that may cause injury, pain, etc. **3 in danger of.** liable to. **4 on the danger list.** critically ill in hospital. ORIG C13 *daunger* power, hence power to inflict injury, from OF *dongier* from L *dominium* ownership
▸ **'dangerless** *adj*

danger money *n* extra money paid to compensate for the risks involved in certain dangerous jobs.

dangerous ('deɪndʒərəs) *adj* causing danger; perilous.
▸ **'dangerously** *adv*

dangle ('dæŋgᵊl) *vb* **dangles, dangling, dangled.** **1** to hang or cause to hang freely: *his legs dangled over the wall.* **2** (*tr*) to display as an enticement. ORIG C16: ?from Danish *dangle,* prob. imit.
▸ **'dangler** *n*

Daniel ★ ('dænjəl) *n* **1** *Old Testament.* **1a** a youth who was taken into the household of Nebuchadnezzar, received guidance and apocalyptic visions from God, and was given divine protection when thrown into the lions' den. **1b** the book that recounts these experiences and visions (in full **The Book of the Prophet Daniel**). **2** (often preceded by *a*) a wise upright person. ORIG sense 2: referring to Daniel in the Apocryphal *Book of Susanna*

Danish ('deɪnɪʃ) *adj* **1** of Denmark, its people, or their language. ◆ *n* **2** the official language of Denmark.

Danish blue *n* a strong-tasting white cheese with blue veins.

★ people and places

Danish pastry *n* a rich puff pastry filled with apple, almond paste, icing, etc.

Danish West Indies ★ *pl n* the former possession of Denmark in the W Lesser Antilles, sold to the US in 1917 and since then named the **Virgin Islands of the United States**.

dank (dæŋk) *adj* (esp. of cellars, caves, etc.) unpleasantly damp and chilly. ORIG C14: prob. from ON
▸ **'dankly** *adv* ▸ **'dankness** *n*

Dankworth ★ ('dæŋkwɜːθ) *n* **John** (**Philip William**). born 1927, British jazz composer and saxophonist: married to Cleo Laine.

Danmark ★ ('danmarg) *n* the Danish name for **Denmark**.

D'Annunzio ★ (*Italian* dan'nuntsjo) *n* **Gabriele** (ga'brjɛːle). 1863–1938, Italian writer and Fascist. His works include the poems in *Alcione* (1904) and the drama *La Figlia di Iorio* (1904).

danseur *French.* (dɑ̃sœr) *or* (*fem*) ***danseuse*** (dɑ̃søz) *n* a ballet dancer.

Dante ★ ('dæntɪ, 'dɑːnteɪ; *Italian* 'dante) *n* full name **Dante Alighieri** (*Italian* ali'gjɛːri). 1265–1321, Italian poet. His works include *La Divina Commedia* (?1309–?1320) and *La Vita Nuova* (?1292).
▸ **Dantean** ('dæntɪən, dæn'tiːən) *or* **Dantesque** (dæn'tɛsk) *adj*

Danton ★ ('dæntən; *French* dɑ̃tɔ̃) *n* **Georges Jacques** (ʒɔrʒ ʒɑk). 1759–94, French revolutionary leader: a founder member of the Committee of Public Safety (1793) and minister of justice (1792–94): guillotined.

Danube ★ ('dænjuːb) *n* a river in central and SE Europe, rising in the Black Forest in Germany and flowing to the Black Sea. Length: 2859 km (1776 miles). German name: **Donau**. Czech name: **Dunaj**. Hungarian name: **Duna**. Serbo-Croat name: **Dunav** ('dunaf). Romanian name: **Dunărea**.
▸ **Danubian** (dæn'juːbɪən) *adj*

Danzig ★ ('dænsɪg; *German* 'dantsɪç) *n* the German name for **Gdańsk**.

dap (dæp) *vb* **daps, dapping, dapped. 1** *Angling.* to fly-fish so that the fly bobs on and off the water. **2** (*intr*) to dip lightly into water. **3** to bounce or cause to bounce. ORIG C17: imit.

daphne ('dæfnɪ) *n* any of various Eurasian ornamental shrubs with shiny evergreen leaves and clusters of small bell-shaped flowers. ORIG via L from Gk: laurel

Daphne ★ ('dæfnɪ) *n Greek myth.* a nymph who was saved from the amorous attentions of Apollo by being changed into a laurel tree.

daphnia ('dæfnɪə) *n* any of several waterfleas having a rounded body enclosed in a transparent shell. ORIG C19: prob. from DAPHNE

Daphnis ★ ('dæfnɪs) *n Greek myth.* a Sicilian shepherd, the son of Hermes and a nymph, who was regarded as the inventor of pastoral poetry.

Da Ponte ★ (*Italian* da 'pɔnte) *n* **Lorenzo** (lo'rɛntso), real name *Emmanuele Conegliano.* 1749–1838, Italian writer; Mozart's librettist for *The Marriage of Figaro* (1786), *Don Giovanni* (1787), and *Cosi fan tutte* (1790).

dapper ('dæpə) *adj* **1** neat in dress and bearing. **2** small and nimble. ORIG C15: from MDu.: active, nimble
▸ **'dapperly** *adv* ▸ **'dapperness** *n*

dapple ('dæp^{ə}l) *vb* **dapples, dappling, dappled. 1** to mark or become marked with spots of a different colour; mottle. ◆ *n* **2** mottled or spotted markings. **3** a dappled horse, etc. ◆ *adj* **4** marked with dapples or spots. ORIG C14: from ?

dapple-grey *n* a horse with a grey coat having spots of darker colour.

Dapsang ★ (dʌp'sʌŋ) *n* another name for **K2**.

darbies ('dɑːbɪz) *pl n Brit.* a slang term for **handcuffs**. ORIG C16: ?from *Father Derby's* (or *Darby's*) *bonds,* a rigid agreement between a usurer and his client

Darby and Joan ('dɑːbɪ) *n* **1** an ideal elderly married couple living in domestic harmony. **2 Darby and Joan Club.** a club for elderly people. ORIG C18: couple in 18th-cent. English ballad

Darcy ★ ('dɑːsɪ) *n* (**James**) **Les**(**lie**). 1895–1917, Australian boxer and folk hero.

Dardanelles ★ (ˌdɑːdə'nɛlz) *n* the strait between the Aegean and the Sea of Marmara, separating European from Asian Turkey. Ancient name: **Hellespont**.

dare (dɛə) *vb* **dares, daring, dared. 1** (*tr*) to challenge (a person to do something) as proof of courage. **2** (can take an infinitive with or without *to*) to be courageous enough to try (to do something). **3** (*tr*) *Rare.* to oppose without fear; defy. **4 I dare say. 4a** (it is) quite possible (that). **4b** probably. ◆ *n* **5** a challenge to do something as proof of courage. **6** something done in response to such a challenge. ORIG OE *durran*
▸ **'darer** *n*

daredevil ('dɛəˌdɛv^{ə}l) *n* **1** a recklessly bold person. ◆ *adj* **2** reckless; daring; bold.
▸ **'dareˌdevilry** *or* **'dareˌdeviltry** *n*

Dar es Salaam ★ ('dɑːr ɛs sə'lɑːm) *n* the chief port of Tanzania, on the Indian Ocean: capital of German East Africa (1891–1916); capital of Tanzania until 1983 when it was replaced by Dodoma; university (1963). Pop.: 1 360 850 (1988).

Darfur ★ (dɑː'fʊə) *n* a region of W Sudan; an independent kingdom until conquered by Egypt in 1874.

Darien ★ ('dɛərɪən, 'dæ-) *n* **1** the E part of the Isthmus of Panama, between the **Gulf of Darien** on the Caribbean coast and the Gulf of San Miguel on the Pacific coast; chiefly within the republic of Panama but extending also into Colombia: site of a disastrous attempt to establish a Scottish colony in 1698. **2 Isthmus of.** the former name of the Isthmus of **Panama**. ◆ Spanish name: **Darién** (da'rjen).

daring ('dɛərɪŋ) *adj* **1** bold or adventurous. ◆ *n* **2** courage in taking risks; boldness.

Dario ★ (*Spanish* da'rio) *n* **Rubén** (ru'βen), real name *Félix Rubén Garcia Sarmiento.* 1867–1916, Nicaraguan poet whose work includes *Prosas Profanas* (1896).

Darius I ★ (də'raɪəs) *n* known as *Darius the Great,* surname *Hystaspis.* ?550–486 B.C., king of Persia (521–486). He led two expeditions against Greece but was defeated at Marathon (490).

Darjeeling ★ (dɑː'dʒiːlɪŋ) *n* **1** a town in NE India, in West Bengal in the Himalayas, at an altitude of about 2250 m (7500 ft). Pop.: 73 090 (1991). **2** a high-quality black tea grown in the mountains around Darjeeling.

dark (dɑːk) *adj* **1** having little or no light. **2** (of a colour) reflecting or transmitting little light: *dark brown.* **3** (of complexion, hair colour, etc.) not fair; swarthy; brunette. **4** gloomy or dismal. **5** sinister; evil: *a dark purpose.* **6** sullen or angry. **7** ignorant or unenlightened: *a dark period in our history.* **8** secret or mysterious. ◆ *n* **9** absence of light; darkness. **10** night or nightfall. **11** a dark place. **12** a state of ignorance (esp. in **in the dark**). ORIG OE *deorc*
▸ **'darkish** *adj* ▸ **'darkly** *adv* ▸ **'darkness** *n*

Dark Ages *pl n European history.* the period from about the late 5th century A.D. to about 1000 A.D., once considered an unenlightened period.

Dark Continent ★ *n* **the.** a term for Africa when it was relatively unexplored by Europeans.

darken ('dɑːkən) *vb* **1** to make or become dark or darker. **2** to make or become gloomy, angry, or sad. **3 darken** (**someone's**) **door.** (*usually used with a negative*) to visit someone: *never darken my door again!*
▸ **'darkener** *n*

dark horse *n* **1** a competitor in a race or contest about whom little is known. **2** a person who reveals little about himself or herself, esp. one who has unexpected talents. **3** *US politics.* a candidate who is unexpectedly nominated or elected.

dark lantern *n* a lantern having a sliding shutter or panel to dim or hide the light.

darkling ('dɑːklɪŋ) *adv, adj Poetic.* in the dark or night. ORIG C15: from DARK + -LING[2]

dark matter *n Astron.* matter known to make up a substantial part of the mass of the universe, but not detectable by its absorption or emission of electromagnetic radiation.

darkroom ('dɑːkˌruːm, -ˌrʊm) *n* a room in which photographs are processed in darkness or safe light.

darksome ('dɑːksəm) *adj Literary.* dark or darkish.

dark star *n* an invisible star known to exist only from observation of its radio, infrared, or other spectrum or of its gravitational effect.

Darlan ★ (*French* darlɑ̃) *n* **Jean Louis Xavier François** (ʒɑ̃ lwi gzavje frɑ̃swa). 1881–1942, French admiral and member of the Vichy government. He cooperated with the Allies after their invasion of North Africa; assassinated.

darling ('dɑːlɪŋ) *n* **1** a person very much loved. **2** a favourite. ◆ *adj* (*prenominal*) **3** beloved. **4** much admired; pleasing: *a darling hat.* ORIG OE *dēorling;* see DEAR, -LING[1]

Darling ★ ('dɑːlɪŋ) *n* **Grace.** 1815–42, British national heroine, famous for her rescue (1838) of some shipwrecked sailors with her father, a lighthouse keeper.

Darling Downs ★ *pl n* a plateau in NE Australia, in SE Queensland: a vast agricultural and stock-raising area.

Darling Range ★ *n* a ridge in SW Western Australia, parallel to the coast. Highest point: about 582 m (1669 ft).

Darling River ★ *n* a river in SE Australia, rising in the Eastern Highlands and flowing southwest to the Murray River. Length: 2740 km (1702 miles).

Darlington ★ ('dɑːlɪŋtən) *n* **1** an industrial town in NE England in S Durham: developed mainly with the opening of the Stockton-Darlington railway (1825). Pop.: 86 767 (1991). **2** a unitary authority in NE England, in Durham. Pop.: 101 106 (1997 est.). Area: 198 sq. km (77 sq. miles).

Darmstadt ★ ('dɑːmstæt; *German* 'darmʃtat) *n* an industrial city in central Germany, in Hesse: former capital of the grand duchy of Hesse-Darmstadt (1567–1945). Pop.: 138 980 (1996 est.).

darn[1] (dɑːn) *vb* **1** to mend (a hole or a garment) with a series of crossing or interwoven stitches. ◆ *n* **2** a patch of darned work on a garment. ORIG C16: prob. from F (dialect) *darner*
▸ **'darner** *n*

darn[2] (dɑːn) *interj, adj, adv, n* a euphemistic word for **damn** (senses 1–5, 12, 13).

darnel ('dɑːnᵊl) *n* any of several grasses that grow as weeds in grain fields in Europe and Asia. ORIG C14: prob. rel. to F (dialect) *darnelle,* from ?

darning ('dɑːnɪŋ) *n* **1** the act of mending a hole using interwoven stitches. **2** garments needing to be darned.

darning needle *n* a long needle with a large eye used for darning.

Darnley ★ ('dɑːnlɪ) *n* **Lord.** title of *Henry Stuart* (or *Stewart*). 1545–67, Scottish nobleman; second husband of Mary, Queen of Scots and father of James I of England. After murdering his wife's secretary, Rizzio (1566), he was assassinated.

dart (dɑːt) *n* **1** a small narrow pointed missile that is thrown or shot, as in the game of darts. **2** a sudden quick movement. **3** *Zool.* a slender pointed structure, as in snails for aiding copulation. **4** a tapered tuck made in dressmaking. ◆ *vb* **5** to move or throw swiftly and suddenly; shoot. ORIG C14: from OF, of Gmc origin
▸ **'darting** *adj*

dartboard ('dɑːtˌbɔːd) *n* a circular piece of wood, cork, etc., used as the target in the game of darts.

darter ('dɑːtə) *n* **1** Also called: **anhinga, snakebird.** any of various aquatic birds of tropical and subtropical inland waters, having a long slender neck and bill. **2** any of various small brightly coloured North American freshwater fish.

Dartford ★ ('dɑːtfəd) *n* a town in SE England, in NW Kent. Pop.: 59 411 (1991).

Dartmoor ★ ('dɑːtˌmʊə) *n* **1** a moorland plateau in SW England, in SW Devon: a national park since 1951. Area: 945 sq. km (365 sq. miles). **2** a prison in SW England, on Dartmoor: England's main prison for long-term convicts. **3** a small strong breed of pony, originally from Dartmoor. **4** a hardy coarse-woolled breed of sheep originally from Dartmoor.

Dartmouth ★ ('dɑːtməθ) *n* **1** a port in SW England, in S Devon: Royal Naval College (1905). Pop.: 5676 (1991). **2** a city in SE Canada, in S Nova Scotia, on Halifax Harbour: oil refineries and shipyards. Pop.: 67 798 (1991).

darts (dɑːts) *n* (*functioning as sing*) any of various competitive games in which darts are thrown at a dartboard.

Darwin[1] ★ ('dɑːwɪn) *n* a port in N Australia, capital of the Northern Territory: destroyed by a cyclone in 1974 but rebuilt on the same site. Pop.: 78 100 (1994). Former name (1869–1911): **Palmerston.**

Darwin[2] ★ ('dɑːwɪn) *n* **1 Charles (Robert).** 1809–82, British naturalist who formulated the theory of evolution, expounded in *On the Origin of Species* (1859) and applied to man in *The Descent of Man* (1871). **2** his grandfather, **Erasmus.** 1731–1802, British physician and poet; author of *Zoonomia* (1794–96), anticipating Lamarck's views on evolution. **3** Sir **George Howard,** son of Charles Darwin. 1845–1912, British astronomer.

Darwinian (dɑː'wɪnɪən) *adj* **1** of or relating to Charles Darwin or his theory of evolution. ◆ *n* **2** a person who accepts, supports, or uses this theory.

Darwinism ('dɑːwɪˌnɪzəm) *or* **Darwinian theory** *n* the theory of the origin of animal and plant species by evolution through a process of natural selection.
▸ **'Darwinist** *n, adj*

dash[1] (dæʃ) *vb* (*mainly tr*) **1** to hurl; crash: *he dashed the cup to the floor.* **2** to mix: *white paint dashed with blue.* **3** (*intr*) to move hastily or recklessly; rush. **4** (usually foll. by *off* or *down*) to write (down) or finish (off) hastily. **5** to frustrate: *his hopes were dashed.* **6** to daunt (someone); discourage. ◆ *n* **7** a sudden quick movement. **8** a small admixture: *coffee with a dash of cream.* **9** a violent stroke or blow. **10** the sound of splashing or smashing. **11** panache; style: *he rides with dash.* **12** Also called: **rule.** the punctuation mark —, used to indicate a sudden change of subject or to enclose a parenthetical remark. **13** the symbol (–) used, in combination with the symbol *dot* (•), in the written representation of Morse and other telegraphic codes. **14** *Athletics.* another word (esp. US and Canad.) for **sprint.** ORIG ME *daschen, dassen,* ?from ON

dash[2] (dæʃ) *interj Inf.* a euphemistic word for **damn** (senses 1, 2).

dashboard ('dæʃˌbɔːd) *n* **1** Also called (Brit.): **fascia.** the instrument panel in a car, boat, or aircraft. **2** *Obs.* a board at the side of a carriage or boat to protect against splashing.

dasher ('dæʃə) *n* **1** one that dashes. **2** *Canad.* the ledge along the top of the boards of an ice hockey rink.

dashiki (dɑː'ʃiːkɪ) *n* a large loose-fitting upper garment worn esp. by Blacks in the US, Africa, and the Caribbean. ORIG C20: of W African origin

dashing ('dæʃɪŋ) *adj* **1** spirited; lively: *a dashing young man.* **2** stylish; showy.

dashlight ('dæʃˌlaɪt) *n* a light that illuminates the dashboard of a car, esp. at night.

Dasht-i-Kavir *or* **Dasht-e-Kavir** ★ (ˌdæʃtiːkæ'vɪə) *n* a salt waste on the central plateau of Iran: a treacherous marsh beneath a salt crust. Also called: **Kavir Desert.**

Dasht-i-Lut *or* **Dasht-e-Lut** ★ (ˌdæʃtiː'luːt) *n* a desert plateau in central and E central Iran.

Dassehra ('dæsɛəræ) *n* an annual Hindu festival celebrated on the 10th lunar day of Navaratri; images of the goddess Durga are immersed in water.

dassie ('dæsɪ) *n* another name for a **hyrax,** esp. the rock hyrax. ORIG C19: from Afrik.

dastardly ('dæstədlɪ) *adj* mean and cowardly. ORIG C15 *dastard* (in the sense: dullard): prob. from ON *dæstr* exhausted, out of breath
▸ **'dastardliness** *n*

dasyure ('dæsɪˌjʊə) *n* **1** any of several small carnivorous marsupials of Australia, New Guinea, and adjacent islands. **2** the ursine dasyure. See **Tasmanian devil.** ORIG C19: from NL, from Gk *dasus* shaggy + *oura* tail

DAT *abbrev. for* digital audio tape.

dat. *abbrev. for* dative.

data ('deɪtə, 'dɑːtə) *pl n* **1** a series of observations, measurements, or facts; information. **2** Also called: **information.** *Computing.* the information operated on by a computer program. ORIG C17: from L, lit.: (things) given, from *dare* to give

> **USAGE NOTE** From a historical point of view only, the word *data* is a plural. In fact, in many cases it is not clear from context if it is being used as a singular or plural, so there is no issue: *when next needed the data can be accessed very quickly.* When it is necessary to specify, the preferred usage nowadays in general language is to treat it as singular, as in: *this data is useful to the government in the planning of housing services.* There are rather more examples in the Bank of English of *these data* than *this data,* with a marked preference for the plural in academic and scientific writing. As regards *data is* versus *data are,* the preference for the plural form overall is even more marked in that kind of writing. When speaking, however, it is best to opt for treating the word as singular, except in precise scientific contexts. The singular form *datum* is comparatively rare in the sense of a single item of data.

database ('deɪtəˌbeɪs) *n* **1** Also called: **data bank.** a store of a large amount of information, esp. in a form that can be handled by a computer. **2** *Inf.* any large store of information: *a database of knowledge.*

data capture *n* any process for converting information into a form that can be handled by a computer.

data mining *n* the gathering of information from pre-existing data stored in a database, such as one held by a supermarket with details of customers' shopping habits.

data pen *n* a device for reading or scanning magnetically coded data on labels, packets, etc.

data processing *n* **a** a sequence of operations performed on data, esp. by a computer, in order to extract information, reorder files, etc. **b** (*as modifier*): *a data-processing centre.*

data protection *n* (in Britain) safeguards for individuals relating to personal data stored on a computer.

data set *n Computing.* another name for **file**[1] (sense 6).

date[1] (deɪt) *n* **1** a specified day of the month. **2** the particular day or year of an event. **3** an inscription on a coin, letter, etc., stating when it was made or written. **4a** an appointment for a particular time, esp. with a person of the opposite sex. **4b** the person with whom the appointment is made. **5** the present moment; now (esp. in **to date, up to date**). ◆ *vb* **dates, dating, dated. 6** (*tr*) to mark (a letter, coin, etc.) with the day, month, or year. **7** (*tr*) to assign a date of occurrence or creation to. **8** (*intr;* foll. by *from* or *back to*) to have originated (at a specified time). **9** (*tr*) to reveal the age of: *that dress dates her.* **10** to make or become old-fashioned: *some good films hardly date at all.* **11** *Inf., chiefly US & Canad.* **11a** to be a boyfriend or girlfriend of (someone of the opposite sex). **11b** to accompany (a member of the opposite sex) on a date. ORIG C14: from OF, from L *dare* to give, as in *epistula data Romae* letter handed over at Rome
▸ **'datable** *or* **'dateable** *adj*

> **USAGE NOTE** See at **year.**

date[2] (deɪt) *n* **1** the fruit of the date palm, having sweet edible flesh and a single large woody seed. **2** short for **date palm.** ORIG C13: from OF, from L, from Gk *daktulos* finger

dated ('deɪtɪd) *adj* **1** unfashionable; outmoded. **2** (of a security) having a fixed date for redemption.

dateless ('deɪtlɪs) *adj* likely to remain fashionable, good, or interesting regardless of age.

dateline ('deɪtˌlaɪn) *n Journalism.* the date and location of a story, placed at the top of an article.

date line *n* (*often caps.*) short for **International Date Line.**

date palm *n* a tall feather palm grown in tropical regions for its sweet edible fruit.

date rape *n* **1** the act or an instance of a man raping a woman while they are on a date together. **2** an act of sexual intercourse regarded as tantamount to rape, esp. if the woman was encouraged to drink excessively or was subjected to undue pressure.

date stamp *n* **1** an adjustable rubber stamp for recording the date. **2** an inked impression made by this.

dating ('deɪtɪŋ) *n* any of several techniques, such as radioactive dating, dendrochronology, or varve dating, for establishing the age of rocks, palaeontological or archaeological specimens, etc.

dating agency *n* an agency that provides introductions to people seeking a companion with similar interests.

dative ('deɪtɪv) *Grammar.* ◆ *adj* **1** denoting a case of nouns, pronouns, and adjectives used to express the indirect object, to identify the recipients, and for other purposes. ◆ *n* **2a** the dative case. **2b** a word or speech element in this case. ORIG C15: from L *datīvus,* from *dare* to give
▸ **datival** (deɪ'taɪvᵊl) *adj* ▸ **'datively** *adv*

datum ('deɪtəm, 'dɑːtəm) *n, pl* **data. 1** a single piece of information; fact. **2** a proposition taken as unquestionable, often in order to construct some theoretical framework upon it. See also **sense datum.** ORIG C17: from L: something given; see DATA

> **USAGE NOTE** See at **data.**

datura (də'tjʊərə) *n* any of various chiefly Indian plants and shrubs with large trumpet-shaped flowers. ORIG C16: from NL, from Hindi

daub (dɔːb) *vb* **1** (*tr*) to smear or spread (paint, mud, etc.), esp. carelessly. **2** (*tr*) to cover or coat (with paint, plaster, etc.) carelessly. **3** to paint (a picture) clumsily or badly. ◆ *n* **4** an unskilful or crude painting. **5** something daubed on, esp. as a wall covering. **6** a smear (of paint, mud, etc.). ORIG C14: from OF *dauber* to paint, whitewash, from L *dealbāre,* from *albāre* to whiten
▸ **'dauber** *n*

Daubigny ★ (*French* dobiɲi) *n* **Charles François** (ʃarl frɑ̃swa). 1817–78, French landscape painter associated with the Barbizon School.

Daudet ★ (*French* dodɛ) *n* **Alphonse** (alfɔ̃s). 1840–97, French novelist, short-story writer, and dramatist: noted particularly for his humorous sketches of Provençal life, as in *Lettres de mon moulin* (1866).

Daugava ★ ('daʊgaˌva) *n* the Latvian name for the Western **Dvina.**

Daugavpils ★ (*Latvian* 'daʊgafˌpils) *n* a city in SE Latvia on the Western Dvina River: founded in 1274 by Teutonic Knights; ruled by Poland (1559–1772) and Russia (1772–1915; 1940–91). Pop.: 118 500 (1996 est.). German name (until 1893): **Dünaburg.** Former Russian name (1893–1920): **Dvinsk.**

daughter ('dɔːtə) *n* **1** a female offspring; a girl or woman in relation to her parents. **2** a female descendant. **3** a female from a certain country, etc., or one closely connected with a certain environment, etc.: *a daughter of the church.* ◆ (*modifier*) **4** *Biol.* denoting a cell or unicellular organism produced by the division of one of its own kind. **5** *Physics.* (of a nuclide) formed from another nuclide by radioactive decay. ORIG OE *dohtor*
▸ **'daughterhood** *n* ▸ **'daughterless** *adj* ▸ **'daughterly** *adj*

daughter-in-law *n, pl* **daughters-in-law.** the wife of one's son.

Daumier ★ (*French* domje) *n* **Honoré** (ɔnɔre). 1808–79, French painter and lithographer, noted particularly for his political and social caricatures.

daunt (dɔːnt) *vb* (*tr; often passive*) **1** to intimidate. **2** to dishearten. ORIG C13: from OF *danter,* changed from *donter* to conquer, from L *domitāre* to tame
▸ **'daunting** *adj* ▸ **'dauntingly** *adv*

dauntless ('dɔːntlɪs) *adj* bold; fearless; intrepid.
▸ **'dauntlessly** *adv* ▸ **'dauntlessness** *n*

dauphin ('dɔːfɪn; *French* dofɛ̃) *n* (1349–1830) the title of the eldest son of the king of France. ORIG C15: from OF: orig. a family name

dauphine ('dɔːfiːn; *French* dofin) *or* **dauphiness** ('dɔːfɪnɪs) *n French history.* the wife of a dauphin.

davenport ('dævən,pɔːt) *n* **1** *Chiefly Brit.* a tall narrow writing desk with drawers. **2** *US & Canad.* a large sofa, esp. one convertible into a bed. ORIG C19: sense 1 supposedly after Captain *Davenport,* who commissioned the first ones

Daventry ★ ('dævəntrɪ) *n* a town in central England, in Northamptonshire: light industries, site of an important international radio transmitter. Pop.: 18 099 (1991).

David ★ ('deɪvɪd) *n* **1** the second king of the Hebrews (about 1000–962 B.C.), who united Israel as a kingdom with Jerusalem as its capital. **2 Elizabeth.** 1914–92, British cookery writer. Her books include *Mediterranean Food* (1950). **3** (*French* david). **Jacques Louis** (ʒɑk lwi). 1748–1825, French neoclassical painter. **4 Saint.** 6th century A.D., Welsh bishop; patron saint of Wales. Feast day: March 1.

David I ★ *n* 1084–1153, king of Scotland (1124–53) who supported his niece Matilda's claim to the English throne and unsuccessfully invaded England on her behalf.

David II ★ *n* 1324–71, king of Scotland (1329–71): he was forced into exile in France (1334–41) by Edward de Baliol; captured following the battle of Neville's Cross (1346), and imprisoned by the English (1346–57).

Davies ★ ('deɪvɪs) *n* **1** Sir **John.** 1569–1626, English poet, author of *Orchestra or a Poem of Dancing* (1596). **2** Sir **Peter Maxwell.** born 1934, British composer whose works include the opera *Taverner* (1967), four symphonies, and a violin concerto (1985). **3** (**William**) **Robertson.** 1913–95, Canadian novelist and dramatist. His novels include *Murther and Walking Spirits* (1991). **4 W(illiam) H(enry).** 1871–1940, Welsh poet, noted also for his *Autobiography of a Super-tramp* (1908).

da Vinci ★ (də 'vɪntʃɪ) *n* See **Leonardo da Vinci.**

Davis ★ ('deɪvɪs) *n* **1 Bette** ('betɪ), real name *Ruth Elizabeth Davis* 1908–89, US film actress, whose films include *Jezebel* (1938) and *Now Voyager* (1942). **2** Sir **Colin** (**Rex**). born 1927, British conductor. **3 Jefferson.** 1808–89, president of the Confederate States of America during the Civil War (1861–65). **4 Joe.** 1901–78, British billiards and snooker player: world champion from 1927 to 1946. **5 John.** Also called: **John Davys.** ?1550–1605, English navigator: discovered the Falkland Islands (1592). **6 Miles** (**Dewey**). 1926–91, US jazz trumpeter and composer. **7 Steve.** born 1957, British snooker player: world champion 1981, 1983–84, 1987–89.

Davisson ★ ('deɪvɪsᵊn) *n* **Clinton Joseph.** 1881–1958, US physicist, noted for his discovery of electron diffraction; shared the Nobel prize for physics 1937.

Davis Strait ★ *n* a strait between Baffin Island, in Canada, and Greenland. ORIG after John DAVIS

davit ('dævɪt, 'deɪ-) *n* a cranelike device, usually one of a pair, fitted with a tackle for suspending or lowering equipment, esp. a lifeboat. ORIG C14: from Anglo-F *daviot,* dim. of *Davi* David

Davos ★ ('dɑːvɒs) *n* a mountain resort in Switzerland: winter sports, site of the Parsenn ski run. Pop.: 10 500 (1990). Height: about 1560 m (5118 ft). Romansh name: **Tarau.**

Davy ★ ('deɪvɪ) *n* Sir **Humphry.** 1778–1829, British chemist who isolated sodium, chlorine, and other elements. He invented the **Davy lamp.**

Davy Jones *n* **1** Also called: **Davy Jones's locker.** the ocean's bottom, esp. when regarded as the grave of those lost or buried at sea. **2** the spirit of the sea. ORIG C18: from ?

Davy lamp *n* See **safety lamp.** ORIG C19: after Sir H. DAVY, who invented it

daw (dɔː) *n* an archaic, dialect, or poetic name for a **jackdaw.** ORIG C15: rel. to OHG *taha*

dawdle ('dɔːdᵊl) *vb* **dawdles, dawdling, dawdled. 1** (*intr*) to be slow or lag behind. **2** (when *tr,* often foll. by *away*) to waste (time); trifle. ORIG C17: from ?
▸ **'dawdler** *n*

Dawes ★ (dɔːz) *n* **Charles Gates.** 1865–1951, US financier and statesman, who devised the Dawes Plan for German reparations after World War I; Nobel peace prize 1925.

Dawkins ★ ('dɔːkɪnz) *n* **Richard.** born 1941, British zoologist and author of *The Selfish Gene* (1976) and *River Out of Eden* (1995).

dawn (dɔːn) *n* **1** daybreak. Related adj: **auroral. 2** the sky when light first appears in the morning. **3** the beginning of something. ◆ *vb* (*intr*) **4** to begin to grow light after the night. **5** to begin to develop or appear. **6** (usually foll. by *on* or *upon*) to begin to become apparent (to). ORIG OE *dagian* to dawn
▸ **'dawn,like** *adj*

dawn chorus *n* the singing of large numbers of birds at dawn.

dawn raid *n Stock Exchange.* an unexpected attempt to acquire a substantial proportion of a company's shares at the start of a day's trading as a preliminary to a takeover bid.

Dawson Creek ★ ('dɔːsᵊn) *n* a town in W Canada, in NE British Columbia: SE terminus of the Alaska Highway. Pop.: 10 981 (1991).

day (deɪ) *n* **1** Also called: **civil day.** the period of time, the **calendar day,** of 24 hours' duration reckoned from one midnight to the next. **2a** the period of light between sunrise and sunset. **2b** (*as modifier*): *the day shift.* **3** the part of a day occupied with regular activity, esp. work. **4** (*sometimes pl*) a period or point in time: *in days gone by; any day now.* **5** the period of time, the **sidereal day,** during which the earth makes one complete revolution on its axis relative to a particular star. **6** the period of time, the **solar day,** during which the earth makes one complete revolution on its axis relative to the sun. **7** the period of time taken by a specified planet to make one complete rotation on its axis: *the Martian day.* **8** (*often cap.*) a day designated for a special observance: *Christmas Day.* **9** a time of success, recognition, etc.: *his day will come.* **10** a struggle or issue at hand: *the day is lost.* **11 all in a day's work.** part of one's normal activity. **12 at the end of the day.** in the final reckoning. **13 call it a day.** to stop work or other activity. **14 day after day.** without respite; relentlessly. **15 day by day.** gradually or progressively. **16 day in, day out.** every day and all day long. **17 day of rest.** the Sabbath; Sunday. **18 every dog has his day.** one's luck will come. **19 in this day and age.** nowadays. **20 that will be the day. 20a** that is most unlikely to happen. **20b** I look forward to that. ◆ Related adj: **diurnal.** ◆ See also **days.** ORIG OE *dæg*

Dayak ('daɪæk) *n, pl* **Dayaks** *or* **Dayak.** a variant spelling of **Dyak.**

Dayan ★ (daɪ'jɑːn) *n* **Moshe** ('mɒʃe). 1915–81, Israeli soldier and statesman; minister of defence (1967; 1969–74) and foreign minister (1977–79).

day bed *n* a narrow bed intended for use as a seat and as a bed.

daybook ('deɪ,bʊk) *n Book-keeping.* a book in which the transactions of each day are recorded as they occur.

dayboy ('deɪ,bɔɪ) *n Brit.* a boy who attends a boarding school daily, but returns home each evening.
▸ **'daygirl** *fem n*

daybreak ('deɪ,breɪk) *n* the time in the morning when light first appears; dawn; sunrise.

daycare ('deɪ,keə) *n Brit. social welfare.* **1** occupation, treatment, or supervision during the working day for people who might be at risk if left on their own. **2** welfare services provided by a local authority, health service, etc., during the day.

daycentre ('deɪ,sentə) *or* **day centre** *n Social welfare.* (in Britain) **1** a building used for daycare or other welfare services. **2** the enterprise itself, including staff, users, and organization.

daydream ('deɪ,driːm) *n* **1** a pleasant dreamlike fantasy indulged in while awake. **2** a pleasant scheme or wish that is unlikely to be fulfilled. ◆ *vb* **3** (*intr*) to indulge in idle fantasy.
▸ **'day,dreamer** *n* ▸ **'day,dreamy** *adj*

Day-Glo *n Trademark.* **a** a brand of fluorescent colouring materials, as of paint. **b** (*as modifier*): *Day-Glo colours.*

day labourer *n* an unskilled worker hired and paid by the day.

Day-Lewis ('deɪ'luːɪs) *or* **Day Lewis** ★ *n* **Cecil.** 1904–72, British poet and (under the pen name *Nicholas Blake*) author of detective stories; poet laureate (1968–72).

daylight ('deɪˌlaɪt) *n* **1** light from the sun. **2** daytime. **3** daybreak. **4 see daylight. 4a** to understand something previously obscure. **4b** to realize that the end of a difficult task is approaching.

daylight robbery *n Inf.* blatant overcharging.

daylights ('deɪˌlaɪts) *pl n* consciousness or wits (esp. in **scare, knock,** or **beat the (living) daylights out of someone**).

daylight-saving time *n* time set usually one hour ahead of the local standard time, widely adopted in the summer to provide extra daylight in the evening.

daylong ('deɪˌlɒŋ) *adj, adv* lasting the entire day; all day.

day release *n Brit.* a system whereby workers are released for part-time education without loss of pay.

day return *n* a reduced fare for a journey (by train, etc.) travelling both ways in one day.

day room *n* a communal living room in a residential institution such as a hospital.

days (deɪz) *adv Inf.* during the day, esp. regularly: *he works days.*

day school *n* **1** a private school taking day students only. **2** a school giving instruction during the daytime.

daytime ('deɪˌtaɪm) *n* the time between dawn and dusk.

day-to-day *adj* routine; everyday.

day trading *n* the practice of buying shares and selling them later the same day, often via the Internet, in order to make a quick profit.
▸ **day trader** *n*

day trip *n* a journey made to and from a place within one day.
▸ **'day-ˌtripper** *n*

Da Yunhe ★ ('dæ 'juːnhə) *n* Pinyin transliteration of the Chinese name for the **Grand Canal** (sense 1).

daze (deɪz) *vb* **dazes, dazing, dazed.** (*tr*) **1** to stun, esp. by a blow or shock. **2** to bewilder or amaze. ◆ *n* **3** a state of stunned confusion or shock (esp. in **in a daze**). ORIG C14: from ON *dasa-*, as in *dasast* to grow weary

dazzle ('dæzᵊl) *vb* **dazzles, dazzling, dazzled. 1** (*usually tr*) to blind or be blinded partially and temporarily by sudden excessive light. **2** (*tr*) to amaze, as with brilliance. ◆ *n* **3** bright light that dazzles. **4** bewilderment caused by glamour, brilliance, etc.: *the dazzle of fame.* ORIG C15: from DAZE
▸ **'dazzler** *n* ▸ **'dazzling** *adj* ▸ **'dazzlingly** *adv*

dazzle gun *n* a weapon consisting of a laser gun used to dazzle enemy pilots.

dB *or* **db** *symbol for* decibel *or* decibels.

DBE *abbrev. for* Dame (Commander of the Order) of the British Empire (a Brit. title).

DBMS *abbrev. for* database management system.

DBS *abbrev. for* direct broadcasting by satellite.

dbx *or* **DBX** *n Trademark. Electronics.* a noise-reduction system that works across the full frequency spectrum.

DC *abbrev. for:* **1** *Music.* da capo. **2** direct current. Cf. **AC. 3** Also: **D.C.** District of Columbia.

DCB *abbrev. for* Dame Commander of the Order of the Bath (a Brit. title).

DCC *abbrev. for* digital compact cassette.

DCM *Brit. mil. abbrev. for* Distinguished Conduct Medal.

DD *abbrev. for:* **1** Doctor of Divinity. **2** Also: **dd.** direct debit.

D-day *n* the day selected for the start of some operation, esp. of the Allied invasion of Europe on June 6, 1944. ORIG C20: from *D(ay)-day*

DDR *abbrev. for* Deutsche Demokratische Republik (the former East Germany; GDR).

DDS *or* **DDSc** *abbrev. for* Doctor of Dental Surgery *or* Science.

DDT *n* dichlorodiphenyltrichloroethane; a colourless odourless substance used as an insecticide. It is now banned in the UK.

de- *prefix forming verbs and verbal derivatives.* **1** removal of or from something: *deforest; dethrone.* **2** reversal of something: *decode; desegregate.* **3** departure from: *decamp.* ORIG from L, from *dē* (prep) from, away from, out of, etc. In compound words of Latin origin, *de-* also means away, away from (*decease*); down (*degrade*); reversal (*detect*); removal (*defoliate*); and is used intensively (*devote*) and pejoratively (*detest*)

deacon ('diːkən) *n Christianity.* **1** (in the Roman Catholic and other episcopal churches) an ordained minister ranking immediately below a priest. **2** (in some other churches) a lay official who assists the minister, esp. in secular affairs. ORIG OE, ult. from Gk *diakonos* servant
▸ **'deaconate** *n* ▸ **'deaconˌship** *n*

deaconess ('diːkənɪs) *n Christianity.* (in the early church and in some modern Churches) a female member of the laity with duties similar to those of a deacon.

deactivate (diː'æktɪˌveɪt) *vb* **deactivates, deactivating, deactivated. 1** (*tr*) to make (a bomb, etc.) harmless or inoperative. **2** (*intr*) to become less radioactive.
▸ **de'actiˌvator** *n*

dead (dɛd) *adj* **1a** no longer alive. **1b** (*as collective n;* preceded by *the*): *the dead.* **2** not endowed with life; inanimate. **3** no longer in use, effective, or relevant: *a dead issue; a dead language.* **4** unresponsive or unaware. **5** lacking in freshness or vitality. **6** lacking activity or excitement: *this place is dead at night.* **7** devoid of physical sensation; numb. **8** resembling death: *a dead sleep.* **9** no longer burning or hot: *dead coals.* **10** (of flowers or foliage) withered; faded. **11** (*prenominal*) (intensifier): *a dead stop.* **12** *Inf.* very tired. **13** *Electronics.* **13a** drained of electric charge. **13b** not connected to a source of potential difference or electric charge. **14** lacking acoustic reverberation: *a dead sound.* **15** *Sport.* (of a ball, etc.) out of play. **16** accurate; precise (esp. in **a dead shot**). **17** lacking resilience or bounce: *a dead ball.* **18** not yielding a return: *dead capital.* **19** (of colours) not glossy or bright. **20** stagnant: *dead air.* **21** *Mil.* shielded from view, as by a geographic feature. **22 dead from the neck up.** *Inf.* stupid. **23 dead to the world.** *Inf.* unaware of one's surroundings, esp. asleep or drunk. ◆ *n* **24** a period during which coldness, darkness, etc. is at its most intense: *the dead of winter.* ◆ *adv* **25** (intensifier): *dead easy; stop dead.* **26 dead on.** exactly right. ORIG OE *dēad*
▸ **'deadness** *n*

dead-and-alive *adj Brit.* (of a place, activity, or person) dull; uninteresting.

dead-ball line *n Rugby.* a line behind the goal line beyond which the ball is out of play.

deadbeat ('dɛdˌbiːt) *n* **1** *Inf.* a lazy or socially undesirable person. **2** *Chiefly US.* **2a** a person who makes a habit of evading his or her responsibilities or debts. **2b** (*as modifier*): *a deadbeat dad.* **3** a high grade escapement used in pendulum clocks. **4** (*modifier*) without recoil.

dead beat *adj Inf.* very tired; exhausted.

dead-cat bounce *n Stock Exchange inf.* a temporary recovery in prices following a substantial fall as a result of speculators buying stocks they have already sold rather than as a result of a genuine reversal of the downward trend.

dead centre *n* **1** the exact top or bottom of the piston stroke in a reciprocating engine or pump. **2** a rod mounted in the tailstock of a lathe to support a workpiece. ◆ Also called: **dead point.**

dead duck *n Sl.* a person or thing doomed to death, failure, etc., esp. because of a mistake.

deaden ('dɛdᵊn) *vb* **1** to make or become less sensitive, intense, lively, etc. **2** (*tr*) to make acoustically less resonant.
▸ **'deadening** *adj*

dead end *n* **1** a cul-de-sac. **2** a situation in which further progress is impossible.

deadeye ('dɛdˌaɪ) *n* **1** *Naut.* either of a pair of disclike wooden blocks, supported by straps in grooves around them, between which a line is rove so as to draw them together to tighten a shroud. **2** *Inf., chiefly US.* an expert marksman.

deadfall ('dɛd,fɔːl) *n* a trap in which a heavy weight falls to crush the prey.

deadhead ('dɛd,hɛd) *n* **1** a person who uses a free ticket, as for the theatre, etc. **2** a train, etc., travelling empty. **3** *US & Canad.* a dull person. **4** *US & Canad.* a totally or partially submerged log floating in a lake, etc. ◆ *vb* **5** (*intr*) *US & Canad.* to drive an empty bus, train, etc. **6** (*tr*) to remove dead flower heads.

Dead Heart ★ *n* (usually preceded by *the*) *Austral.* the remote interior of Australia. ORIG C20: from *The Dead Heart of Australia* (1906) by J. W. Gregory (1864–1932), British geologist

dead heat *n* **a** a race or contest in which two or more participants tie for first place. **b** a tie between two or more contestants in any position.

dead leg *n Inf.* temporary loss of sensation in the leg, caused by a blow to a muscle.

dead letter *n* **1** a law or ordinance that is no longer enforced. **2** a letter that cannot be delivered or returned because it lacks adequate directions.

deadlight ('dɛd,laɪt) *n* **1** *Naut.* **1a** a bull's-eye to admit light to a cabin. **1b** a shutter for sealing off a porthole or cabin window. **2** a skylight designed not to be opened.

deadline ('dɛd,laɪn) *n* a time limit for any activity.

deadlock ('dɛd,lɒk) *n* **1** a state of affairs in which further action between two opposing forces is impossible. **2** a tie between opponents. **3** a lock having a bolt that can be opened only with a key. ◆ *vb* **4** to bring or come to a deadlock.

dead loss *n* **1** a complete loss for which no compensation is paid. **2** *Inf.* a useless person or thing.

deadly ('dɛdlɪ) *adj* **deadlier, deadliest. 1** likely to cause death. **2** *Inf.* extremely boring. ◆ *adv, adj* **3** like death in appearance or certainty.

deadly nightshade *n* a poisonous Eurasian plant having purple bell-shaped flowers and black berries. Also called: **belladonna, dwale.**

deadly sins *pl n* the sins of pride, covetousness, lust, envy, gluttony, anger, and sloth.

dead man's handle *or* **pedal** *n* a safety switch on a piece of machinery that allows operation only while depressed by the operator.

dead march *n* a piece of solemn funeral music played to accompany a procession.

dead-nettle *n* any of several Eurasian plants having leaves resembling nettles but lacking stinging hairs.

deadpan ('dɛd,pæn) *adj, adv* with a deliberately emotionless face or manner.

dead reckoning *n* a method of establishing one's position using the distance and direction travelled rather than astronomical observations.

Dead Sea ★ *n* a lake between Israel and Jordan, 397 m (1302 ft) below sea level: the lowest lake in the world, with no outlet and very high salinity. Area: 1020 sq. km (394 sq. miles).

dead set *adv* **1** absolutely: *he is dead set against going to Spain.* ◆ *n* **2** the motionless position of a dog when pointing towards game. ◆ *adj* **3** (of a hunting dog) in this position.

dead soldier *or* **marine** *n Inf.* an empty beer or spirit bottle.

dead time *n Electronics.* the time immediately following a stimulus, during which an electrical device, component, etc. is insensitive to a further stimulus.

dead weight *n* **1** a heavy weight or load. **2** an oppressive burden. **3** the difference between the loaded and the unloaded weights of a ship. **4** the intrinsic invariable weight of a structure, such as a bridge.

deadwood ('dɛd,wʊd) *n* **1** dead trees or branches. **2** *Inf.* a useless person; encumbrance.

deaf (dɛf) *adj* **1a** partially or totally unable to hear. **1b** (*as collective n;* preceded by *the*)*: the deaf.* **2** refusing to heed. ORIG OE *dēaf*
▸ **'deafness** *n*

> **USAGE NOTE** See at **disabled.**

deaf aid *n* another name for **hearing aid.**

deaf-and-dumb *Offens.* ◆ *adj* **1** unable to hear or speak. ◆ *n* **2** a deaf-mute person.

deafblind ('dɛf,blaɪnd) *adj* **a** unable to hear or see. **b** (*as collective n*; preceded by *the*): *the deafblind.*

> **USAGE NOTE** See at **disabled.**

deafen ('dɛfᵊn) *vb* (*tr*) to make deaf, esp. momentarily, as by a loud noise.
▸ **'deafening** *adj* ▸ **'deafeningly** *adv*

deaf-mute *n* **1** a person who is unable to hear or speak. See also **mute** (sense 7). ◆ *adj* **2** unable to hear or speak. ORIG C19: translation of F *sourd-muet*

> **USAGE NOTE** Nowadays this word would be considered offensive, and should be replaced by *profoundly deaf.*

Deakin ★ ('diːkɪn) *n* **Alfred.** 1856–1919, Australian statesman: prime minister (1903–04; 1905–08; 1909–10).

deal[1] (diːl) *vb* **deals, dealing, dealt. 1** (*intr;* foll. by *in*) to engage in commercially: *to deal in upholstery.* **2** (often foll. by *out*) to apportion or distribute. **3** (*tr*) to give (a blow, etc.) to (someone); inflict. **4** (*intr*) *Sl.* to sell any illegal drug. ◆ *n* **5** *Inf.* a bargain, transaction, or agreement. **6** a particular type of treatment received, esp. as the result of an agreement: *a fair deal.* **7** an indefinite amount (esp. in **good** *or* **great deal**). **8** *Cards.* **8a** the process of distributing the cards. **8b** a player's turn to do this. **8c** a single round in a card game. **9 big deal.** *Sl.* an important person, event, or matter: often used sarcastically. **10 cut a deal.** *Inf., chiefly US.* to come to an arrangement; make a deal. ◆ See also **deal with.** ORIG OE *dǣlan,* from *dǣl* a part; cf. OHG *teil* a part, ON *deild* a share

deal[2] (diːl) *n* **1** a plank of softwood timber, such as fir or pine, or such planks collectively. **2** the sawn wood of various coniferous trees. ◆ *adj* **3** of fir or pine. ORIG C14: from MLow G *dele* plank

Deal ★ (diːl) *n* a town in SE England, in Kent, on the English Channel: two 16th-century castles: tourism, light industries. Pop.: 28 504 (1991).

dealer ('diːlə) *n* **1** a person or firm engaged in commercial purchase and sale; trader: *a car dealer.* **2** *Cards.* the person who distributes the cards. **3** *Sl.* a person who sells illegal drugs.

dealings ('diːlɪŋz) *pl n* (*sometimes sing*) transactions or business relations.

dealt (dɛlt) *vb* the past tense and past participle of **deal**[1].

deal with *vb* (*tr, adv*) **1** to take action on: *to deal with each problem in turn.* **2** to punish: *the headmaster will deal with the culprit.* **3** to treat or be concerned with: *the book deals with architecture.* **4** to conduct oneself (towards others), esp. with regard to fairness. **5** to do business with.

dean (diːn) *n* **1** the chief administrative official of a college or university faculty. **2** (at Oxford and Cambridge universities) a college fellow with responsibility for undergraduate discipline. **3** *Chiefly Church of England.* the head of a chapter of canons and administrator of a cathedral or collegiate church. **4** *RC Church.* the cardinal bishop senior by consecration and head of the college of cardinals. Related adj: **decanal.** See also **rural dean.** ORIG C14: from OF *deien,* from LL *decānus* one set over ten persons, from L *decem* ten

Dean[1] ★ (diːn) *n* **Forest of.** a forest in W England, in Gloucestershire, between the Rivers Severn and Wye: formerly a royal hunting ground.

Dean[2] ★ (diːn) *n* **James (Byron).** 1931–55, US film actor and cult figure; his films include *East of Eden* and *Rebel Without a Cause* (both 1955). He died in a car crash.

deanery ('diːnərɪ) *n, pl* **deaneries. 1** the office or residence of a dean. **2** the group of parishes presided over by a rural dean.

dear (dɪə) *adj* **1** beloved; precious. **2** used in conventional forms of address, as in *Dear Sir.* **3** (*postpositive;* foll. by *to*) important; close. **4a** highly priced. **4b** charging high

prices. **5** appealing. **6 for dear life.** with extreme vigour or desperation. ◆ *interj* **7** used in exclamations of surprise or dismay, such as *Oh dear!* ◆ *n* **8** Also: **dearest.** (*often used in direct address*) someone regarded with affection and tenderness. ◆ *adv* **9** dearly. ORIG OE *dēore*
▸ **'dearness** *n*

dearly ('dɪəlɪ) *adv* **1** very much. **2** affectionately. **3** at a great cost.

dearth (dɜ:θ) *n* an inadequate amount, esp. of food; scarcity. ORIG C13 *derthe,* from *dēr* DEAR

deary *or* **dearie** ('dɪərɪ) *n* **1** (*pl* **dearies**) *Inf.* a term of affection: now often sarcastic or facetious. **2 deary** *or* **dearie me!** an exclamation of surprise or dismay.

death (dɛθ) *n* **1** the permanent end of all functions of life in an organism. **2** an instance of this: *his death ended an era.* **3** a murder or killing. **4** termination or destruction. **5** a state of affairs or an experience considered as terrible as death. **6** a cause or source of death. **7** (*usually cap.*) a personification of death, usually a skeleton or an old man holding a scythe. **8 at death's door.** likely to die soon. **9 catch one's death (of cold).** *Inf.* to contract a severe cold. **10 do to death. 10a** to kill. **10b** to overuse. **11 in at the death. 11a** present when a hunted animal is killed. **11b** present at the finish or climax. **12 like death warmed up.** *Inf.* very ill. **13 like grim death.** as if afraid of one's life. **14 put to death.** to kill deliberately or execute. **15 to death. 15a** until dead. **15b** very much. ◆ Related adjs.: **fatal, lethal, mortal.** ORIG OE *dēath*

death adder *n* a venomous thick-bodied Australian snake.

deathbed ('dɛθ,bɛd) *n* the bed in which a person is about to die.

deathblow ('dɛθ,bləʊ) *n* a thing or event that destroys life or hope, esp. suddenly.

death camp *n* a concentration camp in which the conditions are so brutal that few prisoners survive, or one to which prisoners are sent for execution.

death cap *or* **angel** *n* a poisonous woodland fungus with white gills and a cuplike structure at the base of the stalk.

death certificate *n* a legal document issued by a qualified medical practitioner certifying the death of a person and stating the cause if known.

death duty *n* a tax on property inheritances, in Britain replaced by capital transfer tax in 1975 and since 1986 by inheritance tax. Also called: **estate duty.**

death futures *pl n* life insurance policies of terminally ill people that are bought speculatively for a lump sum by a company, enabling it to collect the proceeds of the policies when the ill people die.

death knell *or* **bell** *n* **1** something that heralds death or destruction. **2** a bell rung to announce a death.

deathless ('dɛθlɪs) *adj* immortal, esp. because of greatness; everlasting.
▸ **'deathlessness** *n*

deathly ('dɛθlɪ) *adj* **1** deadly. **2** resembling death: *a deathly quiet.*

death mask *n* a cast of a dead person's face.

death rate *n* the ratio of deaths in a specified area, group, etc., to the population of that area, group, etc. Also called: **mortality rate.**

death rattle *n* a low-pitched gurgling sound sometimes made by a dying person.

death's-head *n* a human skull or a representation of one.

death's-head moth *n* a European hawk moth having markings resembling a human skull on its upper thorax.

death star *n* a weapon consisting of a flat star-shaped piece of metal with sharpened points that is thrown at an opponent. Also called: **throwing star.**

deathtrap ('dɛθ,træp) *n* a building, vehicle, etc., that is considered very unsafe.

Death Valley ★ *n* a desert valley in E California and W Nevada: the lowest, hottest, and driest area of the US. Lowest point: 86 m (282 ft) below sea level. Area: about 3885 sq. km (1500 sq. miles).

death warrant *n* **1** the official authorization for carrying out a sentence of death. **2 sign one's (own) death warrant.** to cause one's own destruction.

deathwatch ('dɛθ,wɒtʃ) *n* **1** a vigil held beside a dying or dead person. **2 deathwatch beetle.** a beetle whose woodboring larvae are a serious pest. The adult produces a tapping sound that was once supposed to presage death.

death wish *n* (in Freudian psychology) the desire for self-annihilation.

Deauville ★ ('dəʊvi:l; *French* dovil) *n* a town and resort in NW France: casino. Pop.: 4770 (latest est.).

deb (dɛb) *n Inf.* short for **debutante.**

debacle (deɪ'bɑ:kᵊl, dɪ-) *n* **1** a sudden disastrous collapse or defeat; rout. **2** the breaking up of ice in a river, often causing flooding. **3** a violent rush of water carrying along debris. ORIG C19: from F, from OF *desbacler* to unbolt

debag (di:'bæg) *vb* **debags, debagging, debagged.** (*tr*) *Brit. sl.* to remove the trousers from (someone) by force.

debar (dɪ'bɑ:) *vb* **debars, debarring, debarred.** (*tr;* usually foll. by *from*) to exclude from a place, a right, etc.; bar.
▸ **de'barment** *n*

> **USAGE NOTE** See at **disbar.**

debark[1] (dɪ'bɑ:k) *vb* another word for **disembark.** ORIG C17: from F *débarquer,* from *dé-* DIS-[1] + *barque* BARQUE
▸ **debarkation** (,di:bɑ:'keɪʃən) *n*

debark[2] (di:'bɑ:k) *vb* (*tr*) to remove the bark from (a tree). ORIG C18: from DE-+ BARK[2]

debase (dɪ'beɪs) *vb* **debases, debasing, debased.** (*tr*) to lower in quality, character, or value; adulterate. ORIG C16: see DE-, BASE[2]
▸ **de'basement** *n* ▸ **de'baser** *n*

debate (dɪ'beɪt) *n* **1** a formal discussion, as in a legislative body, in which opposing arguments are put forward. **2** discussion or dispute. **3** the formal presentation and opposition of a specific motion, followed by a vote. ◆ *vb* **debates, debating, debated. 4** to discuss (a motion, etc.), esp. in a formal assembly. **5** to deliberate upon (something). ORIG C13: from OF *debatre* to discuss, argue, from L *battuere*
▸ **de'batable** *adj* ▸ **de'bater** *n*

debauch (dɪ'bɔ:tʃ) *vb* **1** (when *tr, usually passive*) to lead into a life of depraved self-indulgence. **2** (*tr*) to seduce (a woman). ◆ *n* **3** an instance or period of extreme dissipation. ORIG C16: from OF *desbaucher* to corrupt, lit.: to shape (timber) roughly, from *bauch* beam, of Gmc origin
▸ **de'baucher** *n* ▸ **de'bauchery** *n*

debauchee (,dɛbɔ:'tʃi:) *n* a man who leads a life of promiscuity and self-indulgence.

debenture (dɪ'bɛntʃə) *n* **1** a long-term bond, bearing fixed interest and usually unsecured, issued by a company or governmental agency. **2** a certificate acknowledging a debt. **3** a customs certificate providing for a refund of excise or import duty. ORIG C15: from L *dēbentur mihi* there are owed to me, from *dēbēre*
▸ **de'bentured** *adj*

debenture stock *n* shares issued by a company, which guarantee a fixed return at regular intervals.

debilitate (dɪ'bɪlɪ,teɪt) *vb* **debilitates, debilitating, debilitated.** (*tr*) to make feeble; weaken. ORIG C16: from L, from *dēbilis* weak
▸ **de,bili'tation** *n* ▸ **de'bilitative** *adj*

debility (dɪ'bɪlɪtɪ) *n, pl* **debilities.** weakness or infirmity.

debit ('dɛbɪt) *n* **1a** acknowledgment of a sum owing by entry on the left side of an account. **1b** the left side of an account. **1c** an entry on this side. **1d** the total of such entries. **1e** (*as modifier*): *a debit balance.* ◆ *vb* **debits, debiting, debited. 2** (*tr*) **2a** to record (an item) as a debit in an account. **2b** to charge (a person or his or her account) with a debt. ORIG C15: from L *dēbitum* DEBT

debit card *n* a card issued by a bank or building society enabling customers to pay for goods or services by inserting it into a computer-controlled device at the place of sale, which is connected through the telephone network to the bank or building society.

debonair *or* **debonnaire** (ˌdɛbəˈnɛə) *adj* **1** suave and refined. **2** carefree; light-hearted. **3** courteous and cheerful. ORIG C13: from OF, from *de bon aire* having a good disposition
▸ ˌ**deboˈnairly** *adv* ▸ ˌ**deboˈnairness** *n*

Deborah ★ (ˈdɛbərə, -brə) *n Old Testament.* **1** a prophetess and judge of Israel who fought the Canaanites (Judges 4, 5). **2** Rebecca's nurse (Genesis 35:8).

debouch (dɪˈbaʊtʃ) *vb* (*intr*) **1** (esp. of troops) to move into a more open space. **2** (of a river, glacier, etc.) to flow into a larger area or body. ORIG C18: from F *déboucher,* from *dé-* DIS-[1] + *bouche* mouth
▸ **deˈbouchment** *n*

Debrett (dəˈbrɛt) *n* a list, considered exclusive, of the British aristocracy. In full: **Debrett's Peerage.** ORIG C19: after J. *Debrett* (c 1750-1822), London publisher who first issued it

debrief (diːˈbriːf) *vb* (*tr*) to elicit a report from (a soldier, diplomat, etc.) after a mission or event.
▸ **deˈbriefing** *n*

debris *or* **débris** (ˈdeɪbrɪ, ˈdɛbrɪ) *n* **1** fragments of something destroyed or broken; rubble. **2** a collection of loose material derived from rocks, or an accumulation of animal or vegetable matter. ORIG C18: from F, from obs. *debrisier* to break into pieces, of Celtic origin

de Broglie ★ (*French* də brɔj) *n* See (Louis Victor de) **Broglie.**

debt (dɛt) *n* **1** something owed, such as money, goods, or services. **2 bad debt.** a debt that has little prospect of being paid. **3** an obligation to pay or perform something. **4** the state of owing something, or of being under an obligation (esp. in **in debt, in (someone's) debt**). ORIG C13: from OF *dette,* from L *dēbitum,* from *dēbēre* to owe, from DE- + *habēre* to have

debt collector *n* a person employed to collect debts for creditors.

debt of honour *n* a debt that is morally but not legally binding.

debtor (ˈdɛtə) *n* a person or commercial enterprise that owes a financial obligation.

debt swap *n* See **swap** (sense 4).

debud (diːˈbʌd) *vb* **debuds, debudding, debudded.** another word for **disbud.**

debug (diːˈbʌg) *vb* **debugs, debugging, debugged.** (*tr*) *Inf.* **1** to locate and remove concealed microphones from (a room, etc.). **2** to locate and remove defects in (a device, system, plan, etc.). **3** to remove insects from. ORIG C20: from DE- + BUG

debunk (diːˈbʌŋk) *vb* (*tr*) *Inf.* to expose the pretensions or falseness of, esp. by ridicule. ORIG C20: from DE- + BUNK[2]
▸ **deˈbunker** *n*

debus (diːˈbʌs) *vb* **debuses, debusing, debused** *or* **debusses, debussing, debussed.** to unload (goods, etc.) or (esp. of troops) to alight from a bus.

Debussy ★ (dəˈbjuːsɪ, ˈdeɪbjuːsɪ; *French* dəbysi) *n* **(Achille) Claude** (klod). 1862–1918, French impressionist composer. His works include *Prélude à l'après-midi d'un faune* (1894) and *La Mer* (1905) for orchestra and the opera *Pelléas et Mélisande* (1902).

debut (ˈdeɪbjuː, ˈdɛbjuː) *n* **1a** the first public appearance of an actor, musician, etc. **1b** (*as modifier*): *debut album.* **2** the presentation of a debutante. ORIG C18: from F, from OF *desbuter* to play first, from *des-* DE- + *but* goal, target

debutante (ˈdɛbjʊˌtɑːnt, -ˌtænt) *n* **1** a young upper-class woman who is formally presented to society. **2** a young woman regarded as being upper-class, wealthy, and frivolous. ORIG C19: from F, from *débuter* to lead off in a game, make one's first appearance; see DEBUT

Debye ★ (*Dutch* deˈbɛiə) *n* **Peter Joseph Wilhelm.** 1884–1966, Dutch chemist, working in the US: Nobel prize for chemistry (1936) for work on dipole moments.

dec. *abbrev. for:* **1** deceased. **2** decimal. **3** decimetre. **4** declaration. **5** declension. **6** declination. **7** decrease. **8** *Music.* decrescendo.

Dec. *abbrev. for* December.

deca-, deka- *or before a vowel* **dec-, dek-** *prefix* denoting ten: *decagon.* In conjunction with scientific units the symbol **da** is used. ORIG from Gk *deka*

decade (ˈdɛkeɪd, dɪˈkeɪd) *n* **1** a period of ten years. **2** a group of ten. ORIG C15: from OF, from LL, from Gk, from *deka* ten
▸ **deˈcadal** *adj*

> **USAGE NOTE** Though this word may be pronounced with the stress on the first or the second syllable, stressing the first syllable is preferable.

decadence (ˈdɛkədəns) *or* **decadency** *n* **1** deterioration, esp. of morality or culture. **2** the state reached through such a process. **3** (*often cap.*) the period or style associated with the 19th-century decadents. ORIG C16: from F, from Med. L *dēcadentia,* lit.: a falling away; see DECAY

decadent (ˈdɛkədənt) *adj* **1** characterized by decline, as in being self-indulgent or morally corrupt. **2** belonging to a period of decline in artistic standards. ◆ *n* **3** a decadent person. **4** (*often cap.*) one of a group of French and English writers of the late 19th century whose works were characterized by refinement of style and a tendency toward the artificial and abnormal.

decaf (ˈdiːkæf) *Inf.* ◆ *n* **1** decaffeinated coffee. ◆ *adj* **2** decaffeinated.

decaffeinate (dɪˈkæfɪˌneɪt) *vb* **decaffeinates, decaffeinating, decaffeinated.** (*tr*) to remove all or part of the caffeine from (coffee, tea, etc.).

decagon (ˈdɛkəˌgɒn) *n* a polygon having ten sides.
▸ **decagonal** (dɪˈkægənᵊl) *adj*

decahedron (ˌdɛkəˈhiːdrən) *n* a solid figure having ten plane faces.
▸ ˌ**decaˈhedral** *adj*

decal (dɪˈkæl, ˈdiːkæl) *n* **1** short for **decalcomania.** ◆ *vb* **decals, decalling, decalled** *or US* **decals, decaling, decaled. 2** to transfer (a design, etc.) by decalcomania.

decalcify (diːˈkælsɪˌfaɪ) *vb* **decalcifies, decalcifying, decalcified.** (*tr*) to remove calcium or lime from (bones, etc.).
▸ **deˈcalciˌfier** *n*

decalcomania (dɪˌkælkəˈmeɪnɪə) *n* **1** the process of transferring a design from prepared paper onto another surface, such as glass or paper. **2** a design so transferred. ORIG C19: from F, from *décalquer,* from *de-* DE- + *calquer* to trace + *-manie* -MANIA

decalitre *or US* **decaliter** (ˈdɛkəˌliːtə) *n* a metric measure of volume equivalent to 10 litres.

Decalogue (ˈdɛkəˌlɒg) *n* another name for the **Ten Commandments.** ORIG C14: from Church L *decalogus,* from Gk, from *deka* ten + *logos* word

decametre *or US* **decameter** (ˈdɛkəˌmiːtə) *n* a metric measure of length equivalent to 10 metres.

decamp (dɪˈkæmp) *vb* (*intr*) **1** to leave a camp; break camp. **2** to depart secretly or suddenly; abscond.
▸ **deˈcampment** *n*

decanal (dɪˈkeɪnᵊl) *adj* **1** of a dean or deanery. **2** on the same side of a cathedral, etc., as the dean; on the S side of the choir. ORIG C18: from Med. L *decānālis, decānus* DEAN

decani (dɪˈkeɪnaɪ) *adj, adv Music.* to be sung by the decanal side of a choir. Cf. **cantoris.** ORIG L: genitive of *decānus*

decant (dɪˈkænt) *vb* **1** to pour (a liquid, such as wine) from one container to another, esp. without disturbing any sediment. **2** (*tr*) to rehouse (people) while their homes are being rebuilt or refurbished. ORIG C17: from Med. L *dēcanthāre,* from *canthus* spout, rim

decanter (dɪˈkæntə) *n* a stoppered bottle, into which a drink is poured for serving.

decapitate (dɪˈkæpɪˌteɪt) *vb* **decapitates, decapitating, decapitated.** (*tr*) to behead. ORIG C17: from LL *dēcapitāre,* from L DE- + *caput* head
▸ **deˌcapiˈtation** *n* ▸ **deˈcapiˌtator** *n*

decapod ('dɛkəˌpɒd) *n* **1** any crustacean having five pairs of walking limbs, as a crab, lobster, shrimp, etc. **2** any cephalopod mollusc having eight short tentacles and two longer ones, as a squid or cuttlefish.
▸ **decapodal** (dɪ'kæpədᵊl), **de'capodan,** *or* **de'capodous** *adj*

decarbonate (diː'kɑːbəˌneɪt) *vb* **decarbonates, decarbonating, decarbonated.** (*tr*) to remove carbon dioxide from.
▸ **deˌcarbon'ation** *n* ▸ **de'carbonˌator** *n*

decarbonize *or* **decarbonise** (diː'kɑːbəˌnaɪz) *vb* **decarbonizes, decarbonizing, decarbonized** *or* **decarbonises, decarbonising, decarbonised.** (*tr*) to remove carbon from (an internal-combustion engine, etc.). Also: **decoke, decarburize.**
▸ **deˌcarboni'zation** *or* **deˌcarboni'sation** *n* ▸ **de'carbonˌizer** *or* **de'carbonˌiser** *n*

decarboxylase (ˌdiːkɑː'bɒksɪˌleɪz) *n* an enzyme that catalyses the removal of carbon dioxide from a compound.

decastyle ('dɛkəˌstaɪl) *n Archit.* a portico consisting of ten columns.

decasyllable ('dɛkəˌsɪləbᵊl) *n* a word or line of verse consisting of ten syllables.
▸ **decasyllabic** (ˌdɛkəsɪ'læbɪk) *adj*

decathlon (dɪ'kæθlɒn) *n* an athletic contest in which each athlete competes in ten different events. ORIG C20: from DECA- + Gk *athlon* contest, prize; see ATHLETE
▸ **de'cathlete** *n*

decay (dɪ'keɪ) *vb* **1** to decline or cause to decline gradually in health, prosperity, excellence, etc.; deteriorate. **2** to rot or cause to rot; decompose. **3** (*intr*) Also: **disintegrate.** *Physics.* **3a** (of an atomic nucleus) to undergo radioactive disintegration. **3b** (of an elementary particle) to transform into two or more different elementary particles. **4** (*intr*) *Physics.* (of a stored charge, magnetic flux, etc.) to decrease gradually when the source of energy has been removed. ◆ *n* **5** the process of decline, as in health, mentality, etc. **6** the state brought about by this process. **7** decomposition. **8** rotten or decayed matter. **9** *Physics.* **9a** See **radioactive decay. 9b** a spontaneous transformation of an elementary particle into two or more different particles. **10** *Physics.* a gradual decrease of a stored charge, current, etc., when the source of energy has been removed. ORIG C15: from OF *decaïr,* from LL *dēcadere,* lit.: to fall away, from L *cadere* to fall
▸ **de'cayable** *adj*

Deccan ★ ('dɛkən) *n* **the. 1** a plateau in S India, between the Eastern Ghats, the Western Ghats, and the Narmada River. **2** the whole Indian peninsula south of the Narmada River.

decease (dɪ'siːs) *n* **1** a more formal word for **death.** ◆ *vb* **deceases, deceasing, deceased. 2** (*intr*) a more formal word for **die**[1]. ORIG C14 (n): from OF, from L *dēcēdere* to depart

deceased (dɪ'siːst) *adj* **a** a more formal word for **dead** (sense 1). **b** (*as n; preceded by the*)*: the deceased.*

deceit (dɪ'siːt) *n* **1** the act or practice of deceiving. **2** a statement, act, or device intended to mislead; fraud; trick. **3** a tendency to deceive. ORIG C13: from OF, from *deceivre* to DECEIVE

deceitful (dɪ'siːtfʊl) *adj* full of deceit.

deceive (dɪ'siːv) *vb* **deceives, deceiving, deceived.** (*tr*) **1** to mislead by deliberate misrepresentation or lies. **2** to delude (oneself). **3** to be unfaithful to (one's sexual partner). **4** *Arch.* to disappoint. ORIG C13: from OF *deceivre,* from L *dēcipere* to ensnare, cheat, from *capere* to take
▸ **de'ceivable** *adj* ▸ **de'ceiver** *n*

decelerate (diː'sɛləˌreɪt) *vb* **decelerates, decelerating, decelerated.** to slow down or cause to slow down. ORIG C19: from DE- + (AC)CELERATE
▸ **deˌceler'ation** *n* ▸ **de'celerˌator** *n*

December (dɪ'sɛmbə) *n* the twelfth month of the year, consisting of 31 days. ORIG C13: from OF, from L: the tenth month (the Roman year orig. began with March), from *decem* ten

decencies ('diːsᵊnsɪz) *pl n* **1 the.** those things that are considered necessary for a decent life. **2** another word for **proprieties,** see **propriety** (sense 3).

decency ('diːsᵊnsɪ) *n, pl* **decencies. 1** conformity to the prevailing standards of propriety, morality, modesty, etc. **2** the quality of being decent.

decennial (dɪ'sɛnɪəl) *adj* **1** lasting for ten years. **2** occurring every ten years. ◆ *n* **3** a tenth anniversary.
▸ **de'cennially** *adv*

decent ('diːsᵊnt) *adj* **1** polite or respectable. **2** proper and suitable; fitting. **3** conforming to conventions of sexual behaviour; not indecent. **4** free of oaths, blasphemy, etc. **5** good or adequate: *a decent wage.* **6** *Inf.* kind; generous. **7** *Inf.* sufficiently clothed to be seen by other people: *are you decent?* ORIG C16: from L *decēns* suitable, from *decēre* to be fitting
▸ **'decently** *adv*

decentralize *or* **decentralise** (diː'sɛntrəˌlaɪz) *vb* **decentralizes, decentralizing, decentralized** *or* **decentralises, decentralising, decentralised. 1** to reorganize into smaller more autonomous units. **2** to disperse (a concentration, as of industry or population).
▸ **de'centralist** *n, adj* ▸ **deˌcentrali'zation** *or* **deˌcentrali'sation** *n*

deception (dɪ'sɛpʃən) *n* **1** the act of deceiving or the state of being deceived. **2** something that deceives; trick.

deceptive (dɪ'sɛptɪv) *adj* likely or designed to deceive; misleading.
▸ **de'ceptively** *adv* ▸ **de'ceptiveness** *n*

decertify (diː'sɜːtɪˌfaɪ) *vb* **decertifies, decertifying, decertified.** (*tr*) to withdraw or remove a certificate or certification from (a person, organization, or country).
▸ **deˌcertifi'cation** *n*

deci- *prefix* denoting one tenth: *decimetre.* Symbol: d ORIG from F *déci-,* from L *decimus* tenth

decibel ('dɛsɪˌbɛl) *n* **1** a unit for comparing two currents, voltages, or power levels, equal to one tenth of a bel. **2** a similar unit for measuring the intensity of a sound. Abbrev.: **dB.**

decide (dɪ'saɪd) *vb* **decides, deciding, decided. 1** (*may take a clause or an infinitive as object;* when *intr,* sometimes foll. by *on* or *about*) to reach a decision: *decide what you want; he decided to go.* **2** (*tr*) to cause to reach a decision. **3** (*tr*) to determine or settle (a contest or question). **4** (*tr*) to influence decisively the outcome of (a contest or question). **5** (*intr;* foll. by *for* or *against*) to pronounce a formal verdict. ORIG C14: from OF, from L *dēcīdere,* lit.: to cut off, from *caedere* to cut
▸ **de'cidable** *adj*

decided (dɪ'saɪdɪd) *adj* (*prenominal*) **1** unmistakable. **2** determined; resolute: *a girl of decided character.*
▸ **de'cidedly** *adv*

decider (dɪ'saɪdə) *n* the point, goal, game, etc., that determines who wins a match or championship.

deciduous (dɪ'sɪdjʊəs) *adj* **1** (of trees and shrubs) shedding all leaves annually at the end of the growing season. Cf. **evergreen. 2** (of antlers, teeth, etc.) being shed at the end of a period of growth. ORIG C17: from L: falling off, from *dēcidere* to fall down, from *cadere* to fall
▸ **de'ciduousness** *n*

decilitre *or US* **deciliter** ('dɛsɪˌliːtə) *n* a metric measure of volume equivalent to one tenth of a litre.

decillion (dɪ'sɪljən) *n* **1** (in Britain, France, and Germany) the number represented as one followed by 60 zeros (10^{60}). **2** (in the US and Canada) the number represented as one followed by 33 zeros (10^{33}). ORIG C19: from L *decem* ten + *-illion* as in *million*
▸ **de'cillionth** *adj*

decimal ('dɛsɪməl) *n* **1** Also called: **decimal fraction.** a fraction that has an unwritten denominator of a power of ten. It is indicated by a decimal point to the left of the numerator: *.2=2/10.* **2** any number used in the decimal system. ◆ *adj* **3a** relating to or using powers of ten. **3b** of the base ten. **4** (*prenominal*) expressed as a decimal. ORIG C17: from Med. L *decimālis* of tithes, from L *decima* a tenth
▸ **'decimally** *adv*

decimal classification *n* another term for **Dewey Decimal System.**

decimal currency *n* a system of currency in which the monetary units are parts or powers of ten.

★ people and places

decimalize *or* **decimalise** (ˈdɛsɪməˌlaɪz) *vb* **decimalizes, decimalizing, decimalized** *or* **decimalises, decimalising, decimalised.** to change (a system, number, etc.) to the decimal system.
▸ **ˌdecimaliˈzation** *or* **ˌdecimaliˈsation** *n*

decimal place *n* **1** the position of a digit after the decimal point. **2** the number of digits to the right of the decimal point.

decimal point *n* a full stop or a raised full stop placed between the integral and fractional parts of a number in the decimal system.

> **USAGE NOTE** Conventions relating to the use of the decimal point are confused. The IX General Conference on Weights and Measures resolved in 1948 that the decimal point should be a point on the line or a comma, but not a centre dot. It also resolved that figures could be grouped in threes about the decimal point, but that no point or comma should be used for this purpose. These conventions are adopted in this dictionary. However, the Decimal Currency Board recommended that for sums of money the centre dot should be used as the decimal point and that the comma should be used as the thousand marker. Moreover, in some countries the position is reversed, the comma being used as the decimal point and the dot as the thousand marker.

decimal system *n* **1** the number system in general use, having a base of ten, in which numbers are expressed by combinations of the ten digits 0 to 9. **2** a system of measurement in which the multiple and submultiple units are related to a basic unit by powers of ten.

decimate (ˈdɛsɪˌmeɪt) *vb* **decimates, decimating, decimated.** (*tr*) **1** to destroy or kill a large proportion of. **2** (esp. in the ancient Roman army) to kill every tenth man of (a mutinous section). ORIG C17: from L *decimāre*, from *decem* ten
▸ **ˌdeciˈmation** *n* ▸ **ˈdeciˌmator** *n*

> **USAGE NOTE** The antiquarian view that this word is only properly used to refer to slaughtering one in ten of a population, because of what it meant in Latin, now seems wilfully obscurantist. Nowadays the word is used not only to describe the destruction of people and animals, but also of institutions: *overseas visitors will stay away in droves, decimating the tourist industry.* When using this word it is advisable to refer to its effects on the whole of something, not on a part: *disease decimated the population*, not *disease decimated most of the population.*

decimetre *or US* **decimeter** (ˈdɛsɪˌmiːtə) *n* one tenth of a metre. Symbol: **dm.**

decipher (dɪˈsaɪfə) *vb* (*tr*) **1** to determine the meaning of (something obscure or illegible). **2** to convert from code into plain text; decode.
▸ **deˈcipherable** *adj* ▸ **deˈcipherment** *n*

decision (dɪˈsɪʒən) *n* **1** a judgment, conclusion, or resolution reached or given; verdict. **2** the act of making up one's mind. **3** firmness of purpose or character; determination. ORIG C15: from OF, from L *dēcīsiō*, lit.: a cutting off; see DECIDE

decision tree *n* a treelike diagram illustrating the choices available to a decision maker, each possible decision and its estimated outcome being shown as a separate branch of the tree.

decisive (dɪˈsaɪsɪv) *adj* **1** influential; conclusive. **2** characterized by the ability to make decisions, esp. quickly; resolute.
▸ **deˈcisively** *adv* ▸ **deˈcisiveness** *n*

deck (dɛk) *n* **1** *Naut.* any of various platforms built into a vessel. **2** a similar platform, as in a bus. **3a** the horizontal platform that supports the turntable and pick-up of a record player. **3b** See **tape deck. 4** *Chiefly US.* a pack of playing cards. **5** *Computing.* a collection of punched cards relevant to a particular program. **6 clear the decks.** *Inf.* to prepare for action, as by removing obstacles. **7 hit the deck.** *Inf.* **7a** to fall to the ground, esp. to avoid injury. **7b** to prepare for action. **7c** to get out of bed. ◆ *vb* (*tr*) **8** (often foll. by *out*) to dress or decorate. **9** to build a deck on (a vessel). **10** *Sl.* to knock (someone) to the floor or ground. ORIG C15: from MDu. *dec* a covering

deck-access *adj* (of a block of flats) having a continuous balcony at each level onto which the front door of each flat opens.

deck chair *n* a folding chair consisting of a wooden frame suspending a length of canvas.

Decker ★ (ˈdɛkə) *n* a variant spelling of (Thomas) **Dekker.**

-decker *adj* (*in combination*) having a certain specified number of levels or layers: *a double-decker bus.*

deck hand *n* **1** a seaman assigned duties on the deck of a ship. **2** (in Britain) a seaman who has seen sea duty for at least one year. **3** a helper aboard a yacht.

decking (ˈdɛkɪŋ) *n* a form of floor covering, used in gardens, made from varnished or stained wooden boards or tiles.

deckle *or* **deckel** (ˈdɛkᵊl) *n* **1** a frame used to contain pulp on the mould in the making of handmade paper. **2** a strap on a paper-making machine that fixes the width of the paper. ORIG C19: from G *Deckel* lid, from *decken* to cover

deckle edge *n* **1** the rough edge of paper made using a deckle, often left as ornamentation. **2** an imitation of this.
▸ **ˈdeckle-ˈedged** *adj*

declaim (dɪˈkleɪm) *vb* **1** to make (a speech, etc.) loudly and in a rhetorical manner. **2** to speak lines from (a play, poem, etc.) with studied eloquence. **3** (*intr;* foll. by *against*) to protest (against) loudly and publicly. ORIG C14: from L *dēclāmāre*, from *clāmāre* to call out
▸ **deˈclaimer** *n* ▸ **declamatory** (dɪˈklæmətərɪ) *adj*

declamation (ˌdɛkləˈmeɪʃən) *n* **1** a rhetorical or emotional speech, made esp. in order to protest; tirade. **2** a speech, verse, etc., that is or can be spoken. **3** the act or art of declaiming.

declaration (ˌdɛkləˈreɪʃən) *n* **1** an explicit or emphatic statement. **2** a formal statement or announcement. **3** the act of declaring. **4** the ruling of a judge or court on a question of law. **5** *Law.* an unsworn statement of a witness admissible in evidence under certain conditions. **6** *Cricket.* the voluntary closure of an innings before all ten wickets have fallen. **7** *Contract bridge.* the final contract. **8** a statement or inventory of goods, etc., submitted for tax assessment.

declarative (dɪˈklærətɪv) *or* **declaratory** (dɪˈklærətərɪ, -trɪ) *adj* making or having the nature of a declaration.
▸ **deˈclaratively** *or* **deˈclaratorily** *adv*

declare (dɪˈklɛə) *vb* **declares, declaring, declared.** (*mainly tr*) **1** (*may take a clause as object*) to make clearly known or announce officially: *war was declared.* **2** to state officially that (a person, fact, etc.) is as specified: *he declared him fit.* **3** (*may take a clause as object*) to state emphatically; assert. **4** to show, reveal, or manifest. **5** (*intr;* often foll. by *for* or *against*) to make known one's choice or opinion. **6** to make a statement of (dutiable goods, etc.). **7** (*also intr*) *Cards.* **7a** to display (cards) on the table so as to add to one's score. **7b** to decide (the trump suit) by making the final bid. **8** (*intr*) *Cricket.* to close an innings voluntarily before all ten wickets have fallen. **9** to authorize payment of (a dividend). ORIG C14: from L *dēclārāre* to make clear, from *clārus* clear
▸ **deˈclarable** *adj* ▸ **deˈclarer** *n*

declassify (diːˈklæsɪˌfaɪ) *vb* **declassifies, declassifying, declassified.** (*tr*) to release (a document or information) from the security list.
▸ **deˌclassifiˈcation** *n*

declension (dɪˈklɛnʃən) *n* **1** *Grammar.* **1a** inflection of nouns, pronouns, or adjectives for case, number, and gender. **1b** the complete set of the inflections of such a word. **2** a decline or deviation. **3** a downward slope. ORIG

C15: from L *dēclīnātiō*, lit.: a bending aside, hence variation; see DECLINE
▸ **de'clensional** *adj*

declination (ˌdɛklɪ'neɪʃən) *n* **1** *Astron.* the angular distance of a star, planet, etc., north or south from the celestial equator. Symbol: δ. **2** the angle made by a compass needle with the direction of the geographical north pole. **3** a refusal, esp. a courteous or formal one.
▸ **ˌdecli'national** *adj*

decline (dɪ'klaɪn) *vb* **declines, declining, declined. 1** to refuse to do or accept (something), esp. politely. **2** (*intr*) to grow smaller; diminish. **3** to slope or cause to slope downwards. **4** (*intr*) to deteriorate gradually. **5** *Grammar.* to list the inflections of (a noun, adjective, or pronoun), or (of a noun, adjective, or pronoun) to be inflected for number, case, or gender. ◆ *n* **6** gradual deterioration or loss. **7** a movement downward; diminution. **8** a downward slope. **9** *Arch.* any slowly progressive disease, such as tuberculosis. ORIG C14: from OF *decliner*, from L *dēclīnāre* to bend away, inflect grammatically
▸ **de'clinable** *adj* ▸ **de'cliner** *n*

declivity (dɪ'klɪvɪtɪ) *n, pl* **declivities.** a downward slope, esp. of the ground. ORIG C17: from L *dēclīvitās*, from DE- + *clīvus* a slope, hill
▸ **de'clivitous** *adj*

declutch (dɪ'klʌtʃ) *vb* (*intr*) to disengage the clutch of a motor vehicle.

decoct (dɪ'kɒkt) *vb* to extract the essence or active principle from (a medicinal or similar substance) by boiling. ORIG C15: see DECOCTION

decoction (dɪ'kɒkʃən) *n* **1** *Pharmacol.* the extraction of the water-soluble substances of a drug or medicinal plants by boiling. **2** the liquor resulting from this. ORIG C14: from OF, from LL, from *dēcoquere* to boil down, from *coquere* to cook

decode (diː'kəʊd) *vb* **decodes, decoding, decoded.** to convert from code into ordinary language.
▸ **de'coder** *n*

decoke (diː'kəʊk) *vb* **decokes, decoking, decoked.** (*tr*) another word for **decarbonize.**

décolletage (ˌdeɪkɒl'tɑːʒ) *n* a low-cut dress or neckline. ORIG C19: from F; see DÉCOLLETÉ

décolleté (deɪ'kɒlteɪ) *adj* **1** (of a woman's garment) low-cut. **2** wearing a low-cut garment. ◆ *n* **3** a low-cut neckline. ORIG C19: from F *décolleter* to cut out the neck (of a dress), from *collet* collar

decolonize *or* **decolonise** (diː'kɒləˌnaɪz) *vb* **decolonizes, decolonizing, decolonized** *or* **decolonises, decolonising, decolonised.** (*tr*) to grant independence to (a colony).
▸ **deˌcoloni'zation** *or* ▸ **deˌcoloni'sation** *n*

decolour (diː'kʌlə), **decolorize,** *or* **decolorise** *vb* **decolorizes, decolorizing, decolorized** *or* **decolorises, decolorising, decolorised.** (*tr*) to deprive of colour.
▸ **deˌcolori'zation** *or* **deˌcolori'sation** *n*

decommission (ˌdiːkə'mɪʃən) *vb* (*tr*) to dismantle or remove from service (a nuclear reactor, weapon, ship, etc. which is no longer required).

decompose (ˌdiːkəm'pəʊz) *vb* **decomposes, decomposing, decomposed. 1** to break down or be broken down into constituent elements by bacterial or fungal action; rot. **2** *Chem.* to break down or cause to break down into simpler chemical compounds. **3** to break up or separate into constituent parts.
▸ **decomposition** (ˌdiːkɒmpə'zɪʃən) *n*

decomposer (ˌdiːkəm'pəʊzə) *n* a person or thing that causes decomposition, esp. any of the organisms, such as bacteria, that do so in an ecosystem.

decompress (ˌdiːkəm'prɛs) *vb* **1** to relieve or be relieved of pressure. **2** to return (a diver, etc.) to a condition of normal atmospheric pressure or to be returned to such a condition.
▸ **ˌdecom'pression** *n*

decompression chamber *n* a chamber in which the pressure of air can be varied slowly for returning people safely from abnormal pressures to atmospheric pressure.

decompression sickness *or* **illness** *n* a disorder characterized by severe pain, cramp, and difficulty in breathing, caused by a sudden and sustained decrease in atmospheric pressure.

decongestant (ˌdiːkən'dʒɛstənt) *adj* **1** relieving congestion, esp. nasal congestion. ◆ *n* **2** a decongestant drug.

deconsecrate (diː'kɒnsɪˌkreɪt) *vb* **deconsecrates, deconsecrating, deconsecrated.** (*tr*) to transfer (a church, etc.) to secular use.
▸ **deˌconse'cration** *n*

deconstruct (ˌdiːkən'strʌkt) *vb* (*tr*) **1** to apply the theories of deconstruction to (a text, film, etc.). **2** to expose or dismantle the existing structure in (a system, organization, etc.).

deconstruction (ˌdiːkən'strʌkʃən) *n* a technique of literary analysis that regards meaning as resulting from the differences between words rather than their reference to the things they stand for.

decontaminate (ˌdiːkən'tæmɪˌneɪt) *vb* **decontaminates, decontaminating, decontaminated.** (*tr*) to render harmless by the removal or neutralization of poisons, radioactivity, etc.
▸ **ˌdeconˌtami'nation** *n*

decontrol (ˌdiːkən'trəʊl) *vb* **decontrols, decontrolling, decontrolled.** (*tr*) to free of restraints or controls, esp. government controls: *to decontrol prices.*

décor *or* **decor** ('deɪkɔː) *n* **1** a style or scheme of interior decoration, furnishings, etc., as in a room or house. **2** stage decoration; scenery. ORIG C19: from F, from *décorer* to DECORATE

decorate ('dɛkəˌreɪt) *vb* **decorates, decorating, decorated. 1** (*tr*) to ornament; adorn. **2** to paint or wallpaper. **3** (*tr*) to confer a mark of distinction, esp. a medal, upon. ORIG C16: from L *decorāre*, from *decus* adornment
▸ **'decorative** *adj*

Decorated style *n* a 14th-century style of English architecture characterized by geometrical tracery and floral decoration.

decoration (ˌdɛkə'reɪʃən) *n* **1** an addition that renders something more attractive or ornate. **2** the act or art of decorating. **3** a medal, etc., conferred as a mark of honour.

decorator ('dɛkəˌreɪtə) *n* **1** *Brit.* a person whose profession is the painting and wallpapering of buildings or their interiors. **2** a person who decorates.

decorous ('dɛkərəs) *adj* characterized by propriety in manners, conduct, etc. ORIG C17: from L, from *decor* elegance
▸ **'decorously** *adv* ▸ **'decorousness** *n*

decorum (dɪ'kɔːrəm) *n* **1** propriety, esp. in behaviour or conduct. **2** a requirement of correct behaviour in polite society. ORIG C16: from L: propriety

decoupage (ˌdeɪkuː'pɑːʒ) *n* the decoration of a surface with cutout shapes or illustrations. ORIG C20: from F, from *découper*, from DE- + *couper* to cut

decoy *n* ('diːkɔɪ, dɪ'kɔɪ). **1** a person or thing used to lure someone into danger. **2** *Mil.* something designed to deceive an enemy. **3** a bird or animal, or an image of one, used to lure game into a trap or within shooting range. **4** a place into which game can be lured for capture. **5** *Canad.* another word for **deke** (sense 2). ◆ *vb* (dɪ'kɔɪ). **6** to lure or be lured by or as if by means of a decoy. **7** (*tr*) *Canad.* another word for **deke** (sense 1). ORIG C17: prob. from Du. *de kooi*, lit.: the cage, from L *cavea* CAGE

decrease *vb* (dɪ'kriːs). **decreases, decreasing, decreased. 1** to diminish or cause to diminish in size, strength, etc. ◆ *n* ('diːkriːs, dɪ'kriːs). **2** a diminution; reduction. **3** the amount by which something has been diminished. ORIG C14: from OF, from L *dēcrescere* to grow less, from DE- + *crescere* to grow
▸ **de'creasing** *adj* ▸ **de'creasingly** *adv*

decree (dɪ'kriː) *n* **1** an edict, law, etc., made by someone in authority. **2** an order or judgment of a court. ◆ *vb* **decrees, decreeing, decreed. 3** to order, adjudge, or ordain by decree. ORIG C14: from OF, from L *dēcrētum* ordinance, from *dēcrētus* decided, p.p. of *dēcernere*

decree absolute *n* the final decree in divorce proceedings, which leaves the parties free to remarry.

decree nisi ('naɪsaɪ) *n* a provisional decree, esp. in divorce proceedings, which will later be made absolute unless cause is shown why it should not.

decrement (ˈdɛkrɪmənt) *n* **1** the act of decreasing; diminution. **2** *Maths.* a negative increment. **3** *Physics.* a measure of the damping of an oscillator or oscillation, expressed by the ratio of amplitudes in successive cycles. ORIG C17: from L *dēcrēmentum,* from *dēcrescere* to DECREASE

decrepit (dɪˈkrɛpɪt) *adj* **1** enfeebled by old age; infirm. **2** broken down or worn out by hard or long use; dilapidated. ORIG C15: from L *dēcrepitus,* from *crepāre* to creak
▸ **deˈcrepiˌtude** *n*

decrescendo (ˌdiːkrɪˈʃɛndəʊ) *n, adj* another word for **diminuendo.** ORIG It., from *decrescere* to DECREASE

decrescent (dɪˈkrɛsənt) *adj* (esp. of the moon) decreasing; waning. ORIG C17: from L *dēcrescēns* growing less; see DECREASE
▸ **deˈcrescence** *n*

decretal (dɪˈkriːtᵊl) *n* **1** *RC Church.* a papal decree; edict on doctrine or church law. ◆ *adj* **2** of or relating to a decree. ORIG C15: from OF, from LL *dēcrētālis;* see DECREE

decriminalize *or* **decriminalise** (diːˈkrɪmɪnᵊˌlaɪz) *vb* **decriminalizes, decriminalizing, decriminalized** *or* **decriminalises, decriminalising, decriminalised.** (*tr*) to remove (an action) from the legal category of criminal offence: *to decriminalize the possession of marijuana.*

decry (dɪˈkraɪ) *vb* **decries, decrying, decried.** (*tr*) **1** to express open disapproval of; disparage. **2** to depreciate by proclamation: *to decry obsolete coinage.* ORIG C17: from OF *descrier,* from *des-* DIS-[1] + *crier* to CRY

decumbent (dɪˈkʌmbənt) *adj* **1** lying down. **2** *Bot.* (of stems) lying flat with the tip growing upwards. ORIG C17: from L, present participle of *dēcumbere* to lie down
▸ **deˈcumbency** *n*

Dedéagach, Dedeagatch, *or* **Dedeağaç** ★ (ˈdɛdeɪɑːˈgɑːtʃ) *n* a former name (until the end of World War I) of **Alexandroúpolis.**

Dedekind ★ (*German* ˈdedəˌkɪnt) *n* (**Julius Wilhelm**) **Richard** (ˈrɪxɑːt). 1831–1916, German mathematician, who devised a way (the **Dedekind cut**) of according irrational and rational numbers the same status.

dedicate (ˈdɛdɪˌkeɪt) *vb* **dedicates, dedicating, dedicated.** (*tr*) **1** (often foll. by *to*) to devote (oneself, one's time, etc.) wholly to a special purpose or cause. **2** (foll. by *to*) to address a book, performance, etc., to a person, cause, etc., as a token of affection or respect. **3** (foll. by *to*) to request or play (a record) on radio for another person as a greeting. **4** to assign or allocate to a particular project, function, etc. **5** to set apart for a deity or for sacred uses. ORIG C15: from L *dēdicāre* to announce, from *dicāre* to make known
▸ **ˈdediˌcator** *n* ▸ **dedicatory** (ˈdɛdɪˌkeɪtərɪ, ˈdɛdɪkətərɪ) *or* **ˈdediˌcative** *adj*

dedicated (ˈdɛdɪˌkeɪtɪd) *adj* **1** devoted to a particular purpose or cause. **2** assigned or allocated to a particular project, function, etc.: *a dedicated transmission line.* **3** *Computing.* designed to fulfil one function.

dedication (ˌdɛdɪˈkeɪʃən) *n* **1** the act of dedicating or being dedicated. **2** an inscription prefixed to a book, etc., dedicating it to a person or thing. **3** wholehearted devotion, esp. to a career, ideal, etc.
▸ **ˌdediˈcational** *adj*

deduce (dɪˈdjuːs) *vb* **deduces, deducing, deduced.** (*tr*) **1** (*may take a clause as object*) to reach (a conclusion) by reasoning; conclude (that); infer. **2** *Arch.* to trace the origin or derivation of. ORIG C15: from L *dēdūcere* to lead away, derive, from DE- + *dūcere* to lead
▸ **deˈducible** *adj*

deduct (dɪˈdʌkt) *vb* (*tr*) to take away or subtract (a number, quantity, part, etc.). ORIG C15: from L *dēductus,* p.p. of *dēdūcere* to DEDUCE

deductible (dɪˈdʌktɪbᵊl) *adj* **1** capable of being deducted. **2** *US.* short for **tax-deductible.** ◆ *n* **3** *Insurance.* the US name for **excess** (sense 5).

deduction (dɪˈdʌkʃən) *n* **1** the act or process of deducting or subtracting. **2** something that is or may be deducted. **3** *Logic.* **3a** a process of reasoning by which a specific conclusion necessarily follows from a set of general premises. **3b** a logical conclusion reached by this process.
▸ **deˈductive** *adj*

Dee ★ (diː) *n* **1** a river in N Wales and NW England, rising in S Gwynedd and flowing east and north to the Irish Sea. Length: about 112 km (70 miles). **2** a river in NE Scotland, rising in the Cairngorms and flowing east to the North Sea. Length: about 140 km (87 miles). **3** a river in S Scotland, flowing south to the Solway Firth. Length: about 80 km (50 miles).

deed (diːd) *n* **1** something that is done or performed; act. **2** a notable achievement. **3** action as opposed to words. **4** *Law.* a legal document signed, witnessed, and delivered to effect a conveyance or transfer of property or to create a legal contract. ◆ *vb* **5** (*tr*) *US.* to convey or transfer (property) by deed. ORIG OE *dēd*

deed box *n* a strong box in which deeds and other documents are kept.

deed poll *n Law.* a deed made by one party only, esp. one by which a person changes his name.

deejay (ˈdiːˌdʒeɪ) *n* an informal name for **disc jockey.** ORIG C20: from the initials DJ (disc jockey)

deem (diːm) *vb* (*tr*) to judge or consider. ORIG OE *dēman*

de-emphasize *or* **de-emphasise** (diːˈɛmfəˌsaɪz) *vb* **de-emphasizes, de-emphasizing, de-emphasized** *or* **de-emphasises, de-emphasising, de-emphasised.** (*tr*) to remove emphasis from.

deemster (ˈdiːmstə) *n* the title of one of the two justices in the Isle of Man. Also called: **dempster.**

de-energize *or* **de-energise** (diːˈɛnədʒaɪz) *vb* **de-energizes, de-energizing, de-energized** *or* **de-energises, de-energising, de-energised.** (*tr*) *Electrical engineering.* to disconnect (an electrical circuit) from its source.
▸ **de-ˌenergiˈzation** *or* **de-ˌenergiˈsation** *n*

deep (diːp) *adj* **1** extending or situated far down from a surface: *a deep pool.* **2** extending or situated far inwards, backwards, or sideways. **3** *Cricket.* far from the pitch: *the deep field.* **4** (*postpositive*) of a specified dimension downwards, inwards, or backwards: *six feet deep.* **5** coming from or penetrating to a great depth. **6** difficult to understand; abstruse. **7** intellectually demanding: *a deep discussion.* **8** of great intensity: *deep trouble.* **9** (*postpositive;* foll. by *in*) absorbed (by); immersed (in): *deep in study.* **10** very cunning; devious. **11** mysterious: *a deep secret.* **12** (of a colour) having an intense or dark hue. **13** low in pitch: *a deep voice.* **14 go off the deep end.** *Inf.* **14a** to lose one's temper; react angrily. **14b** *Chiefly US.* to act rashly. **15 in deep water.** *Inf.* in a tricky position or in trouble. ◆ *n* **16** any deep place on land or under water. **17 the deep. 17a** a poetic term for the **ocean. 17b** *Cricket.* the area of the field relatively far from the pitch. **18** the most profound, intense, or central part: *the deep of winter.* **19** a vast extent, as of space or time. ◆ *adv* **20** far on in time; late: *they worked deep into the night.* **21** profoundly or intensely. **22 deep down.** *Inf.* in reality, esp. as opposed to appearance. ORIG OE *dēop*
▸ **ˈdeeply** *adv* ▸ **ˈdeepness** *n*

deep-discount bond *n* a fixed-interest security that pays little or no interest but is issued at a substantial discount to its redemption value, thus largely substituting capital gain for income.

deepen (ˈdiːpᵊn) *vb* to make or become deep, deeper, or more intense.
▸ **ˈdeepener** *n*

deepfreeze (ˌdiːpˈfriːz) *n* **1** another name for **freezer. 2** storage in a freezer. **3** *Inf.* a state of suspended activity. ◆ *vb* **deep-freeze, deep-freezes, deep-freezing, deep-froze, deep-frozen. 4** (*tr*) to freeze (food) or keep (food) in a freezer.

deep-fry *vb* **deep-fries, deep-frying, deep-fried.** to cook (fish, etc.) in sufficient hot fat to cover the food.

deep-laid *adj* (of a plot or plan) carefully worked out and kept secret.

deep-rooted *or* **deep-seated** *adj* (of ideas, beliefs, etc.) firmly fixed or held; ingrained.

deep-sea *n* (*modifier*) of, found in, or characteristic of the deep parts of the sea.

deep-set *adj* (esp. of eyes) deeply set.

★ people and places

Deep South ★ *n* the SE part of the US, esp. South Carolina, Georgia, Alabama, Mississippi, and Louisiana.

deep space *n* any region of outer space beyond the system of the earth and moon.

deep structure *n Generative grammar.* a representation of a sentence at a level where logical or grammatical relations are made explicit. Cf. **surface structure.**

deep-vein thrombosis *n* a blood clot in one of the major veins, usually in the legs or pelvis. Abbrev.: **DVT.**

deer (dɪə) *n, pl* **deer** *or* **deers.** any of a family of hoofed, ruminant mammals including reindeer, elk, and roe deer, typically having antlers in the male. Related adj: **cervine.** ORIG OE *dēor* beast

deer lick *n* a naturally or artificially salty area of ground where deer come to lick the salt.

deerskin ('dɪəˌskɪn) *n* **a** the hide of a deer. **b** (*as modifier*): *a deerskin jacket.*

deerstalker ('dɪəˌstɔːkə) *n* **1** a person who stalks deer, esp. in order to shoot them. **2** a hat, peaked in front and behind, with earflaps usually tied together on the top.
▸ **'deerˌstalking** *adj, n*

de-escalate (diː'ɛskəˌleɪt) *vb* **de-escalates, de-escalating, de-escalated.** to reduce the level or intensity of (a crisis, etc.) or (of a crisis, etc.) to decrease in level or intensity.
▸ **de-ˌesca'lation** *n*

def (dɛf) *adj Sl.* very good. ORIG C20: ?from *definitive*

def. *abbrev. for:* **1** defective. **2** defence. **3** defendant. **4** deferred. **5** definite. **6** definition.

deface (dɪ'feɪs) *vb* **defaces, defacing, defaced.** (*tr*) to spoil or mar the surface or appearance of; disfigure.
▸ **de'faceable** *adj* ▸ **de'facement** *n* ▸ **de'facer** *n*

de facto (deɪ 'fæktəʊ) *adv* **1** in fact. ◆ *adj* **2** existing in fact, whether legally recognized or not: *a de facto regime.* Cf. **de jure.** ◆ *n, pl* **de factos. 3** *Austral. & NZ.* a de facto wife or husband. ORIG C17: L

defalcate ('diːfælˌkeɪt) *vb* **defalcates, defalcating, defalcated.** (*intr*) *Law.* to misuse or misappropriate property or funds entrusted to one. ORIG C15: from Med. L *dēfalcāre* to cut off, from L DE- + *falx* sickle
▸ **'defalˌcator** *n*

defame (dɪ'feɪm) *vb* **defames, defaming, defamed.** (*tr*) to attack the good name or reputation of; slander; libel. ORIG C14: from OF, from L, from *diffāmāre* to spread by unfavourable report, from *fāma* FAME
▸ **defamation** (ˌdɛfə'meɪʃən) *n* ▸ **defamatory** (dɪ'fæmətərɪ) *adj*

default (dɪ'fɔːlt) *n* **1** a failure to act, esp. a failure to meet a financial obligation or to appear in a court of law at a time specified. **2** absence or lack. **3 by default.** in the absence of opposition or a better alternative: *he became prime minister by default.* **4 in default of.** through or in the lack or absence of. **5 judgment by** *or* **in default.** *Law.* a judgment in the plaintiff's favour when the defendant fails to plead or to appear. **6** (*also* 'diːfɔːlt). *Computing.* **6a** the preset selection of an option offered by a system, which will always be followed except when explicitly altered. **6b** (*as modifier*): *default setting.* ◆ *vb* **7** (*intr;* often foll. by *on* or *in*) to fail to make payment when due. **8** (*intr*) to fail to fulfil an obligation. **9** *Law.* to lose (a case) by failure to appear in court. ORIG C13: from OF *defaute,* from *defaillir* to fail, from Vulgar L *dēfallīre* (unattested) to be lacking

defaulter (dɪ'fɔːltə) *n* **1** a person who defaults. **2** *Chiefly Brit.* a person, esp. a soldier, who has broken the disciplinary code of his service.

defeat (dɪ'fiːt) *vb* (*tr*) **1** to overcome; win a victory over. **2** to thwart or frustrate. **3** *Law.* to render null and void. ◆ *n* **4** a defeating or being defeated. ORIG C14: from OF, from *desfaire* to undo, ruin, from *des-* DIS-[1] + *faire* to do, from L *facere*

defeatism (dɪ'fiːtɪzəm) *n* a ready acceptance or expectation of defeat.
▸ **de'featist** *n, adj*

defecate ('dɛfɪˌkeɪt) *vb* **defecates, defecating, defecated. 1** (*intr*) to discharge waste from the body through the anus. **2** (*tr*) to remove impurities from. ORIG C16: from L *dēfaecāre* to cleanse from dregs, from DE- + *faex* dregs
▸ **ˌdefe'cation** *n* ▸ **'defeˌcator** *n*

defect *n* ('diːfɛkt). **1** a lack of something necessary for completeness; deficiency. **2** an imperfection or blemish. ◆ *vb* (dɪ'fɛkt). **3** (*intr*) to desert one's country, cause, etc., esp. in order to join the opposing forces. ORIG C15: from L, from *dēficere* to forsake, fail
▸ **de'fector** *n*

defection (dɪ'fɛkʃən) *n* **1** abandonment of duty, allegiance, principles, etc. **2** a shortcoming.

defective (dɪ'fɛktɪv) *adj* **1** having a defect or flaw; imperfect. **2** (of a person) below the usual standard or level, esp. in intelligence. **3** *Grammar.* lacking the full range of inflections characteristic of its form class.
▸ **de'fectiveness** *n*

defence *or US* **defense** (dɪ'fɛns) *n* **1** resistance against danger or attack. **2** a person or thing that provides such resistance. **3** a plea, essay, etc., in support of something. **4** a country's military measures or resources. **5** *Law.* a defendant's denial of the truth of the allegations or charge against him or her. **6** *Law.* the defendant and his or her legal advisers collectively. **7** *Sport.* **7a** the action of protecting oneself or part of the playing area against an opponent's attacks. **7b** (usually preceded by *the*) the players in a team whose function is to do this. **8** *American football.* (usually preceded by *the*) **8a** the team that does not have possession of the ball. **8b** the members of a team that play in such circumstances. **9** (*pl*) fortifications. ORIG C13: from OF, from LL *dēfensum,* p.p. of *dēfendere* to DEFEND
▸ **de'fenceless** *or US* **de'fenseless** *adj*

defence mechanism *n* **1** *Psychoanalysis.* an unconscious mental process designed to reduce anxiety or shame. **2** *Physiol.* the protective response of the body against disease.

defend (dɪ'fɛnd) *vb* **1** (*tr*) to protect from harm or danger. **2** (*tr*) to support in the face of criticism, esp. by argument. **3** to represent (a defendant) in court. **4** *Sport.* to guard (one's goal, etc.) against attack. **5** (*tr*) to protect (a title, etc.) against a challenge. ORIG C13: from OF, from L *dēfendere* to ward off, from DE- + *-fendere* to strike
▸ **de'fender** *n*

defendant (dɪ'fɛndənt) *n* **1** a person against whom an action or claim is brought in a court of law. Cf. **plaintiff.** ◆ *adj* **2** defending.

defenestration (diːˌfɛnɪ'streɪʃən) *n* the act of throwing someone out of a window. ORIG C17: from NL *dēfenestrātiō,* from L DE- + *fenestra* window

defensible (dɪ'fɛnsɪbᵊl) *adj* capable of being defended, as in war, an argument, etc.
▸ **deˌfensi'bility** *or* **de'fensibleness** *n*

defensive (dɪ'fɛnsɪv) *adj* **1** intended for defence. **2** rejecting criticisms of oneself. ◆ *n* **3** a position of defence. **4 on the defensive.** in a position of defence, as in being ready to reject criticism.
▸ **de'fensively** *adv*

defer[1] (dɪ'fɜː) *vb* **defers, deferring, deferred.** (*tr*) to delay until a future time; postpone. ORIG C14: from OF *differer* to be different, postpone; see DIFFER
▸ **de'ferment** *or* **de'ferral** *n* ▸ **de'ferrer** *n*

defer[2] (dɪ'fɜː) *vb* **defers, deferring, deferred.** (*intr;* foll. by *to*) to yield to or comply with the wishes or judgments (of). ORIG C15: from L *dēferre,* lit.: to bear down, from DE- + *ferre* to bear

deference ('dɛfərəns) *n* **1** compliance with the wishes of another. **2** courteous regard; respect. ORIG C17: from F *déférence;* see DEFER[2]

deferent[1] ('dɛfərənt) *adj* another word for **deferential.**

deferent[2] ('dɛfərənt) *adj* (esp. of a nerve or duct) conveying an impulse, fluid, etc., down or away; efferent. ORIG C17: from L *dēferre;* see DEFER[2]

deferential (ˌdɛfə'rɛnʃəl) *adj* showing deference; respectful.
▸ **ˌdefer'entially** *adv*

defiance (dɪ'faɪəns) *n* **1** open or bold resistance to authority, opposition, or power. **2** a challenge.
▸ **de'fiant** *adj*

defibrillation (dɪˌfaɪbrɪ'leɪʃən) *n Med.* the application of

★ people and places

an electric current to the heart to restore normal contractions after a heart attack caused by fibrillation.

defibrillator (dɪˈfaɪbrɪˌleɪtə) *n Med.* an apparatus for stopping fibrillation of the heart by application of an electric current.

deficiency (dɪˈfɪʃənsɪ) *n, pl* **deficiencies. 1** the state or quality of being deficient. **2** a lack or insufficiency; shortage. **3** a deficit. **4** *Biol.* the absence of a gene or a region of a chromosome normally present.

deficiency disease *n* **1** *Med.* any condition, such as pellagra, beriberi, or scurvy, produced by a lack of vitamins or other essential substances. **2** *Bot.* any disease caused by lack of essential minerals.

deficient (dɪˈfɪʃənt) *adj* **1** lacking some essential; incomplete; defective. **2** inadequate in quantity or supply; insufficient. ORIG C16: from L *dēficiēns* lacking, from *dēficere* to fall short
▸ **deˈficiently** *adv*

deficit (ˈdɛfɪsɪt, dɪˈfɪsɪt) *n* **1** the amount by which an actual sum is lower than that expected or required. **2a** an excess of liabilities over assets. **2b** an excess of expenditures over revenues. ORIG C18: from L, lit.: there is lacking, from *dēficere*

deficit financing *n* government spending in excess of revenues so that a budget deficit is incurred, which is financed by borrowing.

defile[1] (dɪˈfaɪl) *vb* **defiles, defiling, defiled.** (*tr*) **1** to make foul or dirty; pollute. **2** to taint; corrupt. **3** to damage or sully (someone's reputation, etc.). **4** to make unfit for ceremonial use. **5** to violate the chastity of. ORIG C14: from earlier *defoilen,* from OF *defouler* to trample underfoot, abuse, from DE- + *fouler* to tread upon; see FULL[2]
▸ **deˈfilement** *n*

defile[2] (ˈdiːfaɪl, dɪˈfaɪl) *n* **1** a narrow pass or gorge. **2** a single file of soldiers, etc. ◆ *vb* **defiles, defiling, defiled. 3** (*intr*) to march in single file. ORIG C17: from F, from *défiler* to file off, from *filer* to march in a column, from OF, from L *fīlum* thread

define (dɪˈfaɪn) *vb* **defines, defining, defined.** (*tr*) **1** to state precisely the meaning of (words, terms, etc.). **2** to describe the nature, properties, or essential qualities of. **3** to determine the boundary or extent of. **4** (*often passive*) to delineate the form or outline of: *the shape of the tree was clearly defined by the light behind it.* **5** to fix with precision; specify. ORIG C14: from OF: to determine, from L *dēfīnīre* to set bounds to, from *fīnīre* to FINISH
▸ **deˈfinable** *adj* ▸ **deˈfiner** *n*

definite (ˈdɛfɪnɪt) *adj* **1** clearly defined; exact. **2** having precise limits or boundaries. **3** known for certain. ORIG C15: from L *dēfīnītus* limited, distinct; see DEFINE
▸ **ˈdefiniteness** *n*

> **USAGE NOTE** *Definite* and *definitive* should be carefully distinguished. *Definite* indicates precision and firmness, as in *a definite decision. Definitive* includes these senses but also indicates conclusiveness. *A definite answer* indicates a clear and firm answer to a particular question; *a definitive answer* implies an authoritative resolution of a complex question.

definite article *n Grammar.* a determiner that expresses specificity of reference, such as *the* in English. Cf. **indefinite article.**

definite integral *n* See **integral.**

definitely (ˈdɛfɪnɪtlɪ) *adv* **1** in a definite manner. **2** (*sentence modifier*) certainly: *he said he was coming, definitely.* ◆ *sentence substitute.* **3** unquestionably.

definition (ˌdɛfɪˈnɪʃən) *n* **1** a formal and concise statement of the meaning of a word, phrase, etc. **2** the act of defining. **3** specification of the essential properties of something. **4** the act of making clear or definite. **5** the state of being clearly defined. **6** a measure of the clarity of an optical, photographic, or television image as characterized by its sharpness and contrast.

definitive (dɪˈfɪnɪtɪv) *adj* **1** serving to decide or settle finally. **2** most reliable or authoritative. **3** serving to define or outline. **4** *Zool.* fully developed. **5** (of postage stamps) permanently on sale. ◆ *n* **6** *Grammar.* a word indicating specificity of reference.
▸ **deˈfinitively** *adv*

deflate (diːˈfleɪt) *vb* **deflates, deflating, deflated. 1** to collapse through the release of gas. **2** (*tr*) to take away the self-esteem or conceit from. **3** (*tr*) to take away the enthusiasm or excitement from. **4** *Econ.* to cause deflation of (an economy, the money supply, etc.). ORIG C19: from DE- + (IN)FLATE
▸ **deˈflator** *n*

deflation (diːˈfleɪʃən) *n* **1** the act of deflating or the state of being deflated. **2** *Econ.* a reduction in spending and economic activity resulting in lower levels of output, employment, investment, trade, profits, and prices. **3** the removal of loose rock material, etc., by wind.
▸ **deˈflationary** *adj* ▸ **deˈflationist** *n, adj*

deflect (dɪˈflɛkt) *vb* to turn or cause to turn aside from a course. ORIG C17: from L *dēflectere,* from *flectere* to bend
▸ **deˈflector** *n*

deflection *or* **deflexion** (dɪˈflɛkʃən) *n* **1** a deflecting or being deflected. **2** the amount of deviation. **3** the change in direction of a light beam as it crosses a boundary between two media with different refractive indexes. **4** a deviation of the indicator of a measuring instrument from its zero position.
▸ **deˈflective** *adj*

deflocculate (diːˈflɒkjʊˌleɪt) *vb* **deflocculates, deflocculating, deflocculated.** (*tr*) to cause (an aggregate) to separate into particles.
▸ **deˌflocculˈlation** *n* ▸ **deˈflocculant** *n*

deflower (diːˈflaʊə) *vb* (*tr*) **1** to deprive (esp. a woman) of virginity. **2** to despoil of beauty, innocence, etc. **3** to rob or despoil of flowers.
▸ **ˌdefloˈration** *n*

Defoe ★ (dɪˈfəʊ) *n* **Daniel.** ?1660–1731, English novelist and pamphleteer, noted for his novels *Robinson Crusoe* (1719) and *Moll Flanders* (1722).

defoliant (diːˈfəʊlɪənt) *n* a chemical sprayed or dusted onto trees to cause their leaves to fall, esp. to remove cover from an enemy in warfare.

defoliate (diːˈfəʊlɪˌeɪt) *vb* **defoliates, defoliating, defoliated.** to deprive (a plant) of its leaves. ORIG C18: from Med. L *dēfoliāre,* from L DE- + *folium* leaf
▸ **deˌfoliˈation** *n*

deforest (diːˈfɒrɪst) *vb* (*tr*) to clear of trees. Also: **disforest.**
▸ **deˌforesˈtation** *n*

De Forest ★ (də ˈfɒrɪst) *n* **Lee.** 1873–1961, US inventor of telegraphic, telephonic, and radio equipment: patented the first triode valve (1907).

deform (dɪˈfɔːm) *vb* **1** to make or become misshapen or distorted. **2** (*tr*) to mar the beauty of; disfigure. **3** (*tr*) to subject or be subjected to a stress that causes a change of dimensions. ORIG C15: from L *dēformāre,* from DE- + *forma* shape, beauty
▸ **deˈformable** *adj* ▸ **ˌdeforˈmation** *n*

deformed (dɪˈfɔːmd) *adj* **1** disfigured or misshapen. **2** morally perverted; warped.

deformity (dɪˈfɔːmɪtɪ) *n, pl* **deformities. 1** a deformed condition. **2** *Pathol.* a distortion of an organ or part. **3** a deformed person or thing. **4** a defect, esp. of the mind or morals; depravity.

defraud (dɪˈfrɔːd) *vb* (*tr*) to take away or withhold money, rights, property, etc., from (a person) by fraud; swindle.
▸ **deˈfrauder** *n*

defray (dɪˈfreɪ) *vb* (*tr*) to provide money for (costs, expenses, etc.); pay. ORIG C16: from OF *deffroier* to pay expenses, from *de-* DIS-[1] + *frai* expenditure
▸ **deˈfrayable** *adj* ▸ **deˈfrayal** *or* **deˈfrayment** *n*

defrock (diːˈfrɒk) *vb* (*tr*) to deprive (a person in holy orders) of ecclesiastical status; unfrock.

defrost (diːˈfrɒst) *vb* **1** to make or become free of frost or ice. **2** to thaw, esp. through removal from a deepfreeze.

defroster (diːˈfrɒstə) *n* a device by which a de-icing process, as of a refrigerator, is accelerated.

deft (dɛft) *adj* quick and neat in movement; nimble; dexterous. ORIG C13 (in the sense: gentle): see DAFT
▸ **'deftly** *adv* ▸ **'deftness** *n*

defunct (dɪ'fʌŋkt) *adj* **1** no longer living; dead or extinct. **2** no longer operative or valid. ORIG C16: from L *dēfungī* to discharge (one's obligations), die; see DE-, FUNCTION
▸ **de'functness** *n*

defuse *or US* (*sometimes*) **defuze** (diː'fjuːz) *vb* **defuses, defusing, defused** *or US* (*sometimes*) **defuzes, defuzing, defuzed.** (*tr*) **1** to remove the triggering device of (a bomb, etc.). **2** to remove the cause of tension from (a crisis, etc.).

> **USAGE NOTE** See at **diffuse.**

defy (dɪ'faɪ) *vb* **defies, defying, defied.** (*tr*) **1** to resist openly and boldly. **2** to elude, esp. in a baffling way. **3** *Formal.* to challenge (someone to do something); dare. **4** *Arch.* to invite to do battle or combat. ORIG C14: from OF *desfier*, from *des-* DE- + *fier* to trust, from L *fīdere*
▸ **de'fier** *n*

deg. *abbrev. for* degree.

Degas ★ ('deɪgɑː; *French* dəga) *n* **Hilaire Germain Edgar** (ilɛr ʒɛrmɛ̃ ɛdgar). 1834–1917, French impressionist painter and sculptor, noted for his studies of ballet dancers.

De Gasperi ★ (*Italian* de 'gasperi) *n* **Alcide** (al'tʃiːde). 1881–1954, Italian statesman; prime minister (1945–53).

de Gaulle ★ (*French* də gol) *n* **Charles** (**André Joseph Marie**) (ʃarl). 1890–1970, French general and statesman. During World War II, he founded the Free French movement in England (1940). He was head of the provisional governments (1944–46) and became first president of the Fifth Republic (1959–69).

degauss (diː'gaʊs) *vb* (*tr*) to neutralize by producing an opposing magnetic field.
▸ **de'gausser** *n*

degeneracy (dɪ'dʒɛnərəsɪ) *n, pl* **degeneracies. 1** the act or state of being degenerate. **2** the process of becoming degenerate.

degenerate *vb* (dɪ'dʒɛnəˌreɪt). **degenerates, degenerating, degenerated.** (*intr*) **1** to become degenerate. **2** *Biol.* (of organisms or their parts) to become less specialized or functionally useless. ◆ *adj* (dɪ'dʒɛnərɪt). **3** having declined or deteriorated to a lower mental, moral, or physical level; degraded; corrupt. ◆ *n* (dɪ'dʒɛnərɪt). **4** a degenerate person. ORIG C15: from L, from *dēgener* departing from its kind, ignoble, from DE- + *genus* race
▸ **de'generately** *adv* ▸ **de'generateness** *n* ▸ **de'generative** *adj*

degenerate matter *n Astrophysics.* the highly compressed state of a star's matter when its atoms virtually touch in the final stage of its evolution into a white dwarf.

degeneration (dɪˌdʒɛnə'reɪʃən) *n* **1** the process of degenerating. **2** the state of being degenerate. **3** *Biol.* the loss of specialization, function, or structure by organisms and their parts. **4** impairment or loss of the function and structure of cells or tissues, as by disease or injury. **5** *Electronics.* negative feedback of a signal.

degradable (dɪ'greɪdəbᵊl) *adj* **1** capable of being decomposed chemically or biologically. **2** capable of being degraded.

degradation (ˌdɛgrə'deɪʃən) *n* **1** a degrading or being degraded. **2** a state of degeneration or squalor. **3** some act, constraint, etc., that is degrading. **4** the wearing down of the surface of rocks, cliffs, etc., by erosion. **5** *Chem.* a breakdown of a molecule into atoms or smaller molecules. **6** *Physics.* an irreversible process in which the energy available to do work is decreased. **7** *RC Church.* the permanent unfrocking of a priest.

degrade (dɪ'greɪd) *vb* **degrades, degrading, degraded. 1** (*tr*) to reduce in worth, character, etc.; disgrace. **2** (diː'greɪd) (*tr*) to reduce in rank or status; demote. **3** (*tr*) to reduce in strength, quality, etc. **4** to reduce or be reduced by erosion or down-cutting, as a land surface or bed of a river. **5** *Chem.* to decompose into atoms or smaller molecules. ORIG C14: from LL *dēgradāre*, from L DE- + *gradus* rank, degree
▸ **de'grader** *n*

degrading (dɪ'greɪdɪŋ) *adj* causing humiliation; debasing.
▸ **de'gradingly** *adv*

degree (dɪ'griː) *n* **1** a stage in a scale of relative amount or intensity: *a high degree of competence.* **2** an academic award conferred by a university or college on successful completion of a course or as an honorary distinction (**honorary degree**). **3** any of three categories of seriousness of a burn. **4** (in the US) any of the categories into which a crime is divided according to its seriousness. **5** *Genealogy.* a step in a line of descent. **6** *Grammar.* any of the forms of an adjective used to indicate relative amount or intensity: in English they are *positive, comparative,* and *superlative.* **7** *Music.* any note of a diatonic scale relative to the other notes in that scale. **8** a unit of temperature on a specified scale. Symbol: °. See also **Celsius scale, Fahrenheit scale. 9** a measure of angle equal to one three-hundred-and-sixtieth of the angle traced by one complete revolution of a line about one of its ends. Symbol: °. **10** a unit of latitude or longitude used to define points on the earth's surface. Symbol: °. **11** a unit on any of several scales of measurement, as for specific gravity. Symbol: °. **12** *Maths.* **12a** the highest power or the sum of the powers of any term in a polynomial or by itself: $x^4 + x + 3$ *and* xyz^2 *are of the fourth degree.* **12b** the greatest power of the highest order derivative in a differential equation. **13** *Obs.* a step; rung. **14** *Arch.* a stage in social status or rank. **15 by degrees.** little by little; gradually. **16 one degree under.** *Inf.* off colour; ill. **17 to a degree.** somewhat; rather. ORIG C13: from OF *degre*, from L DE- + *gradus* step

degree of freedom *n* **1** *Chem.* the least number of independently variable properties needed to determine the state of a system. See also **phase rule. 2** one of the independent components of motion (translation, vibration, and rotation) of an atom or molecule.

De Havilland ★ (də 'hævɪlənd) *n* Sir **Geoffrey.** 1882–1965, British aircraft designer.

dehisce (dɪ'hɪs) *vb* **dehisces, dehiscing, dehisced.** (*intr*) (of fruits, anthers, etc.) to burst open spontaneously, releasing seeds, pollen, etc. ORIG C17: from L *dēhiscere* to split open, from DE- + *hiscere* to yawn, gape
▸ **de'hiscent** *adj*

dehorn (diː'hɔːn) *vb* (*tr*) to remove the horns of (cattle, sheep, or goats).

dehumanize *or* **dehumanise** (diː'hjuːməˌnaɪz) *vb* **dehumanizes, dehumanizing, dehumanized** *or* **dehumanises, dehumanising, dehumanised.** (*tr*) **1** to deprive of human qualities. **2** to render mechanical, artificial, or routine.
▸ **deˌhumani'zation** *or* **deˌhumani'sation** *n*

dehumidify (ˌdiːhjuː'mɪdɪˌfaɪ) *vb* **dehumidifies, dehumidifying, dehumidified.** (*tr*) to remove water from (the air, etc.)
▸ **ˌdehuˌmidifi'cation** *n* ▸ **ˌdehu'midiˌfier** *n*

dehydrate (diː'haɪdreɪt, ˌdiːhaɪ'dreɪt) *vb* **dehydrates, dehydrating, dehydrated. 1** to lose or cause to lose water. **2** to lose or deprive of water, as the body or tissues.
▸ **ˌdehy'dration** *n* ▸ **de'hydrator** *n*

dehydrogenate (diː'haɪdrədʒəˌneɪt), **dehydrogenize,** *or* **dehydrogenise** (diː'haɪdrədʒəˌnaɪz) *vb* **dehydrogenates, dehydrogenating, dehydrogenated, dehydrogenizes, dehydrogenizing, dehydrogenized** *or* **dehydrogenises, dehydrogenising, dehydrogenised.** (*tr*) to remove hydrogen from.
▸ **deˌhydroge'nation, deˌhydrogeni'zation,** *or* **deˌhydrogeni'sation** *n*

de-ice (diː'aɪs) *vb* **de-ices, de-icing, de-iced.** to free or be freed of ice.

de-icer (diː'aɪsə) *n* **1** a mechanical or thermal device designed to melt or stop the formation of ice on an aircraft. **2** a substance used for this purpose, esp. an aerosol that can be sprayed on car windscreens to remove ice or frost.

deictic ('daɪktɪk) *adj* **1** *Logic.* proving by direct argument. Cf. **elenctic** (see **elenchus**). ◆ *n* **2** another word for **indexical** (sense 2). ORIG C17: from Gk *deiktikos* concerning proof, from *deiknunai* to show

deify ('diːɪˌfaɪ, 'deɪɪ-) *vb* **deifies, deifying, deified.** (*tr*) **1** to exalt to the position of a god or personify as a god. **2** to

accord divine honour or worship to. ORIG C14: from OF, from LL *deificāre*, from L *deus* god + *facere* to make
▸ ˌ**deifiˈcation** *n* ▸ ˈ**deiˌfier** *n*

Deighton ★ (ˈdeɪtᵊn) *n* **Len.** born 1929, British writer. His books include *The Ipcress File* (1962) and the trilogy *Berlin Game, Mexico Set,* and *London Match* (1983–85).

deign (deɪn) *vb* **1** (*intr*) to think it fit or worthy of oneself (to do something); condescend. **2** (*tr*) *Arch.* to vouchsafe. ORIG C13: from OF, from L *dignārī* to consider worthy, from *dignus*

deindividuation (diːˌɪndɪˌvɪdjuˈeɪʃən) *n Psychol.* the loss of a person's sense of individuality and responsibility.

de-industrialization *or* **de-industrialisation** (diːɪndʌstrɪəlaɪˈzeɪʃən) *n* a decline in importance of a country's manufacturing industry.

de-ionize *or* **de-ionise** (diːˈaɪəˌnaɪz) *vb* **de-ionizes, de-ionizing, de-ionized** *or* **de-ionises, de-ionising, de-ionised.** (*tr*) to remove ions from (water, etc.), esp. by ion exchange.
▸ **deˌioniˈzation** *or* **deˌioniˈsation** *n*

Deirdre ★ (ˈdɪədrɪ) *n Irish myth.* a beautiful girl who was raised by Conchobar to be his wife but eloped with Naoise. When Conchobar treacherously killed Naoise she took her own life: often used to symbolize Ireland. See also **Naoise.**

deism (ˈdiːɪzəm, ˈdeɪ-) *n* belief in the existence of God based on natural reason, without revelation. Cf. **theism.** ORIG C17: from F *déisme,* from L *deus* god
▸ ˈ**deist** *n, adj* ▸ **deˈistic** *or* **deˈistical** *adj* ▸ **deˈistically** *adv*

deity (ˈdeɪɪtɪ, ˈdiː-) *n, pl* **deities. 1** a god or goddess. **2** the state of being divine; godhead. **3** the rank of a god. **4** the nature or character of God. ORIG C14: from OF, from LL *deitās,* from L *deus* god

Deity (ˈdeɪɪtɪ, ˈdiː-) *n* **the.** God.

déjà vu (ˈdeɪʒæ ˈvuː) *n* the experience of perceiving a new situation as if it had occurred before. ORIG from F, lit.: already seen

deject (dɪˈdʒɛkt) *vb* (*tr*) to have a depressing effect on; dispirit; dishearten. ORIG C15: from L *dēicere* to cast down, from DE- + *iacere* to throw

dejected (dɪˈdʒɛktɪd) *adj* miserable; despondent; downhearted.
▸ **deˈjectedly** *adv*

dejection (dɪˈdʒɛkʃən) *n* **1** lowness of spirits; depression. **2a** faecal matter. **2b** defecation.

de jure (deɪ ˈdʒʊəreɪ) *adv* according to law; by right; legally. Cf. **de facto.** ORIG L

deka- *or* **dek-** *combining form.* variants of **deca-.**

deke (diːk) *Canad. sl.* ◆ *vb* **dekes, deking, deked. 1** (*tr*) (in ice hockey or box lacrosse) to draw a defending player out of position by faking a shot or movement. ◆ *n* **2** such a shot or movement. ◆ Also: **decoy.** ORIG C20: from DECOY

Dekker *or* **Decker** ★ (ˈdɛkə) *n* **Thomas.** ?1572–?1632, English dramatist and pamphleteer, noted particularly for his comedy *The Shoemaker's Holiday* (1600).

dekko (ˈdɛkəʊ) *n, pl* **dekkos.** *Brit. sl.* a look; glance. ORIG C19: from Hindi *dekho!* look! from *dekhnā* to see

de Klerk ★ (də ˈklɜːk) *n* **F(rederik) W(illem).** born 1936, South African statesman; president (1989–94); second executive deputy president (1994–97). In 1990 he began to dismantle the apartheid system; shared Nobel peace prize with Nelson Mandela 1993.

de Kooning ★ (də ˈkuːnɪŋ) *n* **Willem.** See (Willem de) **Kooning.**

del (dɛl) *n Maths.* the differential operator $\mathbf{i}(\partial/\partial x) + \mathbf{j}(\partial/\partial y) + \mathbf{k}(\partial/\partial z)$, where **i**, **j**, and **k** are unit vectors in the *x*, *y*, and *z* directions. Symbol: ∇ Also called: **nabla.**

del. *abbrev. for* delegate.

Del. *abbrev. for* Delaware.

Delacroix ★ (*French* dəlakrwa) *n* **(Ferdinand Victor) Eugène** (øʒɛn). 1798–1863, French romantic painter.

Delagoa Bay ★ (ˌdɛləˈgəʊə) *n* an inlet of the Indian Ocean, in S Mozambique. Official name: **Baía de Lourenço Marques.**

de la Mare ★ (də lɑː mɛə) *n* **Walter (John).** 1873–1956, British poet and novelist, noted for *The Listeners and Other Poems* (1912) and *Memoirs of a Midget* (1921).

Delaroche ★ (*French* dəlarɔʃ) *n* **(Hippolyte) Paul** (pɔl). 1797–1859, French painter.

Delaunay ★ (*French* dəlonɛ) *n* **Robert** (rɔbɛr). 1885–1941, French painter.

Delaware[1] (ˈdɛləˌwɛə) *n* **1** (*pl* **Delawares** *or* **Delaware**) a member of a North American Indian people formerly living near the Delaware River **2** the language of this people.

Delaware[2] ★ (ˈdɛləˌwɛə) *n* **1** a state of the northeastern US, on the Delmarva Peninsula: mostly flat and low-lying, with hills in the extreme north and cypress swamps in the extreme south. Capital: Dover. Pop.: 743 603 (1998 est.). Area: 5004 sq. km (1932 sq. miles). Abbrevs.: **Del.** or (with zip code) **DE** **2** a river in the northeastern US, rising in the Catskill Mountains and flowing south into **Delaware Bay,** an inlet of the Atlantic. Length 660 km (410 miles).
▸ ˌ**DelaˈwareanA** *adj*

De La Warr ★ (ˈdɛləˌwɛə) *n* **Baron,** title of *Thomas West,* known as *Lord Delaware.* 1577–1618, English administrator in America; first governor of Virginia (1610).

delay (dɪˈleɪ) *vb* **1** (*tr*) to put off to a later time; defer. **2** (*tr*) to slow up or cause to be late. **3** (*intr*) to be irresolute or put off doing something. **4** (*intr*) to linger; dawdle. ◆ *n* **5** a delaying or being delayed. **6** the interval between one event and another. ORIG C13: from OF, from *des-* off + *laier* to leave, from L *laxāre* to loosen
▸ **deˈlayer** *n*

delayed action *or* **delay action** *n* a device for operating a mechanism, such as a camera shutter, a short time after setting.

delayed drop *n Aeronautics.* a parachute descent in which the opening of the parachute is delayed for a predetermined time.

delayering (diːˈleɪərɪŋ) *n* the process of pruning the administrative structure of a large organization by reducing the number of tiers in its hierarchy.

dele (ˈdiːlɪ) *n, pl* **deles. 1** a sign (δ) indicating that typeset matter is to be deleted. ◆ *vb* **deles, deleing, deled. 2** (*tr*) to mark (matter to be deleted) with a dele. ORIG C18: from L: delete (imperative), from *dēlēre* to destroy, obliterate

delectable (dɪˈlɛktəbᵊl) *adj* highly enjoyable, esp. pleasing to the taste; delightful. ORIG C14: from L *dēlectābilis,* from *dēlectāre* to DELIGHT
▸ **deˈlectableness** *or* **deˌlectaˈbility** *n*

delectation (ˌdiːlɛkˈteɪʃən) *n* pleasure; enjoyment.

delegate *n* (ˈdɛlɪˌgeɪt, -gɪt). **1** a person chosen to act for another or others, esp. at a conference or meeting. ◆ *vb* (ˈdɛlɪˌgeɪt), **delegates, delegating, delegated. 2** to give (duties, powers, etc.) to another as representative; depute. **3** (*tr*) to authorize (a person) as representative. ORIG C14: from L *dēlēgāre* to send on a mission, from *lēgāre* to send, depute
▸ ˈ**delegable** *adj*

delegation (ˌdɛlɪˈgeɪʃən) *n* **1** a person or group chosen to represent another or others. **2** a delegating or being delegated.

de Lesseps ★ (*French* də lɛsɛps) *n* **Vicomte.** title of (Ferdinand Marie) **Lesseps.**

delete (dɪˈliːt) *vb* **deletes, deleting, deleted.** (*tr*) to remove (something printed or written); erase; strike out. ORIG C17: from L *dēlēre* to destroy, obliterate
▸ **deˈletion** *n*

deleterious (ˌdɛlɪˈtɪərɪəs) *adj* harmful; injurious; hurtful. ORIG C17: from NL, from Gk *dēlētērios,* from *dēleisthai* to hurt
▸ ˌ**deleˈteriousness** *n*

Delft ★ (dɛlft) *n* **1** a town in the SW Netherlands, in South Holland province. Pop.: 91 941 (1994). **2** Also called: ˈ**delftware.** tin-glazed earthenware made in Delft since the 17th century, typically having blue decoration on a white ground. **3** a similar earthenware made in England.

Delhi ★ (ˈdɛlɪ) *n* **1** the capital of India, in the N central part, on the Jumna river: consists of **Old Delhi** (a walled city reconstructed in 1639 on the site of former cities of Delhi, which date from the 15th century B.C.) and **New Delhi** to the south, chosen as the capital in 1912, replacing Calcutta; university (1922). Pop. (urban area): 8 419 084 (1991). **2** a Union Territory of N India. Capital: Delhi. Area: 1418 sq. km (553 sq. miles). Pop.: 10 865 000 (1994 est.).

deli ('dɛlɪ) *n, pl* **delis.** an informal word for **delicatessen.**

deliberate *adj* (dɪ'lɪbərɪt). **1** carefully thought out in advance; intentional. **2** careful or unhurried: *a deliberate pace.* ◆ *vb* (dɪ'lɪbəˌreɪt). **deliberates, deliberating, deliberated. 3** to consider (something) deeply; think over. ORIG C15: from L *dēlīberāre,* from *lībrāre* to weigh, from *lībra* scales
▸ **de'liberately** *adv* ▸ **de'liberateness** *n* ▸ **de'liberˌator** *n*

deliberation (dɪˌlɪbə'reɪʃən) *n* **1** careful consideration. **2** (*often pl*) formal discussion, as of a committee. **3** care or absence of hurry.

deliberative (dɪ'lɪbərətɪv) *adj* **1** of or for deliberating: *a deliberative assembly.* **2** characterized by deliberation.
▸ **de'liberatively** *adv* ▸ **de'liberativeness** *n*

Delibes ★ (*French* dəlib) *n* (**Clément Philibert**) **Léo** (leo). 1836–91, French composer, noted for his ballets *Coppélia* (1870) and *Sylvia* (1876), and the opera *Lakmé* (1883).

delicacy ('dɛlɪkəsɪ) *n, pl* **delicacies. 1** fine or subtle quality, character, construction, etc. **2** fragile or graceful beauty. **3** something that is considered choice to eat, such as caviar. **4** fragile construction or constitution. **5** refinement of feeling, manner, or appreciation. **6** fussy or squeamish refinement, esp. in matters of taste, propriety, etc. **7** need for tactful or sensitive handling. **8** sensitivity of response, as of an instrument.

delicate ('dɛlɪkɪt) *adj* **1** fine or subtle in quality, character, construction, etc. **2** having a soft or fragile beauty. **3** (of colour, tone, taste, etc.) pleasantly subtle. **4** easily damaged or injured; fragile. **5** precise or sensitive in action: *a delicate mechanism.* **6** requiring tact. **7** showing regard for the feelings of others. **8** excessively refined; squeamish. ORIG C14: from L *dēlicātus* affording pleasure, from *dēliciae* (pl) delight, pleasure
▸ **'delicately** *adv* ▸ **'delicateness** *n*

delicatessen (ˌdɛlɪkə'tɛsᵊn) *n* **1** a shop selling various foods, esp. unusual or imported foods, already cooked or prepared. **2** such foods. ORIG C19: from G *Delikatessen,* lit.: delicacies, from F *délicatesse*

delicious (dɪ'lɪʃəs) *adj* **1** very appealing, esp. to taste or smell. **2** extremely enjoyable. ORIG C13: from OF, from LL *dēliciōsus,* from L *dēliciae* delights, from *dēlicere* to entice; see DELIGHT
▸ **de'liciously** *adv* ▸ **de'liciousness** *n*

delight (dɪ'laɪt) *vb* **1** (*tr*) to please greatly. **2** (*intr;* foll. by *in*) to take great pleasure (in). ◆ *n* **3** extreme pleasure. **4** something that causes this. ORIG C13: from OF, from *deleitier* to please, from L *dēlectāre,* from *dēlicere* to allure, from DE- + *lacere* to entice
▸ **de'lighted** *adj* ▸ **de'lightedly** *adv*

delightful (dɪ'laɪtful) *adj* giving great delight; very pleasing, beautiful, charming, etc.
▸ **de'lightfully** *adv* ▸ **de'lightfulness** *n*

Delilah ★ (dɪ'laɪlə) *n* **1** Samson's Philistine mistress, who betrayed him (Judges 16). **2** a voluptuous and treacherous woman; temptress.

delimit (di:'lɪmɪt) *or* **delimitate** *vb* **delimits, delimiting, delimited** *or* **delimitates, delimitating, delimitated.** (*tr*) to mark or prescribe the limits or boundaries of.
▸ **deˌlimi'tation** *n* ▸ **de'limitative** *adj*

delineate (dɪ'lɪnɪˌeɪt) *vb* **delineates, delineating, delineated.** (*tr*) **1** to trace the outline of. **2** to represent pictorially; depict. **3** to portray in words; describe. ORIG C16: from L *dēlīneāre* to sketch out, from *līnea* LINE[1]
▸ **deˌline'ation** *n* ▸ **de'lineative** *adj*

delinquency (dɪ'lɪŋkwənsɪ) *n, pl* **delinquencies. 1** an offence or misdeed, esp. one committed by a young person. See **juvenile delinquency. 2** failure or negligence in duty or obligation. **3** a delinquent nature or delinquent behaviour. ORIG C17: from LL *dēlinquentia* fault, offence, from L *dēlinquere* to transgress, from DE- + *linquere* to forsake

delinquent (dɪ'lɪŋkwənt) *n* **1** someone, esp. a young person, guilty of delinquency. ◆ *adj* **2** guilty of an offence or misdeed. **3** failing in or neglectful of duty or obligation. ORIG C17: from L *dēlinquēns* offending; see DELINQUENCY

deliquesce (ˌdɛlɪ'kwɛs) *vb* **deliquesces, deliquescing, deliquesced.** (*intr*) (esp. of certain salts) to dissolve gradually in water absorbed from the air. ORIG C18: from L *dēliquēscere,* from DE- + *liquēscere* to melt, from *liquēre* to be liquid
▸ **ˌdeli'quescence** *n* ▸ **ˌdeli'quescent** *adj*

delirious (dɪ'lɪrɪəs) *adj* **1** affected with delirium. **2** wildly excited, esp. with joy or enthusiasm.
▸ **de'liriously** *adv*

delirium (dɪ'lɪrɪəm) *n, pl* **deliriums** *or* **deliria** (-'lɪrɪə). **1** a state of excitement and mental confusion, often accompanied by hallucinations, caused by high fever, poisoning, brain injury, etc. **2** violent excitement or emotion; frenzy. ORIG C16: from L: madness, from *dēlīrāre,* lit.: to swerve from a furrow, hence be crazy, from DE- + *līra* furrow

delirium tremens ('trɛmɛnz, 'tri:-) *n* a severe psychotic condition occurring in some persons with chronic alcoholism, characterized by delirium, tremor, anxiety, and vivid hallucinations. Abbrevs.: **DT's** (informal), **dt.** ORIG C19: NL, lit.: trembling delirium

delist (di:'lɪst) *vb* (*tr*) **1** to remove from a list. **2** *Stock Exchange.* to remove (a security) from the register of those that may be traded on the recognized market.

Delius ★ ('di:lɪəs) *n* **Frederick.** 1862–1934, British composer. His works include the opera *A Village Romeo and Juliet* (1901), *A Mass of Life* (1905), and the orchestral variations *Brigg Fair* (1907).

deliver (dɪ'lɪvə) *vb* (*mainly tr*) **1** to carry to a destination, esp. to distribute (goods, mail, etc.) to several places. **2** (often foll. by *over* or *up*) to hand over or transfer. **3** (often foll. by *from*) to release or rescue (from captivity, harm, etc.). **4** (*also intr*) **4a** to aid in the birth of (offspring). **4b** to give birth to (offspring). **4c** (usually foll. by *of*) to aid (a female) in the birth (of offspring). **4d** (*passive;* foll. by *of*) to give birth (to offspring). **5** to present (a speech, idea, etc.). **6** to utter: *to deliver a cry of exultation.* **7** to discharge or release (something, such as a blow or shot) suddenly. **8** (*intr*) *Inf.* Also: **deliver the goods.** to produce something promised or expected. **9** *Chiefly US.* to cause (voters, etc.) to support a given candidate, cause, etc. **10 deliver oneself of.** to speak with deliberation or at length. ORIG C13: from OF, from LL *dēlīberāre* to set free, from L DE- + *līberāre* to free
▸ **de'liverable** *adj* ▸ **de'liverer** *n*

deliverance (dɪ'lɪvərəns) *n* **1** a formal expression of opinion. **2** rescue from moral corruption or evil; salvation.

delivery (dɪ'lɪvərɪ) *n, pl* **deliveries. 1a** the act of delivering or distributing goods, mail, etc. **1b** something that is delivered. **2** the act of giving birth to a child. **3** manner or style of utterance, esp. in public speaking: *the chairman had a clear delivery.* **4** the act of giving or transferring or the state of being given or transferred. **5** a rescuing or being rescued; liberation. **6** *Sport.* the act or manner of bowling or throwing a ball. **7** the handing over of property, a deed, etc. **8** *S. African.* the supply of basic services to communities deprived under apartheid.

dell (dɛl) *n* a small, esp. wooded hollow. ORIG OE

della Robbia ★ (*Italian* 'della 'robbja) *n* See (Luca della) **Robbia.**

Deller ★ ('dɛlə) *n* **Alfred** (**George**). 1912–79, British countertenor.

Del Mar ★ (dɛl 'mɑ:) *n* **Norman.** 1919–94, British conductor.

Delmarva Peninsula ★ (dɛl'mɑ:və) *n* a peninsula of the northeast US, between Chesapeake Bay and the Atlantic.

Delors ★ (*French* dəlɔr) *n* **Jacques** (**Lucien Jean**) (ʒɑk). born 1925, French politician and economist, President of the European Commission (1985–94): originator of the **Delors plan** for closer European union.

Delos ★ ('diːlɒs) *n* a Greek island in the SW Aegean Sea, in the Cyclades: a commercial centre in ancient times; the legendary birthplace of Apollo and Artemis. Area: about 5 sq. km (2 sq. miles). Modern Greek name: **Dhílos.**

de los Angeles ★ (*Spanish* de los 'aŋxeles) *n* **Victoria** (bik'torja). born 1923, Spanish soprano.

delouse (diː'laʊs, -'laʊz) *vb* **delouses, delousing, deloused.** (*tr*) to rid (a person or animal) of lice as a sanitary measure.

Delphi ★ ('dɛlfɪ) *n* an ancient Greek city on the S slopes of Mount Parnassus: site of the most famous oracle of Apollo.

Delphic ('dɛlfɪk) *or* **Delphian** *adj* **1** of or relating to the ancient Greek city of Delphi or its oracle or temple. **2** obscure or ambiguous.

Delphic oracle ★ *n* the oracle of Apollo at Delphi that gave answers held by the ancient Greeks to be of great authority but also noted for their ambiguity.

delphinium (dɛl'fɪnɪəm) *n, pl* **delphiniums** *or* **delphinia** (-ɪə). a plant with spikes of blue, pink, or white spurred flowers. See also **larkspur.** ORIG C17: NL, from Gk *delphinion* larkspur, from *delphis* dolphin, referring to the shape of the nectary

del Sarto ★ (*Italian* del 'sarto) *n* See (Andrea del) **Sarto.**

delta ('dɛltə) *n* **1** the fourth letter in the Greek alphabet (Δ or δ). **2** (*cap. when part of name*) the flat alluvial area at the mouth of some rivers where the mainstream splits up into several distributaries. **3** *Maths.* a finite increment in a variable. ORIG C16: via L from Gk, of Semitic origin
▸ **deltaic** (dɛl'teɪɪk) *or* **'deltic** *adj*

delta connection *n* a connection used in a three-phase electrical system in which three elements in series form a triangle, the supply being input and output at the three junctions.

delta particle *n Physics* a very short-lived type of hyperon.

delta ray *n* a particle, esp. an electron, ejected from matter by ionizing radiation.

delta rhythm *or* **wave** *n Physiol.* the normal electrical activity of the cerebral cortex during deep sleep. See also **brain wave.**

delta stock *n* any of the fourth rank of active securities on the London stock exchange. Market makers need not display prices of these securities continuously.

delta wing *n* a triangular swept-back aircraft wing.

deltiology (ˌdɛltɪ'ɒlədʒɪ) *n* the collection and study of postcards. ORIG C20: from Gk *deltion,* dim. of *deltos* a writing tablet + -LOGY
▸ **ˌdelti'ologist** *n*

deltoid ('dɛltɔɪd) *n* a thick muscle of the shoulder that acts to raise the arm. ORIG C18: from Gk *deltoeidēs* triangular, from DELTA

delude (dɪ'luːd) *vb* **deludes, deluding, deluded.** (*tr*) to deceive; mislead; beguile. ORIG C15: from L *dēlūdere* to mock, play false, from DE- + *lūdere* to play
▸ **de'ludable** *adj* ▸ **de'luder** *n*

deluge ('dɛljuːdʒ) *n* **1** a great flood of water. **2** torrential rain. **3** an overwhelming rush or number. ◆ *vb* **deluges, deluging, deluged.** (*tr*) **4** to flood. **5** to overwhelm; inundate. ORIG C14: from OF, from L *dīluvium,* from *dīluere* to wash away, drench, from *di-* DIS-[1] + *-luere,* from *lavere* to wash

Deluge ('dɛljuːdʒ) *n* **the.** another name for the **Flood.**

delusion (dɪ'luːʒən) *n* **1** a mistaken idea, belief, etc. **2** *Psychiatry.* a belief held in the face of evidence to the contrary, that is resistant to all reason. **3** a deluding or being deluded.
▸ **de'lusional** *adj* ▸ **de'lusive** *adj* ▸ **delusory** (dɪ'luːsərɪ) *adj*

de luxe (də 'lʌks, 'lʊks) *adj* **1** rich or sumptuous; superior in quality: *the de luxe model of a car.* ◆ *adv* **2** *Chiefly US.* in a luxurious manner. ORIG C19: from F, lit.: of luxury

delve (dɛlv) *vb* **delves, delving, delved.** (*mainly intr; often foll. by in or into*) **1** to research deeply or intensively (for information, etc.). **2** to search or rummage. **3** to dig or burrow deeply. **4** (*also tr*) *Arch. or Brit. dialect.* to dig. ORIG OE *delfan*
▸ **'delver** *n*

Dem. (in the US) *abbrev. for* Democrat(ic).

demagnetize *or* **demagnetise** (diː'mægnəˌtaɪz) *vb* **demagnetizes, demagnetizing, demagnetized** *or* **demagnetises, demagnetising, demagnetised.** to remove or lose magnetic properties. Also: **degauss.**
▸ **deˌmagneti'zation** *or* **deˌmagneti'sation** *n* ▸ **de'magnetˌizer** *or* **de'magnetˌiser** *n*

demagogue *or US* (*sometimes*) **demagog** ('dɛməˌgɒg) *n* **1** a political agitator who appeals with crude oratory to the prejudice and passions of the mob. **2** (esp. in the ancient world) any popular political leader or orator. ORIG C17: from Gk *dēmagōgos* people's leader, from *dēmos* people + *agein* to lead
▸ **ˌdema'gogic** *adj* ▸ **ˌdema'goguery** *n*

demagogy ('dɛməˌgɒgɪ) *n, pl* **demagogies. 1** demagoguery. **2** rule by a demagogue or by demagogues. **3** a group of demagogues.

demand (dɪ'mɑːnd) *vb* (*tr; may take a clause as object or an infinitive*) **1** to request peremptorily or urgently. **2** to require as just, urgent, etc.: *the situation demands attention.* **3** to claim as a right; exact. **4** *Law.* to make a formal legal claim to (property). ◆ *n* **5** an urgent or peremptory requirement or request. **6** something that requires special effort or sacrifice. **7** the act of demanding something or the thing demanded. **8** an insistent question. **9** *Econ.* **9a** willingness and ability to purchase goods and services. **9b** the amount of a commodity that consumers are willing and able to purchase at a specified price. Cf. **supply**[1] (sense 9). **10** *Law.* a formal legal claim, esp. to real property. **11 in demand.** sought after. **12 on demand.** as soon as requested. ORIG C13: from Anglo-F, from Med. L *dēmandāre,* from L: to commit to, from DE- + *mandāre* to command, entrust
▸ **de'mandable** *adj* ▸ **de'mander** *n*

demand feeding *n* the practice of feeding a baby whenever it is hungry, rather than at set intervals.

demanding (dɪ'mɑːndɪŋ) *adj* requiring great patience, skill, etc.: *a demanding job.*

demarcate ('diːmɑːˌkeɪt) *vb* **demarcates, demarcating, demarcated.** (*tr*) **1** to mark the boundaries, limits, etc., of. **2** to separate; distinguish.
▸ **'demarˌcator** *n*

demarcation *or* **demarkation** (ˌdiːmɑː'keɪʃən) *n* **1** the act of establishing limits or boundaries. **2** a limit or boundary. **3a** a strict separation of the kinds of work performed by members of different trade unions. **3b** (*as modifier*): *demarcation dispute.* **4** separation or distinction (as in **line of demarcation**). ORIG C18: from Sp. *demarcar* to appoint the boundaries of, from *marcar* to mark, from It., of Gmc origin

démarche *French.* (demarʃ) *n* a move, step, or manoeuvre, esp. in diplomatic affairs. ORIG C17: lit.: walk, gait, from OF *demarcher* to tread, trample

dematerialize *or* **dematerialise** (diːmə'tɪərɪəˌlaɪz) *vb* **dematerializes, dematerializing, dematerialized** *or* **dematerialises, dematerialising, dematerialised.** (*intr*) **1** to cease to have material existence, as in science fiction or spiritualism. **2** to vanish.
▸ **demaˌteriali'zation** *or* **demaˌteriali'sation** *n*

deme (diːm) *n* **1** (in ancient Attica) a geographical unit of local government. **2** *Biol.* a group of individuals within a species that possess particular characteristics of cytology, genetics, etc. ORIG C19: from Gk *dēmos* district in local government, the populace

demean[1] (dɪ'miːn) *vb* (*tr*) to lower (oneself) in dignity, status, or character; humble; debase. ORIG C17: see DE-, MEAN[2]

demean[2] (dɪ'miːn) *vb* (*tr*) *Rare.* to behave or conduct (oneself). ORIG C13: from OF, from DE- + *mener* to lead, from L *mināre* to drive (animals), from *minārī* to use threats

demeanour *or US* **demeanor** (dɪ'miːnə) *n* **1** the way a person behaves towards others. **2** bearing or mien. ORIG C15: see DEMEAN[2]

dement (dɪˈmɛnt) *vb* **1** (*intr*) to deteriorate mentally, esp. because of old age. **2** (*tr*) *Rare.* to drive mad; make insane. ORIG C16: from LL *dēmentāre* to drive mad, from L DE- + *mēns* mind

demented (dɪˈmɛntɪd) *adj* mad; insane.
▸ **deˈmentedly** *adv* ▸ **deˈmentedness** *n*

dementia (dɪˈmɛnʃə, -ʃɪə) *n* a state of serious mental deterioration, of organic or functional origin. ORIG C19: from L: madness; see DEMENT

dementia praecox (ˈpriːkɒks) *n* a former name for **schizophrenia.** ORIG C19: NL, lit.: premature dementia

demerara (ˌdɛməˈrɛərə, -ˈrɑːrə) *n* brown crystallized cane sugar from the Caribbean. ORIG C19: after *Demerara,* a region of Guyana

Demerara ★ (ˌdɛməˈrɛərə, -ˈrɑːrə) *n* **the.** a river in Guyana, rising in the central forest area and flowing north to the Atlantic at Georgetown. Length: 346 km (215 miles).

demerit (diːˈmɛrɪt) *n* **1** something that deserves censure. **2** *US & Canad.* a mark given against a student, etc., for failure or misconduct. **3** a fault. ORIG C14 (orig.: worth, desert, ult.: something worthy of blame): from L *dēmerērī* to deserve
▸ **deˌmeriˈtorious** *adj*

demersal (dɪˈmɜːsᵊl) *adj* living or occurring in deep water or on the bottom of a sea or lake. ORIG C19: from L *dēmersus* submerged (from *mergere* to dip) + -AL[1]

demesne (dɪˈmeɪn, -ˈmiːn) *n* **1** land surrounding a house or manor. **2** *Property law.* the possession and use of one's own property or land. **3** realm; domain. **4** a region or district. ORIG C14: from OF *demeine;* see DOMAIN

Demeter ★ (dɪˈmiːtə) *n Greek myth.* the goddess of agricultural fertility and protector of marriage and women. Roman counterpart: **Ceres.**

demi- *prefix* **1** half: *demirelief.* **2** of less than full size, status, or rank: *demigod.* ORIG via F from Med. L, from L *dīmīdius* half, from *dis-* apart + *medius* middle

demigod (ˈdɛmɪˌgɒd) *n* **1a** a being who is part mortal, part god. **1b** a lesser deity. **2** a person with godlike attributes. ORIG C16: translation of L *sēmideus*
▸ **ˈdemiˌgoddess** *fem n*

demijohn (ˈdɛmɪˌdʒɒn) *n* a large bottle with a short narrow neck, often encased in wickerwork. ORIG C18: prob. from F *dame-jeanne,* from *dame* lady + *Jeanne* Jane

demilitarize *or* **demilitarise** (diːˈmɪlɪtəˌraɪz) *vb* **demilitarizes, demilitarizing, demilitarized** *or* **demilitarises, demilitarising, demilitarised.** (*tr*) **1** to remove and prohibit any military presence or function in (an area): *demilitarized zone.* **2** to free of military character, purpose, etc.
▸ **deˌmilitariˈzation** *or* **deˌmilitariˈsation** *n*

De Mille ★ (də ˈmɪl) *n* **Cecil B(lount).** 1881–1959, US film producer and director.

demimondaine (ˌdɛmɪˈmɒndeɪn) *n* a woman of the demimonde. ORIG C19: from F

demimonde (ˌdɛmɪˈmɒnd) *n* **1** (esp. in the 19th century) those women considered to be outside respectable society, esp. on account of sexual promiscuity. **2** any group considered to be not wholly respectable. ORIG C19: from F, lit.: half-world

demise (dɪˈmaɪz) *n* **1** failure or termination. **2** a euphemistic or formal word for **death. 3** *Property law.* a transfer of an estate by lease or on the death of the owner. **4** the transfer of sovereignty to a successor upon the death, abdication, etc., of a ruler (esp. in **demise of the crown**). ◆ *vb* **demises, demising, demised. 5** to transfer or be transferred by inheritance, will, or succession. **6** (*tr*) *Property law.* to transfer for a limited period; lease. **7** (*tr*) to transfer (sovereignty, a title, etc.) ORIG C16: from OF, fem of *demis* dismissed, from *demettre* to send away, from L *dīmittere*
▸ **deˈmisable** *adj*

demi-sec (ˌdɛmɪˈsɛk) *adj* (of wine) medium-dry. ORIG C20: from F, from *demi* half + *sec* dry

demisemiquaver (ˈdɛmɪˌsɛmɪˌkweɪvə) *n Music.* a note having the time value of one thirty-second of a semibreve. Usual US and Canad. name: **thirty-second note.**

demist (diːˈmɪst) *vb* to free or become free of condensation.
▸ **deˈmister** *n*

demitasse (ˈdɛmɪˌtæs) *n* **1** a small cup used to serve coffee, esp. after a meal. **2** the coffee itself. ORIG C19: F, lit.: half-cup

demiurge (ˈdɛmɪˌɜːdʒ) *n* **1** (in the philosophy of Plato) the creator of the universe. **2** (in Gnostic philosophy) the creator of the universe, supernatural but subordinate to the Supreme Being. ORIG C17: from Church L, from Gk *dēmiourgos* skilled workman, lit.: one who works for the people, from *dēmos* people + *ergon* work
▸ **ˌdemiˈurgic** *or* **ˌdemiˈurgical** *adj*

demiveg (ˈdɛmɪˌvɛdʒ) *Inf.* ◆ *n* **1** a person who eats poultry and fish, but no red meat. ◆ *adj* **2** denoting a person who eats poultry and fish, but no red meat. ORIG C20: from DEMI- + VEG(ETARIAN)

demo (ˈdɛməʊ) *n, pl* **demos.** *Inf.* **1** short for **demonstration** (sense 4). **2** a demonstration record or tape.

demo- *or before a vowel* **dem-** *combining form.* indicating people or population: *demography.* ORIG from Gk *dēmos*

demob *Brit. inf.* ◆ *vb* (diːˈmɒb), **demobs, demobbing, demobbed. 1** to demobilize. ◆ *n* (ˈdiːmɒb). **2** demobilization.

demobilize *or* **demobilise** (diːˈməʊbɪˌlaɪz) *vb* **demobilizes, demobilizing, demobilized** *or* **demobilises, demobilising, demobilised.** to disband, as troops, etc.
▸ **deˌmobiliˈzation** *or* **deˌmobiliˈsation** *n*

Demochristian (ˌdɛməʊˈkrɪstʃən) *n* an informal name for a **Christian Democrat.**

democracy (dɪˈmɒkrəsɪ) *n, pl* **democracies. 1** government by the people or their elected representatives. **2** a political or social unit governed ultimately by all its members. **3** the practice or spirit of social equality. **4** a social condition of classlessness and equality. ORIG C16: from F, from LL, from Gk *dēmokratia* government by the people

democrat (ˈdɛməˌkræt) *n* **1** an advocate of democracy. **2** a member or supporter of a democratic party or movement.

Democrat (ˈdɛməˌkræt) *n* (in the US) a member or supporter of the Democratic Party.
▸ **ˌDemoˈcratic** *adj*

democratic (ˌdɛməˈkrætɪk) *adj* **1** of or relating to the principles of democracy. **2** upholding democracy or the interests of the common people. **3** popular with or for the benefit of all.
▸ **ˌdemoˈcratically** *adv*

democratic centralism *n* the Leninist principle that policy should be decided centrally by officials, who are nominally democratically elected.

Democratic Republic of Congo ★ *n* **the.** See **Congo** (sense 1).

democratize *or* **democratise** (dɪˈmɒkrəˌtaɪz) *vb* **democratizes, democratizing, democratized** *or* **democratises, democratising, democratised.** (*tr*) to make democratic.
▸ **deˌmocratiˈzation** *or* **deˌmocratiˈsation** *n*

Democritus ★ (dɪˈmɒkrɪtəs) *n* ?460–?370 B.C., Greek philosopher who developed the atomic theory of matter of his teacher, Leucippus.

démodé *French.* (demɔde) *adj* outmoded. ORIG F, from *dé-* out of + *mode* fashion

demodulate (diːˈmɒdjʊˌleɪt) *vb* **demodulates, demodulating, demodulated.** to carry out demodulation on.
▸ **deˈmoduˌlator** *n*

demodulation (ˌdiːmɒdjʊˈleɪʃən) *n Electronics.* the act or process by which an output wave or signal is obtained having the characteristics of the original modulating wave or signal; the reverse of modulation.

demographic (ˌdɛməˈgræfɪk, ˌdiːmə-) *adj* **1** Also: **demographical.** of or relating to demography. ◆ *n* **2** a section of the population sharing common characteristics, such as age, sex, class, ethnic background, etc.: *this programme appeals to a young demographic.*

demographic timebomb *n Chiefly Brit.* a predicted shortage of school-leavers and consequently of available workers, caused by an earlier drop in the birth rate.

demography (dɪˈmɒgrəfɪ) *n* the scientific study of human populations, esp. of their size, distribution, etc. ORIG C19: from F, from Gk *dēmos* the populace; see -GRAPHY
▸ **deˈmographer** *n*

demoiselle (dəmwɑːˈzɛl) *n* **1** a small crane of central Asia, N Africa, and SE Europe, having a grey plumage with black breast feathers and white ear tufts. **2** a less common name for a **damselfly. 3** a literary word for **damsel.** ORIG C16: from F: young woman; see DAMSEL

demolish (dɪˈmɒlɪʃ) *vb* (*tr*) **1** to tear down or break up (buildings, etc.). **2** to put an end to (an argument, etc.). **3** *Facetious.* to eat up. ORIG C16: from F, from L *dēmōlīrī* to throw down, from DE- + *mōlīrī* to construct, from *mōles* mass
▸ **deˈmolisher** *n*

demolition (ˌdɛməˈlɪʃən, ˌdiː-) *n* **1** a demolishing or being demolished. **2** *Chiefly mil.* destruction by explosives.
▸ **ˌdemoˈlitionist** *n, adj*

demon (ˈdiːmən) *n* **1** an evil spirit or devil. **2** a person, obsession, etc., thought of as evil or cruel. **3** Also called: **daemon, daimon.** an attendant or ministering spirit; genius: *the demon of inspiration.* **4a** a person extremely skilful in or devoted to a given activity, esp. a sport: *a demon at cycling.* **4b** (*as modifier*): *a demon cyclist.* **5** a variant spelling of **daemon** (senses 1, 2). **6** *Austral. & NZ sl.* a detective or policeman, esp. one in plain clothes. ORIG C15: from L *daemōn* (evil) spirit, from Gk *daimōn* spirit, deity, fate
▸ **demonic** (dɪˈmɒnɪk) *adj*

demonetize *or* **demonetise** (diːˈmʌnɪˌtaɪz) *vb* **demonetizes, demonetizing, demonetized** *or* **demonetises, demonetising, demonetised.** (*tr*) **1** to deprive (a metal) of its capacity as a monetary standard. **2** to withdraw from use as currency.
▸ **deˌmonetiˈzation** *or* **deˌmonetiˈsation** *n*

demoniac (dɪˈməʊnɪˌæk) *adj also* **demoniacal** (ˌdiːməˈnaɪəkᵊl). **1** of or like a demon. **2** suggesting inner possession or inspiration. **3** frantic; frenzied. ◆ *n* **4** a person possessed by a demon.
▸ **ˌdemoˈniacally** *adv*

demonism (ˈdiːməˌnɪzəm) *n* **1** belief in the existence and power of demons. **2** another name for **demonology** (sense 1).
▸ **ˈdemonist** *n*

demonize *or* **demonise** (ˌdiːməˌnaɪz) *vb* (*tr*) **1** to make into or like a demon. **2** to subject to demonic influence. **3** to mark out or describe as evil or culpable: *they demonized the enemy in the run-up to war.*

demonolatry (ˌdiːməˈnɒlətrɪ) *n* the worship of demons. ORIG C17: see DEMON, -LATRY

demonology (ˌdiːməˈnɒlədʒɪ) *n* **1** Also called: **demonism.** the study of demons or demonic beliefs. **2** a set of people or things that are disliked or feared: *Adolf Hitler's place in contemporary demonology.*
▸ **ˌdemonˈologist** *n*

demonstrable (ˈdɛmənstrəbᵊl, dɪˈmɒn-) *adj* able to be demonstrated or proved.
▸ **ˌdemonstraˈbility** *n* ▸ **ˈdemonstrably** *adv*

demonstrate (ˈdɛmənˌstreɪt) *vb* **demonstrates, demonstrating, demonstrated. 1** (*tr*) to show or prove, esp. by reasoning, evidence, etc. **2** (*tr*) to evince; reveal the existence of. **3** (*tr*) to explain by experiment, example, etc. **4** (*tr*) to display and explain the workings of (a machine, product, etc.). **5** (*intr*) to manifest support, protest, etc., by public parades or rallies. **6** (*intr*) to be employed as a demonstrator of machinery, etc. **7** (*intr*) *Mil.* to make a show of force. ORIG C16: from L *dēmonstrāre* to point out, from *monstrāre* to show

demonstration (ˌdɛmənˈstreɪʃən) *n* **1** the act of demonstrating. **2** proof or evidence leading to proof. **3** an explanation, illustration, or experiment showing how something works. **4** Also: **demo.** a manifestation of support or protest by public rallies, parades, etc. **5** a manifestation of emotion. **6** a show of military force.
▸ **ˌdemonˈstrational** *adj* ▸ **ˌdemonˈstrationist** *n*

demonstration model *n* a nearly new product, such as a car, that has been used to demonstrate its performance by a dealer and is offered at a discount.

demonstrative (dɪˈmɒnstrətɪv) *adj* **1** tending to express one's feelings easily or unreservedly. **2** (*postpositive;* foll. by *of*) serving as proof; indicative. **3** involving or characterized by demonstration. **4** conclusive. **5** *Grammar.* denoting or belonging to a class of determiners used to point out the individual referent or referents intended, such as *this* and *those.* Cf. **interrogative, relative.** ◆ *n* **6** *Grammar.* a demonstrative word.
▸ **deˈmonstratively** *adv* ▸ **deˈmonstrativeness** *n*

demonstrator (ˈdɛmənˌstreɪtə) *n* **1** a person who demonstrates equipment, machines, products, etc. **2** a person who takes part in a public demonstration.

demoralize *or* **demoralise** (dɪˈmɒrəˌlaɪz) *vb* **demoralizes, demoralizing, demoralized** *or* **demoralises, demoralising, demoralised.** (*tr*) **1** to undermine the morale of; dishearten. **2** to corrupt. **3** to throw into confusion.
▸ **deˌmoraliˈzation** *or* **deˌmoraliˈsation** *n*

Demosthenes ★ (dɪˈmɒsθəˌniːz) *n* 384–322 B.C., Athenian statesman, orator, and lifelong opponent of the power of Macedonia over Greece.

demote (dɪˈməʊt) *vb* **demotes, demoting, demoted.** (*tr*) to lower in rank or position; relegate. ORIG C19: from DE- + (PRO)MOTE
▸ **deˈmotion** *n*

demotic (dɪˈmɒtɪk) *adj* **1** of or relating to the common people; popular. **2** of or relating to a simplified form of hieroglyphics used in ancient Egypt. Cf. **hieratic.** ◆ *n* **3** the demotic script of ancient Egypt. ORIG C19: from Gk *dēmotikos* of the people, from *dēmotēs* a man of the people, commoner
▸ **deˈmotist** *n*

Dempsey ★ (ˈdɛmpsɪ) *n* **Jack.** real name *William Harrison Dempsey.* 1895–1983, US boxer; world heavyweight champion (1919–26).

dempster (ˈdɛmpstə) *n* a variant spelling of **deemster.**

demulcent (dɪˈmʌlsᵊnt) *adj* **1** soothing. ◆ *n* **2** a drug or agent that soothes irritation. ORIG C18: from L *dēmulcēre,* from DE- + *mulcēre* to stroke

demur (dɪˈmɜː) *vb* **demurs, demurring, demurred.** (*intr*) **1** to show reluctance. **2** *Law.* to raise an objection by entering a demurrer. ◆ *n also* **demurral** (dɪˈmʌrəl). **3** the act of demurring. **4** an objection raised. ORIG C13: from OF, from L *dēmorārī,* from *morārī* to delay
▸ **deˈmurrable** *adj*

demure (dɪˈmjʊə) *adj* **1** sedate; decorous; reserved. **2** affectedly modest or prim; coy. ORIG C14: ?from OF *demorer* to delay, linger; ? infl. by *meur* ripe, MATURE
▸ **deˈmurely** *adv* ▸ **deˈmureness** *n*

demurrage (dɪˈmʌrɪdʒ) *n* **1** the delaying of a ship, etc., caused by the charterer's failure to load, unload, etc., before the time of scheduled departure. **2** the extra charge required for such delay. ORIG C14: from OF *demorage, demourage;* see DEMUR

demurrer (dɪˈmʌrə) *n* **1** *Law.* a pleading that admits an opponent's point but denies that it is relevant or valid. **2** any objection raised.

demutualize *or* **demutualise** (diːˈmjuːtjʊəˌlaɪz) *vb* **demutualizes, demutualizing, demutualized** *or* **demutualises, demutualising, demutualised.** (*intr*) (of a mutual savings or life-assurance organization) to convert to a public limited company.
▸ **ˌdemutualiˈzation** *or* **ˌdemutualiˈsation** *n*

demy (dɪˈmaɪ) *n, pl* **demies. 1** a size of printing paper, 17½ by 22½ inches (444.5 × 571.5 mm). **2** a size of writing paper, 15½ by 20 inches (Brit.) (393.7 × 508 mm) or 16 by 21 inches (US) (406.4 × 533.4 mm). ORIG C16: see DEMI-

demystify (diːˈmɪstɪˌfaɪ) *vb* **demystifies, demystifying, demystified.** (*tr*) to remove the mystery from.
▸ **deˌmystifiˈcation** *n*

demythologize *or* **demythologise** (ˌdiːmɪˈθɒləˌdʒaɪz) *vb* **demythologizes, demythologizing, demythologized** *or* **demythologises, demythologising, demythologised.** (*tr*) **1** to eliminate mythical elements from (a piece of writing, esp. the Bible). **2** to restate (a religious message) in rational terms.

den (dɛn) *n* **1** the habitat or retreat of a wild animal; lair. **2** a small or secluded room in a home, often used for carrying on a hobby. **3** a squalid room or retreat. **4** a site or haunt: *a den of vice.* **5** *Scot.* a small wooded valley. ◆ *vb*

dens, denning, denned. 6 *(intr)* to live in or as if in a den. ORIG OE *denn*

Den. *abbrev. for* Denmark.

denar (dɪˈnɑː) *n* the standard monetary unit of (the Former Yugoslav Republic of) Macedonia.

denarius (dɪˈnɛərɪəs) *n, pl* **denarii** (-ˈnɛərɪˌaɪ). **1** a silver coin of ancient Rome, often called a penny in translation. **2** a gold coin worth 25 silver denarii. ORIG C16: from L: coin orig. equal to ten asses, from *dēnārius* (adj) containing ten, from *decem* ten

denary (ˈdiːnərɪ) *adj* **1** calculated by tens; decimal. **2** containing ten parts; tenfold. ORIG C16: from L *dēnārius;* see DENARIUS

denationalize *or* **denationalise** (diːˈnæʃənᵊˌlaɪz) *vb* **denationalizes, denationalizing, denationalized** *or* **denationalises, denationalising, denationalised. 1** to transfer (an industry, etc.) from public to private ownership. **2** to deprive of national character or nationality.
▸ **deˌnationaliˈzation** *or* **deˌnationaliˈsation** *n*

denaturalize *or* **denaturalise** (diːˈnætʃrəˌlaɪz) *vb* **denaturalizes, denaturalizing, denaturalized** *or* **denaturalises, denaturalising, denaturalised.** *(tr)* **1** to deprive of nationality. **2** to make unnatural.
▸ **deˌnaturaliˈzation** *or* **deˌnaturaliˈsation** *n*

denature (diːˈneɪtʃə) *or* **denaturize, denaturise** (diːˈneɪtʃəˌraɪz) *vb* **denatures, denaturing, denatured** *or* **denaturizes, denaturizing, denaturized; denaturises, denaturising, denaturised.** *(tr)* **1** to change the nature of. **2** to change the properties of (a protein), as by the action of acid or heat. **3** to render (something, such as alcohol) unfit for consumption by adding nauseous substances. **4** to render (fissile material) unfit for use in nuclear weapons by addition of an isotope.
▸ **deˈnaturant** *n* ▸ **deˌnaturˈation** *n*

Denbighshire ★ (ˈdɛnbɪˌʃɪə, -ʃə) *n* a county of N Wales, part of Clwyd and Gwynedd (1974–96). Administrative centre: Ruthin. Pop.: 91 585 (1996 est.). Area: 844 sq. km (327 sq. miles).

Den Bosch ★ (dən bɔs) *n* another name for **'s Hertogenbosch.**

Dench ★ (dɛntʃ) *n* Dame **Judi (Olivia).** born 1934, British actress and theatre director.

dendrite (ˈdɛndraɪt) *n* **1** Also called: **dendron.** any of the branched extensions of a nerve cell, which conduct impulses towards the cell body. **2** a branching mosslike crystalline structure in some rocks and minerals. **3** a crystal that has branched during growth. ORIG C18: from Gk *dendritēs* relating to a tree
▸ **dendritic** (dɛnˈdrɪtɪk) *adj*

dendro-, dendri-, *or before a vowel* **dendr-** *combining form.* tree: *dendrochronology.* ORIG NL, from Gk, from *dendron* tree

dendrochronology (ˌdɛndrəʊkrəˈnɒlədʒɪ) *n* the study of the annual rings of trees, used esp. to date past events.

dendrology (dɛnˈdrɒlədʒɪ) *n* the branch of botany that is concerned with the natural history of trees.
▸ **dendrological** (ˌdɛndrəˈlɒdʒɪkᵊl) *or* **ˌdendroˈlogic** *adj*
▸ **denˈdrologist** *n*

dene[1] *or* **dean** (diːn) *n Brit.* a narrow wooded valley. ORIG OE *denu* valley

dene[2] *or* **dean** (diːn) *n Dialect, chiefly southern English.* a sandy stretch of land or dune near the sea. ORIG C13: prob. rel. to OE *dūn* hill

denervate (ˈdɛnəˌveɪt) *vb* **denervates, denervating, denervated.** *(tr)* to deprive (a tissue or organ) of its nerve supply.
▸ **ˌdenerˈvation** *n*

Deneuve ★ (*French* dənøv) *n* **Catherine** (katrin), original name *Catherine Dorléac.* born 1943, French film actress: her films include *Belle de Jour* (1967) and *Indochine* (1992).

dengue (ˈdɛŋgɪ) *or* **dandy** (ˈdændɪ) *n* an acute viral disease transmitted by mosquitoes, characterized by headache, fever, pains in the joints, and skin rash. ORIG C19: from Sp., prob. of African origin

Deng Xiaoping (ˈdʌŋ ˈsjaʊpɪŋ) *or* **Teng Hsiao-ping** ★ *n* 1904–97, Chinese Communist statesman; deputy prime minister of China (1973–76; 1977–80) and dominant figure in the Chinese government from 1977 until his death.

Den Haag ★ (dɛn ˈhaːx) *n* the Dutch name for (The) **Hague.**

deniable (dɪˈnaɪəbᵊl) *adj* able to be denied; questionable.
▸ **deˈniably** *adv*

denial (dɪˈnaɪəl) *n* **1** a refusal to agree or comply with a statement. **2** the rejection of the truth of a proposition, doctrine, etc. **3** a rejection of a request. **4** a refusal to acknowledge; disavowal. **5** a psychological process by which painful truths are not admitted into an individual's consciousness. **6** abstinence; self-denial.

denier[1] *n* **1** (ˈdɛnɪˌeɪ, ˈdɛnjə). a unit of weight used to measure the fineness of silk and man-made fibres, esp. when woven into women's tights, etc. **2** (dəˈnjeɪ, -ˈnɪə). any of several former European coins of various denominations. ORIG C15: from OF: coin, from L *dēnārius* DENARIUS

denier[2] (dɪˈnaɪə) *n* a person who denies.

denigrate (ˈdɛnɪˌgreɪt) *vb* **denigrates, denigrating, denigrated.** *(tr)* to belittle or disparage the character of; defame. ORIG C16: from L *dēnigrāre* to make very black, from *nigrāre,* from *niger* black
▸ **ˌdeniˈgration** *n* ▸ **ˈdeniˌgrator** *n*

denim (ˈdɛnɪm) *n* **1** a hard-wearing twill-weave cotton fabric used for trousers, work clothes, etc. **2** a similar lighter fabric used in upholstery. ORIG C17: from F *(serge) de Nîmes* (serge) of Nîmes, in S France

denims (ˈdɛnɪmz) *pl n* jeans or overalls made of denim.

De Niro ★ (də ˈnɪərəʊ) *n* **Robert.** born 1943, US film actor. His films include *Taxi Driver* (1976), *Raging Bull* (1980), *Awakenings* (1991), and *Analyze This* (1999).

Denis ★ (ˈdɛnɪs; *French* dəni) *n* **Saint.** Also: **Denys.** 3rd century A.D., first bishop of Paris; patron saint of France. Feast day: Oct. 9.

denizen (ˈdɛnɪzən) *n* **1** an inhabitant; resident. **2** *Brit.* an individual permanently resident in a foreign country where he or she enjoys certain rights of citizenship. **3** a plant or animal established in a place to which it is not native. **4** a naturalized foreign word. ORIG C15: from Anglo-F *denisein,* from OF *denzein,* from *denz* within, from L *de intus* from within

Denmark ★ (ˈdɛnmɑːk) *n* a kingdom in N Europe, between the Baltic and the North Sea: consists of the mainland of Jutland and about 100 inhabited islands (chiefly Zealand, Lolland, Funen, Falster, Langeland, and Bornholm); extended its territory throughout the Middle Ages, ruling Sweden until 1523 and Norway until 1814; it was occupied (1940–45) by Germany. It incorporated Greenland as a province from 1953 to 1979; a member of the European Union; an important exporter of dairy produce. Language: Danish. Religion: chiefly Lutheran. Currency: krone. Capital: Copenhagen. Pop.: 5 316 000 (1999 est.). Area: 43 031 sq. km (16 614 sq. miles). Danish name: **Danmark.**

Denmark Strait ★ *n* a channel between SE Greenland and Iceland, linking the Arctic Ocean with the Atlantic.

Denning ★ (ˈdɛnɪŋ) *n* Baron **Alfred Thompson.** 1899–1999, British judge; Master of the Rolls 1962–82.

Dennis ★ (ˈdɛnɪs) *n* **C(larence) J(ames).** 1876–1938, the poet of the Australian larrikin, esp. in *The Songs of a Sentimental Bloke* (1915) and *The Moods of Ginger Mick* (1916).

denominate *vb* (dɪˈnɒmɪˌneɪt). **denominates, denominating, denominated. 1** *(tr)* to give a specific name to; designate. ◆ *adj* (dɪˈnɒmɪnɪt, -ˌneɪt). **2** *Maths.* (of a number) representing a multiple of a unit of measurement: *4 is the denominate number in 4 miles.* ORIG C16: from L *denōminare* from DE- (intensive) + *nōminare* to name

denomination (dɪˌnɒmɪˈneɪʃən) *n* **1** a group having a distinctive interpretation of a religious faith and usually its own organization. **2** a grade or unit in a series of designations of value, weight, measure, etc. **3** a name given to a class or group; classification. **4** the act of giving a name. **5** a name; designation.
▸ **deˌnomiˈnational** *adj*

denominative (dɪˈnɒmɪnətɪv) *adj* **1** giving or constituting a name. **2** *Grammar.* **2a** formed from or having the same form as a noun. **2b** (*as n*): *the verb "to mushroom" is a denominative.*

denominator (dɪˈnɒmɪˌneɪtə) *n* the divisor of a fraction, as 8 in ⅞. Cf. **numerator.**

denotation (ˌdiːnəʊˈteɪʃən) *n* **1** a denoting; indication. **2** a particular meaning given by a sign or symbol. **3** specific meaning as distinguished from suggestive meaning and associations. **4** *Logic.* another word for **extension** (sense 10).

denote (dɪˈnəʊt) *vb* **denotes, denoting, denoted.** (*tr; may take a clause as object*) **1** to be a sign of; designate. **2** (of words, phrases, etc.) to have as a literal or obvious meaning. ORIG C16: from L *dēnotāre* to mark, from *notāre* to mark, NOTE
▸ **deˈnotative** *adj*

denouement (deɪˈnuːmɒn) *or* **dénouement** (*French* denumɑ̃) *n* **1** the clarification or resolution of a plot in a play or other work. **2** final outcome; solution. ORIG C18: from F, lit.: an untying, from OF *desnoer,* from *des-* DE- + *noer* to tie, from L *nōdus* a knot

denounce (dɪˈnaʊns) *vb* **denounces, denouncing, denounced.** (*tr*) **1** to condemn openly or vehemently. **2** to give information against; accuse. **3** to announce formally the termination of (a treaty, etc.). ORIG C13: from OF *denoncier,* from L *dēnuntiāre* to make an official proclamation, threaten, from DE- + *nuntiāre* to announce
▸ **deˈnouncement** *n* ▸ **deˈnouncer** *n*

de novo *Latin.* (diː ˈnəʊvəʊ) *adv* from the beginning; anew.

dense (dɛns) *adj* **1** thickly crowded or closely set. **2** thick; impenetrable. **3** *Physics.* having a high density. **4** stupid; dull. **5** (of a photographic negative) having many dark or exposed areas. ORIG C15: from L *densus* thick
▸ **ˈdensely** *adv* ▸ **ˈdenseness** *n*

densimeter (dɛnˈsɪmɪtə) *n Physics.* any instrument for measuring density.
▸ **densimetric** (ˌdɛnsɪˈmɛtrɪk) *adj* ▸ **denˈsimetry** *n*

density (ˈdɛnsɪtɪ) *n, pl* **densities. 1** the degree to which something is filled or occupied: *high density of building in towns.* **2** stupidity. **3** a measure of the compactness of a substance, expressed as its mass per unit volume. Symbol: ρ. See also **relative density. 4** a measure of a physical quantity per unit of length, area, or volume. **5** *Physics, photog.* a measure of the extent to which a substance or surface transmits or reflects light.

dent (dɛnt) *n* **1** a hollow in a surface, as one made by pressure or a blow. **2** an appreciable effect, esp. of lessening: *a dent in our resources.* ◆ *vb* (*tr*) **3** to make a dent in. ORIG C13 (in the sense: a stroke, blow): var. of DINT

dental (ˈdɛntᵊl) *adj* **1** of or relating to the teeth or dentistry. **2** *Phonetics.* pronounced with the tip of the tongue touching the backs of the upper teeth, as for *t* in French *tout.* ◆ *n* **3** *Phonetics.* a dental consonant. ORIG C16: from Med. L *dentālis,* from L *dens* tooth

dental floss *n* a waxed thread used to remove food particles from between the teeth.

dental plaque *n* a filmy deposit on the surface of a tooth consisting of a mixture of mucus, bacteria, food, etc.

dental surgeon *n* another name for **dentist.**

dentate (ˈdɛnteɪt) *adj* **1** having teeth or toothlike processes. **2** (of leaves) having a toothed margin. ORIG C19: from L *dentātus*
▸ **ˈdentately** *adv*

denti- *or before a vowel* **dent-** *combining form.* indicating a tooth: *dentine.* ORIG from L *dens, dent-*

denticulate (dɛnˈtɪkjʊlɪt, -ˌleɪt) *adj* **1** *Biol.* very finely toothed: *denticulate leaves.* **2** *Arch.* having dentils. ORIG C17: from L *denticulātus* having small teeth

dentifrice (ˈdɛntɪfrɪs) *n* any substance, esp. paste or powder, for use in cleaning the teeth. ORIG C16: from L *dentifricium,* from *dent-, dens* tooth + *fricāre* to rub

dentil (ˈdɛntɪl) *n* one of a set of small square or rectangular blocks evenly spaced to form an ornamental row. ORIG C17: from F, from obs. *dentille* a little tooth, from *dent* tooth

dentine (ˈdɛntiːn) *or* **dentin** (ˈdɛntɪn) *n* the calcified tissue comprising the bulk of a tooth. ORIG C19: from DENTI- + -IN
▸ **ˈdentinal** *adj*

dentist (ˈdɛntɪst) *n* a person qualified to practise dentistry. ORIG C18: from F *dentiste,* from *dent* tooth

dentistry (ˈdɛntɪstrɪ) *n* the branch of medical science concerned with the diagnosis and treatment of disorders of the teeth and gums.

dentition (dɛnˈtɪʃən) *n* **1** the arrangement, type, and number of the teeth in a particular species. **2** the time or process of teething. ORIG C17: from L *dentītiō* a teething

D'Entrecasteaux Islands ★ (*French* dɑ̃trəkasto) *pl n* a group of volcanic islands in the Pacific, off the SE coast of New Guinea: part of Papua New Guinea. Pop.: 49 167 (1990 est.). Area: 3141 sq. km (1213 sq. miles).

denture (ˈdɛntʃə) *n* (*usually pl*) **1** a partial or full set of artificial teeth. **2** *Rare.* a set of natural teeth. ORIG C19: from F, from *dent* tooth + -URE

denuclearize *or* **denuclearise** (dɪˈnjuːklɪəˌraɪz) *vb* **denuclearizes, denuclearizing, denuclearized** *or* **denuclearises, denuclearising, denuclearised.** (*tr*) to deprive (a state, etc.) of nuclear weapons.
▸ **deˌnucleariˈzation** *or* **deˌnucleariˈsation** *n*

denudate (ˈdɛnjʊˌdeɪt, dɪˈnjuːdeɪt) *vb* **denudates, denudating, denudated. 1** a less common word for **denude.** ◆ *adj* **2** denuded.

denude (dɪˈnjuːd) *vb* **denudes, denuding, denuded.** (*tr*) **1** to make bare; strip. **2** to expose (rock) by the erosion of the layers above.
▸ **denudation** (ˌdɛnjʊˈdeɪʃən) *n*

denumerable (dɪˈnjuːmərəbᵊl) *adj Maths.* capable of being put into a one-to-one correspondence with the positive integers; countable.
▸ **deˈnumerably** *adv*

denunciate (dɪˈnʌnsɪˌeɪt) *vb* **denunciates, denunciating, denunciated.** (*tr*) to condemn; denounce. ORIG C16: from L *dēnuntiāre;* see DENOUNCE
▸ **deˈnunciˌator** *n* ▸ **deˈnunciatory** *adj*

denunciation (dɪˌnʌnsɪˈeɪʃən) *n* **1** open condemnation; denouncing. **2** *Law, obsolete.* a charge or accusation of crime made before a public prosecutor or tribunal. **3** a formal announcement of the termination of a treaty.

Denver ★ (ˈdɛnvə) *n* a city in central Colorado: the state capital. Pop.: 497 840 (1996 est.).

Denver boot *n* a slang name for **wheel clamp.** ORIG C20: from DENVER, where the device was first used

deny (dɪˈnaɪ) *vb* **denies, denying, denied.** (*tr*) **1** to declare (a statement, etc.) to be untrue. **2** to reject as false. **3** to withhold. **4** to refuse to fulfil the expectations of: *it is hard to deny a child.* **5** to refuse to acknowledge; disown. **6** to refuse (oneself) things desired. ORIG C13: from OF *denier,* from L *dēnegāre,* from *negāre*

Denys ★ (ˈdɛnɪs; *French* dəni) *n* **Saint.** a variant spelling of (Saint) **Denis.**

deodar (ˈdiːəʊˌdɑː) *n* **1** a Himalayan cedar with drooping branches. **2** the durable fragrant highly valued wood of this tree. ORIG C19: from Hindi, from Sansk. *devadāru,* lit.: wood of the gods

deodorant (diːˈəʊdərənt) *n* **1** a substance applied to the body to suppress or mask the odour of perspiration. **2** any substance for destroying or masking odours.

deodorize *or* **deodorise** (diːˈəʊdəˌraɪz) *vb* **deodorizes, deodorizing, deodorized** *or* **deodorises, deodorising, deodorised.** (*tr*) to remove, disguise, or absorb the odour of, esp. when unpleasant.
▸ **deˌodoriˈzation** *or* **deˌodoriˈsation** *n* ▸ **deˈodorˌizer** *or* **deˈodorˌiser** *n*

deontic (diːˈɒntɪk) *adj Logic.* **a** of such ethical concepts as obligation and permissibility. **b** designating the branch of logic that deals with the formalization of these concepts. ORIG C19: from Gk *deon* duty, from impersonal *dei* it behoves, it is binding
▸ **ˌdeonˈtology** *n*

deoxidize *or* **deoxidise** (diːˈɒksɪˌdaɪz) *vb* **deoxidizes, deoxidizing, deoxidized** *or* **deoxidises, deoxidising, deoxidised. 1**

(*tr*) to remove oxygen atoms from (a compound, molecule, etc.). **2** another word for **reduce** (sense 12).
▸ **de,oxidi'zation** *or* **de,oxidi'sation** *n* ▸ **de'oxi,dizer** *or* **de'oxi,diser** *n*

deoxygenate (diː'ɒksɪdʒɪˌneɪt) *or* **deoxygenize, deoxygenise** (diː'ɒksɪdʒɪˌnaɪz) *vb* **deoxygenates, deoxygenating, deoxygenated** *or* **deoxygenizes, deoxygenizing, deoxygenized; deoxygenises, deoxygenising, deoxygenised.** (*tr*) to remove oxygen from.
▸ **de,oxygen'ation** *n*

deoxyribonuclease (diː'ɒksɪˌraɪbəʊ'njuːklɪeɪz) *n* the full name for **DNAase**.

deoxyribonucleic acid (diːˌɒksɪˌraɪbəʊnjuː'kleɪɪk) *or* **desoxyribonucleic acid** *n* the full name for **DNA**.

dep. *abbrev. for:* **1** department. **2** departure. **3** deposed. **4** deposit. **5** depot. **6** deputy.

Depardieu ★ (*French* dəpardjø) *n* **Gérard** (ʒerar). born 1948, French film actor. His films include *Jean de Florette* (1986), *Cyrano de Bergerac* (1990), and *Green Card* (1991).

depart (dɪ'pɑːt) *vb* (*mainly intr*) **1** to leave. **2** to set forth. **3** (usually foll. by *from*) to differ; vary: *to depart from normal procedure.* **4** (*tr*) to quit (arch., except in **depart this life**). ORIG C13: from OF *departir,* from DE- + *partir* to go away, divide, from L *partīrī* to divide, distribute, from *pars* a part

departed (dɪ'pɑːtɪd) *adj Euphemistic.* **a** dead. **b** (*as sing or collective n;* preceded by *the*): *the departed.*

department (dɪ'pɑːtmənt) *n* **1** a specialized division of a large concern, such as a business, store, or university. **2** a major subdivision of the administration of a government. **3** a branch of learning. **4** an administrative division in several countries, such as France. **5** *Inf.* a specialized sphere of skill or activity: *wine-making is my wife's department.* ORIG C18: from F *département,* from *départir* to divide; see DEPART
▸ **departmental** (ˌdiːpɑːt'mɛntᵊl) *adj*

departmentalize *or* **departmentalise** (ˌdiːpɑːt'mɛntᵊˌlaɪz) *vb* **departmentalizes, departmentalizing, departmentalized** *or* **departmentalises, departmentalising, departmentalised.** (*tr*) to organize into departments, esp. excessively.
▸ **ˌdepartˌmentali'zation** *or* **ˌdepartˌmentali'sation** *n*

department store *n* a large shop divided into departments selling a great many kinds of goods.

departure (dɪ'pɑːtʃə) *n* **1** the act or an instance of departing. **2** a variation from previous custom. **3** a course of action, venture, etc.: *selling is a new departure for him.* **4** *Naut.* the net distance travelled due east or west by a vessel. **5** a euphemistic word for **death.**

depend (dɪ'pɛnd) *vb* (*intr*) **1** (foll. by *on* or *upon*) to put trust (in); rely (on). **2** (usually foll. by *on* or *upon*) to be influenced or determined (by): *it all depends on you.* **3** (foll. by *on* or *upon*) to rely (on) for income, support, etc. **4** (foll. by *from*) *Rare.* to hang down. **5** to be undecided. ORIG C15: from OF, from L *dēpendēre* to hang from, from DE- + *pendēre*

dependable (dɪ'pɛndəbᵊl) *adj* able to be depended on; reliable.
▸ **de,penda'bility** *or* **de'pendableness** *n* ▸ **de'pendably** *adv*

dependant (dɪ'pɛndənt) *n* a person who depends on another person, organization, etc., for support, aid, or sustenance, esp. financial support.

> **USAGE NOTE** *Dependant* is the generally accepted correct spelling in British usage for the noun: *if you are single and have no dependants,...* The adjective should be spelt *dependent: ...tax allowance for dependent* (not *dependant*) *children....* American usage spells both adjective and noun with an *e* in the last syllable.

dependence *or US* (*sometimes*) **dependance** (dɪ'pɛndəns) *n* **1** the state or fact of being dependent, esp. for support or help. **2** reliance; trust; confidence.

dependency *or US* (*sometimes*) **dependancy** (dɪ'pɛndənsɪ) *n, pl* **dependencies** *or US* (*sometimes*) **dependancies. 1** a territory subject to a state on which it does not border. **2** a dependent or subordinate person or thing. **3** *Psychol.* overreliance on another person or on a drug, etc. **4** another word for **dependence.**

dependent *or US* (*sometimes*) **dependant** (dɪ'pɛndənt) *adj* **1** depending on a person or thing for aid, support, etc. **2** (*postpositive;* foll. by *on* or *upon*) influenced or conditioned (by); contingent (on). **3** subordinate; subject. **4** *Obs.* hanging down. ◆ *n* **5** a variant spelling (esp. US) of **dependant.**
▸ **de'pendently** *adv*

> **USAGE NOTE** See at **dependant.**

dependent clause *n Grammar.* another term for **subordinate clause.**

dependent variable *n* a variable in a mathematical equation or statement whose value depends on that taken on by the independent variable.

depersonalize *or* **depersonalise** (dɪ'pɜːsnᵊˌlaɪz) *vb* **depersonalizes, depersonalizing, depersonalized** *or* **depersonalises, depersonalising, depersonalised.** (*tr*) **1** to deprive (a person, organization, etc.) of individual or personal qualities. **2** to cause (someone) to lose his or her sense of identity.
▸ **de,personali'zation** *or* **de,personali'sation** *n*

depict (dɪ'pɪkt) *vb* (*tr*) **1** to represent by drawing, sculpture, painting, etc.; delineate; portray. **2** to represent in words; describe. ORIG C17: from L *dēpingere,* from *pingere* to paint
▸ **de'picter** *or* **de'pictor** *n* ▸ **de'piction** *n* ▸ **de'pictive** *adj*

depilate ('dɛpɪˌleɪt) *vb* **depilates, depilating, depilated.** (*tr*) to remove the hair from. ORIG C16: from L *dēpilāre,* from *pilāre* to make bald, from *pilus* hair
▸ **ˌdepi'lation** *n* ▸ **'depi,lator** *n*

depilatory (dɪ'pɪlətərɪ, -trɪ) *adj* **1** able or serving to remove hair. ◆ *n, pl* **depilatories. 2** a chemical used to remove hair from the body.

deplane (diː'pleɪn) *vb* **deplanes, deplaning, deplaned.** (*intr*) *Chiefly US. & Canad.* to disembark from an aeroplane. ORIG C20: from DE- + PLANE[1]

deplete (dɪ'pliːt) *vb* **depletes, depleting, depleted.** (*tr*) **1** to use up (supplies, money, etc.); exhaust. **2** to empty entirely or partially. ORIG C19: from L *dēplēre* to empty out, from DE- + *plēre* to fill
▸ **de'pletion** *n*

depleted uranium *n* uranium from which most of the radioactive uranium-235 isotope has been removed, used in armour-piercing shells. Abbrev.: **DU.**

depletion layer *n* a region at the interface between dissimilar zones of conductivity in a semiconductor, in which there are few charge carriers.

deplorable (dɪ'plɔːrəbᵊl) *adj* **1** lamentable. **2** worthy of censure or reproach; very bad.
▸ **de'plorably** *adv*

deplore (dɪ'plɔː) *vb* **deplores, deploring, deplored.** (*tr*) **1** to express or feel sorrow about. **2** to express or feel strong disapproval of; censure. ORIG C16: from OF, from L *dēplōrāre* to weep bitterly, from *plōrāre* to weep
▸ **de'ploringly** *adv*

deploy (dɪ'plɔɪ) *vb Chiefly mil.* **1** to adopt or cause to adopt a battle formation. **2** (*tr*) to redistribute (forces) to or within a given area. ORIG C18: from F, from L *displicāre* to unfold; see DISPLAY
▸ **de'ployment** *n*

depolarize *or* **depolarise** (diː'pəʊləˌraɪz) *vb* **depolarizes, depolarizing, depolarized** *or* **depolarises, depolarising, depolarised.** to undergo or cause to undergo a loss of polarity or polarization.
▸ **de,polari'zation** *or* **de,polari'sation** *n*

deponent (dɪ'pəʊnənt) *adj* **1** *Grammar.* (of a verb, esp. in Latin) having the inflectional endings of a passive verb but the meaning of an active verb. ◆ *n* **2** *Grammar.* a deponent verb. **3** *Law.* a person who makes an affidavit or a deposition. ORIG C16: from L *dēpōnēns* putting aside, putting down, from *dēpōnere*

depopulate (dɪ'pɒpjʊˌleɪt) *vb* **depopulates, depopulating, depopulated.** to be or cause to be reduced in population.
▸ **de,popu'lation** *n*

deport (dɪˈpɔːt) *vb* (*tr*) **1** to remove forcibly from a country; expel. **2** to conduct, hold, or behave (oneself) in a specified manner. ORIG C15: from F, from L *dēportāre* to carry away, banish, from DE- + *portāre* to carry
▸ **deˈportable** *adj*

deportation (ˌdiːpɔːˈteɪʃən) *n* the act of expelling someone from a country.

deportee (ˌdiːpɔːˈtiː) *n* a person deported or awaiting deportation.

deportment (dɪˈpɔːtmənt) *n* the manner in which a person behaves, esp. in physical bearing: *military deportment.* ORIG C17: from F, from OF *deporter* to conduct (oneself); see DEPORT

depose (dɪˈpəʊz) *vb* **deposes, deposing, deposed. 1** (*tr*) to remove from an office or position of power. **2** *Law.* to testify or give (evidence, etc.) on oath. ORIG C13: from OF: to put away, put down, from LL *dēpōnere* to depose from office, from L: to put aside

deposit (dɪˈpɒzɪt) *vb* (*tr*) **1** to put or set down, esp. carefully; place. **2** to entrust for safekeeping. **3** to place (money) in a bank or similar institution to earn interest or for safekeeping. **4** to give (money) in part payment or as security. **5** to lay down naturally: *the river deposits silt.* ◆ *n* **6a** an instance of entrusting money or valuables to a bank or similar institution. **6b** the money or valuables so entrusted. **7** money given in part payment or as security. **8** an accumulation of sediments, minerals, coal, etc. **9** any deposited material, such as a sediment. **10** a depository or storehouse. **11 on deposit.** payable as the first instalment, as when buying on hire-purchase. ORIG C17: from Med. L *dēpositāre,* from L *dēpositus* put down

deposit account *n Brit.* a bank account that earns interest and usually requires notice of withdrawal.

depositary (dɪˈpɒzɪtərɪ, -trɪ) *n, pl* **depositaries. 1** a person or group to whom something is entrusted for safety. **2** a variant spelling of **depository.**

deposition (ˌdɛpəˈzɪʃən) *n* **1** *Law.* **1a** the giving of testimony on oath. **1b** the testimony given. **1c** the sworn statement of a witness used in court in his or her absence. **2** the act or an instance of deposing. **3** the act or an instance of depositing. **4** something deposited. ORIG C14: from LL *dēpositiō* a laying down, disposal, burying, testimony

depositor (dɪˈpɒzɪtə) *n* a person who places or has money on deposit, esp. in a bank.

depository (dɪˈpɒzɪtərɪ, -trɪ) *n, pl* **depositories. 1** a store for furniture, valuables, etc.; repository. **2** a variant spelling of **depositary.** ORIG C17 (in the sense: place of a deposit): from Med. L *dēpositōrium;* C18 (in the sense: depositary): see DEPOSIT, -ORY[1]

depot (ˈdɛpəʊ; *US & Canad.* ˈdiːpəʊ) *n* **1** a storehouse or warehouse. **2** *Mil.* **2a** a store for supplies. **2b** a training and holding centre for recruits and replacements. **3** *Chiefly Brit.* a building used for the storage and servicing of buses or railway engines. **4** *US & Canad.* a bus or railway station. ORIG C18: from F *dépôt,* from L *dēpositum* a deposit, trust

deprave (dɪˈpreɪv) *vb* **depraves, depraving, depraved.** (*tr*) to make morally bad; corrupt. ORIG C14: from L *dēprāvāre* to distort, corrupt, from DE- + *prāvus* crooked
▸ **depravation** (ˌdɛprəˈveɪʃən) *n* ▸ **deˈpraved** *adj*

depravity (dɪˈprævɪtɪ) *n, pl* **depravities.** the state or an instance of moral corruption.

deprecate (ˈdɛprɪˌkeɪt) *vb* **deprecates, deprecating, deprecated.** (*tr*) **1** to express disapproval of; protest against. **2** to depreciate; belittle. ORIG C17: from L *dēprecārī* to avert, ward off by entreaty, from DE- + *precārī* to PRAY
▸ **ˈdepreˌcating** *adj* ▸ **ˈdepreˌcatingly** *adv* ▸ **ˌdepreˈcation** *n* ▸ **ˈdeprecative** *adj* ▸ **ˈdepreˌcator** *n*

> **USAGE NOTE** See at **depreciate.**

deprecatory (ˈdɛprɪkətərɪ) *adj* **1** expressing disapproval; protesting. **2** expressing apology; apologetic.
▸ **ˈdeprecatorily** *adv*

depreciate (dɪˈpriːʃɪˌeɪt) *vb* **depreciates, depreciating, depreciated. 1** to reduce or decline in value or price. **2** (*tr*) to lessen the value of by derision, criticism, etc. ORIG C15: from LL *dēpretiāre* to lower the price of, from L DE- + *pretium* PRICE
▸ **deˈpreciˌatingly** *adv* ▸ **depreciatory** (dɪˈpriːʃɪətərɪ) *or* **deˈpreciative** *adj*

> **USAGE NOTE** The form *self-depreciating,* which used to be considered incorrect, is now in quite common use, and is generally agreed to be an acceptable alternative to *self-deprecating.*

depreciation (dɪˌpriːʃɪˈeɪʃən) *n* **1** *Accounting.* **1a** the reduction in value of a fixed asset due to use, obsolescence, etc. **1b** the amount deducted from gross profit to allow for this. **2** the act or an instance of depreciating or belittling. **3** a decrease in the exchange value of a currency brought about by excess supply of that currency under conditions of fluctuating exchange rates.

depredation (ˌdɛprɪˈdeɪʃən) *n* the act or an instance of plundering; pillage. ORIG C15: from LL *dēpraedārī* to ravage

depress (dɪˈprɛs) *vb* (*tr*) **1** to lower in spirits; make gloomy. **2** to weaken the force, or energy of. **3** to lower prices of. **4** to press or push down. ORIG C14: from OF *depresser,* from L *dēprimere* from DE- + *premere* to PRESS[1]
▸ **deˈpressing** *adj* ▸ **deˈpressingly** *adv*

depressant (dɪˈprɛsᵊnt) *adj* **1** *Med.* able to reduce nervous or functional activity. **2** causing gloom; depressing. ◆ *n* **3** a depressant drug.

depressed (dɪˈprɛst) *adj* **1** low in spirits; downcast. **2** lower than the surrounding surface. **3** pressed down or flattened. **4** Also: **distressed.** characterized by economic hardship, such as unemployment: *a depressed area.* **5** lowered in force, intensity, or amount. **6** *Bot., zool.* flattened.

depression (dɪˈprɛʃən) *n* **1** a depressing or being depressed. **2** a sunken place. **3** a mental disorder characterized by feelings of gloom and inadequacy. **4** *Pathol.* an abnormal lowering of the rate of any physiological activity or function. **5** an economic condition characterized by unemployment, low investment, etc.; slump. **6** Also called: **cyclone, low.** *Meteorol.* a body of moving air below normal atmospheric pressure, which often brings rain. **7** (esp. in surveying and astronomy) the angular distance of an object below the horizontal plane.

Depression (dɪˈprɛʃən) *n* (usually preceded by *the*) the worldwide economic depression of the early 1930s, when there was mass unemployment.

depressive (dɪˈprɛsɪv) *adj* **1** tending to depress. **2** *Psychol.* tending to be subject to periods of depression.
▸ **deˈpressively** *adv*

depressor (dɪˈprɛsə) *n* **1** a person or thing that depresses. **2** any muscle that draws down a part. **3** *Med.* an instrument used to press down or aside an organ or part.

depressurize *or* **depressurise** (dɪˈprɛʃəˌraɪz) *vb* **depressurizes, depressurizing, depressurized** *or* **depressurises, depressurising, depressurised.** (*tr*) to reduce the pressure of a gas inside (an enclosed space), as in an aircraft cabin.
▸ **deˌpressuriˈzation** *or* **deˌpressuriˈsation** *n*

deprive (dɪˈpraɪv) *vb* **deprives, depriving, deprived.** (*tr*) **1** (foll. by *of*) to prevent from possessing or enjoying; dispossess (of). **2** *Arch.* to depose; demote. ORIG C14: from OF, from Med. L *dēprīvāre,* from L DE- + *prīvāre* to deprive of
▸ **deˈprival** *n* ▸ **deprivation** (ˌdɛprɪˈveɪʃən) *n*

deprived (dɪˈpraɪvd) *adj* lacking adequate food, shelter, education, etc.: *deprived inner-city areas.*

deprogramme *or esp. US* **deprogram** (diːˈprəʊgræm) *vb* **deprogrammes, deprogramming, deprogrammed** *or esp. US* **deprograms, deprogramming, deprogrammed.** to attempt to reverse the brainwashing of (a person).

dept *abbrev. for* department.

depth (dɛpθ) *n* **1** the distance downwards, backwards, or inwards. **2** the quality of being deep; deepness. **3** intensity of emotion. **4** profundity of moral character; sagacity; integrity. **5** complexity or abstruseness, as of thought. **6** intensity, as of silence, colour, etc. **7** lowness of pitch. **8** (*often pl*) a deep, inner, or remote part, such as an inaccessible region of a country. **9** (*often pl*) the most intense or severe part: *the depths of winter.* **10** (*usually pl*) a low moral state. **11** (*often pl*) a vast space or abyss. **12 beyond** *or* **out of one's depth. 12a** in water deeper than one is tall. **12b** beyond the range of one's competence or understanding. ORIG C14: from *dep* DEEP + -TH[1]

depth charge *or* **bomb** *n* a bomb used to attack submarines that explodes at a preset depth of water.

depth gauge *n* a device attached to a drill bit to prevent the hole from exceeding a predetermined depth.

depth of field *n* the range of distance in front of and behind an object focused by an optical instrument, such as a camera or microscope, within which other objects will also appear sharply defined in the resulting image.

depth psychology *n Psychol.* the study of unconscious motives and attitudes.

depuration (ˌdɛpjuˈreɪʃən) *n* the act or process of eliminating impurities; self-purification. ORIG C17: from F or Med. L, ult. from L *pūrus* pure

deputation (ˌdɛpjuˈteɪʃən) *n* **1** the act of appointing a person or body of people to represent others. **2** a person or body of people so appointed; delegation.

depute *vb* (dɪˈpjuːt), **deputes, deputing, deputed.** (*tr*) **1** to appoint as an agent. **2** to assign (authority, duties, etc.) to a deputy. ◆ *n* (ˈdɛpjuːt). **3** *Scot.* **3a** a deputy. **3b** (*as modifier, usually postpositive*): *a sheriff-depute.* ORIG C15: from OF, from LL *dēputāre* to assign, allot, from L DE- + *putāre* to think, consider

deputize *or* **deputise** (ˈdɛpjuˌtaɪz) *vb* **deputizes, deputizing, deputized** *or* **deputises, deputising, deputised.** to appoint or act as deputy.

deputy (ˈdɛpjutɪ) *n, pl* **deputies. 1a** a person appointed to act on behalf of or represent another. **1b** (*as modifier*): *the deputy chairman.* **2** a member of a legislative assembly in various countries, such as France. ORIG C16: from OF, from *deputer* to appoint; see DEPUTE

De Quincey ★ (də ˈkwɪnsɪ) *n* **Thomas.** 1785–1859, British critic and essayist, noted particularly for his *Confessions of an English Opium Eater* (1821).

der. *abbrev. for:* **1** derivation. **2** derivative.

deracinate (dɪˈræsɪˌneɪt) *vb* **deracinates, deracinating, deracinated.** (*tr*) to pull up by or as if by the roots; uproot. ORIG C16: from OF *desraciner,* from *des-* DIS-[1] + *racine* root, from LL, from L *rādīx* a root
▸ **deˌraciˈnation** *n*

derail (dɪˈreɪl) *vb* to go or cause to go off the rails, as a train, tram, etc.
▸ **deˈrailment** *n*

Derain ★ (*French* dərɛ̃) *n* **André** (ɑ̃dre). 1880–1954, French Fauvist painter.

derange (dɪˈreɪndʒ) *vb* **deranges, deranging, deranged.** (*tr*) **1** to throw into disorder; disarrange. **2** to disturb the action of. **3** to make insane. ORIG C18: from OF *desrengier,* from des- DIS-[1] + *reng* row, order
▸ **deˈrangement** *n*

derby (ˈdɜːrbɪ) *n, pl* **derbies.** the US and Canad. name for **bowler**[2].

Derby[1] (ˈdɑːbɪ; *US* ˈdɜːrbɪ) *n, pl* **Derbies. 1 the.** an annual horse race run at Epsom Downs, Surrey, since 1780. **2** (*usually not cap.*) any of various other horse races. **3 local derby.** a football match between two teams from the same area. ORIG C18: after the twelfth Earl of *Derby* (died 1834), who founded the race in 1780

Derby[2] ★ (ˈdɑːbɪ) *n* **1** a city in central England, in Derbyshire: seat of the University of Derby (1993). Pop.: 223 836 (1991). **2** a unitary authority in central England, in Derbyshire. Pop.: 233 700 (1996 est.). Area: 78 sq. km (30 sq. miles). **3** a firm pale-coloured cheese. **4 sage Derby.** a green-and-white Derby cheese flavoured with sage.

Derby[3] ★ (ˈdɑːbɪ) *n* **Earl of.** title of *Edward George Geoffrey Smith Stanley.* 1799–1869, British statesman; Conservative prime minister (1852; 1858–59; 1866–68).

Derbyshire ★ (ˈdɑːbɪˌʃɪə, -ʃə) *n* a county of N central England: contains the Peak District and several resorts with mineral springs. Administrative centre: Matlock. Pop. (excluding Derby unitary authority): 728 300 (1996 est.). Area (excluding Derby unitary authority): 2551 sq. km (985 sq. miles).

derecognize *or* **derecognise** (diːˈrɛkəgˌnaɪz) *vb* **derecognizes, derecognizing, derecognized** *or* **derecognises, derecognising, derecognised.** (*tr*) to cease to recognize (a trade union) as having special negotiating rights within a company or industry.
▸ **ˌderecogˈnition** *n*

deregulate (diːˈrɛgjuˌleɪt) *vb* **deregulates, deregulating, deregulated.** (*tr*) to remove regulations from.
▸ **deˌreguˈlation** *n*

derelict (ˈdɛrɪlɪkt) *adj* **1** deserted or abandoned, as by an owner, occupant, etc. **2** falling into ruins. **3** neglectful of duty; remiss. ◆ *n* **4** a social outcast or vagrant. **5** property deserted or abandoned by an owner, occupant, etc. **6** a vessel abandoned at sea. **7** a person who is neglectful of duty. ORIG C17: from L, from *dērelinquere* to abandon, from DE- + *relinquere* to leave

dereliction (ˌdɛrɪˈlɪkʃən) *n* **1** conscious or wilful neglect (esp. in **dereliction of duty**). **2** an abandoning or being abandoned. **3** *Law.* accretion of dry land gained by the gradual receding of the sea.

derestrict (ˌdiːrɪˈstrɪkt) *vb* (*tr*) to render or leave free from restriction, esp. a road from speed limits.
▸ **ˌdereˈstriction** *n*

deride (dɪˈraɪd) *vb* **derides, deriding, derided.** (*tr*) to speak of or treat with contempt or ridicule; scoff at. ORIG C16: from L *dērīdēre* to laugh to scorn, from DE- + *rīdēre* to laugh, smile
▸ **deˈrider** *n* ▸ **deˈridingly** *adv*

de rigueur *French.* (də rigœr) *adj* required by etiquette or fashion. ORIG lit.: of strictness

derision (dɪˈrɪʒən) *n* the act of deriding; mockery; scorn. ORIG C15: from LL *dērīsiō,* from L *dērīsus;* see DERIDE
▸ **deˈrisible** *adj*

derisive (dɪˈraɪsɪv) *adj* characterized by derision; mocking; scornful.
▸ **deˈrisively** *adv* ▸ **deˈrisiveness** *n*

derisory (dɪˈraɪsərɪ) *adj* **1** subject to or worthy of derision. **2** another word for **derisive.**

deriv. *abbrev. for:* **1** derivation. **2** derivative. **3** derived.

derivation (ˌdɛrɪˈveɪʃən) *n* **1** a deriving or being derived. **2** the origin or descent of something, such as a word. **3** something derived; a derivative. **4a** the process of deducing a mathematical theorem, formula, etc., as a necessary consequence of a set of accepted statements. **4b** this sequence of statements.
▸ **ˌderiˈvational** *adj*

derivative (dɪˈrɪvətɪv) *adj* **1** derived. **2** based on other sources; not original. ◆ *n* **3** a term, idea, etc., that is based on or derived from another in the same class. **4** a word derived from another word. **5** *Chem.* a compound that is formed from, or can be regarded as formed from, a structurally related compound. **6** *Maths.* **6a** Also called: **differential coefficient, first derivative.** the change of a function, f(x), with respect to an infinitesimally small change in the independent variable, x. **6b** the rate of change of one quantity with respect to another. **7** *Finance.* a financial instrument, such as a futures contract or option, the price of which is largely determined by the commodity, currency, share price, interest rate, etc., to which it is linked.
▸ **deˈrivatively** *adv*

derive (dɪˈraɪv) *vb* **derives, deriving, derived. 1** (usually foll. by *from*) to draw or be drawn (from) in source or origin. **2** (*tr*) to obtain by reasoning; deduce; infer. **3** (*tr*) to trace the source or development of. **4** (usually foll. by *from*) to produce or be produced (from) by a chemical reaction. ORIG C14: from OF: to spring from, from L *dērīvāre* to draw off, from DE- + *rīvus* a stream
▸ **deˈrivable** *adj* ▸ **deˈriver** *n*

derived unit *n* a unit of measurement obtained by multiplication or division of the base units of a system without the introduction of numerical factors.

-derm *n combining form.* indicating skin: *endoderm.* ORIG via F from Gk *derma* skin

★ people and places

derma (ˈdɜːmə) *n* another name for **corium**. Also: **derm**. ORIG C18: NL, from Gk: skin

dermal (ˈdɛːməl) *adj* of or relating to the skin.

dermatitis (ˌdɜːməˈtaɪtɪs) *n* inflammation of the skin.

dermato-, derma- *or before a vowel* **dermat-, derm-** *combining form.* indicating skin: *dermatitis.* ORIG from Gk *derma* skin

dermatology (ˌdɜːməˈtɒlədʒɪ) *n* the branch of medicine concerned with the skin and its diseases.
▸ **dermatological** (ˌdɜːmətəˈlɒdʒɪkᵊl) *adj* ▸ ˌ**dermaˈtologist** *n*

dermis (ˈdɜːmɪs) *n* another name for **corium**. ORIG C19: NL, from EPIDERMIS
▸ ˈ**dermic** *adj*

dernier cri *French.* (dɛrnje kri) *n* **le** (lə). the latest fashion; the last word. ORIG lit.: last cry

derogate (ˈdɛrəˌgeɪt) *vb* **derogates, derogating, derogated. 1** (*intr;* foll. by *from*) to cause to seem inferior; detract. **2** (*intr;* foll. by *from*) to deviate in standard or quality. **3** (*tr*) to cause to seem inferior, etc.; disparage. **4** (*tr*) to curtail the application of (a law or regulation). ORIG C15: from L *dērogāre* to repeal some part of a law, modify it, from DE- + *rogāre* to ask, propose a law
▸ ˌ**deroˈgation** *n* ▸ **derogative** (dɪˈrɒgətɪv) *adj*

derogatory (dɪˈrɒgətərɪ) *adj* tending or intended to detract, disparage, or belittle; intentionally offensive.
▸ **deˈrogatorily** *adv*

derrick (ˈdɛrɪk) *n* **1** a simple crane having lifting tackle slung from a boom. **2** the framework erected over an oil well to enable drill tubes to be raised and lowered. ORIG C17 (in the sense: gallows): from *Derrick,* celebrated hangman at Tyburn, London

Derrida ★ (*French* dɛrɪdɑ) *n* **Jacques** (ʒɑk). born 1930, French philosopher and literary critic, regarded as the founder of deconstruction: author of *L'Écriture et la différence* (1967).

derrière (ˌdɛrɪˈɛə) *n* a euphemistic word for **buttocks**. ORIG C18: lit.: behind (prep), from OF *deriere,* from L *dē retrō* from the back

derring-do (ˈdɛrɪŋˈduː) *n Arch. or literary.* boldness or bold action. ORIG C16: from ME *durring don* daring to do, from *durren* to dare + *don* to do

derringer *or* **deringer** (ˈdɛrɪndʒə) *n* a short-barrelled pocket pistol of large calibre. ORIG C19: after Henry *Deringer,* US gunsmith, who invented it

derris (ˈdɛrɪs) *n* **1** an East Indian woody climbing plant. **2** an insecticide made from its powdered roots. ORIG C19: NL, from Gk: covering, leather, from *deros* skin, hide, from *derein* to skin

Derry ★ (ˈdɛrɪ) *n* **1** Also called: **Londonderry**. a district in NW Northern Ireland, bordering the Irish Republic: textiles, light industry, agriculture. Administrative centre: Londonderry. Pop.: 95 371 (1991). Area: 384 sq. km (148 sq. miles). **2** another name for **Londonderry** (senses 1 and 2).

derv (dɜːv) *n* a Brit. name for **diesel oil** when used for road transport. ORIG C20: from *d(iesel) e(ngine) r(oad) v(ehicle)*

dervish (ˈdɜːvɪʃ) *n* a member of any of various Muslim orders of ascetics, some of which (**whirling dervishes**) are noted for a frenzied, ecstatic, whirling dance. ORIG C16: from Turkish, from Persian *darvīsh* mendicant monk

Derwent ★ (ˈdɜːwənt) *n* **1** a river in S Australia, in S Tasmania, flowing southeast to the Tasman Sea. Length: 172 km (107 miles). **2** a river in N central England, in N Derbyshire, flowing southeast to the River Trent. Length: 96 km (60 miles). **3** a river in N England, in Yorkshire, rising on the North York Moors and flowing south to the River Ouse. Length: 92 km (57 miles). **4** a river in NW England, in Cumbria, rising on the Borrowdale Fells and flowing north and west to the Irish Sea. Length: 54 km (34 miles).

Derwentwater ★ (ˈdɜːwəntˌwɔːtə) *n* a lake in NW England, in Cumbria in the Lake District. Area: about 8 sq. km (3 sq. miles).

DES (in Britain) *abbrev. for* (the former) Department of Education and Science.

Desai ★ (dɛˈsaɪ) *n* **Morarji** (**Ranchhodji**) (məˈrɑːdʒɪ). 1896–1995, Indian statesman. He founded the Janata party in opposition to Indira Gandhi, whom he defeated in the 1977 election; prime minister of India (1977–79).

desalination (diːˌsælɪˈneɪʃən) *or* **desalinization, desalinisation** *n* the process of removing salt, esp. from sea water.

descale (ˌdiːˈskeɪl) *vb* **descales, descaling, descaled.** (*tr*) to remove the hard deposit formed by chemicals in water from (a kettle, pipe, etc.).

descant (ˈdɛskænt) *n* **1** Also called: **discant**. a decorative counterpoint added above a basic melody. **2** a comment or discourse. ◆ *adj* **3** Also: **discant**. of the highest member in common use in a family of musical instruments: *a descant recorder.* ◆ *vb* (*intr*) **4** Also: **discant**. (often foll. by *on* or *upon*) to perform a descant. **5** (often foll. by *on* or *upon*) to discourse or make comments. **6** *Arch.* to sing sweetly. ORIG C14: from OF, from Med. L *discanthus,* from L DIS-[1] + *cantus* song
▸ **desˈcanter** *n*

Descartes ★ (ˈdeɪˌkɑːt; *French* dekart) *n* **René** (rəne). 1596–1650, French philosopher and mathematician. He is regarded as the founder of modern philosophy and of analytic geometry. His works include *Meditationes de Prima Philosophia* (1641) and *Principia Philosophiae* (1644). Related adj: **Cartesian**.

descend (dɪˈsɛnd) *vb* (*mainly intr*) **1** (*also tr*) to move down (a slope, staircase, etc.). **2** to lead or extend down; slope. **3** to move to a lower level, pitch, etc.; fall. **4** (often foll. by *from*) to be connected by a blood relationship (to a dead or extinct individual, species, etc.). **5** to be inherited. **6** to sink or come down in morals or behaviour. **7** (often foll. by *on* or *upon*) to arrive or attack in a sudden or overwhelming way. **8** (of the sun, moon, etc.) to move towards the horizon. ORIG C13: from OF, from L *dēscendere,* from DE- + *scandere* to climb
▸ **desˈcendable** *or* **desˈcendible** *adj*

descendant (dɪˈsɛndənt) *n* **1** a person, animal, or plant when described as descended from an individual, race, species, etc. **2** something that derives from an earlier form. ◆ *adj* **3** a variant spelling of **descendent**.

descendent (dɪˈsɛndənt) *adj* descending.

descender (dɪˈsɛndə) *n* **1** *Printing.* the part of certain lower-case letters, such as j, p, or y, that extends below the body of the letter. **2** a person or thing that descends.

descent (dɪˈsɛnt) *n* **1** the act of descending. **2** a downward slope. **3** a path or way leading downwards. **4** derivation from an ancestor; lineage. **5** a generation in a particular lineage. **6** a decline or degeneration. **7** a movement or passage in degree or state from higher to lower. **8** (often foll. by *on*) a sudden and overwhelming arrival or attack. **9** *Property law.* (formerly) the transmission of real property to the heir.

deschool (ˌdiːˈskuːl) *vb* (*tr*) to separate education from the institution of school and operate through the pupil's life experience as opposed to a set curriculum.

describe (dɪˈskraɪb) *vb* **describes, describing, described.** (*tr*) **1** to give an account or representation of in words. **2** to pronounce or label. **3** to draw a line or figure, such as a circle. ORIG C15: from L *dēscrībere* to copy off, write out, from DE- + *scrībere* to write
▸ **deˈscribable** *adj* ▸ **deˈscriber** *n*

description (dɪˈskrɪpʃən) *n* **1** a statement or account that describes. **2** the act, process, or technique of describing. **3** sort or variety: *reptiles of every description.*

descriptive (dɪˈskrɪptɪv) *adj* **1** characterized by or containing description. **2** *Grammar.* (of an adjective) serving to describe the referent of the noun modified, as for example the adjective *brown* as contrasted with *my.* **3** relating to description or classification rather than explanation or prescription.
▸ **deˈscriptively** *adv* ▸ **deˈscriptiveness** *n*

descry (dɪˈskraɪ) *vb* **descries, descrying, descried.** (*tr*) **1** to catch sight of. **2** to discover by looking carefully. ORIG C14: from OF *descrier* to proclaim, DECRY

desecrate (ˈdɛsɪˌkreɪt) *vb* **desecrates, desecrating, desecrated.** (*tr*) **1** to violate the sacred character of (an object or place) by destructive, blasphemous, or sacrilegious action. **2** to deconsecrate. ORIG C17: from DE- + CONSECRATE
▸ ˈ**deseˌcrator** *or* ˈ**deseˌcrater** *n* ▸ ˌ**deseˈcration** *n*

desegregate (diːˈsɛɡrɪˌɡeɪt) *vb* **desegregates, desegregating, desegregated.** to end racial segregation in (a school or other public institution).
▸ **ˌdesegreˈgation** *n*

deselect (ˌdiːsɪˈlɛkt) *vb* (*tr*) *Brit. politics.* (of a constituency organization) to refuse to select (an existing MP) for reelection.
▸ **ˌdeseˈlection** *n*

desensitize *or* **desensitise** (diːˈsɛnsɪˌtaɪz) *vb* **desensitizes, desensitizing, desensitized** *or* **desensitises, desensitising, desensitised.** (*tr*) to render less sensitive or insensitive: *the patient was desensitized to the allergen.*
▸ **deˌsensitiˈzation** *or* **deˌsensitiˈsation** *n* ▸ **deˈsensiˌtizer** *or* **deˈsensiˌtiser** *n*

desert[1] (ˈdɛzət) *n* **1** a region that is devoid or almost devoid of vegetation, esp. because of low rainfall. **2** an uncultivated uninhabited region. **3** a place which lacks some desirable feature or quality: *a cultural desert.* **4** (*modifier*) of, relating to, or like a desert. ORIG C13: from OF, from Church L *dēsertum,* from L *dēserere* to abandon, lit.: to sever one's links with, from DE- + *serere* to bind together

desert[2] (dɪˈzɜːt) *vb* **1** (*tr*) to abandon (a person, place, etc.) without intending to return, esp. in violation of a promise or obligation. **2** *Mil.* to abscond from (a post or duty) with no intention of returning. **3** (*tr*) to fail (someone) in time of need. ORIG C15: from F *déserter,* from LL *dēsertāre,* from L *dēserere* to forsake; see DESERT[1]
▸ **deˈserted** *adj* ▸ **deˈserter** *n*

desert[3] (dɪˈzɜːt) *n* **1** (*often pl*) just reward or punishment. **2** the state of deserving a reward or punishment. ORIG C13: from OF *deserte,* from *deservir* to DESERVE

desert boots *pl n* ankle-high boots, often of suede, with laces and soft soles.

desertification (dɪˌzɜːtɪfɪˈkeɪʃən) *n* the transformation of fertile land into an arid or semiarid region as a result of intensive farming, soil erosion, etc.

desertion (dɪˈzɜːʃən) *n* **1** a deserting or being deserted. **2** *Law.* wilful abandonment, esp. of one's spouse or children.

desert island *n* a small remote tropical island.

desert pea *n* an Australian trailing leguminous plant with scarlet flowers.

desert rat *n* **1** a jerboa inhabiting the deserts of N Africa. **2** *Brit. inf.* a soldier who served in North Africa with the British 7th Armoured Division in 1941–42.

deserve (dɪˈzɜːv) *vb* **deserves, deserving, deserved. 1** (*tr*) to be entitled to or worthy of; merit. **2** (*intr;* foll. by *of*) *Obs.* to be worthy. ORIG C13: from OF *deservir,* from L *dēservīre* to serve devotedly, from DE- + *servīre* to SERVE

deserved (dɪˈzɜːvd) *adj* rightfully earned; justified; warranted.
▸ **deservedly** (dɪˈzɜːvɪdlɪ) *adv* ▸ **deservedness** (dɪˈzɜːvɪdnɪs) *n*

deserving (dɪˈzɜːvɪŋ) *adj* (often *postpositive* and foll. by *of*) worthy, esp. of praise or reward.
▸ **deˈservingly** *adv* ▸ **deˈservingness** *n*

deshabille (ˌdeɪzæˈbiːl) *or* **dishabille** *n* the state of being partly or carelessly dressed. ORIG C17: from F *déshabillé,* from *dés* DIS-[1] + *habiller* to dress

de Sica ★ (*Italian* de ˈsiːka) *n* **Vittorio** (vitˈtɔːrjo). 1902–74, Italian film actor and director. His films, in the realist tradition, include *Shoeshine* (1946) and *Bicycle Thieves* (1948).

desiccant (ˈdɛsɪkənt) *adj* **1** drying. ◆ *n* **2** a substance that absorbs water and is used to remove moisture. ORIG C17: from L *dēsiccāns* drying up; see DESICCATE

desiccate (ˈdɛsɪˌkeɪt) *vb* **desiccates, desiccating, desiccated. 1** (*tr*) to remove most of the water from; dehydrate. **2** (*tr*) to preserve (food) by removing moisture; dry. **3** (*intr*) to become dried up. ORIG C16: from L *dēsiccāre* to dry up, from DE- + *siccāre,* from *siccus* dry
▸ **ˈdesicˌcated** *adj* ▸ **ˌdesicˈcation** *n*

desiderate (dɪˈzɪdəˌreɪt) *vb* **desiderates, desiderating, desiderated.** (*tr*) to feel the lack of or need for; miss. ORIG C17: from L *dēsīderāre,* from DE- + *sīdus* star; see DESIRE
▸ **deˌsiderˈation** *n*

desideratum (dɪˌzɪdəˈrɑːtəm) *n, pl* **desiderata** (-tə). something lacked and wanted. ORIG C17: from L; see DESIDERATE

design (dɪˈzaɪn) *vb* **1** to work out the structure or form of (something), as by making a sketch or plans. **2** to plan and make (something) artistically or skilfully. **3** (*tr*) to invent. **4** (*tr*) to intend, as for a specific purpose; plan. ◆ *n* **5** a plan or preliminary drawing. **6** the arrangement, elements, or features of an artistic or decorative work: *the design of the desk is Chippendale.* **7** a finished artistic or decorative creation. **8** the art of designing. **9** a plan or project. **10** an intention; purpose. **11** (*often pl;* often foll. by *on* or *against*) a plot, often to gain possession of (something) by illegitimate means. ORIG C16: from L *dēsignāre* to mark out, describe, from DE- + *signāre,* from *signum* a mark
▸ **deˈsignable** *adj*

designate *vb* (ˈdɛzɪɡˌneɪt). **designates, designating, designated.** (*tr*) **1** to indicate or specify. **2** to give a name to; style; entitle. **3** to select or name for an office or duty; appoint. ◆ *adj* (ˈdɛzɪɡnɪt, -ˌneɪt). **4** (*immediately postpositive*) appointed, but not yet in office: *a minister designate.* ORIG C15: from L *dēsignātus* marked out, defined; see DESIGN
▸ **ˈdesigˌnator** *n*

designation (ˌdɛzɪɡˈneɪʃən) *n* **1** something that designates, such as a name. **2** the act of designating or the fact of being designated.

designedly (dɪˈzaɪnɪdlɪ) *adv* by intention or design; on purpose.

designer (dɪˈzaɪnə) *n* **1** a person who devises and executes designs, as for clothes, machines, etc. **2** (*modifier*) designed by and bearing the label of a well-known fashion designer: *designer jeans.* **3** (*modifier*) (of things, ideas, etc.) fashionably trendy: *designer stubble.* **4** (*modifier*) (of cells, chemicals, etc.) designed or produced to perform a specific function or combat a specific problem: *designer insecticide.* **5** a person who devises plots; intriguer.

designer drug *n* **1** *Med.* a synthetic antibiotic designed to be effective against a particular bacterium. **2** a synthetic drug that has the same properties as an illegal narcotic or hallucinogen but can be manufactured legally.

designing (dɪˈzaɪnɪŋ) *adj* artful and scheming.

desirable (dɪˈzaɪərəbᵊl) *adj* **1** worthy of desire: *a desirable residence.* **2** arousing desire, esp. sexual desire; attractive.
▸ **deˌsiraˈbility** *or* **deˈsirableness** *n* ▸ **deˈsirably** *adv*

desire (dɪˈzaɪə) *vb* **desires, desiring, desired.** (*tr*) **1** to wish or long for; crave. **2** to request; ask for. ◆ *n* **3** a wish or longing. **4** an expressed wish; request. **5** sexual appetite. **6** a person or thing that is desired. ORIG C13: from OF, from L *dēsīderāre* to desire earnestly; see DESIDERATE
▸ **deˈsirer** *n*

desirous (dɪˈzaɪərəs) *adj* (usually *postpositive* and foll. by *of*) having or expressing desire (for).

desist (dɪˈzɪst) *vb* (*intr;* often foll. by *from*) to cease, as from an action; stop or abstain. ORIG C15: from OF, from L *dēsistere* to leave off, stand apart, from DE- + *sistere* to stand, halt

desk (dɛsk) *n* **1** a piece of furniture with a writing surface and usually drawers or other compartments. **2** a service counter or table in a public building, such as a hotel. **3** a support for the book from which services are read in a church. **4** the editorial section of a newspaper, etc., responsible for a particular subject: *the news desk.* **5** a music stand shared by two orchestral players. ORIG C14: from Med. L *desca* table, from L *discus* disc, dish

desk-bound *adj* obliged by one's occupation to work sitting at a desk.

desk editor *n* (in a publishing house) an editor responsible for the preparation and checking of manuscripts for printing.

deskill (diːˈskɪl) *vb* (*tr*) **1** to mechanize or computerize (a job) so that little skill is required to do it. **2** to deprive (employees) of the opportunity for skilled work.

desktop (ˈdɛskˌtɒp) *n* (*modifier*) denoting a computer

★ people and places

system, esp. for word processing, that is small enough to use at a desk.

desktop publishing *n* a means of publishing reports, advertising material, etc., to near-typeset quality using a desktop computer and a laser printer. Abbrev.: **DTP**.

desman (ˈdɛsmən) *n, pl* **desmans.** either of two molelike amphibious mammals, the Russian desman or the Pyrenean desman, with dense fur and webbed feet. ORIG C18: from Swedish *desmansråtta,* from *desman* musk + *råtta* rat

Des Moines ★ (də ˈmɔɪn, ˈmɔɪnz) *n* **1** a city in S central Iowa: state capital. Pop.: 193 422 (1996 est.). **2** a river in the N central US, rising in SW Minnesota and flowing southeast to join the Mississippi. Length: 861 km (535 miles).

Desmoulins ★ (*French* dɛmulɛ̃) *n* (**Lucie Simplice**) **Camille** (**Benoît**) (kamij). 1760–94, French revolutionary leader, pamphleteer, and orator.

desolate *adj* (ˈdɛsəlɪt). **1** uninhabited; deserted. **2** made uninhabitable; laid waste; devastated. **3** without friends, hope, or encouragement. **4** dismal; depressing. ◆ *vb* (ˈdɛsəˌleɪt), **desolates, desolating, desolated.** (*tr*) **5** to deprive of inhabitants; depopulate. **6** to lay waste; devastate. **7** to make wretched or forlorn. **8** to forsake or abandon. ORIG C14: from L *dēsōlāre* to leave alone, from DE- + *sōlāre* to make lonely, lay waste, from *sōlus* alone
▸ **ˈdesoˌlater** *or* **ˈdesoˌlator** *n* ▸ **ˈdesolately** *adv* ▸ **ˈdesolateness** *n*

desolation (ˌdɛsəˈleɪʃən) *n* **1** a desolating or being desolated; ruin or devastation. **2** solitary misery; wretchedness. **3** a desolate region.

De Soto ★ (də ˈsəutəu; *Spanish* de ˈsoto) *n* **Hernando** (erˈnando). ?1500–42, Spanish explorer, who discovered the Mississippi River (1541). Also called: **Fernando De Soto** (ferˈnando).

despair (dɪˈspɛə) *vb* **1** (*intr;* often foll. by *of*) to lose or give up hope: *I despair of his coming.* ◆ *n* **2** total loss of hope. **3** a person or thing that causes hopelessness or for which there is no hope. ORIG C14: from OF *despoir* hopelessness, from *desperer* to despair, from L *dēspērāre,* from DE- + *spērāre* to hope

despairing (dɪˈspɛərɪŋ) *adj* hopeless, despondent; feeling or showing despair.
▸ **deˈspairingly** *adv*

despatch (dɪˈspætʃ) *vb* (*tr*), *n* a less common spelling of **dispatch.**
▸ **desˈpatcher** *n*

Despenser ★ (dɪsˈpɛnsə) *n* **Hugh le,** Earl of Winchester. 1262–1326, English statesman, a favourite of Edward II. Together with his son **Hugh,** *the Younger* (?1290–1326), he was executed by the king's enemies.

desperado (ˌdɛspəˈrɑːdəu) *n, pl* **desperadoes** *or* **desperados.** a reckless or desperate person, esp. one ready to commit any violent illegal act. ORIG C17: prob. pseudo-Spanish var. of obs. *desperate* (n)

desperate (ˈdɛspərɪt, -prɪt) *adj* **1** careless of danger, as from despair. **2** (of an act) reckless; risky. **3** used or undertaken as a last resort. **4** critical; very grave: *in desperate need.* **5** (often *postpositive* and foll. by *for*) in distress and having a great need or desire. **6** moved by or showing despair. ORIG C15: from L *dēspērāre* to have no hope; see DESPAIR
▸ **ˈdesperately** *adv* ▸ **ˈdesperateness** *n*

desperation (ˌdɛspəˈreɪʃən) *n* **1** desperate recklessness. **2** the state of being desperate.

despicable (dɪˈspɪkəbᵊl, ˈdɛspɪk-) *adj* worthy of being despised; contemptible; mean. ORIG C16: from LL *dēspicābilis,* from *dēspicārī* to disdain; cf. DESPISE
▸ **deˈspicably** *adv*

despise (dɪˈspaɪz) *vb* **despises, despising, despised.** (*tr*) to look down on with contempt; scorn: *he despises flattery.* ORIG C13: from OF *despire,* from L *dēspicere* to look down, from DE- + *specere* to look
▸ **deˈspiser** *n*

despite (dɪˈspaɪt) *prep* **1** in spite of; undeterred by. ◆ *n* **2** *Arch.* contempt; insult. **3 in despite of.** (*prep*) *Rare.* in spite of. ORIG C13: from OF *despit,* from L *dēspectus* contempt; see DESPISE

despoil (dɪˈspɔɪl) *vb* (*tr*) to deprive by force; plunder; loot. ORIG C13: from OF, from L *dēspoliāre,* from DE- + *spoliāre* to rob (esp. of clothing)
▸ **deˈspoiler** *n* ▸ **deˈspoilment** *n*

despoliation (dɪˌspəulɪˈeɪʃən) *n* **1** plunder or pillage. **2** the state of being despoiled.

despond (dɪˈspɒnd) *vb* (*intr*) **1** to become disheartened; despair. ◆ *n* **2** *Arch.* despondency. ORIG C17: from L *dēspondēre* to promise, make over to, yield, lose heart, from DE- + *spondēre* to promise
▸ **deˈspondingly** *adv*

despondent (dɪˈspɒndənt) *adj* downcast or disheartened; dejected.
▸ **deˈspondence** *or* **deˈspondency** *n* ▸ **deˈspondently** *adv*

despot (ˈdɛspɒt) *n* **1** an absolute or tyrannical ruler. **2** any person in power who acts tyrannically. ORIG C16: from Med. L *despota,* from Gk *despotēs* lord, master
▸ **despotic** (dɛsˈpɒtɪk) *or* **desˈpotical** *adj* ▸ **desˈpotically** *adv*

despotism (ˈdɛspəˌtɪzəm) *n* **1** the rule of a despot; absolute or tyrannical government. **2** arbitrary or tyrannical authority or behaviour.

des Prés *or* **Desprez** ★ (*French* de pre) *n* **Josquin** (ʒɔskɛ̃). ?1450–1521, Flemish Renaissance composer of masses, motets, and chansons.

des res (ˈdɛz ˈrɛz) *n* (in estate agents' jargon) a desirable residence.

Dessau ★ (*German* ˈdɛsau) *n* an industrial city in central Germany, in Saxony-Anhalt: capital of Anhalt state from 1340 to 1918. Pop.: 95 100 (1991).

dessert (dɪˈzɜːt) *n* **1** the sweet, usually last course of a meal. **2** *Chiefly Brit.* (esp. formerly) fruit, dates, nuts, etc., served at the end of a meal. ORIG C17: from F, from *desservir* to clear a table, from *des-* DIS-[1] + *servir* to SERVE

dessertspoon (dɪˈzɜːtˌspuːn) *n* a spoon intermediate in size between a tablespoon and a teaspoon.

destination (ˌdɛstɪˈneɪʃən) *n* **1** the predetermined end of a journey. **2** the end or purpose for which something is created or a person is destined.

destine (ˈdɛstɪn) *vb* **destines, destining, destined.** (*tr*) to set apart (for a certain purpose or person); intend; design. ORIG C14: from OF, from L *dēstināre* to appoint, from DE- + *-stināre,* from *stāre* to stand

destined (ˈdɛstɪnd) *adj* (*postpositive*) **1** foreordained; meant. **2** (usually foll. by *for*) heading (towards a specific destination).

destiny (ˈdɛstɪnɪ) *n, pl* **destinies. 1** the future destined for a person or thing. **2** the predetermined or inevitable course of events. **3** the power that predetermines the course of events. ORIG C14: from OF, from *destiner* to DESTINE

destitute (ˈdɛstɪˌtjuːt) *adj* **1** lacking the means of subsistence; totally impoverished. **2** (*postpositive;* foll. by *of*) completely lacking: *destitute of words.* ORIG C14: from L, from *dēstituere* to leave alone, from *statuere* to place

destitution (ˌdɛstɪˈtjuːʃən) *n* the state of being destitute; utter poverty.

destrier (ˈdɛstrɪə) *n Arch.* a warhorse. ORIG C13: from OF, from *destre* right hand, from L *dextra;* from the fact that a squire led a knight's horse with his right hand

destroy (dɪˈstrɔɪ) *vb* (*mainly tr*) **1** to ruin; spoil. **2** to tear down or demolish. **3** to put an end to. **4** to kill or annihilate. **5** to crush or defeat. **6** (*intr*) to be destructive or cause destruction. ORIG C13: from OF, from L *dēstruere* to pull down, from DE- + *struere* to pile up, build

destroyer (dɪˈstrɔɪə) *n* **1** a small fast lightly armoured but heavily armed warship. **2** a person or thing that destroys.

destruct (dɪˈstrʌkt) *vb* **1** to destroy (one's own missile, etc.) for safety. **2** (*intr*) (of a missile, etc.) to be destroyed, for safety, by those controlling it. ◆ *n* **3** the act of destructing. ◆ *adj* **4** designed to be capable of destroying itself or the object containing it: *destruct mechanism.*

destructible (dɪˈstrʌktɪbᵊl) *adj* capable of being or liable to be destroyed.

destruction (dɪˈstrʌkʃən) *n* **1** the act of destroying or state of being destroyed; demolition. **2** a cause of ruin or means of destroying. ORIG C14: from L *dēstructiō* a pulling down; see DESTROY

destructive (dɪˈstrʌktɪv) *adj* **1** (often *postpositive* and foll. by *of* or *to*) causing or tending to cause the destruction (of). **2** intended to discredit, esp. without positive suggestions or help; negative: *destructive criticism.*
▸ **deˈstructively** *adv* ▸ **deˈstructiveness** *n*

destructive distillation *n* the decomposition of a complex substance, such as wood or coal, by heating it in the absence of air and collecting the volatile products.

destructor (dɪˈstrʌktə) *n* **1** a furnace or incinerator for the disposal of refuse. **2** a device used to blow up a defective missile.

desuetude (dɪˈsjuːɪˌtjuːd, ˈdɛswɪˌtjuːd) *n Formal.* the condition of not being in use or practice; disuse. ORIG C15: from L, from *dēsuescere* to lay aside a habit, from DE- + *suescere* to grow accustomed

desulphurize *or* **desulphurise** (diːˈsʌlfjʊˌraɪz) *vb* **desulphurizes, desulphurizing, desulphurized** *or* **desulphurises, desulphurising, desulphurised.** to free or become free from sulphur.

desultory (ˈdɛsəltərɪ, -trɪ) *adj* **1** passing from one thing to another, esp. in a fitful way; unmethodical; disconnected. **2** random or incidental: *a desultory thought.* ORIG C16: from L: relating to one who vaults or jumps, hence superficial, from *dēsilīre* to jump down, from DE- + *salīre*
▸ **ˈdesultorily** *adv* ▸ **ˈdesultoriness** *n*

Det. *abbrev. for* Detective.

detach (dɪˈtætʃ) *vb* (*tr*) **1** to disengage and separate or remove; unfasten; disconnect. **2** *Mil.* to separate (a small unit) from a larger, esp. for a special assignment. ORIG C17: from OF *destachier,* from *des-* DIS-[1] + *atachier* to ATTACH
▸ **deˈtachable** *adj* ▸ **deˌtachaˈbility** *n*

detached (dɪˈtætʃt) *adj* **1** disconnected or standing apart; not attached: *a detached house.* **2** showing no bias or emotional involvement. **3** *Ophthalmol.* (of the retina) separated from the choroid layer of the eyeball to which it is normally attached, resulting in loss of vision in the affected part.

detachment (dɪˈtætʃmənt) *n* **1** indifference; aloofness. **2** freedom from self-interest or bias; disinterest. **3** the act of detaching something. **4** the condition of being detached; disconnection. **5** *Mil.* **5a** the separation of a small unit from its main body. **5b** the unit so detached. **6** *Canad.* a branch office of a police force.

detail (ˈdiːteɪl) *n* **1** an item that is considered separately; particular. **2** an item that is unimportant: *passengers' comfort was regarded as a detail.* **3** treatment of particulars: *this essay includes too much detail.* **4** items collectively; particulars. **5** a small section or element in a painting, building, statue, etc., esp. when considered in isolation. **6** *Mil.* **6a** the act of assigning personnel for a specific duty. **6b** the personnel selected. **6c** the duty. **7 in detail.** including all or most particulars or items thoroughly. ◆ *vb* (*tr*) **8** to list or relate fully. **9** *Mil.* to select (personnel) for a specific duty. ORIG C17: from F, from OF *detailler* to cut in pieces, from *de-* DIS-[1] + *tailler* to cut

detailed (ˈdiːteɪld) *adj* having many details or giving careful attention to details.

detain (dɪˈteɪn) *vb* (*tr*) **1** to delay; hold back. **2** to confine or hold in custody. ORIG C15: from OF, from L *dētinēre* to hold off, keep back, from DE- + *tenēre* to hold
▸ **deˈtainable** *adj* ▸ **detainee** (ˌdiːteɪˈniː) *n* ▸ **deˈtainment** *n*

detect (dɪˈtɛkt) *vb* (*tr*) **1** to perceive or notice. **2** to discover the existence or presence of (esp. something likely to elude observation). **3** *Obs.* to discover, or reveal (a crime, criminal, etc.). **4** to extract information from (an electromagnetic wave). ORIG C15: from L *dētectus,* from *dētegere* to uncover, from DE- + *tegere* to cover
▸ **deˈtectable** *or* **deˈtectible** *adj*

detection (dɪˈtɛkʃən) *n* **1** the act of discovering or the fact of being discovered. **2** the act or process of extracting information, esp. at audio or video frequencies, from an electromagnetic wave; demodulation.

detective (dɪˈtɛktɪv) *n* **1a** a police officer who investigates crimes. **1b** See **private detective. 1c** (*as modifier*): *a detective story.* ◆ *adj* **2** of or for detection.

detector (dɪˈtɛktə) *n* **1** a person or thing that detects. **2** any mechanical sensing device. **3** *Electronics.* a device used in the detection of radio signals.

detent (dɪˈtɛnt) *n* the locking piece of a mechanism, often spring-loaded to check the movement of a wheel in only one direction. ORIG C17: from OF *destente* a loosening, trigger; see DÉTENTE

détente (deɪˈtɑːnt; *French* detɑ̃t) *n* the relaxing or easing of tension, esp. between nations. ORIG F, lit.: a loosening, from OF *destendre* to release, from *tendre* to stretch

detention (dɪˈtɛnʃən) *n* **1** a detaining or being detained. **2a** custody or confinement, esp. of a suspect awaiting trial. **2b** (*as modifier*): *a detention order.* **3** a form of punishment in which a pupil is detained after school. ORIG C16: from L *dētentiō* a keeping back; see DETAIN

detention centre *n* (formerly) a place in which young persons could be detained for short periods by order of a court.

deter (dɪˈtɜː) *vb* **deters, deterring, deterred.** (*tr*) to discourage (from acting) or prevent (from occurring), usually by instilling fear, doubt, or anxiety. ORIG C16: from L *dēterrēre,* from DE- + *terrēre* to frighten
▸ **deˈterment** *n*

deterge (dɪˈtɜːdʒ) *vb* **deterges, deterging, deterged.** (*tr*) to cleanse: *to deterge a wound.* ORIG C17: from L *dētergēre* to wipe away, from DE- + *tergēre* to wipe

detergent (dɪˈtɜːdʒənt) *n* **1** a cleansing agent, esp. a chemical such as an alkyl sulphonate, widely used in industry, laundering, etc. ◆ *adj* **2** having cleansing power. ORIG C17: from L *dētergēns* wiping off; see DETERGE

deteriorate (dɪˈtɪərɪəˌreɪt) *vb* **deteriorates, deteriorating, deteriorated. 1** to make or become worse; depreciate. **2** (*intr*) to wear away or disintegrate. ORIG C16: from LL *dēteriōrāre,* from L *dēterior* worse
▸ **deˌterioˈration** *n* ▸ **deˈteriorative** *adj*

determinacy (dɪˈtɜːmɪnəsɪ) *n* **1** the quality of being defined or fixed. **2** the condition of being predicted or deduced.

determinant (dɪˈtɜːmɪnənt) *adj* **1** serving to determine. ◆ *n* **2** a factor that influences or determines. **3** *Maths.* a square array of elements that represents the sum of certain products of these elements, used to solve simultaneous equations, in vector studies, etc.

determinate (dɪˈtɜːmɪnɪt) *adj* **1** definitely limited, defined, or fixed. **2** determined. **3** able to be predicted or deduced. **4** *Bot.* having the main and branch stems ending in flowers.
▸ **deˈterminateness** *n*

determination (dɪˌtɜːmɪˈneɪʃən) *n* **1** the act of making a decision. **2** the condition of being determined; resoluteness. **3** an ending of an argument by the decision of an authority. **4** the act of fixing the quality, limit, position, etc., of something. **5** a decision or opinion reached. **6** a resolute movement towards some object or end. **7** *Law.* the termination of an estate or interest. **8** *Law.* the decision reached by a court of justice on a disputed matter.

determinative (dɪˈtɜːmɪnətɪv) *adj* **1** serving to settle or determine; deciding. ◆ *n* **2** a factor, circumstance, etc., that settles or determines.
▸ **deˈterminatively** *adv* ▸ **deˈterminativeness** *n*

determine (dɪˈtɜːmɪn) *vb* **determines, determining, determined. 1** to settle or decide (an argument, question, etc.) conclusively. **2** (*tr*) to conclude, esp. after observation or consideration. **3** (*tr*) to influence; give direction to. **4** (*tr*) to fix in scope, variety, etc.: *the river determined the edge of the property.* **5** to make or cause to make a decision. **6** (*tr*) *Logic.* to define or limit (a notion) by adding or requiring certain features or characteristics. **7** (*tr*) *Geom.* to fix or specify the position or form of. **8** *Chiefly law.* to come or bring to an end, as an estate. ORIG C14: from OF, from L *dētermināre* to set boundaries to, from DE- + *termināre* to limit
▸ **deˈterminable** *adj*

determined (dɪˈtɜːmɪnd) *adj* of unwavering mind; resolute; firm.
▸ **deˈterminedly** *adv*

determiner (dɪˈtɜːmɪnə) *n* **1** a word, such as a number, article, or personal pronoun, that determines (limits) the meaning of a noun phrase, e.g. *their* in 'their black cat'. **2** a person or thing that determines.

determinism (dɪˈtɜːmɪˌnɪzəm) *n* the philosophical doctrine that all events, including human actions, are fully determined by preceding events, and so freedom of choice is illusory. Also called: **necessitarianism.** Cf. **free will.**
▸ **deˈterminist** *n, adj* ▸ **deˌterminˈistic** *adj*

deterrent (dɪˈtɛrənt) *n* **1** something that deters. **2** a weapon, esp. nuclear, held by one state, etc., to deter attack by another. ◆ *adj* **3** tending or used to deter. ORIG C19: from L *dēterrēns* hindering; see DETER
▸ **deˈterrence** *n*

detest (dɪˈtɛst) *vb* (*tr*) to dislike intensely; loathe. ORIG C16: from L *dētestārī* to curse (while invoking a god as witness), from DE- + *testārī*, from *testis* a witness
▸ **deˈtester** *n*

detestable (dɪˈtɛstəbᵊl) *adj* being or deserving to be abhorred or detested.
▸ **deˌtestaˈbility** *or* **deˈtestableness** *n* ▸ **deˈtestably** *adv*

detestation (ˌdiːtɛsˈteɪʃən) *n* **1** intense hatred; abhorrence. **2** a person or thing that is detested.

dethrone (dɪˈθrəʊn) *vb* **dethrones, dethroning, dethroned.** (*tr*) to remove from a throne or deprive of any high position or title.
▸ **deˈthronement** *n* ▸ **deˈthroner** *n*

detonate (ˈdɛtəˌneɪt) *vb* **detonates, detonating, detonated.** to cause (a bomb, mine, etc.) to explode or (of a bomb, mine, etc.) to explode. ORIG C18: from L *dētonāre* to thunder down, from DE- + *tonāre* to THUNDER
▸ **ˌdetoˈnation** *n*

detonator (ˈdɛtəˌneɪtə) *n* **1** a small amount of explosive, as in a percussion cap, used to initiate a larger explosion. **2** a device, such as an electrical generator, used to set off an explosion from a distance. **3** an explosive.

detour (ˈdiːtʊə) *n* **1** a deviation from a direct route or course of action. ◆ *vb* **2** to deviate or cause to deviate from a direct route or course of action. ORIG C18: from F, from OF *destorner* to divert, turn away, from *des-* DE- + *torner* to TURN

detox (ˈdiːˌtɒks) *Inf.* ◆ *n* **1** treatment designed to rid the body of poisonous substances, esp. alcohol and drugs. ◆ *vb* (*intr*) **2** to undergo treatment to rid the body of poisonous substances, esp. alcohol and drugs.

detoxification centre *n* a place that specializes in the treatment of alcoholism or drug addiction.

detoxify (diːˈtɒksɪˌfaɪ) *vb* **detoxifies, detoxifying, detoxified.** (*tr*) **1** to remove poison from. **2** to treat (a person) for alcoholism or drug dependency.
▸ **deˌtoxifiˈcation** *n*

DETR (in Britain) *abbrev. for* Department of Environment, Transport and the Regions.

detract (dɪˈtrækt) *vb* **1** (when *intr*, usually foll. by *from*) to take away a part (of); diminish: *her anger detracts from her beauty.* **2** (*tr*) to distract or divert. **3** (*tr*) *Obs.* to belittle or disparage. ORIG C15: from L *dētractus*, from *dētrahere* to pull away, disparage, from DE- + *trahere* to drag
▸ **deˈtractive** *adj* ▸ **deˈtractor** *n* ▸ **deˈtraction** *n*

> **USAGE NOTE** *Detract* is sometimes wrongly used where *distract* is meant: *a noise distracted* (not *detracted*) *my attention.*

detrain (diːˈtreɪn) *vb* to leave or cause to leave a railway train.
▸ **deˈtrainment** *n*

detriment (ˈdɛtrɪmənt) *n* **1** disadvantage or damage. **2** a cause of disadvantage or damage. ORIG C15: from L *dētrīmentum*, a rubbing off, hence damage, from *dēterere*, from DE- + *terere* to rub

detrimental (ˌdɛtrɪˈmɛntᵊl) *adj* (when *postpositive*, foll. by *to*) harmful; injurious.

detritus (dɪˈtraɪtəs) *n* **1** a loose mass of stones, silt, etc., worn away from rocks. **2** the organic debris formed from the decay of organisms. ORIG C18: from F, from L: a rubbing away; see DETRIMENT
▸ **deˈtrital** *adj*

Detroit ★ (dɪˈtrɔɪt) *n* **1** a city in SE Michigan, on the Detroit River: a major Great Lakes port; largest car-manufacturing centre in the world. Pop.: 1 000 272 (1996 est.). **2** a river in central North America, flowing along the US-Canadian border from Lake St Clair to Lake Erie.

de trop *French.* (də tro) *adj* (*postpositive*) not wanted; in the way. ORIG lit.: of too much

detumescence (ˌdiːtjuˈmɛsəns) *n* the subsidence of a swelling. ORIG C17: from L *dētumescere* to cease swelling, from DE- + *tumescere*, from *tumēre* to swell

deuce[1] (djuːs) *n* **1a** a playing card or dice with two spots. **1b** a throw of two in dice. **2** *Tennis, etc.* a tied score that requires one player to gain two successive points to win the game. ORIG C15: from OF *deus* two, from L *duos*, from *duo* two

deuce[2] (djuːs) *Inf.* ◆ *interj* **1** an expression of annoyance or frustration. ◆ *n* **2 the deuce.** (intensifier) used in such phrases as **what the deuce, where the deuce,** etc. ORIG C17: prob. special use of DEUCE[1] (in the sense: lowest throw at dice)

deuced (ˈdjuːsɪd, djuːst) *Brit. inf.* ◆ *adj* **1** (intensifier) confounded: *he's a deuced idiot.* ◆ *adv* **2** (intensifier): *deuced good luck.*

Deus *Latin.* (ˈdeɪʊs) *n* God. ORIG rel. to Gk *Zeus*

deus ex machina *Latin.* (ˈdeɪʊs ɛks ˈmækɪnə) *n* **1** (in ancient Greek and Roman drama) a god introduced into a play to resolve the plot. **2** any unlikely device serving this purpose. ORIG lit.: god out of a machine

Deut. *Bible. abbrev. for* Deuteronomy.

deuteride (ˈdjuːtəˌraɪd) *n* a compound of deuterium and another element.

deuterium (djuːˈtɪərɪəm) *n* a stable isotope of hydrogen, occurring in natural hydrogen and in heavy water. Symbol: D or ^{2}H; atomic no.: 1; atomic wt.: 2.014. ORIG C20: NL; see DEUTERO-, -IUM; from the fact that it is the second heaviest hydrogen isotope

deuterium oxide *n* the compound D_2O; water in which the normal hydrogen atoms are replaced by deuterium atoms. See also **heavy water.**

deutero-, deuto- *or before a vowel* **deuter-, deut-** *combining form.* second or secondary: *deuterium.* ORIG from Gk *deuteros* second

deuteron (ˈdjuːtəˌrɒn) *n* the nucleus of a deuterium atom.

Deutsch ★ (dɔɪtʃ; *German* dɔytʃ) *n* **Otto Erich** (ˈɔto ˈeːrɪç). 1883–1967, Austrian music historian, noted for his catalogue of Schubert's works (1951).

Deutschland ★ (ˈdɔytʃlant) *n* the German name for **Germany.**

Deutschmark (ˈdɔɪtʃˌmɑːk) *or* **Deutsche Mark** (ˈdɔɪtʃə) *n* the standard monetary unit of Germany.

deutzia (ˈdjuːtsɪə, ˈdɔɪtsɪə) *n* any of various shrubs with white, pink, or purplish flowers in early summer. ORIG C19: NL, after J. *Deutz*, 18th-cent. Du. patron of botany

Deux-Sèvres ★ (*French* døsɛvrə) *n* a department of W France, in Poitou-Charentes region. Capital: Niort. Pop.: 346 612 (1994 est.). Area: 6054 sq. km (2337 sq. miles).

de Valera ★ (də vəˈlɛərə, -ˈlɪə-) *n* **Eamon** (ˈeɪmən). 1882–1975, Irish statesman; president of Sinn Fein (1917) and of the Dáil (1918–22); formed the Fianna Fáil party (1927); prime minister (1937–48; 1951–54; 1957–59) and president (1959–73) of the Irish Republic.

de Valois ★ (də ˈvælwɑː) *n* See (Ninette de) **Valois**[3].

devalue (diːˈvæljuː) *or* **devaluate** (diːˈvæljuːˌeɪt) *vb* **devalues, devaluing, devalued** *or* **devaluates, devaluating, devaluated. 1** to reduce (a currency) or (of a currency) be reduced in exchange value. **2** (*tr*) to reduce the value of.
▸ **deˌvaluˈation** *n*

Devanagari (ˌdeɪvəˈnɑːgərɪ) *n* a syllabic script in which

Sanskrit, Hindi, and other modern languages of India are written. ORIG C18: from Sansk.: alphabet of the gods

devastate ('dɛvəˌsteɪt) *vb* **devastates, devastating, devastated.** (*tr*) **1** to lay waste or make desolate; ravage; destroy. **2** to confound or overwhelm. ORIG C17: from L *dēvastāre,* from DE- + *vastāre* to ravage; rel. to *vastus* waste, empty
▸ **ˌdevasˈtation** *n* ▸ **ˈdevasˌtator** *n*

develop (dɪˈvɛləp) *vb* **1** to come or bring to a later or more advanced or expanded stage; grow or cause to grow gradually. **2** (*tr*) to work out in detail. **3** to disclose or unfold (thoughts, a plot, etc.) gradually or (of thoughts, etc.) to be gradually disclosed or unfolded. **4** to come or bring into existence: *he developed a new faith in God.* **5** (*intr*) to follow as a result of something; ensue: *a row developed after her remarks.* **6** (*tr*) to contract (a disease or illness). **7** (*tr*) to improve the value or change the use of (land). **8** to exploit or make available the natural resources of (a country or region). **9** (*tr*) *Photog.* to treat (exposed film, plate, or paper) with chemical solutions in order to produce a visible image. **10** *Biol.* to progress or cause to progress from simple to complex stages in the growth of an individual or the evolution of a species. **11** (*tr*) to elaborate upon (a musical theme) by varying the melody, key, etc. **12** (*tr*) *Maths.* to expand (a function or expression) in the form of a series. **13** (*tr*) *Geom.* to project or roll out (a surface) onto a plane without stretching or shrinking any element. **14** *Chess.* to bring (a piece) into play from its initial position on the back rank. ORIG C19: from OF *desveloper* to unwrap, from *des-* DIS-[1] + *veloper* to wrap; see ENVELOP
▸ **deˈvelopable** *adj*

developer (dɪˈvɛləpə) *n* **1** a person or thing that develops something, esp. a person who develops property. **2** Also called: **developing agent.** *Photog.* a chemical used to convert the latent image recorded in the emulsion of a film or paper into a visible image.

developing country *n* a poor or non-industrial country that is seeking to develop its resources by industrialization.

development (dɪˈvɛləpmənt) *n* **1** the act or process of growing or developing. **2** the product of developing. **3** a fact or event, esp. one that changes a situation. **4** an area of land that has been developed. **5** the section of a movement, usually in sonata form, in which the basic musical themes are developed. **6** *Chess.* the process of developing pieces.
▸ **deˌvelopˈmental** *adj*

developmental disorder *n Psychiatry.* any condition, such as autism or dyslexia, that appears in childhood and is characterized by delay in the development of one or more psychological functions, such as language skill.

development area *n* (in Britain) an area which has experienced economic depression because of the decline of its main industry or industries, and which is given government assistance to establish new industry.

Devereux ★ ('dɛvərə) *n* **Robert.** See (2nd Earl of) **Essex.**

Devi ★ ('deɪviː) *n* a Hindu goddess and embodiment of the female energy of Siva. ORIG Sansk.: goddess

deviance ('diːvɪəns) *n* **1** Also called: **deviancy.** the act or state of being deviant. **2** *Statistics.* a measure of the degree of fit of a statistical model compared to that of a more complete model.

deviant ('diːvɪənt) *adj* **1** deviating, as from what is considered acceptable behaviour. ◆ *n* **2** a person whose behaviour, esp. sexual behaviour, deviates from what is considered to be acceptable.

deviate *vb* ('diːvɪˌeɪt), **deviates, deviating, deviated. 1** (*usually intr*) to differ or cause to differ, as in belief or thought. **2** (*usually intr*) to turn aside or cause to turn aside. **3** (*intr*) *Psychol.* to depart from an accepted standard. ◆ *n, adj* ('diːvɪɪt). **4** another word for **deviant.** ORIG C17: from LL *dēviāre* to turn aside from the direct road, from DE- + *via* road
▸ **ˈdeviˌator** *n* ▸ **ˈdeviatory** *adj*

deviation (ˌdiːvɪˈeɪʃən) *n* **1** an act or result of deviating. **2** *Statistics.* the difference between an observed value in a series of such values and their arithmetic mean. **3** the error of a compass due to local magnetic disturbances.

device (dɪˈvaɪs) *n* **1** a machine or tool used for a specific task. **2** *Euphemistic.* a bomb. **3** a plan, esp. a clever or evil one; trick. **4** any ornamental pattern or picture, as in embroidery. **5** computer hardware designed for a specific function. **6** a design or figure, used as a heraldic sign, emblem, etc. **7** a particular pattern of words, figures of speech, etc., used in literature to produce an effect on the reader. **8 leave (someone) to his** (*or* **her**) **own devices.** to leave (someone) alone to do as he or she wishes. ORIG C13: from OF *devis* purpose, contrivance & *devise* difference, intention, from *deviser* to divide, control; see DEVISE

devil ('dɛvᵊl) *n* **1** (*often cap.*) *Theol.* the chief spirit of evil and enemy of God, often depicted as a human figure with horns, cloven hoofs, and tail. **2** any subordinate evil spirit. **3** a person or animal regarded as wicked or ill-natured. **4** a person or animal regarded as unfortunate or wretched. **5** a person or animal regarded as daring, mischievous, or energetic. **6** *Inf.* something difficult or annoying. **7** *Christian Science.* an error, lie, or false belief. **8** (in Malaysia) a ghost. **9** a portable furnace or brazier. **10** any of various mechanical devices, such as a machine for making wooden screws or a rag-tearing machine. **11** See **printer's devil. 12** *Law.* (in England) a junior barrister who does work for another in order to gain experience, usually for a half fee. **13** *Meteorol.* a small whirlwind in arid areas that raises dust or sand in a column. **14 between the devil and the deep blue sea.** between equally undesirable alternatives. **15 devil of 15a** *Inf.* (intensifier): *a devil of a fine horse.* **16 give the devil his due.** to acknowledge the talent or success of an unpleasant person. **17 go to the devil. 17a** to fail or become dissipated. **17b** (*interj*) used to express annoyance with the person causing it. **18 (let) the devil take the hindmost.** look after oneself and leave others to their fate. **19 talk** (*or* **speak**) **of the devil!** used when an absent person who has been the subject of conversation appears. **20 the devil!** (intensifier): **20a** used in **what the devil, where the devil,** etc. **20b** an exclamation of anger, surprise, disgust, etc. **21 the devil to pay.** trouble to be faced as a consequence of an action. ◆ *vb* **devils, devilling, devilled** *or US* **devils, deviling, deviled. 22** (*tr*) to prepare (food) by coating with a highly flavoured spiced paste or mixture of condiments before cooking. **23** (*tr*) to tear (rags) with a devil. **24** (*intr*) to serve as a printer's devil. **25** (*intr*) *Chiefly Brit.* to do hackwork, esp. for a lawyer or author. **26** (*tr*) *US inf.* to harass, vex, etc. ORIG OE *dēofol,* from L *diabolus,* from Gk *diabolos* enemy, accuser, slanderer

devilfish ('dɛvᵊlˌfɪʃ) *n, pl* **devilfish** *or* **devilfishes. 1** Also called: **devil ray.** another name for **manta** (the fish). **2** another name for **octopus.**

devilish ('dɛvəlɪʃ) *adj* **1** of, resembling, or befitting a devil; diabolic; fiendish. ◆ *adv, adj* **2** *Inf.* (intensifier): *devilish good food.*
▸ **ˈdevilishly** *adv* ▸ **ˈdevilishness** *n*

devil-may-care *adj* careless or reckless; happy-go-lucky: *a devil-may-care attitude.*

devilment ('dɛvᵊlmənt) *n* devilish or mischievous conduct.

devilry ('dɛvᵊlrɪ) *or* **deviltry** *n, pl* **devilries** *or* **deviltries. 1** reckless or malicious fun or mischief. **2** wickedness. **3** black magic or other forms of diabolism. ORIG C18: from F *diablerie,* from *diable* DEVIL

devil's advocate *n* **1** a person who advocates an opposing or unpopular view, often for the sake of argument. **2** *RC Church.* the official appointed to put the case against the beatification or canonization of a candidate. ORIG translation of NL *advocātus diabolī*

devil's coach-horse *n* a large black beetle with large jaws and ferocious habits.

devil's food cake *n Chiefly US & Canad.* a rich chocolate cake.

Devil's Island ★ *n* one of the three Safety Islands, off the coast of French Guiana: formerly a leper colony, then a French penal colony from 1895 until 1938. Area: less than 2 sq. km (1 sq. mile). French name: **Île du Diable.**

Devine ★ (dəˈviːn) *n* **George (Alexander Cassady).** 1910–65, British stage director and actor: founded (1956) the English Stage Company.

devious ('diːvɪəs) *adj* **1** not sincere or candid; deceitful. **2** (of a route or course of action) rambling; indirect. **3** going astray; erring. ORIG C16: from L *dēvius* lying to one side of the road, from DE- + *via* road
▸ **'deviously** *adv* ▸ **'deviousness** *n*

devise (dɪ'vaɪz) *vb* **devises, devising, devised. 1** to work out or plan (something) in one's mind. **2** (*tr*) *Law.* to dispose of (real property) by will. ◆ *n Law.* **3** a disposition of property by will. **4** a will or clause in a will disposing of real property. ORIG C15: from OF *deviser* to divide, apportion, intend, from L *dīvidere* to DIVIDE
▸ **de'viser** *n*

devitalize *or* **devitalise** (diː'vaɪtəˌlaɪz) *vb* **devitalizes, devitalizing, devitalized** *or* **devitalises, devitalising, devitalised.** (*tr*) to lower or destroy the vitality of; make weak or lifeless.
▸ **deˌvitali'zation** *or* **deˌvitali'sation** *n*

Devizes ★ (də'vaɪzəz) *n* a market town in S England, in Wiltshire: agricultural products. Pop.: 13 205 (1991).

devoid (dɪ'vɔɪd) *adj* (*postpositive;* foll. by *of*) destitute or void (of); free (from). ORIG C15: orig. p.p. of *devoid* (*vb*) to remove, from OF *devoider* from DE- + *voider* to void

devoirs (də'vwɑː) *pl n* (*sometimes sing*) compliments or respects. ORIG C13: from OF: duty, from *devoir* to be obliged to, owe, from L *dēbēre*

devolution (ˌdiːvə'luːʃən) *n* **1** a devolving. **2** a passing onwards or downwards from one stage to another. **3** a transfer of authority from a central government to regional governments. ORIG C16: from Med. L *dēvolūtiō* a rolling down, from L *dēvolvere;* see DEVOLVE
▸ **ˌdevo'lutionary** *adj* ▸ **ˌdevo'lutionist** *n, adj*

devolve (dɪ'vɒlv) *vb* **devolves, devolving, devolved. 1** (foll. by *on, upon, to,* etc.) to pass or cause to pass to a successor or substitute, as duties, power, etc. **2** (*intr;* foll. by *on* or *upon*) *Law.* (of an estate, etc.) to pass to another by operation of law. ORIG C15: from L *dēvolvere* to roll down, fall into, from DE- + *volvere* to roll
▸ **de'volvement** *n*

Devon ★ ('dɛvᵊn) *n* **1** Also called: **Devonshire.** a county of SW England, between the Bristol Channel and the English Channel, including the island of Lundy: hilly, rising to the uplands of Exmoor and Dartmoor, with wooded river valleys and a rugged coastline. Plymouth and Torbay became unitary authorities in 1998. Administrative centre: Exeter. Pop. (excluding unitary authorities): 680 100 (1996 est.). Area (excluding unitary authorities): 6569 sq. km (2536 sq. miles). **2** a breed of large red cattle originally from Devon.

Devonian (də'vəʊnɪən) *adj* **1** of, denoting, or formed in the fourth period of the Palaeozoic era, between the Silurian and Carboniferous periods. **2** of or relating to Devon. ◆ *n* **3 the.** the Devonian period or rock system.

Devonshire ★ ('dɛvᵊnʃɪə, -ʃə) *n* **8th Duke of,** title of *Spencer Compton Cavendish.* 1833–1908, British politician, also known (1858–91) as Lord Hartington. He led the Liberal Party (1874–80) and left it to found the Liberal Unionist Party (1886).

Devonshire split *n* a kind of yeast bun split open and served with cream or jam.

devoré (dəvɒ'reɪ) *n* a velvet fabric with a raised pattern created by disintegrating some of the pile with chemicals. ORIG from F, p.p. of *dévorer* to devour

devote (dɪ'vəʊt) *vb* **devotes, devoting, devoted.** (*tr*) to apply or dedicate (oneself, money, etc.) to some pursuit, cause, etc. ORIG C16: from L *dēvōtus* devoted, solemnly promised, from *dēvovēre* to vow; see DE-, VOW

devoted (dɪ'vəʊtɪd) *adj* **1** feeling or demonstrating loyalty or devotion; devout. **2** (*postpositive;* foll. by *to*) dedicated or consecrated.
▸ **de'votedly** *adv* ▸ **de'votedness** *n*

devotee (ˌdɛvə'tiː) *n* **1** a person ardently enthusiastic about something, such as a sport or pastime. **2** a zealous follower of a religion.

devotion (dɪ'vəʊʃən) *n* **1** (often foll. by *to*) strong attachment (to) or affection (for a cause, person, etc.) marked by dedicated loyalty. **2** religious zeal; piety. **3** (*often pl*) religious observance or prayers.
▸ **de'votional** *adj*

devour (dɪ'vaʊə) *vb* (*tr*) **1** to eat up greedily or voraciously. **2** to waste or destroy; consume. **3** to consume greedily or avidly with the senses or mind. **4** to engulf or absorb. ORIG C14: from OF, from L *dēvorāre* to gulp down, from DE- + *vorāre;* see VORACIOUS
▸ **de'vourer** *n* ▸ **de'vouring** *adj*

devout (dɪ'vaʊt) *adj* **1** deeply religious; reverent. **2** sincere; earnest; heartfelt. ORIG C13: from OF *devot,* from LL *dēvōtus,* from L: faithful; see DEVOTE
▸ **de'voutly** *adv* ▸ **de'voutness** *n*

De Vries ★ (*Dutch* də vriːs) *n* **Hugo** ('hyːxoː). 1848–1935, Dutch botanist, who rediscovered Mendel's laws and developed the mutation theory of evolution.

dew (djuː) *n* **1** drops of water condensed on a cool surface, esp. at night, from vapour in the air. **2** something like this, esp. in freshness: *the dew of youth.* **3** small drops of moisture, such as tears. ◆ *vb* **4** (*tr*) to moisten with or as with dew. ORIG OE *dēaw*

Dewar ★ ('djuːə) *n* **1 Donald.** 1937–2000, Scottish Labour politician; secretary of state for Scotland (1997–99); first minister for Scotland (1999–2000). **2** Sir **James.** 1842–1923, Scottish chemist and physicist: invented the vacuum flask.

dewberry ('djuːbərɪ, -brɪ) *n, pl* **dewberries. 1** any trailing bramble having blue-black fruits. **2** the fruit of any such plant.

dewclaw ('djuːˌklɔː) *n* **1** a nonfunctional claw in dogs. **2** an analogous rudimentary hoof in deer, goats, etc.
▸ **'dewˌclawed** *adj*

dewdrop ('djuːˌdrɒp) *n* a drop of dew.

de Wet ★ (də 'vɛt) *n* **Christian Rudolf.** 1854–1922, Afrikaner military commander and politician, who led the Orange Free State army in the second Boer War (1899–1902). He was imprisoned for treason (1914) after organizing an Afrikaner nationalist rebellion.

Dewey ★ ('djuːɪ) *n* **John.** 1859–1952, US pragmatist philosopher and educator. His works include *Democracy and Education* (1916).

Dewey Decimal System ('djuːɪ) *n* a system of library book classification with ten main subject classes. Also called: **decimal classification.** ORIG C19: after Melvil *Dewey* (1851–1931), US educator

dewlap ('djuːˌlæp) *n* **1** a loose fold of skin hanging from beneath the throat in cattle, dogs, etc. **2** loose skin on an elderly person's throat. ORIG C14 *dewlappe,* from DEW (prob. from an earlier form of different meaning) + LAP[1] (from OE *læppa* hanging flap), ?from ON

DEW line (djuː) *n acronym for* distant early warning line, a network of radar stations situated mainly in Arctic regions of North America.

dew point *n* the temperature at which dew begins to form.

dew pond *n* a shallow pond, usually man made, that is kept full by dew and mist.

dewy ('djuːɪ) *adj* **dewier, dewiest. 1** moist with or as with dew. **2** of or resembling dew. **3** *Poetic.* suggesting, falling, or refreshing like dew: *dewy sleep.*
▸ **'dewily** *adv* ▸ **'dewiness** *n*

dexter ('dɛkstə) *adj* **1** *Arch.* of or located on the right side. **2** (*usually postpositive*) *Heraldry.* of, on, or starting from the right side of a shield from the bearer's point of view and therefore on the spectator's left. ◆ Cf. **sinister.** ORIG C16: from L; cf. Gk *dexios* on the right hand

dexterity (dɛk'stɛrɪtɪ) *n* **1** physical, esp. manual, skill or nimbleness. **2** mental skill or adroitness. ORIG C16: from L *dexteritās* aptness, readiness; see DEXTER

dexterous ('dɛkstrəs) *adj* possessing or done with dexterity.
▸ **'dexterously** *adv* ▸ **'dexterousness** *n*

dextral ('dɛkstrəl) *adj* **1** of or located on the right side, esp. of the body. **2** of a person who prefers to use his or her right foot, hand, or eye; right-handed. **3** (of shells) coiling in an anticlockwise direction from the apex.
▸ **dextrality** (dɛk'strælɪtɪ) *n* ▸ **'dextrally** *adv*

dextran ('dɛkstrən) *n Biochem.* a chainlike polymer of glucose produced by the action of bacteria on sucrose:

used as a substitute for plasma in blood transfusions. ORIG C19: from DEXTRO- + -AN

dextrin ('dɛkstrɪn) *or* **dextrine** ('dɛkstrɪn, -tri:n) *n* any of a group of sticky substances obtained from starch: used as thickening agents in foods and as gums. ORIG C19: from F *dextrine;* see DEXTRO-, -IN

dextro- *or before a vowel* **dextr-** *combining form.* on or towards the right: *dextrorotation.* ORIG from L, from *dexter* on the right side

dextrorotation (ˌdɛkstrəʊrəʊ'teɪʃən) *n* a rotation to the right; clockwise rotation, esp. of the plane of polarization of plane-polarized light. Cf. **laevorotation.**
▸ **dextrorotatory** (ˌdɛkstrəʊ'rəʊtətərɪ, -trɪ) *or* ˌ**dextro'rotary** *adj*

dextrorse ('dɛkstrɔ:s) *or* **dextrorsal** (dɛk'strɔ:səl) *adj* (of some climbing plants) growing upwards in a spiral from left to right or anticlockwise. ORIG C19: from L *dextrorsum* towards the right, from DEXTRO- + *vorsus,* var. of *versus,* from *vertere* to turn
▸ '**dextrorsely** *adv*

dextrose ('dɛkstrəʊz, -trəʊs) *n* a glucose occurring widely in fruit, honey, and in the blood and tissue of animals. Formula: $C_6H_{12}O_6$. Also called: **grape sugar, dextroglucose.**

dextrous ('dɛkstrəs) *adj* a variant spelling of **dexterous.**
▸ '**dextrously** *adv* ▸ '**dextrousness** *n*

Dezhnev ★ (*Russian* dɪʒ'njɔf) *n* **Cape.** a cape in NE Russia, at the E end of Chukotski Peninsula: the northeasternmost point of Asia. Former name: **East Cape.**

DF *abbrev. for* Defender of the Faith.

D/F *or* **DF** *Telecomm.* ◆ *abbrev. for:* **1** direction finder. **2** direction finding.

DFC *abbrev. for* Distinguished Flying Cross.

DfEE (in Britain) *abbrev. for* Department for Education and Employment.

DFM *abbrev. for* Distinguished Flying Medal.

dg *symbol for* decigram.

DH (in Britain) *abbrev. for* Department of Health.

Dhahran ★ (dɑ:'rɑ:n) *n* a town in E Saudi Arabia: site of the original discovery of oil in the country (1938).

Dhaka *or* **Dacca** ★ ('dækə) *n* the capital of Bangladesh, in the E central part: capital of Bengal (1608–39; 1660–1704) and of East Pakistan (1949–71); jute and cotton mills; university (1921). Pop.: 3 839 000 (1991).

dhal, dal, *or* **dholl** (dɑ:l) *n* **1** a tropical African and Asian shrub cultivated for its nutritious pealike seeds. **2** the seed of this shrub. **3** a curry made from lentils or other pulses. ORIG C17: from Hindi, from Sansk. *dal* to split

dharma ('dɑ:mə) *n* **1** *Hinduism.* social custom regarded as a religious and moral duty. **2** *Hinduism.* **2a** the essential principle of the cosmos; natural law. **2b** conduct that conforms with this. **3** *Buddhism.* ideal truth. ORIG Sansk.: habit, usage, law

Dhílos ★ ('ðilɔs) *n* transliteration of the Modern Greek name for **Delos.**

dhobi ('dəʊbɪ) *n, pl* **dhobis.** (in India, E Africa, etc.) a washerman. ORIG C19: from Hindi, from *dhōb* washing

Dhodhekánisos ★ (ðɔðɛ'kanisɔs) *n* a transliteration of the modern Greek name for the **Dodecanese.**

dhoti ('dəʊtɪ), **dhooti, dhootie,** *or* **dhuti** ('du:tɪ) *n, pl* **dhotis.** a long loincloth worn by men in India. ORIG C17: from Hindi

dhow (daʊ) *n* a lateen-rigged coastal Arab sailing vessel. ORIG C19: from Ar.

DHSS (formerly, in Britain) *abbrev. for* Department of Health and Social Security.

DI *abbrev. for* donor insemination.

di. *or* **dia.** *abbrev. for* diameter.

di-[1] *prefix* **1** twice; two; double: *dicotyledon.* **2a** containing two specified atoms or groups of atoms: *carbon dioxide.* **2b** a nontechnical equivalent of **bi-** (sense 5). ORIG via L from Gk, from *dis* twice, double, rel. to *duo* two. Cf. BI-

di-[2] *combining form.* a variant of **dia-** before a vowel: *dioptre.*

dia- *or* **di-** *prefix* **1** through or during: *diachronic.* **2** across: *diactinic.* **3** apart: *diacritic.* ORIG from Gk *dia* through, between, across, by

diabetes (ˌdaɪə'bi:tɪs, -ti:z) *n* any of various disorders, esp. diabetes mellitus, characterized by excessive thirst and excretion of an abnormally large amount of urine. ORIG C16: from L: siphon, from Gk, lit.: a passing through

diabetes mellitus (mə'laɪtəs) *n* a form of diabetes, caused by a deficiency of insulin, in which the body is unable to metabolize sugars. ORIG C18: NL, lit.: honey-sweet diabetes

diabetic (ˌdaɪə'bɛtɪk) *adj* **1** of, relating to, or having diabetes. **2** for the use of diabetics. ◆ *n* **3** a person who has diabetes.

diablerie (dɪ'ɑ:blərɪ) *n* **1** magic or witchcraft connected with devils. **2** esoteric knowledge of devils. **3** devilry; mischief. ORIG C18: from OF, from *diable* devil, from L *diabolus;* see DEVIL

diabolic (ˌdaɪə'bɒlɪk) *adj* **1** of the devil; satanic. **2** extremely cruel or wicked; fiendish. **3** very difficult or unpleasant. ORIG C14: from LL, from Gk *diabolikos,* from *diabolos* DEVIL
▸ ˌ**dia'bolically** *adv* ▸ ˌ**dia'bolicalness** *n*

diabolical (ˌdaɪə'bɒlɪkəl) *adj Inf.* **1** excruciatingly bad. **2** (intensifier): *a diabolical liberty.*
▸ ˌ**dia'bolically** *adv* ▸ ˌ**dia'bolicalness** *n*

diabolism (daɪ'æbəˌlɪzəm) *n* **1a** witchcraft or sorcery. **1b** worship of devils or beliefs concerning them. **2** character or conduct that is devilish.
▸ **di'abolist** *n*

diabolo (dɪ'æbəˌləʊ) *n, pl* **diabolos. 1** a game in which one throws and catches a top on a cord fastened to two sticks. **2** the top used in this. ORIG C20: from It., lit.: devil

diachronic (ˌdaɪə'krɒnɪk) *adj* of, relating to, or studying the development of a phenomenon through time; historical. Cf. **synchronic.** ORIG C19: from DIA- + Gk *khronos* time

diacidic (ˌdaɪə'sɪdɪk) *adj* (of a base) capable of neutralizing two protons with one of its molecules. Also: **diacid.**

diaconal (daɪ'ækənəl) *adj* of or associated with a deacon or the diaconate. ORIG C17: from LL *diāconālis,* from *diāconus* DEACON

diaconate (daɪ'ækənɪt, -ˌneɪt) *n* the office, sacramental status, or period of office of a deacon. ORIG C17: from LL *diāconātus;* see DEACON

diacritic (ˌdaɪə'krɪtɪk) *n* **1** a sign placed above or below a character or letter to indicate that it has a different phonetic value, is stressed, or for some other reason. ◆ *adj* **2** another word for **diacritical.** ORIG C17: from Gk *diakritikos* serving to distinguish, from *diakrinein,* from DIA- + *krinein* to separate

diacritical (ˌdaɪə'krɪtɪkəl) *adj* **1** of or relating to a diacritic. **2** showing up a distinction.

diadem ('daɪəˌdɛm) *n* **1** a royal crown, esp. a light jewelled circlet. **2** royal dignity or power. ORIG C13: from L, from Gk: fillet, royal headdress, from *diadein,* from DIA- + *dein* to bind

diaeresis *or* **dieresis** (daɪ'ɛrɪsɪs) *n, pl* **diaereses** *or* **diereses** (-ˌsi:z). **1** the mark ¨ placed over the second of two adjacent vowels to indicate that it is to be pronounced separately, as in some spellings of *coöperate, naïve,* etc. **2** this mark used for any other purpose, such as to indicate a special pronunciation for a particular vowel. **3** a pause in a line of verse when the end of a foot coincides with the end of a word. ORIG C17: from L, from Gk: a division, from *diairein,* from DIA- + *hairein* to take; cf. HERESY
▸ **diaeretic** *or* **dieretic** (ˌdaɪə'rɛtɪk) *adj*

diag. *abbrev. for* diagram.

Diaghilev ★ (*Russian* 'djagɪlif) *n* **Sergei Pavlovich** (sɪr'gjej 'pavləvitʃ). 1872–1929, Russian ballet impresario. He founded (1909) the *Ballet Russe.*

diagnose ('daɪəgˌnəʊz) *vb* **diagnoses, diagnosing, diagnosed. 1** to determine by diagnosis. **2** (*tr*) to examine (a person or thing), as for a disease.
▸ ˌ**diag'nosable** *adj*

diagnosis (ˌdaɪəg'nəʊsɪs) *n, pl* **diagnoses** (-si:z). **1a** the identification of diseases from the examination of symptoms. **1b** an opinion so reached. **2a** thorough anal-

★ people and places

ysis of facts or problems in order to gain understanding. **2b** an opinion reached through such analysis. ORIG C17: NL, from Gk: a distinguishing, from *diagignōskein*, from *gignōskein* to perceive, KNOW
▸ **diagnostic** (ˌdaɪəgˈnɒstɪk) *adj*

diagonal (daɪˈægənᵊl) *adj* **1** *Maths.* connecting any two vertices that in a polygon are not adjacent and in a polyhedron are not in the same face. **2** slanting; oblique. **3** marked with slanting lines or patterns. ◆ *n* **4** a diagonal line, plane, or pattern. **5** something put, set, or drawn obliquely. ORIG C16: from L, from Gk *diagōnios*, from DIA- + *gōnia* angle
▸ **diˈagonally** *adv*

diagram (ˈdaɪəˌgræm) *n* **1** a sketch or plan demonstrating the form or workings of something. **2** *Maths.* a pictorial representation of a quantity or of a relationship. ◆ *vb* **diagrams, diagramming, diagrammed** *or US* **diagrams, diagraming, diagramed. 3** to show in or as if in a diagram. ORIG C17: from L, from Gk, from *diagraphein*, from *graphein* to write
▸ **diagrammatic** (ˌdaɪəgrəˈmætɪk) *adj*

dial (ˈdaɪəl) *n* **1** the face of a watch, clock, etc., marked with divisions representing units of time. **2** the graduated disc of various measuring instruments. **3a** the control on a radio or television set used to change the station or channel. **3b** the panel on a radio on which the frequency, wavelength, or station is indicated. **4** a numbered disc on a telephone that is rotated a set distance for each digit of a number being called. **5** *Brit.* a slang word for **face.** ◆ *vb* **dials, dialling, dialled** *or US* **dials, dialing, dialed. 6** to try to establish a telephone connection with (a subscriber) by operating the dial or buttons on a telephone. **7** (*tr*) to indicate, measure, or operate with a dial. ORIG C14: from Med. L *diālis* daily, from L *diēs* day
▸ **ˈdialler** *or US* **ˈdialer** *n*

dial. *abbrev. for* dialect(al).

dialect (ˈdaɪəˌlɛkt) *n* **a** a form of a language spoken in a particular geographical area or by members of a particular social class or occupational group, distinguished by its vocabulary, grammar, and pronunciation. **b** a form of a language that is considered inferior. ORIG C16: from L, from Gk *dialektos* speech, dialect, discourse, from *dialegesthai* to converse, from *legein* to talk, speak
▸ **ˌdiaˈlectal** *adj*

dialectic (ˌdaɪəˈlɛktɪk) *n* **1** disputation or debate, esp. when intended to resolve differences between two views. **2** logical argumentation. **3** a variant of **dialectics** (sense 1). **4** *Philosophy.* an interpretive method used by Hegel in which contradictions are resolved at a higher level of truth (synthesis). ◆ *adj* **5** of or relating to logical disputation. ORIG C17: from L, from Gk *dialektikē* (*tekhnē*) (the art) of argument; see DIALECT
▸ **ˌdialecˈtician** *n*

dialectical (ˌdaɪəˈlɛktɪkᵊl) *adj* of or relating to dialectic or dialectics.
▸ **ˌdiaˈlectically** *adv*

dialectical materialism *n* the economic, political, and philosophical system of Marx and Engels that combines traditional materialism and Hegelian dialectic.

dialectics (ˌdaɪəˈlɛktɪks) *n* (*functioning as pl or* (*sometimes*) *sing*) **1** the study of reasoning. **2** a particular methodology or system. **3** the application of the Hegelian dialectic or the rationale of dialectical materialism.

dialling code *n* a sequence of numbers which is dialled for connection with another exchange before an individual subscriber's telephone number is dialled.

dialling tone *or US & Canad.* **dial tone** *n* a continuous sound, either purring or high-pitched, heard over a telephone indicating that a number can be dialled.

dialogue *or US* (*often*) **dialog** (ˈdaɪəˌlɒg) *n* **1** conversation between two or more people. **2** an exchange of opinions; discussion. **3** the lines spoken by characters in drama or fiction. **4** a passage of conversation in a literary or dramatic work. **5** a literary composition in the form of a dialogue. **6** a political discussion between representatives of two nations or groups. ORIG C13: from OF, from L, from Gk, from *dialegesthai*; see DIALECT

dialogue box *or* **dialog box** *n* a small window that may open on a computer screen to prompt the user to enter information or select an option.

dialyse *or US* **dialyze** (ˈdaɪəˌlaɪz) *vb* **dialyses, dialysing, dialysed** *or US* **dialyzes, dialyzing, dialyzed.** (*tr*) to separate by dialysis.
▸ **ˌdialyˈsation** *or US* **ˌdialyˈzation** *n*

dialyser *or US* **dialyzer** (ˈdaɪəˌlaɪzə) *n* a machine that performs dialysis, esp. one that removes impurities from the blood of patients with malfunctioning kidneys; kidney machine.

dialysis (daɪˈælɪsɪs) *n, pl* **dialyses** (-ˌsiːz). **1** the separation of small molecules from large molecules and colloids in a solution by the selective diffusion of the small molecules through a semipermeable membrane. **2** *Med.* the filtering of blood through a semipermeable membrane to remove waste products. ORIG C16: from LL: a separation, from Gk *dialusis*, from *dialuein* to tear apart, dissolve, from *luein* to loosen
▸ **dialytic** (ˌdaɪəˈlɪtɪk) *adj*

diam. *abbrev. for* diameter.

diamagnetic (ˌdaɪəmægˈnɛtɪk) *adj* of, exhibiting, or concerned with diamagnetism.

diamagnetism (ˌdaɪəˈmægnɪˌtɪzəm) *n* the phenomenon exhibited by substances that have a relative permeability less than unity and a negative susceptibility; caused by the orbital motion of electrons in the atoms of the material.

diamanté (ˌdaɪəˈmæntɪ) *adj* **1** decorated with glittering ornaments, such as sequins. ◆ *n* **2** a fabric so covered. ORIG C20: from F, from *diamanter* to adorn with diamonds

diameter (daɪˈæmɪtə) *n* **1a** a straight line connecting the centre of a circle, sphere, etc. with two points on the perimeter or surface. **1b** the length of such a line. **2** the thickness of something, esp. with circular cross section. ORIG C14: from Med. L, from Gk: diameter, diagonal, from DIA- + *metron* measure

diametric (ˌdaɪəˈmɛtrɪk) *or* **diametrical** *adj* **1** Also: **diametral.** of, related to, or along a diameter. **2** completely opposed.

diametrically (ˌdaɪəˈmɛtrɪkəlɪ) *adv* completely; utterly (esp. in **diametrically opposed**).

diamond (ˈdaɪəmənd) *n* **1a** a usually colourless exceptionally hard form of carbon in cubic crystalline form. It is used as a precious stone and for industrial cutting or abrading. **1b** (*as modifier*): *a diamond ring*. **2** *Geom.* a figure having four sides of equal length forming two acute angles and two obtuse angles; rhombus. **3a** a red lozenge-shaped symbol on a playing card. **3b** a card with one or more of these symbols or (*when pl*) the suit of cards so marked. **4** *Baseball.* **4a** the whole playing field. **4b** the square formed by the four bases. ◆ *vb* **5** (*tr*) to decorate with or as with diamonds. ORIG C13: from OF *diamant*, from Med. L *diamas*, from L *adamas* the hardest iron or steel, diamond; see ADAMANT
▸ **diamantine** (ˌdaɪəˈmæntaɪn) *adj*

diamond anniversary *n* a 60th, or occasionally 75th, anniversary.

diamondback (ˈdaɪəmənd,bæk) *n* **1** Also called: **diamondback terrapin** *or* **turtle.** any edible North American terrapin having diamond-shaped markings on the shell. **2** a large North American rattlesnake having diamond-shaped markings.

diamond wedding *n* the 60th, or occasionally the 75th, anniversary of a marriage.

diamorphine (ˌdaɪəˈmɔːfiːn) *n* a technical name for **heroin.**

Diana ★ (daɪˈænə) *n* **1** the virginal Roman goddess of the hunt and the moon. Greek counterpart: **Artemis. 2** title *Diana, Princess of Wales*, original name *Lady Diana Frances Spencer.* 1961–97, she married Charles, Prince of Wales, in 1981; they were divorced in 1996.

dianthus (daɪˈænθəs) *n, pl* **dianthuses.** any Eurasian plant of the widely cultivated genus *Dianthus*, such as the carnation, pink, and sweet william. ORIG C19: NL, from Gk DI-[1] + *anthos* flower

diapason (ˌdaɪəˈpeɪzᵊn) *n Music.* **1** either of two stops (**open** and **stopped diapason**) found throughout the com-

★ people and places

pass of a pipe organ that give it its characteristic tone colour. **2** the compass of an instrument or voice. **3a** a standard pitch used for tuning. **3b** a tuning fork or pitch pipe. **4** (in classical Greece) an octave. ORIG C14: from L: the whole octave, from Gk: (*hē*) *dia pasōn* (*khordōn sumphōnia*) (concord) through all (the notes)

diapause (ˈdaɪəˌpɔːz) *n* a period of suspended development and growth accompanied by decreased metabolism in insects and some other animals. ORIG C19: from Gk *diapausis* pause, from *diapauein* to pause, bring to an end, from DIA- + *pauein* to stop

diaper (ˈdaɪəpə) *n* **1** the US and Canad. word for **nappy**[1]. **2a** a fabric having a pattern of a small repeating design, esp. diamonds. **2b** such a pattern, used as decoration. ◆ *vb* **3** (*tr*) to decorate with such a pattern. ORIG C14: from OF *diaspre,* from Med. L *diasprus* made of diaper, from Med. Gk *diaspros* pure white, from DIA- + *aspros* white, shining

diaphanous (daɪˈæfənəs) *adj* (usually of fabrics) fine and translucent. ORIG C17: from Med. L, from Gk *diaphanēs* transparent, from DIA- + *phainein* to show
▸ **diˈaphanously** *adv*

diaphoresis (ˌdaɪəfəˈriːsɪs) *n* perspiration, esp. when perceptible and excessive. ORIG C17: via LL from Gk, from *diaphorein* to disperse by perspiration, from DIA- + *phorein* to carry

diaphoretic (ˌdaɪəfəˈrɛtɪk) *adj* **1** relating to or causing perspiration. ◆ *n* **2** a diaphoretic drug.

diaphragm (ˈdaɪəˌfræm) *n* **1** *Anat.* any separating membrane, esp. the muscular partition that separates the abdominal and thoracic cavities in mammals. **2** another name for **cap** (sense 11). **3** any thin dividing membrane. **4** Also called: **stop.** a device to control the amount of light entering an optical instrument, such as a camera. **5** a thin vibrating disc used to convert sound signals to electrical signals or vice versa in telephones, etc. ORIG C17: from LL, from Gk, from DIA- + *phragma* fence
▸ **diaphragmatic** (ˌdaɪəfrægˈmætɪk) *adj*

diapositive (ˌdaɪəˈpɒzɪtɪv) *n* a positive transparency.

diarist (ˈdaɪərɪst) *n* a person who writes a diary, esp. one that is subsequently published.

diarrhoea *or esp. US* **diarrhea** (ˌdaɪəˈrɪə) *n* frequent and copious discharge of abnormally liquid faeces. ORIG C16: from LL, from Gk, from *diarrhein,* from DIA- + *rhein* to flow
▸ **ˌdiarˈrhoeal, ˌdiarˈrhoeic** *or esp. US* **ˌdiarˈrheal, ˌdiarˈrheic** *adj*

diary (ˈdaɪərɪ) *n, pl* **diaries. 1** a personal record of daily events, appointments, observations, etc. **2** a book for this. ORIG C16: from L *diārium* daily allocation of food or money, journal, from *diēs* day

Dias *or* **Diaz** ★ (ˈdiːəs; *Portuguese* ˈdiəʃ) *n* **Bartholomeu** (ˌbərtuluˈmeu). ?1450–1500, Portuguese navigator.

Diaspora (daɪˈæspərə) *n* **1a** the dispersion of the Jews after the Babylonian and Roman conquests of Palestine. **1b** the Jewish people and communities outside Israel. **2** (*often not cap.*) a dispersion, as of people originally belonging to one nation. **3** *Caribbean.* the descendants of Sub-Saharan African peoples living anywhere in the Western hemisphere. ORIG C19: from Gk: a scattering, from *diaspeirein,* from DIA- + *speirein* to scatter, sow
▸ **Diasporic** *or* **diasporic** (ˌdaɪəˈspɒrɪk) *adj*

diastalsis (ˌdaɪəˈstælsɪs) *n, pl* **diastalses** (-siːz). *Physiol.* a downward wave of contraction occurring in the intestine during digestion. ORIG C20: NL, from DIA- + (PERI)STALSIS
▸ **ˌdiaˈstaltic** *adj*

diastase (ˈdaɪəˌsteɪs, -ˌsteɪz) *n* any of a group of enzymes that hydrolyse starch to maltose. They are present in germinated barley and in the pancreas. ORIG C19: from F, from Gk *diastasis* a separation
▸ **ˌdiaˈstasic** *adj*

diastole (daɪˈæstəlɪ) *n* the dilation of the chambers of the heart that follows each contraction, during which they refill with blood. Cf. **systole.** ORIG C16: via LL from Gk, from *diastellein* to expand, from DIA- + *stellein* to place, bring together, make ready
▸ **diastolic** (ˌdaɪəˈstɒlɪk) *adj*

diastrophism (daɪˈæstrəˌfɪzəm) *n* the process of movement of the earth's crust that gives rise to mountains, continents, and other large-scale features. ORIG C19: from Gk *diastrophē* a twisting; see DIA-, STROPHE
▸ **diastrophic** (ˌdaɪəˈstrɒfɪk) *adj*

diathermancy (ˌdaɪəˈθɜːmənsɪ) *n, pl* **diathermancies.** the property of transmitting infrared radiation. ORIG C19: from F, from DIA- + Gk *thermansis* heating, from *thermos* hot
▸ **ˌdiaˈthermanous** *adj*

diathermy (ˈdaɪəˌθɜːmɪ) *or* **diathermia** (ˌdaɪəˈθɜːmɪə) *n* local heating of the body tissues with an electric current for medical purposes. ORIG C20: from NL, from DIA- + Gk *thermē* heat

diatom (ˈdaɪətəm) *n* a microscopic unicellular alga having a cell wall impregnated with silica. ORIG C19: from NL, from Gk *diatomos* cut in two, from DIA- + *temnein* to cut

diatomaceous (ˌdaɪətəˈmeɪʃəs) *adj* of or containing diatoms or their fossil remains.

diatomic (ˌdaɪəˈtɒmɪk) *adj* (of a compound or molecule) containing two atoms.

diatomite (daɪˈætəˌmaɪt) *n* a soft whitish rock consisting of the siliceous remains of diatoms.

diatonic (ˌdaɪəˈtɒnɪk) *adj* **1** of, relating to, or based upon any scale of five tones and two semitones produced by playing the white keys of a keyboard instrument. **2** not involving the sharpening or flattening of the notes of the major or minor scale nor the use of such notes as modified by accidentals. ORIG C16: from LL, from Gk, from *diatonos* extending, from DIA- + *teinein* to stretch

diatonic scale *n Music.* the major and minor scales, made up of both tones and semitones.

diatribe (ˈdaɪəˌtraɪb) *n* a bitter or violent criticism or attack. ORIG C16: from L *diatriba* learned debate, from Gk *diatribē* discourse, pastime, from *diatribein* to while away, from DIA- + *tribein* to rub

Díaz de Vivar ★ (*Spanish* ˈdiaθ dɛ biˈβar) *n* **Rodrigo** (rɔˈðriɣo). the original name of (El) **Cid.**

diazepam (daɪˈæzəˌpæm) *n* a chemical compound used as a tranquillizer and muscle relaxant. ORIG C20: from DI-[1] + *azo-* + *ep(oxide)* + *-am*

diazo (daɪˈeɪzəʊ) *adj* **1** of, consisting of, or containing the divalent group, =N:N, or the divalent group, -N:N-. **2** of the reproduction of documents using the bleaching action of ultraviolet radiation on diazonium salts. ◆ *n, pl* **diazos** *or* **diazoes. 3** a document produced by this method.

diazonium (ˌdaɪəˈzəʊnɪəm) *n* (modifier) of, consisting of, or containing the group ArN:N–, where Ar is an aryl group: *a diazonium salt.*

dibasic (daɪˈbeɪsɪk) *adj* **1** (of an acid) containing two acidic hydrogen atoms. **2** (of a salt) derived by replacing two acidic hydrogen atoms.
▸ **dibasicity** (ˌdaɪbeɪˈsɪsɪtɪ) *n*

dibble (ˈdɪbᵊl) *n* **1** Also: **dibber.** a small hand tool used to make holes in the ground for bulbs, seeds, or roots. ◆ *vb* **dibbles, dibbling, dibbled. 2** to make a hole in (the ground) with a dibble. **3** to plant (seeds, etc.) with a dibble. ORIG C15: from ?

dibs (dɪbz) *pl n* **1** another word for **jacks. 2** *Sl.* money. **3** (foll. by *on*) *Inf.* rights (to) or claims (on): used mainly by children. ORIG C18: from *dibstones* game played with knucklebones or pebbles, prob. from *dib* to tap

DiCaprio ★ (dɪˈkæprɪəʊ) *n* **Leonardo.** born 1974, US film actor; his films include *Romeo & Juliet* (1996), *Titanic* (1997), and *The Beach* (2000).

dice (daɪs) *pl n* **1** cubes of wood, plastic, etc., each of whose sides has a different number of spots (1 to 6), used in games of chance. **2** (*functioning as sing*) Also called: **die.** one of these cubes. **3** small cubes as of vegetables, meat, etc. **4 no dice.** *Sl., chiefly US & Canad.* an expression of refusal. ◆ *vb* **dices, dicing, diced. 5** to cut (food, etc.) into small cubes. **6** (*intr*) to gamble or play with dice. **7** (*intr*) to take a chance or risk (esp. in **dice with death**). **8** (*tr*) *Austral. inf.* to abandon or reject. ORIG C14: pl of DIE[2]
▸ **ˈdicer** *n*

dicey (ˈdaɪsɪ) *adj* **dicier, diciest.** *Inf., chiefly Brit.* difficult or dangerous; risky; tricky.

dichloride (daɪˈklɔːraɪd) *n* a compound in which two atoms of chlorine are combined with another atom or group. Also called: **bichloride.**

dichlorodiphenyltrichloroethane (daɪˌklɔːrəʊdaɪˌfiːnaɪltraɪˌklɔːrəʊ'iːθeɪn) *n* the full name for **DDT**.

dichloromethane (daɪˌklɔːrəʊ'miːθeɪn) *n* a noxious colourless liquid widely used as a solvent, e.g. in paint strippers. Formula: CH_2Cl_2. Traditional name: **methylene dichloride.**

dichotomy (daɪ'kɒtəmɪ) *n, pl* **dichotomies. 1** division into two parts or classifications, esp. when they are sharply distinguished or opposed. **2** *Bot.* a simple method of branching by repeated division into two equal parts.
▸ **di'chotomous** *adj*

> **USAGE NOTE** *Dichotomy* should always refer to a division of some kind into two groups. It is sometimes used to refer to a puzzling situation which seems to involve a contradiction, but this use is thought by many to be incorrect, and *dilemma* is often more appropriate.

dichroism ('daɪkrəʊˌɪzəm) *n* a property of a uniaxial crystal of showing a difference in colour when viewed along two different axes (in transmitted white light). Also called: **dichromaticism.** See also **pleochroism.**
▸ **di'chroic** *adj*

dichromate (daɪ'krəʊmeɪt) *n* any salt or ester of dichromic acid. Also called: **bichromate.**

dichromatic (ˌdaɪkrəʊ'mætɪk) *adj* **1** Also: **dichroic.** having two colours. **2** (of animal species) having two different colour varieties. **3** able to perceive only two colours (and mixes of them).
▸ **dichromatism** (daɪ'krəʊməˌtɪzəm) *n*

dichromic (daɪ'krəʊmɪk) *adj* of or involving only two colours; dichromatic.

dick (dɪk) *n Sl.* **1** *Brit.* a fellow or person. **2 clever dick.** *Brit.* an opinionated person; know-all. **3** a taboo word for **penis.** ORIG C16 (meaning: fellow): from *Dick,* familiar form of *Richard,* applied to any fellow, lad, etc.; hence, C19: penis

dickens ('dɪkɪnz) *n Inf.* a euphemistic word for **devil** (used as intensifier in **what the dickens**). ORIG C16: from the name *Dickens*

Dickens ★ ('dɪkɪnz) *n* **Charles** (**John Huffam**), pen name *Boz.* 1812–70, British novelist. His works include *Pickwick Papers* (1837), *Oliver Twist* (1839), *Nicholas Nickleby* (1839), *Old Curiosity Shop* (1840–41), *Martin Chuzzlewit* (1844), *David Copperfield* (1850), *Bleak House* (1853), *Little Dorrit* (1857), and *Great Expectations* (1861).

Dickensian (dɪ'kɛnzɪən) *adj* **1** of Charles Dickens or his novels. **2a** denoting poverty, distress, and exploitation as depicted in the novels of Dickens. **2b** grotesquely comic, as some of the characters of Dickens.

dicker ('dɪkə) *vb* **1** to trade (goods) by bargaining; barter. ◆ *n* **2** a petty bargain or barter. ORIG C12: ult. from L *decuria* company of ten, from *decem* ten

dickhead ('dɪkˌhɛd) *n Sl.* a stupid or despicable man or boy. ORIG C20: from DICK (in the sense: penis) + HEAD

Dickinson ★ ('dɪkɪns^{ə}n) *n* **Emily.** 1830–86, US poet.

dicky[1] *or* **dickey** ('dɪkɪ) *n, pl* **dickies** *or* **dickeys. 1** a false blouse or shirt front. **2** Also called: **dicky bow.** *Brit.* a bow tie. **3** Also called: **dicky-bird, dickeybird.** a child's word for a bird. **4** a folding outside seat at the rear of some early cars. ORIG C18 (in the sense: shirt front): from *Dickey,* dim. of *Dick* (name)

dicky[2] *or* **dickey** ('dɪkɪ) *adj* **dickier, dickiest.** *Brit. inf.* shaky, unsteady, or unreliable: *I feel a bit dicky today.* ORIG C18: ?from *as queer as Dick's hatband* feeling ill

diclinous ('daɪklɪnəs) *adj* (of flowering plants) unisexual. Cf. **monoclinous**
▸ **'diclinism** *n*

dicotyledon (ˌdaɪkɒtɪ'liːd^{ə}n) *n* a flowering plant having two embryonic seed leaves.
▸ **ˌdicoty'ledonous** *adj*

dict. *abbrev. for:* **1** dictation. **2** dictator. **3** dictionary.

dicta ('dɪktə) *n* a plural of **dictum.**

Dictaphone ('dɪktəˌfəʊn) *n Trademark.* a tape recorder designed for recording dictation for subsequent typing.

dictate *vb* (dɪk'teɪt), **dictates, dictating, dictated. 1** to say (letters, speeches, etc.) aloud for mechanical recording or verbatim transcription by another person. **2** (*tr*) to prescribe (commands, etc.) authoritatively. **3** (*intr*) to seek to impose one's will on others. ◆ *n* ('dɪkteɪt). **4** an authoritative command. **5** a guiding principle: *the dictates of reason.* ORIG C17: from L *dictāre* to say repeatedly, order, from *dīcere* to say

dictation (dɪk'teɪʃən) *n* **1** the act of dictating material to be recorded or taken down in writing. **2** the material dictated. **3** authoritative commands or the act of giving them.

dictator (dɪk'teɪtə) *n* **1a** a ruler who is not effectively restricted by a constitution, laws, etc. **1b** an absolute, esp. tyrannical, ruler. **2** (in ancient Rome) a person appointed during a crisis to exercise supreme authority. **3** a person who makes pronouncements, which are regarded as authoritative. **4** a person who behaves in an authoritarian or tyrannical manner.

dictatorial (ˌdɪktə'tɔːrɪəl) *adj* **1** of or characteristic of a dictator. **2** tending to dictate; tyrannical; overbearing.
▸ **ˌdicta'torially** *adv*

dictatorship (dɪk'teɪtəˌʃɪp) *n* **1** the rank, office, or period of rule of a dictator. **2** government by a dictator. **3** a country ruled by a dictator. **4** absolute power or authority.

diction ('dɪkʃən) *n* **1** the choice of words in writing or speech. **2** the manner of enunciating words and sounds. ORIG C15: from L *dictiō* a saying, mode of expression, from *dīcere* to speak, say

dictionary ('dɪkʃənərɪ) *n, pl* **dictionaries. 1a** a book that consists of an alphabetical list of words with their meanings, parts of speech, pronunciations, etymologies, etc. **1b** a similar book giving equivalent words in two or more languages. **2** a reference book listing words or terms and giving information about a particular subject or activity. **3** a collection of information or examples with the entries alphabetically arranged: *a dictionary of quotations.* ORIG C16: from Med. L *dictiōnārium* collection of words, from LL *dictiō* word; see DICTION

dictum ('dɪktəm) *n, pl* **dictums** *or* **dicta. 1** a formal or authoritative statement; pronouncement. **2** a popular saying or maxim. **3** *Law.* See **obiter dictum.** ORIG C16: from L, from *dīcere* to say

did (dɪd) *vb* the past tense of **do**[1].

didactic (dɪ'dæktɪk) *adj* **1** intended to instruct, esp. excessively. **2** morally instructive. **3** (of works of art or literature) containing a political or moral message to which aesthetic considerations are subordinated. ORIG C17: from Gk *didaktikos* skilled in teaching, from *didaskein*
▸ **di'dactically** *adv* ▸ **di'dacticism** *n*

didactics (dɪ'dæktɪks) *n* (*functioning as sing*) the art or science of teaching.

diddle ('dɪd^{ə}l) *vb* **diddles, diddling, diddled.** (*tr*) *Inf.* to cheat or swindle. ORIG C19: back formation from Jeremy *Diddler,* a scrounger in J. Kenney's farce *Raising the Wind* (1803)
▸ **'diddler** *n*

Diderot ★ ('diːdərəʊ; *French* didro) *n* **Denis** (dəni). 1713–84, French philosopher, noted for the *Encyclopédie.*

didgeridoo (ˌdɪdʒərɪ'duː) *n Music.* a native deep-toned Australian wind instrument. ORIG C20: imit.

didn't ('dɪd^{ə}nt) *contraction of* did not.

dido ('daɪdəʊ) *n, pl* **didos** *or* **didoes.** (*usually pl*) *Inf.* an antic; prank; trick. ORIG C19: from ?

Dido ★ ('daɪdəʊ) *n Classical myth.* a princess of Tyre who founded Carthage and became its queen. Virgil tells of her suicide when abandoned by her lover Aeneas.

didst (dɪdst) *vb Arch.* (used with *thou*) a form of the past tense of **do**[1].

didymium (daɪ'dɪmɪəm) *n* a mixture of the metallic rare earths neodymium and praseodymium, once thought to be an element. ORIG C19: from NL, from Gk *didumos* twin + -IUM

die[1] (daɪ) *vb* **dies, dying, died.** (*mainly intr*) **1** (of an organism, organs, etc.) to cease all biological activity permanently. **2** (of something inanimate) to cease to exist. **3**

(often foll. by *away, down,* or *out*) to lose strength, power, or energy, esp. by degrees. **4** (often foll. by *away* or *down*) to become calm; subside. **5** to stop functioning: *the engine died.* **6** to languish, as with love, longing, etc. **7** (usually foll. by *of*) *Inf.* to be nearly overcome (with laughter, boredom, etc.). **8** *Christianity.* to lack spiritual life within the soul. **9** (*tr*) to suffer (a death of a specified kind): *he died a saintly death.* **10 be dying.** (foll. by *for* or an infinitive) to be eager or desperate (for something or to do something). **11 die hard.** to cease to exist after a struggle: *old habits die hard.* **12 die in harness.** to die while still working or active. **13 never say die.** *Inf.* never give up. ◆ See also **die down, die out.** ORIG OE *dīegan,* prob. of Scand. origin

die[2] (daɪ) *n* **1a** a shaped block used to cut or form metal in a drop forge, press, etc. **1b** a tool with a conical hole through which wires, etc. are drawn to reduce their diameter. **2** an internally-threaded tool for cutting external threads. **3** a casting mould. **4** *Archit.* the dado of a pedestal, usually cubic. **5** another name for **dice** (sense 2). **6 the die is cast.** the irrevocable decision has been taken. ORIG C13 *dee,* from OF *de,* ?from Vulgar L *datum* (unattested) a piece in games, from L *dare* to give, play

die-cast *vb* **die-casts, die-casting, die-cast.** (*tr*) to shape or form (an object) by introducing molten metal or plastic into a reusable mould, esp. under pressure.
▸ **'die-ˌcasting** *n*

die down *vb* (*intr, adv*) **1** (of plants) to wither above ground, leaving only the root alive during the winter. **2** to lose strength or power, esp. by degrees. **3** to become calm.

Diefenbaker ★ ('diːfᵊnˌbeɪkə) *n* **John George.** 1895–1979, Canadian Conservative statesman; prime minister (1957–63).

die-hard *n* **1** a person who resists change or who holds onto an untenable position. **2** (*modifier*) obstinately resistant to change.

dieldrin ('diːldrɪn) *n* a crystalline substance, consisting of a chlorinated derivative of naphthalene: a contact insecticide the use of which is now restricted. ORIG C20: from *Diel(s-Al)d(e)r (reaction)* + -IN; Diels & Alder were G chemists

dielectric (ˌdaɪɪ'lɛktrɪk) *n* **1** a substance that can sustain an electric field. **2** a substance of very low electrical conductivity; insulator. ◆ *adj* **3** concerned with or having the properties of a dielectric. ORIG from DIA- + ELECTRIC
▸ **ˌdie'lectrically** *adv*

Dien Bien Phu ★ (ˌdjɛn bjɛn 'fuː) *n* a village in NW Vietnam: French military post during the Indochina War; scene of a major defeat of French forces by the Vietminh (1954).

diene ('daɪiːn) *n Chem.* a hydrocarbon that contains two carbon-to-carbon double bonds in its molecules. ORIG from DI-[1] + -ENE

die out *or* **off** *vb* (*intr, adv*) **1** to die one after another until few or none are left. **2** to become extinct, esp. after a period of gradual decline.

Dieppe ★ (dɪ'ɛp; *French* djɛp) *n* a port and resort in N France, on the English Channel. Pop.: 36 600 (1990).

dieresis (daɪ'ɛrɪsɪs) *n, pl* **diereses** (-ˌsiːz). a variant spelling of **diaeresis.**

diesel ('diːzᵊl) *n* **1** See **diesel engine. 2** a ship, locomotive, lorry, etc., driven by a diesel engine. **3** *Inf.* short for **diesel oil** (*or* **fuel**).

Diesel ★ ('diːzᵊl) *n* **Rudolf** ('ruːdɔlf). 1858–1913, German engineer, who invented the diesel engine (1892).

diesel-electric *n* **1** a locomotive fitted with a diesel engine driving an electric generator that feeds electric traction motors. ◆ *adj* **2** of or relating to such a locomotive or system.

diesel engine *or* **motor** *n* a type of internal-combustion engine in which atomized fuel oil is ignited by compression alone.

diesel oil *or* **fuel** *n* a fuel obtained from petroleum distillation that is used in diesel engines. Also called (Brit.): **derv.**

Dies Irae *Latin.* ('diːeɪz 'ɪəraɪ) *n* **1** a Latin hymn of the 13th century, describing the Last Judgment. It is used in the Mass for the dead. **2** a musical setting of this. ORIG lit.: day of wrath

diesis ('daɪɪsɪs) *n, pl* **dieses** (-ˌsiːz). *Printing.* another name for **double dagger.** ORIG C16: via L from Gk: a quarter tone, lit.: a sending through, from *diienai;* the double dagger was orig. used in musical notation

diestock ('daɪˌstɒk) *n* the device holding the dies used to cut an external screw thread.

diet[1] ('daɪət) *n* **1** a specific allowance or selection of food, esp. prescribed to control weight or for health reasons: *a salt-free diet.* **2** the food and drink that a person or animal regularly consumes. **3** regular activities or occupations. ◆ *vb* **4** (*usually intr*) to follow or cause to follow a dietary regimen. ORIG C13: from OF *diete,* from L *diaeta,* from Gk *diaita* mode of living, from *diaitan* to direct one's own life
▸ **'dieter** *n*

diet[2] ('daɪət) *n* **1** (*sometimes cap.*) a legislative assembly in various countries. **2** (*sometimes cap.*) the assembly of the estates of the Holy Roman Empire. **3** *Scots Law.* a single session of a court. ORIG C15: from Med. L *diēta* public meeting, prob. from L *diaeta* DIET[1] but associated with L *diēs* day

dietary ('daɪətərɪ, -trɪ) *adj* **1** of or relating to a diet. ◆ *n, pl* **dietaries. 2** a regulated diet. **3** a system of dieting.

dietary fibre *n* fibrous substances in fruits and vegetables, such as the structural polymers of cell walls, which aid digestion. Also called: **roughage.**

dietetic (ˌdaɪɪ'tɛtɪk) *or* **dietetical** *adj* **1** denoting or relating to diet. **2** prepared for special dietary requirements.
▸ **ˌdie'tetically** *adv*

dietetics (ˌdaɪɪ'tɛtɪks) *n* (*functioning as sing*) the scientific study and regulation of food intake and preparation.

diethylene glycol *n* a colourless soluble liquid used as an antifreeze and solvent.

dietitian *or* **dietician** (ˌdaɪɪ'tɪʃən) *n* a person who specializes in dietetics.

Dietrich ★ (*German* 'diːtrɪç) *n* **Marlene** (mar'leːnə), real name *Maria Magdalene von Losch.* 1901–92, US actress, born in Germany.

differ ('dɪfə) *vb* (*intr*) **1** (often foll. by *from*) to be dissimilar in quality, nature, or degree (to); vary (from). **2** (often foll. by *from* or *with*) to disagree (with). **3** *Dialect.* to quarrel or dispute. ORIG C14: from L *differre,* to scatter, put off, be different, from *dis-* apart + *ferre* to bear

difference ('dɪfərəns) *n* **1** the state or quality of being unlike. **2** a specific instance of being unlike. **3** a distinguishing mark or feature. **4** a significant change. **5** a disagreement or argument. **6** a degree of distinctness, as between two people or things. **7** Also called: **remainder.** the result of the subtraction of one number, quantity, etc., from another. **8** *Maths.* (of two sets) the set of members of the first that are not members of the second. **9** *Heraldry.* an addition to the arms of a family to represent a younger branch. **10 make a difference. 10a** to have an effect. **10b** to treat differently. **11 split the difference. 11a** to compromise. **11b** to divide a remainder equally. **12 with a difference.** with some distinguishing quality, good or bad.

different ('dɪfərənt) *adj* **1** partly or completely unlike. **2** not identical or the same; other. **3** unusual.
▸ **'differently** *adv* ▸ **'differentness** *n*

USAGE NOTE The constructions *different from, different to,* and *different than* are all found in the works of writers of English during the past. Nowadays, however, the most widely acceptable preposition to use after *different* is *from. Different to* is common in British English, but is considered by some people to be incorrect, or less acceptable. *Different than* is a standard construction in American English. As, however, this structure is not regarded as totally acceptable in British usage, it is preferable either to use *different from: this result is only slightly different from that obtained* *in the US* or to rephrase the sentence: *this result differs only slightly from that in the US.* See also at **disabled.**

differentia (ˌdɪfəˈrɛnʃɪə) *n, pl* **differentiae** (-ʃɪˌiː). *Logic.* a feature by which two subclasses of the same class of named objects can be distinguished. ORIG C19: from L: diversity

differential (ˌdɪfəˈrɛnʃəl) *adj* **1** of, relating to, or using a difference. **2** constituting a difference; distinguishing. **3** *Maths.* involving one or more derivatives or differentials. **4** *Physics, engineering.* relating to, operating on, or based on the difference between two opposing effects, motions, forces, etc. ◆ *n* **5** a factor that differentiates between two comparable things. **6** *Maths.* **6a** an increment in a given function, expressed as the product of the derivative of that function and the corresponding increment in the independent variable. **6b** an increment in a given function of two or more variables, $f(x_1, x_2, \ldots x_n)$, expressed as the sum of the products of each partial derivative and the increment in the corresponding variable. **7** See **differential gear. 8** *Chiefly Brit.* the difference between rates of pay for different types of labour, esp. when forming a pay structure within an industry. **9** (in commerce) a difference in rates, esp. between comparable services.
▸ **ˌdifferˈentially** *adv*

differential calculus *n* the branch of calculus concerned with the study, evaluation, and use of derivatives and differentials.

differential equation *n* an equation containing differentials or derivatives of a function of one independent variable.

differential gear *n* the epicyclic gear mounted in the driving axle of a road vehicle that permits one driving wheel to rotate faster than the other, as when cornering.

differential operator *n* the mathematical operator del, ∇, used in vector analysis.

differentiate (ˌdɪfəˈrɛnʃɪˌeɪt) *vb* **differentiates, differentiating, differentiated. 1** (*tr*) to serve to distinguish between. **2** (when *intr,* often foll. by *between*) to perceive, show, or make a difference (in or between); discriminate. **3** (*intr*) to become dissimilar or distinct. **4** *Maths.* to perform a differentiation on (a quantity, expression, etc.). **5** (*intr*) (of unspecialized cells, etc.) to change during development to more specialized forms.
▸ **ˌdifferˈentiˌator** *n*

differentiation (ˌdɪfəˌrɛnʃɪˈeɪʃən) *n* **1** the act, process, or result of differentiating. **2** *Maths.* an operation used in calculus in which the derivative of a function or variable is determined.

difficult (ˈdɪfɪkᵊlt) *adj* **1** not easy to do; requiring effort. **2** not easy to understand or solve. **3** troublesome: *a difficult child.* **4** not easily convinced, pleased, or satisfied. **5** full of hardships or trials. ORIG C14: back formation from DIFFICULTY
▸ **ˈdifficultly** *adv*

difficulty (ˈdɪfɪkᵊltɪ) *n, pl* **difficulties. 1** the state or quality of being difficult. **2** a task, problem, etc., that is hard to deal with. **3** (*often pl*) a troublesome or embarrassing situation, esp. a financial one. **4** a disagreement. **5** (*often pl*) an objection or obstacle. **6** a trouble or source of trouble; worry. **7** lack of ease; awkwardness. ORIG C14: from L *difficultās,* from *difficilis,* from *dis-* not + *facilis* easy

diffident (ˈdɪfɪdənt) *adj* lacking self-confidence; shy. ORIG C15: from L *diffīdere,* from *dis-* not + *fīdere* to trust
▸ **ˈdiffidence** *n* ▸ **ˈdiffidently** *adv*

diffract (dɪˈfrækt) *vb* to undergo or cause to undergo diffraction.
▸ **difˈfractive** *adj* ▸ **difˈfractively** *adv* ▸ **difˈfractiveness** *n*

diffraction (dɪˈfrækʃən) *n* **1** *Physics.* a deviation in the direction of a wave at the edge of an obstacle in its path. **2** any phenomenon caused by diffraction, such as the formation of light and dark fringes by the passage of light through a small aperture. ORIG C17: from NL *diffractiō* a breaking to pieces, from L *diffringere* to shatter, from *dis-* apart + *frangere* to break

diffuse *vb* (dɪˈfjuːz), **diffuses, diffusing, diffused. 1** to spread in all directions. **2** to undergo or cause to undergo diffusion. **3** to scatter; disperse. ◆ *adj* (dɪˈfjuːs). **4** spread out over a wide area. **5** lacking conciseness. **6** characterized by diffusion. ORIG C15: from L *diffūsus* spread abroad, from *diffundere* to pour forth, from *dis-* away + *fundere* to pour
▸ **diffusely** (dɪˈfjuːslɪ) *adv* ▸ **difˈfuseness** *n* ▸ **diffusible** (dɪˈfjuːzɪbᵊl) *adj*

USAGE NOTE This word is quite commonly misused instead of *defuse,* when talking about calming down a situation.

diffuser *or* **diffusor** (dɪˈfjuːzə) *n* **1** a person or thing that diffuses. **2** a part of a lighting fixture, as a translucent covering, used to scatter the light and prevent glare. **3** a cone, wedge, or baffle placed in front of the diaphragm of a loudspeaker to diffuse the sound waves. **4** a duct, esp. in a wind tunnel or jet engine, that reduces the speed and increases the pressure of the air or fluid. **5** *Photog.* a light-scattering medium, such as a screen of fine fabric, used to reduce the sharpness of shadows and thus soften the lighting. **6** a device attached to a hair dryer that diffuses the warm air as it comes out.

diffusion (dɪˈfjuːʒən) *n* **1** a diffusing or being diffused; dispersion. **2** verbosity. **3** *Physics.* **3a** the random thermal motion of atoms, molecules, etc., in gases, liquids, and some solids. **3b** the transfer of atoms or molecules by their random motion from one part of a medium to another. **4** *Physics.* the transmission or reflection of electromagnetic radiation, esp. light, in which the radiation is scattered in many directions. **5** *Anthropol.* the transmission of social institutions, skills, and myths from one culture to another.

diffusionism (dɪˈfjuːʒənˌɪzəm) *n Anthropol.* the theory that diffusion is responsible for the similarities between different cultures.
▸ **difˈfusionist** *n, adj*

diffusive (dɪˈfjuːsɪv) *adj* characterized by diffusion.
▸ **difˈfusively** *adv* ▸ **difˈfusiveness** *n*

dig (dɪg) *vb* **digs, digging, dug. 1** (when *tr,* often foll. by *up*) to cut into, break up, and turn over or remove (earth, etc.), esp. with a spade. **2** to excavate (a hole, tunnel, etc.) by digging, usually with an implement or (of animals) with claws, etc. **3** (often foll. by *through*) to make or force (one's way): *he dug his way through the crowd.* **4** (*tr;* often foll. by *out* or *up*) to obtain by digging. **5** (*tr;* often foll. by *out* or *up*) to find by effort or searching: *to dig out facts.* **6** (*tr;* foll. by *in* or *into*) to thrust or jab. **7** (*tr;* foll. by *in* or *into*) to mix (compost, etc.) with soil by digging. **8** (*intr;* foll. by *in* or *into*) *Inf.* to begin vigorously to do something. **9** (*tr*) *Inf.* to like, understand, or appreciate. **10** (*intr*) *US sl.* to work hard, esp. for an examination. ◆ *n* **11** the act of digging. **12** a thrust or poke. **13** a cutting remark. **14** *Inf.* an archaeological excavation. **15** *Austral. & NZ inf.* short for **digger** (sense 4). ◆ See also **dig in.** ORIG C13 *diggen,* from ?

digest *vb* (dɪˈdʒɛst, daɪ-). **1** to subject (food) to a process of digestion. **2** (*tr*) to assimilate mentally. **3** *Chem.* to soften or disintegrate by the action of heat, moisture, or chemicals. **4** (*tr*) to arrange in a methodical order; classify. **5** (*tr*) to reduce to a summary. ◆ *n* (ˈdaɪdʒɛst). **6** a comprehensive and systematic compilation of information or material, often condensed. **7** a magazine, periodical, etc., that summarizes news. **8** a compilation of rules of law. ORIG C14: from LL *dīgesta* writings grouped under various heads, from L *dīgerere* to divide, from *di-* apart + *gerere* to bear

Digest (ˈdaɪdʒɛst) *n Roman law.* the books of law compiled by order of Justinian in the sixth century A.D.

digestible (dɪˈdʒɛstɪbᵊl, daɪ-) *adj* capable of being digested.
▸ **diˌgestiˈbility** *n*

digestion (dɪˈdʒɛstʃən, daɪ-) *n* **1** the act or process in living organisms of breaking down food into easily absorbed substances by the action of enzymes, etc. **2** mental assimilation, esp. of ideas. **3** the decomposition of sewage by bacteria. **4** *Chem.* the treatment of material

with heat, solvents, etc., to cause decomposition. ORIG C14: from OF, from L *digestiō* a dissolving, digestion
▸ **di'gestional** *adj*

digestive (dɪ'dʒɛstɪv, daɪ-) *or* **digestant** (daɪ'dʒɛstənt) *adj* **1** relating to, aiding, or subjecting to digestion. ◆ *n* **2** any substance that aids digestion.
▸ **di'gestively** *adv*

digestive biscuit *n* a round semisweet biscuit made from wholemeal flour.

digger ('dɪgə) *n* **1** a person, animal, or machine that digs. **2** a miner. **3** a tool or machine used for excavation. **4** (*sometimes cap.*) *Austral. inf.* an Australian, esp. a soldier: often used as a friendly term of address.

diggings ('dɪgɪŋz) *pl n* **1** (*functioning as pl*) material that has been dug out. **2** (*functioning as sing or pl*) a place where mining has taken place. **3** (*functioning as pl*) *Brit. inf.* a less common name for **digs**.

dight (daɪt) *vb* **dights, dighting, dight** *or* **dighted.** (*tr*) *Arch.* to adorn or equip, as for battle. ORIG OE *dihtan* to compose, from L *dictāre* to DICTATE

Digibox ('dɪdʒɪ,bɒks) *n Trademark.* a device which converts the signals from a digital television broadcast into a form which can be viewed on a standard television set. ORIG C20: from DIGI(TAL) (sense 3) + BOX[1]

dig in *vb* (*adv*) **1** *Mil.* to dig foxholes, trenches, etc. **2** *Inf.* to entrench (oneself). **3** (*intr*) *Inf.* to defend a position firmly, as in an argument. **4** (*intr*) *Inf.* to begin to eat vigorously: *don't wait, just dig in.* **5 dig one's heels in.** *Inf.* to refuse to move or be persuaded.

digit ('dɪdʒɪt) *n* **1** a finger or toe. **2** any of the ten Arabic numerals from 0 to 9. ORIG C15: from L *digitus* toe, finger

digital ('dɪdʒɪtᵊl) *adj* **1** of, resembling, or possessing a digit or digits. **2** performed with the fingers. **3** representing data as a series of numerical values. **4** displaying information as numbers rather than by a pointer moving over a dial. ◆ *n* **5** *Music.* a key on a piano, harpsichord, etc.
▸ **'digitally** *adv*

digital audio tape *n* magnetic tape on which sound is recorded digitally, giving high-fidelity reproduction. Abbrev.: **DAT**.

digital camera *n* a camera that produces digital images, which can be stored on a computer, displayed on a screen, and printed.

digital clock *or* **watch** *n* a clock or watch in which the time is indicated by digits rather than by hands on a dial.

digital compact cassette *n* a magnetic tape cassette on which sound can be recorded in digital format. Abbrev.: **DCC**.

digital computer *n* an electronic computer in which the input is discrete, consisting of numbers, letters, etc. that are represented internally in binary notation.

digitalin (,dɪdʒɪ'teɪlɪn) *n* a poisonous glycoside extracted from digitalis and used in treating heart disease. ORIG C19: from DIGITAL(IS) + -IN

digitalis (,dɪdʒɪ'teɪlɪs) *n* **1** any of a genus of Eurasian plants such as the foxglove, having long spikes of bell-shaped flowers. **2** a drug prepared from the dried leaves of the foxglove: used medicinally as a heart stimulant. ORIG C17: from NL, from L: relating to a finger; based on G *Fingerhut* foxglove, lit.: finger-hat

digitalize *or* **digitalise** ('dɪdʒɪtə,laɪz) *vb* **digitalizes, digitalizing, digitalized** *or* **digitalises, digitalising, digitalised.** (*tr*) another word for **digitize.**

digital mapping *n* a method of preparing maps in which the data is stored in a computer for ease of access and updating.
▸ **digital map** *n*

digital radio *n* **1** radio in which the audio information is transmitted in digital form and decoded at the receiver. **2** a radio set that can receive and decode digital information.

digital recording *n* a sound recording process that converts audio or analogue signals into a series of pulses that correspond to the voltage level.

digital television *n* **1** television in which the picture information is transmitted in digital form and decoded at the receiver. **2** a television set that can receive and decode digital information.

digital versatile disk *n* a disk similar to a CD but with much greater capacity, used for storing and distributing films, multimedia, etc. Also called (esp. formerly): **digital video disk.** Abbrev.: **DVD.**

digital video *n* video output based on digital rather than analogue signals.

digitate ('dɪdʒɪ,teɪt) *or* **digitated** *adj* **1** (of leaves) having the leaflets in the form of a spread hand. **2** (of animals) having digits.
▸ **'digi,tately** *adv* ▸ **,digi'tation** *n*

digitigrade ('dɪdʒɪtɪ,greɪd) *adj* **1** (of dogs, cats, horses, etc.) walking so that only the toes touch the ground. ◆ *n* **2** a digitigrade animal.

digitize *or* **digitise** ('dɪdʒɪ,taɪz) *vb* **digitizes, digitizing, digitized** *or* **digitises, digitising, digitised.** (*tr*) to transcribe (data) into a digital form for processing by a computer.
▸ **,digiti'zation** *or* **,digiti'sation** *n* ▸ **'digi,tizer** *or* **'digi,tiser** *n*

dignified ('dɪgnɪ,faɪd) *adj* characterized by dignity of manner or appearance; stately; noble.
▸ **'digni,fiedly** *adv* ▸ **'digni,fiedness** *n*

dignify ('dɪgnɪ,faɪ) *vb* **dignifies, dignifying, dignified.** (*tr*) **1** to invest with honour or dignity. **2** to add distinction to. **3** to add a semblance of dignity to, esp. by the use of a pretentious name or title. ORIG C15: from OF *dignifier,* from LL *dignificāre,* from L *dignus* worthy + *facere* to make

dignitary ('dɪgnɪtərɪ) *n, pl* **dignitaries.** a person of high official position or rank.

dignity ('dɪgnɪtɪ) *n, pl* **dignities. 1** a formal or stately bearing. **2** the state or quality of being worthy of honour. **3** relative importance; rank. **4** sense of self-importance (often in **stand** (*or* **be**) **on one's dignity, beneath one's dignity**). **5** high rank, esp. in government or the church. ORIG C13: from OF *dignite,* from L *dignitās* merit, from *dignus* worthy

digoxin (daɪ'dʒɒksɪn) *n* a glycoside extracted from digitalis leaves and used in the treatment of heart failure.

digraph ('daɪgrɑːf) *n* a combination of two letters used to represent a single sound such as *gh* in *tough.*
▸ **digraphic** (daɪ'græfɪk) *adj*

digress (daɪ'grɛs) *vb* (*intr*) **1** to depart from the main subject in speech or writing. **2** to wander from one's path. ORIG C16: from L *dīgressus* turned aside, from *dīgredī,* from *dis-* apart + *gradī* to go
▸ **di'gresser** *n* ▸ **di'gression** *n*

digressive (daɪ'grɛsɪv) *adj* characterized by digression.
▸ **di'gressively** *adv* ▸ **di'gressiveness** *n*

digs (dɪgz) *pl n Brit. inf.* lodgings. ORIG C19: from DIGGINGS, ? referring to where one *digs* or works, but see also DIG IN

dihedral (daɪ'hiːdrəl) *adj* **1** having or formed by two intersecting planes. ◆ *n* **2** Also called: **dihedron, dihedral angle.** the figure formed by two intersecting planes. **3** the upward inclination of an aircraft wing in relation to the lateral axis.

Dijon ★ (*French* diʒɔ̃) *n* a city in E France: capital of the former duchy of Burgundy. Pop.: 151 636 (1990).

dik-dik ('dɪk,dɪk) *n* any of several small antelopes inhabiting semiarid regions of Africa. ORIG C19: E African, prob. imit.

dike (daɪk) *n, vb* **dikes, diking, diked.** a variant spelling of **dyke**[1].

diktat ('dɪktɑːt) *n* **1** a decree or settlement imposed, esp. by a ruler or a victorious nation. **2** a dogmatic statement. ORIG from G: dictation, from L *dictātum,* from *dictāre* to DICTATE

dilapidate (dɪ'læpɪ,deɪt) *vb* **dilapidates, dilapidating, dilapidated.** to fall or cause to fall into ruin. ORIG C16: from L *dīlapidāre* to waste, from *dis-* apart + *lapidāre* to stone, from *lapis* stone
▸ **di,lapi'dation** *n*

dilapidated (dɪ'læpɪ,deɪtɪd) *adj* falling to pieces or in a state of disrepair; shabby.

dilate (daɪ'leɪt, dɪ-) *vb* **dilates, dilating, dilated. 1** to make or become wider or larger. **2** (*intr;* often foll. by *on* or *upon*) to speak or write at length. ORIG C14: from L *dīlātāre* to spread out, from *dis-* apart + *lātus* wide

▸ **diˈlatable** *adj* ▸ **diˌlataˈbility** *n* ▸ **diˈlation** *or* **dilatation** (ˌdaɪləˈteɪʃən) *n* ▸ **dilative** (daɪˈleɪtɪv) *adj*

dilatory (ˈdɪlətərɪ, -trɪ) *adj* **1** tending to delay or waste time. **2** intended to waste time or defer action. ORIG C15: from LL *dīlātōrius* inclined to delay, from *differre* to postpone; see DIFFER
▸ **ˈdilatorily** *adv* ▸ **ˈdilatoriness** *n*

dildo *or* **dildoe** (ˈdɪldəʊ) *n, pl* **dildos** *or* **dildoes.** an object used as a substitute for an erect penis. ORIG C16: from ?

dilemma (dɪˈlɛmə, daɪ-) *n* **1** a situation necessitating a choice between two equally undesirable alternatives. **2** a problem that seems incapable of a solution. **3** *Logic.* a type of argument which forces the maintainer of a proposition to accept one of two conclusions each of which contradicts the original assertion. **4 on the horns of a dilemma. 4a** faced with the choice between two equally unpalatable alternatives. **4b** in an awkward situation. ORIG C16: via L from Gk, from DI-[1] + *lēmma* proposition, from *lambanein* to grasp
▸ **dilemmatic** (ˌdɪlɪˈmætɪk) *adj*

> **USAGE NOTE** The use of *dilemma* to refer to a problem that seems incapable of a solution is considered by some people to be incorrect.

dilettante (ˌdɪlɪˈtɑːntɪ) *n, pl* **dilettantes** *or* **dilettanti** (-ˈtɑːntɪ). **1** a person whose interest in a subject is superficial rather than professional. **2** a person who loves the arts. ◆ *adj* **3** of or characteristic of a dilettante. ORIG C18: from It., from *dilettare* to delight, from L *dēlectāre*
▸ **ˌdiletˈtantish** *or* **ˌdiletˈtanteish** *adj* ▸ **ˌdiletˈtantism** *or* **ˌdiletˈteism** *n*

diligence[1] (ˈdɪlɪdʒəns) *n* **1** steady and careful application. **2** proper attention or care. ORIG C14: from L *dīligentia* care

diligence[2] (ˈdɪlɪdʒəns) *n History.* a stagecoach. ORIG C18: from F, shortened from *carosse de diligence,* lit.: coach of speed

diligent (ˈdɪlɪdʒənt) *adj* **1** careful and persevering in carrying out tasks or duties. **2** carried out with care and perseverance: *diligent work.* ORIG C14: from OF, from L *dīligere* to value, from *dis-* apart + *legere* to read
▸ **ˈdiligently** *adv*

dill[1] (dɪl) *n* **1** an aromatic Eurasian plant with umbrella-shaped clusters of yellow flowers. **2** the leaves or fruits of this plant, used for flavouring and in medicine. ORIG OE *dile*

dill[2] (dɪl) *n Austral. & NZ sl.* a fool. ORIG C20: from DILLY[2]

dill pickle *n* a pickled cucumber flavoured with dill.

dilly[1] (ˈdɪlɪ) *n, pl* **dillies.** *Sl., chiefly US & Canad.* a person or thing that is remarkable. ORIG C20: ?from girl's name *Dilly*

dilly[2] (ˈdɪlɪ) *adj* **dillier, dilliest.** *Austral. sl.* silly. ORIG C20: from E dialect, ?from SILLY

dilly bag *n Austral.* a small bag, esp., formerly, one made of plaited grass, etc., often used for carrying food. ORIG from Abor. *dilly* small bag or basket

dilly-dally (ˌdɪlɪˈdælɪ) *vb* **dilly-dallies, dilly-dallying, dilly-dallied.** (*intr*) *Inf.* to loiter or vacillate. ORIG C17: by reduplication from DALLY

dilute (daɪˈluːt) *vb* **dilutes, diluting, diluted. 1** to make or become less concentrated, esp. by adding water or a thinner. **2** to make or become weaker in force, effect, etc. ◆ *adj* **3** *Chem.* **3a** (of a solution, etc.) having a low concentration. **3b** (of a substance) present in solution, esp. a weak solution in water: *dilute acetic acid.* ORIG C16: from L *dīluere,* from *dis-* apart + *-luere,* from *lavāre* to wash
▸ **diˈluter** *n*

dilution (daɪˈluːʃən) *n* **1** the act of diluting or state of being diluted. **2** a diluted solution.

diluvial (daɪˈluːvɪəl, dɪ-) *or* **diluvian** *adj* of or connected with a deluge, esp. with the great Flood described in Genesis. ORIG C17: from LL *dīluviālis,* from L *dīluere* to wash away; see DILUTE

dim (dɪm) *adj* **dimmer, dimmest. 1** badly illuminated. **2** not clearly seen; faint. **3** having weak or indistinct vision. **4** mentally dull. **5** not clear in the mind; obscure: *a dim memory.* **6** lacking in brightness or lustre. **7** unfavourable, gloomy or disapproving (esp. in **take a dim view**). ◆ *vb* **dims, dimming, dimmed. 8** to become or cause to become dim. **9** (*tr*) to cause to seem less bright. **10** the US and Canad. word for **dip** (sense 5). ORIG OE *dimm*
▸ **ˈdimly** *adv* ▸ **ˈdimness** *n*

dim. *abbrev. for:* **1** dimension. **2** Also: **dimin.** *Music.* diminuendo. **3** Also: **dimin.** diminutive.

Dimashq ★ (diːˈmæʃk) *n* an Arabic name for **Damascus.**

Dimbleby ★ (ˈdɪmbᵊlbɪ) *n* **Richard.** 1913–65, British broadcaster.

dime (daɪm) *n* **1** a coin of the US and Canada, worth one tenth of a dollar or ten cents. **2 a dime a dozen.** very cheap or common. ORIG C14: from OF *disme,* from L *decimus* tenth, from *decem* ten

dimenhydrinate (ˌdaɪmɛnˈhaɪdrɪˌneɪt) *n* a crystalline substance, used as an antihistamine and for the prevention of nausea, esp. in travel sickness. ORIG from DI-[1] + ME(THYL) + (AMI)N(E) + *(diphen)hydr(am)in(e)* + -ATE[1]

dime novel *n US.* (formerly) a cheap melodramatic novel, usually in paperback.

dimension (dɪˈmɛnʃən) *n* **1** (*often pl*) a measurement of the size of something in a particular direction, such as the length, width, height, or diameter. **2** (*often pl*) scope; size; extent. **3** aspect: *a new dimension to politics.* **4** *Maths.* the number of coordinates required to locate a point in space. ◆ *vb* **5** (*tr*) *Chiefly US.* to cut to or mark with specified dimensions. ORIG C14: from OF, from L *dīmensiō* an extent, from *dīmētīrī* to measure out, from *mētīrī*
▸ **diˈmensional** *adj* ▸ **diˈmensionless** *adj*

dimer (ˈdaɪmə) *n Chem.* a compound the molecule of which is formed by the linking of two identical molecules. ORIG C20: from DI-[1] + -MER
▸ **dimeric** (daɪˈmɛrɪk) *adj*

dimerize *or* **dimerise** (ˈdaɪməˌraɪz) *vb* **dimerizes, dimerizing, dimerized** *or* **dimerises, dimerising, dimerised.** to react or cause to react to form a dimer.
▸ **ˌdimeriˈzation** *or* **ˌdimeriˈsation** *n*

dimeter (ˈdɪmɪtə) *n Prosody.* a line of verse consisting of two metrical feet or a verse written in this metre.

dimethylformamide (daɪˌmiːθaɪlˈfɔːməˌmaɪd) *n* a colourless liquid widely used as a solvent and sometimes as a catalyst. Formula: $(CH_3)_2NCHO$. Abbrev.: **DMF.**

dimethylsulphoxide (daɪˌmiːθaɪlsʌlˈfɒksaɪd) *n* a liquid used as a solvent and in medicine to improve the penetration of drugs applied to the skin. Abbrev.: **DMSO.**

diminish (dɪˈmɪnɪʃ) *vb* **1** to make or become smaller, fewer, or less. **2** (*tr*) *Archit.* to cause to taper. **3** (*tr*) *Music.* to decrease (a minor or perfect interval) by a semitone. **4** to reduce in authority, status, etc. ORIG C15: blend of *diminuen* to lessen (from L *dēminuere,* from *minuere*) + archaic *minish* to lessen
▸ **diˈminishable** *adj*

diminished (dɪˈmɪnɪʃt) *adj* **1** reduced or lessened; made smaller. **2** *Music.* denoting any minor or perfect interval reduced by a semitone.

diminished responsibility *n Law.* a plea under which mental derangement is submitted as demonstrating lack of criminal responsibility.

diminishing returns *pl n Econ.* progressively smaller increases in output resulting from equal increases in production.

diminuendo (dɪˌmɪnjʊˈɛndəʊ) *Music.* ◆ *n, pl* **diminuendos. 1a** a gradual decrease in loudness. Symbol: > **1b** a musical passage affected by a diminuendo. ◆ *adj* **2** gradually decreasing in loudness. **3** with a diminuendo. ORIG C18: from It., from *diminuire* to DIMINISH

diminution (ˌdɪmɪˈnjuːʃən) *n* **1** reduction; decrease. **2** *Music.* the presentation of the subject of a fugue, etc., in which the note values are reduced in length. ORIG C14: from L *dēminūtiō;* see DIMINISH

diminutive (dɪˈmɪnjʊtɪv) *adj* **1** very small; tiny. **2** *Grammar.* **2a** denoting an affix added to a word to convey the meaning *small* or *unimportant* or to express affection. **2b** denoting a word formed by the addition of a diminutive

affix. ◆ *n* **3** *Grammar.* a diminutive word or affix. **4** a tiny person or thing.
▸ **di'minutively** *adv* ▸ **di'minutiveness** *n*

dimissory (dɪ'mɪsərɪ) *adj* **1** granting permission to be ordained: *a bishop's dimissory letter.* **2** granting permission to depart.

Dimitrovo ★ (di'mitrovo) *n* the former name (1949–62) of **Pernik.**

dimity ('dɪmɪtɪ) *n, pl* **dimities.** a light strong cotton fabric with woven stripes or squares. ORIG C15: from Med. L *dimitum,* from Gk *dimiton,* from DI-[1] + *mitos* thread of the warp

dimmer ('dɪmə) *n* **1** a device for dimming an electric light. **2** (*often pl*) *US.* **2a** a dipped headlight on a road vehicle. **2b** a parking light on a car.

dimorphism (daɪ'mɔːfɪzəm) *n* **1** the occurrence within a plant of two distinct forms of any part. **2** the occurrence in an animal species of two distinct types of individual. **3** a property of certain substances that enables them to exist in two distinct crystalline forms.
▸ **di'morphic** *or* **di'morphous** *adj*

dimple ('dɪmp^{ə}l) *n* **1** a small natural dent, esp. on the cheeks or chin. **2** any slight depression in a surface. ◆ *vb* **dimples, dimpling, dimpled. 3** to make or become dimpled. **4** (*intr*) to produce dimples by smiling. ORIG C13 *dympull*
▸ **'dimply** *adj*

dim sum (ˌdɪm 'sʌm) *n* a Chinese appetizer of steamed dumplings containing various fillings. ORIG Cantonese

dimwit ('dɪmˌwɪt) *n Inf.* a stupid or silly person.
▸ **ˌdim-'witted** *adj* ▸ **ˌdim-'wittedness** *n*

din (dɪn) *n* **1** a loud discordant confused noise. ◆ *vb* **dins, dinning, dinned. 2** (*tr;* usually foll. by *into*) to instil by constant repetition. **3** (*tr*) to subject to a din. **4** (*intr*) to make a din. ORIG OE *dynn*

DIN *n* **1** a formerly used logarithmic expression of the speed of a photographic film, plate, etc.; high-speed films have high numbers. **2** a system of standard plugs, sockets, etc. formerly used for interconnecting domestic audio and video equipment. ORIG C20: from G *D(eutsche) I(ndustrie) N(ormen)* German Industry Standards

dinar ('diːnɑː) *n* the standard monetary unit of Algeria, Bahrain, Bosnia-Herzegovina, Iraq, Jordan, Kuwait, Libya, Sudan, Tunisia, and Yugoslavia. ORIG C17: from Ar., from LGk *dēnarion,* from L *dēnārius* DENARIUS

d'Indy ★ (*French* dɛ̃di) *n* (**Paul Marie Theodore**) **Vincent.** 1851–1931, French composer.

dine (daɪn) *vb* **dines, dining, dined. 1** (*intr*) to eat dinner. **2** (*intr;* often foll. by *on, off,* or *upon*) to make one's meal (of): *the guests dined upon roast beef.* **3** (*tr*) *Inf.* to entertain to dinner (esp. in **wine and dine someone**). ORIG C13: from OF *disner,* from Vulgar L *disjējūnāre* (unattested), from *dis-* not + LL *jējūnāre* to fast

dine out *vb* (*intr, adv*) **1** to dine away from home. **2** (foll. by *on*) to have dinner at the expense of someone else mainly for the sake of one's conversation about (a subject or story).

diner ('daɪnə) *n* **1** a person eating a meal, esp. in a restaurant. **2** *Chiefly US & Canad.* a small cheap restaurant. **3** a fashionable bar, or a section of one, where food is served.

Dinesen ★ ('dɪnɪs^{ə}n) *n* **Isak** ('aɪzək), pen name of *Baroness Karen Blixen.* 1885–1962, Danish author of short stories. Her life story was told in the film *Out of Africa* (1986).

dinette (daɪ'nɛt) *n* an alcove or small area for use as a dining room.

ding (dɪŋ) *vb* **1** to ring, esp. with tedious repetition. **2** (*tr*) another word for **din** (sense 2). ◆ *n* **3** an imitation of the sound of a bell. ORIG C13: prob. imit., but infl. by DIN + RING[2]

dingbat ('dɪŋˌbæt) *n Austral. sl.* a crazy or stupid person.

dingbats ('dɪŋˌbæts) *pl n Austral. & NZ sl.* an attack of nervousness, irritation, or loathing: *he had the dingbats.*

ding-dong *n* **1** the sound of a bell or bells. **2** an imitation of the sound of a bell. **3a** a violent exchange of blows or words. **3b** (*as modifier*): *a ding-dong battle.* ◆ *adj* **4** sounding or ringing repeatedly. ORIG C16: imit.; see DING

dinges ('dɪŋəs) *n S. African inf.* a jocular word for something whose name is unknown or forgotten; thingumabob. ORIG from Afrik., from Du. *dinges* thing

dinghy ('dɪŋɪ, 'dɪŋgɪ) *n, pl* **dinghies.** any small boat, powered by sail, oars, or outboard motor. Also (esp. formerly): **dingy, dingey.** ORIG C19: from Hindi or Bengali *dingi*

dingle ('dɪŋg^{ə}l) *n* a small wooded dell. ORIG C13: from ?

dingo ('dɪŋgəʊ) *n, pl* **dingoes.** a wild dog of Australia, having a yellowish-brown coat and resembling a wolf. ORIG C18: from Abor.

dingy ('dɪndʒɪ) *adj* **dingier, dingiest. 1** lacking light or brightness; drab. **2** dirty; discoloured. ORIG C18: perhaps from an earlier dialect word rel. to OE *dynge* dung
▸ **'dingily** *adv* ▸ **'dinginess** *n*

dining car *n* a railway coach in which meals are served at tables. Also called: **restaurant car.**

dining room *n* a room where meals are eaten.

dinitrogen oxide (daɪ'naɪtrədʒən) *n* the systematic name for **nitrous oxide.**

dinkie ('dɪŋkɪ) *n* **1** an affluent married childless person. ◆ *adj* **2** designed for or appealing to dinkies. ORIG C20: from *d(ouble) i(ncome) n(o) k(ids)* + -IE

dinkum ('dɪŋkəm) *adj Austral. & NZ inf.* **1** genuine or right: *a fair dinkum offer.* **2 dinkum oil.** the truth. ORIG C19: from E dialect: work, from ?

dinky ('dɪŋkɪ) *adj* **dinkier, dinkiest.** *Inf.* **1** *Brit.* small and neat; dainty. **2** *US.* inconsequential; insignificant. ORIG C18: from Scot. & N English dialect *dink* neat, neatly dressed

dinky-di (ˌdɪŋkɪ'daɪ) *adj Austral. inf.* typical: *dinky-di Pom idleness.* ORIG C20: var. of DINKUM

dinner ('dɪnə) *n* **1** a meal taken in the evening. **2** a meal taken at midday, esp. when it is the main meal of the day; lunch. **3** a formal meal or banquet in honour of someone or something. **4** (*as modifier*): *dinner table; dinner hour.* ORIG C13: from OF *disner;* see DINE

dinner dance *n* a formal dinner followed by dancing.

dinner jacket *n* a man's semiformal evening jacket without tails, usually black. US and Canad. name: **tuxedo.**

dinner service *n* a set of matching plates, dishes, etc., suitable for serving a meal.

dinosaur ('daɪnəˌsɔː) *n* **1** any of a large order of extinct reptiles many of which were of gigantic size and abundant in the Mesozoic era. **2** a person or thing that is considered to be out of date. ORIG C19: from NL *dinosaurus,* from Gk *deinos* fearful + *sauros* lizard
▸ **ˌdino'saurian** *adj*

dint (dɪnt) *n* **1 by dint of.** by means or use of: *by dint of hard work.* **2** *Arch.* a blow or a mark made by a blow. ◆ *vb* **3** (*tr*) to mark with dints. ORIG OE *dynt*

dioc. *abbrev. for:* **1** diocesan. **2** diocese.

Dio Cassius ★ ('daɪəʊ 'kæsɪəs) *n* ?155–?230 A.D., Roman historian. His *History of Rome* covers the period of Rome's transition from Republic to Empire.

diocesan (daɪ'ɒsɪs^{ə}n) *adj* **1** of or relating to a diocese. ◆ *n* **2** the bishop of a diocese.

diocese ('daɪəsɪs) *n* the district under the jurisdiction of a bishop. ORIG C14: from OF, from LL *diocēsis,* from Gk *dioikēsis* administration, from *dioikein* to manage a household, from *oikos* house

Dio Chrysostom ★ ('daɪəʊ 'krɪsəstəm) *n* 2nd century A.D., Greek orator and philosopher.

Diocletian ★ (ˌdaɪə'kliːʃən) *n* full name *Gaius Aurelius Valerius Diocletianus.* 245–313 A.D., Roman emperor (284–305), who divided the empire into East and West (293).

diode ('daɪəʊd) *n* **1** a semiconductor device used in circuits for converting alternating current to direct current. **2** the earliest type of electronic valve having two electrodes between which a current can flow only in one direction. ORIG C20: from DI-[1] + -ODE[2]

dioecious (daɪ'iːʃəs) *adj* (of plants) having the male and female reproductive organs on separate plants. ORIG

C18: from NL *Dioecia* name of class, from DI-[1] + Gk *oikia* house

Diogenes ★ (daɪ'ɒdʒɪˌniːz) *n* ?412–?323 B.C., Greek Cynic philosopher.

Diomede Islands ★ ('daɪəˌmiːd) *pl n* two small islands in the Bering Strait, separated by the international date line and by the boundary line between the US and Russia.

Diomedes (ˌdaɪə'miːdiːz), **Diomede,** *or* **Diomed** ★ ('daɪəˌmɛd) *n Greek myth.* a king of Argos, and suitor of Helen, who fought with the Greeks at Troy.

Dionysian (ˌdaɪə'nɪzɪən) *adj* **1** of or relating to Dionysus. **2** (*often not cap.*) wild or orgiastic.

Dionysius ★ (ˌdaɪə'nɪsɪəs) *n* called *the Elder.* ?430–367 B.C., tyrant of Syracuse (405–367).

Dionysus *or* **Dionysos** ★ (ˌdaɪə'naɪsəs) *n* the Greek god of wine, fruitfulness, and vegetation, worshipped in orgiastic rites. He was also known as the bestower of ecstasy and god of the drama, and identified with Bacchus.

Diophantine equation (ˌdaɪəʊ'fæntaɪn) *n* (in number theory) an equation in more than one variable, for which integral solutions are sought. ORIG from DIOPHANTUS

Diophantus ★ (ˌdaɪəʊ'fæntəs) *n* 3rd century A.D., Greek mathematician, noted for his treatise on the theory of numbers, *Arithmetica.*

dioptre *or US* **diopter** (daɪ'ɒptə) *n* a unit for measuring the refractive power of a lens: the reciprocal of the focal length of the lens expressed in metres. ORIG C16: from L *dioptra* optical instrument, from Gk, from *dia-* through + *opsesthai* to see
▸ **di'optral** *adj*

dioptrics (daɪ'ɒptrɪks) *n* (*functioning as sing*) the branch of geometrical optics concerned with the formation of images by lenses. ORIG C20: from DIOPTRE + -ICS

Dior ★ (diː'ɔː; *French* djɔr) *n* **Christian** ('krɪstʃən; *French* kristjɑ̃). 1905–57, French couturier.

diorama (ˌdaɪə'rɑːmə) *n* **1** a miniature three-dimensional scene, in which models of figures are seen against a background. **2** a picture made up of illuminated translucent curtains, viewed through an aperture. **3** a museum display, as of an animal, of a specimen in its natural setting. ORIG C19: from F, from Gk *dia-* through + *horama* view, from *horan* to see
▸ **dioramic** (ˌdaɪə'ræmɪk) *adj*

dioxide (daɪ'ɒksaɪd) *n* any oxide containing two oxygen atoms per molecule, both of which are bonded to an atom of another element.

dioxin (daɪ'ɒksɪn) *n* any of various chemical by-products of the manufacture of certain herbicides and bactericides, esp. the extremely toxic tetrachlorodibenzoparadioxin (TCDD).

dip (dɪp) *vb* **dips, dipping, dipped. 1** to plunge or be plunged quickly or briefly into a liquid, esp. to wet or coat. **2** (*intr*) to undergo a slight decline, esp. temporarily: *sales dipped in November.* **3** (*intr*) to slope downwards. **4** (*intr*) to sink quickly. **5** (*tr*) to switch (car headlights) from the main to the lower beam. US and Canad. word: **dim. 6** (*tr*) **6a** to immerse (sheep, etc.) briefly in a chemical to rid them of or prevent infestation by insects, etc. **6b** to immerse (grain, vegetables, or wood) in a preservative liquid. **7** (*tr*) to dye by immersing in a liquid. **8** (*tr*) to baptize (someone) by immersion. **9** (*tr*) to plate or galvanize (a metal, etc.) by immersion in an electrolyte or electrolytic cell. **10** (*tr*) to scoop up a liquid or something from a liquid in the hands or in a container. **11** to lower or be lowered briefly. **12** (*tr*) to make (a candle) by plunging the wick into melted wax. **13** (*intr*) to plunge a container, the hands, etc., into something, esp. to obtain an object. **14** (*intr*) (of an aircraft) to drop suddenly and then regain height. ◆ *n* **15** the act of dipping or state of being dipped. **16** a brief swim in water. **17a** any liquid chemical in which sheep, etc. are dipped. **17b** any liquid preservative into which objects are dipped. **18** a dye into which fabric is immersed. **19** a depression, esp. in a landscape. **20** something taken up by dipping. **21** a container used for dipping; dipper. **22** a momentary sinking down. **23** the angle of slope of rock strata, etc., from the horizontal plane. **24** the angle between the direction of the earth's magnetic field and the plane of the horizon; the angle that a magnetic needle free to swing in a vertical plane makes with the horizontal. **25** a creamy savoury mixture into which pieces of food are dipped before being eaten. **26** *Surveying.* the angular distance of the horizon below the plane of observation. **27** a candle made by plunging a wick into wax. **28** a momentary loss of altitude when flying. ◆ See also **dip into.** ORIG OE *dyppan*

dip. *or* **Dip.** *abbrev. for* diploma.

DipAD *abbrev. for* Diploma in Art and Design.

DipEd (in Britain) *abbrev. for* Diploma in Education.

diphtheria (dɪp'θɪərɪə) *n* an acute contagious disease caused by a bacillus, producing fever, severe prostration, and difficulty in breathing and swallowing as the result of swelling of the throat and the formation of a false membrane. ORIG C19: NL, from F *diphthérie,* from Gk *diphthera* leather; from the nature of the membrane
▸ **diph'therial, diphtheritic** (ˌdɪpθə'rɪtɪk), *or* **diphtheric** (dɪp'θɛrɪk) *adj*

diphthong ('dɪfθɒŋ) *n* **1** a vowel sound, occupying a single syllable, during the articulation of which the tongue moves continuously from one position to another, as in the pronunciation of *a* in *late.* **2** a digraph or ligature representing a composite vowel such as this, as *ae* in *Caesar.* ORIG C15: from LL *diphthongus,* from Gk *diphthongos,* from DI-[1] + *phthongos* sound
▸ **diph'thongal** *adj*

diphthongize *or* **diphthongise** ('dɪfθɒŋˌaɪz) *vb* **diphthongizes, diphthongizing, diphthongized** *or* **diphthongises, diphthongising, diphthongised.** (*often passive*) to make (a simple vowel) into a diphthong.
▸ **ˌdiphthongi'zation** *or* **ˌdiphthongi'sation** *n*

dip into *vb* (*intr, prep*) **1** to draw upon: *he dipped into his savings.* **2** to dabble (in); play at. **3** to read passages at random from (a book, newspaper, etc.).

diplodocus (ˌdɪpləʊ'dəʊkəs, dɪ'plɒdəkəs) *n, pl* **diplodocuses.** a herbivorous dinosaur characterized by a very long neck and tail and a total body length of 27 metres. ORIG C19: from NL, from Gk *diplo-,* (from *diploos,* from DI-[1] + *-ploos* -fold)+ *dokos* beam

diploid ('dɪplɔɪd) *adj* **1** *Biol.* (of cells or organisms) having paired homologous chromosomes so that twice the haploid number is present. **2** double or twofold. ◆ *n* **3** a diploid cell or organism.
▸ **dip'loidic** *adj*

diploma (dɪ'pləʊmə) *n* **1** a document conferring a qualification, recording success in examinations or successful completion of a course of study. **2** an official document that confers an honour or privilege. ORIG C17: from L: official letter or document, lit.: letter folded double, from Gk

diplomacy (dɪ'pləʊməsɪ) *n, pl* **diplomacies. 1** the conduct of the relations of one state with another by peaceful means. **2** skill in the management of international relations. **3** tact, skill, or cunning in dealing with people. ORIG C18: from F *diplomatie,* from *diplomatique* DIPLOMATIC

diplomat ('dɪpləˌmæt) *n* **1** an official such as an ambassador, engaged in diplomacy. **2** a person who deals with people tactfully or skilfully. ◆ Also called: **diplomatist** (dɪ'pləʊmətɪst).

diplomatic (ˌdɪplə'mætɪk) *adj* **1** of or relating to diplomacy or diplomats. **2** skilled in negotiating, esp. between states or people. **3** tactful in dealing with people. ORIG C18: from F *diplomatique* concerning the documents of diplomacy, from NL *diplōmaticus;* see DIPLOMA
▸ **ˌdiplo'matically** *adv*

diplomatic bag *n* a container or bag in which official mail is sent, free from customs inspection, to and from an embassy or consulate.

diplomatic corps *or* **body** *n* the entire body of diplomats accredited to a given state.

diplomatic immunity *n* the immunity from local jurisdiction and exemption from taxation in the country to which they are accredited afforded to diplomats.

Diplomatic Service *n* **1** (in Britain) the division of the Civil Service which provides diplomats to represent the

UK abroad. **2** (*not caps.*) the equivalent institution of any other country.

dipole ('daɪˌpəʊl) *n* **1** two equal but opposite electric charges or magnetic poles separated by a small distance. **2** a molecule in which the centre of positive charge does not coincide with the centre of negative charge. **3** a directional aerial consisting of two metal rods with a connecting wire fixed between them in the form of a T.
▸ **di'polar** *adj*

dipole moment *n Chem.* a measure of the polarity in a chemical bond or molecule, equal to the product of one charge and the distance between the charges. Symbol: μ

dipper ('dɪpə) *n* **1** a ladle used for dipping. **2** Also called: **water ouzel.** any of a genus of aquatic songbirds that inhabit fast-flowing streams. **3** a person or thing that dips. **4** *Arch.* an Anabaptist. ◆ See also **big dipper.**

dippy ('dɪpɪ) *adj* **dippier, dippiest.** *Sl.* odd, eccentric, or crazy. ORIG C20: from ?

dipsomania (ˌdɪpsəʊ'meɪnɪə) *n* a compulsive desire to drink alcoholic beverages. ORIG C19: NL, from Gk *dipsa* thirst + -MANIA
▸ **ˌdipso'maniac** *n, adj*

dipstick ('dɪpˌstɪk) *n* **1** a graduated rod or strip dipped into a container to indicate the fluid level. **2** *Brit. sl.* a fool.

dip switch *n* a device for dipping car headlights.

dipteran ('dɪptərən) *or* **dipteron** ('dɪptəˌrɒn) *n* **1** any dipterous insect. ◆ *adj* **2** another word for **dipterous** (sense 1).

dipterous ('dɪptərəs) *adj* **1** Also: **dipteran.** of a large order of insects having a single pair of wings and sucking or piercing mouthparts. The group includes flies, mosquitoes, and midges. **2** *Bot.* having two winglike parts. ORIG C18: from Gk *dipteros* two-winged

diptych ('dɪptɪk) *n* **1** a pair of hinged wooden tablets with waxed surfaces for writing. **2** a painting or carving on two hinged panels. ORIG C17: from Gk *diptukhos* folded together, from DI-[1] + *ptukhos* fold

Dirac ★ (dɪ'ræk) *n* **Paul Adrien Maurice.** 1902–84, British physicist, noted for his work on the quantum theory: shared the Nobel prize for physics 1933.

dire ('daɪə) *adj* (*usually prenominal*) **1** Also: **direful.** disastrous; fearful. **2** desperate; urgent: *a dire need.* **3** foreboding disaster; ominous. ORIG C16: from L *dīrus* ominous
▸ **'direly** *adv* ▸ **'direness** *n*

direct (dɪ'rɛkt, daɪ-) *vb* (*mainly tr*) **1** to conduct or control the affairs of. **2** (*also intr*) to give commands or orders with authority to (a person or group). **3** to tell or show (someone) the way to a place. **4** to aim, point, or cause to move towards a goal. **5** to address (a letter, etc.). **6** to address (remarks, etc.). **7** (*also intr*) **7a** to provide guidance to (actors, cameramen, etc.) in a play or film. **7b** to supervise the making or staging of (a film or play). **8** (*also intr*) to conduct (a piece of music or musicians), usually while performing oneself. ◆ *adj* **9** without delay or evasion; straightforward. **10** without turning aside; shortest; straight: *a direct route.* **11** without intervening persons or agencies: *a direct link.* **12** honest; frank. **13** (*usually prenominal*) precise; exact: *a direct quotation.* **14** diametrical: *the direct opposite.* **15** in an unbroken line of descent: *a direct descendant.* **16** (of government, decisions, etc.) by or from the electorate rather than through representatives. **17** *Logic, maths.* (of a proof) progressing from the premises to the conclusion, rather than eliminating the possibility of the falsehood of the conclusion. Cf. **indirect proof. 18** *Astron.* moving from west to east. Cf. **retrograde. 19** of or relating to direct current. **20** *Music.* (of an interval or chord) in root position; not inverted. ◆ *adv* **21** directly; straight. ORIG C14: from L *dīrectus,* from *dīrigere* to guide, from *dis-* apart + *regere* to rule
▸ **di'rectness** *n*

direct access *n* a method of reading data from a computer file without reading through the file from the beginning.

direct action *n* action such as strikes or civil disobedience employed to obtain demands from an employer, government, etc.

direct current *n* a continuous electric current that flows in one direction only.

direct debit *n* an order given to a bank or building society by a holder of an account, instructing it to pay to a specified person or organization any sum demanded by that person or organization. Cf. **standing order.**

direct-grant school *n* (in Britain, formerly) a school financed by endowment, fees, and a state grant conditional upon admittance of a percentage of nonpaying pupils.

direction (dɪ'rɛkʃən, daɪ-) *n* **1** the act of directing or the state of being directed. **2** management, control, or guidance. **3** the work of a stage or film director. **4** the course or line along which a person or thing moves, points, or lies. **5** the place towards which a person or thing is directed. **6** a line of action; course. **7** the name and address on a letter, parcel, etc. **8** *Music.* the process of conducting an orchestra, choir, etc. **9** *Music.* an instruction to indicate tempo, dynamics, mood, etc.

directional (dɪ'rɛkʃənᵊl, daɪ-) *adj* **1** of or relating to a spatial direction. **2** *Electronics.* **2a** having or relating to an increased sensitivity to radio waves, nuclear particles, etc., coming from a particular direction. **2b** (of an aerial) transmitting or receiving radio waves more effectively in some directions than in others. **3** *Physics, electronics.* concentrated in, following, or producing motion in a particular direction.
▸ **diˌrection'ality** *n*

directional drilling *n* a method of drilling for oil in which the well is not drilled vertically, as when a number of wells are to be drilled from a single platform. Also called: **deviated drilling.**

direction finder *n* a device to determine the direction of incoming radio signals, used esp. as a navigation aid.

directions (dɪ'rɛkʃənz, daɪ-) *pl n* (*sometimes sing*) instructions for doing something or for reaching a place.

directive (dɪ'rɛktɪv, daɪ-) *n* **1** an instruction; order. ◆ *adj* **2** tending to direct; directing. **3** indicating direction.

directly (dɪ'rɛktlɪ, daɪ-) *adv* **1** in a direct manner. **2** at once; without delay. **3** (foll. by *before* or *after*) immediately; just. ◆ *conj* **4** (*subordinating*) as soon as.

direct marketing *n* selling goods directly to consumers rather than through retailers, as by mail order, telephone selling, etc. Also called: **direct selling.**

direct object *n Grammar.* a noun, pronoun, or noun phrase whose referent receives the direct action of a verb. For example, *a book* in *They bought Anne a book.*

directoire (dɪ'rɛktwɑː) *adj* (of ladies' knickers) knee-length, with elastic at waist and knees. ORIG C19: after fashions of the period of the French *Directoire* Directorate (1795–99)

director (dɪ'rɛktə, daɪ-) *n* **1** a person or thing that directs, controls, or regulates. **2** a member of the governing board of a business concern. **3** a person who directs the affairs of an institution, trust, etc. **4** the person responsible for the artistic and technical aspects of the making of a film or television programme or the staging of a play. Cf. **producer** (sense 3). **5** *Music.* another word (esp. US) for **conductor.**
▸ **ˌdirec'torial** *adj* ▸ **ˌdi'rectorˌship** *n* ▸ **di'rectress** *fem n*

directorate (dɪ'rɛktərɪt, daɪ-) *n* **1** a board of directors. **2** Also: **directorship.** the position of director.

director-general *n, pl* **directors-general.** the head of a large organization such as the CBI or BBC.

Director of Public Prosecutions *n* (in Britain) an official who, as head of the Crown Prosecution Service, is responsible for conducting all criminal prosecutions initiated by the police. Abbrev.: **DPP.**

director's chair *n* a light wooden folding chair with arm rests and a canvas seat and back, as used by film directors.

directory (dɪ'rɛktərɪ, -trɪ; daɪ-) *n, pl* **directories. 1** a book listing names, addresses, telephone numbers, etc., of individuals or firms. **2** a book giving directions. **3** a book containing the rules to be observed in the forms of worship used in churches. **4** a directorate. **5** *Computing.* an area of a disk, Winchester disk, or floppy disk that contains the names and locations of files currently held on that disk. ◆ *adj* **6** directing.

Directory (dɪˈrɛktərɪ, -trɪ; daɪ-) *n* **the.** *History.* the body of five directors in power in France from 1795 until their overthrow by Napoleon in 1799. Also called: **French Directory.**

direct primary *n US government.* a primary in which voters directly select the candidates who will run for office.

direct selling *n* another name for **direct marketing.**

direct speech *or esp. US* **direct discourse** *n* the reporting of what someone has said or written by quoting his or her exact words.

direct tax *n* a tax paid by the person or organization on which it is levied.

dirge (dɜːdʒ) *n* **1** a chant of lamentation for the dead. **2** the funeral service in its solemn or sung forms. **3** any mourning song or melody. ORIG C13: from L *dīrigē* direct (imperative), opening word of antiphon used in the office of the dead
▸ **ˈdirgeful** *adj*

dirham (ˈdɪəræm) *n* **1** the standard monetary unit of Morocco and the United Arab Emirates. **2** a monetary unit of Kuwait, Libya, Qatar, and Tunisia. **3** any of various N African coins. ORIG C18: from Ar., from L: DRACHMA

dirigible (ˈdɪrɪdʒɪbᵊl) *adj* **1** able to be steered or directed. ◆ *n* **2** another name for **airship.** ORIG C16: from L *dīrigere* to DIRECT
▸ **ˌdirigiˈbility** *n*

dirigisme (diːriːˈʒiːzəm) *n* control by the state of economic and social matters. ORIG C20: from F
▸ **diriˈgiste** *adj*

dirk (dɜːk) *n* **1** a dagger, esp. as formerly worn by Scottish Highlanders. ◆ *vb* **2** (*tr*) to stab with a dirk. ORIG C16: from Scot. *durk,* ?from G *Dolch* dagger

dirndl (ˈdɜːndᵊl) *n* **1** a woman's dress with a full gathered skirt and fitted bodice; originating from Tyrolean peasant wear. **2** a gathered skirt of this kind. ORIG G (Bavarian and Austrian): from *Dirndlkleid,* from *Dirndl* little girl + *Kleid* dress

dirt (dɜːt) *n* **1** any unclean substance, such as mud, etc.; filth. **2** loose earth; soil. **3a** packed earth, gravel, cinders, etc., used to make a racetrack. **3b** (*as modifier*): *a dirt track.* **4** *Mining.* the gravel or soil from which minerals are extracted. **5** a person or thing regarded as worthless. **6** obscene or indecent speech or writing. **7** *Sl.* gossip; scandalous information. **8** moral corruption. **9 do (someone) dirt.** *Sl.* to do something vicious to (someone). **10 eat dirt.** *Sl.* to accept insult without complaining. ORIG C13: from ON *drit* excrement

dirt bike *n* a type of motorbike designed for use over rough ground.

dirt-cheap *adj, adv Inf.* at an extremely low price.

dirt road *n Austral. & NZ.* a road without shingle or any form of sealing.

dirty (ˈdɜːtɪ) *adj* **dirtier, dirtiest. 1** covered or marked with dirt; filthy. **2a** obscene: *dirty books.* **2b** sexually clandestine: *a dirty weekend.* **3** causing one to become grimy: *a dirty job.* **4** (of a colour) not clear and bright. **5** unfair; dishonest. **6** mean; nasty: *a dirty cheat.* **7** scandalous; unkind. **8** revealing dislike or anger. **9** (of weather) rainy or squally; stormy. **10** (of a nuclear weapon) producing a large quantity of radioactive fallout. **11 dirty linen.** *Inf.* intimate secrets, esp. those that might give rise to gossip. **12 dirty work.** unpleasant or illicit activity. ◆ *n* **13 do the dirty on.** *Inf.* to behave meanly towards. ◆ *vb* **dirties, dirtying, dirtied. 14** to make or become dirty; stain; soil.
▸ **ˈdirtily** *adv* ▸ **ˈdirtiness** *n*

dis (dɪs) *vb* a variant spelling of **diss.**

Dis ★ (dɪs) *n* **1** Also called: **Orcus, Pluto.** the Roman god of the underworld. **2** the abode of the dead; underworld. ◆ Greek equivalent: **Hades.**

dis-[1] *prefix* **1** indicating reversal: *disconnect.* **2** indicating negation, lack, or deprivation: *dissimilar; disgrace.* **3** indicating removal or release: *disembowel.* **4** expressing intensive force: *dissever.* ORIG from L *dis-* apart; in some cases, via OF *des-*. In compound words of L origin, *dis-* becomes *dif-* before *f,* and *di-* before some consonants

dis-[2] *combining form.* a variant of **di-**[1] before *s: dissyllable.*

disability (ˌdɪsəˈbɪlɪtɪ) *n, pl* **disabilities. 1** the condition of being physically or mentally impaired. **2** something that disables; handicap. **3** lack of necessary intelligence, strength, etc. **4** an incapacity in the eyes of the law to enter into certain transactions.

disable (dɪsˈeɪbᵊl) *vb* **disables, disabling, disabled.** (*tr*) **1** to make ineffective, unfit, or incapable, as by crippling. **2** to make or pronounce legally incapable. **3** to switch off (an electronic device).
▸ **disˈablement** *n*

disabled (dɪˈseɪbᵊld) *adj* **a** lacking one or more physical powers, such as the ability to walk or to coordinate one's movements. **b** (*as collective n;* preceded by *the*): *the disabled.* See usage note below.

> **USAGE NOTE** The use of *the disabled, the blind,* etc., can be offensive and should be avoided. Instead you should talk about *disabled people, blind people,* etc. An acceptable alternative to the word *disabled* is *differently abled.*

disabuse (ˌdɪsəˈbjuːz) *vb* **disabuses, disabusing, disabused.** (*tr;* usually foll. by *of*) to rid of a mistaken idea; set right.

disadvantage (ˌdɪsədˈvɑːntɪdʒ) *n* **1** an unfavourable circumstance, thing, person, etc. **2** injury, loss, or detriment. **3** an unfavourable situation (esp. in **at a disadvantage**). ◆ *vb* **disadvantages, disadvantaging, disadvantaged. 4** (*tr*) to put at a disadvantage; handicap.

disadvantaged (ˌdɪsədˈvɑːntɪdʒd) *adj* socially or economically deprived or discriminated against.

disadvantageous (ˌdɪsædvɑːnˈteɪdʒəs, dɪsˌædvənˈteɪdʒəs) *adj* unfavourable; detrimental.
▸ **ˌdisadvanˈtageously** *adv* ▸ **ˌdisadvanˈtageousness** *n*

disaffect (ˌdɪsəˈfɛkt) *vb* (*tr; often passive*) to cause to lose loyalty or affection; alienate.
▸ **ˌdisafˈfectedly** *adv* ▸ **ˌdisafˈfection** *n*

disaffiliate (ˌdɪsəˈfɪlɪˌeɪt) *vb* **disaffiliates, disaffiliating, disaffiliated.** to sever an affiliation (with).
▸ **ˌdisafˌfiliˈation** *n*

disafforest (ˌdɪsəˈfɒrɪst) *vb* (*tr*) *Law.* to reduce (land) from the status of a forest to the state of ordinary ground.
▸ **ˌdisafˌforesˈtation** *n*

disaggregate (dɪsˈægrɪˌgeɪt) *vb* **disaggregates, disaggregating, disaggregated. 1** to separate from a group or mass. **2** to divide into parts.
▸ **ˌdisaggreˈgation** *n*

disagree (ˌdɪsəˈgriː) *vb* **disagrees, disagreeing, disagreed.** (*intr;* often foll. by *with*) **1** to dissent in opinion or dispute (about an idea, fact, etc.). **2** to fail to correspond; conflict. **3** to be unacceptable (to) or unfavourable (for): *curry disagrees with me.* **4** to be opposed (to).

disagreeable (ˌdɪsəˈgrɪəbᵊl) *adj* **1** not likable; bad-tempered, esp. disobliging, etc. **2** not to one's liking; unpleasant.
▸ **ˌdisaˈgreeableness** *n* ▸ **ˌdisaˈgreeably** *adv*

disagreement (ˌdɪsəˈgriːmənt) *n* **1** refusal or failure to agree. **2** a failure to correspond. **3** an argument or dispute.

disallow (ˌdɪsəˈlaʊ) *vb* (*tr*) **1** to reject as untrue or invalid. **2** to cancel.
▸ **ˌdisalˈlowable** *adj* ▸ **ˌdisalˈlowance** *n*

disappear (ˌdɪsəˈpɪə) *vb* **1** (*intr*) to cease to be visible; vanish. **2** (*intr*) to go away or become lost, esp. without explanation. **3** (*intr*) to cease to exist; become extinct or lost. **4** (*tr*) (esp. in South and Central America) to arrest secretly and presumably imprison or kill (a member of an opposing political group).
▸ **ˌdisapˈpearance** *n*

disapplication (ˌdɪsæplɪˈkeɪʃən) *n Brit. education.* a provision for exempting schools or individuals from the requirements of the National Curriculum in special circumstances.

disappoint (ˌdɪsəˈpɔɪnt) *vb* (*tr*) **1** to fail to meet the expectations, hopes, etc. of; let down. **2** to prevent the fulfilment of (a plan, etc.); frustrate. ORIG C15 (orig. meaning: to remove from office): from OF *desapointier;* see DIS-[1], APPOINT
▸ ˌ**disapˈpointed** *adj* ▸ ˌ**disapˈpointing** *adj* ▸ ˌ**disapˈpointingly** *adv*

disappointment (ˌdɪsəˈpɔɪntmənt) *n* **1** a disappointing or being disappointed. **2** a person or thing that disappoints.

disapprobation (ˌdɪsæprəʊˈbeɪʃən) *n* moral or social disapproval.

disapproval (ˌdɪsəˈpruːvᵊl) *n* the act or a state or feeling of disapproving; censure.

disapprove (ˌdɪsəˈpruːv) *vb* **disapproves, disapproving, disapproved. 1** (*intr;* often foll. by *of*) to consider wrong, bad, etc. **2** (*tr*) to withhold approval from.
▸ ˌ**disapˈproving** *adj* ▸ ˌ**disapˈprovingly** *adv*

disarm (dɪsˈɑːm) *vb* **1** (*tr*) to remove defensive or offensive capability from (a country, army, etc.). **2** (*tr*) to deprive of weapons. **3** (*tr*) to win the confidence or affection of. **4** (*intr*) (of a nation, etc.) to decrease the size and capability of one's armed forces. **5** (*intr*) to lay down weapons.
▸ **disˈarmer** *n*

disarmament (dɪsˈɑːməmənt) *n* **1** the reduction of fighting capability, as by a nation. **2** a disarming or being disarmed.

disarming (dɪsˈɑːmɪŋ) *adj* tending to neutralize hostility, suspicion, etc.
▸ **disˈarmingly** *adv*

disarrange (ˌdɪsəˈreɪndʒ) *vb* **disarranges, disarranging, disarranged.** (*tr*) to throw into disorder.
▸ ˌ**disarˈrangement** *n*

disarray (ˌdɪsəˈreɪ) *n* **1** confusion, dismay, and lack of discipline. **2** (esp. of clothing) disorderliness; untidiness. ◆ *vb* (*tr*) **3** to throw into confusion. **4** *Arch.* to undress.

disassemble (ˌdɪsəˈsɛmbᵊl) *vb* **disassembles, disassembling, disassembled.** (*tr*) to take apart (a piece of machinery, etc.); dismantle.

disassembler (ˌdɪsəˈsɛmblə) *n Computing.* a computer program that translates machine code into assembly language.

disassociate (ˌdɪsəˈsəʊʃɪˌeɪt, -sɪ-) *vb* **disassociates, disassociating, disassociated.** a less common word for **dissociate.**
▸ ˌ**disasˌsociˈation** *n*

disaster (dɪˈzɑːstə) *n* **1** an occurrence that causes great distress or destruction. **2** a thing, project, etc., that fails or has been ruined. ORIG C16 (orig. in the sense: malevolent astral influence): from It. *disastro,* from *dis-* (pejorative) + *astro* star, ult. from Gk *astron*
▸ **disˈastrous** *adj*

disavow (ˌdɪsəˈvaʊ) *vb* (*tr*) to deny knowledge of, connection with, or responsibility for.
▸ ˌ**disaˈvowal** *n* ▸ **disavowedly** (ˌdɪsəˈvaʊɪdlɪ) *adv*

disband (dɪsˈbænd) *vb* to cease to function or cause to stop functioning, as a unit, group, etc.
▸ **disˈbandment** *n*

disbar (dɪsˈbɑː) *vb* **disbars, disbarring, disbarred.** (*tr*) *Law.* to deprive of the status of barrister; expel from the Bar.
▸ **disˈbarment** *n*

> **USAGE NOTE** *Disbar* should only be used when talking about a barrister, and should not be confused with *debar,* in the sense of 'prevent'.

disbelief (ˌdɪsbɪˈliːf) *n* refusal or reluctance to believe.

disbelieve (ˌdɪsbɪˈliːv) *vb* **disbelieves, disbelieving, disbelieved. 1** (*tr*) to reject as false or lying. **2** (*intr;* usually foll. by *in*) to have no faith (in).
▸ ˌ**disbeˈliever** *n* ▸ ˌ**disbeˈlieving** *adj*

disbud (dɪsˈbʌd) *or* **debud** (diːˈbʌd) *vb* **disbuds, disbudding, disbudded** *or* **debuds, debudding, debudded. 1** to remove superfluous buds from (a plant). **2** *Vet. science.* to remove the horn buds of (calves, lambs, and kids).

disburden (dɪsˈbɜːdᵊn) *vb* **1** to remove a load from. **2** (*tr*) to relieve (one's mind, etc.) of a distressing worry.

disburse (dɪsˈbɜːs) *vb* **disburses, disbursing, disbursed.** (*tr*) to pay out. ORIG C16: from OF *desborser,* from *des-* DIS-[1] + *borser* to obtain money, from *borse* bag, from LL *bursa*
▸ **disˈbursable** *adj* ▸ **disˈbursement** *n* ▸ **disˈburser** *n*

> **USAGE NOTE** *Disburse* is sometimes wrongly used where *disperse* is meant: *the police used water cannon to disperse* (not *disburse*) *the crowd.*

disc (dɪsk) *n* **1** a flat circular plate. **2** something resembling this. **3** a gramophone record. **4** *Anat.* any approximately circular flat structure in the body, esp. an intervertebral disc. **5** the flat receptacle of composite flowers, such as the daisy. **6a** Also called: **parking disc.** a marker or device for display in a parked vehicle showing the time of arrival or the latest permitted time of departure or both. **6b** (*as modifier*)*: disc parking.* **7** *Computing.* a variant spelling of **disk.** ORIG C18: from L *discus* DISCUS
▸ **ˈdiscal** *adj*

> **USAGE NOTE** See at **disk.**

disc. *abbrev. for:* **1** discount. **2** discovered.

discard *vb* (dɪsˈkɑːd). **1** (*tr*) to get rid of as useless or undesirable. **2** *Cards.* to throw out (a card or cards) from one's hand. **3** *Cards.* to play (a card not of the suit led nor a trump) when unable to follow suit. ◆ *n* (ˈdɪskɑːd). **4** a person or thing that has been cast aside. **5** *Cards.* a discarded card. **6** the act of discarding.

disc brake *n* a type of brake in which two pads rub against a flat disc attached to the wheel hub when the brake is applied.

discern (dɪˈsɜːn) *vb* **1** (*tr*) to recognize or perceive clearly. **2** to recognize or perceive (differences). ORIG C14: from OF *discerner,* from L *discernere* to divide, from DIS-[1] apart + *cernere* to separate
▸ **disˈcernible** *adj* ▸ **disˈcernibly** *adv*

discerning (dɪˈsɜːnɪŋ) *adj* having or showing good taste or judgment; discriminating.

discernment (dɪˈsɜːnmənt) *n* keen perception or judgment.

disc flower *or* **floret** *n* any of the small tubular flowers at the centre of the flower head of certain composite plants, such as the daisy.

discharge *vb* (dɪsˈtʃɑːdʒ). **discharges, discharging, discharged. 1** (*tr*) to release or allow to go. **2** (*tr*) to dismiss from or relieve of duty, employment, etc. **3** to fire or be fired, as a gun. **4** to pour forth or cause to pour forth: *the boil discharges pus.* **5** (*tr*) to remove (the cargo) from (a boat, etc.); unload. **6** (*tr*) to perform the duties of or meet the demands of (an office, obligation, etc.). **7** (*tr*) to relieve (oneself) of (a responsibility, debt, etc.). **8** (*intr*) *Physics.* **8a** to lose or remove electric charge. **8b** to form an arc, spark, or corona in a gas. **8c** to take or supply electrical current from a cell or battery. **9** (*tr*) *Law.* to release (a prisoner from custody, etc.). ◆ *n* (ˈdɪstʃɑːdʒ, dɪsˈtʃɑːdʒ). **10** a person or thing that is discharged. **11a** dismissal or release from an office, job, institution, etc. **11b** the document certifying such release. **12** the fulfilment of an obligation or release from a responsibility or liability. **13** the act of removing a load, as of cargo. **14** a pouring forth of a fluid; emission. **15a** the act of firing a projectile. **15b** the volley, bullet, etc., fired. **16** *Law.* **16a** a release, as of a person held under legal restraint. **16b** an annulment, as of a court order. **17** *Physics.* **17a** the act or process of removing or losing charge. **17b** a conduction of electricity through a gas by the formation and movement of electrons and ions in an applied electric field.
▸ **disˈchargeable** *adj* ▸ **disˈcharger** *n*

discharge tube *n Electronics.* an electrical device in which current flow is by electrons and ions in an ionized gas, as in a fluorescent light or neon tube.

disc harrow *n* a harrow with sharp-edged discs used to cut clods on the surface of the soil or to cover seed after planting.

disciple (dɪ'saɪpᵊl) *n* **1** a follower of the doctrines of a teacher or a school of thought. **2** one of the personal followers of Christ (including his 12 apostles) during his earthly life. ORIG OE *discipul,* from L *discipulus* pupil, from *discere* to learn
▸ **dis'ciple,ship** *n* ▸ **discipular** (dɪ'sɪpjʊlə) *adj*

disciplinarian (,dɪsɪplɪ'nɛərɪən) *n* a person who imposes or advocates strict discipline.

disciplinary ('dɪsɪ,plɪnərɪ) *adj* **1** of, promoting, or used for discipline; corrective. **2** relating to a branch of learning.

discipline ('dɪsɪplɪn) *n* **1** training or conditions imposed for the improvement of physical powers, self-control, etc. **2** systematic training in obedience. **3** the state of improved behaviour, etc., resulting from such training. **4** punishment or chastisement. **5** a system of rules for behaviour, etc. **6** a branch of learning or instruction. **7** the laws governing members of a Church. ◆ *vb* **disciplines, disciplining, disciplined.** (*tr*) **8** to improve or attempt to improve the behaviour, orderliness, etc., of by training, conditions, or rules. **9** to punish or correct. ORIG C13: from L *disciplīna* teaching, from *discipulus* DISCIPLE
▸ **'disci,plinable** *adj* ▸ **disciplinal** (,dɪsɪ'plaɪnᵊl) *adj* ▸ **'disci,pliner** *n*

disc jockey *n* a person who announces and plays recorded music, esp. pop music, on a radio programme, etc.

disclaim (dɪs'kleɪm) *vb* **1** (*tr*) to deny or renounce (any claim, connection, etc.). **2** (*tr*) to deny the validity or authority of. **3** *Law.* to renounce or repudiate (a legal claim or right).

disclaimer (dɪs'kleɪmə) *n* a repudiation or denial.

disclose (dɪs'kləʊz) *vb* **discloses, disclosing, disclosed.** (*tr*) **1** to make known. **2** to allow to be seen.
▸ **dis'closer** *n*

disclosure (dɪs'kləʊʒə) *n* **1** something that is disclosed. **2** the act of disclosing; revelation.

disco ('dɪskəʊ) *n, pl* **discos. 1a** an occasion at which people dance to pop records. **1b** (*as modifier*): *disco music.* **2** a nightclub or other public place where such dances are held. **3** mobile equipment for providing music for a disco. ORIG C20: from DISCOTHEQUE

discobolus (dɪs'kɒbələs) *n, pl* **discoboli** (-,laɪ). a discus thrower. ORIG C18: from L, from Gk, from *diskos* DISCUS + *-bolos,* from *ballein* to throw

discography (dɪs'kɒgrəfɪ) *n* a classified list of gramophone records.
▸ **dis'cographer** *n*

discoid ('dɪskɔɪd) *adj also* **discoidal. 1** like a disc. ◆ *n* **2** a disclike object.

discolour *or US* **discolor** (dɪs'kʌlə) *vb* to change in colour; fade or stain.
▸ **dis,color'ation** *or* **dis,colour'ation** *n*

discombobulate (,dɪskəm'bɒbjʊ,leɪt) *vb* **discombobulates, discombobulating, discombobulated.** (*tr*) *Inf., chiefly US & Canad.* to throw into confusion. ORIG C20: prob. a whimsical alteration of DISCOMPOSE or DISCOMFIT

discomfit (dɪs'kʌmfɪt) *vb* (*tr*) **1** to make uneasy or confused. **2** to frustrate the plans or purpose of. **3** *Arch.* to defeat. ORIG C14: from OF *desconfire* to destroy, from *des-* (indicating reversal) + *confire* to make, from L *conficere* to produce
▸ **dis'comfiture** *n*

discomfort (dɪs'kʌmfət) *n* **1** an inconvenience, distress, or mild pain. **2** something that disturbs or deprives of ease. ◆ *vb* **3** (*tr*) to make uncomfortable or uneasy.

discommode (,dɪskə'məʊd) *vb* **discommodes, discommoding, discommoded.** (*tr*) to cause inconvenience to; disturb.
▸ **,discom'modious** *adj*

discompose (,dɪskəm'pəʊz) *vb* **discomposes, discomposing, discomposed.** (*tr*) **1** to disturb the composure of; disconcert. **2** *Now rare.* to disarrange.
▸ **,discom'posure** *n*

disconcert (,dɪskən'sɜːt) *vb* (*tr*) **1** to disturb the composure of. **2** to frustrate or upset.
▸ **,discon'certed** *adj* ▸ **,discon'certing** *adj* ▸ **,discon'certion** *n*

disconformity (,dɪskən'fɔːmɪtɪ) *n, pl* **disconformities. 1** lack of conformity; discrepancy. **2** the junction between two parallel series of stratified rocks.

disconnect (,dɪskə'nɛkt) *vb* (*tr*) to undo or break the connection of or between (something, as a plug and a socket).
▸ **,discon'nection** *n*

disconnected (,dɪskə'nɛktɪd) *adj* **1** not rationally connected; confused or incoherent. **2** not connected or joined.

disconsolate (dɪs'kɒnsəlɪt) *adj* **1** sad beyond comfort; inconsolable. **2** disappointed; dejected. ORIG C14: from Med. L *disconsōlātus,* from DIS-[1] + *consōlātus* comforted
▸ **dis'consolately** *adv* ▸ **dis'consolateness** *or* **dis,conso'lation** *n*

discontent (,dɪskən'tɛnt) *n* **1** Also called: **discontentment.** lack of contentment, as with one's condition or lot in life. ◆ *vb* **2** (*tr*) to make dissatisfied.
▸ **,discon'tented** *adj* ▸ **,discon'tentedness** *n*

discontinue (,dɪskən'tɪnjuː) *vb* **discontinues, discontinuing, discontinued. 1** to come or bring to an end; interrupt or be interrupted; stop. **2** (*tr*) *Law.* to terminate or abandon (an action, suit, etc.).
▸ **,discon'tinuance** *n* ▸ **,discon,tinu'ation** *n*

discontinuity (,dɪskɒntɪ'njuːɪtɪ, dɪs,kɒntɪ-) *n, pl* **discontinuities. 1** lack of rational connection or cohesion. **2** a break or interruption.

discontinuous (,dɪskən'tɪnjʊəs) *adj* characterized by interruptions or breaks; intermittent.
▸ **,discon'tinuously** *adv* ▸ **,discon'tinuousness** *n*

discord *n* ('dɪskɔːd). **1** lack of agreement or harmony. **2** harsh confused mingling of sounds. **3** a combination of musical notes, esp. one containing one or more dissonant intervals. ◆ *vb* (dɪs'kɔːd). **4** (*intr*) to disagree; clash. ORIG C13: from OF *descort,* from *descorder* to disagree, from L *discordāre,* from *discors* at variance, from DIS-[1] + *cor* heart

discordant (dɪs'kɔːdᵊnt) *adj* **1** at variance; disagreeing. **2** harsh in sound; inharmonious.
▸ **dis'cordance** *n* ▸ **dis'cordantly** *adv*

discotheque ('dɪskə,tɛk) *n* the full term for **disco.** ORIG C20: from F *discothèque,* from Gk *diskos* disc + *-o-* + Gk *thēkē* case

discount *vb* (dɪs'kaʊnt, 'dɪskaʊnt). (*mainly tr*) **1** to leave out of account as being unreliable, prejudiced, or irrelevant. **2** to anticipate and make allowance for. **3a** to deduct (an amount or percentage) from the price, cost, etc. **3b** to reduce (the regular price, etc.) by a percentage or amount. **4** to sell or offer for sale at a reduced price. **5** to buy or sell (a bill of exchange, etc.) before maturity, with a deduction for interest. **6** (*also intr*) to loan money on (a negotiable instrument) with a deduction for interest. ◆ *n* ('dɪskaʊnt). **7** a deduction from the full amount of a price or debt. See also **cash discount, trade discount. 8** Also called: **discount rate. 8a** the amount of interest deducted in the purchase or sale of or the loan of money on unmatured negotiable instruments. **8b** the rate of interest deducted. **9** (in the issue of shares) a percentage deducted from the par value to give a reduced amount payable by subscribers. **10** a discounting. **11 at a discount. 11a** below the regular price. **11b** held in low regard. **12** (*modifier*) offering or selling at reduced prices: *a discount shop.*
▸ **dis'countable** *adj* ▸ **'discounter** *n*

discounted cash flow *n* the cash flow of an organization taking into account the future values of benefits and assets in addition to their present values.

discountenance (dɪs'kaʊntɪnəns) *vb* **discountenances, discountenancing, discountenanced.** (*tr*) **1** to make ashamed or confused. **2** to disapprove of. ◆ *n* **3** disapproval.

discount house *n* **1** *Chiefly Brit.* a financial organization engaged in discounting bills of exchange, etc., on a large scale. **2** Also called: **discount store.** *Chiefly US.* a shop offering for sale most of its merchandise at prices below the recommended prices.

discount market *n* the part of the money market consisting of banks, discount houses, and brokers on which bills are discounted.

discourage (dɪsˈkʌrɪdʒ) *vb* **discourages, discouraging, discouraged.** (*tr*) **1** to deprive of the will to persist in something. **2** to inhibit; prevent: *this solution discourages rust.* **3** to oppose by expressing disapproval.
▸ **disˈcouragement** *n* ▸ **disˈcouragingly** *adv*

discourse *n* (ˈdɪskɔːs, dɪsˈkɔːs). **1** verbal communication; talk; conversation. **2** a formal treatment of a subject in speech or writing. **3** a unit of text used by linguists for the analysis of linguistic phenomena that range over more than one sentence. **4** *Arch.* the ability to reason. ◆ *vb* (dɪsˈkɔːs), **discourses, discoursing, discoursed. 5** (*intr;* often foll. by *on* or *upon*) to speak or write (about) formally. **6** (*intr*) to hold a discussion. **7** (*tr*) *Arch.* to give forth (music). ORIG C14: from Med. L *discursus* argument, from L: a running to and fro, from *discurrere,* from DIS-[1] + *currere* to run

discourteous (dɪsˈkɜːtɪəs) *adj* showing bad manners; impolite; rude.
▸ **disˈcourteously** *adv* ▸ **disˈcourteousness** *n*

discourtesy (dɪsˈkɜːtɪsɪ) *n, pl* **discourtesies. 1** bad manners; rudeness. **2** a rude remark or act.

discover (dɪˈskʌvə) *vb* (*tr; may take a clause as object*) **1** to be the first to find or find out about. **2** to learn about for the first time; realize. **3** to find after study or search. **4** to reveal or make known.
▸ **disˈcoverable** *adj* ▸ **disˈcoverer** *n*

discovery (dɪˈskʌvərɪ) *n, pl* **discoveries. 1** the act, process, or an instance of discovering. **2** a person, place, or thing that has been discovered. **3** *Law.* the compulsory disclosure by a party to an action of relevant documents in his possession.

discredit (dɪsˈkrɛdɪt) *vb* (*tr*) **1** to damage the reputation of. **2** to cause to be disbelieved or distrusted. **3** to reject as untrue. ◆ *n* **4** something that causes disgrace. **5** damage to a reputation. **6** lack of belief or confidence.

discreditable (dɪsˈkrɛdɪtəbᵊl) *adj* tending to bring discredit; shameful or unworthy.

discreet (dɪˈskriːt) *adj* **1** careful to avoid embarrassment, esp. by keeping confidences secret; tactful. **2** unobtrusive. ORIG C14: from OF *discret,* from Med. L *discrētus,* from L *discernere* to DISCERN
▸ **disˈcreetly** *adv* ▸ **disˈcreetness** *n*

> **USAGE NOTE** See at **discrete.**

discrepancy (dɪˈskrɛpənsɪ) *n, pl* **discrepancies.** a conflict or variation, as between facts, figures, or claims. ORIG C15: from L *discrepāns,* from *discrepāre* to differ in sound, from DIS-[1] + *crepāre* to be noisy
▸ **disˈcrepant** *adj*

discrete (dɪsˈkriːt) *adj* **1** separate or distinct. **2** consisting of distinct or separate parts. ORIG C14: from L *discrētus* separated; see DISCREET
▸ **disˈcretely** *adv* ▸ **disˈcreteness** *n*

> **USAGE NOTE** This word is quite often used by mistake where *discreet* is intended: *reading is a set of discrete skills; she was discreet* (not *discrete*) *about the affair.*

discretion (dɪˈskrɛʃən) *n* **1** the quality of behaving so as to avoid social embarrassment or distress. **2** freedom or authority to make judgments and to act as one sees fit (esp. in **at one's own discretion, at the discretion of**). **3 age** *or* **years of discretion.** the age at which a person is thought able to manage his or her own affairs.

discretionary (dɪˈskrɛʃənərɪ, -ənrɪ) *or* **discretional** *adj* having or using the ability to decide at one's own discretion: *discretionary powers.*

discretionary trust *n* a trust in which the beneficiaries' shares are not fixed in the trust deed but are left to the discretion of other persons, often the trustees.

discriminate *vb* (dɪˈskrɪmɪˌneɪt). **discriminates, discriminating, discriminated. 1** (*intr;* usually foll. by *in favour of* or *against*) to single out a particular person, group, etc., for special favour or, esp., disfavour. **2** (when *intr,* foll. by *between* or *among*) to recognize or understand the difference (between); distinguish. **3** (*intr*) to constitute or mark a difference. **4** (*intr*) to be discerning in matters of taste. ◆ *adj* (dɪˈskrɪmɪnɪt). **5** showing or marked by discrimination. ORIG C17: from L *discrīmināre* to divide, from *discrīmen* a separation, from *discernere* to DISCERN
▸ **disˈcriminately** *adv*

discriminating (dɪˈskrɪmɪˌneɪtɪŋ) *adj* **1** able to see fine distinctions and differences. **2** discerning in matters of taste. **3** (of a tariff, import duty, etc.) levied at differential rates.

discrimination (dɪˌskrɪmɪˈneɪʃən) *n* **1** unfair treatment of a person, racial group, minority, etc.; action based on prejudice. **2** subtle appreciation in matters of taste. **3** the ability to see fine distinctions and differences.

discriminatory (dɪˈskrɪmɪnətərɪ, -trɪ) *or* **discriminative** (dɪˈskrɪmɪnətɪv) *adj* **1** based on or showing prejudice; biased. **2** capable of making fine distinctions.

discursive (dɪˈskɜːsɪv) *adj* **1** passing from one topic to another; digressive. **2** *Philosophy.* of or relating to knowledge obtained by reason and argument rather than intuition. ORIG C16: from Med. L *discursīvus,* from LL *discursus* DISCOURSE
▸ **disˈcursively** *adv* ▸ **disˈcursiveness** *n*

discus (ˈdɪskəs) *n, pl* **discuses** *or* **disci** (ˈdɪskaɪ). **1** (originally) a circular stone or plate used in throwing competitions by the ancient Greeks. **2** *Field sports.* a similar disc-shaped object with a heavy middle, thrown by athletes. **3** (preceded by *the*) the event or sport of throwing the discus. ORIG C17: from L, from Gk *diskos,* from *dikein* to throw

discuss (dɪˈskʌs) *vb* (*tr*) **1** to have a conversation about; consider by talking over. **2** to treat (a subject) in speech or writing. ORIG C14: from LL *discussus* examined, from *discutere,* from L: to dash to pieces, from DIS-[1] + *quatere* to shake
▸ **disˈcussant** *or* **disˈcusser** *n* ▸ **disˈcussible** *or* **disˈcussable** *adj*

discussion (dɪˈskʌʃən) *n* the examination or consideration of a matter in speech or writing.

disdain (dɪsˈdeɪn) *n* **1** a feeling or show of superiority and dislike; contempt; scorn. ◆ *vb* **2** (*tr; may take an infinitive*) to refuse or reject with disdain. ORIG C13 *dedeyne,* from OF *desdeign,* from *desdeigner* to reject as unworthy, from L *dēdignārī;* see DIS-[1], DEIGN
▸ **disˈdainful** *adj*

disease (dɪˈziːz) *n* **1** any impairment of normal physiological function affecting an organism, esp. a change caused by infection, stress, etc., producing characteristic symptoms; illness or sickness in general. **2** a corresponding condition in plants. **3** any condition likened to this. ORIG C14: from OF *desaise;* see DIS-[1], EASE
▸ **disˈeased** *adj*

diseconomy (ˌdɪsɪˈkɒnəmɪ) *n Econ.* disadvantage, such as lower efficiency or higher costs, resulting from the scale on which an enterprise operates.

disembark (ˌdɪsɪmˈbɑːk) *vb* to land or cause to land from a ship, aircraft, etc.
▸ **disembarkation** (dɪsˌɛmbɑːˈkeɪʃən) *n*

disembarrass (ˌdɪsɪmˈbærəs) *vb* (*tr*) **1** to free from embarrassment, entanglement, etc. **2** to relieve or rid of something burdensome.

disembodied (ˌdɪsɪmˈbɒdɪd) *adj* **1** lacking a body or freed from the body. **2** lacking in substance or any firm relation to reality.

disembody (ˌdɪsɪmˈbɒdɪ) *vb* **disembodies, disembodying, disembodied.** (*tr*) to free from the body or from physical form.
▸ ˌ**disemˈbodiment** *n*

disembogue (ˌdɪsɪmˈbəʊg) *vb* **disembogues, disemboguing, disembogued. 1** (of a river, stream, etc.) to discharge (water) at the mouth. **2** (*intr*) to flow out. ORIG C16: from Sp. *desembocar,* from *des-* DIS-[1] + *embocar* to put into the mouth
▸ ˌ**disemˈboguement** *n*

disembowel (ˌdɪsɪmˈbaʊəl) *vb* **disembowels, disembowelling, disembowelled** *or US* **disembowels, disemboweling, disemboweled.** (*tr*) to remove the entrails of.
▸ ˌ**disemˈbowelment** *n*

disempower (ˌdɪsɪmˈpaʊə) *vb* (*tr*) to deprive (a person) of power or authority.
▸ **ˌdisemˈpowerment** *n*

disenchant (ˌdɪsɪnˈtʃɑːnt) *vb* (*tr*) to free from or as if from an enchantment; disillusion.
▸ **ˌdisenˈchantingly** *adv* ▸ **ˌdisenˈchantment** *n*

disencumber (ˌdɪsɪnˈkʌmbə) *vb* (*tr*) to free from encumbrances.
▸ **ˌdisenˈcumberment** *n*

disenfranchise (ˌdɪsɪnˈfræntʃaɪz) *or* **disfranchise** *vb* **disenfranchises, disenfranchising, disenfranchised** *or* **disfranchises, disfranchising, disfranchised.** (*tr*) **1** to deprive (a person) of the right to vote or other rights of citizenship. **2** to deprive (a place) of the right to send representatives to an elected body. **3** to deprive (a person, place, etc.) of any franchise or right.
▸ **disenfranchisement** (ˌdɪsɪnˈfræntʃɪzmənt) *or* **disˈfranchisement** *n*

disengage (ˌdɪsɪnˈgeɪdʒ) *vb* **disengages, disengaging, disengaged. 1** to release or become released from a connection, obligation, etc. **2** *Mil.* to withdraw (forces) from close action. **3** *Fencing.* to move (one's blade) from one side of an opponent's blade to another in a circular motion.
▸ **ˌdisenˈgaged** *adj* ▸ **ˌdisenˈgagement** *n*

disentangle (ˌdɪsɪnˈtæŋgᵊl) *vb* **disentangles, disentangling, disentangled. 1** to release or become free from entanglement or confusion. **2** (*tr*) to unravel or work out.
▸ **ˌdisenˈtanglement** *n*

disequilibrium (ˌdɪsiːkwɪˈlɪbrɪəm) *n* a loss or absence of equilibrium, esp. in an economy.

disestablish (ˌdɪsɪˈstæblɪʃ) *vb* (*tr*) to deprive (a church, custom, institution, etc.) of established status.
▸ **ˌdisesˈtablishment** *n*

disesteem (ˌdɪsɪˈstiːm) *vb* **1** (*tr*) to think little of. ◆ *n* **2** lack of esteem.

disfavour *or US* **disfavor** (dɪsˈfeɪvə) *n* **1** disapproval or dislike. **2** the state of being disapproved of or disliked. **3** an unkind act. ◆ *vb* **4** (*tr*) to treat with disapproval or dislike.

disfigure (dɪsˈfɪgə) *vb* **disfigures, disfiguring, disfigured.** (*tr*) **1** to spoil the appearance or shape of; deface. **2** to mar the effect or quality of.
▸ **disˈfigurement** *n*

disforest (dɪsˈfɒrɪst) *vb* (*tr*) **1** another word for **deforest. 2** *English law.* a less common word for **disafforest.**
▸ **disˌforesˈtation** *n*

disfranchise (dɪsˈfræntʃaɪz) *vb* another word for **disenfranchise.**

disgorge (dɪsˈgɔːdʒ) *vb* **disgorges, disgorging, disgorged. 1** to throw out (food, etc.) from the throat or stomach; vomit. **2** to discharge or empty of (contents). **3** (*tr*) to yield up unwillingly.
▸ **disˈgorgement** *n*

disgrace (dɪsˈgreɪs) *n* **1** a condition of shame, loss of reputation, or dishonour. **2** a shameful person or thing. **3** exclusion from confidence or trust: *he is in disgrace with his father.* ◆ *vb* **disgraces, disgracing, disgraced.** (*tr*) **4** to bring shame upon. **5** to treat or cause to be treated with disfavour.

disgraceful (dɪsˈgreɪsfʊl) *adj* shameful; scandalous.
▸ **disˈgracefully** *adv*

disgruntle (dɪsˈgrʌntᵊl) *vb* **disgruntles, disgruntling, disgruntled.** (*tr*) to make sulky or discontented. ORIG C17: DIS-[1] + obs. *gruntle* to complain
▸ **disˈgruntled** *adj* ▸ **disˈgruntlement** *n*

disguise (dɪsˈgaɪz) *vb* **disguises, disguising, disguised. 1** to modify the appearance or manner in order to conceal the identity of (someone or something). **2** (*tr*) to misrepresent in order to obscure the actual nature or meaning. ◆ *n* **3** a mask, costume, or manner that disguises. **4** a disguising or being disguised. ORIG C14: from OF *desguisier,* from *des-* DIS-[1] + *guise* manner
▸ **disˈguised** *adj*

disgust (dɪsˈgʌst) *vb* (*tr*) **1** to sicken or fill with loathing. **2** to offend the moral sense of. ◆ *n* **3** a great loathing or distaste. **4 in disgust.** as a result of disgust. ORIG C16: from OF *desgouster,* from *des-* DIS-[1] + *gouster* to taste, from L *gustus* taste
▸ **disˈgustedly** *adv* ▸ **disˈgustedness** *n*

dish (dɪʃ) *n* **1** a container used for holding or serving food, esp. an open shallow container. **2** the food in a dish. **3** a particular kind of food. **4** Also called: **dishful.** the amount contained in a dish. **5** something resembling a dish. **6** a concavity. **7** short for **dish aerial. 8** *Inf.* an attractive person. ◆ *vb* (*tr*) **9** to put into a dish. **10** to make concave. **11** *Brit. inf.* to ruin or spoil. ◆ See also **dish out, dish up.** ORIG OE *disc,* from L *discus* quoit
▸ **ˈdishˌlike** *adj*

dishabille (ˌdɪsæˈbiːl) *n* a variant of **deshabille.**

dish aerial *n* a microwave aerial, used esp. in radar, radio telescopes, and satellite broadcasting (**satellite dish aerial**), consisting of a parabolic reflector. Formal name: **parabolic aerial.** ◆ Also called: **dish antenna.** Often shortened to **dish.**

disharmony (dɪsˈhɑːmənɪ) *n, pl* **disharmonies. 1** lack of accord or harmony. **2** a situation, circumstance, etc., that is inharmonious.
▸ **disharmonious** (ˌdɪshɑːˈməʊnɪəs) *adj*

dishcloth (ˈdɪʃˌklɒθ) *n* a cloth or rag for washing or drying dishes.

dishearten (dɪsˈhɑːtᵊn) *vb* (*tr*) to weaken or destroy the hope, courage, enthusiasm, etc., of.
▸ **disˈhearteningly** *adv* ▸ **disˈheartenment** *n*

dished (dɪʃt) *adj* **1** shaped like a dish. **2** (of wheels) closer to one another at the bottom than at the top. **3** *Inf.* exhausted or defeated.

dishevel (dɪˈʃɛvᵊl) *vb* **dishevels, dishevelling, dishevelled** *or US* **dishevels, disheveling, disheveled.** to disarrange (the hair or clothes) of (someone). ORIG C15: back formation from DISHEVELLED
▸ **diˈshevelment** *n*

dishevelled *or US* **disheveled** (dɪˈʃɛvᵊld) *adj* **1** (esp. of hair) hanging loosely. **2** unkempt; untidy. ORIG C15 *dischevelee,* from OF *deschevelé,* from *des-* DIS-[1] + *chevel* hair, from L *capillus*

dishonest (dɪsˈɒnɪst) *adj* not honest or fair; deceiving or fraudulent.
▸ **disˈhonestly** *adv*

dishonesty (dɪsˈɒnɪstɪ) *n, pl* **dishonesties. 1** lack of honesty. **2** a deceiving act or statement.

dishonour *or US* **dishonor** (dɪsˈɒnə) *vb* (*tr*) **1** to treat with disrespect. **2** to fail or refuse to pay (a cheque, etc.). **3** to cause the disgrace of (a woman) by seduction or rape. ◆ *n* **4** a lack of honour or respect. **5** a state of shame or disgrace. **6** a person or thing that causes a loss of honour. **7** an insult; affront. **8** refusal or failure to accept or pay a commercial paper.

dishonourable *or US* **dishonorable** (dɪsˈɒnərəbᵊl) *adj* **1** characterized by or causing dishonour or discredit. **2** having little or no integrity; unprincipled.
▸ **disˈhonourableness** *or US* **disˈhonorableness** *n* ▸ **disˈhonourably** *or US* **disˈhonorably** *adv*

dish out *vb* (*tr, adv*) **1** *Inf.* to distribute. **2 dish it out.** to inflict punishment.

dishtowel (ˈdɪʃˌtaʊəl) *n* another name (esp. Scot., US and Canad.) for a **tea towel.**

dish up *vb* (*adv*) **1** to serve (a meal, food, etc.). **2** (*tr*) *Inf.* to prepare or present, esp. in an attractive manner.

dishwasher (ˈdɪʃˌwɒʃə) *n* **1** a machine for washing dishes, etc. **2** a person who washes dishes, etc.

dishwater (ˈdɪʃˌwɔːtə) *n* **1** water in which dishes have been washed. **2** something resembling this.

dishy (ˈdɪʃɪ) *adj* **dishier, dishiest.** *Inf., chiefly Brit.* good-looking or attractive.

disillusion (ˌdɪsɪˈluːʒən) *vb* **1** (*tr*) to destroy the ideals, illusions, or false ideas of. ◆ *n also* **disillusionment. 2** the act of disillusioning or the state of being disillusioned.

disincentive (ˌdɪsɪnˈsɛntɪv) *n* **1** something that acts as a deterrent. ◆ *adj* **2** acting as a deterrent: *a disincentive effect on productivity.*

disincline (ˌdɪsɪnˈklaɪn) *vb* **disinclines, disinclining, disinclined.** to make or be unwilling, reluctant, or averse.
▸ **disinclination** (ˌdɪsɪnklɪˈneɪʃən) *n*

disinfect (ˌdɪsɪnˈfɛkt) *vb* (*tr*) to rid of microorganisms potentially harmful to man, esp. by chemical means.
▸ **ˌdisinˈfection** *n*

disinfectant (ˌdɪsɪnˈfɛktənt) *n* an agent that destroys or inhibits the activity of microorganisms that cause disease.

disinfest (ˌdɪsɪnˈfɛst) *vb* (*tr*) to rid of vermin.
▸ **ˌdisinfesˈtation** *n*

disinflation (ˌdɪsɪnˈfleɪʃən) *n Econ.* a reduction or stabilization of the general price level intended to improve the balance of payments without incurring reductions in output, employment, etc.

disinformation (ˌdɪsɪnfəˈmeɪʃən) *n* false information intended to deceive or mislead.

disingenuous (ˌdɪsɪnˈdʒɛnjʊəs) *adj* not sincere; lacking candour.
▸ **ˌdisinˈgenuously** *adv* ▸ **ˌdisinˈgenuousness** *n*

disinherit (ˌdɪsɪnˈhɛrɪt) *vb* (*tr*) **1** *Law.* to deprive (an heir or next of kin) of inheritance or right to inherit. **2** to deprive of a right or heritage.
▸ **ˌdisinˈheritance** *n*

disintegrate (dɪsˈɪntɪˌgreɪt) *vb* **disintegrates, disintegrating, disintegrated. 1** to break or be broken into fragments or parts; shatter. **2** to lose or cause to lose cohesion. **3** (*intr*) to lose judgment or control. **4** *Physics.* **4a** to induce or undergo nuclear fission. **4b** another word for **decay** (sense 3).
▸ **disˌinteˈgration** *n* ▸ **disˈinteˌgrator** *n*

disinter (ˌdɪsɪnˈtɜː) *vb* **disinters, disinterring, disinterred.** (*tr*) **1** to remove or dig up; exhume. **2** to bring to light; expose.
▸ **ˌdisinˈterment** *n*

disinterest (dɪsˈɪntrɪst, -tərɪst) *n* **1** freedom from bias or involvement. **2** lack of interest.

disinterested (dɪsˈɪntrɪstɪd, -tərɪs-) *adj* **1** free from bias or partiality; objective. **2** not interested.
▸ **disˈinterestedly** *adv* ▸ **disˈinterestedness** *n*

> **USAGE NOTE** *Disinterested* is now so commonly used to mean 'not interested' that to avoid ambiguity it is often advisable to replace it by a synonym when the meaning intended is 'impartial, unbiased'. In the Bank of English about 10% of the examples of the word occur followed by *in*, and overall about a third of examples are of this usage.

disintermediation (dɪsˌɪntəˌmiːdɪˈeɪʃən) *n Finance.* the elimination of such financial intermediaries as banks and brokers in transactions between principals, often as a result of deregulation and the use of computing.

disinvest (dɪsɪnˈvɛst) *vb Econ.* **1** (usually foll. by *in*) to remove investment (from). **2** (*intr*) to reduce the capital stock of an economy or enterprise, as by not replacing obsolete machinery.
▸ **ˌdisinˈvestment** *n*

disjoin (dɪsˈdʒɔɪn) *vb* to disconnect or become disconnected; separate.
▸ **disˈjoinable** *adj*

disjoint (dɪsˈdʒɔɪnt) *vb* **1** to take apart or come apart at the joints. **2** (*tr*) to disunite or disjoin. **3** to dislocate or become dislocated. **4** (*tr; usually passive*) to end the unity, sequence, or coherence of.

disjointed (dɪsˈdʒɔɪntɪd) *adj* **1** having no coherence; disconnected. **2** separated at the joint. **3** dislocated.
▸ **disˈjointedly** *adv*

disjunct (ˈdɪsdʒʌŋkt) *n Logic.* one of the propositions in a disjunction.

disjunction (dɪsˈdʒʌŋkʃən) *n* **1** Also called: **disjuncture.** a disconnecting or being disconnected; separation. **2** *Logic.* **2a** the operator that forms a compound sentence from two given sentences and corresponds to the English *or*. **2b** the relation between such sentences.

★ people and places

disjunctive (dɪsˈdʒʌŋktɪv) *adj* **1** serving to disconnect or separate. **2** *Grammar.* denoting a word, esp. a conjunction, that serves to express opposition or contrast: *but* in *She was poor but she was honest.* **3** *Logic.* relating to, characterized by, or containing disjunction. ◆ *n* **4** *Grammar.* a disjunctive word, esp. a conjunction. **5** *Logic.* a disjunctive proposition.
▸ **disˈjunctively** *adv*

disk (dɪsk) *n* **1** a variant spelling (esp. US and Canad.) of **disc. 2** Also called: **magnetic disk, hard disk.** *Computing.* a direct-access storage device consisting of a stack of plates coated with a magnetic layer, the whole assembly rotating rapidly as a single unit.

> **USAGE NOTE** *Disk* is the preferred US spelling of *disc* in all its senses, and is also the majority spelling in the computer industry.

disk drive *n Computing.* the controller and mechanism for reading and writing data on computer disks.

diskette (dɪsˈkɛt) *n* another name for **floppy disk.**

disk operating system *n* an operating system used on a computer system with one or more disk drives. Often shortened to: **DOS.**

dislike (dɪsˈlaɪk) *vb* **dislikes, disliking, disliked. 1** (*tr*) to consider unpleasant or disagreeable. ◆ *n* **2** a feeling of aversion or antipathy.
▸ **disˈlikable** *or* **disˈlikeable** *adj*

dislocate (ˈdɪsləˌkeɪt) *vb* **dislocates, dislocating, dislocated.** (*tr*) **1** to disrupt or shift out of place. **2** to displace from its normal position, esp. a bone from its joint.

dislocation (ˌdɪsləˈkeɪʃən) *n* **1** a displacing or being displaced. **2** the state or condition of being dislocated.

dislodge (dɪsˈlɒdʒ) *vb* **dislodges, dislodging, dislodged.** to remove from or leave a lodging place, hiding place, or previously fixed position.
▸ **disˈlodgment** *or* **disˈlodgement** *n*

disloyal (dɪsˈlɔɪəl) *adj* not loyal or faithful; deserting one's allegiance.
▸ **disˈloyally** *adv*

disloyalty (dɪsˈlɔɪəltɪ) *n, pl* **disloyalties.** the condition or an instance of being unfaithful or disloyal.

dismal (ˈdɪzməl) *adj* **1** causing gloom or depression. **2** causing dismay or terror. **3** of poor quality or a low standard; feeble. ORIG C13: from *dismal* (n) list of 24 unlucky days in the year, from Med. L *diēs malī*, from L *diēs* day + *malus* bad
▸ **ˈdismally** *adv* ▸ **ˈdismalness** *n*

dismantle (dɪsˈmæntᵊl) *vb* **dismantles, dismantling, dismantled.** (*tr*) **1** to take apart. **2** to demolish or raze. **3** to strip of covering. ORIG C17: from OF *desmanteler* to remove a cloak from
▸ **disˈmantlement** *n*

dismast (dɪsˈmɑːst) *vb* (*tr*) to break off the mast or masts of (a sailing vessel).

dismay (dɪsˈmeɪ) *vb* (*tr*) **1** to fill with apprehension or alarm. **2** to fill with depression or discouragement. ◆ *n* **3** consternation or agitation. ORIG C13: from OF *desmaiier* (unattested), from *des-* DIS-[1] + *esmayer* to frighten, ult. of Gmc origin
▸ **disˈmaying** *adj*

dismember (dɪsˈmɛmbə) *vb* (*tr*) **1** to remove the limbs or members of. **2** to cut to pieces. **3** to divide or partition (something, such as an empire).
▸ **disˈmemberment** *n*

dismiss (dɪsˈmɪs) *vb* (*tr*) **1** to remove or discharge from employment or service. **2** to send away or allow to go. **3** to dispel from one's mind; discard. **4** to cease to consider (a subject). **5** to decline further hearing to (a claim or action). **6** *Cricket.* to bowl out a side for a particular number of runs. ORIG C15: from Med. L *dismissus* sent away, from *dīmittere*, from *dī-* DIS-[1] + *mittere* to send
▸ **disˈmissal** *n* ▸ **disˈmissible** *adj* ▸ **disˈmissive** *adj*

dismount (dɪsˈmaʊnt) *vb* **1** to get off a horse, bicycle, etc. **2** (*tr*) to disassemble or remove from a mounting. ◆ *n* **3** the act of dismounting.

Disney ★ (ˈdɪznɪ) *n* **Walt(er Elias).** 1901–66, US film producer, who pioneered animated cartoons: noted esp. for his creations *Mickey Mouse* and *Donald Duck* and films such as *Fantasia* (1940).
▸ **ˌDisneyˈesque** *adj*

Disneyfy (ˈdɪznɪˌfaɪ) *vb* **Disneyfies, Disneyfying, Disneyfied.** (*tr*) to transform (historic places, local customs, etc.) into trivial entertainment for tourists. ORIG C20: from the *Disneyland* amusement park in California
▸ **ˌDisneyfiˈcation** *n*

disobedience (ˌdɪsəˈbiːdɪəns) *n* lack of obedience.

disobedient (ˌdɪsəˈbiːdɪənt) *adj* not obedient; neglecting or refusing to obey.
▸ **ˌdisoˈbediently** *adv*

disobey (ˌdɪsəˈbeɪ) *vb* to neglect or refuse to obey (someone, an order, etc.).
▸ **ˌdisoˈbeyer** *n*

disoblige (ˌdɪsəˈblaɪdʒ) *vb* **disobliges, disobliging, disobliged.** (*tr*) **1** to disregard the desires of. **2** to slight; insult. **3** *Inf.* to cause trouble or inconvenience to.
▸ **ˌdisoˈbliging** *adj*

disorder (dɪsˈɔːdə) *n* **1** a lack of order; confusion. **2** a disturbance of public order. **3** an upset of health; ailment. **4** a deviation from the normal system or order. ◆ *vb* (*tr*) **5** to upset the order of. **6** to disturb the health or mind of.

disorderly (dɪsˈɔːdəlɪ) *adj* **1** untidy; irregular. **2** uncontrolled; unruly. **3** *Law.* violating public peace or order.
▸ **disˈorderliness** *n*

disorderly house *n Law.* an establishment in which unruly behaviour habitually occurs, esp. a brothel or a gaming house.

disorganize *or* **disorganise** (dɪsˈɔːgəˌnaɪz) *vb* **disorganizes, disorganizing, disorganized** *or* **disorganises, disorganising, disorganised.** (*tr*) to disrupt the arrangement, system, or unity of.
▸ **disˌorganiˈzation** *or* **disˌorganiˈsation** *n*

disorientate (dɪsˈɔːrɪɛnˌteɪt) *or* **disorient** *vb* **disorientates, disorientating, disorientated** *or* **disorients, disorienting, disoriented.** (*tr*) **1** to cause (someone) to lose his or her bearings. **2** to perplex; confuse.
▸ **disˌorienˈtation** *n*

disown (dɪsˈəʊn) *vb* (*tr*) to deny any connection with; refuse to acknowledge.
▸ **disˈowner** *n*

disparage (dɪˈspærɪdʒ) *vb* **disparages, disparaging, disparaged.** (*tr*) **1** to speak contemptuously of; belittle. **2** to damage the reputation of. ORIG C14: from OF *desparagier,* from *des-* DIS-[1] + *parage* equality, from L *par* equal
▸ **disˈparagement** *n* ▸ **disˈparaging** *adj*

disparate (ˈdɪspərɪt) *adj* **1** utterly different or distinct in kind. ◆ *n* **2** (*pl*) unlike things or people. ORIG C16: from L *disparāre* to divide, from DIS-[1] + *parāre* to prepare; also infl. by L *dispar* unequal
▸ **ˈdisparately** *adv* ▸ **ˈdisparateness** *n*

disparity (dɪˈspærɪtɪ) *n, pl* **disparities. 1** inequality or difference, as in age, rank, wages, etc. **2** dissimilarity.

dispassionate (dɪsˈpæʃənɪt) *adj* devoid of or uninfluenced by emotion or prejudice; objective; impartial.
▸ **disˈpassionately** *adv*

dispatch *or* **despatch** (dɪˈspætʃ) *vb* (*tr*) **1** to send off promptly, as to a destination or to perform a task. **2** to discharge or complete (a duty, etc.) promptly. **3** *Inf.* to eat up quickly. **4** to murder or execute. ◆ *n* **5** the act of sending off a letter, messenger, etc. **6** prompt action or speed (often in **with dispatch**). **7** an official communication or report, sent in haste. **8** a report sent to a newspaper, etc., by a correspondent. **9** murder or execution. ORIG C16: from It. *dispacciare,* from Provençal *despachar,* from OF *despeechier* to set free, from *des-* DIS-[1] + *-peechier,* ult. from L *pedica* a fetter
▸ **disˈpatcher** *n*

dispatch box *n* a case or box used to hold valuables or documents, esp. official state documents.

dispatch case *n* a case used for carrying papers, documents, books, etc.

dispatch rider *n* a horseman or motorcyclist who carries dispatches.

dispel (dɪˈspɛl) *vb* **dispels, dispelling, dispelled.** (*tr*) to disperse or drive away. ORIG C17: from L *dispellere,* from DIS-[1] + *pellere* to drive
▸ **disˈpeller** *n*

dispensable (dɪˈspɛnsəbᵊl) *adj* **1** not essential; expendable. **2** (of a law, vow, etc.) able to be relaxed.
▸ **disˌpensaˈbility** *n*

dispensary (dɪˈspɛnsərɪ) *n, pl* **dispensaries.** a place where medicine, etc., is dispensed.

dispensation (ˌdɪspɛnˈseɪʃən) *n* **1** the act of distributing or dispensing. **2** something distributed or dispensed. **3** a system or plan of administering or dispensing. **4** *Chiefly RC Church.* permission to dispense with an obligation of church law. **5** any exemption from an obligation. **6a** the ordering of life and events by God. **6b** a religious system or code of prescriptions for life and conduct regarded as of divine origin.
▸ **ˌdispenˈsational** *adj*

dispensatory (dɪˈspɛnsətərɪ, -trɪ) *n, pl* **dispensatories.** a book listing the composition, preparation, and application of various drugs.

dispense (dɪˈspɛns) *vb* **dispenses, dispensing, dispensed. 1** (*tr*) to give out or distribute in portions. **2** (*tr*) to prepare and distribute (medicine), esp. on prescription. **3** (*tr*) to administer (the law, etc.). **4** (*intr;* foll. by *with*) to do away (with) or manage (without). **5** to grant a dispensation to. **6** to exempt or excuse from a rule or obligation. ORIG C14: from Med. L *dispensāre* to pardon, from L *dispendere* to weigh out, from DIS-[1] + *pendere*

dispenser (dɪˈspɛnsə) *n* **1** a device that automatically dispenses a single item or a measured quantity. **2** a person or thing that dispenses.

dispensing optician *n* See **optician.**

dispersal (dɪˈspɜːsᵊl) *n* **1** a dispersing or being dispersed. **2** the spread of animals, plants, or seeds to new areas.

dispersant (dɪsˈpɜːsənt) *n* a liquid or gas used to disperse small particles or droplets, as in an aerosol.

disperse (dɪˈspɜːs) *vb* **disperses, dispersing, dispersed. 1** to scatter; distribute over a wide area. **2** to dissipate. **3** to leave or cause to leave a gathering. **4** to separate or be separated by dispersion. **5** (*tr*) to spread (news, etc.). **6** to separate (particles) throughout a solid, liquid, or gas. ◆ *adj* **7** of or consisting of the particles in a colloid or suspension: *disperse phase.* ORIG C14: from L *dispersus,* from *dispergere* to scatter widely, from DI-[2] + *spargere* to strew
▸ **disˈperser** *n*

USAGE NOTE See at **disburse.**

dispersion (dɪˈspɜːʃən) *n* **1** another word for **dispersal. 2** *Physics.* **2a** the separation of electromagnetic radiation into constituents of different wavelengths. **2b** a measure of the ability of a substance to separate by refraction. **3** *Statistics.* the degree to which values of a frequency distribution are scattered around some central point, usually the arithmetic mean or median. **4** *Chem.* a system containing particles dispersed in a solid, liquid, or gas. **5** *Ecology.* the distribution pattern of a population of animals or plants.

dispirit (dɪˈspɪrɪt) *vb* (*tr*) to lower the spirit of; make downhearted; discourage.
▸ **disˈpirited** *adj* ▸ **disˈpiritedness** *n* ▸ **disˈpiriting** *adj*

displace (dɪsˈpleɪs) *vb* **displaces, displacing, displaced.** (*tr*) **1** to move from the usual or correct location. **2** to remove from office or employment. **3** to occupy the place of; replace; supplant.

displaced person *n* a person forced from his or her home or country, esp. by war or revolution.

displacement (dɪsˈpleɪsmənt) *n* **1** a displacing or being displaced. **2** the weight or volume displaced by a body in a fluid. **3** *Psychoanal.* the transferring of emotional feelings from their original object to one that disguises their real nature. **4** *Maths.* the distance measured in a particular direction from a reference point. Symbol: *s*

displacement activity *n Psychol.* behaviour that occurs typically when there is a conflict of motives and that has no relevance to either motive: e.g. head scratching.

display (dɪˈspleɪ) *vb* **1** (*tr*) to show or make visible. **2** (*tr*) to put out to be seen; exhibit. **3** (*tr*) to disclose; reveal. **4** (*tr*) to flaunt in an ostentatious way. **5** (*tr*) to spread out; unfold. **6** (*tr*) to give prominence to. **7** (*intr*) *Zool.* to engage in a display. ◆ *n* **8** an exhibiting or displaying; show. **9** something exhibited or displayed. **10** an ostentatious exhibition. **11** an arrangement of certain typefaces to give prominence to headings, etc. **12** *Electronics.* **12a** a device capable of representing information visually, as on a cathode-ray tube screen. **12b** the information so presented. **13** *Zool.* a pattern of behaviour by which the animal attracts attention while it is courting the female, defending its territory, etc. **14** (*modifier*) designating typefaces that give prominence to the words they are used to set. ORIG C14: from Anglo-F *despleier* to unfold, from LL *displicāre* to scatter, from DIS-[1] + *plicāre* to fold
▸ **disˈplayer** *n*

displease (dɪsˈpliːz) *vb* **displeases, displeasing, displeased.** to annoy, offend, or cause displeasure to (someone).
▸ **disˈpleasing** *adj* ▸ **disˈpleasingly** *adv*

displeasure (dɪsˈplɛʒə) *n* **1** the condition of being displeased. **2** *Arch.* **2a** pain. **2b** an act or cause of offence.

disport (dɪˈspɔːt) *vb* **1** (*tr*) to indulge (oneself) in pleasure. **2** (*intr*) to frolic or gambol. ◆ *n* **3** *Arch.* amusement. ORIG C14: from Anglo-F *desporter,* from *des-* DIS-[1] + *porter* to carry

disposable (dɪˈspəʊzəbᵊl) *adj* **1** designed for disposal after use: *disposable cups.* **2** available for use if needed: *disposable assets.* ◆ *n* **3** something, such as a baby's nappy, that is designed for disposal. **4** (*pl*) short for **disposable goods.**
▸ **disˌposaˈbility** *or* **disˈposableness** *n*

disposable goods *pl n* consumer goods that are used up a short time after purchase, including perishables, newspapers, clothes, etc. Also called: **disposables.**

disposable income *n* **1** the money a person has available to spend after paying taxes, pension contributions, etc. **2** the total amount of money that the individuals in a community, country, etc., have available to buy consumer goods.

disposal (dɪˈspəʊzᵊl) *n* **1** the act or means of getting rid of something. **2** arrangement in a particular order. **3** a specific method of tending to matters, as in business. **4** the act or process of transferring something to or providing something for another. **5** the power or opportunity to make use of someone or something (esp. in **at one's disposal**).

dispose (dɪˈspəʊz) *vb* **disposes, disposing, disposed.** **1** (*intr;* foll. by *of*) **1a** to deal with or settle. **1b** to give, sell, or transfer to another. **1c** to throw out or away. **1d** to consume, esp. hurriedly. **1e** to kill. **2** to arrange or settle (matters). **3** (*tr*) to make willing or receptive. **4** (*tr*) to place in a certain order. **5** (*tr;* often foll. by *to*) to accustom or condition. ORIG C14: from OF *disposer,* from L *dispōnere* to set in different places, from DIS-[1] + *pōnere* to place
▸ **disˈposer** *n*

disposed (dɪˈspəʊzd) *adj* **a** having an inclination as specified (towards something). **b** (*in combination*): *well-disposed.*

disposition (ˌdɪspəˈzɪʃən) *n* **1** a person's usual temperament or frame of mind. **2** a tendency, inclination, or habit. **3** another word for **disposal** (senses 2–5). **4** *Arch.* manner of placing or arranging.

dispossess (ˌdɪspəˈzɛs) *vb* (*tr*) to take away possession of something, esp. property; expel.
▸ **ˌdisposˈsession** *n* ▸ **ˌdisposˈsessor** *n*

dispraise (dɪsˈpreɪz) *vb* **dispraises, dispraising, dispraised.** **1** (*tr*) to express disapproval or condemnation of. ◆ *n* **2** the disapproval, etc., expressed.
▸ **disˈpraiser** *n*

disproof (dɪsˈpruːf) *n* **1** facts that disprove something. **2** the act of disproving.

disproportion (ˌdɪsprəˈpɔːʃən) *n* **1** lack of proportion or equality. **2** an instance of disparity or inequality. ◆ *vb* **3** (*tr*) to cause to become exaggerated or unequal.
▸ **ˌdisproˈportional** *adj*

disproportionate (ˌdɪsprəˈpɔːʃənɪt) *adj* out of proportion; unequal.
▸ **ˌdisproˈportionately** *adv* ▸ **ˌdisproˈportionateness** *n*

disprove (dɪsˈpruːv) *vb* **disproves, disproving, disproved.** (*tr*) to show (an assertion, claim, etc.) to be incorrect.
▸ **disˈprovable** *adj* ▸ **disˈproval** *n*

disputable (dɪˈspjuːtəbᵊl, ˈdɪspjʊtə-) *adj* capable of being argued; debatable.
▸ **disˌputaˈbility** *or* **disˈputableness** *n* ▸ **disˈputably** *adv*

disputant (dɪˈspjuːtᵊnt, ˈdɪspjʊtənt) *n* **1** a person who argues; contestant. ◆ *adj* **2** engaged in argument.

disputation (ˌdɪspjʊˈteɪʃən) *n* **1** the act or an instance of arguing. **2** a formal academic debate on a thesis. **3** an obsolete word for **conversation.**

disputatious (ˌdɪspjʊˈteɪʃəs) *or* **disputative** (dɪˈspjuːtətɪv) *adj* inclined to argument.
▸ **ˌdispuˈtatiousness** *or* **disˈputativeness** *n*

dispute *vb* (dɪˈspjuːt) **disputes, disputing, disputed.** **1** to argue, debate, or quarrel about (something). **2** (*tr; may take a clause as object*) to doubt the validity, etc., of. **3** (*tr*) to seek to win; contest for. **4** (*tr*) to struggle against; resist. ◆ *n* (dɪˈspjuːt, ˈdɪspjuːt). **5** an argument or quarrel. **6** *Rare.* a fight. ORIG C13: from LL *disputāre* to contend verbally, from L: to discuss, from DIS-[1] + *putāre* to think
▸ **disˈputer** *n*

disqualify (dɪsˈkwɒlɪˌfaɪ) *vb* **disqualifies, disqualifying, disqualified.** (*tr*) **1** to make unfit or unqualified. **2** to make ineligible, as for entry to an examination. **3** to debar from a contest. **4** to deprive of rights, powers, or privileges.
▸ **disˌqualifiˈcation** *n*

disquiet (dɪsˈkwaɪət) *n* **1** a feeling or condition of anxiety or uneasiness. ◆ *vb* **2** (*tr*) to make anxious or upset.
▸ **disˈquieting** *adj*

disquietude (dɪsˈkwaɪɪˌtjuːd) *n* a feeling or state of anxiety or uneasiness.

disquisition (ˌdɪskwɪˈzɪʃən) *n* a formal examination of a subject. ORIG C17: from L *disquīsītiō,* from *disquīrere* to make an investigation, from DIS-[1] + *quaerere* to seek
▸ **ˌdisquiˈsitional** *adj*

Disraeli ★ (dɪzˈreɪlɪ) *n* **Benjamin,** 1st Earl of Beaconsfield. 1804–81, British Tory statesman and novelist; prime minister (1868; 1874–80). He gave coherence to the Tory principles of protectionism and imperialism, was responsible for the Reform Bill (1867) and, as prime minister, bought a controlling interest in the Suez Canal. His novels include *Coningsby* (1844) and *Sybil* (1845).

disregard (ˌdɪsrɪˈgɑːd) *vb* (*tr*) **1** to give little or no attention to; ignore. **2** to treat as unworthy of consideration or respect. ◆ *n* **3** lack of attention or respect.
▸ **ˌdisreˈgardful** *adj*

disremember (ˌdɪsrɪˈmɛmbə) *vb Inf., chiefly US.* to fail to recall.

disrepair (ˌdɪsrɪˈpɛə) *n* the condition of being worn out or in poor working order; a condition requiring repairs.

disreputable (dɪsˈrɛpjʊtəbᵊl) *adj* **1** having or causing a lack of repute. **2** disordered in appearance.
▸ **disˈreputably** *adv*

disrepute (ˌdɪsrɪˈpjuːt) *n* a loss or lack of credit or repute.

disrespect (ˌdɪsrɪˈspɛkt) *n* contempt; rudeness; lack of respect.
▸ **ˌdisreˈspectful** *adj*

disrobe (dɪsˈrəʊb) *vb* **disrobes, disrobing, disrobed.** **1** to undress. **2** (*tr*) to divest of authority, etc.
▸ **disˈrobement** *n*

disrupt (dɪsˈrʌpt) *vb* **1** (*tr*) to throw into turmoil or disorder. **2** (*tr*) to interrupt the progress of. **3** to break or split apart. ORIG C17: from L *disruptus* burst asunder, from *dīrumpere* to dash to pieces, from DIS-[1] + *rumpere* to burst
▸ **disˈrupter** *or* **disˈruptor** *n* ▸ **disˈruption** *n*

disruptive (dɪsˈrʌptɪv) *adj* involving, causing, or tending to cause disruption.

diss *or* **dis** (dɪs) *vb* **disses, dissing, dissed.** *Sl., chiefly US.* to

★ people and places

treat (someone) with contempt. ORIG C20: orig. US Black rap slang, short for DISRESPECT

dissatisfy (dɪs'sætɪs,faɪ) *vb* **dissatisfies, dissatisfying, dissatisfied.** (*tr*) to fail to satisfy; disappoint.
▸ **,dissatis'faction** *n* ▸ **,dissatis'factory** *adj*

dissect (dɪ'sɛkt, daɪ-) *vb* **1** to cut open and examine the structure of (a dead animal or plant). **2** (*tr*) to examine critically and minutely. ORIG C17: from L *dissecāre*, from DIS-[1] + *secāre* to cut
▸ **dis'section** *n* ▸ **dis'sector** *n*

dissected (dɪ'sɛktɪd, daɪ-) *adj* **1** *Bot.* in the form of narrow lobes or segments. **2** *Geol.* cut by erosion into hills and valleys.

disselboom ('dɪsᵊl,bu:m) *n S. African.* the single shaft of a wagon, esp. an ox wagon. ORIG from Du. *dissel* shaft + *boom* beam

dissemble (dɪ'sɛmbᵊl) *vb* **dissembles, dissembling, dissembled. 1** to conceal (one's real motives, emotions, etc.) by pretence. **2** (*tr*) to pretend; simulate. ORIG C15: from earlier *dissimulen*, from L *dissimulāre;* prob. infl. by obs. *semble* to resemble
▸ **dis'semblance** *n* ▸ **dis'sembler** *n*

disseminate (dɪ'sɛmɪ,neɪt) *vb* **disseminates, disseminating, disseminated.** (*tr*) to distribute or scatter about; diffuse. ORIG C17: from L *dissēmināre*, from DIS-[1] + *sēmināre* to sow, from *sēmen* seed
▸ **dis,semi'nation** *n* ▸ **dis'semi,nator** *n*

disseminated sclerosis *n* another name for **multiple sclerosis.**

dissension (dɪ'sɛnʃən) *n* disagreement, esp. when leading to a quarrel. ORIG C13: from L *dissēnsiō*, from *dissentīre* to DISSENT

dissent (dɪ'sɛnt) *vb* (*intr*) **1** to have a disagreement or withhold assent. **2** *Christianity.* to reject the doctrines, beliefs, or practices of an established church, and to adhere to a different system of beliefs. ◆ *n* **3** a difference of opinion. **4** *Christianity.* separation from an established church; Nonconformism. **5** the voicing of a minority opinion in the decision on a case at law. ORIG C16: from L *dissentīre* to disagree, from DIS-[1] + *sentīre* to feel
▸ **dis'senter** *n* ▸ **dis'senting** *adj*

Dissenter (dɪ'sɛntə) *n Christianity, chiefly Brit.* a Nonconformist or a person who refuses to conform to the established church.

dissentient (dɪ'sɛnʃənt) *adj* **1** dissenting, esp. from the opinion of the majority. ◆ *n* **2** a dissenter.
▸ **dis'sentience** *or* **dis'sentiency** *n*

dissertation (,dɪsə'teɪʃən) *n* **1** a written thesis, often based on original research, usually required for a higher degree. **2** a formal discourse. ORIG C17: from L *dissertāre* to debate, from *disserere* to examine, from DIS-[1] + *serere* to arrange
▸ **,disser'tational** *adj*

disserve (dɪs'sɜ:v) *vb* **disserves, disserving, disserved.** (*tr*) *Arch.* to do a disservice to.

disservice (dɪs'sɜ:vɪs) *n* an ill turn; wrong; injury, esp. when trying to help.

dissever (dɪ'sɛvə) *vb* **1** to break off or become broken off. **2** (*tr*) to divide up into parts. ORIG C13: from OF *dessevrer*, from LL DIS-[1] + *sēparāre* to SEPARATE
▸ **dis'severance** *or* **dis'severment** *n*

dissident ('dɪsɪdənt) *adj* **1** disagreeing; dissenting. ◆ *n* **2** a person who disagrees, esp. one who disagrees with the government. ORIG C16: from L *dissidēre* to be remote from, from DIS-[1] + *sedēre* to sit
▸ **'dissidence** *n* ▸ **'dissidently** *adv*

dissimilar (dɪ'sɪmɪlə) *adj* not alike; not similar; different.
▸ **dis'similarly** *adv* ▸ **,dissimi'larity** *n*

dissimilate (dɪ'sɪmɪ,leɪt) *vb* **dissimilates, dissimilating, dissimilated. 1** to make or become dissimilar. **2** (usually foll. by *to*) *Phonetics.* to change or displace (a consonant) or (of a consonant) to be changed to or displaced by (another consonant) so that its manner of articulation becomes less similar to a speech sound in the same word. Thus (r) in the final syllable of French *marbre* is dissimilated to (l) in its English form *marble.* ORIG C19: from DIS-[1] + ASSIMILATE

dissimilation (,dɪsɪmɪ'leɪʃən) *n* **1** the act or an instance of making dissimilar. **2** *Phonetics.* the alteration or omission of a consonant as a result of being dissimilated.

dissimilitude (,dɪsɪ'mɪlɪ,tju:d) *n* **1** dissimilarity; difference. **2** a point of difference.

dissimulate (dɪ'sɪmjʊ,leɪt) *vb* **dissimulates, dissimulating, dissimulated.** to conceal (one's real feelings) by pretence.
▸ **dis,simu'lation** *n* ▸ **dis'simu,lator** *n*

dissipate ('dɪsɪ,peɪt) *vb* **dissipates, dissipating, dissipated. 1** to exhaust or be exhausted by dispersion. **2** (*tr*) to scatter or break up. **3** (*intr*) to indulge in the pursuit of pleasure. ORIG C15: from L *dissipāre* to disperse, from DIS-[1] + *supāre* to throw
▸ **'dissi,pater** *or* **'dissi,pator** *n* ▸ **'dissi,pative** *adj*

dissipated ('dɪsɪ,peɪtɪd) *adj* **1** indulging without restraint in the pursuit of pleasure; debauched. **2** wasted, scattered, or exhausted.

dissipation (,dɪsɪ'peɪʃən) *n* **1** a dissipating or being dissipated. **2** unrestrained indulgence in physical pleasures. **3** excessive expenditure; wastefulness.

dissociate (dɪ'səʊʃɪ,eɪt, -sɪ-) *vb* **dissociates, dissociating, dissociated. 1** to break or cause to break the association between (people, organizations, etc.). **2** (*tr*) to regard or treat as separate or unconnected. **3** to undergo or subject to dissociation.
▸ **dis'sociative** *adj*

dissociation (dɪ,səʊsɪ'eɪʃən, -ʃɪ-) *n* **1** a dissociating or being dissociated. **2** *Chem.* the decomposition of the molecules of a single compound into two or more other compounds, atoms, ions, or radicals. **3** *Psychiatry.* the separation of a group of mental processes or ideas from the rest of the personality, so that they lead an independent existence, as in cases of multiple personality.

dissoluble (dɪ'sɒljʊbᵊl) *adj* a less common word for **soluble.** ORIG C16: from L *dissolūbilis*, from *dissolvere* to DISSOLVE
▸ **dis,solu'bility** *n*

dissolute ('dɪsə,lu:t) *adj* given to dissipation; debauched. ORIG C14: from L *dissolūtus* loose, from *dissolvere* to DISSOLVE
▸ **'disso,lutely** *adv* ▸ **'disso,luteness** *n*

dissolution (,dɪsə'lu:ʃən) *n* **1** separation into component parts; disintegration. **2** destruction by breaking up and dispersing. **3** the termination of a meeting or assembly, such as Parliament. **4** the termination of a formal or legal relationship, such as a business, marriage, etc. **5** the act or process of dissolving.

dissolve (dɪ'zɒlv) *vb* **dissolves, dissolving, dissolved. 1** to go or cause to go into solution. **2** to become or cause to become liquid; melt. **3** to disintegrate or disperse. **4** to come or bring to an end. **5** to dismiss (a meeting, Parliament, etc.) or (of a meeting, etc.) to be dismissed. **6** to collapse or cause to collapse emotionally: *to dissolve into tears.* **7** to lose or cause to lose distinctness. **8** (*tr*) to terminate legally, as a marriage, etc. **9** (*intr*) *Films, television.* to fade out one scene and replace with another to make two scenes merge imperceptibly or slowly overlap. ◆ *n* **10** *Films, television.* a scene filmed or televised by dissolving. ORIG C14: from L *dissolvere* to make loose, from DIS-[1] + *solvere* to release
▸ **dis'solvable** *adj*

dissonance ('dɪsənəns) *or* **dissonancy** *n* **1** a discordant combination of sounds. **2** lack of agreement or consistency. **3** *Music.* **3a** a sensation of harshness and incompleteness associated with certain intervals and chords. **3b** an interval or chord of this kind.

dissonant ('dɪsənənt) *adj* **1** discordant. **2** incongruous or discrepant. **3** *Music.* characterized by dissonance. ORIG C15: from L *dissonāre* to be discordant, from DIS-[1] + *sonāre* to sound

dissuade (dɪ'sweɪd) *vb* **dissuades, dissuading, dissuaded.** (*tr*) **1** (often foll. by *from*) to deter (someone) by persuasion from a course of action, policy, etc. **2** to advise against (an action, etc.). ORIG C15: from L *dissuādēre*, from DIS-[1] + *suādēre* to persuade
▸ **dis'suader** *n* ▸ **dis'suasion** *n* ▸ **dis'suasive** *adj*

dissyllable (dɪˈsɪləbᵊl) *or* **disyllable** *n* a word of two syllables.
▸ **dissyllabic** (ˌdɪsɪˈlæbɪk) *or* **disyllabic** (ˌdaɪsɪˈlæbɪk) *adj*

dissymmetry (dɪˈsɪmɪtrɪ, dɪsˈsɪm-) *n, pl* **dissymmetries. 1** lack of symmetry. **2** the relationship between two objects when one is the mirror image of the other.
▸ **dissymmetric** (ˌdɪsɪˈmɛtrɪk, ˌdɪssɪ-) *or* ˌ**dissymˈmetrical** *adj*

dist. *abbrev. for:* **1** distant. **2** distinguish(ed). **3** district.

distaff (ˈdɪstɑːf) *n* **1** the rod on which flax is wound preparatory to spinning. **2** *Figurative.* women's work. ORIG OE *distæf,* from *dis-* bunch of flax + *stæf* STAFF[1]

distaff side *n* the female side of a family.

distal (ˈdɪstᵊl) *adj Anat.* situated farthest from the centre or point of attachment or origin. ORIG C19: from DISTANT + -AL[1]
▸ **ˈdistally** *adv*

distance (ˈdɪstəns) *n* **1** the space between two points. **2** the length of this gap. **3** the state of being apart in space; remoteness. **4** an interval between two points in time. **5** the extent of progress. **6** a distant place or time. **7** a separation or remoteness in relationship. **8** (preceded by *the*) the most distant or a faraway part of the visible scene. **9** *Horse racing.* **9a** *Brit.* a point on a racecourse 240 yards from the winning post. **9b** *US.* the part of a racecourse that a horse must reach before the winner passes the finishing line in order to qualify for later heats. **10 go the distance. 10a** *Boxing.* to complete a bout without being knocked out. **10b** to be able to complete an assigned task or responsibility. **11 keep one's distance.** to maintain a reserve in respect of another person. **12 middle distance.** halfway between the foreground or the observer and the horizon. ◆ *vb* **distances, distancing, distanced.** (*tr*) **13** to hold or place at a distance. **14** to separate (oneself) mentally from something. **15** to outdo; outstrip.

distance learning *n* a teaching system consisting of video, audio, and written material designed for a person to use in studying a subject at home.

distant (ˈdɪstənt) *adj* **1** far apart in space or time. **2** (*postpositive*) separated in space or time by a specified distance. **3** apart in relationship: *a distant cousin.* **4** coming from or going to a faraway place. **5** remote in manner; aloof. **6** abstracted; absent: *a distant look.* ORIG C14: from L *distāre* to be distant, from DIS-[1] + *stāre* to stand
▸ **ˈdistantly** *adv* ▸ **ˈdistantness** *n*

distaste (dɪsˈteɪst) *n* (often foll. by *for*) a dislike (of); aversion (to).

distasteful (dɪsˈteɪstfʊl) *adj* unpleasant or offensive.
▸ **disˈtastefulness** *n*

distemper[1] (dɪsˈtɛmpə) *n* **1** any of various infectious diseases of animals, esp. **canine distemper,** a highly contagious viral disease of dogs. **2** *Arch.* **2a** a disorder. **2b** disturbance. **2c** discontent. ORIG C14: from LL *distemperāre* to derange the health of, from L DIS-[1] + *temperāre* to mix in correct proportions

distemper[2] (dɪsˈtɛmpə) *n* **1** a technique of painting in which the pigments are mixed with water, glue, size, etc.: used for poster, mural, and scene painting. **2** the paint used in this technique or any of various water-based paints. ◆ *vb* **3** to paint (something) with distemper. ORIG C14: from Med. L *distemperāre* to soak, from L DIS-[1] + *temperāre* to mingle

distend (dɪˈstɛnd) *vb* **1** to expand by or as if by pressure from within; swell; inflate. **2** (*tr*) to stretch out or extend. ORIG C14: from L *distendere,* from DIS-[1] + *tendere* to stretch
▸ **disˈtensible** *adj* ▸ **disˈtension** *or* **disˈtention** *n*

distich (ˈdɪstɪk) *n Prosody.* a unit of two verse lines, usually a couplet. ORIG C16: from Gk *distikhos* having two lines, from DI-[1] + *stikhos* row, line

distil *or US* **distill** (dɪsˈtɪl) *vb* **distils, distilling, distilled** *or US* **distills, distilling, distilled. 1** to subject to or undergo distillation. **2** (sometimes foll. by *out* or *off*) to purify, separate, or concentrate, or be purified, separated, or concentrated by distillation. **3** to obtain or be obtained by distillation. **4** to exude or give off (a substance) in drops. **5** (*tr*) to extract the essence of. ORIG C14: from L *dēstillāre* to distil, from DE- + *stillāre* to drip

distillate (ˈdɪstɪlɪt) *n* **1** the product of distillation. **2** a concentrated essence.

distillation (ˌdɪstɪˈleɪʃən) *n* **1** a distilling. **2** the process of evaporating or boiling a liquid and condensing its vapour. **3** purification or separation of mixtures by using different evaporation rates or boiling points of their components. **4** the process of obtaining the essence or an extract of a substance, usually by heating it in a solvent. **5** a distillate. **6** a concentrated essence.
▸ **disˈtillatory** *adj*

distiller (dɪˈstɪlə) *n* a person or organization that distils, esp. a company that makes spirits.

distillery (dɪˈstɪlərɪ) *n, pl* **distilleries.** a place where alcoholic drinks, etc., are made by distillation.

distinct (dɪˈstɪŋkt) *adj* **1** easily sensed or understood; clear. **2** (when *postpositive,* foll. by *from*) not the same (as); separate (from). **3** not alike; different. **4** sharp; clear. **5** recognizable; definite. **6** explicit; unequivocal. **7** *Bot.* (of parts of a plant) not joined together; separate. ORIG C14: from L *distinctus,* from *distinguere* to DISTINGUISH
▸ **disˈtinctly** *adv* ▸ **disˈtinctness** *n*

distinction (dɪˈstɪŋkʃən) *n* **1** the act or an instance of distinguishing or differentiating. **2** a distinguishing feature. **3** the state of being different or distinguishable. **4** special honour, recognition, or fame. **5** excellence of character; distinctive qualities. **6** distinguished appearance. **7** a symbol of honour or rank.

distinctive (dɪˈstɪŋktɪv) *adj* serving or tending to distinguish; characteristic.
▸ **disˈtinctively** *adv* ▸ **disˈtinctiveness** *n*

distingué *French.* (distɛ̃ge) *adj* distinguished or noble.

distinguish (dɪˈstɪŋgwɪʃ) *vb* (*mainly tr*) **1** (when *intr,* foll. by *between* or *among*) to make, show, or recognize a difference (between or among); differentiate (between). **2** to be a distinctive feature of; characterize. **3** to make out; perceive. **4** to mark for a special honour. **5** to make (oneself) noteworthy. **6** to classify. ORIG C16: from L *distinguere* to separate
▸ **disˈtinguishable** *adj* ▸ **disˈtinguishing** *adj*

distinguished (dɪˈstɪŋgwɪʃt) *adj* **1** noble or dignified in appearance or behaviour. **2** eminent; famous; celebrated.

distort (dɪˈstɔːt) *vb* (*tr*) **1** (*often passive*) to twist or pull out of shape; contort; deform. **2** to alter or misrepresent (facts, etc.). **3** *Electronics.* to reproduce or amplify (a signal) inaccurately. ORIG C16: from L *distortus,* from *distorquēre* to turn different ways, from DIS-[1] + *torquēre* to twist
▸ **disˈtorted** *adj*

distortion (dɪˈstɔːʃən) *n* **1** a distorting or being distorted. **2** something that is distorted. **3** *Electronics.* an undesired change in the shape of an electrical wave or signal resulting in a loss of clarity in radio reception or sound reproduction.
▸ **disˈtortional** *adj*

distract (dɪˈstrækt) *vb* (*tr*) **1** (*often passive*) to draw the attention of (a person) away from something. **2** to divide or confuse the attention of (a person). **3** to amuse or entertain. **4** to trouble greatly. **5** to make mad. ORIG C14: from L *distractus* perplexed, from *distrahere* to pull in different directions, from DIS-[1] + *trahere* to drag

USAGE NOTE See at **detract.**

distracted (dɪˈstræktɪd) *adj* **1** bewildered; confused. **2** mad.
▸ **disˈtractedly** *adv*

distraction (dɪˈstrækʃən) *n* **1** a distracting or being distracted. **2** something that serves as a diversion or entertainment. **3** an interruption; obstacle to concentration. **4** mental turmoil or madness.

distrain (dɪˈstreɪn) *vb Law.* to seize (personal property) as security or indemnity for a debt. ORIG C13: from OF *destreindre,* from L *distringere* to impede, from DIS-[1] + *stringere* to draw tight
▸ **disˈtrainment** *n* ▸ **disˈtrainor** *or* **disˈtrainer** *n*

distraint (dɪˈstreɪnt) *n Law.* the act or process of distraining; distress.

distrait (dɪ'streɪ; *French* distrɛ) *adj* absent-minded; abstracted. ORIG C18: from F, from *distraire* to DISTRACT

distraught (dɪ'strɔːt) *adj* **1** distracted or agitated. **2** *Rare.* mad. ORIG C14: changed from obs. *distract* through influence of obs. *straught,* p.p. of STRETCH

distress (dɪ'strɛs) *vb* (*tr*) **1** to cause mental pain to; upset badly. **2** (*usually passive*) to subject to financial or other trouble. **3** to treat (something, esp. furniture or fabric) in order to make it appear older than it is. **4** *Law.* a less common word for **distrain.** ◆ *n* **5** mental pain; anguish. **6** a distressing or being distressed. **7** physical or financial trouble. **8 in distress.** (of a ship, etc.) in dire need of help. **9** *Law.* **9a** the seizure of property as security for or in satisfaction of a debt, claim, etc.; distraint. **9b** the property thus seized. **9c** (*as modifier*) *US: distress merchandise.* ORIG C13: from OF *destresse,* via Vulgar L, from L *districtus* divided in mind
▸ **dis'tressful** *adj* ▸ **dis'tressing** *adj* ▸ **dis'tressingly** *adv*

distressed (dɪ'strɛst) *adj* **1** much troubled; upset; afflicted. **2** in financial straits; poor. **3** (of furniture, fabric, etc.) having signs of ageing artificially applied. **4** *Econ.* another word for **depressed.**

distress signal *n* a signal by radio, Very light, etc., from a ship in need of immediate assistance.

distribute (dɪ'strɪbjuːt) *vb* **distributes, distributing, distributed.** (*tr*) **1** to give out in shares; dispense. **2** to hand out or deliver. **3** (*often passive*) to spread throughout an area. **4** (*often passive*) to divide into classes or categories. **5** *Printing.* to return (used type) to the correct positions in the typecase. **6** *Logic.* to incorporate in a distributed term of a categorical proposition. **7** *Maths.* to expand an expression containing two operators so as to change the order, as in expressing $a(b + c)$ as $ab + ac$. ORIG C15: from L *distribuere,* from DIS-[1] + *tribuere* to give
▸ **dis'tributable** *adj*

distributed logic *n* a computer system in which remote terminals and electronic devices supplement the main computer by doing some of the computing or decision making.

distributed term *n Logic.* a term applying equally to every member of the class it designates, as *men* in *all men are mortal.*

distribution (ˌdɪstrɪ'bjuːʃən) *n* **1** the act of distributing or the state or manner of being distributed. **2** a thing or portion distributed. **3** arrangement or location. **4** the process of physically satisfying the demand for goods and services. **5** *Econ.* the division of the total income of a community among its members. **6** *Statistics.* the set of possible values of a random variable, considered in terms of theoretical or observed frequency. **7** *Law.* the apportioning of the estate of a deceased intestate. **8** *Law.* the lawful division of the assets of a bankrupt among his or her creditors. **9** *Finance.* **9a** the division of part of a company's profit as a dividend to its shareholders. **9b** the amount paid by dividend in a particular distribution. **10** *Engineering.* the way in which the fuel-air mixture is supplied to each cylinder of a multicylinder internal-combustion engine.
▸ **ˌdistri'butional** *adj*

distributive (dɪ'strɪbjʊtɪv) *adj* **1** characterized by or relating to distribution. **2** *Grammar.* referring separately to the individual people or items in a group, as the words *each* and *every.* ◆ *n* **3** *Grammar.* a distributive word.
▸ **dis'tributively** *adv* ▸ **dis'tributiveness** *n*

distributive law *n Maths, logic.* a theorem asserting that one operator can validly be distributed over another. See **distribute** (sense 7).

distributor (dɪ'strɪbjʊtə) *n* **1** a person or thing that distributes. **2** a wholesaler or middleman engaged in the distribution of a category of goods, esp. to retailers in a specific area. **3** the device in a petrol engine that distributes the high-tension voltage to the sparking plugs.

district ('dɪstrɪkt) *n* **1a** an area of land marked off for administrative or other purposes. **1b** (*as modifier*): *district nurse.* **2** a locality separated by geographical attributes; region. **3** any subdivision of a territory, region, etc. **4** a political subdivision of a county, region, etc., that elects a council responsible for certain local services. ◆ *vb* **5** (*tr*) to divide into districts. ORIG C17: from Med. L *districtus* area of jurisdiction, from L *distringere* to stretch out

district attorney *n* (in the US) the state prosecuting officer in a specified judicial district.

District Court *n* **1** (in Scotland) a court of summary jurisdiction which deals with minor criminal offences. **2** (in the US) **2a** a Federal trial court in each US district. **2b** in some states, a court of general jurisdiction. **3** (in New Zealand) a court lower than a High Court. Formerly called: **magistrates' court.**

district high school *n* (in New Zealand) a school in a rural area providing both primary and secondary education.

district nurse *n* (in Britain) a nurse appointed to attend patients within a particular district, usually in the patients' homes.

District of Columbia ★ *n* a federal district of the eastern US, coextensive with the federal capital, Washington. Pop.: 543 213 (1996 est.). Area: 178 sq. km (69 sq. miles). Abbrevs.: **D.C.** or (with zip code) **DC**

distrust (dɪs'trʌst) *vb* **1** to regard as untrustworthy or dishonest. ◆ *n* **2** suspicion; doubt.
▸ **dis'truster** *n* ▸ **dis'trustful** *adj*

disturb (dɪ'stɜːb) *vb* (*tr*) **1** to intrude on; interrupt. **2** to destroy the quietness or peace of. **3** to disarrange; muddle. **4** (*often passive*) to upset; trouble. **5** to inconvenience; put out. ORIG C13: from L *disturbāre,* from DIS-[1] + *turbāre* to confuse
▸ **dis'turber** *n* ▸ **dis'turbing** *adj* ▸ **dis'turbingly** *adv*

disturbance (dɪ'stɜːbəns) *n* **1** a disturbing or being disturbed. **2** an interruption or intrusion. **3** an unruly outburst or tumult. **4** *Law.* an interference with another's rights. **5** *Geol.* a minor movement of the earth causing a small earthquake. **6** *Meteorol.* a small depression. **7** *Psychiatry.* a mental or emotional disorder.

disturbed (dɪ'stɜːbd) *adj Psychiatry.* emotionally upset, troubled, or maladjusted.

disulphide (daɪ'sʌlfaɪd) *n* any chemical compound containing two sulphur atoms per molecule.

disunite (ˌdɪsjʊ'naɪt) *vb* **disunites, disuniting, disunited. 1** to separate; disrupt. **2** (*tr*) to set at variance; estrange.
▸ **dis'union** *n* ▸ **dis'unity** *n*

disuse (dɪs'juːs) *n* the condition of being unused; neglect (often in **in** *or* **into disuse**).

disutility (ˌdɪsjuː'tɪlɪtɪ) *n, pl* **disutilities.** *Econ.* the shortcomings of a commodity or activity in satisfying human wants. Cf. **utility** (sense 4).

disyllable ('daɪˌsɪləbᵊl) *n* a variant of **dissyllable.**

ditch (dɪtʃ) *n* **1** a narrow channel dug in the earth, usually used for drainage, irrigation, or as a boundary marker. ◆ *vb* **2** to make a ditch in. **3** (*intr*) to edge with a ditch. **4** *Sl.* to crash, esp. deliberately, as to avoid more unpleasant circumstances: *he had to ditch the car.* **5** (*tr*) *Sl.* to abandon. **6** *Sl.* to land (an aircraft) on water in an emergency. **7** (*tr*) *US sl.* to evade. ORIG OE *dīc*
▸ **'ditcher** *n*

ditchwater ('dɪtʃˌwɔːtə) *n* **1** stagnant water, esp. found in ditches. **2 as dull as ditchwater.** very dull; very uninteresting.

dither ('dɪðə) *vb* (*intr*) **1** *Chiefly Brit.* to be uncertain or indecisive. **2** *Chiefly US.* to be in an agitated state. **3** to tremble, as with cold. ◆ *n* **4** *Chiefly Brit.* a state of indecision. **5** a state of agitation. ORIG C17: var. of C14 (N English dialect) *didder,* from ?
▸ **'ditherer** *n* ▸ **'dithery** *adj*

dithyramb ('dɪθɪˌræm, -ˌræmb) *n* **1** (in ancient Greece) a passionate choral hymn in honour of Dionysus. **2** any utterance or a piece of writing that resembles this. ORIG C17: from L *dīthyrambus,* from Gk *dithurambos*
▸ **ˌdithy'rambic** *adj*

dittany ('dɪtənɪ) *n, pl* **dittanies. 1** an aromatic Cretan plant with pink flowers: formerly credited with medicinal properties. **2** a North American plant with purplish flowers. ORIG C14: from OF *ditan,* from L *dictamnus,* from Gk *diktamnon,* ?from *Diktē,* mountain in Crete

ditto ('dɪtəʊ) *n, pl* **dittos. 1** the aforementioned; the above; the same. Used in accounts, lists, etc., to avoid repetition, and symbolized by two small marks („) known as **ditto marks,** placed under the thing repeated. **2** *Inf.* a duplicate. ◆ *adv* **3** in the same way. ◆ *sentence substitute.* **4** *Inf.* used to avoid repeating or to confirm agreement with an immediately preceding sentence. ◆ *vb* **dittos, dittoing, dittoed. 5** (*tr*) to copy; repeat. ORIG C17: from It. (dialect): var. of *detto* said, from *dicere* to say, from L

ditty ('dɪtɪ) *n, pl* **ditties.** a short simple song or poem. ORIG C13: from OF *ditie* poem, from *ditier* to compose, from L *dictāre* to DICTATE

ditty bag *or* **box** *n* a sailor's bag or box for personal belongings or tools. ORIG C19: ?from obs. *dutty* calico, from Hindi *dhōtī* loincloth

ditzy *or* **ditsy** ('dɪtzɪ, 'dɪtsɪ) *adj* **ditzier, ditziest** *or* **ditsier, ditsiest.** *Sl.* silly and scatterbrained. ORIG C20: perhaps from DOTTY + DIZZY

Diu ★ ('diːuː) *n* a small island off the NW coast of India: together with a mainland area, it formed a district of Portuguese India (1535–1961); formerly part of the Indian Union Territory of Goa, Daman, and Diu (1962–87).

diuretic (ˌdaɪju'rɛtɪk) *adj* **1** acting to increase the flow of urine. ◆ *n* **2** a drug or agent that increases the flow of urine. ORIG ME, from LL, from Gk, from *dia-* through + *ourein* to urinate
▸ **diuresis** (ˌdaɪju'riːsɪs) *n*

diurnal (daɪ'ɜːnᵊl) *adj* **1** happening during the day or daily. **2** (of flowers) open during the day and closed at night. **3** (of animals) active during the day. ◆ Cf. **nocturnal.** ORIG C15: from LL *diurnālis,* from L *diurnus,* from *diēs* day
▸ **di'urnally** *adv*

div (dɪv) *n Sl.* a shortened form of **divvy**[1].

div. *abbrev. for:* **1** divide(d). **2** dividend. **3** division. **4** divorce(d).

diva ('diːvə) *n, pl* **divas** *or* **dive** (-vɪ). a highly distinguished female singer; prima donna. ORIG C19: via It. from L: a goddess, from *dīvus* DIVINE

divagate ('daɪvəˌgeɪt) *vb* **divagates, divagating, divagated.** (*intr*) *Rare.* to digress or wander. ORIG C16: from L DI-[2] + *vagārī* to wander
▸ ˌ**diva'gation** *n*

divalent (daɪ'veɪlənt, 'daɪˌveɪ-) *adj Chem.* **1** having a valency of two. **2** having two valencies. ◆ Also: **bivalent.**
▸ **di'valency** *n*

divan (dɪ'væn) *n* **1a** a backless sofa or couch. **1b** a bed resembling such a couch. **2** (esp. formerly) a smoking room. **3a** a Muslim law court, council chamber, or counting house. **3b** a Muslim council of state. ORIG C16: from Turkish *dīvān,* from Persian *dīwān*

dive (daɪv) *vb* **dives, diving, dived** *or US* **dove** (dəuv), **dived.** (*mainly intr*) **1** to plunge headfirst into water. **2** (of a submarine, etc.) to submerge under water. **3** (*also tr*) to fly in a steep nose-down descending path. **4** to rush, go, or reach quickly, as in a headlong plunge: *he dived for the ball.* **5** (*also tr;* foll. by *in* or *into*) to dip or put (one's hand) quickly or forcefully (into). **6** (usually foll. by *in* or *into*) to involve oneself (in something), as in eating food. ◆ *n* **7** a headlong plunge into water. **8** an act or instance of diving. **9** a steep nose-down descent of an aircraft. **10** *Sl.* a disreputable bar or club. **11** *Boxing sl.* the act of a boxer pretending to be knocked down or out. ORIG OE *dȳfan*

dive bomber *n* a military aircraft designed to release its bombs on a target during a steep dive.
▸ **'dive-bomb** *vb* (*tr*)

diver ('daɪvə) *n* **1** a person or thing that dives. **2** a person who works or explores underwater. **3** any of various aquatic birds of northern oceans: noted for skill in diving. US and Canad. name: **loon. 4** any of various other diving birds.

diverge (daɪ'vɜːdʒ) *vb* **diverges, diverging, diverged. 1** to separate or cause to separate and go in different directions from a point. **2** (*intr*) to be at variance; differ. **3** (*intr*) to deviate from a prescribed course. **4** (*intr*) *Maths.* (of a series) to have no limit. ORIG C17: from Med. L *dīvergere,* from L DI-[2] + *vergere* to turn

divergence (daɪ'vɜːdʒəns) *or* **divergency** *n* **1** the act or result of diverging or the amount by which something diverges. **2** the condition of being divergent.

divergent (daɪ'vɜːdʒənt) *adj* **1** diverging or causing divergence. **2** *Maths.* (of a series) having no limit.
▸ **di'vergently** *adv*

> **USAGE NOTE** The use of *divergent* to mean different as in *they hold widely divergent views* is considered by some people to be incorrect.

divergent thinking *n Psychol.* thinking in an unusual and unstereotyped way, for instance to generate several possible solutions to a problem.

divers ('daɪvəz) *determiner Arch. or literary.* various; sundry; some. ORIG C13: from OF, from L *dīversus* turned in different directions

diverse (daɪ'vɜːs, 'daɪvɜːs) *adj* **1** having variety; assorted. **2** distinct in kind. ORIG C13: from L *dīversus;* see DIVERS
▸ **di'versely** *adv*

diversify (daɪ'vɜːsɪˌfaɪ) *vb* **diversifies, diversifying, diversified. 1** (*tr*) to create different forms of; variegate; vary. **2** (of an enterprise) to vary (products, operations, etc.) in order to spread risk, expand, etc. **3** to distribute (investments) among several securities in order to spread risk. ORIG C15: from OF *diversifier,* from Med. L *dīversificāre,* from L *dīversus* DIVERSE + *facere* to make
▸ **diˌversifi'cation** *n*

diversion (daɪ'vɜːʃən) *n* **1** the act of diverting from a specified course. **2** *Chiefly Brit.* an official detour used by traffic when a main route is closed. **3** something that distracts from business, etc.; amusement. **4** *Mil.* a feint attack designed to draw an enemy away from the main attack.
▸ **di'versional** *or* **di'versionary** *adj*

diversity (daɪ'vɜːsɪtɪ) *n* **1** the state or quality of being different or varied. **2** a point of difference.

divert (daɪ'vɜːt) *vb* **1** to turn aside; deflect. **2** (*tr*) to entertain; amuse. **3** (*tr*) to distract the attention of. ORIG C15: from F *divertir,* from L *dīvertere* to turn aside, from DI-[2] + *vertere* to turn
▸ **di'verting** *adj* ▸ **di'vertingly** *adv*

diverticulitis (ˌdaɪvəˌtɪkju'laɪtɪs) *n* inflammation of one or more diverticula, esp. of the colon.

diverticulum (ˌdaɪvə'tɪkjuləm) *n, pl* **diverticula** (-lə). any sac or pouch formed by herniation of the wall of a tubular organ or part, esp. the intestines. ORIG C16: from NL, from L *dēverticulum* by-path, from *dēvertere* to turn aside, from *vertere* to turn

divertimento (dɪˌvɜːtɪ'mɛntəu) *n, pl* **divertimenti** (-tɪ). **1** a piece of entertaining music, often scored for a mixed ensemble and having no fixed form. **2** an episode in a fugue. ORIG C18: from It.

divertissement (dɪ'vɜːtɪsmənt) *n* a brief entertainment or diversion, usually between the acts of a play. ORIG C18: from F: entertainment

Dives ★ ('daɪviːz) *n* **1** a rich man in the parable in Luke 16:19–31. **2** a very rich man.

divest (daɪ'vɛst) *vb* (*tr;* usually foll. by *of*) **1** to strip (of clothes). **2** to deprive or dispossess. ORIG C17: changed from earlier *devest*
▸ **divestiture** (daɪ'vɛstɪtʃə), **divesture** (daɪ'vɛstʃə), *or* **di'vestment** *n*

divi ('dɪvɪ) *n* an alternative spelling of **divvy**[1].

divide (dɪ'vaɪd) *vb* **divides, dividing, divided. 1** to separate into parts; split up. **2** to share or cause to be shared out in parts; distribute. **3** to diverge or cause to diverge in opinion or aim. **4** (*tr*) to keep apart or be a boundary between. **5** (*intr*) to vote by separating into two groups. **6** to categorize; classify. **7** to calculate the quotient of (one number or quantity) and (another number or quantity) by division. **8** (*intr*) to diverge: *the roads divide.* **9** (*tr*) to mark increments of (length, angle, etc.). ◆ *n* **10** *Chiefly US & Canad.* an area of relatively high ground separating drainage basins; watershed. **11** a division; split. ORIG C14: from L *dīvidere* to force apart, from DIS-[1] + *vid-* separate, from the source of *viduus* bereaved

divided (dɪˈvaɪdɪd) *adj* **1** *Bot.* another word for **dissected** (sense 1). **2** split; not united.

dividend (ˈdɪvɪˌdend) *n* **1a** a distribution from the net profits of a company to its shareholders. **1b** a portion of this distribution received by a shareholder. **2** the share of a cooperative society's surplus allocated to members. **3** *Insurance.* a sum of money distributed from a company's net profits to the holders of certain policies. **4** something extra; a bonus. **5** a number or quantity to be divided by another number or quantity. **6** *Law.* the proportion of an insolvent estate payable to the creditors. ORIG C15: from L *dīvidendum* what is to be divided

divider (dɪˈvaɪdə) *n* **1** Also called: **room divider.** a screen or piece of furniture placed so as to divide a room into separate areas. **2** a person or thing that divides. **3** *Electronics.* an electrical circuit with an output that is a well-defined fraction of a given input: *a voltage divider.*

dividers (dɪˈvaɪdəz) *pl n* a type of compass with two pointed arms, used for measuring lines or dividing them.

divination (ˌdɪvɪˈneɪʃən) *n* **1** the art or practice of discovering future events or unknown things, as though by supernatural powers. **2** a prophecy. **3** a guess.
▸ **divinatory** (dɪˈvɪnətərɪ, -trɪ) *adj*

divine (dɪˈvaɪn) *adj* **1** of God or a deity. **2** godlike. **3** of or associated with religion or worship. **4** of supreme excellence or worth. **5** *Inf.* splendid; perfect. ◆ *n* **6** (*often cap.*; preceded by *the*) another term for **God. 7** a priest, esp. one learned in theology. ◆ *vb* **divines, divining, divined. 8** to perceive (something) by intuition. **9** to conjecture (something); guess. **10** to discern (a hidden or future reality) as though by supernatural power. **11** (*tr*) to search for (water, metal, etc.) using a divining rod. ORIG C14: from L *dīvīnus,* from *dīvus* a god
▸ **diˈvinely** *adv* ▸ **diˈviner** *n*

divine office *n* (*sometimes cap.*) the canonical prayers recited daily by priests, etc. Also called: **Liturgy of the Hours.**

divine right of kings *n History.* the concept that the right to rule derives from God and that kings are answerable for their actions to God alone.

diving bell *n* an early diving submersible having an open bottom and being supplied with compressed air.

diving board *n* a platform or springboard from which swimmers may dive.

diving suit *or* **dress** *n* a waterproof suit used by divers, having a heavy detachable helmet and an air supply.

divining rod *n* a forked twig said to move when held over ground in which water, metal, etc., is to be found. Also called: **dowsing rod.**

divinity (dɪˈvɪnɪtɪ) *n, pl* **divinities. 1** the nature of a deity or the state of being divine. **2** a god. **3** (*often cap.*; preceded by *the*) another term for **God. 4** another word for **theology.**

divisible (dɪˈvɪzɪbᵊl) *adj* capable of being divided, usually with no remainder.
▸ **diˌvisiˈbility** *or* **diˈvisibleness** *n* ▸ **diˈvisibly** *adv*

division (dɪˈvɪʒən) *n* **1** a dividing or being divided. **2** the act of sharing out; distribution. **3** something that divides; boundary. **4** one of the parts, groups, etc., into which something is divided. **5** a part of a government, business, etc., that has been made into a unit for administrative or other reasons. **6** a formal vote in Parliament or a similar legislative body. **7** a difference of opinion. **8** (in sports) a section or class organized according to age, weight, skill, etc. **9** a mathematical operation in which the quotient of two numbers or quantities is calculated. Usually written: $a \div b$, a/b, $\frac{a}{b}$. **10** *Army.* a major formation, larger than a brigade but smaller than a corps, containing the necessary arms to sustain independent combat. **11** *Biol.* (in traditional classification systems) a major category of the plant kingdom that contains one or more related classes. Cf. **phylum** (sense 1). ORIG C14: from L *dīvīsiō,* from *dīvidere* to DIVIDE
▸ **diˈvisional** *or* **diˈvisionary** *adj* ▸ **diˈvisionally** *adv*

division sign *n* the symbol ÷, placed between the dividend and the divisor to indicate division, as in $12 \div 6 = 2$.

divisive (dɪˈvaɪsɪv) *adj* tending to cause disagreement or dissension.
▸ **diˈvisively** *adv* ▸ **diˈvisiveness** *n*

divisor (dɪˈvaɪzə) *n* **1** a number or quantity to be divided into another number or quantity (the dividend). **2** a number that is a factor of another number.

divorce (dɪˈvɔːs) *n* **1** the legal dissolution of a marriage. **2** a judicial decree declaring a marriage to be dissolved. **3** a separation, esp. one that is total or complete. ◆ *vb* **divorces, divorcing, divorced. 4** to separate or be separated by divorce; give or obtain a divorce. **5** (*tr*) to remove or separate, esp. completely. ORIG C14: from OF, from L *dīvortium,* from *dīvertere* to separate
▸ **diˈvorceable** *adj*

divorcée (dɪvɔːˈsiː) *or* (*masc*) **divorcé** (dɪˈvɔːseɪ) *n* a person who has been divorced.

divot (ˈdɪvət) *n* a piece of turf dug out of a grass surface, esp. by a golf club or by horses' hooves. ORIG C16: from Scot., from ?

divulge (daɪˈvʌldʒ) *vb* **divulges, divulging, divulged.** (*tr; may take a clause as object*) to make known; disclose. ORIG C15: from L *dīvulgāre,* from DI-[2] + *vulgāre* to spread among people, from *vulgus* the common people
▸ **diˈvulgence** *or* **diˈvulgement** *n* ▸ **diˈvulger** *n*

divvy[1] (ˈdɪvɪ) *Inf.* ◆ *n, pl* **divvies. 1** *Brit.* short for **dividend,** esp. (formerly) one paid by a cooperative society. **2** *US & Canad.* a share; portion. ◆ *vb* **divvies, divvying, divvied. 3** (*tr;* usually foll. by *up*) to divide and share.

divvy[2] (ˈdɪvɪ) *n, pl* **divvies.** *Sl.* a stupid or odd person; misfit. ORIG C20: ? from DEVIANT

Diwali (dɪˈwɑːlɪ) *n* a major Hindu religious festival, honouring Lakshmi, the goddess of wealth. Held over the New Year according to the Vikrama calendar, it is marked by feasting, gifts, and the lighting of lamps.

dixie (ˈdɪksɪ) *n* **1** *Chiefly mil.* a large metal pot for cooking, brewing tea, etc. **2** a mess tin. ORIG C19: from Hindi *degcī,* dim. of *degcā* pot

Dixie (ˈdɪksɪ) *n* **1** Also called: **Dixieland.** the southern states of the US. ◆ *adj* **2** of the southern states of the US. ORIG C19: ?from the nickname of New Orleans, from *dixie* a ten-dollar bill printed there, from F *dix* ten

Dixieland (ˈdɪksɪˌlænd) *n* **1** a form of jazz that originated in New Orleans in the 1920s. **2** a revival of this style in the 1950s. **3** See **Dixie** (sense 1).

DIY *or* **d.i.y.** *Brit., Austral., & NZ abbrev. for* do-it-yourself.

dizzy (ˈdɪzɪ) *adj* **dizzier, dizziest. 1** affected with a whirling or reeling sensation; giddy. **2** mentally confused or bewildered. **3** causing or tending to cause vertigo or bewilderment. **4** *Inf.* foolish or flighty. ◆ *vb* **dizzies, dizzying, dizzied. 5** (*tr*) to make dizzy. ORIG OE *dysig* silly
▸ **ˈdizzily** *adv* ▸ **ˈdizziness** *n*

DJ *or* **dj** (ˈdiːˌdʒeɪ) *n* **1** a variant of **deejay. 2** an informal term for **dinner jacket.**

Djailolo *or* **Jilolo** ★ (dʒaɪˈləʊləʊ) *n* the Dutch name for **Halmahera.**

Djaja ★ (ˈdʒɑːdʒə) *n* a variant spelling of (Mount) **Jaya.**

Djajapura ★ (ˌdʒɑːdʒɑːˈpʊərə) *n* a variant spelling of **Jayapura.**

Djakarta ★ (dʒəˈkɑːtə) *n* a variant spelling of **Jakarta.**

Djambi ★ (ˈdʒæmbɪ) *n* a variant spelling of **Jambi.**

djellaba, djellabah *or* **jellaba, jellabah** (ˈdʒɛləbə) *n* a kind of loose cloak with a hood, worn by men esp. in N Africa and the Middle East. ORIG from Ar. *jallabah*

Djibouti *or* **Jibouti** ★ (dʒɪˈbuːtɪ) *n* **1** a republic in E Africa, on the Gulf of Aden: a French overseas territory (1946–77); became independent in 1977; mainly desert. Official languages: Arabic and French. Currency: Djibouti franc. Capital: Djibouti. Pop.: 669 000 (1999 est.). Area: 23 200 sq. km (8950 sq. miles). **2** the capital of Djibouti, a port on the Gulf of Aden: an outlet for Ethiopian merchandise. Pop.: 383 000 (1995 est).

djinni *or* **djinny** (dʒɪˈniː, ˈdʒɪnɪ) *n, pl* **djinn** (dʒɪn). variant spellings of **jinni.**

dl *symbol for* decilitre.

DLitt *or* **DLit** *abbrev. for:* **1** Doctor of Letters. **2** Doctor of Literature. ORIG L *Doctor Litterarum*

dm *symbol for* decimetre.

DM *abbrev. for* Deutschmark.

DMA *Computing. abbrev. for* direct memory access.

D-mark *or* **D-Mark** *n* short for **Deutschmark**.

DMF *abbrev. for* dimethylformamide.

DMs *Inf. abbrev. for* Doc Martens.

DMus *abbrev. for* Doctor of Music.

DNA *n* deoxyribonucleic acid, the main constituent of the chromosomes of all organisms (except some viruses) in the form of a double helix. DNA is self-replicating and is responsible for the transmission of hereditary characteristics.

DNAase (ˌdiːɛnˈeɪeɪz) *or* **DNase** (ˌdiːɛnˈeɪz) *n* deoxyribonuclease; any of a number of enzymes that hydrolyse DNA.

DNA fingerprinting *or* **profiling** *n* another name for **genetic fingerprinting**.

Dnepropetrovsk ★ (*Russian* dnɪprəprɪˈtrɔfsk) *n* a major industrial city in E central Ukraine, on the Dnieper River. Pop.: 1 147 000 (1996 est.). Former name (1787–1796, 1802–1926): **Yekaterinoslav**.

Dnieper ★ (ˈdniːpə) *n* a river in E Europe, rising in Russia, in the Valdai Hills NE of Smolensk and flowing south to the Black Sea: the third longest river in Europe; a major navigable waterway. Length: 2200 km (1370 miles). Russian name: **Dnepr** (ˈdnjɛpə).

Dniester ★ (ˈdniːstə) *n* a river in E Europe, rising in Ukraine, in the Carpathian Mountains, and flowing generally southeast to the Black Sea. Length: 1411 km (877 miles). Russian name: **Dnestr** (ˈdnjɛstə).

D-notice *n Brit.* an official notice sent to newspapers prohibiting the publication of certain security information. ORIG C20: from their administrative classification letter

do[1] (duː; *unstressed* dʊ, də) *vb* **does, doing, did, done. 1** to perform or complete (a deed or action): *to do a portrait.* **2** (often *intr;* foll. by *for*) to serve the needs of; be suitable for; suffice. **3** (*tr*) to arrange or fix. **4** (*tr*) to prepare or provide; serve: *this restaurant doesn't do lunch on Sundays.* **5** (*tr*) to make tidy, elegant, ready, etc.: *to do one's hair.* **6** (*tr*) to improve (esp. in **do something to** *or* **for**). **7** (*tr*) to find an answer to (a problem or puzzle). **8** (*tr*) to translate or adapt the form or language of: *the book was done into a play.* **9** (*intr*) to conduct oneself: *do as you please.* **10** (*intr*) to fare or manage. **11** (*tr*) to cause or produce: *complaints do nothing to help.* **12** (*tr*) to give or render: *do me a favour.* **13** (*tr*) to work at, esp. as a course of study or a profession. **14** (*tr*) to perform (a play, etc.); act. **15** (*tr*) to mimic or play the part of: *she does a wonderful elderly aunt.* **16** (*tr*) to travel at a specified speed, esp. as a maximum. **17** (*tr*) to travel or traverse (a distance). **18** (takes an infinitive without *to*) used as an auxiliary **18a** before the subject of an interrogative sentence as a way of forming a question: *do you agree?* **18b** to intensify positive statements and commands: *I do like your new house; do hurry!* **18c** before a negative adverb to form negative statements or commands: *do not leave me here alone!* **18d** in inverted constructions: *little did he realize that.* **19** used as an auxiliary to replace an earlier verb or verb phrase: *he likes you as much as I do.* **20** (*tr*) *Inf.* to visit as a sightseer or tourist. **21** (*tr*) to wear out; exhaust. **22** (*intr*) to happen (esp. in **nothing doing**). **23** (*tr*) *Sl.* to serve (a period of time) as a prison sentence. **24** (*tr*) *Inf.* to cheat or swindle. **25** (*tr*) *Sl.* to rob. **26** (*tr*) *Sl.* **26a** to arrest. **26b** to convict of a crime. **27** (*tr*) *Austral. sl.* to spend (money). **28** (*tr*) *Sl., chiefly Brit.* to treat violently; assault. **29** *Sl.* to take or use (a drug). **30** (*tr*) *Taboo sl.* (of a male) to have sexual intercourse with. **31 do or die.** to make a final or supreme effort. **32 make do.** to manage with whatever is available. ◆ *n, pl* **dos** *or* **do's. 33** *Sl.* an act or instance of cheating or swindling. **34** *Inf., chiefly Brit. & NZ.* a formal or festive gathering; party. **35 do's and don'ts.** *Inf.* rules. ◆ See also **do away with, do by,** etc. ORIG OE *dōn*

do[2] (dəʊ) *n, pl* **dos.** a variant spelling of **doh**.

do. *abbrev. for* ditto.

DOA *abbrev. for* dead on arrival.

doable (ˈduːəbᵊl) *adj* capable of being done.

do away with *vb* (*intr, adv + prep*) **1** to kill or destroy. **2** to discard or abolish.

★ people and places

dobbin (ˈdɒbɪn) *n* a name for a horse, esp. a workhorse. ORIG C16: from *Robin,* pet form of *Robert*

Dobell ★ (dəʊˈbɛl) *n* Sir **William.** 1899–1970, Australian portrait and landscape painter.

Doberman pinscher (ˈdəʊbəmən ˈpɪnʃə) *or* **Doberman** *n* a breed of large dog with a glossy black-and-tan coat. Also: **Dobermann.** ORIG C19: after L. *Dobermann* (19th-cent. G dog breeder) who bred it + *Pinscher,* ? after *Pinzgau,* district in Austria

dob in *vb* **dobs, dobbing, dobbed.** (*adv*) *Austral. & NZ sl.* **1** (*tr*) to inform against, esp. to the police. **2** to contribute to a fund.

dobra (ˈdəʊbrə) *n* the standard monetary unit of São Tomé e Principe.

Dobruja ★ (*Bulgarian* ˈdɔbrudʒa) *n* a region of E Europe, between the River Danube and the Black Sea: the north passed to Romania and the south to Bulgaria after the Berlin Congress (1878). Romanian name: **Dobrogea** (doˈbrodʒea).

do by *vb* (*intr, prep*) to treat in the manner specified.

doc (dɒk) *n Inf.* short for **doctor**.

DOC *abbrev. for* Denominazione di Origine Controllata: used of wines. ORIG It., lit.: name of origin controlled

docent (ˈdəʊsᵊnt) *n* a voluntary worker acting as a guide in a museum, art gallery, etc. ORIG C19: from G *Dozent,* from L *docēns* from *docēre* to teach

DOCG *abbrev. for* Denominazione di Origine Controllata Garantita: used of wines. ORIG It., lit: name of origin guaranteed controlled

docile (ˈdəʊsaɪl) *adj* **1** easy to manage or discipline; submissive. **2** *Rare.* easy to teach. ORIG C15: from L *docilis* easily taught, from *docēre* to teach
▸ ˈ**docilely** *adv* ▸ **docility** (dəʊˈsɪlɪtɪ) *n*

dock[1] (dɒk) *n* **1** a wharf or pier. **2** a space between two wharves or piers for the mooring of ships. **3** an area of water that can accommodate a ship and can be closed off to allow regulation of the water level. **4** short for **dry dock. 5 in** *or* **into dock.** *Brit. inf.* **5a** (of people) in hospital. **5b** (of cars, etc.) in a repair shop. **6** *Chiefly US & Canad.* a platform from which lorries, goods trains, etc., are loaded and unloaded. ◆ *vb* **7** to moor or be moored at a dock. **8** to put (a vessel) into, or (of a vessel) to come into a dry dock. **9** (of two spacecraft) to link together in space or link together (two spacecraft) in space. ORIG C14: from MDu. *docke;* ? rel. to L *ducere* to lead

dock[2] (dɒk) *n* **1** the bony part of the tail of an animal. **2** the part of an animal's tail left after the major part of it has been cut off. ◆ *vb* (*tr*) **3** to remove (the tail or part of the tail) of (an animal) by cutting through the bone. **4** to deduct (an amount) from (a person's wages, pension, etc.). ORIG C14: *dok* from ?

dock[3] (dɒk) *n* an enclosed space in a court of law where the accused sits or stands during his trial. ORIG C16: from Flemish *dok* sty

dock[4] (dɒk) *n* any of various weedy plants having greenish or reddish flowers and broad leaves. ORIG OE *docce*

dockage (ˈdɒkɪdʒ) *n* **1** a charge levied upon a vessel for using a dock. **2** facilities for docking vessels. **3** the practice of docking vessels.

docker (ˈdɒkə) *n Brit.* a man employed in the loading or unloading of ships. US and Canad. equivalent: **longshoreman.** Austral. and NZ equivalent: **watersider, wharfie.** See also **stevedore.**

docket (ˈdɒkɪt) *n* **1** *Chiefly Brit.* a piece of paper accompanying or referring to a package or other delivery, stating contents, delivery instructions, etc., sometimes serving as a receipt. **2** *Law.* **2a** a summary of the proceedings in a court. **2b** a register containing this. **3** *Brit.* **3a** a customs certificate declaring that duty has been paid. **3b** a certificate giving particulars of a shipment. **4** a summary of contents, as in a document. **5** *US.* a list of things to be done. **6** *US law.* a list of cases awaiting trial. ◆ *vb* **dockets, docketing, docketed.** (*tr*) **7** to fix a docket to (a package, etc.). **8** *Law.* **8a** to make a summary of (a judgment, etc.). **8b** to abstract and enter in a register. **9** to endorse (a document, etc.) with a summary. ORIG C15: from ?

dockland (ˈdɒkˌlænd) *n* the area around the docks.

dockside ('dɒk,saɪd) *n* an area beside a dock.

dockyard ('dɒk,jɑːd) *n* a naval establishment with docks, workshops, etc., for the building, fitting out, and repair of vessels.

Doc Martens (dɒk 'mɑːtənz) *pl n Trademark.* a brand of lace-up boots with thick lightweight resistant soles. In full: **Doctor Martens.** Abbrev.: **DMs.**

doctor ('dɒktə) *n* **1** a person licensed to practise medicine. **2** a person who has been awarded a higher academic degree in any field of knowledge. **3** *Chiefly US & Canad.* a person licensed to practise dentistry or veterinary medicine. **4** (*often cap.*) Also called: **Doctor of the Church.** a title given to any of several of the early Fathers of the Christian Church. **5** *Angling.* any of various artificial flies. **6** *Inf.* a person who mends or repairs things. **7** *Sl.* a cook on a ship or at a camp. **8** *Arch.* a man, esp. a teacher, of learning. **9** a cool sea breeze blowing in some warm countries: *the Cape doctor.* **10 go for the doctor.** *Austral. sl.* to make a great effort or move very fast. **11 what the doctor ordered.** something needed or desired. ◆ *vb* **12** (*tr*) to give medical treatment to. **13** (*intr*) *Inf.* to practise medicine. **14** (*tr*) to repair or mend. **15** (*tr*) to make different in order to deceive. **16** (*tr*) to adapt. **17** (*tr*) *Inf.* to castrate (a cat, dog, etc.). ORIG C14: from L: teacher, from *docēre* to teach
▸ **'doctoral** *or* **doctorial** (dɒk'tɔːrɪəl) *adj*

doctorate ('dɒktərɪt, -trɪt) *n* the highest academic degree in any field of knowledge.

Doctor of Philosophy *n* a doctorate awarded for original research in any subject except law, medicine, or theology.

doctrinaire (,dɒktrɪ'nɛə) *adj* **1** stubbornly insistent on the observation of the niceties of a theory, esp. without regard to practicality, suitability, etc. **2** theoretical; impractical. ◆ *n* **3** a person who stubbornly attempts to apply a theory without regard to practical difficulties.
▸ **,doctri'nairism** *n* ▸ **,doctri'narian** *n*

doctrine ('dɒktrɪn) *n* **1** a creed or body of teachings of a religious, political, or philosophical group presented for acceptance or belief; dogma. **2** a principle or body of principles that is taught or advocated. ORIG C14: from OF, from L *doctrīna* teaching, from *doctor*; see DOCTOR
▸ **doctrinal** (dɒk'traɪnᵊl) *adj* ▸ **doc'trinally** *adv*

docudrama ('dɒkjʊ,drɑːmə) *n* a film or television programme based on true events, presented in a dramatized form.

document *n* ('dɒkjʊmənt). **1** a piece of paper, booklet, etc., providing information, esp. of an official nature. **2** a piece of text or graphics, such as a letter or article, stored in a computer as a file for manipulation by document processing software. **3** *Arch.* proof. ◆ *vb* ('dɒkjʊ,mɛnt). (*tr*) **4** to record or report in detail, as in the press, on television, etc. **5** to support (statements in a book) with references, etc. **6** to support (a claim, etc.) with evidence. **7** to furnish (a vessel) with documents specifying its registration, dimensions, etc. ORIG C15: from L *documentum* a lesson, from *docēre* to teach

documentary (,dɒkjʊ'mɛntərɪ) *adj* **1** Also: **documental.** consisting of or relating to documents. **2** presenting factual material with few or no fictional additions. ◆ *n, pl* **documentaries. 3** a factual film or television programme about an event, person, etc., presenting the facts with little or no fiction.
▸ **,docu'mentarily** *adv*

documentation (,dɒkjʊmɛn'teɪʃən) *n* **1** the act of supplying with or using documents or references. **2** the documents or references supplied.

document reader *n Computing.* a device that reads and inputs into a computer marks and characters on a special form, as by optical or magnetic character recognition.

docu-soap *or* **docusoap** ('dɒkjʊ,səʊp) *n* a television documentary series in which the lives of the people filmed are presented as entertainment or drama. ORIG C20: from DOCU(MENTARY) + SOAP (OPERA)

dodder[1] ('dɒdə) *vb* (*intr*) **1** to move unsteadily; totter. **2** to shake or tremble, as from age. ORIG C17: var. of earlier *dadder*
▸ **'dodderer** *n* ▸ **'doddery** *adj*

dodder[2] ('dɒdə) *n* any of a genus of rootless parasitic plants lacking chlorophyll and having suckers for drawing nourishment from the host plant. ORIG C13: of Gmc origin

doddle ('dɒdᵊl) *n Brit. inf.* something easily accomplished. ORIG C20: ?from *doddle* (vb) to totter

dodeca- *combining form.* indicating twelve: *dodecaphonic.* ORIG from Gk *dōdeka* twelve

dodecagon (dəʊ'dɛkə,gɒn) *n* a polygon having twelve sides.

dodecahedron (,dəʊdɛkə'hiːdrən) *n* a solid figure having twelve plane faces.
▸ **,dodeca'hedral** *adj*

Dodecanese ★ (,dəʊdɪkə'niːz) *pl n* a group of islands in the SE Aegean Sea, forming a department of Greece: part of the Southern Sporades. Capital: Rhodes. Pop.: 162 439 (1991). Area: 2663 sq. km (1028 sq. miles). Modern Greek name: **Dhodhekánisos.**

dodecaphonic (,dəʊdɛkə'fɒnɪk) *adj* of or relating to the twelve-tone system of serial music.

dodge (dɒdʒ) *vb* **dodges, dodging, dodged. 1** to avoid or attempt to avoid (a blow, discovery, etc.), as by moving suddenly. **2** to evade by cleverness or trickery. **3** (*intr*) *Change-ringing.* to make a bell change places with its neighbour when sounding in successive changes. **4** (*tr*) *Photog.* to lighten or darken (selected areas on a print). ◆ *n* **5** a plan contrived to deceive. **6** a sudden evasive movement. **7** a clever contrivance. **8** *Change-ringing.* the act of dodging. ORIG C16: from ?

Dodge City ★ *n* a city in SW Kansas, on the Arkansas River: famous as a frontier town on the Santa Fe Trail. Pop.: 21 130 (1990).

Dodgem ('dɒdʒəm) *n Trademark.* an electrically propelled vehicle driven and bumped against similar cars in a rink at a funfair.

dodger ('dɒdʒə) *n* **1** a person who evades or shirks. **2** a shifty dishonest person. **3** a canvas shelter on a ship's bridge, etc., to protect the helmsman from bad weather. **4** *Dialect & Austral.* food, esp. bread.

dodgy ('dɒdʒɪ) *adj* **dodgier, dodgiest.** *Brit., Austral. & NZ inf.* **1** risky, difficult, or dangerous. **2** uncertain or unreliable; tricky.

dodo ('dəʊdəʊ) *n, pl* **dodos** *or* **dodoes. 1** any of a now extinct family of flightless birds formerly found on Mauritius. They had a hooked bill and short stout legs. **2** *Inf.* an intensely conservative person who is unaware of changing fashions, ideas, etc. **3** (**as**) **dead as a dodo.** irretrievably defunct or out of date. ORIG C17: from Port. *doudo,* from *duodo* stupid

Dodoma ★ ('dəʊdəmə) *n* a city in central Tanzania, the legislative capital of the country. Pop.: 203 833 (1988).

do down *vb* (*tr, adv*) **1** to belittle or humiliate. **2** to deceive or cheat.

doe (dəʊ) *n, pl* **does** *or* **doe.** the female of the deer, hare, rabbit, and certain other animals. ORIG OE *dā*

Doe (dəʊ) *n* **John.** *Law.* **1** (formerly) the plaintiff in a fictitious action, Doe versus Roe, to test a point of law. See also **Roe. 2** Also: **Jane Doe.** *US.* an unknown or unidentified person.

DOE (in Britain) *abbrev. for* (the former) Department of the Environment.

doek (dʊk) *n S. African inf.* a square of cloth worn mainly by African women to cover the head. ORIG C18: from Afrik.: cloth

Doenitz ★ (*German* 'dø:nɪts) *n* a variant spelling of (Karl) **Dönitz.**

doer ('duːə) *n* **1** a person or thing that does something. **2** an active or energetic person. **3** a thriving animal, esp. a horse.

does (dʌz) *vb* (used with a singular noun or the pronouns *he, she,* or *it*) a form of the present tense (indicative mood) of **do**[1].

doeskin ('dəʊ,skɪn) *n* **1** the skin of a deer, lamb, or sheep. **2** a very supple leather made from this. **3** a heavy smooth cloth.

doff (dɒf) *vb* (*tr*) **1** to take off or lift (one's hat) in saluta-

tion. **2** to remove (clothing). ORIG OE *dōn of;* see DO[1], OFF; cf. DON[1]
▸ ˈ**doffer** *n*

do for *vb (prep) Inf.* **1** *(tr)* to convict of a crime or offence. **2** *(intr)* to cause the ruin, death, or defeat of. **3** *(intr)* to do housework for. **4 do well for oneself.** to thrive or succeed.

dog (dɒg) *n* **1** a domesticated canine mammal occurring in many breeds that show a great variety in size and form. **2** any other carnivore of the dog family, such as the dingo and coyote. **3** the male of animals of the dog family. **4** *(modifier)* spurious, inferior, or useless. **5** a mechanical device for gripping or holding. **6** *Inf.* a fellow; chap. **7** *Inf.* a man or boy regarded as unpleasant or wretched. **8** *Sl.* an unattractive girl or woman. **9** *US & Canad. inf.* something unsatisfactory or inferior. **10** short for **firedog. 11 a dog's chance.** no chance at all. **12 a dog's dinner** *or* **breakfast.** *Inf.* something messy or bungled. **13 a dog's life.** a wretched existence. **14 dog eat dog.** ruthless competition. **15 like a dog's dinner.** dressed smartly or ostentatiously. **16 put on the dog.** *US & Canad. inf.* to behave or dress in an ostentatious manner. ◆ *vb* **dogs, dogging, dogged.** *(tr)* **17** to pursue or follow after with determination. **18** to trouble; plague. **19** to chase with a dog. **20** to grip or secure by a mechanical device. ◆ *adv* **21** *(usually in combination)* thoroughly; utterly: *dog-tired.* ◆ See also **dogs.** ORIG OE *docga,* from ?

dog and bone *n Brit. sl.* a telephone. ORIG rhyming sl. for *phone*

dog biscuit *n* a hard biscuit for dogs.

dog box *n NZ inf.* disgrace; disfavour: *in the dog box.*

dogcart (ˈdɒg,kɑːt) *n* a light horse-drawn two-wheeled vehicle.

dog-catcher *n Now chiefly US & Canad.* a local official whose job is to impound and dispose of stray dogs.

dog collar *n* **1** a collar for a dog. **2** *Inf.* a clerical collar. **3** *Inf.* a tight-fitting necklace.

dog days *pl n* the hot period of the summer reckoned in ancient times from the heliacal rising of Sirius (the Dog Star). ORIG C16: translation of LL *diēs caniculārēs,* translation of Gk *hēmerai kunades*

doge (dəʊdʒ) *n* (formerly) the chief magistrate in the republics of Venice and Genoa. ORIG C16: via F from It. (Venetian dialect), from L *dux* leader

dog-ear *vb* **1** *(tr)* to fold down the corner of (a page). ◆ *n also* **dog's-ear. 2** a folded-down corner of a page.

dog-eared *adj* **1** having dog-ears. **2** shabby or worn.

dog-end *n Inf.* a cigarette end.

dogfight (ˈdɒg,faɪt) *n* **1** close-quarters combat between fighter aircraft. **2** any rough fight.

dogfish (ˈdɒg,fɪʃ) *n, pl* **dogfish** *or* **dogfishes. 1** any of several small sharks. **2** a less common name for the **bowfin.**

dogged (ˈdɒgɪd) *adj* obstinately determined; wilful or tenacious.
▸ ˈ**doggedly** *adv* ▸ ˈ**doggedness** *n*

Dogger Bank ★ (ˈdɒgə) *n* an extensive submerged sandbank in the North Sea between N England and Denmark: fishing ground.

doggerel (ˈdɒgərəl) *or* **dogrel** (ˈdɒgrəl) *n* **1a** comic verse, usually irregular in measure. **1b** *(as modifier): a doggerel rhythm.* **2** nonsense. ORIG C14 *dogerel* worthless, ?from *dogge* DOG

doggish (ˈdɒgɪʃ) *adj* **1** of or like a dog. **2** surly; snappish.

doggo (ˈdɒgəʊ) *adv Brit. inf.* in hiding and keeping quiet (esp. in **lie doggo**). ORIG C19: prob. from DOG

doggone (ˈdɒgɒn) *US & Canad.* ◆ *interj* **1** an exclamation of annoyance, etc. ◆ *adj (prenominal), adv* **2** Also: **doggoned.** another word for **damn.** ORIG C19: euphemism for *God damn*

doggy *or* **doggie** (ˈdɒgɪ) *n, pl* **doggies. 1** a child's word for a **dog.** ◆ *adj* **doggier, doggiest. 2** of, like, or relating to a dog. **3** fond of dogs.

doggy bag *n* a bag in which leftovers from a meal may be taken away, supposedly for the diner's dog.

doggy paddle *or* **doggie paddle** *n, vb* another word for **dog paddle.**

doghouse (ˈdɒg,haʊs) *n* **1** the US and Canad. name for **kennel. 2** *Inf.* disfavour (in **in the doghouse**).

dogie, dogy, *or* **dogey** (ˈdəʊgɪ) *n, pl* **dogies** *or* **dogeys.** *US & Canad.* a motherless calf. ORIG C19: from *dough-guts,* because they were fed on flour-and-water paste

dog in the manger *n* a person who prevents others from using something he or she has no use for.

dog Latin *n* spurious or incorrect Latin.

dogleg (ˈdɒg,lɛg) *n* **1** a sharp bend or angle. ◆ *vb* **doglegs, doglegging, doglegged. 2** *(intr)* to go off at an angle. ◆ *adj* **3** of or with the shape of a dogleg.
▸ **doglegged** (,dɒgˈlɛgɪd, ˈdɒg,lɛgd) *adj*

dogma (ˈdɒgmə) *n, pl* **dogmas** *or* **dogmata** (-mətə). **1** a religious doctrine or system of doctrines proclaimed by ecclesiastical authority as true. **2** a belief, principle, or doctrine or a code of beliefs, principles, or doctrines. ORIG C17: via L from Gk: opinion, from *dokein* to seem good

dogman (ˈdɒgmən) *n, pl* **dogmen.** *Austral.* a person who directs the operation of a crane whilst riding on an object being lifted by it.

dogmatic (dɒgˈmætɪk) *or* **dogmatical** *adj* **1a** (of a statement, opinion, etc.) forcibly asserted as if authoritative and unchallengeable. **1b** (of a person) prone to making such statements. **2** of or constituting dogma. **3** based on assumption rather than observation.
▸ **dogˈmatically** *adv*

dogmatics (dɒgˈmætɪks) *n (functioning as sing)* the study of religious dogmas and doctrines. Also called: **dogmatic** (*or* **doctrinal**) **theology.**

dogmatize *or* **dogmatise** (ˈdɒgmə,taɪz) *vb* **dogmatizes, dogmatizing, dogmatized** *or* **dogmatises, dogmatising, dogmatised.** to say or state (something) in a dogmatic manner.
▸ ˈ**dogmatism** *n* ▸ ˈ**dogmatist** *n*

do-gooder *n Inf.* a well-intentioned person, esp. a naive or impractical one.
▸ ,**do-ˈgooding** *n, adj*

dog paddle *n* **1** a swimming stroke in which the swimmer paddles his or her hands in imitation of a swimming dog. ◆ *vb* **dog-paddle, dog-paddles, dog-paddling, dog-paddled. 2** *(intr)* to swim using the dog paddle. ◆ Also: **doggy paddle** *or* **doggie paddle.**

dog rose *n* a prickly wild European rose that has pink or white scentless flowers. ORIG from belief that its root was effective against the bite of a mad dog

dogs (dɒgz) *pl n* **1** *Sl.* the feet. **2** *Marketing inf.* goods with a low market share, which are unlikely to yield substantial profits. **3 go to the dogs.** *Inf.* to go to ruin physically or morally. **4 let sleeping dogs lie.** to leave things undisturbed. **5 the dogs.** *Brit. inf.* greyhound racing.

Dogs ★ (dɒgz) *n* **Isle of.** a district in the East End of London, bounded on three sides by the River Thames.

dogsbody (ˈdɒgz,bɒdɪ) *Inf.* ◆ *n, pl* **dogsbodies. 1** a person who carries out menial tasks for others. ◆ *vb* **dogsbodies, dogsbodying, dogsbodied.** *(intr)* **2** to act as a dogsbody.

dog's disease *n Austral. inf.* influenza.

dogsled (ˈdɒg,slɛd) *n Chiefly US & Canad.* a sleigh drawn by dogs. Also called (Brit.): **dog sledge.**

Dog Star *n* **the.** another name for **Sirius.**

dog-tired *adj (usually postpositive) Inf.* exhausted.

dogtooth (ˈdɒg,tuːθ) *n, pl* **dogteeth.** *Archit.* a carved ornament in the form of a series of four-cornered pyramids set diagonally and often decorated with leaf shapes along each edge, used in England in the 13th century.

dogtooth violet *n* any of a genus of plants, esp. a European plant with purple flowers.

dogtrot (ˈdɒg,trɒt) *n* a gently paced trot.

dog violet *n* any of three wild violets found in Britain and northern Europe.

dogwatch (ˈdɒg,wɒtʃ) *n* either of two two-hour watches aboard ship, from four to six p.m. or from six to eight p.m.

dogwood (ˈdɒg,wʊd) *n* any of various trees or shrubs, esp. a European shrub with small white flowers and black berries.

dogy ('dəʊgɪ) *n, pl* **dogies.** a variant of **dogie.**

doh (dəʊ) *n Music.* (in tonic sol-fa) the first degree of any major scale. ORIG C18: from It., replacing *ut*; see GAMUT

Doha ★ ('dəʊhɑː, 'dəʊə) *n* the capital and chief port of Qatar, on the E coast of the peninsula. Pop.: 339 471 (1993 est.). Former name: **Bida, El Beda.**

Dohnányi ★ (dɒk'nɑːnjɪ, dɒx-; *Hungarian* 'dohnaːnji) *n* **Ernö** ('ɛrnøː) *or* **Ernst von** (ɛrnst fɔn). 1877–1960, Hungarian composer.

doily *or* **doyley** ('dɔɪlɪ) *n, pl* **doilies** *or* **doileys.** a decorative mat of lace or lacelike paper, etc., laid on plates. ORIG C18: after *Doily,* a London draper

do in *vb* (*tr, adv*) *Sl.* **1** to kill. **2** to exhaust.

doing ('duːɪŋ) *n* **1** an action or the performance of an action: *whose doing is this?* **2** *Inf.* a beating or castigation.

doings ('duːɪŋz) *n* **1** (*functioning as pl*) deeds, actions, or events. **2** (*functioning as sing*) *Inf.* anything of which the name is not known, or euphemistically left unsaid, etc.

do-it-yourself *n* **a** the hobby or process of constructing and repairing things oneself. **b** (*as modifier*): *a do-it-yourself kit.*

dol. *abbrev. for:* **1** *Music.* dolce. **2** (*pl* **dols.**) dollar.

Dolby ('dɒlbɪ) *n Trademark.* any of various specialized electronic circuits, esp. those used in tape recorders for noise reduction in high-frequency signals. ORIG after R. *Dolby* (born 1933), US inventor

dolce ('dɒltʃɪ) *adj, adv Music.* (to be performed) gently and sweetly. ORIG It.

Dolcelatte (ˌdɒltʃiː'lɑːtɪ) *n* a soft creamy blue-veined Italian cheese. ORIG It., lit: sweet milk

dolce vita ('dɒltʃɪ 'viːtə) *n* a life of luxury. ORIG It., lit.: sweet life

doldrums ('dɒldrəmz) *n* **the. 1** a depressed or bored state of mind. **2** a state of inactivity or stagnation. **3** a belt of light winds or calms along the equator. ORIG C19: prob. from OE *dol* DULL, infl. by TANTRUM

dole[1] (dəʊl) *n* **1** (usually preceded by *the*) *Brit. & Austral. inf.* money received from the state while out of work. **2** **on the dole.** *Brit. & Austral. inf.* receiving such money. **3** a small portion of money or food given to a poor person. **4** the act of distributing such portions. **5** *Arch.* fate. ◆ *vb* **doles, doling, doled. 6** (*tr;* usually foll. by *out*) to distribute, esp. in small portions. ORIG OE *dāl* share

dole[2] (dəʊl) *n Arch.* grief or mourning. ORIG C13: from OF, from LL *dolus,* from L *dolēre* to lament

dole-bludger *n Austral. & NZ sl.* a person who draws unemployment benefit without making any attempt to get work.

doleful ('dəʊlfʊl) *adj* dreary; mournful.
▸ **'dolefully** *adv* ▸ **'dolefulness** *n*

dolerite ('dɒləˌraɪt) *n* **1** a dark basic igneous rock; a coarse-grained basalt. **2** any dark igneous rock whose composition cannot be determined with the naked eye. ORIG C19: from F *dolérite,* from Gk *doleros* deceitful; from the difficulty in determining its composition

Dolgellau ★ (dɒl'gɛθlaɪ, *Welsh* dɔl'gɛhla) *n* a market town and tourist centre in NW Wales, in Gwynedd. Pop.: 2396 (1991).

dolichocephalic (ˌdɒlɪkəʊsɪ'fælɪk) *or* **dolichocephalous** (ˌdɒlɪkəʊ'sɛfələs) *adj* having a head much longer than it is broad. ORIG C19: from Gk *dolichos* long + -CEPHALIC

Dolin ★ ('dəʊlɪn) *n* Sir **Anton,** real name *Sydney Healey-Kay.* 1904–83, British ballet dancer and choreographer: cofounder (1949) of the London Festival Ballet.

doll (dɒl) *n* **1** a small model or dummy of a human being, used as a toy. **2** *Sl.* a pretty girl or woman of little intelligence. ORIG C16: prob. from *Doll,* pet name for *Dorothy*

dollar ('dɒlə) *n* **1** the standard monetary unit of the US, divided into 100 cents. **2** the standard monetary unit, comprising 100 cents, of various other countries including: Australia, the Bahamas, Canada, Jamaica, Malaysia, New Zealand, Singapore, Taiwan, and Zimbabwe. ORIG C16: from Low G *daler,* from G *Taler, Thaler,* short for *Joachimsthaler,* coin made from metal mined in *Joachimsthal* Jachymov, town in the Czech Republic

dollarbird ('dɒləˌbɜːd) *n* a bird of S and SE Asia and Australia with a round white spot on each wing.

dollar diplomacy *n Chiefly US.* **1** a foreign policy that encourages and protects commercial and financial involvement abroad. **2** use of financial power as a diplomatic weapon.

Dollfuss ★ (*German* 'dɔlfuːs) *n* **Engelbert** ('ɛŋəlbɛrt). 1892–1934, Austrian chancellor (1932–34); assassinated by Austrian Nazis.

dollop ('dɒləp) *Inf.* ◆ *n* **1** a semisolid lump. **2** a measure or serving. ◆ *vb* **3** (*tr;* foll. by *out*) to serve out (food). ORIG C16: from ?

doll up *vb* (*tr, adv*) *Sl.* to dress in a stylish or showy manner.

dolly ('dɒlɪ) *n, pl* **dollies. 1** a child's word for a **doll. 2** *Films, etc.* a wheeled support on which a camera may be mounted. **3** a cup-shaped anvil used to hold a rivet. **4** *Cricket.* **4a** a simple catch. **4b** a full toss bowled in a slow high arc. **5** Also called: **dolly bird.** *Sl., chiefly Brit.* an attractive and fashionable girl. ◆ *vb* **dollies, dollying, dollied. 6** *Films, etc.* to wheel (a camera) backwards or forwards on a dolly.

dolly mixture *n* **1** a mixture of tiny coloured sweets. **2** one such sweet.

dolma ('dɒlmə) *n, pl* **dolmas** *or* **dolmades** (dɒl'mɑːdiːz). a vine leaf stuffed with a filling of meat and rice. ORIG C19: Turkish *dolma* lit. something filled

dolman sleeve ('dɒlmən) *n* a sleeve that is very wide at the armhole and tapers to a tight wrist. ORIG C19: from *dolman,* a type of Turkish robe, ult. from Turkish *dolamak* to wind

dolmen ('dɒlmɛn) *n* a Neolithic stone formation, consisting of a horizontal stone supported by several vertical stones, and thought to be a tomb. ORIG C19: from F, prob. from OBreton *tol* table, from L *tabula* board + Breton *mēn* stone, of Celtic origin

Dolmetsch ★ ('dɒlmɛtʃ) *n* **Arnold.** 1858–1940, British musician, born in France. He contributed greatly to the revival of interest in early music and instruments.

dolomite ('dɒləˌmaɪt) *n* **1** a mineral consisting of calcium magnesium carbonate. **2** a rock resembling limestone but consisting principally of the mineral dolomite. ORIG C18: after Déodat de *Dolomieu* (1750–1801), F mineralogist
▸ **dolomitic** (ˌdɒlə'mɪtɪk) *adj*

Dolomites ★ ('dɒləˌmaɪts) *pl n* a mountain range in NE Italy: part of the Alps; formed of dolomitic limestone. Highest peak: Marmolada, 3342 m (10 965 ft).

doloroso (ˌdɒlə'rəʊsəʊ) *adj, adv Music.* (to be performed) in a sorrowful manner. ORIG It.

dolorous ('dɒlərəs) *adj* causing or involving pain or sorrow.
▸ **'dolorously** *adv*

dolos ('dɒlɒs) *n, pl* **dolosse.** *S. African.* a knucklebone of a sheep, buck, etc., used esp. by diviners. ORIG from ?

dolour *or US* **dolor** ('dɒlə) *n Poetic.* grief or sorrow. ORIG C14: from L, from *dolēre* to grieve

dolphin ('dɒlfɪn) *n* **1** any of various marine mammals that are typically smaller than whales and larger than porpoises and have a beaklike snout. **2** **river dolphin.** any of various freshwater mammals inhabiting rivers of North and South America and S Asia. **3** Also called: **dorado.** either of two large marine fishes that have an iridescent coloration. **4** *Naut.* a post or buoy for mooring a vessel. ORIG C13: from OF *dauphin,* via L, from Gk *delphin-, delphis*

dolphinarium (ˌdɒlfɪ'nɛərɪəm) *n, pl* **dolphinariums** *or* **dolphinaria** (-ɪə). a pool or aquarium for dolphins, esp. one in which they give public displays.

dolt (dəʊlt) *n* a slow-witted or stupid person. ORIG C16: prob. rel. to OE *dol* stupid
▸ **'doltish** *adj* ▸ **'doltishness** *n*

dom. *abbrev. for:* **1** domain. **2** domestic.

-dom *suffix forming nouns.* **1** state or condition: *freedom.* **2** rank, office, or domain of: *earldom.* **3** a collection of persons: *officialdom.* ORIG OE *-dōm*

Domagk ★ (*German* 'do:mak) *n* **Gerhard** ('ge:rhart). 1895–1964, German biochemist: Nobel prize for medicine (1939) for isolating sulphanilamide.

domain (də'meɪn) *n* **1** land governed by a ruler or government. **2** land owned by one person or family. **3** a field or scope of knowledge or activity. **4** a region having specific characteristics. **5** *Austral. & NZ.* a park or recreation reserve maintained by a public authority, often the government. **6** *Law.* the absolute ownership and right to dispose of land. **7** *Maths.* the set of values of the independent variable of a function for which the functional value exists. **8** *Logic.* another term for **universe of discourse.** **9** *Philosophy.* range of significance. **10** *Physics.* one of the regions in a ferromagnetic solid in which all the atoms have their magnetic moments aligned in the same direction. **11** *Computing.* a group of computers that have the same suffix (**domain name**) in their names on the Internet, specifying the country, type of institution, etc. where they are located. ORIG C17: from F *domaine,* from L *dominium* property, from *dominus* lord

dome (dəʊm) *n* **1** a hemispherical roof or vault. **2** something shaped like this. **3** a slang word for the **head.** ◆ *vb* **domes, doming, domed.** (*tr*) **4** to cover with or as if with a dome. **5** to shape like a dome. ORIG C16: from F, from It. *duomo* cathedral, from L *domus* house
▸ **'dome,like** *adj* ▸ **domical** ('dəʊmɪk°l, 'dɒm-) *adj*

Dome of the Rock ★ *n* a mosque in Jerusalem, Israel, on the Temple Mount: the third most holy place of Islam.

Domesday Book *or* **Doomsday Book** ('du:mz,deɪ) *n History.* the record of a survey of the land of England carried out by the commissioners of William I in 1086.

domestic (də'mɛstɪk) *adj* **1** of the home or family. **2** enjoying or accustomed to home or family life. **3** (of an animal) bred or kept by man as a pet or for purposes such as the supply of food. **4** of one's own country or a specific country: *domestic and foreign affairs.* ◆ *n* **5** a household servant. ORIG C16: from OF *domestique,* from L *domesticus* belonging to the house, from *domus* house
▸ **do'mestically** *adv*

domesticate (də'mɛstɪ,keɪt) *or US* (*sometimes*) **domesticize** (də'mɛstɪ,saɪz) *vb* **domesticates, domesticating, domesticated** *or US* **domesticizes, domesticizing, domesticized.** (*tr*) **1** to bring or keep (wild animals or plants) under control or cultivation. **2** to accustom to home life. **3** to adapt to an environment.
▸ **do'mesticable** *adj* ▸ **do,mesti'cation** *n*

domesticity (,dəʊmɛ'stɪsɪtɪ) *n, pl* **domesticities. 1** home life. **2** devotion to or familiarity with home life. **3** (*usually pl*) a domestic duty or matter.

domestic science *n* the study of cooking, needlework, and other subjects concerned with household skills.

domicile ('dɒmɪ,saɪl) *or* **domicil** ('dɒmɪsɪl) *Formal.* ◆ *n* **1** a dwelling place. **2** a permanent legal residence. **3** *Commerce, Brit.* the place where a bill of exchange is to be paid. ◆ *vb also* **domiciliate** (,dɒmɪ'sɪlɪ,eɪt), **domiciles, domiciling, domiciled** *or* **domiciliates, domiciliating, domiciliated. 4** to establish or be established in a dwelling place. ORIG C15: from L *domicilium,* from *domus* house
▸ **domiciliary** (,dɒmɪ'sɪlɪərɪ) *adj*

dominance ('dɒmɪnəns) *n* control; ascendancy.

dominant ('dɒmɪnənt) *adj* **1** having primary authority or influence; governing; ruling. **2** predominant or primary: *the dominant topic of the day.* **3** occupying a commanding position. **4** *Genetics.* (of a gene) producing the same phenotype in the organism whether its allele is identical or dissimilar. Cf. **recessive. 5** *Music.* of or relating to the fifth degree of a scale. **6** *Ecology.* (of a plant or animal species) more prevalent than any other species and determining the appearance and composition of the community. ◆ *n* **7** *Genetics.* a dominant gene. **8** *Music.* **8a** the fifth degree of a scale. **8b** a key or chord based on this. **9** *Ecology.* a dominant plant or animal in a community.
▸ **'dominantly** *adv*

dominant seventh chord *n Music.* a chord consisting of the dominant and the major third, perfect fifth, and minor seventh above it.

dominate ('dɒmɪ,neɪt) *vb* **dominates, dominating, dominated. 1** to control, rule, or govern. **2** to tower above (surroundings, etc.). **3** (*tr; usually passive*) to predominate in. ORIG C17: from L *dominārī* to be lord over, from *dominus* lord
▸ **'domi,nating** *adj* ▸ **,domi'nation** *n*

dominatrix (,dɒmɪ'neɪtrɪks) *n, pl* **dominatrices** (,dɒmɪnə'traɪsi:z). **1** a woman who is the dominant sexual partner in a sadomasochistic relationship. **2** a dominant woman. ORIG C16: from L, fem of *dominātor,* from *dominārī* to be lord over

dominee ('du:mɪnɪ, 'duə-) *n* (in South Africa) a minister in any of the Afrikaner Churches. ORIG from Afrik., from Du.; cf. DOMINIE

domineer (,dɒmɪ'nɪə) *vb* (*intr;* often foll. by *over*) to act with arrogance or tyranny; behave imperiously. ORIG C16: from Du. *domineren,* from F *dominer* to DOMINATE
▸ **,domi'neering** *adj*

Domingo ★ (də'mɪŋgəʊ; *Spanish* do'miŋgo) *n* **Placido** ('plæsɪdəʊ; *Spanish* 'plaθiðo). born 1941, Spanish operatic tenor.

Dominic ★ ('dɒmɪnɪk) *n* **Saint.** original name *Domingo de Guzman.* ?1170–1221, Spanish priest; founder of the Dominican order. Feast day: Aug. 7.

Dominica ★ (,dɒmɪ'ni:kə, də'mɪnɪkə) *n* a republic in the E Caribbean, comprising a volcanic island in the Windward Islands group; a former British colony; became independent as a member of the Commonwealth in 1978. Official language: English. Religion: mostly Roman Catholic. Currency: East Caribbean dollar. Capital: Roseau. Pop.: 77 000 (1999 est.). Area: 751 sq. km (290 sq. miles). Official name: **Commonwealth of Dominica.**

dominical (də'mɪnɪk°l) *adj* **1** of Jesus Christ as Lord. **2** of Sunday as the Lord's Day. ORIG C15: from LL *dominicālis,* from L *dominus* lord

Dominican[1] (də'mɪnɪkən) *n* **1a** a member of an order of preaching friars founded by Saint Dominic in 1215; a Blackfriar. **1b** a nun of one of the orders founded under his patronage. ◆ *adj* **2** of Saint Dominic or the Dominican order.

Dominican[2] (də'mɪnɪkən) *adj* **1** of or relating to the Dominican Republic or Dominica. ◆ *n* **2** a native or inhabitant of the Dominican Republic or Dominica.

Dominican Republic ★ *n* a republic in the Caribbean, occupying the eastern half of the island of Hispaniola: colonized by the Spanish after its discovery by Columbus in 1492; gained independence from Spain in 1821. It is generally mountainous, dominated by the Cordillera Central, which rises over 3000 m (10 000 ft), with fertile lowlands. Language: Spanish. Religion: mostly Roman Catholic. Currency: peso. Capital: Santo Domingo. Pop.: 8 132 000 (1999 est.). Area: 48 441 sq. km (18 703 sq. miles). Former name (until 1844): **Santo Domingo.**

dominie ('dɒmɪnɪ) *n* **1** a Scots word for **schoolmaster. 2** a minister or clergyman. ORIG C17: from L *dominē,* vocative case of *dominus* lord

dominion (də'mɪnjən) *n* **1** rule; authority. **2** the land governed by one ruler or government. **3** sphere of influence; area of control. **4** a name formerly applied to self-governing divisions of the British Empire. **5 the Dominion.** New Zealand. ORIG C15: from OF, from L *dominium* ownership, from *dominus* master

Dominion Day *n* the former name for **Canada Day.**

domino[1] ('dɒmɪ,nəʊ) *n, pl* **dominoes.** a small rectangular block marked with dots, used in dominoes. ORIG C19: from F, from It., ?from *domino!* master!, said by the winner

domino[2] ('dɒmɪ,nəʊ) *n, pl* **dominoes** *or* **dominos. 1** a large hooded cloak worn with an eye mask at a masquerade. **2** the eye mask worn with such a cloak. ORIG C18: from F or It., prob. from L *dominus* lord, master

Domino ★ ('dɒmɪnəʊ) *n* **Fats.** real name *Antoine Domino.* born 1928, US rhythm-and-blues and rock-and-roll pianist, singer, and songwriter. His singles include "Ain't that a Shame" (1955) and "Blueberry Hill" (1956).

domino effect *n* a series of similar or related events occurring as a direct and inevitable result of one initial event. ORIG C20: alluding to a row of dominoes, each standing on end, all of which fall when one is pushed

dominoes ('dɒmɪˌnəʊz) *n* (*functioning as sing*) any of several games in which dominoes with matching halves are laid together.

Dominus *Latin.* ('dɒmɪnʊs) *n* God or Christ.

Domitian ★ (də'mɪʃən) *n* full name *Titus Flavius Domitianus.* 51–96 A.D., Roman emperor (81–96): instigated a reign of terror (93); assassinated.

Domrémy-la-Pucelle (*French* dɔ̃remilapysɛl) *or* **Domrémy** ★ *n* a village in NE France, in the Vosges: birthplace of Joan of Arc.

don[1] (dɒn) *vb* **dons, donning, donned.** (*tr*) to put on (clothing). ORIG C14: from DO[1] + ON; cf. DOFF

don[2] (dɒn) *n* **1** *Brit.* a member of the teaching staff at a university or college, esp. at Oxford or Cambridge. **2** the head of a student dormitory at certain Canadian universities and colleges. **3** a Spanish gentleman or nobleman. **4** (in the Mafia) the head of the family. **5** *Arch.* a person of rank. ORIG C17: ult. from L *dominus* lord

Don[1] (dɒn) *n* a Spanish title equivalent to *Mr.* ORIG C16: via Sp., from L *dominus* lord

Don[2] ★ (dɒn) *n* **1** a river rising in W Russia, southeast of Tula and flowing generally south to the Sea of Azov: linked by canal to the River Volga. Length: 1870 km (1162 miles). **2** a river in NE Scotland, rising in the Cairngorm Mountains and flowing east to the North Sea. Length: 100 km (62 miles). **3** a river in N central England, rising in S Yorkshire and flowing northeast to the Humber. Length: about 96 km (60 miles).

Doña ('dɒnjə) *n* a Spanish title of address equivalent to *Mrs* or *Madam.* ORIG C17: via Sp., from L *domina*

Donar ★ ('dəʊnɑː; *German* 'doːnar) *n* the Germanic god of thunder, corresponding to Thor in Norse mythology.

donate (dəʊ'neɪt) *vb* **donates, donating, donated.** to give (money, time, etc.), esp. to a charity.
▸ **do'nator** *n*

Donatello ★ (*Italian* dona'tɛllo) *n* real name *Donato di Betto Bardi.* 1386–1466, Florentine Renaissance sculptor, whose work includes the classic bronze *David.*

donation (dəʊ'neɪʃən) *n* **1** the act of donating. **2** a contribution. ORIG C15: from L *dōnātiō* a presenting, from *dōnāre* to give, from *dōnum* gift

donative ('dəʊnətɪv) *n* **1** a gift or donation. **2** a benefice capable of being conferred as a gift. ◆ *adj* **3** of or like a donation. **4** being or relating to a benefice. ORIG C15: from L *dōnātīvum* a donation made to soldiers by a Roman emperor, from *dōnāre* to present

Donatus ★ (dəʊ'nɑːtəs) *n* **1 Aelius** ('iːlɪəs). 4th century A.D., Latin grammarian, who taught Saint Jerome; his textbook *Ars Grammatica* was used throughout the Middle Ages. **2** 4th century A.D., bishop of Carthage; leader of the Donatists, a heretical Christian sect originating in N Africa in 311 A.D.

Donau ★ ('doːnau) *n* the German name for the **Danube.**

Donbass *or* **Donbas** ★ (dɒn'bɑːs) *n* an industrial region of E Ukraine, in the plain of the Rivers Donets and lower Dnieper: the site of a major coalfield. Also called: **Donets Basin.**

Doncaster ★ ('dɒŋkəstə) *n* **1** an industrial town in N England, on the River Don. Pop.: 71 595 (1991). **2** a unitary authority in N England. Pop.: 292 900 (1995 est.). Area: 582 sq. km (225 sq. miles).

donder ('dɒndə) *S. African sl.* ◆ *vb* **1** (*tr*) to beat (someone) up. ◆ *n* **2** a wretch; swine. ORIG from Afrik., from Du. *donderen* to swear, bully

done (dʌn) *vb* **1** the past participle of **do**[1]. **2 be** *or* **have done with.** to end relations with. **3 have done.** to be completely finished: *have you done?* ◆ *interj* **4** an expression of agreement, as on the settlement of a bargain. ◆ *adj* **5** completed. **6** cooked enough. **7** used up. **8** socially acceptable. **9** *Inf.* cheated; tricked. **10 done for.** *Inf.* **10a** dead or almost dead. **10b** in serious difficulty. **11 done in** *or* **up.** *Inf.* exhausted.

donee (dəʊ'niː) *n* a person who receives a gift. ORIG C16: from DON(OR) + -EE

Donegal ★ ('dɒnɪˌgɔːl, ˌdɒnɪ'gɔːl) *n* a county in NW Republic of Ireland, on the Atlantic: mountainous, with a rugged coastline and many offshore islands. County town: Lifford. Pop.: 129 000 (1996). Area: 4830 sq. km (1865 sq. miles).

doner kebab ('dɒnə) *n* a fast-food dish comprising grilled meat and salad served in pitta bread with chilli sauce. ORIG from Turkish *döner* rotating + KEBAB

Donets ★ (*Russian* da'njɛts) *n* a river in E Europe, rising in Russia, in the Kursk steppe, and flowing southeast, through Ukraine, to the Don River. Length: about 1078 km (670 miles).

Donets Basin ★ (də'nɛts) *n* another name for the **Donbass.**

Donetsk ★ (*Russian* da'njɛtsk) *n* a city in E Ukraine: the chief industrial centre of the Donbass; first ironworks founded by a Welshman, John Hughes (1872), after whom the town was named **Yuzovka** (Hughesovka). Pop.: 1 088 000 (1996 est.). Former names (from 1924 until 1961): **Stalin** or **Stalino.**

dong (dɒŋ) *n* **1** an imitation of the sound of a bell. **2** *Austral. & NZ inf.* a heavy blow. ◆ *vb* **3** (*intr*) to make such a sound. **4** *Austral. & NZ inf.* to strike or punch. ORIG C19: imit.

donga ('dɒŋgə) *n S. African & Austral.* a steep-sided gully created by soil erosion. ORIG C19: from Afrik., from Zulu

Dongola ★ ('dɒŋgələ) *n* a small town in the N Sudan, on the Nile: built on the site of Old Dongola, the capital of the Christian Kingdom of Nubia (6th to 14th centuries). Pop.: 5937 (latest est.).

Dongting ('dʊŋ'tɪŋ), **Tungting,** *or* **Tung-t'ing** ★ *n* a lake in S China, in NE Hunan province: main outlet flows to the Yangtze; rice-growing in winter. Area: (in winter) 3900 sq. km (1500 sq. miles).

Dönitz *or* **Doenitz** ★ (*German* 'døːnɪts) *n* **Karl** (karl). 1891–1980, German admiral; commander of the German navy (1943–45); after Hitler's death he surrendered to the Allies.

Donizetti ★ (ˌdɒnɪ'zɛtɪ; *Italian* donid'dzetti) *n* **Gaetano** (gae'taːno). 1797–1848, Italian operatic composer: his works include *Lucia di Lammermoor* (1835), *La Fille du régiment* (1840), and *Don Pasquale* (1843).

donjon ('dʌndʒən, 'dɒn-) *n* the heavily fortified central tower or keep of a medieval castle. Also: **dungeon.** ORIG C14: arch. var. of *dungeon*

Don Juan ★ ('dɒn 'dʒuːən) *n* **1** a legendary Spanish nobleman and philanderer: hero of many poems, plays, and operas. **2** a successful seducer of women.

donkey ('dɒŋkɪ) *n* **1** a long-eared member of the horse family. **2** a stupid or stubborn person. **3 talk the hind leg(s) off a donkey.** to talk endlessly. ORIG C18: ?from *dun* dark + *-key,* as in *monkey*

donkey jacket *n* a thick hip-length jacket, usually navy blue, with a waterproof panel across the shoulders.

donkey's years *pl n Inf.* a long time.

donkey vote *n Austral.* a vote in which the voter's order of preference follows the order in which the candidates are listed.

donkey-work *n* **1** groundwork. **2** drudgery.

Donleavy ★ (dɒn'liːvɪ) *n* **J(ames) P(atrick).** born 1926, Irish novelist, born in the US. His books include *The Ginger Man* (1956), *The Onion Eaters* (1971), and *The Lady who Liked Clean Rest Rooms* (1995).

Donna ('dɒnə) *n* an Italian title of address equivalent to *Madam.* ORIG C17: from It., from L *domina* lady

Donne ★ (dʌn) *n* **John.** 1573–1631, English metaphysical poet and preacher.

donnish ('dɒnɪʃ) *adj* of or resembling a university don, esp. denoting pedantry or fussiness.
▸ **'donnishness** *n*

donnybrook ('dɒnɪˌbrʊk) *n* a rowdy brawl. ORIG C19: after *Donnybrook Fair,* an annual event until 1855 near Dublin

donor ('dəʊnə) *n* **1** a person who makes a donation. **2** *Med.* any person who gives blood, organs, etc., for use in the treatment of another person. **3** the atom supplying both electrons in a coordinate bond. ORIG C15: from OF *doneur,* from L *dōnātor,* from *dōnāre* to give

donor card *n* a card carried to show that the bodily organs specified on it may be used for transplants after the carrier's death.

Don Quixote ('dɒn kiː'həutiː, 'kwɪksət) *n* an impractical idealist. ORIG after the hero of Cervantes' *Don Quixote de la Mancha* (1605)

don't (dəunt) *contraction of* do not.

don't know *n* a person who has no definite opinion, esp. as a response to a questionnaire.

doodah ('duːdɑː) *or US & Canad.* **doodad** ('duːdæd) *n Inf.* an unnamed thing, esp. an object the name of which is unknown or forgotten. ORIG C20: from ?

doodle ('duːdᵊl) *Inf.* ◆ *vb* **doodles, doodling, doodled. 1** to scribble or draw aimlessly. **2** to play or improvise idly. **3** (*intr; often foll. by away*) *US.* to dawdle or waste time. ◆ *n* **4** a shape, picture, etc., drawn aimlessly. ORIG C20: ?from C17: a foolish person, but infl. in meaning by DAWDLE
▸ '**doodler** *n*

doodlebug ('duːdᵊlˌbʌg) *n* **1** another name for the **V-1. 2** a diviner's rod. **3** a US name for an **antlion** (the larva). ORIG C20: prob. from DOODLE + BUG

doo-doo ('duːˌduː) *n US & Canad. inf.* a child's word for **excrement.**

doohickey ('duːˌhɪkɪ) *n US & Canad. inf.* another name for **doodah.**

Doolittle ★ ('duːlɪtᵊl) *n* **Hilda.** known as *H.D.* 1886–1961, US imagist poet and novelist, lived in Europe.

doom (duːm) *n* **1** death or a terrible fate. **2** a judgment. **3** (*sometimes cap.*) another term for the **Last Judgment.** ◆ *vb* **4** (*tr*) to destine or condemn to death or a terrible fate. ORIG OE *dōm*

doomsday *or* **domesday** ('duːmzˌdeɪ) *n* **1** (*sometimes cap.*) the day on which the Last Judgment will occur. **2** any day of reckoning. **3** (*modifier*) characterized by predictions of disaster: *doomsday scenario.* ORIG OE *dōmes dæg* Judgment Day

doona ('duːnə) *n* the Austral. name for **continental quilt.** ORIG from a trademark

door (dɔː) *n* **1** a hinged or sliding panel for closing the entrance to a room, cupboard, etc. **2** a doorway or entrance. **3** a means of access or escape: *a door to success.* **4 lay at someone's door.** to lay (the blame or responsibility) on someone. **5 out of doors.** in or into the open air. **6 show someone the door.** to order someone to leave. ORIG OE *duru*

do-or-die *adj* (*prenominal*) of a determined and sometimes reckless effort to succeed.

door furniture *n* locks, handles, etc., designed for use on doors.

doorjamb ('dɔːˌdʒæm) *n* one of the two vertical members forming the sides of a doorframe. Also called: **doorpost.**

doorkeeper ('dɔːˌkiːpə) *n* a person attending or guarding a door or gateway.

doorman ('dɔːˌmæn, -mən) *n, pl* **doormen.** a man employed to attend the doors of certain buildings.

doormat ('dɔːˌmæt) *n* **1** a mat, placed at an entrance, for wiping dirt from shoes. **2** *Inf.* a person who offers little resistance to ill-treatment.

Doorn ★ (*Dutch* doːrn) *n* a town in the central Netherlands, in Utrecht province: residence of Kaiser William II of Germany from his abdication (1919) until his death (1941).

doornail ('dɔːˌneɪl) *n* (**as**) **dead as a doornail.** dead beyond any doubt.

Doornik ★ ('doːrnɪk) *n* the Flemish name for **Tournai.**

doorsill ('dɔːˌsɪl) *n* a horizontal member of wood, stone, etc., forming the bottom of a doorframe.

doorstep ('dɔːˌstɛp) *n* **1** a step in front of a door. **2** *Inf.* a thick slice of bread. ◆ *vb* **doorsteps, doorstepping, doorstepped.** (*tr*) **3** to canvass (a district or member of the public) by or in the course of door-to-door visiting. **4** (of journalists) to wait outside the house of (someone) in order to obtain an interview or photograph when he or she emerges.

doorstop ('dɔːˌstɒp) *n* **1** any device which prevents an open door from moving. **2** a piece of rubber, etc., fixed to the floor to stop a door striking a wall.

door to door *adj* (**door-to-door** *when prenominal*), *adv* **1** (of selling, etc.) from one house to the next. **2** (of journeys, etc.) direct.

doorway ('dɔːˌweɪ) *n* **1** an opening into a building, room, etc., esp. one that has a door. **2** a means of access or escape: *a doorway to freedom.*

do over *vb* (*tr, adv*) **1** *Inf.* to redecorate. **2** *Brit., Austral. & NZ sl.* to beat up; thrash.

doo-wop ('duːˌwɒp) *n* vocalizing based on rhythm-and-blues harmony. ORIG C20: imit.

dop (dɒp) *n S. African sl.* **1** Cape brandy. **2** a tot of this. ORIG from Afrik., from ?

dope (dəup) *n* **1** any of a number of preparations applied to fabric in order to improve strength, tautness, etc. **2** an additive, such as an antiknock compound added to petrol. **3** a thick liquid, such as a lubricant, applied to a surface. **4** a combustible absorbent material used to hold the nitroglycerine in dynamite. **5** *Sl.* an illegal drug, usually cannabis. **6** a drug administered to a racehorse or greyhound to affect its performance. **7** *Inf.* a stupid or slow-witted person. **8** *Inf.* news or facts, esp. confidential information. ◆ *vb* **dopes, doping, doped.** (*tr*) **9** *Electronics.* to add impurities to (a semiconductor) in order to produce or modify its properties. **10** to apply or add dope to. **11** to administer a drug to (oneself or another). ORIG C19: from Du. *doop* sauce, from *doopen* to dip
▸ '**doper** *n*

dopey *or* **dopy** ('dəupɪ) *adj* **dopier, dopiest. 1** *Sl.* silly. **2** *Inf.* half-asleep or semiconscious, as when under the influence of a drug.

doppelgänger ('dɒpᵊlˌgɛŋə) *n Legend.* a ghostly duplicate of a living person. ORIG from G *Doppelgänger,* lit.: double-goer

Doppler effect ('dɒplə) *n* a change in the apparent frequency of a sound or light wave, etc., as a result of relative motion between the observer and the source. Also called: **Doppler shift.** ORIG C19: after C. J. *Doppler* (1803–53), Austrian physicist

Doráti ★ (də'rɑːtɪ) *n* **Antal** ('æntæl). 1906–88, US conductor and composer.

Dorcas ★ ('dɔːkəs) *n* a charitable woman of Joppa (Acts 9:36–42).

Dorchester ★ ('dɔːtʃɪstə) *n* a town in S England, administrative centre of Dorset: associated with Thomas Hardy, esp. as the Casterbridge of his novels. Pop.: 15 037 (1991). Latin name: **Durnovaria** (ˌdjurnəu'veɪrɪə).

Dordogne ★ (*French* dɔrdɔɲ) *n* **1** a river in SW France, rising in the Auvergne Mountains and flowing southwest and west to join the Garonne river and form the Gironde estuary. Length: 472 km (293 miles). **2** a department of SW France, in Aquitaine region. Capital: Périgueux. Pop.: 388 521 (1994 est.). Area: 9224 sq. km (3597 sq. miles).

Dordrecht ★ (*Dutch* 'dɔrdrɛxt) *n* a port in the SW Netherlands, in South Holland province: chief port of the Netherlands until the 17th century. Pop.: 114 152 (1995 est.). Also called: **Dort.**

Doré ★ (*French* dɔre) *n* (**Paul**) **Gustave** (gystav). 1832–83, French illustrator; he illustrated the Bible, Dante's *Inferno,* and works by Rabelais.

Doric ('dɒrɪk) *adj* **1** of the inhabitants of Doris in ancient Greece or their dialect. **2** of or denoting one of the five classical orders of architecture: characterized by a heavy fluted column and a simple capital. **3** (*sometimes not cap.*) rustic. ◆ *n* **4** one of four chief dialects of Ancient Greek. **5** any rural dialect of English, esp. a Scots one.

Doris[1] ★ ('dɒrɪs) *n* (in ancient Greece) **1** a small landlocked area north of the Gulf of Corinth. Traditionally regarded as the home of the Dorians, it was perhaps settled by some of them during their southward migration. **2** the coastal area of Caria in SW Asia Minor, settled by Dorians.

Doris[2] ★ ('dɒrɪs) *n Greek myth.* a sea nymph.

dork (dɔːk) *n Sl.* a stupid or incompetent person. ORIG C20: from ?

dorm (dɔːm) *n Inf.* short for **dormitory.**

dormant (ˈdɔːmənt) *adj* **1** quiet and inactive, as during sleep. **2** latent or inoperative. **3** (of a volcano) neither extinct nor erupting. **4** *Biol.* alive but in a resting condition with reduced metabolism. **5** (*usually postpositive*) *Heraldry.* (of a beast) in a sleeping position. ORIG C14: from OF *dormant,* from *dormir* to sleep, from L *dormīre*
▸ **ˈdormancy** *n*

dormer (ˈdɔːmə) *n* a construction with a gable roof and a window that projects from a sloping roof. Also called: **dormer window.** ORIG C16: from OF *dormoir,* from L *dormītōrium* DORMITORY

dormie *or* **dormy** (ˈdɔːmɪ) *adj Golf.* as many holes ahead of an opponent as there are still to play: *dormie three.* ORIG C19: from ?

dormitory (ˈdɔːmɪtərɪ, -trɪ) *n, pl* **dormitories. 1** a large room, esp. at a school, containing several beds. **2** *US.* a building, esp. at a college or camp, providing living and sleeping accommodation. **3** (*modifier*) *Brit.* denoting or relating to an area from which most of the residents commute to work (esp. in **dormitory suburb**). ORIG C15: from L *dormītōrium,* from *dormīre* to sleep

Dormobile (ˈdɔːməʊˌbiːl) *n Trademark.* a vanlike vehicle specially equipped for living in while travelling.

dormouse (ˈdɔːˌmaʊs) *n, pl* **dormice.** a small Eurasian rodent resembling a mouse with a furry tail. ORIG C15: *dor-,* ?from OF *dormir* to sleep, (from L *dormīre)* + MOUSE

dorp (dɔːp) *n S. African.* a small town or village. ORIG C16: from Du.

Dorpat ★ (ˈdɔrpat) *n* the German name for **Tartu.**

dorsal (ˈdɔːsᵊl) *adj Anat., zool.* relating to the back or spinal part of the body. ORIG C15: from Med. L *dorsālis,* from L *dorsum* back
▸ **ˈdorsally** *adv*

dorsal fin *n* an unpaired fin on the back of a fish that maintains balance during locomotion.

Dorset ★ (ˈdɔːsɪt) *n* a county in SW England, on the English Channel: mainly hilly but low-lying in the east: Bournemouth and Poole are administered by separate unitary authorities. Administrative centre: Dorchester. Pop. (excluding Bournemouth and Poole): 382 090 (1996 est.). Area (excluding Bournemouth and Poole): 2542 sq. km (981 sq. miles).

Dort ★ (*Dutch* dɔrt) *n* another name for **Dordrecht.**

Dortmund ★ (ˈdɔːtmənd; *German* ˈdɔrtmʊnt) *n* an industrial city in W Germany, in North Rhine-Westphalia at the head of the **Dortmund–Ems Canal**: university 1966. Pop.: 598 840 (1996 est.).

dory[1] (ˈdɔːrɪ) *n, pl* **dories.** any of various spiny-finned food fishes, esp. the John Dory. ORIG C14: from F *dorée* gilded, from LL *deaurāre* to gild, ult. from L *aurum* gold

dory[2] (ˈdɔːrɪ) *n, pl* **dories.** *US & Canad.* a flat-bottomed rowing boat with a high bow, stern, and sides. ORIG C18: from Amerind *dóri* dugout

DOS (dɒs) *n Computers, trademark. acronym for* disk-operating system, often prefixed, as in MS-DOS and PC-DOS; a computer operating system.

dosage (ˈdəʊsɪdʒ) *n* **1** the administration of a drug or agent in prescribed amounts. **2** the optimum therapeutic dose and interval between doses. **3** another name for **dose** (senses 3, 4).

dose (dəʊs) *n* **1** *Med.* a specific quantity of a therapeutic drug or agent taken at any one time or at specified intervals. **2** *Inf.* something unpleasant to experience: *a dose of influenza.* **3** Also called: **dosage.** the total energy of ionizing radiation absorbed by unit mass of material, esp. of living tissue; usually measured in grays (SI unit) or rads. **4** Also called: **dosage.** a small amount of syrup added to wine during bottling. **5** *Sl.* a sexually transmitted infection. ◆ *vb* **doses, dosing, dosed.** (*tr*) **6** to administer a dose to (someone). **7** *Med.* to prescribe (a drug) in appropriate quantities. **8** to add syrup to (wine) during bottling. ORIG C15: from F, from LL *dosis,* from Gk: a giving, from *didonai* to give

dosh (dɒʃ) *n Brit.* a slang word for **money.** ORIG C20: of unknown origin

dosimeter (dəʊˈsɪmɪtə) *n* an instrument for measuring the dose of radiation absorbed by matter or the intensity of a source of radiation.
▸ **dosimetric** (ˌdəʊsɪˈmɛtrɪk) *adj*

dosing strip *n* (in New Zealand) an area set aside for treating dogs suspected of having hydatid disease.

Dos Passos ★ (ˈdɒs ˈpæsɒs) *n* **John** (**Roderigo**). 1896–1970, US novelist, best known for the trilogy *USA* (1930–36).

doss (dɒs) *Brit. sl.* ◆ *vb* **1** (*intr;* often foll. by *down*) to sleep, esp. in a dosshouse. **2** (*intr;* often foll. by *around*) to pass time aimlessly. ◆ *n* **3** a bed, esp. in a dosshouse. **4** another word for **sleep. 5** short for **dosshouse. 6** a task or pastime requiring little effort: *making a film is a bit of a doss.* ORIG C18: from ?

dosser (ˈdɒsə) *n* **1** *Brit. sl.* a person who sleeps in dosshouses. **2** *Brit. sl.* another word for **dosshouse. 3** *Sl.* a lazy person.

dosshouse (ˈdɒsˌhaʊs) *n Brit. sl.* a cheap lodging house, esp. one used by tramps. US name: **flophouse.**

dossier (ˈdɒsɪˌeɪ) *n* a collection of papers about a subject or person. ORIG C19: from F: a file with a label on the back, from *dos* back, from L *dorsum*

dost (dʌst) *vb Arch. or dialect.* (used with *thou)* a singular form of the present tense (indicative mood) of **do**[1].

Dostoevsky, Dostoyevsky, Dostoevski, *or* **Dostoyevski** ★ (ˌdɒstɔɪˈɛfskɪ; *Russian* dəstaˈjɛfskij) *n* **Fyodor Mikhailovich** (ˈfjɔdər miˈxajləvitʃ). 1821–81, Russian novelist. His works include *Crime and Punishment* (1866), *The Idiot* (1868), and *The Brothers Karamazov* (1879–80).

dot[1] (dɒt) *n* **1** a small round mark; spot; point. **2** anything resembling a dot; a small amount. **3** the mark (˙) above the letters *i, j.* **4** *Music.* **4a** the symbol (·) placed after a note or rest to increase its time value by half. **4b** this symbol written above or below a note indicating staccato. **5** *Maths, logic.* **5a** the symbol (.) indicating multiplication or logical conjunction. **5b** a decimal point. **6** the symbol (•) used, in combination with the symbol for *dash* (—), in Morse and other codes. **7 on the dot.** at exactly the arranged time. ◆ *vb* **dots, dotting, dotted. 8** (*tr*) to mark or form with a dot. **9** (*tr*) to scatter or intersperse (as with dots): *bushes dotting the plain.* **10** (*intr*) to make a dot or dots. **11 dot one's i's and cross one's t's.** *Inf.* to pay meticulous attention to detail. ORIG OE *dott* head of a boil
▸ **ˈdotter** *n*

dot[2] (dɒt) *n* a woman's dowry. ORIG C19: from F from L *dōs;* rel. to *dōtāre* to endow, *dāre* to give

dotage (ˈdəʊtɪdʒ) *n* **1** feebleness of mind, esp. as a result of old age. **2** foolish infatuation. ORIG C14: from DOTE + -AGE

dotard (ˈdəʊtəd) *n* a person who is weak-minded, esp. through senility. ORIG C14: from DOTE + -ARD
▸ **ˈdotardly** *adj*

dotcom *or* **dot.com** *n* **a** a company that conducts most of its business on the Internet. **b** (*as modifier*): *dotcom stocks.* ORIG C20: from *.com,* the domain-name suffix of businesses trading on the Internet

dote (dəʊt) *vb* **dotes, doting, doted.** (*intr*) **1** (foll. by *on* or *upon*) to love to an excessive or foolish degree. **2** to be foolish or weak-minded, esp. as a result of old age. ORIG C13: rel. to MDu. *doten* to be silly
▸ **ˈdoter** *n*

doth (dʌθ) *vb Arch. or dialect.* (used with *he, she,* or *it*) a singular form of the present tense of **do**[1].

dot-matrix printer *n Computing.* a printer in which each character is produced by a subset of an array of needles.

dotterel *or* **dottrel** (ˈdɒtrəl) *n* **1** a rare Eurasian plover with white bands around the head and neck. **2** *Dialect.* a person who is foolish or easily duped. ORIG C15 *dotrelle;* see DOTE

dottle (ˈdɒtᵊl) *n* the plug of tobacco left in a pipe after smoking. ORIG C15: dim. of *dot* lump

dotty (ˈdɒtɪ) *adj* **dottier, dottiest. 1** *Sl., chiefly Brit.* feeble-minded; slightly crazy. **2** *Brit. sl.* (foll. by *about*) extremely fond (of). **3** marked with dots. ORIG C19: from DOT[1]
▸ **ˈdottily** *adv* ▸ **ˈdottiness** *n*

★ people and places

Douai ★ ('duːeɪ; *French* dwɛ) *n* an industrial city in N France: a centre for exiled English Catholics in the 16th and 17th centuries. Pop.: 199 562 (1990).

Douala *or* **Duala** ★ (duˈɑːlə) *n* the chief port and largest city in W Cameroon, on the Bight of Bonny. Pop.: 1 200 000 (1992 est.).

Douay Bible *or* **Version** ('duːeɪ) *n* an English translation of the Bible from the Vulgate by Catholic scholars at Douai in 1610.

double ('dʌbᵊl) *adj* (*usually prenominal*) **1** as much again in size, strength, number, etc.: *a double portion.* **2** composed of two equal or similar parts. **3** designed for two users: *a double room.* **4** folded in two; composed of two layers. **5** stooping; bent over. **6** having two aspects; ambiguous: *a double meaning.* **7** false, deceitful, or hypocritical: *a double life.* **8** (of flowers) having more than the normal number of petals. **9** *Music.* **9a** (of an instrument) sounding an octave lower: *a double bass.* **9b** (of time) duple. ◆ *adv* **10** twice over; twofold. **11** two together; two at a time (esp. in **see double**). ◆ *n* **12** twice the number, amount, size, etc. **13** a double measure of spirits. **14** a duplicate or counterpart, esp. a person who closely resembles another; understudy. **15** a ghostly apparition of a living person; doppelgänger. **16** a sharp turn, esp. a return on one's own tracks. **17** *Bridge.* a call that increases certain scoring points if the last preceding bid becomes the contract. **18** *Billiards, etc.* a strike in which the object ball is struck so as to make it rebound against the cushion to an opposite pocket. **19** a bet on two horses in different races in which any winnings from the first race are placed on the horse in the later race. **20a** the narrow outermost ring on a dartboard. **20b** a hit on this ring. **21 at** *or* **on the double. 21a** at twice normal marching speed. **21b** quickly or immediately. ◆ *vb* **doubles, doubling, doubled. 22** to make or become twice as much. **23** to bend or fold (material, etc.). **24** (*tr;* sometimes foll. by *up*) to clench (a fist). **25** (*tr;* often foll. by *together* or *up*) to join or couple. **26** (*tr*) to repeat exactly; copy. **27** (*intr*) to play two parts or serve two roles. **28** (*intr*) to turn sharply; follow a winding course. **29** *Naut.* to sail around (a headland or other point). **30** *Music.* **30a** to duplicate (a part) either in unison or at the octave above or below it. **30b** (*intr;* usually foll. by *on*) to be capable of performing (upon an additional instrument). **31** *Bridge.* to make a call that will double certain scoring points if the preceding bid becomes the contract. **32** *Billiards, etc.* to cause (a ball) to rebound or (of a ball) to rebound from a cushion. **33** (*intr;* foll. by *for*) to act as substitute. **34** (*intr*) to go or march at twice the normal speed. ◆ See also **double back, doubles, double up.** ORIG C13: from OF, from L *duplus* twofold, from *duo* two + *-plus* -FOLD
▸ **'doubler** *n*

double agent *n* a spy employed by two mutually antagonistic countries, companies, etc.

double back *vb* (*intr, adv*) to go back in the opposite direction (esp. in **double back on one's tracks**).

double-bank *vb Austral. & NZ inf.* to carry (a second person) on (a horse, bicycle, etc.). Also: **dub.**

double bar *n Music.* a symbol, consisting of two ordinary bar lines or a single heavy one, that marks the end of a composition or section.

double-barrelled *or US* **double-barreled** *adj* **1** (of a gun) having two barrels. **2** extremely forceful. **3** *Brit.* (of a surname) having hyphenated parts. **4** serving two purposes; ambiguous: *a double-barrelled remark.*

double bass (beɪs) *n* **1** Also called (US): **bass viol.** a stringed instrument, the largest and lowest member of the violin family with a range of almost three octaves. Inf. name: **bass fiddle.** ◆ *adj* **double-bass. 2** of an instrument whose pitch lies below the bass; contrabass.

double bassoon *n Music.* the lowest and largest instrument in the oboe class; contrabassoon.

double-blind *adj* of or denoting an experimental study of a new drug in which neither the experimenters nor the patients know which are the test subjects and which are the controls.

double boiler *n* the US and Canad. name for **double saucepan.**

double-breasted *adj* (of a garment) having overlapping fronts.

double-check *vb* **1** to check again; verify. ◆ *n* **double check. 2** a second examination or verification. **3** *Chess.* a simultaneous check from two pieces.

double chin *n* a fold of fat under the chin.
▸ **ˌdouble-'chinned** *adj*

double concerto *n* a concerto for two solo instruments and orchestra.

double cream *n Brit.* thick cream with a high fat content.

double-cross *vb* **1** (*tr*) to cheat or betray. ◆ *n* **2** the act or an instance of double-crossing; betrayal.
▸ **ˌdouble-'crosser** *n*

double dagger *n* a character (‡) used in printing to indicate a cross-reference. Also called: **diesis, double obelisk.**

double-dealing *n* **a** action characterized by treachery or deceit. **b** (*as modifier*): *double-dealing treachery.*
▸ **ˌdouble-'dealer** *n*

double-decker *n* **1** *Chiefly Brit.* a bus with two passenger decks. **2** *Inf.* **2a** a thing or structure having two decks, layers, etc. **2b** (*as modifier*): *a double-decker sandwich.*

double-declutch *vb* (*intr*) *Brit., Austral, & NZ.* to change to a lower gear in a motor vehicle by first placing the gear lever into neutral before engaging the desired gear. US term: **double-clutch.**

double Dutch *n Brit. inf.* incomprehensible talk; gibberish.

double-edged *adj* **1** acting in two ways. **2** (of a remark, etc.) having two possible interpretations, esp. applicable both for and against, or being malicious though apparently innocuous. **3** (of a knife, etc.) having a cutting edge on either side of the blade.

double entendre (ɑːnˈtɑːndrə) *n* **1** a word, phrase, etc., that can be interpreted in two ways, esp. one having one meaning that is indelicate. **2** the type of humour that depends upon this. ORIG C17: from obs. F: double meaning

double entry *n* **a** a book-keeping system in which any commercial transaction is entered as a debit in one account and as a credit in another. **b** (*as modifier*): *double-entry book-keeping.*

double exposure *n* **1** the act or process of recording two superimposed images on a photographic medium. **2** the photograph resulting from such an act.

double-faced *adj* **1** (of textiles) having a finished nap on each side; reversible. **2** insincere or deceitful.

double feature *n Films.* a programme showing two full-length films. Inf. name (US): **twin bill.**

double first *n Brit.* a first-class honours degree in two subjects.

double glazing *n* **1** two panes of glass in a window, fitted to reduce heat loss, etc. **2** the fitting of glass in such a manner.

double-header *n* **1** a train drawn by two locomotives coupled together. **2** Also called: **twin bill.** *Sport, US & Canad.* two games played consecutively. **3** *Austral. & NZ inf.* a coin with the impression of a head on each side. **4** *Austral. inf.* a double ice-cream cone.

double helix *n* the form of the molecular structure of DNA, consisting of two helical chains coiled around the same axis.

double-jointed *adj* having unusually flexible joints permitting an abnormal degree of motion.

double knitting *n* a widely used medium thickness of knitting wool.

double negative *n* a construction, often considered ungrammatical, in which two negatives are used where one is needed, as in *I wouldn't never have believed it.*

USAGE NOTE There are two contexts where double negatives are found. An adjective with negative force is often used with a negative in order to express a nuance of meaning somewhere between the positive and the negative: *he was a not infrequent visitor; it is not an uncommon sight.* Two negatives are also found together where they reinforce each other rather than conflict: *he never went back, not even to collect his belongings.* These two uses of what is technically a double negative are acceptable. A third case, illustrated by *I shouldn't wonder if it didn't rain today,* has the force of a weak positive statement (*I expect it to rain today*) and is common in informal English.

double-park *vb* to park (a vehicle) alongside or opposite another already parked by the roadside, thereby causing an obstruction.

double pneumonia *n* pneumonia affecting both lungs.

double-quick *adj* **1** very quick; rapid. ◆ *adv* **2** in a very quick or rapid manner.

double-reed *adj* relating to or denoting a wind instrument having two reeds that vibrate against each other.

double refraction *n* the splitting of a ray of unpolarized light into two unequally refracted rays polarized in mutually perpendicular planes. Also called: **birefringence.**

doubles (ˈdʌbəlz) *n* (*functioning as sing or pl*) **a** a game between two pairs of players. **b** (*as modifier*): *a doubles match.*

double saucepan *n Brit.* a cooking utensil consisting of two saucepans: the lower pan is used to boil water to heat food in the upper pan. US and Canad. name: **double boiler.**

double-space *vb* **double-spaces, double-spacing, double-spaced.** to type (copy) with a full space between lines.

double spread *n Printing.* two facing pages of a publication treated as a single unit.

double standard *n* a set of principles that allows greater freedom to one person or group than to another.

double-stop *vb* **double-stops, double-stopping, double-stopped.** to play (two notes or parts) simultaneously on a violin or related instrument.

doublet (ˈdʌblɪt) *n* **1** (formerly) a man's close-fitting jacket, with or without sleeves (esp. in **doublet and hose**). **2a** a pair of similar things, esp. two words deriving ultimately from the same source. **2b** one of such a pair. **3** *Jewellery.* a false gem made by welding or fusing stones together. **4** *Physics.* a closely spaced pair of related spectral lines. **5** (*pl*) two dice each showing the same number of spots on one throw. ORIG C14: from OF, from DOUBLE

double take *n* (esp. in comedy) a delayed reaction by a person to a remark, situation, etc.

double talk *n* **1** rapid speech with a mixture of nonsense syllables and real words; gibberish. **2** empty, deceptive, or ambiguous talk.

doublethink (ˈdʌbəlˌθɪŋk) *n* deliberate, perverse, or unconscious acceptance or promulgation of conflicting facts, principles, etc.

double time *n* **1** a doubled wage rate, paid for working on public holidays, etc. **2** *Music.* two beats per bar. **3** a slow running pace, keeping in step. **4** *US Army.* a fast march.

double up *vb* (*adv*) **1** to bend or cause to bend in two. **2** (*intr*) to share a room or bed designed for one person, family, etc. **3** (*intr*) *Brit.* to use the winnings from one bet as the stake for another. US and Canad. term: **parlay.**

double whammy *n Inf., chiefly US.* a devastating setback made up of two elements.

doubloon (dʌˈbluːn) *n* **1** a former Spanish gold coin. **2** (*pl*) *Sl.* money. ORIG C17: from Sp. *doblón,* from *dobla,* from L *dupla,* fem. of *duplus* twofold

doubly (ˈdʌblɪ) *adv* **1** to or in a double degree, quantity, or measure. **2** in two ways.

Doubs ★ (*French* du) *n* **1** a department of E France, in Franche-Comté region. Capital: Besançon. Pop.: 493 133 (1994 est.). Area: 5258 sq. km (2030 sq. miles). **2** a river in E France, rising in the Jura Mountains, becoming part of the border between France and Switzerland and flowing generally southwest to the Saône River. Length: 430 km (267 miles).

doubt (daʊt) *n* **1** uncertainty about the truth, fact, or existence of something (esp. in **in doubt, without doubt,** etc.). **2** (*often pl*) lack of belief in or conviction about something. **3** an unresolved difficulty, point, etc. **4** *Obs.* fear. **5** **give (someone) the benefit of the doubt.** to presume (someone suspected of guilt) innocent. **6** **no doubt.** almost certainly. ◆ *vb* **7** (*tr; may take a clause as object*) to be inclined to disbelieve. **8** (*tr*) to distrust or be suspicious of. **9** (*intr*) to feel uncertainty or be undecided. **10** (*tr*) *Arch.* to fear. ORIG C13: from OF *douter,* from L *dubitāre*
▸ ˈ**doubtable** *adj* ▸ ˈ**doubter** *n* ▸ ˈ**doubtingly** *adv*

USAGE NOTE When a clause follows *doubt* in an affirmative sentence it was formerly considered correct only to use *whether*: (*I doubt whether he will come*), but nowadays *if* and *that* are also common and acceptable. In negative statements, *doubt* is invariably followed by *that*: *I do not doubt that he is telling the truth.* In such sentences, *but* (*I do not doubt but that he is telling the truth*) is rather rare, and will tend to sound either formal or pompous.

doubtful (ˈdaʊtfʊl) *adj* **1** unlikely; improbable. **2** uncertain: *a doubtful answer.* **3** unsettled; unresolved. **4** of questionable reputation or morality. **5** having reservations or misgivings.
▸ ˈ**doubtfully** *adv* ▸ ˈ**doubtfulness** *n*

USAGE NOTE It was formerly considered correct to use *whether* after *doubtful* (*it is doubtful whether he will come*), but now *if* and *that* are also acceptable.

doubting Thomas *n* a person who insists on proof before he or she will believe anything. ORIG after THOMAS (the apostle), who did not believe that Jesus had been resurrected

doubtless (ˈdaʊtlɪs) *adv also* **doubtlessly** (*sentence modifier*), *sentence substitute.* **1** certainly. **2** probably. ◆ *adj* **3** certain; assured.
▸ ˈ**doubtlessness** *n*

douche (duːʃ) *n* **1** a stream of water directed onto or into the body for cleansing or medical purposes. **2** the application of such a stream of water. **3** an instrument for applying a douche. ◆ *vb* **douches, douching, douched.** **4** to cleanse or treat or be cleansed or treated by means of a douche. ORIG C18: from F, from It. *doccia* pipe

dough (dəʊ) *n* **1** a thick mixture of flour or meal and water or milk, used for making bread, pastry, etc. **2** any similar pasty mass. **3** a slang word for **money.** ORIG OE *dāg*

doughboy (ˈdəʊˌbɔɪ) *n* **1** *US Inf.* an infantryman, esp. in World War I. **2** dough that is boiled or steamed as a dumpling.

doughnut (ˈdəʊnʌt) *n* **1** a small cake of sweetened dough, often ring-shaped, cooked in hot fat. **2** anything shaped like a ring, such as the reaction vessel of a thermonuclear reactor. ◆ *vb* **doughnuts, doughnutting, doughnutted.** **3** (*tr*) *Inf.* (of Members of Parliament) to surround (a speaker) during the televising of Parliament to give the impression that the chamber is crowded or the speaker is well supported.

doughty (ˈdaʊtɪ) *adj* **doughtier, doughtiest.** hardy; resolute. ORIG OE *dohtig*
▸ ˈ**doughtily** *adv* ▸ ˈ**doughtiness** *n*

doughy (ˈdəʊɪ) *adj* **doughier, doughiest.** resembling dough; soft, pallid, or flabby.

Douglas[1] ★ (ˈdʌgləs) *n* the capital of the Isle of Man, a resort on the E coast. Pop.: 23 487 (1996).

Douglas[2] ★ (ˈdʌgləs) *n* **1** **C(lifford) H(ugh).** 1879–1952, British economist, who originated the theory of social credit. **2** **Gavin.** ?1474–1522, Scottish poet, the first British translator of the *Aeneid.* **3** **Keith (Castellain).** 1920–44, British poet noted for his poems in World War II: killed in action. **4** (**George**) **Norman.** 1868–1952, British writer, noted for the novel *South Wind* (1917).

Douglas fir, spruce, *or* **hemlock** *n* a North American pyramidal coniferous tree, widely planted for ornament and for timber. ORIG C19: after David *Douglas* (1798–1834), Scot. botanist

Douglas-Home ★ (ˈdʌɡləsˈhjuːm) *n* Sir **Alexander.** See (Baron Alexander) **Home of the Hirsel.**

Doukhobor *or* **Dukhobor** (ˈduːkəʊˌbɔː) *n* a member of a Russian sect of Christians that originated in the 18th century. In the late 19th century a large number emigrated to W Canada, where most Doukhobors now live. ORIG C19: from Russian *dukhoborets* spirit wrestlers

Dounreay ★ (ˌduːnˈreɪ) *n* the site in N Scotland of a nuclear power station, which contained the world's first fast-breeder reactor (1962–77).

do up *vb* (*adv; mainly tr*) **1** to wrap and make into a bundle: *to do up a parcel.* **2** to beautify or adorn. **3** (*also intr*) to fasten or be fastened. **4** *Inf.* to renovate or redecorate. **5** *Sl.* to assault. **6** *Inf.* to cause the downfall of (a person).

dour (dʊə, ˈdaʊə) *adj* **1** sullen. **2** hard or obstinate. ORIG C14: prob. from L *dūrus* hard
▸ **ˈdourly** *adv* ▸ **ˈdourness** *n*

douroucouli (ˌduːruːˈkuːlɪ) *n* a nocturnal New World monkey of Central and South America with thick fur and large eyes. ORIG from Amerind

douse *or* **dowse** (daʊs) *vb* **douses, dousing, doused** *or* **dowses, dowsing, dowsed. 1** to plunge or be plunged into liquid; duck. **2** (*tr*) to drench with water. **3** (*tr*) to put out (a light, candle, etc.). ◆ *n* **4** an immersion. ORIG C16: ? rel. to obs. *douse* to strike, from ?

dove (dʌv) *n* **1** any of a family of birds having a heavy body, small head, short legs, and long pointed wings. **2** *Politics.* a person opposed to war. **3** a gentle or innocent person: used as a term of endearment. **4a** a greyish-brown colour. **4b** (*as adj*): *dove walls.* ORIG OE *dūfe* (unattested except as a fem proper name)
▸ **ˈdoveˌlike** *adj*

Dove (dʌv) *n* **the.** *Christianity.* a manifestation of the Holy Spirit (John 1:32).

dovecote (ˈdʌvˌkəʊt) *or* **dovecot** (ˈdʌvˌkɒt) *n* a structure for housing pigeons.

Dover ★ (ˈdəʊvə) *n* **1** a port in SE England, in E Kent on the Strait of Dover: the only one of the Cinque Ports that is still important; a stronghold since ancient times and Caesar's first point of attack in the invasion of Britain (55 B.C.). Pop.: 34 179 (1991). **2 Strait of.** a strait between SE England and N France, linking the English Channel with the North Sea. Width: about 32 km (20 miles). French name: **Pas de Calais. 3** a city in the US, the capital of Delaware, founded in 1683: 18th-century buildings. Pop.: 27 630 (1990).

dovetail (ˈdʌvˌteɪl) *n* **1** a wedge-shaped tenon. **2** Also called: **dovetail joint.** a joint containing such tenons. ◆ *vb* **3** (*tr*) to join by means of dovetails. **4** to fit or cause to fit together closely or neatly.

dowager (ˈdaʊədʒə) *n* **1a** a widow possessing property or a title obtained from her husband. **1b** (*as modifier*): *the dowager duchess.* **2** a wealthy or dignified elderly woman. ORIG C16: from OF *douagiere,* from *douage* DOWER

Dowding ★ (ˈdaʊdɪŋ) *n* Baron **Hugh Caswall Tremenheere,** nicknamed *Stuffy.* 1882–1970, British air chief marshal in charge of Fighter Command (1936–40) during the Battle of Britain (1940).

dowdy (ˈdaʊdɪ) *adj* **dowdier, dowdiest. 1** (esp. of a woman or a woman's dress) shabby or old-fashioned. ◆ *n, pl* **dowdies. 2** a dowdy woman. ORIG C14: *dowd* slut, from ?
▸ **ˈdowdily** *adv* ▸ **ˈdowdiness** *n* ▸ **ˈdowdyish** *adj*

dowel (ˈdaʊəl) *n* a wooden or metal peg that fits into two corresponding holes to join two adjacent parts. ORIG C14: from MLow G *dövel* plug, from OHG *tubili*

Dowell ★ (ˈdaʊəl) *n* **Anthony.** born 1943, British ballet dancer. He became director of the Royal Ballet in 1986.

dower (ˈdaʊə) *n* **1** the life interest in a part of her husband's estate allotted to a widow by law. **2** an archaic word for **dowry** (sense 1). **3** a natural gift. ◆ *vb* **4** (*tr*) to endow. ORIG C14: from OF *douaire,* from Med. L *dōtārium,* from L *dōs* gift

dower house *n* a house for the use of a widow, often on her deceased husband's estate.

do with *vb* **1 could** *or* **can do with.** to find useful; benefit from. **2 have to do with.** to be involved in or connected with. **3 to do with.** concerning; related to. **4 what...do with. 4a** to put or place: *what did you do with my coat?* **4b** to handle or treat. **4c** to fill one's time usefully: *she didn't know what to do with herself when the project was finished.*

do without *vb* (*intr*) **1** to forgo; manage without. **2** (*prep*) not to require (uncalled-for comments): *we can do without your criticisms.*

Dow-Jones average (ˈdaʊˈdʒəʊnz) *n US.* a daily index of average stock-exchange prices. ORIG C20: after Charles H. *Dow* (died 1902) & Edward D. *Jones* (died 1920), American financial statisticians

Dowland ★ (ˈdaʊlənd) *n* **John.** ?1563–1626, English lutenist and composer of songs and lute music.

down[1] (daʊn) *prep* **1** used to indicate movement from a higher to a lower position. **2** at a lower or further level or position on, in, or along: *he ran down the street.* ◆ *adv* **3** downwards; at or to a lower level or position. **4** (*particle*) used with many verbs when the result of the verb's action is to lower or destroy its object: *knock down.* **5** (*particle*) used with several verbs to indicate intensity or completion: *calm down.* **6** immediately: *cash down.* **7** on paper: *write this down.* **8** arranged; scheduled. **9** in a helpless position. **10a** away from a more important place. **10b** away from a more northerly place. **10c** (of a member of some British universities) away from the university. **10d** in a particular part of a country: *down south.* **11** *Naut.* (of a helm) having the rudder to windward. **12** reduced to a state of lack or want: *down to the last pound.* **13** lacking a specified amount. **14** lower in price. **15** including all intermediate grades. **16** from an earlier to a later time. **17** to a finer or more concentrated state: *to grind down.* **18** *Sport.* being a specified number of points, goals, etc., behind another competitor, team, etc. **19** (of a person) being inactive, owing to illness: *down with flu.* **20** (*functioning as imperative*) (to dogs): *down, Rover!* **21** (*functioning as imperative*) **down with.** wanting the end of somebody or something: *down with the king!* **22 get down on something.** *Austral. & NZ.* to procure something, esp. in advance of needs or in anticipation of someone else. ◆ *adj* **23** (*postpositive*) depressed. **24** (*prenominal*) of or relating to a train or trains from a more important place or one regarded as higher: *the down line.* **25** (*postpositive*) (of a device, machine, etc., esp. a computer) temporarily out of action. **26** made in cash: *a down payment.* **27 down to.** the responsibility or fault of: *this defeat was down to me.* ◆ *vb* (*tr*) **28** to knock, push, or pull down. **29** to cause to go or come down. **30** *Inf.* to drink, esp. quickly. **31** to bring (someone) down, esp. by tackling. ◆ *n* **32** a descent; downward movement. **33** a lowering or a poor period (esp. in **ups and downs**). **34** (in American football) any of a series of four attempts to advance the ball ten yards. **35 have a down on.** *Inf.* to bear ill will towards. ORIG OE *dūne,* short for *adūne,* var. of *of dūne,* lit.: from the hill

down[2] (daʊn) *n* **1** soft fine feathers. **2** another name for **eiderdown** (sense 1). **3** *Bot.* a fine coating of soft hairs, as on certain leaves, fruits, and seeds. **4** any growth or coating of soft fine hair. ORIG C14: from ON

down[3] (daʊn) *n Arch.* a hill, esp. a sand dune. See also **downs.** ORIG OE *dūn*

Down ★ (daʊn) *n* **1** a historic county of SE Northern Ireland, on the Irish Sea: hilly, rising to the Mountains of Mourne. Area: 2 446 sq. km (952 sq. miles). **2** a district of SE Northern Ireland, bordering the Irish Sea E of Strangford Lough. Administrative centre: Downpatrick. Pop.: 58 008 (1991). Area: 646 sq. km (249 sq. miles).

down and dirty *adj* (**down-and-dirty** *when prenominal*) *Inf., chiefly US.* **1** ruthlessly competitive or underhand: *if Bush gets down and dirty the Governor will give as good as he gets.* **2** uninhibited; frank.

down-and-out *adj* **1** without any means of livelihood; poor and, often, socially outcast. ◆ *n* **2** a person who is destitute and, often, homeless.

downbeat (ˈdaʊnˌbiːt) *n* **1** *Music.* the first beat of a bar or the downward gesture of a conductor's baton indicating this. ◆ *adj Inf.* **2** depressed; gloomy. **3** relaxed.

downcast ('daʊn,kɑːst) *adj* **1** dejected. **2** (esp. of the eyes) directed downwards. ◆ *n* **3** *Mining.* a ventilation shaft.

downer ('daʊnə) *n Sl.* **1** a barbiturate, tranquillizer, or narcotic. **2** a depressing experience. **3** a state of depression.

downfall ('daʊn,fɔːl) *n* **1** a sudden loss of position, health, or reputation. **2** a fall of rain, snow, etc., esp. a sudden heavy one.

downgrade ('daʊn,greɪd) *vb* **downgrades, downgrading, downgraded.** (*tr*) **1** to reduce in importance or value, esp. to demote (a person) to a poorer job. **2** to speak of disparagingly. ◆ *n* **3** *Chiefly US & Canad.* a downward slope. **4 on the downgrade.** waning in importance, health, etc.

downhearted (,daʊn'hɑːtɪd) *adj* discouraged; dejected. ▸ **,down'heartedly** *adv*

downhill ('daʊn'hɪl) *adj* **1** going or sloping down. ◆ *adv* **2** towards the bottom of a hill; downwards. **3 go downhill.** *Inf.* to decline; deteriorate. ◆ *n* **4** the downward slope of a hill; a descent. **5** a skiing race downhill.

downhole ('daʊn,həʊl) *adj* (in the oil industry) denoting any piece of equipment used in the well itself.

downhome (,daʊn'həʊm) *adj Sl., chiefly US.* of, relating to, or reminiscent of rural life, esp. in the southern US; unsophisticated; homely.

Downing Street ★ ('daʊnɪŋ) *n* **1** a street in W central London: official residences of the prime minister of Great Britain and the Chancellor of the Exchequer. **2** the office of the prime minister. ORIG after Sir George *Downing* (1623–84), E statesman

download ('daʊn,ləʊd) *vb* (*tr*) to copy or transfer (data or a program) from one computer's memory to that of another, esp. in a network of computers. ▸ **,down'loadable** *adj*

down-market *adj* relating to commercial products, services, etc., that are cheap, unfashionable, or poor quality.

Downpatrick ★ (,daʊn'pætrɪk) *n* a market town in Northern Ireland: Saint Patrick is said to be buried here. Pop.: 10 257 (1991).

down payment *n* the deposit paid on an item purchased on hire-purchase, mortgage, etc.

downpipe ('daʊn,paɪp) *n Brit. and NZ.* a pipe for carrying rainwater from a roof gutter to ground level. Usual US & Canad. name: **downspout.**

downpour ('daʊn,pɔː) *n* a heavy continuous fall of rain.

downrange ('daʊn'reɪndʒ) *adj, adv* in the direction of the intended flight path of a rocket or missile.

downright ('daʊn,raɪt) *adj* **1** frank or straightforward; blunt. ◆ *adv, adj* (*prenominal*) **2** (intensifier): *downright rude.* ▸ **'down,rightly** *adv* ▸ **'down,rightness** *n*

downs (daʊnz) *pl n* **1** rolling upland, esp. in the chalk areas of S Britain, characterized by lack of trees and used mainly as pasture. **2** *Austral. & NZ.* a flat grassy area, not necessarily of uplands.

Downs ★ (daʊnz) *n* **the. 1** any of various ranges of low chalk hills in S England, esp. the **South Downs** in Sussex. **2** a roadstead off the SE coast of Kent, protected by the Goodwin Sands.

downshifting ('daʊn,ʃɪftɪŋ) *n* the practice of simplifying one's lifestyle and becoming less materialistic. ▸ **'down,shifter** *n*

downside ('daʊn,saɪd) *n* the disadvantageous aspect of a situation: *the downside of twentieth-century living.*

downsize ('daʊn,saɪz) *vb* **downsizes, downsizing, downsized.** (*tr*) **1** to reduce the number of people employed by (a company). **2** to upgrade (a computer system) by replacing a mainframe or minicomputer with a network of microcomputing. Cf. **rightsize.**

Down's syndrome (daʊnz) *n* **a** *Pathol.* a chromosomal abnormality resulting in a flat face and nose, a vertical fold of skin at the inner edge of the eye, and mental retardation. Former name: **mongolism. b** (*as modifier*): *a Down's syndrome baby.* ORIG C19: after John *Langdon-Down* (1828–96), Brit. physician

downstage ('daʊn'steɪdʒ) *Theatre.* ◆ *adv* **1** at or towards the front of the stage. ◆ *adj* **2** of or relating to the front of the stage.

downstairs ('daʊn'stɛəz) *adv* **1** down the stairs; to or on a lower floor. ◆ *n* **2a** a lower or ground floor. **2b** (*as modifier*): *a downstairs room.* **3** *Brit. inf., old-fashioned.* the servants of a household collectively.

downstream ('daʊn'striːm) *adv, adj* in or towards the lower part of a stream; with the current. Cf. **upstream** (sense 1).

downswing ('daʊn,swɪŋ) *n* a statistical downward trend in business activity, the death rate, etc.

downtime ('daʊn,taɪm) *n Commerce.* time during which a computer or machine is not working, as when under repair.

down-to-earth *adj* sensible; practical; realistic.

downtown ('daʊn'taʊn) *Chiefly US, Canad., & NZ.* ◆ *n* **1** the central or lower part of a city, esp. the main commercial area. ◆ *adv* **2** towards, to, or into this area. ◆ *adj* **3** of, relating to, or situated in the downtown area: *a downtown cinema.*

downtrodden ('daʊn,trɒdᵊn) *adj* **1** subjugated; oppressed. **2** trodden down.

downturn ('daʊn,tɜːn) *n* a drop or reduction in the success of a business or economy.

down under *Inf.* ◆ *n* **1** Australia or New Zealand. ◆ *adv* **2** in or to Australia or New Zealand.

downward ('daʊnwəd) *adj* **1** descending from a higher to a lower level, condition, position, etc. **2** descending from a beginning. ◆ *adv* **3** a variant of **downwards.** ▸ **'downwardly** *adv*

downwards ('daʊnwədz) *or* **downward** *adv* **1** from a higher to a lower place, level, etc. **2** from an earlier time or source to a later.

downwind ('daʊn'wɪnd) *adv, adj* in the same direction towards which the wind is blowing; with the wind from behind.

downy ('daʊnɪ) *adj* **downier, downiest. 1** covered with soft fine hair or feathers. **2** light, soft, and fluffy. **3** made from or filled with down. **4** *Brit. sl.* sharp-witted. ▸ **'downiness** *n*

dowry ('daʊərɪ) *n, pl* **dowries. 1** the property brought by a woman to her husband at marriage. **2** a natural talent or gift. ORIG C14: from Anglo-F *douarie,* from Med. L *dōtārium;* see DOWER

dowse (daʊz) *vb* **dowses, dowsing, dowsed.** (*intr*) to search for underground water, minerals, etc., using a divining rod; divine. ORIG C17: from ? ▸ **'dowser** *n*

Dowson ★ ('daʊsᵊn) *n* **Ernest** (**Christopher**). 1867–1900, British Decadent poet noted for his lyric *Cynara.*

doxology (dɒk'sɒlədʒɪ) *n, pl* **doxologies.** a hymn, verse, or form of words in Christian liturgy glorifying God. ORIG C17: from Med. L *doxologia,* from Gk, from *doxologos* uttering praise, from *doxa* praise; see -LOGY ▸ **doxological** (,dɒksə'lɒdʒɪkᵊl) *adj*

doxy ('dɒksɪ) *n, pl* **doxies.** *Arch. sl.* a prostitute or mistress. ORIG C16: prob. from MFlemish *docke* doll

doyen ('dɔɪən) *n* the senior member of a group, profession, or society. ORIG C17: from F, from LL *decānus* leader of a group of ten ▸ **doyenne** (dɔɪ'ɛn) *fem*

doyley ('dɔɪlɪ) *n* a variant spelling of **doily.**

D'Oyly Carte ★ (,dɔɪlɪ 'kɑːt) *n* **Richard.** 1844–1901, British impresario noted for his productions of the operettas of Gilbert and Sullivan.

doz. *abbrev. for* dozen.

doze (dəʊz) *vb* **dozes, dozing, dozed.** (*intr*) **1** to sleep lightly or intermittently. **2** (often foll. by *off*) to fall into a light sleep. ◆ *n* **3** a short sleep. ORIG C17: prob. from ON *dūs* lull ▸ **'dozer** *n*

dozen ('dʌzᵊn) *determiner* **1** (preceded by *a* or a numeral) twelve or a group of twelve. ◆ *n, pl* **dozens** *or* **dozen. 2 by the dozen.** in large quantities. **3 daily dozen.** *Brit.* regular physical exercises. **4 talk nineteen to the dozen.** to talk with-

out stopping. ORIG C13: from OF *douzaine,* from *douze* twelve, from L *duodecim,* from *duo* two + *decem* ten
▸ **'dozenth** *adj*

dozy ('dəʊzɪ) *adj* **dozier, doziest. 1** drowsy. **2** *Brit. inf.* stupid.
▸ **'dozily** *adv* ▸ **'doziness** *n*

DP *abbrev. for:* **1** data processing. **2** displaced person.

DPB (in New Zealand) *abbrev. for* domestic purposes benefit: an allowance paid to single parents.

DPhil *or* **DPh** *abbrev. for* Doctor of Philosophy. Also: **PhD.**

dpi *abbrev. for* dots per inch: a measure of the resolution of a typesetting machine, computer screen, etc.

DPP (in Britain) *abbrev. for* Director of Public Prosecutions.

dpt *abbrev. for:* **1** department. **2** depot.

dr *abbrev. for:* **1** Also: **dr.** dram. **2** debtor.

Dr *abbrev. for:* **1** Doctor. **2** Drive.

DR *abbrev. for* dry riser.

dr. *abbrev. for:* **1** debit. **2** drachma.

drab[1] (dræb) *adj* **drabber, drabbest. 1** dull; dingy. **2** cheerless; dreary. **3** of the colour drab. ◆ *n* **4** a light olive-brown colour. ORIG C16: from OF *drap* cloth, from LL *drappus,* ? of Celtic origin
▸ **'drably** *adv* ▸ **'drabness** *n*

drab[2] (dræb) *Arch.* ◆ *n* **1** a slatternly woman. **2** a whore. ◆ *vb* **drabs, drabbing, drabbed. 3** (*intr*) to consort with prostitutes. ORIG C16: of Celtic origin

Drabble ★ ('dræbᵊl) *n* **Margaret.** born 1939, British novelist and editor. Her novels include *The Needle's Eye* (1972) and *The Gates of Ivory* (1991).

drachm (dræm) *n* **1** Also called: **fluid dram.** *Brit.* one eighth of a fluid ounce. **2** *US.* another name for **dram** (sense 2). **3** another name for **drachma.** ORIG C14: learned var. of DRAM

drachma ('drækmə) *n, pl* **drachmas** *or* **drachmae** (-miː). **1** the standard monetary unit of Greece. **2** *US.* another name for **dram** (sense 2). **3** a silver coin of ancient Greece. ORIG C16: from L, from Gk *drakhmē* a handful, from *drassesthai* to seize

drack *or* **drac** (dræk) *adj Austral. sl.* (of a woman) unattractive. ORIG C20: ?from *Dracula's* daughter

Draco ★ ('dreɪkəʊ) *n* 7th century B.C., Athenian statesman, whose code of laws (621) prescribed death for most offences.

Draconian (dreɪ'kəʊnɪən) *or* **Draconic** (dreɪ'kɒnɪk) *adj* (*sometimes not cap.*) *n* **1** of or relating to Draco or his code of laws. **2** harsh. ▸ **Dra'conianism** *n* ▸ **Dra'conically** *adv*

Dracula ('drækjʊlə) *n* **1** a cruel or bloodthirsty person. **2** a person who preys ruthlessly on others. ORIG C20: from the vampire in Bram Stoker's Gothic novel *Dracula* (1897)

draff (dræf) *n* the residue of husks after fermentation of the grain in brewing, used as cattle fodder. ORIG C13: from ON *draf*

draft (drɑːft) *n* **1** a plan, sketch, or drawing of something. **2** a preliminary outline of a book, speech, etc. **3** another word for **bill of exchange. 4** a demand or drain on something. **5** *US & Austral.* selection for compulsory military service. **6** detachment of military personnel from one unit to another. **7** *Austral. & NZ.* a group of livestock separated from the rest of the herd or flock. ◆ *vb* (*tr*) **8** to draw up an outline or sketch for. **9** to prepare a plan or design of. **10** to detach (military personnel) from one unit to another. **11** *US & Austral.* to select for compulsory military service. **12** *Austral. & NZ.* **12a** to select (cattle or sheep) from a herd or flock. **12b** to select (farm stock) for sale. ◆ *n, vb* **13** the usual US spelling of **draught.** ORIG C16: var. of DRAUGHT
▸ **'drafter** *n*

draftee (drɑːf'tiː) *n US.* a conscript.

drafty ('drɑːftɪ) *adj* **draftier, draftiest.** the usual US spelling of **draughty.**

drag (dræg) *vb* **drags, dragging, dragged. 1** to pull or be pulled with force, esp. along the ground. **2** (*tr; often foll. by away* or *from*) to persuade to come away. **3** to trail or cause to trail on the ground. **4** (*tr*) to move with effort or difficulty. **5** to linger behind. **6** (often foll. by *on* or *out*) to prolong or be prolonged unnecessarily or tediously: *his talk dragged on for hours.* **7** (when *intr,* usually foll. by *for*) to search (the bed of a river, etc.) with a dragnet or hook. **8** (*tr;* foll. by *out* or *from*) to crush (clods) or level (a soil surface) by use of a drag. **9** (of hounds) to follow (a fox or its trail). **10** (*intr*) *Sl.* to draw (on a cigarette, etc.). **11** *Computing.* to move (a graphics image) from one place to another on the screen using a mouse. **12 drag anchor.** (of a vessel) to move away from its mooring because the anchor has failed to hold. **13 drag one's feet** *or* **heels.** *Inf.* to act with deliberate slowness. ◆ *n* **14** the act of dragging or the state of being dragged. **15** an implement, such as a dragnet, dredge, etc., used for dragging. **16** a type of harrow used to crush clods, level soil, etc. **17** a coach with seats inside and out, usually drawn by four horses. **18** a braking device. **19** a person or thing that slows up progress. **20** slow progress or movement. **21** *Aeronautics.* the resistance to the motion of a body passing through a fluid, esp. through air. **22** the trail of scent left by a fox, etc. **23** an artificial trail of scent drawn over the ground for hounds to follow. **24** See **drag hunt. 25** *Inf.* a person or thing that is very tedious. **26** *Sl.* a car. **27** short for **drag race. 28** *Sl.* **28a** women's clothes worn by a man (esp. in **in drag**). **28b** (*as modifier*): *a drag show.* **28c** clothes collectively. **29** *Inf.* a draw on a cigarette, etc. **30** *US sl.* influence. **31** *Chiefly US sl.* a street (esp. in **main drag**). ◆ See also **drag out of, drag up.** ORIG OE *dragan* to DRAW

dragée (dræ'ʒeɪ) *n* **1** a sweet coated with a hard sugar icing. **2** a tiny beadlike sweet used for decorating cakes, etc. **3** a medicinal pill coated with sugar. ORIG C19: from F; see DREDGE[2]

draggle ('drægᵊl) *vb* **draggles, draggling, draggled. 1** to make or become wet or dirty by trailing on the ground; bedraggle. **2** (*intr*) to lag; dawdle. ORIG ME, prob. frequentative of DRAG

drag hunt *n* **1** a hunt in which hounds follow an artificial trail of scent. **2** a club that organizes such hunts.
▸ **'drag-ˌhunt** *vb*

dragnet ('drægˌnɛt) *n* **1** a net used to scour the bottom of a pond, river, etc., as when searching for something. **2** any system of coordinated efforts to track down wanted persons.

dragoman ('drægəʊmən) *n, pl* **dragomans** *or* **dragomen.** (in some Middle Eastern countries, esp. formerly) a professional interpreter or guide. ORIG C14: from F, from It., from Med. Gk *dragoumanos,* from Ar. *targumān,* ult. from Akkadian

dragon ('drægən) *n* **1** a mythical monster usually represented as breathing fire and having a scaly reptilian body, wings, claws, and a long tail. **2** *Inf.* a fierce person, esp. a woman. **3** any of various very large lizards, esp. the Komodo dragon. **4** *Commerce.* a newly industrialized country, esp. one in SE Asia. **5 chase the dragon.** *Sl.* to smoke opium or heroin. ORIG C13: from OF, from L *dracō,* from Gk *drakōn*

dragonet ('drægənɪt) *n* a small fish with spiny fins, a flat head, and a tapering brighty coloured body. ORIG C14 (meaning: small dragon): from F; applied to fish C18

dragonfly ('drægənˌflaɪ) *n, pl* **dragonflies.** a predatory insect having a long slender body and two pairs of iridescent wings that are outspread at rest.

dragon light *n* an extremely powerful light used by police to dazzle and immobilize criminal suspects.

dragonnade (ˌdrægə'neɪd) *n* **1** *History.* the persecution of French Huguenots during the reign of Louis XIV by dragoons quartered in their villages and homes. **2** subjection by military force. ◆ *vb* **dragonnades, dragonnading, dragonnaded. 3** (*tr*) to subject to persecution by military troops. ORIG C18: from F, from *dragon* DRAGOON

dragoon (drə'guːn) *n* **1** (originally) a mounted infantryman armed with a carbine. **2** (*sometimes cap.*) a domestic fancy pigeon. **3a** a type of cavalryman. **3b** (*pl; cap. when part of a name*): *the Royal Dragoons.* ◆ *vb* (*tr*) **4** to coerce; force. **5** to persecute by military force. ORIG C17: from F *dragon* (special use of DRAGON), soldier armed with a carbine

drag out of *vb* (*tr, adv + prep*) to obtain or extract (a confession, statement, etc.), esp. by force. Also: **drag from.**

drag race *n* a type of motor race in which specially built or modified cars or motorcycles are timed over a measured course.
▸ **drag racing** *n*

dragster ('drægstə) *n* a car specially built or modified for drag racing.

drag up *vb (tr, adv) Inf.* **1** to rear (a child) poorly and in an undisciplined manner. **2** to introduce or revive (an unpleasant fact or story).

drain (dreɪn) *n* **1** a pipe or channel that carries off water, sewage, etc. **2** an instance or cause of continuous diminution in resources or energy; depletion. **3** *Surgery.* a device, such as a tube, to drain off pus, etc. **4 down the drain.** wasted. ◆ *vb* **5** (*tr;* often foll. by *off*) to draw off or remove (liquid) from. **6** (*intr;* often foll. by *away*) to flow (away) or filter (off). **7** (*intr*) to dry or be emptied as a result of liquid running off or flowing away. **8** (*tr*) to drink the entire contents of (a glass, etc.). **9** (*tr*) to consume or make constant demands on (resources, energy, etc.); exhaust. **10** (*intr*) to disappear or leave, esp. gradually. **11** (of a river, etc.) to carry off the surface water from (an area). **12** (*intr*) (of an area) to discharge its surface water into rivers, streams, etc. ORIG OE *drēahnian*
▸ **'drainer** *n*

drainage ('dreɪnɪdʒ) *n* **1** the process or a method of draining. **2** a system of watercourses or drains. **3** liquid, sewage, etc., that is drained away.

drainage basin *or* **area** *n* another name for **catchment area.**

draining board *n* a sloping grooved surface at the side of a sink, used for draining washed dishes, etc. Also called: **drainer.**

drainpipe ('dreɪn,paɪp) *n* a pipe for carrying off rainwater, sewage, etc.; downpipe.

drainpipes ('dreɪn,paɪps) *pl n* trousers with very narrow legs, worn esp. by teddy boys in the 1950s.

drake (dreɪk) *n* the male of any duck. ORIG C13: ?from Low G

Drake ★ (dreɪk) *n* Sir **Francis.** ?1540–96, English buccaneer, who sailed round the world (1577–80). He commanded a fleet against the Spanish Armada (1588).

Drakensberg ★ ('drɑːkənz,bɜːg) *n* a mountain range in southern Africa, extending through Lesotho, E South Africa, and Swaziland. Highest peak: Thabana Ntlenyana, 3482 m (11 425 ft). Sotho name: **Quathlamba.**

Dralon ('dreɪlɒn) *n Trademark.* an acrylic fibre fabric used esp. for upholstery.

dram (dræm) *n* **1** one sixteenth of an ounce (avoirdupois). 1 dram is equivalent to 0.0018 kilogram. **2** *US.* one eighth of an apothecaries' ounce; 60 grains. 1 dram is equivalent to 0.0039 kilogram. **3** a small amount of an alcoholic drink, esp. a spirit; tot. **4** the standard monetary unit of Armenia. ORIG C15: from OF *dragme,* from LL *dragma,* from Gk *drakhmē;* see DRACHMA

DRAM *or* **D-RAM** ('diːræm) *n acronym for* dynamic random access memory: **a** a widely used type of random access memory. See **RAM**[1]. **b** a chip containing such a memory.

drama ('drɑːmə) *n* **1** a work to be performed by actors; play. **2** the genre of literature represented by works intended for the stage. **3** the art of the writing and production of plays. **4** a situation that is highly emotional, tragic, or turbulent. ORIG C17: from LL: a play, from Gk: something performed, from *drān* to do

dramatic (drə'mætɪk) *adj* **1** of drama. **2** like a drama in suddenness, emotional impact, etc. **3** striking; effective. **4** acting or performed in a flamboyant way.
▸ **dra'matically** *adv*

dramatic irony *n Theatre.* the irony occurring when the implications of a situation, speech, etc., are understood by the audience but not by the characters in the play.

dramatics (drə'mætɪks) *n* **1** (*functioning as sing or pl*) **1a** the art of acting or producing plays. **1b** dramatic productions. **2** (*usually functioning as pl*) histrionic behaviour.

dramatis personae ('drɑːmətɪs pə'səʊnaɪ) *pl n* (*often functioning as sing*) the characters in a play. ORIG C18: from NL

dramatist ('dræmətɪst) *n* a playwright.

dramatize *or* **dramatise** ('dræmə,taɪz) *vb* **dramatizes, dramatizing, dramatized** *or* **dramatises, dramatising, dramatised. 1** (*tr*) to put into dramatic form. **2** to express (something) in a dramatic or exaggerated way.
▸ **,dramati'zation** *or* **,dramati'sation** *n*

dramaturge ('dræmə,tɜːdʒ) *n* **1** Also called: **dramaturgist.** a dramatist. **2** Also called: **dramaturg.** a literary adviser on the staff of a theatre, film company, etc. ORIG C19: prob. from F, from Gk *dramatourgos* playwright, from DRAMA + *ergon* work

dramaturgy ('dræmə,tɜːdʒɪ) *n* the art and technique of the theatre; dramatics.
▸ **,drama'turgic** *or* **,drama'turgical** *adj*

drank (dræŋk) *vb* the past tense of **drink.**

drape (dreɪp) *vb* **drapes, draping, draped. 1** (*tr*) to hang or cover with material or fabric, usually in folds. **2** to hang or arrange or be hung or arranged, esp. in folds. **3** (*tr*) to place casually and loosely. ◆ *n* **4** (*often pl*) a cloth or hanging that covers something in folds. **5** the way in which fabric hangs. ORIG C15: from OF *draper,* from *drap* piece of cloth; see DRAB[1]

draper ('dreɪpə) *n* **1** *Brit.* a dealer in fabrics and sewing materials. **2** *Arch.* a maker of cloth.

drapery ('dreɪpərɪ) *n, pl* **draperies. 1** fabric or clothing arranged and draped. **2** (*often pl*) curtains or hangings that drape. **3** *Brit.* the occupation or shop of a draper. **4** fabrics and cloth collectively.
▸ **'draperied** *adj*

drapes (dreɪps) *or* **draperies** ('dreɪpərɪz) *pl n Chiefly US & Canad.* curtains, esp. ones of heavy fabric.

drastic ('dræstɪk) *adj* extreme or forceful; severe. ORIG C17: from Gk *drastikos,* from *drān* to do, act
▸ **'drastically** *adv*

drat (dræt) *interj Sl.* an exclamation of annoyance. ORIG C19: prob. alteration of *God rot*

draught *or US* **draft** (drɑːft) *n* **1** a current of air, esp. in an enclosed space. **2a** the act of pulling a load, as by a vehicle or animal. **2b** (*as modifier*): *a draught horse.* **3** the load or quantity drawn. **4** a portion of liquid to be drunk, esp. a dose of medicine. **5** the act or an instance of drinking; a gulp or swallow. **6** the act or process of drawing air, etc., into the lungs. **7** the amount of air, etc., inhaled. **8a** beer, wine, etc., stored in bulk, esp. in a cask. **8b** (*as modifier*): *draught beer.* **8c on draught.** drawn from a cask or keg. **9** any one of the flat discs used in the game of draughts. US and Canad. equivalent: **checker. 10** the depth of a loaded vessel in the water. **11 feel the draught.** to be short of money. ORIG C14: prob. from ON *drahtr,* of Gmc origin

draughtboard ('drɑːft,bɔːd) *n* a square board divided into 64 squares of alternating colours, used for playing draughts or chess.

draughts (drɑːfts) *n* (*functioning as sing*) a game for two players using a draughtboard and 12 draughtsmen each. US and Canad. name: **checkers.** ORIG C14: pl of DRAUGHT (in obs. sense: a chess move)

draughtsman *or US* **draftsman** ('drɑːftsmən) *n, pl* **draughtsmen** *or US* **draftsmen. 1** a person employed to prepare detailed scale drawings of machinery, buildings, etc. **2** a person skilled in drawing. **3** *Brit.* any of the flat discs used in the game of draughts. US and Canad. equivalent: **checker.**
▸ **'draughtsman,ship** *or US* **'draftsman,ship** *n*

draughty *or US* **drafty** ('drɑːftɪ) *adj* **draughtier, draughtiest** *or US* **draftier, draftiest.** characterized by or exposed to draughts of air.
▸ **'draughtily** *or US* **'draftily** *adv* ▸ **'draughtiness** *or US* **'draftiness** *n*

Dravidian (drə'vɪdɪən) *n* **1** a family of languages spoken in S and central India and Sri Lanka, including Tamil, Malayalam, etc. **2** a member of one of the aboriginal races of India, pushed south by the Indo-Europeans and now mixed with them. ◆ *adj* **3** of or denoting this family of languages or these peoples.

★ people and places

draw (drɔː) *vb* **draws, drawing, drew, drawn.** **1** to cause (a person or thing) to move towards or away by pulling. **2** to bring, take, or pull (something) out, as from a drawer, holster, etc. **3** (*tr*) to extract or pull or take out: *to draw teeth.* **4** (*tr; often foll. by off*) to take (liquid) out of a cask, etc., by means of a tap. **5** (*intr*) to move, esp. in a specified direction: *to draw alongside.* **6** (*tr*) to attract: *to draw attention.* **7** (*tr*) to cause to flow: *to draw blood.* **8** to depict or sketch (a figure, picture, etc.) in lines, as with a pencil or pen. **9** (*tr*) to make, formulate, or derive: *to draw conclusions.* **10** (*tr*) to write (a legal document) in proper form. **11** (*tr; sometimes foll. by in*) to suck or take in (air, etc.). **12** (*intr*) to induce or allow a draught to carry off air, smoke, etc. **13** (*tr*) to take or receive from a source: *to draw money from the bank.* **14** (*tr*) to earn: *draw interest.* **15** (*tr*) to write out (a bill of exchange, etc.). **16** (*tr*) to choose at random. **17** (*tr*) to reduce the diameter of (a wire) by pulling it through a die. **18** (*tr*) to shape (metal or glass) by rolling, by pulling through a die, or by stretching. **19** *Archery.* to bend (a bow) by pulling the string. **20** to steep (tea) or (of tea) to steep in boiling water. **21** (*tr*) to disembowel. **22** (*tr*) to cause (pus, etc.) to discharge from an abscess or wound. **23** (*intr*) (of two teams, etc.) to finish a game with an equal number of points, goals, etc.; tie. **24** (*tr*) *Bridge, whist.* to keep leading a suit in order to force out (all outstanding cards). **25** **draw trumps.** *Bridge, whist.* to play the trump suit until the opponents have none left. **26** (*tr*) *Billiards.* to cause (the cue ball) to spin back after a direct impact with another ball. **27** (*tr*) to search (a place) in order to find wild animals, etc., for hunting. **28** *Golf.* to cause (a golf ball) to move with a controlled right-to-left trajectory or (of a golf ball) to veer gradually from right to left. **29** (*tr*) *Naut.* (of a vessel) to require (a certain depth) in which to float. **30** **draw and quarter.** to disembowel and dismember (a person) after hanging. **31** **draw stumps.** *Cricket.* to close play. **32** **draw the shot.** *Bowls.* to deliver the bowl in such a way that it approaches the jack. ◆ *n* **33** the act of drawing. **34** *US.* a sum of money advanced to finance anticipated expenses. **35** *Inf.* an event, act, etc., that attracts a large audience. **36** a raffle or lottery. **37** something taken at random, as a ticket in a lottery. **38** a contest or game ending in a tie. **39** *US & Canad.* a small natural drainage way or gully. ◆ See also **drawback, draw in,** etc. ORIG OE *dragan*

drawback (ˈdrɔːˌbæk) *n* **1** a disadvantage or hindrance. **2** a refund of customs or excise paid on goods that are being exported or used in making goods for export. ◆ *vb* **draw back.** (*intr, adv; often foll. by from*) **3** to retreat; move backwards. **4** to turn aside from an undertaking.

drawbridge (ˈdrɔːˌbrɪdʒ) *n* a bridge that may be raised to prevent access or to enable vessels to pass.

drawee (drɔːˈiː) *n* the person or organization on which an order for payment is drawn.

drawer (ˈdrɔːə) *n* **1** a person or thing that draws, esp. a draughtsman. **2** a person who draws a cheque. See **draw** (sense 15). **3** a person who draws up a commercial paper. **4** *Arch.* a person who draws beer, etc., in a bar. **5** (drɔː). a boxlike container in a chest, table, etc., made for sliding in and out.

drawers (drɔːz) *pl n* a legged undergarment for either sex, worn below the waist.

draw in *vb* (*intr, adv*) **1** (of hours of daylight) to become shorter. **2** (of a train) to arrive at a station.

drawing (ˈdrɔːɪŋ) *n* **1** a picture or plan made by means of lines on a surface, esp. one made with a pencil or pen. **2** a sketch or outline. **3** the art of making drawings; draughtsmanship.

drawing pin *n Brit.* a short tack with a broad smooth head for fastening papers to a drawing board, etc. US and Canad. name: **thumbtack.**

drawing room *n* **1** a room where visitors are received and entertained; living room; sitting room. **2** *Arch.* a formal reception.

drawknife (ˈdrɔːˌnaɪf) *or* **drawshave** *n, pl* **drawknives** *or* **drawshaves.** a tool with two handles, used to shave wood. US name: **spokeshave.**

drawl (drɔːl) *vb* **1** to speak or utter (words) slowly, esp. prolonging the vowel sounds. ◆ *n* **2** the way of speech of someone who drawls. ORIG C16: prob. frequentative of DRAW
▸ ˈ**drawling** *adj*

drawn (drɔːn) *vb* **1** the past participle of **draw.** ◆ *adj* **2** haggard, tired, or tense in appearance.

drawn work *n* ornamental needlework done by drawing threads out of the fabric and using the remaining threads to form lacelike patterns. Also called: **drawn-thread work.**

draw off *vb* (*adv*) **1** (*tr*) to cause (a liquid) to flow from something. **2** to withdraw (troops).

draw on *vb* **1** (*intr, prep*) to use or exploit (a source, fund, etc.). **2** (*intr, adv*) to come near. **3** (*tr, prep*) to withdraw (money) from (an account). **4** (*tr, adv*) to put on (clothes). **5** (*tr, adv*) to lead further; entice.

draw out *vb* (*adv*) **1** to extend. **2** (*tr*) to cause (a person) to talk freely. **3** (*tr;* foll. by *of*) Also: **draw from.** to elicit (information) (from). **4** (*tr*) to withdraw (money) as from a bank account. **5** (*intr*) (of hours of daylight) to become longer. **6** (*intr*) (of a train) to leave a station. **7** (*tr*) to extend (troops) in line. **8** (*intr*) (of troops) to proceed from camp.

drawstring (ˈdrɔːˌstrɪŋ) *n* a cord, etc., run through a hem around an opening, so that when it is pulled tighter, the opening closes.

draw up *vb* (*adv*) **1** to come or cause to come to a halt. **2** (*tr*) **2a** to prepare a draft of (a document, etc.). **2b** to formulate and write out: *to draw up a contract.* **3** (*used reflexively*) to straighten oneself. **4** to form or arrange (a body of soldiers, etc.) in order or formation.

dray[1] (dreɪ) *n* **a** a low cart used for carrying heavy loads. **b** (*in combination*): *a drayman.* ORIG OE *dræge* dragnet

dray[2] (dreɪ) *n* a variant spelling of **drey.**

Drayton ★ (ˈdreɪtᵊn) *n* **Michael.** 1563–1631, English poet. His work includes odes and pastorals, and *Poly-Olbion* (1613–22), on the topography of England.

dread (drɛd) *vb* (*tr*) **1** to anticipate with apprehension or terror. **2** to fear greatly. **3** *Arch.* to be in awe of. ◆ *n* **4** great fear. **5** an object of terror. **6** *Sl.* a Rastafarian. **7** *Arch.* deep reverence. ORIG OE *ondrǣdan*

dreadful (ˈdrɛdfʊl) *adj* **1** extremely disagreeable, shocking, or bad. **2** (intensifier): *a dreadful waste of time.* **3** causing dread; terrifying. **4** *Arch.* inspiring awe.

dreadfully (ˈdrɛdfʊlɪ) *adv* **1** in a shocking or disagreeable manner. **2** (intensifier): *you're dreadfully kind.*

dreadlocks (ˈdrɛdˌlɒks) *pl n Inf.* hair worn in the Rastafarian style of long tightly-curled strands.

dreadnought (ˈdrɛdˌnɔːt) *n* **1** a battleship armed with heavy guns of uniform calibre. **2** an overcoat made of heavy cloth.

dream (driːm) *n* **1a** mental activity, usually an imagined series of events, occurring during sleep. **1b** (*as modifier*): *a dream sequence.* **1c** (*in combination*): *dreamland.* **2a** a sequence of imaginative thoughts indulged in while awake; daydream; fantasy. **2b** (*as modifier*): *a dream world.* **3** a person or thing seen or occurring in a dream. **4** a cherished hope; aspiration. **5** a vain hope. **6** a person or thing that is as pleasant or seemingly unreal as a dream. **7** **go like a dream.** to move, develop, or work very well. ◆ *vb* **dreams, dreaming, dreamed** *or* **dreamt. 8** (*may take a clause as object*) to undergo or experience (a dream or dreams). **9** (*intr*) to indulge in daydreams. **10** (*intr*) to suffer delusions; be unrealistic. **11** (when *intr,* foll. by *of* or *about*) to have an image (of) or fantasy (about) in or as if in a dream. **12** (*intr;* foll. by *of*) to consider the possibility (of). ◆ *adj* **13** too good to be true; ideal: *dream kitchen.* ORIG OE *drēam* song
▸ ˈ**dreamer** *n*

dreamboat (ˈdriːmˌbəʊt) *n Sl.* an ideal or desirable person, esp. one of the opposite sex.

dreamt (drɛmt) *vb* a past tense and past participle of **dream.**

dream team *n Inf.* a group of people regarded as having the perfect combination of talents.

dream ticket *n* a combination of two people, usually candidates in an election, that is considered to be ideal.

Dreamtime (ˈdriːmˌtaɪm) *n* **1** Also called: **alcheringa.** (in the mythology of Australian Aboriginal peoples) a mythical golden age of the past, when the first men were created. **2** *Austral. inf.* any remote period, out of touch with the realities of the present.

dream up *vb (tr, adv)* to invent by ingenuity and imagination: *to dream up an excuse.*

dreamy ('dri:mɪ) *adj* **dreamier, dreamiest. 1** vague or impractical. **2** resembling a dream. **3** relaxing; gentle. **4** *Inf.* wonderful. **5** having dreams, esp. daydreams.
▸ **'dreamily** *adv* ▸ **'dreaminess** *n*

dreary ('drɪərɪ) *adj* **drearier, dreariest. 1** sad or dull. **2** wearying; boring. ◆ Also (literary): **drear.** ORIG OE *drēorig* gory
▸ **'drearily** *adv* ▸ **'dreariness** *n*

dredge[1] (drɛdʒ) *n* **1** a machine used to scoop or suck up material from a riverbed, channel, etc. **2** another name for **dredger.** ◆ *vb* **dredges, dredging, dredged. 3** to remove (material) from a riverbed, etc., by means of a dredge. **4** *(tr)* to search for (a submerged object) with or as if with a dredge; drag. ORIG C16: ? ult. from OE *dragan* to DRAW

dredge[2] (drɛdʒ) *vb* **dredges, dredging, dredged.** to sprinkle or coat (food) with flour, etc. ORIG C16: from OF *dragie,* ?from L *tragēmata* spices, from Gk
▸ **'dredger** *n*

dredger ('drɛdʒə) *n* **1** a vessel used for dredging. **2** another name for **dredge**[1] (sense 1).

dredge up *vb (tr, adv)* **1** *Inf.* to bring to notice, esp. with effort and from an obscure source. **2** to raise, as with a dredge.

dree (dri:) *Scot., literary.* ◆ *vb* **drees, dreeing, dreed. 1** *(tr)* to endure. ◆ *adj* **2** dreary. ORIG OE *drēogan*

D region *or* **layer** *n* the lowest region of the ionosphere, extending from a height of about 60 km to about 90 km.

dregs (drɛgz) *pl n* **1** solid particles that settle at the bottom of some liquids. **2** residue or remains. **3 the dregs.** *Brit. sl.* a despicable person or people. ORIG C14 *dreg,* from ON *dregg*

dreich *or* **dreigh** (dri:x) *adj Scot. dialect.* dreary. ORIG ME *dreig, drih* enduring, from OE *drēog* (unattested)

drench (drɛntʃ) *vb (tr)* **1** to make completely wet; soak. **2** to give liquid medicine to (an animal). ◆ *n* **3** a drenching. **4** a dose of liquid medicine given to an animal. ORIG OE *drencan* to cause to drink
▸ **'drenching** *n, adj*

Drenthe ★ (*Dutch* 'drɛntə) *n* a province of the NE Netherlands: a low plateau, with many raised bogs, partially reclaimed; agricultural, with oil deposits. Capital: Assen. Pop.: 460 800 (1997 est.). Area: 2647 sq. km (1032 sq. miles).

Dresden ★ ('drɛzdᵊn) *n* **1** an industrial city in SE Germany, on the River Elbe: capital of Saxony from the 16th century until 1952 and from 1990; it was severely damaged in the Seven Years' War (1760); the baroque city was almost totally destroyed in World War II by Allied bombing (1945). Pop.: 469 110 (1996 est.). ◆ *adj* **2** relating to, designating, or made of Dresden china.

Dresden china *n* porcelain ware, esp. delicate and elegantly decorative objects and figures of high quality, made at Meissen, near Dresden, since 1710.

dress (drɛs) *vb* **1** to put clothes on; attire. **2** *(intr)* to put on more formal attire. **3** *(tr)* to provide (someone) with clothing; clothe. **4** *(tr)* to arrange merchandise in (a shop window). **5** *(tr)* to arrange (the hair). **6** *(tr)* to apply protective or therapeutic covering to (a wound, sore, etc.). **7** *(tr)* to prepare (food, esp. fowl and fish) by cleaning, gutting, etc. **8** *(tr)* to put a finish on (stone, metal, etc.). **9** *(tr)* to cultivate (land), esp. by applying fertilizer. **10** *(tr)* to trim (trees, etc.). **11** *(tr)* to groom (a horse). **12** *(tr)* to convert (tanned hides) into leather. **13** *Angling.* to tie (a fly). **14** *Mil.* to bring (troops) into line or (of troops) to come into line (esp. in **dress ranks**). **15 dress ship.** *Naut.* to decorate a vessel by displaying signal flags on lines. ◆ *n* **16** a one-piece garment for a woman, consisting of a skirt and bodice. **17** complete style of clothing; costume: *military dress.* **18** *(modifier)* suitable for a formal occasion: *a dress shirt.* **19** outer covering or appearance. ◆ See also **dress down, dress up.** ORIG C14: from OF *drecier,* ult. from L *dīrigere* to DIRECT

dressage ('drɛsɑ:ʒ) *n* **a** the training of a horse to perform manoeuvres in response to the rider's body signals. **b** the manoeuvres performed. ORIG F: preparation, from OF *dresser* to prepare; see DRESS

dress circle *n* a tier of seats in a theatre or other auditorium, usually the first gallery, in which evening dress formerly had to be worn.

dress code *n* a set of rules or guidelines regarding the manner of dress acceptable in an office, restaurant, etc.

dress down *vb (adv)* **1** *(tr) Inf.* to reprimand severely or scold (a person). **2** *(intr)* to dress in casual clothes.

dresser[1] ('drɛsə) *n* **1** a set of shelves, usually also with cupboards, for storing or displaying dishes, etc. **2** *US.* a chest of drawers for storing clothing, often having a mirror on top. ORIG C14 *dressour,* from OF *dreceore,* from *drecier* to arrange; see DRESS

dresser[2] ('drɛsə) *n* **1** a person who dresses in a specified way: *a fashionable dresser.* **2** *Theatre.* a person employed to assist actors with their costumes. **3** a tool used for dressing stone, etc. **4** *Brit.* a person who assists a surgeon during operations. **5** *Brit.* See **window-dresser.**

dressing ('drɛsɪŋ) *n* **1** a sauce for food, esp. for salad. **2** the US and Canad. name for **stuffing** (sense 2). **3** a covering for a wound, etc. **4** fertilizer spread on land. **5** size used for stiffening textiles. **6** the processes in the conversion of hides into leather.

dressing-down *n Inf.* a severe scolding.

dressing gown *n* a full robe worn before dressing or for lounging.

dressing room *n* **1** *Theatre.* a room backstage for an actor to change clothing and to make up. **2** any room used for changing clothes.

dressing station *n Mil.* a first-aid post close to a combat area.

dressing table *n* a piece of bedroom furniture with a mirror and a set of drawers for clothes, cosmetics, etc.

dressmaker ('drɛsˌmeɪkə) *n* a person whose occupation is making clothes, esp. for women.
▸ **'dressˌmaking** *n*

dress parade *n Mil.* a formal parade in dress uniform.

dress rehearsal *n* **1** the last rehearsal of a play, etc., using costumes, lighting, etc., as for the first night. **2** any full-scale practice.

dress shirt *n* a man's evening shirt, worn as part of formal evening dress.

dress suit *n* a man's evening suit, esp. tails.

dress uniform *n Mil.* formal ceremonial uniform.

dress up *vb (adv)* **1** to attire (oneself or another) very smartly or elaborately. **2** to put fancy dress, etc., on. **3** *(tr)* to improve the appearance or impression of: *to dress up the facts.*

dressy ('drɛsɪ) *adj* **dressier, dressiest. 1** (of clothes) elegant. **2** (of persons) dressing stylishly. **3** overelegant.
▸ **'dressiness** *n*

drew (dru:) *vb* the past tense of **draw.**

drey *or* **dray** (dreɪ) *n* a squirrel's nest. ORIG C17: from ?

Dreyfus ★ ('dreɪfəs; *French* drɛfys) *n* **Alfred** (alfrɛd). 1859–1935, French army officer, a Jew whose false imprisonment for treason (1894) raised issues of anti-semitism and militarism that dominated French politics until his release (1906).

dribble ('drɪbᵊl) *vb* **dribbles, dribbling, dribbled. 1** *(usually intr)* to flow or allow to flow in a thin stream or drops; trickle. **2** *(intr)* to allow saliva to trickle from the mouth. **3** (in soccer, basketball, hockey, etc.) to propel (the ball) by repeatedly tapping it with the hand, foot, or a stick. ◆ *n* **4** a small quantity of liquid falling in drops or flowing in a thin stream. **5** a small quantity or supply. **6** an act or instance of dribbling. ORIG C16: frequentative of *drib,* var. of DRIP
▸ **'dribbler** *n* ▸ **'dribbly** *adj*

driblet *or* **dribblet** ('drɪblɪt) *n* a small amount. ORIG C17: from obs. *drib* to fall bit by bit + -LET

dribs and drabs (drɪbz) *pl n Inf.* small sporadic amounts.

dried (draɪd) *vb* the past tense and past participle of **dry.**

drier[1] ('draɪə) *adj* a comparative of **dry.**

drier[2] ('draɪə) *n* a variant spelling of **dryer**[1].

driest ('draɪɪst) *adj* a superlative of **dry**.

drift (drɪft) *vb* (*mainly intr*) **1** (*also tr*) to be carried along as by currents of air or water or (of a current) to carry (a vessel, etc.) along. **2** to move aimlessly from one place or activity to another. **3** to wander away from a fixed course or point; stray. **4** (*also tr*) (of snow, etc.) to accumulate in heaps or to drive (snow, etc.) into heaps. ◆ *n* **5** something piled up by the wind or current, as a snowdrift. **6** tendency or meaning: *the drift of the argument.* **7** a state of indecision or inaction. **8** the extent to which a vessel, aircraft, etc., is driven off course by winds, etc. **9** a general tendency of surface ocean water to flow in the direction of the prevailing winds. **10** a driving movement, force, or influence; impulse. **11** a controlled four-wheel skid used to take bends at high speed. **12** a deposit of sand, gravel, etc., esp. one transported and deposited by a glacier. **13** a horizontal passage in a mine that follows the mineral vein. **14** something, esp. a group of animals, driven along. **15** a steel tool driven into holes to enlarge or align them. **16** an uncontrolled slow change in some operating characteristic of a piece of equipment. **17** *S. African.* a ford. ORIG C13: from ON: snowdrift

driftage ('drɪftɪdʒ) *n* **1** the act of drifting. **2** matter carried along by drifting. **3** the amount by which an aircraft or vessel has drifted.

drifter ('drɪftə) *n* **1** a person or thing that drifts. **2** a person who moves aimlessly from place to place. **3** a boat used for drift-net fishing.

drift ice *n* masses of ice floating in the sea.

drift net *n* a large fishing net that is allowed to drift with the tide or current.

driftwood ('drɪft,wʊd) *n* wood floating on or washed ashore by the sea or other body of water.

drill[1] (drɪl) *n* **1** a machine or tool for boring holes. **2** *Mil.* **2a** training in procedures or movements, as for parades or the use of weapons. **2b** (*as modifier*): *drill hall.* **3** strict and often repetitious training or exercises used in teaching. **4** *Inf.* correct procedure. **5** a marine mollusc that preys on oysters. ◆ *vb* **6** to pierce, bore, or cut (a hole) in (material) with or as if with a drill. **7** to instruct or be instructed in military procedures or movements. **8** (*tr*) to teach by rigorous exercises or training. **9** (*tr*) *Inf.* to riddle with bullets. ORIG C17: from MDu. *drillen*
▸ **'driller** *n*

drill[2] (drɪl) *n* **1** a machine for planting seeds in rows. **2** a furrow in which seeds are sown. **3** a row of seeds planted by means of a drill. ◆ *vb* **4** to plant (seeds) by means of a drill. ORIG C18: from ?; cf. G *Rille* furrow
▸ **'driller** *n*

drill[3] (drɪl) *n* a hard-wearing twill-weave cotton cloth, used for uniforms, etc. ORIG C18: var. of G *Drillich*, from L *trilīx*, from TRI- + *līcium* thread

drill[4] (drɪl) *n* an Old World monkey of W Africa, related to the mandrill. ORIG C17: from a West African word

drilling fluid *n* a fluid, usually consisting of a suspension of clay in water, pumped down when an oil well is being drilled. Also called: **mud**.

drilling platform *n* a structure, either fixed to the sea bed or mobile, which supports the drilling rig, stores, etc., required for drilling an offshore oil well.

drilling rig *n* **1** the complete machinery, equipment, and structures needed to drill an oil well. **2** a mobile drilling platform used for exploratory offshore drilling.

drillmaster ('drɪl,mɑːstə) *n* **1** Also called: **drill sergeant**. a military drill instructor. **2** a person who instructs in a strict manner.

drill press *n* a machine tool for boring holes.

drily *or* **dryly** ('draɪlɪ) *adv* in a dry manner.

drink (drɪŋk) *vb* **drinks, drinking, drank, drunk. 1** to swallow (a liquid). **2** (*tr*) to soak up (liquid); absorb. **3** (*tr; usually* foll. by *in*) to pay close attention to. **4** (*tr*) to bring (oneself) into a certain condition by consuming alcohol. **5** (*tr;* often foll. by *away*) to dispose of or ruin by excessive expenditure on alcohol. **6** (*intr*) to consume alcohol, esp. to excess. **7** (when *intr*, foll. by *to*) to drink (a toast). **8** **drink the health of.** to salute or celebrate with a toast. **9** **drink with the flies.** *Austral. inf.* to drink alone. ◆ *n* **10** liquid suitable for drinking. **11** alcohol or its habitual or excessive consumption. **12** a portion of liquid for drinking; draught. **13** **the drink.** *Inf.* the sea. ORIG OE *drincan*
▸ **'drinkable** *adj* ▸ **'drinker** *n*

drink-driving *n* (*modifier*) of or relating to driving a car after drinking alcohol: *drink-driving offences.*

drinking fountain *n* a device for providing a flow or jet of drinking water, esp. in public places.

drinking-up time *n* (in Britain) a short time for finishing drinks after last orders in a public house.

drinking water *n* water reserved or suitable for drinking.

Drinkwater ★ ('drɪŋk,wɔːtə) *n* **John.** 1882–1937, British writer; author of such plays as *Abraham Lincoln* (1918).

drip (drɪp) *vb* **drips, dripping, dripped. 1** to fall or let fall in drops. ◆ *n* **2** the formation and falling of drops of liquid. **3** the sound made by falling drops. **4** a projection at the edge of a sill or cornice designed to throw water clear of the wall. **5** *Inf.* an inane, insipid person. **6** *Med.* **6a** the apparatus used for the intravenous drop-by-drop administration of a solution. **6b** the solution so administered. ORIG OE *dryppan*, from *dropa* DROP

drip-dry *adj* **1** designating clothing or a fabric that will dry relatively free of creases if hung up when wet. ◆ *vb* **drip-dries, drip-drying, drip-dried. 2** to dry or become dry thus.

drip-feed *vb* **drip-feeds, drip-feeding, drip-fed.** (*tr*) **1** to feed (someone) a liquid drop by drop, esp. intravenously. **2** *Inf.* to fund (a new company) in stages rather than by injecting a large sum at its inception. ◆ *n* **drip feed. 3** another term for **drip** (sense 6).

dripping ('drɪpɪŋ) *n* **1** the fat exuded by roasting meat. **2** (*often pl*) liquid that falls in drops. ◆ *adv* **3** (intensifier): *dripping wet.*

drippy ('drɪpɪ) *adj* **drippier, drippiest. 1** *Inf.* mawkish, insipid, or inane. **2** tending to drip.

drive (draɪv) *vb* **drives, driving, drove, driven. 1** to push, propel, or be pushed or propelled. **2** to guide the movement of (a vehicle, animal, etc.). **3** (*tr*) to compel or urge to work or act, esp. excessively. **4** (*tr*) to goad into a specified attitude or state: *work drove him mad.* **5** (*tr*) to cause (an object) to make (a hole, crack, etc.). **6** to move rapidly by striking or throwing with force. **7** *Sport.* to hit (a ball) very hard and straight. **8** *Golf.* to strike (the ball) with a driver. **9** (*tr*) to chase (game) from cover. **10** to transport or be transported in a vehicle. **11** (*intr*) to rush or dash violently, esp. against an obstacle. **12** (*tr*) to transact with vigour (esp. in **drive a hard bargain**). **13** (*tr*) to force (a component) into or out of its location by means of blows or a press. **14** (*tr*) *Mining.* to excavate horizontally. **15** **drive home. 15a** to cause to penetrate to the fullest extent. **15b** to make clear by special emphasis. ◆ *n* **16** the act of driving. **17** a journey in a driven vehicle. **18** a road for vehicles, esp. a private road leading to a house. **19** vigorous pressure, as in business. **20** a united effort, esp. towards a common goal. **21** *Brit.* a large gathering of persons to play cards, etc. **22** energy, ambition, or initiative. **23** *Psychol.* a motive or interest, such as sex or ambition. **24** a sustained and powerful military offensive. **25a** the means by which force, motion, etc., is transmitted in a mechanism. **25b** (*as modifier*): *a drive shaft.* **26** *Sport.* a hard straight shot or stroke. **27** a search for and chasing of game towards waiting guns. **28** *Electronics.* the signal applied to the input of an amplifier. ORIG OE *drīfan*
▸ **'drivable** *or* **'driveable** *adj*

drive at *vb* (*intr, prep*) *Inf.* to intend or mean: *what are you driving at?*

drive-by shooting *n* an incident in which a person, building, or vehicle is shot at by someone in a moving vehicle. Sometimes shortened to **drive-by**.

drive-in *adj* **1** denoting a public facility or service designed to be used by patrons seated in their cars: *a drive-in bank.* ◆ *n* **2** *Chiefly US & Canad.* a cinema designed to be used in such a manner.

drivel ('drɪvᵊl) *vb* **drivels, drivelling, drivelled** *or US* **drivels, driveling, driveled. 1** to allow (saliva) to flow from the mouth; dribble. **2** (*intr*) to speak foolishly. ◆ *n* **3** foolish

or senseless talk. **4** saliva flowing from the mouth; slaver. ORIG OE *dreflian* to slaver
▸ **'driveller** *or US* **'driveler** *n*

driven ('drɪvᵊn) *vb* the past participle of **drive.**

driver ('draɪvə) *n* **1** a person who drives a vehicle. **2** **in the driver's seat.** in a position of control. **3** a person who drives animals. **4** a mechanical component that exerts a force on another to produce motion. **5** *Golf.* a club, a No. 1 wood, used for tee shots. **6** *Electronics.* a circuit whose output provides the input of another circuit. **7** *Computing.* a computer program that controls a device.
▸ **'driverless** *adj*

drive-thru *n* **a** a takeaway restaurant, bank, etc., designed so that customers can use it without leaving their cars. **b** (*as modifier*): *a drive-thru restaurant.*

drive-time *n* **a** the time of day when many people are driving to or from work, considered as a broadcasting slot. **b** (*as modifier*): *the daily drive-time show.*

driveway ('draɪvˌweɪ) *n* a path for vehicles, often connecting a house with a public road.

driving chain *n Engineering.* a roller chain that transmits power from one toothed wheel to another. Also called: **drive chain.**

driving licence *n* an official document authorizing a person to drive a motor vehicle.

drizzle ('drɪzᵊl) *n* **1** very light rain. ◆ *vb* **drizzles, drizzling, drizzled. 2** (*intr*) to rain lightly. ORIG OE *drēosan* to fall
▸ **'drizzly** *adj*

Drogheda ★ ('drɔɪɪdə) *n* a port in NE Republic of Ireland, in Co. Louth near the mouth of the River Boyne: captured by Cromwell in 1649 and its inhabitants massacred. Pop.: 23 800 (1991).

drogue (drəʊg) *n* **1** any funnel-like device used as a sea anchor. **2a** a small parachute released behind an aircraft to reduce its landing speed. **2b** a small parachute released during the landing of a spacecraft. **3** a device towed behind an aircraft as a target for firing practice. **4** a device on the end of the hose of a tanker aircraft, to assist location of the probe of the receiving aircraft. **5** a windsock. ORIG C18: prob. based ult. on OE *dragan* to DRAW

droll (drəʊl) *adj* amusing in a quaint or odd manner; comical. ORIG C17: from F *drôle* scamp, from MDu.: imp
▸ **'drollness** *n* ▸ **'drolly** *adv*

drollery ('drəʊlərɪ) *n, pl* **drolleries. 1** humour; comedy. **2** *Rare.* a droll act, story, or remark.

Drôme ★ (*French* drom) *n* a department of SE France, in Rhône-Alpes region. Capital: Valence. Pop.: 425 476 (1994 est.). Area: 6561 sq. km (2559 sq. miles).

-drome *n combining form.* **1** a course or race-course: *hippodrome.* **2** a large place for a special purpose: *aerodrome.* ORIG via L from Gk *dromos* race, course

dromedary ('drʌmədərɪ) *n, pl* **dromedaries.** a type of Arabian camel bred for racing and riding, having a single hump. ORIG C14: from LL *dromedārius* (*camēlus*), from Gk *dromas* running

-dromous *adj combining form.* moving or running: *anadromous; catadromous.* ORIG via NL from Gk *-dromos,* from *dromos* a running

drone[1] (drəʊn) *n* **1** a male honeybee whose sole function is to mate with the queen. **2** a person who lives off the work of others. **3** a pilotless radio-controlled aircraft. ORIG OE *drān;* see DRONE[2]

drone[2] (drəʊn) *vb* **drones, droning, droned. 1** (*intr*) to make a monotonous low dull sound. **2** (when *intr,* often foll. by *on*) to utter (words) in a monotonous tone, esp. to talk without stopping. ◆ *n* **3** a monotonous low dull sound. **4** *Music.* a sustained bass note or chord. **5** one of the single-reed pipes in a set of bagpipes. **6** a person who speaks in a low monotonous tone. ORIG C16: rel. to DRONE[1] & MDu. *drōnen,* G *dröhnen*
▸ **'droning** *adj*

drongo ('drɒŋgəʊ) *n, pl* **drongos. 1** any of various songbirds of the Old World tropics, having a glossy black plumage. **2** *Austral. & NZ sl.* a slow-witted person. ORIG C19: from Malagasy

drool (dru:l) *vb* **1** (*intr;* often foll. by *over*) to show excessive enthusiasm (for) or pleasure (in); gloat (over). ◆ *vb, n* **2** another word for **drivel** (senses 1, 2, 4). ORIG C19: prob. alteration of DRIVEL

droop (dru:p) *vb* **1** to sag or allow to sag, as from weakness. **2** (*intr*) to be overcome by weariness. **3** (*intr*) to lose courage. ◆ *n* **4** the act or state of drooping. ORIG C13: from ON *drūpa*
▸ **'drooping** *adj* ▸ **'droopy** *adj*

drop (drɒp) *n* **1** a small quantity of liquid that forms or falls in a spherical mass. **2** a very small quantity of liquid. **3** a very small quantity of anything. **4** something resembling a drop in shape or size. **5** the act or an instance of falling; descent. **6** a decrease in amount or value. **7** the vertical distance that anything may fall. **8** a steep incline or slope. **9** short for **fruit drop. 10** the act of unloading troops, etc., by parachute. **11** (in cable television) a short spur from a trunk cable that feeds signals to an individual house. **12** *Theatre.* See **drop curtain. 13** another word for **trap door** or **gallows. 14** *Chiefly US & Canad.* a slot through which an object can be dropped into a receptacle. **15** *Austral. cricket sl.* a fall of the wicket. **16** See **drop shot. 17** **at the drop of a hat.** without hesitation or delay. **18** **have the drop on** (**someone**). *US & NZ.* to have the advantage over (someone). ◆ *vb* **drops, dropping, dropped. 19** (of liquids) to fall or allow to fall in globules. **20** to fall or allow to fall vertically. **21** (*tr*) to allow to fall by letting go of. **22** to sink or fall or cause to sink to the ground, as from a blow, weariness, etc. **23** (*intr;* foll. by *back, behind,* etc.) to move in a specified manner, direction, etc. **24** (*intr;* foll. by *in, by,* etc.) *Inf.* to pay a casual visit (to). **25** to decrease in amount or value. **26** to sink or cause to sink to a lower position. **27** to make or become less in strength, volume, etc. **28** (*intr*) to decline in health or condition. **29** (*intr; sometimes foll. by into*) to pass easily into a condition: *to drop into a habit.* **30** (*intr*) to move gently as with a current of air. **31** (*tr*) to mention casually: *to drop a hint.* **32** (*tr*) to leave out (a word or letter). **33** (*tr*) to set down (passengers or goods). **34** (*tr*) to send or post: *drop me a line.* **35** (*tr*) to discontinue: *let's drop the matter.* **36** (*tr*) to cease to associate with. **37** (*tr*) *Sl., chiefly US.* to cease to employ. **38** (*tr; sometimes foll. by in, off,* etc.) *Inf.* to leave or deposit. **39** (of animals) to give birth to (offspring). **40** *Sl., chiefly US & Canad.* to lose (money). **41** (*tr*) to lengthen (a hem, etc.). **42** (*tr*) to unload (troops, etc.) by parachute. **43** (*tr*) *Naut.* to sail out of sight of. **44** (*tr*) *Sport.* to omit (a player) from a team. **45** (*tr*) to lose (a game, etc.). **46** (*tr*) *Golf, basketball, etc.* to hit or throw (a ball) into a goal. **47** (*tr*) to hit (a ball) with a drop shot. ◆ *n, vb* **48** *Rugby.* short for **drop kick** or **drop-kick.** ◆ See also **drop off, dropout, drops.** ORIG OE *dropian*

drop curtain *n Theatre.* a curtain that can be raised and lowered onto the stage.

drop-dead *adv Sl.* outstandingly or exceptionally: *drop-dead gorgeous.*

drop forge *n* a device for forging metal between two dies, one of which is fixed, the other acting by gravity or by pressure.
▸ **'drop-ˌforge** *vb* (*tr*)

drop goal *n Rugby.* a goal scored with a drop kick during the run of play.

drop hammer *n* another name for **drop forge.**

drop-in centre *n* (in Britain) a daycentre run by the social services or a charity that clients may attend on an informal basis.

drop kick *n* **1** a kick in which the ball is dropped and kicked as it bounces from the ground. **2** a wrestling attack in which a wrestler leaps in the air and kicks his opponent. ◆ *vb* **drop-kick. 3** to kick (a ball, a wrestling opponent, etc.) by the use of a drop kick.

drop leaf *n* **a** a hinged flap on a table that can be raised to extend the surface. **b** (*as modifier*): *a drop-leaf table.*

droplet ('drɒplɪt) *n* a tiny drop.

drop lock *n Finance.* a variable-rate bank loan that is automatically replaced by a fixed-rate long-term bond if the long-term interest rates fall to a specified level.

drop off *vb* (*adv*) **1** (*intr*) to grow smaller or less. **2** (*tr*) to set down. **3** (*intr*) *Inf.* to fall asleep. ◆ *n* **drop-off. 4** a steep descent. **5** a sharp decrease.

dropout ('drɒpˌaʊt) *n* **1** a student who fails to complete a course. **2** a person who rejects conventional society. **3** **drop-out.** *Rugby.* a drop kick taken to restart play. ◆ *vb* **drop out.** (*intr, adv;* often foll. by *of*) **4** to abandon or withdraw from (a school, job, etc.).

dropper ('drɒpə) *n* **1** a small tube having a rubber bulb at one end for dispensing drops of liquid. **2** a person or thing that drops.

droppings ('drɒpɪŋz) *pl n* the dung of certain animals, such as rabbits, sheep, and birds.

drops (drɒps) *pl n* any liquid medication applied by means of a dropper.

drop scone *n* a flat spongy cake made by dropping a spoonful of batter on a hot griddle.

drop shot *n* **a** *Tennis.* a softly played return that drops abruptly after clearing the net. **b** *Squash.* a shot that stops abruptly after hitting the front wall of the court.

dropsy ('drɒpsɪ) *n* **1** *Pathol.* a condition characterized by an accumulation of watery fluid in the tissues or in a body cavity. **2** *Sl.* a tip or bribe. ORIG C13: from *ydropesie,* from L *hydrōpisis,* from Gk *hudrōps,* from *hudōr* water
▸ **dropsical** ('drɒpsɪkᵊl) *adj*

droshky ('drɒʃkɪ) *or* **drosky** ('drɒskɪ) *n, pl* **droshkies** *or* **droskies.** an open four-wheeled carriage, formerly used in Russia. ORIG C19: from Russian, dim. of *drogi* wagon

drosophila (drɒ'sɒfɪlə) *n, pl* **drosophilas** *or* **drosophilae** (-ˌliː). any of a genus of small flies that are widely used in laboratory genetics studies. Also called: **fruit fly.** ORIG C19: NL, from Gk *drosos* dew + *-phila* -PHILE

dross (drɒs) *n* **1** the scum formed on the surfaces of molten metals. **2** worthless matter; waste. ORIG OE *drōs* dregs
▸ **'drossy** *adj* ▸ **'drossiness** *n*

drought (draʊt) *n* **1** a prolonged period of scanty rainfall. **2** a prolonged shortage. ORIG OE *drūgoth*
▸ **'droughty** *adj*

drove[1] (drəʊv) *vb* the past tense of **drive.**

drove[2] (drəʊv) *n* **1** a herd of livestock being driven together. **2** (*often pl*) a moving crowd of people. ◆ *vb* **droves, droving, droved.** (*tr*) **3** to drive (livestock), usually for a considerable distance. ORIG OE *drāf* herd

drover ('drəʊvə) *n* a person who drives sheep or cattle, esp. to and from market.

drown (draʊn) *vb* **1** to die or kill by immersion in liquid. **2** (*tr*) to get rid of: *he drowned his sorrows in drink.* **3** (*tr*) to drench thoroughly. **4** (*tr;* sometimes foll. by *out*) to render (a sound) inaudible by making a loud noise. ORIG C13: prob. from OE *druncnian*

drowse (draʊz) *vb* **drowses, drowsing, drowsed. 1** to be or cause to be sleepy, dull, or sluggish. ◆ *n* **2** the state of being drowsy. ORIG C16: prob. from OE *drūsian* to sink

drowsy ('draʊzɪ) *adj* **drowsier, drowsiest. 1** heavy with sleepiness; sleepy. **2** inducing sleep; soporific. **3** sluggish or lethargic; dull.
▸ **'drowsily** *adv* ▸ **'drowsiness** *n*

drub (drʌb) *vb* **drubs, drubbing, drubbed.** (*tr*) **1** to beat as with a stick. **2** to defeat utterly, as in a contest. **3** to drum or stamp (the feet). **4** to instil with force or repetition. ◆ *n* **5** a blow, as from a stick. ORIG C17: prob. from Ar. *dáraba* to beat

drubbing ('drʌbɪŋ) *n* **1** a beating. **2** a total defeat.

drudge (drʌdʒ) *n* **1** a person who works hard at wearisome menial tasks. ◆ *vb* **drudges, drudging, drudged. 2** (*intr*) to toil at such tasks. ORIG C16: ?from *druggen* to toil
▸ **'drudger** *n* ▸ **'drudgingly** *adv*

drudgery ('drʌdʒərɪ) *n, pl* **drudgeries.** hard, menial, and monotonous work.

drug (drʌg) *n* **1** any substance used in the treatment, prevention, or diagnosis of disease. Related adj: **pharmaceutical. 2** a chemical substance, esp. a narcotic, taken for the effects it produces. **3 drug on the market.** a commodity available in excess of demand. ◆ *vb* **drugs, drugging, drugged.** (*tr*) **4** to mix a drug with (food, etc.). **5** to administer a drug to. **6** to stupefy or poison with or as if with a drug. ORIG C14: from OF *drogue,* prob. of Gmc origin

drug addict *n* any person who is abnormally dependent on narcotic drugs.

drugget ('drʌgɪt) *n* a coarse fabric used as a protective floor covering, etc. ORIG C16: from F *droguet* useless fabric, from *drogue* trash

druggie ('drʌgɪ) *n Inf.* a drug addict.

druggist ('drʌgɪst) *n* a US and Canad. term for **pharmacist.**

drugstore ('drʌgˌstɔː) *n US & Canad.* a shop where medical prescriptions are made up and a wide variety of goods and sometimes light meals are sold.

druid ('druːɪd) *n* (*sometimes cap.*) **1** a member of an ancient order of priests in Gaul, Britain, and Ireland in the pre-Christian era. **2** a member of any of several modern movements attempting to revive druidism. ORIG C16: from L *druides,* of Gaulish origin
▸ **'druidess** *fem n* ▸ **dru'idic** *or* **dru'idical** *adj* ▸ **'druidˌism** *n*

drum (drʌm) *n* **1** a percussion instrument sounded by striking a membrane stretched across the opening of a hollow cylinder or hemisphere. **2** the sound produced by a drum or any similar sound. **3** an object that resembles a drum in shape, such as a large spool or a cylindrical container. **4** *Archit.* a cylindrical block of stone used to construct the shaft of a column. **5** short for **eardrum. 6** any of various North American fishes that utter a drumming sound. **7** a type of hollow rotor for steam turbines or axial compressors. **8** *Arch.* a drummer. **9 beat the drum for.** *Inf.* to attempt to arouse interest in. **10 the drum.** *Austral. inf.* the necessary information (esp. in **give (someone) the drum**). ◆ *vb* **drums, drumming, drummed. 11** to play (music) on or as if on a drum. **12** to tap rhythmically or regularly. **13** (*tr;* sometimes foll. by *up*) to summon or call by drumming. **14** (*tr*) to instil by constant repetition. ◆ See also **drum up.** ORIG C16: prob. from MDu. *tromme,* imit.

drumbeat ('drʌmˌbiːt) *n* the sound made by beating a drum.

drum brake *n* a type of brake used on the wheels of vehicles, consisting of two shoes that rub against the brake drum when the brake is applied.

drumhead ('drʌmˌhɛd) *n* **1** the part of a drum that is actually struck. **2** the head of a capstan. **3** another name for **eardrum.**

drumlin ('drʌmlɪn) *n* a streamlined mound of glacial drift. ORIG C19: from Irish Gaelic *druim* ridge + *-lin* -LING[1]

drum machine *n* a synthesizer specially programmed to reproduce the sound of drums and other percussion instruments in variable rhythms and combinations selected by the musician; the resulting beat is produced continually until stopped or changed.

drum major *n* the noncommissioned officer, usually of warrant officer's rank, who commands the corps of drums of a military band and who is in command of both the drums and the band when paraded together.

drum majorette *n* a girl who marches at the head of a procession, twirling a baton.

drummer ('drʌmə) *n* **1** a drum player. **2** *Chiefly US.* a travelling salesman.

drumstick ('drʌmˌstɪk) *n* **1** a stick used for playing a drum. **2** the lower joint of the leg of a cooked fowl.

drum up *vb* (*tr, adv*) to obtain (support, business, etc.) by solicitation or canvassing.

drunk (drʌŋk) *adj* **1** intoxicated with alcohol to the extent of losing control over normal functions. **2** overwhelmed by strong influence or emotion. ◆ *n* **3** a person who is drunk. **4** *Inf.* a drinking bout. ORIG OE *druncen,* p.p. of *drincan* to drink

drunkard ('drʌŋkəd) *n* a person who is frequently or habitually drunk.

drunken ('drʌŋkən) *adj* **1** intoxicated. **2** habitually drunk. **3** (*prenominal*) caused by or relating to alcoholic intoxication: *a drunken brawl.*
▸ **'drunkenly** *adv* ▸ **'drunkenness** *n*

drupe (druːp) *n* any fruit that has a fleshy or fibrous part around a stone that encloses a seed, as the peach, plum,

and cherry. ORIG C18: from L *druppa* wrinkled overripe olive, from Gk: olive
▸ **drupaceous** (druː'peɪʃəs) *adj*

drupelet ('druːplɪt) *or* **drupel** ('druːpᵊl) *n* a small drupe, usually one of a number forming a compound fruit.

Druse *or* **Druze** (druːz) *n, pl* **Druse** *or* **Druze. a** a member of a religious sect, mainly living in Syria, Lebanon, and Israel, having certain characteristics in common with Muslims. **b** (*as modifier*): *Druse customs.* ORIG C18: from Arabic *Durūz*, after Ismail al-*Darazi*, 11th-century founder of the sect

dry (draɪ) *adj* **drier, driest** *or* **dryer, dryest. 1** lacking moisture; not damp or wet. **2** having little or no rainfall. **3** not in or under water. **4** having the water drained away or evaporated: *a dry river.* **5** not providing milk: *a dry cow.* **6** (of the eyes) free from tears. **7a** *Inf.* thirsty. **7b** causing thirst. **8** eaten without butter, jam, etc.: *dry toast.* **9** *Electronics* (of a soldered joint) imperfect because the solder has not adhered to the metal. **10** (of wine, etc.) not sweet. **11** not producing a mucous or watery discharge: *a dry cough.* **12** consisting of solid as opposed to liquid substances. **13** without adornment; plain: *dry facts.* **14** lacking interest: *a dry book.* **15** lacking warmth: *a dry greeting.* **16** (of humour) shrewd and keen in an impersonal, sarcastic, or laconic way. **17** *Inf.* opposed to or prohibiting the sale of alcoholic liquor: *a dry country.* ◆ *vb* **dries, drying, dried. 18** (when *intr,* often foll. by *off*) to make or become dry. **19** (*tr*) to preserve (fruit, etc.) by removing the moisture. ◆ *n, pl* **drys** *or* **dries. 20** *Brit. inf.* a Conservative politician who is a hardliner. **21 the dry.** (*sometimes cap.*) *Austral. inf.* the dry season. ◆ See also **dry out, dry up.** ORIG OE *drȳge*
▸ **'dryness** *n*

dryad ('draɪəd, -æd) *n, pl* **dryads** *or* **dryades** (-əˌdiːz). *Greek myth.* a nymph or divinity of the woods. ORIG C14: from L *Dryas,* from Gk *Druas,* from *drus* tree

dry battery *n* an electric battery consisting of two or more dry cells.

dry cell *n* a primary cell in which the electrolyte is in the form of a paste or is treated in some way to prevent it from spilling.

dry-clean *vb* (*tr*) to clean (fabrics, etc.) with a solvent other than water.
▸ **ˌdry-'cleaner** *n* ▸ **ˌdry-'cleaning** *n*

Dryden ★ ('draɪdᵊn) *n* **John.** 1631–1700, English poet and dramatist. His works include *All for Love* (1677) and *Absalom and Achitophel* (1681).

dry dock *n* a dock that can be pumped dry for work on a ship's bottom.

dryer[1] ('draɪə) *n* **1** a person or thing that dries. **2** an apparatus for removing moisture by forced draught, heating, or centrifuging. **3** any of certain chemicals added to oils to accelerate their drying when used in paints, etc.

dryer[2] ('draɪə) *adj* a variant spelling of **drier**[1].

dry fly *n Angling.* **a** an artificial fly designed to be floated on the surface of the water. **b** (*as modifier*): *dry-fly fishing.*

dry hole *n* (in the oil industry) a well which proves unsuccessful.

dry ice *n* solid carbon dioxide used as a refrigerant, and to create billows of smoke in stage shows. Also called: **carbon dioxide snow.**

drying ('draɪɪŋ) *n* the processing of timber until it has a moisture content suitable for the purposes for which it is to be used.

dryly ('draɪlɪ) *adv* a variant spelling of **drily.**

dry measure *n* a unit or system of units for measuring dry goods, such as fruit, grains, etc.

dry out *vb* (*adv*) **1** to make or become dry. **2** to undergo or cause to undergo treatment for alcoholism or drug addiction.

dry point *n* **1** a technique of intaglio engraving with a hard steel needle, without acid, on a copper plate. **2** the sharp steel needle used. **3** the engraving or print produced.

dry riser *n* a vertical pipe, not containing water, having connections on different floors of a building for a fireman's hose to be attached. A fire tender can be connected at the lowest level to make water rise under pressure within the pipe. Abbrev.: **DR.**

dry rot *n* **1** crumbling and drying of timber, bulbs, potatoes, or fruit, caused by certain fungi. **2** any fungus causing this decay. **3** moral degeneration or corruption.

dry run *n* **1** *Mil.* practice in firing without live ammunition. **2** *Inf.* a rehearsal.

drysalter ('draɪˌsɔːltə) *n Obs.* a dealer in dyestuffs and gums, and in dried, tinned, or salted foods and edible oils.

Drysdale ★ ('draɪzdeɪl) *n* Sir **George Russell.** 1912–81, Australian painter, esp. of landscapes.

dry slope *n* an artificial ski slope used for tuition and practice. Also called: **dry-ski slope.**

dry-stone *adj* (of a wall) made without mortar.

dry up *vb* (*adv*) **1** (*intr*) to become barren or unproductive; fail. **2** to dry (dishes, cutlery, etc.) with a tea towel after they have been washed. **3** (*intr*) *Inf.* to stop talking or speaking.

DS *or* **ds** *Music. abbrev. for* dal segno.

DSc *abbrev. for* Doctor of Science.

DSC *Mil. abbrev. for* Distinguished Service Cross.

DSM *Mil. abbrev. for* Distinguished Service Medal.

DSO *Brit. mil. abbrev. for* Distinguished Service Order.

DSS *Brit. abbrev. for:* **1** Department of Social Security. **2** Director of Social Services.

DST *abbrev. for* Daylight Saving Time.

DSW (in New Zealand) *abbrev. for* Department of Social Welfare.

DTI (in Britain) *abbrev. for* Department of Trade and Industry.

DTP *abbrev for* desktop publishing.

DT's *Inf. abbrev. for* delirium tremens.

DU *abbrev. for* depleted uranium.

Du. *abbrev. for* Dutch.

dual ('djuːəl) *adj* **1** relating to or denoting two. **2** twofold; double. **3** (in the grammar of some languages) denoting a form of a word indicating that exactly two referents are being referred to. **4** *Maths, logic.* (of a pair of operators) convertible into one another by the distribution of negation over either. ◆ *n* **5** *Grammar.* **5a** the dual number. **5b** a dual form of a word. ORIG C17: from L *duālis* concerning two, from *duo* two
▸ **'dually** *adv* ▸ **duality** (djuː'ælɪtɪ) *n*

dual carriageway *n Brit.* a road on which traffic travelling in opposite directions is separated by a central strip of turf, etc. US and Canad. name: **divided highway.**

dualism ('djuːəˌlɪzəm) *n* **1** the state of being twofold or double. **2** *Philosophy.* the doctrine that reality consists of two basic types of substance, usually taken to be mind and matter or mental and physical entities. Cf. **monism** (sense 1). **3a** the theory that the universe has been ruled from its origins by two conflicting powers, one good and one evil. **3b** the theory that there are two personalities, one human and one divine, in Christ.
▸ **'dualist** *n* ▸ **dual'istic** *adj*

dub[1] (dʌb) *vb* **dubs, dubbing, dubbed. 1** (*tr*) to invest (a person) with knighthood by tapping on the shoulder with a sword. **2** (*tr*) to invest with a title, name, or nickname. **3** (*tr*) to dress (leather) by rubbing. **4** *Angling.* to dress (a fly). ORIG OE *dubbian*

dub[2] (dʌb) *vb* **dubs, dubbing, dubbed. 1** to alter the soundtrack of (a film, etc.). **2** (*tr*) to provide (a film) with a new soundtrack, esp. in a different language. **3** (*tr*) to provide (a film or tape) with a soundtrack. ◆ *n* **4** the new sounds added. **5** *Music.* a style of record production associated with reggae, involving the use of echo, delay, etc. ORIG C20: shortened from DOUBLE

dub[3] (dʌb) *vb* **dubs, dubbing, dubbed.** *Austral. & NZ inf.* short for **double-bank.**

Dubai ★ (duː'baɪ) *n* a sheikhdom in the NE United Arab Emirates, consisting principally of the port of Dubai, on the Persian Gulf: oilfields. Pop.: 548 000 (1993).

du Barry (djuː 'bærɪ; *French* dy bari) *n* **Comtesse** (kɔ̃tɛs), original name *Marie Jeanne Bécu.* ?1743–93, mistress of Louis XV, guillotined in the French Revolution.

dubbin ★ ('dʌbɪn) *n Brit.* a greasy preparation applied to leather to soften it and make it waterproof. ORIG C18: from *dub* to dress leather

dubbing[1] ('dʌbɪŋ) *n Films.* **1** the replacement of a soundtrack, esp. by one in another language. **2** the combination of several soundtracks. **3** the addition of a soundtrack to a film, etc.

dubbing[2] ('dʌbɪŋ) *n* **1** *Angling.* fibrous material used for the body of an artificial fly. **2** a variant of **dubbin.**

Dubček ★ (*Czech* 'duptʃɛk) *n* **Alexander** ('aleksandᵊr). 1921–92, Czechoslovak statesman. His reforms as first secretary of the Czechoslovak Communist Party (1968–69) prompted the Soviet occupation (1968) and his enforced resignation. Following the uprising of 1989 he was elected chairman of the new parliament.

du Bellay ★ (*French* dy bɛlɛ) *n* See (Joachim du) **Bellay.**

dubiety (dju:'baɪɪtɪ) *n, pl* **dubieties. 1** the state of being doubtful. **2** a doubtful matter. ORIG C18: from LL *dubietās,* from L *dubius* DUBIOUS

dub in *or* **up** *vb* (*adv*) *Sl.* to contribute to the cost of something: *we'll all dub in a fiver for the trip.*

dubious ('dju:bɪəs) *adj* **1** marked by or causing doubt. **2** uncertain; doubtful. **3** of doubtful quality; untrustworthy. **4** not certain in outcome. ORIG C16: from L *dubius* wavering
▸ **'dubiously** *adv* ▸ **'dubiousness** *n*

Dublin ★ ('dʌblɪn) *n* **1** the capital of the Republic of Ireland, on **Dublin Bay**: under English rule from 1171 until 1922; commercial and cultural centre; contains one of the world's largest breweries and exports whiskey, stout, and agricultural produce. Pop.: 480 996 (1996). Gaelic name: **Baile Átha Cliath. 2** a county, comprising four county boroughs, in E Republic of Ireland, in Leinster on the Irish Sea: mountainous in the south. County seat: Dublin. Pop.: 1 057 000 (1996). Area: 922 sq. km (356 sq. miles).
▸ **'Dubliner** *n*

Dublin Bay prawn ('dʌblɪn) *n* a large prawn usually used in a dish of scampi.

dubnium ('dʌb,nɪəm) *n* a synthetic transactinide element produced in minute quantities by bombarding plutonium with high-energy neon ions. Symbol: Du; atomic no. 105. ORIG C20: from *Dubna,* city in Russia where it was first reported

Dubrovnik ★ (du'brɒvnɪk) *n* a port in W Croatia, on the Dalmatian coast: an important commercial centre in the Middle Ages; tourist centre. Pop.: 49 730 (1991). Former Italian name (until 1918): **Ragusa.**

Dubuffet ★ (*French* dybyfɛ) *n* **Jean** (ʒɑ̃). 1901–85, French painter.

ducal ('dju:kᵊl) *adj* of a duke or duchy. ORIG C16: from F, from LL *ducālis* of a leader, from L *dux* leader

ducat ('dʌkət) *n* **1** any of various former European gold or silver coins. **2** (*often pl*) money. ORIG C14: from OF, from OIt. *ducato* coin stamped with the doge's image

Duccio di Buoninsegna ★ (*Italian* 'duttʃo di buonin'seɲɲa) *n* ?1255–?1318, Italian painter; founder of the Sienese school.

duce ('du:tʃɪ) *n* leader. ORIG C20: from It., from L *dux*

Duce (*Italian* 'du:tʃe) *n* **Il** (il). the title assumed by Mussolini as leader of Fascist Italy (1922–43).

Duchamp ★ (*French* dyʃɑ̃) *n* **Marcel** (marsɛl). 1887–1968, US painter and sculptor, born in France.

Duchenne dystrophy (du'ʃɛn) *or* **Duchenne muscular dystrophy** *n* the most common form of muscular dystrophy, usually affecting only boys. ORIG after Guillaume *Duchenne* (1806–75), F neurologist

duchess ('dʌtʃɪs) *n* **1** the wife or widow of a duke. **2** a woman who holds the rank of duke in her own right. ◆ *vb* **3** (*tr*) *Austral. inf.* to overwhelm with flattering attention. ORIG C14: from OF *duchesse*

duchesse ('dʌtʃɪs) *n Austral. & NZ.* a dressing table or chest of drawers with a mirror.

duchy ('dʌtʃɪ) *n, pl* **duchies.** the territory of a duke or duchess; dukedom. ORIG C14: from OF *duche,* from *duc* DUKE

duck[1] (dʌk) *n, pl* **ducks** *or* **duck. 1** any of a family of aquatic birds, esp. those having short legs, webbed feet, and a broad blunt bill. **2** the flesh of this bird, used as food. **3** the female of such a bird, as opposed to the male (drake). **4** Also: **ducks.** *Brit. inf.* dear or darling: used as a term of address. See also **ducky. 5** *Cricket.* a score of nothing by a batsman. **6 like water off a duck's back.** *Inf.* without effect. ORIG OE *dūce* duck, diver; rel. to DUCK[2]

duck[2] (dʌk) *vb* **1** to move (the head or body) quickly downwards or away, esp. to escape observation or evade a blow. **2** to plunge suddenly under water. **3** (when *intr,* often foll. by *out*) *Inf.* to dodge or escape (a person, duty, etc.). **4** (*intr*) *Bridge.* to play a low card rather than try to win a trick. ◆ *n* **5** the act or an instance of ducking. ORIG C14: rel. to OHG *tūhhan* to dive, MDu. *dūken*
▸ **'ducker** *n*

duck[3] (dʌk) *n* a heavy cotton fabric of plain weave, used for clothing, tents, etc. ORIG C17: from MDu. *doek*

duck[4] (dʌk) *n* an amphibious vehicle used in World War II. ORIG C20: from code name DUKW

duck-billed platypus *n* an amphibious egg-laying mammal of E Australia having dense fur, a broad bill and tail, and webbed feet.

duckboard ('dʌk,bɔ:d) *n* a board or boards laid so as to form a path over wet or muddy ground.

ducking stool *n History.* a chair used for punishing offenders by plunging them into water.

duckling ('dʌklɪŋ) *n* a young duck.

ducks and drakes *n* (*functioning as sing*) **1** a game in which a flat stone is bounced across the surface of water. **2 make ducks and drakes of** *or* **play (at) ducks and drakes with.** *Inf.* to use recklessly; squander.

duck's arse *n* a hairstyle in which the hair is swept back to a point at the nape of the neck, resembling a duck's tail. Abbrev.: **DA.**

duck soup *n US sl.* something that is easy to do.

duckweed ('dʌk,wi:d) *n* any of various small stemless aquatic plants that occur floating on still water in temperate regions.

ducky *or* **duckie** ('dʌkɪ) *Inf.* ◆ *n, pl* **duckies. 1** *Brit.* darling or dear: a term of endearment. ◆ *adj* **duckier, duckiest. 2** delightful; fine.

duct (dʌkt) *n* **1** a tube, pipe, or canal by means of which a substance, esp. a fluid or gas, is conveyed. **2** any bodily passage, esp. one conveying secretions or excretions. **3** a narrow tubular cavity in plants. **4** a channel or pipe carrying electric wires. **5** a passage through which air can flow, as in air conditioning. ORIG C17: from L *ductus* a leading (in Med. L: aqueduct), from *dūcere* to lead
▸ **'ductless** *adj*

ductile ('dʌktaɪl) *adj* **1** (of a metal) able to sustain large deformations without fracture and able to be hammered into sheets or drawn out into wires. **2** able to be moulded. **3** easily led or influenced. ORIG C14: from OF, from L *ductilis,* from *dūcere* to lead
▸ **ductility** (dʌk'tɪlɪtɪ) *n*

ductless gland *n Anat.* See **endocrine gland.**

dud (dʌd) *Inf.* ◆ *n* **1** a person or thing that proves ineffectual. **2** a shell, etc., that fails to explode. **3** (*pl*) *Old-fashioned.* clothes or other belongings. ◆ *adj* **4** failing in its purpose or function. ORIG C15 (in the sense: an article of clothing, a thing, used disparagingly): from ?

dude (du:d, dju:d) *n Inf.* **1** *Western US & Canad.* a city dweller, esp. one holidaying on a ranch. **2** *US & Canad.* a dandy. **3** *US & Canad.* any person: often used to any male in direct address. ORIG C19: from ?
▸ **'dudish** *adj* ▸ **'dudishly** *adv*

dude ranch *n US & Canad.* a ranch used as a holiday resort.

dudgeon ('dʌdʒən) *n* anger or resentment (arch., except in **in high dudgeon**). ORIG C16: from ?

Dudley[1] ★ ('dʌdlɪ) *n* **1** a town in W central England, in the West Midlands: clothing and light-engineering industries. Pop.: 192 171 (1991). **2** a unitary authority in

W central England. Pop.: 311 200 (1997 est.). Area: 98 sq. km (38 sq. miles).

Dudley[2] ★ ('dʌdlɪ) *n* **Robert.** See (Earl of) **Leicester.**

due (dju:) *adj* **1** (*postpositive*) immediately payable. **2** (*postpositive*) owed as a debt. **3** fitting; proper. **4** (*prenominal*) adequate or sufficient. **5** (*postpositive*) expected or appointed to be present or arrive. **6 due to.** attributable to or caused by. ◆ *n* **7** something that is owed, required, or due. **8 give (a person) his due.** to give or allow what is deserved or right. ◆ *adv* **9** directly or exactly. ORIG C13: from OF *deu,* from *devoir* to owe, from L *debēre*

USAGE NOTE In usage debates over the years, there can have been few more contentious subjects than the use of *due to* as a compound preposition. It used to be claimed that a sentence such as *the late arrival of the 10.15 from Guildford is due to snow on the lines* was correct, while *the trains are running late due to snow on the lines* was incorrect. The reasoning was that in the first case *due* is being used as an adjective synonymous with 'attributable', followed by *to* and a complement, whereas in the second case there is no explicit noun which *due* as an adjective can be said to modify. Nowadays, while the construction is quite common, it may be advisable in certain types of writing to replace it with an uncontentious alternative, such as *on account of, because of,* or *owing to.*

duel ('dju:əl) *n* **1** a formal prearranged combat with deadly weapons between two people in the presence of seconds, usually to settle a quarrel. **2** a contest or conflict between two persons or parties. ◆ *vb* **duels, duelling, duelled** *or US* **duels, dueling, dueled.** (*intr*) **3** to fight in a duel. **4** to contest closely. ORIG C15: from Med. L *duellum,* from L, poetical var. of *bellum* war; associated with L *duo* two
▸ **'dueller, 'duellist** *or US* **'dueler, 'duelist** *n*

duenna (dju:'ɛnə) *n* (in Spain and Portugal, etc.) an elderly woman retained by a family to act as governess and chaperon to girls. ORIG C17: from Sp. *dueña,* from L *domina* lady

due process of law *n* the administration of justice in accordance with established rules and principles.

dues (dju:z) *pl n* (*sometimes sing*) charges, as for membership of a club or organization; fees.

duet (dju:'ɛt) *n* **1** a musical composition for two performers or voices. **2** a pair of closely connected individuals; duo. ORIG C18: from It. *duetto* a little duet, from *duo* duet, from L: two
▸ **du'ettist** *n*

duff[1] (dʌf) *n* **1** a thick flour pudding boiled in a cloth bag. **2 up the duff.** *Sl.* pregnant. ORIG C19: N English var. of DOUGH

duff[2] (dʌf) *vb* (*tr*) **1** *Sl.* to give a false appearance to (old or stolen goods); fake. **2** (foll. by *up*) *Brit. sl.* to beat (a person) severely. **3** *Austral. sl.* to steal (cattle), altering the brand. **4** *Golf. inf.* to bungle a shot by hitting the ground behind the ball. ◆ *adj* **5** *Brit., Austral., & NZ inf.* bad or useless. ORIG C19: prob. back formation from DUFFER

duffel *or* **duffle** ('dʌfᵊl) *n* **1** a heavy woollen cloth. **2** *Chiefly US & Canad.* equipment or supplies. ORIG C17: after *Duffel,* Belgian town

duffel bag *n* a cylindrical drawstring canvas bag, originally used esp. by sailors for carrying personal articles.

duffel coat *n* a usually knee-length wool coat, usually with a hood and fastened with toggles.

duffer ('dʌfə) *n* **1** *Inf.* a dull or incompetent person. **2** *Sl.* something worthless. **3** *Austral. sl.* **3a** an unproductive mine. **3b** a person who steals cattle. ORIG C19: from ?

Dufy ★ (*French* dyfi) *n* **Raoul** (raul). 1877–1953, French painter.

dug[1] (dʌg) *vb* the past tense and past participle of **dig.**

dug[2] (dʌg) *n* a nipple, teat, udder, or breast. ORIG C16: of Scand. origin

dugong ('du:gɒŋ) *n* a whalelike mammal occurring in shallow tropical waters from E Africa to Australia. ORIG C19: from Malay *duyong*

dugout ('dʌgˌaʊt) *n* **1** a canoe made by hollowing out a log. **2** *Mil.* a covered excavation dug to provide shelter. **3** (at a sports ground) the covered bench where managers, substitutes, etc., sit. **4** (in the Canadian prairies) a reservoir dug on a farm in which water from rain and snow is collected for use in irrigation, watering livestock, etc.

duiker *or* **duyker** ('daɪkə) *n, pl* **duikers, duiker** *or* **duykers, duyker. 1** Also: **duikerbok.** any of various small African antelopes. **2** *S. African.* any of several cormorants, esp. the long-tailed shag. ORIG C18: via Afrik., from Du. *duiker* diver, from *duiken* to dive

Duisburg ★ (*German* 'dy:sbʊrk) *n* an industrial city in NW Germany, in North Rhine-Westphalia at the confluence of the Rivers Rhine and Ruhr: the largest European inland port. Pop.: 535 250 (1996 est.).

Dukas ★ (*French* dyka) *n* **Paul** (pɔl). 1865–1935, French composer noted for the orchestral scherzo *The Sorcerer's Apprentice* (1897).

duke (dju:k) *n* **1** a nobleman of high rank: in the British Isles standing above the other grades of the nobility. **2** the prince or ruler of a small principality or duchy. ORIG C12: from OF *duc,* from L *dux* leader
▸ **'dukedom** *n*

dukes (dju:ks) *pl n Sl.* the fists. ORIG C19: from *Duke of Yorks* rhyming sl. for *forks* (fingers)

dulcet ('dʌlsɪt) *adj* (of a sound) soothing or pleasant; sweet. ORIG C14: from L *dulcis* sweet

dulcimer ('dʌlsɪmə) *n* **1** a tuned percussion instrument consisting of a set of strings stretched over a sounding board and struck with hammers. **2** an instrument used in US folk music, with an elliptical body and usually three strings plucked with a goose quill. ORIG C15: from OF *doulcemer,* from OIt. *dolcimelo,* from *dolce* (from L *dulcis* sweet) + *-melo,* ?from Gk *melos* song

dull (dʌl) *adj* **1** slow to think or understand; stupid. **2** lacking in interest. **3** lacking in perception; insensitive. **4** lacking sharpness. **5** not acute, intense, or piercing. **6** (of weather) not bright or clear. **7** not active, busy, or brisk. **8** lacking in spirit; listless. **9** (of colour) lacking brilliance; sombre. **10** not loud or clear; muffled. ◆ *vb* **11** to make or become dull. ORIG OE *dol*
▸ **'dullish** *adj* ▸ **'dullness** *or* **'dulness** *n* ▸ **'dully** *adv*

dullard ('dʌləd) *n* a dull or stupid person.

dulse (dʌls) *n* any of several seaweeds that occur on rocks and have large red edible fronds. ORIG C17: from OIrish *duilesc* seaweed

Dulwich ★ ('dʌlɪtʃ) *n* a residential district in the Greater London borough of Southwark: site of Dulwich College.

duly ('dju:lɪ) *adv* **1** in a proper manner. **2** at the proper time. ORIG C14: see DUE, -LY[2]

duma *Russian.* ('du:mə) *n Russian history.* **1** (*usually cap.*) the elective legislative assembly established by Tsar Nicholas II in 1905: overthrown in 1917. **2** (before 1917) any official assembly or council. **3** short for **State Duma,** the lower chamber of the Russian parliament. ORIG C20: from *duma* thought, of Gmc origin

Dumas ★ (*French* dyma) *n* **1 Alexandre** (alɛksɑ̃drə), known as *Dumas père.* 1802–70, French writer, noted for his novels *The Count of Monte Cristo* (1844) and *The Three Musketeers* (1844). **2** his son, **Alexandre,** known as *Dumas fils.* 1824–95, French writer, noted esp. for *La Dame aux camélias* (1852). **3 Jean-Baptiste André** (ʒɑ̃batist ɑ̃dre). 1800–84, French chemist.

Du Maurier ★ (du 'mɒrɪˌeɪ) *n* **1** Dame **Daphne.** 1907–89, British novelist; author of *Rebecca* (1938) and *My Cousin Rachel* (1951). **2** her grandfather, **George Louis Palmella Busson** ('pælmɛlə 'bju:sᵊn). 1834–96, British novelist and illustrator; author of *Trilby* (1894). **3** his son, Sir **Gerald (Hubert Edward).** 1873–1934, British actor-manager: father of Daphne Du Maurier.

dumb (dʌm) *adj* **1** lacking the power to speak; mute. **2** lacking the power of human speech: *dumb animals.* **3** temporarily bereft of the power to speak: *struck dumb.* **4** refraining from speech; uncommunicative. **5** producing no sound: *a dumb piano.* **6** made, done, or performed

without speech. **7** *Inf.* **7a** dim-witted. **7b** foolish. ♦ See also **dumb down.** ORIG OE
▸ **'dumbly** *adv* ▸ **'dumbness** *n*

Dumbarton ★ (dʌm'bɑːtᵊn) *n* a town in W Scotland, in West Dunbartonshire near the confluence of the Rivers Leven and Clyde: centred around the **Rock of Dumbarton,** an important stronghold since ancient times; engineering and distilling. Pop.: 21 962 (1991).

Dumbarton Oaks ★ ('dʌmˌbɑːtᵊn) *n* an estate in the District of Columbia in the US: scene of conferences in 1944 concerned with creating the United Nations.

dumbbell ('dʌmˌbɛl) *n* **1** an exercising weight consisting of a short bar with a heavy ball or disc at either end, used for single-arm movements. **2** a small wooden or rubber object of a similar shape used to train dogs in retrieval. **3** *Sl., chiefly US & Canad.* a fool.

dumb down *vb (tr)* to make less intellectually demanding or sophisticated: *the move to dumb down television news.*

dumbfound *or* **dumfound** (dʌm'faʊnd) *vb (tr)* to strike dumb with astonishment; amaze. ORIG C17: from DUMB + (CON)FOUND

dumb show *n* **1** formerly, a part of a play acted in pantomime. **2** meaningful gestures.

dumbstruck ('dʌmˌstrʌk) *adj* temporarily deprived of speech through shock or surprise.

dumbwaiter ('dʌmˌweɪtə) *n* **1** *Brit.* **1a** a stand placed near a dining table to hold food. **1b** a revolving circular tray placed on a table to hold food. US and Canad. name: **lazy Susan. 2** a lift for carrying food, rubbish, etc., between floors.

dumdum ('dʌmˌdʌm) *n* a soft-nosed bullet that expands on impact and inflicts extensive laceration. ORIG C19: after *Dum-Dum,* town near Calcutta where orig. made

dumela (dʊ'mɛla) *sentence substitute. S. African.* hello; good morning. ORIG Sotho

Dumfries ★ (dʌm'friːs) *n* a town in S Scotland on the River Nith, administrative centre of Dumfries and Galloway. Pop.: 32 136 (1991).

Dumfries and Galloway ★ *n* a council area in SW Scotland. Administrative centre: Dumfries. Pop.: 147 900 (1993 est.). Area: 6439 sq. km (2486 sq. miles).

Dumfriesshire ★ (dʌm'friːsˌʃɪə, -ʃə) *n* (until 1975) a county in S Scotland, on the Solway Firth, now part of Dumfries and Galloway.

dummy ('dʌmɪ) *n, pl* **dummies. 1** a figure representing the human form, used for displaying clothes, as a target, etc. **2a** a copy of an object, often lacking some essential feature of the original. **2b** *(as modifier): a dummy drawer.* **3** *Sl.* a stupid person. **4** *Derog., sl.* a person without the power of speech. **5** *Inf.* a person who says or does nothing. **6a** a person who appears to act for himself or herself while acting on behalf of another. **6b** *(as modifier): a dummy buyer.* **7** *Mil.* a weighted round without explosives. **8** *Bridge.* **8a** the hand exposed on the table by the declarer's partner and played by the declarer. **8b** the declarer's partner. **9a** a prototype of a book, indicating the appearance of the finished product. **9b** a designer's layout of a page. **10** *Sport.* a feigned pass or move. **11** *Brit.* a rubber teat for babies to suck or bite on. US and Canad. equivalent: **pacifier. 12** *(modifier)* counterfeit; sham. **13** *(modifier)* (of a card game) played with one hand exposed or unplayed. **14 sell (someone) a dummy.** *Sport.* to trick (an opponent) with a dummy pass. ORIG C16: see DUMB, -Y[3]

dummy run *n* an experimental run; practice; rehearsal.

Du Mont ★ ('djuːˌmɒnt) *n* **Allen Balcom.** 1901–65, US engineer, who developed the cathode-ray tube.

dump (dʌmp) *vb* **1** to drop, fall, or let fall heavily or in a mass. **2** *(tr)* to empty (objects or material) out of a container. **3** to unload or empty (a container), as by overturning. **4** *(tr)* **4a** *Inf.* to dispose of without subtlety or proper care. **4b** to dispose of (nuclear waste). **5** *Commerce.* to market (goods) in bulk and at low prices, esp. abroad, in order to maintain a high price in the home market and obtain a share of the foreign markets. **6** *(tr)* to store (supplies, etc.) temporarily. **7** *(intr) Sl., chiefly US.* to defecate. **8** *(tr) Surfing.* (of a wave) to hurl a swimmer or surfer down. **9** *(tr) Austral. & NZ.* to compact (bales of wool) by hydraulic pressure. **10** *(tr) Computing.* to record (the contents of the memory) on a storage device at a series of points during a computer run. ♦ *n* **11** a place or area where waste materials are dumped. **12** a pile or accumulation of rubbish. **13** the act of dumping. **14** *Inf.* a dirty or unkempt place. **15** *Mil.* a place where weapons, supplies, etc., are stored. **16** *Sl., chiefly US.* an act of defecation. ORIG C14: prob. from ON

dumper ('dʌmpə) *n* **1** a person or thing that dumps. **2** *Surfing.* a wave that hurls a swimmer or surfer down.

dumpling ('dʌmplɪŋ) *n* **1** a small ball of dough cooked and served with stew. **2** a pudding consisting of a round pastry case filled with fruit: *apple dumpling.* **3** *Inf.* a short plump person. ORIG C16: *dump-,* ? var. of LUMP[1] + -LING[1]

dumps (dʌmps) *pl n Inf.* a state of melancholy or depression (esp. in **down in the dumps**). ORIG C16: prob. from MDu. *domp* haze

dump truck *or* **dumper-truck** *n* a small truck used on building sites, having a load-bearing container at the front that can be tipped up to dump the contents.

dumpy ('dʌmpɪ) *adj* **dumpier, dumpiest.** short and plump; squat. ORIG C18: ? rel. to DUMPLING
▸ **'dumpily** *adv* ▸ **'dumpiness** *n*

dun[1] (dʌn) *vb* **duns, dunning, dunned. 1** *(tr)* to press (a debtor) for payment. ♦ *n* **2** a person, esp. a hired agent, who importunes another for the payment of a debt. **3** a demand for payment. ORIG C17: from ?

dun[2] (dʌn) *n* **1** a brownish-grey colour. **2** a horse of this colour. **3** *Angling.* **3a** an immature adult mayfly. **3b** an artificial fly resembling this. ♦ *adj* **dunner, dunnest. 4** of a dun colour. **5** dark and gloomy. ORIG OE *dunn*

Duna ★ ('dunɔ) *n* the Hungarian name for the **Danube.**

Dünaburg ★ ('dyːnabʊrk) *n* the German name (until 1893) for **Daugavpils.**

Dunaj ★ ('dunaj) *n* the Czech name for the **Danube.**

Dunant ★ (*French* dynɑ̃) *n* **Jean Henri** (ʒɑ̃ ɑ̃ri). 1828–1910, Swiss humanitarian, founder of the International Red Cross (1864): shared the Nobel peace prize 1901.

Dunărea ★ ('dunərjɑ) *n* the Romanian name for the **Danube.**

Dunbar[1] ★ (dʌn'bɑː) *n* a port and resort in SE Scotland, in East Lothian: scene of Cromwell's defeat of the Scots (1650). Pop.: 6518 (1991).

Dunbar[2] ★ (dʌn'bɑː) *n* **William.** ?1460–?1520, Scottish poet, noted for his satirical, allegorical, and elegiac works.

Dunbartonshire ★ (dʌn'bɑːtᵊnʃɪə, -ʃə) *n* a historic county of W Scotland, now part of East Dunbartonshire and West Dunbartonshire.

Duncan ★ ('dʌŋkən) *n* **Isadora** (ˌɪzə'dɔːrə). 1878–1927, US dancer and choreographer.

Duncan I ★ ('dʌŋkən) *n* died 1040, king of Scotland (1034–40); killed by Macbeth.

dunce (dʌns) *n* a person who is stupid or slow to learn. ORIG C16: from *Dunses* or *Dunsmen,* term of ridicule applied to the followers of John *Duns Scotus* (?1265–1308), Scot. scholastic theologian, esp. by 16th-cent. humanists

dunce cap *or* **dunce's cap** *n* a conical paper hat, formerly placed on the head of a dull child at school.

Dundalk ★ (dʌn'dɔːk) *n* a town in NE Republic of Ireland, on **Dundalk Bay:** county town of Co. Louth. Pop.: 25 800 (1991).

Dundee[1] ★ (dʌn'diː) *n* **1** a port in E Scotland on the Firth of Tay: formerly a centre of the British jute industry; seat of The University of Dundee (1967). Pop.: 158 981 (1991). **2 City of.** a council area in E Scotland. Pop.: 167 500 (1996 est.). Area: 65 sq. km (25 sq. miles).
▸ **Dundonian** (dʌn'dəʊnɪən) *n, adj*

Dundee[2] ★ (dʌn'diː) *n* **1st Viscount,** title of *John Graham of Claverhouse.* ?1649–89, Scottish Jacobite leader, who died after winning the battle of Killiecrankie.

Dundee cake (dʌn'diː) *n Chiefly Brit.* a fairly rich fruit cake decorated with almonds.

dunderhead ('dʌndəˌhɛd) *n* a slow-witted person. ORIG C17: prob. from Du. *donder* thunder + HEAD
▸ **'dunderˌheaded** *adj*

dune (djuːn) *n* a mound or ridge of drifted sand. ORIG C18: via OF from MDu. *dūne*

Dunedin ★ (dʌn'i:dɪn) *n* a port in New Zealand, on SE South Island: founded (1848) by Scottish settlers. Pop. (urban area): 121 100 (1996).

Dunfermline ★ (dʌn'fɜ:mlɪn) *n* a city in E Scotland, in SW Fife: ruined palace, a former residence of Scottish kings. Pop.: 55 083 (1991).

dung (dʌŋ) *n* **1** excrement, esp. of animals; manure. **2** something filthy. ◆ *vb* **3** (*tr*) to cover with manure. ORIG OE: prison; rel. to OHG *tunc* cellar roofed with dung, ON *dyngja* manure heap

Dungannon ★ (dʌn'gænən) *n* a district of central Northern Ireland, bordering the W shore of Lough Neagh and the Irish Republic: agriculture. Administrative centre: Dungannon. Pop.: 45 428 (1991). Area: 783 sq. km (302 sq. miles)

dungaree (ˌdʌŋgə'ri:) *n* **1** a coarse cotton fabric used chiefly for work clothes, etc. **2** (*pl*) **2a** a suit of workman's overalls made of this material, consisting of trousers with a bib attached. **2b** a casual garment resembling this, usually worn by women or children. **3** (*pl*) *US.* jeans. ORIG C17: from Hindi, after *Dungrī,* district of Bombay, where this fabric originated

Dungeness ★ (ˌdʌndʒə'nɛs) *n* a low shingle headland on the S coast of England, in Kent: two nuclear power stations: automatic lighthouse.

dungeon ('dʌndʒən) *n* **1** a prison cell, often underground. **2** a variant spelling of **donjon**. ORIG C14: from OF *donjon*

dunghill ('dʌŋˌhɪl) *n* **1** a heap of dung. **2** a foul place, condition, or person.

dunk (dʌŋk) *vb* **1** to dip (bread, etc.) in tea, soup, etc., before eating. **2** to submerge or be submerged. ORIG C20: from Pennsylvania Du., from MHG *dunken,* from OHG *dunkōn*
▸ **'dunker** *n*

Dunkerque ★ (*French* dœ̃kɛrk) *n* a port in N France, on the Strait of Dover: scene of the evacuation of British and other Allied troops after the fall of France in 1940; industrial centre. Pop.: 190 879 (1990). English name: **Dunkirk** (dʌn'kɜ:k).

Dún Laoghaire ★ (du:n 'lɪərɪ) *n* a port in E Republic of Ireland, on Dublin Bay. Pop.: 185 400 (1991). Former names: **Dunleary** (until 1821), **Kingstown** (1821–1921).

dunlin ('dʌnlɪn) *n* a small sandpiper of northern and arctic regions, having a brown back and black breast in summer. ORIG C16: DUN[2] + -LING[1]

Dunlop ★ ('dʌnlɒp) *n* **John Boyd.** 1840–1921, Scottish veterinary surgeon, who devised the first successful pneumatic tyre.

dunnage ('dʌnɪdʒ) *n* loose material used for packing cargo. ORIG C14: from ?

dunno (dʌ'nəʊ, də-) *Sl. contraction of* (I) do not know.

dunnock ('dʌnək) *n* another name for a **hedge sparrow**. ORIG C15: from DUN[2] + -OCK

dunny ('dʌnɪ) *n, pl* **dunnies. 1** *Scot. dialect.* a cellar or basement. **2** *Austral. & NZ inf.* a lavatory, esp. one which is outside. ORIG C20: from ?

Dunsinane ★ (dʌn'sɪnən) *n* a hill in central Scotland, in the Sidlaw Hills: the ruined fort at its summit is regarded as Macbeth's castle. Height: 308 m (1012 ft).

> **USAGE NOTE** The pronunciation 'dʌnsɪˌneɪn is used in Shakespeare's *Macbeth* for the purposes of rhyme.

Duns Scotus ★ ('dʌnz 'skɒtəs) *n* **John.** ?1265–1308, Scottish scholastic theologian and Franciscan priest: opposed the theology of St Thomas Aquinas.

Dunstable ★ ('dʌnstəbəl) *n* an industrial town in SE central England, in Bedfordshire. Pop.: 49 666 (1991).

Dunstan ★ ('dʌnstən) *n* **Saint.** ?909–988 A.D., English prelate; archbishop of Canterbury (959–988). Feast day: May 19.

duo ('dju:əʊ) *n, pl* **duos** *or* **dui** ('dju:i:). **1** *Music.* **1a** a pair of performers. **1b** a duet. **2** a pair of actors, etc. **3** *Inf.* a pair of closely connected individuals. ORIG C16: via It. from L: two

duo- *combining form.* indicating two. ORIG from L

duodecimal (ˌdju:əʊ'dɛsɪməl) *adj* **1** relating to twelve or twelfths. ◆ *n* **2** a twelfth. **3** one of the numbers used in a duodecimal number system.
▸ **ˌduo'decimally** *adv*

duodecimo (ˌdju:əʊ'dɛsɪˌməʊ) *n, pl* **duodecimos. 1** Also called: **twelvemo.** a book size resulting from folding a sheet of paper into twelve leaves. **2** a book of this size. ORIG C17: from L *in duodecimō* in twelfth

duodenum (ˌdju:əʊ'di:nəm) *n, pl* **duodena** (-nə) *or* **duodenums.** the first part of the small intestine, between the stomach and the jejunum. ORIG C14: from Med. L, from *intestinum duodenum digitorum* intestine of twelve fingers' length
▸ **ˌduo'denal** *adj*

duologue *or US* (*sometimes*) **duolog** ('dju:əˌlɒg) *n* **1** a part or all of a play in which the speaking roles are limited to two actors. **2** a less common word for **dialogue.**

duopoly (dju'ɒpəlɪ) *n, pl* **duopolies.** a situation in which control of a commodity or service in a particular market is vested in two producers or suppliers.
▸ **duˌopo'listic** *adj*

dup. *abbrev. for* duplicate.

dupe (dju:p) *n* **1** a person who is easily deceived. ◆ *vb* **dupes, duping, duped. 2** (*tr*) to deceive; cheat; fool. ORIG C17: from F, from OF *duppe,* contraction of *de huppe* of (a) hoopoe; from the bird's reputation for stupidity
▸ **'dupable** *adj* ▸ **'duper** *n* ▸ **'dupery** *n*

duple ('dju:pəl) *adj* **1** a less common word for **double. 2** *Music.* (of time or music) having two beats in a bar. ORIG C16: from L *duplus* twofold, double

duplex ('dju:plɛks) *n* **1** *US & Canad.* a duplex apartment or house. **2** *Biochem.* a double-stranded region in a nucleic acid molecule. ◆ *adj* **3** having two parts. **4** having pairs of components of independent but identical function. **5** permitting the transmission of simultaneous signals in both directions. ORIG C19: from L: twofold, from *duo* two + *-plex* -FOLD
▸ **du'plexity** *n*

duplex apartment *n US & Canad.* an apartment on two floors.

duplex house *n US & Canad.* a house divided into two separate dwellings. Also called (US): **semidetached.**

duplicate *adj* ('dju:plɪkɪt). **1** copied exactly from an original. **2** identical. **3** existing as a pair or in pairs. ◆ *n* ('dju:plɪkɪt). **4** an exact copy. **5** something additional of the same kind. **6** two exact copies (esp. in **in duplicate**). ◆ *vb* ('dju:plɪˌkeɪt), **duplicates, duplicating, duplicated.** (*tr*) **7** to make a replica of. **8** to do or make again. **9** to make in a pair; make double. ORIG C15: from L *duplicāre* to double, from *duo* two + *plicāre* to fold
▸ **'duplicable** *adj*

duplication (ˌdju:plɪ'keɪʃən) *n* **1** the act of duplicating or the state of being duplicated. **2** a copy; duplicate. **3** *Genetics.* a mutation in which there are two or more copies of a gene or of a segment of a chromosome.

duplicator ('dju:plɪˌkeɪtə) *n* an apparatus for making replicas of an original, such as a machine using a stencil wrapped on an ink-loaded drum.

duplicity (dju:'plɪsɪtɪ) *n, pl* **duplicities.** deception; double-dealing. ORIG C15: from OF *duplicite,* from LL *duplicitās* a being double, from L DUPLEX

du Pré ★ (du 'preɪ) *n* **Jacqueline.** 1945–87, British cellist. Multiple sclerosis ended her performing career (1973).

Dupré ★ (*French* dypre) *n* **Marcel** (marsɛl). 1886–1971, French organist and composer, noted as an improviser.

Duque de Caxias ★ (*Portuguese* 'du:ke 'də: kə'ʃiəʃ) *n* a city in SE Brazil. Pop.: 325 903 (1991).

Dur. *abbrev. for* Durham.

durable ('djʊərəbəl) *adj* long-lasting; enduring. ORIG C14: from OF, from L *dūrābilis,* from *dūrāre* to last
▸ **ˌdura'bility** *n* ▸ **'durably** *adv*

durable goods *pl n* goods that require infrequent replacement. Also called: **durables.**

dural ('djʊərəl) *adj* relating to or affecting the dura mater.

Duralumin (djʊ'ræljʊmɪn) *n Trademark.* a light strong

aluminium alloy containing copper, silicon, magnesium, and manganese.

dura mater ('djʊərə 'meɪtə) *n* the outermost and toughest of the three membranes covering the brain and spinal cord. Often shortened to **dura.** ORIG C15: from Med. L: hard mother

duramen (djʊ'reɪmɛn) *n* another name for **heartwood.** ORIG C19: from L: hardness, from *dūrāre* to harden

Durán ★ (djʊ'ræn) *n* **Roberto.** born 1951, Panamanian boxer.

durance ('djʊərəns) *n Arch. or literary.* **1** imprisonment. **2** duration. ORIG C15: from OF, from *durer* to last, from L *dūrāre*

Durango ★ (djʊ'ræŋgəʊ; *Spanish* du'raŋgo) *n* **1** a state in N central Mexico: high plateau, with the Sierra Madre Occidental in the west; irrigated agriculture (esp. cotton) and rich mineral resources. Capital: Durango. Pop.: 1 449 036 (1997 est.). Area: 119 648 sq. km (46 662 sq. miles). **2** a city in NW central Mexico, capital of Durango state: mining centre. Pop.: 348 036 (1990). Official name: **Victoria de Durango.**

Durante ★ (də'ræntɪ) *n* **Jimmy**, known as *Schnozzle.* 1893–1980, US comedian.

Duras ★ (*French* dyra) *n* **Marguerite** (margərit), real name *Marguerite Donnadieu.* 1914–96, French novelist born in Indochina. Her works include the script for the film *Hiroshima mon amour* (1960).

duration (djʊ'reɪʃən) *n* the length of time that something lasts or continues. ORIG C14: from Med. L *dūrātiō,* from L *dūrāre* to last
▸ **du'rational** *adj*

durative ('djʊərətɪv) *Grammar.* ◆ *adj* **1** denoting an aspect of verbs that includes the imperfective and the progressive. ◆ *n* **2a** the durative aspect of a verb. **2b** a verb in this aspect.

Durban ★ ('dɜ:bᵊn) *n* a port in E South Africa, in E Natal on the Indian Ocean: University of Natal (1909); resort and industrial centre, with oil refineries, shipbuilding yards, etc. Pop.: 715 669 (1991).

durbar ('dɜ:bɑ:, ˌdɜ:'bɑ:) *n* **a** (formerly) the court of a native ruler or a governor in India. **b** a levee at such a court. ORIG C17: from Hindi *darbār,* from Persian, from *dar* door + *bār* entry, audience

Dürer ★ (*German* 'dy:rər) *n* **Albrecht** ('albrɛçt). 1471–1528, German Renaissance painter and engraver.

duress (djʊ'rɛs, djʊə-) *n* **1** compulsion by use of force or threat; coercion (often in **under duress**). **2** imprisonment. ORIG C14: from OF *duresse,* from L *dūritia* hardness, from *dūrus* hard

Durga Puja (ˌdʊəgə 'pu:dʒə) *n* another name for **Navaratri.** ORIG from Sanskr. *Durga* (Hindu goddess) and *puja* worship

Durham ★ ('dʌrəm) *n* **1** a county of NE England, on the North Sea: rises to the N Pennines in the west: contains three unitary authorities. Administrative centre: Durham. Pop. (excluding unitary authorities): 506 900 (1996). Area (excluding unitary authorities): 2434 sq. km (940 sq. miles). Abbrev.: **Dur. 2** a city in NE England, administrative centre of Co. Durham, on the River Wear: Norman cathedral; 11th-century castle (founded by William the Conqueror), now occupied by The University of Durham (1832). Pop.: 36 937 (1991). **3** a variety of shorthorn cattle.

during ('djʊərɪŋ) *prep* **1** concurrently with (some other activity). **2** within the limit of (a period of time). ORIG C14: from *duren* to last, ult. from L *dūrare* to last

Durkheim ★ ('dɜ:khaɪm; *French* dyrkɛm) *n* **Émile** (emil). 1858–1917, French sociologist, whose pioneering works include *De la Division du travail social* (1893).

durmast *or* **durmast oak** ('dɜ:ˌmɑ:st) *n* a large Eurasian oak tree with lobed leaves and sessile acorns. Also called: **sessile oak.** ORIG C18: prob. from DUN[2] + MAST[2]

durra ('dʌrə) *n* an Old World variety of sorghum, cultivated for grain and fodder. ORIG C18: from Ar. *dhurah* grain

Durrell ★ ('dʌrəl) *n* **1 Gerald (Malcolm)**, 1925–95, British zoologist and writer: his books include *My Family and Other Animals* (1956). **2** his brother, **Lawrence (George).** 1912–90, British poet and novelist; author of *The Alexandria Quartet* of novels, consisting of *Justine* (1957), *Balthazar* (1958), *Mountolive* (1958), and *Clea* (1960).

Dürrenmatt ★ (*German* 'dyrənmat) *n* **Friedrich** ('fri:drɪç). 1921–90, Swiss dramatist and novelist, whose works include the plays *The Visit* (1956) and *The Physicists* (1962).

durry ('dʌrɪ) *n, pl* **durries.** *Austral. sl.* a cigarette. ORIG from *durrie* a type of Indian carpet

durst (dɜ:st) *vb* an archaic past tense of **dare.**

durum *or* **durum wheat** ('djʊərəm) *n* a variety of wheat with a high gluten content, used chiefly to make pastas. ORIG C20: from NL *trīticum dūrum,* lit.: hard wheat

Duse ★ (*Italian* 'du:ze) *n* **Eleonora** (ˌɛlɪə'nɔ:rə). 1858–1924, Italian actress, noted as a tragedienne.

Dushanbe ★ (du:'ʃɑ:nbɪ) *n* the capital of Tajikistan; a cultural centre. Pop.: 524 000 (1994 est.). Former name (1929–61): **Stalinabad.**

dusk (dʌsk) *n* **1** the darker part of twilight. **2** *Poetic.* gloom; shade. ◆ *adj* **3** *Poetic.* shady; gloomy. ◆ *vb* **4** *Poetic.* to make or become dark. ORIG OE *dox*

dusky ('dʌskɪ) *adj* **duskier, duskiest. 1** dark in colour; swarthy or dark-skinned. **2** dim.
▸ **'duskily** *adv* ▸ **'duskiness** *n*

Düsseldorf ★ ('dʊsəlˌdɔ:f; *German* 'dysəldɔrf) *n* an industrial city in W Germany, capital of North Rhine-Westphalia, on the Rhine: commercial centre of the Rhine-Ruhr industrial area. Pop.: 571 030 (1996 est.).

dust (dʌst) *n* **1** dry fine powdery material, such as particles of dirt, earth, or pollen. **2** a cloud of such fine particles. **3a** the mortal body of man. **3b** the corpse of a dead person. **4** the earth; ground. **5** *Inf.* a disturbance; fuss (esp. in **kick up a dust, raise a dust**). **6** something of little worth. **7** short for **gold dust. 8** ashes or household refuse. **9 dust and ashes.** something that is very disappointing. **10 shake the dust off** (*or* **from**) **one's feet.** to depart angrily or contemptuously. **11 throw dust in the eyes of.** to confuse or mislead. ◆ *vb* **12** (*tr*) to sprinkle or cover (something) with (dust or some other powdery substance). **13** to remove dust (from) by wiping, sweeping, or brushing. **14** *Arch.* to make or become dirty with dust. ◆ See also **dust down, dust-up.** ORIG OE *dūst*
▸ **'dustless** *adj*

dustbin ('dʌstˌbɪn) *n* a large, usually cylindrical container for rubbish, esp. one used by a household. US and Canad. names: **garbage can, trash can.**

dust bowl *n* a semiarid area in which the surface soil is exposed to wind erosion.

Dust Bowl ★ *n* **the.** the area of the south central US that became denuded of topsoil by wind erosion during the droughts of the mid-1930s.

dustcart ('dʌstˌkɑ:t) *n* a road vehicle for collecting refuse. US and Canad. name: **garbage truck.**

dust cover *n* **1** another name for **dustsheet. 2** another name for **dust jacket. 3** a Perspex cover for the turntable of a record player.

dust devil *n* a strong miniature whirlwind that whips up dust, litter, leaves, etc., into the air.

dust down *vb* (*tr, adv*). **1** to remove dust from by brushing or wiping. **2** to reprimand severely.
▸ **dusting down** *n*

duster ('dʌstə) *n* **1** a cloth used for dusting. US name: **dust cloth. 2** a machine for blowing out dust. **3** a person or thing that dusts.

dusting-powder *n* fine powder (such as talcum powder) used to absorb moisture, etc.

dust jacket *or* **cover** *n* a removable paper cover used to protect a bound book.

dustman ('dʌstmən) *n, pl* **dustmen.** *Brit.* a man whose job is to collect domestic refuse.

dustpan ('dʌstˌpæn) *n* a short-handled hooded shovel into which dust is swept from floors, etc.

dustsheet ('dʌstˌʃi:t) *n Brit.* a large cloth used to protect furniture from dust.

dust storm *n* a windstorm that whips up clouds of dust.

dust-up *Inf.* ◆ *n* **1** a fight or argument. ◆ *vb* **dust up. 2** (*tr, adv*) to attack (someone).

dusty ('dʌstɪ) *adj* **dustier, dustiest. 1** covered with or involving dust. **2** like dust. **3** (of a colour) tinged with grey; pale. **4 give** (*or* **get**) **a dusty answer.** to give (*or* get) an unhelpful or bad-tempered reply.
▸ **'dustily** *adv* ▸ **'dustiness** *n*

Dutch (dʌtʃ) *n* **1** the language of the Netherlands. **2 the Dutch.** (*functioning as pl*) the natives, citizens, or inhabitants of the Netherlands. **3** See **double Dutch. 4 in Dutch.** *Sl.* in trouble. ◆ *adj* **5** of the Netherlands, its inhabitants, or their language. ◆ *adv* **6 go Dutch.** *Inf.* to share expenses equally.

Dutch auction *n* an auction in which the price is lowered by stages until a buyer is found.

Dutch barn *n Brit.* a farm building consisting of a steel frame and a curved roof.

Dutch courage *n* **1** false courage gained from drinking alcohol. **2** alcoholic drink.

Dutch door *n* the US and Canad. name for **stable door.**

Dutch East Indies ★ *n* **the.** a former name (1798–1945) of **Indonesia.** Also called: **Netherlands East Indies.**

Dutch elm disease *n* a fungal disease of elm trees characterized by withering of the foliage and stems and eventual death of the tree.

Dutch Guiana *or* **Netherlands Guiana** ★ *n* the former name of **Surinam.**

Dutchman ('dʌtʃmən) *n, pl* **Dutchmen. 1** a native, citizen, or inhabitant of the Netherlands. **2** *S. African derog.* an Afrikaner.

Dutch New Guinea ★ *n* a former name (until 1963) of **Irian Jaya.**

Dutch oven *n* **1** an iron or earthenware container with a cover, used for stews, etc. **2** a metal box, open in front, for cooking in front of an open fire.

Dutch treat *n Inf.* an entertainment, meal, etc., where each person pays for himself.

Dutch uncle *n Inf.* a person who criticizes or reproves frankly and severely.

Dutch West Indies ★ *pl n* **the.** a former name of the **Netherlands Antilles.**

duteous ('dju:tɪəs) *adj Formal or arch.* dutiful; obedient.
▸ **'duteously** *adv*

dutiable ('dju:tɪəbᵊl) *adj* (of goods) liable to duty.
▸ **ˌdutia'bility** *n*

dutiful ('dju:tɪfʊl) *adj* **1** exhibiting or having a sense of duty. **2** characterized by or resulting from a sense of duty: *a dutiful answer.*

duty ('dju:tɪ) *n, pl* **duties. 1** a task or action that a person is bound to perform for moral or legal reasons. **2** respect or obedience due to a superior, older persons, etc. **3** the force that binds one morally or legally to one's obligations. **4** a government tax, esp. on imports. **5** *Brit.* **5a** the quantity of work for which a machine is designed. **5b** a measure of the efficiency of a machine. **6a** a job or service allocated. **6b** (*as modifier*): *duty rota.* **7 do duty for.** to act as a substitute for. **8 on** (*or* **off**) **duty.** at (*or* not at) work. ORIG C13: from Anglo-F *dueté,* from OF *deu* DUE

duty-bound *adj* morally obliged.

duty-free *adj, adv* **1** with exemption from customs or excise duties. ◆ *n* **2** goods sold in a duty-free shop.

duty-free shop *n* a shop, esp. one at an airport or on board a ship, that sells perfume, tobacco, etc., at duty-free prices.

duumvir (dju:'ʌmvə) *n, pl* **duumvirs** *or* **duumviri** (-vɪˌri:). **1** *Roman history.* one of two coequal magistrates. **2** either of two men who exercise a joint authority. ORIG C16: from L, from *duo* two + *vir* man
▸ **duumvirate** (dju:'ʌmvɪrɪt) *n*

Duvalier ★ (*French* dyvalje) *n* **1 François** (frɑ̃swa), known as *Papa Doc.* 1907–71, president of Haiti (1957–71). **2** his son, **Jean-Claude** (ʒɑ̃klod), known as *Baby Doc.* born 1951, Haitian statesman; president of Haiti 1971–86; deposed and exiled.

duvet ('du:veɪ) *n* **1** another name for **continental quilt. 2** Also called: **duvet jacket.** a down-filled jacket. ORIG C18: from F, from earlier *dumet,* from OF *dum* DOWN[2]

dux (dʌks) *n* (esp. in Scottish schools) the top pupil in a class or school. ORIG L: leader

DV *abbrev. for:* **1** Deo volente. ORIG L: God willing **2** Douay Version (of the Bible).

DVD *abbrev. for* digital versatile disk or (formerly) digital video disk.

Dvina ★ (*Russian* dvi'na) *n* **1 Northern.** a river in NW Russia, formed by the confluence of the Sukhona and Yug Rivers and flowing northwest to Dvina Bay in the White Sea. Length: 750 km (466 miles). Russian name: **Severnaya Dvina. 2 Western.** a river in E Europe, rising in the Valdai Hills in W Russia, and flowing south and southwest then northwest to the Gulf of Riga in Latvia. Length: 1021 km (634 miles). Russian name: **Zapadnaya Dvina** ('zapədnəjə). Latvian name: **Daugava.**

Dvina Bay *or* **Dvina Gulf** ★ *n* an inlet of the White Sea, off the coast of NW Russia.

Dvinsk ★ (dvinsk) *n* transliteration of the former Russian name for **Daugavpils.**

DVLA *abbrev. for* Driver and Vehicle Licensing Agency.

Dvořák ★ ('dvɔ:ʒæk; *Czech* 'dvɔrʒa:k) *n* **Antonín** ('antɔnji:n), known as *Anton Dvořák.* 1841–1904, Czech composer; noted for the *Symphony No. 9 From the New World* (1893).

DVT *abbrev. for* deep-vein thrombosis.

dwaal (dwɑ:l) *n S. African.* a state of befuddlement; daze. ORIG from Afrik. *dwaal* wander

dwale (dweɪl) *n* another name for **deadly nightshade.** ORIG C14: ?from ON

dwarf (dwɔ:f) *n, pl* **dwarfs** *or* **dwarves** (dwɔ:vz). **1** an abnormally undersized person. **2a** an animal or plant much below the average height for the species. **2b** (*as modifier*): *a dwarf tree.* **3** (in folklore) a small ugly manlike creature, often possessing magical powers. **4** *Astron.* short for **dwarf star.** ◆ *vb* **5** to become or cause to become comparatively small in size, importance, etc. **6** (*tr*) to stunt the growth of. ORIG OE *dweorg*
▸ **'dwarfish** *adj*

dwarf star *n* any unevolved star, such as the sun, lying in the main sequence of the Hertzsprung-Russell diagram. Also called: **main sequence star.** See also **red dwarf, white dwarf.**

dwell (dwɛl) *vb* **dwells, dwelling, dwelt** *or* **dwelled.** (*intr*) **1** *Formal, literary.* to live as a permanent resident. **2** to live (in a specified state): *to dwell in poverty.* ◆ *n* **3** a regular pause in the operation of a machine. ORIG OE *dwellan* to seduce, get lost
▸ **'dweller** *n*

dwelling ('dwɛlɪŋ) *n Formal, literary.* a place of residence.

dwell on *or* **upon** *vb* (*intr, prep*) to think, speak, or write at length about.

dwelt (dwɛlt) *vb* a past tense and past participle of **dwell.**

dwindle ('dwɪndᵊl) *vb* **dwindles, dwindling, dwindled.** to grow or cause to grow less in size, intensity, or number. ORIG C16: from OE *dwīnan* to waste away

Dy *the chemical symbol for* dysprosium.

dyad ('daɪæd) *n* **1** *Maths.* an operator that is the unspecified product of two vectors. **2** an atom or group that has a valency of two. **3** a group of two; couple. ORIG C17: from LL *dyas,* from Gk *duas* two
▸ **dy'adic** *adj*

Dyak *or* **Dayak** ('daɪæk) *n, pl* **Dyaks, Dyak** *or* **Dayaks, Dayak.** a member of a Malaysian people of Borneo. ORIG from Malay: upcountry, from *darat* land

dybbuk ('dɪbək) *n, pl* **dybbuks** *or* **dybbukkim.** *Judaism.* (in folklore) the soul of a dead sinner that has transmigrated into the body of a living person. ORIG from Yiddish: devil, from Heb.

dye (daɪ) *n* **1** a staining or colouring substance. **2** a liquid that contains a colouring material and can be used to stain fabrics, skins, etc. **3** the colour produced by dyeing. ◆ *vb* **dyes, dyeing, dyed. 4** (*tr*) to impart a colour or stain to (fabric, hair, etc.) by or as if by the application of a dye. ORIG OE *dēagian,* from *dēag* a dye
▸ **'dyable** *or* **'dyeable** *adj* ▸ **'dyer** *n*

dyed-in-the-wool *adj* **1** uncompromising or unchanging in attitude, opinion, etc. **2** (of a fabric) made of dyed yarn.

dyeing ('daɪɪŋ) *n* the process or industry of colouring yarns, fabric, etc.

dyestuff ('daɪˌstʌf) *n* a substance that can be used as a dye or which yields a dye.

Dyfed ★ ('dʌvɛd) *n* a former county in SW Wales, formed in 1974 from Cardiganshire, Pembrokeshire, and Carmarthenshire, replaced in 1996 by Pembrokeshire, Carmarthenshire, and Ceredigion.

dying ('daɪɪŋ) *vb* **1** the present participle of **die**[1]. ◆ *adj* **2** relating to or occurring at the moment of death: *a dying wish.*

dyke[1] *or* **dike** (daɪk) *n* **1** an embankment constructed to prevent flooding, keep out the sea, or confine a river to a particular course. **2** a ditch or watercourse. **3** a bank made of earth alongside a ditch. **4** *Scot.* a wall, esp. a drystone wall. **5** a barrier or obstruction. **6** a wall-like mass of igneous rock in older sedimentary rock. **7** *Austral. & NZ inf.* a lavatory. ◆ *vb* **dykes, dyking, dyked. 8** (*tr*) to protect, enclose, or drain (land) with a dyke. ORIG C13: from OE *dic* ditch

dyke[2] *or* **dike** (daɪk) *n Sl.* a lesbian. ORIG C20: from ?

Dylan ★ ('dɪlən) *n* **Bob**, real name *Robert Allen Zimmerman.* born 1941, US rock singer and songwriter. His albums include *Blonde on Blonde* (1966), *Blood on the Tracks* (1974), and *Time Out of Mind* (1997).

dynamic (daɪ'næmɪk) *adj* **1** of or concerned with energy or forces that produce motion, as opposed to *static.* **2** of or concerned with dynamics. **3** Also: **dynamical.** characterized by force of personality, ambition, energy, etc. **4** *Computing.* (of a memory) needing its contents refreshed periodically. ORIG C19: from F *dynamique,* from Gk *dunamikos* powerful, from *dunamis* power, from *dunasthai* to be able
▸ **dy'namically** *adv*

dynamics (daɪ'næmɪks) *n* **1** (*functioning as sing*) the branch of mechanics concerned with the forces that change or produce the motions of bodies. **2** (*functioning as sing*) the branch of mechanics that includes statics and kinetics. **3** (*functioning as sing*) the branch of any science concerned with forces. **4** (*functioning as pl*) those forces that produce change in any field or system. **5** (*functioning as pl*) *Music.* **5a** the various degrees of loudness called for in performance. **5b** directions and symbols used to indicate degrees of loudness.

dynamism ('daɪnəˌmɪzəm) *n* **1** *Philosophy.* any of several theories that attempt to explain phenomena in terms of an immanent force or energy. **2** the forcefulness of an energetic personality.
▸ **'dynamist** *n* ▸ **ˌdyna'mistic** *adj*

dynamite ('daɪnəˌmaɪt) *n* **1** an explosive consisting of nitroglycerine mixed with an absorbent. **2** *Inf.* a spectacular or potentially dangerous person or thing. ◆ *vb* **dynamites, dynamiting, dynamited. 3** (*tr*) to mine or blow up with dynamite. ORIG C19 (coined by Alfred Nobel): from DYNAMO- + -ITE[1]
▸ **'dynaˌmiter** *n*

dynamo ('daɪnəˌməʊ) *n, pl* **dynamos. 1** a device for converting mechanical energy into electrical energy. **2** *Inf.* an energetic hard-working person. ORIG C19: short for *dynamoelectric machine*

dynamo- *or sometimes before a vowel* **dynam-** *combining form.* indicating power: *dynamite.* ORIG from Gk, from *dunamis* power

dynamoelectric (ˌdaɪnəməʊɪ'lɛktrɪk) *or* **dynamoelectrical** *adj* of or concerned with the interconversion of mechanical and electrical energy.

dynamometer (ˌdaɪnə'mɒmɪtə) *n* an instrument for measuring power or force.

dynamotor ('daɪnəˌməʊtə) *n* an electrical machine having two independent armature windings of which one acts as a motor and the other a generator: used to convert direct current into alternating current.

dynast ('dɪnəst, -æst) *n* a ruler, esp. a hereditary one. ORIG C17: from L *dynastēs,* from Gk, from *dunasthai* to be powerful

dynasty ('dɪnəstɪ) *n, pl* **dynasties. 1** a sequence of hereditary rulers. **2** any sequence of powerful leaders of the same family. ORIG C15: via LL from Gk, from *dunastēs* DYNAST
▸ **dynastic** (dɪ'næstɪk) *adj*

dyne (daɪn) *n* the cgs unit of force; the force that imparts an acceleration of 1 centimetre per second per second to a mass of 1 gram. 1 dyne is equivalent to 10^{-5} newton or 7.233×10^{-5} poundal. ORIG C19: from F, from Gk *dunamis* power, force

dys- *prefix* **1** diseased, abnormal, or faulty. **2** difficult or painful. **3** unfavourable or bad. ORIG via L from Gk *dus-*

dysentery ('dɪsᵊntrɪ) *n* infection of the intestine marked by severe diarrhoea with the passage of mucus and blood. ORIG C14: via L from Gk, from *dusentera,* lit.: bad bowels, from DYS- + *enteron* intestine
▸ **dysenteric** (ˌdɪsᵊn'tɛrɪk) *adj*

dysfunction (dɪs'fʌŋkʃən) *n* **1** *Med.* any disturbance or abnormality in the function of an organ or part. **2** (esp. of a family) failure to show the characteristics or fulfil the purposes accepted as normal or beneficial.

dysfunctional (dɪs'fʌŋkʃənᵊl) *adj* **1** *Med.* (of an organ or part) not functioning normally. **2** (esp. of a family) characterized by a breakdown of normal or beneficial relationships between the members of a group.

dysgraphia (dɪs'græfɪə) *n* inability to write correctly, caused by disease of part of the brain.

dyslexia (dɪs'lɛksɪə) *n* a developmental disorder which can cause learning difficulty in one or more of the areas of reading, writing, and numeracy. ORIG C19: NL, from DYS- + *-lexia,* from Gk *lexis* word
▸ **dyslectic** (dɪs'lɛktɪk) *adj* ▸ **dys'lexic** *adj, n*

dysmenorrhoea *or esp. US* **dysmenorrhea** (ˌdɪsmɛnə'rɪə) *n* abnormally difficult or painful menstruation. ORIG C19: from DYS- + Gk *mēn* month + *rhoia* a flowing

dyspepsia (dɪs'pɛpsɪə) *n* indigestion or upset stomach. ORIG C18: from L, from Gk *duspepsia,* from DYS- + *pepsis* digestion

dyspeptic (dɪs'pɛptɪk) *adj* **1** relating to or suffering from dyspepsia. **2** irritable. ◆ *n* **3** a person suffering from dyspepsia.

dysphasia (dɪs'feɪzɪə) *n* a disorder of language caused by a brain lesion.
▸ **dys'phasic** *adj, n*

dysphoria (dɪs'fɔːrɪə) *n* a feeling of being ill at ease. ORIG C20: NL, from Gk DYS- + *-phoria,* from *pherein* to bear

dyspnoea *or US* **dyspnea** (dɪsp'niːə) *n* difficulty in breathing or in catching the breath. ORIG C17: via L from Gk *duspnoia,* from DYS- + *pnoē* breath, from *pnein* to breathe
▸ **dysp'noeal, dysp'noeic** *or US* **dysp'neal, dysp'neic** *adj*

dysprosium (dɪs'prəʊsɪəm) *n* a metallic element of the lanthanide series: used in laser materials and as a neutron absorber in nuclear control rods. Symbol: Dy; atomic no.: 66; atomic wt.: 162.50. ORIG C20: NL, from Gk *dusprositos* difficult to get near + -IUM

dysthymia (dɪs'θaɪmɪə) *n Psychiatry.* the characteristics of the neurotic and introverted, including anxiety, depression, and compulsive behaviour. ORIG C19: NL, from Gk *dusthumia,* from DYS- + *thumos* mind
▸ **dys'thymic** *adj*

dysthymic disorder *n* a psychiatric disorder characterized by generalized depression that lasts for at least a year.

dystrophy ('dɪstrəfɪ) *n* any of various bodily disorders, characterized by wasting of tissues. See also **muscular dystrophy.** ORIG C19: NL *dystrophia,* from DYS- + Gk *trophē* food
▸ **dystrophic** (dɪs'trɒfɪk) *adj*

dz. *abbrev. for* dozen.

Dzaudzhikau ★ (dzəudʒi'kau) *n* the former name (1944–54) of **Ordzhonikidze.**

dzo (zəʊ) *n, pl* **dzos** *or* **dzo.** a variant spelling of **zo.**

Dzungaria ★ (dzuŋ'gɛərɪə, zuŋ-) *n* a variant transliteration of the Chinese name for **Junggar Pendi.**

Ee

e *or* **E** (iː) *n, pl* **e's, E's,** *or* **Es. 1** the fifth letter and second vowel of the English alphabet. **2** any of several speech sounds represented by this letter, as in *he, bet,* or *below.*

e *symbol for:* **1** *Maths.* a transcendental number used as the base of natural logarithms. Approximate value: 2.718 282... **2** electron.

E *symbol for:* **1** *Music.* **1a** the third note of the scale of C major. **1b** the major or minor key having this note as its tonic. **2** earth. **3** East. **4** English. **5** Egypt(ian). **6** *Physics.* **6a** energy. **6b** electromotive force. **7** exa-. **8a** a person without a regular income, or who is dependent on the state on a long-term basis because of unemployment, sickness, old age, etc. **8b** (*as modifier*): *E worker.* ◆ See also **occupation groupings. 9** the drug ecstasy.

e. *abbrev. for* engineer(ing).

E. *abbrev. for* Earl.

e- *prefix* electronic, indicating the involvement of the Internet: *e-mail; e-money.*

E- *prefix* used with numbers indicating a standardized system within the European Union, as of food additives. See also **E number.**

ea. *abbrev. for* each.

each (iːtʃ) *determiner* **1a** every (one) of two or more considered individually: *each day; each person.* **1b** (*as pron*): *each gave according to his ability.* ◆ *adv* **2** for, to, or from each one; apiece: *four apples each.* ORIG OE *ǣlc*

> **USAGE NOTE** *Each* is a singular pronoun and should be used with a singular form of a verb: *each of the candidates was* (not *were*) *interviewed separately.* See also at **either.**

Eadred ★ (ˈɛdrɪd) *n* died 955 A.D., king of England (946–55): regained Northumbria (954) from the Norwegian king Eric Bloodaxe.

eager (ˈiːgə) *adj* **1** (*postpositive;* often foll. by *to* or *for*) impatiently desirous (of); anxious or avid (for). **2** characterized by or feeling expectancy or great desire: *an eager look.* **3** *Arch.* biting; sharp. ORIG C13: from OF *egre,* from L *acer* sharp, keen
▸ ˈ**eagerly** *adv* ▸ ˈ**eagerness** *n*

eager beaver *n Inf.* a person who displays conspicuous diligence.

eagle (ˈiːgᵊl) *n* **1** any of various birds of prey having large broad wings and strong soaring flight. Related adj: **aquiline. 2** a representation of an eagle used as an emblem, etc., esp. representing power: *the Roman eagle.* **3** a standard, seal, etc., bearing the figure of an eagle. **4** *Golf.* a score of two strokes under par for a hole. **5** a former US gold coin worth ten dollars. ◆ *vb* **6** *Golf.* to score two strokes under par for a hole. ORIG C14: from OF *aigle,* from OProvençal *aigla,* from L *aquila*

eagle-eyed *adj* having keen or piercing eyesight.

eagle-hawk *n* a large brown Australian eagle. Also called: **wedge-tailed eagle.**

eagle owl *n* a large Eurasian owl with brownish speckled plumage and large ear tufts.

eaglet (ˈiːglɪt) *n* a young eagle.

Eakins ★ (ˈiːkɪnz) *n* **Thomas.** 1844–1916, US painter of portraits and sporting life: a noted realist.

ealdorman (ˈɔːldəmən) *n, pl* **ealdormen.** an official of Anglo-Saxon England, appointed by the king, and responsible for law and order in his shire and for leading local militia. ORIG OE *ealdor* lord + MAN

Ealing ★ (ˈiːlɪŋ) *n* a borough of W Greater London, formed in 1965 from Acton, Ealing, and Southall. Pop.: 289 800 (1994 est.). Area: 55 sq. km (21 sq. miles).

-ean *suffix forming adjectives and nouns.* a variant of **-an:** *Caesarean.*

ear[1] (ɪə) *n* **1** the organ of hearing and balance in higher vertebrates (see **middle ear**). Related adj: **aural. 2** the outermost cartilaginous part of the ear in mammals, esp. man. **3** the sense of hearing. **4** sensitivity to musical sounds, poetic diction, etc.: *he has an ear for music.* **5** attention; consideration (esp. in **give ear to, lend an ear**). **6** an object resembling the external ear. **7 all ears.** very attentive; listening carefully. **8 a thick ear.** *Inf.* a blow on the ear. **9 fall on deaf ears.** to be ignored or pass unnoticed. **10 in one ear and out the other.** heard but unheeded. **11 keep** (*or* **have**) **one's ear to the ground.** to be or try to be well informed about current trends and opinions. **12 out on one's ear.** *Inf.* dismissed unceremoniously. **13 play by ear. 13a** *Inf.* to act according to the demands of a situation; improvise. **13b** to perform a musical piece on an instrument without written music. **14 turn a deaf ear.** to be deliberately unresponsive. **15 up to one's ears.** *Inf.* deeply involved, as in work or debt. ORIG OE *ēare*
▸ **eared** *adj* ▸ ˈ**earless** *adj*

ear[2] (ɪə) *n* **1** the part of a cereal plant, such as wheat or barley, that contains the seeds, grains, or kernels. ◆ *vb* **2** (*intr*) (of cereal plants) to develop such parts. ORIG OE *ēar*

earache (ˈɪərˌeɪk) *n* pain in the ear.

earbash (ˈɪəˌbæʃ) *vb* (*intr*) *Austral. & NZ sl.* to talk incessantly.
▸ ˈ**ear**ˌ**bashing** *n*

eardrum (ˈɪəˌdrʌm) *n* the nontechnical name for **tympanic membrane.**

earful (ˈɪəfʊl) *n Inf.* **1** something heard or overheard. **2** a rebuke or scolding.

Earhart ★ (ˈɛəˌhɑːt) *n* **Amelia.** 1898–1937, US aviator: the first woman to fly the Atlantic (1928). She disappeared on a Pacific flight (1937).

earl (ɜːl) *n* (in Britain) a nobleman ranking below a marquess and above a viscount. Female equivalent: **countess.** ORIG OE *eorl*
▸ ˈ**earldom** *n*

Earl Grey *n* a variety of China tea flavoured with oil of bergamot.

Earl Marshal *n* an officer of the English peerage who presides over the College of Heralds and organizes royal processions and other important ceremonies.

early (ˈɜːlɪ) *adj, adv* **earlier, earliest. 1** before the expected or usual time. **2** occurring in or characteristic of the first part of a period or sequence. **3** occurring in or characteristic of a period far back in time. **4** occurring in the near future. **5 in the early days.** during the first years of any enterprise, such as marriage. ORIG OE *ǣrlīce,* from *ǣr* ERE + *-līce* -LY[2]
▸ ˈ**earliness** *n*

early closing *n Brit.* the shutting of shops in a town one afternoon each week.

Early English *n* a style of architecture used in England in the 12th and 13th centuries, characterized by lancet arches and plate tracery.

early music *n* **1** music of the Middle Ages and Renaissance, sometimes also including music of the baroque and early classical periods. ◆ (*modifier*) **early-music. 2** of or denoting an approach to musical performance emphasizing the use of period instruments and historically researched scores and playing techniques: *the early-music movement.*

early warning *n* advance notice of some impending event.

earmark (ˈɪəˌmɑːk) *vb* (*tr*) **1** to set aside or mark out for a specific purpose. **2** to make an identification mark on the ear of (a domestic animal). ◆ *n* **3** such a mark of

★ people and places

identification. **4** any distinguishing mark or characteristic.

earmuff ('ɪəˌmʌf) *n* one of a joined pair of pads of fur or cloth for keeping the ears warm.

earn (ɜːn) *vb* **1** to gain or be paid (money or other payment) in return for work or service. **2** (*tr*) to acquire or deserve through behaviour or action. **3** (*tr*) (of securities, investments, etc.) to gain (interest, profit, etc.). ORIG OE *earnian*

earned income *n* income derived from paid employment.

earner ('ɜːnə) *n* **1** a person who earns money. **2** *Sl.* an activity or thing that produces income, esp. illicitly: *a nice little earner.*

earnest[1] ('ɜːnɪst) *adj* **1** serious in mind or intention. **2** characterized by sincerity of intention. **3** demanding or receiving serious attention. ♦ *n* **4 in earnest.** with serious or sincere intentions. ORIG OE *eornost*
▸ **'earnestly** *adv* ▸ **'earnestness** *n*

earnest[2] ('ɜːnɪst) *n* **1** a part of something given in advance as a guarantee of the remainder. **2** Also called: **earnest money.** *Contract law.* something given, usually a nominal sum of money, to confirm a contract. **3** any token of something to follow. ORIG C13: from OF *erres* pledges, pl of *erre* earnest money, from L *arrha,* from *arrabō* pledge, from Gk *arrabon,* from Heb. *'ērābhōn* pledge

earnings ('ɜːnɪŋz) *pl n* **1** money or other payment earned. **2** the profits of an enterprise.

EAROM ('ɪərɒm) *n Computing. acronym for* electrically alterable read only memory.

earphone ('ɪəˌfəʊn) *n* a device for converting electric currents into sound waves, held close to or inserted into the ear.

ear piercing *n* **1** the making of a hole in the lobe of an ear, using a sterilized needle, so that earrings may be worn fastened in the hole. ♦ *adj* **ear-piercing. 2** so loud or shrill as to hurt the ears.

earplug ('ɪəˌplʌg) *n* a piece of soft material placed in the ear to keep out noise or water.

earring ('ɪəˌrɪŋ) *n* an ornament for the ear, usually clipped onto the lobe or fastened through a hole pierced in the lobe.

earshot ('ɪəˌʃɒt) *n* the range or distance within which sound may be heard (esp. in **out of earshot,** etc.)

ear-splitting *adj* so loud or shrill as to hurt the ears.

earth (ɜːθ) *n* **1** (*sometimes cap.*) the third planet from the sun, the only planet on which life is known to exist. Related adjs.: **terrestrial, telluric. 2** the inhabitants of this planet: *the whole earth rejoiced.* **3** the dry surface of this planet; land; ground. **4** the loose soft material on the surface of the ground that consists of disintegrated rock particles, mould, clay, etc.; soil. **5** worldly or temporal matters as opposed to the concerns of the spirit. **6** the hole in which a burrowing animal, esp. a fox, lives. **7** *Chem.* See **rare earth, alkaline earth. 8** Also (US and Canad.): **ground. 8a** a connection between an electric circuit or device and the earth, which is at zero potential. **8b** a terminal to which this connection is made. **9** (*modifier*) *Astrol.* of or relating to a group of three signs of the zodiac: Taurus, Virgo, and Capricorn. **10 come back** *or* **down to earth.** to return to reality from a fantasy or daydream. **11 on earth.** used as an intensifier in **what on earth, who on earth,** etc. **12 run to earth. 12a** to hunt (an animal, esp. a fox) to its earth and trap it there. **12b** to find (someone) after hunting. ♦ *vb* **13** Also (US and Canad.): **ground.** (*tr*) to connect (a circuit, device, etc.) to earth. ♦ See also **earth up.** ORIG OE *eorthe*

earthbound ('ɜːθˌbaʊnd) *adj* **1** confined to the earth. **2** heading towards the earth.

earth closet *n* a type of lavatory in which earth is used to cover excreta.

earthen ('ɜːθən) *adj* (*prenominal*) **1** made of baked clay: *an earthen pot.* **2** made of earth.

earthenware ('ɜːθənˌwɛə) *n* **a** vessels, etc., made of baked clay. **b** (*as adj*): *an earthenware pot.*

earth-grazer *n* an asteroid in an orbit that takes it close to the earth. Also called: **near-earth asteroid.**

earthly ('ɜːθlɪ) *adj* **earthlier, earthliest. 1** of or characteristic of the earth as opposed to heaven; materialistic; worldly. **2** (*usually with a negative*) *Inf.* conceivable or possible (in **not an earthly** (**chance**), etc.).
▸ **'earthliness** *n*

earthman ('ɜːθˌmæn) *n, pl* **earthmen.** (esp. in science fiction) an inhabitant or native of the earth. Also called: **earthling.**

earthnut ('ɜːθˌnʌt) *n* **1** a perennial umbelliferous plant of Europe and Asia, having edible dark brown tubers. **2** any of various plants having an edible root, tuber, or underground pod, such as the peanut or truffle.

earthquake ('ɜːθˌkweɪk) *n* a series of vibrations at the earth's surface caused by movement along a fault plane, volcanic activity, etc. Related adj: **seismic.**

earth science *n* any of various sciences, such as geology and geography, that are concerned with the structure, age, etc., of the earth.

earth up *vb* (*tr, adv*) to cover (part of a plant) with soil to protect from frost, light, etc.

earthward ('ɜːθwəd) *adj* **1** directed towards the earth. ♦ *adv* **2** a variant of **earthwards.**

earthwards ('ɜːθwədz) *or* **earthward** *adv* towards the earth.

earthwork ('ɜːθˌwɜːk) *n* **1** excavation of earth, as in engineering construction. **2** a fortification made of earth.

earthworm ('ɜːθˌwɜːm) *n* any of numerous worms which burrow in the soil and help aerate and break up the ground.

earthy ('ɜːθɪ) *adj* **earthier, earthiest. 1** of, composed of, or characteristic of earth. **2** unrefined, coarse, or crude.
▸ **'earthily** *adv* ▸ **'earthiness** *n*

ear trumpet *n* a trumpet-shaped instrument held to the ear: an old form of hearing aid.

earwax ('ɪəˌwæks) *n* the nontechnical name for **cerumen.**

earwig ('ɪəˌwɪg) *n* **1** any of various insects that typically have an elongated body with small leathery forewings, semicircular membranous hindwings, and curved forceps at the tip of the abdomen. ♦ *vb* **earwigs, earwigging, earwigged. 2** (*intr*) *Inf.* to eavesdrop. **3** (*tr*) *Arch.* to attempt to influence (a person) by private insinuation. ORIG OE *ēarwicga,* from *ēare* ear + *wicga* beetle, insect; prob. from superstition that the insect crept into human ears

earwigging ('ɪəˌwɪgɪŋ) *n Inf.* a scolding or harangue: *I'll give him an earwigging about that.*

ease (iːz) *n* **1** freedom from discomfort, worry, or anxiety. **2** lack of difficulty, labour, or awkwardness. **3** rest, leisure, or relaxation. **4** freedom from poverty; affluence: *a life of ease.* **5** lack of restraint, embarrassment, or stiffness: *ease of manner.* **6 at ease. 6a** *Mil.* (of a standing soldier, etc.) in a relaxed position with the feet apart, rather than at attention. **6b** a command to adopt such a position. **6c** in a relaxed attitude or frame of mind. ♦ *vb* **eases, easing, eased. 7** to make or become less burdensome. **8** (*tr*) to relieve (a person) of worry or care; comfort. **9** (*tr*) to make comfortable or give rest to. **10** (*tr*) to make less difficult; facilitate. **11** to move or cause to move into, out of, etc., with careful manipulation. **12** (when *intr,* often foll. by *off* or *up*) to lessen or cause to lessen in severity, pressure, tension, or strain. **13 ease oneself** *or* **ease nature.** *Arch., euphemistic.* to urinate or defecate. ORIG C13: from OF *aise* ease, opportunity, from L *adjacēns* neighbouring (area); see ADJACENT
▸ **'easeful** *adj*

easel ('iːzᵊl) *n* a frame, usually an upright tripod, for supporting or displaying an artist's canvas, a blackboard, etc. ORIG C17: from Du. *ezel*; ult. from L *asinus* ass

easement ('iːzmənt) *n* **1** *Property law.* the right enjoyed by a landowner of making limited use of his neighbour's land, as by crossing it to reach his own property. **2** the act of easing or something that brings ease.

easily ('iːzɪlɪ) *adv* **1** with ease; without difficulty or exertion. **2** by far; undoubtedly: *easily the best.* **3** probably; almost certainly.

easiness ('iːzɪnɪs) *n* **1** the quality or condition of being easy to accomplish, do, obtain, etc. **2** ease or relaxation of manner; nonchalance.

east (iːst) *n* **1** the direction along a parallel towards the sunrise, at 90° to north; the direction of the earth's rotation. **2 the east.** (*often cap.*) any area lying in or towards the east. Related adj: **oriental. 3** (*usually cap.*) *Cards.* the player or position at the table corresponding to east on the compass. ◆ *adj* **4** situated in, moving towards, or facing the east. **5** (esp. of the wind) from the east. ◆ *adv* **6** in, to, or towards the east. **7 back East.** *Canad.* in or to E Canada, esp. east of Quebec. ◆ Symbol: E ORIG OE *ēast*

East (iːst) *n* **the. 1** the continent of Asia regarded as culturally distinct from Europe and the West; the Orient. **2** the countries under Communist rule and those under Communist rule until *c.* 1991, lying mainly in the E hemisphere. ◆ *adj* **3** of or denoting the eastern part of a specified country, area, etc.

East Africa ★ *n* a region of Africa comprising Kenya, Uganda, and Tanzania.
▸ **East African** *adj, n*

East Anglia ★ *n* **1** a region of E England south of the Wash: consists of Norfolk and Suffolk, and parts of Essex and Cambridgeshire. **2** an Anglo-Saxon kingdom that consisted of Norfolk and Suffolk in the 6th century A.D.; became a dependency of Mercia in the 8th century.
▸ **East Anglian** *adj, n*

East Ayrshire ★ *n* a council area of SE Scotland. Administrative centre: Kilmarnock. Pop.: 123 820 (1996 est.). Area: 1252 sq. km (483 sq. miles).

East Bengal ★ *n* the part of the former Indian province of Bengal assigned to Pakistan in 1947 (now Bangladesh).
▸ **East Bengali** *adj, n*

East Berlin ★ *n* (formerly) the part of Berlin under East German control.
▸ **East Berliner** *n*

eastbound (ˈiːstˌbaʊnd) *adj* going or leading towards the east.

Eastbourne ★ (ˈiːstˌbɔːn) *n* a resort in SE England, in East Sussex on the English Channel. Pop.: 83 200 (1991 est.).

east by north *n* one point on the compass north of east.

east by south *n* one point on the compass south of east.

East Cape ★ *n* **1** the easternmost point of New Guinea, on Milne Bay. **2** the easternmost point of New Zealand, on North Island. **3** the former name for Cape **Dezhnev.**

East China Sea ★ *n* part of the N Pacific, between the E coast of China and the Ryukyu Islands.

East Dunbartonshire ★ *n* a council area of central Scotland. Administrative centre: Kirkintilloch. Pop.: 110 220 (1996 est.). Area: 172 sq. km (66 sq. miles).

East End ★ *n* **the.** a densely populated part of E London containing former industrial and dock areas.
▸ **East Ender** *n*

Easter (ˈiːstə) *n* **1** a festival of the Christian Church commemorating the Resurrection of Christ: falls on the Sunday following the first full moon after the vernal equinox. **2** Also called: **Easter Sunday, Easter Day.** the day on which this festival is celebrated. **3** the period between Good Friday and Easter Monday. ◆ Related adj: **Paschal.** ORIG OE *ēastre*

Easter cactus *n* a Brazilian cactus, *Rhipsalidopsis gaertneri*, widely cultivated as an ornamental for its showy red flowers.

Easter egg *n* **1** an egg given to children at Easter, usually a chocolate egg or a hen's egg with its shell painted. **2** *Computing.* an unexpected entertaining effect in an applications program, initiated when certain actions are carried out, such as pressing certain key combinations.

Easter Island ★ *n* an isolated volcanic island in the Pacific, 3700 km (2300 miles) west of Chile, of which it is a dependency: discovered on Easter Sunday, 1722; annexed by Chile in 1888; noted for the remains of an aboriginal culture, which includes gigantic stone figures. Pop.: 2095 (1989). Area: 166 sq. km (64 sq. miles). Also called: **Rapa Nui.**
▸ **Easter Islander** *n*

easterly (ˈiːstəlɪ) *adj* **1** of or in the east. ◆ *adv, adj* **2** towards the east. **3** from the east: *an easterly wind.* ◆ *n, pl* **easterlies. 4** a wind from the east.

eastern (ˈiːstən) *adj* **1** situated in or towards the east. **2** facing or moving towards the east.

Eastern Cape ★ *n* a province of S South Africa; formed in 1994 from part of the former Cape Province. Capital: Bisho. Pop.: 6 481 300 (1995 est.). Area: 169 000 sq. km (65 483 sq. miles).

Eastern Church *n* **1** any of the Christian Churches of the former Byzantine Empire. **2** any Church owing allegiance to the Orthodox Church. **3** any Church having Eastern forms of liturgy and institutions.

Easterner (ˈiːstənə) *n* (*sometimes not cap.*) a native or inhabitant of the east of any specified region.

Eastern Ghats ★ *pl n* a mountain range in S India, parallel to the Bay of Bengal: united with the Western Ghats by the Nilgiri Hills; forms the E margin of the Deccan plateau.

eastern hemisphere *n* (*often caps.*) **1** that half of the globe containing Europe, Asia, Africa, and Australia, lying east of the Greenwich meridian. **2** the lands in this, esp. Asia.

Eastern Orthodox Church *n* another name for the **Orthodox Church.**

Eastern Townships ★ *n* an area of central Canada, in S Quebec: consists of 11 townships south of the St Lawrence.

Eastertide (ˈiːstəˌtaɪd) *n* the Easter season.

East Flanders ★ *n* a province of W Belgium: low-lying, with reclaimed land in the northeast: textile industries. Capital: Ghent. Pop.: 1 357 576 (1998 est.). Area: 2979 sq. km (1150 sq. miles).

East Germany ★ *n* a former republic in N central Europe: established in 1949 and declared a sovereign state by the Soviet Union in 1954; Communist regime replaced by a multiparty democracy in 1989; reunited with West Germany in 1990. Official name: **German Democratic Republic.** Abbrevs.: **DDR, GDR.** See also **Germany.**
▸ **East German** *adj, n*

East Indian *n* **1** Also called: **Indo-Caribbean.** *Caribbean.* an immigrant to the countries of the Caribbean (West Indies) who is of Indian origin; an Asian West Indian. ◆ *adj* **2** of, relating to, or originating in the East Indies.

East Indies ★ *pl n* **the. 1** the Malay Archipelago, including or excluding the Philippines. **2** SE Asia in general.

easting (ˈiːstɪŋ) *n* **1** *Naut.* the net distance eastwards made by a vessel moving towards the east. **2** *Cartography.* the distance eastwards of a point from a given meridian indicated by the first half of a map grid reference.

East Kilbride ★ (kɪlˈbraɪd) *n* a town in W Scotland, in South Lanarkshire near Glasgow: designated a new town in 1947. Pop.: 70 422 (1991).

Eastleigh ★ (ˈiːstˌliː) *n* a town in S England, in S Hampshire: railway engineering industry. Pop.: 49 934 (1991).

East London ★ *n* a port in S South Africa, on the Indian Ocean. Pop.: 102 325 (1991).

East Lothian ★ *n* a council area and historic county of E central Scotland, formerly part of Lothian region (1975–96). Administrative centre: Haddington. Pop.: 85 640 (1996 est.). Area: 678 sq. km (262 sq. miles).

Eastman ★ (ˈiːstmən) *n* **George.** 1854–1932, US manufacturer of photographic equipment.

east-northeast *n* **1** the point on the compass or the direction midway between northeast and east. ◆ *adj, adv* **2** in, from, or towards this direction.

East Pakistan ★ *n* the former name (until 1971) of **Bangladesh.**
▸ **East Pakistani** *adj, n*

East Prussia ★ *n* a former province of NE Germany on the Baltic Sea: separated in 1919 from the rest of Germany by the Polish Corridor and Danzig: in 1945 Po-

land received the south part, the Soviet Union the north. German name: **Ostpreussen** (ost'prɔysən).
▸ **East Prussian** *adj, n*

East Renfrewshire ★ *n* a council area of W central Scotland, formerly part of Strathclyde region (1975–96). Administrative centre: Giffnock. Pop.: 86 780 (1996 est.). Area: 173 sq. km (67 sq. miles).

East Riding of Yorkshire ★ *n* a county of NE England, a historical division of Yorkshire, formerly part of Humberside (1974–96); includes Hull unitary authority. Administrative centre: Beverley. Pop. (excluding Hull): 308 400 (1996 est.). Area (excluding Hull): 1748 sq. km (675 sq. miles).

east-southeast *n* **1** the point on the compass or the direction midway between east and southeast. ◆ *adj, adv* **2** in, from, or towards this direction.

East Sussex ★ *n* a county of SE England; includes Brighton and Hove unitary authority: mainly undulating agricultural land, with the South Downs and seaside resorts in the south. Administrative centre: Lewes. Pop. (excluding Brighton and Hove): 485 400 (1996 est.). Area (excluding Brighton and Hove): 1795 sq. km (693 sq. miles).

East Timor ★ *n* the eastern part of the island of Timor: declared independence from Portugal in 1975 and annexed by Indonesia in 1976; voted for independence in 1999; now under UN control in transition to full nationhood.

eastward ('i:stwəd) *adj* **1** situated or directed towards the east. ◆ *adv* **2** a variant of **eastwards**. ◆ *n* **3** the eastward part, direction, etc.
▸ **'eastwardly** *adv, adj*

eastwards ('i:stwədz) *or* **eastward** *adv* towards the east.

Eastwood ★ ('i:stwʊd) *n* **Clint**. born 1930, US film actor and director. His films include *The Good The Bad and The Ugly* (1966) and as actor and director *Unforgiven* (1993) and *True Crime* (1999).

easy ('i:zɪ) *adj* **easier, easiest. 1** not requiring much labour or effort; not difficult. **2** free from pain, care, or anxiety. **3** not restricting; lenient: *easy laws.* **4** tolerant and undemanding; easy-going: *an easy disposition.* **5** readily influenced; pliant: *an easy victim.* **6** not constricting; loose: *an easy fit.* **7** not strained or extreme; moderate: *an easy pace.* **8** *Inf.* ready to fall in with any suggestion made; not predisposed: *he is easy about what to do.* **9** *Sl.* sexually available. ◆ *adv* **10** *Inf.* in an easy or relaxed manner. **11 easy does it.** *Inf.* go slowly and carefully; be careful. **12 go easy.** (*usually imperative;* often foll. by *on*) to exercise moderation. **13 stand easy.** *Mil.* a command to soldiers standing at ease that they may relax further. **14 take it easy. 14a** to avoid stress or undue hurry. **14b** to remain calm. ORIG C12: from OF *aisié,* p.p. of *aisier* to relieve, EASE

easy-care *adj* (esp. of a fabric or garment) hard-wearing and requiring no special treatment during washing, etc.

easy chair *n* a comfortable upholstered armchair.

easy-going ('i:zɪ'gəʊɪŋ) *adj* **1** relaxed in manner or attitude; excessively tolerant. **2** moving at a comfortable pace: *an easy-going horse.*

easy meat *n Inf.* **1** someone easily seduced or deceived. **2** something easy.

easy money *n* **1** money made with little effort, sometimes dishonestly. **2** *Commerce.* money that can be borrowed at a low interest rate.

Easy Street *n* (*sometimes not caps.*) *Inf.* a state of financial security.

eat (i:t) *vb* **eats, eating, ate, eaten. 1** to take into the mouth and swallow (food, etc.), esp. after biting and chewing. **2** (*tr;* often foll. by *away* or *up*) to destroy as if by eating: *the damp had eaten away the woodwork.* **3** (often foll. by *into*) to use up or waste: *taxes ate into his inheritance.* **4** (often foll. by *into* or *through*) to make (a hole, passage, etc.) by eating or gnawing: *rats ate through the floor.* **5** to take or have (a meal or meals): *we eat at six.* **6** (*tr*) to include as part of one's diet: *he doesn't eat fish.* **7** (*tr*) *Inf.* to cause to worry: *what's eating you?* ◆ See also **eat out, eats, eat up.** ORIG OE *etan*
▸ **'eater** *n*

eatable ('i:təbᵊl) *adj* fit or suitable for eating; edible.

eatables ('i:təbᵊlz) *pl n* food.

eating ('i:tɪŋ) *n* **1** food, esp. in relation to quality or taste: *this fruit makes excellent eating.* ◆ *adj* **2** suitable for eating uncooked: *eating apples.* **3** relating to or for eating: *an eating house.*

eat out *vb* (*intr, adv*) to eat away from home, esp. in a restaurant.

eats (i:ts) *pl n Inf.* articles of food; provisions.

eat up *vb* (*adv, mainly tr*) **1** (*also intr*) to eat or consume entirely. **2** *Inf.* to listen to with enthusiasm or appreciation: *the audience ate up his every word.* **3** (*often passive*) *Inf.* to affect grossly: *she was eaten up by jealousy.* **4** *Inf.* to travel (a distance) quickly: *we just ate up the miles.*

eau de Cologne (ˌəʊ də kə'ləʊn) *n* See **cologne.** ORIG F, lit.: water of Cologne

eau de nil (ˌəʊ də 'ni:l) *n, adj* (of) a pale yellowish-green colour. ORIG F, lit.: water of (the) Nile

eau de vie (ˌəʊ də 'vi:) *n* brandy or other spirits. ORIG F, lit.: water of life

eaves (i:vz) *pl n* the edge of a roof that projects beyond the wall. ORIG OE *efes*

eavesdrop ('i:vzˌdrɒp) *vb* **eavesdrops, eavesdropping, eavesdropped.** (*intr*) to listen secretly to the private conversation of others. ORIG C17: back formation from *evesdropper,* from OE *yfesdrype* water dripping from the eaves
▸ **'eavesˌdropper** *n*

ebb (ɛb) *vb* (*intr*) **1** (of tide water) to flow back or recede. Cf. **flow** (sense 8). **2** to fall away or decline. ◆ *n* **3a** the flowing back of the tide from high to low water or the period in which this takes place. **3b** (*as modifier*): *the ebb tide.* Cf. **flood** (sense 3). **4 at a low ebb.** in a state of weakness or decline. ORIG OE *ebba*

Ebbinghaus ★ ('ɛbɪŋhaʊs) *n* **Hermann** ('hɛrman). 1850–1909, German experimental psychologist who undertook the first systematic large-scale studies of memory.

Ebbw Vale ★ ('ɛbu: 'veɪl) *n* a town in S Wales, in Blaenau Gwent: a former coal-mining centre. Pop.: 19 484 (1991).

EBCDIC ('ɛpsɪˌdɪk) *n acronym for* extended binary-coded decimal-interchange code: a computer code for representing alphanumeric characters.

Ebert ★ (*German* 'e:bərt) *n* **Friedrich** ('fri:drɪç). 1871–1925, German Social Democratic statesman; first president of the German Republic (1919–25).

ebon ('ɛbᵊn) *adj, n* a poetic word for **ebony.** ORIG C14: from L *hebenus;* see EBONY

ebonite ('ɛbəˌnaɪt) *n* another name for **vulcanite.**

ebonize *or* **ebonise** ('ɛbəˌnaɪz) *vb* **ebonizes, ebonizing, ebonized** *or* **ebonises, ebonising, ebonised.** (*tr*) to stain or otherwise finish in imitation of ebony.

ebony ('ɛbənɪ) *n, pl* **ebonies. 1** any of various tropical and subtropical trees that have hard dark wood. **2** the wood of such a tree. **3a** a black colour. **3b** (*as adj*): *an ebony skin.* ORIG C16 *hebeny,* from LL, from Gk, from *ebenos* ebony, from Egyptian

Ebor. ('i:bɔ:) *abbrev. for* Eboracensis. ORIG L.: (Archbishop) of York

Eboracum ★ (i:'bɒrəkəm, ˌi:bɔ:'rɑ:kəm) *n* the Roman name for **York**[1] (sense 1).

EBRD *abbrev. for* European Bank for Reconstruction and Development.

Ebro ★ ('i:brəʊ; *Spanish* 'eβro) *n* the second largest river in Spain, rising in the Cantabrian Mountains and flowing southeast to the Mediterranean. Length: 910 km (565 miles).

ebullient (ɪ'bʌljənt, ɪ'bʊl-) *adj* **1** overflowing with enthusiasm or excitement. **2** boiling. ORIG C16: from L *ēbullīre* to bubble forth, be boisterous, from *bullīre* to BOIL[1]
▸ **e'bullience** *or* **e'bulliency** *n*

ebulliometer (ɪˌbʌlɪ'ɒmɪtə) *n Physics.* a device used to determine the boiling point of a solution.

ebullition (ˌɛbə'lɪʃən) *n* **1** the process of boiling. **2** a sudden outburst, as of intense emotion. ORIG C16: from LL *ēbullītiō;* see EBULLIENT

EC *abbrev. for:* **1** European Community. **2** (in London postal codes) East Central.

ec- *combining form.* out from; away from: *eccentric; ecdysis.* ORIG from Gk *ek* (before a vowel *ex*) out of, away from; see EX-[1]

ECB *abbrev. for* European Central Bank.

Ecbatana ★ (ɛk'bætənə) *n* an ancient city in Iran, on the site of modern Hamadān; capital of Media and royal residence of the Persians and Parthians.

eccentric (ɪk'sɛntrɪk) *adj* **1** deviating or departing from convention; irregular or odd. **2** situated away from the centre or the axis. **3** not having a common centre: *eccentric circles.* **4** not precisely circular. ◆ *n* **5** a person who deviates from normal forms of behaviour. **6** a device for converting rotary motion to reciprocating motion. ORIG C16: from Med. L *eccentricus,* from Gk *ekkentros,* from *ek-* EX-[1] + *kentron* centre
▸ **ec'centrically** *adv*

eccentricity (ˌɛksɛn'trɪsɪtɪ) *n, pl* **eccentricities. 1** unconventional or irregular behaviour. **2** the state of being eccentric. **3** deviation from a circular path or orbit. **4** *Geom.* a number that expresses the shape of a conic section. **5** the degree of displacement of the geometric centre of a part from the true centre, esp. of the axis of rotation of a wheel.

eccl. *or* **eccles.** *abbrev. for* ecclesiastic(al).

Eccles[1] ★ ('ɛkᵊlz) *n* a town in NW England, in Salford unitary authority, in Greater Manchester. Pop.: 36 000 (1991).

Eccles[2] ★ ('ɛkᵊlz) *n* Sir **John Carew.** 1903–97, Australian physiologist: shared the Nobel prize for physiology (1963) with A. L. Hodgkin and A. F. Huxley for their work on conduction of nervous impulses.

Eccles. *or* **Eccl.** *Bible. abbrev. for* Ecclesiastes.

ecclesiastic (ɪˌkliːzɪ'æstɪk) *n* **1** a clergyman or other person in holy orders. ◆ *adj* **2** of or associated with the Christian Church or clergy.

ecclesiastical (ɪˌkliːzɪ'æstɪkᵊl) *adj* of or relating to the Christian Church.
▸ **ecˌclesi'astically** *adv*

ecclesiasticism (ɪˌkliːzɪ'æstɪˌsɪzəm) *n* exaggerated attachment to the practices or principles of the Christian Church.

ecclesiology (ɪˌkliːzɪ'ɒlədʒɪ) *n* **1** the study of the Christian Church. **2** the study of Church architecture and decoration.
▸ **ecclesiological** (ɪˌkliːzɪə'lɒdʒɪkᵊl) *adj*

eccrine ('ɛkrɪn) *adj* of or denoting glands that secrete externally, esp. the sweat glands. Cf. **apocrine.** ORIG from Gk *ekkrinein,* from *ek-* EC- + *krinein* to separate
▸ **eccrinology** (ˌɛkrɪ'nɒlədʒɪ) *n*

ecdemic (ɛk'dɛmɪk) *adj* not indigenous or endemic; foreign: *an ecdemic disease.*

ecdysis ('ɛkdɪsɪs) *n, pl* **ecdyses** (-ˌsiːz). the periodic shedding of the cuticle in insects and other arthropods or the outer epidermal layer in reptiles. ORIG C19: NL, from Gk *ekdusis,* from *ekduein* to strip, from *ek-* EX-[1] + *duein* to put on

ECG *abbrev. for:* **1** electrocardiogram. **2** electrocardiograph.

echelon ('ɛʃəˌlɒn) *n* **1** a level of command, responsibility, etc. (esp. in **the upper echelons**). **2** *Mil.* **2a** a formation in which units follow one another but are offset sufficiently to allow each unit a line of fire ahead. **2b** a group formed in this way. ◆ *vb* **3** to assemble in echelon. ORIG C18: from F *échelon,* lit.: rung of a ladder, from OF *eschiele* ladder, from L *scāla*

echidna (ɪ'kɪdnə) *n, pl* **echidnas** *or* **echidnae** (-niː). a spine-covered monotreme mammal of Australia and New Guinea, having a long snout and claws. Also called: **spiny anteater.** ORIG C19: from NL, from L: viper, from Gk *ekhidna*

echinoderm (ɪ'kaɪnəʊˌdɜːm) *n* any of various marine invertebrates characterized by tube feet, a calcite body-covering, and a five-part symmetrical body. The group includes the starfish, sea urchins, and sea cucumbers.

echinus (ɪ'kaɪnəs) *n, pl* **echini** (-naɪ). **1** *Archit.* a moulding between the shaft and the abacus of a Doric column. **2** any sea urchin of the genus *Echinus,* such as the Mediterranean edible sea urchin. ORIG C14: from L, from Gk *ekhinos*

echo ('ɛkəʊ) *n, pl* **echoes. 1a** the reflection of sound or other radiation by a reflecting medium, esp. a solid object. **1b** the sound so reflected. **2** a repetition or imitation, esp. an unoriginal reproduction of another's opinions. **3** something that evokes memories. **4** (*sometimes pl*) an effect that continues after the original cause has disappeared: *echoes of the French Revolution.* **5** a person who copies another, esp. one who obsequiously agrees with another's opinions. **6a** the signal reflected by a radar target. **6b** the trace produced by such a signal on a radar screen. ◆ *vb* **echoes, echoing, echoed. 7** to resound or cause to resound with an echo. **8** (*intr*) (of sounds) to repeat or resound by echoes; reverberate. **9** (*tr*) (of persons) to repeat (words, opinions, etc.) in imitation, agreement, or flattery. **10** (*tr*) (of things) to resemble or imitate (another style, an earlier model, etc.). ORIG C14: via L from Gk *ēkhō;* rel. to Gk *ēkhē* sound
▸ **'echoing** *adj* ▸ **'echoless** *adj* ▸ **'echo-ˌlike** *adj*

Echo ★ ('ɛkəʊ) *n Greek myth.* a nymph who, spurned by Narcissus, pined away until only her voice remained.

echocardiography (ˌɛkəʊˌkɑːdɪ'ɒgrəfɪ) *n* examination of the heart using ultrasound techniques.

echo chamber *n* a room with walls that reflect sound. It is used to make acoustic measurements and as a recording studio when echo effects are required. Also called: **reverberation chamber.**

echography (ɛ'kɒgrəfɪ) *n* medical examination of the internal structures of the body by means of ultrasound.

echoic (ɛ'kəʊɪk) *adj* **1** characteristic of or resembling an echo. **2** onomatopoeic; imitative.

echolalia (ˌɛkəʊ'leɪlɪə) *n Psychiatry.* the tendency to repeat mechanically words just spoken by another person. ORIG C19: from NL, from ECHO + Gk *lalia* talk, chatter

echolocation (ˌɛkəʊləʊ'keɪʃən) *n* determination of the position of an object by measuring the time taken for an echo to return from it and its direction.

echo sounder *n* a navigation device that determines depth by measuring the time taken for a pulse of sound to reach the sea bed or a submerged object and for the echo to return.
▸ **echo sounding** *n*

echovirus *or* **ECHO virus** ('ɛkəʊˌvaɪrəs) *n* any of a group of viruses that can cause symptoms of mild meningitis, the common cold, or infections of the intestinal and respiratory tracts. ORIG C20: from initials of *Enteric Cytopathic Human Orphan* ("orphan" because orig. believed to be unrelated to any disease) + VIRUS

Eck ★ (ɛk) *n* **Johann** (jo'han), original name *Johann Mayer.* 1486–1543, German Roman Catholic theologian; opponent of Luther and the Reformation.

Eckert ★ ('ɛkət) *n* **John Presper.** 1919–95, US electronics engineer: built the first electronic computer with John W. Mauchly in 1946.

éclair (eɪ'klɛə, ɪ'klɛə) *n* a finger-shaped cake of choux pastry, usually filled with cream and covered with chocolate. ORIG C19: from F, lit.: lightning (prob. because it does not last long)

eclampsia (ɪ'klæmpsɪə) *n Pathol.* a toxic condition that sometimes develops in the last three months of pregnancy, characterized by high blood pressure, weight gain, and convulsions. ORIG C19: from NL, from Gk *eklampsis* a shining forth

éclat (eɪ'klɑː) *n* **1** brilliant or conspicuous success, effect, etc. **2** showy display; ostentation. **3** social distinction. **4** approval; acclaim; applause. ORIG C17: from F, from *éclater* to burst

eclectic (ɪ'klɛktɪk, ɛ'klɛk-) *adj* **1** selecting from various styles, ideas, methods, etc. **2** composed of elements drawn from a variety of sources, styles, etc. ◆ *n* **3** a person who favours an eclectic approach. ORIG C17: from Gk *eklektikos,* from *eklegein* to select, from *legein* to gather
▸ **e'clectically** *adv* ▸ **e'clecticism** *n*

eclipse (ɪ'klɪps) *n* **1** the total or partial obscuring of one

celestial body by another (**total eclipse** *or* **partial eclipse**). A **solar eclipse** occurs when the moon passes between the sun and the earth; a **lunar eclipse** when the earth passes between the sun and the moon. **2** the period of time during which such a phenomenon occurs. **3** any dimming or obstruction of light. **4** a loss of importance, power, fame, etc., esp. through overshadowing by another. ◆ *vb* **eclipses, eclipsing, eclipsed.** (*tr*) **5** to cause an eclipse of. **6** to cast a shadow upon; obscure. **7** to overshadow or surpass. ORIG C13: back formation from OE *eclypsis,* from L, from Gk *ekleipsis* a forsaking, from *ekleipein* to abandon
► **e'clipser** *n*

eclipsing binary *n* a binary star whose orbital plane lies in or near the line of sight so that one component is regularly eclipsed by its companion.

ecliptic (ɪ'klɪptɪk) *n* **1** *Astron.* **1a** the great circle on the celestial sphere representing the apparent annual path of the sun relative to the stars. **1b** (*as modifier*): *the ecliptic plane.* **2** an equivalent great circle on the terrestrial globe. ◆ *adj* **3** of or relating to an eclipse.
► **e'cliptically** *adv*

eclogue ('ɛklɒg) *n* a pastoral or idyllic poem, usually in the form of a conversation. ORIG C15: from L *ecloga* short poem, collection of extracts, from Gk *eklogē* selection

eclosion (ɪ'kləʊʒən) *n* the emergence of an insect larva from the egg or an adult from the pupal case. ORIG C19: from F, from *éclore* to hatch, ult. from L *exclūdere* to shut out

Eco ★ ('ɛkəʊ) *n* **Umberto.** born 1932, Italian writer. His novels include *The Name of the Rose* (1981) and *The Island of the Day Before* (1995).

eco- *combining form.* denoting ecology or ecological: *ecocide; ecosphere.*

ecocentric (ˌi:kəʊ'sɛntrɪk) *adj* having a serious concern for environmental issues: *ecocentric management.*

ecofriendly ('i:kəʊˌfrɛndlɪ) *adj* having a beneficial effect on the environment or at least not causing environmental damage.

ecol. *abbrev. for:* **1** ecological. **2** ecology.

E. coli (i:'kəʊlaɪ) *n* short for *Escherichia coli*, see ***Escherichia.***

ecological (ˌi:kə'lɒdʒɪkᵊl) *adj* **1** of or relating to ecology. **2** (of a practice, policy, product, etc.) tending to benefit or cause minimal damage to the environment.
► **ˌeco'logically** *adv*

ecology (ɪ'kɒlədʒɪ) *n* **1** the study of the relationships between living organisms and their environment. **2** the set of relationships of a particular organism with its environment. ORIG C19: from G *Ökologie,* from Gk *oikos* house (hence, environment)
► **e'cologist** *n*

e-commerce *or* **ecommerce** ('i:'kɒmɜ:s) *n* business transactions conducted on the Internet. ORIG C20: from E- + COMMERCE

econ. *abbrev. for:* **1** economical. **2** economics. **3** economy.

econometrics (ɪˌkɒnə'mɛtrɪks) *n* (*functioning as sing*) the application of mathematical and statistical techniques to economic theories.
► **eˌcono'metric** *or* **eˌcono'metrical** *adj* ► **econometrician** (ɪˌkɒnəmə'trɪʃən) *or* **econometrist** (ˌi:kə'nɒmətrɪst, -ˌɛkə-) *n*

economic (ˌi:kə'nɒmɪk, ˌɛkə-) *adj* **1** of or relating to an economy, economics, or finance. **2** *Brit.* capable of being produced, operated, etc., for profit; profitable. **3** concerning or affecting material resources or welfare: *economic pests.* **4** concerned with or relating to the necessities of life; utilitarian. **5** a variant of **economical. 6** *Inf.* inexpensive; cheap.

economical (ˌi:kə'nɒmɪkᵊl, ˌɛkə-) *adj* **1** using the minimum required; not wasteful. **2** frugal; thrifty. **3** a variant of **economic** (senses 1–4). **4** *Euphemistic.* deliberately withholding information (esp. in **economical with the truth**).
► **ˌeco'nomically** *adv*

economic indicator *n* a statistical measure representing an economic variable: *the retail price index is an economic indicator of the actual level of prices.*

economic migrant *or* **refugee** *n* a person who emigrates from a poor country to a developed one in the hope of improving his or her standard of living.

economic rationalism *n Austral. & NZ.* an economic policy based on the efficiency of market forces, characterized by minimal government intervention, tax cuts, privatization, and deregulation of labour markets.

economics (ˌi:kə'nɒmɪks, ˌɛkə-) *n* **1** (*functioning as sing*) the social science concerned with the production and consumption of goods and services and the analysis of the commercial activities of a society. **2** (*functioning as pl*) financial aspects.

economic sanctions *pl n* any actions taken by one nation or group of nations to harm the economy of another nation or group, often to force a political change.

economist (ɪ'kɒnəmɪst) *n* a specialist in economics.

economize *or* **economise** (ɪ'kɒnəˌmaɪz) *vb* **economizes, economizing, economized** *or* **economises, economising, economised.** (often foll. by *on*) to limit or reduce (expense, waste, etc.).
► **eˌconomi'zation** *or* **eˌconomi'sation** *n*

economy (ɪ'kɒnəmɪ) *n, pl* **economies. 1** careful management of resources to avoid unnecessary expenditure or waste; thrift. **2** a means or instance of this; saving. **3** sparing, restrained, or efficient use. **4a** the complex of activities concerned with the production, distribution, and consumption of goods and services. **4b** a particular type or branch of this: *a socialist economy.* **5** the management of the resources, finances, income, and expenditure of a community, business enterprise, etc. **6a** a class of travel in aircraft, cheaper and less luxurious than first class. **6b** (*as modifier*): *economy class.* **7** (*modifier*) purporting to offer a larger quantity for a lower price: *economy pack.* **8** the orderly interplay between the parts of a system or structure. ORIG C16: via L from Gk *oikonomia* domestic management, from *oikos* house + *-nomia,* from *nemein* to manage

economy-class syndrome *n* (*not in technical usage*) a deep-vein thrombosis that has developed in the legs or pelvis of a person travelling for a long period of time in cramped conditions. ORIG C20: reference to the restricted legroom of cheaper seats on passenger aircraft

ecosphere ('i:kəʊˌsfɪə, 'ɛkəʊ-) *n* the parts of the universe, esp. on earth, where life can exist.

écossaise (ˌeɪkɒ'seɪz) *n* **1** a lively dance in two-four time. **2** the tune for such a dance. ORIG C19: F, lit.: Scottish (dance)

ecosystem ('i:kəʊˌsɪstəm, 'ɛkəʊ-) *n Ecology.* a system involving the interactions between a community and its nonliving environment. ORIG C20: from ECO- + SYSTEM

ecoterrorist ('i:kəʊˌtɛrərɪst) *n* a person who uses violence in order to achieve environmentalist aims.

ecotourism ('i:kəʊˌtʊərɪzəm) *n* tourism which is designed to contribute to the protection of the environment or at least minimize damage to it, often involving travel to areas of natural interest in developing countries or participation in environmental projects.
► **'ecoˌtourist** *n*

eco-warrior ('i:kəʊˌwɒrɪə) *n Inf.* a person who zealously pursues environmentalist aims.

ecru ('ɛkru:, 'eɪkru:) *n, adj* (of) a greyish-yellow to a light greyish colour. ORIG C19: from F, from *é-* (intensive) + *cru* raw, from L *crūdus;* see CRUDE

ecstasy ('ɛkstəsɪ) *n, pl* **ecstasies. 1** (*often pl*) a state of exalted delight, joy, etc.; rapture. **2** intense emotion of any kind: *an ecstasy of rage.* **3** *Psychol.* overpowering emotion sometimes involving temporary loss of consciousness: often associated with mysticism. **4** *Sl.* 3,4-methylenedioxymethamphetamine: a powerful drug that acts as a stimulant and can produce hallucinations. ORIG C14: from OF via Med. L from Gk *ekstasis* displacement, trance, from *ex-* out + *histanai* to cause to stand

ecstatic (ɛk'stætɪk) *adj* **1** in a trancelike state of rapture or delight. **2** showing or feeling great enthusiasm. ◆ *n* **3** a person who has periods of intense trancelike joy.
► **ec'statically** *adv*

ECT *abbrev. for* electroconvulsive therapy.

ecto- *combining form.* indicating outer, outside. ORIG from Gk *ektos* outside, from *ek, ex* out

ectoblast ('ɛktəʊˌblæst) *n* another name for **ectoderm**.
▸ ˌ**ecto'blastic** *adj*

ectoderm ('ɛktəʊˌdɜːm) *or* **exoderm** *n* the outer germ layer of an animal embryo, which gives rise to epidermis and nervous tissue.
▸ ˌ**ecto'dermal** *or* ˌ**ecto'dermic** *adj*

ectomorph ('ɛktəʊˌmɔːf) *n* a type of person having a body build characterized by thinness, weakness, and a lack of weight.
▸ ˌ**ecto'morphic** *adj* ▸ '**ectoˌmorphy** *n*

-ectomy *n combining form.* indicating surgical excision of a part: *appendectomy.* ORIG from NL *-ectomia,* from Gk *ek-* out + -TOMY

ectopic pregnancy (ɛk'tɒpɪk) *n Pathol.* the abnormal development of a fertilized egg outside the uterus, usually within a Fallopian tube.

ectoplasm ('ɛktəʊˌplæzəm) *n* **1** *Cytology.* the outer layer of cytoplasm. **2** *Spiritualism.* the substance supposedly emanating from the body of a medium during trances.
▸ ˌ**ecto'plasmic** *adj*

ECU (*also* 'eɪkjuː, 'ɛkjuː) *abbrev. for* European Currency Unit.

Ecua. *abbrev. for* Ecuador.

Ecuador ★ ('ɛkwəˌdɔː) *n* a republic in South America, on the Pacific: under the Incas when Spanish colonization began in 1532; gained independence in 1822; declared a republic in 1830. It consists chiefly of a coastal plain in the west, separated from the densely forested upper Amazon basin (Oriente) by ranges and plateaus of the Andes. Official language: Spanish; Quechua is also widely spoken. Religion: Roman Catholic. Currency: US dollar (replacing the sucre in 2000 in an attempt to end an economic crisis). Capital: Quito. Pop.: 12 411 000 (1999 est.). Area: 283 560 sq. km (109 483 sq. miles).
▸ ˌ**Ecua'dorian** *or* ˌ**Ecua'doran** *adj, n*

ecumenical, oecumenical (ˌiːkjʊ'mɛnɪkᵊl, ˌɛk-) *or* **ecumenic, oecumenic** *adj* **1** of or relating to the Christian Church throughout the world, esp. with regard to its unity. **2** tending to promote unity among Churches. ORIG C16: via LL from Gk *oikoumenikos,* from *oikein* to inhabit, from *oikos* house
▸ ˌ**ecu'menically** *or* ˌ**oecu'menically** *adv*

ecumenism (ɪ'kjuːməˌnɪzəm, 'ekjʊm-), **ecumenicism** (ˌiːkjʊ'mɛnɪˌsɪzəm, ˌɛk-) *or* **ecumenicalism** (ˌiːkjʊ'mɛnɪkəˌlɪzəm, ˌɛk-) *n* the aim of unity among all Christian churches throughout the world.

eczema ('ɛksɪmə) *n Pathol.* a skin inflammation with lesions that scale, crust, or ooze a serous fluid, often accompanied by intense itching. ORIG C18: from NL, from Gk *ekzema,* from *ek-* out + *zein* to boil
▸ **eczematous** (ɛk'sɛmətəs) *adj*

ed. *abbrev. for:* **1** edited. **2** (*pl* **eds.**) edition. **3** (*pl* **eds.**) editor. **4** education.

-ed[1] *suffix.* forming the past tense of most English verbs. ORIG OE *-de, -ede, -ode, -ade*

-ed[2] *suffix.* forming the past participle of most English verbs. ORIG OE *-ed, -od, -ad*

-ed[3] *suffix forming adjectives from nouns.* possessing or having the characteristics of: *salaried; red-blooded.* ORIG OE *-ede*

Edam ★ ('iːdæm) *n* **1** a town in the NW Netherlands, in North Holland province, on the IJsselmeer: cheese, light manufacturing. Pop.: 24 572 (1989). **2** a hard round mild-tasting Dutch cheese with a red outside covering.

Edberg ★ ('ɛdbɜːg) *n* **Stefan.** born 1966, Swedish tennis player: Wimbledon champion 1988, 1990.

EDC *abbrev. for* European Defence Community.

Edda ('ɛdə) *n* **1** Also called: **Elder Edda, Poetic Edda.** a 12th-century collection of mythological Old Norse poems. **2** Also called: **Younger Edda, Prose Edda.** a treatise on versification together with a collection of Scandinavian myths, legends, and poems (?1222). ORIG C18: ON
▸ **Eddaic** (e'deɪɪk) *adj*

Eddery ★ ('ɛdərɪ) *n* **Patrick,** known as *Pat.* born 1952, Irish jockey.

Eddington ★ ('ɛdɪŋtən) *n* Sir **Arthur Stanley.** 1882–1944, British astronomer, noted for his research on stars.

eddo ('ɛdəʊ) *n, pl* **eddoes.** another name for **taro.**

eddy ('ɛdɪ) *n, pl* **eddies. 1** a movement in air, water, or other fluid in which the current doubles back on itself causing a miniature whirlwind or whirlpool. **2** a deviation from or disturbance in the main trend of thought, life, etc. ◆ *vb* **eddies, eddying, eddied. 3** to move or cause to move against the main current. ORIG C15: prob. from ON

Eddy ★ ('ɛdɪ) *n* **Mary Baker.** 1821–1910, US religious leader; founder of the Christian Science movement (1866).

eddy current *n* an electric current induced in a massive conductor by an alternating magnetic field.

Eddystone Rocks ★ ('ɛdɪstən) *n* a dangerous group of rocks at the W end of the English Channel, southwest of Plymouth: lighthouse.

Ede ★ ('eɪdə) *n* a city in the central Netherlands, in Gelderland province. Pop.: 98 220 (1994).

Edelman ★ ('ɛdᵊlmən) *n* **Gerald Maurice.** born 1929, US biochemist: he shared the Nobel prize for physiology or medicine (1972) with Rodney Porter for determining the structure of antibodies.

edelweiss ('eɪdᵊlˌvaɪs) *n* a small alpine flowering plant having white woolly oblong leaves and a tuft of floral leaves surrounding the flowers. ORIG C19: G, lit.: noble white

edema (ɪ'diːmə) *n, pl* **edemata** (-mətə). the usual US spelling of **oedema.**

Eden[1] ★ ('iːdᵊn) *n* **1** Also called: **Garden of Eden.** *Bible.* the garden in which Adam and Eve were placed at the Creation. **2** a place or state of great delight or contentment. ORIG C14: from LL, from Heb. *'ēdhen* place of pleasure
▸ **Edenic** (iː'dɛnɪk) *adj*

Eden[2] ★ ('iːdᵊn) *n* Sir (**Robert**) **Anthony,** Earl of Avon. 1897–1977, British Conservative statesman; foreign secretary (1935–38; 1940–45; 1951–55) and prime minister (1955–57). He resigned after the controversy caused by the occupation of the Suez Canal zone by British and French forces (1956).

Eden Project *n* the world's largest greenhouse, built in a disused clay pit near St Austell, Cornwall, to study plant populations in a variety of environments.

edentate (iː'dɛnteɪt) *n* **1** any mammal of the order *Edentata,* of tropical Central and South America, which have few or no teeth. The order includes anteaters, sloths, and armadillos. ◆ *adj* **2** of or relating to the order Edentata. ORIG C19: from L *ēdentātus* lacking teeth, from *ēdentāre* to render toothless, from *e-* out + *dēns* tooth

Edessa ★ (ɪ'dɛsə) *n* **1** an ancient city on the N edge of the Syrian plateau, founded as a Macedonian colony by Seleucus I: a centre of early Christianity. Modern name: **Urfa. 2** a market town in Greece: ancient capital of Macedonia. Pop.: 15 980 (1981). Ancient name: **Aegae** ('iːgiː). Modern Greek name: **Édhessa.**

Edgar ★ ('ɛdgə) *n* **1** 944–975 A.D., king of Mercia and Northumbria (957–975) and of England (959–975). **2** ?1074–1107, king of Scotland (1097–1107), fourth son of Malcolm III. He overthrew his uncle Donald to gain the throne. **3 David.** born 1948, British dramatist, noted for political plays such as *Destiny* (1976) and *Maydays* (1983).

Edgar Atheling ★ ('æθɪlɪŋ) *n* ?1050–?1125, grandson of Edmund II; Anglo-Saxon pretender to the English throne in 1066.

edge (ɛdʒ) *n* **1** a border, brim, or margin. **2** a brink or verge. **3** a line along which two faces or surfaces of a solid meet. **4** the sharp cutting side of a blade. **5** keenness, sharpness, or urgency. **6** force, effectiveness, or incisiveness: *the performance lacked edge.* **7** a ridge. **8 have the edge on** *or* **over.** to have a slight advantage or superiority over. **9 on edge. 9a** nervously irritable; tense. **9b** nervously excited or eager. **10 set (someone's) teeth on edge.** to make (someone) acutely irritated or uncomfortable. ◆ *vb* **edges, edging, edged. 11** (*tr*) to provide an edge or border for. **12** (*tr*) to shape or trim the edge or border of (something). **13** to push (one's way, someone, something, etc.) gradually, esp. edgeways. **14** (*tr*) *Cricket.* to hit

(a bowled ball) with the edge of the bat. **15** (*tr*) to sharpen (a knife, etc.). ORIG OE *ecg*
▸ **'edger** *n*

Edgehill ★ (ˌɛdʒ'hɪl) *n* a ridge in S Warwickshire: site of the indecisive first battle between Charles I and the Parliamentarians (1642) in the Civil War.

edgeways ('ɛdʒˌweɪz) *or esp. US & Canad.* **edgewise** ('ɛdʒˌwaɪz) *adv* **1** with the edge forwards or uppermost. **2** on, by, with, or towards the edge. **3 get a word in edgeways.** (*usually with a negative*) to interrupt a conversation in which someone else is talking incessantly.

Edgeworth ★ ('ɛdʒwɜːθ) *n* **Maria.** 1767–1849, Anglo-Irish novelist: her works include *Castle Rackrent* (1800).

edging ('ɛdʒɪŋ) *n* **1** anything placed along an edge to finish it, esp. as an ornament. **2** the act of making an edge. ◆ *adj* **3** used for making an edge: *edging shears.*

edgy ('ɛdʒɪ) *adj* **edgier, edgiest.** (*usually postpositive*) nervous, irritable, tense, or anxious.
▸ **'edgily** *adv* ▸ **'edginess** *n*

edh (ɛð) *or* **eth** (ɛθ, ɛð) *n* a character of the runic alphabet (ð) used to represent the voiced dental fricative as in *then, mother, bathe.*

Édhessa ★ (*Greek* 'ɛðɛsa) *n* transliteration of the Modern Greek name for **Edessa.**

edible ('ɛdɪbᵊl) *adj* fit to be eaten; eatable. ORIG C17: from LL *edibilis,* from L *edere* to eat
▸ **ˌedi'bility** *n*

edibles ('ɛdɪbᵊlz) *pl n* articles fit to eat; food.

edict ('iːdɪkt) *n* **1** a decree or order issued by any authority. **2** any formal or authoritative command, proclamation, etc. ORIG C15: from L *ēdictum,* from *ēdīcere* to declare
▸ **e'dictal** *adj*

edifice ('ɛdɪfɪs) *n* **1** a building, esp. a large or imposing one. **2** a complex or elaborate institution or organization. ORIG C14: from OF, from L *aedificium,* from *aedificāre* to build; see EDIFY

edify ('ɛdɪˌfaɪ) *vb* **edifies, edifying, edified.** (*tr*) to improve the morality, intellect, etc., of, esp. by instruction. ORIG C14: from OF, from L *aedificāre* to construct, from *aedēs* a dwelling, temple + *facere* to make
▸ **ˌedifi'cation** *n* ▸ **'ediˌfying** *adj*

Edinburgh[1] ★ ('ɛdɪnbərə, -brə) *n* **1** the capital of Scotland, in Lothian region on the S side of the Firth of Forth: became the capital in the 15th century; castle; universities (1583, 1966); commercial and cultural centre, noted for its annual festival. Pop.: 401 910 (1991). **2 City of.** a council area in central Scotland. Pop.: 447 550 (1996 est.). Area: 262 sq. km (101 sq. miles).

Edinburgh[2] ★ ('ɛdɪnbərə, -brə) *n* **Duke of,** title of Prince *Philip Mountbatten.* born 1921, husband of Elizabeth II of Great Britain and Northern Ireland.

Edirne ★ (ɛ'dirnɛ) *n* a city in NW Turkey: a Thracian town, rebuilt and renamed by the Roman emperor Hadrian. Pop.: 117 331 (1995 est.). Former name: **Adrianople.**

Edison ★ ('ɛdɪsᵊn) *n* **Thomas Alva.** 1847–1931, US inventor. His inventions include the phonograph and the incandescent electric lamp.

edit ('ɛdɪt) *vb* **edits, editing, edited.** (*tr*) **1** to prepare (text) for publication by checking and improving its accuracy, clarity, etc. **2** to be in charge of (a publication, esp. a periodical). **3** to prepare (a film, tape, etc.) by rearrangement or selection of material. **4** (*tr*) to modify (a computer file). **5** (often foll. by *out*) to remove, as from a manuscript or film. ORIG C18: back formation from EDITOR

edit. *abbrev. for:* **1** edited. **2** edition. **3** editor.

edition (ɪ'dɪʃən) *n* **1** *Printing.* **1a** the entire number of copies of a book or other publication printed at one time. **1b** a copy from this number: *a first edition.* **2** one of a number of printings of a book or other publication, issued at separate times with alterations, amendments, etc. **3a** an issue of a work identified by its format: *a leather-bound edition.* **3b** an issue of a work identified by its editor or publisher: *the Oxford edition.* ORIG C16: from L *ēditiō* a bringing forth, publishing, from *ēdere* to give out; see EDITOR

editor ('ɛdɪtə) *n* **1** a person who edits written material for publication. **2** a person in overall charge of a newspaper or periodical. **3** a person in charge of one section of a newspaper or periodical: *the sports editor.* **4** *Films.* a person who makes a selection and arrangement of shots. **5** a person in overall control of a television or radio programme that consists of various items. ORIG C17: from LL: producer, exhibitor, from *ēdere* to give out, publish, from *ē-* out + *dāre* to give
▸ **'editorˌship** *n*

editorial (ˌɛdɪ'tɔːrɪəl) *adj* **1** of or relating to editing or editors. **2** of, relating to, or expressed in an editorial. **3** of or relating to the content of a publication. ◆ *n* **4** an article in a newspaper, etc., expressing the opinion of the editor or the publishers.
▸ **ˌedi'torially** *adv*

editorialize *or* **editorialise** (ˌɛdɪ'tɔːrɪəˌlaɪz) *vb* **editorializes, editorializing, editorialized** *or* **editorialises, editorialising, editorialised.** (*intr*) to express an opinion as in an editorial.
▸ **ˌediˌtoriali'zation** *or* **ˌediˌtoriali'sation** *n*

Edmonton ★ ('ɛdməntən) *n* a city in W Canada, capital of Alberta: oil industry. Pop.: 616 741 (1991).

Edmund ★ ('ɛdmənd) *n* **Saint,** also called *Saint Edmund Rich.* 1175–1240, English churchman: archbishop of Canterbury (1234–40). Feast day: Nov. 16.

Edmund I ★ *n* ?922–946 A.D., king of England (940–946).

Edmund II ★ *n* called *Edmund Ironside.* ?980–1016, king of England in 1016. His succession was contested by Canute and they divided the kingdom between them.

EDT (in the US and Canada) *abbrev. for* Eastern Daylight Time.

educate ('ɛdjʊˌkeɪt) *vb* **educates, educating, educated.** (*mainly tr*) **1** (*also intr*) to impart knowledge by formal instruction to (a pupil); teach. **2** to provide schooling for. **3** to improve or develop (a person, taste, skills, etc.). **4** to train for some particular purpose or occupation. ORIG C15: from L *ēducāre* to rear, educate, from *dūcere* to lead
▸ **'educable** *or* **'eduˌcatable** *adj* ▸ **ˌeduca'bility** *or* **ˌeduˌcata'bility** *n* ▸ **'educative** *adj*

educated ('ɛdjʊˌkeɪtɪd) *adj* **1** having an education, esp. a good one. **2** displaying culture, taste, and knowledge; cultivated. **3** (*prenominal*) based on experience or information (esp. in **an educated guess**).

education (ˌɛdjʊ'keɪʃən) *n* **1** the act or process of acquiring knowledge. **2** the knowledge or training acquired by this process. **3** the act or process of imparting knowledge, esp. at a school, college, or university. **4** the theory of teaching and learning. **5** a particular kind of instruction or training: *a university education.*
▸ **ˌedu'cational** *adj* ▸ **ˌedu'cationalist** *or* **ˌedu'cationist** *n*

educator ('ɛdjʊˌkeɪtə) *n* **1** a person who educates; teacher. **2** a specialist in education.

educe (ɪ'djuːs) *vb* **educes, educing, educed.** (*tr*) *Rare.* **1** to evolve or develop. **2** to draw out or elicit (information, solutions, etc.). ORIG C15: from L *ēdūcere,* from *ē-* out + *dūcere* to lead
▸ **e'ducible** *adj* ▸ **eductive** (ɪ'dʌktɪv) *adj*

Edward[1] ★ ('ɛdwəd) *n* **Lake.** a lake in central Africa, between Uganda and the Democratic Republic of Congo in the Great Rift Valley: empties through the Semliki River into Lake Albert. Area: about 2150 sq. km (830 sq. miles). Former official name: **Lake Amin.**

Edward[2] ★ ('ɛdwəd) *n* known as *the Black Prince.* 1330–76, Prince of Wales, the son of Edward III of England. He won victories over the French at Crécy (1346) and Poitiers (1356) in the Hundred Years' War.

Edward I ★ *n* 1239–1307, king of England (1272–1307); son of Henry III. He conquered Wales (1284).

Edward II ★ *n* 1284–1327, king of England (1307–27); son of Edward I. He invaded Scotland but was defeated by Robert Bruce at Bannockburn (1314). He was deposed by his wife Isabella and Roger Mortimer; died in prison.

Edward III ★ *n* 1312–77, king of England (1327–77); son of Edward II. His claim to the French throne in right of his mother Isabella provoked the Hundred Years' War (1337).

Edward IV ★ *n* 1442–83, king of England (1461–70; 1471–83); son of Richard, duke of York. He defeated Henry VI in the Wars of the Roses and became king (1461). In 1470 Henry was restored, but Edward recovered the crown by his victory at Tewkesbury.

Edward V ★ *n* 1470–?83, king of England in 1483; son of Edward IV. He was deposed by his uncle, Richard, Duke of Gloucester (Richard III), and is thought to have been murdered with his brother in the Tower of London.

Edward VI ★ *n* 1537–53, king of England (1547–53), son of Henry VIII and Jane Seymour. His uncle the Duke of Somerset was regent until 1552, when he was executed. Edward then came under the control of Dudley, Duke of Northumberland.

Edward VII ★ *n* 1841–1910, king of Great Britain and Ireland (1901–10); son of Queen Victoria.

Edward VIII ★ *n* 1894–1972, king of Great Britain and Northern Ireland in 1936; son of George V. He abdicated to marry Mrs Wallis Simpson (1896–1986); created Duke of Windsor (1937).

Edwardian (ɛd'wɔːdɪən) *adj* of or characteristic of the reign of Edward VII.
▸ **Ed'wardian,ism** *n*

Edwards ('ɛdwədz) *n* **Jonathan.** born 1966, British athlete: gold medallist in the Olympic triple jump (2000).

Edward the Confessor ★ *n* **Saint.** ?1002–66, king of England (1042–66); son of Ethelred II; founder of Westminster Abbey. Feast day: Oct. 13.

Edward the Elder ★ *n* died 924 A.D., king of England (899–924), son of Alfred the Great.

Edward the Martyr ★ *n* **Saint.** ?963–978 A.D., king of England (975–78), son of Edgar: murdered. Feast day: March 18.

Edwin ★ ('ɛdwɪn) *n* ?585–633 A.D., king of Northumbria (617–633) and overlord of all England except Kent.

-ee *suffix forming nouns.* **1** indicating a recipient of an action (as opposed, esp. in legal terminology, to the agent): *assignee; lessee.* **2** indicating a person in a specified state or condition: *absentee.* **3** indicating a diminutive form of something: *bootee.* ORIG via OF *-é, -ée,* p.p. endings, from L *-ātus, -āta* -ATE[1]

EEC *abbrev. for* (the former) European Economic Community.

EEG *abbrev. for:* **1** electroencephalogram. **2** electroencephalograph.

eel (iːl) *n* **1** any teleost fish such as the European freshwater eel, having a long snakelike body, a smooth slimy skin, and reduced fins. **2** any of various similar animals, such as the mud eel and the electric eel. **3** an evasive or untrustworthy person. ORIG OE *ǣl*
▸ **'eel-,like** *adj* ▸ **'eely** *adj*

eelgrass ('iːl,grɑːs) *n* any of several perennial submerged marine plants having grasslike leaves.

eelpout ('iːl,paʊt) *n* **1** a marine eel-like fish. **2** another name for **burbot.** ORIG OE *ǣlepūte*

eelworm ('iːl,wɜːm) *n* any of various nematode worms, esp. the wheatworm and the vinegar eel.

e'en (iːn) *adv, n Poetic or arch.* contraction of **even**[2] or **evening.**

e'er (ɛə) *adv Poetic or arch.* contraction of **ever.**

-eer *or* **-ier** *suffix.* **1** (*forming nouns*) indicating a person who is concerned with or who does something specified: *auctioneer; engineer; profiteer; mutineer.* **2** (*forming verbs*) to be concerned with something specified: *electioneer.* ORIG from OF *-ier,* from L *-arius* -ARY

eerie ('ɪərɪ) *adj* **eerier, eeriest.** uncannily frightening or disturbing; weird. ORIG C13: orig. Scot. & N English, prob. from OE *earg* cowardly
▸ **'eerily** *adv* ▸ **'eeriness** *n*

EETPU (in Britain) *abbrev. for* Electrical, Electronic, Telecommunications, and Plumbing Union.

eff (ɛf) *vb* **1** euphemism for **fuck** (esp. in **eff off**). **2 eff and blind.** *Sl.* to use obscene language.
▸ **'effing** *n, adj, adv*

efface (ɪ'feɪs) *vb* **effaces, effacing, effaced.** (*tr*) **1** to obliterate or make dim. **2** to make (oneself) inconspicuous or humble. **3** to rub out; erase. ORIG C15: from F *effacer,* lit.: to obliterate the face; see FACE
▸ **ef'faceable** *adj* ▸ **ef'facement** *n* ▸ **ef'facer** *n*

effect (ɪ'fɛkt) *n* **1** something produced by a cause or agent; result. **2** power to influence or produce a result. **3** the condition of being operative (esp. in **in** *or* **into effect**). **4 take effect.** to become operative or begin to produce results. **5** basic meaning or purpose (esp. in **to that effect**). **6** an impression, usually contrived (esp. in **for effect**). **7** a scientific phenomenon: *the Doppler effect.* **8 in effect. 8a** in fact; actually. **8b** for all practical purposes. **9** the overall impression or result. ◆ *vb* **10** (*tr*) to cause to occur; accomplish. ORIG C14: from L *effectus* a performing, tendency, from *efficere* to accomplish, from *facere* to do
▸ **ef'fecter** *n* ▸ **ef'fectible** *adj*

> **USAGE NOTE** It is quite common for *effect* to be mistakenly used where *affect* is intended, in the verb use. With initial *e* the verb is relatively uncommon and rather formal, and is a synonym of 'bring about'. Conversely, the noun is quite often mistakenly written with an initial *a.* The following are correct: *the group is still recovering from the effects of the recession; they really are powerless to effect any change.* The next two examples are incorrect: *the full affects of the shutdown won't be felt for several more days; ...men whose lack of hair doesn't effect their self-esteem.*

effective (ɪ'fɛktɪv) *adj* **1** productive of or capable of producing a result. **2** in effect; operative. **3** impressive: *an effective entrance.* **4** (*prenominal*) actual rather than theoretical. **5** (of a military force, etc.) equipped and prepared for action. ◆ *n* **6** a serviceman equipped and prepared for action.
▸ **ef'fectively** *adv* ▸ **ef'fectiveness** *n*

effects (ɪ'fɛkts) *pl n* **1** Also called: **personal effects.** personal belongings. **2** lighting, sounds, etc., to accompany a stage, film, or broadcast production.

effectual (ɪ'fɛktjʊəl) *adj* **1** capable of or successful in producing an intended result; effective. **2** (of documents, etc.) having legal force.
▸ **ef,fectu'ality** *or* **ef'fectualness** *n*

effectually (ɪ'fɛktjʊəlɪ) *adv* **1** with the intended effect. **2** in effect.

effectuate (ɪ'fɛktjʊ,eɪt) *vb* **effectuates, effectuating, effectuated.** (*tr*) to cause to happen; effect; accomplish.
▸ **ef,fectu'ation** *n*

effeminate (ɪ'fɛmɪnɪt) *adj* (of a man or boy) displaying characteristics regarded as typical of a woman; not manly. ORIG C14: from L *effēmināre* to make into a woman, from *fēmina* woman
▸ **ef'feminacy** *or* **ef'feminateness** *n*

effendi (ɛ'fɛndɪ) *n, pl* **effendis. 1** (in the Ottoman Empire) a title of respect. **2** (in Turkey since 1934) the oral title of address equivalent to *Mr.* ORIG C17: from Turkish *efendi* master, from Mod. Gk *aphentēs,* from Gk *authentēs* lord, doer

efferent ('ɛfərənt) *adj Physiol.* carrying or conducting outwards, esp. from the brain or spinal cord. Cf. **afferent.** ORIG C19: from L *efferre* to bear off, from *ferre* to bear
▸ **'efference** *n*

effervesce (,ɛfə'vɛs) *vb* **effervesces, effervescing, effervesced.** (*intr*) **1** (of a liquid) to give off bubbles of gas. **2** (of a gas) to issue in bubbles from a liquid. **3** to exhibit great excitement, vivacity, etc. ORIG C18: from L *effervescere* to foam up, ult. from *fervēre* to boil, ferment
▸ **,effer'vescingly** *adv*

effervescent (,ɛfə'vɛsᵊnt) *adj* **1** (of a liquid) giving off bubbles of gas. **2** high-spirited; vivacious.
▸ **,effer'vescence** *n*

effete (ɪ'fiːt) *adj* **1** weak or decadent. **2** exhausted; spent. **3** (of animals or plants) no longer capable of reproduction. ORIG C17: from L *effētus* exhausted by bearing, from *fētus* having brought forth; see FETUS
▸ **ef'feteness** *n*

efficacious (ˌɛfɪˈkeɪʃəs) *adj* capable of or successful in producing an intended result; effective. ORIG C16: from L *efficāx* powerful, efficient, from *efficere* to achieve
▸ **efficacy** (ˈɛfɪkəsɪ) *or* **ˌeffiˈcaciousness** *n*

efficiency (ɪˈfɪʃənsɪ) *n, pl* **efficiencies. 1** the quality or state of being efficient. **2** the ratio of the useful work done by a machine, etc., to the energy input, often expressed as a percentage.

efficient (ɪˈfɪʃənt) *adj* **1** functioning or producing effectively and with the least waste of effort; competent. **2** *Philosophy*. producing a direct effect. ORIG C14: from L *efficiēns* effecting

effigy (ˈɛfɪdʒɪ) *n, pl* **effigies. 1** a portrait, esp. as a monument. **2** a crude representation of someone, used as a focus for contempt or ridicule (often in **burn** *or* **hang in effigy**). ORIG C18: from L *effigiēs*, from *effingere* to form, portray, from *fingere* to shape

effleurage (ˌɛflɜːˈrɑːʒ) *n Med.* a light stroking movement used in massage. ORIG C19: from F

effloresce (ˌɛflɔːˈrɛs) *vb* **effloresces, efflorescing, effloresced.** (*intr*) **1** to burst forth as into flower; bloom. **2** to become powdery by loss of water or crystallization. **3** to become encrusted with powder or crystals as a result of chemical change or evaporation. ORIG C18: from L *efflōrēscere* to blossom, from *flōrēscere*, from *flōs* flower

efflorescence (ˌɛflɔːˈrɛsᵊns) *n* **1** a bursting forth or flowering. **2** *Chem., geol.* **2a** the process of efflorescing. **2b** the powdery substance formed as a result of this process. **3** any skin rash or eruption.
▸ **ˌeffloˈrescent** *adj*

effluence (ˈɛfluəns) *or* **efflux** (ˈɛflʌks) *n* **1** the act or process of flowing out. **2** something that flows out.

effluent (ˈɛfluənt) *n* **1** liquid discharged as waste, as from an industrial plant or sewage works. **2** radioactive waste released from a nuclear power station. **3** a stream that flows out of another body of water. **4** something that flows out or forth. ◆ *adj* **5** flowing out or forth. ORIG C18: from L *effluere* to run forth, from *fluere* to flow

effluvium (ɛˈfluːvɪəm) *n, pl* **effluvia** (-vɪə) *or* **effluviums.** an unpleasant smell or exhalation, as of gaseous waste or decaying matter. ORIG C17: from L: a flowing out; see EFFLUENT
▸ **efˈfluvial** *adj*

effort (ˈɛfət) *n* **1** physical or mental exertion. **2** a determined attempt. **3** achievement; creation. ORIG C15: from OF *esfort*, from *esforcier* to force, ult. from L *fortis* strong
▸ **ˈeffortful** *adj* ▸ **ˈeffortless** *adj*

effrontery (ɪˈfrʌntərɪ) *n, pl* **effronteries.** shameless or insolent boldness. ORIG C18: from F, from OF *esfront* barefaced, shameless, from LL *effrons*, lit.: putting forth one's forehead

effulgent (ɪˈfʌldʒənt) *adj* radiant; brilliant. ORIG C18: from L *effulgēre* to shine forth, from *fulgēre* to shine
▸ **efˈfulgence** *n* ▸ **efˈfulgently** *adv*

effuse *vb* (ɪˈfjuːz), **effuses, effusing, effused. 1** to pour or flow out. **2** to spread out; diffuse. ◆ *adj* (ɪˈfjuːs). **3** *Bot.* (esp. of an inflorescence) spreading out loosely. ORIG C16: from L *effūsus* poured out, from *effundere* to shed

effusion (ɪˈfjuːʒən) *n* **1** an unrestrained outpouring in speech or words. **2** the act or process of being poured out. **3** something that is poured out. **4** *Med.* **4a** the escape of blood or other fluid into a body cavity or tissue. **4b** the fluid that has escaped.

effusive (ɪˈfjuːsɪv) *adj* **1** extravagantly demonstrative of emotion; gushing. **2** (of rock) formed by the solidification of magma.
▸ **efˈfusively** *adv* ▸ **efˈfusiveness** *n*

E-FIT (ˈiːˌfɪt) *n Trademark*. **1** a technique that uses computer technology to generate a likeness of a face, used by police to trace people from witnesses' descriptions. **2** an image generated by this technique. ORIG C20: from *E*lectronic *F*acial *I*dentification *T*echnique

EFL *abbrev. for* English as a Foreign Language.

eft (ɛft) *n* a dialect or archaic name for a **newt**. ORIG OE *efeta*

EFTA (ˈɛftə) *n acronym for* European Free Trade Association; established in 1960 to eliminate trade tariffs on industrial products; the current members are Austria, Iceland, Norway, Sweden, and Switzerland.

EFTPOS (ˈɛftpɒs) *n acronym for* electronic funds transfer at point of sale.

EFTS *abbrev. for* electronic funds transfer system.

Eg. *abbrev. for:* **1** Egypt(ian). **2** Egyptology.

e.g., eg, *or* **eg.** *abbrev. for* exempli gratia. ORIG L: for example

> **USAGE NOTE** In careful writing which is not technical, it is best to avoid using this abbreviation and write *for example* instead. In the Bank of English the abbreviation occurs most commonly in magazines and miscellaneous brochures and junk mail, and relatively infrequently in books. There is occasional confusion between *e.g.* and *i.e.* as in *the item just got lost in the system (e.g. stuck at the bottom of a mailbag)*. Here *i.e.* was clearly meant. The correct form of the abbreviation is with two stops, although it is frequently encountered with none, or with one after the *g*.

egad (ɪˈgæd, iːˈgæd) *interj Arch.* a mild oath. ORIG C17: prob. var. of *Ah God!*

egalitarian (ɪˌgælɪˈtɛərɪən) *adj* **1** of or upholding the doctrine of the equality of mankind. ◆ *n* **2** an adherent of egalitarian principles. ORIG C19: alteration of *equalitarian*, through infl. of F *égal* equal
▸ **eˌgaliˈtarianˌism** *n*

Egbert ★ (ˈɛgbɜːt) *n* ?775–839 A.D., king of Wessex (802–839); first overlord of all England (829–830).

Eger ★ *n* **1** (*Hungarian* ˈɛgɛr). a city in N central Hungary. Pop.: 60 000 (1995 est.). **2** (ˈeːgər). the German name for **Cheb**.

egg¹ (ɛg) *n* **1** the oval or round reproductive body laid by the females of birds, reptiles, fishes, insects, and some other animals, consisting of a developing embryo, its food store, and sometimes jelly or albumen, all surrounded by an outer shell or membrane. **2** Also called: **egg cell.** any female gamete; ovum. **3** the egg of the domestic hen used as food. **4** something resembling an egg, esp. in shape. **5 good** (*or* **bad**) **egg.** *Old-fashioned inf.* a good (or bad) person. **6 put** *or* **have all one's eggs in one basket.** to stake everything on a single venture. **7 teach one's grandmother to suck eggs.** *Inf.* to presume to teach someone something that he or she knows already. **8 with egg on one's face.** *Inf.* made to look ridiculous. ORIG C14: from ON *egg*; rel. to OE *ǣg*

egg² (ɛg) *vb* (*tr;* usually foll. by *on*) to urge or incite, esp. to daring or foolish acts. ORIG OE *eggian*

egg-and-spoon race *n* a race in which runners carry an egg balanced in a spoon.

eggbeater (ˈɛgˌbiːtə) *n* **1** Also called: **eggwhisk.** a utensil for beating eggs; whisk. **2** *Chiefly US & Canad.* an informal name for **helicopter**.

egger *or* **eggar** (ˈɛgə) *n* any of various European moths having brown bodies and wings. ORIG C18: from EGG¹, from the egg-shaped cocoon

egghead (ˈɛgˌhɛd) *n Inf.* an intellectual.

eggnog (ˌɛgˈnɒg) *n* a drink made of eggs, milk, sugar, spice, and brandy, rum, or other spirit. Also called: **egg flip.** ORIG C19: from EGG¹ + NOG

eggplant (ˈɛgˌplɑːnt) *n* another name (esp. US, Canad., & Austral.) for **aubergine.**

eggshell (ˈɛgˌʃɛl) *n* **1** the hard porous outer layer of a bird's egg. **2** (*modifier*) (of paint) having a very slight sheen.

eggshell porcelain *or* **china** *n* a very thin translucent porcelain originally from China.

egg tooth *n* (in embryo reptiles) a temporary tooth or (in birds) projection of the beak used for piercing the eggshell.

Egham ★ (ˈɛgəm) *n* a town in S England, in N Surrey on the River Thames. Pop.: 23 816 (1991).

eglantine (ˈɛglənˌtaɪn) *n* another name for **sweetbrier.**

ORIG C14: from OF *aiglent,* ult. from L *acus* needle, from *acer* sharp, keen

EGM *abbrev. for* extraordinary general meeting.

Egmont[1] ★ ('ɛgmɒnt) *n* **Mount.** a mountain in New Zealand, in W central North Island in the **Egmont National Park:** an almost perfect volcanic cone. Height: 2518 m (8261 ft). Maori name: **Taranaki.**

Egmont[2] ★ ('ɛgmɒnt) *n* **Lamoral** (lamo'ral), Count of Egmont, Prince of Gavre. 1522–68, Flemish statesman. He tried to reform the Spanish government of the Netherlands, refused to join William the Silent's rebellion, but was executed for treason.

ego ('iːgəʊ, 'ɛgəʊ) *n, pl* **egos. 1** the self of an individual person; the conscious subject. **2** *Psychoanalysis.* the conscious mind, based on perception of the environment: modifies the antisocial instincts of the id and is itself modified by the conscience (superego). **3** one's image of oneself; morale. **4** egotism; conceit. ORIG C19: from L: I

egocentric (ˌiːgəʊ'sɛntrɪk, ˌɛg-) *adj* **1** regarding everything only in relation to oneself; self-centred. ◆ *n* **2** a self-centred person; egotist.
▸ **ˌegocen'tricity** *n* ▸ **ˌego'centrism** *n*

egoism ('iːgəʊˌɪzəm, 'ɛg-) *n* **1** concern for one's own interests and welfare. **2** *Ethics.* the theory that the pursuit of one's own welfare is the highest good. **3** self-centredness; egotism.
▸ **'egoist** *n* ▸ **ˌego'istic** *or* **ˌego'istical** *adj*

Egoli ★ (ɛ'gəʊlɪ) *n S. African.* an informal name for **Johannesburg.** ORIG from Zulu *eboli* place of gold

egomania (ˌiːgəʊ'meɪnɪə, ˌɛg-) *n Psychiatry.* obsessive love for oneself.
▸ **ˌego'maniˌac** *n* ▸ **egomaniacal** (ˌiːgəʊmə'naɪɪkᵊl, ˌɛg-) *adj*

egotism ('iːgəˌtɪzəm, 'ɛgə-) *n* **1** an inflated sense of self-importance or superiority; self-centredness. **2** excessive reference to oneself. ORIG C18: from L *ego* I + -ISM
▸ **'egotist** *n* ▸ **ˌego'tistic** *or* **ˌego'tistical** *adj*

ego trip *n Inf.* something undertaken to boost or draw attention to a person's own image or appraisal of himself.

egregious (ɪ'griːdʒəs, -dʒɪəs) *adj* **1** outstandingly bad; flagrant. **2** *Arch.* distinguished; eminent. ORIG C16: from L *ēgregius* outstanding (lit.: standing out from the herd), from *ē-* out + *grex* flock, herd
▸ **e'gregiousness** *n*

egress ('iːgrɛs) *n* **1** Also: **egression.** the act of going or coming out; emergence. **2** a way out; exit. **3** the right to go out or depart. ORIG C16: from L *ēgredī* to come forth, depart, from *gradī* to move, step

egret ('iːgrɪt) *n* any of various wading birds similar to herons but usually having white plumage and, in the breeding season, long feathery plumes. ORIG C15: from OF *aigrette,* of Gmc origin

Egypt ★ ('iːdʒɪpt) *n* a republic in NE Africa, on the Mediterranean and Red Sea: its history dates back about 5000 years. Occupied by the British from 1882, it became an independent kingdom in 1922 and a republic in 1953. Over 96 per cent of the total area is desert, with the chief areas of habitation and cultivation in the Nile delta and valley. Cotton is the main export. Official language: Arabic. Official religion: Muslim (Sunni majority). Currency: pound. Capital: Cairo. Pop.: 64 560 000 (1999 est.). Area: 997 739 sq. km (385 229 sq. miles). Official name: **Arab Republic of Egypt.** Former official name (1958–71): **United Arab Republic.**

Egyptian (ɪ'dʒɪpʃən) *adj* **1** of or relating to Egypt, its inhabitants, or their dialect of Arabic. **2** of or characteristic of the ancient Egyptians, their language, or culture. ◆ *n* **3** a native or inhabitant of Egypt. **4** a member of a people who established an advanced civilization in Egypt that flourished from the late fourth millennium B.C. **5** the extinct language of the ancient Egyptians.

Egyptology (ˌiːdʒɪp'tɒlədʒɪ) *n* the study of the archaeology and language of ancient Egypt.
▸ **ˌEgyp'tologist** *n*

eh (eɪ) *interj* an exclamation used to express questioning surprise or to seek the repetition or confirmation of a statement or question.

EHF *abbrev. for* extremely high frequency.

Ehrenburg *or* **Erenburg** ★ ('ɛərənˌbɜːg; *Russian* ɛrɪn'burk) *n* **Ilya Grigorievich** (ilj'ja gri'gɔrjɪvitʃ). 1891–1967, Soviet novelist and journalist. His novel *The Thaw* (1954) was the first published in the Soviet Union to deal with repression under Stalin.

Ehrlich ★ (*German* 'eːrlɪç) *n* **Paul** (paul). 1854–1915, German bacteriologist, noted for his pioneering work in immunology and chemotherapy: Nobel prize for physiology or medicine 1908.

EI *abbrev. for:* **1** East Indian. **2** East Indies.

Eichler ★ (*German* 'aɪçlər) *n* **August Wilhelm** ('aʊgʊst 'vɪlhɛlm). 1839–87, German botanist: devised the system on which modern plant classification is based.

Eichmann ★ (*German* 'aɪçman) *n* **(Karl) Adolf** ('aːdɔlf). 1902–62, Austrian Nazi, who organized the extermination of European Jews; executed in Israel.

eider *or* **eider duck** ('aɪdə) *n* any of several sea ducks of the N hemisphere. See **eiderdown.** ORIG C18: from ON *æthr*

eiderdown ('aɪdəˌdaʊn) *n* **1** the breast down of the female eider duck, used for stuffing pillows, quilts, etc. **2** a thick, warm cover for a bed, enclosing a soft filling.

eidetic (aɪ'dɛtɪk) *adj Psychol.* **1** (of visual, or sometimes auditory, images) very vivid and allowing detailed recall of something previously perceived: thought to be common in children. **2** relating to or subject to such imagery. ORIG C20: from Gk *eidētikos,* from *eidos* shape, form
▸ **ei'detically** *adv*

Eid-ul-Adha ('iːdʊlˌɑːdə) *n* an annual Muslim festival marking the end of the pilgrimage to Mecca. Animals are sacrificed and their meat shared among the poor. ORIG from Ar. *id ul adha* festival of sacrifice

Eid-ul-Fitr ('iːdʊlˌfiːtə) *n* an annual Muslim festival marking the end of Ramadan, involving the exchange of gifts and a festive meal. ORIG from Ar. *id ul fitr* festival of fast-breaking

Eifel ★ ('aɪfᵊl; *German* 'aɪfəl) *n* a plateau region in W Germany, between the River Moselle and the Belgian frontier: quarrying.

Eiffel ★ ('aɪfᵊl; *French* ɛfɛl) *n* **Alexandre Gustave** (alɛksɑ̃drə gystav). 1832–1923, French engineer.

Eiffel Tower ★ ('aɪfᵊl) *n* a tower in Paris: designed by A. G. Eiffel; erected for the 1889 Paris Exposition. Height: 300 m (984 ft), raised in 1959 to 321 m (1052 ft).

Eigen ★ (*German* 'aɪgən) *n* **Manfred.** born 1927, German chemist: shared the Nobel prize for chemistry (1967) for his relaxation technique for studying fast reactions.

Eiger ★ (*German* 'aɪgər) *n* a mountain in central Switzerland, in the Bernese Alps. Height: 3970 m (13 025 ft).

eight (eɪt) *n* **1** the cardinal number that is the sum of one and seven and the product of two and four. **2** a numeral, 8, VIII, etc., representing this number. **3** the amount or quantity that is one greater than seven. **4** something representing, represented by, or consisting of eight units. **5** *Rowing.* **5a** a racing shell propelled by eight oarsmen. **5b** the crew of such a shell. **6** Also called: **eight o'clock.** eight hours after noon or midnight. **7 have one over the eight.** *Sl.* to be drunk. ◆ *determiner* **8a** amounting to eight. **8b** *(as pron): I could only find eight.* ORIG OE *eahta*

eighteen ('eɪ'tiːn) *n* **1** the cardinal number that is the sum of ten and eight and the product of two and nine. **2** a numeral, 18, XVIII, etc., representing this number. **3** the amount or quantity that is eight more than ten. **4** something represented by, representing, or consisting of 18 units. ◆ *determiner* **5a** amounting to eighteen: *eighteen weeks.* **5b** *(as pron): eighteen of them knew.* ORIG OE *eahtatēne*
▸ **'eigh'teenth** *adj, n*

eightfold ('eɪtˌfəʊld) *adj* **1** equal to or having eight times as many or as much. **2** composed of eight parts. ◆ *adv* **3** by eight times as much.

eighth (eɪtθ) *adj* **1** *(usually prenominal)* **1a** coming after the seventh and before the ninth in numbering, position, etc.; being the ordinal number of *eight:* often written 8th. **1b** *(as n): the eighth in line.* ◆ *n* **2a** one of eight equal parts of something. **2b** *(as modifier): an eighth part.* **3** the fraction one divided by eight (1/8). **4** another word for **octave.** ◆ *adv* **5** Also: **eighthly.** after the seventh person, position, event, etc.

eighth note *n Music.* the usual US and Canad. name for **quaver.**

eightsome reel ('eɪtsəm) *n* a Scottish dance for eight people.

eighty ('eɪtɪ) *n, pl* **eighties. 1** the cardinal number that is the product of ten and eight. **2** a numeral, 80, LXXX, etc., representing this number. **3** *(pl)* the numbers 80–89, esp. the 80th to the 89th year of a person's life or of a century. **4** the amount or quantity that is eight times ten. **5** something represented by, representing, or consisting of 80 units. ◆ *determiner* **6a** amounting to eighty: *eighty pages of nonsense.* **6b** *(as pron): eighty are expected.* ORIG OE *eahtatig*
▸ **'eightieth** *adj, n*

Eilat, Elat, *or* **Elath** ★ (eɪ'lɑːt) *n* a port in S Israel, on the Gulf of Aqaba: Israel's only outlet to the Red Sea. Pop.: 26 010 (1989 est.).

eina ('eɪˌnɑː) *interj S. African.* an exclamation of sudden pain. ORIG C19: Afrik., from Khoi

Eindhoven ★ ('aɪntˌhəʊvᵊn, *Dutch* 'ɛinthoːvə) *n* a city in the SE Netherlands, in North Brabant province: radio and electrical industry. Pop.: 197 374 (1996 est.).

Einstein ★ ('aɪnstaɪn) *n* **Albert.** 1879–1955, US physicist and mathematician, born in Germany. He formulated the special theory of relativity (1905) and the general theory of relativity (1916), and made major contributions to the quantum theory, for which he was awarded the Nobel prize for physics in 1921. He was noted also for his work for world peace.
▸ **Ein'steinian** *adj*

einsteinium (aɪn'staɪnɪəm) *n* a radioactive metallic transuranic element artificially produced from plutonium. Symbol: Es; atomic no.: 99; half-life of most stable isotope, ^{252}Es: 276 days. ORIG C20: NL, after Albert EINSTEIN

Einthoven ★ (*Dutch* 'ɛinthoːvə) *n* **Willem** ('wɪləm). 1860–1927, Dutch physiologist. A pioneer of electrocardiography, he was awarded the Nobel prize for physiology or medicine in 1924.

Eire ★ ('ɛərə) *n* **1** the Irish Gaelic name for **Ireland**[1]: often used to mean the **Republic of Ireland. 2** a former name for the **Republic of Ireland** (1937–49).

EIS *abbrev. for* Educational Institute of Scotland.

Eisenach ★ (*German* 'aɪzənax) *n* a city in central Germany, in Thuringia. Pop.: 48 361 (1989 est.).

Eisenhower ★ ('aɪzənˌhaʊə) *n* **Dwight D(avid),** known as *Ike.* 1890–1969, US general and Republican statesman; Supreme Commander of the Allied Expeditionary Force (1943–45) and 34th president of the US (1953–61). He was also Supreme Commander of the combined land forces of NATO (1950–52).

Eisenstadt ★ (*German* 'aɪzənʃtat) *n* a town in E Austria, capital of Burgenland province: Hungarian until 1921. Pop.: 10 506 (1991).

Eisenstein ★ ('aɪzᵊnˌstaɪn; *Russian* ejzɪn'ʃtjejn) *n* **Sergei Mikhailovich** (sɪr'gjej mi'xajləvitʃ). 1898–1948, Soviet film director. His films include *Battleship Potemkin* (1925), *Alexander Nevsky* (1938), and *Ivan the Terrible* (1944).

Eisk *or* **Eysk** ★ (*Russian* jejsk) *n* variant transliterations of the Russian name for **Yeisk.**

eisteddfod (aɪ'stɛdfəd) *n, pl* **eisteddfods** *or* **eisteddfodau** (*Welsh* aɪˌstɛð'vɒdaɪ). any of a number of annual festivals in Wales in which competitions are held in music, poetry, drama, and the fine arts. ORIG C19: from Welsh, lit.: session, from *eistedd* to sit + *-fod,* from *bod* to be

either ('aɪðə, 'iːðə) *determiner* **1a** one or the other (of two). **1b** *(as pron): either is acceptable.* **2** both one and the other: *at either end of the table.* ◆ *conj* **3** *(coordinating)* used preceding two or more possibilities joined by "or". ◆ *adv (sentence modifier)* **4** *(with a negative)* used to indicate that the clause immediately preceding is a partial reiteration of a previous clause: *John isn't a liar, but he isn't exactly honest either.* ORIG OE *ǣgther,* short for *ǣghwæther* each of two; see WHETHER

> **USAGE NOTE** *Either* should be followed by a singular verb: *either is good; either of these books is useful.* Care should be taken to avoid ambiguity when using *either* to mean *both* or *each,* as in the following sentence: *a ship could be moored on either side of the channel.* Agreement between the verb and its subject in *either...or...* constructions follows the pattern for *neither...nor...* See at **neither.**

ejaculate *vb* (ɪ'dʒækjʊˌleɪt), **ejaculates, ejaculating, ejaculated. 1** to eject or discharge (semen) in orgasm. **2** *(tr)* to utter abruptly; blurt out. ◆ *n* (ɪ'dʒækjʊlɪt). **3** another word for **semen.** ORIG C16: from L *ējaculārī* to hurl out, from *jaculum* javelin, from *jacere* to throw
▸ **eˌjacu'lation** *n* ▸ **e'jaculatory** *or* **e'jaculative** *adj*
▸ **e'jacuˌlator** *n*

eject (ɪ'dʒɛkt) *vb* **1** *(tr)* to force out; expel or emit. **2** *(tr)* to compel (a person) to leave; evict. **3** *(tr)* to dismiss, as from office. **4** *(intr)* to leave an aircraft rapidly, using an ejection seat or capsule. ORIG C15: from L *ejicere,* from *jacere* to throw
▸ **e'jection** *n* ▸ **e'jective** *adj* ▸ **e'jector** *n*

ejection seat *or* **ejector seat** *n* a seat, esp. in military aircraft, fired by a cartridge or rocket to eject the occupant in an emergency.

Ekaterinburg ★ (*Russian* jɪkətɪrim'burk) *n* a variant of **Yekaterinburg.**

Ekaterinodar ★ (*Russian* jɪkətɪrina'dar) *n* the former name (until 1920) of **Krasnodar.**

eke (iːk) *sentence connector. Arch.* also; moreover. ORIG OE *eac*

eke out (iːk) *vb (tr, adv)* **1** to make (a supply) last, esp. by frugal use. **2** to support (existence) with difficulty and effort. **3** to add to (something insufficient), esp. with effort. ORIG from obs. *eke* to enlarge

Ekman ★ (*Swedish* 'ɛkman) *n* **Vagn Walfrid** (vaɣᵊn wɑːlfriːd). 1874–1954, Swedish oceanographer: discoverer of the **Ekman Spiral** (a complex interaction on the surface of the sea between wind, rotation of the earth, and friction forces) and the **Ekman layer** (the thin top layer of the sea that flows at 90° to the wind direction).

El Aaiún ★ (ɛl aɪ'juːn) *n* a city in Morocco, in Western Sahara: the capital of the former Spanish Sahara; port facilities at **Playa de El Aaiún,** 20 km (12 miles) away. Pop.: 136 950 (1994).

elaborate *adj* (ɪ'læbərɪt). **1** planned with care and exactness. **2** marked by complexity or detail. ◆ *vb* (ɪ'læbəˌreɪt), **elaborates, elaborating, elaborated. 3** *(intr; usually foll. by on or upon)* to add detail (to an account); expand (upon). **4** *(tr)* to work out in detail; develop. **5** *(tr)* to produce by careful labour. **6** *(tr) Physiol.* to change (food or simple substances) into more complex substances for use in the body. ORIG C16: from L *ēlabōrāre* to take pains, from *labōrāre* to toil
▸ **e'laborateness** *n* ▸ **eˌlabo'ration** *n* ▸ **elaborative** (ɪ'læbərətɪv) *adj* ▸ **e'laboˌrator** *n*

Elagabalus ★ (ˌɛlə'gæbələs, ˌiːlə-) *n* a variant of **Heliogabalus.**

El Alamein *or* **Alamein** ★ (ɛl 'æləˌmeɪn) *n* a village on the N coast of Egypt, about 112 km (70 miles) west of Alexandria: scene of a decisive Allied victory over the Axis forces (1942).

Elam ★ ('iːləm) *n* an ancient kingdom east of the River Tigris: established before 4000 B.C.; probably inhabited by a non-Semitic people.

élan (eɪ'lɑːn) *n* a combination of style and vigour. ORIG C19: from F, from *élancer* to throw forth, ult. from L *lancea* LANCE

eland ('iːlənd) *n* **1** a large spiral-horned antelope inhabiting bushland in eastern and southern Africa. **2 giant eland.** a similar but larger animal of central and W Africa. ORIG C18: via Afrik., from Du. *eland* elk

elapse (ɪ'læps) *vb* **elapses, elapsing, elapsed.** *(intr)* (of time) to pass by. ORIG C17: from L *ēlābī* to slip away

elasmobranch (ɪˈlæsməˌbræŋk) *n* **1** any cartilaginous fish of the subclass *Elasmobranchii,* which includes sharks, rays, and skates. ◆ *adj* **2** of or relating to the *Elasmobranchii.* ORIG C19: from NL *elasmobranchii,* from Gk *elasmos* metal plate + *brankhia* gills

elastane (ɪˈlæsteɪn) *n* a synthetic fibre characterized by its ability to revert to its original shape after being stretched.

elastic (ɪˈlæstɪk) *adj* **1** (of a body or material) capable of returning to its original shape after compression, stretching, or other deformation. **2** capable of adapting to change. **3** quick to recover from fatigue, dejection, etc. **4** springy or resilient. **5** made of elastic. ◆ *n* **6** tape, cord, or fabric containing flexible rubber or similar substance allowing it to stretch and return to its original shape. ORIG C17: from NL *elasticus* impulsive, from Gk *elastikos,* from *elaunein* to beat, drive
▸ **eˈlastically** *adv* ▸ **elasˈticity** *n*

elasticate (ɪˈlæstɪˌkeɪt) *vb* **elasticates, elasticating, elasticated.** (*tr*) to insert elastic into (a fabric or garment).
▸ **eˌlastiˈcation** *n*

elastic band *n* another name for **rubber band.**

elasticize *or* **elasticise** (ɪˈlæstɪˌsaɪz) *vb* **elasticizes, elasticizing, elasticized** *or* **elasticises, elasticising, elasticised. 1** to make elastic. **2** another word for **elasticate.**

elastomer (ɪˈlæstəmə) *n* any material, such as rubber, able to resume its original shape when a deforming force is removed. ORIG C20: from ELASTIC + -MER
▸ **elastomeric** (ɪˌlæstəˈmɛrɪk) *adj*

Elastoplast (ɪˈlæstəˌplɑːst) *n Trademark.* a gauze surgical dressing backed by adhesive tape.

Elat *or* **Elath** ★ (eɪˈlɑːt) *n* variant spellings of **Eilat.**

elate (ɪˈleɪt) *vb* **elates, elating, elated.** (*tr*) to fill with high spirits, exhilaration, pride, or optimism. ORIG C16: from p.p. of L *efferre* to bear away, from *ferre* to carry
▸ **eˈlated** *adj* ▸ **eˈlatedly** *adv* ▸ **eˈlatedness** *n*

elation (ɪˈleɪʃən) *n* joyfulness or exaltation of spirit, as from success, pleasure, or relief.

E layer *n* another name for **E region.**

Elba ★ (ˈɛlbə) *n* a mountainous island off the W coast of Italy, in the Mediterranean: Napoleon Bonaparte's first place of exile (1814–15). Pop.: 27 722 (1991 est.). Area: 223 sq. km (86 sq. miles).

Elbe ★ (ɛlb; *German* ˈɛlbə) *n* a river in central Europe, rising in the N Czech Republic and flowing generally northwest through Germany to the North Sea at Hamburg. Length: 1165 km (724 miles). Czech name: **Labe.**

Elbert ★ (ˈɛlbət) *n* **Mount.** a mountain in central Colorado, in the Sawatch range. Height: 4399 m (14 431 ft).

Elbląg ★ (*Polish* ˈɛlblɔŋk) *n* a port in N Poland: metallurgical industries. Pop.: 128 700 (1996 est.). German name: **Elbing** (ˈɛlbɪŋ).

elbow (ˈɛlbəʊ) *n* **1** the joint between the upper arm and the forearm. **2** the corresponding joint of birds or mammals. **3** the part of a garment that covers the elbow. **4** something resembling an elbow, such as a sharp bend in a road. **5 at one's elbow.** within easy reach. **6 out at elbow(s).** ragged or impoverished. **7 the elbow.** dismissal or rejection. ◆ *vb* **8** to make (one's way) by shoving, jostling, etc. **9** (*tr*) to knock or shove as with the elbow. ORIG OE *elnboga*

elbow grease *n Facetious.* vigorous physical labour, esp. hard rubbing.

elbowroom (ˈɛlbəʊˌruːm, -ˌrʊm) *n* sufficient scope to move or function.

Elbrus ★ (ɪlˈbruːs) *n* a mountain in S W Russia, on the border with Georgia, with two extinct volcanic peaks: the highest mountain in Europe. Height: 5642 m (18 510 ft).

Elburz Mountains ★ (ɛlˈbʊəz) *pl n* a mountain range in N Iran, parallel to the SW and S shores of the Caspian Sea. Highest peak: Mount Demavend, 5601 m (18 376 ft).

El Capitan ★ (ɛl ˌkæpɪˈtæn) *n* a mountain in E central California, in the Sierra Nevada: a monolith with a precipice rising over 1100 m (3600 ft) above the floor of the Yosemite Valley. Height: 2306 m (7564 ft).

Elche ★ (*Spanish* ˈɛltʃe) *n* a town in S Spain, in Valencia: noted for Iberian and Roman archaeological finds and the medieval religious drama performed there annually: fruit growing, esp. dates, pomegranates, figs. Pop.: 192 424 (1995 est.).

El Cid Campeador ★ (*Spanish* ɛl ˈθið kampeaˈðɔr) *n* See (El) **Cid.**

elder[1] (ˈɛldə) *adj* **1** born earlier; senior. Cf. **older. 2** (in certain card games) denoting or relating to the nondealer (the **elder hand**), who has certain advantages in the play. **3** *Arch.* **3a** prior in rank or office. **3b** of a previous time. ◆ *n* **4** an older person; one's senior. **5** *Anthropol.* a senior member of a tribe who has authority. **6** (in certain Protestant Churches) a lay office. **7** another word for **presbyter.** ORIG OE *eldra,* comp. of *eald* OLD
▸ **ˈelderˌship** *n*

elder[2] (ˈɛldə) *n* any of various shrubs or small trees having clusters of small white flowers and red, purple, or black berry-like fruits. Also called: **elderberry.** ORIG OE *ellern*

elderberry (ˈɛldəˌbɛrɪ) *n, pl* **elderberries. 1** the fruit of the elder. **2** another name for **elder**[2].

elder brother *n* one of the senior members of Trinity House.

elderly (ˈɛldəlɪ) *adj* (of people) quite old; past middle age.
▸ **ˈelderliness** *n*

eldest (ˈɛldɪst) *adj* being the oldest, esp. the oldest surviving child of the same parents. ORIG OE *eldesta,* sup. of *eald* OLD

El Dorado (ɛl dɒˈrɑːdəʊ) *n* **1** a fabled city in South America, rich in treasure. **2** Also: **eldorado.** any place of great riches or fabulous opportunity. ORIG C16: from Sp., lit.: the gilded (place)

eldritch *or* **eldrich** (ˈɛldrɪtʃ) *adj Poetic, Scot.* unearthly; weird. ORIG C16: ?from OE *ælf* elf + *rīce* realm

Elea ★ (ˈiːlɪə) *n* (in ancient Italy) a Greek colony on the Tyrrhenian coast of Lucana.

Eleanor of Aquitaine ★ (ˈɛlɪnə, -ˌnɔː) *n* ?1122–1204, queen of France (1137–52) by her marriage to Louis VII and queen of England (1154–89) by her marriage to Henry II; mother of the English kings Richard I and John.

Eleanor of Castile ★ (ˈɛlɪnə, -ˌnɔː) *n* 1246–90, Spanish wife of Edward I of England. **Eleanor Crosses** were erected at each place at which her body rested between Nottingham, where she died, and London, where she is buried.

elect (ɪˈlɛkt) *vb* **1** (*tr*) to choose (someone) to be (a representative or official) by voting. **2** to select; choose. **3** (*tr*) (of God) to predestine for the grace of salvation. ◆ *adj* **4** (*immediately postpositive*) voted into office but not yet installed: *president elect.* **5a** chosen; elite. **5b** (*as collective n; preceded by the*): *the elect.* **6** *Christian theol.* **6a** predestined by God to receive salvation. **6b** (*as collective n; preceded by the*): *the elect.* ORIG C15: from L *ēligere* to select, from *legere* to choose
▸ **eˈlectable** *adj*

elect. *or* **elec.** *abbrev. for:* **1** electric(al). **2** electricity.

election (ɪˈlɛkʃən) *n* **1** the selection by vote of a person or persons for a position, esp. a political office. **2** a public vote. **3** the act or an instance of choosing. **4** *Christian theol.* **4a** the doctrine that God chooses individuals for salvation without reference to faith or works. **4b** the doctrine that God chooses for salvation those who, by grace, persevere in faith and works.

electioneer (ɪˌlɛkʃəˈnɪə) *vb* (*intr*) **1** to be active in a political election or campaign. ◆ *n* **2** a person who engages in this activity.
▸ **eˌlectionˈeering** *n, adj*

elective (ɪˈlɛktɪv) *adj* **1** of or based on selection by vote. **2** selected by vote. **3** having the power to elect. **4** open to choice; optional. ◆ *n* **5** an optional course or hospital placement undertaken by a medical student.
▸ **electivity** (ˌiːlɛkˈtɪvɪtɪ) *or* **eˈlectiveness** *n*

elector (ɪˈlɛktə) *n* **1** someone who is eligible to vote in the election of a government. **2** (*often cap.*) a member of the US electoral college. **3** (*often cap.*) (in the Holy Roman

Empire) any of the German princes entitled to take part in the election of a new emperor.
▸ **e'lectoral** *adj* ▸ **e'lector,ship** *n* ▸ **e'lectress** *fem n*

electoral college *n* (*often cap.*) **1** *US.* a body of electors chosen by the voters who formally elect the president and vice president. **2** any body of electors with similar functions.

electorate (ɪ'lɛktərɪt) *n* **1** the body of all qualified voters. **2** the rank, position, or territory of an elector of the Holy Roman Empire. **3** *Austral. & NZ.* the area represented by a Member of Parliament. **4** *Austral. & NZ.* the voters in a constituency.

Electra ★ (ɪ'lɛktrə) *n Greek myth.* the daughter of Agamemnon and Clytemnestra. She persuaded her brother Orestes to avenge their father by killing his murderess Clytemnestra and her lover Aegisthus.

electret (ɪ'lɛktrət) *n* a permanently polarized dielectric material; its field is similar to that of a permanent magnet. ORIG C20: from *electr(icity + magn)et*

electric (ɪ'lɛktrɪk) *adj* **1** of, derived from, produced by, producing, transmitting, or powered by electricity. **2** (of a musical instrument) amplified electronically. **3** very tense or exciting; emotionally charged. ◆ *n* **4** *Inf.* an electric train, car, etc. **5** (*pl*) an electric circuit or electric appliances. ORIG C17: from NL *electricus* amber-like (because friction causes amber to become charged), from L *ēlectrum* amber, from Gk *ēlektron,* from ?

electrical (ɪ'lɛktrɪk^əl) *adj* of, relating to, or concerned with electricity.
▸ **e'lectrically** *adv*

electrical engineering *n* the branch of engineering concerned with practical applications of electricity.
▸ **electrical engineer** *n*

electric blanket *n* a blanket that contains an electric heating element, used to warm a bed.

electric chair *n* (in the US) **a** an electrified chair for executing criminals. **b** (usually preceded by *the*) execution by this method.

electric circuit *n Physics.* another name for **circuit** (sense 3a).

electric constant *n* the permittivity of free space, which has the value $8.854\ 185 \times 10^{-12}$ farad per metre.

electric discharge *n Physics.* another name for **discharge** (sense 17b).

electric displacement *n Physics.* the charge per unit area displaced across a layer of conductor in an electric field. Symbol: *D* Also called: **electric flux density.**

electric eel *n* an eel-like freshwater fish of N South America, having electric organs in the body.

electric eye *n* another name for **photocell.**

electric field *n* a field of force surrounding a charged particle within which another charged particle experiences a force.

electric flux *n* the amount of electricity displaced across a given area in a dielectric. Symbol: Ψ

electric flux density *n* another name for **electric displacement.**

electric guitar *n* an electrically amplified guitar, used mainly in pop music.

electrician (ɪlɛk'trɪʃən, ˌiːlɛk-) *n* a person whose occupation is the installation, maintenance, and repair of electrical devices.

electricity (ɪlɛk'trɪsɪtɪ, ˌiːlɛk-) *n* **1** any phenomenon associated with stationary or moving electrons, ions, or other charged particles. **2** the science of electricity. **3** an electric current or charge. **4** emotional tension or excitement.

electric motor *n* a device that converts electrical energy to mechanical torque.

electric organ *n* **1** *Music.* **1a** a pipe organ operated by electrical means. **1b** another name for **electronic organ. 2** a group of cells on certain fishes, such as the electric eel, that gives an electric shock to any animal touching them.

electric potential *n* **a** the work required to transfer a unit of positive electric charge from an infinite distance to a given point. **b** the potential difference between the point and some other point. Sometimes shortened to **potential.**

electric ray *n* any ray of tropical and temperate seas, having a flat rounded body and an organ for producing electricity in each fin.

electric shock *n* the physiological reaction, characterized by pain and muscular spasm, to the passage of an electric current through the body. It can affect the respiratory system and heart rhythm. Sometimes shortened to **shock.**

electric susceptibility *n* another name for **susceptibility** (sense 4a).

electrify (ɪ'lɛktrɪˌfaɪ) *vb* **electrifies, electrifying, electrified.** (*tr*) **1** to adapt or equip (a system, device, etc.) for operation by electrical power. **2** to charge with or subject to electricity. **3** to startle or excite intensely.
▸ **e'lectri,fiable** *adj* ▸ **e,lectrifi'cation** *n* ▸ **e'lectri,fier** *n*

electro (ɪ'lɛktrəʊ) *n, pl* **electros.** short for **electroplate** or **electrotype.**

electro- *or sometimes before a vowel* **electr-** *combining form.* **1** electric or electrically: *electrodynamic.* **2** electrolytic: *electrodialysis.* ORIG from NL, from L *ēlectrum* amber, from Gk *ēlektron*

electroacoustic (ɪˌlɛktrəʊə'kuːstɪk) *adj* (of music) combining both computer-generated and acoustic sounds.

electrocardiograph (ɪˌlɛktrəʊ'kɑːdɪəʊˌgrɑːf) *n* an instrument for making tracings (**electrocardiograms**) recording the electrical activity of the heart.
▸ **e,lectro,cardio'graphic** *or* **e,lectro,cardio'graphical** *adj*
▸ **electrocardiography** (ɪˌlɛktrəʊˌkɑːdɪ'ɒgrəfɪ) *n*

electrochemistry (ɪˌlɛktrəʊ'kɛmɪstrɪ) *n* the branch of chemistry concerned with electric cells and electrolysis.
▸ **,electro'chemical** *adj* ▸ **e,lectro'chemist** *n*

electroconvulsive therapy (ɪˌlɛktrəʊkən'vʌlsɪv) *n Med.* the treatment of certain psychotic conditions by passing an electric current through the brain to induce coma or convulsions. See also **shock therapy.**

electrocute (ɪ'lɛktrəˌkjuːt) *vb* **electrocutes, electrocuting, electrocuted.** (*tr*) **1** to kill as a result of an electric shock. **2** *US.* to execute in the electric chair. ORIG C19: from ELECTRO- + (EXE)CUTE
▸ **e,lectro'cution** *n*

electrode (ɪ'lɛktrəʊd) *n* **1** a conductor through which an electric current enters or leaves an electrolyte, an electric arc, or an electronic valve or tube. **2** an element in a semiconducting device that emits, collects, or controls the movement of electrons or holes.

electrodeposit (ɪˌlɛktrəʊdɪ'pɒzɪt) *vb* **1** (*tr*) to deposit (a metal) by electrolysis. ◆ *n* **2** the deposit so formed.
▸ **electrodeposition** (ɪˌlɛktrəʊˌdɛpə'zɪʃən) *n*

electrodynamics (ɪˌlɛktrəʊdaɪ'næmɪks) *n* (*functioning as sing*) the branch of physics concerned with the interactions between electrical and mechanical forces.

electroencephalograph (ɪˌlɛktrəʊɛn'sɛfələˌgrɑːf) *n* an instrument for making tracings (**electroencephalograms**) recording the electrical activity of the brain, usually by means of electrodes placed on the scalp. See also **brain wave.**
▸ **e,lectroen,cephalo'graphic** *adj* ▸ **electroencephalography** (ɪˌlɛktrəʊɛnˌsɛfə'lɒgrəfɪ) *n*

electrolyse *or US* **electrolyze** (ɪ'lɛktrəʊˌlaɪz) *vb* **electrolyses, electrolysing, electrolysed** *or US* **electrolyzes, electrolyzing, electrolyzed.** (*tr*) **1** to decompose (a chemical compound) by electrolysis. **2** to destroy (living tissue, such as hair roots) by electrolysis.
▸ **e'lectro,lyser** *or US* **e'lectro,lyzer** *n*

electrolysis (ɪlɛk'trɒlɪsɪs) *n* **1** the conduction of electricity by an electrolyte, esp. the use of this process to induce chemical changes. **2** the destruction of living tissue, such as hair roots, by an electric current, usually for cosmetic reasons.

electrolyte (ɪ'lɛktrəʊˌlaɪt) *n* **1** a solution or molten substance that conducts electricity. **2a** a chemical compound that dissociates in solution into ions. **2b** any of the ions themselves.

electrolytic (ɪˌlɛktrəʊ'lɪtɪk) *adj* **1** *Physics.* **1a** of, con-

cerned with, or produced by electrolysis or electrodeposition. **1b** of, relating to, or containing an electrolyte. ◆ *n* **2** *Electronics.* Also called: **electrolytic capacitor.** a small capacitor consisting of two electrodes separated by an electrolyte.
▸ **eˌlectroˈlytically** *adv*

electromagnet (ɪˌlɛktrəʊˈmæɡnɪt) *n* a magnet consisting of an iron or steel core wound with a coil of wire, through which a current is passed.

electromagnetic (ɪˌlɛktrəʊmæɡˈnɛtɪk) *adj* **1** of, containing, or operated by an electromagnet. **2** of, relating to, or consisting of electromagnetism. **3** of or relating to electromagnetic radiation.
▸ **eˌlectromagˈnetically** *adv*

electromagnetic radiation *n* radiation consisting of an electric and magnetic field at right angles to each other and to the direction of propagation.

electromagnetics (ɪˌlɛktrəʊmæɡˈnɛtɪks) *n* (*functioning as sing*) *Physics.* another name for **electromagnetism** (sense 2).

electromagnetic spectrum *n* the complete range of electromagnetic radiation from the longest radio waves to the shortest gamma radiation.

electromagnetic unit *n* any unit of a system of electrical cgs units in which the magnetic constant is given the value of unity.

electromagnetic wave *n* a wave of energy propagated in an electromagnetic field.

electromagnetism (ɪˌlɛktrəʊˈmæɡnɪˌtɪzəm) *n* **1** magnetism produced by electric current. **2** Also called: **electromagnetics.** the branch of physics concerned with this magnetism and with the interaction of electric and magnetic fields.

electrometer (ɪlɛkˈtrɒmɪtə, ˌiːlɛk-) *n* an instrument for detecting or measuring a potential difference or charge by the electrostatic forces between charged bodies.
▸ **electrometric** (ɪˌlɛktrəʊˈmɛtrɪk) *or* **eˌlectroˈmetrical** *adj*
▸ **elecˈtrometry** *n*

electromotive (ɪˌlɛktrəʊˈməʊtɪv) *adj* of, concerned with, or producing an electric current.

electromotive force *n Physics.* **a** a source of energy that can cause current to flow in an electrical circuit. **b** the rate at which energy is drawn from this source when unit current flows through the circuit, measured in volts.

electromyography (ɪˌlɛktrəʊmaɪˈɒɡrəfɪ) *n Med.* a technique for recording the electrical activity of muscles: used in the diagnosis of nerve and muscle disorders.

electron (ɪˈlɛktrɒn) *n* an elementary particle in all atoms, orbiting the nucleus in numbers equal to the atomic number of the element. ORIG C19: from ELECTRO- + -ON

electronegative (ɪˌlɛktrəʊˈnɛɡətɪv) *adj* **1** having a negative electric charge. **2** (of an atom, molecule, etc.) tending to attract electrons and form negative ions or polarized bonds.

electron gun *n* a heated cathode for producing and focusing a beam of electrons, used esp. in cathode-ray tubes.

electronic (ɪlɛkˈtrɒnɪk, ˌiːlɛk-) *adj* **1** of, concerned with, using, or operated by devices, such as transistors, in which electrons are conducted through a semiconductor, free space, or gas. **2** of or concerned with electronics. **3** of or concerned with electrons. **4** involving or concerned with the representation, storage, or transmission of information by electronic systems: *electronic mail; electronic shopping.*
▸ **elecˈtronically** *adv*

electronic flash *n Photog.* an electronic device for producing a very bright flash of light by means of an electric discharge in a gas-filled tube.

electronic funds transfer at point of sale *n* a system for debiting a retail sale direct to the customer's bank, building-society, or credit-card account by means of a computer link using the telephone network. The customer inserts his or her debit card or credit card into the computer at the point of sale. Acronym: **EFTPOS.**

electronic ignition *n* any system that uses an electronic circuit to supply the voltage to the sparking plugs of an internal-combustion engine.

electronic keyboard *n* a typewriter keyboard used to operate an electronic device such as a computer.

electronic mail *n* the transmission of information, messages, facsimiles, etc., from one computer terminal to another. Often shortened to **E-mail, e-mail, email.**

electronic music *n* music consisting of sounds produced by electric currents either controlled from an instrument panel or keyboard or prerecorded on magnetic tape.

electronic organ *n Music.* an instrument played by means of a keyboard, in which sounds are produced by electronic or electrical means.

electronic organizer *n* a computerized personal organizer.

electronic point of sale *n* a computerized system for recording sales in retail shops, using a laser scanner at the cash till to read bar codes on the packages of the items sold. The retailer's stock record is automatically adjusted and the customer receives an itemized bill. Acronym: **EPOS.**

electronic publishing *n* the publication of information on magnetic tape, discs, etc., so that it can be accessed by a computer.

electronics (ɪlɛkˈtrɒnɪks, ˌiːlɛk-) *n* **1** (*functioning as sing*) the science and technology concerned with the development, behaviour, and applications of electronic devices and circuits. **2** (*functioning as pl*) the circuits and devices of a piece of electronic equipment.

electronic surveillance *n* **1** the use of such electronic devices as television monitors, video cameras, etc., to prevent burglary, shop lifting, break-ins, etc. **2** monitoring events, conversations, etc. at a distance by electronic means, esp. by such covert means as wire tapping or bugging.

electronic tag *n* another name for **tag**[1] (sense 2).

electronic transfer of funds *n* the transfer of money from one bank or building-society account to another by means of a computer link using the telephone network. Abbrev.: **ETF.**

electron lens *n* a system, such as an arrangement of electrodes or magnets, that produces a field for focusing a beam of electrons.

electron micrograph *n* a photograph of a specimen taken through an electron microscope.

electron microscope *n* a powerful microscope that uses electrons, rather than light, and electron lenses to produce a magnified image.

electron tube *n* an electrical device, such as a valve, in which a flow of electrons between electrodes takes place.

electronvolt (ɪˌlɛktrɒnˈvəʊlt) *n* a unit of energy equal to the work done on an electron accelerated through a potential difference of 1 volt.

electrophoresis (ɪˌlɛktrəʊfəˈriːsɪs) *n* the motion of charged particles in a colloid under the influence of an applied electric field.
▸ **electrophoretic** (ɪˌlɛktrəʊfəˈrɛtɪk) *adj*

electrophorus (ɪlɛkˈtrɒfərəs, ˌiːlɛk-) *n* an apparatus for generating static electricity by induction. ORIG C18: from ELECTRO- + *-phorus,* from Gk, from *pherein* to bear

electroplate (ɪˈlɛktrəʊˌpleɪt) *vb* **electroplates, electroplating, electroplated. 1** (*tr*) to plate (an object) by electrolysis. ◆ *n* **2** electroplated articles collectively, esp. when plated with silver.
▸ **eˈlectroˌplater** *n*

electropositive (ɪˌlɛktrəʊˈpɒzɪtɪv) *adj* **1** having a positive electric charge. **2** (of an atom, molecule, etc.) tending to release electrons and form positive ions or polarized bonds.

electrorheology (ɪˌlɛktrəʊrɪˈɒlədʒɪ) *n* **1** the study of the flow of fluids under the influence of electric fields. **2** the way in which fluid flow is influenced by an electric field.
▸ **eˌlectroˌrheoˈlogical** *adj*

electroscope (ɪ'lɛktrəʊˌskəʊp) *n* an apparatus for detecting an electric charge, typically consisting of a rod holding two gold foils that separate when a charge is applied.
▸ **electroscopic** (ɪˌlɛktrəʊ'skɒpɪk) *adj*

electroshock therapy (ɪ'lɛktrəʊˌʃɒk) *n* another name for **electroconvulsive therapy.**

electrostatics (ɪˌlɛktrəʊ'stætɪks) *n* (*functioning as sing*) the branch of physics concerned with static electricity.
▸ **eˌlectro'static** *adj*

electrostatic unit *n* any unit of a system of electrical cgs units in which the electric constant is given the value of unity.

electrotherapeutics (ɪˌlɛktrəʊˌθɛrə'pju:tɪks) *n* (*functioning as sing*) the branch of medical science concerned with the use of electrotherapy.
▸ **eˌlectroˌthera'peutic** *or* **eˌlectroˌthera'peutical** *adj*

electrotherapy (ɪˌlɛktrəʊ'θɛrəpɪ) *n* treatment in which electric currents are passed through the tissues to stimulate muscle function in paralysed patients.
▸ **eˌlectro'therapist** *n*

electrotype (ɪ'lɛktrəʊˌtaɪp) *n* **1** a duplicate printing plate made by electrolytically depositing a layer of copper or nickel onto a mould of the original. ◆ *vb* **electrotypes, electrotyping, electrotyped. 2** (*tr*) to make an electrotype of (printed matter, etc.).
▸ **e'lectroˌtyper** *n*

electrovalent bond (ɪˌlɛktrəʊ'veɪlənt) *n* a type of chemical bond in which one atom loses an electron to form a positive ion and the other atom gains the electron to form a negative ion. The resulting ions are held together by electrostatic attraction.
▸ **eˌlectro'valency** *n*

electroweak (ɪˌlɛktrəʊ'wi:k) *adj Physics.* involving both electromagnetic interaction and weak interaction.

electrum (ɪ'lɛktrəm) *n* an alloy of gold and silver. ORIG C14: from L, from Gk *ēlektron* amber

electuary (ɪ'lɛktjʊərɪ) *n, pl* **electuaries.** *Med.* a paste taken orally, containing a drug mixed with syrup or honey. ORIG C14: from LL *ēlēctuārium,* prob. from Gk *ekleikton,* from *leikhein* to lick

eleemosynary (ˌɛlɪi:'mɒsɪnərɪ) *adj* **1** of or dependent on charity. **2** given as an act of charity. ORIG C17: from Church L *eleēmosyna* ALMS

elegance ('ɛlɪgəns) *or* **elegancy** *n, pl* **elegances** *or* **elegancies. 1** dignified grace. **2** good taste in design, style, arrangement, etc. **3** something elegant; a refinement.

elegant ('ɛlɪgənt) *adj* **1** tasteful in dress, style, or design. **2** dignified and graceful. **3** cleverly simple; ingenious: *an elegant solution.* ORIG C16: from L *ēlegāns* tasteful; see ELECT

elegiac (ˌɛlɪ'dʒaɪək) *adj* **1** resembling, characteristic of, relating to, or appropriate to an elegy. **2** lamenting; mournful. **3** denoting or written in elegiac couplets (which consist of a dactylic hexameter followed by a dactylic pentameter) or elegiac stanzas (which consist of a quatrain in iambic pentameters with alternate lines rhyming). ◆ *n* **4** (*often pl*) an elegiac couplet or stanza.
▸ **ˌele'giacally** *adv*

elegize *or* **elegise** ('ɛlɪˌdʒaɪz) *vb* **elegizes, elegizing, elegized** *or* **elegises, elegising, elegised. 1** to compose an elegy (in memory of). **2** (*intr*) to write elegiacally.
▸ **'elegist** *n*

elegy ('ɛlɪdʒɪ) *n, pl* **elegies. 1** a mournful poem or song, esp. a lament for the dead. **2** poetry written in elegiac couplets or stanzas. ORIG C16: via F & L from Gk, from *elegos* lament sung to flute accompaniment

Eleia ★ ('i:lɪə) *n* a variant spelling of **Elia**[1].

elem. *abbrev. for:* **1** element(s). **2** elementary.

element ('ɛlɪmənt) *n* **1** any of the 109 known substances that consist of atoms with the same number of protons in their nuclei. **2** one of the fundamental or irreducible components making up a whole. **3** a cause that contributes to a result; factor. **4** any group that is part of a larger unit, such as a military formation. **5** a small amount; hint. **6** a distinguishable section of a social group. **7** the most favourable environment for an animal or plant. **8** the situation in which a person is happiest or most effective (esp. in **in** *or* **out of one's element**). **9** the resistance wire that constitutes the electrical heater in a cooker, heater, etc. **10** one of the four substances thought in ancient and medieval cosmology to constitute the universe (earth, air, water, or fire). **11** (*pl*) atmospheric conditions, esp. wind, rain, and cold. **12** (*pl*) the basic principles. **13** *Christianity.* the bread or wine consecrated in the Eucharist. ORIG C13: from L *elementum* a first principle, element

elemental (ˌɛlɪ'mɛntᵊl) *adj* **1** fundamental; basic. **2** motivated by or symbolic of primitive powerful natural forces or passions. **3** of or relating to earth, air, water, and fire considered as elements. **4** of or relating to atmospheric forces, esp. wind, rain, and cold. **5** of or relating to a chemical element. ◆ *n* **6** *Rare.* a spirit or force that is said to appear in physical form.
▸ **ˌele'mentalˌism** *n*

elementary (ˌɛlɪ'mɛntərɪ) *adj* **1** not difficult; rudimentary. **2** of or concerned with the first principles of a subject; introductory or fundamental. **3** *Chem.* another word for **elemental** (sense 5).
▸ **ˌele'mentariness** *n*

elementary particle *n* any of several entities, such as electrons, neutrons, or protons, that are less complex than atoms.

elementary school *n* **1** *Brit.* a former name for **primary school. 2** *US & Canad.* a state school for the first six to eight years of a child's education.

elenchus (ɪ'lɛŋkəs) *n, pl* **elenchi** (-kaɪ). *Logic.* refutation of an argument by proving the contrary of its conclusion, esp. syllogistically. ORIG C17: from L, from Gk, from *elenkhein* to refute
▸ **e'lenctic** *adj*

elephant ('ɛlɪfənt) *n, pl* **elephants** *or* **elephant.** either of two proboscidean mammals. The **African elephant** is the larger species, with large flapping ears and a less humped back than the **Indian elephant,** of S and SE Asia. ORIG C13: from L, from Gk *elephas* elephant, ivory

elephantiasis (ˌɛlɪfən'taɪəsɪs) *n Pathol.* a complication of chronic filariasis, in which nematode worms block the lymphatic vessels, usually in the legs or scrotum, causing extreme enlargement of the affected area. ORIG C16: via L from Gk, from *elephas* ELEPHANT + -IASIS

elephantine (ˌɛlɪ'fæntaɪn) *adj* **1** denoting, relating to, or characteristic of an elephant or elephants. **2** huge, clumsy, or ponderous.

elephant seal *n* either of two large earless seals, of southern oceans or of the N Atlantic, the males of which have a trunklike snout.

Eleusinian mysteries *pl n* a mystical religious festival, held at Eleusis in classical times, to celebrate the gods Persephone, Demeter, and Dionysus.

Eleusis ★ (ɪ'lu:sɪs) *n* a town in Greece, in Attica about 23 km (14 miles) west of Athens, of which it is now an industrial suburb. Modern Greek name: **Elevsís.**
▸ **Eleusinian** (ˌɛljʊ'sɪnɪən) *n, adj*

elev. *or* **el.** *abbrev. for* elevation.

elevate ('ɛlɪˌveɪt) *vb* **elevates, elevating, elevated.** (*tr*) **1** to move to a higher place. **2** to raise in rank or status. **3** to put in a cheerful mood; elate. **4** to put on a higher cultural plane; uplift. **5** to raise the axis of a gun. **6** to raise the intensity or pitch of (the voice). ORIG C15: from L *ēlevāre,* from *levāre* to raise, from *levis* (adj) light
▸ **'eleˌvatory** *adj*

elevated ('ɛlɪˌveɪtɪd) *adj* **1** raised to or being at a higher level. **2** inflated or lofty; exalted. **3** in a cheerful mood. **4** *Inf.* slightly drunk.

elevation (ˌɛlɪ'veɪʃən) *n* **1** the act of elevating or the state of being elevated. **2** the height of something above a given place, esp. above sea level. **3** a raised area; height. **4** nobleness or grandeur. **5** a drawing to scale of the external face of a building or structure. **6** a ballet dancer's ability to leap high. **7** *Astron.* another name for **altitude** (sense 3). **8** the angle formed between the muzzle of a gun and the horizontal.
▸ **ˌele'vational** *adj*

elevator ('ɛlɪˌveɪtə) *n* **1** a person or thing that elevates. **2**

a mechanical hoist, often consisting of a chain of scoops linked together on a conveyor belt. **3** the US and Canad. name for **lift** (sense 14a). **4** *Chiefly US & Canad.* a granary equipped with an elevator and, usually, facilities for cleaning and grading the grain. **5** a control surface on the tailplane of an aircraft, for making it climb or descend. **6** any muscle that raises a part of the body.

eleven (ɪ'lɛvᵊn) *n* **1** the cardinal number that is the sum of ten and one. **2** a numeral, 11, XI, etc., representing this number. **3** something representing, represented by, or consisting of 11 units. **4** (*functioning as sing or pl*) a team of 11 players in football, cricket, etc. **5** Also called: **eleven o'clock.** eleven hours after noon or midnight. ◆ *determiner* **6a** amounting to eleven. **6b** (*as pron*): *another eleven.* ORIG OE *endleofan*
▸ **e'leventh** *adj, n*

eleven-plus *n* (in Britain, esp. formerly) an examination taken by children aged 10 or 11 that determines the type of secondary education a child will be given.

elevenses (ɪ'lɛvᵊnzɪz) *pl n* (*sometimes functioning as sing*) *Brit. inf.* a light snack taken in mid-morning.

eleventh hour *n* the latest possible time; last minute.

Elevsís ★ (ˌɛlɛf'sis) *n* transliteration of the Modern Greek name for **Eleusis.**

elf (ɛlf) *n, pl* **elves. 1** (in folklore) one of a kind of legendary beings, usually characterized as small, manlike, and mischievous. **2** a mischievous or whimsical child. ORIG OE *ælf*
▸ **'elfish** *or* **'elvish** *adj*

El Faiyûm (ɛl faɪ'ju:m) *or* **Al Faiyûm** ★ (æl faɪ'ju:m) *n* a city in N Egypt: a site of towns going back at least to the 12th dynasty. Pop.: 250 000 (1992 est.).

El Ferrol ★ (*Spanish* ɛl fe'rrɔl) *n* a port in NW Spain, on the Atlantic: fortified naval base, with a deep natural harbour. Pop.: 82 371 (1991). Official name (since 1939): **El Ferrol del Caudillo** (dɛl kau'ðiʎo).

elfin ('ɛlfɪn) *adj* **1** of or like an elf or elves. **2** small, delicate, and charming.

elflock ('ɛlfˌlɒk) *n* a lock of hair, fancifully regarded as having been tangled by the elves.

Elgar ★ ('ɛlgɑ:) *n* Sir **Edward (William).** 1857–1934, British composer, whose works include the *Enigma Variations* (1899), the oratorio *The Dream of Gerontius* (1900), two symphonies, a cello concerto, and a violin concerto.

Elgin ★ ('ɛlgɪn) *n* a market town in NE Scotland, the administrative centre of Moray, on the River Lossie: ruined 13th-century cathedral: distilling, engineering. Pop.: 19 027 (1994).

El Gîza ★ (ɛl 'gi:zə) *n* a city in NE Egypt, on the W bank of the Nile opposite Cairo: nearby are the Great Pyramid of Cheops (Khufu) and the Sphinx. Pop.: 2 144 000 (1992 est.).

Elgon ★ ('ɛlgɒn) *n* **Mount.** an extinct volcano in E Africa, on the Kenya-Uganda border. Height: 4321 m (14 178 ft).

El Greco ★ (ɛl 'grɛkəʊ) *n* real name *Domenikos Theotocopoulos.* 1541–1614, Spanish painter, born in Crete.

Eli ★ ('i:laɪ) *n Old Testament.* the highest priest at Shiloh and teacher of Samuel (I Samuel 1–3).

Elia[1] *or* **Eleia** ★ ('i:lɪə) *n* a department of SW Greece, in the W Peloponnese: in ancient times most of the region formed the state of Elis. Pop.: 179 429 (1991). Area: 2681 sq. km (1035 sq. miles). Modern Greek name: **Ilía.**

Elia[2] ★ ('i:lɪə) *n* the pen name of (Charles) **Lamb.**

Elias ★ (ɪ'laɪəs) *n Bible.* the Douay spelling of **Elijah.**

elicit (ɪ'lɪsɪt) *vb* (*tr*) **1** to give rise to; evoke. **2** to bring to light. ORIG C17: from L *ēlicere*, from *licere* to entice
▸ **e'licitable** *adj* ▸ **eˌlici'tation** *n* ▸ **e'licitor** *n*

elide (ɪ'laɪd) *vb* **elides, eliding, elided.** to undergo or cause to undergo elision. ORIG C16: from L *ēlīdere* to knock, from *laedere* to hit, wound
▸ **e'lidible** *adj*

eligible ('ɛlɪdʒəbᵊl) *adj* **1** fit, worthy, or qualified, as for office. **2** desirable, esp. as a spouse. ORIG C15: from LL *ēligere* to ELECT
▸ **ˌeligi'bility** *n* ▸ **'eligibly** *adv*

Elijah ★ (ɪ'laɪdʒə) *n Old Testament.* a Hebrew prophet of the 9th century B.C., who was persecuted for denouncing Ahab and Jezebel. (I Kings 17–21: 21; II Kings 1–2:18).

Elikón ★ (ɛli'kɔn) *n* transliteration of the Modern Greek name for **Helicon.**

eliminate (ɪ'lɪmɪˌneɪt) *vb* **eliminates, eliminating, eliminated.** (*tr*) **1** to remove or take out. **2** to reject; omit from consideration. **3** to remove (a competitor, team, etc.) from a contest, usually by defeat. **4** *Sl.* to murder in cold blood. **5** *Physiol.* to expel (waste) from the body. **6** *Maths.* to remove (an unknown variable) from simultaneous equations. ORIG C16: from L *ēlīmināre* to turn out of the house, from *e-* out + *līmen* threshold
▸ **e'liminable** *adj* ▸ **eˌlimi'nation** *n* ▸ **e'liminative** *adj*
▸ **e'limiˌnator** *n*

Eliot ★ ('ɛlɪət) *n* **1 George,** real name *Mary Ann Evans.* 1819–80, British novelist, noted for *The Mill on the Floss* (1860), *Silas Marner* (1861), and *Middlemarch* (1872). **2** Sir **John.** 1592–1632, English statesman, a leader of parliamentary opposition to Charles I. **3 T(homas) S(tearns).** 1888–1965, British poet, dramatist, and critic, born in the US. His poetry includes *The Waste Land* (1922) and *Four Quartets* (1943). Among his verse plays are *Murder in the Cathedral* (1935) and *The Confidential Clerk* (1954): Nobel prize for literature 1948.

Elis ★ ('i:lɪs) *n* an ancient city-state of SW Greece, in the NW Peloponnese: site of the ancient Olympic games.

ELISA (ɪ'laɪzə) *n acronym for* enzyme-linked immunosorbent assay: an immunological technique for accurately measuring the amount of a substance, for example in a blood sample.

Elisabeth ★ (ɪ'lɪzəbəθ) *n* a variant spelling of **Elizabeth**[2] (sense 1).

Élisabethville ★ (ɪ'lɪzəbəθˌvɪl) *n* the former name (until 1966) of **Lubumbashi.**

Elisavetgrad ★ (*Russian* jɪliza'vjɛtgrət) *n* a former name (until 1924) of **Kirovograd.**

Elisavetpol ★ (*Russian* jɪliza'vjɛtpəlj) *n* a former name (until 1920) of **Kirovabad.**

Elisha ★ (ɪ'laɪʃə) *n Old Testament.* a Hebrew prophet of the 9th century B.C.: successor of Elijah (II Kings 3–9).

elision (ɪ'lɪʒən) *n* **1** omission of a syllable or vowel from a word. **2** omission of parts of a book, etc. ORIG C16: from L *ēlīdere* to ELIDE

elite *or* **élite** (ɪ'li:t, eɪ-) *n* **1** (*sometimes functioning as pl*) the most powerful, rich, or gifted members of a group, community, etc. **2** a typewriter type size having 12 characters to the inch. ◆ *adj* **3** of or suitable for an elite. ORIG C18: from F, from OF *eslit* chosen, from L *ēligere* to ELECT

elitism (ɪ'li:tɪzəm, eɪ-) *n* **1a** the belief that society should be governed by an elite. **1b** such government. **2** pride in or awareness of being one of an elite group.
▸ **e'litist** *adj, n*

elixir (ɪ'lɪksə) *n* **1** an alchemical preparation supposed to be capable of prolonging life (**elixir of life**) or of transmuting base metals into gold. **2** anything that purports to be a sovereign remedy. **3** a quintessence. **4** a liquid containing a medicine with syrup, glycerine, or alcohol added to mask its unpleasant taste. ORIG C14: from Med. L, from Ar., prob. from Gk *xērion* powder used for drying wounds

Elizabeth[1] ★ (ɪ'lɪzəbəθ) *n* **1** a city in NE New Jersey, on Newark Bay. Pop.: 110 149 (1996 est.). **2** a town in SE South Australia, near Adelaide. Pop.: 34 000 (latest est.).

Elizabeth[2] ★ (ɪ'lɪzəbəθ) *n* **1** Also: **Elisabeth. Saint.** *New Testament.* the wife of Zacharias, mother of John the Baptist, and kinswoman of the Virgin Mary. Feast day: Nov. 5 or 8. **2** pen name *Carmen Sylva.* 1843–1916, queen of Romania (1881–1914) and author. **3** Russian name *Yelizaveta Petrovna.* 1709–62, empress of Russia (1741–62); daughter of Peter the Great. **4** title *the Queen Mother;* original name Lady *Elizabeth Bowes-Lyon.* born 1900, queen of Great Britain and Northern Ireland (1936–52) as the wife of George VI; mother of Elizabeth II.

Elizabeth I ★ *n* 1533–1603, queen of England (1558–1603); daughter of Henry VIII and Anne Boleyn. She established the Church of England (1559), executed Mary

Queen of Scots (1587), and defeated the Spanish Armada (1588).

Elizabeth II ★ *n* born 1926, queen of Great Britain and Northern Ireland from 1952; daughter of George VI.

Elizabethan (ɪˌlɪzəˈbiːθən) *adj* **1** of, characteristic of, or relating to the reigns of Elizabeth I or Elizabeth II. **2** of, relating to, or designating a style of architecture used in England during the reign of Elizabeth I. ◆ *n* **3** a person who lived in England during the reign of Elizabeth I.

Elizabethan sonnet *n* another term for **Shakespearean sonnet.**

Elizabeth of Hungary ★ *n* **Saint.** 1207–31, Hungarian princess who devoted herself to charity and asceticism. Feast day: Nov. 17 and 19.

elk (ɛlk) *n, pl* **elks** *or* **elk. 1** a large deer of N Europe and Asia: also occurs in N America, where it is called a moose. **2 American elk.** another name for **wapiti.** ORIG OE *eolh*

El Khalil ★ (æl xɒˈliːl) *n* transliteration of the Arabic name for **Hebron.**

ell (ɛl) *n* an obsolete unit of length, approximately 45 inches. ORIG OE *eln* forearm (the measure orig. being from elbow to fingertips)

Ellás ★ (ɛˈlas) *n* transliteration of the Modern Greek name for **Greece.**

Ellesmere Island ★ (ˈɛlzmɪə) *n* a Canadian island in the Arctic Ocean: part of the Northwest Territories; mountainous, with many glaciers. Area: 212 688 sq. km (82 119 sq. miles).

Ellesmere Port ★ *n* a port in NW England, in NW Cheshire on the Mersey estuary and Manchester Ship Canal. Pop.: 64 504 (1991).

Ellice Islands ★ (ˈɛlɪs) *pl n* the former name (until 1975) of **Tuvalu.**

Ellington ★ (ˈɛlɪŋtən) *n* **Duke,** nickname of *Edward Kennedy Ellington.* 1899–1974, US jazz composer and pianist.

ellipse (ɪˈlɪps) *n* a closed conic section shaped like a flattened circle and formed by an inclined plane that does not cut the base of the cone. ORIG C18: back formation from ELLIPSIS

ellipsis (ɪˈlɪpsɪs) *n, pl* **ellipses** (-siːz). **1** omission of parts of a word or sentence. **2** *Printing.* a sequence of three dots (...) indicating an omission in text. ORIG C16: from L, from Gk, from *en* in + *leipein* to leave

ellipsoid (ɪˈlɪpsɔɪd) *n* **a** a geometric surface, symmetrical about the three coordinate axes, whose plane sections are ellipses or circles. **b** a solid having this shape.
▸ **ellipsoidal** (ɪlɪpˈsɔɪdᵊl, ˌɛl-) *adj*

ellipsoid of revolution *n* a geometric surface produced by rotating an ellipse about one of its two axes and having circular plane sections perpendicular to the axis of revolution.

elliptical (ɪˈlɪptɪkᵊl) *adj* **1** relating to or having the shape of an ellipse. **2** relating to or resulting from ellipsis. **3** (of speech, literary style, etc.) **3a** very concise, often so as to be obscure or ambiguous. **3b** circumlocutory. ◆ Also (for senses 1 and 2): **elliptic.**
▸ **elˈlipticalness** *n*

Ellis ★ (ˈɛlɪs) *n* (**Henry**) **Havelock** (ˈhævlɒk). 1859–1939, British essayist: author of works on the psychology of sex.

elm (ɛlm) *n* **1** any tree of the genus *Ulmus,* occurring in the N hemisphere, having serrated leaves and winged fruits (samaras). **2** the hard heavy wood of this tree. ORIG OE *elm*

El Mansûra (ɛl mænˈsʊərə) *or* **Al Mansûrah** ★ *n* a city in NE Egypt: scene of a battle (1250) in which the Crusaders were defeated by the Mamelukes and Louis IX of France was captured; cotton-manufacturing centre. Pop.: 371 000 (1992 est.).

El Minya ★ (ɛl ˈmɪnjə) *n* a river port in central Egypt on the Nile. Pop.: 208 000 (1992 est.).

El Misti ★ (ɛl ˈmiːstiː) *n* a volcano in S Peru, in the Andes. Height: 5852 m (19 199 ft).

El Niño (ɛl ˈniːnjəʊ) *n Meteorol.* a warming of the eastern tropical Pacific occurring every few years, which disrupts the local climate and has a wider effect on general weather patterns. ORIG from Sp.: The Child, i.e. Christ, referring to its occurrence around Christmas time

El Obeid ★ (ɛl əʊˈbeɪd) *n* a city in the central Sudan, in Kordofan province: scene of the defeat of a British and Egyptian army by the Mahdi (1883). Pop.: 228 096 (1993).

elocution (ˌɛləˈkjuːʃən) *n* the art of public speaking. ORIG C15: from L *ēloquī,* from *loquī* to speak
▸ **ˌeloˈcutionary** *adj* ▸ **ˌeloˈcutionist** *n*

Elohim ★ (ɛˈləʊhɪm, ˌɛləʊˈhiːm) *n Old Testament.* a Hebrew word for God or gods. ORIG C17: from Heb. *'Elōhim,* pl (to indicate uniqueness) of *'Elōah* God

Elohist (ɛˈləʊhɪst) *n Bible.* the supposed author or authors of the Pentateuch, identified chiefly by the use of the word *Elohim* for God.

elongate (ˈiːlɒŋgeɪt) *vb* **elongates, elongating, elongated. 1** to make or become longer; stretch. ◆ *adj* **2** long and narrow. **3** lengthened or tapered. ORIG C16: from LL *ēlongāre* to keep at a distance, from *ē-* away + L *longē* (adv) far
▸ **ˌelonˈgation** *n*

elope (ɪˈləʊp) *vb* **elopes, eloping, eloped.** (*intr*) to run away secretly with a lover, esp. in order to marry. ORIG C16: from Anglo-F *aloper,* ?from MDu. *lōpen* to run; see LOPE
▸ **eˈlopement** *n* ▸ **eˈloper** *n*

eloquence (ˈɛləkwəns) *n* **1** ease in using language. **2** powerful and effective language. **3** the quality of being persuasive or moving.

eloquent (ˈɛləkwənt) *adj* **1** (of speech, writing, etc.) fluent and persuasive. **2** visibly or vividly expressive: *an eloquent yawn.* ORIG C14: from L *ēloquēns,* from *loquī* to speak
▸ **ˈeloquentness** *n*

El Paso ★ (ɛl ˈpæsəʊ) *n* a city in W Texas, on the Rio Grande opposite Ciudad Juárez, Mexico. Pop.: 599 865 (1996 est.).

El Salvador ★ (ɛl ˈsælvəˌdɔː) *n* a republic in Central America, on the Pacific: colonized by the Spanish from 1524; declared independence in 1841, becoming a republic in 1856. It consists of coastal lowlands rising to a central plateau. Coffee constitutes about half of the total exports. Official language: Spanish. Religion: Roman Catholic. Currency: colón. Capital: San Salvador. Pop.: 5 839 000 (1999 est.). Area: 21 393 sq. km (8236 sq. miles).
▸ **ˌSalvaˈdoran, ˌSalvaˈdorean,** *or* **ˌSalvaˈdorian** *adj, n*

Elsan (ˈɛlsæn) *n Trademark.* a type of portable chemical lavatory. ORIG C20: from initials of *E. L.* Jackson, manufacturer + SAN(ITATION)

Elsass ★ (ˈɛlzas) *n* the German name for **Alsace.**

Elsass-Lothringen ★ (ˈɛlzasˈloːtrɪŋən) *n* the German name for **Alsace-Lorraine.**

else (ɛls) *determiner* (*postpositive; used after an indefinite pronoun or an interrogative*) **1** in addition; more: *there is nobody else here.* **2** other; different: *where else could he be?* ◆ *adv* **3 or else. 3a** if not, then: *go away or else I won't finish my work today.* **3b** or something terrible will result: used as a threat: *sit down, or else!* ORIG OE *elles,* genitive of *el-* strange, foreign

elsewhere (ˌɛlsˈwɛə) *adv* in or to another place; somewhere else. ORIG OE *elles hwǣr;* see ELSE, WHERE

Elsinore ★ (ˈɛlsɪˌnɔː, ˌɛlsɪˈnɔː) *n* the English name for **Helsingør.**

ELT *abbrev. for* English Language Teaching.

Elton ★ (ˈɛltᵊn) *n* **1 Ben.** born 1959, British comedian, scriptwriter, playwright, and novelist; his works include the book and lyrics for the Lloyd Webber musical *The Beautiful Game* (2000). **2 Charles Sutherland.** 1900–91, British zoologist: initiated the study of animal ecology.

eluate (ˈɛljuːˌeɪt) *n* a solution of adsorbed material in the eluant obtained during the process of elution.

elucidate (ɪˈluːsɪˌdeɪt) *vb* **elucidates, elucidating, elucidated.** to make clear (something obscure or difficult); clarify. ORIG C16: from LL *ēlūcidāre* to enlighten; see LUCID
▸ **eˌluciˈdation** *n* ▸ **eˈluciˌdative** *or* **eˈluciˌdatory** *adj*
▸ **eˈluciˌdator** *n*

elude (ɪˈluːd) *vb* **eludes, eluding, eluded.** (*tr*) **1** to escape from or avoid, esp. by cunning. **2** to avoid fulfilment of (a responsibility, obligation, etc.); evade. **3** to escape discov-

ery or understanding by; baffle. ORIG C16: from L *ēlūdere* to deceive, from *lūdere* to play
▸ **e'luder** *n* ▸ **e'lusion** *n*

USAGE NOTE *Elude* is sometimes wrongly used where *allude* is meant: *he was alluding* (not *eluding*) *to his previous visit to the city*.

eluent *or* **eluant** ('ɛljuənt) *n* a solvent used for eluting.

elusive (ɪ'luːsɪv) *adj* **1** difficult to catch. **2** preferring or living in solitude and anonymity. **3** difficult to remember.
▸ **e'lusiveness** *n*

USAGE NOTE See at **illusory**.

elute (iː'luːt, ɪ'luːt) *vb* **elutes, eluting, eluted.** (*tr*) to wash out (a substance) by the action of a solvent, as in chromatography. ORIG C18: from L *ēlūtus* rinsed out, from *luere* to wash, LAVE
▸ **e'lution** *n*

elutriate (ɪ'luːtrɪˌeɪt) *vb* **elutriates, elutriating, elutriated.** (*tr*) to purify or separate (a substance or mixture) by washing and straining or decanting. ORIG C18: from L *ēluere*, from *ē-* out + *lavere* to wash
▸ **eˌlutri'ation** *n*

elver ('ɛlvə) *n* a young eel, esp. one migrating up a river. ORIG C17: var. of *eelfare*, lit.: eel-journey; see EEL, FARE

elves (ɛlvz) *n* the plural of **elf**.

elvish ('ɛlvɪʃ) *adj* a variant of **elfish**: see **elf**.

Ely ★ ('iːlɪ) *n* **1** a cathedral city in E England, in E Cambridgeshire on the River Ouse. Pop.: 10 329 (1991). **2 Isle of.** a former county of E England, part of Cambridgeshire since 1965.

Elysée ★ (eɪ'liːzeɪ) *n* a palace in Paris, in the Champs Elysées: official residence of the president of France.

Elysium ★ (ɪ'lɪzɪəm) *n* **1** Also called: **Elysian fields.** *Greek myth.* the dwelling place of the blessed after death. **2** a state or place of perfect bliss. ORIG C16: from L, from Gk *Ēlusion pedion* Elysian (that is, blessed) fields

elytron ('ɛlɪˌtrɒn) *or* **elytrum** ('ɛlɪtrəm) *n, pl* **elytra** (-trə). either of the horny front wings of beetles and some other insects. ORIG C18: from Gk *elutron* sheath

em (ɛm) *n Printing.* **1** the square of a body of any size of type, used as a unit of measurement. **2** Also called: **pica em, pica.** a unit of measurement in printing, equal to twelve points or one sixth of an inch. ORIG C19: from the name of the letter *M*

em- *prefix* a variant of **en-**[1] and **en-**[2] before *b, m,* and *p*.

'em (əm) *pron* an informal variant of **them.**

emaciate (ɪ'meɪsɪˌeɪt) *vb* **emaciates, emaciating, emaciated.** (*usually tr*) to become or cause to become abnormally thin. ORIG C17: from L, from *macer* thin
▸ **e'maciˌated** *adj* ▸ **eˌmaci'ation** *n*

E-mail, e-mail, *or* **email** ('iːmeɪl) *n* **1** short for **electronic mail.** ◆ *vb* (*tr*) **2** to contact (a person) by electronic mail. **3** to send (a message, document, etc.) by electronic mail.

emanate ('ɛməˌneɪt) *vb* **emanates, emanating, emanated. 1** (*intr;* often foll. by *from*) to issue or proceed from or as from a source. **2** (*tr*) to send forth; emit. ORIG C18: from L *ēmānāre* to flow out, from *mānāre* to flow
▸ **emanative** ('ɛmənətɪv) *adj* ▸ **'emaˌnator** *n* ▸ **'emaˌnatory** *adj*

emanation (ˌɛmə'neɪʃən) *n* **1** an act or instance of emanating. **2** something that emanates or is produced. **3** a gaseous product of radioactive decay.
▸ **ˌema'national** *adj*

emancipate (ɪ'mænsɪˌpeɪt) *vb* **emancipates, emancipating, emancipated.** (*tr*) **1** to free from restriction or restraint, esp. social or legal restraint. **2** (*often passive*) to free from the inhibitions of conventional morality. **3** to liberate (a slave) from bondage. ORIG C17: from L *ēmancipāre* to give independence (to a son), from *mancipāre* to transfer property; see MANCIPLE
▸ **e'manciˌpated** *adj* ▸ **eˌmanci'pation** *n* ▸ **e'manciˌpator** *n*
▸ **emancipatory** (ɪ'mænsɪpətərɪ, -trɪ) *adj*

emasculate *vb* (ɪ'mæskjuˌleɪt), **emasculates, emasculating, emasculated.** (*tr*) **1** to remove the testicles of; castrate; geld. **2** to deprive of vigour, effectiveness, etc. **3** *Bot.* to remove the stamens from (a flower) to prevent self-pollination for the purposes of plant breeding. ◆ *adj* (ɪ'mæskjulɪt, -ˌleɪt). **4** castrated; gelded. **5** Also: **emasculated.** deprived of strength, effectiveness, etc. ORIG C17: from L *ēmasculāre*, from *masculus* male; see MASCULINE
▸ **eˌmascu'lation** *n* ▸ **e'mascuˌlator** *n* ▸ **e'masculatory** *adj*

embalm (ɪm'bɑːm) *vb* (*tr*) **1** to treat (a dead body) with preservatives to retard putrefaction. **2** to preserve or cherish the memory of. **3** *Poetic.* to give a sweet fragrance to. ORIG C13: from OF *embaumer;* see BALM
▸ **em'balmer** *n* ▸ **em'balmment** *n*

embank (ɪm'bæŋk) *vb* (*tr*) to protect, enclose, or confine with an embankment.

embankment (ɪm'bæŋkmənt) *n* a man-made ridge of earth or stone that carries a road or railway or confines a waterway.

embargo (ɛm'bɑːgəu) *n, pl* **embargoes. 1** a government order prohibiting the departure or arrival of merchant ships in its ports. **2** any legal stoppage of commerce. **3** a restraint or prohibition. ◆ *vb* **embargoes, embargoing, embargoed.** (*tr*) **4** to lay an embargo upon. **5** to seize for use by the state. ORIG C16: from Sp., from *embargar*, from L IM- + *barra* BAR[1]

embark (ɛm'bɑːk) *vb* **1** to board (a ship or aircraft). **2** (*intr;* usually foll. by *on* or *upon*) to commence or engage (in) a new project, venture, etc. ORIG C16: via F from OF, from EM- + *barca* boat, BARQUE
▸ **ˌembar'kation** *n*

embarrass (ɪm'bærəs) *vb* (*mainly tr*) **1** to cause to feel confusion or self-consciousness; disconcert. **2** (*usually passive*) to involve in financial difficulties. **3** *Arch.* to complicate. **4** *Arch.* to impede or hamper. ORIG C17 (in the sense: to impede): via F & Sp. from It., from *imbarrare* to confine within bars
▸ **em'barrassed** *adj* ▸ **em'barrassing** *adj* ▸ **em'barrassment** *n*

embassy ('ɛmbəsɪ) *n, pl* **embassies. 1** the residence or place of business of an ambassador. **2** an ambassador and his or her entourage collectively. **3** the position, business, or mission of an ambassador. **4** any important or official mission. ORIG C16: from OF *ambaisada;* see AMBASSADOR

embattle (ɪm'bæt[ə]l) *vb* **embattles, embattling, embattled.** (*tr*) **1** to deploy (troops) for battle. **2** to fortify (a position, town, etc.). **3** to provide with battlements. ORIG C14: from OF *embataillier;* see EN-[1] BATTLE

embay (ɪm'beɪ) *vb* (*tr*) (*usually passive*) **1** to form into a bay. **2** to enclose in or as if in a bay.

embed (ɪm'bɛd) *vb* **embeds, embedding, embedded. 1** (usually foll. by *in*) to fix or become fixed firmly and deeply in a surrounding solid mass. **2** (*tr*) to surround closely. **3** (*tr*) to fix or retain (a thought, idea, etc.) in the mind. ◆ Also: **imbed.**
▸ **em'bedment** *n*

embellish (ɪm'bɛlɪʃ) *vb* (*tr*) **1** to beautify; adorn. **2** to make (a story, etc.) more interesting by adding detail. ORIG C14: from OF *embelir*, from *bel* beautiful, from L *bellus*
▸ **em'bellisher** *n* ▸ **em'bellishment** *n*

ember ('ɛmbə) *n* **1** a glowing or smouldering piece of coal or wood, as in a dying fire. **2** the remains of a past emotion. ORIG OE *ǣmyrge*

Ember days *pl n RC & Anglican Church.* any of four groups in the year of three days (always Wednesday, Friday, and Saturday) of prayer and fasting. ORIG OE *ymbrendǣg*, from *ymb* around + *ryne* a course + *dǣg* day

embezzle (ɪm'bɛz[ə]l) *vb* **embezzles, embezzling, embezzled.** to convert (money or property entrusted to one) fraudulently to one's own use. ORIG C15: from Anglo-F *embeseiller* to destroy, from OF *beseiller* to make away with, from ?
▸ **em'bezzlement** *n* ▸ **em'bezzler** *n*

embitter (ɪm'bɪtə) *vb (tr)* **1** to make (a person) bitter. **2** to aggravate (a hostile feeling, difficult situation, etc.).
▸ **em'bittered** *adj* ▸ **em'bitterment** *n*

emblazon (ɪm'bleɪzᵊn) *vb (tr)* **1** to portray heraldic arms on (a shield, one's notepaper, etc.). **2** to make bright or splendid, as with colours, flowers, etc. **3** to glorify, praise, or extol.
▸ **em'blazonment** *n*

emblem ('ɛmbləm) *n* a visible object or representation that symbolizes a quality, type, group, etc. ORIG C15: from L *emblēma,* from Gk, from *emballein* to insert, from *en* in + *ballein* to throw
▸ **ˌemblem'atic** *or* **ˌemblem'atical** *adj* ▸ **ˌemblem'atically** *adv*

embody (ɪm'bɒdɪ) *vb* **embodies, embodying, embodied.** *(tr)* **1** to give a tangible, bodily, or concrete form to (an abstract concept). **2** to be an example of or express (an idea, principle, etc.). **3** (often foll. by *in*) to collect or unite in a comprehensive whole. **4** to invest (a spiritual entity) with bodily form.
▸ **em'bodiment** *n*

embolden (ɪm'bəʊldᵊn) *vb (tr)* to encourage; make bold.

embolism ('ɛmbəˌlɪzəm) *n* the occlusion of a blood vessel by an embolus. ORIG C14: from Med. L, from LGk *embolismos;* see EMBOLUS
▸ **embolic** (ɛm'bɒlɪk) *adj*

embolus ('ɛmbələs) *n, pl* **emboli** (-ˌlaɪ). material, such as part of a blood clot or an air bubble, that becomes lodged within a small blood vessel and impedes the circulation. ORIG C17: via L from Gk *embolos* stopper; see EMBLEM

embonpoint *French.* (ɑ̃bɔ̃pwɛ̃) *n* **1** plumpness or stoutness. ◆ *adj* **2** plump; stout. ORIG C18: from *en bon point* in good condition

embosom (ɪm'bʊzəm) *vb (tr) Arch.* **1** to enclose or envelop, esp. protectively. **2** to clasp to the bosom; hug. **3** to cherish.

emboss (ɪm'bɒs) *vb* **1** to mould or carve (a decoration) on (a surface) so that it is raised above the surface in low relief. **2** to cause to bulge; make protrude. ORIG C14: from OF *embocer,* from EM- + *boce* BOSS[2]
▸ **em'bossed** *adj* ▸ **em'bosser** *n* ▸ **em'bossment** *n*

embouchure (ˌɒmbʊ'ʃʊə) *n* **1** the mouth of a river or valley. **2** *Music.* **2a** the correct application of the lips and tongue in playing a wind instrument. **2b** the mouthpiece of a wind instrument. ORIG C18: from F, from OF, from *bouche* mouth, from L *bucca* cheek

embower (ɪm'baʊə) *vb (tr) Arch.* to enclose in or as in a bower.

embrace (ɪm'breɪs) *vb* **embraces, embracing, embraced.** *(mainly tr)* **1** *(also intr)* (of a person) to take or clasp (another person) in the arms, or (of two people) to clasp each other, as in affection, greeting, etc.; hug. **2** to accept willingly or eagerly. **3** to take up (a new idea, faith, etc.); adopt. **4** to comprise or include as an integral part. **5** to encircle or enclose. **6** *Rare.* to perceive or understand. ◆ *n* **7** the act of embracing. ORIG C14: from OF, from EM- + *brace* a pair of arms, from L *bracchia* arms
▸ **em'braceable** *adj* ▸ **em'bracement** *n* ▸ **em'bracer** *n*

embrasure (ɪm'breɪʒə) *n* **1** *Fortifications.* an opening or indentation, as in a battlement, for shooting through. **2** a door or window having splayed sides that increase the width of the opening in the interior. ORIG C18: from F, from obs. *embraser* to widen
▸ **em'brasured** *adj*

embrocate ('ɛmbrəʊˌkeɪt) *vb* **embrocates, embrocating, embrocated.** *(tr)* to apply a liniment or lotion to (a part of the body). ORIG C17: from Med. L *embrocha* poultice, from Gk, from *brokhē* a moistening

embrocation (ˌɛmbrəʊ'keɪʃən) *n* a drug or agent for rubbing into the skin; liniment.

embroider (ɪm'brɔɪdə) *vb* **1** to do decorative needlework (upon). **2** to add fictitious or exaggerated detail to (a story, etc.). ORIG C15: from OF *embroder*
▸ **em'broiderer** *n*

embroidery (ɪm'brɔɪdərɪ) *n, pl* **embroideries. 1** decorative needlework done usually on loosely woven cloth or canvas, often being a picture or pattern. **2** elaboration or exaggeration, esp. in writing or reporting; embellishment.

embroil (ɪm'brɔɪl) *vb (tr)* **1** to involve (a person, oneself, etc.) in trouble, conflict, or argument. **2** to throw (affairs, etc.) into a state of confusion or disorder; complicate; entangle. ORIG C17: from F *embrouiller,* from *brouiller* to mingle, confuse
▸ **em'broiler** *n* ▸ **em'broilment** *n*

embryo ('ɛmbrɪˌəʊ) *n, pl* **embryos. 1** an animal in the early stages of development up to birth or hatching. **2** the human product of conception up to approximately the end of the second month of pregnancy. Cf. **fetus. 3** a plant in the early stages of development. **4** an undeveloped or rudimentary state (esp. in **in embryo**). **5** something in an early stage of development. ORIG C16: from LL, from Gk *embruon,* from *bruein* to swell

embryology (ˌɛmbrɪ'ɒlədʒɪ) *n* **1** the scientific study of embryos. **2** the structure and development of the embryo of a particular organism.
▸ **embryological** (ˌɛmbrɪə'lɒdʒɪkᵊl) *or* **ˌembryo'logic** *adj*
▸ **ˌembry'ologist** *n*

embryonic (ˌɛmbrɪ'ɒnɪk) *or* **embryonal** ('ɛmbrɪənᵊl) *adj* **1** of or relating to an embryo. **2** in an early stage; rudimentary; undeveloped.
▸ **ˌembry'onically** *adv*

emcee (ˌɛm'siː) *Inf.* ◆ *n* **1** a master of ceremonies. ◆ *vb* **emcees, emceeing, emceed. 2** to act as master of ceremonies (for or at). ORIG C20: from MC

Emden ★ *(German* 'ɛmdən) *n* a port in NW Germany, in Lower Saxony at the mouth of the River Ems. Pop.: 51 100 (1991).

-eme *suffix forming nouns. Linguistics.* indicating a minimal distinctive unit of a specified type in a language: *morpheme; phoneme.* ORIG C20: via F, abstracted from PHONEME

emend (ɪ'mɛnd) *vb (tr)* to make corrections or improvements in (a text) by critical editing. ORIG C15: from L, from *ē-* out + *mendum* a mistake
▸ **e'mendable** *adj*

emendation (ˌiːmɛn'deɪʃən) *n* **1** a correction or improvement in a text. **2** the act or process of emending.
▸ **'emenˌdator** *n* ▸ **emendatory** (ɪ'mɛndətərɪ, -trɪ) *adj*

emerald ('ɛmərəld, 'ɛmrəld) *n* **1** a green transparent variety of beryl: highly valued as a gem. **2a** its clear green colour. **2b** *(as adj): an emerald carpet.* ORIG C13: from OF *esmeraude,* from L *smaragdus,* from Gk *smaragdos*

Emerald Isle ★ *n* a poetic name for **Ireland**[1].

emerge (ɪ'mɜːdʒ) *vb* **emerges, emerging, emerged.** *(intr; often foll. by from)* **1** to come up to the surface of or rise from water or other liquid. **2** to come into view, as from concealment or obscurity. **3** (foll. by *from*) to come out (of) or live (through (a difficult experience, etc.)). **4** to become apparent. ORIG C17: from L *ēmergere* to rise up from, from *mergere* to dip
▸ **e'mergence** *n* ▸ **e'merging** *adj*

emergency (ɪ'mɜːdʒənsɪ) *n, pl* **emergencies. 1a** an unforeseen or sudden occurrence, esp. of danger demanding immediate action. **1b** *(as modifier): an emergency exit.* **2a** a patient requiring urgent treatment. **2b** *(as modifier): an emergency ward.* **3** *NZ.* a player selected to stand by to replace an injured member of a team; reserve. **4 state of emergency.** a condition, declared by a government, in which martial law applies, usually because of civil unrest or natural disaster.

emergent (ɪ'mɜːdʒənt) *adj* **1** coming into being or notice. **2** (of a nation) recently independent.
▸ **e'mergently** *adv*

emeritus (ɪ'mɛrɪtəs) *adj (usually postpositive)* retired or honourably discharged from full-time work, but retaining one's title on an honorary basis: *a professor emeritus.* ORIG C19: from L, from *merēre* to deserve; see MERIT

emersion (ɪ'mɜːʃən) *n* **1** the act or an instance of emerging. **2** *Astron.* the reappearance of a celestial body after an eclipse or occultation. ORIG C17: from L *ēmersus;* see EMERGE

Emerson ★ ('ɛməsᵊn) *n* **Ralph Waldo** (rælf 'wɔːldəʊ). 1803–82, US poet, essayist, and transcendentalist.

emery ('ɛmərɪ) *n* **a** a hard greyish-black mineral consisting of corundum with either magnetite or haematite: used as an abrasive and polishing agent. **b** (*as modifier*): *emery paper.* ORIG C15: from OF *esmeril,* ult. from Gk *smuris* powder for rubbing

emery board *n* a strip of cardboard or wood with a rough surface of crushed emery, for filing one's nails.

emetic (ɪ'mɛtɪk) *adj* **1** causing vomiting. ◆ *n* **2** an emetic agent or drug. ORIG C17: from LL, from Gk *emetikos,* from *emein* to vomit

emf *or* **EMF** *abbrev. for* electromotive force.

-emia *n combining form.* a US variant of **-aemia.**

emigrant ('ɛmɪgrənt) *n* **a** a person who leaves one place, esp. his or her native country, to settle in another. **b** (*as modifier*): *an emigrant worker.*

emigrate ('ɛmɪˌgreɪt) *vb* **emigrates, emigrating, emigrated.** (*intr*) to leave one place, esp. one's native country, to settle in another. ORIG C18: from L *ēmīgrāre,* from *mīgrāre* to depart, MIGRATE
▸ **ˌemi'gration** *n* ▸ **'emiˌgratory** *adj*

émigré ('ɛmɪˌgreɪ) *n* an emigrant, esp. one forced to leave his or her native country for political reasons. ORIG C18: from F, from *émigrer* to EMIGRATE

Emilia-Romagna ★ (ɪ'miːlɪərəʊ'mænjə; *Italian* e'miːlja-ro'maɲɲa) *n* a region of N central Italy, on the Adriatic: rises from the plains of the Po valley in the north to the Apennines in the south. Capital: Bologna. Pop.: 3 924 456 (1996 est.). Area: 22 123 sq. km (8628 sq. miles).

Eminem ★ (ˌɛmə'nɛm) *n* real name *Marshall Mathers.* born 1972, US White rap singer noted for the controversial lyrics on *The Slim Shady LP* (1999) and *The Marshall Mathers LP* (2000).

eminence ('ɛmɪnəns) *n* **1** a position of superiority or fame. **2** a high or raised piece of ground. ◆ Also: **eminency.** ORIG C17: from F, from L *ēminentia* a standing out; see EMINENT

Eminence ('ɛmɪnəns) *or* **Eminency** *n, pl* **Eminences** *or* **Eminencies.** (preceded by *Your* or *His*) a title used to address or refer to a cardinal.

éminence grise *French.* (eminɑ̃s griz) *n, pl* ***éminences grises*** (eminɑ̃s griz). a person who wields power and influence unofficially or behind the scenes. ORIG lit.: grey eminence, orig. applied to Père Joseph (François Le Clerc du Tremblay; died 1638), F monk, secretary of Cardinal RICHELIEU

eminent ('ɛmɪnənt) *adj* **1** above others in rank, merit, or reputation; distinguished. **2** (*prenominal*) noteworthy or outstanding. **3** projecting or protruding; prominent. ORIG C15: from L *ēminēre* to project, stand out, from *minēre* to stand

eminent domain *n Law.* the right of a state to confiscate private property for public use, payment usually being made in compensation.

emir (ɛ'mɪə) *n* (in the Islamic world) **1** an independent ruler or chieftain. **2** a military commander or governor. **3** a descendant of Mohammed. ORIG C17: via F from Sp., from Ar. *'amīr* commander
▸ **e'mirate** *n*

emissary ('ɛmɪsərɪ, -ɪsrɪ) *n, pl* **emissaries. 1a** an agent sent on a mission, esp. one who represents a government or head of state. **1b** (*as modifier*): *an emissary delegation.* **2** an agent sent on a secret mission, as a spy. ◆ *adj* **3** (of veins) draining blood from sinuses in the dura mater to veins outside the skull. ORIG C17: from L *ēmissārius,* from *ēmittere* to send out; see EMIT

emission (ɪ'mɪʃən) *n* **1** the act of emitting or sending forth. **2** energy, in the form of heat, light, radio waves, etc., emitted from a source. **3** a substance, fluid, etc., that is emitted; discharge. **4** *Physiol.* any bodily discharge, esp. of semen. ORIG C17: from L *ēmissiō,* from *ēmittere* to send forth, EMIT
▸ **e'missive** *adj*

emission spectrum *n* the spectrum or pattern of bright lines or bands seen when the electromagnetic radiation emitted by a substance is passed into a spectrometer.

emissivity (ˌiːmɪ'sɪvɪtɪ, ˌɛm-) *n* a measure of the ability of a surface to radiate energy; the ratio of the radiant flux emitted per unit area to that emitted by a black body at the same temperature.

emit (ɪ'mɪt) *vb* **emits, emitting, emitted.** (*tr*) **1** to give or send forth; discharge. **2** to give voice to; utter. **3** *Physics.* to give off (radiation or particles). ORIG C17: from L *ēmittere* to send out, from *mittere* to send

emitter (ɪ'mɪtə) *n* **1** a person or thing that emits. **2** a substance that emits radiation. **3** the region in a transistor in which the charge-carrying holes or electrons originate.

Emmanuel ★ (ɪ'mænjʊəl) *n* a variant spelling of **Immanuel.**

Emmen ★ ('ɛmən; *Dutch* 'ɛmə) *n* a city in the NE Netherlands, in Drenthe province: a new town developed since World War II. Pop.: 93 476 (1994).

Emmenthal, Emmental ('ɛmənˌtɑːl), *or* **Emmenthaler** *n* a hard Swiss cheese with holes in it. ORIG C20: after *Emmenthal,* valley in Switzerland

Emmet ★ ('ɛmɪt) *n* **Robert.** 1778–1803, Irish nationalist, executed for leading an uprising for Irish independence.

Emmy ('ɛmɪ) *n, pl* **Emmys** *or* **Emmies.** (in the US) one of the statuettes awarded annually for outstanding television performances and productions. ORIG C20: from *Immy,* short for *image orthicon tube*

emollient (ɪ'mɒljənt) *adj* **1** softening or soothing, esp. to the skin. **2** helping to avoid confrontation; calming. ◆ *n* **3** any preparation or substance that has this effect. ORIG C17: from L *ēmollīre* to soften, from *mollis* soft
▸ **e'mollience** *n*

emolument (ɪ'mɒljʊmənt) *n* the profit arising from an office or employment; fees or wages. ORIG C15: from L *ēmolumentum* benefit; orig., fee paid to a miller, from *molere* to grind

emote (ɪ'məʊt) *vb* **emotes, emoting, emoted.** (*intr*) to display exaggerated emotion, as in acting. ORIG C20: back formation from EMOTION
▸ **e'moter** *n*

emoticon (ɪ'məʊtɪˌkɒn) *n* any of several combinations of symbols used in electronic mail to indicate the state of mind of the writer, as in :-) to indicate happiness or :-o to indicate surprise. ORIG C20: from EMOT(ION) + ICON

emotion (ɪ'məʊʃən) *n* any strong feeling, as of joy, sorrow, or fear. ORIG C16: from F, from OF, from L *ēmovere* to disturb, from *movēre* to MOVE

emotional (ɪ'məʊʃənᵊl) *adj* **1** of, characteristic of, or expressive of emotion. **2** readily or excessively affected by emotion. **3** appealing to or arousing emotion. **4** caused or determined by emotion rather than reason: *an emotional argument.*
▸ **eˌmotion'ality** *n*

> **USAGE NOTE** See at **emotive.**

emotionalism (ɪ'məʊʃənəˌlɪzəm) *n* **1** emotional nature or quality. **2** a tendency to yield readily to the emotions. **3** an appeal to the emotions, esp. as to an audience.
▸ **e'motionalist** *n* ▸ **eˌmotional'istic** *adj*

emotionalize *or* **emotionalise** (ɪ'məʊʃənəˌlaɪz) *vb* **emotionalizes, emotionalizing, emotionalized** *or* **emotionalises, emotionalising, emotionalised.** (*tr*) to make emotional; subject to emotional treatment.

emotive (ɪ'məʊtɪv) *adj* **1** tending or designed to arouse emotion. **2** of or characterized by emotion.
▸ **e'motiveness** *or* **ˌemo'tivity** *n*

> **USAGE NOTE** *Emotional* is the more general and neutral word for referring to the emotions and emotional states. *Emotive* has the more restricted meaning of 'tending to arouse emotion', and is often associated with *issues, subjects, language, words.* However, since *emotional* can also mean 'arousing emotion', with certain nouns it is possible to use either word, depending on the slant one wishes to give: *...an emotive/emotional appeal on behalf of the disadvantaged young.*

Emp. *abbrev. for:* **1** Emperor. **2** Empire. **3** Empress.

empanel *or* **impanel** (ɪm'pænᵊl) *vb* **empanels, empanelling, empanelled** *or US* **empanels, empaneling, empaneled** *or* **impanels, impanelling, impanelled** *or US* **impanels, impaneling, impaneled.** (*tr*) *Law.* **1** to enter on a list (names of persons to be summoned for jury service). **2** to select (a jury) from such a list.
▸ **em'panelment** *or* **im'panelment** *n*

empathize *or* **empathise** ('ɛmpə,θaɪz) *vb* **empathizes, empathizing, empathized** *or* **empathises, empathising, empathised.** (*intr*) to engage in or feel empathy.

empathy ('ɛmpəθɪ) *n* **1** the power of understanding and imaginatively entering into another person's feelings. **2** the attribution to an object, such as a work of art, of one's own feelings about it. ORIG C20: from Gk *empatheia* affection, passion
▸ **em'pathic** *or* **,empa'thetic** *adj*

Empedocles ★ (ɛm'pɛdə,kli:z) *n* ?490–430 B.C., Greek philosopher and scientist, who held that the world is composed of four elements, air, fire, earth, and water, which are governed by the opposing forces of love and discord.

emperor ('ɛmpərə) *n* a monarch who rules or reigns over an empire. ORIG C13: from OF, from L *imperāre* to command, from IM- + *parāre* to make ready
▸ **'emperor,ship** *n*

emperor penguin *n* an Antarctic penguin with orange-yellow patches on the neck: the largest penguin, reaching a height of 1.3 m (4 ft).

emphasis ('ɛmfəsɪs) *n, pl* **emphases** (-si:z). **1** special importance or significance. **2** an object, idea, etc., that is given special importance or significance. **3** stress on a particular syllable, word, or phrase in speaking. **4** force or intensity of expression. **5** sharpness or clarity of form or outline. ORIG C16: via L from Gk: meaning, (in rhetoric) significant stress; see EMPHATIC

emphasize *or* **emphasise** ('ɛmfə,saɪz) *vb* **emphasizes, emphasizing, emphasized** *or* **emphasises, emphasising, emphasised.** (*tr*) to give emphasis or prominence to; stress.

emphatic (ɪm'fætɪk) *adj* **1** expressed, spoken, or done with emphasis. **2** forceful and positive; definite; direct. **3** sharp or clear in form, contour, or outline. **4** important or significant; stressed. ORIG C18: from Gk, from *emphainein* to display, from *phainein* to show
▸ **em'phatically** *adv*

emphysema (,ɛmfɪ'si:mə) *n Pathol.* **1** a condition in which the air sacs of the lungs are grossly enlarged, causing breathlessness and wheezing. **2** the abnormal presence of air in a tissue or part. ORIG C17: from NL, from Gk *emphusēma* a swelling up, from *phusan* to blow

empire ('ɛmpaɪə) *n* **1** an aggregate of peoples and territories under the rule of a single person, oligarchy, or sovereign state. **2** any monarchy that has an emperor as head of state. **3** the period during which a particular empire exists. **4** supreme power; sovereignty. **5** a large industrial organization with many ramifications. ORIG C13: from OF, from L, from *imperāre* to command, from *parāre* to prepare

Empire ('ɛmpaɪə) *n* **the. 1** See **British Empire. 2** *French history.* **2a** the period of imperial rule in France from 1804 to 1815 under Napoleon Bonaparte. **2b** Also called: **Second Empire.** the period from 1852 to 1870 when Napoleon III ruled as emperor. ◆ *adj* **3** denoting, characteristic of, or relating to the British Empire. **4** denoting, characteristic of, or relating to either French Empire, esp. the first.

empire-builder *n Inf.* a person who seeks extra power, esp. by increasing the number of his staff.
▸ **'empire-,building** *n, adj*

Empire Day *n* the former name of **Commonwealth Day.**

Empire State ★ *n* nickname of **New York** (state).

empiric (ɛm'pɪrɪk) *n* **1** a person who relies on empirical methods. **2** a medical quack. ◆ *adj* **3** a variant of **empirical.** ORIG C16: from L, from Gk *empeirikos* practised, from *peiran* to attempt

empirical (ɛm'pɪrɪkᵊl) *adj* **1** derived from or relating to experiment and observation rather than theory. **2** (of medical treatment) based on practical experience rather than scientific proof. **3** *Philosophy.* (of knowledge) derived from experience rather than by logic from first principles. **4** of or relating to medical quackery.
▸ **em'piricalness** *n*

empiricism (ɛm'pɪrɪ,sɪzəm) *n* **1** *Philosophy.* the doctrine that all knowledge derives from experience. **2** the use of empirical methods. **3** medical quackery.
▸ **em'piricist** *n, adj*

emplace (ɪm'pleɪs) *vb* **emplaces, emplacing, emplaced.** (*tr*) to put in position.

emplacement (ɪm'pleɪsmənt) *n* **1** a prepared position for a gun or other weapon. **2** the act of putting or state of being put in place. ORIG C19: from F, from obs. *emplacer* to put in position, from PLACE

emplane (ɪm'pleɪn) *vb* **emplanes, emplaning, emplaned.** to board or put on board an aeroplane.

employ (ɪm'plɔɪ) *vb* (*tr*) **1** to engage or make use of the services of (a person) in return for money; hire. **2** to provide work or occupation for; keep busy. **3** to use as a means. ◆ *n* **4** the state of being employed (esp. in **in someone's employ**). ORIG C15: from OF *emploier*, from L *implicāre* to entangle, engage, from *plicāre* to fold
▸ **em'ployable** *adj* ▸ **em,ploya'bility** *n*

employee *or US* **employe** (ɛm'plɔɪi:, ,ɛmplɔɪ'i:) *n* a person who is hired to work for another or for a business, firm, etc., in return for payment.

employer (ɪm'plɔɪə) *n* **1** a person, firm, etc., that employs workers. **2** a person who employs.

employment (ɪm'plɔɪmənt) *n* **1** the act of employing or state of being employed. **2** a person's work or occupation.

employment exchange *n Brit.* a former name for **employment office.**

employment office *n Brit.* any government office established to collect and supply to the unemployed information about job vacancies and to employers information about availability of prospective workers. See also **Jobcentre.**

employment tribunal *n* a tribunal that rules on disputes between employers and employees regarding unfair dismissal, redundancy, etc. Also called: **industrial tribunal.**

emporium (ɛm'pɔ:rɪəm) *n, pl* **emporiums** *or* **emporia** (-rɪə). a large retail shop offering for sale a wide variety of merchandise. ORIG C16: from L, from Gk, from *emporos* merchant, from *poros* a journey

empower (ɪm'paʊə) *vb* (*tr*) **1** to give power or authority to; authorize. **2** to give ability to; enable or permit.
▸ **em'powerment** *n*

empress ('ɛmprɪs) *n* **1** the wife or widow of an emperor. **2** a woman who holds the rank of emperor in her own right. ORIG C12: from OF *empereriz*, from L *imperātrix;* see EMPEROR

Empson ★ ('ɛmpsᵊn) *n* Sir **William.** 1906–84, English poet and critic; author of *Seven Types of Ambiguity* (1930).

empty ('ɛmptɪ) *adj* **emptier, emptiest. 1** containing nothing. **2** without inhabitants; vacant or unoccupied. **3** carrying no load, passengers, etc. **4** without purpose, substance, or value: *an empty life.* **5** insincere or trivial: *empty words.* **6** not expressive or vital; vacant: *an empty look.* **7** *Inf.* hungry. **8** (*postpositive;* foll. by *of*) devoid; destitute. **9** *Inf.* drained of energy or emotion. **10** *Maths, logic.* (of a set or class) containing no members. ◆ *vb* **empties, emptying, emptied. 11** to make or become empty. **12** (when *intr,* foll. by *into*) to discharge (contents). **13** (*tr;* often foll. by *of*) to unburden or rid (oneself). ◆ *n, pl* **empties. 14** an empty container, esp. a bottle. ORIG OE *ǣmtig*
▸ **'emptiable** *adj* ▸ **'emptier** *n* ▸ **'emptily** *adv* ▸ **'emptiness** *n*

empty-handed *adj* **1** carrying nothing in the hands. **2** having gained nothing.

empty-headed *adj* lacking sense; frivolous.

empty-nester (-'nɛstə) *n Inf.* a married person whose children have grown up and left home.

Empty Quarter ★ *n* another name for **Rub' al Khali.**

empyema (ˌɛmpaɪ'iːmə) *n, pl* **empyemata** (-'iːmətə) *or* **empyemas.** a collection of pus in a body cavity, esp. in the chest. ORIG C17: from Med. L, from Gk *empuēma* abscess, from *empuein* to suppurate, from *puon* pus
▸ ˌ**empy'emic** *adj*

empyrean (ˌɛmpaɪ'riːən) *n* **1** *Arch.* the highest part of the heavens, thought in ancient times to contain the pure element of fire and by early Christians to be the abode of God. **2** *Poetic.* the heavens or sky. ◆ *adj also* **empyreal. 3** of or relating to the sky. **4** heavenly or sublime. ORIG C17: from LL, from Gk *empurios* fiery

empyreuma (ˌɛmpɪ'ruːmə) *n, pl* **empyreumata** (-mətə). the smell and taste associated with burning vegetable and animal matter. ORIG C17: from Gk, from *empureuein* to set on fire

Ems ★ (ɛmz) *n* **1** a town in W Germany, in the Rhineland-Palatinate: famous for the **Ems Telegram** (1870), Bismarck's dispatch that led to the outbreak of the Franco-Prussian War. Pop.: 10 250 (latest est.). **2** a river in West Germany, rising in the Teutoburger Wald and flowing generally north to the North Sea. Length: about 370 km (230 miles).

EMS *abbrev. for* European Monetary System.

emu ('iːmjuː) *n* a large Australian flightless bird, similar to the ostrich. ORIG C17: changed from Port. *ema* ostrich, from Arab. *Na-'amah* ostrich

EMU 1 *abbrev. for* European Monetary Union. **2** See **e.m.u.**

e.m.u. *or* **EMU** *abbrev. for* electromagnetic unit.

emu-bob *Austral. inf.* ◆ *vb* **emu-bobs, emu-bobbing, emu-bobbed. 1** (*intr*) to bend over to collect litter or small pieces of wood. ◆ *n* **2** Also called: **emu parade.** a parade of soldiers or schoolchildren for litter collection.
▸ '**emu-**ˌ**bobbing** *n*

emulate ('ɛmjʊˌleɪt) *vb* **emulates, emulating, emulated.** (*tr*) **1** to attempt to equal or surpass, esp. by imitation. **2** to rival or compete with. ORIG C16: from L *aemulus* competing with
▸ '**emulative** *adj* ▸ ˌ**emu'lation** *n* ▸ '**emu**ˌ**lator** *n*

emulous ('ɛmjʊləs) *adj* **1** desiring or aiming to equal or surpass another. **2** characterized by or arising from emulation. ORIG C14: from L; see EMULATE
▸ '**emulousness** *n*

emulsifier (ɪ'mʌlsɪˌfaɪə) *n* an agent that forms an emulsion, esp. a food additive that prevents separation of processed foods.

emulsify (ɪ'mʌlsɪˌfaɪ) *vb* **emulsifies, emulsifying, emulsified.** to make or form into an emulsion.
▸ **e**ˌ**mulsi'fiable** *or* **e'mulsible** *adj* ▸ **e**ˌ**mulsifi'cation** *n*

emulsion (ɪ'mʌlʃən) *n* **1** *Photog.* a light-sensitive coating on a base, such as paper or film, consisting of silver bromide suspended in gelatine. **2** *Chem.* a colloid in which both phases are liquids. **3** a type of paint in which the pigment is suspended in a vehicle that is dispersed in water as an emulsion. **4** *Pharmacol.* a mixture in which an oily medicine is dispersed in another liquid. **5** any liquid resembling milk. ORIG C17: from NL *ēmulsiō*, from L, from *ēmulgēre* to milk out, from *mulgēre* to milk
▸ **e'mulsive** *adj*

emu-wren *n* an Australian wren having long plumy tail feathers.

en (ɛn) *n Printing.* a unit of measurement, half the width of an em.

EN (in Britain) *abbrev. for:* **1** enrolled nurse. **2** English Nature.

en-[1] *or* **em-** *prefix forming verbs.* **1** (*from nouns*) **1a** put in or on: *entomb; enthrone.* **1b** go on or into: *enplane.* **1c** surround or cover with: *enmesh.* **1d** furnish with: *empower.* **2** (*from adjectives and nouns*) cause to be in a certain condition: *enable; enslave.* ORIG via OF from L *in-* IN-[2]

en-[2] *or* **em-** *prefix forming nouns and adjectives.* in; into; inside: *endemic.* ORIG from Gk (often via L); cf. IN-[1], IN-[2]

-en[1] *suffix forming verbs from adjectives and nouns.* cause to be; become; cause to have: *blacken; heighten.* ORIG OE *-n-*, as in *fæst-n-ian* to fasten, of Gmc origin

-en[2] *suffix forming adjectives from nouns.* of; made of; resembling: *ashen; wooden.* ORIG OE *-en*

enable (ɪn'eɪbᵊl) *vb* **enables, enabling, enabled.** (*tr*) **1** to provide (someone) with adequate power, means, opportunity, or authority (to do something). **2** to make possible.
▸ **en'ablement** *n* ▸ **en'abler** *n*

enabling act *n* a legislative act conferring certain specified powers on a person or organization.

enact (ɪn'ækt) *vb* (*tr*) **1** to make into an act or statute. **2** to establish by law; decree. **3** to represent or perform as in a play.
▸ **en'actable** *adj* ▸ **en'active** *or* **en'actory** *adj* ▸ **en'actment** *or* **en'action** *n* ▸ **en'actor** *n*

enamel (ɪ'næməl) *n* **1** a coloured glassy substance, translucent or opaque, fused to the surface of articles made of metal, glass, etc., for ornament or protection. **2** an article or articles ornamented with enamel. **3** an enamel-like paint or varnish. **4** any coating resembling enamel. **5** the hard white substance that covers the crown of each tooth. **6** (*modifier*) decorated or covered with enamel. ◆ *vb* **enamels, enamelling, enamelled** *or US* **enamels, enameling, enameled.** (*tr*) **7** to decorate with enamel. **8** to ornament with glossy variegated colours, as if with enamel. **9** to portray in enamel. ORIG C15: from OF *esmail,* of Gmc origin
▸ **e'nameller, e'namellist** *or US* **e'nameler, e'namelist** *n*
▸ **e'namel**ˌ**work** *n*

enamour *or US* **enamor** (ɪn'æmə) *vb* (*tr; usually passive* and foll. by *of*) to inspire with love; captivate. ORIG C14: from OF, from *amour* love, from L *amor*
▸ **en'amoured** *or US* **en'amored** *adj*

en bloc *French.* (ɑ̃ blɔk) *adv* in a lump or block; as a body or whole; all together.

en brosse *French.* (ɑ̃ brɔs) *adj, adv* (of the hair) cut very short so that the hair stands up stiffly. ORIG lit.: in the style of a brush

enc. *abbrev. for:* **1** enclosed. **2** enclosure.

encamp (ɪn'kæmp) *vb* to lodge or cause to lodge in a camp.

encampment (ɪn'kæmpmənt) *n* **1** the act of setting up a camp. **2** the place where a camp, esp. a military camp, is set up.

encapsulate *or* **incapsulate** (ɪn'kæpsjʊˌleɪt) *vb* **encapsulates, encapsulating, encapsulated** *or* **incapsulates, incapsulating, incapsulated. 1** to enclose or be enclosed as in a capsule. **2** (*tr*) to sum up in a short or concise form.
▸ **en**ˌ**capsu'lation** *or* **in**ˌ**capsu'lation** *n*

encase *or* **incase** (ɪn'keɪs) *vb* **encases, encasing, encased.** (*tr*) to place or enclose as in a case.
▸ **en'casement** *or* **in'casement** *n*

encash (ɪn'kæʃ) *vb* (*tr*) *Brit., formal.* to exchange (a cheque) for cash.
▸ **en'cashable** *adj* ▸ **en'cashment** *n*

encaustic (ɪn'kɒstɪk) *Ceramics, etc.* ◆ *adj* **1** decorated by any process involving burning in colours, esp. by inlaying coloured clays and baking or by fusing wax colours to the surface. ◆ *n* **2** the process of burning in colours. **3** a product of such a process. ORIG C17: from L *encausticus,* from Gk, from *enkaiein* to burn in, from *kaiein* to burn
▸ **en'caustically** *adv*

-ence *or* **-ency** *suffix forming nouns.* indicating an action, state, condition, or quality: *benevolence; residence; patience.* ORIG via OF from L *-entia,* from *-ēns,* present participial ending

enceinte (ɒn'sænt) *adj* another word for **pregnant.** ORIG C17: from F, from L *inciēns* pregnant

Enceladus ★ (ɛn'sɛlədəs) *n Greek myth.* a giant who was punished for his rebellion against the gods by a fatal blow from a stone cast by Athena. He was believed to be buried under Mount Etna in Sicily.

encephalic (ˌɛnsɪ'fælɪk) *adj* of or relating to the brain.

encephalin (ɛn'sɛfəlɪn) *n* a variant of **enkephalin.**

encephalitis (ˌɛnsɛfə'laɪtɪs) *n* inflammation of the brain.
▸ **encephalitic** (ˌɛnsɛfə'lɪtɪk) *adj*

encephalitis lethargica (lɪ'θɑːdʒɪkə) *n* a technical name for **sleeping sickness** (sense 2).

★ people and places

encephalo- *or before a vowel* **encephal-** *combining form.* indicating the brain: *encephalogram; encephalitis.* ORIG from NL, from Gk *enkephalos,* from *en-* in + *kephalē* head

encephalogram (ɛn'sɛfələˌɡræm) *n* **1** an X-ray photograph of the brain, esp. one (a **pneumoencephalogram**) taken after replacing some of the cerebrospinal fluid with air or oxygen. **2** short for **electroencephalogram;** see **electroencephalograph.**

encephalon (ɛn'sɛfəˌlɒn) *n, pl* **encephala** (-lə). a technical name for **brain.** ORIG C18: from NL, from Gk *enkephalos* brain, from EN-[2] + *kephalē* head
▸ **en'cephalous** *adj*

encephalopathy (ˌɛnsɛfə'lɒpəθɪ) *n* any degenerative disease of the brain, often associated with toxic conditions. See also **BSE.**

enchain (ɪn'tʃeɪn) *vb (tr)* **1** to bind with chains. **2** to hold fast or captivate (the attention, etc.).
▸ **en'chainment** *n*

enchant (ɪn'tʃɑːnt) *vb (tr)* **1** to cast a spell on; bewitch. **2** to delight or captivate utterly. ORIG C14: from OF, from L *incantāre,* from *cantāre* to chant
▸ **en'chanted** *adj* ▸ **en'chanter** *n* ▸ **en'chantress** *fem n*

enchanting (ɪn'tʃɑːntɪŋ) *adj* pleasant; delightful.
▸ **en'chantingly** *adv*

enchantment (ɪn'tʃɑːntmənt) *n* **1** the act of enchanting or state of being enchanted. **2** a magic spell. **3** great charm or fascination.

enchase (ɪn'tʃeɪs) *vb* **enchases, enchasing, enchased.** *(tr)* a less common word for **chase**[3]. ORIG C15: from OF *enchasser* to enclose, set, from EN-[1] + *casse* CASE[2]
▸ **en'chaser** *n*

enchilada (ˌɛntʃɪ'lɑːdə) *n* a Mexican dish of a tortilla filled with meat, served with a chilli sauce. ORIG American Sp., from *enchilado,* from *enchilar* to spice with chilli

-enchyma *n combining form.* denoting cellular tissue. ORIG C20: abstracted from PARENCHYMA

encipher (ɪn'saɪfə) *vb (tr)* to convert (a message, etc.) into code or cipher.
▸ **en'cipherer** *n* ▸ **en'cipherment** *n*

encircle (ɪn'sɜːkᵊl) *vb* **encircles, encircling, encircled.** *(tr)* to form a circle around; enclose within a circle; surround.
▸ **en'circlement** *n*

enclave ('ɛnkleɪv) *n* a part of a country entirely surrounded by foreign territory: viewed from the position of the surrounding territories. ORIG C19: from F, from OF *enclaver* to enclose, from Vulgar L *inclāvāre* (unattested) to lock up, from L IN-[2] + *clavis* key

enclitic (ɪn'klɪtɪk) *adj* **1** denoting or relating to a monosyllabic word or form that is treated as a suffix of the preceding word. ◆ *n* **2** an enclitic word or form. ORIG C17: from LL, from Gk, from *enklinein* to cause to lean, from EN-[2] + *klinein* to lean
▸ **en'clitically** *adv*

enclose *or* **inclose** (ɪn'kləʊz) *vb* **encloses, enclosing, enclosed** *or* **incloses, inclosing, inclosed.** *(tr)* **1** to close; hem in; surround. **2** to surround (land) with or as if with a fence. **3** to put in an envelope or wrapper, esp. together with a letter. **4** to contain or hold.
▸ **en'closable** *or* **in'closable** *adj* ▸ **en'closer** *or* **in'closer** *n*

enclosed order *n* a Christian religious order that does not permit its members to go into the outside world.

enclosure *or* **inclosure** (ɪn'kləʊʒə) *n* **1** the act of enclosing or state of being enclosed. **2** an area enclosed as by a fence. **3** the act of appropriating land by setting up a fence, hedge, etc., around it. **4** a fence, wall, etc., that encloses. **5** something enclosed within an envelope or wrapper, esp. together with a letter. **6** *Brit.* a section of a sports ground, racecourse, etc., allotted to certain spectators.

encode (ɪn'kəʊd) *vb* **encodes, encoding, encoded.** *(tr)* to convert (a message) into code.
▸ **en'codement** *n* ▸ **en'coder** *n*

encomiast (ɛn'kəʊmɪˌæst) *n* a person who speaks or writes an encomium. ORIG C17: from Gk, from *enkōmiazein* to utter an ENCOMIUM
▸ **enˌcomi'astic** *or* **enˌcomi'astical** *adj*

encomium (ɛn'kəʊmɪəm) *n, pl* **encomiums** *or* **encomia** (-mɪə). a formal expression of praise; eulogy. ORIG C16: from L, from Gk, from EN-[2] + *kōmos* festivity

encompass (ɪn'kʌmpəs) *vb (tr)* **1** to enclose within a circle; surround. **2** to bring about: *he encompassed the enemy's ruin.* **3** to include entirely or comprehensively.
▸ **en'compassment** *n*

encore ('ɒŋkɔː) *sentence substitute.* **1** again: used by an audience to demand an extra or repeated performance. ◆ *n* **2** an extra or repeated performance given in response to enthusiastic demand. ◆ *vb* **encores, encoring, encored. 3** *(tr)* to demand an extra or repeated performance of (a work, piece of music, etc.) by (a performer). ORIG C18: from F: still, again, ?from L *in hanc hōram* until this hour

encounter (ɪn'kaʊntə) *vb* **1** to come upon or meet casually or unexpectedly. **2** to meet (an enemy, army, etc.) in battle or contest. **3** *(tr)* to be faced with; contend with. ◆ *n* **4** a casual or unexpected meeting. **5** a hostile meeting; contest. ORIG C13: from OF, from Vulgar L *incontrāre* (unattested), from L IN-[2] + *contrā* against, opposite

encounter group *n* a group of people who meet in order to develop self-awareness and mutual understanding by openly expressing their feelings, by confrontation, etc.

encourage (ɪn'kʌrɪdʒ) *vb* **encourages, encouraging, encouraged.** *(tr)* **1** to inspire (someone) with the courage or confidence (to do something). **2** to stimulate (something or someone) by approval or help.
▸ **en'couragement** *n* ▸ **en'courager** *n* ▸ **en'couraging** *adj*
▸ **en'couragingly** *adv*

encroach (ɪn'krəʊtʃ) *vb (intr)* **1** (often foll. by *on* or *upon*) to intrude gradually or stealthily upon the rights, property, etc., of another. **2** to advance beyond certain limits. ORIG C14: from OF *encrochier* to seize, lit.: fasten upon with hooks, of Gmc origin
▸ **en'croacher** *n* ▸ **en'croachment** *n*

encrust *or* **incrust** (ɪn'krʌst) *vb* **1** *(tr)* to cover or overlay with or as with a crust or hard coating. **2** to form or cause to form a crust or hard coating. **3** *(tr)* to decorate lavishly, as with jewels.
▸ **ˌencrus'tation** *or* **ˌincrus'tation** *n*

encumber *or* **incumber** (ɪn'kʌmbə) *vb (tr)* **1** to hinder or impede; hamper. **2** to fill with superfluous or useless matter. **3** to burden with debts, obligations, etc. ORIG C14: from OF, from EN-[1] + *combre* a barrier, from LL *combrus*

encumbrance *or* **incumbrance** (ɪn'kʌmbrəns) *n* **1** a thing that impedes or is burdensome; hindrance. **2** *Law.* a burden or charge upon property, such as a mortgage or lien.

ency., encyc., *or* **encycl.** *abbrev. for* encyclopedia.

-ency *suffix forming nouns.* a variant of **-ence:** *fluency; permanency.*

encyclical (ɛn'sɪklɪkᵊl) *n* **1** a letter sent by the pope to all Roman Catholic bishops. ◆ *adj also* **encyclic. 2** (of letters) intended for general circulation. ORIG C17: from LL, from Gk, from *kuklos* circle

encyclopedia *or* **encyclopaedia** (ɛnˌsaɪkləʊ'piːdɪə) *n* a book, often in many volumes, containing articles, often arranged in alphabetical order, dealing either with the whole range of human knowledge or with one particular subject. ORIG C16: from NL, erroneously for Gk *enkuklios paideia* general education
▸ **enˌcyclo'pedic** *or* **enˌcyclo'paedic** *adj*

encyclopedist *or* **encyclopaedist** (ɛnˌsaɪkləʊ'piːdɪst) *n* a person who compiles or contributes to an encyclopedia.
▸ **enˌcyclo'pedism** *or* **enˌcyclo'paedism** *n*

encyst (ɛn'sɪst) *vb Biol.* to enclose or become enclosed by a cyst, thick membrane, or shell.
▸ **en'cystment** *or* **ˌencys'tation** *n*

end (ɛnd) *n* **1** the extremity of the length of something, such as a road, line, etc. **2** the surface at either extremity of an object. **3** the extreme extent, limit, or degree of something. **4** the most distant place or time that can be imagined: *the ends of the earth.* **5** the time at which something is concluded. **6** the last section or part. **7** a share or

part. **8** (*often pl*) a remnant or fragment (esp. in **odds and ends**). **9** a final state, esp. death; destruction. **10** the purpose of an action or existence. **11** *Sport.* either of the two defended areas of a playing field, rink, etc. **12** *Bowls, etc.* a section of play from one side of the rink to the other. **13 at an end.** exhausted or completed. **14 come to an end.** to become completed or exhausted. **15 have one's end away.** *Sl.* to have sexual intercourse. **16 in the end.** finally. **17 keep one's end up. 17a** to sustain one's part in a joint undertaking. **17b** to hold one's own in an argument, contest, etc. **18 make** (**both**) **ends meet.** to spend no more than the money one has. **19 no end** (**of**). *Inf.* (intensifier): *I had no end of work.* **20 on end.** *Inf.* without pause or interruption. **21 the end.** *Sl.* the worst, esp. something that goes beyond the limits of endurance. ◆ *vb* **22** to bring or come to a finish; conclude. **23** to die or cause to die. **24** (*tr*) to surpass or outdo: *a novel to end all novels.* **25 end it all.** *Inf.* to commit suicide. ◆ See also **end up.** ORIG OE *ende*
▸ **'ender** *n*

end- *combining form.* a variant of **endo-** before a vowel.

-end *suffix forming nouns.* See **-and.**

endamoeba *or US* **endameba** (ˌendəˈmiːbə) *n* variant spellings of **entamoeba.**

endanger (ɪnˈdeɪndʒə) *vb* (*tr*) to put in danger or peril; imperil.
▸ **enˈdangerment** *n*

endangered (ɪnˈdeɪndʒəd) *adj* in danger, esp. of extinction: *an endangered species.*

endear (ɪnˈdɪə) *vb* (*tr*) to cause to be beloved or esteemed.
▸ **enˈdearing** *adj*

endearment (ɪnˈdɪəmənt) *n* something that endears, such as an affectionate utterance.

endeavour *or US* **endeavor** (ɪnˈdɛvə) *vb* **1** to try (to do something). ◆ *n* **2** an effort to do or attain something. ORIG C14 *endeveren,* from EN-[1] + *-deveren* from *dever* duty, from OF *deveir;* see DEVOIRS
▸ **enˈdeavourer** *or US* **enˈdeavorer** *n*

endemic (ɛnˈdɛmɪk) *adj also* **endemial** (ɛnˈdɛmɪəl) *or* **endemical. 1** present within a localized area or peculiar to persons in such an area. ◆ *n* **2** an endemic disease or plant. ORIG C18: from NL *endēmicus,* from Gk *endēmos* native, from EN-[2] + *dēmos* the people
▸ **enˈdemically** *adv* ▸ **ˈendemism** *or* **ˌendeˈmicity** *n*

Enderby Land ★ (ˈɛndəbɪ) *n* part of the coastal region of Antarctica, between Kempland and Queen Maud Land: the westernmost part of the Australian Antarctic Territory; discovered in 1831.

endermic (ɛnˈdɜːmɪk) *adj* (of a medicine, etc.) acting by absorption through the skin. ORIG C19: from EN-[2] + Gk *derma* skin

endgame (ˈɛndˌgeɪm) *n* the closing stage of any of certain games, esp. chess, when there are only a few pieces left in play.

ending (ˈɛndɪŋ) *n* **1** the act of bringing to or reaching an end. **2** the last part of something. **3** the final part of a word, esp. a suffix.

endive (ˈɛndaɪv) *n* a plant cultivated for its crisp curly leaves, which are used in salads. Cf. **chicory.** ORIG C15: from OF, from Med. L, from var. of L *intubus, entubus*

endless (ˈɛndlɪs) *adj* **1** having or seeming to have no end; eternal or infinite. **2** continuing too long or continually recurring. **3** formed with the ends joined.
▸ **ˈendlessness** *n*

endmost (ˈɛndˌməʊst) *adj* nearest the end; most distant.

endo- *or before a vowel* **end-** *combining form.* inside; within: *endocrine.* ORIG from Gk, from *endon* within

endoblast (ˈɛndəʊˌblæst) *n* **1** *Embryol.* a less common name for **endoderm. 2** another name for **hypoblast.**
▸ **ˌendoˈblastic** *adj*

endocarditis (ˌɛndəʊkɑːˈdaɪtɪs) *n* inflammation of the lining of the heart. ORIG C19: from NL, from ENDO- + Gk *kardia* heart + -ITIS
▸ **endocarditic** (ˌɛndəʊkɑːˈdɪtɪk) *adj*

endocarp (ˈɛndəˌkɑːp) *n* the inner layer of the pericarp of a fruit, such as the stone of a peach.
▸ **ˌendoˈcarpal** *or* **ˌendoˈcarpic** *adj*

endocrine (ˈɛndəʊˌkraɪn) *adj also* **ˌendoˈcrinal, endocrinic** (ˌɛndəʊˈkrɪnɪk). **1** of or denoting endocrine glands or their secretions. ◆ *n* **2** an endocrine gland. ORIG C20: from ENDO- + *-crine,* from Gk *krinein* to separate

endocrine gland *n* any of the glands that secrete hormones directly into the bloodstream, e.g. the pituitary, pineal, and thyroid.

endocrinology (ˌɛndəʊkraɪˈnɒlədʒɪ, -krɪ-) *n* the branch of medical science concerned with the endocrine glands and their secretions.
▸ **ˌendocriˈnologist** *n*

endoderm (ˈɛndəʊˌdɜːm) *or* **entoderm** *n* the inner germ layer of an animal embryo, which gives rise to the lining of the digestive and respiratory tracts.
▸ **ˌendoˈdermal, ˌendoˈdermic** *or* **ˌentoˈdermal, ˌentoˈdermic** *adj*

end of steel *n Canad.* **1** a point up to which railway tracks have been laid. **2** a town located at such a point.

endogamy (ɛnˈdɒgəmɪ) *n* **1** *Anthropol.* marriage within one's own tribe or similar unit. **2** pollination between two flowers on the same plant.
▸ **enˈdogamous** *or* **endogamic** (ˌɛndəʊˈgæmɪk) *adj*

endogenous (ɛnˈdɒdʒɪnəs) *adj* **1** *Biol.* developing or originating within an organism or part of an organism. **2** having no apparent external cause: *endogenous depression.*
▸ **enˈdogeny** *n*

endometritis (ˌɛndəʊmɪˈtraɪtɪs) *n* inflammation of the endometrium, which is caused by infection, as by bacteria, foreign bodies, etc.

endometrium (ˌɛndəʊˈmiːtrɪəm) *n, pl* **endometria** (-trɪə). the mucous membrane that lines the uterus. ORIG C19: NL, from ENDO- + Greek *mētra* uterus
▸ **ˌendoˈmetrial** *adj*

endomorph (ˈɛndəʊˌmɔːf) *n* **1** a type of person having a body build characterized by fatness and heaviness. **2** a mineral that naturally occurs enclosed within another mineral.
▸ **ˌendoˈmorphic** *adj* ▸ **ˈendoˌmorphy** *n*

endomorphism (ˌɛndəʊˈmɔːˌfɪzəm) *n Geol.* metamorphism in which changes are induced in cooling molten rock by contact with older rocks.

endophyte (ˈɛndəʊˌfaɪt) *n* any plant, parasitic fungus, or alga that lives within a plant.
▸ **endophytic** (ˌɛndəʊˈfɪtɪk) *adj*

endoplasm (ˈɛndəʊˌplæzəm) *n Cytology.* the inner cytoplasm of a cell.
▸ **ˌendoˈplasmic** *adj*

end organ *n Anat.* the expanded end of a peripheral motor or sensory nerve.

endorphin (ɛnˈdɔːfɪn) *n* any of a class of chemicals occurring in the brain, including enkephalin, which have a similar effect to morphine.

endorsation (ˌɛndɔːˈseɪʃən) *n Canad.* approval or support.

endorse *or* **indorse** (ɪnˈdɔːs) *vb* **endorses, endorsing, endorsed** *or* **indorses, indorsing, indorsed.** (*tr*) **1** to give approval or sanction to. **2** to sign (one's name) on the back of (a cheque, etc.) to specify oneself as payee. **3** *Commerce.* **3a** to sign the back of (a document) to transfer ownership of the rights to a specified payee. **3b** to specify (a sum) as transferable to another as payee. **4** to write (a qualifying comment, etc.) on the back of a document. **5** to sign a document, as when confirming receipt of payment. **6** *Chiefly Brit.* to record a conviction on (a driving licence). ORIG C16: from OF *endosser* to put on the back, from EN-[1] + *dos* back
▸ **enˈdorsable** *or* **inˈdorsable** *adj* ▸ **enˈdorser, enˈdorsor** *or* **inˈdorser, inˈdorsor** *n* ▸ **enˌdorˈsee** *or* **inˌdorˈsee** *n*

endorsement *or* **indorsement** (ɪnˈdɔːsmənt) *n* **1** the act or an instance of endorsing. **2** something that endorses, such as a signature. **3** approval or support. **4** a record of a motoring offence on a driving licence.

endoscope (ˈɛndəʊˌskəʊp) *n* a medical instrument for examining the interior of hollow organs such as the stomach or bowel.
▸ **endoscopic** (ˌɛndəʊˈskɒpɪk) *adj*

★ people and places

endoskeleton (ˌɛndəʊˈskɛlɪtᵊn) *n* an internal skeleton, esp. the bony or cartilaginous skeleton of vertebrates.
▸ ˌ**endo**ˈ**skeletal** *adj*

endosperm (ˈɛndəʊˌspɜːm) *n* the tissue within the seed of a flowering plant that surrounds and nourishes the embryo.
▸ ˌ**endo**ˈ**spermic** *adj*

endothermic (ˌɛndəʊˈθɜːmɪk) *or* **endothermal** *adj* (of a chemical reaction or compound) occurring or formed with the absorption of heat.
▸ ˌ**endo**ˈ**thermically** *adv* ▸ ˌ**endo**ˈ**thermism** *n*

endow (ɪnˈdaʊ) *vb* (*tr*) **1** to provide with or bequeath a source of permanent income. **2** (usually foll. by *with*) to provide (with qualities, characteristics, etc.). ORIG C14: from OF, from EN-[1] + *douer,* from L *dōtāre,* from *dōs* dowry

endowment (ɪnˈdaʊmənt) *n* **1** the income with which an institution, etc., is endowed. **2** the act or process of endowing. **3** (*usually pl*) natural talents or qualities.

endowment assurance *or* **insurance** *n* a form of life insurance that provides for the payment of a specified sum directly to the policyholder at a designated date or to his beneficiary should he die before this date.

endpaper (ˈɛndˌpeɪpə) *n* either of two leaves at the front and back of a book pasted to the inside of the board covers and the first leaf of the book.

end point *n* **1** *Chem.* the point at which a titration is complete. **2** the point at which anything is complete.

end product *n* the final result of a process, series, etc., esp. in manufacturing.

endue *or* **indue** (ɪnˈdjuː) *vb* **endues, enduing, endued** *or* **indues, induing, indued.** (*tr*) (usually foll. by *with*) to invest or provide, as with some quality or trait. ORIG C15: from OF, from L *indūcere,* from *dūcere* to lead

end up *vb* (*adv*) **1** (*copula*) to become eventually; turn out to be. **2** (*intr*) to arrive, esp. by a circuitous or lengthy route or process.

endurance (ɪnˈdjʊərəns) *n* **1** the capacity, state, or an instance of enduring. **2** something endured; a hardship, strain, or privation.

endure (ɪnˈdjʊə) *vb* **endures, enduring, endured. 1** to undergo (hardship, strain, etc.) without yielding; bear. **2** (*tr*) to permit or tolerate. **3** (*intr*) to last or continue to exist. ORIG C14: from OF, from L *indūrāre* to harden, from *dūrus* hard
▸ **en**ˈ**durable** *adj*

enduring (ɪnˈdjʊərɪŋ) *adj* **1** permanent; lasting. **2** having forbearance; long-suffering.
▸ **en**ˈ**duringly** *adv* ▸ **en**ˈ**duringness** *n*

end user *n* **1** (in international trading) the person, organization, or nation that will be the ultimate user of goods such as arms. **2** *Computing.* the ultimate destination of information that is being transferred within a system.

endways (ˈɛndˌweɪz) *or esp. US & Canad.* **endwise** (ˈɛndˌwaɪz) *adv* **1** having the end forwards or upwards. ◆ *adj* **2** vertical or upright. **3** lengthways. **4** standing or lying end to end.

Endymion ★ (ɛnˈdɪmɪən) *n Greek myth.* a handsome youth who was visited every night by the moon goddess Selene, who loved him.

end zone *n American football.* the area behind the goals at each end of the field that the ball must cross for a touchdown to be awarded.

ENE *symbol for* east-northeast.

-ene *n combining form.* (in chemistry) indicating an unsaturated compound containing double bonds: *benzene; ethylene.* ORIG from Gk *-ēnē,* fem. patronymic suffix

enema (ˈɛnɪmə) *n, pl* **enemas** *or* **enemata** (-mətə). *Med.* **1** the introduction of liquid into the rectum to evacuate the bowels, medicate, or nourish. **2** the liquid so introduced. ORIG C15: from NL, from Gk: injection, from *enienai* to send in

enemy (ˈɛnəmɪ) *n, pl* **enemies. 1** a person hostile or opposed to a policy, cause, person, or group. **2a** an armed adversary; opposing military force. **2b** (*as modifier*): *enemy aircraft.* **3a** a hostile nation or people. **3b** (*as modifier*): *an enemy alien.* **4** something that harms or opposes. ◆ Related adj: **inimical.** ORIG C13: from OF, from L *inimīcus* hostile, from IN-[1] + *amīcus* friend

energetic (ˌɛnəˈdʒɛtɪk) *adj* having or showing energy; vigorous.
▸ ˌ**ener**ˈ**getically** *adv*

energize *or* **energise** (ˈɛnəˌdʒaɪz) *vb* **energizes, energizing, energized** *or* **energises, energising, energised. 1** to have or cause to have energy; invigorate. **2** (*tr*) to apply electric current or electromotive force to (a circuit, etc.).
▸ ˈ**ener**ˌ**gizer** *or* ˈ**ener**ˌ**giser** *n*

energy (ˈɛnədʒɪ) *n, pl* **energies. 1** intensity or vitality of action or expression; forcefulness. **2** capacity or tendency for intense activity; vigour. **3** *Physics.* **3a** the capacity of a body or system to do work. **3b** a measure of this capacity, measured in joules (SI units). ORIG C16: from LL, from Gk *energeia* activity, from EN-[2] + *ergon* work

energy band *n Physics.* a range of energies associated with the quantum states of electrons in a crystalline solid.

energy conversion *n* the process of changing one form of energy into another, such as nuclear energy into heat or solar energy into electrical energy.

enervate *vb* (ˈɛnəˌveɪt), **enervates, enervating, enervated. 1** (*tr*) to deprive of strength or vitality. ◆ *adj* (ɪˈnɜːvɪt). **2** deprived of strength or vitality. ORIG C17: from L *ēnervāre* to remove the nerves from, from *nervus* nerve
▸ ˈ**ener**ˌ**vating** *adj* ▸ ˌ**ener**ˈ**vation** *n*

Enesco ★ (ɛˈnɛskəʊ) *n* **Georges** (ʒɔrʒ), original name *George Enescu.* 1881–1955, Romanian violinist and composer.

en famille *French.* (ɑ̃ famij) *adv* **1** with one's family; at home. **2** in a casual way; informally.

enfant terrible *French.* (ɑ̃fɑ̃ tɛriblə) *n, pl* ***enfants terribles*** (ɑ̃fɑ̃ tɛriblə). a person given to unconventional conduct or indiscreet remarks. ORIG C19: lit.: terrible child

enfeeble (ɪnˈfiːbᵊl) *vb* **enfeebles, enfeebling, enfeebled.** (*tr*) to make weak.
▸ **en**ˈ**feeblement** *n* ▸ **en**ˈ**feebler** *n*

en fête *French.* (ɑ̃ fɛt) *adv* dressed for or engaged in a festivity. ORIG C19: lit.: in festival

Enfield ★ (ˈɛnfiːld) *n* a borough of N Greater London: a residential suburb. Pop.: 259 800 (1994 est.). Area: 55 sq. km (31 sq. miles).

enfilade (ˌɛnfɪˈleɪd) *Mil.* ◆ *n* **1** gunfire directed along the length of a position or formation. **2** a position or formation subject to such fire. ◆ *vb* **enfilades, enfilading, enfiladed.** (*tr*) **3** to attack (a position or formation) with enfilade. ORIG C18: from F: suite, from *enfiler* to thread on string, from *fil* thread

enfold *or* **infold** (ɪnˈfəʊld) *vb* (*tr*) **1** to cover by enclosing. **2** to embrace.
▸ **en**ˈ**folder** *or* **in**ˈ**folder** *n* ▸ **en**ˈ**foldment** *or* **in**ˈ**foldment** *n*

enforce (ɪnˈfɔːs) *vb* **enforces, enforcing, enforced.** (*tr*) **1** to ensure obedience to (a law, decision, etc.). **2** to impose (obedience, etc.) as by force. **3** to emphasize or reinforce (an argument, etc.).
▸ **en**ˈ**forceable** *adj* ▸ **en**ˌ**forcea**ˈ**bility** *n* ▸ **enforcedly** (ɪnˈfɔːsɪdlɪ) *adv* ▸ **en**ˈ**forcement** *n* ▸ **en**ˈ**forcer** *n*

enfranchise (ɪnˈfræntʃaɪz) *vb* **enfranchises, enfranchising, enfranchised.** (*tr*) **1** to grant the power of voting to. **2** to liberate, as from servitude. **3** (in England) to invest (a town, city, etc.) with the right to be represented in Parliament.
▸ **en**ˈ**franchisement** *n* ▸ **en**ˈ**franchiser** *n*

ENG *abbrev. for* electronic news gathering: TV news obtained at the point of action by means of modern video equipment.

Eng. *abbrev. for:* **1** England. **2** English.

Engadine ★ (ˈɛŋgəˌdiːn) *n* the upper part of the valley of the River Inn in Switzerland, in Graubünden canton: tourist and winter sports centre.

engage (ɪnˈgeɪdʒ) *vb* **engages, engaging, engaged.** (*mainly tr*) **1** to secure the services of. **2** to secure for use; reserve. **3** to involve (a person or his or her attention) intensely. **4** to attract (the affection) of (a person). **5** to draw (somebody) into conversation. **6** (*intr*) to take part; participate. **7** to promise (to do something). **8** (*also intr*) *Mil.* to begin

an action with (an enemy). **9** to bring (a mechanism) into operation. **10** (*also intr*) to undergo or cause to undergo interlocking, as of the components of a driving mechanism. **11** *Machinery*. to locate (a locking device) in its operative position or to advance (a tool) into a workpiece to commence cutting. ORIG C15: from OF, from EN-[1] + *gage* a pledge; see GAGE[1]
▸ **en'gager** *n*

engagé *or* (*fem*) ***engagée*** *French*. (ãgaʒe) *adj* (of an artist) committed to some ideology.

engaged (ɪn'geɪdʒd) *adj* **1** pledged to be married; betrothed. **2** occupied or busy. **3** *Archit*. built against or attached to a wall or similar structure. **4** (of a telephone line) in use.

engaged tone *n Brit*. a repeated single note heard on a telephone when the number called is already in use.

engagement (ɪn'geɪdʒmənt) *n* **1** a pledge of marriage; betrothal. **2** an appointment or arrangement, esp. for business or social purposes. **3** the act of engaging or condition of being engaged. **4** a promise, obligation, or other condition that binds. **5** a period of employment, esp. a limited period. **6** an action; battle.

engagement ring *n* a ring given by a man to a woman as a token of their betrothal.

engaging (ɪn'geɪdʒɪŋ) *adj* pleasing, charming, or winning.
▸ **en'gagingness** *n*

en garde *French*. (ã gard) *sentence substitute*. **1** on guard; a call to a fencer to adopt a defensive stance in readiness for an attack or bout. ◆ *adj* **2** (of a fencer) in such a stance.

Engels ★ (*German* 'ɛŋəls) *n* **Friedrich** ('fri:drɪç). 1820–95, German socialist leader and political philosopher, in England from 1849. He collaborated with Marx on *The Communist Manifesto* (1848) and his own works include *Condition of the Working Classes in England* (1844).

engender (ɪn'dʒɛndə) *vb* (*tr*) to bring about or give rise to; cause to be born. ORIG C14: from OF, from L *ingenerāre*, from *generāre* to beget

engin. *abbrev. for* engineering.

engine ('ɛndʒɪn) *n* **1** any machine designed to convert energy into mechanical work. **2** a railway locomotive. **3** *Mil*. any piece of equipment formerly used in warfare, such as a battering ram. **4** *Obs*. any instrument or device. ORIG C13: from OF, from L *ingenium* nature, talent, ingenious contrivance, from IN-[2] + *-genium*, rel. to *gignere* to beget, produce

engine driver *n Chiefly Brit*. a man who drives a railway locomotive; train driver.

engineer (ˌɛndʒɪ'nɪə) *n* **1** a person trained in any branch of engineering. **2** the originator or manager of a situation, system, etc. **3** *US & Canad*. the driver of a railway locomotive. **4** an officer responsible for a ship's engines. **5** a member of the armed forces trained in engineering and construction work. ◆ *vb* (*tr*) **6** to originate, cause, or plan in a clever or devious manner. **7** to design, plan, or construct as a professional engineer. ORIG C14 *enginer*, from OF, from *engignier* to contrive, ult. from L *ingenium* skill, talent; see ENGINE

engineering (ˌɛndʒɪ'nɪərɪŋ) *n* the profession of applying scientific principles to the design, construction, and maintenance of engines, cars, machines, etc. (**mechanical engineering**), buildings, bridges, roads, etc. (**civil engineering**), electrical machines and communication systems (**electrical engineering**), chemical plant and machinery (**chemical engineering**), or aircraft (**aeronautical engineering**).

England ★ ('ɪŋglənd) *n* the largest division of Great Britain, bordering on Scotland and Wales: unified in the mid-tenth century and conquered by the Normans in 1066; united with Wales in 1536 and Scotland in 1707; monarchy overthrown in 1649 but restored in 1660. Capital: London. Pop.: 47 058 200 (1991). Area: 130 439 sq. km (50 352 sq. miles). See **United Kingdom, Great Britain**.

English ('ɪŋglɪʃ) *n* **1** the official language of Britain, the US, most of the Commonwealth, and certain other countries. **2 the English**. (*functioning as pl*) the natives or inhabitants of England collectively. **3** (*often not cap*.) the usual US & Canad. term for **side** (in billiards). ◆ *adj* **4** of or relating to the English language. **5** relating to or characteristic of England or the English. ◆ *vb* (*tr*) **6** *Arch*. to translate or adapt into English.
▸ **'Englishness** *n*

English Channel ★ *n* an arm of the Atlantic Ocean between S England and N France, linked with the North Sea by the Strait of Dover. Length: about 560 km (350 miles). Width: between 32 km (20 miles) and 161 km (100 miles).

English horn *n Music*. another name for **cor anglais**.

Englishman ('ɪŋglɪʃmən) *or* (*fem*) **Englishwoman** *n*, *pl* **Englishmen** *or* **Englishwomen**. a native or inhabitant of England.

engorge (ɪn'gɔ:dʒ) *vb* **engorges, engorging, engorged**. (*tr*) **1** *Pathol*. to congest with blood. **2** to eat (food) greedily. **3** to gorge (oneself); glut.
▸ **en'gorgement** *n*

engr *abbrev. for*: **1** engineer. **2** engraver.

engraft *or* **ingraft** (ɪn'grɑ:ft) *vb* (*tr*) **1** to graft (a shoot, bud, etc.) onto a stock. **2** to incorporate in a firm or permanent way; implant.
▸ **ˌengraf'tation, ˌingraf'tation** *or* **en'graftment, in'graftment** *n*

engrain (ɪn'greɪn) *vb* a variant spelling of **ingrain**.

engrave (ɪn'greɪv) *vb* **engraves, engraving, engraved**. (*tr*) **1** to inscribe (a design, writing, etc.) onto (a block, plate, or other printing surface) by carving, etching, or other process. **2** to print (designs or characters) from a plate so made. **3** to fix deeply or permanently in the mind. ORIG C16: from EN-[1] + GRAVE[3], on the model of F *engraver*
▸ **en'graver** *n*

engraving (ɪn'greɪvɪŋ) *n* **1** the art of a person who engraves. **2** a printing surface that has been engraved. **3** a print made from this.

engross (ɪn'grəʊs) *vb* (*tr*) **1** to occupy one's attention completely; absorb. **2** to write or copy (manuscript) in large legible handwriting. **3** *Law*. to write or type out formally (a document) preparatory to execution. ORIG C14 (in the sense: to buy up wholesale); C15 (in the sense: to write in large letters): from L *grossus* thick, GROSS
▸ **en'grossed** *adj* ▸ **en'grossing** *adj* ▸ **en'grossment** *n*

engulf *or* **ingulf** (ɪn'gʌlf) *vb* (*tr*) **1** to immerse, plunge, bury, or swallow up. **2** (*often passive*) to overwhelm.
▸ **en'gulfment** *n*

enhance (ɪn'hɑ:ns) *vb* **enhances, enhancing, enhanced**. (*tr*) to intensify or increase in quality, value, power, etc.; improve; augment. ORIG C14: from OF, from EN-[1] + *haucier* to raise, from Vulgar L *altiāre* (unattested), from L *altus* high
▸ **en'hancement** *n* ▸ **en'hancer** *n*

enharmonic (ˌɛnhɑ:'mɒnɪk) *adj Music*. **1** denoting or relating to a small difference in pitch between two notes, such as A flat and G sharp: not present in instruments of equal temperament, but significant in the intonation of stringed instruments. **2** denoting or relating to enharmonic modulation. ORIG C17: from L, from Gk, from EN-[2] + *harmonia*; see HARMONY
▸ **ˌenhar'monically** *adv*

Enid ★ ('i:nɪd) *n* (in Arthurian legend) the faithful wife of Geraint.

enigma (ɪ'nɪgmə) *n* a person, thing, or situation that is mysterious, puzzling, or ambiguous. ORIG C16: from L, from Gk, from *ainissesthai* to speak in riddles, from *ainos* fable, story
▸ **enigmatic** (ˌɛnɪg'mætɪk) *or* **ˌenig'matical** *adj* ▸ **ˌenig'matically** *adv*

Eniwetok ★ (ˌɛnə'wi:tɒk, ə'ni:wɪˌtɔ:k) *n* an atoll in the W Pacific Ocean, in the NW Marshall Islands: taken by the US from Japan in 1944; became a naval base and later a testing ground for atomic weapons. Pop.: 715 (1988).

enjambment *or* **enjambement** (ɪn'dʒæmmənt) *n* *Prosody*. the running over of a sentence from one line of verse into the next. ORIG C19: from F, lit.: a straddling, from EN-[1] + *jambe* leg; see JAMB
▸ **en'jambed** *adj*

enjoin (ɪn'dʒɔɪn) *vb* (*tr*) **1** to order (someone) to do something. **2** to impose or prescribe (a mode of behaviour, etc.). **3** *Law.* to require (a person) to do or refrain from some act, esp. by an injunction. ORIG C13: from OF *enjoindre,* from L *injungere* to fasten to, from IN-[2] + *jungere* to JOIN
▸ **en'joiner** *n* ▸ **en'joinment** *n*

enjoy (ɪn'dʒɔɪ) *vb* (*tr*) **1** to receive pleasure from; take joy in. **2** to have the benefit of; use. **3** to have as a condition; experience. **4** **enjoy oneself.** to have a good time. ORIG C14: from OF, from EN-[1] + *joir* to find pleasure in, from L *gaudēre* to rejoice
▸ **en'joyable** *adj* ▸ **en'joyableness** *n* ▸ **en'joyably** *adv* ▸ **en'joyer** *n*

enjoyment (ɪn'dʒɔɪmənt) *n* **1** the act or condition of receiving pleasure from something. **2** the use or possession of something that is satisfying. **3** something that provides joy or satisfaction.

enkephalin (ɛn'kɛfəlɪn) *or* **encephalin** (ɛn'sɛfəlɪn) *n* a chemical occurring in the brain, having effects similar to those of morphine.

enkindle (ɪn'kɪndᵊl) *vb* **enkindles, enkindling, enkindled.** (*tr*) **1** to set on fire; kindle. **2** to excite to activity or ardour; arouse.

enlace (ɪn'leɪs) *vb* **enlaces, enlacing, enlaced.** (*tr*) **1** to bind or encircle with or as with laces. **2** to entangle; intertwine.
▸ **en'lacement** *n*

enlarge (ɪn'lɑːdʒ) *vb* **enlarges, enlarging, enlarged. 1** to make or grow larger; increase or expand. **2** (*tr*) to make (a photographic print) of a larger size than the negative. **3** (*intr;* foll. by *on* or *upon*) to speak or write (about) in greater detail.
▸ **en'largeable** *adj* ▸ **en'largement** *n* ▸ **en'larger** *n*

enlighten (ɪn'laɪtᵊn) *vb* (*tr*) **1** to give information or understanding to; instruct. **2** to free from prejudice, superstition, etc. **3** to give spiritual or religious revelation to. **4** *Poetic.* to shed light on.
▸ **en'lightening** *adj*

enlightened (ɪn'laɪtᵊnd) *adj* **1** well-informed, tolerant, and guided by rational thought: *an enlightened administration.* **2** claiming a spiritual revelation of truth.

enlightenment (ɪn'laɪtᵊnmənt) *n* the act or means of enlightening or the state of being enlightened.

Enlightenment (ɪn'laɪtᵊnmənt) *n* **the.** an 18th-century philosophical movement stressing the importance of reason.

enlist (ɪn'lɪst) *vb* **1** to enter or persuade to enter the armed forces. **2** (*tr*) to engage or secure (a person or his or her support) for a venture, cause, etc. **3** (*intr;* foll. by *in*) to enter into or join an enterprise, cause, etc.
▸ **en'lister** *n* ▸ **en'listment** *n*

enlisted man *n US.* a serviceman who holds neither a commission nor a warrant.

enliven (ɪn'laɪvᵊn) *vb* (*tr*) **1** to make active, vivacious, or spirited. **2** to make cheerful or bright; gladden.
▸ **en'livening** *adj* ▸ **en'livenment** *n*

en masse (*French* ɑ̃ mas) *adv* in a group or mass; as a whole; all together. ORIG C19: from F

enmesh (ɪn'mɛʃ) *vb* (*tr*) to catch or involve in or as if in a net or snare; entangle.
▸ **en'meshment** *n*

enmity ('ɛnmɪtɪ) *n, pl* **enmities.** a feeling of hostility or ill will, as between enemies. ORIG C13: from OF; see ENEMY

Ennerdale Water ★ ('ɛnəˌdeɪl) *n* a lake in NW England, in Cumbria in the Lake District. Length: 4 km (2.5 miles).

Ennis ★ ('ɛnɪs) *n* a town in the W Republic of Ireland, county town of Co. Clare. Pop.: 13 750 (1991).

Enniskillen (ˌɛnɪs'kɪlɪn) *or* (*formerly*) **Inniskilling ★** *n* a town in SW Northern Ireland, in Fermanagh, on an island in the River Erne: scene of the defeat of James II's forces in 1689. Pop.: 11 436 (1991).

Ennius ★ ('ɛnɪəs) *n* **Quintus** ('kwɪntəs). 239–169 B.C., Roman epic poet and dramatist.

ennoble (ɪ'nəʊbᵊl) *vb* **ennobles, ennobling, ennobled.** (*tr*) **1** to make noble, honourable, or excellent; dignify; exalt. **2** to raise to a noble rank.
▸ **en'noblement** *n* ▸ **en'nobler** *n* ▸ **en'nobling** *adj*

ennui ('ɒnwiː) *n* a feeling of listlessness and general dissatisfaction resulting from lack of activity or excitement. ORIG C18: from F: apathy, from OF *enui* annoyance, vexation; see ANNOY

Enoch ★ ('iːnɒk) *n Old Testament.* **1** the eldest son of Cain after whom the first city was named (Genesis 4:17). **2** the father of Methuselah: said to have walked with God and to have been taken by God at the end of his earthly life (Genesis 5:24).

enology (iː'nɒlədʒɪ) *n* the usual US spelling of **oenology.**

enormity (ɪ'nɔːmɪtɪ) *n, pl* **enormities. 1** the quality or character of extreme wickedness. **2** an act of great wickedness; atrocity. **3** *Inf.* vastness of size or extent. ORIG C15: from OF, from LL *ēnormitās* hugeness; see ENORMOUS

enormous (ɪ'nɔːməs) *adj* **1** unusually large in size, extent, or degree; immense; vast. **2** *Arch.* extremely wicked; heinous. ORIG C16: from L, from *ē-* out of, away from + *norma* rule, pattern
▸ **e'normously** *adv* ▸ **e'normousness** *n*

Enos ★ ('iːnɒs) *n Old Testament.* a son of Seth (Genesis 4:26; 5:6).

enosis ('ɛnəʊsɪs) *n* the union of Greece and Cyprus: the aim of a group of Greek Cypriots. ORIG C20: Mod. Gk: from Gk *henoun* to unite, from *heis* one

enough (ɪ'nʌf) *determiner* **1a** sufficient to answer a need, demand or supposition. **1b** (*as pron*): *enough is now known.* **2 that's enough!** that will do: used to put an end to an action, speech, performance, etc. ◆ *adv* **3** so as to be sufficient; as much as necessary. **4** (*not used with a negative*) very or quite; rather. **5** (intensifier): *oddly enough.* **6** just adequately; tolerably. ORIG OE *genōh*

en passant (ɒn pæ'sɑːnt) *adv* in passing: in chess, said of capturing a pawn that has made an initial move of two squares. The capture is made as if the captured pawn had moved one square instead of two. ORIG C17: from F

enprint ('ɛnprɪnt) *n* a standard photographic print (5 × 3.5 in.) produced from a negative.

enquire (ɪn'kwaɪə) *vb* **enquires, enquiring, enquired.** a variant of **inquire.**
▸ **en'quirer** *n* ▸ **en'quiry** *n*

enrage (ɪn'reɪdʒ) *vb* **enrages, enraging, enraged.** (*tr*) to provoke to fury; put into a rage.
▸ **en'raged** *adj* ▸ **en'ragement** *n*

en rapport *French.* (ɑ̃ rapɔr) *adj* (*postpositive*), *adv* in sympathy, harmony, or accord.

enrapture (ɪn'ræptʃə) *vb* **enraptures, enrapturing, enraptured.** (*tr*) to fill with delight; enchant.

enrich (ɪn'rɪtʃ) *vb* (*tr*) **1** to increase the wealth of. **2** to endow with fine or desirable qualities. **3** to make more beautiful; adorn; decorate. **4** to improve in quality, colour, flavour, etc. **5** to increase the food value of by adding nutrients. **6** to fertilize (soil). **7** *Physics.* to increase the concentration or abundance of one component or isotope in (a solution or mixture).
▸ **en'riched** *adj* ▸ **en'richment** *n*

Enright ★ ('ɛnraɪt) *n* **D(ennis) J(oseph).** born 1920, British poet, essayist, and editor.

enrol *or US* **enroll** (ɪn'rəʊl) *vb* **enrols** *or US* **enrolls, enrolling, enrolled.** (*mainly tr*) **1** to record or note in a roll or list. **2** (*also intr*) to become or cause to become a member; enlist; register. **3** to put on record.
▸ **ˌenrol'lee** *n* ▸ **en'roller** *n*

enrolment *or US* **enrollment** (ɪn'rəʊlmənt) *n* **1** the act of enrolling or state of being enrolled. **2** a list of people enrolled. **3** the total number of people enrolled.

en route (ɒn 'ruːt) *adv* on or along the way. ORIG C18: from F

Ens. *abbrev. for* Ensign.

ENSA ('ɛnsə) *n acronym for* Entertainments National Service Association.

Enschede ★ (*Dutch* 'ɛnsxədeː) *n* a city in the E Netherlands, in Overijssel province: a major centre of the Dutch cotton industry. Pop.: 147 832 (1996 est.).

ensconce (ɪn'skɒns) *vb* **ensconces, ensconcing, ensconced.** (*tr; often passive*) **1** to establish or settle firmly or comfortably. **2** to place in safety; hide. ORIG C16: see EN-[1], SCONCE[2]

ensemble (ɒn'sɒmbᵊl) *n* **1** all the parts of something considered together. **2** a person's complete costume; outfit. **3** the cast of a play other than the principals. **4** *Music.* a group of soloists singing or playing together. **5** *Music.* the degree of precision and unity exhibited by a group of instrumentalists or singers performing together. **6** the general effect of something made up of individual parts. ◆ *adv* **7** all together or at once. ORIG C15: from F: together, from L, from IN-[2] + *simul* at the same time

enshrine *or* **inshrine** (ɪn'ʃraɪn) *vb* **enshrines, enshrining, enshrined.** (*tr*) **1** to place or enclose as in a shrine. **2** to hold as sacred; cherish; treasure.
▸ **en'shrinement** *n*

enshroud (ɪn'ʃraʊd) *vb* (*tr*) to cover or hide as with a shroud.

ensign ('ɛnsaɪn) *n* **1** (*also* 'ɛnsən). a flag flown by a ship, branch of the armed forces, etc., to indicate nationality, allegiance, etc. See also **Red Ensign, White Ensign. 2** any flag, standard, or banner. **3** a standard-bearer. **4** a symbol or emblem; sign. **5** (in the US Navy) a commissioned officer of the lowest rank. **6** (in the British infantry) a colours bearer. **7** (formerly in the British infantry) a commissioned officer of the lowest rank. ORIG C14: from OF *enseigne*, from L INSIGNIA
▸ **'ensign,ship** *or* **'ensigncy** *n*

ensilage ('ɛnsɪlɪdʒ) *n* **1** the process of ensiling green fodder. **2** a less common name for **silage.**

ensile (ɛn'saɪl, 'ɛnsaɪl) *vb* **ensiles, ensiling, ensiled.** (*tr*) **1** to store and preserve (green fodder) in a silo. **2** to turn (green fodder) into silage by causing it to ferment in a silo. ORIG C19: from F, from Sp., from EN-[1] + *silo* SILO

enslave (ɪn'sleɪv) *vb* **enslaves, enslaving, enslaved.** (*tr*) to make a slave of; subjugate.
▸ **en'slavement** *n* ▸ **en'slaver** *n*

ensnare *or* **insnare** (ɪn'snɛə) *vb* **ensnares, ensnaring, ensnared** *or* **insnares, insnaring, insnared.** (*tr*) **1** to catch or trap as in a snare. **2** to trap or gain power over (someone) by dishonest or underhand means.
▸ **en'snarement** *n* ▸ **en'snarer** *n*

ensue (ɪn'sjuː) *vb* **ensues, ensuing, ensued. 1** (*intr*) to come next or afterwards. **2** (*intr*) to occur as a consequence; result. **3** (*tr*) *Obs.* to pursue. ORIG C14: from Anglo-F, from OF, from EN-[1] + *suivre* to follow, from L *sequī*
▸ **en'suing** *adj*

en suite *French.* (ɑ̃ sɥit) *adv* forming a unit: *a room with bathroom en suite.* ORIG lit.: in sequence

ensure (ɛn'ʃʊə, -'ʃɔː) *or esp. US* **insure** *vb* **ensures, ensuring, ensured** *or US* **insures, insuring, insured.** (*tr*) **1** (*may take a clause as object*) to make certain or sure; guarantee. **2** to make safe or secure; protect.
▸ **en'surer** *n*

ENT *Med. abbrev. for* ear, nose, and throat.

-ent *suffix forming adjectives and nouns.* causing or performing an action or existing in a certain condition; the agent that performs an action: *astringent; dependent.* ORIG from L *-ent-, -ens,* present participial ending

entablature (ɛn'tæblətʃə) *n Archit.* **1** the part of a classical temple above the columns, having an architrave, a frieze, and a cornice. **2** any similar construction. ORIG C17: from F, from It. *intavolatura* something put on a table, hence, something laid flat, from *tavola* table

entablement (ɪn'teɪbᵊlmənt) *n* the platform of a pedestal, above the dado, that supports a statue. ORIG C17: from OF

entail (ɪn'teɪl) *vb* (*tr*) **1** to bring about or impose inevitably: *this task entails careful thought.* **2** *Property law.* to restrict (the descent of an estate) to designated heirs. **3** *Logic.* to have as a necessary consequence. ◆ *n* **4** *Property law.* **4a** the restriction imposed by entailing an estate. **4b** an entailed estate. ORIG C14 *entaillen*, from EN-[1] + *taille* limitation, TAIL[2]
▸ **en'tailer** *n* ▸ **en'tailment** *n*

entamoeba (ˌɛntə'miːbə), **endamoeba** *or US* **entameba, endameba** *n, pl* **entamoebae** (-biː), **entamoebas, endamoebae, endamoebas** *or US* **entamebae, entamebas, endamebae, endamebas.** any parasitic amoeba of the genus *Entamoeba* (or *Endamoeba*) which lives in the intestines of man and causes amoebic dysentery.

entangle (ɪn'tæŋgᵊl) *vb* **entangles, entangling, entangled.** (*tr*) **1** to catch or involve in or as if in a tangle; ensnare or enmesh. **2** to make tangled or twisted; snarl. **3** to make complicated; confuse. **4** to involve in difficulties.
▸ **en'tanglement** *n* ▸ **en'tangler** *n*

entasis ('ɛntəsɪs) *n, pl* **entasises** (-siːz). a slightly convex curve given to the shaft of a column, or similar structure, to correct the illusion of concavity produced by a straight shaft. ORIG C18: from Gk, from *enteinein* to stretch tight, from *teinein* to stretch

Entebbe ★ (ɛn'tɛbɪ) *n* a town in S Uganda, on Lake Victoria: British administrative centre of Uganda (1893–1958); international airport. Pop.: 41 638 (1991).

entellus (ɛn'tɛləs) *n* an Old World monkey of S Asia. ORIG C19: NL, apparently after a character in Virgil's *Aeneid*

entente (*French* ɑ̃tɑ̃t) *n* **1** short for **entente cordiale. 2** the parties to an entente cordiale collectively. ORIG C19: F: understanding

entente cordiale (*French* ɑ̃tɑ̃t kɔrdjal) *n* **1** a friendly understanding between political powers. **2** (*often caps.*) the understanding reached by France and Britain in 1904, over colonial disputes. ORIG C19: F: cordial understanding

enter ('ɛntə) *vb* **1** to come or go into (a place, house, etc.). **2** to penetrate or pierce. **3** (*tr*) to introduce or insert. **4** to join (a party, organization, etc.). **5** (when *intr*, foll. by *into*) to become involved or take part (in). **6** (*tr*) to record (an item) in a journal, account, etc. **7** (*tr*) to record (a name, etc.) on a list. **8** (*tr*) to present or submit: *to enter a proposal.* **9** (*intr*) *Theatre.* to come on stage: used as a stage direction: *enter Juliet.* **10** (when *intr*, often foll. by *into, on,* or *upon*) to begin; start: *to enter upon a new career.* **11** (*intr*; often foll. by *upon*) to come into possession (of). **12** (*tr*) to place (evidence, etc.) before a court of law. ORIG C13: from OF, from L *intrāre*, from *intrā* within
▸ **'enterable** *adj* ▸ **'enterer** *n*

enteric (ɛn'tɛrɪk) *or* **enteral** ('ɛntərəl) *adj* intestinal. ORIG C19: from Gk, from *enteron* intestine

enter into *vb* (*intr, prep*) **1** to be considered as a necessary part of (one's plans, calculations, etc.). **2** to be in sympathy with.

enteritis (ˌɛntə'raɪtɪs) *n* inflammation of the intestine.

entero- *or before a vowel* **enter-** *combining form.* indicating an intestine: *enterovirus; enteritis.* ORIG from NL, from Gk *enteron* intestine

enterobiasis (ˌɛntərəʊ'baɪəsɪs) *n* a disease, common in children, caused by infestation of the large intestine with pinworms. ORIG C20: NL, from *enterobius* (generic name of worm) + -IASIS

enterprise ('ɛntəˌpraɪz) *n* **1** a project or undertaking, esp. one that requires boldness or effort. **2** participation in such projects. **3** readiness to embark on new ventures; boldness and energy. **4a** initiative in business. **4b** (*as modifier*): *the enterprise culture.* **5** a company or firm. ORIG C15: from OF *entreprise* (n), from *entreprendre* from *entre-* between (from L: INTER-) + *prendre* to take, from L *prehendere* to grasp
▸ **'enterˌpriser** *n*

Enterprise Allowance Scheme *n* (in Britain) a scheme to provide a weekly allowance to an unemployed person who wishes to set up a business and is willing to invest a specified amount in it during its first year.

enterprise zone *n* one of several areas in the UK in which industrial development is encouraged by tax and other concessions.

enterprising ('ɛntəˌpraɪzɪŋ) *adj* ready to embark on new ventures; full of boldness and initiative.
▸ **'enterˌprisingly** *adv*

entertain (ˌɛntə'teɪn) *vb* **1** to provide amusement for (a person or audience). **2** to show hospitality to (guests). **3** (*tr*) to hold in the mind. ORIG C15: from OF, from *entre-* mutually + *tenir* to hold

entertainer (ˌɛntəˈteɪnə) *n* **1** a professional performer in public entertainments. **2** any person who entertains.

entertaining (ˌɛntəˈteɪnɪŋ) *adj* serving to entertain or give pleasure; diverting; amusing.

entertainment (ˌɛntəˈteɪnmənt) *n* **1** the act or art of entertaining or state of being entertained. **2** an act, production, etc., that entertains; diversion; amusement.

enthral *or US* **enthrall** (ɪnˈθrɔːl) *vb* **enthrals** *or US* **enthralls, enthralling, enthralled.** (*tr*) **1** to hold spellbound; enchant; captivate. **2** *Obs.* to hold as thrall; enslave.
▸ **enˈthraller** *n* ▸ **enˈthralling** *adj* ▸ **enˈthralment** *or US* **enˈthrallment** *n*

enthrone (ɛnˈθrəʊn) *vb* **enthrones, enthroning, enthroned.** (*tr*) **1** to place on a throne. **2** to honour or exalt. **3** to assign authority to.
▸ **enˈthronement** *n*

enthuse (ɪnˈθjuːz) *vb* **enthuses, enthusing, enthused.** to feel or show or cause to feel or show enthusiasm.

enthusiasm (ɪnˈθjuːzɪˌæzəm) *n* **1** ardent and lively interest or eagerness. **2** an object of keen interest. **3** *Arch.* extravagant religious fervour. ORIG C17: from LL, from Gk, from *enthousiazein* to be possessed by a god, from EN-[2] + *theos* god

enthusiast (ɪnˈθjuːzɪˌæst) *n* **1** a person motivated by enthusiasm; fanatic. **2** *Arch.* one whose zeal for religion is extravagant.
▸ **enˌthusiˈastic** *adj* ▸ **enˌthusiˈastically** *adv*

enthymeme (ˈɛnθɪˌmiːm) *n Logic.* a syllogism in which one or more premises are unexpressed. ORIG C16: via L from Gk *enthumeisthai* to infer, from EN-[2] + *thumos* mind

entice (ɪnˈtaɪs) *vb* **entices, enticing, enticed.** (*tr*) to attract by exciting hope or desire; tempt; allure. ORIG C13: from OF, from Vulgar L *intitiāre* (unattested) to incite
▸ **enˈticement** *n* ▸ **enˈticer** *n* ▸ **enˈticing** *adj* ▸ **enˈticingly** *adv*

entire (ɪnˈtaɪə) *adj* **1** (*prenominal*) whole; complete. **2** (*prenominal*) without reservation or exception. **3** not broken or damaged. **4** undivided; continuous. **5** (of leaves, petals, etc.) having a smooth margin not broken up into teeth or lobes. **6** not castrated: *an entire horse.* **7** *Obs.* unmixed; pure. ◆ *n* **8** an uncastrated horse. ORIG C14: from OF, from L *integer* whole, from IN-[1] + *tangere* to touch
▸ **enˈtireness** *n*

entirely (ɪnˈtaɪəlɪ) *adv* **1** wholly; completely. **2** solely or exclusively.

entirety (ɪnˈtaɪərɪtɪ) *n, pl* **entireties. 1** the state of being entire or whole; completeness. **2** a thing, sum, amount, etc., that is entire; whole; total.

entitle (ɪnˈtaɪtᵊl) *vb* **entitles, entitling, entitled.** (*tr*) **1** to give (a person) the right to do or have something; qualify; allow. **2** to give a name or title to. **3** to confer a title of rank or honour upon. ORIG C14: from OF *entituler*, from LL, from L *titulus* TITLE
▸ **enˈtitlement** *n*

entity (ˈɛntɪtɪ) *n, pl* **entities. 1** something having real or distinct existence. **2** existence or being. ORIG C16: from Med. L, from *ēns* being, from L *esse* to be
▸ **ˈentitative** *adj*

ento- *combining form.* inside; within: *entoderm.* ORIG NL, from Gk *entos* within

entomb (ɪnˈtuːm) *vb* (*tr*) **1** to place in or as if in a tomb; bury; inter. **2** to serve as a tomb for.
▸ **enˈtombment** *n*

entomo- *combining form.* indicating an insect: *entomology.* ORIG from Gk *entomon* insect

entomol. *or* **entom.** *abbrev. for* entomology.

entomology (ˌɛntəˈmɒlədʒɪ) *n* the branch of science concerned with the study of insects.
▸ **ˌentomoˈlogical** *adj* ▸ **ˌentoˈmologist** *n*

entophyte (ˈɛntəʊˌfaɪt) *n Bot.* a variant spelling of **endophyte.**
▸ **entophytic** (ˌɛntəʊˈfɪtɪk) *adj*

entourage (ɒntʊˈrɑːʒ) *n* **1** a group of attendants or retainers; retinue. **2** surroundings. ORIG C19: from F, from *entourer* to surround, from *tour* circuit; see TOUR, TURN

entr'acte (ɒnˈtrækt) *n* **1** an interval between two acts of a play or opera. **2** (esp. formerly) an entertainment during such an interval. ORIG C19: F, lit.: between-act

entrails (ˈɛntreɪlz) *pl n* **1** the internal organs of a person or animal; intestines; guts. **2** the innermost parts of anything. ORIG C13: from OF, from Med. L *intrālia*, changed from L *interānea* intestines

entrain (ɪnˈtreɪn) *vb* to board or put aboard a train.
▸ **enˈtrainment** *n*

entrance[1] (ˈɛntrəns) *n* **1** the act or an instance of entering; entry. **2** a place for entering, such as a door. **3a** the power, liberty, or right of entering. **3b** (*as modifier*): *an entrance fee.* **4** the coming of an actor or other performer onto a stage. ORIG C16: from F, from *entrer* to ENTER

entrance[2] (ɪnˈtrɑːns) *vb* **entrances, entrancing, entranced.** (*tr*) **1** to fill with wonder and delight; enchant. **2** to put into a trance; hypnotize.
▸ **enˈtrancement** *n* ▸ **enˈtrancing** *adj*

entrant (ˈɛntrənt) *n* a person who enters. ORIG C17: from F, lit.: entering, from *entrer* to ENTER

entrap (ɪnˈtræp) *vb* **entraps, entrapping, entrapped.** (*tr*) **1** to catch or snare as in a trap. **2** to trick into danger, difficulty, or embarrassment.
▸ **enˈtrapment** *n* ▸ **enˈtrapper** *n*

entreat *or* **intreat** (ɪnˈtriːt) *vb* **1** to ask (a person) earnestly; beg or plead with; implore. **2** to make an earnest request or petition for (something). **3** an archaic word for **treat** (sense 4). ORIG C15: from OF, from EN-[1] + *traiter* to TREAT
▸ **enˈtreatment** *or* **inˈtreatment** *n*

entreaty (ɪnˈtriːtɪ) *n, pl* **entreaties.** an earnest request or petition; supplication; plea.

entrechat (*French* ɑ̃trəʃa) *n* a leap in ballet during which the dancer repeatedly crosses his or her feet or beats them together. ORIG C18: from F *entrechase*, changed by folk etymology from It. (*capriola*) *intrecciata*, lit.: entwined (caper)

entrecôte (*French* ɑ̃trəkot) *n* a beefsteak cut from between the ribs. ORIG F, from *entre-* INTER- + *côte* rib

entrée (ˈɒntreɪ) *n* **1** a dish served before a main course. **2** *Chiefly US.* the main course of a meal. **3** the power or right of entry. ORIG C18: from F, from *entrer* to ENTER; in cookery, so called because formerly the course was served after an intermediate course called the *relevé* (remove)

entremets (*French* ɑ̃trəmɛ) *n, pl* **entremets** (*French* -mɛ). **1** a dessert. **2** a light dish formerly served between the main course and the dessert. ORIG C18: from F, from OF, from *entre-* between + *mes* dish

entrench *or* **intrench** (ɪnˈtrɛntʃ) *vb* **1** (*tr*) to construct a defensive position by digging trenches around it. **2** (*tr*) to fix or establish firmly. **3** (*intr;* foll. by *on* or *upon*) to trespass or encroach.
▸ **enˈtrenched** *or* **inˈtrenched** *adj* ▸ **enˈtrenchment** *or* **inˈtrenchment** *n*

entrepôt (*French* ɑ̃trəpo) *n* **1** a warehouse for commercial goods. **2a** a trading centre or port at which goods are imported and re-exported without incurring duty. **2b** (*as modifier*): *an entrepôt trade.* ORIG C18: F, from *entreposer*, from *entre* between + *poser* to place; formed on the model of DEPOT

entrepreneur (ˌɒntrəprəˈnɜː) *n* **1** the owner or manager of a business enterprise who, by risk and initiative, attempts to make profits. **2** a middleman or commercial intermediary. ORIG C19: from F, from *entreprendre* to undertake; see ENTERPRISE
▸ **ˌentrepreˈneurial** *adj* ▸ **ˌentrepreˈneurship** *n*

entropy (ˈɛntrəpɪ) *n, pl* **entropies. 1** a thermodynamic quantity that changes in a reversible process by an amount equal to the heat absorbed or emitted divided by the thermodynamic temperature. It is measured in joules per kelvin. **2** lack of pattern or organization; disorder. ORIG C19: from EN-[2] + -TROPE

entrust *or* **intrust** (ɪnˈtrʌst) *vb* (*tr*) **1** (usually foll. by

with) to invest or charge (with a duty, responsibility, etc.). **2** (often foll. by *to)* to put into the care or protection of someone.
▸ **en'trustment** *or* **in'trustment** *n*

entry ('ɛntrɪ) *n, pl* **entries. 1** the act or an instance of entering; entrance. **2** a point or place for entering, such as a door, etc. **3a** the right or liberty of entering. **3b** *(as modifier): an entry permit.* **4** the act of recording an item in a journal, account, etc. **5** an item recorded, as in a diary, dictionary, or account. **6** a person, horse, car, etc., entering a competition or contest. **7** the competitors entering a contest considered collectively. **8** the action of an actor in going on stage. **9** *Property law.* the act of going upon land with the intention of asserting the right to possession. **10** any point in a piece of music at which a performer commences or resumes singing or playing. **11** *Bridge, etc.* a card that enables one to transfer the lead from one's own hand to that of one's partner or to the dummy hand. **12** *Dialect.* a passage between the backs of two rows of houses. ORIG C13: from OF *entree,* p.p. of *entrer* to ENTER

entryism ('ɛntrɪɪzəm) *n* the policy or practice of joining an existing political party with the intention of changing it instead of forming a new party.
▸ **'entryist** *n, adj*

entry-level *adj* **1** (of a job or worker) at the most elementary level in a career structure. **2** (of a product) characterized by being at the most appropriate level for use by a beginner: *an entry-level camera.*

entwine *or* **intwine** (ɪn'twaɪn) *vb* **entwines, entwining, entwined** *or* **intwines, intwining, intwined.** (of two or more things) to twine together or (of one or more things) to twine around (something else).
▸ **en'twinement** *or* **in'twinement** *n*

Enugu ★ (ɛ'nu:gu:) *n* **1** a city in S Nigeria, capital of Enugu state: capital of the former Eastern region and of the breakaway state of Biafra during the Civil War (1967–70): coal-mining. Pop.: 316 100 (1996 est.). **2** a state in S Nigeria. Capital: Enugu. Pop.: 3 534 633 (1995 est.). Area: 12 831 sq. km (4954 sq. miles).

E number *n* any of a series of numbers with the prefix E indicating a specific food additive recognized by the European Union.

enumerate (ɪ'nju:məˌreɪt) *vb* **enumerates, enumerating, enumerated.** *(tr)* **1** to name one by one; list. **2** to determine the number of; count. **3** *Canad.* to compile or enter (a name or names) in a voting list for an area. ORIG C17: from L, from *numerāre* to count, reckon; see NUMBER
▸ **e'numerable** *adj* ▸ **eˌnumer'ation** *n* ▸ **e'numerative** *adj*

enumerator (ɪ'nju:məˌreɪtə) *n* **1** a person or thing that enumerates. **2** *Brit.* a person who issues and retrieves census forms.

enunciable (ɪ'nʌnsɪəbᵊl) *adj* capable of being enunciated.

enunciate (ɪ'nʌnsɪˌeɪt) *vb* **enunciates, enunciating, enunciated. 1** to articulate or pronounce (words), esp. clearly and distinctly. **2** *(tr)* to state precisely or formally. ORIG C17: from L *ēnuntiāre* to declare, from *nuntiāre* to announce
▸ **eˌnunci'ation** *n* ▸ **e'nunciative** *or* **e'nunciatory** *adj*
▸ **e'nunciˌator** *n*

enuresis (ˌɛnjʊ'ri:sɪs) *n* involuntary discharge of urine, esp. during sleep. ORIG C19: from NL, from Gk EN-[2] + *ouron* urine
▸ **enuretic** (ˌɛnjʊ'rɛtɪk) *adj, n*

envelop (ɪn'vɛləp) *vb* **envelops, enveloping, enveloped.** *(tr)* **1** to wrap or enclose as in a covering. **2** to conceal or obscure. **3** to surround (an enemy force). ORIG C14: from OF *envoluper,* from EN-[1] + *voluper, voloper,* from ?
▸ **en'velopment** *n*

envelope ('ɛnvəˌləʊp, 'ɒn-) *n* **1** a flat covering of paper, usually rectangular and with a flap that can be sealed, used to enclose a letter, etc. **2** any covering or wrapper. **3** *Biol.* any enclosing structure, such as a membrane, shell, or skin. **4** the bag enclosing gas in a balloon. **5** *Maths.* a curve or surface that is tangential to each one of a group of curves or surfaces. **6 push the envelope.** *Inf.* to push the boundaries of what is possible. ORIG C18: from F, from *envelopper* to wrap around; see ENVELOP; sense 6 from aeronautics jargon, referring to graphs of aircraft performance

envenom (ɪn'vɛnəm) *vb (tr)* **1** to fill or impregnate with venom; make poisonous. **2** to fill with bitterness or malice.

Enver Pasha ★ ('ɛnvə 'pɑ:ʃə) *n* 1881–1922, Turkish soldier and leader of the Young Turks: minister of war (1914–18).

enviable ('ɛnvɪəbᵊl) *adj* exciting envy; fortunate or privileged.
▸ **'enviableness** *n*

envious ('ɛnvɪəs) *adj* feeling, showing, or resulting from envy. ORIG C13: from Anglo-Norman, ult. from L *invidiōsus* full of envy, INVIDIOUS; see ENVY
▸ **'enviously** *adv* ▸ **'enviousness** *n*

environ (ɪn'vaɪrən) *vb (tr)* to encircle or surround. ORIG C14: from OF *environner* to surround, from EN-[1] + *viron* a circle, from *virer* to turn, VEER

environment (ɪn'vaɪrənmənt) *n* **1** external conditions or surroundings. **2** *Ecology.* the external surroundings in which a plant or animal lives, which influence its development and behaviour. **3** *Computing.* an operating system, program, or integrated suite of programs that provides all the facilities necessary for a particular application: *a word-processing environment.*
▸ **enˌviron'mental** *adj*

environmentalist (ɪnˌvaɪrən'mɛntəlɪst) *n* **1** a specialist in the maintenance of ecological balance and the conservation of the environment. **2** a person concerned with issues that affect the environment, such as pollution.

environs (ɪn'vaɪrənz) *pl n* a surrounding area or region, esp. the suburbs or outskirts of a city.

envisage (ɪn'vɪzɪdʒ) *vb* **envisages, envisaging, envisaged.** *(tr)* **1** to form a mental image of; visualize. **2** to conceive of as a possibility in the future. ORIG C19: from F, from EN-[1] + *visage* face, VISAGE
▸ **en'visagement** *n*

envision (ɪn'vɪʒən) *vb (tr)* to conceive of as a possibility, esp. in the future; foresee.

envoy[1] ('ɛnvɔɪ) *n* **1** Also called: **minister, minister plenipotentiary.** a diplomat ranking between an ambassador and a minister resident. **2** an accredited agent or representative. ORIG C17: from F, from *envoyer* to send, from Vulgar L *inviāre* (unattested) to send on a journey, from IN-[2] + *via* road
▸ **'envoyship** *n*

envoy[2] *or* **envoi** ('ɛnvɔɪ) *n* **1** a brief concluding stanza, notably in ballades. **2** a postscript in other forms of verse or prose. ORIG C14: from OF, from *envoyer* to send; see ENVOY[1]

envy ('ɛnvɪ) *n, pl* **envies. 1** a feeling of grudging or somewhat admiring discontent aroused by the possessions, achievements, or qualities of another. **2** the desire to have something possessed by another; covetousness. **3** an object of envy. ◆ *vb* **envies, envying, envied. 4** to be envious of (a person or thing). ORIG C13: via OF from L *invidia,* from *invidēre* to eye maliciously, from IN-[2] + *vidēre* to see
▸ **'envier** *n* ▸ **'envyingly** *adv*

enwrap *or* **inwrap** (ɪn'ræp) *vb* **enwraps, enwrapping, enwrapped.** *(tr)* **1** to wrap or cover up; envelop. **2** *(usually passive)* to engross or absorb.

enwreath (ɪn'ri:ð) *vb (tr)* to surround or encircle with or as with a wreath or wreaths.

Enzed ★ ('ɛn'zɛd) *n Austral & NZ inf.* **1** New Zealand. **2** Also called: **'En'zedder.** a New Zealander.

enzootic (ˌɛnzəʊ'ɒtɪk) *adj* **1** (of diseases) affecting animals within a limited region. ◆ *n* **2** an enzootic disease. ORIG C19: from EN-[2] + Gk *zōion* animal + -OTIC
▸ **ˌenzo'otically** *adv*

enzyme ('ɛnzaɪm) *n* any of a group of complex proteins produced by living cells, that act as catalysts in specific biochemical reactions. ORIG C19: from Med. Gk *enzumos* leavened, from Gk EN-[2] + *zumē* leaven

▸ **enzymatic** (ˌɛnzaɪˈmætɪk, -zɪ-) *or* **enzymic** (ɛnˈzaɪmɪk, -ˈzɪm-) *adj*

enzyme-linked immunosorbent assay (ˌɪmjʊnəʊˈsɔːbənt) *n* the full name for **ELISA.**

eo- *combining form.* early or primeval: *Eocene; eohippus.* ORIG from Gk, from *ēōs* dawn

EOC *abbrev. for* Equal Opportunities Commission.

Eocene (ˈiːəʊˌsiːn) *adj* **1** of or denoting the second epoch of the Tertiary period, during which hooved mammals appeared. ◆ *n* **2 the.** the Eocene epoch or rock series. ORIG C19: from EO- + -CENE

eohippus (ˌiːəʊˈhɪpəs) *n, pl* **eohippuses.** the earliest horse: an extinct Eocene dog-sized animal. ORIG C19: NL, from EO- + Gk *hippos* horse

Eolithic (ˌiːəʊˈlɪθɪk) *adj* denoting or relating to the early part of the Stone Age, characterized by the use of crude stone tools (**eoliths**).

eon (ˈiːən, ˈiːɒn) *n* **1** the usual US spelling of **aeon. 2** *Geol.* the longest division of geological time, comprising two or more eras.

Eos ★ (ˈiːɒs) *n Greek myth.* the winged goddess of the dawn, the daughter of Hyperion. Roman counterpart: **Aurora.**

eosin (ˈiːəʊsɪn) *or* **eosine** (ˈiːəʊsɪn, -ˌsiːn) *n* **1** a red fluorescent crystalline water-insoluble compound. Its soluble salts are used as dyes. **2** any of several similar dyes. ORIG C19: from Gk *ēōs* dawn + -IN; referring to colour it gives to silk

Eötvös ★ (*Hungarian* ˈøtvøʃ) *n* Baron **Roland von.** 1848–1919, Hungarian physicist noted for his studies of gravity.

-eous *suffix forming adjectives.* relating to or having the nature of: *gaseous.* ORIG from L *-eus*

EP *n* an extended-play gramophone record, usually 7 inches (18 cm) in diameter: a longer recording than a single.

EPA *abbrev. for* eicosapentaenoic acid: a fatty acid, found in certain fish oils, that can reduce blood cholesterol.

epact (ˈiːpækt) *n* **1** the difference in time, about 11 days, between the solar year and the lunar year. **2** the number of days between the beginning of the calendar year and the new moon immediately preceding this. ORIG C16: via LL from Gk *epaktē,* from *epagein* to bring in, intercalate

Epaminondas ★ (ɛˌpæmɪˈnɒndæs) *n* ?418–362 B.C., Greek Theban statesman and general: defeated the Spartans at Leuctra (371) and Mantinea (362) and restored power in Greece to Thebes.

eparch (ˈɛpɑːk) *n* **1** a bishop or metropolitan in the Orthodox Church. **2** a governor of a subdivision of a province of modern Greece. ORIG C17: from Gk *eparkhos,* from *epi-* over, on + -ARCH

▸ **ˈeparchy** *n*

epaulette *or US* **epaulet** (ˈɛpəˌlɛt, -lɪt) *n* a piece of ornamental material on the shoulder of a garment, esp. a military uniform. ORIG C18: from F, from *épaule* shoulder, from L *spatula* shoulder blade

épée (ˈɛpeɪ) *n* a sword similar to the foil but with a heavier blade. ORIG C19: from F: sword, from L *spatha,* from Gk *spathē* blade; see SPADE[1]

▸ **ˈépéeist** *n*

epeirogeny (ˌɛpaɪˈrɒdʒɪnɪ) *or* **epeirogenesis** (ɪˌpaɪrəʊˈdʒɛnɪsɪs) *n* the formation of continents by relatively slow displacements of the earth's crust. ORIG C19: from Gk *ēpeiros* continent + -GENY

▸ **epeirogenic** (ɪˌpaɪrəʊˈdʒɛnɪk) *or* **epeirogenetic** (ɪˌpaɪrəʊdʒɪˈnɛtɪk) *adj*

epergne (ɪˈpɜːn) *n* an ornamental centrepiece for a table, holding fruit, flowers, etc. ORIG C18: prob. from F *épargne* a saving, from *épargner* to economize, of Gmc origin

epexegesis (ɛˌpɛksɪˈdʒiːsɪs) *n, pl* **epexegesises** (-ˌsiːz). *Rhetoric.* **1** the addition of a phrase, clause, or sentence to a text to provide further explanation. **2** the phrase, clause, or sentence added for this purpose. ORIG C17: from Gk; see EPI-, EXEGESIS

▸ **epexegetic** (ɛˌpɛksɪˈdʒɛtɪk) *or* **epˌexeˈgetical** *adj*

Eph. *or* **Ephes.** *Bible. abbrev. for* Ephesians.

ephah *or* **epha** (ˈiːfə) *n* a Hebrew unit of measure equal to approximately one bushel or about 33 litres. ORIG C16: from Heb., from Egyptian

ephedrine *or* **ephedrin** (ɪˈfɛdrɪn, ˈɛfɪˌdriːn, -drɪn) *n* a white crystalline alkaloid used for the treatment of asthma and hay fever. ORIG C19: from NL from L from Gk, from EPI- + *hedra* seat + -INE[2]

ephemera (ɪˈfɛmərə) *n, pl* **ephemeras** *or* **ephemerae** (-əˌriː). **1** a mayfly, esp. one of the genus *Ephemera.* **2** something transitory or short-lived. **3** (*functioning as pl*) collectable items not originally intended to be long-lasting, such as tickets, posters, etc. **4** a plural of **ephemeron.** ORIG C16: see EPHEMERAL

ephemeral (ɪˈfɛmərəl) *adj* **1** transitory; short-lived: *ephemeral pleasure.* ◆ *n* **2** a short-lived organism, such as the mayfly. ORIG C16: from Gk *ephēmeros* lasting only a day, from *hēmera* day

▸ **eˌphemerˈality** *or* **eˈphemeralness** *n*

ephemerid (ɪˈfɛmərɪd) *n* any insect of the order *Ephemeroptera* (or *Ephemerida*), which comprises the mayflies. Also: **ephemeropteran.** ORIG C19: from NL, from Gk *ephēmeros* short-lived + -ID[1]

ephemeris (ɪˈfɛmərɪs) *n, pl* **ephemerides** (ˌɛfɪˈmɛrɪˌdiːz). a table giving the future positions of a planet, comet, or satellite during a specified period. ORIG C16: from L, from Gk: diary, journal; see EPHEMERAL

ephemeron (ɪˈfɛməˌrɒn) *n, pl* **ephemera** (-ərə) *or* **ephemerons.** (*usually pl*). something transitory or short-lived. ORIG C16: see EPHEMERAL

Ephesus ★ (ˈɛfɪsəs) *n* (in ancient Greece) a major trading city on the W coast of Asia Minor: famous for its temple of Artemis (Diana); sacked by the Goths (262 A.D.).

ephod (ˈiːfɒd) *n Bible.* an embroidered vestment worn by priests in ancient Israel. ORIG C14: from Heb.

ephor (ˈɛfɔː) *n, pl* **ephors** *or* **ephori** (-əˌraɪ) (in ancient Greece) a senior magistrate, esp. one of the five Spartan ephors, who wielded effective power. ORIG C16: from Gk, from *ephoran* to supervise, from EPI- + *horan* to look

▸ **ˈephoral** *adj* ▸ **ˈephorate** *n*

Ephraim ★ (ˈiːfreɪɪm) *n Old Testament.* **1a** the younger son of Joseph, who received the principal blessing of his grandfather Jacob (Genesis 48:8–22). **1b** the tribe descended from him. **1c** the territory of this tribe, west of the River Jordan. **2** the northern kingdom of Israel after the kingdom of Solomon had been divided into two.

Ephraimite ★ (ˈiːfreɪɪˌmaɪt) *n* a member of the tribe of Ephraim.

epi-, eph-, *or before a vowel* **ep-** *prefix* **1** upon; above; over: *epidermis; epicentre.* **2** in addition to: *epiphenomenon.* **3** after: *epilogue.* **4** near; close to: *epicalyx.* ORIG from Gk, from *epi* (prep)

epic (ˈɛpɪk) *n* **1** a long narrative poem recounting in elevated style the deeds of a legendary hero. **2** the genre of epic poetry. **3** any work of literature, film, etc., having qualities associated with the epic. **4** an episode in the lives of men in which heroic deeds are performed. ◆ *adj* **5** denoting, relating to, or characteristic of an epic or epics. **6** of heroic or impressive proportions. ORIG C16: from L, from Gk *epikos,* from *epos* speech, word, song

epicalyx (ˌɛpɪˈkeɪlɪks, -ˈkæl-) *n, pl* **epicalyxes** *or* **epicalyces** (-lɪˌsiːz). *Bot.* a series of small sepal-like bracts forming an outer calyx beneath the true calyx in some flowers.

epicanthus (ˌɛpɪˈkænθəs) *n, pl* **epicanthi** (-θaɪ). a fold of skin extending vertically over the inner angle of the eye: characteristic of Mongolian peoples. ORIG C19: NL, from EPI- + L *canthus* corner of the eye, from Gk *kanthos*

▸ **ˌepiˈcanthic** *adj*

epicardium (ˌɛpɪˈkɑːdɪəm) *n, pl* **epicardia** (-dɪə). *Anat.* the innermost layer of the pericardium. ORIG C19: NL, from EPI- + Gk *kardia* heart

▸ **ˌepiˈcardiac** *or* **ˌepiˈcardial** *adj*

epicarp (ˈɛpɪˌkɑːp) *or* **exocarp** *n* the outermost layer of the pericarp of fruits. ORIG C19: from F, from EPI- + Gk *karpos* fruit

epicene (ˈɛpɪˌsiːn) *adj* **1** having the characteristics of

both sexes. **2** of neither sex; sexless. **3** effeminate. **4** *Grammar.* **4a** denoting a noun that may refer to a male or a female. **4b** (in Latin, Greek, etc.) denoting a noun that retains the same gender regardless of the sex of the referent. ORIG C15: from L *epicoenus* of both genders, from Gk *epikoinos* common to many, from *koinos* common
▸ **ˌepiˈcenism** *n*

epicentre *or US* **epicenter** (ˈɛpɪˌsɛntə) *n* the point on the earth's surface immediately above the origin of an earthquake. ORIG C19: from NL, from Gk *epikentros* over the centre, from EPI- + CENTRE
▸ **ˌepiˈcentral** *adj*

Epictetus ★ (ˌɛpɪkˈtiːtəs) *n* ?50–?120 A.D., Greek Stoic philosopher, who stressed self-renunciation and the brotherhood of man.

epicure (ˈɛpɪˌkjʊə) *n* **1** a person who cultivates a discriminating palate for good food and drink. **2** a person devoted to sensual pleasures. ORIG C16: from Med. L *epicūrus,* after EPICURUS
▸ **ˈepicurˌism** *n*

epicurean (ˌɛpɪkjʊˈriːən) *adj* **1** devoted to sensual pleasures, esp. food and drink. **2** suitable for an epicure. ◆ *n* **3** an epicure; gourmet.
▸ **ˌepicuˈreanˌism** *n*

Epicurean (ˌɛpɪkjʊˈriːən) *adj* **1** of or relating to the philosophy of Epicurus. ◆ *n* **2** a follower of the philosophy of Epicurus.
▸ **ˌEpicuˈreanˌism** *n*

Epicurus ★ (ˌɛpɪˈkjʊərəs) *n* 341–270 B.C., Greek philosopher, who held that the highest good is pleasure and that the world is a series of fortuitous combinations of atoms.

epicycle (ˈɛpɪˌsaɪkᵊl) *n* a circle that rolls around the inside or outside of another circle. ORIG C14: from LL, from Gk; see EPI-, CYCLE
▸ **epicyclic** (ˌɛpɪˈsaɪklɪk, -ˈsɪklɪk) *or* **ˌepiˈcyclical** *adj*

epicyclic train *n* a cluster of gears consisting of a central gearwheel, a coaxial gearwheel of greater diameter, and one or more planetary gears engaging with both of them.

epicycloid (ˌɛpɪˈsaɪklɔɪd) *n* the curve described by a point on the circumference of a circle as this circle rolls around the outside of another fixed circle.
▸ **ˌepicyˈcloidal** *adj*

Epidaurus ★ (ˌɛpɪˈdɔːrəs; *Greek* ɛˈpiðavrɔs) *n* an ancient port in Greece, in the NE Peloponnese, in Argolis on the Saronic Gulf.

epideictic (ˌɛpɪˈdaɪktɪk) *adj* designed to display something, esp. the skill of the speaker in rhetoric. Also: **epidictic** (ˌɛpɪˈdɪktɪk). ORIG C18: from Gk, from *epideiknunai* to display, from *deiknunai* to show

epidemic (ˌɛpɪˈdɛmɪk) *adj* **1** (esp. of a disease) attacking or affecting many persons simultaneously in a community or area. ◆ *n* **2** a widespread occurrence of a disease. **3** a rapid development, spread, or growth of something. ORIG C17: from F, via LL from Gk *epidēmia,* lit.: among the people, from EPI- + *dēmos* people
▸ **ˌepiˈdemically** *adv*

epidemiology (ˌɛpɪˌdiːmɪˈɒlədʒɪ) *n* the branch of medical science concerned with the occurrence, distribution, and control of diseases in populations.
▸ **epidemiological** (ˌɛpɪˌdiːmɪəˈlɒdʒɪkᵊl) *adj* ▸ **ˌepiˌdemiˈologist** *n*

epidermis (ˌɛpɪˈdɜːmɪs) *n* **1** the thin protective outer layer of the skin. **2** the outer layer of cells of an invertebrate. **3** the outer protective layer of cells of a plant. ORIG C17: via LL from Gk, from EPI- + *derma* skin
▸ **ˌepiˈdermal, ˌepiˈdermic,** *or* **ˌepiˈdermoid** *adj*

epidiascope (ˌɛpɪˈdaɪəˌskəʊp) *n* an optical device for projecting a magnified image onto a screen.

epididymis (ˌɛpɪˈdɪdɪmɪs) *n, pl* **epididymides** (-dɪˈdɪmɪˌdiːz). *Anat.* a convoluted tube behind each testis, in which spermatozoa are stored and conveyed to the vas deferens. ORIG C17: from Gk *epididumis,* from EPI- + *didumos* twin, testicle

epidural (ˌɛpɪˈdjʊərəl) *adj* **1** Also: **extradural.** upon or outside the dura mater. ◆ *n* **2** Also: **epidural anaesthesia, spinal anaesthesia. 2a** injection of anaesthetic into the space outside the dura mater enveloping the spinal cord. **2b** anaesthesia induced by this method. ORIG C19: from EPI- + DUR(A MATER) + -AL[1]

epigamic (ˌɛpɪˈgæmɪk) *adj Zool.* attractive to the opposite sex: *epigamic coloration.*

epigeal (ˌɛpɪˈdʒiːəl), **epigean,** *or* **epigeous** *adj* **1** of or relating to seed germination in which the cotyledons appear above the ground. **2** living or growing on or close to the surface of the ground. ORIG C19: from Gk *epigeios* of the earth, from EPI- + *gē* earth

epiglottis (ˌɛpɪˈglɒtɪs) *n, pl* **epiglottises** *or* **epiglottides** (-tɪˌdiːz). a thin cartilaginous flap that covers the entrance to the larynx during swallowing, preventing food from entering the trachea.
▸ **ˌepiˈglottal** *or* **ˌepiˈglottic** *adj*

Epigoni ★ (ɪˈpɪgəˌnaɪ) *pl n, sing* **-onus** (-ənəs). *Greek myth.* the descendants of the Seven against Thebes, who undertook a second expedition against the city and eventually captured and destroyed it. ORIG C20: from Gk *epigonoi* those born after

epigram (ˈɛpɪˌgræm) *n* **1** a witty, often paradoxical remark, concisely expressed. **2** a short poem, esp. one having a witty and ingenious ending. ORIG C15: from L *epigramma,* from Gk: inscription, from *graphein* to write
▸ **ˌepigramˈmatic** *adj* ▸ **ˌepigramˈmatically** *adv*

epigrammatize *or* **epigrammatise** (ˌɛpɪˈgræməˌtaɪz) *vb* **epigrammatizes, epigrammatizing, epigrammatized** *or* **epigrammatises, epigrammatising, epigrammatised.** to make an epigram (about).
▸ **ˌepiˈgrammatism** *n* ▸ **ˌepiˈgrammatist** *n*

epigraph (ˈɛpɪˌgrɑːf) *n* **1** a quotation at the beginning of a book, chapter, etc. **2** an inscription on a monument or building. ORIG C17: from Gk; see EPIGRAM
▸ **epigraphic** (ˌɛpɪˈgræfɪk) or **ˌepiˈgraphical** *adj*

epigraphy (ɪˈpɪgrəfɪ) *n* **1** the study of ancient inscriptions. **2** epigraphs collectively.
▸ **eˈpigraphist** *or* **eˈpigrapher** *n*

epilator (ˈɛpɪˌleɪtə) *n* an electrical appliance consisting of a metal spiral head that rotates at high speed, plucking unwanted hair.

epilepsy (ˈɛpɪˌlɛpsɪ) *n* a disorder of the central nervous system characterized by periodic loss of consciousness with or without convulsions. ORIG C16: from LL *epilēpsia,* from Gk, from *epilambanein* to attack, seize

epileptic (ˌɛpɪˈlɛptɪk) *adj* **1** of, relating to, or having epilepsy. ◆ *n* **2** a person who has epilepsy.
▸ **ˌepiˈleptically** *adv*

epilogue (ˈɛpɪˌlɒg) *n* **1a** a speech addressed to the audience by an actor at the end of a play. **1b** the actor speaking this. **2** a short postscript to any literary work. **3** *Brit.* the concluding programme of the day on a radio or television station. ORIG C15: from L, from Gk *epilogos,* from *logos* word, speech
▸ **epilogist** (ɪˈpɪlədʒɪst) *n*

epinephrine (ˌɛpɪˈnɛfrɪn, -riːn) *or* **epinephrin** *n* a US name for **adrenaline.** ORIG C19: from EPI- + *nephro-* + -INE[2]

epiphany (ɪˈpɪfənɪ) *n, pl* **epiphanies. 1** the manifestation of a supernatural or divine reality. **2** any moment of great or sudden revelation.
▸ **epiphanic** (ˌɛpɪˈfænɪk) *adj*

Epiphany (ɪˈpɪfənɪ) *n, pl* **Epiphanies.** a Christian festival held on Jan. 6, commemorating, in the Western Church, the manifestation of Christ to the Magi. ORIG C17: via Church L from Gk *epiphaneia* an appearing, from EPI- + *phainein* to show

epiphenomenon (ˌɛpɪfɪˈnɒmɪnən) *n, pl* **epiphenomenona** (-nə). **1** a secondary or additional phenomenon. **2** *Philosophy.* mind or consciousness regarded as a by-product of the biological activity of the human brain. **3** *Pathol.* an unexpected symptom or occurrence during the course of a disease.
▸ **ˌepipheˈnomenal** *adj*

epiphyte (ˈɛpɪˌfaɪt) *n* a plant that grows on another plant but is not parasitic on it. ORIG C19: via NL from Gk, from EPI- + *phusis* growth
▸ **epiphytic** (ˌɛpɪˈfɪtɪk), **ˌepiˈphytal,** *or* **ˌepiˈphytical** *adj*

Epirus ★ (ɪ'paɪərəs) *n* **1** a region of NW Greece, part of ancient Epirus ceded to Greece after independence in 1830. **2** (in ancient Greece) a region between the Pindus mountains and the Ionian Sea, straddling the modern border with Albania.

Epis. *abbrev. for:* **1** Also: **Episc.** Episcopal *or* Episcopalian. **2** *Bible.* Also: **Epist.** Epistle.

episcopacy (ɪ'pɪskəpəsɪ) *n, pl* **episcopacies. 1** government of a Church by bishops. **2** another word for **episcopate.**

episcopal (ɪ'pɪskəpᵊl) *adj* of, denoting, governed by, or relating to a bishop or bishops. ORIG C15: from Church L, from *episcopus* BISHOP

Episcopal (ɪ'pɪskəpᵊl) *adj* of or denoting the Episcopal Church, an autonomous church of Scotland and the US which is in full communion with the Church of England.

episcopalian (ɪˌpɪskə'peɪlɪən) *adj also* **episcopal. 1** practising or advocating the principle of Church government by bishops. ◆ *n* **2** an advocate of such Church government.
▸ **eˌpiscoˈpalianism** *n*

Episcopalian (ɪˌpɪskə'peɪlɪən) *adj* **1** belonging to or denoting the Episcopal Church. ◆ *n* **2** a member or adherent of this Church.

episcopate (ɪ'pɪskəpɪt, -ˌpeɪt) *n* **1** the office, status, or term of office of a bishop. **2** bishops collectively.

episiotomy (ɪˌpiːzɪ'ɒtəmɪ) *n, pl* **episiotomies.** surgical incision into the perineum during labour to prevent its laceration during childbirth. ORIG C20: from Gk *epision* pubic region + -TOMY

episode ('ɛpɪˌsəʊd) *n* **1** an event or series of events. **2** any of the sections into which a serialized novel or radio or television programme is divided. **3** an incident or sequence that forms part of a narrative but may be a digression from the main story. **4** (in ancient Greek tragedy) a section between two choric songs. **5** *Music.* a contrasting section between statements of the subject, as in a fugue. ORIG C17: from Gk *epeisodion* something added, from *epi-* (in addition) + *eisodios* coming in, from *eis-* in + *hodos* road

episodic (ˌɛpɪ'sɒdɪk) *or* **episodical** *adj* **1** resembling or relating to an episode. **2** divided into episodes. **3** irregular or sporadic.
▸ **ˌepiˈsodically** *adv*

epistaxis (ˌɛpɪ'stæksɪs) *n* the technical name for **nosebleed.** ORIG C18: from Gk: a dropping, from *epistazein* to drop on, from *stazein* to drip

epistemology (ɪˌpɪstɪ'mɒlədʒɪ) *n* the theory of knowledge, esp. the critical study of its validity, methods, and scope. ORIG C19: from Gk *epistēmē* knowledge
▸ **epistemological** (ɪˌpɪstɪmə'lɒdʒɪkᵊl) *adj* ▸ **eˌpisteˈmologist** *n*

epistle (ɪ'pɪsᵊl) *n* **1** a letter, esp. one that is long, formal, or didactic. **2** a literary work in letter form, esp. a verse letter. ORIG OE *epistol,* via L from Gk *epistolē*

Epistle (ɪ'pɪsᵊl) *n* **1** *Bible.* any of the letters of the apostles. **2** a reading from one of the Epistles, part of the Eucharistic service in many Christian Churches.

epistolary (ɪ'pɪstələrɪ) *or* (*arch.*) **epistolatory** *adj* **1** relating to, denoting, conducted by, or contained in letters. **2** (of a novel, etc.) in the form of a series of letters.

epistyle ('ɛpɪˌstaɪl) *n* another name for **architrave** (sense 1). ORIG C17: via L from Gk, from EPI- + *stulos* column, STYLE

epitaph ('ɛpɪˌtɑːf) *n* **1** a commemorative inscription on a tombstone or monument. **2** a commemorative speech or written passage. **3** a final judgment on a person or thing. ORIG C14: via L from Gk, from EPI- + *taphos* tomb
▸ **epitaphic** (ˌɛpɪ'tæfɪk) *adj* ▸ **ˈepiˌtaphist** *n*

epitaxy ('ɛpɪˌtæksɪ) *n* the growth of a layer of one substance on the surface of a crystal so that the layer has the same structure as the underlying crystal.
▸ **epitaxial** (ˌɛpɪ'tæksɪəl) *adj*

epithalamium (ˌɛpɪθə'leɪmɪəm) *or* **epithalamion** *n, pl* **epithalamia** (-mɪə). a poem or song written to celebrate a marriage. ORIG C17: from L, from Gk *epithalamion* marriage song, from *thalamos* bridal chamber
▸ **epithalamic** (ˌɛpɪθə'læmɪk) *adj*

epithelium (ˌɛpɪ'θiːlɪəm) *n, pl* **epitheliums** *or* **epithelia** (-lɪə). an animal cellular tissue covering the external and internal surfaces of the body. ORIG C18: NL, from EPI- + Gk *thēlē* nipple
▸ **ˌepiˈthelial** *adj*

epithet ('ɛpɪˌθɛt) *n* a descriptive word or phrase added to or substituted for a person's name. ORIG C16: from L, from Gk, from *epitithenai* to add, from *tithenai* to put
▸ **ˌepiˈthetic** *or* **ˌepiˈthetical** *adj*

epitome (ɪ'pɪtəmɪ) *n* **1** a typical example of a characteristic or class; embodiment; personification. **2** a summary of a written work; abstract. ORIG C16: via L from Gk, from *epitemnein* to abridge, from EPI- + *temnein* to cut
▸ **epitomical** (ˌɛpɪ'tɒmɪkᵊl) *or* **ˌepiˈtomic** *adj*

epitomize *or* **epitomise** (ɪ'pɪtəˌmaɪz) *vb* **epitomizes, epitomizing, epitomized** *or* **epitomises, epitomising, epitomised.** (*tr*) **1** to be a personification of; typify. **2** to make an epitome of.
▸ **eˈpitomist** *n* ▸ **eˌpitomiˈzation** *or* **eˌpitomiˈsation** *n*

epizootic (ˌɛpɪzəʊ'ɒtɪk) *adj* **1** (of a disease) suddenly and temporarily affecting a large number of animals. ◆ *n* **2** an epizootic disease.

EPNS *abbrev. for* electroplated nickel silver.

epoch ('iːpɒk) *n* **1** a point in time beginning a new or distinctive period. **2** a long period of time marked by some predominant characteristic; era. **3** *Astron.* a precise date to which information relating to a celestial body is referred. **4** a unit of geological time within a period during which a series of rocks is formed. ORIG C17: from NL, from Gk *epokhē* cessation
▸ **epochal** ('ɛpˌɒkᵊl) *adj*

epode ('ɛpəʊd) *n Greek prosody.* **1** the part of a lyric ode that follows the strophe and the antistrophe. **2** a type of lyric poem composed of couplets in which a long line is followed by a shorter one. ORIG C16: via L from Gk, from *epaidein* to sing after, from *aidein* to sing

eponym ('ɛpənɪm) *n* **1** a name, esp. a place name, derived from the name of a real or mythical person. **2** the name of the person from which such a name is derived. ORIG C19: from Gk *epōnumos* giving a significant name
▸ **eˈponymy** *n*

eponymous (ɪ'pɒnɪməs) *adj* **1** (of a person) being the person after whom a literary work, film, etc., is named: *the eponymous heroine in the film of Jane Eyre.* **2** (of a literary work, film, etc.) named after its central character or creator: *The Stooges' eponymous debut album.*
▸ **eˈponymously** *adv*

EPOS ('iːpɒs) *n acronym for* electronic point of sale.

epoxidize *or* **epoxidise** *vb* **epoxidizes, epoxidizing, epoxidized** *or* **epoxidises, epoxidising, epoxidised.** (*tr*) to convert into or treat with an epoxy resin.

epoxy (ɪ'pɒksɪ) *adj Chem.* **1** of, consisting of, or containing an oxygen atom joined to two different groups that are themselves joined to other groups: *epoxy group.* **2** of, relating to, or consisting of an epoxy resin. ◆ *n, pl* **epoxies. 3** short for **epoxy resin.** ORIG C20: from EPI- + OXY-[2]

epoxy *or* **epoxide resin** (ɪ'pɒksaɪd) *n* any of various tough resistant thermosetting synthetic resins containing epoxy groups: used in surface coatings, laminates, and adhesives.

Epping ★ ('ɛpɪŋ) *n* a town in E England, in Essex, on the edge of Epping Forest: a residential centre for London. Pop.: 9922 (1991).

Epping Forest ★ *n* a forest in E England, northeast of London: formerly a royal hunting ground.

eps *abbrev. for* earnings per share.

epsilon ('ɛpsɪˌlɒn) *n* the fifth letter of the Greek alphabet (Ε, ε). ORIG Gk *e psilon,* lit.: simple *e*

Epsom ★ ('ɛpsəm) *n* a town in SE England, in Surrey: famous for its mineral springs and for horse racing. Pop. (with Ewell): 64 405 (1991).

Epsom salts *n* (*functioning as sing or pl*) a medicinal preparation of hydrated magnesium sulphate, used as a purgative, etc. ORIG C18: after EPSOM, where they occur in the water

Epstein ★ ('ɛpstaɪn) *n* Sir **Jacob.** 1880–1959, British sculptor, born in the US of Russo-Polish parents.

equable ('ɛkwəbᵊl) *adj* **1** even-tempered; placid. **2** unvarying; uniform: *an equable climate.* ORIG C17: from L *aequābilis,* from *aequāre* to make equal
▸ ˌ**equa'bility** *or* '**equableness** *n*

equal ('iːkwəl) *adj* **1** (often foll. by *to* or *with*) identical in size, quantity, degree, intensity, etc. **2** having identical privileges, rights, status, etc. **3** having uniform effect or application: *equal opportunities.* **4** evenly balanced or proportioned. **5** (usually foll. by *to*) having the necessary or adequate strength, ability, means, etc. (for). ◆ *n* **6** a person or thing equal to another, esp. in merit, ability, etc. ◆ *vb* **equals, equalling, equalled** *or US* **equals, equaling, equaled. 7** (*tr*) to be equal to; match. **8** (*intr;* usually foll. by *out*) to become equal. **9** (*tr*) to make or do something equal to. ORIG C14: from L *aequālis,* from *aequus* level
▸ '**equally** *adv*

equalitarian (ɪˌkwɒlɪ'tɛərɪən) *adj, n* a less common word for **egalitarian.**
▸ **eˌquali'tarianism** *n*

equality (ɪ'kwɒlɪtɪ) *n, pl* **equalities.** the state of being equal.

equalize *or* **equalise** ('iːkwəˌlaɪz) *vb* **equalizes, equalizing, equalized** *or* **equalises, equalising, equalised. 1** (*tr*) to make equal or uniform. **2** (*intr*) (in sports) to reach the same score as one's opponent or opponents.
▸ ˌ**equali'zation** *or* ˌ**equali'sation** *n*

equal opportunity *n* **a** the offering of employment, pay, or promotion without discrimination as to sex, race, etc. **b** (*as modifier*): *an equal-opportunities employer.*

equal sign *or* **equals sign** *n* the symbol =, used to indicate a mathematical equality.

equanimity (ˌiːkwə'nɪmɪtɪ, ˌɛkwə-) *n* calmness of mind or temper; composure. ORIG C17: from L, from *aequus* even, EQUAL + *animus* mind, spirit
▸ **equanimous** (ɪ'kwænɪməs) *adj*

equate (ɪ'kweɪt) *vb* **equates, equating, equated.** (*mainly tr*) **1** to make or regard as equivalent or similar. **2** *Maths.* to indicate the equality of; form an equation from. **3** (*intr*) to be equal. ORIG C15: from L *aequāre* to make EQUAL
▸ **e'quatable** *adj* ▸ **eˌquata'bility** *n*

equation (ɪ'kweɪʒən, -ʃən) *n* **1** a mathematical statement that two expressions are equal. **2** the act of equating. **3** the state of being equal, equivalent, or equally balanced. **4** a representation of a chemical reaction using symbols of the elements. **5** a situation or problem in which a number of factors need to be considered.
▸ **e'quational** *adj* ▸ **e'quationally** *adv*

equator (ɪ'kweɪtə) *n* **1** the great circle of the earth, equidistant from the poles, dividing the N and S hemispheres. **2** a circle dividing a sphere into two equal parts. **3** *Astron.* See **celestial equator.** ORIG C14: from Med. L (*circulus*) *aequātor* (*diei et noctis*) (circle) that equalizes (the day and night), from L *aequāre* to make EQUAL

equatorial (ˌɛkwə'tɔːrɪəl) *adj* **1** of, like, or existing at or near the equator. **2** *Astron.* of or referring to the celestial equator. **3** (of a telescope) mounted on perpendicular axes, one of which is parallel to the earth's axis. ◆ *n* **4** an equatorial mounting for a telescope.

Equatorial Guinea ★ *n* a republic of W Africa, consisting of Río Muni on the mainland and the island of Bioko in the Gulf of Guinea, with four smaller islands: ceded by Portugal to Spain in 1778; gained independence in 1968. Official languages: Spanish and French. Religion: Roman Catholic majority. Currency: franc. Capital: Malabo. Pop.: 466 000 (1999 est.). Area: 28 049 sq. km (10 830 sq. miles). Former name (until 1964): **Spanish Guinea.**

equerry ('ɛkwərɪ; *at the British court* ɪ'kwɛrɪ) *n, pl* **equerries. 1** an officer attendant upon the British sovereign. **2** (formerly) an officer in a royal household responsible for the horses. ORIG C16: alteration (through infl. of L *equus* horse) of earlier *escuirie,* from OF: stable

equestrian (ɪ'kwɛstrɪən) *adj* **1** of or relating to horses and riding. **2** on horseback; mounted. **3** of, relating to, or composed of knights. ◆ *n* **4** a person skilled in riding and horsemanship. ORIG C17: from L *equestris,* from *equus* horse
▸ **e'questrianˌism** *n*

equi- *combining form.* equal or equally: *equidistant; equilateral.*

equiangular (ˌiːkwɪ'æŋgjʊlə) *adj* having all angles equal.

equidistant (ˌiːkwɪ'dɪstənt) *adj* equally distant.
▸ ˌ**equi'distance** *n* ▸ ˌ**equi'distantly** *adv*

equilateral (ˌiːkwɪ'lætərəl) *adj* **1** having all sides of equal length. ◆ *n* **2** a geometric figure having all sides of equal length. **3** a side that is equal in length to other sides.

equilibrant (ɪ'kwɪlɪbrənt) *n* a force capable of balancing another force.

equilibrate (ˌiːkwɪ'laɪbreɪt, ɪ'kwɪlɪˌbreɪt) *vb* **equilibrates, equilibrating, equilibrated.** to bring to or be in equilibrium; balance. ORIG C17: from LL, from *aequilībris* in balance; see EQUILIBRIUM
▸ ˌ**equili'bration** *n*

equilibrist (ɪ'kwɪlɪbrɪst) *n* a person who performs balancing feats, esp. on a high wire.
▸ **eˌquili'bristic** *adj*

equilibrium (ˌiːkwɪ'lɪbrɪəm) *n, pl* **equilibriums** *or* **equilibria** (-rɪə). **1** a stable condition in which forces cancel one another. **2** a state or feeling of mental balance; composure. **3** any unchanging state of a body, system, etc., resulting from the balance of the influences to which it is subjected. **4** *Physiol.* a state of bodily balance, maintained primarily by receptors in the inner ear. ORIG C17: from L, from *aequi-* EQUI- + *lībra* pound, balance

equine ('ɛkwaɪn) *adj* of, relating to, or resembling a horse. ORIG C18: from L, from *equus* horse

equinoctial (ˌiːkwɪ'nɒkʃəl) *adj* **1** relating to or occurring at either or both equinoxes. **2** *Astron.* of or relating to the celestial equator. ◆ *n* **3** a storm or gale at or near an equinox. **4** another name for **celestial equator.** ORIG C14: from L: see EQUINOX

equinoctial circle *or* **line** *n* another name for **celestial equator.**

equinoctial point *n* either of two points at which the celestial equator intersects the ecliptic.

equinox ('iːkwɪˌnɒks) *n* **1** either of the two occasions, six months apart, when day and night are of equal length. In the N hemisphere the **vernal equinox** occurs around March 21 (Sept. 23 in the S hemisphere). The **autumnal equinox** occurs around Sept. 23 in the N hemisphere (March 21 in the S hemisphere). **2** another name for **equinoctial point.** ORIG C14: from Med. L *equinoxium,* changed from L *aequinoctium,* from *aequi-* EQUI- + *nox* night

equip (ɪ'kwɪp) *vb* **equips, equipping, equipped.** (*tr*) **1** to furnish (with necessary supplies, etc.). **2** (*usually passive*) to provide with abilities, understanding, etc. **3** to dress out; attire. ORIG C16: from OF *eschiper* to embark, fit out (a ship), of Gmc origin
▸ **e'quipper** *n*

equipage ('ɛkwɪpɪdʒ) *n* **1** a horse-drawn carriage, esp. one attended by liveried footmen. **2** the stores and equipment of a military unit. **3** *Arch.* a set of useful articles.

equipment (ɪ'kwɪpmənt) *n* **1** an act or instance of equipping. **2** the items provided. **3** a set of tools, kit, etc., assembled for a specific purpose.

equipoise ('ɛkwɪˌpɔɪz) *n* **1** even balance of weight; equilibrium. **2** a counterbalance; counterpoise. ◆ *vb* **equipoises, equipoising, equipoised. 3** (*tr*) to offset or balance.

equipollent (ˌiːkwɪ'pɒlənt) *adj* **1** equal or equivalent in significance, power, or effect. ◆ *n* **2** something that is equipollent. ORIG C15: from L *aequipollēns* of equal importance, from EQUI- + *pollēre* to be able, be strong
▸ ˌ**equi'pollence** *or* ˌ**equi'pollency** *n*

equisetum (ˌɛkwɪ'siːtəm) *n, pl* **equisetums** *or* **equiseta** (-tə). any plant of the horsetail genus. ORIG C19: NL, from L, from *equus* horse + *saeta* bristle

equitable ('ɛkwɪtəbᵊl) *adj* **1** fair; just. **2** *Law.* relating to or valid in equity, as distinct from common law or statute law. ORIG C17: from F, from *équité* EQUITY
▸ '**equitableness** *n*

equitation (ˌɛkwɪˈteɪʃən) *n* the study and practice of riding and horsemanship. ORIG C16: from L *equitātiō*, from *equitāre* to ride, from *equus* horse

equities (ˈɛkwɪtɪz) *pl n* another name for **ordinary shares.**

equity (ˈɛkwɪtɪ) *n, pl* **equities. 1** the quality of being impartial; fairness. **2** an impartial or fair act, decision, etc. **3** *Law.* a system of jurisprudence founded on principles of natural justice and fair conduct. It supplements common law, as by providing a remedy where none exists at law. **4** *Law.* an equitable right or claim. **5** the interest of ordinary shareholders in a company. **6** the value of a debtor's property in excess of debts to which it is liable. ORIG C14: from OF, from L *aequitās*, from *aequus* level, EQUAL

Equity (ˈɛkwɪtɪ) *n* the actors' trade union.

equity capital *n* the part of the share capital of a company owned by ordinary shareholders or in certain circumstances by other classes of shareholder.

equity-linked policy *n* an insurance or assurance policy in which premiums are invested partially or wholly in ordinary shares for the eventual benefit of the beneficiaries of the policy.

equivalence (ɪˈkwɪvələns) *or* **equivalency** *n* **1** the state of being equivalent. **2** *Logic, maths.* another term for **biconditional.**

equivalent (ɪˈkwɪvələnt) *adj* **1** equal in value, quantity, significance, etc. **2** having the same or a similar effect or meaning. **3** *Logic, maths.* (of two propositions) having a biconditional between them. ◆ *n* **4** something that is equivalent. **5** Also called: **equivalent weight.** the weight of a substance that will combine with or displace 8 grams of oxygen or 1.007 97 grams of hydrogen. ORIG C15: from LL, from L *aequi-* EQUI- + *valēre* to be worth
▸ **eˈquivalently** *adv*

equivocal (ɪˈkwɪvəkᵊl) *adj* **1** capable of varying interpretations; ambiguous. **2** deliberately misleading or vague. **3** of doubtful character or sincerity. ORIG C17: from LL, from L EQUI- + *vōx* voice
▸ **eˌquivoˈcality** *or* **eˈquivocalness** *n*

equivocate (ɪˈkwɪvəˌkeɪt) *vb* **equivocates, equivocating, equivocated.** (*intr*) to use equivocal language, esp. to avoid speaking directly or honestly. ORIG C15: from Med. L, from LL *aequivocus* ambiguous, EQUIVOCAL
▸ **eˈquivoˌcatingly** *adv* ▸ **eˌquivoˈcation** *n* ▸ **eˈquivoˌcator** *n* ▸ **eˈquivocatory** *adj*

er (ə, ɜː) *interj* a sound made when hesitating in speech.

Er *the chemical symbol for* erbium.

ER *abbrev. for:* **1** Elizabeth Regina. ORIG L: Queen Elizabeth **2** Eduardus Rex. ORIG L: King Edward

-er[1] *suffix forming nouns.* **1** a person or thing that performs a specified action: *reader; lighter.* **2** a person engaged in a profession, occupation, etc.: *writer; baker.* **3** a native or inhabitant of: *Londoner; villager.* **4** a person or thing having a certain characteristic: *newcomer; fiver.* ORIG OE *-ere*

-er[2] *suffix.* forming the comparative degree of adjectives (*deeper, freer,* etc.) and adverbs (*faster, slower,* etc.). ORIG OE *-rd, -re* (adj), *-or* (adv)

era (ˈɪərə) *n* **1** a period of time considered as being of a distinctive character; epoch. **2** an extended period of time the years of which are numbered from a fixed point: *the Christian era.* **3** a point in time beginning a new or distinctive period. **4** a major division of geological time, divided into periods. ORIG C17: from L *aera* counters, pl of *aes* brass, pieces of brass money

ERA (ˈɪərə) *n* (in Britain) *acronym for* Education Reform Act: the 1988 act which established the key elements of the National Curriculum and the Basic Curriculum.

eradicate (ɪˈrædɪˌkeɪt) *vb* **eradicates, eradicating, eradicated.** (*tr*) **1** to obliterate. **2** to pull up by the roots. ORIG C16: from L *ērādīcāre* to uproot, from EX-[1] + *rādīx* root
▸ **eˈradicable** *adj* ▸ **eˌradiˈcation** *n* ▸ **eˈradicative** *adj*

erase (ɪˈreɪz) *vb* **erases, erasing, erased. 1** to obliterate or rub out (something written, typed, etc.). **2** (*tr*) to destroy all traces of. **3** to remove (a recording) from (magnetic tape). ORIG C17: from L, from EX-[1] + *rādere* to scratch, scrape
▸ **eˈrasable** *adj*

eraser (ɪˈreɪzə) *n* an object, such as a piece of rubber, for erasing something written, typed, etc.

Erasmus ★ (ɪˈræzməs) *n* **Desiderius** (ˌdɛzɪˈdɪərɪəs), real name *Gerhard Gerhards.* ?1466–1536, Dutch Renaissance humanist.

erasure (ɪˈreɪʒə) *n* **1** the act or an instance of erasing. **2** the place or mark, as on a piece of paper, where something has been erased.

Erato ★ (ˈɛrəˌtəʊ) *n Greek myth.* the Muse of love poetry.

Eratosthenes ★ (ˌɛrəˈtɒsθɪˌniːz) *n* ?276–?194 B.C., Greek mathematician and astronomer, who calculated the circumference of the earth by observing the angle of the sun's rays at different places.

Erbil, Irbil (ˈɜːbɪl), *or* **Arbil** ★ *n* a city in N Iraq: important in Assyrian times. Pop.: 485 968 (1987). Ancient name: **Arbela.**

erbium (ˈɜːbɪəm) *n* a soft malleable silvery-white element of the lanthanide series of metals. Symbol: Er; atomic no.: 68; atomic wt.: 167.26. ORIG C19: from NL, from (*Ytt*)*erb*(*y*), Sweden, where it was first found + -IUM

Erciyas Daği ★ (*Turkish* ˈɛrdʒijɑs dɑːˈi) *n* an extinct volcano in central Turkey. Height 3916 m (12 848 ft).

ERDF *abbrev. for* European Regional Development Fund: a fund to provide money for specific projects for work on the infrastructure in countries of the European Union.

ere (ɛə) *conj, prep* a poetic word for **before.** ORIG OE *ǣr*

Erebus[1] ★ (ˈɛrɪbəs) *n Greek myth.* **1** the god of darkness, son of Chaos and brother of Night. **2** the darkness below the earth, thought to be the abode of the dead or the region they pass through on their way to Hades.

Erebus[2] ★ (ˈɛrɪbəs) *n* **Mount.** a volcano in Antarctica, on Ross Island: discovered by Sir James Ross in 1841 and named after his ship. Height: 3794 m (12 448 ft).

Erechtheum (ɪˈrɛkθɪəm, ˌɛrəkˈθiːəm) *or* **Erechtheion** ★ (ɪˈrɛkθɪən, ˌɛrəkˈθiːən) *n* a temple on the Acropolis at Athens, which has a porch of caryatids.

Erechtheus ★ (ɛˈrɛkθjuːs, -θɪəs) *n Greek myth.* a king of Athens who sacrificed one of his daughters because the oracle at Delphi said this was the only way to win the war against the Eleusinians.

erect (ɪˈrɛkt) *adj* **1** upright in posture or position. **2** *Physiol.* (of the penis, clitoris, or nipples) firm or rigid after swelling with blood, esp. as a result of sexual excitement. **3** (of plant parts) growing vertically or at right angles to the parts from which they arise. ◆ *vb* (*mainly tr*) **4** to put up; build. **5** to raise to an upright position. **6** to found or form; set up. **7** (*also intr*) *Physiol.* to become or cause to become firm or rigid by filling with blood. **8** to exalt. **9** to draw or construct (a line, figure, etc.) on a given line or figure. ORIG C14: from L *ērigere* to set up, from *regere* to control, govern
▸ **eˈrectable** *adj* ▸ **eˈrecter** *or* **eˈrector** *n* ▸ **eˈrectness** *n*

erectile (ɪˈrɛktaɪl) *adj* **1** *Physiol.* (of tissues or organs, such as the penis or clitoris) capable of becoming erect. **2** capable of being erected.
▸ **erectility** (ɪrɛkˈtɪlɪtɪ, ˌiːrɛk-) *n*

erection (ɪˈrɛkʃən) *n* **1** the act of erecting or the state of being erected. **2** a building or construction. **3** *Physiol.* the enlarged state of erectile tissues or organs, esp. the penis, when filled with blood. **4** an erect penis.

E region *or* **layer** *n* a region of the ionosphere, extending from a height of 90 to about 150 kilometres. It reflects radio waves of medium wavelength.

eremite (ˈɛrɪˌmaɪt) *n* a Christian hermit or recluse. ORIG C13: see HERMIT
▸ **eremitic** (ˌɛrɪˈmɪtɪk) or ˌ**ereˈmitical** *adj* ▸ **ˈeremitˌism** *n*

Erenburg ★ (ˈɛərənˌbɜːg; *Russian* ɛrɪnˈburk) *n* a variant spelling of (Ilya Grigorievich) **Ehrenburg.**

erepsin (ɪˈrɛpsɪn) *n* a mixture of proteolytic enzymes secreted by the small intestine. ORIG C20: *er-*, from L *ēripere* to snatch + (P)EPSIN

erethism (ˈɛrɪˌθɪzəm) *n* **1** *Physiol.* an abnormal irritability or sensitivity in any part of the body. **2** *Psychiatry.* **2a** a personality disorder resulting from mercury poisoning. **2b** an abnormal tendency to become aroused quickly, esp. sexually, as the result of a verbal or psychic stimulus. ORIG C18: from F, from Gk, from *erethizein* to excite, irritate

Eretria ★ (ɪ'rɛtrɪə) *n* an ancient city in Greece, on the S coast of Euboea: founded as an Ionian colony; destroyed by the Persians in 490 B.C. following which it never regained its former significance.

Erevan ★ (*Russian* jɪrɪ'van) *n* a variant spelling of **Yerevan.**

erf (ɜːf) *n, pl* **erven** ('ɜːvən). *S. African.* a plot of land, usually urban. ORIG from Afrik., from Du.: inheritance

Erf (ɜːf) *n acronym for* electrorheological fluid: a liquid that thickens or solidifies when an electric current passes and returns to a liquid when the current ceases.

Erfurt ★ (*German* 'ɛrfʊrt) *n* an industrial city in central Germany, the capital of Thuringia: university (1392). Pop.: 211 108 (1996 est.).

erg[1] (ɜːg) *n* the cgs unit of work or energy. ORIG C19: from Gk *ergon* work

erg[2] (ɜːg) *n, pl* **ergs** *or* **areg** (ə'rɛg). an area of shifting sand dunes, esp. in the Sahara Desert in N Africa. ORIG C19: from Ar. *'irj*

ergo ('ɜːgəʊ) *sentence connector.* therefore; hence. ORIG C14: from L: therefore

ergonomic (ˌɜːgə'nɒmɪk) *adj* **1** of or relating to ergonomics. **2** designed to minimize physical effort and discomfort, and hence maximize efficiency.

ergonomics (ˌɜːgə'nɒmɪks) *n* (*functioning as sing*) the study of the relationship between workers and their environment, esp. the equipment they use. ORIG C20: from Gk *ergon* work + (ECO)NOMICS
▸ **ergonomist** (ɜː'gɒnəmɪst) *n*

ergosterol (ɜː'gɒstəˌrɒl) *n* a plant sterol that is converted into vitamin D by the action of ultraviolet radiation.

ergot ('ɜːgət, -gɒt) *n* **1** a disease of cereals and other grasses caused by fungi of the genus *Claviceps.* **2** any fungus causing this disease. **3** the dried fungus, used as the source of certain alkaloids used in medicine. ORIG C17: from F: spur (of a cock), from ?

ergotism ('ɜːgəˌtɪzəm) *n* ergot poisoning, producing either burning pains and eventually gangrene or itching skin and convulsions.

Erhard ★ (*German* 'eːrhart) *n* **Ludwig** ('luːtvɪç). 1897–1977, German statesman: chief architect of the *Wirtschaftswunder* ("economic miracle") of West Germany's recovery after World War II; chancellor (1963–66).

erica ('ɛrɪkə) *n* any shrub of the ericaceous genus *Erica,* including the heaths and some heathers. ORIG C19: via L from Gk *ereikē* heath

ericaceous (ˌɛrɪ'keɪʃəs) *adj* of or relating to the Ericaceae, a family of trees and shrubs with typically bell-shaped flowers: includes heather, rhododendron, azalea, and arbutus.

Ericson *or* **Ericsson** ★ ('ɛrɪksᵊn) *n* **Leif** (liːf). 10th–11th centuries A.D., Norse navigator, who discovered Vinland (?1000), variously identified as the coast of New England, Labrador, or Newfoundland; son of Eric the Red.

Eric the Red ★ ('ɛrɪk) *n* ?940–?1010 A.D., Norse navigator: discovered and colonized Greenland; father of Leif Ericson.

Erie ★ ('ɪərɪ) *n* **1 Lake.** a lake between the US and Canada: the southernmost and the shallowest of the Great Lakes; empties by the Niagara River into Lake Ontario. Area: 25 718 sq. km (9930 sq. miles). **2** a port in NW Pennsylvania, on Lake Erie. Pop.: 105 270 (1996 est.).

Erie Canal ★ *n* a canal in New York State between Albany and Buffalo, linking the Hudson River with Lake Erie. Length: 579 km (360 miles).

erigeron (ɪ'rɪdʒərən, -'rɪg-) *n* any plant of the genus *Erigeron,* whose flowers resemble asters. ORIG C17: via L from Gk, from *ēri* early + *gerōn* old man; from the white down of some species

Eriksson ★ ('ɛrɪksən) *n* **Sven Goran** ('gɒrən). born 1948, Swedish football manager: England national coach from 2001.

Erin ★ ('ɪərɪn, 'ɛərɪn) *n* an archaic or poetic name for **Ireland**[1]. ORIG from Irish Gaelic *Éirinn,* dative of Ireland

Erinyes ★ (ɪ'rɪnɪˌiːz) *pl n, sing* **Erinys** (ɪ'rɪnɪs, ɪ'raɪ-). *Myth.* another name for the **Furies.** ORIG Gk

Eris ★ ('ɛrɪs) *n Greek myth.* the goddess of discord, sister of Ares.

Eritrea ★ (ˌɛrɪ'treɪə) *n* a country in NE Africa, on the Red Sea: became an Italian colony in 1890; federated with Ethiopia (1952–93); after civil war with the Ethiopian government for independence (1961–91), a provisional Eritrean government was established (1991); full independence was gained in 1993. It consists of hot and arid coastal lowlands, rising to the foothills of the Ethiopian highlands. Languages: Arabic, English, Afar, and others. Religions: Muslim and Christian. Currency: nakfa. Capital: Asmara. Pop.: 3 985 000 (1999 est.). Area: 117 400 sq. km (45 300 sq. miles).
▸ ˌ**Eri'trean** *n*

Erivan ★ (*Russian* jɪrɪ'van) *n* a variant spelling of **Yerevan.**

erk (ɜːk) *n Brit. sl.* an aircraftman or naval rating. ORIG C20: ? a corruption of *AC* (aircraftman)

Erlangen ★ (*German* 'ɛrlaŋən) *n* a town in central Germany, in Bavaria: university (1743). Pop.: 101 406 (1996 est.).

Erlanger ★ ('ɜːˌlæŋə) *n* **Joseph.** 1874–1965, US physiologist. He shared a Nobel prize for physiology or medicine (1944) for work on the electrical signs of nervous activity.

ERM *abbrev. for* Exchange Rate Mechanism.

ermine ('ɜːmɪn) *n, pl* **ermines** *or* **ermine. 1** the stoat in northern regions, where it has a white winter coat with a black-tipped tail. **2** the fur of this animal. **3** the dignity or office of a judge, noble, etc., whose state robes are trimmed with ermine. ORIG C12: from OF, from Med. L *Armenius* (*mūs*) Armenian (mouse)

erne *or* **ern** (ɜːn) *n* a fish-eating sea eagle. ORIG OE *earn*

Erne ★ (ɜːn) *n* a river in N central Republic of Ireland, rising in County Cavan and flowing north across the border, through **Upper Lough Erne** and **Lower Lough Erne,** and then west to Donegal Bay. Length: about 96 km (60 miles).

Ernie ('ɜːnɪ) *n* (in Britain) a machine that randomly selects winning numbers of Premium Bonds. ORIG C20: acronym of *E*lectronic *R*andom *N*umber *I*ndicator *E*quipment

Ernst ★ (*German* ɛrnst) *n* **Max** (maks). 1891–1976, German painter, resident in France and the US: developed the technique of collage.

erode (ɪ'rəʊd) *vb* **erodes, eroding, eroded. 1** to grind or wear down or away or become ground or worn down or away. **2** to deteriorate or cause to deteriorate. ORIG C17: from L, from EX-[1] + *rōdere* to gnaw
▸ **e'rodible** *adj*

erogenous (ɪ'rɒdʒɪnəs) *or* **erogenic** (ˌɛrə'dʒɛnɪk) *adj* **1** sensitive to sexual stimulation. **2** arousing sexual desire or giving sexual pleasure. ORIG C19: from Gk *erōs* love, desire + -GENOUS
▸ **erogeneity** (ˌɛrədʒɪ'niːɪtɪ) *n*

Eros ★ ('ɪərɒs, 'ɛrɒs) *n Greek myth.* the god of love, son of Aphrodite. Roman counterpart: **Cupid.**

erosion (ɪ'rəʊʒən) *n* **1** the wearing away of rocks, soil, etc., by the action of water, ice, wind, etc. **2** the act or process of eroding or the state of being eroded.
▸ **e'rosive** *or* **e'rosional** *adj*

erotic (ɪ'rɒtɪk) *adj* **1** of, concerning, or arousing sexual desire or giving sexual pleasure. **2** marked by strong sexual desire or being especially sensitive to sexual stimulation. Also: **erotical.** ORIG C17: from Gk *erōtikos,* from *erōs* love
▸ **e'rotically** *adv*

erotica (ɪ'rɒtɪkə) *pl n* explicitly sexual literature or art. ORIG C19: from Gk: see EROTIC

eroticism (ɪ'rɒtɪˌsɪzəm) *or* **erotism** ('ɛrəˌtɪzəm) *n* **1** erotic quality or nature. **2** the use of sexually arousing or pleasing symbolism in literature or art. **3** sexual excitement or desire.

erotogenic (ɪˌrɒtə'dʒɛnɪk) *adj* originating from or causing sexual stimulation; erogenous.

err (ɜː) *vb* (*intr*) **1** to make a mistake; be incorrect. **2** to deviate from a moral standard. **3** to act with bias, esp. favourable bias: *to err on the right side.* ORIG C14 *erren* to wander, stray, from OF, from L *errāre*

▸ **'errancy** *n*

errand ('ɛrənd) *n* **1** a short trip undertaken to perform a task or commission (esp. in **run errands**). **2** the purpose or object of such a trip. ORIG OE *ǣrende*

errant ('ɛrənt) *adj* (*often postpositive*) **1** *Arch. or literary.* wandering in search of adventure. **2** erring or straying from the right course or accepted standards. ORIG C14: from OF: journeying, from Vulgar L *iterāre* (unattested), from L *iter* journey; infl. by L *errāre* to err

▸ **'errantry** *n*

erratic (ɪ'rætɪk) *adj* **1** irregular in performance, behaviour, or attitude; unpredictable. **2** having no fixed or regular course. ◆ *n* **3** a piece of rock that has been transported from its place of origin, esp. by glacial action. ORIG C14: from L, from *errāre* to wander, err

▸ **er'ratically** *adv*

erratum (ɪ'rɑːtəm) *n, pl* **errata** (-tə). **1** an error in writing or printing. **2** another name for **corrigendum.** ORIG C16: from L: mistake, from *errāre* to err

Er Rif ★ (ɛə 'rɪf) *n* a mountainous region of N Morocco, near the Mediterranean coast.

erroneous (ɪ'rəunɪəs) *adj* based on or containing error; incorrect. ORIG C14 (in the sense: deviating from what is right), from L, from *errāre* to wander

▸ **er'roneousness** *n*

error ('ɛrə) *n* **1** a mistake or inaccuracy. **2** an incorrect belief or wrong judgment. **3** the condition of deviating from accuracy or correctness. **4** deviation from a moral standard; wrongdoing. **5** *Maths, statistics.* a measure of the difference between some quantity and an approximation of it, often expressed as a percentage. ORIG C13: from L, from *errāre* to err

▸ **'error-ˌfree** *adj*

ersatz ('ɛəzæts, 'ɜː-) *adj* **1** made in imitation; artificial. ◆ *n* **2** an ersatz substance or article. ORIG C20: G, from *ersetzen* to substitute

Erse (ɜːs) *n* **1** another name for Irish **Gaelic.** ◆ *adj* **2** of or relating to the Irish Gaelic language. ORIG C14: from Lowland Scots *Erisch* Irish

erst (ɜːst) *adv Arch.* **1** long ago; formerly. **2** at first. ORIG OE *ǣrest* earliest, sup. of *ǣr* early

erstwhile ('ɜːstˌwaɪl) *adj* **1** former; one-time. ◆ *adv* **2** *Arch.* long ago; formerly.

Erté ★ (*French* ɛrte) *n* real name *Romain de Tirtoff.* 1892–1990, French fashion illustrator and designer, born in Russia.

eruct (ɪ'rʌkt) *or* **eructate** *vb* **eructs, eructing, eructed** *or* **eructates, eructating, eructated. 1** to belch. **2** (of a volcano) to pour out (fumes or volcanic matter). ORIG C17: from L, from *ructāre* to belch

▸ **eructation** (ɪˌrʌk'teɪʃən, ˌiːrʌk-) *n*

erudite ('ɛruˌdaɪt) *adj* having or showing extensive scholarship; learned. ORIG C15: from L, from *ērudīre* to polish

▸ **erudition** (ˌɛru'dɪʃən) *or* **'eruˌditeness** *n*

erupt (ɪ'rʌpt) *vb* **1** to eject (steam, water, and volcanic material) violently or (of volcanic material, etc.) to be so ejected. **2** (*intr*) (of a blemish) to appear on the skin. **3** (*intr*) (of a tooth) to emerge through the gum during normal tooth development. **4** (*intr*) to burst forth suddenly and violently. ORIG C17: from L *ēruptus* having burst forth, from *ērumpere,* from *rumpere* to burst

▸ **e'ruptive** *adj* ▸ **e'ruption** *n*

-ery *or* **-ry** *suffix forming nouns.* **1** indicating a place of business or activity: *bakery; refinery.* **2** indicating a class or collection of things: *cutlery.* **3** indicating qualities or actions: *snobbery; trickery.* **4** indicating a practice or occupation: *husbandry.* **5** indicating a state or condition: *slavery.* ORIG from OF *-erie;* see -ER[1], -Y[3]

Erymanthus ★ (ˌɛrɪ'mænθəs) *n* **Mount.** a mountain in SW Greece, in the NW Peloponnese. Height: 2224 m (7297 ft). Modern Greek name: **Erímanthos** (e'rimanθɔs).

erysipelas (ˌɛrɪ'sɪpɪləs) *n* an acute streptococcal infectious disease of the skin, characterized by fever and purplish lesions. ORIG C16: from L, from Gk, from *erusi-* red + *-pelas* skin

erythro- *or before a vowel* **erythr-** *combining form.* red: *erythrocyte.* ORIG from Gk *eruthros* red

erythrocyte (ɪ'rɪθrəuˌsaɪt) *n* a blood cell of vertebrates that transports oxygen and carbon dioxide, combined with haemoglobin.

▸ **erythrocytic** (ɪˌrɪθrəu'sɪtɪk) *adj*

erythromycin (ɪˌrɪθrəu'maɪsɪn) *n* an antibiotic used in treating certain bacterial infections. ORIG C20: from ERYTHRO- + Gk *mukēs* fungus + -IN

erythropoiesis (ɪˌrɪθrəupɔɪ'iːsɪs) *n Physiol.* the formation of red blood cells. ORIG C19: from ERYTHRO- + Gk *poiēs* a making, from *poiein* to make

▸ **erythropoietic** (ɪˌrɪθrəupɔɪ'ɛtɪk) *adj*

Erzgebirge ★ (*German* 'eːrtsgəbɪrgə) *pl n* a mountain range on the border between Germany and the Czech Republic: formerly rich in mineral resources. Highest peak: Mount Klínovec (Keilberg), 1244 m (4081 ft). Czech name: **Krušné Hory.** Also called: **Ore Mountains.**

Erzurum ★ ('ɛəzurum) *n* a city in E Turkey: a strategic centre; scene of two major battles against Russian forces (1877 and 1916); important military base and a closed city to unofficial visitors. Pop.: 247 587 (1995 est.).

Es *the chemical symbol for* einsteinium.

-es *suffix.* **1** a variant of **-s**[1] for nouns ending in *ch, s, sh, z,* postconsonantal *y,* for some nouns ending in a vowel, and nouns in *f* with *v* in the plural: *ashes; heroes; calves.* **2** a variant of **-s**[2] for verbs ending in *ch, s, sh, z,* postconsonantal *y,* or a vowel: *preaches; steadies; echoes.*

Esau ★ ('iːsɔː) *n Bible.* son of Isaac and Rebecca and twin brother of Jacob, to whom he sold his birthright (Genesis 25).

Esbjerg ★ (*Danish* 'ɛsbjɛr) *n* a port in SW Denmark, in Jutland on the North Sea: Denmark's chief fishing port. Pop.: 82 579 (1995 est.).

escadrille (ˌɛskə'drɪl) *n* a French squadron of aircraft, esp. in World War I. ORIG from F: flotilla, from Sp., from *escuadra* SQUADRON

escalade (ˌɛskə'leɪd) *n* **1** an assault using ladders, esp. on a fortification. ◆ *vb* **escalades, escalading, escaladed. 2** to gain access to (a place) by ladders. ORIG C16: from F, from It., from *scalare* to mount, SCALE[3]

escalate ('ɛskəˌleɪt) *vb* **escalates, escalating, escalated.** to increase or be increased in extent, intensity, or magnitude. ORIG C20: back formation from ESCALATOR

▸ **ˌesca'lation** *n*

escalator ('ɛskəˌleɪtə) *n* **1** a moving staircase consisting of stair treads fixed to a conveyor belt. **2** short for **escalator clause.** ORIG C20: orig. a trademark

escalator clause *n* a clause in a contract stipulating an adjustment in wages, prices, etc., in the event of specified changes in conditions, such as a large rise in the cost of living.

escallop (ɛ'skɒləp, ɛ'skæl-) *n, vb* another word for **scallop.**

escalope ('ɛskəˌlɒp) *n* a thin slice of meat, usually veal. ORIG C19: from OF: shell

escapade ('ɛskəˌpeɪd, ˌɛskə'peɪd) *n* **1** an adventure, esp. one that is mischievous or unlawful. **2** a prank; romp. ORIG C17: from F, from OIt., from Vulgar L *excappāre* (unattested) to ESCAPE

escape (ɪ'skeɪp) *vb* **escapes, escaping, escaped. 1** to get away or break free from (confinement, etc.). **2** to manage to avoid (danger, etc.). **3** (*intr;* usually foll. by *from*) (of gases, liquids, etc.) to issue gradually, as from a crack; seep; leak. **4** (*tr*) to elude; be forgotten by: *the figure escapes me.* **5** (*tr*) to be articulated inadvertently or involuntarily from: *a roar escaped his lips.* ◆ *n* **6** the act of escaping or state of having escaped. **7** avoidance of injury, harm, etc. **8a** a means or way of escape. **8b** (*as modifier*): *an escape route.* **9** a means of distraction or relief. **10** a gradual outflow; leakage; seepage. **11** Also called: **escape valve, escape cock.** a valve that releases air, steam, etc., above a certain pressure. **12** a plant originally cultivated but now growing wild. ORIG C14: from OF, from Vulgar

L *excappāre* (unattested) to escape (lit.: to slip out of one's cloak, hence free oneself), from EX-[1] + LL *cappa* cloak
▸ **es'capable** *adj* ▸ **es'caper** *n*

escapee (ɪˌskeɪ'piː) *n* a person who has escaped, esp. an escaped prisoner.

escapement (ɪ'skeɪpmənt) *n* **1** a mechanism consisting of a toothed wheel (**escape wheel**) and anchor, used in timepieces to provide periodic impulses to the pendulum or balance. **2** any similar mechanism that regulates movement. **3** in pianos, the mechanism which allows the hammer to clear the string after striking, so the string can vibrate. **4** *Rare.* an act or means of escaping.

escape road *n* a road provided on a hill for a driver to drive into if his brakes fail or on a bend if he loses control of the turn.

escape velocity *n* the minimum velocity necessary for a body to escape from the gravitational field of the earth or other celestial body.

escapism (ɪ'skeɪpɪzəm) *n* an inclination to retreat from unpleasant reality, as through diversion or fantasy.
▸ **es'capist** *n, adj*

escapologist (ˌɛskə'pɒlədʒɪst) *n* an entertainer who specializes in freeing himself or herself from confinement.
▸ **ˌesca'pology** *n*

escargot *French.* (ɛskargo) *n* a variety of edible snail.

escarpment (ɪ'skɑːpmənt) *n* **1** the long continuous steep face of a ridge or plateau formed by erosion or faulting; scarp. **2** a steep artificial slope made immediately in front of a fortified place. ORIG C19: from F *escarpe;* see SCARP

Escaut ★ (ɛsko) *n* the French name for the **Scheldt.**

-escent *suffix forming adjectives.* beginning to be, do, show, etc.: *convalescent; luminescent.* ORIG via OF from L *-ēscent-*, stem of present participial suffix of *-ēscere,* ending of inceptive verbs
▸ **-escence** *suffix forming nouns.*

eschatology (ˌɛskə'tɒlədʒɪ) *n* the branch of theology concerned with the end of the world. ORIG C19: from Gk *eskhatos* last
▸ **eschatological** (ˌɛskətə'lɒdʒɪkᵊl) *adj* ▸ **ˌescha'tologist** *n*

escheat (ɪs'tʃiːt) *Law.* ◆ *n* **1** (in England before 1926) the reversion of property to the Crown in the absence of legal heirs. **2** *Feudalism.* the reversion of property to the feudal lord in the absence of legal heirs. **3** the property so reverting. ◆ *vb* **4** to take (land) by escheat or (of land) to revert by escheat. ORIG C14: from OF, from *escheoir* to fall to the lot of, from LL *excadere* (unattested), from L *cadere* to fall
▸ **es'cheatable** *adj* ▸ **es'cheatage** *n*

Escherichia (ˌɛʃə'rɪkɪə) *n* a genus of bacteria that form acid and gas in the presence of carbohydrates and are found in the intestines of humans and many animals, esp. *E. coli*, which is sometimes pathogenic and is widely used in genetic research. ORIG C19: after Theodor *Escherich* (1857–1911), G paediatrician

eschew (ɪs'tʃuː) *vb* (*tr*) to keep clear of or abstain from (something disliked, injurious, etc.); shun; avoid. ORIG C14: from OF *eschiver,* of Gmc origin; see SHY[1], SKEW
▸ **es'chewal** *n* ▸ **es'chewer** *n*

eschscholzia *or* **eschscholtzia** (ɪs'kɒlʃə) *n* another name for **California poppy.** ORIG C19: after J. F. von *Eschscholtz* (1793–1831), G botanist

Escoffier ★ (*French* ɛskɔfje) *n* (**Georges**) **Auguste** (ogyst). 1846–1935, French chef.

Escorial (ˌɛskɒrɪ'ɑːl, ɛ'skɔːrɪəl) *or* **Escurial** ★ *n* a village in central Spain, northwest of Madrid: site of an architectural complex containing a monastery, palace, and college, built by Philip II between 1563 and 1584.

escort *n* ('ɛskɔːt). **1** one or more persons, soldiers, vehicles, etc., accompanying another or others for protection, as a mark of honour, etc. **2** a man or youth who accompanies a woman or girl on a social occasion. ◆ *vb* (ɪs'kɔːt). **3** (*tr*) to accompany or attend as an escort. ORIG C16: from F, from It., from *scorgere* to guide, from L *corrigere* to straighten; see CORRECT

escritoire (ˌɛskrɪ'twɑː) *n* a writing desk with compartments and drawers. ORIG C18: from F, from Med. L *scriptōrium* writing room in a monastery, from L *scrībere* to write

escrow ('ɛskrəʊ, ɛ'skrəʊ) *Law.* ◆ *n* **1** money, goods, or a written document, held by a third party pending fulfilment of some condition. **2** the state or condition of being an escrow (esp. in **in escrow**). ◆ *vb* (*tr*) **3** to place (money, a document, etc.) in escrow. ORIG C16: from OF *escroe,* of Gmc origin; see SCREED, SHRED, SCROLL

escudo (ɛ'skuːdəʊ) *n, pl* **escudos. 1** the standard monetary unit of Cape Verde and Portugal. **2** a former standard monetary unit of Chile. **3** an old Spanish silver coin. ORIG C19: Sp., lit.: shield, from L *scūtum*

esculent ('ɛskjʊlənt) *n* **1** any edible substance. ◆ *adj* **2** edible. ORIG C17: from L *ēsculentus* good to eat, from *ēsca* food, from *edere* to eat

Escurial ★ (ɛˌskjʊərɪ'ɑːl, ɛ'skjʊərɪəl) *n* a variant of **Escorial.**

escutcheon (ɪ'skʌtʃən) *n* **1** a shield, esp. a heraldic one that displays a coat of arms. **2** a plate or shield around a keyhole, door handle, etc. **3** the place on the stern of a vessel where the name is shown. **4 blot on one's escutcheon.** a stain on one's honour. ORIG C15: from OF *escuchon,* ult. from L *scūtum* shield
▸ **es'cutcheoned** *adj*

Esdraelon ★ (ˌɛsdreɪ'iːlɒn) *n* a plain in N Israel, east of Mount Carmel. Also called: (Plain of) **Jezreel.**

ESE *symbol for* east-southeast.

-ese *suffix forming adjectives and nouns.* indicating place of origin, language, or style: *Cantonese; Japanese; journalese.*

Eşfahān ★ (ˌɛʃfə'hɑːn) *n* a variant of **Isfahan.**

ESG (*in Britain*) *abbrev. for* Educational Support Grant: a government grant given to a Local Education Authority to fund educational schemes dealing with social issues, such as drug abuse.

Esher ★ ('iːʃə) *n* a town in SE England, in NE Surrey near London: racecourse. Pop.: 46 599 (1991).

esker ('ɛskə) *or* **eskar** ('ɛskɑː, -kə) *n* a long winding ridge of gravel, sand, etc., originally deposited by a meltwater stream running under a glacier. ORIG C19: from OIrish *escir* ridge

Eskilstuna ★ (*Swedish* 'ɛskilstuːna) *n* an industrial city in SE Sweden. Pop.: 89 761 (1994).

Eskimo ('ɛskɪˌməʊ) *n* **1** (*pl* **Eskimos** *or* **Eskimo**) a member of a group of peoples inhabiting N Canada, Greenland, Alaska, and E Siberia. The Eskimos are more properly referred to as the **Inuit. 2** the language of these peoples. ◆ *adj* **3** of or relating to the Eskimos. ORIG C18 *Esquimawes:* rel. to *esquimantsic* (from a native language) eaters of raw flesh

> **USAGE NOTE** *Eskimo* is considered by many people to be offensive, and the term *Inuit* is nowadays preferred.

Eskimo dog *n* a large powerful breed of dog with a long thick coat and curled tail, developed for hauling sledges.

Eskişehir ★ (*Turkish* ɛs'kiʃɛˌhir) *n* an industrial city in NW Turkey: founded around hot springs in Byzantine times. Pop.: 455 285 (1995 est.).

Esky ('ɛskɪ) *n, pl* **Eskies.** (*sometimes not cap.*) *Austral. trademark.* a portable insulated container for keeping food and drink cool. ORIG C20: from ESKIMO, alluding to the Eskimos' cold habitat

ESN *abbrev. for* educationally subnormal; formerly used to designate a person of limited intelligence who needs special schooling.

esophagus (iː'sɒfəgəs) *n* the US spelling of **oesophagus.**

esoteric (ˌɛsəʊ'tɛrɪk) *adj* **1** restricted to or intended for an enlightened or initiated minority. **2** difficult to understand; abstruse. **3** not openly admitted; private. ORIG C17: from Gk, from *esōterō* inner
▸ **ˌeso'terically** *adv* ▸ **ˌeso'teriˌcism** *n*

ESP *abbrev. for* extrasensory perception.

esp. *abbrev. for* especially.

★ people and places

espadrille (ˌɛspəˈdrɪl) *n* a light shoe with a canvas upper, esp. with a braided cord sole. ORIG C19: from F, from Provençal *espardilho*, dim. of *espart* ESPARTO; from use of esparto for the soles

espalier (ɪˈspæljə) *n* **1** an ornamental shrub or fruit tree trained to grow flat, as against a wall. **2** the trellis or framework on which such plants are trained. ◆ *vb* **3** (*tr*) to train (a plant) on an espalier. ORIG C17: from F: trellis, from OIt.: shoulder supports, from *spalla* shoulder

España ★ (esˈpaɲa) *n* the Spanish name for **Spain.**

esparto *or* **esparto grass** (ɛˈspɑːtəʊ) *n, pl* **espartos.** any of various grasses of S Europe and N Africa, used to make ropes, mats, etc. ORIG C18: from Sp., via L from Gk *spartos* a kind of rush

especial (ɪˈspɛʃəl) *adj* (*prenominal*) **1** unusual; notable. **2** applying to one person or thing in particular; specific; peculiar: *he had an especial dislike of relatives.* ORIG C14: from OF, from L *speciālis* individual; see SPECIAL
▸ **esˈpecially** *adv*

Esperanto (ˌɛspəˈræntəʊ) *n* an international artificial language based on words common to the chief European languages. ORIG C19: lit.: the one who hopes, pseudonym of Dr L. L. Zamenhof (1859–1917), its Polish inventor
▸ ˌ**Espeˈrantist** *n, adj*

espial (ɪˈspaɪəl) *n Arch.* **1** the act or fact of being seen or discovered. **2** the act of noticing. **3** the act of spying upon; secret observation.

espionage (ˈɛspɪəˌnɑːʒ) *n* **1** the use of spies to obtain secret information, esp. by governments. **2** the act of spying. ORIG C18: from F, from *espion* spy

Espírito Santo ★ (*Portuguese* ɪʃˈpiritu ˈsəntu) *n* a state of E Brazil, on the Atlantic: swampy coastal plain with mountains in the west; heavily forested. Capital: Vitória. Pop.: 2 802 707 (1996 est.). Area: 45 597 sq. km (17 601 sq. miles).

Espíritu Santo ★ (ɛsˈpɪrɪtuː ˈsæntəʊ) *n* an island in the SW Pacific: the largest and westernmost of the Vanuatu islands. Pop.: 25 581 (1989). Area: 4856 sq. km (1875 sq. miles).

esplanade (ˌɛspləˈneɪd) *n* **1** a long open level stretch of ground for walking along, esp. beside the seashore. Cf. **promenade** (sense 1). **2** an open area in front of a fortified place. ORIG C17: from F, from OIt. *spianata*, from *spianare* to make level, from L *explānāre*; see EXPLAIN

Espoo ★ (*Finnish* ˈɛspoː) *n* a city in S Finland. Pop.: 196 260 (1997 est.).

espousal (ɪˈspaʊzəl) *n* **1** adoption or support: *an espousal of new beliefs.* **2** (*sometimes pl*) *Arch.* a marriage or betrothal ceremony.

espouse (ɪˈspaʊz) *vb* **espouses, espousing, espoused.** (*tr*) **1** to adopt or give support to (a cause, ideal, etc.): *to espouse socialism.* **2** *Arch.* (esp. of a man) to take as spouse; marry. ORIG C15: from OF *espouser*, from L *spōnsāre* to affiance, espouse
▸ **esˈpouser** *n*

espressivo (ˌɛsprɛˈsiːvəʊ) *adv Music.* in an expressive manner. ORIG It.

espresso (ɛˈsprɛsəʊ) *n, pl* **espressos. 1** coffee made by forcing steam or boiling water through ground coffee beans. **2** an apparatus for making coffee in this way. ORIG C20: It., lit.: pressed

esprit (ɛˈspriː) *n* spirit and liveliness, esp. in wit. ORIG C16: from F, from L *spīritus* a breathing, SPIRIT[1]

esprit de corps (ɛˈspriː də ˈkɔː) *n* consciousness of and pride in belonging to a particular group; the sense of shared purpose and fellowship.

espy (ɪˈspaɪ) *vb* **espies, espying, espied.** (*tr*) to catch sight of or perceive; detect. ORIG C14: from OF *espier* to SPY, of Gmc origin
▸ **esˈpier** *n*

Esq. *abbrev. for* esquire.

-esque *suffix forming adjectives.* indicating a specified character, manner, style, or resemblance: *picturesque; Romanesque; statuesque.* ORIG via F from It. *-esco*

Esquiline ★ (ˈɛskwəˌlaɪn) *n* one of the seven hills on which ancient Rome was built.

Esquimau (ˈɛskɪˌməʊ) *n, pl* **Esquimaus** *or* **Esquimau,** *adj* a former spelling of **Eskimo.**

esquire (ɪˈskwaɪə) *n* **1** *Chiefly Brit.* a title of respect, usually abbreviated *Esq.*, placed after a man's name. **2** (in medieval times) the attendant of a knight, subsequently often knighted himself. ORIG C15: from OF *escuier*, from LL *scūtārius* shield bearer, from L *scūtum* shield

ESRC (in Britain) *abbrev. for* Economic and Social Research Council.

ESRO (ˈɛzrəʊ) *n acronym for* European Space Research Organization.

-ess *suffix forming nouns.* indicating a female: *waitress; lioness.* ORIG via OF from LL *-issa*, from Gk

> **USAGE NOTE** The suffix *-ess* in such words as *poetess, authoress* is now often regarded as disparaging; a sexually neutral term *poet, author* is preferred.

Essaouira ★ (ˌɛsəˈwɪərə) *n* a port in SW Morocco on the Atlantic. Pop.: 42 000 (1982). Former name (until 1956): **Mogador.**

essay *n* (ˈɛseɪ; *senses 2, 3 also* ɛˈseɪ). **1** a short literary composition. **2** an attempt; effort. **3** a test or trial. ◆ *vb* (ɛˈseɪ). (*tr*) **4** to attempt or try. **5** to test or try out. ORIG C15: from OF *essai* an attempt, from LL *exagium* a weighing, from L *agere* to do, infl. by *exigere* to investigate

essayist (ˈɛseɪɪst) *n* a person who writes essays.

Essen ★ (*German* ˈɛsən) *n* a city in W Germany, in North Rhine-Westphalia: the leading industrial centre of the Ruhr, with extensive iron and steel factories. Pop.: 614 861 (1996 est.).

essence (ˈɛsəns) *n* **1** the characteristic or intrinsic feature of a thing, which determines its identity; fundamental nature. **2** a perfect or complete form of something. **3** *Philosophy.* the unchanging and unchangeable inward nature of something. **4a** the constituent of a plant, usually an oil, alkaloid, or glycoside, that determines its chemical properties. **4b** an alcoholic solution of such a substance. **5** a substance containing the properties of a plant or foodstuff in concentrated form: *vanilla essence.* **6** a rare word for **perfume. 7 in essence.** essentially; fundamentally. **8 of the essence.** indispensable; vitally important. ORIG C14: from Med. L *essentia*, from L: the being (of something), from *esse* to be

Essene (ˈɛsiːn, ɛˈsiːn) *n Judaism.* a member of an ascetic sect that flourished in Palestine from the second century B.C. to the second century A.D.
▸ **Essenian** (ɛˈsiːnɪən) *or* **Essenic** (ɛˈsɛnɪk) *adj*

essential (ɪˈsɛnʃəl) *adj* **1** vitally important; absolutely necessary. **2** basic; fundamental. **3** absolute; perfect. **4** derived from or relating to an extract of a plant, drug, etc.: *an essential oil.* **5** *Biochem.* (of an amino acid or a fatty acid) necessary for the normal growth of an organism but not synthesized by the organism and therefore required in the diet. **6** *Pathol.* (of a disease) having no obvious external cause: *essential hypertension.* ◆ *n* **7** something fundamental or indispensable.
▸ **essentiality** (ɪˌsɛnʃɪˈælɪtɪ) *or* **esˈsentialness** *n* ▸ **esˈsentially** *adv*

essential element *n Biochem.* any chemical element required by an organism for healthy growth. It may be required in large amounts (**macronutrient**) or in very small amounts (**trace element**).

essentialism (ɪˈsɛnʃəˌlɪzəm) *n Philosophy.* any doctrine that material objects have an essence distinguishable from their attributes and existence.
▸ **esˈsentialist** *n*

essential oil *n* any of various volatile oils in plants, having the odour or flavour of the plant from which they are extracted.

Essequibo ★ (ˌɛsɪˈkwiːbəʊ) *n* a river in Guyana, rising near the Brazilian border and flowing north to the Atlantic: drains over half of Guyana. Length: 1014 km (630 miles).

Essex[1] ★ (ˈɛsɪks) *n* **1** a county of SE England, on the North Sea and the Thames estuary. Southend-on-Sea and Thurrock became independent unitary authorities in 1998. Administrative centre: Chelmsford. Pop. (excluding unitary authorities): 1 281 600 (1996 est.). Area (excluding unitary authorities): 3446 sq. km (1330 sq. miles). **2** an Anglo-Saxon kingdom that in the early 7th century A.D. comprised the modern county of Essex and much of Hertfordshire and Surrey. By the late 8th century, Essex had become a dependency of the kingdom of Mercia.

Essex[2] ★ ('ɛsɪks) *n* **2nd Earl of,** title of *Robert Devereux.* ?1566–1601, English soldier and favourite of Elizabeth I; executed for treason.

Essex Man *n Inf., derog.* a self-made man, esp. of working-class origins, characterized by philistinism and bigoted right-wing views. ORIG C20: from the supposed prevalence of such people in ESSEX[1] (sense 1)

Esslingen ★ ('ɛslɪŋən) *n* a town in SW Germany, on the River Neckar: Gothic church, medieval buildings: wines, light industry. Pop.: 91 685 (1991 est.).

Essonne ★ (*French* ɛsɔn) *n* a department of N France, south of Paris in Île-de-France region: formed in 1964. Capital: Évry. Pop.: 1 141 679 (1994 est.). Area: 1811 sq. km (706 sq. miles).

EST *abbrev. for:* **1** (in the US and Canada) Eastern Standard Time. **2** electric-shock treatment.

est. *abbrev. for:* **1** established. **2** estimate(d).

-est[1] *suffix.* forming the superlative degree of adjectives and adverbs: *fastest.* ORIG OE *-est, -ost*

-est[2] *or* **-st** *suffix.* forming the archaic second person singular present and past indicative tense of verbs: *thou goest; thou hadst.* ORIG OE *-est, -ast*

establish (ɪ'stæblɪʃ) *vb* (*tr*) **1** to make secure or permanent in a certain place, condition, job, etc. **2** to create or set up (an organization, etc.) as on a permanent basis. **3** to prove correct; validate: *establish a fact.* **4** to cause (a principle, theory, etc.) to be accepted: *establish a precedent.* **5** to give (a Church) the status of a national institution. **6** to cause (a person) to become recognized and accepted. **7** (in works of imagination) to cause (a character, place, etc.) to be credible and recognized. ORIG C14: from OF, from L *stabilis* STABLE[2]
▸ **es'tablisher** *n*

Established Church *n* a Church that is officially recognized as a national institution, esp. the Church of England.

establishment (ɪ'stæblɪʃmənt) *n* **1** the act of establishing or state of being established. **2a** a business organization or other large institution. **2b** a place of business. **3** the staff and equipment of an organization. **4** any large organization or system. **5** a household; residence. **6** a body of employees or servants. **7** (*modifier*) belonging to or characteristic of the Establishment.

Establishment (ɪ'stæblɪʃmənt) *n* **the.** a group or class having institutional authority within a society: usually seen as conservative.

estate (ɪ'steɪt) *n* **1** a large piece of landed property, esp. in the country. **2** *Chiefly Brit.* a large area of property development, esp. of new houses or (**trading estate**) of factories. **3** *Law.* **3a** property or possessions. **3b** the nature of interest that a person has in land or other property. **3c** the total extent of the property of a deceased person or bankrupt. **4** Also called: **estate of the realm.** an order or class in a political community, regarded as a part of the body politic: the lords spiritual (**first estate**), lords temporal or peers (**second estate**), and commons (**third estate**). See also **fourth estate. 5** state, period, or position in life: *youth's estate; a poor man's estate.* ORIG C13: from OF *estat,* from L *status* condition, STATE

estate agent *n* **1** *Brit.* an agent concerned with the valuation, management, lease, and sale of property. **2** the administrator of a large landed property; estate manager.

estate car *n Brit.* a car containing a large carrying space, reached through a rear door: usually the back seats fold forward to increase the carrying space.

estate duty *n* another name for **death duty.**

Este ★ ('ɛste) *n* a noble family of Italy founded by Alberto Azzo II (996–1097), who was invested with the town of Este in NE Italy as a fief of the Holy Roman Empire. The family governed Ferrara (13th–16th centuries), Modena, and Reggio (13th–18th centuries).

esteem (ɪ'sti:m) *vb* (*tr*) **1** to have great respect or high regard for. **2** *Formal.* to judge or consider; deem. ◆ *n* **3** high regard or respect; good opinion. **4** *Arch.* judgment; opinion. ORIG C15: from OF *estimer,* from L *aestimāre* ESTIMATE
▸ **es'teemed** *adj*

ester ('ɛstə) *n Chem.* any of a class of compounds produced by reaction between acids and alcohols with the elimination of water. ORIG C19: from G, prob. a contraction of *Essigäther* acetic ether, from *Essig* vinegar (ult. from L *acētum*) + *Äther* ETHER

Esterházy ★ ('ɛstə,hɑ:zɪ) *n* a noble Hungarian family that produced many soldiers, diplomats, and patrons of the arts.

Esth. *Bible. abbrev.for* Esther.

Esther ★ ('ɛstə) *n Old Testament.* **1** a beautiful Jewish woman who became queen of Persia and saved her people from massacre. **2** the book in which this episode is recounted.

esthesia (i:s'θi:zɪə) *n* a US spelling of **aesthesia.**

esthete ('i:sθi:t) *n* a US spelling of **aesthete.**

Esthonia ★ (ɛ'stəunɪə, ɛ'sθəu-) *n* See **Estonia.**

estimable ('ɛstɪməb[ə]l) *adj* worthy of respect; deserving of admiration.
▸ **'estimableness** *n* ▸ **'estimably** *adv*

estimate *vb* ('ɛstɪ,meɪt), **estimates, estimating, estimated. 1** to form an approximate idea of (size, cost, etc.); calculate roughly. **2** (*tr; may take a clause as object*) to form an opinion about; judge. **3** to submit (an approximate price) for (a job) to a prospective client. ◆ *n* ('ɛstɪmɪt). **4** an approximate calculation. **5** a statement of the likely charge for certain work. **6** a judgment; appraisal. ORIG C16: from L *aestimāre* to assess the worth of, from ?
▸ **'esti,mator** *n* ▸ **'estimative** *adj*

estimation (,ɛstɪ'meɪʃən) *n* **1** a considered opinion; judgment. **2** esteem; respect. **3** the act of estimating.

estival (i:'staɪv[ə]l, 'ɛstɪ-) *adj* the usual US spelling of **aestival.**

estivate ('i:stɪ,veɪt, 'ɛs-) *vb* **estivates, estivating, estivated.** (*intr*) the usual US spelling of **aestivate.**

Estonia *or* **Esthonia** ★ (ɛ'stəunɪə, ɛ'sθəu-) *n* a republic on the Gulf of Finland and the Baltic: low-lying with many lakes and forests. It was under Scandinavian and Teutonic rule from the 13th century to 1721, when it passed to Russia: became an independent republic from 1920 to 1940, when it was annexed by the Soviet Union as the Estonian Soviet Socialist Republic: regained independence in 1991. Official language: Estonian. Currency: kroon. Religion: believers are mostly Lutheran. Capital: Tallinn. Pop.: 1 439 000 (1999 est.). Area: 45 227 sq. km (17 462 sq. miles).

Estonian *or* **Esthonian** (ɛ'stəunɪən, ɛ'sθəu-) *adj* **1** of, relating to, or characteristic of Estonia, its people, or their language. ◆ *n* **2** the official language of Estonia. **3** a native or inhabitant of Estonia.

estop (ɪ'stɒp) *vb* **estops, estopping, estopped.** (*tr*) **1** *Law.* to preclude by estoppel. **2** *Arch.* to stop. ORIG C15: from OF *estoper* to plug, ult. from L *stuppa* tow; see STOP
▸ **es'toppage** *n*

estoppel (ɪ'stɒp[ə]l) *n Law.* a rule of evidence whereby a person is precluded from denying the truth of a statement he has previously asserted. ORIG C16: from OF *estoupail* plug; see ESTOP

Estoril ★ (,ɛʃtu'ri:l) *n* a resort in W Portugal, near Lisbon, on the Atlantic Ocean: noted esp. for a famous avenue of palm trees leading to the seafront. Pop.: 24 850 (1991).

estovers (ɛ'stəuvəz) *pl n Law.* necessaries allowed to tenants of land, esp. wood for fuel and repairs. ORIG C15: from Anglo-F., pl of *estover,* from OF *estovoir* to be necessary, from L *est opus* there is need

estradiol (,ɛstrə'daɪɒl, ,i:strə-) *n* the usual US spelling of **oestradiol.**

estrange (ɪ'streɪndʒ) *vb* **estranges, estranging, estranged.** (*tr*) to antagonize or lose the affection of (someone previously friendly); alienate. ORIG C15: from OF *estranger,*

from LL *extrāneāre* to treat as a stranger, from L *extrāneus* foreign
▸ **es'tranged** *adj* ▸ **es'trangement** *n*

Estremadura ★ (*Portuguese* ɪʃtrəmə'ðurə) *n* **1** a region of W Spain: arid and sparsely populated except in the valleys of the Tagus and Guadiana Rivers. Area: 41 593 sq. km (16 059 sq. miles). Spanish name: **Extremadura. 2** a region, formerly a province, in Portugal around Lisbon.

estrogen ('ɛstrədʒən, 'iːstrə-) *n* the usual US spelling of **oestrogen.**

estrus ('ɛstrəs, 'iːstrəs) *n* the usual US spelling of **oestrus.**

estuary ('ɛstjʊərɪ) *n, pl* **estuaries.** the widening channel of a river where it nears the sea. ORIG C16: from L *aestuārium* marsh, channel, from *aestus* tide
▸ **estuarial** (ˌɛstjʊ'ɛərɪəl) *adj* ▸ **'estuarine** *adj*

e.s.u. *or* **ESU** *abbrev. for* electrostatic unit.

E. Sussex *abbrev. for* East Sussex.

ET (in Britain) *abbrev. for* Employment Training: a government scheme offering training in technological and business skills to unemployed people.

-et *suffix of nouns.* small or lesser: *islet; baronet.* ORIG from OF *-et, -ete*

eta ('iːtə) *n* the seventh letter in the Greek alphabet (H, η). ORIG Gk, from Phoenician

ETA *abbrev. for* estimated time of arrival.

e-tail ('iːteɪl) *n* retail conducted on the Internet. ORIG C20: E- + (RE)TAIL
▸ **'e-tailer** *n* ▸ **'e-tailing** *n*

et al. *abbrev. for:* **1** et alibi. ORIG L: and elsewhere **2** et alii. ORIG L: and others

etalon ('ɛtəˌlɒn) *n Physics.* a device used in spectroscopy to measure wavelengths by interference effects produced by multiple reflections between parallel half-silvered glass plates. ORIG C20: F *étalon* a standard of weights & measures

etc. *abbrev. for* et cetera.

et cetera *or* **etcetera** (ɪt 'sɛtrə) *n and vb substitute.* **1** and the rest; and others; and so forth. **2** or the like; or something similar. ORIG from L *et* and + *cetera* the other (things)

> **USAGE NOTE** It is unnecessary to use *and* before *etc.* as the Latin words of which *etc.* is an abbreviation already mean 'and other things'. The repetition of *etc.*, as in *he brought paper, ink, notebooks, etc., etc.*, should be avoided except in spoken or informal contexts.

etceteras (ɪt'sɛtrəz) *pl n* miscellaneous extra things or persons.

etch (ɛtʃ) *vb* **1** (*tr*) to wear away the surface of (a metal, glass, etc.) by the action of an acid. **2** to cut or corrode (a design, etc.) on (a metal or other printing plate) by the action of acid on parts not covered by an acid-resistant coating. **3** (*tr*) to cut as with a sharp implement. **4** (*tr; usually passive*) to imprint vividly. ORIG C17: from Du. *etsen*, from OHG *azzen* to feed, bite
▸ **'etcher** *n*

etching ('ɛtʃɪŋ) *n* **1** the art, act, or process of preparing etched surfaces or of printing designs from them. **2** an etched plate. **3** an impression made from an etched plate.

ETD *abbrev. for* estimated time of departure.

Eteocles ★ (ɪ'tiːəˌkliːz, 'ɛtɪə-) *n Greek myth.* a son of Oedipus and Jocasta. He and his brother, Polynices, were to share the kingdom of Thebes but Eteocles expelled Polynices from Thebes; they killed each other in single combat when Polynices returned as leader of the Seven against Thebes.

eternal (ɪ'tɜːnᵊl) *adj* **1a** without beginning or end; lasting forever. **1b** (*as n*): *the eternal.* **2** (*often cap.*) a name applied to God. **3** unchanged by time; immutable: *eternal truths.* **4** seemingly unceasing. ORIG C14: from LL, from L *aeternus;* rel. to L *aevum* age
▸ **ˌeter'nality** *or* **e'ternalness** *n* ▸ **e'ternally** *adv*

Eternal City ★ *n* **the.** Rome.

eternalize (ɪ'tɜːnəˌlaɪz) *or* **eternize** (ɪ'tɜːnaɪz), **eternalise** *vb* **eternalizes, eternalizing, eternalized** *or* **eternalises, eternalising, eternalised.** (*tr*) **1** to make eternal. **2** to make famous forever; immortalize.
▸ **eˌternali'zation** *or* **eˌterni'zation, eˌternali'sation** *n*

eternal triangle *n* an emotional relationship usually involving three people, two of whom are rival lovers of the third person.

eternity (ɪ'tɜːnɪtɪ) *n, pl* **eternities. 1** endless or infinite time. **2** the quality, state, or condition of being eternal. **3** (*usually pl*) any aspect of life and thought considered timeless. **4** the timeless existence, believed by some to characterize the afterlife. **5** a seemingly endless period of time.

eternity ring *n* a ring given as a token of lasting affection, esp. one set all around with stones to symbolize continuity.

etesian (ɪ'tiːʒɪən) *adj* (of NW winds) recurring annually in the summer in the E Mediterranean. ORIG C17: from L *etēsius* yearly, from Gk *etos* year

ETF *abbrev. for* electronic transfer of funds.

Eth. *abbrev. for:* **1** Ethiopia(n). **2** Ethiopic.

-eth[1] *suffix.* forming the archaic third person singular present indicative tense of verbs: *goeth; taketh.* ORIG OE *-eth, -th*

-eth[2] *suffix forming ordinal numbers.* a variant of **-th**[2]: *twentieth.*

ethanal ('ɛθəˌnæl) *n* the systematic name for **acetaldehyde.**

ethane ('iːθeɪn, 'ɛθ-) *n* a colourless odourless flammable gaseous alkane obtained from natural gas and petroleum: used as a fuel. Formula: C_2H_6. ORIG C19: from ETH(YL)+ -ANE

ethanediol ('iːθeɪnˌdaɪɒl, 'ɛθ-) *n* a colourless soluble liquid used as an antifreeze and solvent. Formula: $C_2H_4(OH)_2$. ORIG C20: from ETHANE + DI-[1] + -OL[1]

ethanoic acid (ˌɛθə'nəʊɪk, ˌiːθə-) *n* the systematic name for **acetic acid.**

ethanol ('ɛθəˌnɒl, 'iːθə-) *n* the systematic name for **alcohol** (sense 1).

Ethelbert ('ɛθəlˌbɜːt) *or* **Æthelbert** ★ ('æθəlˌbɜːt) *n* **Saint.** ?552–616 A.D., king of Kent (560–616): converted to Christianity by St Augustine; issued the earliest known code of English laws. Feast day: Feb. 24 or 25.

Ethelred I ('ɛθəlˌrɛd) *or* **Æthelred** ★ ('æθəlˌrɛd) *n* died 871, king of Wessex (866–71). He led resistance to the Danish invasion of England; died following his victory at Ashdown.

Ethelred II *or* **Æthelred** ★ *n* known as *Ethelred the Unready.* ?968–1016 A.D., king of England (978–1016). He was temporarily deposed by the Danish king Sweyn (1013) but was recalled on Sweyn's death (1014).

Ethelwulf ('ɛθəlˌwʊlf) *or* **Æthelwulf** ★ ('æθəlˌwʊlf) *n* died 858 A.D., king of Wessex (839–858).

ethene ('ɛθiːn) *n* the systematic name for **ethylene.**

ether ('iːθə) *n* **1** Also called: **diethyl ether, ethyl ether, ethoxyethane.** a colourless volatile highly flammable liquid: used as a solvent and anaesthetic. Formula: $C_2H_5OC_2H_5$. **2** any of a class of organic compounds with the general formula ROR′, as in methyl ethyl ether, $CH_3OC_2H_5$. **3** the medium formerly believed to fill all space and to support the propagation of electromagnetic waves. **4** *Greek myth.* the upper atmosphere; clear sky or heaven. ◆ Also (for senses 3 and 4): **aether.** ORIG C17: from L, from Gk *aithein* to burn
▸ **e'theric** *adj*

ethereal (ɪ'θɪərɪəl) *adj* **1** extremely delicate or refined. **2** almost as light as air; airy. **3** celestial or spiritual. **4** of, containing, or dissolved in an ether, esp. diethyl ether. **5** of or relating to the ether. ORIG C16: from L, from Gk *aithēr* ETHER
▸ **eˌthere'ality** *or* **e'therealness** *n*

etherealize *or* **etherealise** (ɪ'θɪərɪəˌlaɪz) *vb* **etherealizes, etherealizing, etherealized** *or* **etherealises, etherealising, etherealised.** (*tr*) **1** to make or regard as being ethereal. **2** to add ether to or make into ether.
▸ **eˌthereali'zation** *or* **eˌthereali'sation** *n*

etherize *or* **etherise** (ˈiːθəˌraɪz) *vb* **etherizes, etherizing, etherized** *or* **etherises, etherising, etherised.** (*tr*) *Obs.* to subject (a person) to the anaesthetic influence of ether fumes; anaesthetize.
▸ **ˌetheriˈzation** *or* **ˌetheriˈsation** *n* ▸ **ˈetherˌizer** *or* **ˈetherˌiser** *n*

Ethernet (ˈiːθəˌnɛt) *n Trademark, computing.* a widely used type of local area network.

ethic (ˈɛθɪk) *n* **1** a moral principle or set of moral values held by an individual or group. ◆ *adj* **2** another word for **ethical.** ORIG C15: from L, from Gk *ēthos* custom

ethical (ˈɛθɪkᵊl) *adj* **1** in accordance with principles of conduct that are considered correct, esp. those of a given profession or group. **2** of or relating to ethics. **3** (of a medicinal agent) available legally only with a doctor's prescription.
▸ **ˈethically** *adv* ▸ **ˈethicalness** *or* **ˌethiˈcality** *n*

ethical investment *n* an investment in a company whose activities or products are not considered by the investor to be unethical.

ethics (ˈɛθɪks) *n* **1** (*functioning as sing*) the philosophical study of the moral value of human conduct and of the rules and principles that ought to govern it. **2** (*functioning as pl*) a code of behaviour considered correct, esp. that of a particular group, profession, or individual. **3** (*functioning as pl*) the moral fitness of a decision, course of action, etc.
▸ **ethicist** (ˈɛθɪsɪst) *n*

Ethiopia ★ (ˌiːθɪˈəʊpɪə) *n* a state in NE Africa, on the Red Sea: consolidated as an empire under Menelik II (1889–1913); federated with Eritrea (1952–93); Emperor Haile Selassie was deposed by the military in 1974 and the monarchy was abolished in 1975. It lies along the Great Rift Valley and consists of deserts in the southeast and northeast and a high central plateau with many rivers (including the Blue Nile) and mountains rising over 4500 m (15 000 ft); the main export is coffee. Language: Amharic. Religion: Christian majority. Currency: birr. Capital: Addis Ababa. Pop.: 59 680 000 (1999 est.). Area: 1 128 215 sq. km (435 614 sq. miles). Former name: **Abyssinia.** See also **Eritrea.**

Ethiopian (ˌiːθɪˈəʊpɪən) *adj* **1** of or relating to Ethiopia, its people, or any of their languages. ◆ *n* **2** a native or inhabitant of Ethiopia. **3** any of the languages of Ethiopia, esp. Amharic. ◆ *n, adj* **4** an archaic word for **Black**[1].

Ethiopic (ˌiːθɪˈɒpɪk, -ˈəʊpɪk) *n* **1** the ancient Semitic language of Ethiopia: a Christian liturgical language. **2** the group of languages developed from this language, including Amharic. ◆ *adj* **3** denoting or relating to this language or group of languages. **4** a less common word for **Ethiopian.**

ethnic (ˈɛθnɪk) *or* **ethnical** *adj* **1** of or relating to a human group having racial, religious, linguistic, and other traits in common. **2** relating to the classification of mankind into groups, esp. on the basis of racial characteristics. **3** denoting or deriving from the cultural traditions of a group of people. **4** characteristic of another culture, esp. a peasant one. ◆ *n* **5** *Chiefly US.* a member of an ethnic group, esp. a minority one. ORIG C14 (in the senses: heathen, Gentile): from LL *ethnicus,* from Gk *ethnos* race
▸ **ˈethnically** *adv* ▸ **ethnicity** (ɛθˈnɪsɪtɪ) *n*

ethnic cleansing *n Euphemistic.* the violent removal by one ethnic group of other ethnic groups from the population of a particular area: used esp. of the activities of Serbs against Croats and Muslims in the former Yugoslavia.

ethno- *combining form.* indicating race, people, or culture. ORIG via F from Gk *ethnos* race

ethnocentrism (ˌɛθnəʊˈsɛnˌtrɪzəm) *n* belief in the intrinsic superiority of the nation, culture, or group to which one belongs.
▸ **ˌethnoˈcentric** *adj* ▸ **ˌethnoˈcentrically** *adv* ▸ **ˌethnocenˈtricity** *n*

ethnography (ɛθˈnɒgrəfɪ) *n* the branch of anthropology that deals with the scientific description of individual human societies.
▸ **ˌethˈnographer** *n* ▸ **ethnographic** (ˌɛθnəʊˈgræfɪk) *or* **ˌethnoˈgraphical** *adj*

ethnology (ɛθˈnɒlədʒɪ) *n* the branch of anthropology that deals with races and peoples, their origins, characteristics, etc.
▸ **ethnologic** (ˌɛθnəˈlɒdʒɪk) *or* **ˌethnoˈlogical** *adj* ▸ **ethˈnologist** *n*

ethnomusicology (ˌɛθnəʊˌmjuːzɪˈkɒlədʒɪ) *n* the study of the origins of music, esp. from non-European cultures.

ethology (ɪˈθɒlədʒɪ) *n* the study of the behaviour of animals in their normal environment. ORIG C17 (in the obs. sense: mimicry): via L from Gk *ēthos* character; current sense, C19
▸ **ethological** (ˌɛθəˈlɒdʒɪkᵊl) *adj* ▸ **eˈthologist** *n*

ethos (ˈiːθɒs) *n* the distinctive character, spirit, and attitudes of a people, culture, era, etc.: *the revolutionary ethos.* ORIG C19: from LL: habit, from Gk

ethyl (ˈiːθaɪl, ˈɛθɪl) *n* (*modifier*) of, consisting of, or containing the monovalent group C_2H_5–. ORIG C19: from ETH(ER) + -YL
▸ **ethylic** (ɪˈθɪlɪk) *adj*

ethyl acetate *n* a colourless volatile flammable liquid ester: used in perfumes and flavourings and as a solvent. Formula: $CH_3COOC_2H_5$.

ethyl alcohol *n* another name for **alcohol** (sense 1).

ethylene (ˈɛθɪˌliːn) *or* **ethene** (ˈɛθiːn) *n* a colourless flammable gaseous alkene used in the manufacture of polythene and other chemicals. Formula: CH_2:CH_2.
▸ **ethylenic** (ˌɛθɪˈliːnɪk) *adj*

ethylene glycol *n* another name for **ethanediol.**

ethylene group *or* **radical** *n Chem.* the divalent group, $-CH_2CH_2-$, derived from ethylene.

ethylene series *n Chem.* another name for **alkene series.**

ethyne (ˈɛθaɪn) *n Chem.* the systematic name for **acetylene.**

ethyne series *n Chem.* another name for **acetylene series.**

etiolate (ˈiːtɪəʊˌleɪt) *vb* **etiolates, etiolating, etiolated. 1** *Bot.* to whiten (a green plant) through lack of sunlight. **2** to become or cause to become pale and weak. ORIG C18: from F *étioler* to make pale, prob. from OF *estuble* straw, from L *stipula*
▸ **ˌetioˈlation** *n*

etiology (ˌiːtɪˈɒlədʒɪ) *n, pl* **etiologies.** a variant spelling of **aetiology.**

etiquette (ˈɛtɪˌkɛt, ˌɛtɪˈkɛt) *n* **1** the customs or rules governing behaviour regarded as correct in social life. **2** a conventional code of practice followed in certain professions or groups. ORIG C18: from F, from OF *estiquette* label, from *estiquier* to attach; see STICK[2]

Etna ★ (ˈɛtnə) *n* **Mount.** an active volcano in E Sicily: the highest volcano in Europe and the highest peak in Italy south of the Alps. Height: 3323 m (10 902 ft).

Eton ★ (ˈiːtᵊn) *n* **1** a town in S England, in Berkshire near the River Thames: site of **Eton College,** a public school for boys founded in 1440. Pop.: 1974 (1991). **2** this college.
▸ **Etonian** (iːˈtəʊnɪən) *adj, n*

Eton collar *n* (formerly) a broad stiff white collar worn outside a boy's jacket.

Eton crop *n* a very short mannish hairstyle worn by women in the 1920s.

Eton jacket *n* (formerly) a boy's waist-length jacket with a V-shaped back, open in front.

Etruria ★ (ɪˈtrʊərɪə) *n* **1** an ancient country of central Italy, between the Rivers Arno and Tiber, roughly corresponding to present-day Tuscany and part of Umbria. **2** a factory established in Staffordshire by Josiah Wedgwood in 1769.

Etruscan (ɪˈtrʌskən) *or* **Etrurian** (ɪˈtrʊərɪən) *n* **1** a member of an ancient people of Etruria whose civilization greatly influenced the Romans. **2** the language of the ancient Etruscans. ◆ *adj* **3** of or relating to Etruria, the Etruscans, their culture, or their language.

et seq. *abbrev. for:* **1** et sequens ORIG L: and the following **2** Also: **et seqq.** et sequentia ORIG L: and those that follow

-ette *suffix of nouns.* **1** small: *cigarette.* **2** female: *majorette.* **3** (esp. in trade names) imitation: *Leatherette.* ORIG from F, fem of -ET

étude ('eɪtjuːd) *n* a short musical composition for a solo instrument, esp. one designed as an exercise or exploiting virtuosity. ORIG C19: from F: STUDY

étui (ɛ'twiː) *n, pl* **étuis.** a small usually ornamented case for holding needles, cosmetics, or other small articles. ORIG C17: F, from OF *estuier* to enclose; see TWEEZERS

etymology (ˌɛtɪ'mɒlədʒɪ) *n, pl* **etymologies. 1** the study of the sources and development of words. **2** an account of the source and development of a word. ORIG C14: via L from Gk; see ETYMON, -LOGY
▸ **etymological** (ˌɛtɪmə'lɒdʒɪkᵊl) *adj* ▸ **ˌety'mologist** *n* ▸ **ˌety'moloˌgize** *or* **ˌety'moloˌgise** *vb*

etymon ('ɛtɪˌmɒn) *n, pl* **etymons** *or* **etyma** (-mə). a form of a word, usually the earliest recorded form or a reconstructed form, from which another word is derived. ORIG C16: via L from Gk *etumon* basic meaning, from *etumos* true, actual

Etzel ★ ('ɛtsᵊl) *n German legend.* a great king who, according to the *Nibelungenlied,* was the second husband of Kriemhild after the death of Siegfried: identified with Attila the Hun. Cf. **Atli.**

Eu *the chemical symbol for* europium.

EU *abbrev. for* European Union.

eu- *combining form.* well, pleasant, or good: *eupeptic; euphony.* ORIG via L from Gk, from *eus* good

Euboea ★ (juː'bɪə) *n* an island in the W Aegean Sea: the largest island after Crete of the Greek archipelago; linked with the mainland by a bridge across the Euripus channel. Capital: Chalcis. Pop.: 188 410 (1981). Area: 3908 sq. km (1509 sq. miles). Modern Greek name: **Évvoia.** Former English name: **Negropont.**
▸ **Eu'boean** *adj, n*

eucalyptus (ˌjuːkə'lɪptəs) *or* **eucalypt** ('juːkəˌlɪpt) *n, pl* **eucalyptuses, eucalypti** (-'lɪptaɪ), *or* **eucalypts.** any tree of the mostly Australian genus *Eucalyptus,* widely cultivated for timber and gum, as ornament, and for the medicinal oil in their leaves (**eucalyptus oil**). ORIG C19: NL, from EU- + Gk *kaluptos* covered, from *kaluptein* to cover, hide

Eucharist ('juːkərɪst) *n* **1** the Christian sacrament in which Christ's Last Supper is commemorated by the consecration of bread and wine. **2** the consecrated elements of bread and wine offered in the sacrament. ORIG C14: via Church L from Gk *eukharistos* thankful, from EU- + *kharis* favour
▸ **ˌEucha'ristic** *or* **ˌEucha'ristical** *adj*

euchre ('juːkə) *n* **1** a US and Canad. card game for two, three, or four players, using a poker pack. **2** an instance of euchring another player. ◆ *vb* **euchres, euchring, euchred.** (*tr*) **3** to prevent (a player) from making his or her contracted tricks. **4** (usually foll. by *out*) *US, Canad., Austral., & NZ inf.* to outwit or cheat. ORIG C19: from ?

Euclid ★ ('juːklɪd) *n* **1** 3rd century B.C., Greek mathematician of Alexandria; author of *Elements,* setting out the principles of geometry. **2** the works of Euclid, esp. his system of geometry.
▸ **Euclidean** *or* **Euclidian** (juː'klɪdɪən) *adj*

eucryphia (juː'krɪfɪə) *n* any of various mostly evergreen trees and shrubs of S America and Australia. ORIG NL, from EU- + Gk *kryphios* covered

eudiometer (ˌjuːdɪ'ɒmɪtə) *n* a graduated glass tube used in the study and volumetric analysis of gas reactions. ORIG C18: from Gk *eudios,* lit.: clear-skied + -METER

Eugène ★ (*French* øʒɛn) *n* **Prince,** title of *François Eugène de Savoie-Carignan.* 1663–1736, Austrian general, born in France: with Marlborough defeated the French at Blenheim (1704) and Malplaquet (1709).

eugenics (juː'dʒɛnɪks) *n* (*functioning as sing*) the study of methods of improving the quality of the human race, esp. by selective breeding. ORIG C19: from Gk *eugenēs* well-born, from EU- + *-genēs* born; see -GEN
▸ **eu'genic** *adj* ▸ **eu'genically** *adv* ▸ **eu'genicist** *n* ▸ **eugenist** ('juːdʒənɪst) *n*

Eugénie ★ (*French* øʒeni) *n* original name *Eugénia Maria de Montijo de Guzman, Comtesse de Téba.* 1826–1920, Empress of France (1853–71) as wife of Napoleon III.

eukaryote *or* **eucaryote** (juː'kærɪəʊt) *n* an organism having cells each with a nucleus within which the genetic material is contained. Cf. **prokaryote.** ORIG from EU- + KARYO- + *-ote* as in *zygote*
▸ **eukaryotic** *or* **eucaryotic** (juˌkærɪ'ɒtɪk) *adj*

Euler ★ (*German* 'ɔɪlər) *n* **1 Leonhard** ('leːɔnhart). 1707–83, Swiss mathematician, noted esp. for his work on the calculus of variation: considered the founder of modern mathematical analysis. **2 Ulf** (**Svante**) **von** (ulf fɔn). 1905–83, Swedish physiologist: shared the Nobel prize (1970) for physiology or medicine.

Euler-Chelpin ★ (*German* 'ɔɪlər'kɛlpiːn) *n* **Hans** (**Karl August**) **von.** 1873–1964, Swedish biochemist, born in Germany: shared the Nobel prize for chemistry (1929) for work on enzymes: father of Ulf von Euler.

eulogize *or* **eulogise** ('juːləˌdʒaɪz) *vb* **eulogizes, eulogizing, eulogized** *or* **eulogises, eulogising, eulogised.** to praise (a person or thing) highly in speech or writing.
▸ **'eulogist, 'euloˌgizer,** *or* **'euloˌgiser** *n* ▸ **ˌeulo'gistic** *or* **ˌeulo'gistical** *adj*

eulogy ('juːlədʒɪ) *n, pl* **eulogies. 1** a speech or piece of writing praising a person or thing, esp. a person who has recently died. **2** high praise or commendation. ◆ Also called (archaic): **eulogium** (juː'ləʊdʒɪəm). ORIG C16: from LL, from Gk: praise, from EU- + -LOGY

Eumenides (juː'mɛnɪˌdiːz) *pl n* another name for the **Furies,** used by the Greeks as a euphemism. ORIG from Gk, lit: the benevolent ones

eunuch ('juːnək) *n* **1** a man who has been castrated, esp. (formerly) for some office such as a guard in a harem. **2** *Inf.* an ineffective man. ORIG C15: via L from Gk *eunoukhos* bedchamber attendant

euonymus (juː'ɒnɪməs) *or* **evonymus** (ɛ'vɒnɪməs) *n* any tree or shrub of the N temperate genus *Euonymus,* such as the spindle tree. ORIG C18: from L: spindle tree, from Gk *euōnumos* fortunately named, from EU- + *onoma* NAME

Eupen and Malmédy ★ (*French* øpɛn; malmedi) *n* a region of Belgium in Liège province: ceded by Germany in 1919. Pop.: 27 675 (1995 est.).

eupepsia (juː'pɛpsɪə) *or* **eupepsy** (juː'pɛpsɪ) *n Physiol.* good digestion. ORIG C18: from NL, from Gk, from EU- + *pepsis* digestion
▸ **eupeptic** (juː'pɛptɪk) *adj*

euphemism ('juːfɪˌmɪzəm) *n* **1** an inoffensive word or phrase substituted for one considered offensive or hurtful. **2** the use of such inoffensive words or phrases. ORIG C17: from Gk, from EU- + *phēmē* speech
▸ **ˌeuphe'mistic** *adj* ▸ **ˌeuphe'mistically** *adv*

euphemize *or* **euphemise** ('juːfɪˌmaɪz) *vb* **euphemizes, euphemizing, euphemized** *or* **euphemises, euphemising, euphemised.** to speak in euphemisms or refer to by means of a euphemism.
▸ **'eupheˌmizer** *or* **'eupheˌmiser** *n*

euphonic (juː'fɒnɪk) *or* **euphonious** (juː'fəʊnɪəs) *adj* **1** denoting or relating to euphony. **2** (of speech sounds) altered for ease of pronunciation.
▸ **eu'phonically** *or* **eu'phoniously** *adv* ▸ **eu'phoniousness** *n*

euphonium (juː'fəʊnɪəm) *n* a brass musical instrument with four valves. ORIG C19: NL, from EUPH(ONY + HARM)ONIUM

euphonize *or* **euphonise** ('juːfəˌnaɪz) *vb* **euphonizes, euphonizing, euphonized** *or* **euphonises, euphonising, euphonised. 1** to make pleasant to hear. **2** to change (speech sounds) so as to facilitate pronunciation.

euphony ('juːfənɪ) *n, pl* **euphonies. 1** the alteration of speech sounds, esp. by assimilation, so as to make them easier to pronounce. **2** a pleasing sound, esp. in speech. ORIG C17: from LL, from Gk, from EU- + *phōnē* voice

euphorbia (juː'fɔːbɪə) *n* any plant of the genus *Euphorbia,* such as the spurges. ORIG C14 *euforbia,* from L *euphorbea* African plant, after *Euphorbus,* first-cent. A.D. Gk physician

euphoria (juːˈfɔːrɪə) *n* a feeling of great elation, esp. when exaggerated. ORIG C19: from Gk: good ability to endure, from EU- + *pherein* to bear
▸ **euphoric** (juːˈfɒrɪk) *adj*

euphoriant (juːˈfɔːrɪənt) *adj* **1** able to produce euphoria. ◆ *n* **2** a euphoriant drug or agent.

euphotic (juːˈfəʊtɪk, -ˈfɒt-) *adj* denoting or relating to the uppermost part of a sea or lake, which receives enough light for photosynthesis to take place. ORIG C20: from EU- + PHOTIC

euphrasy (ˈjuːfrəsɪ) *n, pl* **euphrasies.** another name for **eyebright.** ORIG C15: *eufrasie,* from Med. L, from Gk *euphrasia* gladness, from EU- + *phrēn* mind

Euphrates ★ (juːˈfreɪtiːz) *n* a river in SW Asia, rising in E Turkey and flowing south across Syria and Iraq to join the Tigris, forming the Shatt-al-Arab, which flows to the head of the Persian Gulf: important in ancient times for the extensive irrigation of its valley (in Mesopotamia). Length: 3598 km (2235 miles).

Euphrosyne ★ (juːˈfrɒzɪˌniː) *n Greek myth.* one of the three Graces. ORIG from Gk: mirth, merriment

euphuism (ˈjuːfjuːˌɪzəm) *n* **1** an artificial prose style of the Elizabethan period, marked by extreme use of antithesis, alliteration, and extended similes and allusions. **2** any stylish affectation in speech or writing. ORIG C16: after *Euphues,* prose romance by John LYLY
▸ **ˈeuphuist** *n* ▸ **ˌeuphuˈistic** *or* **ˌeuphuˈistical** *adj*

eur. *or* **Eur.** *abbrev. for* Europe(an).

eur- *combining form.* (*sometimes cap.*) a variant of **euro-** before a vowel.

Eurasia ★ (jʊəˈreɪʃə, -ʒə) *n* the continents of Europe and Asia considered as a whole.

Eurasian (jʊəˈreɪʃən, -ʒən) *adj* **1** of or relating to Eurasia. **2** of mixed European and Asian descent. ◆ *n* **3** a person of mixed European and Asian descent.

Euratom (jʊəˈrætəm) *n* short for **European Atomic Energy Community;** an authority established by the EEC (now the EU) to develop peaceful uses of nuclear energy.

Eure ★ (*French* œr) *n* a department of N France, in Haute-Normandie region. Capital: Évreux. Pop.: 533 731 (1994 est.). Area: 6037 sq. km (2354 sq. miles).

Eure-et-Loir ★ (*French* œrelwar) *n* a department of N central France, in Centre region. Capital: Chartres. Pop.: 409 420 (1994 est.). Area: 5940 sq. km (2317 sq. miles).

eureka (jʊˈriːkə) *interj* an exclamation of triumph on discovering or solving something. ORIG C17: from Gk *heurēka* I have found (it), from *heuriskein* to find; traditionally the exclamation of Archimedes when he realized, during bathing, that the volume of an irregular solid could be calculated by measuring the water displaced when it was immersed

eurhythmic (juːˈrɪðmɪk), **eurhythmical,** *or esp. US* **eurythmic, eurythmical** *adj* **1** having a pleasing and harmonious rhythm, order, or structure. **2** of or relating to eurhythmics. ORIG C19: from L, from Gk, from EU- + *rhuthmos* proportion, RHYTHM

eurhythmics *or esp. US* **eurythmics** (juːˈrɪðmɪks) *n* (*functioning as sing*) **1** a system of training through physical movement to music. **2** dancing of this style. ORIG C20: from EURHYTHMIC
▸ **euˈrhythmy** *or* **euˈrythmy** *n*

Euripides ★ (jʊˈrɪpɪˌdiːz) *n* ?480–406 B.C., Greek tragic dramatist. His plays, 18 of which are extant, include *Alcestis, Medea, Hippolytus, Hecuba, Trojan Women, Electra, Iphigeneia in Tauris, Iphigeneia in Aulis,* and *Bacchae.*

euro (ˈjʊərəʊ) *n, pl* **euros.** the currency unit, divided into 100 cents, of the member countries of the European Union who have adopted European Monetary Union.

euro- (ˈjʊərəʊ) *or before a vowel* **eur-** *combining form.* (*sometimes cap.*) Europe *or* European.

eurobond (ˈjʊərəʊˌbɒnd) *n* (*sometimes cap.*) a bond issued in a eurocurrency.

Eurocentric (ˌjʊərəʊˈsɛntrɪk) *adj* chiefly concerned with or concentrating on Europe and European culture: *the Eurocentric curriculum.*

eurocheque (ˈjʊərəʊˌtʃɛk) *n* (*sometimes cap.*) a cheque drawn on a European bank that can be cashed at any bank or bureau de change displaying the EU sign or that can be used to pay for goods or services at any outlet displaying this sign.

Eurocommunism (ˌjʊərəʊˈkɒmjʊˌnɪzəm) *n* the policies, doctrines, and practices of Communist Parties in Western Europe in the 1970s and 1980s, esp. those rejecting democratic centralism and favouring nonalignment with the Soviet Union and China.
▸ **ˌEuroˈcommunist** *n, adj*

eurocrat (ˈjʊərəˌkræt) *n* (*sometimes cap.*) a member of the administration of the European Union.

eurocurrency (ˈjʊərəʊˌkʌrənsɪ) *n* (*sometimes cap.*) the currency of any country held on deposit in Europe outside its home market: used as a source of short- or medium-term finance because of easy convertibility.

eurodollar (ˈjʊərəʊˌdɒlə) *n* (*sometimes cap.*) a US dollar as part of a European holding. See **eurocurrency.**

euroland (ˈjʊərəʊˌlænd) *n* (*sometimes cap.*) another name for **eurozone.**

euromarket (ˈjʊərəʊˌmɑːkɪt) *n* **1** a market for financing international trade backed by the central banks and commercial banks of the European Union. **2** the European Union treated as one large market for the sale of goods and services.

Euro MP *n Inf.* a member of the European Parliament.

euronote (ˈjʊərəʊˌnəʊt) *n* a form of euro-commercial paper consisting of short-term negotiable bearer notes.

Europa ★ (jʊˈrəʊpə) *n Greek myth.* a Phoenician princess who had three children by Zeus in Crete, where he had taken her after assuming the guise of a white bull. Their offspring were Rhadamanthys, Minos, and Sarpedon.

Europe ★ (ˈjʊərəp) *n* **1** the second smallest continent, forming the W extension of Eurasia: the border with Asia runs from the Urals to the Caspian and the Black Sea. The coastline is generally extremely indented and there are several peninsulas (notably Scandinavia, Italy, and Iberia) and offshore islands (including the British Isles and Iceland). It contains a series of great mountain systems in the south (Pyrenees, Alps, Apennines, Carpathians, Caucasus), a large central plain, and a N region of lakes and mountains in Scandinavia. Pop.: 729 370 000 (1996 est.). Area: about 10 400 000 sq. km (4 000 000 sq. miles). **2** *Brit.* the continent of Europe except for the British Isles: *we're going to Europe for our holiday.* **3** *Brit.* the European Union: *when did Britain go into Europe?*

European (ˌjʊərəˈpɪən) *adj* **1** of or relating to Europe or its inhabitants. **2** native to or derived from Europe. ◆ *n* **3** a native or inhabitant of Europe. **4** a person of European descent. **5** *S. African.* any White person.
▸ **ˌEuroˈpeanˌism** *n*

European Commission *n* the executive body of the European Union, formed in 1967: it initiates legislation, administers funds, and ensures that Union laws are enforced.

European Community *or* **Communities** *n* an economic and political association of European states that came into being in 1967, when the executive and legislative bodies of the European Economic Community merged with those of the European Coal and Steel Community and the European Atomic Energy Community.

European Council *n* a body consisting of the heads of government of the member states of the European Union that meets three times a year to discuss major policy developments.

European Currency Unit *n* See **ECU.**

European Economic Community *n* the former W European economic association created by the Treaty of Rome (1957); in 1967 its executive and legislative bodies merged with those of the European Coal and Steel Community and the European Atomic Energy Community to form the European Community. Informal name: **Common Market.** Abbrev.: **EEC.**

Europeanize *or* **Europeanise** (ˌjʊərəˈpɪəˌnaɪz) *vb* **Europeanizes, Europeanizing, Europeanized** *or* **Europeanises, Europeanising, Europeanised.** (*tr*) **1** to make European. **2** to integrate (a country, economy, etc.) into the European Union.
▸ **ˌEuroˌpeaniˈzation** *or* **ˌEuroˌpeaniˈsation** *n*

European Monetary System *n* the system used in the European Union for stabilizing exchange rates between the currencies of member states. It relies on the Exchange Rate Mechanism and the balance-of-payments support mechanism. Abbrev.: **EMS.**

European Monetary Union *n* the agreement between members of the European Union to establish a common currency. The current participating members are Austria, Belgium, Finland, France, Germany, Greece, Ireland, Italy, Luxembourg, the Netherlands, Portugal, and Spain. Abbrev.: **EMU.**

European Parliament *n* the assembly of the European Union in Strasbourg.

European Union *n* an organization created in 1993 with the aim of achieving closer economic and political union between member states of the European Community. The current members are Austria, Belgium, Denmark, Finland, France, Germany, Greece, Ireland, Italy, Luxembourg, the Netherlands, Portugal, Spain, Sweden, and the UK. Abbrev.: **EU.**

Europhile (ˈjʊərəʊˌfaɪl) (*sometimes not cap.*) ◆ *n* **1** a person who admires Europe, Europeans, or the European Union. ◆ *adj* **2** marked by admiration for Europe, Europeans, or the European Union.

europium (jʊˈrəʊpɪəm) *n* a silvery-white element of the lanthanide series of metals. Symbol: Eu; atomic no.: 63; atomic wt.: 151.96. ORIG C20: after EUROPE + -IUM

Europol (ˈjʊərəʊˌpɒl) *n acronym for* European Police Office, an international organization devoted to fighting cross-border organized crime within the European Union.

Europoort ★ (*Dutch* ˈøːroːpoːrt) *n* a port in the Netherlands near Rotterdam: developed in the 1960s; handles oil.

Eurosceptic (ˈjʊərəʊˌskɛptɪk) (in Britain) ◆ *n* **1** a person who is opposed to closer links with the European Union. ◆ *adj* **2** opposing closer links with the European Union: *Eurosceptic MPs.*

Eurotunnel (ˈjʊərəʊˌtʌnᵊl) *n* another name for **Channel Tunnel.**

eurozone (ˈjʊərəʊˌzəʊn) *n* (*sometimes cap.*) the geographical area containing the countries that are participating in European Monetary Union. Also called: **euroland.**

Eurus ★ (ˈjʊərəs) *n Greek myth.* the east or southeast wind personified. ORIG L, from Gk *euros*

Euryale ★ (jʊˈraɪəlɪ) *n Greek myth.* one of the three Gorgons.

Eurydice ★ (jʊˈrɪdɪsɪ) *n Greek myth.* a dryad married to Orpheus, who sought her in Hades after she died. She would have been able to leave Hades with him had he not broken his pact and looked back at her.

Eurystheus ★ (jʊˈrɪsθjuːs, -θɪəs) *n Greek myth.* a grandson of Perseus, who, through the favour of Hera, inherited the kingship of Mycenae, which Zeus had intended for Hercules.

eurythmics (juːˈrɪðmɪks) *n* a variant spelling (esp. US) of **eurhythmics.**

Eusebio ★ (juːˈseɪbɪəʊ) *n* **Silva Ferreira da** (*Portuguese* ˈsilvə fəˈrrəirə da). born 1942, Portuguese footballer.

Eusebius ★ (juːˈsiːbɪəs) *n* ?265–?340 A.D., bishop of Caesarea: author of a history of the Christian Church to 324 A.D.

Eustachian tube (juːˈsteɪʃən) *n* a tube that connects the middle ear with the pharynx and equalizes the pressure between the two sides of the eardrum. ORIG C18: after Bartolomeo *Eustachio,* 16th-cent. It. anatomist

eustatic (juːˈstætɪk) *adj* denoting or relating to worldwide changes in sea level, caused by the melting of ice sheets, sedimentation, etc. ORIG C20: from Gk, from EU- + STATIC

eutectic (juːˈtɛktɪk) *adj* **1** (of a mixture of substances) having the lowest freezing point of all possible mixtures of the substances. **2** concerned with or suitable for the formation of eutectic mixtures. ◆ *n* **3** a eutectic mixture. **4** the temperature at which a eutectic mixture forms. ORIG C19: from Gk *eutēktos* melting readily, from EU- + *tēkein* to melt

Euterpe ★ (juːˈtɜːpɪ) *n Greek myth.* the Muse of lyric poetry and music.
▸ **Euˈterpean** *adj*

euthanasia (ˌjuːθəˈneɪzɪə) *n* the act of killing someone painlessly, esp. to relieve suffering from an incurable illness. ORIG C17: via NL from Gk: easy death

euthenics (juːˈθɛnɪks) *n* (*functioning as sing*) the study of the control of the environment, esp. with a view to improving the health and living standards of the human race. ORIG C20: from Gk *euthēnein* to thrive
▸ **euˈthenist** *n*

eutrophic (juːˈtrɒfɪk, -ˈtrəʊ-) *adj* (of lakes, etc.) rich in organic and mineral nutrients and supporting an abundant plant life. ORIG C18: prob. from *eutrophy,* from Gk, from *eutrophos* well-fed
▸ **ˈeutrophy** *n*

Euxine Sea ★ (ˈjuːksaɪn) *n* another name for the **Black Sea.**

eV *abbrev. for* electronvolt.

EVA *Astronautics. abbrev. for* extravehicular activity.

evacuate (ɪˈvækjʊˌeɪt) *vb* **evacuates, evacuating, evacuated.** (*mainly tr*) **1** (*also intr*) to withdraw or cause to withdraw (from a place of danger) to a place of safety. **2** to make empty. **3** (*also intr*) *Physiol.* **3a** to eliminate or excrete (faeces). **3b** to discharge (any waste) from (the body). **4** (*tr*) to create a vacuum in (a bulb, flask, etc.). ORIG C16: from L *ēvacuāre* to void, from *vacuus* empty
▸ **eˌvacuˈation** *n* ▸ **eˈvacuative** *adj* ▸ **eˈvacuˌator** *n* ▸ **eˌvacuˈee** *n*

evade (ɪˈveɪd) *vb* **evades, evading, evaded.** (*mainly tr*) **1** to get away from or avoid (imprisonment, captors, etc.). **2** to get around, shirk, or dodge (the law, a duty, etc.). **3** (*also intr*) to avoid answering (a question). ORIG C16: from F, from L *ēvādere* to go forth
▸ **eˈvadable** *adj* ▸ **eˈvader** *n*

evaginate (ɪˈvædʒɪˌneɪt) *vb* **evaginates, evaginating, evaginated.** (*tr*) *Med.* to turn (an organ or part) inside out. ORIG C17: from LL *ēvāgīnare* to unsheathe, from L *vāgīna* sheath

evaluate (ɪˈvæljʊˌeɪt) *vb* **evaluates, evaluating, evaluated.** (*tr*) **1** to ascertain or set the amount or value of. **2** to judge or assess the worth of. ORIG C19: back formation from *evaluation,* from F, from *évaluer;* see VALUE
▸ **eˌvaluˈation** *n* ▸ **eˈvaluative** *adj* ▸ **eˈvaluˌator** *n*

evanesce (ˌɛvəˈnɛs) *vb* **evanesces, evanescing, evanesced.** (*intr*) (of smoke, mist, etc.) to fade gradually from sight; vanish. ORIG C19: from L *ēvānēscere* to disappear; see VANISH

evanescent (ˌɛvəˈnɛsᵊnt) *adj* **1** passing out of sight; fading away; vanishing. **2** ephemeral or transitory.
▸ **ˌevaˈnescence** *n*

evangel (ɪˈvændʒəl) *n* **1** *Arch.* the gospel of Christianity. **2** (*often cap.*) any of the four Gospels of the New Testament. **3** any body of teachings regarded as basic. **4** *US.* an evangelist. ORIG C14: from Church L, from Gk *evangelion* good news, from EU- + *angelos* messenger; see ANGEL

evangelical (ˌiːvænˈdʒɛlɪkᵊl) *Christianity.* ◆ *adj* **1** of or following from the Gospels. **2** denoting or relating to any of certain Protestant sects, which emphasize personal conversion and faith in atonement through the death of Christ as a means of salvation. **3** denoting or relating to an evangelist. ◆ *n* **4** a member of an evangelical sect.
▸ **ˌevanˈgelicalism** *n* ▸ **ˌevanˈgelically** *adv*

evangelism (ɪˈvændʒɪˌlɪzəm) *n* **1** the practice of spreading the Christian gospel. **2** ardent or missionary zeal for a cause.

evangelist (ɪˈvændʒɪlɪst) *n* **1** an occasional preacher, sometimes itinerant. **2** a preacher of the Christian gospel.
▸ **eˌvangeˈlistic** *adj*

Evangelist (ɪˈvændʒɪlɪst) *n* any of the writers of the New Testament Gospels: Matthew, Mark, Luke, or John.

evangelize *or* **evangelise** (ɪˈvændʒɪˌlaɪz) *vb* **evangelizes, evangelizing, evangelized** *or* **evangelises, evangelising, evangelised. 1** to preach the Christian gospel (to). **2** (*intr*) to advocate a cause with the object of making converts.
▸ **eˌvangeliˈzation** *or* **eˌvangeliˈsation** *n* ▸ **eˈvangeˌlizer** *or* **eˈvangeˌliser** *n*

Evans ★ (ˈɛvənz) *n* **1** Sir **Arthur John.** 1851–1941, British archaeologist, whose excavations of the palace of Knossos in Crete provided evidence for the existence of the Minoan civilization. **2** Dame **Edith.** 1888–1976, British actress. **3** Sir **Geraint (Llewellyn)** (ˈgɛraɪnt). 1922–92, Welsh operatic baritone. **4 Herbert McLean.** 1882–1971, US anatomist and embryologist; discoverer of vitamin E (1922).

Evanston ★ (ˈɛvənstən) *n* a city in NE Illinois, on Lake Michigan north of Chicago: Northwestern University (1851). Pop.: 73 233 (1990).

Evansville ★ (ˈɛvənzˌvɪl) *n* a city in SW Indiana, on the Ohio River. Pop.: 123 456 (1996 est.).

evaporate (ɪˈvæpəˌreɪt) *vb* **evaporates, evaporating, evaporated. 1** to change or cause to change from a liquid or solid state to a vapour. **2** to lose or cause to lose liquid by vaporization leaving a more concentrated residue. **3** to disappear or cause to disappear. ORIG C16: from LL, from L *vapor* steam; see VAPOUR
▸ **eˈvaporable** *adj* ▸ **eˌvapoˈration** *n* ▸ **eˈvaporative** *adj* ▸ **eˈvapoˌrator** *n*

evaporated milk *n* thick unsweetened tinned milk from which some of the water has been evaporated.

evasion (ɪˈveɪʒən) *n* **1** the act of evading, esp. a distasteful duty, responsibility, etc., by cunning or by illegal means: *tax evasion.* **2** cunning or deception used to dodge a question, duty, etc.; means of evading. ORIG C15: from LL *ēvāsio*; see EVADE

evasive (ɪˈveɪsɪv) *adj* **1** tending or seeking to evade; not straightforward. **2** avoiding or seeking to avoid trouble or difficulties. **3** hard to catch or obtain; elusive.
▸ **eˈvasively** *adv* ▸ **eˈvasiveness** *n*

eve (iːv) *n* **1** the evening or day before some special event. **2** the period immediately before an event: *the eve of war.* **3** an archaic word for **evening.** ORIG C13: var. of EVEN²

Eve ★ (iːv) *n Old Testament.* the first woman; mother of the human race, fashioned by God from the rib of Adam (Genesis 2:18-25).

Evelyn ★ (ˈiːvlɪn, ˈɛv-) *n* **John.** 1620–1706, English author, noted chiefly for his diary (1640–1706).

even¹ (ˈiːvᵊn) *adj* **1** level and regular; flat. **2** (*postpositive; foll. by with*) on the same level or in the same plane (as). **3** without variation or fluctuation; regular; constant. **4** not readily moved or excited; calm: *an even temper.* **5** equally balanced between two sides: *an even game.* **6** equal or identical in number, quantity, etc. **7a** (of a number) divisible by two. **7b** characterized or indicated by such a number: *the even pages.* Cf. **odd** (sense 4). **8** relating to or denoting two or either of two alternatives, events, etc., that have an equal probability: *an even chance of missing or catching a train.* **9** having no balance of debt; neither owing nor being owed. **10** just and impartial; fair. **11** exact in number, amount, or extent: *an even pound.* **12** equal, as in score; level. **13 even money. 13a** a bet in which the winnings are the same as the amount staked. **13b** (*as modifier*): *the even-money favourite.* **14 get even (with).** *Inf.* to exact revenge (on); settle accounts (with). ◆ *adv* **15** (intensifier; used to suggest that the content of a statement is unexpected or paradoxical): *even an idiot can do that.* **16** (intensifier; used with comparative forms): *even better.* **17** notwithstanding; in spite of. **18** used to introduce a more precise version of a word, phrase, or statement: *he is base, even depraved.* **19** used preceding a clause of supposition or hypothesis to emphasize that whether or not the condition in it is fulfilled, the statement in the main clause remains valid: *even if she died he wouldn't care.* **20** *Arch.* all the way; fully: *I love thee even unto death.* **21 even as.** (*conj*) at the very same moment or in the very same way that. **22 even so.** in spite of any assertion to the contrary: nevertheless. ◆ See also **even out, evens, even up.** ORIG OE *efen*
▸ **ˈevener** *n* ▸ **ˈevenly** *adv* ▸ **ˈevenness** *n*

even² (ˈiːvᵊn) *n* an archaic word for **eve** or **evening.** ORIG OE *ǣfen*

even-handed *adj* fair; impartial.
▸ **ˌeven-ˈhandedly** *adv* ▸ **ˌeven-ˈhandedness** *n*

evening (ˈiːvnɪŋ) *n* **1** the latter part of the day, esp. from late afternoon until nightfall. **2** the latter or concluding period: *the evening of one's life.* **3** the early part of the night spent in a specified way: *an evening at the theatre.* **4** (*modifier*) of, used in, or occurring in the evening: *the evening papers.* ORIG OE *ǣfnung*

evening dress *n* attire for a formal occasion during the evening.

evening primrose *n* any plant of the genus *Oenothera,* typically having yellow flowers that open in the evening.

evening primrose oil *n* an oil, obtained from the seeds of the evening primrose, that is claimed to stimulate the production of prostaglandins.

evenings (ˈiːvnɪŋz) *adv Inf.* in the evening, esp. regularly.

evening star *n* a planet, usually Venus, seen just after sunset during the time that the planet is east of the sun.

even out *vb* (*adv*) to make or become even, as by the removal of bumps, inequalities, etc.

evens (ˈiːvənz) *adj, adv* **1** (of a bet) winning the same as the amount staked if successful. **2** (of a runner) offered at such odds.

evensong (ˈiːvᵊnˌsɒŋ) *n* **1** Also called: **Evening Prayer, vespers.** *Church of England.* the daily evening service. **2** *RC Church, arch.* another name for **vespers.**

event (ɪˈvɛnt) *n* **1** anything that takes place, esp. something important; an incident. **2** the actual or final outcome (esp. in **in the event, after the event**). **3** any one contest in a programme of sporting or other contests. **4 in any event** *or* **at all events.** regardless of circumstances; in any case. **5 in the event of.** in case of; if (such a thing) happens. **6 in the event that.** if it should happen that. ORIG C16: from L *ēvenīre* to come forth, happen

even-tempered *adj* not easily angered or excited; calm.

eventful (ɪˈvɛntfʊl) *adj* full of events.
▸ **eˈventfully** *adv* ▸ **eˈventfulness** *n*

event horizon *n Astron.* the spherical boundary of a black hole: objects passing through it would disappear completely and for ever, as no information can escape across the event horizon from the interior.

eventide (ˈiːvᵊnˌtaɪd) *n Arch. or poetic.* another word for **evening.**

eventide home *n Euphemistic.* an old people's home.

eventing (ɪˈvɛntɪŋ) *n Chiefly Brit.* taking part in equestrian competitions (esp. **three-day events**), usually involving cross-country riding, jumping, and dressage.

eventual (ɪˈvɛntʃʊəl) *adj* **1** (*prenominal*) happening in due course of time; ultimate. **2** *Arch.* contingent or possible.

eventuality (ɪˌvɛntʃʊˈælɪtɪ) *n, pl* **eventualities.** a possible event, occurrence, or result; contingency.

eventually (ɪˈvɛntʃʊəlɪ) *adv* **1** at the very end; finally. **2** (*sentence modifier*) after a long time or long delay: *eventually, he arrived.*

eventuate (ɪˈvɛntʃʊˌeɪt) *vb* **eventuates, eventuating, eventuated.** (*intr*) **1** (often foll. by *in*) to result ultimately (in). **2** to come about as a result.
▸ **eˌventuˈation** *n*

even up *vb* (*adv*) to make or become equal, esp. in respect of claims or debts.

ever (ˈɛvə) *adv* **1** at any time. **2** by any chance; in any case: *how did you ever find out?* **3** at all times; always. **4** in any possible way or manner: *come as fast as ever you can.* **5** *Inf., chiefly Brit.* (intensifier, in **ever so, ever such,** and **ever such a**). **6 is he** *or* **she ever!** *US & Canad. sl.* he *or* she displays the quality concerned in abundance. ◆ See also **forever.** ORIG OE *ǣfre,* from ?

Everest ★ (ˈɛvərɪst) *n* **1 Mount.** a mountain in S Asia on the border between Nepal and Tibet, in the Himalayas: the highest mountain in the world; first climbed by a British expedition (1953). Height: 8850 m (29 035 ft). **2** any high point of ambition or achievement. ORIG C19:

after Sir G. *Everest* (1790–1866), Surveyor-General of India

Everglades ★ ('ɛvəˌgleɪdz) *pl n* **the.** a subtropical marshy region of Florida, south of Lake Okeechobee: contains the **Everglades National Park,** established to preserve the flora and fauna of the swamps. Area: over 13 000 sq. km (5000 sq. miles).

evergreen ('ɛvəˌgri:n) *adj* **1** (of certain trees and shrubs) bearing foliage throughout the year. Cf. **deciduous. 2** remaining fresh and vital. ◆ *n* **3** an evergreen tree or shrub.

evergreen fund *n* a fund that provides capital for new companies and makes regular injections of capital to support their development.

everlasting (ˌɛvə'lɑ:stɪŋ) *adj* **1** never coming to an end; eternal. **2** lasting for an indefinitely long period. **3** lasting so long or occurring so often as to become tedious. ◆ *n* **4** eternity. **5** Also called: **everlasting flower.** another name for **immortelle.**
▸ **ˌever'lastingly** *adv*

evermore (ˌɛvə'mɔ:) *adv* (often preceded by *for*) all time to come.

evert (ɪ'vɜ:t) *vb* (*tr*) to turn (an eyelid or other bodily part) outwards or inside out. ORIG C16: from L *ēvertere* to overthrow, from *vertere* to turn
▸ **e'versible** *adj* ▸ **e'version** *n*

Evert ★ ('ɛvət) *n* **Chris(tine).** born 1954, US tennis player: Wimbledon champion 1974, 1976, and 1981; US champion 1975–78, 1980, and 1982.

every ('ɛvrɪ) *determiner* **1** each one (of the class specified), without exception. **2** (*not used with a negative*) the greatest or best possible: *every hope.* **3** each: used before a noun phrase to indicate the recurrent, intermittent, or serial nature of a thing: *every third day.* **4 every bit.** (used in comparisons with *as*) quite; just; equally. **5 every other.** each alternate; every second. **6 every which way.** *US & Canad.* **6a** in all directions; everywhere. **6b** from all sides. ORIG C15 *everich,* from OE *ǣfre ǣlc,* from *ǣfre* EVER + *ǣlc* EACH

everybody ('ɛvrɪˌbɒdɪ) *pron* every person; everyone.

> **USAGE NOTE** See at **everyone.**

everyday ('ɛvrɪˌdeɪ) *adj* **1** happening each day. **2** commonplace or usual. **3** suitable for or used on ordinary days.

Everyman ('ɛvrɪˌmæn) *n* **1** a medieval English morality play in which the central figure represents mankind. **2** (*often not cap.*) the ordinary person; common man.

everyone ('ɛvrɪˌwʌn, -wən) *pron* every person; everybody.

> **USAGE NOTE** *Everyone* and *everybody* are interchangeable, as are *no one* and *nobody,* and *someone* and *somebody.* Care should be taken to distinguish between *everyone* and *someone* as single words and *every one* and *some one* as two words, the latter form correctly being used to refer to each individual person or thing in a particular group: *every one of them is wrong.*

every one *pron* each person or thing in a group, without exception.

everything ('ɛvrɪˌθɪŋ) *pron* **1** the entirety of a specified or implied class. **2** a great deal, esp. of something very important.

everywhere ('ɛvrɪˌwɛə) *adv* to or in all parts or places.

Evesham ★ ('i:vʃəm) *n* a town in W central England, in E Hereford and Worcester, on the River Avon: scene of the Battle of Evesham in 1265 (Lord Edward's defeat of Simon de Montfort and the barons); centre of the **Vale of Evesham,** famous for market gardens and orchards. Pop.: 17 823 (1991).

Evian ('ɛvɪan) *n Trademark.* a type of bottled natural mineral water. ORIG from *Evian-les-Bains,* town in the French Alps

evict (ɪ'vɪkt) *vb* (*tr*) **1** to expel (a tenant) from property by process of law; turn out. **2** to recover (property or the title to property) by judicial process or by virtue of a superior title. ORIG C15: from LL *ēvincere,* from L: to vanquish utterly
▸ **e'viction** *n* ▸ **e'victor** *n*

evidence ('ɛvɪdəns) *n* **1** ground for belief or disbelief; data on which to base proof or to establish truth or falsehood. **2** a mark or sign that makes evident. **3** *Law.* matter produced before a court of law in an attempt to prove or disprove a point in issue. **4 in evidence.** on display; apparent. ◆ *vb* **evidences, evidencing, evidenced.** (*tr*) **5** to make evident; show clearly. **6** to give proof of or evidence for.

evident ('ɛvɪdənt) *adj* easy to see or understand; apparent. ORIG C14: from L *ēvidēns,* from *vidēre* to see

evidential (ˌɛvɪ'dɛnʃəl) *adj* relating to, serving as, or based on evidence.
▸ **ˌevi'dentially** *adv*

evidently ('ɛvɪdəntlɪ) *adv* **1** without question; clearly. **2** to all appearances; apparently.

evil ('i:vᵊl) *adj* **1** morally wrong or bad; wicked. **2** causing harm or injury. **3** marked or accompanied by misfortune: *an evil fate.* **4** (of temper, disposition, etc.) characterized by anger or spite. **5** infamous: *an evil reputation.* **6** offensive or unpleasant: *an evil smell.* **7** *Sl., chiefly US.* excellent or outstanding. ◆ *n* **8** the quality or an instance of being morally wrong; wickedness. **9** (*sometimes cap.*) a force or power that brings about wickedness or harm. ◆ *adv* **10** (*now usually in combination*) in an evil manner; badly: *evil-smelling.* ORIG OE *yfel*
▸ **'evilly** *adv* ▸ **'evilness** *n*

evildoer ('i:vᵊlˌdu:ə) *n* a person who does evil.
▸ **'evilˌdoing** *n*

evil eye *n* **the. 1** a look or glance superstitiously supposed to have the power of inflicting harm or injury. **2** the power to inflict harm, etc., by such a look.
▸ **ˌevil-'eyed** *adj*

evil-minded *adj* inclined to evil thoughts; malicious or spiteful.
▸ **ˌevil-'mindedly** *adv* ▸ **ˌevil-'mindedness** *n*

evince (ɪ'vɪns) *vb* **evinces, evincing, evinced.** (*tr*) to make evident; show (something) clearly. ORIG C17: from L *ēvincere* to overcome; see EVICT
▸ **e'vincible** *adj*

> **USAGE NOTE** The rather bookish and highfalutin word *evince* is sometimes wrongly used where *evoke* is meant as in: *its very mention is likely to evince a smile of embarrassment* where *evoke* would have been correct.

eviscerate (ɪ'vɪsəˌreɪt) *vb* **eviscerates, eviscerating, eviscerated.** (*tr*) **1** to remove the internal organs of; disembowel. **2** to deprive of meaning or significance. ORIG C17: from L *ēviscerāre,* from *viscera* entrails
▸ **eˌviscer'ation** *n* ▸ **e'viscerˌator** *n*

evocation (ˌɛvə'keɪʃən) *n* the act or an instance of evoking. ORIG C17: from L: see EVOKE
▸ **evocative** (ɪ'vɒkətɪv) *adj*

evoke (ɪ'vəʊk) *vb* **evokes, evoking, evoked.** (*tr*) **1** to call or summon up (a memory, feeling, etc.), esp. from the past. **2** to provoke; elicit. **3** to cause (spirits) to appear; conjure up. ORIG C17: from L *ēvocāre* to call forth, from *vocāre* to call
▸ **evocable** ('ɛvəkəbᵊl) *adj* ▸ **e'voker** *n*

> **USAGE NOTE** See at **evince** and **invoke.**

evolute ('ɛvəˌlu:t) *n* **1** a geometric curve that describes the locus of the centres of curvature of another curve (the **involute**). ◆ *adj* **2** *Biol.* having the margins rolled outwards. ORIG C19: from L *ēvolūtus* unrolled, from *ēvolvere* to roll out, EVOLVE

evolution (ˌi:və'lu:ʃən) *n* **1** *Biol.* a gradual change in the characteristics of a population of animals or plants over successive generations. **2** a gradual development, esp. to a more complex form: *the evolution of modern art.* **3** the act

of throwing off, as heat, gas, vapour, etc. **4** a pattern formed by a series of movements or something similar. **5** an algebraic operation in which the root of a number, expression, etc., is extracted. **6** *Mil.* an exercise carried out in accordance with a set procedure or plan. ORIG C17: from L *ēvolūtiō* an unrolling, from *ēvolvere* to EVOLVE
▸ ˌ**evoˈlutionary** *or* ˌ**evoˈlutional** *adj*

evolutionist (ˌiːvəˈluːʃənɪst) *n* **1** a person who believes in a theory of evolution. ◆ *adj* **2** of or relating to a theory of evolution.
▸ ˌ**evoˈlutionism** *n* ▸ ˌ**evolutionˈistic** *adj*

evolve (ɪˈvɒlv) *vb* **evolves, evolving, evolved. 1** to develop or cause to develop gradually. **2** (of animal or plant species) to undergo evolution of (organs or parts). **3** (*tr*) to yield, emit, or give off (heat, gas, vapour, etc.). ORIG C17: from L *ēvolvere* to unfold, from *volvere* to roll
▸ **eˈvolvable** *adj* ▸ **eˈvolvement** *n*

Évora ★ (*Portuguese* ˈɛvura) *n* a city in S central Portugal: ancient Roman settlement; occupied by the Moors from 712 to 1166; residence of the Portuguese court in 15th and 16th centuries. Pop.: 34 100 (latest est.). Ancient name: **Ebora** (ˈiːbərə).

Évreux ★ (*French* evrø) *n* an industrial town in NW France: severely damaged in World War II; cathedral (12th–16th centuries). Pop.: 51 450 (1990).

Évros ★ (ˈɛvrɔs) *n* transliteration of the Modern Greek name for the **Maritsa**.

Évvoia ★ (ˈɛvia) *n* transliteration of the Modern Greek name for **Euboea**.

evzone (ˈɛvzəʊn) *n* a soldier in an elite Greek infantry regiment. ORIG C19: from Mod. Gk, from Gk *euzōnos*, lit.: well-girt, from EU- + *zōne* girdle

ewe (juː) *n* **a** a female sheep. **b** (*as modifier*): *a ewe lamb.* ORIG OE *ēowu*

ewer (ˈjuːə) *n* a large jug or pitcher with a wide mouth. ORIG C14: from OF *evier*, from L *aquārius* water carrier, from *aqua* water

ex[1] (ɛks) *prep* **1** *Finance.* excluding; without: *ex dividend.* **2** *Commerce.* without charge to the buyer until removed from: *ex warehouse.* ORIG C19: from L: out of, from

ex[2] (ɛks) *n Inf.* (a person's) former wife, husband, etc.

Ex. *Bible. abbrev. for* Exodus.

ex-[1] *prefix* **1** out of; outside of; from: *exclosure; exurbia.* **2** former: *ex-wife.* ORIG from L, from *ex* (prep), identical with Gk *ex, ek*; see EC-

ex-[2] *combining form.* a variant of **exo-** before a vowel: *exergonic.*

exa- *combining form.* **1** denoting 10^{18}: *exametres.* **2** Also: **exbi-**. *Computing.* denoting 2^{60}: *exabyte.* ◆ Symbol: E

USAGE NOTE See at **kilo-**.

exacerbate (ɪgˈzæsəˌbeɪt, ɪkˈsæs-) *vb* **exacerbates, exacerbating, exacerbated.** (*tr*) **1** to make (pain, disease, etc.) more intense; aggravate. **2** to irritate (a person). ORIG C17: from L *exacerbāre* to irritate, from *acerbus* bitter
▸ **exˌacerˈbation** *n*

exact (ɪgˈzækt) *adj* **1** correct in every detail; strictly accurate. **2** precise, as opposed to approximate. **3** (*prenominal*) specific; particular. **4** operating with very great precision. **5** allowing no deviation from a standard; rigorous; strict. **6** based on measurement and the formulation of laws, as opposed to description and classification: *an exact science.* ◆ *vb* (*tr*) **7** to force or compel (payment, etc.); extort: *to exact tribute.* **8** to demand as a right; insist upon. **9** to call for or require. ORIG C16: from L *exactus* driven out, from *exigere* to drive forth, from *agere* to drive
▸ **exˈactable** *adj* ▸ **exˈactness** *n* ▸ **exˈactor** *or* **exˈacter** *n*

exacting (ɪgˈzæktɪŋ) *adj* making rigorous or excessive demands.
▸ **exˈactingness** *n*

exaction (ɪgˈzækʃən) *n* **1** the act or an instance of exacting. **2** an excessive or harsh demand, esp. for money. **3** a sum or payment exacted.

exactitude (ɪgˈzæktɪˌtjuːd) *n* the quality of being exact; precision; accuracy.

exactly (ɪgˈzæktlɪ) *adv* **1** in an exact manner; accurately or precisely. **2** in every respect; just. ◆ *sentence substitute.* **3** just so!, precisely! **4 not exactly.** *Ironical.* not at all; by no means.

exacum (ˈɛksəkəm) *n* any of various Asian flowering herbs. ORIG NL, from EX-[1] + Gk *ago* to arrive

exaggerate (ɪgˈzædʒəˌreɪt) *vb* **exaggerates, exaggerating, exaggerated. 1** to regard or represent as larger or greater, more important or more successful, etc., than is true. **2** (*tr*) to make greater, more noticeable, etc. ORIG C16: from L *exaggerāre* to magnify, from *aggerāre* to heap, from *agger* heap
▸ **exˈaggerˌated** *adj* ▸ **exˌaggerˈation** *n* ▸ **exˈaggerˌator** *n*

ex all *adv, adj Finance.* without the right to any benefits: *shares quoted ex all.*

exalt (ɪgˈzɔːlt) *vb* (*tr*) **1** to elevate in rank, dignity, etc. **2** to praise highly; extol. **3** to stimulate; excite. **4** to fill with joy or delight; elate. ORIG C15: from L *exaltāre* to raise, from *altus* high
▸ **exˈalted** *adj* ▸ **exˈalter** *n*

exaltation (ˌɛgzɔːlˈteɪʃən) *n* **1** the act of exalting or state of being exalted. **2** exhilaration; elation; rapture.

exam (ɪgˈzæm) *n* short for **examination.**

examination (ɪgˌzæmɪˈneɪʃən) *n* **1** the act of examining or state of being examined. **2** *Education.* **2a** written exercises, oral questions, etc., set to test a candidate's knowledge and skill. **2b** (*as modifier*): *an examination paper.* **3** *Med.* **3a** physical inspection of a patient. **3b** laboratory study of secretory or excretory products, tissue samples, etc. **4** *Law.* the formal interrogation of a person on oath.
▸ **exˌamiˈnational** *adj*

examine (ɪgˈzæmɪn) *vb* **examines, examining, examined.** (*tr*) **1** to inspect or scrutinize carefully or in detail; investigate. **2** *Education.* to test the knowledge or skill of (a candidate) in (a subject or activity) by written or oral questions, etc. **3** *Law.* to interrogate (a person) formally on oath. **4** *Med.* to investigate the state of health of (a patient). ORIG C14: from OF, from L *exāmināre* to weigh, from *exāmen* means of weighing
▸ **exˈaminable** *adj* ▸ **exˌamiˈnee** *n* ▸ **exˈaminer** *n* ▸ **exˈamining** *adj*

example (ɪgˈzɑːmpᵊl) *n* **1** a specimen or instance that is typical of its group or set; sample. **2** a person, action, thing, etc., that is worthy of imitation; pattern. **3** a precedent, illustration of a principle, or model. **4** a punishment or the recipient of a punishment intended to serve as a warning. **5 for example.** as an illustration; for instance. ◆ *vb* **examples, exampling, exampled. 6** (*tr; now usually passive*) to present an example of; exemplify. ORIG C14: from OF, from L *exemplum* pattern, from *eximere* to take out

exanthema (ˌɛksænˈθiːmə) *n, pl* **exanthemata** (-ˈθiːmətə) *or* **exanthemas.** a skin rash occurring in a disease such as measles. ORIG C17: via LL from Gk, from *exanthein* to burst forth, from *anthein* to blossom

exasperate (ɪgˈzɑːspəˌreɪt) *vb* **exasperates, exasperating, exasperated.** (*tr*) **1** to cause great irritation or anger to. **2** to cause (something unpleasant) to worsen; aggravate. ORIG C16: from L *exasperāre* to make rough, from *asper* rough
▸ **exˈasperˌatedly** *adv* ▸ **exˈasperˌatingly** *adv* ▸ **exˌasperˈation** *n*

exbi- (ˈeksbɪ) *combining form. Computing.* denoting 2^{60}: *exbibyte.* ORIG C20: from EX(A-) + BI(NARY)

USAGE NOTE See at **kilo-**.

ex cathedra (ɛks kəˈθiːdrə) *adj, adv* **1** with authority. **2** *RC Church.* (of doctrines of faith or morals) defined by the pope as infallibly true, to be accepted by all Catholics. ORIG L, lit.: from the chair

excavate (ˈɛkskəˌveɪt) *vb* **excavates, excavating, excavated. 1** to remove (soil, earth, etc.) by digging; dig out. **2** to make (a hole or tunnel) in (solid matter) by hollowing. **3** to unearth (buried objects) methodically to discover information about the past. ORIG C16: from L *cavāre* to make hollow, from *cavus* hollow
▸ ˌ**excaˈvation** *n* ▸ ˈ**excaˌvator** *n*

exceed (ɪk'siːd) *vb* **1** to be superior (to); excel. **2** (*tr*) to go beyond the limit or bounds of. **3** (*tr*) to be greater in degree or quantity than. ORIG C14: from L *excēdere* to go beyond
▸ **ex'ceedable** *adj* ▸ **ex'ceeder** *n*

exceeding (ɪk'siːdɪŋ) *adj* **1** very great; exceptional or excessive. ◆ *adv* **2** *Arch.* to a great or unusual degree.
▸ **ex'ceedingly** *adv*

excel (ɪk'sɛl) *vb* **excels, excelling, excelled. 1** to be superior to (another or others); surpass. **2** (*intr;* foll. by *in* or *at*) to be outstandingly good or proficient. ORIG C15: from L *excellere* to rise up

excellence ('ɛksələns) *n* **1** the state or quality of excelling or being exceptionally good; extreme merit. **2** an action, feature, etc., in which a person excels.
▸ **'excellent** *adj* ▸ **'excellently** *adv*

Excellency ('ɛksələnsɪ) *or* **Excellence** *n, pl* **Excellencies** *or* **Excellences. 1** (usually preceded by *Your, His,* or *Her*) a title used to address or refer to a high-ranking official, such as an ambassador. **2** *RC Church.* a title of bishops and archbishops in many non-English-speaking countries.

excelsior (ɪk'sɛlsɪˌɔː) *interj, n* **1** excellent: used as a motto and as a trademark for various products. **2** upward. ORIG C19: from L: higher

except (ɪk'sɛpt) *prep* **1** Also: **except for.** other than; apart from. **2 except that.** (*conj*) but for the fact that; were it not true that. ◆ *conj* **3** an archaic word for **unless. 4** *Inf. (not standard in the US)* except that; but for the fact that. ◆ *vb* **5** (*tr*) to leave out; omit; exclude. **6** (*intr;* often foll. by *to*) *Rare.* to take exception; object. ORIG C14: from OF *excepter* to leave out, from L *excipere* to take out

excepting (ɪk'sɛptɪŋ) *prep* **1** except; except for (esp. in **not excepting**). ◆ *conj* **2** an archaic word for **unless.**

> **USAGE NOTE** The use of *excepting* used to be considered by purists acceptable only after *not, only, always,* or *without.* Nowadays it seems to appear after these words largely in books, and is otherwise used as a more highbrow alternative to *except.*

exception (ɪk'sɛpʃən) *n* **1** the act of excepting or fact of being excepted; omission. **2** anything excluded from or not in conformance with a general rule, principle, class, etc. **3** criticism, esp. adverse; objection. **4** *Law.* (formerly) a formal objection in legal proceedings. **5 take exception. 5a** (usually foll. by *to*) to make objections (to); demur (at). **5b** (often foll. by *at*) to be offended (by); be resentful (at).

exceptionable (ɪk'sɛpʃənəbᵊl) *adj* open to or subject to objection; objectionable.
▸ **ex'ceptionableness** *n* ▸ **ex'ceptionably** *adv*

exceptional (ɪk'sɛpʃənᵊl) *adj* **1** forming an exception; not ordinary. **2** having much more than average intelligence, ability, or skill.

excerpt *n* ('ɛksɜːpt). **1** a part or passage taken from a book, speech, etc.; extract. ◆ *vb* (ɛk'sɜːpt). **2** (*tr*) to take (a part or passage) from a book, speech, etc. ORIG C17: from L *excerptum,* lit.: (something) picked out, from *excerpere* to select, from *carpere* to pluck
▸ **ex'cerptible** *adj* ▸ **ex'cerption** *n* ▸ **ex'cerptor** *n*

excess *n* (ɪk'sɛs, 'ɛksɛs). **1** the state or act of going beyond normal, sufficient, or permitted limits. **2** an immoderate or abnormal amount. **3** the amount, number, etc., by which one thing exceeds another. **4** overindulgence or intemperance. **5** *Insurance, chiefly Brit.* a specified contribution towards the cost of a claim, payable by the policyholder. US name: **deductible. 6 in excess of.** of more than; over. **7 to excess.** to an inordinate extent; immoderately. ◆ *adj* ('ɛksɛs, ɪk'sɛs). (*usually prenominal*) **8** more than normal, necessary, or permitted; surplus: *excess weight.* **9** payable as a result of previous underpayment: *excess postage.* ORIG C14: from L *excēdere* to go beyond; see EXCEED

excessive (ɪk'sɛsɪv) *adj* exceeding the normal or permitted limits; immoderate; inordinate.
▸ **ex'cessively** *adv* ▸ **ex'cessiveness** *n*

excess luggage *or* **baggage** *n* luggage that is more in weight or number of pieces than an airline, etc., will carry free.

exchange (ɪks'tʃeɪndʒ) *vb* **exchanges, exchanging, exchanged. 1** (*tr*) to give up or transfer (one thing) for an equivalent. **2** (*tr*) to give and receive (information, ideas, etc.); interchange. **3** (*tr*) to replace (one thing) with another, esp. to replace unsatisfactory goods. **4** to hand over (goods) in return for the equivalent value in kind; barter; trade. ◆ *n* **5** the act or process of exchanging. **6a** anything given or received as an equivalent or substitute for something else. **6b** (*as modifier*): *an exchange student.* **7** an argument or quarrel. **8** Also called: **telephone exchange.** a switching centre in which telephone lines are interconnected. **9** a place where securities or commodities are sold, bought, or traded, esp. by brokers or merchants. **10a** the system by which commercial debts are settled by commercial documents, esp. bills of exchange, instead of by direct payment of money. **10b** the percentage or fee charged for accepting payment in this manner. **11** a transfer or interchange of sums of money of equivalent value, as between different currencies. **12 win** (*or* **lose**) **the exchange.** *Chess.* to win (*or* lose) a rook in return for a bishop or knight. ◆ See also **bill of exchange, exchange rate, labour exchange.** ORIG C14: from Anglo-French *eschaungier,* from Vulgar L *excambiāre* (unattested), from L *cambīre* to barter
▸ **ex'changeable** *adj* ▸ **exˌchangea'bility** *n* ▸ **ex'changeably** *adv* ▸ **ex'changer** *n*

exchange rate *n* the rate at which the currency unit of one country may be exchanged for that of another.

Exchange Rate Mechanism *n* the mechanism used in the European Monetary System in which participating governments commit themselves to maintain the values of their currencies in relation to the ECU. Abbrev.: **ERM.**

exchequer (ɪks'tʃɛkə) *n* **1** (*often cap.*) *Government.* (in Britain and certain other countries) the accounting department of the Treasury. **2** *Inf.* personal funds; finances. ORIG C13 (in the sense: chessboard, counting table): from OF *eschequier,* from *eschec* CHECK

excisable (ɪk'saɪzəbᵊl) *adj* **1** liable to an excise tax. **2** suitable for deletion.

excise[1] *n* ('ɛksaɪz, ɛk'saɪz). **1** Also called: **excise tax.** a tax on goods, such as spirits, produced for the home market. **2** a tax paid for a licence to carry out various trades, sports, etc. **3** *Brit.* that section of the government service responsible for the collection of excise, now the Board of Customs and Excise. ◆ *vb* (ɪk'saɪz), **excises, excising, excised. 4** (*tr*) *Rare.* to compel (a person) to pay excise. ORIG C15: prob. from MDu. *excijs,* prob. from OF *assise* a sitting, assessment, from L *assidēre* to sit beside, assist in judging
▸ **ex'cisable** *adj*

excise[2] (ɪk'saɪz) *vb* **excises, excising, excised.** (*tr*) **1** to delete (a passage, sentence, etc.). **2** to remove (an organ or part) surgically. ORIG C16: from L *excīdere* to cut down
▸ **excision** (ɪk'sɪʒən) *n*

exciseman ('ɛksaɪzˌmæn) *n, pl* **excisemen.** *Brit.* (formerly) a government agent whose function was to collect excise and prevent smuggling.

excitable (ɪk'saɪtəbᵊl) *adj* **1** easily excited; volatile. **2** (esp. of a nerve) ready to respond to a stimulus.
▸ **exˌcita'bility** *or* **ex'citableness** *n*

excitation (ˌɛksɪ'teɪʃən) *n* **1** the act or process of exciting or state of being excited. **2** a means of exciting or cause of excitement. **3** the current in a field coil of a generator, motor, etc., or the magnetizing current in a transformer. **4** the action of a stimulus on an animal or plant organ, inducing it to respond.

excite (ɪk'saɪt) *vb* **excites, exciting, excited.** (*tr*) **1** to arouse (a person), esp. to pleasurable anticipation or nervous agitation. **2** to arouse or elicit (an emotion, response, etc.); evoke. **3** to cause or bring about; stir up. **4** to arouse sexually. **5** *Physiol.* to cause a response in or increase the activity of (an organ, tissue, or part); stimulate. **6** to raise (an atom, molecule, etc.) from the ground state to a higher energy level. **7** to supply electricity to (the coils of a generator or motor) in order to create a magnetic field.

ORIG C14: from L *excīēre* to stimulate, from *ciēre* to set in motion, rouse
▸ **ex'citant** *n* ▸ **ex'citative** *or* **ex'citatory** *adj* ▸ **ex'citer** *or* **ex'citor** *n*

excited (ɪk'saɪtɪd) *adj* **1** emotionally aroused, esp. to pleasure or agitation. **2** characterized by excitement. **3** sexually aroused. **4** (of an atom, molecule, etc.) having an energy level above the ground state.
▸ **ex'citedness** *n*

excitement (ɪk'saɪtmənt) *n* **1** the state of being excited. **2** a person or thing that excites.

exciting (ɪk'saɪtɪŋ) *adj* causing excitement; stirring; stimulating.
▸ **ex'citingly** *adv*

exclaim (ɪk'skleɪm) *vb* to cry out or speak suddenly or excitedly, as from surprise, delight, horror, etc. ORIG C16: from L *exclāmāre,* from *clāmāre* to shout
▸ **ex'claimer** *n*

exclamation (ˌɛkskləˈmeɪʃən) *n* **1** an abrupt or excited cry or utterance; ejaculation. **2** the act of exclaiming.
▸ **ˌexcla'mational** *adj* ▸ **ex'clamatory** *adj*

exclamation mark *or US* **point** *n* **1** the punctuation mark ! used after exclamations and vehement commands. **2** this mark used for any other purpose, as to draw attention to an obvious mistake, in road warning signs, etc.

exclave ('ɛkskleɪv) *n* a part of a country entirely surrounded by foreign territory: viewed from the position of the home country. ORIG C20: from EX-[1] + *-clave,* on the model of ENCLAVE

exclosure (ɪk'skləʊʒə) *n* an area of land fenced round to keep out unwanted animals.

exclude (ɪk'sklu:d) *vb* **excludes, excluding, excluded.** (*tr*) **1** to keep out; prevent from entering. **2** to bar (someone) from access to or participation in: *to exclude from school.* **3** to reject or not consider; leave out. **4** to expel forcibly; eject. ORIG C14: from L *exclūdere,* from *claudere* to shut
▸ **ex'cludable** *or* **ex'cludible** *adj* ▸ **ex'cluder** *n*

exclusion (ɪk'sklu:ʒən) *n* the act or an instance of excluding or the state of being excluded.
▸ **ex'clusionary** *adj*

exclusion principle *n* See **Pauli exclusion principle.**

exclusive (ɪk'sklu:sɪv) *adj* **1** excluding all else; rejecting other considerations, events, etc. **2** belonging to a particular individual or group and to no other; not shared. **3** belonging to or catering for a privileged minority, esp. a fashionable clique. **4** (*postpositive;* foll. by *to*) limited (to); found only (in). **5** single; unique; only. **6** separate and incompatible. **7** (*immediately postpositive*) not including the numbers, dates, letters, etc., mentioned. **8** (*postpositive;* foll. by *of*) except (for); not taking account (of). **9** *Logic.* (of a disjunction) true if only one rather than both of its component propositions is true. ◆ *n* **10** an exclusive story; a story reported in only one newspaper.
▸ **ex'clusively** *adv* ▸ **exclusivity** (ˌɛksklu:'sɪvɪtɪ) *or* **ex'clusiveness** *n*

exclusive OR circuit *or* **gate** *n Electronics.* a computer logic circuit having two or more input wires and one output wire and giving a high-voltage output signal if a low-voltage signal is fed to one or more, but not all, of the input wires. Cf. **OR circuit.**

excommunicate *RC Church.* ◆ *vb* (ˌɛkskə'mju:nɪˌkeɪt), **excommunicates, excommunicating, excommunicated. 1** (*tr*) to sentence (a member of the Church) to exclusion from the communion of believers and from the privileges and public prayers of the Church. ◆ *adj* (ˌɛkskə'mju:nɪkɪt, -ˌkeɪt). **2** having incurred such a sentence. ◆ *n* (ˌɛkskə'mju:nɪkɪt, -ˌkeɪt). **3** an excommunicated person. ORIG C15: from LL *excommūnicāre,* lit.: to exclude from the community, from L *commūnis* COMMON
▸ **ˌexcomˌmuni'cation** *n* ▸ **ˌexcom'muniˌcator** *n*

excoriate (ɪk'skɔ:rɪˌeɪt) *vb* **excoriates, excoriating, excoriated.** (*tr*) **1** to strip the skin from (a person or animal). **2** to denounce vehemently. ORIG C15: from LL *excoriāre* to strip, flay, from L *corium* skin, hide
▸ **exˌcori'ation** *n*

excrement ('ɛkskrɪmənt) *n* waste matter discharged from the body, esp. faeces; excreta. ORIG C16: from L *excernere* to sift, EXCRETE
▸ **excremental** (ˌɛkskrɪ'mɛnt°l) *or* **excrementitious** (ˌɛkskrɪmɛn'tɪʃəs) *adj*

excrescence (ɪk'skrɛs°ns) *n* a projection or protuberance, esp. an outgrowth from an organ or part of the body.
▸ **ex'crescent** *adj* ▸ **excrescential** (ˌɛkskrɪ'sɛnʃəl) *adj*

excreta (ɪk'skri:tə) *pl n* waste matter, such as urine, faeces, or sweat, discharged from the body. ORIG C19: NL, from L: see EXCRETE
▸ **ex'cretal** *adj*

excrete (ɪk'skri:t) *vb* **excretes, excreting, excreted. 1** to discharge (waste matter, such as urine, sweat, or faeces) from the body. **2** (of plants) to eliminate (waste matter) through the leaves, roots, etc. ORIG C17: from L *excernere* to separate, discharge, from *cernere* to sift
▸ **ex'creter** *n* ▸ **ex'cretion** *n* ▸ **ex'cretive** *or* **ex'cretory** *adj*

excruciate (ɪk'skru:ʃɪˌeɪt) *vb* **excruciates, excruciating, excruciated.** (*tr*) to inflict mental suffering on; torment. ORIG C16: from L *excruciāre,* from *cruciāre* to crucify, from *crux* cross

excruciating (ɪk'skru:ʃɪˌeɪtɪŋ) *adj* **1** unbearably painful; agonizing. **2** intense; extreme. **3** *Inf.* irritating; trying. **4** *Humorous.* very bad: *an excruciating pun.*

exculpate ('ɛkskʌlˌpeɪt, ɪk'skʌlpeɪt) *vb* **exculpates, exculpating, exculpated.** (*tr*) to free from blame or guilt; vindicate or exonerate. ORIG C17: from Med. L, from L EX-[1] + *culpa* fault, blame
▸ **ˌexcul'pation** *n* ▸ **ex'culpatory** *adj*

excursion (ɪk'skɜ:ʃən, -ʒən) *n* **1** a short outward and return journey, esp. for sightseeing, etc.; outing. **2** a group going on such a journey. **3** (*modifier*) of or relating to reduced rates offered on certain journeys by rail: *an excursion ticket.* **4** a digression or deviation; diversion. **5** (formerly) a raid or attack. ORIG C16: from L *excursiō* an attack, from *excurrere* to run out, from *currere* to run
▸ **ex'cursionist** *n*

excursive (ɪk'skɜ:sɪv) *adj* **1** tending to digress. **2** involving detours; rambling. ORIG C17: from L *excursus,* from *excurrere* to run forth
▸ **ex'cursively** *adv* ▸ **ex'cursiveness** *n*

excuse *vb* (ɪk'skju:z), **excuses, excusing, excused.** (*tr*) **1** to pardon or forgive. **2** to seek pardon or exemption for (a person, esp. oneself). **3** to make allowances for: *to excuse someone's ignorance.* **4** to serve as an apology or explanation for; justify: *her age excuses her.* **5** to exempt from a task, obligation, etc. **6** to dismiss or allow to leave. **7** to seek permission for (someone, esp. oneself) to leave. **8 be excused.** *Euphemistic.* to go to the lavatory. **9 excuse me!** an expression used to catch someone's attention or to apologize for an interruption, disagreement, etc. ◆ *n* (ɪk'skju:s). **10** an explanation offered in defence of some fault or as a reason for not fulfilling an obligation, etc. **11** *Inf.* an inferior example of something; makeshift substitute: *she is a poor excuse for a hostess.* **12** the act of excusing. ORIG C13: from L, from EX-[1] + *causa* cause, accusation
▸ **ex'cusable** *adj* ▸ **ex'cusableness** *n* ▸ **ex'cusably** *adv*

excuse-me *n* a dance in which a person may take another's partner.

ex-directory *adj Chiefly Brit.* not listed in a telephone directory, by request, and not disclosed to inquirers.

ex dividend *adj, adv* without the right to the current dividend: *to quote shares ex dividend.*

exeat ('ɛksɪət) *n Brit.* **1** leave of absence from school or some other institution. **2** a bishop's permission for a priest to leave his diocese in order to take up an appointment elsewhere. ORIG C18: L, lit.: he may go out, from *exīre*

exec. *abbrev. for:* **1** executive. **2** executor.

execrable ('ɛksɪkrəb°l) *adj* **1** deserving to be execrated; abhorrent. **2** of very poor quality. ORIG C14: from L: see EXECRATE
▸ **'execrableness** *n* ▸ **'execrably** *adv*

execrate ('ɛksɪˌkreɪt) *vb* **execrates, execrating, execrated. 1** (*tr*) to loathe; detest; abhor. **2** (*tr*) to denounce; deplore. **3**

to curse (a person or thing); damn. ORIG C16: from L *exsecrārī* to curse, from EX-[1] + *-secrārī* from *sacer* SACRED
▸ ,**exe'cration** *n* ▸ **'exe,crative** *or* **'exe,cratory** *adj*

execute ('ɛksɪ,kju:t) *vb* **executes, executing, executed.** (*tr*) **1** to put (a condemned person) to death; inflict capital punishment upon. **2** to carry out; complete. **3** to perform; accomplish; effect. **4** to make or produce: *to execute a drawing.* **5** to carry into effect (a judicial sentence, the law, etc.). **6** *Law.* to render (a deed, etc.) effective, as by signing, sealing, and delivering. **7** to carry out the terms of (a contract, will, etc.). ORIG C14: from OF *executer,* back formation from *executeur* EXECUTOR
▸ **'exe,cutable** *adj* ▸ **executant** (ɪg'zɛkjʊtənt) *n* ▸ **'exe,cuter** *n*

execution (,ɛksɪ'kju:ʃən) *n* **1** the act or process of executing. **2** the carrying out or undergoing of a sentence of death. **3** the style or manner in which something is accomplished or performed; technique. **4a** the enforcement of the judgment of a court of law. **4b** the writ ordering such enforcement.

executioner (,ɛksɪ'kju:ʃənə) *n* an official charged with carrying out the death sentence passed upon a condemned person.

executive (ɪg'zɛkjʊtɪv) *n* **1** a person or group responsible for the administration of a project, activity, or business. **2a** the branch of government responsible for carrying out laws, decrees, etc. **2b** any administration. ◆ *adj* **3** having the function of carrying plans, orders, laws, etc., into effect. **4** of or relating to an executive. **5** *Inf.* very expensive or exclusive: *executive housing.*
▸ **ex'ecutively** *adv*

Executive Council *n* (in Australia and New Zealand) a body of ministers of the Crown presided over by the governor or governor-general that formally approves cabinet decisions, etc.

executive director *n* a member of the board of directors of a company who is also an employee (usually full-time) and who often has a specified area of responsibility, such as finance or production. Cf. **nonexecutive director.**

executive officer *n* the second-in-command of any of certain military units.

executor (ɪg'zɛkjʊtə) *n* **1** *Law.* a person appointed by a testator to carry out his will. **2** a person who executes. ORIG C14: from Anglo-F *executour,* from L *execūtor*
▸ **ex,ecu'torial** *adj* ▸ **ex'ecutory** *adj* ▸ **ex'ecutor,ship** *n*

executrix (ɪg'zɛkjʊtrɪks) *n, pl* **executrices** (ɪg,zɛkju'traɪsi:z) *or* **executrixes.** *Law.* a female executor.

exegesis (,ɛksɪ'dʒi:sɪs) *n, pl* **exegeses** (-si:z). explanation or critical interpretation of a text, esp. of the Bible. ORIG C17: from Gk, from *exēgeisthai* to interpret, from EX-[1] + *hēgeisthai* to guide
▸ **exegetic** (,ɛksɪ'dʒɛtɪk) *adj*

exegete ('ɛksɪ,dʒi:t) *or* **exegetist** (,ɛksɪ'dʒi:tɪst, -'dʒɛt-) *n* a person who practises exegesis.

exemplar (ɪg'zɛmplə, -plɑ:) *n* **1** a person or thing to be copied or imitated; model. **2** a typical specimen or instance; example. ORIG C14: from L, from *exemplum* EXAMPLE

exemplary (ɪg'zɛmplərɪ) *adj* **1** fit for imitation; model. **2** serving as a warning; admonitory. **3** representative; typical.
▸ **ex'emplarily** *adv* ▸ **ex'emplariness** *n*

exemplary damages *pl n Law.* damages awarded to a plaintiff above the value of actual loss sustained so that they serve also as a punishment to the defendant.

exemplify (ɪg'zɛmplɪ,faɪ) *vb* **exemplifies, exemplifying, exemplified.** (*tr*) **1** to show by example. **2** to serve as an example of. **3** *Law.* to make an official copy of (a document) under seal. ORIG C15: via OF from Med. L *exemplificāre,* from L *exemplum* EXAMPLE + *facere* to make
▸ **ex'empli,fiable** *adj* ▸ **ex,emplifi'cation** *n* ▸ **ex'emplifi,cative** *adj* ▸ **ex'empli,fier** *n*

exempt (ɪg'zɛmpt) *vb* **1** (*tr*) to release from an obligation, tax, etc.; excuse. ◆ *adj* **2a** freed from or not subject to an obligation, tax, etc.; excused. **2b** (*in combination*): *tax-exempt.* ◆ *n* **3** a person who is exempt. ORIG C14: from L *exemptus* removed, from *eximere* to take out, from *emere* to buy, obtain
▸ **ex'emption** *n*

exequies ('ɛksɪkwɪz) *pl n, sing* **exequy.** the rites and ceremonies used at funerals. ORIG C14: from L *exequiae* (pl) funeral procession, rites, from *exequī* to follow to the end

exercise ('ɛksə,saɪz) *vb* **exercises, exercising, exercised.** (*mainly tr*) **1** to put into use; employ. **2** (*intr*) to take exercise or perform exercises. **3** to practise using in order to develop or train. **4** to perform or make use of: *to exercise one's rights.* **5** to bring to bear: *to exercise one's influence.* **6** (*often passive*) to occupy the attentions of, esp. so as to worry or vex: *to be exercised about a decision.* **7** *Mil.* to carry out or cause to carry out simulated combat, manoeuvres, etc. ◆ *n* **8** physical exertion, esp. for development, training, or keeping fit. **9** mental or other activity or practice, esp. to develop a skill. **10** a set of movements, tasks, etc., designed to train, improve, or test one's ability: *piano exercises.* **11** a performance or work of art done as practice or to demonstrate a technique. **12** the performance of a function: *the exercise of one's rights.* **13** (*usually pl*) *Mil.* a manoeuvre or simulated combat operation. **14** *Gymnastics.* a particular event, such as the horizontal bar. ORIG C14: from OF, from L, from *exercēre* to drill, from EX-[1] + *arcēre* to ward off
▸ **'exer,cisable** *adj* ▸ **'exer,ciser** *n*

exercise bike *or* **cycle** *n* a stationary exercise machine that is pedalled like a bicycle as a method of increasing cardiovascular fitness.

exercise book *n* a notebook used by pupils and students.

exercise price *n Stock Exchange.* the price at which the holder of a traded option may exercise his right to buy (or sell) a security.

exert (ɪg'zɜ:t) *vb* (*tr*) **1** to use (influence, authority, etc.) forcefully or effectively. **2** to apply (oneself) diligently; make a strenuous effort. ORIG C17 (in the sense: push forth, emit): from L *exserere* to thrust out, from EX-[1] + *serere* to bind together, entwine
▸ **ex'ertion** *n* ▸ **ex'ertive** *adj*

Exeter ★ ('ɛksɪtə) *n* a city in SW England, administrative centre of Devon; university (1955). Pop.: 94 717 (1991).

exeunt ('ɛksɪ,ʌnt) *Latin.* they go out: used as a stage direction.

exeunt omnes ('ɒmneɪz) *Latin.* they all go out: used as a stage direction.

exfoliate (ɛks'fəʊlɪ,eɪt) *vb* **exfoliates, exfoliating, exfoliated.** (of bark, skin, minerals, etc.) to peel off in layers, flakes, or scales. ORIG C17: from LL *exfoliāre* to strip off leaves, from L *folium* leaf
▸ **ex,foli'ation** *n* ▸ **ex'foliative** *adj*

ex gratia ('greɪʃə) *adj* given as a favour or gratuitously where no legal obligation exists: *an ex gratia payment.* ORIG NL, lit.: out of kindness

exhale (ɛks'heɪl, ɪg'zeɪl) *vb* **exhales, exhaling, exhaled. 1** to expel (breath, smoke, etc.) from the lungs; breathe out. **2** to give off (air, fumes, etc.) or (of air, etc.) to be given off. ORIG C14: from L *exhālāre,* from *hālāre* to breathe
▸ **ex'halable** *adj* ▸ **,exha'lation** *n*

exhaust (ɪg'zɔ:st) *vb* (*mainly tr*) **1** to drain the energy of; tire out. **2** to deprive of resources, etc. **3** to deplete totally; consume. **4** to empty (a container) by drawing off or pumping out (the contents). **5** to develop or discuss thoroughly so that no further interest remains. **6** to remove gas from (a vessel, etc.) in order to reduce pressure or create a vacuum. **7** (*intr*) (of steam or other gases) to be emitted or to escape from an engine after being expanded. ◆ *n* **8** gases ejected from an engine as waste products. **9** the expulsion of expanded gas or steam from an engine. **10a** the parts of an engine through which exhausted gases or steam pass. **10b** (*as modifier*): *exhaust pipe.* ORIG C16: from L *exhaustus* made empty, from *exhaurīre* to draw out, from *haurīre* to draw, drain
▸ **ex'hausted** *adj* ▸ **ex'haustible** *adj* ▸ **ex'hausting** *adj*

exhaustion (ɪg'zɔ:stʃən) *n* **1** extreme tiredness. **2** the condition of being used up. **3** the act of exhausting or the state of being exhausted.

★ people and places

exhaustive (ɪg'zɔːstɪv) *adj* **1** comprehensive; thorough. **2** tending to exhaust.
▸ **ex'haustively** *adv* ▸ **ex'haustiveness** *n*

exhibit (ɪg'zɪbɪt) *vb* (*mainly tr*) **1** (*also intr*) to display (something) to the public. **2** to manifest; display; show. **3** *Law.* to produce (a document or object) in court as evidence. ◆ *n* **4** an object or collection exhibited to the public. **5** *Law.* a document or object produced in court as evidence. ORIG C15: from L *exhibēre* to hold forth, from *habēre* to have
▸ **ex'hibitor** *n* ▸ **ex'hibitory** *adj*

exhibition (ˌɛksɪ'bɪʃən) *n* **1** a public display of art, skills, etc. **2** the act of exhibiting or the state of being exhibited. **3 make an exhibition of oneself.** to behave so foolishly that one excites notice or ridicule. **4** *Brit.* an allowance or scholarship awarded to a student at a university or school.

exhibitioner (ˌɛksɪ'bɪʃənə) *n Brit.* a student who has been awarded an exhibition.

exhibitionism (ˌɛksɪ'bɪʃəˌnɪzəm) *n* **1** a compulsive desire to attract attention to oneself, esp. by exaggerated behaviour. **2** a compulsive desire to expose one's genital organs publicly.
▸ **ˌexhi'bitionist** *n* ▸ **ˌexhiˌbition'istic** *adj*

exhibitive (ɪg'zɪbɪtɪv) *adj* (*usually postpositive* and foll. by *of*) illustrative or demonstrative.

exhilarate (ɪg'zɪləˌreɪt) *vb* **exhilarates, exhilarating, exhilarated.** (*tr*) to make lively and cheerful; elate. ORIG C16: from L *exhilarāre,* from *hilarāre* to cheer
▸ **ex'hilaˌrating** *adj* ▸ **exˌhila'ration** *n* ▸ **ex'hilarative** *adj*

exhort (ɪg'zɔːt) *vb* to urge or persuade (someone) earnestly; advise strongly. ORIG C14: from L *exhortārī,* from *hortārī* to urge
▸ **ex'hortative** *or* **ex'hortatory** *adj* ▸ **ˌexhor'tation** *n* ▸ **ex'horter** *n*

exhume (ɛks'hjuːm) *vb* **exhumes, exhuming, exhumed.** (*tr*) **1** to dig up (something buried, esp. a corpse); disinter. **2** to reveal; disclose. ORIG C18: from Med. L, from L EX-[1] + *humāre* to bury, from *humus* the ground
▸ **exhumation** (ˌɛkshju'meɪʃən) *n* ▸ **ex'humer** *n*

ex hypothesi (ɛks haɪ'pɒθəsɪ) *adv* in accordance with the hypothesis stated. ORIG C17: NL

exigency ('ɛksɪdʒənsɪ, ɪg'zɪdʒənsɪ) *or* **exigence** ('ɛksɪdʒəns) *n, pl* **exigencies** *or* **exigences. 1** urgency. **2** (*often pl*) an urgent demand; pressing requirement. **3** an emergency.

exigent ('ɛksɪdʒənt) *adj* **1** urgent; pressing. **2** exacting; demanding. ORIG C15: from L *exigere* to drive out, weigh out, from *agere* to drive, compel

exiguous (ɪg'zɪgjuəs, ɪk'sɪg-) *adj* scanty or slender; meagre. ORIG C17: from L *exiguus,* from *exigere* to weigh out; see EXIGENT
▸ **exiguity** (ˌɛksɪ'gjuːɪtɪ) *or* **ex'iguousness** *n*

exile ('ɛgzaɪl, 'ɛksaɪl) *n* **1** a prolonged, usually enforced absence from one's home or country. **2** the official expulsion of a person from his or her native land. **3** a person banished or living away from his or her home or country; expatriate. ◆ *vb* **exiles, exiling, exiled. 4** (*tr*) to expel from home or country, esp. by official decree; banish. ORIG C13: from L *exsilium* banishment, from *exsul* banished person
▸ **exilic** (ɛg'zɪlɪk, ɛk'sɪlɪk) *adj*

exist (ɪg'zɪst) *vb* (*intr*) **1** to have being or reality; be. **2** to eke out a living; stay alive. **3** to be living; live. **4** to be present under specified conditions or in a specified place. ORIG C17: from L *exsistere* to step forth, from EX-[1] + *sistere* to stand
▸ **ex'istent** *adj* ▸ **ex'isting** *adj*

USAGE NOTE See at **extant.**

existence (ɪg'zɪstəns) *n* **1** the fact or state of existing; being. **2** the continuance or maintenance of life; living, esp. in adverse circumstances. **3** something that exists; a being or entity. **4** everything that exists.

existential (ˌɛgzɪ'stɛnʃəl) *adj* **1** of or relating to existence, esp. human existence. **2** *Philosophy.* known by experience rather than reason. **3** of a formula or proposition asserting the existence of at least one object fulfilling a given condition. **4** of or relating to existentialism.

existentialism (ˌɛgzɪ'stɛnʃəˌlɪzəm) *n* a modern philosophical movement stressing personal experience and responsibility and their demands on the individual, who is seen as a free agent in a deterministic and seemingly meaningless universe.
▸ **ˌexis'tentialist** *adj, n*

exit ('ɛgzɪt, 'ɛksɪt) *n* **1** a way out. **2** the act or an instance of going out. **3a** the act of leaving or right to leave a particular place. **3b** (*as modifier*): *an exit visa.* **4** departure from life; death. **5** *Theatre.* the act of going offstage. **6** *Brit.* a point at which vehicles may leave or join a motorway. ◆ *vb* **exits, exiting, exited. 7** (*intr*) to go away or out; depart. **8** (*intr*) *Theatre.* to go offstage: used as a stage direction: *exit Hamlet.* **9** *Computing.* to leave (a computer program or system). ORIG C17: from L *exitus* a departure, from *exīre* to go out, from EX-[1] + *īre* to go

exitance ('ɛksɪtəns) *n* a measure of the ability of a surface to emit radiation. ORIG C20: from EXIT + -ANCE

exit poll *n* a poll taken by asking people how they voted in an election as they leave a polling station.

ex libris (ɛks 'liːbrɪs) *prep* **1** from the collection or library of. ◆ *n* **ex-libris,** *pl* **ex-libris. 2** a bookplate bearing the owner's name, coat of arms, etc. ORIG C19: from L, lit.: from the books (of)

Exmoor ★ ('ɛksˌmʊə, -ˌmɔː) *n* a high moorland in SW England, in W Somerset and N Devon: largely forested until the 19th century, now chiefly grazing ground for Exmoor ponies, sheep, and red deer.

Exmouth ★ ('ɛksməθ) *n* a town in SW England, in Devon, at the mouth of the River Exe: tourism, fishing. Pop.: 28 414 (1991).

ex new *adv, adj* (of shares, etc.) without the right to take up any scrip issue or rights issue. Cf. **cum new.**

exo- *combining form.* external, outside, or beyond: *exothermal.* ORIG from Gk *exō* outside

exobiology (ˌɛksəubaɪ'ɒlədʒɪ) *n* another name for **astrobiology.**
▸ **ˌexobi'ologist** *n*

exocarp ('ɛksəuˌkɑːp) *n* another name for **epicarp.**

exocrine ('ɛksəuˌkraɪn, -krɪn) *adj* **1** of or relating to exocrine glands or their secretions. ◆ *n* **2** an exocrine gland. ORIG C20: EXO- + *-crine* from Gk *krinein* to separate

exocrine gland *n* any gland, such as a salivary or sweat gland, that secretes its products through a duct onto an epithelial surface.

Exod. *Bible. abbrev. for* Exodus.

exodus ('ɛksədəs) *n* the act or an instance of going out. ORIG C17: via L from Gk *exodos,* from EX-[1] + *hodos* way

Exodus ('ɛksədəs) *n* **1 the.** the departure of the Israelites from Egypt. **2** the second book of the Old Testament, recounting the events connected with this.

ex officio ('ɛks ə'fɪʃɪəu, ə'fɪsɪəu) *adv, adj* by right of position or office. ORIG L

exogamy (ɛk'sɒgəmɪ) *n Anthropol., sociol.* marriage outside one's own tribe or similar unit.
▸ **ex'ogamous** *or* **exogamic** (ˌɛksəu'gæmɪk) *adj*

exogenous (ɛk'sɒdʒɪnəs) *adj* **1** having an external origin. **2** *Biol.* **2a** originating outside an organism. **2b** of or relating to external factors, such as light, that influence an organism. **3** *Psychiatry* (of a mental illness) caused by external factors.

exon ('ɛksɒn) *n Brit.* one of the four officers who command the Yeomen of the Guard. ORIG C17: a pronunciation spelling of F *exempt* EXEMPT

exonerate (ɪg'zɒnəˌreɪt) *vb* **exonerates, exonerating, exonerated.** (*tr*) **1** to absolve from blame or a criminal charge. **2** to relieve from an obligation. ORIG C16: from L *exonerāre* to free from a burden, from *onus* a burden
▸ **exˌoner'ation** *n* ▸ **ex'onerative** *adj* ▸ **ex'onerˌator** *n*

exophthalmos (ˌɛksɒf'θælmɒs), **exophthalmus** (ˌɛksɒf'θælməs), *or* **exophthalmia** (ˌɛksɒf'θælmɪə) *n* abnormal protrusion of the eyeball, as caused by

hyperthyroidism. ORIG C19: via NL from Gk, from EX-[1] + *ophthalmos* eye
▸ **ˌexophˈthalmic** *adj*

exorbitant (ɪgˈzɔ:bɪtənt) *adj* (of prices, demands, etc.) excessive; extravagant; immoderate. ORIG C15: from LL *exorbitāre* to deviate, from L *orbita* track
▸ **exˈorbitance** *n* ▸ **exˈorbitantly** *adv*

exorcize *or* **exorcise** (ˈɛksɔ:ˌsaɪz) *vb* **exorcizes, exorcizing, exorcized** *or* **exorcises, exorcising, exorcised.** (*tr*) to expel (evil spirits) from (a person or place), by adjurations and religious rites. ORIG C15: from LL, from Gk, from EX-[1] + *horkizein* to adjure
▸ **ˈexorcism** *n* ▸ **ˈexorcist** *n* ▸ **ˈexorˌcizer** *or* **ˈexorˌciser** *n*

exordium (ɛkˈsɔ:dɪəm) *n, pl* **exordiums** *or* **exordia** (-dɪə). an introductory part or beginning, esp. of an oration or discourse. ORIG C16: from L, from *exōrdīrī* to begin, from *ōrdīrī* to begin
▸ **exˈordial** *adj*

exoskeleton (ˌɛksəʊˈskɛlɪtən) *n* the protective or supporting structure covering the outside of the body of many animals, such as the thick cuticle of arthropods.
▸ **ˌexoˈskeletal** *adj*

exosphere (ˈɛksəʊˌsfɪə) *n* the outermost layer of the earth's atmosphere. It extends from about 400 kilometres above the earth's surface.

exothermic (ˌɛksəʊˈθɜ:mɪk) *or* **exothermal** *adj* (of a chemical reaction or compound) occurring or formed with the evolution of heat.
▸ **ˌexoˈthermically** *or* **ˌexoˈthermally** *adv*

exotic (ɪgˈzɒtɪk) *adj* **1** originating in a foreign country, esp. one in the tropics; not native: *an exotic plant.* **2** having a strange or bizarre allure, beauty, or quality. ◆ *n* **3** an exotic person or thing. ORIG C16: from L, from Gk *exōtikos* foreign, from *exō* outside
▸ **exˈotically** *adv* ▸ **exˈotiˌcism** *n* ▸ **exˈoticness** *n*

exotica (ɪgˈzɒtɪkə) *pl n* exotic objects, esp. when forming a collection. ORIG C19: L, neuter pl of *exōticus;* see EXOTIC

exotic dancer *n* a striptease or belly dancer.

expand (ɪkˈspænd) *vb* **1** to make or become greater in extent, volume, size, or scope. **2** to spread out; unfold; stretch out. **3** (*intr;* often foll. by *on*) to enlarge or expatiate (on a story, topic, etc.). **4** (*intr*) to become increasingly relaxed, friendly, or talkative. **5** *Maths.* to express (a function or expression) as the sum or product of terms. ORIG C15: from L *expandere* to spread out
▸ **exˈpandable** *adj*

expanded (ɪkˈspændɪd) *adj* (of a plastic) having been foamed during manufacture by a gas to make a light packaging material or heat insulator: *expanded polystyrene.*

expanded metal *n* an open mesh of metal used for reinforcing brittle or friable materials and in fencing.

expander (ɪkˈspændə) *n* **1** a device for exercising and developing the muscles of the body. **2** an electronic device for increasing the variations in signal amplitude in a transmission system according to a specified law.

expanse (ɪkˈspæns) *n* **1** an uninterrupted surface of something that extends, esp. over a wide area; stretch. **2** expansion or extension. ORIG C17: from NL *expansum* the heavens, from L *expansus* spread out, from *expandere* to expand

expansible (ɪkˈspænsəbəl) *adj* able to expand or be expanded.
▸ **exˌpansiˈbility** *n*

expansion (ɪkˈspænʃən) *n* **1** the act of expanding or the state of being expanded. **2** something expanded. **3** the degree or amount by which something expands. **4** an increase or development, esp. in the activities of a company. **5** the increase in the dimensions of a body or substance when subjected to an increase in temperature, internal pressure, etc.
▸ **exˈpansionary** *adj*

expansionism (ɪkˈspænʃəˌnɪzəm) *n* the doctrine or practice of expanding the economy or territory of a country.
▸ **exˈpansionist** *n, adj* ▸ **exˌpansionˈistic** *adj*

expansive (ɪkˈspænsɪv) *adj* **1** able or tending to expand or characterized by expansion. **2** wide; extensive. **3** friendly, open, or talkative. **4** grand or extravagant.
▸ **exˈpansiveness** *n*

expansivity (ˌɛkspænˈsɪvɪtɪ) *n* the fractional increase in length or volume of a substance or body on being heated through a one degree rise in temperature; coefficient of expansion.

ex parte (ɛks ˈpɑ:tɪ) *adj Law.* (of an application in a judicial proceeding) on behalf of one side or party only: *an ex parte injunction.*

expat (ˌɛksˈpæt) *n, adj Inf.* short for **expatriate.**

expatiate (ɪkˈspeɪʃɪˌeɪt) *vb* **expatiates, expatiating, expatiated.** (*intr*) **1** (foll. by *on* or *upon*) to enlarge (on a theme, topic, etc.); elaborate (on). **2** *Rare.* to wander about. ORIG C16: from L *exspatiārī* to digress, from *spatiārī* to walk about
▸ **exˌpatiˈation** *n* ▸ **exˈpatiˌator** *n*

expatriate *adj* (ɛksˈpætrɪɪt, -ˌeɪt). **1** resident outside one's native country. **2** exiled or banished from one's native country. ◆ *n* (ɛksˈpætrɪɪt, -ˌeɪt). **3** a person living outside his native country **4** an exile; expatriate person. ◆ *vb* (ɛksˈpætrɪˌeɪt), **expatriates, expatriating, expatriated.** (*tr*) **5** to exile (oneself) from one's native country or cause (another) to go into exile. ORIG C18: from Med. L, from L EX-[1] + *patria* native land
▸ **exˌpatriˈation** *n*

expect (ɪkˈspɛkt) *vb* (*tr; may take a clause as object or an infinitive*) **1** to regard as likely; anticipate. **2** to look forward to or be waiting for. **3** to decide that (something) is necessary; require: *the teacher expects us to work late.* ◆ See also **expecting.** ORIG C16: from L *exspectāre* to watch for, from *spectāre* to look at
▸ **exˈpectable** *adj*

expectancy (ɪkˈspɛktənsɪ) *or* **expectance** *n* **1** something expected, esp. on the basis of a norm or average: *his life expectancy was 30 years.* **2** anticipation; expectation. **3** the prospect of a future interest or possession.

expectant (ɪkˈspɛktənt) *adj* **1** expecting, anticipating, or hopeful. **2** having expectations, esp. of possession of something. **3** pregnant. ◆ *n* **4** a person who expects something.
▸ **exˈpectantly** *adv*

expectation (ˌɛkspɛkˈteɪʃən) *n* **1** the act or state of expecting or the state of being expected. **2** (*usually pl*) something looked forward to, whether feared or hoped for. **3** an attitude of expectancy or hope. **4** *Statistics.* **4a** the numerical probability that an event will occur. **4b** another term for **expected value.**

expected frequency *n Statistics.* the number of occasions on which an event may be presumed to occur on average in a given number of trials.

expected value *n Statistics.* the sum or integral of all possible values of a random variable, or any given function of it, multiplied by the respective probabilities of the values of the variable.

expecting (ɪkˈspɛktɪŋ) *adj Inf.* pregnant.

expectorant (ɪkˈspɛktərənt) *Med.* ◆ *adj* **1** promoting the secretion, liquefaction, or expulsion of sputum from the respiratory passages. ◆ *n* **2** an expectorant drug or agent.

expectorate (ɪkˈspɛktəˌreɪt) *vb* **expectorates, expectorating, expectorated.** to cough up and spit out (sputum from the respiratory passages). ORIG C17: from L *expectorāre,* lit.: to drive from the breast, expel, from *pectus* breast
▸ **exˌpectoˈration** *n* ▸ **exˈpectoˌrator** *n*

expediency (ɪkˈspi:dɪənsɪ) *or* **expedience** *n, pl* **expediencies** *or* **expediences. 1** appropriateness; suitability. **2** the use of or inclination towards methods that are advantageous rather than fair or just. **3** another word for **expedient** (sense 3).

expedient (ɪkˈspi:dɪənt) *adj* **1** suitable to the circumstances; appropriate. **2** inclined towards methods that are advantageous rather than fair or just. ◆ *n also* **expediency. 3** something suitable or appropriate, esp. during an urgent situation. ORIG C14: from L *expediēns* setting free; see EXPEDITE

expedite (ˈɛkspɪˌdaɪt) *vb* **expedites, expediting, expedited.**

(*tr*) **1** to hasten or assist the progress of. **2** to do or process with speed and efficiency. ORIG C17: from L *expedīre,* lit.: to free the feet (as from a snare), hence, liberate, from EX-[1] + *pēs* foot
▸ **'expe,diter** *or* **'expe,ditor** *n*

expedition (,ɛkspɪ'dɪʃən) *n* **1** an organized journey or voyage, esp. for exploration or for a scientific or military purpose. **2** the people and equipment comprising an expedition. **3** promptness; dispatch. ORIG C15: from L *expedīre* to prepare, EXPEDITE
▸ **,expe'ditionary** *adj*

expeditious (,ɛkspɪ'dɪʃəs) *adj* characterized by or done with speed and efficiency; prompt; quick.
▸ **,expe'ditiously** *adv* ▸ **,expe'ditiousness** *n*

expel (ɪk'spɛl) *vb* **expels, expelling, expelled.** (*tr*) **1** to eject or drive out with force. **2** to deprive of participation in or membership of a school, club, etc. ORIG C14: from L *expellere* to drive out, from *pellere* to thrust, drive
▸ **ex'pellable** *adj* ▸ **expellee** (,ɛkspɛ'liː) *n* ▸ **ex'peller** *n*

expellant *or* **expellent** (ɪk'spɛlənt) *adj* **1** forcing out or able to force out. ◆ *n* **2** a medicine used to expel undesirable substances or organisms from the body.

expend (ɪk'spɛnd) *vb* (*tr*) **1** to spend; disburse. **2** to consume or use up. ORIG C15: from L *expendere,* from *pendere* to weigh
▸ **ex'pender** *n*

expendable (ɪk'spɛndəb[ə]l) *adj* **1** that may be expended or used up. **2** able to be sacrificed to achieve an objective, esp. a military one. ◆ *n* **3** something expendable.
▸ **ex,penda'bility** *n*

expenditure (ɪk'spɛndɪtʃə) *n* **1** something expended, esp. money. **2** the act of expending.

expense (ɪk'spɛns) *n* **1** a particular payment of money; expenditure. **2** money needed for individual purchases; cost; charge. **3** (*pl*) money spent in the performance of a job, etc., usually reimbursed by an employer or allowable against tax. **4** something requiring money for its purchase or upkeep. **5 at the expense of.** to the detriment of. ORIG C14: from LL, from L *expēnsus* weighed out; see EXPEND

expense account *n* **1** an arrangement by which an employee's expenses are refunded by his employer or deducted from his income for tax purposes. **2** a record of such expenses.

expensive (ɪk'spɛnsɪv) *adj* high-priced; costly; dear.
▸ **ex'pensiveness** *n*

experience (ɪk'spɪərɪəns) *n* **1** direct personal participation or observation. **2** a particular incident, feeling, etc., that a person has undergone. **3** accumulated knowledge, esp. of practical matters. ◆ *vb* **experiences, experiencing, experienced.** (*tr*) **4** to participate in or undergo. **5** to be moved by; feel. ORIG C14: from L *experīrī* to prove; rel. to L *perīculum* PERIL
▸ **ex'perienceable** *adj*

experienced (ɪk'spɪərɪənst) *adj* having become skilful or knowledgeable from extensive participation or observation.

experiential (ɪk,spɪərɪ'ɛnʃəl) *adj Philosophy.* relating to or derived from experience; empirical.

experiment *n* (ɪk'spɛrɪmənt). **1** a test or investigation, esp. one planned to provide evidence for or against a hypothesis. **2** the act of conducting such an investigation or test; research. **3** an attempt at something new or original. ◆ *vb* (ɪk'spɛrɪ,mɛnt). **4** (*intr*) to make an experiment or experiments. ORIG C14: from L *experīmentum* proof, trial, from *experīrī* to test; see EXPERIENCE
▸ **ex'peri,menter** *n*

experimental (ɪk,spɛrɪ'mɛnt[ə]l) *adj* **1** relating to, based on, or having the nature of experiment. **2** based on or derived from experience; empirical. **3** tending to experiment. **4** tentative or provisional.
▸ **ex,peri'mentalism** *n*

experimentation (ɪk,spɛrɪmɛn'teɪʃən) *n* the act, process, or practice of experimenting.

expert ('ɛkspɜːt) *n* **1** a person who has extensive skill or knowledge in a particular field. ◆ *adj* **2** skilful or knowledgeable. **3** of, involving, or done by an expert: *an expert job.* ORIG C14: from L *expertus* known by experience; see EXPERIENCE
▸ **'expertly** *adv* ▸ **'expertness** *n*

expertise (,ɛkspɜː'tiːz) *n* special skill, knowledge, or judgment; expertness. ORIG C19: from F: expert skill, from EXPERT

expiate ('ɛkspɪ,eɪt) *vb* **expiates, expiating, expiated.** (*tr*) to atone for (sin or wrongdoing); make amends for. ORIG C16: from L *expiāre,* from *pius* dutiful; see PIOUS
▸ **'expiable** *adj* ▸ **,expi'ation** *n* ▸ **'expi,ator** *n*

expiatory ('ɛkspɪətərɪ, -trɪ) *adj* **1** capable of making expiation. **2** offered in expiation.

expiration (,ɛkspɪ'reɪʃən) *n* **1** the finish of something; expiry. **2** the act, process, or sound of breathing out.

expire (ɪk'spaɪə) *vb* **expires, expiring, expired. 1** (*intr*) to finish or run out; come to an end. **2** to breathe out (air). **3** (*intr*) to die. ORIG C15: from OF, from L *exspīrāre* to breathe out, from *spīrāre* to breathe
▸ **ex'pirer** *n*

expiry (ɪk'spaɪərɪ) *n, pl* **expiries. 1a** a coming to an end, esp. of a contract period; termination. **1b** (*as modifier*): *the expiry date.* **2** death.

explain (ɪk'spleɪn) *vb* **1** (when *tr, may take a clause as object*) to make (something) comprehensible, esp. by giving a clear and detailed account of it. **2** (*tr*) to justify or attempt to justify (oneself) by reasons for one's actions. ORIG C15: from L *explānāre* to flatten, from *plānus* level
▸ **ex'plainable** *adj* ▸ **ex'plainer** *n*

explain away *vb* (*tr, adv*) to offer excuses or reasons for (bad conduct, mistakes, etc.).

explanation (,ɛksplə'neɪʃən) *n* **1** the act or process of explaining. **2** something that explains. **3** a clarification of disputed points.

explanatory (ɪk'splænətərɪ, -trɪ) *or* **explanative** *adj* serving or intended to serve as an explanation.
▸ **ex'planatorily** *adv*

expletive (ɪk'spliːtɪv) *n* **1** an exclamation or swearword; an oath or sound expressing emotion rather than meaning. **2** any syllable, word, or phrase conveying no independent meaning, esp. one inserted in verse for the sake of metre. ◆ *adj also* **expletory** (ɪk'spliːtərɪ, -trɪ). **3** without particular meaning, esp. when filling out a line of verse. ORIG C17: from LL *explētīvus* for filling out, from *explēre,* from *plēre* to fill

explicable ('ɛksplɪkəb[ə]l, ɪk'splɪk-) *adj* capable of being explained.

explicate ('ɛksplɪ,keɪt) *vb* **explicates, explicating, explicated.** (*tr*) *Formal.* **1** to make clear or explicit; explain. **2** to formulate or develop (a theory, hypothesis, etc.). ORIG C16: from L *explicāre* to unfold
▸ **,expli'cation** *n*

explicit (ɪk'splɪsɪt) *adj* **1** precisely and clearly expressed, leaving nothing to implication; fully stated. **2** leaving little to the imagination; graphically detailed. **3** openly expressed without reservations; unreserved. ORIG C17: from L *explicitus* unfolded
▸ **ex'plicitly** *adv* ▸ **ex'plicitness** *n*

explode (ɪk'spləʊd) *vb* **explodes, exploding, exploded. 1** to burst or cause to burst with great violence, esp. through detonation of an explosive; blow up. **2** to destroy or be destroyed in this manner. **3** (of a gas) to undergo or cause (a gas) to undergo a sudden violent expansion, as a result of a fast exothermic chemical or nuclear reaction. **4** (*intr*) to react suddenly or violently with emotion, etc. **5** (*intr*) (esp. of a population) to increase rapidly. **6** (*tr*) to show (a theory, etc.) to be baseless. ORIG C16: from L *explōdere* to drive off by clapping
▸ **ex'ploder** *n*

exploded view *n* a drawing or photograph of a mechanism that shows its parts separately, usually indicating their relative positions.

exploit *n* ('ɛksplɔɪt). **1** a notable deed or feat, esp. one that is heroic. ◆ *vb* (ɪk'splɔɪt). (*tr*) **2** to take advantage of (a person, situation, etc.) for one's own ends. **3** to make the best use of. ORIG C14: from OF: accomplishment, from L *explicitum* (something) unfolded, from *explicāre* to EXPLICATE

▸ **exˈploitable** *adj* ▸ **ˌexploiˈtation** *n* ▸ **exˈploitive** *or* **exˈploitative** *adj*

exploration (ˌɛkspləˈreɪʃən) *n* **1** the act or process of exploring. **2** an organized trip into unfamiliar regions, esp. for scientific purposes.
▸ **exploratory** (ɪkˈsplɒrətərɪ, -trɪ) *or* **exˈplorative** *adj*

explore (ɪkˈsplɔː) *vb* **explores, exploring, explored. 1** (*tr*) to examine or investigate, esp. systematically. **2** to travel into (unfamiliar regions), esp. for scientific purposes. **3** (*tr*) *Med.* to examine (an organ or part) for diagnostic purposes. ORIG C16: from L, from EX-[1] + *plōrāre* to cry aloud; prob. from the shouts of hunters sighting prey
▸ **exˈplorer** *n*

explosion (ɪkˈspləʊʒən) *n* **1** the act or an instance of exploding. **2** a violent release of energy resulting from a rapid chemical or nuclear reaction. **3** a sudden or violent outburst of activity, noise, emotion, etc. **4** a rapid increase, esp. in a population. ORIG C17: from L *explōsiō*, from *explōdere* to EXPLODE

explosive (ɪkˈspləʊsɪv) *adj* **1** of, involving, or characterized by explosion. **2** capable of exploding or tending to explode. **3** potentially violent or hazardous: *an explosive situation.* ◆ *n* **4** a substance capable of exploding or tending to explode.
▸ **exˈplosiveness** *n*

expo (ˈɛkspəʊ) *n, pl* **expos.** short for **exposition** (sense 3).

exponent (ɪkˈspəʊnənt) *n* **1** (usually foll. by *of*) a person or thing that acts as an advocate (of an idea, cause, etc.). **2** a person or thing that explains or interprets. **3** a performer or artist. **4** Also called: **power, index.** *Maths.* a number or variable placed as a superscript to another number or quantity to indicate the number of times the designated number or quantity should appear in a repeated multiplication, as in $x^3 = x \times x \times x$, where 3 is the exponent. ◆ *adj* **5** offering a declaration, explanation, or interpretation. ORIG C16: from L *expōnere* to set out, expound

exponential (ˌɛkspəʊˈnɛnʃəl) *adj* **1** *Maths.* (of a function, curve, etc.) of or involving numbers or quantities raised to an exponent, esp. e^x. **2** *Maths.* raised to the power of e, the base of natural logarithms. **3** of or involving an exponent or exponents. **4** *Inf.* very rapid. ◆ *n* **5** *Maths.* an exponential function, etc.

exponential distribution *n Statistics.* a continuous single-parameter distribution used esp. when making statements about the length of life of materials or times between random events.

export *n* (ˈɛkspɔːt). **1** (*often pl*) **1a** goods (**visible exports**) or services (**invisible exports**) sold to a foreign country or countries. **1b** (*as modifier*): *an export licence.* ◆ *vb* (ɪkˈspɔːt, ˈɛkspɔːt). **2** to sell (goods or services) or ship (goods) to a foreign country. **3** (*tr*) to transmit or spread (an idea, institution, etc.) abroad. ORIG C15: from L *exportāre* to carry away
▸ **exˈportable** *adj* ▸ **exˌportaˈbility** *n* ▸ **ˌexporˈtation** *n*
▸ **exˈporter** *n*

export reject *n* an article that fails to meet a standard of quality required for export and that is sold on the home market.

expose (ɪkˈspəʊz) *vb* **exposes, exposing, exposed.** (*tr*) **1** to display for viewing; exhibit. **2** to bring to public notice; disclose. **3** to divulge the identity of; unmask. **4** (foll. by *to*) to make subject or susceptible (to attack, criticism, etc.). **5** to abandon (a child, etc.) in the open to die. **6** (foll. by *to*) to introduce (to) or acquaint (with). **7** *Photog.* to subject (a film or plate) to light, X-rays, etc. **8 expose oneself.** to display one's sexual organs in public. ORIG C15: from OF *exposer*, from L *expōnere* to set out
▸ **exˈposable** *adj* ▸ **exˈposal** *n* ▸ **exˈposer** *n*

exposé (ɛksˈpəʊzeɪ) *n* the act or an instance of bringing a scandal, crime, etc., to public notice.

exposed (ɪkˈspəʊzd) *adj* **1** not concealed; displayed for viewing. **2** without shelter from the elements. **3** susceptible to attack or criticism; vulnerable.

exposition (ˌɛkspəˈzɪʃən) *n* **1** a systematic, usually written statement about or explanation of a subject. **2** the act of expounding or setting forth information or a viewpoint. **3** a large public exhibition, esp. of industrial products or arts and crafts. **4** the act of exposing or the state of being exposed. **5** *Music.* the first statement of the subjects or themes of a movement in sonata form or a fugue. **6** *RC Church.* the exhibiting of the consecrated Eucharistic Host or a relic for public veneration. ORIG C14: from L *expositiō* a setting forth, from *expōnere* to display
▸ **ˌexpoˈsitional** *adj*

expositor (ɪkˈspɒzɪtə) *n* a person who expounds.

expository (ɪkˈspɒzɪtərɪ, -trɪ) *or* **expositive** *adj* of or involving exposition; explanatory.

ex post facto (ɛks pəʊst ˈfæktəʊ) *adj* having retrospective effect. ORIG C17: from L *ex* from + *post* afterwards + *factus* done, from *facere* to do

expostulate (ɪkˈspɒstjʊˌleɪt) *vb* **expostulates, expostulating, expostulated.** (*intr;* usually foll. by *with*) to argue or reason (with), esp. in order to dissuade. ORIG C16: from L *expostulāre* to require, from *postulāre* to demand; see POSTULATE
▸ **exˌpostuˈlation** *n* ▸ **exˈpostuˌlator** *n*

exposure (ɪkˈspəʊʒə) *n* **1** the act of exposing or the condition of being exposed. **2** the position or outlook of a house, building, etc.: *a southern exposure.* **3** lack of shelter from the weather, esp. the cold. **4** a surface that is exposed. **5** *Photog.* **5a** the act of exposing a film or plate to light, X-rays, etc. **5b** an area on a film or plate that has been exposed. **6** *Photog.* **6a** the intensity of light falling on a film or plate multiplied by the time for which it is exposed. **6b** a combination of lens aperture and shutter speed used in taking a photograph. **7** appearance before the public, as in a theatre, on television, etc.

exposure meter *n Photog.* an instrument for measuring the intensity of light so that suitable camera settings can be determined. Also called: **light meter.**

expound (ɪkˈspaʊnd) *vb* (when *intr,* foll. by *on* or *about*) to explain or set forth (an argument, theory, etc.) in detail. ORIG C13: from OF, from L *expōnere* to set forth, from *pōnere* to put
▸ **exˈpounder** *n*

express (ɪkˈsprɛs) *vb* (*tr*) **1** to transform (ideas) into words; utter; verbalize. **2** to show or reveal. **3** to communicate (emotion, etc.) without words, as through music, painting, etc. **4** to indicate through a symbol, formula, etc. **5** to squeeze out: *to express the juice from an orange.* **6 express oneself.** to communicate one's thoughts or ideas. ◆ *adj* (*prenominal*) **7** clearly indicated; explicitly stated. **8** done or planned for a definite reason; particular. **9** of or designed for rapid transportation of people, mail, etc.: *express delivery.* ◆ *n* **10a** a system for sending mail, money, etc., rapidly. **10b** mail, etc., conveyed by such a system. **10c** *Chiefly US & Canad.* an enterprise operating such a system. **11** Also: **express train.** a fast train stopping at no or only a few stations between its termini. ◆ *adv* **12** by means of express delivery. ORIG C14: from L *expressus,* lit.: squeezed out, hence, prominent, from *exprimere* to force out, from EX-[1] + *premere* to press
▸ **exˈpresser** *n* ▸ **exˈpressible** *adj*

expression (ɪkˈsprɛʃən) *n* **1** the act or an instance of transforming ideas into words. **2** a manifestation of an emotion, feeling, etc., without words. **3** communication of emotion through music, painting, etc. **4** a look on the face that indicates mood or emotion. **5** the choice of words, intonation, etc., in communicating. **6** a particular phrase used conventionally to express something. **7** the act or process of squeezing out a liquid. **8** *Maths.* a variable, function, or some combination of these.
▸ **exˈpressional** *adj* ▸ **exˈpressionless** *adj*

expressionism (ɪkˈsprɛʃəˌnɪzəm) *n* (*sometimes cap.*) an artistic and literary movement originating in the early 20th century, which sought to express emotions rather than to represent external reality: characterized by symbolism and distortion.
▸ **exˈpressionist** *n, adj* ▸ **exˌpressionˈistic** *adj*

expression mark *n* one of a set of musical directions, usually in Italian, indicating how a piece or passage is to be performed.

expressive (ɪkˈsprɛsɪv) *adj* **1** of, involving, or full of expression. **2** (*postpositive;* foll. by *of*) indicative or sugges-

tive (of). **3** having a particular meaning or force; significant.
▸ **ex'pressiveness** *n*

expressly (ɪk'sprɛslɪ) *adv* **1** for an express purpose. **2** plainly, exactly, or unmistakably.

expresso (ɪk'sprɛsəʊ) *n, pl* **expressos.** a variant of **espresso.**

expressway (ɪk'sprɛsˌweɪ) *n* a motorway.

expropriate (ɛks'prəuprɪˌeɪt) *vb* **expropriates, expropriating, expropriated.** (*tr*) to deprive (an owner) of (property), esp. by taking it for public use. ORIG C17: from Med. L *expropriāre* to deprive of possessions, from *proprius* own
▸ **exˌpropri'ation** *n* ▸ **ex'propriˌator** *n*

expulsion (ɪk'spʌlʃən) *n* the act of expelling or the fact or condition of being expelled. ORIG C14: from L *expulsiō* a driving out, from *expellere* to EXPEL
▸ **ex'pulsive** *adj*

expunge (ɪk'spʌndʒ) *vb* **expunges, expunging, expunged.** (*tr*) to delete or erase; blot out; obliterate. ORIG C17: from L *expungere* to blot out, from *pungere* to prick
▸ **expunction** (ɪk'spʌŋkʃən) *n* ▸ **ex'punger** *n*

expurgate ('ɛkspəˌgeɪt) *vb* **expurgates, expurgating, expurgated.** (*tr*) to amend (a book, text, etc.) by removing (offensive sections). ORIG C17: from L *expurgāre* to clean out, from *purgāre* to purify; see PURGE
▸ **ˌexpur'gation** *n* ▸ **'expurˌgator** *n*

exquisite (ɪk'skwɪzɪt, 'ɛkskwɪzɪt) *adj* **1** possessing qualities of unusual delicacy and craftsmanship. **2** extremely beautiful. **3** outstanding or excellent. **4** sensitive; discriminating. **5** fastidious and refined. **6** intense or sharp in feeling. ◆ *n* **7** *Obs.* a dandy. ORIG C15: from L *exquīsītus* excellent, from *exquīrere* to search out, from *quaerere* to seek
▸ **ex'quisitely** *adv* ▸ **ex'quisiteness** *n*

ex-serviceman or (*fem*) **ex-servicewoman** *n, pl* **ex-servicemen** or **ex-servicewomen.** a person who has served in the armed forces.

extant (ɛk'stænt, 'ɛkstənt) *adj* still in existence; surviving. ORIG C16: from L *exstāns* standing out, from *exstāre,* from *stāre* to stand

> **USAGE NOTE** According to some, *extant* should properly only be used where there is a connotation of survival, often against all odds: *the oldest extant document dates from 1492.* Where the phrase *in existence* can be substituted, using *extant* would on this view be incorrect: *in existence* (not *extant*) *for nearly 15 years, they have been consistently one of the finest rock bands on the planet.* In practice, however, the distinct meanings of the two phrases often overlap: *these beasts, the largest primates on the planet and the greatest of the great apes, are man's closest living relatives and the only extant primate with which we share close physical characteristics.*

extemporaneous (ɪkˌstɛmpə'reɪnɪəs) or **extemporary** (ɪk'stɛmpərərɪ) *adj* **1** spoken, performed, etc., without preparation; extempore. **2** done in a temporary manner; improvised.
▸ **exˌtempo'raneously** or **ex'temporarily** *adv* ▸ **exˌtempo'raneousness** or **ex'temporariness** *n*

extempore (ɪk'stɛmpərɪ) *adv, adj* without planning or preparation. ORIG C16: from L *ex tempore* instantaneously, from EX-[1] out of + *tempus* time

extemporize or **extemporise** (ɪk'stɛmpəˌraɪz) *vb* **extemporizes, extemporizing, extemporized** or **extemporises, extemporising, extemporised. 1** to perform, speak, or compose (an act, speech, music, etc.) without preparation. **2** to use a temporary solution; improvise.
▸ **exˌtempori'zation** or **exˌtempori'sation** *n* ▸ **ex'tempoˌrizer** or **ex'tempoˌriser** *n*

extend (ɪk'stɛnd) *vb* **1** to draw out or be drawn out; stretch. **2** to last or cause to last for a certain time. **3** (*intr*) to reach a certain point in time or distance. **4** (*intr*) to exist or occur. **5** (*tr*) to increase (a building, etc.) in size; add to or enlarge. **6** (*tr*) to broaden the meaning or scope of: *the law was extended.* **7** (*tr*) to present or offer. **8** to stretch forth (an arm, etc.). **9** (*tr*) to lay out (a body) at full length. **10** (*tr*) to strain or exert (a person or animal) to the maximum. **11** (*tr*) to prolong (the time) for payment of (a debt or loan), completion of (a task), etc. ORIG C14: from L *extendere* to stretch out, from *tendere* to stretch
▸ **ex'tendible** or **ex'tendable** *adj* ▸ **exˌtendi'bility** or **exˌtenda'bility** *n*

extended family *n Sociol., anthropol.* the nuclear family together with relatives, often spanning three or more generations.

extended-play *adj* denoting an EP record.

extender (ɪk'stɛndə) *n* **1** a person or thing that extends. **2** a substance added to paints to give body and decrease their rate of settlement. **3** a substance added to glues and resins to dilute them or to modify their viscosity.

extensible (ɪk'stɛnsɪbᵊl) or **extensile** (ɪk'stɛnsaɪl) *adj* capable of being extended.
▸ **exˌtensi'bility** or **ex'tensibleness** *n*

extension (ɪk'stɛnʃən) *n* **1** the act of extending or the condition of being extended. **2** something that can be extended or that extends another object. **3** the length, range, etc., over which something is extended. **4** an additional telephone set connected to the same telephone line as another set. **5** a room or rooms added to an existing building. **6** a delay in the date originally set for payment of a debt or completion of a contract. **7** the property of matter by which it occupies space. **8a** the act of straightening or extending an arm or leg. **8b** its position after being straightened or extended. **9a** a service by which the facilities of an educational establishment, library, etc., are offered to outsiders. **9b** (*as modifier*): *a university extension course.* **10** *Logic.* the class of entities to which a given word correctly applies. ORIG C14: from LL *extensiō* a stretching out; see EXTEND
▸ **ex'tensional** *adj* ▸ **exˌtension'ality** or **ex'tensionalˌism** *n*

extensive (ɪk'stɛnsɪv) *adj* **1** having a large extent, area, degree, etc. **2** widespread. **3** *Agriculture.* involving or farmed with minimum expenditure of capital or labour, esp. depending on a large extent of land. Cf. **intensive** (sense 3). **4** of or relating to logical extension.
▸ **ex'tensiveness** *n*

extensor (ɪk'stɛnsə, -sɔː) *n* any muscle that stretches or extends an arm, leg, or other bodily part. Cf. **flexor.** ORIG C18: from NL, from L *extensus* stretched out

extent (ɪk'stɛnt) *n* **1** the range over which something extends; scope. **2** an area or volume. ORIG C14: from OF, from L *extentus* extensive, from *extendere* to EXTEND

extenuate (ɪk'stɛnjuˌeɪt) *vb* **extenuates, extenuating, extenuated.** (*tr*) **1** to represent (an offence, fault, etc.) as being less serious than it appears, as by showing mitigating circumstances. **2** to cause to be or appear less serious; mitigate. **3** *Arch.* **3a** to emaciate or weaken. **3b** to dilute or thin out. ORIG C16: from L *extenuāre* to make thin, from *tenuis* thin, frail
▸ **ex'tenuˌating** *adj* ▸ **exˌtenu'ation** *n* ▸ **ex'tenuˌator** *n*

exterior (ɪk'stɪərɪə) *n* **1** a part, surface, or region that is on the outside. **2** the outward behaviour or appearance of a person. **3** a film or scene shot outside a studio. ◆ *adj* **4** of, situated on, or suitable for the outside. **5** coming or acting from without. ORIG C16: from L, comp. of *exterus* on the outside, from *ex* out of
▸ **ex'teriorly** *adv*

exterior angle *n* **1** an angle of a polygon contained between one side extended and the adjacent side. **2** any of the four angles made by a transversal that are outside the region between the two intersected lines.

exteriorize or **exteriorise** (ɪk'stɪərɪəˌraɪz) *vb* **exteriorizes, exteriorizing, exteriorized** or **exteriorises, exteriorising, exteriorised.** (*tr*) **1** *Surgery.* to expose (an attached organ or part) outside the body. **2** another word for **externalize.**
▸ **exˌteriori'zation** or **exˌteriori'sation** *n*

exterminate (ɪk'stɜːmɪˌneɪt) *vb* **exterminates, exterminating, exterminated.** (*tr*) to destroy (living things, esp. pests

or vermin) completely; annihilate; eliminate. ORIG C16: from L *extermināre* to drive away, from *terminus* boundary
▸ **ex'terminable** *adj* ▸ **ex,termi'nation** *n* ▸ **ex'termi,nator** *n*

external (ɪk'stɜːnᵊl) *adj* **1** of, situated on, or suitable for the outside; outer. **2** coming or acting from without. **3** of or involving foreign nations. **4** of, relating to, or designating a medicine that is applied to the outside of the body. **5** *Anat.* situated on or near the outside of the body. **6** (of a student) studying a university subject extramurally. **7** *Philosophy.* (of objects, etc.) taken to exist independently of a perceiving mind. ◆ *n* **8** (*often pl*) an external circumstance or aspect, esp. one that is superficial. **9** *Austral.* an extramural student. ORIG C15: from L *externus* outward, from *exterus* on the outside, from *ex* out of
▸ **ex'ternally** *adv* ▸ **,exter'nality** *n*

externalize *or* **externalise** (ɪk'stɜːnə,laɪz) *vb* **externalizes, externalizing, externalized** *or* **externalises, externalising, externalised.** (*tr*) **1** to make external; give outward shape to. **2** *Psychol.* to attribute (one's feelings) to one's surroundings.
▸ **ex,ternali'zation** *or* **ex,ternali'sation** *n*

extinct (ɪk'stɪŋkt) *adj* **1** (of an animal or plant species) having died out. **2** quenched or extinguished. **3** (of a volcano) no longer liable to erupt; inactive. ORIG C15: from L *exstinctus* quenched, from *exstinguere* to EXTINGUISH

extinction (ɪk'stɪŋkʃən) *n* **1** the act of making extinct or the state of being extinct. **2** the act of extinguishing or the state of being extinguished. **3** complete destruction; annihilation. **4** *Physics.* reduction of the intensity of radiation as a result of absorption or scattering by matter.

extinguish (ɪk'stɪŋgwɪʃ) *vb* (*tr*) **1** to put out or quench (a light, flames, etc.). **2** to remove or destroy entirely; annihilate. **3** *Arch.* to eclipse or obscure. ORIG C16: from L *exstinguere*, from *stinguere* to quench
▸ **ex'tinguishable** *adj* ▸ **ex'tinguisher** *n* ▸ **ex'tinguishment** *n*

extirpate ('ɛkstə,peɪt) *vb* **extirpates, extirpating, extirpated.** (*tr*) **1** to remove or destroy completely. **2** to pull up or out; uproot. ORIG C16: from L *exstirpāre* to root out, from *stirps* root, stock
▸ **,extir'pation** *n* ▸ **'extir,pator** *n*

extol *or US* **extoll** (ɪk'stəʊl) *vb* **extols** *or US* **extolls, extolling, extolled.** (*tr*) to praise lavishly; exalt. ORIG C15: from L *extollere* to elevate, from *tollere* to raise
▸ **ex'toller** *n* ▸ **ex'tolment** *n*

extort (ɪk'stɔːt) *vb* (*tr*) **1** to secure (money, favours, etc.) by intimidation, violence, or the misuse of authority. **2** to obtain by importunate demands. ORIG C16: from L *extortus* wrenched out, from *extorquēre* to wrest away, from *torquēre* to twist, wrench
▸ **ex'tortion** *n* ▸ **ex'tortioner, ex'tortionist,** *or* **ex'torter** *n*
▸ **ex'tortive** *adj*

extortionate (ɪk'stɔːʃənɪt) *adj* **1** (of prices, etc.) excessive; exorbitant. **2** (of persons) using extortion.
▸ **ex'tortionately** *adv*

extra ('ɛkstrə) *adj* **1** being more than what is usual or expected; additional. ◆ *n* **2** a person or thing that is additional. **3** something for which an additional charge is made. **4** an additional edition of a newspaper, esp. to report a new development. **5** *Films.* a person temporarily engaged, usually for crowd scenes. **6** *Cricket.* a run not scored from the bat, such as a wide, no-ball, or bye. ◆ *adv* **7** unusually; exceptionally: *an extra fast car.* ORIG C18: ? shortened from EXTRAORDINARY

extra- *prefix* outside or beyond an area or scope: *extrasensory; extraterritorial.* ORIG from L *extrā* outside, beyond, from *extera,* from *exterus* outward

extra cover *n Cricket.* a fielding position between cover and mid-off.

extract *vb* (ɪk'strækt). (*tr*) **1** to pull out or uproot by force. **2** to remove or separate. **3** to derive (pleasure, information, etc.) from some source. **4** to deduce or develop (a doctrine, policy, etc.). **5** *Inf.* to extort (money, etc.). **6** to obtain (a substance) from a mixture or material by a process, such as digestion, distillation, mechanical separation, etc. **7** to cut out or copy out (an article, passage, etc.) from a publication. **8** to determine the value of (the root of a number). ◆ *n* ('ɛkstrækt). **9** something extracted, such as a passage from a book, etc. **10** a preparation containing the active principle or concentrated essence of a material. ORIG C15: from L *extractus* drawn forth, from *extrahere,* from *trahere* to drag
▸ **ex'tractable** *adj* ▸ **ex,tracta'bility** *n* ▸ **ex'tractive** *adj*

USAGE NOTE *Extract* is occasionally wrongly used where *extricate* would be better: *he will find it difficult extricating* (not *extracting*) *himself from this situation.* The main difference between the two words is that while both can be used to refer to removing oneself from a physical situation, *extricate* has stronger overtones of difficulty, and is primarily used with *oneself.* The idea of 'entanglement' present in the Latin root is also there in *intricate.*

extraction (ɪk'strækʃən) *n* **1** the act of extracting or the condition of being extracted. **2** something extracted. **3** the act or an instance of extracting a tooth. **4** origin or ancestry.

extractor (ɪk'stræktə) *n* **1** a person or thing that extracts. **2** an instrument for pulling something out or removing tight-fitting components. **3** short for **extractor fan.**

extractor fan *or* **extraction fan** *n* a fan used in kitchens, bathrooms, workshops, etc., to remove stale air or fumes.

extracurricular (,ɛkstrəkə'rɪkjʊlə) *adj* **1** taking place outside the normal school timetable. **2** beyond the regular duties, schedule, etc.

extradite ('ɛkstrə,daɪt) *vb* **extradites, extraditing, extradited.** (*tr*) **1** to surrender (an alleged offender) for trial to a foreign state. **2** to procure the extradition of. ORIG C19: back formation from EXTRADITION
▸ **'extra,ditable** *adj*

extradition (,ɛkstrə'dɪʃən) *n* the surrender of an alleged offender to the state where the alleged offence was committed. ORIG C19: from F, from L *trāditiō* a handing over

extrados (ɛk'streɪdɒs) *n, pl* **extrados** (-dəʊz) *or* **extradoses.** *Archit.* the outer curve of an arch or vault. ORIG C18: from F, from EXTRA- + *dos* back

extradural (,ɛkstrə'djʊərəl) *adj* another word for **epidural** (sense 1).

extragalactic (,ɛkstrəgə'læktɪk) *adj* occurring or existing beyond the Galaxy.

extramarital (,ɛkstrə'mærɪtᵊl) *adj* (esp. of sexual relations) occurring outside marriage.

extramural (,ɛkstrə'mjʊərəl) *adj* **1** connected with but outside the normal courses of a university, college, etc. **2** beyond the boundaries or walls of a city, castle, etc.

extraneous (ɪk'streɪnɪəs) *adj* **1** not essential. **2** not pertinent; irrelevant. **3** coming from without. **4** not belonging. ORIG C17: from L *extrāneus* external, from *extrā* outside
▸ **ex'traneousness** *n*

extraordinary (ɪk'strɔːdᵊnrɪ) *adj* **1** very unusual or surprising. **2** not in an established manner or order. **3** employed for particular purposes. **4** (*usually postpositive*) (of an official, etc.) additional or subordinate. ORIG C15: from L *extraordinārius* beyond what is usual; see ORDINARY
▸ **ex'traordinarily** *adv* ▸ **ex'traordinariness** *n*

extraordinary general meeting *n* a meeting specially called to discuss an important item of a company's business. It may be called by a group of shareholders or by the directors. Abbrev.: **EGM.**

extrapolate (ɪk'stræpə,leɪt) *vb* **extrapolates, extrapolating, extrapolated. 1** *Maths.* to estimate (a value of a function etc.) beyond the known values, by the extension of a curve. Cf. **interpolate** (sense 4). **2** to infer (something) by using but not strictly deducing from known facts. ORIG C19: EXTRA- + *-polate,* as in INTERPOLATE
▸ **ex,trapo'lation** *n* ▸ **ex'trapolative** *or* **ex'trapolatory** *adj*
▸ **ex'trapo,lator** *n*

extrasensory (ˌɛkstrəˈsɛnsərɪ) *adj* of or relating to extrasensory perception.

extrasensory perception *n* the supposed ability of certain individuals to obtain information about the environment without the use of normal sensory channels.

extraterritorial (ˌɛkstrəˌtɛrɪˈtɔːrɪəl) *or* **exterritorial** *adj* **1** beyond the limits of a country's territory. **2** of, relating to, or possessing extraterritoriality.

extraterritoriality (ˌɛkstrəˌtɛrɪˌtɔːrɪˈælɪtɪ) *n* **1** the privilege granted to some aliens, esp. diplomats, of being exempt from the jurisdiction of the state in which they reside. **2** the right of a state to exercise authority in certain circumstances beyond the limits of its territory.

extra time *n Sport.* an additional period played at the end of a match, to compensate for time lost through injury or (in certain circumstances) to allow the teams to achieve a conclusive result.

extravagance (ɪkˈstrævɪgəns) *n* **1** excessive outlay of money; wasteful spending. **2** immoderate or absurd speech or behaviour.

extravagant (ɪkˈstrævɪgənt) *adj* **1** spending money excessively or immoderately. **2** going beyond usual bounds; unrestrained. **3** ostentatious; showy. **4** exorbitant in price; overpriced. ORIG C14: from Med. L *extravagāns,* from L EXTRA- + *vagārī* to wander

extravaganza (ɪkˌstrævəˈgænzə) *n* **1** an elaborately staged light entertainment. **2** any lavish or fanciful display, literary composition, etc. ORIG C18: from It.: extravagance

extravasate (ɪkˈstrævəˌseɪt) *vb* **extravasates, extravasating, extravasated.** *Pathol.* to cause (blood or lymph) to escape or (of blood or lymph) to escape into the surrounding tissues from their proper vessels. ORIG C17: from L EXTRA- + *vās* vessel
▸ **exˌtravaˈsation** *n*

extravehicular (ˌɛkstrəvɪˈhɪkjʊlə) *adj* occurring or used outside a spacecraft, either in space or on the surface of a planet.

extraversion (ˌɛkstrəˈvɜːʃən) *n* a variant spelling of **extroversion.**
▸ **ˈextraˌvert** *n, adj*

extra virgin *adj* (of olive oil) of the highest quality, extracted by cold pressing rather than chemical treatment.

Extremadura ★ (estremaˈðura) *n* the Spanish name for **Estremadura.**

extreme (ɪkˈstriːm) *adj* **1** being of a high or of the highest degree or intensity. **2** exceeding what is usual or reasonable; immoderate. **3** very strict or severe; drastic. **4** (*prenominal*) farthest or outermost. ◆ *n* **5** the highest or furthest degree (often in **in the extreme, go to extremes**). **6** (*often pl*) either of the two limits or ends of a scale or range. **7** *Maths.* the first or last term of a series or a proportion. ORIG C15: from L *extrēmus* outermost, from *exterus* on the outside; see EXTERIOR
▸ **exˈtremely** *adv* ▸ **exˈtremeness** *n*

> **USAGE NOTE** See at **very.**

extreme unction *n RC Church.* the former name for **anointing of the sick.**

extremist (ɪkˈstriːmɪst) *n* **1** a person who favours immoderate or fanatical methods, esp. in being politically radical. ◆ *adj* **2** of or characterized by immoderate or excessive actions, opinions, etc.
▸ **exˈtremism** *n*

extremity (ɪkˈstrɛmɪtɪ) *n, pl* **extremities. 1** the farthest or outermost point or section. **2** the greatest degree. **3** an extreme condition or state, as of adversity. **4** a limb, such as a leg or wing, or the end of such a limb. **5** (*usually pl*) *Arch.* a drastic or severe measure.

extricate (ˈɛkstrɪˌkeɪt) *vb* **extricates, extricating, extricated.** (*tr*) to remove or free from complication, hindrance, or difficulty; disentangle. ORIG C17: from L *extrīcāre* to disentangle
▸ **ˈextricable** *adj* ▸ **ˌextriˈcation** *n*

> **USAGE NOTE** See at **extract.**

extrinsic (ɛkˈstrɪnsɪk) *adj* **1** not contained or included within; extraneous. **2** originating or acting from outside. ORIG C16: from LL *extrinsecus* (adj) outward, from L (adv), ult. from *exter* outward + *secus* alongside
▸ **exˈtrinsically** *adv*

extroversion *or* **extraversion** (ˌɛkstrəˈvɜːʃən) *n Psychol.* the directing of one's interest outwards, esp. towards social contacts. ORIG C17: from *extro-* (var. of EXTRA-, contrasting with *intro-*) + *-version,* from L *vertere* to turn
▸ **ˌextroˈversive** *or* **ˌextraˈversive** *adj*

extrovert *or* **extravert** (ˈɛkstrəˌvɜːt) *Psychol.* ◆ *n* **1** a person concerned more with external reality than inner feelings. ◆ *adj* **2** of or characterized by extroversion. ORIG C20: from *extro-* (var. of EXTRA-, contrasting with *intro-*) + *-vert,* from L *vertere* to turn
▸ **ˈextroˌverted** *or* **ˈextraˌverted** *adj*

extrude (ɪkˈstruːd) *vb* **extrudes, extruding, extruded.** (*tr*) **1** to squeeze or force out. **2** to produce (moulded sections of plastic, metal, etc.) by ejection from a shaped nozzle or die. **3** to chop up or pulverize (an item of food) and re-form it to look like a whole. ORIG C16: from L *extrūdere* to thrust out, from *trūdere* to push, thrust
▸ **exˈtruded** *adj*

extrusion (ɪkˈstruːʒən) *n* **1** the act or process of extruding. **2a** the movement of magma through volcano craters and cracks in the earth's crust, forming igneous rock. **2b** any igneous rock formed in this way. **3** anything formed by the process of extruding.
▸ **exˈtrusive** *adj*

exuberant (ɪgˈzjuːbərənt) *adj* **1** abounding in vigour and high spirits. **2** lavish or effusive; excessively elaborate. **3** growing luxuriantly or in profusion. ORIG C15: from L *exūberāns,* from *ūberāre* to be fruitful
▸ **exˈuberance** *n*

exuberate (ɪgˈzjuːbəˌreɪt) *vb* **exuberates, exuberating, exuberated.** (*intr*) *Rare.* **1** to be exuberant. **2** to abound. ORIG C15: from L *exūberāre* to be abundant; see EXUBERANT

exude (ɪgˈzjuːd) *vb* **exudes, exuding, exuded. 1** to release or be released through pores, incisions, etc., as sweat or sap. **2** (*tr*) to make apparent by mood or behaviour. ORIG C16: from L *exsūdāre,* from *sūdāre* to sweat
▸ **exudation** (ˌɛksjʊˈdeɪʃən) *n*

exult (ɪgˈzʌlt) *vb* (*intr*) **1** to be joyful or jubilant, esp. because of triumph or success. **2** (often foll. by *over*) to triumph (over). ORIG C16: from L *exsultāre* to jump or leap for joy, from *saltāre* to leap
▸ **exultation** (ˌɛgzʌlˈteɪʃən) *n* ▸ **exˈultingly** *adv*

exultant (ɪgˈzʌltənt) *adj* elated or jubilant, esp. because of triumph or success.
▸ **exˈultantly** *adv*

exurbia (ɛksˈɜːbɪə) *n Chiefly US.* the region outside the suburbs of a city, consisting of residential areas (**exurbs**) occupied predominantly by rich commuters (**exurbanites**). ORIG C20: from EX-[1] + L *urbs* city
▸ **exˈurban** *adj*

exuviate (ɪgˈzjuːvɪˌeɪt) *vb* **exuviates, exuviating, exuviated.** to shed (a skin or similar outer covering). ORIG C17: from L *exuere* to strip off
▸ **exˌuviˈation** *n*

-ey *suffix.* a variant of **-y**[1] and **-y**[2].

Eyam ★ (ˈiːəm) *n* a village in N central England, in Derbyshire. When plague reached the village in 1665 the inhabitants isolated themselves to prevent it spreading further: as a result, most of them died.

eyas (ˈaɪəs) *n* a nestling hawk or falcon, esp. one reared for falconry. ORIG C15: mistaken division of earlier *a nyas,* from OF *niais* nestling, from L *nīdus* nest

eye[1] (aɪ) *n* **1** the organ of sight of animals. Related adjs.: **ocular, ophthalmic. 2** (*often pl*) the ability to see; sense of vision. **3** the external part of an eye, often including the area around it. **4** a look, glance, expression, or gaze. **5** a sexually inviting or provocative look (esp. in **give (someone) the (glad) eye, make eyes at**). **6** attention or observation (often in **catch someone's eye, keep an eye on, cast an eye over**). **7** ability to recognize, judge, or appreciate. **8** (*often pl*) opinion, judgment, point of view, or authority: *in the eyes of the law.* **9** a structure or marking resembling

an eye, such as the bud on a potato tuber or a spot on a butterfly wing. **10** a small loop or hole, as at one end of a needle. **11** a small area of low pressure and calm in the centre of a storm, hurricane, or tornado. **12 electric eye.** another name for **photocell.** **13 all eyes.** *Inf.* acutely vigilant or observant. **14 (all) my eye.** *Inf.* rubbish; nonsense. **15 an eye for an eye.** retributive or vengeful justice; retaliation. **16 get one's eye in.** *Chiefly sport.* to become accustomed to the conditions, light, etc., with a consequent improvement in one's performance. **17 go eyes out.** *Austral. & NZ.* to make every possible effort. **18 half an eye.** a modicum of perceptiveness. **19 have eyes for.** to be interested in. **20 in one's mind's eye.** pictured within the mind; imagined or remembered vividly. **21 in the public eye.** exposed to public curiosity or publicity. **22 keep an eye open** *or* **out (for).** to watch with special attention (for). **23 keep one's eyes peeled** (*or* **skinned**). to watch vigilantly (for). **24 lay, clap,** *or* **set eyes on.** (*usually with a negative*) to see. **25 look (someone) in the eye.** to look openly and without shame or embarrassment at (someone). **26 make sheep's eyes (at).** *Old-fashioned.* to ogle amorously. **27 more than meets the eye.** hidden motives, meaning, or facts. **28 see eye to eye (with).** to agree (with). **29 turn a blind eye to** *or* **close one's eyes to.** to pretend not to notice or to ignore deliberately. **30 up to one's eyes (in).** extremely busy (with). **31 with** *or* **having an eye to.** (*prep*) **31a** regarding; with reference to. **31b** with the intention or purpose of. **32 with one's eyes open.** in the full knowledge of all relevant facts. **33 with one's eyes shut.** **33a** with great ease, esp. as a result of thorough familiarity. **33b** without being aware of all the facts. ◆ *vb* **eyes, eyeing** *or* **eying, eyed.** (*tr*) **34** to look at carefully or warily. **35** Also: **eye up.** to look at in a manner indicating sexual interest; ogle. ORIG OE *ēage*
▸ **'eyeless** *adj* ▸ **'eye,like** *adj*

eye² (aɪ) *n* another word for **nye.**

eyeball ('aɪ,bɔːl) *n* **1** the entire ball-shaped part of the eye. **2 eyeball to eyeball.** in close confrontation. ◆ *vb* **3** (*tr*) *Sl.* to stare at.

eyebank ('aɪ,bæŋk) *n* a place in which corneas are stored for use in corneal grafts.

eyebath ('aɪ,bɑːθ) *n* a small vessel for applying medicated or cleansing solutions to the eye. Also called (US and Canad.): **eyecup.**

eyeblack ('aɪ,blæk) *n* another name for **mascara.**

eyebright ('aɪ,braɪt) *n* an annual plant having small white-and-purple flowers: formerly used in the treatment of eye disorders.

eyebrow ('aɪ,braʊ) *n* **1** the transverse bony ridge over each eye. **2** the arch of hair that covers this ridge. **3 raise an eyebrow.** to give rise to doubt or disapproval.

eyebrow pencil *n* a cosmetic in pencil form for applying colour and shape to the eyebrows.

eye-catching *adj* tending to attract attention; striking.

eye contact *n* a direct look between two people; meeting of eyes.

eyed (aɪd) *adj* **a** having an eye or eyes (as specified). **b** (*in combination*): *brown-eyed.*

eye dog *n NZ.* a dog trained to control sheep by staring fixedly at them. Also called: **strong-eye dog.**

eyeful ('aɪfʊl) *n Inf.* **1** a view, glance, or gaze. **2** a beautiful or attractive sight, esp. a woman.

eyeglass ('aɪ,glɑːs) *n* **1** a lens for aiding or correcting defective vision, esp. a monocle. **2** another word for **eyepiece** or **eyebath.**

eyeglasses ('aɪ,glɑːsɪz) *pl n Now chiefly US.* another word for **spectacles.**

eyehole ('aɪ,həʊl) *n* **1** a hole through which a rope, hook, etc., is passed. **2** the cavity that contains the eyeball. **3** another word for **peephole.**

eyelash ('aɪ,læʃ) *n* **1** any one of the short curved hairs that grow from the edge of the eyelids. **2** a row or fringe of these hairs.

eyelet ('aɪlɪt) *n* **1** a small hole for a lace, cord, or hook to be passed through. **2** a small metal ring or tube reinforcing an eyehole in fabric. **3** a small opening, such as a peephole. **4** *Embroidery.* a small hole with finely stitched edges. **5** a small eye or eyelike marking. ◆ *vb* **6** (*tr*) to supply with an eyelet or eyelets. ORIG C14: from OF *oillet,* lit.: a little eye, from *oill* eye, from L *oculus* eye

eyelevel ('aɪ,lɛvᵊl) *adj* level with a person's eyes when looking straight ahead: *an eyelevel grill.*

eyelid ('aɪ,lɪd) *n* either of the two muscular folds of skin that can be moved to cover the exposed portion of the eyeball.

eyeliner ('aɪ,laɪnə) *n* a cosmetic used to outline the eyes.

eye-opener *n Inf.* **1** something startling or revealing. **2** *US & Canad.* an alcoholic drink taken early in the morning.

eyepiece ('aɪ,piːs) *n* the lens or lenses in an optical instrument nearest the eye of the observer.

eye rhyme *n* a rhyme involving words that are similar in spelling but not in sound, such as *stone* and *none.*

eye shadow *n* a coloured cosmetic put around the eyes.

eyeshot ('aɪ,ʃɒt) *n* range of vision; view.

eyesight ('aɪ,saɪt) *n* the ability to see; faculty of sight.

eyesore ('aɪ,sɔː) *n* something very ugly.

eyespot ('aɪ,spɒt) *n* **1** a small area of light-sensitive pigment in some simple organisms. **2** an eyelike marking, as on a butterfly wing.

eyestrain ('aɪ,streɪn) *n* fatigue or irritation of the eyes, resulting from excessive use or uncorrected defects of vision.

Eyetie ('aɪtaɪ) *n, adj Brit. sl., offensive.* Italian. ORIG C20: from jocular mispronunciation of *Italian*

eyetooth (,aɪ'tuːθ) *n, pl* **eyeteeth.** **1** either of the two canine teeth in the upper jaw. **2 give one's eyeteeth for.** to go to any lengths to achieve or obtain (something).

eyewash ('aɪ,wɒʃ) *n* **1** a lotion for the eyes. **2** *Inf.* nonsense; rubbish.

eyewitness ('aɪ,wɪtnɪs) *n* a person present at an event who can describe what happened.

eyot (aɪt) *n Brit., obs. except in place names.* island. ORIG var. of AIT

Eyre¹ ★ (ɛə) *n* **Lake.** a shallow salt lake in NE central South Australia, about 11 m (35 ft) below sea level. Area: 9600 sq. km (3700 sq. miles). ORIG C19: after E. J. EYRE

Eyre² ★ (ɛə) *n* **1 Edward John.** 1815–1901, British explorer and colonial administrator. He was governor of Jamaica (1864–66); his authorization of 400 executions led to his recall. **2 Richard.** born 1943, British theatre director: director of the Royal National Theatre (1988–97).

Eyre Peninsula ★ *n* a peninsula of South Australia, between the Great Australian Bight and Spencer Gulf.

eyrie ('ɪərɪ, 'ɛərɪ, 'aɪərɪ) *or* **aerie** *n* **1** the nest of an eagle or other bird of prey, built in a high inaccessible place. **2** any high isolated position or place. ORIG C16: from Med. L *airea,* from L *ārea* open field, hence, nest

eyrir ('eɪrɪə) *n, pl* **aurar** ('ɔɪrɑː). an Icelandic monetary unit worth one hundredth of a krona. ORIG ON: ounce (of silver), money; rel. to L *aureus* golden

Eysenck ★ ('aɪzɛŋk) *n* **Hans Jürgen** (hænz 'jɜːgən). 1916–97, British psychologist, born in Germany, who developed a theory of personality based on heredity.

Ez. *or* **Ezr.** *Bible. abbrev. for* Ezra.

Ezek. *Bible. abbrev. for* Ezekiel.

Ezekiel ★ (ɪ'ziːkɪəl) *n Old Testament.* **1** a Hebrew prophet of the 6th century B.C., exiled to Babylon in 597 B.C. **2** the book containing his oracles, which describe the downfall of Judah and Jerusalem and their subsequent restoration. Douay spelling: **Ezechiel.**

e-zine ('iː,ziːn) *n* a magazine available only in electronic form, for example on the World Wide Web.

Ezra ★ ('ɛzrə) *n Old Testament.* **1** a Jewish priest of the 5th century B.C., who was sent from Babylon by the Persian king Artaxerxes I to reconstitute observance of the Jewish law and worship in Jerusalem after the captivity. **2** the book recounting his efforts to perform this task.

Ff

f *or* **F** (ɛf) *n, pl* **f's, F's,** *or* **Fs. 1** the sixth letter of the English alphabet. **2** a speech sound represented by this letter, as in *fat.*

f *symbol for:* **1** *Music.* forte: an instruction to play loudly. **2** *Physics.* frequency. **3** *Maths.* function (of). **4** *Physics.* femto-.

f, f/, *or* **f:** *symbol for* f-number.

F *symbol for:* **1** *Music.* **1a** the fourth note of the scale of C major. **1b** the major or minor key having this note as its tonic. **2** Fahrenheit. **3** farad(s). **4** *Chem.* fluorine. **5** *Physics.* force. **6** franc(s). **7** *Genetics.* a generation of filial offspring, F_1 being the first generation of offspring.

f. *or* **F.** *abbrev. for:* **1** fathom(s). **2** female. **3** *Grammar.* feminine. **4** (*pl* **ff.** *or* **FF.**) folio. **5** (*pl* **ff.**) following (page).

F- (of US military aircraft) *abbrev. for* fighter.

fa (fɑː) *n Music.* the syllable used in the fixed system of solmization for the note F. ORIG C14: see GAMUT

FA (in Britain) *abbrev. for* Football Association.

f.a. *or* **FA** *abbrev. for* fanny adams.

FAB *abbrev. for* fuel air bomb.

Fabergé ★ (ˈfæbəˌʒeɪ) *n* **Peter Carl.** 1846–1920, Russian goldsmith and jeweller, known for the golden Easter eggs he created for the Russian and other royal families.

Fabian (ˈfeɪbɪən) *adj* **1** of or resembling the delaying tactics of Q. Fabius Maximus; cautious. ◆ *n* **2** a member of or sympathizer with the Fabian Society. ORIG C19: from L *Fabiānus* of Fabius
▸ **ˈFabiaˌnism** *n*

Fabian Society *n* an association of British socialists advocating the establishment of socialism by gradual reforms.

Fabius Maximus ★ (ˈfeɪbɪəs ˈmæksɪməs) *n* full name *Quintus Fabius Maximus Verrucosus,* called *Cunctator* (the delayer). died 203 B.C., Roman general and statesman. As commander of the Roman army during the Second Punic War, he withstood Hannibal by his strategy of harassing the Carthaginians while avoiding a pitched battle.

fable (ˈfeɪbᵊl) *n* **1** a short moral story, esp. one with animals as characters. **2** a false, fictitious, or improbable account. **3** a story or legend about supernatural or mythical characters or events. **4** legends or myths collectively. ◆ *vb* **fables, fabling, fabled. 5** to relate or tell (fables). **6** (*intr*) to tell lies. **7** (*tr*) to talk about or describe in the manner of a fable. ORIG C13: from L *fābula* story, narrative, from *fārī* to speak, say
▸ **ˈfabler** *n*

fabled (ˈfeɪbᵊld) *adj* **1** made famous in fable. **2** fictitious.

fabliau (ˈfæblɪˌəʊ) *n, pl* **fabliaux** (ˈfæblɪˌəʊz). a comic usually ribald verse tale, popular in France in the 12th and 13th centuries. ORIG C19: from F: a little tale, from *fable* tale

Fablon (ˈfæblən, -lɒn) *n Trademark.* a brand of adhesive-backed plastic material used to cover and decorate shelves, worktops, etc.

Fabre ★ (*French* fabrə) *n* **Jean Henri** (ʒɑ̃ ɑ̃ri). 1823–1915, French entomologist; author of many works on insect life, esp. *Souvenirs Entomologiques* (1879–1907). Nobel prize for literature 1910.

fabric (ˈfæbrɪk) *n* **1** any cloth made from yarn or fibres by weaving, knitting, felting, etc. **2** the texture of a cloth. **3** a structure or framework: *the fabric of society.* **4** a style or method of construction. **5** *Rare.* a building. ORIG C15: from L *fabrica* workshop, from *faber* craftsman

fabricate (ˈfæbrɪˌkeɪt) *vb* **fabricates, fabricating, fabricated.** (*tr*) **1** to make, build, or construct. **2** to devise or concoct (a story, etc.). **3** to fake or forge. ORIG C15: from L, from *fabrica* workshop; see FABRIC
▸ **ˌfabriˈcation** *n* ▸ **ˈfabriˌcator** *n*

Fabry ★ (*French* fabri) *n* **Charles** (ʃarl). 1867–1945, French physicist: discovered ozone in the upper atmosphere.

fabulist (ˈfæbjʊlɪst) *n* **1** a person who invents or recounts fables. **2** a person who lies.

fabulous (ˈfæbjʊləs) *adj* **1** almost unbelievable; astounding; legendary: *fabulous wealth.* **2** *Inf.* extremely good: *a fabulous time at the party.* **3** of, relating to, or based upon fable: *a fabulous beast.* ORIG C15: from L *fābulōsus* celebrated in fable, from *fābula* FABLE
▸ **ˈfabulously** *adv* ▸ **ˈfabulousness** *n*

Fac. *abbrev. for* Faculty.

façade *or* **facade** (fəˈsɑːd, fæ-) *n* **1** the face of a building, esp. the main front. **2** a front or outer appearance, esp. a deceptive one. ORIG C17: from F, from It., from *faccia* FACE

face (feɪs) *n* **1a** the front of the head from the forehead to the lower jaw. **1b** (*as modifier*): *face flannel.* **2a** the expression of the countenance: *a sad face.* **2b** a distorted expression, esp. to indicate disgust. **3** *Inf.* make-up (esp. in **put one's face on**). **4** outward appearance: *the face of the countryside is changing.* **5** appearance or pretence (esp. in **put a bold, good, bad,** etc., **face on**). **6** dignity (esp. in **lose** *or* **save face**). **7** *Inf.* impudence or effrontery. **8** the main side of an object, building, etc., or the front: *a cliff face.* **9** the marked surface of an instrument, esp. the dial of a timepiece. **10** the functional or working side of an object, as of a tool or playing card. **11a** the exposed area of a mine from which coal, ore, etc., may be mined. **11b** (*as modifier*): *face worker.* **12** the uppermost part or surface: *the face of the earth.* **13** Also called: **side.** any one of the plane surfaces of a crystal or other solid figure. **14** Also called: **typeface.** *Printing.* **14a** the printing surface of any type character. **14b** the style or design of the character on the type. **15** *NZ.* the exposed slope of a hill. **16** *Brit. sl.* a well-known or important person. **17 in (the) face of.** despite. **18 on the face of it.** to all appearances. **19 set one's face against.** to oppose with determination. **20 show one's face.** to make an appearance. **21 to someone's face.** in someone's presence: *I told him the truth to his face.* ◆ *vb* **faces, facing, faced. 22** (when *intr,* often foll. by *to, towards,* or *on*) to look or be situated or placed (in a specified direction): *the house faces onto the square.* **23** to be opposite: *facing page 9.* **24** (*tr*) to be confronted by: *he faces many problems.* **25** (*tr*) to provide with a surface of a different material. **26** to dress the surface of (stone or other material). **27** (*tr*) to expose (a card) with the face uppermost. **28** *Mil.* to order (a formation) to turn in a certain direction or (of a formation) to turn as required: *right face!* ◆ See also **face down, face up to.** ORIG C13: from OF, from Vulgar L *facia* (unattested), from L *faciēs* form

face card *n* the usual US and Canad. term for **court card.**

face cloth *or* **face flannel** *n Brit.* a small piece of cloth used to wash the face and hands. US equivalent: **washcloth.**

facedown (ˈfeɪsdaʊn) *n Inf.* another word for **face-off** (sense 2).

face down *vb* (*tr, adv*) to confront and force (someone or something) to back down.

faceless (ˈfeɪslɪs) *adj* **1** without a face. **2** without identity; anonymous.
▸ **ˈfacelessness** *n*

face-lift *n* **1** a cosmetic surgical operation for tightening sagging skin and smoothing wrinkles on the face. **2** any improvement or renovation. ◆ *vb* (*tr*) **3** to improve the appearance of, as by a face-lift.

face-off *n* **1** *Ice hockey.* the method of starting a game, in which the referee drops the puck, etc. between two opposing players. **2** Also called **facedown.** a confrontation, esp. one in which each party attempts to make the other back down. ◆ *vb* **face off.** (*intr, adv*) **3** to start play by a face-off.

face powder *n* a cosmetic powder worn to make the face look less shiny, softer, etc.

facer ('feɪsə) *n* **1** a person or thing that faces. **2** *Brit. inf.* a difficulty or problem.

face-saving *adj* maintaining dignity or prestige.
▸ **'face-ˌsaver** *n*

facet ('fæsɪt) *n* **1** any of the surfaces of a cut gemstone. **2** an aspect or phase, as of a subject or personality. ◆ *vb* **facets, faceting** *or* **facetting, faceted** *or* **facetted. 3** (*tr*) to cut facets in (a gemstone). ORIG C17: from F *facette* a little FACE

facetiae (fə'siːʃɪˌiː) *pl n* **1** humorous or witty sayings. **2** obscene or coarsely witty books. ORIG C17: from L: jests, pl of *facētia* witticism, from *facētus* elegant

facetious (fə'siːʃəs) *adj* **1** characterized by love of joking. **2** jocular or amusing, esp. at inappropriate times: *facetious remarks.* ORIG C16: from OF *facetieux,* from *facetie* witticism; see FACETIAE
▸ **fa'cetiously** *adv* ▸ **fa'cetiousness** *n*

face to face *adv, adj* (**face-to-face** *as adj*) **1** opposite one another. **2** in confrontation.

face up to *vb* (*intr, adv + prep*) to accept (an unpleasant fact, reality, etc.).

face value *n* **1** the value written or stamped on the face of a commercial paper or coin. **2** apparent worth or value.

facia ('feɪʃɪə) *n* a variant spelling of **fascia.**

facial ('feɪʃəl) *adj* **1** of or relating to the face. ◆ *n* **2** a beauty treatment for the face involving massage and cosmetic packs.
▸ **'facially** *adv*

-facient *suffix forming adjectives and nouns.* indicating a state or quality: *absorbefacient.* ORIG from L *facient-, faciēns,* present participle of *facere* to do

facies ('feɪʃɪˌiːz) *n, pl* **facies. 1** the general form and appearance of an individual or a group. **2** the characteristics of a rock or rocks reflecting their appearance and conditions of formation. **3** *Med.* the general facial expression of a patient. ORIG C17: from L: appearance, FACE

facile ('fæsaɪl) *adj* **1** easy to perform or achieve. **2** working or moving easily or smoothly. **3** superficial: *a facile solution.* ORIG C15: from L *facilis* easy, from *facere* to do
▸ **'facilely** *adv* ▸ **'facileness** *n*

facilitate (fə'sɪlɪˌteɪt) *vb* **facilitates, facilitating, facilitated.** (*tr*) to assist the progress of.
▸ **faˌcili'tation** *n*

facility (fə'sɪlɪtɪ) *n, pl* **facilities. 1** ease of action or performance. **2** ready skill or ease deriving from practice or familiarity. **3** (*often pl*) the means or equipment facilitating the performance of an action. **4** *Rare.* easy-going disposition. **5** (*usually pl*) a euphemistic word for **lavatory.** ORIG C15: from L *facilitās,* from *facilis* easy; see FACILE

facing ('feɪsɪŋ) *n* **1** a piece of material used esp. to conceal the seam of a garment and prevent fraying. **2** (*usually pl*) the collar, cuffs, etc., of the jacket of a military uniform. **3** an outer layer or coat of material applied to the surface of a wall.

facsimile (fæk'sɪmɪlɪ) *n* **1** an exact copy or reproduction. **2** an image produced by facsimile transmission; fax. ◆ *vb* **facsimiles, facsimileing, facsimiled. 3** (*tr*) to make an exact copy of. ORIG C17: from L *fac simile!* make something like it!, from *facere* to make + *similis* similar, like

facsimile transmission *n* an international system of transmitting a written, printed, or pictorial document over the telephone system by scanning it photoelectrically and reproducing the image xerographically after transmission. Often shortened to **fax.**

fact (fækt) *n* **1** an event or thing known to have happened or existed. **2** a truth verifiable from experience or observation. **3** a piece of information: *get me all the facts of this case.* **4** (*often pl*) *Law.* an actual event, happening, etc., as distinguished from its legal consequences. **5 after** (*or* **before**) **the fact.** *Criminal law.* after (or before) the commission of the offence. **6 as a matter of fact, in fact, in point of fact.** in reality or actuality. **7 fact of life.** an inescapable truth, esp. an unpleasant one. See also **facts of life.** ORIG C16: from L *factum* something done, from *factus* made, from *facere* to do, make

faction[1] ('fækʃən) *n* **1** a group of people forming a minority within a larger body, esp. a dissentious group. **2** strife or dissension within a group. ORIG C16: from L *factiō* a making, from *facere* to do, make
▸ **'factional** *adj*

faction[2] ('fækʃən) *n* a television programme, film, or literary work comprising a dramatized presentation of actual events. ORIG C20: a blend of FACT & FICTION

faction fight *n* conflict between different groups within a larger body, esp. in S Africa a fight between Blacks of different tribes.

factious ('fækʃəs) *adj* given to, producing, or characterized by faction.
▸ **'factiously** *adv*

factitious (fæk'tɪʃəs) *adj* **1** artificial rather than natural. **2** not genuine; sham: *factitious enthusiasm.* ORIG C17: from L *factīcius,* from *facere* to do, make
▸ **fac'titiously** *adv* ▸ **fac'titiousness** *n*

factitive ('fæktɪtɪv) *adj Grammar.* denoting a verb taking a direct object as well as a noun in apposition, as for example *elect* in *They elected John president,* where *John* is the direct object and *president* is the complement. ORIG C19: from NL, from L *factitāre* to do frequently, from *facere* to do, make

factoid ('fæktɔɪd) *n* a piece of unreliable information believed to be true because of the way it is presented or repeated in print. ORIG C20: coined by Norman MAILER, from FACT + -OID

factor ('fæktə) *n* **1** an element or cause that contributes to a result. **2** *Maths.* one of two or more integers or polynomials whose product is a given integer or polynomial: *2 and 3 are factors of 6.* **3** (foll. by identifying numeral) *Med.* any of several substances that participate in the clotting of blood: *factor VIII.* **4** a person who acts on another's behalf, esp. one who transacts business for another. **5** former name for a **gene. 6** *Commercial law.* a person to whom goods are consigned for sale and who is paid a commission. **7** (in Scotland) the manager of an estate. ◆ *vb* **8** (*intr*) to engage in the business of a factor. ORIG C15: from L: one who acts, from *facere* to do, make
▸ **'factorable** *adj* ▸ **'factorship** *n*

> **USAGE NOTE** Purists maintain that *factor* (sense 1) should only be used to refer to something which contributes to a result. It should not be used to refer to a part of something, such as a plan or arrangement; instead a word such as *component* or *element* should be used.

factor VIII *n* a protein that participates in the clotting of blood. It is extracted from donated serum and used in the treatment of haemophilia.

factorial (fæk'tɔːrɪəl) *Maths.* ◆ *n* **1** the product of all the positive integers from one up to and including a given integer: *factorial four is 1 × 2 × 3 × 4.* ◆ *adj* **2** of or involving factorials or factors.
▸ **fac'torially** *adv*

factorize *or* **factorise** ('fæktəˌraɪz) *vb* **factorizes, factorizing, factorized** *or* **factorises, factorising, factorised.** (*tr*) *Maths.* to resolve (an integer or polynomial) into factors.
▸ **ˌfactori'zation** *or* **ˌfactori'sation** *n*

factory ('fæktərɪ) *n, pl* **factories. a** a building or group of buildings containing a plant assembly for the manufacture of goods. **b** (*as modifier*): *a factory worker.* ORIG C16: from LL *factorium;* see FACTOR
▸ **'factory-ˌlike** *adj*

factory farm *n* a farm in which animals are intensively reared using modern industrial methods.
▸ **factory farming** *n*

factory outlet *or* **factory shop** *n* a usually low-rent site leased by a factory to sell its end-of-line or damaged stock direct to the customer at reduced prices.

factory ship *n* a vessel that processes fish supplied by a fleet.

factotum (fæk'təʊtəm) *n* a person employed to do all kinds of work. ORIG C16: from Med. L, from L *fac!* do! + *tōtum,* from *tōtus* (adj) all

facts and figures *pl n* details.

factsheet ('fækt,ʃi:t) *n* a printed sheet containing information relating to items covered in a television or radio programme.

facts of life *pl n* **the.** the details of sexual behaviour and reproduction.

factual ('fæktʃʊəl) *adj* **1** of, relating to, or characterized by facts. **2** real; actual.
▸ **'factually** *adv* ▸ **'factualness** *or* **,factu'ality** *n*

facula ('fækjʊlə) *n, pl* **faculae** (-,li:). any of the bright areas on the sun's surface, usually appearing just before a sunspot. ORIG C18: from L: little torch, from *fax* torch
▸ **'facular** *adj*

facultative ('fækəltətɪv) *adj* **1** empowering but not compelling the doing of an act. **2** that may or may not occur. **3** *Biol.* able to exist under more than one set of environmental conditions. **4** of or relating to a faculty.
▸ **'facultatively** *adv*

faculty ('fækəltɪ) *n, pl* **faculties. 1** one of the inherent powers of the mind or body, such as memory, sight, or hearing. **2** any ability or power, whether acquired or inherent. **3** a conferred power or right. **4a** a department within a university or college devoted to a particular branch of knowledge. **4b** the staff of such a department. **4c** *Chiefly US & Canad.* all the teaching staff at a university, school, etc. **5** all members of a learned profession. ORIG C14 (in the sense: department of learning): from L *facultās* capability; rel. to L *facilis* easy

FA Cup *n Soccer.* (in England and Wales) **1** an annual knockout competition among member teams of the Football Association. **2** the trophy itself.

fad (fæd) *n Inf.* **1** an intense but short-lived fashion. **2** a personal idiosyncrasy. ORIG C19: from ?
▸ **'faddish** *or* **'faddy** *adj*

Fadden ★ ('fædən) *n* Sir **Arthur William.** 1895–1973, Australian statesman; prime minister of Australia (1941).

fade (feɪd) *vb* **fades, fading, faded. 1** to lose or cause to lose brightness, colour, or clarity. **2** (*intr*) to lose vigour or youth. **3** (*intr;* usually foll. by *away* or *out*) to vanish slowly. **4a** to decrease the brightness or volume of (a television or radio programme) or (of a television programme, etc.) to decrease in this way. **4b** to decrease the volume of (a sound) in a recording system or (of a sound) to be so reduced in volume. **5** (*intr*) (of the brakes of a vehicle) to lose power. **6** to cause (a golf ball) to veer from a straight line or (of a golf ball) to veer from a straight flight. ◆ *n* **7** the act or an instance of fading. ORIG C14: from *fade* (adj) dull, from OF, from Vulgar L *fatidus* (unattested), prob. blend of L *vapidus* VAPID + L *fatuus* FATUOUS
▸ **'fadeless** *adj* ▸ **'fadedness** *n* ▸ **'fader** *n*

fade-in *n* **1** *Films.* an optical effect in which a shot appears gradually out of darkness. ◆ *vb* **fade in.** (*adv*) **2** to increase or cause to increase gradually, as vision or sound in a film or broadcast.

fade-out *n* **1** *Films.* an optical effect in which a shot slowly disappears into darkness. **2** a gradual and temporary loss of a radio or television signal. **3** a slow or gradual disappearance. ◆ *vb* **fade out.** (*adv*) **4** to decrease or cause to decrease gradually, as vision or sound in a film or broadcast.

faeces *or esp. US* **feces** ('fi:si:z) *pl n* bodily waste matter discharged through the anus. ORIG C15: from L *faecēs,* pl. of *faex* sediment, dregs
▸ **faecal** *or esp. US* **fecal** ('fi:kəl) *adj*

Faenza ★ (*Italian* fa'ɛntsa) *n* a city in N Italy, in Emilia-Romagna: famous in the 15th and 16th centuries for its majolica earthenware, esp. faïence. Pop.: 54 050 (1990).

faerie *or* **faery** ('feɪərɪ, 'fɛərɪ) *n, pl* **faeries.** *Arch. or poetic.* **1** the land of fairies. ◆ *adj, n* **2** a variant spelling of **fairy.**

Faeroes *or* **Faroes** ★ ('fɛərəʊz) *pl n* a group of 21 basalt islands in the North Atlantic between Iceland and the Shetland Islands: a self-governing community within the kingdom of Denmark; fishing. Capital: Thorshavn. Pop.: 43 719 (1994). Area: 1400 sq. km (540 sq. miles). Also called: **Faeroe Islands** or **Faroe Islands.**

Faeroese *or* **Faroese** (,fɛərəʊ'i:z) *adj* **1** of or characteristic of the Faeroes, their inhabitants, or their language. ◆ *n* **2** the language of the Faeroes, closely related to Icelandic. **3** (*pl* **Faeroese** *or* **Faroese**) a native or inhabitant of the Faeroes.

faff (fæf) *vb* (*intr;* often foll. by *about*) *Brit. inf.* to dither or fuss. ORIG C19: from ?

Fafnir ★ ('fæfnɪə, 'fæv-) *n Norse myth.* the son of Hreidmar, whom he killed to gain the cursed treasure of Andvari. He became a dragon and was slain by Sigurd while guarding the treasure.

fag[1] (fæg) *n* **1** *Inf.* a boring or wearisome task. **2** *Brit.* (esp. formerly) a young public school boy who performs menial chores for an older boy or prefect. ◆ *vb* **fags, fagging, fagged. 3** (when *tr,* often foll. by *out*) *Inf.* to become or cause to become exhausted by hard work **4** (*usually intr*) *Brit.* to do or cause to do menial chores in a public school. ORIG C18: from ?

fag[2] (fæg) *n Brit. sl.* a cigarette. ORIG C16 (in the sense: something hanging loose, flap): from ?

fag[3] (fæg) *n Sl., chiefly US & Canad.* short for **faggot**[2].

fag end *n* **1** the last and worst part. **2** *Brit. inf.* the stub of a cigarette. ORIG C17: see FAG[2]

faggot[1] *or esp. US* **fagot** ('fægət) *n* **1** a bundle of sticks or twigs, esp. when used as fuel. **2** a bundle of iron bars, esp. to be forged into wrought iron. **3** a ball of chopped meat bound with herbs and bread and eaten fried. ◆ *vb* (*tr*) **4** to collect into a bundle or bundles. **5** *Needlework.* to do faggoting on (a garment, etc.). ORIG C14: from OF, ?from Gk *phakelos* bundle

faggot[2] ('fægət) *n Sl., chiefly US & Canad.* a male homosexual. ORIG C20: special use of FAGGOT[1]

faggoting *or esp. US* **fagoting** ('fægətɪŋ) *n* **1** decorative needlework done by tying vertical threads together in bundles. **2** a decorative way of joining two hems by criss-cross stitches.

fag hag *n US sl., usually derog.* a heterosexual woman who prefers the company of homosexual men.

fah *n Music.* (in tonic sol-fa) the fourth degree of any major scale. ORIG C14: later variant of *fa;* see GAMUT

Fah. *or* **Fahr.** *abbrev. for* Fahrenheit.

Fahd ibn Abdul Aziz ★ (fɑ:d 'ɪbən 'æbdʊl ə'zi:z) *n* born 1923, king of Saudi Arabia from 1982.

Fahrenheit[1] ('færən,haɪt) *adj* of or measured according to the Fahrenheit scale of temperature. Symbol: F

Fahrenheit[2] ★ (*German* 'fa:rənhait) *n* **Gabriel Daniel** ('ga:brie:l 'da:nie:l). 1686–1736, German physicist, who invented the mercury thermometer and devised the temperature scale that bears his name.

Fahrenheit scale *n* a scale of temperatures in which 32° represents the melting point of ice and 212° represents the boiling point of pure water under standard atmospheric pressure. Cf. **Celsius scale.**

Faial *or* **Fayal** ★ (*Portuguese* fə'jal) *n* an island in the central Azores archipelago. Chief town: Horta. Area: 171 sq. km (66 sq. miles).

faïence (faɪ'ɑ:ns, feɪ-) *n* tin-glazed earthenware, usually that of French, German, Italian, or Scandinavian origin. ORIG C18: from F, strictly: pottery from FAENZA

fail (feɪl) *vb* **1** to be unsuccessful in an attempt (at something or to do something). **2** (*intr*) to stop operating or working properly: *the steering failed suddenly.* **3** to judge or be judged as being below the officially accepted standard required in (a course, examination, etc.). **4** (*tr*) to prove disappointing or useless to (someone). **5** (*tr*) to neglect or be unable (to do something). **6** (*intr*) to prove insufficient in quantity or extent. **7** (*intr*) to weaken. **8** (*intr*) to go bankrupt. ◆ *n* **9** a failure to attain the required standard. **10 without fail.** definitely. ORIG C13: from OF *faillir,* ult. from L *fallere* to disappoint

failing ('feɪlɪŋ) *n* **1** a weak point. ◆ *prep* **2** (*used to express a*

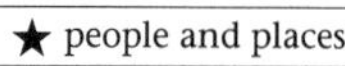

condition) in default of: *failing a solution, the problem will have to wait until Monday.*

fail-safe *adj* **1** designed to return to a safe condition in the event of a failure or malfunction. **2** safe from failure; foolproof.

failure ('feɪljə) *n* **1** the act or an instance of failing. **2** a person or thing that is unsuccessful or disappointing. **3** nonperformance of something required or expected: *failure to attend will be punished.* **4** cessation of normal operation: *a power failure.* **5** an insufficiency: *a crop failure.* **6** a decline or loss, as in health. **7** the fact of not reaching the required standard in an examination, test, etc. **8** bankruptcy.

fain (feɪn) *adv* **1** (usually with *would*) *Arch.* gladly: *she would fain be dead.* ◆ *adj* **2** *Obs.* **2a** willing. **2b** compelled. ORIG OE *fægen;* see FAWN[2]

faint (feɪnt) *adj* **1** lacking clarity, brightness, volume, etc. **2** lacking conviction or force: *faint praise.* **3** feeling dizzy or weak as if about to lose consciousness. **4** timid (esp. in **faint-hearted**). **5 not the faintest** (**idea** *or* **notion**). no idea whatsoever: *I haven't the faintest.* ◆ *vb* (*intr*) **6** to lose consciousness, as through weakness. **7** *Arch. or poetic.* to become weak, esp. in courage. ◆ *n* **8** a sudden spontaneous loss of consciousness caused by an insufficient supply of blood to the brain. ORIG C13: from OF, from *faindre* to be idle
▸ **'faintish** *adj* ▸ **'faintly** *adv* ▸ **'faintness** *n*

fair[1] (fɛə) *adj* **1** free from discrimination, dishonesty, etc. **2** in conformity with rules or standards: *a fair fight.* **3** (of the hair or complexion) light in colour. **4** beautiful to look at. **5** quite good: *a fair piece of work.* **6** unblemished; untainted. **7** (of the tide or wind) favourable to the passage of a vessel. **8** fine or cloudless. **9** pleasant or courteous. **10** apparently good or valuable: *fair words.* **11 fair and square.** in a correct or just way. ◆ *adv* **12** in a fair way: *act fair, now!* **13** absolutely or squarely; quite. ◆ *vb* **14** (*intr*) *Dialect.* (of the weather) to become fine. ◆ *n* **15** *Arch.* a person or thing that is beautiful or valuable. ORIG OE *fæger*
▸ **'fairish** *adj* ▸ **'fairness** *n*

fair[2] (fɛə) *n* **1** a travelling entertainment with sideshows, rides, etc. **2** a gathering of producers of and dealers in a given class of products to facilitate business: *a book fair.* **3** a regular assembly at a specific place for the sale of goods, esp. livestock. ORIG C13: from OF *feire,* from LL *fēria* holiday, from L *fēriae* days of rest

Fairbanks[1] ★ ('fɛə,bæŋks) *n* a city in central Alaska, at the terminus of the Alaska Highway. Pop.: 30 800 (1990).

Fairbanks[2] ★ ('fɛə,bæŋks) *n* **1 Douglas** (**Elton**), real name *Julius Ullman.* 1883–1939, US film actor and producer. **2** his son, **Douglas, Jnr.** 1909–2000, US film actor.

Fairfax ★ ('fɛəfæks) *n* **Thomas,** 3rd Baron Fairfax. 1612–71, English general and statesman: commanded the Parliamentary army (1645–50), defeating Charles I at Naseby (1645). He was instrumental in restoring Charles II to the throne (1660).

fair game *n* a legitimate object for ridicule or attack.

fairground ('fɛə,graʊnd) *n* an open space used for a fair or exhibition.

fairing[1] ('fɛərɪŋ) *n* an external metal structure fitted around parts of an aircraft, car, etc., to reduce drag. ORIG C20: from *fair* to streamline + -ING[1]

fairing[2] ('fɛərɪŋ) *n Arch.* a present, esp. from a fair.

Fair Isle *n* an intricate multicoloured pattern knitted with Shetland wool into various garments, such as sweaters. ORIG C19: after one of the Shetland Islands where this type of pattern originated

fairly ('fɛəlɪ) *adv* **1** (*not used with a negative*) moderately. **2** as deserved; justly. **3** (*not used with a negative*) positively: *the hall fairly rang with applause.*

fair-minded *adj* just or impartial.
▸ **,fair-'mindedness** *n*

fair play *n* **1** an established standard of decency, etc. **2** abidance by this standard.

fair sex *n* **the.** women collectively.

fair-spoken *adj* civil, courteous, or elegant in speech.
▸ **,fair-'spokenness** *n*

fair trade *n* **a** the practice of benefiting producers in the developing world by buying directly from them at a guaranteed price. **b** (*as modifier*): *fair-trade coffee.*

fairway ('fɛə,weɪ) *n* **1** (on a golf course) the avenue approaching a green bordered by rough. **2** *Naut.* the navigable part of a river, harbour, etc.

fair-weather *adj* **1** suitable for use in fair weather only. **2** not reliable in situations of difficulty: *fair-weather friend.*

fairy ('fɛərɪ) *n, pl* **fairies. 1** an imaginary supernatural being, usually represented in diminutive human form and characterized as having magical powers. **2** *Sl.* a male homosexual. ◆ *adj* (*prenominal*) **3** of a fairy or fairies. **4** resembling a fairy or fairies. ORIG C14: from OF *faerie* fairyland, from *feie* fairy, from L *Fāta* the Fates; see FATE, FAY
▸ **'fairy-,like** *adj*

fairy cycle *n* a child's bicycle.

fairyfloss ('fɛərɪ,flɒs) *n* the Australian word for **candyfloss.**

fairy godmother *n* a benefactress, esp. an unknown one.

fairyland ('fɛərɪ,lænd) *n* **1** the imaginary domain of the fairies. **2** a fantasy world, esp. one resulting from a person's wild imaginings.

fairy lights *pl n* small coloured electric bulbs strung together and used as decoration, esp. on a Christmas tree.

fairy penguin *n* a small penguin with a bluish head and back, found on the Australian coast. Also called: **little** or **blue penguin.**

fairy ring *n* a ring of dark luxuriant vegetation in grassy ground corresponding to the outer edge of an underground fungal mycelium.

fairy tale *or* **story** *n* **1** a story about fairies or other mythical or magical beings. **2** a highly improbable account.

fairy-tale *adj* **1** of or relating to a fairy tale. **2** resembling a fairy tale, esp. in being extremely happy or fortunate: *a fairy-tale ending.* **3** highly improbable: *a fairy-tale account.*

Faisal I *or* **Feisal I** ★ ('faɪsᵊl) *n* 1885–1933, king of Syria (1920) and first king of Iraq (1921–33): a leader of the Arab revolt against the Turks.

Faisal II *or* **Feisal II** ★ *n* 1935–58, last king of Iraq (1939–58).

Faisalabad ★ (faɪ'ʒɑːlə,bɑːd) *n* a city in NE Pakistan: commercial and manufacturing centre of a cotton- and wheat-growing region; university (1961). Pop.: 1 875 000 (1995 est.). Former name (until 1979): **Lyallpur.**

Faisal Ibn Abdul Aziz ★ ('ɪbᵊn 'æbdʊl ə'ziːz) *n* 1905–75, king of Saudi Arabia (1964–75).

fait accompli *French.* (fɛt akɔ̃pli) *n, pl* ***faits accomplis*** (fɛz akɔ̃pli). something already done and beyond alteration. ORIG lit.: accomplished fact

faith (feɪθ) *n* **1** strong or unshakeable belief in something, esp. without proof. **2** a specific system of religious beliefs: *the Jewish faith.* **3** *Christianity.* trust in God and in his actions and promises. **4** a conviction of the truth of certain doctrines of religion. **5** complete confidence or trust in a person, remedy, etc. **6** loyalty, as to a person or cause (esp. in **keep faith, break faith**). **7 bad faith.** dishonesty. **8 good faith.** honesty. **9** (*modifier*) using or relating to the supposed ability to cure bodily ailments by means of religious faith: *a faith healer.* ◆ *interj* **10** *Arch.* indeed. ORIG C12: from Anglo-F *feid,* from L *fidēs* trust, confidence

faithful ('feɪθfʊl) *adj* **1** remaining true or loyal. **2** maintaining sexual loyalty to one's lover or spouse. **3** consistently reliable: *a faithful worker.* **4** reliable or truthful. **5** accurate in detail: *a faithful translation.* ◆ *n* **6 the faithful. 6a** the believers in a religious faith, esp. Christianity. **6b** any group of loyal and steadfast followers.
▸ **'faithfully** *adv* ▸ **'faithfulness** *n*

faithless ('feɪθlɪs) *adj* **1** unreliable or treacherous. **2** dishonest or disloyal. **3** lacking religious faith.
▸ **'faithlessness** *n*

Faiyûm *or* **Fayum** ★ (faɪ'juːm) *n* See **El Faiyûm.**

fajitas (fə'hiːtəz) *pl n* a Mexican dish of soft tortillas wrapped round fried strips of meat, vegetables, etc. ORIG Mexican Sp.

fake (feɪk) *vb* **fakes, faking, faked. 1** (*tr*) to cause (something inferior or not genuine) to appear more valuable or real by fraud or pretence. **2** to pretend to have (an illness, emotion, etc.). ◆ *n* **3** an object, person, or act that is not genuine; sham. ◆ *adj* **4** not genuine. ORIG C18: prob. ult. from It. *facciare* to make or do
▸ **'faker** *n* ▸ **'fakery** *n*

fakir ('feɪkɪə, fə'kɪə) *n* **1** a member of any religious order of Islam. **2** a Hindu ascetic mendicant. ORIG C17: from Ar. *faqīr* poor

falafel *or* **felafel** (fə'lɑːfəl) *n* a ball or cake of ground spiced chickpeas, deep-fried and often served with pitta bread. ORIG C20: from Arabic *felāfil*

Falange ('fælændʒ) *n* the Fascist movement founded in Spain in 1933. ORIG Sp.: PHALANX
▸ **Fa'langist** *n, adj*

falcate ('fælkeɪt) *or* **falciform** ('fælsɪˌfɔːm) *adj Biol.* shaped like a sickle. ORIG C19: from L *falcātus*, from *falx* sickle

falchion ('fɔːltʃən, 'fɔːlʃən) *n* **1** a short and slightly curved medieval sword. **2** an archaic word for **sword.** ORIG C14: from It., from *falce*, from L *falx* sickle

falcon ('fɔːlkən, 'fɔːkən) *n* **1** a diurnal bird of prey such as the gyrfalcon, peregrine falcon, etc., having pointed wings and a long tail. **2a** any of these or related birds, trained to hunt small game. **2b** the female of such a bird (cf. **tercel**). ORIG C13: from OF, from LL *falcō* hawk, prob. of Gmc origin; ? rel. to L *falx* sickle

falconet ('fɔːlkəˌnɛt, 'fɔːkə-) *n* **1** any of various small falcons. **2** a small light cannon used from the 15th to 17th centuries.

falconry ('fɔːlkənrɪ, 'fɔːkən-) *n* the art of keeping falcons and training them to return from flight to a lure or to hunt quarry.
▸ **'falconer** *n*

falderal ('fældəˌræl) *or* **folderol** ('fɒldəˌrɒl) *n* **1** a showy but worthless trifle. **2** foolish nonsense. **3** a nonsensical refrain in old songs.

Faldo ★ ('fældəʊ) *n* **Nick.** born 1957, British golfer: won the British Open Championship (1987, 1990, 1992) and the US Masters (1989, 1990, 1996).

faldstool ('fɔːldˌstuːl) *n* a backless seat, sometimes capable of being folded, used by bishops and certain other prelates. ORIG C11 *fyldestol*, prob. a translation of Med. L *faldistolium* folding stool, of Gmc origin; cf. OHG *faldstuol*

Falerii ★ (fə'lɪərɪˌaɪ) *n* an ancient city of S Italy, in Latium: important in pre-Roman times.

Falkirk ★ ('fɔːlkɜːk) *n* **1** a town in Scotland, the administrative centre of Falkirk council area: scene of Edward I's defeat of Wallace (1298) and Prince Charles Edward's defeat of General Hawley (1746); iron works. Pop.: 35 610 (1991). **2** a council area in central Scotland: created in 1996 from part of Central Region. Administrative centre: Falkirk. Pop.: 142 610 (1996 est.). Area: 299 sq. km (115 sq. miles).

Falkland Islands ★ ('fɔːlklənd) *pl n* a group of over 100 islands in the S Atlantic: a United Kingdom overseas territory; invaded by Argentina, who had long laid claim to the islands, on 2 April 1982; recaptured by a British expeditionary force on 14 June 1982. Chief town: Stanley. Pop.: 2121 (1991). Area: about 12 200 sq. km (4700 sq. miles). Spanish name: **Islas Malvinas.**

Falkland Islands Dependencies ★ *pl n* a group of almost uninhabited islands south of the Falkland Islands: consisting of the South Sandwich Islands and South Georgia: part of the United Kingdom overseas territory of the Falkland Islands. Area: 4090 sq. km (1580 sq. miles).

Falkner ★ ('fɔːknə) *n* a variant spelling of (William) **Faulkner.**

fall (fɔːl) *vb* **falls, falling, fell, fallen.** (*mainly intr*) **1** to descend by the force of gravity from a higher to a lower place. **2** to drop suddenly from an erect position. **3** to collapse to the ground, esp. in pieces. **4** to become less or lower in number, quality, etc.: *prices fell.* **5** to become lower in pitch. **6** to extend downwards: *her hair fell to her waist.* **7** to be badly wounded or killed. **8** to slope in a downward direction. **9** to yield to temptation or sin. **10** to diminish in status, estimation, etc. **11** to yield to attack: *the city fell under the assault.* **12** to lose power: *the government fell after the riots.* **13** to pass into or take on a specified condition: *to fall asleep.* **14** to adopt a despondent expression: *her face fell.* **15** to be averted: *her gaze fell.* **16** to come by chance or presumption: *suspicion fell on the butler.* **17** to occur; take place: *night fell.* **18** (foll. by *back, behind,* etc.) to move in a specified direction. **19** to occur at a specified place: *the accent falls on the last syllable.* **20** (foll. by *to*) to be inherited (by): *the estate falls to the eldest son.* **21** (often foll. by *into, under,* etc.) to be classified: *the subject falls into two main areas.* **22** to issue forth: *a curse fell from her lips.* **23** (*tr*) *Dialect, Austral. & NZ.* to fell (trees). **24** *Cricket.* (of a batsman's wicket) to be taken by the bowling side: *the sixth wicket fell for 96.* **25 fall short. 25a** to prove inadequate. **25b** (often foll. by *of*) to fail to reach or measure up to (a standard). ◆ *n* **26** an act or instance of falling. **27** something that falls: *a fall of snow.* **28** *Chiefly US.* autumn. **29** the distance that something falls: *a hundred-foot fall.* **30** a sudden drop from an upright position. **31** (*often pl*) **31a** a waterfall or cataract. **31b** (*cap. when part of a name*): *Niagara Falls.* **32** a downward slope or decline. **33** a decrease in value, number, etc. **34** a decline in status or importance. **35** a capture or overthrow: *the fall of the city.* **36** *Machinery, naut.* the end of a tackle to which power is applied to hoist it. **37** Also called: **pinfall.** *Wrestling.* a scoring move, pinning both shoulders of one's opponent to the floor for a specified period. **38a** the birth of an animal. **38b** the animals produced at a single birth. ◆ See also **fall about, fall away,** etc. ORIG OE *feallan*: cf. FELL[2]

Fall (fɔːl) *n* **the.** *Theol.* Adam's sin of disobedience and the state of innate sinfulness ensuing from this for himself and all mankind.

Falla ★ (*Spanish* 'faʎa) *n* **Manuel de** (ma'nwɛl de). 1876–1946, Spanish composer and pianist, composer of the opera *La Vida Breve* (1905), the ballet *The Three-Cornered Hat* (1919), guitar and piano music, and songs.

fall about *vb* (*intr, adv*) to laugh in an uncontrolled manner: *we fell about at the sight.*

fallacious (fə'leɪʃəs) *adj* **1** containing or involving a fallacy. **2** tending to mislead. **3** delusive or disappointing.
▸ **fal'laciously** *adv*

fallacy ('fæləsɪ) *n, pl* **fallacies. 1** an incorrect or misleading notion or opinion based on inaccurate facts or invalid reasoning. **2** unsound reasoning. **3** the tendency to mislead. **4** *Logic.* an error in reasoning that renders an argument logically invalid. ORIG C15: from L, from *fallax* deceitful, from *fallere* to deceive

fall apart *vb* (*intr adv*) **1** to break owing to long use or poor construction: *the chassis is falling apart.* **2** to become disorganized and ineffective: *since you resigned, the office has fallen apart.*

fall away *vb* (*intr, adv*) **1** (of friendship, etc.) to be withdrawn. **2** to slope down.

fall back *vb* (*intr, adv*) **1** to recede or retreat. **2** (foll. by *on* or *upon*) to have recourse (to). ◆ *n* **fall-back. 3** a retreat. **4** a reserve, esp. money, that can be called upon in need. **5a** anything to which one can have recourse as a second choice. **5b** (*as modifier*): *a fall-back position.*

fall behind *vb* (*intr, adv*) **1** to drop back; fail to keep up. **2** to be in arrears, as with a payment.

fall down *vb* (*intr, adv*) **1** to drop suddenly or collapse. **2** (often foll. by *on*) *Inf.* to fail.

fallen ('fɔːlən) *vb* **1** the past participle of **fall.** ◆ *adj* **2** having sunk in reputation or honour: *a fallen woman.* **3** killed in battle with glory.

fallen arch *n* collapse of the arch formed by the instep of the foot, resulting in flat feet.

fall for *vb* (*intr, prep*) **1** to become infatuated with (a person). **2** to allow oneself to be deceived by (a lie, trick, etc.).

fall guy *n Inf.* **1** a person who is the victim of a confidence trick. **2** a scapegoat.

fallible ('fælɪbᵊl) *adj* **1** capable of being mistaken. **2** liable to mislead. ORIG C15: from Med. L *fallibilis,* from L *fallere* to deceive
▸ ˌ**falliˈbility** *n*

fall in *vb* (*intr, adv*) **1** to collapse. **2** to adopt a military formation, esp. as a soldier taking his place in a line. **3** (of a lease) to expire. **4** (often foll. by *with*) **4a** to meet and join. **4b** to agree with or support a person, suggestion, etc.

falling sickness *or* **evil** *n* a former name (nontechnical) for **epilepsy**.

falling star *n* an informal name for **meteor**.

Fall Line ★ *n* a natural junction, running parallel to the E coast of the US, between the hard rocks of the Appalachians and the softer coastal plain, along which rivers form falls and rapids.

fall off *vb* (*intr*) **1** to drop unintentionally to the ground from (a high object, bicycle, etc.), esp. after losing one's balance. **2** (*adv*) to diminish in size, intensity, etc. ◆ *n* **fall-off. 3** a decline or drop.

fall on *vb* (*intr, prep*) **1** Also: **fall upon.** to attack or snatch (an army, booty, etc.). **2 fall on one's feet.** to emerge unexpectedly well from a difficult situation.

Fallopian tube (fəˈləʊpɪən) *n* either of a pair of slender tubes through which ova pass from the ovaries to the uterus in female mammals. ORIG C18: after Gabriello *Fallopio* (1523–62), It. anatomist who first described the tubes

fallout (ˈfɔːlˌaʊt) *n* **1** the descent of radioactive material following a nuclear explosion. **2** any particles that so descend. **3** secondary consequences. ◆ *vb* **fall out.** (*intr, adv*) **4** *Inf.* to disagree. **5** (*intr*) to occur. **6** *Mil.* to leave a disciplinary formation.

fallow¹ (ˈfæləʊ) *adj* **1** (of land) left unseeded after being ploughed to regain fertility for a crop. **2** (of an idea, etc.) undeveloped, but potentially useful. ◆ *n* **3** land treated in this way. ◆ *vb* **4** (*tr*) to leave (land) unseeded after ploughing it. ORIG OE *fealga*
▸ ˈ**fallowness** *n*

fallow² (ˈfæləʊ) *n, adj* (of) a light yellowish-brown colour. ORIG OE *fealu*

fallow deer *n* either of two species of deer, one of which is native to the Mediterranean region and the other to Persia. The summer coat is reddish with white spots.

fall through *vb* (*intr, adv*) to fail.

fall to *vb* (*intr*) **1** (*adv*) to begin some activity, as eating, working, or fighting. **2** (*prep*) to devolve on (a person): *the task fell to me.*

Falmouth ★ (ˈfælməθ) *n* a port and resort in SW England, in S Cornwall. Pop.: 20 297 (1991).

false (fɔːls) *adj* **1** not in accordance with the truth or facts. **2** irregular or invalid: *a false start.* **3** untruthful or lying: *a false account.* **4** artificial; fake: *false teeth.* **5** being or intended to be misleading or deceptive: *a false rumour.* **6** treacherous: *a false friend.* **7** based on mistaken or irrelevant ideas or facts: *a false argument.* **8** (*prenominal*) (esp. of plants) superficially resembling the species specified: *false hellebore.* **9** serving to supplement or replace, often temporarily: *a false keel.* **10** *Music.* (of a note, interval, etc.) out of tune. ◆ *adv* **11** in a false or dishonest manner (esp. in **play** (**someone**) **false**). ORIG OE *fals*
▸ ˈ**falsely** *adv* ▸ ˈ**falseness** *n*

false colour *n* colour used in a computer or photographic display to help in interpreting the image, as in the use of red to show high temperatures and blue to show low temperatures in an infrared image converter.

false dawn *n* light appearing just before sunrise.

false diamond *n* any of a number of semiprecious stones that resemble diamond, such as zircon and white topaz.

falsehood (ˈfɔːlsˌhʊd) *n* **1** the quality of being untrue. **2** an untrue statement; lie. **3** the act of deceiving or lying.

false imprisonment *n Law.* the restraint of a person's liberty without lawful authority.

false pretences *pl n* a misrepresentation used to obtain anything, such as trust or affection (esp. in **under false pretences**).

false ribs *pl n* any of the lower five pairs of ribs in man, not attached directly to the breastbone.

false step *n* **1** an unwise action. **2** a stumble; slip.

falsetto (fɔːlˈsetəʊ) *n, pl* **falsettos.** a form of vocal production used by male singers to extend their range upwards by limiting the vibration of the vocal cords. ORIG C18: from It., from *falso* false

falsies (ˈfɔːlsɪz) *pl n Inf.* pads of soft material, such as foam rubber, worn to exaggerate the size of a woman's breasts.

falsify (ˈfɔːlsɪˌfaɪ) *vb* **falsifies, falsifying, falsified.** (*tr*) **1** to make (a report, evidence, etc.) false or inaccurate by alteration, esp. in order to deceive. **2** to prove false. ORIG C15: from OF, from LL, from L *falsus* FALSE + *facere* to do, make
▸ ˈ**falsiˌfiable** *adj* ▸ **falsification** (ˌfɔːlsɪfɪˈkeɪʃən) *n*

falsity (ˈfɔːlsɪtɪ) *n, pl* **falsities. 1** the state of being false or untrue. **2** a lie or deception.

Falstaffian (fɔːlˈstɑːfɪən) *adj* jovial, plump, and dissolute. ORIG C19: after Sir John *Falstaff,* a character in Shakespeare's play *Henry IV*

Falster ★ (ˈfɑːlstə) *n* an island in the Baltic Sea, part of SE Denmark. Chief town: Nykøbing. Pop.: 42 846 (1990). Area: 513 sq. km (198 sq. miles).

falter (ˈfɔːltə) *vb* **1** (*intr*) to be hesitant, weak, or unsure. **2** (*intr*) to move unsteadily or hesitantly. **3** to utter haltingly or hesitantly. ◆ *n* **4** hesitancy in speech or action. **5** a quavering sound. ORIG C14: prob. from ON
▸ ˈ**falterer** *n* ▸ ˈ**falteringly** *adv*

Falun ★ (ˌfɑːˈlʌn) *n* a city in central Sweden: iron and pyrites mines. Pop.: 55 014 (1994).

Famagusta ★ (ˌfæməˈgʊstə) *n* a port in E Cyprus, on **Famagusta Bay:** became one of the richest cities in Christendom in the 14th century. Pop.: 67 167 (1994).

fame (feɪm) *n* **1** the state of being widely known or recognized. **2** *Arch.* rumour or public report. ◆ *vb* **fames, faming, famed. 3** (*tr; now usually passive*) to make famous: *he was famed for his ruthlessness.* ORIG C13: from L *fāma* report; rel. to *fārī* to say

familial (fəˈmɪlɪəl) *adj* **1** of or relating to the family. **2** occurring in the members of a family: *a familial disease.*

familiar (fəˈmɪlɪə) *adj* **1** well-known: *a familiar figure.* **2** frequent or customary: *a familiar excuse.* **3** (*postpositive;* foll. by *with*) acquainted. **4** friendly; informal. **5** close; intimate. **6** more intimate than is acceptable; presumptuous. ◆ *n* **7** Also called: **familiar spirit.** a supernatural spirit supposed to attend and aid a witch, wizard, etc. **8** a person attached to the household of the pope or a bishop, who renders service in return for support. **9** a friend. ORIG C14: from L *familiāris* domestic, from *familia* FAMILY
▸ **faˈmiliarly** *adv* ▸ **faˈmiliarness** *n*

familiarity (fəˌmɪlɪˈærɪtɪ) *n, pl* **familiarities. 1** knowledge, as of a subject or place. **2** close acquaintanceship. **3** undue intimacy. **4** (*sometimes pl*) an instance of unwarranted intimacy.

familiarize *or* **familiarise** (fəˈmɪljəˌraɪz) *vb* **familiarizes, familiarizing, familiarized** *or* **familiarises, familiarising, familiarised.** (*tr*) **1** to make (oneself or someone else) familiar, as with a particular subject. **2** to make (something) generally known.
▸ **faˌmiliariˈzation** *or* **faˌmiliariˈzatiˈsation** *n*

famille *French.* (famij) *n* a type of Chinese porcelain characterized either by a design on a background of yellow (***famille jaune***) or black (***famille noire***) or by a design in which the predominant colour is pink (***famille rose***) or green (***famille verte***). ORIG C19: lit.: family

family (ˈfæmɪlɪ, ˈfæmlɪ) *n, pl* **families. 1a** a primary social group consisting of parents and their offspring. **1b** (*as modifier*): *a family unit.* **2** one's wife or husband and one's children. **3** one's children, as distinguished from one's husband or wife. **4** a group descended from a common ancestor. **5** all the persons living together in one household. **6** any group of related things or beings, esp. when scientifically categorized. **7** *Biol.* any of the taxonomic

★ people and places

groups into which an order is divided and which contains one or more genera. **8** a group of historically related languages assumed to derive from one original language. **9** *Maths.* a group of curves or surfaces whose equations differ from a given equation only in the values assigned to one or more constants. **10 in the family way.** *Inf.* pregnant. ORIG C15: from L *familia* a household, servants of the house, from *famulus* servant

family allowance *n* **1** (in Britain) a former name for **child benefit. 2** (*caps.*) the Canadian equivalent of **child benefit.**

family Bible *n* a large Bible in which births, marriages, and deaths of the members of a family are recorded.

Family Compact *n Canad.* **1 the.** the ruling oligarchy in Upper Canada in the early 19th century. **2** (*often not cap.*) any influential clique.

family credit *n* (formerly, in Britain) a means-tested allowance paid to families who have at least one dependent child and whose earnings from full-time work are low. It replaced **family income supplement.**

family man *n* a man who is married and has children, esp. one who is devoted to his family.

family name *n* a surname, esp. when regarded as representing the family honour.

family planning *n* the control of the number of children in a family and of the intervals between them, esp. by the use of contraceptives.

family support *n NZ.* a means-tested allowance for families in need.

family therapy *n* a form of psychotherapy in which the members of a family participate, with the aim of improving communications between them and the ways in which they relate to each other.

family tree *n* a chart showing the genealogical relationships and lines of descent of a family. Also called: **genealogical tree.**

famine ('fæmɪn) *n* **1** a severe shortage of food, as through crop failure or overpopulation. **2** acute shortage of anything. **3** violent hunger. ORIG C14: from OF, via Vulgar L, from L *famēs* hunger

famish ('fæmɪʃ) *vb* (*now usually passive*) to be or make very hungry or weak. ORIG C14: from OF, from L *famēs* FAMINE

famous ('feɪməs) *adj* **1** known to or recognized by many people. **2** *Inf.* excellent; splendid. ORIG C14: from L *fāmōsus;* see FAME
▸ **'famously** *adv* ▸ **'famousness** *n*

fan[1] (fæn) *n* **1** any device for creating a current of air by movement of a surface or number of surfaces, esp. a rotating device consisting of a number of blades attached to a central hub. **2** any of various hand-agitated devices for cooling oneself, esp. a collapsible semicircular series of flat segments of paper, ivory, etc. **3** something shaped like such a fan, such as the tail of certain birds. **4** *Agriculture.* a kind of basket formerly used for winnowing grain. ♦ *vb* **fans, fanning, fanned.** (*mainly tr*) **5** to cause a current of air to blow upon, as by means of a fan: *to fan one's face.* **6** to agitate or move (air, etc.) with or as if with a fan. **7** to make fiercer, more ardent, etc.: *fan one's passion.* **8** (*also intr; often foll. by out*) to spread out or cause to spread out in the shape of a fan. **9** to winnow (grain) by blowing the chaff away from it. ORIG OE *fann,* from L *vannus*
▸ **'fanlike** *adj* ▸ **'fanner** *n*

fan[2] (fæn) *n* **1** an ardent admirer of a pop star, football team, etc. **2** a devotee of a sport, hobby, etc. ORIG C17, re-formed C19: from FAN(ATIC)
▸ **'fandom** *n*

Fanagalo ('fænəgələʊ) *or* **Fanakalo** *n* (in South Africa) a Zulu-based pidgin with English and Afrikaans components. ORIG C20: from Fanagalo *fana ga lo,* lit.: to be like this

fanatic (fə'nætɪk) *n* **1** a person whose enthusiasm or zeal for something is extreme or beyond normal limits. **2** *Inf.* a person devoted to a particular hobby or pastime. ♦ *adj* **3** a variant of **fanatical.** ORIG C16: from L *fānāticus* belonging to a temple, hence, inspired by a god, frenzied, from *fānum* temple

fanatical (fə'nætɪkᵊl) *adj* surpassing what is normal or accepted in enthusiasm for or belief in something.
▸ **fa'natically** *adv*

fanaticism (fə'nætɪˌsɪzəm) *n* wildly excessive or irrational devotion, dedication, or enthusiasm.

fan belt *n* the belt that drives a cooling fan in a car engine.

fancied ('fænsɪd) *adj* **1** imaginary; unreal. **2** thought likely to win or succeed: *a fancied runner.*

fancier ('fænsɪə) *n* **1** a person with a special interest in something. **2** a person who breeds special varieties of plants or animals: *a pigeon fancier.*

fanciful ('fænsɪfʊl) *adj* **1** not based on fact: *fanciful notions.* **2** made or designed in a curious, intricate, or imaginative way. **3** indulging in or influenced by fancy.
▸ **'fancifully** *adv* ▸ **'fancifulness** *n*

fan club *n* **1** an organized group of admirers of a particular pop singer, film star, etc. **2 be a member of someone's fan club.** *Inf.* to approve of someone strongly.

fancy ('fænsɪ) *adj* **fancier, fanciest. 1** ornamented or decorative: *fancy clothes.* **2** requiring skill to perform: *a fancy dance routine.* **3** capricious or illusory. **4** (often used ironically) superior in quality. **5** higher than expected: *fancy prices.* **6** (of a domestic animal) bred for particular qualities. ♦ *n, pl* **fancies. 7** a sudden capricious idea. **8** a sudden or irrational liking for a person or thing. **9** the power to conceive and represent decorative and novel imagery, esp. in poetry. **10** an idea or thing produced by this. **11** a mental image. **12** *Music.* a composition for solo lute, keyboard, etc., current during the 16th and 17th centuries. **13 the fancy.** *Arch.* those who follow a particular sport, esp. prize fighting. ♦ *vb* **fancies, fancying, fancied.** (*tr*) **14** to picture in the imagination. **15** to imagine: *I fancy it will rain.* **16** (*often used with a negative*) to like: *I don't fancy your chances!* **17** (*reflexive*) to have a high or ill-founded opinion of oneself. **18** *Inf.* to have a wish for: *she fancied some chocolate.* **19** *Brit. inf.* to be physically attracted to (another person). **20** to breed (animals) for particular characteristics. ♦ *interj* **21** Also: **fancy that!** an exclamation of surprise. ORIG C15 *fantsy,* shortened from *fantasie;* see FANTASY
▸ **'fancily** *adv* ▸ **'fanciness** *n*

fancy dress *n* **a** costume worn at masquerades, etc., representing an historical figure, etc. **b** (*as modifier*): *a fancy-dress ball.*

fancy-free *adj* having no commitments.

fancy goods *pl n* small decorative gifts.

fancy man *n Sl.* **1** a woman's lover. **2** a pimp.

fancy woman *n Sl.* a mistress or prostitute.

fancywork ('fænsɪˌwɜːk) *n* any ornamental needlework, such as embroidery or crochet.

fan dance *n* a dance in which large fans are manipulated in front of the body, partially revealing or suggesting nakedness.

fandangle (fæn'dæŋgᵊl) *n Inf.* **1** elaborate ornament. **2** nonsense. ORIG C19: ?from FANDANGO

fandango (fæn'dæŋgəʊ) *n, pl* **fandangos. 1** an old Spanish courtship dance in triple time. **2** a piece of music composed for or in the rhythm of this dance. ORIG C18: from Sp., from ?

fane (feɪn) *n Arch. or poetic.* a temple or shrine. ORIG C14: from L *fānum*

fanfare ('fænfɛə) *n* **1** a flourish or short tune played on brass instruments. **2** an ostentatious flourish or display. ORIG C17: from F, back formation from *fanfarer,* from Sp, from *fanfarron* boaster, from Ar. *farfār* garrulous

fang (fæŋ) *n* **1** the long pointed hollow or grooved tooth of a venomous snake through which venom is injected. **2** any large pointed tooth, esp. the canine tooth of a carnivorous mammal. **3** the root of a tooth. **4** (*usually pl*) *Brit. inf.* a tooth. ORIG OE *fang* what is caught, prey
▸ **fanged** *adj* ▸ **'fangless** *adj*

Fangio ★ (*Spanish* 'faŋxjo) *n* **Juan Manuel** (xwan ma'nwɛl). 1911–95, Argentinian racing driver who won the World Championship five times between 1951 and 1957.

fan heater *n* a space heater consisting of an electrically heated element with an electrically driven fan to disperse the heat.

fanjet ('fæn,dʒɛt) *n* another name for **turbofan**.

fanlight ('fæn,laɪt) *n* **1** a semicircular window over a door or window, often having sash bars like the ribs of a fan. **2** a small rectangular window over a door. US name: **transom**.

fan mail *n* mail sent to a famous person, such as a pop musician or film star, by admirers.

fanny ('fænɪ) *n, pl* **fannies.** *Sl.* **1** *Taboo, Brit.* the female genitals. **2** *Chiefly US & Canad.* the buttocks. ORIG C20: ?from *Fanny,* pet name from *Frances*

fanny adams *n Brit. sl.* **1** (usually preceded by *sweet*) absolutely nothing at all. **2** *Chiefly naut.* (formerly) tinned meat. ORIG C19: from the name of a young murder victim whose body was cut up into small pieces. For sense 1: a euphemism for *fuck all*

fantail ('fæn,teɪl) *n* **1** a breed of domestic pigeon having a large tail that can be opened like a fan. **2** an Old World flycatcher of Australia, New Zealand, and SE Asia, having a broad fan-shaped tail. **3** a tail shaped like an outspread fan. **4** an auxiliary sail on the upper portion of a windmill. **5** *US.* a part of the deck projecting aft of the sternpost of a ship.
▸ **'fan-,tailed** *adj*

fan-tan *n* **1** a Chinese gambling game. **2** a card game played in sequence, the winner being the first to use up all his cards. ORIG C19: from Chinese (Cantonese) *fan t'an* repeated divisions, from *fan* times + *t'an* division

fantasia (fæn'teɪzɪə) *n* **1** any musical composition of a free or improvisatory nature. **2** a potpourri of popular tunes woven loosely together. ORIG C18: from It.: fancy; see FANTASY

fantasist ('fæntəsɪst) *n* **1** a person who indulges in fantasies. **2** a person who writes literary or musical fantasies.

fantasize *or* **fantasise** ('fæntə,saɪz) *vb* **fantasizes, fantasizing, fantasized** *or* **fantasises, fantasising, fantasised. 1** (when *tr,* takes a clause as object) to conceive extravagant or whimsical ideas, images, etc. **2** (*intr*) to conceive pleasant mental images.

fantastic (fæn'tæstɪk) *adj also* **fantastical. 1** strange or fanciful in appearance, conception, etc. **2** created in the mind; illusory. **3** unrealistic: *fantastic plans.* **4** incredible or preposterous: *a fantastic verdict.* **5** *Inf.* very large or extreme: *a fantastic fortune.* **6** *Inf.* very good; excellent. **7** of or characterized by fantasy. **8** capricious; fitful. ORIG C14 *fantastik* imaginary, via LL from Gk *phantastikos* capable of imagining, from *phantazein* to make visible
▸ **fan,tasti'cality** *or* **fan'tasticalness** *n* ▸ **fan'tastically** *adv*

fantasy *or* **phantasy** ('fæntəsɪ) *n, pl* **fantasies** *or* **phantasies. 1a** imagination unrestricted by reality. **1b** (*as modifier*): *a fantasy world.* **2** a creation of the imagination, esp. a weird or bizarre one. **3** *Psychol.* a series of pleasing mental images, usually serving to fulfil a need not gratified in reality. **4** a whimsical or far-fetched notion. **5** an illusion or phantom. **6** a highly elaborate imaginative design or creation. **7** *Music.* another word for **fantasia. 8** literature, etc., having a large fantasy content. **9** (*modifier*) of or relating to a competition, often in a newspaper, in which a participant selects players for an imaginary ideal team, and points are awarded according to the actual performances of the chosen players: *fantasy football.* ◆ *vb* **fantasies, fantasying, fantasied** *or* **phantasies, phantasying, phantasied. 10** a less common word for **fantasize.** ORIG C14 *fantasie,* from L, from Gk *phantazein* to make visible

Fantin-Latour ★ (*French* fɑ̃tɛ̃latur) *n* (**Ignace**) **Henri** (**Joseph Théodore**) (ɑ̃ri). 1836–1904, French painter, noted for his still lifes and portrait groups.

fan vaulting *n Archit.* vaulting having ribs that radiate like those of a fan and spring from the top of a capital. Also called: **palm vaulting.**

fanzine ('fæn,ziːn) *n* a magazine produced by amateurs for fans of a specific interest, pop group, etc. ORIG C20: from FAN[2] + (MAGA)ZINE

FAO *abbrev. for:* **1** Food and Agriculture Organization (of the United Nations). **2** for the attention of.

f.a.q. *abbrev. for:* **1** *Commerce.* fair average quality. **2** free alongside quay.

FAQ *Computing. abbrev. for* frequently asked question *or* questions; a question or set of questions with answers, designed to give basic information about a particular topic.

far (fɑː) *adv* **farther** *or* **further, farthest** *or* **furthest. 1** at, to, or from a great distance. **2** at or to a remote time: *far in the future.* **3** to a considerable degree: *a far better plan.* **4 as far as. 4a** to the degree or extent that. **4b** to the distance or place of. **4c** *Inf.* with reference to; as for. **5 by far.** by a considerable margin. **6 far and away.** by a very great margin. **7 far and wide.** everywhere. **8 far be it from me.** on no account: *far be it from me to tell you what to do.* **9 go far. 9a** to be successful: *your son will go far.* **9b** to be sufficient or last long: *the wine didn't go far.* **10 go too far.** to exceed reasonable limits. **11 so far. 11a** up to the present moment. **11b** up to a certain point, extent, degree, etc. ◆ *adj* (*prenominal*) **12** remote in space or time: *in the far past.* **13** extending a great distance. **14** more distant: *the far end of the room.* **15 far from.** in a degree, state, etc. remote from: *he is far from happy.* ORIG OE *feorr*
▸ **'farness** *n*

farad ('færəd) *n Physics.* the derived SI unit of electric capacitance; the capacitance of a capacitor between the plates of which a potential of 1 volt is created by a charge of 1 coulomb. Symbol: F ORIG C19: see FARADAY

faraday ('færə,deɪ) *n* a quantity of electricity, used in electrochemical calculations, equivalent to unit amount of substance of electrons. Symbol: *F* ORIG C20: after Michael FARADAY

Faraday ★ ('færə,deɪ) *n* **Michael.** 1791–1867, English physicist and chemist who discovered electromagnetic induction, leading to the invention of the dynamo. He also carried out research into the principles of electrolysis.

faradic (fə'rædɪk) *adj* of or concerned with an intermittent alternating current such as that induced in the secondary winding of an induction coil. ORIG C19: from F *faradique;* from Michael FARADAY

farandole ('færən,dəʊl) *n* **1** a lively dance from Provence. **2** a piece of music composed for or in the rhythm of this dance. ORIG C19: from F, from Provençal *farandoulo,* from ?

faraway ('fɑːrə,weɪ) *adj* (**far away** *when postpositive*). **1** very distant. **2** absent-minded.

farce (fɑːs) *n* **1** a broadly humorous play based on the exploitation of improbable situations. **2** the genre of comedy represented by works of this kind. **3** a ludicrous situation or action. **4** another name for **forcemeat.** ORIG C14 (in the sense: stuffing): from OF, from L *farcīre* to stuff, interpolate passages (in the mass, in religious plays, etc.)

farcical ('fɑːsɪkᵊl) *adj* **1** absurd. **2** of or relating to farce.
▸ **,farci'cality** *n* ▸ **'farcically** *adv*

fardel ('fɑːdᵊl) *n Arch.* a bundle or burden. ORIG C13: from OF *farde,* ult. from Ar. *fardah*

fare (fɛə) *n* **1** the sum charged or paid for conveyance in a bus, train, etc. **2** a paying passenger, esp. when carried by taxi. **3** a range of food and drink. ◆ *vb* **fares, faring, fared.** (*intr*) **4** to get on (as specified): *he fared well.* **5** (with *it* as a subject) to happen as specified: *it fared badly with him.* **6** *Arch.* to eat: *we fared sumptuously.* **7** (often foll. by *forth*) *Arch.* to travel. ORIG OE *faran*
▸ **'farer** *n*

Far East *n* **the.** the countries of E Asia, including China, Japan, North and South Korea, E Siberia, Indonesia, Malaysia, and the Philippines: sometimes extended to include all territories east of Afghanistan.
▸ **Far Eastern** *adj*

fare stage *n* **1** a section of a bus journey for which a set charge is made. **2** the bus stop marking the end of such a section.

farewell (,fɛə'wɛl) *sentence substitute.* **1** goodbye; adieu. ◆ *n* **2** a parting salutation. **3** an act of departure. **4** (*modifier*) expressing leave-taking: *a farewell speech.*

far-fetched *adj* unlikely.

far-flung *adj* **1** widely distributed. **2** far distant; remote.

Fargo ★ ('fɑːgəʊ) *n* **William.** 1818–81, US businessman: founded (1852) with Henry Wells the express mail service Wells, Fargo and Company.

farina (fə'riːnə) *n* **1** flour or meal made from any kind of cereal grain. **2** *Chiefly Brit.* starch. ORIG C18: from L *fār* spelt, coarse meal

farinaceous (ˌfærɪ'neɪʃəs) *adj* **1** consisting or made of starch. **2** having a mealy texture or appearance. **3** containing starch: *farinaceous seeds.*

farm (fɑːm) *n* **1a** a tract of land, usually with house and buildings, cultivated as a unit or used to rear livestock. **1b** (*as modifier*): *farm produce.* **1c** (*in combination*): *farmland.* **2** a unit of land or water devoted to the growing or rearing of some particular type of vegetable, fruit, animal, or fish: *a fish farm.* **3** an installation for storage or disposal: *a sewage farm.* ♦ *vb* **4** (*tr*) **4a** to cultivate (land). **4b** to rear (stock, etc.) on a farm. **5** (*intr*) to engage in agricultural work, esp. as a way of life. **6** (*tr*) to look after a child for a fixed sum. **7** to collect the moneys due and retain the profits from (a tax district, business, etc.) for a specified period. ♦ See also **farm out.** ORIG C13: from OF *ferme* rented land, ult. from L *firmāre* to settle
▸ '**farmable** *adj*

farmed (fɑːmd) *adj* (of fish and game) reared on a farm rather than caught in the wild.

farmer ('fɑːmə) *n* **1** a person who operates or manages a farm. **2** a person who obtains the right to collect and retain a tax, rent, etc., on payment of a fee.

Farmer ★ ('fɑːmə) *n* **John.** ?1565–1605, English madrigal composer and organist.

farmer's lung *n* inflammation of the alveoli of the lungs caused by an allergic response to fungal spores in hay.

farm hand *n* a person who is hired to work on a farm.

farmhouse ('fɑːmˌhaʊs) *n* a house attached to a farm, esp. the dwelling from which the farm is managed.

farming ('fɑːmɪŋ) *n* **a** the business or skill of agriculture. **b** (*as modifier*): *farming methods.*

farm out *vb* (*tr, adv*) **1** to send (work) to be done by another person, firm, etc. **2** to put (a child, etc.) into the care of a private individual. **3** to lease to another for a fee the right to collect (taxes).

farmstead ('fɑːmˌstɛd) *n* a farm or the part of a farm comprising its main buildings together with adjacent grounds.

farmyard ('fɑːmˌjɑːd) *n* an area surrounded by or adjacent to farm buildings.

Farnborough ★ ('fɑːnbərə, -brə) *n* a town in S England, in NE Hampshire: military base, with an aeronautical research centre. Pop.: 52 535 (1991).

Farnese ★ (*Italian* far'neːse) *n* **1 Alessandro** (ales'sandro). original name of (Pope) **Paul III. 2 Alessandro.** duke of Parma and Piacenza. 1545–92, Italian general, statesman, and diplomat in the service of Philip II of Spain. As governor of the Netherlands (1578–92), he successfully suppressed revolts against Spanish rule.

Far North *n* **the.** the Arctic and sub-Arctic regions of the world.

faro ('fɛərəʊ) *n* a gambling game in which players bet against the dealer on what cards he will turn up. ORIG C18: prob. spelling var. of *Pharoah*

Faroes ★ ('fɛərəʊz) *n* a variant spelling of **Faeroes.**
▸ **Faroese** (ˌfɛərəʊ'iːz) *adj, n*

far-off *adj* (**far off** *when postpositive*). remote in space or time; distant.

farouche *French.* (faruʃ) *adj* sullen or shy. ORIG C18: from F, from OF, from LL *forasticus* from without, from L *foras* out of doors

Farouk I *or* **Faruk I** ★ (fə'ruːk) *n* 1920–65, last king of Egypt (1936–52). He was forced to abdicate (1952).

far-out *Sl.* ♦ *adj* (**far out** *when postpositive*) **1** bizarre or avant-garde. **2** wonderful. ♦ *interj* **far out. 3** an expression of amazement or delight.

Farquhar ★ ('fɑːkwə, -kə) *n* **George.** 1678–1707, Irish-born dramatist; author of comedies such as *The Recruiting Officer* (1706) and *The Beaux' Stratagem* (1707).

Farquhar Islands ★ *pl n* an island group in the Indian Ocean: administratively part of the Seychelles.

farrago (fə'rɑːgəʊ) *n, pl* **farragos** *or* **farragoes.** a hotchpotch. ORIG C17: from L: mash for cattle (hence, a mixture), from *fār* spelt
▸ **farraginous** (fə'rædʒɪnəs) *adj*

far-reaching *adj* extensive in influence, effect, or range.

Farrell ★ ('færəl) *n* **1 J(ames) G(ordon).** 1935–79, British novelist: author of *The Siege of Krishnapur* (1973) and *The Singapore Grip* (1978). **2 James T(homas).** 1904–79, US writer. His works include the trilogy *Young Lonigan* (1932), *The Young Manhood of Studs Lonigan* (1934), and *Judgment Day* (1935).

farrier ('færɪə) *n Chiefly Brit.* **1** a person who shoes horses. **2** another name for **veterinary surgeon.** ORIG C16: from OF, from L *ferrārius* smith, from *ferrum* iron
▸ '**farriery** *n*

farrow ('færəʊ) *n* **1** a litter of piglets. ♦ *vb* **2** (of a sow) to give birth to (a litter). ORIG OE *fearh*

far-seeing *adj* having shrewd judgment.

Farsi ('fɑːsɪ) *n* a language spoken in Iran.

far-sighted *adj* **1** possessing prudence and foresight. **2** another word for **long-sighted.**
▸ ˌ**far-'sightedly** *adv* ▸ ˌ**far-'sightedness** *n*

fart (fɑːt) *Taboo.* ♦ *n* **1** an emission of intestinal gas from the anus. **2** *Sl.* a contemptible person. ♦ *vb* (*intr*) **3** to break wind. **4 fart about** *or* **around.** *Sl.* **4a** to behave foolishly. **4b** to waste time. ORIG ME *farten*

farther ('fɑːðə) *adv* **1** to or at a greater distance in space or time. **2** in addition. ♦ *adj* **3** more distant or remote in space or time. **4** additional. ORIG C13: see FAR, FURTHER

> **USAGE NOTE** *Farther, farthest, further,* and *furthest* can all be used to refer to literal distance, but *further* and *furthest* are used for figurative senses denoting greater or additional amount, time, etc.: *further to my letter. Further* and *furthest* are also preferred for figurative distance.

farthermost ('fɑːðəˌməʊst) *adj* most distant or remote.

farthest ('fɑːðɪst) *adv* **1** to or at the greatest distance in space or time. ♦ *adj* **2** most distant in space or time. **3** most extended. ORIG C14 *ferthest,* from *ferther* FURTHER

farthing ('fɑːðɪŋ) *n* **1** a former British bronze coin worth a quarter of an old penny: withdrawn in 1961. **2** something of negligible value; jot. ORIG OE *fēorthing* from *fēortha* FOURTH + -ING[1]

farthingale ('fɑːðɪŋˌgeɪl) *n* a hoop or framework worn under skirts, esp. in the Elizabethan period, to shape and spread them. ORIG C16: from F *verdugale,* from OSp. *verdugado,* from *verdugo* rod

Faruk I ★ (fə'ruːk) *n* a variant spelling of **Farouk I.**

fasces ('fæsiːz) *pl n, sing* **fascis** (-sɪs). **1** (in ancient Rome) one or more bundles of rods containing an axe with its blade protruding; a symbol of a magistrate's power. **2** (in modern Italy) such an object used as the symbol of Fascism. ORIG C16: from L, pl of *fascis* bundle

fascia *or* **facia** ('feɪʃɪə) *n, pl* **fasciae** *or* **faciae** (-ʃɪˌiː). **1** the flat surface above a shop window. **2** *Archit.* a flat band or surface, esp. a part of an architrave. **3** ('fæʃɪə). fibrous connective tissue occurring in sheets between muscles. **4** *Biol.* a distinctive band of colour, as on an insect or plant. **5** *Brit.* the outer panel which covers the dashboard of a motor vehicle. ORIG C16: from L: band: rel. to *fascis* bundle
▸ '**fascial** *or* '**facial** *adj*

fasciate ('fæʃɪˌeɪt) *or* **fasciated** *adj* **1** *Bot.* (of stems and branches) abnormally flattened due to coalescence. **2** (of birds, insects, etc.) marked by bands of colour. ORIG C17: prob. from NL *fasciātus* (unattested) having bands; see FASCIA

fascicle ('fæsɪkᵊl) *n* **1** a bundle of branches, leaves, etc. **2** Also called: **fasciculus.** *Anat.* a small bundle of fibres, esp.

nerve fibres. ORIG C15: from L *fasciculus* a small bundle, from *fascis* a bundle
▸ **'fascicled** *adj* ▸ **fascicular** (fə'sɪkjulə) *or* **fasciculate** (fə'sɪkju,leɪt) *adj* ▸ **fas,cicu'lation** *n*

fascicule ('fæsɪ,kju:l) *n* one part of a printed work that is published in instalments. Also called: **fascicle, fasciculus.**

fascinate ('fæsɪ,neɪt) *vb* **fascinates, fascinating, fascinated.** (*mainly tr*) **1** to attract and delight by arousing interest: *his stories fascinated me for hours.* **2** to render motionless, as by arousing terror or awe. **3** *Arch.* to put under a spell. ORIG C16: from L, from *fascinum* a bewitching
▸ **,fasci'nation** *n*

fascinating ('fæsɪ,neɪtɪŋ) *adj* **1** arousing great interest. **2** enchanting or alluring.

fascinator ('fæsɪ,neɪtə) *n Rare.* a lace or crocheted head covering for women.

Fascism ('fæʃɪzəm) *n* **1** the political movement, doctrine, system, or regime of Benito Mussolini in Italy. Fascism encouraged militarism and nationalism, organizing the country along hierarchical authoritarian lines. **2** (*sometimes not cap.*) any ideology or movement modelled on or inspired by this. **3** *Inf.* (*often not cap.*) any doctrine, system, or practice, regarded as authoritarian, militaristic, or extremely right-wing. ORIG C20: from It. *fascismo,* from *fascio* political group, from L *fascis* bundle; see FASCES

Fascist ('fæʃɪst) *n* **1** a supporter or member of a Fascist movement. **2** (*sometimes not cap.*) any person regarded as having right-wing authoritarian views. ◆ *adj* **3** characteristic of or relating to Fascism.

fashion ('fæʃən) *n* **1a** style in clothes, behaviour, etc., esp. the latest style. **1b** (*as modifier*): *a fashion magazine.* **2** (*modifier*) designed to be in the current fashion. **3a** manner of performance: *in a striking fashion.* **3b** (*in combination*): *crab-fashion.* **4** a way of life that revolves around the activities, dress, interests, etc., that are most fashionable. **5** shape or form. **6** sort; kind. **7 after** *or* **in a fashion.** in some manner, but not very well: *I mended it, after a fashion.* **8 of fashion.** of high social standing. ◆ *vb* (*tr*) **9** to give a particular form to. **10** to make suitable or fitting. **11** *Obs.* to contrive. ORIG C13 *facioun* form, manner, from OF *faceon,* from L, from *facere* to make
▸ **'fashioner** *n*

fashionable ('fæʃənəbᵊl) *adj* **1** conforming to fashion; in vogue. **2** of or patronized by people of fashion: *a fashionable café.* **3** (usually foll. by *with*) patronized (by).
▸ **,fashiona'bility** *or* **'fashionableness** *n* ▸ **'fashionably** *adv*

fashion plate *n* **1** an illustration of the latest fashion in dress. **2** a fashionably dressed person.

fashion victim *n Inf.* a person who slavishly follows fashion.

Fassbinder ★ (*German* 'fasbɪndər) *n* **Rainer Werner** ('rainər 'vɛrnər). 1946–82, German film director. His films include *Fear Eats the Soul* (1974) and *The Marriage of Maria Braun* (1978).

fast¹ (fɑ:st) *adj* **1** acting or moving or capable of acting or moving quickly. **2** accomplished in or lasting a short time: *a fast visit.* **3** (*prenominal*) adapted to or facilitating rapid movement: *the fast lane of a motorway.* **4** (of a clock, etc.) indicating a time in advance of the correct time. **5** given to an active dissipated life. **6** of or characteristic of such activity: *a fast life.* **7** not easily moved; firmly fixed; secure. **8** firmly fastened or shut. **9** steadfast; constant (esp. in **fast friends**). **10** *Sport.* (of a playing surface, running track, etc.) conducive to rapid speed, as of a ball used on it or of competitors racing on it. **11** that will not fade or change colour readily. **12** proof against fading. **13** *Photog.* **13a** requiring a relatively short time of exposure to produce a given density: *a fast film.* **13b** permitting a short exposure time: *a fast shutter.* **14 a fast one.** *Inf.* a deceptive or unscrupulous trick (esp. in **pull a fast one**). **15 fast worker.** a person who achieves results quickly, esp. in seductions. ◆ *adv* **16** quickly; rapidly. **17** soundly; deeply: *fast asleep.* **18** firmly; tightly. **19** in quick succession. **20** in advance of the correct time: *my watch is running fast.* **21** in a reckless or dissipated way. **22 fast by** *or* **beside.** *Arch.* close by. **23 play fast and loose.** *Inf.* to behave in an insincere or unreliable manner. ORIG OE *fæst* strong, tight

fast² (fɑ:st) *vb* **1** (*intr*) to abstain from eating all or certain foods or meals, esp. as a religious observance. ◆ *n* **2a** an act or period of fasting. **2b** (*as modifier*): *a fast day.* ORIG OE *fæstan*
▸ **'faster** *n*

fastback ('fɑ:st,bæk) *n* a car having a back that forms one continuous slope from roof to rear.

fast-breeder reactor *n* a nuclear reactor that uses little or no moderator and produces more fissionable material than it consumes.

fasten ('fɑ:sᵊn) *vb* **1** to make or become fast or secure. **2** to make or become attached or joined. **3** to close or become closed by fixing firmly in place, locking, etc. **4** (*tr;* foll. by *in* or *up*) to enclose or imprison. **5** (*tr;* usually foll. by *on*) to cause (blame, a nickname, etc.) to be attached (to). **6** (usually foll. by *on* or *upon*) to direct or be directed in a concentrated way. **7** (*intr;* usually foll. by *on*) to take a firm hold (of). ORIG OE *fæstnian; see* FAST¹
▸ **'fastener** *n*

fastening ('fɑ:sᵊnɪŋ) *n* something that fastens, such as a clasp or lock.

fast food *n* **a** food, esp. hamburgers, fried chicken, etc., that is prepared and served very quickly. **b** (*as modifier*): *a fast-food restaurant.*

fast-forward *n* **1** (*sometimes not hyphenated*) the control on a tape deck or video recorder used to wind the tape or video forwards at speed. **2** *Inf.* a state of urgency or rapid progress: *put the deal into fast-forward.* ◆ *vb* (*tr*) **3** to wind (a tape, etc.) forward using the fast-forward control. **4** *Inf.* **4a** to deal with or dispatch (something) rapidly: *fast-forward this to the press.* **4b** to skip (something): *fast-forward the small talk and get down to business.*

fastidious (fæ'stɪdɪəs) *adj* **1** hard to please. **2** excessively particular about details. **3** exceedingly delicate. ORIG C15: from L *fastīdiōsus* scornful, from *fastīdium* loathing, from *fastus* pride + *taedium* weariness
▸ **fas'tidiously** *adv* ▸ **fas'tidiousness** *n*

fastigiate (fæ'stɪdʒɪɪt) *or* **fastigiated** *adj Biol.* (of parts or organs) united in a tapering group. ORIG C17: from Med. L *fastīgiātus* lofty, from L *fastīgium* height

fast lane *n* **1** the outside lane on a motorway for vehicles overtaking or travelling at high speed. **2** *Inf.* the quickest but most competitive route to success.

fastness ('fɑ:stnɪs) *n* **1** a stronghold; fortress. **2** the state or quality of being firm or secure. ORIG OE *fæstnes;* see FAST¹

fast track *n* **1a** the quickest or most direct route or system. **1b** (*as modifier*): *fast-track executives; a fast-track procedure for libel claims.* ◆ *vb* **fast-track.** (*tr*) **2** to speed up the progress of (a project or person).
▸ **,fast-'tracker** *n*

fat (fæt) *n* **1** any of a class of naturally occurring soft greasy solids that are present in some plants and animals, and are used in making soap and paint and in the food industry. **2** vegetable or animal tissue containing fat. **3** corpulence, obesity, or plumpness. **4** the best or richest part of something. **5 the fat is in the fire.** an irrevocable action has been taken from which dire consequences are expected. **6 the fat of the land.** the best that is obtainable. ◆ *adj* **fatter, fattest. 7** having much or too much flesh or fat. **8** consisting of or containing fat; greasy. **9** profitable; lucrative. **10** affording great opportunities: *a fat part in the play.* **11** fertile or productive: *a fat land.* **12** thick, broad, or extended: *a fat log of wood.* **13** *Sl.* very little or none (in **a fat chance, a fat lot of good,** etc.). ◆ *vb* **fats, fatting, fatted. 14** to make or become fat; fatten. ORIG OE *fǣtt,* p.p. of *fǣtan* to cram
▸ **'fatless** *adj* ▸ **'fatly** *adv* ▸ **'fatness** *n* ▸ **'fattish** *adj*

fatal ('feɪtᵊl) *adj* **1** resulting in death: *a fatal accident.* **2** bringing ruin. **3** decisively important. **4** inevitable. ORIG C14: from OF or L from L *fātum;* see FATE
▸ **'fatally** *adv*

fatalism ('feɪtə,lɪzəm) *n* **1** the philosophical doctrine that all events are predetermined so that man is powerless to alter his destiny. **2** the acceptance of and submission to this doctrine.
▸ **'fatalist** *n* ▸ **,fatal'istic** *adj*

fatality (fə'tælɪtɪ) *n, pl* **fatalities. 1** an accident or disaster

★ people and places

resulting in death. **2** a person killed in an accident or disaster. **3** the power of causing death or disaster. **4** the quality or condition of being fated. **5** something caused by fate.

fate (feɪt) *n* **1** the ultimate agency that predetermines the course of events. **2** the inevitable fortune that befalls a person or thing. **3** the end or final result. **4** death, destruction, or downfall. ◆ *vb* **fates, fating, fated. 5** (*tr; usually passive*) to predetermine: *he was fated to lose.* ORIG C14: from L *fātum* oracular utterance, from *fārī* to speak

fated (ˈfeɪtɪd) *adj* **1** destined. **2** doomed to death or destruction.

fateful (ˈfeɪtfʊl) *adj* **1** having important consequences. **2** bringing death or disaster. **3** controlled by or as if by fate. **4** prophetic.
▸ **ˈfatefully** *adv* ▸ **ˈfatefulness** *n*

Fates ★ (feɪts) *pl n* **1** *Greek myth.* the three goddesses who control the destinies of the lives of man, which are likened to skeins of thread that they spin, measure out, and at last cut. See **Atropos, Clotho, Lachesis. 2** *Norse myth.* another name for the **Norns** (see **Norn**[1]).

fat farm *n Sl.* a health farm or similar establishment to which people go to lose weight.

fathead (ˈfætˌhɛd) *n Inf.* a stupid person; fool.
▸ **ˈfatˌheaded** *adj*

father (ˈfɑːðə) *n* **1** a male parent. **2** a person who founds a line or family; forefather. **3** any male acting in a paternal capacity. **4** (*often cap.*) a respectful term of address for an old man. **5** a male who originates something: *the father of modern psychology.* **6** a leader of an association, council, etc.: *a city father.* **7** *Brit.* the eldest or most senior member in a union, profession, etc. **8** (*often pl*) a senator in ancient Rome. ◆ *vb* (*tr*) **9** to procreate or generate (offspring). **10** to create, found, etc. **11** to act as a father to. **12** to acknowledge oneself as father or originator of. **13** (foll. by *on* or *upon*) to impose or foist upon. ORIG OE *fæder*
▸ **ˈfatherhood** *n* ▸ **ˈfatherless** *adj* ▸ **ˈfather-ˌlike** *adj*

Father (ˈfɑːðə) *n* **1** God, esp. when considered as the first person of the Christian Trinity. **2** any of the early writers on Christian doctrine. **3** a title used for Christian priests.

father confessor *n* **1** *Christianity.* a priest who hears confessions. **2** any person to whom one tells private matters.

father-in-law *n, pl* **fathers-in-law.** the father of one's wife or husband.

fatherland (ˈfɑːðəˌlænd) *n* **1** a person's native country. **2** the country of a person's ancestors.

fatherly (ˈfɑːðəlɪ) *adj* of, resembling, or suitable to a father, esp. in kindliness, encouragement, etc.
▸ **ˈfatherliness** *n*

Father's Day *n* a day observed in honour of fathers; in Britain the third Sunday in June.

fathom (ˈfæðəm) *n* **1** a unit of length equal to six feet (1.829 metres), used to measure depths of water. ◆ *vb* (*tr*) **2** to measure the depth of, esp. with a sounding line. **3** to penetrate (a mystery, problem, etc.). ORIG OE *fæthm*
▸ **ˈfathomable** *adj*

Fathometer (fəˈðɒmɪtə) *n Trademark.* a type of echo sounder used for measuring the depth of water.

fathomless (ˈfæðəmlɪs) *adj* another word for **unfathomable.**
▸ **ˈfathomlessness** *n*

fatigue (fəˈtiːg) *n* **1** physical or mental exhaustion due to exertion. **2** a tiring activity or effort. **3** *Physiol.* the temporary inability of an organ or part to respond to a stimulus because of overactivity. **4** the weakening of a material subjected to alternating stresses, esp. vibrations. **5** the temporary inability to respond to a situation resulting from overexposure to it: *compassion fatigue.* **6** any of the mainly domestic duties performed by military personnel, esp. as a punishment. **7** (*pl*) special clothing worn by military personnel to carry out such duties. ◆ *vb* **fatigues, fatiguing, fatigued. 8** to make or become weary or exhausted. ORIG C17: from F, from *fatiguer* to tire, from L *fatīgāre*
▸ **fatigable** *or* **fatiguable** (ˈfætɪgəbᵊl) *adj*

Fatima ★ (ˈfætɪmə) *n* ?606–632 A.D., daughter of Mohammed; wife of Ali.

Fátima ★ (*Portuguese* ˈfatimə) *n* a village in central Portugal: Roman Catholic shrine and pilgrimage centre.

Fatshan ★ (ˈfɑːtˈʃɑːn) *n* a variant transliteration of the Chinese name for **Foshan.**

fatshedera (fætsˈhɛdərə) *n* a hybrid plant with five-lobed leaves. ORIG from NL, from *Fatsia japonica* + *Hedera hibernica*

fatsia (ˈfætsɪə) *n* an evergreen hardy shrub. Also known as the **false castor-oil plant.** ORIG from NL

fatso (ˈfætsəʊ) *n Sl.* a fat person.

fat-soluble *adj* soluble in substances, such as ether, chloroform, and oils. Fat-soluble compounds are often insoluble in water.

fat stock *n* livestock fattened and ready for market.

fatten (ˈfætᵊn) *vb* **1** to grow or cause to grow fat or fatter. **2** (*tr*) to cause (an animal or fowl) to become fat by feeding it. **3** (*tr*) to make fuller or richer. **4** (*tr*) to enrich (soil).
▸ **ˈfattening** *adj*

fatty (ˈfætɪ) *adj* **fattier, fattiest. 1** containing or derived from fat. **2** greasy; oily. **3** (esp. of tissues, organs, etc.) characterized by the excessive accumulation of fat. ◆ *n, pl* **fatties. 4** *Inf.* a fat person.
▸ **ˈfattily** *adv* ▸ **ˈfattiness** *n*

fatty acid *n* an aliphatic carboxylic acid, esp. one found in lipids, such as palmitic acid, stearic acid, and oleic acid.

fatty degeneration *n Pathol.* the abnormal formation of tiny globules of fat within the cytoplasm of a cell.

fatuity (fəˈtjuːɪtɪ) *n, pl* **fatuities. 1** inanity. **2** a fatuous remark, act, sentiment, etc.
▸ **faˈtuitous** *adj*

fatuous (ˈfætjʊəs) *adj* complacently or inanely foolish. ORIG C17: from L *fatuus;* rel. to *fatiscere* to gape
▸ **ˈfatuously** *adv* ▸ **ˈfatuousness** *n*

fatwa *or* **fatwah** (ˈfætwə) *n* a religious decree issued by a Muslim leader. ORIG Ar.

fauces (ˈfɔːsiːz) *n, pl* **fauces.** *Anat.* the area between the cavity of the mouth and the pharynx. ORIG C16: from L: throat
▸ **faucal** (ˈfɔːkᵊl) *or* **faucial** (ˈfɔːʃəl) *adj*

faucet (ˈfɔːsɪt) *n* **1** a tap fitted to a barrel. **2** the US name for **tap**[2] (sense 1). ORIG C14: from OF from Provençal *falsar* to bore

Faulkner *or* **Falkner** ★ (ˈfɔːknə) *n* **William.** 1897–1962, US writer. His novels include *The Sound and the Fury* (1929), *Light in August* (1932), and *The Reivers* (1962). Nobel prize for literature 1949.

fault (fɔːlt) *n* **1** a failing or defect; flaw. **2** a mistake or error. **3** a misdeed. **4** responsibility for a mistake or misdeed. **5** *Electronics.* a defect in a circuit, component, or line, such as a short circuit. **6** *Geol.* a fracture in the earth's crust resulting in the relative displacement of the rocks on either side of it. **7** *Tennis, squash, etc.* an invalid serve. **8** (in showjumping) a penalty mark given for failing to clear, or refusing, a fence, etc. **9 at fault.** guilty of error; culpable. **10 find fault (with).** to seek out minor imperfections or errors (in). **11 to a fault.** excessively. ◆ *vb* **12** *Geol.* to undergo or cause to undergo a fault. **13** (*tr*) to criticize or blame. **14** (*intr*) to commit a fault. ORIG C13: from OF *faute* ult. from L *fallere* to fail

fault-finding *n* **1** continual criticism. ◆ *adj* **2** given to finding fault.
▸ **ˈfault-ˌfinder** *n*

faultless (ˈfɔːltlɪs) *adj* perfect or blameless.
▸ **ˈfaultlessly** *adv* ▸ **ˈfaultlessness** *n*

faulty (ˈfɔːltɪ) *adj* **faultier, faultiest.** defective or imperfect.
▸ **ˈfaultily** *adv* ▸ **ˈfaultiness** *n*

faun (fɔːn) *n* (in Roman legend) a rural deity represented as a man with a goat's ears, horns, tail, and hind legs. ORIG C14: back formation from *Faunes* (pl), from L *Faunus* deity of forests
▸ **ˈfaunˌlike** *adj*

fauna (ˈfɔːnə) *n, pl* **faunas** *or* **faunae** (-niː). **1** all the animal life of a given place or time. **2** a descriptive list of such

animals. ORIG C18: from NL, from LL *Fauna* a goddess of living things
▸ ˈ**faunal** *adj*

Faunus ★ (ˈfɔːnəs) *n* an ancient Italian deity of pastures and forests, later identified with the Greek Pan.

Fauré ★ (ˈfɔːreɪ; *French* fore) *n* **Gabriel** (**Urbain**) (gabriɛl). 1845–1924, French composer, noted for his song settings, piano music, and *Messe de Requiem* (1887).

Faust (faʊst) *or* **Faustus** ★ (ˈfaʊstəs) *n German legend.* a magician and alchemist who sells his soul to the devil in exchange for knowledge and power.
▸ ˈ**Faustian** *adj*

Fauvism (ˈfəʊvɪzəm) *n* a form of expressionist painting characterized by the use of bright colours and simplified forms. ORIG C20: from F, from *fauve* wild beast
▸ **Fauve** *n, adj* ▸ ˈ**Fauvist** *n, adj*

faux pas (fəʊ pɑː) *n, pl* **faux pas** (fəʊ pɑːz). a social blunder. ORIG C17: from F: false step

fave (feɪv) *adj, n Inf.* short for **favourite** (senses 1, 2).

favour *or US* **favor** (ˈfeɪvə) *n* **1** an approving attitude; goodwill. **2** an act performed out of goodwill or mercy. **3** prejudice and partiality. **4** a condition of being regarded with approval (esp. in **in favour, out of favour**). **5** a token of love, goodwill, etc. **6** a small gift or toy given to a guest at a party. **7** *History.* a badge or ribbon worn or given to indicate loyalty. **8 find favour with.** to be approved of by someone. **9 in favour of. 9a** approving. **9b** to the benefit of. **9c** (of a cheque, etc.) made out to. **9d** in order to show preference for. ◆ *vb* (*tr*) **10** to regard with especial kindness. **11** to treat with partiality. **12** to support; advocate. **13** to oblige. **14** to help; facilitate. **15** *Inf.* to resemble: *he favours his father.* **16** to wear habitually: *she favours red.* **17** to treat gingerly: *a footballer favouring an injured leg.* ORIG C14: from L, from *favēre* to protect
▸ ˈ**favourer** *or US* ˈ**favorer** *n*

favourable *or US* **favorable** (ˈfeɪvərəbᵊl) *adj* **1** advantageous, encouraging or promising. **2** giving consent.
▸ ˈ**favourably** *or US* ˈ**favorably** *adv*

-favoured *adj* (*in combination*) having an appearance (as specified): *ill-favoured.*

favourite *or US* **favorite** (ˈfeɪvərɪt) *adj* **1** (*prenominal*) most liked. ◆ *n* **2** a person or thing regarded with especial preference or liking. **3** *Sport.* a competitor thought likely to win. ORIG C16: from It., from *favorire* to favour, from L *favēre*

favouritism *or US* **favoritism** (ˈfeɪvərɪˌtɪzəm) *n* the practice of giving special treatment to a person or group.

Fawcett ★ (ˈfɔːsɪt) *n* Dame **Millicent Garrett.** 1847–1929, British suffragette.

Fawkes ★ (fɔːks) *n* **Guy.** 1570–1606, English conspirator, executed for his part in the Gunpowder Plot to blow up King James I and the Houses of Parliament (1605). Effigies of him (guys) are burnt in Britain on Guy Fawkes Day (Nov. 5).

fawn[1] (fɔːn) *n* **1** a young deer of either sex aged under one year. **2a** a light greyish-brown colour. **2b** (*as adj*): *a fawn raincoat.* ◆ *vb* **3** (of deer) to bear (young). ORIG C14: from OF, from L *fētus* offspring; see FETUS
▸ ˈ**fawn**ˌ**like** *adj*

fawn[2] (fɔːn) *vb* (*intr;* often foll. by *on* or *upon*) **1** to seek attention and admiration (from) by cringing and flattering. **2** (of animals, esp. dogs) to try to please by a show of extreme friendliness. ORIG OE *fægnian* to be glad, from *fægen* glad; see FAIN
▸ ˈ**fawner** *n* ▸ ˈ**fawning** *adj*

fax (fæks) *n* **1** short for **facsimile transmission. 2** a message or document sent by facsimile transmission. **3** Also called: **fax machine, facsimile machine.** a machine which transmits and receives exact copies of documents. ◆ *vb* **4** (*tr*) to send (a message or document) by facsimile transmission.

fay (feɪ) *n* a fairy or sprite. ORIG C14: from OF *feie,* ult. from L *fātum* FATE

Fayal ★ (*Portuguese* fəˈial) *n* a variant spelling of **Faial.**

Fayum ★ (faɪˈjuːm) *n* See **El Faiyûm.**

faze (feɪz) *vb* **fazes, fazing, fazed.** (*tr*) *Inf.* to disconcert; worry; disturb. ORIG C19: var. of arch. *feeze* to beat off

FBA *abbrev. for* Fellow of the British Academy.

FBI (in the US) *abbrev. for* Federal Bureau of Investigation; an agency responsible for investigating violations of Federal laws.

FC (in Britain) *abbrev. for:* **1** Football Club. **2** Free Church.

fcap *abbrev. for* foolscap.

F clef *n* another name for **bass clef.**

FD *abbrev. for* Fidei Defensor. ORIG L: Defender of the Faith

FDR *abbrev. for* Franklin Delano Roosevelt.

Fe *the chemical symbol for* iron. ORIG from NL *ferrum*

fealty (ˈfiːəltɪ) *n, pl* **fealties.** (in feudal society) the loyalty sworn to one's lord on becoming his vassal. ORIG C14: from OF, from L *fidēlitās* FIDELITY

fear (fɪə) *n* **1** a feeling of distress, apprehension, or alarm caused by impending danger, pain, etc. **2** a cause of this feeling. **3** awe; reverence: *fear of God.* **4** concern; anxiety. **5** possibility; chance. **6 for fear of, that** *or* **lest.** to forestall or avoid. **7 no fear.** certainly not. ◆ *vb* **8** to be afraid (to do something) or of (a person or thing). **9** (*tr*) to revere; respect. **10** (*tr; takes a clause as object*) to be sorry: *I fear that you have not won.* **11** (*intr;* foll. by *for*) to feel anxiety about something. ORIG OE *fǣr*
▸ ˈ**fearless** *adj* ▸ ˈ**fearlessly** *adv* ▸ ˈ**fearlessness** *n*

fearful (ˈfɪəfʊl) *adj* **1** afraid. **2** causing fear. **3** *Inf.* very unpleasant: *a fearful cold.*
▸ ˈ**fearfully** *adv* ▸ ˈ**fearfulness** *n*

fearsome (ˈfɪəsəm) *adj* **1** frightening. **2** timorous; afraid.
▸ ˈ**fearsomely** *adv*

feasibility study *n* a study designed to determine the practicability of a system or plan.

feasible (ˈfiːzəbᵊl) *adj* **1** able to be done or put into effect; possible. **2** likely; probable. ORIG C15: from Anglo-F *faisable,* from *faire* to do, from L *facere*
▸ ˌ**feasi**ˈ**bility** *n* ▸ ˈ**feasibly** *adv*

feast (fiːst) *n* **1** a large and sumptuous meal. **2** a periodic religious celebration. **3** something extremely pleasing: *a feast for the eyes.* **4 movable feast.** a festival of variable date. ◆ *vb* **5** (*intr*) **5a** to eat a feast. **5b** (usually foll. by *on*) to enjoy the eating (of): *to feast on cakes.* **6** (*tr*) to give a feast to. **7** (*intr;* foll. by *on*) to take great delight (in): *to feast on beautiful paintings.* **8** (*tr*) to regale or delight: *to feast one's eyes.* ORIG C13: from OF, from L *festa,* neuter pl (later assumed to be fem sing) of *festus* joyful; rel. to L *fānum* temple, *fēriae* festivals
▸ ˈ**feaster** *n*

Feast of Dedication *n* a literal translation of **Chanukah.**

Feast of Lights *n* an English name for **Chanukah.**

Feast of Tabernacles *n* a literal translation of **Sukkoth.**

Feast of Weeks *n* a literal translation of **Shavuot.**

feat (fiːt) *n* a remarkable, skilful, or daring action. ORIG C14: from Anglo-F *fait,* from L *factum* deed; see FACT

feather (ˈfɛðə) *n* **1** any of the flat light waterproof structures forming the plumage of birds, each consisting of a hollow shaft having a vane of barbs on either side. **2** something resembling a feather, such as a tuft of hair or grass. **3** *Archery.* **3a** a bird's feather or artificial substitute fitted to an arrow to direct its flight. **3b** the feathered end of an arrow. **4** *Rowing.* the position of an oar turned parallel to the water between strokes. **5** condition of spirits; fettle: *in fine feather.* **6** something of negligible value: *I don't care a feather.* **7 feather in one's cap.** a cause for pleasure at one's achievements. ◆ *vb* **8** (*tr*) to fit, cover, or supply with feathers. **9** *Rowing.* to turn (an oar) parallel to the water during recovery between strokes, in order to lessen wind resistance. **10** to change the pitch of (an aircraft propeller) so that the chord lines of the blades are in line with the airflow. **11** (*intr*) (of a bird) to grow feathers. **12 feather one's nest.** to provide oneself with comforts. ORIG OE *fether*
▸ ˈ**feathering** *n* ▸ ˈ**feather-**ˌ**like** *adj* ▸ ˈ**feathery** *adj*

feather bed *n* **1** a mattress filled with feathers or down. ◆ *vb* **featherbed, featherbeds, featherbedding, featherbedded. 2** (*tr*) to pamper; spoil.

featherbedding ('fɛðəˌbɛdɪŋ) *n* the practice of limiting production or of overmanning in order to prevent redundancies or create jobs.

featherbrain ('fɛðəˌbreɪn) *or* **featherhead** *n* a frivolous or forgetful person.
▸ **'featherˌbrained** *or* **'featherˌheaded** *adj*

featheredge ('fɛðərˌɛdʒ) *n* a board or plank that tapers to a thin edge at one side.

featherstitch ('fɛðəˌstɪtʃ) *n* **1** a zigzag embroidery stitch. ◆ *vb* **2** to decorate (cloth) with featherstitch.

featherweight ('fɛðəˌweɪt) *n* **1a** something very light or of little importance. **1b** (*as modifier*): *featherweight considerations.* **2a** a professional boxer weighing 118–126 pounds (53.5–57 kg). **2b** an amateur boxer weighing 54–57 kg (119–126 pounds). **3** an amateur wrestler weighing usually 127–137 pounds (58–62 kg).

feature ('fiːtʃə) *n* **1** any one of the parts of the face, such as the nose, chin, or mouth. **2** a prominent or distinctive part, as of a landscape, book, etc. **3** the principal film in a programme at a cinema. **4** an item or article appearing regularly in a newspaper, magazine, etc.: *a gardening feature.* **5** Also called: **feature story.** a prominent story in a newspaper, etc.: *a feature on prison reform.* **6** a programme given special prominence on radio or television. **7** *Arch.* general form. ◆ *vb* **features, featuring, featured. 8** (*tr*) to have as a feature or make a feature of. **9** to give prominence to (an actor, famous event, etc.) in a film or (of an actor, etc.) to have prominence in a film. **10** (*tr*) *Arch.* to draw the main features or parts of. ORIG C14: from Anglo-F *feture,* from L *factūra* a making, from *facere* to make
▸ **'featureless** *adj*

-featured *adj* (*in combination*) having features as specified: *heavy-featured.*

Feb. *abbrev. for* February.

febri- *combining form.* indicating fever: *febrifuge.* ORIG from L *febris* fever

febrifuge ('fɛbrɪˌfjuːdʒ) *n* **1** any drug or agent for reducing fever. ◆ *adj* **2** serving to reduce fever. ORIG C17: from Med. L *febrifugia* feverfew; see FEBRI-, -FUGE
▸ **febrifugal** (fɪ'brɪfjʊgᵊl) *adj*

febrile ('fiːbraɪl) *adj* of or relating to fever; feverish. ORIG C17: from Medical L *febrīlis,* from L *febris* fever
▸ **febrility** (fɪ'brɪlɪtɪ) *n*

February ('fɛbrʊərɪ) *n, pl* **Februaries.** the second month of the year, consisting of 28 or (in a leap year) 29 days. ORIG C13: from L *Februārius mēnsis* month of expiation, from *februa* Roman festival of purification held on February 15, from pl of *februum* a purgation

feces ('fiːsiːz) *pl n* the usual US spelling of **faeces.**
▸ **fecal** ('fiːkᵊl) *adj*

Fechner ★ (*German* 'fɛçnər) *n* **Gustav Theodor** ('gustaf 'teːodoːər). 1801–87, German physicist, philosopher, and psychologist, noted particularly for his work on psychophysics, *Elemente der Psychophysik* (1860).

feckless ('fɛklɪs) *adj* feeble; weak; ineffectual. ORIG C16: from obs. *feck* value, effect + -LESS
▸ **'fecklessly** *adv* ▸ **'fecklessness** *n*

feculent ('fɛkjʊlənt) *adj* **1** filthy or foul. **2** of or containing waste matter. ORIG C15: from L *faeculentus;* see FAECES
▸ **'feculence** *n*

fecund ('fiːkənd, 'fɛk-) *adj* **1** fertile. **2** intellectually productive. ORIG C14: from L *fēcundus*
▸ **fecundity** (fɪ'kʌndɪtɪ) *n*

fecundate ('fiːkənˌdeɪt, 'fɛk-) *vb* **fecundates, fecundating, fecundated.** (*tr*) **1** to make fruitful. **2** to fertilize. ORIG C17: from L *fēcundāre* to fertilize
▸ **ˌfecun'dation** *n*

fed[1] (fɛd) *vb* **1** the past tense and past participle of **feed. 2 fed to death** *or* **fed (up) to the (back) teeth.** *Inf.* bored or annoyed.

fed[2] (fɛd) *n US sl.* an agent of the FBI.

Fed (fɛd) *n* short for **Federal Reserve System.**

Fed. *or* **fed.** *abbrev. for:* **1** Federal. **2** Federation. **3** Federated.

fedayee (fə'dɑːjiː) *n, pl* **fedayeen** (-jiːn). **a** (*sometimes cap.*) (in Arab states) a commando, esp. one fighting against Israel. **b** (esp. in Iran and Afghanistan) a member of a guerrilla organization. ORIG from Ar. *fidā'i* one who risks his life in a cause, from *fidā'* redemption

federal ('fɛdərəl) *adj* **1** of or relating to a form of government or a country in which power is divided between one central and several regional governments. **2** of or relating to the central government of a federation. ORIG C17: from L *foedus* league
▸ **'federaˌlism** *n* ▸ **'federalist** *n, adj* ▸ **'federally** *adv*

Federal ('fɛdərəl) *adj* **1** characteristic of or supporting the Union government during the American Civil War. ◆ *n* **2** a supporter of the Union government during the American Civil War.

Federal Government *n* the national government of a federated state, such as the Canadian national government located in Ottawa.

federalize *or* **federalise** ('fɛdərəˌlaɪz) *vb* **federalizes, federalizing, federalized** *or* **federalises, federalising, federalised.** (*tr*) **1** to unite in a federal union. **2** to subject to federal control.
▸ **ˌfederali'zation** *or* **ˌfederali'sation** *n*

Federal Republic of Germany ★ *n* the official name of **Germany,** formerly of West Germany.

Federal Reserve System *n* (in the US) a banking system consisting of twelve **Federal Reserve Banks** and their member banks. It performs functions similar to those of the Bank of England.

federate *vb* ('fɛdəˌreɪt), **federates, federating, federated. 1** to unite or cause to unite in a federal union. ◆ *adj* ('fɛdərɪt). **2** federal; federated.
▸ **'federative** *adj*

Federated Malay States ★ *pl n* See **Malay States.**

federation (ˌfɛdə'reɪʃən) *n* **1** the act of federating. **2** the union of several provinces, states, etc., to form a federal union. **3** a political unit formed in such a way. **4** any league, alliance, or confederacy.

Federation of Rhodesia and Nyasaland ★ *n* a federation (1953–63) of Northern Rhodesia, Southern Rhodesia, and Nyasaland.

fedora (fɪ'dɔːrə) *n* a soft felt brimmed hat, usually with a band. ORIG C19: allegedly after *Fédora* (1882), play by Victorien Sardou (1831–1908)

fed up *adj* (*usually postpositive*) *Inf.* annoyed or bored: *I'm fed up with your conduct.*

fee (fiː) *n* **1** a payment asked by professional people or public servants for their services: *school fees.* **2** a charge made for a privilege: *an entrance fee.* **3** *Property law.* an interest in land capable of being inherited. The interest can be with unrestricted rights of disposal (**fee simple**) or with restricted rights to one class of heirs (**fee tail**). **4** (in feudal Europe) the land granted by a lord to his vassal. **5 in fee.** *Law.* (of land) in absolute ownership. ◆ *vb* **fees, feeing, feed. 6** *Rare.* to give a fee to. **7** *Chiefly Scot.* to hire for a fee. ORIG C14: from OF *fie,* of Gmc origin; see FIEF

feeble ('fiːbᵊl) *adj* **1** lacking in physical or mental strength. **2** unconvincing: *feeble excuses.* **3** easily influenced. ORIG C12: from OF *feble, fleible,* from L *flēbilis* to be lamented, from *flēre* to weep
▸ **'feebleness** *n* ▸ **'feebly** *adv*

feeble-minded *adj* **1** lacking in intelligence. **2** mentally defective.

feed (fiːd) *vb* **feeds, feeding, fed.** (*mainly tr*) **1** to give food to: *to feed the cat.* **2** to give as food: *to feed meat to the cat.* **3** (*intr*) to eat food: *the horses feed at noon.* **4** to provide food for. **5** to gratify; satisfy. **6** (*also intr*) to supply (a machine, furnace, etc.) with (the necessary materials or fuel) for its operation, or (of such materials) to flow or move forwards into a machine, etc. **7** *Theatre, inf.* to cue (an actor, esp. a comedian) with lines. **8** *Sport.* to pass a ball to (a team-mate). **9** (*also intr; foll. by on or upon*) to eat or cause to eat. ◆ *n* **10** the act or an instance of feeding. **11** food, esp. that of animals or babies. **12** the process of supplying a machine or furnace with a material or fuel. **13** the quantity of material or fuel so supplied. **14** *Theatre, inf.* a performer, esp. a straight man, who provides cues. **15** *Inf.* a meal. ORIG OE *fēdan*
▸ **'feedable** *adj*

feedback ('fiːd,bæk) *n* **1** information or an opinion in response to an inquiry, proposal, etc. **2a** the return of part of the output of an electronic circuit, device, or mechanical system to its input. In **negative feedback** a rise in output energy reduces the input energy; in **positive feedback** an increase in output energy reinforces the input energy. **2b** that part of the output signal fed back into the input. **3** the return of part of the sound output of a loudspeaker to the microphone or pick-up, so that a high-pitched whistle is produced. **4** the whistling noise so produced. **5** the effect of a product or action in a cyclic biological reaction on another stage in the same reaction.

feeder ('fiːdə) *n* **1** a person or thing that feeds or is fed. **2** a child's feeding bottle or bib. **3** a person or device that feeds the working material into a system or machine. **4** a tributary channel. **5** a road, service, etc., that links secondary areas to the main traffic network. **6** a power line for transmitting electrical power from a generating station to a distribution network.

feeding bottle *n* a bottle fitted with a rubber teat from which infants suck liquids.

feel (fiːl) *vb* **feels, feeling, felt. 1** to perceive (something) by touching. **2** to have a physical or emotional sensation of (something): *to feel anger.* **3** (*tr*) to examine (something) by touch. **4** (*tr*) to find (one's way) by testing or cautious exploration. **5** (*copula*) to seem in respect of the sensation given: *it feels warm.* **6** to sense (esp. in **feel (it) in one's bones**). **7** to consider; believe; think. **8** (*intr;* foll. by *for*) to show sympathy or compassion (towards): *I feel for you in your sorrow.* **9** (*tr;* often foll. by *up*) *Sl.* to pass one's hands over the sexual organs of. **10 feel like.** to have an inclination (for something or doing something): *I don't feel like going to the pictures.* **11 feel up to.** (*usually used with a negative or in a question*) to be fit enough for (something or doing something): *I don't feel up to going out.* ◆ *n* **12** the act or an instance of feeling. **13** the quality of or an impression from something perceived through feeling: *a homely feel.* **14** the sense of touch. **15** an instinctive aptitude; knack: *she's got a feel for this sort of work.* ORIG OE *fēlan*

feeler ('fiːlə) *n* **1** a person or thing that feels. **2** an organ in certain animals, such as an antenna, that is sensitive to touch. **3** a remark designed to probe the reactions or intentions of others.

feeler gauge *n* a thin metal strip of known thickness used to measure a narrow gap or to set a gap between two parts.

feel-good *adj* causing or characterized by a feeling of self-satisfaction: *feel-good factor.*

feeling ('fiːlɪŋ) *n* **1** the sense of touch. **2a** the ability to experience physical sensations, such as heat, etc. **2b** the sensation so experienced. **3** a state of mind. **4** a physical or mental impression: *a feeling of warmth.* **5** fondness; sympathy: *to have a great deal of feeling for someone.* **6** a sentiment: *a feeling that the project is feasible.* **7** an emotional disturbance, esp. anger or dislike: *a lot of bad feeling.* **8** intuitive appreciation and understanding: *a feeling for words.* **9** sensibility in the performance of something. **10** (*pl*) emotional or moral sensitivity (esp. in **hurt** *or* **injure the feelings of**). **11 have feelings for.** to be emotionally or sexually attracted to. ◆ *adj* **12** sentient; sensitive. **13** expressing or containing emotion.
▸ **'feelingly** *adv*

feet (fiːt) *n* **1** the plural of **foot. 2 at (someone's) feet.** as someone's disciple. **3 be run** *or* **rushed off one's feet.** to be very busy. **4 carry** *or* **sweep off one's feet.** to fill with enthusiasm. **5 feet of clay.** a weakness that is not widely known. **6 have** (*or* **keep**) **one's feet on the ground.** to be practical and reliable. **7 on one's** *or* **its feet. 7a** standing up. **7b** in good health. **8 stand on one's own feet.** to be independent.

feign (feɪn) *vb* **1** to pretend: *to feign innocence.* **2** (*tr*) to invent: *to feign an excuse.* **3** (*tr*) to copy; imitate. ORIG C13: from OF, from L *fingere* to form, shape, invent
▸ **'feigningly** *adv*

feijoa (fiː'dʒəʊə) *n* **1** an evergreen shrub of South America. **2** the fruit of this shrub. ORIG C19: NL, after J. da Silva *Feijo,* 19th-cent. Sp. botanist

Feininger ★ ('faɪnɪŋə) *n* **Lyonel.** 1871–1956, US artist, who worked at the Bauhaus, noted for his use of superimposed translucent planes of colour.

feint[1] (feɪnt) *n* **1** a mock attack or movement designed to distract an adversary, as in boxing, fencing, etc. **2** a misleading action or appearance. ◆ *vb* **3** (*intr*) to make a feint. ORIG C17: from F, from OF *feindre* to FEIGN

feint[2] (feɪnt) *n Printing.* a narrow rule used in the production of ruled paper. ORIG C19: var. of FAINT

Feisal ★ ('faɪsᵊl) *n* a variant spelling of **Faisal.**

feisty ('faɪstɪ) *adj* **feistier, feistiest.** *Inf.* **1** lively, resilient, and self-reliant. **2** *US & Canad.* frisky. **3** *US & Canad.* irritable. ORIG C19: dialect *feist, fist* small dog

felafel (fə'lɑːfəl) *n* a variant spelling of **falafel.**

feldspar ('fɛld,spɑː, 'fɛl,spɑː) *or* **felspar** *n* any of a group of hard rock-forming minerals consisting of aluminium silicates of potassium, sodium, calcium, or barium: the principal constituents of igneous rocks. ORIG C18: from G, from *Feld* field + *Spat(h)* SPAR[3]
▸ **feldspathic** (fɛld'spæθɪk, fɛl'spæθ-) *or* **fel'spathic** *adj*

felicitate (fɪ'lɪsɪ,teɪt) *vb* **felicitates, felicitating, felicitated.** to congratulate.
▸ **fe,lici'tation** *n* ▸ **fe'lici,tator** *n*

felicitous (fɪ'lɪsɪtəs) *adj* **1** well-chosen; apt. **2** possessing an agreeable style. **3** marked by happiness.
▸ **fe'licitously** *adv*

felicity (fɪ'lɪsɪtɪ) *n, pl* **felicities. 1** happiness. **2** a cause of happiness. **3** an appropriate expression or style. **4** the display of such expressions or style. ORIG C14: from L *fēlīcitās* happiness, from *fēlix* happy

feline ('fiːlaɪn) *adj* **1** of, relating to, or belonging to a family of predatory mammals, including cats, lions, leopards, and cheetahs, having a round head and retractile claws. **2** resembling or suggestive of a cat, esp. in stealth or grace. ◆ *n* **3** any member of the cat family; a cat. ORIG C17: from L, from *fēlēs* cat
▸ **'felinely** *adv* ▸ **felinity** (fɪ'lɪnɪtɪ) *n*

Felixstowe ★ ('fiːlɪk,stəʊ) *n* a port and resort in E England, in Suffolk: ferry connections to Rotterdam and Zeebrugge. Pop.: 28 606 (1991).

fell[1] (fɛl) *vb* the past tense of **fall.**

fell[2] (fɛl) *vb* (*tr*) **1** to cut or knock down: *to fell a tree.* **2** *Needlework.* to fold under and sew flat (the edges of a seam). ◆ *n* **3** *US & Canad.* the timber felled in one season. **4** a seam finished by felling. ORIG OE *fellan;* cf. FALL
▸ **'feller** *n*

fell[3] (fɛl) *adj* **1** *Arch.* cruel or fierce. **2** *Arch.* destructive or deadly. **3 one fell swoop.** a single hasty action or occurrence. ORIG C13 *fel,* from OF: cruel, from Med. L *fellō* villain; see FELON[1]

fell[4] (fɛl) *n* an animal skin or hide. ORIG OE

fell[5] (fɛl) *n* (*often pl*) *Scot. & N English.* **a** a mountain, hill, or moor. **b** (*in combination*): *fell-walking.* ORIG C13: from ON *fjall;* rel. to OHG *felis* rock

fellah ('fɛlə) *n, pl* **fellahs, fellahin,** *or* **fellaheen** (,fɛlə'hiːn). a peasant in Arab countries. ORIG C18: from Ar., dialect var. of *fallāh,* from *falaha* to cultivate

fellatio (fɪ'leɪʃɪəʊ) *n* a sexual activity in which the penis is stimulated by the mouth. ORIG C19: NL, from L *fellāre* to suck

Felling ★ ('fɛlɪŋ) *n* a town in NE England, in Gateshead unitary authority, Tyne and Wear; formerly noted for coal mining. Pop.: 35 053 (1991).

Fellini ★ (fə'liːnɪ; *Italian* fel'liːni) *n* **Federico** (fede'riːko). 1920–93, Italian film director. His films include *La Dolce Vita* (1959), *Satyricon* (1969), and *Intervista* (1987).

felloe ('fɛləʊ) *or* **felly** ('fɛlɪ) *n, pl* **felloes** *or* **fellies.** a segment or the whole rim of a wooden wheel to which the spokes are attached. ORIG OE *felge*

fellow ('fɛləʊ) *n* **1** a man or boy. **2** an informal word for **boyfriend. 3** *Inf.* one or oneself: *a fellow has to eat.* **4** a person considered to be of little worth. **5a** (*often pl*) a companion; associate. **5b** (*as modifier*): *fellow travellers.* **6** a member of the governing body at any of various universities or colleges. **7** a postgraduate student employed, esp. for a fixed period, to undertake research. **8a** a person in the same group, class, or condition: *the surgeon asked* *his fellows.* **8b** (*as modifier*): *a fellow sufferer.* **9** one of a pair; counterpart; mate. ORIG OE *fēolaga*

Fellow ('fɛləʊ) *n* a member of any of various learned societies: *Fellow of the British Academy.*

fellow feeling *n* **1** mutual sympathy or friendship. **2** an opinion held in common.

fellowship ('fɛləʊˌʃɪp) *n* **1** the state of sharing mutual interests, activities, etc. **2** a society of people sharing mutual interests, activities, etc. **3** companionship; friendship. **4** the state or relationship of being a fellow. **5** *Education.* **5a** a financed research post providing study facilities, privileges, etc., often in return for teaching services. **5b** an honorary title carrying certain privileges awarded to a postgraduate student.

fellow traveller *n* **1** a companion on a journey. **2** a non-Communist who sympathizes with Communism.

felon[1] ('fɛlən) *n* **1** *Criminal law.* (formerly) a person who has committed a felony. ◆ *adj* **2** *Arch.* evil. ORIG C13: from OF: villain, from Med. L *fellō,* from ?

felon[2] ('fɛlən) *n* a purulent inflammation of the end joint of a finger. ORIG C12: from Med. L *fellō,* ?from L *fel* poison

felonious (fɪ'ləʊnɪəs) *adj* **1** *Criminal law.* of, involving, or constituting a felony. **2** *Obs.* wicked.
▸ **fe'loniously** *adv* ▸ **fe'loniousness** *n*

felony ('fɛlənɪ) *n, pl* **felonies.** *Criminal law.* (formerly) a serious crime, such as murder or arson.

felspar ('fɛlˌspɑː) *n* a variant spelling (esp. Brit.) of **feldspar.**
▸ **felspathic** (fɛl'spæθɪk) *adj*

felt[1] (fɛlt) *vb* the past tense and past participle of **feel.**

felt[2] (fɛlt) *n* **1** a matted fabric of wool, hair, etc., made by working the fibres together under pressure or by heat or chemical action. **2** any material, such as asbestos, made by a similar process of matting. ◆ *vb* **3** (*tr*) to make into or cover with felt. **4** (*intr*) to become matted. ORIG OE

felt-tip pen *n* a pen whose writing point is made from pressed fibres. Also called: **fibre-tip pen.**

felucca (fɛ'lʌkə) *n* a narrow lateen-rigged vessel of the Mediterranean. ORIG C17: from It., prob. from obs. Sp. *faluca,* prob. from Ar. *fulūk* ships, from Gk, from *ephelkein* to tow

fem. *abbrev. for:* **1** female. **2** feminine.

female ('fiːmeɪl) *adj* **1** of, relating to, or designating the sex producing gametes (ova) that can be fertilized by male gametes (spermatozoa). **2** of or characteristic of a woman. **3** for or composed of women or girls: *a female choir.* **4** (of reproductive organs such as the ovary and carpel) capable of producing female gametes. **5** (of flowers) lacking, or having nonfunctional, stamens. **6** having an internal cavity into which a projecting male counterpart can be fitted: *a female thread.* ◆ *n* **7** a female animal or plant. ORIG C14: from earlier *femelle* (infl. by *male*), from L *fēmella* a young woman, from *fēmina* a woman
▸ **'femaleness** *n*

female impersonator *n* a male theatrical performer who acts as a woman.

feminine ('fɛmɪnɪn) *adj* **1** suitable to or characteristic of a woman. **2** possessing qualities or characteristics considered typical of or appropriate to a woman. **3** effeminate; womanish. **4** *Grammar.* **4a** denoting or belonging to a gender of nouns that includes all kinds of referents as well as some female animate referents. **4b** (*as n*): *German* Zeit *"time" and* Ehe *"marriage" are feminines.* ORIG C14: from L, from *fēmina* woman
▸ **'femininely** *adv* ▸ **ˌfemi'ninity** *or* **'feminineness** *n*

feminism ('fɛmɪˌnɪzəm) *n* a doctrine or movement that advocates equal rights for women.
▸ **'feminist** *n, adj*

feminize *or* **feminise** ('fɛmɪˌnaɪz) *vb* **feminizes, feminizing, feminized** *or* **feminises, feminising, feminised. 1** to make or become feminine. **2** to cause (a male animal) to develop female characteristics.
▸ **ˌfemini'zation** *or* **ˌfemini'sation** *n*

femme fatale *French.* (fam fatal) *n, pl* ***femmes fatales*** (fam fatal). an alluring or seductive woman, esp. one who causes men to love her to their own distress. ORIG fatal woman

femto- *prefix* denoting 10^{-15}: *femtometer.* Symbol: f ORIG from Danish or Norwegian *femten* fifteen

femur ('fiːmə) *n, pl* **femurs** *or* **femora** ('fɛmərə). **1** the longest thickest bone of the human skeleton, with the pelvis above and the knee below. Nontechnical name: **thighbone. 2** the corresponding bone in other vertebrates or the corresponding segment of an insect's leg. ORIG C18: from L: thigh
▸ **'femoral** *adj*

fen (fɛn) *n* low-lying flat land that is marshy or artificially drained. ORIG OE *fenn*
▸ **'fenny** *adj*

fence (fɛns) *n* **1** a structure that serves to enclose an area such as a garden or field, usually made of posts of timber, concrete, or metal connected by wire netting, rails, or boards. **2** *Sl.* a dealer in stolen property. **3** an obstacle for a horse to jump in steeplechasing or showjumping. **4** *Machinery.* a guard or guide, esp. in a circular saw or plane. **5** (**sit**) **on the fence.** (to be) unable or unwilling to commit oneself. ◆ *vb* **fences, fencing, fenced. 6** (*tr*) to construct a fence on or around (a piece of land, etc.). **7** (*tr;* foll. by *in* or *off*) to close (in) or separate (off) with or as if with a fence: *he fenced in the livestock.* **8** (*intr*) to fight using swords or foils. **9** (*intr*) to evade a question or argument. **10** (*intr*) *Sl.* to receive stolen property. ORIG C14 *fens,* shortened from *defens* DEFENCE
▸ **'fenceless** *adj* ▸ **'fencer** *n*

fencible ('fɛnsəbᵊl) *n* (formerly) a person who undertook military service in immediate defence of his homeland only.

fencing ('fɛnsɪŋ) *n* **1** the practice, art, or sport of fighting with foils, épées, sabres, etc. **2a** wire, stakes, etc., used as fences. **2b** fences collectively.

fend (fɛnd) *vb* **1** (*intr;* foll. by *for*) to give support (to someone, esp. oneself). **2** (*tr;* usually foll. by *off*) to ward off or turn aside (blows, questions, etc.). ◆ *n* **3** *Scot. & N English dialect.* a shift or effort. ORIG C13 *fenden,* shortened from *defenden* to DEFEND

fender ('fɛndə) *n* **1** a low metal frame which confines falling coals to the hearth. **2** *Chiefly US.* a metal frame fitted to the front of locomotives to absorb shock, etc. **3** a cushion-like device, such as a car tyre hung over the side of a vessel to reduce damage resulting from collision. **4** the US and Canad. name for the wing of a car.

Fénelon ★ (*French* fenlɔ̃) *n* **François de Salignac de La Mothe** (frɑ̃swa də saliɲak də la mɔt). 1651–1715, French theologian, author of *Maximes des saints* (1697) and *Les aventures de Télémaque* (1699), criticizing the government of Louis XIV.

fenestra (fɪ'nɛstrə) *n, pl* **fenestrae** (-triː). **1** *Biol.* a small opening, esp. either of two openings between the middle and inner ears. **2** *Zool.* a transparent marking or spot, as on the wings of moths. **3** *Archit.* a window or window-like opening in the outside wall of a building. ORIG C19: via NL from L: wall opening, window

fenestrated (fɪ'nɛstreɪtɪd, 'fɛnɪˌstreɪtɪd) *or* **fenestrate** *adj* **1** *Archit.* having windows. **2** *Biol.* perforated or having fenestrae.

fenestration (ˌfɛnɪ'streɪʃən) *n* **1** the arrangement of windows in a building. **2** an operation to restore hearing by making an artificial opening into the labyrinth of the ear.

feng shui ('fʌŋ 'ʃweɪ) *n* the Chinese art of determining the most propitious design and placement of a grave, building, room, etc., so that the maximum harmony is achieved between the flow of chi of the environment and that of the user, believed to bring good fortune. ORIG C20: from Chinese *feng* wind + *shui* water

Fenian ('fiːnɪən, 'fiːnjən) *n* **1** (formerly) a member of an Irish revolutionary organization founded in the US in the 19th century to fight for an independent Ireland. ◆ *adj* **2** of or relating to the Fenians. ORIG C19: from Irish Gaelic *fēinne,* after *Fiann* Irish folk hero
▸ **'Fenianism** *n*

fennec ('fɛnɛk) *n* a very small nocturnal fox inhabiting

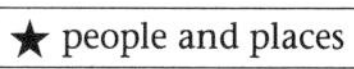

deserts of N Africa and Arabia, having enormous ears. ORIG C18: from Ar. *fenek* fox

fennel ('fɛnᵊl) *n* a strong-smelling yellow-flowered umbelliferous plant whose seeds, feathery leaves, and bulbous aniseed-flavoured root are used in cookery. ORIG OE *fenol*

Fenrir ('fɛnrɪə), **Fenris** ('fɛnrɪs), *or* **Fenriswolf** ★ ('fɛnrɪs,wʊlf) *n Norse myth.* an enormous wolf, fathered by Loki, which killed Odin.

Fens ★ (fɛnz) *pl n* **the.** a flat low-lying area of E England, west and south of the Wash: consisted of marshes until reclaimed in the 17th to 19th centuries.

Fenton ★ ('fɛntᵊn) *n* **James** (**Martin**). born 1949, British poet and journalist. His poetry includes the collections *A German Requiem* (1980) and *Out of Danger* (1993).

fenugreek ('fɛnjʊ,gri:k) *n* an annual heavily scented Mediterranean leguminous plant with hairy stems and white flowers. ORIG OE *fēnogrēcum*

feoff (fi:f) *History.* ◆ *n* **1** a variant spelling of **fief.** ◆ *vb* **2** (*tr*) to invest with a benefice or fief. ORIG C13: from Anglo-F: a FIEF
▸ **'feoffee** *n* ▸ **'feoffment** *n* ▸ **'feoffor** *or* **'feoffer** *n*

-fer *n combining form.* indicating a person or thing that bears something specified: *crucifer; conifer.* ORIG from L, from *ferre* to bear

feral ('fɪərəl) *adj* **1** (of animals and plants) existing in a wild or uncultivated state. **2** savage; brutal. ORIG C17: from Med. L, from L, from *ferus* savage

fer-de-lance (,fɛədə'lɑ:ns) *n* a large highly venomous tropical American snake with a greyish-brown mottled coloration. ORIG C19: from F, lit.: iron (head) of a lance

Ferdinand ★ ('fɜ:dɪ,nænd; *German* 'fɛrdinant) *n* See **Franz Ferdinand.**

Ferdinand I ★ ('fɜ:dɪ,nænd) *n* **1** known as *Ferdinand the Great.* ?1016–65, king of Castile (1035–65) and León (1037–65): achieved control of the Moorish kings of Saragossa, Seville, and Toledo. **2** 1503–64, king of Hungary and Bohemia (1526–64); Holy Roman Emperor (1558–64), bringing years of religious warfare to an end. **3** 1751–1825, king of the Two Sicilies (1816–25); king of Naples (1759–1806; 1815–25), as Ferdinand IV, being dispossessed by Napoleon (1806–15). **4** 1793–1875, king of Hungary (1830–48) and emperor of Austria (1835–48); abdicated after the Revolution of 1848 in favour of his nephew, Franz Josef I. **5** 1861–1948, ruling prince of Bulgaria (1887–1908) and tsar from 1908 until his abdication in 1918. **6** 1865–1927, king of Romania (1914–27); sided with the Allies in World War I.

Ferdinand II ★ *n* **1** 1578–1637, Holy Roman Emperor (1619–37); king of Bohemia (1617–19; 1620–37) and of Hungary (1617–37). His anti-Protestant policies led to the Thirty Years' War. **2** title as king of Aragon and Sicily of **Ferdinand V.**

Ferdinand III ★ *n* **1** 1608–57, Holy Roman Emperor (1637–57) and king of Hungary (1625–57); son of Ferdinand II. **2** title as king of Naples of **Ferdinand V.**

Ferdinand V ★ *n* known as *Ferdinand the Catholic.* 1452–1516, king of Castile (1474–1504); as Ferdinand II, king of Aragon (1479–1516) and Sicily (1468–1516); as Ferdinand III, king of Naples (1504–16). His marriage to Isabella I of Castile (1469) led to the union of Aragon and Castile and his reconquest of Granada from the Moors (1492) completed the unification of Spain. He introduced the Inquisition (1478), expelled the Jews from Spain (1492), and financed Columbus' voyage to the New World.

Ferdinand VII ★ *n* 1784–1833, king of Spain (1808; 1814–33). He precipitated the Carlist Wars by excluding his brother Don Carlos as his successor.

feretory ('fɛrɪtərɪ, -trɪ) *n, pl* **feretories.** *Chiefly RC Church.* **1** a shrine, usually portable, for a saint's relics. **2** the chapel in which a shrine is kept. ORIG C14: from MF *fiertre,* from L *feretrum* a bier, from Gk, from *pherein* to bear

Fergana *or* **Ferghana** ★ (fə'gɑ:nə) *n* **1** a region of W central Asia, surrounded by high mountains and accessible only from the west; mainly in Uzbekistan and partly in Tajikistan and Kyrgyzstan. **2** the chief city of this region, in E Uzbekistan. Pop.: 191 000 (1993 est.).

Fergus ★ ('fɜ:gəs) *n* (in Irish legend) a warrior king of Ulster, who was supplanted by Conchobar.

feria ('fɪərɪə) *n, pl* **ferias** *or* **feriae** (-rɪ,i:). *RC Church.* a weekday, other than Saturday, on which no feast occurs. ORIG C19: from LL: day of the week (as in *prīma fēria* Sunday), sing of L *fēriae* festivals
▸ **'ferial** *adj*

Ferlinghetti ★ (,fɜ:lɪŋ'gɛtɪ) *n* **Lawrence.** born 1920, US poet of the Beat Generation. His poetry includes the collection *Pictures of the Gone World* (1955).

Fermanagh ★ (fə'mænə) *n* a district and historic county of SW Northern Ireland, bordering the Irish Republic: contains the Upper and Lower Lough Erne. Administrative centre: Enniskillen. Pop.: 54 033 (1991). Area (excluding water): 1700 sq. km (656 sq. miles).

Fermat ★ (fɜ:'mæt; *French* fɛrma) *n* **Pierre de** (pjɛr də). 1601–65, French mathematician, regarded as the founder of the modern theory of numbers.

fermata (fə'mɑ:tə) *n, pl* **fermatas** *or* **fermate** (-tɪ). *Music.* another word for **pause** (sense 5). ORIG from It., from *fermare* to stop, from L *firmāre* to establish

ferment *n* ('fɜ:mɛnt). **1** any agent or substance, such as a bacterium, mould, yeast, or enzyme, that causes fermentation. **2** another word for **fermentation. 3** commotion; unrest. ◆ *vb* (fə'mɛnt). **4** to undergo or cause to undergo fermentation. **5** to stir up or seethe with excitement. ORIG C15: from L *fermentum* yeast, from *fervēre* to seethe
▸ **fer'mentable** *adj*

USAGE NOTE See at **foment.**

fermentation (,fɜ:mɛn'teɪʃən) *n* a chemical reaction in which an organic molecule splits into simpler substances, esp. the conversion of sugar to ethyl alcohol by yeast.
▸ **fer'mentative** *adj*

fermentation lock *n* a valve placed on the top of bottles of fermenting wine to allow bubbles to escape.

fermi ('fɜ:mɪ) *n* a unit of length used in nuclear physics equal to 10^{-15} metre. ORIG C20: after Enrico FERMI

Fermi ★ ('fɜ:mɪ; *Italian* 'fɛrmi) *n* **Enrico** (en'ri:ko). 1901–54, Italian nuclear physicist, in the US from 1939. He was awarded a Nobel prize for physics (1938) for his work on nuclear bombardment; headed the group that produced the first controlled nuclear reaction (1942).

fermion ('fɜ:mɪ,ɒn) *n* any of a group of elementary particles, such as a nucleon, that has half-integral spin and obeys the Pauli exclusion principle. Cf. **boson.** ORIG C20: after Enrico FERMI; see -ON

fermium ('fɜ:mɪəm) *n* a transuranic element artificially produced by neutron bombardment of plutonium. Symbol: Fm; atomic no.: 100; half-life of most stable isotope, ^{257}Fm: 80 days (approx.). ORIG C20: after Enrico FERMI

Fermor ★ ('fɜ:mɔ:) *n* **Patrick** (**Michael**) **Leigh.** born 1915, British author, noted for the travel books *A Time of Gifts* (1977) and *Between the Woods and the Water* (1986).

fern (fɜ:n) *n* **1** a plant having roots, stems, and fronds and reproducing by spores formed in structures (sori) on the fronds. **2** any of certain similar but unrelated plants, such as the sweet fern. ORIG OE *fearn*
▸ **'ferny** *adj*

Fernandel ★ (*French* fɛrnɑ̃dɛl) *n* real name *Fernand Joseph Désiré Contandin.* 1903–71, French comic film actor.

Fernando de Noronha ★ (*Portuguese* fer'nəndu di no'roɲa) *n* a volcanic island in the S Atlantic northeast of Cape São Roque: constitutes a federal territory of Brazil; a penal colony since the 18th century and inhabited by military personnel. Area: 26 sq. km (10 sq. miles).

Fernando Po ★ (fə'nændəʊ pəʊ) *n* a former name (until 1973) of **Bioko.**

fernbird ('fɜ:n,bɜ:d) *n* a New Zealand swamp bird with a fernlike tail.

ferocious (fə'rəʊʃəs) *adj* savagely fierce or cruel: *a ferocious tiger.* ORIG C17: from L *ferox* fierce, warlike
▸ **ferocity** (fə'rɒsɪtɪ) *n*

-ferous *adj combining form.* bearing or producing: *coniferous.* ORIG from -FER + -OUS

Ferrara ★ (fəˈrɑːrə; *Italian* ferˈrara) *n* a city in N Italy, in Emilia–Romagna: a centre of the Renaissance under the House of Este; university (1391). Pop.: 135 135 (1996 est.).

Ferrari ★ (fəˈrɑːrɪ; *Italian* ferˈraːri) *n* **Enzo** (ˈɛntso). 1898–1988, Italian designer and manufacturer of racing cars.

ferrate (ˈfɛreɪt) *n* a salt containing the divalent ion, FeO_4^{2-}. ORIG C19: from L *ferrum* iron

ferret (ˈfɛrɪt) *n* **1** a domesticated albino variety of the polecat bred for hunting rats, rabbits, etc. **2** an assiduous searcher. ◆ *vb* **ferrets, ferreting, ferreted. 3** to hunt (rabbits, rats, etc.) with ferrets. **4** (*tr; usually foll. by out*) to drive from hiding: *to ferret out snipers.* **5** (*tr; usually foll. by out*) to find by persistent investigation. **6** (*intr*) to search around. ORIG C14: from OF *furet,* from L *fur* thief
▸ **ˈferreter** *n* ▸ **ˈferrety** *adj*

ferri- *combining form.* indicating the presence of iron, esp. in the trivalent state: *ferricyanide; ferriferous.* Cf. **ferro-**. ORIG from L *ferrum* iron

ferriage (ˈfɛrɪɪdʒ) *n* **1** transportation by ferry. **2** the fee charged for passage on a ferry.

ferric (ˈfɛrɪk) *adj* of or containing iron in the trivalent state; designating an iron(III) compound. ORIG C18: from L *ferrum* iron

ferric oxide *n* a red crystalline insoluble oxide of iron that occurs as haematite and rust, used as a pigment and metal polish (**jeweller's rouge**), and as a sensitive coating on magnetic tape. Formula: Fe_2O_3. Systematic name: **iron(III) oxide.**

Ferrier ★ (ˈfɛrɪə) *n* **Kathleen.** 1912–53, British contralto.

ferrimagnetism (ˌfɛrɪˈmægnɪˌtɪzəm) *n* a phenomenon exhibited by certain substances, such as ferrites, in which the magnetic moments of neighbouring ions are nonparallel and unequal in magnitude.
▸ **ferrimagnetic** (ˌfɛrɪmægˈnɛtɪk) *adj*

Ferris wheel (ˈfɛrɪs) *n* a fairground wheel having seats freely suspended from its rim. ORIG C19: after G.W.G. *Ferris* (1859–96), American engineer

ferrite (ˈfɛraɪt) *n* any of a class of nonconducting magnetic mixed-oxide ceramics.

ferrite-rod aerial *n* a type of aerial, normally used in radio reception, consisting of a small coil of wire mounted on a ferromagnetic ceramic core, the coil serving as a tuning inductance.

ferro- *combining form.* **1** indicating a property of iron or the presence of iron: *ferromagnetism.* **2** indicating the presence of iron in the divalent state: *ferrocyanide.* Cf. **ferri-**. ORIG from L *ferrum* iron

ferrocene (ˈfɛrəʊˌsiːn) *n* a reddish-orange compound in which the molecules have an iron atom sandwiched between two cyclopentadiene rings. Formula: $Fe(C_5H_5)_2$. ORIG C20: from FERRO- + C(YCLOPENTADI)ENE

ferroconcrete (ˌfɛrəʊˈkɒŋkriːt) *n* another name for **reinforced concrete.**

Ferrol ★ (*Spanish* fɛˈrrɔl) *n* See **El Ferrol.**

ferromagnetism (ˌfɛrəʊˈmægnɪˌtɪzəm) *n* the phenomenon exhibited by substances, such as iron, that have relative permeabilities much greater than unity and increasing magnetization with applied magnetizing field. Certain of these substances retain their magnetization in the absence of the applied field.
▸ **ferromagnetic** (ˌfɛrəʊmægˈnɛtɪk) *adj*

ferromanganese (ˌfɛrəʊˈmæŋgəˌniːz) *n* an alloy of iron and manganese, used in making additions of manganese to cast iron and steel.

ferrous (ˈfɛrəs) *adj* of or containing iron in the divalent state; designating an iron(II) compound. ORIG C19: from FERRI- + -OUS

ferrous sulphate *n* an iron salt usually obtained as greenish crystals: used in inks, tanning, etc. Formula: $FeSO_4$. Systematic name: **iron(II) sulphate.** Also called: **copperas.**

ferruginous (fɛˈruːdʒɪnəs) *adj* **1** (of minerals, rocks, etc.) containing iron: *a ferruginous clay.* **2** rust-coloured. ORIG C17: from L *ferrūgineus* of a rusty colour, from *ferrum* iron

ferrule (ˈfɛruːl) *n* **1** a metal ring, tube, or cap placed over the end of a stick or post for added strength or to increase wear. **2** a small length of tube, etc., esp. one used for making a joint. ORIG C17: from ME *virole,* from OF, from L, from *viria* bracelet; infl. by L *ferrum* iron

ferry (ˈfɛrɪ) *n, pl* **ferries. 1** Also called: **ferryboat.** a vessel for transporting passengers and usually vehicles across a body of water, esp. as a regular service. **2a** such a service. **2b** (*in combination*): *a ferryman.* **3** the delivering of aircraft by flying them to their destination. ◆ *vb* **ferries, ferrying, ferried. 4** to transport or go by ferry. **5** to deliver (an aircraft) by flying it to its destination. **6** (*tr*) to convey (passengers, goods, etc.). ORIG OE *ferian* to carry, bring

fertile (ˈfɜːtaɪl) *adj* **1** capable of producing offspring. **2a** (of land) capable of sustaining an abundant growth of plants. **2b** (of farm animals) capable of breeding stock. **3** *Biol.* capable of undergoing growth and development: *fertile seeds; fertile eggs.* **4** producing many offspring; prolific. **5** highly productive: *a fertile brain.* **6** *Physics.* (of a substance) able to be transformed into fissile or fissionable material. ORIG C15: from L *fertilis,* from *ferre* to bear
▸ **ˈfertilely** *adv* ▸ **ˈfertileness** *n*

Fertile Crescent *n* an area of fertile land in the Middle East, extending around the Rivers Tigris and Euphrates in a semicircle from Israel to the Persian Gulf.

fertility (fɜːˈtɪlɪtɪ) *n* **1** the ability to produce offspring. **2** the state or quality of being fertile.

fertility drug *n* any of a group of preparations used to stimulate ovulation in women hitherto infertile.

fertilize *or* **fertilise** (ˈfɜːtɪˌlaɪz) *vb* **fertilizes, fertilizing, fertilized** *or* **fertilises, fertilising, fertilised.** (*tr*) **1** to provide (an animal, plant, etc.) with sperm or pollen to bring about fertilization. **2** to supply (soil or water) with nutrients to aid the growth of plants. **3** to make fertile.
▸ **ˌfertiliˈzation** *or* **ˌfertiliˈsation** *n*

fertilizer *or* **fertiliser** (ˈfɜːtɪˌlaɪzə) *n* **1** any substance, such as manure, added to soil or water to increase its productivity. **2** an object or organism that fertilizes an animal or plant.

ferula (ˈfɛrʊlə) *n, pl* **ferulas** *or* **ferulae** (-ˌliː). a large umbelliferous plant having thick stems and dissected leaves. ORIG C14: from L: giant fennel

ferule (ˈfɛruːl) *n* **1** a flat piece of wood, such as a ruler, used in some schools to cane children on the hand. ◆ *vb* **ferules, feruling, feruled. 2** (*tr*) *Rare.* to punish with a ferule. ORIG C16: from L *ferula* giant fennel

fervent (ˈfɜːvənt) *or* **fervid** (ˈfɜːvɪd) *adj* **1** intensely passionate; ardent. **2** *Arch. or poetic.* burning or glowing. ORIG C14: from L *fervēre* to boil, glow
▸ **ˈfervency** *n* ▸ **ˈfervently** *or* **ˈfervidly** *adv*

USAGE NOTE While both *fervent* and *fervid* come from the same root and share the meaning 'intense, ardent', the first has largely positive connotations, and is associated with *hopes, wishes, beliefs* and *admirers, supporters, fans.* The second, apart from being used less often than the first, is chiefly negative: *...in the fervid politics of New York city.* A *fervent kiss* from an admirer would probably be welcome; a *fervid* one would not.

fervour *or US* **fervor** (ˈfɜːvə) *n* **1** great intensity of feeling or belief. **2** *Rare.* intense heat. ORIG C14: from L *fervor* heat, from *fervēre* to glow, boil

Fès (fɛs) *or* **Fez** ★ *n* a city in N central Morocco, traditional capital of the north: became an independent kingdom in the 11th century, at its height in the 14th century; religious centre; university (850). Pop.: 564 000 (1993 est.).

fescue (ˈfɛskjuː) *or* **fescue grass** *n* a widely cultivated pasture and lawn grass, having stiff narrow leaves. ORIG C14: from OF *festu,* ult. from L *festūca* stem, straw

fess (fɛs) *vb* (*intr;* foll. by *up*) *Inf., chiefly US.* to make a confession. ORIG C19: shortened from CONFESS

fesse *or* **fess** (fɛs) *n Heraldry.* an ordinary consisting of a horizontal band across a shield. ORIG C15: from Anglo-F, from L *fascia* band, fillet

fest (fɛst) *n* **a** a meeting or event at which the emphasis is on a particular activity: *a fashion fest*. **b** (*in combination*): *schmaltz-fest; lovefest*. ORIG C19: from G *Fest* festival

festal ('fɛstᵊl) *adj* another word for **festive**. ORIG C15: from L *festum* holiday
▸ **'festally** *adv*

fester ('fɛstə) *vb* **1** to form or cause to form pus. **2** (*intr*) to become rotten; decay. **3** to become or cause to become bitter, irritated, etc., esp. over a long period of time. ◆ *n* **4** a small ulcer or sore containing pus. ORIG C13: from OF *festre* suppurating sore, from L: FISTULA

festival ('fɛstɪvᵊl) *n* **1** a day or period set aside for celebration or feasting, esp. one of religious significance. **2** any occasion for celebration. **3** an organized series of special events and performances: *a festival of drama*. **4** *Arch.* a time of revelry. **5** (*modifier*) relating to or characteristic of a festival. ORIG C14: from Church L *fēstivālis* of a feast, from L *festīvus* FESTIVE

Festival Hall ★ *n* a concert hall in London, on the South Bank of the Thames: built for the 1951 Festival of Britain; completed 1964–65. Official name: **Royal Festival Hall**.

festive ('fɛstɪv) *adj* appropriate to or characteristic of a holiday, etc. ORIG C17: from L *festīvus* joyful, from *festus* of a FEAST
▸ **'festively** *adv*

festivity (fɛs'tɪvɪtɪ) *n, pl* **festivities**. **1** merriment characteristic of a festival, etc. **2** any festival or other celebration. **3** (*pl*) celebrations.

festoon (fɛ'stu:n) *n* **1** a decorative chain of flowers, ribbons, etc., suspended in loops. **2** a carved or painted representation of this, as in architecture, furniture, or pottery. ◆ *vb* (*tr*) **3** to decorate or join together with festoons. **4** to form into festoons. ORIG C17: from F, from It. *festone* ornament for a feast, from *festa* FEAST

festoon blind *n* a window blind consisting of vertical rows of horizontally gathered fabric that may be drawn up to form a series of ruches.

feta ('fɛtə) *n* a white sheep or goat cheese popular in Greece. ORIG Mod. Gk, from the phrase *turi pheta*, from *turi* cheese + *pheta*, from It. *fetta* a slice

fetal *or* **foetal** ('fi:tᵊl) *adj* of, relating to, or resembling a fetus.

fetal alcohol syndrome *n* a condition in newborn babies caused by excessive intake of alcohol by the mother during pregnancy: characterized by various defects including mental retardation.

fetch[1] (fɛtʃ) *vb* (*mainly tr*) **1** to go after and bring back: *to fetch help*. **2** to cause to come; bring or draw forth. **3** (*also intr*) to cost or sell for (a certain price): *the table fetched six hundred pounds*. **4** to utter (a sigh, groan, etc.). **5** *Inf.* to deal (a blow, slap, etc.). **6** (used esp. as a command to dogs) to retrieve (an object thrown, etc.). **7 fetch and carry**. to perform menial tasks or run errands. ◆ *n* **8** the reach, stretch, etc., of a mechanism. **9** a trick or stratagem. ORIG OE *feccan*
▸ **'fetcher** *n*

fetch[2] (fɛtʃ) *n* the ghost or apparition of a living person. ORIG C18: from ?

fetching ('fɛtʃɪŋ) *adj Inf.* **1** attractively befitting. **2** charming.

fetch up *vb* (*adv*) **1** (*intr; usually foll. by at or in*) *Inf.* to arrive (at) or end up (in): *to fetch up in New York*. **2** *Sl.* to vomit (food, etc.).

fête *or* **fete** (feɪt) *n* **1** a gala, bazaar, or similar entertainment, esp. one held outdoors in aid of charity. **2** a feast day or holiday, esp. one of religious significance. ◆ *vb* **fêtes, fêting, fêted** *or* **fetes, feting, feted**. **3** (*tr*) to honour or entertain with or as if with a fête ORIG C18: from F: FEAST

fetid *or* **foetid** ('fɛtɪd, 'fi:-) *adj* having a stale nauseating smell, as of decay. ORIG C16: from L, from *fētēre* to stink; rel. to *fūmus* smoke
▸ **'fetidly** *or* **'foetidly** *adv* ▸ **'fetidness** *or* **'foetidness** *n*

fetish ('fɛtɪʃ, 'fi:tɪʃ) *n* **1** something, esp. an inanimate object, that is believed to have magical powers. **2a** a form of behaviour involving fetishism. **2b** any object that is involved in fetishism. **3** any object, activity, etc., to which one is excessively devoted. ORIG C17: from F, from Port. *feitiço* (n) sorcery, from adj: artificial, from L *factīcius* made by art, FACTITIOUS

fetishism ('fɛtɪˌʃɪzəm, 'fi:-) *n* **1** a condition in which the handling of an inanimate object or a part of the body other than the sexual organs is a source of sexual satisfaction. **2** belief in or recourse to a fetish for magical purposes.
▸ **'fetishist** *n* ▸ **ˌfetish'istic** *adj*

fetlock ('fɛtˌlɒk) *n* **1** a projection behind and above a horse's hoof. **2** Also called: **fetlock joint**. the joint at this part of the leg. **3** the tuft of hair growing from this part. ORIG C14 *fetlak*

fetor *or* **foetor** ('fi:tə) *n* an offensive stale or putrid odour. ORIG C15: from L, from *fētēre* to stink

fetter ('fɛtə) *n* **1** (*often pl*) a chain or bond fastened round the ankle. **2** (*usually pl*) a check or restraint. ◆ *vb* (*tr*) **3** to restrict or confine. **4** to bind in fetters. ORIG OE *fetor*

fettle ('fɛtᵊl) *vb* **fettles, fettling, fettled**. (*tr*) **1** to line or repair (the walls of a furnace). **2** *Brit. dialect.* **2a** to prepare or arrange (a thing, oneself, etc.). **2b** to repair or mend (something). ◆ *n* **3** state of health, spirits, etc. (esp. in **in fine fettle**). ORIG C14 (in the sense: to put in order): back formation from *fetled* girded up, from OE *fetel* belt

fettler ('fɛtlə) *n* a person employed to maintain railway tracks.

fetus *or* **foetus** ('fi:təs) *n, pl* **fetuses** *or* **foetuses**. the embryo of a mammal in the later stages of development, esp. a human embryo from the end of the second month of pregnancy until birth. ORIG C14: from L: offspring

feu (fju:) *n* **1** *Scot. legal history.* **1a** a feudal tenure of land for which rent was paid in money or grain instead of by the performance of military service. **1b** the land so held. **2** *Scots Law.* a right to the use of land in return for a fixed annual payment (**feu duty**). ORIG C15: from OF; see FEE

Feuchtwanger ★ (*German* 'fɔɪçtvaŋər) *n* **Lion** ('li:ɒn). 1884–1958, German novelist and dramatist, lived in the US (1940–58): noted for his novel *Jew Süss* (1925).

feud[1] (fju:d) *n* **1** long and bitter hostility between two families, clans, or individuals. **2** a quarrel or dispute. ◆ *vb* **3** (*intr*) to carry on a feud. ORIG C13 *fede*, from OF, from OHG *fēhida*; rel. to OE *fæhth* hostility; see FOE
▸ **'feudist** *n*

feud[2] *or* **feod** (fju:d) *n Feudal law.* land held in return for service. ORIG C17: from Med. L *feodum*, of Gmc origin; see FEE

feudal ('fju:dᵊl) *adj* **1** of or characteristic of feudalism or its institutions. **2** of or relating to a fief. **3** *Disparaging.* old-fashioned. ORIG C17: from Med. L, from *feudum* FEUD[2]

feudalism ('fju:dəˌlɪzəm) *n* the legal and social system that evolved in W Europe in the 8th and 9th centuries, in which vassals were protected and maintained by their lords, usually through the granting of fiefs, and were required to serve under them in war. Also called: **feudal system**.
▸ **'feudalist** *n* ▸ **ˌfeudal'istic** *adj*

feudality (fju:'dælɪtɪ) *n, pl* **feudalities**. **1** the state or quality of being feudal. **2** a fief or fee.

feudalize *or* **feudalise** ('fju:dəˌlaɪz) *vb* **feudalizes, feudalizing, feudalized** *or* **feudalises, feudalising, feudalised**. (*tr*) to create feudal institutions in (a society, etc.).
▸ **ˌfeudali'zation** *or* **ˌfeudali'sation** *n*

feudatory ('fju:dətərɪ) (in feudal Europe) ◆ *n, pl* **feudatories**. **1** a person holding a fief; vassal. ◆ *adj* **2** relating to or characteristic of the relationship between lord and vassal. ORIG C16: from Med. L *feudātor*

Feuerbach ★ (*German* 'fɔɪərbax) *n* **Ludwig Andreas** ('lu:tvɪç an'dre:as). 1804–72, German materialist philosopher: in *The Essence of Christianity* (1841), translated into English by George Eliot (1853), he maintained that God is merely an outward projection of man's inner self.

feuilleton (*French* fœjtɔ̃) *n* **1** the part of a European newspaper carrying reviews, serialized fiction, etc. **2**

such a review or article. ORIG C19: from F, from *feuillet* sheet of paper, dim. of *feuille* leaf, from L *folium*

fever ('fiːvə) *n* **1** an abnormally high body temperature, accompanied by a fast pulse rate, dry skin, etc. Related adj: **febrile. 2** any of various diseases, such as yellow fever or scarlet fever, characterized by a high temperature. **3** intense nervous excitement. ◆ *vb* **4** (*tr*) to affect with or as if with fever. ORIG OE *fēfor,* from L *febris*
▸ **'fevered** *adj*

feverfew ('fiːvəˌfjuː) *n* a bushy European strong-scented perennial plant with white flower heads, formerly used medicinally. ORIG OE *feferfuge,* from LL, from L *febris* fever + *fugāre* to put to flight

feverish ('fiːvərɪʃ) *or* **feverous** *adj* **1** suffering from fever. **2** in a state of restless excitement. **3** of, caused by, or causing fever.
▸ **'feverishly** *or* **'feverously** *adv*

fever pitch *n* a state of intense excitement.

fever therapy *n* a former method of treating disease by raising the body temperature.

few (fjuː) *determiner* **1a** hardly any: *few men are so cruel.* **1b** (*as pronoun; functioning as pl*): *many are called but few are chosen.* **2** (preceded by *a*) **2a** a small number of: *a few drinks.* **2b** (*as pronoun; functioning as pl*): *a few of you.* **3 a good few.** *Inf.* several. **4 few and far between. 4a** widely spaced. **4b** scarce. **5 not** *or* **quite a few.** *Inf.* several. ◆ *n* **6 the few.** a small number of people considered as a class: *the few who fell at Thermopylae.* ORIG OE *fēawa*
▸ **'fewness** *n*

USAGE NOTE See at **less.**

fey (feɪ) *adj* **1** interested in or believing in the supernatural. **2** clairvoyant; visionary. **3** *Chiefly Scot.* fated to die; doomed. **4** *Chiefly Scot.* in a state of high spirits. ORIG OE *fǣge* marked out for death
▸ **'feyness** *n*

Feydeau ★ (*French* fɛdo) *n* **Georges** (ʒɔrʒ). 1862–1921, French dramatist, noted for his farces, esp. *La Dame de chez Maxim* (1899) and *Occupe-toi d'Amélie* (1908).

Feynman ★ ('faɪnmən) *n* **Richard.** 1918–88, US physicist, noted for his research on quantum electrodynamics; shared the Nobel prize for physics in 1965.

fez (fɛz) *n, pl* **fezzes.** an originally Turkish brimless felt or wool cap, shaped like a truncated cone. ORIG C19: via F from Turkish, from FÈS

Fez ★ (fɛz) *n* a variant of **Fès.**

Fezzan ★ (fɛ'zɑːn) *n* a region of SW Libya, in the Sahara: a former province (until 1963).

ff *Music. symbol for* fortissimo.

ff. **1** *abbrev. for* folios. **2** *symbol for* and the following (pages, lines, etc.).

Ffestiniog ★ (fes'tɪnɪɒg) *n* a town in N Wales, in Gwynedd: tourist attractions include former slate quarries and a narrow-gauge railway at nearby Blaenau Ffestiniog. Pop.: 800 (latest est.).

FI *abbrev. for* Falkland Islands.

fiacre (fɪ'ɑːkrə) *n* a small four-wheeled horse-drawn carriage. ORIG C17: after the Hotel de St *Fiacre,* Paris, where these vehicles were first hired out

fiancé *or* (*fem*) **fiancée** (fɪ'ɒnseɪ) *n* a person who is engaged to be married. ORIG C19: from F, from OF *fiancier* to promise, betroth, from *fiance* a vow, from *fier* to trust, from L *fīdere*

Fianna ★ ('fiːənə) *pl n* a legendary band of Irish warriors noted for their heroic exploits, attributed to the 2nd and 3rd centuries A.D. Also called: **Fenians.**

fiasco (fɪ'æskəʊ) *n, pl* **fiascos** *or* **fiascoes.** a complete failure, esp. one that is ignominious or humiliating. ORIG C19: from It., lit.: FLASK; sense development obscure

fiat ('faɪət) *n* **1** official sanction. **2** an arbitrary order or decree. ORIG C17: from L, lit.: let it be done

fib (fɪb) *n* **1** a trivial and harmless lie. ◆ *vb* **fibs, fibbing, fibbed. 2** (*intr*) to tell such a lie. ORIG C17: ?from *fibble-fable* an unlikely story; see FABLE
▸ **'fibber** *n*

Fibonacci ★ (*Italian* fibo'nattʃi) *n* **Leonardo** (leo'nardo), also called *Leonardo of Pisa.* ?1170–?1250, Italian mathematician: popularized the decimal system in Europe.

Fibonacci sequence *or* **series** (ˌfɪbə'nɑːtʃɪ) *n* the infinite sequence of numbers, 0, 1, 1, 2, 3, 5, 8, etc., in which each member (**Fibonacci number**) is the sum of the previous two. ORIG after Leonardo FIBONACCI

fibre *or US* **fiber** ('faɪbə) *n* **1** a natural or synthetic filament that may be spun into yarn, such as cotton or nylon. **2** cloth or other material made from such yarn. **3** a long fine continuous thread or filament. **4** the texture of any material or substance. **5** essential substance or nature. **6** strength of character (esp. in **moral fibre**). **7** *Bot.* **7a** a narrow elongated thick-walled cell. **7b** a very small root or twig. **8** a fibrous substance, such as bran, as part of someone's diet: *dietary fibre.* ORIG C14: from L *fibra* filament, entrails
▸ **'fibred** *or US* **'fibered** *adj*

fibreboard *or US* **fiberboard** ('faɪbəˌbɔːd) *n* a building material made of compressed wood or other plant fibres.

fibreglass *or US* **fiberglass** ('faɪbəˌglɑːs) *n* **1** material consisting of matted fine glass fibres, used as insulation in buildings, etc. **2** a light strong material made by bonding fibreglass with a synthetic resin; used for car bodies, etc.

fibre optics *or US* **fiber optics** *n* (*functioning as sing*) the transmission of information modulated on light down very thin flexible fibres of glass. See also **optical fibre.**
▸ **ˌfibre-'optic** *or US* **ˌfiber-'optic** *adj*

fibrescope *or US* **fiberscope** ('faɪbəˌskəʊp) *n* a medical instrument using fibre optics used to examine internal organs, such as the stomach.

fibril ('faɪbrɪl) *or* **fibrilla** (faɪ'brɪlə) *n, pl* **fibrils** *or* **fibrillae** (-'brɪliː). **1** a small fibre or part of a fibre. **2** *Biol.* a root hair. ORIG C17: from NL *fibrilla* a little FIBRE
▸ **fi'brillar** *or* **fi'brillose** *adj*

fibrillation (ˌfaɪbrɪ'leɪʃən, ˌfɪb-) *n* **1** a local and uncontrollable twitching of muscle fibres. **2** irregular twitchings of the muscular wall of the heart.

fibrin ('fɪbrɪn) *n* a white insoluble elastic protein formed from fibrinogen when blood clots: forms a network that traps red cells and platelets.

fibrinogen (fɪ'brɪnədʒən) *n* a soluble protein in blood plasma, converted to fibrin by the action of the enzyme thrombin when blood clots.

fibro ('faɪbrəʊ) *n Austral. inf.* **a** short for **fibrocement. b** (*as modifier*): *a fibro shack.*

fibro- *combining form.* **1** indicating fibrous tissue: *fibrosis.* **2** indicating fibre: *fibrocement.* ORIG from L *fibra* FIBRE

fibrocement (ˌfaɪbrəʊsɪ'mɛnt) *n* cement combined with asbestos fibre, used esp. in sheets for building.

fibroid ('faɪbrɔɪd) *adj* **1** *Anat.* (of structures or tissues) containing or resembling fibres. ◆ *n* **2** a benign tumour, composed of fibrous and muscular tissue, occurring in the wall of the uterus and often causing heavy menstruation.

fibroin ('faɪbrəʊɪn) *n* a tough elastic protein that is the principal component of spiders' webs and raw silk.

fibroma (faɪ'brəʊmə) *n, pl* **fibromata** (-mətə) *or* **fibromas.** a benign tumour derived from fibrous connective tissue.

fibrosis (faɪ'brəʊsɪs) *n* the formation of an abnormal amount of fibrous tissue in an organ or part.

fibrositis (ˌfaɪbrə'saɪtɪs) *n* inflammation of white fibrous tissue, esp. that of muscle sheaths.

fibrous ('faɪbrəs) *adj* consisting of or resembling fibres: *fibrous tissue.*
▸ **'fibrously** *adv*

fibula ('fɪbjʊlə) *n, pl* **fibulae** (-ˌliː) *or* **fibulas. 1** the outer and thinner of the two bones between the knee and ankle of the human leg. Cf. **tibia. 2** the corresponding bone in other vertebrates. **3** a metal brooch resembling a safety pin. ORIG C17: from L: clasp, prob. from *figere* to fasten
▸ **'fibular** *adj*

-fic *suffix forming adjectives.* making or producing: *honorific.* ORIG from L *-ficus,* from *facere* to do, make

fiche (fiːʃ) *n* See **microfiche, ultrafiche.**

fichu (ˈfiːʃuː) *n* a woman's shawl worn esp. in the 18th century. ORIG C19: from F: small shawl, from *ficher* to fix with a pin, from L *figere* to fasten, FIX

fickle (ˈfɪkᵊl) *adj* changeable in purpose, affections, etc. ORIG OE *ficol* deceitful
▸ ˈ**fickleness** *n*

fictile (ˈfɪktaɪl) *adj* **1** moulded or capable of being moulded from clay. **2** made of clay by a potter. ORIG C17: from L *fictilis* that can be moulded, from *fingere* to shape

fiction (ˈfɪkʃən) *n* **1** literary works invented by the imagination, such as novels or short stories. **2** an invented story or explanation. **3** the act of inventing a story. **4** *Law.* something assumed to be true for the sake of convenience, though probably false. ORIG C14: from L *fictiō* a fashioning, hence something imaginary, from *fingere* to shape
▸ ˈ**fictional** *adj* ▸ ˈ**fictionally** *adv* ▸ ˈ**fictive** *adj*

fictionalize *or* **fictionalise** (ˈfɪkʃənəˌlaɪz) *vb* **fictionalizes, fictionalizing, fictionalized** *or* **fictionalises, fictionalising, fictionalised.** (*tr*) to make into fiction.
▸ ˌ**fictionaliˈzation** *or* ˌ**fictionaliˈsation** *n*

fictitious (fɪkˈtɪʃəs) *adj* **1** not genuine or authentic: *to give a fictitious address.* **2** of, related to, or characteristic of fiction.
▸ **ficˈtitiously** *adv* ▸ **ficˈtitiousness** *n*

fid (fɪd) *n Naut.* **1** a spike for separating strands of rope in splicing. **2** a wooden or metal bar for supporting the topmast. ORIG C17: from ?

-fid *adj combining form.* divided into parts or lobes: *bifid.* ORIG from L *-fidus,* from *findere* to split

fiddle (ˈfɪdᵊl) *n* **1** *Inf. or disparaging.* the violin. **2** a violin played as a folk instrument. **3** *Naut.* a small railing around the top of a table to prevent objects from falling off it. **4** *Brit. inf.* an illegal transaction or arrangement. **5** *Brit. inf.* a manually delicate or tricky operation. **6 at** *or* **on the fiddle.** *Inf.* engaged in an illegal or fraudulent undertaking. **7 fit as a fiddle.** *Inf.* in very good health. **8 play second fiddle.** *Inf.* to play a minor part. ◆ *vb* **fiddles, fiddling, fiddled. 9** to play (a tune) on the fiddle. **10** (*intr;* often foll. by *with*) to make aimless movements with the hands. **11** (when *intr,* often foll. by *about* or *around*) *Inf.* to waste (time). **12** (often foll. by *with*) *Inf.* to interfere (with). **13** *Inf.* to contrive to do (something) by illicit means or deception. **14** (*tr*) *Inf.* to falsify (accounts, etc.). ORIG OE *fithele;* see VIOLA[1]

fiddle-faddle (ˈfɪdᵊlˌfædᵊl) *n, interj* **1** trivial matter; nonsense. ◆ *vb* **fiddle-faddles, fiddle-faddling, fiddle-faddled. 2** (*intr*) to fuss or waste time. ORIG C16: reduplication of FIDDLE
▸ ˈ**fiddle-ˌfaddler** *n*

fiddler (ˈfɪdlə) *n* **1** a person who plays the fiddle. **2** See **fiddler crab. 3** *Inf.* a petty rogue.

fiddler crab *n* any of various burrowing crabs of American coastal regions, the males of which have one of their pincer-like claws enlarged. ORIG C19: referring to the rapid fiddling movement of the enlarged anterior claw of the males, used to attract females

fiddlestick (ˈfɪdᵊlˌstɪk) *n* **1** *Inf.* a violin bow. **2** any trifle. **3 fiddlesticks!** an expression of annoyance or disagreement.

fiddling (ˈfɪdlɪŋ) *adj* **1** trifling or insignificant. **2** another word for **fiddly.**

fiddly (ˈfɪdlɪ) *adj* **fiddlier, fiddliest.** small and awkward to do or handle.

Fidei Defensor *Latin.* (ˈfaɪdɪˌaɪ dɪˈfɛnsɔː) *n* defender of the faith; a title given to Henry VIII by Pope Leo X, and appearing on British coins as FID DEF (before decimalization) or FD (after decimalization).

fidelity (fɪˈdɛlɪtɪ) *n, pl* **fidelities. 1** devotion to duties, obligations, etc. **2** loyalty or devotion, as to a person or cause. **3** faithfulness to one's spouse, lover, etc. **4** accuracy in reporting detail. **5** *Electronics.* the degree to which an amplifier or radio accurately reproduces the characteristics of the input signal. ORIG C15: from L, from *fidēs* faith, loyalty

fidget (ˈfɪdʒɪt) *vb* **1** (*intr*) to move about restlessly. **2** (*intr;* often foll. by *with*) to make restless or uneasy movements (with something). **3** (*tr*) to cause to fidget. ◆ *n* **4** (*often pl*) a state of restlessness or unease: *he's got the fidgets.* **5** a person who fidgets. ORIG C17: from earlier *fidge,* prob. from ON *fikjast* to desire eagerly
▸ ˈ**fidgety** *adj*

fiducial (fɪˈdjuːʃɪəl) *adj* **1** *Physics, etc.* used as a standard of reference or measurement: *a fiducial point.* **2** of or based on trust or faith. ORIG C17: from LL *fīdūciālis,* from L *fīdūcia* confidence, from *fīdere* to trust

fiduciary (fɪˈduːʃɪərɪ) *Law.* ◆ *n, pl* **fiduciaries. 1** a person bound to act for another's benefit, as a trustee. ◆ *adj* **2a** having the nature of a trust. **2b** of or relating to a trust or trustee. ORIG C17: from L *fīdūciārius* relating to something held in trust, from *fīdūcia* trust

fiduciary issue *n* an issue of banknotes not backed by gold.

fie (faɪ) *interj Obs. or facetious.* an exclamation of distaste or mock dismay. ORIG C13: from OF *fi,* from L *fī,* exclamation of disgust

fief *or* **feoff** (fiːf) *n* (in feudal Europe) the property or fee granted to a vassal for his maintenance by his lord in return for service. ORIG C17: from OF *fie,* of Gmc origin; cf. OE *fēo* cattle, money, L *pecus* cattle, *pecūnia* money, Gk *pokos* fleece

fiefdom (ˈfiːfdəm) *n* **1** (in feudal Europe) the property owned by a lord. **2** an area over which a person or organization exerts authority or influence.

field (fiːld) *n* **1** an open tract of uncultivated grassland; meadow. **2** a piece of land cleared of trees and undergrowth used for pasture or growing crops: *a field of barley.* **3** a limited or marked off area on which any of various sports, athletic competitions, etc., are held: *a soccer field.* **4** an area that is rich in minerals or other natural resources: *a coalfield.* **5** short for **battlefield** or **airfield. 6** the mounted followers that hunt with a pack of hounds. **7a** all the runners in a race or competitors in a competition. **7b** the runners in a race or competitors in a competition excluding the favourite. **8** *Cricket.* the fielders collectively, esp. with regard to their positions. **9** a wide or open expanse: *a field of snow.* **10a** an area of human activity: *the field of human knowledge.* **10b** a sphere or division of knowledge, etc.: *his field is physics.* **11** a place away from the laboratory, office, library, etc., where practical work is done. **12** the surface or background, as of a flag, coin, or heraldic shield, on which a design is displayed. **13** Also called: **field of view.** the area within which an object may be observed with a telescope, etc. **14** *Physics.* See **field of force. 15** *Maths.* a set of entities, such as numbers, subject to two binary operations, addition and multiplication, such that the set is a commutative group under addition and the set, minus the zero, is a commutative group under multiplication. **16** *Computing.* a set of one or more characters comprising a unit of information. **17 play the field.** *Inf.* to disperse one's interests or attentions among a number of activities, people, or objects. **18 take the field.** to begin or carry on activity, esp. in sport or military operations. **19** (*modifier*) *Mil.* of or relating to equipment, personnel, etc., specifically trained for operations in the field: *a field gun.* ◆ *vb* **20** (*tr*) *Sport.* to stop, catch, or return (the ball) as a fielder. **21** (*tr*) *Sport.* to send (a player or team) onto the field to play. **22** (*intr*) *Sport.* (of a player or team) to act or take turn as a fielder or fielders. **23** (*tr*) to enter (a person) in a competition: *each party fielded a candidate.* **24** (*tr*) *Inf.* to deal with or handle: *to field a question.* ORIG OE *feld*

Field ★ (fiːld) *n* **John.** 1782–1837, Irish composer and pianist, lived in Russia from 1803: invented the nocturne.

field artillery *n* artillery capable of deployment in support of front-line troops, due mainly to its mobility.

field day *n* **1** a day spent in some special outdoor activity, such as nature study. **2** *Mil.* a day devoted to manoeuvres or exercises, esp. before an audience. **3** *Inf.* a day or time of exciting activity: *the children had a field day with their new toys.*

field effect transistor *n* a unipolar transistor in which the transverse application of an electric field produces amplification.

★ people and places

fielder ('fi:ldə) *n Cricket, etc.* **a** a player in the field. **b** a member of the fielding side.

field event *n* a competition, such as the discus, etc., that takes place on a field or similar area as opposed to those on the running track.

fieldfare ('fi:ld,fɛə) *n* a large Old World thrush having a pale grey head, brown wings and back, and a blackish tail. ORIG OE *feldefare;* see FIELD, FARE

field glasses *pl n* another name for **binoculars.**

field goal *n* **1** *Basketball.* a goal scored while the ball is in normal play rather than from a free throw. **2** *American & Canadian football.* a score of three points made by kicking the ball through the opponent's goalposts above the crossbar.

field hockey *n US & Canad.* hockey played on a field, as distinguished from ice hockey.

field hospital *n* a temporary hospital set up near a battlefield for emergency treatment.

Fielding ★ ('fi:ldɪŋ) *n* **1 Helen.** born 1958, British humorous writer: author of the novels *Bridget Jones's Diary* (1996) and *The Edge of Reason* (1999). **2 Henry.** 1707–54, English novelist and dramatist, noted particularly for his picaresque novel *Tom Jones* (1749) and for *Joseph Andrews* (1742), which starts as a parody of Richardson's *Pamela:* also noted as an enlightened magistrate and a founder of the Bow Street runners (1749).

field magnet *n* a permanent magnet or an electromagnet that produces the magnetic field in a generator, electric motor, or similar device.

field marshal *n* an officer holding the highest rank in certain armies.

fieldmouse ('fi:ld,maus) *n, pl* **fieldmice.** a nocturnal mouse inhabiting woods, fields, and gardens of the Old World that has yellowish-brown fur.

field officer *n* an officer holding the rank of major, lieutenant colonel, or colonel.

field of force *n* the region of space surrounding a body, such as a charged particle or a magnet, within which it can exert a force on a similar body not in contact with it.

Fields ★ (fi:ldz) *n* **1** Dame **Gracie.** real name *Grace Stansfield.* 1898–1979, British singer and entertainer. **2 W. C.** real name *William Claude Dukenfield.* 1880–1946, US film actor.

fieldsman ('fi:ldzmən) *n, pl* **fieldsmen.** *Cricket.* another name for **fielder.**

field sports *pl n* sports carried on in the countryside, such as hunting or fishing.

field tile *n Brit. & NZ.* an earthenware drain used in farm drainage.

field trial *n* (*often pl*) a test to display performance, efficiency, or durability, as of a vehicle or invention.

field trip *n* an expedition, as by a group of students, to study something at first hand.

field winding ('waɪndɪŋ) *n* the current-carrying coils on a field magnet that produce the magnetic field intensity required to set up the electrical excitation in a generator or motor.

fieldwork ('fi:ld,wɜ:k) *n Mil.* a temporary structure used in fortifying a place or position.

field work *n* an investigation or search for material, data, etc., made in the field as opposed to the classroom or laboratory.
▸ **field worker** *n*

fiend (fi:nd) *n* **1** an evil spirit. **2** a cruel, brutal, or spiteful person. **3** *Inf.* **3a** a person who is intensely interested in or fond of something: *a fresh-air fiend.* **3b** an addict: *a drug fiend.* ORIG OE *fēond*

fiendish ('fi:ndɪʃ) *adj* **1** of or like a fiend. **2** diabolically wicked or cruel. **3** *Inf.* extremely difficult or unpleasant: *a fiendish problem.*

fierce (fɪəs) *adj* **1** having a violent and unrestrained nature: *a fierce dog.* **2** wild or turbulent in force, action, or intensity: *a fierce storm.* **3** intense or strong: *fierce competition.* **4** *Inf.* very unpleasant. ORIG C13: from OF *fiers,* from L *ferus*
▸ **'fiercely** *adv* ▸ **'fierceness** *n*

fiery ('faɪərɪ) *adj* **fierier, fieriest. 1** of, containing, or composed of fire. **2** resembling fire in heat, colour, ardour, etc.: *a fiery speaker.* **3** easily angered or aroused: *a fiery temper.* **4** (of food) producing a burning sensation: *a fiery curry.* **5** (of the skin or a sore) inflamed. **6** flammable.
▸ **'fierily** *adv* ▸ **'fieriness** *n*

Fiesole[1] ★ (*Italian* 'fiɛ:zole) *n* a town in central Italy, in Tuscany near Florence: Etruscan and Roman remains. Pop.: 4000 (1987 est.). Ancient name: **Faesulae** ('fi:sʊli:).

Fiesole[2] ★ (*Italian* 'fiɛ:zole) *n* **Giovanni da** (dʒo'vanni da). the monastic name of (Fra) **Angelico.**

fiesta (fɪ'ɛstə) *n* (esp. in Spain and Latin America) **1** a religious festival or celebration. **2** a holiday or carnival. ORIG Sp., from L *festa;* see FEAST

FIFA ('fi:fə) *n acronym for* Fédération Internationale de Football Association. ORIG from F

fife (faɪf) *n* **1** a small high-pitched flute similar to the piccolo, used esp. in military bands. ◆ *vb* **fifes, fifing, fifed. 2** to play (music) on a fife. ORIG C16: from OHG *pfīfa;* see PIPE[1]
▸ **'fifer** *n*

Fife[1] ★ (faɪf) *n* a council area and historic county of E central Scotland, bordering on the North Sea between the Firths of Tay and Forth: coastal lowlands in the north and east, with several ranges of hills; mainly agricultural. Administrative centre: Glenrothes. Pop.: 352 100 (1994 est.). Area: 1305 sq. km (504 sq. miles).

Fife[2] ★ (faɪf) *n* **Duncan.** See (Duncan) **Phyfe.**

FIFO ('faɪfəʊ) *n acronym for* first in, first out (as an accounting principle in costing stock). Cf. **LIFO.**

fifteen ('fɪf'ti:n) *n* **1** the cardinal number that is the sum of ten and five. **2** a numeral, 15, XV, etc., representing this number. **3** something represented by, representing, or consisting of 15 units. **4** a Rugby Union (football) team. ◆ *determiner* **5a** amounting to fifteen: *fifteen jokes.* **5b** (*as pronoun*): *fifteen of us danced.* ORIG OE *fīftēne*
▸ **'fif'teenth** *adj, n*

fifth (fɪfθ) *adj* (*usually prenominal*) **1a** coming after the fourth in order, position, etc. Often written 5th. **1b** (*as n*): *he came on the fifth.* ◆ *n* **2a** one of five equal parts of an object, quantity, etc. **2b** (*as modifier*): *a fifth part.* **3** the fraction equal to one divided by five (1/5). **4** *Music.* **4a** the interval between one note and another five notes away from it in a diatonic scale. **4b** one of two notes constituting such an interval in relation to the other. ◆ *adv* **5** Also: **fifthly.** after the fourth person, position, event, etc. ◆ *sentence connector.* **6** Also: **fifthly.** as the fifth point. ORIG OE *fifta*

fifth column *n* **1** (originally) a group of Falangist sympathizers in Madrid during the Spanish Civil War who were prepared to join the insurgents marching on the city. **2** any group of hostile infiltrators.
▸ **fifth columnist** *n*

fifth wheel *n* **1** a spare wheel for a four-wheeled vehicle. **2** a superfluous or unnecessary person or thing.

fifty ('fɪftɪ) *n, pl* **fifties. 1** the cardinal number that is the product of ten and five. **2** a numeral, 50, L, etc., representing this number. **3** something represented by, representing, or consisting of 50 units. ◆ *determiner* **4a** amounting to fifty: *fifty people.* **4b** (*as pronoun*): *fifty should be sufficient.* ORIG OE *fīftig*
▸ **'fiftieth** *adj, n*

fifty-fifty *adj, adv Inf.* in equal parts.

fig (fɪg) *n* **1** a tree or shrub in which the flowers are borne inside a pear-shaped receptacle. **2** the fruit of any of these trees, which develops from the receptacle and has sweet flesh containing numerous seedlike structures. **3** (*used with a negative*) something of negligible value: *I don't care a fig for your opinion.* ORIG C13: from OF, from *figa,* from L *ficus* fig tree

fig. *abbrev. for:* **1** figurative(ly). **2** figure.

fight (faɪt) *vb* **fights, fighting, fought. 1** to oppose or struggle against (an enemy) in battle. **2** to oppose or struggle against (a person, cause, etc.) in any manner. **3** (*tr*) to engage in or carry on (a battle, contest, etc.). **4** (when *intr,* often foll. by *for*) to uphold or maintain (a cause, etc.) by fighting or struggling: *to fight for freedom.* **5** (*tr*) to make or achieve (a way) by fighting. **6** to engage (another or others) in combat. **7 fight it out.** to contend until a decisive result is obtained. **8 fight shy.** to keep aloof from. ◆ *n* **9** a battle, struggle, or physical combat. **10** a quarrel, dispute, or contest. **11** resistance (esp. in **to put up a fight**). **12** a boxing match. ◆ See also **fight off.** ORIG OE *feohtan*

fighter ('faɪtə) *n* **1** a person who fights, esp. a professional boxer. **2** a person who has determination. **3** *Mil.* an armed aircraft designed for destroying other aircraft.

fighter-bomber *n* an aircraft that combines the roles of fighter and bomber.

fighting chance *n* a slight chance of success dependent on a struggle.

fighting cock *n* **1** a gamecock. **2** a pugnacious person.

fighting fish *n* any of various tropical fishes of the genus *Betta,* esp. the Siamese fighting fish.

fight off *vb (tr, adv)* **1** to repulse; repel. **2** to struggle to avoid or repress: *to fight off a cold.*

fight-or-flight *n (modifier)* involving or relating to an involuntary response to stress in which the hormone adrenaline is secreted into the blood in readiness for physical action, such as fighting or running away.

fig leaf *n* **1** a leaf from a fig tree. **2** a representation of a fig leaf used in sculpture, etc. to cover the genitals of nude figures. **3** a device to conceal something regarded as shameful.

figment ('fɪgmənt) *n* a fantastic notion or fabrication: *a figment of the imagination.* ORIG C15: from LL *figmentum* a fiction, from L *fingere* to shape

figurant ('fɪgjʊrənt) *n* a ballet dancer who does group work but no solo roles. ORIG C18: from F, from *figurer* to represent, appear, FIGURE
▸ **figurante** (ˌfɪgjʊ'rɒnt) *fem n*

figuration (ˌfɪgə'reɪʃən) *n* **1** *Music.* **1a** the employment of characteristic patterns of notes, esp. in variations on a theme. **1b** florid ornamentation. **2** the act or an instance of representing figuratively, as by means of allegory. **3** a figurative representation. **4** the act of decorating with a design.

figurative ('fɪgərətɪv) *adj* **1** involving a figure of speech; not literal; metaphorical. **2** using or filled with figures of speech. **3** representing by means of an emblem, likeness, etc.
▸ **'figuratively** *adv* ▸ **'figurativeness** *n*

figure ('fɪgə) *n* **1** any written symbol other than a letter, esp. a whole number. **2** another name for **digit** (sense 2). **3** an amount expressed numerically: *a figure of £1800 was suggested.* **4** *(pl)* calculations with numbers: *he's good at figures.* **5** visible shape or form; outline. **6** the human form: *a girl with a slender figure.* **7** a slim bodily shape (esp. in **keep** *or* **lose one's figure**). **8** a character or personage: *a figure in politics.* **9** the impression created by a person through behaviour (esp. in **to cut a fine, bold,** etc., **figure**). **10a** a person as impressed on the mind. **10b** *(in combination): father-figure.* **11** a representation in painting or sculpture, esp. of the human form. **12** an illustration or diagram in a text. **13** a representative object or symbol. **14** a pattern or design, as in wood. **15** a predetermined set of movements in dancing or skating. **16** *Geom.* any combination of points, lines, curves, or planes. **17** *Logic.* one of four possible arrangements of the terms in the major and minor premises of a syllogism that give the same conclusion. **18** *Music.* **18a** a numeral written above or below a note in a part. **18b** a characteristic short pattern of notes. ◆ *vb* **figures, figuring, figured. 19** (when *tr,* often foll. by *up*) to calculate or compute (sums, amounts, etc.). **20** *(tr; usually takes a clause as object) Inf., US, Canad., & NZ.* to consider. **21** *(tr)* to represent by a diagram or illustration. **22** *(tr)* to pattern or mark with a design. **23** *(tr)* to depict or portray in a painting, etc. **24** *(tr)* to imagine. **25** *(tr) Music.* to decorate (a melody line or part) with ornamentation. **26** *(intr;* usually foll. by *in)* to be included: *his name figures in the article.* **27** *(intr) Inf.* to accord with expectation: *it figures that he wouldn't come.* ◆ See also **figure out.** ORIG C13: from L *figūra* a shape, from *fingere* to mould
▸ **'figurer** *n*

figured ('fɪgəd) *adj* **1** depicted as a figure in painting or sculpture. **2** decorated with a design. **3** having a form. **4** *Music.* **4a** ornamental. **4b** (of a bass part) provided with numerals indicating accompanying harmonies.

figured bass (beɪs) *n* a shorthand method of indicating a thorough-bass part in which each bass note is accompanied by figures indicating the intervals to be played in the chord above it.

figurehead ('fɪgəˌhɛd) *n* **1** a person nominally having a prominent position, but no real authority. **2** a carved bust on the bow of some sailing vessels.

figure of speech *n* an expression of language, such as metaphor, by which the literal meaning of a word is not employed.

figure out *vb (tr, adv; may take a clause as object) Inf.* **1** to calculate. **2** to understand.

figure skating *n* **1** ice skating in which the skater traces outlines of selected patterns. **2** the whole art of skating, as distinct from skating at speed.
▸ **figure skater** *n*

figurine (ˌfɪgə'riːn) *n* a small carved or moulded figure; statuette. ORIG C19: from F, from It. *figurina* a little FIGURE

figwort ('fɪgˌwɜːt) *n* a plant related to the foxglove having square stems and small greenish flowers.

Fiji ★ ('fiːdʒiː, fiː'dʒiː) *n* **1** an independent republic (within the British Commonwealth 1970–87 and from 1997), consisting of 844 islands (chiefly Viti Levu and Vanua Levu) in the SW Pacific: a British colony (1874–1970); the large islands are of volcanic origin, surrounded by coral reefs; smaller ones are of coral. Official language: English. Religion: Christian and Hindu. Currency: dollar. Capital: Suva. Pop.: 813 000 (1999 est.). Area: 18 272 sq. km (7055 sq. miles). ◆ *n, adj* **2** another word for **Fijian.**

Fijian (fiː'dʒiːən) *n* **1** a member of the indigenous people inhabiting Fiji. **2** the language of this people, belonging to the Malayo-Polynesian family. ◆ *adj* **3** of or characteristic of Fiji or its inhabitants. ◆ Also: **Fiji.**

filagree ('fɪləˌgriː) *n, adj* a less common spelling of **filigree.**

filament ('fɪləmənt) *n* **1** the thin wire, usually tungsten, inside a light bulb that emits light when heated to incandescence by an electric current. **2** *Electronics.* a high-resistance wire forming the cathode in some valves. **3** a single strand of a natural or synthetic fibre. **4** *Bot.* the stalk of a stamen. **5** any slender structure or part. ORIG C16: from NL, from Med. L *filāre* to spin, from L *filum* thread
▸ **filamentary** (ˌfɪlə'mɛntərɪ) *or* ˌ**fila'mentous** *adj*

filaria (fɪ'lɛərɪə) *n, pl* **filariae** (-ɪˌiː). a parasitic nematode worm that lives in the blood of vertebrates and is transmitted by insects: the cause of filariasis. ORIG C19: NL (former name of genus), from L *filum* thread
▸ **fi'larial** *adj*

filariasis (ˌfɪlə'raɪəsɪs, fɪˌlɛərɪ'eɪsɪs) *n* a disease common in tropical and subtropical countries resulting from infestation of the lymphatic system with nematode worms transmitted by mosquitoes: characterized by inflammation. See also **elephantiasis.** ORIG C19: from NL; see FILARIA

filbert ('fɪlbət) *n* **1** any of several N temperate shrubs that have edible rounded brown nuts. **2** Also called: **hazelnut, cobnut.** the nut of any of these shrubs. ORIG C14: after St *Philbert,* 7th-century Frankish abbot, because the nuts are ripe around his feast day, Aug. 22

filch (fɪltʃ) *vb (tr)* to steal or take in small amounts. ORIG C16 *filchen* to steal, attack, ?from OE *gefylce* band of men
▸ **'filcher** *n*

file[1] (faɪl) *n* **1** a folder, box, etc., used to keep documents or other items in order. **2** the documents, etc., kept in this way. **3** documents or information about a specific subject, person, etc. **4** a line of people in marching formation, one behind another. **5** any of the eight vertical rows of squares on a chessboard. **6** *Computing.* a named collection of information, in the form of text, programs, graphics, etc., held on a permanent storage device, such as a magnetic disk. **7 on file.** recorded or catalogued for reference, as in a file. ◆ *vb* **files, filing, filed. 8** to place (a document, etc.) in a file. **9** *(tr)* to place (a legal docu-

ment) on public or official record. **10** (*tr*) to bring (a suit, esp. a divorce suit) in a court of law. **11** (*tr*) to submit (copy) to a newspaper. **12** (*intr*) to march or walk in a file or files: *the ants filed down the hill.* ORIG C16 (in the sense: string on which documents are hung): from OF, from Med. L *fīlāre;* see FILAMENT
▸ **'filer** *n*

file² (faɪl) *n* **1** a hand tool consisting of a steel blade with small cutting teeth on some or all of its faces. It is used for shaping or smoothing. ◆ *vb* **files, filing, filed. 2** (*tr*) to shape or smooth (a surface) with a file. ORIG OE *fīl*
▸ **'filer** *n*

filefish ('faɪlˌfɪʃ) *n, pl* **filefish** *or* **filefishes.** any tropical triggerfish having a narrow compressed body and a very long dorsal spine. ORIG C18: referring to its file-like scales

filename ('faɪlˌneɪm) *n* an arrangement of characters that enables a computer system to permit the user to have access to a particular file.

file server *n Computing.* the central unit of a local area network that controls its operation and provides access to separately stored data files.

filet ('fɪlɪt, 'fɪleɪ) *n* a variant spelling of **fillet** (senses 1–3). ORIG C20: from F: net, from OF, from *fil* thread, from L *fīlum*

filet mignon ('fɪleɪ 'miːnjɒn) *n* a small tender boneless cut of beef. ORIG from F, lit.: dainty fillet

filial ('fɪljəl) *adj* **1** of, resembling, or suitable to a son or daughter: *filial affection.* **2** *Genetics.* designating any of the generations following the parental generation. ORIG C15: from LL *fīliālis,* from L *fīlius* son
▸ **'filially** *adv*

filibeg *or* **philibeg** ('fɪlɪˌbɛg) *n* the kilt worn by Scottish Highlanders. ORIG C18: from Scot. Gaelic *fēileadhbeag,* from *fēileadh* kilt + *beag* small

filibuster ('fɪlɪˌbʌstə) *n* **1** the process of obstructing legislation by means of delaying tactics. **2** Also called: **filibusterer.** a legislator who engages in such obstruction. **3** a freebooter or military adventurer, esp. in a foreign country. ◆ *vb* **4** to obstruct (legislation) with delaying tactics. **5** (*intr*) to engage in unlawful military action. ORIG C16: from Sp., from F *flibustier,* prob. from Du. *vrijbuiter* pirate, lit.: one plundering freely; see FREEBOOTER
▸ **'filiˌbusterer** *n*

filigree ('fɪlɪˌgriː) *or* **filagree** *n* **1** delicate ornamental work of twisted gold, silver, or other wire. **2** any fanciful delicate ornamentation. ◆ *adj* **3** made of or as if with filigree. ORIG C17: from earlier *filigreen,* from F *filigrane,* from L *fīlum* thread + *grānum* GRAIN
▸ **'filiˌgreed** *adj*

filings ('faɪlɪŋz) *pl n* shavings or particles removed by a file: *iron filings.*

Filipino (ˌfɪlɪ'piːnəʊ) *n* **1** (*pl* **Filipinos**) Also (fem): **Filipina.** a native or inhabitant of the Philippines. **2** another name for **Tagalog.** ◆ *adj* **3** of or relating to the Philippines or their inhabitants.

fill (fɪl) *vb* (*mainly tr;* often foll. by *up*) **1** (*also intr*) to make or become full: *to fill up a bottle.* **2** to occupy the whole of: *the party filled the house.* **3** to plug (a gap, crevice, etc.). **4** to meet (a requirement or need) satisfactorily. **5** to cover (a page or blank space) with writing, drawing, etc. **6** to hold and perform the duties of (an office or position). **7** to appoint or elect an occupant to (an office or position). **8** (*also intr*) to swell or cause to swell with wind, as in manoeuvring the sails of a sailing vessel. **9** *Chiefly US & Canad.* to put together the necessary materials for (a prescription or order). **10 fill the bill.** *Inf.* to serve or perform adequately. ◆ *n* **11** material such as gravel, stones, etc., used to bring an area of ground up to a required level. **12 one's fill.** the quantity needed to satisfy one. ◆ See also **fill in, fill out,** etc. ORIG OE *fyllan*

filler ('fɪlə) *n* **1** a person or thing that fills. **2** an object or substance used to add weight or size to something or to fill in a gap. **3** a paste, used for filling in cracks, holes, etc., in a surface before painting. **4** the inner portion of a cigar. **5** *Journalism.* articles, photographs, etc., to fill space between more important articles in a newspaper or magazine.

fillet ('fɪlɪt) *n* **1a** Also called: **fillet steak.** a strip of boneless meat. **1b** the boned side of a fish. **2** a narrow strip of any material. **3** a thin strip of ribbon, lace, etc., worn in the hair or around the neck. **4** a narrow flat moulding, esp. one between other mouldings. **5** a narrow band between flutings on the shaft of a column. **6** *Heraldry.* a horizontal division of a shield. **7** a narrow decorative line, impressed on the cover of a book. ◆ *vb* **fillets, filleting, filleted.** (*tr*) **8** to cut or prepare (meat or fish) as a fillet. **9** to cut fillets from (meat or fish). **10** to bind or decorate with or as if with a fillet. ◆ Also (for senses 1–3): **filet.** ORIG C14: from OF *filet,* from *fil* thread, from L *fīlum*

fill in *vb* (*adv*) **1** (*tr*) to complete (a form, drawing, etc.). **2** (*intr*) to act as a substitute. **3** (*tr*) to put material into (a hole or cavity), esp. so as to make it level with a surface. **4** (*tr*) *Inf.* to inform with facts or news. ◆ *n* **fill-in. 5** a substitute.

filling ('fɪlɪŋ) *n* **1** the substance or thing used to fill a space or container: *pie filling.* **2** *Dentistry.* any of various substances (metal, plastic, etc.) for inserting into the prepared cavity of a tooth. **3** *Chiefly US.* the weft in weaving. ◆ *adj* **4** (of food or a meal) substantial and satisfying.

filling station *n* a place where petrol and other supplies for motorists are sold.

fillip ('fɪlɪp) *n* **1** something that adds stimulation or enjoyment. **2** the action of holding a finger towards the palm with the thumb and suddenly releasing it outwards to produce a snapping sound. **3** a quick blow or tap made by this. ◆ *vb* **4** (*tr*) to stimulate or excite. **5** (*tr*) to strike or project sharply with a fillip. **6** (*intr*) to make a fillip. ORIG C15 *philippe,* imit.

Fillmore ★ ('fɪlmɔː) *n* **Millard.** 1800–74, 13th president of the US (1850-53); a leader of the Whig Party.

fill out *vb* (*adv*) **1** to make or become fuller, thicker, or rounder. **2** to make more substantial. **3** (*tr*) *Chiefly US & Canad.* to fill in (a form, etc.).

fill up *vb* (*adv*) **1** (*tr*) to complete (a form, application, etc.). **2** to make or become full. ◆ *n* **fill-up. 3** the act of filling something completely, esp. the petrol tank of a car.

filly ('fɪlɪ) *n, pl* **fillies.** a female horse or pony under the age of four. ORIG C15: from ON *fylja;* see FOAL

film (fɪlm) *n* **1a** a sequence of images of moving objects photographed by a camera and providing the optical illusion of continuous movement when projected onto a screen. **1b** a form of entertainment, etc., composed of such a sequence of images. **1c** (*as modifier*): *film techniques.* **2** a thin flexible strip of cellulose coated with a photographic emulsion, used to make negatives and transparencies. **3** a thin coating or layer. **4** a thin sheet of any material, as of plastic for packaging. **5** a fine haze, mist, or blur. **6** a gauzy web of filaments or fine threads. ◆ *vb* **7a** to photograph with a cine camera. **7b** to make a film of (a screenplay, event, etc.). **8** (often foll. by *over*) to cover or become covered or coated with a film. ORIG OE *filmen* membrane

filmic ('fɪlmɪk) *adj* **1** of or relating to films or the cinema. **2** suggestive of films or the cinema.
▸ **'filmically** *adv*

film noir (nwɑː) *n* a type of gangster thriller, made esp. in the 1940s in Hollywood, characterized by stark lighting, an involved plot, and an atmosphere of cynicism and corruption. ORIG C20: F, lit.: black film

filmography (fɪl'mɒgrəfɪ) *n* **1** a list of the films made by a particular director, actor, etc. **2** any writing that deals with films or the cinema.

filmset ('fɪlmˌsɛt) *vb* **filmsets, filmsetting, filmset.** (*tr*) *Brit.* to set (type matter) by filmsetting.
▸ **'filmˌsetter** *n*

filmsetting ('fɪlmˌsɛtɪŋ) *n Brit., printing.* typesetting by exposing type characters onto photographic film from which printing plates are made.

film speed *n* **1** the sensitivity to light of a photographic film, specified in terms of the film's ISO rating. **2** the rate at which the film passes through a motion picture camera or projector.

film strip *n* a strip of film composed of different images projected separately as slides.

filmy ('fɪlmɪ) *adj* **filmier, filmiest. 1** transparent or gauzy. **2** hazy; blurred.
▸ **'filmily** *adv* ▸ **'filminess** *n*

filo ('fiːləʊ) *n* a type of Greek flaky pastry in very thin sheets. ORIG C20: Mod. Gk *phullon* leaf

Filofax ('faɪləʊˌfæks) *n Trademark.* a type of loose-leaf ring binder with sets of different-coloured paper, used as a portable personal filing system, including appointments, addresses, etc.

filter ('fɪltə) *n* **1** a porous substance, such as paper or sand, that allows fluid to pass but retains suspended solid particles. **2** any device containing such a porous substance for separating suspensions from fluids. **3** any of various porous substances built into the mouth end of a cigarette or cigar for absorbing impurities such as tar. **4** any electronic, optical, or acoustic device that blocks signals or radiations of certain frequencies while allowing others to pass. **5** any transparent disc of gelatine or glass used to eliminate or reduce the intensity of given frequencies from the light leaving a lamp, entering a camera, etc. **6** *Brit.* a traffic signal at a road junction which permits vehicles to turn either left or right when the main signals are red. ◆ *vb* **7** (often foll. by *out*) to remove or separate (suspended particles, etc.) from (a liquid, gas, etc.) by the action of a filter. **8** (*tr*) to obtain by filtering. **9** (*intr;* foll. by *through*) to pass (through a filter or something like a filter). **10** (*intr*) to flow slowly; trickle. ORIG C16 *filtre,* from Med. L *filtrum* piece of felt used as a filter, of Gmc origin

filterable ('fɪltərəbᵊl) *or* **filtrable** ('fɪltrəbᵊl) *adj* **1** capable of being filtered. **2** (of most viruses and certain bacteria) capable of passing through the pores of a fine filter.

filter bed *n* a layer of sand or gravel in a tank or reservoir through which a liquid is passed so as to purify it.

filter feeding *n Zool.* a method of feeding in some aquatic animals, such as whalebone whales, in which minute food particles are filtered from the surrounding water.
▸ **filter feeder** *n*

filter out *or* **through** *vb* (*intr, adv*) to become known gradually; leak.

filter paper *n* a porous paper used for filtering liquids.

filter tip *n* **1** an attachment to the mouth end of a cigarette for trapping impurities such as tar during smoking. **2** a cigarette having such an attachment.
▸ **'filter-ˌtipped** *adj*

filth (fɪlθ) *n* **1** foul or disgusting dirt; refuse. **2** extreme physical or moral uncleanliness. **3** vulgarity or obscenity. **4 the filth.** *Derog. sl.* the police. ORIG OE *fӯlth*

filthy ('fɪlθɪ) *adj* **filthier, filthiest. 1** very dirty or obscene. **2** offensive or vicious: *that was a filthy trick to play.* **3** *Inf., chiefly Brit.* extremely unpleasant: *filthy weather.* ◆ *adv* **4** extremely; disgustingly (esp. in **filthy rich**).
▸ **'filthily** *adv* ▸ **'filthiness** *n*

filtrate ('fɪltreɪt) *n* **1** a liquid or gas that has been filtered. ◆ *vb* **filtrates, filtrating, filtrated. 2** to filter. ORIG C17: from Med. L *filtrāre* to FILTER
▸ **fil'tration** *n*

fin (fɪn) *n* **1** any of the firm appendages that are the organs of locomotion and balance in fishes and some other aquatic animals. **2** a part or appendage that resembles a fin. **3a** *Brit.* a vertical surface to which the rudder is attached at the rear of an aeroplane. **3b** a tail surface fixed to a rocket or missile to give stability. **4** *Naut.* a fixed or adjustable blade projecting under water from the hull of a vessel to give it stability or control. **5** a projecting rib to dissipate heat from the surface of an engine cylinder or radiator. ◆ *vb* **fins, finning, finned. 6** (*tr*) to provide with fins. ORIG OE *finn*
▸ **'finless** *adj* ▸ **finned** *adj*

fin. *abbrev. for:* **1** finance. **2** financial.

Fin. *abbrev. for:* **1** Finland. **2** Finnish.

finable *or* **fineable** ('faɪnəbᵊl) *adj* liable to a fine.
▸ **'finableness** *or* **'fineableness** *n*

finagle (fɪ'neɪgᵊl) *vb* **finagles, finagling, finagled.** *Inf.* **1** (*tr*) to get or achieve by craftiness or persuasion. **2** to use trickery on (a person). ORIG C20: ?from dialect *fainaigue* cheat
▸ **fi'nagler** *n*

final ('faɪnᵊl) *adj* **1** of or occurring at the end; last. **2** having no possibility of further discussion, action, or change: *a final decree of judgment.* **3** relating to or constituting an end or purpose: *a final clause may be introduced by "in order to".* **4** *Music.* another word for **perfect** (sense 9b). ◆ *n* **5** a last thing; end. **6** a deciding contest between the winners of previous rounds in a competition. ◆ See also **finals.** ORIG C14: from L *fīnālis,* from *fīnis* limit, boundary

finale (fɪ'nɑːlɪ) *n* **1** the concluding part of any performance or presentation. **2** the closing section or movement of a musical composition. ORIG C18: from It., n use of adj *finale,* from L *fīnālis* FINAL

finalist ('faɪnəlɪst) *n* a contestant who has reached the last stage of a competition.

finality (faɪ'nælɪtɪ) *n, pl* **finalities. 1** the condition or quality of being final or settled: *the finality of death.* **2** a final or conclusive act.

finalize *or* **finalise** ('faɪnəˌlaɪz) *vb* **finalizes, finalizing, finalized** *or* **finalises, finalising, finalised. 1** (*tr*) to put into final form; settle: *to finalize plans for the merger.* **2** to reach agreement on a transaction.
▸ **ˌfinali'zation** *or* **ˌfinali'sation** *n*

finally ('faɪnəlɪ) *adv* **1** at last; eventually. **2** at the end or final point; lastly. **3** completely; conclusively. ◆ *sentence connector.* **4** in the end; lastly: *finally, he put his tie on.* **5** as the last or final point.

finals ('faɪnᵊlz) *pl n* **1** the deciding part of a competition. **2** *Education.* the last examinations in an academic or professional course.

finance (fɪ'næns, 'faɪnæns) *n* **1** the system of money, credit, etc., esp. with respect to government revenues and expenditures. **2** funds or the provision of funds. **3** (*pl*) financial condition. ◆ *vb* **finances, financing, financed. 4** (*tr*) to provide or obtain funds or credit for. ORIG C14: from OF, from *finer* to end, settle by payment

finance company *or* **house** *n* an enterprise engaged in the loan of money against collateral, esp. one specializing in the financing of hire-purchase contracts.

financial (fɪ'nænʃəl, faɪ-) *adj* **1** of or relating to finance or finances. **2** of or relating to persons who manage money, capital, or credit. **3** *Austral. & NZ inf.* having money; in funds. **4** *Austral. & NZ.* (of a club member) fully paid-up.
▸ **fi'nancially** *adv*

financial futures *pl n* futures in a stock-exchange index, currency exchange rate, or interest rate enabling banks, building societies, brokers, and speculators to hedge their involvement in these markets.

Financial Ombudsman *n* any of five British ombudsmen: the **Banking Ombudsman**, set up in 1986 to investigate complaints from banking customers; the **Building Society Ombudsman**, set up in 1987 to investigate complaints from building society customers; the **Insurance Ombudsman**, set up in 1981 to investigate complaints by policyholders (since 1988 this ombudsman has also operated a **Unit Trust Ombudsman** scheme); the **Investment Ombudsman**, set up in 1989 to investigate complaints by investors (the **Personal Investment Authority Ombudsman** is responsible for investigating complaints by personal investors); and the **Pensions Ombudsman**, set up in 1993 to investigate complaints regarding pension schemes.

financial year *n Brit.* **1** any annual period at the end of which a firm's accounts are made up. **2** the annual period ending April 5, over which Budget estimates are made by the British Government. ◆ US and Canad. equivalent: **fiscal year.**

financier (fɪ'nænsɪə, faɪ-) *n* a person who is engaged in large-scale financial operations.

financing gap *n* the difference between a country's requirements for foreign exchange to finance its debts and imports and its income from overseas.

finback ('fɪnˌbæk) *n* another name for **rorqual.**

finch (fɪntʃ) *n* any of various songbirds having a short stout bill for feeding on seeds, such as the bullfinch, chaffinch, siskin, and canary. ORIG OE *finc*

Finchley ★ ('fɪntʃlɪ) *n* a residential district of N London, part of the Greater London borough of Barnet from 1965.

find (faɪnd) *vb* **finds, finding, found.** (*mainly tr*) **1** to meet with or discover by chance. **2** to discover or obtain, esp. by search or effort: *to find happiness.* **3** (*may take a clause as object*) to realize: *he found that nobody knew.* **4** (*may take a clause as object*) to consider: *I find this wine a little sour.* **5** to look for and point out (something to be criticized). **6** (*also intr*) *Law.* to determine an issue and pronounce a verdict (upon): *the court found the accused guilty.* **7** to regain (something lost or not functioning): *to find one's tongue.* **8** to reach (a target): *the bullet found its mark.* **9** to provide, esp. with difficulty: *we'll find room for you too.* **10** to be able to pay: *I can't find that amount of money.* **11 find oneself.** to realize and accept one's true character; discover one's vocation. **12 find one's feet.** to become capable or confident. ◆ *n* **13** a person, thing, etc., that is found, esp. a valuable discovery. ORIG OE *findan*

finder ('faɪndə) *n* **1** a person or thing that finds. **2** *Physics.* a small telescope fitted to a more powerful larger telescope. **3** *Photog.* short for **viewfinder. 4 finders keepers.** *Inf.* whoever finds something has the right to keep it.

fin de siècle *French.* (fɛ̃ də sjɛklə) *n* **1** the end of the 19th century. ◆ *adj* ***fin-de-siècle.*** **2** of or relating to the close of the 19th century. **3** decadent, esp. in artistic tastes.

finding ('faɪndɪŋ) *n* **1** a thing that is found or discovered. **2** *Law.* the conclusion reached after a judicial inquiry; verdict.

find out *vb* (*adv*) **1** to gain knowledge of (something); learn. **2** to detect the crime, deception, etc., of (someone).

fine[1] (faɪn) *adj* **1** very good of its kind: *a fine speech.* **2** superior in skill or accomplishment: *a fine violinist.* **3** (of weather) clear and dry. **4** enjoyable or satisfying: *a fine time.* **5** (*postpositive*) *Inf.* quite well: *I feel fine.* **6** satisfactory; acceptable: *that's fine by me.* **7** of delicate composition or careful workmanship: *fine crystal.* **8** (of precious metals) pure or having a high degree of purity: *fine silver.* **9** discriminating: *a fine eye for antique brasses.* **10** abstruse or subtle: *a fine point.* **11** very thin or slender: *fine hair.* **12** very small: *fine print.* **13** (of edges, blades, etc.) sharp; keen. **14** ornate, showy, or smart. **15** good-looking: *a fine young woman.* **16** polished, elegant, or refined: *a fine gentleman.* **17** *Cricket.* (of a fielding position) oblique to and behind the wicket: *fine leg.* **18** (*prenominal*) *Inf.* disappointing or terrible: *a fine mess.* ◆ *adv* **19** *Inf.* all right: *that suits me fine.* **20** finely. ◆ *vb* **fines, fining, fined. 21** to make or become finer; refine. **22** (often foll. by *down* or *away*) to make or become smaller. ORIG C13: from OF *fin,* from L *fīnis* end, boundary, as in *fīnis honōrum* the highest degree of honour
▸ **'finely** *adv* ▸ **'fineness** *n*

fine[2] (faɪn) *n* **1** a certain amount of money exacted as a penalty: *a parking fine.* **2** a payment made by a tenant at the start of his or her tenancy to reduce his or her subsequent rent; premium. **3 in fine. 3a** in short. **3b** in conclusion. ◆ *vb* **fines, fining, fined. 4** (*tr*) to impose a fine on. ORIG C12 (in the sense: conclusion, settlement): from OF *fin;* see FINE[1]

fine[3] ('fiːneɪ) *n Music.* the point at which a piece is to end. ORIG It., from L *fīnis* end

fine art *n* **1** art produced chiefly for its aesthetic value. **2** (*often pl*) any of the fields in which such art is produced, such as painting, sculpture, and engraving.

fine-draw *vb* **fine-draws, fine-drawing, fine-drew, fine-drawn.** (*tr*) to sew together so finely that the join is scarcely noticeable.

fine-drawn *adj* **1** (of arguments, distinctions, etc.) precise or subtle. **2** (of wire, etc.) drawn out until very fine.

fine-grained *adj* (of wood, leather, etc.) having a fine smooth even grain.

finery[1] ('faɪnərɪ) *n* elaborate or showy decoration, esp. clothing and jewellery.

finery[2] ('faɪnərɪ) *n, pl* **fineries.** a hearth for converting cast iron into wrought iron. ORIG C17: from OF *finerie,* from *finer* to refine; see FINE[1]

fines herbes (*French* finz ɛrb) *pl n* a mixture of finely chopped herbs, used to flavour omelettes, salads, etc.

finespun ('faɪn'spʌn) *adj* **1** spun or drawn out to a fine thread. **2** excessively subtle or refined.

finesse (fɪ'nɛs) *n* **1** elegant skill in style or performance. **2** subtlety and tact in handling difficult situations. **3** *Bridge, whist.* an attempt to win a trick when opponents hold a high card in the suit led by playing a lower card. **4** a trick, artifice, or strategy. ◆ *vb* **finesses, finessing, finessed. 5** to bring about with finesse. **6** to play (a card) as a finesse. ORIG C15: from OF, from *fin* fine, delicate; see FINE[1]

fine-tooth comb *or* **fine-toothed comb** *n* **1** a comb with fine teeth set closely together. **2 go over** (*or* **through**) **with a fine-tooth**(**ed**) **comb.** to examine very thoroughly.

fine-tune *vb* **fine-tunes, fine-tuning, fine-tuned.** (*tr*) to make fine adjustments to (something) in order to obtain optimum performance.

Fingal's Cave ★ ('fɪŋgəlz) *n* a cave in W Scotland, on Staffa Island in the Inner Hebrides: basaltic pillars. Length: 69 m (227 ft). Height: 36 m (117 ft).

finger ('fɪŋgə) *n* **1a** any of the digits of the hand, often excluding the thumb. **1b** (*as modifier*): *a finger bowl.* **1c** (*in combination*): *a fingernail.* Related adj: **digital. 2** the part of a glove made to cover a finger. **3** something that resembles a finger in shape or function: *a finger of land.* **4** the length or width of a finger used as a unit of measurement. **5** a quantity of liquid in a glass, etc., as deep as a finger is wide. **6 get** *or* **pull one's finger out.** *Brit. inf.* to begin or speed up activity, esp. after initial delay. **7 have a** (*or* **one's**) **finger in the pie. 7a** to have an interest in or take part in some activity. **7b** to meddle or interfere. **8 lay** *or* **put one's finger on.** to indicate or locate accurately. **9 not lift** (*or* **raise**) **a finger.** (*foll. by an infinitive*) not to make any effort (to do something). **10 twist** *or* **wrap around one's little finger.** to have easy and complete control or influence over. **11 put the finger on.** *Inf.* to inform on or identify, esp. for the police. ◆ *vb* **12** (*tr*) to touch or manipulate with the fingers; handle. **13** (*tr*) *Inf., chiefly US.* to identify as a criminal or suspect. **14** to use one's fingers in playing (an instrument, such as a piano or clarinet). **15** to indicate on (a composition or part) the fingering required by a pianist, etc. ORIG OE
▸ **'fingerless** *adj*

fingerboard ('fɪŋgəˌbɔːd) *n* the long strip of hard wood on a violin, guitar, etc. upon which the strings are stopped by the fingers.

finger bowl *n* a small bowl filled with water for rinsing the fingers at the table after a meal.

finger buffet ('bʊfeɪ) *n* a buffet meal at which food that may be picked up in the fingers (**finger food**), such as canapés or vol-au-vents, is served.

fingered ('fɪŋgəd) *adj* **1** marked or dirtied by handling. **2a** having a finger or fingers. **2b** (*in combination*): *red-fingered.* **3** (of a musical part) having numerals indicating the fingering.

fingering ('fɪŋgərɪŋ) *n* **1** the technique or art of using one's fingers in playing a musical instrument, esp. the piano. **2** the numerals in a musical part indicating this.

fingerling ('fɪŋgəlɪŋ) *n* a very young fish, esp. the parr of salmon or trout.

fingermark ('fɪŋgəˌmɑːk) *n* a mark left by dirty or greasy fingers on paintwork, walls, etc.

fingernail ('fɪŋgəˌneɪl) *n* a thin horny translucent plate covering part of the dorsal surface of the end joint of each finger.

finger painting *n* the process or art of painting with **finger paints** of starch, glycerine, and pigments, using the fingers, hand, or arm.

finger post *n* a signpost showing a pointing finger or hand.

fingerprint ('fɪŋgəˌprɪnt) *n* **1** an impression of the pattern of ridges on the surface of the end joint of each finger and thumb. **2** any unique identifying characteristic.

◆ *vb* (*tr*) **3** to take an inked impression of the fingerprints of (a person). **4** to take a sample of (a person's) DNA.

fingerstall ('fɪŋgəˌstɔːl) *n* a protective covering for a finger. Also called: **cot**.

fingertip ('fɪŋgəˌtɪp) *n* **1** the end joint or tip of a finger. **2** **at one's fingertips.** readily available.

finial ('faɪnɪəl) *n* **1** an ornament on top of a spire, etc., esp. in the form of a fleur-de-lys. **2** an ornament at the top of a piece of furniture, etc. ORIG C14: from *finial* (adj), var. of FINAL

finicky ('fɪnɪkɪ) *or* **finicking** *adj* **1** excessively particular; fussy. **2** overelaborate. ORIG C19: from *finical,* from FINE[1]

finis ('fɪnɪs) *n* the end; finish: used at the end of books, films, etc. ORIG C15: from L

finish ('fɪnɪʃ) *vb* (*mainly tr*) **1** to bring to an end; conclude or stop. **2** (*intr;* sometimes foll. by *up*) to be at or come to the end; use up. **3** to bring to a desired or complete condition. **4** to put a particular surface texture on (wood, cloth, etc.). **5** (often foll. by *off*) to destroy or defeat completely. **6** to train (a person) in social graces and talents. **7** (*intr;* foll. by *with*) to end a relationship or association. ◆ *n* **8** the final or last stage or part; end. **9** the death or absolute defeat of a person or one side in a conflict: *a fight to the finish.* **10** the surface texture or appearance of wood, cloth, etc.: *a rough finish.* **11** a thing, event, etc., that completes. **12** completeness and high quality of workmanship. **13** *Sport.* ability to sprint at the end of a race. ORIG C14: from OF, from L *fīnīre;* see FINE[1]
▸ '**finished** *adj* ▸ '**finisher** *n*

finishing school *n* a private school for girls that teaches social graces.

Finistère ★ (ˌfɪnɪ'stɛə; *French* finistɛr) *n* a department of NW France, at the tip of the Breton peninsula. Capital: Quimper. Pop.: 840 103 (1994 est.). Area: 7029 sq. km (2741 sq. miles).

Finisterre ★ (ˌfɪnɪ'stɛə) *n* **1** **Cape.** a headland in NW Spain: the westernmost point of the Spanish mainland. **2** an English name for **Finistère.**

finite ('faɪnaɪt) *adj* **1** bounded in magnitude or spatial or temporal extent. **2** *Maths, logic.* having a countable number of elements. **3** limited or restricted in nature: *human existence is finite.* **4** denoting any form of a verb inflected for grammatical features such as person, number, and tense. ORIG C15: from L *fīnītus* limited, from *fīnīre* to limit, end
▸ '**finitely** *adv* ▸ '**finiteness** *or* **finitude** ('faɪnɪˌtjuːd) *n*

fink (fɪŋk) *n Sl., chiefly US & Canad.* **1** a strikebreaker. **2** an unpleasant or contemptible person. ORIG C20: from ?

Finland ★ ('fɪnlənd) *n* **1** a republic in N Europe, on the Baltic Sea: ceded to Russia by Sweden in 1809; gained independence in 1917; Soviet invasion successfully withstood in 1939–40, with the loss of Karelia; a member of the European Union. It is generally low-lying, with about 50 000 lakes, extensive forests, and peat bogs. Official languages: Finnish and Swedish. Religion: Christian (Lutheran) majority. Currency: markka and euro. Capital: Helsinki. Pop.: 5 167 000 (1999 est.). Area: 337 000 sq. km (130 120 sq. miles). Finnish name: **Suomi.** **2** **Gulf of.** an arm of the Baltic Sea between Finland, Estonia, and Russia.

Finlandization *or* **Finlandisation** (ˌfɪnləndaɪ'zeɪʃən) *n* neutralization of a small country by a superpower, using conciliation rather than confrontation, as the former Soviet Union did in relation to Finland.

Finlay ★ ('fɪnlɪ) *n* **Carlos Juan** (*Spanish* 'karlɔs xwan). 1833–1915, Cuban physician: discovered that the mosquito was the vector of yellow fever.

Finn[1] (fɪn) *n* a native, inhabitant, or citizen of Finland. ORIG OE *Finnas* (pl)

Finn[2] ★ (fɪn) *n* known as *Finn MacCool.* (in Irish legend) chief of the Fianna, father of the heroic poet Ossian.

finnan haddock ('fɪnən) *or* **haddie** ('hædɪ) *n* smoked haddock. ORIG C18: *finnan* after *Findon,* a village in NE Scotland

Finney ★ ('fɪnɪ) *n* **1** **Albert.** born 1936, British actor. **2** **Tom.** born 1922, British footballer: won 76 international caps.

Finnic ('fɪnɪk) *n* **1** one of the two branches of the Finno-Ugric family of languages, including Finnish and several languages of NE Europe. ◆ *adj* **2** of or relating to this group of languages or to the Finns.

Finnish ('fɪnɪʃ) *adj* **1** of or characteristic of Finland, the Finns, or their language. ◆ *n* **2** the official language of Finland, belonging to the Finno-Ugric family.

Finnmark ★ ('fɪnˌmɑːk) *n* a county of N Norway: the largest, northernmost, and least populated county; mostly a barren plateau. Capital: Vadsø. Pop.: 76 502 (1996 est.). Area: 48 649 sq. km (18 779 sq. miles).

Finno-Ugric ('fɪnəʊ'uːgrɪk, -'juː-) *or* **Finno-Ugrian** *n* **1** a family of languages spoken in Scandinavia, E Europe, and W Asia, including Finnish, Estonian, and Hungarian. ◆ *adj* **2** of, relating to, speaking, or belonging to this family of languages.

finny ('fɪnɪ) *adj* **finnier, finniest.** **1** *Poetic.* relating to or containing many fishes. **2** having or resembling a fin or fins.

fino ('fiːnəʊ) *n* a very dry sherry. ORIG Sp.: FINE[1]

Finsen ★ (*Danish* 'fensən) *n* **Niels Ryberg** (neːls 'ryber). 1860–1904, Danish physician; founder of phototherapy: Nobel prize for physiology or medicine 1903.

Finsteraarhorn ★ (*German* ˌfɪnstər'aːrhɔrn) *n* a mountain in S central Switzerland: highest peak in the Bernese Alps. Height: 4274 m (14 022 ft).

fiord (fjɔːd) *n* a variant spelling of **fjord.**

fioriture (ˌfjɔːrɪ'tʊəreɪ) *pl n Music.* flourishes; embellishments. ORIG C19: It, from *fiorire* to flower

fipple ('fɪpᵊl) *n* a wooden plug forming a flue in the end of a pipe, as the mouthpiece of a recorder. ORIG C17: from ?

fipple flute *n* an end-blown flute provided with a fipple, such as the recorder or flageolet.

fir (fɜː) *n* **1** any of a genus of pyramidal coniferous trees having single needle-like leaves and erect cones. **2** any of various other related trees, such as the Douglas fir. **3** the wood of any of these trees. ORIG OE *furh*

Firbank ★ ('fɜːbæŋk) *n* (**Arthur Annesley**) **Ronald.** 1886–1926, British novelist, whose works include *Valmouth* (1919), *The Flower beneath the Foot* (1923), and *Concerning the Eccentricities of Cardinal Pirelli* (1926).

Firdausi (fɪə'daʊsɪ) *or* **Firdusi** ★ (fɪə'duːsɪ) *n* pen name of *Abul Qasim Mansur.* ?935–1020 A.D., Persian poet; author of *Shah Nama* (*The Book of Kings*).

fire ('faɪə) *n* **1** the state of combustion in which inflammable material burns, producing heat, flames, and often smoke. **2a** a mass of burning coal, wood, etc., used esp. in a hearth to heat a room. **2b** (*in combination*): *firelighter.* **3** a destructive conflagration, as of a forest, building, etc. **4** a device for heating a room, etc. **5** something resembling a fire in light or brilliance: *a diamond's fire.* **6** the act of discharging weapons, artillery, etc. **7** a burst or rapid volley: *a fire of questions.* **8** intense passion; ardour. **9** liveliness, as of imagination, etc. **10** fever and inflammation. **11** a severe trial or torment (esp. in **go through fire and water**). **12** **between two fires.** under attack from two sides. **13** **catch fire.** to ignite. **14** **on fire.** **14a** in a state of ignition. **14b** ardent or eager. **15** **open fire.** to start firing a gun, artillery, etc. **16** **play with fire.** to be involved in something risky. **17** **set fire to** *or* **set on fire.** **17a** to ignite. **17b** to arouse or excite. **18** **under fire.** being attacked, as by weapons or by harsh criticism. **19** (*modifier*) *Astrol.* of or relating to a group of three signs of the zodiac, Aries, Leo, and Sagittarius. ◆ *vb* **fires, firing, fired.** **20** to discharge (a firearm or projectile), or (of a firearm, etc.) to be discharged. **21** to detonate (an explosive charge or device), or (of such a charge or device) to be detonated. **22** (*intr*) (of an engine) to start working; ignite. **23** (*tr*) *Inf.* to dismiss from employment. **24** (*tr*) *Ceramics.* to bake in a kiln to harden the clay, etc. **25** to kindle or be kindled. **26** (*tr*) to provide with fuel: *oil fires the heating system.* **27** (*tr*) to subject to heat. **28** (*tr*) to heat slowly so as to dry. **29** (*tr*) to arouse to strong emotion. **30** to glow or cause to glow. ◆ *sentence substitute.* **31** a cry to warn others of a fire. **32** the order to begin firing a gun, artillery, etc. ORIG OE *fȳr*
▸ '**firer** *n*

★ people and places

fire alarm *n* a device to give warning of fire, esp. a bell, siren, or hooter.

fire appliance *n* another name for fire engine.

firearm ('faɪər,ɑːm) *n* a weapon from which a projectile can be discharged by an explosion caused by igniting gunpowder, etc.

fireback ('faɪə,bæk) *n* an ornamental iron slab against the back wall of a hearth.

fireball ('faɪə,bɔːl) *n* **1** a ball-shaped discharge of lightning. **2** the region of hot ionized gas at the centre of a nuclear explosion. **3** *Astron.* a large bright meteor. **4** *Sl.* an energetic person.

fire blight *n* a disease of apples, pears, and similar fruit trees, caused by a bacterium and characterized by blackening of the blossoms and leaves.

fireboat ('faɪə,bəut) *n* a motor vessel equipped with fire-fighting apparatus.

firebomb ('faɪə,bɒm) *n* another name for **incendiary** (sense 6).

firebox ('faɪə,bɒks) *n* the furnace chamber of a boiler in a steam locomotive.

firebrand ('faɪə,brænd) *n* **1** a piece of burning wood. **2** a person who causes unrest.

firebreak ('faɪə,breɪk) *n* a strip of open land in forest or prairie, serving to arrest the advance of a fire.

firebrick ('faɪə,brɪk) *n* a refractory brick made of fire clay, used for lining furnaces, flues, etc.

fire brigade *n Chiefly Brit.* an organized body of firefighters.

firebug ('faɪə,bʌg) *n Inf.* a person who deliberately sets fire to property.

fire clay *n* a heat-resistant clay used in the making of firebricks, furnace linings, etc.

fire company *n* **1** an insurance company selling policies relating to fire risk. **2** *US.* an organized body of firemen.

fire control *n Mil.* the procedures by which weapons are brought to engage a target.

firecracker ('faɪə,krækə) *n* a small cardboard container filled with explosive powder.

firecrest ('faɪə,krest) *n* a small European warbler having a crown striped with yellow, black, and white.

firedamp ('faɪə,dæmp) *n* an explosive mixture of hydrocarbons, chiefly methane, formed in coal mines. See also **afterdamp**.

firedog ('faɪə,dɒg) *n* either of a pair of metal stands used to support logs in an open fire.

fire door *n* **1** a door made of noncombustible material that prevents a fire spreading within a building. **2** a similar door leading to the outside of a building that can be easily opened from inside; emergency exit.

fire-eater *n* **1** a performer who simulates the swallowing of fire. **2** a belligerent person.

fire engine *n* a vehicle that carries firemen and fire-fighting equipment to a fire.

fire escape *n* a means of evacuating persons from a building in the event of fire.

fire-extinguisher *n* a portable device for extinguishing fires, usually consisting of a canister with a directional nozzle used to direct a spray of water, etc., onto the fire.

firefighter ('faɪə,faɪtə) *n* a person who assists in extinguishing fires and rescuing those endangered by them, usually a public employee or trained volunteer.
▸ **'fire-,fighting** *n, adj*

firefly ('faɪə,flaɪ) *n, pl* **fireflies.** a nocturnal beetle common in warm and tropical regions, having luminescent abdominal organs.

fireguard ('faɪə,gɑːd) *n* a meshed frame put before an open fire to protect against falling logs, sparks, etc.

fire hall *n Canad.* a fire station.

fire hydrant *n* a hydrant for use as an emergency supply for fighting fires.

fire insurance *n* insurance covering damage or loss caused by fire or lightning.

fire irons *pl n* metal fireside implements, such as poker, shovel, and tongs.

firelock ('faɪə,lɒk) *n* **1** an obsolete type of gunlock with a priming mechanism ignited by sparks. **2** a gun or musket having such a lock.

fireman ('faɪəmən) *n, pl* **firemen. 1** a man who fights fires; firefighter. **2a** (on steam locomotives) the man who stokes the fire. **2b** (on diesel and electric locomotives) the driver's assistant. **3** a man who tends furnaces; stoker.

Firenze ★ (fi'rɛntse) *n* the Italian name for **Florence.**

fire opal *n* an orange-red translucent variety of opal, valued as a gemstone.

fireplace ('faɪə,pleɪs) *n* **1** an open recess at the base of a chimney, etc., for a fire; hearth. **2** *Austral.* an authorized place or installation for outside cooking, esp. by a roadside.

fireplug ('faɪə,plʌg) *n* another name (esp. US and NZ) for **fire hydrant.**

fire power *n Mil.* **1** the amount of fire that can be delivered by a unit or weapon. **2** the capability of delivering fire.

fireproof ('faɪə,pruːf) *adj* **1** capable of resisting damage by fire. ◆ *vb* **2** (*tr*) to make resistant to fire.

fire raiser *n* a person who deliberately sets fire to property, etc.
▸ **fire raising** *n*

fire sale *n* **1** a sale of goods at reduced prices after a fire at a shop or factory. **2** any instance of offering goods or assets at greatly reduced prices to ensure a quick sale.

fire screen *n* **1** a decorative screen placed in the hearth when there is no fire. **2** a screen placed before a fire to protect the face.

fire ship *n* a vessel loaded with explosives and used, esp. formerly, as a bomb by igniting it and directing it to drift among an enemy's warships.

fireside ('faɪə,saɪd) *n* **1** the hearth. **2** family life; the home.

fire station *n* a building where fire-fighting vehicles and equipment are stationed and where firefighters on duty wait. Also called (US): **firehouse, station house.**

firestorm ('faɪə,stɔːm) *n* an uncontrollable blaze sustained by violent winds that are drawn into the column of rising hot air over the burning area: often the result of heavy bombing.

fire trail *n Austral.* a permanent track cleared through the bush to provide access for fire-fighting.

firetrap ('faɪə,træp) *n* a building that would burn easily or one without fire escapes.

firewall ('faɪə,wɔːl) *n* **1** a fireproof wall or partition used to impede the progress of a fire. **2** *Computing.* a computer system that isolates another computer from the Internet in order to prevent unauthorized access.

firewater ('faɪə,wɔːtə) *n* any strong spirit, esp. whisky.

fireweed ('faɪə,wiːd) *n* any of various plants that appear as first vegetation in burnt-over areas.

firework ('faɪə,wɜːk) *n* a device, such as a Catherine wheel or rocket, in which combustible materials are ignited and produce coloured flames, sparks, and smoke.

fireworks ('faɪə,wɜːks) *pl n* **1** a show in which large numbers of fireworks are let off. **2** *Inf.* an exciting exhibition, as of musical virtuosity or wit. **3** *Inf.* a burst of temper.

firing ('faɪərɪŋ) *n* **1** the process of baking ceramics, etc., in a kiln. **2** the act of stoking a fire or furnace. **3** a discharge of a firearm. **4** something used as fuel, such as coal or wood.

firing line *n* **1** *Mil.* the positions from which fire is delivered. **2** the leading or most advanced position in an activity.

firkin ('fɜːkɪn) *n* **1** a small wooden barrel. **2** *Brit.* a unit of capacity equal to nine gallons. ORIG C14 *fir,* from MDu. *vierde* FOURTH + -KIN

firm[1] (fɜːm) *adj* **1** not soft or yielding to a touch or pres-

sure. **2** securely in position; stable or stationary. **3** decided; settled. **4** enduring or steady. **5** having determination or strength. **6** (of prices, markets, etc.) tending to rise. ◆ *adv* **7** in a secure or unyielding manner: *he stood firm.* ◆ *vb* **8** (sometimes foll. by *up*) to make or become firm. ORIG C14: from L *firmus*
▸ **'firmly** *adv* ▸ **'firmness** *n*

firm² (fɜːm) *n* **1** a business partnership. **2** any commercial enterprise. **3** a team of doctors and their assistants. **4 the.** (*often cap.*) *Sl.* any organized group of people, such as intelligence agents, criminals, or football hooligans. ORIG C16 (in the sense: signature): from Sp. *firma* signature, from *firmar* to sign, from L *firmāre* to confirm, from *firmus* firm

firmament ('fɜːməmənt) *n* the expanse of the sky; heavens. ORIG C13: from LL *firmāmentum* sky (considered as fixed above the earth), from L: prop, support, from *firmāre* to make FIRM¹

firmware ('fɜːmˌwɛə) *n Computing.* a series of fixed instructions built into the hardware of a computer that can be changed only if the hardware itself is modified in some way.

first (fɜːst) *adj* (*usually prenominal*) **1a** coming before all others. **1b** (*as n*): *I was the first to arrive.* **2** preceding all others in numbering or counting order; the ordinal number of *one*. Often written: 1st. **3** rated, graded, or ranked above all other levels. **4** denoting the lowest forward ratio of a gearbox in a motor vehicle. **5** *Music.* **5a** denoting the highest part assigned to one of the voice parts in a chorus or one of the sections of an orchestra: *the first violins.* **5b** denoting the principal player in a specific orchestral section: *he plays first horn.* **6 first thing.** as the first action of the day: *I'll see you first thing tomorrow.* ◆ *n* **7** the beginning; outset: *I couldn't see at first because of the mist.* **8** *Education, chiefly Brit.* an honours degree of the highest class. Full term: **first-class honours degree. 9** the lowest forward ratio of a gearbox in a motor vehicle. ◆ *adv* **10** Also: **firstly.** before anything else in order, time, importance, etc.: *do this first.* **11 first and last.** on the whole. **12 from first to last.** throughout. **13** for the first time: *I've loved you since I first saw you.* **14** (*sentence modifier*) in the first place or beginning of a series of actions. ORIG OE *fyrest*

first aid *n* **a** immediate medical assistance given in an emergency. **b** (*as modifier*): *first-aid box.*

first-born *adj* **1** eldest of the children in a family. ◆ *n* **2** the eldest child in a family.

first class *n* **1** the class or grade of the best or highest value, quality, etc. ◆ *adj* (**first-class** *when prenominal*) **2** of the best or highest class or grade: *a first-class citizen.* **3** excellent. **4** of or denoting the most comfortable class of accommodation in a hotel, aircraft, train, etc. **5** (in Britain) of mail that is processed most quickly. ◆ *adv* **first-class. 6** by first-class mail, means of transportation, etc.

first-day cover *n Philately.* an envelope postmarked on the first day of the issue of its stamps.

first-degree burn *n Pathol.* the least severe type of burn, in which the skin surface is red and painful.

first-foot *Chiefly Scot.* ◆ *n also* **first-footer. 1** the first person to enter a household in the New Year. ◆ *vb* **2** to enter (a house) as first-foot.
▸ **'first-'footing** *n*

first fruits *pl n* **1** the first results or profits of an undertaking. **2** fruit that ripens first.

first-hand *adj, adv* **1** from the original source: *he got the news first-hand.* **2 at first hand.** directly.

first lady *n* (*often caps.*) (in the US) the wife or official hostess of a state governor or a president.

firstling ('fɜːstlɪŋ) *n* the first, esp. the first offspring.

first-loss policy *n* an insurance policy for goods in which a total loss is extremely unlikely and the insurer agrees to provide cover for a sum less than the total value of the property.

firstly ('fɜːstlɪ) *adv* another word for **first.**

first mate *n* an officer second in command to the captain of a merchant ship.

First Minister *n* **1** the chief minister of the Northern Ireland Assembly. **2** the chief minister of the Scottish Parliament.

first mortgage *n* a mortgage that has priority over other mortgages on the same property.

first name *n* a name given to a person at birth, as opposed to a surname. Also called: **Christian name, forename, given name.**

First Nation *n Canad.* a formally recognized group of Indians on a reserve.

first night *n* **a** the first public performance of a play, etc. **b** (*as modifier*): *first-night nerves.*

first offender *n* a person convicted of a criminal offence for the first time.

first officer *n* **1** another name for **first mate. 2** the member of an aircraft crew who is second in command to the captain.

first-past-the-post *n* (*modifier*) of a voting system in which a candidate may be elected by a simple majority.

first person *n* a grammatical category of pronouns and verbs used by the speaker to refer to or talk about himself.

first-rate *adj* **1** of the best or highest rated class or quality. **2** *Inf.* very good; excellent.

first reading *n* the introduction of a bill into a legislative assembly.

first refusal *n* the right to buy something before it is offered to others.

First Secretary *n* the chief minister of the National Assembly for Wales.

first-strike *adj* (of a nuclear missile) intended for use in an opening attack calculated to destroy the enemy's nuclear weapons.

first water *n* **1** the finest quality of diamond or other precious stone. **2** the highest grade or best quality.

firth (fɜːθ) *or* **frith** *n* a narrow inlet of the sea, esp. in Scotland. ORIG C15: from ON *fjörthr* FJORD

fiscal ('fɪskᵊl) *adj* **1** of or relating to government finances, esp. tax revenues. **2** of or involving financial matters. ◆ *n* **3a** (in some countries) a public prosecutor. **3b** *Scot.* short for **procurator fiscal.** ORIG C16: from L *fiscālis* concerning the state treasury, from *fiscus* public money
▸ **'fiscally** *adv*

fiscal year *n* the US and Canad. term for **financial year.**

Fischer ★ (*German* 'fɪʃər) *n* **1 Emil Hermann** ('eːmiːl 'hɛrman). 1852–1919, German chemist, noted for his work on synthetic sugars: Nobel prize for chemistry 1902. **2 Ernst Otto** (ɛrnst 'ɔto). 1918–94, German chemist: shared the Nobel prize for chemistry (1973) for work on inorganic complexes. **3 Hans** (hans). 1881–1945, German chemist, noted for his work on chlorophyll, haemin, and the porphyrins: Nobel prize for chemistry 1930. **4** ('fɪʃə). **Robert James,** known as *Bobby.* born 1943, US chess player; world champion 1972–75.

Fischer-Dieskau ★ (*German* -'diːskau) *n* **Dietrich** ('diːtrɪç). born 1925, German baritone.

fish (fɪʃ) *n, pl* **fish** *or* **fishes. 1a** any of a large group of cold-blooded aquatic vertebrates having jaws, gills, and usually fins and a skin covered in scales: includes the sharks, rays, teleosts, lungfish, etc. **1b** (*in combination*): *fishpond.* Related adj: **piscine. 2** any of various similar but jawless vertebrates, such as the hagfish and lamprey. **3** (*not in technical use*) any of various aquatic invertebrates, such as the cuttlefish and crayfish. **4** the flesh of fish used as food. **5** *Inf.* a person of little emotion or intelligence: *a poor fish.* **6 drink like a fish.** to drink (esp. alcohol) to excess. **7 have other fish to fry.** to have other activities to do, esp. more important ones. **8 like a fish out of water.** out of one's usual place. **9 make fish of one and flesh of another.** *Irish.* to discriminate unfairly between people. **10 neither fish, flesh, nor fowl.** neither this nor that. ◆ *vb* **11** (*intr*) to attempt to catch fish, as with a line and hook or with nets, traps, etc. **12** (*tr*) to fish in (a particular area of water). **13** to search (a body of water) for something or to search for something, esp. in a body of water. **14** (*intr;* foll. by *for*) to seek something indirectly: *to fish for compliments.* ◆ See also **fish out.** ORIG OE *fisc*
▸ **'fishˌlike** *adj*

fish and chips *n* fish fillets coated with batter and deep-fried, eaten with potato chips.

fish cake *n* a fried flattened ball of flaked fish mixed with mashed potatoes.

fisher ('fɪʃə) *n* **1** a fisherman. **2** Also called: **pekan. 2a** a large North American marten having dark brown fur. **2b** the fur of this animal.

Fisher ★ ('fɪʃə) *n* **1 Andrew.** 1862–1928, Australian statesman, born in Scotland: prime minister (1908–09; 1910–13; 1914–15). **2 Saint John.** ?1469–1535, English prelate and scholar: executed for refusing to acknowledge Henry VIII as supreme head of the church. Feast day: June 22. **3 John Arbuthnot,** 1st Baron Fisher of Kilverstone. 1841–1920, British admiral; First Sea Lord (1904–10; 1914–15); introduced the dreadnought.

fisherman ('fɪʃəmən) *n, pl* **fishermen. 1** a person who fishes as a profession or for sport. **2** a vessel used for fishing.

fishery ('fɪʃərɪ) *n, pl* **fisheries. 1a** the industry of catching, processing, and selling fish. **1b** a place where this is carried on. **2** a place where fish are reared. **3** a fishing ground.

Fishes ('fɪʃɪz) *n* **the.** the constellation Pisces, the twelfth sign of the zodiac.

fisheye lens ('fɪʃ,aɪ) *n Photog.* a lens of small focal length, having a highly curved protruding front element that covers an angle of view of almost 180°.

fishfinger ('fɪʃ'fɪŋgə) *or US & Canad.* **fish stick** *n* an oblong piece of filleted or minced fish coated in breadcrumbs.

Fishguard ★ ('fɪʃ,gɑːd) *n* a port and resort in SW Wales, in Pembrokeshire: ferry connections to Cork and Rosslare. Pop.: 2679 (1991).

fish hawk *n* another name for the **osprey.**

fish-hook *n* a sharp hook used in angling, esp. one with a barb.

fishing ('fɪʃɪŋ) *n* **a** the occupation of catching fish. **b** (*as modifier*): *a fishing match.*

fishing ground *n* an area of water that is good for fishing.

fishing rod *n* a long tapered flexible pole for use with a fishing line and, usually, a reel.

fish joint *n* a connection formed by fishplates at the meeting point of two rails, beams, etc.

fishmeal ('fɪʃ,miːl) *n* ground dried fish used as feed for farm animals, as a fertilizer, etc.

fishmonger ('fɪʃ,mʌŋgə) *n Chiefly Brit.* a retailer of fish.

fishnet ('fɪʃ,nɛt) *n* **a** an open mesh fabric resembling netting. **b** (*as modifier*): *fishnet tights.*

fish out *vb* (*tr, adv*) to find or extract (something): *to fish keys out of a pocket.*

fishplate ('fɪʃ,pleɪt) *n* a flat piece of metal joining one rail or beam to the next, esp. on railway tracks.

fishtail ('fɪʃ,teɪl) *n* **1** an aeroplane manoeuvre in which the tail is moved from side to side to reduce speed. **2** a nozzle having a long narrow slot at the top, placed over a Bunsen burner to produce a thin fanlike flame.

fishwife ('fɪʃ,waɪf) *n, pl* **fishwives. 1** a woman who sells fish. **2** a coarse scolding woman.

fishy ('fɪʃɪ) *adj* **fishier, fishiest. 1** of, involving, or suggestive of fish. **2** abounding in fish. **3** *Inf.* suspicious, doubtful, or questionable. **4** dull and lifeless: *a fishy look.*
▸ **'fishily** *adv*

fissile ('fɪsaɪl) *adj* **1** *Brit.* capable of undergoing nuclear fission. **2** fissionable. **3** tending to split or capable of being split. ORIG C17: from L, from *fissus* split

fission ('fɪʃən) *n* **1** the act or process of splitting or breaking into parts. **2** *Biol.* a form of asexual reproduction involving a division into two or more equal parts. **3** short for **nuclear fission.** ORIG C19: from L *fissiō* a cleaving
▸ **'fissionable** *adj*

fission-track dating *n* the dating of samples of minerals by comparing the tracks in them made by fission fragments of the uranium nuclei they contain, before and after irradiation by neutrons.

fissiparous (fɪ'sɪpərəs) *adj Biol.* reproducing by fission.
▸ **fis'siparously** *adv*

fissure ('fɪʃə) *n* **1** any long narrow cleft or crack, esp. in a rock. **2** a weakness or flaw. **3** *Anat.* a narrow split or groove that divides an organ such as the brain, lung, or liver into lobes. ◆ *vb* **fissures, fissuring, fissured. 4** to crack or split apart. ORIG C14: from Medical L *fissūra,* from L *fissus* split

fist (fɪst) *n* **1** a hand with the fingers clenched into the palm, as for hitting. **2** Also called: **fistful.** the quantity that can be held in a fist or hand. **3** *Inf.* handwriting. **4** an informal word for **index** (sense 9). ◆ *vb* **5** (*tr*) to hit with the fist. ORIG OE *fȳst*

fisticuffs ('fɪstɪ,kʌfs) *pl n* combat with the fists. ORIG C17: prob. from *fisty* with the fist + CUFF[2]

fistula ('fɪstjʊlə) *n, pl* **fistulas** *or* **fistulae** (-,liː). *Pathol.* an abnormal opening between one hollow organ and another or between a hollow organ and the surface of the skin, caused by ulceration, malformation, etc. ORIG C14: from L: pipe, tube, hollow reed, ulcer
▸ **'fistulous** *or* **'fistular** *adj*

fit[1] (fɪt) *vb* **fits, fitting, fitted** *or US* **fit. 1** to be appropriate or suitable for (a situation, etc.). **2** to be of the correct size or shape for (a container, etc.). **3** (*tr*) to adjust in order to render appropriate. **4** (*tr*) to supply with that which is needed. **5** (*tr*) to try clothes on (someone) in order to make adjustments if necessary. **6** (*tr*) to make competent or ready. **7** (*tr*) to locate with care. **8** (*intr*) to correspond with the facts or circumstances. ◆ *adj* **fitter, fittest. 9** appropriate. **10** having the right qualifications; qualifying. **11** in good health. **12** worthy or deserving. **13** (*foll. by an infinitive*) *Inf.* ready (to); strongly disposed (to): *she was fit to scream.* ◆ *n* **14** the manner in which something fits. **15** the act or process of fitting. **16** *Statistics.* the correspondence between observed and predicted characteristics of a distribution or model. ◆ See also **fit in, fit out.** ORIG C14: prob. from MDu. *vitten;* rel. to ON *fitja* to knit
▸ **'fitly** *adv* ▸ **'fittable** *adj*

fit[2] (fɪt) *n* **1** *Pathol.* a sudden attack or convulsion, such as an epileptic seizure. **2** a sudden spell of emotion: *a fit of anger.* **3** an impulsive period of activity or lack of activity. **4 have** *or* **throw a fit.** *Inf.* to become very angry. **5 in** *or* **by fits and starts.** in spasmodic spells. ORIG OE *fitt* conflict

fitch (fɪtʃ) *n* **1** a polecat. **2** the fur of the polecat. ORIG C16: prob. from *ficheux,* from OF, from ?

fitful ('fɪtfʊl) *adj* characterized by or occurring in irregular spells.
▸ **'fitfully** *adv*

fit in *vb* **1** (*tr*) to give a place or time to. **2** (*intr, adv*) to belong or conform, esp. after adjustment: *he didn't fit in with their plans.*

fitment ('fɪtmənt) *n* **1** *Machinery.* an accessory attached to an assembly of parts. **2** *Chiefly Brit.* a detachable part of the furnishings of a room.

fitness ('fɪtnɪs) *n* **1** the state of being fit. **2** *Biol.* **2a** the degree of adaptation of an organism to its environment, determined by its genetic constitution. **2b** the ability of an organism to produce viable offspring capable of surviving to the next generation.

fit out *vb* (*tr, adv*) to equip.

fitted ('fɪtɪd) *adj* **1** designed for excellent fit: *a fitted suit.* **2** (of a carpet) cut or sewn to cover a floor completely. **3a** (of furniture) built to fit a particular space: *a fitted cupboard.* **3b** (of a room) equipped with fitted furniture: *a fitted kitchen.* **4** (of sheets) having ends that are elasticated and shaped to fit tightly over a mattress.

fitter ('fɪtə) *n* **1** a person who fits a garment, esp. when it is made for a particular person. **2** a person who is skilled in the assembly and adjustment of machinery, esp. of a specified sort.

fitting ('fɪtɪŋ) *adj* **1** appropriate or proper. ◆ *n* **2** an accessory or part: *an electrical fitting.* **3** (*pl*) furnishings or accessories in a building. **4** work carried out by a fitter. **5** the act of trying on clothes so that they can be adjusted to fit.
▸ **'fittingly** *adv*

Fittipaldi ★ (,fɪtɪ'pældɪ) *n* **Emerson.** born 1946, Brazilian motor-racing driver: world champion in 1972 and 1974.

Fitzgerald ★ (fɪts'dʒerəld) *n* **1 Edward.** 1809–83, British poet, noted for his translation of the *Rubáiyát of Omar Khayyám* (1859). **2 Ella.** 1918–96, US jazz singer. **3 F(rancis) Scott (Key).** 1896–1940, US writer, noted for his novels *The Great Gatsby* (1925) and *Tender is the Night* (1934). **4 Garret.** born 1926, Irish politician; leader of Fine Gael Party (1977–87); prime minister of the Republic of Ireland (1981–82; and 1982–87).

Fitzgerald-Lorentz contraction *n Physics.* the contraction that a moving body exhibits when its velocity approaches that of light. ORIG C19: after G. F. *Fitzgerald* (1851–1901), Irish physicist, and H. A. LORENTZ

Fitzrovia ★ (fɪts'rəʊvɪə) *n Inf.* the district north of Oxford Street, London, around Fitzroy Square and its pubs, noted in the 1930s and 40s as a haunt of poets.

Fitzsimmons ★ (ˌfɪt'sɪmənz) *n* **Bob.** 1862–1917, New Zealand boxer, born in England: world middleweight (1891–97), heavyweight (1897–99), and light-heavyweight (1903–05) champion.

Fiume ★ ('fju:me) *n* the Italian name for **Rijeka.**

five (faɪv) *n* **1** the cardinal number that is the sum of four and one. **2** a numeral, 5, V, etc., representing this number. **3** the amount or quantity that is one greater than four. **4** something representing, represented by, or consisting of five units, such as a playing card with five symbols on it. **5 five o'clock.** five hours after noon or midnight. ◆ *determiner* **6a** amounting to five: *five nights.* **6b** (*as pronoun*): *choose any five you like.* ◆ See also **fives.** ORIG OE *fīf*

five-a-side *n* a version of soccer with five players on each side.

five-eighth *n Austral. & NZ.* a rugby player positioned between the halfbacks and three-quarters.

five-finger *n* any of various plants having five-petalled flowers or five lobed leaves, such as cinquefoil and Virginia creeper.

fivefold ('faɪvˌfəʊld) *adj* **1** equal to or having five times as many or as much. **2** composed of five parts. ◆ *adv* **3** by or up to five times as many or as much.

Five Nations *pl n* (formerly) a confederacy of N American Indian peoples consisting of the Cayugas, Mohawks, Oneidas, Onondagas, and Senecas. See also **Six Nations.**

five-o'clock shadow *n* beard growth visible late in the day on a man's shaven face.

fivepins ('faɪvˌpɪnz) *n* (*functioning as sing*) a bowling game using five pins, played esp. in Canada.
▸ **'fiveˌpin** *adj*

fiver ('faɪvə) *n Brit. inf.* a five-pound note.

fives (faɪvz) *n* (*functioning as sing*) a ball game similar to squash but played with bats or the hands.

Five Towns ★ *n* **the.** the name given in his fiction by Arnold Bennett to the Potteries towns (actually six in number) of Burslem, Fenton, Hanley, Longton, Stoke-upon-Trent, and Tunstall, now part of the city of Stoke-on-Trent.

Five-Year Plan *n* (in socialist economies) a government plan for economic development over a period of five years.

fix (fɪks) *vb* (*mainly tr*) **1** (*also intr*) to make or become firm, stable, or secure. **2** to attach or place permanently. **3** (often foll. by *up*) to settle definitely; decide. **4** to hold or direct (eyes, etc.) steadily: *he fixed his gaze on the woman.* **5** to call to attention or rivet. **6** to make rigid: *to fix one's jaw.* **7** to place or ascribe: *to fix the blame.* **8** to mend or repair. **9** *Inf.* to provide or be provided with: *how are you fixed for supplies?* **10** *Inf.* to influence (a person, etc.) unfairly, as by bribery. **11** *Sl.* to take revenge on. **12** *Inf.* to give (someone) his or her just deserts: *that'll fix him.* **13** *Inf., chiefly US & Canad.* to prepare: *to fix a meal.* **14** *Dialect or inf.* to spay or castrate (an animal). **15** *Photog.* to treat (a film, plate, or paper) with fixer to make permanent the image rendered visible by developer. **16** to convert (atmospheric nitrogen) into nitrogen compounds, as in the manufacture of fertilizers or the action of bacteria in the soil. **17** to reduce (a substance) to a solid state or a less volatile state. **18** (*intr*) *Sl.* to inject a narcotic drug. ◆ *n* **19** *Inf.* a predicament; dilemma. **20** the ascertaining of the navigational position, as of a ship, by radar, etc. **21** *Sl.* an intravenous injection of a narcotic such as heroin. ◆ See also **fix up.** ORIG C15: from Med. L *fixāre*, from L *fixus* fixed, from L *fīgere*
▸ **'fixable** *adj*

fixate (fɪk'seɪt) *vb* **fixates, fixating, fixated. 1** to become or cause to become fixed. **2** *Psychol.* to engage in fixation. **3** (*tr; usually passive*) *Inf.* to obsess. ORIG C19: from L *fixus* fixed + -ATE[1]

fixation (fɪk'seɪʃən) *n* **1** the act of fixing or the state of being fixed. **2** a preoccupation or obsession. **3** *Psychol.* **3a** the situation of being set in a certain way of thinking or acting. **3b** a strong attachment of a person to another person or an object in early life. **4** *Chem.* the conversion of nitrogen in the air into a compound, esp. a fertilizer. **5** the reduction of a substance to a nonvolatile or solid form.

fixative ('fɪksətɪv) *adj* **1** serving or tending to fix. ◆ *n* **2** a fluid sprayed over drawings to prevent smudging or one that fixes tissues and cells for microscopic study. **3** a substance added to a liquid, such as a perfume, to make it less volatile.

fixed (fɪkst) *adj* **1** attached or placed so as to be immovable. **2** stable: *fixed prices.* **3** steadily directed: *a fixed expression.* **4** established as to relative position: *a fixed point.* **5** always at the same time: *a fixed holiday.* **6** (of ideas, etc.) firmly maintained. **7** (of an element) held in chemical combination: *fixed nitrogen.* **8** (of a substance) nonvolatile. **9** arranged. **10** *Inf.* equipped or provided for, as with money, possessions, etc. **11** *Inf.* illegally arranged: *a fixed trial.*
▸ **fixedly** ('fɪksɪdlɪ) *adv* ▸ **'fixedness** *n*

fixed assets *pl n* nontrading business assets of a relatively permanent nature, such as plant, fixtures, or goodwill. Also called: **capital assets.**

fixed oil *n* a natural animal or vegetable oil that is not volatile: a mixture of esters of fatty acids.

fixed-point representation *n Computing.* the representation of numbers by a single set of digits such that the radix point has a predetermined location. Cf. **floating-point representation.**

fixed satellite *n* a satellite revolving in a stationary orbit so that it appears to remain over a fixed point on the earth's surface.

fixed star *n* an extremely distant star whose position appears to be almost stationary over a long period of time.

fixer ('fɪksə) *n* **1** a person or thing that fixes. **2** *Photog.* a solution used to dissolve unexposed silver halides after developing. **3** *Sl.* a person who makes arrangements, esp. by underhand or illegal means.

fixing ('fɪksɪŋ) *n* a means of attaching one thing to another, as a pipe to a wall, a slate to a roof, etc.

fixity ('fɪksɪtɪ) *n, pl* **fixities. 1** the state or quality of being fixed. **2** a fixture.

fixture ('fɪkstʃə) *n* **1** an object firmly fixed in place, esp. a household appliance. **2** a person or thing regarded as fixed in a particular place or position. **3** *Property law.* an article attached to land and regarded as part of it. **4** *Chiefly Brit.* **4a** a sports match or social occasion. **4b** the date of such an event. ORIG C17: from LL *fixūra* a fastening (with *-t-* by analogy with *mixture*)

fix up *vb* (*tr, adv*) **1** to arrange: *let's fix up a date.* **2** (often foll. by *with*) to provide: *I'm sure we can fix you up with a room.*

fizgig ('fɪzˌgɪg) *n* **1** a frivolous or flirtatious girl. **2** a firework that fizzes as it moves. ORIG C16: prob. from obs. *fise* a breaking of wind + *gig* girl

fizz (fɪz) *vb* (*intr*) **1** to make a hissing or bubbling sound. **2** (of a drink) to produce bubbles of carbon dioxide. ◆ *n* **3** a hissing or bubbling sound. **4** the bubbly quality of a drink; effervescence. **5** any effervescent drink. ORIG C17: imit.
▸ **'fizzy** *adj* ▸ **'fizziness** *n*

fizzle ('fɪzᵊl) *vb* **fizzles, fizzling, fizzled.** (*intr*) **1** to make a hissing or bubbling sound. **2** (often foll. by *out*) *Inf.* to fail or die out, esp. after a promising start. ◆ *n* **3** a hissing or bubbling sound. **4** *Inf.* a failure. ORIG C16: prob. from obs. *fist* to break wind

fjord *or* **fiord** (fjɔːd) *n* a long narrow inlet of the sea between high steep cliffs, common in Norway. ORIG C17: from Norwegian, from ON *fjörthr;* see FIRTH, FORD

FL *abbrev. for:* **1** Flight Lieutenant. **2** Florida.

fl. *abbrev. for:* **1** floor. **2** floruit. **3** fluid.

Fl. *abbrev. for:* **1** Flanders. **2** Flemish.

Fla. *abbrev. for* Florida.

flab (flæb) *n* unsightly or unwanted fat on the body. ORIG C20: back formation from FLABBY

flabbergast (ˈflæbəˌgɑːst) *vb* (*tr; usually passive*) *Inf.* to amaze utterly; astound. ORIG C18: from ?

flabby (ˈflæbɪ) *adj* **flabbier, flabbiest. 1** loose or yielding: *flabby muscles.* **2** having flabby flesh, esp. through being overweight. **3** lacking vitality; weak. ORIG C17: alteration of *flappy* from FLAP + -Y[1]; cf. Du. *flabbe* drooping lip
▸ **ˈflabbiness** *n*

flaccid (ˈflæksɪd) *adj* lacking firmness; soft and limp. ORIG C17: from L *flaccidus,* from *flaccus*
▸ **flacˈcidity** *n*

flacon (*French* flakɔ̃) *n* a small stoppered bottle, esp. used for perfume. ORIG C19: from F; see FLAGON

flag[1] (flæg) *n* **1** a piece of cloth, esp. bunting, often attached to a pole or staff, decorated with a design and used as an emblem, symbol, or standard or as a means of signalling. **2** a small piece of paper, etc., sold on flag days. **3** the conspicuously marked or shaped tail of a deer or of certain dogs. **4** anything used like a flag to attract attention, esp. a code inserted into a computer file to distinguish certain information. **5** *Brit., Austral., & NZ.* the part of a taximeter that is raised when a taxi is for hire. **6 show the flag. 6a** to assert a claim by military presence. **6b** *Inf.* to make an appearance. ◆ *vb* **flags, flagging, flagged.** (*tr*) **7** to decorate or mark with a flag or flags. **8** (often foll. by *down*) to warn or signal (a vehicle) to stop. **9** to send or communicate (messages, information, etc.) by flag. ORIG C16: from ?
▸ **ˈflagger** *n*

flag[2] (flæg) *n* **1** any of various plants that have long swordlike leaves, esp. an iris (**yellow flag**). **2** the leaf of any such plant. ORIG C14: prob. from ON

flag[3] (flæg) *vb* **flags, flagging, flagged.** (*intr*) **1** to hang down; droop. **2** to become weak or tired. ORIG C16: from ?

flag[4] (flæg) *n* **1** short for **flagstone.** ◆ *vb* **flags, flagging, flagged. 2** (*tr*) to furnish (a floor, etc.) with flagstones.

flag day *n Brit.* a day on which money is collected by a charity and small flags or emblems are given to contributors.

flagellant (ˈflædʒɪlənt, fləˈdʒɛlənt) *or* **flagellator** (ˈflædʒɪˌleɪtə) *n* a person who whips himself or herself or others either as part of a religious penance or for sexual gratification. ORIG C16: from L *flagellāre* to whip, from FLAGELLUM

flagellate *vb* (ˈflædʒɪˌleɪt), **flagellates, flagellating, flagellated. 1** (*tr*) to whip; flog. ◆ *adj* (ˈflædʒɪlɪt), *also* **flagellated. 2** possessing one or more flagella. **3** whiplike. ◆ *n* (ˈflædʒɪlɪt). **4** a flagellate organism.
▸ **ˌflagelˈlation** *n*

flagellum (fləˈdʒɛləm) *n, pl* **flagella** (-lə) *or* **flagellums. 1** *Biol.* a long whiplike outgrowth from a cell that acts as an organ of locomotion: occurs in some protozoans, gametes, etc. **2** *Bot.* a long thin shoot or runner. ORIG C19: from L: a little whip, from *flagrum* a whip, lash
▸ **flaˈgellar** *adj*

flageolet[1] (ˌflædʒəˈlɛt) *n* a high-pitched musical instrument of the recorder family. ORIG C17: from F, modification of OF *flajolet* a little flute, from Vulgar L *flabeolum* (unattested), from L *flāre* to blow

flageolet[2] *or* **flageolet bean** (ˌflædʒəˈlɛt) *n* the pale green immature seed of a haricot bean, cooked and eaten as a vegetable. ORIG C19: from F *fageolet,* from L *phaseolus* bean; ? infl. by FLAGEOLET[1]

flag fall *n Austral.* the minimum charge for hiring a taxi, to which the rate per kilometre is added.

flag of convenience *n* a national flag flown by a ship registered in that country to gain financial or legal advantage.

flag of truce *n* a white flag indicating an invitation to an enemy to negotiate.

flagon (ˈflægən) *n* **1** a large bottle of wine, cider, etc. **2** a vessel having a handle, spout, and narrow neck. ORIG C15: from OF *flascon,* from LL *flascō,* prob. of Gmc origin; see FLASK

flagpole (ˈflægˌpəʊl) *or* **flagstaff** (ˈflægˌstɑːf) *n, pl* **flagpoles, flagstaffs** *or* **flagstaves** (-ˌsteɪvz). a pole or staff on which a flag is hoisted and displayed.

flagrant (ˈfleɪgrənt) *adj* openly outrageous. ORIG C15: from L *flagrāre* to blaze, burn
▸ **ˈflagrancy** *n* ▸ **ˈflagrantly** *adv*

flagrante delicto (fləˈgræntɪ dɪˈlɪktəʊ) *adv* See **in flagrante delicto.**

flagship (ˈflægˌʃɪp) *n* **1** a ship, esp. in a fleet, aboard which the commander of the fleet is quartered. **2** the most important ship belonging to a shipping company. **3** the item in a group considered most important esp. in establishing a public image: *costume drama is the flagship of the BBC.*

Flagstad ★ (ˈflægstæd; *Norwegian* ˈflaksta) *n* **Kirsten** (ˈçirstən). 1895–1962, Norwegian operatic soprano, noted particularly for her interpretations of Wagner.

flagstone (ˈflægˌstəʊn) *n* **1** a hard fine-textured rock that can be split up into slabs for paving. **2** a slab of such a rock. ORIG C15 *flag* (in the sense: sod, turf), from ON *flaga* slab; cf. OE *flæcg* plaster, poultice

flag-waving *n Inf.* an emotional appeal intended to arouse patriotic feeling.
▸ **ˈflagˌwaver** *n*

Flaherty ★ (ˈflɑːhətɪ) *n* **Robert** (**Joseph**). 1884–1951, US film director, his work includes *Nanook of the North* (1922) and *Elephant Boy* (1935).

flail (fleɪl) *n* **1** an implement used for threshing grain, consisting of a wooden handle with a free-swinging metal or wooden bar attached to it. ◆ *vb* **2** (*tr*) to beat with or as if with a flail. **3** to thresh about: *with arms flailing.* ORIG C12 *fleil,* ult. from LL *flagellum* flail, from L: whip

flair (flɛə) *n* **1** natural ability; talent. **2** perceptiveness. **3** *Inf.* stylishness or elegance: *to dress with flair.* ORIG C19: from F, lit.: sense of smell, from OF: scent, ult. from L *frāgrāre* to smell sweet; see FRAGRANT

flak (flæk) *n* **1** anti-aircraft fire or artillery. **2** *Inf.* adverse criticism. ORIG C20: from G *Fl(ieger)a(bwehr)k(anone),* lit.: aircraft defence gun

flake[1] (fleɪk) *n* **1** a small thin piece or layer chipped off or detached from an object or substance. **2** a small piece or particle: *a flake of snow.* **3** *Archaeol.* a fragment removed by chipping from a larger stone used as a tool or weapon. **4** *Chiefly US sl.* an eccentric, crazy, or unreliable person. ◆ *vb* **flakes, flaking, flaked. 5** to peel or cause to peel off in flakes. **6** to cover or become covered with or as with flakes. **7** (*tr*) to form into flakes. ORIG C14: from ON

flake[2] (fleɪk) *n* a rack or platform for drying fish. ORIG C14: from ON *flaki;* rel. to Du. *vlaak* hurdle

flake out *vb* (*intr, adv*) *Inf.* to collapse or fall asleep as through extreme exhaustion.

flake white *n* a pigment made from flakes of white lead.

flak jacket *n* a reinforced jacket for protection against gunfire or shrapnel worn by soldiers, policemen, etc.

flaky (ˈfleɪkɪ) *adj* **flakier, flakiest. 1** like or made of flakes. **2** tending to break easily into flakes. **3** Also spelt: **flakey.** *US sl.* eccentric; crazy.
▸ **ˈflakily** *adv* ▸ **ˈflakiness** *n*

flambé (ˈflɑːmbeɪ) **1** *adj* (of food, such as steak or pancakes) served in flaming brandy ◆ *vb* **flambés, flambéing, flambéed. 2** (*tr*) to serve (food) in such a manner. ORIG F, p.p. of *flamber* to FLAME

flambeau (ˈflæmbəʊ) *n, pl* **flambeaux** (-bəʊ, -bəʊz) *or* **flambeaus.** a burning torch, as used in night processions, etc. ORIG C17: from OF: torch, lit.: a little flame, from *flambe* FLAME

★ people and places

Flamborough Head ★ ('flæmbərə, -brə) *n* a chalk promontory in NE England, on the coast of the East Riding of Yorkshire.

flamboyant (flæm'bɔɪənt) *adj* **1** elaborate or extravagant; showy. **2** rich or brilliant in colour. **3** exuberant or ostentatious. **4** of the French Gothic style of architecture characterized by flamelike tracery and elaborate carving. ORIG C19: from F: flaming, from *flamboyer* to FLAME
▸ **flam'boyance** *or* **flam'boyancy** *n* ▸ **flam'boyantly** *adv*

flame (fleɪm) *n* **1** a hot usually luminous body of burning gas emanating in flickering streams from burning material or produced by a jet of ignited gas. **2** (*often pl*) the state or condition of burning with flames: *to burst into flames.* **3** a brilliant light. **4a** a strong reddish-orange colour. **4b** (*as adj*): *a flame carpet.* **5** intense passion or ardour. **6** *Inf.* a lover or sweetheart (esp. in **an old flame**). **7** *Inf.* an abusive message sent by electronic mail. ◆ *vb* **flames, flaming, flamed. 8** to burn or cause to burn brightly. **9** (*intr*) to become red or fiery: *his face flamed with anger.* **10** (*intr*) to become angry or excited. **11** (*tr*) to apply a flame to (something). **12** *Inf.* to send an abusive message by electronic mail. ORIG C14: from Anglo-F, from OF *flambe,* from L *flammula* a little flame, from *flamma* flame
▸ **'flame,like** *adj* ▸ **'flamy** *adj*

flame gun *n* a type of flame-thrower for destroying garden weeds, etc.

flamen ('fleɪmɛn) *n, pl* **flamens** *or* **flamines** ('flæmɪ,ni:z). (in ancient Rome) any of 15 priests who each served a particular deity. ORIG C14: from L; prob. rel. to OE *blōtan* to sacrifice, Gothic *blotan* to worship

flamenco (flə'mɛŋkəʊ) *n, pl* **flamencos. 1** a type of dance music for vocal soloist and guitar, characterized by sad mood. **2** the dance performed to such music. ORIG from Sp.: like a Gipsy, lit.: Fleming, from MDu. *Vlaminc* Fleming

flameout ('fleɪm,aʊt) *n* the failure of an aircraft jet engine in flight due to extinction of the flame.

flame-thrower *n* a weapon that ejects a stream or spray of burning fluid.

flame tree *n* any of various tropical trees with red or orange flowers.

flaming ('fleɪmɪŋ) *adj* **1** burning with or emitting flames. **2** glowing brightly. **3** intense or ardent: *a flaming temper.* **4** *Inf.* (intensifier): *you flaming idiot.*

flamingo (flə'mɪŋgəʊ) *n, pl* **flamingos** *or* **flamingoes.** a large wading bird having a pink-and-red plumage and downward-bent bill and inhabiting brackish lakes. ORIG C16: from Port., from Provençal, from L *flamma* flame + Gmc suffix *-ing* denoting descent from; cf. -ING[3]

Flaminian Way ★ (flə'mɪnɪən) *n* an ancient road in Italy, extending north from Rome to Rimini: constructed in 220 B.C. by Gaius Flaminius. Length: over 322 km (200 miles). Latin name: **Via Flaminia.**

Flamininus ★ (,flæmɪ'naɪnəs) *n* **Titus Quinctius** ('taɪtəs 'kwɪŋktɪəs). ?230–?174 B.C., Roman general and statesman: defeated Macedonia (197) and proclaimed the independence of the Greek states (196).

Flaminius ★ (flə'mɪnɪəs) *n* **Gaius** ('gaɪəs). died 217 B.C., Roman statesman and general: built the Flaminian Way; defeated by Hannibal at Trasimene (217).

flammable ('flæməb[ə]l) *adj* readily combustible; inflammable.
▸ **,flamma'bility** *n*

> **USAGE NOTE** *Flammable* and *inflammable* are interchangeable when used of the properties of materials. *Flammable* is, however, often preferred for warning labels as there is less likelihood of misunderstanding (*inflammable* being sometimes taken to mean *not flammable*). *Inflammable* is preferred in figurative contexts: *this could prove to be an inflammable situation.*

Flamsteed ★ ('flæm,sti:d) *n* **John.** 1646–1719, English astronomer: the first Astronomer Royal and first director of the Royal Observatory, Greenwich (1675).

flan (flæn) *n* **1** an open pastry or sponge tart filled with fruit or a savoury mixture. **2** a piece of metal ready to receive the die or stamp in the production of coins. ORIG C19: from F, from OF *flaon,* from LL *fladō* flat cake, of Gmc origin

Flanders ★ ('flɑ:ndəz) *n* a powerful medieval principality in the SW part of the Low Countries, now in the Belgian provinces of East and West Flanders, the Netherlands province of Zeeland, and the French department of the Nord; scene of battles in many wars.

flange (flændʒ) *n* **1** a radially projecting collar or rim on an object for strengthening it or for attaching it to another object. **2** a flat outer face of a rolled-steel joist. ◆ *vb* **flanges, flanging, flanged. 3** (*tr*) to provide (a component) with a flange. ORIG C17: prob. changed from earlier *flaunche* curved segment at side of a heraldic field, from F *flanc* FLANK
▸ **flanged** *adj* ▸ **'flangeless** *adj*

flank (flæŋk) *n* **1** the side of a man or animal between the ribs and the hip. **2** a cut of beef from the flank. **3** the side of anything, such as a mountain or building. **4** the side of a naval or military formation. ◆ *vb* **5** (when *intr,* often foll. by *on* or *upon*) to be located at the side of (an object, etc.). **6** *Mil.* to position or guard on or beside the flank of (a formation, etc.). ORIG C12: from OF *flanc,* of Gmc origin

flanker ('flæŋkə) *n* **1** one of a detachment of soldiers detailed to guard the flanks. **2** a fortification used to protect a flank. **3** Also called: **flank forward.** *Rugby.* another name for **winger.**

flannel ('flæn[ə]l) *n* **1** a soft light woollen fabric with a slight nap, used for clothing, etc. **2** (*pl*) trousers or other garments made of flannel. **3** *Brit.* a small piece of cloth used to wash the face and hands; face flannel. US and Canad. equivalent: **washcloth. 4** *Brit. inf.* indirect or evasive talk. ◆ *vb* **flannels, flannelling, flannelled** *or US* **flannels, flanneling, flanneled.** (*tr*) **5** to cover or wrap with flannel. **6** to rub or polish with flannel. **7** *Brit. inf.* to flatter. ORIG C14: prob. var. of *flanen* sackcloth, from Welsh, from *gwlân* wool
▸ **'flannelly** *adj*

flannelette (,flæn[ə]'lɛt) *n* a cotton imitation of flannel.

flap (flæp) *vb* **flaps, flapping, flapped. 1** to move (wings or arms) up and down, esp. in or as if in flying, or (of wings or arms) to move in this way. **2** to move or cause to move noisily back and forth or up and down: *the curtains flapped in the breeze.* **3** (*intr*) *Inf.* to become agitated or flustered. **4** to deal (a person or thing) a blow with a broad flexible object. ◆ *n* **5** the action, motion, or noise made by flapping: *with one flap of its wings the bird was off.* **6** a piece of material, etc., attached at one edge and usually used to cover an opening, as on a tent, envelope, or pocket. **7** a blow dealt with a flat object. **8** a movable surface fixed to an aircraft wing that increases lift during takeoff and drag during landing. **9** *Inf.* a state of panic or agitation. ORIG C14: prob. imit.

flapdoodle ('flæp,du:d[ə]l) *n Sl.* foolish talk; nonsense. ORIG C19: from ?

flapjack ('flæp,dʒæk) *n* **1** a chewy biscuit made with rolled oats. **2** *Chiefly US & Canad.* another word for **pancake.**

flapper ('flæpə) *n* (in the 1920s) a young woman, esp. one flaunting her unconventional behaviour.

flare (flɛə) *vb* **flares, flaring, flared. 1** to burn or cause to burn with an unsteady or sudden bright flame. **2** to burn off excess gas or oil. **3** to spread or cause to spread outwards from a narrow to a wider shape. ◆ *n* **4** an unsteady flame. **5** a sudden burst of flame. **6a** a blaze of light or fire used to illuminate, signal distress, alert, etc. **6b** the device producing such a blaze. **7** a spreading shape or anything with a spreading shape: *a skirt with a flare.* **8** an open flame used to burn off unwanted gas at an oil well. **9** *Astron.* short for **solar flare.** ORIG C16 (to spread out): from ?

flares (flɛəz) *pl n Inf.* trousers with legs that widen below the knee.

flare-up *n* **1** a sudden burst of fire or light. **2** *Inf.* a sudden burst of emotion or violence. ◆ *vb* **flare up.** (*intr, adv*). **3**

to burst suddenly into fire or light. **4** *Inf.* to burst into anger.

flash (flæʃ) *n* **1** a sudden short blaze of intense light or flame: *a flash of sunlight.* **2** a sudden occurrence or display, esp. one suggestive of brilliance: *a flash of understanding.* **3** a very brief space of time: *over in a flash.* **4** Also called: **newsflash.** a short news announcement concerning a new event. **5** Also called: **patch.** *Chiefly Brit.* an insignia or emblem worn on a uniform, vehicle, etc., to identify its military formation. **6** a sudden rush of water down a river or watercourse. **7** *Photog., inf.* short for **flashlight** (sense 2). **8** (*modifier*) involving, using, or produced by a flash of heat, light, etc.: *flash distillation.* **9 flash in the pan.** a project, person, etc., that enjoys only short-lived success. ◆ *adj* **10** *Inf.* ostentatious or vulgar. **11** sham or counterfeit. **12** *Inf.* relating to or characteristic of the criminal underworld. **13** brief and rapid: *flash freezing.* ◆ *vb* **14** to burst or cause to burst suddenly or intermittently into flame. **15** to emit or reflect or cause to emit or reflect light suddenly or intermittently. **16** (*intr*) to move very fast: *he flashed by on his bicycle.* **17** (*intr*) to come rapidly (into the mind or vision). **18** (*intr;* foll. by *out* or *up*) to appear like a sudden light. **19a** to signal or communicate very fast: *to flash a message.* **19b** to signal by use of a light, such as car headlights. **20** (*tr*) *Inf.* to display ostentatiously: *to flash money around.* **21** (*tr*) *Inf.* to show suddenly and briefly. **22** (*intr*) *Brit. sl.* to expose oneself indecently. **23** to send a sudden rush of water down (a river, etc.), or to carry (a vessel) down by this method. ORIG C14 (in the sense: to rush, as of water): from ?
▸ **'flasher** *n*

flashback ('flæʃ,bæk) *n* a transition in a novel, film, etc., to an earlier scene or event.

flashboard ('flæʃ,bɔːd) *n* a board or boarding that is placed along the top of a dam to increase its height and capacity.

flashbulb ('flæʃ,bʌlb) *n Photog.* a small expendable glass light bulb formerly used to produce a bright flash of light.

flashbulb memory *n Psychol.* the clear recollections that a person may have of the circumstances associated with a dramatic event.

flash burn *n Pathol.* a burn caused by momentary exposure to intense radiant heat.

flash card *n* a card on which are written or printed words for children to look at briefly, used as an aid to learning.

flashcube ('flæʃ,kjuːb) *n* a boxlike camera attachment, holding four flashbulbs, that turns so that each flashbulb can be used.

flash flood *n* a sudden short-lived torrent, usually caused by a heavy storm, esp. in desert regions.

flashgun ('flæʃ,gʌn) *n* a type of electronic flash, attachable to or sometimes incorporated in a camera, that emits a very brief flash of light when the shutter is open.

flashing ('flæʃɪŋ) *n* a weatherproof material, esp. thin sheet metal, used to cover the valleys between the slopes of a roof, the junction between a chimney and a roof, etc.

flashlight ('flæʃ,laɪt) *n* **1** another word (esp. US and Canad.) for **torch. 2** *Photog.* the brief bright light emitted by an electronic flash unit. Often shortened to **flash.**

flash point *n* **1** the lowest temperature at which the vapour above a liquid can be ignited in air. **2** a critical time or place beyond which a situation will inevitably erupt into violence.

flashy ('flæʃɪ) *adj* **flashier, flashiest. 1** brilliant and dazzling, esp. for a short time or in a superficial way. **2** cheap and ostentatious.
▸ **'flashily** *adv* ▸ **'flashiness** *n*

flask (flɑːsk) *n* **1** a bottle with a narrow neck, esp. used in a laboratory or for wine, oil, etc. **2** Also called: **hip flask.** a small flattened container of glass or metal designed to be carried in a pocket, esp. for liquor. **3** See **vacuum flask.** ORIG C14: from OF, from Med. L *flasca, flasco,* ? of Gmc origin; cf. OE *flasce, flaxe*

flat¹ (flæt) *adj* **flatter, flattest. 1** horizontal; level: *a flat roof.* **2** even or smooth, without projections or depressions: *a flat surface.* **3** lying stretched out at full length: *he lay flat on the ground.* **4** having little depth or thickness: *a flat dish.* **5** (*postpositive;* often foll. by *against*) having a surface or side in complete contact with another surface: *flat against the wall.* **6** (of a tyre) deflated. **7** (of shoes) having an unraised heel. **8** *Chiefly Brit.* **8a** (of races, racetracks, or racecourses) not having obstacles to be jumped. **8b** of, relating to, or connected with flat racing as opposed to steeplechasing and hurdling. **9** without qualification; total: *a flat denial.* **10** fixed: *a flat rate.* **11** (*prenominal or immediately postpositive*) neither more nor less; exact: *he did the journey in thirty minutes flat.* **12** unexciting: *a flat joke.* **13** without variation or resonance; monotonous: *a flat voice.* **14** (of beer, sparkling wines, etc.) having lost effervescence, as by exposure to air. **15** (of trade, business, etc.) commercially inactive. **16** (of a battery) fully discharged. **17** (of a print, photograph, or painting) lacking contrast. **18** (of paint) without gloss or lustre. **19** (of lighting) diffuse. **20** *Music.* **20a** (*immediately postpositive*) denoting a note of a given letter name (or the sound it represents) that has been lowered in pitch by one chromatic semitone: *B flat.* **20b** (of an instrument, voice, etc.) out of tune by being too low in pitch. Cf. **sharp** (sense 12). **21** *Phonetics.* **flat a.** the vowel sound of *a* as in the usual US or S Brit. pronunciation of *hand, cat.* ◆ *adv* **22** in or into a prostrate, level, or flat state or position: *he held his hand out flat.* **23** completely or utterly; absolutely. **24** exactly; precisely: *in three minutes flat.* **25** *Music.* **25a** lower than a standard pitch. **25b** too low in pitch: *she sings flat.* Cf. **sharp** (sense 17). **26 fall flat (on one's face).** to fail to achieve a desired effect. **27 flat out.** *Inf.* **27a** with the maximum speed or effort. **27b** totally exhausted. ◆ *n* **28** a flat object, surface, or part. **29** (*often pl*) a low-lying tract of land, esp. a marsh or swamp. **30** (*often pl*) a mud bank exposed at low tide. **31** *Music.* **31a** an accidental that lowers the pitch of a note by one chromatic semitone. Usual symbol: ♭ **31b** a note affected by this accidental. Cf. **sharp** (sense 18). **32** *Theatre.* a wooden frame covered with painted canvas, etc., used to form part of a stage setting. **33** a punctured car tyre. **34** (*often cap.;* preceded by *the*) *Chiefly Brit.* **34a** flat racing, esp. as opposed to steeplechasing and hurdling. **34b** the season of flat racing. **35** *US & Canad.* a shallow box used for holding plants, etc. ◆ *vb* **flats, flatting, flatted. 36** to make or become flat. ORIG C14: from ON *flatr*
▸ **'flatly** *adv* ▸ **'flatness** *n* ▸ **'flattish** *adj*

flat² (flæt) *n* **1** a set of rooms comprising a residence entirely on one floor of a building. Usual US and Canad. name: **apartment.** ◆ *vb* **2** (*intr*) *Austral. & NZ inf.* to live in a flat with other people. ORIG OE *flett* floor, hall, house

flatbed lorry ('flæt,bɛd) *n* a lorry with a flat platform for its body.

flatbed scanner *n Computing.* a computer-controlled device that electronically scans images placed on its flat glass, to produce digitized images for use in desktop publishing, etc.

flatboat ('flæt,bəʊt) *n* any boat with a flat bottom, usually for transporting goods on a canal.

flatette (,flæt'ɛt) *n Austral.* a very small flat.

flatfish ('flæt,fɪʃ) *n, pl* **flatfish** *or* **flatfishes.** any of an order of marine spiny-finned fish including the halibut, plaice, turbot, and sole, all of which have a flat body which has both eyes on the uppermost side.

flatfoot ('flæt,fʊt) *n* **1** Also called: **splayfoot.** a condition in which the instep arch of the foot is flattened. **2** (*pl* **flatfoots** *or* **flatfeet**) a slang word (usually derogatory) for a **policeman.**

flat-footed (,flæt'fʊtɪd) *adj* **1** having flatfoot. **2** *Inf.* **2a** awkward. **2b** downright. **3** *Inf.* off guard (often in **catch flat-footed**).
▸ **,flat-'footedly** *adv* ▸ **,flat-'footedness** *n*

flathead ('flæt,hɛd) *n, pl* **flathead** *or* **flatheads.** a Pacific food fish which resembles the gurnard.

flatiron ('flæt,aɪən) *n* (formerly) an iron for pressing clothes that was heated by being placed on a stove, etc.

flatlet ('flætlɪt) *n* a flat having only a few rooms.

flatmate ('flæt,meɪt) *n* a person with whom one shares a flat.

flat racing *n* **a** the racing of horses on racecourses without jumps. **b** (*as modifier*): *the flat-racing season.*

flat spin *n* **1** an aircraft spin in which the longitudinal axis is more nearly horizontal than vertical. **2** *Inf.* a state of confusion; dither.

flat spot *n* **1** *Engineering.* a region of poor acceleration over a narrow range of throttle openings, caused by a weak mixture in the carburettor. **2** any narrow region of poor performance in a mechanical device.

flatten ('flætᵊn) *vb* **1** (sometimes foll. by *out*) to make or become flat or flatter. **2** (*tr*) *Inf.* **2a** to knock down or injure. **2b** to crush or subdue. **3** (*tr*) *Music.* to lower the pitch of (a note) by one chromatic semitone.
▸ **'flattener** *n*

flatter ('flætə) *vb* **1** to praise insincerely, esp. in order to win favour or reward. **2** to show to advantage: *that dress flatters her.* **3** (*tr*) to make to appear more attractive, etc., than in reality. **4** to gratify the vanity of (a person). **5** (*tr*) to encourage, esp. falsely. **6** (*tr*) to deceive (oneself): *I flatter myself that I am the best.* ORIG C13: prob. from OF *flater* to lick, fawn upon, of Frankish origin
▸ **'flatterable** *adj* ▸ **'flatterer** *n*

flattery ('flætərɪ) *n, pl* **flatteries. 1** the act of flattering. **2** excessive or insincere praise.

flattie ('flætɪ) *n NZ inf.* a flounder or other flatfish.

flatties ('flætɪz) *pl n* shoes with flat heels.

flat top *n* a style of haircut in which the hair is cut shortest on the top of the head so that it stands up from the scalp and appears flat from the crown to the forehead.

flatulent ('flætjʊlənt) *adj* **1** suffering from or caused by an excessive amount of gas in the alimentary canal. **2** generating excessive gas in the alimentary canal. **3** pretentious. ORIG C16: from NL *flātulentus,* from L *flatus,* from *flāre* to breathe, blow
▸ **'flatulence** *or* **'flatulency** *n* ▸ **'flatulently** *adv*

flatus ('fleɪtəs) *n, pl* **flatuses.** gas generated in the alimentary canal. ORIG C17: from L: a blowing, from *flāre* to breathe, blow

flatworm ('flætˌwɜːm) *n* any parasitic or free-living invertebrate of the phylum *Platyhelminthes,* including flukes and tapeworms, having a flattened body.

Flaubert ★ ('fləʊbɛə; *French* flobɛr) *n* **Gustave** (gystav). 1821–80, French writer. His works include *Madame Bovary* (1857), for which he was prosecuted (and acquitted) on charges of immorality, *L'Éducation sentimentale* (1869), *La Tentation de Saint Antoine* (1874), and *Trois contes* (1877).

flaunt (flɔːnt) *vb* **1** to display (possessions, oneself, etc.) ostentatiously. **2** to wave or cause to wave freely. ◆ *n* **3** the act of flaunting. ORIG C16: ? of Scand. origin

> **USAGE NOTE** *Flaunt* is sometimes wrongly used where *flout* is meant: *they must be prevented from flouting* (not *flaunting*) *the law.*

flautist ('flɔːtɪst) *or US & Canad.* **flutist** ('fluːtɪst) *n* a player of the flute. ORIG C19: from It. *flautista,* from *flauto* FLUTE

flavescent (flə'vɛsᵊnt) *adj* turning yellow; yellowish. ORIG C19: from L *flāvēscere* to become yellow

flavin *or* **flavine** ('fleɪvɪn) *n* **1** a heterocyclic ketone that forms the nucleus of certain natural yellow pigments, such as riboflavin. **2** any yellow pigment based on flavin. ORIG C19: from L *flāvus* yellow

flavine ('fleɪvɪn) *n* another name for **acriflavine hydrochloride.**

flavone ('fleɪvəʊn) *n* **1** a crystalline compound occurring in plants. **2** any of a class of yellow plant pigments derived from flavone. ORIG C19: from G, from L *flāvus* yellow + -ONE

flavoprotein (ˌfleɪvəʊ'prəʊtiːn) *n* any of a group of enzymes that contain a derivative of riboflavin linked to a protein and catalyse oxidation in cells.

flavour *or US* **flavor** ('fleɪvə) *n* **1** taste perceived in food or liquid in the mouth. **2** a substance added to food, etc., to impart a specific taste. **3** a distinctive quality or atmosphere. **4** *Physics.* a property of quarks that distinguishes different types. ◆ *vb* **5** (*tr*) to impart a flavour or quality to. ORIG C14: from OF *flaour,* from LL *flātor* (unattested) bad smell, breath, from L *flāre* to blow
▸ **'flavourless** *or US* **'flavorless** *adj* ▸ **'flavourful** *or US* **'flavorful** *adj*

flavour enhancer *n* a food additive, such as monosodium glutamate, used to intensify the flavour of foods.

flavouring *or US* **flavoring** ('fleɪvərɪŋ) *n* a substance used to impart a particular flavour to food.

flaw[1] (flɔː) *n* **1** an imperfection or blemish. **2** a crack or rift. **3** *Law.* an invalidating defect in a document or proceeding. ◆ *vb* **4** to make or become blemished or imperfect. ORIG C14: prob. from ON *flaga* stone slab
▸ **'flawless** *adj*

flaw[2] (flɔː) *n* a sudden short gust of wind; squall. ORIG C16: of Scand. origin

flax (flæks) *n* **1** a herbaceous plant or shrub that has blue flowers and is cultivated for its seeds (flaxseed) and for the fibres of its stems. **2** the fibre of this plant, made into thread and woven into linen fabrics. **3** any of various similar plants. **4** *NZ.* a swamp plant producing a fibre that is used by Maoris for clothing, baskets, etc. ORIG OE *fleax*

flaxen ('flæksən) *adj* **1** of or resembling flax. **2** of a soft yellow colour: *flaxen hair.*

Flaxman ★ ('flæksmən) *n* **John.** 1755–1826, British neoclassical sculptor and draughtsman, noted for his monuments and his illustrations for the *Iliad* and the *Odyssey.*

flaxseed ('flæksˌsiːd) *n* the seed of the flax plant, which yields linseed oil. Also called: **linseed.**

flay (fleɪ) *vb* (*tr*) **1** to strip off the skin or covering of, esp. by whipping. **2** to attack with savage criticism. ORIG OE *flēan*
▸ **'flayer** *n*

flea (fliː) *n* **1** a small wingless parasitic blood-sucking jumping insect living on the skin of mammals and birds. **2 flea in one's ear.** *Inf.* a sharp rebuke. ORIG OE *flēah*

fleabane ('fliːˌbeɪn) *n* any of several plants, including one having purplish tubular flower heads with orange centres and one having yellow daisy-like flower heads, that are reputed to ward off fleas.

fleabite ('fliːˌbaɪt) *n* **1** the bite of a flea. **2** a slight or trifling annoyance or discomfort.

flea-bitten *adj* **1** bitten by or infested with fleas. **2** *Inf.* shabby or decrepit.

flea market *n* an open-air market selling cheap and often second-hand goods.

fleapit ('fliːˌpɪt) *n Inf.* a shabby cinema or theatre.

fleawort ('fliːˌwɜːt) *n* **1** any of various plants with yellow daisy-like flowers and rosettes of downy leaves. **2** a Eurasian plantain whose seeds were formerly used as a flea repellent.

flèche (fleɪʃ, flɛʃ) *n* a slender spire, esp. over the intersection of the nave and transept ridges of a church roof. Also called: **spirelet.** ORIG C18: from F: spire (lit.: arrow), prob. of Gmc origin

fleck (flɛk) *n* **1** a small marking or streak. **2** a speck: *a fleck of dust.* ◆ *vb* **3** (*tr*) Also: **flecker.** to speckle. ORIG C16: prob. from ON *flekkr* stain, spot

Flecker ★ ('flɛkə) *n* **James Elroy.** 1884–1915, British poet and dramatist; author of *Hassan* (1922).

fled (flɛd) *vb* the past tense and past participle of **flee.**

fledge (flɛdʒ) *vb* **fledges, fledging, fledged.** (*tr*) **1** to feed and care for (a young bird) until it is able to fly. **2** Also called: **fletch.** to fit (something, esp. an arrow) with a feather or feathers. **3** to cover or adorn with or as if with feathers. ORIG OE *-flycge,* as in *unflycge* unfledged; see FLY[1]

fledgling *or* **fledgeling** ('flɛdʒlɪŋ) *n* **1** a young bird that has grown feathers. **2** a young and inexperienced person.

flee (fliː) *vb* **flees, fleeing, fled. 1** to run away from (a place, danger, etc.). **2** (*intr*) to run or move quickly. ORIG OE *flēon*
▸ **'fleer** *n*

fleece (fliːs) *n* **1** the coat of wool that covers the body of a sheep or similar animal. **2** the wool removed from a single sheep. **3** something resembling a fleece. **4** sheepskin or a fabric with soft pile, used as a lining for coats, etc. **5a** a warm polyester fabric with a brushed nap, used for outdoor garments. **5b** a jacket or top made from such a fabric. ◆ *vb* **fleeces, fleecing, fleeced.** (*tr*) **6** to defraud or charge exorbitantly. **7** another term for **shear** (sense 1). ORIG OE *flēos*

fleecie ('fli:sɪ) *n NZ.* a person who collects fleeces after shearing and prepares them for baling. Also called: **fleece-oh.**

fleecy ('fli:sɪ) *adj* **fleecier, fleeciest.** of or resembling fleece.
► **'fleecily** *adv*

fleer (flɪə) *Arch.* ◆ *vb* **1** to scoff; sneer. ◆ *n* **2** a derisory glance. ORIG C14: from ON; cf. Norwegian *flire* to snigger

fleet[1] (fli:t) *n* **1** a number of warships organized as a tactical unit. **2** all the warships of a nation. **3** a number of aircraft, ships, buses, etc., operating together or under the same ownership. ORIG OE *flēot*

fleet[2] (fli:t) *adj* **1** rapid in movement; swift. **2** *Poetic.* fleeting. ◆ *vb* **3** (*intr*) to move rapidly. **4** (*tr*) *Obs.* to cause (time) to pass rapidly. ORIG prob. OE *flēotan* to float, glide rapidly
► **'fleetly** *adv* ► **'fleetness** *n*

Fleet ★ (fli:t) *n* **the. 1** a stream that formerly ran into the Thames between Ludgate Hill and Fleet Street and is now a covered sewer. **2** Also called: **Fleet Prison.** a former London prison, used esp. for holding debtors.

Fleet Air Arm *n* the aviation branch of the Royal Navy.

fleet chief petty officer *n* a noncommissioned officer in the Royal Navy comparable in rank to a warrant officer in the army or the Royal Air Force.

fleeting ('fli:tɪŋ) *adj* rapid and transient: *a fleeting glimpse of the sea.*
► **'fleetingly** *adv*

fleet rate *or* **rating** *n* a reduced rate quoted by an insurance company to underwrite the risks to a fleet of vehicles, aircraft, etc.

Fleet Street ★ *n* **1** a street in central London in which many newspaper offices were formerly situated. **2** British journalism or journalists collectively.

Fleetwood ★ ('fli:tˌwʊd) *n* a fishing port in NW England, in Lancashire. Pop.: 27 227 (1991).

Flémalle ★ (*French* flemal) *n* **Master of.** See (Robert) **Campin.**

Fleming[1] ('flɛmɪŋ) *n* a native or inhabitant of Flanders or of Flemish-speaking Belgium.

Fleming[2] ★ ('flɛmɪŋ) *n* **1** Sir **Alexander.** 1881–1955, Scottish bacteriologist: discovered lysozyme (1922) and penicillin (1928): shared the Nobel prize for physiology or medicine in 1945. **2 Ian (Lancaster).** 1908–64, British author of spy novels; creator of the agent James Bond. **3** Sir **John Ambrose.** 1849–1945, British electrical engineer: invented the thermionic valve (1904).

Flemish ('flɛmɪʃ) *n* **1** one of the two official languages of Belgium. **2 the Flemish.** (*functioning as pl*) the Flemings collectively. ◆ *adj* **3** of or characteristic of Flanders, the Flemings, or their language.

Flemish Brabant ★ *n* a province of central Belgium, formed in 1995 from the N part of Brabant province. Pop.: 1 007 882 (1998 est.). Area: 2106 sq. km (813 sq. miles).

Flensburg ★ (*German* 'flɛnsbʊrk) *n* a port in N Germany, in Schleswig-Holstein: taken from Denmark by Prussia in 1864; voted to remain German in 1920. Pop.: 87 240 (1991).

flense (flɛns), **flench** (flɛntʃ), *or* **flinch** (flɪntʃ) *vb* **flenses, flensing, flensed** *or* **flenches, flenching, flenched** *or* **flinches, flinching, flinched.** (*tr*) to strip (a whale, seal, etc.) of (its blubber or skin). ORIG C19: from Danish *flense;* rel. to Du. *flensen*

flesh (flɛʃ) *n* **1** the soft part of the body of an animal or human, esp. muscular tissue, as distinct from bone and viscera. **2** *Inf.* excess weight; fat. **3** *Arch.* the edible tissue of animals as opposed to that of fish or, sometimes, fowl. **4** the thick soft part of a fruit or vegetable. **5** the human body and its physical or sensual nature as opposed to the soul or spirit. Related adj: **carnal. 6** mankind in general. **7** animate creatures in general. **8** one's own family; kin (esp. in **one's own flesh and blood**). **9a** a yellowish-pink colour. **9b** (*as adj*): *flesh tights.* **10 in the flesh.** in person; actually present. **11 press the flesh.** *Inf.* to shake hands, usually with large numbers of people, esp. as a political campaigning ploy. ◆ *vb* **12** (*tr*) *Hunting.* to stimulate the hunting instinct of (hounds or falcons) by giving them small quantities of raw flesh. **13** *Arch. or poetic.* to accustom or incite to bloodshed or battle by initial experience. **14** to fatten; fill out. ORIG OE *flǣsc*

fleshings ('flɛʃɪŋz) *pl n* flesh-coloured tights.

fleshly ('flɛʃlɪ) *adj* **fleshlier, fleshliest. 1** relating to the body; carnal: *fleshly desire.* **2** worldly as opposed to spiritual. **3** fat.
► **'fleshliness** *n*

flesh out *vb* (*adv*) **1** (*tr*) to give substance to (an argument, description, etc.). **2** (*intr*) to expand or become more substantial.

fleshpots ('flɛʃˌpɒts) *pl n Often facetious.* **1** luxurious living. **2** places where bodily desires are gratified. ORIG C16: from the Biblical use as applied to Egypt (Exodus 16:3)

flesh wound (wu:nd) *n* a wound affecting superficial tissues.

fleshy ('flɛʃɪ) *adj* **fleshier, fleshiest. 1** plump. **2** related to or resembling flesh. **3** *Bot.* (of some fruits, etc.) thick and pulpy.
► **'fleshiness** *n*

fletcher ('flɛtʃə) *n* a person who makes arrows. ORIG C14: from OF *flechier,* from *fleche* arrow; see FLÈCHE

Fletcher ★ ('flɛtʃə) *n* **John.** 1579–1625, English Jacobean dramatist, noted for his romantic tragicomedies written in collaboration with Francis Beaumont, esp. *Philaster* (1610) and *The Maid's Tragedy* (1611).

fleur-de-lys *or* **fleur-de-lis** (ˌflɜ:də'li:) *n, pl* **fleurs-de-lys** *or* **fleurs-de-lis** (ˌflɜ:də'li:z). **1** *Heraldry.* a charge representing a lily with three distinct petals. **2** another name for **iris** (sense 2). ORIG C19: from OF *flor de lis,* lit.: lily flower

fleurette *or* **fleuret** (flʊə'rɛt) *n* an ornament or motif resembling a flower. ORIG C19: F, lit.: a small flower, from *fleur* flower

Fleury ★ (*French* flœri) *n* **André Hercule de** (ɑ̃dre ɛrkyl də). 1653–1743, French cardinal and statesman: Louis XV's chief adviser and virtual ruler of France (1726–43).

flew (flu:) *vb* the past tense of **fly**[1].

flews (flu:z) *pl n* the fleshy hanging upper lip of a bloodhound or similar dog. ORIG C16: from ?

flex (flɛks) *n* **1** *Brit.* a flexible insulated electric cable, used esp. to connect appliances to mains. US and Canad. name: **cord.** ◆ *vb* **2** to bend or be bent: *he flexed his arm.* **3** to contract (a muscle) or (of a muscle) to contract. **4** (*intr*) to work flexitime. ORIG C16: from L *flexus* bent, winding, from *flectere* to bend, bow

flexible ('flɛksɪbᵊl) *adj* **1** Also **flexile** ('flɛksaɪl). able to be bent easily without breaking. **2** adaptable or variable: *flexible working hours.* **3** able to be persuaded easily.
► ˌ**flexi'bility** *n* ► **'flexibly** *adv*

flexion ('flɛkʃən) *or* **flection** *n* **1** the act of bending a joint or limb. **2** the condition of the joint or limb so bent.
► **'flexional** *adj*

flexitime ('flɛksɪˌtaɪm) *n* a system permitting flexibility of working hours at the beginning or end of the day, provided an agreed period (**core time**) is spent at work. Also called: **flextime.**

flexor ('flɛksə) *n* any muscle whose contraction serves to bend a joint or limb. Cf. **extensor.** ORIG C17: NL; see FLEX

flexuous ('flɛksjʊəs) *adj* full of bends or curves; winding. ORIG C17: from L *flexuōsus* full of bends, tortuous, from *flexus* a bending; see FLEX
► **'flexuously** *adv*

flexure ('flɛkʃə) *n* **1** the act of flexing or the state of being flexed. **2** a bend, turn, or fold.

flex-wing *n Aeronautics.* a collapsible fabric delta wing, as used with hang-gliders.

flibbertigibbet ('flɪbətɪˌdʒɪbɪt) *n* an irresponsible, silly, or gossipy person. ORIG C15: from ?

flick[1] (flɪk) *vb* **1** (*tr*) to touch with or as if with the finger or hand in a quick jerky movement. **2** (*tr*) to propel or remove by a quick jerky movement, usually of the fingers or hand. **3** to move or cause to move quickly or jerkily. **4** (*intr;* foll. by *through*) to read or look at (a book, etc.) quickly or idly. ◆ *n* **5** a tap or quick stroke with the fingers, a whip, etc. **6** the sound made by such a stroke. **7** a fleck or particle. **8 give (someone) the flick.** to dismiss (someone) from consideration. ORIG C15: imit.; cf. F *flicflac*

flick[2] (flɪk) *n Sl.* **1** a cinema film. **2 the flicks.** the cinema: *what's on at the flicks tonight?*

flicker[1] ('flɪkə) *vb* **1** (*intr*) to shine with an unsteady or intermittent light. **2** (*intr*) to move quickly to and fro. **3** (*tr*) to cause to flicker. ◆ *n* **4** an unsteady or brief light or flame. **5** a swift quivering or fluttering movement. ORIG OE *flicorian*

flicker[2] ('flɪkə) *n* a North American woodpecker which has a yellow undersurface to the wings and tail. ORIG C19: ? imit. of the bird's call

flick knife *n* a knife with a retractable blade that springs out when a button is pressed.

flier ('flaɪə) *n* a variant spelling of **flyer.**

flight[1] (flaɪt) *n* **1** the act, skill, or manner of flying. **2** a journey made by a flying animal or object. **3** a group of flying birds or aircraft: *a flight of swallows.* **4** the basic tactical unit of a military air force. **5** a journey through space, esp. of a spacecraft. **6** an aircraft flying on a scheduled journey. **7** a soaring mental journey above or beyond the normal everyday world: *a flight of fancy.* **8** a single line of hurdles across a track in a race. **9** a feather or plastic attachment fitted to an arrow or dart to give it stability in flight. **10** a set of steps or stairs between one landing or floor and the next. ◆ *vb* (*tr*) **11** *Sport.* to cause (a ball, dart, etc.) to float slowly towards its target. **12** to shoot (a bird) in flight. **13** to fledge (an arrow or dart). ORIG OE *flyht*

flight[2] (flaɪt) *n* **1** the act of fleeing or running away, as from danger. **2 put to flight.** to cause to run away. **3 take (to) flight.** to run away; flee. ORIG OE *flyht* (unattested)

flight attendant *n* a person who attends to the needs of passengers on a commercial flight.

flight deck *n* **1** the crew compartment in an airliner. **2** the upper deck of an aircraft carrier from which aircraft take off.

flightless ('flaɪtlɪs) *adj* (of certain birds and insects) unable to fly. See also **ratite.**

flight lieutenant *n* an officer holding a commissioned rank senior to a flying officer and junior to a squadron leader in the Royal Air Force.

flight path *n* the course through the air of an aircraft, rocket, or projectile.

flight recorder *n* an electronic device fitted to an aircraft for collecting and storing information concerning its performance in flight. It is often used to determine the cause of a crash. Also called: **black box.**

flight sergeant *n* a noncommissioned officer in the Royal Air Force, junior in rank to that of master aircrew.

flight simulator *n* a ground-training device that reproduces exactly the conditions experienced on the flight deck of an aircraft.

flighty ('flaɪtɪ) *adj* **flightier, flightiest. 1** frivolous and irresponsible. **2** mentally erratic or wandering.
► '**flightiness** *n*

flimflam ('flɪmˌflæm) *Inf.* ◆ *n* **1a** nonsense; rubbish; foolishness. **1b** (*as modifier*): *flimflam arguments.* **2** a deception; trick; swindle. ◆ *vb* **flimflams, flimflamming, flimflammed. 3** (*tr*) to deceive; trick; swindle; cheat. ORIG C16: prob. of Scand. origin
► '**flimˌflammer** *n*

flimsy ('flɪmzɪ) *adj* **flimsier, flimsiest. 1** not strong or substantial: *a flimsy building.* **2** light and thin: *a flimsy dress.* **3** unconvincing; weak: *a flimsy excuse.* ◆ *n* **4** thin paper used for making carbon copies of a letter, etc. **5** a copy made on such paper. ORIG C17: from ?
► '**flimsiness** *n*

flinch (flɪntʃ) *vb* (*intr*) **1** to draw back suddenly, as from pain, shock, etc.; wince. **2** (often foll. by *from*) to avoid contact (with): *he never flinched from his duty.* ORIG C16: from OF *flenchir;* rel. to MHG *lenken* to bend, direct
► '**flinchingly** *adv*

flinders ('flɪndəz) *pl n Rare.* small fragments or splinters (esp. in **fly into flinders**). ORIG C15: prob. from ON; cf. Norwegian *flindra* thin piece of stone

Flinders Island ★ ('flɪndəz) *n* an island off the coast of NE Tasmania: the largest of the Furneaux Islands. Pop.: 1100 (latest est.). Area: 2077 sq. km (802 sq. miles).

Flinders Range ★ *n* a mountain range in E South Australia, between Lake Torrens and Lake Frome. Highest peak: 1188 m (3898 ft).

fling (flɪŋ) *vb* **flings, flinging, flung.** (*mainly tr*) **1** to throw, esp. with force or abandon. **2** to put or send without warning or preparation: *to fling someone into jail.* **3** (*also intr*) to move (oneself or a part of the body) with abandon or speed. **4** (usually foll. by *into*) to apply (oneself) diligently and with vigour (to). **5** to cast aside: *she flung away her scruples.* ◆ *n* **6** the act or an instance of flinging. **7** a period or occasion of unrestrained or extravagant behaviour. **8** any of various vigorous Scottish reels full of leaps and turns, such as the Highland fling. **9** a trial; try: *to have a fling at something different.* ORIG C13: from ON
► '**flinger** *n*

flint (flɪnt) *n* **1** an impure greyish-black form of quartz that occurs in chalk. It produces sparks when struck with steel and is used in the manufacture of pottery and road-construction materials. Formula: SiO_2. **2** any piece of flint, esp. one used as a primitive tool or for striking fire. **3** a small cylindrical piece of an iron alloy, used in cigarette lighters. **4** Also called: **flint glass.** colourless glass other than plate glass. ORIG OE

Flint ★ (flɪnt) *n* **1** a town in NE Wales, in Flintshire, on the Dee estuary. Pop.: 11 737 (1991). **2** a city in SE Michigan. Pop.: 134 881 (1996 est.).

flintlock ('flɪntˌlɒk) *n* **1** an obsolete gunlock in which the charge is ignited by a spark produced by a flint in the hammer. **2** a firearm having such a lock.

Flintshire ★ ('flɪntˌʃɪə, -ʃə) *n* a county of NE Wales: became part of Clwyd in 1974, reinstated with new borders in 1996. Administrative centre: Mold. Pop.: 145 000 (1996 est.). Area: 437 sq. km (169 sq. miles).

flinty ('flɪntɪ) *adj* **flintier, flintiest. 1** of or resembling flint. **2** hard or cruel; unyielding.
► '**flintily** *adv* ► '**flintiness** *n*

flip (flɪp) *vb* **flips, flipping, flipped. 1** to throw (something light or small) carelessly or briskly. **2** to throw or flick (an object such as a coin) so that it turns or spins in the air. **3** to flick: *to flip a crumb across the room.* **4** (foll. by *through*) to read or look at (a book, etc.) quickly, idly, or incompletely. **5** (*intr*) to make a snapping movement or noise with the finger and thumb. **6** (*intr*) *Sl.* to fly into a rage or an emotional outburst (also in **flip one's lid, flip one's top, flip out**). ◆ *n* **7** a snap or tap, usually with the fingers. **8** a rapid jerk. **9** any alcoholic drink containing beaten egg. ◆ *adj* **10** *Inf.* flippant or pert. ORIG C16: prob. imit.; see FILLIP

flip chart *n* a pad, containing large sheets of paper that can be easily turned over, mounted on a stand and used to present reports, data, etc.

flip-flop *n* **1** a backward handspring. **2** Also called: **bistable.** an electronic device or circuit that can assume either of two states by the application of a suitable pulse. **3** *Inf., chiefly US.* a complete change of opinion, policy, etc. **4** a repeated flapping noise. **5** Also called (esp. US, Austral., and Canad.): **thong.** a rubber-soled sandal attached to the foot by a thong between the big toe and the next toe. ◆ *vb* **flip-flops, flip-flopping, flip-flopped.** (*intr*) **6** *Inf., chiefly US.* to have a complete change of opinion, policy, etc. **7** to move with repeated flaps. ORIG C16: reduplication of FLIP

flippant ('flɪpənt) *adj* **1** marked by inappropriate levity; frivolous. **2** impertinent; saucy. ORIG C17: ?from FLIP
► '**flippancy** *n* ► '**flippantly** *adv*

flipper ('flɪpə) *n* **1** the flat broad limb of seals, whales, etc., specialized for swimming. **2** (*often pl*) either of a pair of rubber paddle-like devices worn on the feet as an aid in swimming.

flip side *n* **1** another term for **B-side**. **2** another, less familiar, aspect of a person or thing.

flirt (flɜːt) *vb* **1** (*intr*) to behave or act amorously without emotional commitment. **2** (*intr;* usually foll. by *with*) to deal playfully or carelessly (with something dangerous or serious): *the motorcyclist flirted with death.* **3** (*intr;* usually foll. by *with*) to toy (with): *to flirt with the idea of leaving.* **4** (*intr*) to dart; flit. **5** (*tr*) to flick or toss. ◆ *n* **6** a person who acts flirtatiously. ORIG C16: from ?
▸ **'flirter** *n* ▸ **'flirty** *adj*

flirtation (flɜː'teɪʃən) *n* **1** behaviour intended to arouse sexual feelings or advances without emotional commitment. **2** any casual involvement.

flirtatious (flɜː'teɪʃəs) *adj* **1** given to flirtation. **2** expressive of playful sexual invitation: *a flirtatious glance.*
▸ **flir'tatiously** *adv*

flit (flɪt) *vb* **flits, flitting, flitted.** (*intr*) **1** to move along rapidly and lightly. **2** to fly rapidly and lightly. **3** to pass quickly: *a memory flitted into his mind.* **4** *Scot. & N English dialect.* to move house. **5** *Brit. inf.* to depart hurriedly and stealthily in order to avoid obligations. ◆ *n* **6** the act or an instance of flitting. **7** *Brit. inf.* a hurried and stealthy departure in order to avoid obligations. ORIG C12: from ON *flytja* to carry
▸ **'flitter** *n*

flitch (flɪtʃ) *n* **1** a side of pork salted and cured. **2** a piece of timber cut lengthways from a tree trunk. ORIG OE *flicce;* cf. FLESH

flitter ('flɪtə) *vb* a less common word for **flutter**.

flittermouse ('flɪtə,maʊs) *n, pl* **flittermice.** a dialect name for **bat**[2] (sense 1). ORIG C16: translation of G *Fledermaus*

float (fləʊt) *vb* **1** to rest or cause to rest on the surface of a fluid or in a fluid or space without sinking: *oil floats on water.* **2** to move or cause to move buoyantly, lightly, or freely across a surface or through air, water, etc. **3** to move about aimlessly, esp. in the mind: *thoughts floated before him.* **4** (*tr*) **4a** to launch or establish (a commercial enterprise, etc.). **4b** to offer for sale (stock or bond issues, etc.) on the stock market. **5** (*tr*) *Finance.* to allow (a currency) to fluctuate against other currencies in accordance with market forces. **6** (*tr*) to flood, inundate, or irrigate (land). ◆ *n* **7** something that floats. **8** *Angling.* an indicator attached to a baited line that sits on the water and moves when a fish bites. **9** a small hand tool with a rectangular blade used for smoothing plaster, etc. **10** Also called: **paddle**. a blade of a paddle wheel. **11** *Brit.* a buoyant garment or device to aid a person in staying afloat. **12** a structure fitted to the underside of an aircraft to allow it to land on water. **13** a motor vehicle used to carry a tableau or exhibit in a parade, esp. a civic parade. **14** a small delivery vehicle, esp. one powered by batteries: *a milk float.* **15** *Austral. & NZ.* a vehicle for transporting horses. **16** a sum of money used by shopkeepers to provide change at the start of the day's business. **17** the hollow floating ball of a ballcock. ORIG OE *flotian;* see FLEET[2]
▸ **'floatable** *adj* ▸ **,floata'bility** *n* ▸ **'floaty** *adj*

floatage ('fləʊtɪdʒ) *n* a variant spelling of **flotage**.

floatation (fləʊ'teɪʃən) *n* a variant spelling of **flotation**.

floatel (fləʊ'tel) *n* a variant spelling of **flotel**.

floater ('fləʊtə) *n* **1** a person or thing that floats. **2** a dark spot that appears in one's vision as a result of dead cells or cell fragments in the eye. **3** *US & Canad.* a person of no fixed political opinion. **4** *US inf.* a person who often changes employment, residence, etc.

float glass *n* polished glass made by floating molten glass on liquid metal in a reservoir.

floating ('fləʊtɪŋ) *adj* **1** having little or no attachment. **2** (of an organ or part) displaced from the normal position or abnormally movable: *a floating kidney.* **3** uncommitted or unfixed: *floating voters.* **4** *Finance.* **4a** (of capital) available for current use. **4b** (of debt) short-term and unfunded, usually raised to meet current expenses. **4c** (of a currency) free to fluctuate against other currencies in accordance with market forces.
▸ **'floatingly** *adv*

floating-point representation *n Computing.* the representation of numbers by two sets of digits (*a, b*), the set *a* indicating the significant digits, the set *b* giving the position of the radix point. Also called: **floating decimal point representation.** Cf. **fixed-point representation.**

floating rib *n* any rib of the lower two pairs of ribs in man, which are not attached to the breastbone.

floats (fləʊts) *pl n Theatre.* another word for **footlights**.

flob (flɒb) *vb* **flobs, flobbing, flobbed.** (*intr*) *Brit. sl.* to spit. ORIG C20: from?

flocculate ('flɒkjʊ,leɪt) *vb* **flocculates, flocculating, flocculated.** to form or be formed into an aggregated flocculent mass.
▸ **,floccu'lation** *n*

flocculent ('flɒkjʊlənt) *adj* **1** like wool; fleecy. **2** *Chem.* aggregated in woolly cloudlike masses: *a flocculent precipitate.* **3** *Biol.* covered with tufts or flakes. ORIG C19: from L *floccus* FLOCK[2] + -ULENT
▸ **'flocculence** *n*

flocculus ('flɒkjʊləs) *n, pl* **flocculi** (-,laɪ). **1** Also called: **plage**. a cloudy marking on the sun's surface. It consists of calcium when lighter than the surroundings and of hydrogen when darker. **2** *Anat.* a tiny prominence on each side of the cerebellum.

flock[1] (flɒk) *n* (*sometimes functioning as pl*) **1** a group of animals of one kind, esp. sheep or birds. **2** a large number of people. **3** a body of Christians regarded as the pastoral charge of a priest, bishop, etc. ◆ *vb* (*intr*) **4** to gather together or move in a flock. **5** to go in large numbers: *people flocked to the church.* ORIG OE *flocc*

flock[2] (flɒk) *n* **1** a tuft, as of wool, hair, cotton, etc. **2** waste from fabrics such as cotton or wool used for stuffing mattresses, etc. **3** Also called: **flocking**. very small tufts of wool applied to fabrics, wallpaper, etc., to give a raised pattern. ORIG C13: from OF *floc,* from L *floccus*
▸ **'flocky** *adj*

Flodden ★ ('flɒdᵊn) *n* a hill in Northumberland where invading Scots were defeated by the English in 1513 and James IV of Scotland was killed. Also called: **Flodden Field.**

floe (fləʊ) *n* See **ice floe**. ORIG C19: prob. from Norwegian *flo* slab, layer, from ON; see FLAW[1]

flog (flɒg) *vb* **flogs, flogging, flogged.** **1** (*tr*) to beat harshly, esp. with a whip, strap, etc. **2** *Brit. sl.* to sell. **3** (*intr*) to make progress by painful work. **4 flog a dead horse.** *Chiefly Brit.* **4a** to harp on some long discarded subject. **4b** to pursue the solution of a problem long realized to be insoluble. ORIG C17: prob. from L *flagellāre;* see FLAGELLANT
▸ **'flogger** *n*

flong (flɒŋ) *n Printing.* a material used for making moulds in stereotyping. ORIG C20: var. of FLAN

flood (flʌd) *n* **1a** the inundation of land that is normally dry through the overflowing of a body of water, esp. a river. **1b** the state of a river that is at an abnormally high level. Related adj: **diluvial**. **2** a great outpouring or flow: *a flood of words.* **3a** the rising of the tide from low to high water. **3b** (*as modifier*): *the flood tide.* Cf. **ebb** (sense 3). **4** *Theatre.* short for **floodlight**. ◆ *vb* **5** (of water) to inundate or submerge (land) or (of land) to be inundated or submerged. **6** to fill or be filled to overflowing, as with a flood. **7** (*intr*) to flow; surge: *relief flooded through him.* **8** to supply an excessive quantity of petrol to (a carburettor or petrol engine) or (of a carburettor, etc.) to be supplied with such an excess. **9** (*intr*) to overflow. **10** (*intr*) to bleed profusely from the uterus, as following childbirth. ORIG OE *flōd;* see FLOW, FLOAT

Flood (flʌd) *n Old Testament.* **the.** the flood from which Noah and his family and livestock were saved in the ark (Genesis 7–8).

floodgate ('flʌd,geɪt) *n* **1** Also called: **head gate, water gate.** a gate in a sluice that is used to control the flow of water. **2** (*often pl*) a control or barrier against an outpouring or flow.

flooding ('flʌdɪŋ) *n* **1** *Psychol.* a method of eliminating anxiety in a given situation, by exposing a person to the situation until the anxiety subsides. **2** *Pathol.* excessive bleeding from the uterus.

★ people and places

floodlight ('flʌd,laɪt) *n* **1** a broad intense beam of artificial light, esp. as used in the theatre or to illuminate the exterior of buildings. **2** the lamp producing such light. ◆ *vb* **floodlights, floodlighting, floodlit. 3** (*tr*) to illuminate as by floodlight.

flood plain *n* the flat area bordering a river, composed of sediment deposited during flooding.

floor (flɔː) *n* **1** Also called: **flooring.** the inner lower surface of a room. **2** a storey of a building: *the second floor.* **3** a flat bottom surface in or on any structure: *a dance floor.* **4** the bottom surface of a tunnel, cave, sea, etc. **5** that part of a legislative hall in which debate and other business is conducted. **6** the right to speak in a legislative body (esp. in **get, have,** *or* **be given the floor**). **7** the room in a stock exchange where trading takes place. **8** the earth; ground. **9** a minimum price charged or paid. **10 take the floor.** to begin dancing on a dance floor. ◆ *vb* **11** to cover with or construct a floor. **12** (*tr*) to knock to the floor or ground. **13** (*tr*) *Inf.* to disconcert, confound, or defeat. ORIG OE *flōr*

floorboard ('flɔː,bɔːd) *n* one of the boards forming a floor.

flooring ('flɔːrɪŋ) *n* **1** the material used in making a floor. **2** another word for **floor** (sense 1).

floor manager *n* **1** the stage manager of a television programme. **2** a person in overall charge of one floor of a large shop.

floor plan *n* a drawing to scale of the arrangement of rooms on one floor of a building.

floor show *n* a series of entertainments, such as singing and dancing, performed in a nightclub.

floozy, floozie, *or* **floosie** ('fluːzɪ) *n, pl* **floozies** *or* **floosies.** *Sl.* a disreputable woman. ORIG C20: from ?

flop (flɒp) *vb* **flops, flopping, flopped. 1** (*intr*) to bend, fall, or collapse loosely or carelessly: *his head flopped backwards.* **2** (when *intr,* often foll. by *into, onto,* etc.) to fall, cause to fall, or move with a sudden noise. **3** (*intr*) *Inf.* to fail: *the scheme flopped.* **4** (*intr*) to fall flat onto the surface of water. **5** (*intr;* often foll. by *out*) *Sl.* to go to sleep. ◆ *n* **6** the act of flopping. **7** *Inf.* a complete failure. ORIG C17: var. of FLAP

floppy ('flɒpɪ) *adj* **floppier, floppiest. 1** limp or hanging loosely. ◆ *n, pl* **floppies. 2** short for **floppy disk.**
▸ **'floppily** *adv* ▸ **'floppiness** *n*

floppy disk *n* a flexible magnetic disk that stores information and can be used to store data in the memory of a digital computer.

flops *abbrev.* (*sometimes caps.*) *for* floating-point operations per second: a measure of computer processing power.

flora ('flɔːrə) *n, pl* **floras** *or* **florae** (-riː). **1** all the plant life of a given place or time. **2** a descriptive list of such plants, often including a key for identification. ORIG C18: from NL, from FLORA

Flora ★ ('flɔːrə) *n* the Roman goddess of flowers. ORIG C16: from L, from *flōs* flower

floral ('flɔːrəl) *adj* **1** decorated with or consisting of flowers or patterns of flowers. **2** of or associated with flowers.
▸ **'florally** *adv*

Florence ★ ('flɒrəns) *n* a city in central Italy, on the River Arno in Tuscany: became an independent republic in the 14th century; under Austrian and other rule intermittently from 1737 to 1859; capital of Italy 1865–70. It was the major cultural and artistic centre of the Renaissance and is still one of the world's chief art centres. Pop.: 383 594 (1996 est.). Ancient name: **Florentia** (flɒ'rɛntsɪə, -rɛntɪə). Italian name: **Firenze.**

Florentine ('flɒrən,taɪn) *adj* **1** of or relating to Florence, in Italy. ◆ *n* **2** a native or inhabitant of Florence.

Flores ★ ('flɔːrɛs) *n* **1** an island in Indonesia, one of the Lesser Sunda Islands, between the Flores Sea and the Savu Sea: mountainous, with active volcanoes and unexplored forests. Chief town: Ende. Area: 17 150 sq. km (6622 sq. miles). **2** (*also Portuguese* 'florɪʃ). an island in the Atlantic, the westernmost of the Azores. Chief town: Santa Cruz. Area: 142 sq. km (55 sq. miles).

florescence (flɔː'rɛsəns) *n* the process, state, or period of flowering. ORIG C18: from NL, from L *flōrēscere* to come into flower

Flores Sea ★ *n* a part of the Pacific Ocean in Indonesia between Celebes and the Lesser Sunda Islands.

floret ('flɔːrɪt) *n* a small flower, esp. one of many making up the head of a composite flower. ORIG C17: from OF, from *flor* FLOWER

Florey ★ ('flɔːrɪ) *n* **Howard Walter,** Baron Florey. 1898–1968, British pathologist: shared the Nobel prize for physiology or medicine (1945) for work on penicillin.

Florianópolis ★ (*Portuguese* floriə'nɔpulis) *n* a port in S Brazil, capital of Santa Caterina state, on the W coast of Santa Caterina Island. Pop.: 191 664 (1991).

floriated *or* **floreated** ('flɔːrɪ,eɪtɪd) *adj Archit.* having ornamentation based on flowers and leaves. ORIG C19: from L *flōs* FLOWER

floribunda (,flɔːrɪ'bʌndə) *n* any of several varieties of cultivated hybrid roses whose flowers grow in large sprays. ORIG C19: from NL, fem of *flōribundus* flowering freely

floriculture ('flɔːrɪ,kʌltʃə) *n* the cultivation of flowering plants.
▸ **,flori'cultural** *adj* ▸ **,flori'culturist** *n*

florid ('flɒrɪd) *adj* **1** having a red or flushed complexion. **2** excessively ornate; flowery: *florid architecture.* ORIG C17: from L *flōridus* blooming
▸ **flo'ridity** *n* ▸ **'floridly** *adv*

Florida ★ ('flɒrɪdə) *n* **1** a state of the southeastern US, between the Atlantic and the Gulf of Mexico: consists mostly of a low-lying peninsula ending in the **Florida Keys,** a chain of small islands off the coast of S Florida, extending southwest for over 160 km (100 miles). Capital: Tallahassee. Pop.: 14 915 980 (1998 est.). Area: 143 900 sq. km (55 560 sq. miles). Abbrevs.: **Fla.** or (with zip code) **FL 2 Straits of.** a sea passage between the Florida Keys and Cuba, linking the Atlantic with the Gulf of Mexico.
▸ **Flo'ridian** *adj*

floriferous (flɔː'rɪfərəs) *adj* bearing or capable of bearing many flowers.

florin ('flɒrɪn) *n* **1** a former British coin, originally silver, equivalent to ten (new) pence. **2** (formerly) another name for **guilder** (sense 1). ORIG C14: from F, from OIt. *fiorino* Florentine coin, from *fiore* flower, from L *flōs*

florist ('flɒrɪst) *n* a person who grows or deals in flowers.

floristic (flɒ'rɪstɪk) *adj* of or relating to flowers or a flora.
▸ **flo'ristically** *adv*

-florous *adj combining form.* indicating number or type of flowers: *tubuliflorous.*

floruit *Latin.* ('flɒruːɪt) *vb* (he or she) flourished: used to indicate the period when a figure, whose birth and death dates are unknown, was most active.

floss (flɒs) *n* **1** the mass of fine silky fibres obtained from cotton and similar plants. **2** any similar fine silky material. **3** untwisted silk thread used in embroidery, etc. **4** See **dental floss.** ◆ *vb* **5** (*tr*) to clean (between one's teeth) with dental floss. ORIG C18: ?from OF *flosche* down

flossy ('flɒsɪ) *adj* **flossier, flossiest.** consisting of or resembling floss.

flotage *or* **floatage** ('fləʊtɪdʒ) *n* **1** the act or state of floating. **2** power or ability to float. **3** flotsam.

flotation *or* **floatation** (fləʊ'teɪʃən) *n* **1a** the launching or financing of a commercial enterprise by bond or share issues. **1b** the raising of a loan or new capital by bond or share issues. **2** power or ability to float. **3** Also called: **froth flotation.** a process to concentrate the valuable ore in low-grade ores by using induced differences in surface tension to carry the valuable fraction to the surface.

flotel *or* **floatel** (fləʊ'tɛl) *n* a rig used for accommodation of workers in off-shore oil fields. ORIG C20: FLO(ATING) + (HO)TEL

flotilla (flə'tɪlə) *n* a small fleet or a fleet of small vessels. ORIG C18: from Sp., from F *flotte,* ult. from ON *floti*

flotsam ('flɒtsəm) *n* **1** wreckage from a ship found floating. Cf. **jetsam. 2** odds and ends (esp. in **flotsam and jet-**

sam). **3** vagrants. ORIG C16: from Anglo-F *floteson*, from *floter* to FLOAT

flounce[1] (flaʊns) *vb* **flounces, flouncing, flounced. 1** (*intr; often foll. by about, away, out,* etc.) to move or go with emphatic movements. ◆ *n* **2** the act of flouncing. ORIG C16: of Scand. origin

flounce[2] (flaʊns) *n* an ornamental gathered ruffle sewn to a garment by its top edge. ORIG C18: from OF, from *froncir* to wrinkle, of Gmc origin

flounder[1] (ˈflaʊndə) *vb* (*intr*) **1** to move with difficulty, as in mud. **2** to make mistakes. ◆ *n* **3** the act of floundering. ORIG C16: prob. a blend of FOUNDER[2] + BLUNDER; ? infl. by FLOUNDER[2]

> **USAGE NOTE** *Flounder* is sometimes wrongly used where *founder* is meant: *the project foundered (not floundered) because of lack of funds.*

flounder[2] (ˈflaʊndə) *n, pl* **flounder** *or* **flounders.** a European flatfish having a greyish-brown body covered with prickly scales: an important food fish. ORIG C14: from ON

flour (ˈflaʊə) *n* **1** a powder, which may be either fine or coarse, prepared by grinding the meal of a grass, esp. wheat. **2** any finely powdered substance. ◆ *vb* (*tr*) **3** to make (grain, etc.) into flour. **4** to dredge or sprinkle (food or utensils) with flour. ORIG C13 *flur* finer portion of meal, FLOWER
► **ˈfloury** *adj*

flourish (ˈflʌrɪʃ) *vb* **1** (*intr*) to thrive; prosper. **2** (*intr*) to be at the peak of condition. **3** (*intr*) to be healthy: *plants flourish in the light.* **4** to wave or cause to wave in the air with sweeping strokes. **5** to display or make a display. **6** to play (a fanfare, etc.) on a musical intrument. ◆ *n* **7** the act of waving or brandishing. **8** a showy gesture: *he entered with a flourish.* **9** an ornamental embellishment in writing. **10** a display of ornamental language or speech. **11** a grandiose passage of music. ORIG C13: from OF, ult. from L *flōrēre* to flower, from *flōs* a flower
► **ˈflourisher** *n*

flout (flaʊt) *vb* (when *intr,* usually foll. by *at*) to show contempt (for). ORIG C16: ?from ME *flouten* to play the flute, from OF *flauter*
► **ˈfloutingly** *adv*

> **USAGE NOTE** See at **flaunt.**

flow (fləʊ) *vb* (*mainly intr*) **1** (of liquids) to move or be conveyed as in a stream. **2** (of blood) to circulate around the body. **3** to move or progress freely as if in a stream: *the crowd flowed into the building.* **4** to be produced continuously and effortlessly: *ideas flowed from her pen.* **5** to be marked by smooth or easy movement. **6** to hang freely or loosely: *her hair flowed down her back.* **7** to be present in abundance: *wine flows at their parties.* **8** (of tide water) to advance or rise. Cf. **ebb** (sense 1). **9** (of rocks such as slate) to yield to pressure so that the structure and arrangement of the constituent minerals are altered. ◆ *n* **10** the act, rate, or manner of flowing: *a fast flow.* **11** a continuous stream or discharge. **12** continuous progression. **13** the advancing of the tide. **14** *Scot.* **14a** a marsh or swamp. **14b** an inlet or basin of the sea. **14c** (*cap. when part of a name*): *Scapa Flow.* ORIG OE *flōwan*

flow chart *or* **sheet** *n* a diagrammatic representation of the sequence of operations in an industrial process, computer program, etc.

Flow Country ★ *n* an area of moorland and peat bogs in northern Scotland known for its wildlife, now partly afforested.

flower (ˈflaʊə) *n* **1a** a bloom or blossom on a plant. **1b** a plant that bears blooms or blossoms. **2** the reproductive structure of angiosperm plants, consisting of stamens and carpels surrounded by petals and sepals. In some plants it is brightly coloured and attracts insects for pollination. Related adj: **floral. 3** any similar reproductive structure in other plants. **4** the prime; peak: *in the flower of his youth.* **5** the choice or finest product, part, or representative. **6** a decoration or embellishment. **7** (*pl*) fine powder, usually produced by sublimation: *flowers of sulphur.* ◆ *vb* **8** (*intr*) to produce flowers; bloom. **9** (*intr*) to reach full growth or maturity. **10** (*tr*) to deck or decorate with flowers or floral designs. ORIG C13: from OF *flor,* from L *flōs*
► **ˈflowerless** *adj* ► **ˈflower-ˌlike** *adj*

flowered (ˈflaʊəd) *adj* **1** having flowers. **2** decorated with flowers or a floral design.

floweret (ˈflaʊərɪt) *n* another name for **floret.**

flower girl *n* a girl or woman who sells flowers in the street.

flowering (ˈflaʊərɪŋ) *adj* (of certain species of plants) capable of producing conspicuous flowers.

flowerpot (ˈflaʊəˌpɒt) *n* a pot in which plants are grown.

flower power *n Inf.* a youth cult of the late 1960s advocating peace and love; associated with drug-taking. Its adherents were known as **flower children** or **flower people.**

flowery (ˈflaʊərɪ) *adj* **1** abounding in flowers. **2** decorated with flowers or floral patterns. **3** like or suggestive of flowers. **4** (of language or style) elaborate.
► **ˈfloweriness** *n*

flown (fləʊn) *vb* the past participle of **fly**[1].

flow-on *n Austral. & NZ.* **a** a wage or salary increase granted to one group of workers as a consequence of a similar increase granted to another group. **b** (*as modifier*): *a flow-on effect.*

fl. oz. *abbrev. for* fluid ounce.

flu (fluː) *n Inf.* **1** (often preceded by *the*) short for **influenza. 2** any of various viral infections, esp. a respiratory or intestinal infection.

fluctuate (ˈflʌktjʊˌeɪt) *vb* **fluctuates, fluctuating, fluctuated. 1** to change or cause to change position constantly. **2** (*intr*) to rise and fall like a wave. ORIG C17: from L, from *fluctus* a wave, from *fluere* to flow
► **ˈfluctuant** *adj* ► **ˌfluctuˈation** *n*

flue (fluː) *n* a shaft, tube, or pipe, esp. as used in a chimney, to carry off smoke, gas, etc. ORIG C16: from ?

fluent (ˈfluːənt) *adj* **1** able to speak or write a specified foreign language with facility. **2** spoken or written with facility. **3** graceful in motion or shape. **4** flowing or able to flow freely. ORIG C16: from L: flowing, from *fluere* to flow
► **ˈfluency** *n* ► **ˈfluently** *adv*

flue pipe *or* **flue** *n* an organ pipe whose sound is produced by the passage of air across a fissure in the side, as distinguished from a **reed pipe.**

fluff (flʌf) *n* **1** soft light particles, such as the down or nap of cotton or wool. **2** any light downy substance. **3** *Inf.* a mistake, esp. in speaking or reading lines or performing music. **4** *Inf.* a young woman (esp. in **a bit of fluff**). ◆ *vb* **5** to make or become soft and puffy. **6** *Inf.* to make a mistake in performing (an action, music, etc.). ORIG C18: ?from *flue* downy matter

fluffy (ˈflʌfɪ) *adj* **fluffier, fluffiest. 1** of, resembling, or covered with fluff. **2** soft and light.
► **ˈfluffily** *adv* ► **ˈfluffiness** *n*

flugelhorn (ˈfluːgəlˌhɔːn) *n* a type of valved brass instrument consisting of a tube of conical bore with a cup-shaped mouthpiece, used esp. in brass bands. ORIG G, from *Flügel* wing + *Horn* HORN

fluid (ˈfluːɪd) *n* **1** a substance, such as a liquid or gas, that can flow, has no fixed shape, and offers little resistance to an external stress. ◆ *adj* **2** capable of flowing and easily changing shape. **3** of or using a fluid or fluids. **4** constantly changing or apt to change. **5** flowing. ORIG C15: from L, from *fluere* to flow
► **ˈfluidal** *adj* ► **fluˈidity** *or* **ˈfluidness** *n*

fluidics (fluːˈɪdɪks) *n* (*functioning as sing*) the study and use of systems in which the flow of fluids in tubes simulates the flow of electricity in conductors.
► **fluˈidic** *adj*

fluidize *or* **fluidise** (ˈfluːɪˌdaɪz) *vb* **fluidizes, fluidizing, fluidized** *or* **fluidises, fluidising, fluidised.** (*tr*) to make fluid, esp. to make (solids) fluid by pulverizing them so that they can be transported in gas as if they were liquids.
► **ˌfluidiˈzation** *or* **ˌfluidiˈsation** *n*

★ people and places

fluid mechanics *n* (*functioning as sing*) the study of the mechanical and flow properties of fluids, esp. as they apply to practical engineering. Also called: **hydraulics.**

fluid ounce *n* **1** *Brit.* a unit of capacity equal to one twentieth of an Imperial pint. **2** *US.* a unit of capacity equal to one sixteenth of a US pint.

fluke[1] (fluːk) *n* **1** a flat bladelike projection at the end of the arm of an anchor. **2** either of the two lobes of the tail of a whale. **3** the barb of a harpoon, arrow, etc. ORIG C16: ? a special use of FLUKE[3] (in the sense: a flounder)

fluke[2] (fluːk) *n* **1** an accidental stroke of luck. **2** any chance happening. ◆ *vb* **flukes, fluking, fluked. 3** (*tr*) to gain, make, or hit by a fluke. ORIG C19: from ?

fluke[3] (fluːk) *n* any parasitic flatworm, such as the blood fluke and liver fluke. ORIG OE *flōc;* rel. to ON *flōki* flounder

fluky *or* **flukey** (ˈfluːkɪ) *adj* **flukier, flukiest.** *Inf.* **1** done or gained by an accident, esp. a lucky one. **2** variable; uncertain.
▸ **ˈflukiness** *n*

flume (fluːm) *n* **1** a ravine through which a stream flows. **2** a narrow artificial channel made for providing water for power, floating logs, etc. **3** a slide in the form of a long and winding tube with a stream of water running through it that descends into a purpose-built pool. ◆ *vb* **flumes, fluming, flumed. 4** (*tr*) to transport (logs) in a flume. ORIG C12: from OF, ult. from L *flūmen* stream, from *fluere* to flow

flummery (ˈflʌmərɪ) *n, pl* **flummeries. 1** *Inf.* meaningless flattery. **2** *Chiefly Brit.* a cold pudding of oatmeal, etc. ORIG C17: from Welsh *llymru*

flummox (ˈflʌməks) *vb* (*tr*) to perplex or bewilder. ORIG C19: from ?

flung (flʌŋ) *vb* the past tense and past participle of **fling.**

flunitrazepam (ˌfluːnaɪˈtræzəˌpæm) *n* a drug similar to diazepam, used in treating long-term insomnia.

flunk (flʌŋk) *vb Inf., US, Canad., & NZ.* **1** to fail or cause to fail to reach the required standard in (an examination, course, etc.). **2** (*intr;* foll. by *out*) to be dismissed from a school. ORIG C19: ?from FLINCH + FUNK[1]

flunky *or* **flunkey** (ˈflʌŋkɪ) *n, pl* **flunkies** *or* **flunkeys. 1** a servile person. **2** a person who performs menial tasks. **3** *Usually derog.* a manservant in livery. ORIG C18: from ?

fluor (ˈfluːɔː) *n* another name for **fluorspar.** ORIG C17: from L: a flowing; so called from its use as a metallurgical flux

fluor- *combining form.* a variant of **fluoro-** before a vowel: *fluorine.*

fluoresce (ˌflʊəˈrɛs) *vb* **fluoresces, fluorescing, fluoresced.** (*intr*) to exhibit fluorescence. ORIG C19: back formation from FLUORESCENCE

fluorescence (ˌflʊəˈrɛsəns) *n* **1** *Physics.* **1a** the emission of light or other radiation from atoms or molecules that are bombarded by particles, such as electrons, or by radiation from a separate source. **1b** such an emission of photons that ceases as soon as the bombarding radiation is discontinued. **2** the radiation emitted as a result of fluorescence. Cf. **phosphorescence.** ORIG C19: FLUOR + *-escence* (as in *opalescence*)
▸ ˌ**fluoˈrescent** *adj*

fluorescent lamp *n* a type of lamp in which ultraviolet radiation from an electrical gas discharge causes a thin layer of phosphor on a tube's inside surface to fluoresce.

fluoridate (ˈflʊərɪˌdeɪt) *vb* **fluoridates, fluoridating, fluoridated.** to subject (water) to fluoridation.

fluoridation (ˌflʊərɪˈdeɪʃən) *n* the addition of fluorides to the public water supply as a protection against tooth decay.

fluoride (ˈflʊəˌraɪd) *n* **1** any salt of hydrofluoric acid, containing the fluoride ion, F^-. **2** any compound containing fluorine, such as methyl fluoride.

fluorinate (ˈflʊərɪˌneɪt) *vb* **fluorinates, fluorinating, fluorinated.** to treat or combine with fluorine.
▸ ˌ**fluoriˈnation** *n*

fluorine (ˈflʊəriːn) *n* a toxic pungent pale yellow gas of the halogen group that is the most electronegative and reactive of all the elements: used in the production of uranium, fluorocarbons, and other chemicals. Symbol: F; atomic no.: 9; atomic wt.: 18.998.

fluorite (ˈflʊəraɪt) *n* the US and Canad. name for **fluorspar.**

fluoro- *or before a vowel* **fluor-** *combining form.* **1** indicating the presence of fluorine: *fluorocarbon.* **2** indicating fluorescence: *fluoroscope.*

fluorocarbon (ˌflʊərəʊˈkɑːbᵊn) *n* any compound derived by replacing all or some of the hydrogen atoms in hydrocarbons by fluorine atoms. Many of them are used as lubricants, solvents, coatings, and aerosol propellants. See also **Freon, CFC.**

fluorometer (ˌflʊəˈrɒmɪtə) *or* **fluorimeter** (ˌflʊəˈrɪmɪtə) *n* a device for detecting and measuring ultraviolet radiation by determining the amount of fluorescence that it produces from a phosphor.

fluoroscope (ˈflʊərəˌskəʊp) *n* a device consisting of a fluorescent screen and an X-ray source that enables an X-ray image of an object, person, or part to be observed directly.

fluoroscopy (flʊəˈrɒskəpɪ) *n* examination of a person or object by means of a fluoroscope.

fluorosis (flʊəˈrəʊsɪs) *n* fluoride poisoning, due to ingestion of too much fluoride.

fluorspar (ˈflʊəˌspɑː), **fluor,** *or US & Canad.* **fluorite** *n* a white or colourless soft mineral, sometimes fluorescent or tinted by impurities, consisting of calcium fluoride (CaF) in crystalline form: the chief ore of fluorine.

flurry (ˈflʌrɪ) *n, pl* **flurries. 1** a sudden commotion. **2** a light gust of wind or rain or fall of snow. ◆ *vb* **flurries, flurrying, flurried. 3** to confuse or bewilder or be confused or bewildered. ORIG C17: from obs. *flurr* to scatter, ? formed on analogy with HURRY

flush[1] (flʌʃ) *vb* **1** to blush or cause to blush. **2** to flow or flood or cause to flow or flood with or as if with water. **3** to glow or shine or cause to glow or shine with a rosy colour. **4** to send a volume of water quickly through (a pipe, etc.) or into (a toilet) for the purpose of cleansing, etc. **5** (*tr; usually passive*) to excite or elate. ◆ *n* **6** a rosy colour, esp. in the cheeks. **7** a sudden flow or gush, as of water. **8** a feeling of excitement or elation: *the flush of success.* **9** freshness: *the flush of youth.* **10** redness of the skin, as from the effects of a fever, alcohol, etc. ORIG C16: (in the sense: to gush forth): ?from FLUSH[3]
▸ **ˈflusher** *n*

flush[2] (flʌʃ) *adj* (*usually postpositive*) **1** level or even with another surface. **2** directly adjacent; continuous. **3** *Inf.* having plenty of money. **4** *Inf.* abundant or plentiful, as money. **5** full to the brim. ◆ *adv* **6** so as to be level or even. **7** directly or squarely. ◆ *vb* (*tr*) **8** to cause (surfaces) to be on the same level or in the same plane. ◆ *n* **9** a period of fresh growth of leaves, shoots, etc. ORIG C18: prob. from FLUSH[1] (in the sense: spring out)
▸ **ˈflushness** *n*

flush[3] (flʌʃ) *vb* (*tr*) to rouse (game, etc.) and put to flight. ORIG C13 *flusshen,* ? imit.

flush[4] (flʌʃ) *n* (in poker and similar games) a hand containing only one suit. ORIG C16: from OF, from L *fluxus* FLUX

Flushing ★ (ˈflʌʃɪŋ) *n* a port in the SW Netherlands, in Zeeland province, on Walcheren Island, at the mouth of the West Scheldt river: the first Dutch city to throw off Spanish rule (1572). Pop.: 43 947 (1989). Dutch name: **Vlissingen.**

fluster (ˈflʌstə) *vb* **1** to make or become nervous or upset. ◆ *n* **2** a state of confusion or agitation. ORIG C15: from ON

flute (fluːt) *n* **1** a wind instrument consisting of an open cylindrical tube of wood or metal having holes in the side stopped either by the fingers or by pads controlled by keys. The breath is directed across a mouth hole cut in the side. **2** *Archit.* a rounded shallow concave groove on the shaft of a column, pilaster, etc. **3** a tall narrow wineglass. ◆ *vb* **flutes, fluting, fluted. 4** to produce or utter (sounds) in the manner or tone of a flute. **5** (*tr*) to make grooves or furrows in. ORIG C14: from OF *flahute,* from Vulgar L *flabeolum* (unattested); ? also infl. by OF *laut* lute
▸ **ˈfluteˌlike** *adj* ▸ **ˈfluty** *adj*

fluting ('flu:tɪŋ) *n* a design or decoration of flutes on a column, pilaster, etc.

flutist ('flu:tɪst) *n Now chiefly US & Canad.* a variant spelling of **flautist**.

flutter ('flʌtə) *vb* **1** to wave or cause to wave rapidly. **2** (*intr*) (of birds, butterflies, etc.) to flap the wings. **3** (*intr*) to move, esp. downwards, with an irregular motion. **4** (*intr*) *Pathol.* (of the heart) to beat abnormally rapidly, esp. in a regular rhythm. **5** to be or make nervous or restless. **6** (*intr*) to move about restlessly. ◆ *n* **7** a quick flapping or vibrating motion. **8** a state of nervous excitement or confusion. **9** excited interest; stir. **10** *Brit. inf.* a modest bet or wager. **11** *Pathol.* an abnormally rapid beating of the heart, esp. in a regular rhythm. **12** *Electronics.* a slow variation in pitch in a sound-reproducing system, similar to wow but occurring at higher frequencies. **13** a potentially dangerous oscillation of an aircraft, or part of an aircraft. **14** Also called: **flutter tonguing.** *Music.* a method of sounding a wind instrument, esp. the flute, with a rolling movement of the tongue. ORIG OE *floterian* to float to and fro
▸ **'flutterer** *n* ▸ **'fluttery** *adj*

fluvial ('flu:vɪəl) *adj* of or occurring in a river: *fluvial deposits.* ORIG C14: from L, from *fluvius* river, from *fluere* to flow

flux (flʌks) *n* **1** a flow or discharge. **2** continuous change; instability. **3** a substance, such as borax or salt, that gives a low melting-point mixture with a metal oxide to assist in fusion. **4** *Metallurgy.* a chemical used to increase the fluidity of refining slags. **5** *Physics.* **5a** the rate of flow of particles, energy, or a fluid, such as that of neutrons (**neutron flux**) or of light energy (**luminous flux**). **5b** the strength of a field in a given area: *magnetic flux.* **6** *Pathol.* an excessive discharge of fluid from the body, such as watery faeces in diarrhoea. ◆ *vb* **7** to make or become fluid. **8** (*tr*) to apply flux to (a metal, soldered joint, etc.). ORIG C14: from L *fluxus* a flow, from *fluere* to flow

flux density *n Physics.* the amount of flux per unit of cross-sectional area.

fluxion ('flʌkʃən) *n Maths., obs.* the rate of change of a function, especially the instantaneous velocity of a moving body; derivative. ORIG C16: from LL *fluxiō* a flowing

fly[1] (flaɪ) *vb* **flies, flying, flew, flown. 1** (*intr*) (of birds, aircraft, etc.) to move through the air in a controlled manner using aerodynamic forces. **2** to travel over (an area of land or sea) in an aircraft. **3** to operate (an aircraft or spacecraft). **4** to float, flutter, or be displayed in the air or cause to float, etc., in this way: *they flew the flag.* **5** to transport or be transported by or through the air by aircraft, wind, etc. **6** (*intr*) to move or be moved very quickly, or suddenly: *the door flew open.* **7** (*intr*) to pass swiftly: *time flies.* **8** to escape from (an enemy, place, etc.); flee. **9** (*intr;* may be foll. by *at* or *upon*) to attack a person. **10 fly a kite. 10a** to procure money by an accommodation bill. **10b** to release information or take a step in order to test public opinion. **11 fly high.** *Inf.* **11a** to have a high aim. **11b** to prosper or flourish. **12 let fly.** *Inf.* **12a** to lose one's temper (with a person): *she really let fly at him.* **12b** to shoot or throw (an object). ◆ *n, pl* **flies. 13** (*often pl*) Also called: **fly front.** a closure that conceals a zip, buttons, or other fastening, by having one side overlapping, as on trousers. **14** Also called: **fly sheet. 14a** a flap forming the entrance to a tent. **14b** a piece of canvas drawn over the ridgepole of a tent to form an outer roof. **15** short for **flywheel. 16a** the outer edge of a flag. **16b** the distance from the outer edge of a flag to the staff. **17** *Brit.* a light one-horse covered carriage formerly let out on hire. **18** (*pl*) *Theatre.* the space above the stage out of view of the audience, used for storing scenery, etc. **19** *Rare.* the act of flying. ORIG OE *flēogan*
▸ **'flyable** *adj*

fly[2] (flaɪ) *n, pl* **flies. 1** any dipterous insect, esp. the housefly, characterized by active flight. **2** any of various similar but unrelated insects, such as the caddis fly, firefly, and dragonfly. **3** *Angling.* a lure made from a fish-hook dressed with feathers, tinsel, etc., to resemble any of various flies or nymphs: used in fly-fishing. **4 fly in the ointment.** *Inf.* a slight flaw that detracts from value or enjoyment. **5 fly on the wall. 5a** a person who watches others, while not being noticed himself. **5b** (*as modifier*): *a fly-on-the-wall documentary.* **6 there are no flies on him, her,** etc. *Inf.* he, she, etc., is no fool. ORIG OE *flēoge*
▸ **'flyless** *adj*

fly[3] (flaɪ) *adj Sl., chiefly Brit.* knowing and sharp; smart. ORIG C19: from ?

fly agaric *n* a woodland fungus having a scarlet cap with white warts and white gills: poisonous but rarely fatal. ORIG so named from its use as a poison on flypaper

fly ash *n* fine solid particles of ash carried into the air during combustion.

flyaway ('flaɪə,weɪ) *adj* **1** (of hair or clothing) loose and fluttering. **2** frivolous or flighty; giddy.

flyblow ('flaɪ,bləʊ) *vb* **flyblows, flyblowing, flyblew, flyblown. 1** (*tr*) to contaminate, esp. with the eggs or larvae of the blowfly; taint. ◆ *n* **2** (*usually pl*) the eggs or young larva of a blowfly.

flyblown ('flaɪ,bləʊn) *adj* **1** covered with flyblows. **2** contaminated; tainted.

flybook ('flaɪ,bʊk) *n* a small case or wallet used by anglers for storing artificial flies.

flyby ('flaɪ,baɪ) *n, pl* **flybys.** a flight past a particular position or target, esp. the close approach of a spacecraft to a planet or satellite.

fly-by-night *Inf.* ◆ *adj* **1** unreliable or untrustworthy, esp. in finance. ◆ *n* **2** an untrustworthy person, esp. one who departs secretly or by night to avoid paying debts.

flycatcher ('flaɪ,kætʃə) *n* **1** a small insectivorous songbird of the Old World having a small slender bill fringed with bristles. **2** an American passerine bird.

fly-drive *adj, adv* describing a type of package-deal holiday in which the price includes outward and return flights and car hire while away.

flyer *or* **flier** ('flaɪə) *n* **1** a person or thing that flies or moves very fast. **2** an aviator or pilot. **3** *Inf.* a large flying leap. **4** a rectangular step in a straight flight of stairs. Cf. **winder** (sense 5). **5** *Athletics inf.* a flying start. **6** *Chiefly US.* a speculative business transaction. **7** a small handbill.

fly-fish *vb* (*intr*) *Angling.* to fish using artificial flies as lures.
▸ **'fly-,fishing** *n*

fly half *n Rugby.* another name for **stand-off half.**

flying ('flaɪɪŋ) *adj* **1** (*prenominal*) hurried; fleeting: *a flying visit.* **2** (*prenominal*) designed for fast action. **3** (*prenominal*) moving or passing quickly on or as if on wings: *flying hours.* **4** hanging, waving, or floating freely: *flying hair.* ◆ *n* **5** the act of piloting, navigating, or travelling in an aircraft. **6** (*modifier*) relating to, accustomed to, or adapted for flight: *a flying machine.*

flying boat *n* a seaplane in which the fuselage consists of a hull that provides buoyancy.

flying bridge *n* an auxiliary bridge of a vessel.

flying buttress *n* a buttress supporting a wall or other structure by an arch that transmits the thrust outwards and downwards.

flying colours *pl n* conspicuous success; triumph: *he passed his test with flying colours.*

flying doctor *n* (in areas of sparse or scattered population) a doctor who visits patients by aircraft.

flying fish *n* a fish common in warm and tropical seas, having enlarged winglike pectoral fins used for gliding above the surface of the water.

flying fox *n* **1** any large fruit bat of tropical Africa and Asia. **2** *Austral. & NZ.* a cable mechanism used for transportation across a river, gorge, etc.

flying gurnard *n* a marine spiny-finned gurnard-like fish having enlarged fan-shaped pectoral fins used to glide above the surface of the sea.

flying jib *n* the jib set furthest forward or outboard on a vessel with two or more jibs.

flying lemur *n* either of the two arboreal mammals of S and SE Asia that resemble lemurs but have a fold of skin between the limbs enabling movement by gliding leaps.

flying officer *n* an officer holding commissioned rank senior to a pilot officer but junior to a flight lieutenant in the British and certain other air forces.

flying phalanger *n* a nocturnal arboreal phalanger of E Australia and New Guinea, moving with gliding leaps using folds of skin between the hind limbs and forelimbs.

flying picket *n* (in industrial disputes) a member of a group of pickets organized to be able to move quickly from place to place.

flying saucer *n* any unidentified disc-shaped flying object alleged to come from outer space.

flying squad *n* a small group of police, soldiers, etc., ready to move into action quickly.

flying squirrel *n* a nocturnal rodent of Asia and North America, related to the squirrel. Furry folds of skin between the forelegs and hind legs enable these animals to move by gliding leaps.

flying start *n* **1** (in sprinting) a start by a competitor anticipating the starting signal. **2** a start to a race in which the competitor is already travelling at speed as he passes the starting line. **3** any promising beginning. **4** an initial advantage.

flying wing *n* **1** an aircraft consisting mainly of one large wing or tailplane and no fuselage. **2** (in Canadian football) the twelfth player, who has a variable position behind the scrimmage line.

flyleaf ('flaɪˌliːf) *n, pl* **flyleaves.** the inner leaf of the endpaper of a book, pasted to the first leaf.

Flynn ★ (flɪn) *n* **1 Errol.** 1909–59, Australian actor, who was noted for his swashbuckling roles; his films included *Captain Blood* (1935), *The Adventures of Robin Hood* (1938), and *Too Much Too Soon* (1958). **2** Rev. **John.** 1880–1951, founder of the Australian flying doctor service.

flyover ('flaɪˌəʊvə) *n* **1** *Brit.* an intersection of two roads at which one is carried over the other by a bridge. **2** the US name for **fly-past.**

flypaper ('flaɪˌpeɪpə) *n* paper with a sticky and poisonous coating, usually hung from the ceiling to trap flies.

fly-past *n* a ceremonial flight of aircraft over a given area.

flyposting ('flaɪˌpəʊstɪŋ) *n* the posting of advertising or political posters, etc., in unauthorized places.

flyscreen ('flaɪˌskriːn) *n* a wire-mesh screen over a window to prevent flies entering a room.

fly sheet *n* **1** another term for **fly**[1] (sense 14). **2** a short handbill.

flyspeck ('flaɪˌspɛk) *n* **1** the small speck of the excrement of a fly. **2** a small spot or speck. ◆ *vb* **3** (*tr*) to mark with flyspecks.

fly spray *n* a liquid used to destroy flies and other insects, sprayed from an aerosol.

fly-tipping *n* the deliberate dumping of rubbish in an unauthorized place.

flytrap ('flaɪˌtræp) *n* **1** any of various insectivorous plants. **2** a device for catching flies.

fly way *n* the usual route used by birds when migrating.

flyweight ('flaɪˌweɪt) *n* **1a** a professional boxer weighing not more than 112 pounds (51 kg). **1b** an amateur boxer weighing 48–51 kg (106–112 pounds). **2** an amateur wrestler weighing 107–115 pounds (49–52 kg).

flywheel ('flaɪˌwiːl) *n* a heavy wheel that stores kinetic energy and smooths the operation of a reciprocating engine by maintaining a constant speed of rotation over the whole cycle.

fm *abbrev. for:* **1** fathom. **2** from.

Fm *the chemical symbol for* fermium.

FM *abbrev. for:* **1** frequency modulation. **2** Field Marshal.

f-number, f number, f-stop, *or* **f stop** *n Photog.* the numerical value of the relative aperture. If the relative aperture is f8, 8 is the f-number.

Fo ★ (fəʊ) *n* **Dario** ('dærɪəʊ). born 1926, Italian playwright and actor. His plays include *The Accidental Death of an Anarchist* (1970) and *The Tricks of the Trade* (1991): Nobel prize for literature 1997.

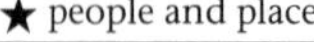

FO *abbrev. for:* **1** *Army.* Field Officer. **2** *Air Force.* Flying Officer. **3** Foreign Office.

fo. *abbrev. for* folio.

foal (fəʊl) *n* **1** the young of a horse or related animal. ◆ *vb* **2** to give birth to (a foal). ORIG OE *fola*

foam (fəʊm) *n* **1** a mass of small bubbles of gas formed on the surface of a liquid, such as the froth produced by a solution of soap or detergent in water. **2** frothy saliva sometimes formed in and expelled from the mouth, as in rabies. **3** the frothy sweat of a horse or similar animal. **4a** any of a number of light cellular solids made by creating bubbles of gas in the liquid material: used as insulation and packaging. **4b** (*as modifier*): *foam rubber; foam plastic.* ◆ *vb* **5** to produce or cause to produce foam; froth. **6** (*intr*) to be very angry (esp. in **foam at the mouth**). ORIG OE *fām*
► 'foamless *adj*

foamy ('fəʊmɪ) *adj* **foamier, foamiest.** of, resembling, consisting of, or covered with foam.

fob[1] (fɒb) *n* **1** a chain or ribbon by which a pocket watch is attached to a waistcoat. **2** any ornament hung on such a chain. **3** a small pocket in a man's waistcoat, etc., for holding a watch. ORIG C17: prob. of Gmc origin

fob[2] (fɒb) *vb* **fobs, fobbing, fobbed.** (*tr*) *Arch.* to cheat. ORIG C15: prob. from G *foppen* to trick

fob[3] (fɒb) *n NZ sl.* a Pacific Islander who has newly arrived in New Zealand. ORIG C20: *f(resh) o(ff the) b(oat)*

f.o.b. *or* **FOB** *Commerce. abbrev. for* free on board.

fob off *vb* (*tr, adv*) **1** to trick (a person) with lies or excuses. **2** to dispose of (goods) by trickery.

focal ('fəʊkᵊl) *adj* **1** of or relating to a focus. **2** situated at or measured from the focus.

focalize *or* **focalise** ('fəʊkəˌlaɪz) *vb* **focalizes, focalizing, focalized** *or* **focalises, focalising, focalised.** a less common word for **focus.**
► ˌfocaliˈzation *or* ˌfocaliˈsation *n*

focal length *or* **distance** *n* the distance from the focal point of a lens or mirror to the reflecting surface of the mirror or the centre point of the lens.

focal plane *n* the plane that is perpendicular to the axis of a lens or mirror and passes through the focal point.

focal point *n* the point on the axis of a lens or mirror to which parallel rays of light converge or from which they appear to diverge after refraction or reflection. Also called: **focus.**

Foch ★ (*French* fɔʃ) *n* **Ferdinand** (fɛrdinɑ̃). 1851–1929, marshal of France; commander in chief of Allied armies on the Western front in World War I (1918).

fo'c's'le *or* **fo'c'sle** ('fəʊksᵊl) *n* a variant spelling of **forecastle.**

focus ('fəʊkəs) *n, pl* **focuses** *or* **foci** (-saɪ). **1** a point of convergence of light or sound waves, etc., or a point from which they appear to diverge. **2** another name for **focal point** or **focal length. 3** *Optics.* the state of an optical image when it is distinct and clearly defined or the state of an instrument producing this image: *the telescope is out of focus.* **4** a point upon which attention, activity, etc., is concentrated. **5** *Geom.* a fixed reference point on the concave side of a conic section, used when defining its eccentricity. **6** the point beneath the earth's surface at which an earthquake originates. **7** *Pathol.* the main site of an infection. ◆ *vb* **focuses, focusing, focused** *or* **focusses, focussing, focussed. 8** to bring or come to a focus or into focus. **9** (*tr;* often foll. by *on*) to concentrate. ORIG C17: via NL from L: hearth, fireplace
► 'focuser *n*

focus group *n* a group of people gathered by a market research company to discuss and assess a product or service.

focus puller *n Films.* the member of a camera crew who adjusts the focus of the lens as the camera is tracked in or out.

fodder ('fɒdə) *n* **1** bulk feed for livestock, esp. hay, straw, etc. ◆ *vb* **2** (*tr*) to supply (livestock) with fodder. ORIG OE *fōdor*

foe (fəʊ) *n Formal or literary.* another word for **enemy.** ORIG OE *fāh* hostile

FoE *or* **FOE** *abbrev. for* Friends of the Earth.

foehn (fɜːn; *German* føːn) *n Meteorol.* a variant spelling of **föhn.**

foeman (ˈfəʊmən) *n, pl* **foemen.** *Arch. & poetic.* an enemy in war; foe.

foetal (ˈfiːtᵊl) *adj* a variant spelling of **fetal.**

foetid (ˈfɛtɪd, ˈfiː-) *adj* a variant spelling of **fetid.**
▸ ˈ**foetidly** *adv* ▸ ˈ**foetidness** *n*

foetus (ˈfiːtəs) *n, pl* **foetuses.** a variant spelling of **fetus.**

fog[1] (fɒg) *n* **1** a mass of droplets of condensed water vapour suspended in the air, often greatly reducing visibility. **2** a cloud of any substance in the atmosphere reducing visibility. **3** a state of mental uncertainty. **4** *Photog.* a blurred area on a developed negative, print, or transparency. ◆ *vb* **fogs, fogging, fogged. 5** to envelop or become enveloped with or as if with fog. **6** to confuse or become confused. **7** *Photog.* to produce fog on (a negative, print, or transparency) or (of a negative, print, or transparency) to be affected by fog. **8** (*tr*) to treat (an infested area) with insecticide in the form of a spray. ORIG C16: ? back formation from *foggy* damp, boggy, from FOG[2]

fog[2] (fɒg) *n* a second growth of grass after the first mowing. ORIG C14: prob. from ON

fog bank *n* a distinct mass of fog, esp. at sea.

fogbound (ˈfɒgˌbaʊnd) *adj* prevented from operation by fog: *the airport was fogbound.*

fogbow (ˈfɒgˌbəʊ) *n* a faint arc of light sometimes seen in a fog bank.

fogey *or* **fogy** (ˈfəʊgɪ) *n, pl* **fogeys** *or* **fogies.** an extremely fussy or conservative person (esp. in **old fogey**). ORIG C18: from ?
▸ ˈ**fogeyish** *or* ˈ**fogyish** *adj*

Foggia ★ (*Italian* ˈfɔddʒa) *n* a city in SE Italy, in Apulia: seat of Emperor Frederick II; centre for Carbonari revolutionary societies in the revolts of 1820, 1848, and 1860. Pop.: 156 032 (1996 est.).

fogging machine *n Caribbean.* a mechanical device, usually mounted on a tractor or other vehicle, used to spray an area with insecticide.

foggy (ˈfɒgɪ) *adj* **foggier, foggiest. 1** thick with fog. **2** obscure or confused. **3 not the foggiest (idea** *or* **notion).** no idea whatsoever: *I haven't the foggiest.*
▸ ˈ**fogginess** *n*

foghorn (ˈfɒgˌhɔːn) *n* **1** a mechanical instrument sounded at intervals to serve as a warning to vessels in fog. **2** *Inf.* a loud deep resounding voice.

fog signal *n* a signal used to warn railway engine drivers in fog, consisting of a detonator placed on the line.

föhn *or* **foehn** (fɜːn; *German* føːn) *n* a warm dry wind blowing down the northern slopes of the Alps. ORIG G, from OHG, from L *favōnius;* rel. to *fovēre* to warm

foible (ˈfɔɪbᵊl) *n* **1** a slight peculiarity or minor weakness; idiosyncrasy. **2** the most vulnerable part of a sword's blade, from the middle to the tip. ORIG C17: from obs. F, from obs. adj: FEEBLE

foie gras (*French* fwa grɑ) *n* See **pâté de foie gras.**

foil[1] (fɔɪl) *vb* (*tr*) **1** to baffle or frustrate (a person, attempt, etc.). **2** *Hunting.* (of hounds, hunters, etc.) to obliterate the scent left by a hunted animal or (of a hunted animal) to run back over its own trail. ◆ *n* **3** *Arch.* a setback or defeat. ORIG C13 *foilen* to trample, from OF, *fuler* tread down
▸ ˈ**foilable** *adj*

foil[2] (fɔɪl) *n* **1** metal in the form of very thin sheets: *tin foil.* **2** the thin metallic sheet forming the backing of a mirror. **3** a thin leaf of shiny metal set under a gemstone to add brightness or colour. **4** a person or thing that gives contrast to another. **5** *Archit.* a small arc between cusps. **6** short for **hydrofoil.** ◆ *vb* (*tr*) **7** Also: **foliate.** *Archit.* to ornament (windows, etc.) with foils. ORIG C14: from OF, from L *folia* leaves

foil[3] (fɔɪl) *n* a light slender flexible sword tipped by a button. ORIG C16: from ?

foist (fɔɪst) *vb* (*tr*) **1** (often foll. by *off* or *on*) to sell or pass off (something, esp. an inferior article) as genuine, valuable, etc. **2** (usually foll. by *in* or *into*) to insert surreptitiously or wrongfully. ORIG C16: prob. from obs. Du. *vuisten* to enclose in one's hand, from MDu. *vuist* fist

Fokine ★ (*Russian* ˈfɔkin; *French* fɔkin) *n* **Michel** (miʃɛl). 1880–1942, US choreographer, born in Russia; worked with Diaghilev as director of the Ballet Russe (1909–15).

Fokker ★ (ˈfɒkə; *Dutch* ˈfɔkər) *n* **Anthony Herman Gerard** (ɑnˈtoːniː ˈhɛrman ˈxeːrɑrt). 1890–1939, Dutch aircraft manufacturer, born in Java; had German factories to make World War I aircraft. Moved to US (1922).

FOL (in New Zealand) *abbrev. for* Federation of Labour.

fol. *abbrev. for:* **1** folio. **2** following.

fold[1] (fəʊld) *vb* **1** to bend or be bent double so that one part covers another. **2** (*tr*) to bring together and intertwine (the arms, legs, etc.). **3** (*tr*) (of birds, insects, etc.) to close (the wings) together from an extended position. **4** (*tr;* often foll. by *up* or *in*) to enclose in or as if in a surrounding material. **5** (*tr;* foll. by *in*) to clasp (a person) in the arms. **6** (*tr;* usually foll. by *round, about,* etc.) to wind (around); entwine. **7** Also: **fold in.** (*tr*) to mix (a whisked mixture) with other ingredients by gently turning one part over the other with a spoon. **8** (*intr;* often foll. by *up*) *Inf.* to collapse; fail: *the business folded.* ◆ *n* **9** a piece or section that has been folded: *a fold of cloth.* **10** a mark, crease, or hollow made by folding. **11** a hollow in undulating terrain. **12** a bend in stratified rocks that results from movements within the earth's crust. **13** a coil, as in a rope, etc. ORIG OE *fealdan*
▸ ˈ**foldable** *adj*

fold[2] (fəʊld) *n* **1a** a small enclosure or pen for sheep or other livestock, where they can be gathered. **1b** a flock of sheep. **2** a church or the members of it. ◆ *vb* **3** (*tr*) to gather or confine (sheep, etc.) in a fold. ORIG OE *falod*

-fold *suffix forming adjectives and adverbs.* having so many parts or being so many times as much or as many: *threehundredfold.* ORIG OE *-fald, -feald*

foldaway (ˈfəʊldəˌweɪ) *adj* (*prenominal*) (of a bed, etc.) able to be folded away when not in use.

folded dipole *n* a type of aerial consisting of two parallel dipoles connected together at their outer ends and fed at the centre of one of them. The length is usually half the operating wavelength.

folder (ˈfəʊldə) *n* **1** a binder or file for holding loose papers, etc. **2** a folded circular. **3** a person or thing that folds.

folderol (ˈfɒldəˌrɒl) *n* a variant spelling of **falderal.**

folding door *n* a door in the form of two or more vertical hinged leaves that can be folded one against another.

folding money *n Inf.* paper money.

foley *or* **foley artist** (ˈfəʊlɪ) *n Films.* the US name for **footsteps editor.** ORIG C20: after the inventor of the technique

foliaceous (ˌfəʊlɪˈeɪʃəs) *adj* **1** having the appearance of the leaf of a plant. **2** bearing leaves or leaflike structures. **3** *Geol.* consisting of thin layers. ORIG C17: from L *foliāceus*

foliage (ˈfəʊlɪɪdʒ) *n* **1** the green leaves of a plant. **2** sprays of leaves used for decoration. **3** an ornamental leaflike design. ORIG C15: from OF *fuellage,* from *fuelle* leaf; infl. in form by L *folium*

foliar (ˈfəʊlɪə) *adj* of or relating to a leaf or leaves. ORIG C19: from F, from L *folium* leaf

foliate *adj* (ˈfəʊlɪɪt, -ˌeɪt). **1a** relating to, possessing, or resembling leaves. **1b** (*in combination*): *trifoliate.* ◆ *vb* (ˈfəʊlɪˌeɪt), **foliates, foliating, foliated. 2** (*tr*) to ornament with foliage or with leaf forms such as foils. **3** to hammer or cut (metal) into thin plates or foil. **4** (*tr*) to number the leaves of (a book, etc.). Cf. **paginate. 5** (*intr*) (of plants) to grow leaves. ORIG C17: from L *foliātus* leaved, leafy

foliation (ˌfəʊlɪˈeɪʃən) *n* **1** *Bot.* **1a** the process of producing leaves. **1b** the state of being in leaf. **1c** the arrangement of leaves in a leaf bud. **2** *Archit.* ornamentation consisting of cusps and foils. **3** the consecutive numbering of the leaves of a book. **4** *Geol.* the arrangement of the constituents of a rock in leaflike layers, as in schists.

folic acid (ˈfəʊlɪk) *n* any of a group of vitamins of the B complex, used in the treatment of anaemia. Also called:

folacin. ORIG C20: from L *folium* leaf; so called because it may be obtained from green leaves

folio ('fəʊlɪəʊ) *n, pl* **folios. 1** a sheet of paper folded in half to make two leaves for a book. **2** a book of the largest common size made up of such sheets. **3a** a leaf of paper numbered on the front side only. **3b** the page number of a book. **4** *Law.* a unit of measurement of the length of legal documents, determined by the number of words, generally 72 or 90 in Britain and 100 in the US. ♦ *adj* **5** relating to or having the format of a folio: *a folio edition.* ORIG C16: from L phrase *in foliō* in a leaf, from *folium* leaf

folk (fəʊk) *n, pl* **folk** *or* **folks. 1** (*functioning as pl; often pl in form*) people in general, esp. those of a particular group or class: *country folk.* **2** (*functioning as pl; usually pl in form*) *Inf.* members of a family. **3** (*functioning as sing*) *Inf.* short for **folk music. 4** a people or tribe. **5** (*modifier*) originating from or traditional to the common people of a country: *a folk song.* ORIG OE *folc*
▸ **'folkish** *adj*

folk dance *n* **1** any of various traditional rustic dances. **2** a piece of music composed for or in the rhythm of such a dance.
▸ **folk dancing** *n*

Folkestone ★ ('fəʊkstən) *n* a port and resort in SE England, in E Kent. Pop.: 45 587 (1991).

folk etymology *n* the gradual change in the form of a word through the influence of a more familiar word or phrase with which it becomes associated, as for example *sparrow-grass* for *asparagus.*

folkie *or* **folky** ('fəʊkɪ) *n, pl* **folkies.** *Inf.* a devotee of folk music.

folklore ('fəʊk,lɔː) *n* **1** the unwritten literature of a people as expressed in folk tales, songs, etc. **2** the body of stories and legends attached to a particular place, group, etc.: *rugby folklore.* **3** study of folkloric materials.
▸ **'folk,loric** *adj* ▸ **'folk,lorist** *n, adj*

folk medicine *n* medicine as practised among rustic communities and primitive peoples, consisting typically of the use of herbal remedies.

folk music *n* **1** music that is passed on from generation to generation. **2** any music composed in this idiom.

folk-rock *n* a style of rock music influenced by folk.

folk song *n* **1** a song which has been handed down among the common people. **2** a modern song which reflects the folk idiom.

folksy ('fəʊksɪ) *adj* **folksier, folksiest. 1** of or like ordinary people; sometimes used derogatorily to describe affected simplicity. **2** *Inf., chiefly US.* friendly; affable.

folk tale *or* **story** *n* a tale or legend originating among a people and becoming part of an oral tradition.

folk weave *n* a type of fabric with a loose weave.

follicle ('fɒlɪkᵊl) *n* **1** any small sac or cavity in the body having an excretory, secretory, or protective function: *a hair follicle.* **2** *Bot.* a dry fruit that splits along one side only to release its seeds. ORIG C17: from L *folliculus* small bag, from *follis* pair of bellows, leather money-bag
▸ **follicular** (fɒ'lɪkjʊlə), **folliculate** (fɒ'lɪkjʊ,leɪt), *or* **fol'licu,lated** *adj*

follow ('fɒləʊ) *vb* **1** to go or come after in the same direction. **2** (*tr*) to accompany: *she followed her sister everywhere.* **3** to come after as a logical or natural consequence. **4** (*tr*) to keep to the course or track of: *she followed the towpath.* **5** (*tr*) to act in accordance with: *to follow instructions.* **6** (*tr*) to accept the ideas or beliefs of (a previous authority, etc.): *he followed Donne in most of his teachings.* **7** to understand (an explanation, etc.): *the lesson was difficult to follow.* **8** to watch closely or continuously: *she followed his progress.* **9** (*tr*) to have a keen interest in: *to follow athletics.* **10** (*tr*) to help in the cause of: *the men who followed Napoleon.* ORIG OE *folgian*

follower ('fɒləʊə) *n* **1** a person who accepts the teachings of another: *a follower of Marx.* **2** an attendant. **3** a supporter, as of a sport or team. **4** (esp. formerly) a male admirer.

following ('fɒləʊɪŋ) *adj* **1a** (*prenominal*) about to be mentioned, specified, etc.: *the following items.* **1b** (*as n*)*: will the following please raise their hands?* **2** (of winds, currents, etc.) moving in the same direction as a vessel. ♦ *n* **3** a group of supporters or enthusiasts: *he attracted a large following.* ♦ *prep* **4** as a result of: *he was arrested following a tip-off.*

follow-on *Cricket.* ♦ *n* **1** an immediate second innings forced on a team scoring a prescribed number of runs fewer than its opponents in the first innings. ♦ *vb* **follow on. 2** (*intr, adv*) (of a team) to play a follow-on.

follow out *vb* (*tr, adv*) to implement (an idea or action) to a conclusion.

follow through *vb* (*adv*) **1** *Sport.* to complete (a stroke or shot) by continuing the movement to the end of its arc. **2** (*tr*) to pursue (an aim) to a conclusion. ♦ *n* **follow-through. 3** the act of following through.

follow up *vb* (*tr, adv*) **1** to pursue or investigate (a person, etc.) closely. **2** to continue (action) after a beginning, esp. to increase its effect. ♦ *n* **follow-up. 3a** something done to reinforce an initial action. **3b** (*as modifier*)*: a follow-up letter.* **4** *Med.* an examination of a patient at intervals after treatment.

folly ('fɒlɪ) *n, pl* **follies. 1** the state or quality of being foolish. **2** a foolish action, idea, etc. **3** a building in the form of a castle, temple, etc., built to satisfy a fancy or conceit. **4** (*pl*) *Theatre.* an elaborately costumed revue. ORIG C13: from OF *folie* madness, from *fou* mad; see FOOL[1]

foment (fə'mɛnt) *vb* (*tr*) **1** to encourage or instigate (trouble, discord, etc.). **2** *Med.* to apply heat and moisture to (a part of the body) to relieve pain. ORIG C15: from LL, from L *fōmentum* a poultice, ult. from *fovēre* to foster
▸ **fomentation** (,fəʊmɛn'teɪʃən) *n* ▸ **fo'menter** *n*

> **USAGE NOTE** Both *foment* and *ferment* can be used to talk about stirring up trouble: *he was accused of fomenting/fermenting unrest.* Only *ferment* can be used intransitively or as a noun: *his anger continued to ferment* (not *foment*)*; rural areas were unaffected by the ferment in the cities.*

fond (fɒnd) *adj* **1** (*postpositive;* foll. by *of*) having a liking (for). **2** loving; tender. **3** indulgent: *a fond mother.* **4** (of hopes, wishes, etc.) cherished but unlikely to be realized: *he had fond hopes of starting his own firm.* **5** *Arch. or dialect.* **5a** foolish. **5b** credulous. ORIG C14 *fonned,* from *fonne* a fool
▸ **'fondly** *adv* ▸ **'fondness** *n*

Fonda ★ ('fɒndə) *n* **1 Henry.** 1905–82, US film actor. His films include *The Grapes of Wrath* (1940), *Twelve Angry Men* (1957), and *On Golden Pond* (1981). **2** his daughter **Jane.** born 1937, US film actress. Her films include *Klute* (1971), *Julia* (1977), and *The China Syndrome* (1979).

fondant ('fɒndənt) *n* **1** a thick flavoured paste of sugar and water, used in sweets and icings. **2** a sweet made of this mixture. ♦ *adj* **3** (of a colour) soft, pastel. ORIG C19: from F, lit.: melting, from *fondre* to melt, from L *fundere;* see FOUND[3]

fondle ('fɒndᵊl) *vb* **fondles, fondling, fondled.** (*tr*) to touch or stroke tenderly. ORIG C17: from (obs.) vb *fond* to fondle; see FOND
▸ **'fondler** *n*

fondue ('fɒndjuː; *French* fɔ̃dy) *n* a Swiss dish, consisting of melted cheese into which small pieces of bread are dipped. ORIG C19: from F, fem of *fondu* melted; see FONDANT

Fonseca ★ (*Spanish* fɔn'seka) *n* **Gulf of.** an inlet of the Pacific Ocean in W Central America.

font¹ (fɒnt) *n* **1a** a large bowl for baptismal water. **1b** a receptacle for holy water. **2** the reservoir for oil in an oil lamp. **3** *Arch. or poetic.* a fountain or well. ORIG OE, from Church L *fons,* from L: fountain

font² (fɒnt) *n Printing.* another name (esp. US and Canad.) for **fount²**.

Fontainebleau ★ ('fɒntɪn,bləʊ; *French* fɔ̃tɛnblo) *n* a town in N France, in the **Forest of Fontainebleau:** famous for its palace (now a museum), one of the largest royal residences in France, built largely by Francis I (16th century). Pop.: 18 753 (1982).

fontanelle *or chiefly US* **fontanel** (,fɒntə'nɛl) *n Anat.*

any of the soft membranous gaps between the bones of the skull in a fetus or infant. ORIG C16 (in the sense: hollow between muscles): from OF *fontanele,* lit.: a little spring, from *fontaine* FOUNTAIN

Fonteyn ★ (fɒn'teɪn) *n* Dame **Margot**. real name *Margaret Hookham.* 1919–91, British ballerina.

Foochow ★ ('fu:'tʃaʊ) *n* a variant transliteration of the Chinese name for **Fuzhou**.

food (fu:d) *n* **1** any substance that can be ingested by a living organism and metabolized into energy and body tissue. Related adj: **alimentary**. **2** nourishment in more or less solid form: *food and drink.* **3** anything that provides mental nourishment or stimulus. ORIG OE *fōda*

food additive *n* any of various natural or synthetic substances, such as salt or citric acid, used in the commercial processing of food as preservatives, antioxidants, emulsifiers, etc.

food chain *n Ecology.* a series of organisms in a community, each member of which feeds on another in the chain and is in turn eaten.

foodie *or* **foody** ('fu:dɪ) *n, pl* **foodies**. a person having an enthusiastic interest in the preparation and consumption of good food.

food poisoning *n* an acute illness caused by food that is either naturally poisonous or contaminated by bacteria.

food processor *n Cookery.* an electric domestic appliance for automatic chopping, grating, blending, etc.

foodstuff ('fu:dˌstʌf) *n* any material, substance, etc., that can be used as food.

food value *n* the relative degree of nourishment obtained from different foods.

fool[1] (fu:l) *n* **1** a person who lacks sense or judgement. **2** a person who is made to appear ridiculous. **3** (formerly) a professional jester living in a royal or noble household. **4** *Obs.* an idiot or imbecile: *the village fool.* **5 play** *or* **act the fool**. to deliberately act foolishly. ◆ *vb* **6** (*tr*) to deceive (someone), esp. in order to make him or her look ridiculous. **7** (*intr;* foll. by *with, around with,* or *about with*) *Inf.* to act or play (with) irresponsibly or aimlessly. **8** (*intr*) to speak or act in a playful or jesting manner. **9** (*tr;* foll. by *away*) to squander; fritter. ◆ *adj* **10** *US inf.* short for **foolish**. ORIG C13: from OF *fol* mad person, from LL *follis* empty-headed fellow, from L: bellows

fool[2] (fu:l) *n Chiefly Brit.* a dessert made from a purée of fruit with cream. ORIG C16: ?from FOOL[1]

foolery ('fu:lərɪ) *n, pl* **fooleries**. **1** foolish behaviour. **2** an instance of this.

foolhardy ('fu:lˌhɑ:dɪ) *adj* **foolhardier, foolhardiest**. heedlessly rash or adventurous. ORIG C13: from OF, from *fol* foolish + *hardi* bold
▸ **'fool,hardily** *adv* ▸ **'fool,hardiness** *n*

foolish ('fu:lɪʃ) *adj* **1** unwise; silly. **2** resulting from folly or stupidity. **3** ridiculous or absurd. **4** weak-minded; simple.
▸ **'foolishly** *adv* ▸ **'foolishness** *n*

foolproof ('fu:lˌpru:f) *adj Inf.* **1** proof against failure. **2** (esp. of machines, etc.) proof against human misuse, error, etc.

foolscap ('fu:lzˌkæp) *n Chiefly Brit.* a size of writing or printing paper, 13½ by 17 inches. ORIG C17: see FOOL[1], CAP; so called from the watermark formerly used on this kind of paper

fool's cap *n* **1** a hood or cap with bells or tassels, worn by court jesters. **2** a dunce's cap.

fool's errand *n* a fruitless undertaking.

fool's gold *n* any of various yellow minerals, esp. pyrite, that can be mistaken for gold.

fool's paradise *n* illusory happiness.

fool's-parsley *n* an evil-smelling Eurasian umbelliferous plant with small white flowers.

foot (fʊt) *n, pl* **feet**. **1** the part of the vertebrate leg below the ankle joint that is in contact with the ground during standing and walking. Related adj: **pedal**. **2** the part of a garment covering a foot. **3** any of various organs of locomotion or attachment in invertebrates, including molluscs. **4** *Bot.* the lower part of some plants or plant structures. **5** a unit of length equal to one third of a yard or 12 inches. 1 foot is equivalent to 0.3048 metre. **6** any part resembling a foot in form or function: *the foot of a chair.* **7** the lower part of something; bottom: *the foot of a hill.* **8** the end of a series or group: *the foot of the list.* **9** manner of walking or moving: *a heavy foot.* **10a** infantry, esp. in the British army. **10b** (*as modifier*): *a foot soldier.* **11** any of various attachments on a sewing machine that hold the fabric in position. **12** *Prosody.* a group of two or more syllables in which one syllable has the major stress, forming the basic unit of poetic rhythm. **13 my foot!** an expression of disbelief, often of the speaker's own preceding statement. **14 of foot**. *Arch.* in manner of movement: *fleet of foot.* **15 one foot in the grave**. *Inf.* near to death. **16 on foot**. **16a** walking or running. **16b** astir; afoot. **17 put a foot wrong**. to make a mistake. **18 put one's best foot forward**. **18a** to try to do one's best. **18b** to hurry. **19 put one's foot down**. *Inf.* to act firmly. **20 put one's foot in it**. *Inf.* to blunder. **21 under foot**. on the ground; beneath one's feet. ◆ *vb* **22** to dance to music (esp. in **foot it**). **23** (*tr*) to walk over or set foot on (esp. in **foot it**). **24** (*tr*) to pay the entire cost of (esp. in **foot the bill**). ORIG OE *fōt* ◆ See also **feet**.
▸ **'footless** *adj*

> **USAGE NOTE** In front of another noun, the plural for the unit of length is *foot: a 20-foot putt; his 70-foot ketch. Foot* can also be used instead of *feet* when mentioning a quantity and in front of words like *tall*: *four foot of snow; he is at least six foot tall.*

Foot ★ (fʊt) *n* **Michael** (**Mackintosh**). born 1913, British Labour politician; secretary of state for employment (1974–76); leader of the House of Commons (1976–79); leader of the Labour Party (1980–83).

footage ('fʊtɪdʒ) *n* **1** a length or distance measured in feet. **2** the extent of film material shot and exposed.

foot-and-mouth disease *n* an acute highly infectious viral disease of cattle, pigs, sheep, and goats, characterized by the formation of vesicular eruptions in the mouth and on the feet.

football ('fʊtˌbɔ:l) *n* **1a** any of various games played with a round or oval ball and usually based on two teams competing to kick, head, carry, or otherwise propel the ball into each other's goal, territory, etc. **1b** (*as modifier*): *a football supporter.* **2** the ball used in any of these games or their variants. **3** a problem, issue, etc., that is continually passed from one group or person to another as a pretext for argument.
▸ **'foot,baller** *n*

footboard ('fʊtˌbɔ:d) *n* **1** a board for a person to stand or rest his feet on. **2** a treadle or foot-operated lever on a machine. **3** a vertical board at the foot of a bed.

footbridge ('fʊtˌbrɪdʒ) *n* a narrow bridge for the use of pedestrians.

-footed *adj* **1** having a foot or feet as specified: *four-footed.* **2** having a tread as specified: *heavy-footed.*

footer[1] ('fʊtə) *n* (*in combination*) a person or thing of a specified length or height in feet: *a six-footer.*

footer[2] ('fʊtə) *n Brit. inf.* short for **football** (the game).

footfall ('fʊtˌfɔ:l) *n* the sound of a footstep.

foot fault *n Tennis.* a fault that occurs when the server fails to keep both feet behind the baseline until he has served.

foothill ('fʊtˌhɪl) *n* (*often pl*) a relatively low hill at the foot of a mountain.

foothold ('fʊtˌhəʊld) *n* **1** a ledge or other place affording a secure grip, as during climbing. **2** a secure position from which further progress may be made.

footing ('fʊtɪŋ) *n* **1** the basis or foundation on which something is established: *the business was on a secure footing.* **2** the relationship or status existing between two persons, groups, etc. **3** a secure grip by or for the feet. **4** the lower part of a foundation of a column, wall, building, etc.

footle ('fu:tᵊl) *vb* **footles, footling, footled**. (*intr;* often foll. by

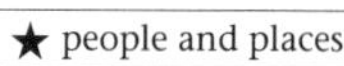

around or *about*) *Inf.* to loiter aimlessly. ORIG C19: prob. from F *foutre* to copulate with, from L *futuere*
▸ 'footling *adj*

footlights ('fʊtˌlaɪts) *pl n Theatre.* lights set in a row along the front of the stage floor.

footloose ('fʊtˌluːs) *adj* **1** free to go or do as one wishes. **2** restless: *to feel footloose.*

footman ('fʊtmən) *n, pl* **footmen. 1** a male servant, esp. one in livery. **2** (formerly) a foot soldier.

footnote ('fʊtˌnəʊt) *n* **1** a note printed at the bottom of a page, to which attention is drawn by means of a mark in the text. ◆ *vb* **footnotes, footnoting, footnoted. 2** (*tr*) to supply (a page, etc.) with footnotes.

footpad ('fʊtˌpæd) *n Arch.* a robber or highwayman, on foot rather than horseback.

footpath ('fʊtˌpɑːθ) *n* **1** a narrow path for walkers only. **2** *Chiefly Austral. & NZ.* another word for **pavement.**

footplate ('fʊtˌpleɪt) *n Chiefly Brit.* a platform in the cab of a locomotive on which the crew stand to operate the controls.

foot-pound-second *n* See **fps units.**

footprint ('fʊtˌprɪnt) *n* an indentation or outline of the foot of a person or animal on a surface.

footrest ('fʊtˌrɛst) *n* something that provides a support for the feet, such as a low stool, rail, etc.

foot rot *n Vet. science.* See **rot** (sense 10).

footsie ('fʊtsɪ) *n Inf.* flirtation involving the touching together of feet, etc.

Footsie ('fʊtsɪ) *n Brit. inf.* the Financial Times Stock Exchange 100 index. See **FT Index** (sense 2).

foot soldier *n* an infantryman.

footsore ('fʊtˌsɔː) *adj* having sore or tired feet, esp. from much walking.
▸ 'footˌsoreness *n*

footstep ('fʊtˌstɛp) *n* **1** the action of taking a step in walking. **2** the sound made by walking. **3** the distance covered with a step. **4** a footmark. **5** a single stair. **6 follow in someone's footsteps.** to continue the example of another.

footsteps editor *n Brit. films.* the technician who adds sound effects, such as doors closing, rain falling, etc., during the postproduction sound-dubbing process. US name: **foley** *or* **foley artist.**

footstool ('fʊtˌstuːl) *n* a low stool used for supporting or resting the feet of a seated person.

footwear ('fʊtˌwɛə) *n* anything worn to cover the feet.

footwork ('fʊtˌwɜːk) *n* **1** the use of the feet, esp. in sports, dancing, etc. **2** *Inf.* clever manoeuvring: *deft political footwork.* **3** *Inf.* preliminary groundwork: *many estate agents do the footwork; you only need to visit.*

footy *or* **footie** ('fʊtɪ) *n Inf.* **a** football. **b** (*as modifier*): *footy boots.*

fop (fɒp) *n* a man who is excessively concerned with fashion and elegance. ORIG C15: rel. to G *foppen* to trick
▸ 'foppery *n* ▸ 'foppish *adj*

for (fɔː; *unstressed* fə) *prep* **1** directed or belonging to: *there's a phone call for you.* **2** to the advantage of: *I only did it for you.* **3** in the direction of: *heading for the border.* **4** over a span of (time or distance): *working for six days.* **5** in favour of: *vote for me.* **6** in order to get or achieve: *I do it for money.* **7** designed to meet the needs of: *these kennels are for puppies.* **8** at a cost of: *I got it for hardly any money.* **9** such as explains or results in: *his reason for changing his job was not given.* **10** in place of: *a substitute for the injured player.* **11** because of: *she wept for pure relief.* **12** with regard or consideration to the usual characteristics of: *it's cool for this time of year.* **13** concerning: *desire for money.* **14** as being: *I know that for a fact.* **15** at a specified time: *a date for the next evening.* **16** to do or partake of: *an appointment for supper.* **17** in the duty or task of: *that's for him to say.* **18** to allow of: *too big a job for us to handle.* **19** despite: *she's a good wife, for all her nagging.* **20** in order to preserve, retain, etc.: *to fight for survival.* **21** as a direct equivalent to: *word for word.* **22** in order to become or enter: *to train for the priesthood.* **23** in recompense for: *I paid for it last week.* **24 for it.** *Brit. inf.* liable for punishment or blame: *you'll be for it if she catches you.* ◆ *conj* **25** (*coordinating*) because; seeing that: *I couldn't stay, for the area was violent.* ORIG OE

for- *prefix* **1** indicating rejection or prohibition: *forbid.* **2** indicating falsity: *forswear.* **3** used to give intensive force: *forlorn.* ORIG OE *for-*

forage ('fɒrɪdʒ) *n* **1** food for horses or cattle, esp. hay or straw. **2** the act of searching for food or provisions. ◆ *vb* **forages, foraging, foraged. 3** to search (the countryside or a town) for food, etc. **4** (*intr*) *Mil.* to carry out a raid. **5** (*tr*) to obtain by searching about. **6** (*tr*) to give food or other provisions to. **7** (*tr*) to feed (cattle or horses) with such food. ORIG C14: from OF *fourrage,* prob. of Gmc origin
▸ 'forager *n*

forage cap *n* a soldier's undress cap.

foramen (fɒ'reɪmɛn) *n, pl* **foramina** (-'ræmɪnə) *or* **foramens.** a natural hole, esp. one in a bone. ORIG C17: from L, from *forāre* to bore, pierce

foraminifer (ˌfɒrə'mɪnɪfə) *n* a protozoan of the phylum *Foraminifera,* having a shell with numerous openings through which the cytoplasmic processes protrude. ORIG C19: from NL, from FORAMEN + -FER

forasmuch as (fərəz'mʌtʃ) *conj* (*subordinating*) *Arch. or legal.* seeing that.

foray ('fɒreɪ) *n* **1** a short raid or incursion. ◆ *vb* **2** to raid or ravage (a town, district, etc.). ORIG C14: from *forrayen* to pillage, from OF, from *fuerre* fodder

forbade (fə'bæd, -'beɪd) *or* **forbad** (fə'bæd) *vb* the past tense of **forbid.**

forbear[1] (fɔː'bɛə) *vb* **forbears, forbearing, forbore, forborne. 1** (when *intr,* often foll. by *from* or an infinitive) to cease or refrain (from doing something). **2** *Arch.* to tolerate (misbehaviour, etc.). ORIG OE *forberan*

forbear[2] ('fɔːˌbɛə) *n* a variant spelling of **forebear.**

forbearance (fɔː'bɛərəns) *n* **1** the act of forbearing. **2** self-control; patience.

Forbes ★ (fɔːbz) *n* **George William.** 1869–1947, New Zealand statesman; prime minister (1930–35).

forbid (fə'bɪd) *vb* **forbids, forbidding, forbade** *or* **forbad, forbidden** *or* **forbid.** (*tr*) **1** to prohibit (a person) in a forceful or authoritative manner (from doing or having something). **2** to make impossible. **3** to shut out or exclude. ORIG OE *forbēodan;* see FOR-, BID
▸ for'bidder *n*

> **USAGE NOTE** It was formerly considered incorrect to talk of *forbidding* someone *from* doing something, but in modern usage either *from* or *to* can be used: *he was forbidden from entering/to enter the building.*

forbidden (fə'bɪdᵊn) *adj* **1** not permitted by order or law. **2** *Physics.* involving a change in quantum numbers that is not permitted by certain rules derived from quantum mechanics.

Forbidden City ★ *n* **the. 1** Lhasa, Tibet: once famed for its inaccessibility and hostility to strangers. **2** a walled section of Beijing, China, enclosing the Imperial Palace and associated buildings of the former Chinese Empire.

forbidden fruit *n* any pleasure or enjoyment regarded as illicit, esp. sexual indulgence.

forbidding (fə'bɪdɪŋ) *adj* **1** hostile or unfriendly. **2** dangerous or ominous.

forbore (fɔː'bɔː) *vb* the past tense of **forbear**[1].

forborne (fɔː'bɔːn) *vb* the past participle of **forbear**[1].

force[1] (fɔːs) *n* **1** strength or energy; power: *the force of the blow.* **2** exertion or the use of exertion against a person or thing that resists. **3** *Physics.* **3a** a dynamic influence that changes a body from a state of rest to one of motion or changes its rate of motion. **3b** a static influence that produces a strain in a body or system. Symbol: *F* **4a** intellectual, political, or moral influence or strength: *the force of his argument.* **4b** a person or thing with such influence: *he was a force in the land.* **5** vehemence or intensity: *she spoke with great force.* **6** a group of persons organized for military or police functions: *armed forces.* **7** (*sometimes cap.;*

preceded by *the*) *Inf.* the police force. **8** a group of persons organized for particular duties or tasks: *a workforce.* **9** *Criminal law.* violence unlawfully committed or threatened. **10 in force. 10a** (of a law) having legal validity. **10b** in great strength or numbers. ◆ *vb* **forces, forcing, forced.** (*tr*) **11** to compel or cause (a person, group, etc.) to do something through effort, superior strength, etc. **12** to acquire or produce through effort, superior strength, etc.: *to force a confession.* **13** to propel or drive despite resistance. **14** to break down or open (a lock, door, etc.). **15** to impose or inflict: *he forced his views on them.* **16** to cause (plants or farm animals) to grow or fatten artificially at an increased rate. **17** to strain to the utmost: *to force the voice.* **18** to rape. **19** *Cards.* **19a** to compel a player by the lead of a particular suit to play (a certain card). **19b** (in bridge) to induce (a bid) from one's partner. ORIG C13: from OF, from Vulgar L *fortia* (unattested), from L *fortis* strong
▸ **'forceable** *adj* ▸ **'forceless** *adj* ▸ **'forcer** *n*

force² (fɔːs) *n* (in N England) a waterfall. ORIG C17: from ON *fors*

forced (fɔːst) *adj* **1** done because of force: *forced labour.* **2** false or unnatural: *a forced smile.* **3** due to an emergency or necessity: *a forced landing.*

force de frappe *French* (fɔrs də frap) *n* a military strike force, esp. the independent nuclear strike force of France. ORIG C20: lit.: striking force

force-feed *vb* **force-feeds, force-feeding, force-fed.** (*tr*) to force (a person or animal) to eat or swallow food.

forceful ('fɔːsful) *adj* **1** powerful. **2** persuasive or effective.
▸ **'forcefully** *adv* ▸ **'forcefulness** *n*

forcemeat ('fɔːsˌmiːt) *n* a mixture of chopped ingredients used for stuffing. Also called: **farce.** ORIG C17: from *force* (see FARCE) + MEAT

forceps ('fɔːsɪps) *n, pl* **forceps. 1a** a surgical instrument in the form of a pair of pincers, used esp. in the delivery of babies. **1b** (*as modifier*): *a forceps baby.* **2** any part of an organism shaped like a forceps. ORIG C17: from L, from *formus* hot + *capere* to seize

force pump *n* a pump that ejects fluid under pressure. Cf. **lift pump.**

Forces ('fɔːsɪz) *pl n* (usually preceded by *the*) the armed services of a nation.

forcible ('fɔːsəbᵊl) *adj* **1** done by, involving, or having force. **2** convincing or effective: *a forcible argument.*
▸ **'forcibly** *adv*

ford (fɔːd) *n* **1** a shallow area in a river that can be crossed by car, on horseback, etc. ◆ *vb* **2** (*tr*) to cross (a river, brook, etc.) over a shallow area. ORIG OE
▸ **'fordable** *adj*

Ford ★ (fɔːd) *n* **1 Ford Madox** ('mædəks), real name *Ford Madox Hueffer.* 1873–1939, British writer; works include *The Good Soldier* (1915) and the war tetralogy *Parade's End* (1924–28). **2 Gerald R(udolph).** born 1913, US politician; 38th president of the US (1974–77). **3 Harrison.** born 1942, US film actor. His films include *Star Wars* (1977), *Raiders of the Lost Ark* (1981), *Air Force One* (1997), and *Random Hearts* (1999). **4 Henry.** 1863–1947, US car manufacturer, who pioneered mass production. **5 John.** 1586–?1639, English dramatist; author of such tragedies as *'Tis Pity She's a Whore* (1633). **6 John,** real name *Sean O'Feeney.* 1895–1973, US film director, esp. of Westerns such as *Stagecoach* (1939).

fore¹ (fɔː) *adj* **1** (*usually in combination*) located at, in, or towards the front: *the forelegs of a horse.* ◆ *n* **2** the front part. **3** something located at, or towards the front. **4 fore and aft.** located at both ends of a vessel: *a fore-and-aft rig.* **5 to the fore.** to the front or conspicuous position. ◆ *adv* **6** at or towards a ship's bow. **7** *Obs.* before. ◆ *prep, conj* **8** a less common word for **before.** ORIG OE

fore² (fɔː) *sentence substitute.* (in golf) a warning shout made by a player about to make a shot. ORIG C19: prob. short for BEFORE

fore- *prefix* **1** before in time or rank: *forefather.* **2** at or near the front: *forecourt.* ORIG OE, from *fore* (adv)

fore-and-after *n Naut.* **1** any vessel with a fore-and-aft rig. **2** a double-ended vessel.

forearm¹ ('fɔːrˌɑːm) *n* the part of the arm from the elbow to the wrist. ORIG C18: from FORE- + ARM¹

forearm² (fɔːr'ɑːm) *vb* (*tr*) to prepare or arm (someone) in advance. ORIG C16: from FORE- + ARM²

forebear *or* **forbear** ('fɔːˌbɛə) *n* an ancestor.

forebode (fɔː'bəud) *vb* **forebodes, foreboding, foreboded. 1** to warn of or indicate (an event, result, etc.) in advance. **2** to have a premonition of (an event).

foreboding (fɔː'bəudɪŋ) *n* **1** a feeling of impending evil, disaster, etc. **2** an omen or portent. ◆ *adj* **3** presaging something.

forebrain ('fɔːˌbreɪn) *n* the nontechnical name for **prosencephalon.**

forecast ('fɔːˌkɑːst) *vb* **forecasts, forecasting, forecast** *or* **forecasted. 1** to predict or calculate (weather, events, etc.), in advance. **2** (*tr*) to serve as an early indication of. ◆ *n* **3** a statement of probable future weather calculated from meteorological data. **4** a prediction. **5** the practice or power of forecasting.
▸ **'foreˌcaster** *n*

forecastle, fo'c's'le, *or* **fo'c'sle** ('fəuksᵊl) *n* the part of a vessel at the bow where the crew is quartered.

foreclose (fɔː'kləuz) *vb* **forecloses, foreclosing, foreclosed. 1** *Law.* to deprive (a mortgagor, etc.) of the right to redeem (a mortgage or pledge). **2** (*tr*) to shut out; bar. **3** (*tr*) to prevent or hinder. ORIG C15: from OF, from *for-* out + *clore* to close, from L *claudere*
▸ **fore'closable** *adj* ▸ **foreclosure** (fɔː'kləuʒə) *n*

forecourt ('fɔːˌkɔːt) *n* **1** a courtyard in front of a building, as one in a filling station. **2** the section of the court in tennis, badminton, etc., between the service line and the net.

foredoom (fɔː'duːm) *vb* (*tr*) to doom or condemn beforehand.

forefather ('fɔːˌfɑːðə) *n* an ancestor, esp. a male.
▸ **'foreˌfatherly** *adj*

forefinger ('fɔːˌfɪŋgə) *n* the finger next to the thumb. Also called: **index finger.**

forefoot ('fɔːˌfut) *n, pl* **forefeet.** either of the front feet of a quadruped.

forefront ('fɔːˌfrʌnt) *n* **1** the extreme front. **2** the position of most prominence or action.

foregather *or* **forgather** (fɔː'gæðə) *vb* (*intr*) **1** to gather together. **2** (foll. by *with*) to socialize.

forego¹ (fɔː'gəu) *vb* **foregoes, foregoing, forewent, foregone.** to precede in time, place, etc. ORIG OE *foregān*

forego² (fɔː'gəu) *vb* **foregoes, foregoing, forewent, foregone.** (*tr*) a variant spelling of **forgo.**

foregoing (fɔː'gəuɪŋ) *adj* (*prenominal*) (esp. of writing or speech) going before; preceding.

foregone (fɔː'gɒn, 'fɔːˌgɒn) *adj* gone or completed; past.
▸ **fore'goneness** *n*

foregone conclusion *n* an inevitable result or conclusion.

foreground ('fɔːˌgraund) *n* **1** the part of a scene situated towards the front or nearest to the viewer. **2** a conspicuous position.

forehand ('fɔːˌhænd) *adj* (*prenominal*) **1** *Tennis, squash, etc.* (of a stroke) made with the palm of the hand facing the direction of the stroke. ◆ *n* **2** *Tennis, squash, etc.* **2a** a forehand stroke. **2b** the side on which such strokes are made. **3** the part of a horse in front of the saddle.

forehead ('fɒrɪd, 'fɔːˌhɛd) *n* the part of the face between the natural hairline and the eyes. Related adj: **frontal.** ORIG OE *forhēafod*

foreign ('fɒrɪn) *adj* **1** of, located in, or coming from another country, area, people, etc.: *a foreign resident.* **2** dealing or concerned with another country, area, people, etc.: *a foreign office.* **3** not pertinent or related: *a matter foreign to the discussion.* **4** not familiar; strange. **5** in an abnormal place or position: *foreign matter.* ORIG C13: from OF, from Vulgar L *forānus* (unattested) on the outside, from L *foris* outside
▸ **'foreignness** *n*

foreign affairs *pl n* matters abroad that involve the homeland, such as relations with another country.

★ people and places

foreigner ('fɒrɪnə) *n* **1** a person from a foreign country. **2** an outsider. **3** something from a foreign country, such as a ship or product.

foreign minister *or* **secretary** *n* (*often caps.*) a cabinet minister who is responsible for a country's dealings with other countries. US equivalent: **secretary of state.**

foreign office *n* the ministry of a country or state that is concerned with dealings with other states. US equivalent: **State Department.**

foreknowledge (fɔː'nɒlɪdʒ) *n* knowledge of a thing before it exists or occurs; prescience.
▸ **fore'know** *vb* ▸ **fore'knowable** *adj*

foreland ('fɔːlənd) *n* **1** a headland, cape, or promontory. **2** land lying in front of something, such as water.

foreleg ('fɔːˌlɛg) *n* either of the front legs of a horse, sheep, or other quadruped.

forelimb ('fɔːˌlɪm) *n* either of the front or anterior limbs of a four-limbed vertebrate.

forelock ('fɔːˌlɒk) *n* a lock of hair growing or falling over the forehead.

foreman ('fɔːmən) *n, pl* **foremen. 1** a person, often experienced, who supervises other workmen. **2** *Law.* the principal juror, who presides at the deliberations of a jury.

Foreman ★ ('fɔːmən) *n* **George.** born 1949, US boxer: WBA world heavyweight champion (1973–74); he regained the title in 1994 but had it withdrawn in 1995 when he refused to fight a challenger; remained WBU champion until 1997.

foremast ('fɔːˌmɑːst; *Naut.* 'fɔːməst) *n* the mast nearest the bow on vessels with two or more masts.

foremost ('fɔːˌməʊst) *adj, adv* first in time, place, rank, etc. ORIG OE, from *forma* first

forename ('fɔːˌneɪm) *n* another term for **first name.**

forenamed ('fɔːˌneɪmd) *adj* (*prenominal*) named or mentioned previously; aforesaid.

forenoon ('fɔːˌnuːn) *n* the daylight hours before or just before noon.

forensic (fə'rɛnsɪk) *adj* used in, or connected with a court of law: *forensic science.* ORIG C17: from L *forēnsis* public, from FORUM
▸ **fo'rensically** *adv*

forensic medicine *n* the use of medical knowledge, esp. pathology, for the purposes of the law, as in determining the cause of death. Also called: **medical jurisprudence.**

foreordain (ˌfɔːrɔː'deɪn) *vb* (*tr; may take a clause as object*) to determine (events, etc.) in the future.
▸ **foreordination** (ˌfɔːrɔːdɪ'neɪʃən) *n*

forepaw ('fɔːˌpɔː) *n* either of the front feet of most land mammals that do not have hoofs.

foreplay ('fɔːˌpleɪ) *n* mutual sexual stimulation preceding sexual intercourse.

forequarter ('fɔːˌkwɔːtə) *n* the front portion, including the leg, of half of a carcass, as of beef.

forequarters ('fɔːˌkwɔːtəz) *pl n* the part of the body of a horse, etc. that consists of the forelegs, shoulders, and adjoining parts.

forerun (fɔː'rʌn) *vb* **foreruns, forerunning, foreran, forerun.** (*tr*) **1** to serve as a herald for. **2** to precede. **3** to forestall.

forerunner ('fɔːˌrʌnə) *n* **1** a person or thing that precedes another. **2** a person or thing coming in advance to herald the arrival of someone or something. **3** an omen; portent.

foresail ('fɔːˌseɪl; *Naut.* 'fɔːsᵊl) *n Naut.* **1** the aftermost headsail of a fore-and-aft rigged vessel. **2** the lowest sail set on the foremast of a square-rigged vessel.

foresee (fɔː'siː) *vb* **foresees, foreseeing, foresaw, foreseen.** (*tr; may take a clause as object*) to see or know beforehand: *he did not foresee that.*
▸ **fore'seeable** *adj* ▸ **fore'seer** *n*

foreshadow (fɔː'ʃædəʊ) *vb* (*tr*) to show, indicate, or suggest in advance; presage.

foreshank ('fɔːˌʃæŋk) *n* **1** the top of the front leg of an animal. **2** a cut of meat from this part.

foresheet ('fɔːˌʃiːt) *n* **1** the sheet of a foresail. **2** (*pl*) the part forward of the foremost thwart of a boat.

foreshock ('fɔːˌʃɒk) *n Chiefly US.* a relatively small earthquake heralding the arrival of a much larger one.

foreshore ('fɔːˌʃɔː) *n* **1** the part of the shore that lies between the limits for high and low tides. **2** the part of the shore that lies just above the high water mark.

foreshorten (fɔː'ʃɔːtᵊn) *vb* (*tr*) to represent (a line, form, object, etc.) as shorter than actual length in order to give an illusion of recession or projection.

foreshow (fɔː'ʃəʊ) *vb* **foreshows, foreshowing, foreshowed; foreshown** *or* **foreshowed.** (*tr*) *Arch.* to indicate in advance.

foresight ('fɔːˌsaɪt) *n* **1** provision for or insight into future problems, needs, etc. **2** the act or ability of foreseeing. **3** the act of looking forward. **4** *Surveying.* a reading taken looking forwards. **5** the front sight on a firearm.
▸ ˌ**fore'sighted** *adj* ▸ ˌ**fore'sightedly** *adv* ▸ ˌ**fore'sightedness** *n*

foreskin ('fɔːˌskɪn) *n Anat.* the nontechnical name for **prepuce.**

forest ('fɒrɪst) *n* **1** a large wooded area having a thick growth of trees and plants. **2** the trees of such an area. **3** *NZ.* an area planted with pines or similar trees, not native trees. Cf. **bush**[1] (sense 4). **4** something resembling a large wooded area, esp. in density: *a forest of telegraph poles.* **5** *Law.* (formerly) an area of woodland, esp. one owned by the sovereign and set apart as a hunting ground. **6** (*modifier*) of, involving, or living in a forest or forests: *a forest glade.* ◆ *vb* **7** (*tr*) to create a forest. ORIG C13: from OF, from Med. L *forestis* unfenced woodland, from L *foris* outside
▸ **'forested** *adj*

forestall (fɔː'stɔːl) *vb* (*tr*) **1** to delay, stop, or guard against beforehand. **2** to anticipate. **3** to buy up merchandise for profitable resale. ORIG C14 *forestallen* to waylay, from OE, from *fore-* in front of + *steall* place
▸ **fore'staller** *n* ▸ **fore'stalment** *n*

forestation (ˌfɒrɪ'steɪʃən) *n* the planting of trees over a wide area.

forestay ('fɔːˌsteɪ) *n Naut.* an adjustable stay leading from the truck of the foremast to the deck, for controlling the bending of the mast.

forester ('fɒrɪstə) *n* **1** a person skilled in forestry or in charge of a forest. **2** a person or animal that lives in a forest. **3** (*cap.*) a member of the Ancient Order of Foresters, a friendly society.

Forester ★ ('fɒrɪstə) *n* **C(ecil) S(cott).** 1899–1966, English novelist; creator of Captain Horatio Hornblower in a series of novels on the Napoleonic Wars.

forest park *n NZ.* a recreational reserve which may include bush and exotic trees.

forestry ('fɒrɪstrɪ) *n* **1** the science of planting and caring for trees. **2** the planting and management of forests. **3** *Rare.* forest land.

foretaste ('fɔːˌteɪst) *n* an early but limited experience of something to come.

foretell (fɔː'tɛl) *vb* **foretells, foretelling, foretold.** (*tr; may take a clause as object*) to tell or indicate (an event, a result, etc.) beforehand.

forethought ('fɔːˌθɔːt) *n* **1** advance consideration or deliberation. **2** thoughtful anticipation of future events.

foretoken *n* ('fɔːˌtəʊkən). **1** a sign of a future event. ◆ *vb* (fɔː'təʊkən). **2** (*tr*) to foreshadow.

foretop ('fɔːˌtɒp; *Naut.* 'fɔːtəp) *n Naut.* a platform at the top of the foremast.

fore-topgallant (ˌfɔːtɒp'gælənt; *Naut.* ˌfɔːtə'gælənt) *adj Naut.* of, relating to, or being the topmost portion of a foremast.

fore-topmast (fɔː'tɒpˌmɑːst; *Naut.* fɔː'tɒpməst) *n Naut.* a mast stepped above a foremast.

fore-topsail (fɔː'tɒpˌseɪl; *Naut.* fɔː'tɒpsᵊl) *n Naut.* a sail set on a fore-topmast.

forever (fɔː'rɛvə, fə-) *adv* **1** Also: **for ever.** without end; everlastingly. **2** at all times. **3** *Inf.* for a very long time: *he went on speaking forever.* ◆ *n* **forever. 4** (*as object*) *Inf.* a very long time: *it took him forever to reply.*

> **USAGE NOTE** *Forever* and *for ever* can both be used to say that something is without end. For all other meanings, *forever* is the preferred form.

for evermore *or* **forevermore** (fɔːˌrɛvəˈmɔː, fə-) *adv* a more emphatic or emotive term for **forever.**

forewarn (fɔːˈwɔːn) *vb (tr)* to warn beforehand.
▸ **foreˈwarner** *n*

forewent (fɔːˈwɛnt) *vb* the past tense of **forego.**

forewing (ˈfɔːˌwɪŋ) *n* either wing of the anterior pair of an insect's two pairs of wings.

foreword (ˈfɔːˌwɜːd) *n* an introductory statement to a book. ORIG C19: literal translation of G *Vorwort*

forfaiting (ˈfɔːˌfeɪtɪŋ) *n* the financial service of discounting, without recourse, a promissory note, bill of exchange, letter of credit, etc., received from an overseas buyer by an exporter; a form of debt discounting. ORIG C20: from F *forfaire* to forfeit or surrender

Forfar ★ (ˈfɔːfər, -fɑː) *n* a market town in E Scotland, the administrative centre of Angus council area: site of a castle, residence of Scottish kings between the 11th and 14th centuries. Pop.: 12 961 (1991).

forfeit (ˈfɔːfɪt) *n* **1** something lost or given up as a penalty for a fault, mistake, etc. **2** the act of losing or surrendering something in this manner. **3** *Law.* something confiscated as a penalty for an offence, etc. **4** *(sometimes pl)* **4a** a game in which a player has to give up an object, perform a specified action, etc., if he commits a fault. **4b** an object so given up. ◆ *vb (tr)* **5** to lose or be liable to lose in consequence of a mistake, fault, etc. **6** *Law.* to confiscate as punishment. ◆ *adj* **7** surrendered or liable to be surrendered as a penalty. ORIG C13: from OF *forfet* offence, from *forfaire* to commit a crime, from Med. L, from L *foris* outside + *facere* to do
▸ **ˈforfeiter** *n*

forfeiture (ˈfɔːfɪtʃə) *n* **1** something forfeited. **2** the act of forfeiting or paying a penalty.

forfend *or* **forefend** (fɔːˈfɛnd) *vb (tr)* **1** *US.* to protect or secure. **2** *Obs.* to prevent.

forgather (fɔːˈgæðə) *vb* a variant spelling of **foregather.**

forgave (fəˈgeɪv) *vb* the past tense of **forgive.**

forge¹ (fɔːdʒ) *n* **1** a place in which metal is worked by heating and hammering; smithy. **2** a hearth or furnace used for heating metal. ◆ *vb* **forges, forging, forged. 3** *(tr)* to shape (metal) by heating and hammering. **4** *(tr)* to form, make, or fashion (objects, etc.). **5** *(tr)* to invent or devise (an agreement, etc.). **6** to make a fraudulent imitation of (a signature, etc.) or to commit forgery. ORIG C14: from OF *forgier* to construct, from L *fabricāre,* from *faber* craftsman
▸ **ˈforger** *n*

forge² (fɔːdʒ) *vb* **forges, forging, forged.** *(intr)* **1** to move at a steady pace. **2 forge ahead.** to increase speed. ORIG C17: from ?

forgery (ˈfɔːdʒərɪ) *n, pl* **forgeries. 1** the act of reproducing something for a fraudulent purpose. **2** something forged, such as an antique. **3** *Criminal law.* **3a** the false making or altering of a document, such as a cheque, etc., or any tape or disc storing information, with intent to defraud. **3b** something forged.

forget (fəˈgɛt) *vb* **forgets, forgetting, forgot, forgotten** *or* *(Arch. or dialect)* **forgot. 1** (when *tr, may take a clause as object or an infinitive*) to fail to recall (someone or something once known). **2** *(tr; may take a clause as object or an infinitive)* to neglect, either as the result of an unintentional error or intentionally. **3** *(tr)* to leave behind by mistake. **4 forget oneself. 4a** to act in an improper manner. **4b** to be unselfish. **4c** to be deep in thought. ORIG OE *forgietan*
▸ **forˈgettable** *adj* ▸ **forˈgetter** *n*

forgetful (fəˈgɛtful) *adj* **1** tending to forget. **2** *(often postpositive;* foll. by *of)* inattentive (to) or neglectful (of).
▸ **forˈgetfully** *adv* ▸ **forˈgetfulness** *n*

forget-me-not *n* a temperate low-growing plant having clusters of small blue flowers.

forgive (fəˈgɪv) *vb* **forgives, forgiving, forgave, forgiven. 1** to cease to blame (someone or something). **2** to grant pardon for (a mistake, etc.). **3** *(tr)* to free (someone) from penalty. **4** *(tr)* to free from the obligation of (a debt, etc.). ORIG OE *forgiefan*
▸ **forˈgivable** *adj* ▸ **forˈgiver** *n*

forgiveness (fəˈgɪvnɪs) *n* **1** the act of forgiving or the state of being forgiven. **2** willingness to forgive.

forgiving (fəˈgɪvɪŋ) *adj* willing to forgive.

forgo *or* **forego** (fɔːˈgəʊ) *vb* **forgoes, forgoing, forwent, forgone.** *(tr)* to give up or do without. ORIG OE *forgān*

forgot (fəˈgɒt) *vb* **1** the past tense of **forget. 2** *Arch. or dialect.* a past participle of **forget.**

forgotten (fəˈgɒtᵊn) *vb* a past participle of **forget.**

forint *(Hungarian* ˈforint) *n* the standard monetary unit of Hungary. ORIG from Hungarian, from It. *fiorino* FLORIN

fork (fɔːk) *n* **1** a small usually metal implement consisting of two, three, or four long thin prongs on the end of a handle, used for lifting food to the mouth, etc. **2** a similar-shaped agricultural tool, used for lifting, digging, etc. **3** a pronged part of any machine, device, etc. **4** (of a road, river, etc.) **4a** a division into two or more branches. **4b** the point where the division begins. **4c** such a branch. ◆ *vb* **5** *(tr)* to pick up, dig, etc., with a fork. **6** *(tr) Chess.* to place (two enemy pieces) under attack with one of one's own pieces. **7** *(intr)* to be divided into two or more branches. **8** to take one or other branch at a fork in a road, etc. ORIG OE *forca,* from L *furca*

forked (fɔːkt) *adj* **1a** having a fork or forklike parts. **1b** *(in combination): two-forked.* **2** zigzag: *forked lightning.*
▸ **forkedly** (ˈfɔːkɪdlɪ) *adv*

fork-lift truck *n* a vehicle having two power-operated horizontal prongs that can be raised and lowered for transporting and unloading goods. Sometimes shortened to **fork-lift.**

fork out, over, *or* **up** *vb (adv) Sl.* to pay (money, goods, etc.), esp. with reluctance.

forlorn (fəˈlɔːn) *adj* **1** miserable or cheerless. **2** forsaken. **3** *(postpositive;* foll. by *of)* bereft: *forlorn of hope.* **4** desperate: *the last forlorn attempt.* ORIG OE *forloren* lost, from *forlēosan* to lose
▸ **forˈlornness** *n*

forlorn hope *n* **1** a hopeless enterprise. **2** a faint hope. **3** *Obs.* a group of soldiers assigned to an extremely dangerous duty. ORIG C16 (in the obs. sense): changed (by folk etymology) from Du. *verloren hoop* lost troop, from *verloren,* p.p. of *verliezen* to lose + *hoop* troop (lit.: heap)

form (fɔːm) *n* **1** the shape or configuration of something as distinct from its colour, texture, etc. **2** the particular mode, appearance, etc., in which a thing or person manifests itself: *water in the form of ice.* **3** a type or kind: *imprisonment is a form of punishment.* **4** a printed document, esp. one with spaces in which to insert facts or answers: *an application form.* **5** physical or mental condition, esp. good condition, with reference to ability to perform: *off form.* **6** the previous record of a horse, athlete, etc., esp. with regard to fitness. **7** *Brit. sl.* a criminal record. **8** a fixed mode of artistic expression or representation in literary, musical, or other artistic works: *sonata form.* **9** a mould, frame, etc., that gives shape to something. **10** *Education, chiefly Brit.* a group of children who are taught together. **11** behaviour or procedure, esp. as governed by custom or etiquette: *good form.* **12** formality or ceremony. **13** a prescribed set or order of words, terms, etc., as in a religious ceremony or legal document. **14** *Philosophy.* **14a** the structure of anything as opposed to its content. **14b** essence as opposed to matter. **15** See **logical form. 16** *Brit., Austral., & NZ.* a bench, esp. one that is long, low, and backless. **17** a hare's nest. **18** any of the various ways in which a word may be spelt or inflected. ◆ *vb* **19** to give shape or form to or to take shape or form, esp. a particular shape. **20** to come or bring into existence: *a scum formed.* **21** to make or construct or be made or constructed. **22** to construct or develop in the mind: *to form an opinion.* **23** *(tr)* to train or mould by instruction or example. **24** *(tr)* to acquire or develop: *to form a habit.* **25** *(tr)* to be an element of or constitute: *this plank will form a bridge.* **26** *(tr)* to organize: *to form a club.* ORIG C13: from OF, from L *forma* shape, model

-form *adj combining form.* having the shape or form of or

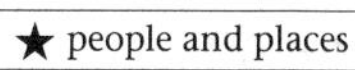
★ people and places

resembling: *cruciform; vermiform.* ORIG from NL *-formis,* from L, from *fōrma* FORM

formal ('fɔːməl) *adj* **1** of or following established forms, conventions, etc.: *a formal document.* **2** characterized by observation of conventional forms of ceremony, behaviour, etc.: *a formal dinner.* **3** methodical or stiff. **4** suitable for occasions organized according to conventional ceremony: *formal dress.* **5** denoting idiom, vocabulary, etc., used by educated speakers and writers of a language. **6** acquired by study in academic institutions. **7** symmetrical in form: *a formal garden.* **8** of or relating to the appearance, form, etc., of something as distinguished from its substance. **9** logically deductive: *formal proof.* **10** denoting a second-person pronoun in some languages: *in French the pronoun "vous" is formal, while "tu" is informal.* ORIG C14: from L *formālis*
▸ **'formally** *adv* ▸ **'formalness** *n*

formaldehyde (fɔː'mældɪˌhaɪd) *n* a colourless poisonous irritating gas with a pungent characteristic odour, used as formalin and in the manufacture of synthetic resins. Formula: HCHO. Systematic name: **methanal.** ORIG C19: FORM(IC) + ALDEHYDE; on the model of G *Formaldehyd*

formalin ('fɔːməlɪn) *n* a solution of formaldehyde in water, used as a disinfectant, preservative for biological specimens, etc.

formalism ('fɔːməˌlɪzəm) *n* **1** scrupulous or excessive adherence to outward form at the expense of content. **2** the mathematical or logical structure of a scientific argument as distinguished from its subject matter. **3** *Theatre.* a stylized mode of production. **4** (in Marxist criticism, etc.) excessive concern with artistic technique at the expense of social values, etc.
▸ **'formalist** *n* ▸ **ˌformal'istic** *adj*

formality (fɔː'mælɪtɪ) *n, pl* **formalities. 1** a requirement of custom, etiquette, etc. **2** the quality of being formal or conventional. **3** strict or excessive observance of ceremony, etc.

formalize *or* **formalise** ('fɔːməˌlaɪz) *vb* **formalizes, formalizing, formalized** *or* **formalises, formalising, formalised. 1** to be or make formal. **2** (*tr*) to make official or valid. **3** (*tr*) to give a definite shape or form to.
▸ **ˌformali'zation** *or* **ˌformali'sation** *n*

formal language *n* any of various languages designed for use in fields such as mathematics, logic, or computer programming, the symbols and formulas of which stand in precisely specified syntactic and semantic relations to one another.

formal logic *n* the study of systems of deductive argument in which symbols are used to represent precisely defined categories of expressions.

Forman ★ ('fɔːmən) *n* **Miloš** ('miːləʊʃ). born 1932, Czech film director working in the USA since 1968. His films include *One Flew over the Cuckoo's Nest* (1976), *Amadeus* (1985), and *Man on the Moon* (2000).

formant ('fɔːmənt) *n Acoustics, phonetics.* any of the constituents of a sound, esp. a vowel sound, that impart to the sound its own special quality, tone colour, or timbre.

format ('fɔːmæt) *n* **1** the general appearance of a publication, including type style, paper, binding, etc. **2** style, plan, or arrangement, as of a television programme. **3** *Computing.* **3a** the defined arrangement of data encoded in a file or, for example, on magnetic disk or CD-ROM, that is essential for the correct recording and recovery of data on different devices. **3b** the arrangement of text on printed output or on a display screen. ◆ *vb* **formats, formatting, formatted.** (*tr*) **4** to arrange (a book, page, etc.) into a specified format. ORIG C19: via F from G, from L *liber formātus* volume formed

formation (fɔː'meɪʃən) *n* **1** the act of giving or taking form or existence. **2** something that is formed. **3** the manner in which something is arranged. **4a** a formal arrangement of a number of persons or things acting as a unit, such as a troop of soldiers or a football team. **4b** (*as modifier*): *formation dancing.* **5** a series of rocks with certain characteristics in common.

formative ('fɔːmətɪv) *adj* **1** of or relating to formation, development, or growth: *formative years.* **2** shaping; moulding: *a formative experience.* **3** functioning in the formation of derived, inflected, or compound words. ◆ *n* **4** an inflectional or derivational affix.
▸ **'formatively** *adv* ▸ **'formativeness** *n*

Formby ★ ('fɔːmbɪ) *n* **George.** Real name *George Booth.* 1904–61, British comedian. He made many musical films in the 1930s, accompanying his songs on the ukulele.

form class *n* **1** another term for **part of speech. 2** a group of words distinguished by common inflections, such as the weak verbs of English.

forme *or US* **form** (fɔːm) *n Printing.* type matter, blocks, etc., assembled in a chase and ready for printing. ORIG C15: from F: FORM

former[1] ('fɔːmə) *adj* (*prenominal*) **1** belonging to or occurring in an earlier time: *former glory.* **2** having been at a previous time: *a former colleague.* **3** denoting the first or first mentioned of two. ◆ *n* **4 the former.** the first or first mentioned of two: distinguished from *latter.*

former[2] ('fɔːmə) *n* **1** a person or thing that forms or shapes. **2** *Electrical engineering.* a tool for giving a coil or winding the required shape.

formerly ('fɔːməlɪ) *adv* at or in a former time; in the past.

formic ('fɔːmɪk) *adj* **1** of, relating to, or derived from ants. **2** of, containing, or derived from formic acid. ORIG C18: from L *formīca* ant; the acid occurs naturally in ants

Formica (fɔː'maɪkə) *n Trademark.* any of various laminated plastic sheets used esp. for heat-resistant surfaces.

formic acid *n* a colourless corrosive liquid carboxylic acid found in some insects, esp. ants, and many plants: used in the manufacture of insecticides. Formula: HCOOH. Systematic name: **methanoic acid.**

formidable ('fɔːmɪdəbᵊl) *adj* **1** arousing or likely to inspire fear or dread. **2** extremely difficult to defeat, overcome, manage, etc. **3** tending to inspire awe or admiration because of great size, excellence, etc. ORIG C15: from L, from *formīdāre* to dread, from *formīdō* fear
▸ **'formidably** *adv*

formless ('fɔːmlɪs) *adj* without a definite shape or form; amorphous.
▸ **'formlessly** *adv*

form letter *n* a single copy of a letter that has been mechanically reproduced in large numbers for circulation.

Formosa ★ (fɔː'məʊsə) *n* the former name of **Taiwan.**

Formosa Strait ★ *n* an arm of the Pacific between Taiwan and mainland China, linking the East and South China Seas. Also called: **Taiwan Strait.**

formula ('fɔːmjʊlə) *n, pl* **formulas** *or* **formulae** (-ˌliː). **1** an established form or set of words, as used in religious ceremonies, legal proceedings, etc. **2** *Maths., physics.* a general relationship, principle, or rule stated, often as an equation, in the form of symbols. **3** *Chem.* a representation of molecules, radicals, ions, etc., expressed in the symbols of the atoms of their constituent elements. **4a** a method, pattern, or rule for doing or producing something, often one proved to be successful. **4b** (*as modifier*): *formula fiction.* **5** *US & Canad.* a prescription for making up a medicine, baby's food, etc. **6** *Motor racing.* the category in which a type of car competes, judged according to engine size, weight, and fuel capacity. ORIG C17: from L: dim. of *forma* FORM
▸ **formulaic** (ˌfɔːmjʊ'leɪɪk) *adj*

Formula One *n* **1** the top class of professional motor racing. **2** the most important world championship in motor racing.

formularize *or* **formularise** ('fɔːmjʊləˌraɪz) *vb* **formularizes, formularizing, formularized** *or* **formularises, formularising, formularised.** a less common word for **formulate** (sense 1).

formulary ('fɔːmjʊlərɪ) *n, pl* **formularies. 1** a book of prescribed formulas, esp. relating to religious procedure or doctrine. **2** a formula. **3** *Pharmacol.* a book containing a list of pharmaceutical products with their formulas. ◆ *adj* **4** of or relating to a formula.

formulate ('fɔːmjʊˌleɪt) *vb* **formulates, formulating, formulated.** (*tr*) **1** to put into or express in systematic terms; express in or as if in a formula. **2** to devise.
▸ **ˌformu'lation** *n*

formwork ('fɔːmˌwɜːk) *n* an arrangement of wooden boards, etc., used to shape concrete while it is setting.

fornicate ('fɔːnɪˌkeɪt) *vb* **fornicates, fornicating, fornicated.** (*intr*) to commit fornication. ORIG C16: from LL *fornicārī*, from L *fornix* vault, brothel situated therein
▸ **'forniˌcator** *n*

fornication (ˌfɔːnɪ'keɪʃən) *n* **1** voluntary sexual intercourse outside marriage. **2** *Bible.* sexual immorality in general, esp. adultery.

Forrest ★ ('fɒrɪst) *n* **John,** 1st Baron Forrest. 1847–1918, Australian statesman and explorer; first premier of Western Australia (1890–1901).

forsake (fə'seɪk) *vb* **forsakes, forsaking, forsook, forsaken.** (*tr*) **1** to abandon. **2** to give up (something valued or enjoyed). ORIG OE *forsacan*
▸ **for'saker** *n*

forsaken (fə'seɪkən) *vb* **1** the past participle of **forsake.** ◆ *adj* **2** completely deserted or helpless.
▸ **for'sakenly** *adv* ▸ **for'sakenness** *n*

forsook (fə'sʊk) *vb* the past tense of **forsake.**

forsooth (fə'suːθ) *adv Arch.* in truth; indeed. ORIG OE *forsōth*

Forster ★ ('fɔːstə) *n* **E(dward) M(organ).** 1879–1970, English novelist, short-story writer, and essayist. His best-known novels are *A Room with a View* (1908), *Howard's End* (1910), and *A Passage to India* (1924), in all of which he stresses the need for sincerity and sensitivity in human relationships and criticizes English middle-class values.

forswear (fɔː'swɛə) *vb* **forswears, forswearing, forswore, forsworn. 1** (*tr*) to reject or renounce with determination or as upon oath. **2** (*tr*) to deny or disavow absolutely or upon oath. **3** to perjure (oneself). ORIG OE *forswearian*
▸ **for'swearer** *n*

forsworn (fɔː'swɔːn) *vb* the past participle of **forswear.**
▸ **for'swornness** *n*

Forsyth ★ (fɔː'saɪθ) *n* **1 Bill.** born 1947, Scottish screenwriter and film director. His films include *Gregory's Girl* (1981), *Local Hero* (1983), and *Rebecca's Daughters* (1992). **2 Frederick.** born 1938, British thriller writer. His books include *The Day of the Jackal* (1970), *The Odessa File* (1972), and *The Fourth Protocol* (1984).

forsythia (fɔː'saɪθɪə) *n* a shrub native to China, Japan, and SE Europe but widely cultivated for its showy yellow bell-shaped flowers, which appear in spring before the foliage. ORIG C19: NL, after William *Forsyth* (1737–1804), E botanist

fort (fɔːt) *n* **1** a fortified enclosure, building, or position able to be defended against an enemy. **2 hold the fort.** *Inf.* to guard something temporarily. ORIG C15: from OF, from *fort* (adj) strong, from L *fortis*

fort. *abbrev. for:* **1** fortification. **2** fortified.

Fortaleza ★ (*Portuguese* forta'leza) *n* a port in NE Brazil, capital of Ceará state. Pop.: 2 660 000 (1995). Also called: **Ceará.**

Fort-de-France ★ (*French* fɔrdəfrɑ̃s) *n* the capital of Martinique, a port on the W coast: commercial centre of the French Antilles. Pop.: 104 000 (1995 est.).

forte[1] (fɔːt, 'fɔːteɪ) *n* **1** something at which a person excels: *cooking is my forte.* **2** *Fencing.* the stronger section of a sword, between the hilt and the middle. ORIG C17: from F, from *fort* (adj) strong, from L *fortis*

forte[2] ('fɔːtɪ) *Music.* ◆ *adj, adv* **1** loud or loudly. Symbol: f ◆ *n* **2** a loud passage in music. ORIG C18: from It., from L *fortis* strong

forte-piano (ˌfɔːtɪ'pjɑːnəʊ) *Music.* ◆ *adj, adv* **1** loud and then immediately soft. Symbol: fp ◆ *n* **2** a note played in this way.

forth (fɔːθ) *adv* **1** forward in place, time, order, or degree. **2** out, as from concealment or inaction. **3** away, as from a place or country. **4 and so forth.** and so on. ◆ *prep* **5** *Arch.* out of. ORIG OE

Forth ★ (fɔːθ) *n* **1 Firth of.** an inlet of the North Sea in SE Scotland: spanned by a cantilever railway bridge 1600 m (almost exactly 1 mile) long (1889), and by a road bridge (1964). **2** a river in central Scotland, flowing generally SE to the Firth of Forth. Length: about 104 km (65 miles).

forthcoming (ˌfɔːθ'kʌmɪŋ) *adj* **1** approaching in time: *the forthcoming debate.* **2** about to appear: *his forthcoming book.* **3** available or ready. **4** open or sociable.

forthright *adj* ('fɔːθˌraɪt). **1** direct and outspoken. ◆ *adv* (ˌfɔːθ'raɪt, 'fɔːθˌraɪt), *also* **forthrightly. 2** in a direct manner; frankly. **3** at once.
▸ **'forthˌrightness** *n*

forthwith (ˌfɔːθ'wɪθ) *adv* at once.

fortification (ˌfɔːtɪfɪ'keɪʃən) *n* **1** the act, art, or science of fortifying or strengthening. **2a** a wall, mound, etc., used to fortify a place. **2b** such works collectively.

fortify ('fɔːtɪˌfaɪ) *vb* **fortifies, fortifying, fortified.** (*mainly tr*) **1** (*also intr*) to make (a place) defensible, as by building walls, etc. **2** to strengthen physically, mentally, or morally. **3** to add alcohol to (wine), in order to produce sherry, port, etc. **4** to increase the nutritious value of (a food), as by adding vitamins. **5** to confirm: *to fortify an argument.* ORIG C15: from OF, from LL, from L *fortis* strong + *facere* to make
▸ **'fortiˌfiable** *adj* ▸ **'fortiˌfier** *n*

fortissimo (fɔː'tɪsɪˌməʊ) *Music.* ◆ *adj, adv* **1** very loud. Symbol: ff ◆ *n* **2** a very loud passage in music. ORIG C18: from It., from L, from *fortis* strong

fortitude ('fɔːtɪˌtjuːd) *n* strength and firmness of mind. ORIG C15: from L *fortitūdō* courage

Fort Knox ★ (nɒks) *n* a military reservation in N Kentucky: site of the US Gold Bullion Depository. Pop.: 38 277 (1989 est.).

Fort Lamy ★ ('fɔːt 'lɑːmɪ; *French* fɔr lami) *n* the former name (until 1973) of **Ndjamena.**

fortnight ('fɔːtˌnaɪt) *n* a period of 14 consecutive days; two weeks. ORIG OE *fēowertīene niht* fourteen nights

fortnightly ('fɔːtˌnaɪtlɪ) *Chiefly Brit.* ◆ *adj* **1** occurring or appearing once each fortnight. ◆ *adv* **2** once a fortnight. ◆ *n, pl* **fortnightlies. 3** a publication issued at intervals of two weeks.

Fortran ('fɔːtræn) *n* a high-level computer programming language for mathematical and scientific purposes. ORIG C20: from *for(mula) tran(slation)*

fortress ('fɔːtrɪs) *n* **1** a large fort or fortified town. **2** a place or source of refuge or support. ◆ *vb* **3** (*tr*) to protect. ORIG C13: from OF, from Med. L *fortalitia,* from L *fortis* strong

Fort Sumter ★ ('sʌmtə) *n* a fort in SE South Carolina, guarding Charleston Harbour. Its capture by Confederate forces (1861) was the first action of the Civil War.

fortuitous (fɔː'tjuːɪtəs) *adj* happening by chance, esp. by a lucky chance. ORIG C17: from L *fortuitus* happening by chance, from *fors* chance, luck
▸ **for'tuitously** *adv*

fortuity (fɔː'tjuːɪtɪ) *n, pl* **fortuities. 1** a chance or accidental occurrence. **2** chance or accident.

Fortuna ★ (fɔː'tjuːnə) *n* the Roman goddess of fortune and good luck. Greek counterpart: **Tyche.**

fortunate ('fɔːtʃənɪt) *adj* **1** having good luck. **2** occurring by or bringing good fortune or luck.
▸ **'fortunately** *adv*

fortune ('fɔːtʃən) *n* **1** an amount of wealth or material prosperity, esp. a great amount. **2 small fortune.** a large sum of money. **3** a power or force, often personalized, regarded as being responsible for human affairs. **4** luck, esp. when favourable. **5** (*often pl*) a person's destiny. ◆ *vb* **fortunes, fortuning, fortuned. 6** (*intr*) *Arch.* to happen by chance. ORIG C13: from OF, from L, from *fors* chance

fortune-hunter *n* a person who seeks to secure a fortune, esp. through marriage.

fortune-teller *n* a person who makes predictions about the future as by looking into a crystal ball, etc.
▸ **'fortune-ˌtelling** *adj, n*

Fort William ★ *n* a town in W Scotland, in Highland council area at the head of Loch Linnhe: tourist centre; the fort itself, built in 1655 and renamed after William III in 1690, was demolished in 1866. Pop.: 10 391 (1991).

Fort Worth ★ (wɜːθ) *n* a city in N Texas, at the junction of the Clear and West forks of the Trinity River: aircraft works, electronics. Pop.: 479 716 (1996 est.).

forty (ˈfɔːtɪ) *n, pl* **forties. 1** the cardinal number that is the product of ten and four. **2** a numeral, 40, XL, etc., representing this number. **3** something representing, represented by, or consisting of 40 units. ◆ *determiner* **4a** amounting to forty: *forty thieves.* **4b** (*as pronoun*): *there were forty in the herd.* ORIG OE *fēowertig*
▸ ˈ**fortieth** *adj, n*

forty-five *n* a gramophone record played at 45 revolutions per minute.

Forty-Five *n* **the.** *British history.* another name for the **Jacobite Rebellion** of 1745–46. See **Young Pretender.**

forty-niner *n* (*sometimes cap.*) *US history.* a prospector who took part in the California gold rush of 1849.

forty winks *n* (*functioning as sing or pl*) *Inf.* a short light sleep; nap.

forum (ˈfɔːrəm) *n, pl* **forums** *or* **fora** (-rə). **1** a meeting for the open discussion of subjects of public interest. **2** a medium for open discussion, such as a magazine. **3** a public meeting place for open discussion. **4** a court; tribunal. **5** *S. African.* a pressure group of leaders or representatives, esp. Black leaders or representatives. **6** (in ancient Italy) an open space serving as a city's marketplace and centre of public business. ORIG C15: from L: public place

Forum *or* **Forum Romanum** ★ (rəʊˈmɑːnəm) *n* **the.** the main forum of ancient Rome.

forward (ˈfɔːwəd) *adj* **1** directed or moving ahead. **2** lying or situated in or near the front part of something. **3** presumptuous, pert, or impudent. **4** well developed or advanced, esp. in physical or intellectual development. **5a** of or relating to the future or favouring change. **5b** (*in combination*): *forward-looking.* **6** (*often postpositive*) *Arch.* ready, eager, or willing. **7** *Commerce.* relating to fulfilment at a future date. ◆ *n* **8** an attacking player in any of various sports, such as soccer. ◆ *adv* **9** a variant of **forwards. 10** (ˈfɔːwəd; *Naut.* ˈfɒrəd). towards the front or bow of an aircraft or ship. **11** into a position of being subject to public scrutiny: *the witness came forward.* ◆ *vb* (*tr*) **12** to send forward or pass on to an ultimate destination: *the letter was forwarded.* **13** to advance or promote: *to forward one's career.* ORIG OE *foreweard*
▸ ˈ**forwarder** *n* ▸ ˈ**forwardly** *adv* ▸ ˈ**forwardness** *n*

forwards (ˈfɔːwədz) *or* **forward** *adv* **1** towards or at a place ahead or in advance, esp. in space but also in time. **2** towards the front.

forwent (fɔːˈwɛnt) *vb* the past tense of **forgo.**

forza (ˈfɔːtsə) *n Music.* force. ORIG C19: It., lit.: force

Foshan (ˈfɔːˈʃɑːn) *or* **Fatshan** ★ *n* a city in SE China, in W Guangdong province. Pop.: 303 160 (1990 est). Also called: **Namhoi.**

fossa (ˈfɒsə) *n, pl* **fossae** (-siː). an anatomical depression or hollow area. ORIG C19: from L: ditch, from *fossus* dug up, from *fodere* to dig up

fosse *or* **foss** (fɒs) *n* a ditch or moat, esp. one dug as a fortification. ORIG C14: from OF, from L *fossa;* see FOSSA

Fosse Way ★ (fɒs) *n* a Roman road in Britain between Lincoln and Exeter, with a fosse on each side.

fossick (ˈfɒsɪk) *vb Austral. & NZ.* **1** (*intr*) to search for gold or precious stones in abandoned workings, rivers, etc. **2** to rummage or search for (something): *to fossick around for.* ORIG C19: Austral., prob. from E dialect *fussock* to bustle about, from FUSS
▸ ˈ**fossicker** *n*

fossil (ˈfɒsᵊl) *n* **1a** a relic or representation of a plant or animal that existed in a past geological age, occurring in the form of mineralized bones, shells, etc. **1b** (*as modifier*): *fossil insects.* **2** *Inf., derog.* a person, idea, thing, etc., that is outdated or incapable of change. **3** *Linguistics.* a form once current but now appearing only in one or two special contexts. ORIG C17: from L *fossilis* dug up, from *fodere* to dig

fossil fuel *n* any naturally occurring fuel, such as coal, and natural gas, formed by the decomposition of prehistoric organisms.

fossiliferous (ˌfɒsɪˈlɪfərəs) *adj* (of sedimentary rocks) containing fossils.

fossilize *or* **fossilise** (ˈfɒsɪˌlaɪz) *vb* **fossilizes, fossilizing, fossilized** *or* **fossilises, fossilising, fossilised. 1** to convert or be converted into a fossil. **2** to become or cause to become antiquated or inflexible.
▸ ˌ**fossiliˈzation** *or* ˌ**fossiliˈsation** *n*

fossorial (fɒˈsɔːrɪəl) *adj* (of the forelimbs and skeleton of burrowing animals) adapted for digging. ORIG C19: from Med. L, from L *fossor* digger, from *fodere* to dig

foster (ˈfɒstə) *vb* (*tr*) **1** to promote the growth or development of. **2** to bring up (a child, etc.). **3** to cherish (a plan, hope, etc.) in one's mind. **4** *Chiefly Brit.* **4a** to place (a child) in the care of foster parents. **4b** to bring up under fosterage. ◆ *adj* **5** indicating relationship through fostering and not through birth: *foster child, foster mother.* **6** of or involved in the rearing of a child by persons other than his natural parents: *foster home.* ORIG OE *fōstrian* to feed, from *fōstor* FOOD
▸ ˈ**fosterer** *n* ▸ ˈ**fostering** *n*

Foster ★ (ˈfɒstə) *n* **1 Jodie.** born 1962, US film actress and director: her films include *Taxi Driver* (1976), *Little Man Tate* (1991; also directed), and *Anna and the King* (1999). **2 Norman,** Baron. born 1935, British architect. His works include the Willis Faber building (1978) in Ipswich, Hong Kong airport, China (1998), and the renovated Reichstag, Berlin (1999). **3 Stephen Collins.** 1826–64, US composer of songs such as *The Old Folks at Home* and *Oh Susanna.*

fosterage (ˈfɒstərɪdʒ) *n* **1** the act of caring for a foster child. **2** the state of being a foster child. **3** the act of encouraging.

Fotheringhay ★ (ˈfɒðərɪŋˌgeɪ) *n* a village in E England, in NE Northamptonshire: ruined castle, scene of the imprisonment and execution of Mary Queen of Scots (1587).

Foucault ★ (*French* fuko) *n* **1 Jean Bernard Léon** (ʒɑ̃ bɛrnar leɔ̃). 1819–68, French physicist. He determined the speed of light, devised a pendulum to demonstrate the rotation of the earth, and invented the gyroscope. **2 Michel** (miʃɛl). 1926–84, French philosopher. His publications include *Histoire de la folie* (1961) and *Les Mots et les choses* (1966).

Foucquet ★ (*French* fukɛ) *n* a variant spelling of (Nicolas) **Fouquet.**

fought (fɔːt) *vb* the past tense and past participle of **fight.**

foul (faʊl) *adj* **1** offensive to the senses; revolting. **2** stinking. **3** charged with or full of dirt or offensive matter. **4** (of food) putrid; rotten. **5** morally or spiritually offensive. **6** obscene; vulgar: *foul language.* **7** unfair: *to resort to foul means.* **8** (esp. of weather) unpleasant or adverse. **9** blocked or obstructed with dirt or foreign matter: *a foul drain.* **10** (of the bottom of a vessel) covered with barnacles that slow forward motion. **11** *Inf.* unsatisfactory; bad: *a foul book.* ◆ *n* **12** *Sport.* **12a** a violation of the rules. **12b** (*as modifier*): *a foul blow.* **13** an entanglement or collision, esp. in sailing or fishing. ◆ *vb* **14** to make or become polluted. **15** to become or cause to become entangled. **16** (*tr*) to disgrace. **17** to become or cause to become clogged. **18** (*tr*) *Naut.* (of underwater growth) to cling to (the bottom of a vessel) so as to slow its motion. **19** (*tr*) *Sport.* to commit a foul against (an opponent). **20** (*intr*) *Sport.* to infringe the rules. **21** to collide (with a boat, etc.). ◆ *adv* **22** in a foul manner. **23 fall foul of. 23a** come into conflict with. **23b** *Naut.* to come into collision with. ORIG OE *fūl*
▸ ˈ**foully** *adv* ▸ ˈ**foulness** *n*

foulard (fuːˈlɑːd) *n* a soft light fabric of plain-weave or twill-weave silk or rayon, usually with a printed design. ORIG C19: from F, from ?

Foulness ★ (faʊlˈnɛs) *n* a flat marshy island in SE England, in Essex north of the Thames estuary.

foul play *n* **1** violent or treacherous conduct, esp. murder. **2** a violation of the rules in a game or sport.

foul up *vb* (*adv*) **1** (*tr*) to bungle. **2** (*tr*) to contaminate. **3** to be or cause to be blocked, choked, or entangled. ◆ *n* **foul-up. 4** a state of confusion or muddle caused by bungling.

found[1] (faʊnd) *vb* **1** the past tense and past participle of **find.** ◆ *adj* **2** furnished or fitted out. **3** *Brit.* with meals, heating, etc., provided without extra charge.

found[2] (faʊnd) *vb* **1** (*tr*) to bring into being or establish (something, such as an institution, etc.). **2** (*tr*) to build or establish the foundation of. **3** (*also intr;* foll. by *on* or *upon*) to have a basis (in). ORIG C13: from OF, from L, from *fundus* bottom

found[3] (faʊnd) *vb* (*tr*) **1** to cast (a material, such as metal or glass) by melting and pouring into a mould. **2** to make (articles) in this way. ORIG C14: from OF, from L *fundere* to melt

foundation (faʊn'deɪʃən) *n* **1** that on which something is founded. **2** (*often pl*) a construction below the ground that distributes the load of a building, wall, etc. **3** the base on which something stands. **4** the act of founding or establishing or the state of being founded or established. **5** an endowment for the support of an institution such as a school. **6** an institution supported by an endowment, often one that provides funds for charities, research, etc. **7** a cosmetic used as a base for make-up.
▸ **foun'dational** *adj*

foundation garment *n* a woman's undergarment worn to shape and support the figure. Also called: **foundation.**

foundation stone *n* a stone laid at a ceremony to mark the foundation of a new building.

foundation subjects *pl n Brit. education.* the subjects studied as part of the National Curriculum, including the compulsory core subjects.

founder[1] ('faʊndə) *n* a person who establishes an institution, society, etc. ORIG C14: see FOUND[2]

founder[2] ('faʊndə) *vb* (*intr*) **1** (of a ship, etc.) to sink. **2** to break down or fail: *the project foundered.* **3** to sink into or become stuck in soft ground. **4** to collapse. **5** (of a horse) to stumble or go lame. ORIG C13: from OF *fondrer* to submerge, from L *fundus* bottom

> **USAGE NOTE** *Founder* is sometimes wrongly used where *flounder* is meant: *this unexpected turn of events left him floundering* (not *foundering*).

founder[3] ('faʊndə) *n* **a** a person who makes metal castings. **b** (*in combination*): *an iron founder.* ORIG C15: see FOUND[3]

foundling ('faʊndlɪŋ) *n* an abandoned infant whose parents are not known. ORIG C13 *foundeling;* see FIND

foundry ('faʊndrɪ) *n, pl* **foundries.** a place in which metal castings are produced. ORIG C17: from OF, from *fondre;* see FOUND[3]

fount[1] (faʊnt) *n* **1** *Poetic.* a spring or fountain. **2** source. ORIG C16: back formation from FOUNTAIN

fount[2] (faʊnt, fɒnt) *n Printing.* a complete set of type of one style and size. Also called (esp. US and Canad.): **font.** ORIG C16: from OF *fonte* a founding, casting, from Vulgar L *funditus* (unattested) a casting, from L *fundere* to melt

fountain ('faʊntɪn) *n* **1** a jet or spray of water or some other liquid. **2** a structure from which such a jet or a number of such jets spurt. **3** a natural spring of water, esp. the source of a stream. **4** a stream, jet, or cascade of sparks, lava, etc. **5** a principal source. **6** a reservoir, as for oil in a lamp. ORIG C15: from OF, from LL, from L *fons* spring, source
▸ **'fountained** *adj*

fountainhead ('faʊntɪn,hɛd) *n* **1** a spring that is the source of a stream. **2** a principal or original source.

fountain pen *n* a pen the nib of which is supplied with ink from a cartridge or a reservoir in its barrel.

Fouqué ★ (*German* fu'ke:) *n* **Friedrich Heinrich Karl** ('fri:drɪç 'hainrɪç karl), Baron de la Motte. 1777–1843, German romantic writer; author of *Undine* (1811).

Fouquet ★ (*French* fukɛ) *n* **1 Jean** (ʒɑ̃). ?1420–?80, French painter and miniaturist. **2** Also: **Foucquet. Nicolas** (nikɔlɑ), *Marquis de Belle-Isle.* 1615–80, French statesman; superintendent of finance (1653–61) under Louis XIV; imprisoned for embezzlement.

Fouquier-Tinville ★ (*French* fukjetɛ̃vil) *n* **Antoine Quentin** (ɑ̃twan kɑ̃tɛ̃). 1746–95, French revolutionary; as public prosecutor (1793–94) during the Reign of Terror, he sanctioned the guillotining of Robespierre and many others.

four (fɔː) *n* **1** the cardinal number that is the sum of three and one. **2** a numeral, 4, IV, etc., representing this number. **3** something representing, represented by, or consisting of four units, such as a playing card with four symbols on it. **4** Also called: **four o'clock.** four hours after noon or midnight. **5** *Cricket.* **5a** a shot that crosses the boundary after hitting the ground. **5b** the four runs scored for such a shot. **6** *Rowing.* **6a** a racing shell propelled by four oarsmen. **6b** the crew of such a shell. ◆ *determiner* **7a** amounting to four: *four times.* **7b** (*as pronoun*): *four are ready.* ORIG OE *fēower*

four-by-four *n* a vehicle equipped with four-wheel drive.

four flush *n* a useless poker hand, containing four of a suit and one odd card.

fourfold ('fɔː,fəʊld) *adj* **1** equal to or having four times as many or as much. **2** composed of four parts. ◆ *adv* **3** by or up to four times as many or as much.

Fourier ★ ('fʊərɪ,eɪ; *French* furje) *n* **1** (**François Marie**) **Charles** (ʃarl). 1772–1837, French social reformer: propounded a system of cooperatives in *Le Nouveau monde industriel* (1829–30). **2 Jean Baptiste Joseph** (ʒɑ̃ batist ʒozɛf). 1768–1830, French mathematician and Egyptologist, noted for the method of analysis named after him.

four-in-hand *n* **1** a road vehicle drawn by four horses and driven by one driver. **2** a four-horse team. **3** *US.* a long narrow tie tied in a flat slipknot with the ends dangling.

four-leaf clover *or* **four-leaved clover** *n* a clover with four leaves rather than three, supposed to bring good luck.

four-letter word *n* any of several short English words referring to sex or excrement: regarded generally as offensive or obscene.

Fournier ★ (*French* furnje) *n* See **Alain-Fournier.**

four-o'clock *n* a tropical American plant, cultivated for its tubular yellow, red, or white flowers that open in late afternoon. Also called: **marvel-of-Peru.**

four-poster *n* a bed with posts at each corner supporting a canopy and curtains.

fourscore (,fɔː'skɔː) *determiner* an archaic word for **eighty.**

foursome ('fɔːsəm) *n* **1** a set or company of four. **2** Also called: **four-ball.** *Golf.* a game between two pairs of players.

foursquare (,fɔː'skwɛə) *adv* **1** squarely; firmly. ◆ *adj* **2** solid and strong. **3** forthright. **4** a rare word for **square.**

four-stroke *adj* designating an internal-combustion engine in which the piston makes four strokes for every explosion.

fourteen ('fɔː'tiːn) *n* **1** the cardinal number that is the sum of ten and four. **2** a numeral, 14, XIV, etc., representing this number. **3** something represented by or consisting of 14 units. ◆ *determiner* **4a** amounting to fourteen: *fourteen cats.* **4b** (*as pronoun*): *the fourteen who remained.* ORIG OE *fēowertīene*
▸ **'four'teenth** *adj, n*

fourth (fɔːθ) *adj* (*usually prenominal*) **1a** coming after the third in order, position, time, etc. Often written: 4th. **1b** (*as n*): *the fourth in succession.* **2** denoting the highest forward ratio of a gearbox in most motor vehicles. ◆ *n* **3** *Music.* **3a** the interval between one note and another four notes away from it in a diatonic scale. **3b** one of two notes constituting such an interval in relation to the other. **4** the fourth forward ratio of a gearbox in a motor vehicle, usually the highest gear in cars. **5** a less common word for **quarter** (sense 2). ◆ *adv also:* **fourthly. 6** after the third person, position, event, etc. ◆ *sentence connector. also:* **fourthly. 7** as the fourth point.

fourth dimension *n* **1** the dimension of time, which in addition to three spatial dimensions specifies the position of a point or particle. **2** the concept in science fic-

tion of a dimension in addition to three spatial dimensions.
▸ ˌ**fourth-diˈmensional** *adj*

fourth estate *n* (*sometimes caps.*) journalists or their profession; the press.

four-wheel drive *n* a system used in motor vehicles in which all four wheels are connected to the source of power.

fovea (ˈfəʊvɪə) *n, pl* **foveae** (-vɪˌiː). *Anat.* any small pit or depression in the surface of a bodily organ or part. ORIG C19: from L: a small pit

Fowey ★ (fɔɪ) *n* a resort and fishing village in SW England, in Cornwall, linked administratively with St Austell in 1968. Pop.: 1939 (1991).

fowl (faʊl) *n* **1** Also called: **domestic fowl.** a domesticated gallinaceous bird occurring in many varieties. **2** any other bird that is used as food or hunted as game. **3** the flesh or meat of fowl, esp. of chicken. **4** an archaic word for any **bird.** ◆ *vb* **5** (*intr*) to hunt or snare wildfowl. ORIG OE *fugol*
▸ ˈ**fowler** *n* ▸ ˈ**fowling** *n, adj*

Fowler ★ (ˈfaʊlə) *n* **Henry Watson.** 1858–1933, English lexicographer and grammarian; compiler of *Modern English Usage* (1926).

Fowles ★ (faʊlz) *n* **John.** born 1926, British novelist. His books include *The Collector* (1963), *The French Lieutenant's Woman* (1969), and *The Tree* (1991).

Fowliang *or* **Fou-liang** ★ (ˈfuːˈljæŋ) *n* a variant transliteration of the Chinese name for **Jingdezhen.**

fowl pest *n* an acute and usually fatal viral disease of domestic fowl, characterized by discoloration of the comb and wattles.

fox (fɒks) *n, pl* **foxes** *or* **fox. 1** any canine mammal of the genus *Vulpes* and related genera. They are mostly predators and have a pointed muzzle and a bushy tail. **2** the fur of any of these animals, usually reddish-brown or grey in colour. **3** a person who is cunning and sly. ◆ *vb* **4** (*tr*) *Inf.* to perplex: *to fox a person with a problem.* **5** to cause (paper, wood, etc.) to become discoloured with spots, or (of paper, etc.) to become discoloured. **6** (*tr*) to trick; deceive. **7** (*intr*) to act deceitfully or craftily. ORIG OE
▸ ˈ**foxˌlike** *adj*

Fox ★ (fɒks) *n* **1 Charles James.** 1749–1806, British Whig statesman. He advocated abolition of the slave trade. **2 George.** 1624–91, English religious leader; founder (1647) of the Society of Friends (Quakers). **3** Sir **William.** 1812–93, New Zealand statesman, born in England: prime minister (1856; 1861–62; 1869–72; 1873).

Foxe ★ (fɒks) *n* **John.** 1516–87, English Protestant clergyman; author of *History of the Acts and Monuments of the Church* (1563), popularly known as the *Book of Martyrs.*

Foxe Basin ★ *n* an arm of the Atlantic in NE Canada, between Melville Peninsula and Baffin Island.

foxfire (ˈfɒksˌfaɪə) *n* a luminescent glow emitted by certain fungi on rotting wood.

foxglove (ˈfɒksˌglʌv) *n* a plant having spikes of purple or white thimble-like flowers. The soft wrinkled leaves are a source of digitalis. ORIG OE

foxhole (ˈfɒksˌhəʊl) *n Mil.* a small pit dug to provide shelter against hostile fire.

foxhound (ˈfɒksˌhaʊnd) *n* a breed of short-haired hound, usually kept for hunting foxes.

fox hunt *n* **1a** the hunting of foxes with hounds. **1b** an instance of this. **2** an organization for fox hunting within a particular area.
▸ ˈ**fox-ˌhunter** *n* ▸ ˈ**fox-ˌhunting** *n*

foxtail (ˈfɒksˌteɪl) *n* any grass of Europe, Asia, and South America, having soft cylindrical spikes of flowers: cultivated as a pasture grass.

Fox Talbot ★ (ˈtɔːlbət) *n* **William Henry.** 1800–77, British physicist; a pioneer of photography.

fox terrier *n* either of two breeds of small tan-black-and-white terrier, the wire-haired and the smooth.

foxtrot (ˈfɒksˌtrɒt) *n* **1** a ballroom dance in quadruple time, combining short and long steps in various sequences. ◆ *vb* **foxtrots, foxtrotting, foxtrotted. 2** (*intr*) to perform this dance.

foxy (ˈfɒksɪ) *adj* **foxier, foxiest. 1** of or resembling a fox, esp. in craftiness. **2** of a reddish-brown colour. **3** (of paper, etc.) spotted, esp. by mildew. **4** *Sl.* sexy; sexually attractive.
▸ ˈ**foxily** *adv* ▸ ˈ**foxiness** *n*

foyer (ˈfɔɪeɪ, ˈfɔɪə) *n* a hall, lobby, or anteroom, as in a hotel, theatre, cinema, etc. ORIG C19: from F: fireplace, from Med. L, from L *focus* fire

fp *Music. abbrev. for* forte-piano.

FP *abbrev. for:* **1** fire plug. **2** former pupil. **3** Also: **fp.** freezing point.

FPA *abbrev. for* Family Planning Association.

fps *abbrev. for:* **1** feet per second. **2** foot-pound-second. **3** *Photog.* frames per second.

fps units *pl, n* an Imperial system of units based on the foot, pound, and second as the units of length, mass, and time.

Fr *abbrev. for:* **1** *Christianity:* **1a** Father. **1b** Frater. ORIG L: brother **2** *the chemical symbol for* francium.

fr. *abbrev. for:* **1** fragment. **2** franc. **3** from.

Fr. *abbrev. for:* **1** France. **2** French.

Fra (frɑː) *n* brother: a title given to an Italian monk or friar. ORIG It., short for *frate* brother, from L *frāter* BROTHER

fracas (ˈfrækɑː) *n* a noisy quarrel; brawl. ORIG C18: from F, from *fracasser* to shatter, from L *frangere* to break, infl. by *quassāre* to shatter

fractal (ˈfræktəl) *n* any of various irregular and fragmented shapes or surfaces that are generated by a series of successive subdivisions. ORIG C20: from L *frāctus,* p.p. of *frangere* to break

fraction (ˈfrækʃən) *n* **1** *Maths.* a ratio of two expressions or numbers other than zero. **2** any part or subdivision. **3** a small piece; fragment. **4** *Chem.* a component of a mixture separated by fractional distillation. **5** *Christianity.* the formal breaking of the bread in Communion. ORIG C14: from LL, from L *fractus* broken, from *frangere* to break
▸ ˈ**fractional** *adj* ▸ ˈ**fractionˌize** *or* ˈ**fractionˌise** *vb*

fractional crystallization *n Chem.* the process of separating the components of a solution on the basis of their different solubilities, by means of evaporating the solution until the least soluble component crystallizes out.

fractional distillation *n* the process of separating the constituents of a liquid mixture by heating it and condensing separately the components according to their different boiling points. Sometimes shortened to **distillation.**

fractionate (ˈfrækʃəˌneɪt) *vb* **fractionates, fractionating, fractionated. 1** to separate or cause to separate into constituents. **2** (*tr*) *Chem.* to obtain (a constituent of a mixture) by a fractional process.
▸ ˌ**fractionˈation** *n*

fractious (ˈfrækʃəs) *adj* **1** irritable. **2** unruly. ORIG C18: from (obs.) *fraction* discord + -OUS
▸ ˈ**fractiously** *adv* ▸ ˈ**fractiousness** *n*

fracture (ˈfræktʃə) *n* **1** the act of breaking or the state of being broken. **2a** the breaking or cracking of a bone or the tearing of a cartilage. **2b** the resulting condition. **3** a division, split, or breach. **4** *Mineralogy.* **4a** the characteristic appearance of the surface of a freshly broken mineral or rock. **4b** the way in which a mineral or rock naturally breaks. ◆ *vb* **fractures, fracturing, fractured. 5** to break or cause to break. **6** to break or crack (a bone) or (of a bone) to become broken or cracked. ORIG C15: from OF, from L, from *frangere* to break
▸ ˈ**fractural** *adj*

fraenum *or* **frenum** (ˈfriːnəm) *n, pl* **fraena** *or* **frena** (-nə). a fold of membrane or skin, such as the fold beneath the tongue. ORIG C18: from L: bridle

fragile (ˈfrædʒaɪl) *adj* **1** able to be broken easily. **2** in a weakened physical state. **3** delicate; light: *a fragile touch.* **4** slight; tenuous. ORIG C17: from L *fragilis,* from *frangere* to break
▸ ˈ**fragilely** *adv* ▸ **fragility** (frəˈdʒɪlɪtɪ) *n*

fragment *n* ('frægmənt). **1** a piece broken off or detached. **2** an incomplete piece: *fragments of a novel.* **3** a scrap; bit. ◆ *vb* (fræg'mɛnt). **4** to break or cause to break into fragments. ORIG C15: from L *fragmentum,* from *frangere* to break
▸ ˌ**fragmen'tation** *n*

fragmentary ('frægməntərɪ) *adj* made up of fragments; disconnected. Also: **fragmental.**

Fragonard ★ (*French* fragɔnar) *n* **Jean-Honoré** (ʒɑ̃ ɔnɔre). 1732–1806, French painter of French court life.

fragrance ('freɪgrəns) *or* **fragrancy** *n, pl* **fragrances** *or* **fragrancies. 1** a pleasant or sweet odour. **2** the state of being fragrant.

fragrant ('freɪgrənt) *adj* having a pleasant or sweet smell. ORIG C15: from L, from *frāgrāre* to emit a smell
▸ '**fragrantly** *adv*

frail[1] (freɪl) *adj* **1** physically weak and delicate. **2** fragile: *a frail craft.* **3** easily corrupted or tempted. ORIG C13: from OF *frele,* from L *fragilis,* FRAGILE

frail[2] (freɪl) *n* **1** a rush basket for figs or raisins. **2** a quantity of raisins or figs equal to between 50 and 75 pounds. ORIG C13: from OF *fraiel,* from ?

frailty ('freɪltɪ) *n, pl* **frailties. 1** physical or moral weakness. **2** (*often pl*) a fault symptomatic of moral weakness.

framboesia *or US* **frambesia** (fræm'biːzɪə) *n Pathol.* another name for **yaws.** ORIG C19: from NL, from F *framboise* raspberry; from its raspberry-like excrescences

frame (freɪm) *n* **1** an open structure that gives shape and support to something, such as the ribs of a ship's hull or an aircraft's fuselage or the beams of a building. **2** an enclosing case or border into which something is fitted: *the frame of a picture.* **3** the system around which something is built up: *the frame of government.* **4** the structure of the human body. **5** a condition; state (esp. in **frame of mind**). **6a** one of a series of exposures on film used in making motion pictures. **6b** an exposure on a film used in still photography. **7** a television picture scanned by one or more electron beams at a particular frequency. **8** *Snooker, etc.* **8a** the wooden triangle used to set up the balls. **8b** the balls when set up. **8c** a single game finished when all the balls have been potted. **9** short for **cold frame. 10** one of the sections of which a beehive is composed, esp. one designed to hold a honeycomb. **11** *Statistics.* an enumeration of a population for the purposes of sampling. **12** *Sl.* another word for **frame-up. 13** *Obs.* shape; form. ◆ *vb* **frames, framing, framed.** (*mainly tr*) **14** to construct by fitting parts together. **15** to draw up the plans or basic details for: *to frame a policy.* **16** to compose or conceive: *to frame a reply.* **17** to provide, support, or enclose with a frame: *to frame a picture.* **18** to form (words) with the lips, esp. silently. **19** *Sl.* to conspire to incriminate (someone) on a false charge. ORIG OE *framiae* to avail
▸ '**frameless** *adj* ▸ '**framer** *n*

Frame ★ (freɪm) *n* **Janet.** born 1924, New Zealand writer: author of the novels *Owls Do Cry* (1957) and *Faces in the Water* (1961), the collection of verse *The Pocket Mirror* (1967), and volumes of autobiography including *An Angel at My Table* (1984).

frame house *n* a house that has a timber framework and cladding.

frame of reference *n* **1** *Sociol.* a set of standards that determines and sanctions behaviour. **2** any set of planes or curves, such as the three coordinate axes, used to locate a point in space.

frame-up *n Sl.* **1** a conspiracy to incriminate someone on a false charge. **2** a plot to bring about a dishonest result, as in a contest.

framework ('freɪmˌwɜːk) *n* **1** a structural plan or basis of a project. **2** a structure or frame supporting or containing something.

franc (fræŋk; *French* frɑ̃) *n* **1** the standard monetary unit of France, French dependencies, and Monaco, divided into 100 centimes. Also called: **French franc. 2** the standard monetary and currency unit, comprising 100 centimes, of various countries including Belgium, the Central African Republic, Congo-Brazzaville, Gabon, Guinea, Liechtenstein, Luxembourg, Mauritania, Niger, Senegal, Switzerland, Togo, etc. **3** a Moroccan monetary unit worth one hundredth of a dirham. ORIG C14: from OF; from L *Rex Francōrum* King of the Franks, inscribed on 14th-century francs

France[1] ★ (frɑːns) *n* a republic in W Europe, between the English Channel, the Mediterranean, and the Atlantic: the largest country wholly in Europe; became a republic in 1793 after the French Revolution and an empire in 1804 under Napoleon; reverted to a monarchy (1815–48), followed by the Second Republic (1848–52), the Second Empire (1852–70), the Third Republic (1870–1940), and the Fourth and Fifth Republics (1946 and 1958); a member of the European Union. It is generally flat or undulating in the north and west and mountainous in the south and east. Official language: French. Religion: mostly Roman Catholic. Currency: franc and euro. Capital: Paris. Pop.: 59 087 000 (1999 est.). Area: (including Corsica) 551 600 sq. km (212 973 sq. miles). Related adj: **Gallic.**

France[2] ★ (*French* frɑ̃s) *n* **Anatole** (anatɔl), real name *Anatole François Thibault.* 1844–1924, French writer. His works include *Le Crime de Sylvestre Bonnard* (1881) and *La Révolte des anges* (1914): Nobel prize for literature 1921.

Francesca ★ (*Italian* fran'tʃeska) *n* See **Piero della Francesca.**

Franche-Comté ★ (*French* frɑ̃ʃkɔ̃te) *n* a region of E France, covering the Jura and the low country east of the Saône: part of the Kingdom of Burgundy (6th cent. A.D.–1137); autonomous as the Free County of Burgundy (1137–1384); under Burgundian rule again (1384–1477) and Hapsburg rule (1493–1674); annexed by France (1678).

franchise ('fræntʃaɪz) *n* **1** (usually preceded by *the*) the right to vote, esp. for representatives in a legislative body. **2** any exemption, privilege, or right granted to an individual or group by a public authority. **3** *Commerce.* authorization granted by a manufacturing enterprise to a distributor to market the manufacturer's products. **4** the full rights of citizenship. ◆ *vb* **franchises, franchising, franchised. 5** (*tr*) *Commerce, chiefly US & Canad.* to grant (a person, firm, etc.) a franchise. ORIG C13: from OF, from *franchir* to set free, from *franc* free
▸ ˌ**franchi'see** *n* ▸ **franchisement** ('fræntʃɪzmənt) *n* ▸ '**franchiser** *n*

Francis ★ ('frɑːnsɪs) *n* **1 Dick,** full name *Richard Stanley Francis.* born 1920, British thriller writer, formerly a jockey. His books include *Dead Cert* (1962), *The Edge* (1988), and *Come to Grief* (1995). **2** Sir **Philip.** 1740–1818, British politician; probable author of the *Letters of Junius* (1769–72).

Francis I ★ *n* **1** 1494–1547, king of France (1515–47). His reign was dominated by his rivalry with Emperor Charles V for the control of Italy. He was a noted patron of the arts and learning. **2** 1708–65, duke of Lorraine (1729–37), grand duke of Tuscany (1737–65), and Holy Roman Emperor (1745–65). His marriage (1736) to Maria Theresa led to the War of the Austrian Succession (1740–48). **3** title as emperor of Austria of **Francis II.**

Francis II ★ *n* **1** 1544–60, king of France (1559–60); son of Henry II and Catherine de' Medici; first husband of Mary, Queen of Scots. **2** 1768–1835, last Holy Roman Emperor (1792–1806) and, as Francis I, first emperor of Austria (1804–35). The Holy Roman Empire was dissolved (1806) following his defeat by Napoleon at Austerlitz.

Franciscan (fræn'sɪskən) *n* **a** a member of a Christian religious order of friars or nuns tracing their origins back to Saint Francis of Assisi. **b** (*as modifier*): *a Franciscan friary.*

Francis of Assisi ★ *n* **Saint.** original name *Giovanni di Bernardone.* ?1181–1226, Italian monk; founder of the Franciscan order. According to tradition, he was the first person to exhibit the stigmata (1224). Feast day: Oct. 4.

Francis of Sales ★ (seɪlz; *French* sal) *n* **Saint.** 1567–1622, French ecclesiastic and theologian; bishop of Geneva (1602–22) and an opponent of Calvinism; author of *Introduction to a Devout Life* (1609) and founder of the Order of the Visitation (1610). Feast day: Jan. 24.

Francis Xavier ★ ('zeɪvɪə) *n* **Saint.** See (Saint Francis) **Xavier.**

francium ('frænsɪəm) *n* an unstable radioactive element of the alkali-metal group, occurring in minute amounts in uranium ores. Symbol: Fr; atomic no.: 87; half-life of most stable isotope, ^{223}Fr: 22 minutes. ORIG C20: from NL, from FRANCE + -IUM; because first found in France

francize *or* **francise** ('frænsaɪz) *vb* **francizes, francizing, francized** *or* **francises, francising, francised.** *Canad.* to make or become French-speaking.
▸ ˌ**franciˈzation** *or* ˌ**franciˈsation** *n*

Franck ★ *n* **1** (*French* frɑ̃k). **César** (**Auguste**) (sezar). 1822–90, French composer, born in Belgium. His works include a violin sonata, a string quartet, the *Symphony in D Minor* (1888), and much organ music. **2** (fræŋk). **James.** 1882–1964, US physicist, born in Germany: shared a Nobel prize for physics (1925) for work on the quantum theory.

Franco ★ ('fræŋkəʊ; *Spanish* 'fraŋko) *n* **Francisco** (fran'θisko), called *el Caudillo.* 1892–1975, Spanish general and statesman; head of state (1939–1975). He was commander-in-chief of the Falangists in the Spanish Civil War (1936–39), defeating the republican government and establishing a dictatorship (1939).

Franco- ('fræŋkəʊ-) *combining form.* indicating France or French: *Franco-Prussian.* ORIG from Med. L *Francus,* from LL: FRANK[1]

francolin ('fræŋkəʊlɪn) *n* an African or Asian partridge. ORIG C17: from F, from OIt. *francolino,* from ?

Franconia ★ (fræŋ'kəʊnɪə) *n* a medieval duchy of Germany, inhabited by the Franks from the 7th century, now chiefly in Bavaria, Hesse, and Baden-Württemberg.

Francophobe ('fræŋkəʊˌfəʊb) *n* **1** a person who hates or fears France or its people. **2** *Canad.* a person who hates or fears Canadian Francophones.

Francophone ('fræŋkəʊˌfəʊn) (*often not cap.*) ◆ *n* **1** a person who speaks French, esp. a native speaker. ◆ *adj* **2** speaking French as a native language. **3** using French as a lingua franca.

frangible ('frændʒɪbᵊl) *adj* breakable or fragile. ORIG C15: from OF, ult. from L *frangere* to break
▸ ˌ**frangiˈbility** *or* ˈ**frangibleness** *n*

frangipane ('frændʒɪˌpeɪn) *n* **1** a pastry filled with cream and flavoured with almonds. **2** a variant of **frangipani** (the perfume).

frangipani (ˌfrændʒɪ'pɑːnɪ) *n, pl* **frangipanis** *or* **frangipani. 1** a tropical American shrub cultivated for its waxy white or pink flowers, which have a sweet overpowering scent. **2** a perfume prepared from this plant or resembling the odour of its flowers. **3 native frangipani.** *Austral.* an Australian evergreen tree with large fragrant yellow flowers. ORIG C17: via F from It.: perfume for scenting gloves, after the Marquis Muzio *Frangipani,* 16th-century Roman nobleman who invented it

Franglais *French.* (frɑ̃glɛ) *n* informal French containing a high proportion of English. ORIG C20: from *français* French + *anglais* English

frank (fræŋk) *adj* **1** honest and straightforward in speech or attitude: *a frank person.* **2** outspoken or blunt. **3** open and avowed: *frank interest.* ◆ *vb* (*tr*) **4** *Chiefly Brit.* to put a mark on (a letter, etc.), either cancelling the postage stamp or in place of a stamp, ensuring free carriage. **5** to mark (a letter, etc.) with an official mark or signature, indicating the right of free delivery. **6** to facilitate or assist (a person) to enter easily. **7** to obtain immunity for (a person). ◆ *n* **8** an official mark or signature affixed to a letter, etc., ensuring free delivery or delivery without stamps. ORIG C13: from OF, from Med. L *francus* free; identical with FRANK[1] (in Frankish Gaul only members of this people enjoyed full freedom)
▸ ˈ**frankable** *adj* ▸ ˈ**franker** *n* ▸ ˈ**frankness** *n*

Frank[1] (fræŋk) *n* a member of a group of West Germanic peoples who spread from the east in the late 4th century A.D., gradually conquering most of Gaul and Germany. ORIG OE *Franca;* ?from the name of a Frankish weapon (cf. OE *franca* javelin)

Frank[2] ★ (*Dutch* fraŋk) *n* **Anne.** 1929–45, German Jewish girl, whose *Diary* (1947) recorded the experiences of her family while in hiding from the Nazis in Amsterdam (1942–44). They were betrayed and she died in a concentration camp.

franked investment income *n* dividends from one UK company received by another on which the paying company has paid corporation tax.

Frankenstein ('fræŋkɪnˌstaɪn) *n* **1** a person who creates something that brings about his or her ruin. **2** Also called: **Frankenstein's monster.** a thing that destroys its creator. ORIG C19: after Baron *Frankenstein,* who created a destructive monster from parts of corpses in the novel by Mary Shelley (1818)
▸ ˌ**Frankenˈsteinian** *adj*

Frankenstein food *n Facetious.* any foodstuff that has been genetically modified. ORIG C20: from FRANKENSTEIN, alluding to its unnatural origin

Frankfort ★ ('fræŋkfət) *n* **1** a city in N Kentucky: the state capital. Pop.: 25 535 (1990). **2** *Now rare.* an English spelling of **Frankfurt.**

Frankfurt (**am Main**) (*German* 'fraŋkfʊrt (am 'main)) ★ *n* a city in central Germany, in Hesse on the Main River: a Roman settlement in the 1st century; a free imperial city (1372–1806); seat of the federal assembly (1815–66); university (1914); trade fairs since the 13th century. Pop.: 650 055 (1996 est.).

Frankfurt (**an der Oder**) (*German* 'fraŋkfʊrt (an der 'oːdər)) ★ *n* a city in E Germany on the Polish border: member of the Hanseatic League (1368–1450). Pop.: 85 360 (1991).

frankfurter ('fræŋkˌfɜːtə) *n* a smoked sausage, made of finely minced pork or beef. ORIG C20: short for G *Frankfurter Wurst* sausage from FRANKFURT AM MAIN

Frankfurter ('fræŋkˌfɜːtə) *n* an inhabitant or native of Frankfurt.

frankincense ('fræŋkɪnˌsɛns) *n* an aromatic gum resin obtained from trees of the genus *Boswellia,* which occur in Asia and Africa. ORIG C14: from OF *franc* free, pure + *encens* INCENSE[1]; see FRANK

Frankish ('fræŋkɪʃ) *n* **1** the ancient West Germanic language of the Franks. ◆ *adj* **2** of or relating to the Franks or their language.

franklin ('fræŋklɪn) *n* (in 14th- and 15th-century England) a substantial landholder of free but not noble birth. ORIG C13: from Anglo-F, from OF *franc* free, on the model of CHAMBERLAIN

Franklin ★ ('fræŋklɪn) *n* **1 Benjamin.** 1706–90, American statesman, scientist, and author. He helped draw up the Declaration of Independence (1776) and, as ambassador to France (1776–85), he negotiated an alliance with France. As a scientist, he is noted for his invention of the lightning conductor. **2** Sir **John.** 1786–1847, British explorer of the Arctic: lieutenant-governor of Van Diemen's Land (now Tasmania) (1836–43). **3 Rosalind.** 1920–58, British x-ray crystallographer. She contributed to the discovery of the structure of DNA.

frankly ('fræŋklɪ) *adv* **1** (*sentence modifier*) to be honest. **2** in a frank manner.

frantic ('fræntɪk) *adj* **1** distracted with fear, pain, joy, etc. **2** marked by or showing frenzy: *frantic efforts.* ORIG C14: from OF, from L *phrenēticus* mad
▸ ˈ**frantically** *or* ˈ**franticly** *adv*

Franz Ferdinand ★ (*German* frants 'fɛrdinant) *n* English name *Francis Ferdinand.* 1863–1914, archduke of Austria; heir apparent of Franz Josef I. His assassination contributed to the outbreak of World War I.

Franz Josef I ★ (*German* frants 'joːzɛf) *n* English name *Francis Joseph I.* 1830–1916, emperor of Austria (1848–1916) and king of Hungary (1867–1916).

Franz Josef Land ★ *n* an archipelago of over 100 islands in the Arctic Ocean, administratively part of Russia. Area: about 21 000 sq. km (8000 sq. miles). Russian name: **Zemlya Frantsa Iosifa** (zji'mlja 'frantsə 'jɔsifə).

frappé ('fræpeɪ) *n* **1** a drink consisting of a liqueur, etc., poured over crushed ice. ◆ *adj* **2** (*postpositive*) (esp. of drinks) chilled. ORIG C19: from F, from *frapper* to strike, hence, chill

Fraser[1] ★ ('freɪzə) *n* a river in SW Canada, in S central British Columbia, flowing northwest, south, and west through spectacular canyons in the Coast Mountains to the Strait of Georgia. Length: 1370 km (850 miles).

Fraser[2] ★ ('freɪzə) *n* **1 (John) Malcolm.** born 1930, Australian statesman; prime minister (1975–83). **2 Peter.** 1884–1950, New Zealand statesman, born in Scotland; prime minister (1940–49).

frater ('freɪtə) *n Arch.* a refectory. ORIG C13: from OF *fraiteur,* from *refreitor,* from LL *rēfectōrium* REFECTORY

fraternal (frə'tɜːnᵊl) *adj* **1** of or suitable to a brother; brotherly. **2** of a fraternity. **3** designating twins of the same or opposite sex that developed from two separate fertilized ova. Cf. **identical** (sense 3). ORIG C15: from L, from *frāter* brother
▸ **fra'ternalism** *n*

fraternity (frə'tɜːnɪtɪ) *n, pl* **fraternities. 1** a body of people united in interests, aims, etc.: *the teaching fraternity.* **2** brotherhood. **3** *US & Canad.* a secret society joined by male students, functioning as a social club.

fraternize *or* **fraternise** ('frætəˌnaɪz) *vb* **fraternizes, fraternizing, fraternized** *or* **fraternises, fraternising, fraternised.** (*intr;* often foll. by *with*) to associate on friendly terms.
▸ **ˌfraterni'zation** *or* **ˌfraterni'sation** *n* ▸ **'fraterˌnizer** *or* **'fraterˌniser** *n*

fratricide ('frætrɪˌsaɪd, 'freɪ-) *n* **1** the act of killing one's brother. **2** a person who kills his or her brother. ORIG C15: from L, from *frater* brother + -CIDE
▸ **ˌfratri'cidal** *adj*

Frau (fraʊ) *n, pl* **Frauen** ('fraʊən) *or* **Fraus.** a married German woman: usually used as a title equivalent to *Mrs.* ORIG from OHG *frouwa*

fraud (frɔːd) *n* **1** deliberate deception, trickery, or cheating intended to gain an advantage. **2** an act or instance of such deception. **3** *Inf.* a person who acts in a false or deceitful way. ORIG C14: from OF, from L *fraus* deception

fraudster ('frɔːdstə) *n* a swindler.

fraudulent ('frɔːdjʊlənt) *adj* **1** acting with or having the intent to deceive. **2** relating to or proceeding from fraud. ORIG C15: from L *fraudulentus* deceitful
▸ **'fraudulence** *n* ▸ **'fraudulently** *adv*

Frauenfeld ★ (*German* 'frauənfelt) *n* a town in NE Switzerland, capital of Thurgau canton. Pop.: 19 402 (1990).

fraught (frɔːt) *adj* **1** (*usually postpositive* and foll. by *with*) filled or charged: *a venture fraught with peril.* **2** *Inf.* showing or producing tension or anxiety. ORIG C14: from MDu. *vrachten,* from *vracht* FREIGHT

Fräulein (*German* 'frɔylaɪn) *n, pl* **Fräulein** *or English* **Fräuleins.** an unmarried German woman: often used as a title equivalent to *Miss.* ORIG from MHG *vrouwelīn,* dim. of *vrouwe* lady

Fraunhofer ★ ('fraʊnhəʊfə; *German* 'fraunhoːfər) *n* **Joseph von** ('joːzɛf fɔn). 1787–1826, German physicist who investigated spectra of the sun, planets, and stars, and improved telescopes and other optical instruments.

Fraunhofer lines *pl n* a set of dark lines appearing in the continuous emission spectrum of the sun.

fraxinella (ˌfræksɪ'nɛlə) *n* another name for **gas plant.** ORIG C17: from NL: a little ash tree, from L *frāxinus* ash

fray[1] (freɪ) *n* **1** a noisy quarrel. **2** a fight or brawl. ORIG C14: short for AFFRAY

fray[2] (freɪ) *vb* **1** to wear or cause to wear away into loose threads, esp. at an edge or end. **2** to make or become strained or irritated. **3** to rub or chafe (another object). ORIG C14: from F *frayer* to rub, from L *fricāre* to rub

Fray Bentos ★ (ˌfreɪ 'bɛntɒs) *n* a port in W Uruguay, on the River Uruguay: noted for meat-packing. Pop.: 21 400 (1995 est.).

Frazer ★ ('freɪzə) *n* Sir **James George.** 1854–1941, Scottish anthropologist; author of many works on religion and magic, esp. *The Golden Bough* (1890).

Frazier ★ ('freɪʒə) *n* **Joe.** born 1944, US boxer: won the world heavyweight title in 1970.

frazil ('freɪzɪl) *n* small pieces of ice that form in water moving turbulently enough to prevent the formation of a sheet of ice. ORIG C19: from Canad. F, from F *fraisil* cinders, ult. from L *fax* torch

frazzle ('fræzᵊl) *Inf.* ◆ *vb* **frazzles, frazzling, frazzled. 1** to make or become exhausted or weary. ◆ *n* **2** the state of being frazzled or exhausted. **3 to a frazzle.** completely (esp. in **burnt to a frazzle**). ORIG C19: prob. from ME *faselen* to fray, from *fasel* fringe; infl. by FRAY[2]

freak (friːk) *n* **1** a person, animal, or plant that is abnormal or deformed. **2a** an object, event, etc., that is abnormal. **2b** (*as modifier*): *a freak storm.* **3** a personal whim or caprice. **4** *Inf.* a person who acts or dresses in a markedly unconventional way. **5** *Inf.* a person who is ardently fond of something specified: *a jazz freak.* ◆ *vb* **6** See **freak out.** ORIG C16: from ?
▸ **'freakish** *adj* ▸ **'freaky** *adj*

freak out *vb* (*adv*) *Inf.* to be or cause to be in a heightened emotional state.

freckle ('frɛkᵊl) *n* **1** a small brownish spot on the skin developed by exposure to sunlight. **2** any small area of discoloration. ◆ *vb* **freckles, freckling, freckled. 3** to mark or become marked with freckles or spots. ORIG C14: from ON *freknur*
▸ **'freckled** *or* **'freckly** *adj*

Fredericia ★ (*Danish* freðə'redsja) *n* a port in Denmark, in E Jutland at the N end of the Little Belt. Pop.: 28 000 (1990).

Frederick I ★ ('frɛdrɪk) *n* **1** See **Frederick Barbarossa. 2** 1657–1713, first king of Prussia (1701–13); son of Frederick William.

Frederick II ★ *n* **1** 1194–1250, Holy Roman Emperor (1220–50), king of Germany (1212–50), and king of Sicily (1198–1250). **2** See **Frederick the Great.**

Frederick III ★ *n* **1** 1415–93, Holy Roman Emperor (1452–93) and, as Frederick IV, king of Germany (1440–93). **2** called *the Wise.* 1463–1525, elector of Saxony (1486–1525). He protected Martin Luther in Wartburg Castle after the Diet of Worms (1521).

Frederick IV ★ *n* See **Frederick III** (sense 1).

Frederick V ★ *n* called *the Winter King.* 1596–1632, elector of the Palatinate (1610–23) and king of Bohemia (1619–20). He led the revolt of Bohemian Protestants at the beginning of the Thirty Years' War.

Frederick IX ★ *n* 1899–1972, king of Denmark (1947–72).

Frederick Barbarossa ★ (ˌbɑːbə'rɒsə) *n* official title *Frederick I.* ?1123–90, Holy Roman Emperor (1155–90), king of Germany (1152–90). His attempt to assert imperial rights in Italy ended in his defeat at Legnano (1176) and the independence of the Lombard cities (1183).

Frederick the Great ★ *n* official title *Frederick II.* 1712–86, king of Prussia (1740–86); son of Frederick William I. He gained Silesia during the War of Austrian Succession (1740–48) and established Prussia as a European power.

Frederick William ★ *n* called *the Great Elector.* 1620–88, elector of Brandenburg (1640–88).

Frederick William I ★ *n* 1688–1740, king of Prussia (1713–40); son of Frederick I: reformed the Prussian army.

Frederick William III ★ *n* 1770–1840, king of Prussia (1797–1840).

Frederick William IV ★ *n* 1795–1861, king of Prussia (1840–61). He submitted to the 1848 Revolution but refused the imperial crown offered by the Frankfurt Parliament (1849). In 1857 he became insane and his brother, William I, became regent (1858–61).

Fredericton ★ ('frɛdrɪktən) *n* a city in SE Canada, capital of New Brunswick, on the St John River. Pop.: 45 364 (1991).

Frederiksberg ★ (*Danish* frɛðregs'bɛr) *n* a city in E Denmark, within the area of greater Copenhagen: founded in 1651 by King Frederick III. Pop.: 88 002 (1995 est.).

Fredrikstad ★ (*Norwegian* 'frɛdrikstad) *n* a port in SE Norway at the entrance to Oslo Fjord. Pop.: 26 546 (1990).

free (friː) *adj* **freer, freest. 1** able to act at will; not under compulsion or restraint. **2a** not enslaved or confined. **2b** (*as n*): *land of the free.* **3** (*often postpositive* and foll. by *from*)

not subject (to) or restricted (by some regulation, constraint, etc.): *free from pain.* **4** (of a country, etc.) autonomous or independent. **5** exempt from external direction: *free will.* **6** not subject to conventional constraints: *free verse.* **7** not exact or literal: *a free translation.* **8** provided without charge: *free entertainment.* **9** *Law.* (of property) **9a** not subject to payment of rent or performance of services; freehold. **9b** not subject to any burden or charge; unencumbered. **10** (*postpositive;* often foll. by *of* or *with*) ready or generous in using or giving: *free with advice.* **11** not occupied or in use; available: *a free cubicle.* **12** (of a person) not busy. **13** open or available to all. **14** without charge to the subscriber or user: *freepost; freephone.* **15** not fixed or joined; loose: *the free end of a chain.* **16** without obstruction or impediment: *free passage.* **17** *Chem.* chemically uncombined: *free nitrogen.* **18** *Logic.* denoting an occurrence of a variable not bound by a quantifier. Cf. **bound**[1] (sense 8). **19** (of routines in figure skating competitions) chosen by the competitor. **20** (of jazz) totally improvised. **21 for free.** *Nonstandard.* without charge or cost. **22 free and easy.** casual or tolerant; easygoing. **23 make free with.** to behave too familiarly towards. ◆ *adv* **24** in a free manner; freely. **25** without charge or cost. **26** *Naut.* with the wind blowing from the quarter. ◆ *vb* **frees, freeing, freed.** (*tr*) **27** to set at liberty; release. **28** to remove obstructions or impediments from. **29** (often foll. by *of* or *from*) to relieve or rid (of obstacles, pain, etc.). ORIG OE *frēo*
▸ **'freely** *adv* ▸ **'freeness** *n*

-free *adj combining form.* free from: *trouble-free; lead-free petrol.*

free alongside ship *adj* (of a shipment of goods) delivered to the dock without charge to the buyer, but excluding the cost of loading onto the vessel. Cf. **free on board.**

free association *n Psychoanal.* a method of exploring a person's unconscious by eliciting words and thoughts that are associated with key words provided by a psychoanalyst.

freebase ('fri:ˌbeɪs) *Sl.* ◆ *n* **1** cocaine that has been refined by heating it in ether or some other solvent. ◆ *vb* **freebases, freebasing, freebased. 2** to refine (cocaine) in this way. **3** to smoke or inhale the fumes from (refined cocaine).

freebie ('fri:bɪ) *n Sl.* something provided without charge.

freeboard ('fri:ˌbɔ:d) *n* the space or distance between the deck of a vessel and the waterline.

freebooter ('fri:ˌbu:tə) *n* a person, such as a pirate, living from plunder. ORIG C16: from Du., from *vrijbuit* booty; see FILIBUSTER
▸ **'freeboot** *vb* (*intr*)

freeborn ('fri:ˌbɔ:n) *adj* **1** not born in slavery. **2** of or suitable for people not born in slavery.

Free Church *n Chiefly Brit.* any Protestant Church, esp. the Presbyterian, other than the Established Church.

free city *n* a sovereign or autonomous city.

freedman ('fri:dˌmæn) *n, pl* **freedmen.** a man who has been freed from slavery.

freedom ('fri:dəm) *n* **1** personal liberty, as from slavery, serfdom, etc. **2** liberation, as from confinement or bondage. **3** the quality or state of being free, esp. to enjoy political and civil liberties. **4** (usually foll. by *from*) exemption or immunity: *freedom from taxation.* **5** the right or privilege of unrestricted use or access: *the freedom of a city.* **6** autonomy, self-government, or independence. **7** the power or liberty to order one's own actions. **8** *Philosophy.* the quality, esp. of the will or the individual, of not being totally constrained. **9** ease or frankness of manner: *she talked with complete freedom.* **10** excessive familiarity of manner. **11** ease and grace, as of movement. ORIG OE *frēodōm*

freedom fighter *n* a militant revolutionary.

free energy *n* a thermodynamic property that expresses the capacity of a system to perform work under certain conditions.

free enterprise *n* an economic system in which commercial organizations compete for profit with little state control.

free fall *n* **1** free descent of a body in which the gravitational force is the only force acting on it. **2** the part of a parachute descent before the parachute opens.

free flight *n* the flight of a rocket, missile, etc., when its engine has ceased to produce thrust.

free-for-all *n Inf.* **1** a disorganized brawl or argument, usually involving all those present. **2a** a contest, discussion, etc., that is open to everyone. **2b** (*as modifier*): *a free-for-all contest.*

free-form *adj Arts.* freely flowing, spontaneous.

free hand *n* **1** unrestricted freedom to act (esp. in **give (someone) a free hand**). ◆ *adj, adv* **freehand. 2** (done) by hand without the use of guiding instruments: *a freehand drawing.*

free-handed *adj* generous or liberal; unstinting.
▸ **ˌfree-'handedly** *adv*

freehold ('fri:ˌhəʊld) *Property law.* ◆ *n* **1a** tenure by which land is held in fee simple, fee tail, or for life. **1b** an estate held by such tenure. ◆ *adj* **2** relating to or having the nature of freehold.
▸ **'freeholder** *n*

free house *n Brit.* a public house not bound to sell only one brewer's products.

free kick *n Soccer.* a place kick awarded for a foul or infringement.

freelance ('fri:ˌlɑ:ns) *n* **1a** Also called: **freelancer.** a self-employed person, esp. a writer or artist, who is hired to do specific assignments. **1b** (*as modifier*): *a freelance journalist.* **2** (in medieval Europe) a mercenary soldier or adventurer. ◆ *vb* **freelances, freelancing, freelanced. 3** to work as a freelance on (an assignment, etc.). ◆ *adv* **4** as a freelance. ORIG C19 (in sense 2): later applied to politicians, writers, etc.

free-living *adj* **1** given to ready indulgence of the appetites. **2** (of animals and plants) not parasitic.
▸ **ˌfree-'liver** *n*

freeloader ('fri:ˌləʊdə) *n Sl.* a person who habitually depends on others for food, shelter, etc.

free love *n* the practice of sexual relationships without fidelity to a single partner.

freeman ('fri:mən) *n, pl* **freemen. 1** a person who is not a slave. **2** a person who enjoys political and civil liberties. **3** a person who enjoys a privilege, such as the freedom of a city.

free market *n* **a** an economic system that allows supply and demand to regulate prices, wages, etc., rather than government policy. **b** (*as modifier*): *a free-market economy.*

freemartin ('fri:ˌmɑ:tɪn) *n* the female of a pair of twin calves of unlike sex that is imperfectly developed and sterile. ORIG C17: from ?

Freemason ('fri:ˌmeɪsᵊn) *n* a member of the widespread secret order, constituted in London in 1717, of **Free and Accepted Masons,** pledged to brotherly love, faith, and charity. Sometimes shortened to **Mason.**

freemasonry ('fri:ˌmeɪsᵊnrɪ) *n* natural or tacit sympathy and understanding.

Freemasonry ('fri:ˌmeɪsᵊnrɪ) *n* **1** the institutions, rites, practices, etc., of Freemasons. **2** Freemasons collectively.

free on board *adj* (of a shipment of goods) delivered on board ship or other carrier without charge to the buyer. Cf. **free alongside ship.**

free port *n* **1** a port open to all commercial vessels on equal terms. **2** a port that permits the duty-free entry of foreign goods intended for re-export.

free radical *n* an atom or group of atoms containing at least one unpaired electron and existing for a brief period of time before reacting to produce a stable molecule.

free-range *adj Chiefly Brit.* kept or produced in natural conditions: *free-range eggs.*

free-select *vb* (*tr*) *Austral. history.* to select (areas of crown land) and acquire the freehold by a series of annual payments.
▸ **'free-se'lection** *n* ▸ **'free-se'lector** *n*

freesia ('fri:zɪə) *n* a plant of Southern Africa, cultivated for its white, yellow, or pink tubular fragrant flowers.

ORIG C19: NL, after F. H. T. *Freese* (died 1876), G physician

free skating *n* either of two parts in a figure-skating competition in which the skater chooses the sequence of figures and the music and which are judged on technique and artistic presentation. The short programme consists of specified movements and the long programme is entirely the skater's own choice.

free space *n* a region that has no gravitational and electromagnetic fields. It is used as an absolute standard and was formerly referred to as a vacuum.

free-spoken *adj* speaking frankly or without restraint.
▸ **ˌfree-ˈspokenly** *adv*

freestanding (ˌfriːˈstændɪŋ) *adj* not attached to or supported by another object.

Free State *n* a province of central South Africa; replaced Orange Free State in 1994. Capital: Bloemfontein. Pop.: 2 782 500 (1995 est.). Area: 129 480 sq. km (49 992 sq. miles).

freestone (ˈfriːˌstəʊn) *n* **1** any fine-grained stone, esp. sandstone or limestone, that can be worked in any direction without breaking. **2** *Bot.* a fruit, such as a peach, in which the flesh separates readily from the stone.

freestyle (ˈfriːˌstaɪl) *n* **1** a competition or race, as in swimming, in which each participant may use a style of his or her choice instead of a specified style. **2a** **International freestyle.** an amateur style of wrestling with an agreed set of rules. **2b** Also called: **all-in wrestling.** a style of professional wrestling with no internationally agreed set of rules.

freethinker (ˌfriːˈθɪŋkə) *n* a person who forms his or her ideas and opinions independently of authority or accepted views, esp. in matters of religion.
▸ **free thought** *n*

Freetown ★ (ˈfriːˌtaʊn) *n* the capital and chief port of Sierra Leone: founded in 1787 for slaves freed and destitute in England. Pop.: 669 000 (1990 est.).

free trade *n* **1** international trade that is free of such government interference as protective tariffs. **2** *Arch.* smuggling.

free verse *n* unrhymed verse without a metrical pattern.

freeware (ˈfriːˌwɛə) *n* computer software that may be distributed and used without payment.

freeway (ˈfriːˌweɪ) *n US.* **1** an expressway. **2** a major road that can be used without paying a toll.

freewheel (ˌfriːˈwiːl) *n* **1** a ratchet device in the rear hub of a bicycle wheel that permits the wheel to rotate freely while the pedals are stationary. ◆ *vb* **2** (*intr*) to coast on a bicycle using the freewheel.

free will *n* **1a** the apparent human ability to make choices that are not externally determined. **1b** the doctrine that such human freedom of choice is not illusory. Cf. **determinism.** **2** the ability to make a choice without outside coercion: *he left of his own free will.*

Free World *n* **the.** the non-Communist countries collectively.

freeze (friːz) *vb* **freezes, freezing, froze, frozen.** **1** to change (a liquid) into a solid as a result of a reduction in temperature, or (of a liquid) to solidify in this way. **2** (when *intr,* sometimes foll. by *over* or *up*) to cover, clog, or harden with ice, or become so covered, clogged, or hardened. **3** to fix fast or become fixed (to something) because of the action of frost. **4** (*tr*) to preserve (food) by subjection to extreme cold, as in a freezer. **5** to feel or cause to feel the sensation or effects of extreme cold. **6** to die or cause to die of extreme cold. **7** to become or cause to become paralysed, fixed, or motionless, esp. through fear, shock, etc. **8** (*tr*) to cause (moving film) to stop at a particular frame. **9** to make or become formal, haughty, etc., in manner. **10** (*tr*) to fix (prices, incomes, etc.) at a particular level. **11** (*tr*) to forbid by law the exchange, liquidation, or collection of (loans, assets, etc.). **12** (*tr*) to stop (a process) at a particular stage of development. **13** (*intr;* foll. by *onto*) *Inf., chiefly US.* to cling. ◆ *n* **14** the act of freezing or state of being frozen. **15** *Meteorol.* a spell of temperatures below freezing point, usually over a wide area. **16** the fixing of incomes, prices, etc., by legislation. ◆ *sentence substitute.* **17** *Chiefly US.* a command to stop instantly or risk being shot. ORIG OE *frēosan*
▸ **ˈfreezable** *adj*

freeze-dry *vb* **freeze-dries, freeze-drying, freeze-dried.** (*tr*) to preserve (a substance) by rapid freezing and subsequently drying in a vacuum.

freeze-frame *n* **1** *Films, television.* a single frame of a film repeated to give an effect like a still photograph. **2** *Video.* a single frame of a video recording viewed as a still by stopping the tape. ◆ *vb* **3** (*tr*) to make a freeze-frame of (an image).

freeze out *vb* (*tr, adv*) *Inf.* to exclude, as by unfriendly behaviour, etc.

freezer (ˈfriːzə) *n* an insulated cold-storage cabinet for long-term storage of perishable foodstuffs. Also called: **deepfreeze.**

freeze-up *n US & Canad. inf.* **a** the freezing of lakes, rivers, etc., in autumn or early winter. **b** the time of year when this occurs.

freezing (ˈfriːzɪŋ) *adj Inf.* extremely cold.

freezing point *n* the temperature below which a liquid turns into a solid.

freezing works *n Austral. & NZ.* a slaughterhouse at which animal carcasses are frozen for export.

Frege ★ (*German* ˈfreːgə) *n* **Gottlob.** 1848–1925, German logician and philosopher, who laid the foundations of modern formal logic and semantics in his *Begriffsschrift* (1879).

Freiburg ★ (*German* ˈfraibʊrk) *n* **1** a city in SW Germany, in SW Baden-Württemberg: under Austrian rule (1368–1805); university (1457). Pop.: 199 273 (1996 est.). Official name: **Freiburg im Breisgau** (ɪm ˈbraisgau). **2** the German name for **Fribourg.**

freight (freɪt) *n* **1a** commercial transport that is slower and cheaper than express. **1b** the price charged for such transport. **1c** goods transported by this means. **1d** (*as modifier*): *freight transport.* **2** *Chiefly Brit.* a ship's cargo or part of it. ◆ *vb* (*tr*) **3** to load with goods for transport. ORIG C16: from MDu *vrecht,* var. of *vracht*

freightage (ˈfreɪtɪdʒ) *n* **1** the commercial conveyance of goods. **2** the goods so transported. **3** the price charged for such conveyance.

freighter (ˈfreɪtə) *n* **1** a ship or aircraft designed for transporting cargo. **2** a person concerned with the loading of a ship.

freightliner (ˈfreɪtˌlaɪnə) *n Trademark.* a type of goods train carrying containers that can be transferred onto lorries or ships.

Fremantle ★ (ˈfriːˌmæntᵊl) *n* a port in SW Western Australia, on the Indian Ocean. Pop.: 24 010 (1986).

French[1] (frɛntʃ) *n* **1** the official language of France: also an official language of Switzerland, Belgium, Canada, and certain other countries. Historically, French is an Indo-European language belonging to the Romance group. **2 the French.** (*functioning as pl*) the natives, citizens, or inhabitants of France collectively. ◆ *adj* **3** relating to, denoting, or characteristic of France, the French, or their language. **4** (in Canada) of French Canadians. ORIG OE *Frencisc* French, Frankish
▸ **ˈFrenchness** *n*

French[2] ★ (frɛntʃ) *n* Sir **John Denton Pinkstone,** 1st Earl of Ypres. 1852–1925, British field marshal in World War I: commanded the British Expeditionary Force in France and Belgium (1914–15); Lord Lieutenant of Ireland (1918–21).

French bread *n* white bread in a long slender loaf that has a crisp brown crust.

French Cameroons ★ *pl n* the part of Cameroon formerly administered by France (1919–60).

French Canada ★ *n* the areas of Canada, esp. in the province of Quebec, where French Canadians predominate.

French Canadian *n* **1** a Canadian citizen whose native language is French. ◆ *adj* **French-Canadian.** **2** of or relating to French Canadians or their language.

French chalk *n* a variety of talc used to mark cloth, remove grease stains, or as a dry lubricant.

French doors *pl n* the US and Canad. name for **French windows.**

French dressing *n* a salad dressing made from oil and vinegar with seasonings; vinaigrette.

French Equatorial Africa ★ *n* the former French overseas territories of Chad, Gabon, Middle Congo, and Ubangi-Shari (1910–58).

French fried potatoes *pl n* a more formal name for chips. Often shortened to **French fries, fries.**

French Guiana ★ *n* a French overseas region in NE South America, on the Atlantic: colonized by the French in about 1637; tropical forests. Capital: Cayenne. Pop.: 90 500 (1988 est.). Area: about 91 000 sq. km (23 000 sq. miles).
▸ **French Guianese** *or* **Guianan** *adj, n*

French Guinea ★ *n* a former French territory of French West Africa: became independent as Guinea in 1958.

French horn *n Music.* a valved brass instrument with a funnel-shaped mouthpiece and a tube of conical bore coiled into a spiral.

Frenchify ('frɛntʃɪˌfaɪ) *vb* **Frenchifies, Frenchifying, Frenchified.** *Inf.* to make or become French in appearance, etc.

French India ★ *n* a former French overseas territory in India, including Chandernagore and Pondicherry: restored to India between 1949 and 1954.

French Indochina ★ *n* the territories of SE Asia that were colonized by France and held mostly until 1954: included Cochin China, Annam, and Tonkin (now largely Vietnam), Cambodia, Laos, and Kuang-Chou Wan (returned to China in 1945, now Zhanjiang).

French kiss *n* a kiss involving insertion of the tongue into the partner's mouth.

French knickers *pl n* women's wide-legged underpants.

French leave *n* an unauthorized or unannounced absence or departure. ORIG C18: alluding to a custom in France of leaving without saying goodbye to one's host or hostess

French letter *n Brit.* a slang term for **condom.**

Frenchman ('frɛntʃmən) *n, pl* **Frenchmen.** a native, citizen, or inhabitant of France.
▸ **'French,woman** *fem n*

French Morocco ★ *n* a former French protectorate in NW Africa, united in 1956 with Spanish Morocco and Tangier to form the kingdom of Morocco.

French mustard *n* a mild mustard paste made with vinegar rather than water.

French North Africa ★ *n* the former French possessions of Algeria, French Morocco, and Tunisia.

French Oceania ★ *n* a former name (until 1958) of **French Polynesia.**

French polish *n* **1** a varnish for wood consisting of shellac dissolved in alcohol. **2** the gloss finish produced by this polish.

French-polish *vb* to treat with French polish or give a French polish (to).

French Polynesia ★ *n* a French Overseas Territory in the S Pacific Ocean, including the Society Islands, the Tuamotu group, the Gambier group, the Tubuai Islands, and the Marquesas Islands. Capital: Papeete, on Tahiti. Pop.: 191 400 (1988 est.). Area: about 4000 sq. km (1500 sq. miles). Former name (until 1958): **French Oceania.**

French seam *n* a seam in which the edges are not visible.

French Somaliland ★ *n* a former name (until 1967) of **Djibouti.**

French Southern and Antarctic Territories ★ *pl n* a French overseas territory, comprising Adélie Land in Antarctica and the islands of Amsterdam and St Paul and the Kerguelen and Crozet archipelagos in the S Indian Ocean.

French Sudan ★ *n* a former name (1898–1959) of **Mali.**

French toast *n* **1** *Brit.* toast cooked on one side only. **2** bread dipped in beaten egg and lightly fried.

French Togoland ★ *n* a former United Nations Trust Territory in W Africa, administered by France (1946–60), now the independent republic of Togo.

French West Africa ★ *n* a former group (1895–1958) of French Overseas Territories: consisted of Senegal, Mauritania, French Sudan, Burkina-Faso, Niger, French Guinea, Côte d'Ivoire, and Benin.

French windows *pl n (sometimes sing) Brit.* a pair of casement windows extending to floor level and opening onto a balcony, garden, etc.

frenetic (frɪ'nɛtɪk) *adj* distracted or frantic. ORIG C14: via OF, from L, from Gk, from *phrenitis* insanity, from *phrēn* mind
▸ **fre'netically** *adv*

frenum ('friːnəm) *n, pl* **frena** (-nə). a variant spelling (esp. US) of **fraenum.**

frenzy ('frɛnzɪ) *n, pl* **frenzies. 1** violent mental derangement. **2** wild excitement or agitation. **3** a bout of wild or agitated activity: *a frenzy of preparations.* ◆ *vb* **frenzies, frenzying, frenzied. 4** *(tr)* to drive into a frenzy. ORIG C14: from OF, from LL *phrēnēsis* madness, from LGk, ult. from Gk *phrēn* mind
▸ **'frenzied** *adj*

Freon ('friːˌɒn) *n Trademark.* any of a group of chemically unreactive gaseous or liquid derivatives of methane in which hydrogen atoms have been replaced by chlorine and fluorine atoms: used as aerosol propellants, refrigerants, and solvents.

freq. *abbrev. for:* **1** frequent(ly). **2** frequentative.

frequency ('friːkwənsɪ) *n, pl* **frequencies. 1** the state of being frequent. **2** the number of times that an event occurs within a given period. **3** *Physics.* the number of times that a periodic function or vibration repeats itself in a specified time, often 1 second. It is usually measured in hertz. **4** *Statistics.* **4a** the number of individuals in a class (**absolute frequency**). **4b** the ratio of this number to the total number of individuals under survey (**relative frequency**). **5** *Ecology.* the number of individuals of a species within a given area. ORIG C16: from L, from *frequēns* crowded

frequency distribution *n Statistics.* the function of the distribution of a sample corresponding to the probability density function of the underlying population and tending to it as the sample size increases.

frequency modulation *n* a method of transmitting information using a radio-frequency carrier wave. The frequency of the carrier wave is varied in accordance with the amplitude of the input signal, the amplitude of the carrier remaining unchanged. Cf. **amplitude modulation.**

frequent *adj* ('friːkwənt). **1** recurring at short intervals. **2** habitual. ◆ *vb* (frɪ'kwɛnt). **3** *(tr)* to visit repeatedly or habitually. ORIG C16: from L *frequēns* numerous
▸ **,frequen'tation** *n* ▸ **fre'quenter** *n* ▸ **'frequently** *adv*

frequentative (frɪ'kwɛntətɪv) *Grammar.* ◆ *adj* **1** denoting an aspect of verbs in some languages used to express repeated or habitual action. **2** (in English) denoting a verb or an affix meaning repeated action, such as the verb *wrestle,* from *wrest.* ◆ *n* **3** a frequentative verb or affix.

fresco ('frɛskəʊ) *n, pl* **frescoes** *or* **frescos. 1** a very durable method of wall-painting using watercolours on wet plaster. **2** a painting done in this way. ORIG C16: from It.: fresh plaster, from *fresco* (adj) fresh, cool, of Gmc origin

Frescobaldi ★ (*Italian* fresko'baldi) *n* **Girolamo** (dʒi'rɔːlamo). 1583–1643, Italian composer, noted esp. for his organ and harpsichord music.

fresh (frɛʃ) *adj* **1** newly made, harvested, etc.: *fresh bread; fresh strawberries.* **2** newly acquired, found, etc.: *fresh publications.* **3** novel; original: *a fresh outlook.* **4** most recent: *fresh developments.* **5** further; additional: *fresh supplies.* **6** not canned, frozen, or otherwise preserved: *fresh fruit.* **7** (of water) not salt. **8** bright or clear: *a fresh morning.* **9**

★ people and places

chilly or invigorating: *a fresh breeze.* **10** not tired; alert. **11** not worn or faded: *fresh colours.* **12** having a healthy or ruddy appearance. **13** newly or just arrived: *fresh from the presses.* **14** youthful or inexperienced. **15** *Inf.* presumptuous or disrespectful; forward. ◆ *n* **16** the fresh part or time of something. **17** another name for **freshet.** ◆ *adv* **18** in a fresh manner. ORIG OE *fersc* fresh, unsalted
▸ **'freshly** *adv* ▸ **'freshness** *n*

fresh breeze *n* a wind of force 5 on the Beaufort scale, blowing at speeds between 19 and 24 mph.

freshen ('frɛʃən) *vb* **1** to make or become fresh or fresher. **2** (often foll. by *up*) to refresh (oneself), esp. by washing. **3** (*intr*) (of the wind) to increase.

fresher ('frɛʃə) *or* **freshman** ('frɛʃmən) *n, pl* **freshers** *or* **freshmen.** a first-year student at college or university.

freshet ('frɛʃɪt) *n* **1** the sudden overflowing of a river caused by heavy rain or melting snow. **2** a stream of fresh water emptying into the sea.

freshwater ('frɛʃˌwɔːtə) *n* (*modifier*) **1** of or living in fresh water. **2** (esp. of a sailor who has not sailed on the sea) inexperienced. **3** *US.* little known: *a freshwater school.*

fresnel ('freɪnɛl) *n* a unit of frequency equivalent to 10^{12} hertz. ORIG C20: after A. J. FRESNEL

Fresnel ★ (*French* frɛnɛl) *n* **Augustin Jean** (ogystɛ̃ ʒɑ̃). 1788–1827, French physicist: worked on the interference of light, contributing to the wave theory of light.

Fresno ★ ('frɛznəʊ) *n* a city in central California, in the San Joaquin Valley. Pop.: 396 011 (1996 est.).

fret[1] (frɛt) *vb* **frets, fretting, fretted. 1** to distress or be distressed. **2** to rub or wear away. **3** to feel or give annoyance or vexation. **4** to eat away or be eaten away, as by chemical action. **5** (*tr*) to make by wearing away; erode. ◆ *n* **6** a state of irritation or anxiety. ORIG OE *fretan* to eat

fret[2] (frɛt) *n* **1** a repetitive geometrical figure, esp. one used as an ornamental border. **2** such a pattern made in relief; fretwork. ◆ *vb* **frets, fretting, fretted. 3** (*tr*) to ornament with fret or fretwork. ORIG C14: from OF *frete* interlaced design used on a shield, prob. of Gmc origin
▸ **'fretless** *adj*

fret[3] (frɛt) *n* any of several small metal bars set across the fingerboard of a musical instrument of the lute, guitar, or viol family at various points along its length so as to produce the desired notes. ORIG C16: from ?
▸ **'fretless** *adj*

fretboard ('frɛtbɔːd) *n* a fingerboard with frets on a stringed instrument.

fretful ('frɛtfʊl) *adj* peevish, irritable, or upset.
▸ **'fretfully** *adv* ▸ **'fretfulness** *n*

fret saw *n* a fine-toothed saw with a long thin narrow blade, used for cutting designs in thin wood or metal.

fretwork ('frɛtˌwɜːk) *n* decorative geometrical carving or openwork.

Freud ★ (frɔɪd) *n* **1 Anna.** 1895–1982, Austrian psychiatrist: daughter of Sigmund Freud and pioneer of child psychoanalysis. **2 Lucian.** born 1922, British painter; grandson of Sigmund Freud. **3 Sigmund** ('sɪgmənd; *German* 'ziːkmʊnt). 1856–1939, Austrian psychiatrist; originator of psychoanalysis. His works include *The Interpretation of Dreams* (1900) and *The Ego and the Id* (1923).

Freudian ('frɔɪdɪən) *adj* **1** of or relating to Sigmund Freud or his ideas. ◆ *n* **2** a person who follows or believes in the basic ideas of Sigmund Freud.
▸ **'Freudianˌism** *n*

Freudian slip *n* any action, such as a slip of the tongue, that may reveal an unconscious thought.

Frey (freɪ) *or* **Freyr** ★ (freɪə) *n Norse myth.* the god of earth's fertility and dispenser of prosperity.

Freya *or* **Freyja** ★ ('freɪə) *n Norse myth.* the goddess of love and fecundity, sister of Frey.

Freytag ★ (*German* 'fraitaːk) *n* **Gustav** ('gʊstaf). 1816–95, German novelist and dramatist; author of the comedy *Die Journalisten* (1853) and *Soll und Haben* (1855).

Fri. *abbrev. for* Friday.

friable ('fraɪəbᵊl) *adj* easily broken up; crumbly. ORIG C16: from L, from *friāre* to crumble
▸ **ˌfria'bility** *or* **'friableness** *n*

friar ('fraɪə) *n* a member of any of various chiefly mendicant religious orders of the Roman Catholic Church. ORIG C13 *frere,* from OF: brother, from L *frāter* BROTHER

friar's balsam *n* a compound containing benzoin, mixed with hot water and used as an inhalant to relieve colds and sore throats.

friary ('fraɪərɪ) *n, pl* **friaries.** *Christianity.* a convent or house of friars.

Fribourg ★ (*French* fribur) *n* **1** a canton in W Switzerland. Capital: Fribourg. Pop.: 222 227 (1995 est.). Area: 1676 sq. km (645 sq. miles). **2** a town in W Switzerland, capital of Fribourg canton: university (1889). Pop.: 35 000 (1989). ◆ German name: **Freiburg.**

fricandeau ('frɪkənˌdəʊ) *n, pl* **fricandeaus** *or* **fricandeaux** (-ˌdəʊz). a larded and braised veal fillet. ORIG C18: from OF, prob. based on FRICASSEE

fricassee (ˌfrɪkə'siː, 'frɪkəsɪ) *n* **1** stewed meat, esp. chicken or veal, served in a thick white sauce. ◆ *vb* **fricassees, fricasseeing, fricasseed. 2** (*tr*) to prepare (meat, etc.) as a fricassee. ORIG C16: from OF, from *fricasser* to fricassee

fricative ('frɪkətɪv) *n* **1** a consonant produced by partial occlusion of the airstream, such as (f) or (z). ◆ *adj* **2** relating to or denoting a fricative. ORIG C19: from NL, from L *fricāre* to rub

friction ('frɪkʃən) *n* **1** a resistance encountered when one body moves relative to another body with which it is in contact. **2** the act, effect, or an instance of rubbing one object against another. **3** disagreement or conflict. ORIG C16: from F, from L *frictiō* a rubbing, from *fricāre* to rub
▸ **'frictional** *adj* ▸ **'frictionless** *adj*

Friday ('fraɪdɪ) *n* **1** the sixth day of the week; fifth day of the working week. **2** See **man Friday.** ORIG OE *Frīgedæg*

fridge (frɪdʒ) *n* short for **refrigerator.**

fried (fraɪd) *vb* the past tense and past participle of **fry**[1].

Friedan ★ ('friːdən) *n* **Betty.** born 1921, US feminist, founder and first president (1966–70) of the National Organization for Women. Her books include *The Feminine Mystique* (1963) and *The Fountain of Life* (1993).

Friedman ★ ('friːdmən) *n* **Milton.** born 1912. US economist, particularly associated with monetarism and an advocate of free market capitalism.
▸ **'Friedmanˌite** *n, adj*

Friedrich ★ (*German* 'friːdrɪç) *n* **Caspar David** ('kaspar 'daːfɪt). 1774–1840, German landscape painter.

friend (frɛnd) *n* **1** a person known well to another and regarded with liking, affection, and loyalty. **2** an acquaintance or associate. **3** an ally in a fight or cause. **4** a fellow member of a party, society, etc. **5** a patron or supporter. **6 be friends (with).** to be friendly (with). **7 make friends (with).** to become friendly (with). ◆ *vb* **8** (*tr*) an archaic word for **befriend.** ORIG OE *frēond*
▸ **'friendless** *adj* ▸ **'friendship** *n*

Friend (frɛnd) *n* a member of the Religious Society of Friends; Quaker.

friend at court *n* an influential acquaintance who can promote one's interests.

friendly ('frɛndlɪ) *adj* **friendlier, friendliest. 1** showing or expressing liking, goodwill, or trust. **2** on the same side; not hostile. **3** tending or disposed to help or support: *a friendly breeze helped them escape.* ◆ *n, pl* **friendlies. 4** Also: **friendly match.** *Sport.* a match played for its own sake.
▸ **'friendlily** *adv* ▸ **'friendliness** *n*

-friendly *adj combining form.* helpful, easy, or good for the person or thing specified: *ozone-friendly.*

friendly fire *n Mil.* firing by one's own side, esp. when it harms one's own personnel.

Friendly Islands ★ *pl n* another name for **Tonga.**

friendly society *n Brit.* an association of people who pay regular dues or other sums in return for old-age pensions, sickness benefits, etc.

Friends of the Earth *n* an organization of environmentalists and conservationists.

frier ('fraɪə) *n* a variant spelling of **fryer.** See **fry**[1].

fries (fraɪz) *pl n* short for **French fried potatoes**; chips.

Friese-Greene ★ (ˌfriːzˈgriːn) *n* **William.** 1855–1921, British photographer. He invented (with Mortimer Evans) the first practicable motion-picture camera.

Friesian (ˈfriːʒən) *n* **1** *Brit.* any of several breeds of black-and-white dairy cattle having a high milk yield. **2** see **Frisian.**

Friesland ★ (ˈfriːzlənd; *Dutch* ˈfriːslɑnt) *n* **1** a province of the N Netherlands, on the IJsselmeer and the North Sea: includes four of the West Frisian Islands. Capital: Leeuwarden. Pop.: 615 000 (1997 est.). Area: 3319 sq. km (1294 sq. miles). Official name: **Fryslân. 2** an area comprising the province of Friesland in the Netherlands along with the regions of East Friesland and North Friesland in Germany.

frieze[1] (friːz) *n* **1** *Archit.* **1a** the horizontal band between the architrave and cornice of a classical entablature. **1b** the upper part of the wall of a room, below the cornice. **2** any ornamental band on a wall. ORIG C16: from F *frise,* ?from Med. L *frisium,* changed from L *Phrygium* Phrygian (work), from Phrygia, famous for embroidery in gold

frieze[2] (friːz) *n* a heavy woollen fabric used for coats, etc. ORIG C15: from OF, from MDu. ?from *Vriese* Frisian

frigate (ˈfrɪgɪt) *n* **1** a medium-sized square-rigged warship of the 18th and 19th centuries. **2a** *Brit.* a warship smaller than a destroyer. **2b** *US.* (formerly) a warship larger than a destroyer. **2c** *US.* a small escort vessel. ORIG C16: from F *frégate,* from It. *fregata,* from ?

frigate bird *n* a bird of tropical and subtropical seas, having a long bill, a wide wingspan, and a forked tail.

Frigg (frɪg) *or* **Frigga** ★ (ˈfrɪgə) *n Norse myth.* the wife of Odin; goddess of the heavens and married love.

fright (fraɪt) *n* **1** sudden fear or alarm. **2** a sudden alarming shock. **3** *Inf.* a horrifying or ludicrous person or thing: *she looks a fright.* **4 take fright.** to become frightened. ◆ *vb* **5** a poetic word for **frighten.** ORIG OE *fryhto*

frighten (ˈfraɪtᵊn) *vb* (*tr*) **1** to terrify; scare. **2** to drive or force to go (away, off, out, in, etc.) by making afraid.
▸ **ˈfrightener** *n* ▸ **ˈfrighteningly** *adv*

frightful (ˈfraɪtfʊl) *adj* **1** very alarming or horrifying. **2** unpleasant, annoying, or extreme: *a frightful hurry.*
▸ **ˈfrightfully** *adv* ▸ **ˈfrightfulness** *n*

frigid (ˈfrɪdʒɪd) *adj* **1** formal or stiff in behaviour or temperament. **2** (esp. of women) lacking sexual responsiveness. **3** characterized by physical coldness: *a frigid zone.* ORIG C15: from L *frigidus* cold, from *frīgēre* to be cold
▸ **friˈgidity** *or* **ˈfrigidness** *n* ▸ **ˈfrigidly** *adv*

Frigid Zone *n* the cold region inside the Arctic or Antarctic Circle where the sun's rays are very oblique.

frijol (*Spanish* friˈxol) *n, pl* **frijoles** (*Spanish* -ˈxoles). a variety of bean extensively cultivated for food in Mexico. ORIG C16: from Sp., ult. from L *phaseolus,* from Gk *phasēlos* bean with edible pod

frill (frɪl) *n* **1** a gathered, ruched, or pleated strip of cloth sewn on at one edge only, as on garments, as ornament, or to give extra body. **2** a ruff of hair or feathers around the neck of a dog or bird or a fold of skin around the neck of a reptile or amphibian. **3** (*often pl*) *Inf.* a superfluous or pretentious thing or manner; affectation: *he made a plain speech with no frills.* ◆ *vb* **4** (*tr*) to adorn or fit with a frill or frills. **5** to form into a frill or frills. ORIG C14: ? of Flemish origin
▸ **ˈfrilliness** *n* ▸ **ˈfrilly** *adj*

frilled lizard *n* a large arboreal insectivorous Australian lizard having an erectile fold of skin around the neck.

fringe (frɪndʒ) *n* **1** an edging consisting of hanging threads, tassels, etc. **2a** an outer edge; periphery. **2b** (*as modifier*): *a fringe area.* **3** (*modifier*) unofficial; not conventional in form: *fringe theatre.* **4** *Chiefly Brit.* a section of the front hair cut short over the forehead. **5** an ornamental border. **6** *Physics.* any of the light and dark bands produced by diffraction or interference of light. ◆ *vb* **fringes, fringing, fringed.** (*tr*) **7** to adorn with a fringe or fringes. **8** to be a fringe for. ORIG C14: from OF *frenge,* ult. from L *fimbria* fringe, border
▸ **ˈfringeless** *adj*

fringe benefit *n* an additional advantage, esp. a benefit provided by an employer to supplement an employee's regular pay.

fringing reef *n* a coral reef close to the shore to which it is attached, having a steep seaward edge.

Frink ★ (frɪŋk) *n* Dame **Elisabeth.** 1930–93, British sculptor.

frippery (ˈfrɪpərɪ) *n, pl* **fripperies. 1** ornate or showy clothing or adornment. **2** ostentation. **3** trifles; trivia. ORIG C16: from OF, from *frepe* frill, rag, from Med. L *faluppa* a straw, splinter, from ?

Frisbee (ˈfrɪzbɪ) *n Trademark.* a light plastic disc thrown with a spinning motion for recreation or in competition.

Frisch ★ (frɪʃ) *n* **1 Karl von** (*German* karl fɔn). 1886–1982, Austrian zoologist; studied animal behaviour, esp. of bees; shared the Nobel prize for physiology or medicine 1973. **2 Max** (*German* maks). 1911–91, Swiss dramatist and novelist. His works include the play *Biedermann und die Brandstifter* (1953) and the novel *Stiller* (1954). **3 Otto.** 1904–79, British nuclear physicist, born in Austria, who contributed to the development of the first atomic bomb. **4 Ragnar** (**Anton Kittil**) (*Norwegian* ˈrɑːŋnɑːr). 1895–1973, Norwegian economist, who pioneered the study of econometrics: shared the first Nobel prize for economics (1969).

Frisches Haff ★ (ˈfrɪʃəs haf) *n* the German name for **Vistula** (sense 2).

Frisian (ˈfrɪʒən) *or* **Friesian** *n* **1** a language spoken in the NW Netherlands, parts of N Germany, and some of the adjacent islands. **2** a speaker of this language or a native or inhabitant of Friesland. ◆ *adj* **3** of or relating to this language, its speakers, or the peoples and culture of Friesland. ORIG C16: from L *Frīsiī* people of northern Germany

Frisian Islands ★ *pl n* a chain of islands in the North Sea along the coasts of the Netherlands, Germany, and Denmark: separated from the mainland by shallows.

frisk (frɪsk) *vb* **1** (*intr*) to leap, move about, or act in a playful manner. **2** (*tr*) (esp. of animals) to whisk or wave briskly: *the dog frisked its tail.* **3** (*tr*) *Inf.* to search (someone) by feeling for concealed weapons, etc. ◆ *n* **4** a playful antic or movement. **5** *Inf.* an instance of frisking a person. ORIG C16: from OF *frisque,* of Gmc origin
▸ **ˈfrisker** *n*

frisky (ˈfrɪskɪ) *adj* **friskier, friskiest.** lively, high-spirited, or playful.
▸ **ˈfriskily** *adv*

frisson *French.* (frisɔ̃) *n* a shiver; thrill. ORIG C18 (but in common use only from C20): lit.: shiver

frit (frɪt) *n* **1a** the basic materials, partially or wholly fused, for making glass, glazes for pottery, enamel, etc. **1b** a glassy substance used in some soft-paste porcelain. ◆ *vb* **frits, fritting, fritted. 2** (*tr*) to fuse (materials) in making frit. ORIG C17: from It. *fritta,* lit.: fried, from *friggere* to fry, from L *frīgere*

fritillary (frɪˈtɪlərɪ) *n, pl* **fritillaries. 1** a liliaceous plant having purple or white drooping bell-shaped flowers, typically marked in a chequered pattern. **2** any of various butterflies having brownish wings chequered with black and silver. ORIG C17: from NL *fritillāria,* from L *fritillus* dice box; prob. with reference to the markings

fritter[1] (ˈfrɪtə) *vb* (*tr*) **1** (usually foll. by *away*) to waste: *to fritter away time.* **2** to break into small pieces. ORIG C18: prob. from obs. *fitter* to break into small pieces, ult. from OE *fitt* a piece

fritter[2] (ˈfrɪtə) *n* a piece of food, such as apple, that is dipped in batter and fried in deep fat. ORIG C14: from OF, from L *frictus* fried, from *frīgere* to fry

Friuli ★ (*Italian* friˈuːli) *n* a historic region of SW Europe, between the Carnic Alps and the Gulf of Venice: the W part (**Venetian Friuli**) was ceded by Austria to Italy in 1866 and **Eastern Friuli** in 1919; in 1947 Eastern Friuli (except Gorizia) was ceded to Yugoslavia.

Friuli-Venezia Giulia ★ (*Italian* ˈdʒuːlja) *n* a region of NE Italy, formed in 1947 from **Venetian Friuli** and part of **Eastern Friuli.** Capital: Trieste. Pop.: 1 188 897 (1996 est.). Area: 7851 sq. km (3031 sq. miles).

★ people and places

frivolous ('frɪvələs) *adj* **1** not serious or sensible in content, attitude, or behaviour. **2** unworthy of serious or sensible treatment: *frivolous details.* ORIG C15: from L *frīvolus*
▸ '**frivolously** *adv* ▸ '**frivolousness** *or* **frivolity** (frɪ'vɒlɪtɪ) *n*

frizz (frɪz) *vb* **1** (of the hair, nap, etc.) to form or cause (the hair, etc.) to form tight curls or crisp tufts. ◆ *n* **2** hair that has been frizzed. **3** the state of being frizzed. ORIG C19: from F *friser* to curl

frizzle[1] ('frɪzᵊl) *vb* **frizzles, frizzling, frizzled. 1** to form (the hair) into tight crisp curls. ◆ *n* **2** a tight curl. ORIG C16: prob. rel. to OE *frīs* curly

frizzle[2] ('frɪzᵊl) *vb* **frizzles, frizzling, frizzled. 1** to scorch or be scorched, esp. with a sizzling noise. **2** (*tr*) to fry (bacon, etc.) until crisp. ORIG C16: prob. blend of FRY[1] + SIZZLE

frizzy ('frɪzɪ) *or* **frizzly** ('frɪzlɪ) *adj* **frizzier, frizziest** *or* **frizzlier, frizzliest.** (of the hair) in tight crisp wiry curls.
▸ '**frizziness** *or* '**frizzliness** *n*

fro (frəʊ) *adv* back or from. ORIG C12: from ON *frā*

Frobisher ★ ('frəʊbɪʃə) *n* Sir **Martin.** ?1535–94, English navigator and explorer: made three unsuccessful voyages in search of the Northwest Passage (1576; 1577; 1578), visiting Labrador and Baffin Island.

Frobisher Bay ★ *n* **1** an inlet of the Atlantic in NE Canada, in the SE coast of Baffin Island. **2** the former name of **Iqaluit.**

frock (frɒk) *n* **1** a girl's or woman's dress. **2** a loose garment of several types, such as a peasant's smock. **3** a wide-sleeved outer garment worn by members of some religious orders. ◆ *vb* **4** (*tr*) to invest (a person) with the office of a cleric. ORIG C14: from OF *froc*

frock coat *n* a man's single- or double-breasted skirted coat, as worn in the 19th century.

Fröding ★ (*Swedish* 'frø:diŋ) *n* **Gustaf** ('gustav). 1860–1911, Swedish poet. His popular lyric verse includes the collections *Guitar and Concertina* (1891), *New Poems* (1894), and *Splashes and Rags* (1896).

Froebel *or* **Fröbel** ★ *n* (*German* 'frø:bəl). **1 Friedrich (Wilhelm August)** ('fri:drɪç). 1782–1852, German educator: founded the first kindergarten (1840). ◆ *adj* ('frəʊbᵊl). **2** of, denoting, or relating to a system of kindergarten education developed by him or to the training and qualification of teachers to use this system.

frog[1] (frɒg) *n* **1** an insectivorous amphibian, having a short squat tailless body with a moist smooth skin and very long hind legs specialized for hopping. **2** any of various similar amphibians, such as the tree frog. **3** any spiked object that is used to support plant stems in a flower arrangement. **4 a frog in one's throat.** phlegm on the vocal cords that affects one's speech. ORIG OE *frogga*
▸ '**froggy** *adj*

frog[2] (frɒg) *n* **1** (*often pl*) a decorative fastening of looped braid or cord, as on a military uniform. **2** an attachment on a belt to hold the scabbard of a sword, etc. ORIG C18: ? ult. from L *floccus* tuft of hair
▸ **frogged** *adj* ▸ '**frogging** *n*

frog[3] (frɒg) *n* a tough elastic horny material in the centre of the sole of a horse's foot. ORIG C17: from ?

frog[4] (frɒg) *n* a plate of iron or steel to guide train wheels over an intersection of railway lines. ORIG C19: from ?; ? a special use of FROG[1]

Frog (frɒg) *or* **Froggy** ('frɒgɪ) *n, pl* **Frogs** *or* **Froggies.** *Brit. sl.* a derogatory word for a French person.

froghopper ('frɒg,hɒpə) *n* any small leaping insect whose larvae secrete a protective spittle-like substance around themselves.

frogman ('frɒgmən) *n, pl* **frogmen.** a swimmer equipped with a rubber suit, flippers, and breathing equipment for working underwater.

frogmarch ('frɒg,mɑ:tʃ) *Chiefly Brit.* ◆ *n* **1** a method of carrying a resisting person in which each limb is held and the victim is carried horizontally and face downwards. **2** any method of making a person move against his will. ◆ *vb* **3** (*tr*) to carry in a frogmarch or cause to move forward unwillingly.

frogmouth ('frɒg,maʊθ) *n* a nocturnal insectivorous bird of SE Asia and Australia, similar to the nightjars.

frogspawn ('frɒg,spɔ:n) *n* a mass of fertilized frogs' eggs surrounded by a protective nutrient jelly.

frog spit *or* **spittle** *n* **1** another name for **cuckoo spit. 2** a foamy mass of threadlike green algae floating on ponds.

Froissart ★ (*French* frwasar) *n* **Jean** (ʒɑ̃). ?1333–?1400, French chronicler and poet, noted for his *Chronique.*

frolic ('frɒlɪk) *n* **1** a light-hearted entertainment or occasion. **2** light-hearted activity; gaiety. ◆ *vb* **frolics, frolicking, frolicked. 3** (*intr*) to caper about. ◆ *adj* **4** *Arch.* full of fun; gay. ORIG C16: from Du. *vrolijk,* from MDu. *vro* happy
▸ '**frolicker** *n*

frolicsome ('frɒlɪksəm) *adj* merry and playful.
▸ '**frolicsomely** *adv*

from (frɒm; *unstressed* frəm) *prep* **1** used to indicate the original location, situation, etc.: *from behind the bushes.* **2** in a period of time starting at: *he lived from 1910 to 1970.* **3** used to indicate the distance between two things or places: *a hundred miles from here.* **4** used to indicate a lower amount: *from five to fifty pounds.* **5** showing the model of: *painted from life.* **6** used with the gerund to mark prohibition, etc.: *nothing prevents him from leaving.* **7** because of: *exhausted from his walk.* ORIG OE *fram*

fromage frais ('frɒmɑ:ʒ 'freɪ; *French* frɔmaʒ frɛ) *n* a low-fat soft cheese with a smooth light texture. ORIG F, lit.: fresh cheese

Frome ★ (frəʊm) *n* **Lake.** a shallow salt lake in NE South Australia: intermittently filled with water. Length: 100 km (60 miles). Width: 48 km (30 miles).

Fromm ★ (frɒm) *n* **Erich** ('ɛrɪk). 1900–80, US psychologist and philosopher, born in Germany. His works include *The Art of Loving* (1956) and *To Have and To Be* (1976).

frond (frɒnd) *n* **1** the compound leaf of a fern. **2** the leaf of a palm. ORIG C18: from L *frōns*

front (frʌnt) *n* **1** that part or side that is forward, or most often seen or used. **2** a position or place directly before or ahead: *a fountain stood at the front of the building.* **3** the beginning, opening, or first part. **4** the position of leadership: *in the front of scientific knowledge.* **5** land bordering a lake, street, etc. **6** land along a seashore or large lake, esp. a promenade. **7** *Mil.* **7a** the total area in which opposing armies face each other. **7b** the space in which a military unit is operating: *to advance on a broad front.* **8** *Meteorol.* the dividing line or plane between two air masses of different origins. **9** outward aspect or bearing, as when dealing with a situation: *a bold front.* **10** *Inf.* a business or other activity serving as a respectable cover for another, usually criminal, organization. **11** Also called: **front man.** a nominal leader of an organization etc.; figurehead. **12** *Inf.* outward appearance of rank or wealth. **13** a particular field of activity: *on the wages front.* **14** a group of people with a common goal: *a national liberation front.* **15** a false shirt front; a dicky. **16** *Arch.* the forehead or the face. ◆ *adj* (*prenominal*) **17** of, at, or in the front: *a front seat.* **18** *Phonetics.* of or denoting a vowel articulated with the tongue brought forward, as for the sound of *ee* in English *see* or *a* in English *hat.* ◆ *vb* **19** (when *intr,* foll. by *on* or *onto*) to face (onto): *this house fronts the river.* **20** (*tr*) to be a front of or for. **21** (*tr*) to appear as a presenter in a television show. **22** (*tr*) to be the lead singer or player in (a band). **23** (*tr*) to confront. **24** to supply a front for. **25** (*intr;* often foll. by *up*) *Austral. inf.* to appear (at): *to front up at the police station.* ORIG C13 (in the sense: forehead, face): from L *frōns* forehead, foremost part
▸ '**frontless** *adj*

frontage ('frʌntɪdʒ) *n* **1** the façade of a building or the front of a plot of ground. **2** the extent of the front of a shop, plot of land, etc. **3** the direction in which a building faces.

frontal ('frʌntᵊl) *adj* **1** of, at, or in the front. **2** of or relating to the forehead: *frontal artery.* ◆ *n* **3** a decorative hanging for the front of an altar. ORIG C14 (in the sense: adornment for forehead, altarcloth): via OF *frontel,* from L *frōns* forehead
▸ '**frontally** *adv*

frontal lobe *n Anat.* the anterior portion of each cerebral hemisphere.

front bench *n* **1** *Brit.* **1a** the foremost bench of either the Government or Opposition in the House of Commons. **1b** the leadership (**frontbenchers**) of either group, who occupy this bench. **2** the leadership of the government or opposition in various legislative assemblies.

front-end *adj* (of money, costs, etc.) required or incurred in advance of a project in order to get it under way.

frontier ('frʌntɪə, frʌn'tɪə) *n* **1a** the region of a country bordering on another or a line, barrier, etc., marking such a boundary. **1b** (*as modifier*): *a frontier post.* **2** *US.* the edge of the settled area of a country. **3** (*often pl*) the limit of knowledge in a particular field: *the frontiers of physics have been pushed back.* ORIG C14: from OF, from *front* (in the sense: part which is opposite)

frontiersman ('frʌntɪəzmən, frʌn'tɪəz-) *or* (*fem*) **frontierswoman** (-ˌwʊmən) *n, pl* **frontiersmen** *or* **frontierswomen.** (formerly) a person living on a frontier, esp. in a newly pioneered territory of the US.

frontispiece ('frʌntɪsˌpiːs) *n* **1** an illustration facing the title page of a book. **2** the principal façade of a building. **3** a pediment over a door, window, etc. ORIG C16 *frontispice,* from F, from LL *frontispicium* façade, from L *frōns* forehead + *specere* to look at; infl. by PIECE

frontlet ('frʌntlɪt) *n Judaism.* a phylactery attached to the forehead. ORIG C15: from OF *frontelet* a little FRONTAL

front line *n* **1** *Military.* **1a** the most advanced military units in a battle. **1b** (*modifier*): of, relating to, or suitable for the military front line: *frontline troops.* **2** (*modifier*) close to a hostile country or scene of armed conflict: *the frontline states.*

front loader *n* a washing machine with a door at the front which opens one side of the drum into which washing is placed.

front-page *n* (*modifier*) important enough to be put on the front page of a newspaper.

frontrunner ('frʌntˌrʌnə) *n Inf.* the leader or a favoured contestant in a race, election, etc.

frontrunning ('frʌntˌrʌnɪŋ) *n Stock Exchange.* the practice by market makers of using advance information provided by their own investment analysts before it has been given to clients.

frost (frɒst) *n* **1** a white deposit of ice particles, esp. one formed on objects out of doors at night. **2** an atmospheric temperature of below freezing point, characterized by the production of this deposit. **3 degrees of frost.** degrees below freezing point. **4** *Inf.* something given a cold reception; failure. **5** *Inf.* coolness of manner. **6** the act of freezing. ◆ *vb* **7** to cover or be covered with frost. **8** (*tr*) to give a frostlike appearance to (glass, etc.), as by means of a fine-grained surface. **9** (*tr*) *Chiefly US & Canad.* to decorate (cakes, etc.) with icing or frosting. **10** (*tr*) to kill or damage (crops, etc.) with frost. ORIG OE *frost*

Frost ★ (frɒst) *n* **Robert (Lee).** 1874–1963, US poet, noted for his lyrical verse on country life in New England. His books include *A Boy's Will* (1913), *North of Boston* (1914), and *New Hampshire* (1923).

frostbite ('frɒstˌbaɪt) *n* destruction of tissues, esp. those of the fingers, ears, toes, and nose, by freezing.
▸ **'frostˌbitten** *adj*

frosted ('frɒstɪd) *adj* **1** covered or injured by frost. **2** covered with icing, as a cake. **3** (of glass, etc.) having a surface roughened to prevent clear vision through it.

frost hollow *n* a depression in a hilly area in which cold air collects, becoming very cold at night.

frosting ('frɒstɪŋ) *n* **1** another word (esp. US and Canad.) for **icing. 2** a rough or matt finish on glass, silver, etc.

frosty ('frɒstɪ) *adj* **frostier, frostiest. 1** characterized by frost: *a frosty night.* **2** covered by or decorated with frost. **3** lacking warmth or enthusiasm: *the new plan had a frosty reception.*
▸ **'frostily** *adv* ▸ **'frostiness** *n*

froth (frɒθ) *n* **1** a mass of small bubbles of air or a gas in a liquid, produced by fermentation, etc. **2** a mixture of saliva and air bubbles formed at the lips in certain diseases, such as rabies. **3** trivial ideas or entertainment. ◆ *vb* **4** to produce or cause to produce froth. **5** (*tr*) to give out in the form of froth. ORIG C14: from ON *frotha* or *frauth*
▸ **'frothy** *adj* ▸ **'frothily** *adv*

Froude ★ (fruːd) *n* **1 James Anthony.** 1818–94, British historian; author of a controversial biography (1882–84) of Carlyle. **2** his brother **William.** 1810–79, British civil engineer.

froufrou ('fruːˌfruː) *n* a swishing sound, as made by a long silk dress. ORIG C19: from F, imit.

froward ('frəʊəd) *adj Arch.* obstinate; contrary. ORIG C14: see FRO, -WARD
▸ **'frowardly** *adv* ▸ **'frowardness** *n*

frown (fraʊn) *vb* **1** (*intr*) to draw the brows together and wrinkle the forehead, esp. in worry, anger, or concentration. **2** (*intr;* foll. by *on* or *upon*) to look disapprovingly (upon). **3** (*tr*) to express (worry, etc.) by frowning. ◆ *n* **4** the act of frowning. **5** a show of dislike or displeasure. ORIG C14: from OF *froigner,* of Celtic origin
▸ **'frowner** *n* ▸ **'frowningly** *adv*

frowst (fraʊst) *n Brit. inf.* a hot and stale atmosphere; fug. ORIG C19: back formation from *frowsty* musty, stuffy, var. of FROWZY

frowsty ('fraʊstɪ) *adj* **frowstier, frowstiest.** ill-smelling; stale; musty.
▸ **'frowstiness** *n*

frowzy *or* **frowsy** ('fraʊzɪ) *adj* **frowzier, frowziest,** *or* **frowsier, frowsiest. 1** untidy or unkempt in appearance. **2** ill-smelling; frowsty. ORIG C17: from ?
▸ **'frowziness** *or* **'frowsiness** *n*

froze (frəʊz) *vb* the past tense of **freeze.**

frozen ('frəʊzᵊn) *vb* **1** the past participle of **freeze.** ◆ *adj* **2** turned into or covered with ice. **3** killed or stiffened by extreme cold. **4** (of a region or climate) icy or snowy. **5** (of food) preserved by a freezing process. **6a** (of prices, wages, etc.) arbitrarily pegged at a certain level. **6b** (of business assets) not convertible into cash. **7** frigid or disdainful in manner. **8** motionless or unyielding: *he was frozen with horror.*
▸ **'frozenly** *adv*

frozen shoulder *n Pathol.* painful stiffness in a shoulder joint.

FRS (in Britain) *abbrev. for* Fellow of the Royal Society.

FRSNZ *abbrev. for* Fellow of the Royal Society of New Zealand.

fructify ('frʌktɪˌfaɪ) *vb* **fructifies, fructifying, fructified. 1** to bear or cause to bear fruit. **2** to make or become fruitful. ORIG C14: from OF, from LL *frūctificāre,* from L *frūctus* fruit + *facere* to produce
▸ **ˌfructifi'cation** *n* ▸ **fruc'tiferous** *adj* ▸ **'fructiˌfier** *n*

fructose ('frʌktəʊs) *n* a white crystalline sugar occurring in many fruits. Formula: $C_6H_{12}O_6$. ORIG C19: from L *frūctus* fruit + -OSE[2]

frugal ('fruːgᵊl) *adj* **1** practising economy; thrifty. **2** not costly; meagre. ORIG C16: from L, from *frūgī* useful, temperate, from *frux* fruit
▸ **fru'gality** *n* ▸ **'frugally** *adv*

frugivorous (fruː'dʒɪvərəs) *adj* fruit-eating. ORIG C18: from *frugi-* (as in FRUGAL) + -VOROUS

fruit (fruːt) *n* **1** *Bot.* the ripened ovary of a flowering plant, containing one or more seeds. It may be dry, as in the poppy, or fleshy, as in the peach. **2** any fleshy part of a plant that supports the seeds and is edible, such as the strawberry. **3** any plant product useful to man, including grain, vegetables, etc. **4** (*often pl*) the result or consequence of an action or effort. **5** *Arch.* offspring of man or animals. **6** *Inf., chiefly US & Canad.* a male homosexual. ◆ *vb* **7** to bear or cause to bear fruit. ORIG C12: from OF, from L *frūctus* enjoyment, fruit, from *fruī* to enjoy
▸ **'fruitˌlike** *adj*

fruit bat *n* a large Old World bat occurring in tropical and subtropical regions and feeding on fruit.

fruitcake ('fruːtˌkeɪk) *n* a rich cake containing mixed dried fruit, lemon peel, etc.

fruit drop *n* **1** the premature shedding of fruit from a tree before fully ripe. **2** a boiled sweet with a fruity flavour.

fruiterer ('fru:tərə) *n Chiefly Brit.* a fruit dealer or seller.

fruit fly *n* **1** a small dipterous fly which feeds on and lays its eggs in plant tissues. **2** any dipterous fly of the genus *Drosophila*. See **drosophila**.

fruitful ('fru:tfʊl) *adj* **1** bearing fruit in abundance. **2** productive or prolific. **3** producing results or profits: *a fruitful discussion.*
▸ **'fruitfully** *adv* ▸ **'fruitfulness** *n*

fruition (fru:'ɪʃən) *n* **1** the attainment of something worked for or desired. **2** enjoyment of this. **3** the act or condition of bearing fruit. ORIG C15: from LL, from L *fruī* to enjoy

fruitless ('fru:tlɪs) *adj* **1** yielding nothing or nothing of value; unproductive. **2** without fruit.
▸ **'fruitlessly** *adv* ▸ **'fruitlessness** *n*

fruit machine *n Brit.* a gambling machine that pays out when certain combinations of diagrams, usually of fruit, appear on a dial.

fruit salad *n* a dessert consisting of sweet fruits cut up and served in a syrup.

fruit sugar *n* another name for **fructose**.

fruit tree *n* any tree that bears edible fruit.

fruity ('fru:tɪ) *adj* **fruitier, fruitiest. 1** of or resembling fruit. **2** (of a voice) mellow or rich. **3** *Inf., chiefly Brit.* erotically stimulating; salacious. **4** *Inf., chiefly US & Canad.* homosexual.
▸ **'fruitily** *adv* ▸ **'fruitiness** *n*

frumenty ('fru:məntɪ) *or* **furmenty** *n Brit.* a kind of porridge made from hulled wheat boiled with milk, sweetened, and spiced. ORIG C14: from OF, from *frument* grain, from L *frūmentum*

frump (frʌmp) *n* a woman who is dowdy, drab, or unattractive. ORIG C16 (in the sense: to be sullen; C19: dowdy woman): from MDu. *verrompelen* to wrinkle
▸ **'frumpy** *or* **'frumpish** *adj*

Frunze ★ (*Russian* 'frunzɪ) *n* the former name (until 1991) of **Bishkek**.

frustrate (frʌ'streɪt) *vb* **frustrates, frustrating, frustrated.** (*tr*) **1** to hinder or prevent (the efforts, plans, or desires) of. **2** to upset, agitate, or tire. ◆ *adj* **3** *Arch.* frustrated or thwarted. ORIG C15: from L *frustrāre* to cheat, from *frustrā* in error
▸ **frus'tration** *n*

frustrated (frʌ'streɪtɪd) *adj* having feelings of dissatisfaction or lack of fulfilment.

frustum ('frʌstəm) *n, pl* **frustums** *or* **frusta** (-tə). *Geom.* **a** the part of a solid, such as a cone or pyramid, contained between the base and a plane parallel to the base that intersects the solid. **b** the part of such a solid contained between two parallel planes intersecting the solid. ORIG C17: from L: piece

fry[1] (fraɪ) *vb* **fries, frying, fried. 1** (when *tr*, sometimes foll. by *up*) to cook or be cooked in fat, oil, etc., usually over direct heat. **2** *Sl., chiefly US.* to kill or be killed by electrocution. ◆ *n, pl* **fries. 3** a dish of something fried, esp. the offal of a specified animal: *pig's fry.* **4 fry-up.** *Brit. inf.* the act of preparing a mixed fried dish or the dish itself. ORIG C13: from OF *frire*, from L *frīgere* to fry
▸ **'fryer** *or* **'frier** *n*

fry[2] (fraɪ) *pl n* **1** the young of various species of fish. **2** the young of certain other animals, such as frogs. ORIG C14 (in the sense: young, offspring): from OF *freier* to spawn, from L *fricāre* to rub

Fry ★ (fraɪ) *n* **1 Christopher.** born 1907, English dramatist; author of the verse dramas *A Phoenix Too Frequent* (1946), *The Lady's Not For Burning* (1948), *Venus Observed* (1950), and *One Thing More* (1986). **2 Elizabeth.** 1780–1845, English prison reformer and Quaker. **3 Roger Eliot.** 1866–1934, English art critic and painter who helped to introduce the postimpressionists to Britain. His books include *Vision and Design* (1920) and *Cézanne* (1927).

frying pan *n* **1** a long-handled shallow pan used for frying. **2 out of the frying pan into the fire.** from a bad situation to a worse one.

FSB *abbrev. for* the Russian Federal Security Service, founded in 1995. ORIG C20: from Russian *Federalnaya sluzhba bezopasnosti*

f-stop ('ɛf,stɒp) *n* any of the settings for the f-number of a camera.

ft. *abbrev. for* foot *or* feet.

FTAA *abbrev. for* Free Trade Area of the Americas.

fth. *or* **fthm.** *abbrev. for* fathom.

FT Index *abbrev. for:* **1** Financial Times Industrial Ordinary Share Index: an index designed to show the general trend in share prices, produced daily by the *Financial Times* newspaper. **2** Financial Times Stock Exchange 100 Index: an index produced by the *Financial Times* based on an average of 100 securities and giving the best indication of daily movements. Also: **FTSE Index.** Informal name: **Footsie.**

FTP *abbrev.* (*sometimes not caps.*) *for* file transfer protocol: the standard mechanism used to transfer files between computer systems or across the Internet.

Fuad I ★ (fu:'ɑ:d) *n* original name *Ahmed Fuad Pasha.* 1868–1936, sultan of Egypt (1917–22) and king (1922–36).

Fu-chou ★ ('fu:'tʃaʊ) *n* a variant transliteration of the Chinese name for **Fuzhou**.

Fuchs ★ (fʊks, fu:ks) *n* **1 Klaus Emil** (*German* klaus 'e:mi:l). 1911–88, German physicist, who became a British citizen (1942) and was imprisoned (1950–59) for giving secret atomic information to the Soviet Union. **2** Sir **Vivian Ernest.** 1908–99, British explorer and geologist: led the Commonwealth Trans-Antarctic Expedition (1955–58).

fuchsia ('fju:ʃə) *n* **1** a shrub widely cultivated for its showy drooping purple, red, or white flowers. **2a** a reddish-purple to purplish-pink colour. **2b** (*as adj*): *a fuchsia dress.* ORIG C18: from NL, after Leonhard *Fuchs* (1501–66), G botanist

fuchsin ('fu:ksɪn) *or* **fuchsine** ('fu:ksi:n, -sɪn) *n* an aniline dye forming a red solution in water: used as a textile dye and a biological stain. ORIG C19: from FUCHS(IA) + -IN; from its similarity in colour to the flower

fuck (fʌk) *Taboo.* ◆ *vb* **1** to have sexual intercourse with (someone). ◆ *n* **2** an act of sexual intercourse. **3** *Sl.* a partner in sexual intercourse. **4 not care** *or* **give a fuck.** not to care at all. ◆ *interj* **5** *Offens.* an expression of strong disgust or anger. ORIG C16: of Gmc origin

fuck off *Offens. taboo sl.* ◆ *interj* **1** a forceful expression of dismissal or contempt. ◆ *vb* **2** (*intr, adv*) to go away. ◆ *adj* **3** (*prenominal*) very large or impressive: *a huge fuck-off cigar.*

fucus ('fju:kəs) *n, pl* **fuci** (-saɪ) *or* **fucuses.** a seaweed of the genus *Fucus*, having greenish-brown slimy fronds. ORIG C16: from L: rock lichen, from Gk *phukos* seaweed, of Semitic origin

fuddle ('fʌdᵊl) *vb* **fuddles, fuddling, fuddled. 1** (*tr; often passive*) to cause to be confused or intoxicated. ◆ *n* **2** a muddled or confused state. ORIG C16: from ?

fuddy-duddy ('fʌdɪ,dʌdɪ) *n, pl* **fuddy-duddies.** *Inf.* a person, esp. an elderly one, who is extremely conservative or dull. ORIG C20: from ?

fudge[1] (fʌdʒ) *n* a soft variously flavoured sweet made from sugar, butter, etc. ORIG C19: from ?

fudge[2] (fʌdʒ) *n* **1** foolishness; nonsense. ◆ *interj* **2** a mild exclamation of annoyance. ORIG C18: from ?

fudge[3] (fʌdʒ) *n* **1** a small section of type matter in a box in a newspaper allowing late news to be included without the whole page having to be remade. **2** the late news so inserted. **3** an unsatisfactory compromise reached to evade a difficult problem or controversial issue. ◆ *vb* **fudges, fudging, fudged. 4** (*tr*) to make or adjust in a false or clumsy way. **5** (*tr*) to misrepresent; falsify. **6** to evade (a problem, issue, etc.). ORIG C19: ? rel. to arch. *fadge* to agree, succeed

fuel (fjʊəl) *n* **1** any substance burned as a source of heat or power, such as coal or petrol. **2** the material, containing a fissile substance such as uranium-235, that produces energy in a nuclear reactor. **3** something that nourishes or builds up emotion, action, etc. ◆ *vb* **fuels, fuelling, fuelled** *or US* **fuels, fueling, fueled. 4** to supply with or receive fuel. ORIG C14: from OF, from *feu* fire, ult. from L *focus* hearth

fuel air bomb *n* a type of bomb that spreads a cloud of gas, which is then detonated, over the target area, causing extensive destruction.

fuel cell *n* a cell in which chemical energy is converted directly into electrical energy.

fuel injection *n* a system for introducing fuel directly into the combustion chambers of an internal-combustion engine without the use of a carburettor.

fuel oil *n* a liquid petroleum product used as a substitute for coal in industrial furnaces, ships, and locomotives.

Fuentes ★ (*Spanish* 'fwentes) *n* **Carlos** ('karlɔs). born 1928, Mexican writer. His novels include *The Death of Artemio Cruz* (1962), *Terra Nostra* (1975), *The Old Gringo* (1985), and *Cristóbal Nonato* (1987).

fug (fʌg) *n Chiefly Brit.* a hot, stale, or suffocating atmosphere. ORIG C19: ? var. of FOG[1]
▸ **'fuggy** *adj*

fugacity (fjuː'gæsɪtɪ) *n Thermodynamics.* a property of a gas that expresses its tendency to escape or expand.

Fugard ★ ('fuːgɑːd) *n* **Athol** ('æθəl). born 1932, South African dramatist and director. His plays include *The Blood-Knot* (1961), *Sizwe Banzi is Dead* (1972), and *Sign of Hope* (1992).

-fuge *n combining form.* indicating an agent or substance that expels or drives away: *vermifuge.* ORIG from L *fugāre* to expel

fugitive ('fjuːdʒɪtɪv) *n* **1** a person who flees. **2** a thing that is elusive or fleeting. ◆ *adj* **3** fleeing, esp. from arrest or pursuit. **4** not permanent; fleeting. ORIG C14: from L, from *fugere* to take flight
▸ **'fugitively** *adv*

fugleman ('fjuːgᵊlmən) *n, pl* **fuglemen. 1** (formerly) a soldier used as an example for those learning drill. **2** a leader or example. ORIG C19: from G *Flügelmann,* from *Flügel* wing + *Mann* MAN

fugue (fjuːg) *n* **1** a musical form consisting of a theme repeated a fifth above or a fourth below the continuing first statement. **2** *Psychiatry.* a dreamlike altered state of consciousness, during which a person may lose his memory and wander away. ORIG C16: from F, from It. *fuga,* from L: a running away
▸ **'fugal** *adj*

Führer *or* ***Fuehrer*** *German.* ('fyːrər) *n* a leader: applied esp. to Adolf Hitler while he was Chancellor. ORIG G, from *führen* to lead

Fuji ★ ('fuːdʒɪ) *n* **Mount.** an extinct volcano in central Japan, in S central Honshu: the highest mountain in Japan, famous for its symmetrical snow-capped cone. Height: 3776 m (12 388 ft). Also called: **Fujiyama, Fuji-san.**

Fujian *or* **Fukien** ★ ('fuː'kjɛn) *n* **1** a province of SE China: mountainous and forested, drained chiefly by the Min River; noted for the production of flower-scented teas. Capital: Fuzhou. Pop.: 32 820 000 (1997 est.). Area: 123 000 sq. km (47 970 sq. miles). **2** any of the Chinese dialects of this province.

Fukuoka ★ (ˌfuːkuː'əʊkə) *n* an industrial city and port in SW Japan, in N Kyushu: an important port in ancient times; site of Kyushu university. Pop.: 1 284 741 (1995).

-ful *suffix.* **1** (*forming adjectives*) full of or characterized by: *painful; restful.* **2** (*forming adjectives*) able or tending to: *useful.* **3** (*forming nouns*) indicating as much as will fill the thing specified: *mouthful.* ORIG OE *-ful, -full,* from FULL[1]

> **USAGE NOTE** Where the amount held by a spoon, etc., is used as a rough unit of measurement, the correct form is *spoonful*, etc.: *take a spoonful of this medicine every day. Spoon full* is used in a sentence such as *he held out a spoon full of dark liquid,* where *full of* describes the spoon. A plural form such as *spoonfuls* is preferred by many speakers and writers to *spoonsful.*

fulcrum ('fʊlkrəm, 'fʌl-) *n, pl* **fulcrums** *or* **fulcra** (-krə). **1** the pivot about which a lever turns. **2** something that supports or sustains; prop. ORIG C17: from L: foot of a couch, from *fulcire* to prop up

fulfil *or US* **fulfill** (fʊl'fɪl) *vb* **fulfils, fulfilling, fulfilled** *or US* **fulfills, fulfilling, fulfilled.** (*tr*) **1** to bring about the completion or achievement of (a desire, promise, etc.). **2** to carry out or execute (a request, etc.). **3** to conform with or satisfy (regulations, etc.). **4** to finish or reach the end of. **5 fulfil oneself.** to achieve one's potential or desires. ORIG OE *fulfyllan*
▸ **ful'filment** *or US* **ful'fillment** *n*

fulgent ('fʌldʒənt) *adj Poetic.* shining brilliantly; gleaming. ORIG C15: from L *fulgēre* to shine

fulgurate ('fʌlgjʊˌreɪt) *vb* **fulgurates, fulgurating, fulgurated.** (*intr*) *Rare.* to flash like lightning. ORIG C17: from L, from *fulgur* lightning

fulgurite ('fʌlgjʊˌraɪt) *n* glassy mineral matter found in sand and rock, formed by the action of lightning. ORIG C19: from L *fulgur* lightning

Fulham ★ ('fʊləm) *n* a district of the Greater London borough of Hammersmith and Fulham (since 1965): contains **Fulham Palace** (16th century), residence of the Bishop of London.

fuliginous (fjuː'lɪdʒɪnəs) *adj* **1** sooty or smoky. **2** of the colour of soot. ORIG C16: from LL *fūlīginōsus* full of soot, from L *fūlīgō* soot

full[1] (fʊl) *adj* **1** holding or containing as much as possible. **2** abundant in supply, quantity, number, etc.: *full of energy.* **3** having consumed enough food or drink. **4** (esp. of the face or figure) rounded or plump. **5** (*prenominal*) complete: *a full dozen.* **6** (*prenominal*) with all privileges, rights, etc.: *a full member.* **7** (*prenominal*) having the same parents: *a full brother.* **8** filled with emotion or sentiment: *a full heart.* **9** (*postpositive;* foll. by *of*) occupied or engrossed (with): *full of his own projects.* **10** *Music.* **10a** powerful or rich in volume and sound. **10b** completing a piece or section; concluding: *a full close.* **11** (of a garment, esp. a skirt) containing a large amount of fabric. **12** (of sails, etc.) distended by wind. **13** (of wine, such as a burgundy) having a heavy body. **14** (of a colour) rich; saturated. **15** *Inf.* drunk. **16 full of oneself.** full of pride or conceit. **17 full up.** filled to capacity. **18 in full swing.** at the height of activity: *the party was in full swing.* ◆ *adv* **19a** completely; entirely. **19b** (*in combination*): *full-fledged.* **20** directly; right: *he hit him full in the stomach.* **21** very; extremely (esp. in **full well**). ◆ *n* **22** the greatest degree, extent, etc. **23 in full.** without omitting or shortening: *we paid in full for our mistake.* **24 to the full.** thoroughly; fully. ◆ *vb* **25** (*tr*) *Needlework.* to gather or tuck. **26** (*intr*) (of the moon) to be fully illuminated. ORIG OE
▸ **'fullness** *or esp. US* **'fulness** *n*

full[2] (fʊl) *vb* (of cloth, yarn, etc.) to become or to make (cloth, yarn, etc.) more compact during manufacture through shrinking and pressing. ORIG C14: from OF *fouler,* ult. from L *fullō* a FULLER

fullback ('fʊlˌbæk) *n Soccer, hockey, rugby.* **a** a defensive player. **b** the position held by this player.

full-blooded *adj* **1** (esp. of horses) of unmixed ancestry. **2** having great vigour or health; hearty.
▸ **ˌfull-'bloodedness** *n*

full-blown *adj* **1** characterized by the fullest, strongest, or best development. **2** in full bloom.

full board *n* accommodation at a hotel, etc., that includes all meals.

full-bodied *adj* having a full rich flavour or quality.

full-court press *n Basketball.* the tactic of harrying the opposing team in all areas of the court, as opposed to the more usual practice of trying to defend one's own basket.

full dress *n* **a** a formal style of dress, such as white tie and tails for a man. **b** (*as modifier*): *full-dress uniform.*

full employment *n* a state in which the labour force and other economic resources of a country are utilized to their maximum extent.

fuller ('fʊlə) *n* a person who fulls cloth for a living. ORIG OE *fullere*

Fuller ★ ('fʊlə) *n* **1** (**Richard**) **Buckminster.** 1895–1983, US architect and engineer: developed the geodesic dome. **2**

Roy (**Broadbent**). 1912–91, British poet, whose collections of poetry include *The Middle of a War* (1942), *A Lost Season* (1944), and *Epitaphs and Occasions* (1949). **3 Thomas.** 1608–61, English clergyman and antiquarian; author of *The Worthies of England* (1662).

fullerene ('fʊləˌriːn) *n* short for **buckminsterfullerene.**

fuller's earth *n* a natural absorbent clay used, after heating, for clarifying oils and fats, fulling cloth, etc.

full face *adj* facing towards the viewer, with the entire face visible.

full-fledged *adj* See **fully fledged.**

full-frontal *Inf.* ◆ *adj* **1** (of a nude person or a photograph of a nude person) exposing the genitals to full view. **2** all-out; unrestrained. ◆ *n* **full frontal. 3** a full-frontal photograph.

full house *n* **1** *Poker.* a hand with three cards of the same value and another pair. **2** a theatre, etc., filled to capacity. **3** (in bingo, etc.) the set of numbers needed to win.

full-length *n* (*modifier*) **1** showing the complete length. **2** not abridged.

full moon *n* one of the four phases of the moon when the moon is visible as a fully illuminated disc.

full monty ('mɒntɪ) *n* **the.** *Inf.* something in its entirety. ORIG from ?

full nelson *n* a wrestling hold in which a wrestler places both arms under his opponent's arms from behind and exerts pressure on the back of the neck.

full-on *adj Inf.* complete; unrestrained: *full-on military intervention; full-on hard rock.*

full sail *adv* **1** at top speed. ◆ *adj* (*postpositive*), *adv* **2** with all sails set.

full-scale *n* (*modifier*) **1** (of a plan, etc.) of actual size. **2** using all resources; all-out.

full stop *or* **full point** *n* the punctuation mark (.) used at the end of a sentence that is not a question or exclamation, after abbreviations, etc. Also called (esp. US and Canad.): **period.**

full time *n* the end of a football or other match.

full-time *adj* **1** for the entire time appropriate to an activity: *a full-time job.* ◆ *adv* **full time. 2** on a full-time basis: *he works full time.* ◆ Cf. **part-time.**
▸ ˌ**full-'timer** *n*

full toss *or* **full pitch** *n Cricket.* a bowled ball that reaches the batsman without bouncing.

fully ('fʊlɪ) *adv* **1** to the greatest degree or extent. **2** amply; adequately: *they were fully fed.* **3** at least: *it was fully an hour before she came.*

fully fashioned *adj* (of stockings, knitwear, etc.) shaped and seamed so as to fit closely.

fully fledged *or* **full-fledged** *adj* **1** (of a young bird) having acquired adult feathers, enabling it to fly. **2** developed to the fullest degree. **3** of full rank or status.

fulmar ('fʊlmə) *n* a heavily built short-tailed oceanic bird of polar regions. ORIG C17: of Scand. origin

fulminate ('fʌlmɪˌneɪt) *vb* **fulminates, fulminating, fulminated. 1** (*intr;* often foll. by *against*) to make severe criticisms or denunciations; rail. **2** to explode with noise and violence. ◆ *n* **3** any salt or ester of **fulminic acid,** an isomer of cyanic acid, which is used as a detonator. ORIG C15: from Med. L, from L, from *fulmen* lightning that strikes
▸ '**fulminant** *adj* ▸ ˌ**fulmi'nation** *n* ▸ '**fulmiˌnatory** *adj*

fulsome ('fʊlsəm) *adj* **1** excessive or insincere, esp. in an offensive or distasteful way: *fulsome compliments.* **2** *Not standard.* extremely complimentary. **3** *Inf.* full, rich, or abundant: *a fulsome figure; a fulsome flavour; fulsome detail.*
▸ '**fulsomely** *adv* ▸ '**fulsomeness** *n*

> **USAGE NOTE** The use of *fulsome* to mean 'extremely complimentary' or 'full, rich, or abundant' is common in journalism, but should be avoided in other kinds of writing.

Fulton ★ ('fʊltᵊn) *n* **Robert.** 1765–1815, US engineer and inventor: designed the first commercially successful steamboat (1807) and the first steam warship (1814).

fulvous ('fʌlvəs) *adj* of a dull brownish-yellow colour. ORIG C17: from L *fulvus* reddish yellow

fumarole ('fjuːməˌrəʊl) *n* a vent in or near a volcano from which hot gases, esp. steam, are emitted. ORIG C19: from F, from LL *fūmāriolum* smoke hole, from L *fūmus* smoke

fumble ('fʌmbᵊl) *vb* **fumbles, fumbling, fumbled. 1** (*intr;* often foll. by *for* or *with*) to grope about clumsily or blindly, esp. in searching. **2** (*intr;* foll. by *at* or *with*) to finger or play with, esp. in an absent-minded way. **3** to say or do awkwardly: *he fumbled the introduction badly.* **4** to fail to catch or grasp (a ball, etc.) cleanly. ◆ *n* **5** the act of fumbling. ORIG C16: prob. of Scand. origin
▸ '**fumbler** *n* ▸ '**fumblingly** *adv*

fume (fjuːm) *vb* **fumes, fuming, fumed. 1** (*intr*) to be overcome with anger or fury. **2** to give off (fumes) or (of fumes) to be given off, esp. during a chemical reaction. **3** (*tr*) to fumigate. ◆ *n* **4** (*often pl*) a pungent or toxic vapour, gas, or smoke. **5** a sharp or pungent odour. ORIG C14: from OF *fum,* from L *fūmus* smoke, vapour
▸ '**fumeless** *adj* ▸ '**fumingly** *adv* ▸ '**fumy** *adj*

fumed (fjuːmd) *adj* (of wood, esp. oak) having a dark colour and distinctive grain from exposure to ammonia fumes.

fumigant ('fjuːmɪgənt) *n* a substance used for fumigating.

fumigate ('fjuːmɪˌgeɪt) *vb* **fumigates, fumigating, fumigated.** to treat (something contaminated or infected) with fumes or smoke. ORIG C16: from L, from *fūmus* smoke + *agere* to drive
▸ ˌ**fumi'gation** *n* ▸ '**fumiˌgator** *n*

fuming sulphuric acid *n* a mixture of acids, made by dissolving sulphur trioxide in concentrated sulphuric acid. Also called: **oleum.**

fumitory ('fjuːmɪtərɪ) *n, pl* **fumitories.** any plant of the genus *Fumaria* having spurred flowers and formerly used medicinally. ORIG C14: from OF, from Med. L *fūmus terrae,* lit.: smoke of the earth

fun (fʌn) *n* **1** a source of enjoyment, amusement, diversion, etc. **2** pleasure, gaiety, or merriment. **3** jest or sport (esp. in **in** *or* **for fun**). **4 fun and games.** *Ironic or facetious.* frivolous or hetic activity. **5 make fun of** *or* **poke fun at.** to ridicule or deride. **6** (*modifier*) full of amusement, diversion, gaiety, etc.: *a fun sport.* ORIG C17: ?from obs. *fon* to make a fool of; see FOND

funambulist (fjuː'næmbjʊlɪst) *n* a tightrope walker. ORIG C18: from L, from *fūnis* rope + *ambulāre* to walk
▸ **fu'nambulism** *n*

Funchal ★ (*Portuguese* fũ'ʃal) *n* the capital and chief port of the Madeira Islands, on the S coast of Madeira. Pop.: 44 111 (1987).

function ('fʌŋkʃən) *n* **1** the natural action of a person or thing: *the function of the kidneys is to filter waste products from the blood.* **2** the intended purpose of a person or thing in a specific role: *the function of a hammer is to hit nails into wood.* **3** an official or formal social gathering or ceremony. **4** a factor dependent upon another or other factors. **5** Also called: **map, mapping.** *Maths, logic.* a relation between two sets that associates a unique element (the value) of the second (the range) with each element (the argument) of the first (the domain). Symbol: $f(x)$. The value of $f(x)$ for $x=2$ is $f(2)$. ◆ *vb* (*intr*) **6** to operate or perform as specified. **7** (foll. by *as*) to perform the action or role (of something or someone else): *a coin may function as a screwdriver.* ORIG C16: from L *functiō,* from *fungī* to perform

functional ('fʌŋkʃənᵊl) *adj* **1** of, involving, or containing a function or functions. **2** practical rather than decorative; utilitarian. **3** capable of functioning; working. **4** *Med.* affecting a function of an organ without structural change.
▸ '**functionally** *adv*

functional food *n* food containing additives that provide extra nutritional value. Also called: **nutraceutical.**

functionalism ('fʌŋkʃənəˌlɪzəm) *n* **1** the theory of de-

sign that the form of a thing should be determined by its use. **2** any doctrine that stresses purpose.
▸ **'functionalist** *n, adj*

functionary ('fʌŋkʃənərɪ) *n, pl* **functionaries.** a person acting in an official capacity, as for a government; an official.

fund (fʌnd) *n* **1** a reserve of money, etc., set aside for a certain purpose. **2** a supply or store of something; stock: *it exhausted his fund of wisdom.* ◆ *vb (tr)* **3** to furnish money to in the form of a fund. **4** to place or store up in a fund. **5** to convert (short-term floating debt) into long-term debt bearing fixed interest and represented by bonds. **6** to accumulate a fund for the discharge of (a recurrent liability): *to fund a pension plan.* ◆ See also **funds.** ORIG C17: from L *fundus* the bottom, piece of land
▸ **'funder** *n*

fundament ('fʌndəmənt) *n Euphemistic or facetious.* the buttocks. ORIG C13: from L, from *fundāre* to FOUND[2]

fundamental (ˌfʌndə'mɛnt°l) *adj* **1** of, involving, or comprising a foundation; basic. **2** of, involving, or comprising a source; primary. **3** *Music.* denoting or relating to the principal or lowest note of a harmonic series. ◆ *n* **4** a principle, law, etc., that serves as the basis of an idea or system. **5a** the principal or lowest note of a harmonic series. **5b** the bass note of a chord in root position.
▸ **ˌfundamen'tality** *n* ▸ **ˌfunda'mentally** *adv*

fundamental interaction *n* any of the four basic interactions that occur in nature: the gravitational, electromagnetic, strong, and weak interactions.

fundamentalism (ˌfʌndə'mɛntəˌlɪzəm) *n* **1** *Christianity.* the view that the Bible is divinely inspired and is therefore literally true. **2** *Islam.* a movement favouring strict observance of the teachings of the Koran and Islamic law.
▸ **ˌfunda'mentalist** *n, adj*

fundamental particle *n* another name for **elementary particle.**

fundamental unit *n* one of a set of unrelated units that form the basis of a system of units. For example, the metre, kilogram, and second are fundamental SI units.

funded debt *n* that part of the British national debt that the government is not obliged to repay by a fixed date.

fundholding ('fʌndˌhəʊldɪŋ) *n* (formerly, in the National Health Service in Britain) the system enabling general practitioners to receive a fixed budget from which to pay for primary care, drugs, and non-urgent hospital treatment for patients; abolished in 1999.
▸ **'fundˌholder** *n*

fundi ('fʊndi:) *n S. African.* an expert. ORIG C20: from Nguni *umfundisi* teacher

fundraiser ('fʌndˌreɪzə) *n* **1** a person engaged in fundraising. **2** an event held to raise money for a cause.

fundraising ('fʌndˌreɪzɪŋ) *n* **1** the activity involved in raising money for a cause. ◆ *adj* **2** of, for, or related to fundraising.

funds (fʌndz) *pl n* **1** money that is readily available. **2** British government securities representing national debt.

fundus ('fʌndəs) *n, pl* **fundi** (-daɪ). *Anat.* the base of an organ or the part farthest away from its opening. ORIG C18: from L, lit.: the bottom

Fundy ★ ('fʌndɪ) *n* **Bay of.** an inlet of the Atlantic in SE Canada, between S New Brunswick and W Nova Scotia: remarkable for its swift tides of up to 21 m (70 ft).

Funen ★ ('fu:nən) *n* the second largest island of Denmark, between the Jutland peninsula and the island of Sjælland. Pop.: 605 868 (1995 est.). Area: 3481 sq. km (1344 sq. miles). Danish name: **Fyn.** German name: **Fünen.**

funeral ('fju:nərəl) *n* **1a** a ceremony at which a dead person is buried or cremated. **1b** *(as modifier): funeral service.* **2** a procession of people escorting a corpse to burial. **3** *Inf.* concern; affair: *it's your funeral.* ORIG C14: from Med. L, from LL, from L *fūnus* funeral
▸ **'funerary** *adj*

funeral director *n* an undertaker.

funeral parlour *n* a place where the dead are prepared for burial or cremation. Usual US name: **funeral home.**

funereal (fju:'nɪərɪəl) *adj* suggestive of a funeral; gloomy or mournful. Also: **funebrial.** ORIG C18: from L *fūnereus*
▸ **fu'nereally** *adv*

funfair ('fʌnˌfɛə) *n Brit.* an amusement park or fairground.

fungible ('fʌndʒɪb°l) *n Law.* (*often pl*) moveable perishable goods of a sort that may be estimated by number or weight, such as grain, wine, etc. ORIG C18: from Med. L *fungibilis,* from L *fungī* to perform
▸ **ˌfungi'bility** *n*

fungicide ('fʌndʒɪˌsaɪd) *n* a substance or agent that destroys or is capable of destroying fungi.
▸ **ˌfungi'cidal** *adj*

fungoid ('fʌŋgɔɪd) *adj* resembling a fungus or fungi.

fungous ('fʌŋgəs) *adj* appearing suddenly and spreading quickly like a fungus.

fungus ('fʌŋgəs) *n, pl* **fungi** ('fʌŋgaɪ, 'fʌndʒaɪ, 'fʌndʒɪ) *or* **funguses. 1** any member of a kingdom of organisms, formerly classified as plants, that lack chlorophyll, leaves, true stems, and roots, reproduce by spores, and live as saprotrophs or parasites. **2** something resembling a fungus, esp. in suddenly growing. **3** *Pathol.* any soft tumorous growth. ORIG C16: from L: mushroom, fungus
▸ **'fungal** *adj*

funicular (fju:'nɪkjʊlə) *n* **1** Also called: **funicular railway.** a railway up the side of a mountain, consisting of two cars at either end of a cable passing round a driving wheel at the summit. ◆ *adj* **2** relating to or operated by a rope, etc. ORIG C17: from L, from *fūnis* rope

funk[1] (fʌŋk) *Inf., chiefly Brit.* ◆ *n* **1** Also called: **blue funk.** a state of nervousness, fear, or depression. **2** a coward. ◆ *vb* **3** to flinch from (responsibility, etc.) through fear. **4** *(tr; usually passive)* to make afraid. ORIG C18: university sl., ? rel. to *funk* to smoke

funk[2] (fʌŋk) *n* a type of polyrhythmic Black dance music with heavy syncopation. ORIG C20: back formation from FUNKY

Funk ★ (fʌŋk) *n* **Casimir** ('kæzɪˌmɪə). 1884–1967, US biochemist, born in Poland: studied and named vitamins.

funky ('fʌŋkɪ) *adj* **funkier, funkiest.** *Inf.* (of jazz, pop, etc.) passionate; soulful. ORIG C20: from *funk* to smoke (tobacco), ? alluding to music that was smelly, that is, earthy

funnel ('fʌn°l) *n* **1** a hollow utensil with a wide mouth tapering to a small hole, used for pouring liquids, etc., into a narrow-necked vessel. **2** something resembling this in shape or function. **3** a smokestack for smoke and exhaust gases, as on a steam locomotive. ◆ *vb* **funnels, funnelling, funnelled** *or US* **funnels, funneling, funneled. 4** to move or cause to move or pour through or as if through a funnel. ORIG C15: from OProvençal *fonilh,* ult. from L *infundibulum,* from *infundere* to pour in
▸ **'funnel-ˌlike** *adj*

funnel-web *n Austral.* a large poisonous black spider that constructs funnel-shaped webs.

funny ('fʌnɪ) *adj* **funnier, funniest. 1** causing amusement or laughter; humorous. **2** peculiar; odd. **3** suspicious or dubious (esp. in **funny business**). **4** *Inf.* faint or ill. ◆ *n, pl* **funnies. 5** *Inf.* a joke or witticism.
▸ **'funnily** *adv* ▸ **'funniness** *n*

funny bone *n* the area near the elbow where the ulnar nerve is close to the surface of the skin: when it is struck, a sharp tingling sensation is experienced.

fun run *n* a long run or part-marathon run for exercise and pleasure, often by large numbers of people.

fuoco (fu:'əʊkəʊ) *Music.* ◆ *n* **1** fire. ◆ *adv, adj* **2 con fuoco.** in a fiery manner. ORIG C19: It., lit.: fire

fur (fɜ:) *n* **1** the dense coat of fine silky hairs on such mammals as the cat and mink. **2a** the dressed skin of certain fur-bearing animals, with the hair left on. **2b** *(as modifier): a fur coat.* **3** a garment made of fur, such as a stole. **4** a pile fabric made in imitation of animal fur. **5** *Heraldry.* any of various stylized representations of animal pelts used in coats of arms. **6 make the fur fly.** to cause

a scene or disturbance. **7** *Inf.* a whitish coating on the tongue, caused by excessive smoking, illness, etc. **8** *Brit.* a whitish-grey deposit precipitated from hard water onto the insides of pipes, kettles, etc. ◆ *vb* **furs, furring, furred. 9** (*tr*) to line or trim a garment, etc., with fur. **10** (often foll. by *up*) to cover or become covered with a furlike lining or deposit. ORIG C14: from OF *forrer* to line a garment, from *fuerre* sheath, of Gmc origin
▸ **'furless** *adj*

fur. *abbrev. for* furlong.

furbelow ('fɜːbɪˌləʊ) *n* **1** a flounce, ruffle, or other ornamental trim. **2** (*often pl*) showy ornamentation. ◆ *vb* **3** (*tr*) to put a furbelow on (a garment, etc.). ORIG C18: by folk etymology from F dialect *farbella* a frill

furbish ('fɜːbɪʃ) *vb* (*tr*) **1** to make bright by polishing. **2** (often foll. by *up*) to renovate; restore. ORIG C14: from OF *fourbir* to polish, of Gmc origin
▸ **'furbisher** *n*

furcate ('fɜːkeɪt) *vb* **furcates, furcating, furcated. 1** to divide into two parts. ◆ *adj* **2** forked: *furcate branches.* ORIG C19: from LL, from L *furca* a fork
▸ **fur'cation** *n*

furfuraceous (ˌfɜːfjʊ'reɪʃəs) *adj* **1** relating to or resembling bran. **2** *Med.* resembling dandruff. ORIG C17: from L *furfur* bran, scurf + -ACEOUS

Furies ('fjʊərɪz) *pl n, sing* **Fury.** *Classical myth.* the snake-haired goddesses of vengeance, usually three in number, who pursued unpunished criminals. Also called: **Erinyes, Eumenides.**

furioso (ˌfjʊərɪ'əʊsəʊ) *Music.* ◆ *adj, adv* **1** in a frantically rushing manner. ◆ *n* **2** a passage or piece to be performed in this way. ORIG C19: It., lit.: furious

furious ('fjʊərɪəs) *adj* **1** extremely angry or annoyed. **2** violent or unrestrained, as in speed, energy, etc.
▸ **'furiously** *adv* ▸ **'furiousness** *n*

furl (fɜːl) *vb* **1** to roll up (an umbrella, flag, etc.) neatly and securely or (of an umbrella, flag, etc.) to be rolled up in this way. ◆ *n* **2** the act or an instance of furling. **3** a single rolled-up section. ORIG C16: from OF, from *ferm* tight (from L *firmus* FIRM[1]) + *lier* to bind, from L *ligāre*
▸ **'furlable** *adj*

furlong ('fɜːˌlɒŋ) *n* a unit of length equal to 220 yards (201.168 metres). ORIG OE *furlang,* from *furh* furrow + *lang* long

furlough ('fɜːləʊ) *n* **1** leave of absence from military duty. ◆ *vb* (*tr*) **2** to grant a furlough to. ORIG C17: from Du. *verlof,* from *ver-* FOR- + *lof* leave, permission

furnace ('fɜːnɪs) *n* **1** an enclosed chamber in which heat is produced to destroy refuse, smelt or refine ores, etc. **2** a very hot place. ORIG C13: from OF, from L *fornax* oven, furnace

Furness ★ ('fɜːnɪs) *n* a region in NW England in Cumbria, forming a peninsula between the Irish Sea and Morecambe Bay.

furnish ('fɜːnɪʃ) *vb* (*tr*) **1** to provide (a house, room, etc.) with furniture, etc. **2** to equip with what is necessary. **3** to supply: *the records furnished the information.* ORIG C15: from OF *fournir,* of Gmc origin
▸ **'furnisher** *n*

furnishings ('fɜːnɪʃɪŋz) *pl n* furniture, carpets, etc., with which a room or house is furnished.

furniture ('fɜːnɪtʃə) *n* **1** the movable articles that equip a room, house, etc. **2** the equipment necessary for a ship, factory, etc. **3** *Printing.* lengths of wood, plastic, or metal, used in assembling formes to surround the type. ◆ See also **door furniture, street furniture.** ORIG C16: from F, from *fournir* to equip

Furnivall ★ ('fɜːnɪvəl) *n* **Frederick James.** 1825–1910, British philologist: founder of the Early English Text Society and one of the founders of the *Oxford English Dictionary.*

furore (fjʊ'rɔːrɪ) *or esp. US* **furor** ('fjʊərɔː) *n* **1** a public outburst; uproar. **2** a sudden widespread enthusiasm; craze. **3** frenzy; rage. ORIG C15: from L: frenzy, from *furere* to rave

furphy ('fɜːfɪ) *n, pl* **furphies.** *Austral. sl.* a rumour or fictitious story. ORIG C20: from *Furphy* carts (used for water or sewage in World War I), made at a foundry established by the Furphy family

Furphy ★ ('fɜːfɪ) *n* **Joseph,** pen name *Tom Collins.* 1843–1912, Australian author. His works include the novels *Such is Life* (1903) and *The Buln-Buln and the Brolga* (1948).

furred (fɜːd) *adj* **1** made of, lined with, or covered in fur. **2** wearing fur. **3** (of animals) having fur. **4** another word for **furry** (sense 3). **5** provided with furring strips. **6** (of a pipe, kettle, etc.) lined with hard lime.

furrier ('fʌrɪə) *n* a person whose occupation is selling, making, or repairing fur garments. ORIG C14: *furour,* from OF *fourrer* to trim with FUR
▸ **'furriery** *n*

furring ('fɜːrɪŋ) *n* **1** short for **furring strip. 2** the formation of fur on the tongue. **3** trimming of animal fur, as on a coat.

furring strip *n* a strip of wood or metal fixed to a wall, floor, or ceiling to provide a surface for the fixing of plasterboard, floorboards, etc.

furrow ('fʌrəʊ) *n* **1** a long narrow trench made in the ground by a plough. **2** any long deep groove, esp. a deep wrinkle on the forehead. ◆ *vb* **3** to develop or cause to develop furrows or wrinkles. **4** to make a furrow or furrows in (land). ORIG OE *furh*
▸ **'furrower** *n* ▸ **'furrowless** *adj* ▸ **'furrowy** *adj*

furry ('fɜːrɪ) *adj* **furrier, furriest. 1** covered with fur or something furlike. **2** of, relating to, or resembling fur. **3** Also: **furred.** (of the tongue) coated with whitish cellular debris.
▸ **'furrily** *adv* ▸ **'furriness** *n*

Fur Seal Islands ★ *pl n* another name for the **Pribilof Islands.**

further ('fɜːðə) *adv* **1** in addition; furthermore. **2** to a greater degree or extent. **3** to or at a more advanced point. **4** to or at a greater distance in time or space. ◆ *adj* **5** additional; more. **6** more distant or remote in time or space. ◆ *vb* **7** (*tr*) to assist the progress of. ◆ See also **far, furthest.** ORIG OE *furthor*

> **USAGE NOTE** See at **farther.**

furtherance ('fɜːðərəns) *n* **1** the act of furthering. **2** something that furthers.

further education *n* (in Britain) formal education beyond school other than at a university or polytechnic.

furthermore ('fɜːðəˌmɔː) *adv* in addition; moreover.

furthermost ('fɜːðəˌməʊst) *adj* most distant; furthest.

furthest ('fɜːðɪst) *adv* **1** to the greatest degree or extent. **2** to or at the greatest distance in time or space; farthest. ◆ *adj* **3** most distant or remote in time or space; farthest.

furtive ('fɜːtɪv) *adj* characterized by stealth; sly and secretive. ORIG C15: from L *furtīvus* stolen, from *furtum* a theft, from *fūr* a thief
▸ **'furtively** *adv* ▸ **'furtiveness** *n*

Furtwängler ★ (*German* 'fʊrtvɛŋlər) *n* **Wilhelm** ('vɪlhɛlm). 1886–1954, German conductor.

furuncle ('fjʊərʌŋkəl) *n Pathol.* the technical name for **boil**[2]. ORIG C17: from L *fūrunculus* pilferer, sore, from *fūr* thief
▸ **furuncular** (fjʊ'rʌŋkjʊlə) *or* **fu'runculous** *adj*

furunculosis (fjʊˌrʌŋkjʊ'ləʊsɪs) *n* **1** a skin condition characterized by the presence of multiple boils. **2** a disease of salmon and trout caused by a bacterium.

fury ('fjʊərɪ) *n, pl* **furies. 1** violent or uncontrolled anger. **2** an outburst of such anger. **3** uncontrolled violence: *the fury of the storm.* **4** a person, esp. a woman, with a violent temper. **5** See **Furies. 6 like fury.** *Inf.* violently; furiously. ORIG C14: from L, from *furere* to be furious

furze (fɜːz) *n* another name for **gorse.** ORIG OE *fyrs*
▸ **'furzy** *adj*

fuscous ('fʌskəs) *adj* of a brownish-grey colour. ORIG C17: from L *fuscus* dark, swarthy, tawny

fuse[1] *or chiefly US* **fuze** (fjuːz) *n* **1** a lead of combustible black powder (**safety fuse**), or a lead containing an explosive (**detonating fuse**), used to fire an explosive charge. **2**

any device by which an explosive charge is ignited. ◆ *vb* **fuses, fusing, fused** *or chiefly US* **fuzes, fuzing, fuzed. 3** (*tr*) to equip with such a fuse. ORIG C17: from It. *fuso* spindle, from L *fūsus*
▸ **'fuseless** *adj*

fuse² (fju:z) *vb* **fuses, fusing, fused. 1** to unite or become united by melting, esp. by the action of heat. **2** to become or cause to become liquid, esp. by the action of heat. **3** to join or become combined. **4** (*tr*) to equip (a plug, etc.) with a fuse. **5** *Brit.* to fail or cause to fail as a result of the blowing of a fuse: *the lights fused.* ◆ *n* **6** a protective device for safeguarding electric circuits, etc., containing a wire that melts and breaks the circuit when the current exceeds a certain value. ORIG C17: from L *fūsus* melted, cast, from *fundere* to pour out; sense 5 infl. by FUSE[1]

fusee *or* **fuzee** (fju:'zi:) *n* **1** (in early clocks and watches) a spirally grooved spindle, functioning as an equalizing force on the unwinding of the mainspring. **2** a friction match with a large head. ORIG C16: from F *fusée* spindleful of thread, from OF *fus* spindle, from L *fūsus*

fuselage ('fju:zɪˌlɑ:ʒ) *n* the main body of an aircraft. ORIG C20: from F, from *fuseler* to shape like a spindle, from OF *fusel* spindle

fusel oil *or* **fusel** ('fju:zᵊl) *n* a poisonous by-product formed in the distillation of fermented liquors and used as a source of amyl alcohols. ORIG C19: from G *Fusel* bad spirits

Fushih *or* **Fu-shih** ★ ('fu:'ʃi:) *n* another name for **Yanan.**

Fushun ★ ('fu:'ʃʌn) *n* a city in NE China, in central Liaoning province near Shenyang: situated on one of the richest coalfields in the world; site of the largest thermal power plant in NE Asia. Pop.: 1 350 000 (1991 est.).

fusible ('fju:zəbᵊl) *adj* capable of being fused or melted.
▸ **ˌfusi'bility** *n* ▸ **'fusibly** *adv*

fusiform ('fju:zɪˌfɔ:m) *adj* elongated and tapering at both ends. ORIG C18: from L *fūsus* spindle

fusil ('fju:zɪl) *n* a light flintlock musket. ORIG C16 (in the sense: steel for a tinderbox): from OF, from Vulgar L *focīlis* (unattested), from L *focus* fire

fusilier (ˌfju:zɪ'lɪə) *n* **1** (formerly) an infantryman armed with a light musket. **2** Also: **fusileer. 2a** a soldier, esp. a private, serving in any of certain British or other infantry regiments. **2b** (*pl; cap. when part of a name*): *the Royal Welch Fusiliers.* ORIG C17: from F; see FUSIL

fusillade (ˌfju:zɪ'leɪd) *n* **1** a rapid continual discharge of firearms. **2** a sudden outburst, as of criticism. ◆ *vb* **fusillades, fusillading, fusilladed. 3** (*tr*) to attack with a fusillade. ORIG C19: from F, from *fusiller* to shoot; see FUSIL

fusion ('fju:ʒən) *n* **1** the act or process of fusing or melting together. **2** the state of being fused. **3** something produced by fusing. **4** a kind of popular music that is a blend of two or more styles, such as jazz and funk. **5** See **nuclear fusion. 6** a coalition of political parties. **7** (*modifier*) relating to a style of cooking that combines traditional Western techniques and ingredients with those used in Eastern cuisine: *fusion cuisine; fusion food.* ORIG C16: from L *fūsiō* a pouring out, melting, from *fundere* to pour out, FOUND[3]

fusion bomb *n* a type of bomb in which most of the energy is provided by nuclear fusion. Also called: **thermonuclear bomb, fission-fusion bomb.**

fuss (fʌs) *n* **1** nervous activity or agitation, esp. when unnecessary. **2** complaint or objection: *he made a fuss over the bill.* **3** an exhibition of affection or admiration: *they made a great fuss over the new baby.* **4** a quarrel. ◆ *vb* **5** (*intr*) to worry unnecessarily. **6** (*intr*) to be excessively concerned over trifles. **7** (when *intr,* usually foll. by *over*) to show great or excessive concern, affection, etc. (for). **8** (*tr*) to bother (a person). ORIG C18: from ?
▸ **'fusser** *n*

fusspot ('fʌsˌpɒt) *n Brit. inf.* a person who fusses unnecessarily.

fussy ('fʌsɪ) *adj* **fussier, fussiest. 1** inclined to fuss over minor points. **2** very particular about detail. **3** characterized by overelaborate detail.
▸ **'fussily** *adv* ▸ **'fussiness** *n*

fustanella (ˌfʌstə'nɛlə) *n* a white knee-length pleated skirt worn by men in Greece and Albania. ORIG C19: from It., from Mod. Gk *phoustani,* prob. from It. *fustagno* FUSTIAN

fustian ('fʌstɪən) *n* **1a** a hard-wearing fabric of cotton mixed with flax or wool. **1b** (*as modifier*): *a fustian jacket.* **2** pompous talk or writing. ◆ *adj* **3** cheap; worthless. **4** bombastic. ORIG C12: from OF, from Med. L *fustāneum,* from L *fustis* cudgel

fustic ('fʌstɪk) *n* **1** Also called: **old fustic.** a large tropical American tree. **2** the yellow dye obtained from the wood of this tree. **3** any of various trees or shrubs that yield a similar dye, esp. a European sumach (**young fustic**). ORIG C15: from F *fustoc,* from Sp., from Ar. *fustuq,* from Gk *pistakē* pistachio tree

fusty ('fʌstɪ) *adj* **fustier, fustiest. 1** smelling of damp or mould. **2** old-fashioned in attitude. ORIG C14: from *fust* wine cask, from OF: cask, from L *fūstis* cudgel
▸ **'fustily** *adv* ▸ **'fustiness** *n*

fut. *abbrev. for* future.

futhark ('fu:θɑ:k) *or* **futhorc, futhork** ('fu:θɔ:k) *n* a phonetic alphabet consisting of runes. ORIG C19: from the first six letters: *f, u, th, a, r, k*

futile ('fju:taɪl) *adj* **1** having no effective result; unsuccessful. **2** pointless; trifling. **3** inane or foolish. ORIG C16: from L *futtilis* pouring out easily, from *fundere* to pour out
▸ **'futilely** *adv* ▸ **futility** (fju:'tɪlɪtɪ) *n*

futon ('fu:ˌtɒn) *n* a Japanese padded quilt, laid on the floor as a bed. ORIG C19: from Japanese

futtock ('fʌtək) *n Naut.* one of the ribs in the frame of a wooden vessel. ORIG C13: ? var. of *foothook*

future ('fju:tʃə) *n* **1** the time yet to come. **2** undetermined events that will occur in that time. **3** the condition of a person or thing at a later date: *the future of the school is undecided.* **4** likelihood of later improvement: *he has a future as a singer.* **5** *Grammar.* **5a** a tense of verbs used when the action or event described is to occur after the time of utterance. **5b** a verb in this tense. **6 in future.** from now on. ◆ *adj* **7** that is yet to come or be. **8** of or expressing time yet to come. **9** (*prenominal*) destined to become. **10** *Grammar.* in or denoting the future as a tense of verbs. ◆ See also **futures.** ORIG C14: from L *fūtūrus* about to be, from *esse* to be
▸ **'futureless** *adj*

future perfect *Grammar.* ◆ *adj* **1** denoting a tense of verbs describing an action that will have been performed by a certain time. ◆ *n* **2a** the future perfect tense. **2b** a verb in this tense.

futures ('fju:tʃəz) *pl n* **a** commodities or other financial products bought or sold at an agreed price for delivery at a specified future date. See also **financial futures. b** (*as modifier*): *futures contract; futures market.*

future value *n* the value that a sum of money invested at compound interest will have after a specified period.

futurism ('fju:tʃəˌrɪzəm) *n* an artistic movement that arose in Italy in 1909 to replace traditional aesthetic values with the characteristics of the machine age.
▸ **'futurist** *n, adj*

futuristic (ˌfju:tʃə'rɪstɪk) *adj* **1** denoting or relating to design, etc., that is thought likely to be fashionable at some future time. **2** of or relating to futurism.
▸ **ˌfutur'istically** *adv*

futurity (fju:'tjʊərɪtɪ) *n, pl* **futurities. 1** a less common word for **future. 2** the quality of being in the future. **3** a future event.

futurology (ˌfju:tʃə'rɒlədʒɪ) *n* the study or prediction of the future of mankind.
▸ **ˌfutur'ologist** *n*

fuze (fju:z) *n, vb* **fuzes, fuzing, fuzed.** *Chiefly US.* a variant spelling of **fuse**[1].

fuzee (fju:'zi:) *n* a variant spelling of **fusee.**

Fuzhou ('fu:'dʒəʊ), **Foochow,** *or* **Fuchou** ★ *n* a port in SE China, capital of Fujian province on the Min Jiang: one of the original five treaty ports (1842). Pop.: 874 809 (1990 est.).

fuzz¹ (fʌz) *n* **1** a mass or covering of fine or curly hairs, fibres, etc. **2** a blur. ◆ *vb* **3** to make or become fuzzy. **4** to make or become indistinct. ORIG C17: ?from Low G *fussig* loose

fuzz² (fʌz) *n* a slang word for **police** or **policeman.** ORIG C20: from ?

fuzzy (ˈfʌzɪ) *adj* **fuzzier, fuzziest. 1** of, resembling, or covered with fuzz. **2** unclear or distorted. **3** (of the hair) tightly curled or very wavy.
▸ ˈ**fuzzily** *adv* ▸ ˈ**fuzziness** *n*

fuzzy logic *n* a branch of logic that allows degrees of imprecision in reasoning and knowledge to be represented in such a way that the information can be processed by computer.

fuzzy-wuzzy (ˈfʌzɪˌwʌzɪ) *n, pl* **fuzzy-wuzzies.** *Offens. arch. sl.* a Black fuzzy-haired native of any of various countries.

fwd *abbrev. for* forward.

f-word *n* **the.** (*sometimes cap.*) a euphemistic way of referring to the word **fuck.** ORIG from F(UCK) + WORD

FX (ˈɛfˈɛks) *pl n Films, inf.* short for **special effects.** ORIG C20: a phonetic respelling of EFFECTS

-fy *suffix forming verbs.* to make or become: *beautify.* ORIG from OF *-fier,* from L *-ficāre,* from *-ficus* -FIC

Fylde ★ (faɪld) *n* a region in NW England in Lancashire between the Wyre and Ribble estuaries.

fylfot (ˈfaɪlfɒt) *n* a rare word for **swastika.** ORIG C16 (apparently meaning: a sign or device for the lower part or foot of a painted window): from *fillen* to fill + *fot* foot

Fyn ★ (*Danish* fyːn) *n* the Danish name for **Funen.**

FYROM *abbrev. for* Former Yugoslav Republic of Macedonia.

Gg

g *or* **G** (dʒiː) *n, pl* **g's, G's,** *or* **Gs. 1** the seventh letter of the English alphabet. **2** a speech sound represented by this letter, usually either as in *grass,* or as in *page.*

g *symbol for:* **1** gallon(s). **2** gram(s). **3** grav. **4** acceleration of free fall (due to gravity).

G *symbol for:* **1** *Music.* **1a** the fifth note of the scale of C major. **1b** the major or minor key having this note as its tonic. **2** gauss. **3** gravitational constant. **4** *Physics.* conductance. **5** *Biochem.* guanine. **6** German. **7** giga-. **8** good. **9** *Sl., chiefly US.* grand (a thousand dollars or pounds). **10** (in Australia) **10a** general exhibition (used to describe a category of film certified as suitable for viewing by anyone). **10b** (*as modifier*): *a G film.*

G. *or* **g.** *abbrev. for:* **1** gauges. **2** gelding. **3** guilder(s). **4** guinea(s). **5** Gulf.

G3 *abbrev. for* Group of Three.

G5 *abbrev. for* Group of Five.

G7 *abbrev. for* Group of Seven.

G8 *abbrev. for* Group of Eight.

G10 *abbrev. for* Group of Ten.

G24 *abbrev. for* Group of Twenty-Four.

G77 *abbrev. for* Group of Seventy-Seven.

Ga *the chemical symbol for* gallium.

GA *abbrev. for:* **1** General Assembly (of the United Nations). **2** general average. **3** Georgia.

Ga. *abbrev. for* Georgia.

gab (gæb) *Inf.* ◆ *vb* **gabs, gabbing, gabbed. 1** (*intr*) to talk excessively or idly; gossip. ◆ *n* **2** idle or trivial talk. **3 gift of the gab.** ability to speak glibly or persuasively. ORIG C18: prob. from Irish Gaelic *gob* mouth
▸ **'gabber** *n*

gabardine *or* **gaberdine** ('gæbəˌdiːn, ˌgæbə'diːn) *n* **1** a twill-weave worsted, cotton, or spun-rayon fabric. **2** an ankle-length loose coat or frock worn by men, esp. by Jews, in the Middle Ages. **3** any of various other garments made of gabardine, esp. a child's raincoat. ORIG C16: from OF *gauvardine* pilgrim's garment, from MHG *wallewart* pilgrimage

gabble ('gæbəl) *vb* **gabbles, gabbling, gabbled. 1** to utter (words, etc.) rapidly and indistinctly; jabber. **2** (*intr*) (of geese, etc.) to utter rapid cackling noises. ◆ *n* **3** rapid and indistinct speech or noises. ORIG C17: from MDu. *gabbelen,* imit.
▸ **'gabbler** *n*

gabbro ('gæbrəʊ) *n, pl* **gabbros.** a dark coarse-grained igneous rock consisting of feldspar, pyroxene, and often olivine. ORIG C19: from It., prob. from L *glaber* smooth, bald

gabby ('gæbɪ) *adj* **gabbier, gabbiest.** *Inf.* inclined to chatter; talkative.

Gaberones ★ (ˌgæbə'rəʊnɛs) *n* the former name for **Gaborone.**

Gabès ★ ('gɑːbɛs; *French* gabɛs) *n* **1** a port in E Tunisia. Pop.: 98 800 (1994). **2 Gulf of.** an inlet of the Mediterranean on the E coast of Tunisia. Ancient name: **Syrtis Minor.** Arabic name: **Qabis.**

gabfest ('gæbˌfɛst) *n Inf., chiefly US & Canad.* **1** prolonged gossiping or conversation. **2** an informal gathering for conversation. ORIG C19: from GAB + FEST

gabion ('geɪbɪən) *n* **1** a cylindrical metal container filled with stones, used in the construction of underwater foundations. **2** a wickerwork basket filled with stones or earth, used (esp. formerly) as part of a fortification. ORIG C16: from F: basket, from It., from *gabbia* cage, from L *cavea;* see CAGE

gable ('geɪbəl) *n* **1** the triangular upper part of a wall between the sloping ends of a pitched roof (**gable roof**). **2** a triangular ornamental feature, esp. as used over a door or window. ORIG C14: OF, prob. from ON *gafl*
▸ **'gabled** *adj*

Gable ★ ('geɪbəl) *n* (**William**) **Clark.** 1901–60, US film actor. His films include *It Happened One Night* (1934), *San Francisco* (1936), *Gone with the Wind* (1939), and *The Misfits* (1960).

gable end *n* the end wall of a building on the side which is topped by a gable.

Gabo ★ ('gɑːbəʊ, -bə) *n* **Naum** (naʊm), original name *Naum Neemia Pevsner.* 1890–1977, US sculptor, born in Russia: a leading constructivist.

Gabon ★ (gə'bɒn; *French* gabɔ̃) *n* a republic in W central Africa, on the Atlantic: settled by the French in 1839; made part of the French Congo in 1888; became independent in 1960; almost wholly forested. Official language: French. Religion: Christian and animist. Currency: franc. Capital: Libreville. Pop.: 1 226 000 (1999 est.). Area: 267 675 sq. km (103 350 sq. miles).
▸ **Gabonese** (ˌgæbə'niːz) *adj, n*

gaboon (gə'buːn) *n* a dark mahogany-like wood from an African tree, used in plywood, for furniture, and as a veneer. ORIG C20: altered from GABON

gaboon viper *n* a large venomous viper of African rainforests. It has brown and purple markings and hornlike projections on its snout.

Gabor ★ (gə'bɔː) *n* **Dennis.** 1900–79, British electrical engineer, born in Hungary. He invented holography: Nobel prize for physics 1971.

Gaborone ★ (ˌgæbə'rəʊnɪ) *n* the capital of Botswana (since 1964), in the extreme southeast. Pop.: 182 000 (1995 est.). Former name: **Gaberones.**

Gabriel[1] ★ ('geɪbrɪəl) *n Bible.* one of the archangels, the messenger of good news (Daniel 8:16–26; Luke 1:11–20, 26–38).

Gabriel[2] ★ (*French* gabriɛl) *n* **Jacques-Ange** (ʒakɑ̃ʒ). 1698–1782, French architect: designed the Petit Trianon at Versailles.

Gabrieli (*Italian* ga'brjɛːle) *or* **Gabrielli** ★ (ga'brjɛlli) *n* **1 Andrea** (an'drɛːa). 1520–86, Italian organist and composer; chief organist of St Mark's, Venice. **2** his nephew, **Giovanni** (dʒo'vanni). 1558–1612, Italian organist and composer.

gaby ('geɪbɪ) *n, pl* **gabies.** *Arch. or dialect.* a simpleton. ORIG C18: from ?

gad (gæd) *vb* **gads, gadding, gadded. 1** (*intr;* often foll. by *about* or *around*) to go out in search of pleasure; gallivant. ◆ *n* **2** carefree adventure (esp. in **on the gad**). ORIG C15: back formation from obs. *gadling* companion, from OE, from *gæd* fellowship
▸ **'gadder** *n*

Gad ★ (gæd) *n Old Testament.* **1a** Jacob's sixth son, whose mother was Zilpah, Leah's maid. **1b** the Israelite tribe descended from him. **1c** the territory of this tribe, lying to the east of the Jordan and extending southwards from the Sea of Galilee. **2** a prophet and admonisher of David (I Samuel 22; II Samuel 24).

gadabout ('gædəˌbaʊt) *n Inf.* a person who restlessly seeks amusement, etc.

Gadarene ('gædəˌriːn) *adj* relating to or engaged in a headlong rush. ORIG C19: via LL from Gk *Gadarēnos,* of Gadara (Palestine), alluding to the Gadarene swine (Matthew 8:28ff.)

Gaddafi *or* **Qaddafi** ★ (gə'dɑːfɪ) *n* **Moamar al** ('məʊəˌmɑː æl). born 1942, Libyan army officer and statesman; head of state from 1969.

gadfly ('gædˌflaɪ) *n, pl* **gadflies. 1** any of various large dipterous flies, esp. the horsefly, that annoy livestock by

★ people and places

sucking their blood. **2** a constantly irritating person. ORIG C16: from *gad* sting + FLY[2]

gadget ('gædʒɪt) *n* **1** a small mechanical device or appliance. **2** any object that is interesting for its ingenuity. ORIG C19: ?from F *gâchette* lock catch, dim. of *gâche* staple

gadgetry ('gædʒɪtrɪ) *n* **1** gadgets collectively. **2** use of or preoccupation with gadgets.

gadoid ('geɪdɔɪd) *adj* **1** of or belonging to an order of marine soft-finned fishes typically having the pectoral and pelvic fins close together and small cycloid scales. The group includes cod and hake. ◆ *n* **2** any gadoid fish. ORIG C19: from NL *Gadidae,* from *gadus* cod; see -OID

gadolinium (ˌgædə'lɪnɪəm) *n* a ductile malleable silvery-white ferromagnetic element of the lanthanide series of metals. Symbol: Gd; atomic no.: 64; atomic wt.: 157.25. ORIG C19: NL, after Johan *Gadolin* (1760–1852), Finnish mineralogist

gadroon *or* **godroon** (gə'dru:n) *n* a decorative moulding composed of a series of convex flutes and curves, used esp. as an edge to silver articles. ORIG C18: from F *godron,* ?from OF *godet* cup, goblet

Gadsden Purchase ★ ('gædzdən) *n* an area of about 77 000 sq. km (30 000 sq. miles) in present-day Arizona and New Mexico, bought by the US from Mexico for 10 million dollars in 1853. The purchase was negotiated by James Gadsden (1788–1858), US diplomat.

gadwall ('gædˌwɔ:l) *n, pl* **gadwalls** *or* **gadwall.** a duck related to the mallard. The male has a grey body and black tail. ORIG C17: from ?

gadzooks (gæd'zu:ks) *interj Arch.* a mild oath. ORIG C17: ?from *God's hooks* (the nails of the cross) from *Gad* arch. euphemism for God

Gaea ('dʒi:ə), **Gaia,** *or* **Ge** ★ *n Greek myth.* the goddess of the earth, who bore Uranus and by him Oceanus, Cronus, and the Titans. ORIG from Gk *gaia* earth

Gael (geɪl) *n* a person who speaks a Gaelic language, esp. a Highland Scot or an Irishman. ORIG C19: from Gaelic *Gaidheal*
▸ **'Gaeldom** *n*

Gaelic ('geɪlɪk, 'gæ-) *n* **1** any of the closely related languages of the Celts in Ireland, Scotland, or the Isle of Man. ◆ *adj* **2** of, denoting, or relating to the Celtic people of Ireland, Scotland, or the Isle of Man or their language or customs.

Gaelic coffee *n* another name for **Irish coffee.**

Gaeltacht ('gɛ:ltəxt) *n* any of the regions in Ireland in which Irish Gaelic is the vernacular speech. ORIG C20: from Irish Gaelic

gaff[1] (gæf) *n* **1** *Angling.* a stiff pole with a stout prong or hook attached for landing large fish. **2** *Naut.* a boom hoisted aft of a mast to support a fore-and-aft sail. **3** a metal spur fixed to the leg of a gamecock. ◆ *vb* **4** (*tr*) *Angling.* to hook or land (a fish) with a gaff. ORIG C13: from F *gaffe,* from Provençal *gaf* boat hook

gaff[2] (gæf) *n* **1** *Sl.* nonsense. **2 blow the gaff.** *Brit. sl.* to divulge a secret. ORIG C19: from ?

gaffe (gæf) *n* a social blunder, esp. a tactless remark. ORIG C19: from F

gaffer ('gæfə) *n* **1** an old man: often used affectionately or patronizingly. **2** *Inf., chiefly Brit.* a boss, foreman, or owner of a factory, etc. **3** *Inf.* the senior electrician on a television or film set. ORIG C16: from GODFATHER

gag[1] (gæg) *vb* **gags, gagging, gagged. 1** (*tr*) to stop up (a person's mouth), esp. with a piece of cloth, etc., to prevent him or her from speaking or crying out. **2** (*tr*) to suppress or censor (free expression, information, etc.). **3** to retch or cause to retch. **4** (*intr*) to struggle for breath; choke. ◆ *n* **5** a piece of cloth, rope, etc., stuffed into or tied across the mouth. **6** any restraint on or suppression of information, free speech, etc. **7** *Parliamentary procedure.* another word for **closure** (sense 4). ORIG C15 *gaggen;* ? imit. of a gasping sound

gag[2] (gæg) *Inf.* ◆ *n* **1** a joke or humorous story, esp. one told by a professional comedian. **2** a hoax, practical joke, etc. ◆ *vb* **gags, gagging, gagged. 3** (*intr*) to tell jokes or funny stories, as comedians in nightclubs, etc. ORIG C19: ? special use of GAG[1]

gaga ('gɑ:gɑ:) *adj Inf.* **1** senile; doting. **2** slightly crazy. ORIG C20: from F, imit.

Gagarin ★ (*Russian* ga'garin) *n* **Yuri** ('jurɪ). 1934–68, Soviet cosmonaut: made the first manned space flight (1961).

gage[1] (geɪdʒ) *n* **1** something deposited as security against the fulfilment of an obligation; pledge. **2** (formerly) a glove or other object thrown down to indicate a challenge to combat. ◆ *vb* **gages, gaging, gaged. 3** (*tr*) *Arch.* to stake, pledge, or wager. ORIG C14: from OF, of Gmc origin

gage[2] (geɪdʒ) *n* short for **greengage.**

gage[3] (geɪdʒ) *n, vb* **gages, gaging, gaged.** *US.* a variant spelling (esp. in technical senses) of **gauge.**

Gage ★ (geɪdʒ) *n* **Thomas.** 1721–87, British general and governor in America; commander in chief of British forces at Bunker Hill (1775).

gaggle ('gæg[ə]l) *vb* **gaggles, gaggling, gaggled. 1** (*intr*) (of geese) to cackle. ◆ *n* **2** a flock of geese. **3** *Inf.* a disorderly group of people. ORIG C14: of Gmc origin; imit.

Gaia ★ ('gaɪə) *n* a variant of **Gaea.**

Gaia hypothesis *or* **theory** *n* the theory that the earth and everything on it constitutes a single self-regulating living entity.

gaiety ('geɪətɪ) *n, pl* **gaieties. 1** the state or condition of being merry, bright, or lively. **2** festivity; merrymaking. **3** bright appearance.

> **USAGE NOTE** See at **gay.**

Gaillard Cut ★ (gɪl'jɑ:d, 'geɪlɑ:d) *n* the SE section of the Panama Canal, cut through Culebra Mountain. Length: about 13 km (8 miles). Former name: **Culebra Cut.** ORIG C19: after David Du Bose *Gaillard* (1859–1913), US army engineer in charge of the work

gaillardia (geɪ'lɑ:dɪə) *n* a plant of the composite family having ornamental flower heads with yellow or red rays and purple discs. ORIG C19: from NL, after *Gaillard* de Marentonneau, 18th-cent. F amateur botanist

gaily ('geɪlɪ) *adv* **1** in a gay manner; merrily. **2** with bright colours; showily.

gain (geɪn) *vb* **1** (*tr*) to acquire (something desirable); obtain. **2** (*tr*) to win in competition: *to gain the victory.* **3** to increase, improve, or advance: *the car gained speed.* **4** (*tr*) to earn (a wage, living, etc.). **5** (*intr;* usually foll. by *on* or *upon*) **5a** to get nearer (to) or catch up (on). **5b** to get farther away (from). **6** (*tr*) (esp. of ships) to get to; reach: *the steamer gained port.* **7** (of a timepiece) to operate too fast, so as to indicate a time ahead of the true time. ◆ *n* **8** something won, acquired, earned, etc.; profit; advantage. **9** an increase in size, amount, etc. **10** the act of gaining; attainment; acquisition. **11** Also called: **amplification.** *Electronics.* the ratio of the output signal of an amplifier to the input signal, usually measured in decibels. ORIG C15: from OF *gaaignier,* of Gmc origin

gainer ('geɪnə) *n* **1** a person or thing that gains. **2** a type of dive in which the diver leaves the board facing forward and completes a full backward somersault to enter the water feet first with his back to the diving board.

gainful ('geɪnfʊl) *adj* profitable; lucrative.
▸ **'gainfully** *adv* ▸ **'gainfulness** *n*

gainsay (geɪn'seɪ) *vb* **gainsays, gainsaying, gainsaid.** (*tr*) *Arch. or literary.* to deny (an allegation, statement, etc.); contradict. ORIG C13 *gainsaien,* from *gain-* AGAINST + *saien* to SAY
▸ **gain'sayer** *n*

Gainsborough ★ ('geɪnzbərə, -brə) *n* **Thomas.** 1727–88, British landscape and portrait painter.

'gainst *or* **gainst** (genst, geɪnst) *prep Poetic.* short for **against.**

Gaiseric ★ ('gaɪzərɪk) *n* a variant of **Genseric.**

gait (geɪt) *n* **1** manner of walking or running. **2** (used esp. of horses and dogs) the pattern of footsteps at a particular speed, as the walk, canter, etc. ◆ *vb* **3** (*tr*) to teach (a horse) a particular gait. ORIG C16: var. of GATE

gaiter ('geɪtə) *n* (*often pl*) **1** a cloth or leather covering for the leg or ankle. **2** Also called: **spat.** a similar covering extending from the ankle to the instep. ORIG C18: from F *guêtre,* prob. of Gmc origin

Gaitskell ★ ('geɪtskɪl) *n* **Hugh** (**Todd Naylor**). 1906–63, British politician; leader of the Labour Party (1955–63).

Gaius ('gaɪəs) *or* **Caius** ★ *n* **1** ?110–?180 A.D., Roman jurist. His *Institutes* were later used as the basis for those of Justinian. **2 Gaius Caesar.** See **Caligula.**

gal (gæl) *n Sl.* a girl.

gal. *or* **gall.** *abbrev. for* gallon.

Gal. *Bible. abbrev. for* Galatians.

gala ('gɑːlə, 'geɪlə) *n* **1a** a celebration; festive occasion. **1b** (*as modifier*): *a gala occasion.* **2** *Chiefly Brit.* a sporting occasion involving competitions in several events: *a swimming gala.* ORIG C17: from F or It., from OF *gale,* from *galer* to make merry, prob. of Gmc origin

galactic (gə'læktɪk) *adj* **1** *Astron.* of or relating to a galaxy, esp. the Galaxy. **2 galactic plane.** the plane passing through the spiral arms of the Galaxy, contained by the great circle of the celestial sphere (**galactic equator**) and perpendicular to an imaginary line joining opposite points (**galactic poles**) on the celestial sphere. **3** *Med.* of or relating to milk. ORIG C19: from Gk *galaktikos;* see GALAXY

galactic halo *n Astron.* a spheroidal aggregation of globular clusters, individual stars, dust, and gas that surrounds the Galaxy.

galago (gə'lɑːgəʊ) *n, pl* **galagos.** another name for **bushbaby.** ORIG C19: from NL, ?from Wolof *golokh* monkey

galah (gə'lɑː) *n* **1** an Australian cockatoo, having grey wings, back, and crest, and a pink body. **2** *Austral. sl.* a fool or simpleton. ORIG C19: from Abor.

Galahad ★ ('gælə,hæd) *n* **1 Sir.** (in Arthurian legend) the most virtuous knight of the Round Table. **2** a pure or noble man.

galantine ('gælən,tiːn) *n* a cold dish of meat or poultry, which is boned, cooked, then pressed and glazed. ORIG C14: from OF, from Med. L *galatina,* prob. from L *gelātus* frozen, set

Galápagos Islands ★ (gə'læpəgəs; *Spanish* ga'lapaɣɔs) *pl n* a group of 15 islands in the Pacific west of Ecuador, of which they form a province: discovered (1535) by the Spanish; main settlement on San Cristóbal. Pop.: 13 976 (1996 est.). Area: 7844 sq. km (3028 sq. miles). Official Spanish name: **Archipiélago de Colón.**

Galashiels ★ (,gælə'ʃiːlz) *n* a town in SE Scotland, in central Scottish Borders. Pop.: 13 753 (1997).

Galata ★ ('gælətə) *n* a port in NW Turkey, a suburb and the chief business section of Istanbul.

Galatea ★ (,gælə'tɪə) *n Greek myth.* a statue of a maiden brought to life by Aphrodite in response to the prayers of the sculptor Pygmalion, who had fallen in love with his creation.

Galaţi ★ (*Romanian* ga'latsj) *n* an inland port in SE Romania, on the River Danube. Pop.: 326 728 (1994 est.).

Galatia ★ (gə'leɪʃə, -ʃɪə) *n* an ancient region in central Asia Minor, conquered by Gauls 278–277 B.C.: later a Roman province.
▸ **Ga'latian** *adj, n*

galaxy ('gæləksɪ) *n, pl* **galaxies. 1** any of a vast number of star systems held together by gravitational attraction. **2** a splendid gathering, esp. one of famous or distinguished people. ORIG C14 (in the sense: the Milky Way): from Med. L *galaxia,* from L, from Gk, from *gala* milk

Galaxy ('gæləksɪ) *n* **the.** the spiral galaxy that contains the solar system about three fifths of the distance from its centre. Also called: the **Milky Way System.**

galbanum ('gælbənəm) *n* a bitter aromatic gum resin extracted from any of several Asian umbelliferous plants. ORIG C14: from L, from Gk, from Heb. *helbenāh*

Galbraith ★ (gæl'breɪθ) *n* **John Kenneth.** born 1908, US economist and diplomat born in Canada; author of *The Affluent Society* (1958).
▸ **Gal'braithian** *adj*

gale (geɪl) *n* **1** a strong wind, specifically one of force 8 on the Beaufort scale or 39–46 mph. **2** (*often pl*) a loud outburst, esp. of laughter. **3** *Arch. & poetic.* a gentle breeze. ORIG C16: from ?

galea ('geɪlɪə) *n, pl* **galeae** (-lɪ,iː). a part shaped like a helmet, such as the petals of certain flowers. ORIG C18: from L: helmet
▸ **'gale,ate** *or* **'gale,ated** *adj*

Galen ★ ('geɪlən) *n* Latin name *Claudius Galenus.* ?130–?200 A.D., Greek physician, anatomist, and physiologist. He codified existing medical knowledge and his authority continued until the Renaissance.

galena (gə'liːnə) *or* **galenite** (gə'liːnaɪt) *n* a soft heavy bluish-grey or black mineral consisting of lead sulphide: the chief source of lead. Formula: PbS. ORIG C17: from L: lead ore

Galenic (geɪ'lɛnɪk, gə-) *adj* of or relating to Galen or his teachings or methods.

Galicia ★ *n* **1** (gə'lɪʃɪə, -'lɪʃə). a region of E central Europe on the N side of the Carpathians, now in SE Poland and Ukraine. **2** (*Spanish* ga'liθja). an autonomous region and former kingdom of NW Spain, on the Bay of Biscay and the Atlantic. Pop.: 2 720 761 (1994 est.).
▸ **Galician** (gə'lɪʃɪən, -ʃən) *adj, n*

Galilean[1] (,gælɪ'liːən) *n* **1** a native or inhabitant of Galilee. **2 the.** an epithet of Jesus Christ. ◆ *adj* **3** of Galilee.

Galilean[2] (,gælɪ'leɪən) *adj* of or relating to Galileo.

Galilee ★ ('gælɪ,liː) *n* **1 Sea of.** Also called: Lake **Tiberias,** Lake **Kinneret.** a lake in NE Israel, 209 m (686 ft) below sea level, through which the River Jordan flows. Area: 165 sq. km (64 sq. miles). **2** a northern region of Israel: scene of Christ's early ministry.

Galileo ★ (,gælɪ'leɪəʊ) *n* full name *Galileo Galilei.* 1564–1642, Italian mathematician, astronomer, and physicist. He perfected the refracting telescope, which led to his discovery of Jupiter's satellites. He was forced by the Inquisition to recant his support of the Copernican system.

galingale ('gælɪŋ,geɪl) *or* **galangal** (gə'læŋgᵊl) *n* a European plant with rough-edged leaves, reddish spikelets of flowers, and aromatic roots. ORIG C13: from OF, from Ar., from Chinese

galiot *or* **galliot** ('gælɪət) *n* **1** a small swift galley formerly sailed on the Mediterranean. **2** a ketch formerly used along the coasts of Germany and the Netherlands. ORIG C14: from OF, from It., from Med. L *galea* GALLEY

galipot ('gælɪ,pɒt) *n* a resin obtained from several species of pine. ORIG C18: from F, from ?

gall[1] (gɔːl) *n* **1** *Inf.* impudence. **2** bitterness; rancour. **3** something bitter or disagreeable. **4** *Physiol.* an obsolete term for **bile.** See also **gall bladder.** ORIG from ON, replacing OE *gealla*

gall[2] (gɔːl) *n* **1** a sore on the skin caused by chafing. **2** something that causes vexation or annoyance. **3** irritation; exasperation. ◆ *vb* **4** to abrade (the skin, etc.) as by rubbing. **5** (*tr*) to irritate or annoy; vex. ORIG C14: of Gmc origin; rel. to OE *gealla* sore on a horse, & ? to GALL[1]

gall[3] (gɔːl) *n* an abnormal outgrowth in plant tissue caused by certain parasitic insects, fungi, or bacteria. ORIG C14: from OF, from L *galla*

gall. *or* **gal.** *abbrev. for* gallon.

gallant *adj* ('gælənt). **1** brave and high-spirited; courageous and honourable: *a gallant warrior.* **2** (gə'lænt, 'gælənt). (of a man) attentive to women; chivalrous. **3** imposing; dignified; stately: *a gallant ship.* **4** *Arch.* showy in dress. ◆ *n* ('gælənt, gə'lænt). *Arch.* **5** a woman's lover or suitor. **6** a dashing or fashionable young man, esp. one who pursues women. **7** a brave, high-spirited, or adventurous man. ◆ *vb* (gə'lænt, 'gælənt). *Rare.* **8** (when *intr,* usually foll. by *with*) to court or flirt (with). ORIG C15: from OF, from *galer* to make merry, from *gale* enjoyment, of Gmc origin
▸ **'gallantly** *adv*

gallantry ('gæləntrɪ) *n, pl* **gallantries. 1** conspicuous courage, esp. in war. **2** polite attentiveness to women. **3** a gallant action, speech, etc.

gall bladder *n* a muscular sac, attached to the right lobe of the liver, that stores bile.

Galle ★ (gɔːl) *n* a port in SW Sri Lanka. Pop.: 84 000 (1990). Former name: **Point de Galle.**

galleass (ˈgælɪˌæs) *n* a three-masted galley used as a warship in the Mediterranean from the 15th to the 18th centuries. ORIG C16: from F, from It., from Med. L *galea* GALLEY

galleon (ˈgælɪən) *n* a large sailing ship having three or more masts, used as a warship or trader from the 15th to the 18th centuries. ORIG C16: from Sp. *galeón,* from F, from OF *galie* GALLEY

gallery (ˈgælərɪ) *n, pl* **galleries. 1** a room or building for exhibiting works of art. **2** a covered passageway open on one side or on both sides. **3** a balcony running along or around the inside wall of a church, hall, etc. **4** *Theatre.* **4a** an upper floor that projects from the rear and contains the cheapest seats. **4b** the seats there. **4c** the audience seated there. **5** a long narrow room, esp. one used for a specific purpose: *a shooting gallery.* **6** an underground passage, as in a mine, etc. **7** a small ornamental railing, esp. one surrounding the top of a desk, table, etc. **8** any group of spectators, as at a golf match. **9** a glass-fronted soundproof room overlooking a television studio, used for lighting, etc. **10 play to the gallery.** to try to gain popular favour, esp. by crude appeals. ORIG C15: from OF, from Med. L, prob. from *galilea* galilee, porch or chapel at entrance to medieval church
▸ ˈ**galleried** *adj*

galley (ˈgælɪ) *n* **1** any of various kinds of ship propelled by oars or sails used in ancient or medieval times. **2** the kitchen of a ship, boat, or aircraft. **3** any of various long rowing boats. **4** *Printing.* **4a** a tray for holding composed type. **4b** short for **galley proof.** ORIG C13: from OF *galie,* from Med. L *galea,* from Gk *galaia,* from ?

galley proof *n* a printer's proof, esp. one taken from type in a galley, used to make corrections before the matter has been split into pages. Often shortened to **galley.**

galley slave *n* **1** a criminal or slave condemned to row in a galley. **2** *Inf.* a drudge.

gallfly (ˈgɔːlˌflaɪ) *n, pl* **gallflies.** any of several small insects that produce galls in plant tissues.

Gallia ★ (ˈgælɪə) *n* the Latin name of **Gaul.**

galliard (ˈgæljəd) *n* **1** a spirited dance in triple time for two persons, popular in the 16th and 17th centuries. **2** a piece of music composed for or in the rhythm of this dance. ORIG C14: from OF *gaillard* valiant, ? of Celtic origin

Gallic (ˈgælɪk) *adj* **1** of or relating to France. **2** of or relating to ancient Gaul or the Gauls.

gallic acid *n* a colourless crystalline compound obtained from tannin: used as a tanning agent and in making inks and paper. ORIG C18: from F *gallique;* see GALL[3]

Gallicism (ˈgælɪˌsɪzəm) *n* a word or idiom borrowed from French.

Gallicize *or* **Gallicise** (ˈgælɪˌsaɪz) *vb* **Gallicizes, Gallicizing, Gallicized** *or* **Gallicises, Gallicising, Gallicised.** to make or become French in attitude, language, etc.

galligaskins (ˌgælɪˈgæskɪnz) *pl n* **1** loose wide breeches or hose, esp. as worn by men in the 17th century. **2** leather leggings, as worn in the 19th century. ORIG C16: from obs. F, from It. *grechesco* Greek, from L *Graecus*

gallimaufry (ˌgælɪˈmɔːfrɪ) *n, pl* **gallimaufries.** a jumble; hotchpotch. ORIG C16: from F *galimafrée* ragout, hash, from ?

gallinacean (ˌgælɪˈneɪʃən) *n* any gallinaceous bird.

gallinaceous (ˌgælɪˈneɪʃəs) *adj* of, relating to, or belonging to an order of birds, including domestic fowl, pheasants, grouse, etc., having a heavy rounded body, short bill, and strong legs. ORIG C18: from L, from *gallīna* hen

Gallinas Point ★ (gɑːˈjiːnəs) *n* a cape in NE Colombia: the northernmost point of South America. Spanish name: **Punta Gallinas** (ˈpunta gaˈʎinas).

galling (ˈgɔːlɪŋ) *adj* irritating, exasperating, or bitterly humiliating.
▸ ˈ**gallingly** *adv*

gallinule (ˈgælɪˌnjuːl) *n* any of various aquatic birds, typically having a dark plumage, red bill, and a red shield above the bill. ORIG C18: from NL *Gallīnula,* from L *gallīna* hen

galliot (ˈgælɪət) *n* a variant spelling of **galiot.**

Gallipoli ★ (gəˈlɪpəlɪ) *n* **1** a peninsula in NW Turkey, between the Dardanelles and the Gulf of Saros: scene of a costly but unsuccessful Allied campaign in 1915. **2** a port in NW Turkey, at the entrance to the Sea of Marmara: historically important for its strategic position. Pop.: 16 751 (1985 est.). Turkish name: **Gelibolu.**

gallipot (ˈgælɪˌpɒt) *n* a small earthenware pot used by pharmacists as a container for ointments, etc. ORIG C16: prob. from GALLEY + POT[1]; because imported in galleys

gallium (ˈgælɪəm) *n* a silvery metallic element that is liquid for a wide temperature range. It is used in high-temperature thermometers and low-melting alloys. **Gallium arsenide** is a semiconductor. Symbol: Ga; atomic no.: 31; atomic wt.: 69.72. ORIG C19: from NL, from L *gallus* cock, translation of F *coq* in the name of its discoverer, *Lecoq* de Boisbaudran, 19th-cent. F chemist

gallivant (ˈgælɪˌvænt) *vb* (*intr*) to go about in search of pleasure, etc.; gad about. ORIG C19: ? whimsical from GALLANT

Gällivare ★ (*Swedish* ˈjɛlivɑːrə) *n* a town in N Sweden, within the Arctic Circle: iron mines. Pop.: 22 400 (1990).

galliwasp (ˈgælɪˌwɒsp) *n* a lizard of the Caribbean. ORIG C18: from ?

gallnut (ˈgɔːlˌnʌt) *or* **gall-apple** *n* a type of plant gall that resembles a nut.

Gallo- (ˈgæləʊ) *combining form.* denoting Gaul or France: *Gallo-Roman.* ORIG from L *Gallus* a Gaul

gallon (ˈgælən) *n* **1** Also called: **imperial gallon.** *Brit.* a unit of capacity equal to 277.42 cubic inches. 1 Brit. gallon is equivalent to 1.20 US gallons or 4.55 litres. **2** *US.* a unit of capacity equal to 231 cubic inches. 1 US gallon is equivalent to 0.83 imperial gallon or 3.79 litres. **3** (*pl*) *Inf.* great quantities. ORIG C13: from ONorthern F *galon* (OF *jalon*), ? of Celtic origin

gallonage (ˈgælənɪdʒ) *n* a capacity measured in gallons.

galloon (gəˈluːn) *n* a narrow band of cord, embroidery, silver or gold braid, etc., used on clothes and furniture. ORIG C17: from F, from OF *galonner* to trim with braid, from ?

gallop (ˈgæləp) *vb* **gallops, galloping, galloped. 1** (*intr*) (of a horse or other quadruped) to run fast with a two-beat stride in which all four legs are off the ground at once. **2** to ride (a horse, etc.) at a gallop. **3** (*intr*) to move, read, progress, etc., rapidly. ◆ *n* **4** the fast two-beat gait of horses. **5** an instance of galloping. ORIG C16: from OF *galoper,* from ?
▸ ˈ**galloper** *n*

Galloway ★ (ˈgæləˌweɪ) *n* **1** an area of SW Scotland, on the Solway Firth: consists of the former counties of Kirkcudbright and Wigtown, now part of Dumfries and Galloway; in the west is a large peninsula, the **Rhinns of Galloway,** with the **Mull of Galloway,** a promontory, at the south end of it (the southernmost point of Scotland). Related adj: **Galwegian. 2** a breed of hardy cattle, usually black, originally bred in Galloway.

gallows (ˈgæləʊz) *n, pl* **gallowses** *or* **gallows. 1** a wooden structure usually consisting of two upright posts with a crossbeam, used for hanging criminals. **2** any timber structure resembling this. **3 the gallows.** execution by hanging. ORIG C13: from ON *galgi,* replacing OE *gealga*

gallows bird *n Inf.* a person considered deserving of hanging.

gallows humour *n* sinister and ironic humour.

gallows tree *or* **gallow tree** *n* another name for **gallows** (sense 1).

gallsickness (ˈgɔːlˌsɪknɪs) *n* a disease of cattle and sheep, caused by infection with rickettsiae, resulting in anaemia and jaundice. Also called: **anaplasmosis.**

gallstone (ˈgɔːlˌstəʊn) *n* a small hard concretion formed in the gall bladder or its ducts.

Gallup ★ (ˈgæləp) *n* **George Horace.** 1901–84, US statistician: devised the Gallup Poll.

Gallup Poll *n* a sampling of the views of a representative cross section of the population, used esp. as a means of forecasting voting.

gall wasp *n* any small solitary wasp that produces galls in plant tissue.

galoot *or* **galloot** (gə'lu:t) *n Sl., chiefly US.* a clumsy or uncouth person. ORIG C19: from ?

galop ('gæləp) *n* **1** a 19th-century dance in quick duple time. **2** a piece of music for this dance. ORIG C19: from F; see GALLOP

galore (gə'lɔ:) *determiner (immediately postpositive)* in great numbers or quantity: *there were daffodils galore in the park.* ORIG C17: from Irish Gaelic *go leór* to sufficiency

galoshes *or* **goloshes** (gə'lɒʃɪz) *pl n (sometimes sing)* a pair of waterproof overshoes. ORIG C14 (in the sense: wooden shoe): from OF, from LL *gallicula* Gallic shoe

Galsworthy ★ ('gɔ:lz,wɜ:ðɪ) *n* **John.** 1867–1933, British novelist and dramatist, noted for *The Forsyte Saga* (1906–28): Nobel prize for literature 1932.

Galton ★ ('gɔ:ltən) *n* Sir **Francis.** 1822–1911, British explorer and scientist noted for his researches in heredity, meteorology, and statistics.

galumph (gə'lʌmpf, -'lʌmf) *vb (intr) Inf.* to leap or move about clumsily or joyfully. ORIG C19 (coined by Lewis Carroll): prob. a blend of GALLOP + TRIUMPH

Galvani ★ (*Italian* gal'va:ni) *n* **Luigi** (lu'i:dʒi). 1737–98, Italian physiologist: observed that muscles contracted on contact with dissimilar metals. This led to the galvanic cell and the electrical theory of muscle control.

galvanic (gæl'vænɪk) *adj* **1** of, producing, or concerned with an electric current, esp. a direct current produced chemically. **2** *Inf.* resembling the effect of an electric shock; convulsive, startling, or energetic.
▸ **gal'vanically** *adv*

galvanism ('gælvə,nɪzəm) *n* **1** *Obs.* electricity, esp. when produced by chemical means as in a cell or battery. **2** *Med.* treatment involving the application of electric currents to tissues. ORIG C18: via F from It. *galvanismo,* after GALVANI

galvanize *or* **galvanise** ('gælvə,naɪz) *vb* **galvanizes, galvanizing, galvanized** *or* **galvanises, galvanising, galvanised.** *(tr)* **1** to stimulate to action; excite; startle. **2** to cover (iron, steel, etc.) with a protective zinc coating. **3** to stimulate by application of an electric current.
▸ **,galvani'zation** *or* **,galvani'sation** *n*

galvanized iron *or* **galvanised iron** *n Building trades.* iron, esp. a sheet of corrugated iron, covered with a protective coating of zinc.

galvano- *combining form.* indicating a galvanic current: *galvanometer.*

galvanometer (,gælvə'nɒmɪtə) *n* any sensitive instrument for detecting or measuring small electric currents.
▸ **galvanometric** (,gælvənəʊ'mɛtrɪk, gæl,vænəʊ-) *adj*
▸ **,galva'nometry** *n*

Galway ★ ('gɔ:lweɪ) *n* **1** a county of W Republic of Ireland, in S Connacht, on **Galway Bay** and the Atlantic: it has a deeply indented coastline and many offshore islands, including the Aran Islands. County town: Galway. Pop.: 189 000 (1996). Area: 5939 sq. km (2293 sq. miles). **2** a port in W Ireland, county town of Co. Galway, on Galway Bay: important fisheries (esp. for salmon). Pop.: 50 853 (1991).

gam (gæm) *n Sl.* a leg. ORIG C18: from F *jambe* leg

Gama ★ ('gɑ:mə) *n* **Vasco da** ('væskəʊ də). ?1469–1524, Portuguese navigator, who discovered the sea route from Portugal to India around the Cape of Good Hope (1498).

Gambetta ★ (gæm'bɛtə; *French* gɑ̃bɛta) *n* **Léon** (leɔ̃). 1838–82, French statesman; prime minister (1881–82). He organized resistance during the Franco-Prussian War (1870–71) and was a founder of the Third Republic (1871).

Gambia ★ ('gæmbɪə) *n* **The.** a republic in W Africa, entirely surrounded by Senegal except for an outlet to the Atlantic: sold to English merchants by the Portuguese in 1588; became a British colony in 1843; gained independence and joined the Commonwealth in 1965; joined with Senegal in 1982 to form the Confederation of Senegambia; consists of a strip of land about 16 km (10 miles) wide, on both banks of the **Gambia River,** extending inland for about 480 km (300 miles). Official language: English. Religion: Muslim majority. Currency: dalasi. Capital: Banjul. Pop.: 1 136 000 (1999 est.). Area: 11 295 sq. km (4361 sq. miles).
▸ **'Gambian** *adj, n*

gambier *or* **gambir** ('gæmbɪə) *n* an astringent resinous substance obtained from a tropical Asian plant: used as an astringent and tonic and in tanning. ORIG C19: from Malay

Gambier Islands ★ ('gæmbɪə) *pl n* a group of islands in the S Pacific Ocean, in French Polynesia. Chief settlement: Rikitéa. Pop.: 582 (1988). Area: 30 sq. km (11 sq. miles).

gambit ('gæmbɪt) *n* **1** *Chess.* an opening move in which a chessman, usually a pawn, is sacrificed to secure an advantageous position. **2** an opening comment, manoeuvre, etc., intended to secure an advantage. ORIG C17: from F, from It. *gambetto* a tripping up, from *gamba* leg

gamble ('gæmb^{ə}l) *vb* **gambles, gambling, gambled. 1** *(intr)* to play games of chance to win money, etc. **2** to risk or bet (money, etc.) on the outcome of an event, sport, etc. **3** *(intr; often foll. by on)* to act with the expectation of: *to gamble on its being a sunny day.* **4** (often foll. by *away*) to lose by or as if by betting; squander. ◆ *n* **5** a risky act or venture. **6** a bet or wager. ORIG C18: prob. var. of GAME[1]
▸ **'gambler** *n* ▸ **'gambling** *n*

gamboge (gæm'bəʊdʒ, -'bu:ʒ) *n* **1a** a gum resin used as the source of a yellow pigment and as a purgative. **1b** the pigment made from this resin. **2 gamboge tree.** any of several tropical Asian trees that yield this resin. ORIG C18: from NL *gambaugium,* from CAMBODIA, where first found

gambol ('gæmb^{ə}l) *vb* **gambols, gambolling, gambolled** *or US* **gambols, gamboling, gamboled. 1** *(intr)* to skip or jump about in a playful manner; frolic. ◆ *n* **2** a playful antic; frolic. ORIG C16: from F *gambade;* see JAMB

gambrel ('gæmbrəl) *n* **1** the hock of a horse or similar animal. **2** short for **gambrel roof.** ORIG C16: from OF, from *gambe* leg

gambrel roof *n* **1** *Chiefly Brit.* a hipped roof having a small gable at both ends. **2** *Chiefly US & Canad.* a roof having two slopes on both sides, the lower slopes being steeper than the upper.

game[1] (geɪm) *n* **1** an amusement or pastime; diversion. **2** a contest with rules, the result being determined by skill, strength, or chance. **3** a single period of play in such a contest, sport, etc. **4** the score needed to win a contest. **5** a single contest in a series; match. **6** *(pl; often cap.)* an event consisting of various sporting contests, esp. in athletics: *Olympic Games.* **7** equipment needed for playing certain games. **8** short for **computer game. 9** style or ability in playing a game. **10** a scheme, proceeding, etc., practised like a game: *the game of politics.* **11** an activity undertaken in a spirit of levity; joke: *marriage is just a game to him.* **12a** wild animals, including birds and fish, hunted for sport, food, or profit. **12b** *(as modifier): game laws.* **13** the flesh of such animals, used as food. **14** an object of pursuit; quarry; prey (esp. in **fair game**). **15** *Inf.* work or occupation. **16** *Inf.* a trick, strategy, or device: *I can see through your little game.* **17** *Sl., chiefly Brit.* prostitution (esp. in **on the game**). **18 give the game away.** to reveal one's intentions or a secret. **19 make (a) game of.** to make fun of; ridicule; mock. **20 play the game.** to behave fairly or in accordance with the rules. **21 the game is up.** there is no longer a chance of success. ◆ *adj* **22** *Inf.* full of fighting spirit; plucky; brave. **23** (usually foll. by *for*) *Inf.* prepared or ready; willing: *I'm game for a try.* ◆ *vb* **games, gaming, gamed. 24** *(intr)* to play games of chance for money, stakes, etc.; gamble. ORIG OE *gamen*
▸ **'gamely** *adv* ▸ **'gameness** *n*

game[2] (geɪm) *adj* a less common word for **lame** (esp. in **game leg**). ORIG C18: prob. from Irish *cam* crooked

gamecock ('geɪm,kɒk) *n* a cock bred and trained for fighting. Also called: **fighting cock.**

game fish *n* any fish providing sport for the angler.

gamekeeper (ˈgeɪmˌkiːpə) *n* a person employed to take care of game, as on an estate.

gamelan (ˈgæmɪˌlæn) *n* a type of percussion orchestra common in the East Indies. ORIG from Javanese

game laws *pl n* laws governing the hunting and preservation of game.

game plan *n* **1** a strategy. **2** a plan of campaign, esp. in politics.

game point *n Tennis, etc.* a stage at which winning one further point would enable one player or side to win a game.

gamer (ˈgeɪmə) *n* a person who plays a computer game or participates in a role-playing game.

gamesmanship (ˈgeɪmzmənˌʃɪp) *n Inf.* the art of winning games or defeating opponents by cunning practices without actually cheating.

gamesome (ˈgeɪmsəm) *adj* full of merriment; sportive. ▸ **ˈgamesomeness** *n*

gamester (ˈgeɪmstə) *n* a person who habitually plays games for money; gambler.

gametangium (ˌgæmɪˈtændʒɪəm) *n, pl* **gametangia** (-dʒɪə). *Biol.* an organ or cell in which gametes are produced, esp. in algae and fungi. ORIG C19: NL, from GAMETO- + Gk *angeion* vessel

gamete (ˈgæmiːt, gəˈmiːt) *n* a haploid germ cell that fuses with another during fertilization. ORIG C19: from NL, from Gk *gametē* wife, from *gamos* marriage
▸ **gametic** (gəˈmɛtɪk) *adj*

gamete intrafallopian transfer (ˌɪntrəfəˈləʊpɪən) *n* See **GIFT**.

game theory *n* mathematical theory concerned with the optimum choice of strategy in situations involving a conflict of interest.

gameto- *or sometimes before a vowel* **gamet-** *combining form.* gamete: *gametophyte.*

gametophyte (gəˈmiːtəʊˌfaɪt) *n* the plant body, in species showing alternation of generations, that produces the gametes.
▸ **gametophytic** (ˌgæmɪtəʊˈfɪtɪk) *adj*

gamey *or* **gamy** (ˈgeɪmɪ) *adj* **gamier, gamiest. 1** having the smell or flavour of game, esp. high game. **2** *Inf.* spirited; plucky; brave.
▸ **ˈgamily** *adv* ▸ **ˈgaminess** *n*

gamin (ˈgæmɪn) *n* a street urchin. ORIG from F

gamine (ˈgæmiːn) *n* a slim and boyish girl or young woman; an elfish tomboy. ORIG from F

gaming (ˈgeɪmɪŋ) *n* **a** gambling on games of chance. **b** *(as modifier): gaming house.*

gamma (ˈgæmə) *n* **1** the third letter in the Greek alphabet (Γ, γ). **2** the third in a group or series. ORIG C14: from Gk

gamma distribution *n Statistics.* a continuous two-parameter distribution from which the chi-square and exponential distributions are derived.

gamma globulin *n* any of a group of proteins in blood plasma that includes most known antibodies.

gamma radiation *n* electromagnetic radiation of shorter wavelength and higher energy than X-rays.

gamma-ray astronomy *n* the investigation of cosmic gamma rays, such as those from quasars.

gamma-ray burster *n Astron.* a distant event involving a very bright burst of light and gamma rays lasting a few seconds, possibly caused by a supernova or by the collision of neutron stars.

gamma rays *pl n* streams of gamma radiation.

gamma stock *n* any of the third rank of active securities on the London stock exchange. Prices displayed by market makers are given as an indication rather than an offer to buy or sell.

gammer (ˈgæmə) *n Rare, chiefly Brit.* a dialect word for an old woman: now chiefly humorous or contemptuous. ORIG C16: prob. from GODMOTHER or GRANDMOTHER

gammon[1] (ˈgæmən) *n* **1** a cured or smoked ham. **2** the hindquarter of a side of bacon, cooked either whole or in rashers. ORIG C15: from OF *gambon,* from *gambe* leg

gammon[2] (ˈgæmən) *n* **1** a double victory in backgammon in which one player throws off all his pieces before his opponent throws any. ◆ *vb* **2** *(tr)* to score such a victory over. ORIG C18: prob. special use of ME *gamen* GAME[1]

gammon[3] (ˈgæmən) *Brit. inf.* ◆ *n* **1** deceitful nonsense; humbug. ◆ *vb* **2** to deceive (a person). ORIG C18: ? special use of GAMMON[1]

gammy (ˈgæmɪ) *adj* **gammier, gammiest.** *Brit. sl.* (esp. of the leg) malfunctioning, injured, or lame; game. ORIG C19: dialect var. of GAME[2]

gamo- *or before a vowel* **gam-** *combining form.* **1** indicating sexual union or reproduction: *gamogenesis.* **2** united or fused: *gamopetalous.* ORIG from Gk *gamos* marriage

gamopetalous (ˌgæməʊˈpɛtələs) *adj* (of flowers) having petals that are united or partly united, as the primrose.

gamp (gæmp) *n Brit. inf.* an umbrella. ORIG C19: after Mrs Sarah *Gamp,* a nurse in Dickens' *Martin Chuzzlewit,* who carried a faded cotton umbrella

gamut (ˈgæmət) *n* **1** entire range or scale, as of emotions. **2** *Music.* **2a** a scale, esp. (in medieval theory) one starting on the G on the bottom line of the bass staff. **2b** the whole range of notes. **3** *Physics.* the range of chromaticities that can be obtained by mixing three colours. ORIG C14: from Med. L, from *gamma,* the lowest note of the hexachord as established by Guido d'Arezzo + *ut* (now, *doh*), the first of the notes of the scale *ut, re, mi, fa, sol, la, si*

-gamy *n combining form.* denoting marriage or sexual union: *bigamy.* ORIG from Gk, from *gamos* marriage
▸ **-gamous** *adj combining form.*

Gance ★ (*French* gɑ̃s) *n* **Abel** (abɛl). 1889–1981, French film director, whose works include *J'accuse* (1919, 1937) and *Napoléon* (1927).

Gand ★ (gɑ̃) *n* the French name for **Ghent**.

gander (ˈgændə) *n* **1** a male goose. **2** *Inf.* a quick look (esp. in **take** (*or* **have**) **a gander**). **3** *Inf.* a simpleton. ORIG OE *gandra, ganra*

Gandhi ★ (ˈgændɪ) *n* **1** Mrs **Indira** (**Priyadarshini**) (ɪnˈdɪərə, ˈɪndərə), daughter of Jawaharlal Nehru. 1917–84, Indian stateswoman; prime minister of India (1966–77; 1980–84); assassinated. **2 Mohandas Karamchand** (ˌməʊhənˈdʌs ˌkʌrəmˈtʃʌnd), known as *Mahatma Gandhi.* 1869–1948, Indian political and spiritual leader. He played a major part in India's struggle for home rule and was frequently imprisoned by the British for civil disobedience. He advocated passive resistance and attempted to unite Muslims and Hindus; assassinated. **3 Rajiv** (ræˈdʒiːv), son of Indira Gandhi. 1944–91, Indian statesman; prime minister of India (1984–89); assassinated. **4 Sonia,** widow of Ravi. born 1946, leader of the Congress Party from 1998.

Gandhian (ˈgændɪən) *adj* **1** of or relating to Mahatma Gandhi or his ideas. ◆ *n* **2** a follower of Gandhi or his ideas.

G & S *abbrev. for* Gilbert and Sullivan

Gandzha ★ (*Russian* ganˈdʒa) *n* a city in NW Azerbaijan: annexed by the Russians in 1804; centre of a cotton-growing region. Pop.: 282 200 (1991 est.). Former names: **Yelisavetpol** (1813–1920), **Kirovabad** (1935–91).

Ganesa ★ (gæˈniːsə) *n* the Hindu god of prophecy, represented as having an elephant's head.

gang[1] (gæŋ) *n* **1** a group of people who associate together or act as an organized body, esp. for criminal or illegal purposes. **2** an organized group of workmen. **3** a series of similar tools arranged to work simultaneously in parallel. ◆ *vb* **4** to form into, become part of, or act as a gang.
◆ See also **gang up.** ORIG OE: journey

gang[2] (gæŋ) *n* a variant spelling of **gangue.**

gang[3] (gæŋ) *vb (intr) Scot.* to go or walk. ORIG OE *gangan*

gangbang (ˈgæŋˌbæŋ) *n Sl.* an instance of sexual intercourse between one woman and several men one after the other, esp. against her will.

gang-banger *n US sl.* a member of a street gang.
▸ **ˈgang-ˌbanging** *n*

ganger (ˈgæŋə) *n Chiefly Brit.* the foreman of a gang of labourers.

Ganges ★ (ˈgændʒiːz) *n* the great river of N India and

central Bangladesh: rises in two headstreams in the Himalayas and flows southeast to Allahabad, where it is joined by the Jumna; continues southeast into Bangladesh, where it enters the Bay of Bengal in a great delta; the most sacred river to Hindus, with many places of pilgrimage, esp. Varanasi. Length: 2507 km (1557 miles). Hindi name: **Ganga** (ˈgʌŋgə, ˈgɑːŋ-).
▸ **Gangetic** (gænˈdʒɛtɪk) *adj*

gangland (ˈgæŋˌlænd, -lənd) *n* the criminal underworld.

gangling (ˈgæŋglɪŋ) *or* **gangly** *adj* tall, lanky, and awkward in movement. ORIG see GANG[3]

ganglion (ˈgæŋglɪən) *n, pl* **ganglia** (-glɪə) *or* **ganglions. 1** an encapsulated collection of nerve-cell bodies, usually located outside the brain and spinal cord. **2** any concentration or centre of energy, activity, or strength. **3** a cystic tumour on a tendon sheath. ORIG C17: from LL: swelling, from Gk: cystic tumour
▸ ˈ**gangliar** *adj* ▸ ˌ**gangliˈonic** *or* ˈ**gangliˌated** *adj*

gangplank (ˈgæŋˌplæŋk) *or* **gangway** *n Naut.* a portable bridge for boarding and leaving a vessel at dockside.

gangrene (ˈgæŋgriːn) *n* **1** death and decay of tissue due to an interrupted blood supply, disease, or injury. ◆ *vb* **gangrenes, gangrening, gangrened. 2** to become or cause to become affected with gangrene. ORIG C16: from L, from Gk *gangraina* an eating sore
▸ **gangrenous** (ˈgæŋgrɪnəs) *adj*

gang-saw *n* a multiple saw used in a timber mill to cut planks from logs.

gangsta rap (ˈgæŋstə) *n* a style of rap music, usually characterized by songs about Black street gangs in the US, with nihilistic and misogynistic lyrics. ORIG C20: phonetic rendering of GANGSTER
▸ **gangsta rapper** *n*

gangster (ˈgæŋstə) *n* a member of an organized gang of criminals.

Gangtok ★ (ˈgʌŋtɒk) *n* a city in NE India: capital of Sikkim state. Pop.: 24 970 (1991).

gangue *or* **gang** (gæŋ) *n* valueless and undesirable material in an ore. ORIG C19: from F, from G *Gang* vein of metal, course

gang up *vb* (*intr, adv;* often foll. by *on* or *against*) *Inf.* to combine in a group (against).

gangway (ˈgæŋˌweɪ) *n* **1** another word for **gangplank. 2** an opening in a ship's side to take a gangplank. **3** *Brit.* an aisle between rows of seats. **4** temporary planks over mud, as on a building site. ◆ *sentence substitute.* **5** clear a path!

ganister *or* **gannister** (ˈgænɪstə) *n* a refractory siliceous sedimentary rock occurring beneath coal seams: used for lining furnaces. ORIG C20: from ?

gannet (ˈgænɪt) *n* **1** any of several heavily built marine birds having a long stout bill and typically white plumage with dark markings. **2** *Sl.* a greedy person. ORIG OE *ganot*

ganoid (ˈgænɔɪd) *adj* **1** (of the scales of certain fishes) consisting of an inner bony layer and an outer layer of an enamel-like substance (**ganoin**). **2** denoting fishes, including the sturgeon, having such scales. ◆ *n* **3** a ganoid fish. ORIG C19: from F, from Gk *ganos* brightness + -OID

Gansu (ˈgænˈsuː) *or* **Kansu** ★ *n* a province of NW China, between Tibet and Inner Mongolia: mountainous, with desert regions; forms a corridor, the Old Silk Road, much used in early and medieval times for trade with Turkestan, India, and Persia. Capital: Lanzhou. Pop.: 24 940 000 (1997 est.). Area: 366 500 sq. km (141 500 sq. miles).

gantry (ˈgæntrɪ) *n, pl* **gantries. 1** a bridgelike framework used to support a travelling crane, signals over a railway track, etc. **2** Also called: **gantry scaffold.** the framework tower used to attend to a large rocket on its launch pad. **3** a supporting framework for a barrel. **4a** the area behind a bar where bottles, esp. spirit bottles mounted in optics, are kept. **4b** the range or quality of the spirits on display there. ORIG C16 (in the sense: wooden platform for barrels): from OF *chantier,* from Med. L, from L *canthērius* supporting frame, pack ass

Gantt chart (gænt) *n* a chart showing, in horizontal lines, activity planned to take place during specified periods, which are indicated in vertical bands. ORIG C20: named after Henry L. *Gantt* (1861–1919), US management consultant

Ganymede ★ (ˈgænɪˌmiːd) *n Classical myth.* a beautiful Trojan youth who was abducted by Zeus to Olympus and made the cupbearer of the gods.

Gao ★ (ˈgɑːəʊ, gaʊ) *n* a town in E Mali, on the River Niger: a small river port. Pop.: 54 874 (1987).

gaol (dʒeɪl) *n, vb* (*tr*) *Brit.* a variant spelling of **jail.**
▸ ˈ**gaoler** *n*

Gaoxiong (ˈgaʊˈʃjɒŋ) *or* **Kaohsiung** ★ *n* a city in SW Taiwan, on the South China Sea: the chief port of the island. Pop.: 1 434 907 (1997 est.). Japanese name: **Takao.**

gap (gæp) *n* **1** a break or opening in a wall, fence, etc. **2** a break in continuity; interruption; hiatus. **3** a break in a line of hills or mountains affording a route through. **4** *Chiefly US.* a gorge or ravine. **5** a divergence or difference; disparity: *the generation gap.* **6** *Electronics.* **6a** a break in a magnetic circuit that increases the inductance and saturation point of the circuit. **6b** See **spark gap. 7 bridge, close, fill,** *or* **stop a gap.** to remedy a deficiency. ◆ *vb* **gaps, gapping, gapped. 8** (*tr*) to make a breach or opening in. ORIG C14: from ON *gap* chasm
▸ ˈ**gappy** *adj*

gape (geɪp) *vb* **gapes, gaping, gaped.** (*intr*) **1** to stare in wonder, esp. with the mouth open. **2** to open the mouth wide, esp. involuntarily, as in yawning. **3** to be or become wide open: *the crater gaped under his feet.* ◆ *n* **4** the act of gaping. **5** a wide opening. **6** the width of the widely opened mouth of a vertebrate. **7** a stare of astonishment. ORIG C13: from ON *gapa*
▸ ˈ**gaper** *n* ▸ ˈ**gaping** *adj*

gapes (geɪps) *n* (*functioning as sing*) **1** a disease of young domestic fowl, characterized by gaping and caused by parasitic worms (**gapeworms**). **2** *Inf.* a fit of yawning.

gap year *n* a year's break taken by a student between leaving school and starting further education.

gar (gɑː) *n, pl* **gar** *or* **gars.** short for **garpike.**

garage (ˈgærɑːʒ, -rɪdʒ) *n* **1** a building used to house a motor vehicle. **2** a commercial establishment in which motor vehicles are repaired, serviced, bought, and sold, and which usually also sells motor fuels. ◆ *vb* **garages, garaging, garaged. 3** (*tr*) to put into or keep in a garage. ORIG C20: from F, from OF: to protect, from OHG *warōn*

garage band *n* a rough-and-ready amateurish rock group. ORIG ?from the practice of such bands rehearsing in a garage

garage sale *n* a sale of personal belongings or household effects held at a person's home, usually in the garage.

garb (gɑːb) *n* **1** clothes, esp. the distinctive attire of an occupation: *clerical garb.* **2** style of dress; fashion. **3** external appearance, covering, or attire. ◆ *vb* **4** (*tr*) to clothe; attire. ORIG C16: from OF: graceful contour, from OIt. *garbo* grace, prob. of Gmc origin

garbage (ˈgɑːbɪdʒ) *n* **1** worthless, useless, or unwanted matter. **2** another word (esp. US and Canad.) for **rubbish. 3** *Computing.* invalid data. **4** *Inf.* nonsense. ORIG C15: prob. from Anglo-F *garbelage* removal of discarded matter, from ?

garble (ˈgɑːbᵊl) *vb* **garbles, garbling, garbled.** (*tr*) **1** to jumble (a story, quotation, etc.), esp. unintentionally. **2** to distort the meaning of (an account, text, etc.), as by making misleading omissions; corrupt. ◆ *n* **3a** the act of garbling. **3b** garbled matter. ORIG C15: from OIt. *garbellare* to strain, sift, from Ar., from LL *crībellum* small sieve
▸ ˈ**garbler** *n*

Garbo ★ (ˈgɑːbəʊ) *n* **Greta** (ˈgrɛtə), real name *Greta Lovisa Gustafson.* 1905–90, US film actress, born in Sweden. Her films include *Anna Karenina* (1935) and *Camille* (1936).

garboard (ˈgɑːˌbɔːd) *n Naut.* the bottommost plank of a vessel's hull. Also called: **garboard strake.** ORIG C17: from Du. *gaarboord,* prob. from MDu. *gaderen* to GATHER + *boord* BOARD

garbology (gɑːˈbɒlədʒɪ) *n Chiefly US.* **1** analysis of refuse as a means of investigating the lifestyle of the person or

people who produced it. **2** the study of waste disposal. ORIG C20: from GARBAGE + -OLOGY
▸ **gar'bologist** *n*

García Lorca ★ (*Spanish* gar'θia 'lorka) *n* See (Federico García) **Lorca.**

García Márquez ★ (*Spanish* gar'sia mar'kes) *n* **Gabriel** (ga'βrjel). born 1928, Colombian writer. His works include the novel *One Hundred Years of Solitude* (1967) and the factual *News of a Kidnapping* (1996). Nobel prize for literature 1982.

garçon *French.* (garsɔ̃) *n* a waiter or male servant, esp. if French. ORIG C19: from OF *gars* lad, prob. of Gmc origin

Gard ★ (*French* gar) *n* a department of S France, in Languedoc-Roussillon region. Capital: Nîmes. Pop.: 605 847 (1994 est.). Area: 5881 sq. km (2294 sq. miles).

garda ('gɑːrdə) *n, pl* **gardaí** ('gɑːrdɪ). a member of the **Garda Síochána,** the police force of the Republic of Ireland.

Garda ★ ('gɑːdə) *n* **Lake.** a lake in N Italy: the largest lake in the country. Area: 370 sq. km (143 sq. miles).

garden ('gɑːdᵊn) *n* **1** *Brit.* **1a** an area of land, usually planted with grass, trees, flowerbeds, etc., adjoining a house. US and Canad. word: **yard. 1b** (*as modifier*): *a garden chair.* **2a** an area of land used for the cultivation of ornamental plants, herbs, fruit, vegetables, trees, etc. **2b** (*as modifier*): *garden tools.* Related adj: **horticultural. 3** (*often pl*) such an area of land that is open to the public, sometimes part of a park: *botanical gardens.* **4** a fertile and beautiful region. **5 lead (a person) up the garden path.** *Inf.* to mislead or deceive. ◆ *vb* **6** to work in, cultivate, or take care of (a garden, plot of land, etc.). ORIG C14: from OF *gardin,* of Gmc origin
▸ **'gardener** *n* ▸ **'gardening** *n*

garden centre *n* a place where gardening tools and equipment, plants, seeds, etc., are sold.

garden city *n Brit.* a planned town of limited size surrounded by a rural belt.

gardenia (gɑː'diːnɪə) *n* **1** any evergreen shrub or tree of the Old World tropical genus *Gardenia,* cultivated for their large fragrant waxlike typically white flowers. **2** the flower of any of these shrubs. ORIG C18: NL, after Dr Alexander *Garden* (1730–91), American botanist

gardening leave *n Brit. inf.* a period during which an employee who is about to leave a company continues to receive a salary but does not work.

Garden of Eden ★ *n* the full name for **Eden**[1].

garderobe ('gɑːdˌrəʊb) *n Arch.* **1** a wardrobe or its contents. **2** a private room. **3** a privy. ORIG C14: from F, from *garder* to keep + *robe* dress, clothing; see WARDROBE

Gardiner ★ ('gɑːdnə) *n* **Stephen.** ?1483–1555, English bishop and statesman; lord chancellor (1553–55). He opposed Protestantism, supporting the anti-Reformation policies of Mary I.

Gardner ★ ('gɑːdnə) *n* **Ava.** 1922–90, US film actress. Her films include *The Killers* (1946), *The Sun also Rises* (1957), and *The Night of the Iguana* (1964).

Garfield ★ ('gɑːˌfiːld) *n* **James Abram.** 1831–81, 20th president of the US (1881); assassinated in office.

garfish ('gɑːˌfɪʃ) *n, pl* **garfish** *or* **garfishes. 1** another name for **garpike** (sense 1). **2** an elongated marine teleost fish with long toothed jaws: related to the flying fishes. ORIG OE *gār* spear + FISH

garganey ('gɑːgənɪ) *n* a small Eurasian duck closely related to the mallard. The male has a white stripe over each eye. ORIG C17: from It. dialect *garganei,* imit.

gargantuan (gɑː'gæntjʊən) *adj* (*sometimes cap.*) huge; enormous. ORIG after *Gargantua,* a giant in Rabelais' satire *Gargantua and Pantagruel* (1534)

> **USAGE NOTE** Some people think that *gargantuan* should only be used to describe things connected with food: *a gargantuan meal; his gargantuan appetite.* Nevertheless, the word is now widely used as a synonym of 'colossal'.

gargle ('gɑːgᵊl) *vb* **gargles, gargling, gargled. 1** to rinse the mouth and throat with (a liquid, esp. a medicinal fluid) by slowly breathing out through the liquid. ◆ *n* **2** the liquid used for gargling. **3** the sound produced by gargling. ORIG C16: from OF, from *gargouille* throat, ? imit.

gargoyle ('gɑːˌgɔɪl) *n* **1** a waterspout carved in the form of a grotesque face or creature and projecting from a roof gutter. **2** a person with a grotesque appearance. ORIG C15: from OF *gargouille* gargoyle, throat; see GARGLE

garibaldi (ˌgærɪ'bɔːldɪ) *n Brit.* a type of biscuit having a layer of currants in the centre.

Garibaldi ★ (ˌgærɪ'bɔːldɪ) *n* **Giuseppe** (*Italian* dʒu'zɛppe). 1807–82, Italian patriot; a leader of the Risorgimento. He conquered Sicily and Naples for the emerging kingdom of Italy (1860).

garish ('gɛərɪʃ) *adj* gay or colourful in a crude manner; gaudy. ORIG C16: from earlier *gaure* to stare + -ISH
▸ **'garishly** *adv* ▸ **'garishness** *n*

garland ('gɑːlənd) *n* **1** a wreath of flowers, leaves, etc., worn round the head or neck or hung up. **2** a collection of short literary pieces, such as poems; anthology. ◆ *vb* **3** (*tr*) to adorn with a garland or garlands. ORIG C14: from OF *garlande,* ? of Gmc origin

Garland ★ ('gɑːlənd) *n* **Judy,** real name *Frances Gumm.* 1922–69, US singer and film actress. Her films include *The Wizard of Oz* (1939) and *A Star is Born* (1954).

garlic ('gɑːlɪk) *n* **1** a hardy widely cultivated Asian alliaceous plant having whitish flowers. **2** the bulb of this plant, made up of small segments (cloves) that have a strong odour and pungent taste and are used in cooking. ORIG OE *gārlēac,* from *gār* spear + *lēac* LEEK
▸ **'garlicky** *adj*

garment ('gɑːmənt) *n* **1** (*often pl*) an article of clothing. **2** outer covering. ◆ *vb* **3** (*tr; usually passive*) to cover or clothe. ORIG C14: from OF *garniment,* from *garnir* to equip; see GARNISH

garner ('gɑːnə) *vb* (*tr*) **1** to gather or store as in a granary. ◆ *n* **2** an archaic word for **granary. 3** *Arch.* a place for storage. ORIG C12: from OF: granary, from L *grānārium,* from *grānum* grain

Garner ★ ('gɑːnə) *n* **Erroll.** 1921–77, US jazz pianist and composer.

garnet ('gɑːnɪt) *n* any of a group of hard glassy red, yellow, or green minerals consisting of silicates in cubic crystalline form: used as a gemstone and abrasive. ORIG C13: from OF, from *grenat* (adj) red, from *pome grenate* POMEGRANATE

garnish ('gɑːnɪʃ) *vb* (*tr*) **1** to decorate; trim. **2** to add something to (food) in order to improve its appearance or flavour. **3** *Law.* **3a** to serve with notice of proceedings; warn. **3b** to attach (a debt). ◆ *n* **4** a decoration; trimming. **5** something, such as parsley, added to a dish for its flavour or decorative effect. ORIG C14: from OF *garnir* to adorn, equip, of Gmc origin
▸ **'garnisher** *n*

garnishee (ˌgɑːnɪ'ʃiː) *Law.* ◆ *n* **1** a person upon whom a garnishment has been served. ◆ *vb* **garnishees, garnisheeing, garnisheed.** (*tr*) **2** to attach (a debt or other property) by garnishment. **3** to serve (a person) with a garnishment.

garnishment ('gɑːnɪʃmənt) *n* **1** decoration or embellishment. **2** *Law.* **2a** a notice or warning. **2b** *Obs.* a summons to court proceedings already in progress. **2c** a notice warning a person holding money or property belonging to a debtor whose debt has been attached to hold such property until directed by the court to apply it.

garniture ('gɑːnɪtʃə) *n* decoration or embellishment. ORIG C16: from F, from *garnir* to GARNISH

Garonne ★ (*French* garɔn) *n* a river in SW France, rising in the central Pyrenees in Spain and flowing northeast then northwest into the Gironde estuary. Length: 580 km (360 miles).

garpike ('gɑːˌpaɪk) *n* **1** Also called: **garfish, gar.** any primitive freshwater elongated bony fish of North and Central America, having very long toothed jaws and a body covering of thick scales. **2** another name for **garfish** (sense 2).

garret ('gærɪt) *n* another word for **attic** (sense 1). ORIG

C14: from OF: watchtower, from *garir* to protect, of Gmc origin

garret window *n* a skylight that lies along the slope of the roof.

Garrick ★ ('gærɪk) *n* **David.** 1717–79, British actor and theatre manager.

garrison ('gærɪsᵊn) *n* **1** the troops who maintain and guard a base or fortified place. **2** the place itself. ◆ *vb* **3** (*tr*) to station (troops) in (a fort, etc.). ORIG C13: from OF, from *garir* to defend, of Gmc origin

garron ('gærən) *n* a small sturdy pony bred and used chiefly in Scotland and Ireland. ORIG C16: from Gaelic *gearran*

garrotte *or* **garotte** (gə'rɒt) *n* **1** a Spanish method of execution by strangulation. **2** the device, usually an iron collar, used in such executions. **3** *Obs.* strangulation of one's victim while committing robbery. ◆ *vb* **garrottes, garrotting, garrotted** *or* **garottes, garotting, garotted.** (*tr*) **4** to execute by means of the garrotte. **5** to strangle, esp. in order to commit robbery. ORIG C17: from Sp. *garrote,* ?from OF *garrot* cudgel; from ?
▸ **gar'rotter** *or* **ga'rotter** *n*

garrulous ('gærʊləs) *adj* **1** given to constant chatter; talkative. **2** wordy or diffuse. ORIG C17: from L, from *garrīre* to chatter
▸ **'garrulously** *adv* ▸ **'garrulousness** *or* **garrulity** (gæ'ru:lɪtɪ) *n*

garryowen (ˌgærɪ'əʊɪn) *n* (in rugby union) another term for **up-and-under.** ORIG from *Garryowen* RFC, Ireland

garter ('gɑ:tə) *n* **1** a band, usually of elastic, worn round the leg to hold up a sock or stocking. **2** the US and Canad. word for **suspender.** ◆ *vb* **3** (*tr*) to fasten or secure as with a garter. ORIG C14: from OF *gartier,* from *garet* bend of the knee, prob. of Celtic origin

Garter ('gɑ:tə) *n* **the. 1 Order of the Garter.** the highest order of British knighthood, open to women since 1987. **2** (*sometimes not cap.*) **2a** the badge of this Order. **2b** membership of this Order.

garter snake *n* a nonvenomous North American snake, typically marked with longitudinal stripes.

garter stitch *n* knitting in which all the rows are knitted in plain stitch.

garth (gɑ:θ) *n* **1** a courtyard surrounded by a cloister. **2** *Arch.* a yard or garden. ORIG C14: from ON *garthr*

Gary ★ ('gærɪ) *n* a port in NW Indiana, on Lake Michigan: a major world steel producer. Pop.: 110 975 (1996 est.).

gas (gæs) *n, pl* **gases** *or* **gasses. 1** a substance in a physical state in which it does not resist change of shape and will expand indefinitely to fill any container. Cf. **liquid** (sense 1), **solid** (sense 1). **2** any substance that is gaseous at room temperature and atmospheric pressure. **3** any gaseous substance that is above its critical temperature and therefore not liquefiable by pressure alone. Cf. **vapour** (sense 2). **4a** a fossil fuel in the form of a gas, used as a source of domestic and industrial heat. **4b** (*as modifier*): *a gas cooker; gas fire.* **5** a gaseous anaesthetic, such as nitrous oxide. **6** *Mining.* firedamp or the explosive mixture of firedamp and air. **7** the usual US, Canad., Austral., and NZ word for **petrol,** a shortened form of **gasoline. 8 step on the gas.** *Inf.* **8a** to accelerate a motor vehicle. **8b** to hurry. **9** a toxic, etc., substance in suspension in air used against an enemy, etc. **10** *Inf.* idle talk or boasting. **11** *Sl.* a delightful or successful person or thing: *his latest record is a gas.* **12** *US.* an informal name for **flatus.** ◆ *vb* **gases** *or* **gasses, gassing, gassed. 13** (*tr*) to provide or fill with gas. **14** (*tr*) to subject to gas fumes, esp. so as to asphyxiate or render unconscious. **15** (*intr;* foll. by *to*) *Inf.* to talk in an idle or boastful way (to a person). ORIG C17 (coined by J. B. van Helmont (1577–1644), Flemish chemist): from Gk *khaos* atmosphere

gasbag ('gæsˌbæg) *n Inf.* a person who talks in a voluble way, esp. about unimportant matters.

gas chamber *or* **oven** *n* an airtight room into which poison gas is introduced to kill people or animals.

gas chromatography *n* a technique for analysing a mixture of volatile substances in which the mixture is carried by an inert gas through a column packed with a selective adsorbent or absorbent and a detector records on a moving strip the conductivity of the gas leaving the tube.

Gascon ('gæskən) *n* **1** a native or inhabitant of Gascony. **2** the dialect of French spoken in Gascony. ◆ *adj* **3** of or relating to Gascony, its inhabitants, or their dialect of French.

gasconade (ˌgæskə'neɪd) *Rare.* ◆ *n* **1** boastful talk or bluster. ◆ *vb* **gasconades, gasconading, gasconaded. 2** (*intr*) to boast, brag, or bluster. ORIG C18: from F, from *gasconner* to chatter, boast like a GASCON

gas constant *n* **1** another name for **universal gas constant. 2** the universal gas constant divided by the molar mass of a specified gas.

Gascony ★ ('gæskənɪ) *n* a former province of SW France. French name: **Gascogne** (gaskɔɲ).

gas-cooled reactor *n* a nuclear reactor using a gas as the coolant.

gas-discharge tube *n Electronics.* any tube in which an electric discharge takes place through a gas.

gaseous ('gæsɪəs, -ʃəs, -ʃɪəs, 'geɪ-) *adj* of, concerned with, or having the characteristics of a gas.
▸ **'gaseousness** *n*

gas equation *n* an equation relating the product of the pressure and the volume of an ideal gas to the product of its thermodynamic temperature and the gas constant.

gas gangrene *n* gangrene resulting from infection of a wound by anaerobic bacteria that cause gas bubbles in the surrounding tissues.

gas guzzler *n Sl., chiefly US.* a car that consumes large quantities of petrol.

gash (gæʃ) *vb* **1** (*tr*) to make a long deep cut in; slash. ◆ *n* **2** a long deep cut. ORIG C16: from OF *garser* to scratch, from Vulgar L, from Gk *kharassein*

gasholder ('gæsˌhəʊldə) *n* **1** Also called: **gasometer.** a large tank for storing coal gas or natural gas prior to distribution to users. **2** any vessel for storing or measuring a gas.

gasify ('gæsɪˌfaɪ) *vb* **gasifies, gasifying, gasified.** to make into or become a gas.
▸ **ˌgasifi'cation** *n*

Gaskell ★ ('gæskᵊl) *n* **Mrs.** married name of *Elizabeth Cleghorn Stevenson.* 1810–65, British novelist, whose books include *Mary Barton* (1848) and *Cranford* (1853).

gasket ('gæskɪt) *n* **1** a compressible packing piece of paper, rubber, asbestos, etc., sandwiched between the faces of a metal joint to provide a seal. **2** *Naut.* a piece of line used as a sail stop. ORIG C17 (in the sense: rope lashing a furled sail): prob. from F *garcette* rope's end, lit.: little girl, from OF

gaslight ('gæsˌlaɪt) *n* **1** a type of lamp in which the illumination is produced by an incandescent mantle heated by a jet of gas. **2** the light produced by such a lamp.

gasman ('gæsˌmæn) *n, pl* **gasmen.** a man employed to read household gas meters, supervise gas fittings, etc.

gas mantle *n* a mantle for use in a gaslight. See **mantle** (sense 4).

gas mask *n* a mask fitted with a chemical filter to enable the wearer to breathe air free of poisonous or corrosive gases.

gas meter *n* an apparatus for measuring and recording the amount of gas passed through it.

gasoline *or* **gasolene** ('gæsəˌli:n) *n* a US and Canad. name for **petrol.**

gasometer (gæs'ɒmɪtə) *n* a nontechnical name for **gasholder.**

gasp (gɑ:sp) *vb* **1** (*intr*) to draw in the breath sharply or with effort, esp. in expressing awe, horror, etc. **2** (*intr;* foll. by *after* or *for*) to crave. **3** (*tr;* often foll. by *out*) to utter breathlessly. ◆ *n* **4** a short convulsive intake of breath. **5 at the last gasp. 5a** at the point of death. **5b** at the last moment. ORIG C14: from ON *geispa* to yawn

Gaspar ★ ('gæspə, 'gæspɑ:) *n* a variant of **Caspar.**

Gaspé Peninsula ★ (gæ'speɪ; *French* gaspe) *n* a peninsula in E Canada, in SE Quebec between the St Lawrence

★ people and places

River and New Brunswick: mountainous and wooded with many lakes and rivers. Area: about 29 500 sq. km (11 400 sq. miles). Also called: **the Gaspé**.

gasper ('gɑːspə) *n* **1** a person who gasps. **2** *Brit. dated sl.* a cheap cigarette.

gas plant *n* an aromatic white-flowered Eurasian plant that emits vapour capable of being ignited. Also called: **burning bush, dittany, fraxinella**.

gas ring *n* a circular assembly of gas jets, used esp. for cooking.

Gasser ★ ('gæsə) *n* **Herbert Spencer**. 1888–1963, US physiologist: shared a Nobel prize for physiology or medicine (1944) for work on electrical signs of nervous activity.

gassy ('gæsɪ) *adj* **gassier, gassiest**. **1** filled with, containing, or resembling gas. **2** *Inf.* full of idle or vapid talk.
▸ **'gassiness** *n*

gasteropod ('gæstərəˌpɒd) *n, adj* a variant spelling of **gastropod**.

gas thermometer *n* a device for measuring temperature by observing the pressure of gas at a constant volume or the volume of a gas kept at a constant pressure.

gastric ('gæstrɪk) *adj* of, relating to, near, or involving the stomach.

gastric juice *n* a digestive fluid secreted by the stomach, containing hydrochloric acid, pepsin, rennin, etc.

gastric ulcer *n* an ulcer of the mucous membrane lining the stomach.

gastritis (gæs'traɪtɪs) *n* inflammation of the stomach.

gastro- *or often before a vowel* **gastr-** *combining form*. stomach: *gastroenteritis; gastritis*. ORIG from Gk *gastēr*

gastrocolic (ˌgæstrəʊ'kɒlɪk) *adj* of or relating to the stomach and colon: *gastrocolic reflex*.

gastroenteritis (ˌgæstrəʊˌentə'raɪtɪs) *n* inflammation of the stomach and intestines.

gastrointestinal (ˌgæstrəʊɪn'testɪn°l) *adj* of or relating to the stomach and intestinal tract.

gastronome ('gæstrəˌnəʊm), **gastronomer** (gæs'trɒnəmə), *or* **gastronomist** *n* less common words for **gourmet**.

gastronomy (gæs'trɒnəmɪ) *n* the art of good eating. ORIG C19: from F, from Gk, from *gastēr* stomach; see -NOMY
▸ **gastronomic** (ˌgæstrə'nɒmɪk) *or* **ˌgastro'nomical** *adj*
▸ **ˌgastro'nomically** *adv*

gastropod ('gæstrəˌpɒd) *or* **gasteropod** *n* any of a class of molluscs typically having a flattened muscular foot for locomotion and a head that bears stalked eyes. The class includes the snails, whelks, and slugs.
▸ **gastropodan** (gæs'trɒpəd°n) *adj, n*

gastroscope ('gæstrəˌskəʊp) *n* a medical instrument for examining the interior of the stomach.

gastrula ('gæstrʊlə) *n, pl* **gastrulas** *or* **gastrulae** (-ˌliː). a saclike animal embryo consisting of three layers of cells surrounding a central cavity with a small opening to the exterior. ORIG C19: NL: little stomach, from Gk *gastēr* belly

gas turbine *n* an internal-combustion engine in which the expanding gases emerging from one or more combustion chambers drive a turbine.

gasworks ('gæsˌwɜːks) *n* (*functioning as sing*) a plant in which gas, esp. coal gas, is made.

gat (gæt) *vb Arch.* a past tense of **get**.

gate (geɪt) *n* **1** a movable barrier, usually hinged, for closing an opening in a wall, fence, etc. **2** an opening to allow passage into or out of an enclosed place. **3** any means of entrance or access. **4** a mountain pass or gap, esp. one providing entry into another country or region. **5a** the number of people admitted to a sporting event or entertainment. **5b** the total entrance money received from them. **6** *Electronics.* a logic circuit having one or more input terminals and one output terminal, the output being switched between two voltage levels determined by the combination of input signals. **7** a component in a motion-picture camera or projector that holds each frame flat and momentarily stationary behind the lens. **8** a slotted metal frame that controls the positions of the gear lever in a motor vehicle. ◆ *vb* **gates, gating, gated**. **9** (*tr*) *Brit.* to restrict (a student) to the school or college grounds as a punishment. ORIG OE *geat*

gâteau ('gætəʊ) *n, pl* **gâteaux** (-təʊz). a rich cake usually layered with cream and elaborately decorated. ORIG F: cake

gate-crash *vb Inf.* to gain entry to (a party, concert, etc.) without invitation or payment.
▸ **'gate-ˌcrasher** *n*

gatefold ('geɪtˌfəʊld) *n* an oversize page in a book or magazine that is folded in. Also called: **foldout**.

gatehouse ('geɪtˌhaʊs) *n* **1** a building at or above a gateway, used by a porter or guard, or, formerly, as a fortification. **2** a small house at the entrance to the grounds of a country mansion.

gatekeeper ('geɪtˌkiːpə) *n* **1** a person who has charge of a gate and controls who may pass through it. **2** a manager in a large organization who controls the flow of information, esp. to parent and subsidiary companies. **3** any of several Eurasian butterflies having brown-bordered orange wings.

gate-leg table *or* **gate-legged table** *n* a table with one or two leaves supported by a hinged leg swung out from the frame.

gatepost ('geɪtˌpəʊst) *n* **1a** the post on which a gate is hung. **1b** the post to which a gate is fastened when closed. **2 between you, me, and the gatepost**. confidentially.

Gates ★ (geɪts) *n* **1 Bill**, full name *William Henry Gates*. born 1955, US computer-software executive; founder (1976) of Microsoft Corporation. **2 Horatio**. ?1728–1806, American Revolutionary general: defeated the British at Saratoga (1777).

Gateshead ★ ('geɪtsˌhɛd) *n* **1** a port in NE England, in Tyne and Wear: engineering works. Pop.: 83 159 (1991). **2** a unitary authority in NE England. Pop.: 201 100 (1996 est.). Area: 142 sq. km (55 sq. miles).

gateway ('geɪtˌweɪ) *n* **1** an entrance that may be closed by or as by a gate. **2** a means of entry or access: *Bombay, gateway to India*. **3** *Computing.* hardware and software that connect incompatible computer networks.

Gath ★ (gæθ) *n Old Testament.* one of the five cities of the Philistines, from which Goliath came (I Samuel 17:4) and near which Saul fell in battle (II Samuel 1:20). Douay spelling: **Geth** (gɛθ).

gather ('gæðə) *vb* **1** to assemble or cause to assemble. **2** to collect or be collected gradually; muster. **3** (*tr*) to learn from information given; conclude or assume. **4** (*tr*) to pick or harvest (flowers, fruit, etc.). **5** (*tr*) to bring close (to). **6** to increase or cause to increase gradually, as in force, speed, intensity, etc. **7** to contract (the brow) or (of the brow) to become contracted into wrinkles; knit. **8** (*tr*) to assemble (sections of a book) in the correct sequence for binding. **9** (*tr*) to prepare or make ready: *to gather one's wits*. **10** to draw (material) into a series of small tucks or folds. **11** (*intr*) (of a boil or other sore) to come to a head; form pus. ◆ *n* **12a** the act of gathering. **12b** the amount gathered. **13** a small fold in material, as made by a tightly pulled stitch; tuck. ORIG OE *gadrian*
▸ **'gatherer** *n*

gathering ('gæðərɪŋ) *n* **1** a group of people, things, etc., that are gathered together; assembly. **2** *Sewing.* a series of gathers in material. **3** *Inf.* **3a** the formation of pus in a boil. **3b** the pus so formed. **4** *Printing.* an informal name for **section** (sense 16).

Gatling gun ('gætlɪŋ) *n* a machine gun equipped with a rotating cluster of barrels that are fired in succession. ORIG C19: after R. J. *Gatling* (1818–1903), its US inventor

GATT (gæt) *n acronym for* General Agreement on Tariffs and Trade: a multilateral international treaty signed in 1947 to promote trade; replaced in 1995 by the World Trade Organization.

Gatún Lake ★ (*Spanish* ga'tun) *n* a lake in Panama, part of the Panama Canal: formed in 1912 on the completion of the **Gatún Dam** across the Chagres River. Area: 424 sq. km (164 sq. miles).

gauche (gəʊʃ) *adj* lacking ease of manner; tactless. ORIG

C18: F: awkward, left, from OF *gauchir* to swerve, ult. of Gmc origin
▸ **'gauchely** *adv* ▸ **'gaucheness** *n*

gaucherie (ˌgəʊʃəˈriː, ˈgəʊʃərɪ) *n* **1** the quality of being gauche. **2** a gauche act.

gaucho (ˈgaʊtʃəʊ) *n, pl* **gauchos.** a cowboy of the South American pampas, usually one of mixed Spanish and Indian descent. ORIG C19: from American Sp., prob. from Quechuan *wáhcha* orphan, vagabond

gaud (gɔːd) *n* an article of cheap finery. ORIG C14: prob. from OF *gaudir* to be joyful, from L *gaudēre*

Gaudí ★ (ˈgaʊdɪ; *Spanish* gauˈði) *n* **Antonio** (anˈtonjo). 1852–1926, Spanish architect, an exponent of Art Nouveau in Europe.

Gaudier-Brzeska ★ (*French* godjebʒɛska) *n* **Henri** (ɑ̃ri), original name *Henri Gaudier.* 1891–1915, French vorticist sculptor.

gaudy[1] (ˈgɔːdɪ) *adj* **gaudier, gaudiest.** bright or colourful in a crude or vulgar manner. ORIG C16: from GAUD
▸ **'gaudily** *adv* ▸ **'gaudiness** *n*

gaudy[2] (ˈgɔːdɪ) *n, pl* **gaudies.** *Brit.* a celebratory feast held at some schools and colleges. ORIG C16: from L *gaudium* joy, from *gaudēre* to rejoice

gauge *or* **gage** (geɪdʒ) *vb* **gauges, gauging, gauged** *or* **gages, gaging, gaged.** (*tr*) **1** to measure or determine the amount, quantity, size, condition, etc., of. **2** to estimate or appraise; judge. **3** to check for conformity or bring into conformity with a standard measurement, etc. ◆ *n* **4** a standard measurement, dimension, capacity, or quantity. **5** any of various instruments for measuring a quantity: *a pressure gauge.* **6** any of various devices used to check for conformity with a standard measurement. **7** a standard or means for assessing; test; criterion. **8** scope, capacity, or extent. **9** the diameter of the barrel of a gun, esp. a shotgun. **10** the thickness of sheet metal or the diameter of wire. **11** the distance between the rails of a railway track. **12** the distance between two wheels on the same axle of a vehicle, truck, etc. **13** *Naut.* the position of a vessel in relation to the wind and another vessel. **14** a measure of the fineness of woven or knitted fabric. **15** the width of motion-picture film or magnetic tape. ◆ *adj* **16** (of a pressure measurement) measured on a pressure gauge that registers zero at atmospheric pressure. ORIG C15: from OF, prob. of Gmc origin
▸ **'gaugeable** *or* **'gageable** *adj*

gauge boson *n Physics.* a boson that mediates the interaction between elementary particles. There are four types: photons for electromagnetic interactions, gluons for strong interactions, intermediate vector bosons for weak interactions, and gravitons for gravitational interactions.

gauge theory *n Physics.* a type of theory of elementary particles designed to explain the strong, weak, and electromagnetic interactions in terms of exchange of virtual particles.

Gauguin ★ (*French* gogɛ̃) *n* **Paul** (pɔl). 1848–1903, French postimpressionist painter who worked in the South Pacific from 1891.

Gauhati ★ (gauˈhɑːtɪ) *n* a city in NE India, in Assam on the River Brahmaputra: centre of British administration in Assam (1826–74). Pop.: 584 342 (1991).

Gaul ★ (gɔːl) *n* **1** an ancient region of W Europe corresponding to N Italy, France, Belgium, part of Germany, and the S Netherlands: divided into Cisalpine Gaul, which became a Roman province before 100 B.C., and Transalpine Gaul, which was conquered by Julius Caesar (58–51 B.C.). Latin name: **Gallia.** **2** a native of ancient Gaul. **3** a Frenchman.

Gauleiter (ˈgauˌlaɪtə) *n* **1** a provincial governor in Germany under Hitler. **2** (*sometimes not cap.*) a person in a position of petty authority who behaves in an overbearing manner. ORIG G, from *Gau* district + *Leiter* leader

Gaulish (ˈgɔːlɪʃ) *n* **1** the extinct Celtic language of the pre-Roman Gauls. ◆ *adj* **2** of ancient Gaul, the Gauls, or their language.

Gaulle ★ (gəʊl, gɔːl; *French* gol) *n* **Charles de.** See (Charles) **de Gaulle.**

gaunt (gɔːnt) *adj* **1** bony and emaciated in appearance. **2** (of places) bleak or desolate. ORIG C15: ?from ON
▸ **'gauntly** *adv* ▸ **'gauntness** *n*

gauntlet[1] (ˈgɔːntlɪt) *n* **1** a medieval armoured leather glove. **2** a heavy glove with a long cuff. **3 take up** (*or* **throw down**) **the gauntlet.** to accept (*or* offer) a challenge. ORIG C15: from OF *gantelet,* dim. of *gant* glove, of Gmc origin

gauntlet[2] (ˈgɔːntlɪt) *n* **1** a punishment in which the victim is forced to run between two rows of men who strike at him as he passes: formerly a military punishment. **2 run the gauntlet. 2a** to suffer this punishment. **2b** to endure an onslaught, as of criticism. **3** a testing ordeal. ORIG C15: changed (through infl. of GAUNTLET[1]) from earlier *gantlope,* from Swedish *gatlopp* passageway

gaur (ˈgaʊə) *n* a large wild ox of mountainous regions of S Asia. ORIG C19: from Hindi, from Sansk. *gāūra*

gauss (gaʊs) *n, pl* **gauss.** the cgs unit of magnetic flux density. 1 gauss is equivalent to 10^{-4} tesla. ORIG after K. F. GAUSS

Gauss ★ (*German* gaus) *n* **Karl Friedrich** (karl ˈfriːdrɪç). 1777–1855, German mathematician: developed the theory of numbers and applied mathematics to astronomy, electricity and magnetism, and geodesy.
▸ **Gaussian** (ˈgaʊsɪən) *adj*

Gaussian distribution *n* another name for **normal distribution.**

Gauteng ★ (xauˈtɛŋ) *n* a province of N South Africa; formed in 1994 from part of the former Transvaal. Capital: Johannesburg. Pop.: 7 048 300 (1995 est.). Area: 18 810 sq. km (7262 sq. miles).

Gautier ★ (*French* gotje) *n* **Théophile** (teɔfil). 1811–72, French poet, novelist, and critic.

gauze (gɔːz) *n* **1** a transparent cloth of loose weave. **2** a surgical dressing of muslin or similar material. **3** any thin openwork material, such as wire. **4** a fine mist or haze. ORIG C16: from F *gaze,* ?from GAZA, where it was believed to originate

gauzy (ˈgɔːzɪ) *adj* **gauzier, gauziest.** resembling gauze; thin and transparent.
▸ **'gauzily** *adv* ▸ **'gauziness** *n*

Gavaskar ★ (gæˈvæskɑː) *n* **Sunil Manohar** (ˈsʊnɪl ˈmænəʊhɑː). born 1949, Indian cricketer. He captained India 1978–83 and 1984–85.

gave (geɪv) *vb* the past tense of **give.**

gavel (ˈgævᵊl) *n* a small hammer used by a chairman, auctioneer, etc., to call for order or attention. ORIG C19: from ?

gavial (ˈgeɪvɪəl), **gharial,** *or* **garial** (ˈgærɪəl) *n* a large fish-eating Indian crocodile with a very long slender snout. ORIG C19: from F, from Hindi

Gävle ★ (*Swedish* ˈjɛːvlə) *n* a port in E Sweden, on an inlet of the Gulf of Bothnia. Pop.: 90 270 (1994).

gavotte *or* **gavot** (gəˈvɒt) *n* **1** an old formal dance in quadruple time. **2** a piece of music composed for or in the rhythm of this dance. ORIG C17: from F, from Provençal, from *gavot* mountaineer, dweller in the Alps (where the dance originated)

gawk (gɔːk) *n* **1** a clumsy stupid person; lout. ◆ *vb* **2** (*intr*) to stare in a stupid way; gape. ORIG C18: from ODanish *gaukr;* prob. rel. to GAPE

gawky (ˈgɔːkɪ) *adj* **gawkier, gawkiest.** clumsy or ungainly; awkward. Also: **gawkish.**
▸ **'gawkily** *adv* ▸ **'gawkiness** *n*

gawp *or* **gaup** (gɔːp) *vb* (*intr;* often foll. by *at*) *Brit. sl.* to stare stupidly; gape. ORIG C14 *galpen;* prob. rel. to OE *gielpan* to boast, YELP
▸ **'gawper** *n*

gay (geɪ) *adj* **1a** homosexual. **1b** of or for homosexuals: *a gay club.* **2** carefree and merry: *a gay temperament.* **3** brightly coloured; brilliant: *a gay hat.* **4** given to pleasure, esp. in social entertainment: *a gay life.* ◆ *n* **5** a homosexual. ORIG C13: from OF *gai,* from OProvençal, of Gmc origin
▸ **'gayness** *n*

★ people and places

> **USAGE NOTE** *Gayness* is used in the great majority of cases to refer to the state of being homosexual. The noun which refers to the state of being carefree and merry is *gaiety*.

Gay ★ (geɪ) *n* **John.** 1685–1732, English poet and dramatist; author of *The Beggar's Opera* (1728).

Gaya ★ ('gɑːjə, 'gaɪə) *n* a city in NE India, in central Bihar: Hindu place of pilgrimage and one of the holiest sites of Buddhism. Pop.: 291 675 (1991).

Gaye ★ (geɪ) *n* **Marvin.** 1939–84, US singer and songwriter known for the song "I Heard It Through the Grapevine" and a number of albums, including *Midnight Love* (1982): shot and killed by his father.

Gay-Lussac ★ ('geɪ'luːsæk; *French* gelysak) *n* **Joseph Louis** (ʒozɛf lwi). 1778–1850, French physicist and chemist: discovered the law of combining gases named after him (1808).

Gaza ★ ('gɑːzə) *n* a city in the Gaza Strip: a Philistine city in biblical times. It was under Egyptian administration from 1949 until occupied by Israel (1967). Pop.: 293 000 (1990 est.). Arabic name: **Ghazzah.**

gazania (gæ'zeɪnɪə) *n* any of a genus of S. African plants of the composite family having large showy flowers. ORIG ? after Theodore of *Gaza* (1398–1478), who translated the botanical works of Theophrastus into Latin

Gazankulu ★ (ˌgazaŋ'kuːluː) *n* (formerly) a Bantu homeland in South Africa, consisting of four exclaves in Transvaal; reintegrated into South Africa in 1994. Capital: Giyani.

Gaza Strip ★ *n* a coastal region on the SE corner of the Mediterranean, formerly part of Palestine: administered by Egypt (1949–56, 1957–67); occupied by Israel since 1967; granted autonomy in 1993 and administered by the Palestinian National Authority from 1994. Pop.: 748 400 (1993).

gaze (geɪz) *vb* **gazes, gazing, gazed. 1** (*intr*) to look long and fixedly, esp. in wonder. ◆ *n* **2** a fixed look. ORIG C14: from Swedish dialect *gasa* to gape at
▸ **'gazer** *n*

gazebo (gə'ziːbəʊ) *n, pl* **gazebos** *or* **gazeboes.** a summer-house, garden pavilion, or belvedere, sited to command a view. ORIG C18: ? a pseudo-Latin coinage based on GAZE

gazelle (gə'zɛl) *n, pl* **gazelles** *or* **gazelle.** any small graceful usually fawn-coloured antelope of Africa and Asia. ORIG C17: from OF, from Ar. *ghazāl*

gazette (gə'zɛt) *n* **1** a newspaper or official journal. **2** *Brit.* an official document containing public notices, appointments, etc. ◆ *vb* **gazettes, gazetting, gazetted. 3** (*tr*) *Brit.* to announce or report (facts or an event) in a gazette. ORIG C17: from F, from It., from Venetian dialect *gazeta* news-sheet costing one *gazet*, small copper coin

gazetteer (ˌgæzɪ'tɪə) *n* **1** a book or section of a book that lists and describes places. **2** *Arch.* a writer for a gazette.

Gaziantep ★ (ˌgɑːziːɑːn'tɛp) *n* a city in S Turkey: base for Ibrahim Pasha's campaign against the Turks (1839) and centre of Turkish resistance to French forces (1921). Pop.: 730 435 (1995 est.). Former name (until 1921): **Aintab.**

gazpacho (gəz'pɑːtʃəʊ, gæs-) *n* a Spanish soup made from tomatoes, peppers, etc., and served cold. ORIG from Sp.

gazump (gə'zʌmp) *Brit.* ◆ *vb* **1** to raise the price of something, esp. a house, after agreeing a price verbally with (an intending buyer). **2** (*tr*) to swindle or overcharge. ◆ *n* **3** an instance of gazumping. ORIG C20: from ?
▸ **ga'zumper** *n*

gazunder (gə'zʌndə) *Brit.* ◆ *vb* **1** to reduce an offer on a property immediately before exchanging contracts, having previously agreed to a higher price with (the seller). ◆ *n* **2** an act or instance of gazundering. ORIG C20: modelled on GAZUMP
▸ **ga'zunderer** *n*

GB *abbrev. for* Great Britain.

GBE *abbrev. for* (Knight or Dame) Grand Cross of the British Empire (a Brit. title).

GBH *abbrev. for* grievous bodily harm.

GC *abbrev. for* George Cross (a Brit. award for bravery).

GCB *abbrev. for* (Knight) Grand Cross of the Bath (a Brit. title).

gcd *or* **GCD** *abbrev. for* greatest common divisor.

GCE (in Britain) *abbrev. for* General Certificate of Education: a public examination in specified subjects taken as qualifying examinations for entry into a university, college, etc. The GCSE has replaced it at O level. See also **A level, S level.**

GCHQ (in Britain) *abbrev. for* Government Communications Headquarters.

G clef *n* another name for **treble clef.**

GCMG *abbrev. for* (Knight or Dame) Grand Cross of the Order of St Michael and St George (a Brit. title).

GCSE (in Britain) *abbrev. for* General Certificate of Secondary Education: a public examination in specified subjects for 16-year-old schoolchildren. It replaced GCE O level and CSE.

GCVO *abbrev. for* (Knight or Dame) Grand Cross of the Royal Victorian Order (a Brit. title).

Gd *the chemical symbol for* gadolinium.

Gdańsk ★ (*Polish* gdajinsk) *n* **1** the chief port of Poland, on the Baltic: a member of the Hanseatic league; under Prussian rule (1793–1807 and 1814–1919); a free city under the League of Nations from 1919 until annexed by Germany in 1939; returned to Poland in 1945. Pop.: 462 800 (1996 est.). German name: **Danzig. 2 Bay of.** a wide inlet of the Baltic Sea on the N coast of Poland.

g'day *or* **gidday** (gə'daɪ) *sentence substitute.* an Australian and NZ informal variant of **good day.**

Gdns *abbrev. for* Gardens.

GDR *abbrev. for* German Democratic Republic (East Germany; DDR).

Gdynia ★ (*Polish* 'gdɪnja) *n* a port in N Poland, near Gdańsk: developed 1924–39 as the outlet for trade through the Polish Corridor; naval base. Pop.: 251 400 (1996 est.).

Ge[1] ★ (dʒiː) *n* another name for **Gaea.**

Ge[2] *the chemical symbol for* germanium.

gean (giːn) *n* a white-flowered tree of the rose family of Europe, W Asia, and N Africa; the ancestor of the cultivated sweet cherries.

gear (gɪə) *n* **1** a toothed wheel that engages with another toothed wheel or with a rack in order to change the speed or direction of transmitted motion. **2** a mechanism for transmitting motion by gears. **3** the engagement or specific ratio of a system of gears: *in gear; high gear.* **4** personal belongings. **5** equipment and supplies for a particular operation, sport, etc. **6** *Naut.* all equipment or appurtenances belonging to a certain vessel, sailor, etc. **7** short for **landing gear. 8** *Inf.* up-to-date clothes and accessories. **9** *Sl.* drugs of any type. **10** a less common word for **harness** (sense 1). **11 out of gear.** out of order; not functioning properly. ◆ *vb* **12** (*tr*) to adjust or adapt (one thing) so as to fit in or work with another: *to gear our output to current demand.* **13** (*tr*) to equip with or connect by gears. **14** (*intr*) to be in or come into gear. **15** (*tr*) to equip with a harness. ORIG C13: from ON *gervi*

gearbox ('gɪəˌbɒks) *n* **1** the metal casing within which a train of gears is sealed. **2** this metal casing and its contents, esp. in a motor vehicle.

gearing ('gɪərɪŋ) *n* **1** an assembly of gears designed to transmit motion. **2** the act or technique of providing gears to transmit motion. **3** Also called: **capital gearing.** *Accounting, Brit.* the ratio of a company's debt capital to its equity capital. US word: **leverage.**

gear lever *or US & Canad.* **gearshift** ('gɪəˌʃɪft) *n* a lever used to move gearwheels relative to each other, esp. in a motor vehicle.

gear train *n Engineering.* a system of gears that transmits power from one shaft to another.

gearwheel ('gɪəˌwiːl) *n* another name for **gear** (sense 1).

Geber ★ (ˈdʒiːbə) *n* Latinized form of Jabir, assumed in honour of Jabir ibn Hayyan by a 14th-century alchemist, probably Spanish: he described the preparation of nitric and sulphuric acids.

gecko (ˈgɛkəʊ) *n, pl* **geckos** *or* **geckoes.** a small insectivorous terrestrial lizard of warm regions. ORIG C18: from Malay *ge'kok,* imit.

gee[1] (dʒiː) *interj* **1** Also: **gee up!** an exclamation, as to a horse or draught animal, to encourage it to turn to the right, go on, or go faster. ◆ *vb* **gees, geeing, geed. 2** (usually foll. by *up*) to move (an animal, esp. a horse) ahead; urge on. **3** (foll. by *up*) to encourage (someone) to greater effort or activity. ORIG C17: from ?

gee[2] (dʒiː) *interj US & Canad. inf.* a mild exclamation of surprise, admiration, etc. Also: **gee whizz.** ORIG C20: euphemism for JESUS

Gee ★ (dʒiː) *n* **Maurice.** born 1931, New Zealand novelist.

geebung (ˈdʒiːbʌŋ) *n* **1** any of several Australian trees or shrubs with edible but tasteless fruit. **2** the fruit of these trees. ORIG from Abor.

geek (giːk) *n Sl.* **1** a boring or unattractive social misfit. **2** a person who is preoccupied with or very knowledgeable about computing. **3** a degenerate. ORIG C19: prob. from Scot. *geck* fool
▸ ˈ**geeky** *adj*

geelbek (ˈxiːlˌbɛk) *n S. African.* an edible marine fish with yellow jaws. Also called: **Cape salmon.** ORIG from Afrik. *geel* yellow + *bek* mouth

Geelong ★ (dʒəˈlɒŋ) *n* a port in SE Australia, in S Victoria on Port Phillip Bay. Pop.: 152 600 (1995 est.).

geese (giːs) *n* the plural of **goose**[1].

geezer (ˈgiːzə) *n Inf.* a man. ORIG C19: prob. from dialect pronunciation of GUISER

Gehenna ★ (gɪˈhɛnə) *n* **1** *Old Testament.* the valley below Jerusalem, where children were sacrificed and, later, unclean things were burnt. **2** *New Testament, Judaism.* a place where the wicked are punished after death. **3** a place or state of pain and torment. ORIG C16: from LL, from Gk, from Heb. *Gê' Hinnōm,* lit.: valley of Hinnom, symbolic of hell

Geiger counter *or* **Geiger-Müller counter** (ˈgaɪgə ˈmʊlə) *n* an instrument for detecting and measuring the intensity of ionizing radiation. ORIG C20: after Hans *Geiger* and W. *Müller* (20th-cent.), G physicists

geisha (ˈgeɪʃə) *n, pl* **geisha** *or* **geishas.** a professional female companion for men in Japan, trained in music, dancing, and the art of conversation. ORIG C19: from Japanese, from Ancient Chinese

Geissler tube (ˈgaɪslə) *n* a glass or quartz vessel for maintaining an electric discharge in a low-pressure gas as a source of visible or ultraviolet light for spectroscopy, etc. ORIG C19: after Heinrich *Geissler* (1814–79), G mechanic

gel (dʒɛl) *n* **1** a semirigid jelly-like colloid in which a liquid is dispersed in a solid: *nondrip paint is a gel.* **2** a jelly-like substance applied to the hair before styling in order to retain the style. ◆ *vb* **gels, gelling, gelled. 3** to become or cause to become a gel. **4** a variant spelling of **jell.** ORIG C19: from GELATINE

gelatine (ˈdʒɛləˌtiːn) *or* **gelatin** (ˈdʒɛlətɪn) *n* **1** a colourless or yellowish water-soluble protein prepared by boiling animal hides and bones: used in foods, glue, photographic emulsions, etc. **2** an edible jelly made of this substance. ORIG C19: from F *gélatine,* from Med. L, from L *gelāre* to freeze

gelatinize *or* **gelatinise** (dʒɪˈlætɪˌnaɪz) *vb* **gelatinizes, gelatinizing, gelatinized** *or* **gelatinises, gelatinising, gelatinised. 1** to make or become gelatinous. **2** (*tr*) *Photog.* to coat (glass, paper, etc.) with gelatine.
▸ **geˌlatiniˈzation** *or* ▸ **geˌlatiniˈsation** *n*

gelatinous (dʒɪˈlætɪnəs) *adj* **1** consisting of or resembling jelly; viscous. **2** of, containing, or resembling gelatine.
▸ **geˈlatinously** *adv* ▸ **geˈlatinousness** *n*

gelation[1] (dʒɪˈleɪʃən) *n* the act or process of freezing a liquid. ORIG C19: from L *gelātiō* a freezing; see GELATINE

gelation[2] (dʒɪˈleɪʃən) *n* the act or process of forming into a gel. ORIG C20: from GEL

geld (gɛld) *vb* **gelds, gelding, gelded** *or* **gelt** (gɛlt). (*tr*) **1** to castrate (a horse or other animal). **2** to deprive of virility or vitality; emasculate; weaken. ORIG C13: from ON, from *geldr* barren

Gelderland *or* **Guelderland** ★ (ˈgɛldəˌlænd; *Dutch* ˈxɛldərlɑnt) *n* a province of the E Netherlands: formerly a duchy, belonging successively to several different European powers. Capital: Arnhem. Pop.: 1 886 100 (1997 est.). Area: 5014 sq. km (1955 sq. miles). Also called: **Guelders.**

gelding (ˈgɛldɪŋ) *n* a castrated male horse. ORIG C14: from ON *geldingr;* see GELD, -ING[1]

Geldof ★ (ˈgɛldɒf) *n* **Bob,** full name *Robert Frederick Zenon Geldof.* born 1954, Irish rock singer: lead vocalist with the Boomtown Rats (1977–86): organizer of the Band Aid charity for famine relief in Africa. He received an honorary knighthood in 1986.

Gelée ★ (*French* ʒəle) *n* **Claude** (klod). the original name of **Claude Lorrain.**

Gelibolu ★ (gɛˈlibəlu) *n* the Turkish name for **Gallipoli.**

gelid (ˈdʒɛlɪd) *adj* very cold, icy, or frosty. ORIG C17: from L *gelidus,* from *gelu* frost
▸ **geˈlidity** *n*

gelignite (ˈdʒɛlɪgˌnaɪt) *n* a type of dynamite in which the nitrogelatine is absorbed in a base of wood pulp and potassium or sodium nitrate. Also called (informal): **gelly.** ORIG C19: from GEL(ATINE) + L *ignis* fire + -ITE[1]

Gelligaer ★ (*Welsh* ˌgɛhliːˈgaɪr) *n* a town in S Wales, in Caerphilly county borough. Pop.: 15 906 (1991).

Gell-Mann ★ (ˌgɛlˈmæn) *n* **Murray.** born 1929, US physicist, noted for his research on elementary particles: Nobel prize for physics in 1969.

Gelsenkirchen ★ (*German* gɛlzənˈkɪrçən) *n* an industrial city in W Germany, in North Rhine-Westphalia. Pop.: 291 164 (1996 est.).

gem (dʒɛm) *n* **1** a precious or semiprecious stone used in jewellery as a decoration; jewel. **2** a person or thing held to be a perfect example; treasure. ◆ *vb* **gems, gemming, gemmed. 3** (*tr*) to set or ornament with gems. ORIG C14: from OF, from L *gemma* bud, precious stone
▸ ˈ**gemˌlike** *adj* ▸ ˈ**gemmy** *adj*

Gemara (gɛˈmɑːrə; *Hebrew* gɛmaˈra) *n Judaism.* the later main part of the Talmud, being a commentary on the Mishnah: the primary source of Jewish religious law. ORIG C17: from Aramaic *gemārā* completion

geminate *adj* (ˈdʒɛmɪnɪt, -ˌneɪt) *also* **geminated. 1** combined in pairs; doubled: *a geminate leaf.* ◆ *vb* (ˈdʒɛmɪˌneɪt), **geminates, geminating, geminated. 2** to arrange or be arranged in pairs: *the "t"s in "fitted" are geminated.* ORIG C17: from L *gemināre* to double, from *geminus* twin
▸ ˈ**geminately** *adv* ▸ ˌ**gemiˈnation** *n*

Gemini (ˈdʒɛmɪˌnaɪ, -ˌniː) *n* **1** *Astron.* a zodiacal constellation in the N hemisphere containing the stars Castor and Pollux. **2** *Classical myth.* another name for **Castor and Pollux. 3** *Astrol.* Also called: the **Twins.** the third sign of the zodiac. The sun is in this sign between about May 21 and June 20.

gemma (ˈdʒɛmə) *n, pl* **gemmae** (-miː). **1** a small asexual reproductive structure in mosses, etc., that becomes detached from the parent and develops into a new individual. **2** *Zool.* another name for **gemmule.** ORIG C18: from L: bud, GEM

gemmate (ˈdʒɛmeɪt) *adj* **1** (of some plants and animals) having or reproducing by gemmae. ◆ *vb* **gemmates, gemmating, gemmated. 2** (*intr*) to produce or reproduce by gemmae.
▸ **gemˈmation** *n*

gemmiparous (dʒɛˈmɪpərəs) *adj* (of plants and animals) reproducing by gemmae or buds. Also: **gemmiferous.**

gemmule (ˈdʒɛmjuːl) *n* **1** *Zool.* a cell or mass of cells produced asexually by sponges and developing into a new individual; bud. **2** *Bot.* a small gemma. ORIG C19: from F, from L *gemmula* a little bud; see GEM

gemology *or* **gemmology** (dʒɛˈmɒlədʒɪ) *n* the branch of mineralogy concerned with gems and gemstones. ▸ **gemological** *or* **gemmological** (ˌdʒɛməˈlɒdʒɪkᵊl) *adj* ▸ **gemˈologist** *or* **gemˈmologist** *n*

gemsbok *or* **gemsbuck** (ˈgɛmzˌbʌk) *n, pl* **gemsbok, gemsboks** *or* **gemsbuck, gemsbucks.** an oryx of southern Africa, marked with a broad black band along its flanks. ORIG C18: from Afrik., from G *Gemsbock,* from *Gemse* chamois + *Bock* BUCK[1]

gemstone (ˈdʒɛmˌstəʊn) *n* a precious or semiprecious stone, esp. one cut and polished.

gen (dʒɛn) *n Brit., Austral., & NZ inf.* information: *give me the gen on your latest project.* See also **gen up.** ORIG C20: from *gen(eral information)*

gen. *abbrev. for:* **1** gender. **2** general(ly). **3** generic. **4** genitive. **5** genus.

Gen. *abbrev. for:* **1** General. **2** *Bible.* Genesis.

-gen *suffix forming nouns.* **1** producing or that which produces: *hydrogen.* **2** something produced: *carcinogen.* ORIG via F *-gène,* from Gk *-genēs* born

Genck ★ (*Flemish* xɛŋk) *n* a variant spelling of **Genk.**

gendarme (ˈʒɒndɑːm) *n* **1** a member of the police force in France or in countries influenced or controlled by France. **2** a sharp pinnacle of rock on a mountain ridge. ORIG C16: from F, from *gens d'armes* people of arms

gendarmerie *or* **gendarmery** (ʒɒnˈdɑːmərɪ) *n* **1** the whole corps of gendarmes. **2** the headquarters of a body of gendarmes.

gender (ˈdʒɛndə) *n* **1** a set of two or more grammatical categories into which the nouns of certain languages are divided. **2** any of the categories, such as masculine, feminine, neuter, or common, within such a set. **3** *Inf.* the state of being male, female, or neuter. **4** *Inf.* all the members of one sex: *the female gender.* ORIG C14: from OF, from L *genus* kind

gender-bender *n Inf.* a person who adopts an androgynous style of dress, hair, etc.

gene (dʒiːn) *n* a unit of heredity composed of DNA occupying a fixed position on a chromosome and transmitted from parent to offspring during reproduction. ORIG C20: from G *Gen,* shortened from *Pangen;* see PAN-, -GEN

-gene *suffix forming nouns.* a variant of **-gen.**

genealogy (ˌdʒiːnɪˈælədʒɪ) *n, pl* **genealogies. 1** the direct descent of an individual or group from an ancestor. **2** the study of the evolutionary development of animals and plants from earlier forms. **3** a chart showing the relationships and descent of an individual, group, etc. ORIG C13: from OF, from LL, from Gk, from *genea* race ▸ **genealogical** (ˌdʒiːnɪəˈlɒdʒɪkᵊl) *adj* ▸ **ˌgeneaˈlogically** *adv* ▸ **ˌgeneˈalogist** *n*

gene bank *n Bot.* a collection of seeds, plants, tissue cultures, etc., of potentially useful species, esp. species containing genes of significance to the breeding of crops.

gene clone *n* See **clone** (sense 2).

genecology (ˌdʒɛnɪˈkɒlədʒɪ) *n* the study of the gene frequency of a species in relation to its population distribution within a particular environment.

gene library *n* a collection of gene clones that represents the genetic material of an organism: used in genetic engineering.

gene pool *n* the total of all the genes and their alleles in a population of a plant or animal species.

genera (ˈdʒɛnərə) *n* a plural of **genus.**

general (ˈdʒɛnərəl, ˈdʒɛnrəl) *adj* **1** common; widespread. **2** of, applying to, or participated in by all or most of the members of a group, category, or community. **3** relating to various branches of an activity, profession, etc.; not specialized: *general office work.* **4** including various or miscellaneous items: *general knowledge; a general store.* **5** not specific as to detail; overall: *a general description.* **6** not definite; vague: *the general idea.* **7** applicable or true in most cases; usual. **8** (*prenominal or immediately postpositive*) having superior or extended authority or rank: *general manager; consul general.* ◆ *n* **9** an officer of a rank senior to lieutenant general, esp. one who commands a large military formation. **10** any person acting as a leader and applying strategy or tactics. **11** a general condition or principle: opposed to *particular.* **12** a title for the head of a religious order, congregation, etc. **13** *Arch.* the people; public. **14 in general.** generally; mostly or usually. ORIG C13: from L *generālis* of a particular kind, from *genus* kind

general anaesthetic *n* See **anaesthesia.**

General Assembly *n* **1** the deliberative assembly of the United Nations. Abbrev.: **GA. 2** the supreme governing body of certain religious denominations, esp. of the Presbyterian Church.

general average *n Insurance.* loss or damage to a ship or its cargo that is shared among the shipowners and all the cargo owners. Abbrev.: **GA.** Cf. **particular average.**

General Certificate of Education *n* See **GCE.**

General Certificate of Secondary Education *n* See **GCSE.**

general election *n* **1** an election in which representatives are chosen in all constituencies of a state. **2** *US.* a final election from which successful candidates are sent to a legislative body. **3** *US & Canad.* a national, state, or provincial election.

generalissimo (ˌdʒɛnərəˈlɪsɪˌməʊ, ˌdʒɛnrə-) *n, pl* **generalissimos.** a supreme commander of combined military, naval, and air forces. ORIG C17: from It., sup. of *generale* GENERAL

generality (ˌdʒɛnəˈrælɪtɪ) *n, pl* **generalities. 1** a principle or observation having general application. **2** the state or quality of being general. **3** *Arch.* the majority.

generalization *or* **generalisation** (ˌdʒɛnrəlaɪˈzeɪʃən) *n* **1** a principle, theory, etc., with general application. **2** the act or an instance of generalizing. **3** *Logic.* the derivation of a general statement from a particular one, formally by prefixing a quantifier and replacing a subject term by a bound variable. If the quantifier is universal (**universal generalization**) the argument is not in general valid; if it is existential (**existential generalization**) it is valid.

generalize *or* **generalise** (ˈdʒɛnrəˌlaɪz) *vb* **generalizes, generalizing, generalized** *or* **generalises, generalising, generalised. 1** to form (general principles or conclusions) from (detailed facts, experience, etc.); infer. **2** (*intr*) to think or speak in generalities, esp. in a prejudiced way. **3** (*tr; usually passive*) to cause to become widely used or known.

generally (ˈdʒɛnrəlɪ) *adv* **1** usually; as a rule. **2** commonly or widely. **3** without reference to specific details or facts; broadly.

general practitioner *n* a physician who does not specialize but has a medical practice (**general practice**) in which he treats all illnesses. Informal name: **family doctor.** Abbrev.: **GP.**

general-purpose *adj* having a range of uses; not restricted to one function.

generalship (ˈdʒɛnrəlˌʃɪp) *n* **1** the art or duties of exercising command of a major military formation or formations. **2** tactical or administrative skill.

general staff *n* officers assigned to advise commanders in the planning and execution of military operations.

general strike *n* a strike by all or most of the workers of a country, province, city, etc.

General Synod *n* the governing body, under Parliament, of the Church of England, made up of the bishops and elected clerical and lay representatives.

generate (ˈdʒɛnəˌreɪt) *vb* **generates, generating, generated.** (*mainly tr*) **1** to produce or bring into being; create. **2** (*also intr*) to produce (electricity). **3** to produce (a substance) by a chemical process. **4** *Maths, linguistics.* to provide a precise criterion for membership in (a set). **5** *Geom.* to trace or form by moving a point, line, or plane in a specific way: *circular motion of a line generates a cylinder.* ORIG C16: from L *generāre* to beget, from *genus* kind ▸ **ˈgenerable** *adj*

generation (ˌdʒɛnəˈreɪʃən) *n* **1** the act or process of bringing into being; production or reproduction, esp. of offspring. **2** a successive stage in natural descent of people or animals or the individuals produced at each stage. **3** the average time between two such generations of a species: about 35 years for humans. **4** all the people of approximately the same age, esp. when considered as sharing certain attitudes, etc. **5** production of electricity, heat, etc. **6** (*modifier, in combination*) **6a** belonging to a generation specified as having been born in or as having parents, grandparents, etc., born in a given country: *a third-generation American.* **6b** belonging to a specified stage of development in manufacture: *a second-generation computer.*

generation gap *n* the years separating one generation from the next, esp. when regarded as representing the difference in outlook and the lack of understanding between them.

Generation X *n* members of the generation of people born between the mid-1960s and the mid-1970s who are highly educated and underemployed, reject consumer culture, and have little hope for the future. ORIG C20: from the novel *Generation X: Tales for an Accelerated Culture* by Douglas Coupland

generative ('dʒɛnərətɪv) *adj* **1** of or relating to the production of offspring, parts, etc. **2** capable of producing or originating.

generative grammar *n* a description of a language in terms of explicit rules that ideally generate all and only the grammatical sentences of the language.

generator ('dʒɛnəˌreɪtə) *n* **1** *Physics.* **1a** any device for converting mechanical energy into electrical energy. **1b** a device for producing a voltage electrostatically. **2** an apparatus for producing a gas. **3** a person or thing that generates.

generatrix ('dʒɛnəˌreɪtrɪks) *n, pl* **generatrices** ('dʒɛnəˌreɪtrɪˌsiːz). a point, line, or plane moved in a specific way to produce a geometric figure.

generic (dʒɪ'nɛrɪk) *adj* **1** applicable or referring to a whole class or group; general. **2** *Biol.* of, relating to, or belonging to a genus: *the generic name.* **3** (of a drug, food product, etc.) not having a trademark. ORIG C17: from F; see GENUS
▸ **ge'nerically** *adv*

generic advertising *n* advertising designed to promote a class of product rather than a particular brand.

generosity (ˌdʒɛnə'rɒsɪtɪ) *n, pl* **generosities. 1** willingness and liberality in giving away one's money, time, etc.; magnanimity. **2** freedom from pettiness in character and mind. **3** a generous act. **4** abundance; plenty.

generous ('dʒɛnərəs, 'dʒɛnrəs) *adj* **1** willing and liberal in giving away one's money, time, etc.; munificent. **2** free from pettiness in character and mind. **3** full or plentiful: *a generous portion.* **4** (of wine) rich in alcohol. ORIG C16: via OF from L *generōsus* nobly born, from *genus* race
▸ **'generously** *adv* ▸ **'generousness** *n*

genesis ('dʒɛnɪsɪs) *n, pl* **geneses** (-ˌsiːz). a beginning or origin of anything. ORIG OE: via L from Gk; rel. to Gk *gignesthai* to be born

Genesis ('dʒɛnɪsɪs) *n* the first book of the Old Testament recounting the Creation of the world.

-genesis *n combining form.* indicating genesis, development, or generation: *parthenogenesis.* ORIG NL, from L: GENESIS
▸ **-genetic** *or* **-genic** *adj combining form.*

genet[1] ('dʒɛnɪt) *or* **genette** (dʒɪ'nɛt) *n* **1** an agile catlike mammal of Africa and S Europe, having thick spotted fur and a very long tail. **2** the fur of such an animal. ORIG C15: from OF, from Ar. *jarnayt*

genet[2] ('dʒɛnɪt) *n* an obsolete spelling of **jennet.**

Genet ★ (*French* ʒənɛ) *n* **Jean** (ʒɑ̃). 1910–86, French writer; his novels include *Notre-Dame des Fleurs* (1944) and his plays *Le Balcon* (1956).

gene therapy *n* the replacement or alteration of defective genes in order to prevent the occurrence of such inherited diseases as haemophilia. Effected by genetic engineering techniques, it is still at an early stage of development.

genetic (dʒɪ'nɛtɪk) *or* **genetical** *adj* of or relating to genetics, genes, or the origin of something. ORIG C19: from GENESIS
▸ **ge'netically** *adv*

genetically modified *adj* denoting or derived from an organism whose DNA has been altered for the purpose of improvement or correction of defects: *genetically modified food.* Abbrev.: **GM.**
▸ **genetic modification** *n*

genetic code *n Biochem.* the order in which the four nitrogenous bases of DNA are arranged in the molecule, which determines the type and amount of protein synthesized in the cell.

genetic counselling *n* the provision of advice for couples with a history of inherited disorders who wish to have children, including the likelihood of having affected children, the course and management of the disorder, etc.

genetic engineering *n* alteration of the DNA of a cell as a means of manufacturing animal proteins, making improvements to plants and animals bred by man, etc.

genetic fingerprint *n* the pattern of DNA unique to each individual, that can be analysed in a sample of blood, saliva, or tissue: used as a means of identification.
▸ **genetic fingerprinting** *n*

genetic map *n* a graphic representation of the order of genes within chromosomes by means of detailed analysis of the DNA. See also **chromosome map.**
▸ **genetic mapping** *n*

genetics (dʒɪ'nɛtɪks) *n* **1** (*functioning as sing*) the study of heredity and variation in organisms. **2** (*functioning as pl*) the genetic features and constitution of a single organism, species, or group.
▸ **ge'neticist** *n*

Geneva ★ (dʒɪ'niːvə) *n* **1** a city in SW Switzerland, in the Rhône valley on Lake Geneva: centre of Calvinism; headquarters of the International Red Cross (1864), the International Labour Office (1925), the League of Nations (1929–46), the World Health Organization, and the European office of the United Nations; banking centre. Pop.: 173 549 (1996 est.). **2** a canton in SW Switzerland. Capital: Geneva. Pop.: 380 000 (1988 est.). Area: 282 sq. km (109 sq. miles). ◆ French name: **Genève;** German name: **Genf. 3 Lake.** a lake between SW Switzerland and E France: fed and drained by the River Rhône, it is the largest of the Alpine lakes; the surface is subject to changes of level. Area: 580 sq. km (224 sq. miles). French name: **Lac Léman.** German name: **Genfersee.**

Geneva bands *pl n* a pair of white lawn or linen strips hanging from the front of the neck or collar of some ecclesiastical and academic robes. ORIG C19: after GENEVA, where orig. worn by Swiss Calvinist clergy

Geneva Convention *n* the international agreement, first formulated in 1864 at Geneva, establishing a code for wartime treatment of the sick or wounded: revised and extended to cover maritime warfare and prisoners of war.

Geneva gown *n* a black gown with wide sleeves worn by Protestant clerics. ORIG C19: after GENEVA; see GENEVA BANDS

Genevan (dʒɪ'niːvᵊn) *or* **Genevese** (ˌdʒɛnə'viːz) *adj* **1** of, relating to, or characteristic of Geneva. **2** of, adhering to, or relating to the teachings of Calvin or the Calvinists. ◆ *n, pl* **Genevans** *or* **Genevese. 3** a native or inhabitant of Geneva. **4** a less common name for a **Calvinist.**

Geneva protocol *n* the agreement in 1925 to ban the use of asphyxiating, poisonous, or other gases in war. It does not ban the development or manufacture of such gases.

Genève ★ (*French* ʒənɛv) *n* the French name for **Geneva** (senses 1, 2).

Geneviève ★ ('dʒɛnɪˌviːv; *French* ʒənvjɛv) *n* **Saint.** ?422–?512 A.D., French nun; patron saint of Paris. Feast day: Jan. 3.

Genf ★ (gɛnf) *n* the German name for **Geneva** (senses 1, 2).

Genfersee ★ ('gɛnfərzeː) *n* the German name for (Lake) **Geneva.**

Genghis Khan ★ ('dʒɛŋgɪs kɑːn) *n* original name *Temuchin* or *Temujin.* ?1162–1227, Mongol ruler, whose empire stretched from the Black Sea to the Pacific. Also called: **Jinghis Khan, Jenghis Khan.**

genial[1] ('dʒiːnjəl, -nɪəl) *adj* **1** cheerful, easy-going, and warm in manner. **2** pleasantly warm, so as to give life,

growth, or health. ORIG C16: from L *geniālis* relating to birth or marriage, from *genius* tutelary deity; see GENIUS
▸ **geniality** (ˌdʒiːnɪˈælɪtɪ) *n* ▸ **ˈgenially** *adv*

genial[2] (dʒɪˈniːəl) *adj Anat.* of or relating to the chin. ORIG C19: from Gk, from *genus* jaw

genic (ˈdʒɛnɪk) *adj* of or relating to a gene or genes.

-genic *adj combining form.* **1** relating to production or generation: *carcinogenic.* **2** suited to or suitable for: *photogenic.* ORIG from -GEN + -IC

genie (ˈdʒiːnɪ) *n* **1** (in fairy tales and stories) a servant who appears by magic and fulfils a person's wishes. **2** another word for **jinni.** ORIG C18: from F, from Ar. *jinni* demon, infl. by L *genius* attendant spirit; see GENIUS

genista (dʒɪˈnɪstə) *n* any of a genus of leguminous deciduous shrubs, usually having yellow, often fragrant, flowers; broom. ORIG C17: from L

genital (ˈdʒɛnɪtᵊl) *adj* **1** of or relating to the sexual organs or to reproduction. **2** *Psychoanal.* relating to the mature stage of psychosexual development. ORIG C14: from L *genitālis* concerning birth, from *gignere* to beget

genital herpes *n* a sexually transmitted disease caused by the herpes simplex virus, in which painful blisters occur in the genital region.

genitals (ˈdʒɛnɪtᵊlz) *or* **genitalia** (ˌdʒɛnɪˈteɪlɪə, -ˈteɪljə) *pl n* the external sexual organs.

genitive (ˈdʒɛnɪtɪv) *Grammar.* ◆ *adj* **1** denoting a case of nouns, pronouns, and adjectives in inflected languages used to indicate a relation of ownership or association. ◆ *n* **2a** the genitive case. **2b** a word or speech element in this case. ORIG C14: from L *genetīvus* relating to birth, from *gignere* to produce
▸ **genitival** (ˌdʒɛnɪˈtaɪvᵊl) *adj*

genitourinary (ˌdʒɛnɪtəʊˈjʊərɪnərɪ) *adj* of or relating to both the reproductive and excretory organs; urogenital: *genitourinary medicine.*

genius (ˈdʒiːnɪəs, -njəs) *n, pl* **geniuses** *or* (*for senses 5, 6*) **genii** (ˈdʒiːnɪˌaɪ). **1** a person with exceptional ability, esp. of a highly original kind. **2** such ability. **3** the distinctive spirit of a nation, era, language, etc. **4** a person considered as exerting influence of a certain sort: *an evil genius.* **5** *Roman myth.* **5a** the guiding spirit who attends a person from birth to death. **5b** the guardian spirit of a place. **6** (*usually pl*) *Arabic myth.* a demon; jinn. ORIG C16: from L, from *gignere* to beget

genizah (gɛˈniːzə) *n, pl* **genizahs** *or* **genizoth** (gɛˈniːzəθ). *Judaism.* a repository for sacred objects which can no longer be used but which may not be destroyed. ORIG C19: from Heb., lit.: a hiding place

Genk *or* **Genck** ★ (*Flemish* xɛŋk) *n* a town in NE Belgium, in Limburg province: coal-mining. Pop.: 61 996 (1995 est.).

genoa (ˈdʒɛnəʊə) *n Yachting.* a large jib sail.

Genoa ★ (ˈdʒɛnəʊə) *n* a port in NW Italy, capital of Liguria, on the **Gulf of Genoa:** Italy's main port; an independent commercial city with many colonies in the Middle Ages; university (1243); heavy industries. Pop.: 659 116 (1996 est.). Italian name: **Genova.**

genocide (ˈdʒɛnəʊˌsaɪd) *n* the policy of deliberately killing a nationality or ethnic group. ORIG C20: from Gk *genos* race + -CIDE
▸ ˌ**genoˈcidal** *adj*

Genoese (ˌdʒɛnəʊˈiːz) *or* **Genovese** (ˌdʒɛnəˈviːz) *n, pl* **Genoese** *or* **Genovese. 1** a native or inhabitant of Genoa. ◆ *adj* **2** of or relating to Genoa or its inhabitants.

genome (ˈdʒɛˌnəʊm) *n* the complete set of haploid chromosomes that an organism passes on to its offspring in its reproductive cells. ORIG C20: from GEN(E) + (CHROMOS)OME

genotype (ˈdʒɛnəʊˌtaɪp) *n* **1** the genetic constitution of an organism. **2** a group of organisms with the same genetic constitution.
▸ **genotypic** (ˌdʒɛnəʊˈtɪpɪk) *adj*

-genous *adj combining form.* **1** yielding or generating: *erogenous.* **2** generated by or issuing from: *endogenous.* ORIG from -GEN + -OUS

Genova ★ (ˈdʒɛːnova) *n* the Italian name for **Genoa.**

genre (ˈʒɑːnrə) *n* **1a** kind, category, or sort, esp. of literary or artistic work. **1b** (*as modifier*): *genre fiction.* **2** a category of painting in which incidents from everyday life are depicted. ORIG C19: from F, from OF *gendre;* see GENDER

gens (dʒɛnz) *n, pl* **gentes** (ˈdʒɛntiːz). **1** (in ancient Rome) any of a group of families, having a common name and claiming descent from a common ancestor in the male line. **2** *Anthropol.* a group based on descent in the male line. ORIG C19: from L: race

Genseric (ˈgɛnsərɪk, ˈdʒɛn-) *or* **Gaiseric** ★ *n* ?390–477 A.D., king of the Vandals (428–77). He seized Roman lands, esp. extensive parts of N Africa, and sacked Rome (455).

gent (dʒɛnt) *n Inf.* short for **gentleman.**

Gent ★ (xɛnt) *n* the Flemish name for **Ghent.**

genteel (dʒɛnˈtiːl) *adj* **1** affectedly proper or refined; excessively polite. **2** respectable, polite, and well-bred. **3** appropriate to polite or fashionable society. ORIG C16: from F *gentil* well-born; see GENTLE
▸ **genˈteelly** *adv* ▸ **genˈteelness** *n*

gentian (ˈdʒɛnʃən) *n* **1** any plant of the genus *Gentiana,* having blue, yellow, white, or red showy flowers. **2** the bitter-tasting roots of the yellow gentian, which can be used as a tonic. ORIG C14: from L *gentiāna;* ? after *Gentius,* a second-century B.C. Illyrian king, reputedly the first to use it medicinally

gentian violet *n* a greenish crystalline substance that forms a violet solution in water, used as an indicator, antiseptic, and in the treatment of burns.

Gentile[1] (ˈdʒɛntaɪl) *n* **1** a person, esp. a Christian, who is not a Jew. **2** a Christian, as contrasted with a Jew. **3** a person who is not a member of one's own church: used esp. by Mormons. **4** a heathen or pagan. ◆ *adj* **5** of or relating to a race or religion that is not Jewish. **6** Christian, as contrasted with Jewish. **7** not being a member of one's own church: used esp. by Mormons. **8** pagan or heathen. ORIG C15 *gentil,* from LL *gentīlis,* from L: one belonging to the same tribe

Gentile[2] ★ (*Italian* dʒenˈtiːle) *n* **Giovanni** (dʒoˈvanni). 1875–1944, Italian Idealist philosopher and Fascist politician: minister of education (1922–24).

Gentile da Fabriano ★ (*Italian* da faˈbrjaːno) *n* original name *Niccolo di Giovanni di Massio.* ?1370–1427, Italian painter. His works include the *Adoration of the Magi* (1423).

gentility (dʒɛnˈtɪlɪtɪ) *n, pl* **gentilities. 1** respectability and polite good breeding. **2** affected politeness. **3** noble birth or ancestry. **4** people of noble birth. ORIG C14: from OF, from L *gentīlitās* relationship of those belonging to the same tribe or family; see GENS

gentle (ˈdʒɛntᵊl) *adj* **1** having a mild or kindly nature or character. **2** soft or temperate; mild; moderate. **3** gradual: *a gentle slope.* **4** easily controlled; tame. **5** *Arch.* of good breeding; noble: *gentle blood.* **6** *Arch.* gallant, chivalrous. ◆ *vb* **gentles, gentling, gentled.** (*tr*) **7** to tame or subdue (a horse, etc.). **8** to appease or mollify. ◆ *n* **9** a maggot, esp. when used as bait in fishing. ORIG C13: from OF *gentil* noble, from L *gentīlis* belonging to the same family; see GENS
▸ **ˈgentleness** *n* ▸ **ˈgently** *adv*

gentle breeze *n* a wind of force 3 on the Beaufort scale, blowing at 8-12 mph.

gentlefolk (ˈdʒɛntᵊlˌfəʊk) *or* **gentlefolks** *pl n* persons regarded as being of good breeding.

gentleman (ˈdʒɛntᵊlmən) *n, pl* **gentlemen. 1** a man regarded as having qualities of refinement associated with a good family. **2** a man who is cultured, courteous, and well-educated. **3** a polite name for a man. **4** the personal servant of a gentleman (esp. in **gentleman's gentleman**).
▸ **ˈgentlemanly** *adj* ▸ **ˈgentlemanliness** *n*

gentleman-farmer *n, pl* **gentlemen-farmers. 1** a person who engages in farming but does not depend on it for his living. **2** a person who owns farmland but does not farm it personally.

gentlemen's agreement *or* **gentleman's agreement** *n* an understanding or arrangement based on honour and not legally binding.

★ people and places

gentlewoman ('dʒɛntᵊl,wʊmən) *n, pl* **gentlewomen. 1** *Arch.* a woman regarded as being of good family or breeding; lady. **2** (formerly) a woman in personal attendance on a high-ranking lady.

gentrification (,dʒɛntrɪfɪ'keɪʃən) *n Brit.* a process by which middle-class people take up residence in a traditionally working-class area, changing its character. ORIG C20: from *gentrify* (to become GENTRY)
▸ **'gentri,fier** *n*

gentry ('dʒɛntrɪ) *n* **1** *Brit.* persons just below the nobility in social rank. **2** people of a particular class, esp. one considered to be inferior. ORIG C14: from OF *genterie,* from *gentil* GENTLE

gents (dʒɛnts) *n (functioning as sing) Brit. inf.* a men's public lavatory.

genuflect ('dʒɛnjʊ,flɛkt) *vb (intr)* **1** to act in a servile or deferential manner. **2** *RC Church.* to bend one or both knees as a sign of reverence. ORIG C17: from Med. L, from L *genu* knee + *flectere* to bend
▸ **,genu'flection** *or (esp. Brit.)* **,genu'flexion** *n* ▸ **'genu,flector** *n*

genuine ('dʒɛnjʊɪn) *adj* **1** not fake or counterfeit; original; real; authentic. **2** not pretending; frank; sincere. **3** being of authentic or original stock. ORIG C16: from L *genuīnus* inborn, hence (in LL) authentic
▸ **'genuinely** *adv* ▸ **'genuineness** *n*

gen up *vb* **gens, genning, genned.** *(adv; often passive;* when *intr,* usually foll. by *on) Brit. inf.* to make or become fully conversant (with).

genus ('dʒiːnəs) *n, pl* **genera** *or* **genuses. 1** *Biol.* any of the taxonomic groups into which a family is divided and which contains one or more species. **2** *Logic.* a class of objects or individuals that can be divided into two or more groups or species. **3** a class, group, etc., with common characteristics. ORIG C16: from L: race

-geny *n combining form.* origin or manner of development: *phylogeny.* ORIG from Gk, from *-genēs* born
▸ **-genic** *adj combining form.*

geo- *combining form.* indicating earth: *geomorphology.* ORIG from Gk, from *gē* earth

geocentric (,dʒiːəʊ'sɛntrɪk) *adj* **1** having the earth at its centre. **2** measured as from the centre of the earth.
▸ **,geo'centrically** *adv*

geochronology (,dʒiːəʊkrə'nɒlədʒɪ) *n* the branch of geology concerned with ordering and dating events in the earth's history.
▸ **geochronological** (,dʒiːəʊ,krɒnə'lɒdʒɪkᵊl) *adj*

geode ('dʒiːəʊd) *n* a cavity, usually lined with crystals, within a rock mass or nodule. ORIG C17: from L *geōdēs* a precious stone, from Gk: earthlike; see GEO-, -ODE[1]
▸ **geodic** (dʒɪ'ɒdɪk) *adj*

geodesic (,dʒiːəʊ'dɛsɪk, -'diː-) *adj* **1** Also: **geodetic.** relating to the geometry of curved surfaces. ◆ *n* **2** Also called: **geodesic line.** the shortest line between two points on a curved surface.

geodesic dome *n* a light structural framework arranged as a set of polygons in the form of a shell.

geodesy (dʒɪ'ɒdɪsɪ) *n* the branch of science concerned with determining the exact position of geographical points and the shape and size of the earth. ORIG C16: from F, from Gk *geōdaisia,* from GEO- + *daiein* to divide
▸ **ge'odesist** *n*

geodetic (,dʒiːəʊ'dɛtɪk) *adj* **1** of or relating to geodesy. **2** another word for **geodesic.**
▸ **,geo'detically** *adv*

Geoffrey of Monmouth ★ ('dʒɛfrɪ) *n* ?1100–54, Welsh bishop and chronicler; author of *Historia Regum Britanniae,* the chief source of Arthurian legends.

geog. *abbrev. for:* **1** geographer. **2** geographic(al). **3** geography.

geographical mile *n* a former name for **nautical mile.**

geography (dʒɪ'ɒgrəfɪ) *n, pl* **geographies. 1** the study of the natural features of the earth's surface, including topography, climate, soil, vegetation, etc., and man's response to them. **2** the natural features of a region.
▸ **ge'ographer** *n* ▸ **geographical** (,dʒɪə'græfɪkᵊl) *or* **,geo'graphic** *adj* ▸ **,geo'graphically** *adv*

geoid ('dʒiːɔɪd) *n* **1** a hypothetical surface that corresponds to mean sea level and extends under the continents. **2** the shape of the earth.

geol. *abbrev. for:* **1** geologic(al). **2** geologist. **3** geology.

geology (dʒɪ'ɒlədʒɪ) *n* **1** the scientific study of the origin, structure, and composition of the earth. **2** the geological features of a district or country.
▸ **geological** (,dʒɪə'lɒdʒɪkᵊl) *or* **,geo'logic** *adj* ▸ **,geo'logically** *adv* ▸ **ge'ologist** *n*

geom. *abbrev. for:* **1** geometric(al). **2** geometry.

geomagnetism (,dʒiːəʊ'mægnɪ,tɪzəm) *n* **1** the magnetic field of the earth. **2** the branch of physics concerned with this.
▸ **geomagnetic** (,dʒiːəʊmæg'nɛtɪk) *adj*

geometric (,dʒɪə'mɛtrɪk) *or* **geometrical** *adj* **1** of, relating to, or following the methods and principles of geometry. **2** consisting of, formed by, or characterized by points, lines, curves, or surfaces. **3** (of design or ornamentation) composed predominantly of simple geometric forms, such as circles, triangles, etc.
▸ **,geo'metrically** *adv*

geometric mean *n* the average value of a set of *n* integers, terms, or quantities, expressed as the *n*th root of their product.

geometric progression *n* **1** a sequence of numbers, each of which differs from the succeeding one by a constant ratio, as 1, 2, 4, 8, ... Cf. **arithmetic progression. 2 geometric series.** such numbers written as a sum.

geometrid (dʒɪ'ɒmɪtrɪd) *n* any of a family of moths, the larvae of which are called measuring worms, inchworms, or loopers. ORIG C19: from NL, from L, from Gk *geometrēs* land measurer, from the looping gait of the larvae

geometry (dʒɪ'ɒmɪtrɪ) *n* **1** the branch of mathematics concerned with the properties, relationships, and measurement of points, lines, curves, and surfaces. **2** a shape, configuration, or arrangement. ORIG C14: from L, from Gk, from *geōmetrein* to measure the land
▸ **ge,ome'trician** *n*

geomorphology (,dʒiːəʊmɔː'fɒlədʒɪ) *n* the branch of geology that is concerned with the structure, origin, and development of the topographical features of the earth's crust.
▸ **geomorphological** (,dʒiːəʊ,mɔːfə'lɒdʒɪkᵊl) *or* **,geo,morpho'logic** *adj*

geophysics (,dʒiːəʊ'fɪzɪks) *n (functioning as sing)* the study of the earth's physical properties and of the physical processes acting upon, above, and within the earth. It includes seismology, meteorology, and oceanography.
▸ **,geo'physical** *adj* ▸ **,geo'physicist** *n*

geopolitics (,dʒiːəʊ'pɒlɪtɪks) *n* **1** *(functioning as sing)* the study of the effect of geographical factors on politics. **2** *(functioning as pl)* the combination of geographical and political factors affecting a country or area. **3** *(functioning as pl)* politics as they affect the whole world; global politics.
▸ **geopolitical** (,dʒiːəʊpə'lɪtɪkᵊl) *adj*

Geordie ('dʒɔːdɪ) *Brit.* ◆ *n* **1** a person who comes from or lives in Tyneside. **2** the dialect spoken by these people. ◆ *adj* **3** of or relating to these people or their dialect. ORIG C19: a dim. of *George*

George (dʒɔːdʒ) ★ *n* **1 David Lloyd.** See **Lloyd George. 2 Henry.** 1839–97, US economist: advocated a single tax on land values. **3 Saint.** died ?303 A.D., Christian martyr, the patron saint of England; the hero of a legend in which he slew a dragon. Feast day: April 23.

George I ★ *n* 1660–1727, first Hanoverian king of Great Britain and Ireland (1714–27) and elector of Hanover (1698–1727).

George II ★ *n* **1** 1683–1760, king of Great Britain and Ireland and elector of Hanover (1727–60); son of George I. His victory over the French at Dettingen (1743) in the War of the Austrian Succession was the last appearance on a battlefield by a British king. **2** 1890–1947, king of Greece (1922–24; 1935–47). He was overthrown by the republicans (1924) and exiled during the German occupation of Greece (1941–45).

George III ★ *n* 1738–1820, king of Great Britain and Ireland (1760–1820) and of Hanover (1814–20). During his reign the American colonies were lost. He became insane in 1811, and his son acted as regent for the rest of the reign.

George IV ★ *n* 1762–1830, king of Great Britain and Ireland and also of Hanover (1820–30); regent (1811–20).

George V ★ *n* 1865–1936, king of Great Britain and Northern Ireland and emperor of India (1910–36).

George VI ★ *n* 1895–1952, king of Great Britain and Northern Ireland (1936–52) and emperor of India (1936–47). The second son of George V, he succeeded to the throne after the abdication of his brother, Edward VIII.

George Cross *n* a British award for bravery, esp. of civilians. Abbrev.: **GC**.

Georgetown ★ (ˈdʒɔːdʒˌtaʊn) *n* **1** the capital and chief port of Guyana, at the mouth of the Demerara River: became capital of the Dutch colonies of Essequibo and Demerara in 1784; seat of the University of Guyana. Pop.: 254 000 (1995 est.). Former name (until 1812): **Stabroek**. **2** the capital of the Cayman Islands: a port on Grand Cayman Island. Pop.: 16 600 (1995 est.).

George Town ★ *n* a port in NW Malaysia, capital of Penang state, in NE Penang Island: the first chartered city of the Malayan federation. Pop.: 219 376 (1991). Also called: **Penang**.

georgette *or* **georgette crepe** (dʒɔːˈdʒɛt) *n* a thin silk or cotton crepe fabric. ORIG C20: from Mme *Georgette,* a F modiste

Georgia ★ (ˈdʒɔːdʒjə) *n* **1** a republic in NW Asia, on the Black Sea: an independent kingdom during the middle ages, it was divided by Turkey and Persia in 1555; became part of Russia in 1918 and a separate Soviet republic in 1936; its independence was recognized internationally in 1992. It is rich in minerals and has hydroelectric resources. Official language: Georgian. Religion: believers are mainly Christian or Muslim. Currency: lari. Capital: Tbilisi. Pop.: 5 449 000 (1999 est.). Area: 69 493 sq. km (26 831 sq. miles). **2** a state of the southeastern US, on the Atlantic: consists of coastal plains with forests and swamps, rising to the Cumberland Plateau and the Appalachians in the northwest. Capital: Atlanta. Pop.: 7 642 207 (1998 est.). Area: 152 489 sq. km (58 876 sq. miles). Abbrevs.: **Ga.** or (with zip code) **GA**.

Georgian (ˈdʒɔːdʒjən) *adj* **1** of or relating to any or all of the four kings who ruled Great Britain from 1714 to 1830, or to their reigns. **2** of or relating to George V of Great Britain or his reign (1910–36): *the Georgian poets.* **3** of or relating to Georgia, its people, or their language. **4** of or relating to the American State of Georgia or its inhabitants. **5** (of furniture, architecture, etc.) in or imitative of the style prevalent in Britain during the 18th century. ◆ *n* **6** the official language of Georgia, belonging to the South Caucasian family. **7** a native or inhabitant of Georgia. **8** a native or inhabitant of the American State of Georgia.

Georgian Bay ★ *n* a bay in S central Canada, in Ontario, containing many small islands: the NE part of Lake Huron. Area: 15 000 sq. km (5800 sq. miles).

geostatics (ˌdʒiːəʊˈstætɪks) *n* (*functioning as sing*) the branch of physics concerned with the statics of rigid bodies, esp. the balance of forces within the earth.

geostationary (ˌdʒiːəʊˈsteɪʃənərɪ) *adj* (of a satellite, etc.) in a circular equatorial orbit in which it circles the earth once in 24 hours so that it appears stationary in relation to the earth's surface.

geostrophic (ˌdʒiːəʊˈstrɒfɪk) *adj* of, relating to, or caused by the force produced by the rotation of the earth: *geostrophic wind.*

geosynchronous (ˌdʒiːəʊˈsɪŋkrənəs) *n* (of a satellite) in an orbit in which it circles the earth once in 24 hours.

geosyncline (ˌdʒiːəʊˈsɪŋklaɪn) *n* a broad elongated depression in the earth's crust.

geotextile (ˌdʒiːəʊˈtɛkstaɪl) *n* any strong synthetic fabric used in civil engineering, as to retain an embankment.

geothermal (ˌdʒiːəʊˈθɜːməl) *or* **geothermic** *adj* of or relating to the heat in the interior of the earth.

geotropism (dʒɪˈɒtrəˌpɪzəm) *n* the response of a plant part to the stimulus of gravity. Plant stems, which grow upwards irrespective of the position in which they are placed, show **negative geotropism.**
▸ **geotropic** (ˌdʒiːəʊˈtrɒpɪk) *adj*

Ger. *abbrev. for:* **1** German. **2** Germany.

Gera ★ (*German* ˈgeːra) *n* an industrial city in S Germany, in Thuringia. Pop.: 123 555 (1996 est.).

geranium (dʒɪˈreɪnɪəm) *n* **1** a cultivated plant of the genus *Pelargonium* having scarlet, pink, or white showy flowers. See also **pelargonium. 2** any plant such as cranesbill and herb Robert, having divided leaves and pink or purplish flowers. ORIG C16: from L: cranesbill, from Gk, from *geranos* CRANE

Gérard ★ (*French* ʒerar) *n* **François** (**Pascal Simon**) (frɑ̃swa), Baron. 1770–1837, French painter, court painter to Napoleon I and Louis XVIII.

gerbera (ˈdʒɜːbərə) *n* a genus of African or Asian plants belonging to the composite family, esp. the Transvaal daisy. ORIG C19: from NL, after T. *Gerber* (died 1743), G naturalist

gerbil *or* **gerbille** (ˈdʒɜːbɪl) *n* a burrowing rodent inhabiting hot dry regions of Asia and Africa. ORIG C19: from F, from NL *gerbillus* a little JERBOA

gerfalcon (ˈdʒɜːˌfɔːlkən, -ˌfɔːkən) *n* a variant spelling of **gyrfalcon.**

geriatric (ˌdʒɛrɪˈætrɪk) *adj* **1** of or relating to geriatrics or to elderly people. **2** *Inf.* old, decrepit, or useless. ◆ *n* **3** an elderly person. ORIG C20: from Gk *gēras* old age + IATRIC

geriatrics (ˌdʒɛrɪˈætrɪks) *n* (*functioning as sing*) the branch of medical science concerned with the diagnosis and treatment of diseases affecting elderly people.
▸ **ˌgeriaˈtrician** *n*

Géricault ★ (*French* ʒeriko) *n* (**Jean Louis André**) **Théodore** (teɔdɔr). 1791–1824, French romantic painter.

Gerlachovka ★ (*Czech* ˈgɛrlaxɔfka) *n* a mountain in N Slovakia, in the Tatra Mountains: the highest peak of the Carpathian Mountains. Height: 2663 m (8737 ft).

germ (dʒɜːm) *n* **1** a microorganism, esp. one that produces disease. **2** (*often pl*) the rudimentary or initial form of something: *the germs of revolution.* **3** a simple structure that is capable of developing into a complete organism. ORIG C17: from F, from L *germen* sprout, seed

german (ˈdʒɜːmən) *adj* **1** (used in combination) **1a** having the same parents as oneself: *a brother-german.* **1b** having a parent that is a brother or sister of either of one's own parents: *cousin-german.* **2** a less common word for **germane.** ORIG C14: via OF, from L *germānus* of the same race, from *germen* sprout, offshoot

German (ˈdʒɜːmən) *n* **1** the official language of Germany and Austria and one of the official languages of Switzerland. **2** a native, inhabitant, or citizen of Germany. **3** a person whose native language is German. ◆ *adj* **4** denoting, relating to, or using the German language. **5** relating to, denoting, or characteristic of any German state or its people.

German Democratic Republic ★ *n* (formerly) the official name of **East Germany.** Abbrevs.: **GDR, DDR.**

germander (dʒɜːˈmændə) *n* any of several plants of Europe, having two-lipped flowers with a very small upper lip. ORIG C15: from Med. L, ult. from Gk *khamai* on the ground + *drus* oak tree

germane (dʒɜːˈmeɪn) *adj* (*postpositive;* usually foll. by *to*) related (to the topic being considered); akin; relevant. ORIG var. of GERMAN
▸ **gerˈmanely** *adv* ▸ **gerˈmaneness** *n*

German East Africa ★ *n* a former German territory in E Africa, consisting of Tanganyika and Ruanda-Urundi: divided in 1919 between Great Britain and Belgium; now in Tanzania, Rwanda, and Burundi.

Germanic (dʒɜːˈmænɪk) *n* **1** a branch of the Indo-European family of languages that includes English, Dutch, German, the Scandinavian languages, and Gothic. Abbrev.: **Gmc. 2** Also called: **Proto-Germanic.** the unrecorded language from which all of these languages developed. ◆ *adj* **3** of, denoting, or relating to this group of languages. **4** of, relating to, or characteristic of the German language or any people that speaks a Germanic language. **5** (formerly) of the German people.

Germanicus Caesar ★ (dʒɜːˈmænɪkəs) *n* 15 B.C.–19 A.D., Roman general; nephew of the emperor Tiberius; waged decisive campaigns against the Germans (14–16).

germanium (dʒɜːˈmeɪnɪəm) *n* a brittle crystalline grey element that is a semiconducting metalloid: used in transistors, and to strengthen alloys. Symbol: Ge; atomic no.: 32; atomic wt.: 72.59. ORIG C19: NL, after GERMANY

German measles *n* (*functioning as sing*) a nontechnical name for **rubella**.

German Ocean ★ *n* a former name for the **North Sea**.

German shepherd dog *n* another name for **Alsatian**.

German silver *n* another name for **nickel silver**.

Germany ★ (ˈdʒɜːmənɪ) *n* a country in central Europe: in the Middle Ages the centre of the Holy Roman Empire; dissolved into numerous principalities; united under the leadership of Prussia in 1871 after the Franco-Prussian War; became a republic with reduced size in 1919 after being defeated in World War I; under the dictatorship of Hitler from 1933 to 1945; defeated in World War II and divided by the Allied Powers into four zones, which became established as East and West Germany in the late 1940s; reunified in 1990: a member of the European Union. It is flat and low-lying in the north with plateaus and uplands (including the Black Forest and Bavarian Alps) in the centre and south. Official language: German. Religion: Christian with a Protestant majority. Currency: Deutschmark and euro. Capital: Berlin, some government offices have not yet been transferred from Bonn. Pop.: 82 100 000 (1999). Area: 357 041 sq. km (137 825 sq. miles). German name: **Deutschland**. Official name: **Federal Republic of Germany**. Related adj: **Teutonic**.

germ cell *n* a sexual reproductive cell.

germicide (ˈdʒɜːmɪˌsaɪd) *n* any substance that kills germs.
▸ **ˌgermiˈcidal** *adj*

germinal (ˈdʒɜːmɪnᵊl) *adj* **1** of, relating to, or like germs or a germ cell. **2** of or in the earliest stage of development. ORIG C19: from NL, from L *germen* bud; see GERM
▸ **ˈgerminally** *adv*

germinate (ˈdʒɜːmɪˌneɪt) *vb* **germinates, germinating, germinated. 1** to cause (seeds or spores) to sprout or (of seeds or spores) to sprout. **2** to grow or cause to grow; develop. **3** to come or bring into existence; originate: *the idea germinated with me.* ORIG C17: from L *germināre* to sprout; see GERM
▸ **ˈgerminative** *adj* ▸ **ˌgermiˈnation** *n* ▸ **ˈgermiˌnator** *n*

Germiston ★ (ˈdʒɜːmɪstən) *n* a city in South Africa, southeast of Johannesburg: industrial centre, with the world's largest gold refinery, serving the Witwatersrand mines. Pop.: 134 005 (1991).

germ plasm *n* **a** the part of a germ cell that contains hereditary material. **b** the germ cells collectively.

germ warfare *n* the military use of disease-spreading bacteria against an enemy.

Gerona ★ (*Spanish* xeˈrona) *n* a city in NE Spain: city walls and 14th-century cathedral; often besieged, in particular by the French (1809). Pop.: 67 578 (1986). Ancient name: **Gerunda** (dʒəˈruːndə).

Geronimo ★ (dʒəˈrɒnɪˌməʊ) *n* **1** 1829–1909, Apache Indian chieftain: led a campaign against the White settlers until his capture in 1886. ◆ *interj* **2** *US.* a shout given by paratroopers as they jump into battle.

gerontology (ˌdʒerɒnˈtɒlədʒɪ) *n* the scientific study of ageing and the problems associated with elderly people.
▸ **gerontological** (ˌdʒerɒntəˈlɒdʒɪkᵊl) *adj* ▸ **ˌgeronˈtologist** *n*

-gerous *adj combining form.* bearing or producing: *armigerous.* ORIG from L *-ger* bearing + -OUS

gerrymander (ˈdʒerɪˌmændə) *vb* **1** to divide the constituencies of (a voting area) so as to give one party an unfair advantage. **2** to manipulate or adapt to one's advantage. ◆ *n* **3** an act or result of gerrymandering. ORIG C19: from Elbridge *Gerry,* US politician + (SALA)MANDER; from the salamander-like outline of an electoral district reshaped (1812) for political purposes while Gerry was governor of Massachusetts

Gers ★ (*French* ʒɛr) *n* a department of SW France, in Midi-Pyrénées region. Capital: Auch. Pop.: 172 622 (1994 est.). Area: 6291 sq. km (2453 sq. miles).

Gershwin ★ (ˈgɜːʃwɪn) *n* **1 George,** original name *Jacob Gershvin.* 1898–1937, US composer: incorporated jazz into such works as *Rhapsody in Blue* (1924) and the opera *Porgy and Bess* (1935). **2** his brother, **Ira,** original name *Israel Gershvin.* 1896–1983, US song lyricist.

gerund (ˈdʒerənd) *n* a noun formed from a verb, ending in *-ing,* denoting an action or state: *the living is easy.* ORIG C16: from LL, from L *gerundum* something to be carried on, from *gerere* to wage
▸ **gerundial** (dʒɪˈrʌndɪəl) *adj*

gerundive (dʒɪˈrʌndɪv) *n* **1** (in Latin grammar) an adjective formed from a verb, expressing the desirability, etc., of the activity denoted by the verb. ◆ *adj* **2** of or relating to the gerund or gerundive. ORIG C17: from LL, from *gerundium* GERUND
▸ **gerundival** (ˌdʒerənˈdaɪvᵊl) *adj*

Geryon ★ (ˈgerɪən) *n Greek myth.* a winged monster with three bodies joined at the waist, killed by Hercules, who stole the monster's cattle as his tenth labour.

gesso (ˈdʒesəʊ) *n* **1** a white ground of plaster and size, used to prepare panels or canvas for painting or gilding. **2** any white substance, esp. plaster of Paris, that forms a ground when mixed with water. ORIG C16: from It.: chalk, GYPSUM

gest *or* **geste** (dʒest) *n Arch.* **1** a notable deed or exploit. **2** a tale of adventure or romance, esp. in verse. ORIG C14: from OF, from L *gesta* deeds, from *gerere* to carry out

Gestalt psychology (gəˈʃtælt) *n* a system of thought that regards all mental phenomena as being arranged in patterns or structures (**gestalts**) perceived as a whole and not merely as the sum of their parts. ORIG C20: from G *Gestalt* form

Gestapo (geˈstɑːpəʊ) *n* the secret state police in Nazi Germany. ORIG from G *Ge(heime) Sta(ats)po(lizei),* lit.: secret state police

gestate (ˈdʒesteɪt) *vb* **gestates, gestating, gestated. 1** (*tr*) to carry (developing young) in the uterus during pregnancy. **2** (*tr*) to develop (a plan or idea) in the mind. **3** (*intr*) to be in the process of gestating. ORIG C19: from L p.p. of *gestare,* from *gerere* to bear
▸ **gesˈtation** *n*

gesticulate (dʒeˈstɪkjʊˌleɪt) *vb* **gesticulates, gesticulating, gesticulated.** to express by or make gestures. ORIG C17: from L, from *gesticulus* (unattested except in LL) gesture, from *gerere* to bear, conduct
▸ **geˌsticuˈlation** *n* ▸ **geˈsticulative** *adj* ▸ **gesˈticuˌlator** *n*
▸ **gesˈticulatory** *adj*

gesture (ˈdʒestʃə) *n* **1** a motion of the hands, head, or body to express or emphasize an idea or emotion. **2** something said or done as a formality or as an indication of intention. ◆ *vb* **gestures, gesturing, gestured. 3** to express by or make gestures; gesticulate. ORIG C15: from Med. L *gestūra* bearing, from L *gestus,* p.p. of *gerere* to bear
▸ **ˈgestural** *adj*

get (get) *vb* **gets, getting, got; got** *or esp. US* **gotten.** (*mainly tr*) **1** to come into possession of; receive or earn. **2** to bring or fetch. **3** to contract or be affected by: *he got a chill.* **4** to capture or seize: *the police got him.* **5** (*also intr*) to become or cause to become or act as specified: *to get one's hair cut; get wet.* **6** (*intr;* foll. by a preposition or adverbial particle) to succeed in going, coming, leaving, etc.: *get off the bus.* **7** (*takes an infinitive*) to manage or contrive: *how did you get to be captain?* **8** to make ready or prepare: *to get a meal.* **9** to hear, notice, or understand: *I didn't get your meaning.* **10** to learn or master by study. **11** (*intr;* often foll. by *to*) to come (to) or arrive (at): *we got home safely; to get to London.* **12** to catch or enter: *to get a train.* **13** to induce or persuade: *get him to leave.* **14** to reach by calculation: *add 2 and 2 and you will get 4.* **15** to receive (a broadcast signal). **16** to communicate with (a person or place), as by telephone. **17** (*also intr;* foll. by *to*) *Inf.* to have an emotional effect (on): *that music really gets me.* **18** *Inf.* to annoy or irritate: *her voice gets me.* **19** *Inf.* to bring a person into a difficult position from which he or she cannot escape. **20** *Inf.* to puzzle; baffle. **21** *Inf.* to hit: *the blow got him in the back.* **22** *Inf.* to be revenged on, esp. by killing. **23** *Inf.* to have the better of: *your extravagant habits will get you in the end.* **24** (*intr;* foll. by present participle) *Inf.* to begin: *get moving.* **25** (used as a command) *Inf.* go! leave now! **26** *Arch.* to beget or conceive. **27** **get with child.** *Arch.* to make pregnant. ◆ *n* **28** *Rare.* the act of begetting. **29** *Rare.* something begotten; offspring. **30** *Brit. sl.* a variant of **git.** ◆ See also **get about, get across,** etc. ORIG OE *gietan* ▸ **'getable** *or* **'gettable** *adj* ▸ **'getter** *n*

USAGE NOTE See at **off.**

GeT *abbrev. for* Greenwich Electronic Time.

get about *or* **around** *vb* (*intr, adv*) **1** to move around, as when recovering from an illness. **2** to be socially active. **3** (of news, rumour, etc.) to become known; spread.

get across *vb* **1** to cross or cause to cross. **2** (*adv*) to be or cause to be understood.

get at *vb* (*intr, prep*) **1** to gain access to. **2** to mean or intend: *what are you getting at?* **3** to irritate or annoy persistently; criticize: *she is always getting at him.* **4** to influence or seek to influence, esp. illegally by bribery, intimidation, etc.: *someone had got at the witness before the trial.*

get away *vb* (*adv, mainly intr*) **1** to make an escape; leave. **2** to make a start. **3** **get away with. 3a** to steal and escape with (money, goods, etc.). **3b** to do (something wrong, illegal, etc.) without being discovered or punished. ◆ *interj* **4** an exclamation indicating mild disbelief. ◆ *n* **getaway. 5** the act of escaping, esp. by criminals. **6** a start or acceleration. **7** a short holiday away from home. **8** (*modifier*) used for escaping: *a getaway car.*

get back *vb* (*adv*) **1** (*tr*) to recover or retrieve. **2** (*intr;* often foll. by *to*) to return, esp. to a former position or activity. **3** (*intr;* foll. by *at*) to retaliate (against); wreak vengeance (on). **4** **get one's own back.** *Inf.* to obtain one's revenge.

get by *vb* **1** to pass; go past or overtake. **2** (*intr, adv*) *Inf.* to manage, esp. in spite of difficulties. **3** (*intr*) to be accepted or permitted: *that book will never get by the authorities.*

Gethsemane ★ (gɛθ'sɛmənɪ) *n New Testament.* the garden in Jerusalem where Christ was betrayed on the night before his Crucifixion (Matthew 26:36–56).

get in *vb* (*mainly adv*) **1** (*intr*) to enter a car, train, etc. **2** (*intr*) to arrive, esp. at one's home or place of work. **3** (*tr*) to bring in or inside: *get the milk in.* **4** (*tr*) to insert or slip in: *he got his suggestion in before anyone else.* **5** (*tr*) to gather or collect (crops, debts, etc.). **6** to be elected or cause to be elected. **7** (*intr*) to obtain a place at university, college, etc. **8** (foll. by *on*) to join or cause to join (an activity or organization).

get off *vb* **1** (*intr, adv*) to escape the consequences of an action: *he got off very lightly.* **2** (*adv*) to be or cause to be acquitted: *a good lawyer got him off.* **3** (*adv*) to depart or cause to depart: *to get the children off to school.* **4** (*intr*) to descend (from a bus, train, etc.); dismount: *she got off at the terminus.* **5** to move or cause to move to a distance (from): *get off the field.* **6** (*tr, adv*) to remove; take off: *get your coat off.* **7** (*adv*) to go or send to sleep. **8** (*adv*) to send (letters) or (of letters) to be sent. **9** **get off with.** *Brit. inf.* to establish an amorous or sexual relationship (with).

get on *vb* (*mainly adv*) **1** Also (*when prep*): **get onto.** to board or cause or help to board (a bus, train, etc.). **2** (*tr*) to dress in (clothes as specified). **3** (*intr*) to grow late or (of time) to elapse: *it's getting on and I must go.* **4** (*intr*) (of a person) to grow old. **5** (*intr;* foll. by *for*) to approach (a time, age, amount, etc.): *she is getting on for seventy.* **6** (*intr*) to make progress, manage, or fare: *how did you get on in your exam?* **7** (*intr;* often foll. by *with*) to establish a friendly relationship: *he gets on well with other people.* **8** (*intr;* foll. by *with*) to continue to do: *get on with your homework!*

get out *vb* (*adv*) **1** to leave or escape or cause to leave or escape: used in the imperative when dismissing a person. **2** to make or become known; publish or be published. **3** (*tr*) to express with difficulty. **4** (*tr;* often foll. by *of*) to extract (information or money) (from a person): *to get a confession out of a criminal.* **5** (*tr*) to gain or receive something, esp. something of significance or value. **6** (foll. by *of*) to avoid or cause to avoid: *she always gets out of swimming.* **7** *Cricket.* to dismiss or be dismissed.

get over *vb* **1** to cross or surmount (something). **2** (*intr, prep*) to recover from (an illness, shock, etc.). **3** (*intr, prep*) to overcome or master (a problem). **4** (*intr, prep*) to appreciate fully: *I just can't get over seeing you again.* **5** (*tr, adv*) to communicate effectively. **6** (*tr, adv;* sometimes foll. by *with*) to bring (something necessary but unpleasant) to an end: *let's get this job over with quickly.*

get round *or* **around** *vb* (*intr*) **1** (*prep*) to circumvent or overcome. **2** (*prep*) *Inf.* to have one's way with; cajole: *that girl can get round anyone.* **3** (*prep*) to evade (a law or rules). **4** (*adv;* foll. by *to*) to reach or come to at length: *I'll get round to that job in an hour.*

get through *vb* **1** to succeed or cause or help to succeed in an examination, test, etc. **2** to bring or come to a destination, esp. after overcoming problems: *we got through the blizzards to the survivors.* **3** (*intr, adv*) to contact, as by telephone. **4** (*intr, prep*) to use, spend, or consume (money, supplies, etc.). **5** to complete or cause to complete (a task, process, etc.): *to get a bill through Parliament.* **6** (*adv;* foll. by *to*) to reach the awareness and understanding (of a person): *I just can't get the message through to him.*

get-together *n* **1** *Inf.* a small informal meeting or social gathering. ◆ *vb* **get together.** (*adv*) **2** (*tr*) to gather or collect. **3** (*intr*) (of people) to meet socially. **4** (*intr*) to discuss, esp. in order to reach an agreement.

Getty ★ ('gɛtɪ) *n* **J(ean) Paul.** 1892–1976, US oil executive, millionaire, and art collector.

Gettysburg ★ ('gɛtɪz,bɜːg) *n* a small town in S Pennsylvania, southwest of Harrisburg: scene of a crucial battle (1863) during the American Civil War, in which Meade's Union forces defeated Lee's Confederate army; site of the national cemetery dedicated by President Lincoln. Pop.: 7194 (1980).

get up *vb* (*mainly adv*) **1** to wake and rise from one's bed or cause to wake and rise from bed. **2** (*intr*) to rise to one's feet; stand up. **3** (*also prep*) to ascend or cause to ascend. **4** to increase or cause to increase in strength: *the wind got up at noon.* **5** (*tr*) *Inf.* to dress (oneself) in a particular way, esp. elaborately. **6** (*tr*) *Inf.* to devise or create: *to get up an entertainment for Christmas.* **7** (*tr*) *Inf.* to study or improve one's knowledge of: *I must get up my history.* **8** (*intr;* foll. by *to*) *Inf.* to be involved in: *he's always getting up to mischief.* ◆ *n* **get-up.** *Inf.* **9** a costume or outfit. **10** the arrangement or production of a book, etc.

get-up-and-go *n Inf.* energy or drive.

Getz ★ (gets) *n* **Stanley,** known as *Stan.* 1927–91, US jazz saxophonist.

geum ('dʒiːəm) *n* any herbaceous plant of the rose type, having compound leaves and red, orange, yellow, or white flowers. ORIG C19: NL, from L: herb bennet, avens

gewgaw ('gjuːgɔː, 'guː-) *n* a showy but valueless trinket. ORIG C15: from ?

geyser ('giːzə; *US* 'gaɪzər) *n* **1** a spring that discharges steam and hot water. **2** *Brit.* a domestic gas water heater. ORIG C18: from Icelandic *Geysir,* from ON *geysa* to gush

Gezira ★ (dʒə'zɪərə) *n* a region of the E central Sudan between the Blue and White Niles: site of a large-scale irrigation system.

G-force *n* the force of gravity.

Ghana ★ ('gɑːnə) *n* a republic in W Africa, on the Gulf of Guinea: a powerful empire from the 4th to the 13th centuries; a major source of gold and slaves for Europeans after 1471; British colony of the Gold Coast established in 1874; united with British Togoland in 1957 and became a republic and a member of the Commonwealth in 1960. Official language: English. Religions: Christian, Muslim, and animist. Currency: cedi. Capital: Accra. Pop.: 18 888 000 (1999 est.). Area: 238 539 sq. km (92 100 sq. miles). ▸ **Ghanaian** (gɑː'neɪən) *or* **'Ghanian** *adj, n*

gharry *or* **gharri** ('gærɪ) *n, pl* **gharries.** a horse-drawn vehicle used in India. ORIG C19: from Hindi *gārī*

ghastly ('gɑːstlɪ) *adj* **ghastlier, ghastliest. 1** *Inf.* very bad or unpleasant. **2** deathly pale; wan. **3** *Inf.* extremely unwell; ill. **4** terrifying; horrible. ♦ *adv* **5** unhealthily; sickly: *ghastly pale.* ORIG OE *gāstlīc* spiritual
▸ **'ghastliness** *n*

ghat (gɔːt) *n* (in India) **1** stairs or a passage leading down to a river. **2** a mountain pass. **3** a place of cremation. ORIG C17: from Hindi, from Sansk.

Ghats ★ (gɔːts) *pl n* See **Eastern Ghats** and **Western Ghats.**

Ghazali ★ ('gɑːzˌɑːlɪ) *n* **al-**. 1058–1111, Muslim theologian and mystic.

ghazi ('gɑːzɪ) *n, pl* **ghazis. 1** a Muslim fighter against infidels. **2** (*often cap.*) a Turkish warrior of high rank. ORIG C18: from Ar., from *ghazā* he made war

Ghazzah ★ ('gɑːzə, 'gʌzə) *n* transliteration of the Arabic name for **Gaza.**

ghee (giː) *n* a clarified butter used in Indian cookery. ORIG C17: from Hindi *ghī*, from Sansk. *ghri* sprinkle

Ghent ★ (gent) *n* an industrial city and port in NW Belgium, capital of East Flanders province, at the confluence of the Rivers Lys and Scheldt: formerly famous for its cloth industry; university (1816). Pop.: 226 464 (1996 est.). Flemish name: **Gent.** French name: **Gand.**

gherkin ('gɜːkɪn) *n* **1** the small immature fruit of any of various cucumbers, used for pickling. **2a** a tropical American climbing plant. **2b** its small spiny edible fruit. ORIG C17: from Du., dim. of *gurk*, ult. from Gk *angourion*

ghetto ('gɛtəʊ) *n, pl* **ghettos** *or* **ghettoes. 1** a densely populated slum area of a city inhabited by a socially and economically deprived minority. **2** an area or community that is segregated or isolated. **3** an area in a European city in which Jews were formerly required to live. ORIG C17: from It., ?from *borghetto*, dim. of *borgo* settlement outside a walled city, or from *ghetto* foundry, because one occupied the site of the later Venetian ghetto

ghettoblaster ('gɛtəʊˌblɑːstə) *n Inf.* a large portable cassette or CD recorder with built-in speakers.

ghettoize *or* **ghettoise** ('gɛtəʊˌaɪz) *vb* **ghettoizes, ghettoizing, ghettoized** *or* **ghettoises, ghettoising, ghettoised.** (*tr*) to confine or restrict to a particular area, activity, or category: *to ghettoize women as housewives.*
▸ **ˌghettoi'zation** *or* **ˌghettoi'sation** *n*

Ghiberti ★ (*Italian* gi'bɛrti) *n* **Lorenzo** (lo'rɛntso). 1378–1455, Italian sculptor, painter, and goldsmith: noted for the baptistry doors of Florence Cathedral.

ghillie ('gɪlɪ) *n* a variant spelling of **gillie.**

Ghirlandaio *or* **Ghirlandajo** ★ (*Italian* girlan'daːjo) *n* **Domenico** (do'meːniko). original name *Domenico Bigordi.* 1449–94, Italian painter of frescoes.

ghost (gəʊst) *n* **1** the disembodied spirit of a dead person, supposed to haunt the living as a pale or shadowy vision; phantom. Related adj: **spectral. 2** a haunting memory: *the ghost of his former life rose up before him.* **3** a faint trace or possibility of something; glimmer: *a ghost of a smile.* **4** the spirit; soul (archaic, except in **the Holy Ghost**). **5** *Physics.* **5a** a faint secondary image produced by an optical system. **5b** a similar image on a television screen. **6** (*modifier*) falsely recorded as doing a particular job or fulfilling a particular function in order that some benefit, esp. money, may be obtained: *a ghost worker.* **7 give up the ghost.** to die. ♦ *vb* **8** See **ghostwrite. 9** (*tr*) to haunt. **10** (*intr*) to move effortlessly and smoothly, esp. unnoticed: *he ghosted into the penalty area.* ORIG OE *gāst*
▸ **'ghostˌlike** *adj* ▸ **'ghostly** *adj*

ghost town *n* a deserted town, esp. one in the western US that was formerly a boom town.

ghost word *n* a word that has entered the language through the perpetuation, in dictionaries, etc., of an error.

ghostwrite ('gəʊstˌraɪt) *vb* **ghostwrites, ghostwriting, ghostwrote, ghostwritten.** to write (an article, etc.) on behalf of a person who is then credited as the author. Often shortened to **ghost.**
▸ **'ghostˌwriter** *n*

ghoul (guːl) *n* **1** a malevolent spirit or ghost. **2** a person interested in morbid or disgusting things. **3** a person who robs graves. **4** (in Muslim legend) an evil demon thought to eat corpses. ORIG C18: from Ar. *ghūl*, from *ghāla* he seized
▸ **'ghoulish** *adj* ▸ **'ghoulishly** *adv* ▸ **'ghoulishness** *n*

GHQ *Mil. abbrev. for* General Headquarters.

ghyll (gɪl) *n* a variant spelling of **gill**[3].

Gi *symbol for* gibi-.

GI *US inf.* ♦ *n* **1** (*pl* **GIs** *or* **GI's**) a soldier in the US Army, esp. an enlisted man. ♦ *adj* **2** conforming to US Army regulations. ORIG C20: abbrev. of *government issue*

gi. *abbrev. for* gill (unit of measure).

Giacometti ★ (*Italian* dʒako'metti) *n* **Alberto** (al'bɛrto). 1901–66, Swiss sculptor and painter, noted for his long skeletal statues.

Giambologna ★ (*Italian* dʒambo'loɲɲa) *n*, original name *Giovanni da Bologna* or *Jean de Boulogne.* 1529–1608, Italian mannerist sculptor, born in Flanders.

giant ('dʒaɪənt) *n* **1** Also (fem): **giantess** ('dʒaɪəntɪs). a mythical figure of superhuman size and strength, esp. in folklore or fairy tales. **2** a person or thing of exceptional size, reputation, etc. ♦ *adj* **3** remarkably or supernaturally large. ORIG C13: from OF *geant*, from L *gigās, gigant-*, from Gk

giant hogweed *n* a species of cow parsley that grows up to 3½ metres (10 ft) and whose irritant hairs and sap can cause a severe reaction.

giantism ('dʒaɪənˌtɪzəm) *n* another term for **gigantism** (sense 1).

giant panda *n* See **panda** (sense 1).

Giant's Causeway ★ *n* a promontory of columnar basalt on the N coast of Northern Ireland, in Antrim: consists of several thousand pillars, mostly hexagonal, that were formed by the rapid cooling of lava and the inward contraction of the lava flow.

giant slalom *n Skiing.* a type of slalom in which the course is longer and the obstacles are further apart than in a standard slalom.

giant star *n* any of a class of stars that have swelled and brightened as they approach the end of their life, their energy supply having changed.

giaour ('dʒaʊə) *n* a derogatory term for a non-Muslim, esp. a Christian. ORIG C16: from Turkish: unbeliever, from Persian *gaur*

gib (gɪb) *n* **1** a metal wedge, pad, or thrust bearing, esp. a brass plate let into a steam engine crosshead. ♦ *vb* **gibs, gibbing, gibbed. 2** (*tr*) to fasten or supply with a gib. ORIG C18: from ?

Gib (dʒɪb) *n* an informal name for **Gibraltar.**

gibber[1] ('dʒɪbə) *vb* **1** to utter rapidly and unintelligibly; prattle. **2** (*intr*) (of monkeys and related animals) to make characteristic chattering sounds. ORIG C17: imit.

gibber[2] ('gɪbə) *n Austral.* **1** a stone or boulder. **2** (*modifier*) of or relating to a dry flat area of land covered with wind-polished stones: *gibber plains.* ORIG C19: from Abor.

Gibberd ★ ('gɪbəd) *n* Sir **Frederick.** 1908–84, British architect and town planner. His buildings include the Liverpool Roman Catholic cathedral (1960–67).

gibberellin (ˌdʒɪbə'rɛlɪn) *n* any of several plant hormones whose main action is to cause elongation of the stem. ORIG C20: from NL *Gibberella*, lit.: a little hump, from L *gibber* hump + -IN

gibberish ('dʒɪbərɪʃ) *n* **1** rapid chatter. **2** incomprehensible talk; nonsense.

gibbet ('dʒɪbɪt) *n* **1a** a wooden structure resembling a gallows, from which the bodies of executed criminals were formerly hung to public view. **1b** a gallows. ♦ *vb* (*tr*) **2** to put to death by hanging on a gibbet. **3** to hang (a corpse) on a gibbet. **4** to expose to public ridicule. ORIG C13: from OF: gallows, lit.: little cudgel, from *gibe* cudgel; from ?

gibbon ('gɪbᵊn) *n* a small agile arboreal anthropoid ape inhabiting forests in S Asia. ORIG C18: from F, prob. from an Indian dialect word

Gibbon ★ ('gɪbᵊn) *n* **1 Edward.** 1737–94, British historian; author of *The History of the Decline and Fall of the Roman Empire* (1776–88). **2 Lewis Grassic** ('græsɪk), real name *James Leslie Mitchell.* 1901–35, Scottish writer: best known for his trilogy of novels *A Scots Quair* (1932–34).

Gibbons ★ (ˈɡɪbᵊnz) *n* **1 Grinling.** 1648–1721, English sculptor and woodcarver. **2 Orlando.** 1583–1625, English organist and composer, esp. of anthems, motets, and madrigals.

gibbous (ˈɡɪbəs) *or* **gibbose** (ˈɡɪbəʊs) *adj* **1** (of the moon or a planet) more than half but less than fully illuminated. **2** hunchbacked. **3** bulging. ORIG C17: from LL *gibbōsus* humpbacked, from L *gibba* hump
▸ **ˈgibbously** *adv* ▸ **ˈgibbousness** *or* **gibbosity** (ɡɪˈbɒsɪtɪ) *n*

Gibbs ★ (ɡɪbz) *n* **1 James.** 1682–1754, British architect; his buildings include St Martin's-in-the-Fields, London (1722–26), and the Radcliffe Camera, Oxford (1737–49). **2 Josiah Willard.** 1839–1903, US physicist and mathematician: founder of chemical thermodynamics.

gibe[1] *or* **jibe** (dʒaɪb) *vb* **gibes, gibing, gibed** *or* **jibes, jibing, jibed. 1** to make jeering or scoffing remarks (at); taunt. ◆ *n* **2** a derisive or provoking remark. ORIG C16: ?from OF *giber* to treat roughly, from ?
▸ **ˈgiber** *or* **ˈjiber** *n*

gibe[2] (dʒaɪb) *vb* **gibes, gibing, gibed,** *n Naut.* a variant spelling of **gybe.**

Gibeon ★ (ˈɡɪbɪən) *n* an ancient town of Palestine: the excavated site of what are thought to be its remains lies about 9 kilometres (6 miles) northwest of Jerusalem.

gibi- (ˈɡɪbɪ) *prefix Computing.* denoting 2^{30}: *gibibyte.* Also: **giga-**. Symbol: Gi ORIG C20:from GI(GA-) + BI(NARY)

> **USAGE NOTE** See at **kilo-**.

giblets (ˈdʒɪblɪts) *pl n* (*sometimes sing*) the gizzard, liver, heart, and neck of a fowl. ORIG C14: from OF *gibelet* stew of game birds, prob. from *gibier* game, of Gmc origin

Gibraltar ★ (dʒɪˈbrɔːltə) *n* **1 City of.** a city on the **Rock of Gibraltar,** a limestone promontory at the tip of S Spain: settled by Moors in 711 and taken by Spain in 1462; ceded to Britain in 1713; a British crown colony (1830–1969), now a United Kingdom overseas territory; a naval and air base of strategic importance. Pop.: 27 100 (1997 est.). Area: 6.5 sq. km (2.5 sq. miles). Ancient name: **Calpe. 2 Strait of.** a narrow strait between the S tip of Spain and the NW tip of Africa, linking the Mediterranean with the Atlantic.
▸ **Gibraltarian** (ˌdʒɪbrɔːlˈtɛərɪən) *adj, n*

Gibran ★ (dʒɪˈbrɑːn) *n* **Kahlil** (ˈkɑːliːl). 1883–1931, Syro-Lebanese poet and painter, resident in the US after 1910; author of *The Prophet* (1923).

Gibson ★ (ˈɡɪbsən) *n* **Mel.** born 1956, Australian film actor, born in the US; his films include *Mad Max* (1979), *Braveheart* (1996; also directed), and *What Women Want* (2000).

Gibson Desert ★ (ˈɡɪbsən) *n* a desert in W central Australia, between the Great Sandy Desert and the Victoria Desert: salt marshes, salt lakes, and scrub. Area: about 220 000 sq. km (85 000 sq. miles).

gidday (ɡəˈdaɪ) *sentence substitute.* a variant spelling of **g'day.**

giddy (ˈɡɪdɪ) *adj* **giddier, giddiest. 1** affected with a reeling sensation and feeling as if about to fall; dizzy. **2** causing or tending to cause vertigo. **3** impulsive; scatterbrained. ◆ *vb* **giddies, giddying, giddied. 4** to make or become giddy. ORIG OE *gydig* mad, frenzied, possessed by God; rel. to GOD
▸ **ˈgiddily** *adv* ▸ **ˈgiddiness** *n*

Gide ★ (*French* ʒid) *n* **André** (ɑ̃dre). 1869–1951, French writer. His novels include *L'Immoraliste* (1902) and *Les Faux-Monnayeurs* (1926): Nobel prize for literature 1947.

Gideon ★ (ˈɡɪdɪən) *n Old Testament.* a Hebrew judge who led the Israelites to victory over their Midianite oppressors (Judges 6:11–8:35).

gidgee *or* **gidjee** (ˈɡɪdʒiː) *n Austral.* **1** a small acacia tree yielding useful timber. **2** a spear made of this. ORIG C19: from Abor.

gie (ɡiː) *vb* **gies, gi'ing, gi'ed.** a Scot. word for **give.**

Gielgud ★ (ˈɡiːlɡʊd) *n* Sir **John.** 1904–2000, leading British actor and director.

Giessen ★ (*German* ˈɡiːsən) *n* a city in central Germany, in Hesse: university (1607). Pop.: 71 750 (1989 est.).

GIF (fɪf) *n Computing.* **a** a standard compressed file format used for pictures. **b** a picture held in this format. ORIG C20:from *g(raphic) i(nterchange) f(ormat)*

gift (ɡɪft) *n* **1** something given; a present. **2** a special aptitude, ability, or power; talent. **3** the power or right to give or bestow (esp. in **in the gift of, in (someone's) gift**). **4** the act or process of giving. **5 look a gift-horse in the mouth.** (*usually negative*) to find fault with a free gift or chance benefit. ◆ *vb* (*tr*) **6** to present (something) as a gift to (a person). ORIG OE *gift* payment for a wife, dowry; see GIVE

GIFT (ɡɪft) *n acronym for* gamete intrafallopian transfer: a technique, similar to IVF, that enables some women who cannot conceive to bear children.

gifted (ˈɡɪftɪd) *adj* having or showing natural talent or aptitude: *a gifted musician.*
▸ **ˈgiftedly** *adv* ▸ **ˈgiftedness** *n*

gift of tongues *n* an utterance, partly or wholly unintelligible, produced under the influence of ecstatic religious emotion. Also called: **glossolalia.**

giftwrap (ˈɡɪftˌræp) *vb* **giftwraps, giftwrapping, giftwrapped.** to wrap (a gift) attractively.

Gifu ★ (ˈɡiːˈfuː) *n* a city in Japan, on central Honshu: hot springs. Pop.: 407 145 (1995).

gig[1] (ɡɪɡ) *n* **1** a light two-wheeled one-horse carriage without a hood. **2** *Naut.* a light tender for a vessel. **3** a long light rowing boat, used esp. for racing. ◆ *vb* **gigs, gigging, gigged. 4** (*intr*) to travel in a gig. ORIG C13 (in the sense: flighty girl, spinning top): ?from ON

gig[2] (ɡɪɡ) *n* **1** a cluster of barbless hooks drawn through a shoal of fish to try to impale them. ◆ *vb* **gigs, gigging, gigged. 2** to catch (fish) with a gig. ORIG C18: ? shortened from obs. *fishgig* or *fizgig* kind of harpoon

gig[3] (ɡɪɡ) *n* **1** a job, esp. a single booking for jazz or pop musicians. **2** the performance itself. ◆ *vb* **gigs, gigging, gigged. 3** (*intr*) to perform at a gig or gigs. ORIG C20: from ?

giga- (ˈɡɪɡə, ˈɡaɪɡə) *prefix* **1** denoting 10^9: *gigahertz.* **2** Also: **gibi-**. *Computing.* denoting 2^{30}: *gigabyte.* ◆ Symbol: G ORIG from Gk *gigas* GIANT

> **USAGE NOTE** See at **kilo-**.

gigaflop (ˈɡaɪɡəˌflɒp) *n Computing.* a measure of processing speed, consisting of a thousand million floating-point operations a second. ORIG C20: from GIGA- + *flo(ating) p(oint)*

gigantic (dʒaɪˈɡæntɪk) *adj* **1** very large; enormous. **2** Also: **gigantesque** (ˌdʒaɪɡænˈtɛsk). of or suitable for giants. ORIG C17: from Gk *gigantikos,* from *gigas* GIANT
▸ **giˈgantically** *adv*

gigantism (ˈdʒaɪɡænˌtɪzəm, dʒaɪˈɡæntɪzəm) *n* **1** Also called: **giantism.** excessive growth of the entire body, caused by overproduction of growth hormone by the pituitary gland. **2** the state or quality of being gigantic.

giggle (ˈɡɪɡᵊl) *vb* **giggles, giggling, giggled. 1** (*intr*) to laugh nervously or foolishly. ◆ *n* **2** such a laugh. **3** *Inf.* something or someone that causes amusement. ORIG C16: imit.
▸ **ˈgiggler** *n* ▸ **ˈgiggling** *adj, n* ▸ **ˈgiggly** *adj*

Gigli ★ (*Italian* ˈdʒiʎʎi) *n* **Beniamino** (benjaˈmiːno). 1890–1957, Italian operatic tenor.

gigolo (ˈʒɪɡəˌləʊ) *n, pl* **gigolos. 1** a man who is kept by a woman, esp. an older woman. **2** a man who is paid to dance with or escort women. ORIG C20: from F, back formation from *gigolette* girl for hire as a dancing partner, prostitute, ult. from *gigue* a fiddle

gigot (ˈdʒɪɡət) *n* **1** a leg of lamb or mutton. **2** a leg-of-mutton sleeve. ORIG C16: from OF: leg, a small fiddle, from *gigue* a fiddle, of Gmc origin

gigue (ʒiːɡ) *n* a piece of music, usually in six-eight time, incorporated into the classical suite. ORIG C17: from F, from It. *giga,* lit.: a fiddle; see GIGOT

Gijón ★ (giːˈhɔːn; *Spanish* xiˈxɔn) *n* a port in NW Spain, on the Bay of Biscay: capital of the kingdom of Asturias until 791. Pop.: 270 867 (1995 est.). Ancient name: **Gigia.**

Gila monster (ˈhiːlə) *n* a large venomous brightly coloured lizard inhabiting deserts of the southwestern US and Mexico. ORIG C19: after the *Gila,* a river in New Mexico and Arizona

gilbert ('gɪlbət) *n* the cgs unit of magnetomotive force. Symbol: Gb, Gi ORIG C19: after William GILBERT

Gilbert ★ ('gɪlbət) *n* **1 Grove Karl.** 1843–1918, US geologist who pioneered the study of river development. **2** Sir **Humphrey.** ?1539–83, English navigator: founded the colony at St John's, Newfoundland (1583). **3 William.** 1540–1603, English physician and physicist, noted for his study of terrestrial magnetism in *De Magnete* (1600). **4** Sir **W(illiam) S(chwenck).** 1836–1911, British dramatist, humorist, and librettist. He collaborated (1871–96) with Arthur Sullivan on such comic operettas as *The Pirates of Penzance* (1879) and *The Mikado* (1885).

Gilbert Islands ★ *pl n* a group of islands in the W Pacific: with Banaba, the Phoenix Islands, and three of the Line Islands they constitute the independent state of Kiribati; until 1975 they formed part of the British colony of **Gilbert and Ellice Islands;** achieved full independence in 1979. Pop.: 67 508 (1990). Area: 295 sq. km (114 sq. miles).

gild[1] (gɪld) *vb* **gilds, gilding, gilded** *or* **gilt.** (*tr*) **1** to cover with or as if with gold. **2 gild the lily. 2a** to adorn unnecessarily something already beautiful. **2b** to praise someone inordinately. **3** to give a falsely attractive or valuable appearance to. ORIG OE *gyldan,* from *gold* GOLD
▸ **'gilder** *n*

gild[2] (gɪld) *n* a variant spelling of **guild.**

gilding ('gɪldɪŋ) *n* **1** the act or art of applying gilt to a surface. **2** the surface so produced. **3** another word for **gilt**[1] (sense 2).

Gilead[1] ★ ('gɪlɪ,æd) *n* a historic mountainous region east of the River Jordan, rising over 1200 m (4000 ft).

Gilead[2] ★ ('gɪlɪ,æd) *n Old Testament.* a grandson of Manasseh; ancestor of the Coileadites (Numbers 26: 29–30).

Giles ★ (dʒaɪlz) *n* **1 Saint.** 7th century A.D., Greek hermit in France; patron saint of cripples, beggars, and lepers. Feast day: Sept. 1. **2 William Ernest Powell.** 1835–97, Australian explorer, born in England. He was noted for his exploration of the western desert (1875–76).

gilet (dʒɪ'leɪ) *n* a garment resembling a waistcoat. ORIG C20: F, lit.: waistcoat

gill[1] (gɪl) *n* **1** the respiratory organ in many aquatic animals. **2** any of the radiating leaflike spore-producing structures on the undersurface of the cap of a mushroom. ORIG C14: from ON
▸ **gilled** *adj*

gill[2] (dʒɪl) *n* a unit of liquid measure equal to one quarter of a pint. ORIG C14: from OF *gille* vat, tub, from LL *gillō,* from ?

gill[3] *or* **ghyll** (gɪl) *n Dialect.* **1** a narrow stream; rivulet. **2** a wooded ravine. ORIG C11: from ON *gil* steep-sided valley

Gill ★ (gɪl) *n* **(Arthur) Eric (Rowton).** 1882–1940, British sculptor and typographer: his sculptures include the *Stations of the Cross* in Westminster Cathedral, London.

Gillespie ★ (gɪ'lɛspɪ) *n* **Dizzy,** nickname of *John Birks Gillespie.* 1917–93, US jazz trumpeter.

gillie, ghillie, *or* **gilly** ('gɪlɪ) *n, pl* **gillies** *or* **ghillies.** *Scot.* **1** an attendant or guide for hunting or fishing. **2** (formerly) a Highland chieftain's male attendant. ORIG C17: from Scot. Gaelic *gille* boy, servant

Gillingham ★ ('dʒɪlɪŋəm) *n* a town in SE England, in N Kent on the Medway estuary: former dockyards. Pop.: 94 923 (1991).

Gillray ★ ('gɪlreɪ) *n* **James.** 1757–1815, British caricaturist.

gills (gɪlz) *pl n* **1** (*sometimes sing*) the wattle of birds such as domestic fowl. **2** the cheeks and jowls of a person. **3 green about the gills.** *Inf.* looking or feeling nauseated.

gillyflower *or* **gilliflower** ('dʒɪlɪ,flaʊə) *n* **1** any of several plants having fragrant flowers, such as the stock and wallflower. **2** an archaic name for **carnation.** ORIG C14: from *gilofre,* from OF *girofle,* from Med. L, from Gk: clove tree, from *karuon* nut + *phullon* leaf

Gilolo ★ (dʒaɪ'ləʊləʊ, dʒɪ-) *n* See **Halmahera.**

gilt[1] (gɪlt) *vb* **1** a past tense and past participle of **gild**[1]. ◆ *n* **2** gold or a substance simulating it, applied in gilding. **3** another word for **gilding** (senses 1, 2). **4** superficial or false appearance of excellence. **5** a gilt-edged security. **6 take the gilt off the gingerbread.** to destroy the part of something that gives it its appeal. ◆ *adj* **7** covered with or as if with gold or gilt; gilded.

gilt[2] (gɪlt) *n* a young female pig, esp. one that has not had a litter. ORIG C15: from ON *gyltr*

gilt-edged *adj* **1** denoting government securities on which interest payments will certainly be met and that will certainly be repaid at par on the due date. **2** of the highest quality: *the last track on the album is a gilt-edged classic.* **3** (of books, papers, etc.) having gilded edges.

gimbals ('dʒɪmbᵊlz, 'gɪm-) *pl n* a device, consisting of two or three pivoted rings at right angles to each other, that provides free suspension in all planes for a compass, chronometer, etc. Also called: **gimbal ring.** ORIG C16: var. of earlier *gimmal,* from OF *gemel* double finger ring, from L *gemellus,* dim. of *geminus* twin

gimcrack ('dʒɪm,kræk) *adj* **1** cheap; shoddy. ◆ *n* **2** a cheap showy trifle or gadget. ORIG C18: from C14 *gibecrake* little ornament, from ?
▸ **'gim,crackery** *n*

gimlet ('gɪmlɪt) *n* **1** a small hand tool consisting of a pointed spiral tip attached at right angles to a handle, used for boring small holes in wood. **2** *US.* a cocktail consisting of half gin or vodka and half lime juice. ◆ *vb* **3** (*tr*) to make holes in (wood) using a gimlet. ◆ *adj* **4** penetrating; piercing (esp. in **gimlet-eyed**). ORIG C15: from OF *guimbelet,* of Gmc origin, see WIMBLE

gimmick ('gɪmɪk) *n Inf.* **1** something designed to attract extra attention, interest, or publicity. **2** any clever device, gadget, or stratagem, esp. one used to deceive. ORIG C20: orig. US sl., from ?
▸ **'gimmickry** *n* ▸ **'gimmicky** *adj*

gimp *or* **guimpe** (gɪmp) *n* a tapelike trimming. ORIG C17: prob. from Du. *gimp,* from ?

gin[1] (dʒɪn) *n* an alcoholic drink obtained by distillation of the grain of malted barley, rye, or maize, flavoured with juniper berries. ORIG C18: from Du. *genever,* via OF from L *jūniperus* JUNIPER

gin[2] (dʒɪn) *n* **1** a primitive engine in which a vertical shaft is turned by horses driving a horizontal beam in a circle. **2** Also called: **cotton gin.** a machine of this type used for separating seeds from raw cotton. **3** a trap for catching small mammals, consisting of a noose of thin strong wire. ◆ *vb* **gins, ginning, ginned.** (*tr*) **4** to free (cotton) of seeds with a gin. **5** to trap or snare (game) with a gin. ORIG C13 *gyn,* from ENGINE

gin[3] (gɪn) *vb* **gins, ginning, gan** (gæn), **gun** (gʌn). an archaic word for **begin.**

gin[4] (dʒɪn) *n Austral. offens. sl.* an Aboriginal woman. ORIG C19: from Abor.

ginger ('dʒɪndʒə) *n* **1** any of several plants of the East Indies, cultivated throughout the tropics for their spicy hot-tasting underground stems. **2** the underground stem of this plant, which is used fresh or powdered as a flavouring or crystallized as a sweetmeat. **3a** a reddish-brown or yellowish-brown colour. **3b** (*as adj*): *ginger hair.* **4** *Inf.* liveliness; vigour. ORIG C13: from OF *gingivre,* ult. from Sansk. *śṛṅgaveram,* from *śṛṅga-* horn + *vera-* body, referring to its shape
▸ **'gingery** *adj*

ginger ale *n* a sweetened effervescent nonalcoholic drink flavoured with ginger extract.

ginger beer *n* a slightly alcoholic drink made by fermenting a mixture of syrup and root ginger.

gingerbread ('dʒɪndʒə,brɛd) *n* **1** a moist brown cake, flavoured with ginger and treacle. **2a** a biscuit, similarly flavoured, cut into various shapes. **2b** (*as modifier*): *gingerbread man.* **3** an elaborate but unsubstantial ornamentation.

ginger group *n Chiefly Brit.* a group within a party, association, etc., that enlivens or radicalizes its parent body.

gingerly ('dʒɪndʒəlɪ) *adv* **1** in a cautious, reluctant, or timid manner. ◆ *adj* **2** cautious, reluctant, or timid. ORIG C16: ?from OF *gensor* dainty, from *gent* of noble birth; see GENTLE

ginger nut *or* **snap** *n* a crisp biscuit flavoured with ginger.

★ people and places

gingham ('gɪŋəm) *n* a cotton fabric, usually woven of two coloured yarns in a checked or striped design. ORIG C17: from F, from Malay *ginggang* striped cloth

gingili ('dʒɪndʒɪlɪ) *n* **1** the oil obtained from sesame seeds. **2** another name for **sesame.** ORIG C18: from Hindi *jingalī*

gingiva ('dʒɪndʒɪvə, dʒɪn'dʒaɪvə) *n, pl* **gingivae** (-dʒɪ,viː, -'dʒaɪviː). *Anat.* the technical name for the **gum**². ORIG from L
▸ **'gingival** *adj*

gingivitis (,dʒɪndʒɪ'vaɪtɪs) *n* inflammation of the gums.

ginglymus ('dʒɪŋglɪməs, 'gɪŋ-) *n, pl* **ginglymi** (-,maɪ). *Anat.* a hinge joint. ORIG C17: NL, from Gk *ginglumos* hinge

gink (gɪŋk) *n Sl.* a man or boy, esp. one considered to be odd. ORIG C20: from ?

ginkgo ('gɪŋkgəʊ) *or* **gingko** ('gɪŋkəʊ) *n, pl* **ginkgoes** *or* **gingkoes.** a widely planted ornamental Chinese tree with fan-shaped deciduous leaves and fleshy yellow fruit. Also called: **maidenhair tree.** ORIG C18: from Japanese, from Ancient Chinese: silver + apricot

ginormous (dʒaɪ'nɔːməs) *adj Inf.* very large. ORIG C20: blend of *giant* or *gigantic* & *enormous*

gin palace (dʒɪn) *n* (formerly) a gaudy drinking house.

gin rummy (dʒɪn) *n* a version of rummy in which a player may go out if the odd cards outside his sequences total less than ten points. ORIG C20: from GIN¹ + RUMMY

Ginsberg ★ ('gɪnzbɜːg) *n* **Allen.** 1926–97, US poet of the Beat Generation. His poetry includes *Howl* (1956).

ginseng ('dʒɪnsɛŋ) *n* **1** either of two plants of China or of North America, whose forked aromatic roots are used medicinally. **2** the root of either of these plants or a substance obtained from the roots, believed to possess tonic and energy-giving properties. ORIG C17: from Mandarin Chinese *jen shen*

Ginzburg ★ (*Italian* 'gindzburg) *n* **Natalia** (nata'liːa). 1916–91, Italian writer. Her books include *The Road to the City* (1942) and *Family Sayings* (1963).

Gioconda (*Italian* dʒo'konda) *n* **1 La.** Also called: **Mona Lisa.** the portrait by Leonardo da Vinci of a young woman with an enigmatic smile. **2** (*modifier*) mysterious or enigmatic. ORIG It.: the smiling (lady)

giocoso (dʒə'kəʊzəʊ) *adj Music.* jocose. ORIG It.

Giorgione ★ (*Italian* dʒor'dʒoːne) *n* **Il.** original name *Giorgio Barbarelli.* ?1478–1511, Italian painter of the Venetian school.

Giotto ★ (*Italian* 'dʒɔtto) *n* also known as *Giotto di Bondone.* ?1267–1337, Florentine painter of the early Renaissance.

gip (dʒɪp) *vb* **gips, gipping, gipped. 1** a variant spelling of **gyp**¹. ♦ *n* **2** a variant spelling of **gyp**².

Gippsland ★ ('gɪps,lænd) *n* a fertile region of SE Australia, in SE Victoria, extending east along the coast from Melbourne to the New South Wales border. Area: 35 200 sq. km (13 600 sq. miles).

Gipsy ('dʒɪpsɪ) *n, pl* **Gipsies.** (*sometimes not cap.*) a variant spelling of **Gypsy.**

gipsy moth *n* a variant spelling of **gypsy moth.**

giraffe (dʒɪ'rɑːf, -'ræf) *n, pl* **giraffes** *or* **giraffe.** a large ruminant mammal inhabiting savannas of tropical Africa: the tallest mammal, with very long legs and neck. ORIG C17: from It. *giraffa,* from Ar. *zarāfah,* prob. of African origin

Giraldus Cambrensis ★ (dʒɪ'rældəs kæm'brɛnsɪs) *n* literary name of *Gerald de Barri.* ?1146–?1223, Welsh chronicler and churchman.

girandole ('dʒɪrən,dəʊl) *n* **1** a branched wall candleholder. **2** an earring or pendant having a central gem surrounded by smaller ones. **3** a revolving firework. **4** *Artillery.* a group of connected mines. ORIG C17: from F, from It. *girandola,* from L *gȳrāre* to GYRATE

girasol *or* **girasole** ('dʒɪrə,sɒl, -,səʊl) *n* a type of opal that has a red or pink glow; fire opal. ORIG C16: from It., from *girare* to revolve (see GYRATE) + *sole* the sun

Giraud ★ (*French* ʒiro) *n* **Henri Honoré** (ɑ̃ri ɔnɔre). 1879–1949, French general, who commanded French forces in North Africa (1942–43).

Giraudoux ★ (*French* ʒirodu) *n* (**Hyppolyte**) **Jean** (ʒɑ̃). 1882–1944, French dramatist. His works include the novel *Suzanne et le Pacifique* (1921) and the play *Amphitryon 38* (1929).

gird¹ (gɜːd) *vb* **girds, girding, girded** *or* **girt.** (*tr*) **1** to put a belt, girdle, etc., around (the waist or hips). **2** to bind or secure with or as if with a belt: *to gird on one's armour.* **3** to surround; encircle. **4** to prepare (oneself) for action (esp. in **gird (up) one's loins**). ORIG OE *gyrdan,* of Gmc origin

gird² (gɜːd) *N English dialect.* ♦ *vb* **1** (when *intr,* foll. by *at*) to jeer (at someone); mock. ♦ *n* **2** a taunt; gibe. ORIG C13 *girden* to strike, cut, from ?

girder ('gɜːdə) *n* a large beam, esp. one made of steel, used in the construction of bridges, buildings, etc.

girdle¹ ('gɜːdᵊl) *n* **1** a woman's elastic corset covering the waist to the thigh. **2** anything that surrounds or encircles. **3** a belt or sash. **4** *Jewellery.* the outer edge of a gem. **5** *Anat.* any encircling structure or part. **6** the mark left on a tree trunk after the removal of a ring of bark. ♦ *vb* **girdles, girdling, girdled.** (*tr*) **7** to put a girdle on or around. **8** to surround or encircle. **9** to remove a ring of bark from (a tree). ORIG OE *gyrdel,* of Gmc origin; see GIRD¹

girdle² ('gɜːdᵊl) *n Scot. & N English dialect.* another word for **griddle.**

Girgenti ★ (*Italian* dʒir'dʒɛnti) *n* a former name (until 1927) of **Agrigento.**

girl (gɜːl) *n* **1** a female child from birth to young womanhood. **2** a young unmarried woman; lass; maid. **3** *Inf.* a sweetheart or girlfriend. **4** *Inf.* a woman of any age. **5** a female employee, esp. a female servant. **6** *S. African derog.* a Black female servant. ORIG C13: from ?; ? rel. to Low G *Göre* boy, girl
▸ **'girlish** *adj*

girlfriend ('gɜːl,frɛnd) *n* **1** a female friend with whom a person is romantically or sexually involved. **2** any female friend.

Girl Guide *n* See **Guide.**

girlhood ('gɜːl,hʊd) *n* the state or time of being a girl.

girlie *or* **girly** ('gɜːlɪ) *adj* **1** *Inf.* featuring nude or scantily dressed women: *a girlie magazine.* **2** suited to or designed to appeal to young women: *a real girlie night out.*

giro ('dʒaɪrəʊ) *n, pl* **giros. 1** a system of transferring money within a financial organization, such as a bank or post office, directly from the account of one person into that of another. **2** *Brit. inf.* an unemployment benefit or income support payment by giro cheque. ORIG C20: ult. from Gk *guros* circuit

Gironde ★ (*French* ʒirɔ̃d) *n* **1** a department of SW France, in Aquitaine region. Capital: Bordeaux. Pop.: 1 259 579 (1994 est.). Area: 10 726 sq. km (4183 sq. miles). **2** an estuary in SW France, formed by the confluence of the Rivers Garonne and Dordogne. Length: 72 km (45 miles).

girt¹ (gɜːt) *vb* a past tense and past participle of **gird**¹.

girt² (gɜːt) *vb* **1** (*tr*) to bind or encircle; gird. **2** to measure the girth of (something).

girth (gɜːθ) *n* **1** the distance around something; circumference. **2** a band around a horse's belly to keep the saddle in position. ♦ *vb* **3** (usually foll. by *up*) to fasten a girth on (a horse). **4** (*tr*) to encircle or surround. ORIG C14: from ON *gjörth* belt; see GIRD¹

Gisborne ★ ('gɪzbən) *n* a port in N New Zealand, on E North Island on Poverty Bay. Pop.: 31 700 (1994).

Giscard d'Estaing ★ (*French* ʒiskardɛstɛ̃) *n* **Valéry** (valeri). born 1926, French politician; minister of finance and economic affairs (1962–66; 1969–74); president (1974–81).

Gish ★ (gɪʃ) *n* **1 Dorothy.** 1898–1968, US actress, chiefly in silent films. **2** her sister, **Lillian.** 1896–1993, US actress, noted for her roles in such silent films as *The Birth of a Nation* (1915) and *Intolerance* (1916).

Gissing ★ ('gɪsɪŋ) *n* **George (Robert).** 1857–1903, British novelist. His works include *New Grub Street* (1891).

gist (dʒɪst) *n* the point or substance of an argument, speech, etc. ORIG C18: from Anglo-F, as in *cest action gist en* this action consists in, lit.: lies in, from OF *gésir,* from L *jacēre*

git (gɪt) *n Brit. sl.* **1** a contemptible person, often a fool. **2** a bastard. ORIG C20: from GET (in the sense: *to beget,* hence a bastard, fool)

gîte (ʒiːt) *n* a self-catering holiday cottage for let in France. ORIG C20: F

gittern (ˈgɪtɜːn) *n* an obsolete medieval stringed instrument resembling the guitar. ORIG C14: from OF, ult. from OSp. *guitarra* GUITAR; see CITTERN

Giulini ★ (*Italian* dʒuˈliːni) *n* **Carlo Maria** (ˈkarlo maˈriːa). born 1914, Italian orchestral conductor, esp. of opera.

Giulio Romano ★ (*Italian* ˈdʒuːljo roˈmaːno) *n* ?1499–1546, Italian architect and painter; a founder of mannerism.

giusto (ˈdʒuːstəʊ) *adj Music.* (of tempo) exact; strict. ORIG It.

give (gɪv) *vb* **gives, giving, gave, given.** (*mainly tr*) **1** (*also intr*) to present or deliver voluntarily (something that is one's own) to another. **2** (often foll. by *for*) to transfer (something that is one's own, esp. money) to the possession of another as part of an exchange: *to give fifty pounds for a painting.* **3** to place in the temporary possession of another: *I gave him my watch while I went swimming.* **4** (when *intr,* foll. by *of*) to grant, provide, or bestow: *give me some advice.* **5** to administer: *to give a reprimand.* **6** to award or attribute: *to give blame, praise,* etc. **7** to be a source of: *he gives no trouble.* **8** to impart or communicate: *to give news.* **9** to utter or emit: *to give a shout.* **10** to perform, make, or do: *the car gave a jolt.* **11** to sacrifice or devote: *he gave his life for his country.* **12** to surrender: *to give place to others.* **13** to concede or yield: *I will give you this game.* **14** (*intr*) *Inf.* to happen: *what gives?* **15** (often foll. by *to*) to cause; lead: *she gave me to believe that she would come.* **16** to perform or present as an entertainment: *to give a play.* **17** to act as a host of (a party, etc.). **18** (*intr*) to yield or break under force or pressure: *this surface will give if you sit on it.* **19 give as good as one gets.** to respond to verbal or bodily blows to at least an equal extent as those received. **20 give or take.** plus or minus: *three thousand people came, give or take a few hundred.* **21 give it up for** (**someone**). *Sl.* to applaud (someone). ◆ *n* **22** tendency to yield under pressure; resilience. ◆ See also **give away, give in,** etc. ORIG OE *giefan* ▸ **ˈgivable** *or* **ˈgiveable** *adj* ▸ **ˈgiver** *n*

give-and-take *n* **1** mutual concessions, shared benefits, and cooperation. **2** a smoothly flowing exchange of ideas and talk. ◆ *vb* **give and take.** (*intr*) **3** to make mutual concessions.

give away *vb* (*tr, adv*) **1** to donate or bestow as a gift, prize, etc. **2** to sell very cheaply. **3** to reveal or betray. **4** to fail to use (an opportunity) through folly or neglect. **5** to present (a bride) formally to her husband in a marriage ceremony. ◆ *n* **giveaway. 6** a betrayal or disclosure esp. when unintentional. **7** (*modifier*) **7a** very cheap (esp. in **giveaway prices**). **7b** free of charge: *a giveaway property magazine.*

give in *vb* (*adv*) **1** (*intr*) to yield; admit defeat. **2** (*tr*) to submit or deliver (a document).

given (ˈgɪvᵊn) *vb* **1** the past participle of **give.** ◆ *adj* **2** (*postpositive;* foll. by *to*) tending (to); inclined or addicted (to). **3** specific or previously stated. **4** assumed as a premise. **5** *Maths.* known or determined independently: *a given volume.* **6** (on official documents) issued or executed, as on a stated date.

given name *n* another term (esp. US) for **first name.**

give off *vb* (*tr, adv*) to emit or discharge: *the mothballs gave off an acrid odour.*

give out *vb* (*adv*) **1** (*tr*) to emit or discharge. **2** (*tr*) to publish or make known: *the chairman gave out that he would resign.* **3** (*tr*) to hand out or distribute: *they gave out free chewing gum.* **4** (*intr*) to become exhausted; fail: *the supply of candles gave out.*

give over *vb* (*adv*) **1** (*tr*) to transfer, esp. to the care or custody of another. **2** (*tr*) to assign or resign to a specific purpose or function: *the day was given over to pleasure.* **3** *Inf.* to cease (an activity): *give over fighting, will you!*

give up *vb* (*adv*) **1** to abandon hope (for). **2** (*tr*) to renounce (an activity, belief, etc.): *I have given up smoking.* **3** (*tr*) to relinquish or resign from: *he gave up the presidency.* **4** (*tr; usually reflexive*) to surrender: *the escaped convict gave himself up.* **5** (*intr*) to admit one's defeat or inability to do something. **6** (*tr; often passive or reflexive*) to devote completely (to): *she gave herself up to caring for the sick.*

Gîza ★ (ˈgiːzə) *n* See **El Gîza.**

gizmo *or* **gismo** (ˈgɪzməʊ) *n, pl* **gizmos, gismos.** *Sl.* a device; gadget. ORIG C20: from ?

gizzard (ˈgɪzəd) *n* **1** the thick-walled part of a bird's stomach, in which hard food is broken up. **2** *Inf.* the stomach and entrails generally. ORIG C14: from OF *guisier* fowl's liver, from L *gigēria* entrails of poultry when cooked, from ?

Gk *abbrev. for* Greek.

glabella (gləˈbɛlə) *n, pl* **glabellae** (-liː). *Anat.* a smooth elevation of the frontal bone just above the bridge of the nose. ORIG C19: NL, from L, from *glaber* bald, smooth ▸ **glaˈbellar** *adj*

glabrous (ˈgleɪbrəs) *adj Biol.* without hair or a similar growth; smooth. ORIG C17 *glabrous,* from L *glaber*

glacé (ˈglæsɪ) *adj* **1** crystallized or candied: *glacé cherries.* **2** covered in icing. **3** (of leather, silk, etc.) having a glossy finish. ◆ *vb* **glacés, glacéing, glacéed. 4** (*tr*) to ice or candy (cakes, fruits, etc.). ORIG C19: from F *glacé,* lit.: iced, from *glacer* to freeze, from L *glaciēs* ice

glacial (ˈgleɪsɪəl, -ʃəl) *adj* **1** characterized by the presence of masses of ice. **2** relating to, caused by, or deposited by a glacier. **3** extremely cold; icy. **4** cold or hostile in manner. **5** (of a chemical compound) of or tending to form crystals that resemble ice. ▸ **ˈglacially** *adv*

glacial acetic acid *n* pure acetic acid.

glacial period *n* **1** any period of time during which a large part of the earth's surface was covered with ice, due to the advance of glaciers. **2** (*often caps.*) the Pleistocene epoch. ◆ Also called: **glacial epoch, ice age.**

glaciate (ˈgleɪsɪˌeɪt) *vb* **glaciates, glaciating, glaciated. 1** to cover or become covered with glaciers or masses of ice. **2** (*tr*) to subject to the effects of glaciers, such as denudation and erosion. ▸ **ˌglaciˈation** *n*

glacier (ˈglæsɪə, ˈgleɪs-) *n* a slowly moving mass of ice originating from an accumulation of snow. ORIG C18: from F (dialect), from OF *glace* ice, from LL, from L *glaciēs* ice

glaciology (ˌglæsɪˈɒlədʒɪ, ˌgleɪ-) *n* the study of the distribution, character, and effects of glaciers. ▸ **glaciological** (ˌglæsɪəˈlɒdʒɪkᵊl, ˌgleɪ-) *adj* ▸ **ˌglaciˈologist** *n*

glacis (ˈglæsɪs, ˈglæsɪ, ˈgleɪ-) *n, pl* **glacises** *or* **glacis** (-iːz, -ɪz). **1** a slight incline; slope. **2** an open slope in front of a fortified place. ORIG C17: from F, from OF *glacier* to freeze, slip, from L, from *glaciēs* ice

glad[1] (glæd) *adj* **gladder, gladdest. 1** happy and pleased; contented. **2** causing happiness or contentment. **3** (*postpositive;* foll. by *to*) very willing: *he was glad to help.* **4** (*postpositive;* foll. by *of*) happy or pleased to have: *glad of her help.* ◆ *vb* **glads, gladding, gladded. 5** (*tr*) an archaic word for **gladden.** ORIG OE *glæd* ▸ **ˈgladly** *adv* ▸ **ˈgladness** *n*

glad[2] (glæd) *n Inf.* short for **gladiolus.**

Gladbeck ★ (*German* ˈglatbɛk) *n* a city in NW Germany, in North Rhine-Westphalia. Pop.: 79 190 (1989 est.).

gladden (ˈglædᵊn) *vb* to make or become glad and joyful. ▸ **ˈgladdener** *n*

glade (gleɪd) *n* an open place in a forest; clearing. ORIG C16: from ?; ? rel. to GLAD[1] (in obs. sense: bright); see GLEAM

glad eye *n Inf.* an inviting or seductive glance (esp. in **give** (**someone**) **the glad eye**).

gladiator (ˈglædɪˌeɪtə) *n* **1** (in ancient Rome) a man trained to fight in arenas to provide entertainment. **2** a person who supports and fights publicly for a cause. ORIG C16: from L: swordsman, from *gladius* sword ▸ **gladiatorial** (ˌglædɪəˈtɔːrɪəl) *adj*

gladiolus (ˌglædɪˈəʊləs) *n, pl* **gladiolus, gladioli** (-laɪ), *or* **gladioluses.** any plant of a widely cultivated genus having sword-shaped leaves and spikes of funnel-shaped brightly coloured flowers. Also called: **gladiola.** ORIG C16: from L: a small sword, sword lily, from *gladius* a sword

glad rags *pl n Inf.* best clothes or clothes used on special occasions.

gladsome ('glædsəm) *adj* an archaic word for **glad**[1].
▸ **'gladsomely** *adv* ▸ **'gladsomeness** *n*

Gladstone ★ ('glædstən) *n* **William Ewart.** 1809–98, British statesman. He became leader of the Liberal Party in 1867 and was prime minister (1868–74; 1880–85; 1886; 1892–94).

Gladstone bag *n* a piece of hand luggage consisting of two equal-sized hinged compartments. ORIG C19: after W. E. GLADSTONE

Glagolitic (ˌglægə'lɪtɪk) *adj* of, relating to, or denoting a Slavic alphabet whose invention is attributed to Saint Cyril. ORIG C19: from NL, from Serbo-Croat *glagolica* the Glagolitic alphabet

glair (glɛə) *n* **1** white of egg, esp. when used as a size or adhesive. **2** any substance resembling this. ◆ *vb* **3** (*tr*) to apply glair to (something). ORIG C14: from OF *glaire*, from Vulgar L *clāria* (unattested) CLEAR, from L *clārus*
▸ **'glairy** *or* **'glaireous** *adj*

glam (glæm) *adj Inf.* short for **glamorous.**

Glamorgan (glə'mɔːgən) *or* **Glamorganshire** ★ (glə'mɔːgənˌʃɪə, -ʃə) *n* a former county of SE Wales, now administered by Swansea county and six county boroughs.

glamorize, glamorise, *or US (sometimes)* **glamourize** ('glæməˌraɪz) *vb* **glamorizes, glamorizing, glamorized; glamorises, glamorising, glamorised** *or US (sometimes)* **glamourizes, glamourizing, glamourized.** (*tr*) to cause to be or seem glamorous; romanticize or beautify.
▸ **ˌglamori'zation** *or* **ˌglamori'sation** *n*

glamorous ('glæmərəs) *adj* **1** possessing glamour; alluring and fascinating. **2** beautiful and smart, esp. in a showy way: *a glamorous woman.*
▸ **'glamorously** *adv*

glamour *or US (sometimes)* **glamor** ('glæmə) *n* **1** charm and allure; fascination. **2a** fascinating or voluptuous beauty. **2b** (*as modifier*): *a glamour girl.* **3** *Arch.* a magic spell; charm. ORIG C18: Scot. var. of GRAMMAR (hence a magic spell, because occult practices were popularly associated with learning)

glance[1] (glɑːns) *vb* **glances, glancing, glanced. 1** (*intr*) to look hastily or briefly. **2** (*intr; foll. by over, through,* etc.) to look over briefly: *to glance through a report.* **3** (*intr*) to reflect, glint, or gleam: *the sun glanced on the water.* **4** (*intr; usually foll. by off*) to depart (from an object struck) at an oblique angle: *the arrow glanced off the tree.* ◆ *n* **5** a hasty or brief look; peep. **6** a flash or glint of light; gleam. **7** the act or an instance of an object glancing off another. **8** a brief allusion. ORIG C15: from *glacen* to strike obliquely, from OF *glacier* to slide (see GLACIS)
▸ **'glancing** *adj* ▸ **'glancingly** *adv*

> **USAGE NOTE** *Glance* is sometimes wrongly used where *glimpse* is meant: *he caught a glimpse* (not *glance*) *of her making her way through the crowd.*

glance[2] (glɑːns) *n* any mineral having a metallic lustre. ORIG C19: from G *Glanz* brightness, lustre

gland[1] (glænd) *n* **1** a cell or organ in man and other animals that synthesizes chemical substances and secretes them for the body to use or eliminate, either through a duct (exocrine gland) or directly into the bloodstream (endocrine gland). **2** a structure, such as a lymph node, that resembles a gland in form. **3** a cell or organ in plants that synthesizes and secretes a particular substance. ORIG C17: from L *glāns* acorn

gland[2] (glænd) *n* a device that prevents leakage of fluid along a rotating shaft or reciprocating rod passing between areas of high and low pressure. It often consists of a flanged metal sleeve bedding into a stuffing box. ORIG C19: from ?

glanders ('glændəz) *n* (*functioning as sing*) a highly infectious bacterial disease of horses, sometimes communicated to man, characterized by inflammation and ulceration of the mucous membranes of the air passages, skin and lymph glands. ORIG C16: from OF *glandres*, from L *glandulae*, lit.: little acorns, from *glāns* acorn; see GLAND[1]

glandular ('glændjʊlə) *or* **glandulous** ('glændjʊləs) *adj* of, relating to, containing, functioning as, or affecting a gland. ORIG C18: from L *glandula*, lit.: a little acorn; see GLANDERS
▸ **'glandularly** *or* **'glandulously** *adv*

glandular fever *n* another name for **infectious mononucleosis.**

glandule ('glændjuːl) *n* a small gland.

glans (glænz) *n, pl* **glandes** ('glændiːz). *Anat.* any small rounded body or glandlike mass, such as the head of the penis (**glans penis**). ORIG C17: from L: acorn; see GLAND[1]

glare (glɛə) *vb* **glares, glaring, glared. 1** (*intr*) to stare angrily; glower. **2** (*tr*) to express by glowering. **3** (*intr*) (of light, colour, etc.) to be very bright and intense. **4** (*intr*) to be dazzlingly ornamented or garish. ◆ *n* **5** an angry stare. **6** a dazzling light or brilliance. **7** garish ornamentation or appearance. ORIG C13: prob. from MLow G, MDu. *glaren* to gleam

glaring ('glɛərɪŋ) *adj* **1** conspicuous: *a glaring omission.* **2** dazzling or garish.
▸ **'glaringly** *adv* ▸ **'glaringness** *n*

Glarus ★ (*German* 'glaːrʊs) *n* **1** an Alpine canton of E central Switzerland. Capital: Glarus. Pop.: 39 388 (1995 est.). Area 684 sq. km (264 sq. miles). **2** a town in E central Switzerland, the capital of Glarus canton. Pop.: 5541 (1990). ◆ French name: **Glaris** (glari).

Glaser ★ ('gleɪzə) *n* **Donald Arthur.** born 1926, US physicist: invented the bubble chamber; Nobel prize for physics 1960.

Glasgow ★ ('glɑːzgəʊ, 'glæz-) *n* **1** a city in W central Scotland, in City of Glasgow council area on the River Clyde: the largest city in Scotland; centre of a major industrial region, formerly an important port; seat of The University of Glasgow (1451), The University of Strathclyde (1964), and Glasgow Caledonian University (1992). Pop.: 662 954 (1991). Related adj: **Glaswegian. 2 City of.** a council area in W Scotland. Pop.: 623 850 (1996 est.). Area: 175 sq. km (68 sq. miles).

glasnost ('glæsˌnɒst) *n* the policy of public frankness and accountability developed in the former Soviet Union under the leadership of Mikhail Gorbachov. ORIG C20: Russian, lit.: publicity, openness

glass (glɑːs) *n* **1a** a hard brittle transparent or translucent noncrystalline solid, consisting of metal silicates or similar compounds. It is made from a fused mixture of oxides, such as lime, silicon dioxide, phosphorus pentoxide, etc. **1b** (*as modifier*): *a glass bottle.* Related adj: **vitreous. 2** something made of glass, esp. a drinking vessel, a barometer, or a mirror. **3** Also called: **glassful.** the amount or volume contained in a drinking glass: *he drank a glass of wine.* **4** glassware collectively. **5** See **fibreglass.** ◆ *vb* **6** (*tr*) to cover with, enclose in, or fit with glass. ORIG OE *glæs*
▸ **'glassless** *adj* ▸ **'glassˌlike** *adj*

Glass ★ (glɑːs) *n* **Philip.** born 1937, US avant-garde composer: his works include *Music in Fifths* (1970) and *Monsters of Grace* (1998).

glass-blowing *n* the process of shaping a mass of molten glass by blowing air into it through a tube.
▸ **'glass-ˌblower** *n*

glass ceiling *n* a situation in which progress, esp. promotion, appears to be possible but restrictions or discrimination create a barrier that prevents it.

glasses ('glɑːsɪz) *pl n* a pair of lenses for correcting faulty vision, in a frame that rests on the bridge of the nose and hooks behind the ears. Also called: **spectacles, eyeglasses.**

glass fibre *n* another name for **fibreglass.**

glass harmonica *n* a musical instrument of the 18th century consisting of a set of glass bowls of graduated pitches, played by rubbing the fingers over the moistened rims or by a keyboard mechanism. Sometimes shortened to **harmonica.** Also called: **musical glasses.**

glasshouse ('glɑːsˌhaʊs) *n* **1** *Brit.* a glass building, esp. a greenhouse, used for growing plants in protected or controlled conditions. **2** *Inf., chiefly Brit.* a military detention centre.

glassine (glæ'siːn) *n* a glazed translucent paper.

glass snake *n* any snakelike lizard of Europe, Asia, or North America, with vestigial hind limbs and a tail that breaks off easily.

glassware ('glɑːsˌwɛə) *n* articles made of glass, esp. drinking glasses.

glass wool *n* fine spun glass massed into a wool-like bulk, used in insulation, filtering, etc.

glasswort ('glɑːsˌwɜːt) *n* **1** any plant of salt marshes having fleshy stems and scalelike leaves: formerly used as a source of soda for glass-making. **2** another name for **saltwort**.

glassy ('glɑːsɪ) *adj* **glassier, glassiest. 1** resembling glass, esp. in smoothness or transparency. **2** void of expression, life, or warmth: *a glassy stare.*
▸ **'glassily** *adv* ▸ **'glassiness** *n*

Glastonbury ★ ('glæstənbərɪ, -brɪ) *n* a town in SW England, in Somerset: remains of prehistoric lake villages; the reputed burial place of King Arthur; site of a ruined Benedictine abbey, probably the oldest in England. Pop.: 7747 (1991).

Glaswegian (glæz'wiːdʒən) *adj* **1** of or relating to Glasgow or its inhabitants. ◆ *n* **2** a native or inhabitant of Glasgow. ORIG C19: infl. by NORWEGIAN

Glauber's salt ('glaʊbəz) *or* **Glauber salt** *n* the crystalline decahydrate of sodium sulphate: used in making glass, detergents, and pulp. ORIG C18: after J. R. *Glauber* (1604–68), G chemist

Glauce ★ ('glɔːsɪ) *n Greek myth.* **1** the second bride of Jason, murdered on her wedding day by Medea, whom Jason had deserted. **2** a sea nymph, one of the Nereids.

glaucoma (glɔː'kəʊmə) *n* a disease of the eye in which increased pressure within the eyeball causes impaired vision, sometimes progressing to blindness. ORIG C17: from L, from Gk, from *glaukos;* see GLAUCOUS
▸ **glau'comatous** *adj*

glaucous ('glɔːkəs) *adj* **1** *Bot.* covered with a waxy or powdery bloom. **2** bluish-green. ORIG C17: from L *glaucus* silvery, bluish-green, from Gk *glaukos*

glaze (gleɪz) *vb* **glazes, glazing, glazed. 1** (*tr*) to fit or cover with glass. **2** (*tr*) *Ceramics.* to cover with a vitreous solution, rendering impervious to liquid. **3** (*tr*) to cover (foods) with a shiny coating by applying beaten egg, sugar, etc. **4** (*tr*) to make glossy or shiny. **5** (when *intr,* often foll. by *over*) to become or cause to become glassy: *his eyes were glazing over.* ◆ *n* **6** *Ceramics.* **6a** a vitreous coating. **6b** the substance used to produce such a coating. **7** a smooth lustrous finish on a fabric produced by applying various chemicals. **8** something used to give a glossy surface to foods: *a syrup glaze.* ORIG C14 *glasen,* from *glas* GLASS
▸ **glazed** *adj* ▸ **'glazer** *n*

glaze ice *n Brit.* a thin clear layer of ice caused by the freezing of rain in the air or by refreezing after a thaw.

glazier ('gleɪzɪə) *n* a person who fits windows, doors, etc., with glass.
▸ **'glaziery** *n*

glazing ('gleɪzɪŋ) *n* **1** the surface of a glazed object. **2** glass fitted, or to be fitted, in a door, frame, etc.

Glazunov ★ ('glæzunɒf; *Russian* glәzu'nɔf) *n* **Aleksandr Konstantinovich** (alɪk'sandr kәnstan'tinәvitʃ). 1865–1936, Russian composer, in France from 1928. A pupil of Rimsky-Korsakov, his works include eight symphonies and concertos for piano and for violin.

GLC *abbrev. for* Greater London Council; abolished 1986.

gleam (gliːm) *n* **1** a small beam or glow of light, esp. reflected light. **2** a brief or dim indication: *a gleam of hope.* ◆ *vb* (*intr*) **3** to send forth or reflect a beam of light. **4** to appear, esp. briefly. ORIG OE *glǣm*
▸ **'gleaming** *adj* ▸ **'gleamingly** *adv* ▸ **'gleamy** *adj*

glean (gliːn) *vb* **1** to gather (something) slowly and carefully in small pieces: *to glean information.* **2** to gather (the useful remnants of a crop) from the field after harvesting. ORIG C14: from OF *glener,* from LL *glennāre,* prob. of Celtic origin
▸ **'gleaner** *n*

gleanings ('gliːnɪŋz) *pl n* the useful remnants of a crop that can be gathered from the field after harvesting.

glebe (gliːb) *n* **1** *Brit. history.* land granted to a clergyman as part of his benefice. **2** *Poetic.* land, esp. for growing things. ORIG C14: from L *glaeba*

glee (gliː) *n* **1** great merriment or delight, often caused by someone else's misfortune. **2** a type of song originating in 18th-century England, sung by three or more unaccompanied voices. ORIG OE *gléo*

glee club *n Now chiefly US & Canad.* a society organized for the singing of choral music.

gleeful ('gliːfʊl) *adj* full of glee; merry.
▸ **'gleefully** *adv* ▸ **'gleefulness** *n*

gleeman ('gliːmən) *n, pl* **gleemen.** *Obs.* a minstrel.

Gleiwitz ★ ('glaɪvɪts) *n* the German name for **Gliwice.**

glen (glɛn) *n* a narrow and deep mountain valley, esp. in Scotland or Ireland. ORIG C15: from Scot. Gaelic *gleann,* from OIrish *glend*

Glen Albyn ★ ('ælbɪn, 'ɔːl-) *n* another name for the **Great Glen.**

Glencoe ★ (glɛn'kəʊ) *n* a glen in W Scotland, in S Highland: site of a massacre of Macdonalds by Campbells and English troops (1692).

Glendower ★ (glɛn'daʊə) *n* **Owen,** Welsh name *Owain Glyndŵr.* ?1350–?1416, Welsh chieftain, who led a revolt against Henry IV's rule in Wales (1400–15).

glengarry (glɛn'gærɪ) *n, pl* **glengarries.** a brimless Scottish cap with a crease down the crown, often with ribbons at the back. Also called: **glengarry bonnet.** ORIG C19: after *Glengarry,* Scotland

Glen More ★ (mɔː) *n* another name for the **Great Glen.**

Glenn ★ (glɛn) *n* **John.** born 1921, US astronaut and politician. The first American to orbit the earth (Feb., 1962), he later became a senator. In 1998, as a passenger aboard the space shuttle, he became the oldest person to have gone into space.

Glenrothes ★ (glɛn'rɒθɪs) *n* a new town in E central Scotland, the administrative centre of Fife: founded in 1948. Pop.: 38 650 (1991).

glia ('gliːə) *n* the delicate web of connective tissue that surrounds and supports nerve cells. Also called: **neuroglia.**
▸ **'glial** *adj*

glib (glɪb) *adj* **glibber, glibbest.** fluent and easy, often in an insincere or deceptive way. ORIG C16: prob. from MLow G *glibberich* slippery
▸ **'glibly** *adv* ▸ **'glibness** *n*

glide (glaɪd) *vb* **glides, gliding, glided. 1** to move or cause to move easily without jerks or hesitations. **2** (*intr*) to pass slowly or without perceptible change: *to glide into sleep.* **3** to cause (an aircraft) to come into land without engine power, or (of an aircraft) to land in this way. **4** (*intr*) to fly a glider. **5** (*intr*) *Music.* to execute a portamento from one note to another. **6** (*intr*) *Phonetics.* to produce a glide. ◆ *n* **7** a smooth easy movement. **8a** any of various dances featuring gliding steps. **8b** a step in such a dance. **9** a manoeuvre in which an aircraft makes a gentle descent without engine power. **10** the act or process of gliding. **11** *Music.* a portamento or slur. **12** *Phonetics.* a transitional sound as the speech organs pass from the articulatory position of one speech sound to that of the next. ORIG OE *glīdan*
▸ **'glidingly** *adv*

glide path *or* **glide slope** *n* the path of an aircraft as it descends to land.

glider ('glaɪdə) *n* **1** an aircraft capable of gliding and soaring in air currents without the use of an engine. **2** a person or thing that glides.

glide time *n* the NZ term for **flexitime.**

glimmer ('glɪmə) *vb* (*intr*) **1** (of a light) to glow faintly or flickeringly. **2** to be indicated faintly: *hope glimmered in his face.* ◆ *n* **3** a glow or twinkle of light. **4** a faint indication. ORIG C14: cf. MHG *glimmern*
▸ **'glimmeringly** *adv*

glimpse (glɪmps) *n* **1** a brief or incomplete view: *to catch a glimpse of the sea.* **2** a vague indication. **3** *Arch.* a glimmer of light. ◆ *vb* **glimpses, glimpsing, glimpsed. 4** (*tr*) to catch sight of momentarily. ORIG C14: of Gmc origin; cf. MHG *glimsen* to glimmer
▸ **'glimpser** *n*

> **USAGE NOTE** *Glimpse* is sometimes wrongly used where *glance* is meant: *he gave a quick glance* (not *glimpse*) at his watch.

Glinka ★ (*Russian* 'glinkə) *n* **Mikhail Ivanovich** (mixa'il i'vanəvitʃ). 1803–57, Russian composer. His operas include *Russlan and Ludmilla* (1842).

glint (glɪnt) *vb* **1** to gleam or cause to gleam brightly. ◆ *n* **2** a bright gleam or flash. **3** brightness or gloss. **4** a brief indication. ORIG C15: prob. from ON

glioma (glaɪ'əʊmə) *n, pl* **gliomata** (-mətə) *or* **gliomas**. a tumour of the brain and spinal cord, composed of glia cells and fibres. ORIG C19: from NL, from Gk *glia* glue + -OMA

glissade (glɪ'sɑːd, -'seɪd) *n* **1** a gliding step in ballet. **2** a controlled slide down a snow slope. ◆ *vb* **glissades, glissading, glissaded. 3** (*intr*) to perform a glissade. ORIG C19: from F, from *glisser* to slip, from OF *glicier*, of Frankish origin

glissando (glɪ'sændəʊ) *n, pl* **glissandi** (-diː) *or* **glissandos**. a rapidly executed series of notes, each of which is discretely audible. ORIG C19: prob. It. var. of GLISSADE

glisten ('glɪsᵊn) *vb* (*intr*) **1** (of a wet or glossy surface) to gleam by reflecting light. **2** (of light) to reflect with brightness: *the sunlight glistens on wet leaves.* ◆ *n* **3** *Rare.* a gleam or gloss. ORIG OE *glisnian*

glister ('glɪstə) *vb, n* an archaic word for **glitter**. ORIG C14: prob. from MDu. *glisteren*

glitch (glɪtʃ) *n* **1** a sudden instance of malfunctioning in an electronic system. **2** a change in the rotation rate of a pulsar. ORIG C20: from ?

glitter ('glɪtə) *vb* (*intr*) **1** (of a hard, wet, or polished surface) to reflect light in bright flashes. **2** (of light) to be reflected in bright flashes. **3** (usually foll. by *with*) to be decorated or enhanced by the glamour (of): *the show glitters with famous actors.* ◆ *n* **4** sparkle or brilliance. **5** show and glamour. **6** tiny pieces of shiny decorative material. **7** *Canad.* Also called: **silver thaw**. ice formed from freezing rain. ORIG C14: from ON *glitra*
▸ **'glitteringly** *adv* ▸ **'glittery** *adj*

glitterati (ˌglɪtə'rɑːtiː) *pl n Inf.* the leaders of society, esp. the rich and beautiful. ORIG C20: from GLITTER + *-ati* as in LITERATI

glitzy ('glɪtsɪ) *adj* **glitzier, glitziest**. *Sl.* showily attractive; flashy or glittery. ORIG C20: prob. via Yiddish from G *glitzern* to glitter

Gliwice ★ (*Polish* gli'vitsɛ) *n* an industrial city in S Poland. Pop.: 214 000 (1996 est.). German name: **Gleiwitz**.

gloaming ('gləʊmɪŋ) *n Scot. or poetic.* twilight or dusk. ORIG OE *glōmung*, from *glōm*

gloat (gləʊt) *vb* **1** (*intr*; often foll. by *over*) to dwell (on) with malevolent smugness or exultation. ◆ *n* **2** the act of gloating. ORIG C16: prob. of Scand. origin; cf. ON *glotta* to grin, MHG *glotzen* to stare
▸ **'gloater** *n*

glob (glɒb) *n Inf.* a rounded mass of some thick fluid substance. ORIG C20: prob. from GLOBE, infl. by BLOB

global ('gləʊbᵊl) *adj* **1** covering or relating to the whole world. **2** comprehensive; total.
▸ **'globally** *adv*

globalization *or* **globalisation** (ˌgləʊbᵊlaɪ'zeɪʃən) *n* **1** the process enabling financial and investment markets to operate internationally, largely as a result of deregulation and improved communications. **2** the process by which a company, etc., expands to operate internationally.

globalize *or* **globalise** ('gləʊbᵊˌlaɪz) *vb* **globalizes, globalizing, globalized** *or* **globalises, globalising, globalised**. (*tr*) to put into effect or spread worldwide.

global product *n* a commercial product, such as Coca Cola, that is marketed throughout the world under the same brand name.

global warming *n* an increase in the average temperature worldwide believed to be caused by the greenhouse effect.

globe (gləʊb) *n* **1** a sphere on which a map of the world is drawn. **2 the globe**. the world; the earth. **3** a planet or some other astronomical body. **4** an object shaped like a sphere, such as a glass lampshade or fishbowl. **5** an orb, usually of gold, symbolic of sovereignty. **6** *Austral., NZ, & S. African.* an electric light bulb. ◆ *vb* **globes, globing, globed. 7** to form or cause to form into a globe. ORIG C16: from OF, from L *globus*
▸ **'globeˌlike** *adj*

globefish ('gləʊbˌfɪʃ) *n, pl* **globefish** *or* **globefishes**. another name for **puffer**.

globeflower ('gləʊbˌflaʊə) *n* a plant having pale yellow, white, or orange globe-shaped flowers.

globetrotter ('gləʊbˌtrɒtə) *n* a habitual worldwide traveller, esp. a tourist.
▸ **'globeˌtrotting** *n, adj*

globigerina (gləʊˌbɪdʒə'raɪnə) *n, pl* **globigerinas** *or* **globigerinae** (-niː). **1** a marine protozoan having a rounded shell with spiny processes. **2 globigerina ooze**. a deposit on the ocean floor consisting of the shells of these protozoans. ORIG C19: from NL, from L *globus* GLOBE + *gerere* to bear

globoid ('gləʊbɔɪd) *adj* **1** shaped like a globe. ◆ *n* **2** a globoid body.

globose ('gləʊbəʊs, gləʊ'bəʊs) *or* **globous** ('gləʊbəs) *adj* spherical or approximately spherical. ORIG C15: from L *globōsus*; see GLOBE
▸ **'globosely** *adv*

globular ('glɒbjʊlə) *or* **globulous** *adj* **1** shaped like a globe or globule. **2** having or consisting of globules.

globule ('glɒbjuːl) *n* a small globe, esp. a drop of liquid. ORIG C17: from L *globulus*, dim. of *globus* GLOBE

globulin ('glɒbjʊlɪn) *n* any of a group of simple proteins that are generally insoluble in water but soluble in salt solutions.

glockenspiel ('glɒkənˌspiːl, -ˌʃpiːl) *n* a percussion instrument consisting of a set of tuned metal plates played with a pair of small hammers. ORIG C19: G, from *Glocken* bells + *Spiel* play

glomerate ('glɒmərɪt) *adj* **1** gathered into a compact rounded mass. **2** *Anat.* (esp. of glands) conglomerate in structure. ORIG C18: from L *glomerāre*, from *glomus* ball
▸ **ˌglome'ration** *n*

glomerule ('glɒməˌruːl) *n Bot.* an inflorescence in the form of a ball-like cluster of flowers. ORIG C18: from NL *glomerulus*

Glomma ★ (*Norwegian* 'glɔma) *n* a river in SE Norway, rising near the border with Sweden and flowing generally south to the Skagerrak: the largest river in Scandinavia; important for hydroelectric power and floating timber. Length: 588 km (365 miles).

gloom (gluːm) *n* **1** partial or total darkness. **2** a state of depression or melancholy. **3** an appearance or expression of despondency or melancholy. **4** *Poetic.* a dim or dark place. ◆ *vb* **5** (*intr*) to look sullen or depressed. **6** to make or become dark or gloomy. ORIG C14 *gloumben* to look sullen

gloomy ('gluːmɪ) *adj* **gloomier, gloomiest. 1** dark or dismal. **2** causing depression or gloom: *gloomy news.* **3** despairing; sad.
▸ **'gloomily** *adv* ▸ **'gloominess** *n*

gloop (gluːp) *or esp. US* **glop** (glɒp) *n Inf.* any messy sticky fluid or substance. ORIG C20: from ?
▸ **'gloopy** *or esp. US* **'gloppy** *adj*

gloria ('glɔːrɪə) *n* a halo or nimbus, esp. as represented in art. ORIG C16: from L: GLORY

Gloria ('glɔːrɪə, -ˌɑː) *n* **1** any of several doxologies beginning with the word *Gloria*. **2** a musical setting of one of these.

glorify ('glɔːrɪˌfaɪ) *vb* **glorifies, glorifying, glorified**. (*tr*) **1** to make glorious. **2** to make more splendid; adorn. **3** to worship, exalt, or adore. **4** to extol. **5** to cause to seem more splendid or imposing than reality.
▸ **ˌglorifi'cation** *n*

gloriole ('glɔːrɪˌəʊl) *n* another name for a **halo**. ORIG C19: from L *glōriola*, lit.: a small GLORY

glorious ('glɔːrɪəs) *adj* **1** having or full of glory; illustri-

ous. **2** conferring glory or renown: *a glorious victory.* **3** brilliantly beautiful. **4** delightful or enjoyable.
▸ **'gloriously** *adv* ▸ **'gloriousness** *n*

glory ('glɔːrɪ) *n, pl* **glories. 1** exaltation, praise, or honour. **2** something that brings or is worthy of praise (esp. in **crowning glory**). **3** thanksgiving, adoration, or worship: *glory be to God.* **4** pomp; splendour: *the glory of the king's reign.* **5** radiant beauty; resplendence: *the glory of the sunset.* **6** the beauty and bliss of heaven. **7** a state of extreme happiness or prosperity. **8** another word for **halo** or **nimbus.** ◆ *vb* **glories, glorying, gloried. 9** (*intr;* often foll. by *in*) to triumph or exalt. ◆ *interj* **10** *Inf.* a mild interjection to express pleasure or surprise (often **glory be!**). ORIG C13: from OF *glorie,* from L *glōria,* from ?

glory box *n Austral. & NZ.* (esp. formerly) a box in which a young woman stores clothes, etc., in preparation for marriage.

glory hole *n* **1** a cupboard or storeroom, esp. one which is very untidy. **2** *Naut.* another term for **lazaretto** (sense 1).

Glos *abbrev. for* Gloucestershire.

gloss[1] (glɒs) *n* **1a** lustre or sheen, as of a smooth surface. **1b** (*as modifier*): *gloss paint.* **2** a superficially attractive appearance. **3** a cosmetic used to give a sheen. ◆ *vb* **4** to give a gloss to or obtain a gloss. **5** (*tr;* often foll. by *over*) to hide under a deceptively attractive surface or appearance. ORIG C16: prob. of Scand. origin
▸ **'glosser** *n*

gloss[2] (glɒs) *n* **1** a short or expanded explanation or interpretation of a word, expression, or foreign phrase in the margin or text of a manuscript, etc. **2** an intentionally misleading explanation. **3** short for **glossary.** ◆ *vb* (*tr*) **4** to add glosses to. **5** (often foll. by *over*) to give a false or misleading interpretation of. ORIG C16: from L *glōssa* unusual word requiring explanatory note, from Ionic Gk

glossary ('glɒsərɪ) *n, pl* **glossaries.** an alphabetical list of terms peculiar to a field of knowledge with explanations. ORIG C14: from LL *glossārium;* see GLOSS[2]
▸ **glossarial** (glɒ'sɛərɪəl) *adj* ▸ **'glossarist** *n*

glosseme ('glɒsiːm) *n* the smallest meaningful unit of a language, such as stress, form, etc. ORIG C20: from Gk; see GLOSS[2], -EME

glossitis (glɒ'saɪtɪs) *n* inflammation of the tongue.
▸ **glossitic** (glɒ'sɪtɪk) *adj*

glosso- *or before a vowel* **gloss-** *combining form.* indicating a tongue or language: *glossolaryngeal.* ORIG from Gk *glossa* tongue

glossolalia (ˌglɒsə'leɪlɪə) *n* another term for **gift of tongues.** ORIG C19: NL, from GLOSSO- + Gk *lalein* to babble

glossy ('glɒsɪ) *adj* **glossier, glossiest. 1** smooth and shiny; lustrous. **2** superficially attractive; plausible. **3** (of a magazine) lavishly produced on shiny paper. ◆ *n, pl* **glossies. 4** Also called (US): **slick.** an expensively produced magazine, printed on shiny paper and containing high-quality colour photography. **5** a photograph printed on paper that has a smooth shiny surface.
▸ **'glossily** *adv* ▸ **'glossiness** *n*

glottal ('glɒtᵊl) *adj* **1** of or relating to the glottis. **2** *Phonetics.* articulated or pronounced at or with the glottis.

glottal stop *n* a plosive speech sound produced by tightly closing the glottis and allowing the air pressure to build up before opening the glottis, causing the air to escape with force.

glottis ('glɒtɪs) *n, pl* **glottises** *or* **glottides** (-tɪˌdiːz). the vocal apparatus of the larynx, consisting of the two true vocal cords and the opening between them. ORIG C16: from NL, from Gk, from Attic form of Ionic *glōssa* tongue; see GLOSS[2]

Gloucester[1] ★ ('glɒstə) *n* a city in SW England, administrative centre of Gloucestershire, on the River Severn; cathedral (founded 1100). Pop.: 104 800 (1993 est.). Latin name: **Glevum** ('gliːvʊm).

Gloucester[2] ★ ('glɒstə) *n* **1 Humphrey,** Duke of. 1391–1447, English soldier and statesman; son of Henry IV. He acted as protector during Henry VI's minority (1422–29) and was noted for his patronage of humanists. **2 Duke of.** See **Richard III. 3 Duke of.** See **Thomas of Woodstock.**

Gloucestershire ★ ('glɒstəˌʃɪə, -ʃə) *n* a county of SW England, situated around the lower Severn valley: contains the Forest of Dean and the main part of the Cotswold Hills; includes the unitary authority of South Gloucestershire. Administrative centre: Gloucester. Pop. (excluding South Gloucestershire): 552 700 (1995 est.). Area (excluding South Gloucestershire): 2643 sq. km (1020 sq. miles). Abbrev.: **Glos.**

glove (glʌv) *n* **1** (*often pl*) a shaped covering for the hand with individual sheaths for the fingers and thumb, made of leather, fabric, etc. **2** any of various large protective hand covers worn in sports, such as a boxing glove. ◆ *vb* **gloves, gloving, gloved. 3** (*tr*) to cover or provide with or as if with gloves. ORIG OE *glōfe*

glove box *n* a closed box in which toxic or radioactive substances can be handled by an operator who places his hands through protective gloves sealed to the box.

glove compartment *n* a small compartment in a car dashboard for the storage of miscellaneous articles.

glover ('glʌvə) *n* a person who makes or sells gloves.

glow (gləʊ) *n* **1** light emitted by a substance or object at a high temperature. **2** a steady even light without flames. **3** brilliance of colour. **4** brightness of complexion. **5** a feeling of wellbeing or satisfaction. **6** intensity of emotion. ◆ *vb* (*intr*) **7** to emit a steady even light without flames. **8** to shine intensely, as if from great heat. **9** to be exuberant, as from excellent health or intense emotion. **10** to experience a feeling of wellbeing or satisfaction: *to glow with pride.* **11** (esp. of the complexion) to show a strong bright colour, esp. red. **12** to be very hot. ORIG OE *glōwan*

glow discharge *n* a silent luminous discharge of electricity through a low-pressure gas.

glower ('glaʊə) *vb* **1** (*intr*) to stare hard and angrily. ◆ *n* **2** a sullen or angry stare. ORIG C16: prob. of Scand. origin
▸ **'gloweringly** *adv*

glowing ('gləʊɪŋ) *adj* **1** emitting light without flames: *glowing embers.* **2** warm and rich in colour: *glowing shades of gold and orange.* **3** flushed and rosy: *glowing cheeks.* **4** displaying or indicative of extreme pride or emotion: *a glowing account of his son's achievements.*

glow-worm *n* a European beetle, the females and larvae of which bear luminescent organs producing a soft greenish light.

gloxinia (glɒk'sɪnɪə) *n* any of several tropical plants cultivated for their large white, red, or purple bell-shaped flowers. ORIG C19: after Benjamin P. *Gloxin,* 18th-cent. G physician & botanist

gloze (gləʊz) *vb* **glozes, glozing, glozed.** *Arch.* **1** (*tr;* often foll. by *over*) to explain away; minimize the effect or importance of. **2** to make explanatory notes or glosses on (a text). **3** to use flattery (on). ORIG C13: from OF *glosser* to comment; see GLOSS[2]

Gluck ★ (*German* glʊk) *n* **Christoph Willibald von** ('krɪstɔf 'vɪlibalt fɔn). 1714–87, German composer, esp. of operas, including *Orfeo ed Euridice* (1762) and *Alceste* (1767).

glucose ('gluːkəʊz, -kəʊs) *n* **1** a white crystalline sugar, the most abundant form being dextrose. Formula: $C_6H_{12}O_6$. **2** a yellowish syrup obtained by incomplete hydrolysis of starch: used in confectionery, fermentation, etc. ORIG C19: from F, from Gk *gleukos* sweet wine; rel. to Gk *glukus* sweet

glucoside ('gluːkəʊˌsaɪd) *n Biochem.* any of a large group of glycosides that yield glucose on hydrolysis.
▸ **glucosidic** (ˌgluːkəʊ'sɪdɪk) *adj*

glue (gluː) *n* **1** any natural or synthetic adhesive, esp. a sticky gelatinous substance prepared by boiling animal products such as bones, skin, and horns. **2** any other sticky or adhesive substance. ◆ *vb* **glues, gluing** *or* **glueing, glued. 3** (*tr*) to join or stick together as with glue. ORIG C14: from OF *glu,* from LL *glūs*
▸ **'glueˌlike** *adj* ▸ **'gluer** *n* ▸ **'gluey** *adj*

glue ear *n* accumulation of fluid in the middle ear in children, caused by infection and resulting in deafness.

glue-sniffing *n* the practice of inhaling the fumes of certain types of glue to produce intoxicating or hallucinatory effects.
▸ **'glue-ˌsniffer** *n*

★ people and places

gluhwein ('glu:ˌvaɪn) *n* mulled wine. ORIG G

glum (glʌm) *adj* **glummer, glummest.** silent or sullen, as from gloom. ORIG C16: var. of GLOOM
▸ **'glumly** *adv* ▸ **'glumness** *n*

glume (glu:m) *n Bot.* one of a pair of dry membranous bracts at the base of the spikelet of grasses. ORIG C18: from L *glūma* husk of corn
▸ **glu'maceous** *adj*

gluon ('glu:ɒn) *n* a hypothetical particle believed to be exchanged between quarks in order to bind them together to form particles. ORIG C20: coined from GLUE + -ON

glut (glʌt) *n* **1** an excessive amount, as in the production of a crop. **2** the act of glutting or state of being glutted. ◆ *vb* **gluts, glutting, glutted.** (*tr*) **3** to feed or supply beyond capacity. **4** to supply (a market, etc.) with a commodity in excess of the demand for it. ORIG C14: prob. from OF *gloutir,* from L *gluttīre;* see GLUTTON[1]

glutamic acid (glu:'tæmɪk) *n* an amino acid, occurring in proteins.

gluten ('glu:tᵊn) *n* a protein present in cereal grains, esp. wheat. ORIG C16: from L: GLUE
▸ **'glutenous** *adj*

gluteus (glʊ'ti:əs) *n, pl* **glutei** (-'ti:aɪ). any one of the three large muscles that form the human buttock. ORIG C17: from NL, from Gk *gloutos* buttock, rump
▸ **glu'teal** *adj*

glutinous ('glu:tɪnəs) *adj* resembling glue in texture; sticky.
▸ **'glutinously** *adv*

glutton[1] ('glʌtᵊn) *n* **1** a person devoted to eating and drinking to excess; greedy person. **2** a person who has or appears to have a voracious appetite for something: *a glutton for punishment.* ORIG C13: from OF *glouton,* from L from *gluttīre* to swallow
▸ **'gluttonous** *adj* ▸ **'gluttonously** *adv*

glutton[2] ('glʌtᵊn) *n* another name for **wolverine.** ORIG C17: from GLUTTON[1], apparently translating G *Vielfrass* great eater

gluttony ('glʌtənɪ) *n* the act or practice of eating to excess.

glyceride ('glɪsəˌraɪd) *n* any fatty-acid ester of glycerol.

glycerine ('glɪsəri:n, ˌglɪsə'ri:n) *or* **glycerin** ('glɪsərɪn) *n* another name (not in technical usage) for **glycerol.** ORIG C19: from F, from Gk *glukeros* sweet + *-ine* -IN; rel. to Gk *glukus* sweet

glycerol ('glɪsəˌrɒl) *n* a colourless odourless syrupy liquid: a by-product of soap manufacture, used as a solvent, antifreeze, plasticizer, and sweetener (**E422**). Formula: $CH_2OHCHOHCH_2OH$. ORIG C19: from GLYCER(IN) + -OL[1]

glycine ('glaɪsi:n, glaɪ'si:n) *n* a white sweet crystalline amino acid occurring in most proteins. ORIG C19: GLYCO- + -INE[2]

glyco- *or before a vowel* **glyc-** *combining form.* sugar: *glycogen.* ORIG from Gk *glukus* sweet

glycogen ('glaɪkəʊdʒən) *n* a polysaccharide consisting of glucose units: the form in which carbohydrate is stored in animals.
▸ **glycogenic** (ˌglaɪkəʊ'dʒenɪk) *adj* ▸ **ˌglyco'genesis** *n*

glycol ('glaɪkɒl) *n* another name (not in technical usage) for **ethanediol.**

glycolic acid (glaɪ'kɒlɪk) *n* a colourless crystalline compound found in sugar cane and sugar beet: used in the manufacture of pharmaceuticals, pesticides, and plasticizers.

glycolysis (glaɪ'kɒlɪsɪs) *n Biochem.* the breakdown of glucose by enzymes with the liberation of energy.

glycoside ('glaɪkəʊˌsaɪd) *n* any of a group of substances derived from simple sugars by replacing the hydroxyl group by another group.
▸ **glycosidic** (ˌglaɪkəʊ'sɪdɪk) *adj*

glycosuria (ˌglaɪkəʊ'sjʊərɪə) *n* the presence of excess sugar in the urine, as in diabetes. ORIG C19: from NL, from F *glycose* GLUCOSE + -URIA

Glyndebourne ★ ('glaɪndˌbɔ:n) *n* an estate in SE England, in East Sussex: site of an annual festival of opera, founded in 1934 by John Christie (1882–1962).

glyph (glɪf) *n* **1** a carved channel or groove, esp. a vertical one. **2** *Now rare.* another word for **hieroglyphic.** ORIG C18: from F, from Gk, from *gluphein* to carve
▸ **'glyphic** *adj*

glyphosate ('glaɪfəʊˌseɪt) *n* a systemic nonselective herbicide used in certain commercial weedkillers.

glyptic ('glɪptɪk) *adj* of or relating to engraving or carving, esp. on precious stones. ORIG C19: from F, from Gk, from *gluphein* to carve

glyptodont ('glɪptəˌdɒnt) *n* an extinct mammal of South America which resembled the giant armadillo. ORIG C19: from Gk *gluptos* carved + -ODONT

GM *abbrev. for:* **1** general manager. **2** genetically modified. **3** (in Britain) George Medal. **4** Grand Master. **5** grant-maintained.

G-man *n, pl* **G-men. 1** *US sl.* an FBI agent. **2** *Irish.* a political detective.

Gmc *abbrev. for* Germanic.

GMO *abbrev. for* genetically modified organism.

GMT *abbrev. for* Greenwich Mean Time.

GMWU (in Britain) *abbrev. for* National Union of General and Municipal Workers.

gnarl (nɑ:l) *n* **1** any knotty swelling on a tree. ◆ *vb* **2** (*tr*) to knot or cause to knot. ORIG C19: back formation from *gnarled*

gnarled (nɑ:ld) *or* **gnarly** *adj* **1** having gnarls: *the gnarled trunk of the old tree.* **2** (esp. of hands) rough, twisted, and weather-beaten.

gnash (næʃ) *vb* **1** to grind (the teeth) together, as in pain or anger. **2** (*tr*) to bite or chew as by grinding the teeth. ◆ *n* **3** the act of gnashing the teeth. ORIG C15: prob. from ON; cf. *gnastan* gnashing of teeth

gnat (næt) *n* any of various small fragile biting two-winged insects. ORIG OE *gnætt*

gnathic ('næθɪk) *adj Anat.* of or relating to the jaw. ORIG C19: from Gk *gnathos* jaw

-gnathous *adj combining form.* indicating or having a jaw of a specified kind: *prognathous.* ORIG from NL, from Gk *gnathos* jaw

gnaw (nɔ:) *vb* **gnaws, gnawing, gnawed; gnawed** *or* **gnawn. 1** (when *intr,* often foll. by *at* or *upon*) to bite (at) or chew (upon) constantly so as to wear away little by little. **2** (*tr*) to form by gnawing: *to gnaw a hole.* **3** to cause erosion of (something). **4** (when *intr,* often foll. by *at*) to cause constant distress or anxiety (to). ◆ *n* **5** the act or an instance of gnawing. ORIG OE *gnagan*

gnawing ('nɔ:ɪŋ) *n* a dull persistent pang or pain, esp. of hunger.

gneiss (naɪs) *n* any coarse-grained metamorphic rock that is banded or foliated. ORIG C18: from G *Gneis,* prob. from MHG *ganeist* spark
▸ **'gneissic, 'gneissoid,** *or* **'gneissose** *adj*

gnocchi ('nɒkɪ) *pl n* dumplings made of pieces of semolina pasta, or sometimes potato, served with sauce. ORIG It., pl of *gnocco* lump, prob. of Gmc origin

gnome (nəʊm) *n* **1** one of a species of legendary creatures, usually resembling small misshapen old men, said to live in the depths of the earth and guard buried treasure. **2** the statue of a gnome, esp. in a garden. **3** a very small or ugly person. **4** *Facetious or derog.* an international banker or financier (esp. in **gnomes of Zürich**). ORIG C18: from F, from NL *gnomus,* coined by Paracelsus (1493-1541), Swiss alchemist, from ?
▸ **'gnomish** *adj*

gnomic ('nəʊmɪk, 'nɒm-) *adj* of or relating to aphorisms; pithy.
▸ **'gnomically** *adv*

gnomon ('nəʊmɒn) *n* **1** the stationary arm that projects the shadow on a sundial. **2** a geometric figure remaining after a parallelogram has been removed from one corner of a larger parallelogram. ORIG C16: from L, from Gk: interpreter, from *gignōskein* to know
▸ **gno'monic** *adj*

-gnosis *n combining form.* (esp. in medicine) recognition or knowledge: *diagnosis.* ORIG via L from Gk: knowledge ▸ **-gnostic** *adj combining form.*

gnostic ('nɒstɪk) *adj* of, relating to, or possessing knowledge, esp. spiritual knowledge.

Gnostic ('nɒstɪk) *n* **1** an adherent of Gnosticism. ◆ *adj* **2** of or relating to Gnostics or to Gnosticism. ORIG C16: from LL, from Gk *gnōstikos* relating to knowledge

Gnosticism ('nɒstɪˌsɪzəm) *n* a religious movement characterized by a belief in intuitive spiritual knowledge: regarded as a heresy by the Christian Church.

gnotobiotic (ˌnəʊtəʊbaɪ'ɒtɪk) *adj* of or pertaining to germ-free conditions, esp. in a laboratory in which animals are injected with known strains of organisms. ORIG C20: from Gk *gnōtos*, from *gignōskein* to know + BIOTIC

GNP *abbrev. for* gross national product.

gnu (nuː) *n, pl* **gnus** *or* **gnu.** either of two sturdy antelopes inhabiting the savannas of Africa, having an oxlike head and a long tufted tail. Also called: **wildebeest.** ORIG C18: from Xhosa *nqu*

GNVQ (in Britain) *abbrev. for* general national vocational qualification: a qualification which rewards the development of skills likely to be of use to employers.

go (gəʊ) *vb* **goes, going, went, gone.** (*mainly intr*) **1** to move or proceed, esp. to or from a point or in a certain direction: *go home.* **2** (*tr; takes an infinitive,* often with *to* omitted or replaced by *and*) to proceed towards a particular person or place with some specified purpose: *I must go and get that book.* **3** to depart: *we'll have to go at eleven.* **4** to start, as in a race: often used in commands. **5** to make regular journeys: *this train service goes to the east coast.* **6** to operate or function effectively: *the radio won't go.* **7** (*copula*) to become: *his face went red.* **8** to make a noise as specified: *the gun went bang.* **9** to enter into a specified state or condition: *to go into hysterics.* **10** to be or continue to be in a specified state or condition: *to go in rags; to go in poverty.* **11** to lead, extend, or afford access: *this route goes to the north.* **12** to proceed towards an activity: *to go to sleep.* **13** (*tr; takes an infinitive*) to serve or contribute: *this letter goes to prove my point.* **14** to follow a course as specified; fare: *the lecture went badly.* **15** to be applied or allotted to a particular purpose or recipient: *his money went on drink.* **16** to be sold: *the necklace went for three thousand pounds.* **17** to be ranked; compare: *this meal is good as my meals go.* **18** to blend or harmonize: *these chairs won't go with the rest of your furniture.* **19** (foll. by *by* or *under*) to be known (by a name or disguise). **20** to have a usual or proper place: *those books go on this shelf.* **21** (of music, poetry, etc.) to be sounded; expressed, etc.: *how does that song go?* **22** to fail or give way: *my eyesight is going.* **23** to break down or collapse abruptly: *the ladder went at the critical moment.* **24** to die: *the old man went at 2 a.m.* **25** (often foll. by *by*) **25a** (of time, etc.) to elapse: *the hours go by so slowly.* **25b** to travel past: *the train goes by her house.* **25c** to be guided (by). **26** to occur: *happiness does not always go with riches.* **27** to be eliminated, abolished, or given up: *this entry must go to save space.* **28** to be spent or finished: *all his money has gone.* **29** to attend: *go to school.* **30** to join a stated profession: *go on the stage.* **31** (foll. by *to*) to have recourse (to); turn: *to go to arbitration.* **32** (foll. by *to*) to subject or put oneself (to): *she goes to great pains to please him.* **33** to proceed, esp. up to or beyond certain limits: *you will go too far one day and then you will be punished.* **34** to be acceptable or tolerated: *anything goes.* **35** to carry the weight of final authority: *what the boss says goes.* **36** (*tr*) *Nonstandard.* to say: *Then she goes, "Give it to me!" and she just snatched it.* **37** (foll. by *into*) to be contained in: *four goes into twelve three times.* **38** (often foll. by *for*) to endure or last out: *we can't go for much longer without water.* **39** (*tr*) *Cards.* to bet or bid: *I go two hearts.* **40 be going.** to intend or be about to start (to do or be doing something): often used as an alternative future construction: *what's going to happen to us?* **41 go and.** *Inf.* to be so foolish or unlucky as to: *then she had to go and lose her hat.* **42 go it.** *Sl.* to do something or move energetically. **43 go it alone.** *Inf.* to act or proceed without allies or help. **44 go one better.** *Inf.* to surpass or outdo (someone). **45 let go. 45a** to relax one's hold (on); release. **45b** to discuss or consider no further. **46 let oneself go. 46a** to act in an uninhibited manner. **46b** to lose interest in one's appearance, manners, etc. **47 to go. 47a** remaining. **47b** *US & Canad. inf.* (of food served by a restaurant) for taking away. ◆ *n, pl* **goes. 48** the act of going. **49a** an attempt or try: *he had a go at the stamp business.* **49b** an attempt at stopping a person suspected of a crime: *the police are not always in favour of the public having a go.* **49c** an attack, esp. verbal: *she had a real go at them.* **50** a turn: *it's my go next.* **51** *Inf.* the quality of being active and energetic: *she has much more go than I have.* **52** *Inf.* hard or energetic work: *it's all go.* **53** *Inf.* a successful venture or achievement: *he made a go of it.* **54** *Inf.* a bargain or agreement. **55 from the word go.** *Inf.* from the very beginning. **56 no go.** *Inf.* impossible; abortive or futile: *it's no go, I'm afraid.* **57 on the go.** *Inf.* active and energetic. ◆ *adj* **58** (*postpositive*) *Inf.* functioning properly and ready for action: esp. used in astronautics: *all systems are go.* ◆ See also **go about, go against,** etc. ORIG OE *gān*

Goa ★ ('gəʊə) *n* a state on the W coast of India: a Portuguese overseas territory from 1510 until annexed by India in 1961. Pop.: 1 235 000 (1994 est.). Area: 3702 sq. km (1430 sq. miles).

go about *vb* (*intr*) **1** (*prep*) to busy oneself with: *to go about one's duties.* **2** (*prep*) to tackle (a problem or task). **3** to circulate (in): *there's a lot of flu going about.* **4** (*adv*) (of a sailing ship) to change from one tack to another.

goad (gəʊd) *n* **1** a sharp pointed stick for urging on cattle, etc. **2** anything that acts as a spur or incitement. ◆ *vb* **3** (*tr*) to drive as if with a goad; spur; incite. ORIG OE *gād*, of Gmc origin

Goa, Daman, and Diu ★ *n* a former Union Territory of India consisting of the widely separated districts of Goa and Daman and the island of Diu. Capital: Panaji. Area: 3814 sq. km (1472 sq. miles).

go against *vb* (*intr, prep*) **1** to be contrary to (principles or beliefs). **2** to be unfavourable to (a person): *the case went against him.*

go-ahead *n* **1** (usually preceded by *the*) *Inf.* permission to proceed. ◆ *adj* **2** enterprising or ambitious.

goal (gəʊl) *n* **1** the aim or object towards which an endeavour is directed. **2** the terminal point of a journey or race. **3** (in various sports) the net, basket, etc., into or over which players try to propel the ball, puck, etc., to score. **4** *Sport.* **4a** a successful attempt at scoring. **4b** the score so made. **5** (in soccer, hockey, etc.) the position of goalkeeper. ORIG C16: ? rel. to ME *gol* boundary, OE *gǣlan* to hinder
▸ **'goalless** *adj*

goalball ('gəʊlˌbɔːl) *n* **1** a game played by two teams who compete to score goals by throwing a ball that emits sound when in motion. Players are blindfolded during play. **2** the ball used in this game.

goalie ('gəʊlɪ) *n Inf.* short for **goalkeeper.**

goalkeeper ('gəʊlˌkiːpə) *n Sport.* a player in the goal whose duty is to prevent the ball, puck, etc., from entering or crossing it.

goal kick *n Soccer.* a kick taken from the six-yard line by the defending team after the ball has been put out of play by an opposing player.

goal line *n Sport.* the line marking each end of the pitch, on which the goals stand.

go along *vb* (*intr, adv;* often foll. by *with*) to refrain from disagreement; assent.

goalpost ('gəʊlˌpəʊst) *n* **1** either of two upright posts supporting the crossbar of a goal. **2 move the goalposts.** to change the target required during negotiations, etc.

goanna (gəʊ'ænə) *n* any of various Australian monitor lizards. ORIG C19: from IGUANA

goat (gəʊt) *n* **1** any sure-footed agile ruminant mammal with hollow horns, naturally inhabiting rough stony ground in Europe, Asia, and N Africa. **2** *Inf.* a lecherous man. **3** a foolish person. **4 get (someone's) goat.** *Sl.* to cause annoyance to (someone). ORIG OE *gāt*
▸ **'goatish** *adj*

Goat (gəʊt) *n* **the.** the constellation Capricorn, the tenth sign of the zodiac.

go at *vb* (*intr, prep*) **1** to make an energetic attempt at (something). **2** to attack vehemently.

goatee (ɡəʊ'tiː) *n* a pointed tuftlike beard on the chin. ORIG C19: from GOAT + *-ee* (see -Y[2])

goatherd ('ɡəʊt,hɜːd) *n* a person employed to tend or herd goats.

goatsbeard *or* **goat's-beard** ('ɡəʊts,bɪəd) *n* **1** Also called: **Jack-go-to-bed-at-noon.** a Eurasian plant of the composite family, with woolly stems and large heads of yellow rayed flowers. **2** an American plant with long spikes of small white flowers.

goatskin ('ɡəʊt,skɪn) *n* **1** the hide of a goat. **2** something made from the hide of a goat, such as leather or a container for wine.

goatsucker ('ɡəʊt,sʌkə) *n* the US and Canad. name for **nightjar.**

go-away bird *n S. African.* a common name for a grey-plumaged **lourie.**

gob[1] (ɡɒb) *n* **1** a lump or chunk, esp. of a soft substance. **2** (*often pl*) *Inf.* a great quantity or amount. **3** *Inf.* a globule of spittle or saliva. **4** a lump of molten glass used to make a piece of glassware. ◆ *vb* **gobs, gobbing, gobbed. 5** (*intr*) *Brit. inf.* to spit. ORIG C14: from OF *gobe* lump, from *gober;* see GOBBET

gob[2] (ɡɒb) *n* a slang word (esp. Brit.) for the **mouth.** ORIG C16: ?from Gaelic *gob*

go back *vb* (*intr, adv*) **1** to return. **2** (often foll. by *to*) to originate (in): *the links with France go back to the Norman Conquest.* **3** (foll. by *on*) to change one's mind about; repudiate (esp. in **go back on one's word**).

gobbet ('ɡɒbɪt) *n* a chunk, lump, or fragment, esp. of raw meat. ORIG C14: from OF *gobet,* from *gober* to gulp down

Gobbi ★ (*Italian* 'ɡɔbbi) *n* **Tito** ('tiːto). 1915–84, Italian operatic baritone.

gobble[1] ('ɡɒbᵊl) *vb* **gobbles, gobbling, gobbled. 1** (when *tr,* often foll. by *up*) to eat or swallow (food) hastily and in large mouthfuls. **2** (*tr;* often foll. by *up*) *Inf.* to snatch. ORIG C17: prob. from GOB[1]

gobble[2] ('ɡɒbᵊl) *n* **1** the loud rapid gurgling sound made by male turkeys. ◆ *vb* **gobbles, gobbling, gobbled. 2** (*intr*) (of a turkey) to make this sound. ORIG C17: prob. imit.

gobbledegook *or* **gobbledygook** ('ɡɒbᵊl dɪ,ɡuːk) *n* pretentious or unintelligible jargon, such as that used by officials. ORIG C20: whimsical formation from GOBBLE[2]

gobbler ('ɡɒblə) *n Inf.* a male turkey.

Gobelin ('ɡəʊbəlɪn; *French* ɡɔblɛ̃) *adj* **1** of or resembling tapestry made at the Gobelins' factory in Paris, having vivid pictorial scenes. ◆ *n* **2** a tapestry of this kind. ORIG C19: from the *Gobelin* family, who founded the factory

go-between *n* a person who acts as agent or intermediary for two people or groups in a transaction or dealing.

Gobi ★ ('ɡəʊbɪ) *n* a desert in E Asia, mostly in Mongolia and the Inner Mongolian Autonomous Region of China: sometimes considered to include all the arid regions east of the Pamirs and north of the plateau of Tibet and the Great Wall of China: one of the largest deserts in the world. Length: about 1600 km (1000 miles). Width: about 1000 km (625 miles). Average height: 900 m (3000 ft). Chinese name: **Shamo.**
▸ **'Gobian** *adj*

Gobind Singh ('ɡəʊbɪnd 'sɪŋ) *or* **Govind Singh** ★ ('ɡəʊvɪnd 'sɪŋ) *n* 1666–1708, tenth and last guru of the Sikhs (1675–1708): assassinated.

goblet ('ɡɒblɪt) *n* **1** a vessel for drinking, with a base and stem but without handles. **2** *Arch.* a large drinking cup. ORIG C14: from OF *gobelet* a little cup, ult. of Celtic origin

goblin ('ɡɒblɪn) *n* (in folklore) a small grotesque supernatural creature, regarded as malevolent towards human beings. ORIG C14: from OF, from MHG *kobolt;* cf. COBALT

gobo ('ɡəʊbəʊ) *n, pl* **gobos** *or* **goboes.** a shield placed round a microphone to exclude unwanted sounds, or round a camera lens, etc., to reduce the incident light. ORIG C20: from ?

gobshite ('ɡɒb,ʃaɪt) *n Irish taboo sl.* a stupid person. ORIG C20: from GOB[2] + *shite* excrement; see SHIT

gobsmacked ('ɡɒb,smækt) *adj Brit. sl.* astounded; astonished. ORIG C20: from GOB[2] + SMACK

goby ('ɡəʊbɪ) *n, pl* **goby** *or* **gobies.** a small spiny-finned fish of coastal or brackish waters, having a large head, an elongated tapering body, and the ventral fins modified as a sucker. ORIG C18: from L *gōbius* gudgeon from Gk *kōbios*

go-by *n Sl.* a deliberate snub or slight (esp. in **give (a person) the go-by**).

go by *vb* (*intr*) **1** to pass: *as the years go by.* **2** (*prep*) to be guided by: *in the darkness we could only go by the stars.* **3** (*prep*) to use as a basis for forming an opinion or judgment: *it's wise not to go only by appearances.*

go-cart *n* See **kart.**

god (ɡɒd) *n* **1** a supernatural being, who is worshipped as the controller of some part of the universe or some aspect of life in the world or is the personification of some force. **2** an image, idol, or symbolic representation of such a deity. **3** any person or thing to which excessive attention is given: *money was his god.* **4** a man who has qualities regarded as making him superior to other men. **5** (*pl*) the gallery of a theatre. ORIG OE *god*

God ★ (ɡɒd) *n* **1** the sole Supreme Being, eternal, spiritual, and transcendent, who is the Creator and ruler of all and is infinite in all attributes; the object of worship in monotheistic religions. ◆ *interj* **2** an oath or exclamation used to indicate surprise, annoyance, etc. (and in such expressions as **My God!** or **God Almighty!**).

Godard ★ (*French* ɡɔdar) *n* **Jean-Luc** (ʒɑ̃lyk). born 1930, French film director and writer. His works include *À bout de souffle* (1960) and *Hélas pour moi* (1993).

Godavari ★ (ɡəʊ'dɑːvərɪ) *n* a river in central India, rising in the Western Ghats and flowing southeast to the Bay of Bengal: extensive delta, linked by canal with the Krishna delta; a sacred river to Hindus. Length: about 1500 km (900 miles).

godchild ('ɡɒd,tʃaɪld) *n, pl* **godchildren.** a person who is sponsored by adults at baptism.

Goddard ★ ('ɡɒdɑːd) *n* **Robert Hutchings.** 1882–1945, US physicist. He made the first workable liquid-fuelled rocket.

goddaughter ('ɡɒd,dɔːtə) *n* a female godchild.

goddess ('ɡɒdɪs) *n* **1** a female divinity. **2** a woman who is adored or idealized, esp. by a man.

Gödel ★ ('ɡɜːdᵊl) *n* **Kurt** (kʊrt). 1906–78, US logician and mathematician, born in Austria-Hungary. He showed (**Gödel's proof**) that in a formal axiomatic system, such as logic or mathematics, it is impossible to prove consistency without using methods from outside the system.

Goderich ★ ('ɡəʊdrɪtʃ) *n* **Viscount,** title of *Frederick John Robinson,* 1st Earl of Ripon. 1782–1859, British statesman; prime minister (1827–28).

Godesberg ★ (*German* 'ɡoːdəsbɛrk) *n* a town and spa in W Germany, in North Rhine-Westphalia on the Rhine: a SE suburb of Bonn. Official name: **Bad Godesberg.**

godetia (ɡə'diːʃə) *n* any plant of the American genus *Godetia,* esp. one grown as a showy-flowered annual garden plant. ORIG C19: after C. H. *Godet* (died 1879), Swiss botanist

godfather ('ɡɒd,fɑːðə) *n* **1** a male godparent. **2** the head of a Mafia family or other criminal ring. **3** an originator or leading exponent: *the godfather of South African pop.*

godfather offer *n Inf.* a takeover bid pitched so high that the management of the target company is unable to dissuade shareholders from accepting it. ORIG from the 1972 film *The Godfather,* in which a character was made an offer he could not refuse

God-fearing *adj* pious; devout.

godforsaken ('ɡɒdfə,seɪkən) *adj* (*sometimes cap.*) **1** (*usually prenominal*) desolate; dreary; forlorn. **2** wicked.

Godhead ('ɡɒd,hɛd) *n* (*sometimes not cap.*) **1** the essential nature and condition of being God. **2 the Godhead.** God.

godhood ('ɡɒd,hʊd) *n* the state of being divine.

Godiva ★ (ɡə'daɪvə) *n* **Lady.** ?1040–1080, wife of Leofric, Earl of Mercia. According to legend, she rode naked through Coventry to obtain remission for the townspeople from the heavy taxes imposed by her husband.

godless ('ɡɒdlɪs) *adj* **1** wicked or unprincipled. **2** lacking a god. **3** refusing to acknowledge God.
▸ **'godlessly** *adv* ▸ **'godlessness** *n*

godlike ('gɒd,laɪk) *adj* resembling or befitting a god or God; divine.

godly ('gɒdlɪ) *adj* **godlier, godliest.** having a religious character; pious; devout.
▸ **'godliness** *n*

godmother ('gɒd,mʌðə) *n* a female godparent.

Godolphin ★ (gə'dɒlfɪn) *n* **Sidney.** 1st Earl of Godolphin. 1645–1712, English statesman; as Lord Treasurer, he managed the financing of Marlborough's campaigns in the War of the Spanish Succession.

godown ('gəʊ,daʊn) *n* (in the East, esp. in India) a warehouse. ORIG C16: from Malay *godong*

go down *vb* (*intr, mainly adv*) **1** (*also prep*) to move or lead to or as if to a lower place or level; sink, decline, decrease, etc. **2** to be defeated; lose. **3** to be remembered or recorded (esp. in **go down in history**). **4** to be received: *his speech went down well.* **5** (of food) to be swallowed. **6** *Brit.* to leave a college or university at the end of a term. **7** (usually foll. by *with*) to fall ill; be infected. **8** (of a celestial body) to sink or set. **9 go down on.** *Taboo sl.* to perform cunnilingus or fellatio on.

godparent ('gɒd,pɛərənt) *n* a person who stands sponsor to another at baptism.

God's acre *n Literary.* a churchyard or burial ground. ORIG C17: translation of G *Gottesacker*

godsend ('gɒd,sɛnd) *n* a person or thing that comes unexpectedly but is particularly welcome. ORIG C19: from C17 *God's send,* alteration of *goddes sand* God's message, from OE *sand;* see SEND

godslot ('gɒd,slɒt) *n Inf.* a time in a television or radio schedule traditionally reserved for religious broadcasts.

godson ('gɒd,sʌn) *n* a male godchild.

Godspeed ('gɒd'spiːd) *sentence substitute, n* an expression of good wishes for a person's success and safety. ORIG C15: from *God spede* may God prosper (you)

godsquad ('gɒd,skwɒd) *n Inf., derog.* any group of evangelical Christians, members of which are regarded as intrusive and exuberantly pious.

Godthaab ★ (*Danish* 'gɔdhɔːb) *n* the former name for **Nuuk.**

Godunov ★ ('gɒdə,nɒf, 'gʊd-; *Russian* gədu'nɔf) *n* **Boris Fyodorovich** (ba'ris 'fjɔdərəvitʃ). ?1551–1605, Russian regent (1584–98) and tsar (1598–1605).

Godwin ★ ('gɒdwɪn) *n* **1** died 1053, Earl of Wessex. He was chief adviser to Canute and Edward the Confessor. His son succeeded Edward to the throne as Harold II. **2 Mary.** See (Mary) **Wollstonecraft. 3 William.** 1756–1836, British political philosopher and novelist, noted for his *An Enquiry concerning Political Justice* (1793).

Godwin Austen ★ *n* another name for **K2.**

godwit ('gɒdwɪt) *n* a large shore bird of the sandpiper family having long legs and a long upturned bill. ORIG C16: from ?

Goebbels ★ (*German* 'gœbəls) *n* **Paul Joseph** (paul 'joːzɛf). 1897–1945, German Nazi politician; minister of propaganda (1933–45).

goer ('gəʊə) *n* **1a** a person who attends something regularly. **1b** (*in combination*): *filmgoer.* **2** a person or thing that goes, esp. one that goes very fast. **3** an energetic person. **4** *Austral. inf.* an acceptable or feasible idea, proposal, etc.

Goering ★ (*German* 'gøːrɪŋ) *n* See (Hermann Wilhelm) **Göring.**

Goethe ★ (*German* 'gøːtə) *n* **Johann Wolfgang von** (jo'han 'vɔlfgaŋ fɔn). 1749–1832, German writer, who settled in Weimar in 1775. His early works of the *Sturm und Drang* period include the play *Götz von Berlichingen* (1773) and the novel *The Sorrows of Young Werther* (1774). Later works include the *Wilhelm Meister* novels (1796–1829) and the drama *Faust* (1808; 1832).

go-faster stripe *n Inf.* a decorative line, often suggestive of high speed, on the bodywork of a car.

gofer ('gəʊfə) *n Sl.* a person who runs errands. ORIG C20: from GO + FOR

goffer ('gəʊfə) *vb* (*tr*) **1** to press pleats into (a frill). **2** to decorate (the edges of a book). ◆ *n* **3** an ornamental frill made by pressing pleats. **4** the decoration formed by goffering books. **5** the iron or tool used in making goffers. ORIG C18: from F *gaufrer* to impress a pattern, from *gaufre,* from MLow G *wāfel;* see WAFFLE[1], WAFER

go for *vb* (*intr, prep*) **1** to go somewhere in order to have or fetch: *he went for a drink.* **2** to seek to obtain: *I'd go for that job if I were you.* **3** to prefer or choose; like: *I really go for that new idea of yours.* **4** to make a physical or verbal attack on. **5** to be considered to be of a stated importance or value: *his twenty years went for nothing when he was made redundant.* **6 go for it.** *Inf.* to make the maximum effort to achieve a particular goal.

Gog and Magog ★ (gɒg; 'meɪgɒg) *n* **1** *Old Testament.* a hostile prince and the land from which he comes to attack Israel (Ezekiel 38). **2** *New Testament.* two kings, who are to attack the Church in a climactic battle, but are then to be destroyed by God (Revelation 20:8–10). **3** *Brit. folklore.* two giants, the only survivors of a race of giants destroyed by Brutus, the legendary founder of Britain.

go-getter *n Inf.* an ambitious enterprising person.
▸ **,go-'getting** *adj*

gogga ('xɒxə) *n S. African inf.* any small animal that crawls or flies, esp. an insect. ORIG C20: from Khoikhoi *xoxon* insects collectively

goggle ('gɒg[ə]l) *vb* **goggles, goggling, goggled. 1** (*intr*) to stare fixedly, as in astonishment. **2** to cause (the eyes) to roll or bulge or (of the eyes) to roll or bulge. ◆ *n* **3** a bulging stare. **4** (*pl*) spectacles, often of coloured glass or covered with gauze: used to protect the eyes. ORIG C14: from *gogelen* to look aside, from ?; see AGOG
▸ **'goggle-,eyed** *adj*

gogglebox ('gɒg[ə]l,bɒks) *n Brit. sl.* a television set.

Gogh ★ (gɒx; *Dutch* xɔx) *n* See (Vincent) **van Gogh.**

Go-Go *n* a form of soul music originating in Washington, DC, characterized by the use of funk rhythms and a brass section.

go-go dancer *n* a dancer, usually scantily dressed, who performs rhythmic and often erotic modern dance routines, esp. in a nightclub.

Gogol ★ ('gəʊgɒl; *Russian* 'gɔgəlj) *n* **Nikolai Vasilievich** (nika'laj va'siljɪvitʃ). 1809–52, Russian writer. His works include the play *The Government Inspector* (1836).

Gogra ★ ('gɒgrə) *n* a river in N India, rising in Tibet, in the Himalayas, and flowing southeast through Nepal as the Karnali, then through Uttar Pradesh to join the Ganges. Length: about 1000 km (600 miles).

Goiânia ★ (gɔɪ'ɑːnɪə; *Portuguese* go'jənja) *n* a city in central Brazil, capital of Goiás state: planned in 1933 to replace the old capital, Goiás; two universities. Pop.: 1 033 000 (1995).

Goiás ★ (*Portuguese* gɔ'jas) *n* a state of central Brazil, in the Brazilian Highlands: contains Brasília, the capital of Brazil. Capital: Goiânia. Pop.: 4 514 967 (1996). Area: 341 289 sq. km (131 772 sq. miles).

Goidelic (gɔɪ'dɛlɪk) *n* **1** the N group of Celtic languages, consisting of Irish Gaelic, Scottish Gaelic, and Manx. ◆ *adj* **2** of, relating to, or characteristic of this group of languages. ORIG C19: from OIrish *Goidel* a Celt, from OWelsh, from *gwydd* savage

go in *vb* (*intr, adv*) **1** to enter. **2** (*prep*) See **go into. 3** (of the sun) to become hidden behind a cloud. **4 go in for. 4a** to enter as a competitor or contestant. **4b** to adopt as an activity, interest, or guiding principle: *she went in for nursing.*

going ('gəʊɪŋ) *n* **1** a departure or farewell. **2** the condition of a surface such as a road or field with regard to walking, riding, etc.: *muddy going.* **3** *Inf.* speed, progress, etc.: *we made good going on the trip.* ◆ *adj* **4** thriving (esp. in **a going concern**). **5** current or accepted: *the going rate.* **6** (*postpositive*) available: *the best going.*

going-over *n, pl* **goings-over.** *Inf.* **1** a check, examination, or investigation. **2** a castigation or thrashing.

goings-on *pl n Inf.* **1** actions or conduct, esp. when regarded with disapproval. **2** happenings or events, esp. when mysterious or suspicious.

go into *vb* (*intr, prep*) **1** to enter. **2** to start a career in: *to go* *into publishing.* **3** to investigate or examine. **4** to discuss: *we won't go into that now.* **5** to be admitted to, esp. temporarily: *she went into hospital.* **6** to enter a specified state: *she went into fits of laughter.*

goitre *or US* **goiter** ('gɔɪtə) *n Pathol.* a swelling of the thyroid gland, in some cases nearly doubling the size of the neck. ORIG C17: from F, from OF *goitron* ult. from L *guttur* throat
▸ **'goitred** *or US* **'goitered** *adj* ▸ **'goitrous** *adj*

go-kart *or* **go-cart** *n* See **kart**.

Golan Heights ★ ('gəʊ,læn) *pl n* a range of hills in the Middle East, possession of which is disputed between Israel and Syria: under Syrian control until 1967 when they were stormed by Israeli forces; Jewish settlements have since been established. Highest peak: 2224 m (7297 ft).

Golconda ★ (gɒl'kɒndə) *n* **1** a ruined town and fortress in S central India, in W Andhra Pradesh near Hyderabad city: capital of one of the five Muslim kingdoms of the Deccan from 1512 to 1687, then annexed to the Mogul empire; renowned for its diamonds. **2** (*sometimes not cap.*) a source of wealth or riches, esp. a mine.

gold (gəʊld) *n* **1a** a dense inert bright yellow element that is the most malleable and ductile metal, occurring in rocks and alluvial deposits: used as a monetary standard and in jewellery, dentistry, and plating. Symbol: Au; atomic no.: 79; atomic wt.: 196.97. Related adj: **auric. 1b** (*as modifier*): *a gold mine.* **2** a coin or coins made of this metal. **3** money; wealth. **4** something precious, beautiful, etc., such as a noble nature (esp. in **heart of gold**). **5a** a deep yellow colour, sometimes with a brownish tinge. **5b** (*as adj*): *a gold carpet.* **6** short for **gold medal**. ORIG OE *gold*

Gold ★ (gəʊld) *n* **Thomas.** born 1920, Austrian-born astronomer, working in England and the US: with Bondi and Hoyle he proposed the steady-state theory of the universe.

gold card *n* a credit card issued by credit-card companies to favoured clients, entitling them to high unsecured overdrafts, some insurance cover, etc.

Gold Coast ★ *n* **1** the former name (until 1957) of **Ghana. 2** a line of resort towns and beaches in E Australia, extending for over 30 km (20 miles) along the SE coast of Queensland.

goldcrest ('gəʊld,krɛst) *n* a small Old World warbler having a greenish plumage and a bright yellow-and-black crown.

gold-digger *n* **1** a person who prospects or digs for gold. **2** *Inf.* a woman who uses her sexual attractions to accumulate gifts and wealth.

gold disc *n* **1** (in Britain) an LP record certified to have sold 100 000 copies or a single certified to have sold 400 000 copies. **2** (in the US) an LP record or single certified to have sold 500 000 copies.

gold dust *n* gold in the form of small particles or powder.

golden ('gəʊldən) *adj* **1** of the yellowish colour of gold: *golden hair.* **2** made from or largely consisting of gold: *a golden statue.* **3** happy or prosperous: *golden days.* **4** (*sometimes cap.*) (of anniversaries) the 50th in a series: *Golden Jubilee; golden wedding.* **5** *Inf.* very successful or destined for success: *the golden girl of tennis.* **6** extremely valuable or advantageous: *a golden opportunity.*
▸ **'goldenly** *adv* ▸ **'goldenness** *n*

golden age *n* **1** *Classical myth.* the first and best age of mankind, when existence was happy, prosperous, and innocent. **2** the most flourishing and outstanding period, esp. in the history of an art or nation: *the golden age of poetry.*

golden eagle *n* a large eagle of mountainous regions of the N hemisphere, having a plumage that is golden brown on the back.

goldeneye ('gəʊldən,aɪ) *n, pl* **goldeneyes** *or* **goldeneye.** either of two black-and-white diving ducks of northern regions.

Golden Fleece *n Greek myth.* the fleece of a winged ram stolen by Jason and the Argonauts.

Golden Gate ★ *n* a strait between the Pacific and San Francisco Bay: crossed by the **Golden Gate Bridge,** with a central span of 1280 m (4200 ft).

golden goal *n Soccer.* (in certain competitions) the first goal scored in extra time, which wins the match for the team scoring it.

golden goose *n* a goose in folklore that laid a golden egg every day until its greedy owner killed it in an attempt to get all the gold at once.

golden handcuffs *pl n* payments deferred over a number of years that induce a person to stay with a particular company or in a particular job.

golden handshake *n Inf.* a sum of money given to an employee, either on retirement or as compensation for loss of employment.

golden hello *n* a payment made to a sought-after recruit on signing a contract of employment with a company.

Golden Horn ★ *n* an inlet of the Bosporus in NW Turkey, forming the harbour of Istanbul. Turkish name: **Haliç.**

golden hour *n* the first hour after a serious accident, when it is crucial that the victim receives medical treatment in order to have a chance of surviving.

golden mean *n* **1** the middle course between extremes. **2** another term for **golden section.**

golden number *n* a number between 1 and 19, used to indicate the position of any year in the Metonic cycle: so called from its importance in fixing the date of Easter.

golden parachute *n Inf.* a clause in the employment contract of a senior executive providing for special benefits if the executive's employment is terminated as a result of a takeover.

golden retriever *n* a breed of retriever with a silky wavy coat of a golden colour.

goldenrod (,gəʊldən'rɒd) *n* a plant of the composite family of North America, Europe, and Asia, having spikes of small yellow flowers.

golden rule *n* **1** any of a number of rules of fair conduct, such as *Whatsoever ye would that men should do to you, do ye even so to them* (Matthew 7:12). **2** any important principle: *a golden rule of sailing is to wear a life jacket.* **3** another name for **rule of three.**

golden section *or* **mean** *n* the proportion of the two divisions of a straight line such that the smaller is to the larger as the larger is to the sum of the two.

golden share *n* a share in a company that controls at least 51% of the voting rights, esp. one retained by the UK government in some privatization issues.

Golden Starfish *n* an award given to a bathing beach that meets EU standards of cleanliness but that does not provide facilities.

golden syrup *n Brit.* a light golden-coloured treacle produced by the evaporation of cane sugar juice, used to flavour cakes, puddings, etc.

Golden Triangle ★ *n* **the.** an opium-producing area of SE Asia, comprising parts of Myanmar, Laos, and Thailand.

golden wattle *n* **1** an Australian yellow-flowered plant that yields a useful gum and bark. **2** any of several similar and related Australian plants.

goldfinch ('gəʊld,fɪntʃ) *n* a common European finch, the adult of which has a red-and-white face and yellow-and-black wings.

goldfish ('gəʊld,fɪʃ) *n, pl* **goldfish** *or* **goldfishes.** a freshwater fish of E Europe and Asia, esp. China, widely introduced as a pond or aquarium fish. It resembles the carp and has a typically golden or orange-red coloration.

gold foil *n* thin gold sheet that is thicker than gold leaf.

Golding ★ ('gəʊldɪŋ) *n* Sir **William** (**Gerald**). 1911–93, British writer, his novels include *Lord of the Flies* (1954), *Rites of Passage* (1980), and *Fire Down Below* (1989). Nobel prize for literature 1983.

gold leaf *n* very thin gold sheet produced by rolling or hammering gold and used for gilding woodwork, etc.

gold medal *n* a medal of gold, awarded to the winner of a competition or race.

Goldoni ★ (*Italian* gol'do:ni) *n* **Carlo** ('karlo). 1707–93, Italian dramatist; author of over 250 plays in Italian or French, including *La Locandiera* (1753).

gold plate *n* **1** a thin coating of gold, usually produced by electroplating. **2** vessels or utensils made of gold.
▸ **ˌgold-'plate** *vb (tr)*

gold reserve *n* the gold reserved by a central bank to support domestic credit expansion, to cover balance of payments deficits, and to protect currency.

gold rush *n* a large-scale migration of people to a territory where gold has been found.

Goldschmidt ★ ('gəʊldˌʃmɪt) *n* **Richard Benedikt.** 1878–1958, US geneticist, born in Germany.

goldsmith ('gəʊldˌsmɪθ) *n* **1** a dealer in articles made of gold. **2** an artisan who makes such articles.

Goldsmith ★ ('gəʊldˌsmɪθ) *n* **Oliver.** ?1730–74, Irish writer. His works include the novel *The Vicar of Wakefield* (1766), the poem *The Deserted Village* (1770), and the comedy *She Stoops to Conquer* (1773).

gold standard *n* a monetary system in which the unit of currency is defined with reference to gold.

Goldwyn ★ ('gəʊldwɪn) *n* **Samuel,** original name *Samuel Goldfish.* 1882–1974, US film producer, born in Poland.

golf (gɒlf) *n* **1** a game played on a large open course, the object of which is to hit a ball using clubs, with as few strokes as possible, into each of usually 18 holes. ◆ *vb* **2** *(intr)* to play golf. ORIG C15: ?from MDu. *colf* CLUB
▸ **'golfer** *n*

golf ball *n* **1** a small resilient, usually white, ball of either two-piece or three-piece construction, the former consisting of a solid inner core with a thick covering of toughened material, the latter consisting of a liquid centre, rubber-wound core, and a thin layer of balata. **2** (in some electric typewriters) a small detachable metal sphere, around the surface of which type characters are arranged.

golf club *n* **1** any of various long-shafted clubs with wood or metal heads used to strike a golf ball. **2a** an association of golf players, usually having its own course and facilities. **2b** the premises of such an association.

golf course *or* **links** *n* an area of ground laid out for the playing of golf.

Golgi ★ (*Italian* 'gɔldʒi) *n* **Camillo** (ka'millo). 1844–1926, Italian neurologist and histologist, noted for his discovery in animal cells of the bodies known by his name: shared the Nobel prize for physiology or medicine 1906.

Golgotha ★ ('gɒlgəθə) *n* **1** another name for **Calvary. 2** *(sometimes not cap.) Now rare.* a place of burial. ORIG C17: from LL, from Gk, from Aramaic, based on Heb. *gulgōleth* skull

Goliath ★ (gə'laɪəθ) *n Bible.* a Philistine giant who was killed by David with a stone from his sling (I Samuel 17).

golliwog ('gɒlɪˌwɒg) *n* a soft doll with a black face, usually made of cloth or rags. ORIG C19: from a doll in a series of American children's books

gollop ('gɒləp) *vb* **gollops, golloping, golloped.** to eat or drink (something) quickly or greedily. ORIG dialect var. of GULP

golly ('gɒlɪ) *interj* an exclamation of mild surprise. ORIG C19: orig. a euphemism for GOD

goloshes (gə'lɒʃɪz) *pl n* a less common spelling of **galoshes.**

Gomel ★ (*Russian* 'gɔmɪlj) *n* an industrial city in SE Belarus: belonged to Lithuania until 1772. Pop.: 512 000 (1996 est.).

Gomorrah *or* **Gomorrha ★** (gə'mɒrə) *n* **1** *Old Testament.* one of two ancient cities near the Dead Sea, the other being Sodom, that were destroyed by God as a punishment for the wickedness of their inhabitants (Genesis 19:24). **2** any place notorious for vice and depravity.
▸ **Go'morrean** *or* **Go'morrhean** *adj*

Gomulka ★ (*Polish* gɔ'muwka) *n* **Władysław** (vwa'diswaf). 1905–82, Polish statesman; first secretary of the Polish Communist Party (1956–70).

-gon *n combining form.* indicating a figure having a specified number of angles: *pentagon.* ORIG from Gk *-gōnon,* from *gōnia* angle

gonad ('gɒnæd) *n* an animal organ in which gametes are produced, such as a testis or an ovary. ORIG C19: from NL *gonas,* from Gk *gonos* seed
▸ **'gonadal** *or* **gonadial** (gɒ'neɪdɪəl) *adj*

gonadotrophin (ˌgɒnədəʊ'trəʊfɪn) *or* **gonadotropin** (-'trəʊpɪn) *n* any of several hormones that stimulate the gonads. See also **HCG.**
▸ **gonadotrophic** (ˌgɒnədəʊ'trɒfɪk) *or* **ˌgonado'tropic** *adj*

Gonaïves ★ (*French* gɔnaiv) *n* a port in W Haiti, on the **Gulf of Gonaïves;** scene of the proclamation of Haiti's independence (1804). Pop.: 63 291 (1992).

Goncharov ★ (*Russian* gəntʃɪ'rɔf) *n* **Ivan Aleksandrovich** (i'van alɪk'sandrəvitʃ). 1812–91, Russian novelist: his best-known work is *Oblomov* (1859).

Goncourt ★ (*French* gɔ̃kur) *n* **Edmond Louis Antoine Huot de** (ɛdmɔ̃ lwi ɑ̃twan yo də), 1822–96, and his brother, **Jules Alfred Huot de** (ʒyl alfrɛd), 1830–70, French writers, noted for their collaboration, esp. on their *Journal,* and for the Académie Goncourt founded by Edmond's will.

Gondar ★ ('gɒndɑ:) *n* a city in NW Ethiopia: capital of Ethiopia from the 17th century until 1868. Pop.: 166 593 (1994 est.).

gondola ('gɒndələ) *n* **1** a long narrow flat-bottomed boat with a high ornamented stem: traditionally used on the canals of Venice. **2a** a car or cabin suspended from an airship or balloon. **2b** a moving cabin suspended from a cable across a valley, etc. **3** a flat-bottomed barge used on canals and rivers of the US. **4** *US & Canad.* a low open flat-bottomed railway goods wagon. **5** a set of island shelves in a self-service shop: used for displaying goods. **6** *Canad.* a broadcasting booth built close to the roof of an ice-hockey stadium. ORIG C16: from It. (dialect), from Med. L, ? ult. from Gk *kondu* drinking vessel

gondolier (ˌgɒndə'lɪə) *n* a man who propels a gondola.

Gondwanaland ★ (gɒnd'wɑ:nəˌlænd) *n* one of the two ancient supercontinents comprising chiefly what are now Africa, South America, Australia, Antarctica, and the Indian subcontinent. ORIG C19: from *Gondwana,* region in central north India, where the rock series was orig. found

gone (gɒn) *vb* **1** the past participle of **go.** ◆ *adj (usually postpositive)* **2** ended; past. **3** lost; ruined. **4** dead. **5** spent; consumed; used up. **6** *Inf.* faint or weak. **7** *Inf.* having been pregnant (for a specified time): *six months gone.* **8** (usually foll. by *on*) *Sl.* in love (with).

goner ('gɒnə) *n Sl.* a person or thing beyond help or recovery, esp. a person who is about to die.

gonfalon ('gɒnfələn) *n* **1** a banner hanging from a crossbar, used esp. by certain medieval Italian republics. **2** a battle flag suspended crosswise on a staff, usually having a serrated edge. ORIG C16: from OIt., from OF, of Gmc origin

gong (gɒŋ) *n* **1** a percussion instrument consisting of a metal platelike disc struck with a soft-headed drumstick. **2** a rimmed metal disc, hollow metal hemisphere, or metal strip, tube, or wire that produces a note when struck. **3** a fixed saucer-shaped bell, as on an alarm clock, struck by a mechanically operated hammer. **4** *Brit. sl.* a medal, esp. a military one. ◆ *vb* **5** *(intr)* to sound a gong. **6** *(tr)* (of traffic police) to summon (a driver) to stop by sounding a gong. ORIG C17: from Malay, imit.

goniometer (ˌgəʊnɪ'ɒmɪtə) *n* **1** an instrument for measuring the angles between the faces of a crystal. **2** an instrument used to determine the bearing of a distant radio station. ORIG C18: via F from Gk *gōnia* angle
▸ **goniometric** (ˌgəʊnɪə'metrɪk) *adj* ▸ **ˌgoni'ometry** *n*

-gonium *n combining form.* indicating a seed or reproductive cell: *archegonium.* ORIG from NL, from Gk *gonos* seed

gonococcus (ˌgɒnəʊ'kɒkəs) *n, pl* **gonococci** (-'kɒkaɪ, -'kɒki:). a spherical bacterium that causes gonorrhoea.

gonorrhoea *or esp. US* **gonorrhea** (ˌgɒnə'rɪə) *n* an infectious venereal disease characterized by a discharge of

mucus and pus from the urethra or vagina. ORIG C16: from L, from Gk *gonos* semen + *rhoia* flux
▶ ˌ**gonorˈrhoeal** *or esp. US* ˌ**gonorˈrheal** *adj*

-gony *n combining form.* genesis, origin, or production: *cosmogony.* ORIG from L, from Gk, from *gonos* seed, procreation

González Márquez ★ (*Spanish* gɔnˈθaleθ ˈmarkeθ) *n* **Felipe** (feˈlipe). born 1942, Spanish statesman; prime minister of Spain (1982–96).

gonzo (ˈgɒnzəʊ) *Sl.* ◆ *adj* **1** wild or crazy. **2** (of journalism) focusing on the eccentric personality or lifestyle of the reporter as much as on the events reported. ◆ *n, pl* **gonzos. 3** a wild or crazy person. ORIG C20: coined by Hunter S. Thompson, US journalist, ? from It., lit.: fool, or Sp. *ganso* idiot (lit.: goose)

goo (guː) *n Inf.* **1** a sticky substance. **2** coy or sentimental language or ideas. ORIG C20: from ?

Gooch ★ (guːtʃ) *n* **Graham** (**Alan**). born 1953, English cricketer; captain of England (1988, 1989–93).

good (gʊd) *adj* **better, best. 1** having admirable, pleasing, superior, or positive qualities; not negative, bad, or mediocre: *a good teacher.* **2a** morally excellent or admirable; virtuous; righteous: *a good man.* **2b** (*as collective n; preceded by the*): *the good.* **3** suitable or efficient for a purpose: *a good winter coat.* **4** beneficial or advantageous: *vegetables are good for you.* **5** not ruined or decayed: *the meat is still good.* **6** kindly or generous: *you are good to him.* **7** valid or genuine: *I would not do this without good reason.* **8** honourable or held in high esteem: *a good family.* **9** financially secure, sound, or safe: *a good investment.* **10** (of a draft, etc.) drawn for a stated sum. **11** (of debts) expected to be fully paid. **12** clever, competent, or talented: *he's good at science.* **13** obedient or well-behaved: *a good dog.* **14** reliable, safe, or recommended: *a good make of clothes.* **15** affording material pleasure: *the good life.* **16** having a well-proportioned or generally fine appearance: *a good figure.* **17** complete; full: *I took a good look round the house.* **18** propitious; opportune: *a good time to ask for a rise.* **19** satisfying or gratifying: *a good rest.* **20** comfortable: *did you have a good night?* **21** newest or of the best quality: *keep the good plates for guests.* **22** fairly large, extensive, or long: *a good distance away.* **23** sufficient; ample: *we have a good supply of food.* **24 a good one. 24a** an unbelievable assertion. **24b** a very funny joke. **25 as good as.** virtually; practically: *it's as good as finished.* **26 good and.** *Inf.* (intensifier): *good and mad.* ◆ *interj* **27** an exclamation of approval, agreement, pleasure, etc. ◆ *n* **28** moral or material advantage or use; benefit or profit: *for the good of our workers; what is the good of worrying?* **29** positive moral qualities; goodness; virtue; righteousness; piety. **30** (*sometimes cap.*) moral qualities seen as an abstract entity: *we must pursue the Good.* **31** a good thing. **32 for good** (**and all**). forever; permanently: *I have left them for good.* **33 good for** *or* **on you.** well done, well said, etc.: a term of congratulation. **34 make good. 34a** to recompense or repair damage or injury. **34b** to be successful. **34c** to prove the truth of (a statement or accusation). **34d** to secure and retain (a position). **34e** to effect or fulfil (something intended or promised). ◆ See also **goods.** ORIG OE *gōd*
▶ ˈ**goodish** *adj*

Good Book *n* a name for the **Bible.**

goodbye (ˌgʊdˈbaɪ) *sentence substitute.* **1** farewell: a conventional expression used at leave-taking or parting with people. ◆ *n* **2** a leave-taking; parting: *they prolonged their goodbyes.* **3** a farewell: *they said goodbyes to each other.* ORIG C16: from *God be with ye*

good day *sentence substitute.* a conventional expression of greeting or farewell used during the day.

good-for-nothing *n* **1** an irresponsible or worthless person. ◆ *adj* **2** irresponsible; worthless.

Good Friday *n* the Friday before Easter, observed as a commemoration of the Crucifixion of Jesus.

Good Hope ★ *n* **Cape of.** See **Cape of Good Hope.**

good-humoured *adj* being in or expressing a pleasant, tolerant, and kindly state of mind.
▶ ˌ**good-ˈhumouredly** *adv*

goodies (ˈgʊdɪz) *pl n* any objects, rewards, etc., considered particularly desirable.

good-looking *adj* handsome or pretty.

goodly (ˈgʊdlɪ) *adj* **goodlier, goodliest. 1** considerable: *a goodly amount of money.* **2** *Obs.* attractive, pleasing, or fine.
▶ ˈ**goodliness** *n*

goodman (ˈgʊdmən) *n, pl* **goodmen.** *Arch.* **1** a husband. **2** a man not of gentle birth: used as a title. **3** a master of a household.

Goodman ★ (ˈgʊdmən) *n* **Benny,** full name *Benjamin David Goodman.* 1909–86, US jazz clarinettist and bandleader, who helped to create swing.

good morning *sentence substitute.* a conventional expression of greeting or farewell used in the morning.

good-natured *adj* of a tolerant and kindly disposition.
▶ ˌ**good-ˈnaturedly** *adv*

goodness (ˈgʊdnɪs) *n* **1** the state or quality of being good. **2** generosity; kindness. **3** moral excellence; piety; virtue. **4** what is good in something; essence. ◆ *interj* **5** a euphemism for **God:** used as an exclamation of surprise.

goodness of fit *n Statistics.* the extent to which observed sample values of a variable approximate to values derived from a theoretical density.

good night *sentence substitute.* a conventional expression of farewell, used in the evening or at night, esp. when departing to bed.

good-oh *or* **good-o** (ˈgʊdˈəʊ) *interj Brit. & Austral. inf.* an exclamation of pleasure, agreement, etc.

good oil *n* (usually preceded by *the*) *Austral. sl.* true or reliable facts, information, etc.

goods (gʊdz) *pl n* **1** possessions and personal property. **2** (*sometimes sing*) *Econ.* commodities that are tangible, usually movable, and generally not consumed at the same time as they are produced. **3** articles of commerce; merchandise. **4** *Chiefly Brit.* **4a** merchandise when transported, esp. by rail; freight. **4b** (*as modifier*): *a goods train.* **5 the goods. 5a** *Inf.* that which is expected or promised: *to deliver the goods.* **5b** *Sl.* the real thing. **5c** *US & Canad. sl.* incriminating evidence (esp. in **have the goods on someone**).

Good Samaritan ★ *n* **1** *New Testament.* a figure in one of Christ's parables (Luke 10:30–37) who is an example of compassion towards those in distress. **2** a kindly person who helps another in difficulty or distress.

Good Shepherd *n New Testament.* a title given to Jesus Christ in John 10:11–12.

good-sized *adj* quite large.

good-tempered *adj* of a kindly and generous disposition.

good turn *n* a helpful and friendly act; favour.

goodwife (ˈgʊdˌwaɪf) *n, pl* **goodwives.** *Arch.* **1** the mistress of a household. **2** a woman not of gentle birth: used as a title.

goodwill (ˌgʊdˈwɪl) *n* **1** benevolence, approval, and kindly interest. **2** willingness or acquiescence. **3** an intangible asset of an enterprise reflecting its commercial reputation, customer connections, etc.

Goodwin Sands ★ (ˈgʊdwɪn) *pl n* a dangerous stretch of shoals at the entrance to the Strait of Dover: separated from the E coast of Kent by the Downs roadstead.

Goodwood ★ (ˈgʊdˌwʊd) *n* an area in SE England, in Sussex: site of a famous racecourse and of **Goodwood House,** built 1780–1800.

goody[1] (ˈgʊdɪ) *interj* **1** a child's exclamation of pleasure. ◆ *n, pl* **goodies. 2** short for **goody-goody. 3** *Inf.* the hero in a film, book, etc. **4** See **goodies.**

goody[2] (ˈgʊdɪ) *n, pl* **goodies.** *Arch. or literary.* a married woman of low rank: used as a title: *Goody Two-Shoes.* ORIG C16: from GOODWIFE

Goodyear ★ (ˈgʊdˌjɪə) *n* **Charles.** 1800–60, US inventor of vulcanized rubber.

goody-goody *n, pl* **goody-goodies. 1** *Inf.* a smugly virtuous or sanctimonious person. ◆ *adj* **2** smug and sanctimonious.

gooey (ˈguːɪ) *adj* **gooier, gooiest.** *Inf.* **1** sticky, soft, and often sweet. **2** oversweet and sentimental.
▶ ˈ**gooily** *adv*

★ people and places

goof (gu:f) *Inf.* ◆ *n* **1** a foolish error. **2** a stupid person. ◆ *vb* **3** to bungle (something); botch. **4** (*intr; often foll. by about or around*) to fool (around); mess (about). ORIG C20: prob. from (dialect) *goff* simpleton, from OF *goffe* clumsy, from It. *goffo,* from ?

go off *vb* (*intr*) **1** (*adv*) (of power, a water supply, etc.) to cease to be available or functioning: *the lights suddenly went off.* **2** (*adv*) to explode. **3** (*adv*) to occur as specified: *the meeting went off well.* **4** to leave (a place): *the actors went off stage.* **5** (*adv*) (of a sensation) to gradually cease to be felt. **6** (*adv*) to fall asleep. **7** (*adv*) (of concrete, mortar, etc.) to harden. **8** (*adv*) *Brit. inf.* (of food, etc.) to become stale or rotten. **9** (*prep*) *Brit. inf.* to cease to like.

goofy ('gu:fɪ) *adj* **goofier, goofiest.** *Inf.* foolish; silly. ▸ **'goofily** *adv* ▸ **'goofiness** *n*

goog (gʊg) *n Austral. sl.* an egg. ORIG ?from Du. *oog*

googly ('gu:glɪ) *n, pl* **googlies.** *Cricket.* an off break bowled with a leg break action. ORIG C20: Austral. from ?

Goolagong ★ ('gu:lə,gɒŋ) *n* **Evonne.** See (Evonne) **Cawley.**

Goole ★ (gu:l) *n* an inland port in NE England, in the East Riding of Yorkshire at the confluence of the Ouse and Don Rivers, 75 km (47 miles) from the North Sea. Pop.: 19 410 (1991).

goolie *or* **gooly** ('gu:lɪ) *n, pl* **goolies. 1** (*usually pl*) *Taboo sl.* a testicle. **2** *Austral. sl.* a stone or pebble. ORIG from Hindi *goli* ball

goon (gu:n) *n* **1** a stupid or deliberately foolish person. **2** *US inf.* a thug hired to commit acts of violence or intimidation, esp. in an industrial dispute. ORIG C20: partly from dialect *gooney* fool, partly after the character Alice the *Goon,* created by E. C. Segar (1894–1938), American cartoonist

go on *vb* (*intr, mostly adv*) **1** to continue or proceed. **2** to happen: *there's something peculiar going on here.* **3** (*prep*) to ride on, esp. as a treat: *children love to go on donkeys at the seaside.* **4** *Theatre.* to make an entrance on stage. **5** to talk excessively; chatter. **6** to continue talking, esp. after a short pause. **7** to criticize or nag: *stop going on at me all the time!* ◆ *sentence substitute.* **8** I don't believe what you're saying.

gooney bird ('gu:nɪ) *n* an informal name for **albatross,** esp. the black-footed albatross. ORIG C19 *gony* (orig. sailors' sl.), prob. from dialect *gooney* fool, from ?

goop (gu:p) *n US & Canad. sl.* **1** a rude or ill-mannered person. **2** any sticky or semiliquid substance. ORIG C20: coined by G. Burgess (1866–1951), American humorist ▸ **'goopy** *adj*

goorie *or* **goory** ('gu:rɪ) *n, pl* **goories.** *NZ inf.* a mongrel dog. ORIG from Maori *kuri*

goosander (gu:'sændə) *n* a common merganser (a duck) of Europe and North America, having a dark head and white body in the male. ORIG C17: prob. from GOOSE[1] + ON *önd* (genitive *andar*) duck

goose[1] (gu:s) *n, pl* **geese. 1** any of various web-footed long-necked birds typically larger and less aquatic than ducks. They are gregarious and migratory. **2** the female of such a bird, as opposed to the male (gander). **3** *Inf.* a silly person. **4** (*pl* **gooses**) a pressing iron with a long curving handle, used esp. by tailors. **5** the flesh of the goose, used as food. **6 cook someone's goose.** *Inf.* **6a** to spoil someone's chances or plans completely. **6b** to bring about someone's downfall. **7 kill the goose that lays the golden eggs.** See **golden goose.** ORIG OE *gōs*

goose[2] (gu:s) *Sl.* ◆ *vb* **gooses, goosing, goosed. 1** (*tr*) to prod (a person) playfully in the bottom. ◆ *n, pl* **gooses. 2** such a prod. ORIG C19: from GOOSE[1], prob. from a comparison with the jabbing of a goose's bill

gooseberry ('gʊzbərɪ, -brɪ) *n, pl* **gooseberries. 1** a Eurasian shrub having ovoid yellow-green or red-purple berries. **2a** the berry of this plant. **2b** (*as modifier*): *gooseberry jam.* **3** *Brit. inf.* an unwanted single person, esp. a third person with a couple (often in **play gooseberry**).

goose flesh *n* the bumpy condition of the skin induced by cold, fear, etc., caused by contraction of the muscles at the base of the hair follicles with consequent erection of papillae. Also called: **goose bumps, goose pimples, goose skin.**

goosefoot ('gu:s,fʊt) *n, pl* **goosefoots.** any typically weedy plant having small greenish flowers and leaves shaped like a goose's foot.

goosegog ('gʊzgɒg) *n Brit.* a dialect or informal word for **gooseberry.** ORIG from *goose* in GOOSEBERRY + *gog,* var. of GOB[1]

goosegrass ('gu:s,grɑ:s) *n* another name for **cleavers.**

gooseneck ('gu:s,nɛk) *n* something, such as a jointed pipe, in the form of the neck of a goose.

goose step *n* **1** a military march step in which the leg is swung rigidly to an exaggerated height. ◆ *vb* **goose-step, goose-steps, goose-stepping, goose-stepped. 2** (*intr*) to march in goose step.

Goossens ★ ('gu:sənz) *n* **1** Sir **Eugene.** 1893–1962, British composer and conductor, born in Belgium. **2** his brother, **Leon.** 1896–1988, British oboist.

go out *vb* (*intr, adv*) **1** to depart from a room, house, country, etc. **2** to cease to illuminate, burn, or function: *the fire has gone out.* **3** to cease to be fashionable or popular: *that style went out ages ago!* **4** (of a broadcast) to be transmitted. **5** to go to entertainments, social functions, etc. **6** (usually foll. by *with* or *together*) to associate (with a person of the opposite sex) regularly. **7** (of workers) to begin to strike. **8** *Card games, etc.* to get rid of the last card, token, etc., in one's hand.

go over *vb* (*intr*) **1** to be received in a specified manner: *the concert went over very well.* **2** (*prep*) Also: **go through.** to examine and revise as necessary: *he went over the accounts.* **3** (*prep*) to check and repair: *can you go over my car, please?* **4** (*prep*) Also: **go through.** to rehearse: *I'll go over my lines before the play.*

gopak ('gəʊ,pæk) *n* a spectacular high-leaping Russian peasant dance for men. ORIG from Russian

Go-Ped ('gəʊ,pɛd) *n Trademark.* a motorized vehicle consisting of a low footboard on wheels, steered by handlebars.

gopher ('gəʊfə) *n* **1** Also called: **pocket gopher.** a burrowing rodent of North and Central America, having a thickset body, short legs, and cheek pouches. **2** another name for **ground squirrel. 3** a burrowing tortoise of SE North America. ORIG C19: from earlier *megopher* or *magopher,* from ?

Gorakhpur ★ ('gɔ:rək,pʊə) *n* a city in N India, in SE Uttar Pradesh: formerly an important Muslim garrison. Pop.: 505 566 (1991).

goral ('gɔ:rəl) *n* a small goat antelope inhabiting mountainous regions of S Asia. ORIG C19: from Hindi, prob. from Sansk.

Gorbachov *or* **Gorbachev** ★ ('gɔ:bə,tʃɒf; *Russian* gərba'tʃɔf) *n* **Mikhail Sergeevich** (mixa'il sɪr'gjejɪvitʃ). born 1931, Soviet statesman; general secretary of the Soviet Communist Party (1985–91): president (1988–91); resigned as president on dissolution of Soviet Union. Nobel peace prize 1990.

Gorbals ★ ('gɔ:bᵊlz) *n* **the.** a district of Glasgow, formerly known for its slums.

Gordian knot ('gɔ:dɪən) *n* **1** (in Greek legend) a complicated knot, tied by King Gordius of Phrygia, that Alexander the Great cut with a sword. **2** a complicated and intricate problem (esp. in **cut the Gordian knot**).

Gordimer ★ ('gɔ:dɪmə) *n* **Nadine.** born 1923, South African novelist. Her books include *The Lying Days* (1952), *The Conservationist* (1974), *July's People* (1981), and *The House Gun* (1998): Nobel prize for literature 1991.

Gordon ★ ('gɔ:dᵊn) *n* **1 Adam Lindsay.** 1833–70, Australian poet and horseman, born in the Azores, who developed the bush ballad, esp. in *Bush Ballads and Galloping Rhymes* (1870). **2 Charles George,** known as *Chinese Gordon.* 1833–85, British general and administrator. He helped to crush the Taiping rebellion (1863–64), and was governor of the Sudan (1877–80), returning in 1884 to aid Egyptian forces against the Mahdi. He was killed in the siege of Khartoum. **3** Lord **George.** 1751–93, British religious agitator, who led the Protestant opposition to legislation relieving Roman Catholics of certain disabilities, which culminated in the Gordon riots (1780). **4 George Hamilton.** See (4th Earl of) **Aberdeen.**

gore[1] (gɔː) *n* **1** blood shed from a wound, esp. when coagulated. **2** *Inf.* killing, fighting, etc. ORIG OE *gor* dirt

gore[2] (gɔː) *vb* **gores, goring, gored.** (*tr*) (of an animal, such as a bull) to pierce or stab (a person or another animal) with a horn or tusk. ORIG C16: prob. from OE *gār* spear

gore[3] (gɔː) *n* **1** a tapering or triangular piece of material used in making a shaped skirt, umbrella, etc. ◆ *vb* **gores, goring, gored. 2** (*tr*) to make into or with a gore or gores. ORIG OE *gāra*
▸ **gored** *adj*

Gore ★ (gɔː) *n* **Al(bert) Jr.** born 1948, US Democrat politician; vice president of the US (1993–2001).

gorge (gɔːdʒ) *n* **1** a deep ravine, esp. one through which a river runs. **2** the contents of the stomach. **3** feelings of disgust or resentment (esp. in **one's gorge rises**). **4** an obstructing mass: *an ice gorge.* **5** *Fortifications.* a narrow rear entrance to a work. **6** *Arch.* the throat or gullet. ◆ *vb* **gorges, gorging, gorged. 7** to swallow (food) ravenously. **8** (*tr*) to stuff (oneself) with food. ORIG C14: from OF *gorger* to stuff, from *gorge* throat, from LL *gurga,* from L *gurges* whirlpool

gorgeous (ˈgɔːdʒəs) *adj* **1** strikingly beautiful or magnificent: *a gorgeous array; a gorgeous girl.* **2** *Inf.* extremely pleasing, fine, or good: *gorgeous weather.* ORIG C15: from OF *gorgias* elegant, from *gorge;* see GORGE
▸ **ˈgorgeously** *adv* ▸ **ˈgorgeousness** *n*

gorget (ˈgɔːdʒɪt) *n* **1** a collar-like piece of armour worn to protect the throat. **2** a part of a wimple worn by women to cover the throat and chest, esp. in the 14th century. **3** a band of distinctive colour on the throat of an animal, esp. a bird. ORIG C15: from OF, from *gorge;* see GORGE

Gorgio (ˈgɔːdʒɪəʊ) *n, pl* **Gorgios.** the Gypsy name for a non-Gypsy. ORIG C19: from Romany

Gorgon (ˈgɔːgən) *n* **1** *Greek myth.* any of three winged monstrous sisters who had live snakes for hair, huge teeth, and brazen claws. **2** (*often not cap.*) *Inf.* a fierce or unpleasant woman. ORIG via L *Gorgō* from Gk, from *gorgos* terrible

gorgonian (gɔːˈgəʊnɪən) *n* any of various corals having a horny or calcareous branching skeleton, such as the sea fans and red corals.

Gorgonzola (ˌgɔːgənˈzəʊlə) *n* a semihard blue-veined cheese of sharp flavour, made from pressed milk. ORIG C19: after *Gorgonzola,* It. town where it originated

Gorica ★ (ˈgɔritsa) *n* the Serbo-Croat name for **Gorizia.**

gorilla (gəˈrɪlə) *n* **1** the largest anthropoid ape, inhabiting the forests of central W Africa. It is stocky with a short muzzle and coarse dark hair. **2** *Inf.* a large, strong, and brutal-looking man. ORIG C19: NL, from Gk *Gorillai,* an African tribe renowned for their hirsute appearance

Göring *or* **Goering** ★ (*German* ˈgøːrɪŋ) *n* **Hermann Wilhelm** (ˈhɛrman ˈvɪlhɛlm). 1893–1946, German Nazi leader and field marshal. He founded the Gestapo and mobilized Germany for war. Sentenced to death at Nuremberg, he committed suicide.

Gorizia ★ (*Italian* goˈrittsja) *n* a city in NE Italy, in Friuli-Venezia Giulia, on the Isonzo River: cultural centre under the Hapsburgs. Pop.: 39 230 (1990). German name: **Görz.** Serbo-Croat name: **Gorica.**

Gorki[1] *or* **Gorky** ★ (*Russian* ˈgɔrjkij) *n* the former name (1932–91) of **Nizhni Novgorod.**

Gorki[2] *or* **Gorky** ★ (*Russian* ˈgɔrjkij) *n* **Maxim** (makˈsim), pen name of *Aleksey Maximovich Peshkov.* 1868–1936, Russian writer. His works include the play *The Lower Depths* (1902) and the novel *Mother* (1907).

Gorky ★ (ˈgɔːkɪ) *n* **Arshile** (ˈɑːʃiːl). 1904–48, US abstract expressionist painter, born in Armenia.

Görlitz ★ (*German* ˈgœrlɪts) *n* a city in E Germany, in Saxony, on the Neisse River; formerly in East Germany: divided in 1945, the area on the E bank of the river becoming the Polish town of **Zgorzelec.** Pop.: 70 450 (1991).

Gorlovka ★ (*Russian* ˈgɔrləfkə) *n* a city in SE Ukraine, in the centre of the Donets Basin: a major coal-mining centre. Pop.: 322 000 (1996 est.).

gormand (ˈgɔːmənd) *n* a less common spelling of **gourmand.**

gormandize *or* **gormandise** (ˈgɔːmənˌdaɪz) *vb* **gormandizes, gormandizing, gormandized** *or* **gormandises, gormandising, gormandised.** to eat (food) greedily and voraciously.
▸ **ˈgormandˌizer** *or* **ˈgormandˌiser** *n*

gormless (ˈgɔːmlɪs) *adj Brit. inf.* stupid; dull. ORIG C19: var. of C18 *gaumless,* from dialect *gome,* from OE *gom, gome,* from ON *gaumr* heed

Gorno-Altai Republic ★ (ˈgɔːnəʊælˈtaɪ, -ˈæltaɪ) *n* a constituent republic of S Russia: mountainous, rising over 4350 m (14 500 ft) in the Altai Mountains of the south. Capital: Gorno-Altaisk. Pop.: 202 000 (1996 est.). Area: 92 600 sq. km (35 740 sq. miles). Also called: **Altai Republic.**

Gorno-Badakhshan Autonomous Republic ★ (-bəˈdækʃɑːn) *n* an administrative division of Tajikistan: the region is generally mountainous and inaccessible. Capital: Khorog. Pop.: 167 100 (1991 est.). Area: 63 700 sq. km (24 590 sq. miles). Also called: **Badakhshan.**

go round *vb* (*intr*) **1** (*adv*) to be sufficient: *are there enough sweets to go round?* **2** to circulate (in): *measles is going round the school.* **3** to be long enough to encircle: *will that belt go round you?*

gorse (gɔːs) *n* an evergreen shrub which has yellow flowers and thick green spines instead of leaves. Also called: **furze, whin.** ORIG OE *gors*
▸ **ˈgorsy** *adj*

Gorton ★ (ˈgɔːtᵊn) *n* Sir **John Grey.** born 1911, Australian statesman; prime minister (1968–71).

gory (ˈgɔːrɪ) *adj* **gorier, goriest. 1** horrific or bloodthirsty: *a gory story.* **2** involving bloodshed and killing: *a gory battle.* **3** covered in gore.
▸ **ˈgorily** *adv* ▸ **ˈgoriness** *n*

Görz ★ (gœrts) *n* the German name for **Gorizia.**

gosh (gɒʃ) *interj* an exclamation of mild surprise or wonder. ORIG C18: euphemistic for GOD

goshawk (ˈgɒsˌhɔːk) *n* a large hawk of Europe, Asia, and North America, having a bluish-grey back and wings and paler underparts: used in falconry. ORIG OE *gōshafoc;* see GOOSE[1], HAWK[1]

Goshen ★ (ˈgəʊʃən) *n* **1** a region of ancient Egypt, east of the Nile delta: granted to Jacob and his descendants by the king of Egypt and inhabited by them until the Exodus (Genesis 45:10). **2** a place of comfort and plenty.

gosling (ˈgɒzlɪŋ) *n* **1** a young goose. **2** an inexperienced or youthful person. ORIG C15: from ON *gæslingr;* rel. to Danish *gäsling;* see GOOSE[1], -LING[1]

go-slow *n* **1** *Brit.* a deliberate slackening of the rate of production by organized labour as a tactic in industrial conflict. US and Canad. equivalent: **slowdown.** ◆ *vb* **go slow. 2** (*intr*) to work deliberately slowly as a tactic in industrial conflict.

gospel (ˈgɒspᵊl) *n* **1** Also called: **gospel truth.** an unquestionable truth: *to take someone's word as gospel.* **2** a doctrine maintained to be of great importance. **3** Black religious music originating in the churches of the Southern states of the United States. **4** the message or doctrine of a religious teacher. **5a** the story of Christ's life and teachings as narrated in the Gospels. **5b** the good news of salvation in Jesus Christ. **5c** (*as modifier*): *the gospel story.* ORIG OE *gōdspell,* from *gōd* GOOD + *spell* message; see SPELL[2]

Gospel (ˈgɒspᵊl) *n* **1** any of the first four books of the New Testament, namely Matthew, Mark, Luke, and John. **2** a reading from one of these in a religious service.

Gosport ★ (ˈgɒsˌpɔːt) *n* a town in S England, in Hampshire on Portsmouth harbour: naval base since the 16th century. Pop.: 67 802 (1991).

gossamer (ˈgɒsəmə) *n* **1** a gauze or silk fabric of the very finest texture. **2** a filmy cobweb often seen on foliage or floating in the air. **3** anything resembling gossamer in fineness or filminess. ORIG C14 (in sense 2): prob. from *gos* GOOSE[1] + *somer* SUMMER; the phrase refers to *St Martin's summer,* a period in November when goose was tradi-

tionally eaten; from the prevalence of the cobweb in the autumn
▸ **'gossamery** *adj*

Gosse ★ (gɒs) *n* Sir **Edmund William.** 1849–1928, British writer, noted for his autobiographical *Father and Son* (1907).

gossip ('gɒsɪp) *n* **1** casual and idle chat. **2** a conversation involving malicious chatter or rumours about other people. **3** Also called: **gossipmonger.** a person who habitually talks about others, esp. maliciously. **4** light easy communication: *to write a letter full of gossip.* **5** *Arch.* a close woman friend. ◆ *vb* **gossips, gossiping, gossiped. 6** (*intr;* often foll. by *about*) to talk casually or maliciously (about other people). ORIG OE *godsibb* godparent, from GOD + SIB; came to be applied esp. to a woman's female friends at the birth of a child, hence a woman fond of light talk
▸ **'gossiper** *n* ▸ **'gossipy** *adj*

gossypol ('gɒsɪˌpɒl) *n* a toxic crystalline pigment that is a constituent of cottonseed oil. ORIG C19: from Mod. L *gossypium* cotton plant + -OL[1]

got (gɒt) *vb* **1** the past tense and past participle of **get. 2 have got. 2a** to possess. **2b** (*takes an infinitive*) used as an auxiliary to express compulsion: *I've got to get a new coat.*

Göta ★ (*Swedish* 'jø:ta) *n* a river in S Sweden, draining Lake Vänern and flowing south-southwest to the Kattegat: forms part of the **Göta Canal,** which links Göteborg in the west with Stockholm in the east. Length: 93 km (58 miles).

Göteborg (*Swedish* jœtə'bɔrj) *or* **Gothenburg** ★ *n* a port in SW Sweden, at the mouth of the Göta River: the largest port and second largest city in the country; developed through the Swedish East India Company and grew through Napoleon's continental blockade and with the opening of the Göta Canal (1832); university (1891). Pop.: 454 016 (1997 est.).

Goth (gɒθ) *n* **1** a member of an East Germanic people from Scandinavia who settled south of the Baltic early in the first millennium A.D. They moved on to the Ukrainian steppes and raided and later invaded many parts of the Roman Empire from the 3rd to the 5th century. **2** a rude or barbaric person. ORIG C14: from LL (pl) *Gothī* from Gk *Gothoi*

Gotha ★ ('gəʊθə; *German* 'go:ta) *n* a town in central Germany, in Thuringia on the N edge of the Thuringian forest: capital of Saxe-Coburg-Gotha (1826–1918); noted for the *Almanach de Gotha* (a record of the royal and noble houses of Europe, first published in 1764). Pop.: 57 360 (1989 est.).

Gothenburg ★ ('gɒθənˌbɜ:g) *n* the English name for **Göteborg.**

Gothic ('gɒθɪk) *adj* **1** denoting, relating to, or resembling the style of architecture that was used in W Europe from the 12th to the 16th centuries, characterized by the lancet arch, the ribbed vault, and the flying buttress. See also **Gothic Revival. 2** of or relating to the style of sculpture, painting, or other arts as practised in W Europe from the 12th to the 16th centuries. **3** (*sometimes not cap.*) of or relating to a literary style characterized by gloom, the grotesque, and the supernatural, popular esp. in the late 18th century: when used of modern literature, films, etc., sometimes spelt: **Gothick. 4** of, relating to, or characteristic of the Goths or their language. **5** (*sometimes not cap.*) primitive and barbarous in style, behaviour, etc. **6** of or relating to the Middle Ages. ◆ *n* **7** Gothic architecture or art. **8** the extinct language of the ancient Goths, known mainly from fragments of a translation of the Bible made in the 4th century by Bishop Wulfila. **9** Also called (esp. Brit): **black letter.** a family of heavy script typefaces.
▸ **'Gothically** *adv*

Gothic Revival *n* a Gothic style of architecture popular between the late 18th and late 19th centuries, exemplified by the Houses of Parliament in London (1840). Also called: **neogothic.**

go through *vb* (*intr*) **1** (*adv*) to be approved or accepted: *the amendment went through.* **2** (*prep*) to consume; exhaust: *we went through our supplies in a day.* **3** (*prep*) Also: **go over.** to examine: *he went through the figures.* **4** (*prep*) to suffer: *she went through tremendous pain.* **5** (*prep*) Also: **go over.** to rehearse: *let's just go through the details again.* **6** (*prep*) to search: *she went through the cupboards.* **7** (*adv;* foll. by *with*) to come or bring to a successful conclusion, often by persistence.

Gotland ('gɒtlənd; *Swedish* 'gɔtlant), **Gothland** ('gɒθlənd) *or* **Gottland** ★ ('gɒtlənd) *n* an island in the Baltic Sea, off the SE coast of Sweden: important trading centre since the Bronze Age; long disputed between Sweden and Denmark, finally becoming Swedish in 1645; tourism and agriculture now important. Capital: Visby. Pop. (including associated islands): 58 237 (1994 est.). Area: 3140 sq. km (1212 sq. miles).

go together *vb* (*intr, adv*) **1** to be mutually suited; harmonize: *the colours go well together.* **2** *Inf.* (of two people) to have a romantic or sexual relationship: *they had been going together for two years.*

gotten ('gɒtᵊn) *vb Chiefly US.* a past participle of **get.**

Götterdämmerung (ˌgɒtə'dɛməˌrʊŋ) *n German myth.* the twilight of the gods; their ultimate destruction in a battle with the forces of evil.

Gottfried von Strassburg ★ (*German* 'gɔtfri:t fɔn 'ʃtra:sbʊrk) *n* early 13th-century German poet; author of the incomplete epic *Tristan and Isolde,* the basis of Wagner's opera.

Göttingen ★ (*German* 'gœtɪŋən) *n* a city in central Germany, in Lower Saxony: important member of the Hanseatic League (14th century); university, founded in 1734 by George II of England. Pop.: 126 253 (1996 est.).

gouache (gʊ'ɑ:ʃ) *n* **1** Also called: **body colour.** a painting technique using opaque watercolour in which the pigments are bound with glue and lighter tones contain white. **2** the paint used in this technique. **3** a painting done by this method. ORIG C19: from F, from It. *guazzo* puddle, from L, from *aqua* water

Gouda ★ ('gaʊdə; *Dutch* 'xɔuda:) *n* **1** a town in the W Netherlands, in South Holland province: important medieval cloth trade; famous for its cheese. Pop.: 69 917 (1994). **2** a large round Dutch cheese, mild and similar in taste to Edam.

gouge (gaʊdʒ) *vb* **gouges, gouging, gouged.** (*mainly tr*) **1** (usually foll. by *out*) to scoop or force (something) out of its position. **2** (sometimes foll. by *out*) to cut (a hole or groove) in (something) with a sharp instrument or tool. **3** *US & Canad. inf.* to extort from. **4** (*also intr*) *Austral.* to dig for (opal). ◆ *n* **5** a type of chisel with a blade that has a concavo-convex section. **6** a mark or groove made as with a gouge. **7** *US & Canad. inf.* extortion; swindling. ORIG C15: from F, from LL *gulbia* a chisel, of Celtic origin
▸ **'gouger** *n*

goujon ('gu:ʒɒn) *n* a small strip of fish or chicken, coated in breadcrumbs and deep-fried. ORIG F, lit.: gudgeon

goulash ('gu:læʃ) *n* **1** Also called: **Hungarian goulash.** a rich stew, originating in Hungary, made of beef, lamb, or veal highly seasoned with paprika. **2** *Bridge.* a method of dealing in threes and fours without first shuffling the cards, to produce freak hands. ORIG C19: from Hungarian *gulyás hus* herdsman's meat

Gould ★ (gu:ld) *n* **1 Benjamin Apthorp.** 1824–96, US astronomer: the first to use the telegraph to determine longitudes; founded the *Astronomical Journal* (1849). **2 Glenn.** 1932–82, Canadian pianist.

go under *vb* (*intr, mainly adv*) **1** (*also prep*) to sink below (a surface). **2** to be overwhelmed: *the firm went under in the economic crisis.*

Gounod ★ ('gu:nəʊ; *French* guno) *n* **Charles François** (ʃarl frɑ̃swa). 1818–93, French composer of the operas *Faust* (1859) and *Romeo and Juliet* (1867).

go up *vb* (*intr, mainly adv*) **1** (*also prep*) to move or lead as to a higher place or level; rise; increase: *prices are always going up.* **2** to be destroyed: *the house went up in flames.* **3** *Brit.* to go or return (to college or university) at the beginning of a term or academic year.

gourami ('gʊərəmɪ) *n, pl* **gourami** *or* **gouramis. 1** a large SE Asian labyrinth fish used for food. **2** any of various other labyrinth fishes, many of which are brightly coloured and popular aquarium fishes. ORIG from Malay *gurami*

gourd (gʊəd) *n* **1** the fruit of any of various plants of the cucumber family, esp. the bottle gourd and some squashes, whose dried shells are used for ornament, drinking cups, etc. **2** any plant that bears this fruit. **3** a bottle or flask made from the dried shell of the bottle gourd. ORIG C14: from OF *gourde,* ult. from L *cucurbita*

gourmand ('gʊəmənd) *or* **gormand** *n* a person devoted to eating and drinking, esp. to excess. ORIG C15: from OF *gourmant,* from ?
▸ **'gourmand,ism** *n*

gourmet ('gʊəmeɪ) *n* a person who cultivates a discriminating palate for the enjoyment of good food and drink. ORIG C19: from F, from OF *gromet* serving boy

gout (gaʊt) *n* **1** a metabolic disease characterized by painful inflammation of certain joints, esp. of the big toe, caused by deposits of sodium urate. **2** *Arch.* a drop or splash, esp. of blood. ORIG C13: from OF, from L *gutta* a drop
▸ **'gouty** *adj* ▸ **'goutily** *adv* ▸ **'goutiness** *n*

Gov. *or* **gov.** *abbrev. for:* **1** government. **2** governor.

govern ('gʌvᵊn) *vb* (*mainly tr*) **1** (*also intr*) to direct and control the actions, affairs, policies, functions, etc., of (an organization, nation, etc.); rule. **2** to exercise restraint over; regulate or direct: *to govern one's temper.* **3** to decide or determine (something): *his injury governed his decision to avoid sports.* **4** to control the speed of (an engine, machine, etc.) using a governor. **5** (of a word) to determine the inflection of (another word): *Latin nouns govern adjectives that modify them.* ORIG C13: from OF, from L *gubernāre* to steer, from Gk *kubernan*
▸ **'governable** *adj*

governance ('gʌvənəns) *n* **1** government, control, or authority. **2** the action, manner, or system of governing.

governess ('gʌvənɪs) *n* a woman teacher employed in a private household to teach and train the children.

government ('gʌvənmənt, 'gʌvəmənt) *n* **1** the exercise of political authority over the actions, affairs, etc., of a political unit, people, etc.; the action of governing; political rule and administration. **2** the system or form by which a community, etc., is ruled: *tyrannical government.* **3a** the executive policy-making body of a political unit, community, etc.; ministry or administration. **3b** (*cap. when of a specific country*): *the British Government.* **4a** the state and its administration: *blame it on the government.* **4b** (*as modifier*): *a government agency.* **5** regulation; direction. **6** *Grammar.* the determination of the form of one word by another word.
▸ **governmental** (ˌgʌvən'mɛntᵊl, ˌgʌvə'mɛntᵊl) *adj* ▸ **ˌgovern'mentally** *adv*

governor ('gʌvənə) *n* **1** a person who governs. **2** the ruler or chief magistrate of a colony, province, etc. **3** the representative of the Crown in a British colony. **4** *Brit.* the senior administrator of a society, prison, etc. **5** the chief executive of any state in the US. **6** a device that controls the speed of an engine, esp. by regulating the supply of fuel. **7** *Brit. inf.* a name or title of respect for a father, employer, etc.
▸ **'governor,ship** *n*

governor general *n, pl* **governors general** *or* **governor generals.** **1** the representative of the Crown in a dominion of the Commonwealth or a British colony; vicegerent. **2** *Brit.* a governor with jurisdiction or precedence over other governors.
▸ **ˌgovernor-'general,ship** *n*

Govt *or* **govt** *abbrev. for* government.

Gower[1] ★ ('gaʊə) *n* **the.** a peninsula in S Wales, in Swansea county in the Bristol Channel: mainly agricultural with several resorts.

Gower[2] ★ ('gaʊə) *n* **1 David (Ivon).** born 1957, English cricketer: captained England (1984–86; 1989). **2 John.** ?1330–1408, English poet, noted particularly for his tales of love, the *Confessio Amantis.*

go with *vb* (*intr, prep*) **1** to accompany. **2** to blend or harmonize: *that new wallpaper goes well with the furniture.* **3** to be a normal part of: *three acres of land go with the house.* **4** (of two people of the opposite sex) to associate frequently with each other.

go without *vb* (*intr*) *Chiefly Brit.* to be denied or deprived of (something, esp. food): *if you don't like your tea you can go without.*

gowk (gaʊk) *n Scot. & N English dialect.* **1** a fool. **2** a cuckoo. ORIG from ON *gaukr* cuckoo

gown (gaʊn) *n* **1** any of various outer garments, such as a woman's elegant or formal dress, a dressing robe, or a protective garment, esp. one worn by surgeons during operations. **2** a loose wide garment indicating status, such as worn by academics. **3** the members of a university as opposed to the other residents of the university town. ◆ *vb* **4** (*tr*) to supply with or dress in a gown. ORIG C14: from OF, from LL *gunna* garment made of leather or fur, of Celtic origin

goy (gɔɪ) *n, pl* **goyim** ('gɔɪɪm) *or* **goys.** a Jewish word for a **Gentile.** ORIG from Yiddish, from Heb. *goi* people
▸ **'goyish** *adj*

Goya ★ ('gɔɪə; *Spanish* 'goja) *n* **Francisco de** (fran'θisko de), full name *Francisco José de Goya y Lucientes.* 1746–1828, Spanish painter and etcher; court painter to Charles IV of Spain (1799).

GP *abbrev. for:* **1** Gallup Poll. **2** *Music.* general pause. **3** general practitioner. **4** (in Britain) graduated pension. **5** Grand Prix.

GPMU (in Britain) *abbrev. for* Graphical, Paper and Media Union.

GPO *abbrev. for* general post office.

GPS *abbrev. for* Global Positioning System: a satellite-based navigation system.

Gr. *abbrev. for:* **1** Grecian. **2** Greece. **3** Greek.

Graafian follicle ('grɑːfɪən) *n* a fluid-filled vesicle in the mammalian ovary containing a developing egg cell. ORIG C17: after R. de *Graaf* (1641–73), Du. anatomist

grab (græb) *vb* **grabs, grabbing, grabbed.** **1** to seize hold of (something). **2** (*tr*) to seize illegally or unscrupulously. **3** (*tr*) to arrest; catch. **4** (*tr*) *Inf.* to catch the attention or interest of; impress. ◆ *n* **5** the act or an instance of grabbing. **6** a mechanical device for gripping objects, esp. the hinged jaws of a mechanical excavator. **7** something that is grabbed. ORIG C16: prob. from MLow G or MDu. *grabben*
▸ **'grabber** *n*

grab bag *n* **1** a collection of miscellaneous things. **2** *US, Canad., & Austral.* a bag or other container from which gifts are drawn at random.

grabby ('græbɪ) *adj* **grabbier, grabbiest.** **1** grasping or avaricious. **2** seizing the attention: *a grabby headline; a grabby performance.*

Gracchus ★ ('grækəs) *n* **Tiberius Sempronius** (taɪ'bɪərɪəs sɛm'prəʊnɪəs). ?163–133 B.C., and his younger brother, **Gaius Sempronius** ('gaɪəs), 153–121 B.C., known as *the Gracchi.* Roman tribunes and reformers. Tiberius attempted to redistribute public land among the poor but was murdered in the ensuing riot. Violence again occurred when the reform was revived by Gaius, and he too was killed.

grace (greɪs) *n* **1** elegance and beauty of movement, form, expression, or proportion. **2** a pleasing or charming quality. **3** goodwill or favour. **4** a delay granted for the completion of a task or payment of a debt. **5** a sense of propriety and consideration for others. **6** (*pl*) **6a** affectation of manner (esp. in **airs and graces**). **6b in (someone's) good graces.** regarded favourably and with kindness by (someone). **7** mercy; clemency. **8** *Christian theol.* **8a** the free and unmerited favour of God shown towards man. **8b** the divine assistance given to man in spiritual rebirth. **8c** the condition of being favoured or sanctified by God. **8d** an unmerited gift, favour, etc., granted by God. **9** a short prayer recited before or after a meal to give thanks for it. **10** *Music.* a melodic ornament or decoration. **11 with (a) bad grace.** unwillingly or grudgingly. **12 with (a) good grace.** willingly or cheerfully. ◆ *vb* **graces, gracing, graced.** **13** (*tr*) to add elegance and beauty to: *flowers graced the room.* **14** (*tr*) to honour or favour: *to grace a party with one's presence.* **15** to ornament or decorate (a melody, part, etc.) with nonessential notes. ORIG C12: from OF, from L *grātia,* from *grātus* pleasing

Grace[1] (greɪs) *n* (preceded by *your, his,* or *her*) a title used to address or refer to a duke, duchess, or archbishop.

Grace[2] ★ (greɪs) *n* **W(illiam) G(ilbert).** 1848–1915, English cricketer.

grace-and-favour *n* (*modifier*) *Brit.* (of a house, flat, etc.) owned by the sovereign and granted free of rent to a person to whom the sovereign wishes to express gratitude.

graceful ('greɪsfʊl) *adj* characterized by beauty of movement, style, form, etc.
▸ **'gracefully** *adv* ▸ **'gracefulness** *n*

graceless ('greɪslɪs) *adj* **1** lacking manners. **2** lacking elegance.
▸ **'gracelessly** *adv* ▸ **'gracelessness** *n*

grace note *n Music.* a note printed in small type to indicate that it is melodically and harmonically nonessential.

Graces ★ ('greɪsɪz) *pl n Greek myth.* three sister goddesses, givers of charm and beauty.

gracious ('greɪʃəs) *adj* **1** characterized by or showing kindness and courtesy. **2** condescendingly courteous, benevolent, or indulgent. **3** characterized by or suitable for a life of elegance, ease, and indulgence: *gracious living.* **4** merciful or compassionate. ◆ *interj* **5** an expression of mild surprise or wonder.
▸ **'graciously** *adv* ▸ **'graciousness** *n*

grackle ('græk[ə]l) *n* **1** an American songbird of the oriole family, having a dark iridescent plumage. **2** any of various starlings, such as the Indian grackle or hill myna. ORIG C18: from NL, from L *grāculus* jackdaw

grad. *abbrev. for:* **1** *Maths.* gradient. **2** *Education.* graduate(d).

gradate (grə'deɪt) *vb* **gradates, gradating, gradated. 1** to change or cause to change imperceptibly, as from one colour, tone, or degree to another. **2** (*tr*) to arrange in grades or ranks.

gradation (grə'deɪʃən) *n* **1** a series of systematic stages; gradual progression. **2** (*often pl*) a stage or degree in such a series or progression. **3** the act or process of arranging or forming in stages, grades, etc., or of progressing evenly. **4** (in painting, drawing, or sculpture) transition from one colour, tone, or surface to another through a series of very slight changes. **5** *Linguistics.* any change in the quality or length of a vowel within a word indicating certain distinctions, such as inflectional or tense differentiations. See **ablaut.**
▸ **gra'dational** *adj*

grade (greɪd) *n* **1** a position or degree in a scale, as of quality, rank, size, or progression: *high-grade timber.* **2** a group of people or things of the same category. **3** *Chiefly US.* a military or other rank. **4** a stage in a course of progression. **5** a mark or rating indicating achievement or the worth of work done, as at school. **6** *US & Canad.* a unit of pupils of similar age or ability taught together at school. **7 make the grade.** *Inf.* **7a** to reach the required standard. **7b** to succeed. ◆ *vb* **grades, grading, graded. 8** (*tr*) to arrange according to quality, rank, etc. **9** (*tr*) to determine the grade of or assign a grade to. **10** (*intr*) to achieve or deserve a grade or rank. **11** to change or blend (something) gradually; merge. **12** (*tr*) to level (ground, a road, etc.) to a suitable gradient. ORIG C16: from F, from L *gradus* step, from *gradī* to step

-grade *adj combining form.* indicating a kind or manner of movement or progression: *plantigrade; retrograde.* ORIG via F from L *-gradus,* from *gradus* a step, from *gradī* to walk

gradely ('greɪdlɪ) *adj* **gradelier, gradeliest.** *Midland English dialect.* fine; excellent. ORIG C13: from ON *greidhligr,* from *greidhr* ready

grader ('greɪdə) *n* **1** a person or thing that grades. **2** a machine that levels earth, rubble, etc., as in road construction.

gradient ('greɪdɪənt) *n* **1** Also called (esp. US): **grade.** a part of a railway, road, etc., that slopes upwards or downwards; inclination. **2** Also called (esp. US and Canad.): **grade.** a measure of such a slope, esp. the ratio of the vertical distance between two points on the slope to the horizontal distance between them. **3** *Physics.* a measure of the change of some physical quantity, such as temperature or electric potential, over a specified distance. **4** *Maths.* (of a curve) the slope of the tangent at any point on a curve with respect to the horizontal axis. ◆ *adj* **5** sloping uniformly. ORIG C19: from L *gradiēns* stepping, from *gradī* to go

gradin ('greɪdɪn) *or* **gradine** (grə'di:n) *n* **1** a ledge above or behind an altar for candles, etc., to stand on. **2** one of a set of steps or seats arranged on a slope, as in an amphitheatre. ORIG C19: from F, from It. *gradino,* dim. of *grado* a step

gradual ('grædjʊəl) *adj* **1** occurring, developing, moving, etc., in small stages: *a gradual improvement in health.* **2** not steep or abrupt: *a gradual slope.* ◆ *n* **3** (*often cap.*) *Christianity.* **3a** an antiphon usually from the Psalms, sung or recited immediately after the epistle at Mass. **3b** a book of plainsong containing the words and music of the parts of the Mass that are sung by the cantors and choir. ORIG C16: from Med. L: relating to steps, from L *gradus* a step
▸ **'gradually** *adv* ▸ **'gradualness** *n*

gradualism ('grædjʊə,lɪzəm) *n* **1** the policy of seeking to change something gradually, esp. in politics. **2** the theory that explains major changes in fossils, rock strata, etc., in terms of gradual evolutionary processes rather than sudden violent catastrophes.
▸ **'gradualist** *n, adj* ▸ **,gradual'istic** *adj*

graduand ('grædjʊ,ænd) *n Chiefly Brit.* a person who is about to graduate. ORIG C19: from Med. L gerundive of *graduārī* to GRADUATE

graduate *n* ('grædjʊɪt). **1** a person who has been awarded a first degree from a university or college. **2** *US & Canad.* a student who has completed a course of studies at a high school and received a diploma. ◆ *vb* ('grædjʊ,eɪt), **graduates, graduating, graduated. 3** to receive or cause to receive a degree or diploma. **4** *Chiefly US & Canad.* to confer a degree, diploma, etc., upon. **5** (*tr*) to mark (a thermometer, flask, etc.) with units of measurement; calibrate. **6** (*tr*) to arrange or sort into groups according to type, quality, etc. **7** (*intr; often foll. by to*) to change by degrees (from something to something else). ORIG C15: from Med. L *graduārī* to take a degree, from L *gradus* a step
▸ **'gradu,ator** *n*

graduated pension *n* (in Britain) a national pension scheme in which employees' contributions are scaled in accordance with their wage rate.

graduation (,grædjʊ'eɪʃən) *n* **1** the act of graduating or the state of being graduated. **2** the ceremony at which school or college degrees and diplomas are conferred. **3** a mark or division or all the marks or divisions that indicate measure on an instrument or vessel.

Graeae ('gri:i:) *or* **Graiae** ★ *pl n Greek myth.* three aged sea deities, having only one eye and one tooth among them, guardians of their sisters, the Gorgons.

Graecism *or esp. US* **Grecism** ('gri:sɪzəm) *n* **1** Greek characteristics or style. **2** admiration for or imitation of these, as in sculpture or architecture. **3** a form of words characteristic of the idiom of the Greek language.

Graeco- *or esp. US* **Greco-** ('gri:kəʊ, 'grɛkəʊ) *combining form.* Greek: *Graeco-Roman.*

Graeco-Roman *or esp. US* **Greco-Roman** *adj* of, characteristic of, or relating to Greek and Roman influences.

Graf ★ (græf) *n* **Steffi.** born 1969, German tennis player: Wimbledon champion 1988, 1989, 1991, 1992, 1993, 1995, and 1996; retired in 1999.

graffiti (græ'fi:tɪ) *pl n* (*sometimes functioning as sing*) drawings, messages, etc., often obscene, scribbled on the walls of public lavatories, advertising posters, etc. ORIG C19: see GRAFFITO

graffito (græ'fi:təʊ) *n, pl* **graffiti** (-tɪ). **1** *Archaeol.* any inscription or drawing scratched onto a surface, esp. rock or pottery. **2** See **graffiti.** ORIG C19: from It.: a little scratch, from L *graphium* stylus, from Gk *grapheion;* see GRAFT[1]

graft[1] (grɑ:ft) *n* **1** *Horticulture.* **1a** a small piece of plant tissue (the scion) that is made to unite with an established plant (the stock), which supports and nourishes it. **1b** the plant resulting from the union of scion and stock. **1c** the point of union between the scion and the stock. **2** *Surgery.* a piece of tissue transplanted from a donor or from the patient's own body to an area of the body in need of the tissue. **3** the act of joining one thing to an-

other as by grafting. ◆ *vb* **4** *Horticulture.* **4a** to induce (a plant or part of a plant) to unite with another part or (of a plant or part of a plant) to unite in this way. **4b** to produce (fruit, flowers, etc.) by this means or (of fruit, etc.) to grow by this means. **5** to transplant (tissue) or (of tissue) to be transplanted. **6** to attach or incorporate or become attached or incorporated: *to graft a happy ending onto a sad tale.* ORIG C15: from OF *graffe,* from Med. L *graphium,* from L: stylus, from Gk *grapheion,* from *graphein* to write
▸ **'grafting** *n*

graft² (grɑːft) *n* **1** *Inf.* work (esp. in **hard graft**). **2a** the acquisition of money, power, etc., by dishonest or unfair means, esp. by taking advantage of a position of trust. **2b** something gained in this way. **2c** a payment made to a person profiting by such a practice. ◆ *vb* **3** (*intr*) *Inf.* to work, esp. hard. **4** to acquire by or practise graft. ORIG C19: from ?
▸ **'grafter** *n*

Graham ★ ('greɪəm) *n* **1 Martha.** 1893–1991, US dancer and choreographer. **2 Thomas.** 1805–69, British physicist: proposed **Graham's law** (1831) of diffusion and coined the terms osmosis, crystalloids, and colloids. **3 William Franklin,** known as *Billy.* born 1918, US evangelist.

Grahame ★ ('greɪəm) *n* **Kenneth.** 1859–1932, British author, noted for the children's classic *The Wind in the Willows* (1908).

Graham Land ★ *n* the N part of the Antarctic Peninsula: became part of the British Antarctic Territory in 1962 (formerly part of the Falkland Islands Dependencies).

Graiae ★ ('greiːiː, 'graɪiː) *pl n* a variant of **Graeae.**

Graian Alps ★ ('greɪən, 'graɪ-) *pl n* the N part of the Western Alps, in France and NW Piedmont, Italy. Highest peak: Gran Paradiso, 4061 m (13 323 ft).

Grail (greɪl) *n* See **Holy Grail.**

grain (greɪn) *n* **1** the small hard seedlike fruit of a grass, esp. a cereal plant. **2** a mass of such fruits, esp. when gathered for food. **3** the plants, collectively, from which such fruits are harvested. **4** a small hard particle: *a grain of sand.* **5a** the general direction or arrangement of the fibres, layers, or particles in wood, leather, stone, etc. **5b** the pattern or texture resulting from such an arrangement. **6** the relative size of the particles of a substance: *sugar of fine grain.* **7** the granular texture of a rock, mineral, etc. **8** the outer layer of a hide or skin from which the hair or wool has been removed. **9** the smallest unit of weight in the avoirdupois, Troy, and apothecaries' systems: equal to 0.0648 gram. **10** the threads or direction of threads in a woven fabric. **11** *Photog.* any of a large number of particles in a photographic emulsion. **12** cleavage lines in crystalline material. **13** *Chem.* any of a large number of small crystals forming a solid. **14** a very small amount: *a grain of truth.* **15** natural disposition, inclination, or character (esp. in **go against the grain**). **16** *Astronautics.* a homogeneous mass of solid propellant in a form designed to give the required combustion characteristics for a particular rocket. **17** (not in technical usage) kermes or a red dye made from this insect. ◆ *vb* (*mainly tr*) **18** (*also intr*) to form grains or cause to form into grains; granulate; crystallize. **19** to give a granular or roughened appearance or texture to. **20** to paint, stain, etc., in imitation of the grain of wood or leather. **21a** to remove the hair or wool from (a hide or skin) before tanning. **21b** to raise the grain pattern on (leather). ORIG C13: from OF, from L *grānum*

grain alcohol *n* ethanol containing about 10 per cent of water, made by the fermentation of grain.

grain elevator *n* a machine for raising grain to a higher level, esp. one having an endless belt fitted with scoops.

Grainger ★ ('greɪndʒə) *n* **Percy Aldridge.** 1882–1961, Australian pianist, composer, and collector of folk music.

graining ('greɪnɪŋ) *n* **1** the pattern or texture of the grain of wood, leather, etc. **2** the process of painting, printing, staining, etc., a surface in imitation of a grain. **3** a surface produced by such a process.

grainy ('greɪnɪ) *adj* **grainier, grainiest. 1** resembling, full of, or composed of grain; granular. **2** resembling the grain of wood, leather, etc. **3** *Photog.* having poor definition because of large grain size.
▸ **'graininess** *n*

grallatorial (ˌgrælə'tɔːrɪəl) *adj* of or relating to long-legged wading birds. ORIG C19: from NL, from L *grallātor* one who walks on stilts, from *grallae* stilts

gram¹ (græm) *n* a metric unit of mass equal to one thousandth of a kilogram. Symbol: g ORIG C18: from F *gramme,* from LL *gramma,* from Gk: small weight, from *graphein* to write

gram² (græm) *n* **1** any of several leguminous plants whose seeds are used as food in India. **2** the seed of any of these plants. ORIG C18: from Port. *gram* (modern spelling: *grão*), from L *grānum* GRAIN

gram. *abbrev. for:* **1** grammar. **2** grammatical.

-gram *n combining form.* indicating a drawing or something written or recorded: *hexagram; telegram.* ORIG from L *-gramma,* from Gk, from *gramma* letter & *grammē* line

gram atom *or* **gram-atomic weight** *n* an amount of an element equal to its atomic weight expressed in grams: now replaced by the mole.

gramineous (grə'mɪnɪəs) *adj* **1** of, relating to, or belonging to the grass family. **2** resembling a grass; grasslike. ◆ Also: **graminaceous** (ˌgræmɪ'neɪʃəs). ORIG C17: from L, from *grāmen* grass

graminivorous (ˌgræmɪ'nɪvərəs) *adj* (of animals) feeding on grass. ORIG C18: from L *grāmen* grass + -VOROUS

grammar ('græmə) *n* **1** the branch of linguistics that deals with syntax and morphology, sometimes also phonology and semantics. **2** the abstract system of rules in terms of which a person's mastery of his native language can be explained. **3** a systematic description of the grammatical facts of a language. **4** a book containing an account of the grammatical facts of a language or recommendations as to rules for the proper use of a language. **5** the use of language with regard to its correctness or social propriety, esp. in syntax: *the teacher told him to watch his grammar.* ORIG C14: from OF, from L, from Gk *grammatikē* (*tekhnē*) the grammatical (art), from *grammatikos* concerning letters, from *gramma* letter

grammarian (grə'mɛərɪən) *n* **1** a person whose occupation is the study of grammar. **2** the author of a grammar.

grammar school *n* **1** *Brit.* (esp. formerly) a state-maintained secondary school providing an education with an academic bias. **2** *US.* another term for **elementary school. 3** *Austral.* a private school, esp. one controlled by a church. **4** *NZ.* a secondary school forming part of the public education system.

grammatical (grə'mætɪkᵊl) *adj* **1** of or relating to grammar. **2** (of a sentence) well formed; regarded as correct.
▸ **gram'matically** *adv* ▸ **gram'maticalness** *n*

gram molecule *or* **gram-molecular weight** *n* an amount of a compound equal to its molecular weight expressed in grams: now replaced by the mole. See **mole³**.

Grammy ('græmɪ) *n, pl* **Grammys** *or* **Grammies.** (in the US) one of the gold-plated discs awarded annually for outstanding achievement in the record industry. ORIG C20: from GRAM(OPHONE) + *-my* as in EMMY

gramophone ('græməˌfəʊn) *n* **1a** Also called: **record player.** a device for reproducing the sounds stored on a record: now usually applied to the early type that uses an acoustic horn. US and Canad. word: **phonograph. 1b** (*as modifier*): *a gramophone record.* **2** the technique of recording sound on disc: *the gramophone has made music widely available.* ORIG C19: orig. a trademark, ? based on an inversion of *phonogram;* see PHONO-, -GRAM

Grampian Mountains ★ ('græmpɪən) *pl n* **1** a mountain system of central Scotland, extending from the southwest to the northeast and separating the Highlands from the Lowlands. Highest peak: Ben Nevis, 1343 m (4406 ft). **2** a mountain range in SE Australia, in W Victoria. ◆ Also called: **the Grampians.**

Grampian Region ★ *n* a former (1975–96) local government region in NE Scotland.

grampus ('græmpəs) *n, pl* **grampuses. 1** a widely distributed slaty-grey dolphin with a blunt snout. **2** another name for **killer whale.** ORIG C16: from OF *graspois,* from *gras* fat (from L *crassus*) + *pois* fish (from L *piscis*)

Gram's method (græmz) *n Bacteriol.* **1** a technique used to classify bacteria by staining them with a violet iodine solution. **2 Gram-positive** (*or* **Gram-negative**). *adj* denoting bacteria that do (*or* do not) retain this stain. ORIG C19: after H. C. J. *Gram* (1853–1938), Danish physician

gran (græn) *n* an informal word for **grandmother.**

Granada ★ (grəˈnɑːdə) *n* **1** a former kingdom of S Spain, in Andalusia: founded in the 13th century and divided in 1833 into the present-day provinces of Granada, Almería, and Málaga. **2** a city in S Spain, in Andalusia: capital of the Moorish kingdom of Granada from 1238 to 1492 and a great commercial and cultural centre, containing the Alhambra palace (13th and 14th centuries); university (1531). Pop.: 272 738 (1995 est.). **3** a city in SW Nicaragua, on the NW shore of Lake Nicaragua: the oldest city in the country, founded in 1523 by Córdoba; attacked frequently by pirates in the 17th century. Pop.: 74 396 (1995 est.).

granadilla (ˌgrænəˈdɪlə) *n* **1** any of various passionflowers that have edible egg-shaped fleshy fruit. **2** Also called: **passion fruit.** the fruit of such a plant. ORIG C18: from Sp., dim. of *granada* pomegranate, from LL *grānātum*

Granados ★ (*Spanish* graˈnaðɔs) *n* **Enrique** (enˈrrike), full name *Enrique Granados y Campina.* 1867–1916, Spanish composer.

granary (ˈgrænərɪ; *US* ˈgreɪnərɪ) *n, pl* **granaries. 1** a building for storing threshed grain. **2** a region that produces a large amount of grain. ◆ *adj* **3** (*cap.*) *Trademark.* (of bread, flour, etc.) containing malted wheat grain. ORIG C16: from L *grānārium,* from *grānum* GRAIN

Gran Canaria ★ (graŋ kaˈnarja) *n* the Spanish name for **Grand Canary.**

Gran Chaco ★ (*Spanish* gran ˈtʃako) *n* a plain of S central South America, between the Andes and the Paraguay River in SE Bolivia, E Paraguay, and N Argentina: huge swamps and scrub forest. Area: about 780 000 sq. km (300 000 sq. miles). Often shortened to: **Chaco.**

grand (grænd) *adj* **1** large or impressive in size, extent, or consequence: *grand mountain scenery.* **2** characterized by or attended with magnificence or display; sumptuous: *a grand feast.* **3** of great distinction or pretension; dignified or haughty. **4** designed to impress: *grand gestures.* **5** very good; wonderful. **6** comprehensive; complete: *a grand total.* **7** worthy of respect; fine: *a grand old man.* **8** large or impressive in conception or execution: *grand ideas.* **9** most important; chief: *the grand arena.* ◆ *n* **10** See **grand piano. 11** (*pl* **grand**) *Sl.* a thousand pounds or dollars. ORIG C16: from OF, from L *grandis*
▸ **ˈgrandly** *adv* ▸ **ˈgrandness** *n*

grand- *prefix* (in designations of kinship) one generation removed in ascent or descent: *grandson; grandfather.* ORIG from F *grand-,* on the model of L *magnus* in such phrases as *avunculus magnus* great-uncle

grandad, granddad (ˈgrænˌdæd) *or* **grandaddy, granddaddy** (ˈgrænˌdædɪ) *n, pl* **grandads, granddads** *or* **grandaddies, granddaddies.** informal words for **grandfather.**

grandam (ˈgrændəm, -dæm) *or* **grandame** (ˈgrændeɪm, -dəm) *n* an archaic word for **grandmother.** ORIG C13: from Anglo-F *grandame,* from OF GRAND- + *dame* lady, mother

grandaunt (ˈgrændˌɑːnt) *n* another name for **great-aunt.**

Grand Bahama ★ *n* an island in the Atlantic, in the W Bahamas. Pop.: 40 898 (1990). Area: 1114 sq. km (430 sq. miles).

Grand Banks ★ *pl n* a part of the continental shelf in the Atlantic, extending for about 560 km (350 miles) off the SE coast of Newfoundland: meeting place of the cold Labrador Current and the warm Gulf Stream, producing frequent fogs and rich fishing grounds.

Grand Canal ★ *n* **1** a canal in E China, extending north from Hangzhou to Tianjin: the longest canal in China, now partly silted up; central section, linking the Yangtze and Yellow Rivers, finished in 486 B.C.; north section finished by Kublai Khan between 1282 and 1292. Length: about 1600 km (1000 miles). Chinese name: **Da Yunhe. 2** a canal in Venice, forming the main water thoroughfare: noted for its bridges, the Rialto, and the fine palaces along its banks.

Grand Canary ★ *n* an island in the Atlantic, in the Canary Islands: part of the Spanish province of Las Palmas. Capital: Las Palmas. Pop.: 631 000 (latest est.). Area: 1533 sq. km (592 sq. miles). Spanish name: **Gran Canaria.**

Grand Canyon ★ *n* a gorge of the Colorado River in N Arizona, extending from its junction with the Little Colorado River to Lake Mead; cut by vertical river erosion through the multicoloured strata of a high plateau; partly contained in the **Grand Canyon National Park,** covering 2610 sq. km (1008 sq. miles). Length: 451 km (280 miles). Width: 6 km (4 miles) to 29 km (18 miles). Greatest depth: over 1.5 km (1 mile).

grandchild (ˈgrænˌtʃaɪld) *n, pl* **grandchildren.** the son or daughter of one's child.

Grand Coulee ★ (ˈkuːlɪ) *n* a canyon in central Washington State, over 120 m (400 ft) deep, at the N end of which is situated the **Grand Coulee Dam,** on the Columbia River. Height of dam: 168 m (550 ft). Length of dam: 1310 m (4300 ft).

granddaughter (ˈgrænˌdɔːtə) *n* a daughter of one's son or daughter.

grand duchess *n* **1** the wife or widow of a grand duke. **2** a woman who holds the rank of grand duke in her own right.

grand duchy *n* the territory, state, or principality of a grand duke or grand duchess.

grand duke *n* **1** a prince or nobleman who rules a territory, state, or principality. **2** a son or a male descendant in the male line of a Russian tsar. **3** a medieval Russian prince who ruled over other princes.

grande dame *French.* (grɑ̃d dam) *n* a woman regarded as the most experienced, prominent, or venerable member of her profession, etc.

grandee (grænˈdiː) *n* **1** a Spanish or Portuguese prince or nobleman of the highest rank. **2** a person of high station. ORIG C16: from Sp. *grande*

Grande-Terre ★ (*French* grɑ̃dtɛr) *n* a French island in the Caribbean, in the Lesser Antilles: one of the two main islands which constitute Guadeloupe. Chief town: Pointe-à-Pitre.

grandeur (ˈgrændʒə) *n* **1** personal greatness, esp. when based on dignity, character, or accomplishments. **2** magnificence; splendour. **3** pretentious or bombastic behaviour.

Grand Falls ★ *pl n* the former name (until 1965) of **Churchill Falls.**

grandfather (ˈgrænˌfɑːðə, ˈgrænd-) *n* **1** the father of one's father or mother. **2** (*often pl*) a male ancestor. **3** (*often cap.*) a familiar term of address for an old man.
▸ **ˈgrandˌfatherly** *adj*

grandfather clock *n* a long-pendulum clock in a tall standing wooden case.

Grand Guignol *French.* (grɑ̃ giɲɔl) *n* **a** a brief sensational play intended to horrify. **b** (*modifier*) of or like plays of this kind. ORIG C20: after *Le Grand Guignol,* a small theatre in Montmartre, Paris

grandiloquent (grænˈdɪləkwənt) *adj* inflated, pompous, or bombastic in style or expression. ORIG C16: from L *grandiloquus,* from *grandis* great + *loquī* to speak
▸ **granˈdiloquence** *n* ▸ **granˈdiloquently** *adv*

grandiose (ˈgrændɪˌəʊs) *adj* **1** pretentiously grand or stately. **2** imposing in conception or execution. ORIG C19: from F, from It., from *grande* great; see GRAND
▸ **ˈgrandiˌosely** *adv* ▸ **grandiosity** (ˌgrændɪˈɒsɪtɪ) *n*

grand jury *n Law.* (esp. in the US and, now rarely, in Canada) a jury summoned to inquire into accusations of crime and ascertain whether the evidence is adequate to found an indictment. Abolished in Britain in 1948.

grand larceny *n* **1** (formerly, in England) the theft of property valued at over 12 pence. Abolished in 1827. **2** (in some states of the US) the theft of property of which the value is above a specified figure.

grandma (ˈgrænˌmɑː), **grandmama,** *or* **grand-**

mamma ('grænmə,mɑː) *n* informal words for **grandmother.**

grand mal (grɒn mæl) *n* a form of epilepsy characterized by loss of consciousness for up to five minutes and violent convulsions. Cf. **petit mal.** ORIG F: great illness

Grandma Moses ★ *n* the nickname of (Anna Mary Robertson) **Moses.**

Grand Manan ★ (mə'næn) *n* a Canadian island, off the SW coast of New Brunswick: separated from the coast of Maine by the **Grand Manan Channel.** Area: 147 sq. km (57 sq. miles).

grandmaster ('grænd,mɑːstə) *n* **1** *Chess.* one of the top chess players of a particular country. **2** a leading exponent of any of various arts.

Grand Master *n* the title borne by the head of any of various societies, orders, and other organizations, such as the Templars, Freemasons, or the various martial arts.

grandmother ('græn,mʌðə, 'grænd-) *n* **1** the mother of one's father or mother. **2** (*often pl*) a female ancestor.
▸ **'grand,motherly** *adj*

Grand National *n* **the.** an annual steeplechase run at Aintree, Liverpool, since 1839.

grandnephew ('græn,nɛvjuː, -,nɛfjuː, 'grænd-) *n* another name for **great-nephew.**

grandniece ('græn,niːs, 'grænd-) *n* another name for **great-niece.**

grand opera *n* an opera that has a serious plot and is entirely in musical form, with no spoken dialogue.

grandpa ('græn,pɑː) *or* **grandpapa** ('grænpə,pɑː) *n* informal words for **grandfather.**

grandparent ('græn,pɛərənt, 'grænd-) *n* the father or mother of either of one's parents.

grand piano *n* a form of piano in which the strings are arranged horizontally.

Grand Pré ★ (grɒn preɪ; *French* grɑ̃ pre) *n* a village in SE Canada, in W Nova Scotia: setting of Longfellow's *Evangeline.*

Grand Prix (grɒn priː; *French* grɑ̃ pri) *n* **1** any of a series of formula motor races to determine the annual Driver's World Championship. **2** a very important competitive event in various other sports, such as athletics, snooker, or powerboating. ORIG F: great prize

Grand Rapids ★ *n* (*functioning as sing*) a city in SW Michigan: electronics, car parts. Pop.: 188 242 (1996 est.).

grandsire ('græn,saɪə, 'grænd-) *n* an archaic word for **grandfather.**

grand slam *n* **1** *Bridge, etc.* the winning of 13 tricks by one player or side or the contract to do so. Cf. **little slam. 2** the winning of all major competitions in a season, esp. in tennis and golf. **3** (*often caps.*) *Rugby union.* the winning of all the games in the annual Six Nations Championship involving Scotland, England, Wales, Ireland, France, and Italy.

grandson ('grænsʌn, 'grænd-) *n* a son of one's son or daughter.

grandstand ('græn,stænd, 'grænd-) *n* **1** a terraced block of seats commanding the best view at racecourses, football pitches, etc. **2** the spectators in a grandstand.

grand tour *n* **1** (formerly) an extended tour through the major cities of Europe, esp. one undertaken by a rich or aristocratic Englishman to complete his education. **2** *Inf.* an extended sightseeing trip, tour of inspection, etc.

granduncle ('grænd,ʌŋkəl) *n* another name for **great-uncle.**

grand unified theory *n Physics.* any of a number of theories of elementary particles and fundamental interactions designed to explain the electromagnetic, strong, and weak interactions in terms of a single mathematical formalism. Abbrev.: **GUT.**

Grand Union Canal ★ *n* a canal in S England linking London and the Midlands: opened in 1801.

grange (greɪndʒ) *n* **1** *Chiefly Brit.* a farm, esp. a farmhouse or country house with its various outbuildings. **2** *Arch.* a granary or barn. ORIG C13: from Anglo-F *graunge,* from Med. L *grānica,* from L *grānum* GRAIN

Grangemouth ★ ('greɪndʒmaʊθ, -məθ) *n* a port in Scotland, in Falkirk council area: now Scotland's second port, with oil refineries, shipyards, and chemical industries. Pop.: 18 739 (1991).

Granicus ★ (grə'naɪkəs) *n* an ancient river in NW Asia Minor where Alexander the Great won his first major battle against the Persians (334 B.C.).

granite ('grænɪt) *n* **1** a light-coloured coarse-grained acid plutonic igneous rock consisting of quartz and feldspars: widely used for building. **2** great hardness, endurance, or resolution. ORIG C17: from It. *granito* grained, from *grano* grain, from L *grānum*
▸ **granitic** (grə'nɪtɪk) *adj*

graniteware ('grænɪt,wɛə) *n* **1** iron vessels coated with enamel of a granite-like appearance. **2** a type of pottery with a speckled glaze.

granivorous (græ'nɪvərəs) *adj* (of animals) feeding on seeds and grain.
▸ **granivore** ('grænɪ,vɔː) *n*

granny *or* **grannie** ('grænɪ) *n, pl* **grannies. 1** informal words for **grandmother. 2** *Inf.* an irritatingly fussy person. **3** See **granny knot.**

granny bond *n Brit. inf.* a savings scheme available originally only to people over retirement age.

granny farm *n Derog. sl.* an old people's home, esp. one that charges high fees and offers poor care.

granny flat *n* self-contained accommodation within or built onto a house, suitable for an elderly parent.

granny knot *or* **granny's knot** *n* a reef knot with the ends crossed the wrong way, making it liable to slip or jam.

Gran Paradiso ★ (*Italian* gram para'diːzo) *n* a mountain in NW Italy, in NW Piedmont: the highest peak of the Graian Alps. Height: 4061 m (13 323 ft).

grant (grɑːnt) *vb* (*tr*) **1** to consent to perform or fulfil: *to grant a wish.* **2** (*may take a clause as object*) to permit as a favour, indulgence, etc.: *to grant an interview.* **3** (*may take a clause as object*) to acknowledge the validity of; concede: *I grant what you say is true.* **4** to bestow, esp. in a formal manner. **5** to transfer (property) to another, esp. by deed; convey. **6 take for granted. 6a** to accept or assume without question: *one takes certain amenities for granted.* **6b** to fail to appreciate the value, merit, etc., of (a person). ◆ *n* **7** a sum of money provided by a government, local authority, or public fund to finance educational study, building repairs, overseas aid, etc. **8** a privilege, right, etc., that has been granted. **9** the act of granting. **10** a transfer of property by deed; conveyance. ORIG C13: from OF *graunter,* from Vulgar L *credentāre* (unattested), from L *crēdere* to believe
▸ **'grantable** *adj* ▸ **'granter** *or* (*Law*) **'grantor** *n*

Grant ★ (grɑːnt) *n* **1 Cary,** real name *Alexander Archibald Leach.* 1904–86, US film actor, born in England. His films include *The Philadelphia Story* (1940) and *Arsenic and Old Lace* (1944). **2 Duncan (James Corrowr).** 1885–1978, British painter. **3 Ulysses S(impson),** real name *Hiram Ulysses Grant.* 1822–85, 18th president of the US (1869–77); commander in chief of Union forces in the American Civil War (1864–65).

Granta ★ ('græntə, 'grɑːntə) *n* the original name, still in use locally, for the River Cam.

grantee (grɑːn'tiː) *n Law.* a person to whom a grant is made.

Granth (grʌnt) *n* the sacred scripture of the Sikhs. ORIG from Hindi, from Sansk. *grantha* a book

Grantham ★ ('grænθəm) *n* a town in E England, in Lincolnshire: birthplace of Sir Isaac Newton and Margaret Thatcher. Pop.: 33 243 (1991).

grant-in-aid *n, pl* **grants-in-aid.** a sum of money granted by one government to a lower level of government for a programme, etc.

grant-maintained *adj* (**grant maintained** *when postpositive*) (of schools or educational institutions) funded directly by central government.

gran turismo ('græn tʊə'rɪzməʊ) *n, pl* **gran turismos.** See **GT.** ORIG C20: from It.

granular ('grænjʊlə) *adj* **1** of, like, or containing granules. **2** having a grainy surface.
▸ **granularity** (ˌgrænjʊ'lærɪtɪ) *n* ▸ **'granularly** *adv*

granulate ('grænjʊˌleɪt) *vb* **granulates, granulating, granulated. 1** (*tr*) to make into grains: *granulated sugar.* **2** to make or become roughened in surface texture.
▸ **ˌgranu'lation** *n* ▸ **'granulative** *adj* ▸ **'granuˌlator** *or* **'granuˌlater** *n*

granule ('grænju:l) *n* a small grain. ORIG C17: from LL *grānulum* a small GRAIN

granulocyte ('grænjʊləˌsaɪt) *n* any of a group of unpigmented blood cells having cytoplasmic granules that take up various dyes.

Granville ★ ('grænvɪl) *n* **1st Earl,** title of *John Carteret.* 1690–1763, British statesman: secretary of state (1742–44); a leading opponent of Walpole.

Granville-Barker ★ (-'bɑ:kə) *n* **Harley.** 1877–1946, British dramatist, theatre director, and critic, noted particularly for his *Prefaces to Shakespeare* (1927–47).

grape (greɪp) *n* **1** the fruit of the grapevine, which has a purple or green skin and sweet flesh: eaten raw, dried to make raisins, currants, or sultanas, or used for making wine. **2** See **grapevine** (sense 1). **3 the grape.** *Inf.* wine. **4** See **grapeshot.** ORIG C13: from OF *grape* bunch of grapes, of Gmc origin; rel. to CRAMP[2], GRAPPLE
▸ **'grapey** *or* **'grapy** *adj*

grapefruit ('greɪpˌfru:t) *n, pl* **grapefruit** *or* **grapefruits. 1** a tropical or subtropical evergreen tree. **2** the large round edible fruit of this tree, which has yellow rind and juicy slightly bitter pulp.

grape hyacinth *n* any of various Eurasian bulbous plants of the lily family with clusters of rounded blue flowers resembling tiny grapes.

grapeshot ('greɪpˌʃɒt) *n* ammunition for cannons consisting of a cluster of iron balls that scatter after firing.

grape sugar *n* another name for **dextrose.**

grapevine ('greɪpˌvaɪn) *n* **1** any of several vines of E Asia, widely cultivated for its fruit (grapes). **2** *Inf.* an unofficial means of relaying information, esp. from person to person.

graph (grɑ:f) *n* **1** Also called: **chart.** a drawing depicting the relation between certain sets of numbers or quantities by means of a series of dots, lines, etc., plotted with reference to a set of axes. **2** *Maths.* a drawing depicting a functional relation between two or three variables by means of a curve or surface containing only those points whose coordinates satisfy the relation. **3** *Linguistics.* a symbol in a writing system not further subdivisible into other such symbols. ◆ *vb* **4** (*tr*) to draw or represent in a graph. ORIG C19: short for *graphic formula*

-graph *n combining form.* **1** an instrument that writes or records: *telegraph.* **2** a writing, record, or drawing: *autograph; lithograph.* ORIG via L from Gk, from *graphein* to write
▸ **-graphic** *or* **-graphical** *adj combining form.* ▸ **-graphically** *adv combining form.*

grapheme ('græfi:m) *n Linguistics.* the complete class of letters or combinations of letters that represent one speech sound: for instance, the *f* in *full,* the *gh* in *cough,* and the *ph* in *photo* are members of the same grapheme. ORIG C20: from Gk *graphēma* a letter
▸ **gra'phemically** *adv*

-grapher *n combining form.* **1** indicating a person skilled in a subject: *geographer; photographer.* **2** indicating a person who writes or draws in a specified way: *stenographer; lithographer.*

graphic ('græfɪk) *or* **graphical** *adj* **1** vividly or clearly described: *a graphic account of the disaster.* **2** of or relating to writing: *graphic symbols.* **3** *Maths.* using, relating to, or determined by a graph: *a graphic representation of the figures.* **4** of or relating to the graphic arts. **5** *Geol.* having or denoting a texture resembling writing: *graphic granite.* ORIG C17: from L *graphicus,* from Gk *graphikos,* from *graphein* to write
▸ **'graphically** *adv* ▸ **'graphicness** *n*

graphicacy ('græfɪkəsɪ) *n* the ability to understand and use maps, symbols, etc. ORIG C20: formed on the model of *literacy*

graphical user interface *n* an interface between a user and a computer system that allows the user to operate the system by means of pictorial devices, such as menus and icons.

graphic arts *pl n* any of the fine or applied visual arts based on drawing or the use of line, esp. illustration and printmaking of all kinds.

graphic equalizer *n* a tone control that enables the output signal of an audio amplifier to be adjusted in each of a series of frequency bands by means of sliding contacts.

graphic novel *n* a novel in the form of a comic strip.

graphics ('græfɪks) *n* **1** (*functioning as sing*) the process or art of drawing in accordance with mathematical principles. **2** (*functioning as sing*) the study of writing systems. **3** (*functioning as pl*) the drawings, photographs, etc., in a magazine or book, or in a television or film production. **4** (*functioning as pl*) *Computing.* information displayed in the form of diagrams, graphs, etc.

graphite ('græfaɪt) *n* a blackish soft form of carbon used in pencils, electrodes, as a lubricant, as a moderator in nuclear reactors, and, in carbon fibre form, for tough lightweight sports equipment. ORIG C18: from G *Graphit,* from Gk *graphein* to write + -ITE[1]
▸ **graphitic** (grə'fɪtɪk) *adj*

graphology (græ'fɒlədʒɪ) *n* **1** the study of handwriting, esp. to analyse the writer's character. **2** *Linguistics.* the study of writing systems.
▸ **ˌgrapho'logical** *adj* ▸ **gra'phologist** *n*

graph paper *n* paper printed with intersecting lines for drawing graphs, diagrams, etc.

-graphy *n combining form.* **1** indicating a form of writing, representing, etc.: *calligraphy; photography.* **2** indicating an art or descriptive science: *choreography; oceanography.* ORIG via L from Gk, from *graphein* to write

grapnel ('græpnᵊl) *n* **1** a device with a multiple hook at one end and attached to a rope, which is thrown or hooked over a firm mooring to secure an object attached to the other end of the rope. **2** a light anchor for small boats. ORIG C14: from OF *grapin,* from *grape* a hook; see GRAPE

grappa ('græpə) *n* a spirit distilled from the fermented remains of grapes after pressing. ORIG It.: grape stalk, of Gmc origin; see GRAPE

Grappelli *or* **Grappelly** ★ (grə'pɛlɪ) *n* **Stéphane** ('stɛfᵊn). 1908–97, French jazz violinist: with Django Reinhardt, he led the Quintet of the Hot Club of France (1934–39).

grapple ('græpᵊl) *vb* **grapples, grappling, grappled. 1** to come to grips with (one or more persons), esp. to struggle in hand-to-hand combat. **2** (*intr;* foll. by *with*) to cope or contend: *to grapple with a financial problem.* **3** (*tr*) to secure with a grapple. ◆ *n* **4** any form of hook or metal instrument by which something is secured, such as a grapnel. **5a** the act of gripping or seizing, as in wrestling. **5b** a grip or hold. ORIG C16: from OF *grappelle* a little hook, from *grape* hook; see GRAPNEL
▸ **'grappler** *n*

grappling iron *or* **hook** *n* a grapnel, esp. one used for securing ships.

graptolite ('græptəˌlaɪt) *n* an extinct Palaeozoic colonial animal: a common fossil. ORIG C19: from Gk *graptos* written, from *graphein* to write + -LITE

Grasmere ★ ('grɑ:sˌmɪə) *n* a village in NW England, in Cumbria at the head of **Lake Grasmere**: home of William Wordsworth and of Thomas de Quincey.

grasp (grɑ:sp) *vb* **1** to grip (something) firmly as with the hands. **2** (when *intr,* often foll. by *at*) to struggle, snatch, or grope (for). **3** (*tr*) to understand, esp. with effort. ◆ *n* **4** the act of grasping. **5** a grip or clasp, as of a hand. **6** total rule or possession. **7** understanding; comprehension. ORIG C14: from Low G *grapsen;* rel. to OE *græppian* to seize
▸ **'graspable** *adj* ▸ **'grasper** *n*

grasping ('grɑ:spɪŋ) *adj* greedy; avaricious.
▸ **'graspingly** *adv* ▸ **'graspingness** *n*

grass (grɑːs) *n* **1** any of a family of plants having jointed stems sheathed by long narrow leaves, flowers in spikes, and seedlike fruits. The family includes cereals, bamboo, etc. **2** such plants collectively, in a lawn, meadow, etc. Related adj: **verdant. 3** ground on which such plants grow; a lawn, field, etc. **4** ground on which animals are grazed; pasture. **5** a slang word for **marijuana. 6** *Brit. sl.* a person who informs, esp. on criminals. **7 let the grass grow under one's feet.** to squander time or opportunity. ◆ *vb* **8** to cover or become covered with grass. **9** to feed or be fed with grass. **10** (*tr*) to spread (cloth, etc.) out on grass for drying or bleaching in the sun. **11** (*intr;* usually foll. by *on*) *Brit. sl.* to inform, esp. to the police. ◆ See also **grass up.** ORIG OE *græs*
▸ **'grass,like** *adj*

Grass ★ (*German* gras) *n* **Günter** (**Wilhelm**) ('gyntər). born 1927, German writer, noted particularly for his novels *The Tin Drum* (1959) and *The Rat* (1986), his other books include *Too Far Afield* (2000): Nobel prize for literature 1999.

grass hockey *n* in W Canada, field hockey, as contrasted with ice hockey.

grasshopper ('grɑːs,hɒpə) *n* an insect having hind legs adapted for leaping: typically terrestrial, feeding on plants, and producing a ticking sound by rubbing the hind legs against the leathery forewings.

grassland ('grɑːs,lænd) *n* **1** land, such as a prairie, on which grass predominates. **2** land reserved for natural grass pasture.

grass roots *pl n* **1** ordinary people as distinct from the active leadership of a group or organization, esp. a political party. **2** the essentials.

grass snake *n* **1** a harmless nonvenomous European snake having a brownish-green body with variable markings. **2** any of several similar related European snakes.

grass tree *n* **1** Also called: **blackboy.** an Australian plant of the lily family, having a woody stem, stiff grasslike leaves, and a spike of small white flowers. **2** any of several similar Australasian plants.

grass up *vb* (*tr, adv*) *Sl.* to inform on (someone), esp. to the police.

grass widow *or* (*masc*) **grass widower** *n* a person whose spouse is regularly away for a short period. ORIG C16: ? an allusion to a grass bed as representing an illicit relationship

grassy ('grɑːsɪ) *adj* **grassier, grassiest.** covered with, containing, or resembling grass.
▸ **'grassiness** *n*

grate[1] (greɪt) *vb* **grates, grating, grated. 1** (*tr*) to reduce to small shreds by rubbing against a rough or sharp perforated surface: *to grate carrots.* **2** to scrape (an object) against something or (objects) together, producing a harsh rasping sound, or (of objects) to scrape with such a sound. **3** (*intr;* foll. by *on* or *upon*) to annoy. ORIG C15: from OF *grater* to scrape, of Gmc origin
▸ **'grater** *n*

grate[2] (greɪt) *n* **1** a framework of metal bars for holding fuel in a fireplace, stove, or furnace. **2** a less common word for **fireplace. 3** another name for **grating**[1]. ◆ *vb* **4** (*tr*) to provide with a grate or grates. ORIG C14: from OF, from L *crātis* hurdle

grateful ('greɪtful) *adj* **1** thankful for gifts, favours, etc.; appreciative. **2** showing gratitude: *a grateful letter.* **3** favourable or pleasant: *a grateful rest.* ORIG C16: from obs. *grate,* from L *grātus* + -FUL
▸ **'gratefully** *adv* ▸ **'gratefulness** *n*

Gratian ★ ('greɪʃɪən) *n* Latin name *Flavius Gratianus.* 359–383 A.D., Roman emperor (367–383): ruled with his father Valentinian I (367–375); ruled the Western Roman Empire with his brother Valentinian II (375-83); appointed Theodosius I emperor of the Eastern Roman Empire (379).

graticule ('grætɪ,kjuːl) *n* **1** the grid of intersecting lines of latitude and longitude on which a map is drawn. **2** another name for **reticle.** ORIG C19: from F, from L *crāticula,* from *crātis* wickerwork

gratify ('grætɪ,faɪ) *vb* **gratifies, gratifying, gratified.** (*tr*) **1** to satisfy or please. **2** to yield to or indulge (a desire, whim, etc.). ORIG C16: from L *grātificārī,* from *grātus* grateful + *facere* to make
▸ **,gratifi'cation** *n* ▸ **'grati,fier** *n* ▸ **'grati,fying** *adj* ▸ **'grati,fyingly** *adv*

gratin (*French* gratɛ̃) See **au gratin.**

grating[1] ('greɪtɪŋ) *n* a framework of metal bars in the form of a grille set into a wall, pavement, etc., serving as a cover or guard but admitting air and sometimes light. Also called: **grate.**

grating[2] ('greɪtɪŋ) *adj* **1** (of sounds) harsh and rasping. **2** annoying; irritating. ◆ *n* **3** (*often pl*) something produced by grating.
▸ **'gratingly** *adv*

gratis ('greɪtɪs, 'grætɪs, 'grɑːtɪs) *adv, adj* (*postpositive*) without payment; free of charge. ORIG C15: from L: out of kindness, from *grātiīs,* ablative pl of *grātia* favour

gratitude ('grætɪ,tjuːd) *n* a feeling of thankfulness, as for gifts or favours. ORIG C16: from Med. L *grātitūdō,* from L *grātus* GRATEFUL

gratuitous (grə'tjuːɪtəs) *adj* **1** given or received without payment or obligation. **2** without cause; unjustified. ORIG C17: from L *grātuītus* from *grātia* favour
▸ **gra'tuitously** *adv* ▸ **gra'tuitousness** *n*

gratuity (grə'tjuːɪtɪ) *n, pl* **gratuities. 1** a gift or reward, usually of money, for services rendered; tip. **2** *Mil.* a financial award granted for long or meritorious service.

gratulatory ('grætjulətərɪ) *adj* expressing congratulation. ORIG C16: from L *grātulārī* to congratulate

Graubünden ★ (*German* grau'byndən) *n* an Alpine canton of E Switzerland: the largest of the cantons, but sparsely populated. Capital: Chur. Pop.: 184 300 (1994 est.). Area: 7109 sq. km (2773 sq. miles). Italian name: **Grigioni.** Romansch name: **Grishun.** French name: **Grisons.**

grav (græv) *n* a unit of acceleration equal to the standard acceleration of free fall. 1 grav is equivalent to 9.806 65 metres per second per second. Symbol: g

gravadlax ('grævəd,læks) *n* another name for **gravlax.**

gravamen (grə'veɪmɛn) *n, pl* **gravamina** (-'væmɪnə). **1** *Law.* that part of an accusation weighing most heavily against an accused. **2** *Law.* the substance or material grounds of a complaint. **3** a rare word for **grievance.** ORIG C17: from LL: trouble, from L *gravis* heavy

grave[1] (greɪv) *n* **1** a place for the burial of a corpse, esp. beneath the ground and usually marked by a tombstone. Related adj: **sepulchral. 2** something resembling a grave or resting place: *the ship went to its grave.* **3** (often preceded by *the*) a poetic term for **death. 4 make** (**someone**) **turn in his grave.** to do something that would have shocked or distressed a person now dead. ORIG OE *græf*

grave[2] (greɪv) *adj* **1** serious and solemn: *a grave look.* **2** full of or suggesting danger: *a grave situation.* **3** important; crucial: *grave matters of state.* **4** (of colours) sober or dull. **5** (grɑːv). *Phonetics.* of or relating to an accent (`) over vowels, denoting a pronunciation with lower or falling musical pitch (as in ancient Greek), with certain special quality (as in French), or in a manner that gives the vowel status as a syllable (as in English *agèd*). ◆ *n* **6** (*also* grɑːv). a grave accent. ORIG C16: from OF, from L *gravis*
▸ **'gravely** *adv* ▸ **'graveness** *n*

grave[3] (greɪv) *vb* **graves, graving, graved; graved** *or* **graven.** (*tr*) *Arch.* **1** to carve or engrave. **2** to fix firmly in the mind. ORIG OE *grafan*

grave[4] ('grɑːveɪ) *adj Music.* solemn. ORIG It.

grave clothes (greɪv) *pl n* the wrappings in which a dead body is interred.

gravel ('grævᵊl) *n* **1** a mixture of rock fragments and pebbles that is coarser than sand. **2** *Pathol.* small rough calculi in the kidneys or bladder. ◆ *vb* **gravels, gravelling, gravelled** *or US* **gravels, graveling, graveled.** (*tr*) **3** to cover with gravel. **4** to confound or confuse. **5** *US inf.* to annoy or disturb. ORIG C13: from OF *gravele,* dim. of *grave,* ? of Celtic origin

gravel-blind *adj Literary.* almost completely blind. ORIG C16: from GRAVEL + BLIND

gravelly ('grævəlɪ) *adj* **1** consisting of or abounding in gravel. **2** of or like gravel. **3** (esp. of a voice) harsh and grating.

graven ('greɪvᵊn) *vb* **1** a past participle of **grave**³. ◆ *adj* **2** strongly fixed.

Gravenhage ★ (xra:vən'ha:xə) *n* **'s.** a Dutch name for (The) **Hague.**

graven image *n Chiefly Bible.* a carved image used as an idol.

graver ('greɪvə) *n* any of various engraving or sculpting tools, such as a burin.

Graves¹ (grɑ:v) *n* (*sometimes not cap.*) a white or red wine from the district around Bordeaux, France.

Graves² **★** (greɪvz) *n* **Robert** (**Ranke**). 1895–1985, British writer, whose works include his autobiography, *Goodbye to All That* (1929), and the historical novels *I, Claudius* (1934) and *Claudius the God* (1934).

Gravesend ★ (ˌgreɪvz'ɛnd) *n* a river port in SE England, in NW Kent on the Thames. Pop.: 51 435 (1991).

gravestone ('greɪvˌstəʊn) *n* a stone marking a grave.

graveyard ('greɪvˌjɑ:d) *n* a place for graves; a burial ground, esp. a small one or one in a churchyard.

graveyard shift *n US.* the working shift between midnight and morning.

graveyard slot *n Television.* the hours from late night until early morning when the number of people watching television is at its lowest.

gravid ('grævɪd) *adj* the technical word for **pregnant.** ORIG C16: from L *gravidus,* from *gravis* heavy

gravimeter (grə'vɪmɪtə) *n* **1** an instrument for measuring the earth's gravitational field at points on its surface. **2** an instrument for measuring relative density. ORIG C18: from F *gravimètre,* from L *gravis* heavy
▸ **gra'vimetry** *n*

gravimetric (ˌgrævɪ'mɛtrɪk) *adj* **1** of, concerned with, or using measurement by weight. **2** *Chem.* of analysis of quantities by weight.

graving dock *n* another term for **dry dock.**

gravitas ('grævɪˌtæs) *n* seriousness or solemnity, esp. of conduct or demeanour; weight or authority. ORIG C20: from L *gravitās* weight, from *gravis* heavy

gravitate ('grævɪˌteɪt) *vb* **gravitates, gravitating, gravitated.** (*intr*) **1** *Physics.* to move under the influence of gravity. **2** (usually foll. by *to* or *towards*) to be influenced or drawn, as by strong impulses. **3** to sink or settle.
▸ **'graviˌtater** *n* ▸ **'graviˌtative** *adj*

gravitation (ˌgrævɪ'teɪʃən) *n* **1** the force of attraction that bodies exert on one another as a result of their mass. **2** any process or result caused by this interaction. ◆ Also called: **gravity.**
▸ **ˌgravi'tational** *adj* ▸ **ˌgravi'tationally** *adv*

gravitational constant *n* the factor relating force to mass and distance in Newton's law of gravitation. Symbol: *G*

gravitational field *n* the field of force surrounding a body of finite mass in which another body would experience an attractive force that is proportional to the product of the masses and inversely proportional to the square of the distance between them.

gravitational mass *n* the mass of a body expressed in terms of the gravitational force between it and the earth. Cf. **inertial mass.**

graviton ('grævɪˌtɒn) *n* a postulated quantum of gravitational energy, usually considered to be a particle with zero charge and rest mass and a spin of 2.

gravity ('grævɪtɪ) *n, pl* **gravities. 1** the force of attraction that moves or tends to move bodies towards the centre of a celestial body, such as the earth or moon. **2** the property of being heavy or having weight. **3** another name for **gravitation. 4** seriousness or importance, esp. as a consequence of an action or opinion. **5** manner or conduct that is solemn or dignified. **6** lowness in pitch. **7** (*modifier*) of or relating to gravity or gravitation or their effects: *gravity feed.* ORIG C16: from L *gravitās* weight, from *gravis* heavy

gravity wave *n Physics.* **1** a wave propagated in a gravitational field, predicted to occur as a result of an accelerating mass. **2** a surface wave on water or other liquid propagated because of the weight of liquid in the crests. ◆ Also called: **gravitational wave.**

gravlax ('grævˌlæks) *or* **gravadlax** *n* dry-cured salmon, marinated in salt, sugar, and spices, as served in Scandinavia. ORIG C20: from Norwegian, from *grav* grave (because the salmon is left to ferment) + *laks* or Swedish *lax* salmon

gravure (grə'vjʊə) *n* **1** a method of intaglio printing using a plate with many small etched recesses. See also **rotogravure. 2** See **photogravure. 3** matter printed by this process. ORIG C19: from F, from *graver* to engrave

gravy ('greɪvɪ) *n, pl* **gravies. 1a** the juices that exude from meat during cooking. **1b** the sauce made by thickening and flavouring such juices. **2** *Sl.* money or gain acquired with little effort, esp. above that needed for ordinary living. ORIG C14: from OF *gravé,* from ?

gravy boat *n* a small often boat-shaped vessel for serving gravy or other sauces.

gray¹ (greɪ) *adj, n, vb* a variant spelling (now esp. US) of **grey.**

gray² (greɪ) *n* the derived SI unit of the absorbed dose of ionizing radiation: equal to 1 joule per kilogram. Symbol: Gy ORIG C20: after L. H. *Gray,* Brit. radiobiologist

Gray ★ (greɪ) *n* **1 Simon** (**James Holiday**). born 1936, British writer: his plays include *Butley* (1971), *The Common Pursuit* (1988), and *Hidden Laughter* (1990). **2 Thomas.** 1716–71, British poet, best known for his *Elegy written in a Country Churchyard* (1751).

grayling ('greɪlɪŋ) *n, pl* **grayling** *or* **graylings. 1** a freshwater food fish of the salmon family of the N hemisphere, having a long spiny dorsal fin, a silvery back, and greyish-green sides. **2** any of various European butterflies having grey or greyish-brown wings.

Graz ★ (*German* gra:ts) *n* an industrial city in SE Austria, capital of Styria province: the second largest city in the country. Pop.: 237 810 (1991).

graze¹ (greɪz) *vb* **grazes, grazing, grazed. 1** to allow (animals) to consume the vegetation on (an area of land), or (of animals) to feed thus. **2** (*tr*) to tend (livestock) while at pasture. **3** (*intr*) *Inf.* to eat snacks throughout the day rather than formal meals. **4** (*intr*) *US.* to pilfer and eat sweets, vegetables, etc., from supermarket shelves while shopping. ORIG OE *grasian,* from *græs* GRASS

graze² (greɪz) *vb* **grazes, grazing, grazed. 1** (when *intr,* often foll. by *against* or *along*) to brush or scrape (against) gently, esp. in passing. **2** (*tr*) to break the skin of (a part of the body) by scraping. ◆ *n* **3** the act of grazing. **4** a scrape or abrasion made by grazing. ORIG C17: prob. special use of GRAZE¹

grazier ('greɪzɪə) *n* a rancher or farmer who rears or fattens cattle or sheep on grazing land.

grazing ('greɪzɪŋ) *n* **1** the vegetation on pastures that is available for livestock to feed upon. **2** the land on which this is growing.

grazioso (ˌgrɑ:tsɪ'əʊsəʊ) *adj Music.* graceful. ORIG It.

grease (gri:s, gri:z) *n* **1** animal fat in a soft or melted condition. **2** any thick fatty oil, esp. one used as a lubricant for machinery, etc. ◆ *vb* **greases, greasing, greased.** (*tr*) **3** to soil, coat, or lubricate with grease. **4 grease the palm** (*or* **hand**) **of.** *Sl.* to bribe; influence by giving money to. ORIG C13: from OF *craisse,* from L *crassus* thick
▸ **'greaser** *n*

grease gun *n* a device for forcing grease through nipples into bearings.

grease monkey *n Inf.* a mechanic, esp. one who works on cars or aircraft.

grease nipple *n* a metal nipple designed to engage with a grease gun for injecting grease into a bearing, etc.

greasepaint ('gri:sˌpeɪnt) *n* **1** a waxy or greasy substance used as make-up by actors. **2** theatrical make-up.

greaseproof paper ('gri:sˌpru:f) *n* any paper that is resistant to penetration by greases and oils.

greasy ('gri:sɪ, -zɪ) *adj* **greasier, greasiest. 1** coated or soiled with or as if with grease. **2** composed of or full of grease. **3** resembling grease. **4** unctuous or oily in manner.
▸ **'greasily** *adv* ▸ **'greasiness** *n*

greasy wool *n* untreated wool still retaining the lanolin; used for waterproof clothing.

great (greɪt) *adj* **1** relatively large in size or extent; big. **2** relatively large in number; having many parts or members: *a great assembly.* **3** of relatively long duration: *a great wait.* **4** of larger size or more importance than others of its kind: *the great auk.* **5** extreme or more than usual: *great worry.* **6** of significant importance or consequence: *a great decision.* **7a** of exceptional talents or achievements; remarkable: *a great writer.* **7b** (*as n*): *the great; one of the greats.* **8** doing or exemplifying (something) on a large scale: *she's a great reader.* **9** arising from or possessing idealism in thought, action, etc.; heroic: *great deeds.* **10** illustrious or eminent: *a great history.* **11** impressive or striking: *a great show of wealth.* **12** active or enthusiastic: *a great walker.* **13** (often foll. by *at*) skilful or adroit: *a great carpenter; you are great at singing.* **14** *Inf.* excellent; fantastic. ◆ *n* **15** Also called: **great organ.** the principal manual on an organ. ORIG OE *grēat*
▸ ˈ**greatly** *adv* ▸ ˈ**greatness** *n*

great- *prefix* **1** being the parent of a person's grandparent (in the combinations **great-grandfather, great-grandmother, great-grandparent**). **2** being the child of a person's grandchild (in the combinations **great-grandson, great-granddaughter, great-grandchild**).

great auk *n* a large flightless auk, extinct since the middle of the 19th century.

great-aunt *or* **grandaunt** *n* an aunt of one's father or mother; sister of one's grandfather or grandmother.

Great Australian Bight ★ *n* a wide bay of the Indian Ocean, in S Australia, extending from Cape Pasley to the Eyre Peninsula: notorious for storms.

Great Barrier Reef ★ *n* a coral reef in the Coral Sea, off the NE coast of Australia, extending for about 2000 km (1250 miles) from the Torres Strait along the coast of Queensland; the largest coral reef in the world.

Great Basin ★ *n* a semiarid region of the western US, between the Wasatch and the Sierra Nevada Mountains, having no drainage to the ocean: includes Nevada, W Utah, and parts of E California, S Oregon, and Idaho. Area: about 490 000 sq. km (189 000 sq. miles).

Great Bear *n* **the.** the English name for **Ursa Major.**

Great Bear Lake ★ *n* a lake in NW Canada, in the Northwest Territories: the largest freshwater lake entirely in Canada; drained by the **Great Bear River,** which flows to the Mackenzie River. Area: 31 792 sq. km (12 275 sq. miles).

Great Belt ★ *n* a strait in Denmark, between Zealand and Funen islands, linking the Kattegat with the Baltic. Danish name: **Store Bælt.**

Great Britain ★ *n* England, Wales, and Scotland including those adjacent islands governed from the mainland (i.e. excluding the Isle of Man and the Channel Islands). The United Kingdom of Great Britain was formed by the Act of Union (1707), although the term Great Britain had been in use since 1603, when James VI of Scotland became James I of England (including Wales). Later unions created the United Kingdom of Great Britain and Ireland (1801) and the United Kingdom of Great Britain and Northern Ireland (1922). Pop.: 56 388 200 (1992 est.). Area: 229 523 sq. km (88 619 sq. miles). See also **United Kingdom.**

great circle *n* a circular section of a sphere that has a radius equal to that of the sphere.

greatcoat (ˈgreɪtˌkəʊt) *n* a heavy overcoat.

Great Dane *n* one of a very large breed of dog with a short smooth coat.

Great Dividing Range ★ *pl n* a series of mountain ranges and plateaus roughly parallel to the E coast of Australia, in Queensland, New South Wales, and Victoria; the highest range is the Australian Alps, in the south.

Greater Antilles ★ *pl n* **the.** a group of islands in the Caribbean, including Cuba, Jamaica, Hispaniola, and Puerto Rico.

Greater London ★ *n* See **London**[1] (sense 2).

Greater Manchester ★ *n* a metropolitan county of NW England, administered since 1986 by the unitary authorities of Wigan, Bolton, Bury, Rochdale, Salford, Manchester, Oldham, Trafford, Stockport, and Tameside. Area: 1286 sq. km (496 sq. miles).

Greater Sunda Islands ★ *pl n* a group of islands in the W Malay Archipelago, forming the larger part of the Sunda Islands: consists of Borneo, Sumatra, Java, and Sulawesi.

Great Glen ★ *n* **the.** a fault valley across the whole of Scotland, extending southwest from the Moray Firth in the east to Loch Linnhe and containing Loch Ness and Loch Lochy. Also called: **Glen More, Glen Albyn.**

great gross *n* a unit of quantity equal to one dozen gross (or 1728).

great-hearted *adj* benevolent or noble; magnanimous.
▸ ˌ**great-**ˈ**heartedness** *n*

Great Indian Desert ★ *n* another name for the **Thar Desert.**

Great Lakes ★ *pl n* a group of five lakes in central North America with connecting waterways: the largest group of lakes in the world: consists of Lakes Superior, Huron, Erie, and Ontario, which are divided by the border between the US and Canada and Lake Michigan, which is wholly in the US; constitutes the most important system of inland waterways in the world, discharging through the St Lawrence into the Atlantic. Total length: 3767 km (2340 miles). Area: 246 490 sq. km (95 170 sq. miles).

great-nephew *or* **grandnephew** *n* a son of one's nephew or niece; grandson of one's brother or sister.

great-niece *or* **grandniece** *n* a daughter of one's nephew or niece; grand-daughter of one's brother or sister.

Great Ouse ★ *n* See **Ouse** (sense 1).

Great Plains ★ *pl n* a vast region of North America east of the Rocky Mountains, extending from the lowlands of the Mackenzie River (Canada), south to the Big Bend of the Rio Grande.

Great Red Spot *n* a large long-lived oval feature, south of Jupiter's equator, that is an anticyclonic disturbance in the atmosphere.

Great Rift Valley ★ *n* the most extensive rift in the earth's surface, extending from the Jordan valley in Syria to Mozambique; marked by a chain of steep-sided lakes, volcanoes, and escarpments.

Great Russian *n* **1** *Linguistics.* the technical name for **Russian. 2** a member of the chief East Slavonic people of Russia. ◆ *adj* **3** of or relating to this people or their language.

Greats (greɪts) *pl n* (at Oxford University) **1** the Honour School of Literae Humaniores, involving the study of Greek and Roman history and literature and philosophy. **2** the final examinations at the end of this course.

Great Saint Bernard Pass ★ *n, usually abbreviated to* **Great St Bernard Pass.** a pass over the W Alps, between SW central Switzerland and N Italy: noted for the hospice at the summit, founded in the 11th century. Height: 2469 m (8100 ft).

Great Salt Lake ★ *n* a shallow salt lake in NW Utah, in the Great Basin at an altitude of 1260 m (4200 ft): the area has fluctuated from less than 2500 sq. km (1000 sq. miles) to over 5000 sq. km (2000 sq. miles).

Great Sandy Desert ★ *n* **1** a desert in NW Australia. Area: about 415 000 sq. km (160 000 sq. miles). **2** the English name for the **Rub' al Khali.**

great seal *n* (*often caps.*) the principal seal of a nation, sovereign, etc., used to authenticate documents of the highest importance.

Great Slave Lake ★ *n* a lake in NW Canada, in the Northwest Territories: drained by the Mackenzie River into the Arctic Ocean. Area: 28 440 sq. km (10 980 sq. miles).

Great Slave River ★ *n* another name for the **Slave River.**

Great Smoky Mountains *or* **Great Smokies** ★ *pl n* the W part of the Appalachians, in W North Carolina and E Tennessee. Highest peak: Clingman's Dome, 2024 m (6642 ft).

Great Stour ★ *n* See **Stour.**

great tit *n* a Eurasian tit with yellow-and-black underparts and a black-and-white head.

great-uncle *or* **granduncle** *n* an uncle of one's father or mother; brother of one's grandfather or grandmother.

Great Victoria Desert ★ *n* a desert in S Australia, in SE Western Australia and W South Australia. Area: 323 750 sq. km (125 000 sq. miles).

Great Wall of China ★ *n* a defensive wall in N China, extending from W Gansu to the Gulf of Liaodong: constructed in the 3rd century B.C. as a defence against the Mongols; substantially rebuilt in the 15th century. Length: over 2400 km (1500 miles). Average height: 6 m (20 ft). Average width: 6 m (20 ft).

Great War *n* another name for **World War I.**

Great Yarmouth ★ ('jɑːməθ) *n* a port and resort in E England, in E Norfolk. Pop.: 56 190 (1991).

greave (griːv) *n* (*often pl*) a piece of armour worn to protect the shin. ORIG C14: from OF *greve*, ?from *graver* to part the hair, of Gmc origin

grebe (griːb) *n* an aquatic bird, such as the great crested grebe and little grebe, similar to the divers but with lobate rather than webbed toes and a vestigial tail. ORIG C18: from F *grèbe*, from ?

Grecian ('griːʃən) *adj* **1** (esp. of beauty or architecture) conforming to Greek ideals. ◆ *n* **2** a scholar of Greek. ◆ *adj, n* **3** another word for **Greek.**

Grecism ('griːˌsɪzəm) *n* a variant spelling (esp. US) of **Graecism.**

Greco ★ ('grɛkəʊ) *n* **El.** See **El Greco.**

Greco- ('griːkəʊ, 'grɛkəʊ) *combining form.* a variant (esp. US) of **Graeco-**.

Greece ★ (griːs) *n* a republic in SE Europe, occupying the S part of the Balkan Peninsula and many islands in the Ionian and Aegean Seas; site of two of Europe's earliest civilizations (the Minoan and Mycenaean); in the classical era divided into many small independent city-states, the most important being Athens and Sparta; part of the Roman and Byzantine Empires; passed under Turkish rule in the late Middle Ages; became an independent kingdom in 1827; taken over by a military junta (1967–74); the monarchy was abolished in 1973; became a republic in 1975; a member of the European Union. Official language: Greek. Official religion: Eastern (Greek) Orthodox. Currency: drachma and euro. Capital: Athens. Pop.: 10 561 000 (1999 est.). Area: 131 944 sq. km (50 944 sq. miles). Modern Greek name: **Ellás.** Related adj: **Hellenic.**

greed (griːd) *n* **1** excessive consumption of or desire for food. **2** excessive desire, as for wealth or power. ORIG C17: back formation from GREEDY

greedy ('griːdɪ) *adj* **greedier, greediest. 1** excessively desirous of food or wealth, esp. in large amounts; voracious. **2** (*postpositive;* foll. by *for*) eager (for): *a man greedy for success.* ORIG OE *grǣdig*
▸ **'greedily** *adv* ▸ **'greediness** *n*

greegree ('griːgriː) *n* a variant spelling of **grigri.**

Greek (griːk) *n* **1** the official language of Greece, constituting the Hellenic branch of the Indo-European family of languages. **2** a native or inhabitant of Greece or a descendant of such a native. **3** a member of the Greek Orthodox Church. **4** *Inf.* anything incomprehensible (esp. in **it's (all) Greek to me**). ◆ *adj* **5** denoting, relating to, or characteristic of Greece, the Greeks, or the Greek language; Hellenic. **6** of, relating to, or designating the Greek Orthodox Church.
▸ **'Greekness** *n*

Greek cross *n* a cross with each of the four arms of the same length.

Greek fire *n* a Byzantine weapon consisting of an unknown mixture that caught fire when wetted.

Greek gift *n* a gift given with the intention of tricking and causing harm to the recipient. ORIG C19: in allusion to Virgil's *Aeneid* ii 49; see also TROJAN HORSE

Greek Orthodox Church *n* **1** Also called: **Greek Church.** the established Church of Greece, governed by the holy synod of Greece, in which the Metropolitan of Athens has primacy of honour. **2** another name for **Orthodox Church.**

green (griːn) *n* **1** any of a group of colours, such as that of fresh grass, that lie between yellow and blue in the visible spectrum. Related adj: **verdant. 2** a dye or pigment of or producing these colours. **3** something of the colour green. **4** a small area of grassland, esp. in the centre of a village. **5** an area of smooth turf kept for a special purpose: *a putting green.* **6** (*pl*) **6a** the edible leaves and stems of certain plants, eaten as a vegetable. **6b** freshly cut branches of ornamental trees, shrubs, etc., used as a decoration. **7** (*sometimes cap.*) a person, esp. a politician, who supports environmentalist issues. ◆ *adj* **8** of the colour green. **9** greenish in colour or having parts or marks that are greenish. **10** (*sometimes cap.*) of or concerned with conservation of natural resources and improvement of the environment: used esp. in a political context. **11** vigorous; not faded: *a green old age.* **12** envious or jealous. **13** immature, unsophisticated, or gullible. **14** characterized by foliage or green plants: *a green wood; a green salad.* **15** (formerly) denoting a unit of account that is adjusted in accordance with fluctuations between the currencies of the EU nations and is used to make payments to agricultural producers within the EU: *green pound.* **16** fresh, raw, or unripe: *green bananas.* **17** unhealthily pale in appearance: *he was green after his boat trip.* **18** (of meat) not smoked or cured: *green bacon.* **19** (of timber) freshly felled; not dried or seasoned. ◆ *vb* **20** to make or become green. ORIG OE *grēne*
▸ **'greenish** *or* **'greeny** *adj* ▸ **'greenly** *adv* ▸ **'greenness** *n*

Green ★ (griːn) *n* **1 Henry,** real name *Henry Vincent Yorke.* 1905–73, British novelist: author of *Living* (1929), *Loving* (1945), and *Back* (1946). **2 John Richard.** 1837–83, British historian; author of *A Short History of the English People* (1874). **3 T(homas) H(ill).** 1836–82, British idealist philosopher. His chief work, *Prolegomena to Ethics,* was unfinished at his death.

Greenaway ★ ('griːnəˌweɪ) *n* **1 Kate.** 1846–1901, British painter, noted as an illustrator of children's books. **2 Peter.** born 1942, British film director, his films include *The Draughtsman's Contract* (1982) and *Eight and a Half Women* (1999).

greenback ('griːnˌbæk) *n US.* **1** *Inf.* a legal-tender US currency note. **2** *Sl.* a dollar bill.

green ban *n Austral.* a trade-union ban on any development that might be considered harmful to the environment.

green bean *n* any bean plant, such as the French bean, having narrow green edible pods.

green belt *n* a zone of farmland, parks, and open country surrounding a town or city.

Green Cross Code *n Brit.* a code for children giving rules for road safety.

Greene ★ (griːn) *n* **Graham.** 1904–91, British writer; his works include the novels *Brighton Rock* (1938), *The Power and the Glory* (1940), and *The Captain and the Enemy* (1988) and the literary thrillers *The Third Man* (1950) and *Our Man in Havana* (1958).

greenery ('griːnərɪ) *n, pl* **greeneries.** green foliage, esp. when used for decoration.

green-eyed *adj* **1** jealous or envious. **2 the green-eyed monster.** jealousy or envy.

greenfield ('griːnˌfiːld) *n* (*modifier*). denoting or located in a rural area which has not previously been built on.

greenfinch ('griːnˌfɪntʃ) *n* a European finch the male of which has a dull green plumage with yellow patches on the wings and tail.

green fingers *pl n* considerable talent or ability to grow plants.

greenfly ('griːnˌflaɪ) *n, pl* **greenflies.** a greenish aphid commonly occurring as a pest on garden and crop plants.

greengage ('griːnˌgeɪdʒ) *n* **1** a cultivated variety of plum tree with edible green plumlike fruits. **2** the fruit of this tree. ORIG C18: GREEN + *-gage,* after Sir W. *Gage* (1777–1864), E botanist who brought it from France

greengrocer (ˈgriːnˌgrəʊsə) *n Chiefly Brit.* a retail trader in fruit and vegetables.
▸ **ˈgreenˌgrocery** *n*

Greenham Common ★ (ˈgriːnəm) *n* a village in Berkshire, near Newbury; site of a US missile base and, since 1981, a camp of women protesters against nuclear weapons: the base had been closed by 1991 but a small number of women stayed at the site until 2000.

greenheart (ˈgriːnˌhɑːt) *n* **1** Also called: **bebeeru.** a tropical American tree that has dark green durable wood. **2** any of various similar trees. **3** the wood of any of these trees.

greenhorn (ˈgriːnˌhɔːn) *n* **1** an inexperienced person, esp. one who is extremely gullible. **2** *Chiefly US.* a newcomer. ORIG C17: orig. an animal with *green* (that is, young) horns

greenhouse (ˈgriːnˌhaʊs) *n* **1** a building with glass walls and roof for the cultivation of plants under controlled conditions. ◆ *adj* **2** relating to or contributing to the greenhouse effect: *greenhouse gases, such as carbon dioxide.*

greenhouse effect *n* **1** an effect occurring in greenhouses, etc., in which ultraviolet radiation from the sun passes through the glass warming the contents, the infrared radiation from inside being trapped by the glass. **2** the application of this effect to a planet's atmosphere, esp. the warming up of the earth as man-made carbon dioxide in the atmosphere traps the infrared radiation emitted by the earth's surface. The greenhouse effect is made more serious by damage to the ozone layer, which permits more ultraviolet radiation to reach the earth.

greenie (ˈgriːnɪ) *n Austral. inf.* a conservationist.

greenkeeper (ˈgriːnˌkiːpə) *n* a person responsible for maintaining a golf course or bowling green.

Greenland ★ (ˈgriːnlənd) *n* a large island, lying mostly within the Arctic Circle off the NE coast of North America: first settled by Icelanders in 986; resettled by Danes from 1721 onwards; integral part of Denmark (1953–79); granted internal autonomy 1979; mostly covered by an icecap up to 3300 m (11 000 ft) thick, with ice-free coastal strips and coastal mountains; the population is largely Eskimo, with a European minority; fishing, hunting, and mining. Capital: Nuuk. Pop.: 55 117 (1993). Area: 2 175 600 sq. km (840 000 sq. miles). Danish name: **Grønland.** Greenlandic name: **Kalallit Nunaat.**
▸ **ˈGreenlander** *n* ▸ **Greenlandic** (ˌgriːnˈlændɪk) *adj*

Greenland Sea ★ *n* the S part of the Arctic Ocean, off the NE coast of Greenland.

Greenland whale *n* another name for **bowhead.**

green leek *n* any of several Australian parrots with a green or mostly green plumage.

green light *n* **1** a signal to go, esp. a green traffic light. **2** permission to proceed with a project, etc. ◆ *vb* **greenlight, greenlights, greenlighting, greenlighted.** (*tr*) **3** to permit (a project, etc.) to proceed.

greenmail (ˈgriːnˌmeɪl) *n* (esp. in the US) the practice of a company buying sufficient shares in another company to threaten takeover and making a quick profit as a result of the threatened company buying back its shares at a higher price.

green monkey disease *n* another name for **Marburg disease.**

Green Mountains ★ *pl n* a mountain range in E North America, extending from Canada through Vermont into W Massachusetts: part of the Appalachian system. Highest peak: Mount Mansfield, 1338 m (4393 ft).

Greenock ★ (ˈgriːnək) *n* a port in SW Scotland, in Inverclyde on the Firth of Clyde: shipbuilding and other marine industries. Pop.: 50 013 (1991).

Greenough ★ (ˈgriːnəʊ) *n* **George Bellas.** 1778–1855, British geologist, founder of the Geological Society of London.

green paper *n* (*often caps.*) (in Britain) a government document containing policy proposals to be discussed, esp. by Parliament.

Green Party *n* a political party whose policies are based on concern for the environment.

Greenpeace (ˈgriːnˌpiːs) *n* a conservationist organization founded in 1971: members take active but nonviolent measures against what are regarded as threats to environmental safety, such as the dumping of nuclear waste at sea.

green pepper *n* the green unripe fruit of the sweet pepper, eaten raw or cooked.

green pound *n* a unit of account used in calculating Britain's contributions to and payments from the Community Agricultural Fund of the EU. See also **green** (sense 15).

Green River ★ *n* a river in the western US, rising in W central Wyoming and flowing south into Utah, east through NW Colorado, re-entering Utah before joining the Colorado River. Length: 1175 km (730 miles).

greenroom (ˈgriːnˌruːm, -ˌrʊm) *n* (esp. formerly) a backstage room in a theatre where performers may rest or receive visitors. ORIG C18: prob. from its original colour

greensand (ˈgriːnˌsænd) *n* an olive-green sandstone consisting mainly of quartz and glauconite.

Greensboro ★ (ˈgriːnzbərə, -brə) *n* a city in N central North Carolina. Pop.: 195 426 (1996 est.).

greenshank (ˈgriːnˌʃæŋk) *n* a large European sandpiper with greenish legs and a slightly upturned bill.

greensickness (ˈgriːnˌsɪknɪs) *n* an informal name for **chlorosis.**

greenstick fracture (ˈgriːnˌstɪk) *n* a fracture in children in which the bone is partly bent and splinters only on the convex side of the bend. ORIG C20: alluding to the similar way in which a green stick splinters

greenstone (ˈgriːnˌstəʊn) *n* **1** any basic dark green igneous rock. **2** a variety of jade formerly used in New Zealand by Maoris for ornaments and tools, now used for jewellery.

greensward (ˈgriːnˌswɔːd) *n Arch. or literary.* fresh green turf or an area of such turf.

green tea *n* a sharp tea made from tea leaves that have been dried quickly without fermenting.

green turtle *n* a mainly tropical edible turtle, with greenish flesh.

green-wellie *n* (*modifier*) characterizing or belonging to the upper-class set devoted to hunting, shooting, and fishing: *the green-wellie brigade.*

Greenwich ★ (ˈgrɪnɪdʒ, -ɪtʃ, ˈgrɛn-) *n* a Greater London borough on the Thames: site of a Royal Naval College, the original Royal Observatory designed by Christopher Wren (1675), and the Millennium Dome; seat of the University of Greenwich (1992); accepted internationally as the prime meridian of longitude since 1884, and the basis of Greenwich Mean Time. Pop.: 212 200 (1994 est.). Area: 46 sq. km (18 sq. miles).

Greenwich Electronic Time *n* an international time standard designed for electronic commerce on the Internet.

Greenwich Mean Time *or* **Greenwich Time** *n* mean solar time on the 0° meridian passing through Greenwich, England, measured from midnight: formerly a standard time in Britain and a basis for calculating times throughout most of the world, it has been replaced by an atomic timescale. See **universal time.** Abbrev.: **GMT.**

> **USAGE NOTE** The name *Greenwich Mean Time* is ambiguous, having been measured from mean midday in astronomy up to 1925, and is not used for scientific purposes. It is generally and incorrectly used in the sense of *universal coordinated time*, an atomic timescale available since 1972 from broadcast signals, in addition to the earliest sense of *universal time*, adopted internationally in 1928 as the name for GMT measured from midnight.

Greenwich Village ★ (ˈgrɛnɪtʃ, ˈgrɪn-) *n* a part of New York City in the lower west side of Manhattan; traditionally the home of many artists and writers.

greenwood (ˈgriːnˌwʊd) *n* a forest or wood when the leaves are green.

Greer ★ ('grɪə) *n* **Germaine.** born 1939, Australian writer and feminist. Her books include *The Female Eunuch* (1970) *Sex and Destiny* (1984), and *The Whole Woman* (1998).

greet[1] (gri:t) *vb* (*tr*) **1** to meet or receive with expressions of gladness or welcome. **2** to send a message of friendship to. **3** to receive in a specified manner: *her remarks were greeted by silence.* **4** to become apparent to: *the smell of bread greeted him.* ORIG OE *grētan*
▸ **'greeter** *n*

greet[2] (gri:t) *Scot. or dialect.* ◆ *vb* **1** (*intr*) to weep; lament. ◆ *n* **2** weeping; lamentation. ORIG from OE *grētan,* N dialect var. of *grǣtan*

greeting ('gri:tɪŋ) *n* **1** the act or an instance of welcoming or saluting on meeting. **2** (*often pl*) **2a** an expression of friendly salutation. **2b** (*as modifier*): *a greetings card.*

gregarious (grɪ'gɛərɪəs) *adj* **1** enjoying the company of others. **2** (of animals) living together in herds or flocks. **3** (of plants) growing close together. **4** of or characteristic of crowds or communities. ORIG C17: from L, from *grex* flock
▸ **gre'gariously** *adv* ▸ **gre'gariousness** *n*

Gregorian calendar (grɪ'gɔ:rɪən) *n* the revision of the Julian calendar introduced in 1582 by Pope Gregory XIII and still in force, whereby the ordinary year is made to consist of 365 days.

Gregorian chant *n* another name for **plainsong.**

Gregorian telescope *n* a type of reflecting astronomical telescope with a concave secondary mirror and the eyepiece set in the centre of the parabolic primary mirror. ORIG C18: after J. *Gregory* (died 1675), Scot. mathematician

Gregory ★ ('grɛgərɪ) *n* Lady (**Isabella**) **Augusta** (**Persse**). 1852–1932, Irish dramatist; a founder and director of the Abbey Theatre, Dublin.

Gregory I ★ *n* **Saint,** known as *Gregory the Great.* ?540–604 A.D., pope (590–604). He strengthened papal authority and appointed Saint Augustine missionary to England. Feast day: March 12 or Sept. 3.

Gregory VII ★ *n* **Saint,** monastic name *Hildebrand.* ?1020–85, pope (1073–85), who did much to reform abuses in the Church. His assertion of papal supremacy was opposed by the Holy Roman Emperor Henry IV, whom he excommunicated (1076). He was driven into exile when Henry captured Rome (1084). Feast day: May 25.

Gregory XIII ★ *n* 1502–85, pope (1572–85). He promoted the Counter-Reformation and founded seminaries. His reformed (Gregorian) calendar was issued in 1582.

Gregory of Tours ★ *n* **Saint.** ?538–?594 A.D., Frankish bishop and historian. His *Historia Francorum* is the chief source of knowledge of 6th-century Gaul. Feast day: Nov. 17.

gremial ('gri:mɪəl) *n RC Church.* a cloth spread upon the lap of a bishop when seated during Mass. ORIG C17: from L *gremium* lap

gremlin ('grɛmlɪn) *n* **1** an imaginary imp jokingly said to be responsible for mechanical troubles in aircraft, esp. in World War II. **2** any mischievous troublemaker. ORIG C20: from ?

Grenada ★ (grɛ'neɪdə) *n* an island state in the Caribbean, in the Windward Islands: formerly a British colony (1783–1967); since 1974 an independent state within the Commonwealth; occupied by US troops (1983–85); mainly agricultural. Official language: English. Religion: Christian majority. Currency: East Caribbean dollar. Capital: St George's. Pop.: 101 000 (1999 est.). Area: 344 sq. km (133 sq. miles).
▸ **Gre'nadian** *n, adj*

grenade (grɪ'neɪd) *n* **1** a small container filled with explosive thrown by hand or fired from a rifle. **2** a sealed glass vessel that is thrown and shatters to release chemicals, such as tear gas. ORIG C16: from F, from Sp.: pomegranate, from LL, from L *grānātus* seedy; see GRAIN

grenadier (ˌgrɛnə'dɪə) *n* **1** *Mil.* **1a** (in the British Army) a member of the senior regiment of infantry in the Household Brigade. **1b** (formerly) a member of a special formation, usually selected for strength and height. **1c** (formerly) a soldier trained to throw grenades. **2** any of various deep-sea fish, typically having a large head and a long tapering tail. ORIG C17: from F; see GRENADE

grenadine[1] (ˌgrɛnə'di:n) *n* a light thin fabric of silk, wool, rayon, or nylon, used for dresses, etc. ORIG C19: from F

grenadine[2] (ˌgrɛnə'di:n, 'grɛnəˌdi:n) *n* a syrup made from pomegranate juice, used as a sweetening and colouring agent in various drinks. ORIG C19: from F: a little pomegranate; see GRENADE

Grenadines ★ (ˌgrɛnə'di:nz, 'grɛnəˌdi:nz) *pl n* **the.** a chain of about 600 islets in the Caribbean, part of the Windward Islands, extending for about 100 km (60 miles) between St Vincent and Grenada and divided administratively between the two states. Largest island: Carriacou.

Grendel ★ ('grɛndᵊl) *n* (in Old English legend) a man-eating monster defeated by the hero Beowulf.

Grenfell ★ ('grɛnfəl) *n* **Joyce,** real name *Joyce Irene Phipps.* 1910–79, British comedy actress and writer.

Grenoble ★ (grə'nəʊbᵊl; *French* grənɔblə) *n* a city in SE France, on the Isère River: university (1339). Pop.: 153 973 (1990).

Grenville ★ ('grɛnvɪl) *n* **1 George.** 1712–70, British statesman; prime minister (1763–65). His policy of taxing the American colonies precipitated the War of Independence. **2** Sir **Richard.** ?1541–91, English naval commander. He was fatally wounded during a battle with a fleet of Spanish treasure ships. **3 William Wyndham,** Baron Grenville, son of George Grenville. 1759–1834, British statesman; prime minister (1806–07).

Gresham ★ ('grɛʃəm) *n* Sir **Thomas.** ?1519–79, English financier, who founded the Royal Exchange in London (1568).

Gresham's law *or* **theorem** *n* the economic hypothesis that bad money drives good money out of circulation; the superior currency will tend to be hoarded and the inferior will thus dominate the circulation. ORIG C16: after Sir T. GRESHAM

gressorial (grɛ'sɔ:rɪəl) *or* **gressorious** *adj* **1** (of the feet of certain birds) specialized for walking. **2** (of birds, such as the ostrich) having such feet. ORIG C19: from NL, from *gressus* having walked, from *gradī* to step

Gretna Green ★ ('grɛtnə) *n* a village in S Scotland, in Dumfries and Galloway on the border with England: famous smithy where eloping couples were married by the blacksmith from 1754 until 1940, when such marriages were made illegal. Pop.: 3149 (1991).

Gretzky ★ ('grɛtski) *n* **Wayne.** born 1961, Canadian ice-hockey player.

Greville ★ ('grɛvɪl) *n* **Fulke** (fʊlk), 1st Baron Brooke. 1554–1628, English poet, writer, politician, and diplomat: Chancellor of the Exchequer (1614–22); author of *The Life of the Renowned Sir Philip Sidney* (1652).

grew (gru:) *vb* the past tense of **grow.**

grey *or US* **gray** (greɪ) *adj* **1** of a neutral tone, intermediate between black and white, that has no hue and reflects and transmits only a little light. **2** greyish in colour or having greyish marks. **3** dismal or dark, esp. from lack of light; gloomy. **4** conventional or dull, esp. in character or opinion. **5** having grey hair. **6** of or relating to people of middle age or above: *grey power.* **7** ancient; venerable. ◆ *n* **8** any of a group of grey tones. **9** grey cloth or clothing. **10** an animal, esp. a horse, that is grey or whitish. ◆ *vb* **11** to become or make grey. ORIG OE *grǣg*
▸ **'greyish** *or US* **'grayish** *adj* ▸ **'greyly** *or US* **'grayly** *adv*
▸ **'greyness** *or US* **'grayness** *n*

Grey ★ (greɪ) *n* **1 Charles,** 2nd Earl Grey. 1764–1845, British statesman. As Whig prime minister (1830–34), he carried the Reform Bill of 1832 and the bill for the abolition of slavery throughout the British Empire (1833). **2** Sir **Edward,** 1st Viscount Grey of Fallodon. 1862–1933, British statesman; foreign secretary (1905–16). **3** Sir **George.** 1812–98, British statesman and colonial administrator; prime minister of New Zealand (1877–79). **4**

Lady **Jane.** 1537–54, queen of England (July 9–19, 1553); great-granddaughter of Henry VII. Her father-in-law, the Duke of Northumberland, persuaded Edward VI to alter the succession in her favour, but after ten days as queen she was imprisoned and later executed. **5 Zane.** 1875–1939, US author of Westerns, including *Riders of the Purple Sage* (1912).

grey area *n* **1** an area or part of something existing between two extremes and having mixed characteristics of both. **2** an area, situation, etc., lacking clearly defined characteristics.

greybeard *or US* **graybeard** ('greɪˌbɪəd) *n* **1** an old man, esp. a sage. **2** a large stoneware or earthenware jar or jug for spirits.

grey eminence *n* the English equivalent of ***éminence grise.***

Grey Friar *n* a Franciscan friar.

greyhen ('greɪˌhɛn) *n* the female of the black grouse.

greyhound ('greɪˌhaʊnd) *n* a tall slender fast-moving breed of dog.

grey knight *n Inf.* an ambiguous intervener in a takeover battle, who makes a counterbid for the shares of the target company without having made his intentions clear. Cf. **black knight, white knight.**

greylag *or* **greylag goose** ('greɪˌlæg) *n* a large grey Eurasian goose: the ancestor of many domestic breeds of goose. US spelling: **graylag.** ORIG C18: from GREY + LAG[1], from its migrating later than other species

grey market *n* **1** trade in newly-issued shares before they have been formally listed and traded on the Stock Exchange. **2** a practice in which supermarkets buy excess stock of branded goods from other retailers at a low margin and then sell them at discounted prices.

grey matter *n* **1** the greyish tissue of the brain and spinal cord, containing nerve cell bodies and fibres. **2** *Inf.* brains or intellect.

grey squirrel *n* a grey-furred squirrel, native to E North America but now widely established.

greywacke ('greɪˌwækə) *n* any dark sandstone or grit having a matrix of clay minerals. ORIG C19: partial translation of G *Grauwacke;* see WACKE

grey water *n* water that has been used for one purpose but can be used again for another without repurification (e.g. bathwater, which can be used to water plants).

grey wolf *n* another name for **timber wolf.**

grid (grɪd) *n* **1** See **gridiron. 2** a network of horizontal and vertical lines superimposed over a map, building plan, etc., for locating points. **3** a grating consisting of parallel bars. **4 the grid.** the national network of transmission lines, pipes, etc., by which electricity, gas, or water is distributed. **5** Also called: **control grid.** *Electronics.* an electrode usually consisting of a cylindrical mesh of wires, that controls the flow of electrons between the cathode and anode of a valve. **6** See **starting grid. 7** a plate in an accumulator that carries the active substance. **8** any interconnecting system of links: *the bus service formed a grid across the country.* ORIG C19: back formation from GRIDIRON

grid bias *n* the fixed voltage applied between the control grid and cathode of a valve.

griddle ('grɪdᵊl) *n* **1** Also called: **girdle.** *Brit.* a thick round iron plate with a half hoop handle over the top, for making scones, etc. **2** any flat heated surface, esp. on the top of a stove, for cooking food. ◆ *vb* **griddles, griddling, griddled. 3** (*tr*) to cook (food) on a griddle. ORIG C13: from OF *gridil,* from LL *crātīculum* (unattested) fine wickerwork; see GRILL

griddlecake ('grɪdᵊlˌkeɪk) *n* another name for **drop scone.**

gridiron ('grɪdˌaɪən) *n* **1** a utensil of parallel metal bars, used to grill meat, fish, etc. **2** any framework resembling this utensil. **3** a framework above the stage in a theatre from which suspended scenery, lights, etc., are manipulated. **4a** the field of play in American football. **4b** an informal name for **American football.** ◆ Often shortened to **grid.** ORIG C13 *gredire,* ? a var. (through influence of *ire* IRON) of *gredile* GRIDDLE

gridlock ('grɪdˌlɒk) *Chiefly US.* ◆ *n* **1** obstruction of urban traffic caused by queues of vehicles forming across junctions and causing further queues to form in the intersecting streets. **2** a point in a dispute at which no agreement can be reached: *political gridlock.* ◆ *vb* **3** (*tr*) (of traffic) to block or obstruct (an area).

grief (griːf) *n* **1** deep or intense sorrow, esp. at the death of someone. **2** something that causes keen distress. **3** *Brit. & S. African inf.* trouble or annoyance: *I got grief for leaving early.* **4 come to grief.** *Inf.* to end unsuccessfully or disastrously. ORIG C13: from Anglo-F *gref,* from *grever* to GRIEVE

Grieg ★ (griːg) *n* **Edvard** (**Hagerup**) ('ɛdvard). 1843–1907, Norwegian composer. His works include the music for *Peer Gynt* (1876), a piano concerto, and many songs.

Grierson ★ ('grɪəsᵊn) *n* **John.** 1898–1972, Scottish film director. He coined the noun *documentary;* his *Industrial Britain* (1931) and *Song of Ceylon* (1934) are notable examples.

grievance ('griːvᵊns) *n* **1** a real or imaginary wrong causing resentment and regarded as grounds for complaint. **2** a feeling of resentment or injustice at having been unfairly treated. ORIG C15 *grevance,* from OF, from *grever* to GRIEVE

grieve (griːv) *vb* **grieves, grieving, grieved.** to feel or cause to feel great sorrow or distress, esp. at the death of someone. ORIG C13: from OF *grever,* from L *gravāre* to burden, from *gravis* heavy
▸ **'griever** *n* ▸ **'grieving** *n, adj*

grievous ('griːvəs) *adj* **1** very severe or painful: *a grievous injury.* **2** very serious; heinous: *a grievous sin.* **3** showing or marked by grief. **4** causing great pain or suffering.
▸ **'grievously** *adv* ▸ **'grievousness** *n*

grievous bodily harm *n Criminal law.* serious injury caused by one person to another.

griffin ('grɪfɪn), **griffon,** *or* **gryphon** *n* a winged monster with an eagle-like head and the body of a lion. ORIG C14: from OF *grifon,* from L *grȳphus,* from Gk *grups,* from *grupos* hooked

Griffith ★ ('grɪfɪθ) *n* **1 Arthur.** 1872–1922, Irish journalist and nationalist: founder of Sinn Féin (1905); president of the Irish Free State (1922). **2 D**(**avid Lewelyn**) **W**(**ark**). 1875–1948, US film director and producer, noted for *The Birth of a Nation* (1915).

Griffith-Joyner ★ (-'dʒɔɪnə) *n* **Florence,** known as *Flojo.* 1959–98, US sprinter, winner of three gold medals at the 1988 Olympic Games.

griffon[1] ('grɪfᵊn) *n* **1** any of various small wire-haired breeds of dog, originally from Belgium. **2** a large vulture of Africa, S Europe, and SW Asia, having a pale plumage with black wings. ORIG C19: from F: GRIFFIN

griffon[2] ★ ('grɪfᵊn) *n* a variant of **griffin.**

grifter ('grɪftə) *n Sl., chiefly US.* a petty criminal or gambler. ORIG C20: a blend of GR(AFT)[2] (sense 2) + DRIFTER (sense 2)

Grigioni ★ (gri'dʒoːni) *n* the Italian name for **Graubünden.**

grigri, gris-gris, *or* **greegree** ('griːgriː) *n, pl* **grigris, gris-gris** (-griːz) *or* **greegrees.** an African talisman, amulet, or charm. ORIG of African origin

grill (grɪl) *vb* **1** to cook (meat, etc.) by direct heat, as under a grill or over a hot fire, or (of meat, etc.) to be cooked in this way. Usual US and Canad. word: **broil. 2** (*tr; usually passive*) to torment with or as if with extreme heat: *the travellers were grilled by the scorching sun.* **3** (*tr*) *Inf.* to subject to insistent or prolonged questioning. ◆ *n* **4** a device with parallel bars of thin metal on which meat, etc., may be cooked by a fire; gridiron. **5** a device on a cooker that radiates heat downwards for grilling meat, etc. **6** food cooked by grilling. **7** See **grillroom.** ORIG C17: from F *gril* gridiron, from L *crātīcula* fine wickerwork; see GRILLE
▸ **grilled** *adj* ▸ **'griller** *n*

grillage ('grɪlɪdʒ) *n* an arrangement of beams and crossbeams used as a foundation on soft ground. ORIG C18: from F, from *griller* to furnish with a grille

grille *or* **grill** (grɪl) *n* **1** a framework, esp. of metal bars arranged to form an ornamental pattern, used as a screen or partition. **2** Also called: **radiator grille.** a grating that admits cooling air to the radiator of a motor vehicle. **3** a metal or wooden openwork grating used as a screen or divider. **4** a protective screen, usually plastic or metal, in front of the loudspeaker in a radio, record player, etc. ORIG C17: from OF, from L *crātīcula* fine hurdlework, from *crātis* a hurdle

grillroom ('grɪlˌruːm, -ˌrʊm) *n* a restaurant where grilled steaks and other meat are served.

grilse (grɪls) *n, pl* **grilses** *or* **grilse.** a young salmon that returns to fresh water after one winter in the sea. ORIG C15 *grilles* (pl), from ?

grim (grɪm) *adj* **grimmer, grimmest. 1** stern; resolute: *grim determination.* **2** harsh or formidable in manner or appearance. **3** harshly ironic or sinister: *grim laughter.* **4** cruel, severe, or ghastly: *a grim accident.* **5** *Arch. or poetic.* fierce: *a grim warrior.* **6** *Inf.* unpleasant. ORIG OE *grimm*
▸ **'grimly** *adv* ▸ **'grimness** *n*

grimace (grɪ'meɪs) *n* **1** an ugly or distorted facial expression, as of wry humour, disgust, etc. ◆ *vb* **grimaces, grimacing, grimaced. 2** (*intr*) to contort the face. ORIG C17: from F, of Gmc origin; rel. to Sp. *grimazo* caricature
▸ **gri'macer** *n*

Grimaldi ★ (grɪ'mɔːldɪ) *n* **Joseph.** 1779–1837, British actor, noted as a clown in pantomime.

grimalkin (grɪ'mælkɪn, -'mɔːl-) *n* **1** an old cat, esp. an old female cat. **2** a crotchety or shrewish old woman. ORIG C17: from GREY + *malkin,* dim. of female name *Maud*

grime (graɪm) *n* **1** dirt, soot, or filth, esp. when ingrained. ◆ *vb* **grimes, griming, grimed. 2** (*tr*) to make dirty or coat with filth. ORIG C15: from MDu. *grime*
▸ **'grimy** *adj* ▸ **'griminess** *n*

Grimm ★ (grɪm) *n* **Jakob Ludwig Karl** ('jaːkɔp 'luːtvɪç karl), 1785–1863, and his brother, **Wilhelm Karl** ('vɪlhɛlm karl), 1786–1859, German philologists and folklorists, who collaborated on *Grimm's Fairy Tales* (1812–22) and began a German dictionary. Jakob is noted also for his *Deutsche Grammatik* (1819–37), in which he formulated the law named after him.

Grimsby ★ ('grɪmzbɪ) *n* a fishing port in E England, in North East Lincolnshire. Pop.: 90 703 (1991).

grin (grɪn) *vb* **grins, grinning, grinned. 1** to smile with the lips drawn back revealing the teeth or express (something) by such a smile: *to grin a welcome.* **2** (*intr*) to draw back the lips revealing the teeth, as in a snarl or grimace. **3 grin and bear it.** *Inf.* to suffer trouble or hardship without complaint. ◆ *n* **4** a broad smile. **5** a snarl or grimace. ORIG OE *grennian*
▸ **'grinning** *adj, n*

grind (graɪnd) *vb* **grinds, grinding, ground. 1** to reduce or be reduced to small particles by pounding or abrading: *to grind corn.* **2** (*tr*) to smooth, sharpen, or polish by friction or abrasion. **3** to scrape or grate together (two things, esp. the teeth) with a harsh rasping sound or (of such objects) to be scraped together. **4** (*tr; foll. by out*) to speak or say something in a rough voice. **5** (*tr; often foll. by down*) to hold down; oppress; tyrannize. **6** (*tr*) to operate (a machine) by turning a handle. **7** (*tr; foll. by out*) to produce in a routine or uninspired manner: *he ground out his weekly article for the paper.* **8** (*intr*) *Inf.* to study or work laboriously. ◆ *n* **9** *Inf.* laborious or routine work or study. **10** a specific grade of pulverization, as of coffee beans: *coarse grind.* **11** the act or sound of grinding. ORIG OE *grindan*
▸ **'grindingly** *adv*

Grindelwald ★ (*German* 'grɪndəlvalt) *n* a valley and resort in central Switzerland, in the Bernese Oberland: mountaineering centre, with the Wetterhorn and the Eiger nearby.

grinder ('graɪndə) *n* **1** a person who grinds, esp. one who grinds cutting tools. **2** a machine for grinding. **3** a molar tooth.

grindstone ('graɪndˌstəʊn) *n* **1a** a machine having a circular block of stone rotated for sharpening tools or grinding metal. **1b** the stone used in this machine. **1c** any stone used for sharpening; whetstone. **2 keep** *or* **have one's nose to the grindstone.** to work hard and perseveringly.

gringo ('grɪŋgəʊ) *n, pl* **gringos.** a person from an English-speaking country: used as a derogatory term by Latin Americans. ORIG C19: from Sp.: foreigner, prob. from *griego* Greek, hence an alien

grip (grɪp) *n* **1** the act or an instance of grasping and holding firmly: *he lost his grip on the slope.* **2** Also called: **handgrip.** the strength or pressure of such a grasp, as in a handshake. **3** the style or manner of grasping an object, such as a tennis racket. **4** understanding, control, or mastery of a subject, problem, etc. **5** a person who manoeuvres the cameras in a film or television studio. **6 get** *or* **come to grips.** (often foll. by *with*) **6a** to deal with (a problem or subject). **6b** to tackle (an assailant). **7** Also called: **handgrip.** a part by which an object is grasped; handle. **8** Also called: **handgrip.** a travelling bag or holdall. **9** See **hairgrip. 10** any device that holds by friction, such as certain types of brake. ◆ *vb* **grips, gripping, gripped. 11** to take hold of firmly or tightly, as by a clutch. **12** to hold the interest or attention of: *the thrilling performance gripped the audience.* ORIG OE *gripe* grasp
▸ **'gripper** *n* ▸ **'gripping** *adj*

gripe (graɪp) *vb* **gripes, griping, griped. 1** (*intr*) *Inf.* to complain, esp. in a persistent nagging manner. **2** to cause sudden intense pain in the intestines of (a person) or (of a person) to experience this pain. **3** *Arch.* to clutch; grasp. **4** (*tr*) *Arch.* to afflict. ◆ *n* **5** (*usually pl*) a sudden intense pain in the intestines; colic. **6** *Inf.* a complaint or grievance. **7** *Now rare.* **7a** the act of gripping. **7b** a firm grip. **7c** a device that grips. ORIG OE *grīpan*
▸ **'griper** *n*

Gripe Water *n Brit., trademark.* a solution given to infants to relieve colic.

grippe *or* **grip** (grɪp) *n* a former name for **influenza.** ORIG C18: from F *grippe,* from *gripper* to seize, of Gmc origin; see GRIP

Griqualand East ★ ('griːkwəˌlænd, 'grɪk-) *n* an area of central South Africa: settled in 1861 by Griquas led by Adam Kok III; annexed to the Cape in 1879; part of the Transkei (1903–94); now incorporated into the Eastern Cape. Chief town: Kokstad. Area: 17 100 sq. km (6602 sq. miles).

Griqualand West ★ *n* an area of NW South Africa, north of the Orange river: settled after 1803 by the Griquas; annexed by the British in 1871 following a dispute with the Orange Free State; became part of the Cape Colony in 1880; now incorporated into the Northern Cape. Chief town: Kimberley. Area: 39 360 sq. km (15 197 sq. miles).

Gris ★ (*Spanish* gris) *n* **Juan** (xwan). 1887–1927, Spanish cubist painter, resident in France from 1906.

grisaille (grɪ'zeɪl) *n* **1** a technique of monochrome painting in shades of grey, imitating the effect of relief. **2** a painting, stained-glass window, etc., in this manner. ORIG C19: from F, from *gris* grey

griseofulvin (ˌgrɪzɪəʊ'fʊlvɪn) *n* an antibiotic used to treat fungal infections of the skin and hair. ORIG C20: from NL, ult. from Med. L *griseus* grey + L *fulvus* reddish-yellow

grisette (grɪ'zɛt) *n* (esp. formerly) a French working girl. ORIG C18: from F, from grey fabric used for dresses, from *gris* grey

gris-gris ('griːgriː) *n, pl* **gris-gris** (-griːz). a variant spelling of **grigri.**

Grisham ★ ('grɪʃəm) *n* **John.** born 1955, US novelist and lawyer; his legal thrillers, many of which have been filmed, include *A Time to Kill* (1989), *The Pelican Brief* (1992), and *A Painted House* (2001).

Grishun ★ (griː'ʃuːn) *n* the Romansch name for **Graubünden.**

grisly ('grɪzlɪ) *adj* **grislier, grisliest.** causing horror or dread; gruesome. ORIG OE *grislic*
▸ **'grisliness** *n*

> **USAGE NOTE** See at **grizzly.**

Grisons ★ (grizɔ̃) *n* the French name for **Graubünden.**

grist (grɪst) *n* **1a** grain intended to be or that has been ground. **1b** the quantity of such grain processed in one grinding. **2** *Brewing.* malt grains that have been cleaned and cracked. **3 grist to** (*or* **for**) **the** (*or* **one's**) **mill.** anything that can be turned to profit or advantage. ORIG OE *grīst*

gristle ('grɪsᵊl) *n* cartilage, esp. when in meat. ORIG OE *gristle*
▸ **'gristly** *adj* ▸ **'gristliness** *n*

grit (grɪt) *n* **1** small hard particles of sand, earth, stone, etc. **2** Also called: **gritstone.** any coarse sandstone that can be used as a grindstone or millstone. **3** indomitable courage, toughness, or resolution. ◆ *vb* **grits, gritting, gritted. 4** to clench or grind together (two objects, esp. the teeth). **5** to cover (a surface, such as icy roads) with grit. ORIG OE *grēot*
▸ **'gritter** *n*

Grit (grɪt) *n, adj Canad.* an informal word for **Liberal.**

grits (grɪts) *pl n* **1** hulled or coarsely ground grain. **2** *US.* See **hominy grits.** ORIG OE *grytt*

gritty ('grɪtɪ) *adj* **grittier, grittiest. 1** courageous; hardy; resolute. **2** of, like, or containing grit.
▸ **'grittily** *adv* ▸ **'grittiness** *n*

grizzle[1] ('grɪzᵊl) *vb* **grizzles, grizzling, grizzled. 1** to make or become grey. ◆ *n* **2** a grey colour. **3** grey hair. ORIG C15: from OF *grisel,* from *gris,* of Gmc origin

grizzle[2] ('grɪzᵊl) *vb* **grizzles, grizzling, grizzled.** (*intr*) *Inf., chiefly Brit.* (esp. of a child) to fret; whine. ORIG C18: of Gmc origin
▸ **'grizzler** *n*

grizzled ('grɪzᵊld) *adj* **1** streaked or mixed with grey; grizzly. **2** having grey hair.

grizzly ('grɪzlɪ) *adj* **grizzlier, grizzliest. 1** somewhat grey; grizzled. ◆ *n, pl* **grizzlies. 2** See **grizzly bear.**

> **USAGE NOTE** *Grizzly* is sometimes wrongly used where *grisly* is meant: *a grisly* (not *grizzly*) *murder.*

grizzly bear *n* a variety of the brown bear, formerly widespread in W North America; its brown fur has cream or white tips on the back, giving a grizzled appearance. Often shortened to **grizzly.**

groan (grəʊn) *n* **1** a prolonged stressed dull cry expressive of agony, pain, or disapproval. **2** a loud harsh creaking sound, as of a tree bending in the wind. **3** *Inf.* a grumble or complaint, esp. a persistent one. ◆ *vb* **4** to utter (low inarticulate sounds) expressive of pain, grief, disapproval, etc. **5** (*intr*) to make a sound like a groan. **6** (*intr;* usually foll. by *beneath* or *under*) to be weighed down (by) or suffer greatly (under). **7** (*intr*) *Inf.* to complain or grumble. ORIG OE *grānian*
▸ **'groaner** *n* ▸ **'groaning** *adj, n* ▸ **'groaningly** *adv*

groat (grəʊt) *n* an obsolete English silver coin worth four pennies. ORIG C14: from MDu. *groot,* from MLow G *gros,* from Med. L (*denarius*) *grossus* thick (coin); see GROSCHEN

groats (grəʊts) *pl n* the hulled and crushed grain of oats, wheat, or certain other cereals. ORIG OE *grot* particle

grocer ('grəʊsə) *n* a dealer in foodstuffs and other household supplies. ORIG C15: from OF *grossier,* from *gros* large; see GROSS

groceries ('grəʊsərɪz) *pl n* merchandise, esp. foodstuffs, sold by a grocer.

grocery ('grəʊsərɪ) *n, pl* **groceries.** the business or premises of a grocer.

Grodno ★ (*Russian* 'grɔdnə) *n* a city in W Belarus, on the Neman River: part of Poland (1921–39); an industrial centre. Pop.: 301 000 (1996 est.).

grog (grɒg) *n* **1** diluted spirit, usually rum, as an alcoholic drink. **2** *Austral. & NZ inf.* alcoholic drink in general, esp. spirits. ORIG C18: from Old *Grog,* nickname of Edward Vernon (1684–1757), Brit. admiral, who in 1740 issued naval rum diluted with water; his nickname arose from his grogram cloak

groggy ('grɒgɪ) *adj* **groggier, groggiest.** *Inf.* **1** dazed or staggering, as from exhaustion, blows, or drunkenness. **2** faint or weak.
▸ **'groggily** *adv* ▸ **'grogginess** *n*

grogram ('grɒgrəm) *n* a coarse fabric of silk, wool, or silk mixed with wool or mohair, often stiffened with gum, formerly used for clothing. ORIG C16: from F *gros grain* coarse grain; see GROSGRAIN

groin (grɔɪn) *n* **1** the depression or fold where the legs join the abdomen. **2** *Euphemistic.* the genitals, esp. the testicles. **3** a variant spelling (esp. US) of **groyne. 4** *Archit.* a curved arris formed where two intersecting vaults meet. ◆ *vb* **5** (*tr*) *Archit.* to provide or construct with groins. ORIG C15: ?from E *grynde* abyss

grommet ('grɒmɪt) *or* **grummet** *n* **1** a ring of rubber or plastic or a metal eyelet designed to line a hole to prevent a cable or pipe passed through it from chafing. **2** *Med.* a small tube inserted into the eardrum in cases of glue ear in order to allow air to enter the middle ear. **3** *Austral. inf.* a young or inexperienced surfer. ORIG C15: from obs. F *gourmette* chain linking the ends of a bit, from *gourmer* bridle, from ?

Gromyko ★ (*Russian* gra'mikə) *n* **Andrei Andreyevich** (an'drjej an'drjejɪvitʃ). 1909–89, Soviet statesman and diplomat; foreign minister (1957–85); president (1985–88).

Groningen ★ ('grəʊnɪŋən; *Dutch* 'xro:nɪŋə) *n* **1** a province in the NE Netherlands: mainly agricultural. Capital: Groningen. Pop.: 558 100 (1997 est.). Area: 2336 sq. km (902 sq. miles). **2** a city in the NE Netherlands, capital of Groningen province. Pop.: 169 627 (1996 est.).

Grønland ★ ('grœnlan) *n* the Danish name for **Greenland.**

groom (gru:m, grʊm) *n* **1** a person employed to clean and look after horses. **2** See **bridegroom. 3** any of various officers of a royal or noble household. **4** *Arch.* a male servant. ◆ *vb* (*tr*) **5** to make or keep (clothes, appearance, etc.) clean and tidy. **6** to rub down, clean, and smarten (a horse, dog, etc.). **7** to train or prepare for a particular task, occupation, etc.: *to groom someone for the Presidency.* ORIG C13 *grom* manservant; ? rel. to OE *grōwan* to GROW

groomsman ('gru:mzmən, 'grʊmz-) *n, pl* **groomsmen.** a man who attends the bridegroom at a wedding, usually the best man.

groove (gru:v) *n* **1** a long narrow channel or furrow, esp. one cut into wood by a tool. **2** the spiral channel in a gramophone record. **3** a settled existence, routine, etc., to which one is suited or accustomed. **4** *Dated sl.* an experience, event, etc., that is groovy. **5 in the groove. 5a** *Jazz.* playing well and apparently effortlessly, with a good beat, etc. **5b** *US.* fashionable. ◆ *vb* **grooves, grooving, grooved. 6** (*tr*) to form or cut a groove in. **7** (*intr*) *Dated sl.* to enjoy oneself or feel in rapport with one's surroundings. **8** (*intr*) *Jazz.* to play well, with a good beat, etc. ORIG C15: from obs. Du. *groeve,* of Gmc origin

groovy ('gru:vɪ) *adj* **groovier, grooviest.** *Sl., often jocular.* attractive, fashionable, or exciting.

grope (grəʊp) *vb* **gropes, groping, groped. 1** (*intr;* usually foll. by *for*) to feel or search about uncertainly (for something) with the hands. **2** (*intr;* usually foll. by *for* or *after*) to search uncertainly or with difficulty (for a solution, answer, etc.). **3** (*tr*) to find (one's way) by groping. **4** (*tr*) *Sl.* to fondle the body of (someone) for sexual gratification. ◆ *n* **5** the act of groping. ORIG OE *grāpian*
▸ **'gropingly** *adv*

groper ('grəʊpə) *or* **grouper** *n, pl* **groper, gropers** *or* **grouper, groupers.** a large marine fish of warm and tropical seas. ORIG C17: from Port. *garupa,* prob. from a South American Indian word

Gropius ★ ('grəʊpɪəs) *n* **Walter.** 1883–1969, US architect, born in Germany. He founded (1919) and directed (1919–28) the Bauhaus in Germany. His buildings include the Fagus factory at Alfeld (1911).

Gros ★ (*French* gro) *n* Baron **Antoine Jean** (ãtwan ʒã). 1771–1835, French painter, noted for his battle scenes.

grosbeak ('grəʊs,bi:k, 'grɒs-) *n* any of various finches that have a massive powerful bill. ORIG C17: from F *grosbec,* from OF *gros* large, thick + *bec* BEAK[1]

groschen ('grəʊʃən) *n, pl* **groschen. 1** an Austrian monetary unit worth one hundredth of a schilling. **2** a German coin worth ten pfennigs. **3** a former German silver coin. ORIG C17: from G: alteration of MHG *grosse,* from Med. L (*denarius*) *grossus* thick (penny); see GROSS, GROAT

grosgrain ('grəʊ,greɪn) *n* a heavy ribbed silk or rayon fabric or tape for trimming clothes, etc. ORIG C19: from F *gros grain* coarse grain; see GROSS, GRAIN

gros point ('grəʊ 'pɔɪnt; *French* gro pwɛ̃) *n* **1** a needlepoint stitch covering two horizontal and two vertical threads. **2** work done in this stitch. ORIG OF: large point

gross (grəʊs) *adj* **1** repellently or excessively fat or bulky. **2** with no deductions for expenses, tax, etc.; total: *gross sales.* Cf. **net**². **3** (of personal qualities, tastes, etc.) conspicuously coarse or vulgar. **4** obviously or exceptionally culpable or wrong; flagrant: *gross inefficiency.* **5** lacking in perception, sensitivity, or discrimination: *gross judgments.* **6** (esp. of vegetation) dense; thick; luxuriant. ◆ *n* **7** (*pl* **gross**). a unit of quantity equal to 12 dozen. **8** (*pl* **grosses**). **8a** the entire amount. **8b** the great majority. ◆ *interj* **9** *Sl.* an exclamation indicating disgust. ◆ *vb* (*tr*) **10** to earn as total revenue, before deductions for expenses, tax, etc. ORIG C14: from OF *gros* large, from LL *grossus* thick
▸ **'grossly** *adv* ▸ **'grossness** *n*

gross domestic product *n* the total value of all goods and services produced domestically by a nation during a year. It is equivalent to gross national product minus net investment incomes from foreign nations. Abbrev.: **GDP**.

Grosseteste ★ ('grəʊsˌtɛst) *n* **Robert.** ?1175–1253, English prelate and scholar; bishop of Lincoln (1235–53).

gross national product *n* the total value of all final goods and services produced annually by a nation. Abbrev.: **GNP**.

gross profit *n Accounting.* the difference between total revenue from sales and the total cost of purchases or materials, with an adjustment for stock.

Grosswardein ★ (groːsvar'daɪn) *n* the German name for **Oradea**.

gross weight *n* total weight of an article inclusive of the weight of the container and packaging.

Grosz ★ (grəʊs; *German* grɔs) *n* **George.** 1893–1959, German painter, in the US from 1932, whose works satirized German militarism.

grot (grɒt) *n Sl.* rubbish; dirt. ORIG C20: from GROTTY

Grote ★ (grəʊt) *n* **George.** 1794–1871, English historian, noted particularly for his *History of Greece* (1846–56).

grotesque (grəʊ'tɛsk) *adj* **1** strangely or fantastically distorted; bizarre. **2** of or characteristic of the grotesque in art. **3** absurdly incongruous; in a ludicrous context. ◆ *n* **4** a 16th-century decorative style in which parts of human, animal, and plant forms are distorted and mixed. **5** a decorative device, as in painting or sculpture, in this style. **6** *Printing.* the family of 19th-century sans serif display types. **7** any grotesque person or thing. ORIG C16: from F, from OIt. (*pittura*) *grottesca* cave painting, from *grotta* cave; see GROTTO
▸ **gro'tesquely** *adv* ▸ **gro'tesqueness** *n* ▸ **gro'tesquery** *or* **gro'tesquerie** *n*

Grotius ★ ('grəʊtɪəs) *n* **Hugo,** original name *Huig de Groot.* 1583–1645, Dutch jurist and statesman, whose *De Jure Belli ac Pacis* (1625) is regarded as the foundation of modern international law.
▸ **'Grotian** *adj*

grotto ('grɒtəʊ) *n, pl* **grottoes** *or* **grottos. 1** a small cave, esp. one with attractive features. **2** a construction in the form of a cave, esp. as in landscaped gardens during the 18th century. ORIG C17: from OIt. *grotta,* from LL *crypta* vault; see CRYPT

grotty ('grɒtɪ) *adj* **grottier, grottiest.** *Brit. sl.* **1** nasty or unattractive. **2** of poor quality or in bad condition. ORIG C20: from GROTESQUE

grouch (graʊtʃ) *Inf.* ◆ *vb* (*intr*) **1** to complain; grumble. ◆ *n* **2** a complaint, esp. a persistent one. **3** a person who is always grumbling. ORIG C20: from obs. *grutch,* from OF *grouchier* to complain; see GRUDGE
▸ **'grouchy** *adj* ▸ **'grouchily** *adv* ▸ **'grouchiness** *n*

ground¹ (graʊnd) *n* **1** the land surface. **2** earth or soil. **3** (*pl*) the land around a dwelling house or other building. **4** (*sometimes pl*) an area of land given over to a purpose: *football ground.* **5** land having a particular characteristic: *high ground.* **6** matter for consideration or debate; field of research or inquiry: *the report covered a lot of ground.* **7** a position or viewpoint, as in an argument or controversy (esp. in **give ground, hold, stand,** *or* **shift one's ground**). **8** position or advantage, as in a subject or competition (esp. in **gain ground, lose ground,** etc.). **9** (*often pl*) reason; justification: *grounds for complaint.* **10** *Arts.* **10a** the prepared surface applied to a wall, canvas, etc., to prevent it reacting with or absorbing the paint. **10b** the background of a painting against which the other parts of a work of art appear superimposed. **11a** the first coat of paint applied to a surface. **11b** (*as modifier*): *ground colour.* **12** the bottom of a river or the sea. **13** (*pl*) sediment or dregs, esp. from coffee. **14** *Chiefly Brit.* the floor of a room. **15** *Cricket.* the area from the popping crease back past the stumps, in which a batsman may legally stand. **16** *Electrical.* the usual US and Canad. word for **earth** (sense 8). **17 break new ground.** to do something that has not been done before. **18 common ground.** an agreed basis for identifying issues in an argument. **19 cut the ground from under someone's feet.** to anticipate someone's action or argument and thus make it irrelevant or meaningless. **20** (**down**) **to the ground.** *Brit. inf.* completely; absolutely: *it suited him down to the ground.* **21 home ground.** a familiar area or topic. **22 into the ground.** beyond what is requisite or can be endured; to exhaustion. **23** (*modifier*) on or concerned with the ground: *ground frost; ground forces.* ◆ *vb* **24** (*tr*) to put or place on the ground. **25** (*tr*) to instruct in fundamentals. **26** (*tr*) to provide a basis or foundation for; establish. **27** (*tr*) to confine (an aircraft, pilot, etc.) to the ground. **28** (*tr*) to confine (a teenager) to the house as a punishment. **29** the usual US and Canad. word for **earth** (sense 13). **30** (*tr*) *Naut.* to run (a vessel) aground. **31** (*intr*) to hit or reach the ground. ORIG OE *grund*

ground² (graʊnd) *vb* **1** the past tense and past participle of **grind.** ◆ *adj* **2** having the surface finished, thickness reduced, or an edge sharpened by grinding. **3** reduced to fine particles by grinding.

groundage ('graʊndɪdʒ) *n Brit.* a fee levied on a vessel entering a port or anchored off a shore.

groundbait ('graʊndˌbeɪt) *n Angling.* bait, such as bread or maggots, thrown into an area of water to attract fish.

ground bass (beɪs) *n Music.* a short melodic bass line that is repeated over and over again.

ground-breaking *adj* innovative: *a ground-breaking novel.*

ground control *n* **1** the personnel, radar, computers, etc., on the ground that monitor the progress of aircraft or spacecraft. **2** a system for feeding radio messages to an aircraft pilot to enable him to make a blind landing.

ground cover *n* dense low herbaceous plants and shrubs that grow over the surface of the ground.

ground elder *n* a widely naturalized Eurasian umbelliferous plant with white flowers and creeping underground stems. Also called: **bishop's weed, goutweed.**

ground floor *n* **1** the floor of a building level or almost level with the ground. **2 get in on the ground floor.** *Inf.* to be in a project, undertaking, etc., from its inception.

ground frost *n* the condition resulting from a temperature reading of 0°C or below on a thermometer in contact with a grass surface.

ground glass *n* **1** glass that has a rough surface produced by grinding, used for diffusing light. **2** glass in the form of fine particles produced by grinding, used as an abrasive.

groundhog ('graʊndˌhɒg) *n* another name for **woodchuck.**

grounding ('graʊndɪŋ) *n* a foundation, esp. the basic general knowledge of a subject.

ground ivy *n* a creeping or trailing Eurasian aromatic herbaceous plant with scalloped leaves and purplish-blue flowers.

groundless ('graʊndlɪs) *adj* without reason or justification: *his suspicions were groundless.*
▸ **'groundlessly** *adv* ▸ **'groundlessness** *n*

groundling ('graʊndlɪŋ) *n* **1** any animal or plant that lives close to the ground or at the bottom of a lake, river, etc. **2** (in Elizabethan theatre) a spectator standing in the yard in front of the stage and paying least. **3** a person on the ground as distinguished from one in an aircraft.

groundnut ('graʊnd,nʌt) *n* **1** a North American climbing leguminous plant with small edible underground tubers. **2** the tuber of this plant. **3** *Brit.* another name for **peanut**.

ground plan *n* **1** a drawing of the ground floor of a building, esp. one to scale. **2** a preliminary or basic outline.

ground rule *n* a procedural or fundamental principle.

groundsel ('graʊnsəl) *n* any of certain plants of the composite family, esp. a Eurasian weed with heads of small yellow flowers. ORIG OE, from *gundeswilge,* from *gund* pus + *swelgan* to swallow; after its use in poultices

groundsheet ('graʊnd,ʃi:t) *n* a waterproof rubber, plastic, or polythene sheet placed on the ground in a tent, etc., to keep out damp.

groundsill ('graʊnd,sɪl) *n* a joist forming the lowest member of a timber frame. Also called: **ground plate**.

groundsman ('graʊndzmən) *n, pl* **groundsmen**. a person employed to maintain a sports ground, park, etc.

groundspeed ('graʊnd,spi:d) *n* the speed of an aircraft relative to the ground.

ground squirrel *n* a burrowing rodent resembling a chipmunk and occurring in North America, E Europe, and Asia. Also called: **gopher**.

groundswell ('graʊnd,swel) *n* **1** a considerable swell of the sea, often caused by a distant storm or earthquake. **2** a rapidly developing general feeling or opinion.

ground water *n* underground water that is held in the soil and in pervious rocks.

groundwork ('graʊnd,wɜ:k) *n* **1** preliminary work as a foundation or basis. **2** the ground or background of a painting, etc.

ground zero *n* a point on the ground directly below the centre of a nuclear explosion.

group (gru:p) *n* **1** a number of persons or things considered as a collective unit. **2a** a number of persons bound together by common social standards, interests, etc. **2b** *(as modifier): group behaviour.* **3** a small band of players or singers, esp. of pop music. **4** a number of animals or plants considered as a unit because of common characteristics, habits, etc. **5** an association of companies under a single ownership and control. **6** two or more figures or objects forming a design in a painting or sculpture. **7** a military formation comprising complementary arms and services: *a brigade group.* **8** an air force organization of higher level than a squadron. **9** Also called: **radical**. *Chem.* two or more atoms that are bound together in a molecule and behave as a single unit: *a methyl group* $-CH_3$. **10** a vertical column of elements in the periodic table that all have similar electronic structures, properties, and valencies: *the halogen group.* **11** *Maths.* a set under an operation involving any two members of the set such that the set is closed, associative, and contains both an identity and the inverse of each member. **12** See **blood group**. ◆ *vb* **13** to arrange or place (things, people, etc.) in or into a group, or (of things, etc.) to form into a group. ORIG C17: from F *groupe,* of Gmc origin; cf. It. *gruppo;* see CROP

group captain *n* an officer holding commissioned rank senior to a wing commander but junior to an air commodore in the RAF and certain other air forces.

group dynamics *n (functioning as sing) Psychol.* a field of social psychology concerned with the nature of human groups, their development, and their interactions.

grouper ('gru:pə) *n* a variant spelling of **groper**.

groupie ('gru:pɪ) *n Sl.* **1** an ardent fan of a celebrity, esp. a girl who follows the members of a pop group on tour in order to have sexual relations with them. **2** an enthusiastic follower of some activity: *a political groupie.*

Group of Eight *n* the Group of Seven nations and Russia, whose heads of government meet to discuss economic matters and international relations. Abbrev.: **G8**.

Group of Five *n* France, Japan, the UK, the US, and Germany acting as a group to stabilize their currency exchange rates. Abbrev.: **G5**.

Group of Seven *n* the seven leading industrial nations excepting Russia, i.e. Canada, France, Germany, Italy, Japan, the UK, and the US, whose heads of government and finance ministers meet regularly to coordinate economic policy. Abbrev.: **G7**.

Group of Seventy-Seven *n* the developing countries of the world. Abbrev.: **G77**.

Group of Ten *n* the ten nations who met in Paris in 1961 to arrange the special drawing rights of the IMF; Belgium, Canada, France, Italy, Japan, the Netherlands, Sweden, the UK, the US, and West Germany. Also called: **Paris Club**. Abbrev.: **G10**.

Group of Three *n* Japan, the US, and Germany, regarded as the largest industrialized nations. Abbrev.: **G3**.

Group of Twenty-Four *n* the twenty-four richest industrial countries of the world. Abbrev.: **G24**.

group practice *n* a group of doctors who together run a general practice.

group therapy *n Psychol.* the simultaneous treatment of a number of individuals who are brought together to share their problems in group discussion.

groupuscule ('gru:pə,skju:l) *n Usually derog.* a small group within a political party or movement. ORIG C20: a blend of GROUP + *corpuscule;* see CORPUSCLE

groupware ('gru:p,wɛə) *n* software that enables a group of computers to work together, so that users may access shared files, exchange messages, etc.

grouse[1] (graʊs) *n, pl* **grouse** *or* **grouses**. a game bird occurring mainly in the N hemisphere, having a stocky body and feathered legs and feet. ORIG C16: from ?

grouse[2] (graʊs) *vb* **grouses, grousing, groused. 1** *(intr)* to grumble; complain. ◆ *n* **2** a persistent complaint. ORIG C19: from ?

▸ **'grouser** *n*

grouse[3] (graʊs) *adj Austral. & NZ sl.* fine; excellent. ORIG from ?

grout (graʊt) *n* **1** a thin mortar for filling joints between tiles, masonry, etc. **2** a fine plaster used as a finishing coat. **3** *(pl)* sediment or dregs. ◆ *vb* **4** *(tr)* to fill (joints) or finish (walls, etc.) with grout. ORIG OE *grūt*

▸ **'grouter** *n*

grove (grəʊv) *n* **1** a small wooded area. **2** a road lined with houses and trees, esp. in a suburban area. ORIG OE *grāf*

grovel ('grɒvᵊl) *vb* **grovels, grovelling, grovelled** *or US* **grovels, groveling, groveled**. *(intr)* **1** to humble or abase oneself, as in making apologies or showing respect. **2** to lie or crawl face downwards, as in fear or humility. **3** (often foll. by *in*) to indulge or take pleasure (in sensuality or vice). ORIG C16: back formation from obs. *groveling* (adv), from ME *on grufe* on the face, of Scand. origin; see -LING[2]

▸ **'groveller** *or US* **,groveler** *n*

Groves ★ (grəʊvz) *n* Sir **Charles**. 1915–92, British orchestral conductor.

grow (grəʊ) *vb* **grows, growing, grew, grown. 1** (of an organism or part of an organism) to increase in size or develop (hair, leaves, or other structures). **2** *(intr;* usually foll. by *out of* or *from)* to originate, as from an initial cause or source: *the federation grew out of the Empire.* **3** *(intr)* to increase in size, number, degree, etc.: *the population is growing rapidly.* **4** *(intr)* to change in length or amount in a specified direction: *some plants grow downwards.* **5** *(copula; may take an infinitive)* (esp. of emotions, physical states, etc.) to develop or come into existence or being gradually: *to grow cold.* **6** *(intr;* foll. by *together)* to be joined gradually by or as by growth. **7** (when *intr,* foll. by *with)* to become covered with a growth: *the path grew with weeds.* **8** to produce (plants) by controlling or encouraging their growth, esp. for home consumption or on a commercial basis. ◆ See also **grow into, grow on,** etc. ORIG OE *grōwan*

▸ **'growable** *adj* ▸ **'grower** *n*

grow bag *n* a plastic bag containing a sterile growing medium that enables a plant to be grown to full size in it, usually for one season only. ORIG C20: from *Gro-bag,* trademark for the first ones marketed

growing pains *pl n* **1** pains in muscles or joints sometimes experienced by growing children. **2** difficulties besetting a new enterprise in its early stages.

grow into *vb* (*intr, prep*) to become big or mature enough for: *clothes big enough for him to grow into.*

growl (graʊl) *vb* **1** (of animals, esp. when hostile) to utter (sounds) in a low inarticulate manner: *the dog growled.* **2** to utter (words) in a gruff or angry manner. **3** (*intr*) to make sounds suggestive of an animal growling: *the thunder growled.* ◆ *n* **4** the act or sound of growling. ORIG C18: from earlier *grolle,* from OF *grouller* to grumble
▸ ˈ**growler** *n*

grown (grəʊn) *adj* **a** developed or advanced: *fully grown.* **b** (*in combination*): *half-grown.*

grown-up *adj* **1** having reached maturity; adult. **2** suitable for or characteristic of an adult. ◆ *n* **3** an adult.

grow on *vb* (*intr, prep*) to become progressively more acceptable or pleasant to.

grow out of *vb* (*intr, adv + prep*) to become too big or mature for: *she soon grew out of her girlish ways.*

growth (grəʊθ) *n* **1** the process or act of growing. **2** an increase in size, number, significance, etc. **3** something grown or growing: *a new growth of hair.* **4** a stage of development: *a full growth.* **5** any abnormal tissue, such as a tumour. **6** (*modifier*) of, relating to, causing, or characterized by growth: *a growth industry; growth hormone.*

growth curve *n* a curve on a graph in which a variable is plotted against time to illustrate the growth of the variable.

grow up *vb* (*intr, adv*) **1** to reach maturity; become adult. **2** to come into existence; develop.

groyne *or esp. US* **groin** (grɔɪn) *n* a wall or jetty built out from a riverbank or seashore to control erosion. Also called: **spur, breakwater.** ORIG C16: ?from OF *groign* snout, promontory

Grozny ★ (*Russian* ˈgrɔznij) *n* a city in S Russia, capital of Chechenia: almost destroyed by fighting between Chechen separatists and Russian troops, who occupied the city in 2000; formerly a major oil centre. Pop.: 364 000 (1993 est.).

grub (grʌb) *vb* **grubs, grubbing, grubbed. 1** (when *tr,* often foll. by *up* or *out*) to search for and pull up (roots, stumps, etc.) by digging in the ground. **2** to dig up the surface of (ground, soil, etc.), esp. to clear away roots, stumps, etc. **3** (*intr;* often foll. by *in* or *among*) to search carefully. **4** (*intr*) to work unceasingly, esp. at a dull task. ◆ *n* **5** the short legless larva of certain insects, esp. beetles. **6** *Sl.* food; victuals. **7** a person who works hard, esp. in a dull plodding way. ORIG C13: of Gmc origin; cf. OHG *grubilōn* to dig
▸ ˈ**grubber** *n*

grubby (ˈgrʌbɪ) *adj* **grubbier, grubbiest. 1** dirty; slovenly. **2** mean; beggarly. **3** infested with grubs.
▸ ˈ**grubbily** *adv* ▸ ˈ**grubbiness** *n*

grub screw *n* a small headless screw used to secure a sliding component in position.

grubstake (ˈgrʌbˌsteɪk) *US & Canad. inf.* ◆ *n* **1** supplies provided for a prospector on the condition that the donor has a stake in any finds. ◆ *vb* **grubstakes, grubstaking, grubstaked.** (*tr*) **2** to furnish with such supplies. **3** to supply (a person) with a stake in a gambling game.
▸ ˈ**grubˌstaker** *n*

Grub Street *n* **1** a former street in London frequented by literary hacks and needy authors. **2** the world or class of literary hacks, etc. ◆ *adj also* **Grubstreet. 3** (*sometimes not cap.*) relating to or characteristic of hack literature.

grudge (grʌdʒ) *n* **1** a persistent feeling of resentment, esp. one due to an insult or injury. **2** (*modifier*) planned or carried out in order to settle a grudge: *a grudge fight.* ◆ *vb* **grudges, grudging, grudged. 3** (*tr*) to give unwillingly. **4** to feel resentful or envious about (someone else's success, etc.). ORIG C15: from OF *grouchier* to grumble, prob. of Gmc origin
▸ ˈ**grudging** *adj* ▸ ˈ**grudgingly** *adv*

gruel (ˈgruːəl) *n* a drink or thin porridge made by boiling meal, esp. oatmeal, in water or milk. ORIG C14: from OF, of Gmc origin

gruelling *or US* **grueling** (ˈgruːəlɪŋ) *adj* **1** extremely severe or tiring. ◆ *n* **2** *Inf.* a severe or tiring experience, esp. punishment. ORIG C19: from obs. *gruel* (vb) to punish

gruesome (ˈgruːsəm) *adj* inspiring repugnance and horror; ghastly. ORIG C16: orig. Northern E and Scot., of Scand. origin
▸ ˈ**gruesomely** *adv* ▸ ˈ**gruesomeness** *n*

gruff (grʌf) *adj* **1** rough or surly in manner, speech, etc. **2** (of a voice, bark, etc.) low and throaty. ORIG C16: orig. Scot., from Du. *grof,* of Gmc origin; rel. to OE *hrēof*
▸ ˈ**gruffly** *adv* ▸ ˈ**gruffness** *n*

grumble (ˈgrʌmbᵊl) *vb* **grumbles, grumbling, grumbled. 1** to utter (complaints) in a nagging way. **2** (*intr*) to make low rumbling sounds. ◆ *n* **3** a complaint. **4** a low rumbling sound. ORIG C16: from MLow G *grommelen,* of Gmc origin
▸ ˈ**grumbler** *n* ▸ ˈ**grumblingly** *adv* ▸ ˈ**grumbly** *adj*

grumbling appendix *n Inf.* a condition in which the appendix causes intermittent pain or discomfort but appendicitis has not developed.

grummet (ˈgrʌmɪt) *n* a variant of **grommet.**

grump (grʌmp) *Inf.* ◆ *n* **1** a surly or bad-tempered person. **2** (*pl*) a sulky or morose mood (esp. in **have the grumps**). ◆ *vb* **3** (*intr*) to complain or grumble. ORIG C18: dialect: surly remark, prob. imit.

grumpy (ˈgrʌmpɪ) *or* **grumpish** *adj* **grumpier, grumpiest.** peevish; sulky. ORIG C18: from GRUMP + -Y[1]
▸ ˈ**grumpily** *or* ˈ**grumpishly** *adv* ▸ ˈ**grumpiness** *or* ˈ**grumpishness** *n*

Grundy (ˈgrʌndɪ) *n* a narrow-minded person who keeps critical watch on the propriety of others. ORIG C18: after Mrs *Grundy,* the character in T. Morton's play *Speed the Plough* (1798)
▸ ˈ**Grundyˌism** *n* ▸ ˈ**Grundyist** *or* ˈ**Grundyite** *n*

Grünewald ★ (*German* ˈgryːnəvalt) *n* **Matthias** (maˈtiːas), original name *Mathis Gothardt.* ?1470–1528, German painter.

grunge (grʌndʒ) *n* **1** *US sl.* dirt or rubbish. **2** a style of rock music originating in the US in the late 1980s, featuring a distorted guitar sound. **3** a deliberately untidy and uncoordinated fashion style. ORIG C20: possibly a coinage imitating GRIME + SLUDGE

grungy (ˈgrʌndʒɪ) *adj* **grungier, grungiest. 1** *Sl., chiefly US & Canad.* squalid, seedy, grotty. **2** (of pop music) characterized by a loud fuzzy guitar sound. ORIG from ?

grunion (ˈgrʌnjən) *n* a Californian marine fish that spawns on beaches. ORIG C20: prob. from Sp. *gruñón* a grunter

grunt (grʌnt) *vb* **1** (*intr*) (esp. of pigs and some other animals) to emit a low short gruff noise. **2** (when *tr, may take a clause as object*) to express something gruffly: *he grunted his answer.* ◆ *n* **3** the characteristic low short gruff noise of pigs, etc., or a similar sound, as of disgust. **4** any of various mainly tropical marine fishes that utter a grunting sound when caught. ORIG OE *grunnettan,* prob. imit.; cf. OHG *grunnizōn, grunni* moaning
▸ ˈ**grunter** *n*

Gruyère *or* **Gruyère cheese** (ˈgruːjɛə) *n* a hard flat whole-milk cheese, pale yellow in colour and with holes. ORIG C19: after *Gruyère,* Switzerland, where it originated

gr. wt. *abbrev. for* gross weight.

gryphon ★ (ˈgrɪfᵊn) *n* a variant of **griffin.**

grysbok (ˈgraɪsˌbɒk) *n* either of two small antelopes of central and southern Africa, having small straight horns. ORIG C18: Afrik., from Du. *grijs* grey + *bok* BUCK[1]

GS *abbrev. for:* **1** General Secretary. **2** General Staff.

GST (in New Zealand) *abbrev. for* goods and services tax.

G-string *n* **1** a piece of cloth worn by striptease artistes covering the pubic area and attached to a narrow waistband. **2** a strip of cloth attached to the front and back of a waistband and covering the loins. **3** *Music.* a string tuned to G.

G-suit *n* a close-fitting garment that is worn by the crew of high-speed aircraft and can be pressurized to prevent blackout during manoeuvres. ORIG C20: from *g(ravity) suit*

GSVQ (in Britain) *abbrev. for* General Scottish Vocational Qualification: the Scottish equivalent of GNVQ.

GT *abbrev. for* gran turismo: a touring car; usually a fast sports car with a hard fixed roof.

gtd *abbrev. for* guaranteed.

Guadalajara ★ (ˌgwɑːdəlǝˈhɑːrə; *Spanish* gwaðalaˈxara) *n* **1** a city in W Mexico, capital of Jalisco state: centre of the Indian slave trade until its abolition, declared here in 1810; two universities (1792 and 1935). Pop.: 1 650 042 (1990). **2** a city in central Spain, in New Castile. Pop.: 67 200 (1991).

Guadalcanal ★ (ˌgwɑːdəlkəˈnæl; *Spanish* gwaðalkaˈnal) *n* a mountainous island in the SW Pacific, the largest of the Solomon Islands: under British protection until 1978; occupied by the Japanese (1942–43). Pop.: 59 064 (1996 est.). Area: 6475 sq. km (2500 sq. miles).

Guadalquivir ★ (ˌgwɑːdəlkwɪˈvɪə; *Spanish* gwaðalkiˈβir) *n* the chief river of S Spain, rising in the Sierra de Segura and flowing west and southwest to the Gulf of Cádiz: navigable by ocean-going vessels to Seville. Length: 560 km (348 miles).

Guadalupe Hidalgo ★ (ˌgwɑːdəˈluːp hɪˈdælgəʊ; *Spanish* gwaðaˈlupe iˈðalγo) *n* a city in central Mexico, northwest of Mexico City: became the foremost pilgrimage centre in the Americas after an Indian convert reported seeing a vision of the Virgin Mary here in 1531. Pop.: 535 332 (1990). Former name (1931–71): **Gustavo A. Madero.**

Guadeloupe ★ (ˌgwɑːdəˈluːp) *n* an overseas region of France in the E Caribbean, in the Leeward Islands, formed by the islands of Basse Terre and Grande Terre and their five dependencies. Capital: Basse-Terre. Pop.: 424 000 (1999 est.). Area: 1780 sq. km (687 sq. miles).

Guadiana ★ (*Spanish* gwaˈðjana; *Portuguese* gwəˈðjənə) *n* a river in SW Europe, rising in S central Spain and flowing west, then south as part of the border between Spain and Portugal, to the Gulf of Cádiz. Length: 578 km (359 miles).

guaiacum (ˈgwaɪəkəm) *n* **1** any of a family of tropical American evergreen trees such as the lignum vitae. **2** the hard heavy wood of any of these trees. **3** a brownish resin obtained from the lignum vitae, used medicinally and in making varnishes. ORIG C16: NL, from Sp. *guayaco,* of Amerind origin

Guam ★ (gwɑːm) *n* an island in the N Pacific, the largest and southernmost of the Marianas: belonged to Spain from the 17th century until 1898, when it was ceded to the US; site of naval and air force bases. Capital: Agaña. Pop.: 133 152 (1990). Area: 541 sq. km (209 sq. miles). ▸ **Guamanian** (gwɑːˈmeɪnɪən) *n, adj*

Guanabara ★ (*Portuguese* gwənaˈbara) *n* (until 1975) a state of SE Brazil, on the Atlantic and **Guanabara Bay**, now amalgamated with the state of Rio de Janeiro.

guanaco (gwɑːˈnɑːkəʊ) *n, pl* **guanacos.** a cud-chewing South American mammal closely related to the domesticated llama. ORIG C17: from Sp., from Quechuan *huanacu*

Guanajuato ★ (*Spanish* gwanaˈxwato) *n* **1** a state of central Mexico, on the great central plateau: mountainous in the north, with fertile plains in the south; important mineral resources. Capital: Guanajuato. Pop.: 4 478 673 (1997 est.). Area: 30 588 sq. km (11 810 sq. miles). **2** a city in central Mexico, capital of Guanajuato state: founded in 1554, it became one of the world's richest silver-mining centres. Pop.: 113 580 (1990).

Guangdong (ˈgwæŋˈdʊŋ) *or* **Kwangtung** ★ *n* a province of SE China, on the South China Sea: includes the Leizhou Peninsula, with densely populated river valleys; the only true tropical climate in China. Capital: Canton. Pop.: 70 510 000 (1997 est.). Area: 197 100 sq. km (76 100 sq. miles).

Guangxi Zhuang Autonomous Region (ˈgwæŋˈsiː ˈdʒwæŋ) *or* **Kwangsi-Chuang Autonomous Region** ★ *n* an administrative division of S China: the least developed of Chinese regions. Capital: Nanning. Pop.: 46 330 000 (1997 est.). Area: 220 400 sq. km (85 100 sq. miles).

Guangzhou ★ (ˈgwæŋˈdzəʊ) *n* the Pinyin transliteration of the Chinese name for **Canton.**

guanine (ˈgwɑːniːn, ˈguːəˌniːn) *n* a white almost insoluble compound: one of the purine bases in nucleic acids. ORIG C19: from GUANO + -INE[2]

guano (ˈgwɑːnəʊ) *n, pl* **guanos. 1** the dried excrement of fish-eating sea birds, deposited in rocky coastal regions of South America: used as a fertilizer. **2** any similar but artificially produced fertilizer. ORIG C17: from Sp., from Quechuan *huano* dung

Guantánamo ★ (*Spanish* gwanˈtanamo) *n* a city in SE Cuba, on **Guantánamo Bay**: site of a US naval base. Pop.: 207 796 (1994 est.).

Guaporé ★ (*Portuguese* gwapoˈrɛ) *n* **1** a river in W central South America, rising in SW Brazil and flowing northwest as part of the border between Brazil and Bolivia, to join the Mamoré River. Length: 1750 km (1087 miles). Spanish name: **Iténez. 2** the former name (until 1956) of **Rondônia.**

Guarani (ˌgwɑːrəˈniː) *n* **1** (*pl* **Guarani** *or* **Guaranis**) a member of a South American Indian people of Paraguay, S Brazil, and Bolivia. **2** the language of this people.

guarantee (ˌgærənˈtiː) *n* **1** a formal assurance, esp. in writing, that a product, service, etc., will meet certain standards or specifications. **2** *Law.* a promise, esp. a collateral agreement, to answer for the debt, default, or miscarriage of another. **3a** a person, company, etc., to whom a guarantee is made. **3b** a person, company, etc., who gives a guarantee. **4** a person who acts as a guarantor. **5** something that makes a specified condition or outcome certain. **6** a variant spelling of **guaranty.** ◆ *vb* **guarantees, guaranteeing, guaranteed.** (*mainly tr*) **7** (*also intr*) to take responsibility for (someone else's debts, obligations, etc.). **8** to serve as a guarantee for. **9** to secure or furnish security for: *a small deposit will guarantee any dress.* **10** (usually foll. by *from* or *against*) to undertake to protect or keep secure, as against injury, loss, etc. **11** to ensure: *good planning will guarantee success.* **12** (*may take a clause as object or an infinitive*) to promise or make certain. ORIG C17: ?from Sp. *garante* or F *garant,* of Gmc origin; cf. WARRANT

guarantor (ˌgærənˈtɔː) *n* a person who gives or is bound by a guarantee or guaranty; surety.

guaranty (ˈgærəntɪ) *n, pl* **guaranties. 1** a pledge of responsibility for fulfilling another person's obligations in case of that person's default. **2** a thing given or taken as security for a guaranty. **3** the act of providing security. **4** a person who acts as a guarantor. ◆ *vb* **guaranties, guarantying, guarantied. 5** a variant spelling of **guarantee.** ORIG C16: from OF *garantie,* var. of *warantie,* of Gmc origin; see WARRANTY

guard (gɑːd) *vb* **1** to watch over or shield (a person or thing) from danger or harm; protect. **2** to keep watch over (a prisoner or other potentially dangerous person or thing), as to prevent escape. **3** (*tr*) to control: *to guard one's tongue.* **4** (*intr;* usually foll. by *against*) to take precautions. **5** to control entrance and exit through (a gate, door, etc.). **6** (*tr*) to provide (machinery, etc.) with a device to protect the operator. **7** (*tr*) **7a** *Chess, cards.* to protect or cover (a chessman or card) with another. **7b** *Curling, bowling.* to protect or cover (a stone or bowl) by placing one's own stone or bowl between it and another player. ◆ *n* **8** a person or group who keeps a protecting, supervising, or restraining watch or control over people, such as prisoners, things, etc. Related adj: **custodial. 9** a person or group of people, such as soldiers, who form a ceremonial escort. **10** *Brit.* the official in charge of a train. **11a** the act or duty of protecting, restraining, or supervising. **11b** (*as modifier*): *guard duty.* **12** a device, part, or attachment on an object, such as a weapon or machine tool, designed to protect the user against injury. **13** anything that provides or is intended to provide protection: *a guard against infection.* **14** *Sport.* an article of light tough material worn to protect any of various parts of the body. **15** the posture of defence or readiness in fencing, boxing, cricket, etc. **16 mount guard. 16a** (of a sentry, etc.) to begin to keep watch. **16b** (with *over*) to take a protective or defensive stance (towards something). **17 off (one's) guard.** having one's defences down; unpre-

pared. **18 on (one's) guard.** prepared to face danger, difficulties, etc. **19 stand guard.** (of a sentry, etc.) to keep watch. ORIG C15: from OF, from *garder* to protect, of Gmc origin; see WARD
▸ **'guarder** *n*

Guardafui ★ (ˌgwɑːdəˈfuːɪ) *n* **Cape.** a cape at the NE tip of Somalia, extending into the Indian Ocean.

guarded (ˈgɑːdɪd) *adj* **1** protected or kept under surveillance. **2** prudent, restrained, or noncommittal: *a guarded reply.*
▸ **'guardedly** *adv* ▸ **'guardedness** *n*

guard hair *n* any of the coarse hairs that form the outer fur in certain mammals.

guardhouse (ˈgɑːdˌhaʊs) *or* **guardroom** (ˈgɑːdˌruːm, -rʊm) *n Mil.* a building serving as headquarters for military police and in which military prisoners are detained.

Guardi ★ (*Italian* ˈgwardi) *n* **Francesco** (franˈtʃesko). 1712–93, Venetian landscape painter.

guardian (ˈgɑːdɪən) *n* **1** one who looks after, protects, or defends: *the guardian of public morals.* **2** *Law.* someone legally appointed to manage the affairs of a person incapable of acting for himself, as a minor or person of unsound mind. ◆ *adj* **3** protecting or safeguarding.
▸ **'guardianˌship** *n*

Guardian Angels *pl n* vigilante volunteers who patrol the New York Underground and elsewhere, wearing red berets, to deter violent crime.

guard ring *n* **1** Also called: **keeper ring.** a ring worn to prevent another from slipping off the finger. **2** an electrode used to counteract distortion of the electric fields at the edges of other electrodes.

Guards (gɑːdz) *pl n* (esp. in European armies) any of various regiments responsible for ceremonial duties and, formerly, the protection of the head of state: *the Life Guards.*

guardsman (ˈgɑːdzmən) *n, pl* **guardsmen. 1** (in Britain) a member of a Guards battalion or regiment. **2** (in the US) a member of the National Guard. **3** a guard.

guard's van *n Railways, Brit. & NZ.* the van in which the guard travels, usually attached to the rear of a train. US and Canad. equivalent: **caboose.**

Guarneri (gwɑːˈnɪərɪ; *Italian* gwarˈnɛːri), **Guarnieri** (*Italian* gwarˈnjɛːri), *or* **Guarnerius ★** (gwɑːˈnɛərɪəs) *n, pl* **Guarneris, Guarnieris,** *or* **Guarneriuses. 1** an Italian family of 17th- and 18th-century violin-makers. **2** any violin made by a member of this family.

Guat. *abbrev. for* Guatemala.

Guatemala ★ (ˌgwɑːtəˈmɑːlə) *n* a republic in Central America: original Maya Indians conquered by the Spanish in 1523; became the centre of Spanish administration in Central America; gained independence and was annexed to Mexico in 1821, becoming an independent republic in 1839. Official language: Spanish. Religion: Roman Catholic majority. Currency: quetzal. Capital: Guatemala City. Pop.: 11 090 000 (1999 est.). Area: 108 889 sq. km (42 042 sq. miles).
▸ **ˌGuateˈmalan** *adj, n*

Guatemala City ★ *n* the capital of Guatemala, in the southeast: founded in 1776 to replace the former capital, Antigua Guatemala, after an earthquake; university (1676). Pop.: 1 167 495 (1995).

guava (ˈgwɑːvə) *n* **1** any of various tropical American trees, grown esp. for their edible fruit. **2** the fruit of such a tree, having yellow skin and pink pulp. ORIG C16: from Sp. *guayaba,* from a South American Indian word

Guayaquil ★ (*Spanish* gwajaˈkil) *n* a port in W Ecuador: the largest city in the country and its chief port; university (1867). Pop.: 1 973 880 (1997 est.).

guayule (gwəˈjuːlɪ) *n* **1** a bushy shrub of the southwestern US. **2** rubber derived from the sap of this plant. ORIG from American Sp., from Nahuatl *cuauhuli,* from *cuahuitl* tree + *uli* gum

gubbins (ˈgʌbɪnz) *n* **1** (*functioning as sing*) an object of little value. **2** (*functioning as sing*) a small gadget. **3** (*functioning as pl*) odds and ends; rubbish. **4** (*functioning as sing*) a silly person. ORIG C16 (meaning: fragments): from obs. *gobbon*

gubernatorial (ˌgjuːbənəˈtɔːrɪəl, ˌguː-) *adj Chiefly US.* of or relating to a governor. ORIG C18: from L *gubernātor* governor

guddle (ˈgʌdᵊl) *Scot.* ◆ *vb* **guddles, guddling, guddled. 1** to catch (fish) by groping with the hands under the banks or stones of a stream. ◆ *n* **2** a muddle; confusion. ORIG C19: from ?

gudgeon[1] (ˈgʌdʒən) *n* **1** a small slender European freshwater fish with a barbel on each side of the mouth: used as bait by anglers. **2** any of various other fishes, such as the goby. **3** *Sl.* a person who is easy to trick or cheat. ◆ *vb* **4** (*tr*) *Sl.* to trick or cheat. ORIG C15: from OF *gougon,* prob. from L *gōbius;* see GOBY

gudgeon[2] (ˈgʌdʒən) *n* **1** the female or socket portion of a pinned hinge. **2** *Naut.* one of two or more looplike sockets, fixed to the transom of a boat, into which the pintles of a rudder are fitted. ORIG C14: from OF *goujon,* ?from LL *gulbia* chisel

gudgeon pin *n Brit.* the pin through the skirt of a piston in an internal-combustion engine, to which the little end of the connecting rod is attached. US and Canad. name: **wrist pin.**

Gudrun (ˈgʊdruːn), **Guthrun** (ˈgʊðruːn), *or* **Kudrun ★** (ˈkʊdruːn) *n Norse myth.* the wife of Sigurd and, after his death, of Atli, whom she slew for his murder of her brother Gunnar. She corresponds to Kriemhild in the *Nibelungenlied.*

guelder-rose (ˈgɛldəˌrəʊz) *n* a Eurasian shrub with clusters of white flowers and small red fruits. ORIG C16: from Du. *geldersche roos,* from *Gelderland* or *Gelders,* province of Holland

Guelders ★ (ˈgɛldəz) *n* another name for **Gelderland.**

Guelph ★ (gwɛlf) *n* a city in Canada, in SE Ontario. Pop.: 87 976 (1991).

guenon (gəˈnɒn) *n* a slender agile Old World monkey inhabiting wooded regions of Africa and having long hind limbs and tail and long hair surrounding the face. ORIG C19: from F, from ?

guerdon (ˈgɜːdᵊn) *Poetic.* ◆ *n* **1** a reward or payment. ◆ *vb* **2** (*tr*) to give a guerdon to. ORIG C14: from OF *gueredon,* of Gmc origin; final element infl. by L *dōnum* gift

Guernica ★ (gɜːˈniːkə, ˈgɜːnɪkə; *Spanish* gɛrˈnika) *n* a town in N Spain: formerly the seat of a Basque parliament; destroyed in 1937 by German bombers during the Spanish Civil War, an event depicted in one of Picasso's most famous paintings. Pop.: 16 378 (1989).

Guernsey ★ (ˈgɜːnzɪ) *n* **1** an island in the English Channel: the second largest of the Channel Islands, which, with Alderney and Sark, Herm, Jethou, and some islets, forms the bailiwick of Guernsey; finance, market gardening, dairy farming, and tourism. Capital: St Peter Port. Pop.: 58 867 (1991). Area: 63 sq. km (24.5 sq. miles). **2** a breed of dairy cattle producing rich creamy milk, originating from the island of Guernsey. **3** (*sometimes not cap.*) a seaman's knitted woollen sweater. **4** (*not cap.*) *Austral.* a sleeveless woollen shirt or jumper worn by a football player. **5 get a guernsey.** *Austral.* to be selected or gain recognition for something.

Guerrero ★ (*Spanish* gɛˈrrɛro) *n* a mountainous state of S Mexico, on the Pacific: rich mineral resources. Capital: Chilpancingo. Pop.: 2 994 365 (1997 est.). Area: 63 794 sq. km (24 631 sq. miles).

guerrilla *or* **guerilla** (gəˈrɪlə) *n* **a** a member of an irregular usually politically motivated armed force that combats stronger regular forces. **b** (*as modifier*): *guerrilla warfare.* ORIG C19: from Sp., dim. of *guerra* WAR

guess (gɛs) *vb* (*when tr, may take a clause as object*) **1** (when *intr,* often foll. by *at* or *about*) to form or express an uncertain estimate or conclusion (about something), based on insufficient information: *guess what we're having for dinner.* **2** to arrive at a correct estimate of (something) by guessing: *he guessed my age.* **3** *Inf., chiefly US & Canad.* to believe, think, or suppose (something): *I guess I'll go now.* ◆ *n* **4** an estimate or conclusion arrived at by guessing: *a bad guess.* **5** the act of guessing. ORIG C13: prob. from ON
▸ **'guesser** *n*

guesstimate *or* **guestimate** *Inf.* ◆ *n* ('gestɪmɪt). **1** an estimate calculated mainly or only by guesswork. ◆ *vb* ('gestɪˌmeɪt), **guesstimates, guesstimating, guesstimated.** (*tr*) **2** to form a guesstimate of.

guesswork ('gesˌwɜːk) *n* **1** a set of conclusions, estimates, etc., arrived at by guessing. **2** the process of making guesses.

guest (gest) *n* **1** a person who is entertained, taken out to eat, etc., and paid for by another. **2a** a person who receives hospitality at the home of another. **2b** (*as modifier*): *the guest room.* **3a** a person who receives the hospitality of a government, establishment, or organization. **3b** (*as modifier*): *a guest speaker.* **4a** an actor, contestant, entertainer, etc., taking part as a visitor in a programme in which there are also regular participants. **4b** (*as modifier*): *a guest appearance.* **5** a patron of a hotel, boarding house, restaurant, etc. ◆ *vb* **6** (*intr*) (in theatre and broadcasting) to be a guest: *to guest on a show.* ORIG OE *giest* guest, stranger, enemy

guest beer *n* a draught beer stocked by a bar, often for a limited period, in addition to its usual range.

guesthouse ('gestˌhaʊs) *n* a private home or boarding house offering accommodation.

guest rope *n Naut.* any line trailed over the side of a vessel as a convenience for boats drawing alongside, as an aid in towing, etc.

Guevara ★ (gəˈvɑːrə; *Spanish* geˈβara) *n* **Ernesto** (ɛrˈnesto), known as *Che Guevara.* 1928–67, Latin American politician and soldier, born in Argentina. He developed guerrilla warfare as a tool for revolution and was instrumental in Castro's victory in Cuba (1959): killed while training guerrillas in Bolivia.

guff (gʌf) *n Sl.* ridiculous or insolent talk. ORIG C19: imit. of empty talk

guffaw (gʌˈfɔː) *n* **1** a crude and boisterous laugh. ◆ *vb* **2** to laugh or express (something) in this way. ORIG C18: imit.

Guggenheim Museum ★ ('gʊgənˌhaɪm) *n* **1** a museum of modern art in New York: designed by Frank Lloyd Wright (1956–59). **2** a museum of modern art in Bilbao, Spain, designed by Frank O. Gehry (born 1929).

Guiana (gaɪˈænə, gɪˈɑːnə) *or* **The Guianas** ★ *n* a region of NE South America, including Guyana, Surinam, French Guiana, and the **Guiana Highlands** (largely in SE Venezuela and partly in N Brazil). Area: about 1 787 000 sq. km (690 000 sq. miles).
▸ **Guianese** (ˌgaɪəˈniːz, ˌgɪə-) *or* **Guianan** (gaɪˈænən, gɪˈɑːnən) *adj, n*

guidance ('gaɪdᵊns) *n* **1** leadership, instruction, or direction. **2a** counselling or advice on educational, vocational, or psychological matters. **2b** (*as modifier*): *the marriage-guidance counsellor.* **3** something that guides. **4** any process by which the flight path of a missile is controlled in flight.

guide (gaɪd) *vb* **guides, guiding, guided. 1** to lead the way for (a person). **2** to control the movement or course of (an animal, vehicle, etc.) by physical action; steer. **3** to supervise or instruct (a person). **4** (*tr*) to direct the affairs of (a person, company, nation, etc.). **5** (*tr*) to advise or influence (a person) in his or her standards or opinions: *let truth guide you.* ◆ *n* **6a** a person, animal, or thing that guides. **6b** (*as modifier*): *a guide dog.* **7** a person, usually paid, who conducts tour expeditions, etc. **8** a model or criterion, as in moral standards or accuracy. **9** Also called: **guidebook.** a handbook with information for visitors to a place. **10** a book that instructs or explains the fundamentals of a subject or skill. **11** any device that directs the motion of a tool or machine part. **12** a mark, sign, etc., that points the way. **13a** *Naval.* a ship in a formation used as a reference for manoeuvres. **13b** *Mil.* a soldier stationed to one side of a column or line to regulate alignment, show the way, etc. ORIG C14: from (O)F *guider,* of Gmc origin
▸ **'guidable** *adj* ▸ **'guider** *n*

Guide (gaɪd) *n* (*sometimes not cap.*) a member of an organization for girls equivalent to the Scouts. US equivalent: **Girl Scout.**

guided missile *n* a missile, esp. one that is rocket-propelled, having a flight path controlled either by radio signals or by internal preset or self-actuating homing devices.

guide dog *n* a dog that has been specially trained to accompany someone who is blind, enabling the blind person to move about safely.

guideline ('gaɪdˌlaɪn) *n* a principle put forward to set standards or determine a course of action.

guidepost ('gaɪdˌpəʊst) *n* **1** a sign on a post by a road indicating directions. **2** a principle or guideline.

Guider ('gaɪdə) *n* (*sometimes not cap.*) a woman leader of a company of Guides or of a pack of Brownie Guides.

Guido d'Arezzo ★ (*Italian* ˈgwiːdo daˈrettso) *n* ?995–?1050 A.D., Italian Benedictine monk and musical theorist: reputed inventor of solmization.

guidon ('gaɪdᵊn) *n* **1** a small pennant, used as a marker or standard, esp. by cavalry regiments. **2** the man or vehicle that carries this. ORIG C16: from F, from OProvençal *guidoo,* from *guida* GUIDE

Guienne *or* **Guyenne** ★ (*French* gɥijɛn) *n* a former province of SW France: formed, with Gascony, the duchy of Aquitaine during the 12th century.

guild *or* **gild** (gɪld) *n* **1** an organization, club, or fellowship. **2** (esp. in medieval Europe) an association of men sharing the same interests, such as merchants or artisans: formed for mutual aid and protection and to maintain craft standards. ORIG C14: from ON; cf. *gjald* payment, *gildi* guild; rel. to OE *gield* offering, OHG *gelt* money
▸ **'guildsman, 'gildsman** *or* (*fem*) **'guildswoman, 'gildswoman** *n*

guilder ('gɪldə) *or* **gulden** *n, pl* **guilders, guilder** *or* **guldens, gulden. 1** Also: **gilder, florin.** the standard monetary unit of the Netherlands, divided into 100 cents. **2** any of various former gold or silver coins of Germany, Austria, or the Netherlands. ORIG C15: from MDu. *gulden,* lit.: GOLDEN

Guildford ★ ('gɪlfəd) *n* a town in S England, the administrative centre of Surrey: cathedral (1936–68); seat of the University of Surrey (1966). Pop.: 65 998 (1991).

guildhall ('gɪldˌhɔːl) *n Brit.* **a** the hall of a guild or corporation. **b** a town hall.

guile (gaɪl) *n* clever or crafty character or behaviour. ORIG C18: from OF *guile,* of Gmc origin; see WILE
▸ **'guileful** *adj* ▸ **'guilefully** *adv* ▸ **'guilefulness** *n* ▸ **'guileless** *adj* ▸ **'guilelessly** *adv* ▸ **'guilelessness** *n*

Guilin ('gweɪˈlɪn), **Kweilin,** *or* **Kuei-lin** ★ *n* a city in S China, in Guangxi Zhuang AR on the Li River: noted for the unusual caves and formations of the surrounding karst scenery; trade and manufacturing centre. Pop.: 364 130 (1990 est.).

Guillaume de Lorris ★ (*French* gijom də lɔris) *n* 13th century, French poet who wrote the first 4058 lines of the allegorical romance, the *Roman de la rose,* continued by Jean de Meung.

guillemot ('gɪlɪˌmɒt) *n* a northern oceanic diving bird having a black-and-white plumage and long narrow bill. ORIG C17: from F, dim. of *Guillaume* William

guilloche (gɪˈlɒʃ) *n* an ornamental border with a repeating pattern of two or more interwoven wavy lines, as in architecture. ORIG C19: from F: tool used in ornamental work, ?from *Guillaume* William

guillotine *n* ('gɪləˌtiːn). **1a** a device for beheading persons, consisting of a weighted blade set between two upright posts. **1b the guillotine.** execution by this instrument. **2** a device for cutting or trimming sheet material, such as paper or sheet metal, consisting of a slightly inclined blade that descends onto the sheet. **3** a surgical instrument for removing tonsils, growths in the throat, etc. **4** (in Parliament, etc.) a form of closure under which a bill is divided into compartments, groups of which must be completely dealt with each day. ◆ *vb* (ˌgɪləˈtiːn), **guillotines, guillotining, guillotined.** (*tr*) **5** to behead (a person) by guillotine. **6** (in Parliament, etc.) to limit debate on (a bill, motion, etc.) by the guillotine. ORIG C18: from F, after Joseph Ignace *Guillotin* (1738–1814), F physician, who advocated its use in 1789
▸ **ˌguilloˈtiner** *n*

guilt (gɪlt) *n* **1** the fact or state of having done wrong or committed an offence. **2** responsibility for a criminal or moral offence deserving punishment or a penalty. **3** remorse or self-reproach caused by feeling that one is responsible for a wrong or offence. **4** *Arch.* sin or crime. ORIG OE *gylt,* from ?

guiltless (ˈgɪltlɪs) *adj* free of all responsibility for wrongdoing or crime; innocent.
▸ **ˈguiltlessly** *adv* ▸ **ˈguiltlessness** *n*

guilty (ˈgɪltɪ) *adj* **guiltier, guiltiest. 1** responsible for an offence or misdeed. **2** *Law.* having committed an offence or adjudged to have done so: *the accused was found guilty.* **3** of, showing, or characterized by guilt.
▸ **ˈguiltily** *adv* ▸ **ˈguiltiness** *n*

guimpe (gɪmp) *n* a variant spelling of **gimp.**

Guin. *abbrev. for* Guinea.

guinea (ˈgɪnɪ) *n* **1a** a British gold coin taken out of circulation in 1813, worth 21 shillings. **1b** the sum of 21 shillings (1.05), still used in quoting professional fees. **2** See **guinea fowl.** ORIG C16: the coin was orig. made of gold from Guinea

Guinea ★ (ˈgɪnɪ) *n* **1** a republic in West Africa, on the Atlantic: established as the colony of French Guinea in 1890 and became an independent republic in 1958. Official language: French. Religion: Muslim majority and animist. Currency: Guinean franc of 100 cauris. Capital: Conakry. Pop.: 7 539 000 (1999 est.). Area: 245 855 sq. km (94 925 sq. miles). **2** (formerly) the coastal region of West Africa, between Cape Verde and Namibe (formerly Moçâmedes; Angola): divided by a line of volcanic peaks into **Upper Guinea** (between The Gambia and Cameroon) and **Lower Guinea** (between Cameroon and S Angola). **3 Gulf of.** a large inlet of the S Atlantic on the W coast of Africa, extending from Cape Palmas, Liberia, to Cape Lopez, Gabon: contains two large bays, the Bight of Biafra and the Bight of Benin, separated by the Niger delta.
▸ **ˈGuinean** *adj, n*

Guinea-Bissau ★ *n* a republic in West Africa, on the Atlantic: first discovered by the Portuguese in 1446 and of subsequent importance in the slave trade; made a colony in 1879; became an independent republic in 1974. Official language: Portuguese; Cape Verde creole is widely spoken. Religion: animist majority and Muslim. Currency: peso. Capital: Bissau. Pop.: 1 235 000 (1999 est.). Area: 36 125 sq. km (13 948 sq. miles). Former name (until 1974): **Portuguese Guinea.**

guinea fowl *or* **guinea** *n* a domestic fowl of Africa and SW Asia, having a dark plumage mottled with white, a naked head and neck, and a heavy rounded body.

guinea hen *n* a guinea fowl, esp. a female.

guinea pig *n* **1** a domesticated cavy, commonly kept as a pet and used in scientific experiments. **2** a person or thing used for experimentation. ORIG C17: from ?

Guinevere (ˈgwɪnɪˌvɪə), **Guenevere** (ˈgwɛnɪˌvɪə), *or* **Guinever** ★ (ˈgwɪnɪvə) *n* (in Arthurian legend) the wife of King Arthur and paramour of Lancelot.

Guinness ★ (ˈgɪnɪs) *n* Sir **Alec.** 1914–2000, British actor. His films include *The Bridge on the River Kwai* (1957) and his TV roles include Le Carré's George Smiley.

guipure (gɪˈpjʊə) *n* **1** Also called: **guipure lace.** any of many types of heavy lace that have their pattern connected by threads, rather than supported on a net mesh. **2** a heavy corded trimming; gimp. ORIG C19: from OF, from *guiper* to cover with cloth, of Gmc origin

guise (gaɪz) *n* **1** semblance or pretence: *under the guise of friendship.* **2** external appearance in general. **3** *Arch.* manner or style of dress. ORIG C13: from OF *guise,* of Gmc origin

guising (ˈgaɪzɪŋ) *n* (in Scotland and N England) the practice or custom of disguising oneself in fancy dress, often with mask, and visiting people's houses, esp. at Halloween.
▸ **ˈguiser** *n*

guitar (gɪˈtɑː) *n* a plucked stringed instrument originating in Spain, usually having six strings, a flat sounding board with a circular sound hole in the centre, a flat back, and a fretted fingerboard. ORIG C17: from Sp. *guitarra,* from Ar. *qītār,* from Gk: CITHARA
▸ **guiˈtarist** *n*

Guitry ★ (*French* gitri) *n* **Sacha** (saʃa). 1885–1957, French actor, dramatist, and film director, born in Russia: plays include *Nono* (1905).

Guiyang (ˈgweɪˈjæŋ), **Kweiyang,** *or* **Kuei-yang** ★ *n* a city in S China, capital of Guizhou province: reached by rail in 1959, with subsequent industrial growth. Pop.: 1 530 000 (1991 est.).

Guizhou (ˈgweɪˈdʒəʊ), **Kweichow,** *or* **Kueichou** ★ *n* a province of SW China, between the Yangtze and Xi Rivers: a high plateau. Capital: Guiyang. Pop.: 36 060 000 (1997 est.). Area: 174 000 sq. km (69 278 sq. miles).

Guizot ★ (*French* gizo) *n* **François Pierre Guillaume** (frɑ̃swa pjɛr gijom). 1787–1874, French statesman and historian. As chief minister (1840–48), his reactionary policies contributed to the revolution of 1848.

Gujarat *or* **Gujerat** ★ (ˌgudʒəˈrɑːt) *n* **1** a state of W India: formed in 1960 from the N and W parts of Bombay State; one of India's most industrialized states. Capital: Gandhinagar. Pop.: 44 235 000 (1994 est.). Area: 196 024 sq. km (75 268 sq. miles). **2** a region of W India, north of the Narmada River: generally includes the areas north of Bombay city where Gujarati is spoken.

Gujranwala ★ (guːdʒˈrɑːnˌwʌlə) *n* a city in NE Pakistan: textile manufacturing. Pop.: 1 663 000 (1995 est.).

Gulag (ˈguːlæg) *n* **1** (formerly) the central administrative department of the Soviet security service, responsible for maintaining prisons and labour camps. **2** (*not cap.*) any system used to silence dissidents. ORIG C20: from Russian *G(lavnoye) U(pravleniye Ispravitelno-Trudovykh) Lag(erei)* Main Administration for Corrective Labour Camps

Gulbenkian ★ (gʊlˈbɛŋkɪən) *n* **1 Calouste Sarkis** (kæˈluːst ˈsɑːkɪz). 1869–1955, British industrialist, born in Turkey. He endowed the international Gulbenkian Foundation for the advancement of the arts, science, and education. **2** his son, **Nubar Sarkis** (ˈnuːbɑː ˈsɑːkɪz). 1896–1972, British industrialist, diplomat, and philanthropist.

gulch (gʌltʃ) *n US & Canad.* a narrow ravine cut by a fast stream. ORIG C19: from ?

gulden (ˈgʊldᵊn) *n, pl* **guldens** *or* **gulden.** a variant of **guilder.**

Gülek Bogaz ★ (guːˈlɛk bəʊˈgɑːz) *n* the Turkish name for the **Cilician Gates.**

gules (gjuːlz) *adj* (*usually postpositive*), *n Heraldry.* red. ORIG C14: from OF *gueules* red fur worn around the neck, from *gole* throat, from L *gula* GULLET

gulf (gʌlf) *n* **1** a large deep bay. **2** a deep chasm. **3** something that divides or separates, such as a lack of understanding. **4** something that engulfs, such as a whirlpool. ◆ *vb* **5** (*tr*) to swallow up; engulf. ORIG C14: from OF *golfe,* from It. *golfo,* from Gk *kolpos*

Gulf ★ (gʌlf) *n* **the. 1** the Persian Gulf. **2** *Austral.* **2a** the Gulf of Carpentaria. **2b** (*modifier*) of, relating to, or adjoining the Gulf: *Gulf country.* **3** *NZ.* the Hauraki Gulf.

Gulf States ★ *pl n* **the. 1** the oil-producing states around the Persian Gulf: Iran, Iraq, Kuwait, Saudi Arabia, Bahrain, Qatar, the United Arab Emirates, and Oman. **2** the states of the US that border on the Gulf of Mexico: Alabama, Florida, Louisiana, Mississippi, and Texas.

Gulf Stream *n* a relatively warm ocean current flowing northeastwards from the Gulf of Mexico towards NW Europe. Also called: **North Atlantic Drift.**

Gulf War *n* **1** the war (1991) between US-led UN forces and Iraq, following Iraq's invasion of Kuwait. **2** See **Iran-Iraq War.**

Gulf War syndrome *n* a group of various debilitating symptoms experienced by many soldiers who served in the Gulf War of 1991. It is claimed to be associated with damage to the central nervous system, caused by exposure to pesticides containing organophosphates.

gulfweed (ˈgʌlfˌwiːd) *n* a brown seaweed having air bladders and forming dense floating masses in tropical

Atlantic waters, esp. the Gulf Stream. Also called: **sargasso, sargasso weed.**

gull[1] (gʌl) *n* an aquatic bird such as the common gull or mew having long pointed wings, short legs, and a mostly white plumage. ORIG C15: of Celtic origin

gull[2] (gʌl) *Arch.* ◆ *n* **1** a person who is easily fooled or cheated. ◆ *vb* **2** (*tr*) to fool, cheat, or hoax. ORIG C16: ?from dialect *gull* unfledged bird, prob. from *gul,* from ON *gulr* yellow

gullet (ˈgʌlɪt) *n* **1** a less formal name for the **oesophagus. 2** the throat or pharynx. ORIG C14: from OF *goulet,* dim. of *goule,* from L *gula* throat

gullible (ˈgʌlɪbᵊl) *adj* easily taken in or tricked.
▸ **ˌgulliˈbility** *n* ▸ **ˈgullibly** *adv*

gully *or* **gulley** (ˈgʌlɪ) *n, pl* **gullies** *or* **gulleys. 1** a channel or small valley, esp. one cut by heavy rainwater. **2** *NZ.* a bush-clad small valley. **3** *Cricket.* **3a** a fielding position between the slips and point. **3b** a fielder in this position. ◆ *vb* **gullies, gullying, gullied** *or* **gulleys, gulleying, gulleyed. 4** (*tr*) to make channels in (the ground, sand, etc.). ORIG C16: from F *goulet* neck of a bottle; see GULLET

gulp (gʌlp) *vb* **1** (*tr;* often foll. by *down*) to swallow rapidly, esp. in large mouthfuls. **2** (*tr;* often foll. by *back*) to stifle or choke: *to gulp back sobs.* **3** (*intr*) to swallow air convulsively because of nervousness, surprise, etc. **4** (*intr*) to make a noise, as when swallowing too quickly. ◆ *n* **5** the act of gulping. **6** the quantity taken in a gulp. ORIG C15: from MDu. *gulpen,* imit.
▸ **ˈgulper** *n* ▸ **ˈgulpingly** *adv* ▸ **ˈgulpy** *adj*

gum[1] (gʌm) *n* **1** any of various sticky substances that exude from certain plants, hardening on exposure to air and dissolving or forming viscous masses in water. **2** any of various products, such as adhesives, that are made from such substances. **3** any sticky substance used as an adhesive; mucilage; glue. **4** See **chewing gum, bubble gum,** and **gumtree. 5** *NZ.* See **kauri gum. 6** *Chiefly Brit.* a gumdrop. ◆ *vb* **gums, gumming, gummed. 7** to cover or become covered, clogged, or stiffened as with gum. **8** (*tr*) to stick together or in place with gum. **9** (*intr*) to emit or form gum. ◆ See also **gum up.** ORIG C14: from OF *gomme,* from L *gummi,* from Gk *kommi,* from Egyptian *kemai*

gum[2] (gʌm) *n* the fleshy tissue that covers the jawbones around the bases of the teeth. Technical name: **gingiva.** Related adj: **gingival.** ORIG OE *gōma* jaw

gum ammoniac *n* another name for **ammoniac.**

gum arabic *n* a gum exuded by certain acacia trees, used in the manufacture of ink, food thickeners, pills, emulsifiers, etc. Also called: **gum acacia.**

gumbo (ˈgʌmbəʊ) *n, pl* **gumbos.** *US.* **1** the mucilaginous pods of okra. **2** another name for **okra. 3** a soup or stew thickened with okra pods. **4** a fine soil in the W prairies that becomes muddy when wet. ORIG C19: from Louisiana F *gombo,* of Bantu origin

gumboil (ˈgʌmˌbɔɪl) *n* an abscess on the gums.

gumboots (ˈgʌmˌbuːts) *pl n* another name for **Wellington boots** (sense 1).

gum-digger *n NZ.* a person who digs for fossilized kauri gum in a **gum-field,** an area where it is found buried.

gumdrop (ˈgʌmˌdrɒp) *n* a small jelly-like sweet containing gum arabic and various colourings and flavourings. Also called (esp. Brit.): **gum.**

gummy[1] (ˈgʌmɪ) *adj* **gummier, gummiest. 1** sticky or tacky. **2** consisting of, coated with, or clogged by gum or a similar substance. **3** producing gum. ORIG C14: from GUM[1] + -Y[1]
▸ **ˈgumminess** *n*

gummy[2] (ˈgʌmɪ) *adj* **gummier, gummiest. 1** toothless. ◆ *n, pl* **gummies. 2** Also called: **gummy shark.** *Austral.* a small crustacean-eating shark with flat crushing teeth. ORIG C20: from GUM[2] + -Y[1]

gum nut *n Austral.* the hardened seed container of the gumtree *Eucalyptus gummifera.*

gumption (ˈgʌmpʃən) *n Inf.* **1** *Brit.* common sense or resourcefulness. **2** initiative or courage. ORIG C18: orig. Scot., from ?

gum resin *n* a mixture of resin and gum obtained from various plants and trees.

gumtree (ˈgʌmˌtriː) *n* **1** any of various trees that yield gum, such as the eucalyptus, sweet gum, and sour gum. Sometimes shortened to **gum. 2 up a gumtree.** *Inf.* in a very awkward position; in difficulties.

gum up *vb* (*tr, adv*) **1** to cover, dab, or stiffen with gum. **2** *Inf.* to make a mess of; bungle (often in **gum up the works**).

gun (gʌn) *n* **1a** a weapon with a metallic tube or barrel from which a missile is discharged, usually by force of an explosion. It may be portable or mounted. **1b** (*as modifier*): *a gun barrel.* **2** the firing of a gun as a salute or signal, as in military ceremonial. **3** a member of or a place in a shooting party or syndicate. **4** any device used to project something under pressure: *a spray gun.* **5** *US sl.* an armed criminal; gunman. **6** *Austral. & NZ sl.* **6a** an expert. **6b** (*as modifier*): *a gun shearer.* **7 give it the gun.** *Sl.* to increase speed, effort, etc., to a considerable or maximum degree. **8 go great guns.** *Sl.* to act or function with great speed, intensity, etc. **9 jump** *or* **beat the gun. 9a** (of a runner, etc.) to set off before the starting signal is given. **9b** *Inf.* to act prematurely. **10 stick to one's guns.** *Inf.* to maintain one's opinions or intentions in spite of opposition. ◆ *vb* **guns, gunning, gunned. 11** (when *tr,* often foll. by *down*) to shoot (someone) with a gun. **12** (*tr*) to press hard on the accelerator of (an engine): *to gun the engine.* **13** (*intr*) to hunt with a gun. ◆ See also **gun for.** ORIG C14: prob. from a female pet name, from the Scand. name *Gunnhildr* (from ON *gunnr* war + *hildr* war)

gunboat (ˈgʌnˌbəʊt) *n* a small shallow-draft vessel carrying mounted guns and used by coastal patrols, etc.

gunboat diplomacy *n* diplomacy conducted by threats of military intervention.

guncotton (ˈgʌnˌkɒtᵊn) *n* cellulose nitrate containing a relatively large amount of nitrogen: used as an explosive.

gun dog *n* **1** a dog trained to work with a hunter or gamekeeper, esp. in retrieving, pointing at, or flushing game. **2** a dog belonging to any breed adapted to these activities.

gunfight (ˈgʌnˌfaɪt) *n Chiefly US.* a fight between persons using firearms.
▸ **ˈgunˌfighter** *n*

gunfire (ˈgʌnˌfaɪə) *n* **1** the firing of one or more guns, esp. when done repeatedly. **2** the use of firearms, as contrasted with other military tactics.

gun for *vb* (*intr, prep*) **1** to search for in order to reprimand, punish, or kill. **2** to try earnestly for: *he was gunning for promotion.*

gunge (gʌndʒ) *Inf.* ◆ *n* **1** sticky, rubbery, or congealed matter. ◆ *vb* **gunges, gunging, gunged. 2** (*tr; usually passive;* foll. by *up*) to block or encrust with gunge; clog. ORIG C20: imit., ? infl. by GOO & SPONGE
▸ **ˈgungy** *adj*

gunk (gʌŋk) *n Inf.* slimy, oily, or filthy matter. ORIG C20: ? imit.

gunlock (ˈgʌnˌlɒk) *n* the mechanism in some firearms that causes the charge to be exploded.

gunman (ˈgʌnmən) *n, pl* **gunmen. 1** a man armed with a gun, esp. unlawfully. **2** a man skilled with a gun.

gunmetal (ˈgʌnˌmɛtᵊl) *n* **1** a type of bronze containing copper, tin, and zinc. **2a** a dark grey colour. **2b** (*as adj*): *gunmetal chiffon.*

Gunn ★ (gʌn) *n* **Thom(son William).** born 1929, British poet resident in the US. His works include *Fighting Terms* (1954), *Jack Straw's Castle* (1976), and *The Man with Night Sweats* (1992).

Gunnar ★ (ˈgunɑː) *n Norse myth.* brother of Gudrun and husband of Brynhild, won for him by Sigurd. He corresponds to Gunther in the *Nibelungenlied.*

gunnel[1] (ˈgʌnᵊl) *n* any eel-like fish occurring in coastal regions of northern seas. ORIG C17: from ?

gunnel[2] (ˈgʌnᵊl) *n* a variant spelling of **gunwale.**

Gunnell ★ (ˈgʌnᵊl) *n* **Sally.** born 1966, English hurdler; Olympic gold medallist (1992).

gunner (ˈgʌnə) *n* **1** a serviceman who works with, uses, or specializes in guns. **2** *Naval.* (formerly) a warrant officer responsible for the training of gun crews, their performance in action, and accounting for ammunition. **3**

(in the British Army) an artilleryman, esp. a private. **4** a person who hunts with a rifle or shotgun.

gunnery ('gʌnərɪ) *n* **1** the art and science of the efficient design and use of ordnance, esp. artillery. **2** guns collectively. **3** the use and firing of guns.

gunny ('gʌnɪ) *n, pl* **gunnies.** *Chiefly US.* **1** a coarse hard-wearing fabric usually made from jute and used for sacks, etc. **2** Also called: **gunny sack.** a sack made from this fabric. ORIG C18: from Hindi, from Sansk. *gōnī* sack, prob. of Dravidian origin

gunplay ('gʌn,pleɪ) *n Chiefly US.* the use of firearms, as by criminals, etc.

gunpoint ('gʌn,pɔɪnt) *n* **1** the muzzle of a gun. **2 at gunpoint.** being under or using the threat of being shot.

gunpowder ('gʌn,paʊdə) *n* an explosive mixture of potassium nitrate, charcoal, and sulphur: used in time fuses and in fireworks.

gun room *n* **1** (esp. in the Royal Navy) the mess allocated to junior officers. **2** a room where guns are stored.

gunrunning ('gʌn,rʌnɪŋ) *n* the smuggling of guns and ammunition or other weapons of war into a country.
► **'gun,runner** *n*

gunshot ('gʌn,ʃɒt) *n* **1a** shot fired from a gun. **1b** (*as modifier*): *gunshot wounds.* **2** the range of a gun. **3** the shooting of a gun.

gunslinger ('gʌn,slɪŋə) *n Sl.* a gunfighter or gunman, esp. in the Old West.

gunsmith ('gʌn,smɪθ) *n* a person who makes or repairs firearms, esp. portable guns.

gunstock ('gʌn,stɒk) *n* the wooden handle or support to which is attached the barrel of a rifle.

Gunter ★ ('gʌntə) *n* **Edmund.** 1581–1626, English mathematician and astronomer, who invented various measuring instruments.

Gunter's chain *n Surveying.* a measuring chain 22 yards in length, or this length as a unit. ORIG C17: after E. GUNTER

Gunther ★ ('gʊntə) *n* (in the *Nibelungenlied*) a king of Burgundy, allied with Siegfried, who won for him his wife Brunhild. He corresponds to Gunnar in Norse mythology.

Guntur ★ (gʊn'tʊə) *n* a city in E India, in central Andhra Pradesh: founded by the French in the 18th century; ceded to Britain in 1788. Pop.: 471 051 (1991).

gunwale *or* **gunnel** ('gʌnᵊl) *n Naut.* the top of the side of a boat or ship. ORIG C15: from GUN + WALE from its use to support guns

gunyah ('gʌnjə) *n Austral.* a bush hut or shelter. ORIG C19: from Abor.

guppy ('gʌpɪ) *n, pl* **guppies.** a small brightly coloured freshwater fish of N South America and the Caribbean: a popular aquarium fish. ORIG C20: after R. J. L. *Guppy,* 19th-cent. clergyman of Trinidad who first presented specimens to the British Museum

Gurdjieff ★ ('gɜːdjɛf) *n* **Georgei Ivanovitch.** ?1877–1949, Russian mystic: founded a teaching centre in Paris (1922).

gurdwara ('gɜːdwɑːrə) *n* a Sikh place of worship. ORIG C20: from Punjabi *gurduārā,* from Sansk. *guru* teacher + *dvārā* door

gurgle ('gɜːgᵊl) *vb* **gurgles, gurgling, gurgled.** (*intr*) **1** (of liquids, esp. of streams, etc.) to make low bubbling noises when flowing. **2** to utter low throaty bubbling noises, esp. as a sign of contentment: *the baby gurgled with delight.* ◆ *n* **3** the act or sound of gurgling. ORIG C16: ?from Vulgar L *gurgulāre,* from L *gurguliō* gullet

Gurkha ('gɜːkə) *n* **1** a member of a Hindu people, descended from Brahmins and Rajputs, living chiefly in Nepal. **2** a member of a Gurkha regiment in the Indian or British army.

gurnard ('gɜːnəd) *or* **gurnet** ('gɜːnɪt) *n, pl* **gurnard, gurnards** *or* **gurnet, gurnets.** a European marine fish having a heavily armoured head and finger-like pectoral fins. ORIG C14: from OF *gornard,* from *grognier* to grunt, from L *grunnīre*

guru ('gʊruː, 'guːruː) *n* **1** a Hindu or Sikh religious teacher or leader, giving personal spiritual guidance to his disciples. **2** *Often derog.* a leader or chief theoretician of a movement, esp. a spiritual or religious cult. **3** *Often facetious.* a leading authority in a particular field: *a cricketing guru.* ORIG C17: from Hindi *gurū,* from Sansk. *guruh* weighty

gush (gʌʃ) *vb* **1** to pour out or cause to pour out suddenly and profusely, usually with a rushing sound. **2** to act or utter in an overeffusive, affected, or sentimental manner. ◆ *n* **3** a sudden copious flow or emission, esp. of liquid. **4** something that flows out or is emitted. **5** an extravagant and insincere expression of admiration, sentiment, etc. ORIG C14: prob. imit.; cf. ON *gjósa*
► **'gushing** *adj* ► **'gushingly** *adv*

gusher ('gʌʃə) *n* **1** a person who gushes, as in being effusive or sentimental. **2** something, such as a spurting oil well, that gushes.

gushy ('gʌʃɪ) *adj* **gushier, gushiest.** *Inf.* displaying excessive admiration or sentimentality.
► **'gushily** *adv* ► **'gushiness** *n*

gusset ('gʌsɪt) *n* **1** an inset piece of material used esp. to strengthen or enlarge a garment. **2** a triangular metal plate for strengthening a corner joist. ◆ *vb* **3** (*tr*) to put a gusset in (a garment). ORIG C15: from OF *gousset* a piece of mail, dim. of *gousse* pod, from ?
► **'gusseted** *adj*

gust (gʌst) *n* **1** a sudden blast of wind. **2** a sudden rush of smoke, sound, etc. **3** an outburst of emotion. ◆ *vb* **4** (*intr*) to blow in gusts. ORIG C16: from ON *gustr;* rel. to *gjōsa* to GUSH; see GEYSER

gustation (gʌ'steɪʃən) *n* the act of tasting or the faculty of taste. ORIG C16: from L *gustātiō,* from *gustāre* to taste
► **gustatory** ('gʌstətərɪ) *adj*

Gustavo A. Madero ★ (*Spanish* gus'taβo a ma'ðero) *n* the former name (1931–71) of **Guadalupe Hidalgo.**

Gustavus I ★ (gʊ'stɑːvəs) *n* called *Gustavus Vasa.* ?1496–1560, king of Sweden (1523–60). He was elected king after driving the Danes from Sweden (1520–23).

Gustavus II ★ *n* See **Gustavus Adolphus.**

Gustavus VI ★ *n* title of *Gustaf Adolf.* 1882–1973, king of Sweden (1950–73).

Gustavus Adolphus (ə'dɒlfəs) *or* **Gustavus II ★** *n* 1594–1632, king of Sweden (1611–32). He waged successful wars with Denmark, Russia, and Poland and in the Thirty Years' War led a Protestant army: killed at the battle of Lützen.

gusto ('gʌstəʊ) *n* vigorous enjoyment, zest, or relish: *the aria was sung with great gusto.* ORIG C17: from Sp.: taste, from L *gustus* a tasting

gusty ('gʌstɪ) *adj* **gustier, gustiest. 1** blowing in gusts or characterized by blustery weather: *a gusty wind.* **2** given to sudden outbursts, as of emotion.
► **'gustily** *adv* ► **'gustiness** *n*

gut (gʌt) *n* **1a** the lower part of the alimentary canal; intestine. **1b** the entire alimentary canal. Related adj: **visceral. 2** (*often pl*) the bowels or entrails, esp. of an animal. **3** *Sl.* the belly; paunch. **4** See **catgut. 5** a silky fibrous substance extracted from silkworms, used in the manufacture of fishing tackle. **6** a narrow channel or passage. **7** (*pl*) *Inf.* courage, willpower, or daring; forcefulness. **8** (*pl*) *Inf.* the essential part: *the guts of a problem.* ◆ *vb* **guts, gutting, gutted.** (*tr*) **9** to remove the entrails from (fish, etc.). **10** (esp. of fire) to destroy the inside of (a building). **11** to take out the central points of (an article, etc.), esp. in summary form. ◆ *adj* **12** *Inf.* instinctive, basic, or fundamental: *a gut feeling; capital punishment is a gut issue.* ORIG OE *gutt;* rel. to *gēotan* to flow

GUT (gʌt) *n acronym for* grand unified theory.

Gutenberg ★ ('guːtᵊn,bɜːg; *German* 'guːtənbɛrk) *n* **Johann** (jo'han), original name *Johannes Gensfleisch.* ?1398–1468, German printer; inventor of printing by movable type.

Gütersloh ★ (*German* 'gyːtərsloː) *n* a town in NW Germany, in North Rhine-Westphalia. Pop.: 83 400 (1989 est.).

Guthrie ★ ('gʌθrɪ) *n* **1 Samuel.** 1782–1848, US chemist: invented percussion priming powder and a punch lock for exploding it, and discovered chloroform (1831). **2** Sir (**William**) **Tyrone.** 1900–71, British theatrical director. **3** **Woody,** full name *Woodrow Wilson Guthrie.* 1912–67, US folk singer and songwriter.

Guthrun ★ ('gʊðru:n) *n* a variant of **Gudrun.**

gutless ('gʌtlɪs) *adj Inf.* lacking courage or determination.

gut reaction *n* the first, instinctive, reaction to a situation.

gutsy ('gʌtsɪ) *adj* **gutsier, gutsiest.** *Sl.* **1** gluttonous; greedy. **2** full of courage or boldness. **3** passionate; lusty.

gutta-percha ('gʌtə'pɜ:tʃə) *n* **1** any of several tropical trees with leathery leaves. **2** a whitish rubber substance derived from the coagulated milky latex of any of these trees: used in electrical insulation and dentistry. ORIG C19: from Malay *getah* gum + *percha* tree that produces it

guttate ('gʌteɪt) *adj Biol.* (esp. of plants) covered with small drops or droplike markings. ORIG C19: from L *guttātus* dappled, from *gutta* a drop

gutted ('gʌtɪd) *adj Inf.* disappointed and upset.

gutter ('gʌtə) *n* **1** a channel along the eaves or on the roof of a building, used to collect and carry away rainwater. **2** a channel running along the kerb or the centre of a road to collect and carry away rainwater. **3** either of the two channels running parallel to a tenpin bowling lane. **4** *Printing.* the white space between the facing pages of an open book. **5** *Surfing.* a dangerous deep channel formed by currents and waves. **6 the gutter.** a poverty-stricken, degraded, or criminal environment. ◆ *vb* **7** (*tr*) to make gutters in. **8** (*intr*) to flow in a stream. **9** (*intr*) (of a candle) to melt away as the wax forms channels and runs down in drops. **10** (*intr*) (of a flame) to flicker and be about to go out. ORIG C13: from Anglo-F *goutiere,* from OF *goute* a drop, from L *gutta*
▸ **'guttering** *n*

gutter press *n* the section of the popular press that seeks sensationalism in its coverage.

guttersnipe ('gʌtə,snaɪp) *n* a child who spends most of his or her time in the streets, esp. in a slum area.

guttural ('gʌtərəl) *adj* **1** *Anat.* of or relating to the throat. **2** *Phonetics.* pronounced in the throat or the back of the mouth. **3** raucous. ◆ *n* **4** *Phonetics.* a guttural consonant. ORIG C16: from NL *gutturālis,* from L *guttur* gullet
▸ **'gutturally** *adv*

gut-wrenching *adj Inf.* causing great distress or suffering: *gut-wrenching scenes.*

guy[1] (gaɪ) *n* **1** *Inf.* a man or youth. **2** *Brit.* a crude effigy of Guy Fawkes, usually made of old clothes stuffed with straw or rags, that is burnt on top of a bonfire on Guy Fawkes Day. **3** *Brit.* a person in shabby or ludicrously odd clothes. **4** (*pl*) *Inf.* persons of either sex. ◆ *vb* **5** (*tr*) to make fun of; ridicule. ORIG C19: short for Guy FAWKES

guy[2] (gaɪ) *n* **1** a rope, chain, wire, etc., for anchoring an object in position or for steadying or guiding it. ◆ *vb* **2** (*tr*) to anchor, steady, or guide with a guy or guys. ORIG C14: prob. from Low G; cf. OF *guie* guide, from *guier* to GUIDE

Guyana ★ (gaɪ'ænə) *n* a republic in NE South America, on the Atlantic: colonized chiefly by the Dutch in the 17th and 18th centuries; became a British colony in 1831 and an independent republic within the Commonwealth in 1966. Official language: English. Religions: Christian and Hindu. Currency: dollar. Capital: Georgetown. Pop.: 787 000 (1999 est.). Area: about 215 000 sq. km (83 000 sq. miles). Former name (until 1966): **British Guiana.**
▸ **Guyanese** (,gaɪə'ni:z) *or* **Guy'anan** *adj, n*

Guyenne ★ (*French* gɥijɛn) *n* a variant spelling of **Guienne.**

Guzmán Blanco ★ (*Spanish* guð'man 'blaŋko) *n* **Antonio** (an'tonjo). 1829–99, Venezuelan statesman; president (1873–77; 1879–84; 1886–87). He was virtual dictator of Venezuela from 1870 until his overthrow (1889).

guzzle ('gʌzᵊl) *vb* **guzzles, guzzling, guzzled.** to consume (food or drink) excessively or greedily. ORIG C16: from ?
▸ **'guzzler** *n*

Gwalior ★ ('gwɑ:lɪ,ɔ:) *n* **1** a city in N central India, in Madhya Pradesh: built around the fort, which dates from before 525; industrial and commercial centre. Pop.: 690 765 (1991). **2** a former princely state of central India, established in the 18th century: merged with Madhya Bharat in 1948, which in turn merged with Madhya Pradesh in 1956.

Gwent ★ (gwɛnt) *n* a former (1974–96) county of SE Wales.

Gweru ★ ('gweɪru:) *n* a city in central Zimbabwe. Pop.: 124 735 (1992). Former name (until 1982): **Gwelo** ('gwi:ləʊ).

Gwyn ★ (gwɪn) *n* **Nell,** original name *Eleanor Gwynne.* 1650–87, English actress; mistress of Charles II.

Gwynedd ★ ('gwɪnɛð) *n* a county of NW Wales, formed in 1974 from Anglesey, Caernarvonshire, part of Denbighshire, and most of Merionethshire, reorganized in 1996 and lost Anglesey and areas in the NE: it is generally mountainous with many lakes, much of it lying in the Snowdonia National Park. Administrative centre: Caernarfon. Pop.: 118 005 (1996 est.). Area: 2550 sq. km (869 sq. miles).

gybe, gibe, *or* **jibe** (dʒaɪb) *Naut.* ◆ *vb* **gybes, gybing, gybed, gibes, gibing, gibed** *or* **jibes, jibing, jibed. 1** (*intr*) (of a fore-and-aft sail) to shift suddenly from one side of the vessel to the other when running before the wind. **2** to cause (a sailing vessel) to gybe or (of a sailing vessel) to undergo gybing. ◆ *n* **3** an instance of gybing. ORIG C17: from obs. Du. *gijben* (now *gijpen*), from ?

gym (dʒɪm) *n, adj* short for **gymnasium, gymnastics, gymnastic.**

gymkhana (dʒɪm'kɑ:nə) *n* **1** *Chiefly Brit.* an event in which horses and riders display skill and aptitude in various races and contests. **2** (in Anglo-India) a place providing sporting and athletic facilities. ORIG C19: from Hindi *gend-khānā,* lit.: ball house

gymnasium (dʒɪm'neɪzɪəm) *n, pl* **gymnasiums** *or* **gymnasia** (-zɪə). **1** a large room or hall equipped with bars, weights, ropes, etc., for physical training. **2** (in various European countries) a secondary school that prepares pupils for university. ORIG C16: from L: school for gymnastics, from Gk *gumnasion,* from *gumnazein* to exercise naked

gymnast ('dʒɪmnæst) *n* a person who is skilled or trained in gymnastics.

gymnastic (dʒɪm'næstɪk) *adj* of, like, or involving gymnastics.
▸ **gym'nastically** *adv*

gymnastics (dʒɪm'næstɪks) *n* **1** (*functioning as sing*) practice or training in exercises that develop physical strength and agility or mental capacity. **2** (*functioning as pl*) gymnastic exercises.

gymno- *combining form.* naked, bare, or exposed: *gymnosperm.* ORIG from Gk *gumnos* naked

gymnosperm ('dʒɪmnəʊ,spɜ:m, 'gɪm-) *n* any seed-bearing plant in which the ovules are borne naked on open scales, which are often arranged in cones; any conifer or related plant. Cf. **angiosperm.**
▸ **,gymno'spermous** *adj*

gympie ('gɪmpɪ) *n* a tall Australian tree with stinging hairs on its leaves. Also: **nettle tree.**

gym shoe *n* another name for **plimsoll.**

gymslip ('dʒɪm,slɪp) *n* a tunic or pinafore dress worn by schoolgirls, often part of a school uniform.

gyn- *combining form.* a variant of **gyno-** before a vowel.

gynaeco- *or US* **gyneco-** *combining form.* relating to women; female: *gynaecology.* ORIG from Gk, from *gunē, gunaik-* woman, female

gynaecology *or US* **gynecology** (,gaɪnɪ'kɒlədʒɪ) *n* the branch of medicine concerned with diseases and conditions specific to women.
▸ **gynaecological** (,gaɪnɪkə'lɒdʒɪkᵊl), **,gynaeco'logic** *or US* **,gyneco'logical, ,gyneco'logic** *adj* ▸ **,gynae'cologist** *or US* **,gyne'cologist** *n*

gynandromorph (dʒɪ'nændrəʊ,mɔ:f, gaɪ-) *n* an abnormal organism, esp. an insect, that has both male and female physical characteristics.

gynandrous (dʒaɪ'nændrəs, gaɪ-) *adj* (of flowers such as the orchid) having the stamens and styles united in a column. ORIG C19: from Gk *gunandros* of uncertain sex, from *gunē* woman + *anēr* man

gyno- *or before a vowel* **gyn-** *combining form.* **1** relating to women; female: *gynarchy.* **2** denoting a female reproductive organ: *gynophore.* ORIG from Gk, from *gunē* woman

gynoecium, gynaeceum, *or esp. US* **gynecium** (dʒaɪ'ni:sɪəm, gaɪ-) *n, pl* **gynoecia, gynaecea** *or esp. US* **gynecia** (-sɪə). the carpels of a flowering plant collectively. ORIG C18: NL, from Gk *gunaikeion* women's quarters, from *gunaik-, gunē* woman + *-eion,* suffix indicating place

gynophore ('dʒaɪnəʊˌfɔː, 'gaɪ-) *n* a stalk in some plants that bears the gynoecium above the level of the other flower parts.

-gynous *adj combining form.* **1** of or relating to women or females: *androgynous; misogynous.* **2** relating to female organs: *epigynous.* ORIG from NL, from Gk, from *gunē* woman
▸ **-gyny** *n combining form.*

Györ ★ (*Hungarian* djøːr) *n* an industrial town in NW Hungary: medieval Benedictine abbey. Pop.: 127 000 (1997 est.).

gyp[1] *or* **gip** (dʒɪp) *Sl.* ◆ *vb* **gyps, gypping, gypped** *or* **gips, gipping, gipped. 1** (*tr*) to swindle, cheat, or defraud. ◆ *n* **2** an act of cheating. **3** a person who gyps. ORIG C18: back formation from GYPSY

gyp[2] *or* **gip** (dʒɪp) *n Brit. & NZ sl.* severe pain; torture: *his arthritis gave him gyp.* ORIG C19: prob. a contraction of *gee up!;* see GEE[1]

gyp[3] (dʒɪp) *n* a college servant at the universities of Cambridge or Durham. ORIG C18: ?from obs. *gippo* scullion

gypsophila (dʒɪp'sɒfɪlə) *n* any of a Mediterranean genus of plants, having small white or pink fragrant flowers. ORIG C18: NL, from Gk *gupsos* chalk + *philos* loving

gypsum ('dʒɪpsəm) *n* a mineral consisting of hydrated calcium sulphate that occurs in sedimentary rocks and clay and is used principally in making plasters and cements, esp. plaster of Paris. Formula: $CaSO_4.2H_2O$. ORIG C17: from L, from Gk *gupsos* chalk, plaster, cement, of Semitic origin
▸ **gypseous** ('dʒɪpsɪəs) *adj*

Gypsy *or* **Gipsy** ('dʒɪpsɪ) *n, pl* **Gypsies** *or* **Gipsies.** (*sometimes not cap.*) **1a** a member of a people scattered throughout Europe and North America, who maintain a nomadic way of life in industrialized societies. They migrated from NW India about the 9th century onwards. **1b** (*as modifier*): *a Gypsy fortune-teller.* **2** the language of the Gypsies; Romany. **3** a person who looks or behaves like a Gypsy. ORIG C16: from EGYPTIAN, since they were thought to have come orig. from Egypt
▸ **'Gypsyish** *or* **'Gipsyish** *adj*

gypsy moth *or* **gipsy moth** *n* a European moth whose caterpillars are pests on deciduous trees.

gyrate *vb* (dʒaɪ'reɪt), **gyrates, gyrating, gyrated. 1** (*intr*) to rotate or spiral, esp. about a fixed point or axis. ◆ *adj* ('dʒaɪrɪt). **2** *Biol.* curved or coiled into a circle. ORIG C19: from LL *gȳrāre,* from L *gȳrus* circle, from Gk *guros*
▸ **gy'ration** *n* ▸ **gy'rator** *n* ▸ **gyratory** ('dʒaɪrətərɪ) *adj*

gyre ('dʒaɪə) *Chiefly literary.* ◆ *n* **1** a circular or spiral movement or path. **2** a ring, circle, or spiral. ◆ *vb* **gyres, gyring, gyred. 3** (*intr*) to whirl. ORIG C16: from L *gȳrus* circle, from Gk *guros*

gyrfalcon *or* **gerfalcon** ('dʒɜːˌfɔːlkən, -ˌfɔːkən) *n* a very large rare falcon of northern and arctic regions. ORIG C14: from OF *gerfaucon,* ?from ON *geirfalki,* from *geirr* spear + *falki* falcon

gyro ('dʒaɪrəʊ) *n, pl* **gyros. 1** See **gyrocompass. 2** See **gyroscope.**

gyro- *or before a vowel* **gyr-** *combining form.* **1** indicating rotating or gyrating motion: *gyroscope.* **2** indicating a gyroscope: *gyrocompass.* ORIG via L from Gk, from *guros* circle

gyrocompass ('dʒaɪrəʊˌkʌmpəs) *n* a nonmagnetic compass that uses a motor-driven gyroscope to indicate true north.

gyrodyne ('dʒaɪrəʊˌdaɪn) *n* an aircraft that uses a powered rotor to take off and manoeuvre, but uses autorotation when cruising.

gyromagnetic (ˌdʒaɪrəʊmæg'nɛtɪk) *adj* of or caused by magnetic properties resulting from the spin of a charged particle, such as an electron.

gyroscope ('dʒaɪrəˌskəʊp) *n* a device containing a disc rotating on an axis that can turn freely in any direction so that the disc maintains the same orientation irrespective of the movement of the surrounding structure.
▸ **gyroscopic** (ˌdʒaɪrə'skɒpɪk) *adj* ▸ **ˌgyro'scopically** *adv*

gyrostabilizer *or* **gyrostabiliser** (ˌdʒaɪrəʊ'steɪbɪˌlaɪzə) *n* a gyroscopic device used to stabilize the rolling motion of a ship.

gyve (dʒaɪv) *Arch.* ◆ *vb* **gyves, gyving, gyved. 1** (*tr*) to shackle or fetter. ◆ *n* **2** (*usually pl*) fetter. ORIG C13: from ?

Hh

h *or* **H** (eɪtʃ) *n, pl* **h's, H's,** *or* **Hs. 1** the eighth letter of the English alphabet. **2** a speech sound represented by this letter. **3a** something shaped like an H. **3b** (*in combination*): *an H-beam.*

h *symbol for:* **1** *Physics.* Planck constant. **2** hecto-. **3** hour.

H *symbol for:* **1** *Chem.* hydrogen. **2** *Physics.* magnetic field strength. **3** *Electronics.* henry. **4** (on Brit. pencils, signifying degree of hardness of lead) hard.

h. *or* **H.** *abbrev. for:* **1** harbour. **2** height. **3** high. **4** hour. **5** hundred. **6** husband.

ha[1] *or* **hah** (hɑː) *interj* **1** an exclamation expressing derision, triumph, surprise, etc. **2** (*reiterated*) a representation of the sound of laughter.

ha[2] *symbol for* hectare.

Haakon VII ★ (ˈhɑːkɒn) *n* 1872–1957, king of Norway (1905–57). During the Nazi occupation of Norway (1940–45), he led Norwegian resistance from England.

haar (hɑː) *n Eastern Brit.* a cold sea mist or fog off the North Sea. ORIG C17: rel. to Du. dialect *harig* damp

Haarlem ★ (*Dutch* ˈhaːrlɛm) *n* a city in the W Netherlands, capital of North Holland province. Pop.: 147 617 (1996 est.).

Hab. *Bible. abbrev. for* Habakkuk.

Habakkuk ★ (ˈhæbəkək) *n Old Testament.* **1** a Hebrew prophet. **2** the book containing his oracles and canticle.

Habana ★ (aˈβana) *n* the Spanish name for **Havana.**

habanera (ˌhæbəˈnɛərə) *n* **1** a slow Cuban dance in duple time. **2** a piece of music for this dance. ORIG from Sp. *danza habanera* dance from Havana

habeas corpus (ˈheɪbɪəs ˈkɔːpəs) *n Law.* a writ ordering a person to be brought before a court or judge, esp. so that the court may ascertain whether his detention is lawful. ORIG C15: from the opening of the L writ, lit.: you may have the body

haberdasher (ˈhæbəˌdæʃə) *n* **1** *Brit.* a dealer in small articles for sewing, such as buttons and ribbons. **2** *US.* a men's outfitter. ORIG C14: from Anglo-F *hapertas* small items of merchandise, from ?

haberdashery (ˈhæbəˌdæʃərɪ) *n, pl* **haberdasheries.** the goods or business kept by a haberdasher.

habergeon (ˈhæbədʒən) *n* a light sleeveless coat of mail worn in the 14th century under the plated hauberk. ORIG C14: from OF *haubergeon* a little HAUBERK

Haber process (ˈhɑːbə) *n* an industrial process for producing ammonia by reacting atmospheric nitrogen with hydrogen at high pressure and temperature in the presence of a catalyst. ORIG after Fritz *Haber* (1868–1934), G chemist

habiliment (həˈbɪlɪmənt) *n* (*often pl*) dress or attire. ORIG C15: from OF *habillement,* from *habiller* to dress

habilitate (həˈbɪlɪˌteɪt) *vb* **habilitates, habilitating, habilitated. 1** (*tr*) *US.* to equip and finance (a mine). **2** (*intr*) to qualify for office. ORIG C17: from Med. L *habilitāre* to make fit, from L *habilitās* aptness
▸ **haˌbiliˈtation** *n*

habit (ˈhæbɪt) *n* **1** a tendency or disposition to act in a particular way. **2** established custom, usual practice, etc. **3** *Psychol.* a learned behavioural response to a particular situation. **4** mental disposition or attitude: *a good working habit of mind.* **5a** a practice or substance to which a person is addicted: *drink has become a habit with him.* **5b** the state of being dependent on something, esp. a drug. **6** *Bot., zool.* method of growth, type of existence, or general appearance: *a burrowing habit.* **7** the customary apparel of a particular occupation, rank, etc., now esp. the costume of a nun or monk. **8** Also called: **riding habit.** a woman's riding dress. ◆ *vb* **habits, habiting, habited.** (*tr*) **9** to clothe. **10** an archaic word for **inhabit.** ORIG C13: from L *habitus* custom, from *habēre* to have

habitable (ˈhæbɪtəbᵊl) *adj* able to be lived in.
▸ **ˌhabitaˈbility** *or* **ˈhabitableness** *n* ▸ **ˈhabitably** *adv*

habitant (ˈhæbɪtᵊnt) *n* **1** a less common word for **inhabitant. 2a** an early French settler in Canada or Louisiana. **2b** a descendant of these settlers, esp. a farmer.

habitat (ˈhæbɪˌtæt) *n* **1** the natural home of an animal or plant. **2** the place in which a person, group, class, etc., is normally found. ORIG C18: from L: it inhabits, from *habitāre* to dwell, from *habēre* to have

habitation (ˌhæbɪˈteɪʃən) *n* **1** a dwelling place. **2** occupation of a dwelling place.

habit-forming *adj* tending to become a habit or addiction.

habitual (həˈbɪtjʊəl) *adj* **1** (*usually prenominal*) done or experienced regularly and repeatedly: *the habitual Sunday walk.* **2** (*usually prenominal*) by habit: *a habitual drinker.* **3** customary; usual.
▸ **haˈbitually** *adv* ▸ **haˈbitualness** *n*

habituate (həˈbɪtjʊˌeɪt) *vb* **habituates, habituating, habituated. 1** to accustom; make used to. **2** *US & Canad. arch.* to frequent.
▸ **haˌbituˈation** *n*

habitude (ˈhæbɪˌtjuːd) *n Rare.* habit; tendency.

habitué (həˈbɪtjʊˌeɪ) *n* a frequent visitor to a place. ORIG C19: from F, from *habituer* to frequent

Habsburg ★ (ˈhaːpsbʊrk) *n* the German name for **Hapsburg.**

HAC *abbrev. for* Honourable Artillery Company.

hachure (hæˈʃjʊə) *n* shading of short lines drawn on a relief map to indicate gradients. ORIG C19: from F, from *hacher* to chop up

hacienda (ˌhæsɪˈɛndə) *n* (in Spain or Spanish-speaking countries) **1a** a ranch or large estate. **1b** any substantial manufacturing establishment in the country. **2** the main house on such a ranch or establishment. ORIG C18: from Sp., from L *facienda* things to be done, from *facere* to do

hack[1] (hæk) *vb* **1** (when *intr,* usually foll. by *at* or *away*) to chop (at) roughly or violently. **2** to cut and clear (a way), as through undergrowth. **3** (in sport, esp. rugby) to foul (an opposing player) by kicking his shins. **4** (*intr*) to cough in short dry bursts. **5** (*tr*) to cut (a story, article, etc.) in a damaging way. **6** (*intr;* usually foll. by *into*) to manipulate a computer program skilfully, esp. to gain unauthorized access to another computer system. **7** (*tr*) *Sl.* to tolerate or cope with: *I joined the army but I couldn't hack it.* ◆ *n* **8** a cut or gash. **9** any tool used for shallow digging, such as a mattock or pick. **10** a chopping blow. **11** a dry spasmodic cough. **12** a kick on the shins, as in rugby. ORIG OE *haccian*

hack[2] (hæk) *n* **1** a horse kept for riding. **2** an old or overworked horse. **3** a horse kept for hire. **4** *Brit.* a country ride on horseback. **5** a drudge. **6** a person who produces mediocre literary work. **7** *US inf.* **7a** a cab driver. **7b** a taxi. ◆ *vb* **8** *Brit.* to ride (a horse) cross-country for pleasure. **9** (*tr*) *Inf.* to write (an article, etc.) in the manner of a hack. ◆ *adj* **10** (*prenominal*) banal, mediocre, or unoriginal: *hack writing.* ORIG C17: short for HACKNEY

hack[3] (hæk) *n* **1** a rack used for fodder for livestock. **2** a board on which meat is placed for a hawk. **3** a pile or row of unfired bricks stacked to dry. ORIG C16: var. of HATCH[2]

hackamore (ˈhækəˌmɔː) *n US & NZ.* a rope or rawhide halter used for unbroken foals. ORIG C19: from Sp. *jáquima* headstall, ult. from Ar. *shaqīmah*

hackberry (ˈhækˌbɛrɪ) *n, pl* **hackberries. 1** an American tree having edible cherry-like fruits. **2** the fruit. ORIG C18: var. of **C16** *hagberry,* of Scand. origin

hacker (ˈhækə) *n* **1** a person that hacks. **2** *Sl.* a computer fanatic, esp. one who through a personal computer

★ people and places

breaks into the computer system of a company, government, etc.

hackery ('hækərɪ) *n* **1** *Ironic.* journalism; hackwork. **2** *Inf.* a variant of **hacking**[2].

hacking[1] ('hækɪŋ) *adj* (of a cough) harsh, dry, and spasmodic.

hacking[2] ('hækɪŋ) *n* the practice of gaining illegal access to a computer system.

hackle ('hækᵊl) *n* **1** any of the long slender feathers on the neck of poultry and other birds. **2** *Angling.* parts of an artificial fly made from hackle feathers, representing the legs and sometimes the wings of a real fly. **3** a feathered ornament worn in the headdress of some British regiments. **4** a steel flax comb. ◆ *vb* **hackles, hackling, hackled.** (*tr*) **5** to comb (flax) using a hackle. ORIG C15: *hakell* prob. from OE

hackles ('hækᵊlz) *pl n* **1** the hairs on the back of the neck and the back of a dog, cat, etc., which rise when the animal is angry or afraid. **2** anger or resentment: *to make one's hackles rise.*

hackney ('hæknɪ) *n* **1** a compact breed of harness horse with a high-stepping trot. **2** a coach or carriage that is for hire. **3** a popular term for **hack**[2] (sense 1). ◆ *vb* **4** (*tr; usually passive*) to make commonplace and banal by too frequent use. ORIG C14: prob. after HACKNEY, where horses were formerly raised

Hackney ★ ('hæknɪ) *n* a borough of NE Greater London: formed in 1965 from the former boroughs of Shoreditch, Stoke Newington, and Hackney; nearby are **Hackney Marshes,** the largest recreation ground in London. Pop.: 192 500 (1994 est.). Area: 19 sq. km (8 sq. miles).

hackneyed ('hæknɪd) *adj* used so often as to be trite, dull, and stereotyped.

hacksaw ('hækˌsɔː) *n* a handsaw for cutting metal, with a blade in a frame under tension.

hackwork ('hækˌwɜːk) *n* undistinguished literary work produced to order.

had (hæd) *vb* the past tense and past participle of **have.**

haddock ('hædək) *n, pl* **haddocks** *or* **haddock.** a North Atlantic gadoid food fish similar to but smaller than the cod. ORIG C14: from ?

hade (heɪd) *Geol.* ◆ *n* **1** the angle made to the vertical by the plane of a fault or vein. ◆ *vb* **hades, hading, haded. 2** (*intr*) to incline from the vertical. ORIG C18: from ?

hadedah ('hɑːdɪˌdɑː) *n* a large grey-green S. African ibis. ORIG imit.

Hades ('heɪdiːz) *n* **1** *Greek myth.* **1a** the underworld abode of the souls of the dead. **1b** Pluto, the god of the underworld. **2** (*often not cap.*) hell.

Hadhramaut *or* **Hadramaut** ★ (ˌhɑːdrə'mɔːt) *n* a plateau region of the S Arabian Peninsula, in SE Yemen on the Indian Ocean; formerly in South Yemen: corresponds roughly to the former East Aden Protectorate. Area: about 151 500 sq. km (58 500 sq. miles).

Hadith ('hædɪθ, hɑː'diːθ) *n* the body of tradition about Mohammed and his followers. ORIG Ar.

hadj (hædʒ) *n* a variant spelling of **hajj.**

hadji ('hædʒɪ) *n, pl* **hadjis.** a variant spelling of **hajji.**

Hadlee ★ ('hædlɪ) *n* Sir **Richard** (**John**). born 1951, New Zealand cricketer.

hadn't ('hædᵊnt) *contraction of* had not.

Hadrian ('heɪdrɪən) *or* **Adrian** ★ *n* Latin name *Publius Aelius Hadrianus.* 76–138 A.D., Roman emperor (117–138); adopted son and successor of Trajan. He codified Roman law.

Hadrian's Wall ★ *n* a fortified Roman wall, of which substantial parts remain, extending across N England from the Solway Firth to the mouth of the River Tyne. It was built in 120–123 A.D. on the orders of the emperor Hadrian as a defence against the N British tribes.

hadron ('hædrɒn) *n* an elementary particle capable of taking part in a strong nuclear interaction. ORIG C20: from Gk *hadros* heavy, from *hadēn* enough + -ON
▸ **had'ronic** *adj*

hadst (hædst) *vb Arch. or dialect.* (used with the pronoun *thou*) a singular form of the past tense (indicative mood) of **have.**

haecceity (hɛk'siːɪtɪ, hiːk-) *n, pl* **haecceities.** *Philosophy.* the property that uniquely identifies an object. ORIG C17: from Med. L *haecceitas,* lit.: thisness, from *haec,* fem. of *hic* this

Haeckel ★ (*German* 'hɛkəl) *n* **Ernst Heinrich** (ɛrnst 'haɪnrɪç). 1834–1919, German biologist and philosopher.
▸ **Haeckelian** (hɛ'kiːlɪən) *adj*

haem *or US* **heme** (hiːm) *n Biochem.* a complex red organic pigment containing ferrous iron, present in haemoglobin. ORIG C20: from HAEMATIN

haem- *combining form.* a variant of **haemo-** before a vowel. Also (US): **hem-.**

haemal *or US* **hemal** ('hiːməl) *adj* **1** of the blood. **2** denoting or relating to the region of the body containing the heart.

haematemesis *or US* **hematemesis** (ˌhiːmə'tɛmɪsɪs) *n* vomiting of blood, esp. as the result of a bleeding ulcer. ORIG C19: from HAEMATO- + Gk *emesis* vomiting

haematic *or US* **hematic** (hiː'mætɪk) *adj* relating to, acting on, having the colour of, or containing blood. Also: **haemic** *or US* **hemic.**

haematin *or US* **hematin** ('hɛmətɪn, 'hiː-) *n Biochem.* a dark bluish or brownish pigment obtained by the oxidation of haem.

haematite ('hiːməˌtaɪt, 'hɛm-) *n* a variant spelling of **hematite.**

haemato- *or before a vowel* **haemat-** *combining form.* indicating blood: *haematology.* Also: **haemo-** or (US) **hemato-, hemat-, hemo-.** ORIG from Gk *haima, haimat-* blood

haematocrit *or US* **hematocrit** ('hɛmətəʊkrɪt, 'hiː-) *n* **1** a centrifuge for separating blood cells from plasma. **2** the ratio of the volume occupied by these cells, esp. the red cells, to the total volume of blood, expressed as a percentage. ORIG C20: from HAEMATO- + *-crit,* from Gk *kritēs* judge, from *krinein* to separate

haematology *or US* **hematology** (ˌhiːmə'tɒlədʒɪ) *n* the branch of medical science concerned with diseases of the blood.
▸ **haematologic** (ˌhiːmətə'lɒdʒɪk), ˌ**haemato'logical** *or US* ˌ**hemato'logic,** ˌ**hemato'logical** *adj*

haematoma *or US* **hematoma** (ˌhiːmə'təʊmə) *n, pl* **haematomas, haematomata** *or US* **hematomas, hematomata** (-mətə). *Pathol.* a tumour of clotted blood.

haematuria *or US* **hematuria** (ˌhiːmə'tjʊərɪə) *n Pathol.* the presence of blood or red blood cells in the urine.

-haemia *or esp. US* **-hemia** *n combining form.* variants of **-aemia.**

haemo-, haema-, *or before a vowel* **haem-** *combining form.* denoting blood. Also: (US) **hemo-, hema-,** or **hem-.** ORIG from Gk *haima* blood

haemocyanin *or US* **hemocyanin** (ˌhiːməʊ'saɪənɪn) *n* a blue copper-containing respiratory pigment in crustaceans and molluscs that functions as haemoglobin.

haemocytometer *or US* **hemocytometer** (ˌhiːməʊsaɪ'tɒmɪtə) *n Med.* an apparatus for counting the number of cells in a quantity of blood.

haemodialysis *or US* **hemodialysis** (ˌhiːməʊdaɪ'ælɪsɪs) *n, pl* **haemodialyses** *or US* **hemodialyses** (-ˌsiːz). *Med.* the filtering of circulating blood through a membrane in an apparatus (**haemodialyser** or **artificial kidney**) to remove waste products: performed in cases of kidney failure. ORIG C20: from HAEMO- + DIALYSIS

haemoglobin *or US* **hemoglobin** (ˌhiːməʊ'gləʊbɪn) *n* a protein that gives red blood cells their characteristic colour. It combines reversibly with oxygen and is thus very important in the transportation of oxygen to tissues. ORIG C19: shortened from *haematoglobulin:* see HAEMATIN + GLOBULIN

haemolysis (hɪ'mɒlɪsɪs), **haematolysis** (ˌhiːmə'tɒlɪsɪs) *or US* **hemolysis, hematolysis** *n, pl* **haemolyses, haematolyses** *or US* **hemolyses, hematolyses** (-ˌsiːz). the disintegration of red blood cells, with the release of haemoglobin.
▸ **haemolytic** *or US* **hemolytic** (ˌhiːməʊ'lɪtɪk) *adj*

haemophilia *or US* **hemophilia** (ˌhiːməʊˈfɪlɪə) *n* an inheritable disease, usually affecting only males, characterized by loss or impairment of the normal clotting ability of blood.
► **ˌhaemoˈphiliac** *or US* **ˌhemoˈphiliac** *n* ► **ˌhaemoˈphilic** *or US* **ˌhemoˈphilic** *adj*

haemoptysis *or US* **hemoptysis** (hɪˈmɒptɪsɪs) *n, pl* **haemoptyses** *or US* **hemoptyses** (-ˌsiːz). spitting or coughing up of blood, as in tuberculosis. ORIG C17: from HAEMO- + *-ptysis,* from Gk *ptyein* to spit

haemorrhage *or US* **hemorrhage** (ˈhɛmərɪdʒ) *n* **1** profuse bleeding from ruptured blood vessels. **2** a steady or severe loss or depletion of resources, staff, etc. ◆ *vb* **haemorrhages, haemorrhaging, haemorrhaged** *or US* **hemorrhages, hemorrhaging, hemorrhaged. 3** (*intr*) to bleed profusely. ORIG C17: from L *haemorrhagia;* see HAEMO-, -RRHAGIA

haemorrhoids *or US* **hemorrhoids** (ˈhɛməˌrɔɪdz) *pl n Pathol.* swollen and twisted veins in the region of the anus. Nontechnical name: **piles.** ORIG C14: from L *haemorrhoidae* (pl), from Gk, from *haimorrhoos* discharging blood, from *haimo-* HAEMO- + *rhein* to flow
► **ˌhaemorˈrhoidal** *or US* **ˌhemorˈrhoidal** *adj*

haemostasis *or US* **hemostasis** (ˌhiːməʊˈsteɪsɪs) *n* the stopping of bleeding or of blood circulation, as during a surgical operation. ORIG C18: from NL, from HAEMO- + Gk *stasis* a standing still
► **ˌhaemoˈstatic** *or US* **ˌhemoˈstatic** *adj*

haemostat *or US* **hemostat** (ˈhiːməʊˌstæt) *n* a surgical instrument or chemical agent that retards or stops bleeding.

haeremai (ˈhaɪrəˌmaɪ) *NZ.* ◆ *sentence substitute.* **1** an expression of greeting or welcome. ◆ *n* **2** the act of saying "haeremai". ORIG C18: Maori, lit.: come hither

Ha-erh-pin ★ (ˈhɑːˈɛəˈpɪn) *n* transliteration of the Chinese name for **Harbin.**

hafiz (ˈhɑːfɪz) *n Islam.* **1** a title for a person who knows the Koran by heart. **2** the guardian of a mosque. ORIG from Persian, from Ar., from *hafiza* to guard

hafnium (ˈhæfnɪəm) *n* a bright metallic element found in zirconium ores. Symbol: Hf; atomic no.: 72; atomic wt.: 178.49. ORIG C20: NL, after *Hafnia,* L name of Copenhagen + -IUM

haft (hɑːft) *n* **1** the handle of an axe, knife, etc. ◆ *vb* **2** (*tr*) to provide with a haft. ORIG OE *hæft*

hag[1] (hæg) *n* **1** an unpleasant or ugly old woman. **2** a witch. **3** short for **hagfish.** ORIG OE *hægtesse* witch
► **ˈhaggish** *adj*

hag[2] (hæg) *n Scot. & N English dialect.* **1** a firm spot in a bog. **2** a soft place in a moor. ORIG C13: from ON

Hag. *Bible. abbrev. for* Haggai.

Hagar ★ (ˈheɪgɑː, -gə) *n Old Testament.* an Egyptian maid of Sarah, who bore Ishmael to Abraham, Sarah's husband.

Hagen[1] ★ (ˈhɑːgən) *n* (in the *Nibelungenlied*) Siegfried's killer, who in turn is killed by Siegfried's wife, Kriemhild.

Hagen[2] ★ (*German* ˈhaːgən) *n* an industrial city in NW Germany, in North Rhine-Westphalia. Pop.: 212 003 (1996 est.).

Hagen[3] ★ (ˈheɪgən) *n* **Walter.** 1892–1969, US golfer.

hagfish (ˈhægˌfɪʃ) *n, pl* **hagfish** *or* **hagfishes.** an eel-like marine vertebrate having a round sucking mouth and feeding on the tissues of other animals and on dead organic material.

Haggadah *or* **Haggodoh** (həˈgɑːdə) *n, pl* **Haggadahs, Haggadas** *or* **Haggadoth** (hægəˈdəʊt). *Judaism.* **a** a book containing the order of service of the traditional Passover meal. **b** the narrative of the Exodus from Egypt that constitutes the main part of that service. ◆ See also **Seder.** ORIG C19: from Heb.: story, from *hagged* to tell
► **haggadic** (həˈgædɪk, -ˈgɑː-) *adj*

Haggai ★ (ˈhægeɪˌaɪ) *n Old Testament.* **1** a Hebrew prophet, whose oracles are usually dated between August and December of 520 B.C. **2** the book in which these oracles are contained, chiefly concerned with the rebuilding of the Temple after the Exile. Douay spelling: **Aggeus** (əˈdʒiːəs).

haggard (ˈhægəd) *adj* **1** careworn or gaunt, as from anxiety or starvation. **2** wild or unruly. **3** (of a hawk) having reached maturity in the wild before being caught. ◆ *n* **4** *Falconry.* a haggard hawk. ORIG C16: from OF *hagard,* ? rel. to HEDGE
► **ˈhaggardly** *adv* ► **ˈhaggardness** *n*

Haggard ★ (ˈhægəd) *n* Sir **H(enry) Rider.** 1856–1925, British author of romantic adventure stories, including *King Solomon's Mines* (1885).

haggis (ˈhægɪs) *n* a Scottish dish made from sheep's or calf's offal, oatmeal, suet, and seasonings boiled in a skin made from the animal's stomach. ORIG C15: ?from *haggen* to HACK[1]

haggle (ˈhægᵊl) *vb* **haggles, haggling, haggled.** (*intr;* often foll. by *over*) to bargain or wrangle (over a price, terms of an agreement, etc.); barter. ORIG C16: of Scand. origin
► **ˈhaggler** *n*

hagio- *or before a vowel* **hagi-** *combining form.* indicating a saint, saints, or holiness: *hagiography.* ORIG via LL from Gk, from *hagios* holy

Hagiographa (ˌhægɪˈɒgrəfə) *n* the third of the three main parts into which the books of the Old Testament are divided in Jewish tradition (the other two parts being the Law and the Prophets).

hagiographer (ˌhægɪˈɒgrəfə) *or* **hagiographist** *n* **1** a person who writes about the lives of the saints. **2** one of the writers of the Hagiographa.

hagiography (ˌhægɪˈɒgrəfɪ) *n, pl* **hagiographies. 1** the writing of the lives of the saints. **2** a biography that idealizes or idolizes its subject.
► **hagiographic** (ˌhægɪəˈgræfɪk) *or* **ˌhagioˈgraphical** *adj*

hagiolatry (ˌhægɪˈɒlətrɪ) *n* worship or veneration of saints.

hagiology (ˌhægɪˈɒlədʒɪ) *n, pl* **hagiologies.** literature concerned with the lives and legends of saints.
► **hagiological** (ˌhægɪəˈlɒdʒɪkᵊl) *adj* ► **ˌhagiˈologist** *n*

hag-ridden *adj* tormented or worried, as if by a witch.

Hague[1] ★ (heɪg) *n* **The.** the seat of government of the Netherlands and the capital of South Holland province, situated about 3 km (2 miles) from the North Sea. Pop.: 442 105 (1995). Dutch names: **'s Gravenhage, Den Haag.**

Hague[2] ★ (heɪg) *n* **William Jefferson.** born 1961, British politician; leader of the Conservative party from 1997.

hah (hɑː) *interj* a variant spelling of **ha**[1].

ha-ha[1] (ˈhɑːˈhɑː) *or* **haw-haw** (ˈhɔːˈhɔː) *interj* **1** a representation of the sound of laughter. **2** an exclamation expressing derision, mockery, etc.

ha-ha[2] (ˈhɑːhɑː) *or* **haw-haw** (ˈhɔːhɔː) *n* a wall or other boundary marker that is set in a ditch so as not to interrupt the landscape. ORIG C18: from F *haha,* prob. based on *ha!* ejaculation denoting surprise

Hahn ★ (*German* haːn) *n* **1 Kurt** (kʊrt). 1886–1974, German educationalist; escaped to Britain during the Nazi era, where he founded Gordonstoun School (1935) and helped to establish the Duke of Edinburgh's award scheme. **2 Otto** (ˈɔto). 1879–1968, German physicist: discovered the element protactinium with Meitner (1917); with Strassmann, demonstrated the nuclear fission of uranium when it is bombarded with neutrons: Nobel prize for chemistry 1944.

Hahnemann ★ (*German* ˈhaːnəman) *n* (**Christian Friedrich**) **Samuel** (ˈzaːmueːl). 1755–1843, German physician; founder of homeopathy.

hahnium (ˈhɑːnɪəm) *n* the former name for **hassium.** ORIG C20: after Otto HAHN

Haidar Ali ★ (ˈhaɪdər ˈɑːlɪ) *n* a variant spelling of **Hyder Ali.**

Haifa ★ (ˈhaɪfə) *n* a port in NW Israel, near Mount Carmel, on the Bay of Acre: Israel's chief port, with an oil refinery and other heavy industry. Pop.: 255 300 (1997 est.).

Haig ★ (heɪg) *n* **Douglas,** 1st Earl Haig. 1861–1928, British field marshal; commander in chief of the British forces in France and Flanders (1915–18).

haik *or* **haick** (haɪk, heɪk) *n* a traditional Arabian outer garment for the head and body. ORIG C18: from Ar.

haiku ('haɪku:) *or* **hokku** ('hɒku:) *n, pl* **haiku** *or* **hokku.** an epigrammatic Japanese verse form in 17 syllables. ORIG from Japanese, from *hai* amusement + *ku* verse

hail[1] (heɪl) *n* **1** small pellets of ice falling from cumulonimbus clouds when there are strong rising air currents. **2** a storm of such pellets. **3** words, ideas, missiles, etc., directed with force and in great quantity: *a hail of abuse.* ◆ *vb* **4** (*intr;* with *it* as subject) to be the case that hail is falling. **5** (often with *it* as subject) to fall or cause to fall as or like hail. ORIG OE *hægl*

hail[2] (heɪl) *vb* (*mainly tr*) **1** to greet, esp. enthusiastically: *the crowd hailed the actress with joy.* **2** to acclaim or acknowledge: *they hailed him as their hero.* **3** to attract the attention of by shouting or gesturing: *to hail a taxi.* **4** (*intr;* foll. by *from*) to be a native of: *she hails from India.* ◆ *n* **5** the act or an instance of hailing. **6** a distance across which one can attract attention (esp. in **within hail**). ◆ *sentence substitute.* **7** *Poetic.* an exclamation of greeting. ORIG C12: from ON *heill* healthy

Haile Selassie ★ ('haɪlɪ sə'læsɪ) *n* title of *Ras Tafari Makonnen.* 1892–1975, emperor of Ethiopia (1930–36; 1941–74). During the Italian occupation of Ethiopia (1936–41), he lived in exile in England: deposed 1974.

hail-fellow-well-met *adj* genial and familiar, esp. in an offensive or ingratiating way.

Hail Mary *n* **1** Also called: **Ave Maria.** *RC Church.* a prayer to the Virgin Mary, based on the salutations of the angel Gabriel (Luke 1:28) and Elizabeth (Luke 1:42) to her. **2** *American football sl.* a very long high pass into the end zone, made in the final seconds of a half or of a game.

Hailsham of St Marylebone ★ ('heɪlʃəm) *n* **Quintin (McGarel) Hogg,** Baron. born 1907, British Conservative politician; Lord Chancellor (1970–74; 1979–87). He renounced his viscountcy in 1963 when he made an unsuccessful bid for the Conservative Party leadership; he became a life peer in 1970.

hailstone ('heɪl,stəʊn) *n* a pellet of hail.

hailstorm ('heɪl,stɔ:m) *n* a storm during which hail falls.

Hailwood ★ ('heɪlwʊd) *n* **Mike,** full name *Stanley Michael Bailey Hailwood.* 1940–81, British racing motorcyclist.

Hainan ('haɪ'næn) *or* **Hainan Tao** ★ (taʊ) *n* an island and province in the South China Sea, separated from the mainland of S China by **Hainan Strait:** part of Guangdong province until 1988; China's second largest offshore island. Pop.: 7 430 000 (1997 est.). Area: 33 572 sq. km (12 962 sq. miles).

Hainaut *or* **Hainault** ★ (*French* ɛno) *n* a province of SW Belgium: stretches from the Flanders Plain in the north to the Ardennes in the south. Capital: Mons. Pop.: 1 282 783 (1998 est.). Area: 3797 sq. km (1466 sq. miles).

Haiphong ★ ('haɪ'fɒŋ) *n* a port in N Vietnam, on the Red River delta: a major industrial centre. Pop.: 783 133 (1992 est.).

hair (hɛə) *n* **1** any of the threadlike structures that grow from follicles beneath the skin of mammals. **2** a growth of such structures, as on an animal's body, which helps prevent heat loss. **3** *Bot.* any threadlike outgrowth, such as a root hair. **4** a fabric made from the hair of some animals. **5** another word for **hair's-breadth:** *to lose by a hair.* **6** **get in someone's hair.** *Inf.* to annoy someone persistently. **7** **hair of the dog (that bit one).** an alcoholic drink taken as an antidote to a hangover. **8** **keep your hair on!** *Brit. inf.* keep calm. **9** **let one's hair down.** to behave without reserve. **10** **not turn a hair.** to show no surprise, anger, fear, etc. **11** **split hairs.** to make petty and unnecessary distinctions. ORIG OE *hær*
▸ **'hairless** *adj* ▸ **'hair,like** *adj*

haircloth ('hɛə,klɒθ) *n* a cloth woven from horsehair, used (esp. formerly) in upholstery, etc.

haircut ('hɛə,kʌt) *n* **1** the act of cutting the hair. **2** the style in which hair has been cut.

hairdo ('hɛə,du:) *n, pl* **hairdos.** the arrangement of a person's hair, esp. after styling and setting.

hairdresser ('hɛə,drɛsə) *n* **1** a person whose business is cutting, dyeing, and arranging hair. **2** a hairdresser's establishment. ◆ Related adj: **tonsorial.**
▸ **'hair,dressing** *n*

-haired *adj* having hair as specified: *long-haired.*

hair gel *n* a preparation used in hair styling.

hairgrip ('hɛə,grɪp) *n Chiefly Brit.* a small tightly bent metal hair clip. Also called (US, Canad., and NZ): **bobby pin** or (NZ) **hairclip.**

hairline ('hɛə,laɪn) *n* **1** the natural margin formed by hair on the head. **2a** a very narrow line. **2b** (*as modifier*): *a hairline crack.*

hairline fracture *n* a very fine crack in a bone.

hairnet ('hɛə,nɛt) *n* any of several kinds of light netting worn over the hair to keep it in place.

hairpiece ('hɛə,pi:s) *n* **1** a wig or toupee. **2** a section of extra hair attached to a woman's real hair to give it greater bulk or length.

hairpin ('hɛə,pɪn) *n* **1** a thin double-pronged pin used to fasten the hair. **2** (*modifier*) (esp. of a bend in a road) curving very sharply.

hair-raising *adj* inspiring horror; terrifying.

hair's-breadth *n* **a** a very short or imperceptible margin or distance. **b** (*as modifier*): *a hair's-breadth escape.*

hair shirt *n* **1** a shirt made of haircloth worn next to the skin as a penance. **2** a secret trouble or affliction.

hair slide *n* a hinged clip with a tortoiseshell, bone, or similar back, used to fasten a girl's hair.

hairsplitting ('hɛə,splɪtɪŋ) *n* **1** the making of petty distinctions. ◆ *adj* **2** occupied with or based on petty distinctions.
▸ **'hair,splitter** *n*

hairspring ('hɛə,sprɪŋ) *n* a fine spiral spring in some timepieces which, in combination with the balance wheel, controls the timekeeping.

hairstreak ('hɛə,stri:k) *n* a small butterfly having fringed wings with narrow white streaks.

hairstyle ('hɛə,staɪl) *n* a particular mode of arranging the hair.
▸ **'hair,stylist** *n*

hair trigger *n* **1** a trigger of a firearm that responds to very slight pressure. **2** *Inf.* any mechanism, reaction, etc., set in operation by slight provocation.

hairy ('hɛərɪ) *adj* **hairier, hairiest. 1** covered with hair. **2** *Sl.* **2a** difficult or problematic. **2b** dangerous or exciting.
▸ **'hairiness** *n*

Haiti ★ ('heɪtɪ, hɑ:'i:tɪ) *n* **1** a republic occupying the W part of the island of Hispaniola in the Caribbean, the E part consisting of the Dominican Republic: ceded by Spain to France in 1697 and became one of the richest colonial possessions in the world, with numerous plantations; slaves rebelled under Toussaint L'Ouverture in 1793 and defeated the French; taken over by the US (1915–41) after long political and economic chaos; under the authoritarian regimes of François Duvalier (1957–71) and his son Jean-Claude Duvalier (1971–86); in 1991, following three military regimes, Jean-Bertrand Aristide was democratically elected but was deposed; in 1994, aided by the US military, he returned to power. Official languages: French and Haitian creole. Religions: Roman Catholic and voodoo. Currency: gourde. Capital: Port-au-Prince. Pop.: 6 884 000 (1999 est.). Area: 27 749 sq. km (10 714 sq. miles). **2** a former name for **Hispaniola.**
▸ **Haitian** ('heɪʃɪən, hɑ:'i:ʃən) *adj, n*

Haitink ★ ('haɪ,tɪŋk) *n* **Bernard.** born 1929, Dutch orchestral conductor; received an honorary knighthood in 1977.

hajj *or* **hadj** (hædʒ) *n* the pilgrimage to Mecca that every Muslim is required to make at least once. ORIG from Ar.

hajji, hadji, *or* **haji** ('hædʒɪ) *n, pl* **hajjis, hadjis,** *or* **hajis. 1** a Muslim who has made a pilgrimage to Mecca: also used as a title. **2** a Christian who has visited Jerusalem.

haka ('hɑ:kə) *n NZ.* **1** a Maori war chant accompanied by gestures. **2** a similar performance by, for instance, a rugby team.

hake (heɪk) *n, pl* **hake** *or* **hakes. 1** a gadoid food fish of the

N hemisphere, having an elongated body with a large head and two dorsal fins. **2** a similar North American fish. ORIG C15: ?from ON *haki* hook

hakea ('hɑːkɪə, 'heɪkɪə) *n* any shrub or tree of the Australian genus *Hakea,* having a hard woody fruit and often yielding a useful wood. ORIG C19: NL, after C. L. von *Hake* (died 1818), G botanist

hakim *or* **hakeem** (hɑː'kiːm) *n* **1** a Muslim judge, ruler, or administrator. **2** a Muslim physician. ORIG C17: from Ar., from *hakama* to rule

Hakluyt ★ ('hækluːt) *n* **Richard.** ?1552–1616, English geographer, who compiled *The Principal Navigations, Voyages, and Discoveries of the English Nation* (1589).

Hakodate ★ (ˌhɑːkəʊ'dɑːteɪ) *n* a port in N Japan, on S Hokkaido: fishing industry and shipbuilding. Pop.: 298 868 (1995).

Halakah *or* **Halacha** (ˌhɑːlə'kɑː, hə'lɑːkə) *n* that part of traditional Jewish literature concerned with the law, as contrasted with Haggadah. ORIG C19: from Heb.: way, from *hālakh* to go
▸ **Halakic** *or* **Halachic** (hə'lækɪk) *adj*

halal *or* **hallal** (hɑː'lɑːl) *n* **1** meat from animals that have been killed according to Muslim law. ◆ *adj* **2** of or relating to such meat: *a halal butcher.* ◆ *vb* **halals, halalling, halalled** *or* **hallals, hallalling, hallalled.** (*tr*) **3** to kill (animals) according to Muslim law. ORIG from Ar.: lawful

halation (hə'leɪʃən) *n Photog.* fogging usually seen as a bright ring surrounding a source of light. ORIG C19: from HALO + -ATION

halberd ('hælbəd) *or* **halbert** ('hælbət) *n* a weapon consisting of a long shaft with an axe blade and a pick, topped by a spearhead: used in 15th- and 16th-century warfare. ORIG C15: from OF *hallebarde,* from MHG *helm* handle + *barde* axe
▸ **ˌhalber'dier** *n*

Halberstadt ★ (*German* 'halbərʃtat) *n* a town in central Germany, in Saxony-Anhalt: industrial centre noted for its historic buildings. Pop.: 47 500 (1989 est.).

halcyon ('hælsɪən) *adj* **1** peaceful, gentle, and calm. **2** **halcyon days. 2a** a fortnight of calm weather during the winter solstice. **2b** a period of peace and happiness. ◆ *n* **3** *Greek myth.* a fabulous bird associated with the winter solstice. **4** a poetic name for the **kingfisher.** ORIG C14: from L *alcyon,* from Gk *alkuōn* kingfisher, from ?

Haldane ★ ('hɔːldeɪn) *n* **1 J(ohn) B(urdon) S(anderson).** 1892–1964, British biochemist, geneticist, and writer on science. **2** his father, **John Scott.** 1860–1936, British physiologist, noted for his research into industrial diseases. **3** his brother, **Richard Burdon,** 1st Viscount Haldane of Cloan. 1856–1928, British statesman and jurist; secretary of state for war (1905–12).

hale[1] (heɪl) *adj* healthy and robust (esp. in **hale and hearty**). ORIG OE *hæl* WHOLE
▸ **'haleness** *n*

hale[2] (heɪl) *vb* **hales, haling, haled.** (*tr*) to pull or drag. ORIG C13: from OF *haler,* of Gmc origin
▸ **'haler** *n*

Hale ★ (heɪl) *n* **1 George Ellery.** 1868–1938, US astronomer: invented the spectroheliograph. **2** Sir **Matthew.** 1609–76, English judge and scholar; Lord Chief Justice (1671–76).

Haleakala ★ (ˌhɑːliːˌɑːkɑː'lɑː) *n* a volcano in Hawaii, on E Maui Island. Height: 3057 m (10 032 ft). Area of crater: 49 sq. km (19 sq. miles). Depth of crater: 829 m (2720 ft).

Halesowen ★ (ˌheɪlz'əʊɪn) *n* a town in W central England, in Dudley unitary authority, in the SW West Midlands. Pop.: 57 918 (1991).

Haley ★ ('heɪlɪ) *n* **Bill,** full name *William John Clifton Haley.* 1925–81, US rock-and-roll singer.

half (hɑːf) *n, pl* **halves** (hɑːvz). **1a** either of two equal or corresponding parts that together comprise a whole. **1b** a quantity equalling such a part: *half a dozen.* **2** half a pint, esp. of beer. **3** *Scot.* a small drink of spirits, esp. whisky. **4** *Football, hockey, etc.* the half of the pitch regarded as belonging to one team. **5** *Golf.* an equal score with an opponent. **6** (in various games) either of two periods of play separated by an interval. **7** a half-price ticket on a bus, etc. **8** short for **half-hour. 9** *Sport.* short for **halfback. 10** *Obs.* a half-year period. **11 by halves.** (*used with a negative*) without being thorough: *we don't do things by halves.* **12 go halves.** (often foll. by *on, in,* etc.) **12a** to share expenses. **12b** to share the whole amount (of something): *to go halves on an orange.* ◆ *determiner* **13a** being a half or approximately a half: *half the kingdom.* **13b** (*as pron; functioning as sing or pl*): *half of them came.* ◆ *adj* **14** not perfect or complete: *he only did a half job on it.* ◆ *adv* **15** to the amount or extent of a half. **16** to a great amount or extent. **17** partially; to an extent. **18 by half.** to an excessive degree: *he's too arrogant by half.* **19 half two,** etc. *Inf.* 30 minutes after two o'clock, etc. **20 have half a mind to.** to have a vague intention to. **21 not half.** *Inf.* **21a** not in any way: *he's not half clever enough.* **21b** *Brit.* very: *he isn't half stupid.* **21c** yes, indeed. ORIG OE *healf*

half- *prefix* **1** one of two equal parts: *half-moon.* **2** related through one parent only: *half-brother.* **3** not completely; partly: *half-hardy.*

half-and-half *n* **1** a mixture of half one thing and half another thing. **2** a drink consisting of equal parts of beer and stout, or equal parts of bitter and mild.

halfback ('hɑːfˌbæk) *n* **1** *Soccer.* any of three players positioned behind the line of forwards and in front of the fullbacks. **2** *Rugby.* either the scrum half or the stand-off half. **3** any of certain similar players in other team sports.

half-baked *adj* **1** insufficiently baked. **2** *Inf.* foolish; stupid. **3** *Inf.* poorly planned.

halfbeak ('hɑːfˌbiːk) *n* a marine and freshwater teleost fish having an elongated body with a short upper jaw and a long protruding lower jaw.

half-binding *n* a type of bookbinding in which the backs are bound in one material and the sides in another.

half-blood *n* **1a** the relationship between individuals having only one parent in common. **1b** an individual having such a relationship. **2** a less common name for a **half-breed.**
▸ **ˌhalf-'blooded** *adj*

half board *n* accommodation at a hotel, etc., that includes breakfast and one main meal. Also called: **demi-pension.**

half-boot *n* a boot reaching to the midcalf.

half-bottle *n* a bottle of spirits or wine that contains half the quantity of a standard bottle.

half-breed *n* **1** *Offens.* a person whose parents are of different races, esp. the offspring of a White person and an American Indian. ◆ *adj also* **half-bred. 2** of, relating to, or designating offspring of people or animals of different races or breeds.

half-brother *n* the son of either of one's parents by another partner.

half-butt *n* a snooker cue that is longer than an ordinary cue.

half-caste ◆ *Offens. n* **1** a person having parents of different races, esp. the offspring of a European and an Indian. ◆ *adj* **2** of, relating to, or designating such a person.

half-century *n* **1** a period of 50 years. **2** a score or grouping of 50: *he scored his first half-century for England.*

half-cock *n* **1** the halfway position of a firearm's hammer when the trigger is cocked by the hammer and the hammer cannot reach the primer to fire the weapon. **2** **go off at half-cock** *or* **half-cocked.** to fail as a result of inadequate preparation or premature starting.

half-crown *n* a former British coin worth two shillings and sixpence (12½p). Also called: **half-a-crown.**

half-cut *adj Brit. sl.* rather drunk.

half-dozen *n* six.

half gainer *n* a type of dive in which the diver completes a half backward somersault to enter the water headfirst facing the diving board.

half-hardy *adj* (of a cultivated plant) able to survive out of doors except during severe frost.

half-hearted *adj* without enthusiasm or determination.
▸ **ˌhalf-'heartedly** *adv*

half-hitch *n* a knot made by passing the end of a piece of rope around itself and through the loop thus made.

half-hour *n* **1** a period of 30 minutes. **2** the point of time 30 minutes after the beginning of an hour.
▸ ˌ**half-ˈhourly** *adv, adj*

half-hunter *n* a watch with a hinged lid in which a small circular opening or crystal allows the approximate time to be read.

half landing *n* a landing halfway up a flight of stairs.

half-life *n* the time taken for half of the atoms in a radioactive material to undergo decay.

half-light *n* a dim light, as at dawn or dusk.

half-mast *n* the lower than normal position to which a flag is lowered on a mast as a sign of mourning.

half measure *n* (*often pl*) an inadequate measure or action; compromise.

half-moon *n* **1** the moon at first or last quarter when half its face is illuminated. **2** the time at which a half-moon occurs. **3** something shaped like a half-moon.

half-nelson *n* a wrestling hold in which a wrestler places an arm under one of his opponent's arms from behind and exerts pressure with his palm on the back of his opponent's neck.

half-note *n* the usual US name for **minim** (sense 2).

halfpenny *or* **ha'penny** (ˈheɪpnɪ, *for sense 1* ˈhɑːfˌpɛnɪ) *n* **1** (*pl* **halfpennies** *or* **ha'pennies**) a small British coin worth half a new penny (withdrawn 1985). **2** (*pl* **halfpennies** *or* **ha'pennies**) an old British coin worth half an old penny. **3** (*pl* **halfpence**) something of negligible value.
▸ **halfpennyworth** *or* **ha'p'orth** (ˈheɪpəθ) *n*

half-pie *adj NZ inf.* ill planned; not properly thought out: *a half-pie scheme.* ORIG from Maori *pai* good

half-pint *n Sl.* a small or insignificant person.

half-plate *or* **half-print** *n Photog.* a size of plate measuring 6½ × 4½ inches.

half-rotten *adj* partially rotted or decomposed.

half seas over *adj Brit. inf.* drunk.

half-section *n Engineering.* a scale drawing of a section through a symmetrical object that shows only half the object.

half-sister *n* the daughter of either of one's parents by another partner.

half-size *n* any size, esp. in clothing, that is halfway between two sizes.

half-sole *n* a sole from the shank of a shoe to the toe.

half term *n Brit. education.* a short holiday midway through an academic term.

half-timbered *or* **half-timber** *adj* (of a building) having an exposed timber framework filled with brick, stone, or plastered laths, as in Tudor architecture.
▸ ˌ**half-ˈtimbering** *n*

half-time *n Sport.* **a** a rest period between the two halves of a game. **b** (*as modifier*): *the half-time score.*

half-title *n* **1** the short title of a book as printed on the right-hand page preceding the title page. **2** a title on a separate page preceding a section of a book.

halftone (ˈhɑːfˌtəʊn) *n* **1** a process used to reproduce an illustration by photographing it through a fine screen to break it up into dots. **2** the print obtained. **3** *Music.* the usual US and Canad. name for **semitone.**

half-track *n* a vehicle with caterpillar tracks on the wheels that supply motive power only.

half-truth *n* a partially true statement intended to mislead.
▸ ˌ**half-ˈtrue** *adj*

half volley *n Sport.* a stroke or shot in which the ball is hit immediately after it bounces.

halfway (ˌhɑːfˈweɪ) *adv, adj* **1** at or to half the distance. **2** in or of an incomplete manner. **3 meet halfway.** to compromise with.

halfway house *n* **1** a place to rest midway on a journey. **2** the halfway point in any progression. **3** a centre or hostel designed to facilitate the readjustment to private life of released prisoners, mental patients, etc.

halfwit (ˈhɑːfˌwɪt) *n* **1** a feeble-minded person. **2** a foolish or inane person.
▸ ˌ**halfˈwitted** *adj*

half-year *n* a period of six months.

halibut (ˈhælɪbət) *n, pl* **halibuts** *or* **halibut.** the largest flatfish: a dark green North Atlantic species that is a very important food fish. ORIG C15: from *hali* HOLY (because it was eaten on holy days) + *butte* flat-fish, from MDu.

Haliç ★ (haˈliːtʃ) *n* the Turkish name for the **Golden Horn.**

Halicarnassus ★ (ˌhælɪkɑːˈnæsəs) *n* a Greek colony on the SW coast of Asia Minor: one of the major Hellenistic cities.
▸ ˌ**Halicarˈnassian** *adj*

halide (ˈhælaɪd) *or* **halid** (ˈhælɪd) *n* a binary compound containing a halogen atom or ion in combination with a more electropositive element.

Halifax[1] ★ (ˈhælɪˌfæks) *n* **1** a port in SE Canada, capital of Nova Scotia, on the Atlantic: founded in 1749 as a British stronghold. Pop.: 114 455 (1991). **2** a town in N England, in Calderdale, West Yorkshire: textiles. Pop.: 91 069 (1991).

Halifax[2] ★ (ˈhælɪˌfæks) *n* **1 Charles Montagu,** Earl of Halifax. 1661–1715, British statesman; founder of the National Debt (1692) and the Bank of England (1694). **2 Edward Frederick Lindley Wood,** Earl of Halifax. 1881–1959, British Conservative statesman. He was viceroy of India (1926–31), foreign secretary (1938–40), and ambassador to the US (1941–46).

Haligonian (ˌhælɪˈgəʊnɪən) *n* **1** a native or inhabitant of Halifax, Canada. ◆ *adj* **2** of or relating to Halifax, Canada.

halite (ˈhælaɪt) *n* a mineral consisting of sodium chloride in cubic crystalline form, occurring in sedimentary beds and dried salt lakes: an important source of table salt. Also called: **rock salt.** ORIG C19: from NL *halītes,* from Gk *hals* salt + -ITE[2]

halitosis (ˌhælɪˈtəʊsɪs) *n* the state or condition of having bad breath. ORIG C19: NL, from L *hālitus* breath, from *hālāre* to breathe

hall (hɔːl) *n* **1** a room serving as an entry area. **2** (*sometimes cap.*) a building for public meetings. **3** (*often cap.*) the great house of an estate; manor. **4** a large building or room used for assemblies, dances, etc. **5** a residential building, esp. in a university; hall of residence. **6a** a large room, esp. for dining, in a college or university. **6b** a meal eaten in this room. **7** the large room of a house, castle, etc. **8** *US & Canad.* a corridor into which rooms open. **9** (*often pl*) *Inf.* short for **music hall.** ORIG OE *heall*

Hall ★ (hɔːl) *n* **1 Charles Martin.** 1863–1914, US chemist: discovered the electrolytic process for producing aluminium. **2** Sir **John.** 1824–1907, New Zealand statesman, born in England: prime minister of New Zealand (1879–82). **3** Sir **Peter.** born 1930, British stage director: director of the Royal Shakespeare Company (1960–73) and of the National Theatre (1973–88). **4** (**Marguerite**) **Radclyffe.** 1883–1943, British novelist. Her treatment of a lesbian theme in the novel *The Well of Loneliness* (1928) led to an obscenity trial.

Halle ★ (*German* ˈhalə) *n* a city in E central Germany, in Saxony-Anhalt, on the River Saale: early saltworks; a Hanseatic city in the late Middle Ages; university (1694). Pop.: 282 784 (1996 est.). Official name: **Halle an der Saale** (an der ˈzaːlə).

Hallé ★ (ˈhæleɪ) *n* Sir **Charles,** original name *Karl Hallé.* 1819–95, German conductor and pianist, in Britain from 1848. In 1857 he founded the Hallé Orchestra in Manchester.

hallelujah, halleluiah (ˌhælɪˈluːjə), *or* **alleluia** (ˌælɪˈluːjə) *interj* **1** an exclamation of praise to God. ◆ *n* **2** an exclamation of "Hallelujah". **3** a musical composition that uses the word *Hallelujah* as its text. ORIG C16: from Heb. *hellēl* to praise + *yāh* the Lord

Haller ★ (*German* ˈhalər) *n* **Albrecht von** (ˈalbrɛçt fɔn). 1708–77, Swiss biologist: founder of experimental physiology.

Halley ★ (ˈhælɪ) *n* **Edmund.** 1656–1742, English astronomer and mathematician. He predicted the return of the comet now known as **Halley's comet.**

halliard ('hæljəd) *n* a variant spelling of **halyard.**

Hall-Jones ★ ('hɔːl'dʒəunz) *n* Sir **William.** 1851–1936, New Zealand statesman, born in England: prime minister of New Zealand (1906).

hallmark ('hɔːlˌmɑːk) *n* **1** *Brit.* an official series of marks stamped by the London Guild of Goldsmiths on gold, silver, or platinum articles to guarantee purity, date of manufacture, etc. **2** a mark of authenticity or excellence. **3** an outstanding feature. ◆ *vb* **4** (*tr*) to stamp with or as if with a hallmark. ORIG C18: after Goldsmiths' *Hall* in London, where items were graded and stamped

hallo (hə'ləu) *sentence substitute, n* **1** a variant spelling of **hello.** ◆ *sentence substitute, n, vb* **2** a variant spelling of **halloo.**

halloo (hə'luː), **hallo,** *or* **halloa** (hə'ləu) *sentence substitute.* **1** a shout to attract attention, esp. to call hounds at a hunt. ◆ *n, pl* **halloos, hallos,** *or* **halloas. 2** a shout of "halloo". ◆ *vb* **halloos, hallooing, hallooed; hallos, halloing, halloed;** *or* **halloas, halloaing, halloaed. 3** to shout. **4** (*tr*) to urge on (dogs) with shouts. ORIG C16: ? var. of *hallow* to encourage hounds by shouting

hallow ('hæləu) *vb* (*tr*) **1** to consecrate or set apart as being holy. **2** to venerate as being holy. ORIG OE *hālgian,* from *hālig* HOLY
▸ **'hallower** *n*

hallowed ('hæləud; *liturgical* 'hæləuɪd) *adj* **1** set apart as sacred. **2** consecrated or holy.

Halloween *or* **Hallowe'en** (ˌhæləu'iːn) *n* the eve of All Saints' Day celebrated on Oct. 31; Allhallows Eve. ORIG C18: see ALLHALLOWS, EVEN²

hall stand *or esp. US* **hall tree** *n* a piece of furniture for hanging coats, hats, etc., on.

Hallstatt ('hælstæt) *adj* of a late Bronze Age culture extending from central Europe to Britain and lasting from the 9th to the 5th century B.C. ORIG C19: after *Hallstatt,* Austrian village where remains were found

hallucinate (hə'luːsɪˌneɪt) *vb* **hallucinates, hallucinating, hallucinated.** (*intr*) to experience hallucinations. ORIG C17: from L *ālūcinārī* to wander in mind
▸ **hal'luciˌnator** *n*

hallucination (həˌluːsɪ'neɪʃən) *n* the alleged perception of an object when no object is present, occurring under hypnosis, in some mental disorders, etc.
▸ **hal'lucinatory** *adj*

hallucinogen (hə'luːsɪnəˌdʒɛn) *n* any drug that induces hallucinations.
▸ **hallucinogenic** (həˌluːsɪnə'dʒɛnɪk) *adj*

hallux ('hæləks) *n* the first digit on the hind foot of a mammal, bird, reptile, or amphibian; the big toe of man. ORIG C19: NL, from LL *allex* big toe

hallway ('hɔːlˌweɪ) *n* a hall or corridor.

halm (hɔːm) *n* a variant spelling of **haulm.**

halma ('hælmə) *n* a board game in which players attempt to transfer their pieces from their own to their opponents' bases. ORIG C19: from Gk *halma* leap

Halmahera ★ (ˌhælmə'hɪərə) *n* an island in NE Indonesia, the largest of the Moluccas: consists of four peninsulas enclosing three bays; mountainous and forested. Area: 17 780 sq. km (6865 sq. miles). Dutch name: **Djailola.**

Halmstad ★ (*Swedish* 'halmstɑːd) *n* a port in SW Sweden, on the Kattegat. Pop.: 83 080 (1994).

halo ('heɪləu) *n, pl* **haloes** *or* **halos. 1** a disc or ring of light around the head of an angel, saint, etc., as in painting. **2** the aura surrounding a famous or admired person, thing, or event. **3** a circle of light around the sun or moon, caused by the refraction of light by particles of ice. ◆ *vb* **haloes** *or* **halos, haloing, haloed. 4** to surround with or form a halo. ORIG C16: from Med. L, from L *halōs* circular threshing floor, from Gk

halogen ('hæləˌdʒɛn) *n* any of the chemical elements fluorine, chlorine, bromine, iodine, and astatine. They are all monovalent and readily form negative ions. ORIG C19: from Swedish, from Gk *hals* salt + -GEN
▸ **halogenous** (hə'lɒdʒɪnəs) *adj*

halogenate ('hælədʒəˌneɪt) *vb* **halogenates, halogenating, halogenated.** *Chem.* to treat or combine with a halogen.
▸ ˌ**halogen'ation** *n*

haloid ('hælɔɪd) *Chem.* ◆ *adj* **1** derived from a halogen: *a haloid salt.* ◆ *n* **2** a compound containing halogen atoms in its molecules.

halon ('hælɒn) *n* any of a class of chemical compounds derived from hydrocarbons by replacing one or more hydrogen atoms by bromine atoms and other hydrogen atoms by other halogen atoms (chlorine, fluorine, or iodine).

Hals ★ (*Dutch* hɑls) *n* **Frans** (frɑns). ?1580–1666, Dutch portrait and genre painter: his works include *The Laughing Cavalier* (1624).

Hälsingborg ★ (*Swedish* hɛlsiŋ'bɔrj) *n* the former name (until 1971) of **Helsingborg.**

halt¹ (hɔːlt) *n* **1** an interruption or end to movement or progress. **2** *Chiefly Brit.* a minor railway station, without permanent buildings. **3 call a halt (to).** to put an end (to); stop. ◆ *n, sentence substitute.* **4** a command to halt, esp. as an order when marching. ◆ *vb* **5** to come or bring to a halt. ORIG C17: from *to make halt,* translation of G *halt machen,* from *halten* to stop

halt² (hɔːlt) *vb* (*intr*) **1** (esp. of verse) to falter or be defective. **2** to be unsure. **3** *Arch.* to be lame. ◆ *adj* **4** *Arch.* **4a** lame. **4b** (*as collective n;* preceded by *the*): *the halt.* ORIG OE *healt* lame

halter ('hɔːltə) *n* **1** headgear for a horse, usually with a rope for leading. **2** Also: **halterneck.** a style of woman's top fastened behind the neck and waist, leaving the back and arms bare. **3** a rope having a noose for hanging a person. **4** death by hanging. ◆ *vb* (*tr*) **5** to put on a halter. **6** to hang (someone). ORIG OE *hælfter*

haltere ('hæltɪə) *n, pl* **halteres** (hæl'tɪəriːz). one of a pair of short projections in dipterous insects that are modified hind wings, used for maintaining equilibrium during flight. ORIG C18: from Gk *haltēres* (pl) hand-held weights used as balancers or to give impetus in leaping, from *hallesthai* to leap

halting ('hɔːltɪŋ) *adj* **1** hesitant: *halting speech.* **2** lame.
▸ **'haltingly** *adv*

Halton ★ ('hɔːltən) *n* a unitary authority in NE England, in Cheshire. Pop.: 123 000 (1996 est.).

halvah, halva ('hælvɑː), *or* **halavah** ('hæləvɑː) *n* an Eastern sweetmeat made of honey and containing sesame seeds, nuts, etc. ORIG from Yiddish *halva,* ult. from Ar. *halwā*

halve (hɑːv) *vb* **halves, halving, halved.** (*mainly tr*) **1** to divide into two approximately equal parts. **2** to share equally. **3** (*also intr*) to reduce by half, as by cutting. **4** *Golf.* to take the same number of strokes on (a hole or round) as one's opponent. ORIG OE *hielfan*

halyard *or* **halliard** ('hæljəd) *n Naut.* a line for hoisting or lowering a sail, flag, or spar. ORIG C14 *halier,* infl. by YARD¹; see HALE²

ham¹ (hæm) *n* **1** the part of the hindquarters of a pig between the hock and the hip. **2** the meat of this part. **3** *Inf.* the back of the leg above the knee. ORIG OE *hamm*

ham² (hæm) *n* **1** *Theatre, inf.* **1a** an actor who overacts or relies on stock gestures. **1b** overacting or clumsy acting. **1c** (*as modifier*): *a ham actor.* **2** *Inf.* a licensed amateur radio operator. ◆ *vb* **hams, hamming, hammed. 3** *Inf.* to overact. ORIG C19: special use of HAM¹; in some senses prob. infl. by AMATEUR

Hama ★ ('hɑːmɑː) *n* a city in W Syria, on the Orontes River: an early Hittite settlement; famous for its huge water wheels, used for irrigation since the Middle Ages. Pop.: 229 000 (1992 est.). Biblical name: **Hamath.**

Hamadān *or* **Hamedān** ★ ('hæməˌdæn) *n* city in W central Iran, at an altitude of over 1830 m (6000 ft): changed hands several times from the 17th century between Iraq, Persia, and Turkey; trading centre. Pop.: 406 070 (1994 est.).

hamadryad (ˌhæmə'draɪæd) *n* **1** *Classical myth.* a nymph who inhabits a tree and dies with it. **2** another name for **king cobra.** ORIG C14: from L *Hamādryas,* from Gk *Hamadruas,* from *hama* together with + *drus* tree

hamadryas (ˌhæmə'draɪəs) *n* a baboon of Arabia and NE Africa, having long silvery hair on the head, neck, and chest. ORIG C19: via NL from L; see HAMADRYAD

Hamamatsu ★ (ˌhæmə'mætsuː) *n* a city in central Japan, in S central Honshu: cotton textiles and musical instruments. Pop.: 561 568 (1995).

hamba ('hæmbə) *sentence substitute. S. African, usually offens.* go away; be off. ORIG from a Bantu language, from *ukuttamba* to go

Hamburg ★ ('hæmbɜːg) *n* a city-state and port in NW Germany, on the River Elbe: the largest port in Germany; a founder member of the Hanseatic League; became a free imperial city in 1510 and a state of the German empire in 1871; university (1919); extensive shipyards. Pop.: 1 708 500 (1996 est.).

hamburger ('hæmˌbɜːgə) *n* a cake of minced beef, often served in a bread roll. Also called: **beefburger.** ORIG C20: from *Hamburger steak* (steak in the fashion of HAMBURG)

hame (heɪm) *n* either of the two curved bars holding the traces of the harness, attached to the collar of a draught animal. ORIG C14: from MDu. *hame*

Hameln ★ (*German* 'haːməln) *n* an industrial town in N Germany, in Lower Saxony on the Weser River: famous for the legend of the Pied Piper (supposedly took place in 1284). Pop.: 57 640 (1989 est.). English name: **Hamelin** ('hæməlɪn, 'hæmlɪn).

Hamersley Range ★ ('hæməzlɪ) *n* a mountain range in N Western Australia: iron-ore deposits. Highest peak: 1236 m (4056 ft).

ham-fisted *or* **ham-handed** *adj Inf.* lacking dexterity or elegance; clumsy.

Hamhung *or* **Hamheung** ★ ('hɑːm'hʊŋ) *n* an industrial city in central North Korea: commercial and governmental centre of NE Korea during the Yi dynasty (1392–1910). Pop.: 701 000 (1987 est.).

Hamilcar Barca ★ (hæ'mɪlkɑː 'bɑːkə, 'hæmɪlˌkɑː) *n* died ?228 B.C., Carthaginian general; father of Hannibal. He held command (247–41) during the first Punic War and established Carthaginian influence in Spain (237–?228).

Hamilton[1] ★ ('hæməltən) *n* **1** a port in central Canada, in S Ontario on Lake Ontario: iron and steel industry. Pop.: 318 499 (1991). **2** a city in New Zealand, on central North Island. Pop. (urban area): 106 700 (1996). **3** a town in S Scotland, in South Lanarkshire near Glasgow. Pop.: 49 991 (1991). **4** the capital and chief port of Bermuda. Pop.: 1100 (1994 est.). **5** the former name of the **Churchill** River in Labrador.

Hamilton[2] ★ ('hæməltən) *n* **1 Alexander.** ?1757–1804, American statesman. He was a leader of the Federalists and as first secretary of the Treasury (1789–95) established a federal bank. **2** Lady **Emma.** ?1765–1815, mistress of Viscount Nelson. **3** Sir **William Rowan.** 1805–65, Irish mathematician.

Hamitic (hæ'mɪtɪk, hə-) *n* **1** a group of N African languages related to Semitic. ◆ *adj* **2** denoting or belonging to this group of languages. **3** denoting or characteristic of the Hamites, a group of peoples of N Africa, including the ancient Egyptians, supposedly descended from Noah's son Ham.

hamlet ('hæmlɪt) *n* a small village, esp. (in Britain) one without its own church. ORIG C14: from OF *hamelet,* dim. of *hamel,* from *ham,* of Gmc origin

Hamlyn ★ ('hæmlɪn) *n* Baron **Paul.** born 1926, British businessman and publisher.

Hamm ★ (*German* ham) *n* an industrial city in NW Germany, in North Rhine-Westphalia: a Hanse town from 1417; severely damaged in World War II. Pop.: 183 408 (1996 est.).

Hammarskjöld ★ ('hæməˌʃʊld; *Swedish* 'hamarʃœld) *n* **Dag** (**Hjalmar Agne Carl**) (dɑːg). 1905–61, Swedish statesman; secretary-general of the United Nations (1953–61): Nobel peace prize 1961.

hammer ('hæmə) *n* **1** a hand tool consisting of a heavy usually steel head held transversely on the end of a handle, used for driving in nails, etc. **2** any tool or device with a similar function, such as the striking head on a bell. **3** a power-driven striking tool, esp. one used in forging. **4** a part of a gunlock that strikes the primer or percussion cap when the trigger is pulled. **5** *Athletics.* **5a** a heavy metal ball attached to a flexible wire: thrown in competitions. **5b** the sport of throwing the hammer. **6** an auctioneer's gavel. **7** a device on a piano that is made to strike a string or group of strings causing them to vibrate. **8** *Anat.* the nontechnical name for **malleus. 9 go under the hammer.** to be offered for sale by an auctioneer. **10 hammer and tongs.** with great effort or energy. **11 on someone's hammer.** *Austral. & NZ sl.* persistently demanding and critical of someone. ◆ *vb* **12** to strike or beat with or as if with a hammer. **13** (*tr*) to shape with or as if with a hammer. **14** (*tr;* foll. by *in* or *into*) to force (facts, ideas, etc.) into (someone) through constant repetition. **15** (*intr*) to feel or sound like hammering. **16** (*intr;* often foll. by *away*) to work at constantly. **17** (*tr*) *Brit.* to criticize severely. **18** (*tr*) *Inf.* to defeat. **19** (*tr*) *Stock Exchange.* **19a** to announce the default of (a member). **19b** to cause prices of (securities, the market, etc.) to fall by bearish selling. ORIG OE *hamor*
▸ **'hammer-ˌlike** *adj*

hammer and sickle *n* the emblem on the flag of the former Soviet Union, representing the industrial workers and the peasants respectively.

hammer beam *n* either of a pair of short horizontal beams that project from opposite walls to support arched braces and struts.

Hammerfest ★ (*Norwegian* 'hamərfɛst) *n* a port in N Norway, on the W coast of Kvalöy Island: the northernmost town in Europe, with uninterrupted daylight from May 17 to July 29 and no sun between Nov. 21 and Jan. 21; fishing and tourist centre. Pop.: 6900 (1991).

hammerhead ('hæməˌhɛd) *n* **1** a shark having a flattened hammer-shaped head. **2** a tropical African wading bird having a dark plumage and a long backward-pointing crest. **3** a large African fruit bat with a hammer-shaped muzzle.
▸ **'hammerˌheaded** *adj*

hammerlock ('hæməˌlɒk) *n* a wrestling hold in which a wrestler twists his opponent's arm upwards behind his back.

hammer out *vb* (*tr, adv*) **1** to shape or remove with or as if with a hammer. **2** to settle or reconcile (differences, problems, etc.).

Hammersmith and Fulham ★ ('hæməˌsmɪθ) *n* a borough of Greater London on the River Thames: established in 1965 by the amalgamation of Fulham and Hammersmith. Pop.: 156 600 (1994 est.). Area: 16 sq. km (6 sq. miles).

Hammerstein II ★ ('hæməˌstaɪn) *n* **Oscar.** 1895–1960, US librettist and songwriter: collaborated with the composer Richard Rodgers in musicals such as *South Pacific* (1949) and *The Sound of Music* (1959).

hammertoe ('hæməˌtəʊ) *n* a deformity causing the toe to be bent in a clawlike arch.

Hammett ★ ('hæmət) *n* **Dashiell** (də'ʃiːl). 1894–1961, US writer of such detective novels as *The Maltese Falcon* (1930) and *The Thin Man* (1932).

hammock ('hæmək) *n* a length of canvas, net, etc., suspended at the ends and used as a bed. ORIG C16: from Sp. *hamaca,* from Amerind

Hammond[1] ★ ('hæmənd) *n* a city in NW Indiana, adjacent to Chicago. Pop.: 80 081 (1996 est.).

Hammond[2] ★ ('hæmənd) *n* **1** Dame **Joan.** 1912–96, Australian operatic singer, born in New Zealand. **2 Walter Reginald,** known as *Wally.* 1903–65, English cricketer. An all-rounder, he played for England 85 times between 1928 and 1946.

Hammurabi (ˌhæmʊ'rɑːbɪ) *or* **Hammurapi** ★ *n* ?18th century B.C., king of Babylonia; promulgator of one of the earliest known codes of law.

hammy ('hæmɪ) *adj* **hammier, hammiest.** *Inf.* **1** (of an actor) tending to overact. **2** (of a play, performance, etc.) overacted or exaggerated.

Hampden ★ ('hæmpdən, 'hæmdən) *n* **John.** 1594–1643, English statesman; one of the leaders of the Parliamentary opposition to Charles I.

hamper[1] ('hæmpə) *vb* **1** (*tr*) to prevent the progress or free movement of. ◆ *n* **2** *Naut.* gear aboard a vessel that, though essential, is often in the way. ORIG C14: from ?; ? rel. to OE *hamm* enclosure, *hemm* HEM[1]

hamper[2] ('hæmpə) *n* **1** a large basket, usually with a cover. **2** *Brit.* a selection of food and drink packed in a hamper or other container. ORIG C14: var. of earlier *hanaper* a small basket, from OF, of Gmc origin

Hampshire[1] ★ ('hæmp,ʃɪə, -ʃə) *n* a county of S England, on the English Channel: includes two unitary authorities; crossed by the **Hampshire Downs** and the South Downs, with the New Forest in the southwest and many prehistoric and Roman remains. Administrative centre: Winchester. Pop. (excluding Portsmouth and Southampton): 1 222 100 (1996 est.). Area (excluding Portsmouth and Southampton): 3689 sq. km (1424 sq. miles). Abbrev.: **Hants.**

Hampshire[2] ★ ('hæmpʃə) *n* Sir **Stuart.** born 1914, British philosopher.

Hampstead ★ ('hæmpstɪd) *n* a residential district in N London: part of the Greater London borough of Camden since 1965; nearby is **Hampstead Heath**, a popular recreation area.

Hampton[1] ★ ('hæmptən) *n* **1** a city in SE Virginia, on the harbour of **Hampton Roads** on Chesapeake Bay. Pop.: 138 757 (1996 est.). **2** a district of the Greater London borough of Richmond-upon-Thames, on the River Thames: famous for **Hampton Court Palace** (built in 1515 by Cardinal Wolsey).

Hampton[2] ★ ('hæmptən) *n* **1 Christopher James.** born 1946, British playwright. **2 Lionel.** 1913–96, US jazz-band leader and vibraphone player.

hamster ('hæmstə) *n* a Eurasian burrowing rodent having a stocky body, short tail, and cheek pouches: a popular pet. ORIG C17: from G, from OHG *hamustro*, of Slavic origin

hamstring ('hæm,strɪŋ) *n* **1** one of the tendons at the back of the knee. **2** the large tendon at the back of the hind leg of a horse, etc. ◆ *vb* **hamstrings, hamstringing, hamstrung.** (*tr*) **3** to cripple by cutting the hamstring of. **4** to thwart. ORIG C16: HAM[1] + STRING

Hamsun ★ (*Norwegian* 'hamsun) *n* **Knut** (knu:t), pen name of *Knut Pedersen.* 1859–1952, Norwegian novelist, whose works include *The Growth of the Soil* (1917): Nobel prize for literature 1920.

hamulus ('hæmjuləs) *n, pl* **hamuli** (-,laɪ). *Biol.* a hook or hooklike process, between the fore and hind wings of a bee. ORIG C18: from L: a little hook, from *hāmus* hook

Han[1] ★ (hæn) *n* **1** the imperial dynasty that ruled China for most of the time from 206 B.C. to 221 A.D., expanding its territory and developing its bureaucracy. **2** the Chinese people as contrasted to Mongols, Manchus, etc.

Han[2] ★ (hæn) *n* a river in E central China, rising in S Shaanxi and flowing southeast through Hubei to the Yangtze River at Wuhan. Length: about 1450 km (900 miles).

Hanau ★ (*German* 'ha:nau) *n* a city in central Germany, in Hesse east of Frankfurt am Main: a centre of the jewellery industry. Pop.: 84 420 (1989 est.).

Han Cities ★ *pl n* a group of three cities in E central China, in SE Hubei at the confluence of the Han and Yangtze Rivers: Hanyang, Hankow, and Wuchang; united in 1950 to form the conurbation of Wuhan, the capital of Hubei province.

Hancock ★ ('hænkɒk) *n* **1 Anthony John**, known as *Tony.* 1924–68, British comedian, noted for his radio series *Hancock's Half Hour.* **2 John.** 1737–93, American statesman; first signatory of the Declaration of Independence.

hand (hænd) *n* **1** the prehensile part of the body at the end of the arm, consisting of a thumb, four fingers, and a palm. Related adj: **manual. 2** the corresponding part in animals. **3** something resembling this in shape or function. **4a** the cards dealt in one round of a card game. **4b** a player holding such cards. **4c** one round of a card game. **5** agency or influence: *the hand of God.* **6** a part in something done: *he had a hand in the victory.* **7** assistance: *to give someone a hand.* **8** a pointer on a dial, indicator, or gauge, esp. on a clock. **9** acceptance or pledge of partnership, as in marriage. **10** a position indicated by its location to the side of an object or the observer: *on the right hand.* **11** a contrastive aspect, condition, etc.: *on the other hand.* **12** source or origin: *a story heard at third hand.* **13** a person, esp. one who creates something: *a good hand at painting.* **14** a manual worker. **15** a member of a ship's crew: *all hands on deck.* **16** a person's handwriting: *the letter was in his own hand.* **17** a round of applause: *give him a hand.* **18** a characteristic way of doing something: *the hand of a master.* **19** a unit of length equalling four inches, used for measuring the height of horses. **20** a cluster of bananas. **21** (*modifier*) **21a** of or involving the hand: *a hand grenade.* **21b** carried in or worn on the hand: *hand luggage.* **21c** operated by hand: *a hand drill.* **22** (*in combination*) made by hand rather than machine: *hand-sewn.* **23 a free hand.** freedom to do as desired. **24 a hand's turn.** (*usually used with a negative*) a small amount of work: *he hasn't done a hand's turn.* **25 a heavy hand.** tyranny or oppression: *he ruled with a heavy hand.* **26 a high hand.** a dictatorial manner. **27 by hand. 27a** by manual rather than mechanical means. **27b** by messenger or personally: *the letter was delivered by hand.* **28 force someone's hand.** to force someone to act. **29 from hand to mouth. 29a** in poverty: *living from hand to mouth.* **29b** without preparation or planning. **30 hand and foot.** in all ways possible; completely: *they waited on him hand and foot.* **31 hand in glove.** in close association. **32 hand over fist.** steadily and quickly: *he makes money hand over fist.* **33 hold one's hand.** to stop or postpone a planned action or punishment. **34 hold someone's hand.** to support, help, or guide someone, esp. by giving sympathy. **35 in hand. 35a** under control. **35b** receiving attention. **35c** available in reserve. **35d** with deferred payment: *he works a week in hand.* **36 keep one's hand in.** to maintain a limited involvement in an activity so as to preserve one's proficiency at it. **37 (near) at hand.** very close, esp. in time. **38 on hand.** close by; present. **39 out of hand. 39a** beyond control. **39b** without reservation or deeper examination: *he condemned him out of hand.* **40 show one's hand.** to reveal one's stand, opinion, or plans. **41 take in hand.** to discipline; control. **42 throw one's hand in.** to give up a venture, game, etc. **43 to hand.** accessible. **44 try one's hand.** to attempt to do something. ◆ *vb* (*tr*) **45** to transmit or offer by the hand or hands. **46** to help or lead with the hand. **47** *Naut.* to furl (a sail). **48 hand it to someone.** to give credit to someone. ◆ See also **hand down, hand in,** etc., **hands.** ORIG OE *hand*
▸ **'handless** *adj*

handbag ('hænd,bæg) *n* **1** Also called: **bag, purse** (US and Canad.), **pocketbook** (chiefly US). a woman's small bag carried to contain personal articles. **2** a small suitcase that can be carried by hand.

handball ('hænd,bɔ:l) *n* **1** a game in which two teams of seven players try to throw a ball into their opponent's goal. **2** a game in which two or four people strike a ball against a wall with the hand. **3** *Soccer.* the offence committed when a player other than a goalkeeper in his or her own penalty area touches the ball with a hand. ◆ *vb* **4** *Australian Rules football.* to pass (the ball) with a blow of the fist.

handbarrow ('hænd,bærəu) *n* a flat tray for transporting loads, usually carried by two men.

handbill ('hænd,bɪl) *n* a small printed notice for distribution by hand.

handbook ('hænd,buk) *n* a reference book listing brief facts on a subject or place or directions for maintenance or repair, as of a car.

handbrake ('hænd,breɪk) *n* **1** a brake operated by a hand lever. **2** the lever that operates the handbrake.

handbrake turn *n* a turn sharply reversing the direction of a vehicle by speedily applying the handbrake while turning the steering wheel.

handbreadth ('hænd,bretθ, -,bredθ) *or* **hand's-breadth** *n* the width of a hand used as an indication of length.

h and c *abbrev. for* hot and cold (water).

handcart ('hænd,kɑ:t) *n* a simple cart, usually with one or two wheels, pushed or drawn by hand.

handcraft ('hænd,krɑ:ft) *n* **1** another word for **handicraft.** ◆ *vb* **2** (*tr*) to make by handicraft.
▸ **'hand,crafted** *adj*

handcuff ('hænd,kʌf) *vb* **1** (*tr*) to put handcuffs on (a person); manacle. ◆ *n* **2** (*pl*) a pair of locking metal rings joined by a short bar or chain for securing prisoners, etc.

hand down *vb* (*tr, adv*) **1** to bequeath. **2** to pass (an outgrown garment) on from one member of a family to a younger one. **3** *US & Canad. law.* to announce (a verdict).

-handed *adj* of, for, or using a hand or hands as specified: *left-handed; a four-handed game of cards.*

Handel ★ ('hændᵊl) *n* **George Frederick.** German name *Georg Friedrich Händel.* 1685–1759, German composer, resident in England, noted particularly for his oratorios, including the *Messiah* (1741) and *Samson* (1743), 40 operas, and 12 concerti grossi.

handful ('hændfʊl) *n, pl* **handfuls. 1** the amount or number that can be held in the hand. **2** a small number or quantity. **3** *Inf.* a person or thing difficult to manage or control.

handgun ('hænd,gʌn) *n US & Canad.* a firearm that can be fired with one hand, such as a pistol.

hand-held *adj* **1** held in position by the hand. **2** (of a film camera) held rather than mounted, as in close-up action shots. **3** (of a computer) able to be held in the hand. ◆ *n* **4** a computer that can be held in the hand; a palmtop computer.

handicap ('hændɪ,kæp) *n* **1** something that hampers or hinders. **2a** a contest, esp. a race, in which competitors are given advantages or disadvantages of weight, distance, etc., in an attempt to equalize their chances. **2b** the advantage or disadvantage prescribed. **3** *Golf.* the number of strokes by which a player's averaged score exceeds par for the course. **4** any disability or disadvantage resulting from physical, mental, or social impairment or abnormality. ◆ *vb* **handicaps, handicapping, handicapped.** (*tr*) **5** to be a hindrance or disadvantage to. **6** to assign a handicap to. **7** to organize (a contest) by handicapping. ORIG C17: prob. from *hand in cap,* a lottery game in which players drew forfeits from a cap or deposited money in it
► **'handi,capper** *n*

handicapped ('hændɪ,kæpt) *adj* **1a** physically or mentally disabled. **1b** (*as collective n; preceded by the*): *the handicapped.* **2** (of a competitor) assigned a handicap.

handicraft ('hændɪ,krɑːft) *n* **1** skill in working with the hands. **2** a particular skill performed with the hands, such as weaving. **3** the work so produced. ◆ Also called: **handcraft.** ORIG C15: changed from HANDCRAFT through infl. of HANDIWORK

hand in *vb* (*tr, adv*) to return or submit (something, such as an examination paper).

handiwork ('hændɪ,wɜːk) *n* **1** work produced by hand. **2** the result of the action or endeavours of a person or thing. ORIG OE *handgeweorc,* from HAND + *ge-* (collective prefix) + *weorc* WORK

handkerchief ('hæŋkətʃɪf, -tʃiːf) *n* a small square of soft absorbent material carried and used to wipe the nose, etc.

handle ('hændᵊl) *n* **1** the part of a utensil, drawer, etc., designed to be held in order to move, use, or pick up the object. **2** *Sl.* a person's name or title. **3** *CB radio.* a slang name for **call sign. 4** an excuse for doing something: *his background served as a handle for their mockery.* **5** the quality, as of textiles, perceived by feeling. **6** *NZ.* a glass beer mug with a handle. **7 fly off the handle.** *Inf.* to become suddenly extremely angry. ◆ *vb* **handles, handling, handled.** (*mainly tr*) **8** to hold, move, or touch with the hands. **9** to operate using the hands: *the boy handled the reins well.* **10** to control: *my wife handles my investments.* **11** to manage successfully: *a secretary must be able to handle clients.* **12** to discuss (a theme, subject, etc.). **13** to deal with in a specified way: *I was handled with great tact.* **14** to trade or deal in (specified merchandise). **15** (*intr*) to react in a specified way to operation: *the car handles well on bends.* ORIG OE
► **'handled** *adj* ► **'handling** *n*

handlebar moustache ('hændᵊl,bɑː) *n* a bushy extended moustache with curled ends.

handlebars ('hændᵊl,bɑːz) *pl n* (*sometimes sing*) a metal tube having its ends curved to form handles, used for steering a bicycle, etc.

handler ('hændlə) *n* **1** a person who trains and controls an animal, esp. a police dog. **2** the trainer or second of a boxer.

Handley Page ★ ('hændlɪ) *n* Sir **Frederick.** See (Sir Frederick Handley) **Page.**

handmade (,hænd'meɪd) *adj* made by hand, not by machine, esp. with care or craftsmanship.

handmaiden ('hænd,meɪdᵊn) *or* **handmaid** *n* **1** a person or thing that serves a useful but subordinate purpose. **2** *Arch.* a female servant.

hand-me-down *n Inf.* **1** something, esp. an outgrown garment, passed down from one person to another. **2** anything that has already been used by another.

hand-off *Rugby.* ◆ *n* **1** the act of warding off an opposing player with the open hand. ◆ *vb* **hand off. 2** (*tr, adv*) to ward off thus.

hand on *vb* (*tr, adv*) to pass to the next in a succession.

hand organ *n* another name for **barrel organ.**

hand-out *n* **1** clothing, food, or money given to a needy person. **2** a leaflet, free sample, etc., given out to publicize something. **3** a statement distributed to the press or an audience to confirm or replace an oral presentation. ◆ *vb* **hand out. 4** (*tr, adv*) to distribute.

hand over *vb* **1** (*tr, adv*) to surrender possession of; transfer. ◆ *n* **handover. 2** a transfer; surrender.

hand-pick *vb* (*tr*) to select with great care, as for a special job.
► **,hand-'picked** *adj*

handrail ('hænd,reɪl) *n* a rail alongside a stairway, etc., to provide support.

hands (hændz) *pl n* **1** power or keeping: *your welfare is in his hands.* **2** Also called: **handling.** *Soccer.* the infringement of touching the ball with the hand or arm. **3 change hands.** to pass from the possession of one person to another. **4 hands down.** without effort; easily. **5 have one's hands full. 5a** to be completely occupied. **5b** to be beset with problems. **6 have one's hands tied.** to be unable to act. **7 lay hands on** *or* **upon. 7a** to get possession of. **7b** to beat up; assault. **7c** to find. **7d** *Christianity.* to place hands on (someone) in order to confirm or ordain. **8 off one's hands.** for which one is no longer responsible. **9 on one's hands. 9a** for which one is responsible: *I've got too much on my hands to help.* **9b** to spare: *time on my hands.* **10 wash one's hands of.** to have nothing more to do with; refuse to accept responsibility for.

handsaw ('hænd,sɔː) *n* any saw for use in one hand only.

hand's-breadth *n* another name for **handbreadth.**

handsel *or* **hansel** ('hænsᵊl) *Arch. or dialect.* ◆ *n* **1** a gift for good luck at the beginning of a new year, new venture, etc. ◆ *vb* **handsels, handselling, handselled** *or* **hansels, hanselling, hanselled;** *or US* **handsels, handseling, handseled** *or* **hansels, hanseling, hanseled.** (*tr*) **2** to give a handsel to (a person). **3** to inaugurate. ORIG OE *handselen* delivery into the hand

handset ('hænd,sɛt) *n* a telephone mouthpiece and earpiece mounted as a single unit.

handshake ('hænd,ʃeɪk) *n* the act of grasping and shaking a person's hand, as when being introduced or agreeing on a deal.

hands-off *adj* **1** (of a machine, device, etc.) without need of manual operation. **2** denoting a policy, etc., of deliberate noninvolvement: *a hands-off strategy towards industry.*

handsome ('hænsəm) *adj* **1** (of a man) good-looking. **2** (of a woman) fine-looking in a dignified way. **3** well-proportioned; stately: *a handsome room.* **4** liberal: *a handsome allowance.* **5** gracious or generous: *a handsome action.* ORIG C15 *handsom* easily handled
► **'handsomely** *adv* ► **'handsomeness** *n*

hands-on *adj* involving practical experience of equipment, etc.: *hands-on training in computing.*

handspring ('hænd,sprɪŋ) *n* a gymnastic feat in which a person starts from a standing position and leaps forwards or backwards into a handstand and then onto his feet.

handstand ('hænd,stænd) *n* the act of supporting the body on the hands in an upside-down position.

hand-to-hand *adj, adv* at close quarters.

hand-to-mouth *adj, adv* with barely enough money or food to satisfy immediate needs.

handwork ('hænd,wɜːk) *n* work done by hand rather than by machine.
▸ **'hand,worked** *adj*

handwriting ('hænd,raɪtɪŋ) *n* **1** writing by hand rather than by typing or printing. **2** a person's characteristic writing style: *that is in my handwriting.*
▸ **'hand,written** *adj*

handy ('hændɪ) *adj* **handier, handiest. 1** conveniently within reach. **2** easy to handle or use. **3** skilful with one's hands.
▸ **'handily** *adv* ▸ **'handiness** *n*

Handy ★ ('hændɪ) *n* **W**(**illiam**) **C**(**hristopher**). 1873–1958, US blues musician and songwriter, esp. noted for the song "St Louis Blues".

handy dog *n NZ.* a farm dog that can perform a number of different tasks.

handyman ('hændɪ,mæn) *n, pl* **handymen.** a man employed to do or skilled in odd jobs, etc.

hanepoot ('hɑːnə,pɔːt) *n S. African.* a kind of grape for eating or wine making. ORIG from Du.

hang (hæŋ) *vb* **hangs, hanging, hung. 1** to fasten or be fastened from above, esp. by a cord, chain, etc. **2** to place or be placed in position as by a hinge so as to allow free movement: *to hang a door.* **3** (*intr;* sometimes foll. by *over*) to be suspended; hover: *a pall of smoke hung over the city.* **4** (*intr;* sometimes foll. by *over*) to threaten. **5** (*intr*) to be or remain doubtful (esp. in **hang in the balance**). **6** (*p.t. & p.p.* **hanged**) to suspend or be suspended by the neck until dead. **7** (*tr*) to decorate, furnish, or cover with something suspended. **8** (*tr*) to fasten to a wall: *to hang wallpaper.* **9** to exhibit or be exhibited in an art gallery, etc. **10** to droop or allow to droop: *to hang one's head.* **11** (of cloth, clothing, etc.) to drape, fall, or flow: *her skirt hangs well.* **12** (*tr*) to suspend (game such as pheasant) so that it becomes slightly decomposed and therefore more tasty. **13** (of a jury) to prevent or be prevented from reaching a verdict. **14** (*p.t. & p.p.* **hanged**) *Sl.* to damn or be damned: used in mild curses or interjections. **15** (*intr*) to pass slowly (esp. in **time hangs heavily**). **16 hang fire.** to be delayed or to procrastinate. ◆ *n* **17** the way in which something hangs. **18** (*usually used with a negative*) *Sl.* a damn: *I don't care a hang.* **19 get the hang of.** *Inf.* **19a** to understand the technique of doing something. **19b** to perceive the meaning of. ◆ See also **hang about, hang back,** etc. ORIG OE *hangian*

hang about *or* **around** *vb* (*intr*) **1** to waste time; loiter. **2** (*adv;* foll. by *with*) to frequent the company (of someone).

hangar ('hæŋə) *n* a large building for storing and maintaining aircraft. ORIG C19: from F: shed, ?from Med. L *angārium* shed used as a smithy, from ?

hang back *vb* (*intr, adv;* often foll. by *from*) to be reluctant to go forward or carry on.

Hangchow ★ ('hæŋ'dʒəʊ) *n* a variant transliteration of the Chinese name for **Hangzhou.**

hangdog ('hæŋ,dɒg) *adj* downcast, furtive, or guilty in appearance or manner.

hanger ('hæŋə) *n* **1a** any support, such as a peg or loop, on or by which something may be hung. **1b** See **coat hanger. 2a** a person who hangs something. **2b** (*in combination*): *paperhanger.* **3** a type of dagger worn on a sword belt. **4** *Brit.* a wood on a steep hillside.

hanger-on *n, pl* **hangers-on.** a sycophantic follower or dependant.

hang-glider *n* an unpowered aircraft consisting of a large wing made of cloth or plastic stretched over a light framework from which the pilot hangs in a harness.
▸ **'hang-,gliding** *n*

hangi ('hʌŋiː) *n NZ.* **1** an open-air cooking pit. **2** the food cooked in it. **3** the social gathering at the resultant meal. ORIG from Maori

hang in *vb* (*intr, prep*) *Inf., chiefly US & Canad.* to persist: *just hang in there for a bit longer.*

hanging ('hæŋɪŋ) *n* **1a** the putting of a person to death by suspending the body by the neck. **1b** (*as modifier*): *a hanging offence.* **2** (*often pl*) a decorative drapery hung on a wall or over a window. ◆ *adj* **3** not supported from below; suspended. **4** undecided; still under discussion. **5** projecting downwards; overhanging. **6** situated on a steep slope. **7** (*prenominal*) given to issuing death sentences: *a hanging judge.*

Hanging Gardens of Babylon ★ *n* (in ancient Babylon) gardens, probably planted on terraces of a ziggurat: one of the Seven Wonders of the World.

hanging valley *n Geog.* a tributary valley entering a main valley at a much higher level because of overdeepening of the main valley, esp. by glacial erosion.

hangman ('hæŋmən) *n, pl* **hangmen.** an official who carries out a sentence of hanging.

hangnail ('hæŋ,neɪl) *n* a piece of skin torn away from, but still attached to, the base or side of a fingernail. ORIG C17: from OE *angnægl,* from *enge* tight + *nægl* nail; infl. by HANG

hang on *vb* (*intr*) **1** (*adv*) to continue or persist, esp. with effort or difficulty. **2** (*adv*) to grasp or hold. **3** (*prep*) to depend on: *everything hangs on this deal.* **4** (*prep*) Also: **hang onto, hang upon.** to listen attentively to. **5** (*adv*) *Inf.* to wait: *hang on for a few minutes.*

hang out *vb* (*adv*) **1** to suspend, be suspended, or lean. **2** (*intr*) *Inf.* to frequent a place. **3 let it all hang out.** *Inf., chiefly US.* **3a** to relax completely in an unassuming way. **3b** to act or speak freely. ◆ *n* **hang-out. 4** *Inf.* a place that one frequents.

hangover ('hæŋ,əʊvə) *n* **1** the delayed aftereffects of drinking too much alcohol. **2** a person or thing left over from or influenced by a past age.

Hang Seng Index (hæŋ sɛŋ) *n* an index of share prices based on an average of 33 stocks quoted on the Hong Kong Stock Exchange. ORIG name of a Hong Kong bank

hang together *vb* (*intr, adv*) **1** to be cohesive or united. **2** to be consistent: *your statements don't quite hang together.*

Hanguk ★ ('hæn'gʊk) *n* the Korean name for **South Korea.**

hang up *vb* (*adv*) **1** (*tr*) to put on a hook, hanger, etc. **2** to replace (a telephone receiver) on its cradle at the end of a conversation. **3** (*tr; usually passive;* usually foll. by *on*) *Inf.* to cause to have an emotional or psychological preoccupation or problem: *he's really hung up on his mother.* ◆ *n* **hang-up.** *Inf.* **4** an emotional or psychological preoccupation or problem. **5** a persistent cause of annoyance.

Hangzhou ('hæŋ'dʒəʊ) *or* **Hangchow** ★ *n* a port in E China, capital of Zhejiang province, on **Hangzhou Bay** (an inlet of the East China Sea), at the foot of the Eye of Heaven Mountains: regarded by Marco Polo as the finest city in the world; seat of two universities (1927, 1959). Pop.: 1 340 000 (1991 est.).

hank (hæŋk) *n* **1** a loop, coil, or skein, as of rope. **2** *Naut.* a ringlike fitting that can be opened to admit a stay for attaching the luff of a sail. **3** a unit of measurement of cloth, such as a length of 840 yards (767 m) of cotton or 560 yards (512 m) of worsted yarn. ORIG C13: from ON

hanker ('hæŋkə) *vb* (foll. by *for, after,* or an infinitive) to have a yearning. ORIG C17: prob. from Du. dialect *hankeren*
▸ **'hankering** *n*

Hankow *or* **Han-k'ou** ★ ('hæn'kaʊ) *n* a former city in SE China, in SE Hubei at the confluence of the Han and Yangtze Rivers: one of the Han Cities; merged with Hanyang and Wuchang in 1950 to form the conurbation of Wuhan.

Hanks ★ (hæŋks) *n* **Tom.** born 1956, US film actor: his films include *Forrest Gump* (1994), *Saving Private Ryan* (1998), and *The Green Mile* (2000).

hanky *or* **hankie** ('hæŋkɪ) *n, pl* **hankies.** *Inf.* short for **handkerchief.**

hanky-panky ('hæŋkɪ'pæŋkɪ) *n Inf.* **1** dubious or foolish behaviour. **2** illicit sexual relations. ORIG C19: var. of HOCUS-POCUS

Hannah ★ (ˈhænə) *n Old Testament.* the woman who gave birth to Samuel (I Samuel 1–2).

Hannibal ★ (ˈhænɪbᵊl) *n* 247–182 B.C., Carthaginian general; son of Hamilcar Barca. He commanded the Carthaginian army in the Second Punic War (218–201). After capturing Sagunto in Spain, he invaded Italy (218), crossing the Alps with an army of about 40 000 men and defeated the Romans. In 203 he was recalled to defend Carthage and was defeated by Scipio, later being forced into exile; committed suicide to avoid capture.

Hannover ★ (*German* haˈnoːfər) *n* a city in N Germany, capital of Lower Saxony: capital of the kingdom of Hannover (1815–66); situated on the Mittelland Canal. Pop.: 523 147 (1996 est.). English spelling: **Hanover.**

Hanoi ★ (hæˈnɔɪ) *n* the capital of Vietnam, on the Red River: became capital of Tonkin in 1802, French Indochina in 1887, Vietnam in 1945, and North Vietnam (1954–75); university (1917); industrial centre. Pop.: 2 154 900 (1993 est.).

Hanover[1] ★ (ˈhænəʊvə) *n* the English spelling of **Hannover.**

Hanover[2] (ˈhænəʊvə) *n* **1** a princely house of Germany (1692–1815), the head of which succeeded to the British throne as George I in 1714. **2** the royal house of Britain (1714–1901).
▸ ˌ**Hanoˈverian** *adj, n*

Hansard (ˈhænsɑːd) *n* **1** the official verbatim report of the proceedings of the British Parliament. **2** a similar report kept by the Canadian House of Commons and other legislative bodies. ORIG C19: after L. *Hansard* (1752–1828) and his descendants, who compiled the reports until 1889

Hanse (hæns) *n* **1** a medieval guild of merchants. **2** a fee paid by the new members of a medieval trading guild. **3** another name for the **Hanseatic League.** ORIG C12: of Gmc origin
▸ **Hanseatic** (ˌhænsɪˈætɪk) *adj*

Hanseatic League *n* a commercial organization of towns in N Germany formed in the mid-14th century to protect and control trade.

hansel (ˈhænsᵊl) *n, vb* a variant spelling of **handsel.**

hansom (ˈhænsəm) *n* (*sometimes cap.*) a two-wheeled one-horse carriage with a fixed hood. The driver sits on a high outside seat at the rear. Also called: **hansom cab.** ORIG C19: after its designer J. A. *Hansom* (1803–82)

hantavirus (ˈhæntəˌvaɪrəs) *n* any member of a genus of viruses that infect rodents and can be transmitted to humans, in whom they can cause kidney damage or respiratory disease. ORIG C20: after the *Hantaan* river, South Korea

Hants (hænts) *abbrev. for* Hampshire.

Hanukkah (ˈhɑːnəkə, -nʊˌkɑː) *n* a variant of **Chanukah.**

Hanuman (ˌhʌnʊˈmɑːn) *n* **1** (*pl* **Hanumans**) another word for **entellus** (the monkey). **2** the monkey chief of Hindu mythology. ORIG from Hindi, from Sansk. *hanumant* having (conspicuous) jaws, from *hanu* jaw

Hanyang *or* **Han-yang** ★ (ˈhænˈjæŋ) *n* a former city in SE China, in SE Hubei at the confluence of the Han and Yangtze Rivers: one of the Han Cities; merged with Hankow and Wuchang in 1950 to form the conurbation of Wuhan.

hap (hæp) *Arch.* ◆ *n* **1** luck; chance. **2** an occurrence. ◆ *vb* **haps, happing, happed. 3** (*intr*) to happen. ORIG C13: from ON *happ* good luck

ha'penny (ˈheɪpnɪ) *n, pl* **ha'pennies.** *Brit.* a variant spelling of **halfpenny.**

haphazard (hæpˈhæzəd) *adv, adj* **1** at random. ◆ *adj* **2** careless.
▸ **hapˈhazardly** *adv* ▸ **hapˈhazardness** *n*

hapless (ˈhæplɪs) *adj* unfortunate; wretched.
▸ ˈ**haplessly** *adv* ▸ ˈ**haplessness** *n*

haplography (hæpˈlɒgrəfɪ) *n, pl* **haplographies.** the accidental omission of a letter or syllable which recurs, as in spelling *endodontics* as *endontics.* ORIG C19: from Gk, from *haplous* single + -GRAPHY

haploid (ˈhæplɔɪd) *Biol.* ◆ *adj* **1** (esp. of gametes) having a single set of unpaired chromosomes. ◆ *n* **2** a haploid cell or organism. ORIG C20: from Gk *haploeidēs,* from *haplous* single
▸ ˈ**haploidy** *n*

haplology (hæpˈlɒlədʒɪ) *n* omission of a repeated occurrence of a sound or syllable in fluent speech, as for example in the pronunciation of *library* as (ˈlaɪbrɪ).

haply (ˈhæplɪ) *adv* (*sentence modifier*) an archaic word for **perhaps.**

happen (ˈhæpᵊn) *vb* **1** (*intr*) to take place; occur. **2** (*intr;* foll. by *to*) (of some unforeseen event, esp. death) to fall to the lot (of): *if anything happens to me it'll be your fault.* **3** (*tr*) to chance (to be or do something): *I happen to know him.* **4** (*tr; takes a clause as object*) to be the case, esp. by chance: *it happens that I know him.* ◆ *adv, sentence substitute.* **5** *N English dialect.* another word for **perhaps.** ORIG C14: see HAP, -EN[1]

USAGE NOTE See at **occur.**

happening (ˈhæpənɪŋ, ˈhæpnɪŋ) *n* **1** an event. **2** an improvised or spontaneous performance consisting of bizarre events. ◆ *adj* **3** *Inf.* fashionable and up-to-the-minute.

happen on *or* **upon** *vb* (*intr; prep*) to find by chance.

happy (ˈhæpɪ) *adj* **happier, happiest. 1** feeling or expressing joy; pleased. **2** willing: *I'd be happy to show you around.* **3** causing joy or gladness. **4** fortunate: *the happy position of not having to work.* **5** aptly expressed; appropriate: *a happy turn of phrase.* **6** (*postpositive*) *Inf.* slightly intoxicated. ORIG C14: see HAP, -Y[1]
▸ ˈ**happily** *adv* ▸ ˈ**happiness** *n*

happy event *n Inf.* the birth of a child.

happy-go-lucky *adj* carefree or easy-going.

happy hour *n* a period during which some public houses, bars, restaurants, etc., charge reduced prices.

happy hunting ground *n* **1** (in Amerind legend) the paradise to which a person passes after death. **2** a productive or profitable area to explore.

happy medium *n* a course or state that avoids extremes.

Hapsburg ★ (ˈhæpsˌbɜːg) *n* a German princely family founded by Albert, count of Hapsburg (1153). From 1440 to 1806, they ruled the Holy Roman Empire almost uninterruptedly and provided rulers for Austria, Spain, Hungary, Bohemia, etc. The line continued as the royal house of **Hapsburg-Lorraine,** ruling in Austria (1806–48) and Austria-Hungary (1848–1918). German name: **Habsburg.**

haptic (ˈhæptɪk) *adj* relating to or based on the sense of touch. ORIG C19: from Gk, from *haptein* to touch

hapuka *or* **hapuku** (həˈpuːkə, ˈhɑːpʊkə) *n NZ.* another name for **groper.** ORIG from Maori

hara-kiri (ˌhærəˈkɪrɪ) *or* **hari-kari** (ˌhærɪˈkɑːrɪ) *n* (formerly, in Japan) ritual suicide by disembowelment when disgraced or under sentence of death. Also called: **seppuku.** ORIG C19: from Japanese, from *hara* belly + *kiri* cutting

Harald I ★ (ˈhærəld) *n* called *Harald Fairhair.* ?850–933, first king of Norway: his rule caused emigration to the British Isles.

Harald III ★ *n* surname *Hardraade.* 1015–66, king of Norway (1047–66); invaded England (1066) and died at the battle of Stamford Bridge.

harangue (həˈræŋ) *vb* **harangues, haranguing, harangued. 1** to address (a person or crowd) in an angry, vehement, or forcefully persuasive way. ◆ *n* **2** a loud, forceful, or angry speech. ORIG C15: from OF, from OIt. *aringa* public speech, prob. of Gmc origin
▸ **haˈranguer** *n*

Harappa ★ (həˈræpə) *n* an ancient city in the Punjab in NW Pakistan: one of the centres of the Indus civilization that flourished from 2500 to 1700 B.C.; probably destroyed by Indo-European invaders.
▸ **Haˈrappan** *adj, n*

Harar *or* **Harrer** ★ (ˈhɑːrə) *n* a city in E Ethiopia: former capital of the Muslim state of Adal. Pop.: 122 932 (1994 est.).

Harare ★ (hə'rɑːrɪ) *n* the capital of Zimbabwe, in the northeast: University of Zimbabwe (1957); industrial and commercial centre. Pop.: 1 184 169 (1992). Former name (until 1982): **Salisbury.**

harass ('hærəs, hə'ræs) *vb (tr)* to trouble, torment, or confuse by continual persistent attacks, questions, etc. ORIG C17: from F *harasser,* var. of OF *harer* to set a dog on, of Gmc origin
▸ **'harassed** *adj* ▸ **'harassment** *n*

Harbin ★ (hɑː'biːn, -'bɪn) *n* a city in NE China, capital of Heilongjiang province on the Songhua River: founded by the Russians in 1897; centre of tsarist activities after the October Revolution in Russia (1917). Pop.: 2 830 000 (1991 est.). Also called: **Ha-erh-pin.**

harbinger ('hɑːbɪndʒə) *n* **1** a person or thing that announces or indicates the approach of something; forerunner. ◆ *vb* **2** *(tr)* to announce the approach or arrival of. ORIG C12: from OF *herbergere,* from *herberge* lodging, from OSaxon

harbour *or US* **harbor** ('hɑːbə) *n* **1** a sheltered port. **2** a place of refuge or safety. ◆ *vb* **3** *(tr)* to give shelter to: *to harbour a criminal.* **4** *(tr)* to maintain secretly: *to harbour a grudge.* **5** to shelter (a vessel) in a harbour or (of a vessel) to seek shelter. ORIG OE *herebeorg,* from *here* army + *beorg* shelter

harbourage *or US* **harborage** ('hɑːbərɪdʒ) *n* shelter or refuge, as for a ship.

harbour master *n* an official in charge of a harbour.

hard (hɑːd) *adj* **1** firm or rigid. **2** toughened; not soft or smooth: *hard skin.* **3** difficult to do or accomplish: *a hard task.* **4** difficult to understand: *a hard question.* **5** showing or requiring considerable effort or application: *hard work.* **6** demanding: *a hard master.* **7** harsh; cruel: *a hard fate.* **8** inflicting pain, sorrow, or hardship: *hard times.* **9** tough or violent: *a hard man.* **10** forceful: *a hard knock.* **11** cool or uncompromising: *we took a long hard look at our profit factor.* **12** indisputable; real: *hard facts.* **13** *Chem.* (of water) impairing the formation of a lather by soap. **14** practical, shrewd, or calculating: *he is a hard man in business.* **15** harsh: *hard light.* **16a** (of currency) in strong demand, esp. as a result of a good balance of payments situation. **16b** (of credit) difficult to obtain; tight. **17** (of alcoholic drink) being a spirit rather than a wine, beer, etc. **18** (of a drug) highly addictive. **19** *Physics.* (of radiation) having high energy and the ability to penetrate solids. **20** *Chiefly US.* (of goods) durable. **21** short for **hard-core. 22** *Phonetics.* (not in technical usage) denoting the consonants *c* and *g* when they are pronounced as in *cat* and *got.* **23a** heavily fortified. **23b** (of nuclear missiles) located underground. **24** politically extreme: *the hard left.* **25** *Brit. & NZ inf.* incorrigible or disreputable (esp. in **a hard case**). **26 a hard nut to crack. 26a** a person not easily won over. **26b** a thing not easily done or understood. **27 hard by.** close by. **28 hard of hearing.** slightly deaf. **29 hard up.** *Inf.* **29a** in need of money. **29b** (foll. by *for*) in great need (of): *hard up for suggestions.* ◆ *adv* **30** with great energy, force, or vigour: *the team always played hard.* **31** as far as possible: *hard left.* **32** earnestly or intently: *she thought hard about the formula.* **33** with great intensity: *his son's death hit him hard.* **34** (foll. by *on, upon, by,* or *after*) close; near: *hard on his heels.* **35** (foll. by *at*) assiduously; devotedly. **36a** with effort or difficulty: *their victory was hard won.* **36b** *(in combination)*: *hard-earned.* **37** slowly: *prejudice dies hard.* **38 go hard with.** to cause pain or difficulty to (someone). **39 hard put (to it).** scarcely having the capacity (to do something). ◆ *n* **40** *Brit.* a roadway across a foreshore. **41** *Sl.* hard labour. **42** *Taboo sl.* an erection of the penis (esp. in **get** or **have a hard on**). ORIG OE *heard*
▸ **'hardness** *n*

hard and fast *adj* (**hard-and-fast** *when prenominal*). (of rules, etc.) invariable or strict.

hardback ('hɑːd,bæk) *n* **1** a book with covers of cloth, cardboard, or leather. ◆ *adj* **2** Also: **casebound, hardbound, hardcover.** of or denoting a hardback or the publication of hardbacks.

hard-bitten *adj Inf.* tough and realistic.

hardboard ('hɑːd,bɔːd) *n* a thin stiff sheet made of compressed sawdust and wood pulp bound together under heat and pressure.

hard-boiled *adj* **1** (of an egg) boiled until solid. **2** *Inf.* **2a** tough, realistic. **2b** cynical.

hard card *n* a hard disk, mounted on a card, that can be added to a personal computer.

hard cash *n* money or payment in money, as opposed to payment by cheque, credit, etc.

hard coal *n* another name for **anthracite.**

hard copy *n* computer output printed on paper, as contrasted with machine-readable output such as magnetic tape.

hardcore ('hɑːd,kɔː) *n* **1** a style of rock music characterized by short fast songs with minimal melody and aggressive delivery. **2** a type of dance music with a very fast beat.

hard core *n* **1** the members of a group who form an intransigent nucleus resisting change. **2** material, such as broken stones, used to form a foundation for a road, etc. ◆ *adj* **hard-core. 3** (of pornography) describing or depicting sexual acts in explicit detail. **4** extremely committed or fanatical: *a hard-core Communist.*

hard disk *n Computing.* a disk of rigid magnetizable material that is used to store data for computers: it is permanently mounted in its disk drive and usually has a storage capacity of a few gigabytes.

Hardecanute ★ ('hɑːdɪkə,njuːt) *n* a variant of **Harthacanute.**

harden ('hɑːdᵊn) *vb* **1** to make or become hard or harder; freeze, stiffen, or set. **2** to make or become tough or unfeeling. **3** to make or become stronger or firmer. **4** *(intr) Commerce.* **4a** (of prices, a market, etc.) to cease to fluctuate. **4b** (of price) to rise higher.
▸ **'hardener** *n*

Hardenberg ★ (*German* 'hardənbɛrk) *n* **Friedrich von** ('friːdrɪç fɔn). the original name of **Novalis.**

hardened ('hɑːdᵊnd) *adj* **1** rigidly set, as in a mode of behaviour. **2** toughened; seasoned.

harden off *vb (tr, adv)* to cause (plants) to become resistant to cold, frost, etc., by gradually exposing them to such conditions.

hard feeling *n (often pl; often used with a negative)* resentment; ill will: *no hard feelings?*

hard hat *n* **1** a hat made of a hard material for protection, worn esp. by construction workers, equestrians, etc. **2** *Inf., chiefly US.* a construction worker.

hard-headed *adj* tough, realistic, or shrewd; not moved by sentiment.

hardhearted (,hɑːd'hɑːtɪd) *adj* unkind or intolerant.
▸ **,hard'heartedness** *n*

Hardicanute ★ ('hɑːdɪkə,njuːt) *n* a variant of **Harthacanute.**

Hardie ★ ('hɑːdɪ) *n* **(James) Keir** (kɪə). 1856–1915, British Labour leader and politician, born in Scotland; the first parliamentary leader of the Labour Party.

hardihood ('hɑːdɪ,hʊd) *n* courage or daring.

Harding ★ ('hɑːdɪŋ) *n* **Warren G(amaliel).** 1865–1923, 29th president of the US (1921–23).

hard labour *n Criminal law.* (formerly) the penalty of compulsory physical labour imposed in addition to a sentence of imprisonment.

hard landing *n* **1** a landing by a rocket or spacecraft in which the vehicle is destroyed on impact. **2** a solution to a problem, esp. an economic problem, that involves hardship.

hard line *n* an uncompromising course or policy.
▸ **,hard'liner** *n*

hardly ('hɑːdlɪ) *adv* **1** scarcely; barely: *we hardly knew the family.* **2** only just: *he could hardly hold the cup.* **3** *Often used ironically.* not at all: *he will hardly incriminate himself.* **4** with difficulty. **5** *Rare.* harshly or cruelly.

USAGE NOTE See at **scarcely.**

hard-nosed *adj Inf.* tough, shrewd, and practical.

Hardouin Mansart ★ (*French* ardwɛ̃ mɑ̃sar) *n* See (Jules Hardouin) **Mansart.**

hard pad *n* (in dogs) an abnormal increase in the thickness of the foot pads: one of the clinical signs of canine distemper. See **distemper**[1].

hard palate *n* the anterior bony portion of the roof of the mouth.

hardpan (ˈhɑːdˌpæn) *n* a hard impervious layer of clay below the soil.

hard paste *n* **a** porcelain made with kaolin and petuntse, of Chinese origin and made in Europe from the early 18th century. **b** (*as modifier*): *hard-paste porcelain.*

hard-pressed *adj* **1** in difficulties. **2** subject to severe competition or attack. **3** closely pursued.

hard rock *n* rhythmically simple rock music that is very loud.

hard sauce *n* another name for **brandy butter.**

hard science *n* one of the natural or physical sciences, such as physics, chemistry, biology, geology, or astronomy.
▸ **hard scientist** *n*

hard sell *n* an aggressive insistent technique of selling or advertising.

hard-shell *adj also* **hard-shelled. 1** *Zool.* having a shell or carapace that is thick, heavy, or hard. **2** *US.* strictly orthodox.

hardship (ˈhɑːdʃɪp) *n* **1** conditions of life difficult to endure. **2** something that causes suffering or privation.

hard shoulder *n Brit.* a surfaced verge running along the edge of a motorway for emergency stops.

hardtack (ˈhɑːdˌtæk) *n* a kind of hard saltless biscuit, formerly eaten esp. by sailors as a staple aboard ship. Also called: **ship's biscuit, sea biscuit.**

hardtop (ˈhɑːdˌtɒp) *n* a car with a metal or plastic roof that is sometimes detachable.

hardware (ˈhɑːdˌwɛə) *n* **1** metal tools, implements, etc., esp. cutlery or cooking utensils. **2** *Computing.* the physical equipment used in a computer system, such as the central processing unit, peripheral devices, and memory. Cf. **software. 3** mechanical equipment, components, etc. **4** heavy military equipment, such as tanks and missiles. **5** *Inf.* a gun.

hard-wired *adj* **1** (of a circuit or instruction) permanently wired into a computer, replacing separate software. **2** (of human behaviour) innate; not learned: *humans have a hard-wired ability for acquiring language.*

hardwood (ˈhɑːdˌwʊd) *n* **1** the wood of any of numerous broad-leaved trees, such as oak, beech, ash, etc., as distinguished from the wood of a conifer. **2** any tree from which this wood is obtained.

hardy (ˈhɑːdɪ) *adj* **hardier, hardiest. 1** having or demanding a tough constitution; robust. **2** bold; courageous. **3** foolhardy; rash. **4** (of plants) able to live out of doors throughout the winter. ORIG C13: from OF *hardi,* p.p. of *hardir* to become bold, of Gmc origin; cf. OE *hierdan* to HARDEN, ON *hertha,* OHG *herten*
▸ **ˈhardily** *adv* ▸ **ˈhardiness** *n*

Hardy ★ (ˈhɑːdɪ) *n* **1 Oliver.** See **Laurel and Hardy. 2 Thomas.** 1840–1928, British writer; his novels set in his native Dorset, include *Far from the Madding Crowd* (1874), *Tess of the d'Urbervilles* (1891), and *Jude the Obscure* (1895).

hare (hɛə) *n, pl* **hares** *or* **hare. 1** a solitary mammal which is larger than a rabbit, has longer ears and legs, and lives in a shallow nest (form). **2 run with the hare and hunt with the hounds.** to be on good terms with both sides. **3 start a hare.** to raise a topic for conversation. ◆ *vb* **hares, haring, hared. 4** (*intr;* often foll. by *off, after,* etc.) *Brit. inf.* to run fast or wildly. ORIG OE *hara*
▸ **ˈhareˌlike** *adj*

Hare ★ (hɛə) *n* **1** Sir **David.** born 1947, British dramatist and theatre director: his plays include *Plenty* (1978) and *The Judas Kiss* (1998). **2 William.** 19th century, Irish murderer and body snatcher; associate of William Burke.

hare and hounds *n* (*functioning as sing*) a game in which certain players (**hares**) run across country scattering pieces of paper that the other players (**hounds**) follow in an attempt to catch the hares.

harebell (ˈhɛəˌbɛl) *n* a N temperate plant having slender stems and leaves, and bell-shaped blue flowers.

harebrained *or* **hairbrained** (ˈhɛəˌbreɪnd) *adj* rash, foolish, or badly thought out.

Hare Krishna (ˈhɑːrɪ ˈkrɪʃnə) *n* **1** a Hindu sect devoted to a form of Hinduism (**Krishna Consciousness**) based on the worship of the god Krishna. **2** (*pl* **Hare Krishnas**) a member or follower of this sect. ORIG C20: from Hindi, literally: Lord Krishna (vocative): the opening words of a sacred verse often chanted in public by adherents of the movement

harelip (ˈhɛəˌlɪp) *n* a congenital cleft or fissure in the midline of the upper lip, resembling the cleft upper lip of a hare, often occurring with cleft palate.
▸ **ˈhareˌlipped** *adj*

harem (ˈhɛərəm, hɑːˈriːm) *or* **hareem** (hɑːˈriːm) *n* **1** the part of an Oriental house reserved strictly for wives, concubines, etc. **2** a Muslim's wives and concubines collectively. **3** a group of female animals that are the mates of a single male. ORIG C17: from Ar. *harīm* forbidden (place)

hare's-foot *n* a plant that grows on sandy soils in Europe and NW Asia and has downy heads of white or pink flowers.

Harfleur ★ (ˈhɑːflɜː; *French* arflœr) *n* a port in N France, in the Seine-Maritime department: important centre in the Middle Ages. Pop.: 9700 (latest est.).

Hargeisa ★ (hɑːˈgeɪsə) *n* a city in NW Somalia: former capital of British Somaliland (1941–60); trading centre for nomadic herders. Pop.: 400 000 (1987 est.).

Hargreaves ★ (ˈhɑːgriːvz) *n* **James.** died 1778, English inventor of the spinning jenny.

haricot (ˈhærɪkəʊ) *n* a variety of French bean with light-coloured edible seeds, which can be dried and stored. ORIG C17: from F, ?from Amerind

Harijan (ˈhʌrɪdʒən) *n* a member of certain classes in India, formerly considered inferior and untouchable. ORIG Hindi, lit.: man of God (so called by Mahatma Gandhi)

hari-kari (ˌhærɪˈkɑːrɪ) *n* a non-Japanese variant spelling of **hara-kiri.**

Haringey ★ (ˈhærɪŋˌgeɪ) *n* a borough of N Greater London. Pop.: 212 300 (1994 est.). Area: 30 sq. km (12 sq. miles).

hark (hɑːk) *vb* (*intr; usually imperative*) to listen; pay attention. ORIG OE *heorcnian* to HEARKEN

hark back *vb* (*intr, adv*) to return to an earlier subject in speech or thought.

harken (ˈhɑːkən) *vb* a variant spelling (esp. US) of **hearken.**
▸ **ˈharkener** *n*

harl (hɑːl) *n Angling.* a variant of **herl.**

Harlech ★ (ˈhɑːlək) *n* a town in N Wales, in Gwynedd: noted for its ruined 13th-century castle overlooking Cardigan Bay: tourism. Pop.: 1233 (1991).

Harlem ★ (ˈhɑːləm) *n* a district of New York City, in NE Manhattan: now largely a Black ghetto.

harlequin (ˈhɑːlɪkwɪn) *n* **1** (*sometimes cap.*) *Theatre.* a stock comic character originating in the commedia dell'arte; the foppish lover of Columbine in the English harlequinade. He is usually represented in diamond-patterned multicoloured tights, wearing a black mask. **2** a clown or buffoon. ◆ *adj* **3** varied in colour or decoration. ORIG C16: from OF *Herlequin, Hellequin* leader of band of demon horsemen

harlequinade (ˌhɑːlɪkwɪˈneɪd) *n* **1** (*sometimes cap.*) *Theatre.* a play in which harlequin has a leading role. **2** buffoonery.

Harley ★ (ˈhɑːlɪ) *n* **Robert,** 1st Earl of Oxford. 1661–1724, British statesman; head of the government (1710–14), negotiated the treaty of Utrecht (1713).

Harley Street ★ *n* a street in central London famous for its large number of medical specialists' consulting rooms.

harlot ('hɑːlət) *n* a prostitute. ORIG C13: from OF *herlot* rascal, from ?
▸ **'harlotry** *n*

Harlow[1] ★ ('hɑːləʊ) *n* a town in SE England, in W Essex: designated a new town in 1947. Pop.: 74 629 (1991).

Harlow[2] ★ ('hɑːləʊ) *n* **Jean**, real name *Harlean Carpentier*. 1911–37, US film actress, whose films include *Hell's Angels* (1930) and *Bombshell* (1933).

harm (hɑːm) *n* **1** physical or mental injury. **2** moral wrongdoing. ◆ *vb* **3** (*tr*) to injure physically, morally, or mentally. ORIG OE *hearm*

harmattan (hɑː'mætᵊn) *n* a dry dusty wind from the Sahara blowing towards the W African coast. ORIG C17: from native African language *haramata*, ?from Ar. *harām* forbidden thing; see HAREM

harmful ('hɑːmfʊl) *adj* causing or tending to cause harm; injurious.
▸ **'harmfully** *adv*

harmless ('hɑːmlɪs) *adj* **1** not causing or tending to cause harm. **2** unlikely to annoy or worry people: *a harmless sort of man.*
▸ **'harmlessly** *adv*

harmonic (hɑː'mɒnɪk) *adj* **1** of, producing, or characterized by harmony; harmonious. **2** *Music.* of or belonging to harmony. **3** *Maths.* **3a** capable of expression in the form of sine and cosine functions. **3b** of or relating to numbers whose reciprocals form an arithmetic progression. **4** *Physics.* of or concerned with a harmonic or harmonics. ◆ *n* **5** *Physics, music.* a component of a periodic quantity, such as a musical tone, with a frequency that is an integral multiple of the fundamental frequency. **6** *Music.* (not in technical use) overtone. ◆ See also **harmonics.** ORIG C16: from L *harmonicus* relating to HARMONY
▸ **har'monically** *adv*

harmonica (hɑː'mɒnɪkə) *n* **1** Also called: **mouth organ.** a small wind instrument in which reeds of graduated lengths set into a metal plate enclosed in a narrow oblong box are made to vibrate by blowing and sucking. **2** See **glass harmonica.** ORIG C18: from L *harmonicus* relating to HARMONY

harmonic analysis *n* the representation of a periodic function by means of the summation and integration of simple trigonometric functions.

harmonic mean *n* the reciprocal of the arithmetic mean of the reciprocals of a set of specified numbers: the harmonic mean of 2, 3, and 4 is 3/ (½ + ⅓ + ¼) = 36/13.

harmonic minor scale *n Music.* a minor scale modified from the natural by the sharpening of the seventh degree.

harmonic motion *n* a periodic motion in which the displacement is symmetrical about a point or a periodic motion that is composed of such motions.

harmonic progression *n* a sequence of numbers whose reciprocals form an arithmetic progression, as 1, ½, ⅓, ….

harmonics (hɑː'mɒnɪks) *n* **1** (*functioning as sing*) the science of musical sounds and their acoustic properties. **2** (*functioning as pl*) the overtones of a fundamental note, as produced by lightly touching the string of a stringed instrument at one of its node points while playing.

harmonic series *n* **1** *Maths.* a series whose terms are in harmonic progression, as in 1 + ½ + ⅓ + …. **2** *Acoustics.* the series of tones with frequencies strictly related to one another and to the fundamental tone, as obtained by touching lightly the node points of a string while playing it.

harmonious (hɑː'məʊnɪəs) *adj* **1** (esp. of colours or sounds) fitting together well. **2** having agreement. **3** tuneful or melodious.

harmonist ('hɑːmənɪst) *n* **1** a person skilled in the art and techniques of harmony. **2** a person who combines and collates parallel narratives.

harmonium (hɑː'məʊnɪəm) *n* a musical keyboard instrument in which air from pedal-operated bellows causes the reeds to vibrate. ORIG C19: from F, from *harmonie* HARMONY

harmonize *or* **harmonise** ('hɑːməˌnaɪz) *vb* **harmonizes, harmonizing, harmonized** *or* **harmonises, harmonising, harmonised. 1** to make or become harmonious. **2** (*tr*) *Music.* to provide a harmony for (a tune, etc.). **3** (*intr*) to sing in harmony, as with other singers. **4** to collate parallel narratives.
▸ **ˌharmoni'zation** *or* **ˌharmoni'sation** *n*

harmony ('hɑːmənɪ) *n, pl* **harmonies. 1** agreement in action, opinion, feeling, etc. **2** order or congruity of parts to their whole or to one another. **3** agreeable sounds. **4** *Music.* **4a** any combination of notes sounded simultaneously. **4b** the vertically represented structure of a piece of music. Cf. **melody** (sense 1b). **4c** the art or science concerned with combinations of chords. **5** a collation of parallel narratives, esp. of the four Gospels. ORIG C14: from L *harmonia* concord of sounds, from Gk: harmony, from *harmos* a joint

Harmsworth ★ ('hɑːmzwɜːθ) *n* **1 Alfred Charles William.** See (Viscount) **Northcliffe. 2 Harold Sydney.** See (1st Viscount) **Rothermere.**

harness ('hɑːnɪs) *n* **1** an arrangement of straps fitted to a draught animal in order that the animal can be attached to and pull a cart. **2** something resembling this, esp. for attaching something to the body: *a parachute harness.* **3** *Weaving.* the part of a loom that raises and lowers the warp threads. **4** *Arch.* armour. **5 in harness.** at one's routine work. ◆ *vb* (*tr*) **6** to put a harness on (a horse). **7** (usually foll. by *to*) to attach (a draught animal) to (a cart, etc.). **8** to control so as to employ the energy or potential power of: *to harness the atom.* **9** to equip with armour. ORIG C13: from OF *harneis* baggage, prob. from ON *hernest* (unattested), from *herr* army + *nest* provisions
▸ **'harnesser** *n*

harness race *n Horse racing.* a trotting or pacing race for horses pulling sulkies.

Harney Peak ★ ('hɑːnɪ) *n* a mountain in SW South Dakota: the highest peak in the Black Hills. Height: 2207 m (7242 ft).

Harold I ★ ('hærəld) *n* surname *Harefoot.* died 1040, king of England (1037–40); son of Canute.

Harold II ★ *n* ?1022–66, king of England (1066); son of Earl Godwin and successor of Edward the Confessor. His claim to the throne was disputed by William the Conqueror, who defeated him at the Battle of Hastings (1066).

harp (hɑːp) *n* **1** a large triangular plucked stringed instrument consisting of a soundboard connected to an upright pillar by means of a curved crossbar from which the strings extend downwards. ◆ *vb* (*intr*) **2** to play the harp. **3** (foll. by *on* or *upon*) to speak or write in a persistent and tedious manner. ORIG OE *hearpe*
▸ **'harper** *or* **'harpist** *n*

Harper's Ferry ★ ('hɑːpəz) *n* a village in NE West Virginia, at the confluence of the Potomac and Shenandoah Rivers: site of an arsenal seized by John Brown (1859). Pop.: 308 (1990).

harpoon (hɑː'puːn) *n* **1a** a barbed missile attached to a long cord and hurled or fired from a gun when hunting whales, etc. **1b** (*as modifier*): *a harpoon gun.* ◆ *vb* **2** (*tr*) to spear with or as if with a harpoon. ORIG C17: prob. from Du. *harpoen*, from OF *harpon* clasp, ? of Scand. origin
▸ **har'pooner** *or* **ˌharpoon'eer** *n*

harp seal *n* a brownish-grey North Atlantic and Arctic seal, having a dark mark on its back.

harpsichord ('hɑːpsɪˌkɔːd) *n* a horizontally strung stringed keyboard instrument, triangular in shape, with strings plucked by pivoted plectra mounted on jacks. ORIG C17: from NL *harpichordium*, from LL *harpa* HARP + L *chorda* CHORD[1]
▸ **'harpsiˌchordist** *n*

harpy ('hɑːpɪ) *n, pl* **harpies.** a cruel grasping woman. ORIG C16: from L *Harpyia*, from Gk *Harpuiai* the Harpies, lit.: snatchers, from *harpazein* to seize

Harpy ('hɑːpɪ) *n, pl* **Harpies.** *Greek myth.* a ravenous creature with a woman's head and trunk and a bird's wings and claws.

harquebus ('hɑːkwɪbəs) *n, pl* **harquebuses.** a variant spelling of **arquebus.**

Harrer ★ ('hɑːrə) *n* a variant spelling of **Harar.**

harridan ('hærɪdᵊn) *n* a scolding old woman; nag. ORIG C17: from ?; ? rel. to F *haridelle,* lit.: broken-down horse

harrier[1] ('hærɪə) *n* **1** a person or thing that harries. **2** a diurnal bird of prey having broad wings and long legs and tail.

harrier[2] ('hærɪə) *n* **1** a smallish breed of hound used originally for hare-hunting. **2** a cross-country runner. ORIG C16: from HARE + -ER[1]; infl. by HARRIER[1]

Harriman ★ ('hærɪmən) *n* **W(illiam) Averell.** 1891–1986, US diplomat: negotiated the Nuclear Test Ban Treaty with the Soviet Union (1963); governor of New York (1955–58).

Harris[1] ★ ('hærɪs) *n* the S part of the island of Lewis with Harris, in the Outer Hebrides. Pop.: (including Lewis) 23 390 (1981). Area: 500 sq. km (193 sq. miles).

Harris[2] ★ ('hærɪs) *n* **1** Sir **Arthur Travers,** known as *Bomber Harris.* 1892–1984, British air marshal. He was commander-in-chief of Bomber Command of the RAF (1942–45). **2 Frank.** 1856–1931, British writer and journalist; his books include his autobiography *My Life and Loves* (1923–27) and *Contemporary Portraits* (1915–30). **3 Joel Chandler.** 1848–1908, US writer; creator of Uncle Remus. **4 Roy.** 1898–1979, US composer, esp. of orchestral and choral music.

Harrisburg ★ ('hærɪsˌbɜːg) *n* a city in S Pennsylvania, on the Susquehanna River: the state capital. Pop.: 53 430 (1992 est.).

Harrison ★ ('hærɪsᵊn) *n* **1 Benjamin.** 1833–1901, 23rd president of the US (1889–93). **2 George.** born 1943, British rock singer, guitarist, and songwriter: a member of the Beatles (1962–70). **3 Rex (Carey).** 1908–90, British actor. His many films include *Major Barbara* (1940) and *My Fair Lady* (1964). **4 William Henry.** 1773–1841, 9th president of the US (1841); grandfather of Benjamin Harrison.

Harris Tweed *n Trademark.* a loose-woven tweed made in the Outer Hebrides.

Harrogate ★ ('hærəgɪt) *n* a town in N England, in North Yorkshire: a spa. Pop.: 66 178 (1991).

harrow ('hærəʊ) *n* **1** any of various implements used to level the ground, stir the soil, break up clods, destroy weeds, etc., in soil. ◆ *vb* (*tr*) **2** to draw a harrow over (land). **3** to distress; vex. ORIG C13: from ON
▸ **'harrower** *n* ▸ **'harrowing** *adj*

Harrow ★ ('hærəʊ) *n* a borough of NW Greater London; site of an English boys' public school founded in 1571 at **Harrow-on-the-Hill,** a part of this borough. Pop.: 210 300 (1994 est.). Area: 51 sq. km (20 sq. miles).
▸ **Harrovian** (hə'rəʊvɪən) *adj, n*

harrumph (hə'rʌmf) *vb* (*intr*) *Chiefly US & Canad.* to clear or make the noise of clearing the throat.

harry ('hærɪ) *vb* **harries, harrying, harried. 1** (*tr*) to harass; worry. **2** to ravage (a town, etc.), esp. in war. ORIG OE *hergian;* rel. to *here* army, ON *herja* to lay waste

harsh (hɑːʃ) *adj* **1** rough or grating to the senses. **2** stern, severe, or cruel. ORIG C16: prob. of Scand. origin
▸ **'harshly** *adv* ▸ **'harshness** *n*

hart (hɑːt) *n, pl* **harts** *or* **hart.** the male of the deer, esp. the red deer aged five years or more. ORIG OE *heorot*

Hart ★ (hɑːt) *n* **Lorenz** ('lɒrᵊnz). 1895–1943, US lyricist: collaborated with Richard Rodgers in writing musicals.

hartal (hɑː'tɑːl) *n* (in India) the act of closing shops or suspending work, esp. in political protest. ORIG C20: from Hindi *hartāl,* from *hāt* shop + *tālā* bolt for a door, from Sansk.

Harte ★ (hɑːt) *n* **(Francis) Bret.** 1836–1902, US writer, noted for his sketches of Californian gold miners, such as *The Luck of Roaring Camp* (1870).

hartebeest ('hɑːtɪˌbiːst) *or* **hartbeest** ('hɑːtˌbiːst) *n* either of two large African antelopes having an elongated muzzle, lyre-shaped horns, and a fawn-coloured coat. ORIG C18: via Afrik. from Du.; see HART, BEAST

Hartford ★ ('hɑːtfəd) *n* a port in central Connecticut, on the Connecticut River: the state capital. Pop.: 133 086 (1996 est.).

Harthacanute ('hɑːθəkəˌnjuːt), **Hardecanute,** *or* **Hardicanute** ★ *n* ?1019–42, king of Denmark (1035–42) and of England (1040–42); son of Canute.

Hartington ★ ('hɑːtɪŋtən) *n* **Lord.** See (8th Duke of) **Devonshire.**

Hartlepool ★ ('hɑːtlɪˌpuːl) *n* **1** a port in NE England, in Co. Durham, on the North Sea: greatly enlarged in 1967 by its amalgamation with West Hartlepool; engineering, clothing, food processing. Pop.: 87 310 (1991). **2** a unitary authority in NE England, in Co. Durham. Pop.: 92 100 (1996 est.). Area: 93 sq. km (36 sq. miles).

Hartley ★ ('hɑːtlɪ) *n* **1 David.** 1705–57, English philosopher and physician. In *Observations of Man* (1749) he introduced the theory of psychological associationism. **2 L(eslie) P(oles).** 1895–1972, British novelist. His novels include the trilogy *The Shrimp and the Anemone* (1944), *The Sixth Heaven* (1946), and *Eustace and Hilda* (1947).

Hartnell ★ ('hɑːtnᵊl) *n* Sir **Norman.** 1901–79, British couturier.

hartshorn ('hɑːtsˌhɔːn) *n* an obsolete name for **sal volatile.** ORIG OE *heortes horn* hart's horn (formerly a chief source of ammonia)

hart's-tongue *n* an evergreen Eurasian fern with narrow undivided fronds.

harum-scarum ('hɛərəm'skɛərəm) *adj, adv* **1** in a reckless way or of a reckless nature. ◆ *n* **2** a person who is impetuous or rash. ORIG C17: ?from *hare* (in obs. sense: harass) + *scare,* var. of STARE

Harun al-Rashid ★ (hæ'ruːn 'ælræ'ʃiːd) *n* ?763–809 A.D., Abbasid caliph of Islam (786–809), whose court at Baghdad was idealized in the *Arabian Nights.*

haruspex (hə'rʌspɛks) *n, pl* **haruspices** (hə'rʌspɪˌsiːz). (in ancient Rome) a priest who practised divination, esp. by examining the entrails of animals. ORIG C16: from L, prob. from *hīra* gut + *specere* to look
▸ **haruspicy** (hə'rʌspɪsɪ) *n*

harvest ('hɑːvɪst) *n* **1** the gathering of a ripened crop. **2** the crop itself. **3** the season for gathering crops. **4** the product of an effort, action, etc.: *a harvest of love.* ◆ *vb* **5** to gather (a ripened crop) from (the place where it has been growing). **6** (*tr*) to receive (consequences). ORIG OE *hærfest*
▸ **'harvesting** *n*

harvester ('hɑːvɪstə) *n* **1** a person who harvests. **2** a harvesting machine, esp. a combine harvester.

harvest home *n* **1** the bringing in of the harvest. **2** *Chiefly Brit.* a harvest supper.

harvestman ('hɑːvɪstmən) *n, pl* **harvestmen. 1** a person engaged in harvesting. **2** Also called (US and Canad.): **daddy-longlegs.** an arachnid having a small rounded body and very long thin legs.

harvest moon *n* the full moon occurring nearest to the autumnal equinox.

harvest mouse *n* a very small reddish-brown Eurasian mouse inhabiting cornfields, hedgerows, etc.

Harvey ★ ('hɑːvɪ) *n* **William.** 1578–1657, English physician who discovered the mechanism of blood circulation.

Harwell ★ ('hɑːˌwɛl) *n* a village in S England, in Oxfordshire: atomic research station (1947).

Harwich ★ ('hærɪtʃ) *n* a port in SE England, in NE Essex on the North Sea. Pop.: 18 436 (1991).

Haryana ★ (hər'jɑːnə) *n* a state of NE India, formed in 1966 from the Hindi-speaking parts of the state of Punjab. Capital: Chandigarh (shared with Punjab). Pop.: 17 925 000 (1994 est.). Area: 44 506 sq. km (17 182 sq. miles).

Harz *or* **Harz Mountains** ★ (hɑːts) *pl n* a range of wooded hills in central Germany, between the Rivers Weser and Elbe: source of many legends. Highest peak: Brocken, 1142 m (3746 ft).

has (hæz) *vb* (used with *he, she, it,* or a singular noun) a form of the present tense (indicative mood) of **have.**

has-been *n Inf.* a person or thing that is no longer popular, successful, effective, etc.

Hasdrubal ★ ('hæzdrʊbᵊl) *n* died 207 B.C., Carthaginian general: commanded the Carthaginian army in Spain

(218–211); joined his brother Hannibal in Italy and was killed at the Metaurus.

Hašek ★ (*Czech* 'haʃɛk) *n* **Jaroslav** ('jarɔslaf). 1883–1923, Czech novelist and short-story writer; author of *The Good Soldier Schweik* (1923).

hash[1] (hæʃ) *n* **1** a dish of diced cooked meat, vegetables, etc., reheated in a sauce. **2** a reuse or rework of old material. **3 make a hash of.** *Inf.* to mess up or destroy. **4 settle someone's hash.** *Inf.* to subdue or silence someone. ◆ *vb* (*tr*) **5** to chop into small pieces. **6** to mess up. ORIG C17: from OF *hacher* to chop up, from *hache* HATCHET

hash[2] (hæʃ) *n Sl.* short for **hashish.**

Hashemite Kingdom of Jordan ★ ('hæʃɪˌmaɪt) *n* the official name of **Jordan.**

hashish ('hæʃiːʃ, -ɪʃ) *or* **hasheesh** *n* a resinous extract of the dried flower tops of the female hemp plant, used as a hallucinogenic. See also **cannabis.** ORIG C16: from Ar. *hashīsh* hemp

haslet ('hæzlɪt) *or* **harslet** *n* a loaf of cooked minced pig's offal, eaten cold. ORIG C14: from OF *hastelet* piece of spit-roasted meat, from *haste* spit, of Gmc origin

hasn't ('hæzᵊnt) *contraction of* has not.

hasp (hɑːsp) *n* **1** a metal fastening consisting of a hinged strap with a slot that fits over a staple and is secured by a pin, bolt, or padlock. ◆ *vb* **2** (*tr*) to secure (a door, window, etc.) with a hasp. ORIG OE *hæpse*

Hassan II ★ (hæ'sɑːn, 'hæsᵊn) *n* 1929–99, king of Morocco (1961–99).

Hasselt ★ (*Flemish* 'hɑsəlt; *French* asɛlt) *n* a market town in E Belgium, capital of Limbourg province. Pop.: 67 486 (1995 est.).

Hassid ('hæsɪd) *n* a variant spelling of **Chassid.**

hassium ('hæsɪəm) *n* a synthetic element produced in small quantities by high-energy ion bombardment. Symbol: Hs; atomic no. 108. Former name: **hahnium.** ORIG C20: from L, from HESSE[1], German state where it was discovered

hassle ('hæsᵊl) *Inf.* ◆ *n* **1** a great deal of trouble. **2** a prolonged argument. ◆ *vb* **hassles, hassling, hassled. 3** (*tr*) to cause annoyance or trouble to (someone); harass. **4** (*intr*) to quarrel or wrangle. ORIG C20: from ?

hassock ('hæsək) *n* **1** a firm upholstered cushion used for kneeling on, esp. in church. **2** a thick clump of grass. ORIG OE *hassuc* matted grass

hast (hæst) *vb Arch. or dialect.* (used with the pronoun *thou*) a singular form of the present tense (indicative mood) of **have.**

hastate ('hæsteɪt) *adj* (of a leaf) having a pointed tip and two outward-pointing lobes at the base. ORIG C18: from L *hastātus,* from *hasta* spear

haste (heɪst) *n* **1** speed, esp. in an action. **2** the act of hurrying in a careless manner. **3** a necessity for hurrying; urgency. **4 make haste.** to hurry. ◆ *vb* **hastes, hasting, hasted. 5** a poetic word for **hasten.** ORIG C14: from OF *haste,* of Gmc origin

hasten ('heɪsᵊn) *vb* **1** (*may take an infinitive*) to hurry or cause to hurry; rush. **2** (*tr*) to be anxious (to say something).
▸ **'hastener** *n*

Hastings[1] ★ ('heɪstɪŋz) *n* **1** a port in SE England, in East Sussex on the English Channel: near the site of the **Battle of Hastings** (1066), in which William the Conqueror defeated King Harold; chief of the Cinque Ports. Pop.: 81 139 (1991). **2** a town in New Zealand, on E North Island: centre of a rich agricultural and fruit-growing region. Pop. (urban area): 58 700 (1995 est.).

Hastings[2] ★ ('heɪstɪŋz) *n* **Warren.** 1732–1818, British administrator in India; governor general of Bengal (1773–85). He was impeached by parliament (1788) on charges of corruption; acquitted in 1795.

hasty ('heɪstɪ) *adj* **hastier, hastiest. 1** rapid; swift; quick. **2** excessively or rashly quick. **3** short-tempered. **4** showing irritation or anger: *hasty words.*
▸ **'hastily** *adv* ▸ **'hastiness** *n*

hat (hæt) *n* **1** a head covering, esp. one with a brim and a shaped crown. **2** *Inf.* a role or capacity. **3 I'll eat my hat.** *Inf.* I will be greatly surprised if (something that proves me wrong) happens. **4 keep (something) under one's hat.** to keep (something) secret. **5 pass** (*or* **send**) **the hat round.** to collect money, as for a cause. **6 take off one's hat to.** to admire or congratulate. **7 talk through one's hat. 7a** to talk foolishly. **7b** to deceive or bluff. ◆ *vb* **hats, hatting, hatted. 8** (*tr*) to supply (a person, etc.) with a hat or put a hat on (someone). ORIG OE *hætt*
▸ **'hatless** *adj*

hatband ('hætˌbænd) *n* a band or ribbon around the base of the crown of a hat.

hatbox ('hætˌbɒks) *n* a box or case for a hat.

hatch[1] (hætʃ) *vb* **1** to cause (the young of various animals, esp. birds) to emerge from the egg or (of young birds, etc.) to emerge from the egg. **2** to cause (eggs) to break and release the fully developed young or (of eggs) to break and release the young animal within. **3** (*tr*) to contrive or devise (a scheme, plot, etc.). ◆ *n* **4** the act or process of hatching. **5** a group of newly hatched animals. ORIG C13: of Gmc origin

hatch[2] (hætʃ) *n* **1** a covering for a hatchway. **2a** short for **hatchway. 2b** a door in an aircraft or spacecraft. **3** Also called: **serving hatch.** an opening in a wall separating a kitchen from a dining area. **4** the lower half of a divided door. **5** a sluice in a dam, dyke, or weir. **6 down the hatch.** *Sl.* (used as a toast) drink up! **7 under hatches. 7a** below decks. **7b** out of sight. **7c** dead. ORIG OE *hæcc*

hatch[3] (hætʃ) *vb Drawing, engraving, etc.* to mark (a figure, etc.) with fine parallel or crossed lines to indicate shading. ORIG C15: from OF *hacher* to chop, from *hache* HATCHET
▸ **'hatching** *n*

hatch[4] (hætʃ) *n Inf.* short for **hatchback.**

hatchback ('hætʃˌbæk) *n* **1** a sloping rear end of a car having a single door that is lifted to open. **2** a car having such a rear end.

hatchery ('hætʃərɪ) *n, pl* **hatcheries.** a place where eggs are hatched under artificial conditions.

hatchet ('hætʃɪt) *n* **1** a short axe used for chopping wood, etc. **2** a tomahawk. **3** (*modifier*) of narrow dimensions and sharp features: *a hatchet face.* **4 bury the hatchet.** to cease hostilities and become reconciled. ORIG C14: from OF *hachette,* from *hache* axe, of Gmc origin

hatchet job *n Inf.* a malicious or devastating verbal or written attack.

hatchet man *n Inf.* **1** a person carrying out unpleasant assignments for an employer or superior. **2** a severe or malicious critic.

hatchling ('hætʃlɪŋ) *n* a young animal that has newly emerged from the egg. ORIG C19: from HATCH[1] + -LING[1]

hatchment ('hætʃmənt) *n Heraldry.* a diamond-shaped tablet displaying the coat of arms of a dead person. ORIG C16: changed from earlier use of *achievement* in this sense

hatchway ('hætʃˌweɪ) *n* **1** an opening in the deck of a vessel to provide access below. **2** a similar opening in a wall, floor, ceiling, or roof.

hate (heɪt) *vb* **hates, hating, hated. 1** to dislike (something) intensely; detest. **2** (*intr*) to be unwilling (to be or do something). ◆ *n* **3** intense dislike. **4** *Inf.* a person or thing that is hated (esp. in **pet hate**). **5** (*modifier*) expressing or arousing feelings of hatred: *hate mail.* ORIG OE *hatian*
▸ **'hateable** *or* **'hatable** *adj* ▸ **'hater** *n*

hateful ('heɪtfʊl) *adj* **1** causing or deserving hate; loathsome; detestable. **2** *Arch.* full of hate.
▸ **'hatefully** *adv* ▸ **'hatefulness** *n*

Hatfield ★ ('hætˌfiːld) *n* a market town in S central England, in Hertfordshire, with a new town of the same name built on the outskirts; seat of the University of Hertfordshire (1992). Pop.: 31 104 (1991).

hath (hæθ) *vb Arch. or dialect.* (used with the pronouns *he, she,* or *it* or a singular noun) a form of the present tense (indicative mood) of **have.**

Hathaway ★ ('hæθəˌweɪ) *n* **Anne.** ?1557–1623, wife of William Shakespeare.

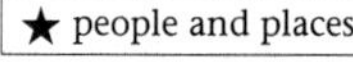

Hathor ★ ('hæθɔ:) *n* (in ancient Egyptian religion) the mother of Horus and goddess of creation.
▸ **Hathoric** (hæ'θɔ:rɪk, -'θɒr-) *adj*

hatred ('heɪtrɪd) *n* intense dislike; enmity.

Hatshepsut (hæt'ʃɛpsu:t) *or* **Hatshepset** ★ *n* queen of Egypt of the 18th dynasty (?1512–1482 B.C.), who built a temple at Deir el Bahri near Thebes.

hat stand *or esp. US* **hat tree** *n* a pole equipped with hooks for hanging up hats, etc.

hatter ('hætə) *n* **1** a person who makes and sells hats. **2** **mad as a hatter.** eccentric.

Hatteras ★ ('hætərəs) *n* **Cape.** a promontory off the E coast of North Carolina, on **Hatteras Island,** which is situated between Pamlico Sound and the Atlantic: known as the "Graveyard of the Atlantic" for its danger to shipping.

Hattersley ★ ('hætəzlɪ) *n* **Roy** (**Sydney George**), Baron Hattersley of Sparkbrook. born 1932, British Labour politician; deputy leader of the Labour Party (1983–92), shadow home secretary (1987–92).

hat trick *n* **1** *Cricket.* the achievement of a bowler in taking three wickets with three successive balls. **2** any achievement of three successive points, victories, etc.

hauberk ('hɔ:bɜ:k) *n* a long coat of mail, often sleeveless. ORIG C13: from OF *hauberc,* of Gmc origin; cf. OHG *halsberc,* OE *healsbeorg,* from *heals* neck + *beorg* protection

Haughey ★ ('hɔ:xɪ; *Irish* 'hʌhi:) *n* **Charles James.** born 1925, Irish politician; leader of the Fianna Fáil party; prime minister of the Republic of Ireland (1979–81; 1982; 1987–92).

haughty ('hɔ:tɪ) *adj* **haughtier, haughtiest.** having or showing arrogance. ORIG C16: from OF *haut* lofty, from L *altus* high
▸ **'haughtily** *adv* ▸ **'haughtiness** *n*

haul (hɔ:l) *vb* **1** to drag (something) with effort. **2** (*tr*) to transport, as in a lorry. **3** *Naut.* to alter the course of (a vessel), esp. so as to sail closer to the wind. **4** (*intr*) *Naut.* (of the wind) to blow from a direction nearer the bow. ◆ *n* **5** the act of dragging with effort. **6** (esp. of fish) the amount caught at a single time. **7** something that is hauled. **8** the goods obtained from a robbery. **9** a distance of hauling or travelling. **10** the amount of a contraband seizure: *arms haul, drugs haul.* ORIG C16: from OF *haler,* of Gmc origin
▸ **'hauler** *n*

haulage ('hɔ:lɪdʒ) *n* **1** the act or labour of hauling. **2** a rate or charge levied for the transportation of goods, esp. by rail.

haulier ('hɔ:ljə) *n* **1** *Brit.* a person or firm that transports goods by road. **2** a mine worker who conveys coal from the workings to the foot of the shaft.

haulm *or* **halm** (hɔ:m) *n* **1** the stalks of beans, peas, potatoes, grasses, etc., collectively. **2** a single stem of such a plant. ORIG OE *healm*

haul up *vb* (*adv*) **1** (*tr*) *Inf.* to call to account or criticize. **2** *Naut.* to sail (a vessel) closer to the wind.

haunch (hɔ:ntʃ) *n* **1** the human hip or fleshy hindquarter of an animal. **2** the leg and loin of an animal, used for food. **3** *Archit.* the part of an arch between the impost and apex. ORIG C13: from OF *hanche;* rel. to Sp., It. *anca,* of Gmc origin

haunt (hɔ:nt) *vb* **1** to visit (a person or place) in the form of a ghost. **2** (*tr*) to recur to (the memory, thoughts, etc.): *he was haunted by the fear of insanity.* **3** to visit (a place) frequently. **4** to associate with (someone) frequently. ◆ *n* **5** (*often pl*) a place visited frequently. **6** a place to which animals habitually resort for food, drink, shelter, etc. ORIG C13: from OF *hanter,* of Gmc origin

haunted ('hɔ:ntɪd) *adj* **1** frequented or visited by ghosts. **2** (*postpositive*) obsessed or worried.

haunting ('hɔ:ntɪŋ) *adj* **1** (of memories) poignant or persistent. **2** poignantly sentimental; eerily evocative.
▸ **'hauntingly** *adv*

Hauptmann ★ (*German* 'hauptman) *n* **Gerhart** ('ge:rhart). 1862–1946, German naturalist and writer. His works include the drama *The Weavers* (1892): Nobel prize for literature 1912.

Hauraki Gulf ★ (hau'rækɪ) *n* an inlet of the Pacific in New Zealand, on the N coast of North Island.

Hausa ('hausə) *n* **1** (*pl* **Hausas** *or* **Hausa**) a member of a Negroid people of W Africa, living chiefly in N Nigeria. **2** the language of this people, widely used as a trading language throughout W Africa.

hausfrau ('haus,frau) *n* a German housewife. ORIG G, from *Haus* house + *Frau* woman, wife

Haussmann ★ (*French* osman) *n* **Georges-Eugène** (ʒɔrʒøʒɛn), Baron. 1809–91, French town planner, noted for his rebuilding of Paris.

hautboy ('əubɔɪ) *n* **1** a strawberry with large fruit. **2** an archaic word for **oboe.** ORIG C16: from F *hautbois,* from *haut* high + *bois* wood, of Gmc origin

haute couture *French.* (ot kutyr) *n* high fashion. ORIG lit.: high dressmaking

haute cuisine *French.* (ot kwizin) *n* high-class cooking. ORIG lit.: high cookery

haute école *French.* (ot ekɔl) *n* the classical art of riding. ORIG lit.: high school

Haute-Garonne ★ (*French* otgarɔn) *n* a department of SW France, in Midi-Pyrénées region. Capital: Toulouse. Pop.: 985 030 (1994 est.). Area: 6367 sq. km (2483 sq. miles).

Haute-Loire ★ (*French* otlwar) *n* a department of S central France, in Auvergne region. Capital: Le Puy. Pop.: 206 578 (1994 est.). Area: 5001 sq. km (1950 sq. miles).

Haute-Marne ★ (*French* otmarn) *n* a department of NE France, in Champagne-Ardenne region. Capital: Chaumont. Pop.: 200 240 (1994 est.). Area: 6257 sq. km (2440 sq. miles).

Haute-Normandie ★ (*French* otnɔrmɑ̃di) *n* a region of NW France, on the English Channel: generally fertile and flat. Pop.: 1 773 704 (1994 est.).

Hautes-Alpes ★ (*French* otzalp) *n* a department of SE France in Provence-Alpes-Côte d'Azur region. Capital: Gap. Pop.: 118 220 (1994 est.). Area: 5643 sq. km (2201 sq. miles).

Haute-Saône ★ (*French* otson) *n* a department of E France, in Franche-Comté region. Capital: Vesoul. Pop.: 229 448 (1994 est.). Area: 5375 sq. km (2096 sq. miles).

Haute-Savoie ★ (*French* otsavwa) *n* a department of E France, in Rhône-Alpes region. Capital: Annecy. Pop.: 613 176 (1994 est.). Area: 4958 sq. km (1934 sq. miles).

Hautes-Pyrénées ★ (*French* otpirene) *n* a department of SW France, in Midi-Pyrénées region. Capital: Tarbes. Pop.: 223 840 (1994 est.). Area: 4534 sq. km (1768 sq. miles).

hauteur (əu'tɜ:) *n* pride; haughtiness. ORIG C17: from F, from *haut* high; see HAUGHTY

Haute-Vienne ★ (*French* otvjɛn) *n* a department of W central France, in Limousin region. Capital: Limoges. Pop.: 355 524 (1994 est.). Area: 5555 sq. km (2166 sq. miles).

haut monde *French.* (o mɔ̃d) *n* high society. ORIG lit.: high world

Haut-Rhin ★ (*French* orɛ̃) *n* a department of E France in Alsace region. Capital: Colmar. Pop.: 693 135 (1994 est.). Area: 3566 sq. km (1377 sq. miles).

Hauts-de-Seine ★ (*French* odəsɛn) *n* a department of N central France, in Île-de-France region just west of Paris: formed in 1964. Capital: Nanterre. Pop.: 1 403 463 (1994 est.). Area: 175 sq. km (68 sq. miles).

Havana ★ (hə'vænə) *n* the capital of Cuba, a port in the northwest on the Gulf of Mexico: the largest city in the Caribbean, founded in 1514 as San Cristóbal de la Habana by Diego Velásquez. Pop.: 2 241 000 (1995 est.). Spanish name: **Habana.**

Havana cigar *n* any of various cigars manufactured in Cuba, known esp. for their high quality. Also: **Havana.**

Havant ★ ('hævᵊnt) *n* a market town in S England, in SE Hampshire. Pop.: 46 510 (1991).

have (hæv) *vb* **has, having, had.** (*mainly tr*) **1** to be in possession of; own: *he has two cars.* **2** to possess as a quality or attribute: *he has dark hair.* **3** to receive, take, or obtain: *she had a present; have a look.* **4** to hold in the mind: *to have an* idea. **5** to possess a knowledge of: *I have no German.* **6** to experience: *to have a shock.* **7** to suffer from: *to have a cold.* **8** to gain control of or advantage over: *you have me on that point.* **9** (*usually passive*) *Sl.* to cheat or outwit: *he was had by that dishonest salesman.* **10** (foll. by *on*) to exhibit (mercy, etc., towards). **11** to take part in: *to have a conversation.* **12** to arrange or hold: *to have a party.* **13** to cause, compel, or require to (be, do, or be done): *have my shoes mended.* **14** (takes an infinitive with *to*) used as an auxiliary to express compulsion or necessity: *I had to run quickly to escape him.* **15** to eat, drink, or partake of. **16** *Taboo sl.* to have sexual intercourse with. **17** (*used with a negative*) to tolerate or allow: *I won't have all this noise.* **18** to state or assert: *rumour has it that they will marry.* **19** to place: *I'll have the sofa in this room.* **20** to receive as a guest: *to have people to stay.* **21** to be pregnant with or bear (offspring). **22** (*takes a past participle*) used as an auxiliary to form compound tenses expressing completed action: *I have gone; I had gone.* **23 had rather** *or* **sooner.** to consider preferable that: *I had rather you left at once.* **24 have had it.** *Inf.* **24a** to be exhausted, defeated, or killed. **24b** to have lost one's last chance. **24c** to become unfashionable. **25 have it away** (*or* **off**). *Taboo, Brit. sl.* to have sexual intercourse. **26 have it so good.** to have so many material benefits. **27 have to do with. 27a** to have dealings with. **27b** to be of relevance to. **28 let (someone) have it.** *Sl.* to launch an attack on (someone). ◆ *n* **29** (*usually pl*) *Inf.* a person or group in possession of wealth, security, etc.: *the haves and the have-nots.* ◆ See also **have at, have on,** etc. ORIG OE *habban*

have-a-go *adj Inf.* (of members of the public at the scene of a crime) intervening physically in an attempt to catch or thwart a criminal, esp. one who is armed: *a have-a-go pensioner.*

have at *vb* (*intr, prep*) *Arch.* to make an opening attack on, esp. in fencing.

Havel[1] ★ (*German* 'ha:fəl) *n* a river in E Germany, flowing south to Berlin, then west and north to join the River Elbe. Length: about 362 km (225 miles).

Havel[2] ★ (*Czech* 'havɛl) *n* **Václav** ('va:tslaf). born 1936, Czech dramatist and statesman: founder of the Civil Forum movement for political change: president of Czechoslovakia (1990–93; president of the Czech Republic from 1993. His plays include *Redevelopment* (1989).

havelock ('hævlɒk) *n* a light-coloured cover for a service cap with a flap extending over the back of the neck to protect the head and neck from the sun. ORIG C19: after Sir H. *Havelock* (1795–1857), E general in India

haven ('heɪvᵊn) *n* **1** a harbour or other sheltered place for shipping. **2** a place of safety; shelter. ◆ *vb* **3** (*tr*) to shelter as in a haven. ORIG OE *hæfen,* from ON *höfn*

have-not *n* (*usually pl*) a person or group in possession of relatively little material wealth.

haven't ('hævᵊnt) *contraction of* have not.

have on *vb* (*tr*) **1** (*usually adv*) to wear. **2** (*usually adv*) to have a commitment: *what does your boss have on this afternoon?* **3** (*adv*) *Inf.* to trick or tease (a person). **4** (*prep*) to have available (information, esp. when incriminating) about (a person).

have out *vb* (*tr, adv*) **1** to settle (a matter) or come to (a final decision), esp. by fighting or by frank discussion (often in **have it out**). **2** to have extracted or removed.

haver ('heɪvə) *vb* (*intr*) **1** *Scot. & N English dialect.* to babble; talk nonsense. **2** to dither. ◆ *n* **3** (*usually pl*) *Scot.* nonsense. ORIG C18: from ?

Havering ★ ('heɪvərɪŋ) *n* a borough of NE Greater London, formed in 1965 from Romford and Hornchurch (both previously in Essex). Pop.: 231 700 (1994 est.). Area: 120 sq. km (46 sq. miles).

haversack ('hævəˌsæk) *n* a canvas bag for provisions or equipment, carried on the back or shoulder. ORIG C18: from F *havresac,* from G *Habersack* oat bag, from OHG *habaro* oats + *Sack* SACK[1]

haversine ('hævəˌsaɪn) *n* half the value of the versed sine. ORIG C19: combination of *half* + *versed* + *sine*[1]

have up *vb* (*tr, adv; usually passive*) to cause to appear for trial: *he was had up for breaking and entering.*

havildar ('hævɪlˌdɑ:) *n* a noncommissioned officer in the Indian army, equivalent in rank to sergeant. ORIG C17: from Hindi, from Persian *hawāldār* one in charge

havoc ('hævək) *n* **1** destruction; devastation; ruin. **2** *Inf.* confusion; chaos. **3 cry havoc.** *Arch.* to give the signal for pillage and destruction. **4 play havoc.** (often foll. by *with*) to cause a great deal of damage, distress, or confusion (to). ORIG C15: from OF *havot* pillage, prob. of Gmc origin

Havre ★ ('hɑ:vrə; *French* ɑvrə) *n* See **Le Havre.**

haw[1] (hɔ:) *n* **1** the fruit of the hawthorn. **2** another name for **hawthorn.** ORIG OE *haga,* identical with *haga* hedge

haw[2] (hɔ:) *n, interj* **1** an inarticulate utterance, as of hesitation, embarrassment, etc.; hem. ◆ *vb* **2** (*intr*) to make this sound. ORIG C17: imit.

haw[3] (hɔ:) *n* the nictitating membrane of a horse or other domestic animal. ORIG C15: from ?

Hawaii ★ (hə'waɪɪ) *n* a state of the US in the central Pacific, consisting of over 20 volcanic islands and atolls, including Hawaii, Maui, Oahu, Kauai, and Molokai: discovered by Captain Cook in 1778; annexed by the US in 1898; naval base at Pearl Harbor attacked by the Japanese in 1941, a major cause of US entry into World War II; became a state in 1959. Capital: Honolulu. Pop.: 1 193 001 (1998 est.). Area: 16 640 sq. km (6425 sq. miles). Former name: **Sandwich Islands.** Abbrevs: **Ha.** or (with zip code) **HI**
▸ **Ha'waiian** *adj, n*

Hawaiki ★ ('hɑ:waɪki:) *n NZ.* a legendary Pacific island from which the Maoris migrated to New Zealand by canoe. ORIG Maori

Hawes Water ★ (hɔ:z) *n* a lake in NW England, in the Lake District: provides part of Manchester's water supply; extended by damming from 4 km (2.5 miles) to 6 km (4 miles).

hawfinch ('hɔ:ˌfɪntʃ) *n* an uncommon European finch having a very stout bill.

Haw-Haw ★ ('hɔ:ˌhɔ:) *n* **Lord.** See (William) **Joyce.**

Hawick ★ ('hɔ:ɪk) *n* a town in SE Scotland, in S central Scottish Borders: knitwear industry. Pop.: 15 812 (1991).

hawk[1] (hɔ:k) *n* **1** any of various diurnal birds of prey of the family Accipitridae, typically having short rounded wings and a long tail. **2** a person who advocates or supports war or warlike policies. Cf. **dove** (sense 2). **3** a ruthless or rapacious person. ◆ *vb* **4** (*intr*) to hunt with falcons, hawks, etc. **5** (*intr*) (of falcons or hawks) to fly in quest of prey. **6** to pursue or attack on the wing, as a hawk. ORIG OE *hafoc*
▸ **'hawking** *n* ▸ **'hawkish** *adj* ▸ **'hawkˌlike** *adj*

hawk[2] (hɔ:k) *vb* **1** to offer (goods) for sale, as in the street. **2** (*tr;* often foll. by *about*) to spread (news, gossip, etc.). ORIG C16: back formation from HAWKER[1]

hawk[3] (hɔ:k) *vb* **1** (*intr*) to clear the throat noisily. **2** (*tr*) to force (phlegm, etc.) up from the throat. ORIG C16: imit.

hawk[4] (hɔ:k) *n* a small square board with a handle underneath, for carrying wet mortar. Also called: **mortarboard.** ORIG from ?

Hawke ★ (hɔ:k) *n* **Robert (James Lee),** known as *Bob.* born 1929, Australian statesman; prime minister of Australia (1983–91).

hawker[1] ('hɔ:kə) *n* a person who travels from place to place selling goods. ORIG C16: prob. from MLow G *hōker,* from *hōken* to peddle; see HUCKSTER

hawker[2] ('hɔ:kə) *n* a person who hunts with hawks, falcons, etc. ORIG OE *hafecere*

hawk-eyed *adj* **1** having extremely keen sight. **2** vigilant, watchful, or observant.

Hawking ★ ('hɔ:kɪŋ) *n* **Stephen William.** born 1942, British physicist. Stricken with a progressive nervous disease since the 1960s, he has nevertheless been a leader in cosmological theory. His *A Brief History of Time* (1987) was a bestseller.

Hawkins ★ ('hɔ:kɪnz) *n* **1 Coleman.** 1904–69, US jazz saxophonist. **2** Sir **John.** 1532–95, English naval commander and slave trader, treasurer of the navy (1577–89); commander of a squadron in the fleet that defeated the Spanish Armada (1588).

hawk moth *n* any of various moths having long narrow wings and powerful flight, with the ability to hover over flowers when feeding from the nectar.

Hawks ★ (hɔːks) *n* **Howard (Winchester)**. 1896–1977, US film director. His films include *Sergeant York* (1941) and *The Big Sleep* (1946).

hawksbill turtle *or* **hawksbill** (ˈhɔːksˌbɪl) *n* a small tropical turtle with a hooked beaklike mouth: a source of tortoiseshell.

Hawksmoor ★ (ˈhɔːksˌmɔː) *n* **Nicholas.** 1661–1736, English architect. His designs include All Souls', Oxford, and a number of London churches.

hawkweed (ˈhɔːkˌwiːd) *n* a hairy plant with clusters of dandelion-like flowers.

Haworth[1] ★ (ˈhaʊəθ) *n* a village in N England, in West Yorkshire: home of Charlotte, Emily, and Anne Brontë. Pop.: 4956 (1991).

Haworth[2] ★ (ˈhaʊəθ) *n* Sir **Walter Norman.** 1883–1950, British biochemist, who shared the Nobel prize for chemistry (1937) for synthesizing ascorbic acid (vitamin C).

hawse (hɔːz) *n Naut.* **1** the part of the bows of a vessel where the hawseholes are. **2** short for **hawsehole** or **hawsepipe. 3** the distance from the bow of an anchored vessel to the anchor. **4** the arrangement of port and starboard anchor ropes when a vessel is riding on both anchors. ORIG C14: from earlier *halse,* prob. from ON *háls* neck, ship's bow

hawsehole (ˈhɔːzˌhəʊl) *n Naut.* one of the holes in the upper part of the bows of a vessel through which the anchor ropes pass.

hawsepipe (ˈhɔːzˌpaɪp) *n Naut.* a strong metal pipe through which an anchor rope passes.

hawser (ˈhɔːzə) *n Naut.* a large heavy rope. ORIG C14: from Anglo-F *hauceour,* from OF *haucier* to hoist, ult. from L *altus* high

hawthorn (ˈhɔːˌθɔːn) *n* any of various thorny trees or shrubs of a N temperate genus, having white or pink flowers and reddish fruits (haws). Also called (in Britain): **may, may tree, mayflower.** ORIG OE *haguthorn,* from *haga* hedge + *thorn* thorn

Hawthorne ★ ((ˈhɔːˌθɔːn) *n* **Nathaniel.** US novelist and short-story writer: his works include the novels *The Scarlet Letter* (1850) and *The House of the Seven Gables* (1851) and the children's stories *Tanglewood Tales* (1853).

hay (heɪ) *n* **1a** grass, clover, etc., cut and dried as fodder. **1b** (*in combination*): *a hayfield.* **2 hit the hay.** *Sl.* to go to bed. **3 make hay of.** to throw into confusion. **4 make hay while the sun shines.** to take full advantage of an opportunity. **5 roll in the hay.** *Inf.* sexual intercourse or heavy petting. ◆ *vb* **6** to cut, dry, and store (grass, etc.) as fodder. ORIG OE *hieg*

Hay ★ (heɪ) *n* **Will.** 1888–1949, British music-hall comedian, who later starred in films, such as *Oh, Mr Porter!* (1937).

haybox (ˈheɪˌbɒks) *n* an airtight box full of hay used for cooking preheated food by retained heat.

haycock (ˈheɪˌkɒk) *n* a small cone-shaped pile of hay left in the field until dry.

Haydn ★ (ˈhaɪdᵊn) *n* **1 (Franz) Joseph** (*German* ˈjoːzɛf). 1732–1809, Austrian composer. His works include the oratorios *The Creation* (1796–98) and *The Seasons* (1798–1801), 104 symphonies, piano music, and string quartets. **2** his brother, **(Johann) Michael** (*German* ˈmɪçael). 1737–1806, Austrian composer, esp. of Church music.

Hayek ★ (ˈhaɪɛk) *n* **Friedrich August von** (*German* ˈfriːdrɪç ˈaʊgʊst fɔn). 1899–1992, British economist and political philosopher, born in Austria; shared the Nobel prize for economics 1974.

Hayes ★ (heɪz) *n* **Rutherford B(irchard).** 1822–93, 19th president of the US (1877–81).

hay fever *n* an allergic reaction to pollen, dust, etc., characterized by sneezing, runny nose, and watery eyes due to inflammation of the mucous membranes of the eyes and nose.

haymaker (ˈheɪˌmeɪkə) *n* **1** a person who helps to cut, turn, or carry hay. **2** either of two machines, one designed to crush stems of hay, the other to break and bend them, in order to cause more rapid and even drying. **3** *Boxing sl.* a wild swinging punch.
▸ **ˈhayˌmaking** *adj, n*

haymow (ˈheɪˌmaʊ) *n* **1** a part of a barn where hay is stored. **2** a quantity of hay stored.

hayseed (ˈheɪˌsiːd) *n* **1** seeds or fragments of grass or straw. **2** *US & Canad. inf., derog.* a yokel.

haystack (ˈheɪˌstæk) *or* **hayrick** *n* a large pile of hay, esp. one built in the open air and covered with thatch.

haywire (ˈheɪˌwaɪə) *adj* (*postpositive*) *Inf.* **1** (of things) not functioning properly. **2** (of people) erratic or crazy. ORIG C20: from the disorderly tangle of wire removed from bales of hay

hazard (ˈhæzəd) *n* **1** exposure or vulnerability to injury, loss, etc. **2 at hazard.** at risk; in danger. **3** a thing likely to cause injury, etc. **4** *Golf.* an obstacle such as a bunker, a road, rough, water, etc. **5** chance; accident. **6** a gambling game played with two dice. **7** *Real Tennis.* **7a** the receiver's side of the court. **7b** one of the winning openings. **8** *Billiards.* a scoring stroke made either when a ball other than the striker's is pocketed (**winning hazard**) or the striker's cue ball itself (**losing hazard**). ◆ *vb* (*tr*) **9** to risk. **10** to venture (an opinion, guess, etc.). **11** to expose to danger. ORIG C13: from OF *hasard,* from Ar. *az-zahr* the die

hazard lights *pl n* the indicator lights of a motor vehicle when flashing simultaneously to indicate that the vehicle is stationary and temporarily obstructing the traffic. Also called: **hazard warning lights, hazards.**

hazardous (ˈhæzədəs) *adj* **1** involving great risk. **2** depending on chance.
▸ **ˈhazardously** *adv* ▸ **ˈhazardousness** *n*

hazard warning device *n* an appliance fitted to a motor vehicle that operates the hazard lights.

haze[1] (heɪz) *n* **1** *Meteorol.* reduced visibility in the air as a result of condensed water vapour, dust, etc., in the atmosphere. **2** obscurity of perception, feeling, etc. ◆ *vb* **hazes, hazing, hazed. 3** (when *intr,* often foll. by *over*) to make or become hazy. ORIG C18: back formation from HAZY

haze[2] (heɪz) *vb* **hazes, hazing, hazed.** (*tr*) **1** *Chiefly US & Canad.* to subject (fellow students) to ridicule or abuse. **2** *Naut.* to harass with humiliating tasks. ORIG C17: from ?

hazel (ˈheɪzᵊl) *n* **1** Also called: **cob.** any of several shrubs of a N temperate genus, having edible rounded nuts. **2** the wood of any of these trees. **3** short for **hazelnut. 4a** a light yellowish-brown colour. **4b** (*as adj*): *hazel eyes.* ORIG OE *hæsel*

hazelhen (ˈheɪzᵊlˌhɛn) *n* a European woodland gallinaceous bird with a speckled brown plumage and slightly crested crown.

hazelnut (ˈheɪzᵊlˌnʌt) *n* the nut of a hazel shrub, having a smooth shiny hard shell. Also called: **filbert,** (Brit.) **cobnut, cob.**

Hazlitt ★ (ˈhæzlɪt) *n* **William.** 1778–1830, British critic and essayist: works include *Table Talk* (1821) and *The Plain Speaker* (1826).

hazy (ˈheɪzɪ) *adj* **hazier, haziest.** misty; indistinct; vague. ORIG C17: from ?
▸ **ˈhazily** *adv* ▸ **ˈhaziness** *n*

Hb *symbol for* haemoglobin.

HB (on Brit. pencils) *symbol for* hard-black: denoting a medium-hard lead.

HBC *abbrev. for* Hudson's Bay Company.

HBM (in Britain) *abbrev. for* His (*or* Her) Britannic Majesty.

H-bomb *n* short for **hydrogen bomb.**

HC *abbrev. for:* **1** Holy Communion. **2** (in Britain) House of Commons.

HCF *or* **hcf** *abbrev. for* highest common factor.

HCG *abbrev. for* human chorionic gonadotrophin; a hormone produced by the placenta during pregnancy: its presence in the urine is used as the basis of most pregnancy tests.

hcp *abbrev. for* handicap.

HD *abbrev. for* heavy duty.

hdqrs *abbrev. for* headquarters.

HDTV *abbrev. for* high definition television.

he (hiː; *unstressed* iː) *pron* (*subjective*) **1** refers to a male person or animal. **2** refers to an indefinite antecedent such as *whoever* or *anybody: everybody can do as he likes.* **3** refers to a person or animal of unknown or unspecified sex: *a member may vote as he sees fit.* ◆ *n* **4a** a male person or animal. **4b** (*in combination*): *he-goat.* **5** (in children's play) another name for **tag**[2] (sense 1), **it** (sense 7). ORIG OE *hē*

He *the chemical symbol for* helium.

HE *abbrev. for:* **1** high explosive. **2** His Eminence. **3** His (*or* Her) Excellency.

head (hɛd) *n* **1** the upper or front part of the body in vertebrates, including man, that contains and protects the brain, eyes, mouth, nose, and ears. Related adj: **cephalic. 2** the corresponding part of an invertebrate animal. **3** something resembling a head in form or function, such as the top of a tool. **4a** the person commanding most authority within a group, organization, etc. **4b** (*as modifier*): *head buyer.* **4c** (*in combination*): *headmaster.* **5** the position of leadership or command. **6** the most forward part of a thing; front: *the head of a queue.* **7** the highest part of a thing; upper end: *the head of the pass.* **8** the froth on the top of a glass of beer. **9** aptitude, intelligence, and emotions (esp. in **over one's head, lose one's head,** etc.): *she has a good head for figures.* **10** (*pl* **head**) a person or animal considered as a unit: *the show was two pounds per head; six hundred head of cattle.* **11** the head considered as a measure: *he's a head taller than his mother.* **12** *Bot.* **12a** a dense inflorescence such as that of the daisy. **12b** any other compact terminal part of a plant, such as the leaves of a cabbage. **13** a culmination or crisis (esp. in **bring** or **come to a head**). **14** the pus-filled tip or central part of a pimple, boil, etc. **15** the source of a river or stream. **16** (*cap. when part of a name*) a headland or promontory. **17** the obverse of a coin, usually bearing a portrait of the head of a monarch, etc. **18** a main point of an argument, discourse, etc. **19** (*often pl*) a headline or heading. **20** (*often pl*) *Naut.* a lavatory. **21** the taut membrane of a drum, tambourine, etc. **22a** the height of the surface of liquid above a specific point, esp. as a measure of the pressure at that point: *a head of four feet.* **22b** pressure of water, caused by height or velocity, measured in terms of a vertical column of water. **22c** any pressure: *a head of steam in the boiler.* **23** *Sl.* **23a** a person who regularly takes drugs, esp. LSD or cannabis. **23b** (*in combination*): *an acidhead.* **24** *Mining.* a road driven into the coalface. **25a** the terminal point of a route. **25b** (*in combination*): *railhead.* **26** a device on a turning or boring machine equipped with one or more cutting tools held to the work by this device. **27 cylinder head.** See **cylinder** (sense 4). **28** an electromagnet that can read, write, or erase information on a magnetic medium, used in computers, tape recorders, etc. **29** *Inf.* short for **headmaster** *or* **headmistress. 30** a narrow margin of victory (esp. in (**win**) **by a head**). **31** *Inf.* short for **headache. 32 bite** *or* **snap someone's head off.** to speak sharply to someone. **33 give someone** (*or* **something**) **his** (*or* **her** *or* **its**) **head. 33a** to allow a person greater freedom or responsibility. **33b** to allow a horse to gallop by lengthening the reins. **34 go to one's head. 34a** to make one dizzy or confused, as might an alcoholic drink. **34b** to make one conceited: *his success has gone to his head.* **35 head and shoulders above.** greatly superior to. **36 head over heels. 36a** turning a complete somersault. **36b** completely; utterly (esp. in **head over heels in love**). **37 hold up one's head.** to be unashamed. **38 keep one's head.** to remain calm. **39 keep one's head above water.** to manage to survive difficulties, esp. financial ones. **40 make head or tail of.** (*used with a negative*) to attempt to understand (a problem, etc.). **41 off** (*or* **out of**) **one's head.** *Sl.* insane or delirious. **42 on one's** (**own**) **head.** at a one's (own) risk or responsibility. **43 over someone's head. 43a** without a person in the obvious position being considered: *the graduate was promoted over the heads of several of his seniors.* **43b** without consulting a person in the obvious position but referring to a higher authority: *he went straight to the director, over the head of his immediate boss.* **43c** beyond a person's comprehension. **44 put** (**our, their,** etc.) **heads together.** *Inf.* to consult together. **45 take it into one's head.** to conceive a notion (to do something). **46 turn someone's head.** to make someone vain, conceited, etc. ◆ *vb* **47** (*tr*) to be at the front or top of: *to head the field.* **48** (*tr;* often foll. by *up*) to be in the commanding or most important position. **49** (often foll. by *for*) to go or cause to go (towards): *where are you heading?* **50** to turn or steer (a vessel) as specified: *to head into the wind.* **51** *Soccer.* to propel (the ball) by striking it with the head. **52** (*tr*) to provide with or be a head or heading for. **53** (*tr*) to cut the top branches or shoots off a tree or plant. **54** (*intr*) to form a head, as a plant. **55** (*intr;* often foll. by *in*) (of streams, rivers, etc.) to originate or rise. ◆ See also **head off, heads.** ORIG OE *hēafod*
▸ **'headless** *adj* ▸ **'head,like** *adj*

Head ★ (hɛd) *n* **Edith.** 1907–81, US dress designer: won many Oscars for her Hollywood film-costume designs.

-head *n combining form.* indicating a person having a preoccupation as specified: *breadhead.*

headache ('hɛd,eɪk) *n* **1** a continuous pain in the head. **2** *Inf.* any cause of worry, difficulty, or annoyance.
▸ **'head,achy** *adj*

headband ('hɛd,bænd) *n* **1** a ribbon or band worn around the head. **2** a narrow cloth band attached to the top of the spine of a book for protection or decoration.

headbang ('hɛd,bæŋ) *vb* (*intr*) *Sl.* to nod one's head violently to the beat of heavy-metal rock music.

head-banger *n Sl.* **1** a heavy-metal rock fan. **2** a crazy or stupid person.

headboard ('hɛd,bɔːd) *n* a vertical board or terminal at the head of a bed.

head-butt *vb* (*tr*) **1** to strike (someone) deliberately with the head. ◆ *n* **head butt. 2** an act or an instance of deliberately striking someone with the head.

headdress ('hɛd,drɛs) *n* any head covering, esp. an ornate one or one denoting a rank.

headed ('hɛdɪd) *adj* **1a** having a head or heads. **1b** (*in combination*): *two-headed; bullet-headed.* **2** having a heading: *headed notepaper.*

header ('hɛdə) *n* **1** a machine that trims the heads from castings, forgings, etc., or one that forms heads, as in wire, to make nails. **2** a person who operates such a machine. **3** Also called: **header tank.** a reservoir that maintains a gravity feed or a static fluid pressure in an apparatus. **4** a brick or stone laid across a wall so that its end is flush with the outer surface. **5** the action of striking a ball with the head. **6** *Inf.* a headlong fall or dive.

headfirst ('hɛd'fɜːst) *adj, adv* **1** with the head foremost; headlong. ◆ *adv* **2** rashly.

headgear ('hɛd,gɪə) *n* **1** a hat. **2** any part of a horse's harness that is worn on the head. **3** the hoisting mechanism at the pithead of a mine.

headguard ('hɛd,gɑːd) *n* a lightweight helmet-like piece of equipment worn to protect the head in various sports.

head-hunting *n* **1** the practice among certain peoples of removing the heads of slain enemies and preserving them as trophies. **2** *US sl.* the destruction or neutralization of political opponents. **3** (of a company or corporation) the recruitment of, or a drive to recruit, new high-level personnel, esp. in management or in specialist fields.
▸ **'head-,hunter** *n*

heading ('hɛdɪŋ) *n* **1** a title for a page, chapter, etc. **2** a main division, as of a speech. **3** *Mining.* **3a** a horizontal tunnel. **3b** the end of such a tunnel. **4** the angle between the direction of an aircraft and a specified meridian, often due north. **5** the compass direction parallel to the keel of a vessel. **6** the act of heading.

headland *n* **1** ('hɛdlənd). a narrow area of land jutting out into a sea, lake, etc. **2** ('hɛd,lænd). a strip of land along the edge of an arable field left unploughed to allow space for machines.

headlight ('hɛd,laɪt) *or* **headlamp** *n* a powerful light, equipped with a reflector and attached to the front of a motor vehicle, etc.

headline ('hɛd,laɪn) *n* **1a** a phrase at the top of a newspaper or magazine article indicating the subject of the article, usually in larger and heavier type. **1b** a line at the top of a page indicating the title, page number, etc. **2 hit the headlines.** to become prominent in the news. **3** (*usu-*

ally pl) the main points of a television or radio news broadcast, read out before the full broadcast. ◆ *vb* **headlines, headlining, headlined. 4** (*tr*) to furnish (a story or page) with a headline. **5** to have top billing (in).

headlong (ˈhɛdˌlɒŋ) *adv, adj* **1** with the head foremost; headfirst. **2** with great haste. ◆ *adj* **3** *Arch.* (of slopes, etc.) very steep; precipitous.

headman (ˈhɛdmən) *n, pl* **headmen. 1** *Anthropol.* a chief or leader. **2** a foreman or overseer.

headmaster (ˌhɛdˈmɑːstə) *or* (*fem*) **headmistress** *n* the principal of a school.

headmost (ˈhɛdˌməʊst) *adj* foremost.

head off *vb* (*tr, adv*) **1** to intercept and force to change direction. **2** to prevent or forestall.

head-on *adv, adj* **1** front foremost: *a head-on collision.* **2** with directness or without compromise: *in his usual head-on fashion.*

headphones (ˈhɛdˌfəʊnz) *pl n* an electrical device consisting of two earphones held in position by a flexible metallic strap passing over the head. Informal name: **cans.**

headpiece (ˈhɛdˌpiːs) *n* **1** *Printing.* a decorative band at the top of a page, etc. **2** a helmet. **3** *Arch.* the intellect.

headpin (ˈhɛdˌpɪn) *n Tenpin bowling.* another word for **kingpin** (sense 2).

headquarters (ˌhɛdˈkwɔːtəz) *pl n* (*sometimes functioning as sing*) **1** any centre from which operations are directed, as in the police. **2** a military formation comprising the commander and his staff. ◆ Abbrev.: **HQ, h.q.**

headrace (ˈhɛdˌreɪs) *n* a channel that carries water to a water wheel, turbine, etc.

headrest (ˈhɛdˌrɛst) *n* a support for the head, as on a dentist's chair or car seat.

head restraint *n* an adjustable support for the head, attached to a car seat, to prevent the neck from being jolted backwards sharply in the event of a crash or sudden stop.

headroom (ˈhɛdˌrʊm, -ˌruːm) *or* **headway** *n* the height of a bridge, room, etc.; clearance.

heads (hɛdz) *interj, adv* with the obverse side of a coin uppermost, esp. if it has a head on it: used as a call before tossing a coin.

headscarf (ˈhɛdˌskɑːf) *n, pl* **headscarves.** a scarf for the head, often worn tied under the chin.

headset (ˈhɛdˌsɛt) *n* a pair of headphones, esp. with a microphone attached.

headship (ˈhɛdʃɪp) *n* **1** the position or state of being a leader; command. **2** *Brit.* the position of headmaster or headmistress of a school.

headshrinker (ˈhɛdˌʃrɪŋkə) *n* **1** a slang name for **psychiatrist.** Often shortened to **shrink. 2** a head-hunter who shrinks the heads of his victims.

headsman (ˈhɛdzmən) *n, pl* **headsmen.** (formerly) an executioner who beheaded condemned persons.

headstall (ˈhɛdˌstɔːl) *n* the part of a bridle that fits round a horse's head.

head start *n* an initial advantage in a competitive situation.

headstock (ˈhɛdˌstɒk) *n* the part of a machine that supports and transmits the drive.

headstone (ˈhɛdˌstəʊn) *n* **1** a memorial stone at the head of a grave. **2** *Archit.* another name for **keystone.**

headstream (ˈhɛdˌstriːm) *n* a stream that is the source or a source of a river.

headstrong (ˈhɛdˌstrɒŋ) *adj* **1** self-willed; obstinate. **2** (of an action) heedless; rash.

head-to-head *Inf.* ◆ *adj* **1** in direct competition. ◆ *n* **2** a competition involving two people, teams, etc.

head-up display *n* a projection of readings from instruments onto a windscreen, enabling a pilot or driver to see them without moving his eyes.

head voice *or* **register** *n* the high register of the human voice, in which the vibrations of sung notes are felt in the head.

headwaters (ˈhɛdˌwɔːtəz) *pl n* the tributary streams of a river in the area in which it rises.

headway (ˈhɛdˌweɪ) *n* **1** motion forward: *the vessel made no headway.* **2** progress: *he made no headway with the problem.* **3** another name for **headroom. 4** the interval between consecutive trains, buses, etc., on the same route.

headwind (ˈhɛdˌwɪnd) *n* a wind blowing directly against the course of an aircraft or ship.

headword (ˈhɛdˌwɜːd) *n* a key word placed at the beginning of a line, paragraph, etc., as in a dictionary entry.

headwork (ˈhɛdˌwɜːk) *n* **1** mental work. **2** the ornamentation of the keystone of an arch.

heady (ˈhɛdɪ) *adj* **headier, headiest. 1** (of alcoholic drink) intoxicating. **2** strongly affecting the senses; extremely exciting. **3** rash; impetuous.
▸ **ˈheadily** *adv* ▸ **ˈheadiness** *n*

heal (hiːl) *vb* **1** to restore or be restored to health. **2** (*intr; often foll. by over or up*) (of a wound) to repair by natural processes, as by scar formation. **3** (*tr*) to cure (a disease or disorder). **4** to restore or be restored to friendly relations, harmony, etc. ORIG OE *hǣlan;* see HALE[1], WHOLE
▸ **ˈhealer** *n* ▸ **ˈhealing** *n, adj*

Healey ★ (ˈhiːlɪ) *n* **Denis (Winston),** Baron Healey. born 1917, British Labour politician; Chancellor of the Exchequer (1974–79); deputy leader of the Labour Party (1980–83).

Healy ★ (ˈhiːlɪ) *n* **Ian.** born 1964, Australian cricketer who holds the record for the number of wicketkeeping dismissals in world test matches.

health (hɛlθ) *n* **1** the state of being bodily and mentally vigorous and free from disease. **2** the general condition of body and mind: *in poor health.* **3** the condition of any unit, society, etc.: *the economic health of a nation.* **4** a toast to a person. **5** (*modifier*) of or relating to food or other goods reputed to be beneficial to the health: *health food.* **6** (*modifier*) of or relating to health: *health care; health service.* ORIG OE *hǣlth;* rel. to *hāl* HALE[1]

health centre *n* (in Britain) premises providing health care for a local community and usually housing a group practice, nursing staff, a child-health clinic, etc.

health farm *n* a residential establishment, often in the country, visited by those who wish to improve their health by losing weight, eating health foods, taking exercise, etc.

health food *n* **a** food eaten for its alleged benefits to health, esp. fruit, vegetables, etc., that are organically grown, high in dietary fibre, and without additives. **b** (*as modifier*): *a health-food shop.*

healthful (ˈhɛlθfʊl) *adj* a less common word for **healthy** (senses 1–3).

health salts *pl n* magnesium sulphate or similar salts taken as a mild laxative.

health visitor *n* (in Britain) a nurse employed by a district health authority to visit people in their homes and give help and advice on health and social welfare, esp. to mothers of preschool children, and to handicapped and elderly people.

healthy (ˈhɛlθɪ) *adj* **healthier, healthiest. 1** enjoying good health. **2** sound: *the company's finances are not very healthy.* **3** conducive to health. **4** indicating soundness of body or mind: *a healthy appetite.* **5** *Inf.* considerable: *a healthy sum.*
▸ **ˈhealthily** *adv* ▸ **ˈhealthiness** *n*

Heaney ★ (ˈhiːnɪ) *n* **Seamus (Justin)** (ˈʃeɪməs). born 1939, Irish poet and critic, born in Northern Ireland. His works include *Death of a Naturalist* (1966), *The Spirit Level* (1996), and a translation of *Beowulf* (1999): Nobel prize for literature 1995.

heap (hiːp) *n* **1** a collection of articles or mass of material gathered in a pile. **2** (*often pl;* usually foll. by *of*) *Inf.* a large number or quantity. **3** *Inf.* a thing that is very old, unreliable, etc.: *the car was a heap.* ◆ *adv* **4 heaps.** (intensifier): *he was heaps better.* ◆ *vb* **5** (often foll. by *up* or *together*) to collect or be collected into or as if into a pile. **6** (*tr;* often foll. by *with, on,* or *upon*) to load (with) abundantly: *to heap with riches.* ORIG OE *hēap*

hear (hɪə) *vb* **hears, hearing, heard** (hɜːd). **1** (*tr*) to perceive (a

sound) with the sense of hearing. **2** (*tr; may take a clause as object*) to listen to: *did you hear what I said?* **3** (when *intr,* sometimes foll. by *of* or *about;* when *tr, may take a clause as object*) to be informed (of); receive information (about). **4** *Law.* to give a hearing to (a case). **5** (when *intr,* usually foll. by *of* and used with a negative) to listen (to) with favour, assent, etc.: *she wouldn't hear of it.* **6** (*intr;* foll. by *from*) to receive a letter (from). **7 hear! hear!** an exclamation of approval. **8 hear tell (of).** *Dialect.* to be told (about). ORIG OE *hieran*
▸ **'hearer** *n*

Heard and McDonald Islands ★ (hɜːd; məkˈdɒnəld) *pl n* a group of islands in the S Indian Ocean: an external territory of Australia from 1947. Area: 412 sq. km (159 sq. miles).

hearing (ˈhɪərɪŋ) *n* **1** the sense by which sound is perceived. **2** an opportunity to be listened to. **3** the range within which sound can be heard; earshot. **4** the investigation of a matter by a court of law, esp. the preliminary inquiry into an indictable crime by magistrates.

hearing aid *n* a device for assisting the hearing of partially deaf people, typically a small battery-powered amplifier worn in or behind the ear. Also called: **deaf aid.**

hearing dog *n* a dog that has been specially trained to help deaf or partially deaf people by alerting them to such sounds as a ringing doorbell, an alarm, etc.

hearken *or US (sometimes)* **harken** (ˈhɑːkən) *vb Arch.* to listen to (something). ORIG OE *heorcnian*

hear out *vb* (*tr, adv*) to listen in regard to every detail and give a proper or full hearing to.

hearsay (ˈhɪəˌseɪ) *n* gossip; rumour.

hearsay evidence *n Law.* evidence based on what has been reported to a witness by others rather than what he has himself observed.

hearse (hɜːs) *n* a vehicle, such as a car or carriage, used to carry a coffin to the grave. ORIG C14: from OF *herce,* from L *hirpex* harrow

Hearst ★ (hɜːst) *n* **William Randolph.** 1863–1951, US newspaper publisher.

heart (hɑːt) *n* **1** the hollow muscular organ in vertebrates whose contractions propel the blood through the circulatory system. Related adj: **cardiac. 2** the corresponding organ in invertebrates. **3** this organ considered as the seat of emotions, esp. love. **4** emotional mood: *a change of heart.* **5** tenderness or pity: *you have no heart.* **6** courage or spirit. **7** the most central part: *the heart of the city.* **8** the most important part: *the heart of the matter.* **9** (of vegetables, such as cabbage) the inner compact part. **10** the breast: *she held him to her heart.* **11** a dearly loved person: *dearest heart.* **12** a conventionalized representation of the heart, having two rounded lobes at the top meeting in a point at the bottom. **13a** a red heart-shaped symbol on a playing card. **13b** a card with one or more of these symbols or (*when pl*) the suit of cards so marked. **14** a fertile condition in land (esp. in **in good heart**). **15 after one's own heart.** appealing to one's own disposition or taste. **16 break one's** (*or* **someone's**) **heart.** to grieve (or cause to grieve) very deeply, esp. through love. **17 by heart.** by committing to memory. **18 eat one's heart out.** to brood or pine with grief or longing. **19 from (the bottom of) one's heart.** very sincerely or deeply. **20 have a change of heart.** to experience a profound change of outlook, attitude, etc. **21 have one's heart in one's mouth** (*or* **throat**). to be full of apprehension, excitement, or fear. **22 have one's heart in the right place.** to be kind, thoughtful, or generous. **23 have the heart.** (*usually used with a negative*) to have the necessary will, callousness, etc. (to do something): *I didn't have the heart to tell him.* **24 heart of hearts.** the depths of one's conscience or emotions. **25 heart of oak.** a brave person. **26 lose heart.** to become despondent or disillusioned (over something). **27 lose one's heart to.** to fall in love with. **28 set one's heart on.** to have as one's ambition to obtain; covet. **29 take heart.** to become encouraged. **30 take to heart.** to take seriously or be upset about. **31 wear one's heart on one's sleeve.** to show one's feelings openly. **32 with all one's heart.** very willingly. ◆ *vb* (*intr*) **33** (of vegetables) to form a heart. ◆ See also **hearts.** ORIG OE *heorte*

heartache (ˈhɑːtˌeɪk) *n* intense anguish or mental suffering.

heart attack *n* any sudden severe instance of abnormal heart functioning, esp. coronary thrombosis.

heartbeat (ˈhɑːtˌbiːt) *n* one complete pulsation of the heart.

heart block *n* impaired conduction of the impulse that regulates the heartbeat, resulting in a lack of coordination between the beating of the atria and the ventricles.

heartbreak (ˈhɑːtˌbreɪk) *n* intense and overwhelming grief, esp. through disappointment in love.
▸ **ˈheartˌbreaker** *n* ▸ **ˈheartˌbreaking** *adj*

heartburn (ˈhɑːtˌbɜːn) *n* a burning sensation beneath the breastbone caused by irritation of the oesophagus. Technical names: **cardialgia, pyrosis.**

-hearted *adj* having a heart or disposition as specified: *cold-hearted; heavy-hearted.*

hearten (ˈhɑːtᵊn) *vb* to make or become cheerful.
▸ **ˈheartening** *adj*

heart failure *n* **1** a condition in which the heart is unable to pump an adequate amount of blood to the tissues. **2** sudden cessation of the heartbeat, resulting in death.

heartfelt (ˈhɑːtˌfɛlt) *adj* sincerely and strongly felt.

hearth (hɑːθ) *n* **1a** the floor of a fireplace, esp. one that extends outwards into the room. **1b** (*as modifier*): *hearth rug.* **2** this as a symbol of the home, etc. **3** the bottom part of a metallurgical furnace in which the molten metal is produced or contained. ORIG OE *heorth*

hearthstone (ˈhɑːθˌstəʊn) *n* **1** a stone that forms a hearth. **2** soft stone used (esp. formerly) to clean and whiten floors, steps, etc.

heartily (ˈhɑːtɪlɪ) *adv* **1** thoroughly or vigorously. **2** in a sincere manner.

heartland (ˈhɑːtˌlænd) *n* the central or most important region of a country or continent.

heartless (ˈhɑːtlɪs) *adj* unkind or cruel.
▸ **ˈheartlessly** *adv* ▸ **ˈheartlessness** *n*

heart-lung machine *n* a machine used to maintain the circulation and oxygenation of the blood during heart surgery.

heart-rending *adj* causing great mental pain and sorrow.
▸ **ˈheart-ˌrendingly** *adv*

hearts (hɑːts) *n* (*functioning as sing*) a card game in which players must avoid winning tricks containing hearts or the queen of spades. Also called: **Black Maria.**

heart-searching *n* examination of one's feelings or conscience.

heartsease *or* **heart's-ease** (ˈhɑːtsˌiːz) *n* **1** another name for the **wild pansy. 2** peace of mind.

heartsick (ˈhɑːtˌsɪk) *adj* deeply despondent.
▸ **ˈheartˌsickness** *n*

heartstrings (ˈhɑːtˌstrɪŋz) *pl n Often facetious.* deep emotions. ORIG C15: orig. referring to the tendons supposed to support the heart

heart-throb *n* **1** an object of infatuation. **2** a heartbeat.

heart-to-heart *adj* **1** (esp. of a conversation) concerned with personal problems or intimate feelings. ◆ *n* **2** an intimate conversation.

heart-warming *adj* **1** pleasing; gratifying. **2** emotionally moving.

heartwood (ˈhɑːtˌwʊd) *n* the central core of dark hard wood in tree trunks, consisting of nonfunctioning xylem tissue that has become blocked with resins, tannins, and oils.

hearty (ˈhɑːtɪ) *adj* **heartier, heartiest. 1** warm and unreserved in manner. **2** vigorous and heartfelt: *hearty dislike.* **3** healthy and strong (esp. in **hale and hearty**). **4** substantial and nourishing. ◆ *n, pl* **hearties.** *Inf.* **5** a comrade, esp. a sailor. **6** a vigorous sporting man: *a rugby hearty.*
▸ **ˈheartiness** *n*

heat (hiːt) *n* **1** the energy transferred as a result of a difference in temperature. Related adjs.: **thermal, calorific. 2** the sensation caused by heat energy; warmth. **3** the state of being hot. **4** hot weather: *the heat of summer.* **5** intensity of feeling: *the heat of rage.* **6** pressure: *the political heat on the government over the economy.* **7** the most intense part: *the heat of the battle.* **8** a period of sexual excitement in female mammals that occurs at oestrus. **9** *Sport.* **9a** a preliminary eliminating contest in a competition. **9b** a single section of a contest. **10** *Sl.* police activity after a crime: *the heat is off.* **11** *Sl., chiefly US.* criticism or abuse: *he took a lot of heat for that mistake.* **12 in the heat of the moment.** without pausing to think. **13 on** *or* **in heat. 13a** Also: **in season.** (of some female mammals) sexually receptive. **13b** in a state of sexual excitement. ◆ *vb* **14** to make or become hot or warm. **15** to make or become excited or intense. ORIG OE *hǣtu*

heat barrier *n* another name for **thermal barrier.**

heat capacity *n* the heat required to raise the temperature of a substance by unit temperature interval under specified conditions.

heat death *n Thermodynamics.* the condition of any closed system when its total entropy is a maximum and it has no available energy. If the universe is a closed system it should eventually reach this state.

heated (ˈhiːtɪd) *adj* **1** made hot. **2** impassioned or highly emotional.
▸ **ˈheatedly** *adv*

heat engine *n* an engine that converts heat energy into mechanical energy.

heater (ˈhiːtə) *n* **1** any device for supplying heat, such as a convector. **2** *US sl.* a pistol. **3** *Electronics.* a conductor carrying a current that indirectly heats the cathode in some types of valve.

heat exchanger *n* a device for transferring heat from one fluid to another without allowing them to mix.

heat exhaustion *n* a condition resulting from exposure to intense heat, characterized by dizziness, abdominal cramp, and prostration.

heath (hiːθ) *n* **1** *Brit.* a large open area, usually with sandy soil and scrubby vegetation, esp. heather. **2** Also called: **heather.** a low-growing evergreen shrub having small bell-shaped typically pink or purple flowers. **3** any of several heathlike plants, such as sea heath. ORIG OE *hǣth*
▸ **ˈheathˌlike** *adj* ▸ **ˈheathy** *adj*

Heath ★ (hiːθ) *n* **Edward (Richard George).** born 1916, British statesman; leader of the Conservative Party (1965–75); prime minister (1970–74).

heathen (ˈhiːðən) *n, pl* **heathens** *or* **heathen. 1** a person who does not acknowledge the God of Christianity, Judaism, or Islam; pagan. **2** an uncivilized or barbaric person. ◆ *adj* **3** irreligious; pagan. **4** uncivilized; barbaric. **5** of or relating to heathen peoples or their customs and beliefs. ORIG OE *hǣthen*
▸ **ˈheathendom** *n* ▸ **ˈheathenism** *or* **ˈheathenry** *n*

heathenize *or* **heathenise** (ˈhiːðəˌnaɪz) *vb* **heathenizes, heathenizing, heathenized** *or* **heathenises, heathenising, heathenised.** to render or become heathen.

heather (ˈhɛðə) *n* **1** Also called: **ling, heath.** a low-growing evergreen Eurasian shrub that grows in dense masses on open ground and has clusters of small bell-shaped typically pinkish-purple flowers. **2** a purplish-red to pinkish-purple colour. ◆ *adj* **3** of a heather colour. **4** of or relating to interwoven yarns of mixed colours: *heather mixture.* ORIG C14: orig. Scot. & N English, prob. from HEATH
▸ **ˈheathery** *adj*

Heath Robinson *adj* (of a mechanical device) absurdly complicated in design and having a simple function. ORIG C20: after (William) *Heath Robinson* (1872–1944), British cartoonist

heating (ˈhiːtɪŋ) *n* **1** a device or system for supplying heat, esp. central heating, to a building. **2** the heat supplied.

heat pump *n* a device for extracting heat from a source and delivering it elsewhere at a higher temperature.

heat rash *n* a nontechnical name for **miliaria.**

heat-seeking *adj* (of a missile, detecting device, etc.) able to detect a source of heat, as from an aircraft engine: *a heat-seeking missile.*
▸ **heat seeker** *n*

heat shield *n* a coating or barrier for shielding from excessive heat, such as that experienced by a spacecraft on re-entry into the earth's atmosphere.

heat sink *n* **1** a metal plate designed to conduct and radiate heat from an electrical component. **2** a layer within the outer skin of high-speed aircraft to absorb heat.

heatstroke (ˈhiːtˌstrəʊk) *n* a condition resulting from prolonged exposure to intense heat, characterized by high fever.

heat-treat *vb* (*tr*) to apply heat to (a metal or alloy) in one or more temperature cycles to give it desirable properties.
▸ **heat treatment** *n*

heat wave *n* **1** a continuous spell of abnormally hot weather. **2** an extensive slow-moving air mass at a relatively high temperature.

heave (hiːv) *vb* **heaves, heaving, heaved** *or* **hove. 1** (*tr*) to lift or move with a great effort. **2** (*tr*) to throw (something heavy) with effort. **3** to utter (sounds) noisily or unhappily: *to heave a sigh.* **4** to rise and fall or cause to rise and fall heavily. **5** (*p.t. & p.p.* **hove**) *Naut.* **5a** to move or cause to move in a specified direction: *to heave in sight.* **5b** (*intr*) (of a vessel) to pitch or roll. **6** (*tr*) to displace (rock strata, etc.) in a horizontal direction. **7** (*intr*) to retch. ◆ *n* **8** the act of heaving. **9** a horizontal displacement of rock strata at a fault. ◆ See also **heave to, heaves.** ORIG OE *hebban*
▸ **ˈheaver** *n*

heave-ho *interj* a sailors' cry, as when hoisting anchor.

heaven (ˈhɛvᵊn) *n* **1** (*sometimes cap.*) *Christianity.* **1a** the abode of God and the angels. **1b** a state of communion with God after death. **2** (*usually pl*) the firmament surrounding the earth. **3** (in various mythologies) a place, such as Elysium or Valhalla, to which those who have died in the gods' favour are brought to dwell in happiness. **4** a place or state of happiness. **5** (*sing or pl; sometimes cap.*) God or the gods, used in exclamatory phrases: *for heaven's sake.* **6 move heaven and earth.** to do everything possible (to achieve something). ORIG OE *heofon*

heavenly (ˈhɛvᵊnlɪ) *adj* **1** *Inf.* wonderful. **2** of or occurring in space: *a heavenly body.* **3** holy.
▸ **ˈheavenliness** *n*

heavenward (ˈhɛvᵊnwəd) *adj* **1** directed towards heaven or the sky. ◆ *adv* **2** Also **heavenwards.** towards heaven or the sky.

heaves (hiːvz) *n* (*functioning as sing or pl*) a chronic respiratory disorder of animals of the horse family, of unknown cause. Also called: **broken wind.**

heave to *vb* (*adv*) to stop (a vessel) or (of a vessel) to stop, as by trimming the sails, etc.

Heaviside ★ (ˈhɛvɪˌsaɪd) *n* **Oliver.** 1850–1925, British physicist. Independently of Kennelly, he predicted (1902) the existence of the Heaviside layer; he also contributed to telegraphy.

Heaviside layer *n* another name for **E region** (of the ionosphere). ORIG C20: after O. HEAVISIDE

heavy (ˈhɛvɪ) *adj* **heavier, heaviest. 1** of comparatively great weight. **2** having a relatively high density: *lead is a heavy metal.* **3** great in yield, quality, or quantity: *heavy traffic.* **4** considerable: *heavy emphasis.* **5** hard to bear or fulfil: *heavy demands.* **6** sad or dejected: *heavy at heart.* **7** coarse or broad: *heavy features.* **8** (of soil) having a high clay content; cloggy. **9** solid or fat: *heavy legs.* **10** (of an industry) engaged in the large-scale complex manufacture of capital goods or extraction of raw materials. **11** serious; grave. **12** *Mil.* **12a** equipped with large weapons, armour, etc. **12b** (of guns, etc.) of a large and powerful type. **13** (of a syllable) having stress or accentuation. **14** dull and uninteresting: *a heavy style.* **15** prodigious: *a heavy drinker.* **16** (of cakes, etc.) insufficiently leavened. **17** deep and loud: *a heavy thud.* **18** (of music, literature, etc.) **18a** dramatic and powerful. **18b** not immediately comprehensible or appealing. **19** *Sl.* (of rock music) having a powerful beat; hard. **20** burdened: *heavy with child.* **21 heavy on.** *Inf.* using large quantities of: *this car is very heavy on petrol.* **22** clumsy and slow: *heavy going.* **23** cloudy or overcast: *heavy skies.* **24** not easily digestible: *a heavy meal.* **25** (of an element or compound) being or containing an isotope with greater atomic weight than

★ people and places

that of the naturally occurring element: *heavy water.* **26** (of the going on a racecourse) soft and muddy. **27** *Sl.* using, or prepared to use, violence or brutality. ◆ *n, pl* **heavies. 28a** a villainous role. **28b** an actor who plays such a part. **29** *Mil.* **29a** a large fleet unit, esp. an aircraft carrier or battleship. **29b** a large piece of artillery. **30** (*usually pl; often preceded by the*) *Inf.* a serious newspaper: *the Sunday heavies.* **31** *Inf.* a heavyweight boxer, wrestler, etc. **32** *Sl.* a man hired to threaten violence or deter others by his presence. ◆ *adv* **33a** in a heavy manner; heavily: *time hangs heavy.* **33b** (*in combination*): *heavy-laden.* ORIG OE *hefig*
▸ **'heavily** *adv* ▸ **'heaviness** *n*

heavy-duty *n* (*modifier*) made to withstand hard wear, bad weather, etc.

heavy-handed *adj* **1** clumsy. **2** harsh and oppressive.
▸ **ˌheavy-'handedly** *adv*

heavy-hearted *adj* sad; melancholy.

heavy hitter *n Inf.* another name for **big hitter** (sense 2).

heavy hydrogen *n* another name for **deuterium.**

heavy metal *n* a type of rock music characterized by high volume, a driving beat, and extended guitar solos, often with violent, nihilistic, and misogynistic lyrics.

heavy middleweight *n* a professional wrestler weighing 177–187 pounds (81–85 kg).

heavy spar *n* another name for **barytes.**

heavy water *n* water that has been electrolytically decomposed to reduce the amount of normal hydrogen present and enrich it in deuterium in the form D_2O or HDO. See also **deuterium oxide.**

heavyweight ('hɛvɪˌweɪt) *n* **1** a person or thing that is heavier than average. **2a** a professional boxer weighing more than 175 pounds (79 kg). **2b** an amateur boxer weighing more than 81 kg (179 pounds). **3a** a professional wrestler weighing over 209 pounds (95 kg). **3b** an amateur wrestler weighing over 220 pounds (100kg). **4** *Inf.* an important or highly influential person.

Heb. *or* **Hebr.** *abbrev. for:* **1** Hebrew (language). **2** *Bible.* Hebrews.

Hebbel ★ (*German* 'hɛbəl) *n* **Christian Friedrich** ('krɪstian 'fri:drɪç). 1813–63, German dramatist and lyric poet; his major plays include the trilogy *Die Nibelungen* (1862).

hebdomadal (hɛb'dɒmədᵊl) *adj* weekly. ORIG C18: from L, from Gk *hebdomas* seven (days), from *hepta* seven

Hebe ★ ('hi:bɪ) *n Greek myth.* the goddess of youth and spring, daughter of Zeus and Hera and wife of Hercules.

Hebei ('hʌ'beɪ), **Hopeh,** *or* **Hopei** ★ *n* a province of NE China, on the Gulf of Chihli: important for the production of winter wheat, cotton, and coal. Capital: Shijiazhuang. Pop.: 65 250 000 (1997 est.). Area: 202 700 sq. km (79 053 sq. miles).

hebetate ('hɛbɪˌteɪt) *adj* **1** (of plant parts) having a blunt or soft point. ◆ *vb* **hebetates, hebetating, hebetated. 2** *Rare.* to make or become blunted. ORIG C16: from L *hebetāre* to make blunt, from *hebes* blunt
▸ **ˌhebe'tation** *n*

Hebraic (hɪ'breɪɪk) *or* **Hebraical** *adj* of, relating to, or characteristic of the Hebrews or their language or culture.
▸ **He'braically** *adv*

Hebraism ('hi:breɪˌɪzəm) *n* a linguistic usage, custom, or other feature borrowed from or particular to the Hebrew language, or to the Jewish people or their culture.
▸ **'Hebraist** *n* ▸ **'Hebraˌize** *or* **'Hebraˌise** *vb*

Hebrew ('hi:bru:) *n* **1** the ancient language of the Hebrews, revived as the official language of Israel. **2** a member of an ancient Semitic people claiming descent from Abraham; an Israelite. **3** *Arch. or offens.* a Jew. ◆ *adj* **4** of or relating to the Hebrews or their language. **5** *Arch. or offens.* Jewish. ORIG C13: from OF *Ebreu,* ult. from Heb. *'ibhrī* one from beyond (the river)

Hebrews ('hi:bru:z) *n* (*functioning as sing*) a book of the New Testament.

Hebrides ★ ('hɛbrɪˌdi:z) *pl n* **the.** a group of over 500 islands off the W coast of Scotland: separated by the North Minch, Little Minch, and the Sea of the Hebrides: the chief islands are Skye, Raasay, Rhum, Eigg, Coll, Tiree, Mull, Jura, Colonsay, and Islay (**Inner Hebrides**), and Lewis with Harris, North Uist, Benbecula, South Uist, and Barra (**Outer Hebrides**). Also called: **Western Isles.**
▸ **ˌHebri'dean** *or* **Hebridian** (hɛ'brɪdɪən) *adj, n*

Hebron ★ ('hɛbrɒn, 'hi:-) *n* a city in the West Bank: famous for the Haram, which includes the cenotaphs of Abraham and Sarah, Isaac and Rebecca, and Jacob and Leah. Pop.: 80 000 (1990 est.). Arabic name: **El Khalil.**

Hecate *or* **Hekate** ★ ('hɛkətɪ) *n Greek myth.* a goddess of the underworld.

hecatomb ('hɛkəˌtəʊm, -ˌtu:m) *n* **1** (in ancient Greece or Rome) any great public sacrifice and feast, originally one in which 100 oxen were sacrificed. **2** a great sacrifice. ORIG C16: from L *hecatombē,* from Gk, from *hekaton* hundred + *bous* ox

heck (hɛk) *interj* a mild exclamation of surprise, irritation, etc. ORIG C19: euphemistic for *hell*

heckelphone ('hɛkəlˌfəʊn) *n Music.* a type of bass oboe. ORIG C20: after W. *Heckel* (1856-1909), G inventor

heckle ('hɛkᵊl) *vb* **heckles, heckling, heckled. 1** to interrupt (a public speaker, etc.) by comments, questions, or taunts. **2** (*tr*) Also: **hackle, hatchel.** to comb (hemp or flax). ◆ *n* **3** an instrument for combing flax or hemp. ORIG C15: N English & East Anglian form of HACKLE
▸ **'heckler** *n*

hectare ('hɛktɑ:) *n* one hundred ares (10 000 square metres or 2.471 acres). Symbol: ha ORIG C19: from F; see HECTO-, ARE[2]

hectic ('hɛktɪk) *adj* **1** characterized by extreme activity or excitement. **2** associated with or symptomatic of tuberculosis (esp. in **hectic fever, hectic flush**). ◆ *n* **3** a hectic fever or flush. **4** *Rare.* a person who is consumptive. ORIG C14: from LL *hecticus,* from Gk *hektikos* habitual, from *hexis* state, from *ekhein* to have
▸ **'hectically** *adv*

hecto- *or before a vowel* **hect-** *prefix* denoting 100: *hectogram.* Symbol: h ORIG via F from Gk *hekaton* hundred

hectog *abbrev. for* hectogram.

hectogram *or* **hectogramme** ('hɛktəʊˌgræm) *n* one hundred grams (3.527 ounces). Symbol: hg

hectograph ('hɛktəʊˌgrɑ:f) *n* **1** a process for copying type or manuscript from a glycerine-coated gelatine master to which the original has been transferred. **2** a machine using this process.

hector ('hɛktə) *vb* **1** to bully or torment. ◆ *n* **2** a blustering bully. ORIG C17: after HECTOR, in the sense: a bully

Hector ★ ('hɛktə) *n Classical myth.* a son of King Priam of Troy, who was killed by Achilles.

Hecuba ★ ('hɛkjubə) *n Classical myth.* the wife of King Priam of Troy, and mother of Hector and Paris.

he'd (hi:d; *unstressed* i:d, hɪd, ɪd) *contraction of* he had *or* he would.

heddle ('hɛdᵊl) *n* one of a set of frames of vertical wires on a loom, each wire having an eye through which a warp thread can be passed. ORIG OE *hefeld* chain

hedera ('hɛdərə) *n* the genus name of **ivy** (sense 1). ORIG L

hedge (hɛdʒ) *n* **1** a row of shrubs or bushes forming a boundary. **2** a barrier or protection against something. **3** the act or a method of reducing the risk of loss on an investment, etc. **4** a cautious or evasive statement. **5** (*as modifier*) low, inferior, or illiterate: *hedge priest.* ◆ *vb* **hedges, hedging, hedged. 6** (*tr*) to enclose or separate with or as if with a hedge. **7** (*intr*) to make or maintain a hedge. **8** (*tr; often foll. by in, about,* or *around*) to hinder or restrict. **9** (*intr*) to evade decision, esp. by making noncommittal statements. **10** (*tr*) to guard against the risk of loss in (a bet, etc.), esp. by laying bets with other bookmakers. **11** (*intr*) to protect against loss through future price fluctuations, as by investing in futures. ORIG OE *hecg*
▸ **'hedger** *n* ▸ **'hedging** *n*

hedge fund *n* a largely unregulated speculative fund, which offers substantial returns for high-risk investments.

hedgehog ('hɛdʒˌhɒg) *n* a small nocturnal Old World mammal having a protective covering of spines on the back.

hedgehop ('hɛdʒˌhɒp) *vb* **hedgehops, hedgehopping, hedgehopped.** (*intr*) (of an aircraft) to fly close to the ground, as in crop spraying.
▸ **'hedgeˌhopping** *n, adj*

hedgerow ('hɛdʒˌrəʊ) *n* a hedge of shrubs or low trees, esp. one bordering a field.

hedge sparrow *n* a small brownish European songbird. Also called: **dunnock.**

Hedjaz ★ (hiː'dʒæz) *n* a variant spelling of **Hejaz.**

hedonics (hiː'dɒnɪks) *n* (*functioning as sing*) **1** the branch of psychology concerned with the study of pleasant and unpleasant sensations. **2** (in philosophy) the study of pleasure.

hedonism ('hiːdᵊˌnɪzəm, 'hɛd-) *n* **1** *Ethics.* **1a** the doctrine that moral value can be defined in terms of pleasure. **1b** the doctrine that the pursuit of pleasure is the highest good. **2** indulgence in sensual pleasures. ORIG C19: from Gk *hēdonē* pleasure
▸ **ˌhedon'istic** *adj* ▸ **'hedonist** *n*

-hedron *n combining form.* indicating a solid having a specified number of surfaces: *tetrahedron.* ORIG from Gk *-edron* -sided, from *hedra* seat, base
▸ **-hedral** *adj combining form.*

heebie-jeebies ('hiːbɪ'dʒiːbɪz) *pl n* **the.** *Sl.* apprehension and nervousness. ORIG C20: coined by W. De Beck (1890–1942), American cartoonist

heed (hiːd) *n* **1** careful attention; notice: *to take heed.* ◆ *vb* **2** to pay close attention to (someone or something). ORIG OE *hēdan*
▸ **'heedful** *adj* ▸ **'heedfully** *adv* ▸ **'heedfulness** *n*

heedless ('hiːdlɪs) *adj* taking no notice; careless or thoughtless.
▸ **'heedlessly** *adv* ▸ **'heedlessness** *n*

heehaw (ˌhiː'hɔː) *interj* an imitation or representation of the braying sound of a donkey.

heel¹ (hiːl) *n* **1** the back part of the human foot. **2** the corresponding part in other vertebrates. **3** the part of a stocking, etc., designed to fit the heel. **4** the outer part of a shoe underneath the heel. **5** the end or back section of something: *the heel of a loaf.* **6** *Horticulture.* the small part of the parent plant that remains attached to a young shoot cut for propagation. **7** the back part of a golf club head where it bends to join the shaft. **8** *Sl.* a contemptible person. **9 at** (*or* **on**) **one's heels.** following closely. **10 down at heel. 10a** shabby or worn. **10b** slovenly. **11 kick** (*or* **cool**) **one's heels.** to wait or be kept waiting. **12 take to one's heels.** to run off. **13 to heel.** under control, as a dog walking by a person's heel. ◆ *vb* **14** (*tr*) to repair or replace the heel of (a shoe, etc.). **15** (*tr*) *Golf.* to strike (the ball) with the heel of the club. **16** to follow at the heels of (a person). ORIG OE *hēla*
▸ **'heelless** *adj*

heel² (hiːl) *vb* **1** (of a vessel) to lean over; list. ◆ *n* **2** inclined position from the vertical. ORIG OE *hieldan*

heelball ('hiːlˌbɔːl) *n* **a** a mixture of beeswax and lampblack used by shoemakers to blacken the edges of heels and soles. **b** a similar substance used to take rubbings, esp. brass rubbings.

heeler ('hiːlə) *n* **1** *US.* See **ward heeler. 2** a person or thing that heels. **3** *Austral. & NZ.* a dog that herds cattle, etc., by biting at their heels.

heel in *vb* (*tr, adv*) to insert (cuttings, shoots, etc.) into the soil before planting to keep them moist.

heeltap ('hiːlˌtæp) *n* **1** a layer of leather, etc., in the heel of a shoe. **2** a small amount of alcoholic drink left at the bottom of a glass.

Heerlen ★ ('hɪələn; *Dutch* 'heːrlə) *n* a city in the SE Netherlands, in Limburg province: industrial centre of a coal-mining region. Pop.: 95 794 (1994).

Hefei ('hʌ'feɪ) *or* **Hofei** ★ *n* a city in SE China, capital of Anhui province: administrative and commercial centre in a rice- and cotton-growing region. Pop.: 1 000 000 (1991 est.).

heft (hɛft) *vb* (*tr*) *Brit. dialect. & US inf.* **1** to assess the weight of (something) by lifting. **2** to lift. ◆ *n* **3** weight. **4** *US.* the main part. ORIG C19: prob. from HEAVE, by analogy with *thieve, theft, cleave, cleft*

hefty ('hɛftɪ) *adj* **heftier, heftiest.** *Inf.* **1** big and strong. **2** characterized by vigour or force: *a hefty blow.* **3** bulky or heavy. **4** sizable; involving a large amount of money: *a hefty bill.*
▸ **'heftily** *adv*

Hegel ★ ('heɪgᵊl) *n* **Georg Wilhelm Friedrich** (ge'ɔrk 'vɪlhɛlm 'friːdrɪç). 1770–1831, German philosopher, whose views are expounded in *The Phenomenology of Mind* (1807).
▸ **Hegelian** (hɪ'geɪlɪən, heɪ'giː-) *adj* ▸ **He'gelianˌism** *n*

hegemony (hɪ'gɛmənɪ) *n, pl* **hegemonies.** ascendancy or domination of one power or state within a league, confederation, etc. ORIG C16: from Gk *hēgemonia,* from *hēgemōn* leader, from *hēgeisthai* to lead
▸ **hegemonic** (ˌhɛgə'mɒnɪk) *adj*

Hegira *or* **Hejira** ('hɛdʒɪrə) *n* **1** the flight of Mohammed from Mecca to Medina in 622 A.D.; the starting point of the Muslim era. **2** the Muslim era itself. **3** (*often not cap.*) an emigration, escape, or flight. ORIG C16: from Med. L, from Ar. *hijrah* emigration or flight

Heidegger ★ (*German* 'haidɛgər) *n* **Martin** ('martiːn). 1889–1976, German existentialist philosopher: he expounded his system in *Being and Time* (1927).

Heidelberg ★ ('haɪdᵊlˌbɜːg; *German* 'haidəlbɛrk) *n* a city in SW Germany, in NW Baden-Württemberg on the River Neckar: capital of the Palatinate from the 13th century until 1719; famous castle (begun in the 12th century) and university (1386), the oldest in Germany. Pop.: 130 781 (1996 est.).

heifer ('hɛfə) *n* a young cow. ORIG OE *heahfore*

Heifetz ★ ('haɪfɪts) *n* **Jascha** ('jæʃə). 1901–87, US violinist, born in Russia.

heigh-ho ('heɪ'həʊ) *interj* an exclamation of weariness, surprise, or happiness.

height (haɪt) *n* **1** the vertical distance from the bottom of something to the top. **2** the vertical distance of a place above sea level. **3** relatively great altitude. **4** the topmost point; summit. **5** *Astron.* the angular distance of a celestial body above the horizon. **6** the period of greatest intensity: *the height of the battle.* **7** an extreme example: *the height of rudeness.* **8** (*often pl*) an area of high ground. ORIG OE *hīehthu;* see HIGH

heighten ('haɪtᵊn) *vb* to make or become higher or more intense.
▸ **'heightened** *adj*

height of land *n US & Canad.* a watershed.

Heilbronn ★ (*German* hail'brɔn) *n* a city in SW Germany, in N Baden-Württemberg on the River Neckar. Pop.: 121 509 (1996 est.).

Heilongjiang ('heɪ'lʊŋdʒaɪ'æŋ) *or* **Heilungkiang** ★ ('heɪ'lʊŋ'kjæŋ, -kaɪ'æŋ) *n* a province of NE China, in Manchuria: coal-mining, with placer gold in some rivers. Capital: Harbin. Pop.: 37 510 000 (1997 est.). Area: 464 000 sq. km (179 000 sq. miles).

Heilong Jiang ★ ('heɪ'lʊŋ dʒaɪ'æŋ) *n* the Pinyin transliteration of the Chinese name for the **Amur.**

Heimdall, Heimdal ('heɪmˌdɑːl), *or* **Heimdallr** ★ ('heɪmˌdɑːlə) *n Norse myth.* the god of light and the dawn, and the guardian of the rainbow bridge Bifrost.

Heine ★ (*German* 'hainə) *n* **Heinrich** ('hainrɪç). 1797–1856, German poet and essayist, whose chief poetic work is *Das Buch der Lieder* (1827). Many of his poems have been set to music, notably by Schubert and Schumann.

Heinkel ★ (*German* 'haınkᵊl) *n* **Ernst Heinrich** (ɛrnst 'hainrɪç). 1888–1958, German aircraft designer. His company provided many military aircraft in World Wars I and II, including the first jet-powered plane.

heinous ('heɪnəs, 'hiː-) *adj* evil; atrocious. ORIG C14: from OF *haineus,* from *haine* hatred, of Gmc origin
▸ **'heinously** *adv*

heir (ɛə) *n* **1** the person legally succeeding to all property of a deceased person. **2** any person or thing that carries

on some tradition, circumstance, etc., from a forerunner. ORIG C13: from OF, from L *hērēs*
▸ '**heirdom** *or* '**heirship** *n*

heir apparent *n, pl* **heirs apparent.** a person whose right to succeed to certain property cannot be defeated, provided such person survives his ancestor.

heiress ('ɛərɪs) *n* **1** a woman who inherits or expects to inherit great wealth. **2** a female heir.

heirloom ('ɛəˌluːm) *n* **1** an object that has been in a family for generations. **2** an item of personal property inherited in accordance with the terms of a will. ORIG C15: from HEIR + *lome* tool; see LOOM[1]

heir presumptive *n Property law.* a person who expects to succeed to an estate but whose right may be defeated by the birth of one nearer in blood to the ancestor.

Heisenberg ★ ('haɪzᵊnˌbɜːg; *German* 'haizənbɛrk) *n* **Werner Karl** ('vɛrnər karl). 1901–76, German physicist. He contributed to quantum mechanics and formulated the uncertainty principle (1927): Nobel prize for physics 1932.

heist (haɪst) *Sl., chiefly US & Canad.* ◆ *n* **1** a robbery. ◆ *vb* **2** (*tr*) to steal. ORIG var. of HOIST

Heitler ★ (*German* 'haitlər) *n* **Walter** ('valtər). 1904–81, German physicist, noted for his work on chemical bonds.

Hejaz, Hedjaz, *or* **Hijaz** ★ (hiː'dʒæz) *n* a region of W Saudi Arabia, along the Red Sea and the Gulf of Aqaba: formerly an independent kingdom; united with Nejd in 1932 to form Saudi Arabia.

Hejira ('hɛdʒɪrə) *n* a variant spelling of **Hegira.**

Hekate ★ ('hɛkətɪ) *n* a variant spelling of **Hecate.**

Hekla ★ ('hɛklə) *n* a volcano in SW Iceland: several craters, with the last eruption in 1970. Height: 1491 m (4892 ft).

Hel (hɛl) *or* **Hela** ★ ('hɛlɑː) *n Norse myth.* **1** the goddess of the dead. **2** the underworld realm of the dead.

held (hɛld) *vb* the past tense and past participle of **hold**[1].

Helen ★ ('hɛlɪn) *n Greek myth.* the beautiful daughter of Zeus and Leda, whose abduction by Paris from her husband Menelaus caused the Trojan War.

Helena[1] ★ ('hɛlənə) *n* a city in W Montana: the state capital. Pop.: 24 569 (1990).

Helena[2] ★ ('hɛlənə) *n* **Saint.** ?248–?328 A.D., Roman empress, mother of Constantine I. After converting to Christianity (313) she made a pilgrimage to the Holy Land (?326). Feast day: May 21.

helenium (hɛ'liːnɪəm) *n* a perennial garden plant with yellow, bronze, or crimson flowers. ORIG from Gk *helenion* name of a plant

Helgoland ★ ('hɛlgolant) *n* the German name for **Heligoland.**

heliacal rising (hɪ'laɪəkᵊl) *n* **1** the rising of a celestial object at the same time as the sun. **2** the date at which such a celestial object first becomes visible. ORIG C17: from LL *hēliacus* relating to the sun, from Gk, from *hēlios* sun

helianthemum (hiːlɪ'ænθəməm) *n* any of a genus of dwarf shrubs with brightly coloured flowers: often grown in rockeries. ORIG from Gk *helios* sun + *anthemon* flower

helianthus (ˌhiːlɪ'ænθəs) *n, pl* **helianthuses.** a plant of the composite family having large yellow daisy-like flowers with yellow, brown, or purple centres. ORIG C18: NL, from Gk *hēlios* sun + *anthos* flower

helical ('hɛlɪkᵊl) *adj* of or like a helix; spiral.

helical gear *n* a gearwheel having the tooth form generated on a helical path about the axis of the wheel.

helices ('hɛlɪˌsiːz) *n* a plural of **helix.**

helichrysum (ˌhɛlɪ'kraɪzəm) *n* any plant of the genus *Helichrysum,* whose flowers retain their shape and colour when dried. ORIG C16: from L, from Gk, from *helix* spiral + *khrusos* gold

helicoid ('hɛlɪˌkɔɪd) *adj* **1** *Biol.* shaped like a spiral: *a helicoid shell.* ◆ *n* **2** *Geom.* any surface resembling that of a screw thread.

helicon ('hɛlɪkən) *n* a bass tuba made to coil over the shoulder of a band musician. ORIG C19: prob. from HELICON; associated with Gk *helix* spiral

Helicon ★ ('hɛlɪkən) *n* a mountain in Greece, in Boeotia: location of the springs of Hippocrene and Aganippe, believed by the Ancient Greeks to be the source of poetic inspiration and the home of the Muses. Height: 1749 m (5738 ft). Modern Greek name: **Elikón.**

helicopter ('hɛlɪˌkɒptə) *n* an aircraft capable of hover, vertical flight, and horizontal flight in any direction. Most get their lift and propulsion from overhead rotating blades. ORIG C19: from F, from Gk *helix* spiral + *pteron* wing

helicopter gunship *n* a large heavily armed helicopter used for ground attack.

Heligoland ★ ('hɛlɪgəʊˌlænd) *n* a small island in the North Sea, one of the North Frisian Islands, separated from the coast of NW Germany by **Heligoland Bight:** administratively part of the German state of Schleswig-Holstein: a large island in early medieval times, now eroded to an area of about 150 hectares (380 acres); ceded by Britain to Germany in 1890 in exchange for Zanzibar. German name: **Helgoland.**

helio- *or before a vowel* **heli-** *combining form.* indicating the sun: *heliocentric.* ORIG from Gk, from *hēlios* sun

heliocentric (ˌhiːlɪəʊ'sɛntrɪk) *adj* **1** having the sun at its centre. **2** measured from or in relation to the sun.
▸ ˌ**helio'centrically** *adv*

Heliogabalus (ˌhiːlɪəʊ'gæbələs) *or* **Elagabalus** ★ *n* original name *Varius Avitus Bassianus.* ?204–222 A.D., Roman emperor (218–222); notorious for his debauchery.

heliograph ('hiːlɪəʊˌgrɑːf) *n* **1** an instrument with mirrors and a shutter used for sending messages in Morse code by reflecting the sun's rays. **2** a device used to photograph the sun.
▸ ˌ**heli'ography** *n*

heliometer (ˌhiːlɪ'ɒmɪtə) *n* a refracting telescope used to determine angular distances between celestial bodies.
▸ ˌ**heli'ometry** *n*

heliopause ('hiːlɪəʊˌpɔːz) *n* the region of space beyond the sun's magnetic field.

Heliopolis ★ (ˌhiːlɪ'ɒpəlɪs) *n* **1** (in ancient Egypt) a city near the apex of the Nile delta: a centre of sun worship. Ancient Egyptian name: **On. 2** the Ancient Greek name for **Baalbek.**

heliopsis (ˌhɛlɪ'ɒpsɪs) *n* a perennial plant with yellow daisy-like flowers.

Helios ★ ('hiːlɪˌɒs) *n Greek myth.* the god of the sun, who drove his chariot daily across the sky. Roman counterpart: **Sol.**

heliostat ('hiːlɪəʊˌstæt) *n* an astronomical instrument used to reflect the light of the sun in a constant direction.
▸ ˌ**helio'static** *adj*

heliotrope ('hiːlɪəˌtrəʊp, 'hɛljə-) *n* **1** any plant of the genus *Heliotropium,* esp. the South American variety, cultivated for its small fragrant purple flowers. **2a** a bluish-violet to purple colour. **2b** (*as adj*): *a heliotrope dress.* **3** another name for **bloodstone.** ORIG C17: from L *hēliotropium,* from Gk, from *hēlios* sun + *trepein* to turn

heliotropism (ˌhiːlɪ'ɒtrəˌpɪzəm) *n* the growth of a plant in response to the stimulus of sunlight.
▸ **heliotropic** (ˌhiːlɪəʊ'trɒpɪk) *adj*

heliport ('hɛlɪˌpɔːt) *n* an airport for helicopters. ORIG C20: from HELI(COPTER) + PORT[1]

helium ('hiːlɪəm) *n* a very light nonflammable colourless odourless element that is an inert gas, occurring in certain natural gases. Symbol: He; atomic no.: 2; atomic wt.: 4.0026. ORIG C19: NL, from HELIO- + -IUM; because first detected in the solar spectrum

helix ('hiːlɪks) *n, pl* **helices** *or* **helixes. 1** a spiral. **2** the incurving fold that forms the margin of the external ear. **3** another name for **volute** (sense 2). **4** any terrestrial mollusc of the genus *Helix,* including the garden snail. ORIG C16: from L, from Gk: spiral; prob. rel. to Gk *helissein* to twist

hell (hɛl) *n* **1** (*sometimes cap.*) *Christianity.* **1a** the place or state of eternal punishment of the wicked after death. **1b** forces of evil regarded as residing there. **2** (*sometimes cap.*) (in various religions and cultures) the abode of the spirits of the dead. **3** pain, extreme difficulty, etc. **4** *Inf.* a cause of such suffering: *war is hell.* **5** *US & Canad.* high spirits or mischievousness. **6** *Now rare.* a gambling house. **7** (**come**) **hell or high water.** *Inf.* whatever difficulties may arise. **8 for the hell of it.** *Inf.* for the fun of it. **9 from hell.** *Inf.* denoting a person or thing that is particularly bad or alarming: *job from hell.* **10 give someone hell.** *Inf.* **10a** to give someone a severe reprimand or punishment. **10b** to be a source of torment to someone. **11 hell for leather.** at great speed. **12 hell to pay.** *Inf.* serious consequences, as of a foolish action. **13 the hell.** *Inf.* **13a** (intensifier): used in such phrases as **what the hell. 13b** an expression of strong disagreement: *the hell I will.* ◆ *interj* **14** *Inf.* an exclamation of anger, surprise, etc. ORIG OE *hell*

he'll (hi:l; *unstressed* i:l, hɪl, ɪl) *contraction of* he will *or* he shall.

hellacious (hɛ'leɪʃəs) *adj US sl.* **1** remarkable; horrifying. **2** wonderful; excellent. ORIG C20: from HELL + *-acious* as in AUDACIOUS

Helladic (hɛ'lædɪk) *adj* of or relating to the Bronze Age civilization that flourished about 2900 to 1100 B.C. on the Greek mainland and islands.

Hellas ★ ('hɛləs) *n* transliteration of the Ancient Greek name for Greece.

hellbent (ˌhɛl'bɛnt) *adj* (*postpositive;* foll. by *on*) *Inf.* strongly or rashly intent.

hellcat ('hɛlˌkæt) *n* a spiteful fierce-tempered woman.

Helle ★ ('hɛlɪ) *n Greek myth.* a daughter of King Athamas, who was borne away with her brother Phrixus on the golden winged ram. She fell from its back and was drowned in the Hellespont. See also **Phrixus, Golden Fleece.**

hellebore ('hɛlɪˌbɔ:) *n* **1** any plant of the Eurasian genus *Helleborus,* typically having showy flowers and poisonous parts. See also **Christmas rose. 2** any of various plants that yield alkaloids used in the treatment of heart disease. ORIG C14: from Gk *helleboros,* from ?

Hellen ★ ('hɛlɪn) *n* (in Greek legend) a Thessalian king and eponymous ancestor of the Hellenes.

Hellene ('hɛli:n) *or* **Hellenian** (hɛ'li:nɪən) *n* another name for a **Greek.**

Hellenic (hɛ'lɛnɪk, -'li:-) *adj* **1** of or relating to the ancient or modern Greeks or their language. **2** of or relating to ancient Greece or the Greeks of the classical period (776–323 B.C.). Cf. **Hellenistic.** ◆ *n* **3** the Greek language in its various ancient and modern dialects.

Hellenism ('hɛlɪˌnɪzəm) *n* **1** the principles, ideals, and pursuits associated with classical Greek civilization. **2** the spirit or national character of the Greeks. **3** imitation of or devotion to the culture of ancient Greece.
▸ **'Hellenist** *n*

Hellenistic (ˌhɛlɪ'nɪstɪk) *or* **Hellenistical** *adj* **1** characteristic of or relating to Greek civilization in the Mediterranean world, esp. from the death of Alexander the Great (323 B.C.) to the defeat of Antony and Cleopatra (30 B.C.). **2** of or relating to the Greeks or to Hellenism.
▸ **ˌHellen'istically** *adv*

Hellenize *or* **Hellenise** ('hɛlɪˌnaɪz) *vb* **Hellenizes, Hellenizing, Hellenized** *or* **Hellenises, Hellenising, Hellenised.** to make or become like the ancient Greeks.
▸ **ˌHelleni'zation** *or* **ˌHelleni'sation** *n*

Heller ★ ('hɛlə) *n* **Joseph.** 1923–99, US novelist. His works include *Catch 22* (1961) and *Closing Time* (1994).

Helles ★ ('hɛlɪs) *n* **Cape.** a cape in NW Turkey, at the S end of the Gallipoli Peninsula.

Hellespont ★ ('hɛlɪˌspɒnt) *n* the ancient name for the **Dardanelles.**

hellfire ('hɛlˌfaɪə) *n* **1** the torment of hell, envisaged as eternal fire. **2** (*modifier*) characterizing sermons that emphasize this.

hellion ('hɛljən) *n Chiefly US inf.* a rowdy person, esp. a child; troublemaker. ORIG C19: prob. from dialect *hallion* rogue, from ?

hellish ('hɛlɪʃ) *adj* **1** of or resembling hell. **2** wicked; cruel. **3** *Inf.* very unpleasant. ◆ *adv* **4** *Brit. inf.* (intensifier): *a hellish good idea.*

Hellman ★ ('hɛlmən) *n* **Lillian.** 1905–84, US dramatist. Her works include the play *The Little Foxes* (1939) and the autobiographical *Scoundrel Time* (1976).

hello, hallo, *or* **hullo** (hɛ'ləʊ, hə-; 'hɛləʊ) *sentence substitute.* **1** an expression of greeting. **2** a call used to attract attention. **3** an expression of surprise. ◆ *n, pl* **hellos, hallos** *or* **hullos. 4** the act of saying or calling "hello". ORIG C19: see HOLLO

Hell's Angel *n* a member of a motorcycle gang who typically dress in Nazi-style paraphernalia and are noted for their lawless behaviour.

helm[1] (hɛlm) *n* **1** *Naut.* **1a** the wheel or entire apparatus by which a vessel is steered. **1b** the position of the helm: that is, on the side of the keel opposite from that of the rudder. **2** a position of leadership or control (esp. in **at the helm**). ◆ *vb* **3** (*tr*) to steer. ORIG OE *helma*
▸ **'helmsman** *n*

helm[2] (hɛlm) *n* an archaic or poetic word for **helmet.** ORIG OE *helm*

Helmand ★ ('hɛlmənd) *n* a river in S Asia, rising in E Afghanistan and flowing generally southwest to a marshy lake, Hamun Helmand, on the border with Iran. Length: 1400 km (870 miles).

helmet ('hɛlmɪt) *n* **1** a piece of protective or defensive armour for the head worn by soldiers, policemen, firemen, divers, etc. See also **crash helmet, pith helmet. 2** *Biol.* a part or structure resembling a helmet, esp. the upper part of the calyx of certain flowers. ORIG C15: from OF, dim. of *helme,* of Gmc origin
▸ **'helmeted** *adj*

Helmholtz ★ (*German* 'hɛlmhɔlts) *n* Baron **Hermann Ludwig Ferdinand von** ('hɛrman 'lu:tvɪç 'fɛrdinant fɔn). 1821–94, German physiologist and physicist: helped to establish the conservation of energy and invented the ophthalmoscope (1850).

helminth ('hɛlmɪnθ) *n* any parasitic worm, esp. a nematode or fluke. ORIG C19: from Gk *helmins* parasitic worm
▸ **hel'minthic** *or* **helminthoid** ('hɛlmɪnˌθɔɪd, hɛl'mɪnθɔɪd) *adj*

helminthiasis (ˌhɛlmɪn'θaɪəsɪs) *n* infestation of the body with parasitic worms. ORIG C19: from NL, from Gk *helminthian* to be infested with worms

Helmont ★ (*Flemish* 'hɛlmɔnt) *n* **Jean Baptiste van** (ʒɑ̃ batist vɑn). 1577–1644, Flemish chemist and physician. He was the first to distinguish gases.

Héloïse ★ ('ɛləʊˌi:z; *French* elɔiz) *n* ?1101–64, pupil, mistress, and wife of Abelard.

helot ('hɛlət, 'hi:-) *n* **1** (*cap.*) (in ancient Sparta) a member of the class of serfs owned by the state. **2** a serf or slave. ORIG C16: from L *Hēlotēs,* from Gk *Heilōtes,* alleged to have meant orig.: inhabitants of Helos, who, after its conquest, were serfs of the Spartans
▸ **'helotism** *n* ▸ **'helotry** *n*

help (hɛlp) *vb* **1** to assist (someone to do something), esp. by sharing the work, cost, or burden of something. **2** to alleviate the burden of (someone else) by giving assistance. **3** (*tr*) to assist (a person) to go in a specified direction: *help the old lady up.* **4** to contribute to: *to help the relief operations.* **5** to improve (a situation, etc.): *crying won't help.* **6** (*tr;* preceded by *can, could,* etc.; *usually used with a negative*) **6a** to refrain from: *we can't help wondering who he is.* **6b** (usually foll. by *it*) to be responsible for: *I can't help it if it rains.* **7** to alleviate (an illness, etc.). **8** (*tr*) to serve (a customer). **9** (*tr;* foll. by *to*) **9a** to serve (someone with food, etc.) (usually in **help oneself**). **9b** to provide (oneself with) without permission. **10 cannot help but.** to be unable to do anything else except: *I cannot help but laugh.* **11 so help me. 11a** on my honour. **11b** no matter what: *so help me, I'll get revenge.* ◆ *n* **12** the act of helping or being helped, or a person or thing that helps. **13a** a person hired for a job, esp. a farm worker or domestic servant. **13b** (*functioning as sing*) several employees collectively. **14** a remedy: *there's no help for it.* ◆ *sentence substitute.* **15** used to ask for assistance. ◆ See also **help out.** ORIG OE *helpan*
▸ **'helper** *n*

★ people and places

helpful (ˈhɛlpfʊl) *adj* giving help.
▸ ˈ**helpfully** *adv* ▸ ˈ**helpfulness** *n*

helping (ˈhɛlpɪŋ) *n* a single portion of food.

helping hand *n* assistance: *many people lent a helping hand in making arrangements.*

helpless (ˈhɛlplɪs) *adj* **1** unable to manage independently. **2** made weak: *they were helpless from giggling.*
▸ ˈ**helplessly** *adv* ▸ ˈ**helplessness** *n*

helpline (ˈhɛlpˌlaɪn) *n* a telephone line operated by a charitable organization for people in distress or by a commercial organization to provide information.

Helpmann ★ (ˈhɛlpmən) *n* Sir **Robert.** 1909–86, Australian ballet dancer and choreographer: his ballets include *Miracle in the Gorbals* (1944) and *Yugen* (1965).

helpmate (ˈhɛlpˌmeɪt) *n* a companion and helper, esp. a wife.

helpmeet (ˈhɛlpˌmiːt) *n* a less common word for **helpmate.** ORIG C17: from *an helpe meet* (suitable) *for him* Genesis 2:18

help out *vb* (*adv*) to assist, esp. by sharing the burden or cost of something with (another person).

Helsingborg ★ (*Swedish* hɛlsiŋˈbɔrj) *n* a port in SW Sweden, on the Sound opposite Helsingør, Denmark: changed hands several times between Denmark and Sweden, finally becoming Swedish in 1710; shipbuilding. Pop.: 114 866 (1997 est.). Former name (until 1971): **Hälsingborg.**

Helsingør ★ (*Danish* hɛlsenˈøːr) *n* a port in NE Denmark, in NE Zealand: site of Kronborg Castle (16th century), famous as the scene of Shakespeare's *Hamlet.* Pop.: 56 855 (1995). English name: **Elsinore.**

Helsinki ★ (ˈhɛlsɪŋkɪ, hɛlˈsɪŋ-) *n* the capital of Finland, a port in the south on the Gulf of Finland: founded by Gustavus I of Sweden in 1550; replaced Turku as capital in 1812, while under Russian rule; university. Pop.: 532 053 (1997 est.). Swedish name: **Helsingfors** (hɛlsɪŋˈfɔrs).

helter-skelter (ˈhɛltəˈskɛltə) *adj* **1** haphazard or careless. ◆ *adv* **2** in a helter-skelter manner. ◆ *n* **3** *Brit.* a high spiral slide, as at a fairground. **4** disorder. ORIG C16: prob. imit.

helve (hɛlv) *n* the handle of a hand tool such as an axe or pick. ORIG OE *hielfe*

Helvellyn ★ (hɛlˈvɛlɪn) *n* a mountain in NW England, in the Lake District. Height: 950 m (3118 ft).

Helvetia ★ (hɛlˈviːʃə) *n* **1** the Latin name for Switzerland. **2** a Roman province in central Europe (1st century B.C. to the 5th century A.D.), corresponding to part of S Germany and parts of W and N Switzerland.

Helvetian (hɛlˈviːʃən) *adj* **1** Swiss. ◆ *n* **2** a native or citizen of Switzerland.

Helvétius ★ (hɛlˈviːʃɪəs; *French* ɛlvesjys) *n* **Claude Adrien** (klod adriɛ). 1715–71, French philosopher. His chief work was *De l'Esprit* (1758).

hem[1] (hɛm) *n* **1** an edge to a piece of cloth, made by folding the raw edge under and stitching it down. **2** short for **hemline.** ◆ *vb* **hems, hemming, hemmed.** (*tr*) **3** to provide with a hem. **4** (usually foll. by *in, around,* or *about*) to enclose or confine. ORIG OE *hemm*
▸ ˈ**hemmer** *n*

hem[2] (hɛm) *n, interj* **1** a representation of the sound of clearing the throat, used to gain attention, etc. ◆ *vb* **hems, hemming, hemmed. 2** (*intr*) to utter this sound. **3 hem** (*or* **hum**) **and haw.** to hesitate in speaking.

he-man *n, pl* **he-men.** *Inf.* a strongly built muscular man.

hematite *or* **haematite** (ˈhɛmətaɪt, ˈhiːm-) *n* a red, grey, or black mineral, found as massive beds and in veins and igneous rocks. It is the chief source of iron. Composition: iron (ferric) oxide. Crystal structure: hexagonal (rhombohedral). ORIG C16: via L from Gk *haimatitēs* resembling blood, from *haima* blood
▸ **hematitic** *or* **haematitic** (ˌhɛməˈtɪtɪk, ˌhiː-) *adj*

hemato- *or before a vowel* **hemat-** *combining form.* US variants of **haemato-.**

Hemel Hempstead ★ (ˈhɛməl ˈhɛmstɪd) *n* a town in SE England, in W Hertfordshire: designated a new town in 1947. Pop.: 79 235 (1991).

hemeralopia (ˌhɛmərəˈləʊpɪə) *n* inability to see clearly in bright light. Nontechnical name: **day blindness.** ORIG C18: NL, from Gk, from *hēmera* day + *alaos* blind + *ōps* eye

hemerocallis (hɛmərˈɒkælɪs) *n* a N temperate plant with large funnel-shaped orange flowers: each single flower lasts for only one day. Also called: **day lily.** ORIG C17: from Gk *hēmera* day + *kallos* beauty

hemi- *prefix* half: *hemicycle; hemisphere.* ORIG from L, from Gk *hēmi-*

-hemia *n combining form.* a US variant of **-aemia.**

hemidemisemiquaver (ˌhɛmɪˌdɛmɪˈsɛmɪˌkweɪvə) *n Music.* a note having the time value of one sixty-fourth of a semibreve. Usual US & Canad. name: **sixty-fourth note.**

Hemingway ★ (ˈhɛmɪŋˌweɪ) *n* **Ernest.** 1899–1961, US writer. His novels include *A Farewell to Arms* (1929) and *For Whom the Bell Tolls* (1940): Nobel prize for literature 1954.

hemiplegia (ˌhɛmɪˈpliːdʒɪə) *n* paralysis of one side of the body.
▸ ˌ**hemiˈplegic** *adj*

hemipode (ˈhɛmɪˌpəʊd) *n* a small quail-like bird occurring in tropical and subtropical regions of the Old World. Also called: **button quail.**

hemipteran (hɪˈmɪptərən) *n* any hemipterous insect. ORIG C19: from HEMI- + Gk *pteron* wing

hemipterous (hɪˈmɪptərəs) *adj* of or belonging to a large order of insects having sucking or piercing mouthparts.

hemisphere (ˈhɛmɪˌsfɪə) *n* **1** one half of a sphere. **2a** half of the terrestrial globe, divided into **northern** and **southern hemispheres** by the equator or into **eastern** and **western hemispheres** by some meridians, usually 0° and 180°. **2b** a map or projection of one of the hemispheres. **3** *Anat.* short for **cerebral hemisphere,** a half of the cerebrum.
▸ **hemispheric** (ˌhɛmɪˈsfɛrɪk) *or* ˌ**hemiˈspherical** *adj*

hemistich (ˈhɛmɪˌstɪk) *n Prosody.* a half line of verse.

hemline (ˈhɛmˌlaɪn) *n* the level to which the hem of a skirt or dress hangs.

hemlock (ˈhɛmˌlɒk) *n* **1** an umbelliferous poisonous Eurasian plant having finely divided leaves, spotted stems, and small white flowers. **2** a poisonous drug derived from this plant. **3** Also called: **hemlock spruce.** a coniferous tree of North America and Asia. ORIG OE *hymlic*

hemo- *combining form.* a US variant of **haemo-.**

hemp (hɛmp) *n* **1** Also called: **cannabis, marijuana.** an Asian plant having tough fibres, deeply lobed leaves, and small greenish flowers. See also **Indian hemp. 2** the fibre of this plant, used to make canvas, rope, etc. **3** any of several narcotic drugs obtained from some varieties of this plant, esp. from Indian hemp. ORIG OE *hænep*
▸ ˈ**hempen** *or* ˈ**hempˌlike** *adj*

hemstitch (ˈhɛmˌstɪtʃ) *n* **1** a decorative edging stitch, usually for a hem, in which the cross threads are stitched in groups. ◆ *vb* **2** to decorate (a hem, etc.) with hemstitches.

hen (hɛn) *n* **1** the female of any bird, esp. of the domestic fowl. **2** the female of certain other animals, such as the lobster. **3** *Scot. dialect.* a term of address used to women. ORIG OE *henn*

Henan (ˈhʌˈnæn) *or* **Honan** ★ *n* a province of N central China: the chief centre of early Chinese culture; mainly agricultural (the largest wheat-producing province in China). Capital: Zhengzhou. Pop.: 92 430 000 (1997 est.).

henbane (ˈhɛnˌbeɪn) *n* a poisonous Mediterranean plant with sticky hairy leaves: yields the drug hyoscyamine.

hence (hɛns) *sentence connector.* **1** for this reason; therefore. ◆ *adv* **2** from this time: *a year hence.* **3** *Arch.* from here; away. ◆ *sentence substitute.* **4** *Arch.* begone! away! ORIG OE *hionane*

henceforth (ˈhɛnsˈfɔːθ), **henceforwards,** *or* **henceforward** *adv* from now on.

henchman (ˈhɛntʃmən) *n, pl* **henchmen. 1** a faithful attendant or supporter. **2** *Arch.* a squire; page. ORIG C14 *hengestman,* from OE *hengest* stallion + MAN

hendeca- *combining form.* eleven: *hendecagon; hendecasyllable.* ORIG from Gk *hendeka,* from *hen,* neuter of *heis* one + *deka* ten

hendecagon (hɛnˈdɛkəgən) *n* a polygon having 11 sides.
▸ **hendecagonal** (ˌhɛndɪˈkægənᵊl) *adj*

hendecasyllable (ˈhɛndɛkəˌsɪləbᵊl) *n Prosody.* a verse line of 11 syllables. ORIG C18: from Gk

Henderson ★ (ˈhɛndəsᵊn) *n* **Arthur.** 1863–1935, British Labour politician. Foreign secretary (1929–31); Nobel peace prize 1934.

hendiadys (hɛnˈdaɪədɪs) *n* a rhetorical device by which two nouns joined by a conjunction are used instead of a noun and a modifier, as in *to run with fear and haste* instead of *to run with fearful haste.* ORIG C16: from Med. L, from Gk *hen dia duoin,* lit.: one through two

Hendrix ★ (ˈhɛndrɪks) *n* **Jimi,** full name *James Marshall Hendrix.* 1942–70, US rock guitarist, singer, and songwriter. His recordings include "Purple Haze" (1967) and *Are you Experienced?* (1967).

Hendry ★ (ˈhɛndrɪ) *n* **Stephen.** born 1969, British snooker player: world champion 1990, 1992–96, and 1999.

henequen, henequin, *or* **heniquen** (ˈhɛnɪkɪn) *n* **1** an agave plant that is native to Mexico. **2** the fibre of this plant, used in making rope, twine, and coarse fabrics. ORIG C19: from American Sp. *henequén,* prob. of Amerind origin

henge (hɛndʒ) *n* a circular monument, often containing a circle of stones, dating from the Neolithic and Bronze Ages. ORIG back formation from *Stonehenge,* site of important megalithic ruins on Salisbury Plain, S England

Hengelo ★ (*Dutch* ˈhɛŋəloː) *n* a city in the E Netherlands, in Overijssel province on the Twente Canal: industrial centre, esp. for textiles. Pop.: 77 514 (1994).

Hengist ★ (ˈhɛŋgɪst) *n* died ?488 A.D., a leader, with his brother Horsa, of the first Jutish settlers in Britain; he is thought to have conquered Kent (?455).

Hengyang ★ (ˈhɛŋˈjæŋ) *n* a city in SE central China, in Hunan province on the Xiang River. Pop.: 487 148 (1990 est.).

hen harrier *n* a common harrier that nests in marshes and open land.

henhouse (ˈhɛnˌhaʊs) *n* a coop for hens.

Henie ★ (ˈhɛnɪ) *n* **Sonja** (ˈsɒnjə). 1912–69, Norwegian figure-skater.

Henley-on-Thames ★ (ˈhɛnlɪ-) *n* a town in S England, in SE Oxfordshire on the River Thames: a riverside resort with an annual regatta. Pop.: 10 558 (1991). Often shortened to **Henley.**

henna (ˈhɛnə) *n* **1** a shrub or tree of Asia and N Africa. **2** a reddish dye obtained from the powdered leaves of this plant, used as a cosmetic and industrial dye. **3a** a reddish-brown colour. **3b** (*as adj*): *henna tresses.* ◆ *vb* **hennas, hennaing, hennaed. 4** (*tr*) to dye with henna. ORIG C16: from Ar. *hinnāʼ;* see ALKANET

hen night *n Inf.* a party for women only, esp. held for a woman shortly before she is married. Cf. **hen party, stag night.**

henotheism (ˈhɛnəʊθiːˌɪzəm) *n* the worship of one deity (of several) as the special god of one's family, clan, or tribe. ORIG C19: from Gk *heis* one + *theos* god
▸ ˌ**henotheˈistic** *adj*

hen party *n Inf.* a party at which only women are present. Cf. **hen night, stag night.**

henpeck (ˈhɛnˌpɛk) *vb* (*tr*) (of a woman) to harass or torment (a man, esp. her husband) by persistent nagging.
▸ **ˈhenˌpecked** *adj*

Henrietta Maria ★ (ˌhɛnrɪˈɛtə məˈriːə) *n* 1609–69, queen of England (1625–49), the wife of Charles I; daughter of Henry IV of France. Her Roman Catholicism contributed to the unpopularity of the crown in the period leading to the Civil War.

henry (ˈhɛnrɪ) *n, pl* **henry, henries,** *or* **henrys.** the derived SI unit of electric inductance; the inductance of a closed circuit in which an emf of 1 volt is produced when the current varies uniformly at the rate of 1 ampere per second. Symbol: H ORIG C19: after Joseph HENRY

Henry ★ (ˈhɛnrɪ) *n* **1 Joseph.** 1797–1878, US physicist. He discovered the principle of electromagnetic induction independently of Faraday and constructed the first electromagnetic motor (1829). **2 Patrick.** 1736–99, American statesman, a leading opponent of British rule during the War of American Independence.

Henry I ★ *n* 1068–1135, king of England (1100–35) and duke of Normandy (1106–35); son of William the Conqueror: crowned in the absence of his elder brother, Robert II, duke of Normandy; conquered Normandy (1106).

Henry II ★ *n* **1** 1133–89, first Plantagenet king of England (1154–89): extended his Anglo-French domains and instituted judicial and financial reforms. His attempts to control the church were opposed by Becket. **2** 1519–59, king of France (1547–59); husband of Catherine de' Medici. He recovered Calais from the English (1558) and suppressed the Huguenots.

Henry III ★ *n* **1** 1207–72, king of England (1216–72); son of John. His incompetent rule provoked the second Barons' War (1264–67), during which he was captured by Simon de Montfort. **2** 1551–89, king of France (1574–89). He plotted the massacre of Huguenots on St Bartholomew's Day (1572) with his mother Catherine de' Medici, thus exacerbating the religious wars in France.

Henry IV ★ *n* **1** 1050–1106, Holy Roman Emperor (1084–1105) and king of Germany (1056–1105). He was excommunicated by Pope Gregory VII, whom he deposed (1084). **2** surnamed *Bolingbroke.* 1367–1413, first Lancastrian king of England (1399–1413); son of John of Gaunt: deposed Richard II (1399) and suppressed rebellions led by Owen Glendower and the Earl of Northumberland. **3** known as *Henry of Navarre.* 1553–1610, first Bourbon king of France (1589–1610). He obtained toleration for the Huguenots with the Edict of Nantes (1598) and restored prosperity to France following the religious wars (1562–98).

Henry V ★ *n* 1387–1422, king of England (1413–22); son of Henry IV. He defeated the French at the Battle of Agincourt (1415), conquered Normandy (1419), and was recognized as heir to the French throne (1420).

Henry VI ★ *n* 1421–71, last Lancastrian king of England (1422–61; 1470–71); son of Henry V. His weak rule was blamed for the loss by 1453 of all his possessions in France except Calais; from 1454 he suffered periods of insanity, which contributed to the outbreak of the Wars of the Roses (1455–85). He was deposed by Edward IV (1461) but was briefly restored to the throne (1470).

Henry VII ★ *n* 1457–1509, first Tudor king of England (1485–1509). He came to the throne (1485) after defeating Richard III at the Battle of Bosworth Field, ending the Wars of the Roses. Royal power and the prosperity of the country greatly increased during his reign.

Henry VIII ★ *n* 1491–1547, king of England (1509–47); second son of Henry VII. The declaration that his marriage to Catherine of Aragon was invalid and his marriage to Anne Boleyn (1533) precipitated the Act of Supremacy, making Henry supreme head of the Church in England. Anne Boleyn was executed (1536) and Henry subsequently married Jane Seymour, Anne of Cleves, Catherine Howard, and Catherine Parr.

Henryson ★ (ˈhɛnrɪsᵊn) *n* **Robert.** ?1430–?1506, Scottish poet. His works include *Testament of Cresseid* (1593) and the 13 *Moral Fables of Esope the Phrygian.*

Henry the Navigator ★ *n* 1394–1460, prince of Portugal, noted for his patronage of Portuguese voyages of exploration.

Henslowe ★ (ˈhɛnzləʊ) *n* **Philip.** died 1616, English theatre manager, noted also for his diary.

Henze ★ (*German* ˈhɛntsə) *n* **Hans Werner** (hans ˈvɛrnər). born 1926, German composer, whose works include the operas *The Stag King* (1956) and *Das verratene Meer* (1990) and the oratorio *The Raft of the Medusa* (1968).

hep (hɛp) *adj* **hepper, heppest.** *Sl.* an earlier word for **hip**[4].

heparin (ˈhɛpərɪn) *n* a polysaccharide, containing sulphate groups, present in most body tissues: an anticoagulant used in the treatment of thrombosis. ORIG C20: from Gk *hēpar* the liver + -IN

hepatic (hɪˈpætɪk) *adj* **1** of the liver. **2** having the colour of liver. ◆ *n* **3** any of various drugs for use in treating diseases of the liver. ORIG C15: from L *hēpaticus,* from Gk *hēpar* liver

hepatica (hɪˈpætɪkə) *n* a woodland plant of a N temperate genus, having three-lobed leaves and white, mauve, or pink flowers. ORIG C16: from Med. L: liverwort, from L *hēpaticus* of the liver

hepatitis (ˌhɛpəˈtaɪtɪs) *n* inflammation of the liver.

hepatitis A *n* a form of hepatitis caused by a virus transmitted in contaminated food or drink.

hepatitis B *n* a form of hepatitis caused by a virus transmitted by infected blood (as in transfusions), contaminated hypodermic needles, sexual contact, or by contact with any other body fluid. Former name: **serum hepatitis.**

hepatitis C *n* a form of hepatitis caused by a virus that is transmitted in the same ways as that responsible for hepatitis B. Former name: **non-A, non-B hepatitis.**

Hepburn ★ (ˈhɛpˌbɜːn) *n* **Katharine.** born 1909, US film actress, whose films include *The Philadelphia Story* (1940), *The African Queen* (1951), *The Lion in Winter* (1968), and *On Golden Pond* (1981).

Hephaestus (hɪˈfiːstəs) *or* **Hephaistos** ★ (hɪˈfaɪstɒs) *n Greek myth.* the lame god of fire and metal-working. Roman counterpart: **Vulcan.**

Hepplewhite (ˈhɛpᵊlˌwaɪt) *adj* of or in a style of ornamental and carved 18th-century English furniture. ORIG C18: after George *Hepplewhite* (1727–86), E cabinetmaker

hepta- *or before a vowel* **hept-** *combining form.* seven: *heptameter.* ORIG from Gk

heptad (ˈhɛptæd) *n* a group or series of seven. ORIG C17: from Gk *heptas* seven

heptagon (ˈhɛptəgən) *n* a polygon having seven sides.
▸ **heptagonal** (hɛpˈtægənᵊl) *adj*

heptahedron (ˌhɛptəˈhiːdrən) *n* a solid figure having seven plane faces.
▸ **ˌheptaˈhedral** *adj*

heptameter (hɛpˈtæmɪtə) *n Prosody.* a verse line of seven metrical feet.
▸ **heptametrical** (ˌhɛptəˈmɛtrɪkᵊl) *adj*

heptane (ˈhɛpteɪn) *n* an alkane which is found in petroleum and used as an anaesthetic. ORIG C19: from HEPTA- + -ANE, because it has seven carbon atoms

heptarchy (ˈhɛptɑːkɪ) *n, pl* **heptarchies. 1** government by seven rulers. **2** the seven kingdoms into which Anglo-Saxon England is thought to have been divided from about the 7th to the 9th centuries A.D.
▸ **ˈheptarch** *n* ▸ **hepˈtarchic** *or* **hepˈtarchal** *adj*

heptathlon (hɛpˈtæθlɒn) *n* an athletic contest for women in which each athlete competes in seven different events. ORIG C20: from HEPTA- + Gk *athlon* contest
▸ **hepˈtathlete** *n*

heptavalent (hɛpˈtævələnt, ˌhɛptəˈveɪlənt) *adj Chem.* having a valency of seven.

Hepworth ★ (ˈhɛpwəθ) *n* Dame **Barbara.** 1903–75, British sculptor of abstract works.

her (hɜː; *unstressed* hə, ə) *pron* (*objective*) **1** refers to a female person or animal: *he loves her.* **2** refers to things personified as feminine or traditionally to ships and nations. ◆ *determiner* **3** of, belonging to, or associated with her: *her hair.* ORIG OE *hire,* genitive & dative of *hēo* SHE, fem. of *hē* HE

> **USAGE NOTE** See at **me**[1].

Hera *or* **Here** ★ (ˈhɪərə) *n Greek myth.* the queen of the Olympian gods and sister and wife of Zeus. Roman counterpart: **Juno.**

Heraclea ★ (ˌhɛrəˈkliːə) *n* any of several ancient Greek colonies. The most famous is the S Italian site where Pyrrhus of Epirus defeated the Romans (280 B.C.).

Heracleides *or* **Heraclides of Pontus** ★ (ˌhɛrəˈklaɪdiːz; ˈpɒntəs) *n* ?390 B.C.–?322 B.C., Greek astronomer and philosopher: the first to state that the earth rotates on its axis.

Heracles *or* **Herakles** ★ (ˈhɛrəˌkliːz) *n* the usual name (in Greek) for **Hercules.**
▸ **ˌHeraˈclean** *or* **ˌHeraˈklean** *adj*

Heraclitus ★ (ˌhɛrəˈklaɪtəs) *n* ?535–?475 B.C., Greek philosopher, who held that fire is the primordial substance.

Heraclius ★ (həˈræklɪəs) *n* ?575–641 A.D., Byzantine emperor, who restored the Holy Cross to Jerusalem (629).

Herakleion *or* **Heraklion** ★ (*Greek* heˈraːkliɔn) *n* a variant of **Iráklion.**

herald (ˈhɛrəld) *n* **1** a person who announces important news. **2** *Often literary.* a forerunner; harbinger. **3** the intermediate rank of heraldic officer, between king-of-arms and pursuivant. **4** (in the Middle Ages) an official at a tournament. ◆ *vb* (*tr*) **5** to announce publicly. **6** to precede or usher in. ORIG C14: from OF *herault,* of Gmc origin

heraldic (hɛˈrældɪk) *adj* of or relating to heraldry or heralds.
▸ **heˈraldically** *adv*

heraldry (ˈhɛrəldrɪ) *n, pl* **heraldries. 1** the study concerned with the classification of armorial bearings, the tracing of genealogies, etc. **2** armorial bearings, insignia, etc. **3** the show and ceremony of heraldry.
▸ **ˈheraldist** *n*

Herat ★ (hɛˈræt) *n* a city in NW Afghanistan, on the Hari Rud River: on the site of several ancient cities; at its height as a cultural centre in the 15th century. Pop.: 186 800 (1990 est.).

Hérault ★ (*French* ero) *n* a department of S France, in Languedoc-Roussillon region. Capital: Montpellier. Pop.: 853 594 (1994 est.). Area: 6224 sq. km (2427 sq. miles).

herb (hɜːb; *US* ɜːrb) *n* **1** a plant whose aerial parts do not persist above ground at the end of the growing season; herbaceous plant. **2** any of various usually aromatic plants, such as parsley and rosemary, that are used in cookery and medicine. ORIG C13: from OF *herbe,* from L *herba* grass, green plants
▸ **ˈherbˌlike** *adj* ▸ **ˈherby** *adj*

herbaceous (hɜːˈbeɪʃəs) *adj* **1** designating or relating to plants that are fleshy as opposed to woody: *a herbaceous plant.* **2** (of petals and sepals) green and leaflike.

herbaceous border *n* a flower bed that contains perennials rather than annuals.

herbage (ˈhɜːbɪdʒ) *n* **1** herbaceous plants collectively, esp. the edible parts on which cattle, sheep, etc., graze. **2** the vegetation of pasture land; pasturage.

herbal (ˈhɜːbᵊl) *adj* **1** of herbs. ◆ *n* **2** a book describing the properties of plants.

herbalist (ˈhɜːbᵊlɪst) *n* **1** a person who grows or specializes in the use of herbs, esp. medicinal herbs. **2** (formerly) a descriptive botanist.

herbarium (hɜːˈbɛərɪəm) *n, pl* **herbariums** *or* **herbaria** (-ɪə). **1** a collection of dried plants that are mounted and classified systematically. **2** a room, etc., in which such a collection is kept.

herb bennet (ˈbɛnɪt) *n* a Eurasian and N African plant with yellow flowers. Also called: **wood avens, bennet.** ORIG from OF *herbe benoite,* lit.: blessed herb, from Med. L *herba benedicta*

Herbert ★ (ˈhɜːbət) *n* **George.** 1593–1633, English Metaphysical poet. His chief work is *The Temple: Sacred Poems and Private Ejaculations* (1633).

herbicide (ˈhɜːbɪˌsaɪd) *n* a chemical that destroys plants, esp. one used to control weeds.

herbivore (ˈhɜːbɪˌvɔː) *n* **1** an animal that feeds on grass and other plants. **2** *Inf.* a liberal, idealistic, or nonmaterialistic person. ORIG C19: from NL *herbivora* grass-eaters
▸ **herˈbivorous** *adj*

herb Paris ('pærɪs) *n, pl* **herbs Paris.** a Eurasian woodland plant with a whorl of four leaves and a solitary yellow flower. ORIG C16: from Med. L *herba paris,* lit.: herb of a pair: because the four leaves on the stalk look like a true lovers' knot

herb Robert ('rɒbət) *n, pl* **herbs Robert.** a low-growing N temperate plant with strongly scented divided leaves and small purplish flowers. ORIG C13: from Med. L *herba Roberti* herb of Robert, prob. after St *Robert,* 11th-cent. F ecclesiastic

Hercegovina ★ (*Serbo-Croat* 'hɛrtsɛgɔvina) *n* a variant of **Herzegovina.**

Herculaneum ★ (ˌhɜːkjʊ'leɪnɪəm) *n* an ancient city in SW Italy, of marked Greek character, on the S slope of Vesuvius: buried along with Pompeii by an eruption of the volcano (79 A.D.). Excavation has uncovered well preserved streets, houses, etc.

herculean (ˌhɜːkjʊ'liːən) *adj* **1** requiring tremendous effort, strength, etc. **2** (*sometimes cap.*) resembling Hercules in strength, courage, etc.

Hercules ('hɜːkjʊˌliːz), **Heracles,** *or* **Herakles** ★ *n* **1** Also called: **Alcides.** *Classical myth.* a hero noted for his great strength, courage, and for the performance of twelve immense labours. **2** a man of outstanding strength or size.

herd[1] (hɜːd) *n* **1** a large group of mammals living and feeding together, esp. cattle. **2** *Often disparaging.* a large group of people. ◆ *vb* **3** to collect or be collected into or as if into a herd. ORIG OE *heord*

herd[2] (hɜːd) *n* **1a** *Arch. or dialect.* a man who tends livestock; herdsman. **1b** (*in combination*): *goatherd.* ◆ *vb* (*tr*) **2** to drive forwards in a large group. **3** to look after (livestock). ORIG OE *hirde:* see HERD[1]

herd instinct *n Psychol.* the inborn tendency to associate with others and follow the group's behaviour.

herdsman ('hɜːdzmən) *n, pl* **herdsmen.** *Chiefly Brit.* a person who breeds or cares for cattle or (rarely) other livestock. US equivalent: **herder.**

here (hɪə) *adv* **1** in, at, or to this place, point, case, or respect: *we come here every summer; here comes Roy.* **2 here and there.** at several places in or throughout an area. **3 here's to.** a formula used in proposing a toast to someone or something. **4 neither here nor there.** of no relevance or importance. ◆ *n* **5** this place or point: *they leave here tonight.* ORIG OE *hēr*

hereabouts ('hɪərəˌbaʊts) *or* **hereabout** *adv* in this region or neighbourhood.

hereafter (ˌhɪər'ɑːftə) *adv* **1** *Formal or law.* in a subsequent part of this document, matter, case, etc. **2** a less common word for **henceforth. 3** at some time in the future. **4** in a future life after death. ◆ *n* (usually preceded by *the*) **5** life after death. **6** the future.

hereat (ˌhɪər'æt) *adv Arch.* because of this.

hereby (ˌhɪə'baɪ) *adv* (used in official statements, etc.) by means of or as a result of this.

hereditable (hɪ'rɛdɪtəb^əl) *adj* a less common word for **heritable.**
▸ **heˌredita'bility** *n*

hereditament (ˌhɛrɪ'dɪtəmənt) *n Property law.* any kind of property capable of being inherited.

hereditary (hɪ'rɛdɪtərɪ, -trɪ) *adj* **1** of or denoting factors that can be transmitted genetically from one generation to another. **2** *Law.* **2a** descending to succeeding generations by inheritance. **2b** transmitted according to established rules of descent. **3** derived from one's ancestors; traditional: *hereditary feuds.*
▸ **he'reditarily** *adv* ▸ **he'reditariness** *n*

heredity (hɪ'rɛdɪtɪ) *n, pl* **heredities. 1** the transmission from one generation to another of genetic factors that determine individual characteristics. **2** the sum total of the inherited factors in an organism. ORIG C16: from OF *heredite,* from L *hērēditās* inheritance; see HEIR

Hereford ★ ('hɛrɪfəd) *n* **1** a city in W England, the administrative centre of Herefordshire, on the River Wye: trading centre for agricultural produce; cathedral (begun 1079). Pop.: 54 326 (1991). **2** a hardy breed of beef cattle characterized by a red body, red and white head, and white markings.

Hereford and Worcester ★ *n* a former county of the W Midlands of England, formed in 1974 from the historic counties of Herefordshire and Worcestershire minus a small area of NW Worcestershire: it was abolished in 1998 when these counties became independent unitary authorities.

Herefordshire ★ ('hɛrɪfədˌʃɪə, -ʃə) *n* a county of W England, formerly part of Hereford and Worcester (1974–98). Drained chiefly by the River Wye, it is mainly agricultural (esp. fruit and cattle). Administrative centre: Hereford. Pop.: 166 750 (1998 est.). Area: 2180 sq. km (842 sq. miles).

herein (ˌhɪər'ɪn) *adv* **1** *Formal or law.* in or into this place, thing, document, etc. **2** *Rare.* in this respect, circumstance, etc.

hereinafter (ˌhɪərɪn'ɑːftə) *adv Formal or law.* from this point on in this document, etc.

hereinto (ˌhɪər'ɪntuː) *adv Formal or law.* into this place, circumstance, etc.

hereof (ˌhɪər'ɒv) *adv Formal or law.* of or concerning this.

hereon (ˌhɪər'ɒn) *adv* an archaic word for **hereupon.**

heresiarch (hɪ'riːzɪˌɑːk) *n* the leader or originator of a heretical movement or sect.

heresy ('hɛrəsɪ) *n, pl* **heresies. 1a** an opinion contrary to the orthodox tenets of a religious body. **1b** the act of maintaining such an opinion. **2** any belief that is or is thought to be contrary to official or established theory. **3** adherence to unorthodox opinion. ORIG C13: from OF *eresie,* from LL, from L: sect, from Gk, from *hairein* to choose

heretic ('hɛrətɪk) *n* **1** *Now chiefly RC Church.* a person who maintains beliefs contrary to the established teachings of his Church. **2** a person who holds unorthodox opinions in any field.
▸ **heretical** (hɪ'rɛtɪk^əl) *adj* ▸ **he'retically** *adv*

hereto (ˌhɪə'tuː) *adv Formal or law.* to this place, thing, matter, document, etc.

heretofore (ˌhɪətʊ'fɔː) *adv Formal or law.* until now; before this time.

hereunder (ˌhɪər'ʌndə) *adv Formal or law.* **1** (in documents, etc.) below this; subsequently; hereafter. **2** under the terms or authority of this.

hereupon (ˌhɪərə'pɒn) *adv* **1** following immediately after this; at this stage. **2** *Formal or law.* upon this thing, point, subject, etc.

Hereward ★ ('hɛrɪwəd) *n* called *Hereward the Wake.* 11th-century Anglo-Saxon rebel, who defended the Isle of Ely against William the Conqueror (1070–71): a subject of many legends.

herewith (ˌhɪə'wɪð, -'wɪθ) *adv Formal.* together with this: *we send you herewith your statement of account.*

heriot ('hɛrɪət) *n* (in medieval England) a death duty paid by villeins and free tenants to their lord, often consisting of the dead man's best beast or chattel. ORIG OE *heregeatwa,* from *here* army + *geatwa* equipment

Herisau ★ (*German* 'heːrizau) *n* a town in NE Switzerland, capital of Appenzell Outer Rhodes demicanton. Pop.: 14 955 (1987).

heritable ('hɛrɪtəb^əl) *adj* **1** capable of being inherited; inheritable. **2** *Chiefly law.* capable of inheriting. ORIG C14: from OF, from *heriter* to INHERIT
▸ **ˌherita'bility** *n* ▸ **'heritably** *adv*

heritage ('hɛrɪtɪdʒ) *n* **1** something inherited at birth. **2** anything that has been transmitted from the past or handed down by tradition. **3** the evidence of the past, such as historical sites, and the unspoilt natural environment, considered as the inheritance of present-day society. **4** *Law.* any property, esp. land, that by law has descended or may descend to an heir. ORIG C13: from OF; see HEIR

herl (hɜːl) *or* **harl** *n Angling.* **1** the barb or barbs of a feather, used to dress fishing flies. **2** an artificial fly dressed with such barbs. ORIG C15: from MLow G *herle,* from ?

Hermannstadt ★ ('hɛrmanʃtat) *n* the German name for **Sibiu.**

hermaphrodite (hɜː'mæfrəˌdaɪt) *n* **1** *Biol.* an animal or flower that has both male and female reproductive organs. **2** a person having both male and female sexual characteristics. **3** a person or thing in which two opposite qualities are combined. ◆ *adj* **4** having the characteristics of a hermaphrodite. ORIG C15: from L *hermaphrodītus,* from Gk, after HERMAPHRODITUS
▸ **herˌmaphro'ditic** *or* **herˌmaphro'ditical** *adj* ▸ **her'maphroditˌism** *n*

hermaphrodite brig *n* a sailing vessel with two masts, rigged square on the foremast and fore-and-aft on the aftermast.

Hermaphroditus ★ (hɜːˌmæfrə'daɪtəs) *n Greek myth.* a son of Hermes and Aphrodite who merged with the nymph Salmacis to form one body.

hermeneutic (ˌhɜːmɪ'njuːtɪk) *or* **hermeneutical** *adj* **1** of or relating to the interpretation of Scripture. **2** interpretive.
▸ ˌ**herme'neutically** *adv*

hermeneutics (ˌhɜːmɪ'njuːtɪks) *n (functioning as sing)* **1** the science of interpretation, esp. of Scripture. **2** *Philosophy.* **2a** the study and interpretation of human behaviour and social institutions. **2b** (in existentialist thought) discussion of the purpose of life. ORIG C18: from Gk *hermēneutikos* expert in interpretation, from *hermēneuein* to interpret, from ?

Hermes ★ ('hɜːmiːz) *n Greek myth.* the messenger and herald of the gods; the divinity of commerce, cunning, theft, travellers, and rascals. He was represented as wearing winged sandals. Roman counterpart: **Mercury.**

Hermes Trismegistus ★ (ˌtrɪsmə'dʒɪstəs) *n* a Greek name for the Egyptian god Thoth, credited with various works on mysticism and magic. ORIG Gk: Hermes thrice-greatest

hermetic (hɜː'mɛtɪk) *or* **hermetical** *adj* **1a** (of a seal) airtight. **1b** (of a vessel, etc.) sealed so as to be airtight. **2** of or relating to alchemy or other forms of ancient science: *the hermetic arts.* **3** esoteric or recondite. **4** hidden or protected from the outside world: *the hermetic world of Vatican politics.* ORIG C17: from Med. L *hermēticus* belonging to HERMES TRISMEGISTUS, traditionally the inventor of a magic seal
▸ **her'metically** *adv*

hermit ('hɜːmɪt) *n* **1** one of the early Christian recluses. **2** any person living in solitude. ORIG C13: from OF *hermite,* from LL, from Gk *erēmitēs* living in the desert, from *erēmos* lonely
▸ **her'mitic** *or* **her'mitical** *adj*

hermitage ('hɜːmɪtɪdʒ) *n* **1** the abode of a hermit. **2** any retreat.

hermit crab *n* a small soft-bodied crustacean living in and carrying about the empty shells of whelks or similar molluscs.

Hermon ★ ('hɜːmən) *n* **Mount.** a mountain on the border between Lebanon and SW Syria, in the Anti-Lebanon Range: represented the NE limits of Israeli conquests under Moses and Joshua. Height: 2814 m (9232 ft).

Hermosillo ★ (*Spanish* ɛrmo'siʎo) *n* a city in NW Mexico, capital of Sonora state, on the Sonora River: university (1938); winter resort and commercial centre for an agricultural and mining region. Pop.: 406 417 (1990).

Hermoupolis ★ (hɜː'muːpəlɪs) *n* a port in Greece, capital of Cyclades department, on the E coast of Syros Island. Pop.: 14 115 (1981).

Herne ★ (*German* 'hɛrnə) *n* an industrial city in W Germany, in North Rhine-Westphalia, in the Ruhr on the Rhine-Herne Canal. Pop.: 179 897 (1996 est.).

hernia ('hɜːnɪə) *n, pl* **hernias** *or* **herniae** (-nɪˌiː). the projection of an organ or part through the lining of the cavity in which it is normally situated, esp. the intestine through the front wall of the abdominal cavity. Also called: **rupture.** ORIG C14: from L
▸ **'hernial** *adj* ▸ **'herniˌated** *adj*

hero ('hɪərəʊ) *n, pl* **heroes. 1** a man distinguished by exceptional courage, nobility, etc. **2** a man who is idealized for possessing superior qualities in any field. **3** *Classical myth.* a being of extraordinary strength and courage, often the offspring of a mortal and a god. **4** the principal male character in a novel, play, etc. ORIG C14: from L *hērōs,* from Gk

Hero[1] ★ ('hɪərəʊ) *n Greek myth.* a priestess of Aphrodite, who killed herself when her lover Leander drowned while swimming the Hellespont to visit her.

Hero[2] ('hɪərəʊ) *or* **Heron** ★ *n* 1st century A.D., Greek mathematician and inventor.

Herod ★ ('hɛrəd) *n* called *the Great.* ?73–4 B.C., king of Judaea (37–4); according to the New Testament he ordered the Massacre of the Innocents.

Herod Agrippa I ★ *n* 10 B.C.–44 A.D., king of Judaea (41–44), grandson of Herod (the Great). A friend of Caligula and Claudius, he imprisoned Saint Peter and executed Saint James.

Herod Agrippa II ★ *n* died ?93 A.D., king of territories in N Palestine (50–?93 A.D.). He presided (60) at the trial of Saint Paul and sided with the Roman authorities in the Jewish rebellion of 66.

Herod Antipas ★ ('æntɪˌpæs) *n* died ?40 A.D., tetrarch of Galilee and Peraea (4 B.C.–40 A.D.); son of Herod the Great. At the instigation of his wife Herodias, he ordered the execution of John the Baptist.

Herodias ★ (hɛ'rəʊdɪˌæs) *n* ?14 B.C. –?40 A.D., niece and wife of Herod Antipas and mother of Salome, whom she persuaded to ask for the head of John the Baptist. Her ambition led to the banishment of her husband.

Herodotus ★ (hɪ'rɒdətəs) *n* called *the Father of History.* ?485–?425 B.C., Greek historian, whose *History* records the events of the wars between the Greeks and the Persians (490–479).

heroic (hɪ'rəʊɪk) *or* **heroical** *adj* **1** of, like, or befitting a hero. **2** courageous but desperate. **3** treating of heroes and their deeds. **4** of or resembling the heroes of classical mythology. **5** (of language, manner, etc.) extravagant. **6** *Prosody.* of or resembling heroic verse. **7** (of the arts, esp. sculpture) larger than life-size; smaller than colossal.
▸ **he'roically** *adv*

heroic age *n* the period in an ancient culture, when legendary heroes are said to have lived.

heroic couplet *n Prosody.* a verse form consisting of two rhyming lines in iambic pentameter.

heroics (hɪ'rəʊɪks) *pl n* **1** *Prosody.* short for **heroic verse. 2** extravagant or melodramatic language, behaviour, etc.

heroic verse *n Prosody.* a type of verse suitable for epic or heroic subjects, such as the classical hexameter or the French Alexandrine.

heroin ('hɛrəʊɪn) *n* a white bitter-tasting crystalline powder derived from morphine: a highly addictive narcotic. ORIG C19: coined in G as a trademark, prob. from HERO, referring to its aggrandizing effect on the personality

heroine ('hɛrəʊɪn) *n* **1** a woman possessing heroic qualities. **2** a woman idealized for possessing superior qualities. **3** the main female character in a novel, play, film, etc.

heroism ('hɛrəʊˌɪzəm) *n* the state or quality of being a hero.

heron ('hɛrən) *n* any of various wading birds having a long neck, slim body, and a plumage that is commonly grey or white. ORIG C14: from OF *hairon,* of Gmc origin

Heron ★ ('hɪərɒn) *n* a variant of **Hero**[2].

heronry ('hɛrənrɪ) *n, pl* **heronries.** a colony of breeding herons.

Herophilus ★ (hɪə'rɒfɪləs) *n* died ?280 B.C., Greek anatomist in Alexandria. He distinguished sensory from motor nerves.

hero worship *n* **1** admiration for heroes or idealized persons. **2** worship by the ancient Greeks and Romans of heroes. ◆ *vb* **hero-worship, hero-worships, hero-worshipping, hero-worshipped** *or US* **hero-worships, hero-worshiping, hero-worshiped. 3** *(tr)* to feel admiration or adulation for.
▸ **'hero-ˌworshipper** *or US* **'hero-ˌworshiper** *n*

herpes ('hɜːpiːz) *n* any of several inflammatory diseases

of the skin, esp. herpes simplex. ORIG C17: via L from Gk, from *herpein* to creep
▸ **herpetic** (hɜːˈpɛtɪk) *adj, n*

herpes simplex (ˈsɪmplɛks) *n* an acute viral disease characterized by formation of clusters of watery blisters, esp. on the lips or the genitals. See **cold sore, genital herpes.** ORIG NL: simple herpes

herpes zoster (ˈzɒstə) *n* a technical name for **shingles.** ORIG NL: girdle herpes, from HERPES + Gk *zōstēr* girdle

herpetology (ˌhɜːpɪˈtɒlədʒɪ) *n* the study of reptiles and amphibians. ORIG C19: from Gk *herpeton* creeping animal
▸ **herpetologic** (ˌhɜːpɪtəˈlɒdʒɪk) *or* ˌ**herpetoˈlogical** *adj*

Herr (*German* hɛr) *n, pl* **Herren** (ˈhɛrən). a German man: used before a name as a title equivalent to *Mr.* ORIG G, from OHG *herro* lord

Herrenvolk *German.* (ˈhɛrənfɔlk) *n* a race, nation, or group, such as the Germans or Nazis as viewed by Hitler, believed by themselves to be superior to other races. Also called: **master race.** ORIG lit.: master race, from *Herren,* pl. of HERR + *Volk* folk

Herrick ★ (ˈhɛrɪk) *n* **Robert.** 1591–1674, English poet. His chief work is the *Hesperides* (1648).

herring (ˈhɛrɪŋ) *n, pl* **herrings** *or* **herring.** an important food fish of northern seas, having an elongated body covered with large silvery scales. ORIG OE *hǣring*

herringbone (ˈhɛrɪŋˌbəʊn) *n* **1a** a pattern consisting of two or more rows of short parallel strokes slanting in alternate directions to form a series of zigzags. **1b** (*as modifier*): *a herringbone pattern.* **2** *Skiing.* a method of ascending a slope by walking with the skis pointing outwards and one's weight on the inside edges. ◆ *vb* **herringbones, herringboning, herringboned. 3** to decorate (textiles, brickwork, etc.) with herringbone. **4** (*intr*) *Skiing.* to ascend a slope in herringbone fashion.

herring gull *n* a common gull that has a white plumage with black-tipped wings.

Herriot ★ *n* **1** (*French* ɛrjo) **Édouard** (edwar). 1872–1957, French Radical statesman and writer; premier (1924–25; 1932). **2** (ˈhɛrɪət) **James.** real name *James Alfred Wight.* 1916–95, British veterinary surgeon and writer.

hers (hɜːz) *pron* **1** something or someone belonging to her: *hers is the nicest dress; that cat is hers.* **2 of hers.** belonging to her. ORIG C14 *hires;* see HER

Herschel ★ (ˈhɜːʃəl) *n* **1** Sir **John Frederick William.** 1792–1871, British astronomer. He discovered and catalogued over 525 nebulae and star clusters. **2** his father, Sir **William,** original name *Friedrich Wilhelm Herschel.* 1738–1822, British astronomer, born in Germany. He constructed a reflecting telescope and discovered the planet Uranus (1781).

herself (həˈsɛlf) *pron* **1a** the reflexive form of *she* or *her.* **1b** (intensifier): *the queen herself signed.* **2** (*preceded by a copula*) her normal self: *she looks herself again.*

Herstmonceux *or* **Hurstmonceux** ★ (ˈhɜːstmənˌsuː, -ˌsəʊ) *n* a village in S England, in E Sussex north of Eastbourne: 15th-century castle, site of the Royal Observatory, which was transferred from Greenwich between 1948 and 1958, until 1990.

Hertford ★ (ˈhɑːtfəd) *n* a town in SE England, administrative centre of Hertfordshire. Pop.: 21 665 (1991).

Hertfordshire ★ (ˈhɑːtfədˌʃɪə, -ʃə) *n* a county of S England, bordering on Greater London in the south: mainly low-lying, with the Chiltern Hills in the northwest; largely agricultural; expanding light industries, esp. in the new towns. Administrative centre: Hertford. Pop.: 1 015 800 (1996 est.). Area: 1634 sq. km (631 sq. miles).

Hertogenbosch ★ (*Dutch* hɛrtoːxənˈbɔs) *n* **'s.** See **'s Hertogenbosch.**

Herts (hɑːts) *abbrev. for* Hertfordshire.

hertz (hɜːts) *n, pl* **hertz.** the derived SI unit of frequency; the frequency of a periodic phenomenon that has a periodic time of 1 second; 1 cycle per second. Symbol: Hz ORIG C20: after H. R. HERTZ

Hertz ★ (hɜːts; *German* hɛrts) *n* **1 Gustav** (ˈgustaf). 1887–1975, German physicist. His research with Franck provided evidence to support the quantum theory: they shared the Nobel prize for physics (1925). **2 Heinrich Rudolph** (ˈhainrɪç ˈruːdɔlf). 1857–94, German physicist; the first to produce electromagnetic waves artificially.
▸ ˈ**Hertzian** *adj*

Hertzian wave *n* an electromagnetic wave with a frequency in the range from about 3×10^{10} hertz to about 1.5×10^{5} hertz. ORIG C19: after H. R. HERTZ

Hertzog ★ (ˈhɜːtsɒg) *n* **James Barry Munnik.** 1866–1942, South African statesman; prime minister (1924–39): founded the Nationalist Party (1913), advocating South African independence from Britain.

Hertzsprung-Russell diagram (ˈhɜːtsspr ʌŋˈrʌsᵊl) *n* a graph in which the spectral types of stars are plotted against their absolute magnitudes. Stars fall into different groupings in different parts of the graph. ORIG C20: after E. *Hertzsprung* (1873–1967), Danish astronomer, and H. N. *Russell* (1877–1957), US astronomer

Herzegovina (ˌhɜːtsəgəʊˈviːnə) *or* **Hercegovina** ★ *n* a region of Bosnia-Herzegovina: originally under Austro-Hungarian rule; was part of the province of Bosnia-Herzegovina (1878), which became a constituent republic of Yugoslavia (1946–91).

Herzl ★ (*German* ˈhɛrtsəl) *n* **Theodor** (ˈteːodoːr). 1860–1904, Austrian writer, born in Hungary; founder of the Zionist movement.

Herzog ★ (*German* ˈhɛrtsoːk) *n* **1 Roman.** born 1934, German politician; president of Germany from 1994. **2 Werner** (ˈvɛrnər). born 1942, German film director. His films include *Signs of Life* (1967) and *Scream from Stone* (1991).

he's (hiːz) *contraction of* he is *or* he has.

Heseltine ★ (ˈhɛzᵊlˌtaɪn) *n* **1 Michael** (**Ray Dibden**). born 1933, British Conservative politician; deputy prime minister (1995–97). **2 Philip Arnold.** See (Peter) **Warlock.**

Hesiod ★ (ˈhɛsɪˌɒd) *n* 8th century B.C., Greek poet. His complete extant works are the *Works and Days* and the *Theogony.*
▸ ˌ**Hesiˈodic** *adj*

Hesione ★ (hɪˈsaɪənɪ) *n Greek myth.* daughter of King Laomedon, rescued by Hercules from a sea monster.

hesitant (ˈhɛzɪtᵊnt) *adj* wavering, hesitating, or irresolute.
▸ ˈ**hesitantly** *adv*

hesitate (ˈhɛzɪˌteɪt) *vb* **hesitates, hesitating, hesitated.** (*intr*) **1** to be slow in acting; be uncertain. **2** to be reluctant (to do something). **3** to stammer or pause in speaking. ORIG C17: from L *haesitāre,* from *haerēre* to cling to
▸ **hesitancy** (ˈhɛzɪtᵊnsɪ) *or* ˌ**hesiˈtation** *n* ▸ ˈ**hesiˌtatingly** *adv*

Hesperia ★ (hɛˈspɪərɪə) *n* a poetic name used by the ancient Greeks for Italy and by the Romans for Spain or beyond. ORIG L, from Gk: land of the west, from *hesperos* western

Hesperian (hɛˈspɪərɪən) *adj* **1** *Poetic.* western. **2** of or relating to the Hesperides or Islands of the Blessed.

Hesperides ★ (hɛˈspɛrɪˌdiːz) *pl n Greek myth.* **1** the daughters of Hesperus, nymphs who kept watch with a dragon over the garden of the golden apples in the Islands of the Blessed. **2** (*functioning as sing*) the gardens themselves. **3** another name for the **Islands of the Blessed.**
▸ **Hesperidian** (ˌhɛspəˈrɪdɪən) *or* ˌ**Hesperˈidean** *adj*

hesperidium (ˌhɛspəˈrɪdɪəm) *n Bot.* the fruit of citrus plants, in which the flesh consists of fluid-filled hairs and is protected by a tough rind. ORIG C19: NL; alluding to the fruit in the garden of the HESPERIDES

Hesperus (ˈhɛspərəs) *n* an evening star, esp. Venus. ORIG from L, from Gk, from *hesperos* western

Hess ★ (hɛs) *n* **1** Dame **Myra.** 1890–1965, British pianist. **2** (**Walther Richard**) **Rudolf** (ˈruːdɔlf). 1894–1987, German Nazi leader. He made a secret flight to Scotland (1941) to negotiate peace; later sentenced to life imprisonment at Nuremberg (1946); committed suicide. **3 Victor Francis.** 1883–1964, US physicist, born in Austria: investigated cosmic rays: shared the Nobel prize for physics (1936).

Hesse[1] ★ (hɛs) *n* a state of E central Germany, formed in 1945 from the former Prussian province of Hesse-Nassau and part of the former state of Hesse; part of

West Germany until 1990. Capital: Wiesbaden. Pop.: 6 016 300 (1996 est.). Area: 21 111 sq. km (8151 sq. miles). German name: **Hessen** (ˈhɛsᵊn).

Hesse[2] ★ (hɛs; *German* ˈhɛsə) *n* **Hermann** (ˈhɛrman). 1877–1962, German writer. His novels include *Steppenwolf* (1927) and *The Glass Bead Game* (1943): Nobel prize for literature 1946.

Hesse-Nassau ★ *n* a former province of Prussia, now part of the state of Hesse, Germany.

hessian (ˈhɛsɪən) *n* a coarse jute fabric similar to sacking. ORIG C18: from HESSIAN

Hessian (ˈhɛsɪən) *n* **1** a native or inhabitant of Hesse. **2** a Hessian soldier in any of the mercenary units of the British Army in the War of American Independence or the Napoleonic Wars. ◆ *adj* **3** of Hesse or its inhabitants.

Hessian fly *n* a small dipterous fly whose larvae damage wheat, barley, and rye. ORIG C18: thought to have been introduced into America by Hessian soldiers

hest (hɛst) *n* an archaic word for **behest.** ORIG OE *hǣs*

Hestia ★ (ˈhɛstɪə) *n Greek myth.* the goddess of the hearth. Roman counterpart: **Vesta.**

hetaera (hɪˈtɪərə) *or* **hetaira** (hɪˈtaɪrə) *n, pl* **hetaerae** (-ˈtɪəriː) *or* **hetairai** (-ˈtaɪraɪ). (esp. in ancient Greece) a prostitute, esp. an educated courtesan. ORIG C19: from Gk *hetaira* concubine

hetaerism (hɪˈtɪərɪzəm) *or* **hetairism** (hɪˈtaɪrɪzəm) *n* **1** the state of being a concubine. **2** *Sociol., anthropol.* a social system attributed to some primitive societies, in which women are communally shared.

hetero- *combining form.* other, another, or different: *heterosexual.* ORIG from Gk *heteros* other

heteroclite (ˈhɛtərəˌklaɪt) *adj also* **heteroclitic** (ˌhɛtərəˈklɪtɪk). **1** (esp. of the form of a word) irregular or unusual. ◆ *n* **2** an irregularly formed word. ORIG C16: from LL *heteroclitus* declining irregularly, from Gk, from HETERO- + *klinein* to inflect

heterocyclic (ˌhɛtərəʊˈsaɪklɪk, -ˈsɪk-) *adj* (of an organic compound) containing a closed ring of atoms, at least one of which is not a carbon atom.

heterodox (ˈhɛtərəʊˌdɒks) *adj* **1** at variance with established or accepted doctrines or beliefs. **2** holding unorthodox opinions. ORIG C17: from Gk *heterodoxos,* from HETERO- + *doxa* opinion
▸ **ˈheteroˌdoxy** *n*

heterodyne (ˈhɛtərəʊˌdaɪn) *vb* **heterodynes, heterodyning, heterodyned. 1** *Electronics.* to combine by modulation (two alternating signals) to produce two signals having frequencies corresponding to the sum and the difference of the original frequencies. ◆ *adj* **2** produced by, operating by, or involved in heterodyning two signals.

heteroecious (ˌhɛtəˈriːʃəs) *adj* (of parasites) undergoing different stages of the life cycle on different host species. ORIG from HETERO- + *-oecious,* from Gk *oikia* house
▸ **heteroecism** (ˌhɛtəˈriːˌsɪzəm) *n*

heterogamete (ˌhɛtərəʊgæˈmiːt) *n* a gamete that differs in size and form from the one with which it unites in fertilization.

heterogamy (ˌhɛtəˈrɒgəmɪ) *n* **1** a type of sexual reproduction in which the gametes differ in both size and form. **2** a condition in which different types of reproduction occur in successive generations of an organism. **3** the presence of both male and female flowers in one inflorescence.
▸ **ˌheterˈogamous** *adj*

heterogeneous (ˌhɛtərəʊˈdʒiːnɪəs) *adj* **1** composed of unrelated parts. **2** not of the same type. ORIG C17: from Med. L *heterogeneus,* from Gk, from HETERO- + *genos* sort
▸ **heterogeneity** (ˌhɛtərəʊdʒɪˈniːɪtɪ) *or* **ˌheteroˈgeneousness** *n*

heterogony (ˌhɛtəˈrɒgənɪ) *n* **1** *Biol.* the alternation of parthenogenetic and sexual generations in rotifers and similar animals. **2** the condition in plants, such as the primrose, of having flowers that differ from each other in the length of their stamens and styles.
▸ **ˌheterˈogonous** *adj*

heterologous (ˌhɛtəˈrɒləgəs) *adj* **1** *Pathol.* designating cells or tissues not normally present in a particular part of the body. **2** differing in structure or origin.
▸ **ˌheterˈology** *n*

heteromerous (ˌhɛtəˈrɒmərəs) *adj Biol.* having parts that differ, esp. in number.

heteromorphic (ˌhɛtərəʊˈmɔːfɪk) *or* **heteromorphous** *adj Biol.* **1** differing from the normal form. **2** (esp. of insects) having different forms at different stages of the life cycle.
▸ **ˌheteroˈmorphism** *n*

heteronomous (ˌhɛtəˈrɒnɪməs) *adj* **1** subject to an external law. **2** (of parts of an organism) differing in the manner of growth, development, or specialization.
▸ **ˌheterˈonomy** *n*

heteronym (ˈhɛtərəʊˌnɪm) *n* one of two or more words pronounced differently but spelt alike: *the two English words spelt "bow" are heteronyms.* Cf. **homograph.** ORIG C17: from LGk *heteronumos,* from Gk HETERO- + *onoma* name

heterophyllous (ˌhɛtərəʊˈfɪləs, ˌhɛtəˈrɒfɪləs) *adj* having more than one type of leaf on the same plant.
▸ **ˈheteroˌphylly** *n*

heteropterous (ˌhɛtəˈrɒptərəs) *or* **heteropteran** *adj* of or belonging to a suborder of hemipterous insects, including bedbugs, water bugs, etc., in which the forewings are membranous but have leathery tips. ORIG C19: from NL *Heteroptera,* from HETERO- + Gk *pteron* wing

heterosexism (ˌhɛtərəʊˈsɛkˌsɪzəm) *n* discrimination on the basis of sexual orientation, practised by heterosexuals against homosexuals.
▸ **heteroˈsexist** *adj, n*

heterosexual (ˌhɛtərəʊˈsɛksjʊəl) *n* **1** a person who is sexually attracted to the opposite sex. ◆ *adj* **2** of or relating to heterosexuality.
▸ **ˌheteroˌsexuˈality** *n*

heterotaxis (ˌhɛtərəʊˈtæksɪs) *or* **heterotaxy** *n* an abnormal or asymmetrical arrangement of parts, as of the organs of the body.

heterotrophic (ˌhɛtərəʊˈtrɒfɪk) *adj* (of animals and some plants) using complex organic compounds to manufacture their own organic constituents. ORIG C20: from HETERO- + Gk *trophikos* concerning food, from *trophē* nourishment
▸ **ˈheteroˌtroph** *n*

heterozygote (ˌhɛtərəʊˈzaɪgəʊt) *n* an animal or plant that is heterozygous; a hybrid.

heterozygous (ˌhɛtərəʊˈzaɪgəs) *adj Genetics.* (of an organism) having dissimilar alleles for any one gene: *heterozygous for eye colour.*

hetman (ˈhɛtmən) *n, pl* **hetmans.** an elected leader of the Cossacks. Also called: **ataman.** ORIG C18: from Polish, from G *Hauptmann* headman

het up *adj Inf.* angry; excited: *don't get het up.* ORIG C19: from dialect p.p. of HEAT

heuchera (ˈhɔɪkərə) *n* a North American shrub with red or pink flowers and ornamental foliage. ORIG after J. H. *Heucher* (1677–1747), G botanist

heuristic (hjʊəˈrɪstɪk) *adj* **1** helping to learn; guiding in investigation. **2** (of a method of teaching) allowing pupils to learn things for themselves. **3a** *Maths, science, philosophy.* using or obtained by exploration of possibilities rather than by following set rules. **3b** *Computing.* denoting a rule of thumb for solving a problem without the exhaustive application of an algorithm: *a heuristic solution.* ◆ *n* **4** (*pl*) the science of heuristic procedure. ORIG C19: from NL *heuristicus,* from Gk *heuriskein* to discover
▸ **heuˈristically** *adv*

Hevesy ★ (*Hungarian* ˈhɛvɛʃi) *n* **Georg von** (ˈgeːɔrg fɔn). 1885–1966, Hungarian chemist; worked on radioactive tracing and, with D. Coster, discovered hafnium (1923): Nobel prize for chemistry 1943.

hew (hjuː) *vb* **hews, hewing, hewed, hewed** *or* **hewn. 1** to strike (something, esp. wood) with cutting blows, as with an axe. **2** (*tr;* often foll. by *out*) to carve from a substance. **3** (*tr;* often foll. by *away, off,* etc.) to sever from a larger portion. **4** (*intr;* often foll. by *to*) *US & Canad.* to conform. ORIG OE *hēawan*
▸ **ˈhewer** *n*

★ people and places

Hewish ★ (ˈhjuːɪʃ) *n* **Antony.** born 1924, British radio astronomer, helped to discover pulsars (1967): shared the Nobel prize for physics 1974.

hex[1] (hɛks) *n* **a** short for **hexadecimal (notation). b** (*as modifier*): *hex code.*

hex[2] (hɛks) *US & Canad. inf.* ◆ *vb* **1** (*tr*) to bewitch. ◆ *n* **2** an evil spell. **3** a witch. ORIG C19: via Pennsylvania Du. from G *Hexe* witch, from MHG *hecse,* ?from OHG *hagzissa*

hex. *abbrev. for:* **1** hexachord. **2** hexagon(al).

hexa- *or before a vowel* **hex-** *combining form.* six: *hexachord; hexameter.* ORIG from Gk, from *hex* SIX

hexachlorophene (ˌhɛksəˈklɔːrəfiːn) *n* an insoluble white bactericidal substance used in antiseptic soaps, deodorants, etc. Formula: $(C_6HCl_3OH)_2CH_2$.

hexachord (ˈhɛksəˌkɔːd) *n* (in medieval musical theory) any of three diatonic scales based upon C, F, and G, each consisting of six notes, from which solmization was developed.

hexad (ˈhɛksæd) *n* a group or series of six. ORIG C17: from Gk *hexas,* from *hex* six

hexadecane (ˈhɛksədɛˌkeɪn, ˌhɛksəˈdɛkeɪn) *n* the systematic name for **cetane.**

hexadecanoic acid (ˌhɛksəˌdɛkəˈnəʊɪk) *n* the systematic name for **palmitic acid.**

hexadecimal notation *or* **hexadecimal** (ˌhɛksəˈdɛsɪməl) *n* a number system having a base 16; the symbols for the numbers 0 – 9 are the same as those used in the decimal system, and the numbers 10 – 15 are usually represented by the letters A – F. The system is used as a convenient way of representing the internal binary code of a computer.

hexagon (ˈhɛksəgən) *n* a polygon having six sides.
▸ **hexˈagonal** *adj*

hexagram (ˈhɛksəˌgræm) *n* a star-shaped figure formed by extending the sides of a regular hexagon to meet at six points.

hexahedron (ˌhɛksəˈhiːdrən) *n* a solid figure having six plane faces.
▸ **ˌhexaˈhedral** *adj*

hexameter (hɛkˈsæmɪtə) *n Prosody.* **1** a verse line consisting of six metrical feet. **2** (in Greek and Latin epic poetry) a verse line of six metrical feet, of which the first four are usually dactyls or spondees, the fifth almost always a dactyl, and the sixth a spondee or trochee.
▸ **hexametric** (ˌhɛksəˈmɛtrɪk) *or* **ˌhexaˈmetrical** *adj*

hexane (ˈhɛkseɪn) *n* a liquid alkane found in petroleum and used as a solvent. Formula: C_6H_{14}. ORIG C19: from HEXA- + -ANE

hexapla (ˈhɛksəplə) *n* an edition of the Old Testament compiled by Origen (?185–?254 A.D.), Christian theologian, containing six versions of the text. ORIG C17: from Gk *hexaploos* sixfold
▸ **ˈhexaplar** *adj*

hexapod (ˈhɛksəˌpɒd) *n* an insect.

hexavalent (ˌhɛksəˈveɪlənt) *adj Chem.* having a valency of six. Also: **sexivalent.**

hexose (ˈhɛksəʊs, -əʊz) *n* a monosaccharide, such as glucose, that contains six carbon atoms per molecule.

hey (heɪ) *interj* **1** an expression indicating surprise, dismay, discovery, etc. **2 hey presto!** an exclamation used by conjurors to herald the climax of a trick. ORIG C13: imit.

heyday (ˈheɪˌdeɪ) *n* the time of most power, popularity, vigour, etc. ORIG C16: prob. based on HEY

Heyer ★ (ˈheɪə) *n* **Georgette.** 1902–74, British historical novelist and writer of detective stories.

Heyerdahl ★ (*Norwegian* ˈhɛiərdaːl) *n* **Thor** (tɔː). born 1914, Norwegian anthropologist. In 1947 he demonstrated that the Polynesians could have been migrants from South America, by sailing from Peru to the Pacific Islands of Tuamotu in the *Kon-Tiki,* a balsawood raft. DNA testing in the late 1990s indicated that such a migration did not actually take place.

Heysham ★ (ˈheɪʃəm) *n* a port in NW England, in NW Lancashire. Pop. (with Morecambe): 46 657 (1991).

Heywood[1] ★ (ˈheɪˌwʊd) *n* a town in NW England, in Greater Manchester near Bury. Pop.: 29 286 (1991).

Heywood[2] ★ (ˈheɪˌwʊd) *n* **1 John.** ?1497–?1580, English dramatist. **2 Thomas.** ?1574–1641, English dramatist, noted for his *A Woman Killed with Kindness* (1607).

Hezekiah ★ (ˌhɛzəˈkaɪə) *n* a king of Judah ?715–?687 B.C., noted for his religious reforms (II Kings 18–19). Douay spelling: **Ezechias.** ORIG from Heb. *hizqīyyāhū* God has strengthened

hf *abbrev. for* half.

Hf *the chemical symbol for* hafnium.

HF *or* **h.f.** *abbrev. for* high frequency.

hg *abbrev. for* hectogram.

Hg *the chemical symbol for* mercury. ORIG from NL *hydrargyrum*

HG *abbrev. for* His (*or* Her) Grace.

hgt *abbrev. for* height.

HGV (formerly, in Britain) *abbrev. for* heavy goods vehicle.

HH *abbrev. for:* **1** His (*or* Her) Highness. **2** His Holiness (title of the Pope). ◆ **3.** (on Brit. pencils) *symbol for* double hard.

hi (haɪ) *sentence substitute.* an informal word for **hello.** ORIG C20: prob. from *how are you?*

HI *abbrev. for:* **1** Hawaii (state). **2** Hawaiian Islands.

Hialeah ★ (ˌhaɪəˈliːə) *n* a city in SE Florida, near Miami: racetrack. Pop.: 204 684 (1996 est.).

hiatus (haɪˈeɪtəs) *n, pl* **hiatuses** *or* **hiatus. 1** (esp. in manuscripts) a break or interruption in continuity. **2** a break between adjacent vowels in the pronunciation of a word. ORIG C16: from L: gap, cleft, from *hiāre* to gape

hiatus hernia *n* protrusion of part of the stomach through the diaphragm at the oesophageal opening.

Hiawatha ★ (ˌhaɪəˈwɒθə) *n* a 16th-century Onondaga Indian chief: credited with the organization of the Five Nations.

Hib (hɪb) *n acronym for* Haemophilus influenzae type b: a vaccine against a type of bacterial meningitis, administered to children.

hibachi (hɪˈbɑːtʃɪ) *n* a portable brazier for heating and cooking food. ORIG from Japanese, from *hi* fire + *bachi* bowl

hibakusha (hɪˈbɑːkʊʃə) *n, pl* **hibakusha** *or* **hibakushas.** a survivor of either of the atomic-bomb attacks on Hiroshima and Nagasaki in 1945. ORIG C20: from Japanese, from *hibaku* bombed + *-sha* -person

hibernal (haɪˈbɜːnᵊl) *adj* of or occurring in winter. ORIG C17: from L *hībernālis,* from *hiems* winter

hibernate (ˈhaɪbəˌneɪt) *vb* **hibernates, hibernating, hibernated.** (*intr*) **1** (of some animals) to pass the winter in a dormant condition with metabolism greatly slowed down. **2** to cease from activity. ORIG C19: from L *hībernāre* to spend the winter, from *hībernus* of winter
▸ **ˌhiberˈnation** *n* ▸ **ˈhiberˌnator** *n*

Hibernia ★ (haɪˈbɜːnɪə) *n* the Roman name for Ireland: used poetically in later times.
▸ **Hiˈbernian** *adj, n*

Hibernicism (haɪˈbɜːnɪˌsɪzəm) *n* an Irish expression, idiom, trait, custom, etc.

Hiberno- (haɪˈbɜːnəʊ) *combining form.* denoting Irish or Ireland: *Hiberno-English.*

hibiscus (hɪˈbɪskəs) *n, pl* **hibiscuses.** any plant of the chiefly tropical and subtropical genus *Hibiscus,* cultivated for its large brightly coloured flowers. ORIG C18: from L, from Gk *hibiskos* marsh mallow

hiccup (ˈhɪkʌp) *n* **1** a spasm of the diaphragm producing a sudden breathing in of air resulting in a characteristic sharp sound. **2** (*pl*) the state of having such spasms. **3** *Inf.* a minor difficulty. ◆ *vb* **hiccups, hiccuping, hiccuped** *or* **hiccups, hiccupping, hiccupped. 4** (*intr*) to make a hiccup or hiccups. **5** (*tr*) to utter with a hiccup. ◆ Also: **hiccough** (ˈhɪkʌp). ORIG C16: imit.

hic jacet *Latin.* (hɪk ˈjækɛt) (on gravestones, etc.) here lies.

hick (hɪk) *n Inf., chiefly US & Canad.* a country bumpkin. ORIG C16: after *Hick,* familiar form of *Richard*

Hickok ★ ('hɪkɒk) *n* **James Butler,** known as *Wild Bill Hickok.* 1837–76, US frontiersman and marshal.

hickory ('hɪkərɪ) *n, pl* **hickories. 1** a tree of a chiefly North American genus having nuts with edible kernels and hard smooth shells. **2** the hard tough wood of this tree. ORIG C17: ult. from Algonquian *pawcohiccora* food made from ground hickory nuts

hid (hɪd) *vb* the past tense and a past participle of **hide**[1].

hidalgo (hɪ'dælgəʊ) *n, pl* **hidalgos.** a member of the lower nobility in Spain. ORIG C16: from Sp., from OSp. *fijo dalgo* nobleman, from L *filius* son + *dē* of + *aliquid* something

Hidalgo ★ (hɪ'dælgəʊ; *Spanish* i'ðalyo) *n* a state of central Mexico: consists of a high plateau, with the Sierra Madre Oriental in the north and east; ancient remains of Teltec culture (at Tula); mineral resources. Capital: Pachuca. Pop.: 2 166 122 (1997 est.). Area: 20 987 sq. km (8103 sq. miles).

hidden ('hɪdᵊn) *vb* **1** a past participle of **hide**[1]. ◆ *adj* **2** concealed or obscured: *a hidden cave; a hidden meaning.*

hidden agenda *n* a hidden motive or intention behind an overt action, policy, etc.

hide[1] (haɪd) *vb* **hides, hiding, hid, hidden** *or* **hid. 1** to conceal (oneself or an object) from view or discovery: *to hide a pencil; to hide from the police.* **2** (*tr*) to obscure: *clouds hid the sun.* **3** (*tr*) to keep secret. **4** (*tr*) to turn (one's eyes, etc.) away. ◆ *n* **5** *Brit.* a place of concealment, usually disguised to appear as part of the natural environment, used by hunters, birdwatchers, etc. US and Canad. equivalent: **blind.** ORIG OE *hȳdan*
▸ **'hider** *n*

hide[2] (haɪd) *n* **1** the skin of an animal, either tanned or raw. **2** *Inf.* the human skin. ◆ *vb* **hides, hiding, hided. 3** (*tr*) *Inf.* to flog. ORIG OE *hȳd*

hide[3] (haɪd) *n* an obsolete Brit. land measure, varying from about 60 to 120 acres. ORIG OE *hīgid*

hide-and-seek *or US, Canad., & Scot.* **hide-and-go-seek** *n* a game in which one player covers his or her eyes while the others hide, and then tries to find them.

hideaway ('haɪdəˌweɪ) *n* a hiding place or secluded spot.

hidebound ('haɪdˌbaʊnd) *adj* **1** restricted by petty rules, a conservative attitude, etc. **2** (of cattle, etc.) having the skin closely attached to the flesh as a result of poor feeding.

hideous ('hɪdɪəs) *adj* **1** extremely ugly; repulsive. **2** terrifying and horrific. ORIG C13: from OF *hisdos,* from *hisde* fear; from ?
▸ **'hideously** *adv* ▸ **'hideousness** *n*

hide-out *n* a hiding place, esp. a remote place used by outlaws, etc.; hideaway.

hiding[1] ('haɪdɪŋ) *n* **1** the state of concealment: *in hiding.* **2** **hiding place.** a place of concealment.

hiding[2] ('haɪdɪŋ) *n Inf.* a flogging; beating.

hidrosis (hɪ'drəʊsɪs) *n* a technical word for **perspiration** or **sweat.** ORIG C18: via NL from Gk, from *hidrōs* sweat
▸ **hidrotic** (hɪ'drɒtɪk) *adj*

hidy-hole *or* **hidey-hole** *n Inf.* a hiding place.

hie (haɪ) *vb* **hies, hieing** *or* **hying, hied.** *Arch. or poetic.* to hurry; speed. ORIG OE *hīgian* to strive

hierarch ('haɪəˌrɑːk) *n* **1** a high priest. **2** a person at a high level in a hierarchy.
▸ **ˌhier'archal** *adj*

hierarchy ('haɪəˌrɑːkɪ) *n, pl* **hierarchies. 1** a system of persons or things arranged in a graded order. **2** a body of persons in holy orders organized into graded ranks. **3** the collective body of those so organized. **4** a series of ordered groupings within a system, such as the arrangement of plants into classes, orders, etc. **5** government by a priesthood. ORIG C14: from Med. L *hierarchia,* from LGk, from *hierarkhēs* high priest; see HIERO-, -ARCHY
▸ **ˌhier'archical** *or* **ˌhier'archic** *adj* ▸ **'hierˌarchism** *n*

hieratic (ˌhaɪə'rætɪk) *adj* **1** of priests. **2** of a cursive form of hieroglyphics used by priests in ancient Egypt. **3** of styles in art that adhere to certain fixed types, as in ancient Egypt. ◆ *n* **4** the hieratic script of ancient Egypt. ORIG C17: from L *hierāticus,* from Gk, from *hiereus* priest
▸ **ˌhier'atically** *adv*

hiero- *or before a vowel* **hier-** *combining form.* holy or divine: *hierarchy.* ORIG from Gk, from *hieros* holy

hieroglyphic (ˌhaɪərə'glɪfɪk) *adj also* **hieroglyphical. 1** of or relating to a form of writing using picture symbols, esp. as used in ancient Egypt. **2** difficult to decipher. ◆ *n also* **hieroglyph. 3** a picture or symbol representing an object, concept, or sound. **4** a symbol that is difficult to decipher. ORIG C16: from LL *hieroglyphicus,* from Gk, from HIERO- + *gluphē,* from *gluphein* to carve
▸ **ˌhiero'glyphically** *adv*

hieroglyphics (ˌhaɪərə'glɪfɪks) *n* (*functioning as sing or pl*) **1** a form of writing, esp. as used in ancient Egypt, in which pictures or symbols are used to represent objects, concepts, or sounds. **2** difficult or undecipherable writing.

Hieronymus ★ (ˌhaɪə'rɒnɪməs) *n* **Eusebius** (juː'siːbɪəs). the Latin name of (Saint) **Jerome.**
▸ **Hieronymic** (ˌhaɪərə'nɪmɪk) *or* **ˌHiero'nymian** *adj*

hierophant ('haɪərəˌfænt) *n* **1** (in ancient Greece) a high priest of religious mysteries. **2** a person who interprets esoteric mysteries. ORIG C17: from LL *hierophanta,* from Gk, from HIERO- + *phainein* to reveal
▸ **ˌhiero'phantic** *adj*

hi-fi ('haɪˌfaɪ) *n Inf.* **1a** short for **high fidelity. 1b** (*as modifier*): *hi-fi equipment.* **2** a set of high-quality sound-reproducing equipment.

higgledy-piggledy ('hɪgᵊldɪ'pɪgᵊldɪ) *Inf.* ◆ *adj, adv* **1** in a jumble. ◆ *n* **2** a muddle.

high (haɪ) *adj* **1** being a relatively great distance from top to bottom; tall: *a high building.* **2** situated at a relatively great distance above sea level: *a high plateau.* **3** (*postpositive*) being a specified distance from top to bottom: *three feet high.* **4** extending from or performed at an elevation: *a high dive.* **5** (*in combination*) coming up to a specified level: *knee-high.* **6** being at its peak: *high noon.* **7** of greater than average height: *a high collar.* **8** greater than normal in intensity or amount: *a high wind; high mileage.* **9** (of sound) acute in pitch. **10** (of latitudes) relatively far north or south from the equator. **11** (of meat) slightly decomposed, regarded as enhancing the flavour of game. **12** very important: *the high priestess.* **13** exalted in style or character: *high drama.* **14** expressing contempt or arrogance: *high words.* **15** elated; cheerful: *high spirits.* **16** *Inf.* being in a state of altered consciousness induced by alcohol, narcotics, etc. **17** *Inf.* overexcited: *by Christmas the children are high.* **18** luxurious or extravagant: *high life.* **19** advanced in complexity: *high finance.* **20** (of a gear) providing a relatively great forward speed for a given engine speed. **21** *Phonetics.* denoting a vowel whose articulation is produced by raising the tongue, such as for the *ee* in *see* or *oo* in *moon.* **22** (*cap. when part of a name*) formal and elaborate: *High Mass.* **23** (*usually cap.*) relating to the High Church. **24** *Cards.* having a relatively great value in a suit. **25 high and dry.** stranded; destitute. **26 high and mighty.** *Inf.* arrogant. **27 high opinion.** a favourable opinion. ◆ *adv* **28** at or to a height: *he jumped high.* **29** in a high manner. **30** *Naut.* close to the wind with sails full. ◆ *n* **31** a high place or level. **32** *Inf.* a state of altered consciousness induced by alcohol, narcotics, etc. **33** another word for **anticyclone. 34 on high. 34a** at a height. **34b** in heaven. ORIG OE *hēah*

High Arctic ★ *n* the regions of Canada, esp. the northern islands, within the Arctic Circle.

highball ('haɪˌbɔːl) *n Chiefly US.* a long iced drink consisting of spirits with soda water, etc.

highborn ('haɪˌbɔːn) *adj* of noble birth.

highboy ('haɪˌbɔɪ) *n US & Canad.* a tallboy.

highbrow ('haɪˌbraʊ) *Often disparaging.* ◆ *n* **1** a person of scholarly and erudite tastes. ◆ *adj also* **highbrowed. 2** appealing to highbrows.

highchair ('haɪˌtʃɛə) *n* a long-legged chair for a child, esp. one with a table-like tray.

High Church *n* **1** the party or movement within the Church of England stressing continuity with Catholic

Christendom, the authority of bishops, and the importance of sacraments. ◆ *adj* **High-Church.** **2** of or relating to this party or movement.
▸ ˈ**High-ˈChurchman** *n*

high-class *adj* **1** of very good quality: *a high-class grocer.* **2** belonging to or exhibiting the characteristics of an upper social class.

high-coloured *adj* (of the complexion) deep red or purplish; florid.

high comedy *n* comedy set largely among cultured and articulate people and featuring witty dialogue.

high commissioner *n* the senior diplomatic representative sent by one Commonwealth country to another instead of an ambassador.

high country *n* (often preceded by *the*) *NZ.* sheep pastures in the foothills of the Southern Alps, New Zealand.

High Court *n* **1** Also called: **High Court of Justice.** (in England) the supreme court dealing with civil law cases. **2** (in Australia) the highest court of appeal, deciding esp. constitutional issues. **3** (in New Zealand) a court of law that is superior to a District Court. Former name: **Supreme Court.**

high definition television *n* a television system using 1000 or more scanning lines and a higher field repetition rate. Abbrev.: **HDTV.**

high-energy physics *n* (*functioning as sing*) another name for **particle physics.**

higher (ˈhaɪə) *adj* **1** the comparative of **high.** ◆ *n* (*usually cap.*) (in Scotland) **2a** the advanced level of the Scottish Certificate of Education. **2b** (*as modifier*): *Higher Latin.* **3** a pass in a subject at Higher level: *she has four Highers.*

higher education *n* education and training at colleges, universities, etc.

higher mathematics *n* (*functioning as sing*) mathematics that is more abstract than normal arithmetic, algebra, geometry, and trigonometry.

higher-rate tax *n* (in Britain) a rate of income tax that is higher than the basic rate and becomes payable on taxable income in excess of a specified limit.

Higher Still *n* a system of courses and qualifications introduced in Scotland to replace Highers and National Certificate modules, covering both academic and vocational subjects.

higher-up *n Inf.* a person of higher rank or in a superior position.

highest common factor *n* the largest number or quantity that is a factor of each member of a group of numbers or quantities.

high explosive *n* an extremely powerful chemical explosive, such as TNT or gelignite.

highfalutin (ˌhaɪfəˈluːtɪn) *or* **highfaluting** *adj Inf.* pompous or pretentious. ORIG C19: from HIGH + *-falutin,* ? var. of *fluting,* from FLUTE

high fidelity *n* **a** the reproduction of sound using electronic equipment that gives faithful reproduction with little or no distortion. **b** (*as modifier*): *a high-fidelity amplifier.* ◆ Often shortened to **hi-fi.**

high-five *n Sl.* a gesture of greeting or congratulation in which two people slap raised right palms together.

high-flown *adj* extravagant or pretentious in conception or intention: *high-flown ideas.*

high-flyer *or* **high-flier** *n* **1** a person who is extreme in aims, ambition, etc. **2** a person of great ability, esp. in a career.
▸ ˌ**high-ˈflying** *adj, n*

high frequency *n* a radio frequency lying between 30 and 3 megahertz. Abbrev.: **HF.**

High German *n* the standard German language, historically developed from the form of West Germanic spoken in S Germany.

high-handed *adj* tactlessly overbearing and inconsiderate.
▸ ˌ**high-ˈhandedness** *n*

high-hat *Inf.* ◆ *adj* **1** snobbish and arrogant. ◆ *vb* **high-hats, high-hatting, high-hatted.** (*tr*) **2** *Chiefly US & Canad.* to treat in a snobbish or offhand way. ◆ *n* **3** a snobbish person.

high hurdles *n* (*functioning as sing*) a race in which competitors leap over hurdles 42 inches (107 cm) high.

high-impact *adj* (*prenominal*) **1** (of a plastic or other material) able to withstand great force or shock. **2** (of aerobic or other exercise) placing great stress on various areas of the body. **3** *Inf.* having great effect: *high-impact sound.*

highjack (ˈhaɪˌdʒæk) *vb, n* a less common spelling of **hijack.**
▸ ˈ**highˌjacker** *n*

high jump *n* **1** (usually preceded by *the*) an athletic event in which a competitor has to jump over a high bar. **2 be for the high jump.** *Brit. inf.* to be liable to receive a severe reprimand or punishment.
▸ **high jumper** *n* ▸ **high jumping** *n*

high-key *adj* (of a painting, etc.) having a predominance of light tones or colours. Cf. **low-key** (sense 3).

highland (ˈhaɪlənd) *n* **1** relatively high ground. **2** (*modifier*) of or relating to a highland.
▸ ˈ**highlander** *n*

Highland ★ (ˈhaɪlənd) *n* **1** a council area in N Scotland, formed in 1975 as Highland Region and reorganized in 1996. Administrative centre: Inverness. Pop.: 206 900 (1996 est.). Area: 25 149 sq. km (9710 sq. miles). **2** (*modifier*) of or denoting the Highlands of Scotland.
▸ ˈ**Highlander** *n*

Highland cattle *n* a breed of cattle with shaggy reddish-brown hair and long horns.

Highland dress *n* **1** the historical costume including the plaid and kilt, of Highland clansmen and soldiers. **2** a modern version of this worn for formal occasions.

Highland fling *n* a vigorous Scottish solo dance.

Highland Games *n* (*functioning as sing or pl*) a meeting in which competitions in sport, piping, and dancing are held: originating in the Highlands of Scotland.

Highlands ★ (ˈhaɪləndz) *n* **the. 1a** the part of Scotland that lies to the northwest of the great fault that runs from Dumbarton to Stonehaven. **1b** a mountainous region of NW Scotland: distinguished by Gaelic culture. **2** (*often not cap.*) the highland region of any country.

high-level *adj* (of conferences, talks, etc.) involving very important people.

high-level language *n Computing.* a programming language that resembles natural language or mathematical notation and is designed to reflect the requirements of a problem.

high-level waste *n* high-activity radioactive waste, such as spent nuclear fuel, needing cooling for several decades before disposal. Cf. **intermediate-level waste, low-level waste.**

highlight (ˈhaɪˌlaɪt) *n* **1** an area of the lightest tone in a painting, photograph, etc. **2** Also called: **high spot.** the most exciting or memorable part or time. **3** (*pl*) a lightened or brightened effect produced in the hair by bleaching selected strands. ◆ *vb* (*tr*) **4** *Painting, photog., etc.* to mark with light tone. **5** to bring emphasis to. **6** to produce highlights in (the hair).

highlighter (ˈhaɪˌlaɪtə) *n* **1** a cosmetic cream or powder applied to the face to highlight the cheekbones, eyes, etc. **2** a fluorescent felt-tip pen used as a marker to emphasize a section of text without obscuring it.

highly (ˈhaɪlɪ) *adv* **1** (intensifier): *highly disappointed.* **2** with great approbation: *we spoke highly of it.* **3** in a high position: *placed highly in class.* **4** at or for a high cost.

highly strung *or US & Canad.* **high-strung** *adj* tense and easily upset; excitable; nervous.

High Mass *n* a solemn and elaborate sung Mass.

high-minded *adj* **1** having or characterized by high moral principles. **2** *Arch.* arrogant; haughty.
▸ ˌ**high-ˈmindedness** *n*

highness (ˈhaɪnɪs) *n* the condition of being high.

Highness (ˈhaɪnɪs) *n* (preceded by *Your, His,* or *Her*) a title used to address or refer to a royal person.

high-octane *adj* **1** (of petrol) having a high octane number. **2** *Inf.* dynamic, forceful, or intense: *high-octane drive and efficiency.*

high-pass filter *n Electronics.* a filter that transmits all frequencies above a specified value, attenuating frequencies below this value.

high-pitched *adj* **1** pitched high in tone. **2** (of a roof) having steeply sloping sides. **3** (of an argument, style, etc.) lofty or intense.

high-powered *adj* **1** (of an optical instrument or lens) having a high magnification. **2** dynamic and energetic; highly capable.

high-pressure *adj* **1** having, using, or designed to withstand pressure above normal. **2** *Inf.* (of selling) persuasive in an aggressive and persistent manner.

high priest *n* **1** *Bible.* the priest of highest rank who alone was permitted to enter the holy of holies of the Temple. **2** Also (fem): **high priestess.** the head of a cult.
▸ **high priesthood** *n*

high profile *n* a position or attitude characterized by a deliberate seeking of prominence or publicity.

high-rise *adj* **1** (*prenominal*) of or relating to a building that has many storeys, esp. one used for flats or offices: *a high-rise block.* ◆ *n* **2** a high-rise building.

high-risk *adj* (*prenominal*) denoting a group, part, etc., that is particularly subject to a danger.

highroad (ˈhaɪˌrəʊd) *n* **1** a main road; highway. **2** (usually preceded by *the*) the sure way: *the highroad to fame.*

high school *n* **1** *Brit.* another term for **grammar school. 2** *US, Canad., NZ, & Scot.* a secondary school.

high seas *pl n* (*sometimes sing*) the open seas, outside the jurisdiction of any one nation.

high season *n* the most popular time of year at a holiday resort, etc.

Highsmith ★ (ˈhaɪˌsmɪθ) *n* **Patricia.** 1921–95, US author of crime fiction. Her novels include *Strangers on a Train* (1950) and *Ripley's Game* (1974).

high-sounding *adj* another term for **high-flown.**

high-spirited *adj* vivacious, bold, or lively.
▸ **ˌhigh-ˈspiritedness** *n*

High Street *n* (*often not cap.; usually preceded by the*) *Brit.* the main street of a town, usually where the principal shops are situated.

high table *n* (*sometimes cap.*) the table in the dining hall of a school, college, etc., at which the principal teachers, fellows, etc., sit.

hightail (ˈhaɪˌteɪl) *vb* (*intr*) *Inf., chiefly US & Canad.* to go or move in a great hurry.

High Tatra ★ *n* another name for the **Tatra Mountains.**

high tea *n Brit.* See **tea** (sense 4b).

high tech (tɛk) *n* a variant spelling of **hi tech.**

high technology *n* any type of sophisticated industrial process, esp. electronic.

high-tension *n* (*modifier*) carrying or operating at a relatively high voltage.

high tide *n* **1** the tide at its highest level. **2** a culminating point.

high time *Inf.* ◆ *adv* **1** the latest possible time: *it's high time you left.* ◆ *n* **2** Also: **high old time.** an enjoyable and exciting time.

high-toned *adj* **1** having a superior social, moral, or intellectual quality. **2** affectedly superior. **3** high in tone.

high tops *pl n* training shoes that reach to above the ankles.

high treason *n* an act of treason directly affecting a sovereign or state.

high-up *n Inf.* a person who holds an important or influential position.

highveld (ˈhaɪˌfɛlt) *n* **the.** the high grassland region of NE South Africa.

high water *n* **1** another name for **high tide. 2** the state of any stretch of water at its highest level, as during a flood. ◆ Abbrev.: **HW.**

high-water mark *n* **1** the level reached by sea water at high tide or by other stretches of water in flood. **2** the highest point.

highway (ˈhaɪˌweɪ) *n* **1** a public road that all may use. **2** *Now chiefly US & Canad. except in legal contexts.* a main road, esp. one that connects towns. **3** a direct path or course.

Highway Code *n* (in Britain) an official booklet giving guidance to users of public roads.

highwayman (ˈhaɪweɪmən) *n, pl* **highwaymen.** (formerly) a robber, usually on horseback, who held up travellers on public roads.

high wire *n* a tightrope stretched high in the air for balancing acts.

High Wycombe ★ (ˈwɪkəm) *n* a town in S central England, in S Buckinghamshire: furniture industry. Pop.: 71 718 (1991).

HIH *abbrev. for* His (*or* Her) Imperial Highness.

hijack *or* **highjack** (ˈhaɪˌdʒæk) *vb* **1** (*tr*) to seize or divert (a vehicle or the goods it carries) while in transit: *to hijack an aircraft.* ◆ *n* **2** the act or an instance of hijacking.
ORIG C20: from ?
▸ **ˈhiˌjacker** *or* **ˈhighˌjacker** *n*

Hijaz ★ (hiːˈdʒæz) *n* a variant spelling of **Hejaz.**

hike (haɪk) *vb* **hikes, hiking, hiked. 1** (*intr*) to walk a long way, usually for pleasure, esp. in the country. **2** (usually foll. by *up*) to pull or be pulled; hitch. **3** (*tr;* usually foll. by *up*) to raise (prices). ◆ *n* **4** a long walk. **5** a rise in price. ORIG C18: from ?
▸ **ˈhiker** *n*

hilarious (hɪˈlɛərɪəs) *adj* very funny. ORIG C19: from L *hilaris* glad, from Gk *hilaros*
▸ **hiˈlariously** *adv* ▸ **hiˈlariousness** *n*

hilarity (hɪˈlærɪtɪ) *n* mirth and merriment.

Hilary of Poitiers ★ (ˈhɪlərɪ) *n* **Saint.** ?315–?367 A.D., French bishop, an opponent of Arianism. Feast day: Jan. 13 or 14.

Hilary term *n* the spring term at Oxford University, the Inns of Court, and some other educational establishments. ORIG C16: after Saint HILARY of Poitiers

Hilbert ★ (*German* ˈhɪlbərt) *n* **David** (ˈdaːfɪt). 1862–1943, German mathematician, who made outstanding contributions to the theories of number fields and invariants and to geometry.

Hildebrand ★ (ˈhɪldəˌbrænd) *n* the monastic name of **Gregory VII.**
▸ **ˌHildeˈbrandian** *adj, n* ▸ **ˈHildeˌbrandine** *adj*

Hildegard of Bingen ★ (ˈhɪldəgɑːd; ˈbɪŋən) *n* **Saint.** 1098–1179, German abbess, poet, composer, and mystic.

Hildesheim ★ (*German* ˈhɪldəshaɪm) *n* a city in N central Germany, in Lower Saxony: a member of the Hanseatic League. Pop.: 106 101 (1996 est.).

hill (hɪl) *n* **1a** a natural elevation of the earth's surface, less high or craggy than a mountain. **1b** (*in combination*): *a hillside.* **2a** a heap or mound. **2b** (*in combination*): *a dunghill.* **3** an incline; slope. **4 over the hill. 4a** *Inf.* beyond one's prime. **4b** *Mil. sl.* absent without leave or deserting. ◆ *vb* (*tr*) **5** to form into a hill. **6** to cover or surround with a heap of earth. ORIG OE *hyll*
▸ **ˈhilly** *adj*

Hill ★ (hɪl) *n* **1 Archibald Vivian.** 1886–1977, British biochemist, noted for his research into heat loss in muscle contraction: shared the Nobel prize for physiology or medicine (1922). **2 Damon Graham Devereux,** son of Graham Hill. born 1960, British motor-racing driver. **3 Geoffrey (William).** born 1932, British poet: his books include *King Log* (1968) and *The Triumph of Love* (1999). **4 Graham.** 1929–75, British motor-racing driver. **5 Octavia.** 1838–1912, British housing reformer; a founder of the National Trust. **6** Sir **Rowland.** 1795–1879, British originator of the penny postage.

Hilla ★ (ˈhɪlə) *n* a market town in central Iraq, on a branch of the Euphrates: built partly of bricks from the nearby site of Babylon. Pop.: 268 834 (1987). Also called: **Al Hillah.**

Hillary ★ (ˈhɪlərɪ) *n* Sir **Edmund.** born 1919, New Zealand explorer and mountaineer. He was the first to reach the summit of Mount Everest (1953); New Zealand ambassador to India (1984–89).

hillbilly ('hɪlˌbɪlɪ) *n, pl* **hillbillies. 1** *Usually disparaging.* an unsophisticated person, esp. from the mountainous areas in the southeastern US. **2** another name for **country and western.** ORIG C20: from HILL + *Billy* (the nickname)

Hillel ★ ('hɪlɛl, -ləl) *n* ?60 B.C.–?9 A.D., rabbi, born in Babylonia; president of the Sanhedrin. He was the first to formulate principles of biblical interpretation.

Hilliard ★ ('hɪlɪəd) *n* **Nicholas.** 1537–1619, English miniaturist, esp. of portraits.

Hillingdon ★ ('hɪlɪŋdən) *n* a residential borough of W Greater London. Pop.: 243 000 (1994 est.). Area: 110 sq. km (43 sq. miles).

hillock ('hɪlək) *n* a small hill or mound. ORIG C14 *hilloc*
▸ **'hillocked** *or* **'hillocky** *adj*

hills (hɪlz) *pl n* **1 as old as the hills.** very old. **2 the.** a hilly and often remote region.

hill station *n* (in northern India, etc.) a settlement or resort at a high altitude.

hilt (hɪlt) *n* **1** the handle or shaft of a sword, dagger, etc. **2 to the hilt.** to the full. ORIG OE

hilum ('haɪləm) *n, pl* **hila** (-lə). *Bot.* a scar on a seed marking its point of attachment to the seed stalk. ORIG C17: from L: trifle

Hilversum ★ ('hɪlvəsəm; *Dutch* 'hɪlvərsym) *n* a city in the central Netherlands, in North Holland province: Dutch radio and television centre. Pop.: 84 213 (1994).

him (hɪm; *unstressed* ɪm) *pron* (*objective*) refers to a male person or animal: *they needed him; she baked him a cake; not him again!* ORIG OE *him,* dative of *hē* HE

> **USAGE NOTE** See at **me**[1].

HIM *abbrev. for* His (*or* Her) Imperial Majesty.

Himachal Pradesh ★ (hɪ'mɑːtʃəl prɑː'dɛʃ) *n* a state of N India, in the W Himalayas: rises to about 6700 m (22 000 ft) and is densely forested. Capital: Simla. Pop.: 5 530 000 (1994 est.). Area: 55 658 sq. km (21 707 sq. miles).

Himalayas ★ (ˌhɪmə'leɪəz, hɪ'mɑːljəz) *pl n* **the.** a vast mountain system in S Asia, extending 2400 km (1500 miles) from Kashmir (west) to Assam (east), between the valleys of the Rivers Indus and Brahmaputra: covers most of Nepal, Sikkim, Bhutan, and the S edge of Tibet; the highest range in the world, with several peaks over 7500 m (25 000 ft). Highest peak: Mount Everest, 8848 m (29 028 ft).
▸ **ˌHima'layan** *adj*

himation (hɪ'mætɪˌɒn) *n, pl* **himatia** (-ɪə). (in ancient Greece) a cloak draped around the body. ORIG C19: from Gk, from *heima* dress, from *hennunai* to clothe

Himeji ★ ('hiːmɛˌdʒiː) *n* a city in central Japan, on W Honshu: cotton textile centre. Pop.: 470 986 (1995).

Himmler ★ (*German* 'hɪmlər) *n* **Heinrich** ('hainrɪç). 1900–45, German Nazi leader, head of the SS and the Gestapo (1936–45); committed suicide.

Hims ★ (hɪmz) *n* a former name of **Homs.**

himself (hɪm'sɛlf; *medially often* ɪm'sɛlf) *pron* **1a** the reflexive form of *he* or *him.* **1b** (intensifier): *the king himself waved to me.* **2** (*preceded by a copula*) his normal self: *he seems himself once more.* ORIG OE *him selfum,* dative sing of *hē self;* see HE, SELF

Hinayana (ˌhiːnə'jɑːnə) *n* any of various early forms of Buddhism. ORIG from Sansk., from *hīna* lesser + *yāna* vehicle

Hinckley ★ ('hɪŋklɪ) *n* a town in central England, in Leicestershire. Pop.: 40 608 (1991 est.).

hind[1] (haɪnd) *adj* **hinder, hindmost** *or* **hindermost.** (*prenominal*) (esp. of parts of the body) situated at the back: *a hind leg.* ORIG OE *hindan* at the back, rel. to G *hinten*

hind[2] (haɪnd) *n, pl* **hinds** *or* **hind. 1** the female of the deer, esp. the red deer when aged three years or more. **2** any of several marine fishes related to the groper. ORIG OE *hind*

hind[3] (haɪnd) *n* (formerly) **1** a simple peasant. **2** (in Scotland and N England) a skilled farm worker. **3** a steward. ORIG OE *hīne,* from *hīgna,* genitive pl of *hīgan* servants

Hindemith ★ (*German* 'hɪndəmɪt) *n* **Paul** (paul). 1895–1963, German composer and musical theorist, who opposed the twelve-tone technique. His works include the song cycle *Das Marienleben* (1923) and the opera *Mathis der Maler* (1938).

Hindenburg[1] ★ ('hɪndənbʊrk) *n* the German name for **Zabrze.**

Hindenburg[2] ★ ('hɪndənˌbɜːg; *German* 'hɪndənbʊrk) *n* **Paul von Beneckendorff und von** (paul fən 'bɛnəkəndɔrf ʊnt fən). 1847–1934, German field marshal and statesman; president (1925–34). During World War I he directed German strategy.

hinder[1] ('hɪndə) *vb* **1** to be or get in the way of (someone or something); hamper. **2** (*tr*) to prevent. ORIG OE *hindrian*

hinder[2] ('haɪndə) *adj* (*prenominal*) situated at or further towards the back; posterior. ORIG OE

Hindi ('hɪndɪ) *n* **1** a language or group of dialects of N central India. See also **Hindustani. 2** a formal literary dialect of this language, the official language of India. **3** a person whose native language is Hindi. ORIG C18: from Hindi, from *Hind* India, from OPersian *Hindu* the river Indus

hindmost ('haɪndˌməʊst) *or* **hindermost** ('hɪndəˌməʊst) *adj* furthest back; last.

Hindoo ('hɪnduː, hɪn'duː) *n, pl* **Hindoos,** *adj* an older spelling of **Hindu.**
▸ **'Hindooˌism** *n*

hindquarter ('haɪndˌkwɔːtə) *n* **1** one of the two back quarters of a carcass of beef, lamb, etc. **2** (*pl*) the rear, esp. of a four-legged animal.

hindrance ('hɪndrəns) *n* **1** an obstruction or snag; impediment. **2** the act of hindering.

hindsight ('haɪndˌsaɪt) *n* **1** the ability to understand, after something has happened, what should have been done. **2** a firearm's rear sight.

Hindu ('hɪnduː, hɪn'duː) *n, pl* **Hindus. 1** a person who adheres to Hinduism. **2** an inhabitant or native of Hindustan or India. ◆ *adj* **3** relating to Hinduism, Hindus, or India. ORIG C17: from Persian *Hindū,* from *Hind* India; see HINDI

Hinduism ('hɪndʊˌɪzəm) *n* the complex of beliefs and customs comprising the dominant religion of India, characterized by the worship of many gods, a caste system, belief in reincarnation, etc.

Hindu Kush ★ (kʊʃ, kuːʃ) *pl n* a mountain range in central Asia, extending about 800 km (500 miles) east from the Koh-i-Baba Mountains of central Afghanistan to the Pamirs. Highest peak: Tirich Mir, 7690 m (25 230 ft).

Hindustan ★ (ˌhɪndʊ'stɑːn) *n* **1** the land of the Hindus, esp. India north of the Deccan and excluding Bengal. **2** the general area around the Ganges where Hindi is the predominant language. **3** the areas of India where Hinduism predominates, as contrasted with those areas where Islam predominates.

Hindustani (ˌhɪndʊ'stɑːnɪ) *n* **1** the dialect of Hindi spoken in Delhi: used as a lingua franca throughout India. **2** all the spoken forms of Hindi and Urdu considered together. ◆ *adj* **3** of or relating to these languages or Hindustan.

Hines ★ (haɪnz) *n* **Earl,** known as *Earl "Fatha" Hines.* 1905–83, US jazz pianist and songwriter.

hinge (hɪndʒ) *n* **1** a device for holding together two parts such that one can swing relative to the other. **2** a natural joint, such as the knee joint, that functions in only one plane. **3** a similar structure in invertebrate animals, such as the joint between the two halves of a bivalve shell. **4** something on which events, opinions, etc., turn. **5** Also called: **mount.** *Philately.* a small transparent strip of gummed paper for affixing a stamp to a page. ◆ *vb* **hinges, hinging, hinged. 6** (*tr*) to fit a hinge to (something). **7** (*intr; usually foll. by on or upon*) to depend (on). **8** (*intr*) to hang or turn on or as if on a hinge. ORIG C13: prob. of Gmc origin
▸ **hinged** *adj*

hinny[1] ('hɪnɪ) *n, pl* **hinnies.** the sterile hybrid offspring of a male horse and a female donkey. ORIG C19: from L *hinnus,* from Gk *hinnos*

hinny[2] ('hɪnɪ) *n Scot. & N English dialect.* a term of endearment, esp. for a woman. ORIG var. of HONEY

Hi-NRG (ˌhaɪ'ɛnədʒɪ) *n* a type of dance music, originating in the late 1980s, that has a very fast tempo and a strong beat. ORIG C20: from HIGH + ENERGY

hint (hɪnt) *n* **1** a suggestion given in an indirect or subtle manner. **2** a helpful piece of advice. **3** a small amount; trace. ◆ *vb* **4** (when *intr,* often foll. by *at;* when *tr, takes a clause as object*) to suggest indirectly. ORIG C17: from ?

hinterland ('hɪntəˌlænd) *n* **1** land lying behind something, esp. a coast or the shore of a river. **2** remote or undeveloped areas. **3** an area near and dependent on a large city, esp. a port. ORIG C19: from G, from *hinter* behind + *land* LAND

hip[1] (hɪp) *n* **1** (*often pl*) either side of the body below the waist and above the thigh. **2** another name for **pelvis** (sense 1). **3** short for **hip joint. 4** the angle formed where two sloping sides of a roof meet. ORIG OE *hype*
▸ **'hipless** *adj*

hip[2] (hɪp) *n* the berry-like brightly coloured fruit of a rose plant. Also called: **rosehip.** ORIG OE *héopa*

hip[3] (hɪp) *interj* an exclamation used to introduce cheers (in **hip, hip, hurrah**). ORIG C18: from ?

hip[4] (hɪp) *adj* **hipper, hippest.** *Sl.* **1** aware of or following the latest trends. **2** (*often postpositive;* foll. by *to*) informed (about). ORIG var. of earlier *hep*

hip bath *n* a portable bath in which the bather sits.

hipbone ('hɪpˌbəʊn) *n* the nontechnical name for **innominate bone.**

hip flask *n* a small metal flask for spirits, etc.

hip-hop ('hɪpˌhɒp) *n* a US pop culture movement of the 1980s comprising rap music, graffiti, and break dancing.

hip joint *n* the ball-and-socket joint that connects each leg to the trunk of the body.

Hipparchus ★ (hɪ'pɑːkəs) *n* **1** 2nd century B.C., Greek astronomer. He discovered the precession of the equinoxes, calculated the length of the solar year, and developed trigonometry. **2** died 514 B.C., tyrant of Athens (527–514).

hippeastrum (ˌhɪpɪ'æstrəm) *n* any plant of a South American genus cultivated for their large funnel-shaped typically red flowers. ORIG C19: NL, from Gk *hippeus* knight + *astron* star

hipped[1] (hɪpt) *adj* **1a** having a hip or hips. **1b** (*in combination*)*: broad-hipped.* **2** (esp. of cows, sheep, etc.) having an injury to the hip, such as a dislocation. **3** *Archit.* having a hip or hips: *hipped roof.*

hipped[2] (hɪpt) *adj* (*often postpositive;* foll. by *on*) *US & Canad. dated sl.* very enthusiastic. ORIG C20: from HIP[4]

hippie *n, pl* **hippies.** a variant of **hippy**[1].

hippo ('hɪpəʊ) *n, pl* **hippos.** *Inf.* short for **hippopotamus.**

hippocampus (ˌhɪpəʊ'kæmpəs) *n, pl* **hippocampi** (-paɪ). **1** a mythological sea creature with the forelegs of a horse and the tail of a fish. **2** any of various small sea fishes with a horselike head; sea horse. **3** an area of cerebral cortex that forms a ridge in the floor of the brain, which in cross section has the shape of a sea horse. It functions as part of the limbic system. ORIG C16: from L, from Gk *hippos* horse + *kampos* a sea monster

hippocras ('hɪpəʊˌkræs) *n* an old English drink of wine flavoured with spices. ORIG C14 *ypocras,* from OF: HIPPOCRATES, prob. referring to a filter called *Hippocrates' sleeve*

Hippocrates ★ (hɪ'pɒkrəˌtiːz) *n* ?460–?377 B.C., Greek physician, commonly regarded as the father of medicine.
▸ **Hippocratic** (ˌhɪpəʊ'krætɪk) *or* ˌ**Hippo'cratical** *adj*

Hippocratic oath *n* an oath taken by a doctor to observe a code of medical ethics derived from that of Hippocrates.

Hippocrene ★ ('hɪpəʊˌkriːn, ˌhɪpəʊ'kriːnɪ) *n* a spring on Mount Helicon in Greece, said to engender poetic inspiration. ORIG C17: via L from Gk *hippos* horse + *krēnē* spring
▸ ˌ**Hippo'crenian** *adj*

hippodrome ('hɪpəˌdrəʊm) *n* **1** a music hall, variety theatre, or circus. **2** (in ancient Greece or Rome) an open-air course for horse and chariot races. ORIG C16: from L *hippodromos,* from Gk *hippos* horse + *dromos* race

hippogriff *or* **hippogryph** ('hɪpəʊˌgrɪf) *n* a monster with a griffin's head, wings, and claws and a horse's body. ORIG C17: from It. *ippogrifo,* from *ippo-* horse (from Gk) + *grifo* GRIFFIN

Hippolyta (hɪ'pɒlɪtə) *or* **Hippolyte** ★ (hɪ'pɒlɪˌtiː) *n Greek myth.* a queen of the Amazons, slain by Hercules in battle for her belt, which he obtained as his ninth labour.

Hippolytus ★ (hɪ'pɒlɪtəs) *n Greek myth.* a son of Theseus, killed after his stepmother Phaedra falsely accused him of raping her.
▸ **Hip'polytan** *adj*

Hippomenes ★ (hɪ'pɒmɪˌniːz) *n Greek myth.* the husband, in some traditions, of Atalanta.

hippopotamus (ˌhɪpə'pɒtəməs) *n, pl* **hippopotamuses** *or* **hippopotami** (-ˌmaɪ). a very large gregarious mammal living in or around the rivers of tropical Africa. ORIG C16: from L, from Gk: river horse, from *hippos* horse + *potamos* river

Hippo Regius ★ ('hɪpəʊ 'riːdʒɪəs) *n* an ancient Numidian city, adjoining present-day Annaba, Algeria. Often shortened to **Hippo.**

hippy[1] *or* **hippie** ('hɪpɪ) *n, pl* **hippies.** (esp. during the 1960s) a person whose behaviour, dress, use of drugs, etc., implies a rejection of conventional values. ORIG C20: see HIP[4]

hippy[2] ('hɪpɪ) *adj* **hippier, hippiest.** *Inf.* (esp. of a woman) having large hips.

hip roof *n* a roof having sloping ends and sides.

hipster ('hɪpstə) *n* **1** *Sl., now rare.* **1a** an enthusiast of modern jazz. **1b** an outmoded word for **hippy**[1]. **2** (*modifier*) (of trousers) cut so that the top encircles the hips.

hipsters ('hɪpstəz) *pl n Brit.* trousers cut so that the top encircles the hips. Usual US word: **hip-huggers.**

Hiram ★ ('haɪərəm) *n* 10th century B.C., king of Tyre, who supplied Solomon with materials and craftsmen for the building of the Temple (II Samuel 5:11; I Kings 5:1–18).

hircine ('hɜːsaɪn, -sɪn) *adj* **1** *Arch.* of or like a goat. **2** *Literary.* lascivious. ORIG C17: from L *hircīnus,* from *hircus* goat

hire ('haɪə) *vb* **hires, hiring, hired.** (*tr*) **1** to acquire the temporary use of (a thing) or the services of (a person) in exchange for payment. **2** to employ (a person) for wages. **3** (often foll. by *out*) to provide (something) or the services of (oneself or others) for payment, usually for an agreed period. **4** (foll. by *out*) *Chiefly Brit.* to pay independent contractors for (work to be done). ◆ *n* **5a** the act of hiring or the state of being hired. **5b** (*as modifier*)*: a hire car.* **6** the price for a person's services or the temporary use of something. **7 for** *or* **on hire.** available for hire. ORIG OE *hȳrian*
▸ **'hirable** *or* **'hireable** *adj* ▸ **'hirer** *n*

hireling ('haɪəlɪŋ) *n Derog.* a person who works only for money. ORIG OE *hȳrling*

hire-purchase *n Brit.* a system in which a buyer takes possession of merchandise on payment of a deposit and completes the purchase by paying a series of instalments while the seller retains ownership until the final instalment is paid. Abbrev.: **HP, h.p.** US and Canad. equivalents: **installment plan, instalment plan.**

Hirohito ★ (ˌhɪərəʊ'hiːtəʊ) *n* 1901–89, emperor of Japan 1926–89. In 1946 he became a constitutional monarch.

Hiroshige ★ (ˌhɪərəʊ'ʃiːgeɪ) *n* **Ando** ('ɑːndəʊ). 1797–1858, Japanese artist, esp. of colour wood-block prints.

Hiroshima ★ (ˌhɪrɒ'ʃiːmə, hɪ'rɒʃɪmə) *n* a port in SW Japan, on SW Honshu on the delta of the Ota River: largely destroyed on August 6, 1945, by the first atomic bomb to be used in warfare, dropped by the US, which killed over 75 000 of its inhabitants. Pop.: 1 108 868 (1995).

Hirst ★ (hɜːst) *n* **Damien.** born 1965, British artist.

hirsute (ˈhɜːsjuːt) *adj* **1** covered with hair. **2** (of plants) covered with long but not stiff hairs. **3** (of a person) having long, thick, or untrimmed hair. ORIG C17: from L *hirsūtus* shaggy
▸ ˈ**hirsuteness** *n*

his (hɪz; *unstressed* ɪz) *determiner* **1a** of, belonging to, or associated with him: *his knee; I don't like his being out so late.* **1b** (*as pron*): *his is on the left; that book is his.* **2 his and hers.** for a man and woman respectively. ◆ *pron* **3 of his.** belonging to him. ORIG OE *his,* genitive of *hē* HE & of *hit* IT

Hispania ★ (hɪˈspænɪə) *n* the Iberian peninsula in the Roman world. ORIG L *Hispania* Spain

Hispanic (hɪˈspænɪk) *adj* **1** of or derived from Spain or the Spanish. ◆ *n* **2** *US.* a US citizen of Latin-American descent.
▸ **Hisˈpanicism** *n*

Hispaniola ★ (ˌhɪspənˈjəʊlə; *Spanish* ispaˈɲola) *n* the second largest island in the Caribbean, in the Greater Antilles: divided politically into Haiti and the Dominican Republic; discovered in 1492 by Christopher Columbus, who named it La Isla Española. Area: 18 703 sq. km (29 418 sq. miles). Former name: **Santo Domingo.**

hispid (ˈhɪspɪd) *adj Biol.* covered with stiff hairs or bristles. ORIG C17: from L *hispidus* bristly

hiss (hɪs) *n* **1** a sound like that of a prolonged *s.* **2** such a sound as an exclamation of derision, contempt, etc. ◆ *vb* **3** (*intr*) to produce or utter a hiss. **4** (*tr*) to express with a hiss. **5** (*tr*) to show derision or anger towards (a speaker, performer, etc.) by hissing. ORIG C14: imit.

Hiss ★ (hɪs) *n* **Alger** (ˈældʒə). 1904–96, US politician: imprisoned (1950–54) for perjury in connection with alleged espionage activities.

hist (hɪst) *interj* an exclamation used to attract attention or as a warning to be silent.

histamine (ˈhɪstəˌmiːn) *n* an amine released by the body tissues in allergic reactions, causing irritation. ORIG C20: from HIST- + AMINE
▸ **histaminic** (ˌhɪstəˈmɪnɪk) *adj*

histo- *or before a vowel* **hist-** *combining form.* indicating animal or plant tissue: *histology; histochemistry.* ORIG from Gk, from *histos* web

histogenesis (ˌhɪstəʊˈdʒɛnɪsɪs) *n* the formation of tissues and organs from undifferentiated cells.
▸ **histogenetic** (ˌhɪstəʊdʒəˈnɛtɪk) *or* ˌ**histoˈgenic** *adj*

histogram (ˈhɪstəˌɡræm) *n* a statistical graph that represents the frequency of values of a quantity by vertical rectangles of varying heights and widths. ORIG C20: ?from HISTO(RY) + -GRAM

histology (hɪˈstɒlədʒɪ) *n* the study of the tissues of an animal or plant.
▸ **histological** (ˌhɪstəˈlɒdʒɪkᵊl) *or* ˌ**histoˈlogic** *adj*

histolysis (hɪˈstɒlɪsɪs) *n* the disintegration of organic tissues.
▸ **histolytic** (ˌhɪstəˈlɪtɪk) *adj*

historian (hɪˈstɔːrɪən) *n* a person who writes or studies history, esp. one who is an authority on it.

historic (hɪˈstɒrɪk) *adj* **1** famous in history; significant. **2** *Linguistics.* (of Latin, Greek, or Sanskrit verb tenses) referring to past time.

> **USAGE NOTE** A distinction is usually made between *historic* (important, significant) and *historical* (pertaining to history): *a historic decision; a historical perspective.*

historical (hɪˈstɒrɪkᵊl) *adj* **1** belonging to or typical of the study of history: *historical methods.* **2** concerned with events of the past: *historical accounts.* **3** based on or constituting factual material as distinct from legend or supposition. **4** based on history: *a historical novel.* **5** occurring in history.
▸ **hisˈtorically** *adv*

> **USAGE NOTE** See at **historic.**

historical-cost accounting *n* a method of accounting that values assets at the original cost. In times of high inflation profits can be overstated. Cf. **current-cost accounting.**

historical linguistics *n* (*functioning as sing*) the study of language as it changes in the course of time.

historical present *n* the present tense used to narrate past events, employed for effect or in informal use, as in *a week ago I see this accident.*

historicism (hɪˈstɒrɪˌsɪzəm) *n* **1** the belief that natural laws govern historical events. **2** the doctrine that each period of history has its own beliefs and values inapplicable to any other. **3** excessive emphasis on history, past styles, etc.
▸ **hisˈtoricist** *n, adj*

historicity (ˌhɪstəˈrɪsɪtɪ) *n* historical authenticity.

historiographer (hɪˌstɔːrɪˈɒɡrəfə) *n* **1** a historian, esp. one concerned with historical method. **2** a historian employed to write the history of a group or public institution.
▸ **hiˌstoriˈography** *n*

history (ˈhɪstərɪ) *n, pl* **histories. 1** a record or account of past events, developments, etc. **2** all that is preserved of the past, esp. in written form. **3** the discipline of recording and interpreting past events. **4** past events, esp. when considered as an aggregate. **5** an event in the past, esp. one that has been reduced in importance: *their quarrel was just history.* **6** the past, previous experiences, etc., of a thing or person: *the house had a strange history.* **7** a play that depicts historical events. **8** a narrative relating the events of a character's life: *the history of Joseph Andrews.* ORIG C15: from L *historia,* from Gk: inquiry, from *historein* to narrate, from *histōr* judge

histrionic (ˌhɪstrɪˈɒnɪk) *adj* **1** excessively dramatic or artificial: *histrionic gestures.* **2** *Now rare.* dramatic. ◆ *n* **3** (*pl*) melodramatic displays of temperament. **4** *Rare.* (*pl; functioning as sing*) dramatics. ORIG C17: from LL *histriōnicus,* from L *histriō* actor
▸ ˌ**histriˈonically** *adv*

hit (hɪt) *vb* **hits, hitting, hit.** (*mainly tr*) **1** (*also intr*) to deal (a blow) to (a person or thing); strike. **2** to come into violent contact with: *the car hit the tree.* **3** to strike with a missile: *to hit a target.* **4** to knock or bump: *I hit my arm on the table.* **5** to propel by striking: *to hit a ball.* **6** *Cricket.* to score (runs). **7** to affect (a person, place, or thing), esp. suddenly or adversely: *his illness hit his wife very hard.* **8** to reach: *unemployment hit a new high.* **9** to experience: *I've hit a slight snag here.* **10** *Sl.* to murder (a rival criminal) in fulfilment of an underworld vendetta. **11** *Inf.* to set out on: *let's hit the road.* **12** *Inf.* to arrive: *he will hit town tomorrow.* **13** *Inf., chiefly US & Canad.* to demand or request from: *he hit me for a pound.* **14 hit the bottle.** *Sl.* to drink an excessive amount of alcohol. ◆ *n* **15** an impact or collision. **16** a shot, blow, etc., that reaches its object. **17** an apt, witty, or telling remark. **18** *Inf.* **18a** a person or thing that gains wide appeal: *she's a hit with everyone.* **18b** (*as modifier*): *a hit record.* **19** *Inf.* a stroke of luck. **20** *Sl.* **20a** a murder carried out as the result of an underworld vendetta. **20b** (*as modifier*): *a hit squad.* **21** *Computing sl.* a single visit to a website. **22 make a hit with.** *Inf.* to make a favourable impression on. ◆ See also **hit off, hit on, hit out.** ORIG OE *hittan,* from ON *hitta*
▸ ˈ**hitter** *n*

Hitachi ★ (hɪˈtætʃɪ) *n* a city in Japan, in E Honshu: a centre of the electronics industry. Pop.: 199 241 (1995).

hit-and-miss *adj Inf.* random; haphazard: *a hit-and-miss affair; the technique is very hit and miss.* Also: **hit or miss.**

hit-and-run *adj* (*prenominal*) **1** denoting a motor-vehicle accident in which the driver leaves the scene without stopping to give assistance, inform the police, etc. **2** (of an attack, raid, etc.) relying on surprise allied to a rapid departure from the scene of operations: *hit-and-run tactics.*

hitch (hɪtʃ) *vb* **1** to fasten or become fastened with a knot or tie. **2** (*tr;* often foll. by *up*) to pull up (the trousers, etc.)

with a quick jerk. **3** (*intr*) *Chiefly US.* to move in a halting manner. **4** (*tr; passive*) *Sl.* to marry (esp. in **get hitched**). **5** *Inf.* to obtain (a ride) by hitchhiking. ◆ *n* **6** an impediment or obstacle, esp. one that is temporary or minor. **7** a knot that can be undone by pulling against the direction of the strain that holds it. **8** a sudden jerk: *he gave it a hitch and it came loose.* **9** *Inf.* a ride obtained by hitchhiking. ORIG C15: from ?
▸ **'hitcher** *n*

Hitchcock ★ ('hɪtʃ,kɒk) *n* Sir **Alfred (Joseph)**. 1899–1980, British film director, noted for his suspense films, such as *The Thirty-Nine Steps* (1935), *Psycho* (1960), and *The Birds* (1963).
▸ **,Hitch'cockian** *adj*

hitchhike ('hɪtʃ,haɪk) *vb* **hitchhikes, hitchhiking, hitchhiked.** (*intr*) to travel by obtaining free lifts in motor vehicles.
▸ **'hitch,hiker** *n*

hi tech *or* **high tech** (tɛk) *n* **1** short for **high technology. 2** a style of interior design using features of industrial equipment. ◆ *adj* **hi-tech** *or* **high-tech. 3** designed for or using high technology. **4** of or in the interior design style. ◆ Cf. **low tech.**

hither ('hɪðə) *adv* **1** to or towards this place (esp. in **come hither**). **2 hither and thither.** this way and that, as in confusion. ◆ *adj* **3** *Arch. or dialect.* (of a side or part) nearer; closer. ORIG OE *hider*

hithermost ('hɪðə,məʊst) *adj Now rare.* nearest to this place or in this direction.

hitherto (,hɪðə'tu:) *adv, adj* until this time: *hitherto, there have been no problems; hitherto private aristocratic homes.*

Hitler ★ ('hɪtlə) *n* **1 Adolf** ('a:dɔlf). 1889–1945, German dictator, born in Austria. As president of the National Socialist German Workers' Party (Nazi party), he attempted to overthrow the government of Bavaria (1923); imprisoned, but eventually became chancellor of Germany (1933), transforming it into the Third Reich. He established concentration camps to exterminate the Jews, annexed (1938) Austria and Czechoslovakia, and invaded Poland (1939), which precipitated World War II; committed suicide. **2** a person who displays dictatorial characteristics.

Hitlerism ('hɪtlə,rɪzəm) *n* the policies, principles, and methods of the Nazi party as developed by Adolf Hitler.

hit list *n Inf.* **1** a list of people to be murdered: *a terrorist hit list.* **2** a list of targets to be eliminated in some way: *a hit list of pits to be closed.*

hit man *n* a hired assassin.

hit off *vb* **1** (*tr, adv*) to represent or mimic accurately. **2 hit it off with.** *Inf.* to have a good relationship with.

hit on *vb* (*prep*) **1** (*tr*) to discover unexpectedly or guess correctly. Also: **hit upon. 2** (*tr*) *US & Canad.* to make sexual advances to.

hit out *vb* (*intr, adv; often foll. by at*) **1** to direct blows forcefully and vigorously. **2** to make a verbal attack (upon someone).

Hittite ('hɪtaɪt) *n* **1** a member of an ancient people of Anatolia, who built a great empire in N Syria and Asia Minor in the second millennium B.C. **2** the extinct language of this people. ◆ *adj* **3** of or relating to this people, their civilization, or their language.

hit wicket *n Cricket.* an instance of a batsman breaking the wicket with the bat or a part of the body while playing a stroke and so being out.

HIV *abbrev. for* human immunodeficiency virus; the cause of AIDS.

hive (haɪv) *n* **1** a structure in which social bees live. **2** a colony of social bees. **3** a place showing signs of great industry (esp. in **a hive of activity**). **4** a teeming multitude. ◆ *vb* **hives, hiving, hived. 5** to cause (bees) to collect or (of bees) to collect inside a hive. **6** to live or cause to live in or as if in a hive. **7** (*tr; often foll. by up or away*) to store, esp. for future use. ORIG OE *hȳf*

hive off *vb* (*adv*) **1** to transfer or be transferred from a larger group or unit. **2** (*usually tr*) to transfer (profitable activities of a nationalized industry) back to private ownership.

hives (haɪvz) *n* (*functioning as sing or pl*) *Pathol.* a nontechnical name for **urticaria.** ORIG C16: from ?

hiya ('haɪjə, ,haɪ'jɑ:) *sentence substitute.* an informal term of greeting. ORIG C20: shortened from *how are you?*

hl *abbrev. for* hectolitre.

HL (in Britain) *abbrev. for* House of Lords.

hm *symbol for* hectometre.

h'm (*spelling pron* hmmm) *interj* used to indicate hesitation, doubt, assent, pleasure, etc.

HM *abbrev. for:* **1** His (*or* Her) Majesty. **2** headmaster; headmistress.

HMAS *abbrev. for* His (*or* Her) Majesty's Australian Ship.

HMCS *abbrev. for* His (*or* Her) Majesty's Canadian Ship.

HMI (in Britain) *abbrev. for* His (*or* Her) Majesty's Inspector; a government official who examines and supervises schools.

Hmong (hmɒŋ) *n, pl* **Hmongs** or **Hmong. 1** a member of a people living in mountain villages in parts of SE Asia. **2** the language of this people.

H.M.S. *or* **HMS** *abbrev. for:* **1** His (*or* Her) Majesty's Service. **2** His (*or* Her) Majesty's Ship.

HMSO (in Britain) *abbrev. for* (the former) His (*or* Her) Majesty's Stationery Office.

HNC (in Britain) *abbrev. for* Higher National Certificate; a qualification recognized by many national technical and professional institutions.

HND (in Britain) *abbrev. for* Higher National Diploma; a qualification in technical subjects equivalent to a degree.

ho[1] (həʊ) *interj* **1** Also: **ho-ho.** an imitation or representation of a deep laugh. **2** an exclamation used to attract attention, etc. ORIG C13: imit.

ho[2] (həʊ) *n US Black sl.* a derogatory term for a woman. ORIG C20: from Black or Southern US pronunciation of WHORE

Ho *the chemical symbol for* holmium.

hoar (hɔ:) *n* **1** short for **hoarfrost.** ◆ *adj* **2** *Rare.* covered with hoarfrost. **3** *Arch.* a poetic variant of **hoary.** ORIG OE *hār*

hoard (hɔ:d) *n* **1** an accumulated store hidden away for future use. **2** a cache of ancient coins, etc. ◆ *vb* **3** to accumulate (a hoard). ORIG OE *hord*
▸ **'hoarder** *n*

hoarding ('hɔ:dɪŋ) *n* **1** Also called (esp. US and Canad.): **billboard.** a large board used for displaying advertising posters, as by a road. **2** a temporary wooden fence erected round a building or demolition site. ORIG C19: from C15 *hoard* fence, from OF *hourd* palisade, of Gmc origin

hoarfrost ('hɔ:,frɒst) *n* a deposit of needle-like ice crystals formed on the ground by direct condensation at temperatures below freezing point. Also called: **white frost.**

hoarhound ('hɔ:,haʊnd) *n* a variant spelling of **horehound.**

hoarse (hɔ:s) *adj* **1** gratingly harsh in tone. **2** having a husky voice, as through illness, shouting, etc. ORIG C14: from ON
▸ **'hoarsely** *adv* ▸ **'hoarseness** *n*

hoarsen ('hɔ:sᵊn) *vb* to make or become hoarse.

hoary ('hɔ:rɪ) *adj* **hoarier, hoariest. 1** having grey or white hair. **2** white or whitish-grey in colour. **3** ancient or venerable.
▸ **'hoariness** *n*

hoatzin (həʊ'ætsɪn) *n* a unique South American bird with clawed wing digits in the young. ORIG C17: from American Sp., from Nahuatl *uatzin* pheasant

hoax (həʊks) *n* **1** a deception, esp. a practical joke. ◆ *vb* **2** (*tr*) to deceive or play a joke on (someone). ORIG C18: prob. from HOCUS
▸ **'hoaxer** *n*

hob[1] (hɒb) *n* **1** the flat top part of a cooking stove, or a separate flat surface, containing hotplates or burners. **2** a shelf beside an open fire, for keeping kettles, etc., hot. **3**

a steel pattern used in forming a mould or die in cold metal. ORIG C16: var. of obs. *hubbe;* ? rel. to HUB

hob[2] (hɒb) *n* **1** a hobgoblin or elf. **2 raise** *or* **play hob.** *US inf.* to cause mischief. **3** a male ferret. ORIG C14: var. of *Rob,* short for *Robin* or *Robert*

Hobart ★ ('həʊbɑːt) *n* a port in Australia, capital of the state of Tasmania on the estuary of the Derwent: natural harbour; University of Tasmania (1890). Pop.: 194 700 (1995 est.).

Hobbema ★ ('hɒbɪmə; *Dutch* 'hɔbəmaː) *n* **Meindert** ('maɪndərt). 1638–1709, Dutch painter of peaceful landscapes, usually including a watermill.

Hobbes ★ (hɒbz) *n* **Thomas.** 1588–1679, English political philosopher. Best known for the *Leviathan* (1651).

hobbit ('hɒbɪt) *n* one of an imaginary race of half-size people living in holes. ORIG C20: coined by J. R. R. Tolkien, with the meaning "hole-builder"

hobble ('hɒbᵊl) *vb* **hobbles, hobbling, hobbled. 1** (*intr*) to walk with a lame awkward movement. **2** (*tr*) to fetter the legs of (a horse) in order to restrict movement. **3** (*intr*) to progress with difficulty. ◆ *n* **4** a strap, rope, etc., used to hobble a horse. **5** a limping gait. ◆ Also (for senses 2, 4): **hopple.** ORIG C14: prob. from Low G
▸ **'hobbler** *n*

hobbledehoy (ˌhɒbᵊldɪ'hɔɪ) *n* a clumsy or bad-mannered youth. ORIG C16: from earlier *hobbard de hoy,* from ?

Hobbs ★ (hɒbz) *n* Sir **John Berry,** known as *Jack Hobbs.* 1882–1963, British cricketer: scored 197 centuries.

hobby[1] ('hɒbɪ) *n, pl* **hobbies. 1** an activity pursued in spare time for pleasure or relaxation. **2** *Arch.* a small horse. **3** short for **hobbyhorse** (sense 1). **4** an early form of bicycle, without pedals. ORIG C14 *hobyn,* prob. var. of name *Robin*
▸ **'hobbyist** *n*

hobby[2] ('hɒbɪ) *n, pl* **hobbies.** any of several small Old World falcons. ORIG C15: from OF *hobet,* from *hobe* falcon

hobbyhorse ('hɒbɪˌhɔːs) *n* **1** a toy consisting of a stick with a figure of a horse's head at one end. **2** a rocking horse. **3** a figure of a horse attached to a performer's waist in a morris dance, etc. **4** a favourite topic (esp. in **on one's hobbyhorse**). ORIG C16: from HOBBY[1], orig. a small horse; then generalized to apply to any pastime

hobgoblin (ˌhɒb'gɒblɪn) *n* **1** a mischievous goblin. **2** a bogey; bugbear. ORIG C16: from HOB[2] + GOBLIN

hobnail ('hɒbˌneɪl) *n* **a** a short nail with a large head for protecting the soles of heavy footwear. **b** (*as modifier*): *hobnail boots.* ORIG C16: from HOB[1] (in archaic sense: peg) + NAIL
▸ **'hobˌnailed** *adj*

hobnob ('hɒbˌnɒb) *vb* **hobnobs, hobnobbing, hobnobbed.** (*intr;* often foll. by *with*) **1** to socialize or talk informally. **2** *Obs.* to drink (with). ORIG C18: from *hob or nob* to drink to one another in turns, ult. from OE *habban* to HAVE + *nabban* not to have

hobo ('həʊbəʊ) *n, pl* **hobos** *or* **hoboes.** *Chiefly US & Canad.* **1** a tramp; vagrant. **2** a migratory worker. ORIG C19 (US): from ?
▸ **'hoboism** *n*

Hoboken ★ ('həʊbəʊkən) *n* a city in N Belgium, in Antwerp province, on the River Scheldt. Pop.: 35 000 (latest est.).

Hobson's choice ('hɒbsᵊnz) *n* the choice of taking what is offered or nothing at all. ORIG C16: after Thomas *Hobson* (1544–1631), E liveryman who gave his customers no choice but had them take the nearest horse

Hochhuth ★ (*German* 'hoːxhuːt) *n* **Rolf** (rɔlf). born 1933, Swiss dramatist. His best-known works are the controversial documentary drama *The Representative* (1963), on the papacy's attitude to the Jews in World War II, *Soldiers* (1967), and *Wessis in Weimar* (1992).

Ho Chi Minh ★ ('həʊ 'tʃiː 'mɪn) *n* original name *Nguyen That Tan.* 1890–1969, Vietnamese statesman; president of North Vietnam (1954–69). He headed the Vietminh (1941), which won independence for Vietnam from the French (1954).

Ho Chi Minh City ★ *n* a port in S Vietnam, 97 km (60 miles) from the South China Sea, on the Saigon River: captured by the French in 1859; merged with adjoining Cholon in 1932; capital of the former Republic of Vietnam (South Vietnam) from 1954 to 1976; university (1917); US headquarters during the Vietnam War. Pop.: 4 322 300 (1993 est.). Former name (until 1976): **Saigon.**

hock[1] (hɒk) *n* **1** the joint at the tarsus of a horse or similar animal, corresponding to the human ankle. ◆ *vb* **2** another word for **hamstring.** ORIG C16: short for *hockshin,* from OE *hōhsinu* heel sinew

hock[2] (hɒk) *n* any of several white wines from the German Rhine. ORIG C17: short for obs. *hockamore* from G *Hochheimer*

hock[3] (hɒk) *Inf., chiefly US & Canad.* ◆ *vb* **1** (*tr*) to pawn or pledge. ◆ *n* **2** the state of being in pawn. **3 in hock. 3a** in prison. **3b** in debt. **3c** in pawn. ORIG C19: from Du. *hok* prison, debt

hockey ('hɒkɪ) *n* **1** Also called (esp. US and Canad.): **field hockey.** a game played on a field by two opposing teams of 11 players each, who try to hit a ball into their opponents' goal using long sticks curved at the end. **2** See **ice hockey.** ORIG C19: from earlier *hawkey,* from ?

Hockney ★ ('hɒknɪ) *n* **David.** born 1937, British painter, known for his etchings, portraits, and paintings of aquatic themes.

hocus ('həʊkəs) *vb* **hocuses, hocusing, hocused** *or* **hocuses, hocussing, hocussed.** (*tr*) *Now rare.* **1** to trick. **2** to stupefy, esp. with a drug. **3** to drug (a drink).

hocus-pocus ('həʊkəs'pəʊkəs) *n* **1** trickery or chicanery. **2** an incantation used by conjurors or magicians. **3** conjuring skill. ◆ *vb* **hocus-pocuses, hocus-pocusing, hocus-pocused** *or* **hocus-pocuses, hocus-pocussing, hocus-pocussed. 4** to deceive or trick (someone). ORIG C17: ? dog Latin invented by jugglers

hod (hɒd) *n* **1** an open wooden box attached to a pole, for carrying bricks, mortar, etc. **2** a tall narrow coal scuttle. ORIG C14: ?from C13 dialect *hot,* from OF *hotte* pannier, prob. of Gmc origin

Hodeida ★ (hɒ'deɪdə) *n* a port in N Yemen, on the Red Sea; formerly in North Yemen. Pop.: 155 100 (latest est.).

hodgepodge ('hɒdʒˌpɒdʒ) *n* a variant spelling (esp. US and Canad.) of **hotchpotch.**

Hodgkin ★ ('hɒdʒkɪn) *n* **1** Sir **Alan Lloyd.** 1914–98, British physiologist. With A. F. Huxley, he explained the conduction of nervous impulses: shared the Nobel prize for physiology or medicine (1963). **2 Dorothy Crowfoot.** 1910–94, British chemist and crystallographer, who determined the three-dimensional structure of insulin: Nobel prize for chemistry (1964).

Hodgkin's disease *n* a malignant disease, a form of lymphoma, characterized by enlargement of the lymph nodes, spleen, and liver. ORIG C19: after Thomas *Hodgkin* (1798–1866), London physician, who first described it

hodograph ('hɒdəˌgrɑːf) *n* a curve of which the radius vector represents the velocity of a moving particle. ORIG C19: from Gk *hodos* way + -GRAPH

hodometer (hɒ'dɒmɪtə) *n* another name for **odometer.**
▸ **ho'dometry** *n*

hoe (həʊ) *n* **1** any of several kinds of long-handled hand implement used to till the soil, weed, etc. ◆ *vb* **hoes, hoeing, hoed. 2** to dig, scrape, weed, or till (surface soil) with or as if with a hoe. ORIG C14: via OF *houe,* of Gmc origin
▸ **'hoer** *n*

hoedown ('həʊˌdaʊn) *n US & Canad.* **1** a boisterous square dance. **2** a party at which hoedowns are danced.

Hoek van Holland ★ ('huːk fɑn 'hɔlɑnt) *n* the Dutch name for the **Hook of Holland.**

Hofei ★ ('həʊ'feɪ) *n* a variant transliteration of the Chinese name for **Hefei.**

Hoffman ★ ('hɒfmən) *n* **Dustin** (**Lee**) born 1937, US actor. His films include *Midnight Cowboy* (1969), *Rain Man* (1989), and *Wag the Dog* (1998).

Hofmannsthal ★ (*German* 'hoːfmanstaːl) *n* **Hugo von**

('huːgo fɔn). 1874–1929, Austrian poet and dramatist, noted as the librettist for Richard Strauss's operas.

Hofuf ★ (huˈfuːf) *n* another name for **Al Hufuf**.

hog (hɒg) *n* **1** a domesticated pig, esp. a castrated male. **2** *US & Canad.* any mammal of the family Suidae; pig. **3** Also: **hogg.** *Austral. dialect.* another name for **hogget**. **4** *Inf.* a greedy person. **5 go the whole hog.** *Sl.* to do something thoroughly or unreservedly. ◆ *vb* **hogs, hogging, hogged.** (*tr*) **6** *Sl.* to take more than one's share of. **7** to arch (the back) like a hog. **8** to cut (the mane) of (a horse) very short. ORIG OE *hogg*, of Celtic origin
▸ **ˈhogger** *n* ▸ **ˈhogˌlike** *adj*

hogan (ˈhəʊgən) *n* a wooden dwelling covered with earth, typical of the Navaho Indians of North America. ORIG of Amerind origin

Hogarth ★ (ˈhəʊgɑːθ) *n* **William.** 1697–1764, English engraver and painter. His engravings satirizing the vices and affectations of his age, include *A Rake's Progress* (1735) and *Marriage à la Mode* (1745).
▸ **Hoˈgarthian** *adj*

hogback (ˈhɒgˌbæk) *n* **1** Also called: **hog's back.** a narrow ridge with steep sides. **2** *Archaeol.* a tomb with sloping sides.

hogfish (ˈhɒgˌfɪʃ) *n, pl* **hogfish** *or* **hogfishes.** a wrasse that occurs in the Atlantic. The head of the male resembles a pig's snout.

Hogg ★ (hɒg) *n* **1 James,** known as *the Ettrick Shepherd.* 1770–1835, Scottish writer. His works include the poems *The Queen's Wake* (1813) and the novel *The Confessions of a Justified Sinner* (1824). **2 Quintin.** See (1st Baron) **Hailsham of St Marylebone.**

hogget (ˈhɒgɪt) *n Dialect, Austral. & NZ.* a young sheep that has yet to be sheared. Also: **hog, hogg.**

hoggish (ˈhɒgɪʃ) *adj* selfish, gluttonous, or dirty.

Hogmanay (ˌhɒgməˈneɪ) *n* (*sometimes not cap.*) New Year's Eve in Scotland. ORIG C17: ?from Norman F *hoguinane,* from OF *aguillanneuf* a New Year's Eve gift

hognose snake (ˈhɒgˌnəʊz) *n* a North American nonvenomous snake that has a trowel-shaped snout and inflates its body when alarmed. Also called: **puff adder.**

hogshead (ˈhɒgzˌhɛd) *n* **1** a unit of capacity, used esp. for alcoholic beverages. It has several values. **2** a large cask. ORIG C14: from ?

hogtie (ˈhɒgˌtaɪ) *vb* **hogties, hogtying, hogtied.** (*tr*) *Chiefly US.* **1** to tie together the legs or the arms and legs of. **2** to impede, hamper, or thwart.

hogwash (ˈhɒgˌwɒʃ) *n* **1** *Inf.* nonsense. **2** pigswill.

hogweed (ˈhɒgˌwiːd) *n* any of several coarse weedy plants.

Hohenlohe ★ (ˈhəʊənˌləʊə; *German* hoːənˈloːə) *n* **Chlodwig** (ˈkloːtvɪç), Prince of Hohenlohe-Schillingsfürst. 1819–1901, Prussian statesman; chancellor of the German empire (1894–1900).

Hohenstaufen ★ (ˈhəʊənˌʃtaʊfən; *German* hoːənˈʃtaufən) *n* a German princely family that provided rulers of Germany (1138–1208, 1215–54), Sicily (1194–1268), and the Holy Roman Empire (1138–1254).

Hohenzollern ★ (ˈhəʊənˌzɒlən; *German* hoːənˈtsɔlərn) *n* a German noble family, the younger (Franconian) branch of which provided rulers of Brandenburg (1417–1701) and Prussia (1701–1918). The last kings of Prussia (1871–1918) were also emperors of Germany.

Hohhot (ˈhɒˈhɒt), **Huhehot,** *or* **Hu-ho-hao-t'e** ★ *n* a city in N China, capital of Inner Mongolia Autonomous Region (since 1954) and capital of the former Suiyüan province; Inner Mongolia University (1957). Pop.: 652 534 (1990 est.).

ho-hum (ˈhəʊˌhʌm) *adj Inf.* lacking interest or inspiration; dull; mediocre: *a ho-hum collection of new releases.*

hoick *or* **hoik** (hɔɪk) *vb* to rise or raise abruptly and sharply. ORIG C20: prob. from HIKE

hoi polloi (ˈhɔɪ pəˈlɔɪ) *n* **the.** *Often derog.* the masses; common people. ORIG Gk, lit.: the many

hoist (hɔɪst) *vb* **1** (*tr*) to raise or lift up, esp. by mechanical means. ◆ *n* **2** any apparatus or device for hoisting. **3** the act of hoisting. **4** *Naut.* a group of signal flags. **5** the inner edge of a flag next to the staff. ORIG C16: var. of *hoise,* prob. from Low G
▸ **ˈhoister** *n*

hoity-toity (ˌhɔɪtɪˈtɔɪtɪ) *adj Inf.* arrogant or haughty. ORIG C17: rhyming compound based on C16 *hoit* to romp, from ?

hokey cokey (ˈhəʊkɪ ˈkəʊkɪ) *n* a dance routine performed to a cockney song of the same name.

Hokkaido ★ (hɒˈkaɪdəʊ) *n* the second largest and northernmost of the four main islands of Japan, separated from Honshu by the Tsugaru Strait and from the island of Sakhalin, Russia, by La Pérouse Strait: constitutes an autonomous administrative division. Capital: Sapporo. Pop.: 5 692 000 (1995). Area: 78 508 sq. km (30 312 sq. miles).

hokonui (ˌhəʊkəˈnuːiː) *n NZ.* illicit whisky. ORIG from *Hokonui,* district of Southland region, NZ

hokum (ˈhəʊkəm) *n Sl., chiefly US & Canad.* **1** claptrap; bunk. **2** obvious or hackneyed material of a sentimental nature in a play, film, etc. ORIG C20: prob. a blend of HOCUS-POCUS & BUNKUM

Hokusai ★ (ˈhəʊkuˌsaɪ, ˌhəʊkuˈsaɪ) *n* **Katsushika** (ˌkætsuːˈʃiːkə). 1760–1849, Japanese artist.

Holarctic (həʊˈlɑːktɪk) *adj* of or denoting a zoogeographical region consisting of the entire arctic regions. ORIG C19: from HOLO- + ARCTIC

Holbein ★ (*German* ˈhɔlbain) *n* **1 Hans** (hans), known as *Holbein the Elder.* 1465–1524, German painter. **2** his son, **Hans,** known as *Holbein the Younger.* 1497–1543, German painter and engraver; court painter to Henry VIII of England (1536–43), noted for his portraits.

hold[1] (həʊld) *vb* **holds, holding, held.** **1** to have or keep (an object) with or within the hands, arms, etc.; clasp. **2** (*tr*) to support: *to hold a drowning man's head above water.* **3** to maintain or be maintained in a specified state: *to hold firm.* **4** (*tr*) to set aside or reserve: *they will hold our tickets until tomorrow.* **5** (when *intr, usually used in commands*) to restrain or be restrained from motion, action, departure, etc.: *hold that man until the police come.* **6** (*intr*) to remain fast or unbroken: *that cable won't hold much longer.* **7** (*intr*) (of the weather) to remain dry and bright. **8** (*tr*) to keep the attention of. **9** (*tr*) to engage in or carry on: *to hold a meeting.* **10** (*tr*) to have the ownership, possession, etc., of: *he holds a law degree; who's holding the ace?* **11** (*tr*) to have the use of or responsibility for: *to hold office.* **12** (*tr*) to have the capacity for: *the carton will hold eight books.* **13** (*tr*) to be able to control the outward effects of drinking beer, spirits, etc. **14** (often foll. by *to* or *by*) to remain or cause to remain committed (to): *hold him to his promise.* **15** (*tr; takes a clause as object*) to claim: *he holds that the theory is incorrect.* **16** (*intr*) to remain relevant, valid, or true: *the old philosophies don't hold nowadays.* **17** (*tr*) to consider in a specified manner: *I hold him very dear.* **18** (*tr*) to defend successfully: *hold the fort against the attack.* **19** (sometimes foll. by *on*) *Music.* to sustain the sound of (a note) throughout its specified duration. **20** (*tr*) *Computing.* to retain (data) in a storage device after copying onto another storage device or location. **21 hold (good) for.** to apply or be relevant to: *the same rules hold for everyone.* **22 there is no holding him** *or* **her.** this person is so spirited that he or she cannot be restrained. ◆ *n* **23** the act or method of holding fast or grasping. **24** something to hold onto, as for support or control. **25** an object or device that holds fast or grips something else. **26** controlling influence: *she has a hold on him.* **27** a short pause. **28** a prison or a cell in a prison. **29** *Wrestling.* a way of seizing one's opponent. **30** *Music.* a pause or fermata. **31a** a tenure, esp. of land. **31b** (*in combination*): *freehold.* **32** *Arch.* a fortified place. **33 no holds barred.** all limitations removed. ◆ See also **hold back, hold down,** etc. ORIG OE *healdan*
▸ **ˈholdable** *adj*

hold[2] (həʊld) *n* the space in a ship or aircraft for storing cargo. ORIG C16: var. of HOLE

holdall (ˈhəʊldˌɔːl) *n Brit.* a large strong bag or basket. Usual US and Canad. name: **carryall.**

hold back *vb* (*adv*) **1** to restrain or be restrained. **2** (*tr*) to withhold: *he held back part of the payment.*

hold down *vb* (*tr, adv*) **1** to restrain or control. **2** *Inf.* to manage to retain or keep possession of: *to hold down two jobs at once.*

holder ('həʊldə) *n* **1** a person or thing that holds. **2a** a person who has possession or control of something. **2b** (*in combination*): *householder.* **3** *Law.* a person who has possession of a bill of exchange, cheque, or promissory note that he is legally entitled to enforce.

Hölderlin ★ (*German* 'hœldərli:n) *n* **Friedrich** ('fri:drɪç). 1770–1843, German poet, whose works include the poem *Menon's Lament for Diotima* and the novel *Hyperion* (1797–99).

holdfast ('həʊld,fɑ:st) *n* **1** the act of gripping strongly. **2** any device used to secure an object, such as a hook, clamp, etc. **3** the organ of attachment of a seaweed or related plant.

hold forth *vb* (*adv*) **1** (*intr*) to speak for a long time or in public. **2** (*tr*) to offer (an attraction or enticement).

hold in *vb* (*tr, adv*) **1** to curb, control, or keep in check. **2** to conceal (feelings).

holding ('həʊldɪŋ) *n* **1** land held under a lease. **2** (*often pl*) property to which the holder has legal title, such as land, stocks, shares, and other investments. **3** *Sport.* the obstruction of an opponent with the hands or arms, esp. in boxing. ◆ *adj* **4** *Austral. inf.* in funds; having money.

holding company *n* a company with controlling shareholdings in one or more other companies.

holding operation *n* a plan or procedure devised to prolong the existing situation.

holding paddock *n Austral. & NZ.* a paddock in which cattle or sheep are kept temporarily, as before shearing, etc.

holding pattern *n* the oval or circular path of an aircraft flying around an airport awaiting permission to land.

hold off *vb* (*adv*) **1** (*tr*) to keep apart or at a distance. **2** (*intr;* often foll. by *from*) to refrain (from doing something).

hold on *vb* (*intr, adv*) **1** to maintain a firm grasp. **2** to continue or persist. **3** (foll. by *to*) to keep or retain: *hold on to those stamps as they'll soon be valuable.* **4** *Inf.* to keep a telephone line open. ◆ *sentence substitute.* **5** *Inf.* stop! wait!

hold out *vb* (*adv*) **1** (*tr*) to offer. **2** (*intr*) to last or endure. **3** (*intr*) to continue to stand firm, as a person refusing to succumb to persuasion. **4** *Chiefly US.* to withhold (something due). **5 hold out for.** to wait patiently for (the fulfilment of one's demands). **6 hold out on.** *Inf.* to keep from telling (a person) some important information.

hold over *vb* (*tr, mainly adv*) **1** to defer or postpone. **2** (*prep*) to intimidate (a person) with (a threat).

hold-up *n* **1** a robbery, esp. an armed one. **2** a delay; stoppage. ◆ *vb* **hold up.** (*tr, adv*) **3** to delay; hinder. **4** to support. **5** to waylay in order to rob, esp. using a weapon. **6** to exhibit or present.

hold with *vb* (*intr, prep*) to support; approve of.

hole (həʊl) *n* **1** an area hollowed out in a solid. **2** an opening in or through something. **3** an animal's burrow. **4** *Inf.* an unattractive place, such as a town. **5** a fault (esp. in **pick holes in**). **6** *Sl.* a difficult and embarrassing situation. **7** the cavity in various games into which the ball must be thrust. **8** (on a golf course) **8a** each of the divisions of a course (usually 18) represented by the distance between the tee and a green. **8b** the score made in striking the ball from the tee into the hole. **9** *Physics.* a vacancy in a nearly full band of quantum states of electrons in a semiconductor or an insulator. Under the action of an electric field holes behave as carriers of positive charge. **10 in holes.** so worn as to be full of holes. **11 make a hole in.** to consume or use a great amount of (food, drink, money, etc.). ◆ *vb* **holes, holing, holed. 12** to make a hole or holes in (something). **13** (when *intr,* often foll. by *out*) *Golf.* to hit (the ball) into the hole. ORIG OE *hol*
▸ **'holey** *adj*

hole-and-corner *adj* (*usually prenominal*) *Inf.* furtive or secretive.

hole in one *n Golf.* a shot from the tee that finishes in the hole. Also (esp. US): **ace.**

hole in the heart *n* a defect of the heart in which there is an abnormal opening in any of the walls dividing the four heart chambers.

hole in the wall *n Inf.* **1** *Chiefly Brit.* another name for **cash dispenser. 2** a small dingy place, esp. one that is difficult to find.

hole up *vb* (*intr, adv*) **1** (of an animal) to hibernate. **2** *Inf.* to hide or remain secluded.

Holguín ★ (*Spanish* ɔl'ɣin) *n* a city in NE Cuba, in Holguín province: trading centre. Pop.: 242 085 (1994 est.).

Holi ('həʊlɪ) *n* a Hindu spring festival, celebrated for two to five days, commemorating Krishna's dalliance with the cowgirls. Bonfires are lit and coloured powder and water thrown over celebrants. ORIG after *Holika,* legendary female demon

-holic *suffix forming noun* indicating desire for or dependence on; *workaholic; chocoholic.* ORIG C20: abstracted from (*alco*)*holic*

holiday ('hɒlɪ,deɪ) *n* **1** (*often pl*) *Chiefly Brit.* a period in which a break is taken from work or studies for rest, travel, or recreation. US and Canad. word: **vacation. 2** a day on which work is suspended by law or custom, such as a religious festival, bank holiday, etc. Related adj: **ferial.** ◆ *vb* **3** (*intr*) *Chiefly Brit.* to spend a holiday. ORIG OE *hāligdæg,* lit.: holy day

Holiday ★ ('hɒlɪ,deɪ) *n* **Billie.** real name *Eleanora Fagan;* known as *Lady Day.* 1915–59, US jazz singer.

holiday camp *n Brit.* a place, esp. one at the seaside, providing accommodation, recreational facilities, etc., for holiday-makers.

holiday-maker *n Brit.* a person who goes on holiday. US and Canad. equivalents: **vacationer, vacationist.**

holily ('həʊlɪlɪ) *adv* in a holy, devout, or sacred manner.

holiness ('həʊlɪnɪs) *n* the state or quality of being holy.

Holiness ('həʊlɪnɪs) *n* (preceded by *His* or *Your*) a title reserved for the pope.

Holinshed ('hɒlɪnʃɛd) *or* **Holingshed** ★ *n* **Raphael.** died ?1580, English chronicler. His *Chronicles of England, Scotland, and Ireland* (1577) provided material for Shakespeare's plays.

holism ('həʊlɪzəm) *n* **1** any doctrine that a system may have properties over and above those of its parts and their organization. **2** (in medicine) the consideration of the complete person in the treatment of disease. ORIG C20: from HOLO- + -ISM
▸ **ho'listic** *adj*

Holkar State ★ (hɒl'kɑ:) *n* a former state of central India, ruled by the Holkar dynasty of Maratha rulers of Indore (18th century until 1947).

holland ('hɒlənd) *n* a coarse linen cloth. ORIG C15: after HOLLAND, where it was made

Holland[1] ★ ('hɒlənd) *n* **1** another name for the **Netherlands. 2** a county of the Holy Roman Empire, corresponding to the present-day North and South Holland provinces of the Netherlands. **3 Parts of.** an area in E England constituting a former administrative division of Lincolnshire.

Holland[2] ★ ('hɒlənd) *n* Sir **Sidney George.** 1893–1961, New Zealand statesman; prime minister of New Zealand (1949–57).

hollandaise sauce (,hɒlən'deɪz, 'hɒlən,deɪz) *n* a rich sauce of egg yolks, butter, vinegar, etc. ORIG C19: from F *sauce hollandaise* Dutch sauce

Hollandia ★ (hɒ'lændɪə) *n* a former name of **Jayapura.**

Hollands ('hɒləndz) *n* (*functioning as sing*) Dutch gin, often sold in stone bottles. ORIG C18: from Du. *hollandsch genever*

holler ('hɒlə) *Inf.* ◆ *vb* **1** to shout or yell (something). ◆ *n* **2** a shout; call. ORIG var. of C16 *hollow,* from *holla,* from F *holà* stop! (lit.: ho there!)

hollo ('hɒləʊ) *or* **holla** ('hɒlə) *n, pl* **hollos** *or* **hollas,** *interj* **1** a cry for attention, or of encouragement. ◆ *vb* **2** (*intr*) to shout. ORIG C16: from F *holà* ho there!

hollow ('hɒləʊ) *adj* **1** having a hole or space within; not solid. **2** having a sunken area; concave. **3** deeply set: *hollow cheeks.* **4** (of sounds) as if resounding in a hollow

place. **5** without substance or validity. **6** hungry or empty. **7** insincere; cynical. ♦ *adv* **8 beat (someone) hollow.** *Brit. inf.* to defeat thoroughly. ♦ *n* **9** a cavity, opening, or space in or within something. **10** a depression in the land. ♦ *vb* (often foll. by *out,* usually when *tr*) **11** to make or become hollow. **12** to form (a hole, cavity, etc.) or (of a hole, etc.) to be formed. ORIG C12: from *holu,* inflected form of OE *holh* cave
▸ **'hollowly** *adv* ▸ **'hollowness** *n*

hollow-eyed *adj* with the eyes appearing to be sunk into the face, as from excessive fatigue.

holly ('hɒlɪ) *n, pl* **hollies. 1** a tree or shrub having bright red berries and shiny evergreen leaves with prickly edges. **2** its branches, used for Christmas decorations. **3 holly oak.** another name for **holm oak.** ORIG OE *holegn*

Holly ★ ('hɒlɪ) *n* **Buddy.** real name *Charles Harden Holley.* 1936–59, US rock-and-roll singer, guitarist, and songwriter. His hits include "That'll be the Day" (1957) and "Peggy Sue" (1957).

hollyhock ('hɒlɪˌhɒk) *n* a tall plant with stout hairy stems and spikes of white, yellow, red, or purple flowers. Also called (US): **rose mallow.** ORIG C16: from HOLY + *hock,* from OE *hoc* mallow

Hollywood ★ ('hɒlɪˌwʊd) *n* **1** a NW suburb of Los Angeles, California: centre of the US film industry. Pop.: 127 894 (1996 est.). **2a** the US film industry. **2b** (*as modifier*): *a Hollywood star.*

holm[1] (həʊm) *n Dialect, chiefly northwestern English.* **1** an island in a river or lake. **2** low flat land near a river. ORIG OE *holm* sea, island

holm[2] (həʊm) *n* **1** short for **holm oak. 2** *Chiefly Brit.* a dialect word for **holly.** ORIG C14: var. of obs. *holin,* from OE *holegn* holly

Holmes ★ (həʊmz) *n* **1 Oliver Wendell.** 1809–94, US author, esp. of humorous essays, such as *The Autocrat of the Breakfast Table* (1858). **2** his son, **Oliver Wendell.** 1841–1935, US jurist.

holmium ('hɒlmɪəm) *n* a malleable silver-white metallic element of the lanthanide series. Symbol: Ho; atomic no.: 67; atomic wt.: 164.93. ORIG C19: from NL *Holmia* Stockholm

holm oak *n* an evergreen Mediterranean oak tree with prickly leaves resembling holly. Also called: **holm, holly oak, ilex.**

holo- *or before a vowel* **hol-** *combining form.* whole or wholly: *holograph.* ORIG from Gk *holos*

holocaust ('hɒləˌkɔːst) *n* **1** great destruction or loss of life or the source of such destruction, esp. fire. **2** (*usually cap.*) **the.** the mass murder of some six million European Jews by the Germans during World War II. **3** a rare word for **burnt offering.** ORIG C13: from LL *holocaustum* whole burnt offering, from Gk, from HOLO- + *kaiein* to burn

Holocene ('hɒləˌsiːn) *adj* **1** of, denoting, or formed in the second and most recent epoch of the Quaternary period, which began 10 000 years ago. ♦ *n* **2 the.** the Holocene epoch or rock series. ♦ Also: **Recent.**

Holofernes ★ (ˌhɒlə'fɜːniːz, hə'lɒfəˌniːz) *n* the Assyrian general, who was killed by the biblical heroine Judith.

hologram ('hɒləˌgræm) *n* a photographic record produced by illuminating the object with coherent light (as from a laser) and, without using lenses, exposing a film to light reflected from this object and to a direct beam of coherent light. When interference patterns on the film are illuminated by the coherent light a three-dimensional image is produced.

holograph ('hɒləˌgrɑːf) *n* a book or document handwritten by its author; original manuscript; autograph.

holography (hɒ'lɒgrəfɪ) *n* the science or practice of producing holograms.
▸ **holographic** (ˌhɒlə'græfɪk) *adj* ▸ **ˌholo'graphically** *adv*

holohedral (ˌhɒlə'hiːdrəl) *adj* (of a crystal) exhibiting all the planes required for the symmetry of the crystal system.

holophytic (ˌhɒlə'fɪtɪk) *adj* (of plants) capable of synthesizing their food from inorganic molecules, esp. by photosynthesis.

holothurian (ˌhɒlə'θjʊərɪən) *n* **1** an echinoderm of the class *Holothuroidea,* having a leathery elongated body with a ring of tentacles around the mouth. ♦ *adj* **2** of the *Holothuroidea.* ORIG C19: from NL *Holothūria,* name of type genus, from L: water polyp, from Gk, from ?

hols (hɒlz) *pl n Brit. school sl.* holidays.

Holst ★ (həʊlst) *n* **Gustav (Theodore).** 1874–1934, English composer. His works include operas, choral music, and orchestral music such as the suite *The Planets* (1917).

Holstein ★ (*German* 'hɔlʃtain) *n* a region of N Germany, in S Schleswig-Holstein: in early times a German duchy of Saxony; became a duchy of Denmark in 1474; finally incorporated into Prussia in 1866.

holster ('həʊlstə) *n* a sheathlike leather case for a pistol, attached to a belt or saddle. ORIG C17: via Du., of Gmc origin

holt[1] (həʊlt) *n Arch. or poetic.* a wood or wooded hill. ORIG OE *holt*

holt[2] (həʊlt) *n* the lair of an animal, esp. an otter. ORIG C16: from HOLD[1]

Holt ★ (həʊlt) *n* **Harold Edward.** 1908–67, Australian statesman; prime minister (1966–67); believed drowned.

holy ('həʊlɪ) *adj* **holier, holiest. 1** of or associated with God or a deity; sacred. **2** endowed or invested with extreme purity. **3** devout or virtuous. **4 holier-than-thou.** offensively sanctimonious or self-righteous. ♦ *n, pl* **holies. 5** a sacred place. ORIG OE *hālig, hǣlig*

Holy City ★ *n* **the. 1** Jerusalem, esp. when regarded as the focal point of the religions of Judaism, Christianity, or Islam. **2** *Christianity.* heaven regarded as the perfect counterpart of Jerusalem. **3** any city regarded as especially sacred by a particular religion.

Holy Communion *n* **1** the celebration of the Eucharist. **2** the consecrated elements.

holy day *n* a day on which a religious festival is observed.

Holy Father *n RC Church.* the pope.

Holy Ghost *n* another name for the **Holy Spirit.**

Holy Grail *n* **1** Also called: **Grail, Sangraal.** (in medieval legend) the bowl used by Jesus at the Last Supper. It was brought to Britain by Joseph of Arimathea, where it became the quest of many knights. **2** *Inf.* any desired ambition or goal: *the Holy Grail of infrared astronomy.* ORIG C14: *grail* from OF *graal,* from Med. L *gradālis* bowl, from ?

Holyhead ★ ('hɒlɪˌhɛd) *n* a port in NW Wales, in Anglesey; the chief town of Holy Island. Pop.: 11 796 (1991).

Holy Island ★ *n* **1** Also called: **Lindisfarne.** an island off the NE coast of Northumberland, site of a monastery founded by St Aidan in 635. **2** an island off NW Anglesey. Area: about 62 sq. km (24 sq. miles).

Holy Land ★ *n* **the.** another name for Palestine.

Holyoake ★ ('həʊlɪˌəʊk) *n* Sir **Keith Jacka.** 1904–83, New Zealand politician; prime minister (1957; 1960–72); governor general (1977–80).

holy of holies *n* **1** any place of special sanctity. **2** (*cap.*) the innermost compartment of the Jewish tabernacle, where the Ark was enshrined.

holy orders *pl n* **1** the sacrament whereby a person is admitted to the Christian ministry. **2** the grades of the Christian ministry. **3** the status of an ordained Christian minister.

Holy Roman Empire *n* the complex of European territories under the rule of the Frankish or German king who bore the title of Roman emperor, beginning with the coronation of Charlemagne in 800 A.D.

Holy Scripture *n* another term for **Scripture.**

Holy See *n RC Church.* **1** the see of the pope as bishop of Rome. **2** the Roman curia.

Holy Spirit *n Christianity.* the third person of the Trinity. Also called: **Holy Ghost.**

holystone ('həʊlɪˌstəʊn) *n* **1** a soft sandstone used for scrubbing the decks of a vessel. ♦ *vb* **holystones, holystoning, holystoned. 2** (*tr*) to scrub (a vessel's decks) with a holystone. ORIG C19: ?from its being used in a kneeling position

holy synod *n* the governing body of any of the Orthodox Churches.

holy water *n* water that has been blessed by a priest for use in symbolic rituals of purification.

Holy Week *n* the week preceding Easter Sunday.

Holy Willie ('wɪlɪ) *n* a person who is hypocritically pious. ORIG C18: from Burns' *Holy Willie's Prayer*

Holy Writ *n* another term for **Scripture.**

homage ('hɒmɪdʒ) *n* **1** a public show of respect or honour towards someone or something (esp. in **pay** *or* **do homage to**). **2** (in feudal society) the act of respect and allegiance made by a vassal to his lord. ORIG C13: from OF, from *home* man, from L *homo*

homburg ('hɒmbɜːg) *n* a man's hat of soft felt with a dented crown and a stiff upturned brim. ORIG C20: after *Homburg,* in Germany, where orig. made

home (həʊm) *n* **1** the place where one lives. **2** a house or other dwelling. **3** a family or other group living in a house. **4** a person's country, city, etc., esp. viewed as a birthplace or a place dear to one. **5** the habitat of an animal. **6** the place where something is invented, founded, or developed. **7** a building or organization set up to care for people in a certain category, such as orphans, the aged, etc. **8** *Sport.* one's own ground: *the match is at home.* **9a** the objective towards which a player strives in certain sports. **9b** an area where a player is safe from attack. **10 a home from home.** a place other than one's own home where one can be at ease. **11 at home. 11a** in one's own home or country. **11b** at ease. **11c** giving an informal party at one's own home. **12 at home in, on,** *or* **with.** familiar with. **13 home and dry.** *Brit. sl.* definitely safe or successful. Austral. and NZ equivalent: **home and hosed. 14 near home.** concerning one deeply. ◆ *adj* (*usually prenominal*) **15** of one's home, country, etc.; domestic. **16** (of an activity) done in one's house: *home taping.* **17** *Sport.* relating to one's own ground: *a home game.* **18** *US.* central; principal: *the company's home office.* ◆ *adv* **19** to or at home: *I'll be home tomorrow.* **20** to or on the point. **21** to the fullest extent: *hammer the nail home.* **22 bring home to. 22a** to make clear to. **22b** to place the blame on. **23 nothing to write home about.** *Inf.* of no particular interest: *the film was nothing to write home about.* ◆ *vb* **homes, homing, homed. 24** (*intr*) (of birds and other animals) to return home accurately from a distance. **25** (often foll. by *in on* or *onto*) to direct or be directed onto a point or target, esp. by automatic navigational aids. **26** to send or go home. **27** (*tr*) to furnish with a home. **28** (*intr;* often foll. by *in* or *in on*) to be directed towards a goal, target, etc. ORIG OE *hām*

USAGE NOTE See at **hone.**

Home ★ (hjuːm) *n* **Baron.** See (Baron) **Home of the Hirsel.**

home-alone *adj Inf.* (esp. of a young child) left in a house, flat, etc., unattended.

home banking *n* a system whereby a person at home or in an office can use a computer with a modem to call up information from a bank or to transfer funds electronically.

homeboy ('həʊmˌbɔɪ) *n Sl., chiefly US.* **1** a close friend. **2** a person from one's home town or neighbourhood. **3** a member of a neighbourhood gang. ORIG C20: US rap-music usage
▸ **'homeˌgirl** *fem n*

home-brew *n* **1** a beer or other alcoholic drink brewed at home rather than commercially. **2** *Canad. inf.* a professional football player who was born in Canada and is not an import.
▸ **ˌhome-'brewed** *adj*

homecoming ('həʊmˌkʌmɪŋ) *n* **1** the act of coming home. **2** *US.* an annual celebration held by a university, college, or school for former students.

Home Counties ★ *pl n* the counties surrounding London.

home economics *n* (*functioning as sing or pl*) the study of diet, budgeting, child care, and other subjects concerned with running a home.

home farm *n Brit.* (esp. formerly) a farm attached to and providing food for a large country house.

Home Guard *n* a volunteer part-time military force recruited to defend the United Kingdom in World War II.

home help *n Brit.* a woman employed, esp. by a local authority, to do housework in a person's home. NZ equivalent: **home aid.**

homeland ('həʊmˌlænd) *n* **1** the country in which one lives or was born. **2** the official name for a **Bantustan.**

homeless ('həʊmlɪs) *adj* **a** having nowhere to live. **b** (*as collective n;* preceded by *the*): *the homeless.*
▸ **'homelessness** *n*

homely ('həʊmlɪ) *adj* **homelier, homeliest. 1** characteristic of or suited to the ordinary home; unpretentious. **2** (of a person) **2a** *Brit.* warm and domesticated. **2b** *Chiefly US & Canad.* plain.
▸ **'homeliness** *n*

home-made *adj* **1** (esp. of foods) made at home or on the premises, esp. of high quality ingredients. **2** crudely fashioned.

homeo-, homoeo-, *or* **homoio-** *combining form.* like or similar: *homeomorphism.* ORIG from L *homoeo-,* from Gk *homoio-,* from *homos* same

Home Office *n Brit. government.* the department responsible for the maintenance of law and order, and all other domestic affairs not assigned to another department.

Home of the Hirsel ★ ('hɜːsəl) *n* Baron, title of *Sir Alec Douglas-Home,* formerly 14th Earl of Home. 1903–95, British Conservative statesman: he renounced his earldom to become prime minister (1963–64); foreign secretary (1970–74).

homeopathy *or* **homoeopathy** (ˌhəʊmɪ'ɒpəθɪ) *n* a method of treating disease by the use of small amounts of a drug that, in healthy persons, produces symptoms similar to those of the disease being treated.
▸ **homeopathic** *or* **homoeopathic** (ˌhəʊmɪə'pæθɪk) *adj*
▸ **homeopathist, homoeopathist** (ˌhəʊmɪ'ɒpəθɪst) *or* **homeopath, homoeopath** ('həʊmɪəˌpæθ) *n*

homeostasis *or* **homoeostasis** (ˌhəʊmɪəʊ'steɪsɪs) *n* **1** the maintenance of metabolic equilibrium within an animal by a tendency to compensate for disrupting changes. **2** the maintenance of equilibrium within a social group, person, etc.

homeowner ('həʊmˌəʊnə) *n* a person who owns the house in which he or she lives.
▸ **ˌhome'ownership** *n*

home page *n Computing.* (on a website) the main document relating to an individual or an institution that provides introductory information about a website with links to the actual details of services or information provided.

homer ('həʊmə) *n* a homing pigeon.

Homer ★ ('həʊmə) *n* c. 800 B.C., Greek poet to whom are attributed the *Iliad* and the *Odyssey*: it is thought that he was born on the island of Chios and was blind.

Homeric (həʊ'merɪk) *adj* **1** of, relating to, or resembling Homer or his poems. **2** imposing or heroic.

home rule *n* **1** self-government, esp. in domestic affairs. **2** the partial autonomy sometimes granted to a national minority or a colony.

Home Secretary *n Brit. government.* the head of the Home Office.

homesick ('həʊmˌsɪk) *adj* depressed or melancholy at being away from home and family.
▸ **'homeˌsickness** *n*

homespun ('həʊmˌspʌn) *adj* **1** having plain or unsophisticated character. **2** woven or spun at home. ◆ *n* **3** cloth made at home or made of yarn spun at home.

homestead ('həʊmˌstɛd, -stɪd) *n* **1** a house or estate and the adjoining land, buildings, etc., esp. a farm. **2** (in the US) a house and adjoining land designated by the owner as his fixed residence and exempt under the homestead laws from seizure and forced sale for debts. **3** (in western Canada) a piece of land granted to a settler by the federal government. **4** *Austral. & NZ.* (on a sheep or cattle station) the owner's or manager's residence; in New Zealand, the term includes all outbuildings.

Homestead Act *n* **1** an act passed by the US Congress in 1862 making available to settlers 160-acre tracts of public land for cultivation. **2** (in Canada) a similar act passed by the Canadian Parliament in 1872.

homesteader ('həʊmˌstɛdə) *n US and Canad.* a person who possesses land under a homestead law.

homestead law *n* (in the US and Canada) any of various laws conferring privileges on owners of homesteads.

home straight *n* **1** *Horse racing.* the section of a racecourse forming the approach to the finish. **2** the final stage of an undertaking. ◆ Also (chiefly US): **home stretch.**

home truth *n* (*often pl*) an unpleasant fact told to a person about himself or herself.

home unit *n Austral. & NZ.* a self-contained residence which is part of a series of similar residences. Often shortened to **unit.**

homeward ('həʊmwəd) *adj* **1** going home. **2** (of a voyage, etc.) returning to the home port. ◆ *adv also* **homewards. 3** towards home.

homework ('həʊmˌwɜːk) *n* **1** school work done at home. **2** any preparatory study. **3** work done at home for pay.

homey ('həʊmɪ) *adj* **homier, homiest.** a variant spelling (esp. US) of **homy.**
▸ **'homeyness** *n*

homicide ('hɒmɪˌsaɪd) *n* **1** the killing of a human being by another person. **2** a person who kills another. ORIG C14: from OF, from L *homo* man + *caedere* to slay
▸ **ˌhomi'cidal** *adj*

homiletics (ˌhɒmɪ'lɛtɪks) *n* (*functioning as sing*) the art of preaching or writing sermons. ORIG C17: from Gk *homilētikos* cordial, from *homilein;* see HOMILY

homily ('hɒmɪlɪ) *n, pl* **homilies. 1** a sermon. **2** moralizing talk or writing. ORIG C14: from Church L *homīlia,* from Gk: discourse, from *homilein* to converse with, from *homilos* crowd, from *homou* together + *ilē* crowd
▸ **ˌhomi'letic** *adj* ▸ **'homilist** *n*

homing ('həʊmɪŋ) *n* (*modifier*) **1** *Zool.* relating to the ability to return home after travelling great distances. **2** (of an aircraft, missile, etc.) capable of guiding itself onto a target.

homing pigeon *n* any breed of pigeon developed for its homing instinct, used for racing. Also called: **homer.**

hominid ('hɒmɪnɪd) *n* **1** any primate of the family Hominidae, which includes modern man (*Homo sapiens*) and the extinct precursors of man. ◆ *adj* **2** of or belonging to the Hominidae. ORIG C19: via NL from L *homo* man + -ID[1]

hominoid ('hɒmɪˌnɔɪd) *adj* **1** of or like man; manlike. **2** of or belonging to the primate superfamily that includes the anthropoid apes and man. ◆ *n* **3** a hominoid animal. ORIG C20: from L *homin-, homo* man + -OID

hominy ('hɒmɪnɪ) *n Chiefly US.* coarsely ground maize prepared as a food by boiling in milk or water. ORIG C17: prob. of Algonquian origin

hominy grits *pl n US.* finely ground hominy.

homo ('həʊməʊ) *n, pl* **homos.** *Inf., derog.* short for **homosexual.**

Homo ('həʊməʊ) *n* a genus of hominids including modern man (see ***Homo sapiens***) and several extinct species of primitive man. ORIG L: man

homo- *combining form.* same or like: *homologous; homosexual.* ORIG via L from Gk *homos* same

homocyclic (ˌhəʊməʊ'saɪklɪk) *adj* (of a chemical compound) containing a closed ring of atoms of the same kind, esp. carbon atoms.

homocysteine (ˌhəʊməʊ'sɪstɪˌiːn) *n* an amino acid occurring as an intermediate in the metabolism of methionine. Elevated levels in the blood may indicate increased risk of cardiovascular disease.

homoeo- *combining form.* a variant of **homeo-.**

homogamy (hɒ'mɒgəmɪ) *n* **1** a condition in which all the flowers of an inflorescence are either of the same sex or hermaphrodite. **2** the maturation of the anthers and stigmas at the same time, ensuring self-pollination.
▸ **ho'mogamous** *adj*

homogeneous (ˌhəʊmə'dʒiːnɪəs, ˌhɒm-) *adj* **1** composed of similar or identical parts or elements. **2** of uniform nature. **3** similar in kind or nature. **4** *Maths.* containing terms of the same degree with respect to all the variables, as in $x^2 + 2xy + y^2$.
▸ **homogeneity** (ˌhəʊməʊdʒɪ'niːɪtɪ, ˌhɒm-) *n* ▸ **ˌhomo'geneousness** *n*

homogenize *or* **homogenise** (hɒ'mɒdʒɪˌnaɪz) *vb* **homogenizes, homogenizing, homogenized** *or* **homogenises, homogenising, homogenised. 1** (*tr*) to break up the fat globules in (milk or cream) so that they are evenly distributed. **2** to make or become homogeneous.
▸ **hoˌmogeni'zation** *or* **hoˌmogeni'sation** *n* ▸ **ho'mogeˌnizer** *or* **ho'mogeˌniser** *n*

homogenous (hə'mɒdʒɪnəs) *adj* of, relating to, or exhibiting homogeny.

homogeny (hɒ'mɒdʒɪnɪ) *n Biol.* similarity in structure because of common ancestry. ORIG C19: from Gk *homogeneia* community of origin, from *homogenēs* of the same kind

homograph ('hɒməˌgrɑːf) *n* one of a group of words spelt in the same way but having different meanings.
▸ **ˌhomo'graphic** *adj*

homoiothermic (həʊˌmɔɪə'θɜːmɪk) *or* **homothermal** (ˌhəʊməʊ'θɜːməl, ˌhɒm-) *adj* having a constant body temperature, usually higher than the temperature of the surroundings; warm-blooded.
▸ **ho'moioˌthermy** *or* **'homoˌthermy** *n*

homologize *or* **homologise** (hɒ'mɒləˌdʒaɪz) *vb* **homologizes, homologizing, homologized** *or* **homologises, homologising, homologised.** to be, show to be, or make homologous.

homologous (həʊ'mɒləgəs, hɒ-), **homological** (ˌhəʊ-mə'lɒdʒɪkᵊl, ˌhɒm-), *or* **homologic** *adj* **1** having a related or similar position, structure, etc. **2** *Biol.* (of organs and parts) having the same evolutionary origin but different functions: *the wing of a bat and the paddle of a whale are homologous.*
▸ **ˌhomo'logically** *adv* ▸ **'homoˌlogue** *or US* (*sometimes*) **'homolog** *n*

homology (həʊ'mɒlədʒɪ) *n, pl* **homologies.** the condition of being homologous. ORIG C17: from Gk *homologia* agreement, from *homologos* agreeing, from HOMO- + *legein* to speak

homolosine projection (hɒ'mɒləˌsaɪn) *n* a map projection of the world on which the oceans are distorted to allow for greater accuracy in representing the continents. ORIG C20: from Gk *homologos* agreeing + SINE[1]

homomorphism (ˌhəʊməʊ'mɔːfɪzəm, ˌhɒm-) *or* **homomorphy** *n Biol.* similarity in form.
▸ **ˌhomo'morphic** *or* **ˌhomo'morphous** *adj*

homonym ('hɒmənɪm) *n* **1** one of a group of words spelt in the same way but having different meanings. Cf. **homograph, homophone. 2** *Biol.* a specific or generic name that has been used for two or more different organisms. ORIG C17: from L *homōnymum,* from Gk, from *homōnumos* of the same name; see HOMO-, -ONYM
▸ **ˌhomo'nymic** *or* **ho'monymous** *adj*

homophobia (ˌhəʊməʊ'fəʊbɪə) *n* intense hatred or fear of homosexuals or homosexuality. ORIG C20: from HOMO(SEXUAL) + -PHOBIA
▸ **'homoˌphobe** *n* ▸ **ˌhomo'phobic** *adj*

homophone ('hɒməˌfəʊn) *n* **1** one of a group of words pronounced in the same way but differing in meaning or spelling or both, as *bear* and *bare.* **2** a written letter or combination of letters that represents the same speech sound as another: *"ph" is a homophone of "f".*

homophonic (ˌhɒmə'fɒnɪk) *adj* of or relating to music in which the parts move together rather than exhibit individual rhythmic independence.

homopterous (həʊ'mɒptərəs) *or* **homopteran** *adj* of or belonging to a suborder of hemipterous insects having wings of a uniform texture held over the back at rest. ORIG C19: from Gk *homopteros,* from HOMO- + *pteron* wing

Homo sapiens ('sæpɪˌɛnz) *n* the specific name of modern man; the only extant species of the genus *Homo*. This species also includes some extinct types of primitive man, such as Cro-Magnon man. ORIG NL, from L *homo* man + *sapiens* wise

homosexual (ˌhəʊməʊ'sɛksjʊəl, ˌhɒm-) *n* **1** a person who is sexually attracted to members of the same sex. ◆ *adj* **2** of or relating to homosexuals or homosexuality. **3** of or relating to the same sex.

homosexuality (ˌhəʊməʊˌsɛksjʊ'ælɪtɪ, ˌhɒm-) *n* sexual attraction to or sexual relations with members of the same sex.

homozygote (ˌhəʊməʊ'zaɪgəʊt) *n* an animal or plant that is homozygous and breeds true to type.
▸ **homozygotic** (ˌhəʊməʊzaɪ'gɒtɪk) *adj*

homozygous (ˌhəʊməʊ'zaɪgəs) *adj Genetics*. (of an organism) having identical alleles for any one gene: *these two fruit flies are homozygous for red eye colour.*

Homs (hɒms) *or* **Hums** ★ (hʊms) *n* a city in W Syria, near the Orontes River: important in Roman times as the capital of Phoenicia-Lebanesia. Pop.: 644 204 (1994 est.). Ancient name: **Emesa** ('ɛmɛsə). Former name: **Hims**.

homunculus (hɒ'mʌŋkjʊləs) *n, pl* **homunculi** (-ˌlaɪ). a miniature man; midget. Also called: **homuncule** (həʊ'mʌŋkjuːl). ORIG C17: from L, dim. of *homo* man
▸ **ho'muncular** *adj*

homy *or esp. US* **homey** ('həʊmɪ) *adj* **homier, homiest.** like a home; cosy.
▸ **'hominess** *or esp. US* **'homeyness** *n*

hon. *abbrev. for:* **1** honorary. **2** honourable.

Hon. *abbrev. for* Honourable (title).

Honan ★ ('həʊ'næn) *n* a variant transliteration of the Chinese name for **Henan**.

honcho ('hɒntʃəʊ) *n, pl* **honchos.** *Inf., chiefly US.* the person in charge; the boss. ORIG C20: from Japanese *han'chō* group leader

Hond. *abbrev. for* Honduras.

Hondo ★ ('hɒndəʊ) *n* another name for **Honshu**.

Honduras ★ (hɒn'djʊərəs) *n* **1** a republic in Central America: an early centre of Mayan civilization; colonized by the Spanish from 1524 onwards; gained independence in 1821. Official language: Spanish; English is also widely spoken. Religion: Roman Catholic majority. Currency: lempira. Capital: Tegucigalpa. Pop.: 6 281 000 (1999 est.). Area: 112 088 sq. km (43 277 sq. miles). **2 Gulf of.** an inlet of the Caribbean, on the coasts of Honduras, Guatemala, and Belize.
▸ **Hon'duran** *adj, n*

hone (həʊn) *n* **1** a fine whetstone for sharpening. ◆ *vb* **hones, honing, honed. 2** (*tr*) to sharpen or polish with or as if with a hone. ORIG OE *hān* stone

> **USAGE NOTE** *Hone* is sometimes wrongly used where *home* is meant: *this device makes it easier to home in on* (not *hone in on*) *the target.*

Honecker ★ (*German* 'hɒːnɛkər) *n* **Erich** ('eːrɪç). 1912–94, German statesman; head of state of East Germany (1976–89).

Honegger ★ ('hɒnɪgə; *French* ɔnɛgɛr) *n* **Arthur** (artyr). 1892–1955, French composer, one of Les Six. His works include the oratorio *King David* (1921) and *Pacific 231* (1924) for orchestra.

honest ('ɒnɪst) *adj* **1** not given to lying, cheating, stealing, etc.; trustworthy. **2** not false or misleading; genuine. **3** just or fair: *honest wages.* **4** characterized by sincerity: *an honest appraisal.* **5** without pretensions: *honest farmers.* **6** *Arch.* (of a woman) respectable. **7 honest broker.** a mediator in disputes, esp. international ones. **8 make an honest woman of.** to marry (a woman, esp. one who is pregnant) to prevent scandal. ORIG C13: from OF *honeste,* from L *honestus* distinguished, from *honōs* HONOUR

honestly ('ɒnɪstlɪ) *adv* **1** in an honest manner. **2** (intensifier): *I honestly don't believe it.*

honesty ('ɒnɪstɪ) *n, pl* **honesties. 1** the condition of being honest. **2** *Arch.* virtue or respect. **3** Also called: **moonwort, satinpod.** a purple-flowered European plant cultivated for its flattened silvery pods, which are used for indoor decoration.

honey ('hʌnɪ) *n* **1** a sweet viscid substance made by bees from nectar and stored in their nests or hives as food. **2** anything that is sweet or delightful. **3** (*often cap.*) *Chiefly US & Canad.* a term of endearment. **4** *Inf., chiefly US & Canad.* something very good of its kind. ◆ *vb* **honeys, honeying, honeyed. 5** (*tr*) to sweeten with or as if with honey. **6** (often foll. by *up*) to talk to (someone) in a flattering way. ORIG OE *huneg*
▸ **'honey-ˌlike** *adj*

honey badger *n* another name for **ratel**.

honeybee ('hʌnɪˌbiː) *n* any of various social bees widely domesticated as a source of honey and beeswax. Also called: **hive bee.**

honey buzzard *n* a common European bird of prey having broad wings and a typically dull brown plumage with white-streaked underparts.

honeycomb ('hʌnɪˌkəʊm) *n* **1** a waxy structure, constructed by bees in a hive, that consists of adjacent hexagonal cells in which honey is stored, eggs are laid, and larvae develop. **2** something resembling this in structure. **3** *Zool.* another name for **reticulum** (sense 2). ◆ *vb* (*tr*) **4** to pierce with holes, cavities, etc. **5** to permeate: *honeycombed with spies.*

honey creeper *n* a small tropical American songbird having a slender downward-curving bill and feeding on nectar.

honeydew ('hʌnɪˌdjuː) *n* **1** a sugary substance excreted by aphids and similar insects. **2** a similar substance exuded by certain plants.

honeydew melon *n* a variety of muskmelon with a smooth greenish-white rind and sweet greenish flesh.

honey-eater ('hʌnɪˌiːtə) *n* a small Australasian songbird having a downward-curving bill and a brushlike tongue specialized for extracting nectar from flowers.

honeyed *or* **honied** ('hʌnɪd) *adj Poetic.* **1** flattering or soothing. **2** made sweet or agreeable: *honeyed words.* **3** full of honey.

honey guide *n* a small bird inhabiting tropical forests of Africa and Asia and feeding on beeswax, honey, and insects.

honeymoon ('hʌnɪˌmuːn) *n* **1** a holiday taken by a newly married couple. **2** a holiday considered to resemble a honeymoon: *a second honeymoon.* **3** the early, usually calm period of a relationship or enterprise. ◆ *vb* **4** (*intr*) to take a honeymoon. ORIG C16: traditionally explained as an allusion to the feelings of married couples as changing with the phases of the moon
▸ **'honeyˌmooner** *n*

honeypot ('hʌnɪˌpɒt) *n* **1** a container for honey. **2** something that attracts in great numbers: *Cornwall is a honeypot for tourists.*

honeysuckle ('hʌnɪˌsʌk^{ə}l) *n* **1** a temperate climbing shrub with fragrant white, yellow, or pink tubular flowers. **2** any of various Australian trees or shrubs of the genus *Banksia,* having flowers in dense spikes. ORIG OE *hunigsūce,* from HONEY + SUCK

honeytrap ('hʌnɪˌtræp) *n Inf.* a scheme in which a victim is lured into a compromising sexual situation that provides the opportunity for blackmail.

Hong Kong ★ ('hɒŋ 'kɒŋ) *n* **1** a Special Administrative Region of S China, with some autonomy; formerly a British Crown Colony: consists of Hong Kong Island, leased by China to Britain (1842–1997), Kowloon Peninsula, Stonecutters Island, the New Territories (mainland), leased by China in 1898 for a 99-year period, and over 230 small islands; important entrepôt trade and manufacturing centre, esp. for textiles and other consumer goods; university (1912). Pop.: 6 885 000 (1999 est.). Area: 1046 sq. km (404 sq. miles). **2** an island in Hong Kong, south of Kowloon Peninsula: contains the former colonial capital, Victoria. Pop.: 996 183 (latest est.). Area: 75 sq. km (29 sq. miles).

Hong-wu ('hɒŋ'wuː) *or* **Hung-wu** ★ *n* title of *Chu Yuan-Zhang* (or *Chu Yüan-Chang*), 1328–98, first emperor

(1368–98) of the Ming dynasty, uniting China under his rule by 1382.

Hong Xiu Quan ('hɒŋ 'ʃju: 'tʃwɑ:n) *or* **Hung Hsiu-ch'uan** ★ *n* 1814–64, Chinese religious leader and revolutionary. Claiming (1851) to be Christ's brother, he led the Taiping rebellion; committed suicide.

Honiara ★ (ˌhəʊnɪ'ɑ:rə) *n* the capital of the Solomon Islands, on NW Guadalcanal Island. Pop.: 43 643 (1996 est.).

honk (hɒŋk) *n* **1** a representation of the sound made by a goose. **2** any sound resembling this, esp. a motor horn. **3** *Brit. & Austral. sl.* a bad smell. ◆ *vb* **4** to make or cause (something) to make such a sound. **5** (*intr*) *Brit. sl.* to vomit. **6** (*intr*) *Brit. & Austral. sl.* to have a bad smell.

honky ('hɒŋkɪ) *n, pl* **honkies.** *Derog. sl., chiefly US.* a White man or White men collectively. ORIG C20: from ?

honky-tonk ('hɒŋkɪˌtɒŋk) *n* **1** *US & Canad. sl.* a cheap disreputable nightclub, bar, etc. **2a** a style of ragtime piano-playing, esp. on a tinny-sounding piano. **2b** (*as modifier*): *honky-tonk music.* ORIG C19: rhyming compound based on HONK

Honolulu ★ (ˌhɒnə'lu:lu:) *n* a port in Hawaii, on S Oahu Island: the state capital. Pop.: 423 475 (1996 est.).

honorarium (ˌɒnə'rɛərɪəm) *n, pl* **honorariums** *or* **honoraria** (-ɪə). a fee paid for a nominally free service. ORIG C17: from L: something presented on being admitted to a post of HONOUR

honorary ('ɒnərərɪ) *adj* (*usually prenominal*) **1a** held or given only as an honour, without the normal privileges or duties: *an honorary degree.* **1b** (of a secretary, treasurer, etc.) unpaid. **2** having such a position or title. **3** depending on honour rather than legal agreement.

honorific (ˌɒnə'rɪfɪk) *adj* **1** showing respect. **2a** (of a pronoun, verb inflection, etc.) indicating the speaker's respect for the addressee. **2b** (*as n*): *a Japanese honorific.*
▸ **ˌhonor'ifically** *adv*

honour *or US* **honor** ('ɒnə) *n* **1** personal integrity; allegiance to moral principles. **2a** fame or glory. **2b** a person who wins this for his country, school, etc. **3** (*often pl*) great respect, esteem, etc., or an outward sign of this. **4** (*often pl*) high or noble rank. **5** a privilege or pleasure: *it is an honour to serve you.* **6** a woman's chastity. **7a** *Bridge, etc.* any of the top five cards in a suit or any of the four aces at no trumps. **7b** *Whist.* any of the top four cards. **8** *Golf.* the right to tee off first. **9** **in honour bound.** under a moral obligation. **10** **in honour of.** out of respect for. **11** **on one's honour.** on the pledge of one's word or good name. ◆ *vb* (*tr*) **12** to hold in respect. **13** to show courteous behaviour towards. **14** to worship. **15** to confer a distinction upon. **16** to accept and then pay when due (a cheque, draft, etc.). **17** to keep (one's promise); fulfil (a previous agreement). **18** to bow or curtsy to (one's dancing partner). ORIG C12: from OF *onor,* from L *honor* esteem

Honour ('ɒnə) *n* (preceded by *Your, His,* or *Her*) a title used to or of certain judges.

honourable *or US* **honorable** ('ɒnərəbᵊl) *adj* **1** possessing or characterized by high principles. **2** worthy of honour or esteem. **3** consistent with or bestowing honour.
▸ **'honourably** *or US* **'honorably** *adv*

Honourable *or US* **Honorable** ('ɒnərəbᵊl) *adj* (*prenominal*) **the.** a title of respect placed before a name: used of various officials in the English-speaking world, as a courtesy title in Britain for the children of certain peers, and in Parliament by one member speaking of another. Abbrev.: **Hon.**

honours *or US* **honors** ('ɒnəz) *pl n* **1** observances of respect. **2** (*often cap.*) **2a** (in a university degree course) a rank of the highest academic standard. **2b** (*as modifier*): *an honours degree.* Abbrev.: **Hons. 3** a high mark awarded for an examination; distinction. **4** **do the honours.** to serve as host or hostess. **5** **last** (*or* **funeral**) **honours.** observances of respect at a funeral. **6** **military honours.** ceremonies performed by troops in honour of royalty, at the burial of an officer, etc.

honours of war *pl n Mil.* the honours granted by the victorious to the defeated, esp. as of marching out with all arms and flags flying.

Honshu ★ ('hɒnʃu:) *n* the largest of the four main islands of Japan, between the Pacific and the Sea of Japan; regarded as the Japanese mainland; includes a number of offshore islands and contains most of the main cities. Pop.: 100 995 000 (1995). Area: 230 448 sq. km (88 976 sq. miles). Also called: **Hondo.**

hooch *or* **hootch** (hu:tʃ) *n Inf., chiefly US & Canad.* alcoholic drink, esp. illicitly distilled spirits. ORIG C20: of Amerind origin, *Hootchinoo,* name of a tribe that distilled a type of liquor

Hooch *or* **Hoogh** ★ (hu:tʃ; *Dutch* ho:x) *n* **Pieter de** ('pi:tər də). 1629–?1684, Dutch genre painter.

hood[1] (hʊd) *n* **1** a loose head covering either attached to a cloak or coat or made as a separate garment. **2** something resembling this in shape or use. **3** the US and Canad. name for **bonnet** (of a car). **4** the folding roof of a convertible car. **5** a hoodlike garment worn over an academic gown, indicating its wearer's degree and university. **6** *Biol.* a hoodlike structure, such as the fold of skin on the head of a cobra. ◆ *vb* **7** (*tr*) to cover with or as if with a hood. ORIG OE *hōd*
▸ **'hoodˌlike** *adj*

hood[2] (hʊd) *n Sl.* short for **hoodlum.**

Hood ★ (hʊd) *n* **1** **Robin.** See **Robin Hood. 2** **Samuel,** 1st Viscount. 1724–1816, British admiral. **3** **Thomas.** 1799–1845, British poet and humorist.

-hood *suffix forming nouns.* **1** indicating state or condition: *manhood.* **2** indicating a body of persons: *knighthood; priesthood.* ORIG OE *-hād*

hooded ('hʊdɪd) *adj* **1** covered with, having, or shaped like a hood. **2** (of eyes) having heavy eyelids that appear to be half closed.

hooded crow *n* a crow that has a grey body and black head, wings, and tail. Also called (Scot.): **hoodie** ('hʊdɪ), **hoodie crow.**

hoodlum ('hu:dləm) *n* **1** a petty gangster. **2** a lawless youth. ORIG C19: ?from Southern G *Haderlump* ragged good-for-nothing

hoodman-blind (ˌhʊdmən'blaɪnd) *n Brit., arch.* blind man's buff.

hoodoo ('hu:du:) *n, pl* **hoodoos. 1** a variant of **voodoo. 2** *Inf.* a person or thing that brings bad luck. **3** *Inf.* bad luck. ◆ *vb* **hoodoos, hoodooing, hoodooed. 4** (*tr*) *Inf.* to bring bad luck to.

hoodwink ('hʊdˌwɪŋk) *vb* (*tr*) **1** to dupe; trick. **2** *Obs.* to cover or hide. ORIG C16: orig., to cover the eyes with a hood, blindfold

hooey ('hu:ɪ) *n, interj Sl.* nonsense. ORIG C20: from ?

hoof (hu:f) *n, pl* **hooves** *or* **hoofs. 1a** the horny covering of the end of the foot in the horse, deer, and all other ungulate mammals. **1b** (*in combination*): *a hoofbeat.* Related adj: **ungular. 2** the foot of an ungulate mammal. **3** a hoofed animal. **4** *Facetious.* a person's foot. **5** **on the hoof. 5a** (of livestock) alive. **5b** in an impromptu manner: *he did his thinking on the hoof.* ◆ *vb* **6** **hoof it.** *Sl.* **6a** to walk. **6b** to dance. ORIG OE *hōf*
▸ **hoofed** *adj*

hoofer ('hu:fə) *n Sl.* a professional dancer.

Hoogh ★ (*Dutch* ho:x) *n* See (Pieter de) **Hooch.**

Hooghly ★ ('hu:glɪ) *n* a river in NE India, in West Bengal: the westernmost and commercially most important channel by which the River Ganges enters the Bay of Bengal. Length: 232 km (144 miles).

hoo-ha ('hu:ˌhɑ:) *n* a noisy commotion or fuss. ORIG C20: from ?

hook (hʊk) *n* **1** a curved piece of material, usually metal, used to suspend, hold, or pull something. **2** short for **fish-hook. 3** a trap or snare. **4** something resembling a hook in design or use. **5a** a sharp bend, esp. in a river. **5b** a sharply curved spit of land. **6** *Boxing.* a short swinging blow delivered with the elbow bent. **7** *Cricket.* a shot in which the ball is hit square on the leg side with the bat held horizontally. **8** *Golf.* a shot that causes the ball to go to the player's left. **9** a hook-shaped stroke used in writing, such as a part of a letter extending above or below the line. **10** *Music.* a stroke added to the stem of a note to indicate time values shorter than a crotchet. **11** a sickle. **12** *Naut.* an anchor. **13** **by hook or** (**by**) **crook.** by any means.

14 hook, line, and sinker. *Inf.* completely: *he fell for it hook, line, and sinker.* **15 off the hook.** *Sl.* free from obligation or guilt. **16 sling one's hook.** *Brit. sl.* to leave. ◆ *vb* **17** (often foll. by *up*) to fasten or be fastened with or as if with a hook or hooks. **18** (*tr*) to catch (something, such as a fish) on a hook. **19** to curve like or into the shape of a hook. **20** (*tr*) to make (a rug) by hooking yarn through a stiff fabric backing with a special instrument. **21** *Boxing.* to hit (an opponent) with a hook. **22** *Cricket, etc.* to play (a ball) with a hook. **23** *Rugby.* to obtain and pass (the ball) backwards from a scrum, using the feet. **24** (*tr*) *Sl.* to steal. ORIG OE *hōc*
▸ **'hook,like** *adj*

hookah *or* **hooka** ('hʊkə) *n* an oriental pipe for smoking marijuana, tobacco, etc., consisting of one or more long flexible stems connected to a container of water or other liquid through which smoke is drawn and cooled. Also called: **hubble-bubble, water pipe.** ORIG C18: from Ar. *huqqah*

Hooke ★ (hʊk) *n* **Robert.** 1635–1703, English physicist and inventor. He formulated Hooke's law (1678), built the first Gregorian telescope, and invented a balance spring.

hooked (hʊkt) *adj* **1** bent like a hook. **2** having a hook or hooks. **3** caught or trapped. **4** a slang word for **married. 5** *Sl.* addicted to a drug. **6** (often foll. by *on*) obsessed (with).

hooker ('hʊkə) *n* **1** a person or thing that hooks. **2** *Sl.* a prostitute. **3** *Rugby.* the central forward in the front row of a scrum.

Hooke's law *n* the principle that the stress imposed on a solid is directly proportional to the strain produced, within the elastic limit. ORIG C18: after R. HOOKE

Hook of Holland ★ *n* **the. 1** a cape on the SW coast of the Netherlands, in South Holland province. **2** a port on this cape. ◆ Dutch name: **Hoek van Holland.**

hook-up *n* **1** the contact of an aircraft in flight with the refuelling hose of a tanker aircraft. **2** an alliance or relationship. **3** the linking of broadcasting equipment or stations to transmit a special programme. ◆ *vb* **hook up** (*adv*). **4** to connect (two or more people or things).

hookworm ('hʊk,wɜːm) *n* any of various parasitic bloodsucking worms which cause disease. They have hooked mouthparts and enter their hosts by boring through the skin. Cf. **ancylostomiasis.**

hooky *or* **hookey** ('hʊkɪ) *n Inf., chiefly US, Canad., & NZ.* truancy, usually from school (esp. in **play hooky**). ORIG C20: ?from *hook it* to escape

hooligan ('huːlɪgən) *n Sl.* a rough lawless young person. ORIG C19: ? var. of *Houlihan,* Irish surname
▸ **'hooliganism** *n*

hoon (huːn) *n Austral. & NZ sl.* a loutish youth; hooligan. ORIG from ?

hoop¹ (huːp) *n* **1** a rigid circular band of metal or wood. **2** something resembling this. **3** a band of iron that holds the staves of a barrel together. **4** a child's toy shaped like a hoop and rolled on the ground or whirled around the body. **5** *Croquet.* any of the iron arches through which the ball is driven. **6a** a light curved frame to spread out a skirt. **6b** (*as modifier*): *a hoop skirt.* **7** *Basketball.* the round metal frame to which the net is attached to form the basket. **8** a large ring through which performers or animals jump. **9 go** *or* **be put through the hoop.** to be subjected to an ordeal. ◆ *vb* **10** (*tr*) to surround with or as if with a hoop. ORIG OE *hōp*
▸ **hooped** *adj*

hoop² (huːp) *n, vb* a variant spelling of **whoop.**

hoopla ('huːplɑː) *n* **1** *Brit.* a fairground game in which a player tries to throw a hoop over an object and so win it. **2** *US & Canad. sl.* **2a** noise; bustle. **2b** nonsense; ballyhoo. ORIG C20: see WHOOP, LA²

hoopoe ('huːpuː) *n* an Old World bird having a pinkish-brown plumage with black-and-white wings and an erectile crest. ORIG C17: from earlier *hoopoop,* imit.

hoop pine *n* a fast-growing timber tree of Australia having rough bark with hooplike cracks around the trunk and branches.

hooray (huː'reɪ) *interj, n, vb* **1** a variant spelling of **hurrah.** ◆ *sentence substitute.* **2** Also: **hooroo** (huː'ruː). *Austral. & NZ.* cheerio.

Hooray Henry ('huː,reɪ 'hɛnrɪ) *n, pl* **Hooray Henries** *or* **Hooray Henrys.** a young upper-class man, often with affectedly hearty voice and manners. Sometimes shortened to **Hooray.**

hoosegow *or* **hoosgow** ('huːsgaʊ) *n US.* a slang word for **jail.** ORIG C20: from Mexican Sp. *jusgado* prison, from Sp.: court of justice, ult. from L *judex* a JUDGE

hoot¹ (huːt) *n* **1** the mournful wavering cry of some owls. **2** a similar sound, such as that of a train whistle. **3** a jeer of derision. **4** *Inf.* an amusing person or thing. ◆ *vb* **5** (often foll. by *at*) to jeer or yell (something) contemptuously (at someone). **6** (*tr*) to drive (speakers, actors on stage, etc.) off by hooting. **7** (*intr*) to make a hoot. **8** (*intr*) *Brit.* to blow a horn. ORIG C13 *hoten,* imit.

hoot² (huːt) *n Austral. & NZ.* a slang word for **money.** ORIG from Maori *utu* price

hootenanny ('huːtᵊ,nænɪ) *or* **hootnanny** ('huːt,nænɪ) *n, pl* **hootenannies** *or* **hootnannies.** *US & Canad.* an informal performance by folk singers. ORIG C20: from ?

hooter ('huːtə) *n Chiefly Brit.* **1** a person or thing that hoots, esp. a car horn. **2** *Sl.* a nose.

Hoover¹ ('huːvə) *n* **1** *Trademark.* a type of vacuum cleaner. ◆ *vb* (*usually not cap.*) **2** to vacuum-clean (a carpet, etc.). **3** (*tr*; often foll. by *up*) to consume or dispose of (something) quickly and completely: *he hoovered up his grilled fish.*

Hoover² ★ ('huːvə) *n* **1 Herbert** (**Clark**). 1874–1964, US statesman; 31st president of the US (1929–33). He organized relief for Europe during and after World War I. **2 J**(**ohn**) **Edgar.** 1895–1972, US lawyer: director of the FBI (1924–72).

Hoover Dam ★ *n* a dam in the western US, on the Colorado River on the border between Nevada and Arizona; forms Lake Mead. Height: 222 m (727 ft). Length: 354 m (1180 ft). Former name (1933–47): **Boulder Dam.**

hooves (huːvz) *n* a plural of **hoof.**

hop¹ (hɒp) *vb* **hops, hopping, hopped. 1** (*intr*) to jump forwards or upwards on one foot. **2** (*intr*) (esp. of frogs, birds, etc.) to move forwards in short jumps. **3** (*tr*) to jump over. **4** (*intr*) *Inf.* to move quickly (in, on, out of, etc.): *hop on a bus.* **5** (*tr*) *Inf.* to cross (an ocean) in an aircraft. **6** (*tr*) *US & Canad. inf.* to travel by means of: *he hopped a train to Chicago.* **7** (*intr*) another word for **limp¹** (senses 1 and 2). **8 hop it** (*or* **off**). *Brit. sl.* to go away. ◆ *n* **9** the act or an instance of hopping. **10** *Inf.* an informal dance. **11** *Inf.* a trip, esp. in an aircraft. **12 on the hop.** *Inf.* **12a** active or busy. **12b** *Brit.* unawares or unprepared. ORIG OE *hoppian*

hop² (hɒp) *n* **1** a climbing plant which has green conelike female flowers and clusters of small male flowers. **2 hop garden.** a field of hops. **3** *Obs. sl.* opium or any other narcotic drug. ◆ See also **hops.** ORIG C15: from MDu. *hoppe*

hope (həʊp) *n* **1** (*sometimes pl*) a feeling of desire for something and confidence in the possibility of its fulfilment: *his hope for peace was justified.* **2** a reasonable ground for this feeling: *there is still hope.* **3** a person or thing that gives cause for hope. **4** a thing, situation, or event that is desired: *my hope is that prices will fall.* **5 not a hope** *or* **some hope.** used ironically to express little confidence that expectations will be fulfilled. ◆ *vb* **hopes, hoping, hoped. 6** (*tr; takes a clause as object or an infinitive*) to desire (something) with some possibility of fulfilment: *I hope to tell you.* **7** (*intr*; often foll. by *for*) to have a wish. **8** (*tr; takes a clause as object*) to trust or believe: *we hope that this is satisfactory.* ORIG OE *hopa*

Hope ★ (həʊp) *n* **1 Anthony,** real name *Sir Anthony Hope Hawkins.* 1863–1933, British novelist; author of *The Prisoner of Zenda* (1894). **2 Bob,** real name *Leslie Townes Hope.* born 1903, US comedian, born in England. His films include *Road to Morocco* (1942) and *The Paleface* (1947): awarded an honorary knighthood in 1998.

hope chest *n* the US and Canad. name for **bottom drawer.**

hopeful ('həʊpfʊl) *adj* **1** having or expressing hope. **2** in-

spiring hope; promising. ◆ *n* **3** a person considered to be on the brink of success (esp. in **a young hopeful**).
▸ **'hopefulness** *n*

hopefully ('həʊpfʊlɪ) *adv* **1** in a hopeful manner. **2** *Inf.* it is hoped: *hopefully they will be married soon.*

> **USAGE NOTE** Objecting to the use of *hopefully* to mean *it is hoped that* is one of the great shibboleths of recent debate on correct usage. It first came into current use in America in the 1960s and rapidly established itself elsewhere, presumably because it filled a useful structural gap, replacing as it does a complete clause. In this way it is no different from other sentence adverbials of the kind *unfortunately*, which can be paraphrased as a clause containing the adjective and modifying the whole sentence.

Hopeh *or* **Hopei** ★ ('həʊ'peɪ) *n* a variant transliteration of the Chinese name for **Hebei.**

hopeless ('həʊplɪs) *adj* **1** having or offering no hope. **2** impossible to solve. **3** unable to learn, function, etc. **4** *Inf.* without skill or ability.
▸ **'hopelessly** *adv* ▸ **'hopelessness** *n*

Hopi ('həʊpɪ) *n* **1** (*pl* **Hopis** *or* **Hopi**) a member of a North American Indian people of NE Arizona. **2** the language of this people. ORIG from Hopi *Hópi* peaceful

Hopkins ★ ('hɒpkɪnz) *n* **1** Sir **Anthony.** born 1937, US actor born in Wales: his films include *The Silence of the Lambs* (1991) and *Meet Joe Black* (1999). **2** Sir **Frederick Gowland** ('gaʊlənd). 1861–1947, British biochemist, who pioneered research into vitamins: shared the Nobel prize for physiology or medicine (1929). **3 Gerard Manley.** 1844–89, British poet and Jesuit priest.

hoplite ('hɒplaɪt) *n* (in ancient Greece) a heavily armed infantryman. ORIG C18: from Gk *hoplitēs,* from *hoplon* weapon, from *hepein* to prepare

hopper ('hɒpə) *n* **1** a person or thing that hops. **2** a funnel-shaped reservoir from which solid materials can be discharged into a receptacle below, esp. for feeding fuel to a furnace, loading a truck, etc. **3** a machine used for picking hops. **4** any of various long-legged hopping insects. **5** an open-topped railway truck for loose minerals, etc., unloaded through doors on the underside. **6** *S. African.* another name for **cocopan. 7** *Computing.* a device for holding punched cards and feeding them to a card reader.

hopping ('hɒpɪŋ) *adv* **hopping mad.** in a terrible rage.

hops (hɒps) *pl n* the dried flowers of the hop plant, used to give a bitter taste to beer.

hopsack ('hɒp,sæk) *n* **1** a roughly woven fabric of wool, cotton, etc., used for clothing. **2** Also called: **hopsacking.** a coarse fabric used for bags, etc., made generally of hemp or jute.

hopscotch ('hɒp,skɒtʃ) *n* a children's game in which a player throws a small stone or other object to land in one of a pattern of squares marked on the ground and then hops over to it to pick it up. ORIG C19: HOP[1] + SCOTCH[1]

Horace ★ ('hɒrɪs) *n* Latin name *Quintus Horatius Flaccus.* 65–8 B.C., Roman poet and satirist: his verse includes the lyrics in the *Epodes* and the *Odes,* the *Epistles* and *Satires,* and the *Ars Poetica.*

Horae ★ ('hɔːriː) *pl n Classical myth.* the goddesses of the seasons. Also called: **the Hours.** ORIG L: hours

horary ('hɔːrərɪ) *adj Arch.* **1** relating to the hours. **2** hourly. ORIG C17: from Med. L *hōrārius,* from L *hora*

Horatian (hə'reɪʃən) *adj* of, relating to, or characteristic of Horace or his poetry.

Horatius Cocles ★ (hɒ'reɪʃɪəs 'kəʊkliːz) *n* a legendary Roman hero of the 6th century B.C., who defended a bridge over the Tiber against Lars Porsena.

horde (hɔːd) *n* **1** a vast crowd; throng; mob. **2** a nomadic group of people, esp. an Asiatic group. **3** a large moving mass of animals, esp. insects. ORIG C16: from Polish *horda,* from Turkish *ordū* camp

Hordern ★ ('hɔːdən) *n* Sir **Michael** (**Murray**). 1911–95, British actor.

Horeb ★ ('hɔːrɛb) *n Bible.* a mountain, probably Mount Sinai.

horehound *or* **hoarhound** ('hɔː,haʊnd) *n* a downy herbaceous Old World plant with small white flowers that contain a bitter juice formerly used as a cough medicine and flavouring. ORIG OE *hārhūne,* from *hār* grey + *hūne* horehound, from ?

horizon (hə'raɪzᵊn) *n* **1** Also called: **visible horizon, apparent horizon.** the apparent line that divides the earth and the sky. **2** *Astron.* **2a** Also called: **sensible horizon.** the circular intersection with the celestial sphere of the plane tangential to the earth at the position of the observer. **2b** Also called: **celestial horizon.** the great circle on the celestial sphere, the plane of which passes through the centre of the earth and is parallel to the sensible horizon. **3** the range or limit of scope, interest, knowledge, etc. **4** a layer of rock within a stratum that has a particular composition by which the stratum may be dated. ORIG C14: from L, from Gk *horizōn kuklos* limiting circle, from *horizein* to limit

horizontal (,hɒrɪ'zɒntᵊl) *adj* **1** parallel to the plane of the horizon; level; flat. **2** of or relating to the horizon. **3** in a plane parallel to that of the horizon. **4** applied uniformly to all members of a group. **5** *Econ.* relating to identical stages of commercial activity: *horizontal integration.* ◆ *n* **6** a horizontal plane, position, line, etc.
▸ **,horizon'tality** *n* ▸ **,hori'zontally** *adv*

horizontal bar *n Gymnastics.* a raised bar on which swinging and vaulting exercises are performed.

hormone ('hɔːməʊn) *n* **1** a chemical substance produced in an endocrine gland and transported in the blood to a certain tissue, on which it exerts a specific effect. **2** an organic compound produced by a plant that is essential for growth. **3** any synthetic substance having the same effects. ORIG C20: from Gk *hormōn,* from *horman* to stir up, from *hormē* impulse
▸ **hor'monal** *adj*

hormone replacement therapy *n* treatment with oestrogens (and usually progestogens) to control menopausal symptoms and in the prevention of osteoporosis. Abbrev.: **HRT.**

Hormuz (hɔː'muːz, 'hɔːmʌz) *or* **Ormuz** ★ *n* an island off the SE coast of Iran, in the **Strait of Hormuz**: ruins of the ancient city of Hormuz, a major trading centre in the Middle Ages. Area: about 41 sq. km (16 sq. miles).

horn (hɔːn) *n* **1** either of a pair of permanent bony outgrowths on the heads of cattle, antelopes, etc. **2** the outgrowth from the nasal bone of a rhinoceros, consisting of a mass of fused hairs. **3** any hornlike projection, such as the eyestalk of a snail. **4** the antler of a deer. **5a** the constituent substance, mainly keratin, of horns, hooves, etc. **5b** (*in combination*): *horn-rimmed spectacles.* **6** a container or device made from this substance or an artificial substitute: *a drinking horn.* **7** an object resembling a horn in shape, such as a cornucopia. **8** a primitive musical wind instrument made from horn. **9** any musical instrument consisting of a pipe or tube of brass fitted with a mouthpiece. See **French horn, cor anglais. 10** *Jazz sl.* any wind instrument. **11a** a device for producing a warning or signalling noise. **11b** (*in combination*): *a foghorn.* **12** (*usually pl*) the imaginary hornlike parts formerly supposed to appear on the forehead of a cuckold. **13a** a hollow conical device coupled to a gramophone to control the direction and quality of the sound. **13b** a similar device attached to an electrical loudspeaker, esp. in a public-address system. **14** a stretch of land or water shaped like a horn. **15** *Brit. taboo sl.* an erection of the penis. ◆ *vb* (*tr*) **16** to provide with a horn or horns. **17** to gore or butt with a horn. **18** to remove or shorten the horns of (cattle, etc.). ◆ See also **horn in.** ORIG OE
▸ **horned** *adj* ▸ **'hornless** *adj*

Horn ★ (hɔːn) *n* **Cape.** See **Cape Horn.**

hornbeam ('hɔːn,biːm) *n* **1** a tree of Europe and Asia having smooth grey bark and hard white wood. **2** its wood. ◆ Also called: **ironwood.** ORIG C14: from HORN + BEAM, referring to its tough wood

hornbill ('hɔːn,bɪl) *n* a bird of tropical Africa and Asia, having a very large bill with a basal bony protuberance.

hornblende ('hɔːn,blɛnd) *n* a mineral of the amphibole

group consisting of the aluminium silicates of calcium, sodium, magnesium, and iron: varies in colour from green to black. ORIG C18: from G *Horn* horn + BLENDE

hornbook ('hɔːnˌbʊk) *n* a page bearing a religious text or the alphabet, held in a frame with a thin window of horn over it.

horned toad *or* **lizard** *n* a small insectivorous burrowing lizard inhabiting desert regions of America, having a flattened toadlike body covered with spines.

horned viper *n* a venomous snake that occurs in desert regions of N Africa and SW Asia and has a small horny spine above each eye.

hornet ('hɔːnɪt) *n* **1** any of various large social wasps that can inflict a severe sting. **2 hornet's nest.** a strongly unfavourable reaction (often in **stir up a hornet's nest**). ORIG OE *hyrnetu*

horn in *vb* (*intr, adv;* often foll. by *on*) *Sl.* to interrupt or intrude.

Horn of Africa ★ *n* a region of NE Africa, comprising Somalia and adjacent territories.

horn of plenty *n* another term for **cornucopia.**

hornpipe ('hɔːnˌpaɪp) *n* **1** an obsolete reed instrument with a mouthpiece made of horn. **2** an old British solo dance to a hornpipe accompaniment, traditionally performed by sailors. **3** a piece of music for such a dance.

hornswoggle ('hɔːnˌswɒgᵊl) *vb* **hornswoggles, hornswoggling, hornswoggled.** (*tr*) *Sl.* to cheat or trick; bamboozle. ORIG C19: from ?

horny ('hɔːnɪ) *adj* **hornier, horniest. 1** of, like, or hard as horn. **2** having a horn or horns. **3** *Sl.* **3a** sexually aroused. **3b** provoking or intended to provoke sexual arousal. **3c** sexually eager or lustful.
▸ **'horniness** *n*

horologe ('hɒrəˌlɒdʒ) *n* a rare word for **timepiece.** ORIG C14: from L *hōrologium,* from Gk *hōrologion,* from *hōra* HOUR + *-logos* from *legein* to tell

horologist (hɒ'rɒlədʒɪst) *or* **horologer** *n* a person skilled in horology.

horology (hɒ'rɒlədʒɪ) *n* the art or science of making timepieces or of measuring time.
▸ **horologic** (ˌhɒrə'lɒdʒɪk) *or* **ˌhoro'logical** *adj*

horoscope ('hɒrəˌskəʊp) *n* **1** the prediction of a person's future based on zodiacal data for the time of birth. **2** the configuration of the planets, sun, and moon in the sky at a particular moment. **3** a diagram showing the positions of the planets, sun, moon, etc., at a particular time and place. ORIG OE *horoscopus,* from L, from Gk *hōroskopos,* from *hōra* HOUR + -SCOPE
▸ **horoscopic** (ˌhɒrə'skɒpɪk) *adj* ▸ **horoscopy** (hɒ'rɒskəpɪ) *n*

Horowitz ★ ('hɒrəvɪts) *n* **Vladimir** ('vlædɪmɪə). 1904–89, Russian pianist, in the US from 1928.

horrendous (hɒ'rɛndəs) *adj* another word for **horrific.** ORIG C17: from L *horrendus* fearful, from *horrēre* to bristle, shudder, tremble; see HORROR
▸ **hor'rendously** *adv*

horrible ('hɒrɪbᵊl) *adj* **1** causing horror; dreadful. **2** disagreeable. **3** *Inf.* cruel or unkind. ORIG C14: via OF from L *horribilis,* from *horrēre* to tremble
▸ **'horribleness** *n* ▸ **'horribly** *adv*

horrid ('hɒrɪd) *adj* **1** disagreeable; unpleasant: *a horrid meal.* **2** repulsive or frightening. **3** *Inf.* unkind. ORIG C16 (in the sense: bristling, shaggy): from L *horridus* prickly, from *horrēre* to bristle
▸ **'horridly** *adv* ▸ **'horridness** *n*

horrific (hɒ'rɪfɪk, hə-) *adj* provoking horror; horrible.
▸ **hor'rifically** *adv*

horrify ('hɒrɪˌfaɪ) *vb* **horrifies, horrifying, horrified.** (*tr*) **1** to cause feelings of horror in; terrify. **2** to shock greatly.
▸ **ˌhorrifi'cation** *n* ▸ **'horriˌfied** *adj* ▸ **'horriˌfying** *adj*
▸ **'horriˌfyingly** *adv*

horripilation (hɒˌrɪpɪ'leɪʃən) *n Physiol.* a technical name for **goose flesh.** ORIG C17: from LL *horripilātiō* a bristling, from L *horrēre* to stand on end + *pilus* hair

horror ('hɒrə) *n* **1** extreme fear; terror; dread. **2** intense hatred. **3** (*often pl*) a thing or person causing fear, loathing, etc. **4** (*modifier*) having a frightening subject: *a horror film.* ORIG C14: from L: a trembling with fear

horrors ('hɒrəz) *pl n* **1** *Sl.* a fit of depression or anxiety. **2** *Inf.* See **delirium tremens.** ◆ *interj* **3** an expression of dismay, sometimes facetious.

Horsa ★ ('hɔːsə) *n* died ?455 A.D., leader, with his brother Hengist, of the first Jutish settlers in Britain. See also **Hengist.**

hors de combat *French.* (ɔr də kɔ̃ba) *adj* (*postpositive*), *adv* disabled or injured. ORIG lit.: out of (the) fight

hors d'oeuvre (ɔː 'dɜːvr) *n, pl* **hors d'oeuvre** *or* **hors d'oeuvres** ('dɜːvr). an appetizer, usually served before the main meal. ORIG C18: from F, lit.: outside the work

horse (hɔːs) *n* **1** a solid-hoofed, herbivorous, domesticated mammal used for draught work and riding. Related adj: **equine. 2** the adult male of this species; stallion. **3 wild horse.** another name for **Przewalski's horse. 4** (*functioning as pl*) horsemen, esp. cavalry: *a regiment of horse.* **5** Also called: **buck.** *Gymnastics.* a padded apparatus on legs, used for vaulting, etc. **6** a narrow board supported by a pair of legs at each end, used as a frame for sawing or as a trestle, barrier, etc. **7** a contrivance on which a person may ride and exercise. **8** a slang word for **heroin. 9** *Mining.* a mass of rock within a vein of ore. **10** *Naut.* a rod, rope, or cable, fixed at the ends, along which something may slide; traveller. **11** *Inf.* short for **horsepower. 12** (*modifier*) drawn by a horse or horses: *a horse cart.* **13 a horse of another** *or* **a different colour.** a completely different topic, argument, etc. **14 be** (*or* **get**) **on one's high horse.** *Inf.* to act disdainfully aloof. **15 hold one's horses.** to restrain oneself. **16 horses for courses.** a policy, course of action, etc. modified slightly to take account of special circumstances without departing in essentials from the original. **17 the horse's mouth.** the most reliable source. ◆ *vb* **horses, horsing, horsed. 18** (*tr*) to provide with a horse or horses. **19** to put or be put on horseback. ORIG OE *hors*
▸ **'horseˌlike** *adj*

horse around *or* **about** *vb* (*intr, adv*) *Inf.* to indulge in horseplay.

horseback ('hɔːsˌbæk) *n* **a** a horse's back (esp. in **on horseback**). **b** *Chiefly US.* (*as modifier*): *horseback riding.*

horsebox ('hɔːsˌbɒks) *n Brit.* a van or trailer used for carrying horses.

horse brass *n* a decorative brass ornament, originally attached to a horse's harness.

horse chestnut *n* **1** a tree having palmate leaves, erect clusters of white, pink, or red flowers, and brown shiny inedible nuts enclosed in a spiky bur. **2** Also called: **conker.** the nut of this tree. ORIG C16: from its having been used in the treatment of respiratory disease in horses

horseflesh ('hɔːsˌflɛʃ) *n* **1** horses collectively. **2** the flesh of a horse, esp. edible horse meat.

horsefly ('hɔːsˌflaɪ) *n, pl* **horseflies.** a large stout-bodied dipterous fly, the female of which sucks the blood of mammals, esp. horses, cattle, and man. Also called: **gadfly, cleg.**

horsehair ('hɔːsˌhɛə) *n* hair taken chiefly from the tail or mane of a horse, used in upholstery and for fabric, etc.

horsehide ('hɔːsˌhaɪd) *n* **1** the hide of a horse. **2** leather made from this hide.

horse latitudes *pl n Naut.* the latitudes near 30°N or 30°S at sea, characterized by baffling winds, calms, and high barometric pressure. ORIG C18: referring either to the high mortality of horses on board ship in these latitudes or to *dead horse* (nautical slang: advance pay), which sailors expected to work off by this stage of a voyage

horse laugh *n* a coarse or raucous laugh.

horseleech ('hɔːsˌliːtʃ) *n* **1** any of several large carnivorous freshwater leeches. **2** an archaic name for a **veterinary surgeon.**

horse mackerel *n* **1** Also called: **scad.** a mackerel-like fish of European Atlantic waters, with a row of bony scales along the lateral line. Sometimes called (US): **saurel. 2** any of various large tunnies or related fishes.

horseman ('hɔːsmən) *n, pl* **horsemen. 1** a person skilled in riding. **2** a person who rides a horse.
▸ **'horseman,ship** *n* ▸ **'horse,woman** *fem n*

horse mushroom *n* a large edible mushroom, with a white cap and greyish gills.

Horsens ★ (*Danish* 'hɔrsəns) *n* a port in Denmark, in E Jutland at the head of **Horsens Fjord.** Pop.: 55 252 (1995).

horse pistol *n* a large holstered pistol formerly carried by horsemen.

horseplay ('hɔːs,pleɪ) *n* rough or rowdy play.

horsepower ('hɔːs,paʊə) *n* an fps unit of power, equal to 550 foot-pounds per second (equivalent to 745.7 watts). Abbrev.: **HP, h.p.**

horseradish ('hɔːs,rædɪʃ) *n* a coarse Eurasian plant cultivated for its thick white pungent root, which is ground and combined with vinegar, etc., to make a sauce.

horse sense *n* another term for **common sense.**

horseshoe ('hɔːs,ʃuː) *n* **1** a piece of iron shaped like a U nailed to the underside of the hoof of a horse to protect the soft part of the foot: commonly thought to be a token of good luck. **2** an object of similar shape.

horseshoe bat *n* any of numerous large-eared Old World bats with a fleshy growth around the nostrils, used in echolocation.

horseshoe crab *n* a marine arthropod of North America and Asia, having a rounded heavily armoured body with a long pointed tail. Also called: **king crab.**

horsetail ('hɔːs,teɪl) *n* **1** a plant having jointed stems with whorls of small dark toothlike leaves and producing spores within conelike structures at the tips of the stems. **2** a stylized horse's tail formerly used as the emblem of a pasha.

horse trading *n* shrewd bargaining.

horsewhip ('hɔːs,wɪp) *n* **1** a whip, usually with a long thong, used for managing horses. ◆ *vb* **horsewhips, horsewhipping, horsewhipped. 2** (*tr*) to flog with such a whip.
▸ **'horse,whipper** *n*

horsey *or* **horsy** ('hɔːsɪ) *adj* **horsier, horsiest. 1** of or relating to horses: *a horsey smell.* **2** dealing with or devoted to horses. **3** like a horse: *a horsey face.*
▸ **'horsily** *adv* ▸ **'horsiness** *n*

horst (hɔːst) *n* a ridge of land that has been forced upwards between two parallel faults. ORIG C20: from G *Horst* thicket

Horta ★ (*Portuguese* 'ɔrtə) *n* a port in the Azores, on the SE coast of Fayal Island.

hortatory ('hɔːtətərɪ) *or* **hortative** ('hɔːtətɪv) *adj* tending to exhort; encouraging. ORIG C16: from LL *hortātōrius,* from L *hortārī* to EXHORT
▸ **hor'tation** *n* ▸ **'hortatorily** *or* **'hortatively** *adv*

Hortense ★ (*French* ɔrtɑ̃s) *n* See (Eugénie Hortense de) **Beauharnais.**

Horthy ★ (*Hungarian* 'horti) *n* **Miklós** ('miklo:ʃ), full name *Horthy de Nagybánya.* 1868–1957, Hungarian admiral: suppressed Kun's Communist republic (1919); regent of Hungary (1920–44).

horticulture ('hɔːtɪ,kʌltʃə) *n* the art or science of cultivating gardens. ORIG C17: from L *hortus* garden + CULTURE; cf. AGRICULTURE
▸ **,horti'cultural** *adj* ▸ **,horti'culturalist** *or* **,horti'culturist** *n*

Horus ★ ('hɔːrəs) *n* a solar god of Egyptian mythology, usually depicted with a falcon's head. ORIG via LL from Gk *Hōros,* from Egyptian *Hur* hawk

Hos. *Bible. abbrev. for* Hosea.

hosanna ★ (həʊ'zænə) *interj* an exclamation of praise, esp. one to God. ORIG OE *osanna,* via LL from Gk, from Heb. *hōshi 'āh nnā* save now, we pray

hose[1] (həʊz) *n* **1** a flexible pipe, for conveying a liquid or gas. ◆ *vb* **hoses, hosing, hosed. 2** (sometimes foll. by *down*) to wash, water, or sprinkle (a person or thing) with or as if with a hose. ORIG C15: later use of HOSE[2]

hose[2] (həʊz) *n, pl* **hose** *or* **hosen** ('həʊzᵊn). **1** stockings, socks, and tights collectively. **2** *History.* a man's garment covering the legs and reaching up to the waist. **3 half-hose.** socks. ORIG OE *hosa*

Hosea ★ (həʊ'zɪə) *n Old Testament.* **1** a Hebrew prophet of the 8th century B.C. **2** the book containing his oracles.

hoser ('həʊzə) *n Canad. sl.* a gauche or uncouth person. ORIG C20: ?from N American slang *hose* to trick, copulate

hosier ('həʊzɪə) *n* a person who sells stockings, etc.

hosiery ('həʊzɪərɪ) *n* stockings, socks, and knitted underclothing collectively.

hospice ('hɒspɪs) *n* **1** a nursing home that specializes in caring for the terminally ill. **2** *Arch.* a place of shelter for travellers, esp. one kept by a monastic order. ORIG C19: from F, from L *hospitium* hospitality, from *hospes* guest

hospitable ('hɒspɪtəbᵊl, hɒ'spɪt-) *adj* **1** welcoming to guests or strangers. **2** fond of entertaining. ORIG C16: from Med. L *hospitāre* to receive as a guest, from L *hospes* guest
▸ **'hospitableness** *n* ▸ **'hospitably** *adv*

hospital ('hɒspɪtᵊl) *n* **1** an institution for the medical or psychiatric care and treatment of patients. **2** (*modifier*) having the function of a hospital: *a hospital ship.* **3** a repair shop for something specified: *a dolls' hospital.* **4** *Arch.* a charitable home, hospice, or school. ORIG C13: from Med. L *hospitāle* hospice, from L, from *hospes* guest

Hospitalet ★ (*Spanish* ɔspita'let) *n* a city in NE Spain, a SW suburb of Barcelona. Pop.: 262 501 (1995 est.).

hospitality (,hɒspɪ'tælɪtɪ) *n, pl* **hospitalities.** kindness in welcoming strangers or guests.

hospitality suite *n* a room or suite, as at a conference, where free drinks are offered.

hospitalize *or* **hospitalise** ('hɒspɪtə,laɪz) *vb* **hospitalizes, hospitalizing, hospitalized** *or* **hospitalises, hospitalising, hospitalised.** (*tr*) to admit or send (a person) into a hospital.
▸ **,hospitali'zation** *or* **,hospitali'sation** *n*

hospitaller *or US* **hospitaler** ('hɒspɪtələ) *n* a person, esp. a member of certain religious orders, dedicated to hospital work, ambulance services, etc. ORIG C14: from OF *hospitalier,* from Med. L, from *hospitāle* hospice; see HOSPITAL

Hospitaller *or US* **Hospitaler** ('hɒspɪtələ) *n* a member of the order of the Knights Hospitallers.

hospital pass *n Inf.* **1** *Sport.* a pass made to a team mate who is in a position such that he or she will be tackled heavily as soon as the ball is received. **2** a task or project that will inevitably result in heavy criticism for the person to whom it has been assigned.

host[1] (həʊst) *n* **1** a person who receives or entertains guests, esp. in his or her own home. **2a** a country or organization which provides facilities for and receives visitors to an event. **2b** (*as modifier*): *the host nation.* **3** the compere of a show or television programme. **4** *Biol.* **4a** an animal or plant that supports a parasite. **4b** an animal into which tissue is experimentally grafted. **5** *Computing.* a computer that is connected to others on a network. **6** the owner or manager of an inn. ◆ *vb* **7** to be the host of (a party, programme, etc.): *to host one's own show.* ORIG C13: from F *hoste,* from L *hospes* guest

host[2] (həʊst) *n* **1** a great number; multitude. **2** an archaic word for **army.** ORIG C13: from OF *hoste,* from L *hostis* stranger

Host (həʊst) *n Christianity.* the wafer of unleavened bread consecrated in the Eucharist. ORIG C14: from OF *oiste,* from L *hostia* victim

hosta ('hɒstə) *n* a plant cultivated esp. for its ornamental foliage. ORIG C19: NL, after N. T. *Host* (1761–1834), Austrian physician

hostage ('hɒstɪdʒ) *n* **1** a person held as a security or pledge or to be ransomed, exchanged for prisoners, etc. **2** the state of being held as a hostage. **3** any security or pledge. **4 give hostages to fortune.** to place oneself in a position in which misfortune may strike through the loss of what one values most. ORIG C13: from OF, from *hoste* guest

hostel ('hɒstᵊl) *n* **1** a building providing overnight accommodation, as for homeless people. **2** See **youth hostel. 3** *Brit.* a supervised lodging house for nurses, workers, etc. **4** *Arch.* another word for **hostelry.** ORIG C13: from OF, from Med. L *hospitāle* hospice; see HOSPITAL

hosteller *or US* **hosteler** (ˈhɒstələ) *n* **1** a person who stays at youth hostels. **2** an archaic word for **innkeeper**.

hostelling *or US* **hosteling** (ˈhɒstəlɪŋ) *n* the practice of staying at youth hostels when travelling.

hostelry (ˈhɒstəlrɪ) *n, pl* **hostelries**. *Arch. or facetious.* an inn.

hostess (ˈhəʊstɪs) *n* **1** a woman acting as host. **2** a woman who receives and entertains patrons of a club, restaurant, etc. **3** See **air hostess**.

hostile (ˈhɒstaɪl) *adj* **1** antagonistic; opposed. **2** of or relating to an enemy. **3** unfriendly. ORIG C16: from L *hostīlis,* from *hostis* enemy
▸ ˈ**hostilely** *adv*

hostility (hɒˈstɪlɪtɪ) *n, pl* **hostilities**. **1** enmity. **2** an act expressing enmity. **3** (*pl*) fighting; warfare.

hostler (ˈɒslə) *n* a variant (esp. Brit.) of **ostler**.

hot (hɒt) *adj* **hotter, hottest**. **1** having a relatively high temperature. **2** having a temperature higher than desirable. **3** causing a sensation of bodily heat. **4** causing a burning sensation on the tongue: *a hot curry.* **5** expressing or feeling intense emotion, such as anger or lust. **6** intense or vehement. **7** recent; new: *hot from the press.* **8** *Ball games.* (of a ball) thrown or struck hard, and so difficult to respond to. **9** much favoured: *a hot favourite.* **10** *Inf.* having a dangerously high level of radioactivity. **11** *Sl.* stolen or otherwise illegally obtained. **12** *Sl.* (of people) being sought by the police. **13** (of a colour) intense; striking: *hot pink.* **14** following closely: *hot on the scent.* **15** *Inf.* at a dangerously high electric potential. **16** *Sl.* good (esp. in **not so hot**). **17** *Jazz sl.* arousing great excitement by inspired improvisation, strong rhythms, etc. **18** *Inf.* dangerous or unpleasant (esp. in **make it hot for someone**). **19** (in various games) very near the answer. **20** *Metallurgy.* (of a process) at a sufficiently high temperature for metal to be in a soft workable state. **21** *Austral. inf.* (of a price, etc.) excessive. **22 hot on.** *Inf.* **22a** very severe: *the police are hot on drunk drivers.* **22b** particularly knowledgeable about. **23 hot under the collar.** *Inf.* aroused with anger, annoyance, etc. **24 in hot water.** *Inf.* in trouble. ◆ *adv* **25** in a hot manner; hotly. ◆ See also **hots, hot up**. ORIG OE *hāt*
▸ ˈ**hotly** *adv* ▸ ˈ**hotness** *n* ▸ ˈ**hottish** *adj*

hot air *n Inf.* empty and usually boastful talk.

Hotan (ˈhəʊˈtæn), **Hotien,** *or* **Ho-t'ien** ★ (ˈhəʊˈtjɛn) *n* **1** an oasis in W China, in the Taklimakan Shamo desert of central Xinjiang Uygur Autonomous Region, around the seasonal Hotan River. **2** the chief town of this oasis, situated at the foot of the Kunlun Mountains. Pop.: 71 600 (1986 est.). Also called: **Khotan, Hetian**.

hotbed (ˈhɒtˌbɛd) *n* **1** a glass-covered bed of soil, usually heated, for propagating plants, forcing early vegetables, etc. **2** a place offering ideal conditions for the growth of an idea, activity, etc., esp. one considered bad.

hot-blooded *adj* **1** passionate or excitable. **2** (of a horse) being of thoroughbred stock.

hot button *n Inf.* **a** a controversial subject or issue that is likely to arouse strong emotions. **b** (*as modifier*): *the hot-button issue of abortion.*

hotchpotch (ˈhɒtʃˌpɒtʃ) *or esp. US & Canad.* **hodgepodge** *n* **1** a jumbled mixture. **2** a thick soup or stew. ORIG C15: var. of *hotchpot* from OF, from *hocher* to shake + POT[1]

hot cross bun *n* a yeast bun marked with a cross and traditionally eaten on Good Friday.

hot desking (ˈdɛskɪŋ) *n* the practice of not assigning permanent desks in a workplace, so that employees may work at any available desk.

hot dog[1] *n* a sausage, esp. a frankfurter, usually served hot in a long roll split lengthways. ORIG C20: from the supposed resemblance of the sausage to a dachshund

hot dog[2] *n* **1** *Chiefly US.* a person who performs showy acrobatic manoeuvres when skiing or surfing. ◆ *vb* **hot-dog, hot-dogs, hot-dogging, hot-dogged**. **2** (*intr*) to perform a series of manoeuvres in skiing, surfing, etc.

hotel (həʊˈtɛl) *n* a commercially run establishment providing lodging and usually meals for guests and often containing a public bar. ORIG C17: from F *hôtel,* from OF *hostel;* see HOSTEL

hotelier (hɒˈtɛljeɪ) *n* an owner or manager of one or more hotels.

hotel ship *n* an accommodation barge anchored near an oil production rig.

hot flush *or US* **hot flash** *n* a sudden unpleasant hot feeling experienced by menopausal women.

hotfoot (ˈhɒtˌfʊt) *adv* with all possible speed.

hothead (ˈhɒtˌhɛd) *n* an excitable person.

hot-headed *adj* impetuous, rash, or hot-tempered.
▸ ˌ**hot-ˈheadedness** *n*

hothouse (ˈhɒtˌhaʊs) *n* **1a** a greenhouse in which the temperature is maintained at a fixed level. **1b** (*as modifier*): *a hothouse plant.* **2a** an environment that encourages rapid development. **2b** (*as modifier*): *a hothouse atmosphere.* **3** (*modifier*) *Inf., often disparaging.* sensitive or delicate: *a hothouse temperament.*

Hotien *or* **Ho-t'ien** ★ (ˈhəʊˈtjɛn) *n* a variant transliteration of the Chinese name for **Hotan**.

hot key *n Computing.* a single key on the keyboard of a computer which carries out a series of commands.

hotline (ˈhɒtˌlaɪn) *n* **1** a direct telephone, teletype, or other communications link between heads of government, etc., for emergency use. **2** any such direct line kept for urgent use.

hot link *n Computing.* a word or phrase in a hypertext document that can be selected to access additional information.

hot money *n* capital that is transferred from one financial centre to another seeking the best opportunity for short-term gain.

hotplate (ˈhɒtˌpleɪt) *n* **1** an electrically heated plate on a cooker or one set into a working surface. **2** a portable device on which food can be kept warm.

hotpot (ˈhɒtˌpɒt) *n* **1** *Brit.* a casserole covered with a layer of potatoes. **2** *Austral. sl.* a heavily backed horse.

hot potato *n Sl.* a delicate or awkward matter.

hot-press *n* **1** a machine for applying a combination of heat and pressure to give a smooth surface to paper, to express oil from it, etc. ◆ *vb* **2** (*tr*) to subject (paper, cloth, etc.) to such a process.

hot rod *n* a car with an engine that has been radically modified to produce increased power.

hots (hɒts) *pl n* **the**. *Sl.* intense sexual desire; lust (esp. in the phrase **have the hots for** (**someone**)).

hot seat *n* **1** *Inf.* a difficult or dangerous position. **2** *US.* a slang term for **electric chair**.

hot spot *n* **1** an area of potential violence. **2** a lively nightclub. **3** any local area of high temperature in a part of an engine, etc. **4** *Med.* **4a** a small area on the surface or within a body with an exceptionally high level of radioactivity or of some chemical or mineral considered harmful. **4b** a similar area that generates an abnormal amount of heat, as revealed by thermography.

hot spring *n* a natural spring of mineral water at 21°C (70°F) or above, found in areas of volcanic activity. Also called: **thermal spring**.

hotspur (ˈhɒtˌspɜː) *n* an impetuous or fiery person. ORIG C15: from HOTSPUR

Hotspur ★ (ˈhɒtˌspɜː) *n* **Harry**. nickname of (Sir Henry) **Percy**.

hot stuff *n Inf.* **1** a person, object, etc., considered important, attractive, etc. **2** a pornographic or erotic book, play, film, etc.

Hottentot (ˈhɒtᵊnˌtɒt) *n* another name for **Khoikhoi**.

hotting (ˈhɒtɪŋ) *n Inf.* the practice of stealing fast cars and putting on a show of skilful but dangerous driving.
▸ ˈ**hotter** *n*

hot up *vb* **hots, hotting, hotted**. (*adv*) *Inf.* **1** to make or become more exciting, active, or intense. **2** (*tr*) another term for **soup up**.

hot-water bottle *n* a receptacle now usually made of rubber, designed to be filled with hot water and used for warming a bed.

hot-wire *vb* **hot-wires, hot-wiring, hot-wired**. (*tr*) *Sl.* to start the engine of (a motor vehicle) by bypassing the ignition switch.

Houdini ★ (huːˈdiːnɪ) *n* **Harry,** real name *Ehrich Weiss.* 1874–1926, US magician and escapologist.

Houdon ★ (*French* udɔ̃) *n* **Jean Antoine** (ʒɑ̃ ɑ̃twan). 1741–1828, French neoclassical portrait sculptor.

hough (hɒk) *Brit.* ◆ *n* **1** a variant of **hock**[1]. ◆ *vb* (*tr*) **2** to hamstring (cattle, horses, etc.). ORIG C14: from OE *hōh* heel

Houghton-le-Spring ★ (ˈhaʊtᵊnləˈsprɪŋ) *n* a town in N England, in Sunderland, E Tyne and Wear: coal-mining. Pop.: 35 100 (1991).

hound (haʊnd) *n* **1a** any of several breeds of dog used for hunting. **1b** (*in combination*): *a deerhound.* **2** a dog, esp. one regarded as annoying. **3** a despicable person. **4** (in hare and hounds) a runner who pursues a hare. **5** *Sl., chiefly US & Canad.* an enthusiast. **6 ride to hounds** *or* **follow the hounds.** to take part in a fox hunt. **7 the hounds.** a pack of foxhounds, etc. ◆ *vb* (*tr*) **8** to pursue relentlessly. **9** to urge on. ORIG OE *hund*
▸ **ˈhounder** *n*

hound's-tongue *n* a plant which has small reddish-purple flowers and spiny fruits. Also called: **dog's-tongue.** ORIG OE *hundestunge,* translation of L *cynoglōssos,* from Gk, from *kuōn* dog + *glōssa* tongue; referring to the shape of its leaves

hound's-tooth check *n* a pattern of broken or jagged checks, esp. on cloth. Also called: **dog's-tooth check, dog-tooth check.**

Hounslow ★ (ˈhaʊnzləʊ) *n* a borough of Greater London, on the River Thames: site of London's first civil airport (1919). Pop.: 202 700 (1994 est.). Area: 59 sq. km (23 sq. miles).

Houphouet-Boigny ★ (*French* ufwɛbwaɲi) *n* **Félix** (feliks). 1905–93, Côte d'Ivoire statesman; president (1960–93).

hour (ˈaʊə) *n* **1** a period of time equal to 3600 seconds; 1/24th of a calendar day. Related adj: **horary. 2** any of the points on the face of a timepiece that indicate intervals of 60 minutes. **3** the time. **4** the time allowed for or used for something: *lunch hour.* **5** a special moment: *our finest hour.* **6** the distance covered in an hour: *we live an hour away.* **7** *Astron.* an angular measurement of right ascension equal to 15° or a 24th part of the celestial equator. **8 one's last hour.** the time of one's death. **9 the hour.** an exact number of complete hours: *the bus leaves on the hour.* ◆ See also **hours.** ORIG C13: from OF *hore,* from L *hōra,* from Gk: season

hour circle *n* a great circle on the celestial sphere passing through the celestial poles and a specified point, such as a star.

hourglass (ˈaʊəˌglɑːs) *n* **1** a device consisting of two transparent chambers linked by a narrow channel, containing a quantity of sand that takes a specified time to trickle from one chamber to the other. **2** (*modifier*) well-proportioned with a small waist: *an hourglass figure.*

hour hand *n* the pointer on a timepiece that indicates the hour.

houri (ˈhʊərɪ) *n, pl* **houris. 1** (in Muslim belief) any of the nymphs of Paradise. **2** any alluring woman. ORIG C18: from F, from Persian, from Ar. *hūr,* pl. of *haurā'* woman with dark eyes

hourly (ˈaʊəlɪ) *adj* **1** of, occurring, or done every hour. **2** done in or measured by the hour: *an hourly rate.* **3** continual or frequent. ◆ *adv* **4** every hour. **5** at any moment.

hours (ˈaʊəz) *pl n* **1** a period regularly appointed for work, etc. **2** one's times of rising and going to bed: *he keeps late hours.* **3 till all hours.** until very late. **4** an indefinite time. **5** *RC Church.* Also called: **canonical hours. 5a** the seven times of the day laid down for the recitation of the prayers of the divine office. **5b** the prayers recited at these times.

Hours ★ (aʊəz) *pl n* another word for the **Horae.**

house *n* (haʊs), *pl* **houses** (ˈhaʊzɪz). **1a** a building used as a home; dwelling. **1b** (*as modifier*): *house dog.* **2** the people present in a house. **3a** a building for some specific purpose. **3b** (*in combination*): *a schoolhouse.* **4** (*often cap.*) a family or dynasty: *the House of York.* **5a** a commercial company: *a publishing house.* **5b** (*as modifier*): *a house journal.* **6** a legislative body. **7** a quorum in such a body (esp. in **make a house**). **8** a dwelling for a religious community. **9** *Astrol.* any of the 12 divisions of the zodiac. **10** any of several divisions of a large school. **11** a hotel, restaurant, club, etc., or the management of such an establishment. **12** (*modifier*) (of wine) sold unnamed by a restaurant, at a lower price than wines specified on the wine list: *the house red.* **13** the audience in a theatre or cinema. **14** an informal word for **brothel. 15** a hall in which a legislative body meets. **16** See **full house. 17** *Naut.* any structure or shelter on the weather deck of a vessel. **18 bring the house down.** *Theatre.* to win great applause. **19 like a house on fire.** *Inf.* very well. **20 on the house.** (usually of drinks) paid for by the management of the hotel, bar, etc. **21 put one's house in order.** to settle or organize one's affairs. **22 safe as houses.** *Brit.* very secure. ◆ *vb* (haʊz), **houses, housing, housed. 23** (*tr*) to provide with or serve as accommodation. **24** to give or receive lodging. **25** (*tr*) to contain or cover; protect. **26** (*tr*) to fit (a piece of wood) into a mortise, etc. ORIG OE *hūs*
▸ **ˈhouseless** *adj*

house agent *n Brit.* another name for **estate agent.**

house arrest *n* confinement to one's own home rather than in prison.

houseboat (ˈhaʊsˌbəʊt) *n* a stationary boat or barge used as a home.

housebound (ˈhaʊsˌbaʊnd) *adj* unable to leave one's house because of illness, injury, etc.

housebreaking (ˈhaʊsˌbreɪkɪŋ) *n Criminal law.* the act of entering a building as a trespasser for an unlawful purpose. Assimilated with burglary (1968).
▸ **ˈhouseˌbreaker** *n*

housecoat (ˈhaʊsˌkəʊt) *n* a woman's loose robelike informal garment.

house-craft *n* skill in domestic management.

housefly (ˈhaʊsˌflaɪ) *n, pl* **houseflies.** a common dipterous fly that frequents human habitations, spreads disease, and lays its eggs in carrion, decaying vegetables, etc.

household (ˈhaʊsˌhəʊld) *n* **1** the people living together in one house. **2** (*modifier*) relating to the running of a household: *household management.*

householder (ˈhaʊsˌhəʊldə) *n* a person who owns or rents a house.
▸ **ˈhouseˌholderˌship** *n*

household name *or* **word** *n* a person or thing that is very well known.

housekeeper (ˈhaʊsˌkiːpə) *n* a person, esp. a woman, employed to run a household.

housekeeping (ˈhaʊsˌkiːpɪŋ) *n* **1** the running of a household. **2** money allotted for this. **3** general maintenance as of records, data, etc., in an organization.

houseleek (ˈhaʊsˌliːk) *n* an Old World plant which has a rosette of succulent leaves and pinkish flowers: grows on walls.

house lights *pl n* the lights in the auditorium of a theatre, cinema, etc.

housemaid (ˈhaʊsˌmeɪd) *n* a girl or woman employed to do housework, esp. one who is resident in the household.

housemaid's knee *n* inflammation and swelling of the bursa in front of the kneecap, caused esp. by constant kneeling on a hard surface. Technical name: **prepatellar bursitis.**

houseman (ˈhaʊsmən) *n, pl* **housemen.** *Med.* a junior doctor who is a member of the medical staff of a hospital. US and Canad. equivalent: **intern.**

house martin *n* a Eurasian swallow with a forked tail.

house mouse *n* any of various greyish mice, a common household pest in most parts of the world.

House music *or* **House** *n* a type of disco music of the late 1980s, based on funk, with fragments of other recordings edited in electronically.

House of Assembly *n* a legislative assembly or the lower chamber of such an assembly.

house of cards *n* **1** a tiered structure created by balancing playing cards on their edges. **2** an unstable situation, etc.

House of Commons *n* (in Britain, Canada, etc.) the lower chamber of Parliament.

house of correction *n* (formerly) a place of confinement for persons convicted of minor offences.

house of ill repute *or* **ill fame** *n* a euphemistic name for **brothel.**

House of Keys *n* the lower chamber of the legislature of the Isle of Man.

House of Lords *n* (in Britain) the upper chamber of Parliament, composed of the peers of the realm.

House of Representatives *n* **1** (in the US) the lower chamber of Congress, or of many state legislatures. **2** (in Australia) the lower chamber of Parliament. **3** the sole chamber of New Zealand's Parliament.

houseparent ('haʊsˌpɛərənt) *n* a person in charge of the welfare of a group of children in an institution.

house party *n* **1** a party, usually in a country house, at which guests are invited to stay for several days. **2** the guests who are invited.

house plant *n* a plant that can be grown indoors.

house-proud *adj* proud of the appearance, cleanliness, etc., of one's house, sometimes excessively so.

houseroom ('haʊsˌrʊm, -ˌruːm) *n* **1** room for storage or lodging. **2 give (something) houseroom.** (*used with a negative*) to have or keep (something) in one's house.

house-sit *vb* **house-sits, house-sitting, house-sat.** (*intr*) to live in and look after a house during the absence of its owner or owners.
▸ **'house-ˌsitter** *n*

Houses of Parliament ★ *n* (in Britain) **1** the building in which the House of Commons and the House of Lords assemble. **2** these two chambers considered together.

house sparrow *n* a small Eurasian bird, now established in North America and Australia. It has a brown plumage with grey underparts. Also called (US): **English sparrow.**

housetop ('haʊsˌtɒp) *n* **1** the roof of a house. **2 proclaim from the housetops.** to announce (something) publicly.

house-train *vb* (*tr*) *Brit.* to train (pets) to urinate and defecate outside the house.
▸ **'house-ˌtrained** *adj*

house-warming *n* a party given after moving into a new home.

housewife *n, pl* **housewives. 1** ('haʊsˌwaɪf). a woman who keeps house. **2** ('hʌzɪf). Also called: **hussy, huswife.** *Chiefly Brit.* a small sewing kit.
▸ **housewifery** ('haʊsˌwɪfərɪ) *n* ▸ **'housewifely** *adj*

housework ('haʊsˌwɜːk) *n* the work of running a home, such as cleaning, cooking, etc.

housey-housey ('haʊsɪ'haʊsɪ) *n* another name for **bingo** or **lotto.** ORIG C20: from the cry of "house!" shouted by the winner, prob. from FULL HOUSE

housing[1] ('haʊzɪŋ) *n* **1a** houses collectively. **1b** (*as modifier*): *a housing problem.* **2** the act of providing with accommodation. **3** a hole or slot made in one wooden member to receive another. **4** a part designed to contain or support a component or mechanism: *a wheel housing.*

housing[2] ('haʊzɪŋ) *n* (*often pl*) *Arch.* another word for **trappings** (sense 2). ORIG C14: from OF *houce* covering, of Gmc origin

housing estate *n* a planned area of housing, often with its own shops and other amenities.

housing scheme *n* a local-authority housing estate. Often shortened to **scheme.**

Housman ★ ('haʊsmən) *n* **A(lfred) E(dward).** 1859–1936, British poet and classical scholar, author of *A Shropshire Lad* (1896) and *Last Poems* (1922).

Houston ★ ('hjuːstən) *n* an inland port in SE Texas, linked by the **Houston Ship Canal** to the Gulf of Mexico and the Gulf Intracoastal Waterway: capital of the Republic of Texas (1837–39; 1842–45); site of the Manned Spacecraft Center (1964). Pop.: 1 744 058 (1996 est.).

hove (həʊv) *vb Chiefly naut.* a past tense and past participle of **heave.**

Hove ★ (həʊv) *n* a town and resort in S England, in East Sussex adjoining Brighton. Pop.: 67 602 (1991).

hovel ('hɒvᵊl) *n* **1** a ramshackle dwelling place. **2** an open shed for livestock, carts, etc. **3** the conical building enclosing a kiln. ORIG C15: from ?

hover ('hɒvə) *vb* (*intr*) **1** to remain suspended in one place. **2** (of certain birds, esp. hawks) to remain in one place in the air by rapidly beating the wings. **3** to linger uncertainly. **4** to be in a state of indecision. ◆ *n* **5** the act of hovering. ORIG C14: *hoveren,* var. of *hoven,* from ?
▸ **'hoverer** *n*

hovercraft ('hɒvəˌkrɑːft) *n* a vehicle that is able to travel across both land and water on a cushion of air.

hover fly *n* a dipterous fly with a hovering flight.

hoverport ('hɒvəˌpɔːt) *n* a port for hovercraft.

hovertrain ('hɒvəˌtreɪn) *n* a train that moves over a concrete track and is supported by a cushion of air supplied by powerful fans.

how (haʊ) *adv* **1** in what way? by what means?: *how did it happen?* Also used in indirect questions: *tell me how he did it.* **2** to what extent?: *how tall is he?* **3** how good? how well? what...like?: *how did she sing?* **4 and how!** (intensifier) very much so! **5 how about?** used to suggest something: *how about a cup of tea?* **6 how are you?** what is your state of health? **7 how come?** *Inf.* what is the reason (that)?: *how come you told him?* **8 how's that? 8a** what is your opinion? **8b** *Cricket.* Also written: **howzat** (haʊ'zæt). (an appeal to the umpire) is the batsman out? **9 how now?** *or* **how so?** *Arch.* what is the meaning of this? **10** in whatever way: *do it how you wish.* ◆ *n* **11** the way a thing is done: *the how of it.* ORIG OE *hu*

Howard ★ ('haʊəd) *n* **1 Catherine.** ?1521–42, fifth wife of Henry VIII of England; beheaded. **2 Charles,** Lord Howard of Effingham and 1st Earl of Nottingham. 1536–1624, Lord High Admiral of England (1585–1618). He commanded the fleet that defeated the Spanish Armada (1588). **3** Sir **Ebenezer.** 1850–1928, British town planner, who introduced garden cities. **4 Henry.** See (Earl of) **Surrey. 5 John.** 1726–90, British prison reformer. **6 John Winston.** born 1939, Australian politician; prime minister of Australia from 1996. **7 Leslie,** real name *Leslie Howard Stainer.* 1890–1943, British actor of Hungarian descent. His films include *Gone With the Wind* (1939). **8 Michael.** born 1941, British Conservative politician; home secretary (1993–97). **9 Trevor.** 1916–88, British actor. His films include *Brief Encounter* (1946), *The Third Man* (1949), and *White Mischief* (1987).

howbeit (haʊ'biːɪt) *Arch.* ◆ *sentence connector.* **1** however. ◆ *conj* **2** (*subordinating*) though; although.

howdah ('haʊdə) *n* a seat for riding on an elephant's back, esp. one with a canopy. ORIG C18: from Hindi *haudah,* from Ar. *haudaj* load carried by elephant or camel

how do you do *sentence substitute.* **1** a formal greeting said by people who are being introduced to each other. ◆ *n* **how-do-you-do. 2** *Inf.* a difficult situation.

howdy ('haʊdɪ) *sentence substitute. Chiefly US.* an informal word for **hello.** ORIG C16: from *how d'ye do*

Howe ★ (haʊ) *n* **1 Elias.** 1819–67, US inventor of the sewing machine (1846). **2 Howe of Aberavon,** Baron, title of *(Richard Edward) Geoffrey Howe.* born 1926, British Conservative politician; Chancellor of the Exchequer (1979–83); foreign secretary (1983–89); deputy prime minister (1984–90). **3 Richard,** 4th Viscount Howe. 1726–99, British admiral: served (1776–78) in the War of American Independence, winning the Battle of the Glorious First of June (1794). **4** his brother, **William,** 5th Viscount Howe. 1729–1814, British general; commander in chief (1776–78) of British forces in the War of American Independence.

Howel Dda ★ ('haʊəl 'ðɑː) *n* a variant of **Hywel Dda.**

however (haʊ'ɛvə) *sentence connector.* **1** still; nevertheless. **2** on the other hand; yet. ◆ *adv* **3** by whatever means. **4** (*used with adjectives of quantity or degree*) no matter how: *however long it takes, finish it.* **5** an emphatic form of **how** (sense 1).

howitzer ('haʊɪtsə) *n* a cannon having a short barrel with a low muzzle velocity and a steep angle of fire. ORIG C16: from Du. *houwitser,* from G, from Czech *houfnice* stone-sling

howl (haʊl) *n* **1** a long plaintive cry characteristic of a wolf or hound. **2** a similar cry of pain or sorrow. **3** a prolonged outburst of laughter. **4** *Electronics.* an unwanted high-pitched sound produced by a sound-producing system as a result of feedback. ◆ *vb* **5** to express in a howl or utter such cries. **6** (*intr*) (of the wind, etc.) to make a wailing noise. **7** (*intr*) *Inf.* to shout or laugh. ORIG C14: *houlen*

Howland Island ★ ('haʊlənd) *n* a small island in the central Pacific, near the equator northwest of Phoenix Island: US airfield. Area: 2.6 sq. km (1 sq. mile).

howl down *vb* (*tr, adv*) to prevent (a speaker) from being heard by shouting disapprovingly.

howler ('haʊlə) *n* **1** Also called: **howler monkey**. a large New World monkey inhabiting tropical forests in South America and having a loud howling cry. **2** *Inf.* a glaring mistake. **3** a person or thing that howls.

howling ('haʊlɪŋ) *adj* (*prenominal*) *Inf.* (intensifier): *a howling success; a howling error.*

Howlin' Wolf ★ ('haʊlɪn) *n* real name *Chester Burnett.* 1910–76, US blues singer and songwriter.

Howrah ★ ('haʊrə) *n* an industrial city in E India, on the Hooghly River opposite Calcutta. Pop.: 950 435 (1991).

howsoever (ˌhaʊsəʊ'ɛvə) *sentence connector, adv* a less common word for **however**.

Howson ★ ('haʊsᵊn) *n* **Peter** (**John**). born 1958, British artist who worked in Glasgow and is noted for portraying social issues: he was an official war artist for the Imperial War Museum in Bosnia (1993–95) and Kosovo (1999).

how-to *adj* (of a book or guide) giving basic instructions to the lay person on how to do or make something: *a how-to book on carpentry.*

howzit ('haʊzɪt) *sentence substitute. S. African.* an informal term of greeting. ORIG C20: from *how is it?*

Hoxha ★ (*Albanian* 'hodʒa) *n* **Enver** ('emver). 1908–85, Albanian statesman: founded the Albanian Communist Party in 1941 and was its first secretary (1954–85).

hoy[1] (hɔɪ) *n Naut.* **1** a freight barge. **2** a coastal fishing and trading vessel used during the 17th and 18th centuries. ORIG C15: from MDu. *hoei*

hoy[2] (hɔɪ) *interj* a cry used to attract attention or drive animals. ORIG C14: var. of HEY

hoya ('hɔɪə) *n* any plant of the genus *Hoya,* of E Asia and Australia, esp. the waxplant. ORIG C19: after Thomas *Hoy* (died 1821), E gardener

hoyden *or* **hoiden** ('hɔɪdᵊn) *n* a wild boisterous girl; tomboy. ORIG C16: ?from MDu. *heidijn* heathen
▸ '**hoydenish** *or* '**hoidenish** *adj*

Hoylake ★ ('hɔɪˌleɪk) *n* a town and resort in NW England, in Merseyside on the Irish Sea. Pop.: 25 554 (1991).

Hoyle[1] (hɔɪl) *n* an authoritative book of rules for card games. ORIG after Edmond *Hoyle,* 18th-cent. E authority on games, its compiler

Hoyle[2] ★ (hɔɪl) *n* Sir **Fred.** born 1915, British astronomer and writer: his books include *The Nature of the Universe* (1950), *Frontiers of Astronomy* (1955), and science-fiction writings.

HP *abbrev. for:* **1** *Brit.* hire-purchase. **2** horsepower. **3** high pressure. **4** (in Britain) Houses of Parliament. ◆ Also (for senses 1–3): **h.p.**

HPV *abbrev. for* human papilloma virus.

HQ *or* **h.q.** *abbrev. for* headquarters.

hr *abbrev. for* hour.

Hradec Králové ★ (*Czech* 'hradɛts 'kraːlɔvɛː) *n* a town in the N Czech Republic, on the Elbe River. Pop.: 100 528 (1996 est.). German name: **Königgrätz.**

HRH *abbrev. for* His (*or* Her) Royal Highness.

HRT *abbrev. for* hormone replacement therapy.

Hrvatska ★ ('hrvaːtskaː) *n* the Serbo-Croat name for **Croatia.**

HS (in Britain) *abbrev. for* Home Secretary.

HSH *abbrev. for* His (*or* Her) Serene Highness.

Hsi ★ (ʃiː) *n* a variant spelling of **Xi.**

Hsia Kuei ★ ('ʃjɑː 'kweɪ) *n* a variant spelling of **Xia Gui.**

Hsia-men ★ ('ʃjɑː'mɛn) *n* a transliteration of the modern Chinese name for **Amoy.**

Hsian ★ (ʃjɑːn) *n* a variant transliteration of the Chinese name for **Xi An.**

Hsiang ★ (ʃjɑːŋ) *n* a variant transliteration of the Chinese name for **Xiang.**

Hsin-hai-lien ★ ('ʃɪn'haɪ'ljɛn) *n* a variant transliteration of the Chinese name of **Lianyungang.**

Hsining ★ ('ʃiː'nɪŋ) *n* a variant transliteration of the Chinese name for **Xining.**

Hsinking ★ ('ʃɪn'kɪŋ) *n* the former name (1932–45) of **Changchun.**

Hsüan T'ung ★ ('ʃwɑːn 'tʊŋ) *n* a variant transliteration of the Chinese name for **Xuan-tong.**

Hsü-chou ★ ('ʃuː'tʃaʊ) *n* a variant transliteration of the Chinese name for **Xuzhou.**

ht *abbrev. for* height.

HT *Physics. abbrev. for* high tension.

HTLV *abbrev. for* human T-cell lymphotropic virus: any one of a family of viruses that cause certain rare human diseases in the T-cells. HTLV-III was an early name for the AIDS virus.

HTML *abbrev. for* hypertext markup language: a text description language that is used for electronic publishing, esp. on the World Wide Web.

HTTP *abbrev. for* hypertext transfer protocol, used esp. on the World Wide Web. See also **hypertext.**

Hua Guo Feng ('hwɑː gwəʊ 'fɛʃ) *or* **Hua Kuo-feng** ★ ('hwɑː kwəʊ'fɛŋ) *n* born c 1920, Chinese Communist statesman; prime minister of China 1976–80.

Huainan ★ ('hwaɪ'næn) *n* a city in E China, in Anhui province north of Hefei. Pop.: 1 200 000 (1991 est.).

Huambo ★ (*Portuguese* 'wambu) *n* a town in central Angola: designated by the Portuguese as the future capital of the country. Pop.: 400 000 (1995 est.). Former name (1928–73): **Nova Lisboa.**

Huang Hai ★ ('hwæŋ 'haɪ) *n* the Pinyin transliteration of the Chinese name for the **Yellow Sea.**

Huang Ho ★ ('hwæŋ 'həʊ) *n* the Pinyin transliteration of the Chinese name for the **Yellow River.**

Huáscar ★ (*Spanish* uas'kar) *n* died 1533, Inca ruler (1525–33): murdered by his half brother Atahualpa.

Huascarán (*Spanish* uaska'ran) *or* **Huascán** ★ (*Spanish* uas'kan) *n* an extinct volcano in W Peru, in the Peruvian Andes: the highest peak in Peru; avalanche in 1962 killed over 3000 people. Height: 6768 m (22 205 ft).

hub (hʌb) *n* **1** the central portion of a wheel, propeller, fan, etc., through which the axle passes. **2** the focal point. ORIG C17: prob. var. of HOB[1]

hub-and-spoke *n* (*modifier*) denoting a method of organizing intercontinental air traffic in which one major airport is used as a feeder for local airports. Sometimes shortened to **hub.**

Hubble ★ ('hʌbᵊl) *n* **Edwin Powell.** 1889–1953, US astronomer, noted for his investigations of nebulae and the recession of the galaxies.

hubble-bubble ('hʌbᵊl'bʌbᵊl) *n* **1** another name for **hookah. 2** turmoil. **3** a gargling sound. ORIG C17: rhyming jingle based on BUBBLE

Hubble's law *n Astron.* a law stating that the velocity of recession of a galaxy is proportional to its distance from the observer. ORIG C20: after E. P. HUBBLE

Hubble telescope *n* a telescope launched into orbit around the earth in 1990 to provide information about the universe.

hubbub ('hʌbʌb) *n* **1** a confused noise of many voices. **2** tumult; uproar. ORIG C16: prob. from Irish *hooboobbes*

hubby (ˈhʌbɪ) *n, pl* **hubbies.** an informal word for **husband.** ORIG C17: by shortening and altering

hubcap (ˈhʌbˌkæp) *n* a cap fitting over the hub of a wheel.

Hubei (ˈhuːˈbeɪ), **Hupeh,** *or* **Hupei** ★ *n* a province of central China: low-lying with many lakes. Capital: Wuhan. Pop.: 58 730 000 (1997 est.). Area: 187 500 sq. km (72 394 sq. miles).

Hubli ★ (ˈhuːblɪ) *n* a city in W India, in NW Mysore: incorporated with Dharwar in 1961; educational and trading centre. Pop. (with Dharwar): 648 298 (1991).

hubris (ˈhjuːbrɪs) *n* **1** pride or arrogance. **2** (in Greek tragedy) ambition, arrogance, etc., ultimately causing the transgressor's ruin. ORIG C19: from Gk
▸ **huˈbristic** *adj*

huckaback (ˈhʌkəˌbæk) *n* a coarse absorbent linen or cotton fabric used for towels, etc. Also: **huck** (hʌk). ORIG C17: from ?

huckleberry (ˈhʌkᵊlˌbɛrɪ) *n, pl* **huckleberries. 1** an American shrub having edible dark blue berries. **2** the fruit of this shrub. **3** a Brit. name for **whortleberry** (sense 1,2). ORIG C17: prob. var. of *hurtleberry,* from ?

huckster (ˈhʌkstə) *n* **1** a person who uses aggressive or questionable methods of selling. **2** *Now rare.* a person who sells small articles or fruit in the street. **3** *US.* a person who writes for radio or television advertisements. ◆ *vb* **4** (*tr*) to peddle. **5** (*tr*) to sell or advertise aggressively or questionably. **6** to haggle (over). ORIG C12: ?from MDu. *hoekster,* from *hoeken* to carry on the back

Huddersfield ★ (ˈhʌdəzˌfiːld) *n* a town in N England, in West Yorkshire on the River Colne: textile industry; seat of the University of Huddersfield (1992). Pop.: 143 726 (1991).

huddle (ˈhʌdᵊl) *n* **1** a heaped or crowded mass of people or things. **2** *Inf.* a private or impromptu conference (esp. in **go into a huddle**). ◆ *vb* **huddles, huddling, huddled. 3** to crowd or nestle closely together. **4** (often foll. by *up*) to hunch (oneself), as through cold. **5** (*intr*) *Inf.* to confer privately. **6** (*tr*) *Chiefly Brit.* to do (something) in a careless way. **7** (*tr*) *Rare.* to put on (clothes) hurriedly. ORIG C16: from ?; cf. ME *hoderen* to wrap up
▸ **ˈhuddler** *n*

Huddleston ★ (ˈhʌdᵊlstən) *n* **Trevor.** 1913–98, British prelate; suffragan bishop of Stepney (1968–78) and bishop of Mauritius (1978–83); president of the Anti-Apartheid Movement (1981–94).

Hudson ★ (ˈhʌdsən) *n* **1 Henry.** died 1611, English navigator: he explored the Hudson River (1609) and Hudson Bay (1610), where his crew mutinied and cast him adrift to die. **2 W(illiam) H(enry).** 1841–1922, British naturalist and novelist, born in Argentina, noted esp. for his romance *Green Mansions* (1904) and the autobiographical *Far Away and Long Ago* (1918).

Hudson Bay ★ *n* an inland sea in NE Canada: linked with the Atlantic by **Hudson Strait;** the S extension forms James Bay; discovered in 1610 by Henry Hudson. Area (excluding James Bay): 647 500 sq. km (250 000 sq. miles).

Hudson River ★ *n* a river in E New York State, flowing generally south into Upper New York Bay: linked to the Great Lakes, the St Lawrence Seaway, and Lake Champlain by the New York State Barge Canal and the canalized Mohawk River. Length: 492 km (306 miles).

hue (hjuː) *n* **1** the attribute of colour that enables an observer to classify it as red, blue, etc., and excludes white, black, and grey. **2** a shade of a colour. **3** aspect: *a different hue on matters.* ORIG OE *hīw* beauty
▸ **hued** *adj*

Hué ★ (*French* ɥe) *n* a port in central Vietnam, on the delta of the **Hué River** near the South China Sea: former capital of the kingdom of Annam, of French Indochina (1883–1946), and of Central Vietnam (1946–54). Pop.: 219 149 (1992 est.).

hue and cry *n* **1** (formerly) the pursuit of a suspected criminal with loud cries in order to raise the alarm. **2** any loud public outcry. ORIG C16: from Anglo-F *hu et cri,* from OF *hue* outcry, from *hu!* shout of warning + *cri* CRY

Huelva ★ (*Spanish* ˈwɛlβa) *n* a port in SW Spain, between the estuaries of the Odiel and Tinto Rivers: exports copper and other ores. Pop.: 145 712 (1995 est.).

Huesca ★ (*Spanish* ˈueska) *n* a city in NE Spain: Roman town, site of Quintus Sertorius' school (76 B.C.); 15th-century cathedral and ancient palace of Aragonese kings. Pop.: 50 020 (1991). Latin name: **Osca** (ˈɒskə).

huff (hʌf) *n* **1** a passing mood of anger or pique (esp. in **in a huff**). ◆ *vb* **2** to make or become angry or resentful. **3** (*intr*) to blow or puff heavily. **4** Also: **blow.** *Draughts.* to remove (an opponent's draught) from the board for failure to make a capture. **5** (*tr*) *Obs.* to bully. **6 huffing and puffing.** empty threats or objections: bluster. ORIG C16: imit.; cf. PUFF
▸ **ˈhuffish** *or* **ˈhuffy** *adj* ▸ **ˈhuffily** *or* **ˈhuffishly** *adv*

Hufuf ★ (hʊˈfuːf) *n* See **Al Hufuf.**

hug (hʌg) *vb* **hugs, hugging, hugged.** (*mainly tr*) **1** (*also intr*) to clasp tightly, usually with affection; embrace. **2** to keep close to a shore, kerb, etc. **3** to cling to (beliefs, etc.); cherish. **4** to congratulate (oneself). ◆ *n* **5** a tight or fond embrace. ORIG C16: prob. of Scand. origin
▸ **ˈhuggable** *adj*

huge (hjuːdʒ) *adj* extremely large. ORIG C13: from OF *ahuge,* from ?
▸ **ˈhugely** *adv* ▸ **ˈhugeness** *n*

hugger-mugger (ˈhʌgəˌmʌgə) *n* **1** confusion. **2** *Rare.* secrecy. ◆ *adj, adv Arch.* **3** with secrecy. **4** in confusion. ◆ *vb Obs.* **5** (*tr*) to keep secret. **6** (*intr*) to act secretly. ORIG C16: from ?

Huggins ★ (ˈhʌgɪnz) *n* Sir **William.** 1824–1910, British astronomer, who used spectroscopy to discover the red shift in stellar spectra.

Hugh Capet ★ (ˈhjuː ˈkæpɪt, ˈkeɪpɪt) *n* See (Hugh) **Capet.**

Hughes ★ (hjuːz) *n* **1 Howard.** 1905–76, US industrialist, aviator, and film producer. **2 Richard** (**Arthur Warren**). 1900–76, British novelist. He wrote *A High Wind in Jamaica* (1929) and *The Fox in the Attic* (1961). **3 Robert.** born 1938, Australian writer and art critic: maker of a number of films and series for television including *The Shock of the New* (1980) and *American Visions* (1996). **4 Ted.** 1930–98, British poet: his works include *The Hawk in the Rain* (1957), *Birthday Letters* (1998), and a translation of the *Oresteia* (published posthumously in 1999); poet laureate (1984–98). **5 Thomas.** 1822–96, British novelist; author of *Tom Brown's Schooldays* (1857).

Hughie (ˈhjuːɪ) *n Austral. & NZ inf.* the god of rain and of surf (esp. in the phrases **send her down, Hughie!, send 'em up, Hughie!**).

Hugo ★ (ˈhjuːgəʊ; *French* ygo) *n* **Victor** (**Marie**) (viktɔr). 1802–85, French writer and leader of the romantic movement in France. His works include the verse *Les Feuilles d'automne* (1831), the novel *Les Misérables* (1862), and the play *Ruy Blas* (1838).

Huguenot (ˈhjuːgəˌnəʊ, -ˌnɒt) *n* **1** a French Calvinist, esp. of the 16th or 17th centuries. ◆ *adj* **2** designating the French Protestant Church. ORIG C16: from F, from Genevan dialect *eyguenot* one who opposed annexation by Savoy, ult. from Swiss G *Eidgenoss* confederate

huh (*spelling pron* hʌ) *interj* an exclamation of derision, bewilderment, inquiry, etc.

Huhehot (ˌhuːhɪˈhɒt ˌhuːɪ-) *or* **Hu-ho-hao-t'e** ★ (ˌhuːhəʊhaʊˈteɪ) *n* a variant transliteration of the Chinese name for **Hohhot.**

huhu (ˈhuːhuː) *n* a New Zealand beetle with a hairy body. ORIG from Maori

hui (ˈhuːɪ) *n NZ.* **1** a Maori social gathering. **2** *Inf.* any party. ORIG from Maori

huia (ˈhuɪjə) *n* an extinct New Zealand bird, prized by early Maoris for its distinctive tail feathers. ORIG from Maori

hula (ˈhuːlə) *or* **hula-hula** *n* a Hawaiian dance performed by a woman. ORIG from Hawaiian

Hula Hoop *n Trademark.* a light hoop that is whirled around the body by movements of the waist and hips.

hulk (hʌlk) *n* **1** the body of an abandoned vessel. **2** *Disparaging.* a large or unwieldy vessel. **3** *Disparaging.* a large ungainly person or thing. **4** (*often pl*) the hull of a ship, used as a storehouse, etc., or (esp. in 19th-century Britain) as a prison. ORIG OE *hulc,* from Med. L *hulca,* from Gk *holkas* barge, from *helkein* to tow

hulking ('hʌlkɪŋ) *adj* big and ungainly.

hull (hʌl) *n* **1** the main body of a vessel, tank, etc. **2** the outer covering of a fruit or seed. **3** the calyx at the base of a strawberry, raspberry, or similar fruit. **4** the outer casing of a missile, rocket, etc. ◆ *vb* **5** to remove the hulls from (fruit or seeds). **6** (*tr*) to pierce the hull of (a vessel, tank, etc.). ORIG OE *hulu*

Hull[1] ★ (hʌl) *n* **1** a port in NE England: the largest fishing port in Britain; seat of The University of Hull (1954) and the Humberside campus of the University of Lincolnshire and Humberside. Pop.: 310 636 (1991). Official name: **Kingston upon Hull. 2** a city in SE Canada, in SW Quebec on the River Ottawa: a centre of the timber trade and associated industries. Pop.: 60 707 (1991).

Hull[2] ★ (hʌl) *n* **Cordell** (ˌkɔːˈdɛl). 1871–1955, US statesman; secretary of state (1933–44). He helped to found the U.N.: Nobel peace prize 1945.

hullabaloo *or* **hullaballoo** (ˌhʌləbəˈluː) *n, pl* **hullabaloos** *or* **hullaballoos.** loud confused noise; commotion. ORIG C18: ?from HALLO + Scot. *baloo* lullaby

hullo (hʌˈləʊ) *sentence substitute, n* a variant spelling of **hello.**

hum (hʌm) *vb* **hums, humming, hummed.** (*intr*) **1** to make a low continuous vibrating sound. **2** (of a person) to sing with the lips closed. **3** to utter an indistinct sound of hesitation; hem. **4** *Inf.* to be in a state of feverish activity. **5** *Brit. & Irish sl.* to smell unpleasant. **6 hum and haw.** See **hem**[2] (sense 3). ◆ *n* **7** a low continuous murmuring sound. **8** *Electronics.* an undesired low-frequency noise in the output of an amplifier or receiver. ◆ *interj, n* **9** an indistinct sound of hesitation, embarrassment, etc.; hem. ORIG C14: imit.

human ('hjuːmən) *adj* **1** of or relating to mankind: *human nature.* **2** consisting of people: *a human chain.* **3** having the attributes of man as opposed to animals, divine beings, or machines: *human failings.* **4a** kind or considerate. **4b** natural. ◆ *n* **5** a human being; person. ORIG C14: from L *hūmānus;* rel. to L *homō* man
▸ **'humanness** *n*

human being *n* a member of any of the races of *Homo sapiens;* person; man, woman, or child.

humane (hjuːˈmeɪn) *adj* **1** characterized by kindness, sympathy, etc. **2** inflicting as little pain as possible: *a humane killing.* **3** civilizing or liberal: *humane studies.* ORIG C16: var. of HUMAN
▸ **huˈmanely** *adv* ▸ **huˈmaneness** *n*

Human Genome Project *n* a 15-year international project to produce a map of all the human genes on their chromosomes: due to be completed in 2003.

human interest *n* (in a newspaper story, etc.) reference to individuals and their emotions, sometimes from exploitative motives.

humanism ('hjuːməˌnɪzəm) *n* **1** the rejection of religion in favour of a belief in the advancement of humanity by its own efforts. **2** (*often cap.*) a cultural movement of the Renaissance, based on classical studies. **3** interest in the welfare of people.
▸ **'humanist** *n* ▸ **ˌhumanˈistic** *adj*

humanitarian (hjuːˌmænɪˈtɛərɪən) *adj* **1** having the interests of mankind at heart. ◆ *n* **2** a philanthropist.
▸ **huˌmaniˈtarianism** *n*

humanity (hjuːˈmænɪtɪ) *n, pl* **humanities. 1** the human race. **2** the quality of being human. **3** kindness or mercy. **4** (*pl; usually preceded by the*) the study of literature, philosophy, and the arts, esp. of Ancient Greece and Rome.

humanize *or* **humanise** ('hjuːməˌnaɪz) *vb* **humanizes, humanizing, humanized** *or* **humanises, humanising, humanised. 1** to make or become human. **2** to make or become humane.
▸ **ˌhumaniˈzation** *or* **ˌhumaniˈsation** *n*

humankind (ˌhjuːmənˈkaɪnd) *n* the human race; humanity.

USAGE NOTE See at **mankind.**

humanly ('hjuːmənlɪ) *adv* **1** by human powers or means. **2** in a human or humane manner.

human nature *n* the qualities common to humanity, esp. with reference to human weakness.

humanoid ('hjuːməˌnɔɪd) *adj* **1** like a human being in appearance. ◆ *n* **2** a being with human rather than anthropoid characteristics. **3** (in science fiction) a robot or creature resembling a human being.

human papilloma virus *n* any of a class of viruses that cause tumours, including warts, in humans. Certain strains have been implicated as a cause of cervical cancer. Abbrev.: **HPV.**

human rights *pl n* the rights of individuals to liberty, justice, etc.

Humber ★ ('hʌmbə) *n* an estuary in NE England, into which flow the Rivers Ouse and Trent: flows east into the North Sea; navigable for large ocean-going ships as far as Hull; crossed by the **Humber Bridge** (1981), a single-span suspension bridge with a main span of 1410 m (4626 ft). Length: 64 km (40 miles).

Humberside ★ ('hʌmbəˌsaɪd) *n* a former county of N England around the Humber estuary, formed in 1974 and replaced by four unitary authorities in 1996.

humble ('hʌmbᵊl) *adj* **1** conscious of one's failings. **2** unpretentious; lowly: *a humble cottage; my humble opinion.* **3** deferential or servile. ◆ *vb* **humbles, humbling, humbled.** (*tr*) **4** to cause to become humble; humiliate. **5** to lower in status. ORIG C13: from OF, from L *humilis* low, from *humus* the ground
▸ **'humbleness** *n* ▸ **'humbly** *adv*

humblebee ('hʌmbᵊlˌbiː) *n* another name for the **bumblebee.** ORIG C15: rel. to MDu. *hommel* bumblebee, OHG *humbal*

humble pie *n* **1** (formerly) a pie made from the heart, entrails, etc., of a deer. **2 eat humble pie.** to be forced to behave humbly; be humiliated. ORIG C17: earlier *an umble pie,* by mistaken word division from *a numble pie,* from *numbles* offal of a deer, ult. from L *lumbulus* a little loin

Humboldt ★ ('hʌmbəʊlt; *German* 'hʊmbɔlt) *n* **1** Baron (**Friedrich Heinrich**) **Alexander von** (alɛˈksandər fɔn). 1769–1859, German scientist, who explored in Central and South America (1799–1804). **2** his brother, Baron (**Karl**) **Wilhelm von** ('vɪlhɛlm fɔn). 1767–1835, German philologist and educational reformer.

humbug ('hʌmˌbʌg) *n* **1** a person or thing that deceives. **2** nonsense. **3** *Brit.* a hard boiled sweet, usually having a striped pattern. ◆ *vb* **humbugs, humbugging, humbugged. 4** to cheat or deceive (someone). ORIG C18: from ?
▸ **'humˌbugger** *n* ▸ **'humˌbuggery** *n*

humdinger ('hʌmˌdɪŋə) *n Sl.* an excellent person or thing. ORIG C20: from ?

humdrum ('hʌmˌdrʌm) *adj* **1** ordinary; dull. ◆ *n* **2** a monotonous routine, task, or person. ORIG C16: rhyming compound, prob. based on HUM

Hume ★ (hjuːm) *n* **1** (**George**) **Basil.** 1923–99, British Roman Catholic Benedictine monk and cardinal; archbishop of Westminster (1976–99). **2 David.** 1711–76, Scottish empiricist philosopher, economist, and historian, who believed that human knowledge is restricted to that which can be perceived by the senses. His works include *A Treatise of Human Nature* (1740) and *An Enquiry concerning the Principles of Morals* (1751). **3 John.** born 1937, Northern Irish politician; leader of the Social Democratic and Labour party from 1979: awarded the Nobel peace prize with David Trimble in 1998 for his role in the Northern Irish peace settlement.
▸ **'Humism** *n*

humectant (hjuːˈmɛktənt) *adj* **1** producing moisture. ◆ *n* **2** a substance added to another to keep it moist. ORIG C17: from L *ūmectāre* to wet, from *ūmēre* to be moist

humerus ('hjuːmərəs) *n, pl* **humeri** (-məˌraɪ). **1** the bone that extends from the shoulder to the elbow in man. **2** the corresponding bone in other vertebrates. ORIG C17: from L *umerus;* rel. to Gothic *ams* shoulder, Gk *ōmos*
▸ **'humeral** *adj*

humid ('hjuːmɪd) *adj* moist; damp. ORIG C16: from L *ūmidus,* from *ūmēre* to be wet
▸ **'humidly** *adv* ▸ **'humidness** *n*

humidex ('hjuːmɪˌdɛks) *n Canad.* an index of discomfort showing the combined effect of humidity and temperature.

humidify (hjuːˈmɪdɪˌfaɪ) *vb* **humidifies, humidifying, humidified.** (*tr*) to make (air, etc.) humid or damp.
▸ **huˌmidifiˈcation** *n* ▸ **huˈmidiˌfier** *n*

humidity (hjuːˈmɪdɪtɪ) *n* **1** dampness. **2** a measure of the amount of moisture in the air.

humidor (ˈhjuːmɪˌdɔː) *n* a humid place or container for storing cigars, tobacco, etc.

humify (ˈhjuːmɪˌfaɪ) *vb* **humifies, humifying, humified.** to convert or be converted into humus.
▸ **ˌhumifiˈcation** *n*

humiliate (hjuːˈmɪlɪˌeɪt) *vb* **humiliates, humiliating, humiliated.** (*tr*) to lower or hurt the dignity or pride of. ORIG C16: from LL *humiliāre,* from L *humilis* HUMBLE
▸ **huˈmiliˌatingly** *adv* ▸ **huˌmiliˈation** *n* ▸ **huˈmiliˌator** *n*

humility (hjuːˈmɪlɪtɪ) *n, pl* **humilities.** the state or quality of being humble.

Hummel ★ (ˈhʊməl) *n* **Johann Nepomuk** (joˈhan ˈneːpomʊk). 1778–1837, German composer and pianist.

hummingbird (ˈhʌmɪŋˌbɜːd) *n* a very small American bird having a brilliant iridescent plumage, long slender bill, and wings specialized for very powerful vibrating flight.

hummock (ˈhʌmək) *n* **1** a hillock; knoll. **2** a ridge or mound of ice in an ice field. **3** *Chiefly southern US.* a wooded area lying above the level of an adjacent marsh. ORIG C16: from ?; cf. HUMP
▸ **ˈhummocky** *adj*

hummus *or* **houmous** (ˈhʊməs) *n* a creamy dip originating in the Middle East, made from puréed chickpeas. ORIG from Turkish *humus*

> **USAGE NOTE** Avoid confusion with **humus.**

humoral (ˈhjuːmərəl) *adj* **1** *Immunol.* denoting or relating to a type of immunity caused by free antibodies circulating in the blood. **2** *Obs.* of or relating to the four bodily fluids (humours).

humoresque (ˌhjuːməˈrɛsk) *n* a short lively piece of music. ORIG C19: from G *Humoreske,* ult. from E HUMOUR

humorist (ˈhjuːmərɪst) *n* a person who acts, speaks, or writes in a humorous way.

humorous (ˈhjuːmərəs) *adj* **1** funny; comical; amusing. **2** displaying or creating humour.
▸ **ˈhumorously** *adv* ▸ **ˈhumorousness** *n*

humour *or US* **humor** (ˈhjuːmə) *n* **1** the quality of being funny. **2** Also called: **sense of humour.** the ability to appreciate or express that which is humorous. **3** situations, speech, or writings that are humorous. **4a** a state of mind; mood. **4b** (*in combination*): *good humour.* **5** temperament or disposition. **6** a caprice or whim. **7** any of various fluids in the body: *aqueous humour.* **8** Also called: **cardinal humour.** *Arch.* any of the four bodily fluids (blood, phlegm, choler or yellow bile, melancholy or black bile) formerly thought to determine emotional and physical disposition. **9 out of humour.** in a bad mood. ◆ *vb* (*tr*) **10** to gratify; indulge: *he humoured the boy's whims.* **11** to adapt oneself to: *to humour someone's fantasies.* ORIG C14: from L *humor* liquid; rel. to L *ūmēre* to be wet
▸ **ˈhumourless** *or US* **ˈhumorless** *adj*

hump (hʌmp) *n* **1** a rounded protuberance or projection. **2** a rounded deformity of the back, consisting of a spinal curvature. **3** a rounded protuberance on the back of a camel or related animal. **4 the hump.** *Brit. inf.* a fit of sulking. ◆ *vb* **5** to form or become a hump; hunch; arch. **6** (*tr*) *Sl.* to carry or heave. **7** *Taboo sl.* to have sexual intercourse with (someone). ORIG C18: prob. from earlier *humpbacked*
▸ **ˈhumpy** *adj*

humpback (ˈhʌmpˌbæk) *n* **1** another word for **hunchback. 2** Also called: **humpback whale.** a large whalebone whale with a humped back and long flippers. **3** a Pacific salmon, the male of which has a humped back. **4** Also: **humpback bridge.** *Brit.* a road bridge having a sharp incline and decline and usually a narrow roadway. ORIG C17: alteration of earlier *crumpbacked,* ? infl. by HUNCHBACK
▸ **ˈhumpˌbacked** *adj*

Humperdinck ★ (*German* ˈhʊmpərdɪŋk) *n* **Engelbert** (ˈɛŋəlbɛrt). 1854–1921, German composer, esp. of operas, including *Hansel and Gretel* (1893).

humph (*spelling pron* hʌmf) *interj* an exclamation of annoyance, indecision, etc.

Humphrey ★ (ˈhʌmfrɪ) *n* **Duke.** See (Humphrey, Duke of) **Gloucester.**

Humphreys Peak ★ (ˈhʌmfrɪz) *n* a mountain in N central Arizona, in the San Francisco Peaks: the highest peak in the state. Height: 3862 m (12 670 ft).

Humphries ★ (ˈhʌmfrɪz) *n* (**John**) **Barry.** born 1934, Australian comic actor and writer, best known for creating the character Dame Edna Everage.

humpty dumpty (ˈhʌmptɪ ˈdʌmptɪ) *n, pl* **humpty dumpties.** *Chiefly Brit.* **1** a short fat person. **2** a person or thing that once broken cannot be mended. ORIG C18: from the nursery rhyme *Humpty Dumpty*

humpy (ˈhʌmpɪ) *n, pl* **humpies.** *Austral.* a primitive hut. ORIG C19: from Abor.

Hums ★ (hʊms) *n* a variant of **Homs.**

humus (ˈhjuːməs) *n* a dark brown or black colloidal mass of partially decomposed organic matter in the soil. It improves the fertility and water retention of the soil. ORIG C18: from L: soil

> **USAGE NOTE** Avoid confusion with **hummus.**

Hun (hʌn) *n, pl* **Huns** *or* **Hun. 1** a member of any of several Asiatic nomadic peoples who dominated much of Asia and E Europe from before 300 B.C., invading the Roman Empire in the 4th and 5th centuries A.D. **2** *Inf.* (esp. in World War I) a derogatory name for a **German. 3** *Inf.* a vandal. ORIG OE *Hūnas,* from LL *Hūnī,* from Turkish *Hun-yü*
▸ **ˈHunnish** *adj* ▸ **ˈHunˌlike** *adj*

Hunan ★ (ˈhuːˈnæn) *n* a province of S China, between the Yangtze River and the Nan Ling Mountains: drained chiefly by the Xiang and Yüan Rivers; valuable mineral resources. Capital: Changsha. Pop.: 64 650 000 (1997 est.). Area: 210 500 sq. km (82 095 sq. miles).

hunch (hʌntʃ) *n* **1** an intuitive guess or feeling. **2** another word for **hump. 3** a lump or large piece. ◆ *vb* **4** to draw (oneself or a part of the body) up or together. **5** (*intr; usually foll. by up*) to sit in a hunched position. ORIG C16: from ?

hunchback (ˈhʌntʃˌbæk) *n* **1** a person having an abnormal curvature of the spine. **2** such a curvature. ◆ Also called: **humpback.** ORIG C18: from earlier *hunchbacked*
▸ **ˈhunchˌbacked** *adj*

hundred (ˈhʌndrəd) *n, pl* **hundreds** *or* **hundred. 1** the cardinal number that is the product of ten and ten; five score. **2** a numeral, 100, C, etc., representing this number. **3** (*often pl*) a large but unspecified number, amount, or quantity. **4** (*pl*) the 100 years of a specified century: *in the sixteen hundreds.* **5** something representing, represented by, or consisting of 100 units. **6** *Maths.* the position containing a digit representing that number followed by two zeros: *in 4376, 3 is in the hundred's place.* **7** an ancient division of a county. ◆ *determiner* **8** amounting to or approximately a hundred: *a hundred reasons for that.* ORIG OE
▸ **ˈhundredth** *adj, n*

hundreds and thousands *pl n* tiny beads of coloured sugar, used in decorating cakes, etc.

hundredweight (ˈhʌndrədˌweɪt) *n, pl* **hundredweights** *or* **hundredweight. 1** Also called: **long hundredweight.** *Brit.* a unit of weight equal to 112 pounds (50.802 kg). **2** Also called: **short hundredweight.** *US & Canad.* a unit of weight equal to 100 pounds (45.359 kg). **3** Also called: **metric hundredweight.** a metric unit of weight equal to 50 kilograms. ◆ Abbrev. (for senses 1, 2): **cwt.**

hung (hʌŋ) *vb* **1** the past tense and past participle of **hang** (except in the sense of *to execute*). ◆ *adj* **2** (of a political party, jury, etc.) not having a majority: *a hung parlia-*

ment. **3 hung over.** *Inf.* suffering from the effects of a hangover. **4 hung up.** *Sl.* **4a** impeded by some difficulty or delay. **4b** emotionally disturbed. **5 hung up on.** *Sl.* obsessively interested in.

Hung. *abbrev. for:* **1** Hungarian. **2** Hungary.

Hungarian (hʌŋˈɡɛərɪən) *n* **1** the official language of Hungary, also spoken in Romania and elsewhere, belonging to the Finno-Ugric family. **2** a native, inhabitant, or citizen of Hungary. ◆ *adj* **3** of or relating to Hungary, its people, or their language. ◆ Cf. **Magyar.**

Hungary ★ (ˈhʌŋɡərɪ) *n* a republic in central Europe: Magyars first unified under Saint Stephen, the first Hungarian king (1001–38); taken by the Hapsburgs from the Turks at the end of the 17th century; gained autonomy with the establishment of the dual monarchy of Austria-Hungary (1867) and became a republic in 1918; passed under Communist control in 1949; a popular rising in 1956 was suppressed by Soviet troops; democracy replaced Communism in 1989 after mass protests. It consists chiefly of the Middle Danube basin and plains. Official language: Hungarian. Religion: Christian majority. Currency: forint. Capital: Budapest. Pop.: 10 065 000 (1999 est.). Area: 93 030 sq. km (35 919 sq. miles). Hungarian name: **Magyarország.**

hunger (ˈhʌŋɡə) *n* **1** a feeling of emptiness or weakness induced by lack of food. **2** desire or craving: *hunger for a woman.* ◆ *vb* **3** (*intr;* usually foll. by *for* or *after*) to have a great appetite or desire (for). ORIG OE

hunger march *n* a procession of protest or demonstration, esp. by the unemployed.

hunger strike *n* a voluntary fast undertaken, usually by a prisoner, as a means of protest.
▸ **hunger striker** *n*

Hung Hsiu-ch'uan ★ (ˈhʌŋ ˈʃjuːˈtʃwɑːn) *n* a variant of **Hong Xiu Quan.**

Hungnam ★ (ˌhʊŋˈnæm) *n* a port in E North Korea, on the Sea of Japan southeast of Hamhung. Pop.: 260 000 (latest est.).

hungry (ˈhʌŋɡrɪ) *adj* **hungrier, hungriest. 1** desiring food. **2** (*postpositive;* foll. by *for*) having a craving, desire, or need (for). **3** expressing or appearing to express greed, craving, or desire. **4** lacking fertility; poor. **5** *Austral. & NZ.* greedy; mean. **6** *NZ.* (of timber) dry and bare.
▸ **ˈhungrily** *adv* ▸ **ˈhungriness** *n*

Hung-wu ★ (ˈhʌŋ ˈwuː) *n* a variant of **Hong-wu.**

hunk (hʌŋk) *n* **1** a large piece. **2** *Sl.* a sexually attractive man. ORIG C19: prob. rel. to Flemish *hunke*

hunkers (ˈhʌŋkəz) *pl n* haunches. ORIG C18: from ?

hunky-dory (ˌhʌŋkɪˈdɔːrɪ) *adj Inf.* very satisfactory; fine. ORIG C20: from ?

hunt (hʌnt) *vb* **1** to seek out and kill (animals) for food or sport. **2** (*intr;* often foll. by *for*) to search (for): *to hunt for a book.* **3** (*tr*) to use (hounds, horses, etc.) in the pursuit of wild animals, game, etc.: *to hunt a pack of hounds.* **4** (*tr*) to search (country) to hunt game, etc.: *to hunt the parkland.* **5** (*tr;* often foll. by *down*) to track diligently so as to capture: *to hunt down a criminal.* **6** (*tr; usually passive*) to persecute; hound. **7** (*intr*) (of a gauge indicator, etc.) to oscillate about a mean value or position. **8** (*intr*) (of an aircraft, rocket, etc.) to oscillate about a flight path or its course axis. ◆ *n* **9** the act or an instance of hunting. **10** chase or search, esp. of animals. **11** the area of a hunt. **12** a party or institution organized for the pursuit of wild animals, esp. for sport. **13** the members of such a party or institution. **14 in the hunt.** *Inf.* having a chance of success: *that result keeps us in the hunt.* ORIG OE *huntian*

Hunt ★ (hʌnt) *n* **1** (**William**) **Holman** (ˈhəʊlmən). 1827–1910, British painter; a founder of the Pre-Raphaelite Brotherhood (1848). **2** (**Henry Cecil**) **John,** Baron. 1910–98, British army officer, who planned and led the first successful Everest ascent (1953). **3** (**James Henry**) **Leigh.** 1784–1859, British poet and essayist.

huntaway (ˈhʌntəˌweɪ) *n NZ.* a sheepdog trained to drive sheep forward by barking on command and able to respond to commands from a distance.

hunted (ˈhʌntɪd) *adj* harassed: *a hunted look.*

hunter (ˈhʌntə) *n* **1** a person or animal that seeks out and kills or captures game. Fem.: **huntress** (ˈhʌntrɪs). **2a** a person who looks diligently for something. **2b** (*in combination*): *a fortune-hunter.* **3** a specially bred horse used in hunting, characterized by strength and stamina. **4** a watch with a hinged metal lid or case (**hunting case**) to protect the crystal.

hunter-killer *adj* denoting a type of submarine designed and equipped to pursue and destroy enemy craft.

hunter's moon *n* the full moon following the harvest moon.

hunting (ˈhʌntɪŋ) *n* **a** the pursuit and killing or capture of wild animals, regarded as a sport. **b** (*as modifier*): *hunting lodge.*

Huntingdon[1] ★ (ˈhʌntɪŋdən) *n* a town in E central England, in Cambridgeshire: birthplace of Oliver Cromwell. Pop. (with Godmanchester): 15 575 (1991).

Huntingdon[2] ★ (ˈhʌntɪŋdən) *n* **Selina,** Countess of Huntingdon. 1707–91, British religious leader, who founded a Calvinistic Methodist sect.

Huntingdonshire ★ (ˈhʌntɪŋdənˌʃɪə, -ʃə) *n* (until 1974) a former county of E England, now part of Cambridgeshire.

hunting horn *n* a long straight metal tube with a flared end, used in giving signals in hunting.

Huntington's disease (ˈhʌntɪŋtənz) *n* a hereditary form of chorea associated with progressive dementia. Former name: **Huntington's chorea.** ORIG after G. *Huntington* (1850–1916), US physician

huntsman (ˈhʌntsmən) *n, pl* **huntsmen. 1** a person who hunts. **2** a person who trains hounds, beagles, etc., and manages them during a hunt.

Huntsville ★ (ˈhʌntsvɪl) *n* a city in NE Alabama: space-flight and guided-missile research centre. Pop.: 170 424 (1996 est.).

Huon pine (ˈhjuːɒn) *n* a tree of Australasia, SE Asia, and Chile, with scalelike leaves and cup-shaped berry-like fruits. ORIG after the *Huon* River, Tasmania

Hupeh *or* **Hupei** ★ (ˈxuːˈpeɪ) *n* a variant transliteration of the Chinese name for **Hubei.**

Hurd ★ (hɜːd) *n* **Douglas** (**Richard**), Baron Hurd of Westwell. born 1930, British Conservative politician; home secretary (1985–89); foreign secretary (1989–95).

hurdle (ˈhɜːdᵊl) *n* **1a** *Athletics.* one of a number of light barriers over which runners leap in certain events. **1b** a low barrier used in certain horse races. **2** an obstacle: *the next hurdle in his career.* **3** a light framework of interlaced osiers, etc., used as a temporary fence. **4** a sledge on which criminals were dragged to their executions. ◆ *vb* **hurdles, hurdling, hurdled. 5** to jump (a hurdle). **6** (*tr*) to surround with hurdles. **7** (*tr*) to overcome. ORIG OE *hyrdel*
▸ **ˈhurdler** *n*

hurdy-gurdy (ˈhɜːdɪˈɡɜːdɪ) *n, pl* **hurdy-gurdies.** any mechanical musical instrument, such as a barrel organ. ORIG C18. rhyming compound, prob. imit.

hurl (hɜːl) *vb* (*tr*) **1** to throw with great force. **2** to utter with force; yell: *to hurl insults.* ◆ *n* **3** the act of hurling. ORIG C13: prob. imit.

hurling (ˈhɜːlɪŋ) *or* **hurley** *n* a traditional Irish game resembling hockey, played with sticks and a ball between two teams of 15 players.

hurly-burly (ˈhɜːlɪˈbɜːlɪ) *n, pl* **hurly-burlies.** confusion or commotion. ORIG C16: from earlier *hurling and burling,* rhyming phrase based on *hurling* in obs. sense of uproar

Huron ★ (ˈhjʊərən) *n* **1 Lake.** a lake in North America, between the US and Canada: the second largest of the Great Lakes. Area: 59 570 sq. km (23 000 sq. miles). **2** (*pl* **Hurons** *or* **Huron**) a member of a North American Indian people formerly living in the region east of Lake Huron. **3** the Iroquoian language of this people.

hurrah (hʊˈrɑː), **hooray** (huːˈreɪ), *or* **hurray** (hʊˈreɪ) *interj, n* **1** a cheer of joy, victory, etc. ◆ *vb* **2** to shout "hurrah". ORIG C17: prob. from G *hurra;* cf. HUZZAH

hurricane (ˈhʌrɪkᵊn) *n* **1** a severe, often destructive storm, esp. a tropical cyclone. **2** a wind of force 12 on the Beaufort scale, with speeds over 72 mph. ORIG C16: from Sp. *huracán,* of Amerind origin, from *hura* wind

hurricane deck *n* a ship's deck that is covered by a light deck as a sunshade.

hurricane lamp *n* a paraffin lamp with a glass covering. Also called: **storm lantern.**

hurried ('hʌrɪd) *adj* performed with great haste.
▸ '**hurriedly** *adv* ▸ '**hurriedness** *n*

hurry ('hʌrɪ) *vb* **hurries, hurrying, hurried. 1** (*intr;* often foll. by *up*) to hasten; rush. **2** (*tr;* often foll. by *along*) to speed up the completion, progress, etc., of. ◆ *n* **3** haste. **4** urgency or eagerness. **5 in a hurry.** *Inf.* **5a** easily: *you won't beat him in a hurry.* **5b** willingly: *we won't go there again in a hurry.* ORIG C16 *horyen,* prob. imit.

hurst (hɜːst) *n Arch.* **1** a wood. **2** a sandbank. ORIG OE *hyrst*

Hurstmonceux ★ ('hɜːstmən,suː, -,səʊ) *n* a variant spelling of **Herstmonceux.**

hurt (hɜːt) *vb* **hurts, hurting, hurt. 1** (*tr*) to cause physical pain to (someone or something). **2** (*tr*) to cause emotional pain or distress to (someone). **3** to produce a painful sensation in (someone): *the bruise hurts.* **4** (*intr*) *Inf.* to feel pain. ◆ *n* **5** physical or mental pain or suffering. **6** a wound, cut, or sore. **7** damage or injury; harm. ◆ *adj* **8** injured or pained: *a hurt knee; a hurt look.* ORIG C12 *hurten* to hit, from OF *hurter* to knock against, prob. of Gmc origin

hurtful ('hɜːtful) *adj* causing distress or injury: *to say hurtful things.*
▸ '**hurtfully** *adv*

hurtle ('hɜːtᵊl) *vb* **hurtles, hurtling, hurtled.** to project or be projected very quickly, noisily, or violently. ORIG C13 *hurtlen,* from *hurten* to strike; see HURT

Hus ★ (*Czech* hʊs) *n* **Jan** (jan). the Czech name of (John) **Huss.**

Husain ★ (hʊ'seɪn, -'saɪn) *n* **1** ?629–680 A.D., Islamic caliph, the son of Ali and Fatima and the grandson of Mohammed. **2** a variant spelling of **Hussein.**

husband ('hʌzbənd) *n* **1** a woman's partner in marriage. **2** *Arch.* a manager of an estate. ◆ *vb* **3** to manage or use (resources, finances, etc.) thriftily. **4** (*tr*) *Arch.* to find a husband for. **5** (*tr*) *Obs.* to till (the soil). ORIG OE *hūsbonda,* from ON *hūsbōndi,* from *hūs* house + *bōndi* one who has a household
▸ '**husbander** *n*

husbandman ('hʌzbəndmən) *n, pl* **husbandmen.** *Arch.* a farmer.

husbandry ('hʌzbəndrɪ) *n* **1** farming, esp. when regarded as a science, skill, or art. **2** management of affairs and resources.

Husein ibn-Ali ★ (hʊ'seɪn 'ɪbᵊn'ɑːlɪ, -'ælɪ, hʊ'saɪn) *n* 1856–1931, first king of Hejaz (1916–24): initiated the Arab revolt against the Turks (1916–18); forced to abdicate by ibn-Saud.

hush (hʌʃ) *vb* **1** to make or become silent; quieten; soothe. ◆ *n* **2** stillness; silence. ◆ *interj* **3** a plea or demand for silence. ORIG C16: prob. from earlier *husht* quiet!, the *-t* being thought to indicate a past participle
▸ **hushed** *adj*

hushaby ('hʌʃə,baɪ) *interj* **1** used in quietening a baby or child to sleep. ◆ *n, pl* **hushabies. 2** a lullaby. ORIG C18: from HUSH + *by,* as in BYE-BYES

hush-hush *adj Inf.* (esp. of official work, documents, etc.) secret; confidential.

hush money *n Sl.* money given to a person to ensure that something is kept secret.

hush up *vb* (*tr, adv*) to suppress information or rumours.

husk (hʌsk) *n* **1** the external green or membranous covering of certain fruits and seeds. **2** any worthless outer covering. ◆ *vb* **3** (*tr*) to remove the husk from. ORIG C14: prob. based on MDu. *huusken* little house, from *hūs* house

husky¹ ('hʌskɪ) *adj* **huskier, huskiest. 1** (of a voice, utterance, etc.) slightly hoarse or rasping. **2** of or containing husks. **3** *Inf.* big and strong. ORIG C19: prob. from HUSK, from the toughness of a corn husk
▸ '**huskily** *adv* ▸ '**huskiness** *n*

husky² ('hʌskɪ) *n, pl* **huskies. 1** a breed of Arctic sled dog with a thick dense coat, pricked ears, and a curled tail. **2** *Canad. sl.* **2a** a member of the Inuit people. **2b** their language. ORIG C19: prob. based on ESKIMO

Huss ★ (hʌs) *n* **John,** Czech name *Jan Hus.* ?1372–1415, Bohemian religious reformer. Influenced by Wycliffe, he anticipated the Reformation by denouncing Church doctrines. His death at the stake precipitated the Hussite wars.

Hussain ★ (hʊ'seɪn) *n* **Nasser** ('næsə). born 1968, British cricketer, born in India; plays for Essex and for England (from 1989; captain from 1999).

hussar (hʊ'zɑː) *n* **1** a member of any of various light cavalry regiments, renowned for their elegant dress. **2** a Hungarian horseman of the 15th century. ORIG C15: from Hungarian *huszár* hussar, formerly freebooter, ult. from OIt. *corsaro* CORSAIR

Hussein ★ (hʊ'seɪn) *n* **1** Also: **Husain.** 1935–99, king of Jordan (1952–99). **2 Saddam** (sæ'dæm). born 1937, Iraqi politician: president of Iraq from 1979. He led Iraq into the Iran-Iraq War (1980–88) and the Gulf War (1991).

Husserl ★ (*German* 'hʊsərl) *n* **Edmund** ('ɛtmʊnt). 1859–1938, German philosopher; founder of phenomenology.

Hussite ('hʌsaɪt) *n* **1** an adherent of the ideas of John Huss or a member of the movement initiated by him. ◆ *adj* **2** of or relating to John Huss, his teachings, etc.
▸ '**Hussitism** *n*

hussy ('hʌsɪ, -zɪ) *n, pl* **hussies.** *Contemptuous.* a shameless or promiscuous woman. ORIG C16 (in the sense: housewife): from *hussif* HOUSEWIFE

hustings ('hʌstɪŋz) *n* (*functioning as pl or sing*) **1** *Brit.* (before 1872) the platform on which candidates were nominated for Parliament and from which they addressed the electors. **2** the proceedings at a parliamentary election. ORIG C11: from ON *hūsthing,* from *hūs* HOUSE + *thing* assembly

hustle ('hʌsᵊl) *vb* **hustles, hustling, hustled. 1** to shove or crowd (someone) roughly. **2** to move hurriedly or furtively: *he hustled her out of sight.* **3** (*tr*) to deal with hurriedly: *to hustle legislation through.* **4** *Sl.* to obtain (something) forcefully. **5** *US & Canad. sl.* (of procurers and prostitutes) to solicit. ◆ *n* **6** an instance of hustling. ORIG C17: from Du. *husselen* to shake, from MDu. *hutsen*
▸ '**hustler** *n*

Huston ★ ('hjuːstᵊn) *n* **John.** 1906–87, US film director. His films include *The Treasure of the Sierra Madre* (1947), *The African Queen* (1951), and *The Dead* (1987).

hut (hʌt) *n* **1** a small house or shelter. ◆ *vb* **huts, hutting, hutted. 2** to furnish with or live in a hut. ORIG C17: from F *hutte,* of Gmc origin
▸ '**hut,like** *adj*

hutch (hʌtʃ) *n* **1** a cage, usually of wood and wire mesh, for small animals. **2** *Inf., derog.* a small house. **3** a cart for carrying ore. ORIG C14 *hucche,* from OF *huche,* from Med. L *hutica,* from ?

hutment ('hʌtmənt) *n Chiefly mil.* a number or group of huts.

Hutton ★ ('hʌtᵊn) *n* **1 James.** 1726–97, Scottish geologist, regarded as the founder of modern geology. **2** Sir **Leonard,** known as *Len Hutton.* 1916–90, English cricketer.

Huxley ★ ('hʌkslɪ) *n* **1 Aldous** (**Leonard**) ('ɔːldəs). 1894–1963, British writer, noted for his novel *Brave New World* (1932). **2** his half-brother, Sir **Andrew Fielding,** born 1917, British biologist: noted for his research into the transmission of nerve impulses; shared Nobel prize for physiology or medicine (1963). **3** brother of Aldous, Sir **Julian** (**Sorrel**). 1887–1975, British biologist; first director-general of UNESCO (1946–48). His works include *Essays of a Biologist* (1923). **4** their grandfather, **Thomas Henry.** 1825–95, British biologist, the leading exponent of Darwin's theory of evolution; his works include *Evolution and Ethics* (1893).

Hu Yaobang ★ ('xuː jaʊ'bɑːŋ) *n* 1915–89, Chinese statesman; leader of the Chinese Communist Party (1981–87).

Huygens ★ ('haɪgənz; *Dutch* 'hœixəns) *n* **Christiaan** ('kristiː,aːn). 1629–95, Dutch physicist: first formulated the wave theory of light.

Huysmans ★ (*French* ɥismɑ̃s) *n* **Joris Karl** (ʒɔris karl). 1848–1907, French novelist of the Decadent school, whose works include *À rebours* (1884).

huzzah (həˈzɑː) *interj, n, vb* an archaic word for **hurrah.** ORIG C16: from ?

HV *or* **h.v.** *abbrev. for* high voltage.

Hwange ★ (ˈhwæŋgeɪ) *n* a town in W Zimbabwe: coal mines. Pop.: 40 000 (1989 est.). Former name (until 1982): **Wankie.**

Hwang Hai ★ (ˈwæŋ ˈhaɪ) *n* a variant transliteration of the Chinese name for the **Yellow Sea.**

Hwang Ho ★ (ˈwæŋ ˈhəʊ) *n* a variant transliteration of the Chinese name for the **Yellow River.**

HWM *abbrev. for* high-water mark.

hwyl (ˈhuːɪl) *n* emotional fervour, as in the recitation of poetry. ORIG C19: Welsh

hyacinth (ˈhaɪəsɪnθ) *n* **1** any plant of the Mediterranean genus *Hyacinthus,* esp. a cultivated variety having a thick flower stalk bearing bell-shaped fragrant flowers. **2** the flower or bulb of such a plant. **3** any similar plant, such as the grape hyacinth. **4** Also called: **jacinth.** a reddish transparent variety of the mineral zircon, used as a gemstone. **5a** any of the varying colours of the hyancinth flower or stone. **5b** (*as adj*): *hyacinth eyes.* ORIG C16: from L *hyacinthus,* from Gk *huakinthos*
▸ ˌ**hyaˈcinthine** *adj*

Hyacinthus ★ (ˌhaɪəˈsɪnθəs) *n Greek myth.* a youth beloved of Apollo and inadvertently killed by him. At the spot where the youth died, Apollo caused a flower to grow.

Hyades[1] (ˈhaɪəˌdiːz) *pl n* an open cluster of stars in the constellation Taurus, formerly believed to bring rain when they rose with the sun. ORIG C16: via L from Gk *huades,* ?from *huein* to rain

Hyades[2] ★ (ˈhaɪəˌdiːz) *pl n Greek myth.* seven nymphs, daughters of Atlas, whom Zeus placed among the stars after death.

hyaena (haɪˈiːnə) *n* a variant spelling of **hyena.**

hyaline (ˈhaɪəlɪn) *adj Biol.* clear and translucent, as a common type of cartilage. ORIG C17: from LL *hyalinus,* from Gk, from *hualos* glass

hyalite (ˈhaɪəˌlaɪt) *n* a clear and colourless variety of opal in globular form.

hyaloid (ˈhaɪəˌlɔɪd) *adj Anat., zool.* clear and transparent; hyaline. ORIG C19: from Gk *hualoeidēs*

hyaloid membrane *n* the delicate transparent membrane enclosing the vitreous humour of the eye.

hybrid (ˈhaɪbrɪd) *n* **1** an animal or plant resulting from a cross between genetically unlike individuals; usually sterile. **2** anything of mixed ancestry. **3** a word, part of which is derived from one language and part from another, such as *monolingual.* ◆ *adj* **4** denoting or being a hybrid; of mixed origin. ORIG C17: from L *hibrida* offspring of a mixed union (human or animal)
▸ ˈ**hybridism** *n* ▸ **hyˈbridity** *n*

hybrid computer *n* a computer that uses both analogue and digital techniques.

hybridize *or* **hybridise** (ˈhaɪbrɪˌdaɪz) *vb* **hybridizes, hybridizing, hybridized** *or* **hybridises, hybridising, hybridised.** to produce or cause to produce hybrids; crossbreed.
▸ ˌ**hybridiˈzation** *or* ˌ**hybridiˈsation** *n*

hybridoma (ˌhaɪbrɪˈdəʊmə) *n* a hybrid cell formed by the fusion of two different types of cell, esp. one capable of producing antibodies fused with an immortal tumour cell. ORIG C20: from HYBRID + -OMA

hybrid vigour *n Biol.* the increased size, strength, etc., of a hybrid as compared to either of its parents. Also called: **heterosis.**

hydatid (ˈhaɪdətɪd) *n* **1** a large bladder containing encysted larvae of the tapeworm *Echinococcus:* causes serious disease in man. **2** Also called: **hydatid cyst.** a sterile fluid-filled cyst produced in man and animals during infestation by *Echinococcus* larval forms. ORIG C17: from Gk *hudatis* watery vesicle, from *hudōr, hudat-* water

Hyde[1] ★ (haɪd) *n* a town in NW England, in Tameside, in E Greater Manchester; textiles, footwear, engineering. Pop.: 30 666 (1991).

Hyde[2] ★ (haɪd) *n* **1 Douglas.** 1860–1949, Irish scholar and author; first president of Eire (1938–45). **2 Edward.** See (1st Earl of) **Clarendon.**

Hyde Park ★ *n* a park in W central London: popular for open-air meetings.

Hyderabad ★ (ˈhaɪdərəˌbɑːd, -ˌbæd, ˈhaɪdrə-) *n* **1** a city in S central India, capital of Andhra Pradesh state and capital of former Hyderabad state; university (1918). Pop.: 3 145 939 (1991). **2** a former state of S India: divided in 1956 between the states of Andhra Pradesh, Mysore, and Maharashtra. **3** a city in SW Pakistan, on the River Indus: seat of the University of Sind (1947). Pop.: 800 000 (latest est.).

Hyder Ali *or* **Haidar Ali** ★ (ˈhaɪdər ˈɑːlɪ) *n* 1722–82, Indian ruler of Mysore (1766–82), who waged two wars against the British in India (1767–69; 1780–82).

hydr- *combining form.* a variant of **hydro-** before a vowel.

hydra (ˈhaɪdrə) *n, pl* **hydras** *or* **hydrae** (-driː). **1** a freshwater coelenterate in which the body is a slender polyp with tentacles around the mouth. **2** a persistent trouble or evil. ORIG C16: from L, from Gk *hudra* water serpent

Hydra ★ (ˈhaɪdrə) *n Greek myth.* a monster with nine heads, each of which, when struck off, was replaced by two new ones.

hydracid (haɪˈdræsɪd) *n* an acid, such as hydrochloric acid, that does not contain oxygen.

hydrangea (haɪˈdreɪndʒə) *n* a shrub or tree of an Asian and American genus cultivated for their large clusters of white, pink, or blue flowers. ORIG C18: from NL, from Gk *hudōr* water + *angeion* vessel: prob. from the cup-shaped fruit

hydrant (ˈhaɪdrənt) *n* an outlet from a water main, usually an upright pipe with a valve attached, from which water can be tapped for fighting fires, etc. ORIG C19: from HYDRO- + -ANT

hydrate (ˈhaɪdreɪt) *n* **1** a chemical compound containing water that is chemically combined with a substance. **2** a crystalline chemical compound containing weakly bound water molecules. ◆ *vb* **hydrates, hydrating, hydrated.** **3** to undergo or cause to undergo treatment or impregnation with water.
▸ **hyˈdration** *n* ▸ ˈ**hydrator** *n*

hydrated (ˈhaɪdreɪtɪd) *adj* (of a compound) chemically bonded to water molecules.

hydraulic (haɪˈdrɒlɪk) *adj* **1** operated by pressure transmitted through a pipe by a liquid, such as water or oil. **2** of or employing liquids in motion. **3** of hydraulics. **4** hardening under water: *hydraulic cement.* ORIG C17: from L *hydraulicus,* from Gk *hudraulikos,* from *hudraulos* water organ, from HYDRO- + *aulos* pipe
▸ **hyˈdraulically** *adv*

hydraulic brake *n* a type of brake, used in motor vehicles, in which the braking force is transmitted from the brake pedal to the brakes by a liquid under pressure.

hydraulic coupling *n* another name for **torque converter.**

hydraulic press *n* a press that utilizes liquid pressure to enable a small force applied to a small piston to produce a large force on a larger piston.

hydraulic ram *n* **1** the larger or working piston of a hydraulic press. **2** a form of water pump utilizing the kinetic energy of running water to provide static pressure to raise water to a reservoir higher than the source.

hydraulics (haɪˈdrɒlɪks) *n* (*functioning as sing*) another name for **fluid mechanics.**

hydraulic suspension *n* a system of motor-vehicle suspension using hydraulic members, often with hydraulic compensation between front and rear systems (**hydroelastic suspension**).

hydrazine (ˈhaɪdrəˌziːn, -zɪn) *n* a colourless liquid made from sodium hypochlorite and ammonia: used as a rocket fuel. Formula: N_2H_4. ORIG C19: from HYDRO- + AZO + -INE[2]

hydric (ˈhaɪdrɪk) *adj* **1** of or containing hydrogen. **2** containing or using moisture.

hydride ('haɪdraɪd) *n* any compound of hydrogen with another element.

hydrilla (haɪ'drɪlə) *n* a type of underwater aquatic weed that was introduced from Asia into the south US, where it has become a serious problem, choking fish and hindering navigation. ORIG C20: NL, prob. from L *hydra*: see HYDRA

hydriodic acid (ˌhaɪdrɪ'ɒdɪk) *n* a solution of hydrogen iodide in water: a strong acid. ORIG C19: from HYDRO- + IODIC

hydro[1] ('haɪdrəʊ) *n, pl* **hydros.** *Brit.* (esp. formerly) a hotel or resort, often near a spa, offering facilities for hydropathic treatment.

hydro[2] ('haɪdrəʊ) *adj* **1** short for **hydroelectric.** ♦ *n* **2** a Canadian name for **electricity.**

Hydro ('haɪdrəʊ) *n* (esp. in Canada) a hydroelectric power company or board.

hydro- *or sometimes before a vowel* **hydr-** *combining form.* **1** indicating water or fluid: *hydrodynamics.* **2** indicating hydrogen in a chemical compound: *hydrochloric acid.* **3** indicating a hydroid: *hydrozoan.* ORIG from Gk *hudōr* water

hydrobromic acid (ˌhaɪdrəʊ'brəʊmɪk) *n* a solution of hydrogen bromide in water: a strong acid.

hydrocarbon (ˌhaɪdrəʊ'kɑːbᵊn) *n* any organic compound containing only carbon and hydrogen.

hydrocele ('haɪdrəʊˌsiːl) *n* an abnormal collection of fluid in any saclike space.

hydrocephalus (ˌhaɪdrəʊ'sɛfələs) *or* **hydrocephaly** (ˌhaɪdrəʊ'sɛfəlɪ) *n* accumulation of cerebrospinal fluid within the ventricles of the brain because its normal outlet has been blocked by congenital malformation or disease. Nontechnical name: **water on the brain.**
▸ **hydrocephalic** (ˌhaɪdrəʊsɛ'fælɪk) *or* ˌ**hydro'cephalous** *adj*

hydrochloric acid (ˌhaɪdrə'klɒrɪk) *n* a solution of hydrogen chloride in water: a strong acid used in many industrial and laboratory processes.

hydrochloride (ˌhaɪdrə'klɔːraɪd) *n* a quaternary salt formed by the addition of hydrochloric acid to an organic base.

hydrocyanic acid (ˌhaɪdrəʊsaɪ'ænɪk) *n* another name for **hydrogen cyanide.**

hydrodynamics (ˌhaɪdrəʊdaɪ'næmɪks, -dɪ-) *n* (*functioning as sing*) the branch of science concerned with the mechanical properties of fluids, esp. liquids. Also called: **hydromechanics.**

hydroelastic suspension (ˌhaɪdrəʊɪ'læstɪk) *n* See **hydraulic suspension.**

hydroelectric (ˌhaɪdrəʊɪ'lɛktrɪk) *adj* **1** generated by the pressure of falling water: *hydroelectric power.* **2** of the generation of electricity by water pressure: *a hydroelectric scheme.*
▸ **hydroelectricity** (ˌhaɪdrəʊɪlɛk'trɪsɪtɪ) *n*

hydrofluoric acid (ˌhaɪdrəʊfluː'ɒrɪk) *n* a solution of hydrogen fluoride in water: a strong acid that attacks glass.

hydrofoil ('haɪdrəˌfɔɪl) *n* **1** a fast light vessel the hull of which is raised out of the water on one or more pairs of fixed vanes. **2** any of these vanes.

hydroforming ('haɪdrəʊˌfɔːmɪŋ) *n* **1** *Chem.* the catalytic reforming of petroleum to increase the proportion of aromatic and branched-chain hydrocarbons. **2** *Engineering.* a forming process in which a metal is shaped by a punch forced against a die, consisting of a flexible bag containing a fluid.

hydrogen ('haɪdrɪdʒən) *n* **a** a flammable colourless gas that is the lightest and most abundant element in the universe. It occurs in water and in most organic compounds. Symbol: H; atomic no.: 1; atomic wt.: 1.007 94. **b** (*as modifier*): *hydrogen bomb.* ORIG C18: from F *hydrogène,* from HYDRO- + -GEN; because its combustion produces water
▸ **hydrogenous** (haɪ'drɒdʒɪnəs) *adj*

hydrogenate ('haɪdrədʒɪˌneɪt, haɪ'drɒdʒɪˌneɪt) *vb* **hydrogenates, hydrogenating, hydrogenated.** to undergo or cause to undergo a reaction with hydrogen: *to hydrogenate ethylene.*
▸ ˌ**hydrogen'ation** *n*

hydrogen bomb *n* a type of bomb in which energy is released by fusion of hydrogen nuclei to give helium nuclei. The energy required to initiate the fusion is provided by the detonation of an atomic bomb, which is surrounded by a hydrogen-containing substance. Also called: **H-bomb.**

hydrogen bond *n* a weak chemical bond between an electronegative atom, such as fluorine, oxygen, or nitrogen, and a hydrogen atom bound to another electronegative atom.

hydrogen bromide *n* **1** a colourless pungent gas used in organic synthesis. Formula: HBr. **2** an aqueous solution of hydrogen bromide; hydrobromic acid.

hydrogen carbonate *n* another name for **bicarbonate.**

hydrogen chloride *n* **1** a colourless pungent corrosive gas obtained by the action of sulphuric acid on sodium chloride: used in making vinyl chloride and other organic chemicals. Formula: HCl. **2** an aqueous solution of hydrogen chloride; hydrochloric acid.

hydrogen cyanide *n* a colourless poisonous liquid with a faint odour of bitter almonds. It forms prussic acid in aqueous solution and is used for making plastics and as a war gas. Formula: HCN. Also called: **hydrocyanic acid.**

hydrogen fluoride *n* **1** a colourless poisonous corrosive gas or liquid made by reaction between calcium fluoride and sulphuric acid: used as a fluorinating agent and catalyst. Formula: HF. **2** an aqueous solution of hydrogen fluoride; hydrofluoric acid.

hydrogen iodide *n* **1** a colourless poisonous corrosive gas obtained by a catalysed reaction between hydrogen and iodine vapour: used in making iodides. Formula HI. **2** an aqueous solution of this gas; hydriodic acid.

hydrogen ion *n* an ionized hydrogen atom, occurring in aqueous solutions of acids; proton. Formula: H^+.

hydrogenize *or* **hydrogenise** ('haɪdrədʒɪˌnaɪz, haɪ'drɒdʒɪˌnaɪz) *vb* **hydrogenizes, hydrogenizing, hydrogenized** *or* **hydrogenises, hydrogenising, hydrogenised.** a variant of **hydrogenate.**

hydrogen peroxide *n* a colourless oily unstable liquid used as a bleach and as an oxidizer in rocket fuels. Formula: H_2O_2.

hydrogen sulphide *n* a colourless poisonous gas with an odour of rotten eggs. Formula: H_2S. Also called: **sulphuretted hydrogen.**

hydrography (haɪ'drɒgrəfɪ) *n* the study, surveying, and mapping of the oceans, seas, and rivers.
▸ **hy'drographer** *n* ▸ **hydrographic** (ˌhaɪdrə'græfɪk) *adj*

hydroid ('haɪdrɔɪd) *adj* **1** of or relating to the *Hydroida,* an order of hydrozoan coelenterates that have the polyp phase dominant. **2** having or consisting of hydra-like polyps. ♦ *n* **3** a hydroid colony or individual.

hydrokinetics (ˌhaɪdrəʊkɪ'nɛtɪks, -kaɪ-) *n* (*functioning as sing*) the branch of science concerned with the behaviour and properties of fluids in motion. Also called: **hydrodynamics.**

hydrolase ('haɪdrəˌleɪz) *n* an enzyme that controls hydrolysis.

hydrology (haɪ'drɒlədʒɪ) *n* the study of the distribution, conservation, use, etc., of the water of the earth and its atmosphere.
▸ **hydrological** (ˌhaɪdrə'lɒdʒɪkᵊl) *adj* ▸ **hy'drologist** *n*

hydrolyse *or US* **hydrolyze** ('haɪdrəˌlaɪz) *vb* **hydrolyses, hydrolysing, hydrolysed** *or US* **hydrolyzes, hydrolyzing, hydrolyzed.** to subject to or undergo hydrolysis.

hydrolysis (haɪ'drɒlɪsɪs) *n* a chemical reaction in which a compound reacts with water to produce other compounds.
▸ **hydrolytic** (ˌhaɪdrə'lɪtɪk) *adj*

hydrolyte ('haɪdrəˌlaɪt) *n* a substance subjected to hydrolysis.

hydromel ('haɪdrəʊˌmɛl) *n Arch.* another word for **mead** (the drink). ORIG C15: from L, from Gk *hudromeli,* from HYDRO- + *meli* honey

hydrometer (haɪ'drɒmɪtə) *n* an instrument for measuring the relative density of a liquid.
▸ **hydrometric** (ˌhaɪdrəʊ'mɛtrɪk) *or* ˌ**hydro'metrical** *adj*

hydronaut ('haɪdrəʊˌnɔːt) *n US Navy.* a person trained to operate deep submergence vessels. ORIG C20: from Gk, from HYDRO- + *-naut,* as in *astronaut*

hydropathy (haɪ'drɒpəθɪ) *n* a pseudoscientific method of treating disease by the use of large quantities of water both internally and externally.
▸ **hydropathic** (ˌhaɪdrəʊ'pæθɪk) *adj*

hydrophilic (ˌhaɪdrəʊ'fɪlɪk) *adj Chem.* tending to dissolve in, mix with, or be wetted by water: *a hydrophilic colloid.*
▸ **hydrophile** ('haɪdrəʊˌfaɪl) *n*

hydrophobia (ˌhaɪdrə'fəʊbɪə) *n* **1** another name for **rabies. 2** a fear of drinking fluids, esp. that of a person with rabies, because of painful spasms when trying to swallow.
▸ **ˌhydro'phobic** *adj*

hydrophone ('haɪdrəˌfəʊn) *n* an electroacoustic transducer that converts sound travelling through water into electrical oscillations.

hydrophyte ('haɪdrəʊˌfaɪt) *n* a plant that grows only in water or very moist soil.

hydroplane ('haɪdrəʊˌpleɪn) *n* **1** a motorboat equipped with hydrofoils or with a shaped bottom that raises its hull out of the water at high speeds. **2** an attachment to an aircraft to enable it to glide along the surface of the water. **3** another name for a **seaplane. 4** a horizontal vane on the hull of a submarine for controlling its vertical motion. ◆ *vb* **hydroplanes, hydroplaning, hydroplaned. 5** *(intr)* (of a boat) to rise out of the water in the manner of a hydroplane.

hydroponics (ˌhaɪdrəʊ'pɒnɪks) *n (functioning as sing)* a method of cultivating plants by growing them in gravel, etc., through which water containing dissolved inorganic nutrient salts is pumped. ORIG C20: from HYDRO- + *(geo)ponics* science of agriculture
▸ **ˌhydro'ponic** *adj* ▸ **ˌhydro'ponically** *adv*

hydropower ('haɪdrəʊˌpaʊə) *n* hydroelectric power.

hydroquinone (ˌhaɪdrəʊkwɪ'nəʊn) *or* **hydroquinol** (ˌhaɪdrəʊ'kwɪnɒl) *n* a white crystalline soluble phenol used as a photographic developer.

hydrosphere ('haɪdrəˌsfɪə) *n* the watery part of the earth's surface, including oceans, lakes, water vapour in the atmosphere, etc.

hydrostatics (ˌhaɪdrəʊ'stætɪks) *n (functioning as sing)* the branch of science concerned with the mechanical properties and behaviour of fluids that are not in motion.
▸ **ˌhydro'static** *adj*

hydrotherapeutics (ˌhaɪdrəʊˌθɛrə'pjuːtɪks) *n (functioning as sing)* the branch of medical science concerned with hydrotherapy.

hydrotherapy (ˌhaɪdrəʊ'θɛrəpɪ) *n Med.* the treatment of certain diseases by the application of water, esp. by exercising in water to mobilize stiff joints or strengthen weak muscles.

hydrothermal (ˌhaɪdrəʊ'θɜːməl) *adj* of or relating to the action of water under conditions of high temperature, esp. in forming rocks.

hydrotropism (haɪ'drɒtrəˌpɪzəm) *n* the directional growth of plants in response to the stimulus of water.

hydrous ('haɪdrəs) *adj* containing water.

hydrovane ('haɪdrəʊˌveɪn) *n* a vane on a seaplane conferring stability on water (a sponson) or facilitating take-off (a hydrofoil).

hydroxide (haɪ'drɒksaɪd) *n* **1** a base or alkali containing the ion OH^-. **2** any compound containing an -OH group.

hydroxy (haɪ'drɒksɪ) *adj* (of a chemical compound) containing one or more hydroxyl groups. ORIG C19: HYDRO- + OXY(GEN)

hydroxyl (haɪ'drɒksɪl) *n (modifier)* of, consisting of, or containing the monovalent group -OH or the ion OH^-: *a hydroxyl group or radical.*

hydroxytryptamine (haɪˌdrɒksɪ'trɪptəˌmiːn) *n* 5-hydroxytryptamine: another name for **serotonin.** Abbrev.: **5HT.**

hydrozoan (ˌhaɪdrəʊ'zəʊən) *n* **1** any coelenterate of the class *Hydrozoa,* which includes the hydra and the Portuguese man-of-war. ◆ *adj* **2** of the *Hydrozoa.*

hyena *or* **hyaena** (haɪ'iːnə) *n* any of several long-legged carnivorous doglike mammals such as the spotted or laughing hyena, of Africa and S Asia. ORIG C16: from Med. L, from L *hyaena,* from Gk, from *hus* hog
▸ **hy'enic** *or* **hy'aenic** *adj*

Hygeia ★ (haɪ'dʒiːə) *n* the Greek goddess of health.
▸ **Hy'geian** *adj*

hygiene ('haɪdʒiːn) *n* **1** Also called: **hygienics.** the science concerned with the maintenance of health. **2** clean or healthy practices or thinking: *personal hygiene.* ORIG C18: from NL *hygiēna,* from Gk *hugieinē,* from *hugiēs* healthy

hygienic (haɪ'dʒiːnɪk) *adj* promoting health or cleanliness; sanitary.
▸ **hy'gienically** *adv*

hygienics (haɪ'dʒiːnɪks) *n (functioning as sing)* another word for **hygiene** (sense 1).

hygienist ('haɪdʒiːnɪst) *n* a person skilled in the practice of hygiene.

hygro- *or before a vowel* **hygr-** *combining form.* indicating moisture: *hygrometer.* ORIG from Gk *hugros* wet

hygrometer (haɪ'grɒmɪtə) *n* any of various instruments for measuring humidity.
▸ **hygrometric** (ˌhaɪgrə'mɛtrɪk) *adj*

hygrophyte ('haɪgrəˌfaɪt) *n* any plant that grows in wet or waterlogged soil.
▸ **hygrophytic** (ˌhaɪgrə'fɪtɪk) *adj*

hygroscope ('haɪgrəˌskəʊp) *n* any device that indicates the humidity of the air without necessarily measuring it.

hygroscopic (ˌhaɪgrə'skɒpɪk) *adj* (of a substance) tending to absorb water from the air.
▸ **ˌhygro'scopically** *adv*

hying ('haɪɪŋ) *vb* a present participle of **hie.**

hyla ('haɪlə) *n* a tree frog of tropical America. ORIG C19: from NL, from Gk *hulē* forest

hylomorphism (ˌhaɪlə'mɔːfɪzəm) *n* the philosophical doctrine that identifies matter with the first cause of the universe.

hylozoism (ˌhaɪlə'zəʊɪzəm) *n* the philosophical doctrine that life is one of the properties of matter. ORIG C17: from Gk *hulē* wood, matter + *zōē* life

hymen ('haɪmɛn) *n Anat.* a fold of mucous membrane that partly covers the entrance to the vagina and is usually ruptured when sexual intercourse takes place for the first time. ORIG C17: from Gk: membrane
▸ **'hymenal** *adj*

Hymen ★ ('haɪmɛn) *n* the Greek and Roman god of marriage.

hymeneal (ˌhaɪmɛ'niːəl) *adj* **1** *Chiefly poetic.* of or relating to marriage. ◆ *n* **2** a wedding song or poem.

hymenopteran (ˌhaɪmɪ'nɒptərən) *or* **hymenopteron** *n, pl* **hymenopterans, hymenoptera** (-tərə), *or* **hymenopterons.** any hymenopterous insect.

hymenopterous (ˌhaɪmɪ'nɒptərəs) *adj* of or belonging to an order of insects, including bees, wasps, and ants, having two pairs of membranous wings. ORIG C19: from Gk *humenopteros* membrane wing; see HYMEN, -PTEROUS

Hymettus ★ (haɪ'mɛtəs) *n* a mountain in SE Greece, in Attica east of Athens: famous for its marble and for honey. Height: 1032 m (3386 ft). Modern Greek name: **Imittós.**
▸ **Hy'mettian** *or* **Hy'mettic** *adj*

hymn (hɪm) *n* **1** a Christian song of praise sung to God or a saint. **2** a similar song praising other gods, a nation, etc. ◆ *vb* **3** to express (praises, thanks, etc.) by singing hymns. ORIG C13: from L *hymnus,* from Gk *humnos*
▸ **hymnic** ('hɪmnɪk) *adj*

hymnal ('hɪmnᵊl) *n* **1** Also: **hymn book.** a book of hymns. ◆ *adj* **2** of, relating to, or characteristic of hymns.

hymnody ('hɪmnədɪ) *n* **1** the composition or singing of hymns. **2** hymns collectively. ◆ Also called: **hymnology.** ORIG C18: from Med. L *hymnōdia,* from Gk, from *humnōidein,* from HYMN + *aeidein* to sing

hymnology (hɪm'nɒlədʒɪ) *n* **1** the study of hymn composition. **2** another word for **hymnody.**
▸ **hym'nologist** *n*

hyoid ('haɪɔɪd) *adj* of or relating to the **hyoid bone,** the horseshoe-shaped bone that lies at the base of the tongue. ORIG C19: from NL *hyoïdes,* from Gk *huoeidēs* having the shape of the letter UPSILON, from *hu* upsilon + -OID

hyoscine ('haɪəˌsiːn) *n* another name for **scopolamine.** ORIG C19: from *huosc(yamus)* a medicinal plant + -INE²; see HYOSCYAMINE

hyoscyamine (ˌhaɪə'saɪəˌmiːn) *n* a poisonous alkaloid occurring in henbane and related plants: used in medicine. ORIG C19: from NL, from Gk *huoskuamos* (from *hus* pig + *kuamos* bean) + AMINE

hyp. *abbrev. for:* **1** hypotenuse. **2** hypothesis. **3** hypothetical.

hypaethral *or US* **hypethral** (hɪ'piːθrəl, haɪ-) *adj* (esp. of a classical temple) having no roof. ORIG C18: from L *hypaethrus* uncovered, from Gk, from HYPO- + *aithros* clear sky

hypallage (haɪ'pæləˌdʒiː) *n Rhetoric.* a figure of speech in which the natural relations of two words in a statement are interchanged, as in *the fire spread the wind.* ORIG C16: via LL from Gk *hupallagē,* from HYPO- + *allassein* to exchange

Hypatia ★ (haɪ'peɪʃɪə) *n* died 415 A.D., Neo-Platonist philosopher and politician, who lectured at Alexandria. She was murdered by a Christian mob.

hype¹ (haɪp) *Sl.* ◆ *n* **1** an intensive or exaggerated publicity or sales promotion. **2** a deception or racket. ◆ *vb* **hypes, hyping, hyped. 3** (*tr*) to market or promote (a product) using intensive or exaggerated publicity. ORIG C20: from ?

hype² (haɪp) *Sl.* ◆ *n* **1** a hypodermic needle or injection. ◆ *vb* **hypes, hyping, hyped. 2** (*intr;* usually foll. by *up*) to inject oneself with a drug. **3** (*tr*) to stimulate artificially or excite. ORIG C20: shortened from HYPODERMIC

hyped up *adj Sl.* stimulated or excited by or as if by the effect of a stimulating drug.

hyper ('haɪpə) *adj Inf.* overactive; overexcited. ORIG C20: prob. independent use of HYPER-

hyper- *prefix* **1** above, over, or in excess: *hypercritical.* **2** denoting an abnormal excess: *hyperacidity.* **3** indicating that a chemical compound contains a greater than usual amount of an element: *hyperoxide.* ORIG from Gk *huper* over

hyperacidity (ˌhaɪpərə'sɪdɪtɪ) *n* excess acidity of the gastrointestinal tract, esp. the stomach, producing a burning sensation.

hyperactive (ˌhaɪpər'æktɪv) *adj* abnormally active.
▸ **ˌhyperac'tivity** *n*

hyperaemia *or US* **hyperemia** (ˌhaɪpər'iːmɪə) *n Pathol.* an excessive amount of blood in an organ or part.

hyperaesthesia *or US* **hyperesthesia** (ˌhaɪpəriːs'θiːzɪə) *n Pathol.* increased sensitivity of any of the sense organs.
▸ **hyperaesthetic** *or US* **hyperesthetic** (ˌhaɪpəriːs'θɛtɪk) *adj*

hyperbaton (haɪ'pɜːbəˌtɒn) *n Rhetoric.* a figure of speech in which the normal order of words is reversed, as in *cheese I love.* ORIG C16: via L from Gk, lit.: an overstepping, from HYPER- + *bainein* to step

hyperbola (haɪ'pɜːbələ) *n, pl* **hyperbolas** *or* **hyperbole** (-ˌliː). a conic section formed by a plane that cuts both bases of a cone: it consists of two branches asymptotic to two intersecting fixed lines. ORIG C17: from Gk *huperbolē,* lit.: excess, extravagance, from HYPER- + *ballein* to throw

hyperbole (haɪ'pɜːbəlɪ) *n* a deliberate exaggeration used for effect: *he embraced her a thousand times.* ORIG C16: from Gk, from HYPER- + *bolē,* from *ballein* to throw
▸ **hy'perbolism** *n*

hyperbolic (ˌhaɪpə'bɒlɪk) *or* **hyperbolical** *adj* **1** of a hyperbola. **2** *Rhetoric.* of a hyperbole.
▸ **ˌhyper'bolically** *adv*

hyperbolic function *n* any of a group of functions of an angle expressed as a relationship between the distances of a point on a hyperbola to the origin and to the coordinate axes.

hyperbolize *or* **hyperbolise** (haɪ'pɜːbəˌlaɪz) *vb* **hyperbolizes, hyperbolizing, hyperbolized** *or* **hyperbolises, hyperbolising, hyperbolised.** to express (something) by means of hyperbole.

hyperboloid (haɪ'pɜːbəˌlɔɪd) *n* a geometric surface consisting of one sheet, or of two sheets separated by a finite distance, whose sections parallel to the three coordinate planes are hyperbolas or ellipses.

Hyperborean ★ (ˌhaɪpə'bɔːrɪən) *n* **1** *Greek myth.* one of a people believed to have lived beyond the North Wind in a sunny land. **2** an inhabitant of the extreme north. ◆ *adj* **3** (*sometimes not cap.*) of or relating to the extreme north. ORIG C16: from L *hyperboreus,* from Gk, from HYPER- + *Boreas* the north wind

hypercharge ('haɪpəˌtʃɑːdʒ) *n* a property of baryons that is used to account for the absence of certain strong interaction decays.

hypercholesterolaemia *or US* **hypercholesterolemia** (ˌhaɪpəkəˌlɛstərɒl'iːmɪə) *n* the condition of having high levels of cholesterol in the blood, predisposing to atherosclerosis of the coronary arteries.

hypercorrect (ˌhaɪpəkə'rɛkt) *adj* **1** excessively correct or fastidious. **2** resulting from or characterized by hypercorrection.

hypercorrection (ˌhaɪpəkə'rɛkʃən) *n* a mistaken correction to text or speech made through a desire to avoid nonstandard pronunciation or grammar: *"between you and I" is a hypercorrection of "between you and me."*

hypercritical (ˌhaɪpə'krɪtɪkᵊl) *adj* excessively or severely critical.
▸ **ˌhyper'critically** *adv*

hyperfocal distance (ˌhaɪpə'fəʊkᵊl) *n* the distance from a camera lens to the point beyond which all objects appear sharp and clearly defined.

hyperglycaemia *or US* **hyperglycemia** (ˌhaɪpəglaɪ'siːmɪə) *n Pathol.* an abnormally large amount of sugar in the blood. ORIG C20: from HYPER- + GLYCO- + -AEMIA
▸ **ˌhypergly'caemic** *or US* **ˌhypergly'cemic** *adj*

hypergolic (ˌhaɪpə'gɒlɪk) *adj* (of a rocket fuel) able to ignite spontaneously on contact with an oxidizer. ORIG C20: from G *Hypergol* (?from HYP(ER-) + ERG¹ + -OL²) + -IC

hypericum (haɪ'pɛrɪkəm) *n* any herbaceous plant or shrub of the temperate genus *Hypericum.* See **rose of Sharon, Saint John's wort.** ORIG C16: via L from Gk *hupereikon,* from HYPER- + *ereikē* heath

hyperinflation (ˌhaɪpəɪn'fleɪʃən) *n* an extremely high level of inflation (with price rises of 50 percent per month), often involving social disorder.

Hyperion ★ (haɪ'pɪərɪən) *n Greek myth.* a Titan, son of Uranus and Gaea, father of Helios (sun), Selene (moon), and Eos (dawn).

hyperlink ('haɪpəˌlɪŋk) *n* **1** a word, phrase, picture, icon, etc., in a computer document on which a user may click to move to another part of the document or to another document. ◆ *vb* **2** (*tr*) to link (files) in this way. ◆ Often shortened to **link.**

hypermarket ('haɪpəˌmɑːkɪt) *n Brit.* a huge self-service store, usually built on the outskirts of a town. ORIG C20: translation of F *hypermarché*

hypermedia ('haɪpəˌmiːdɪə) *n* computer software and hardware that allows users to interact with text, graphics, sound, and video, each of which can be accessed from within any of the others. Cf. **hypertext.**

hypermetropia (ˌhaɪpəmɪ'trəʊpɪə) *or* **hypermetropy** (ˌhaɪpə'mɛtrəpɪ) *n Pathol.* a variant of **hyperopia.** ORIG C19: from Gk *hupermetros* beyond measure (from HYPER- + *metron* measure) + -OPIA

hyperon ('haɪpəˌrɒn) *n Physics.* any baryon that is not a nucleon. ORIG C20: from HYPER- + -ON

hyperopia (ˌhaɪpə'rəʊpɪə) *n* inability to see near objects clearly because the images received by the eye are focused behind the retina; long-sightedness.
▸ **hyperopic** (ˌhaɪpə'rɒpɪk) *adj*

hyperphysical (ˌhaɪpə'fɪzɪkᵊl) *adj* beyond the physical; supernatural or immaterial.

hyperpyrexia (ˌhaɪpəpaɪˈrɛksɪə) *n Pathol.* an extremely high fever, with a temperature of 41°C (106°F) or above.

hypersensitive (ˌhaɪpəˈsɛnsɪtɪv) *adj* **1** having unduly vulnerable feelings. **2** abnormally sensitive to an allergen, a drug, or other agent.
▸ **ˌhyperˈsensitiveness** *or* **ˌhyperˌsensiˈtivity** *n*

hypersonic (ˌhaɪpəˈsɒnɪk) *adj* concerned with or having a velocity of at least five times that of sound in the same medium under the same conditions.
▸ **ˌhyperˈsonics** *n*

hyperspace (ˌhaɪpəˈspeɪs) *n* **1** *Maths.* space having more than three dimensions. **2** (in science fiction) a theoretical dimension within which conventional space-time relationship does not apply.

hypersthene (ˈhaɪpəˌsθiːn) *n* a green, brown, or black pyroxene mineral. ORIG C19: from HYPER- + Gk *sthenos* strength

hypertension (ˌhaɪpəˈtɛnʃən) *n Pathol.* abnormally high blood pressure.
▸ **hypertensive** (ˌhaɪpəˈtɛnsɪv) *adj, n*

hypertext (ˈhaɪpəˌtɛkst) *n* computer software and hardware that allows users to create, store, and view text and move between related items easily and in a nonsequential way.

hyperthermia (ˌhaɪpəˈθɜːmɪə) *or* **hyperthermy** (ˌhaɪpəˈθɜːmɪ) *n Pathol.* a variant of **hyperpyrexia.**
▸ **ˌhyperˈthermal** *adj*

hyperthermophile (ˌhaɪpəˈθɜːməυˌfaɪl) *n* an organism, esp. a bacterium, that lives at high temperatures (above 80°C), found in some hot springs.
▸ **hyperthermophilic** (ˌhaɪpəˌθɜːməυˈfɪlɪk) *adj*

hyperthyroidism (ˌhaɪpəˈθaɪrɔɪˌdɪzəm) *n* overproduction of thyroid hormone by the thyroid gland, causing nervousness, insomnia, and sensitivity to heat.
▸ **ˌhyperˈthyriod** *adj, n*

hypertonic (ˌhaɪpəˈtɒnɪk) *adj* **1** (esp. of muscles) being in a state of abnormally high tension. **2** (of a solution) having a higher osmotic pressure than that of a specified solution.

hypertrophy (haɪˈpɜːtrəfɪ) *n, pl* **hypertrophies. 1** enlargement of an organ or part resulting from an increase in the size of the cells. ◆ *vb* **hypertrophies, hypertrophying, hypertrophied. 2** to undergo or cause to undergo this condition.

hyperventilation (ˌhaɪpəˌvɛntɪˈleɪʃən) *n* an increase in the rate of breathing, sometimes resulting in cramp and dizziness.
▸ **ˌhyperˈventiˌlate** *vb*

hypha (ˈhaɪfə) *n, pl* **hyphae** (-fiː). any of the filaments that constitute the body (mycelium) of a fungus. ORIG C19: from NL, from Gk *huphē* web
▸ **ˈhyphal** *adj*

hyphen (ˈhaɪfᵊn) *n* **1** the punctuation mark **hyphen**, used to separate parts of compound words, to link the words of a phrase, and between syllables of a word split between two consecutive lines. ◆ *vb* **2** (*tr*) another word for **hyphenate.** ORIG C17: from LL (meaning: the combining of two words), from Gk *huphen* (adv) together, from HYPO- + *heis* one

hyphenate (ˈhaɪfᵊˌneɪt) *vb* **hyphenates, hyphenating, hyphenated.** (*tr*) to separate (words, etc.) with a hyphen.
▸ **ˌhyphenˈation** *n*

hyphenated (ˈhaɪfᵊˌneɪtɪd) *adj* **1** containing or linked with a hyphen. **2** *Chiefly US.* having a nationality denoted by a hyphenated word: *Irish-American.*

hypno- *or before a vowel* **hypn-** *combining form.* **1** indicating sleep: *hypnopaedia.* **2** relating to hypnosis: *hypnotherapy.* ORIG from Gk *hupnos* sleep

hypnoid (ˈhɪpˌnɔɪd) *or* **hypnoidal** (hɪpˈnɔɪdᵊl) *adj Psychol.* of or relating to a state resembling sleep or hypnosis.

hypnology (hɪpˈnɒlədʒɪ) *n Psychol.* the study of sleep and hypnosis.
▸ **hypˈnologist** *n*

hypnopaedia (ˌhɪpnəυˈpiːdɪə) *n* the learning of lessons heard during sleep. ORIG C20: from HYPNO- + Gk *paideia* education

hypnopompic (ˌhɪpnəυˈpɒmpɪk) *adj Psychol.* relating to the state existing between sleep and full waking, characterized by the persistence of dreamlike imagery. ORIG C20: from HYPNO- + Gk *pompē* a sending forth, escort + -IC

Hypnos ★ (ˈhɪpnɒs) *n Greek myth.* the god of sleep. Roman counterpart: **Somnus.** Cf. **Morpheus.** ORIG Gk: sleep

hypnosis (hɪpˈnəυsɪs) *n, pl* **hypnoses** (-siːz). an artificially induced state of relaxation and concentration in which deeper parts of the mind become more accessible.

hypnotherapy (ˌhɪpnəυˈθɛrəpɪ) *n* the use of hypnosis in the treatment of emotional and psychogenic problems.
▸ **ˌhypnoˈtherapist** *n*

hypnotic (hɪpˈnɒtɪk) *adj* **1** of or producing hypnosis or sleep. **2** (of a person) susceptible to hypnotism. ◆ *n* **3** a drug that induces sleep. **4** a person susceptible to hypnosis. ORIG C17: from LL *hypnōticus,* from Gk, from *hupnoun* to put to sleep, from *hupnos* sleep
▸ **hypˈnotically** *adv*

hypnotism (ˈhɪpnəˌtɪzəm) *n* **1** the scientific study and practice of hypnosis. **2** the process of inducing hypnosis.
▸ **ˈhypnotist** *n*

hypnotize *or* **hypnotise** (ˈhɪpnəˌtaɪz) *vb* **hypnotizes, hypnotizing, hypnotized** *or* **hypnotises, hypnotising, hypnotised.** (*tr*) **1** to induce hypnosis in (a person). **2** to charm or beguile; fascinate.
▸ **ˌhypnotiˈzation** *or* **ˌhypnotiˈsation** *n* ▸ **ˈhypnoˌtizer** *or* **ˈhypnoˌtiser** *n*

hypo[1] (ˈhaɪpəυ) *n* short for **hyposulphite.** ORIG C19

hypo[2] (ˈhaɪpəυ) *n, pl* **hypos.** *Inf.* short for **hypodermic syringe.**

hypo- *or before a vowel* **hyp-** *prefix* **1** beneath or below: *hypodermic.* **2** lower: *hypogastrium.* **3** less than; denoting a deficiency: *hypothyroid.* **4** indicating that a chemical compound contains an element in a lower oxidation state than usual: *hypochlorous acid.* ORIG from Gk, from *hupo* under

hypoallergenic (ˌhaɪpəυˌæləˈdʒɛnɪk) *adj* (of cosmetics, earrings, etc.) not likely to cause an allergic reaction.

hypoblast (ˈhaɪpəˌblæst) *n Embryol.* the inner layer of an embryo at an early stage of development that becomes the endoderm.

hypocaust (ˈhaɪpəˌkɔːst) *n* an ancient Roman heating system in which hot air circulated under the floor and between double walls. ORIG C17: from L *hypocaustum,* from Gk, from *hupokaiein* to light a fire beneath, from HYPO- + *kaiein* to burn

hypocentre (ˈhaɪpəυˌsɛntə) *n* the point immediately below the centre of explosion of a nuclear bomb. Also called: **ground zero.**

hypochlorite (ˌhaɪpəˈklɔːraɪt) *n* any salt or ester of hypochlorous acid.

hypochlorous acid (ˌhaɪpəˈklɔːrəs) *n* an unstable acid known only in solution and in the form of its salts: a strong oxidizing and bleaching agent. Formula: HOCl.

hypochondria (ˌhaɪpəˈkɒndrɪə) *n* chronic abnormal anxiety concerning the state of one's health. Also called: **hypochondriasis** (ˌhaɪpəkɒnˈdraɪəsɪs). ORIG C18: from LL: abdomen, supposedly the seat of melancholy, from Gk, from *hupokhondrios,* from HYPO- + *khondros* cartilage

hypochondriac (ˌhaɪpəˈkɒndrɪˌæk) *n* **1** a person suffering from hypochondria. ◆ *adj also* **hypochondriacal** (ˌhaɪpəkɒnˈdraɪəkᵊl). **2** relating to or suffering from hypochondria.

hypocorism (haɪˈpɒkəˌrɪzəm) *n* a pet name, esp. one using a diminutive affix: *"Sally" is a hypocorism for "Sarah".* ORIG C19: from Gk *hupo-korisma,* from *hupokorizesthai* to use pet names, from *hypo-* beneath + *korizesthai,* from *korē* girl, *koros* boy
▸ **hypocoristic** (ˌhaɪpəkɔːˈrɪstɪk) *adj*

hypocotyl (ˌhaɪpəˈkɒtɪl) *n* the part of an embryo plant between the cotyledons and the radicle. ORIG C19: from HYPO- + COTYL(EDON)

hypocrisy (hɪˈpɒkrəsɪ) *n, pl* **hypocrisies. 1** the practice of professing standards, beliefs, etc., contrary to one's real character or actual behaviour. **2** an act or instance of this.

hypocrite (ˈhɪpəkrɪt) *n* a person who pretends to be

what he or she is not. ORIG C13: from OF *ipocrite,* via LL from Gk *hupokritēs* one who plays a part, from *hupokrinein* to feign, from *krinein* to judge
▸ ˌ**hypo'critical** *adj* ▸ ˌ**hypo'critically** *adv*

hypocycloid (ˌhaɪpə'saɪklɔɪd) *n* a curve described by a point on the circumference of a circle as the circle rolls around the inside of a fixed coplanar circle.
▸ ˌ**hypocy'cloidal** *adj*

hypodermic (ˌhaɪpə'dɜːmɪk) *adj* **1** of or relating to the region of the skin beneath the epidermis. **2** injected beneath the skin. ◆ *n* **3** a hypodermic syringe or needle. **4** a hypodermic injection.
▸ ˌ**hypo'dermically** *adv*

hypodermic syringe *n Med.* a type of syringe consisting of a hollow cylinder, usually of glass or plastic, a tightly fitting piston, and a hollow needle (**hypodermic needle**), used for withdrawing blood samples, etc.

hypodermis (ˌhaɪpə'dɜːmɪs) *or* **hypoderm** *n* **1** *Bot.* a layer of thick-walled supportive or water-storing cells beneath the epidermis in some plants. **2** *Zool.* the epidermis of arthropods, annelids, etc. ORIG C19: from HYPO- + EPIDERMIS

hypogastrium (ˌhaɪpə'gæstrɪəm) *n, pl* **hypogastria** (-trɪə). *Anat.* the lower front central region of the abdomen. ORIG C17: from NL, from Gk *hupogastrion,* from HYPO- + *gastrion,* dim. of *gastēr* stomach

hypogeal (ˌhaɪpə'dʒiːəl) *or* **hypogeous** *adj* occurring or living below the surface of the ground. ORIG C19: from L *hypogēus,* from Gk, from HYPO- + *gē* earth

hypogene ('haɪpəˌdʒiːn) *adj* formed or originating beneath the surface of the earth.

hypogeum (ˌhaɪpə'dʒiːəm) *n, pl* **hypogea** (-'dʒiːə). an underground vault, esp. one used for burials. ORIG C18: from L, from Gk *hupogeion;* see HYPOGEAL

hypoid gear ('haɪpɔɪd) *n* a gear having a tooth form generated by a hypocycloidal curve. ORIG C20: *hypoid,* shortened from HYPOCYCLOID

hyponasty ('haɪpəˌnæstɪ) *n* increased growth of the lower surface of a plant part, resulting in an upward bending of the part.
▸ ˌ**hypo'nastic** *adj*

hypophosphate (ˌhaɪpə'fɒsfeɪt) *n* any salt or ester of hypophosphoric acid.

hypophosphite (ˌhaɪpə'fɒsfaɪt) *n* any salt of hypophosphorous acid.

hypophosphoric acid (ˌhaɪpəfɒs'fɒrɪk) *n* a tetrabasic acid produced by the slow oxidation of phosphorus in moist air. Formula: $H_4P_2O_6$.

hypophosphorous acid (ˌhaɪpə'fɒsfərəs) *n* a monobasic acid and a reducing agent. Formula: H_3PO_2.

hypophysis (haɪ'pɒfɪsɪs) *n, pl* **hypophyses** (-ˌsiːz). the technical name for **pituitary gland.** ORIG C18: from Gk: outgrowth, from HYPO- + *phuein* to grow
▸ **hypophyseal** *or* **hypophysial** (ˌhaɪpə'fɪzɪəl, haɪˌpɒfɪ'sɪəl) *adj*

hypostasis (haɪ'pɒstəsɪs) *n, pl* **hypostases** (-ˌsiːz). **1** *Metaphysics.* the essential nature of a substance. **2** *Christianity.* **2a** any of the three persons of the Godhead. **2b** the one person of Christ in which the divine and human natures are united. **3** the accumulation of blood in an organ or part as the result of poor circulation. ORIG C16: from LL: substance, from Gk *hupostasis* foundation, from *huphistasthai,* from HYPO- + *histanai* to cause to stand
▸ **hypostatic** (ˌhaɪpə'stætɪk) *or* ˌ**hypo'statical** *adj*

hypostyle ('haɪpəʊˌstaɪl) *adj* **1** having a roof supported by columns. ◆ *n* **2** a building constructed in this way.

hyposulphite (ˌhaɪpə'sʌlfaɪt) *n* another name for **sodium thiosulphate,** esp. when used as a photographic fixer. Often shortened to **hypo.**

hyposulphurous acid (ˌhaɪpə'sʌlfərəs) *n* an unstable acid known only in solution: a powerful reducing agent. Formula $H_2S_2O_4$.

hypotension (ˌhaɪpəʊ'tɛnʃən) *n Pathol.* abnormally low blood pressure.
▸ **hypotensive** (ˌhaɪpəʊ'tɛnsɪv) *adj*

hypotenuse (haɪ'pɒtɪˌnjuːz) *n* the side in a right-angled triangle that is opposite the right angle. Abbrev.: **hyp.** ORIG C16: from L *hypotēnūsa,* from Gk *hupoteinousa grammē* subtending line, from HYPO- + *teinein* to stretch

hypothalamus (ˌhaɪpə'θæləməs) *n, pl* **hypothalami** (-ˌmaɪ). a neural control centre at the base of the brain, concerned with hunger, thirst, satiety, and other autonomic functions.
▸ **hypothalamic** (ˌhaɪpəθə'læmɪk) *adj*

hypothec (haɪ'pɒθɪk) *n Roman & Scots Law.* a charge on property in favour of a creditor. ORIG C16: from LL *hypotheca,* from Gk *hupothēkē* pledge, from *hupotithenai* to deposit as a security, from HYPO- + *tithenai* to place

hypothecate (haɪ'pɒθɪˌkeɪt) *vb* **hypothecates, hypothecating, hypothecated.** (*tr*) **1** *Law.* to pledge (personal property or a ship) as security for a debt without transferring possession or title. **2** to reserve (the proceeds) from (a tax or duty) for use in a particular way: *we intend to hypothecate the penny on income tax for education.*
▸ **hyˌpothe'cation** *n* ▸ **hy'potheˌcator** *n*

hypothermia (ˌhaɪpəʊ'θɜːmɪə) *n* **1** *Pathol.* an abnormally low body temperature, as induced in the elderly by exposure to cold weather. **2** *Med.* the intentional reduction of normal body temperature to reduce the patient's metabolic rate.

hypothesis (haɪ'pɒθɪsɪs) *n, pl* **hypotheses** (-ˌsiːz). **1** a suggested explanation for a group of facts or phenomena, either accepted as a basis for further verification (**working hypothesis**) or accepted as likely to be true. **2** an assumption used in an argument; supposition. ORIG C16: from Gk, from *hupotithenai* to propose, lit.: put under; see HYPO-, THESIS
▸ **hy'pothesist** *n*

hypothesize *or* **hypothesise** (haɪ'pɒθɪˌsaɪz) *vb* **hypothesizes, hypothesizing, hypothesized** *or* **hypothesises, hypothesising, hypothesised.** to form or assume as a hypothesis.
▸ **hy'potheˌsizer** *or* **hy'potheˌsiser** *n*

hypothetical (ˌhaɪpə'θɛtɪkᵊl) *or* **hypothetic** *adj* **1** having the nature of a hypothesis. **2** assumed or thought to exist. **3** *Logic.* another word for **conditional** (sense 3).
▸ ˌ**hypo'thetically** *adv*

hypothyroidism (ˌhaɪpəʊ'θaɪrɔɪˌdɪzəm) *n Pathol.* **1** insufficient production of thyroid hormones by the thyroid gland. **2** any disorder, such as cretinism or myxoedema, resulting from this.
▸ ˌ**hypo'thyroid** *n, adj*

hypotonic (ˌhaɪpə'tɒnɪk) *adj* **1** *Pathol.* (of muscles) lacking normal tone or tension. **2** (of a solution) having a lower osmotic pressure than that of a specified solution.

hypoxia (haɪ'pɒksɪə) *n* deficiency in the amount of oxygen delivered to the body tissues. ORIG C20: from HYPO- + OXY-[2] + -IA
▸ **hypoxic** (haɪ'pɒksɪk) *adj*

Hypsilantis *or* **Hypsilantes** ★ (*Greek* ˌipsi'landis) *n* variants of **Ypsilanti.**

hypso- *or before a vowel* **hyps-** *combining form.* indicating height: *hypsometry.* ORIG from Gk *hupsos*

hypsography (hɪp'sɒgrəfɪ) *n* the scientific study and mapping of the earth's topography above sea level.

hypsometer (hɪp'sɒmɪtə) *n* **1** an instrument for measuring altitudes by determining the boiling point of water at a given altitude. **2** any instrument used to calculate the heights of trees by triangulation.

hypsometry (hɪp'sɒmɪtrɪ) *n* (in mapping) the establishment of height above sea level.

hyrax ('haɪræks) *n, pl* **hyraxes** *or* **hyraces** ('haɪrəˌsiːz). any of various agile herbivorous mammals of Africa and SW Asia. They resemble rodents but have feet with hooflike toes. Also called: **dassie.** ORIG C19: from NL, from Gk *hurax* shrewmouse

Hyrcania ★ (hɜː'keɪnɪə) *n* an ancient district of Asia, southeast of the Caspian Sea.
▸ **Hyr'canian** *adj*

hyssop ('hɪsəp) *n* **1** a widely cultivated Asian plant with spikes of small blue flowers and aromatic leaves, used as a condiment and in perfumery and folk medicine. **2** a

Biblical plant, used for sprinkling in the ritual practices of the Hebrews. ORIG OE *ysope,* from L *hyssōpus,* from Gk *hussōpos,* of Semitic origin

hysterectomy (ˌhɪstəˈrɛktəmɪ) *n, pl* **hysterectomies.** surgical removal of the uterus.

hysteresis (ˌhɪstəˈriːsɪs) *n Physics.* the lag in a variable property of a system with respect to the effect producing it as this effect varies, esp. the phenomenon in which the magnetic induction of a ferromagnetic material lags behind the changing external field. ORIG from Gk *husterēsis,* from *husteros* coming after
▸ **hysteretic** (ˌhɪstəˈrɛtɪk) *adj*

hysteresis loop *n* a closed curve showing the variation of the magnetic induction of a ferromagnetic material with the external magnetic field producing it, when this field is changed through a complete cycle.

hysteria (hɪˈstɪərɪə) *n* **1** a mental disorder characterized by emotional outbursts and, often, symptoms such as paralysis. **2** any frenzied emotional state, esp. of laughter or crying. ORIG C19: from NL, from L *hystericus* HYSTERIC

hysteric (hɪˈstɛrɪk) *n* **1** a hysterical person. ◆ *adj* **2** hysterical. ORIG C17: from L *hystericus,* lit.: of the womb, from Gk, from *hustera* womb; from the belief that hysteria in women originated in disorders of the womb

hysterical (hɪˈstɛrɪkᵊl) *adj* **1** suggesting hysteria: *hysterical cries.* **2** suffering from hysteria. **3** *Inf.* wildly funny.
▸ **hysˈterically** *adv*

hysterics (hɪˈstɛrɪks) *n* (*functioning as pl or sing*) **1** an attack of hysteria. **2** *Inf.* wild uncontrollable bursts of laughter.

hystero- *or before a vowel* **hyster-** *combining form.* the uterus: *hysterectomy.* ORIG from Gk *hustera* womb

hysteron proteron (ˈhɪstəˌrɒn ˈprɒtəˌrɒn) *n* **1** *Logic.* a fallacious argument in which the proposition to be proved is assumed as a premise. **2** *Rhetoric.* a figure of speech in which the normal order of two sentences, clauses, etc., is reversed: *bred and born* (for *born and bred*). ORIG C16: from LL, from Gk *husteron proteron* the latter (placed as) former

hystricomorph (hɪˈstraɪkəʊˌmɔːf) *n* **1** any rodent of the suborder *Hystricomorpha,* which includes porcupines, cavies, agoutis, and chinchillas. ◆ *adj also* **hystricomorphic** (hɪˌstraɪkəʊˈmɔːfɪk). **2** of the *Hystricomorpha.* ORIG C19: from L *hystrix* porcupine, from Gk *hustrix*

Hywel Dda *or* **Howel Dda** ★ (ˈhaʊəl ˈðɑː) *n* known as *Hywel the Good.* died 950 A.D., Welsh prince. He united S and N Wales and codified Welsh law.

Hz *symbol for* hertz.

Ii

i *or* **I** (aɪ) *n, pl* **i's, I's,** *or* **Is. 1** the ninth letter and third vowel of the English alphabet. **2** any of several speech sounds represented by this letter. **3a** something shaped like an I. **3b** *(in combination): an I-beam.*

i *symbol for* the imaginary number √–1.

I[1] (aɪ) *pron (subjective)* refers to the speaker or writer. ORIG C12: from OE *ic;* cf. OSaxon *ik,* OHG *ih,* Sansk. *ahám*

I[2] *symbol for:* **1** *Chem.* iodine. **2** *Physics.* current. **3** *Physics.* isospin. ◆ **4** *the Roman numeral for* one. See **Roman numerals.**

I. *abbrev. for:* **1** Independence. **2** Independent. **3** Institute. **4** International. **5** Island; Isle.

Ia. *or* **IA** *abbrev. for* Iowa.

-ia *suffix forming nouns.* **1** in place names: *Columbia.* **2** in names of diseases: *pneumonia.* **3** in words denoting condition or quality: *utopia.* **4** in names of botanical genera and zoological classes: *Reptilia.* **5** in collective nouns borrowed from Latin: *regalia.* ORIG (for senses 1–4), from L & Gk, suffix of fem nouns; (for sense 5) from L, neuter pl suffix

IAA *abbrev. for* indoleacetic acid.

IAEA *abbrev. for* International Atomic Energy Agency.

-ial *suffix forming adjectives.* of or relating to: *managerial.* ORIG from L *-iālis,* adj. suffix; cf. -AL[1]

iamb (ˈaɪæm, ˈaɪæmb) *or* **iambus** (aɪˈæmbəs) *n, pl* **iambs, iambi** (aɪˈæmbaɪ), *or* **iambuses.** *Prosody.* **1** a metrical foot of two syllables, a short one followed by a long one. **2** a line of verse of such feet. ORIG C19 *iamb,* from C16 *iambus,* from L, from Gk *iambos*

iambic (aɪˈæmbɪk) *Prosody.* ◆ *adj* **1** of, relating to, or using an iamb. **2** (in Greek literature) denoting a satirical verse written in iambs. ◆ *n* **3** a metrical foot, line, or stanza consisting of iambs. **4** an ancient Greek satirical verse written in iambs.

-ian *suffix.* a variant of **-an:** *Etonian.* ORIG from L *-iānus*

-iana *suffix forming nouns.* a variant of **-ana.**

IAP *abbrev. for* Internet access provider.

Iaşi ★ (*Romanian* ˈjaʃj) *n* a city in NE Romania: capital of Moldavia (1565–1859); university (1860). Pop.: 337 643 (1993 est.). German name: **Jassy.**

-iasis *or* **-asis** *n combining form.* (in medicine) indicating a diseased condition: *psoriasis.* Cf. **-osis** (sense 2). ORIG from NL, from Gk, suffix of action

IATA (aɪˈɑːtə, iːˈɑːtə) *n acronym for* International Air Transport Association.

-iatrics *n combining form.* indicating medical care or treatment: *paediatrics.* ORIG C19: from Gk, from *iasthai* to heal

iatrogenic (aɪˌætrəʊˈdʒɛnɪk) *adj Med.* (of an illness) induced in a patient as the result of a physician's action.
▸ **iatrogenicity** (aɪˌætrəʊdʒɪˈnɪsɪtɪ) *n*

-iatry *n combining form.* indicating healing or medical treatment: *psychiatry.* Cf. **-iatrics.** ORIG from NL *-iatria,* from Gk *iatreia* the healing art, from *iatros* healer, physician
▸ **-iatric** *adj combining form.*

IBA (in Britain) *abbrev. for* Independent Broadcasting Authority.

Ibadan ★ (ɪˈbædᵊn) *n* a city in SW Nigeria, capital of Oyo state: university (1948). Pop.: 1 365 000 (1995 est.).

Ibagué ★ (*Spanish* iβaˈɣe) *n* a city in W central Colombia. Pop.: 346 632 (1995 est.).

I-beam *n* a rolled steel joist or a girder with a cross section in the form of a capital *I.*

Ibarruri ★ (*Spanish* iˈβarruri) *n* **Dolores** (doˈlores). real name of (La) **Pasionaria.**

Iberia ★ (aɪˈbɪərɪə) *n* **1** the Iberian Peninsula. **2** an ancient region south of the Caucasus in central Asia, corresponding approximately to present-day Georgia.

Iberian (aɪˈbɪərɪən) *n* **1** a member of a group of ancient Caucasoid peoples who inhabited the Iberian Peninsula, in classical times. **2** a native or inhabitant of the Iberian Peninsula; a Spaniard or Portuguese. **3** a native or inhabitant of ancient Iberia. ◆ *adj* **4** relating to the pre-Roman peoples of the Iberian Peninsula or of Caucasian Iberia. **5** of or relating to the Iberian Peninsula, its inhabitants, or any of their languages.

Iberian Peninsula ★ *n* a peninsula of SW Europe, occupied by Spain and Portugal.

iberis (aɪˈbɪərɪs) *n* any of various Mediterranean plants with white, lilac, or purple flowers. Also called: **candytuft.** ORIG from Gk *ibēris* pepperwort

Ibert ★ (*French* ibɛr) *n* **Jacques** (**François Antoine**) (ʒak). 1890–1962, French composer; his works include the humorous orchestral *Divertissement* (1930).

ibex (ˈaɪbɛks) *n, pl* **ibexes, ibices** (ˈɪbɪˌsiːz, ˈaɪ-), *or* **ibex.** any of three species of wild goat of mountainous regions of Europe, Asia, and North Africa, having large backward-curving horns. ORIG C17: from L: chamois

ibid. *or* **ib.** (referring to a book, etc., previously cited) *abbrev. for* ibidem. ORIG L: in the same place

ibis (ˈaɪbɪs) *n, pl* **ibises** *or* **ibis.** any of various wading birds such as the sacred ibis, that occur in warm regions and have a long thin down-curved bill. ORIG C14: via L from Gk, from Egyptian *hby*

Ibiza *or* **Iviza** ★ (*Spanish* iˈβiθa) *n* **1** a Spanish island in the W Mediterranean, one of the Balearic Islands: hilly, with a rugged coast; tourism. Pop.: 45 000 (1986). Area: 541 sq. km (209 sq. miles). **2** the capital of Ibiza, a port on the south of the island. Pop.: 16 000 (latest est.).

-ible *suffix forming adjectives.* a variant of **-able.**
▸ **-ibly** *suffix forming adverbs.* ▸ **-ibility** *suffix forming nouns.*

ibn-Rushd ★ (ˌɪbᵊnˈrʊʃt) *n* the Arabic name of **Averroës.**

ibn-Saud ★ (ˌɪbᵊnˈsaʊd) *n* **Abdul-Aziz** (æbˈdʊlæˈziːz). 1880–1953, first king of Saudi Arabia (1932–53).

ibn-Sina ★ (ˌɪbᵊnˈsiːnə) *n* the Arabic name of **Avicenna.**

Ibo *or* **Igbo** (ˈiːbəʊ) *n* **1** (*pl* **Ibos** *or* **Ibo**) a member of a Negroid people of W Africa, living in S Nigeria. **2** their language, belonging to the Niger-Congo family.

Ibrahim Pasha ★ (ˌɪbrəˈhiːm ˈpɑːʃə) *n* 1789–1848, Albanian general; son of Mehemet Ali, whom he succeeded as viceroy of Egypt (1848).

IBRD *abbrev. for* International Bank for Reconstruction and Development (the World Bank).

Ibsen ★ (ˈɪbsən) *n* **Henrik** (ˈhɛnrɪk). 1828–1906, Norwegian dramatist and poet. After his early verse plays *Brand* (1866) and *Peer Gynt* (1867), he began the series of social dramas in prose, including *A Doll's House* (1879), *Ghosts* (1881), and *The Wild Duck* (1886), which have had a profound influence on modern drama. His later plays, such as *Hedda Gabler* (1890) and *The Master Builder* (1892), are more symbolic.

ibuprofen (aɪˈbjuːˌprəʊfɛn) *n* a drug that relieves pain and reduces inflammation: used to treat arthritis and muscular strains.

i/c *abbrev. for:* **1** in charge (of). **2** internal combustion.

-ic *suffix forming adjectives.* **1** of, relating to, or resembling: *periodic.* See also **-ical. 2** (in chemistry) indicating that an element is chemically combined in the higher of two possible valence states: *ferric.* Cf. **-ous** (sense 2). ORIG from L *-icus* or Gk *-ikos; -ic* also occurs in nouns that represent a substantive use of adjectives (*magic*) and in nouns borrowed directly from L or Gk (*critic, music*)

Içá ★ (ˈiːsɑː; *Portuguese* iˈsa) *n* the Brazilian part of the **Putumayo River.**

★ people and places

ICA *abbrev. for:* **1** (in Britain) Institute of Contemporary Arts. **2** Institute of Chartered Accountants.

-ical *suffix forming adjectives.* a variant of **-ic**, but having a less literal application than corresponding adjectives ending in *-ic: economical.* ORIG from L *-icālis*
▸ **-ically** *suffix forming adverbs.*

ICAO *abbrev. for* International Civil Aviation Organization.

Icaria ★ (aɪˈkɛərɪə, ɪ-) *n* a Greek island in the Aegean Sea, in the Southern Sporades group. Area: 256 sq. km (99 sq. miles). Modern Greek name: **Ikaría.** Also called: **Nikaria.**

Icarian Sea ★ (aɪˈkɛərɪən, ɪ-) *n* the part of the Aegean Sea between the islands of Patmos and Leros and the coast of Asia Minor, where, according to legend, Icarus fell into the sea.

Icarus ★ (ˈɪkərəs, ˈaɪ-) *n Greek myth.* the son of Daedalus, with whom he escaped from Crete, flying with wings made of wax and feathers. Heedless of his father's warning he flew too near the sun, causing the wax to melt, and fell into the Aegean and drowned.

ICBM *abbrev. for* intercontinental ballistic missile: a missile with a range greater than 5550 km.

ice (aɪs) *n* **1** water in the solid state, formed by freezing liquid water. Related adj: **glacial.** **2** a portion of ice cream. **3** *Sl.* a diamond or diamonds. **4** *Sl.* a concentrated and highly potent form of methamphetamine with dangerous side effects. **5 break the ice. 5a** to relieve shyness, etc., esp. between strangers. **5b** to be the first of a group to do something. **6 on ice.** in abeyance; pending. **7 on thin ice.** unsafe; vulnerable. ◆ *vb* **ices, icing, iced. 8** (often foll. by *up, over,* etc.) to form ice; freeze. **9** (*tr*) to mix with ice or chill (a drink, etc.). **10** (*tr*) to cover (a cake, etc.) with icing. ORIG OE *īs*
▸ **iced** *adj*

ICE (in Britain) *abbrev. for* Institution of Civil Engineers.

Ice. *abbrev. for* Iceland(ic).

ice age *n* another name for **glacial period.**

ice axe *n* a light axe used by mountaineers for cutting footholds in ice.

ice bag *n* a waterproof bag used as an ice pack.

iceberg (ˈaɪsbɜːg) *n* **1** a large mass of ice floating in the sea. **2 tip of the iceberg.** the small visible part of something, esp. a problem, that is much larger. **3** *Sl., chiefly US.* a person considered to have a cold or reserved manner. ORIG C18: prob. part translation of MDu. *ijsberg* ice mountain; cf. Norwegian *isberg*

iceberg lettuce *n* a type of lettuce with very crisp pale leaves tightly enfolded.

iceblink (ˈaɪsˌblɪŋk) *n* a reflected glare in the sky over an ice field. Also called: **blink.**

icebound (ˈaɪsˌbaʊnd) *adj* covered or made immobile by ice; frozen in: *an icebound ship.*

icebox (ˈaɪsˌbɒks) *n* **1** a compartment in a refrigerator for storing or making ice. **2** an insulated cabinet packed with ice for storing food. **3** a US and Canad. name for **refrigerator.**

icebreaker (ˈaɪsˌbreɪkə) *n* **1** Also called: **iceboat.** a vessel with a reinforced bow for breaking up the ice in bodies of water. **2** a device for breaking ice into smaller pieces. **3** something intended to relieve shyness between strangers.

icecap (ˈaɪsˌkæp) *n* a thick mass of glacial ice that permanently covers an area, such as the polar regions or the peak of a mountain.

ice cream *n* a sweetened frozen liquid, made from cream, milk, or a custard base, flavoured in various ways.

ice dance *n* any of a number of dances, mostly based on ballroom dancing, performed by a couple skating on ice.
▸ **ice dancer** *n* ▸ **ice dancing** *n*

icefall (ˈaɪsˌfɔːl) *n* a steep part of a glacier that resembles a frozen waterfall.

ice field *n* **1** a large ice floe. **2** a large mass of ice permanently covering an extensive area of land.

ice floe *n* a sheet of ice, of variable size, floating in the sea. See also **ice field** (sense 1).

ice hockey *n* a game played on ice by two teams wearing skates, who try to propel a flat puck into their opponents' goal with long sticks.

ice house *n* a building for storing ice.

Içel ★ (iːˈtʃɛl) *n* another name for **Mersin.**

Icel. *abbrev. for* Iceland(ic).

Iceland ★ (ˈaɪslənd) *n* an island republic in the N Atlantic, regarded as part of Europe: settled by Norsemen, who established a legislative assembly in 930; under Danish rule (1380–1918); gained independence in 1918 and became a republic in 1944; contains large areas of glaciers, snowfields, and lava beds with many volcanoes and hot springs (the chief source of domestic heat); inhabited chiefly along the SW coast. The economy is based largely on fishing. Official language: Icelandic. Official religion: mostly Lutheran. Currency: krona. Capital: Reykjavik. Pop.: 276 000 (1999 est.). Area: 102 828 sq. km (39 702 sq. miles).

Icelander (ˈaɪslændə, ˈaɪsləndə) *n* a native or inhabitant of Iceland.

Icelandic (aɪsˈlændɪk) *adj* **1** of or relating to Iceland, its people, or their language. ◆ *n* **2** the official language of Iceland.

Iceland poppy *n* any of various arctic poppies with white or yellow nodding flowers.

Iceland spar *n* a pure transparent variety of calcite with double-refracting crystals.

ice lolly *n Brit. inf.* a water ice or an ice cream on a stick. Also called: **lolly.**

ice pack *n* **1** a bag or folded cloth containing ice, applied to a part of the body to reduce swelling, etc. **2** another name for **pack ice. 3** a sachet containing a gel that retains its temperature for an extended period of time, used esp. in cool bags.

ice pick *n* a pointed tool used for breaking ice.

ice plant *n* a low-growing plant of southern Africa, with fleshy leaves covered with icelike hairs and pink or white rayed flowers.

ice point *n* the temperature at which a mixture of ice and water are in equilibrium at a pressure of one atmosphere. It is 0° on the Celsius scale and 32° on the Fahrenheit scale. Cf. **steam point.**

ice sheet *n* a thick layer of ice covering a large area of land for a long time, esp. the layer that covered much of the N hemisphere during the last glacial period.

ice shelf *n* a thick mass of ice that is permanently attached to the land but projects into and floats on the sea.

ice skate *n* **1** a boot having a steel blade fitted to the sole to enable the wearer to glide over ice. **2** the steel blade on such a boot. ◆ *vb* **ice-skate, ice-skates, ice-skating, ice-skated. 3** (*intr*) to glide over ice on ice skates.
▸ **ˈice-ˌskater** *n*

ice station *n* a scientific research station in polar regions, where ice movement, weather, and environmental conditions are monitored.

Ichang *or* **I-ch'ang** ★ (ˈiːˈtʃæŋ) *n* a variant transliteration of the Chinese name of **Yichang.**

IChemE *abbrev. for* Institution of Chemical Engineers.

I Ching (ˈiː ˈtʃɪŋ) *n* an ancient Chinese book of divination and a source of Confucian and Taoist philosophy.

ichneumon (ɪkˈnjuːmən) *n* a mongoose of Africa and S Europe, having greyish-brown speckled fur. ORIG C16: via L from Gk, lit.: tracker, hunter, from *ikhneuein* to track, from *ikhnos* a footprint; so named from the animal's alleged ability to locate the eggs of crocodiles

ichneumon fly *or* **wasp** *n* any hymenopterous insect whose larvae are parasitic in caterpillars and other insect larvae.

ichnography (ɪkˈnɒgrəfɪ) *n* **1** the art of drawing ground plans. **2** the ground plan of a building. ORIG C16: from L, from Gk, from *ikhnos* trace, track
▸ **ichnographic** (ˌɪknəˈgræfɪk) *or* **ˌichnoˈgraphical** *adj*

ichor (ˈaɪkɔː) *n* **1** *Greek myth.* the fluid said to flow in the veins of the gods. **2** *Pathol.* a foul-smelling watery discharge from a wound or ulcer. ORIG C17: from Gk *ikhōr,* from ?
▸ **ˈichorous** *adj*

ichthyo- *or before a vowel* **ichthy-** *combining form.* indicating or relating to fishes: *ichthyology.* ORIG from L, from Gk *ikhthus* fish

ichthyoid ('ɪkθɪˌɔɪd) *adj also* **ichthyoidal. 1** resembling a fish. ◆ *n* **2** a fishlike vertebrate.

ichthyology (ˌɪkθɪ'ɒlədʒɪ) *n* the study of fishes.
▸ **ichthyologic** (ˌɪkθɪə'lɒdʒɪk) *or* ˌ**ichthyo'logical** *adj*
▸ ˌ**ichthy'ologist** *n*

ichthyosaur ('ɪkθɪəˌsɔː) *or* **ichthyosaurus** (ˌɪkθɪə'sɔːrəs) *n, pl* **ichthyosaurs, ichthyosauruses,** *or* **ichthyosauri** (-'sɔːraɪ). an extinct marine Mesozoic reptile which had a porpoise-like body with dorsal and tail fins and paddle-like limbs. See also **plesiosaur.**

ichthyosis (ˌɪkθɪ'əʊsɪs) *n* a congenital disease in which the skin is coarse, dry, and scaly.
▸ **ichthyotic** (ˌɪkθɪ'ɒtɪk) *adj*

ICI *abbrev. for* Imperial Chemical Industries.

-ician *suffix forming nouns.* indicating a person skilled or involved in a subject or activity: *physician; beautician.* ORIG from F *-icien;* see -IC, -IAN

icicle ('aɪsɪkᵊl) *n* a hanging spike of ice formed by the freezing of dripping water. ORIG C14: from ICE + *ickel,* from OE *gicel* icicle, rel. to ON *jökull* glacier

icing ('aɪsɪŋ) *n* **1** Also (esp. US and Canad.): **frosting.** a sugar preparation, variously flavoured and coloured, for coating and decorating cakes, etc. **2 icing on the cake** any unexpected extra or bonus. **3** the formation of ice, as on a ship, due to the freezing of moisture in the atmosphere.

icing sugar *n Brit.* a very finely ground sugar used for icings, confections, etc. US term: **confectioners' sugar.**

icky ('ɪkɪ) *adj* **ickier, ickiest.** *Inf., chiefly US.* **1** sticky. **2** excessively sentimental or emotional.
▸ '**ickiness** *n*

icon *or* **ikon** ('aɪkɒn) *n* **1** a representation of Christ or a saint, esp. one painted in oil on a wooden panel in a traditional Byzantine style and venerated in the Eastern Church. **2** an image, picture, etc. **3** a symbol resembling or analogous to the thing it represents. **4** a person regarded as a sex symbol or as a symbol of a belief or cultural movement. **5** a pictorial representation of a facility available on a computer that can be implemented by a cursor rather than by a textual instruction. ORIG C16: from L, from Gk *eikōn* image, from *eikenai* to be like

Iconium ★ (aɪ'kəʊnɪəm) *n* the ancient name for **Konya.**

icono- *or before a vowel* **icon-** *combining form.* indicating an image or likeness: *iconology.*

iconoclast (aɪ'kɒnəˌklæst) *n* **1** a person who attacks established or traditional concepts, principles, etc. **2a** a destroyer of religious images or objects. **2b** an adherent of a heretical iconoclastic movement within the Greek Orthodox Church from 725 to 842 A.D. ORIG C16: from LL, from LGk *eikonoklastes,* from *eikōn* icon + *klastes* breaker
▸ **iˌcono'clastic** *adj* ▸ **i'conoˌclasm** *n*

iconography (ˌaɪkɒ'nɒgrəfɪ) *n, pl* **iconographies. 1a** the symbols used in a work of art. **1b** the conventional significance attached to such symbols. **2** a collection of pictures of a particular subject. **3** the representation of the subjects of icons or portraits, esp. on coins.
▸ ˌ**ico'nographer** *n* ▸ **iconographic** (aɪˌkɒnə'græfɪk) *or* **iˌcono'graphical** *adj*

iconolatry (ˌaɪkɒ'nɒlətrɪ) *n* the worship of icons as idols.
▸ ˌ**ico'nolater** *n* ▸ ˌ**ico'nolatrous** *adj*

iconology (ˌaɪkɒ'nɒlədʒɪ) *n* **1** the study of icons. **2** icons collectively. **3** the symbolic representation of icons.
▸ **iconological** (aɪˌkɒnə'lɒdʒɪkᵊl) *adj* ▸ ˌ**ico'nologist** *n*

iconoscope (aɪ'kɒnəˌskəʊp) *n* a television camera tube in which an electron beam scans a surface, converting an optical image into electrical pulses.

iconostasis (ˌaɪkəʊ'nɒstəsɪs) *or* **iconostas** (aɪ'kɒnəˌstæs) *n, pl* **iconostases** (ˌaɪkəʊ'nɒstəˌsiːz *or* aɪ'kɒnəˌstæsɪz). *Eastern Church.* a screen with doors and with icons set in tiers, which separates the sanctuary from the nave. ORIG C19: Church L, from LGk *eikonostasion* shrine, lit.: area where images are placed, from *icono-* + *histanai* to stand

icosahedron (ˌaɪkəsə'hiːdrən) *n, pl* **icosahedrons** *or* **icosahedra** (-drə). a solid figure having 20 faces. ORIG C16: from Gk, from *eikosi* twenty + *-edron* -HEDRON
▸ ˌ**icosa'hedral** *adj*

-ics *suffix forming nouns; functioning as sing* **1** indicating a science, art, or matters relating to a particular subject: *politics.* **2** indicating certain activities: *acrobatics.* ORIG pl. of *-ic,* representing L *-ica,* from Gk *-ika*

Ictinus ★ (ɪk'taɪnəs) *n* 5th century B.C., Greek architect, who designed the Parthenon with Callicrates.

ictus ('ɪktəs) *n, pl* **ictuses** *or* **ictus. 1** *Prosody.* metrical or rhythmic stress in verse feet, as contrasted with the stress accent on words. **2** *Med.* a sudden attack or stroke. ORIG C18: from L *icere* to strike
▸ '**ictal** *adj*

ICU *abbrev. for* intensive care unit.

icy ('aɪsɪ) *adj* **icier, iciest. 1** made of, covered with, or containing ice. **2** resembling ice. **3** freezing or very cold. **4** cold or reserved in manner; aloof.
▸ '**icily** *adv* ▸ '**iciness** *n*

id (ɪd) *n Psychoanal.* the primitive instincts and energies in the unconscious mind that, modified by the ego and the superego, underlie all psychic activity. ORIG C20: NL, from L: it; used to render G *Es*

ID *abbrev. for:* **1** Idaho. **2** identification. **3** Also: **i.d.** intradermal(ly).

id. *abbrev. for* idem.

Id. *abbrev. for* Idaho.

I'd (aɪd) *contraction of* I had *or* I would.

-id[1] *suffix forming nouns and adjectives.* indicating members of a zoological family: *cyprinid.* ORIG from NL *-idae* or *-ida,* from Gk *-idēs* suffix indicating offspring

-id[2] *suffix forming nouns.* a variant of **-ide.**

Ida ★ ('aɪdə) *n* **Mount. 1** a mountain in central Crete: the highest on the island; in ancient times associated with the worship of Zeus. Height: 2456 m (8057 ft). Modern Greek name: **Idhi. 2** a mountain in NW Turkey, southeast of the site of ancient Troy. Height: 1767 m (5797 ft). Turkish name: **Kaz Daği.**

IDA *abbrev. for* International Development Association.

-idae *suffix forming plural proper nouns.* indicating names of zoological families: *Felidae.* ORIG NL, from L, from Gk *-idai,* suffix indicating offspring

Idaho ★ ('aɪdəˌhəʊ) *n* a state of the northwestern US: consists chiefly of ranges of the Rocky Mountains, with the Snake River basin in the south; important for agriculture (**Idaho potatoes**), livestock, and silver-mining. Capital: Boise. Pop.: 1 228 684 (1998 est.). Area: 216 413 sq. km (83 557 sq. miles). Abbrevs.: **Id., Ida.,** or (with zip code) **ID**
▸ '**Idaˌhoan** *adj, n*

-ide *or* **-id** *suffix forming nouns.* **1** (*added to the combining form of the nonmetallic or electronegative elements*) indicating a binary compound: *sodium chloride.* **2** indicating an organic compound derived from another: *acetanilide.* **3** indicating one of a class of compounds or elements: *peptide.* ORIG from G *-id,* from F *oxide* OXIDE, based on the suffix of *acide* ACID

idea (aɪ'dɪə) *n* **1** any product of mental activity; thought. **2** the thought of something: *the idea appals me.* **3** a belief; opinion. **4** a scheme, intention, plan, etc. **5** a vague notion; inkling: *he had no idea of the truth.* **6** a person's conception of something: *her idea of honesty is not the same as mine.* **7** significance or purpose: *the idea of the game is to discover the murderer.* **8** *Philosophy.* **8a** an immediate object of thought or perception. **8b** (*sometimes cap.*) (in Plato) the universal essence or archetype of any class of things or concepts. **9 get ideas.** to become ambitious, restless, etc. **10 not one's idea of.** not what one regards as (hard work, a holiday, etc.). **11 that's an idea.** that is worth considering. **12 the very idea!** that is preposterous, unreasonable, etc. ORIG C16: via LL from Gk: model, notion, from *idein* to see

> **USAGE NOTE** It is usually considered correct to say that someone has *the idea of doing* something, rather than *the idea to do it: he had the idea of taking* (not *the idea to take*) *a short holiday.*

ideal (aɪ'dɪəl) *n* **1** a conception of something that is perfect. **2** a person or thing considered to represent perfection. **3** something existing only as an idea. **4** a pattern or model, esp. of ethical behaviour. ◆ *adj* **5** conforming to an ideal. **6** of, involving, or existing in the form of an idea. **7** *Philosophy.* **7a** of or relating to a highly desirable and possible state of affairs. **7b** of or relating to idealism.
▸ **i'deally** *adv* ▸ **i'dealness** *n*

ideal element *n* any element added to a mathematical theory in order to eliminate special cases. The ideal element i = √–1 allows all algebraic equations to be solved.

ideal gas *n* a hypothetical gas which obeys Boyle's law exactly at all temperatures and pressures, and which has internal energy that depends only upon the temperature.

idealism (aɪ'dɪəˌlɪzəm) *n* **1** belief in or pursuance of ideals. **2** the tendency to represent things in their ideal forms, rather than as they are. **3** *Philosophy.* the doctrine that material objects and the external world do not exist in reality, but are creations of the mind. Cf. **materialism.**
▸ **i'dealist** *n* ▸ **iˌdeal'istic** *adj* ▸ **iˌdeal'istically** *adv*

idealize *or* **idealise** (aɪ'dɪəˌlaɪz) *vb* **idealizes, idealizing, idealized** *or* **idealises, idealising, idealised. 1** to consider or represent (something) as ideal. **2** (*tr*) to portray as ideal; glorify. **3** (*intr*) to form an ideal or ideals.
▸ **iˌdeali'zation** *or* **iˌdeali'sation** *n* ▸ **i'dealˌizer** *or* **i'dealˌiser** *n*

idée fixe *French.* (ide fiks) *n, pl* ***idées fixes*** (ide fiks). a fixed idea; obsession.

idem *Latin.* ('aɪdɛm, 'ɪdɛm) *pron, adj* the same: used to refer to an article, chapter, etc., previously cited.

identic (aɪ'dɛntɪk) *adj Diplomacy.* (esp. of opinions expressed by two or more governments) having the same wording or intention regarding another power.

identical (aɪ'dɛntɪkᵊl) *adj* **1** being the same: *we got the identical hotel room as last year.* **2** exactly alike or equal. **3** designating either or both of a pair of twins of the same sex who developed from a single fertilized ovum that split into two. Cf. **fraternal** (sense 3). ORIG C17: from Med. L *identicus,* from L *idem* the same
▸ **i'dentically** *adv*

identification (aɪˌdɛntɪfɪ'keɪʃən) *n* **1** the act of identifying or the state of being identified. **2a** something that identifies a person or thing. **2b** (*as modifier*): *an identification card.* **3** *Psychol.* **3a** the process of recognizing specific objects as the result of remembering. **3b** the process by which one incorporates aspects of another person's personality. **3c** the transferring of a response from one situation to another because the two bear similar features.

identification parade *n* a group of persons, including one suspected of a crime, assembled for the purpose of discovering whether a witness can identify the suspect.

identify (aɪ'dɛntɪˌfaɪ) *vb* **identifies, identifying, identified.** (*mainly tr*) **1** to prove or recognize as being a certain person or thing; determine the identity of. **2** to consider as the same or equivalent. **3** (*also intr;* often foll. by *with*) to consider (oneself) as similar to another. **4** to determine the taxonomic classification of (a plant or animal). **5** (*intr;* usually foll. by *with*) *Psychol.* to engage in identification.
▸ **i'dentiˌfiable** *adj* ▸ **i'dentiˌfiableness** *n* ▸ **i'dentiˌfier** *n*

Identikit (aɪ'dɛntɪˌkɪt) *n Trademark.* **1a** a set of transparencies of typical facial characteristics that can be superimposed on one another to build up a picture of a person sought by the police. **1b** (*as modifier*): *an Identikit picture.* **2** (*modifier*) artificially created by copying different elements in an attempt to form a whole: *an Identikit pop group.*

identity (aɪ'dɛntɪtɪ) *n, pl* **identities. 1** the state of having unique identifying characteristics. **2** the individual characteristics by which a person or thing is recognized. **3** the state of being the same in nature, quality, etc.: *linked by the identity of their tastes.* **4** the state of being the same as a person or thing described or known: *the identity of the stolen goods was soon established.* **5** *Maths.* **5a** an equation that is valid for all values of its variables, as in $(x - y)(x + y) = x^2 - y^2$. Often denoted by the symbol ≡. **5b** Also called: **identity element.** a member of a set that when operating on another member, *x*, produces that member *x*: the identity for multiplication of numbers is 1 since $x.1 = 1.x = x$. **6** *Logic.* the relationship between an object and itself. **7** *Austral. inf.* **7a** a well-known local person; figure: *a Barwidgee identity.* **7b** an eccentric; character: *an old identity in the town.* **8** *NZ.* a well-known person. ORIG C16: from LL *identitās,* from L *idem* the same

identity card *n* a card that establishes a person's identity, esp. one issued to all members of the population in wartime, to the staff of an organization, etc.

ideo- *combining form.* of or indicating idea or ideas: *ideology.* ORIG from F *idéo-,* from Gk *idea* IDEA

ideogram ('ɪdɪəʊˌgræm) *or* **ideograph** ('ɪdɪəʊˌgrɑːf) *n* **1** a sign or symbol, used in a writing system such as that of China, that directly represents a concept or thing, rather than a word for it. **2** any graphic sign or symbol, such as % or &.

ideography (ˌɪdɪ'ɒgrəfɪ) *n* the use of ideograms to communicate ideas.

ideology (ˌaɪdɪ'ɒlədʒɪ) *n, pl* **ideologies. 1** a body of ideas that reflects the beliefs of a nation, political system, class, etc. **2** speculation that is imaginary or visionary. **3** the study of the nature and origin of ideas.
▸ **ideological** (ˌaɪdɪə'lɒdʒɪkᵊl) *or* **ˌideo'logic** *adj* ▸ **ˌideo'logically** *adv* ▸ **ˌide'ologist** *or* **'ideoˌlogue** *n*

ides (aɪdz) *n* (*functioning as sing*) (in the Roman calendar) the 15th day in March, May, July, and October and the 13th day of each other month. ORIG C15: from OF, from L *īdūs* (pl), from ?

id est *Latin.* ('ɪd 'ɛst) the full form of **i.e.**

Idhi ★ ('iði) *n* a transliteration of the Modern Greek name for (Mount) **Ida** (sense 1).

idiocy ('ɪdɪəsɪ) *n, pl* **idiocies. 1** (*not in technical usage*) severe mental retardation. **2** foolishness; stupidity. **3** a foolish act or remark.

idiom ('ɪdɪəm) *n* **1** a group of words whose meaning cannot be predicted from the constituent words: (*It was raining*) *cats and dogs.* **2** linguistic usage that is grammatical and natural to native speakers. **3** the characteristic vocabulary or usage of a specific human group or subject. **4** the characteristic artistic style of an individual, school, etc. ORIG C16: from L *idiōma* peculiarity of language, from Gk *idios* private, separate
▸ **idiomatic** (ˌɪdɪə'mætɪk) *adj* ▸ **ˌidio'matically** *adv*

idiosyncrasy (ˌɪdɪəʊ'sɪŋkrəsɪ) *n, pl* **idiosyncrasies. 1** a tendency, type of behaviour, etc., of a person; quirk. **2** the composite physical or psychological make-up of a person. **3** an abnormal reaction of an individual to specific foods, drugs, etc. ORIG C17: from Gk, from *idios* private, separate + *sunkrasis* mixture, temperament
▸ **idiosyncratic** (ˌɪdɪəʊsɪŋ'krætɪk) *adj* ▸ **ˌidiosyn'cratically** *adv*

idiot ('ɪdɪət) *n* **1** a person with severe mental retardation. **2** a foolish or senseless person. ORIG C13: from L *idiōta* ignorant person, from Gk *idiōtēs* private person, ignoramus

idiot board *n* a slang name for **Autocue.**

idiot box *n Sl.* a television set.

idiotic (ˌɪdɪ'ɒtɪk) *adj* of or resembling an idiot; foolish; senseless.
▸ **ˌidi'otically** *adv*

idiot savant ('iːdjəʊ sæ'vɑ̃, 'ɪdɪət 'sævənt) *n, pl* **idiots savants** ('iːdjəʊ sæ'vɑ̃) *or* **idiot savants.** a person of limited mental or social capabilities who performs brilliantly at some specialized intellectual task.

idiot tape *n Computing.* a tape that prints out information in a continuous stream, with no line breaks.

idle ('aɪdᵊl) *adj* **1** unemployed or unoccupied; inactive. **2** not operating or being used. **3** (of money) not used to earn interest, etc. **4** not wanting to work; lazy. **5** (*usually prenominal*) frivolous or trivial: *idle pleasures.* **6** ineffective or powerless; vain. **7** without basis; unfounded. ◆ *vb* **idles, idling, idled. 8** (when *tr,* often foll. by *away*) to waste or pass (time) fruitlessly or inactively. **9** (*intr*) (of a shaft, etc.) to turn without doing useful work. **10** (*intr*) (of an

engine) to run at low speed with the transmission disengaged. ORIG OE *īdel*
▸ **'idleness** *n* ▸ **'idly** *adv*

idle pulley *or* **idler pulley** *n* a freely rotating pulley used to control the tension or direction of a belt. Also called: **idler.**

idler ('aɪdlə) *n* **1** a person who idles. **2** another name for **idle pulley** or **idle wheel.**

idle wheel *n* a gearwheel interposed between two others to transmit torque without changing the direction of rotation or the velocity ratio. Also called: **idler.**

idol ('aɪdᵊl) *n* **1** a material object that is worshipped as a god. **2** *Christianity, Judaism.* any being (other than the one God) to which divine honour is paid. **3** a person who is revered, admired, or highly loved. ORIG C13: from LL, from L: image, from Gk, from *eidos* shape, form

idolatry (aɪ'dɒlətrɪ) *n* **1** the worship of idols. **2** great devotion or reverence.
▸ **i'dolater** *n or* **i'dolatress** *fem n* ▸ **i'dolatrous** *adj*

idolize *or* **idolise** ('aɪdəˌlaɪz) *vb* **idolizes, idolizing, idolized** *or* **idolises, idolising, idolised. 1** (*tr*) to admire or revere greatly. **2** (*tr*) to worship as an idol. **3** (*intr*) to worship idols.
▸ **ˌidoli'zation** *or* **ˌidoli'sation** *n* ▸ **'idolˌizer** *or* **'idolˌiser** *n*

idolum (ɪ'dəʊləm) *n* **1** a mental picture; idea. **2** a false idea; fallacy. ORIG C17: from L: IDOL

Idomeneus ★ (aɪ'dɒmɪˌnjuːs) *n Greek myth.* a king of Crete who fought on the Greek side in the Trojan War.

IDP *abbrev. for* integrated data processing.

Idun ('iːdʊn) *or* **Ithunn** ★ *n Norse myth.* the goddess of spring who guarded the apples that kept the gods eternally young; wife of Bragi.

idyll *or US* (*sometimes*) **idyl** ('ɪdɪl) *n* **1** a poem or prose work describing an idealized rural life, pastoral scenes, etc. **2** a charming or picturesque scene or event. **3** a piece of music with a pastoral character. ORIG C17: from L, from Gk *eidullion,* from *eidos* shape, (literary) form
▸ **i'dyllic** *adj* ▸ **i'dyllically** *adv*

IE *abbrev. for* Indo-European (languages).

i.e. *abbrev. for* id est. ORIG L: that is (to say); in other words

USAGE NOTE See at **e.g.**

-ie *suffix forming nouns.* a variant of **-y**[2]: *groupie.*

IEE *abbrev. for* Institution of Electrical Engineers.

Ieper ★ ('iːpər) *n* the Flemish name for **Ypres.**

-ier *suffix forming nouns.* a variant of **-eer:** *brigadier.* ORIG from OE *-ere* -ER[1] or (in some words) from OF *-ier,* from L *-ārius* -ARY

Ieyasu ★ (ˌiːjɛ'jɑːsuː) *n* a variant spelling of (Tokugawa) **Iyeyasu.**

if (ɪf) *conj* (*subordinating*) **1** in case that, or on condition that: *if you try hard it might work.* **2** used to introduce an indirect question. In this sense, *if* approaches the meaning of *whether.* **3** even though: *an attractive if awkward girl.* **4a** used to introduce expressions of desire, with *only: if I had only known.* **4b** used to introduce exclamations of surprise, dismay, etc.: *if this doesn't top everything!* ◆ *n* **5** an uncertainty or doubt: *the big if is whether our plan will work.* **6** a condition or stipulation: *I won't have any ifs or buts.* ORIG OE *gif*

IF *or* **i.f.** *Electronics. abbrev. for* intermediate frequency.

IFA *abbrev. for* independent financial adviser.

IFC *abbrev. for* International Finance Corporation.

Ife ★ ('iːfɪ) *n* a town in W central Nigeria: one of the largest and oldest Yoruba towns; university (1961); centre of the cocoa trade. Pop.: 289 500 (1995 est.).

-iferous *suffix forming adjectives.* containing or yielding: *carboniferous.*

iffy ('ɪfɪ) *adj* **iffier, iffiest.** *Inf.* uncertain or subject to contingency. ORIG C20: from IF + -Y[1]

Ifni ★ (*Spanish* 'ifni) *n* a former Spanish province in S Morocco, on the Atlantic: returned to Morocco in 1969.

IFS *abbrev. for* Irish Free State (now called Republic of Ireland).

-ify *suffix forming verbs.* a variant of **-fy:** *intensify.*
▸ **-ification** *suffix forming nouns.*

Igbo ('iːbəʊ) *n, pl* **igbo** *or* **igbos.** a variant spelling of **Ibo.**

IGC *abbrev. for* intergovernmental conference (esp. in the European Union).

Igdrasil ★ ('ɪgdrəsɪl) *n* a variant spelling of **Yggdrasil.**

igloo *or* **iglu** ('ɪgluː) *n, pl* **igloos** *or* **iglus. 1** a dome-shaped Eskimo house, built of blocks of solid snow. **2** a hollow made by a seal in the snow over its breathing hole in the ice. ORIG C19: from Eskimo *igdlu* house

Ignatius ★ (ɪg'neɪʃɪəs) *n* **Saint,** surnamed *Theophorus.* died ?110 A.D., bishop of Antioch. His seven letters, written on his way to his martyrdom in Rome, give valuable insight into the early Christian Church. Feast day: Oct. 17 or Dec. 17 or 20.

Ignatius Loyola ★ (lɔɪ'əʊlə) *n* **Saint.** 1491–1556, Spanish ecclesiastic. He founded the Society of Jesus (1534) and was its first general (1541–56). His *Spiritual Exercises* (1548) remains the manual for training Jesuits. Feast day: July 31.

igneous ('ɪgnɪəs) *adj* **1** (of rocks) derived from magma or lava that has solidified on or below the earth's surface. **2** of or relating to fire. ORIG C17: from L *igneus* fiery, from *ignis* fire

ignis fatuus ('ɪgnɪs 'fætjʊəs) *n, pl* **ignes fatui** ('ɪgniːz 'fætjʊˌaɪ). another name for **will-o'-the-wisp.** ORIG C16: from Med. L, lit.: foolish fire

ignite (ɪg'naɪt) *vb* **ignites, igniting, ignited. 1** to catch fire or set fire to; burn or cause to burn. **2** (*tr*) *Chem.* to heat strongly. ORIG C17: from L, from *ignis* fire
▸ **ig'nitable** *or* **ig'nitible** *adj* ▸ **igˌnita'bility** *or* **igˌniti'bility** *n*
▸ **ig'niter** *n*

ignition (ɪg'nɪʃən) *n* **1** the act or process of initiating combustion. **2** the process of igniting the fuel in an internal-combustion engine. **3** (preceded by *the*) the devices used to ignite the fuel in an internal-combustion engine.

ignition coil *n* an induction coil that supplies the high voltage to the sparking plugs on an internal-combustion engine.

ignition key *n* the key used in a motor vehicle to turn the switch that connects the battery to the ignition system.

ignitron (ɪg'naɪtrɒn, 'ɪgnɪˌtrɒn) *n* a rectifier controlled by a subsidiary electrode, the igniter, partially immersed in a mercury cathode. A current passed between igniter and cathode forms a hot spot sufficient to strike an arc between cathode and anode. ORIG C20: from *igniter* + ELECTRON

ignoble (ɪg'nəʊbᵊl) *adj* **1** dishonourable; base; despicable. **2** of low birth or origins; humble; common. **3** of low quality; inferior. ORIG C16: from L, from IN-[1] + OL *gnōbilis* NOBLE
▸ **ˌigno'bility** *or* **ig'nobleness** *n* ▸ **ig'nobly** *adv*

ignominy ('ɪgnəˌmɪnɪ) *n, pl* **ignominies. 1** disgrace or public shame; dishonour. **2** a cause of disgrace; a shameful act. ORIG C16: from L *ignōminia* disgrace, from *ig-* (see IN-[2]) + *nōmen* name, reputation
▸ **ˌigno'minious** *adj* ▸ **ˌigno'miniously** *adv* ▸ **ˌigno'miniousness** *n*

ignoramus (ˌɪgnə'reɪməs) *n, pl* **ignoramuses.** an ignorant person; fool. ORIG C16: from legal L, lit.: we have no knowledge of, from L *ignōrāre* to be ignorant of; see IGNORE; modern usage originated from use of *Ignoramus* as the name of an unlettered lawyer in a play by G. Ruggle, 17th-century E dramatist

ignorance ('ɪgnərəns) *n* lack of knowledge, information, or education; the state of being ignorant.

ignorant ('ɪgnərənt) *adj* **1** lacking in knowledge or education; unenlightened. **2** (*postpositive;* often foll. by *of*) lacking in awareness or knowledge (of): *ignorant of the law.* **3** resulting from or showing lack of knowledge or awareness: *an ignorant remark.*
▸ **'ignorantly** *adv*

ignore (ɪg'nɔː) *vb* **ignores, ignoring, ignored.** (*tr*) to fail or re-

fuse to notice; disregard. ORIG C17: from L *ignōrāre* not to know, from *ignārus* ignorant of
▸ **ig'norer** *n*

Iguaçú *or* **Iguassú** ★ (*Portuguese* igua'su) *n* a river in SE South America, rising in S Brazil and flowing west to join the Paraná River, forming part of the border between Brazil and Argentina. Length: 1200 km (745 miles).

Iguaçú Falls ★ *n* a waterfall on the border between Brazil and Argentina, on the Iguaçú River: divided into hundreds of separate falls by forested rocky islands. Width: about 4 km (2.5 miles). Height: 82 m (269 ft).

iguana (ɪ'gwɑːnə) *n* either of two large tropical American arboreal herbivorous lizards, esp. the common iguana, having a greyish-green body with a row of spines along the back. ORIG C16: from Sp., from S Amerind *iwana*
▸ **i'guanian** *n, adj*

iguanodon (ɪ'gwɑːnəˌdɒn) *n* a massive herbivorous long-tailed bipedal dinosaur common in Europe and N Africa in Jurassic and Cretaceous times. ORIG C19: NL, from IGUANA + Gk *odōn* tooth

IHC (in New Zealand) *abbrev. for* intellectually handicapped child.

IHS the first three letters of the name Jesus in Greek (ΙΗΣΟΥΣ), often used as a Christian emblem.

IJssel *or* **Yssel** ★ ('aɪsᵊl; *Dutch* 'ɛisəl) *n* a river in the central Netherlands: a distributary of the Rhine, flowing north to the IJsselmeer. Length: 116 km (72 miles).

Ikaría ★ (ika'ria) *n* a transliteration of the Modern Greek name for **Icaria**.

ikat ('iːkæt) *n* a method of creating patterns in fabric by tie-dyeing the yarn before weaving. ORIG C20: from Malay, lit.: to tie, bind

ikebana (ˌiːkə'bɑːnə) *n* the Japanese decorative art of flower arrangement.

Ikeja ★ (ɪ'keɪjə) *n* a town in SW Nigeria, capital of Lagos state: residential and industrial suburb of Lagos. Pop.: 63 870 (latest est.).

Ikhnaton ★ (ɪk'nɑːtən) *n* a variant of **Akhenaten**.

ikon ('aɪkɒn) *n* a variant spelling of **icon**.

IL *abbrev. for* Illinois.

il- *prefix* a variant of **in-**[1] and **in-**[2] before *l*.

-ile *or* **-il** *suffix forming adjectives and nouns.* indicating capability, liability, or a relationship with something: *agile; juvenile.* ORIG via F from L or directly from L *-ilis*
▸ **-ility** *suffix forming nouns.*

Île-de-France ★ (*French* ildəfrɑ̃s) *n* **1** a region of N France, in the Paris Basin: part of the duchy of France in the 10th century. **2** a former name (1715–1810) for **Mauritius**.

Île du Diable ★ (il dy djɑblə) *n* the French name for **Devil's Island**.

ileitis (ˌɪlɪ'aɪtɪs) *n* inflammation of the ileum.

ileostomy (ˌɪlɪ'ɒstəmɪ) *n, pl* **ileostomies**. the surgical formation of a permanent opening through the abdominal wall into the ileum.

Îles Comores ★ (il kɔmɔr) *n* the French name for the **Comoros**.

Îles du Salut ★ (il dy saly) *n* the French name for the **Safety Islands**.

Ilesha ★ (ɪ'leɪʃə) *n* a town in W Nigeria. Pop.: 369 000 (1995 est.).

Îles Mascareignes ★ (il maskarɛɲ) *n* the French name for the **Mascarene Islands**.

Îles sous le Vent ★ (il su lə vɑ̃) *n* the French name for the **Leeward Islands** (sense 3).

ileum ('ɪlɪəm) *n* the part of the small intestine between the jejunum and the caecum. ORIG C17: NL, from L *īlium, īleum* flank, groin, from ?
▸ **'ileˌac** *adj*

ilex ('aɪlɛks) *n* **1** any of a genus of trees or shrubs such as the holly and inkberry. **2** another name for the **holm oak**. ORIG C16: from L

Ilia ★ ('ɪlɪə) *n* (in Roman legend) the daughter of Aeneas and Lavinia, who, according to some traditions, was the mother of Romulus and Remus. See also **Rhea Silvia**.

Ilía ★ (i'lia) *n* a transliteration of the Modern Greek name for **Elia**[1].

Iliamna ★ (ˌɪlɪ'æmnə) *n* **1** a lake in SW Alaska: the largest lake in Alaska. Length: about 130 km (80 miles). Width: 40 km (25 miles). **2** a volcano in SW Alaska, northwest of Iliamna Lake. Height: 3076 m (10 092 ft).

Iligan ★ (ɪ'liːgən) *n* a city in the Philippines, a port on the N coast of Mindanao. Pop.: 209 639 (1994 est.).

Ilion ★ ('ɪlɪən) *n* a transliteration of the Greek name for ancient **Troy**.

ilium ('ɪlɪəm) *n, pl* **ilia** (-ɪə). the uppermost and widest of the three sections of the hipbone.

Ilium ★ ('ɪlɪəm) *n* the Latin name for ancient **Troy**.

ilk (ɪlk) *n* **1** a type; class; sort (esp. in **of that, his,** etc., **ilk**): *people of that ilk should not be allowed here.* **2 of that ilk.** *Scot.* of the place of the same name: to indicate that the person is laird of the place named: *Moncrieff of that ilk.* ORIG OE *ilca* the same family, same kind

> **USAGE NOTE** Although the use of *ilk* to mean 'a type or class' is sometimes condemned as being the result of a misunderstanding of the Scottish expression *of that ilk*, it is nevertheless well established and generally acceptable.

Ilkeston ★ ('ɪlkɪstən) *n* a town in N central England, in SE Derbyshire. Pop.: 35 134 (1991).

Ilkley ★ ('ɪlklɪ) *n* a town in N England, in West Yorkshire: nearby is **Ilkley Moor** (to the south). Pop.: 13 530 (1991).

ill (ɪl) *adj* **worse, worst. 1** (*usually postpositive*) not in good health; sick. **2** characterized by or intending harm, etc.; hostile: *ill deeds.* **3** causing pain, harm, adversity, etc. **4** ascribing or imputing evil to something referred to: *ill repute.* **5** promising an unfavourable outcome; unpropitious: *an ill omen.* **6** harsh; lacking kindness: *ill will.* **7** not up to an acceptable standard; faulty: *ill manners.* **8 ill at ease.** unable to relax; uncomfortable. ◆ *n* **9** evil or harm; misfortune; trouble. **10** a mild disease. ◆ *adv* **11** badly: *the title ill befits him.* **12** with difficulty; hardly: *he can ill afford the money.* **13** not rightly: *he ill deserves such good fortune.* ORIG C11 (in the sense: evil): from ON *illr* bad

ill. *abbrev. for:* **1** illustrated. **2** illustration.

Ill. *abbrev. for* Illinois.

I'll (aɪl) *contraction of* I will *or* I shall.

ill-advised *adj* **1** acting without reasonable care or thought: *you would be ill-advised to sell your house now.* **2** badly thought out; not or insufficiently considered: *an ill-advised plan of action.*
▸ **ill-advisedly** (ˌɪləd'vaɪzɪdlɪ) *adv*

ill-affected *adj* (often foll. by *towards*) not well disposed; disaffected.

Illampu ★ (*Spanish* iʎam'pu) *n* one of the two peaks of Mount **Sorata**.

ill-assorted *adj* badly matched; incompatible.

illative (ɪ'leɪtɪv) *adj* **1** relating to inference; inferential. **2** *Grammar.* denoting a word or morpheme used to signal inference, for example *so* or *therefore.* **3** (esp. in Finnish grammar) denoting a case of nouns expressing a relation of motion or direction, usually translated by *into* or *towards.* ◆ *n* **4** *Grammar.* **4a** the illative case. **4b** an illative word or speech element. ORIG C16: from LL *illātīvus* inferring, concluding
▸ **il'latively** *adv*

Illawarra ★ (ˌɪlə'wɒrə) *n* **1** a coastal district of E Australia, in S New South Wales. Pop.: 359 600 (1993). **2** an Australian breed of shorthorn dairy cattle noted for its high milk yield and ability to survive on poor pastures.

ill-bred *adj* badly brought up; lacking good manners.
▸ **ˌill-'breeding** *n*

ill-considered *adj* done without due consideration; not thought out: *an ill-considered decision.*

ill-defined *adj* imperfectly defined; having no clear outline.

ill-disposed *adj* (often foll. by *towards*) not kindly disposed.

Ille-et-Vilaine ★ (*French* ilevilɛn) *n* a department of NW France, in E Brittany. Capital: Rennes. Pop.: 832 882 (1994 est.). Area: 6992 sq. km (2727 sq. miles).

illegal (ɪˈliːgᵊl) *adj* **1** forbidden by law; unlawful; illicit. **2** unauthorized or prohibited by a code of official or accepted rules. ◆ *n* **3** a person who has entered or attempted to enter a country illegally.
▸ **ilˈlegally** *adv* ▸ **ˌilleˈgality** *n*

illegible (ɪˈlɛdʒɪbᵊl) *adj* unable to be read or deciphered.
▸ **ilˌlegiˈbility** *or* **ilˈlegibleness** *n* ▸ **ilˈlegibly** *adv*

illegitimate (ˌɪlɪˈdʒɪtɪmɪt) *adj* **1a** born of parents who were not married to each other at the time of birth; bastard. **1b** occurring outside marriage: *of illegitimate birth.* **2** illegal; unlawful. **3** contrary to logic; incorrectly reasoned. ◆ *n* **4** an illegitimate person; bastard.
▸ **ˌilleˈgitimacy** *or* **ˌilleˈgitimateness** *n* ▸ **ˌilleˈgitimately** *adv*

ill-fated *adj* doomed or unlucky.

ill-favoured *adj* **1** unattractive or repulsive in appearance; ugly. **2** disagreeable or objectionable.
▸ **ˌill-ˈfavouredly** *adv* ▸ **ˌill-ˈfavouredness** *n*

ill feeling *n* hostile feeling; animosity.

ill-founded *adj* not founded on true or reliable premises; unsubstantiated.

ill-gotten *adj* obtained dishonestly or illegally (esp. in **ill-gotten gains**).

ill humour *n* a disagreeable or sullen mood; bad temper.
▸ **ˌill-ˈhumoured** *adj* ▸ **ˌill-ˈhumouredly** *adv*

illiberal (ɪˈlɪbərəl) *adj* **1** narrow-minded; prejudiced; bigoted; intolerant. **2** not generous; mean. **3** lacking in culture or refinement.
▸ **ilˌliberˈality** *n* ▸ **ilˈliberally** *adv*

Illich ★ (ˈɪlɪtʃ) *n* **Ivan.** born 1926. US teacher and writer, born in Austria. His books include *Deschooling Society* (1971) and *Medical Nemesis* (1975).

illicit (ɪˈlɪsɪt) *adj* **1** another word for **illegal. 2** not allowed or approved by common custom, rule, or standard: *illicit sexual relations.*
▸ **ilˈlicitly** *adv* ▸ **ilˈlicitness** *n*

Illimani ★ (*Spanish* iʎiˈmani) *n* a mountain in W Bolivia, in the Andes near La Paz. Height: 6882 m (22 580 ft).

illimitable (ɪˈlɪmɪtəbᵊl) *adj* limitless; boundless.
▸ **ilˌlimitaˈbility** *or* **ilˈlimitableness** *n*

Illinois ★ (ˌɪlɪˈnɔɪ) *n* **1** a state of the N central US, in the Midwest: consists of level prairie crossed by the Illinois and Kaskaskia Rivers; mainly agricultural. Capital: Springfield. Pop.: 12 045 326 (1998 est.). Area: 144 858 sq. km (55 930 sq. miles). Abbrevs.: **Ill.** or (with zip code) **IL** **2** a river in Illinois, flowing SW to the Mississippi. Length: 439 km (273 miles).
▸ **Illinoisan** (ˌɪlɪˈnɔɪən), **Illinoian** (ˌɪlɪˈnɔɪən), *or* **Illinoisian** (ˌɪlɪˈnɔɪzɪən) *n, adj*

illiterate (ɪˈlɪtərɪt) *adj* **1** unable to read and write. **2** violating accepted standards in reading and writing: *an illiterate scrawl.* **3** uneducated, ignorant, or uncultured: *scientifically illiterate.* ◆ *n* **4** an illiterate person.
▸ **ilˈliteracy** *or* **ilˈliterateness** *n* ▸ **ilˈliterately** *adv*

ill-judged *adj* rash; ill-advised.

ill-mannered *adj* having bad manners; rude; impolite.
▸ **ˌill-ˈmanneredly** *adv*

ill-natured *adj* naturally unpleasant and mean.
▸ **ˌill-ˈnaturedly** *adv* ▸ **ˌill-ˈnaturedness** *n*

illness (ˈɪlnɪs) *n* **1** a disease or indisposition; sickness. **2** a state of ill health.

illogical (ɪˈlɒdʒɪkᵊl) *adj* **1** characterized by lack of logic; senseless or unreasonable. **2** disregarding logical principles.
▸ **illogicality** (ɪˌlɒdʒɪˈkælɪtɪ) *or* **ilˈlogicalness** *n* ▸ **ilˈlogically** *adv*

ill-starred *adj* unlucky; unfortunate; ill-fated.

ill temper *n* bad temper; irritability.
▸ **ˌill-ˈtempered** *adj* ▸ **ˌill-ˈtemperedly** *adv*

ill-timed *adj* occurring at or planned for an unsuitable time.

ill-treat *vb* (*tr*) to behave cruelly or harshly towards; misuse; maltreat.
▸ **ˌill-ˈtreatment** *n*

illuminance (ɪˈluːmɪnəns) *n* the luminous flux incident on unit area of a surface. Sometimes called: **illumination.** Cf. **irradiance.**

illuminant (ɪˈluːmɪnənt) *n* **1** something that provides or gives off light. ◆ *adj* **2** giving off light; illuminating.

illuminate *vb* (ɪˈluːmɪˌneɪt), **illuminates, illuminating, illuminated. 1** (*tr*) to throw light in or into; light up. **2** (*tr*) to make easily understood; clarify. **3** to adorn, decorate, or be decorated with lights. **4** (*tr*) to decorate (a letter, etc.) by the application of colours, gold, or silver. **5** (*intr*) to become lighted up. ◆ *adj* (ɪˈluːmɪnɪt, -ˌneɪt). **6** *Arch.* made clear or bright with light. ◆ *n* (ɪˈluːmɪnɪt, -ˌneɪt). **7** a person who claims to have special enlightenment. ORIG C16: from L *illūmināre* to light up, from *lūmen* light
▸ **ilˈlumiˌnating** *adj* ▸ **ilˈluminative** *adj* ▸ **ilˈlumiˌnator** *n*

illuminati (ɪˌluːmɪˈnɑːtiː) *pl n, sing* **illuminato** (-təʊ). **1** a group of persons claiming exceptional enlightenment on some subject, esp. religion. **2** (*cap.*) any of several groups of illuminati, esp. in 18th-century France and Bavaria or 16th-century Spain. ORIG C16: from L, lit.: the enlightened ones, from *illūmināre* to ILLUMINATE

illumination (ɪˌluːmɪˈneɪʃən) *n* **1** the act of illuminating or the state of being illuminated. **2** a source of light. **3** (*often pl*) *Chiefly Brit.* a light or lights used as decoration in streets, parks, etc. **4** spiritual or intellectual enlightenment; insight or understanding. **5** the act of making understood; clarification. **6** decoration in colours, gold, or silver used on some manuscripts. **7** *Physics.* another name (not in technical usage) for **illuminance.**

illumine (ɪˈluːmɪn) *vb* **illumines, illumining, illumined.** a literary word for **illuminate.** ORIG C14: from L *illūmināre* to make light
▸ **ilˈluminable** *adj*

ill-use *vb* (ˈɪlˈjuːz), **ill-uses, ill-using, ill-used. 1** to use badly or cruelly; abuse; maltreat. ◆ *n* (ˈɪlˈjuːs), *also* **ill-usage. 2** harsh or cruel treatment; abuse.

illusion (ɪˈluːʒən) *n* **1** a false appearance or deceptive impression of reality: *the mirror gives an illusion of depth.* **2** a false or misleading perception or belief; delusion. **3** *Psychol.* a perception that is not true to reality, having been altered subjectively in the mind of the perceiver. See also **hallucination.** ORIG C14: from L *illūsiō* deceit, from *illūdere* to sport with, from *ludus* game
▸ **ilˈlusionary** *or* **ilˈlusional** *adj* ▸ **ilˈlusioned** *adj*

illusionism (ɪˈluːʒəˌnɪzəm) *n* **1** *Philosophy.* the doctrine that the external world exists only in illusory sense perceptions. **2** the use of highly illusory effects in art.

illusionist (ɪˈluːʒənɪst) *n* **1** a person given to illusions; visionary; dreamer. **2** *Philosophy.* a person who believes in illusionism. **3** an artist who practises illusionism. **4** a conjuror; magician.
▸ **ilˌlusionˈistic** *adj*

illusory (ɪˈluːsərɪ) *or* **illusive** (ɪˈluːsɪv) *adj* producing or based on illusion; deceptive or unreal.
▸ **ilˈlusorily** *adv* ▸ **ilˈlusoriness** *n*

> **USAGE NOTE** *Illusive* is sometimes wrongly used where *elusive* is meant: *they fought hard, but victory remained elusive* (not *illusive*).

illust. *or* **illus.** *abbrev. for:* **1** illustrated. **2** illustration.

illustrate (ˈɪləˌstreɪt) *vb* **illustrates, illustrating, illustrated. 1** to clarify or explain by use of examples, analogy, etc. **2** (*tr*) to be an example of. **3** (*tr*) to explain or decorate (a book, text, etc.) with pictures. ORIG C16: from L, from *lustrāre* to purify, brighten; see LUSTRUM
▸ **ˈillusˌtrative** *adj* ▸ **ˈillusˌtrator** *n*

illustration (ˌɪləˈstreɪʃən) *n* **1** pictorial matter used to explain or decorate a text. **2** an example: *an illustration of his ability.* **3** the act of illustrating or the state of being illustrated.
▸ **ˌillusˈtrational** *adj*

illustrious (ɪˈlʌstrɪəs) *adj* **1** of great renown; famous and distinguished. **2** glorious or great: *illustrious deeds.* ORIG

C16: from L *illustris* bright, famous, from *illustrāre* to make light; see ILLUSTRATE
▸ **il'lustriously** *adv* ▸ **il'lustriousness** *n*

ill will *n* hostile feeling; enmity; antagonism.

Illyria ★ (ɪ'lɪərɪə) *n* an ancient region of uncertain boundaries on the E shore of the Adriatic Sea, including parts of present-day Croatia, Montenegro, and Albania.
▸ **I'llyrian** *adj, n*

Illyricum ★ (ɪ'lɪərɪkəm) *n* a Roman province founded after 168 B.C., based on the coastal area of Illyria.

Ilmen ★ ('ɪlmən) *n* **Lake.** a lake in NW Russia, in the Novgorod Region: drains through the Volkhov River into Lake Ladoga. Area: between 780 sq. km (300 sq. miles) and 2200 sq. km (850 sq. miles), according to the season.

ILO *abbrev. for* International Labour Organisation.

Iloilo ★ (ˌiːləʊ'iːləʊ) *n* a port in the W central Philippines, on SE Panay Island. Pop.: 302 200 (1994 est.).

Ilorin ★ (ɪ'lɒrɪn) *n* a city in W Nigeria, capital of Kwara state: agricultural trade centre. Pop.: 464 000 (1995 est.).

Ilyushin ★ (*Russian* ilj'uʃin) *n* **Sergei Vladimirovich** (sɪr'jej vla'dimirəvitʃ). 1894–1977, Soviet aircraft designer.

IM *abbrev. for* **1** intramuscular(ly). Also **i.m. 2** instant messaging; used esp. in e-mails, text messages, etc. ORIG C20

I'm (aɪm) *contraction of* I am.

im- *prefix* a variant of **in-**[1] and **in-**[2] before *b, m,* and *p.*

image ('ɪmɪdʒ) *n* **1** a representation or likeness of a person or thing, esp. in sculpture. **2** an optically formed reproduction of an object, such as one formed by a lens or mirror. **3** a person or thing that resembles another closely; double or copy. **4** a mental picture; idea produced by the imagination. **5** the personality presented to the public by a person, organization, etc.: *a politician's image.* **6** the pattern of light that is focused onto the retina. **7** *Psychol.* the mental experience of something that is not immediately present to the senses, often involving memory. See also **imagery. 8** a personification of a specified quality; epitome: *the image of good breeding.* **9** a mental picture or association of ideas evoked in a literary work. **10** a figure of speech such as a simile or metaphor. ◆ *vb* **images, imaging, imaged.** (*tr*) **11** to picture in the mind; imagine. **12** to make or reflect an image of. **13** to project or display on a screen, etc. **14** to portray or describe. **15** to be an example or epitome of; typify. ORIG C13: from OF *imagene,* from L *imāgō* copy, representation; rel. to L *imitārī* to IMITATE
▸ **'imageable** *adj* ▸ **'imageless** *adj*

image converter *or* **tube** *n* an electronic device that converts an invisible image, esp. one formed by X-rays, into an image that is visible on a fluorescent screen.

image enhancement *n* a method of improving the definition of a video picture by a computer program which reduces the lowest grey values to black and the highest to white: used for pictures from microscopes, surveillance cameras, and scanners.

image intensifier *or* **tube** *n* any of various devices for amplifying the intensity of an optical image, sometimes used in conjunction with an image converter.

image orthicon *n* a television camera tube in which electrons, emitted from a surface in proportion to the intensity of the incident light, are focused onto the target causing secondary emission of electrons.

image processing *n* the manipulation or modification of a digitized image, esp. to improve its quality.

imagery ('ɪmɪdʒrɪ, -dʒərɪ) *n, pl* **imageries. 1** figurative or descriptive language in a literary work. **2** images collectively. **3** *Psychol.* **3a** the materials or general processes of the imagination. **3b** the characteristic kind of mental images formed by a particular individual. See also **image** (sense 7), **imagination** (sense 1).

image tube *n* another name for **image converter** or **image intensifier.**

imaginary (ɪ'mædʒɪnərɪ, -dʒɪnrɪ) *adj* **1** existing in the imagination; unreal; illusory. **2** *Maths.* involving or containing imaginary numbers.
▸ **im'aginarily** *adv*

imaginary number *n* any complex number of the form $a + ib$, where b is not zero and $i = \sqrt{-1}$.

imagination (ɪˌmædʒɪ'neɪʃən) *n* **1** the faculty or action of producing ideas, esp. mental images of what is not present or has not been experienced. **2** mental creative ability. **3** the ability to deal resourcefully with unexpected or unusual problems, circumstances, etc.

imaginative (ɪ'mædʒɪnətɪv) *adj* **1** produced by or indicative of a creative imagination. **2** having a vivid imagination.
▸ **im'aginatively** *adv* ▸ **im'aginativeness** *n*

imagine (ɪ'mædʒɪn) *vb* **imagines, imagining, imagined. 1** (when *tr, may take a clause as object*) to form a mental image of. **2** (when *tr, may take a clause as object*) to think, believe, or guess. **3** (*tr; takes a clause as object*) to suppose; assume: *I imagine he'll come.* **4** (*tr; takes a clause as object*) to believe without foundation: *he imagines he knows the whole story.* ORIG C14: from L *imāginārī* to fancy, picture mentally, from *imāgō* likeness; see IMAGE
▸ **im'aginable** *adj* ▸ **im'aginably** *adv* ▸ **im'aginer** *n*

imagism ('ɪmɪˌdʒɪzəm) *n* an early 20th-century poetic movement, advocating the use of ordinary speech and the precise presentation of images.
▸ **'imagist** *n, adj* ▸ **ˌimag'istic** *adj*

imago (ɪ'meɪgəʊ) *n, pl* **imagoes** *or* **imagines** (ɪ'mædʒəˌniːz). **1** an adult sexually mature insect. **2** *Psychoanal.* an idealized image of another person, usually a parent, carried in the unconscious. ORIG C18: NL, from L: likeness

imam (ɪ'mɑːm) *or* **imaum** (ɪ'mɑːm, ɪ'mɔːm) *n Islam.* **1** a leader of congregational prayer in a mosque. **2** a caliph, as leader of a Muslim community. **3** any of a succession of Muslim religious leaders regarded by their followers as divinely inspired. ORIG C17: from Ar.: leader

imamate (ɪ'mɑːmeɪt) *n Islam.* **1** the region or territory governed by an imam. **2** the office, rank, or period of office of an imam.

imbalance (ɪm'bæləns) *n* a lack of balance, as in emphasis, proportion, etc.: *the political imbalance of the programme.*

imbecile ('ɪmbɪˌsiːl, -ˌsaɪl) *n* **1** *Psychol.* a person of very low intelligence (IQ of 25 to 50). **2** *Inf.* an extremely stupid person; dolt. ◆ *adj also* **imbecilic** (ˌɪmbɪ'sɪlɪk). **3** of or like an imbecile; mentally deficient; feeble-minded. **4** stupid or senseless: *an imbecile thing to do.* ORIG C16: from L *imbēcillus* feeble (physically or mentally)
▸ **'imbeˌcilely** *or* **ˌimbe'cilically** *adv* ▸ **ˌimbe'cility** *n*

imbed (ɪm'bɛd) *vb* **imbeds, imbedding, imbedded.** a less common spelling of **embed.**

imbibe (ɪm'baɪb) *vb* **imbibes, imbibing, imbibed. 1** to drink (esp. alcoholic drinks). **2** *Literary.* to take in or assimilate (ideas, etc.): *to imbibe the spirit of the Renaissance.* **3** (*tr*) to take in as if by drinking: *to imbibe fresh air.* **4** to absorb or cause to absorb liquid or moisture; assimilate or saturate. ORIG C14: from L *imbibere,* from *bibere* to drink
▸ **im'biber** *n*

imbricate *adj* ('ɪmbrɪkɪt, -ˌkeɪt), *also* **imbricated. 1** *Archit.* relating to or having tiles, shingles, or slates that overlap. **2** (of leaves, scales, etc.) overlapping each other. ◆ *vb* ('ɪmbrɪˌkeɪt), **imbricates, imbricating, imbricated. 3** (*tr*) to decorate with a repeating pattern resembling scales or overlapping tiles. ORIG C17: from L *imbricāre* to cover with overlapping tiles, from *imbrex* pantile
▸ **'imbricately** *adv* ▸ **ˌimbri'cation** *n*

imbroglio (ɪm'brəʊlɪˌəʊ) *n, pl* **imbroglios. 1** a confused or perplexing political or interpersonal situation. **2** *Obs.* a confused heap; jumble. ORIG C18: from It., from *imbrogliare* to confuse, EMBROIL

Imbros ★ ('ɪmbrəs) *n* a Turkish island in the NE Aegean Sea, west of the Gallipoli Peninsula: occupied by Greece (1912–14) and Britain (1914–23). Area: 280 sq. km (108 sq. miles). Turkish name: **Imroz.**

imbrue (ɪm'bruː) *vb* **imbrues, imbruing, imbrued.** (*tr*) *Rare.* **1** to stain, esp. with blood. **2** to permeate or impregnate. ORIG C15: from OF *embreuver,* from L *imbibere* to IMBIBE
▸ **im'bruement** *n*

imbue (ɪm'bjuː) *vb* **imbues, imbuing, imbued.** (*tr;* usually foll. by *with*) **1** to instil or inspire (with ideals, principles, etc.). **2** *Rare.* to soak, esp. with dye, etc. ORIG C16: from L *imbuere* to stain, accustom
▸ **im'buement** *n*

IMechE *abbrev. for* Institution of Mechanical Engineers.

IMF *abbrev. for* International Monetary Fund.

IMHO *abbrev. for*: in my humble opinion; used esp. in e-mails, text messages etc.

Imhotep ★ (ɪmˈhəʊtɛp) *n* c. 2600 B.C., Egyptian physician and architect. After his death he was worshipped as a god; the Greeks identified him with Asclepius.

imit. *abbrev. for:* **1** imitation. **2** imitative.

imitate (ˈɪmɪˌteɪt) *vb* **imitates, imitating, imitated.** (*tr*) **1** to try to follow the manner, style, etc., of or take as a model: *many writers imitated the language of Shakespeare.* **2** to pretend to be or to impersonate, esp. for humour; mimic. **3** to make a copy or reproduction of; duplicate. ORIG C16: from L *imitārī;* see IMAGE
▸ **imitable** (ˈɪmɪtəbᵊl) *adj* ▸ **ˌimitaˈbility** *n* ▸ **ˈimiˌtator** *n*

imitation (ˌɪmɪˈteɪʃən) *n* **1** the act or practice of imitating; mimicry. **2** an instance or product of imitating, such as a copy of the manner of a person; impression. **3a** a copy of a genuine article; counterfeit. **3b** (*as modifier*): *imitation jewellery.* **4** *Music.* the repetition of a phrase or figure in one part after its appearance in another, as in a fugue.
▸ **ˌimiˈtational** *adj*

imitative (ˈɪmɪtətɪv) *adj* **1** imitating or tending to copy. **2** characterized by imitation. **3** copying or reproducing an original, esp. in an inferior manner: *imitative painting.* **4** another word for **onomatopoeic.**
▸ **ˈimitatively** *adv* ▸ **ˈimitativeness** *n*

Imittós ★ (ˌimiˈtɔs) *n* a transliteration of the Modern Greek name for **Hymettus.**

immaculate (ɪˈmækjʊlɪt) *adj* **1** completely clean; extremely tidy: *his clothes were immaculate.* **2** completely flawless, etc.: *an immaculate rendering of the symphony.* **3** morally pure; free from sin or corruption. **4** *Biol.* with no spots or markings. ORIG C15: from L, from IM- (not) + *macula* blemish
▸ **imˈmaculacy** *or* **imˈmaculateness** *n* ▸ **imˈmaculately** *adv*

Immaculate Conception *n Christian theol., RC Church.* the doctrine that the Virgin Mary was conceived without any stain of original sin.

immanent (ˈɪmənənt) *adj* **1** existing, operating, or remaining within; inherent. **2** (of God) present throughout the universe. ORIG C16: from L *immanēre* to remain in
▸ **ˈimmanence** *or* **ˈimmanency** *n* ▸ **ˈimmanently** *adv*
▸ **ˈimmanenˌtism** *n*

Immanuel *or* **Emmanuel** ★ (ɪˈmænjʊəl) *n Bible.* the child whose birth was foretold by Isaiah (Isaiah 7:14) and who in Christian tradition is identified with Jesus. ORIG from Heb. *ʻimmānūʼel,* lit.: God with us

immaterial (ˌɪməˈtɪərɪəl) *adj* **1** of no real importance; inconsequential. **2** not formed of matter; incorporeal; spiritual.
▸ **ˌimmaˌteriˈality** *n* ▸ **ˌimmaˈterially** *adv*

immaterialism (ˌɪməˈtɪərɪəˌlɪzəm) *n Philosophy.* the doctrine that the material world exists only in the mind.
▸ **ˌimmaˈterialist** *n*

immature (ˌɪməˈtjʊə, -ˈtʃʊə) *adj* **1** not fully grown or developed. **2** deficient in maturity; lacking wisdom, insight, emotional stability, etc.
▸ **ˌimmaˈturely** *adv* ▸ **ˌimmaˈturity** *or* **ˌimmaˈtureness** *n*

immeasurable (ɪˈmɛʒərəbᵊl) *adj* incapable of being measured, esp. by virtue of great size; limitless.
▸ **imˌmeasuraˈbility** *or* **imˈmeasurableness** *n* ▸ **imˈmeasurably** *adv*

immediate (ɪˈmiːdɪət) *adj* (*usually prenominal*) **1** taking place or accomplished without delay: *an immediate reaction.* **2** closest or most direct in effect or relationship: *the immediate cause of his downfall.* **3** having no intervening medium; direct in effect: *an immediate influence.* **4** contiguous in space, time, or relationship: *our immediate neighbour.* **5** present; current: *the immediate problem is food.* **6** *Philosophy.* of or relating to a concept that is directly known or intuited. ORIG C16: from Med. L, from L IM- (not) + *mediāre* to be in the middle; see MEDIATE
▸ **imˈmediacy** *or* **imˈmediateness** *n*

immediately (ɪˈmiːdɪətlɪ) *adv* **1** without delay or intervention; at once; instantly. **2** very closely or directly: *this immediately concerns you.* **3** near or close by: *somewhere immediately in this area.* ◆ *conj* **4** (*subordinating*) *Chiefly Brit.* as; as soon as: *immediately he opened the door, there was a gust of wind.*

immemorial (ˌɪmɪˈmɔːrɪəl) *adj* originating in the distant past; ancient (postpositive in **time immemorial**). ORIG C17: from Med. L, from L IM- (not) + *memoria* MEMORY
▸ **ˌimmeˈmorially** *adv*

immense (ɪˈmɛns) *adj* **1** unusually large; huge; vast. **2** without limits; immeasurable. **3** *Inf.* very good; excellent. ORIG C15: from L *immensus,* lit.: unmeasured, from IM- (not) + *mētīrī* to measure
▸ **imˈmensely** *adv* ▸ **imˈmenseness** *n*

immensity (ɪˈmɛnsɪtɪ) *n, pl* **immensities. 1** the state of being immense; vastness; enormity. **2** enormous expanse, distance, or volume. **3** *Inf.* a huge amount: *an immensity of wealth.*

immerse (ɪˈmɜːs) *vb* **immerses, immersing, immersed.** (*tr*) **1** (often foll. by *in*) to plunge or dip into liquid. **2** (*often passive;* often foll. by *in*) to involve deeply; engross: *to immerse oneself in a problem.* **3** to baptize by dipping the whole body into water. ORIG C17: from L *immergere,* from IM- (in) + *mergere* to dip
▸ **imˈmersible** *adj* ▸ **imˈmersion** *n*

immerser (ɪˈmɜːsə) *n* an informal term for **immersion heater.**

immersion heater *n* an electrical device, usually thermostatically controlled, for heating the liquid in which it is immersed, esp. as a fixture in a domestic hot-water tank.

immigrant (ˈɪmɪgrənt) *n* **1a** a person who immigrates. **1b** (*as modifier*): *an immigrant community.* **2** *Brit.* a person who has been settled in a country of which he or she is not a native for less than ten years.

immigrate (ˈɪmɪˌgreɪt) *vb* **immigrates, immigrating, immigrated. 1** (*intr*) to come to a place or country of which one is not a native in order to settle there. **2** (*tr*) to introduce or bring in as an immigrant. ORIG C17: from L *immigrāre* to go into
▸ **ˌimmiˈgration** *n* ▸ **ˈimmiˌgrator** *n* ▸ **ˈimmiˌgratory** *adj*

imminent (ˈɪmɪnənt) *adj* **1** liable to happen soon; impending. **2** *Obs.* overhanging. ORIG C16: from L *imminēre* to project over; rel. to *mons* mountain
▸ **ˈimminence** *n* ▸ **ˈimminently** *adv*

Immingham ★ (ˈɪmɪŋəm) *n* a port in NE England, in North East Lincolnshire: docks opened in 1912, principally for the exporting of coal; now handles chiefly bulk materials, esp. imported iron ore. Pop.: 12 278 (1991).

immiscible (ɪˈmɪsɪbᵊl) *adj* (of liquids) incapable of being mixed: *oil and water are immiscible.*
▸ **imˌmisciˈbility** *n* ▸ **imˈmiscibly** *adv*

immitigable (ɪˈmɪtɪgəbᵊl) *adj Rare.* unable to be mitigated.
▸ **imˌmitigaˈbility** *n* ▸ **imˈmitigably** *adv*

immobile (ɪˈməʊbaɪl) *adj* **1** not moving; motionless. **2** not able to move or be moved; fixed.
▸ **immobility** (ˌɪməʊˈbɪlɪtɪ) *n*

immobilize *or* **immobilise** (ɪˈməʊbɪˌlaɪz) *vb* **immobilizes, immobilizing, immobilized** *or* **immobilises, immobilising, immobilised.** (*tr*) **1** to make immobile: *to immobilize a car.* **2** *Finance.* to convert (circulating capital) into fixed capital.
▸ **imˌmobiliˈzation** *or* **imˌmobiliˈsation** *n* ▸ **imˈmobiˌlizer** *or* **imˈmobiˌliser** *n*

immoderate (ɪˈmɒdərɪt, ɪˈmɒdrɪt) *adj* lacking in moderation; excessive: *immoderate demands.*
▸ **imˈmoderately** *adv* ▸ **imˌmoderˈation** *or* **imˈmoderateness** *n*

immodest (ɪˈmɒdɪst) *adj* **1** indecent, esp. with regard to sexual propriety; improper. **2** bold, impudent, or shameless.
▸ **imˈmodestly** *adv* ▸ **imˈmodesty** *n*

immolate (ˈɪməʊˌleɪt) *vb* **immolates, immolating, immolated.** (*tr*) **1** to kill or offer as a sacrifice, esp. by fire. **2** *Literary.* to sacrifice (something highly valued). ORIG C16: from L *immolāre* to sprinkle an offering with sacrificial meal, sacrifice; see MILL
▸ **ˌimmoˈlation** *n* ▸ **ˈimmoˌlator** *n*

immoral (ɪ'mɒrəl) *adj* **1** transgressing accepted moral rules; corrupt. **2** sexually dissolute; profligate or promiscuous. **3** unscrupulous or unethical: *immoral trading.* **4** tending to corrupt or resulting from corruption: *immoral earnings.*
► **im'morally** *adv*

> **USAGE NOTE** See at **amoral.**

immorality (ˌɪmə'rælɪtɪ) *n, pl* **immoralities. 1** the quality or state of being immoral. **2** immoral behaviour, esp. in sexual matters; licentiousness; promiscuity. **3** an immoral act.

immortal (ɪ'mɔːtᵊl) *adj* **1** not subject to death or decay; having perpetual life. **2** having everlasting fame; remembered throughout time. **3** everlasting; perpetual; constant. **4** of or relating to immortal beings or concepts. ♦ *n* **5** an immortal being. **6** (*often pl*) a person who is remembered enduringly, esp. an author.
► **ˌimmor'tality** *n* ► **im'mortally** *adv*

immortalize *or* **immortalise** (ɪ'mɔːtəˌlaɪz) *vb* **immortalizes, immortalizing, immortalized** *or* **immortalises, immortalising, immortalised.** (*tr*) **1** to give everlasting fame to, as by treating in a literary work: *Macbeth was immortalized by Shakespeare.* **2** to give immortality to.
► **imˌmortali'zation** *or* **imˌmortali'sation** *n* ► **im'mortalˌizer** *or* **im'mortalˌiser** *n*

immortelle (ˌɪmɔː'tɛl) *n* any of various composite plants that retain their colour when dried. Also called: **everlasting.** ORIG C19: from F (*fleur*) *immortelle* everlasting (flower)

immovable *or* **immoveable** (ɪ'muːvəbᵊl) *adj* **1** unable to move or be moved; immobile. **2** unable to be diverted from one's intentions; steadfast. **3** unaffected by feeling; impassive. **4** unchanging; unalterable. **5** (of feasts, etc.) on the same date every year. **6** *Law.* **6a** (of property) not liable to be removed; fixed. **6b** of or relating to immovable property.
► **imˌmova'bility, imˌmovea'bility** *or* **im'movableness, im'moveableness** *n* ► **im'movably** *or* **im'moveably** *adv*

immune (ɪ'mjuːn) *adj* **1** protected against a specific disease by inoculation or as the result of innate or acquired resistance. **2** relating to or conferring immunity: *an immune body* (see **antibody**). **3** (*usually postpositive;* foll. by *to*) unsusceptible (to) or secure (against): *immune to inflation.* **4** exempt from obligation, penalty, etc. ♦ *n* **5** an immune person or animal. ORIG C15: from L *immūnis* exempt from a public service

immune response *n* the reaction of an organism's body to foreign materials (antigens), including the production of antibodies.

immunity (ɪ'mjuːnɪtɪ) *n, pl* **immunities. 1** the ability of an organism to resist disease, either through the activities of specialized blood cells or antibodies produced by them in response to natural exposure or inoculation (**active immunity**) or by the injection of antiserum or the transfer of antibodies from a mother to her baby via the placenta or breast milk (**passive immunity**). See also **acquired immunity, natural immunity. 2** freedom from obligation or duty, esp. exemption from tax, legal liability, etc.

immunize *or* **immunise** ('ɪmjʊˌnaɪz) *vb* **immunizes, immunizing, immunized** *or* **immunises, immunising, immunised.** (*tr*) to make immune, esp. by inoculation.
► **ˌimmuni'zation** *or* **ˌimmuni'sation** *n* ► **'immuˌnizer** *or* **'immuˌniser** *n*

immuno- *or before a vowel* **immun-** *combining form.* indicating immunity or immune: *immunology.*

immunoassay (ˌɪmjʊnəʊ'æseɪ) *n Immunol.* a technique of identifying a substance, esp. a protein, through its action as an antigen.

immunocompromised (ˌɪmjʊnəʊ'kɒmprəmaɪzd) *adj* having an impaired immune system and therefore incapable of an effective immune response, usually as a result of disease, such as AIDS, that damages the immune system.

immunodeficiency (ˌɪmjʊnəʊdɪ'fɪʃənsɪ) *n* a deficiency in or breakdown of a person's immune system.

immunogenic (ˌɪmjʊnəʊ'dʒɛnɪk) *adj* causing or producing immunity or an immune response.
► **ˌimmuno'genically** *adv*

immunoglobulin (ˌɪmjʊnəʊ'glɒbjʊlɪn) *n* any of five classes of proteins, all of which show antibody activity.

immunology (ˌɪmjʊ'nɒlədʒɪ) *n* the branch of biological science concerned with the study of immunity.
► **immunologic** (ˌɪmjʊnə'lɒdʒɪk) *or* **ˌimmuno'logical** *adj* ► **ˌimmuno'logically** *adv* ► **ˌimmu'nologist** *n*

immunoreaction (ɪˌmjuːnəʊrɪ'ækʃən) *n* the reaction between an antigen and its antibody.

immunosuppression (ˌɪmjʊnəʊsə'prɛʃən) *n* medical suppression of the body's immune system, esp. in order to reduce the likelihood of rejection of a transplanted organ.
► **ˌimmunosup'pressant** *n, adj*

immunosuppressive (ˌɪmjʊnəʊsə'prɛsɪv) *n* **1** any drug that lessens the body's rejection, esp. of a transplanted organ. ♦ *adj* **2** of or relating to such a drug.

immunotherapy (ˌɪmjʊnəʊ'θɛrəpɪ) *n* the treatment of disease by stimulating or modifying the immune response.
► **immunotherapeutic** (ˌɪmjʊnəʊˌθɛrə'pjuːtɪk) *adj*

immure (ɪ'mjʊə) *vb* **immures, immuring, immured.** (*tr*) **1** *Arch. or literary.* to enclose within or as if within walls; imprison. **2** to shut (oneself) away from society. ORIG C16: from Med. L, from L IM- (in) + *mūrus* wall
► **im'murement** *n*

immutable (ɪ'mjuːtəbᵊl) *adj* unchanging through time; unalterable; ageless: *immutable laws.*
► **imˌmuta'bility** *or* **im'mutableness** *n*

Imo ★ ('iːməʊ) *n* a state of SE Nigeria, formed in 1976 from part of East-Central State. Capital: Owerri. Pop.: 2 779 028 (1995 est.). Area: 5530 sq. km (2135 sq. miles).

imp (ɪmp) *n* **1** a small demon or devil; mischievous sprite. **2** a mischievous child. ♦ *vb* **3** (*tr*) *Falconry.* to insert new feathers in order to repair (the wing of a falcon). ORIG OE *impa* bud, graft, hence offspring, child, from *impian* to graft

imp. *abbrev. for:* **1** imperative. **2** imperfect. **3** imperial. **4** impersonal. **5** import. **6** importer.

impact *n* ('ɪmpækt). **1** the act of one body, etc., striking another; collision. **2** the force with which one thing hits another. **3** the impression made by an idea, social group, etc. ♦ *vb* (ɪm'pækt). **4** to drive or press (an object) firmly into (another object, thing, etc.) or (of two objects) to be driven or pressed firmly together. **5** to have an impact or strong effect (on). ORIG C18: from L *impactus* pushed against, fastened on, from *impingere* to thrust at, from *pangere* to drive in
► **im'paction** *n*

impacted (ɪm'pæktɪd) *adj* **1** (of a tooth) unable to erupt, esp. because of being wedged against another tooth below the gum. **2** (of a fracture) having the jagged broken ends wedged into each other.

impair (ɪm'pɛə) *vb* (*tr*) to reduce or weaken in strength, quality, etc.: *his hearing was impaired by an accident.* ORIG C14: from OF *empeirer* to make worse, from LL, from L *pēior* worse; see PEJORATIVE
► **im'pairable** *adj* ► **im'pairer** *n* ► **im'pairment** *n*

impala (ɪm'pɑːlə) *n, pl* **impalas** *or* **impala.** an antelope of southern and eastern Africa, having lyre-shaped horns and able to move with enormous leaps. ORIG from Zulu

impale *or* **empale** (ɪm'peɪl) *vb* **impales, impaling, impaled.** (*tr*) **1** (often foll. by *on, upon,* or *with*) to pierce with a sharp instrument: *they impaled his severed head on a spear.* **2** *Heraldry.* to charge (a shield) with two coats of arms placed side by side. ORIG C16: from Med. L, from L IM- (in) + *pālus* PALE[2]
► **im'palement** *or* **em'palement** *n*

impalpable (ɪm'pælpəbᵊl) *adj* **1** imperceptible, esp. to the touch: *impalpable shadows.* **2** difficult to understand; abstruse.
► **imˌpalpa'bility** *n* ► **im'palpably** *adv*

impanel (ɪm'pænᵊl) *vb* **impanels, impanelling, impanelled** *or US* **impanels, impaneling, impaneled.** a variant spelling (esp. US) of **empanel.**
► **im'panelment** *n*

impart (ɪm'pɑ:t) *vb* (*tr*) **1** to communicate (information, etc.); relate. **2** to give or bestow (an abstract quality): *to impart wisdom.* ORIG C15: from OF, from L, from IM- (in) + *partīre* to share, from *pars* part
▸ **im'partable** *adj* ▸ **,impar'tation** *or* **im'partment** *n*

impartial (ɪm'pɑ:ʃəl) *adj* not prejudiced towards or against any particular side; fair; unbiased.
▸ **im,parti'ality** *or* **im'partialness** *n* ▸ **im'partially** *adv*

impartible (ɪm'pɑ:təb^{ə}l) *adj Law.* (of land, an estate, etc.) incapable of partition; indivisible.
▸ **im,parti'bility** *n* ▸ **im'partibly** *adv*

impassable (ɪm'pɑ:səb^{ə}l) *adj* (of terrain, roads, etc.) not able to be travelled through or over.
▸ **im,passa'bility** *or* **im'passableness** *n* ▸ **im'passably** *adv*

impasse (æm'pɑ:s, 'æmpɑ:s) *n* a situation in which progress is blocked; an insurmountable difficulty; stalemate. ORIG C19: from F; see IM-, PASS

impassible (ɪm'pæsəb^{ə}l) *adj Rare.* **1** not susceptible to pain or injury. **2** impassive or unmoved.
▸ **im,passi'bility** *or* **im'passibleness** *n* ▸ **im'passibly** *adv*

impassion (ɪm'pæʃən) *vb* (*tr*) to arouse the passions of; inflame.

impassioned (ɪm'pæʃənd) *adj* filled with passion; fiery; inflamed: *an impassioned appeal.*
▸ **im'passionedly** *adv* ▸ **im'passionedness** *n*

impassive (ɪm'pæsɪv) *adj* **1** not revealing or affected by emotion; reserved. **2** calm; serene; imperturbable.
▸ **im'passively** *adv* ▸ **im'passiveness** *or* **impassivity** (,ɪmpæ'sɪvɪtɪ) *n*

impasto (ɪm'pæstəʊ) *n* **1** paint applied thickly, so that brush marks are evident. **2** the technique of painting in this way. ORIG C18: from It., from *impastare*, from *pasta* PASTE

impatience (ɪm'peɪʃəns) *n* **1** lack of patience; intolerance of or irritability with anything that impedes or delays. **2** restless desire for change and excitement.

impatiens (ɪm'peɪʃɪ,ɛnz) *n, pl* **impatiens.** a plant with explosive pods, such as balsam, touch-me-not, and busy Lizzie. ORIG C18: NL from L: impatient; from the fact that the ripe pods burst open when touched

impatient (ɪm'peɪʃənt) *adj* **1** lacking patience; easily irritated at delay, etc. **2** exhibiting lack of patience. **3** (*postpositive;* foll. by *of*) intolerant (of) or indignant (at): *impatient of indecision.* **4** (*postpositive;* often foll. by *for*) restlessly eager (for *or* to do something).
▸ **im'patiently** *adv*

impeach (ɪm'pi:tʃ) *vb* (*tr*) **1** *Criminal law.* to bring a charge or accusation against. **2** *Brit. criminal law.* to accuse of a crime against the state. **3** *Chiefly US.* to charge (a public official) with an offence committed in office. **4** to challenge or question (a person's honesty, etc.). ORIG C14: from OF, from LL *impedicāre* to entangle, catch, from L IM- (in) + *pedica* a fetter, from *pēs* foot
▸ **im'peachable** *adj* ▸ **im'peachment** *n*

impeccable (ɪm'pɛkəb^{ə}l) *adj* **1** without flaw or error; faultless: *an impeccable record.* **2** *Rare.* incapable of sinning. ORIG C16: from LL *impeccābilis* sinless, from L IM- (not) + *peccāre* to sin
▸ **im,pecca'bility** *n* ▸ **im'peccably** *adv*

impecunious (,ɪmpɪ'kju:nɪəs) *adj* without money; penniless. ORIG C16: from IM- (not) + from L *pecūniōsus* wealthy, from *pecūnia* money
▸ **,impe'cuniously** *adv* ▸ **,impe'cuniousness** *or* **impecuniosity** (,ɪmpɪkju:nɪ'ɒsɪtɪ) *n*

impedance (ɪm'pi:d^{ə}ns) *n* **1** a measure of the opposition to the flow of an alternating current equal to the square root of the sum of the squares of the resistance and the reactance, expressed in ohms. **2** the ratio of the sound pressure in a medium to the rate of alternating flow through a specified surface due to the sound wave. **3** the ratio of the mechanical force to the velocity of the resulting vibration.

impede (ɪm'pi:d) *vb* **impedes, impeding, impeded.** (*tr*) to restrict or retard in action, progress, etc.; obstruct. ORIG C17: from L *impedīre* to hinder, lit.: shackle the feet, from *pēs* foot
▸ **im'peder** *n* ▸ **im'pedingly** *adv*

impediment (ɪm'pɛdɪmənt) *n* **1** a hindrance or obstruction. **2** a physical defect, esp. one of speech, such as a stammer. **3** (*pl* **impediments** *or* **impedimenta** (-'mɛntə)) *Law.* an obstruction to the making of a contract, esp. one of marriage.
▸ **im,pedi'mental** *or* **im,pedi'mentary** *adj*

impedimenta (ɪm,pɛdɪ'mɛntə) *pl n* **1** any objects that impede progress, esp. the baggage and equipment carried by an army. **2** a plural of **impediment** (sense 3). ORIG C16: from L, pl of *impedīmentum* hindrance; see IMPEDE

impel (ɪm'pɛl) *vb* **impels, impelling, impelled.** (*tr*) **1** to urge or force (a person) to an action; constrain or motivate. **2** to push, drive, or force into motion. ORIG C15: from L *impellere* to push against, drive forward
▸ **im'pellent** *n, adj*

impeller (ɪm'pɛlə) *n* the vaned rotating disc of a centrifugal pump, compressor, etc.

impend (ɪm'pɛnd) *vb* (*intr*) **1** (esp. of something threatening) to be imminent. **2** (foll. by *over*) *Rare.* to be suspended; hang. ORIG C16: from L *impendēre* to overhang, from *pendēre* to hang
▸ **im'pendence** *or* **im'pendency** *n* ▸ **im'pending** *adj*

impenetrable (ɪm'pɛnɪtrəb^{ə}l) *adj* **1** incapable of being pierced through or penetrated: *an impenetrable forest.* **2** incapable of being understood; incomprehensible. **3** incapable of being seen through: *impenetrable gloom.* **4** not susceptible to ideas, influence, etc.: *impenetrable ignorance.* **5** *Physics.* (of a body) incapable of occupying the same space as another body.
▸ **im,penetra'bility** *n* ▸ **im'penetrableness** *n* ▸ **im'penetrably** *adv*

impenitent (ɪm'pɛnɪtənt) *adj* not sorry or penitent; unrepentant.
▸ **im'penitence, im'penitency,** *or* **im'penitentness** *n* ▸ **im'penitently** *adv*

imper. *abbrev. for* imperative.

imperative (ɪm'pɛrətɪv) *adj* **1** extremely urgent or important; essential. **2** peremptory or authoritative: *an imperative tone of voice.* **3** Also: **imperatival** (ɪm,pɛrə'taɪv^{ə}l). *Grammar.* denoting a mood of verbs used in giving orders, making requests, etc. ◆ *n* **4** something that is urgent or essential. **5** an order or command. **6** *Grammar.* **6a** the imperative mood. **6b** a verb in this mood. ORIG C16: from LL, from L *imperāre* to command
▸ **im'peratively** *adv* ▸ **im'perativeness** *n*

imperator (,ɪmpə'rɑ:tɔ:) *n* (in ancient Rome) a title bestowed upon generals and, later, emperors. ORIG C16: from L: commander, from *imperāre* to command
▸ **imperatorial** (ɪm,pɛrə'tɔ:rɪəl) *adj* ▸ **,impe'rator,ship** *n*

imperceptible (,ɪmpə'sɛptɪb^{ə}l) *adj* too slight, subtle, gradual, etc., to be perceived.
▸ **,imper,cepti'bility** *or* **,imper'ceptibleness** *n* ▸ **,imper'ceptibly** *adv*

imperceptive (,ɪmpə'sɛptɪv) *adj, also* **impercipient** (,ɪmpə'sɪpɪənt). lacking in perception; obtuse.
▸ **,imper'ception** *n* ▸ **,imper'ceptively** *adv* ▸ **,imper'ceptiveness** *or* **,imper'cipience** *n*

imperf. *abbrev. for:* **1** Also: **impf.** imperfect. **2** (of stamps) imperforate.

imperfect (ɪm'pɜ:fɪkt) *adj* **1** exhibiting or characterized by faults, mistakes, etc.; defective. **2** not complete or finished; deficient. **3** *Grammar.* denoting a tense of verbs used most commonly in describing continuous or repeated past actions or events. **4** *Law.* legally unenforceable. **5** *Music.* **5a** proceeding to the dominant from the tonic, subdominant, or any chord other than the dominant. **5b** of or relating to all intervals other than the fourth, fifth, and octave. Cf. **perfect** (sense 9). ◆ *n* **6** *Grammar.* **6a** the imperfect tense. **6b** a verb in this tense.
▸ **im'perfectly** *adv* ▸ **im'perfectness** *n*

imperfection (,ɪmpə'fɛkʃən) *n* **1** the condition or quality of being imperfect. **2** a fault or defect.

imperfective (,ɪmpə'fɛktɪv) *Grammar.* ◆ *adj* **1** denoting an aspect of the verb to indicate that the action is in progress without regard to its completion. Cf. **perfective.** ◆ *n* **2a** the imperfective aspect of a verb. **2b** a verb in this aspect.
▸ **,imper'fectively** *adv*

imperforate (ɪmˈpɜːfərɪt, -ˌreɪt) *adj* **1** not perforated. **2** (of a postage stamp) not provided with perforation or any other means of separation. **3** *Anat.* without the normal opening.
▸ **imˌperfoˈration** *n*

imperial (ɪmˈpɪərɪəl) *adj* **1** of or relating to an empire, emperor, or empress. **2** characteristic of an emperor; majestic; commanding. **3** exercising supreme authority; imperious. **4** (esp. of products) of a superior size or quality. **5** (*usually prenominal*) (of weights, measures, etc.) conforming to standards legally established in Great Britain. ◆ *n* **6** a book size, esp. 7½ by 11 inches or 11 by 15 inches. **7** a size of writing paper, 23 by 31 inches (US and Canad.) or 22 by 30 inches (Brit.). **8** *US.* **8a** the top of a carriage. **8b** a luggage case carried there. **9** a small tufted beard popularized by the French emperor Napoleon III. **10** a wine bottle holding the equivalent of eight normal bottles. ORIG C14: from LL, from L *imperium* command, authority, empire
▸ **imˈperially** *adv* ▸ **imˈperialness** *n*

imperialism (ɪmˈpɪərɪəˌlɪzəm) *n* **1** the policy or practice of extending a state's rule over other territories. **2** the extension or attempted extension of authority, influence, power, etc., by any person, country, institution, etc.: *cultural imperialism.* **3** a system of imperial government or rule by an emperor. **4** the spirit, character, authority, etc., of an empire.
▸ **imˈperialist** *adj, n* ▸ **imˌperialˈistic** *adj* ▸ **imˌperialˈistically** *adv*

imperil (ɪmˈpɛrɪl) *vb* **imperils, imperilling, imperilled** *or US* **imperils, imperiling, imperiled.** (*tr*) to place in danger or jeopardy; endanger.
▸ **imˈperilment** *n*

imperious (ɪmˈpɪərɪəs) *adj* **1** domineering; overbearing. **2** *Rare.* urgent. ORIG C16: from L, from *imperium* command, power
▸ **imˈperiously** *adv* ▸ **imˈperiousness** *n*

imperishable (ɪmˈpɛrɪʃəb^{ə}l) *adj* **1** not subject to decay or deterioration. **2** not likely to be forgotten: *imperishable truths.*
▸ **imˌperishaˈbility** *or* **imˈperishableness** *n* ▸ **imˈperishably** *adv*

impermanent (ɪmˈpɜːmənənt) *adj* not permanent; fleeting.
▸ **imˈpermanence** *or* **imˈpermanency** *n* ▸ **imˈpermanently** *adv*

impermeable (ɪmˈpɜːmɪəb^{ə}l) *adj* (of a substance) not allowing the passage of a fluid through interstices; not permeable.
▸ **imˌpermeaˈbility** *or* **imˈpermeableness** *n* ▸ **imˈpermeably** *adv*

impermissible (ˌɪmpəˈmɪsɪb^{ə}l) *adj* not permissible; not allowed.
▸ **ˌimperˌmissiˈbility** *n*

impersonal (ɪmˈpɜːsən^{ə}l) *adj* **1** without reference to any individual person; objective: *an impersonal assessment.* **2** devoid of human warmth or sympathy; cold: *an impersonal manner.* **3** not having human characteristics: *an impersonal God.* **4** *Grammar.* (of a verb) having no logical subject: *it is raining.* **5** *Grammar.* (of a pronoun) not denoting a person.
▸ **imˌpersonˈality** *n* ▸ **imˈpersonally** *adv*

impersonalize *or* **impersonalise** (ɪmˈpɜːsənəˌlaɪz) *vb* **impersonalizes, impersonalizing, impersonalized** *or* **impersonalises, impersonalising, impersonalised.** (*tr*) to make impersonal, esp. to rid of such human characteristics as sympathy, etc.; dehumanize.
▸ **imˌpersonaliˈzation** *or* **imˌpersonaliˈsation** *n*

impersonate (ɪmˈpɜːsəˌneɪt) *vb* **impersonates, impersonating, impersonated.** (*tr*) **1** to pretend to be (another person). **2** to imitate the character, mannerisms, etc., of (another person). **3** *Rare.* to play the part or character of. **4** an archaic word for **personify.**
▸ **imˌpersonˈation** *n* ▸ **imˈpersonˌator** *n*

impertinence (ɪmˈpɜːtɪnəns) *or* **impertinency** *n* **1** disrespectful behaviour or language; rudeness; insolence. **2** an impertinent act, gesture, etc. **3** *Rare.* lack of pertinence; irrelevance; inappropriateness.

impertinent (ɪmˈpɜːtɪnənt) *adj* **1** rude; insolent; impudent. **2** irrelevant or inappropriate. ORIG C14: from L *impertinēns* not belonging, from L IM- (not) + *pertinēre* to be relevant; see PERTAIN
▸ **imˈpertinently** *adv*

imperturbable (ˌɪmpɜːˈtɜːbəb^{ə}l) *adj* not easily perturbed; calm; unruffled.
▸ **ˌimperˌturbaˈbility** *or* **ˌimperˈturbableness** *n* ▸ **ˌimperˈturbably** *adv*

impervious (ɪmˈpɜːvɪəs) *or* **imperviable** *adj* **1** not able to be penetrated, as by water, light, etc.; impermeable. **2** (*often postpositive;* foll. by *to*) not able to be influenced (by) or not receptive (to): *impervious to argument.*
▸ **imˈperviously** *adv* ▸ **imˈperviousness** *n*

impetigo (ˌɪmpɪˈtaɪgəʊ) *n* a contagious pustular skin disease. ORIG C16: from L: scabby eruption, from *impetere* to assail; see IMPETUS; for form, cf. VERTIGO
▸ **impetiginous** (ˌɪmpɪˈtɪdʒɪnəs) *adj*

impetuous (ɪmˈpɛtjʊəs) *adj* **1** liable to act without consideration; rash; impulsive. **2** resulting from or characterized by rashness or haste. **3** *Poetic.* moving with great force or violence; rushing: *the impetuous stream hurtled down the valley.* ORIG C14: from LL *impetuōsus* violent; see IMPETUS
▸ **imˈpetuously** *adv* ▸ **imˈpetuousness** *or* **impetuosity** (ɪmˌpɛtjʊˈɒsɪtɪ) *n*

impetus (ˈɪmpɪtəs) *n, pl* **impetuses. 1** an impelling movement or force; incentive or impulse; stimulus. **2** *Physics.* the force that sets a body in motion or that tends to resist changes in a body's motion. ORIG C17: from L: attack, from *impetere* to assail, from IM- (in) + *petere* to make for, seek out

impf. *or* **imperf.** *abbrev. for* imperfect.

Imphal ★ (ɪmˈfɑːl, ˈɪmfəl) *n* a city in NE India, capital of Manipur Territory, on the Manipur River: formerly the seat of the Manipur kings: site of a major Anglo-Indian victory over the Japanese (1944), which was a turning point in the British recovery of Burma (now Myanmar). Pop.: 198 535 (1991).

impi (ˈɪmpɪ) *n, pl* **impi** *or* **impies.** a group of Bantu warriors. ORIG C19: from Zulu

impiety (ɪmˈpaɪɪtɪ) *n, pl* **impieties. 1** lack of reverence or proper respect for a god. **2** any lack of proper respect. **3** an impious act.

impinge (ɪmˈpɪndʒ) *vb* **impinges, impinging, impinged. 1** (*intr;* usually foll. by *on* or *upon*) to encroach or infringe; trespass: *to impinge on someone's time.* **2** (*intr;* usually foll. by *on, against,* or *upon*) to collide (with); strike. ORIG C16: from L *impingere* to drive at, dash against, from *pangere* to fasten, drive in
▸ **imˈpingement** *n* ▸ **imˈpinger** *n*

impious (ˈɪmpɪəs) *adj* **1** lacking piety or reverence for a god. **2** lacking respect; undutiful.
▸ **ˈimpiously** *adv* ▸ **ˈimpiousness** *n*

impish (ˈɪmpɪʃ) *adj* of or like an imp; mischievous.
▸ **ˈimpishly** *adv* ▸ **ˈimpishness** *n*

implacable (ɪmˈplækəb^{ə}l) *adj* **1** incapable of being placated or pacified; unappeasable. **2** inflexible; intractable.
▸ **imˌplacaˈbility** *n* ▸ **imˈplacably** *adv*

implant *vb* (ɪmˈplɑːnt). (*tr*) **1** to inculcate; instil: *to implant sound moral principles.* **2** to plant or embed; infix; entrench. **3** *Surgery.* to graft or insert (a tissue, hormone, etc.) into the body. ◆ *n* (ˈɪmplɑːnt). **4** anything implanted, esp. surgically, such as a tissue graft or hormone.
▸ **ˌimplanˈtation** *n*

implausible (ɪmˈplɔːzəb^{ə}l) *adj* not plausible; provoking disbelief; unlikely.
▸ **imˌplausiˈbility** *or* **imˈplausibleness** *n* ▸ **imˈplausibly** *adv*

implement *n* (ˈɪmplɪmənt). **1** a piece of equipment; tool or utensil: *gardening implements.* **2** a means to achieve a purpose; agent. ◆ *vb* (ˈɪmplɪˌmɛnt). (*tr*) **3** to carry out; put into action: *to implement a plan.* **4** *Rare.* to supply with tools. ORIG C17: from LL *implēmentum,* lit.: a filling up, from L *implēre* to fill up, satisfy, fulfil
▸ **ˌimpleˈmental** *adj* ▸ **ˌimplemenˈtation** *n*

implicate (ˈɪmplɪˌkeɪt) *vb* **implicates, implicating, impli-**

★ people and places

cated. (*tr*) **1** to show to be involved, esp. in a crime. **2** to imply: *his protest implicated censure by the authorities.* **3** *Rare.* to entangle. ORIG C16: from L *implicāre* to involve, from *plicāre* to fold
▸ **implicative** (ɪm'plɪkətɪv) *adj* ▸ **im'plicatively** *adv*

implication (ˌɪmplɪ'keɪʃən) *n* **1** the act of implicating. **2** something that is implied. **3** *Logic.* a relation between two propositions, such that the second can be logically deduced from the first.

implicit (ɪm'plɪsɪt) *adj* **1** not explicit; implied; indirect. **2** absolute and unreserved; unquestioning: *implicit trust.* **3** (when *postpositive,* foll. by *in*) contained or inherent: *to bring out the anger implicit in the argument.* ORIG C16: from L *implicitus,* var. of *implicātus* interwoven; see IMPLICATE
▸ **im'plicitly** *adv* ▸ **im'plicitness** *n*

implied (ɪm'plaɪd) *adj* hinted at or suggested; not directly expressed: *an implied criticism.*

implode (ɪm'pləʊd) *vb* **implodes, imploding, imploded.** to collapse inwards. Cf. **explode.** ORIG C19: from IM- + (EX)PLODE

implore (ɪm'plɔː) *vb* **implores, imploring, implored.** (*tr*) to beg or ask (someone) earnestly (to do something); plead with; beseech; supplicate. ORIG C16: from L *implōrāre,* from IM- + *plōrāre* to bewail
▸ **ˌimplo'ration** *n* ▸ **im'ploratory** *adj* ▸ **im'ploringly** *adv*

imply (ɪm'plaɪ) *vb* **implies, implying, implied.** (*tr; may take a clause as object*) **1** to express or indicate by a hint; suggest. **2** to suggest or involve as a necessary consequence. ORIG C14: from OF *emplier,* from L; see IMPLICATE

> **USAGE NOTE** See at **infer.**

impolder (ɪm'pəʊldə) *or* **empolder** *vb* to make into a polder; reclaim (land) from the sea. ORIG C19: from Du. *inpolderen,* see IN-[2], POLDER

impolite (ˌɪmpə'laɪt) *adj* discourteous; rude.
▸ **ˌimpo'litely** *adv* ▸ **ˌimpo'liteness** *n*

impolitic (ɪm'pɒlɪtɪk) *adj* not politic or expedient; unwise.
▸ **im'politicly** *adv*

imponderable (ɪm'pɒndərəbᵊl, -drəbᵊl) *adj* **1** unable to be weighed or assessed. ◆ *n* **2** something difficult or impossible to assess.
▸ **imˌpondera'bility** *or* **im'ponderableness** *n* ▸ **im'ponderably** *adv*

import *vb* (ɪm'pɔːt, 'ɪmpɔːt). **1** to buy or bring in (goods or services) from a foreign country. **2** (*tr*) to bring in from an outside source: *to import foreign words into the language.* **3** *Rare.* to signify; mean: *to import doom.* ◆ *n* ('ɪmpɔːt). **4** (*often pl*) **4a** goods or services that are bought from foreign countries. **4b** (*as modifier*): *an import licence.* **5** importance: *a man of great import.* **6** meaning. **7** *Inf.* a sportsman or -woman who is not native to the country in which he or she plays. ORIG C15: from L *importāre* to carry in
▸ **im'portable** *adj* ▸ **im'porter** *n*

importance (ɪm'pɔːtᵊns) *n* **1** the state of being important; significance. **2** social status; standing; esteem: *a man of importance.* **3** *Obs.* **3a** meaning or signification. **3b** an important matter. **3c** importunity.

important (ɪm'pɔːtᵊnt) *adj* **1** of great significance or value; outstanding. **2** of social significance; notable; eminent; esteemed: *an important man in the town.* **3** (when postpositive, usually foll. by *to*) of great concern (to); valued highly (by): *your wishes are important to me.* ORIG C16: from OIt., from Med. L *importāre* to signify, be of consequence, from L: to carry in
▸ **im'portantly** *adv*

> **USAGE NOTE** The use of *more importantly* as in *more importantly, the local council is opposed to this proposal* has become very common, but many people still prefer to use *more important.*

importation (ˌɪmpɔː'teɪʃən) *n* **1** the act, business, or process of importing goods or services. **2** an imported product or service.

★ people and places

importunate (ɪm'pɔːtjʊnɪt) *adj* **1** persistent or demanding; insistent. **2** *Rare.* troublesome; annoying.
▸ **im'portunately** *adv* ▸ **im'portunateness** *n*

importune (ɪm'pɔːtjuːn, ˌɪmpɔː'tjuːn) *vb* **importunes, importuning, importuned.** (*tr*) **1** to harass with persistent requests; demand of (someone) insistently. **2** to beg for persistently; request with insistence. ORIG C16: from L *importūnus* tiresome, from *im-* IN-[1] + *-portūnus* as in *opportūnus* OPPORTUNE
▸ **im'portunely** *adv* ▸ **im'portuner** *n* ▸ **ˌimpor'tunity** *or* **im'portunacy** *n*

impose (ɪm'pəʊz) *vb* **imposes, imposing, imposed.** (usually foll. by *on* or *upon*) **1** (*tr*) to establish as something to be obeyed or complied with; enforce. **2** to force (oneself, one's presence, etc.) on others; obtrude. **3** (*intr*) to take advantage, as of a person or quality: *to impose on someone's kindness.* **4** (*tr*) *Printing.* to arrange (pages, type, etc.) in a chase so that the pages will be in the correct order. **5** (*tr*) to pass off deceptively; foist. ORIG C15: from OF, from L *impōnere* to place upon, from *pōnere* to place, set
▸ **im'posable** *adj* ▸ **im'poser** *n*

imposing (ɪm'pəʊzɪŋ) *adj* grand or impressive: *an imposing building.*
▸ **im'posingly** *adv* ▸ **im'posingness** *n*

imposition (ˌɪmpə'zɪʃən) *n* **1** the act of imposing. **2** something imposed unfairly on someone. **3** a task set as a school punishment. **4** the arrangement of pages for printing.

impossibility (ɪmˌpɒsə'bɪlɪtɪ, ˌɪmpɒs-) *n, pl* **impossibilities.** **1** the state or quality of being impossible. **2** something that is impossible.

impossible (ɪm'pɒsəbᵊl) *adj* **1** incapable of being done, undertaken, or experienced. **2** incapable of occurring or happening. **3** absurd or inconceivable; unreasonable. **4** *Inf.* intolerable; outrageous: *those children are impossible.*
▸ **im'possibleness** *n* ▸ **im'possibly** *adv*

impossible figure *n* a picture of an object that at first sight looks three-dimensional but cannot be a two-dimensional projection of a real three-dimensional object, for example a picture of a staircase that re-enters itself while appearing to ascend continuously.

impost[1] ('ɪmpəʊst) *n* **1** a tax, esp. a customs duty. **2** the weight that a horse must carry in a handicap race. ◆ *vb* **3** (*tr*) *US.* to classify (imported goods) according to the duty payable on them. ORIG C16: from Med. L *impostus* tax, from L *impositus* imposed; see IMPOSE
▸ **'imposter** *n*

impost[2] ('ɪmpəʊst) *n Archit.* a member at the top of a column that supports an arch. ORIG C17: from F *imposte,* from L *impositus* placed upon; see IMPOSE

impostor *or* **imposter** (ɪm'pɒstə) *n* a person who deceives others, esp. by assuming a false identity; charlatan. ORIG C16: from LL: deceiver; see IMPOSE

imposture (ɪm'pɒstʃə) *n* the act or an instance of deceiving others, esp. by assuming a false identity. ORIG C16: from F, from LL, from L *impōnere;* see IMPOSE
▸ **impostrous** (ɪm'pɒstrəs) *or* **impostorous** (ɪm'pɒstərəs) *adj*

impotent ('ɪmpətənt) *adj* **1** (when *postpositive,* often takes an infinitive) lacking sufficient strength; powerless. **2** (esp. of males) unable to perform sexual intercourse.
▸ **'impotence** *or* **'impotency** *n* ▸ **'impotently** *adv*

impound (ɪm'paʊnd) *vb* (*tr*) **1** to confine (animals, etc.) in a pound. **2** to take legal possession of (a document, evidence, etc.). **3** to collect (water) in a reservoir or dam.
▸ **im'poundable** *adj* ▸ **im'poundage** *or* **im'poundment** *n* ▸ **im'pounder** *n*

impoverish (ɪm'pɒvərɪʃ) *vb* (*tr*) **1** to make poor or diminish the quality of: *to impoverish society by cutting the grant to the arts.* **2** to deprive (soil, etc.) of fertility. ORIG C15: from OF *empovrir,* from *povre* POOR
▸ **im'poverishment** *n*

impracticable (ɪm'præktɪkəbᵊl) *adj* **1** incapable of being put into practice or accomplished; not feasible. **2** unsuitable for a desired use; unfit.
▸ **imˌpractica'bility** *or* **im'practicableness** *n* ▸ **im'practicably** *adv*

impractical (ɪm'præktɪkᵊl) *adj* **1** not practical or work-

able: *an impractical solution.* **2** not given to practical matters or gifted with practical skills.
▸ **im,practi'cality** *or* **im'practicalness** *n* ▸ **im'practically** *adv*

imprecate ('ɪmprɪ,keɪt) *vb* **imprecates, imprecating, imprecated. 1** (*intr*) to swear or curse. **2** (*tr*) to invoke or bring down (evil, a curse, etc.). ORIG C17: from L *imprecārī* to invoke, from *im-* IN-² + *precārī* to PRAY
▸ **,impre'cation** *n* ▸ **'impre,catory** *adj*

imprecise (,ɪmprɪ'saɪs) *adj* not precise; inexact or inaccurate.
▸ **,impre'cisely** *adv* ▸ **imprecision** (,ɪmprɪ'sɪʒən) *or* **,impre'ciseness** *n*

impregnable¹ (ɪm'prɛgnəbᵊl) *adj* **1** unable to be broken into or taken by force: *an impregnable castle.* **2** unshakable: *impregnable self-confidence.* **3** incapable of being refuted: *an impregnable argument.* ORIG C15 *imprenable,* from OF, from IM- (not) + *prenable* able to be taken, from *prendre* to take
▸ **im,pregna'bility** *n* ▸ **im'pregnably** *adv*

impregnable² (ɪm'prɛgnəbᵊl) *or* **impregnatable** (,ɪmprɛg'neɪtəbᵊl) *adj* able to be impregnated; fertile.

impregnate *vb* ('ɪmprɛg,neɪt), **impregnates, impregnating, impregnated.** (*tr*) **1** to saturate, soak, or infuse. **2** to imbue or permeate; pervade. **3** to cause to conceive; make pregnant; fertilize. **4** to make (land, soil, etc.) fruitful. ◆ *adj* (ɪm'prɛgnɪt, -,neɪt). **5** pregnant or fertilized. ORIG C17: from LL, from L *im-* IN-² + *praegnans* PREGNANT
▸ **,impreg'nation** *n* ▸ **im'pregnator** *n*

impresario (,ɪmprə'sɑːrɪ,əʊ) *n, pl* **impresarios.** the director or manager of an opera, ballet, etc. ORIG C18: from It., lit.: one who undertakes

imprescriptible (,ɪmprɪ'skrɪptəbᵊl) *adj Law.* immune or exempt from prescription.
▸ **,impre,scripti'bility** *n* ▸ **,impre'scriptibly** *adv*

impress¹ *vb* (ɪm'prɛs). (*tr*) **1** to make an impression on; have a strong, lasting, or favourable effect on: *I am impressed by your work.* **2** to produce (an imprint, etc.) by pressure in or on (something): *to impress a seal in wax.* **3** (often foll. by *on*) to stress (something to a person); urge; emphasize. **4** to exert pressure on; press. ◆ *n* ('ɪmprɛs). **5** the act or an instance of impressing. **6** a mark, imprint, or effect produced by impressing. ORIG C14: from L *imprimere* to press into, imprint
▸ **im'presser** *n* ▸ **im'pressible** *adj*

impress² *vb* (ɪm'prɛs). **1** to commandeer or coerce (men or things) into government service; press-gang. ◆ *n* ('ɪmprɛs). **2** the act of commandeering or coercing into government service. ORIG C16: see *im-* IN-², PRESS²

impression (ɪm'prɛʃən) *n* **1** an effect produced in the mind by a stimulus; sensation: *he gave the impression of wanting to help.* **2** an imprint or mark produced by pressing. **3** a vague idea, consciousness, or belief: *I had the impression we had met before.* **4** a strong, favourable, or remarkable effect. **5** the act of impressing or the state of being impressed. **6** *Printing.* **6a** the act, process, or result of printing from type, plates, etc. **6b** the total number of copies of a publication printed at one time. **7** an imprint of the teeth and gums for preparing crowns, dentures, etc. **8** an imitation or impersonation.
▸ **im'pressional** *adj* ▸ **im'pressionally** *adv*

impressionable (ɪm'prɛʃənəbᵊl, -'prɛʃnə-) *adj* easily influenced or characterized by susceptibility to influence: *an impressionable age.*
▸ **im,pressiona'bility** *or* **im'pressionableness** *n*

impressionism (ɪm'prɛʃə,nɪzəm) *n* (*often cap.*) a 19th-century movement in French painting, having the aim of objectively recording experience by a system of fleeting impressions, esp. of natural light.
▸ **im'pressionist** *n*

impressive (ɪm'prɛsɪv) *adj* capable of impressing, esp. by size, magnificence, etc.; awe-inspiring; commanding.
▸ **im'pressively** *adv* ▸ **im'pressiveness** *n*

imprest (ɪm'prɛst) *n* **1** a fund of cash from which a department, etc., pays incidental expenses, topped up periodically from central funds. **2** *Chiefly Brit.* an advance from government funds for some public business or service. ORIG C16: prob. from It. *imprestare* to lend, from L *in-* towards + *praestāre* to pay, from *praestō* at hand; see PRESTO

imprimatur (,ɪmprɪ'meɪtə, -'mɑː-) *n* **1** sanction or approval for something to be printed. **2** *RC Church.* a licence certifying the Church's approval. ORIG C17: NL, lit.: let it be printed

imprint *n* ('ɪmprɪnt). **1** a mark or impression produced by pressure, printing, or stamping. **2** a characteristic mark or indication; stamp: *the imprint of great sadness on his face.* **3a** the publisher's name and address, often with the date of publication, printed in a book, usually on the title page or the verso title page. **3b** the printer's name and address on any printed matter. ◆ *vb* (ɪm'prɪnt). (*tr*) **4** to produce (a mark, impression, etc.) on (a surface) by pressure, printing, or stamping: *to imprint a seal on wax.* **5** to establish firmly; impress: *to imprint the details on one's mind.* **6** to cause (a young animal) to undergo the process of imprinting: *chicks can be imprinted on human beings.*

imprinting (ɪm'prɪntɪŋ) *n* the development in young animals of recognition of and attraction to members of their own species or surrogates.

imprison (ɪm'prɪzən) *vb* (*tr*) to confine in or as if in prison.
▸ **im'prisonment** *n*

improbable (ɪm'prɒbəbᵊl) *adj* not likely or probable; doubtful; unlikely.
▸ **im,proba'bility** *or* **im'probableness** *n* ▸ **im'probably** *adv*

improbity (ɪm'prəʊbɪtɪ) *n, pl* **improbities.** dishonesty, wickedness, or unscrupulousness.

impromptu (ɪm'prɒmptjuː) *adj* **1** unrehearsed; spontaneous. **2** produced or done without care or planning; improvised. ◆ *adv* **3** in a spontaneous or improvised way: *he spoke impromptu.* ◆ *n* **4** something that is impromptu. **5** a short piece of instrumental music, sometimes improvisatory in character. ORIG C17: from F, from L *in promptū* in readiness, from *promptus* (adj) ready, PROMPT

improper (ɪm'prɒpə) *adj* **1** lacking propriety; not seemly. **2** unsuitable for a certain use or occasion; inappropriate. **3** irregular or abnormal.
▸ **im'properly** *adv* ▸ **im'properness** *n*

improper fraction *n* a fraction in which the numerator is greater than the denominator, as 7/6.

impropriate *vb* (ɪm'prəʊprɪ,eɪt), **impropriates, impropriating, impropriated. 1** (*tr*) to transfer (property, rights, etc.) from the Church into lay hands. ◆ *adj* (ɪm'prəʊprɪɪt, -,eɪt). **2** transferred in this way. ORIG C16: from Med. L *impropriāre* to make one's own, from L *im-* IN-² + *propriāre* to APPROPRIATE
▸ **im,propri'ation** *n* ▸ **im'propri,ator** *n*

impropriety (,ɪmprə'praɪɪtɪ) *n, pl* **improprieties. 1** lack of propriety; indecency; indecorum. **2** an improper act or use. **3** the state of being improper.

improve (ɪm'pruːv) *vb* **improves, improving, improved. 1** to make or become better in quality; ameliorate. **2** (*tr*) to make (buildings, land, etc.) more valuable by additions or betterment. **3** (*intr;* usually foll. by *on* or *upon*) to achieve a better standard or quality in comparison (with): *to improve on last year's crop.* ORIG C16: from Anglo-F *emprouer* to turn to profit, from LL *prōde* beneficial, from L *prōdesse* to be advantageous
▸ **im'provable** *adj* ▸ **im,prova'bility** *or* **im'provableness** *n*
▸ **im'prover** *n*

improvement (ɪm'pruːvmənt) *n* **1** the act of improving or the state of being improved. **2** something that improves, esp. an addition or alteration. **3** (*usually pl*) *Austral. & NZ.* a building, etc., on a piece of land, adding to its value.

improvident (ɪm'prɒvɪdənt) *adj* **1** not provident; thriftless, imprudent, or prodigal. **2** heedless or incautious; rash.
▸ **im'providence** *n* ▸ **im'providently** *adv*

improvise ('ɪmprə,vaɪz) *vb* **improvises, improvising, improvised. 1** to perform or make quickly from materials and sources available, without previous planning. **2** to perform (a poem, play, piece of music, etc.), composing as one goes along. ORIG C19: from F, from It., from L *imprōvīsus* unforeseen, from *prōvidēre* to foresee; see PROVIDE

▸ ˈimproˌviser *n* ▸ ˌimproviˈsation *n* ▸ **improvisatory** (ˌɪmprəˈvaɪzətərɪ, -ˈvɪz-, ˌɪmprəvaɪzˈeɪtərɪ) *adj*

imprudent (ɪmˈpruːdᵊnt) *adj* not prudent; rash, heedless, or indiscreet.
▸ **imˈprudence** *n* ▸ **imˈprudently** *adv*

impudence (ˈɪmpjʊdəns) *or* **impudency** *n* **1** the quality of being impudent. **2** an impudent act or statement. ORIG C14: from L *impudēns* shameless

impudent (ˈɪmpjʊdənt) *adj* **1** mischievous, impertinent, or disrespectful. **2** *Obs.* immodest.
▸ **ˈimpudently** *adv* ▸ **ˈimpudentness** *n*

impugn (ɪmˈpjuːn) *vb* (*tr*) to challenge or attack as false; criticize. ORIG C14: from OF, from L *impugnāre* to fight against, attack
▸ **imˈpugnable** *adj* ▸ **imˈpugnment** *n* ▸ **imˈpugner** *n*

impulse (ˈɪmpʌls) *n* **1** an impelling force or motion; thrust; impetus. **2** a sudden desire, whim, or inclination. **3** an instinctive drive; urge. **4** tendency; current; trend. **5** *Physics.* **5a** the product of the average magnitude of a force acting on a body and the time for which it acts. **5b** the change in the momentum of a body as a result of a force acting upon it. **6** *Physiol.* See **nerve impulse. 7 on impulse.** spontaneously or impulsively. ORIG C17: from L *impulsus* a pushing against, incitement, from *impellere* to strike against; see IMPEL

impulse buying *n* the buying of merchandise prompted by a whim.
▸ **impulse buyer** *n*

impulsion (ɪmˈpʌlʃən) *n* **1** the act of impelling or the state of being impelled. **2** motion produced by an impulse; propulsion. **3** a driving force; compulsion.

impulsive (ɪmˈpʌlsɪv) *adj* **1** characterized by actions based on sudden desires, whims, or inclinations: *an impulsive man.* **2** based on emotional impulses or whims; spontaneous. **3** forceful, inciting, or impelling. **4** (of physical forces) acting for a short time; not continuous. **5** (of a sound) brief, loud, and having a wide frequency range.
▸ **imˈpulsively** *adv* ▸ **imˈpulsiveness** *n*

impunity (ɪmˈpjuːnɪtɪ) *n, pl* **impunities. 1** exemption or immunity from punishment, recrimination, or other unpleasant consequences. **2 with impunity.** with no care or heed for such consequences. ORIG C16: from L, from *impūnis* unpunished, from IM- (not) + *poena* punishment

impure (ɪmˈpjʊə) *adj* **1** not pure; combined with something else; tainted or sullied. **2** (in certain religions) ritually unclean. **3** (of a colour) mixed with another colour. **4** of more than one origin or style, as of architecture.
▸ **imˈpurely** *adv* ▸ **imˈpureness** *n*

impurity (ɪmˈpjʊərɪtɪ) *n, pl* **impurities. 1** the quality of being impure. **2** an impure thing, constituent, or element: *impurities in the water.* **3** *Electronics.* a small quantity of an element added to a pure semiconductor crystal to control its electrical conductivity.

impute (ɪmˈpjuːt) *vb* **imputes, imputing, imputed.** (*tr*) **1** to attribute or ascribe (something dishonest or dishonourable) to a person. **2** to attribute to a source or cause: *I impute your success to nepotism.* **3** *Commerce.* to give (a notional value) to goods, etc., when the real value is unknown. ORIG C14: from L, from IM- + *putāre* to think, calculate
▸ **ˌimpuˈtation** *n* ▸ **imˈputative** *adj* ▸ **imˈputer** *n* ▸ **imˈputable** *adj*

Imran Khan ★ (ˈɪmrɑːn ˈkɑːn) *n* full name *Imran Ahmad Khan Niazi.* born 1952, Pakistani cricketer: played for Worcestershire (1971–76) and Sussex from 1977; captained Pakistan (1982–84; 1985–87; 1988–92).

Imroz ★ (ˈimrɔz) *n* the Turkish name for **Imbros.**

IMunE *abbrev. for* Institution of Municipal Engineers.

in (ɪn) *prep* **1** inside; within: *no smoking in the auditorium.* **2** at a place where there is: *in the shade.* **3** indicating a state, situation, or condition: *in silence.* **4** when (a period of time) has elapsed: *return in one year.* **5** using: *written in code.* **6** concerned with, esp. as an occupation: *in journalism.* **7** while or by performing the action of: *in crossing the street he was run over.* **8** used to indicate purpose: *in honour of the king.* **9** (of certain animals) pregnant with: *in calf.* **10** a variant of **into:** *she fell in the water.* **11 have it in one.** (often foll. by an infinitive) to have the ability (to do something). **12 in that** *or* **in so far as.** (*conj*) because or to the extent that: *I regret my remark in that it upset you.* **13 nothing in it.** no difference or interval between two things. ◆ *adv* (*particle*) **14** in or into a particular place; inward or indoors: *come in.* **15** so as to achieve office or power: *Labour got in at the last election.* **16** so as to enclose: *block in.* **17** (in certain games) so as to take one's turn of the play: *you have to get the other side out before you go in.* **18** *NZ.* competing: *you've got to be in to win.* **19** *Brit.* (of a fire) alight. **20** (*in combination*) indicating an activity or gathering: *teach-in; work-in.* **21 in at.** present at (the beginning, end, etc.). **22 in for.** about to be affected by (something, esp. something unpleasant): *you're in for a shock.* **23 in on.** acquainted with or sharing in: *I was in on all his plans.* **24 in with.** associated with; friendly with; regarded highly by. **25 have (got) it in for.** to wish or intend harm towards. ◆ *adj* **26** (*stressed*) fashionable; modish: *the in thing to do.* ◆ *n* **27 ins and outs.** intricacies or complications; details. ORIG OE

In *the chemical symbol for* indium.

in. *abbrev. for* inch(es).

in-[1], **il-, im-,** *or* **ir-** *prefix* **a** not; non-: *incredible; illegal; imperfect; irregular.* **b** lack of: *inexperience.* Cf. **un-**. ORIG from L *in-;* rel. to *ne-, nōn* not

in-[2], **il-, im-,** *or* **ir-** *prefix* **1** in; into; towards; within; on: *infiltrate; immigrate.* **2** having an intensive or causative function: *inflame; imperil.* ORIG from IN (prep, adv)

-in *suffix forming nouns.* **1** indicating a neutral organic compound, including proteins, glucosides, and glycerides: *insulin; tripalmitin.* **2** indicating an enzyme in certain nonsystematic names: *pepsin.* **3** indicating a pharmaceutical substance: *penicillin; aspirin.* **4** indicating a chemical substance in certain nonsystematic names: *coumarin.* ORIG from NL *-ina;* cf. -INE[2]

in absentia *Latin.* (ɪn æbˈsɛntɪə) *adv* in the absence of (someone indicated).

inaccessible (ˌɪnækˈsɛsəbᵊl) *adj* not accessible; unapproachable.
▸ **ˌinacˌcessiˈbility** *or* **ˌinacˈcessibleness** *n* ▸ **ˌinacˈcessibly** *adv*

inaccuracy (ɪnˈækjʊrəsɪ) *n, pl* **inaccuracies. 1** lack of accuracy; imprecision. **2** an error, mistake, or slip.
▸ **inˈaccurate** *adj*

inaction (ɪnˈækʃən) *n* lack of action; idleness; inertia.

inactivate (ɪnˈæktɪˌveɪt) *vb* **inactivates, inactivating, inactivated.** (*tr*) to render inactive.
▸ **inˌactiˈvation** *n*

inactive (ɪnˈæktɪv) *adj* **1** idle or inert; not active. **2** sluggish or indolent. **3** *Mil.* of or relating to persons or equipment not in active service. **4** *Chem.* (of a substance) having little or no reactivity.
▸ **inˈactively** *adv* ▸ **ˌinacˈtivity** *n*

inadequate (ɪnˈædɪkwɪt) *adj* **1** not adequate; insufficient. **2** not capable; lacking.
▸ **inˈadequacy** *n* ▸ **inˈadequately** *adv*

inadvertence (ˌɪnədˈvɜːtᵊns) *or* **inadvertency** *n* **1** lack of attention; heedlessness. **2** an oversight; slip.

inadvertent (ˌɪnədˈvɜːtᵊnt) *adj* **1** failing to act carefully or considerately; inattentive. **2** resulting from heedless action; unintentional.
▸ **ˌinadˈvertently** *adv*

-inae *suffix forming plural proper nouns.* occurring in names of zoological subfamilies: *Felinae.* ORIG NL, from L, fem pl of *-īnus* -INE[1]

inalienable (ɪnˈeɪljənəbᵊl) *adj* not able to be transferred to another; not alienable: *the inalienable rights of the citizen.*
▸ **inˌalienaˈbility** *or* **inˈalienableness** *n* ▸ **inˈalienably** *adv*

inalterable (ɪnˈɔːltərəbᵊl) *adj* not alterable; unalterable.
▸ **inˌalteraˈbility** *or* **inˈalterableness** *n* ▸ **inˈalterably** *adv*

inamorata (ɪnˌæməˈrɑːtə, ˌɪnæmə-) *or* (*masc*) **inamorato** (ɪnˌæməˈrɑːtəʊ, ˌɪnæmə-) *n, pl* **inamoratas** *or* (*masc*) **inamoratos.** a person with whom one is in love; lover. ORIG C17: from It., from *innamorare* to cause to fall in love, from *amore* love, from L *amor*

inane (ɪˈneɪn) *adj* **1** senseless, unimaginative, or empty; unintelligent: *inane remarks.* ◆ *n* **2** *Arch.* something

empty or vacant, esp. the void of space. ORIG C17: from L *inānis* empty
▸ **in'anely** *adv*

inanimate (ɪn'ænɪmɪt) *adj* **1** lacking the qualities of living beings; not animate: *inanimate objects.* **2** lacking any sign of life or consciousness; appearing dead. **3** lacking vitality; dull.
▸ **in'animately** *adv* ▸ **in'animateness** *or* **inanimation** (ɪn,ænɪ'meɪʃən) *n*

inanition (,ɪnə'nɪʃən) *n* **1** exhaustion resulting from lack of food. **2** mental, social, or spiritual weakness or lassitude. ORIG C14: from LL *inānītio* emptiness, from L *inānis* empty; see INANE

inanity (ɪ'nænɪtɪ) *n, pl* **inanities. 1** lack of intelligence or imagination; senselessness; silliness. **2** a senseless action, remark, etc. **3** an archaic word for **emptiness.**

inapposite (ɪn'æpəzɪt) *adj* not appropriate or pertinent; unsuitable.
▸ **in'appositely** *adv* ▸ **in'appositeness** *n*

inapt (ɪn'æpt) *adj* **1** not apt or fitting; inappropriate. **2** lacking skill; inept.
▸ **in'apti,tude** *or* **in'aptness** *n* ▸ **in'aptly** *adv*

inarch (ɪn'ɑːtʃ) *vb* (*tr*) to graft (a plant) by uniting stock and scion while both are still growing independently.

inasmuch as (,ɪnəz'mʌtʃ) *conj* (*subordinating*) **1** in view of the fact that; seeing that; since. **2** to the extent or degree that; in so far as.

inaudible (ɪn'ɔːdəbᵊl) *adj* not loud enough to be heard.
▸ **in,audi'bility** *or* **in'audibleness** *n* ▸ **in'audibly** *adv*

inaugural (ɪn'ɔːgjʊrəl) *adj* **1** characterizing or relating to an inauguration. ◆ *n* **2** a speech made at an inauguration, esp. by a president of the US.

inaugurate (ɪn'ɔːgjʊ,reɪt) *vb* **inaugurates, inaugurating, inaugurated.** (*tr*) **1** to commence officially or formally; initiate. **2** to place in office formally and ceremonially; induct. **3** to open ceremonially; dedicate formally: *to inaugurate a factory.* ORIG C17: from L *inaugurāre,* lit.: to take omens, practise augury, hence to install in office after taking auguries; see IN-², AUGUR
▸ **in,augu'ration** *n* ▸ **in'augu,rator** *n* ▸ **inauguratory** (ɪn'ɔːgjʊrətərɪ, -trɪ) *adj*

in-between *adj* intermediate: *he's at the in-between stage, neither a child nor an adult.*

inboard ('ɪn,bɔːd) *adj* **1** (esp. of a boat's motor or engine) situated within the hull. **2** situated between the wing tip of an aircraft and its fuselage: *an inboard engine.* ◆ *adv* **3** towards the centre line of or within a vessel, aircraft, etc.

inborn ('ɪn'bɔːn) *adj* existing from birth; congenital; innate.

inbred ('ɪn'brɛd) *adj* **1** produced as a result of inbreeding. **2** deeply ingrained; innate: *inbred good manners.*

inbreed ('ɪn'briːd) *vb* **inbreeds, inbreeding, inbred. 1** to breed from unions between closely related individuals, esp. over several generations. **2** (*tr*) to develop within; engender.
▸ **'in'breeding** *n, adj*

in-built *adj* built-in, integral.

inc. *abbrev. for:* **1** including. **2** inclusive. **3** income. **4** increase.

Inc. (esp. US) *abbrev. for* incorporated.

Inca ('ɪŋkə) *n, pl* **Inca** *or* **Incas. 1** a member of a South American Indian people whose empire centred on Peru lasted from about 1100 A.D. to the Spanish conquest in the early 1530s. **2** the language of the Incas. See also **Quechua.** ORIG C16: from Sp., from Quechua *inka* king
▸ **Incan** *adj*

incalculable (ɪn'kælkjʊləbᵊl) *adj* beyond calculation; unable to be predicted or determined.
▸ **in,calcula'bility** *n* ▸ **in'calculably** *adv*

incandesce (,ɪnkæn'dɛs) *vb* **incandesces, incandescing, incandesced.** (*intr*) to make or become incandescent.

incandescent (,ɪnkæn'dɛsᵊnt) *adj* **1** emitting light as a result of being heated; red-hot or white-hot. **2** *Inf.* extremely angry. ORIG C18: from L *incandescere* to become hot, glow, from *candēre* to be white; see CANDID
▸ **,incan'descently** *adv* ▸ **,incan'descence** *n*

incandescent lamp *n* a source of light that contains a heated solid, such as an electrically heated filament.

incantation (,ɪnkæn'teɪʃən) *n* **1** ritual recitation of magic words or sounds. **2** the formulaic words or sounds used; a magic spell. ORIG C14: from LL *incantātiō* an enchanting, from *incantāre* to repeat magic formulas, from L, from IN-² + *cantāre* to sing; see ENCHANT
▸ **,incan'tational** *or* **in'cantatory** *adj*

incapacitate (,ɪnkə'pæsɪ,teɪt) *vb* **incapacitates, incapacitating, incapacitated.** (*tr*) **1** to deprive of power, strength, or capacity; disable. **2** to deprive of legal capacity or eligibility.
▸ **,inca,paci'tation** *n*

incapacity (,ɪnkə'pæsɪtɪ) *n, pl* **incapacities. 1** lack of power, strength, or capacity; inability. **2** *Law.* legal disqualification or ineligibility.

in-car *adj* (of hi-fi equipment, etc.) installed inside a car.

incarcerate (ɪn'kɑːsə,reɪt) *vb* **incarcerates, incarcerating, incarcerated.** (*tr*) to confine or imprison. ORIG C16: from Med. L, from L IN-² + *carcer* prison
▸ **in,carcer'ation** *n* ▸ **in'carcer,ator** *n*

incarnadine (ɪn'kɑːnə,daɪn) *Arch. or literary.* ◆ *vb* **incarnadines, incarnadining, incarnadined. 1** (*tr*) to tinge or stain with red. ◆ *adj* **2** of a pinkish or reddish colour similar to that of flesh or blood. ORIG C16: from F *incarnadin* flesh-coloured, from It., from LL *incarnātus* made flesh, INCARNATE

incarnate *adj* (ɪn'kɑːnɪt, -neɪt). (*usually immediately postpositive*) **1** possessing bodily form, esp. the human form: *a devil incarnate.* **2** personified or typified: *stupidity incarnate.* ◆ *vb* (ɪn'kɑːneɪt), **incarnates, incarnating, incarnated.** (*tr*) **3** to give a bodily or concrete form to. **4** to be representative or typical of. ORIG C14: from LL *incarnāre* to make flesh, from L IN-² + *carō* flesh

incarnation (,ɪnkɑː'neɪʃən) *n* **1** the act of manifesting or state of being manifested in bodily form, esp. human form. **2** a bodily form assumed by a god, etc. **3** a person or thing that typifies or represents some quality, idea, etc.

Incarnation (,ɪnkɑː'neɪʃən) *n Christian theol.* the assuming of a human body by the Son of God.

incarvillea (,ɪnkɑː'vɪlɪə) *n* any of various perennials with pink flowers and pinnate leaves. Also called: **Chinese trumpet flower.** ORIG C18: after Pierre d'*Incarville,* F missionary in China

incase (ɪn'keɪs) *vb* **incases, incasing, incased.** a variant spelling of **encase.**
▸ **in'casement** *n*

incautious (ɪn'kɔːʃəs) *adj* not careful or cautious.
▸ **in'cautiously** *adv* ▸ **in'cautiousness** *or* **in'caution** *n*

incendiary (ɪn'sɛndɪərɪ) *adj* **1** of or relating to the illegal burning of property, goods, etc. **2** tending to create strife, violence, etc. **3** (of a substance) capable of catching fire or burning readily. ◆ *n, pl* **incendiaries. 4** a person who illegally sets fire to property, goods, etc.; arsonist. **5** (esp. formerly) a person who stirs up civil strife, violence, etc.; agitator. **6** Also called: **incendiary bomb.** a bomb that is designed to start fires. **7** an incendiary substance, such as phosphorus. ORIG C17: from L, from *incendium* fire, from *incendere* to kindle
▸ **in'cendia,rism** *n*

incense¹ ('ɪnsɛns) *n* **1** any of various aromatic substances burnt for their fragrant odour, esp. in religious ceremonies. **2** the odour or smoke so produced. **3** any pleasant fragrant odour; aroma. ◆ *vb* **incenses, incensing, incensed. 4** to burn incense in honour of (a deity). **5** (*tr*) to perfume or fumigate with incense. ORIG C13: from OF *encens,* from Church L *incensum,* from L *incendere* to kindle

incense² (ɪn'sɛns) *vb* **incenses, incensing, incensed.** (*tr*) to enrage greatly. ORIG C15: from L *incensus* set on fire, from *incendere* to kindle
▸ **in'censement** *n*

incensory ('ɪnsɛnsərɪ) *n, pl* **incensories.** a less common name for **censer.** ORIG C17: from Med. L *incensorium*

incentive (ɪn'sɛntɪv) *n* **1** a motivating influence; stimulus. **2a** an additional payment made to employees to increase production. **2b** (*as modifier*): *an incentive scheme.* ◆ *adj* **3** serving to incite to action. ORIG C15: from LL, from L: striking up, setting the tune, from *incinere* to sing

incept (ɪn'sɛpt) *vb* (*tr*) **1** (of organisms) to ingest (food). **2** *Brit.* (formerly) to take a master's or doctor's degree at a university. ORIG C19: from L *inceptus* begun, attempted, from *incipere* to begin, take in hand
▸ **in'ceptor** *n*

inception (ɪn'sɛpʃən) *n* the beginning, as of a project or undertaking.

inceptive (ɪn'sɛptɪv) *adj* **1** beginning; incipient; initial. **2** Also called: **inchoative.** *Grammar.* denoting a verb used to indicate the beginning of an action. ◆ *n* **3** *Grammar.* an inceptive verb.
▸ **in'ceptively** *adv*

incertitude (ɪn'sɜːtɪˌtjuːd) *n* **1** uncertainty; doubt. **2** a state of mental or emotional insecurity.

incessant (ɪn'sɛsᵊnt) *adj* not ceasing; continual. ORIG C16: from LL, from L IN-[1] + *cessāre* to CEASE
▸ **in'cessancy** *n* ▸ **in'cessantly** *adv*

incest ('ɪnsɛst) *n* sexual intercourse between two persons who are too closely related to marry. ORIG C13: from L, from IN-[1] + *castus* CHASTE

incestuous (ɪn'sɛstjʊəs) *adj* **1** relating to or involving incest: *an incestuous union.* **2** guilty of incest. **3** resembling incest in excessive or claustrophobic intimacy.
▸ **in'cestuously** *adv* ▸ **in'cestuousness** *n*

inch[1] (ɪntʃ) *n* **1** a unit of length equal to one twelfth of a foot or 0.0254 metre. **2** *Meteorol.* **2a** an amount of precipitation that would cover a surface with water one inch deep. **2b** a unit of pressure equal to a mercury column one inch high in a barometer. **3** a very small distance, degree, or amount. **4 every inch.** in every way; completely: *every inch an aristocrat.* **5 inch by inch.** gradually; little by little. **6 within an inch of one's life.** almost to death. ◆ *vb* **7** to move or be moved very slowly or in very small steps: *the car inched forward.* **8** (*tr*; foll. by *out*) to defeat (someone) by a very small margin. ORIG OE *ynce;* see OUNCE[1]

inch[2] (ɪntʃ) *n Scot. & Irish.* a small island. ORIG C15: from Gaelic *innis* island; cf. Welsh *ynys*

inchoate *adj* (ɪn'kəʊeɪt, -'kəʊɪt). **1** just beginning; incipient. **2** undeveloped; immature; rudimentary. ◆ *vb* (ɪn'kəʊeɪt), **inchoates, inchoating, inchoated.** (*tr*) **3** to begin. ORIG C16: from L *incohāre* to make a beginning, lit.: to hitch up, from IN-[2] + *cohum* yokestrap
▸ **in'choately** *adv* ▸ **in'choateness** *n* ▸ **ˌincho'ation** *n*
▸ **inchoative** (ɪn'kəʊətɪv) *adj*

Inchon *or* **Incheon** ★ ('ɪn'tʃɒn) *n* a port in W South Korea, on the Yellow Sea: the chief port for Seoul: site of a major strategic amphibious assault by UN troops, liberating Seoul (Sept. 15, 1950). Pop.: 2 307 618 (1995). Former name: **Chemulpo.**

inchworm ('ɪntʃˌwɜːm) *n* another name for **measuring worm.**

incidence ('ɪnsɪdəns) *n* **1** degree, extent, or frequency of occurrence; amount: *a high incidence of death from pneumonia.* **2** the act or manner of impinging on or affecting by proximity or influence. **3** *Physics.* the arrival of a beam of light or particles at a surface. See also **angle of incidence. 4** *Geom.* the partial coincidence of two configurations, such as a point on a circle.

incident ('ɪnsɪdənt) *n* **1** a definite occurrence; event. **2** a minor, subsidiary, or related event. **3** a relatively insignificant event that might have serious consequences. **4** a public disturbance. ◆ *adj* **5** (*postpositive;* foll. by *to*) related (to) or dependent (on). **6** (when *postpositive,* often foll. by *to*) having a subsidiary or minor relationship (with). **7** (esp. of a beam of light or particles) arriving at or striking a surface. ORIG C15: from Med. L, from L *incidere,* lit.: to fall into, hence befall, happen

incidental (ˌɪnsɪ'dɛntᵊl) *adj* **1** happening in connection with or resulting from something more important; casual or fortuitous. **2** (*postpositive;* foll. by *to*) found in connection (with); related (to). **3** (*postpositive;* foll. by *upon*) caused (by). **4** occasional or minor: *incidental expenses.* ◆ *n* **5** (*often pl*) a minor expense, event, or action.
▸ **ˌinci'dentalness** *n*

incidentally (ˌɪnsɪ'dɛntəlɪ) *adv* **1** as a subordinate or chance occurrence. **2** (*sentence modifier*) by the way.

incidental music *n* background music for a film, etc.

incinerate (ɪn'sɪnəˌreɪt) *vb* **incinerates, incinerating, incinerated.** to burn up completely; reduce to ashes. ORIG C16: from Med. L, from L IN-[2] + *cinis* ashes
▸ **inˌciner'ation** *n*

incinerator (ɪn'sɪnəˌreɪtə) *n* a furnace or apparatus for incinerating something, esp. refuse.

incipient (ɪn'sɪpɪənt) *adj* just starting to be or happen; beginning. ORIG C17: from L, from *incipere* to begin, take in hand
▸ **in'cipience** *or* **in'cipiency** *n* ▸ **in'cipiently** *adv*

incise (ɪn'saɪz) *vb* **incises, incising, incised.** (*tr*) to produce (lines, a design, etc.) by cutting into the surface of (something) with a sharp tool. ORIG C16: from L *incīdere* to cut into

incision (ɪn'sɪʒən) *n* **1** the act of incising. **2** a cut, gash, or notch. **3** a cut made with a knife during a surgical operation.

incisive (ɪn'saɪsɪv) *adj* **1** keen, penetrating, or acute. **2** biting or sarcastic; mordant: *an incisive remark.* **3** having a sharp cutting edge: *incisive teeth.*
▸ **in'cisively** *adv* ▸ **in'cisiveness** *n*

incisor (ɪn'saɪzə) *n* a chisel-edged tooth at the front of the mouth.

incite (ɪn'saɪt) *vb* **incites, inciting, incited.** (*tr*) to stir up or provoke to action. ORIG C15: from L, from IN-[2] + *citāre* to excite
▸ **ˌinci'tation** *n* ▸ **in'citement** *n* ▸ **in'citer** *n* ▸ **in'citingly** *adv*

incivility (ˌɪnsɪ'vɪlɪtɪ) *n, pl* **incivilities. 1** lack of civility or courtesy; rudeness. **2** an impolite or uncivil act or remark.

incl. *abbrev. for:* **1** including. **2** inclusive.

inclement (ɪn'klɛmənt) *adj* **1** (of weather) stormy, severe, or tempestuous. **2** severe or merciless.
▸ **in'clemency** *n* ▸ **in'clemently** *adv*

inclination (ˌɪnklɪ'neɪʃən) *n* **1** (often foll. by *for, to, towards,* or an infinitive) a particular disposition, esp. a liking; tendency: *I've no inclination for such dull work.* **2** the degree of deviation from a particular plane, esp. a horizontal or vertical plane. **3** a sloping or slanting surface; incline. **4** the act of inclining or the state of being inclined. **5** the act of bowing or nodding the head. **6** another name for **dip** (sense 24).
▸ **ˌincli'national** *adj*

incline *vb* (ɪn'klaɪn), **inclines, inclining, inclined. 1** to deviate from a particular plane, esp. a vertical or horizontal plane; slope or slant. **2** (when *tr,* may take an infinitive) to be disposed or cause to be disposed (towards some attitude or to do something). **3** to bend or lower (part of the body, esp. the head), as in a bow or in order to listen. **4 incline one's ear.** to listen favourably (to). ◆ *n* ('ɪnklaɪn, ɪn'klaɪn). **5** an inclined surface or slope; gradient. ORIG C13: from L *inclīnāre* to cause to lean, from *clīnāre* to bend; see LEAN[1]
▸ **in'clined** *adj* ▸ **in'cliner** *n*

inclined plane *n* a plane whose angle to the horizontal is less than a right angle.

inclinometer (ˌɪnklɪ'nɒmɪtə) *n* an aircraft instrument that indicates the angle an aircraft makes with the horizontal.

inclose (ɪn'kləʊz) *vb* **incloses, inclosing, inclosed.** a less common spelling of **enclose.**
▸ **in'closure** *n*

include (ɪn'kluːd) *vb* **includes, including, included.** (*tr*) **1** to have as contents or part of the contents; be made up of or contain. **2** to add as part of something else; put in as part of a set, group, or category. **3** to contain as a secondary or minor ingredient or element. ORIG C15 (in the sense: to enclose): from L, from IN-[2] + *claudere* to close
▸ **in'cludable** *or* **in'cludible** *adj*

include out *vb* (*tr, adv*) *Inf.* to exclude: *you can include me out of that deal.*

inclusion (ɪn'kluːʒən) *n* **1** the act of including or the state of being included. **2** something included.

inclusion body *n Pathol.* any of the small particles found in cells infected with certain viruses.

inclusive (ɪn'kluːsɪv) *adj* **1** (*postpositive;* foll. by *of*) con-

★ people and places

sidered together (with): *capital inclusive of profit.* **2** (*postpositive*) including the limits specified: *Monday to Friday inclusive.* **3** comprehensive. **4** *Logic.* (of a disjunction) true if at least one of its component propositions is true.
▸ **inˈclusively** *adv* ▸ **inˈclusiveness** *n*

inclusive language *n* language that avoids the use of expressions or words that might be considered to exclude particular groups of people, esp. gender-specific words, such as "man", "mankind", and masculine pronouns, in contexts that could exclude women.

incognito (ˌɪnkɒgˈniːtəʊ, ɪnˈkɒgnɪtəʊ) *or* (*fem*) **incognita** *adv, adj* (*postpositive*) **1** under an assumed name or appearance; in disguise. ◆ *n, pl* **incognitos** *or* (*fem*) **incognitas. 2** a person who is incognito. **3** the assumed name or disguise of such a person. ORIG C17: from It., from L *incognitus* unknown

incognizant (ɪnˈkɒgnɪzənt) *adj* (when *postpositive,* often foll. by *of*) unaware (of).
▸ **inˈcognizance** *n*

incoherent (ˌɪnkəʊˈhɪərənt) *adj* **1** lacking in clarity or organization; disordered. **2** unable to express oneself clearly; inarticulate. **3** *Physics.* (of two or more waves) having the same frequency but not the same phase: *incoherent light.*
▸ **ˌincoˈherently** *adv* ▸ **ˌincoˈherence** *or* **ˌincoˈherency** *n*

income (ˈɪnkʌm, ˈɪnkəm) *n* **1** the amount of monetary or other returns, either earned or unearned, accruing over a given period of time. **2** receipts; revenue. ORIG C13 (in the sense: arrival, entrance): from OE *incumen* a coming in

incomer (ˈɪnkʌmə) *n* a person who comes to live in a place in which he or she was not born.

incomes policy *n* an economic policy that attempts to reduce or control inflation by limiting incomes.

income support *n* (in Britain, formerly) a social security payment for people on very low incomes.

income tax *n* a personal tax levied on annual income subject to certain deductions.

incoming (ˈɪnˌkʌmɪŋ) *adj* **1** coming in; entering. **2** about to come into office; succeeding. **3** (of interest, dividends, etc.) being received; accruing. ◆ *n* **4** the act of coming in; entrance. **5** (*usually pl*) income or revenue.

incommensurable (ˌɪnkəˈmɛnʃərəbᵊl) *adj* **1** incapable of being judged, measured, or considered comparatively. **2** (*postpositive;* foll. by *with*) not in accordance; incommensurate. **3** *Maths.* not having a common factor other than 1, such as 2 and $\sqrt{-5}$. ◆ *n* **4** something incommensurable.
▸ **ˌincomˌmensuraˈbility** *n* ▸ **ˌincomˈmensurably** *adv*

incommensurate (ˌɪnkəˈmɛnʃərɪt) *adj* **1** (when *postpositive,* often foll. by *with*) not commensurate; disproportionate. **2** incommensurable.
▸ **ˌincomˈmensurately** *adv* ▸ **ˌincomˈmensurateness** *n*

incommode (ˌɪnkəˈməʊd) *vb* **incommodes, incommoding, incommoded.** (*tr*) to bother, disturb, or inconvenience. ORIG C16: from L *incommodāre* to be troublesome, from *incommodus* inconvenient; see COMMODE

incommodious (ˌɪnkəˈməʊdɪəs) *adj* **1** insufficiently spacious; cramped. **2** troublesome or inconvenient.
▸ **ˌincomˈmodiously** *adv*

incommodity (ˌɪnkəˈmɒdɪtɪ) *n, pl* **incommodities.** anything that causes inconvenience.

incommunicado (ˌɪnkəˌmjuːnɪˈkɑːdəʊ) *adv, adj* (*postpositive*) deprived of communication with other people, as while in solitary confinement. ORIG C19: from Sp., from *incomunicar* to deprive of communication; see IN-[1], COMMUNICATE

incomparable (ɪnˈkɒmpərəbᵊl, -prəbᵊl) *adj* **1** beyond or above comparison; matchless; unequalled. **2** lacking a basis for comparison; not having qualities or features that can be compared.
▸ **inˌcomparaˈbility** *or* **inˈcomparableness** *n* ▸ **inˈcomparably** *adv*

incompatible (ˌɪnkəmˈpætəbᵊl) *adj* **1** incapable of living or existing together in harmony; conflicting. **2** opposed in nature or quality; inconsistent. **3** *Med.* (esp. of two drugs or two types of blood) incapable of being combined or used together; antagonistic. **4** *Logic.* (of two propositions) unable to be both true at the same time. **5** (of plants) incapable of self-fertilization. ◆ *n* **6** (*often pl*) a person or thing that is incompatible with another.
▸ **ˌincomˌpatiˈbility** *or* **ˌincomˈpatibleness** *n* ▸ **ˌincomˈpatibly** *adv*

incompetent (ɪnˈkɒmpɪtənt) *adj* **1** not possessing the necessary ability, skill, etc., to do or carry out a task; incapable. **2** marked by lack of ability, skill, etc. **3** *Law.* not legally qualified: *an incompetent witness.* ◆ *n* **4** an incompetent person.
▸ **inˈcompetence** *or* **inˈcompetency** *n* ▸ **inˈcompetently** *adv*

incomplete (ˌɪnkəmˈpliːt) *adj* **1** not complete or finished. **2** not completely developed; imperfect.
▸ **ˌincomˈpletely** *adv* ▸ **ˌincomˈpleteness** *or* **ˌincomˈpletion** *n*

incomprehensible (ˌɪnkɒmprɪˈhɛnsəbᵊl, ɪnˈkɒm-) *adj* **1** incapable of being understood; unintelligible. **2** *Archaic.* limitless; boundless.
▸ **ˌincompreˌhensiˈbility** *or* **ˌincompreˈhensibleness** *n* ▸ **ˌincompreˈhensibly** *adv*

inconceivable (ˌɪnkənˈsiːvəbᵊl) *adj* incapable of being conceived, imagined, or considered.
▸ **ˌinconˌceivaˈbility** *or* **ˌinconˈceivableness** *n* ▸ **ˌinconˈceivably** *adv*

inconclusive (ˌɪnkənˈkluːsɪv) *adj* not conclusive or decisive; not finally settled; indeterminate.
▸ **ˌinconˈclusively** *adv* ▸ **ˌinconˈclusiveness** *n*

incongruous (ɪnˈkɒŋgruəs) *or* **incongruent** *adj* **1** (when *postpositive,* foll. by *with* or *to*) incompatible with (what is suitable); inappropriate. **2** containing disparate or discordant elements or parts.
▸ **inˈcongruously** *adv* ▸ **inˈcongruousness** *or* **incongruity** (ˌɪnkɒŋˈgruːɪtɪ) *n*

inconnu (ˈɪnkənjuː, ˈɪnkənuː) *n Canad.* a whitefish of Far Northern waters. ORIG C19: from F, lit: unknown

inconsequential (ˌɪnkɒnsɪˈkwɛnʃəl, ɪnˌkɒn-) *or* **inconsequent** (ɪnˈkɒnsɪkwənt) *adj* **1** not following logically as a consequence. **2** trivial or insignificant. **3** not in a logical sequence; haphazard.
▸ **ˌinconseˌquentiˈality, ˌinconseˈquentialness,** *or* **inˈconsequence** *n* ▸ **ˌinconseˈquentially** *or* **inˈconsequently** *adv*

inconsiderable (ˌɪnkənˈsɪdərəbᵊl) *adj* **1** relatively small. **2** not worthy of consideration; insignificant.
▸ **ˌinconˈsiderableness** *n* ▸ **ˌinconˈsiderably** *adv*

inconsiderate (ˌɪnkənˈsɪdərɪt) *adj* lacking in care or thought for others; thoughtless.
▸ **ˌinconˈsiderately** *adv* ▸ **ˌinconˈsiderateness** *or* **ˌinconˌsiderˈation** *n*

inconsistency (ˌɪnkənˈsɪstənsɪ) *n, pl* **inconsistencies. 1** lack of consistency or agreement; incompatibility. **2** an inconsistent feature or quality.

inconsistent (ˌɪnkənˈsɪstənt) *adj* **1** lacking in consistency, agreement, or compatibility; at variance. **2** containing contradictory elements. **3** irregular or fickle in behaviour or mood. **4** *Logic.* (of a set of propositions) enabling an explicit contradiction to be validly derived.
▸ **ˌinconˈsistently** *adv*

inconsolable (ˌɪnkənˈsəʊləbᵊl) *adj* incapable of being consoled or comforted; disconsolate.
▸ **ˌinconˌsolaˈbility** *or* **ˌinconˈsolableness** *n* ▸ **ˌinconˈsolably** *adv*

inconsonant (ɪnˈkɒnsənənt) *adj* lacking in harmony or compatibility; discordant.
▸ **inˈconsonance** *n* ▸ **inˈconsonantly** *adv*

inconspicuous (ˌɪnkənˈspɪkjuəs) *adj* not easily noticed or seen; not prominent or striking.
▸ **ˌinconˈspicuously** *adv* ▸ **ˌinconˈspicuousness** *n*

incontinent[1] (ɪnˈkɒntɪnənt) *adj* **1** relating to or exhibiting involuntary urination or defecation. **2** lacking in restraint or control, esp. sexually. **3** (foll. by *of*) having little or no control (over). **4** unrestrained; uncontrolled. ORIG C14: from OF, from L, from IN-[1] + *continere* to hold, restrain
▸ **inˈcontinence** *n* ▸ **inˈcontinently** *adv*

incontinent[2] (ɪnˈkɒntɪnənt) *or* **incontinently** *adv* obsolete words for **immediately.** ORIG C15: from LL *in con-*

tinentī tempore, lit.: in continuous time, that is, with no interval

incontrovertible (ˌɪnkɒntrəˈvɜːtəbᵊl, ɪnˌkɒn-) *adj* incapable of being contradicted or disputed; undeniable.
► **ˌincontroˌvertiˈbility** *n* ► **ˌincontroˈvertibly** *adv*

inconvenience (ˌɪnkənˈviːnjəns, -ˈviːnɪəns) *n* **1** the state or quality of being inconvenient. **2** something inconvenient; a hindrance, trouble, or difficulty. ◆ *vb* **3** (*tr*) to cause inconvenience to; trouble or harass.

inconvenient (ˌɪnkənˈviːnjənt, -ˈviːnɪənt) *adj* not convenient; troublesome, awkward, or difficult.
► **ˌinconˈveniently** *adv*

incorporate *vb* (ɪnˈkɔːpəˌreɪt), **incorporates, incorporating, incorporated. 1** to include or be included as a part or member of a united whole. **2** to form a united whole or mass; merge or blend. **3** to form into a corporation or other organization with a separate legal identity. ◆ *adj* (ɪnˈkɔːpərɪt, -prɪt). **4** combined into a whole; incorporated. **5** formed into or constituted as a corporation. ORIG C14 (in the sense: put into the body of something else): from LL *incorporāre* to embody, from L IN-[2] + *corpus* body
► **inˈcorpoˌrated** *adj* ► **inˌcorpoˈration** *n* ► **inˈcorporative** *adj*

incorporeal (ˌɪnkɔːˈpɔːrɪəl) *adj* **1** without material form, body, or substance. **2** spiritual or metaphysical. **3** *Law.* having no material existence but existing by reason of its annexation of something material: *an incorporeal hereditament.*
► **ˌincorˈporeally** *adv* ► **incorporeity** (ɪnˌkɔːpəˈriːɪtɪ) *or* **ˌincorporeˈality** *n*

incorrect (ˌɪnkəˈrekt) *adj* **1** false; wrong: *an incorrect calculation.* **2** not fitting or proper: *incorrect behaviour.*
► **ˌincorˈrectly** *adv* ► **ˌincorˈrectness** *n*

incorrigible (ɪnˈkɒrɪdʒəbᵊl) *adj* **1** beyond correction, reform, or alteration. **2** firmly rooted; ineradicable. ◆ *n* **3** a person or animal that is incorrigible.
► **inˌcorrigiˈbility** *or* **inˈcorrigibleness** *n* ► **inˈcorrigibly** *adv*

incorruptible (ˌɪnkəˈrʌptəbᵊl) *adj* **1** incapable of being corrupted; honest; just. **2** not subject to decay or decomposition.
► **ˌincorˌruptiˈbility** *n* ► **ˌincorˈruptibly** *adv*

incr. *abbrev. for:* **1** increase. **2** increased. **3** increasing.

incrassate *adj* (ɪnˈkræsɪt, -eɪt), *also* **incrassated. 1** *Biol.* thickened or swollen. ◆ *vb* (ɪnˈkræseɪt), **incrassates, incrassating, incrassated. 2** *Obs.* to make or become thicker. ORIG C17: from LL, from L *crassus* thick, dense
► **ˌincrasˈsation** *n*

increase *vb* (ɪnˈkriːs), **increases, increasing, increased. 1** to make or become greater in size, degree, frequency, etc.; grow or expand. ◆ *n* (ˈɪnkriːs). **2** the act of increasing; augmentation. **3** the amount by which something increases. **4 on the increase.** increasing, esp. becoming more frequent. ORIG C14: from OF *encreistre,* from L, from IN-[2] + *crēscere* to grow
► **inˈcreasable** *adj* ► **increasedly** (ɪnˈkriːsɪdlɪ) *or* **inˈcreasingly** *adv* ► **inˈcreaser** *n*

incredible (ɪnˈkrɛdəbᵊl) *adj* **1** beyond belief or understanding; unbelievable. **2** *Inf.* marvellous; amazing.
► **inˌcrediˈbility** *or* **inˈcredibleness** *n* ► **inˈcredibly** *adv*

incredulity (ˌɪnkrɪˈdjuːlɪtɪ) *n* lack of belief; scepticism.

incredulous (ɪnˈkrɛdjʊləs) *adj* (often foll. by *of*) not prepared or willing to believe (something); unbelieving.
► **inˈcredulously** *adv* ► **inˈcredulousness** *n*

increment (ˈɪnkrɪmənt) *n* **1** an increase or addition, esp. one of a series. **2** the act of increasing; augmentation. **3** *Maths.* a small positive or negative change in a variable or function. ORIG C15: from L *incrēmentum* growth, INCREASE
► **incremental** (ˌɪnkrɪˈmɛntᵊl) *adj*

incremental plotter *n* a device that plots graphs on paper from computer-generated instructions.

incriminate (ɪnˈkrɪmɪˌneɪt) *vb* **incriminates, incriminating, incriminated.** (*tr*) **1** to imply or suggest the guilt or error of (someone). **2** to charge with a crime or fault. ORIG C18: from LL *incrīmināre* to accuse, from L *crīmen* accusation; see CRIME
► **inˌcrimiˈnation** *n* ► **inˈcrimiˌnator** *n* ► **inˈcriminatory** *adj*

incrust (ɪnˈkrʌst) *vb* a variant spelling of **encrust.**
► **inˈcrustant** *n, adj* ► **ˌincrusˈtation** *n*

incubate (ˈɪnkjʊˌbeɪt) *vb* **incubates, incubating, incubated. 1** (of birds) to supply (eggs) with heat for their development, esp. by sitting on them. **2** to cause (bacteria, etc.) to develop, esp. in an incubator or culture medium. **3** (*intr*) (of embryos, etc.) to develop in favourable conditions, esp. in an incubator. **4** (*intr*) (of disease germs) to remain inactive in an animal or human before causing disease. **5** to develop gradually; foment or be fomented. ORIG C18: from L *incubāre* to lie upon, hatch, from IN-[2] + *cubāre* to lie down
► **ˌincuˈbation** *n* ► **ˌincuˈbational** *adj* ► **ˈincuˌbative** *or* **ˈincuˌbatory** *adj*

incubation period *n Med.* the time between exposure to an infectious disease and the appearance of the first signs or symptoms.

incubator (ˈɪnkjʊˌbeɪtə) *n* **1** *Med.* an apparatus for housing prematurely born babies until they are strong enough to survive. **2** a container in which birds' eggs can be artificially hatched or bacterial cultures grown. **3** a person, animal, or thing that incubates.

incubus (ˈɪnkjʊbəs) *n, pl* **incubi** (-ˌbaɪ) *or* **incubuses. 1** a demon believed in folklore to have sexual intercourse with sleeping women. Cf. **succubus. 2** something that oppresses or disturbs greatly, esp. a nightmare or obsession. ORIG C14: from LL, from L *incubāre* to lie upon; see INCUBATE

inculcate (ˈɪnkʌlˌkeɪt, ɪnˈkʌlkeɪt) *vb* **inculcates, inculcating, inculcated.** (*tr*) to instil by insistent repetition. ORIG C16: from L *inculcāre* to tread upon, ram down, from IN-[2] + *calcāre* to trample, from *calx* heel
► **ˌinculˈcation** *n* ► **ˈinculˌcator** *n*

inculpate (ˈɪnkʌlˌpeɪt, ɪnˈkʌlpeɪt) *vb* **inculpates, inculpating, inculpated.** (*tr*) to incriminate; cause blame to be imputed to. ORIG C18: from LL, from L *culpāre* to blame, from *culpa* fault, blame
► **ˌinculˈpation** *n* ► **inculpative** (ɪnˈkʌlpətɪv) *or* **inculpatory** (ɪnˈkʌlpətərɪ, -trɪ) *adj*

incumbency (ɪnˈkʌmbənsɪ) *n, pl* **incumbencies. 1** the state or quality of being incumbent. **2** the office, duty, or tenure of an incumbent.

incumbent (ɪnˈkʌmbənt) *adj* **1** *Formal.* (often *postpositive* and foll. by *on* or *upon* and an infinitive) morally binding; obligatory: *it is incumbent on me to attend.* **2** (usually *postpositive* and foll. by *on*) resting or lying (on). **3** (usually *prenominal*) occupying or holding an office. ◆ *n* **4** a person who holds an office, esp. a clergyman holding a benefice. ORIG C16: from L *incumbere* to lie upon, devote one's attention to

incunabula (ˌɪnkjʊˈnæbjʊlə) *pl n, sing* **incunabulum** (-ləm). **1** any book printed before 1500. **2** the earliest stages of something; beginnings. ORIG C19: from L, orig.: swaddling clothes, hence beginnings, from IN-[2] + *cūnābula* cradle
► **ˌincuˈnabular** *adj*

incur (ɪnˈkɜː) *vb* **incurs, incurring, incurred.** (*tr*) **1** to make oneself subject to (something undesirable); bring upon oneself. **2** to run into or encounter. ORIG C16: from L *incurrere* to run into, from *currere* to run
► **inˈcurrable** *adj*

incurable (ɪnˈkjʊərəbᵊl) *adj* **1** (esp. of a disease) not curable; unresponsive to treatment. ◆ *n* **2** a person having an incurable disease.
► **inˌcuraˈbility** *or* **inˈcurableness** *n* ► **inˈcurably** *adv*

incurious (ɪnˈkjʊərɪəs) *adj* not curious; indifferent or uninterested.
► **incuriosity** (ɪnˌkjʊərɪˈɒsɪtɪ) *or* **inˈcuriousness** *n* ► **inˈcuriously** *adv*

incursion (ɪnˈkɜːʃən) *n* **1** a sudden invasion, attack, or raid. **2** the act of running or leaking into; penetration. ORIG C15: from L *incursiō* onset, attack, from *incurrere* to run into; see INCUR
► **incursive** (ɪnˈkɜːsɪv) *adj*

incus (ˈɪŋkəs) *n, pl* **incudes** (ɪnˈkjuːdiːz). the central of the three small bones in the middle ear of mammals. Cf. **malleus, stapes.** ORIG C17: from L: anvil, from *incūdere* to forge

incuse (ɪn'kju:z) *n* **1** a design stamped or hammered onto a coin. ◆ *vb* **incuses, incusing, incused. 2** to impress (a coin) with a design by hammering or stamping. ◆ *adj* **3** stamped or hammered onto a coin. ORIG C19: from L *incūsus* hammered; see INCUS

Ind ★ (ɪnd) *n* **1** a poetic name for **India. 2** an obsolete name for the **Indies.**

ind. *abbrev. for:* **1** independence. **2** independent. **3** index. **4** indicative. **5** indirect. **6** industrial. **7** industry.

Ind. *abbrev. for:* **1** Independent. **2** India. **3** Indian. **4** Indies.

indaba (ɪn'dɑ:bə) *n* **1** (among Bantu peoples of southern Africa) a meeting to discuss a serious topic. **2** *S. African inf.* a matter of concern or for discussion. ORIG C19: from Zulu: topic

indebted (ɪn'dɛtɪd) *adj* (*postpositive*) **1** owing gratitude for help, favours, etc.; obligated. **2** owing money.

indebtedness (ɪn'dɛtɪdnɪs) *n* **1** the state of being indebted. **2** the total of a person's debts.

indecency (ɪn'di:sənsɪ) *n, pl* **indecencies. 1** the state or quality of being indecent. **2** an indecent act, etc.

indecent (ɪn'di:sᵊnt) *adj* **1** offensive to standards of decency, esp. in sexual matters. **2** unseemly or improper (esp. in **indecent haste**).
▸ **in'decently** *adv*

indecent assault *n* the offence of subjecting a person to a form of sexual activity, other than rape, against his or her will.

indecent exposure *n* the offence of indecently exposing one's body in public, esp. the genitals.

indecisive (ˌɪndɪ'saɪsɪv) *adj* **1** (of a person) vacillating; irresolute. **2** not decisive or conclusive.
▸ **ˌinde'cision** *or* **ˌinde'cisiveness** *n* ▸ **ˌinde'cisively** *adv*

indecorum (ˌɪndɪ'kɔ:rəm) *n* lack of decorum; unseemliness.
▸ **in'decorous** *adj*

indeed (ɪn'di:d) (*sentence connector*). **1** certainly; actually: *indeed, it may never happen.* ◆ *adv* **2** (intensifier): *that is indeed amazing.* **3** or rather; what is more: *a comfortable, indeed wealthy family.* ◆ *interj* **4** an expression of doubt, surprise, etc.

indef. *abbrev. for* indefinite.

indefatigable (ˌɪndɪ'fætɪgəbᵊl) *adj* unable to be tired out; unflagging. ORIG C16: from L, from *fatīgāre* to tire
▸ **ˌindeˌfatiga'bility** *n* ▸ **ˌinde'fatigably** *adv*

indefeasible (ˌɪndɪ'fi:zəbᵊl) *adj Law.* not liable to be annulled or forfeited.
▸ **ˌindeˌfeasi'bility** *n* ▸ **ˌinde'feasibly** *adv*

indefensible (ˌɪndɪ'fɛnsəbᵊl) *adj* **1** not justifiable or excusable. **2** capable of being disagreed with; untenable. **3** incapable of defence against attack.
▸ **ˌindeˌfensi'bility** *n* ▸ **ˌinde'fensibly** *adv*

indefinite (ɪn'dɛfɪnɪt) *adj* **1** not certain or determined; unsettled. **2** without exact limits; indeterminate: *an indefinite number.* **3** vague or unclear. **4** in traditional logic, a proposition in which it is not stated whether the subject is universal or particular, as in *men are mortal.*
▸ **in'definitely** *adv* ▸ **in'definiteness** *n*

indefinite article *n Grammar.* a determiner that expresses nonspecificity of reference, such as *a, an,* or *some.*

indehiscent (ˌɪndɪ'hɪsᵊnt) *adj* (of fruits, etc.) not dehiscent; not opening to release seeds, etc.
▸ **ˌinde'hiscence** *n*

indelible (ɪn'dɛlɪbᵊl) *adj* **1** incapable of being erased or obliterated. **2** making indelible marks: *indelible ink.* ORIG C16: from L, from IN-[1] + *delēre* to destroy
▸ **inˌdeli'bility** *or* **in'delibleness** *n* ▸ **in'delibly** *adv*

indelicate (ɪn'dɛlɪkɪt) *adj* **1** coarse, crude, or rough. **2** offensive, embarrassing, or tasteless.
▸ **in'delicacy** *or* **in'delicateness** *n* ▸ **in'delicately** *adv*

indemnify (ɪn'dɛmnɪˌfaɪ) *vb* **indemnifies, indemnifying, indemnified.** (*tr*) **1** to secure against future loss, damage, or liability; give security for; insure. **2** to compensate for loss, etc.; reimburse.
▸ **inˌdemnifi'cation** *n* ▸ **in'demniˌfier** *n*

indemnity (ɪn'dɛmnɪtɪ) *n, pl* **indemnities. 1** compensation for loss or damage; reimbursement. **2** protection or insurance against future loss or damage. **3** legal exemption from penalties incurred through one's acts or defaults. **4** *Canad.* the annual salary paid by the government to a member of Parliament or of a provincial legislature. ORIG C15: from LL, from *indemnis* uninjured, from L IN-[1] + *damnum* damage

indene ('ɪndi:n) *n* a colourless liquid hydrocarbon obtained from coal tar and used in making synthetic resins. Formula: C_9H_8. ORIG C20: from INDOLE + -ENE

indent[1] *vb* (ɪn'dɛnt). (*mainly tr*) **1** to place (written matter, etc.) in from the margin. **2** to cut (a document in duplicate) so that the irregular lines may be matched. **3** *Chiefly Brit.* (in foreign trade) to place an order for (foreign goods). **4** (when *intr,* foll. by *for, on,* or *upon*) *Chiefly Brit.* to make an order on (a source or supply) or for (something). **5** to notch (an edge, border, etc.); make jagged. **6** to bind (an apprentice, etc.) by indenture. ◆ *n* ('ɪnˌdɛnt). *Chiefly Brit.* **7** (in foreign trade) an order for foreign merchandise. **8** an official order for goods. ORIG C14: from OF *endenter,* from EN-[1] + *dent* tooth, from L *dēns*
▸ **in'denter** *or* **in'dentor** *n*

indent[2] *vb* (ɪn'dɛnt). **1** (*tr*) to make a dent or depression in. ◆ *n* ('ɪnˌdɛnt). **2** a dent or depression. ORIG C15: from IN-[2] + DENT

indentation (ˌɪndɛn'teɪʃən) *n* **1** a hollowed, notched, or cut place, as on an edge or on a coastline. **2** a series of hollows, notches, or cuts. **3** the act of indenting or the condition of being indented. **4** Also: **indention, indent.** the leaving of space or the amount of space left between a margin and the start of an indented line.

indention (ɪn'dɛnʃən) *n* another word for **indentation** (sense 4).

indenture (ɪn'dɛntʃə) *n* **1** any deed, contract, or sealed agreement between two or more parties. **2** (formerly) a deed drawn up in duplicate, each part having correspondingly indented edges for identification and security. **3** (*often pl*) a contract between an apprentice and his or her master. **4** a less common word for **indentation.** ◆ *vb* **indentures, indenturing, indentured. 5** (*intr*) to enter into an agreement by indenture. **6** (*tr*) to bind (an apprentice, servant, etc.) by indenture.
▸ **in'dentureˌship** *n*

independence (ˌɪndɪ'pɛndəns) *n* the state or quality of being independent. Also: **independency.**

Independence ★ (ˌɪndɪ'pɛndəns) *n* a city in W Missouri, near Kansas City: starting point for the Santa Fe, Oregon, and California Trails (1831–44). Pop.: 111 669 (1994 est.).

independency (ˌɪndɪ'pɛndənsɪ) *n, pl* **independencies. 1** a territory or state free from the control of any other power. **2** another word for **independence.**

independent (ˌɪndɪ'pɛndənt) *adj* **1** free from control in action, judgment, etc.; autonomous. **2** not dependent on anything else for function, validity, etc.; separate. **3** not reliant on the support, esp. financial support, of others. **4** capable of acting for oneself or on one's own: *a very independent little girl.* **5** providing a large unearned sum towards one's support (esp. in **independent income, independent means**). **6** living on an unearned income. **7** *Maths.* (of a system of equations) not linearly dependent. See also **independent variable. 8** *Logic.* (of two or more propositions) unrelated. ◆ *n* **9** an independent person or thing. **10** a person who is not affiliated to or who acts independently of a political party.
▸ **ˌinde'pendently** *adv*

Independent (ˌɪndɪ'pɛndənt) *Christianity.* ◆ *n* **1** (in England) a member of the Congregational Church. ◆ *adj* **2** of or relating to the Congregational Church.

independent clause *n Grammar.* a main or coordinate clause.

independent school *n* **1** (in Britain) a school that is neither financed nor controlled by the government or local authorities. **2** (in Australia) a school that is not part of the state system.

independent variable *n* a variable in a mathematical equation or statement whose value determines that of the dependent variable: in $y = f(x)$, x is the independent variable.

in-depth *adj* detailed and thorough: *an in-depth study.*

indescribable (ˌɪndɪˈskraɪbəbᵊl) *adj* beyond description; too intense, extreme, etc., for words.
▸ **ˌindeˌscribaˈbility** *n* ▸ **ˌindeˈscribably** *adv*

indestructible (ˌɪndɪˈstrʌktəbᵊl) *adj* incapable of being destroyed; very durable.
▸ **ˌindeˌstructiˈbility** *or* **ˌindeˈstructibleness** *n* ▸ **ˌindeˈstructibly** *adv*

indeterminate (ˌɪndɪˈtɜːmɪnɪt) *adj* **1** uncertain in extent, amount, or nature. **2** not definite; inconclusive: *an indeterminate reply.* **3** unable to be predicted, calculated, or deduced. **4** *Maths.* **4a** having no numerical meaning, as 0/0. **4b** (of an equation) having more than one variable and an unlimited number of solutions.
▸ **ˌindeˈterminacy** *or* **ˌindeˈterminateness** *n* ▸ **ˌindeˈterminately** *adv*

indeterminism (ˌɪndɪˈtɜːmɪˌnɪzəm) *n* the philosophical doctrine that behaviour is not entirely determined by motives.
▸ **ˌindeˈterminist** *n, adj* ▸ **ˌindeˌterminˈistic** *adj*

index (ˈɪndɛks) *n, pl* **indexes** *or* **indices** (-dɪˌsiːz). **1** an alphabetical list of persons, subjects, etc., mentioned in a printed work, usually at the back, and indicating where they are referred to. **2** See **thumb index. 3** *Library science.* a systematic list of book titles or authors' names, giving cross-references and the location of each book; catalogue. **4** an indication, sign, or token. **5** a pointer, needle, or other indicator, as on an instrument. **6** *Maths.* **6a** another name for **exponent** (sense 4). **6b** a number or variable placed as a superscript to the left of a radical sign indicating the root to be extracted, as in $\sqrt[3]{8} = 2$. **7** a numerical scale by means of which levels of the cost of living can be compared with some base number. **8** a number or ratio indicating a specific characteristic, property, etc.: *refractive index.* **9** Also called: **fist.** a printer's mark, ☛ used to indicate notes, paragraphs, etc. ◆ *vb* (*tr*) **10** to put an index in (a book). **11** to enter (a word, item, etc.) in an index. **12** to point out; indicate. **13** to make index-linked. **14** to move (a machine, etc.) so that an operation will be repeated at certain defined intervals. ORIG C16: from L: pointer, hence forefinger, title, index, from *indicāre* to disclose, show; see INDICATE
▸ **ˈindexer** *n*

indexation (ˌɪndɛkˈseɪʃən) *or* **index-linking** *n* the act of making wages, interest rates, etc., index-linked.

index case *n Med.* the first case of a disease.

index finger *n* the finger next to the thumb. Also called: **forefinger.**

index fossil *n* a fossil species that characterizes and is used to delimit a geological zone. Also called: **zone fossil.**

index futures *pl n* a form of financial futures based on projected movements of a share price index, such as the Financial Times Stock Exchange 100 Share Index.

indexical (ɪnˈdɛksɪkᵊl) *adj* **1** arranged as or relating to an index or indexes. ◆ *n* **2** Also called: **deictic.** *Logic, linguistics.* a term whose reference depends on the context of utterance, such as *I, you, here, now,* or *tomorrow.*

Index Librorum Prohibitorum *Latin.* (ˈɪndɛks laɪˈbrɔːrʊm prəʊˌhɪbɪˈtɔːrʊm) *n RC Church.* (formerly) an official list of proscribed books. Often called: **the Index.** ORIG C17, lit.: list of forbidden books

index-linked *adj* (of wages, interest rates, etc.) directly related to the cost-of-living index and rising or falling accordingly.

index number *n Statistics.* a statistic indicating the relative change occurring in the price or value of a commodity or in a general economic variable, with reference to a previous base period conventionally given the number 100.

India ★ (ˈɪndɪə) *n* **1** a republic in S Asia: history dates from the Indus Valley civilization (3rd millennium B.C.); came under British supremacy in 1763 and passed to the British Crown in 1858; nationalist movement arose under Gandhi (1869–1948); Indian subcontinent divided into Pakistan (Muslim) and India (Hindu) in 1947; became a republic within the Commonwealth in 1950. It consists chiefly of the Himalayas, rising over 7500 m (25 000 ft) in the extreme north, the Ganges plain in the north, the Thar Desert in the northwest, the Chota Nagpur plateau in the northeast, and the Deccan Plateau in the south. Official and administrative languages: Hindi and English; each state has its own language. Religion: Hindu majority, Muslim minority. Currency: rupee. Capital: New Delhi. Pop.: 1 000 849 000 (1999 est.). Area: 3 268 100 sq. km (1 261 813 sq. miles). Hindi name: **Bharat. 2** *Communications.* a code word for the letter *i.*

Indiaman (ˈɪndɪəmən) *n, pl* **Indiamen.** (formerly) a merchant ship engaged in trade with India.

Indian (ˈɪndɪən) *n* **1** a native or inhabitant of the Republic of India or a descendant of one. **2** an American Indian. **3** (*not in scholarly usage*) any of the languages of the American Indians. ◆ *adj* **4** of or relating to India, its inhabitants, or any of their languages. **5** of or relating to the American Indians or any of their languages.

Indiana ★ (ˌɪndɪˈænə) *n* a state of the N central US, in the Midwest: consists of an undulating plain, with sand dunes and lakes in the north and limestone caves in the south. Capital: Indianapolis. Pop.: 5 899 195 (1998 est.). Area: 93 491 sq. km (36 097 sq. miles). Abbrevs.: **Ind.** or (with zip code) **IN**
▸ **ˌIndiˈanian** *adj, n*

Indianapolis ★ (ˌɪndɪəˈnæpəlɪs) *n* a city in central Indiana: the state capital. Pop.: 752 279 (1994 est.).

Indian club *n* a bottle-shaped club, usually used in pairs by gymnasts, jugglers, etc.

Indian corn *n* another name for **maize** (sense 1).

Indian Desert ★ *n* another name for the **Thar Desert.**

Indian Empire ★ *n* British India and the Indian states under indirect British control, which gained independence as India and Pakistan in 1947.

Indian file *n* another term for **single file.**

Indian hemp *n* another name for **hemp,** esp. the variety *Cannabis indica,* from which several narcotic drugs are obtained.

Indian ink *or esp. US & Canad.* **India ink** *n* **1** a black pigment made from a mixture of lampblack and a binding agent such as gelatine or glue: usually formed into solid cakes and sticks. **2** a black liquid ink made from this pigment. ◆ Also called: **China ink, Chinese ink.**

Indian list *n Inf.* (in Canada) a list of persons to whom spirits may not be sold.

Indian meal *n* another name for **corn meal.**

Indian Ocean ★ *n* an ocean bordered by Africa in the west, Asia in the north, and Australia in the east and merging with the Antarctic Ocean in the south. Average depth: 3900 m (13 000 ft). Greatest depth (off the Sunda Islands): 7450 m (24 442 ft). Area: about 73 556 000 sq. km (28 400 000 sq. miles).

Indian rope-trick *n* the supposed Indian feat of climbing an unsupported rope.

Indian States and Agencies ★ *pl n* another name for the **Native States.**

Indian summer *n* **1** a period of unusually warm weather in the late autumn. **2** a period of tranquillity or of renewed productivity towards the end of something, esp. a person's life. ORIG orig. US: prob. so named because it was first noted in Amerind regions

Indian Territory ★ *n* the territory established in the early 19th century in present-day Oklahoma, where Indians were forced to settle by the US government. The last remnant was integrated into the new state of Oklahoma in 1907.

Indian tobacco *n* a poisonous North American plant with small pale bell-shaped blue flowers and rounded inflated seed capsules.

India paper *n* a thin soft opaque printing paper originally made in the Orient.

India rubber *n* another name for **rubber**[1] (sense 1).

Indic (ˈɪndɪk) *adj* **1** denoting, belonging to, or relating to a branch of Indo-European consisting of certain languages of India, including Sanskrit, Hindi and Urdu. ◆ *n* **2** this group of languages. ◆ Also: **Indo-Aryan.**

indicate (ˈɪndɪˌkeɪt) *vb* **indicates, indicating, indicated.** (*tr*) **1**

(*may take a clause as object*) to be or give a sign or symptom of; imply: *cold hands indicate a warm heart.* **2** to point out or show. **3** (*may take a clause as object*) to state briefly; suggest. **4** (of instruments) to show a reading of. **5** (*usually passive*) to recommend or require: *surgery seems to be indicated for this patient.* ORIG C17: from L *indicāre* to point out, from IN-[2] + *dicāre* to proclaim; cf. INDEX
▸ **'indi,catable** *adj* ▸ **indicatory** (ɪn'dɪkətərɪ, -trɪ) *adj*

indication (,ɪndɪ'keɪʃən) *n* **1** something that serves to indicate or suggest; sign: *an indication of foul play.* **2** the degree or quantity represented on a measuring instrument or device. **3** the action of indicating. **4** something that is indicated as advisable, necessary, or expedient.

indicative (ɪn'dɪkətɪv) *adj* **1** (*usually postpositive;* foll. by *of*) serving as a sign; suggestive: *indicative of trouble ahead.* **2** *Grammar.* denoting a mood of verbs used chiefly to make statements. ◆ *n* **3** *Grammar.* **3a** the indicative mood. **3b** a verb in the indicative mood. ◆ Abbrev.: **indic.**
▸ **in'dicatively** *adv*

indicator ('ɪndɪ,keɪtə) *n* **1** something that provides an indication, esp. of trends. See **economic indicator.** **2** a device to attract attention, such as the pointer of a gauge or a warning lamp. **3** an instrument that displays certain operating conditions in a machine, such as a gauge showing temperature, etc. **4** a device that registers something, such as the movements of a lift, or that shows information, such as train departure times. **5** Also called: **blinker.** a device for indicating that a motor vehicle is about to turn left or right, esp. two pairs of lights that flash. **6** a delicate measuring instrument used to determine small differences in the height of mechanical components. **7** *Chem.* a substance used to indicate the completion of a chemical reaction, usually by a change of colour. **8** Also called: **indicator species.** *Ecology.* a plant or animal species that thrives only under particular environmental conditions and therefore indicates these conditions where it is found.

indices ('ɪndɪ,si:z) *n* a plural of **index.**

indicia (ɪn'dɪʃɪə) *pl n, sing* **indicium** (-ʃɪəm). distinguishing markings or signs; indications. ORIG C17: from L, pl of *indicium* a notice, from INDEX
▸ **in'dicial** *adj*

indict (ɪn'daɪt) *vb* (*tr*) to charge (a person) with crime, esp. formally in writing; accuse. ORIG C14: alteration of *enditen* to INDITE
▸ **,indict'ee** *n* ▸ **in'dicter** *or* **in'dictor** *n* ▸ **in'dictable** *adj*

USAGE NOTE See at **indite.**

indictment (ɪn'daɪtmənt) *n Criminal law.* **1** a formal written charge of crime formerly referred to and presented on oath by a grand jury. **2** any formal accusation of crime. **3** the act of indicting or the state of being indicted.

indie ('ɪndɪ) *n Inf.* **a** an independent film or record company. **b** (*as modifier*): *an indie producer; the indie charts.*

Indies ★ ('ɪndɪz) *n* **the. 1** the territories of S and SE Asia included in the East Indies, India, and Indochina. **2** See **East Indies. 3** See **West Indies.**

indifference (ɪn'dɪfrəns, -fərəns) *n* **1** the fact or state of being indifferent; lack of care or concern. **2** lack of quality; mediocrity. **3** lack of importance; insignificance.

indifferent (ɪn'dɪfrənt, -fərənt) *adj* **1** (often foll. by *to*) showing no care or concern; uninterested: *he was indifferent to my pleas.* **2** unimportant; immaterial. **3a** of only average or moderate size, extent, quality, etc. **3b** not at all good; poor. **4** showing or having no preferences; impartial. ORIG C14: from L *indifferēns* making no distinction
▸ **in'differently** *adv*

indifferentism (ɪn'dɪfrən,tɪzəm, -fərən-) *n* systematic indifference, esp. in matters of religion.
▸ **in'differentist** *n*

indigenous (ɪn'dɪdʒɪnəs) *adj* (when *postpositive,* foll. by *to*) **1** originating or occurring naturally (in a country, etc.); native. **2** innate (to); inherent (in). ORIG C17: from L *indigenus,* from *indi-* in + *gignere* to beget
▸ **in'digenously** *adv* ▸ **in'digenousness** *n*

indigent ('ɪndɪdʒənt) *adj* **1** so poor as to lack even necessities; very needy. **2** (usually foll. by *of*) *Arch.* lacking (in) or destitute (of). ◆ *n* **3** an impoverished person. ORIG C14: from L *indigēre* to need, from *egēre* to lack
▸ **'indigence** *n* ▸ **'indigently** *adv*

indigestible (,ɪndɪ'dʒɛstəb[ə]l) *adj* **1** incapable of being digested or difficult to digest. **2** difficult to understand or absorb mentally: *an indigestible book.*
▸ **,indi,gesti'bility** *n* ▸ **,indi'gestibly** *adv*

indigestion (,ɪndɪ'dʒɛstʃən) *n* difficulty in digesting food, accompanied by abdominal pain, heartburn, and belching.

indignant (ɪn'dɪgnənt) *adj* feeling or showing indignation. ORIG C16: from L *indignārī* to be displeased with
▸ **in'dignantly** *adv*

indignation (,ɪndɪg'neɪʃən) *n* anger aroused by something felt to be unfair, unworthy, or wrong.

indignity (ɪn'dɪgnɪtɪ) *n, pl* **indignities.** injury to one's self-esteem or dignity; humiliation.

indigo ('ɪndɪ,gəʊ) *n, pl* **indigos** *or* **indigoes. 1** a blue vat dye originally obtained from plants but now made synthetically. **2** any of various leguminous tropical plants, such as the anil, that yield this dye. **3a** any of a group of colours that have the same blue-violet hue; a spectral colour. **3b** (*as adj*): *an indigo rug.* ORIG C16: from Sp. *indico,* via L from Gk *Indikos* of India
▸ **indigotic** (,ɪndɪ'gɒtɪk) *adj*

indigo blue *n, adj* (**indigo-blue** *when prenominal*). the full name for **indigo** (the colour and the dye).

indirect (,ɪndɪ'rɛkt) *adj* **1** deviating from a direct course or line; roundabout; circuitous. **2** not coming as a direct effect or consequence; secondary: *indirect benefits.* **3** not straightforward, open, or fair; devious or evasive.
▸ **,indi'rectly** *adv* ▸ **,indi'rectness** *n*

indirect costs *pl n* another name for **overheads.**

indirection (,ɪndɪ'rɛkʃən) *n* **1** indirect procedure, courses, or methods. **2** lack of direction or purpose; aimlessness. **3** indirect dealing; deceit.

indirect lighting *n* reflected or diffused light from a concealed source.

indirect object *n Grammar.* a noun, pronoun, or noun phrase indicating the recipient or beneficiary of the action of a verb and its direct object, as *John* in the sentence *I bought John a newspaper.*

indirect proof *n Logic, maths.* proof of a conclusion by showing its negation to be self-contradictory. Cf. **direct** (sense 17).

indirect question *n* a question reported in indirect speech, as in *She asked why you came.*

indirect speech *or esp. US* **indirect discourse** *n* the reporting of something said or written by conveying what was meant rather than repeating the exact words, as in the sentence *He said I looked happy* as opposed to *He said to me, "You look happy."* Also called: **reported speech.**

indirect tax *n* a tax levied on goods or services rather than on individuals or companies.

indiscreet (,ɪndɪ'skri:t) *adj* not discreet; imprudent or tactless.
▸ **,indis'creetly** *adv* ▸ **,indis'creetness** *n*

indiscrete (,ɪndɪ'skri:t) *adj* not divisible or divided into parts.

indiscretion (,ɪndɪ'skrɛʃən) *n* **1** the characteristic or state of being indiscreet. **2** an indiscreet act, remark, etc.

indiscriminate (,ɪndɪ'skrɪmɪnɪt) *adj* **1** lacking discrimination or careful choice; random or promiscuous. **2** jumbled; confused.
▸ **,indis'criminately** *adv* ▸ **,indis'criminateness** *n* ▸ **,indis,crimi'nation** *n*

indispensable (,ɪndɪ'spɛnsəb[ə]l) *adj* **1** absolutely necessary; essential. **2** not to be disregarded or escaped: *an indispensable role.* ◆ *n* **3** an indispensable person or thing.
▸ **,indis,pensa'bility** *or* **,indis'pensableness** *n* ▸ **,indis'pensably** *adv*

indispose (,ɪndɪ'spəʊz) *vb* **indisposes, indisposing, indisposed.** (*tr*) **1** to make unwilling or opposed; disincline. **2**

to cause to feel ill. **3** to make unfit (for something or to do something).

indisposed (ˌɪndɪˈspəʊzd) *adj* **1** sick or ill. **2** unwilling. ORIG C15: from L *indispositus* disordered
▸ **indisposition** (ˌɪndɪspəˈzɪʃən) *n*

indisputable (ˌɪndɪˈspjuːtəbᵊl) *adj* beyond doubt; not open to question.
▸ **ˌindisˌputaˈbility** *or* **ˌindisˈputableness** *n* ▸ **ˌindisˈputably** *adv*

indissoluble (ˌɪndɪˈsɒljʊbᵊl) *adj* incapable of being dissolved or broken; permanent.
▸ **ˌindisˈsolubly** *adv*

indistinct (ˌɪndɪˈstɪŋkt) *adj* incapable of being clearly distinguished, as by the eyes, ears, or mind; not distinct.
▸ **ˌindisˈtinctly** *adv* ▸ **ˌindisˈtinctness** *n*

indistinguishable (ˌɪndɪˈstɪŋgwɪʃəbᵊl) *adj* **1** (*often postpositive*; foll. by *from*) identical or very similar (to): *twins indistinguishable from one another.* **2** not easily perceptible; indiscernible.
▸ **ˌindisˌtinguishaˈbility** *or* **ˌindisˈtinguishableness** *n* ▸ **ˌindisˈtinguishably** *adv*

indite (ɪnˈdaɪt) *vb* **indites, inditing, indited.** (*tr*) *Arch.* to write. ORIG C14: from OF *enditer,* from L *indīcere* to declare, from IN-² + *dīcere* to say
▸ **inˈditement** *n* ▸ **inˈditer** *n*

> **USAGE NOTE** *Indite* and *inditement* are sometimes wrongly used where *indict* and *indictment* are meant: *he was indicted* (not *indited*) *for fraud.*

indium (ˈɪndɪəm) *n* a rare soft silvery metallic element associated with zinc ores: used in alloys, electronics, and electroplating. Symbol: In; atomic no.: 49; atomic wt.: 114.82. ORIG C19: NL, from INDIGO + -IUM

individual (ˌɪndɪˈvɪdjʊəl) *adj* **1** of, relating to, characteristic of, or meant for a single person or thing. **2** separate or distinct, esp. from others of its kind; particular: *please mark the individual pages.* **3** characterized by unusual and striking qualities; distinctive. **4** *Obs.* indivisible; inseparable. ◆ *n* **5** a single person, esp. when regarded as distinct from others. **6** *Biol.* a single animal or plant, esp. as distinct from a species. **7** *Inf.* a person: *a most obnoxious individual.* ORIG C15: from Med. L, from L *indīviduus* indivisible, from IN-¹ + *dīvidere* to DIVIDE
▸ **ˌindiˈvidually** *adv*

individualism (ˌɪndɪˈvɪdjʊəˌlɪzəm) *n* **1** the principle of asserting one's independence and individuality; egoism. **2** an individual quirk. **3** another word for **laissez faire** (sense 1). **4** *Philosophy.* the doctrine that only individual things exist.
▸ **ˌindiˈvidualist** *n*

individuality (ˌɪndɪˌvɪdjʊˈælɪtɪ) *n, pl* **individualities. 1** distinctive or unique character or personality: *a work of great individuality.* **2** the qualities that distinguish one person or thing from another; identity. **3** the state or quality of being a separate entity; discreteness.

individualize *or* **individualise** (ˌɪndɪˈvɪdjʊəˌlaɪz) *vb* **individualizes, individualizing, individualized** *or* **individualises, individualising, individualised.** (*tr*) **1** to make or mark as individual or distinctive in character. **2** to consider or treat individually; particularize. **3** to make or modify so as to meet the special requirements of a person.
▸ **ˌindiˌvidualiˈzation** *or* **ˌindiˌvidualiˈsation** *n* ▸ **ˌindiˈvidualˌizer** *or* **ˌindiˈvidualˌiser** *n*

individuate (ˌɪndɪˈvɪdjʊˌeɪt) *vb* **individuates, individuating, individuated.** (*tr*) **1** to give individuality or an individual form to. **2** to distinguish from others of the same species or group; individualize.
▸ **ˌindiˈviduˌator** *n*

indivisible (ˌɪndɪˈvɪzəbᵊl) *adj* **1** unable to be divided. **2** *Maths.* leaving a remainder when divided by a given number.
▸ **ˌindiˌvisiˈbility** *n* ▸ **ˌindiˈvisibly** *adv*

Indo- (ˈɪndəʊ) *combining form.* denoting India or Indian: *Indo-European.*

Indo-Caribbean *adj* **1** denoting or relating to Caribbean people of Indian descent or their culture. ◆ *n* a Caribbean of Indian descent. ◆ Also: **East Indian.**

Indochina *or* **Indo-China** ★ (ˈɪndəʊˈtʃaɪnə) *n* **1** Also called: **Farther India.** a peninsula in SE Asia, between India and China: consists of Myanmar, Thailand, Laos, Cambodia, Vietnam, and Malaysia. **2** the former French colonial possessions of Cochin China, Annam, Tonkin, Laos, and Cambodia.
▸ **ˈIndochiˈnese** *or* **ˈIndo-Chiˈnese** *adj, n*

indoctrinate (ɪnˈdɒktrɪˌneɪt) *vb* **indoctrinates, indoctrinating, indoctrinated.** (*tr*) **1** to teach (a person or group of people) systematically to accept doctrines, esp. uncritically. **2** *Rare.* to instruct.
▸ **inˌdoctriˈnation** *n* ▸ **inˈdoctriˌnator** *n*

Indo-European *adj* **1** denoting, belonging to, or relating to a family of languages that includes English: characteristically marked, esp. in the older languages, such as Latin, by inflection showing gender, number, and case. **2** denoting or relating to the hypothetical parent language of this family, primitive Indo-European. **3** denoting, belonging to, or relating to any of the peoples speaking these languages. ◆ *n* **4** the Indo-European family of languages. **5** the reconstructed hypothetical parent language of this family. ◆ Also (*obs.*): **Indo-Germanic.**

Indo-Iranian *adj* **1** of or relating to the Indic and Iranian branches of the Indo-European family of languages. ◆ *n* **2** this group of languages, sometimes considered as forming a single branch of Indo-European.

indole (ˈɪndəʊl) *or* **indol** (ˈɪndəʊl, -dɒl) *n* a white or yellowish crystalline heterocyclic compound extracted from coal tar and used in perfumery, medicine, and as a flavouring agent. ORIG C19: from IND(IGO) + -OLE¹

indolent (ˈɪndələnt) *adj* **1** disliking work or effort; lazy; idle. **2** *Pathol.* causing little pain: *an indolent tumour.* **3** (esp. of a painless ulcer) slow to heal. ORIG C17: from L *indolēns* not feeling pain, from IN-¹ + *dolēre* to grieve, cause distress
▸ **ˈindolence** *n* ▸ **ˈindolently** *adv*

indomitable (ɪnˈdɒmɪtəbᵊl) *adj* (of courage, pride, etc.) difficult or impossible to defeat or subdue. ORIG C17: from LL, from L *indomitus* untameable, from *domāre* to tame
▸ **inˌdomitaˈbility** *or* **inˈdomitableness** *n* ▸ **inˈdomitably** *adv*

Indonesia ★ (ˌɪndəʊˈniːzɪə) *n* a republic in SE Asia, in the Malay Archipelago, consisting of the main islands of Sumatra, Java and Madura, Bali, Sulawesi (Celebes), Lombok, Sumbawa, Flores, the Moluccas, Timor, part of Borneo (Kalimantan), Irian Jaya, and over 3000 small islands in the Indian and Pacific Oceans: became the Dutch East Indies in 1798; declared independence in 1945; became a republic in 1950. Official language: Bahasa Indonesia. Religion: mostly Muslim. Currency: rupiah. Capital: Jakarta. Pop.: 206 143 000 (1999 est.). Area: 1 919 317 sq. km (741 052 sq. miles). Former names (1798–1945): **Dutch East Indies, Netherlands East Indies.**

Indonesian (ˌɪndəʊˈniːzɪən) *adj* **1** of or relating to Indonesia, its people, or their language. ◆ *n* **2** a native or inhabitant of Indonesia.

indoor (ˈɪnˌdɔː) *adj* (*prenominal*) of, situated in, or appropriate to the inside of a house or other building: *an indoor pool; indoor amusements.*

indoors (ˌɪnˈdɔːz) *adv, adj* (*postpositive*) inside or into a house or other building.

Indore ★ (ɪnˈdɔː) *n* **1** a city in central India, in W Madhya Pradesh. Pop.: 1 091 674 (1991). **2** a former state of central India: became part of Madhya Bharat in 1948, which in turn became part of Madhya Pradesh in 1956.

indorse (ɪnˈdɔːs) *vb* **indorses, indorsing, indorsed.** a variant spelling of **endorse.**

Indra ★ (ˈɪndrə) *n Hinduism.* the most celebrated god of the Rig-Veda, governing the weather and dispensing rain.

indraught *or US* **indraft** (ˈɪnˌdrɑːft) *n* **1** the act of drawing or pulling in. **2** an inward flow, esp. of air.

indrawn (ˌɪnˈdrɔːn) *adj* **1** drawn or pulled in. **2** inward-looking or introspective.

Indre ★ (*French* ɛ̃drə) *n* a department of central France in the Centre region. Capital: Châteauroux. Pop.: 234 531 (1994 est). Area: 6906 sq. km (2693 sq. miles).

Indre-et-Loire ★ (*French* ɛ̃drelwar) *n* a department of W central France in the Centre region: contains many famous châteaux along the Loire. Capital: Tours. Pop.: 543 973 (1994 est.). Area: 6158 sq. km (2402 sq. miles).

indris (ˈɪndrɪs) *or* **indri** (ˈɪndrɪ) *n, pl* **indris. 1** a large Madagascan arboreal lemuroid primate with thick silky fur patterned in black, white, and fawn. **2 woolly indris.** a related nocturnal Madagascan animal with thick grey-brown fur and a long tail. ORIG C19: from F: lemur, from native word *indry!* look! mistaken for the animal's name

indubitable (ɪnˈdjuːbɪtəbᵊl) *adj* incapable of being doubted; unquestionable. ORIG C18: from L, from IN-[1] + *dubitāre* to doubt
▸ **inˈdubitably** *adv*

induce (ɪnˈdjuːs) *vb* **induces, inducing, induced.** (*tr*) **1** (often foll. by an infinitive) to persuade or use influence on. **2** to cause or bring about. **3** *Med.* to initiate or hasten (labour), as by administering a drug to stimulate uterine contractions. **4** *Logic, obs.* to assert or establish (a general proposition, etc.) by induction. **5** to produce (an electromotive force or electrical current) by induction. **6** to transmit (magnetism) by induction. ORIG C14: from L *indūcere* to lead in
▸ **inˈducer** *n* ▸ **inˈducible** *adj*

inducement (ɪnˈdjuːsmənt) *n* **1** the act of inducing. **2** a means of inducing; persuasion; incentive. **3** *Law.* the introductory part that leads up to and explains the matter in dispute.

induct (ɪnˈdʌkt) *vb* (*tr*) **1** to bring in formally or install in an office, place, etc.; invest. **2** (foll. by *to* or *into*) to initiate in knowledge (of). **3** *US.* to enlist for military service. **4** *Physics.* another word for **induce** (senses 5, 6). ORIG C14: from L *inductus* led in, p.p. of *indūcere* to introduce; see INDUCE

inductance (ɪnˈdʌktəns) *n* **1** the property of an electric circuit as a result of which an electromotive force is created by a change of current in the same or in a neighbouring circuit. **2** a component, such as a coil, in an electrical circuit, the main function of which is to produce inductance.

induction (ɪnˈdʌkʃən) *n* **1** the act of inducting or state of being inducted. **2** the act of inducing. **3** (in an internal-combustion engine) the drawing in of mixed air and fuel from the carburettor to the cylinder. **4** *Logic.* **4a** a process of reasoning by which a general conclusion is drawn from a set of premises, based mainly on experience or experimental evidence. **4b** a conclusion reached by this process of reasoning. **5** the process by which electrical or magnetic properties are transferred, without physical contact, from one circuit or body to another. See also **inductance. 6** *Maths.* a method of proving a proposition P(*n*) by showing that it is true for all preceding values of *n* and for *n* + 1. **7a** a formal introduction or entry into an office or position. **7b** (*as modifier*): *induction course.* **8** *US.* the enlistment of a civilian into military service.
▸ **inˈductional** *adj*

induction coil *n* **1** any coil of wire used to introduce inductance into a circuit. **2** another name for **ignition coil.**

induction heating *n* the heating of a conducting material as a result of the electric currents induced in it by an externally applied alternating magnetic field.

induction loop system *n* an electronic system enabling partially deaf people to hear dialogue and sound in theatres, cinemas, etc. Often shortened to **induction loop.**

induction motor *n* a type of electric motor in which an alternating supply fed to the windings of the stator creates a magnetic field that induces a current in the windings of the rotor. Rotation of the rotor results from the interaction of the magnetic field created by the rotor current with the field of the stator.

inductive (ɪnˈdʌktɪv) *adj* **1** relating to or operated by electrical or magnetic induction: *an inductive reactance.* **2** *Logic, maths.* of, relating to, or using induction: *inductive reasoning.* **3** serving to induce or cause.
▸ **inˈductively** *adv* ▸ **inˈductiveness** *n*

inductor (ɪnˈdʌktə) *n* **1** a person or thing that inducts. **2** another name for an **inductance** (sense 2).

indue (ɪnˈdjuː) *vb* **indues, induing, indued.** a variant spelling of **endue.**

indulge (ɪnˈdʌldʒ) *vb* **indulges, indulging, indulged. 1** (when *intr,* often foll. by *in*) to yield to or gratify (a whim or desire for): *to indulge in new clothes.* **2** (*tr*) to yield to the wishes of; pamper: *to indulge a child.* **3** (*tr*) to allow (oneself) the pleasure of something: *he indulged himself.* **4** (*intr*) *Inf.* to take alcoholic drink, esp. to excess. ORIG C17: from L *indulgēre* to concede
▸ **inˈdulger** *n* ▸ **inˈdulgingly** *adv*

indulgence (ɪnˈdʌldʒəns) *n* **1** the act of indulging or state of being indulgent. **2** a pleasure, habit, etc., indulged in; extravagance. **3** liberal or tolerant treatment. **4** something granted as a favour or privilege. **5** *RC Church.* a remission of the temporal punishment for sin after its guilt has been forgiven. **6** Also called: **Declaration of Indulgence.** a royal grant during the reigns of Charles II and James II of England giving Nonconformists and Roman Catholics a measure of religious freedom.

indulgent (ɪnˈdʌldʒənt) *adj* showing or characterized by indulgence.
▸ **inˈdulgently** *adv*

induna (ɪnˈduːnə) *n* (in South Africa) a Black African overseer in a factory, mine, etc. ORIG C20: from Zulu *nduna* an official

indurate *vb* (ˈɪndjuˌreɪt), **indurates, indurating, indurated. 1** to make or become hard or callous. **2** to make or become hardy. ◆ *adj* (ˈɪndjurɪt). **3** hardened, callous, or unfeeling. ORIG C16: from L *indūrāre* to make hard; see ENDURE
▸ ˌ**induˈration** *n* ▸ **ˈinduˌrative** *adj*

Indus ★ (ˈɪndəs) *n* a river in S Asia, rising in SW Tibet in the Kailas Range of the Himalayas and flowing northwest through Kashmir, then southwest across Pakistan to the Arabian Sea: important throughout history, esp. for the Indus Civilization (about 3000 to 1500 B.C.), and for irrigation. Length: about 2900 km (1800 miles).

indusium (ɪnˈdjuːzɪəm) *n, pl* **indusia** (-zɪə). **1** a membranous outgrowth on the undersurface of fern leaves that protects the developing spores. **2** an enveloping membrane, such as the amnion. ORIG C18: NL, from L: tunic, from *induere* to put on
▸ **inˈdusial** *adj*

industrial (ɪnˈdʌstrɪəl) *adj* **1** of, relating to, or derived from industry. **2** employed in industry: *the industrial workforce.* **3** relating to or concerned with workers in industry: *industrial conditions.* **4** used in industry: *industrial chemicals.*
▸ **inˈdustrially** *adv*

industrial action *n Brit.* any action, such as a strike or go-slow, taken by employees in industry to protest against working conditions, etc.

industrial archaeology *n* the study of industrial machines, works, etc. of the past.

industrial design *n* the art or practice of designing any object for manufacture.
▸ **industrial designer** *n*

industrial diamond *n* a small often synthetic diamond, valueless as a gemstone, used in cutting tools, abrasives, etc.

industrial disease *n* any disease to which workers in a particular industry are prone.

industrial espionage *n* attempting to obtain trade secrets by dishonest means, as by telephone- or computer-tapping, infiltration of a competitor's workforce, etc.

industrial estate *n Brit.* another name for **trading estate.** US equivalent: **industrial park.**

industrialism (ɪnˈdʌstrɪəˌlɪzəm) *n* an organization of society characterized by large-scale mechanized manufacturing industry rather than trade, farming, etc.

industrialist (ɪnˈdʌstrɪəlɪst) *n* a person who has a substantial interest in the ownership or control of industrial enterprise.

industrialize *or* **industrialise** (ɪn'dʌstrɪəˌlaɪz) *vb* **industrializes, industrializing, industrialized** *or* **industrialises, industrialising, industrialised. 1** (*tr*) to develop industry on an extensive scale in (a country, region, etc.). **2** (*intr*) (of a country, region, etc.) to undergo the development of industry on an extensive scale.
▸ **inˌdustrialiˈzation** *or* **inˌdustrialiˈsation** *n*

industrial medicine *n* the study and practice of the health care of employees of large organizations.

industrial relations *n* **1** (*functioning as pl*) relations between the employers and employees in an industrial enterprise. **2** (*functioning as sing*) the management of such relations.

Industrial Revolution *n* **the.** the transformation in the 18th and 19th centuries of Britain and other countries into industrial nations.

industrial tribunal *n* a tribunal that rules on disputes between employers and employees regarding unfair dismissal, redundancy, etc.

industrious (ɪn'dʌstrɪəs) *adj* hard-working, diligent, or assiduous.
▸ **inˈdustriously** *adv* ▸ **inˈdustriousness** *n*

industry ('ɪndəstrɪ) *n, pl* **industries. 1** organized economic activity concerned with manufacture, processing of raw materials, or construction. **2** a branch of commercial enterprise concerned with the output of a specified product: *the steel industry.* **3a** industrial ownership and management interests collectively. **3b** manufacturing enterprise collectively, as opposed to agriculture. **4** diligence; assiduity. ORIG C15: from L *industria* diligence, from *industrius* active, from ?

indwell (ɪn'dwɛl) *vb* **indwells, indwelling, indwelt. 1** (*tr*) (of a spirit, principle, etc.) to inhabit; suffuse. **2** (*intr*) to dwell; exist.
▸ **inˈdweller** *n*

Indy, d' ★ (*French* dɛ̃di) *n* **Vincent** (vɛ̃sɑ̃). See (Vincent) **d'Indy.**

Ine ★ ('ɪnə, 'ɪnɪ) *n* died after 726, king of Wessex (688–726).

-ine[1] *suffix forming adjectives.* **1** of, relating to, or belonging to: *saturnine.* **2** consisting of or resembling: *crystalline.* ORIG from L *-īnus,* from Gk *-inos*

-ine[2] *suffix forming nouns.* **1** indicating a halogen: *chlorine.* **2** indicating a nitrogenous organic compound, including amino acids, alkaloids, and certain other bases: *nicotine.* **3** Also: **-in.** indicating a chemical substance in certain nonsystematic names: *glycerine.* **4** indicating a mixture of hydrocarbons: *benzine.* **5** indicating feminine form: *heroine.* ORIG via F from L *-ina* (from *-inus*) and Gk *-inē*

inebriate *vb* (ɪn'iːbrɪˌeɪt), **inebriates, inebriating, inebriated.** (*tr*) **1** to make drunk; intoxicate. **2** to arouse emotionally; make excited. ◆ *n* (ɪn'iːbrɪɪt). **3** a person who is drunk, esp. habitually. ◆ *adj* (ɪn'iːbrɪɪt), *also* **inebriated. 4** drunk, esp. habitually. ORIG C15: from L, from IN-[2] + *ēbriāre* to intoxicate, from *ēbrius* drunk
▸ **inˌebriˈation** *n* ▸ **inebriety** (ˌɪnɪ'braɪɪtɪ) *n*

inedible (ɪn'ɛdɪbᵊl) *adj* not fit to be eaten.
▸ **inˌediˈbility** *n*

ineducable (ɪn'ɛdjʊkəbᵊl) *adj* incapable of being educated, esp. on account of mental retardation.
▸ **inˌeducaˈbility** *n*

ineffable (ɪn'ɛfəbᵊl) *adj* **1** too great or intense to be expressed in words; unutterable. **2** too sacred to be uttered. **3** indescribable; indefinable. ORIG C15: from L, from IN-[1] + *effābilis,* from *fārī* to speak
▸ **inˌeffaˈbility** *or* **inˈeffableness** *n* ▸ **inˈeffably** *adv*

ineffective (ˌɪnɪ'fɛktɪv) *adj* **1** having no effect. **2** incompetent or inefficient.
▸ **ˌinefˈfectively** *adv* ▸ **ˌinefˈfectiveness** *n*

ineffectual (ˌɪnɪ'fɛktʃʊəl) *adj* **1** having no effect or an inadequate effect. **2** lacking in power or forcefulness; impotent: *an ineffectual ruler.*
▸ **ˌinefˌfectuˈality** *or* **ˌinefˈfectualness** *n* ▸ **ˌinefˈfectually** *adv*

inefficacious (ˌɪnɛfɪ'keɪʃəs) *adj* failing to produce the desired effect.
▸ **ˌineffiˈcaciously** *adv* ▸ **inefficacy** (ɪn'ɛfɪkəsɪ), **ˌineffiˈcaciousness,** *or* **inefficacity** (ˌɪnɛfɪ'kæsɪtɪ) *n*

inefficient (ˌɪnɪ'fɪʃənt) *adj* **1** unable to perform a task or function to the best advantage; wasteful or incompetent. **2** unable to produce the desired result.
▸ **ˌinefˈficiency** *n* ▸ **ˌinefˈficiently** *adv*

ineligible (ɪn'ɛlɪdʒəbᵊl) *adj* **1** (often foll. by *for* or an infinitive) not fit or qualified: *ineligible for a grant; ineligible to vote.* ◆ *n* **2** an ineligible person.
▸ **inˌeligiˈbility** *or* **inˈeligibleness** *n* ▸ **inˈeligibly** *adv*

ineluctable (ˌɪnɪ'lʌktəbᵊl) *adj* (esp. of fate) incapable of being avoided; inescapable. ORIG C17: from L, from IN-[1] + *ēluctārī* to escape, from *luctārī* to struggle
▸ **ˌineˌluctaˈbility** *n* ▸ **ˌineˈluctably** *adv*

inept (ɪn'ɛpt) *adj* **1** awkward, clumsy, or incompetent. **2** not suitable, appropriate, or fitting; out of place. ORIG C17: from L *ineptus,* from IN-[1] + *aptus* fitting
▸ **inˈeptiˌtude** *n* ▸ **inˈeptly** *adv* ▸ **inˈeptness** *n*

inequable (ɪn'ɛkwəbᵊl) *adj* **1** uneven. **2** not uniform. **3** changeable.

inequality (ˌɪnɪ'kwɒlɪtɪ) *n, pl* **inequalities. 1** the state or quality of being unequal; disparity. **2** an instance of disparity. **3** lack of smoothness or regularity. **4** social or economic disparity. **5** *Maths.* **5a** a statement indicating that the value of one quantity or expression is not equal to another. **5b** the relation of being unequal. **6** *Astron.* a departure from uniform orbital motion.

inert (ɪn'ɜːt) *adj* **1** having no inherent ability to move or to resist motion. **2** inactive, lazy, or sluggish. **3** having only a limited ability to react chemically; unreactive. ORIG C17: from L *iners* unskilled, from IN-[1] + *ars* skill; see ART[1]
▸ **inˈertly** *adv* ▸ **inˈertness** *n*

inert gas *n* **1** any of the unreactive gaseous elements helium, neon, argon, krypton, xenon, and radon. **2** (loosely) any gas, such as carbon dioxide, that is nonoxidizing.

inertia (ɪn'ɜːʃə, -ʃɪə) *n* **1** the state of being inert; disinclination to move or act. **2** *Physics.* **2a** the tendency of a body to preserve its state of rest or uniform motion unless acted upon by an external force. **2b** an analogous property of other physical quantities that resist change: *thermal inertia.*
▸ **inˈertial** *adj*

inertial guidance *or* **navigation** *n* a method of controlling the flight path of a missile by instruments contained within it.

inertial mass *n* the mass of a body as determined by its momentum, as opposed to the extent to which it responds to the force of gravity. Cf. **gravitational mass.**

inertia-reel seat belt *n* a type of car seat belt in which the belt is free to unwind from a metal drum except when the drum locks as a result of rapid change of velocity.

inertia selling *n* the illegal practice of sending unrequested goods to householders, followed by a bill for the goods if they do not return them.

inescapable (ˌɪnɪ'skeɪpəbᵊl) *adj* incapable of being escaped or avoided.
▸ **ˌinesˈcapably** *adv*

inestimable (ɪn'ɛstɪməbᵊl) *adj* **1** not able to be estimated; immeasurable. **2** of immeasurable value.
▸ **inˌestimaˈbility** *or* **inˈestimableness** *n* ▸ **inˈestimably** *adv*

inevitable (ɪn'ɛvɪtəbᵊl) *adj* **1** unavoidable. **2** sure to happen; certain. ◆ *n* **3** (often preceded by *the*) something that is unavoidable. ORIG C15: from L, from IN-[1] + *ēvītāre* to shun, from *vītāre* to avoid
▸ **inˌevitaˈbility** *or* **inˈevitableness** *n* ▸ **inˈevitably** *adv*

inexcusable (ˌɪnɪk'skjuːzəbᵊl) *adj* not able to be excused or justified.
▸ **ˌinexˌcusaˈbility** *or* **ˌinexˈcusableness** *n* ▸ **ˌinexˈcusably** *adv*

inexhaustible (ˌɪnɪg'zɔːstəbᵊl) *adj* **1** incapable of being

used up; endless. **2** incapable or apparently incapable of becoming tired; tireless.
▸ ˌ**inexˌhaustiˈbility** *n* ▸ ˌ**inexˈhaustibly** *adv*

inexorable (ɪnˈɛksərəbᵊl) *adj* **1** not able to be moved by entreaty or persuasion. **2** relentless. ORIG C16: from L, from IN-[1] + *exōrāre* to prevail upon, from *ōrāre* to pray
▸ **inˌexoraˈbility** *n* ▸ **inˈexorably** *adv*

inexpensive (ˌɪnɪkˈspɛnsɪv) *adj* not expensive; cheap.
▸ ˌ**inexˈpensively** *adv* ▸ ˌ**inexˈpensiveness** *n*

inexperience (ˌɪnɪkˈspɪərɪəns) *n* lack of experience or of the knowledge and understanding derived from experience.
▸ ˌ**inexˈperienced** *adj*

inexpiable (ɪnˈɛkspɪəbᵊl) *adj* **1** incapable of being expiated; unpardonable. **2** *Arch.* implacable.
▸ **inˈexpiableness** *n*

inexplicable (ˌɪnɪkˈsplɪkəbᵊl, ɪnˈɛksplɪkəbᵊl) *adj* not capable of explanation; unexplained.
▸ ˌ**inexplicaˈbility** *n* ▸ ˌ**inexˈplicably** *adv*

in extenso *Latin.* (ɪn ɪkˈstɛnsəʊ) *adv* at full length.

in extremis *Latin.* (ɪn ɪkˈstriːmɪs) *adv* **1** in extremity; in dire straits. **2** at the point of death. ORIG lit.: in the furthest reaches

inextricable (ˌɪnɛksˈtrɪkəbᵊl) *adj* **1** not able to be escaped from: *an inextricable dilemma.* **2** not able to be disentangled, etc.: *an inextricable knot.* **3** extremely involved or intricate.
▸ ˌ**inextricaˈbility** *or* ˌ**inexˈtricableness** *n* ▸ ˌ**inexˈtricably** *adv*

inf. *abbrev. for:* **1** Also: **Inf.** infantry. **2** inferior. **3** infinitive. **4** informal. **5** information.

infallible (ɪnˈfæləbᵊl) *adj* **1** not fallible; not liable to error. **2** not liable to failure; certain; sure: *an infallible cure.* ◆ *n* **3** a person or thing that is incapable of error or failure.
▸ **inˌfalliˈbility** *or* **inˈfallibleness** *n* ▸ **inˈfallibly** *adv*

infamous (ˈɪnfəməs) *adj* **1** having a bad reputation; notorious. **2** causing or deserving a bad reputation; shocking: *infamous conduct.*
▸ ˈ**infamously** *adv* ▸ ˈ**infamousness** *n*

infamy (ˈɪnfəmɪ) *n, pl* **infamies. 1** the state or condition of being infamous. **2** an infamous act or event. ORIG C15: from L *infāmis* of evil repute, from IN-[1] + *fāma* FAME

infancy (ˈɪnfənsɪ) *n, pl* **infancies. 1** the state or period of being an infant; childhood. **2** an early stage of growth or development. **3** infants collectively. **4** the period of life prior to attaining legal majority; minority nonage.

infant (ˈɪnfənt) *n* **1** a child at the earliest stage of its life; baby. **2** *Law.* another word for **minor** (sense 9). **3** *Brit.* a young schoolchild. **4** a person who is beginning or inexperienced in an activity. **5** (*modifier*) **5a** of or relating to young children or infancy. **5b** designed or intended for young children. ◆ *adj* **6** in an early stage of development; nascent: *an infant science.* **7** *Law.* of or relating to the legal status of infancy. ORIG C14: from L *infāns,* lit.: speechless, from IN-[1] + *fārī* to speak
▸ ˈ**infantˌhood** *n*

infanta (ɪnˈfæntə) *n* (formerly) **1** a daughter of a king of Spain or Portugal. **2** the wife of an infante. ORIG C17: from Sp. or Port., fem of INFANTE

infante (ɪnˈfæntɪ) *n* (formerly) a son of a king of Spain or Portugal, esp. one not heir to the throne. ORIG C16: from Sp. or Port., lit.: INFANT

infanticide (ɪnˈfæntɪˌsaɪd) *n* **1** the killing of an infant. **2** the practice of killing newborn infants, still prevalent in some primitive tribes. **3** a person who kills an infant.
▸ **inˌfantiˈcidal** *adj*

infantile (ˈɪnfənˌtaɪl) *adj* **1** like a child in action or behaviour; childishly immature; puerile. **2** of, relating to, or characteristic of infants or infancy. **3** in an early stage of development.
▸ **infantility** (ˌɪnfənˈtɪlɪtɪ) *n*

infantile paralysis *n* a former name for **poliomyelitis.**

infantilism (ɪnˈfæntɪˌlɪzəm) *n* **1** *Psychol.* a condition in which an older child or adult is mentally or physically undeveloped. **2** childish speech; baby talk.

infantry (ˈɪnfəntrɪ) *n, pl* **infantries. a** soldiers or units of soldiers who fight on foot with small arms. **b** (*as modifier*): *an infantry unit.* ORIG C16: from It. *infanteria,* from *infante* boy, foot soldier; see INFANT

infantryman (ˈɪnfəntrɪmən) *n, pl* **infantrymen.** a soldier belonging to the infantry.

infant school *n* (in England and Wales) a school for children aged between 5 and 7.

infarct (ɪnˈfɑːkt) *n* a localized area of dead tissue resulting from obstruction of the blood supply to that part. Also called: **infarction.** ORIG C19: via NL from L *infarctus* stuffed into, from *farcīre* to stuff
▸ **inˈfarcted** *adj*

infatuate *vb* (ɪnˈfætjʊˌeɪt), **infatuates, infatuating, infatuated.** (*tr*) **1** to inspire or fill with foolish, shallow, or extravagant passion. **2** to cause to act foolishly. ◆ *n* (ɪnˈfætjʊɪt, -ˌeɪt). **3** *Literary.* a person who is infatuated. ORIG C16: from L *infatuāre,* from IN-[2] + *fatuus* FATUOUS
▸ **inˌfatuˈation** *n*

infatuated (ɪnˈfætjʊˌeɪtɪd) *adj* (often foll. by *with*) possessed by a foolish or extravagant passion, esp. for another person.

infect (ɪnˈfɛkt) *vb* (*mainly tr*) **1** to cause infection in; contaminate (an organism, wound, etc.) with pathogenic microorganisms. **2** (*also intr*) to affect or become affected with a communicable disease. **3** to taint, pollute, or contaminate. **4** to affect, esp. adversely, as if by contagion. **5** (*also intr*) *Computing.* to affect or become affected with a computer virus. ◆ *adj* **6** *Arch.* contaminated or polluted with or as if with a disease; infected. ORIG C14: from L *inficere* to dip into, stain, from *facere* to make
▸ **inˈfector** *or* **inˈfecter** *n*

infection (ɪnˈfɛkʃən) *n* **1** invasion of the body by pathogenic microorganisms. **2** the resulting condition in the tissues. **3** an infectious disease. **4** the act of infecting or state of being infected. **5** an agent or influence that infects. **6** persuasion or corruption, as by ideas, perverse influences, etc.

infectious (ɪnˈfɛkʃəs) *adj* **1** (of a disease) capable of being transmitted. **2** (of a disease) caused by microorganisms, such as bacteria, viruses, or protozoa. **3** causing or transmitting infection. **4** tending or apt to spread, as from one person to another: *infectious mirth.*
▸ **inˈfectiously** *adv* ▸ **inˈfectiousness** *n*

infectious hepatitis *n* any form of hepatitis caused by viruses. See **hepatitis A, hepatitis B, hepatitis C.**

infectious mononucleosis *n* an acute infectious disease, caused by a virus (**Epstein-Barr virus**), characterized by fever, sore throat, swollen and painful lymph nodes, and abnormal lymphocytes in the blood. Also called: **glandular fever.**

infective (ɪnˈfɛktɪv) *adj* **1** capable of causing infection. **2** a less common word for **infectious.**
▸ **inˈfectively** *adv* ▸ **inˈfectiveness** *n*

infelicity (ˌɪnfɪˈlɪsɪtɪ) *n, pl* **infelicities. 1** unhappiness; misfortune. **2** an instance of bad luck or mischance. **3** something, esp. a remark or expression, that is inapt or inappropriate.
▸ ˌ**infeˈlicitous** *adj*

infer (ɪnˈfɜː) *vb* **infers, inferring, inferred.** (when *tr, may take a clause as object*) **1** to conclude (a state of affairs, supposition, etc.) by reasoning from evidence; deduce. **2** (*tr*) to have or lead to as a necessary or logical consequence; indicate. **3** (*tr*) to hint or imply. ORIG C16: from L *inferre* to bring into, from *ferre* to bear, carry
▸ **inˈferable** *or* **inˈferrable** *adj* ▸ **inˈferrer** *n*

USAGE NOTE The use of *infer* to mean *imply* is becoming more and more common in both speech and writing. There is nevertheless a useful distinction between the two which many people would be in favour of maintaining. To infer means 'to deduce', and is used in the construction *to infer something from something: I in-*

> *ferred from what she said that she had not been well.* To *imply* (sense 1) means 'to suggest, to insinuate' and is normally followed by a clause: *are you implying that I was responsible for the mistake?*

inference ('ɪnfərəns, -frəns) *n* **1** the act or process of inferring. **2** an inferred conclusion, deduction, etc. **3** any process of reasoning from premises to a conclusion. **4** *Logic.* the specific mode of reasoning used.

inferential (ˌɪnfə'rɛnʃəl) *adj* of, relating to, or derived from inference.
▸ **ˌinfer'entially** *adv*

inferior (ɪn'fɪərɪə) *adj* **1** lower in value or quality. **2** lower in rank, position, or status; subordinate. **3** not of the best; mediocre; commonplace. **4** lower in position; situated beneath. **5** (of a plant ovary) situated below the other floral parts. **6** *Astron.* **6a** orbiting between the sun and the earth: *an inferior planet.* **6b** lying below the horizon. **7** *Printing.* (of a character) printed at the foot of an ordinary character. ◆ *n* **8** an inferior person. **9** *Printing.* an inferior character. ORIG C15: from L: lower, from *inferus* low
▸ **inferiority** (ɪnˌfɪərɪ'ɒrɪtɪ) *n* ▸ **in'feriorly** *adv*

inferiority complex *n Psychiatry.* a disorder arising from the conflict between the desire to be noticed and the fear of being humiliated, characterized by aggressiveness or withdrawal into oneself.

infernal (ɪn'fɜːnᵊl) *adj* **1** of or relating to an underworld of the dead. **2** deserving or befitting hell; diabolic; fiendish. **3** *Inf.* irritating; confounded. ORIG C14: from LL, from *infernus* hell, from L (adj): lower, hellish; rel. to L *inferus* low
▸ **ˌinfer'nality** *n* ▸ **in'fernally** *adv*

infernal machine *n Arch.* an explosive device (usually disguised) or booby trap.

inferno (ɪn'fɜːnəʊ) *n, pl* **infernos. 1** (*sometimes cap.;* usually preceded by *the*) hell; the infernal region. **2** any place or state resembling hell, esp. a conflagration. ORIG C19: from It., from LL *infernus* hell

infertile (ɪn'fɛːtaɪl) *adj* **1** not capable of producing offspring; sterile. **2** (of land) not productive; barren.
▸ **in'fertilely** *adv* ▸ **infertility** (ˌɪnfə'tɪlɪtɪ) *n*

infest (ɪn'fest) *vb* (*tr*) **1** to inhabit or overrun in unpleasantly large numbers. **2** (of parasites such as lice) to invade and live on or in (a host). ORIG C15: from L *infestāre* to molest, from *infestus* hostile
▸ **ˌinfes'tation** *n* ▸ **in'fester** *n*

infeudation (ˌɪnfju'deɪʃən) *n History.* **1** (in feudal society) the act of putting a vassal in possession of a fief. **2** the granting of tithes to laymen.

infidel ('ɪnfɪdᵊl) *n* **1** a person who has no religious belief; unbeliever. ◆ *adj* **2** rejecting a specific religion, esp. Christianity or Islam. **3** of or relating to unbelievers or unbelief. ORIG C15: from Med. L, from L (adj): unfaithful, from IN-[1] + *fidēlis* faithful; see FEALTY

infidelity (ˌɪnfɪ'dɛlɪtɪ) *n, pl* **infidelities. 1** lack of faith or constancy, esp. sexual faithfulness. **2** lack of religious faith; disbelief. **3** an act or instance of disloyalty.

infield ('ɪnˌfiːld) *n* **1** *Cricket.* the area of the field near the pitch. Cf. **outfield** (sense 1). **2** *Baseball.* the area of the playing field enclosed by the base lines. **3** *Agriculture.* the part of a farm nearest to the farm buildings.
▸ **'inˌfielder** *n*

infighting ('ɪnˌfaɪtɪŋ) *n* **1** *Boxing.* combat at close quarters in which proper blows are inhibited. **2** intense competition, as between members of an organization.
▸ **'inˌfighter** *n*

infill ('ɪnfɪl) *or* **infilling** ('ɪnfɪlɪŋ) *n* **1** the act of filling or closing gaps, etc., in something, such as a row of buildings. **2** material used to fill a cavity, gap, hole, etc.

infiltrate ('ɪnfɪlˌtreɪt) *vb* **infiltrates, infiltrating, infiltrated. 1** to undergo the process in which a fluid passes into the pores or interstices of a solid; permeate. **2** *Mil.* to pass undetected through (an enemy-held line or position). **3** to gain or cause to gain entrance or access surreptitiously: *they infiltrated the party structure.* ◆ *n* **4** something that infiltrates. ORIG C18: from IN-[2] + FILTRATE
▸ **ˌinfil'tration** *n* ▸ **'infilˌtrative** *adj* ▸ **'infilˌtrator** *n*

infin. *abbrev. for* infinitive.

infinite ('ɪnfɪnɪt) *adj* **1a** having no limits or boundaries in time, space, extent, or magnitude. **1b** (*as n;* preceded by *the*): *the infinite.* **2** extremely or immeasurably great or numerous: *infinite wealth.* **3** all-embracing, absolute, or total: *God's infinite wisdom.* **4** *Maths.* having an unlimited or uncountable number of digits, factors, terms, etc.
▸ **'infinitely** *adv* ▸ **'infiniteness** *n*

infinitesimal (ˌɪnfɪnɪ'tɛsɪməl) *adj* **1** infinitely or immeasurably small. **2** *Maths.* of, relating to, or involving a small change in the value of a variable that approaches zero as a limit. ◆ *n* **3** *Maths.* an infinitesimal quantity.
▸ **ˌinfini'tesimally** *adv*

infinitesimal calculus *n* another name for **calculus** (sense 1).

infinitive (ɪn'fɪnɪtɪv) *n Grammar.* a form of the verb not inflected for grammatical categories such as tense and person and used without an overt subject. In English, the infinitive usually consists of the word *to* followed by the verb.
▸ **infinitival** (ˌɪnfɪnɪ'taɪvᵊl) *adj* ▸ **in'finitively** *or* **ˌinfini'tivally** *adv*

infinitude (ɪn'fɪnɪˌtjuːd) *n* **1** the state or quality of being infinite. **2** an infinite extent, quantity, degree, etc.

infinity (ɪn'fɪnɪtɪ) *n, pl* **infinities. 1** the state or quality of being infinite. **2** endless time, space, or quantity. **3** an infinitely or indefinitely great number or amount. **4** *Maths.* **4a** the concept of a value greater than any finite numerical value. **4b** the reciprocal of zero. **4c** the limit of an infinite sequence of numbers.

infirm (ɪn'fɜːm) *adj* **1a** weak in health or body, esp. from old age. **1b** (*as collective n;* preceded by *the*): *the infirm.* **2** lacking moral certainty; indecisive or irresolute. **3** not stable, sound, or secure: *an infirm structure.* **4** *Law.* (of a law, etc.) lacking legal force; invalid.
▸ **in'firmly** *adv* ▸ **in'firmness** *n*

infirmary (ɪn'fɜːmərɪ) *n, pl* **infirmaries.** a place for the treatment of the sick or injured; hospital.

infirmity (ɪn'fɜːmɪtɪ) *n, pl* **infirmities. 1** the state or quality of being infirm. **2** physical weakness or debility; frailty. **3** a moral flaw or failing.

infix *vb* (ɪn'fɪks, 'ɪnˌfɪks). **1** (*tr*) to fix firmly in. **2** (*tr*) to instil or inculcate. **3** *Grammar.* to insert (an affix) into the middle of a word. ◆ *n* ('ɪnˌfɪks). **4** *Grammar.* an affix inserted into the middle of a word.
▸ **ˌinfix'ation** *or* **infixion** (ɪn'fɪkʃən) *n*

in flagrante delicto (ɪn flə'græntɪ dɪ'lɪktəʊ) *adv Chiefly law.* while committing the offence; red-handed. Also: **flagrante delicto.** ORIG L, lit.: with the crime still blazing

inflame (ɪn'fleɪm) *vb* **inflames, inflaming, inflamed. 1** to arouse or become aroused to violent emotion. **2** (*tr*) to increase or intensify; aggravate. **3** to produce inflammation in (a tissue, organ, or part) or (of a tissue, etc.) to become inflamed. **4** to set or be set on fire. **5** (*tr*) to cause to redden.
▸ **in'flamer** *n*

inflammable (ɪn'flæməbᵊl) *adj* **1** liable to catch fire; flammable. **2** readily aroused to anger or passion. ◆ *n* **3** something that is liable to catch fire.
▸ **inˌflamma'bility** *or* **in'flammableness** *n* ▸ **in'flammably** *adv*

> **USAGE NOTE** See at **flammable.**

inflammation (ˌɪnflə'meɪʃən) *n* **1** the reaction of living tissue to injury or infection, characterized by heat, redness, swelling, and pain. **2** the act of inflaming or the state of being inflamed.

inflammatory (ɪn'flæmətərɪ, -trɪ) *adj* **1** characterized by or caused by inflammation. **2** tending to arouse violence, strong emotion, etc.
▸ **in'flammatorily** *adv*

inflatable (ɪnˈfleɪtəbᵊl) *n* **1** any of various large air-filled objects made of strong plastic or rubber. ◆ *adj* **2** capable of being inflated.

inflate (ɪnˈfleɪt) *vb* **inflates, inflating, inflated. 1** to expand or cause to expand by filling with gas or air. **2** (*tr*) to cause to increase excessively; puff up; swell: *to inflate one's opinion of oneself.* **3** (*tr*) to cause inflation of (prices, money, etc.). **4** (*tr*) to raise in spirits; elate. **5** (*intr*) to undergo economic inflation. ORIG C16: from L *inflāre* to blow into, from *flāre* to blow
▸ **inˈflatedly** *adv* ▸ **inˈflatedness** *n* ▸ **inˈflater** *or* **inˈflator** *n*

inflation (ɪnˈfleɪʃən) *n* **1** the act of inflating or state of being inflated. **2** *Econ.* a progressive increase in the general level of prices brought about by an expansion in demand or the money supply or by autonomous increases in costs. Cf. **reflation. 3** *Inf.* the rate of increase of prices. **4** *Astron.* a very fast expansion of the universe occurring immediately after the big bang, postulated in certain models of the universe (**inflationary universes**) to account for the present distribution of matter.
▸ **inˈflationary** *adj*

inflationary spiral *n* a self-sustaining form of inflation in which a rise in prices generates a wage demand, causing a further price rise and a further wage demand.

inflationism (ɪnˈfleɪʃəˌnɪzəm) *n* the policy of inflation through expansion of the supply of money and credit.
▸ **inˈflationist** *n, adj*

inflect (ɪnˈflɛkt) *vb* **1** *Grammar.* to change (the form of a word) by inflection. **2** (*tr*) to change (the voice) in tone or pitch; modulate. **3** (*tr*) to cause to deviate from a straight or normal line or course; bend. ORIG C15: from L *inflectere* to curve round, alter, from *flectere* to bend
▸ **inˈflectedness** *n* ▸ **inˈflective** *adj* ▸ **inˈflector** *n*

inflection *or* **inflexion** (ɪnˈflɛkʃən) *n* **1** modulation of the voice. **2** *Grammar.* a change in the form of a word, signalling change in such grammatical functions as tense, person, gender, number, or case. **3** an angle or bend. **4** the act of inflecting or the state of being inflected. **5** *Maths.* a change in curvature from concave to convex or vice versa.
▸ **inˈflectional** *or* **inˈflexional** *adj* ▸ **inˈflectionally** *or* **inˈflexionally** *adv* ▸ **inˈflectionless** *or* **inˈflexionless** *adj*

inflexible (ɪnˈflɛksəbᵊl) *adj* **1** not flexible; rigid; stiff. **2** obstinate; unyielding. **3** without variation; unalterable; fixed. ORIG C14: from L *inflexibilis*; see INFLECT
▸ **inˌflexiˈbility** *or* **inˈflexibleness** *n* ▸ **inˈflexibly** *adv*

inflict (ɪnˈflɪkt) *vb* (*tr*) **1** (often foll. by *on* or *upon*) to impose (something unwelcome, such as pain, oneself, etc.). **2** to deal out (blows, lashes, etc.). ORIG C16: from L *inflīgere* to strike (something) against, dash against, from *flīgere* to strike
▸ **inˈflictable** *adj* ▸ **inˈflicter** *or* **inˈflictor** *n* ▸ **inˈfliction** *n*

in-flight *adj* provided during flight in an aircraft: *in-flight entertainment.*

inflorescence (ˌɪnflɔːˈrɛsəns) *n* **1** the part of a plant that consists of the flower-bearing stalks. **2** the arrangement of the flowers on the stalks. **3** the process of flowering; blossoming. ORIG C16: from NL, from LL, from *flōrescere* to bloom
▸ **ˌifloˈrescent** *adj*

inflow (ˈɪnˌfləʊ) *n* **1** something, such as a liquid or gas, that flows in. **2** Also called: **inflowing**. the act of flowing in; influx.

influence (ˈɪnflʊəns) *n* **1** an effect of one person or thing on another. **2** the power of a person or thing to have such an effect. **3** power resulting from ability, wealth, position, etc. **4** a person or thing having influence. **5** *Astrol.* an ethereal fluid regarded as emanating from the stars and affecting a person's future. **6 under the influence.** *Inf.* drunk. ◆ *vb* **influences, influencing, influenced.** (*tr*) **7** to persuade or induce. **8** to have an effect upon (actions, events, etc.); affect. ORIG C14: from Med. L *influentia* emanation of power from the stars, from L *influere* to flow into, from *fluere* to flow
▸ **ˈinfluenceable** *adj* ▸ **ˈinfluencer** *n*

influent (ˈɪnflʊənt) *adj also* **inflowing. 1** flowing in. ◆ *n* **2** something flowing in, esp. a tributary. **3** *Ecology.* an organism that has a major effect on its community.

influential (ˌɪnflʊˈɛnʃəl) *adj* having or exerting influence.
▸ **ˌinfluˈentially** *adv*

influenza (ˌɪnflʊˈɛnzə) *n* a highly contagious viral disease characterized by fever, muscular aches and pains, and inflammation of the respiratory passages. ORIG C18: from It., lit.: INFLUENCE, hence, incursion, epidemic (first applied to influenza in 1743)
▸ **ˌinfluˈenzal** *adj*

influx (ˈɪnˌflʌks) *n* **1** the arrival or entry of many people or things. **2** the act of flowing in; inflow. **3** the mouth of a stream or river. ORIG C17: from LL *influxus*, from *influere;* see INFLUENCE

info (ˈɪnfəʊ) *n Inf.* short for **information.**

infold (ɪnˈfəʊld) *vb* (*tr*) a variant of **enfold.**

inform (ɪnˈfɔːm) *vb* **1** (*tr;* often foll. by *of* or *about*) to give information to; tell. **2** (*tr;* often foll. by *of* or *about*) to make conversant (with). **3** (*intr;* often foll. by *against* or *on*) to give information regarding criminals, to the police, etc. **4** (*tr*) to give form to. **5** (*tr*) to impart some essential or formative characteristic to. **6** (*tr*) to animate or inspire. ORIG C14: from L *informāre* to give form to, describe, from *formāre* to FORM
▸ **inˈformable** *adj*

informal (ɪnˈfɔːməl) *adj* **1** not of a formal, official, or stiffly conventional nature. **2** appropriate to everyday life or use. **3** denoting or characterized by idiom, vocabulary, etc., appropriate to conversational language rather than to formal written language. **4** denoting a second-person pronoun in some languages used when the addressee is regarded as a friend or social inferior.
▸ **inˈformally** *adv*

informality (ˌɪnfɔːˈmælɪtɪ) *n, pl* **informalities. 1** the condition or quality of being informal. **2** an informal act.

informal settlement *n S. African euphemistic.* a squatter camp or shanty town.

informal vote *n Austral. & NZ.* an invalid vote or ballot.

informant (ɪnˈfɔːmənt) *n* a person who gives information.

information (ˌɪnfəˈmeɪʃən) *n* **1** knowledge acquired through experience or study. **2** knowledge of specific and timely events or situations; news. **3** the act of informing or the condition of being informed. **4a** an office, agency, etc., providing information. **4b** (*as modifier*): *information service.* **5** a charge or complaint made before justices of the peace, usually on oath, to institute summary criminal proceedings. **6** *Computing.* **6a** the meaning given to data by the way it is interpreted. **6b** another word for **data** (sense 2).
▸ **ˌinforˈmational** *adj*

information retrieval *n Computing.* the process of recovering information from stored data.

information superhighway *n* **1** the concept of a worldwide network of computers capable of transferring all types of digital information at high speed. **2** another name for the **Internet.** ◆ Also called: **information highway.**

information technology *n* the production, storage, and communication of information using computers, etc.

information theory *n* a collection of mathematical theories concerned with coding, transmitting, storing, retrieving, and decoding information.

informative (ɪnˈfɔːmətɪv) *or* **informatory** *adj* providing information; instructive.
▸ **inˈformatively** *adv* ▸ **inˈformativeness** *n*

informed (ɪnˈfɔːmd) *adj* **1** having much knowledge or education; learned or cultured. **2** based on information: an informed judgment.

informer (ɪnˈfɔːmə) *n* **1** a person who informs against someone, esp. a criminal. **2** a person who provides information.

infotainment (ˌɪnfəʊˈteɪnmənt) *n* (in television) the practice of presenting serious or instructive subjects in a style designed primarily to be entertaining. ORIG C20: from INFO + (ENTER)TAINMENT

infra- *prefix* below; beneath; after: *infrasonic.* ORIG from L *infrā*

infract (ɪn'frækt) *vb* (*tr*) to violate or break (a law, etc.). ORIG C18: from L *infractus* broken off; see INFRINGE
▸ **in'fraction** *n* ▸ **in'fractor** *n*

infra dig ('ɪnfrə 'dɪg) *adj* (*postpositive*) *Inf.* beneath one's dignity. ORIG C19: from L *infrā dignitātem*

infrangible (ɪn'frændʒɪbᵊl) *adj* **1** incapable of being broken. **2** not capable of being violated or infringed. ORIG C16: from LL, from L IN-[1] + *frangere* to break
▸ **inˌfrangi'bility** *or* **in'frangibleness** *n* ▸ **in'frangibly** *adv*

infrared (ˌɪnfrə'rɛd) *n* **1** the part of the electromagnetic spectrum with a longer wavelength than light but a shorter wavelength than radio waves. ◆ *adj* **2** of, relating to, using, or consisting of radiation lying within the infrared.

infrared astronomy *n* the study of radiations from space in the infrared region of the electromagnetic spectrum.

infrared photography *n* photography using film with an emulsion that is sensitive to infrared light, enabling it to be used in dark or misty conditions.

infrasound ('ɪnfrəˌsaʊnd) *n* soundlike waves having a frequency below the audible range, i.e. below about 16 Hz.
▸ **infrasonic** (ˌɪnfrə'sɒnɪk) *adj*

infrastructure ('ɪnfrəˌstrʌktʃə) *n* **1** the basic structure of an organization, system, etc. **2** the stock of fixed capital equipment in a country, including factories, roads, schools, etc., considered as a determinant of economic growth.

infrequent (ɪn'friːkwənt) *adj* rarely happening or present; only occasional.
▸ **in'frequency** *or* **in'frequence** *n* ▸ **in'frequently** *adv*

infringe (ɪn'frɪndʒ) *vb* **infringes, infringing, infringed. 1** (*tr*) to violate or break (a law, agreement, etc.). **2** (*intr;* foll. by *on* or *upon*) to encroach or trespass. ORIG C16: from L *infringere* to break off, from *frangere* to break
▸ **in'fringement** *n* ▸ **in'fringer** *n*

infundibular (ˌɪnfʌn'dɪbjʊlə) *adj* funnel-shaped. ORIG C18: from L *infundibulum* funnel

infuriate *vb* (ɪn'fjʊərɪˌeɪt), **infuriates, infuriating, infuriated. 1** (*tr*) to anger; annoy. ◆ *adj* (ɪn'fjʊərɪɪt). **2** *Arch.* furious. ORIG C17: from Med. L *infuriāre* (vb); see IN-[2], FURY
▸ **in'furiˌating** *adj* ▸ **in'furiˌatingly** *adv*

infuse (ɪn'fjuːz) *vb* **infuses, infusing, infused. 1** (*tr;* often foll. by *into*) to instil or inculcate. **2** (*tr;* foll. by *with*) to inspire; emotionally charge. **3** to soak or be soaked so as to extract flavour or other properties. **4** *Rare.* (foll. by *into*) to pour. ORIG C15: from L *infundere* to pour into
▸ **in'fuser** *n*

infusible[1] (ɪn'fjuːzəbᵊl) *adj* not fusible; not easily melted; having a high melting point. ORIG C16: from IN-[1] + FUSIBLE
▸ **inˌfusi'bility** *or* **in'fusibleness** *n*

infusible[2] (ɪn'fjuːzəbᵊl) *adj* capable of being infused. ORIG C17: from INFUSE + -IBLE
▸ **inˌfusi'bility** *or* **in'fusibleness** *n*

infusion (ɪn'fjuːʒən) *n* **1** the act of infusing. **2** something infused. **3** an extract obtained by soaking.
▸ **infusive** (ɪn'fjuːsɪv) *adj*

infusorian (ˌɪnfjʊ'zɔːrɪən) *Obs.* ◆ *n* **1** any of the microscopic organisms, such as protozoans, found in infusions of organic material. ◆ *adj* **2** of or relating to infusorians. ORIG C18: from NL *Infusoria* former class name; see INFUSE
▸ ˌ**infu'sorial** *adj*

-ing[1] *suffix forming nouns.* **1** (*from verbs*) the action of, process of, result of, or something connected with the verb: *meeting; winnings.* **2** (*from other nouns*) something used in, consisting of, involving, etc.: *tubing; soldiering.* **3** (*from other parts of speech*)*: an outing.* ORIG OE *-ing, -ung*

-ing[2] *suffix.* **1** forming the present participle of verbs: *walking; believing.* **2** forming participial adjectives: *a sinking ship.* **3** forming adjectives not derived from verbs: *swashbuckling.* ORIG ME *-ing, -inde,* from OE *-ende*

-ing[3] *suffix forming nouns.* a person or thing having a certain quality or being of a certain kind: *sweeting; whiting.* ORIG OE *-ing;* rel. to ON *-ingr*

ingather (ɪn'gæðə) *vb* (*tr*) to gather together or in (a harvest, etc.).
▸ **in'gatherer** *n*

Inge ★ (ɪŋ) *n* **William Ralph,** known as *the Gloomy Dean.* 1860–1954, British theologian, noted for his pessimism; dean of St Paul's Cathedral (1911–34).

ingeminate (ɪn'dʒɛmɪˌneɪt) *vb* **ingeminates, ingeminating, ingeminated.** (*tr*) *Rare.* to repeat; reiterate. ORIG C16: from L *ingemināre* to redouble, from IN-[2] + *gemināre* to GEMINATE

Ingenhousz ★ (*Dutch* 'ɪŋənhuːs) *n* **Jan** (jɑn). 1730–99, Dutch plant physiologist and physician, who discovered photosynthesis.

ingenious (ɪn'dʒiːnjəs, -nɪəs) *adj* possessing or done with ingenuity; skilful or clever. ORIG C15: from L, from *ingenium* natural ability; see ENGINE
▸ **in'geniously** *adv* ▸ **in'geniousness** *n*

ingénue (ˌænʒeɪ'njuː) *n* an artless, innocent, or inexperienced girl or young woman. ORIG C19: from F, fem of *ingénu* INGENUOUS

ingenuity (ˌɪndʒɪ'njuːɪtɪ) *n, pl* **ingenuities. 1** inventive talent; cleverness. **2** an ingenious device, act, etc. **3** *Arch.* frankness; candour. ORIG C16: from L *ingenuitās* a freeborn condition, outlook consistent with such a condition, from *ingenuus* native, freeborn (see INGENUOUS); meaning infl. by INGENIOUS

ingenuous (ɪn'dʒɛnjʊəs) *adj* **1** naive, artless, or innocent. **2** candid; frank; straightforward. ORIG C16: from L *ingenuus* freeborn, virtuous, from IN-[2] + *gignere* to beget
▸ **in'genuously** *adv* ▸ **in'genuousness** *n*

ingest (ɪn'dʒɛst) *vb* (*tr*) to take (food or liquid) into the body. ORIG C17: from L *ingerere* to put into, from IN-[2] + *gerere* to carry; see GEST
▸ **in'gestible** *adj* ▸ **in'gestion** *n* ▸ **in'gestive** *adj*

ingle ('ɪŋgᵊl) *n Arch. or dialect.* a fire in a room or a fireplace. ORIG C16: prob. from Scot. Gaelic *aingeal* fire

Ingleborough ★ ('ɪŋgᵊlbərə, -brə) *n* a mountain in N England, in North Yorkshire: potholes. Height: 723 m (2373 ft).

inglenook ('ɪŋgᵊlˌnʊk) *n Brit.* a corner by a fireplace; chimney corner.

ingoing ('ɪnˌgəʊɪŋ) *adj* going in; entering.

Ingolstadt ★ (*German* 'ɪŋgɔlʃtat) *n* a city in S central Germany, in Bavaria on the River Danube: oil-refining. Pop.: 111 979 (1996 est.).

ingot ('ɪŋgət) *n* a piece of cast metal obtained from a mould in a form suitable for storage, etc. ORIG C14: ?from IN-[2] + OE *goten,* p.p. of *geotan* to pour

ingraft (ɪn'grɑːft) *vb* a variant spelling of **engraft.**
▸ **in'graftment** *or* ˌ**ingraf'tation** *n*

ingrain *or* **engrain** *vb* (ɪn'greɪn). (*tr*) **1** to impress deeply on the mind or nature; instil. **2** *Arch.* to dye into the fibre of (a fabric). ◆ *adj* ('ɪnˌgreɪn). **3** (of woven or knitted articles) made of dyed yarn or of fibre that is dyed before being spun into yarn. ◆ *n* ('ɪnˌgreɪn). **4** a carpet made from ingrained yarn. ORIG C18: from *dyed in grain* dyed with kermes through the fibre

ingrained *or* **engrained** (ɪn'greɪnd) *adj* **1** deeply impressed or instilled. **2** (*prenominal*) complete or inveterate; utter. **3** (esp. of dirt) worked into or through the fibre, pores, etc.
▸ **ingrainedly** *or* **engrainedly** (ɪn'greɪnɪdlɪ) *adv* ▸ **in'grainedness** *or* **en'grainedness** *n*

ingrate ('ɪngreɪt, ɪn'greɪt) *Arch.* ◆ *n* **1** an ungrateful person. ◆ *adj* **2** ungrateful. ORIG C14: from L *ingrātus* (adj), from IN-[1] + *grātus* GRATEFUL
▸ **'ingrately** *adv*

ingratiate (ɪn'greɪʃɪˌeɪt) *vb* **ingratiates, ingratiating, ingratiated.** (*tr;* often foll. by *with*) to place (oneself) purposely in the favour (of another). ORIG C17: from L, from IN-[2] + *grātia* grace, favour
▸ **in'gratiˌating** *or* **in'gratiatory** *adj* ▸ **in'gratiˌatingly** *adv* ▸ **inˌgrati'ation** *n*

ingredient (ɪn'griːdɪənt) *n* a component of a mixture, compound, etc., esp. in cooking. ORIG C15: from L *ingrediēns* going into, from *ingredī* to enter; see INGRESS

Ingres ★ (*French* ɛ̃grə) *n* **Jean Auguste Dominique** (ʒɑ̃ ogyst dɔminik). 1780–1867, French classical painter, noted for his draughtsmanship.

ingress (ˈɪngrɛs) *n* **1** the act of going or coming in; an entering. **2** a way in; entrance. **3** the right or permission to enter. ORIG C15: from L *ingressus,* from *ingredī* to go in, from *gradī* to step, go
▸ **ingression** (ɪnˈgrɛʃən) *n*

in-group *n Sociol.* a highly cohesive and relatively closed social group characterized by the preferential treatment reserved for its members.

ingrowing (ˈɪnˌgrəʊɪŋ) *adj* **1** (esp. of a toenail) growing abnormally into the flesh. **2** growing within or into.
▸ **ˈinˌgrowth** *n*

ingrown (ˈɪnˌgrəʊn, ɪnˈgrəʊn) *adj* **1** (esp. of a toenail) grown abnormally into the flesh; covered by adjacent tissues. **2** grown within; native; innate.

inguinal (ˈɪŋgwɪnᵊl) *adj Anat.* of or relating to the groin. ORIG C17: from L *inguinālis,* from *inguen* groin

ingulf (ɪnˈgʌlf) *vb* (*tr*) a variant of **engulf**.

ingurgitate (ɪnˈgɜːdʒɪˌteɪt) *vb* **ingurgitates, ingurgitating, ingurgitated.** to swallow (food, etc.) greedily or in excess. ORIG C16: from L *ingurgitāre* to flood, from IN-[2] + *gurges* abyss
▸ **inˌgurgiˈtation** *n*

Ingushetia ★ (ˌɪŋguːˈʃɛtɪə) *n* an administrative division of S Russia: part of the former Checheno-Ingush Autonomous Republic, which was split into Ingushetia and Chechenia in 1992. Capital: Nazran (a new capital, Magas, is under construction). Pop. (including Chechenia): 1 165 000 (1996 est.). Area (including Chechenia): 19 300 sq. km (7450 sq. miles). Also called: **Ingush Republic** (ˈɪŋguːʃ).

inhabit (ɪnˈhæbɪt) *vb* **inhabits, inhabiting, inhabited.** (*tr*) to live or dwell in; occupy. ORIG C14: from L *inhabitāre,* from *habitāre* to dwell
▸ **inˈhabitable** *adj* ▸ **inˌhabitaˈbility** *n* ▸ **inˌhabiˈtation** *n*

inhabitant (ɪnˈhæbɪtənt) *n* a person or animal that is a permanent resident of a particular place or region.
▸ **inˈhabitancy** *or* **inˈhabitance** *n*

inhalant (ɪnˈheɪlənt) *adj* **1** (esp. of a medicinal preparation) inhaled for its therapeutic effect. **2** inhaling. ◆ *n* **3** an inhalant medicinal preparation.

inhale (ɪnˈheɪl) *vb* **inhales, inhaling, inhaled.** to draw (breath, etc.) into the lungs; breathe in. ORIG C18: from IN-[2] + L *halāre* to breathe
▸ **ˌinhaˈlation** *n*

inhaler (ɪnˈheɪlə) *n* **1** a device for breathing in therapeutic vapours, esp. one for relieving nasal congestion. **2** a person who inhales.

Inhambane ★ (ˌɪnjəmˈbɑːnə) *n* a port in SE Mozambique on an inlet of the Mozambique Channel (**Inhambane Bay**). Pop.: 64 274 (1986).

inhere (ɪnˈhɪə) *vb* **inheres, inhering, inhered.** (*intr;* foll. by *in*) to be an inseparable part (of). ORIG C16: from L *inhaerēre* to stick in, from *haerēre* to stick

inherent (ɪnˈhɪərənt, -ˈhɛr-) *adj* existing as an inseparable part; intrinsic.
▸ **inˈherently** *adv*

inherit (ɪnˈhɛrɪt) *vb* **inherits, inheriting, inherited. 1** to receive (property, etc.) by succession or under a will. **2** (*intr*) to succeed as heir. **3** (*tr*) to possess (a characteristic) through genetic transmission. **4** (*tr*) to receive (a position, etc.) from a predecessor. ORIG C14: from OF *enheriter,* from LL *inhērēditāre* to appoint an heir, from L *hērēs* HEIR
▸ **inˈherited** *adj* ▸ **inˈheritor** *n* ▸ **inˈheritress** *or* **inˈheritrix** *fem n*

inheritable (ɪnˈhɛrɪtəbᵊl) *adj* **1** capable of being transmitted by heredity from one generation to a later one. **2** capable of being inherited. **3** *Rare.* having the right to inherit.
▸ **inˌheritaˈbility** *or* **inˈheritableness** *n* ▸ **inˈheritably** *adv*

inheritance (ɪnˈhɛrɪtəns) *n* **1** *Law.* **1a** hereditary succession to an estate, title, etc. **1b** the right of an heir to succeed on the death of an ancestor. **1c** something that may legally be transmitted to an heir. **2** the act of inheriting. **3** something inherited; heritage. **4** the derivation of characteristics of one generation from an earlier one by heredity.

inheritance tax *n* **1** (in Britain) a tax introduced in 1986 to replace capital transfer tax, consisting of a percentage levied on that part of an inheritance exceeding a specified allowance. **2** (in the US) a state tax imposed on an inheritance according to its size and the relationship of the beneficiary to the deceased.

inhibit (ɪnˈhɪbɪt) *vb* **inhibits, inhibiting, inhibited.** (*tr*) **1** to restrain or hinder (an impulse, desire, etc.). **2** to prohibit, forbid, or prevent. **3** to stop, prevent, or decrease the rate of (a chemical reaction). ORIG C15: from L *inhibēre* to restrain, from IN-[2] + *habēre* to have
▸ **inˈhibitable** *adj* ▸ **inˈhibitive** *or* **inˈhibitory** *adj*

inhibition (ˌɪnɪˈbɪʃən, ˌɪnhɪ-) *n* **1** the act of inhibiting or the condition of being inhibited. **2** *Psychol.* a mental state or condition in which the varieties of expression and behaviour of an individual become restricted. **3** the process of stopping or retarding a chemical reaction. **4** *Physiol.* the suppression of the function or action of an organ or part, as by stimulation of its nerve supply.

inhibitor (ɪnˈhɪbɪtə) *n* **1** Also: **inhibiter.** a person or thing that inhibits. **2** a substance that retards or stops a chemical reaction. **3** *Biochem.* **3a** a substance that inhibits the action of an enzyme. **3b** a substance that inhibits a metabolic or physiological process: *a plant growth inhibitor.*

inhospitable (ɪnˈhɒspɪtəbᵊl, ˌɪnhɒˈspɪt-) *adj* **1** not hospitable; unfriendly. **2** (of a region, an environment, etc.) lacking a favourable climate, terrain, etc.
▸ **inˈhospitableness** *n* ▸ **inˈhospitably** *adv*

in-house *adj, adv* within an organization or group: *an in-house job; the job was done in-house.*

inhuman (ɪnˈhjuːmən) *adj* **1** Also: **inhumane** (ˌɪnhjuːˈmeɪn). lacking humane feelings, such as sympathy, understanding, etc.; cruel; brutal. **2** not human.
▸ **ˌinhuˈmanely** *adv* ▸ **inˈhumanly** *adv* ▸ **inˈhumanness** *n*

inhumanity (ˌɪnhjuːˈmænɪtɪ) *n, pl* **inhumanities. 1** lack of humane qualities. **2** an inhumane act, decision, etc.

inhume (ɪnˈhjuːm) *vb* **inhumes, inhuming, inhumed.** (*tr*) to inter; bury. ORIG C17: from L, from IN-[2] + *humus* ground
▸ **ˌinhuˈmation** *n* ▸ **inˈhumer** *n*

inimical (ɪˈnɪmɪkᵊl) *adj* **1** adverse or unfavourable. **2** not friendly; hostile. ORIG C17: from LL, from *inimīcus,* from IN-[1] + *amīcus* friendly; see ENEMY
▸ **inˈimically** *adv* ▸ **inˈimicalness** *or* **inˌimiˈcality** *n*

inimitable (ɪˈnɪmɪtəbᵊl) *adj* incapable of being duplicated or imitated; unique.
▸ **inˌimitaˈbility** *or* **inˈimitableness** *n* ▸ **inˈimitably** *adv*

iniquity (ɪˈnɪkwɪtɪ) *n, pl* **iniquities. 1** lack of justice or righteousness; wickedness; injustice. **2** a wicked act; sin. ORIG C14: from L, from *inīquus* unfair, from IN-[1] + *aequus* even, level; see EQUAL
▸ **inˈiquitous** *adj* ▸ **inˈiquitously** *adv* ▸ **inˈiquitousness** *n*

initial (ɪˈnɪʃəl) *adj* **1** of, at, or concerning the beginning. ◆ *n* **2** the first letter of a word, esp. a person's name. **3** *Printing.* a large letter set at the beginning of a chapter or work. **4** *Bot.* a cell from which tissues and organs develop by division and differentiation. ◆ *vb* **initials, initialling, initialled** *or US* **initials, initialing, initialed. 5** (*tr*) to sign with one's initials, esp. to indicate approval; endorse. ORIG C16: from L *initiālis* of the beginning, from *initium* beginning, lit.: an entering upon, from *inīre* to go in
▸ **inˈitialer** *or* **inˈitialler** *n* ▸ **inˈitially** *adv*

initialize *or* **initialise** (ɪˈnɪʃəˌlaɪz) *vb* **initializes, initializing, initialized** *or* **initialises, initialising, initialised.** (*tr*) to assign an initial value to (a variable or storage location) in a computer program.
▸ **inˌitialiˈzation** *or* **inˌitialiˈsation** *n*

initiate *vb* (ɪˈnɪʃɪˌeɪt), **initiates, initiating, initiated.** (*tr*) **1** to begin or originate. **2** to accept (new members) into an organization such as a club, through often secret ceremonies. **3** to teach fundamentals to. ◆ *adj* (ɪˈnɪʃɪɪt, -ˌeɪt). **4** initiated; begun. ◆ *n* (ɪˈnɪʃɪɪt, -ˌeɪt). **5** a person who has been initiated, esp. recently. **6** a beginner; novice. ORIG C17: from L *initiāre* (vb), from *initium;* see INITIAL
▸ **inˈitiatory** *adj*

initiation (ɪˌnɪʃɪˈeɪʃən) *n* **1** the act of initiating or the condition of being initiated. **2** the ceremony, often secret, initiating new members into an organization.

initiative (ɪˈnɪʃɪətɪv, -ˈnɪʃətɪv) *n* **1** the first step or action of a matter; commencing move: *a peace initiative.* **2** the right or power to begin or initiate something: *he has the initiative.* **3** the ability or attitude required to begin or initiate something. **4** *Government.* the right of citizens to introduce legislation, etc., in a legislative body, as in Switzerland. **5** **on one's own initiative.** without being prompted. ◆ *adj* **6** of or concerning initiation or serving to initiate; initiatory.
▸ **inˈitiatively** *adv*

initiator (ɪˈnɪʃɪˌeɪtə) *n* **1** a person or thing that initiates. **2** *Chem.* a substance that starts a chain reaction. **3** *Chem.* a very sensitive explosive used in detonators.

inject (ɪnˈdʒɛkt) *vb* (*tr*) **1** *Med.* to introduce (a fluid) into the body (of a person or animal) by means of a syringe. **2** (foll. by *into*) to introduce (a new aspect or element): *to inject humour into a scene.* **3** to interject (a comment, idea, etc.). ORIG C17: from *injicere* to throw in, from *jacere* to throw
▸ **inˈjectable** *adj* ▸ **inˈjector** *n*

injection (ɪnˈdʒɛkʃən) *n* **1** fluid injected into the body, esp. for medicinal purposes. **2** something injected. **3** the act of injecting. **4a** the act or process of introducing fluid under pressure, such as fuel into the combustion chamber of an engine. **4b** (*as modifier*): *injection moulding.*
▸ **inˈjective** *adj*

injunction (ɪnˈdʒʌŋkʃən) *n* **1** *Law.* an instruction or order issued by a court to a party to an action, esp. to refrain from some act. **2** a command, admonition, etc. **3** the act of enjoining. ORIG C16: from LL, from L *injungere* to ENJOIN
▸ **inˈjunctive** *adj* ▸ **inˈjunctively** *adv*

injure (ˈɪndʒə) *vb* **injures, injuring, injured.** (*tr*) **1** to cause physical or mental harm or suffering to; hurt or wound. **2** to offend, esp. by an injustice. ORIG C16: back formation from INJURY
▸ **ˈinjurable** *adj* ▸ **ˈinjured** *adj* ▸ **ˈinjurer** *n*

injurious (ɪnˈdʒʊərɪəs) *adj* **1** causing damage or harm; deleterious; hurtful. **2** abusive, slanderous, or libellous.
▸ **inˈjuriously** *adv* ▸ **inˈjuriousness** *n*

injury (ˈɪndʒərɪ) *n, pl* **injuries. 1** physical damage or hurt. **2** a specific instance of this: *a leg injury.* **3** harm done to a reputation. **4** *Law.* a violation or infringement of another person's rights that causes him or her harm and is actionable at law. ORIG C14: from L *injūria* injustice, wrong, from *injūriōsus* acting unfairly, wrongful, from IN-[1] + *jūs* right

injury time *n Soccer, rugby, etc.* extra playing time added on to compensate for time spent attending to injured players during the match. Also called: **stoppage time.**

injustice (ɪnˈdʒʌstɪs) *n* **1** the condition or practice of being unjust or unfair. **2** an unjust act.

ink (ɪŋk) *n* **1** a fluid or paste used for printing, writing, and drawing. **2** a dark brown fluid ejected into the water for self-concealment by an octopus or related mollusc. ◆ *vb* (*tr*) **3** to mark with ink. **4** to coat (a printing surface) with ink. ORIG C13: from OF *enque,* from LL *encaustum* a purplish-red ink, from Gk *enkauston* purple ink, from *enkaustos* burnt in, from *enkaiein* to burn in; see EN-[2], CAUSTIC
▸ **ˈinker** *n*

Inkatha (ɪnˈkɑːtə) *n* a South African political party; originally a Zulu organization founded in 1975 as a paramilitary group seeking nonracial democracy; won four seats in democratic multiracial elections in 1994. ORIG C20: Zulu name for the grass coil used by Zulu women carrying loads on their heads

inkblot (ˈɪŋkˌblɒt) *n* a patch of ink accidentally or deliberately spilled. Ten such patches, of different shapes, are used in the Rorschach test.

ink-cap *n* any of several saprotrophic fungi whose caps disintegrate into a black inky fluid after the spores mature.

Inkerman ★ (ˈɪŋkəmən; *Russian* inkɪrˈman) *n* a village in Ukraine, in the S Crimea east of Sevastopol: scene of a battle during the Crimean War in which British and French forces defeated the Russians (1854).

inkhorn (ˈɪŋkˌhɔːn) *n* (formerly) a small portable container for ink, usually made from horn.

ink in *vb* (*adv*) **1** (*tr*) to use ink to go over pencil lines in (a drawing). **2** to apply ink to (a printing surface) in preparing to print from it. **3** to arrange or confirm definitely.

inkling (ˈɪŋklɪŋ) *n* a slight intimation or suggestion; suspicion. ORIG C14: prob. from *inclen* to hint at

inkstand (ˈɪŋkˌstænd) *n* a stand or tray on which are kept writing implements and containers for ink.

inkwell (ˈɪŋkˌwɛl) *n* a small container for pen ink, often let into the surface of a desk.

inky (ˈɪŋkɪ) *adj* **inkier, inkiest. 1** resembling ink, esp. in colour; dark or black. **2** of, containing, or stained with ink.
▸ **ˈinkiness** *n*

INLA *abbrev. for* Irish National Liberation Army.

inlaid (ˈɪnˌleɪd, ɪnˈleɪd) *adj* **1** set in the surface, as a design in wood. **2** having such a design or inlay: *an inlaid table.*

inland *adj* (ˈɪnlənd). **1** of or located in the interior of a country or region away from a sea or border. **2** *Chiefly Brit.* operating within a country or region; domestic; not foreign. ◆ *n* (ˈɪnˌlænd, -lənd). **3** the interior of a country or region. ◆ *adv* (ˈɪnˌlænd, -lənd). **4** towards or into the interior of a country or region.
▸ **ˈinlander** *n*

Inland Revenue *n* (in Britain and New Zealand) a government board that administers and collects major direct taxes, such as income tax.

Inland Sea ★ *n* a sea in SW Japan, between the islands of Honshu, Shikoku, and Kyushu. Japanese name: **Seto Naikai.**

in-law *n* **1** a relative by marriage. ◆ *adj* **2** (*postpositive; in combination*) related by marriage: *a father-in-law.* ORIG C19: back formation from *father-in-law,* etc.

inlay *vb* (ɪnˈleɪ), **inlays, inlaying, inlaid.** (*tr*) **1** to decorate (an article, esp. of furniture) by inserting pieces of wood, ivory, etc., into slots in the surface. ◆ *n* (ˈɪnˌleɪ). **2** *Dentistry.* a filling inserted into a cavity and held in position by cement. **3** decoration made by inlaying. **4** an inlaid article, surface, etc.
▸ **ˈinˌlayer** *n*

inlet *n* (ˈɪnˌlɛt). **1** a narrow inland opening of the coastline. **2** an entrance or opening. **3** the act of letting someone or something in. **4** something let in or inserted. **5a** a passage or valve through which a substance, esp. a fluid, enters a machine. **5b** (*as modifier*): *an inlet valve.* ◆ *vb* (ɪnˈlɛt), **inlets, inletting, inlet. 6** (*tr*) to insert or inlay.

inlier (ˈɪnˌlaɪə) *n* an outcrop of rocks that is entirely surrounded by younger rocks.

in-line skate *n* another name for **Rollerblade.**

in loco parentis *Latin.* (ɪn ˈləʊkəʊ pəˈrɛntɪs) in place of a parent: said of a person acting in a parental capacity.

inly (ˈɪnlɪ) *adv Poetic.* inwardly; intimately.

inmate (ˈɪnˌmeɪt) *n* a person who is confined to an institution such as a prison or hospital.

in medias res *Latin.* (ɪn ˈmiːdɪˌæs ˈreɪs) in or into the middle of events or a narrative. ORIG lit.: into the midst of things, taken from a passage in Horace's *Ars Poetica*

in memoriam (ɪn mɪˈmɔːrɪəm) in memory of: used in obituaries, epitaphs, etc. ORIG L

inmost (ˈɪnˌməʊst) *adj* another word for **innermost.**

inn (ɪn) *n* a pub or small hotel providing food and accommodation.

Inn ★ (ɪn) *n* a river in central Europe, rising in Switzerland in Graubünden and flowing northeast through Austria and Bavaria to join the River Danube at Passau: forms part of the border between Austria and Germany. Length: 514 km (319 miles).

innards (ˈɪnədz) *pl n Inf.* **1** the internal organs of the body, esp. the viscera. **2** the interior parts of anything, esp. the working parts. ORIG C19: colloquial var. of *inwards*

innate (ɪˈneɪt, ˈɪneɪt) *adj* **1** existing from birth; congenital; inborn. **2** being an essential part of the character of a

person or thing. **3** instinctive; not learned: *innate capacities.* **4** *Philosophy.* (of ideas) present in the mind before any experience and knowable by pure reason. ORIG C15: from L, from *innascī* to be born in, from *nascī* to be born
▸ **in'nately** *adv* ▸ **in'nateness** *n*

inner ('ɪnə) *adj (prenominal)* **1** being or located further inside: *an inner room.* **2** happening or occurring inside. **3** relating to the soul, mind, spirit, etc. **4** more profound or obscure; less apparent: *the inner meaning.* **5** exclusive or private: *inner regions of the party.* ◆ *n* **6** *Archery.* **6a** the red innermost ring on a target. **6b** a shot which hits this ring.
▸ **'innerly** *adv* ▸ **'innerness** *n*

inner bar *n* **the.** *Brit.* all Queen's or King's Counsel collectively.

inner child *n Psychol.* the part of the psyche that retains feelings as they were experienced in childhood.

inner city *n* **a** the parts of a city in or near its centre, esp. when associated with poverty, substandard housing, etc. **b** *(as modifier)*: *inner-city schools.*

Inner Hebrides ★ *pl n* See **Hebrides.**

inner man *or (fem)* **inner woman** *n* **1** the mind or soul. **2** *Jocular.* the stomach or appetite.

Inner Mongolia ★ *n* an autonomous region of NE China: consists chiefly of the Mongolian plateau, with the Gobi Desert in the north and the Great Wall of China in the south. Capital: Hohhot. Pop.: 23 260 000 (1997 est.). Area: 1 177 500 sq. km (459 225 sq. miles).

innermost ('ɪnəˌməʊst) *adj* **1** being or located furthest within; central. **2** intimate; private.

inner tube *n* an inflatable rubber tube that fits inside a pneumatic tyre casing.

innervate ('ɪnɜːˌveɪt) *vb* **innervates, innervating, innervated.** *(tr)* **1** to supply nerves to (a bodily organ or part). **2** to stimulate (a bodily organ or part) with nerve impulses.
▸ **ˌinner'vation** *n*

innings ('ɪnɪŋz) *n* **1** *(functioning as sing) Cricket, etc.* **1a** the batting turn of a player or team. **1b** the runs scored during such a turn. **2** *(sometimes sing)* a period of opportunity or action.

Inniskilling ★ (ˌɪnɪs'kɪlɪŋ) *n* the former name of **Enniskillen.**

innkeeper ('ɪnˌkiːpə) *n* an owner or manager of an inn.

innocence ('ɪnəsəns) *n* the quality or state of being innocent. Archaic word: **innocency** ('ɪnəsənsɪ). ORIG C14: from L *innocentia* harmlessness, from *innocēns* blameless, from IN-[1] + *nocēre* to hurt

innocent ('ɪnəsənt) *adj* **1** not corrupted or tainted with evil; sinless; pure. **2** not guilty of a particular crime; blameless. **3** *(postpositive;* foll. by *of)* free (of); lacking: *innocent of all knowledge of history.* **4a** harmless or innocuous: *an innocent game.* **4b** not cancerous: *an innocent tumour.* **5** credulous, naive, or artless. **6** simple-minded; slow-witted. ◆ *n* **7** an innocent person, esp. a young child or an ingenuous adult. **8** a simple-minded person; simpleton.
▸ **'innocently** *adv*

Innocent II ★ ('ɪnəsənt) *n* original name *Gregorio Papareschi.* died 1143, pope (1130–43). He condemned Abelard's teachings.

Innocent III ★ *n* original name *Giovanni Lotario de' Conti.* ?1161–1216, pope (1198–1216), under whom the temporal power of the papacy reached its height. He instituted the Fourth Crusade (1202) and a crusade against the Albigenses (1208), and called the fourth Lateran Council (1215).

Innocent IV ★ *n* original name *Sinibaldo de' Fieschi.* died 1254, pope (1243–54); an unrelenting enemy of Emperor Frederick II and his heirs.

innocuous (ɪ'nɒkjuəs) *adj* having little or no adverse or harmful effect; harmless. ORIG C16: from L *innocuus* harmless, from IN-[1] + *nocēre* to harm
▸ **in'nocuously** *adv* ▸ **in'nocuousness** *or* **innocuity** (ˌɪnə'kjuːɪtɪ) *n*

innominate bone (ɪ'nɒmɪnɪt) *n* either of the two bones that form the sides of the pelvis, consisting of the ilium, ischium, and pubis. Nontechnical name: **hipbone.**

innovate ('ɪnəˌveɪt) *vb* **innovates, innovating, innovated.** to invent or begin to apply (methods, ideas, etc.). ORIG C16: from L *innovāre* to renew, from IN-[2] + *novāre* to make new, from *novus* new
▸ **'innoˌvative** *or* **'innoˌvatory** *adj* ▸ **'innoˌvator** *n*

innovation (ˌɪnə'veɪʃən) *n* **1** something newly introduced, such as a new method or device. **2** the act of innovating.
▸ **ˌinno'vational** *adj* ▸ **ˌinno'vationist** *n*

Innsbruck ★ ('ɪnzbrʊk) *n* a city in W Austria, on the River Inn at the foot of the Brenner Pass: tourist centre. Pop.: 118 112 (1991).

innuendo (ˌɪnju'ɛndəʊ) *n, pl* **innuendos** *or* **innuendoes. 1** an indirect or subtle reference, esp. one made maliciously or indicating criticism or disapproval; insinuation. **2** *Law.* (in an action for defamation) an explanation of the construction put upon words alleged to be defamatory where this meaning is not apparent. ORIG C17: from L, lit.: by hinting, from *innuere* to convey by a nod, from IN-[2] + *nuere* to nod

Innuit ('ɪnjuːɪt) *n* a variant spelling of **Inuit.**

innumerable (ɪ'njuːmərəbᵊl, ɪ'njuːmrəbᵊl) *or* **innumerous** *adj* so many as to be uncountable; extremely numerous.
▸ **inˌnumera'bility** *or* **in'numerableness** *n* ▸ **in'numerably** *adv*

innumerate (ɪ'njuːmərɪt) *adj* **1** having neither knowledge nor understanding of mathematics or science. ◆ *n* **2** an innumerate person.
▸ **in'numeracy** *n*

inoculate (ɪ'nɒkjʊˌleɪt) *vb* **inoculates, inoculating, inoculated. 1** to introduce (the causative agent of a disease) into the body in order to induce immunity. **2** *(tr)* to introduce (microorganisms, esp. bacteria) into (a culture medium). **3** *(tr)* to cause to be influenced or imbued, as with ideas. ORIG C15: from L *inoculāre* to implant, from IN-[2] + *oculus* eye, bud
▸ **inˌocu'lation** *n* ▸ **in'oculative** *adj* ▸ **in'ocuˌlator** *n*

inoculum (ɪ'nɒkjʊləm) *or* **inoculant** *n, pl* **inocula** (-lə) *or* **inoculants.** *Med.* the substance used in giving an inoculation. ORIG C20: NL; see INOCULATE

in-off *n Billiards.* a shot that goes into a pocket after striking another ball.

Inönü ★ ('iːnɜːˌnʊ, ˌɪnɜː'nuː) *n* **Ismet** (ɪs'mɛt, 'ɪsmɛt). 1884–1973, Turkish statesman; president of Turkey (1938–50) and prime minister (1923–37; 1961–65).

inoperable (ɪn'ɒpərəbᵊl, -'ɒprə-) *adj* **1** incapable of being implemented or operated. **2** *Surgery.* not suitable for operation without risk, esp. because of metastasis.
▸ **inˌopera'bility** *or* **in'operableness** *n* ▸ **in'operably** *adv*

inordinate (ɪn'ɔːdɪnɪt) *adj* **1** exceeding normal limits; immoderate. **2** unrestrained, as in behaviour or emotion; intemperate. **3** irregular or disordered. ORIG C14: from L *inordinātus* disordered, from IN-[1] + *ordināre* to put in order
▸ **in'ordinacy** *or* **in'ordinateness** *n* ▸ **in'ordinately** *adv*

inorganic (ˌɪnɔː'gænɪk) *adj* **1** not having the structure or characteristics of living organisms; not organic. **2** relating to or denoting chemical compounds that do not contain carbon. **3** not having a system, structure, or ordered relation of parts; amorphous. **4** not resulting from or produced by growth; artificial.
▸ **ˌinor'ganically** *adv*

inorganic chemistry *n* the branch of chemistry concerned with the elements and all their compounds except those containing carbon.

inosculate (ɪn'ɒskjʊˌleɪt) *vb* **inosculates, inosculating, inosculated. 1** *Physiol.* (of small blood vessels) to communicate by anastomosis. **2** to unite or be united so as to be continuous; blend. **3** to intertwine or cause to intertwine. ORIG C17: from IN-[2] + L *ōsculāre* to equip with an opening, from *ōsculum,* dim. of *ōs* mouth
▸ **inˌoscu'lation** *n*

inositol (ɪ'nəʊsɪˌtɒl) *n* a cyclic alcohol, one isomer of which (*i*-inositol) is present in yeast and is a growth factor for some organisms. ORIG C19: from Gk *in-, is* sinew + -OSE[2] + -ITE[1] + -OL[1]

inpatient (ˈɪnˌpeɪʃənt) *n* a patient living in the hospital where he or she is being treated.

in perpetuum *Latin.* (ɪn pɜːˈpɛtjʊəm) forever.

input (ˈɪnˌpʊt) *n* **1** the act of putting in. **2** that which is put in. **3** (*often pl*) a resource required for industrial production, such as capital goods, etc. **4** *Electronics.* the signal or current fed into a component or circuit. **5** *Computing.* the data fed into a computer from a peripheral device. **6** (*modifier*) of or relating to electronic, computer, or other input: *input program.* ◆ *vb* **inputs, inputting, input. 7** (*tr*) to insert (data) into a computer.

input/output *n Computing.* **1** the data or information passed into or out of a computer. **2** (*modifier*) concerned with or relating to such passage of data or information.

inquest (ˈɪnˌkwɛst) *n* **1** an inquiry, esp. into the cause of an unexplained, sudden, or violent death, held by a coroner, in certain cases with a jury. **2** *Inf.* any inquiry or investigation. ORIG C13: from Med. L, from L IN-[2] + *quaesītus* investigation, from *quaerere* to examine

inquietude (ɪnˈkwaɪɪˌtjuːd) *n* restlessness, uneasiness, or anxiety.
▸ **inquiet** (ɪnˈkwaɪət) *adj* ▸ **inˈquietly** *adv*

inquiline (ˈɪnkwɪˌlaɪn) *n* **1** an animal that lives in close association with another animal without harming it. See also **commensal** (sense 1). ◆ *adj* **2** of or living as an inquiline. ORIG C17: from L *inquilīnus* lodger, from IN-[2] + *colere* to dwell
▸ **inquilinous** (ˌɪnkwɪˈlaɪnəs) *adj*

inquire *or* **enquire** (ɪnˈkwaɪə) *vb* **inquires, inquiring, inquired** *or* **enquires, enquiring, enquired. 1a** to seek information (about); ask: *she inquired his age; she inquired about rates of pay.* **1b** (*intr;* foll. by *of*) to ask (a person) for information: *I'll inquire of my aunt when she is coming.* **2** (*intr;* often foll. by *into*) to make a search or investigation. ORIG C13: from L *inquīrere,* from IN-[2] + *quaerere* to seek
▸ **inˈquirer** *or* **enˈquirer** *n* ▸ **inˈquiry** *or* **enˈquiry** *n*

inquisition (ˌɪnkwɪˈzɪʃən) *n* **1** the act of inquiring deeply or searchingly; investigation. **2** a deep or searching inquiry, esp. a ruthless official investigation in order to suppress revolt or root out the unorthodox. **3** an official inquiry, esp. one held by a jury before an officer of the Crown. ORIG C14: from legal L *inquīsītiō,* from *inquīrere* to seek for; see INQUIRE
▸ **ˌinquiˈsitional** *adj* ▸ **ˌinquiˈsitionist** *n*

Inquisition (ˌɪnkwɪˈzɪʃən) *n History.* a judicial institution of the Roman Catholic Church (1232–1820) founded to suppress heresy.

inquisitive (ɪnˈkwɪzɪtɪv) *adj* **1** excessively curious, esp. about the affairs of others; prying. **2** eager to learn; inquiring.
▸ **inˈquisitively** *adv* ▸ **inˈquisitiveness** *n*

inquisitor (ɪnˈkwɪzɪtə) *n* **1** a person who inquires, esp. deeply, searchingly, or ruthlessly. **2** (*often cap.*) an official of the ecclesiastical court of the Inquisition.

inquisitorial (ɪnˌkwɪzɪˈtɔːrɪəl) *adj* **1** of, relating to, or resembling inquisition or an inquisitor. **2** offensively curious; prying. **3** *Law.* denoting criminal procedure in which one party is both prosecutor and judge, or in which the trial is held in secret. Cf. **accusatorial** (sense 2).
▸ **inˌquisiˈtorially** *adv* ▸ **inˌquisiˈtorialness** *n*

inquorate (ɪnˈkwɔːˌreɪt) *adj Brit.* not consisting of or being a quorum: *this meeting is inquorate.*

in re (ɪn ˈreɪ) *prep* in the matter of: used esp. in bankruptcy proceedings. ORIG C17: from L

INRI *abbrev. for* Iesus Nazarenus Rex Iudaeorum (the inscription placed over Christ's head during the Crucifixion). ORIG L: Jesus of Nazareth, King of the Jews

inro (ˈɪnrəʊ) *n, pl* **inro.** a set of small lacquer boxes formerly worn hung from the belt by Japanese men and used to carry medicines, seals, etc.

inroad (ˈɪnˌrəʊd) *n* **1** an invasion or hostile attack; raid or incursion. **2** an encroachment or intrusion.

inrush (ˈɪnˌrʌʃ) *n* a sudden usually overwhelming inward flow or rush; influx.
▸ **ˈinˌrushing** *n, adj*

ins. *abbrev. for:* **1** inches. **2** insulated. **3** insurance.

insane (ɪnˈseɪn) *adj* **1a** mentally deranged; crazy; of unsound mind. **1b** (*as collective n;* preceded by *the*): *the insane.* **2** characteristic of a person of unsound mind: *an insane stare.* **3** irresponsible; very foolish; stupid.
▸ **inˈsanely** *adv* ▸ **inˈsaneness** *n*

insanitary (ɪnˈsænɪtərɪ, -trɪ) *adj* not sanitary; dirty or infected.

insanity (ɪnˈsænɪtɪ) *n, pl* **insanities. 1** relatively permanent disorder of the mind; state or condition of being insane. **2** utter folly; stupidity.

insatiable (ɪnˈseɪʃəbᵊl, -ʃɪə-) *or* **insatiate** (ɪnˈseɪʃɪɪt) *adj* not able to be satisfied; greedy or unappeasable.
▸ **inˌsatiaˈbility** *or* **inˈsatiateness** *n* ▸ **inˈsatiably** *or* **inˈsatiately** *adv*

inscape (ˈɪnskeɪp) *n* the essential inner nature of a person, object, etc. ORIG C19: from IN-[2] + *-scape,* as in LANDSCAPE; coined by Gerard Manley HOPKINS

inscribe (ɪnˈskraɪb) *vb* **inscribes, inscribing, inscribed.** (*tr*) **1** to make, carve, or engrave (writing, letters, etc.) on (a surface such as wood, stone, or paper). **2** to enter (a name) on a list or in a register. **3** to sign one's name on (a book, etc.) before presentation to another person. **4** to draw (a geometric construction) inside another construction so that the two are in contact but do not intersect. ORIG C16: from L *inscrībere;* see INSCRIPTION
▸ **inˈscribable** *adj* ▸ **inˈscribableness** *n* ▸ **inˈscriber** *n*

inscription (ɪnˈskrɪpʃən) *n* **1** something inscribed, esp. words carved or engraved on a coin, tomb, etc. **2** a signature or brief dedication in a book or on a work of art. **3** the act of inscribing. ORIG C14: from L *inscriptiō* a writing upon, from *inscrībere* to write upon, from IN-[2] + *scrībere* to write
▸ **inˈscriptional** *or* **inˈscriptive** *adj* ▸ **inˈscriptively** *adv*

inscrutable (ɪnˈskruːtəbᵊl) *adj* mysterious or enigmatic; incomprehensible. ORIG C15: from LL, from L IN-[1] + *scrūtārī* to examine
▸ **inˌscrutaˈbility** *or* **inˈscrutableness** *n* ▸ **inˈscrutably** *adv*

insect (ˈɪnsɛkt) *n* **1** any of a class of small air-breathing arthropods, having a body divided into head, thorax, and abdomen, three pairs of legs, and (in most species) two pairs of wings. **2** (loosely) any similar invertebrate, such as a spider, tick, or centipede. **3** a contemptible, loathsome, or insignificant person. ORIG C17: from L *insectum* (animal that has been) cut into, insect, from *insecāre,* from IN-[2] + *secāre* to cut
▸ **inˈsectile** *adj* ▸ **ˈinsect-ˌlike** *adj*

insectarium (ˌɪnsɛkˈtɛərɪəm) *or* **insectary** (ɪnˈsɛktərɪ) *n, pl* **insectariums, insectaria** (-ˈtɛərɪə), *or* **insectaries.** a place where living insects are kept, bred, and studied.

insecticide (ɪnˈsɛktɪˌsaɪd) *n* a substance used to destroy insect pests.
▸ **inˌsectiˈcidal** *adj*

insectivore (ɪnˈsɛktɪˌvɔː) *n* **1** any of an order of placental mammals, being typically small, with simple teeth, and feeding on invertebrates. The group includes shrews, moles, and hedgehogs. **2** any animal or plant that derives nourishment from insects.
▸ **ˌinsecˈtivorous** *adj*

insecure (ˌɪnsɪˈkjʊə) *adj* **1** anxious or afraid; not confident or certain. **2** not adequately protected: *an insecure fortress.* **3** unstable or shaky.
▸ **ˌinseˈcurely** *adv* ▸ **ˌinseˈcureness** *n* ▸ **ˌinseˈcurity** *n*

inselberg (ˈɪnzᵊlˌbɜːg) *n* an isolated rocky hill rising abruptly from a flat plain. ORIG from G, from *Insel* island + *Berg* mountain

inseminate (ɪnˈsɛmɪˌneɪt) *vb* **inseminates, inseminating, inseminated.** (*tr*) **1** to impregnate (a female) with semen. **2** to introduce (ideas or attitudes) into the mind of (a person or group). ORIG C17: from L *insēmināre,* from IN-[2] + *sēmināre* to sow, from *sēmen* seed
▸ **inˌsemiˈnation** *n* ▸ **inˈsemiˌnator** *n*

insensate (ɪnˈsɛnseɪt, -sɪt) *adj* **1** lacking sensation or consciousness. **2** insensitive; unfeeling. **3** foolish; senseless.
▸ **inˈsensately** *adv* ▸ **inˈsensateness** *n*

insensible (ɪnˈsɛnsəbᵊl) *adj* **1** lacking sensation or consciousness. **2** (foll. by *of* or *to*) unaware (of) or indifferent

(to): *insensible to suffering.* **3** thoughtless or callous. **4** a less common word for **imperceptible.**
▸ **in,sensi'bility** *or* **in'sensibleness** *n* ▸ **in'sensibly** *adv*

insensitive (ɪn'sɛnsɪtɪv) *adj* **1** lacking sensitivity; unfeeling. **2** lacking physical sensation. **3** (*postpositive*; foll. by *to*) not sensitive (to) or affected (by): *insensitive to radiation.*
▸ **in'sensitively** *adv* ▸ **in'sensitiveness** *or* **in,sensi'tivity** *n*

insentient (ɪn'sɛnʃɪənt) *adj* lacking consciousness or senses; inanimate.
▸ **in'sentience** *n*

inseparable (ɪn'sɛpərəbᵊl, -'sɛprə-) *adj* incapable of being separated or divided.
▸ **in,separa'bility** *or* **in'separableness** *n* ▸ **in'separably** *adv*

insert *vb* (ɪn'sɜːt). (*tr*) **1** to put in or between; introduce. **2** to introduce into text, as in a newspaper; interpolate. ◆ *n* ('ɪnsɜːt). **3** something inserted. **4** Also called: **inset. 4a** a folded section placed in another for binding in with a book. **4b** a printed sheet, esp. one bearing advertising, placed loose between the leaves of a book, periodical, etc. ORIG C16: from L *inserere* to plant in, from IN-[2] + *serere* to join
▸ **in'sertable** *adj* ▸ **in'serter** *n*

insertion (ɪn'sɜːʃən) *n* **1** the act of inserting or something that is inserted. **2** a word, sentence, correction, etc., inserted into text, such as a newspaper. **3** a strip of lace, embroidery, etc., between two pieces of material. **4** *Anat.* the point or manner of attachment of a muscle to the bone that it moves.
▸ **in'sertional** *adj*

in-service *adj* denoting training that is given to employees during the course of employment: *an in-service course.*

insessorial (,ɪnsɛ'sɔːrɪəl) *adj* **1** (of feet or claws) adapted for perching. **2** (of birds) having insessorial feet. ORIG C19: from NL *Insessōrēs* birds that perch, from L: perchers, from *insidēre* to sit upon

inset *vb* (ɪn'sɛt), **insets, insetting, inset. 1** (*tr*) to set or place in or within; insert. ◆ *n* ('ɪn,sɛt). **2** something inserted. **3** *Printing.* **3a** a small map or diagram set within the borders of a larger one. **3b** another name for **insert** (sense 4). **4** a piece of fabric inserted into a garment, as to shape it or for decoration.
▸ **'in,setter** *n*

inshallah (ɪn'ʃælə) *sentence substitute. Islam.* if Allah wills it. ORIG C19: from Ar.

inshore ('ɪn'ʃɔː) *adj* **1** in or on the water, but close to the shore: *inshore weather.* ◆ *adv, adj* **2** towards the shore from the water: *an inshore wind; we swam inshore.*

inside *n* ('ɪn'saɪd). **1** the interior; inner or enclosed part or surface. **2** the side of a path away from the road or adjacent to a wall. **3** (*also pl*) *Inf.* the internal organs of the body, esp. the stomach and bowels. **4 inside of.** in a period of time less than; within. **5 inside out.** with the inside facing outwards. **6 know (something) inside out.** to know thoroughly or perfectly. ◆ *prep* (,ɪn'saɪd). **7** in or to the interior of; within or to within; on the inside of. ◆ *adj* ('ɪn,saɪd). **8** on or of an interior; on the inside: *an inside door.* **9** (*prenominal*) arranged or provided by someone within an organization or building, esp. illicitly: *the raid was an inside job; inside information.* ◆ *adv* (,ɪn'saɪd). **10** within or to within a thing or place; indoors. **11** *Sl.* in or into prison.

USAGE NOTE See at **outside.**

inside job *n Inf.* a crime committed with the assistance of someone associated with the victim.

inside lane *n Athletics.* the inside, and therefore the shortest, route around a circular or oval multi-lane running track.

insider (,ɪn'saɪdə) *n* **1** a member of a specified group. **2** a person with access to exclusive information.

insider dealing *or* **trading** *n* the illegal practice of a person on the Stock Exchange or in some branches of the Civil Service taking advantage of early confidential information in order to deal in shares for personal profit.
▸ **insider dealer** *or* **trader** *n*

insidious (ɪn'sɪdɪəs) *adj* **1** stealthy, subtle, cunning, or treacherous. **2** working in a subtle or apparently innocuous way, but nevertheless deadly: *an insidious illness.* ORIG C16: from L *insidiōsus* cunning, from *insidiae* an ambush, from *insidēre* to sit in
▸ **in'sidiously** *adv* ▸ **in'sidiousness** *n*

insight ('ɪn,saɪt) *n* **1** the ability to perceive clearly or deeply; penetration. **2** a penetrating and often sudden understanding, as of a complex situation or problem. **3** *Psychol.* the capacity for understanding one's own or another's mental processes. **4** *Psychiatry.* the ability to understand one's own problems.
▸ **'in,sightful** *adj*

insignia (ɪn'sɪgnɪə) *n, pl* **insignias** *or* **insignia. 1** a badge or emblem of membership, office, or dignity. **2** a distinguishing sign or mark. ORIG C17: from L: badges, from *insignis* distinguished by a mark, prominent, from IN-[2] + *signum* mark

insignificant (,ɪnsɪg'nɪfɪkənt) *adj* **1** having little or no importance; trifling. **2** almost or relatively meaningless. **3** small or inadequate: *an insignificant wage.* **4** not distinctive in character, etc.
▸ **,insig'nificance** *or* **,insig'nificancy** *n* ▸ **,insig'nificantly** *adv*

insincere (,ɪnsɪn'sɪə) *adj* lacking sincerity; hypocritical.
▸ **,insin'cerely** *adv* ▸ **insincerity** (,ɪnsɪn'sɛrɪtɪ) *n*

insinuate (ɪn'sɪnjʊ,eɪt) *vb* **insinuates, insinuating, insinuated. 1** (*may take a clause as object*) to suggest by indirect allusion, hints, innuendo, etc. **2** (*tr*) to introduce subtly or deviously. **3** (*tr*) to cause (someone, esp. oneself) to be accepted by gradual approaches or manoeuvres. ORIG C16: from L *insinuāre* to wind one's way into, from IN-[2] + *sinus* curve
▸ **in'sinuative** *or* **in'sinuatory** *adj* ▸ **in'sinu,ator** *n*

insinuation (ɪn,sɪnjʊ'eɪʃən) *n* **1** an indirect or devious hint or suggestion. **2** the act or practice of insinuating.

insipid (ɪn'sɪpɪd) *adj* **1** lacking spirit or interest; boring. **2** lacking taste; unpalatable. ORIG C17: from L, from IN-[1] + *sapidus* full of flavour, SAPID
▸ **,insi'pidity** *or* **in'sipidness** *n* ▸ **in'sipidly** *adv*

insist (ɪn'sɪst) *vb* (when *tr, takes a clause as object;* when *intr,* usually foll. by *on* or *upon*) **1** to make a determined demand (for): *he insisted on his rights.* **2** to express a convinced belief (in) or assertion (of). ORIG C16: from L *insistere* to stand upon, urge, from IN-[2] + *sistere* to stand
▸ **in'sister** *n* ▸ **in'sistingly** *adv*

insistent (ɪn'sɪstənt) *adj* **1** making continual and persistent demands. **2** demanding notice or attention; compelling: *the insistent cry of a bird.*
▸ **in'sistence** *or* **in'sistency** *n* ▸ **in'sistently** *adv*

in situ *Latin.* (ɪn 'sɪtjuː) *adv, adj* (*postpositive*) in the natural, original, or appropriate position.

in so far as *or* **insofar as** (,ɪnsəʊ'fɑː) *adv* to the degree or extent that.

insolation (,ɪnsəʊ'leɪʃən) *n* **1** the quantity of solar radiation falling upon a body or planet, esp. per unit area. **2** exposure to the sun's rays. **3** another name for **sunstroke.**

insole ('ɪn,səʊl) *n* **1** the inner sole of a shoe or boot. **2** a loose additional inner sole used to give extra warmth or to make a shoe fit.

insolent ('ɪnsələnt) *adj* impudent or disrespectful. ORIG C14: from L, from IN-[1] + *solēre* to be accustomed
▸ **'insolence** *n* ▸ **'insolently** *adv*

insoluble (ɪn'sɒljʊbᵊl) *adj* **1** incapable of being dissolved; incapable of forming a solution, esp. in water. **2** incapable of being solved.
▸ **in,solu'bility** *or* **in'solubleness** *n* ▸ **in'solubly** *adv*

insolvent (ɪn'sɒlvənt) *adj* **1** having insufficient assets to meet debts and liabilities; bankrupt. **2** of or relating to bankrupts or bankruptcy. ◆ *n* **3** a person who is insolvent; bankrupt.
▸ **in'solvency** *n*

insomnia (ɪn'sɒmnɪə) *n* chronic inability to fall asleep or to enjoy uninterrupted sleep. ORIG C18: from L, from *insomnis* sleepless, from *somnus* sleep
▸ **in'somni,ac** *n, adj* ▸ **in'somnious** *adj*

insomuch (,ɪnsəʊ'mʌtʃ) *adv* **1** (foll. by *as* or *that*) to such an extent or degree. **2** (foll. by *as*) because of the fact (that); inasmuch (as).

insouciant (ɪn'su:sɪənt) *adj* carefree or unconcerned; light-hearted. ORIG C19: from F, from IN-[1] + *souciant* worrying, from *soucier* to trouble, from L *sollicitāre*
▸ **in'souciance** *n* ▸ **in'souciantly** *adv*

inspan (ɪn'spæn) *vb* **inspans, inspanning, inspanned.** (*tr*) *Chiefly S. African.* **1** to harness (animals) to (a vehicle); yoke. **2** to press (people) into service. ORIG C19: from Afrik., from MDu. *inspannen,* from *spannen* to stretch

inspect (ɪn'spɛkt) *vb* (*tr*) **1** to examine closely, esp. for faults or errors. **2** to scrutinize officially (a document, military personnel on ceremonial parade, etc.). ORIG C17: from L *inspicere,* from *specere* to look
▸ **in'spectable** *adj* ▸ **in'spection** *n* ▸ **in'spective** *adj*

inspector (ɪn'spɛktə) *n* **1** a person who inspects, esp. an official who examines for compliance with regulations, standards, etc. **2** a police officer ranking below a superintendent and above a sergeant.
▸ **in'spectoral** *or* **inspectorial** (ˌɪnspɛk'tɔ:rɪəl) *adj* ▸ **in'spector,ship** *n*

inspectorate (ɪn'spɛktərɪt) *n* **1** the office, rank, or duties of an inspector. **2** a body of inspectors. **3** a district under an inspector.

inspiration (ˌɪnspɪ'reɪʃən) *n* **1** stimulation or arousal of the mind, feelings, etc., to special activity or creativity. **2** the state or quality of being so stimulated or aroused. **3** someone or something that causes this state. **4** an idea or action resulting from such a state. **5** the act or process of inhaling; breathing in.

inspiratory (ɪn'spaɪərətərɪ, -trɪ) *adj* of or relating to inhalation or the drawing in of air.

inspire (ɪn'spaɪə) *vb* **inspires, inspiring, inspired. 1** to exert a stimulating or beneficial effect upon (a person, etc.); animate or invigorate. **2** (*tr;* foll. by *with* or *to; may take an infinitive*) to arouse (with a particular emotion or to a particular action); stir. **3** (*tr*) to prompt or instigate; give rise to. **4** (*tr; often passive*) to guide or arouse by divine influence or inspiration. **5** to take or draw (air, gas, etc.) into the lungs; inhale. **6** (*tr*) *Arch.* to breathe into or upon. ORIG C14 (in the sense: to breathe upon, blow into): from L *inspīrāre,* from *spīrāre* to breathe
▸ **in'spirable** *adj* ▸ **in'spirative** *adj* ▸ **in'spirer** *n* ▸ **in'spiringly** *adv*

inspirit (ɪn'spɪrɪt) *vb* (*tr*) to fill with vigour; inspire.
▸ **in'spiriter** *n* ▸ **in'spiriting** *adj* ▸ **in'spiritment** *n*

inspissate (ɪn'spɪseɪt) *vb* **inspissates, inspissating, inspissated.** *Arch.* to thicken, as by evaporation. ORIG C17: from LL *inspissātus* thickened, from L, from *spissus* thick
▸ **ˌinspis'sation** *n* ▸ **'inspis,sator** *n*

inst. *abbrev. for:* **1** instant (this month). **2** instantaneous. **3** instrumental.

Inst. *abbrev. for:* **1** Institute. **2** Institution.

instability (ˌɪnstə'bɪlɪtɪ) *n, pl* **instabilities. 1** lack of stability or steadiness. **2** tendency to variable or unpredictable behaviour.

install *or* **instal** (ɪn'stɔ:l) *vb* **installs** *or* **instals, installing, installed.** (*tr*) **1** to place (equipment) in position and connect and adjust for use. **2** to transfer (computer software) from a distribution file to a permanent location on disk, and prepare it for its particular environment and application. **3** to put in a position, rank, etc. **4** to settle (a person, esp. oneself) in a position or state: *she installed herself in an armchair.* ORIG C16: from Med. L *installāre,* from IN-[2] + *stallum* STALL[1]
▸ **in'staller** *n*

installation (ˌɪnstə'leɪʃən) *n* **1** the act of installing or the state of being installed. **2** a large device, system, or piece of equipment that has been installed.

installment plan *or esp. Canad.* **instalment plan** *n* the US and Canad. name for **hire-purchase.**

instalment *or US* **installment** (ɪn'stɔ:lmənt) *n* **1** one of the portions into which a debt is divided for payment at specified intervals over a fixed period. **2** a portion of something that is issued, broadcast, or published in parts. ORIG C18: from obs. *estallment,* prob. from OF *estaler* to fix, from *estal* something fixed, from OHG *stal* STALL[1]

instance ('ɪnstəns) *n* **1** a case or particular example. **2 for instance.** for or as an example. **3** a specified stage in proceedings; step (in **in the first, second,** etc., **instance**). **4** urgent request or demand (esp. in **at the instance of**). ◆ *vb* **instances, instancing, instanced.** (*tr*) **5** to cite as an example. ORIG C14 (in the sense: case, example): from Med. L *instantia* example, (in the sense: urgency) from L: a being close upon, from *instāns* urgent; see INSTANT

instant ('ɪnstənt) *n* **1** a very brief time; moment. **2** a particular moment or point in time: *at the same instant.* **3 on the instant.** immediately; without delay. ◆ *adj* **4** immediate; instantaneous. **5** (esp. of foods) prepared or designed for preparation with very little time and effort: *instant coffee.* **6** urgent or imperative. **7** (*postpositive*) of the present month: *a letter of the 7th instant.* Abbrev.: **inst.** ORIG C15: from L *instāns,* from *instāre* to be present, press closely, from IN-[2] + *stāre* to stand

instantaneous (ˌɪnstən'teɪnɪəs) *adj* **1** occurring with almost no delay; immediate. **2** happening or completed within a moment: *instantaneous death.*
▸ **ˌinstan'taneously** *adv* ▸ **ˌinstan'taneousness** *or* **instantaneity** (ɪnˌstæntə'ni:ɪtɪ) *n*

instanter (ɪn'stæntə) *adv Law.* without delay; the same day or within 24 hours. ORIG C17: from L: urgently, from *instans* INSTANT

instantly ('ɪnstəntlɪ) *adv* **1** immediately; at once. **2** *Arch.* urgently or insistently.

instar ('ɪnstɑ:) *n* the stage in the development of an insect between any two moults. ORIG C19: NL from L: image

instate (ɪn'steɪt) *vb* **instates, instating, instated.** (*tr*) to place in a position or office; install.
▸ **in'statement** *n*

instead (ɪn'stɛd) *adv* **1** as a replacement, substitute, or alternative. **2 instead of.** (*prep*) in place of or as an alternative to. ORIG C13: from *in stead* in place

instep ('ɪnˌstɛp) *n* **1** the middle section of the human foot, forming the arch between the ankle and toes. **2** the part of a shoe, stocking, etc., covering this. ORIG C16: prob. from IN-[2] + STEP

instigate ('ɪnstɪˌgeɪt) *vb* **instigates, instigating, instigated.** (*tr*) **1** to bring about, as by incitement: *to instigate rebellion.* **2** to urge on to some drastic or unadvisable action. ORIG C16: from L *instīgāre* to incite
▸ **ˌinsti'gation** *n* ▸ **'insti,gative** *adj* ▸ **'insti,gator** *n*

instil *or US* **instill** (ɪn'stɪl) *vb* **instils** *or US* **instills, instilling, instilled.** (*tr*) **1** to introduce gradually; implant or infuse. **2** *Rare.* to pour in or inject in drops. ORIG C16: from L *instillāre* to pour in a drop at a time, from *stillāre* to drip
▸ **in'stiller** *n* ▸ **in'stilment,** *US* **in'stillment,** *or* **ˌinstil'lation** *n*

instinct *n* ('ɪnstɪŋkt). **1** the innate capacity of an animal to respond to a given stimulus in a relatively fixed way. **2** inborn intuitive power. ◆ *adj* (ɪn'stɪŋkt). **3** (*postpositive;* often foll. by *with*) *Rare.* **3a** animated or impelled (by). **3b** imbued or infused (with). ORIG C15: from L *instinctus* roused, from *instinguere* to incite

instinctive (ɪn'stɪŋktɪv) *adj* **1** of, relating to, or resulting from instinct. **2** conditioned so as to appear innate: *an instinctive movement in driving.*
▸ **in'stinctively** *adv*

instinctual (ɪn'stɪŋktjʊəl) *adj* of or pertaining to instinct.
▸ **in'stinctually** *adv*

institute ('ɪnstɪˌtju:t) *vb* **institutes, instituting, instituted.** (*tr*) **1** to organize; establish. **2** to initiate: *to institute a practice.* **3** to establish in a position or office; induct. ◆ *n* **4** an organization founded for particular work, such as education, promotion of the arts, or scientific research. **5** the building where such an organization is situated. **6** something instituted, esp. a rule, custom, or precedent. ORIG C16: from L *instituere,* from *statuere* to place
▸ **'insti,tutor** *or* **'insti,tuter** *n*

institutes ('ɪnstɪˌtju:ts) *pl n* a digest or summary, esp. of laws.

institution (ˌɪnstɪˈtjuːʃən) *n* **1** the act of instituting. **2** an organization or establishment founded for a specific purpose, such as a hospital or college. **3** the building where such an organization is situated. **4** an established custom, law, or relationship in a society or community. **5** Also called: **institutional investor.** a large organization, such as an insurance company or pension fund, that has substantial sums to invest on a stock exchange. **6** *Inf.* a constant feature or practice: *Jones's drink at the bar was an institution.* **7** the appointment of an incumbent to an ecclesiastical office or pastoral charge.
▸ **ˌinstiˈtutionary** *adj*

institutional (ˌɪnstɪˈtjuːʃənᵊl) *adj* **1** of, relating to, or characteristic of institutions. **2** dull, routine, and uniform: *institutional meals.* **3** relating to principles or institutes, esp. of law.
▸ **ˌinstiˈtutionally** *adv* ▸ **ˌinstiˈtutionaˌlism** *n*

institutionalize *or* **institutionalise** (ˌɪnstɪˈtjuːʃənəˌlaɪz) *vb* **institutionalizes, institutionalizing, institutionalized** *or* **institutionalises, institutionalising, institutionalised. 1** (*tr; often passive*) to subject to the deleterious effects of confinement in an institution. **2** (*tr*) to place in an institution. **3** to make or become an institution.
▸ **ˌinstiˌtutionaliˈzation** *or* **ˌinstiˌtutionaliˈsation** *n*

in-store *adj* available within a department store: *in-store banking facilities.*

instruct (ɪnˈstrʌkt) *vb* (*tr*) **1** to direct to do something; order. **2** to teach (someone) how to do (something). **3** to furnish with information; apprise. **4** *Law, chiefly Brit.* (esp. of a client to his or her solicitor or a solicitor to a barrister) to give relevant facts or information to. ORIG C15: from L *instruere* to construct, equip, teach, from *struere* to build
▸ **inˈstructible** *adj*

instruction (ɪnˈstrʌkʃən) *n* **1** a direction; order. **2** the process or act of imparting knowledge; teaching; education. **3** *Computing.* a part of a program consisting of a coded command to the computer to perform a specified function.
▸ **inˈstructional** *adj*

instructions (ɪnˈstrʌkʃənz) *pl n* **1** directions, orders, or recommended rules for guidance, use, etc. **2** *Law.* the facts and details relating to a case given by a client to his solicitor or by a solicitor to a barrister.

instructive (ɪnˈstrʌktɪv) *adj* serving to instruct or enlighten; conveying information.
▸ **inˈstructively** *adv* ▸ **inˈstructiveness** *n*

instructor (ɪnˈstrʌktə) *n* **1** someone who instructs; teacher. **2** *US & Canad.* a university teacher ranking below assistant professor.
▸ **inˈstructorship** *n* ▸ **instructress** (ɪnˈstrʌktrɪs) *fem n*

instrument *n* (ˈɪnstrəmənt). **1** a mechanical implement or tool, esp. one used for precision work. **2** *Music.* any of various contrivances or mechanisms that can be played to produce musical tones or sounds. **3** an important factor or agency in something: *her evidence was an instrument in his arrest.* **4** *Inf.* a person used by another to gain an end; dupe. **5** a measuring device, such as a pressure gauge. **6a** a device or system for use in navigation or control, esp. of aircraft. **6b** (*as modifier*): *instrument landing.* **7** a formal legal document. ◆ *vb* (ˈɪnstrəˌmɛnt). (*tr*) **8** another word for **orchestrate** (sense 1). **9** to equip with instruments. ORIG C13: from L *instrūmentum* tool, from *instruere* to erect, furnish; see INSTRUCT

instrumental (ˌɪnstrəˈmɛntᵊl) *adj* **1** serving as a means or influence; helpful. **2** of, relating to, or characterized by an instrument. **3** played by or composed for musical instruments. **4** *Grammar.* denoting a case of nouns, etc. indicating the instrument used in performing an action, usually using the prepositions *with* or *by means of.* ◆ *n* **5** a piece of music composed for instruments rather than for voices. **6** *Grammar.* the instrumental case.
▸ **ˌinstrumenˈtality** *n* ▸ **ˌinstruˈmentally** *adv*

instrumentalist (ˌɪnstrəˈmɛntəlɪst) *n* a person who plays a musical instrument.

instrumentation (ˌɪnstrəmɛnˈteɪʃən) *n* **1** the instruments specified in a musical score or arrangement. **2** another word for **orchestration. 3** the study of the characteristics of musical instruments. **4** the use of instruments or tools.

instrument panel *or* **board** *n* **1** a panel on which instruments are mounted, as on a car. See also **dashboard. 2** an array of instruments, gauges, etc., mounted to display the condition or performance of a machine.

insubordinate (ˌɪnsəˈbɔːdɪnɪt) *adj* **1** not submissive to authority; disobedient or rebellious. **2** not in a subordinate position or rank. ◆ *n* **3** an insubordinate person.
▸ **ˌinsubˈordinately** *adv* ▸ **ˌinsubˌordiˈnation** *n*

insubstantial (ˌɪnsəbˈstænʃəl) *adj* **1** not substantial; flimsy, tenuous, or slight. **2** imaginary; unreal.
▸ **ˌinsubˌstantiˈality** *n* ▸ **ˌinsubˈstantially** *adv*

insufferable (ɪnˈsʌfərəbᵊl) *adj* intolerable; unendurable.
▸ **inˈsufferableness** *n* ▸ **inˈsufferably** *adv*

insufficiency (ˌɪnsəˈfɪʃənsɪ) *n* **1** Also: **ˌinsufˈficience.** the state of being insufficient. **2** *Pathol.* failure in the functioning of an organ, tissue, etc.: *cardiac insufficiency.*

insufficient (ˌɪnsəˈfɪʃənt) *adj* not sufficient; inadequate or deficient.
▸ **ˌinsufˈficiently** *adv*

insufflate (ˈɪnsʌˌfleɪt) *vb* **insufflates, insufflating, insufflated. 1** (*tr*) to breathe or blow (something) into (a room, area, etc.). **2** *Med.* to blow (air, medicated powder, etc.) into a body cavity. **3** (*tr*) to breathe or blow upon (someone or something) as a ritual or sacramental act.
▸ **ˌinsufˈflation** *n* ▸ **ˈinsufˌflator** *n*

insular (ˈɪnsjulə) *adj* **1** of, relating to, or resembling an island. **2** remote, detached, or aloof. **3** illiberal or narrow-minded. **4** isolated or separated. ORIG C17: from LL, from L *insula* island
▸ **ˈinsularism** *or* **insularity** (ˌɪnsjuˈlærɪtɪ) *n* ▸ **ˈinsularly** *adv*

insulate (ˈɪnsjuˌleɪt) *vb* **insulates, insulating, insulated.** (*tr*) **1** to prevent the transmission of electricity, heat, or sound to or from (a body or device) by surrounding with a nonconducting material. **2** to isolate or detach. ORIG C16: from LL *insulātus* made into an island

insulation (ˌɪnsjuˈleɪʃən) *n* **1** Also: **insulant.** material used to insulate a body or device. **2** the act or process of insulating.

insulator (ˈɪnsjuˌleɪtə) *n* any material or device that insulates, esp. a material with a very low electrical conductivity or thermal conductivity.

insulin (ˈɪnsjulɪn) *n* a protein hormone, secreted in the pancreas by the islets of Langerhans, that controls the concentration of glucose in the blood. ORIG C20: from NL *insula* islet (of the pancreas) + -IN

insult *vb* (ɪnˈsʌlt). (*tr*) **1** to treat, mention, or speak to rudely; offend; affront. ◆ *n* (ˈɪnsʌlt). **2** an offensive or contemptuous remark or action; affront; slight. **3** a person or thing producing the effect of an affront: *some television is an insult to intelligence.* **4** *Med.* an injury or trauma. ORIG C16: from L *insultāre* to jump upon
▸ **inˈsulter** *n*

insuperable (ɪnˈsuːpərəbᵊl, -prəbᵊl, -ˈsjuː-) *adj* incapable of being overcome; insurmountable.
▸ **inˌsuperaˈbility** *n* ▸ **inˈsuperably** *adv*

insupportable (ˌɪnsəˈpɔːtəbᵊl) *adj* **1** incapable of being endured; intolerable; insufferable. **2** incapable of being supported or justified; indefensible.
▸ **ˌinsupˈportableness** *n* ▸ **ˌinsupˈportably** *adv*

insurance (ɪnˈʃuərəns, -ˈʃɔː-) *n* **1a** the act, system, or business of providing financial protection against specified contingencies, such as death, loss, or damage. **1b** the state of having such protection. **1c** Also called: **insurance policy.** the policy providing such protection. **1d** the pecuniary amount of such protection. **1e** the premium payable in return for such protection. **1f** (*as modifier*): *insurance agent; insurance broker; insurance company.* **2** a means of protecting or safeguarding against risk or injury.

insure (ɪnˈʃuə, -ˈʃɔː) *vb* **insures, insuring, insured. 1** (often foll. by *against*) to guarantee or protect (against risk, loss, etc.). **2** (often foll. by *against*) to issue (a person) with an insurance policy or take out an insurance policy (on): *his*

house was heavily insured against fire. **3** a variant spelling (esp. US) of **ensure.** ◆ Also (rare) (for senses 1, 2): **ensure.**
▸ **in'surable** *adj* ▸ **in,sura'bility** *n*

insured (ɪn'ʃʊəd, -'ʃɔːd) *adj* **1** covered by insurance: *an insured risk.* ◆ *n* **2** the person, persons, or organization covered by an insurance policy.

insurer (ɪn'ʃʊərə, -'ʃɔː-) *n* **1** a person or company offering insurance policies in return for premiums. **2** a person or thing that insures.

insurgence (ɪn'sɜːdʒəns) *n* rebellion, uprising, or riot.

insurgent (ɪn'sɜːdʒənt) *adj* **1** rebellious or in revolt, as against a government in power or the civil authorities. ◆ *n* **2** a person who takes part in an uprising or rebellion; insurrectionist. ORIG C18: from L *insurgēns* rising upon or against, from *surgere* to rise
▸ **in'surgency** *n*

insurmountable (,ɪnsə'maʊntəbᵊl) *adj* incapable of being overcome; insuperable.
▸ **,insur,mounta'bility** *or* **,insur'mountableness** *n* ▸ **,insur'mountably** *adv*

insurrection (,ɪnsə'rɛkʃən) *n* the act or an instance of rebelling against a government in power or the civil authorities; insurgency. ORIG C15: from LL *insurrectiō,* from *insurgere* to rise up
▸ **,insur'rectional** *adj* ▸ **,insur'rectionary** *n, adj* ▸ **,insur'rectionist** *n, adj*

int. *abbrev. for:* **1** interest. **2** interior. **3** internal. **4** Also: **Int.** international.

intact (ɪn'tækt) *adj* untouched or unimpaired; left complete or perfect. ORIG C15: from L *intactus* not touched, from *tangere* to touch
▸ **in'tactness** *n*

intaglio (ɪn'tɑːlɪ,əʊ) *n, pl* **intaglios** *or* **intagli** (-ljiː). **1** a seal, gem, etc., ornamented with a sunken or incised design. **2** the art or process of incised carving. **3** a design, figure, or ornamentation carved, engraved, or etched into the surface of the material used. **4** any of various printing techniques using an etched or engraved plate. **5** an incised die used to make a design in relief. ORIG C17: from It., from *intagliare* to engrave, from *tagliare* to cut, from LL *tāliāre;* see TAILOR
▸ **intagliated** (ɪn'tɑːlɪ,eɪtɪd) *adj*

intake ('ɪn,teɪk) *n* **1** a thing or a quantity taken in: *an intake of students.* **2** the act of taking in. **3** the opening through which fluid enters a duct or channel, esp. the air inlet of a jet engine. **4** a ventilation shaft in a mine. **5** a contraction or narrowing: *an intake in a garment.*

intangible (ɪn'tændʒɪbᵊl) *adj* **1** incapable of being perceived by touch; impalpable. **2** imprecise or unclear to the mind: *intangible ideas.* **3** (of property or a business asset) saleable though not possessing intrinsic productive value. ◆ *n* **4** something that is intangible.
▸ **in,tangi'bility** *n* ▸ **in'tangibly** *adv*

intarsia (ɪn'tɑːsɪə) *or* **tarsia** *n* **1** a decorative mosaic of inlaid wood of a style developed in the Italian Renaissance. **2** (in knitting) **2a** an individually worked motif. **2b** the method of knitting blocks of colour in place to create such a pattern. ORIG C19: changed from It. *intarsio*

integer ('ɪntɪdʒə) *n* **1** any rational number that can be expressed as the sum or difference of a finite number of units, as 1, 2, 3, etc. **2** an individual entity or whole unit. ORIG C16: from L: untouched, from *tangere* to touch

integral ('ɪntɪgrəl, ɪn'tɛgrəl) *adj* **1** (often foll. by *to*) being an essential part (of); intrinsic (to). **2** intact; entire. **3** formed of constituent parts; united. **4** *Maths.* **4a** of or involving an integral. **4b** involving or being an integer. ◆ *n* **5** *Maths.* the sum of a large number of infinitesimally small quantities, summed either between stated limits (**definite integral**) or in the absence of limits (**indefinite integral**). **6** a complete thing; whole.
▸ **integrality** (,ɪntɪ'grælɪtɪ) *n* ▸ **'integrally** *adv*

integral calculus *n* the branch of calculus concerned with the determination of integrals (**integration**) and their application to the solution of differential equations.

integrand ('ɪntɪ,grænd) *n* a mathematical function to be integrated. ORIG C19: from L: to be integrated

integrant ('ɪntəgrənt) *adj* **1** part of a whole; integral; constituent. ◆ *n* **2** an integrant part.

integrate *vb* ('ɪntɪ,greɪt), **integrates, integrating, integrated.** **1** to make or be made into a whole; incorporate or be incorporated. **2** (*tr*) to designate (a school, park, etc.) for use by all races or groups; desegregate. **3** to amalgamate or mix (a racial or religious group) with an existing community. **4** *Maths.* to determine the integral of a function or variable. ◆ *adj* ('ɪntɪgrɪt). **5** made up of parts; integrated. ORIG C17: from L *integrāre;* see INTEGER
▸ **integrable** ('ɪntəgrəbᵊl) *adj* ▸ **,integra'bility** *n* ▸ **,inte'gration** *n* ▸ **'inte,grative** *adj*

integrated circuit *n* a very small electronic circuit consisting of an assembly of elements made from a chip of semiconducting material.

integrity (ɪn'tɛgrɪtɪ) *n* **1** adherence to moral principles; honesty. **2** the quality of being unimpaired; soundness. **3** unity; wholeness. ORIG C15: from L *integritās;* see INTEGER

integument (ɪn'tɛgjʊmənt) *n* any outer protective layer or covering, such as a cuticle, seed coat, rind, or shell. ORIG C17: from L *integumentum,* from *tegere* to cover
▸ **in,tegu'mental** *or* **in,tegu'mentary** *adj*

intellect ('ɪntɪ,lɛkt) *n* **1** the capacity for understanding, thinking, and reasoning. **2** a mind or intelligence, esp. a brilliant one: *his intellect is wasted on that job.* **3** *Inf.* a person possessing a brilliant mind; brain. ORIG C14: from L *intellectus* comprehension, from *intellegere* to understand; see INTELLIGENCE
▸ **,intel'lective** *adj* ▸ **,intel'lectively** *adv*

intellection (,ɪntɪ'lɛkʃən) *n* **1** mental activity; thought. **2** an idea or thought.

intellectual (,ɪntɪ'lɛktʃʊəl) *adj* **1** of or relating to the intellect. **2** appealing to or characteristic of people with a developed intellect: *intellectual literature.* **3** expressing or enjoying mental activity. ◆ *n* **4** a person who enjoys mental activity and has highly developed tastes in art, etc. **5** a person who uses his or her intellect. **6** a highly intelligent person.
▸ **,intel,lectu'ality** *or* **,intel'lectualness** *n* ▸ **,intel'lectual,ize** *or* **,intel'lectual,ise** *vb* ▸ **,intel'lectually** *adv*

intellectualism (,ɪntɪ'lɛktʃʊə,lɪzəm) *n* **1** development and exercise of the intellect. **2** *Philosophy.* the doctrine that reason is the ultimate criterion of knowledge.
▸ **,intel'lectualist** *n, adj* ▸ **,intel,lectual'istic** *adj*

intellectual property *n* an intangible asset, such as a copyright or patent.

intelligence (ɪn'tɛlɪdʒəns) *n* **1** the capacity for understanding; ability to perceive and comprehend meaning. **2** *Old-fashioned.* news; information. **3** military information about enemies, spies, etc. **4** a group or department that gathers or deals with such information. **5** (*often cap.*) an intelligent being, esp. one that is not embodied. **6** (*modifier*) of or relating to intelligence: *an intelligence network.* ORIG C14: from L *intellegentia,* from *intellegere* to discern, lit.: to choose between, from INTER- + *legere* to choose
▸ **in,telli'gential** *adj*

intelligence quotient *n* a measure of the intelligence of an individual. The quotient is derived by dividing an individual's mental age by his chronological age and multiplying the result by 100. Abbrev.: **IQ.**

intelligence test *n* any of a number of tests designed to measure a person's mental skills.

intelligent (ɪn'tɛlɪdʒənt) *adj* **1** having or indicating intelligence; clever. **2** indicating high intelligence; perceptive: *an intelligent guess.* **3** (of computerized functions, weapons, etc.) able to initiate or modify action in the light of ongoing events. **4** (*postpositive;* foll. by *of*) *Arch.* having knowledge or information.
▸ **in'telligently** *adv*

intelligent card *n* another name for **smart card.**

intelligentsia (ɪn,tɛlɪ'dʒɛntsɪə) *n* (usually preceded by *the*) the educated or intellectual people in a society or community. ORIG C20: from Russian *intelligentsiya,* from L *intellegentia* INTELLIGENCE

intelligible (ɪn'tɛlɪdʒəbᵊl) *adj* **1** able to be understood; comprehensible. **2** *Philosophy.* capable of being appre-

hended by the mind or intellect alone. ORIG C14: from L *intellegibilis;* see INTELLECT
▸ **in,telligi'bility** *n* ▸ **in'telligibly** *adv*

intemperate (ɪn'tɛmpərɪt, -prɪt) *adj* **1** consuming alcoholic drink habitually or to excess; immoderate. **2** unrestrained: *intemperate rage.* **3** extreme or severe: *an intemperate climate.*
▸ **in'temperance** *or* **in'temperateness** *n* ▸ **in'temperately** *adv*

intend (ɪn'tɛnd) *vb* **1** (*may take a clause as object*) to propose or plan (something or to do something); have in mind; mean. **2** (*tr;* often foll. by *for*) to design or destine (for a certain purpose, person, etc.). **3** (*tr*) to mean to express or indicate: *what do his words intend?* **4** (*intr*) to have a purpose as specified; mean: *he intends well.* ORIG C14: from L *intendere* to stretch forth, give one's attention to, from *tendere* to stretch
▸ **in'tender** *n*

intendancy (ɪn'tɛndənsɪ) *n* **1** the position or work of an intendant. **2** intendants collectively.

intendant (ɪn'tɛndənt) *n* a senior administrator; superintendent or manager.

intended (ɪn'tɛndɪd) *adj* **1** planned or future. ◆ *n* **2** *Inf.* a person whom one is to marry; fiancé or fiancée.

intense (ɪn'tɛns) *adj* **1** of extreme force, strength, degree, or amount: *intense heat.* **2** characterized by deep or forceful feelings: *an intense person.* ORIG C14: from L *intensus* stretched, from *intendere* to stretch out
▸ **in'tensely** *adv* ▸ **in'tenseness** *n*

USAGE NOTE *Intense* is sometimes wrongly used where *intensive* is meant: *the land is under intensive* (not *intense*) *cultivation. Intensely* is sometimes wrongly used where *intently* is meant: *he listened intently* (not *intensely*).

intensifier (ɪn'tɛnsɪ,faɪə) *n* **1** a person or thing that intensifies. **2** a word, esp. an adjective or adverb, that serves to intensify the meaning of the word or phrase that it modifies. **3** a substance, esp. one containing silver or uranium, used to increase the density of a photographic film or plate.

intensify (ɪn'tɛnsɪ,faɪ) *vb* **intensifies, intensifying, intensified. 1** to make or become intense or more intense. **2** (*tr*) to increase the density of (a photographic film or plate).
▸ **in,tensifi'cation** *n*

intension (ɪn'tɛnʃən) *n Logic.* the set of characteristics or properties that distinguish the referent or referents of a given word.
▸ **in'tensional** *adj*

intensity (ɪn'tɛnsɪtɪ) *n, pl* **intensities. 1** the state or quality of being intense. **2** extreme force, degree, or amount. **3** *Physics.* **3a** a measure of field strength or of the energy transmitted by radiation. **3b** (of sound in a specified direction) the average rate of flow of sound energy for one period through unit area at right angles to the specified direction.

intensive (ɪn'tɛnsɪv) *adj* **1** of, relating to, or characterized by intensity: *intensive training.* **2** (*usually in combination*) using one factor of production proportionately more than others, as specified: *capital-intensive; labour-intensive.* **3** *Agriculture.* involving or farmed using large amounts of capital or labour to increase production from a particular area. Cf. **extensive** (sense 3). **4** denoting or relating to a grammatical intensifier. **5** denoting or belonging to a class of pronouns used to emphasize a noun or personal pronoun. **6** of or relating to intension. ◆ *n* **7** an intensifier or intensive pronoun or grammatical construction.
▸ **in'tensively** *adv* ▸ **in'tensiveness** *n*

USAGE NOTE See at **intense.**

intensive care *n* **1** extensive and continuous care provided for an acutely ill patient in a hospital. **2** the unit in which this care is provided; intensive-care unit.

intent (ɪn'tɛnt) *n* **1** something that is intended; aim; purpose; design. **2** the act of intending. **3** *Law.* the will or purpose with which one does an act. **4** implicit meaning; connotation. **5 to all intents and purposes.** for all practical purposes; virtually. ◆ *adj* **6** firmly fixed; determined; concentrated: *an intent look.* **7** (*postpositive;* usually foll. by *on* or *upon*) having the fixed intention (of); directing one's mind or energy (to): *intent on committing a crime.* ORIG C13 (in the sense: intention): from LL *intentus* aim, from L: a stretching out; see INTEND
▸ **in'tently** *adv* ▸ **in'tentness** *n*

USAGE NOTE See at **intense.**

intention (ɪn'tɛnʃən) *n* **1** a purpose or goal; aim: *it is his intention to reform.* **2** *Med.* a natural healing process in which the edges of a wound cling together with no tissue between (**first intention**), or in which the edges adhere with tissue between (**second intention**). **3** (*usually pl*) design or purpose with respect to a proposal of marriage (esp. in **honourable intentions**).

intentional (ɪn'tɛnʃənᵊl) *adj* **1** performed by or expressing intention; deliberate. **2** of or relating to intention or purpose.
▸ **in,tention'ality** *n* ▸ **in'tentionally** *adv*

inter (ɪn'tɜː) *vb* **inters, interring, interred.** (*tr*) to place (a body, etc.) in the earth; bury, esp. with funeral rites. ORIG C14: from OF *enterrer,* from L IN-[2] + *terra* earth

inter- *prefix* **1** between or among: *international.* **2** together, mutually, or reciprocally: *interdependent; interchange.* ORIG from L

interact (,ɪntər'ækt) *vb* (*intr*) to act on or in close relation with each other.

interaction (,ɪntə'rækʃən) *n* **1** a mutual or reciprocal action. **2** *Physics.* the transfer of energy between elementary particles, between a particle and a field, or between fields. See **fundamental interaction.**

interactive (,ɪntər'æktɪv) *adj* **1** allowing or relating to continuous two-way transfer of information between a user and the central point of a communication system, such as a computer or television. **2** (of two or more persons, forces, etc.) acting upon or in close relation with each other; interacting.

inter alia *Latin.* ('ɪntər 'eɪlɪə) *adv* among other things.

interbreed (,ɪntə'briːd) *vb* **interbreeds, interbreeding, interbred. 1** to breed within a single family or strain so as to produce particular characteristics in the offspring. **2** another term for **crossbreed** (sense 1).

interbroker dealer (,ɪntə'brəʊkə) *n Stock Exchange.* a specialist who matches the needs of different market makers and facilitates dealings between them.

intercalary (ɪn'tɜːkələrɪ) *adj* **1** (of a day, month, year, etc.) inserted in the calendar. **2** (of a particular year) having one or more days inserted. **3** inserted, introduced, or interpolated. ORIG C17: from L *intercalārius;* see INTERCALATE

intercalate (ɪn'tɜːkə,leɪt) *vb* **intercalates, intercalating, intercalated.** (*tr*) **1** to insert (one or more days) into the calendar. **2** to interpolate or insert. ORIG C17: from L *intercalāre* to insert, proclaim that a day has been inserted, from INTER- + *calāre* to proclaim
▸ **in,terca'lation** *n* ▸ **in'tercalative** *adj*

intercede (,ɪntə'siːd) *vb* **intercedes, interceding, interceded.** (*intr;* often foll. by *in*) to come between parties or act as mediator or advocate: *to intercede in the strike.* ORIG C16: from L *intercēdere,* from INTER- + *cēdere* to move
▸ **,inter'ceder** *n*

intercensal (,ɪntə'sɛnsəl) *adj* (of population figures, etc.) estimated at a time between official censuses. ORIG C19: from INTER- + *censal,* irregularly formed from CENSUS

intercept *vb* (,ɪntə'sɛpt). (*tr*) **1** to stop, deflect, or seize on the way from one place to another; prevent from arriving or proceeding. **2** *Sport.* to seize or cut off (a pass) on its way from one opponent to another. **3** *Maths.* to cut off, mark off, or bound (some part of a line, curve, plane, or surface). ◆ *n* ('ɪntə,sɛpt). **4** *Maths.* **4a** a point at which two figures intersect. **4b** the distance from the origin to the point at which a line, curve, or surface cuts a coordi-

nate axis. **5** *Sport, US & Canad.* the act of intercepting an opponent's pass. ORIG C16: from L *intercipere* to seize before arrival, from INTER- + *capere* to take
▸ **ˌinterˈception** *n* ▸ **ˌinterˈceptive** *adj*

interceptor *or* **intercepter** (ˌɪntəˈsɛptə) *n* **1** a person or thing that intercepts. **2** a fast highly manoeuvrable fighter aircraft used to intercept enemy aircraft.

intercession (ˌɪntəˈsɛʃən) *n* **1** the act or an instance of interceding. **2** the act of interceding or offering petitionary prayer to God on behalf of others. **3** such petitionary prayer. ORIG C16: from L *intercessio;* see INTERCEDE
▸ **ˌinterˈcessional** *or* **ˌinterˈcessory** *adj* ▸ **ˌinterˈcessor** *n* ▸ **ˌintercesˈsorial** *adj*

interchange *vb* (ˌɪntəˈtʃeɪndʒ), **interchanges, interchanging, interchanged. 1** to change places or cause to change places; alternate; exchange; switch. ◆ *n* (ˈɪntəˌtʃeɪndʒ). **2** the act of interchanging; exchange or alternation. **3** a motorway junction of interconnecting roads and bridges designed to prevent streams of traffic crossing one another.
▸ **ˌinterˈchangeable** *adj* ▸ **ˌinterˌchangeaˈbility** *or* **ˌinterˈchangeableness** *n* ▸ **ˌinterˈchangeably** *adv*

Intercity (ˌɪntəˈsɪtɪ) *adj* (in Britain) *Trademark.* denoting a fast train or passenger rail service, esp. between main towns.

intercom (ˈɪntəˌkɒm) *n Inf.* an internal telephone system for communicating within a building, aircraft, etc. ORIG C20: short for INTERCOMMUNICATION

intercommunicate (ˌɪntəkəˈmjuːnɪˌkeɪt) *vb* **intercommunicates, intercommunicating, intercommunicated.** (*intr*) **1** to communicate mutually. **2** to interconnect, as two rooms, etc.
▸ **ˌintercomˈmunicable** *adj* ▸ **ˌintercomˌmuniˈcation** *n* ▸ **ˌintercomˈmunicative** *adj*

intercommunion (ˌɪntəkəˈmjuːnjən) *n* association between Churches, involving esp. mutual reception of Holy Communion.

intercontinental (ˌɪntəˌkɒntɪˈnɛntᵊl) *adj* travelling between or linking continents.

interconvertible (ˌɪntəkənˈvɜːtɪbᵊl) *adj* (of two or more things) capable of being converted into each other.

intercostal (ˌɪntəˈkɒstᵊl) *adj Anat.* between the ribs: *intercostal muscles.* ORIG C16: via NL from L INTER- + *costa* rib

intercourse (ˈɪntəˌkɔːs) *n* **1** See **sexual intercourse. 2** communication or exchange between individuals; mutual dealings. ORIG C15: from Med. L *intercursus* business, from L *intercurrere* to run between

intercurrent (ˌɪntəˈkʌrənt) *adj* **1** occurring during or in between; intervening. **2** *Pathol.* (of a disease) occurring during the course of another disease.
▸ **ˌinterˈcurrence** *n*

interdependent (ˌɪntədɪˈpɛndənt) *adj* (of two or more things) dependent on each other.

interdict *n* (ˈɪntəˌdɪkt). **1** *RC Church.* the exclusion of a person in a particular place from certain sacraments, although not from communion. **2** *Civil law.* any order made by a court or official prohibiting an act. **3** *Scots Law.* an order having the effect of an injunction. ◆ *vb* (ˌɪntəˈdɪkt). (*tr*) **4** to place under legal or ecclesiastical sanction; prohibit; forbid. **5** *Mil.* to destroy (an enemy's lines of communication) by firepower. ORIG C13: from L *interdictum* prohibition, from *interdīcere* to forbid, from INTER- + *dīcere* to say
▸ **ˌinterˈdiction** *n* ▸ **ˌinterˈdictive** *or* **ˌinterˈdictory** *adj* ▸ **ˌinterˈdictively** *adv* ▸ **ˌinterˈdictor** *n*

interdigitate (ˌɪntəˈdɪdʒɪˌteɪt) *vb* **interdigitates, interdigitating, interdigitated.** (*intr*) to interlock like the fingers of clasped hands. ORIG C19: from INTER- + L *digitus* (see DIGIT) + -ATE[1]

interdisciplinary (ˌɪntəˈdɪsɪˌplɪnərɪ) *adj* involving two or more academic disciplines.

interest (ˈɪntrɪst, -tərɪst) *n* **1** the sense of curiosity about or concern with something or someone. **2** the power of stimulating such a sense: *to have great interest.* **3** the quality of such stimulation. **4** something in which one is interested; a hobby or pursuit. **5** (*often pl*) benefit; advantage: *in one's own interest.* **6** (*often pl*) a right, share, or claim, esp. in a business or property. **7a** a charge for the use of credit or borrowed money. **7b** such a charge expressed as a percentage per time unit of the sum borrowed or used. **8** (*often pl*) a section of a community, etc., whose members have common aims: *the landed interest.* **9 declare an interest.** to make known one's connection, esp. a prejudicial connection, with an affair. ◆ *vb* (*tr*) **10** to arouse or excite the curiosity or concern of. **11** to cause to become involved in something; concern. ORIG C15: from L: it concerns, from *interesse,* from INTER- + *esse* to be

interested (ˈɪntrɪstɪd, -tərɪs-) *adj* **1** showing or having interest. **2** (*usually prenominal*) personally involved or implicated: *the interested parties met to discuss the business.*
▸ **ˈinterestedly** *adv* ▸ **ˈinterestedness** *n*

interesting (ˈɪntrɪstɪŋ, -tərɪs-) *adj* inspiring interest; absorbing.
▸ **ˈinterestingly** *adv* ▸ **ˈinterestingness** *n*

interest-rate futures *pl n* financial futures based on projected movements of interest rates.

interface *n* (ˈɪntəˌfeɪs). **1** *Physical chem.* a surface that forms the boundary between two liquids or chemical phases. **2** a common point or boundary between two things. **3** an electrical circuit linking one device, esp. a computer, with another. ◆ *vb* (ˌɪntəˈfeɪs), **interfaces, interfacing, interfaced. 4** (*tr*) to design or adapt the input and output configurations of (two electronic devices) so that they may work together compatibly. **5** to be an interface (with). **6** to be interactive (with).
▸ **interfacial** (ˌɪntəˈfeɪʃəl) *adj* ▸ **ˌinterˈfacially** *adv*

interfacing (ˈɪntəˌfeɪsɪŋ) *n* **1** a piece of fabric sewn beneath the facing of a garment, usually at the inside of the neck, armholes, etc., to give shape and firmness. **2** another name for **interlining.**

interfere (ˌɪntəˈfɪə) *vb* **interferes, interfering, interfered.** (*intr*) **1** (often foll. by *in*) to interpose, esp. meddlesomely or unwarrantedly; intervene. **2** (often foll. by *with*) to come between or into opposition; hinder. **3** (foll. by *with*) *Euphemistic.* to assault sexually. **4** to strike one against the other, as a horse's legs. **5** *Physics.* to cause or produce interference. ORIG C16: from OF *s'entreferir* to collide, from *entre-* INTER- + *ferir* to strike, from L *ferīre*
▸ **ˌinterˈfering** *adj*

interference (ˌɪntəˈfɪərəns) *n* **1** the act or an instance of interfering. **2** *Physics.* the process in which two or more coherent waves combine to form a resultant wave in which the displacement at any point is the vector sum of the displacements of the individual waves. **3** any undesired signal that tends to interfere with the reception of radio waves.
▸ **interferential** (ˌɪntəfəˈrɛnʃəl) *adj*

interferometer (ˌɪntəfəˈrɒmɪtə) *n Physics.* any acoustic, optical, or microwave instrument that uses interference patterns to make accurate measurements of wavelength, distance, etc.
▸ **interferometric** (ˌɪntəˌfɛrəˈmɛtrɪk) *adj* ▸ **ˌinterˌferoˈmetrically** *adv* ▸ **ˌinterferˈometry** *n*

interferon (ˌɪntəˈfɪərɒn) *n Biochem.* any of a family of proteins made by cells in response to virus infection that prevent the growth of the virus. ORIG C20: from INTERFERE + -ON

interfuse (ˌɪntəˈfjuːz) *vb* **interfuses, interfusing, interfused. 1** to diffuse or mix throughout or become so diffused or mixed; intermingle. **2** to blend or fuse or become blended or fused.
▸ **ˌinterˈfusion** *n*

intergovernmental (ˌɪntəˌgʌvənˈmɛntᵊl) *adj* conducted between or involving two or more governments.

interim (ˈɪntərɪm) *adj* **1** (*prenominal*) temporary, provisional, or intervening: *interim measures to deal with the emergency.* ◆ *n* **2** (usually preceded by *the*) the intervening time; the meantime (esp. in **in the interim**). ◆ *adv* **3** *Rare.* meantime. ORIG C16: from L: meanwhile

interior (ɪnˈtɪərɪə) *n* **1** a part, surface, or region that is inside or on the inside: *the interior of Africa.* **2** inner character or nature. **3** a film or scene shot inside a building, studio, etc. **4** a picture of the inside of a room or building, as in a painting or stage design. **5** the inside of a

building or room, with respect to design and decoration. ◆ *adj* **6** of, situated on, or suitable for the inside; inner. **7** coming or acting from within; internal. **8** of or involving a nation's domestic affairs; internal. **9** (esp. of one's spiritual or mental life) secret or private; not observable. ORIG C15: from L (adj), comp. of *inter* within
▸ **in'teriorly** *adv*

interior angle *n* an angle of a polygon contained between two adjacent sides.

interior decoration *n* **1** the colours, furniture, etc., of the interior of a house, etc. **2** Also called: **interior design.** the art or business of planning the interiors of houses, etc.
▸ **interior decorator** *n*

interiorize *or* **interiorise** (ɪn'tɪərɪəˌraɪz) *vb* **interiorizes, interiorizing, interiorized** *or* **interiorises, interiorising, interiorised.** (*tr*) another word for **internalize.**

interj. *abbrev. for* interjection.

interject (ˌɪntə'dʒɛkt) *vb* (*tr*) to interpose abruptly or sharply; interrupt with; throw in: *she interjected clever remarks.* ORIG C16: from L *interjicere* to place between, from *jacere* to throw
▸ **ˌinter'jector** *n*

interjection (ˌɪntə'dʒɛkʃən) *n* **1** the act of interjecting. **2** a word or phrase that is used in syntactic isolation and that expresses sudden emotion; expletive. Abbrev.: **interj.**
▸ **ˌinter'jectional** *or* **ˌinter'jectory** *adj* ▸ **ˌinter'jectionally** *adv*

Interlaken ★ ('ɪntəˌlɑːkən) *n* a town and resort in central Switzerland, situated between Lakes Brienz and Thun on the River Aar. Pop.: 4900 (1987 est.).

interlard (ˌɪntə'lɑːd) *vb* (*tr*) **1** to scatter thickly in or between; intersperse: *to interlard one's writing with foreign phrases.* **2** to occur frequently in; be scattered in or through: *foreign phrases interlard his writings.*

interlay (ˌɪntə'leɪ) *vb* **interlays, interlaying, interlaid.** (*tr*) to insert (layers) between; interpose.

interleaf ('ɪntəˌliːf) *n, pl* **interleaves.** a blank leaf inserted between the leaves of a book.

interleave (ˌɪntə'liːv) *vb* **interleaves, interleaving, interleaved.** (*tr*) **1** (often foll. by *with*) to intersperse (with), esp. alternately, as the illustrations in a book (with protective leaves). **2** to provide (a book) with blank leaves for notes, etc., or to protect illustrations.

interleukin (ˌɪntə'luːkɪn) *n* a substance extracted from white blood cells that stimulates their activity against infection and may be used to combat some forms of cancer.

interline[1] (ˌɪntə'laɪn) *or* **interlineate** (ˌɪntə'lɪnɪˌeɪt) *vb* **interlines, interlining, interlined** *or* **interlineates, interlineating, interlineated.** (*tr*) to write or print (matter) between the lines of (a text, book, etc.).
▸ **'interˌlining** *or* **ˌinterˌline'ation** *n*

interline[2] (ˌɪntə'laɪn) *vb* **interlines, interlining, interlined.** (*tr*) to provide (a part of a garment) with a second lining, esp. of stiffened material.
▸ **'interˌliner** *n*

interlinear (ˌɪntə'lɪnɪə) *or* **interlineal** *adj* **1** written or printed between lines of text. **2** written or printed with the text in different languages or versions on alternate lines.
▸ **ˌinter'linearly** *or* **ˌinter'lineally** *adv*

interlining ('ɪntəˌlaɪnɪŋ) *n* the material used to interline parts of garments, now often made of reinforced paper.

interlock *vb* (ˌɪntə'lɒk). **1** to join or be joined firmly, as by a mutual interconnection of parts. ◆ *n* ('ɪntəˌlɒk). **2** the act of interlocking or the state of being interlocked. **3** a device, esp. one operated electromechanically, used in a logic circuit to prevent an activity being initiated unless preceded by certain events. **4** a closely knitted fabric. ◆ *adj* **5** closely knitted.
▸ **'interˌlocker** *n*

interlocutor (ˌɪntə'lɒkjʊtə) *n* **1** a person who takes part in a conversation. **2** the man in the centre of a troupe of minstrels who engages the others in talk or acts as announcer. **3** *Scots Law.* a decree by a judge.
▸ **ˌinter'locutress, ˌinter'locutrice,** *or* **ˌinter'locutrix** *fem n*

interlocutory (ˌɪntə'lɒkjʊtərɪ, -trɪ) *adj* **1** *Law.* pronounced during the course of proceedings; provisional: *an interlocutory injunction.* **2** interposed, as into a conversation, narrative, etc. **3** of, relating to, or characteristic of dialogue.
▸ **ˌinter'locutorily** *adv*

interloper ('ɪntəˌləʊpə) *n* **1** an intruder. **2** a person who introduces himself or herself into professional or social circles where he or she does not belong. **3** a person who interferes in matters that are not his or her concern. ORIG C17: from INTER- + *loper*, from MDu. *loopen* to leap
▸ **ˌinter'lope** *vb* (*intr*)

interlude ('ɪntəˌluːd) *n* **1** a period of time or different activity between longer periods, processes, or events; episode or interval. **2** *Theatre.* a short dramatic piece played separately or as part of a longer entertainment, common in 16th-century England. **3** a brief piece of music, dance, etc., given between the sections of another performance. ORIG C14: from Med. L, from L INTER- + *lūdus* play

intermarry (ˌɪntə'mærɪ) *vb* **intermarries, intermarrying, intermarried.** (*intr*) **1** (of different races, religions, etc.) to become connected by marriage. **2** to marry within one's own family, clan, group, etc.
▸ **ˌinter'marriage** *n*

intermediary (ˌɪntə'miːdɪərɪ) *n, pl* **intermediaries. 1** a person who acts as a mediator or agent between parties. **2** something that acts as a medium or means. ◆ *adj* **3** acting as an intermediary. **4** situated, acting, or coming between.

intermediate *adj* (ˌɪntə'miːdɪɪt). **1** occurring or situated between two points, extremes, places, etc.; in between. **2** (of a class, course, etc.) suitable for learners with some degree of skill or competence. ◆ *n* (ˌɪntə'miːdɪɪt). **3** something intermediate. **4** a substance formed during one of the stages of a chemical process before the desired product is obtained. ◆ *vb* (ˌɪntə'miːdɪˌeɪt), **intermediates, intermediating, intermediated. 5** (*intr*) to act as an intermediary or mediator. ORIG C17: from Med. L *intermediāre* to intervene, from L INTER- + *medius* middle
▸ **ˌinter'mediacy** *or* **ˌinter'mediateness** *n* ▸ **ˌinter'mediately** *adv* ▸ **ˌinterˌmedi'ation** *n* ▸ **ˌinter'mediˌator** *n*

intermediate-acting *adj* (of a drug) intermediate in its effects between long- and short-acting drugs. Cf. **long-acting, short-acting.**

intermediate frequency *n Electronics.* the frequency to which the signal carrier frequency is changed in a superheterodyne receiver and at which most of the amplification takes place.

intermediate-level waste *n* radioactive waste material, such as reactor components, that can be mixed with concrete and safely stored in steel drums in deep mines or beneath the seabed in concrete chambers. Cf. **high-level waste, low-level waste.**

intermediate technology *n* technology that implements sophisticated technical ideas using readily available cheap materials and resources, esp. for use in developing countries.

intermediate vector boson *n Physics.* a hypothetical particle believed to mediate the weak interaction between elementary particles.

interment (ɪn'tɜːmənt) *n* burial, esp. with ceremonial rites.

intermezzo (ˌɪntə'mɛtsəʊ) *n, pl* **intermezzos** *or* **intermezzi** (-tsiː). **1** a short piece of instrumental music composed for performance between the acts or scenes of an opera, drama, etc. **2** an instrumental piece either inserted between two longer movements in an extended composition or intended for independent performance. ORIG C19: from It., from LL *intermedium* interval; see INTERMEDIATE

interminable (ɪn'tɜːmɪnəbᵊl) *adj* endless or seemingly endless because of monotony or tiresome length.
▸ **in'terminableness** *n* ▸ **in'terminably** *adv*

intermission (ˌɪntə'mɪʃən) *n* **1** an interval, as between parts of a film, etc. **2** a period between events or activities; pause. **3** the act of intermitting or the state of being

intermitted. ORIG C16: from L, from *intermittere* to INTERMIT
▸ ˌinterˈmissive *adj*

intermit (ˌɪntəˈmɪt) *vb* **intermits, intermitting, intermitted.** to suspend (activity) or (of activity) to be suspended temporarily or at intervals. ORIG C16: from L *intermittere* to leave off, from INTER- + *mittere* to send
▸ ˌinterˈmittor *n*

intermittent (ˌɪntəˈmɪtᵊnt) *adj* occurring occasionally or at regular or irregular intervals; periodic.
▸ ˌinterˈmittence *or* ˌinterˈmittency *n* ▸ ˌinterˈmittently *adv*

intermix (ˌɪntəˈmɪks) *vb* **1** (*tr*) to mix (ingredients, liquids, etc.) together. **2** (*intr*) to become or have the capacity to become combined, joined, etc.

intermixture (ˌɪntəˈmɪkstʃə) *n* **1** the act of intermixing or state of being intermixed. **2** an additional ingredient.

intern *vb* **1** (ɪnˈtɜːn). (*tr*) to detain or confine within a country or a limited area, esp. during wartime. **2** (ˈɪntɜːn). (*intr*) *Chiefly US.* to serve or train as an intern. ◆ *n* (ˈɪntɜːn). **3** another word for **internee. 4** Also: **interne.** the approximate US and Canad. equivalent of **houseman. 5** Also: **interne.** *Chiefly US.* a student teacher. **6** Also: **interne.** *Chiefly US.* a student or recent graduate undergoing practical training in a working environment. ORIG C19: from L *internus* internal
▸ inˈternment *n* ▸ ˈinternship *or* ˈinterneship *n*

internal (ɪnˈtɜːnᵊl) *adj* **1** of, situated on, or suitable for the inside; inner. **2** coming or acting from within; interior. **3** involving the spiritual or mental life; subjective. **4** of or involving a nation's domestic as opposed to foreign affairs. **5** situated within, affecting, or relating to the inside of the body. ◆ *n* **6** *Euphemistic.* a medical examination of the vagina or uterus. ORIG C16: from Med. L, from LL *internus* inward
▸ ˌinterˈnality *or* inˈternalness *n* ▸ inˈternally *adv*

internal-combustion engine *n* a heat engine in which heat is supplied by burning the fuel in the working fluid (usually air).

internal energy *n* the thermodynamic property of a system that changes by an amount equal to the work done on the system when it suffers an adiabatic change.

internalize *or* **internalise** (ɪnˈtɜːnəˌlaɪz) *vb* **internalizes, internalizing, internalized** *or* **internalises, internalising, internalised.** (*tr*) *Psychol., sociol.* to make internal, esp. to incorporate within oneself (values, attitudes, etc.) through learning or socialization. Also: **interiorize.**
▸ inˌternaliˈzation *or* inˌternaliˈsation *n*

internal market *n* a system in which goods and services are sold by the provider to a range of purchasers within the same organization, who compete to establish the price of the product.

internal medicine *n* the branch of medical science concerned with the diagnosis and nonsurgical treatment of disorders of the internal structures of the body.

international (ˌɪntəˈnæʃənᵊl) *adj* **1** of, concerning, or involving two or more nations or nationalities. **2** established by, controlling, or legislating for several nations: *an international court.* **3** available for use by all nations: *international waters.* ◆ *n* **4** *Sport.* **4a** a contest between two national teams. **4b** a member of a national team.
▸ ˌinterˌnationˈality *n* ▸ ˌinterˈnationally *adv*

International (ˌɪntəˈnæʃənᵊl) *n* **1** any of several international socialist organizations, esp. **First International** (1864–76) and **Second International** (1889 until World War I). **2** a member of any of these organizations.

International Atomic Time *n* the scientific standard of time based on the SI unit, the second, used to synchronize the time standards of the major nations. Abbrev.: **TAI.**

International Bank for Reconstruction and Development *n* the official name for the **World Bank.**

International Court of Justice *n* a court established in the Hague, in the Netherlands, to settle disputes brought by nations that are parties to the Statute of the Court. Also called: **World Court.**

International Date Line *n* the line approximately following the 180° meridian from Greenwich on the east side of which the date is one day earlier than on the west.

internationalism (ˌɪntəˈnæʃənəˌlɪzəm) *n* **1** the ideal or practice of cooperation and understanding between nations. **2** the state or quality of being international.
▸ ˌinterˈnationalist *n*

internationalize *or* **internationalise** (ˌɪntəˈnæʃənəˌlaɪz) *vb* **internationalizes, internationalizing, internationalized** *or* **internationalises, internationalising, internationalised.** (*tr*) **1** to make international. **2** to put under international control.
▸ ˌinterˌnationaliˈzation *or* ˌinterˌnationaliˈsation *n*

international law *n* the body of rules generally recognized by civilized nations as governing their conduct towards each other.

International Modernism *n* See **International Style.**

International Phonetic Alphabet *n* a series of signs and letters for the representation of human speech sounds. It is based on the Roman alphabet but supplemented by modified signs or symbols from other writing systems.

International Practical Temperature Scale *n* a temperature scale adopted by international agreement in 1968 based on thermodynamic temperature and using experimental values to define 11 fixed points.

International Space Station Alpha *n* an orbiting space station constructed between 1998 and 2001 with the cooperation of 16 nations, used for scientific and space research.

International Style *or* **Modernism** *n* an architectural style of the 1920s that used cubic forms, large windows, and modern materials.

International Telecommunications Union *n* a special agency of the United Nations, founded in 1947, that is responsible for the international allocation and registration of frequencies for communications and the regulation of telegraph, telephone, and radio services.

interne (ˈɪntɜːn) *n* a variant spelling of **intern** (senses 4, 5, 6).

internecine (ˌɪntəˈniːsaɪn) *adj* **1** mutually destructive or ruinous; maiming both or all sides: *internecine war.* **2** of or relating to slaughter or carnage; bloody. **3** of or involving conflict within a group or organization. ORIG C17: from L, from *internecāre* to destroy, from *necāre* to kill

internee (ˌɪntɜːˈniː) *n* a person who is interned, esp. an enemy citizen in wartime or a terrorism suspect.

Internet (ˈɪntəˌnɛt) *n* **the.** (*also not cap.*) the single worldwide computer network that interconnects other computer networks, on which end-user services, such as World Wide Web sites or data archives, are located, enabling data and other information to be exchanged. Also called: **the Net.**

internist (ˈɪntɜːnɪst, ɪnˈtɜːnɪst) *n* a physician who specializes in internal medicine.

interpellate (ɪnˈtɜːpɛˌleɪt) *vb* **interpellates, interpellating, interpellated.** (*tr*) *Parliamentary procedure.* (in European legislatures) to question (a member of the government) on a point of government policy, often interrupting the business of the day. ORIG C16: from L *interpellāre* to disturb, from INTER- + *pellere* to push
▸ inˌterpelˈlation *n* ▸ inˈterpelˌlator *n*

interpenetrate (ˌɪntəˈpɛnɪˌtreɪt) *vb* **interpenetrates, interpenetrating, interpenetrated. 1** to penetrate (something) thoroughly; pervade. **2** to penetrate each other or one another mutually.
▸ ˌinterˈpenetrable *adj* ▸ ˌinterˈpenetrant *adj* ▸ ˌinterˌpeneˈtration *n* ▸ ˌinterˈpenetrative *adj* ▸ ˌinterˈpenetratively *adv*

interplay (ˈɪntəˌpleɪ) *n* reciprocal and mutual action and reaction, as in circumstances, events, or personal relations.

interpleader (ˌɪntəˈpliːdə) *n Law.* **1** a process by which a person holding money claimed by two or more parties and having no interest in it himself can require the claimants to litigate with each other. **2** a person who interpleads.

Interpol (ˈɪntəˌpɒl) *n acronym for* International Criminal Police Organization, an association of over 100 national police forces, devoted to fighting international crime.

interpolate (ɪnˈtɜːpəˌleɪt) *vb* **interpolates, interpolating, interpolated. 1** to insert or introduce (a comment, passage,

etc.) into (a conversation, text, etc.). **2** to falsify or alter (a text, manuscript, etc.) by the later addition of (material, esp. spurious passages). **3** (*intr*) to make additions, interruptions, or insertions. **4** *Maths.* to estimate (a value of a function) between the values already known or determined. Cf. **extrapolate** (sense 1). ORIG C17: from L *interpolāre* to give a new appearance to
▸ **in'terpo,later** *or* **in'terpo,lator** *n* ▸ **in'terpolative** *adj*

interpose (ˌɪntəˈpəʊz) *vb* **interposes, interposing, interposed.** **1** to put or place between or among other things. **2** to introduce (comments, questions, etc.) into a speech or conversation; interject. **3** to exert or use influence or action in order to alter or intervene in (a situation). ORIG C16: from OF, from L *interpōnere,* from INTER- + *pōnere* to put
▸ **ˌinter'posal** *n* ▸ **ˌinter'poser** *n* ▸ **ˌinterpo'sition** *n*

interpret (ɪnˈtɜːprɪt) *vb* **1** (*tr*) to clarify or explain the meaning of; elucidate. **2** (*tr*) to construe the significance or intention of. **3** (*tr*) to convey the spirit or meaning of (a poem, song, etc.) in performance. **4** (*intr*) to act as an interpreter; translate orally. ORIG C14: from L *interpretārī,* from *interpres* negotiator, one who explains
▸ **in'terpretable** *adj* ▸ **in,terpreta'bility** *or* **in'terpretableness** *n* ▸ **in'terpretably** *adv* ▸ **in'terpretive** *adj*

interpretation (ɪnˌtɜːprɪˈteɪʃən) *n* **1** the act or process of interpreting or explaining; elucidation. **2** the result of interpreting; an explanation. **3** a particular view of an artistic work, esp. as expressed by stylistic individuality in its performance. **4** explanation, as of a historical site, provided by the use of original objects, visual display material, etc.
▸ **in,terpre'tational** *adj*

interpreter (ɪnˈtɜːprɪtə) *n* **1** a person who translates orally from one language into another. **2** a person who interprets the work of others. **3** *Computing.* a program that translates a statement in a source program to machine code and executes it before translating and executing the next statement.
▸ **in'terpretership** *n* ▸ **in'terpretress** *fem n*

interpretive centre *n* (at a historical site, etc.) a building that provides interpretation of the site through a variety of media, such as video displays and exhibitions, and, often, includes facilities such as refreshment rooms.

interregnum (ˌɪntəˈrɛgnəm) *n, pl* **interregnums** *or* **interregna** (-nə). **1** an interval between two reigns, governments, etc. **2** any period in which a state lacks a ruler, government, etc. **3** a period of absence of some control, authority, etc. **4** a gap in a continuity. ORIG C16: from L, from INTER- + *regnum* REIGN
▸ **ˌinter'regnal** *adj*

interrelate (ˌɪntərɪˈleɪt) *vb* **interrelates, interrelating, interrelated.** to place in or come into a mutual or reciprocal relationship.
▸ **ˌinterre'lation** *n* ▸ **ˌinterre'lation,ship** *n*

interrogate (ɪnˈtɛrəˌgeɪt) *vb* **interrogates, interrogating, interrogated.** to ask questions (of), esp. to question (a witness in court, spy, etc.) closely. ORIG C15: from L *interrogāre,* from *rogāre* to ask
▸ **in'terro,gator** *n*

interrogation (ɪnˌtɛrəˈgeɪʃən) *n* **1** the technique, practice, or an instance of interrogating. **2** a question or query. **3** *Telecomm.* the transmission of one or more triggering pulses to a transponder.
▸ **in,terro'gational** *adj*

interrogation mark *n* a less common term for **question mark.**

interrogative (ˌɪntəˈrɒgətɪv) *adj* **1** asking or having the nature of a question. **2** denoting a form or construction used in asking a question. **3** denoting or belonging to a class of words, such as *which* and *whom,* that serve to question which individual referent is intended. ◆ *n* **4** an interrogative word, phrase, sentence, or construction. **5** a question mark.
▸ **ˌinter'rogatively** *adv*

interrogatory (ˌɪntəˈrɒgətərɪ, -trɪ) *adj* **1** expressing or involving a question. ◆ *n, pl* **interrogatories. 2** a question or interrogation.

interrupt (ˌɪntəˈrʌpt) *vb* **1** to break the continuity of (an action, event, etc.) or hinder (a person) by intrusion. **2** (*tr*) to cease to perform (some action). **3** (*tr*) to obstruct (a view, etc.). **4** to prevent or disturb (a conversation, discussion, etc.) by questions, interjections, or comment. ORIG C15: from L *interrumpere,* from INTER- + *rumpere* to break
▸ **ˌinter'ruptible** *adj* ▸ **ˌinter'ruptive** *adj* ▸ **ˌinter'ruptively** *adv* ▸ **ˌinter'rupted** *adj*

interrupted screw *n* a screw with a slot cut into the thread, esp. one used in the breech of some guns permitting both engagement and release of the block by a partial turn of the screw.

interrupter *or* **interruptor** (ˌɪntəˈrʌptə) *n* **1** a person or thing that interrupts. **2** an electromechanical device for opening and closing an electric circuit.

interruption (ˌɪntəˈrʌpʃən) *n* **1** something that interrupts, such as a comment, question, or action. **2** an interval or intermission. **3** the act of interrupting or the state of being interrupted.

interscholastic (ˌɪntəskəˈlæstɪk) *adj* **1** (of sports events, competitions, etc.) occurring between two or more schools. **2** representative of various schools.

intersect (ˌɪntəˈsɛkt) *vb* **1** to divide, cut, or mark off by passing through or across. **2** (esp. of roads) to cross (each other). **3** *Maths.* (often foll. by *with*) to have one or more points in common (with another configuration). ORIG C17: from L *intersecāre* to divide, from INTER- + *secāre* to cut

intersection (ˌɪntəˈsɛkʃən, ˈɪntəˌsɛk-) *n* **1** a point at which things intersect, esp. a road junction. **2** the act of intersecting or the state of being intersected. **3** *Maths.* **3a** a point or set of points common to two or more geometric configurations. **3b** Also called: **product.** the set of elements that are common to two sets. **3c** the operation that yields that set from a pair of given sets.
▸ **ˌinter'sectional** *adj*

intersex (ˈɪntəˌsɛks) *n Zool.* an individual with characteristics intermediate between those of a male and a female.

intersexual (ˌɪntəˈsɛksjʊəl) *adj* **1** occurring or existing between the sexes. **2** relating to or being an intersex.
▸ **ˌinter,sexu'ality** *n* ▸ **ˌinter'sexually** *adv*

interspace *vb* (ˌɪntəˈspeɪs), **interspaces, interspacing, interspaced. 1** (*tr*) to make or occupy a space between. ◆ *n* (ˈɪntəˌspeɪs). **2** space between or among things.
▸ **interspatial** (ˌɪntəˈspeɪʃəl) *adj* ▸ **ˌinter'spatially** *adv*

intersperse (ˌɪntəˈspɜːs) *vb* **intersperses, interspersing, interspersed.** (*tr*) **1** to scatter or distribute among, between, or on. **2** to diversify (something) with other things scattered here and there. ORIG C16: from L *interspargere,* from INTER- + *spargere* to sprinkle
▸ **interspersedly** (ˌɪntəˈspɜːsɪdlɪ) *adv* ▸ **interspersion** (ˌɪntəˈspɜːʃən) *or* **ˌinter'spersal** *n*

interstate (ˈɪntəˌsteɪt) *n US.* a motorway crossing between states.

interstellar (ˌɪntəˈstɛlə) *adj* between or among stars.

interstice (ɪnˈtɜːstɪs) *n* (*usually pl*) **1** a minute opening or crevice between things. **2** *Physics.* the space between adjacent atoms in a crystal lattice. ORIG C17: from L *interstitium* interval, from *intersistere,* from INTER- + *sistere* to stand

interstitial (ˌɪntəˈstɪʃəl) *adj* **1** of or relating to an interstice or interstices. **2** *Physics.* forming or occurring in an interstice: *an interstitial atom.* **3** *Anat., zool.* occurring in the spaces between organs, tissues, etc.: *interstitial cells.* ◆ *n* **4** *Chem.* an atom or ion situated in the interstices of a crystal lattice.
▸ **ˌinter'stitially** *adv*

intertrigo (ˌɪntəˈtraɪgəʊ) *n* chafing between two skin surfaces, as at the armpit. ORIG C18: from INTER- + *-trigo,* from L *terere* to rub

interval (ˈɪntəvəl) *n* **1** the period of time between two events, instants, etc. **2** the distance between two points, objects, etc. **3** a pause or interlude, as between periods of intense activity. **4** *Brit.* a short period between parts of a play, etc.; intermission. **5** *Music.* the difference of pitch between two notes, either sounded simultaneously or in succession as in a musical part. **6** the ratio of the fre-

quencies of two sounds. **7 at intervals. 7a** occasionally or intermittently. **7b** with spaces between. ORIG C13: from L *intervallum,* lit.: space between two palisades, from INTER- + *vallum* palisade
▸ **intervallic** (ˌɪntəˈvælɪk) *adj*

intervene (ˌɪntəˈviːn) *vb* **intervenes, intervening, intervened.** (*intr*) **1** (often foll. by *in*) to take a decisive or intrusive role (in) in order to determine events. **2** (foll. by *in* or *between*) to come or be (among or between). **3** (of a period of time) to occur between events or points in time. **4** (of an event) to disturb or hinder a course of action. **5** *Econ.* to take action to affect the market forces of an economy, esp. to maintain the stability of a currency. **6** *Law.* to interpose and become a party to a legal action between others, esp. in order to protect one's interests. ORIG C16: from L *intervenīre* to come between
▸ **ˌinterˈvener** *or* **ˌinterˈvenor** *n*

intervention (ˌɪntəˈvɛnʃən) *n* **1** an act of intervening. **2** any interference in the affairs of others, esp. by one state in the affairs of another. **3** *Econ.* the action of a central bank in supporting the international value of a currency by buying large quantities of the currency to keep the price up. **4** *Commerce.* the action of the EU in buying up surplus produce when the market price drops to a certain value.

interventionist (ˌɪntəˈvɛnʃənɪst) *adj* **1** of, relating to, or advocating intervention, esp. in order to achieve a policy objective. ◆ *n* **2** a person or state that pursues a policy of intervention.

intervertebral disc (ˌɪntəˈvɜːtɪbrəl) *n* any of the cartilaginous discs between individual vertebrae, acting as shock absorbers.

interview (ˈɪntəˌvjuː) *n* **1** a conversation with or questioning of a person, usually conducted for television or a newspaper. **2** a formal discussion, esp. one in which an employer assesses a job applicant. ◆ *vb* **3** to conduct an interview with (someone). ORIG C16: from OF *entrevue*
▸ **ˌinterviewˈee** *n* ▸ **ˈinterˌviewer** *n*

inter vivos *Latin.* (ˈɪntə ˈviːvɒs) *adj Law.* between living people: *an inter vivos gift.*

interwar (ˌɪntəˈwɔː) *adj* of or happening in the period between World War I and World War II.

intestate (ɪnˈtɛsteɪt, -tɪt) *adj* **1a** (of a person) not having made a will. **1b** (of property) not disposed of by will. ◆ *n* **2** a person who dies without having made a will. ORIG C14: from L *intestātus,* from IN-[1] + *testārī* to bear witness, make a will, from *testis* a witness
▸ **inˈtestacy** *n*

intestine (ɪnˈtɛstɪn) *n* the part of the alimentary canal between the stomach and the anus. See **large intestine, small intestine.** ORIG C16: from L *intestīnum* gut, from *intestīnus* internal, from *intus* within
▸ **intestinal** (ɪnˈtɛstɪnᵊl, ˌɪntɛsˈtaɪnᵊl) *adj*

inti (ˈɪntɪ) *n* a former monetary unit of Peru. ORIG C20: from Quechua

intifada (ˌɪntɪˈfɑːdə) *n* a Palestinian uprising against Israel in the West Bank and Gaza Strip. Two uprisings have occurred, one starting in 1987 and the other in 2000. ORIG C20: from Ar., lit.: uprising

intimacy (ˈɪntɪməsɪ) *n, pl* **intimacies. 1** close or warm friendship or understanding; personal relationship. **2** (*often pl*) *Euphemistic.* sexual relations.

intimate[1] (ˈɪntɪmɪt) *adj* **1** characterized by a close or warm personal relationship: *an intimate friend.* **2** deeply personal, private, or secret. **3** (*often postpositive;* foll. by *with*) *Euphemistic.* having sexual relations (with). **4** (*postpositive;* foll. by *with*) having a deep or unusual knowledge (of). **5** having a friendly, warm, or informal atmosphere: *an intimate nightclub.* **6** of or relating to the essential part or nature of something; intrinsic. ◆ *n* **7** a close friend. ORIG C17: from L *intimus* very close friend, from (adj): innermost, from *intus* within
▸ **ˈintimately** *adv* ▸ **ˈintimateness** *n*

intimate[2] (ˈɪntɪˌmeɪt) *vb* **intimates, intimating, intimated.** (*tr; may take a clause as object*) **1** to hint; suggest. **2** to proclaim; make known. ORIG C16: from LL *intimāre* to proclaim, from L *intimus* innermost
▸ **ˈintiˌmater** *n* ▸ **ˌintiˈmation** *n*

intimidate (ɪnˈtɪmɪˌdeɪt) *vb* **intimidates, intimidating, intimidated.** (*tr*) **1** to make timid or frightened; scare. **2** to discourage, restrain, or silence unscrupulously, as by threats. ORIG C17: from Med. L *intimidāre,* from L IN-[2] + *timidus* fearful, from *timor* fear
▸ **ˌinˈtimiˌdating** *adj* ▸ **inˌtimiˈdation** *n* ▸ **inˈtimiˌdator** *n*

intinction (ɪnˈtɪŋkʃən) *n Christianity.* the practice of dipping the Eucharistic bread into the wine at Holy Communion. ORIG C16: from LL *intinctiō* a dipping in, from L *intingere,* from *tingere* to dip

intitule (ɪnˈtɪtjuːl) *vb* **intitules, intituling, intituled.** (*tr*) *Parliamentary procedure.* (in Britain) to entitle (an Act). ORIG C15: from OF *intituler,* from L *titulus* TITLE

intl *abbrev. for* international.

into (ˈɪntuː; *unstressed* ˈɪntə) *prep* **1** to the interior or inner parts of: *to look into a case.* **2** to the middle or midst of so as to be surrounded by: *into the bushes.* **3** against; up against: *he drove into a wall.* **4** used to indicate the result of a change: *he changed into a monster.* **5** *Maths.* used to indicate a dividend: *three into six is two.* **6** *Inf.* interested or enthusiastically involved in: *I'm really into Freud.*

intonation (ˌɪntəʊˈneɪʃən) *n* **1** the sound pattern of phrases and sentences produced by pitch variation in the voice. **2** the act or manner of intoning. **3** an intoned, chanted, or monotonous utterance; incantation. **4** *Music.* the opening of a piece of plainsong, sung by a soloist. **5** *Music.* the capacity to play or sing in tune.
▸ **ˌintoˈnational** *adj*

intone (ɪnˈtəʊn) *or* **intonate** *vb* **intones, intoning, intoned** *or* **intonates, intonating, intonated. 1** to utter, recite, or sing (a chant, prayer, etc.) in a monotonous or incantatory tone. **2** (*intr*) to speak with a particular or characteristic intonation or tone. **3** to sing (the opening phrase of a psalm, etc.) in plainsong. ORIG C15: from Med. L *intonare,* from IN-[2] + TONE
▸ **inˈtoner** *n*

in toto *Latin.* (ɪn ˈtəʊtəʊ) *adv* totally; entirely.

intoxicant (ɪnˈtɒksɪkənt) *n* **1** anything that causes intoxication. ◆ *adj* **2** causing intoxication.

intoxicate (ɪnˈtɒksɪˌkeɪt) *vb* **intoxicates, intoxicating, intoxicated.** (*tr*) **1** (of an alcoholic drink) to produce in (a person) a state ranging from euphoria to stupor; make drunk; inebriate. **2** to stimulate, excite, or elate so as to overwhelm. **3** (of a drug, etc.) to poison. ORIG C16: from Med. L, from *intoxicāre* to poison, from L *toxicum* poison; see TOXIC
▸ **inˈtoxicable** *adj* ▸ **inˈtoxiˌcating** *adj* ▸ **inˈtoxiˌcatingly** *adv*

intoxication (ɪnˌtɒksɪˈkeɪʃən) *n* **1** drunkenness; inebriation. **2** great elation. **3** the act of intoxicating. **4** poisoning.

intr. *abbrev. for* intransitive.

intra- *prefix* within; inside: *intrastate; intravenous.* ORIG from L *intrā* within; see INTERIOR

Intracoastal Waterway (ˌɪntrəˈkəʊstᵊl) ★ *n* short for **Atlantic Intracoastal Waterway.**

intractable (ɪnˈtræktəbᵊl) *adj* **1** difficult to influence or direct: *an intractable disposition.* **2** (of a problem, illness, etc.) difficult to solve, alleviate, or cure.
▸ **inˌtractaˈbility** *or* **inˈtractableness** *n* ▸ **inˈtractably** *adv*

intradermal (ˌɪntrəˈdɜːməl) *adj* within the skin: *an intradermal injection.* Abbrevs. (esp. of an injection): **ID, i.d.**
▸ **ˌintraˈdermally** *adv*

intrados (ɪnˈtreɪdɒs) *n, pl* **intrados** *or* **intradoses.** *Archit.* the inner curve or surface of an arch. ORIG C18: from F, from INTRA- + *dos* back, from L *dorsum*

intramural (ˌɪntrəˈmjʊərəl) *adj Education, chiefly US & Canad.* operating within or involving those in a single establishment.
▸ **ˌintraˈmurally** *adv*

intramuscular (ˌɪntrəˈmʌskjʊlə) *adj* within a muscle: *an intramuscular injection.* Abbrevs. (esp. of an injection): **IM, i.m.**
▸ **ˌintraˈmuscularly** *adv*

intranet (ˈɪntrəˌnɛt) *n Computing.* an internal network in a company or other organization that makes use of

Internet technology. ORIG C20: INTRA- + NET(WORK) (sense 5), modelled on INTERNET

intrans. *abbrev. for* intransitive.

intransigent (ɪnˈtrænsɪdʒənt) *adj* **1** not willing to compromise; obstinately maintaining an attitude. ◆ *n* **2** an intransigent person, esp. in politics. ORIG C19: from Sp. *los intransigentes* the uncompromising (ones), a name adopted by certain political extremists, from IN-[1] + *transigir* to compromise, from L *transigere* to settle; see TRANSACT
▸ **inˈtransigence** *or* **inˈtransigency** *n* ▸ **inˈtransigently** *adv*

intransitive (ɪnˈtrænsɪtɪv) *adj* **1a** denoting a verb that does not require a direct object: *"to faint" is an intransitive verb.* **1b** (*as n*) such a verb. **2** denoting an adjective or noun that does not require any particular noun phrase as a referent. **3** having the property that if it holds between one argument and a second, and between the second and a third, it must fail to hold between the first and third: *"being the mother of" is an intransitive relation.* ◆ Cf. **transitive.**
▸ **inˈtransitively** *adv* ▸ **inˌtransiˈtivity** *or* **inˈtransitiveness** *n*

intrapreneur (ˌɪntrəprəˈnɜː) *n* a person who while remaining within a larger organization uses entrepreneurial skills to develop a new product or line of business as a subsidiary of the organization. ORIG C20: from INTRA- + (ENTRE)PRENEUR

intrauterine (ˌɪntrəˈjuːtəraɪn) *adj* within the womb.

intrauterine device *n* a metal or plastic device, in the shape of a loop, coil, or ring, inserted into the uterus to prevent conception. Abbrev.: **IUD.**

intravenous (ˌɪntrəˈviːnəs) *adj Anat.* within a vein: *an intravenous injection.* Abbrevs. (esp. of an injection): **IV, i.v.**
▸ **ˌintraˈvenously** *adv*

in-tray *n* a tray for incoming papers, etc., requiring attention.

intrench (ɪnˈtrɛntʃ) *vb* a less common spelling of **entrench.**
▸ **inˈtrencher** *n* ▸ **inˈtrenchment** *n*

intrepid (ɪnˈtrɛpɪd) *adj* fearless; daring; bold. ORIG C17: from L *intrepidus,* from IN-[1] + *trepidus* fearful
▸ **ˌintreˈpidity** *n* ▸ **inˈtrepidly** *adv*

intricate (ˈɪntrɪkɪt) *adj* **1** difficult to understand; obscure; complex; puzzling. **2** entangled or involved: *intricate patterns.* ORIG C15: from L *intrīcāre* to entangle, perplex, from IN-[2] + *trīcae* trifles, perplexities
▸ **ˈintricacy** *or* **ˈintricateness** *n* ▸ **ˈintricately** *adv*

intrigue *vb* (ɪnˈtriːg), **intrigues, intriguing, intrigued. 1** (*tr*) to make interested or curious. **2** (*intr*) to make secret plots or employ underhand methods; conspire. **3** (*intr;* often foll. by *with*) to carry on a clandestine love affair. ◆ *n* (ɪnˈtriːg, ˈɪntriːg). **4** the act or an instance of secret plotting, etc. **5** a clandestine love affair. **6** the quality of arousing interest or curiosity; beguilement. ORIG C17: from F *intriguer,* from It., from L *intrīcāre;* see INTRICATE
▸ **inˈtriguer** *n* ▸ **inˈtriguingly** *adv*

intrinsic (ɪnˈtrɪnsɪk) *or* **intrinsical** *adj* **1** of or relating to the essential nature of a thing; inherent. **2** *Anat.* situated within or peculiar to a part: *intrinsic muscles.* ORIG C15: from LL *intrinsecus* from L, inwardly, from *intrā* within + *secus* alongside
▸ **inˈtrinsically** *adv*

intro (ˈɪntrəʊ) *n, pl* **intros.** *Inf.* short for **introduction.**

intro. *or* **introd.** *abbrev. for:* **1** introduction. **2** introductory.

intro- *prefix* in, into, or inward: *introvert.* ORIG from L *intrō* inwardly, within

introduce (ˌɪntrəˈdjuːs) *vb* **introduces, introducing, introduced.** (*tr*) **1** (often foll. by *to*) to present (someone) by name (to another person). **2** (foll. by *to*) to cause to experience for the first time: *to introduce a visitor to beer.* **3** to present for consideration or approval, esp. before a legislative body: *to introduce a bill in parliament.* **4** to bring in; establish: *to introduce decimal currency.* **5** to present (a radio or television programme, etc.) verbally. **6** (foll. by *with*) to start: *he introduced his talk with some music.* **7** (often foll. by *into*) to insert or inject: *he introduced the needle into his arm.* **8** to place (members of a plant or animal species) in a new environment with the intention of producing a resident breeding population. ORIG C16: from L *intrōdūcere* to bring inside
▸ **ˌintroˈducer** *n* ▸ **ˌintroˈducible** *adj*

introduction (ˌɪntrəˈdʌkʃən) *n* **1** the act of introducing or fact of being introduced. **2** a presentation of one person to another or others. **3** a means of presenting a person to another person, such as a letter of introduction or reference. **4** a preliminary part, as of a book. **5** *Music.* an opening passage in a movement or composition that precedes the main material. **6** a basic or elementary work of instruction, reference, etc.

introductory (ˌɪntrəˈdʌktərɪ, -trɪ) *adj* serving as an introduction; preliminary; prefatory.

introit (ˈɪntrɔɪt) *n RC Church, Church of England.* a short prayer said or sung as the celebrant is entering the sanctuary to celebrate Mass or Holy Communion. ORIG C15: from Church L *introitus* introit, from L: entrance, from *introīre* to go in
▸ **inˈtroital** *adj*

intromit (ˌɪntrəˈmɪt) *vb* **intromits, intromitting, intromitted.** (*tr*) *Rare.* to enter or insert. ORIG C15: from L *intrōmittere* to send in
▸ **ˌintroˈmissible** *adj* ▸ **ˌintroˈmission** *n* ▸ **ˌintroˈmittent** *adj*

introspection (ˌɪntrəˈspɛkʃən) *n* the examination of one's own thoughts, impressions, and feelings. ORIG C17: from L *intrōspicere* to look within
▸ **ˌintroˈspective** *adj* ▸ **ˌintroˈspectively** *adv*

introversion (ˌɪntrəˈvɜːʃən) *n Psychol.* the directing of interest inwards towards one's own thoughts and feelings rather than towards the external world or making social contacts.
▸ **ˌintroˈversive** *or* **ˌintroˈvertive** *adj*

introvert *n* (ˈɪntrəˌvɜːt). **1** *Psychol.* a person prone to introversion. ◆ *adj* (ˈɪntrəˌvɜːt). **2** Also: **introverted.** characterized by introversion. ◆ *vb* (ˌɪntrəˈvɜːt). **3** (*tr*) *Pathol.* to turn (a hollow organ or part) inside out. ORIG C17: see INTRO-, INVERT

intrude (ɪnˈtruːd) *vb* **intrudes, intruding, intruded. 1** (often foll. by *into, on,* or *upon*) to put forward or interpose (oneself, one's views, something) abruptly or without invitation. **2** *Geol.* to force or thrust (molten magma) between solid rocks. ORIG C16: from L *intrūdere* to thrust in
▸ **inˈtruder** *n* ▸ **inˈtrudingly** *adv*

intrusion (ɪnˈtruːʒən) *n* **1** the act or an instance of intruding; an unwelcome visit, etc.: *an intrusion on one's privacy.* **2a** the movement of magma into spaces in the overlying strata to form igneous rock. **2b** any igneous rock formed in this way. **3** *Property law.* an unlawful entry onto land by a stranger after determination of a particular estate of freehold.
▸ **inˈtrusional** *adj*

intrusive (ɪnˈtruːsɪv) *adj* **1** characterized by intrusion or tending to intrude. **2** (of igneous rocks) formed by intrusion. **3** *Phonetics.* relating to or denoting a speech sound that is introduced into a word or piece of connected speech for a phonetic reason.
▸ **inˈtrusively** *adv* ▸ **inˈtrusiveness** *n*

intrust (ɪnˈtrʌst) *vb* a less common spelling of **entrust.**

intubate (ˈɪntjʊˌbeɪt) *vb* **intubates, intubating, intubated.** (*tr*) *Med.* to insert a tube into (a hollow organ).
▸ **ˌintuˈbation** *n*

intuit (ɪnˈtjuːɪt) *vb* **intuits, intuiting, intuited.** to know or discover by intuition.
▸ **inˈtuitable** *adj*

intuition (ˌɪntjʊˈɪʃən) *n* **1** knowledge or belief obtained neither by reason nor perception. **2** instinctive knowledge or belief. **3** a hunch or unjustified belief. ORIG C15: from LL *intuitiō* a contemplation, from L *intuērī* to gaze upon, from *tuērī* to look at
▸ **ˌintuˈitional** *adj* ▸ **ˌintuˈitionally** *adv*

intuitionism (ˌɪntjʊˈɪʃəˌnɪzəm) *or* **intuitionalism** *n Philosophy.* **1** the doctrine that knowledge is acquired primarily by intuition. **2** the theory that the solution to moral problems can be discovered by intuition. **3** the doctrine that external objects are known to be real by intuition.
▸ **ˌintuˈitionist** *or* **ˌintuˈitionalist** *n*

intuitive (ɪn'tjuːɪtɪv) *adj* **1** resulting from intuition: *an intuitive awareness.* **2** of, characterized by, or involving intuition.
▸ **in'tuitively** *adv* ▸ **in'tuitiveness** *n*

intumesce (ˌɪntjʊ'mɛs) *vb* **intumesces, intumescing, intumesced.** (*intr*) to swell. ORIG C18: from L *intumescere,* from *tumescere* to begin to swell, from *tumēre* to swell
▸ **ˌintu'mescence** *n*

intussusception (ˌɪntəssə'sɛpʃən) *n* **1** *Pathol.* the telescoping of one section of the intestinal tract into a lower section. **2** *Biol.* growth in the surface area of a cell by the deposition of new particles between the existing particles of the cell wall. ORIG C18: from L *intus* within + *susceptiō* a taking up

Inuit *or* **Innuit** ('ɪnjuːɪt) *n, pl* **Inuit, Inuits** *or* **Innuit, Innuits.** an Eskimo of North America or Greenland, as distinguished from one from Asia or the Aleutian Islands. ORIG from Eskimo *inuit* people, pl of *inuk* a man

USAGE NOTE See at **Eskimo.**

Inuk ('ɪnʊk) *n Canad.* a member of the Inuit. ORIG from Eskimo *inuk* a man

Inuktitut (ɪ'nʊktɪˌtʊt) *n Canad.* the language of the Inuit; Eskimo. ORIG from Eskimo *inuk* man + *titut* speech

inunction (ɪn'ʌŋkʃən) *n* **1** the application of an ointment to the skin, esp. by rubbing. **2** the ointment so used. **3** the act of anointing; anointment. ORIG C15: from L *inunguere* to anoint, from *unguere;* see UNCTION

inundate ('ɪnʌnˌdeɪt) *vb* **inundates, inundating, inundated.** (*tr*) **1** to cover completely with water; overflow; flood; swamp. **2** to overwhelm, as if with a flood: *to be inundated with requests.* ORIG C17: from L *inundāre,* from *unda* wave
▸ **'inundant** *or* **in'undatory** *adj* ▸ **ˌinun'dation** *n* ▸ **'inunˌdator** *n*

inure *or* **enure** (ɪ'njʊə) *vb* **inures, inuring, inured** *or* **enures, enuring, enured. 1** (*tr; often passive;* often foll. by *to*) to cause to accept or become hardened to; habituate. **2** (*intr*) (esp. of a law, etc.) to come into operation; take effect. ORIG C15 *enuren* to accustom, from *ure* use, from OF *euvre* custom, work, from L *opera* works
▸ **in'urement** *or* **en'urement** *n*

in utero *Latin.* (ɪn 'juːtərəʊ) *adv, adj* in the uterus.

inv. *abbrev. for:* **1** invented. **2** inventor. **3** invoice.

in vacuo *Latin.* (ɪn 'vækjʊˌəʊ) *adv* in a vacuum.

invade (ɪn'veɪd) *vb* **invades, invading, invaded. 1** to enter (a country, territory, etc.) by military force. **2** (*tr*) to occupy in large numbers; overrun; infest. **3** (*tr*) to trespass or encroach upon (privacy, etc.). **4** (*tr*) to enter and spread throughout, esp. harmfully; pervade. ORIG C15: from L *invādere,* from *vādere* to go
▸ **in'vadable** *adj* ▸ **in'vader** *n*

invaginate *vb* (ɪn'vædʒɪˌneɪt), **invaginates, invaginating, invaginated. 1** *Pathol.* to push one section of (a tubular organ or part) back into itself so that it becomes ensheathed. **2** (*intr*) (of the outer layer of an organism or part) to undergo this process. ◆ *adj* (ɪn'vædʒɪnɪt, -ˌneɪt). **3** (of an organ or part) folded back upon itself. ORIG C19: from Med. L *invāgināre,* from L IN-[2] + *vāgīna* sheath
▸ **in'vaginable** *adj* ▸ **inˌvagi'nation** *n*

invalid[1] ('ɪnvəˌliːd, -lɪd) *n* **1a** a person suffering from disablement or chronic ill health. **1b** (*as modifier*): *an invalid chair.* ◆ *adj* **2** suffering from or disabled by injury, sickness, etc. ◆ *vb* (*tr*) **3** to cause to become an invalid; disable. **4** (*often passive;* usually foll. by *out*) *Chiefly Brit.* to require (a member of the armed forces) to retire from active service through wounds or illness. ORIG C17: from L *invalidus* infirm, from IN-[1] + *validus* strong
▸ **invalidity** (ˌɪnvə'lɪdɪtɪ) *n*

invalid[2] (ɪn'vælɪd) *adj* **1** not valid; having no cogency or legal force. **2** *Logic.* (of an argument) having a conclusion that does not follow from the premises. ORIG C16: from Med. L *invalidus* without legal force; see INVALID[1]
▸ **ˌinva'lidity** *or* **in'validness** *n* ▸ **in'validly** *adv*

invalidate (ɪn'vælɪˌdeɪt) *vb* **invalidates, invalidating, invalidated.** (*tr*) **1** to render weak or ineffective (an argument). **2** to take away the legal force or effectiveness of; annul (a contract).
▸ **inˌvali'dation** *n* ▸ **in'valiˌdator** *n*

invaluable (ɪn'væljʊəbᵊl) *adj* having great value that is impossible to calculate; priceless.
▸ **in'valuableness** *n* ▸ **in'valuably** *adv*

Invar (ɪn'vɑː) *n Trademark.* an alloy containing iron, nickel, and carbon. It has a very low coefficient of expansion and is used for the balance springs of watches, etc. ORIG C20: shortened from INVARIABLE

invariable (ɪn'vɛərɪəbᵊl) *adj* **1** not subject to alteration; unchanging. ◆ *n* **2** a mathematical quantity having an unchanging value; a constant.
▸ **inˌvaria'bility** *or* **in'variableness** *n* ▸ **in'variably** *adv*

invariant (ɪn'vɛərɪənt) *Maths.* ◆ *n* **1** an entity, quantity, etc., that is unaltered by a particular transformation of coordinates. ◆ *adj* **2** (of a relationship or a property of a function, configuration, or equation) unaltered by a particular transformation of coordinates.
▸ **in'variance** *or* **in'variancy** *n*

invasion (ɪn'veɪʒən) *n* **1** the act of invading with armed forces. **2** any encroachment or intrusion: *an invasion of rats.* **3** the onset or advent of something harmful, esp. of a disease. **4** *Pathol.* the spread of cancer from its point of origin into surrounding tissues. **5** the movement of plants to an area to which they are not native.

invasive (ɪn'veɪsɪv) *adj* **1** of or relating to an invasion, intrusion, etc. **2** (of surgery) involving making a relatively large incision in the body to gain access to the target of the surgery.

invective (ɪn'vɛktɪv) *n* **1** vehement accusation or denunciation, esp. of a bitterly abusive or sarcastic kind. ◆ *adj* **2** characterized by or using abusive language, bitter sarcasm, etc. ORIG C15: from LL *invectīvus* reproachful, from L *invectus* carried in; see INVEIGH
▸ **in'vectively** *adv* ▸ **in'vectiveness** *n*

inveigh (ɪn'veɪ) *vb* (*intr;* foll. by *against*) to speak with violent or invective language; rail. ORIG C15: from L *invehī,* lit.: to be carried in, hence, assail physically or verbally
▸ **in'veigher** *n*

inveigle (ɪn'viːgᵊl, -'veɪ-) *vb* **inveigles, inveigling, inveigled.** (*tr;* often foll. by *into* or an infinitive) to lead (someone into a situation) or persuade (to do something) by cleverness or trickery; cajole. ORIG C15: from OF *avogler* to blind, deceive, from *avogle* blind, from Med. L *ab oculis* without eyes
▸ **in'veiglement** *n* ▸ **in'veigler** *n*

invent (ɪn'vɛnt) *vb* **1** to create or devise (new ideas, machines, etc.). **2** to make up (falsehoods, etc.); fabricate. ORIG C15: from L *invenīre* to find, come upon
▸ **in'ventable** *adj*

invention (ɪn'vɛnʃən) *n* **1** the act or process of inventing. **2** something that is invented. **3** *Patent law.* the discovery or production of some new or improved process or machine. **4** creative power or ability; inventive skill. **5** *Euphemistic.* a fabrication; lie. **6** *Music.* a short piece consisting of two or three parts usually in imitative counterpoint.
▸ **in'ventional** *adj* ▸ **in'ventionless** *adj*

inventive (ɪn'vɛntɪv) *adj* **1** skilled or quick at contriving; ingenious; resourceful. **2** characterized by inventive skill: *an inventive programme of work.* **3** of or relating to invention.
▸ **in'ventively** *adv* ▸ **in'ventiveness** *n*

inventor (ɪn'vɛntə) *n* a person who invents, esp. as a profession.
▸ **in'ventress** *fem n*

inventory ('ɪnvəntərɪ, -trɪ) *n, pl* **inventories. 1** a detailed list of articles, goods, property, etc. **2** (*often pl*) *Accounting, chiefly US.* **2a** the amount or value of a firm's current assets that consist of raw materials, work in progress, and finished goods; stock. **2b** such assets individually. ◆ *vb* **inventories, inventorying, inventoried. 3** (*tr*) to enter (items) in an inventory; make a list of. ORIG C16: from Med. L *inventōrium;* see INVENT
▸ **'inventoriable** *adj* ▸ **ˌinven'torial** *adj* ▸ **ˌinven'torially** *adv*

Inveraray ★ (ˌɪnvəˈrɛərɪ) *n* a town in W Scotland, in Argyll and Bute: Inveraray Castle is the seat of the Dukes of Argyll. Pop.: 512 (1991).

Invercargill ★ (ˌɪnvəˈkɑːgɪl) *n* a city in New Zealand, on South Island: regional trading centre for sheep and agricultural products. Pop.: 51 600 (1995 est.).

Inverclyde ★ (ˌɪnvəˈklaɪd) *n* a council area of W central Scotland. Administrative centre: Greenock. Pop.: 89 990 (1996 est.). Area: 162 sq. km (63 sq. miles).

Inverness ★ (ˌɪnvəˈnɛs) *n* **1** a city in N Scotland, administrative centre of Highland: tourism and specialized engineering. Pop.: 41 234 (1991). **2** (*sometimes not cap.*) an overcoat with a removable cape.

Inverness-shire ★ (ˌɪnvəˈnɛsˌʃɪə, -ʃə) *n* (until 1975) a county of NW Scotland, now part of Highland.

inverse (ɪnˈvɜːs, ˈɪnvɜːs) *adj* **1** opposite or contrary in effect, sequence, direction, etc. **2** *Maths.* **2a** (of a relationship) containing two variables such that an increase in one results in a decrease in the other. **2b** (of an element) operating on a specified member of a set to produce the identity of the set: *the additive inverse element of x is –x.* **3** (*usually prenominal*) upside-down; inverted: *in an inverse position.* ◆ *n* **4** *Maths.* an inverse element. ORIG C17: from L *inversus,* from *invertere* to INVERT
▸ **inˈversely** *adv*

inverse function *n* a function whose independent variable is the dependent variable of a given trigonometric or hyperbolic function: *the inverse function of* sin *x is* arcsin *y* (*also written* $\sin^{-1}y$).

inversion (ɪnˈvɜːʃən) *n* **1** the act of inverting or state of being inverted. **2** something inverted, esp. a reversal of order, mutual functions, etc.: *an inversion of their previous relationship.* **3** Also: **anastrophe.** *Rhetoric.* the reversal of a normal order of words, as in the phrase *weeping left she sorrowfully.* **4** *Chem.* **4a** the conversion of a dextrorotatory solution of sucrose into a laevorotatory solution of glucose and fructose by hydrolysis. **4b** any similar reaction in which the optical properties of the reactants are opposite to those of the products. **5** *Music.* **5a** the process or result of transposing the notes of a chord such that the root, originally in the bass, is placed in an upper part. **5b** the modification of an interval in which the higher note becomes the lower or the lower one the higher. **6** *Pathol.* abnormal positioning of an organ or part, as in being upside down or turned inside out. **7** *Psychiatry.* **7a** the adoption of the role or characteristics of the opposite sex. **7b** another word for **homosexuality. 8** *Meteorol.* an abnormal condition in which the layer of air next to the earth's surface is cooler than an overlying layer. **9** *Computing.* an operation by which each digit of a binary number is changed to the alternative digit, as *10110* to *01001.*
▸ **inˈversive** *adj*

invert *vb* (ɪnˈvɜːt). **1** to turn or cause to turn upside down or inside out. **2** (*tr*) to reverse in effect, sequence, direction, etc. **3** (*tr*) *Phonetics.* to turn (the tip of the tongue) up and back to pronounce (a speech sound). ◆ *n* (ˈɪnvɜːt). **4** *Psychiatry.* **4a** a person who adopts the role of the opposite sex. **4b** another word for **homosexual. 5** *Archit.* **5a** the lower inner surface of a drain, sewer, etc. **5b** an arch that is concave upwards, esp. one used in foundations. ORIG C16: from L *invertere,* from IN-[2] + *vertere* to turn
▸ **inˈvertible** *adj* ▸ **inˌvertiˈbility** *n*

invertase (ɪnˈvɜːteɪz) *n* an enzyme, occurring in the intestinal juice of animals and in yeasts, that hydrolyses sucrose to glucose and fructose.

invertebrate (ɪnˈvɜːtɪbrɪt, -ˌbreɪt) *n* **1** any animal lacking a backbone, including all species not classified as vertebrates. ◆ *adj also* **invertebral. 2** of, relating to, or designating invertebrates.

inverted comma *n* another term for **quotation mark.**

inverted mordent *n Music.* a melodic ornament consisting of the rapid alternation of a principal note with a note one degree higher.

inverter *or* **invertor** (ɪnˈvɜːtə) *n* any device for converting a direct current into an alternating current.

invert sugar *n* a mixture of fructose and glucose obtained by the inversion of sucrose.

invest (ɪnˈvɛst) *vb* **1** (often foll. by *in*) to lay out (money or capital in an enterprise) with the expectation of profit. **2** (*tr;* often foll. by *in*) to devote (effort, resources, etc., to a project). **3** (*tr;* often foll. by *in* or *with*) *Arch. or ceremonial.* to clothe or adorn (in some garment, esp. the robes of an office). **4** (*tr;* often foll. by *in*) to install formally or ceremoniously (in an official position, rank, etc.). **5** (*tr;* foll. by *in* or *with*) to place (power, authority, etc., in) or provide (with power or authority): *to invest new rights in the monarchy.* **6** (*tr; usually passive;* foll. by *in* or *with*) to provide or endow (a person with qualities, characteristics, etc.). **7** (*tr;* foll. by *with*) *Usually poetic.* to cover or adorn, as if with a coat or garment: *when spring invests the trees with leaves.* **8** (*tr*) *Rare.* to surround with military forces; besiege. **9** (*intr;* foll. by *in*) *Inf.* to purchase; buy. ORIG C16: from Med. L *investīre* to clothe, from L, from *vestīre,* from *vestis* a garment
▸ **inˈvestable** *or* **inˈvestible** *adj* ▸ **inˈvestor** *n*

investigate (ɪnˈvɛstɪˌgeɪt) *vb* **investigates, investigating, investigated.** to inquire into (a situation or problem, esp. a crime or death) thoroughly; examine systematically, esp. in order to discover the truth. ORIG C16: from L *investīgāre* to search after, from IN-[2] + *vestīgium* track; see VESTIGE
▸ **inˈvestiˌgative** *or* **inˈvestigatory** *adj* ▸ **inˈvestiˌgator** *n*

investigation (ɪnˌvɛstɪˈgeɪʃən) *n* the act or process of investigating; a careful search or examination in order to discover facts, etc.

investiture (ɪnˈvɛstɪtʃə) *n* **1** the act of presenting with a title or with the robes and insignia of an office or rank. **2** (in feudal society) the formal bestowal of the possessory right to a fief.
▸ **inˈvestitive** *adj*

investment (ɪnˈvɛstmənt) *n* **1a** the act of investing money. **1b** the amount invested. **1c** an enterprise, asset, etc., in which money is or can be invested. **2a** the act of investing effort, resources, etc. **2b** the amount invested. **3** *Biol.* the outer layer or covering of an organ, part, or organism. **4** a less common word for **investiture** (sense 1). **5** the act of investing or state of being invested, as with an official robe, specific quality, etc. **6** *Rare.* the act of besieging with military forces, works, etc.

investment analyst *n* a specialist in forecasting the prices of stocks and shares.

investment bond *n* a single-premium life-assurance policy in which a fixed sum is invested in an asset-backed fund.

investment trust *n* a financial enterprise that invests its subscribed capital in securities for its investors' benefit.

inveterate (ɪnˈvɛtərɪt) *adj* **1** long established, esp. so as to be deep-rooted or ingrained: *an inveterate feeling of hostility.* **2** (*prenominal*) confirmed in a habit or practice, esp. a bad one; hardened. ORIG C16: from L *inveterātus* of long standing, from *inveterāre* to make old, from IN-[2] + *vetus* old
▸ **inˈveteracy** *n* ▸ **inˈveterately** *adv*

invidious (ɪnˈvɪdɪəs) *adj* **1** incurring or tending to arouse resentment, unpopularity, etc.: *an invidious task.* **2** (of comparisons or distinctions) unfairly or offensively discriminating. ORIG C17: from L *invidiōsus* full of envy, from *invidia* ENVY
▸ **inˈvidiously** *adv* ▸ **inˈvidiousness** *n*

invigilate (ɪnˈvɪdʒɪˌleɪt) *vb* **invigilates, invigilating, invigilated.** (*intr*) **1** *Brit.* to watch examination candidates, esp. to prevent cheating. US word: **proctor. 2** *Arch.* to keep watch. ORIG C16: from L *invigilāre* to watch over; see VIGIL
▸ **inˌvigiˈlation** *n* ▸ **inˈvigiˌlator** *n*

invigorate (ɪnˈvɪgəˌreɪt) *vb* **invigorates, invigorating, invigorated.** (*tr*) to give vitality and vigour to; animate; brace; refresh: *to be invigorated by fresh air.* ORIG C17: from IN-[2] + L *vigor* VIGOUR
▸ **inˈvigorˌating** *adj* ▸ **inˌvigorˈation** *n* ▸ **inˈvigorative** *adj*
▸ **inˈvigorˌator** *n*

invincible (ɪnˈvɪnsəbᵊl) *adj* incapable of being defeated;

unconquerable. ORIG C15: from LL *invincibilis*, from L IN-[1] + *vincere* to conquer
▸ in,vinci'bility *or* in'vincibleness *n* ▸ in'vincibly *adv*

inviolable (ɪn'vaɪələbᵊl) *adj* that must not or cannot be transgressed, dishonoured, or broken; to be kept sacred: *an inviolable oath.*
▸ in,viola'bility *n* ▸ in'violably *adv*

inviolate (ɪn'vaɪəlɪt, -,leɪt) *adj* **1** free from violation, injury, disturbance, etc. **2** a less common word for **inviolable.**
▸ in'violacy *or* in'violateness *n* ▸ in'violately *adv*

invisible (ɪn'vɪzəbᵊl) *adj* **1** not visible; not able to be perceived by the eye: *invisible rays.* **2** concealed from sight; hidden. **3** not easily seen or noticed: *invisible mending.* **4** kept hidden from public view; secret. **5** *Econ.* of or relating to services, such as insurance and freight, rather than goods: *invisible earnings.* ◆ *n* **6** *Econ.* an invisible item of trade; service.
▸ in,visi'bility *or* in'visibleness *n* ▸ in'visibly *adv*

invitation (,ɪnvɪ'teɪʃən) *n* **1a** the act of inviting, such as an offer of entertainment or hospitality. **1b** (*as modifier*): *an invitation race.* **2** the act of enticing or attracting; allurement.

invite *vb* (ɪn'vaɪt), **invites, inviting, invited.** (*tr*) **1** to ask (a person) in a friendly or polite way (to do something, attend an event, etc.). **2** to make a request for, esp. publicly or formally: *to invite applications.* **3** to bring on or provoke; give occasion for: *you invite disaster by your actions.* **4** to welcome or tempt. ◆ *n* ('ɪnvaɪt). **5** *Inf.* an invitation. ORIG C16: from L *invītāre* to invite, entertain
▸ in'viter *n*

inviting (ɪn'vaɪtɪŋ) *adj* tempting; alluring; attractive.
▸ in'vitingness *n*

in vitro (ɪn 'vi:trəʊ) *adv, adj* (of biological processes or reactions) made to occur outside the body of the organism in an artificial environment. ORIG NL, lit.: in glass

in vitro fertilization *n* a technique enabling some women who are unable to conceive to bear children. Egg cells removed from a woman's ovary are fertilized by sperm in vitro; some of the resulting fertilized egg cells are then implanted into her uterus. Abbrev.: **IVF.**

in vivo (ɪn 'vi:vəʊ) *adv, adj* (of biological processes or experiments) occurring or carried out in the living organism. ORIG NL, lit.: in a living (thing)

invocation (,ɪnvə'keɪʃən) *n* **1** the act of invoking or calling upon some agent for assistance. **2** a prayer asking God for help, forgiveness, etc. **3** an appeal for inspiration from a Muse or deity at the beginning of a poem. **4a** the act of summoning a spirit from another world by ritual incantation or magic. **4b** the incantation used in this act.
▸ ,invo'cational *adj* ▸ invocatory (ɪn'vɒkətərɪ, -trɪ) *adj*

invoice ('ɪnvɔɪs) *n* **1** a document issued by a seller to a buyer listing the goods or services supplied and stating the sum of money due. **2** *Rare.* a consignment of invoiced merchandise. ◆ *vb* **invoices, invoicing, invoiced. 3** (*tr*) **3a** to present (a customer, etc.) with an invoice. **3b** to list (merchandise sold) on an invoice. ORIG C16: from earlier *invoyes*, from OF *envois*, pl. of *envoi* message; see ENVOY[1]

invoke (ɪn'vəʊk) *vb* **invokes, invoking, invoked.** (*tr*) **1** to call upon (an agent, esp. God or another deity) for help, inspiration, etc. **2** to put (a law, penalty, etc.) into use: *the union invoked the dispute procedure.* **3** to appeal to (an outside authority) for confirmation, corroboration, etc. **4** to implore or beg (help, etc.). **5** to summon (a spirit, etc.); conjure up. ORIG C15: from L *invocāre* to appeal to, from *vocāre* to call
▸ in'vocable *adj* ▸ in'voker *n*

USAGE NOTE *Invoke* is sometimes wrongly used where *evoke* is meant: *this proposal evoked* (not *invoked*) *a strong reaction.*

involucre ('ɪnvə,lu:kə) *or* **involucrum** (,ɪnvə'lu:krəm) *n, pl* **involucres** *or* **involucra** (-krə). a ring of bracts at the base of an inflorescence. ORIG C16 (in the sense: envelope): from NL *involucrum*, from L: wrapper, from *involvere* to wrap
▸ ,invo'lucral *adj* ▸ ,invo'lucrate *adj*

involuntary (ɪn'vɒləntərɪ, -trɪ) *adj* **1** carried out without one's conscious wishes; not voluntary; unintentional. **2** *Physiol.* (esp. of a movement or muscle) performed or acting without conscious control.
▸ in'voluntarily *adv* ▸ in'voluntariness *n*

involute *adj* ('ɪnvə,lu:t), *also* **involuted. 1** complex, intricate, or involved. **2** *Bot.* (esp. of petals, leaves, etc., in bud) having margins that are rolled inwards. **3** (of certain shells) closely coiled so that the axis is obscured. ◆ *n* ('ɪnvə,lu:t). **4** *Geom.* the curve described by the free end of a thread as it is wound around another curve, the **evolute,** such that its normals are tangential to the evolute. ◆ *vb* (,ɪnvə'lu:t), **involutes, involuting, involuted. 5** (*intr*) to become involute. ORIG C17: from L *involūtus*, from *involvere*; see INVOLVE
▸ 'invo,lutely *adv* ▸ ,invo'lutedly *adv*

involution (,ɪnvə'lu:ʃən) *n* **1** the act of involving or complicating or the state of being involved or complicated. **2** something involved or complicated. **3** *Zool.* degeneration or structural deformation. **4** *Biol.* an involute formation or structure. **5** *Physiol.* reduction in size of an organ or part, as of the uterus following childbirth or as a result of ageing. **6** an algebraic operation in which a number, expression, etc., is raised to a specified power.
▸ ,invo'lutional *adj*

involve (ɪn'vɒlv) *vb* **involves, involving, involved.** (*tr*) **1** to include or contain as a necessary part. **2** to have an effect on; spread to: *the investigation involved many innocent people.* **3** (*often passive;* usually foll. by *in* or *with*) to concern or associate significantly: *many people were involved in the crime.* **4** (*often passive*) to make complicated; tangle. **5** *Rare, often poetic.* to wrap or surround. **6** *Maths, obs.* to raise to a specified power. ORIG C14: from L *involvere* to surround, from IN-[2] + *volvere* to roll
▸ in'volvement *n* ▸ in'volver *n*

invulnerable (ɪn'vʌlnərəbᵊl, -'vʌlnrəbᵊl) *adj* **1** incapable of being wounded, hurt, damaged, etc. **2** incapable of being damaged or captured: *an invulnerable fortress.*
▸ in,vulnera'bility *or* in'vulnerableness *n* ▸ in'vulnerably *adv*

inward ('ɪnwəd) *adj* **1** going or directed towards the middle of or into something. **2** situated within; inside. **3** of, relating to, or existing in the mind or spirit: *inward meditation.* **4** of one's own country or a specific country: *inward investment.* ◆ *adv* **5** a variant of **inwards.** ◆ *n* **6** the inward part; inside.
▸ 'inwardness *n*

inwardly ('ɪnwədlɪ) *adv* **1** within the private thoughts or feelings; secretly. **2** not aloud: *to laugh inwardly.* **3** with reference to the inside or inner part; internally.

inwards *adv* ('ɪnwədz), *also* **inward. 1** towards the interior or middle of something. **2** in, into, or towards the mind or spirit. ◆ *pl n* ('ɪnədz). **3** a variant of **innards** (sense 1).

inweave (ɪn'wi:v) *vb* **inweaves, inweaving, inwove** *or* **inweaved; inwoven** *or* **inweaved.** (*tr*) to weave together into or as if into a design, fabric, etc.

inwrap (ɪn'ræp) *vb* **inwraps, inwrapping, inwrapped.** a less common spelling of **enwrap.**

inwrought (,ɪn'rɔ:t) *adj* **1** worked or woven into material, esp. decoratively. **2** *Rare.* blended with other things.

in-your-face *adj Sl.* aggressive and confrontational: *provocative in-your-face activism.*

Io[1] ★ ('aɪəʊ) *n Greek myth.* a maiden loved by Zeus and turned into a white heifer by either Zeus or Hera.

Io[2] *the chemical symbol for* ionium.

Ioánnina (*Greek* jɔ'anina) *or* **Yanina** ★ *n* a city in NW Greece: belonged to the Serbs (1349–1430) and then the Turks (until 1913); seat of Ali Pasha, the "Lion of Janina", from 1788 to 1822. Pop.: 56 496 (1991 est.). Serbian name: **Janina.**

IOC *abbrev. for* International Olympic Committee.

iodic (aɪ'ɒdɪk) *adj* of or containing iodine, esp. in the pentavalent state.

iodide ('aɪə,daɪd) *n* **1** a salt of hydriodic acid, containing the iodide ion, I^-. **2** a compound containing an iodine atom, such as methyl iodide (iodomethane).

iodine ('aɪə,di:n) *n* a bluish-black element of the halogen group that sublimates into a violet irritating gas. Its compounds are used in medicine and photography and in dyes. The radioisotope **iodine-131** is used in the treatment of thyroid disease. Symbol: I; atomic no.: 53; atomic wt.: 126.90. ORIG C19: from F *iode,* from Gk *iōdēs* rust-coloured, but mistaken as violet-coloured, from *ion* violet

iodize *or* **iodise** (ˈaɪəˌdaɪz) *vb* **iodizes, iodizing, iodized** *or* **iodises, iodising, iodised.** (*tr*) to treat or react with iodine or an iodine compound. Also: **iodate.**
▸ **ˌiodiˈzation** *or* **ˌiodiˈsation** *n* ▸ **ˈioˌdizer** *or* **ˈioˌdiser** *n*

iodoform (aɪˈɒdəˌfɔːm) *n* a yellow crystalline solid made by heating alcohol with iodine and an alkali: used as an antiseptic. Formula: CHI_3. Systematic name: **triiodomethane.**

iodopsin (ˌaɪəˈdɒpsɪn) *n* a violet light-sensitive pigment in the cones of the retina of the eye. See also **rhodopsin.**

IOM *abbrev. for* Isle of Man.

ion (ˈaɪən, -ɒn) *n* an electrically charged atom or group of atoms formed by the loss or gain of one or more electrons. See also **cation, anion.** ORIG C19: from Gk, lit.: going, from *ienai* to go

-ion *suffix forming nouns.* indicating an action, process, or state: *creation; objection.* Cf. **-ation, -tion.** ORIG from L *-iōn-, -io*

Iona ★ (aɪˈəʊnə) *n* an island off the W coast of Scotland, in the Inner Hebrides: site of St Columba's monastery (founded in 563) and an important early centre of Christianity. Area: 854 ha (2112 acres).

Ionesco ★ (ˌiːəˈnɛskəʊ; *French* jɔnɛsko) *n* **Eugène** (øʒɛn). 1912–94, French dramatist, born in Romania; a leading exponent of the theatre of the absurd. His plays include *The Bald Prima Donna* (1950) and *Rhinoceros* (1960).

ion exchange *n* the process in which ions are exchanged between a solution and an insoluble solid, usually a resin. It is used to soften water.

Ionia ★ (aɪˈəʊnɪə) *n* an ancient region of W central Asia Minor, including adjacent Aegean islands: colonized by Greeks in about 1100 B.C.
▸ **Iˈonian** *adj, n*

Ionian Islands ★ *pl n* a group of Greek islands in the Ionian Sea, consisting of Corfu, Cephalonia, Zante, Levkas, Ithaca, Cythera, and Paxos: ceded by Britain to Greece in 1864. Pop.: 193 734 (1991). Area: 2307 sq. km (891 sq. miles).

Ionian Sea ★ *n* the part of the Mediterranean Sea between SE Italy, E Sicily, and Greece.

ionic (aɪˈɒnɪk) *adj* of, relating to, or occurring in the form of ions.

Ionic (aɪˈɒnɪk) *adj* **1** of, denoting, or relating to one of the five classical orders of architecture, characterized by fluted columns and capitals with scroll-like ornaments. **2** of or relating to Ionia, on the coast of Asia Minor, its inhabitants or their dialect of Ancient Greek. ◆ *n* **3** one of four chief dialects of Ancient Greek, the dialect spoken in Ionia.

ionium (aɪˈəʊnɪəm) *n Obs.* a naturally occurring radioisotope of thorium with a mass number of 230. Symbol: Io ORIG C20: from NL

ionization *or* **ionisation** (ˌaɪənaɪˈzeɪʃən) *n* **a** the formation of ions as a result of a chemical reaction, high temperature, electrical discharge, or radiation. **b** (*as modifier*): *ionization temperature.*

ionize *or* **ionise** (ˈaɪəˌnaɪz) *vb* **ionizes, ionizing, ionized** *or* **ionises, ionising, ionised.** to change or become changed into ions.
▸ **ˈionˌizable** *or* **ˈionˌisable** *adj* ▸ **ˈionˌizer** *or* **ˈionˌiser** *n*

ionosphere (aɪˈɒnəˌsfɪə) *n* a region of the earth's atmosphere, extending from about 60 to 1000 km above the earth's surface, in which there is a high concentration of free electrons formed as a result of ionizing radiation entering the atmosphere from space.
▸ **ionospheric** (aɪˌɒnəˈsfɛrɪk) *adj*

iota (aɪˈəʊtə) *n* **1** the ninth letter in the Greek alphabet (Ι, ι), a vowel or semivowel. **2** (*usually used with a negative*) a very small amount; jot (esp. in **not one** *or* **an iota**). ORIG C16: via L from Gk, of Semitic origin

IOU *n* a written promise or reminder to pay a debt. ORIG C17: representing *I owe you*

-ious *suffix forming adjectives from nouns.* characterized by or full of: *suspicious.* ORIG from L *-ius* & *-iōsus* full of

IOW *abbrev. for* Isle of Wight.

Iowa ★ (ˈaɪəʊə) *n* a state of the N central US, in the Midwest: consists of rolling plains crossed by many rivers, with the Missouri forming the western border and the Mississippi the eastern. Capital: Des Moines. Pop.: 2 862 447 (1998 est.). Area: 144 887 sq. km (55 941 sq. miles). Abbrevs.: **Ia.** or (with zip code) **IA**
▸ **ˈIowan** *adj, n*

IPA *abbrev. for* International Phonetic Alphabet.

ipecacuanha (ˌɪpɪˌkækjʊˈænə) *or* **ipecac** (ˈɪpɪˌkæk) *n* **1** a low-growing South American shrub. **2** a drug prepared from the dried roots of this plant, used as a purgative and emetic. ORIG C18: from Port., from Amerind *ipekaaguéne,* from *ipeh* low + *kaa* leaves + *guéne* vomit

Iphigenia ★ (ˌɪfɪdʒɪˈnaɪə) *n Greek myth.* the daughter of Agamemnon, taken by him to be sacrificed to Artemis, who saved her life and made her a priestess.

I-pin ★ (ˈiːˈbɪn) *n* a variant transliteration of the Chinese name for **Yibin.**

IPO *Stock Exchange. abbrev. for* initial public offering.

Ipoh ★ (ˈiːpəʊ) *n* a city in Malaysia, capital of Perak state: tin-mining centre. Pop.: 382 633 (1991).

ipomoea (ˌɪpəˈmɪə, ˌaɪ-) *n* **1** any tropical or subtropical plant, such as the morning-glory, sweet potato, and jalap, having trumpet-shaped flowers. **2** the dried root of a Mexican species which yields a cathartic resin. ORIG C18: NL, from Gk *ips* worm + *homoios* like

ippon (ˈɪpɒn) *n Judo & karate.* a winning point awarded in a sparring competition for a perfectly executed technique. ORIG C20: Japanese, lit.: one point

Ipsambul ★ (ˌɪpsæmˈbuːl) *n* another name for **Abu Simbel.**

ipse dixit *Latin.* (ˈɪpseɪ ˈdɪksɪt) *n* an arbitrary and unsupported assertion. ORIG C16, lit.: he himself said it

ipso facto (ˈɪpsəʊ ˈfæktəʊ) *adv* by that very fact or act. ORIG from L

Ipsus ★ (ˈɪpsəs) *n* an ancient town in Asia Minor, in S Phrygia: site of a decisive battle (301 B.C.) in the Wars of the Diadochi in which Lysimachus and Seleucus defeated Antigonus and Demetrius.

Ipswich ★ (ˈɪpswɪtʃ) *n* a town in E England, administrative centre of Suffolk, at the head of the Orwell estuary: manufactures agricultural and industrial machinery. Pop.: 130 157 (1991).

IQ *abbrev. for* intelligence quotient.

Iqaluit ★ (ɪˈkæluːɪt) *n* a town in N Canada; capital of Nunavut. Former name: **Frobisher Bay.**

Iqbal ★ (ˈɪkbal) *n* Sir **Muhammad** (mʊˈhæməd). 1875–1938, Indian Muslim poet, philosopher, and political leader, who advocated the establishment of separate nations for Indian Hindus and Muslims and is generally regarded as the originator of Pakistan.

Iquique ★ (*Spanish* iˈkike) *n* a port in N Chile: oil refineries. Pop.: 152 592 (1995 est.).

Iquitos ★ (*Spanish* iˈkitɔs) *n* an inland port in NE Peru, on the Amazon 3703 km (2300 miles) from the Atlantic: head of navigation for steamers. Pop.: 274 759 (1993).

Ir *the chemical symbol for* iridium.

Ir. *abbrev. for:* **1** Ireland. **2** Irish.

ir- *prefix* a variant of **in-**[1] and **in-**[2] before *r.*

IRA *abbrev. for* Irish Republican Army.

irade (ɪˈrɑːdɛ) *n* a written edict of a Muslim ruler. ORIG C19: from Turkish: will, from Ar. *irādah*

Iráklion ★ (*Greek* iˈrakliɔn) *n* a port in Greece, in N Crete: former capital of Crete (until 1841); ruled by Venetians (13th–17th centuries). Pop.: 117 167 (1991). Italian name: **Candia.** Also called: **Heraklion, Herakleion.**

Iran ★ (ɪˈrɑːn) *n* a republic in SW Asia, between the Caspian Sea and the Persian Gulf: consists chiefly of a high central desert plateau almost completely surrounded by mountains, a semitropical fertile region along the Cas-

★ people and places

pian coast, and a hot and dry area beside the Persian Gulf. Oil is the most important export. Official language: Farsi (Persian). Official religion: Muslim. Currency: rial. Capital: Tehran. Pop.: 67 172 000 (1999 est.). Area: 1 647 050 sq. km (635 932 sq. miles). Former name (until 1935): **Persia.** Official name: **Islamic Republic of Iran.** See also **Persian Empire.**

Iranian (ɪˈreɪnɪən) *n* **1** a native or inhabitant of Iran. **2** a branch of the Indo-European family of languages, including Persian. **3** the modern Persian language. ◆ *adj* **4** relating to or characteristic of Iran, its inhabitants, or their language; Persian. **5** belonging to or relating to the Iranian branch of Indo-European.

Iran-Iraq War *n* the indecisive war (1980–88) fought by Iran and Iraq, following the Iraqi invasion of disputed border territory in Iran. Also called: **Gulf War.**

Iraq ★ (ɪˈrɑːk) *n* a republic in SW Asia, on the Persian Gulf: coextensive with ancient Mesopotamia; became a British mandate in 1920, independent in 1932, and a republic in 1958; the Iraqi invasion of Kuwait (1990) led to the Gulf War (1991), in which Iraq was defeated by US-led UN forces. It consists chiefly of the mountains of Kurdistan in the northeast, part of the Syrian Desert, and the lower basin of the Rivers Tigris and Euphrates. Oil is the major export. Official language: Arabic; Kurdish is also spoken. Official religion: Muslim. Currency: dinar. Capital: Baghdad. Pop.: 22 427 000 (1999 est.). Area: 438 446 sq. km (169 284 sq. miles).
▸ **Iraqi** (ɪˈrɑːkɪ) *adj, n*

irascible (ɪˈræsɪbᵊl) *adj* **1** easily angered; irritable. **2** showing irritability: *an irascible action.* ORIG C16: from LL *īrascibilis,* from L *īra* anger
▸ **iˌrasciˈbility** *or* **iˈrascibleness** *n* ▸ **iˈrascibly** *adv*

irate (aɪˈreɪt) *adj* **1** incensed with anger; furious. **2** marked by extreme anger: *an irate letter.* ORIG C19: from L *īrātus* enraged, from *īrascī* to be angry
▸ **iˈrately** *adv*

Irbid ★ (ˈɪrbɪd) *n* a town in NW Jordan. Pop.: 208 201 (1994).

Irbil ★ (ˈɪəbɪl) *n* a variant of **Erbil.**

IRBM *abbrev. for* intermediate-range ballistic missile.

ire (ˈaɪə) *n Literary.* anger; wrath. ORIG C13: from OF, from L *īra*
▸ **ˈireful** *adj* ▸ **ˈirefulness** *n*

Ire. *abbrev. for* Ireland.

Ireland[1] ★ (ˈaɪələnd) *n* **1** an island off NW Europe: part of the British Isles, separated from Britain by the North Channel, the Irish Sea, and St George's Channel; large areas of peat bog, with mountains that rise over 900 m (3000 ft) in the southwest and several large lakes. It was conquered by England in the 16th and early 17th centuries and ruled as a dependency until 1801, when it was united with Great Britain until its division in 1921 into the Irish Free State and Northern Ireland. Latin name: **Hibernia. 2 Republic of.** Also called: **Irish Republic, Southern Ireland.** a republic in NW Europe occupying most of Ireland: established as the Irish Free State (a British dominion) in 1921 and declared a republic in 1949; a member of the European Union. Official languages: Irish (Gaelic) and English. Currency: punt and euro. Capital: Dublin. Pop.: 3 736 000 (1999 est.). Area: 70 282 sq. km (27 136 sq. miles). Gaelic name: **Eire.** ◆ See also **Northern Ireland.**

Ireland[2] ★ (ˈaɪələnd) *n* **John (Nicholson).** 1879–1962, British composer, esp. of songs.

irenic, eirenic (aɪˈriːnɪk, -ˈrɛn-) *or* **irenical, eirenical** *adj* tending to conciliate or promote peace. ORIG C19: from Gk *eirēnikos,* from *eirēnē* peace
▸ **iˈrenically** *or* **eiˈrenically** *adv*

Ireton ★ (ˈaɪətᵊn) *n* **Henry.** 1611–51, English Parliamentarian general in the Civil War; son-in-law of Oliver Cromwell. His plan for a constitutional monarchy was rejected by Charles I (1647), whose death warrant he signed; lord deputy of Ireland (1650–51).

Irian Barat ★ (ˈɪərɪən ˈbærɑːt) *n* the former Indonesian name for **Irian Jaya.**

Irian Jaya ★ *n* the W part of the island of New Guinea: formerly under Dutch rule, becoming a province of Indonesia in 1963. Capital: Jayapura. Pop.: 1 956 300 (1995 est.). Area: 416 990 sq. km (161 000 sq. miles). Former names (until 1963): **Dutch New Guinea, Netherlands New Guinea.** English name: **West Irian.**

iridaceous (ˌɪrɪˈdeɪʃəs, ˌaɪ-) *adj* of, relating to, or belonging to the family of monocotyledonous plants, including the iris, having swordlike leaves and showy flowers.

iridescent (ˌɪrɪˈdɛsᵊnt) *adj* displaying a spectrum of colours that shimmer and change due to interference and scattering as the observer's position changes. ORIG C18: from L *irid-* iris + -ESCENT
▸ **ˌiriˈdescence** *n* ▸ **ˌiriˈdescently** *adv*

iridium (aɪˈrɪdɪəm, ɪˈrɪd-) *n* a very hard yellowish-white transition element that is the most corrosion-resistant metal known. It occurs in platinum ores and is used as an alloy with platinum. Symbol: Ir; atomic no.: 77; atomic wt.: 192.2. ORIG C19: NL, from L *irid-* iris + -IUM; from its colourful appearance when dissolving in certain acids

iris (ˈaɪrɪs) *n, pl* **irises** *or* **irides** (ˈaɪrɪˌdiːz, ˈɪrɪ-). **1** the coloured muscular diaphragm that surrounds and controls the size of the pupil of the eye. **2** Also called: **fleur-de-lys.** any iridaceous plant having brightly coloured flowers composed of three petals and three drooping sepals. **3** a poetic word for **rainbow. 4** short for **iris diaphragm.** ORIG C14: from L: rainbow, iris (flower), crystal, from Gk

Iris ★ (ˈaɪrɪs) *n* the goddess of the rainbow along which she travelled to earth as a messenger of the gods.

iris diaphragm *n* an adjustable diaphragm that regulates the amount of light entering an optical instrument, esp. a camera.

Irish (ˈaɪrɪʃ) *adj* **1** of, relating to, or characteristic of Ireland, its people, their Celtic language, or their dialect of English. **2** *Inf. offens.* ludicrous or illogical. ◆ *n* **3 the Irish.** (*functioning as pl*) the natives or inhabitants of Ireland. **4** another name for **Irish Gaelic. 5** the dialect of English spoken in Ireland.

Irish coffee *n* hot coffee mixed with Irish whiskey and topped with double cream.

Irish Free State ★ *n* a former name for the (Republic of) **Ireland** (1921–37).

Irish Gaelic *n* the Goidelic language of the Celts of Ireland, now spoken mainly along the west coast; an official language of the Republic of Ireland since 1921.

Irishman (ˈaɪrɪʃmən) *or* (*fem*) **Irishwoman** *n, pl* **Irishmen** *or* **Irishwomen.** a native or inhabitant of Ireland.

Irish pipes *pl n* another name for **uillean pipes.**

Irish Republic ★ *n* See **Ireland**[1] (sense 2).

Irish Republican Army *n* a militant organization of Irish nationalists founded with the aim of striving for a united independent Ireland by means of guerrilla warfare. Abbrev.: **IRA.**

Irish Sea ★ *n* an arm of the North Atlantic Ocean between Great Britain and Ireland.

Irish stew *n* a stew made of mutton, lamb, or beef, with potatoes, onions, etc.

Irish wolfhound *n* a large breed of hound with a rough thick coat.

iritis (aɪˈraɪtɪs) *n* inflammation of the iris of the eye.
▸ **iritic** (aɪˈrɪtɪk) *adj*

irk (ɜːk) *vb* (*tr*) to irritate, vex, or annoy. ORIG C13 *irken* to grow weary

irksome (ˈɜːksəm) *adj* causing vexation, annoyance, or boredom; troublesome or tedious.
▸ **ˈirksomely** *adv* ▸ **ˈirksomeness** *n*

Irkutsk ★ (*Russian* irˈkutsk) *n* a city in S Russia: situated on the Trans-Siberian railway; university (1918); one of the largest industrial centres in Siberia, esp. for heavy engineering. Pop.: 585 000 (1995 est.).

IRO *abbrev. for:* **1** (in Britain) Inland Revenue Office. **2** International Refugee Organization.

iron (ˈaɪən) *n* **1a** a malleable ductile silvery-white ferromagnetic metallic element. It is widely used for structural and engineering purposes. Symbol: Fe; atomic no.: 26; atomic wt.: 55.847. Related adjs.: **ferric, ferrous.** Related prefix: **ferro-. 1b** (*as modifier*): *iron railings.* **2** any of certain tools or implements made of iron or steel, esp.

for use when hot: *a grappling iron; a soldering iron.* **3** an appliance for pressing fabrics using dry heat or steam, esp. a small electrically heated device with a handle and a weighted flat bottom. **4** any of various golf clubs with metal heads, numbered from 1 to 10 according to the slant of the face. **5** a splintlike support for a malformed leg. **6** great hardness, strength, or resolve: *a will of iron.* **7** **strike while the iron is hot.** to act at an opportune moment. ◆ *adj* **8** very hard, immovable, or implacable: *iron determination.* **9** very strong; extremely robust: *an iron constitution.* **10** cruel or unyielding: *he ruled with an iron hand.* ◆ *vb* **11** to smooth (clothes or fabric) by removing (creases or wrinkles) using a heated iron; press. **12** (*tr*) to furnish or clothe with iron. **13** (*tr*) *Rare.* to place (a prisoner) in irons. ◆ See also **iron out, irons.** ORIG OE *īren*
▸ **ˈironer** *n* ▸ **ˈironless** *adj* ▸ **ˈironˌlike** *adj*

Iron Age *n* **a** the period following the Bronze Age characterized by the extremely rapid spread of iron tools and weapons. **b** (*as modifier*): *an Iron-Age weapon.*

ironbark (ˈaɪənˌbɑːk) *n* any of several Australian eucalyptus trees that have hard rough bark.

ironbound (ˈaɪənˌbaʊnd) *adj* **1** bound with iron. **2** unyielding; inflexible. **3** (of a coast) rocky; rugged.

Iron Chancellor ★ *n* **the.** nickname of (Prince Otto Eduard Leopold von) **Bismarck.**

ironclad *adj* (ˌaɪənˈklæd). **1** covered or protected with iron: *an ironclad warship.* **2** inflexible; rigid: *an ironclad rule.* ◆ *n* (ˈaɪənˌklæd). **3** a large wooden 19th-century warship with armoured plating.

Iron Curtain *n* **1** (formerly) **1a** the guarded border between the countries of the Soviet bloc and the rest of Europe. **1b** (*as modifier*): *Iron Curtain countries.* **2** (*sometimes not caps.*) any barrier that separates communities or ideologies.

Iron Gate *or* **Iron Gates** ★ *n* a gorge of the River Danube on the border between Romania and Yugoslavia. Length: 3 km (2 miles). Romanian name: **Porţile de Fier.**

iron hand *n* harsh or rigorous control; overbearing or autocratic force.

iron horse *n Arch.* a steam-driven railway locomotive.

ironic (aɪˈrɒnɪk) *or* **ironical** *adj* of, characterized by, or using irony.
▸ **iˈronically** *adv* ▸ **iˈronicalness** *n*

ironing (ˈaɪənɪŋ) *n* **1** the act of ironing washed clothes. **2** clothes, etc., that are to be or that have been ironed.

ironing board *n* a board, usually on legs, with a suitable covering on which to iron clothes.

iron lung *n* an airtight metal cylinder enclosing the entire body up to the neck and providing artificial respiration.

iron maiden *n* a medieval instrument of torture, consisting of a hinged case (often shaped in the form of a woman) lined with iron spikes, which was forcibly closed on the victim.

iron man *n Austral.* **1** an event at a surf carnival in which contestants compete at swimming, surfing, running, etc. **2** a participant in such an event.

ironmaster (ˈaɪənˌmɑːstə) *n Brit.* a manufacturer of iron.

ironmonger (ˈaɪənˌmʌŋgə) *n Brit.* a dealer in metal utensils, hardware, locks, etc. US and Canad. equivalent: **hardware dealer.**
▸ **ˈironˌmongery** *n*

iron out *vb* (*tr, adv*) **1** to smooth, using a heated iron. **2** to put right or settle (a problem or difficulty) as a result of negotiations or discussions. **3** *Austral. inf.* to knock unconscious.

iron pyrites (ˈpaɪraɪts) *n* another name for **pyrite.**

iron rations *pl n* emergency food supplies, esp. for military personnel in action.

irons (ˈaɪənz) *pl n* **1** fetters or chains (often in **in** *or* **into irons**). **2** **have several irons in the fire.** to be involved in many projects, etc.

Irons ★ (ˈaɪənz) *n* **Jeremy.** born 1948, British film and stage actor. His films include *The French Lieutenant's Woman* (1981) and *House of the Spirits* (1993).

Ironside ★ (ˈaɪənˌsaɪd) *n* nickname of **Edmund II** of England.

ironsides (ˈaɪənˌsaɪdz) *n* **1** a person with great stamina or resistance. **2** an ironclad ship. **3** (*often cap.*) (in the English Civil War) **3a** the cavalry regiment trained and commanded by Oliver Cromwell. **3b** Cromwell's entire army.

ironstone (ˈaɪənˌstəʊn) *n* **1** any rock consisting mainly of an iron-bearing ore. **2** a tough durable earthenware.

ironware (ˈaɪənˌwɛə) *n* domestic articles made of iron.

ironwood (ˈaɪənˌwʊd) *n* **1** any of various trees, such as hornbeam, that have very hard wood. **2** a Californian rosaceous tree with very hard wood. **3** any of various other trees with hard wood, such as the mopani. **4** the wood of any of these trees.

ironwork (ˈaɪənˌwɜːk) *n* **1** work done in iron, esp. decorative work. **2** the craft or practice of working in iron.

ironworks (ˈaɪənˌwɜːks) *n* (*sometimes functioning as sing*) a building in which iron is smelted, cast, or wrought.

irony[1] (ˈaɪrənɪ) *n, pl* **ironies.** **1** the humorous or mildly sarcastic use of words to imply the opposite of what they normally mean. **2** an instance of this, used to draw attention to some incongruity or irrationality. **3** incongruity between what is expected to be and what actually is, or a situation or result showing such incongruity. **4** See **dramatic irony.** **5** *Philosophy.* See **Socratic irony.** ORIG C16: from L, from Gk *eirōneia,* from *eirōn* dissembler, from *eirein* to speak

irony[2] (ˈaɪənɪ) *adj* of, resembling, or containing iron.

Iroquois (ˈɪrəˌkwɔɪ) *n* **1** (*pl* **Iroquois**) a member of a confederacy of North American Indian tribes formerly living in and around New York State. **2** any of the languages of these people.
▸ **ˌIroˈquoian** *adj*

irradiance (ɪˈreɪdɪəns) *n* the radiant flux incident on unit area of a surface. Also: **irradiation.** Cf. **illuminance.**

irradiate (ɪˈreɪdɪˌeɪt) *vb* **irradiates, irradiating, irradiated.** **1** (*tr*) *Physics.* to subject to or treat with light or other electromagnetic radiation or with beams of particles. **2** (*tr*) to expose (food) to electromagnetic radiation to kill bacteria and retard deterioration. **3** (*tr*) to make clear or bright intellectually or spiritually; illumine. **4** a less common word for **radiate** (sense 1). **5** (*intr*) *Obs.* to become radiant.
▸ **irˈradiˌation** *n* ▸ **irˈradiative** *adj* ▸ **irˈradiˌator** *n*

irrational (ɪˈræʃənᵊl) *adj* **1** inconsistent with reason or logic; illogical; absurd. **2** incapable of reasoning. **3a** *Maths.* (of an equation, etc.) containing one or more variables in irreducible radical form or raised to a fractional power: $\sqrt{(x^2 + 1)} = x^{5/3}$. **3b** (*as n*): *an irrational.*
▸ **irˌrationˈality** *n* ▸ **irˈrationally** *adv*

irrational number *n* any real number that cannot be expressed as the ratio of two integers, such as π.

Irrawaddy ★ (ˌɪrəˈwɒdɪ) *n* the main river in Myanmar, rising in the north in two headstreams and flowing south through the whole length of Myanmar, to enter the Andaman Sea by nine main mouths. Length: 2100 km (1300 miles).

irreclaimable (ˌɪrɪˈkleɪməbᵊl) *adj* not able to be reclaimed.
▸ **ˌirreˌclaimaˈbility** *or* **ˌirreˈclaimableness** *n* ▸ **ˌirreˈclaimably** *adv*

irreconcilable (ɪˈrɛkᵊnˌsaɪləbᵊl, ɪˌrɛkᵊnˈsaɪ-) *adj* **1** not able to be reconciled; uncompromisingly conflicting; incompatible. ◆ *n* **2** a person or thing that is implacably hostile or uncompromisingly opposed. **3** (*usually pl*) one of various principles, ideas, etc., that are incapable of being brought into agreement.
▸ **irˌreconˌcilaˈbility** *or* **irˈreconˌcilableness** *n* ▸ **irˈreconˌcilably** *adv*

irrecoverable (ˌɪrɪˈkʌvərəbᵊl, -ˈkʌvrə-) *adj* **1** not able to be recovered or regained. **2** not able to be remedied or rectified.
▸ **ˌirreˈcoverableness** *n* ▸ **ˌirreˈcoverably** *adv*

irrecusable (ˌɪrɪˈkjuːzəbᵊl) *adj* not able to be rejected or challenged, as evidence, etc.

irredeemable (ˌɪrɪˈdiːməbᵊl) *adj* **1** (of bonds, shares, etc.) without a date of redemption of capital; incapable

of being bought back directly or paid off. **2** (of paper money) not convertible into specie. **3** (of a loss) not able to be recovered; irretrievable. **4** not able to be improved or rectified; irreparable.
► **ˌirreˌdeemaˈbility** *or* **ˌirreˈdeemableness** *n* ► **ˌirreˈdeemably** *adv*

irredentist (ˌɪrɪˈdɛntɪst) *n* **1** (*sometimes cap.*) a person, esp. a member of a 19th-century Italian association, who favours the acquisition of territory that was once part of his country or is considered to have been. ◆ *adj* **2** of or relating to irredentists or their policies. ORIG C19: from It. *irredentista,* from *ir-* IN-[1] + *redento* redeemed, from L *redemptus* bought back; see REDEEM
► **ˌirreˈdentism** *n*

irreducible (ˌɪrɪˈdjuːsɪbᵊl) *adj* **1** not able to be reduced or lessened. **2** not able to be brought to a simpler or reduced form. **3** *Maths.* (of a polynomial) unable to be factorized into polynomials of lower degree, as $(x^2 + 1)$.
► **ˌirreˌduciˈbility** *n* ► **ˌirreˈducibly** *adv*

irrefragable (ɪˈrɛfrəgəbᵊl) *adj* not able to be denied or refuted. ORIG C16: from LL *irrefrāgābilis,* from L *ir-* + *refrāgārī* to resist
► **irˌrefragaˈbility** *or* **irˈrefragableness** *n* ► **irˈrefragably** *adv*

irrefrangible (ˌɪrɪˈfrændʒəbᵊl) *adj* **1** not to be broken or transgressed; inviolable. **2** *Physics.* incapable of being refracted.
► **ˌirreˌfrangiˈbility** *or* **ˌirreˈfrangibleness** *n* ► **ˌirreˈfrangibly** *adv*

irrefutable (ɪˈrɛfjʊtəbᵊl, ˌɪrɪˈfjuːtəbᵊl) *adj* impossible to deny or disprove; incontrovertible.
► **irˌrefutaˈbility** *n* ► **irˈrefutably** *adv*

irreg. *abbrev. for* irregular(ly).

irregular (ɪˈrɛgjʊlə) *adj* **1** lacking uniformity or symmetry; uneven in shape, position, arrangement, etc. **2** not occurring at expected or equal intervals: *an irregular pulse.* **3** differing from the normal or accepted practice or routine; unconventional. **4** (of the formation, inflections, or derivations of a word) not following the usual pattern of formation in a language. **5** of or relating to guerrillas or volunteers not belonging to regular forces: *irregular troops.* **6** (of flowers) having any of their petals differing in size, shape, etc. **7** *US.* (of merchandise) not up to the manufacturer's standards or specifications; imperfect. ◆ *n* **8** a soldier not in a regular army. **9** (*often pl*) *US.* imperfect or flawed merchandise.
► **irˌreguˈlarity** *n* ► **irˈregularly** *adv*

irrelevant (ɪˈrɛləvənt) *adj* not relating or pertinent to the matter at hand.
► **irˈrelevance** *or* **irˈrelevancy** *n* ► **irˈrelevantly** *adv*

irreligion (ˌɪrɪˈlɪdʒən) *n* **1** lack of religious faith. **2** indifference or opposition to religion.
► **ˌirreˈligionist** *n* ► **ˌirreˈligious** *adj* ► **ˌirreˈligiously** *adv* ► **ˌirreˈligiousness** *n*

irremediable (ˌɪrɪˈmiːdɪəbᵊl) *adj* not able to be remedied; incurable or irreparable.
► **ˌirreˈmediableness** *n* ► **ˌirreˈmediably** *adv*

irremissible (ˌɪrɪˈmɪsəbᵊl) *adj* **1** unpardonable; inexcusable. **2** that must be done, as through duty or obligation.
► **ˌirreˌmissiˈbility** *or* **ˌirreˈmissibleness** *n* ► **ˌirreˈmissibly** *adv*

irremovable (ˌɪrɪˈmuːvəbᵊl) *adj* not able to be removed.
► **ˌirreˌmovaˈbility** *n* ► **ˌirreˈmovably** *adv*

irreparable (ɪˈrɛpərəbᵊl, ɪˈrɛprəbᵊl) *adj* not able to be repaired or remedied; beyond repair.
► **irˌreparaˈbility** *or* **irˈreparableness** *n* ► **irˈreparably** *adv*

irreplaceable (ˌɪrɪˈpleɪsəbᵊl) *adj* not able to be replaced: *an irreplaceable antique.*
► **ˌirreˈplaceably** *adv*

irrepressible (ˌɪrɪˈprɛsəbᵊl) *adj* not capable of being repressed, controlled, or restrained.
► **ˌirreˌpressiˈbility** *or* **ˌirreˈpressibleness** *n* ► **ˌirreˈpressibly** *adv*

irreproachable (ˌɪrɪˈprəʊtʃəbᵊl) *adj* not deserving reproach; blameless.
► **ˌirreˌproachaˈbility** *or* **ˌirreˈproachableness** *n* ► **ˌirreˈproachably** *adv*

irresistible (ˌɪrɪˈzɪstəbᵊl) *adj* **1** not able to be resisted or refused; overpowering: *an irresistible impulse.* **2** very fascinating or alluring: *an irresistible woman.*
► **ˌirreˌsistiˈbility** *or* **ˌirreˈsistibleness** *n* ► **ˌirreˈsistibly** *adv*

irresolute (ɪˈrɛzəˌluːt) *adj* lacking resolution; wavering; hesitating.
► **irˈresoˌlutely** *adv* ► **irˈresoˌluteness** *or* **irˌresoˈlution** *n*

irrespective (ˌɪrɪˈspɛktɪv) *adj* **1 irrespective of.** without taking account of; regardless of. ◆ *adv* **2** *Inf.* regardless; without due consideration: *he carried on with his plan irrespective.*
► **ˌirreˈspectively** *adv*

irresponsible (ˌɪrɪˈspɒnsəbᵊl) *adj* **1** not showing or done with due care for the consequences of one's actions or attitudes; reckless. **2** not capable of bearing responsibility.
► **ˌirreˌsponsiˈbility** *or* **ˌirreˈsponsibleness** *n* ► **ˌirreˈsponsibly** *adv*

irresponsive (ˌɪrɪˈspɒnsɪv) *adj* not responsive.
► **ˌirreˈsponsively** *adv* ► **ˌirreˈsponsiveness** *n*

irretrievable (ˌɪrɪˈtriːvəbᵊl) *adj* not able to be retrieved, recovered, or repaired.
► **ˌirreˌtrievaˈbility** *n* ► **ˌirreˈtrievably** *adv*

irreverence (ɪˈrɛvərəns, ɪˈrɛvrəns) *n* **1** lack of due respect or veneration; disrespect. **2** a disrespectful remark or act.
► **irˈreverent** *or* **irˌreveˈrential** *adj* ► **irˈreverently** *adv*

irreversible (ˌɪrɪˈvɜːsəbᵊl) *adj* **1** not able to be reversed: *the irreversible flow of time.* **2** not able to be revoked or repealed; irrevocable. **3** *Chem., physics.* capable of changing or producing a change in one direction only: *an irreversible reaction.*
► **ˌirreˌversiˈbility** *or* **ˌirreˈversibleness** *n* ► **ˌirreˈversibly** *adv*

irrevocable (ɪˈrɛvəkəbᵊl) *adj* not able to be revoked, changed, or undone.
► **irˌrevocaˈbility** *or* **irˈrevocableness** *n* ► **irˈrevocably** *adv*

irrigate (ˈɪrɪˌgeɪt) *vb* **irrigates, irrigating, irrigated. 1** to supply (land) with water by means of artificial canals, etc., esp. to promote the growth of food crops. **2** *Med.* to bathe or wash out (a bodily part, cavity, or wound). **3** (*tr*) to make fertile, fresh, or vital by or as if by watering. ORIG C17: from L *irrigāre,* from *rigāre* to moisten, conduct water
► **ˈirrigable** *adj* ► **ˌirriˈgation** *n* ► **ˈirriˌgative** *adj* ► **ˈirriˌgator** *n*

irritable (ˈɪrɪtəbᵊl) *adj* **1** quickly irritated; easily annoyed; peevish. **2** (of all living organisms) capable of responding to such stimuli as heat, light, and touch. **3** *Pathol.* abnormally sensitive.
► **ˌirritaˈbility** *n* ► **ˈirritableness** *n* ► **ˈirritably** *adv*

irritable bowel syndrome *n Med.* a chronic condition of recurring abdominal pain with constipation or diarrhoea or both.

irritant (ˈɪrɪtənt) *adj* **1** causing irritation; irritating. ◆ *n* **2** something irritant.
► **ˈirritancy** *n*

irritate (ˈɪrɪˌteɪt) *vb* **irritates, irritating, irritated. 1** to annoy or anger (someone). **2** (*tr*) *Biol.* to stimulate (an organism or part) to respond in a characteristic manner. **3** (*tr*) *Pathol.* to cause (a bodily organ or part) to become excessively stimulated, resulting in inflammation, tenderness, etc. ORIG C16: from L *irrītāre* to provoke
► **ˈirriˌtator** *n*

irritation (ˌɪrɪˈteɪʃən) *n* **1** something that irritates. **2** the act of irritating or the condition of being irritated.
► **ˈirriˌtative** *adj*

irrupt (ɪˈrʌpt) *vb* (*intr*) **1** to enter forcibly or suddenly. **2** (of a plant or animal population) to enter a region suddenly and in very large numbers. **3** (of a population) to increase suddenly and greatly. ORIG C19: from L *irrumpere* to rush into, invade, from *rumpere* to break, burst
► **irˈruption** *n* ► **irˈruptive** *adj*

Irtysh *or* **Irtish** ★ (ɪəˈtɪʃ) *n* a river in central Asia, rising in China in the Altai Mountains and flowing west through Kazakhstan, then northwest into Russia to join the Ob River as its chief tributary. Length: 4444 km (2760 miles).

Irvine ★ ('ɜːvɪn) *n* a town on the W coast of Scotland, the administrative centre of North Ayrshire: designated a new town in 1966. Pop.: 32 988 (1991).

Irving ★ ('ɜːvɪŋ) *n* **1** Sir **Henry**. real name *John Henry Brodribb*. 1838–1905, English actor and manager of the Lyceum Theatre in London (1878–1902). **2 Washington.** 1783–1859, US essayist and short-story writer, noted for *The Sketch Book of Geoffrey Crayon* (1820), which contains the stories *Rip Van Winkle* and *The Legend of Sleepy Hollow*.

IRW *abbrev. for:* in the real world; used esp. in e-mails, text messages etc. ORIG C20

is (ɪz) *vb* (used with *he, she, it,* and with singular nouns) a form of the present tense (indicative mood) of **be.** ORIG OE

Is. *abbrev. for:* **1** Also: **Isa.** *Bible.* Isaiah. **2** Island(s) *or* Isle(s).

is- *combining form.* a variant of **iso-** before a vowel: *isentropic.*

ISA ('aɪsə) *n acronym for* individual savings account: a tax-free savings scheme introduced in the UK in 1999.

Isaac ★ ('aɪzək) *n* an Old Testament patriarch, the son of Abraham and Sarah and father of Jacob and Esau (Genesis 17; 21–27).

Isabella ★ (ˌɪzə'bɛlə) *n* original name *Elizabeth Farnese.* 1692–1766, second wife (1714–46) of Philip V of Spain and mother of Charles III of Spain.

Isabella I ★ *n* known as *Isabella the Catholic.* 1451–1504, queen of Castile (1474–1504) and, with her husband, Ferdinand V, joint ruler of Castile and Aragon (1479–1504).

Isabella II ★ *n* 1830–1904, queen of Spain (1833–68), whose accession precipitated the first Carlist war (1833–39). She was deposed in a revolution.

Isabella of France ★ *n* 1292–1358, wife (1308–27) of Edward II of England, whom, aided by her lover, Roger de Mortimer, she deposed; mother of Edward III.

isagogics (ˌaɪsə'gɒdʒɪks) *n* introductory studies, esp. in the history of the Bible. ORIG C19: from L, from Gk, from *eisagein* to introduce, from *eis-* into + *agein* to lead

Isaiah ★ (aɪ'zaɪə) *n Old Testament.* **1** the first of the major Hebrew prophets, who lived in the 8th century B.C. **2** the book of his and others' prophecies.

isallobar (aɪ'sæləˌbɑː) *n* a line on a map connecting places with equal pressure changes.

Isar ★ ('iːzɑː) *n* a river in central Europe, rising in W Austria and flowing generally northeast through S Germany into the Danube. Length: over 260 km (160 miles).

isatin ('aɪsətɪn) *or* **isatine** ('aɪsəˌtiːn) *n* a yellowish-red crystalline compound soluble in hot water, used for the preparation of vat dyes. ORIG C19: from L *isatis* woad + -IN
▸ ˌ**isa'tinic** *adj*

Isauria ★ (aɪ'sɔːrɪə) *n* an ancient district of S central Asia Minor, chiefly on the N slopes of the W Taurus Mountains.
▸ **I'saurian** *adj, n*

ISBN *abbrev. for* International Standard Book Number

Iscariot ★ (ɪ'skærɪət) *n* See **Judas** (Iscariot).

ischaemia *or* **ischemia** (ɪ'skiːmɪə) *n Pathol.* an inadequate supply of blood to an organ or part, as from an obstructed blood flow. ORIG C19: from Gk *iskhein* to restrict, + -AEMIA
▸ **ischaemic** *or* **ischemic** (ɪ'skɛmɪk) *adj*

Ischia ★ ('iːskjɑː, 'ɪskɪə) *n* a volcanic island in the Tyrrhenian Sea, at the N end of the Bay of Naples. Area: 47 sq. km (18 sq. miles).

ischium ('ɪskɪəm) *n, pl* **ischia** (-kɪə). one of the three sections of the hipbone, situated below the ilium. ORIG C17: from L: hip joint, from Gk *iskhion*
▸ **'ischial** *adj*

-ise *suffix forming verbs.* a variant of **-ize.**

> **USAGE NOTE** See at **-ize.**

isentropic (ˌaɪsɛn'trɒpɪk) *adj* having or taking place at constant entropy.

Isère ★ (*French* izɛr) *n* **1** a department of SE France, in Rhône-Alpes region. Capital: Grenoble. Pop.: 1 060 252 (1994 est.). Area: 7904 sq. km (3083 sq. miles). **2** a river in SE France, rising in the Graian Alps and flowing west and southwest to join the River Rhône near Valence. Length: 290 km (180 miles).

Iseult, Yseult (ɪ'suːlt), *or* **Isolde** ★ (ɪ'zəʊldə) *n* (in Arthurian legend) **1** an Irish princess wed to Mark, king of Cornwall, but in love with his knight Tristan. **2** (in another account) the daughter of the king of Brittany, married to Tristan.

Isfahan (ˌɪsfə'hɑːn) *or* **Eşfahān** ★ *n* a city in central Iran: the second largest city in the country; capital of Persia in the 11th century and from 1598 to 1722. Pop.: 1 127 030 (1991). Ancient name: **Aspadana** (ˌæspə'dɑːnə).

-ish *suffix forming adjectives.* **1** of or belonging to a nationality: *Scottish.* **2** *Often derog.* having the manner or qualities of; resembling: *slavish; boyish.* **3** somewhat; approximately: *yellowish; sevenish.* **4** concerned or preoccupied with: *bookish.* ORIG OE *-isc*

Isherwood ★ ('ɪʃəˌwʊd) *n* **Christopher,** full name *Christopher William Bradshaw-Isherwood.* 1904–86, US novelist and dramatist, born in England. His works include the novel *Goodbye to Berlin* (1939) and three verse plays written in collaboration with W. H. Auden.

Ishiguro ★ (ˌɪʃɪ'guːrəʊ) *n* **Kazuo** (kæ'zuːəʊ). born 1954, British novelist, born in Japan. His novels include *An Artist of the Floating World* (1986), *The Remains of the Day* (1989), and *When We Were Orphans* (2000).

Ishmael ★ ('ɪʃmeɪəl) *n* **1** the son of Abraham and Hagar, Sarah's handmaid: the ancestor of 12 Arabian tribes (Genesis 21:8–21; 25:12–18). **2** a bandit chieftain, who defied the Babylonian conquerors of Judah and assassinated the governor appointed by Nebuchadnezzar (II Kings 25:25; Jeremiah 40:13–41:18). **3** *Rare.* an outcast.

Ishtar ★ ('ɪʃtɑː) *n* the principal goddess of the Babylonians and Assyrians; divinity of love, fertility, and war.

Isidore of Seville ★ ('ɪzɪdɔː) *n* **Saint,** Latin name *Isidorus Hispalensis.* ?560–636 A.D., Spanish archbishop and scholar, noted for his *Etymologies,* an encyclopedia. Feast day: April 4.

isinglass ('aɪzɪŋˌglɑːs) *n* **1** a gelatine made from the air bladders of freshwater fish, used as a clarifying agent and adhesive. **2** another name for **mica.** ORIG C16: from MDu. *huysenblase,* lit.: sturgeon bladder; infl. by E GLASS

Isis[1] ★ ('aɪsɪs) *n* the local name for the River Thames at Oxford.

Isis[2] ★ ('aɪsɪs) *n* an ancient Egyptian fertility goddess, usually depicted as a woman with a cow's horns, between which was the disc of the sun; wife and sister of Osiris.

Iskenderun ★ (ɪs'kɛndəˌruːn) *n* a port in S Turkey, on the **Gulf of Iskenderun.** Pop.: 156 800 (1994 est.). Former name: **Alexandretta.**

Isl. *abbrev. for:* **1** Island. **2** Isle.

Islam ('ɪzlɑːm) *n* **1** Also called: **Islamism.** the religion of Muslims, teaching that there is only one God and that Mohammed is his prophet. **2a** Muslims collectively and their civilization. **2b** the countries where the Muslim religion is predominant. ORIG C19: from Ar.: surrender (to God), from *aslama* to surrender
▸ **Is'lamic** *adj*

Islamabad ★ (ɪz'lɑːməˌbɑːd) *n* the capital of Pakistan, in the north on the Potwar Plateau: site chosen in 1959; surrounded by the Capital Territory of Islamabad for 909 sq. km (351 sq. miles). Pop.: 204 364 (1995 est.).

Islamist ('ɪzˌləmɪst) *adj* **1** supporting or advocating Islamic fundamentalism. ◆ *n* **2** a supporter or advocate of Islamic fundamentalism.

Islamize *or* **Islamise** ('ɪzləˌmaɪz) *vb* **Islamizes, Islamizing, Islamized** *or* **Islamises, Islamising, Islamised.** (*tr*) to convert or subject to the influence of Islam.
▸ ˌ**Islami'zation** *or* ˌ**Islami'sation** *n*

island ('aɪlənd) *n* **1** a mass of land that is surrounded by water and is smaller than a continent. **2** something isolated, detached, or surrounded: *a traffic island.* **3** *Anat.* a part, structure, or group of cells distinct in constitution from its immediate surroundings. ◆ Related adj: **insular.** ◆ *vb* (*tr*) *Rare.* **4** to cause to become an island. **5** to inter-

sperse with islands. **6** to place on an island; insulate; isolate. ORIG OE *īgland*
▸ **'island-,like** *adj*

islander ('aɪləndə) *n* a native or inhabitant of an island.

Islands ★ ('aɪləndz) *pl n NZ.* **the.** the islands of the South Pacific.

Islands of the Blessed ★ *pl n Greek myth.* lands where the souls of heroes and good men were taken after death. Also called: **Hesperides.**

island universe *n* a former name for **galaxy.**

Islay ★ ('aɪlə, 'aɪleɪ) *n* an island off the W coast of Scotland: the southernmost of the Inner Hebrides; separated from the island of Jura by the **Sound of Islay.** Pop.: 3500 (latest est.). Area: 606 sq. km (234 sq. miles).

isle (aɪl) *n Poetic except when cap. and part of place name.* an island, esp. a small one. ORIG C13: from OF, from L *insula* island

Isle of Dogs ★ *n* See (Isle of) **Dogs.**

Isle of Man ★ *n* See (Isle of) **Man.**

Isle of Pines ★ *n* the former name of the (Isle of) **Youth.**

Isle of Sheppey ★ *n* See (Isle of) **Sheppey.**

Isle of Wight ★ *n* See (Isle of) **Wight.**

Isle of Youth ★ *n* See (Isle of) **Youth.**

Isle Royale ★ ('rɔɪəl) *n* an island in the northeast US, in NW Lake Superior: forms, with over 100 surrounding islands, **Isle Royale National Park.** Area: 541 sq. km (209 sq. miles).

islet ('aɪlɪt) *n* a small island. ORIG C16: from OF *islette;* see ISLE

islets *or* **islands of Langerhans** ('læŋəˌhæns) *pl n* small groups of endocrine cells in the pancreas that secrete insulin. ORIG C19: after Paul *Langerhans* (1847–88), G physician

Islington ★ ('ɪzlɪŋtən) *n* a borough of N Greater London. Pop.: 175 200 (1994 est.). Area: 16 sq. km (6 sq. miles).

ism ('ɪzəm) *n Inf., often derog.* an unspecified doctrine, system, or practice.

-ism *suffix forming nouns.* **1** indicating an action, process, or result: *criticism.* **2** indicating a state or condition: *paganism.* **3** indicating a doctrine, system, or body of principles and practices: *Leninism; spiritualism.* **4** indicating behaviour or a characteristic quality: *heroism.* **5** indicating a characteristic usage, esp. of a language: *Scotticism.* **6** indicating prejudice on the basis specified: *sexism; ageism.* ORIG from OF *-isme,* from L *-ismus,* from Gk *-ismos*

Ismaili *or* **Isma'ili** (ˌɪzmɑːˈiːlɪ) *n Islam.* **1** a Shiah sect whose adherents believe that Ismail, son of the sixth imam, was the rightful seventh imam. **2** a member of this sect.

Ismailia ★ (ˌɪzmaɪˈlɪə) *n* a city in NE Egypt, on the Suez Canal: founded in 1863 by the former Suez Canal Company; devastated by Israeli troops in the October War (1973). Pop.: 255 000 (1992 est.).

Ismail Pasha ★ (ˌɪzmɑːˈiːl ˈpɑːʃə) *n* 1830–95, viceroy (1863–66) and khedive (1867–79) of Egypt, who brought his country close to bankruptcy. He was forced to submit to Anglo-French financial control (1876) and to abdicate (1879).

isn't ('ɪzᵊnt) *contraction of* is not.

ISO[1] ('aɪ'ɛs'əʊ) *n* International Organization for Standardization. ORIG from Gk *isos* equal; often wrongly thought to be an abbreviation for *International Standards Organization*

ISO[2] *abbrev. for:* Imperial Service Order (a Brit. decoration).

iso- *or before a vowel* **is-** *combining form.* **1** equal or identical: *isomagnetic.* **2** indicating that a chemical compound is an isomer of a specified compound: *isobutane.* ORIG from Gk *isos* equal

isobar ('aɪsəʊˌbɑː) *n* **1** a line on a map connecting places of equal atmospheric pressure, usually reduced to sea level for purposes of comparison, at a given time or period. **2** *Physics.* any of two or more atoms that have the same mass number but different atomic numbers. Cf. **isotope.** ORIG C19: from Gk *isobarēs* of equal weight
▸ **ˌiso'baric** *adj* ▸ **'isobarˌism** *n*

isobutene (ˌaɪsəʊ'bjuːtiːn) *n* a colourless gas used in the manufacture of synthetic rubber.

isocheim *or* **isochime** ('aɪsəʊˌkaɪm) *n* a line on a map connecting places with the same mean winter temperature. Cf. **isothere.** ORIG C19: from ISO- + Gk *kheima* winter weather
▸ **ˌiso'cheimal** *or* **ˌiso'chimal** *adj*

isochronal (aɪ'sɒkrənᵊl) *or* **isochronous** *adj* **1** having the same duration; equal in time. **2** occurring at equal time intervals; having a uniform period of vibration. ORIG C17: from NL, from Gk *isokhronos,* from ISO- + *khronos* time
▸ **i'sochronally** *or* **i'sochronously** *adv* ▸ **i'sochroˌnism** *n*

isoclinal (ˌaɪsəʊ'klaɪnᵊl) *or* **isoclinic** (ˌaɪsəʊ'klɪnɪk) *adj* **1** sloping in the same direction and at the same angle. **2** *Geol.* (of folds) having limbs that are parallel to each other. ◆ *n* **3** Also: **isocline, isoclinal line.** an imaginary line connecting points on the earth's surface having equal angles of magnetic dip.

isocline ('aɪsəʊˌklaɪn) *n* **1** a series of rock strata with isoclinal folds. **2** another name for **isoclinal** (sense 3).

Isocrates ★ (aɪ'sɒkrəˌtiːz) *n* 436–338 B.C., Athenian rhetorician and teacher.

isodynamic (ˌaɪsəʊdaɪ'næmɪk) *adj Physics.* **1** having equal force or strength. **2** of or relating to an imaginary line on the earth's surface connecting points of equal magnetic intensity.

isogeotherm (ˌaɪsəʊ'dʒiːəʊˌθɜːm) *n* an imaginary line below the surface of the earth connecting points of equal temperature.
▸ **ˌisoˌgeo'thermal** *or* **ˌisoˌgeo'thermic** *adj*

isogloss ('aɪsəʊˌglɒs) *n* a line drawn on a map around the area in which a linguistic feature is to be found.
▸ **ˌiso'glossal** *or* **ˌiso'glottic** *adj*

isogonic (ˌaɪsəʊ'gɒnɪk) *or* **isogonal** (aɪ'sɒgənᵊl) *adj* **1** *Maths.* having, making, or involving equal angles. ◆ *n* **2** Also called: **isogonic line, isogonal line, isogone.** *Physics.* an imaginary line connecting points on the earth's surface having equal magnetic declination.

isohel ('aɪsəʊˌhɛl) *n* a line on a map connecting places with an equal period of sunshine. ORIG C20: from ISO- + Gk *hēlios* sun

isohyet (ˌaɪsəʊ'haɪɪt) *n* a line on a map connecting places having equal rainfall. ORIG C19: from ISO- + *-hyet,* from Gk *huetos* rain

isolate *vb* ('aɪsəˌleɪt), **isolates, isolating, isolated.** (*tr*) **1** to place apart; cause to be alone. **2** *Med.* to quarantine (a person or animal) having a contagious disease. **3** to obtain (a compound) in an uncombined form. **4** to obtain pure cultures of (bacteria, esp. those causing a particular disease). **5** *Electronics.* to prevent interaction between (circuits, components, etc.); insulate. ◆ *n* ('aɪsəlɪt). **6** an isolated person or group. ORIG C19: back formation from *isolated,* via It. from L *insulātus,* lit.: made into an island
▸ **'isolable** *adj* ▸ **ˌisola'bility** *n* ▸ **'isoˌlator** *n* ▸ **ˌiso'lation** *n*

isolationism (ˌaɪsə'leɪʃəˌnɪzəm) *n* **1** a policy of nonparticipation in or withdrawal from international affairs. **2** an attitude favouring such a policy.
▸ **ˌiso'lationist** *n, adj*

Isolde ★ (i'zɔldə) *n* the German name of **Iseult.**

isomer ('aɪsəmə) *n* **1** *Chem.* a compound that exhibits isomerism with one or more other compounds. **2** *Physics.* a nuclide that exhibits isomerism with one or more other nuclides.
▸ **isomeric** (ˌaɪsə'mɛrɪk) *adj*

isomerism (aɪ'sɒməˌrɪzəm) *n* **1** the existence of two or more compounds having the same molecular formula but a different arrangement of atoms. **2** the existence of two or more nuclides having the same atomic numbers and mass numbers but different energy states.

isomerous (aɪ'sɒmərəs) *adj* (of flowers) having floral whorls with the same number of parts.

isometric (ˌaɪsəʊ'mɛtrɪk) *adj also* **isometrical. 1** having equal dimensions or measurements. **2** *Physiol.* of or relating to muscular contraction that does not produce

shortening of the muscle. **3** (of a crystal or system of crystallization) having three mutually perpendicular equal axes. **4** (of a method of projecting a drawing in three dimensions) having the three axes equally inclined and all lines drawn to scale. ◆ *n* **5** Also called: **isometric drawing.** a drawing made in this way. ORIG C19: from Gk *isometria*
▸ ˌ**iso'metrically** *adv*

isometrics (ˌaɪsəʊ'mɛtrɪks) *n* (*functioning as sing*) physical exercise involving isometric contraction of muscles.

isomorphism (ˌaɪsəʊ'mɔːˌfɪzəm) *n* **1** *Biol.* similarity of form, as in different generations of the same life cycle. **2** *Chem.* the existence of two or more substances of different composition in a similar crystalline form. **3** *Maths.* a one-to-one correspondence between the elements of two or more sets, such as those of Arabic and Roman numerals.
▸ '**isoˌmorph** *n* ▸ ˌ**iso'morphic** *or* ˌ**iso'morphous** *adj*

isopleth ('aɪsəʊˌplɛθ) *n* a line on a map connecting places registering the same amount or ratio of some geographical, etc. phenomenon. ORIG C20: from Gk *isoplēthēs* equal in number, from ISO- + *plēthos* multitude

isopod ('aɪsəʊˌpɒd) *n* a crustacean, such as the woodlouse, in which the body is flattened.
▸ **isopodan** (aɪ'sɒpədən) *or* **i'sopodous** *adj*

isoprene ('aɪsəʊˌpriːn) *n* a colourless volatile liquid with a penetrating odour: used in making synthetic rubbers. Formula: CH_2:C(CH_3)CH:CH_2. Systematic name: **methylbuta-1,3-diene.** ORIG C20: from ISO- + PR(OPYL) + -ENE

isopteran (aɪ'sɒptərən) *n, pl* **isopterans** *or* **isoptera** (-tərə). **1** any of an order of insects having two pairs of wings equal in size: comprises the termites. ◆ *adj also* **isopterous. 2** of, relating to, or belonging to this order. ORIG C19: from NL, from ISO- + Gk *pteron* wing

ISO rating *n Photog.* a classification of film speed in which a doubling of the ISO number represents a doubling in sensitivity; for example, ISO 400 film requires half the exposure of ISO 200 under the same conditions. The system uses identical numbers to the obsolete ASA rating. ORIG C20: from ISO[1]

isosceles (aɪ'sɒsɪˌliːz) *adj* (of a triangle) having two sides of equal length. ORIG C16: from LL, from Gk, from ISO- + *skelos* leg

isoseismal (ˌaɪsəʊ'saɪzməl) *adj* **1** of or relating to equal intensity of earthquake shock. ◆ *n* **2** a line on a map connecting points at which earthquake shocks are of equal intensity. ◆ Also: **isoseismic.**

isostasy (aɪ'sɒstəsɪ) *n* the state of balance which sections of the earth's lithosphere are thought ultimately to achieve when the vertical forces upon them remain unchanged. If a section is loaded as by ice, it slowly subsides. If a section is reduced in mass, as by erosion, it slowly rises. ORIG C19: ISO- + *-stasy,* from Gk *stasis* a standing
▸ **isostatic** (ˌaɪsəʊ'stætɪk) *adj*

isothere ('aɪsəʊˌθɪə) *n* a line on a map linking places of equal mean summer temperature. Cf. **isocheim.** ORIG C19: from ISO- + Gk *theros* summer
▸ **isotheral** (aɪ'sɒθərəl) *adj*

isotherm ('aɪsəʊˌθɜːm) *n* **1** a line on a map linking places of equal temperature. **2** *Physics.* a curve on a graph that connects points of equal temperature. ◆ Also called: **isothermal, isothermal line.**

isothermal (ˌaɪsəʊ'θɜːməl) *adj* **1** (of a process or change) taking place at constant temperature. **2** of or relating to an isotherm. ◆ *n* **3** another word for **isotherm.**
▸ ˌ**iso'thermally** *adv*

isotonic (ˌaɪsəʊ'tɒnɪk) *adj* **1** *Physiol.* (of two or more muscles) having equal tension. **2** (of a drink) designed to replace the fluid and salts lost from the body during strenuous exercise. **3** Also: **isosmotic.** (of two solutions) having the same osmotic pressure, commonly having physiological osmotic pressure. Cf. **hypertonic, hypotonic.**
▸ **isotonicity** (ˌaɪsəʊtəʊ'nɪsɪtɪ) *n*

isotope ('aɪsəˌtəʊp) *n* one of two or more atoms with the same atomic number that contain different numbers of neutrons. ORIG C20: from ISO- + Gk *topos* place
▸ **isotopic** (ˌaɪsə'tɒpɪk) *adj* ▸ ˌ**iso'topically** *adv* ▸ **isotopy** (aɪ'sɒtəpɪ) *n*

isotropic (ˌaɪsəʊ'trɒpɪk) *or* **isotropous** (aɪ'sɒtrəpəs) *adj* **1** having uniform physical properties in all directions. **2** *Biol.* not having predetermined axes: *isotropic eggs.*
▸ ˌ**iso'tropically** *adv* ▸ **i'sotropy** *n*

ISP *abbrev. for* Internet service provider.

I-spy *n* a game in which one player specifies the initial letter of the name of an object that he or she can see, which the other players then try to guess.

Israel ★ ('ɪzreɪəl, -rɪəl) *n* **1** a republic in SW Asia, on the Mediterranean Sea: established in 1948, in the former British mandate of Palestine, as a primarily Jewish state; disputes with Arab neighbours, who did not recognize Israel, erupted into full-scale wars in 1949, 1956, 1967 (the Six Day War), and 1973 (the Yom Kippur War). In 1993 Israel agreed to grant autonomy to the West Bank and Gaza Strip in a peace deal with the PLO. Official languages: Hebrew and Arabic. Religion: Jewish majority, Muslim and Christian minorities. Currency: shekel. Capital: Jerusalem (international recognition withheld: UN recognized capital: Tel Aviv). Pop.: 5 934 000 (1999 est.). Area (including Golan Heights and East Jerusalem): 21 946 sq. km (8473 sq. miles). **2a** the ancient kingdom of the 12 Hebrew tribes at the SE end of the Mediterranean. **2b** the kingdom in the N part of this region formed by the ten northern tribes of Israel in the 10th century B.C. and destroyed by the Assyrians in 721 B.C.

Israeli (ɪz'reɪlɪ) *n, pl* **Israelis** *or* **Israeli. 1** a citizen or inhabitant of the state of Israel. ◆ *adj* **2** of or relating to the state of Israel or its inhabitants.

Israelite ('ɪzrɪəˌlaɪt, -rə-) *n* **1** *Bible.* a member of the ethnic group claiming descent from Jacob; a Hebrew. **2** a member of any of various Christian sects who regard themselves as God's chosen people. **3** an archaic word for a **Jew.**

Issachar ★ ('ɪsəˌkɑː) *n Old Testament.* **1** the fifth son of Jacob by his wife Leah (Genesis 30:17–18). **2** the tribe descended from this patriarch. **3** the territory of this tribe.

Issigonis ★ (ˌɪsɪ'gəʊnɪs) *n* Sir **Alec** (**Arnold Constantine**). 1906–88, British car designer born in Smyrna. He is noted for his designs for the Morris Minor (1948) and the Mini (1959).

issuance ('ɪʃjʊəns) *n* the act of issuing.

issue ('ɪʃjuː) *n* **1** the act of sending or giving out something; supply; delivery. **2** something issued; an edition of stamps, a magazine, etc. **3** the number of identical items, such as banknotes or shares in a company, that become available at a particular time. **4** the act of emerging; outflow; discharge. **5** something flowing out, such as a river. **6** a place of outflow; outlet. **7** the descendants of a person; offspring; progeny. **8** a topic of interest or discussion. **9** an important subject requiring a decision. **10** an outcome or consequence; result. **11** *Pathol.* discharge from a wound. **12** *Law.* the matter remaining in dispute between the parties to an action after the pleadings. **13** the yield from or profits arising out of land or other property. **14 at issue. 14a** under discussion. **14b** in disagreement. **15 force the issue.** to compel decision on some matter. **16 join issue.** to join in controversy. **17 take issue.** to disagree. ◆ *vb* **issues, issuing, issued. 18** to come forth or emerge or cause to come forth or emerge. **19** to publish or deliver (a newspaper, magazine, etc.). **20** (*tr*) to make known or announce. **21** (*intr*) to originate or proceed. **22** (*intr*) to be a consequence; result. **23** (*intr; foll. by in*) to end or terminate. **24** (*tr*) (foll. by *with*) to supply officially (with). ORIG C13: from OF *eissue* way out, from *eissir* to go out, from L *exīre*
▸ '**issuable** *adj* ▸ '**issuer** *n*

issue price *n Stock Exchange.* the price at which a new issue of shares is offered to the public.

Issus ★ ('ɪsəs) *n* an ancient town in S Asia Minor, in Cilicia north of present-day Iskenderun: scene of a battle (333 B.C.) in which Alexander the Great defeated the Persians.

Issyk-Kul ★ (*Russian* is'sik'kulj) *n* a lake in NE Kyrgyzstan in the Tian Shan mountains, at an altitude of

1609 m (5280 ft): one of the largest mountain lakes in the world. Area: 6200 sq. km (2390 sq. miles).

-ist *suffix.* **1** (*forming nouns*) a person who performs a certain action or is concerned with something specified: *motorist; soloist.* **2** (*forming nouns*) a person who practises in a specific field: *physicist.* **3** (*forming nouns and adjectives*) a person who advocates a particular doctrine, system, etc., or relating to such a person or the doctrine advocated: *socialist.* **4** (*forming nouns and adjectives*) a person characterized by a specified trait, tendency, etc., or relating to such a person or trait: *purist.* **5** (*forming nouns and adjectives*) a person who is prejudiced on the basis specified: *sexist; ageist.* ORIG via OF from L *-ista, -istēs,* from Gk *-istēs*

Istanbul ★ (ˌɪstænˈbuːl) *n* a port in NW Turkey, on the western (European) shore of the Bosporus: the largest city in Turkey; founded in about 660 B.C. by Greeks; refounded by Constantine the Great in 330 A.D. as the capital of the Eastern Roman Empire; taken by the Turks in 1453 and remained capital of the Ottoman Empire until 1922; industrial centre for shipbuilding, textiles, etc. Pop.: 7 615 500 (1994 est.). Ancient name: **Byzantium.** Former name (330–1926): **Constantinople.**

isthmian (ˈɪsθmɪən) *adj* relating to or situated in an isthmus.

isthmus (ˈɪsməs) *n, pl* **isthmuses** *or* **isthmi** (-maɪ). **1** a narrow strip of land connecting two relatively large land areas. **2** *Anat.* **2a** a narrow band of tissue connecting two larger parts of a structure. **2b** a narrow passage connecting two cavities. ORIG C16: from L, from Gk *isthmos*
▸ ˈ**isthmoid** *adj*

-istic *suffix forming adjectives.* equivalent to a combination of **-ist** and **-ic** but in some words having a less specific or literal application and sometimes a mildly pejorative force, as compared with corresponding adjectives ending in **-ist**: *communistic; impressionistic.* ORIG from L *-isticus,* from Gk *istikos*

istle (ˈɪstlɪ) *or* **ixtle** *n* a fibre obtained from various tropical American agave and yucca trees used in making carpets, cord, etc. ORIG C19: from Mexican Sp. *ixtle,* from Amerind *ichtli*

Istria ★ (ˈɪstrɪə) *n* a peninsula in the N Adriatic Sea: passed from Italy to Yugoslavia (except for Trieste) in 1947 and to Croatia in 1991.
▸ ˈ**Istrian** *n, adj*

it (ɪt) *pron* (*subjective or objective*) **1** refers to a nonhuman, animal, plant, or inanimate thing, or sometimes to a small baby: *it looks dangerous; give it a bone.* **2** refers to an unspecified or implied antecedent or to a previous or understood clause, phrase, etc.: *it is impossible; I knew it.* **3** used to represent human life or experience in respect of the present situation: *how's it going? I've had it; to brazen it out.* **4** used as a formal subject (or object), referring to a following clause, phrase, or word: *it helps to know the truth; I consider it dangerous to go on.* **5** used in the nominative as the formal grammatical subject of impersonal verbs: *it is raining; it hurts.* **6** (used as complement with *be*) *Inf.* the crucial or ultimate point: *the steering failed and I thought that was it.* ◆ *n* **7** (in children's games) the player whose turn it is to try to touch another. **8** *Inf.* **8a** sexual intercourse. **8b** sex appeal. **9** *Inf.* a desirable quality or ability: *he's really got it.* ORIG OE *hit*

IT *abbrev. for* information technology.

It. *abbrev. for:* **1** Italian. **2** Italy.

i.t.a. *or* **ITA** *abbrev. for* initial teaching alphabet, a partly phonetic alphabet used to teach reading.

ital. *abbrev. for* italic.

Ital. *abbrev. for:* **1** Italian. **2** Italy.

Italia ★ (iˈtaːlja) *n* the Italian name for **Italy.**

Italian (ɪˈtæljən) *n* **1** the official language of Italy and one of the official languages of Switzerland. **2** a native or inhabitant of Italy or a descendant of one. ◆ *adj* **3** relating to, denoting, or characteristic of Italy, its inhabitants, or their language.

Italianate (ɪˈtæljənɪt, -ˌneɪt) *or* **Italianesque** *adj* Italian in style or character.

Italian East Africa ★ *n* a former Italian territory in E Africa, formed in 1936 from the possessions of Eritrea, Italian Somaliland, and Ethiopia: taken by British forces in 1941.

Italian Somaliland ★ *n* a former Italian colony in E Africa, united with British Somaliland in 1960 to form the independent republic of Somalia.

italic (ɪˈtælɪk) *adj* **1** Also: **Italian.** of, relating to, or denoting a style of handwriting with the letters slanting to the right. **2** of, relating to, or denoting a style of printing type modelled on this, chiefly used to indicate emphasis, a foreign word, etc. Cf. **roman.** ◆ *n* **3** (*often pl*) italic type or print. ORIG C16 (after an edition of Virgil (1501) printed in Venice and dedicated to Italy): from L *Italicus* of Italy, from Gk *Italikos*

Italic (ɪˈtælɪk) *n* **1** a branch of the Indo-European family of languages that includes many of the ancient languages of Italy. ◆ *adj* **2** denoting, relating to, or belonging to this group of languages, esp. the extinct ones.

italicize *or* **italicise** (ɪˈtælɪˌsaɪz) *vb* **italicizes, italicizing, italicized** *or* **italicises, italicising, italicised. 1** to print (textual matter) in italic type. **2** (*tr*) to underline (words, etc.) with a single line to indicate italics.
▸ **iˌtaliciˈzation** *or* **iˌtaliciˈsation** *n*

Italy ★ (ˈɪtəlɪ) *n* a republic in S Europe, occupying a peninsula in the Mediterranean between the Tyrrhenian and the Adriatic Seas, with the islands of Sardinia and Sicily to the west: first united under the Romans but became fragmented into numerous political units in the Middle Ages; united kingdom proclaimed in 1861; under the dictatorship of Mussolini (1922–43); became a republic in 1946; a member of the European Union. It is generally mountainous, with the Alps in the north and the Apennines running the length of the peninsula. Official language: Italian. Religion: Roman Catholic majority. Currency: lira and euro. Capital: Rome. Pop.: 57 723 000 (1999 est.). Area: 301 247 sq. km (116 312 sq. miles). Italian name: **Italia.**

ITC (in Britain) *abbrev. for* Independent Television Commission.

itch (ɪtʃ) *n* **1** an irritation or tickling sensation of the skin causing a desire to scratch. **2** a restless desire. **3** any skin disorder, such as scabies, characterized by intense itching. ◆ *vb* (*intr*) **4** to feel or produce an irritating or tickling sensation. **5** to have a restless desire (to do something). **6 have itchy feet.** to be restless; have a desire to travel. **7 itching palm.** a grasping nature; avarice. ORIG OE *gīccean*
▸ ˈ**itchy** *adj* ▸ ˈ**itchiness** *n*

-ite[1] *suffix forming nouns.* **1** a native or inhabitant of: *Israelite.* **2** a follower or advocate of; a supporter of a group: *Luddite; labourite.* **3** (in biology) indicating a division of a body or organ: *somite.* **4** indicating a mineral or rock: *nephrite; peridotite.* **5** indicating a commercial product: *vulcanite.* ORIG via L *-ita* from Gk *-itēs* or directly from Gk

-ite[2] *suffix forming nouns.* indicating a salt or ester of an acid having a name ending in *-ous: a nitrite is a salt of nitrous acid.* ORIG from F, arbitrary alteration of -ATE[1]

item *n* (ˈaɪtəm). **1** a thing or unit, esp. included in a list or collection. **2** *Book-keeping.* an entry in an account. **3** a piece of information, detail, or note: *a news item.* **4** *Inf.* two people having a romantic or sexual relationship. ◆ *vb* (ˈaɪtəm). **5** (*tr*) *Arch.* to itemize. ◆ *adv* (ˈaɪtɛm). **6** likewise; also. ORIG C14 (adv) from L: in like manner

itemize *or* **itemise** (ˈaɪtəˌmaɪz) *vb* **itemizes, itemizing, itemized** *or* **itemises, itemising, itemised.** (*tr*) to put on a list or make a list of.
▸ ˌ**itemiˈzation** *or* ˌ**itemiˈsation** *n* ▸ ˈ**itemˌizer** *or* ˈ**itemˌiser** *n*

Iténez ★ (iˈteneθ) *n* the Spanish name for the **Guaporé.**

iterate (ˈɪtəˌreɪt) *vb* **iterates, iterating, iterated.** (*tr*) to say or do again. ORIG C16: from L *iterāre,* from *iterum* again
▸ ˈ**iterant** *adj* ▸ ˌ**iterˈation** *n* ▸ ˈ**iterative** *adj*

Ithaca ★ (ˈɪθəkə) *n* a Greek island in the Ionian Sea, the smallest of the Ionian Islands: regarded as the home of Homer's Odysseus. Area: 93 sq. km (36 sq. miles). Modern Greek name: **Itháki** (iˈθaki).
▸ ˈ**Ithacan** *n, adj*

Ithunn ★ (ˈiːðʊn) *n* a variant of **Idun.**

itinerancy (ɪ'tɪnərənsɪ, aɪ-) *or* **itineracy** *n* **1** the act of itinerating. **2** *Chiefly Methodist Church.* the system of appointing a minister to a circuit of churches or chapels. **3** itinerants collectively.

itinerant (ɪ'tɪnərənt, aɪ-) *adj* **1** itinerating. **2** working for a short time in various places, esp. as a casual labourer. ◆ *n* **3** an itinerant worker or other person. ORIG C16: from LL *itinerārī* to travel, from L *iter* a journey
▸ **i'tinerantly** *adv*

itinerary (aɪ'tɪnərərɪ, ɪ-) *n, pl* **itineraries. 1** a plan or line of travel; route. **2** a record of a journey. **3** a guidebook for travellers. ◆ *adj* **4** of or relating to travel or routes of travel.

itinerate (aɪ'tɪnəˌreɪt, ɪ-) *vb* **itinerates, itinerating, itinerated.** (*intr*) to travel from place to place.
▸ **iˌtiner'ation** *n*

-itis *suffix forming nouns.* **1** indicating inflammation of a specified part: *tonsillitis.* **2** *Inf.* indicating a preoccupation with or imaginary condition of illness caused by: *computeritis; telephonitis.* ORIG NL, from Gk, fem of *-itēs* belonging to

it'll ('ɪtᵊl) *contraction of* it will *or* it shall.

Ito ★ ('i:təʊ) *n* Prince **Hirobumi** (ˌhɪərə'bu:mɪ). 1841–1909, Japanese statesman; premier (1884–88; 1892–96; 1898; 1900–01). He led the movement to modernize Japan and helped to draft the Meiji constitution (1889); assassinated.

ITO *abbrev. for* International Trade Organization.

-itol *suffix forming nouns.* indicating that certain chemical compounds are alcohols containing two or more hydroxyl groups: *inisitol; sorbitol.* ORIG from -ITE[2] + -OL[1]

its (ɪts) *determiner* **a** of, belonging to, or associated in some way with it: *its left rear wheel; I can see its logical consequence.* **b** (*as pronoun*): *each town claims its is the best.*

it's (ɪts) *contraction of* it is *or* it has.

itself (ɪt'sɛlf) *pron* **1a** the reflexive form of **it. 1b** (intensifier): *even the money itself won't convince me.* **2** (*preceded by a copula*) its normal or usual self: *my cat doesn't seem itself these days.*

itsy-bitsy ('ɪtsɪ'bɪtsɪ) *or* **itty-bitty** ('ɪtɪ'bɪtɪ) *adj Inf.* very small; tiny. ORIG C20: baby talk alteration of *little bit*

ITU *abbrev. for:* **1** intensive therapy unit. **2** International Telecommunications Union.

ITV (in Britain) *abbrev. for* Independent Television.

-ity *suffix forming nouns.* indicating state or condition: *technicality.* ORIG from OF *-ite,* from L *-itās*

IU *abbrev. for:* **1** immunizing unit. **2** international unit.

IU(C)D *abbrev. for* intrauterine (contraceptive) device.

Iulus ★ (aɪ'ju:ləs) *n Roman myth.* **1** another name for **Ascanius. 2** the son of Ascanius, founder of the Julian gens or clan.

-ium *or sometimes* **-um** *suffix forming nouns.* **1** indicating a metallic element: *platinum; barium.* **2** (in chemistry) indicating groups forming positive ions: *ammonium chloride, hydroxonium ion.* **3** indicating a biological structure: *syncytium.* ORIG NL, from L, from Gk *-ion,* dim. suffix

i.v. *abbrev. for:* **1** initial velocity. **2** Also: **IV.** intravenous(ly).

Ivan III ★ ('aɪvən) *n* known as *Ivan the Great.* 1440–1505, grand duke of Muscovy (1462–1505). He expanded Muscovy by conquest, defeated the Tatars (1480), and assumed the title of Ruler of all Russia (1472).

Ivan IV ★ *n* known as *Ivan the Terrible.* 1530–84, grand duke of Muscovy (1533–47) and first tsar of Russia (1547–84). He conquered Kazan (1552), Astrakhan (1556), and Siberia (1581), but was defeated by Poland in the Livonian War (1558–82) after which his rule became increasingly oppressive.

Ivanovo ★ (*Russian* ɪ'vanəvə) *n* a city in W central Russia, on the Uvod River: a major textile centre. Pop.: 474 000 (1995 est.). Former name (1871–1932): **Ivanovo-Voznesensk** (-vəznɪ'sjensk).

I've (aɪv) *contraction of* I have.

-ive *suffix.* **1** (*forming adjectives*) indicating a tendency, inclination, character, or quality: *divisive; festive; massive.* **2** (*forming nouns of adjectival origin*): *detective; expletive.* ORIG from L *-īvus*

Ives ★ (aɪvz) *n* **1 Charles Edward.** 1874–1954, US composer, noted for his innovative use of polytonality, polyrhythms, and quarter tones. His works include five symphonies, chamber music, and songs. **2 Frederick Eugene.** 1856–1937, US inventor of halftone photography.

IVF *abbrev. for* in vitro fertilization.

ivied ('aɪvɪd) *adj* covered with ivy.

Iviza ★ (*Spanish* i'βiθa) *n* a variant spelling of **Ibiza.**

Ivorian (aɪ'vɔ:rɪən) *n* **1** a native or inhabitant of the Côte d'Ivoire. ◆ *adj* **2** of or relating to the Côte d'Ivoire or its inhabitants.

ivories ('aɪvərɪz, -vrɪz) *pl n Sl.* **1** the keys of a piano. **2** billiard balls. **3** another word for **teeth. 4** another word for **dice.**

ivory ('aɪvərɪ, -vrɪ) *n, pl* **ivories. 1a** a hard smooth creamy white variety of dentine that makes up a major part of the tusks of elephants and walruses. **1b** (*as modifier*): *ivory ornaments.* **2** a tusk made of ivory. **3a** a yellowish-white colour; cream. **3b** (*as adj*): *ivory shoes.* **4** a substance resembling elephant tusk. **5** an ornament, etc., made of ivory. **6 black ivory.** *Obs.* Black slaves collectively. ORIG C13: from OF, from L *evoreus* made of ivory, from *ebur* ivory
▸ **'ivory-ˌlike** *adj*

Ivory ★ ('aɪvərɪ) *n* **James.** born 1928, US film director. With the producer Ismael Merchant, his films include *Shakespeare Wallah* (1964), *A Room With a View* (1986), *The Remains of the Day* (1993), and *A Soldier's Daughter Never Cries* (1998).

ivory black *n* a black pigment obtained by grinding charred scraps of ivory in oil.

Ivory Coast ★ *n* **the.** the former name (until 1986) of **Côte d'Ivoire.**

ivory nut *n* **1** the seed of the ivory palm, which contains an ivory-like substance used to make buttons, etc. **2** any similar seed from other palms. ◆ Also called: **vegetable ivory.**

ivory tower ('taʊə) *n* **a** seclusion or remoteness of attitude regarding problems, everyday life, etc. **b** (*as modifier*): *ivory-tower aestheticism.*
▸ **ˌivory-'towered** *adj*

ivorywood ('aɪvərɪˌwʊd) *n* **1** the yellowish-white wood of an Australian tree, used for engraving, inlaying, and turnery. **2** the tree itself.

IVR *abbrev. for* International Vehicle Registration.

ivy ('aɪvɪ) *n, pl* **ivies. 1** a woody climbing or trailing plant having lobed evergreen leaves and black berry-like fruits. **2** any of various other climbing or creeping plants, such as poison ivy and ground ivy. ORIG OE *īfig*
▸ **'ivy-ˌlike** *adj*

iwi ('i:wi:) *n NZ.* a Maori tribe. ORIG Maori

Iwo ★ ('i:wəʊ) *n* a city in SW Nigeria. Pop.: 353 000 (1995 est.).

Iwo Jima ★ ('dʒi:mə) *n* an island in the W Pacific, about 1100 km (700 miles) south of Japan: one of the Volcano Islands; scene of prolonged fighting between US and Japanese forces until taken by the US in 1945; returned to Japan in 1968. Area: 20 sq. km (8 sq. miles).

IWW *abbrev. for* Industrial Workers of the World.

ixia ('ɪksɪə) *n* an iridaceous plant of southern Africa, having showy ornamental funnel-shaped flowers. ORIG C18: NL from Gk *ixos* mistletoe

Ixion ★ (ɪk'saɪən) *n Greek myth.* a Thessalian king punished by Zeus for his love of Hera by being bound to a perpetually revolving wheel.
▸ **Ixionian** (ˌɪksɪ'əʊnɪən) *adj*

Ixtaccihuatl *or* **Iztaccihuatl** ★ (ˌi:stək'si:wətᵊl) *n* a dormant volcano in central Mexico, southeast of Mexico City. Height: (central peak) 5286 m (17 342 ft).

ixtle ('ɪkstlɪ, 'ɪst-) *n* a variant spelling of **istle.**

Iyeyasu *or* **Ieyasu** ★ (ˌi:jeɪ'jɑ:su:) *n* **Tokugawa** (ˌtɒku:'gɑ:wə). 1542–1616, Japanese general and statesman; founder of the Tokugawa shogunate (1603–1867).

★ people and places

izard (ˈɪzəd) *n* (esp. in the Pyrenees) another name for **chamois.**

-ize *or* **-ise** *suffix forming verbs.* **1** to cause to become, resemble, or agree with: *legalize.* **2** to become; change into: *crystallize.* **3** to affect in a specified way; subject to: *hypnotize.* **4** to act according to some practice, principle, policy, etc.: *economize.* ORIG from OF *-iser,* from LL *-izāre,* from Gk *-izein*

> **USAGE NOTE** In Britain and the US *-ize* is the preferred ending for many verbs, but *-ise* is equally acceptable in British English. Certain words (chiefly those not formed by adding the suffix to an existing word) are, however, always spelt with *-ise* in both Britain and the US: *advertise, revise.*

Izetbegović ★ (ˌɪzətˈbɛgəvɪtʃ) *n* **Alija** (ˈæljə). born 1925, Bosnia-Herzegovinan politician; president (1992–2000).

Izhevsk ★ (*Russian* iˈʒɛfsk) *n* an industrial city in central Russia, capital of the Udmurt Republic. Pop.: 654 000 (1995 est.).

Izmir ★ (ˈɪzmɪə) *n* a port in W Turkey, on the **Gulf of Izmir:** the third largest city in the country; university (1955). Pop.: 1 985 300 (1994 est.). Former name: **Smyrna.**

Izmit ★ (ˈɪzmɪt) *n* a town in NW Turkey, on the **Gulf of Izmit.** Pop.: 275 800 (1994 est.).

Iznik ★ (ɪzˈnɪk) *n* the modern Turkish name of **Nicaea.**

Iztaccihuatl ★ (ˌiːstəkˈsiːwətᵊl) *n* a variant spelling of **Ixtaccihuatl.**

★ people and places

Jj

j *or* **J** (dʒeɪ) *n, pl* **j's, J's,** *or* **Js. 1** the tenth letter of the English alphabet. **2** a speech sound represented by this letter.

j *symbol for:* **1** *Maths.* the unit vector along the *y*-axis. **2** the imaginary number √–1.

J *symbol for:* **1** current density. **2** *Cards.* jack. **3** joule(s).

J. *abbrev. for:* **1** Journal. **2** (*pl* **JJ.**) Judge. **3** (*pl* **JJ.**) Justice.

jab (dʒæb) *vb* **jabs, jabbing, jabbed. 1** to poke or thrust sharply. **2** to strike with a quick short blow or blows. ◆ *n* **3** a sharp poke or stab. **4** a quick short blow. **5** *Inf.* an injection: *polio jabs.* ORIG C19: orig. Scot. var. of JOB
▸ **'jabbing** *adj*

Jabalpur *or* **Jubbulpore** ★ (ˌdʒʌbəl'pʊə) *n* a city in central India, in central Madhya Pradesh. Pop.: 741 927 (1991).

jabber ('dʒæbə) *vb* **1** to speak or say rapidly, incoherently, and without making sense; chatter. ◆ *n* **2** such talk. ORIG C15: imit.

jabberwocky ('dʒæbəˌwɒkɪ) *n* nonsensical writing or speech. ORIG C19: coined by Lewis Carroll as the title of a poem in *Through the Looking Glass* (1871)

Jabir ibn Hayyan ★ ('dʒɑːbɪə 'ɪbᵊn hɑː'jɑːn) *n* ?721–?815. Arab alchemist, whose works were esteemed by later alchemists.

jabiru ('dʒæbɪˌruː) *n* **1** a large white tropical American stork with a dark naked head and a dark bill. **2** Also called: **black-necked stork, policeman bird.** a large Australian stork, having a white plumage, dark green back and tail, and red legs. **3** another name for **saddlebill.** ORIG C18: via Port., of Amerind origin

jabot ('ʒæbəʊ) *n* a frill or ruffle on the breast or throat of a garment. ORIG C19: from F: bird's crop, jabot

jaçana (ˌʒɑːsə'nɑː, ˌdʒæ-) *n* a bird of tropical and subtropical marshy regions, having long legs and very long toes that enable walking on floating plants. ORIG C18: from Port., of Amerind origin, from *jasaná*

jacaranda (ˌdʒækə'rændə) *n* **1** a tropical American tree having fernlike leaves and pale purple flowers and widely cultivated in temperate areas of Australia. **2** the fragrant ornamental wood of this tree. **3** any of several related or similar trees or their wood. ORIG C18: from Port., of Amerind origin, from *yacarandá*

jacaré ('dʒækəˌreɪ) *n* another name for **cayman.** ORIG C18: from Port., of Amerind origin

jacinth ('dʒæsɪnθ) *n* another name for **hyacinth** (sense 4). ORIG C13: from Med. L *jacinthus,* from L *hyacinthus* plant, precious stone; see HYACINTH

jack (dʒæk) *n* **1** a man or fellow. **2** a sailor. **3** the male of certain animals, esp. of the ass or donkey. **4** a mechanical or hydraulic device for exerting a large force, esp. to raise a heavy weight such as a motor vehicle. **5** any of several mechanical devices that replace manpower, such as a contrivance for rotating meat on a spit. **6** one of four playing cards in a pack, one for each suit; knave. **7** *Bowls.* a small usually white bowl at which the players aim with their own bowls. **8** *Electrical engineering.* a female socket with two or more terminals designed to receive a male plug (**jack plug**) that either makes or breaks the circuit or circuits. **9** a flag, esp. a small flag flown at the bow of a ship indicating the ship's nationality. **10** a part of the action of a harpsichord, consisting of a fork-shaped device on the end of a pivoted lever on which a plectrum is mounted. **11a** any of various tropical and subtropical fishes. **11b** an immature pike. **12** Also called: **jackstone.** one of the pieces used in the game of jacks. **13** *US.* a slang word for **money. 14 every man jack.** everyone without exception. **15 the jack.** *Austral. sl.* syphilis. ◆ *adj* **16** *Austral. sl.* tired or fed up (esp. in **be jack of something**). ◆ *vb* **17** (*tr*) to lift or push (an object) with a jack. ◆ See also **jack in, jack up.** ORIG C16 *jakke,* var. of *Jankin,* dim. of *John*

Jack (dʒæk) *n* **I'm all right, Jack.** *Brit. inf.* a remark indicating smug and complacent selfishness.

jackal ('dʒækɔːl) *n* **1** any of several African or S Asian mammals closely related to the dog, having long legs and pointed ears and muzzle: they are predators and carrion-eaters. **2** a person who does menial tasks for another. ORIG C17: from Turkish, from Persian, from Sansk. *srgāla*

jackanapes ('dʒækəˌneɪps) *n* (*functioning as sing*) **1** a conceited impertinent person. **2** a mischievous child. **3** *Arch.* a monkey. ORIG C16: var. of *Jakken-apes,* lit.: Jack of the ape, nickname of William de la Pole (1396–1450), first Duke of Suffolk, whose badge showed an ape's ball and chain

jackass ('dʒækˌæs) *n* **1** a male donkey. **2** a fool. ORIG C18: from JACK (male) + ASS[1]

jackboot ('dʒækˌbuːt) *n* **1** an all-leather military boot, extending up to or above the knee. **2** authoritarian rule or behaviour.
▸ **'jackˌbooted** *adj*

jackdaw ('dʒækˌdɔː) *n* a large Eurasian bird, related to the crow, having a black and dark grey plumage: noted for its thieving habits. ORIG C16: from JACK + *daw,* obs. name for jackdaw

jackeroo *or* **jackaroo** (ˌdʒækə'ruː) *n, pl* **jackeroos** *or* **jackaroos.** *Austral. inf.* a novice on a sheep or cattle station. ORIG C19: from JACK + (KANG)AROO

jacket ('dʒækɪt) *n* **1** a short coat, esp. one that is hip-length and has a front opening and sleeves. **2** something that resembles this: *a life jacket.* **3** any exterior covering or casing, such as the insulating cover of a boiler. **4** See **dust jacket. 5a** the skin of a baked potato. **5b** (*as modifier*): *jacket potatoes.* **6** *Oil industry.* the support structure, esp. the legs, of an oil platform. ◆ *vb* **7** (*tr*) to put a jacket on (someone or something). ORIG C15: from OF *jaquet* short jacket, from *jacque* peasant, from *Jacques* James
▸ **'jacketed** *adj*

Jack Frost *n* a personification of frost.

Jackie *or* **Jacky** ('dʒækɪ) *n, pl* **Jackies.** *Austral. offens. sl.* **1** a native Australian. **2** native Australians collectively. **3 sit up like Jackie.** to sit bolt upright, esp. cheekily.

jack in *vb* (*tr, adv*) *Sl.* to abandon or leave (an attempt or enterprise).

jack-in-office *n* a self-important petty official.

jack-in-the-box *n, pl* **jack-in-the-boxes** *or* **jacks-in-the-box.** a toy consisting of a figure on a compressed spring in a box, which springs out when the lid is opened.

Jack Ketch (kɛtʃ) *n Brit. arch.* a hangman. ORIG C18: after *John Ketch* (died 1686), public executioner in England

jackknife ('dʒækˌnaɪf) *n, pl* **jackknives. 1** a knife with the blade pivoted to fold into a recess in the handle. **2** a former name for a type of dive in which the diver bends at the waist in midair; forward pike dive. ◆ *vb* **jackknifes, jackknifing, jackknifed.** (*intr*) **3** (of an articulated lorry) to go out of control in such a way that the trailer swings round at an angle to the tractor.

Jacklin ★ ('dʒæklɪn) *n* **Tony,** full name *Anthony Jacklin.* born 1944. British golfer: won the British Open Championship (1969) and the US Open Championship (1970).

jack of all trades *n, pl* **jacks of all trades.** a person who undertakes many different kinds of work.

jack-o'-lantern *n* **1** a lantern made from a hollowed pumpkin, which has holes cut in it to represent a human face. **2** a will-o'-the-wisp.

★ people and places

jack plane *n* a carpenter's plane, usually with a wooden body, used for rough planing of timber.

jack plug *n* See **jack** (sense 8).

jackpot ('dʒæk,pɒt) *n* **1** any large prize, kitty, or accumulated stake that may be won in gambling. **2 hit the jackpot. 2a** to win a jackpot. **2b** *Inf.* to achieve great success, esp. through luck. ORIG C20: prob. from JACK (playing card) + POT[1]

jack rabbit *n* any of various W North American hares having long hind legs and large ears. ORIG C19: shortened from *jackass-rabbit,* referring to its long ears

Jack Robinson ('rɒbɪnsən) *n* **before you could** (*or* **can**) **say Jack Robinson.** extremely quickly or suddenly.

Jack Russell ('rʌsᵊl) *n* a small short-legged terrier having a white coat with tan, black, or lemon markings. ORIG after John *Russell* (1795-1883), E clergyman who developed the breed

jacks (dʒæks) *n* (*functioning as sing*) a game in which bone, metal, or plastic pieces (**jackstones**) are thrown and then picked up between bounces of a small ball or throws of another piece (the **jack**). ORIG C19: shortened from *jackstones,* var. of *checkstones* pebbles

jacksie *or* **jacksy** ('dʒæksɪ) *n, pl* **jacksies.** *Brit. sl.* the buttocks or anus. Also: **jaxie, jaxy.** ORIG C19: ? from JACK

jacksnipe ('dʒæk,snaɪp) *n, pl* **jacksnipe** *or* **jacksnipes.** a small Eurasian short-billed snipe.

Jackson[1] ★ ('dʒæksən) *n* a city in and state capital of Mississippi, on the Pearl River. Pop.: 193 097 (1994 est.).

Jackson[2] ★ ('dʒæksən) *n* **1 Andrew.** 1767–1845, US statesman, general, and lawyer; seventh president of the US (1829–37). He became a national hero after successfully defending New Orleans from the British (1815). During his administration the national debt was fully paid off. **2 Glenda.** born 1936, British stage and film actress. Her films include *Women in Love* (1969) and *A Touch of Class* (1972); became a Labour MP in 1992. **3 Jesse** (**Louis**). born 1941, US Democrat politician; Black campaigner for minority rights. **4 Michael** (**Joe**). born 1958, US pop singer, lead vocalist with the Jacksons (originally the Jackson 5) (1969–86). His solo albums include *Thriller* (1982) and *Bad* (1984). **5 Thomas Jonathan,** known as *Stonewall Jackson.* 1824–63, Confederate general in the American Civil War, in command at the first Battle of Bull Run (1861).

Jacksonville ★ ('dʒæksən,vɪl) *n* a port in NE Florida: the leading commercial centre of the southeast. Pop.: 665 070 (1994 est.).

jackstraws ('dʒæk,strɔːz) *n* (*functioning as sing*) another name for **spillikins.**

Jack Tar *n Now chiefly literary.* a sailor.

Jack the Ripper ★ *n* an unidentified murderer who killed at least seven prostitutes in London's East End between August and November 1888.

jack up *vb* (*adv*) **1** (*tr*) to increase (prices, salaries, etc.). **2** (*tr*) to raise an object, such as a car, with or as with a jack. **3** (*intr*) *Sl.* to inject oneself with a drug. **4** (*intr*) *Austral. inf.* to refuse to comply. **5** (*tr*) *NZ.* to organize or procure, esp. through unorthodox channels.

Jacob ★ ('dʒeɪkəb) *n Old Testament.* the son of Isaac, twin brother of Esau, and father of the twelve patriarchs of Israel.

Jacobean (,dʒækə'bɪən) *adj* **1** *History.* relating to James I of England or to the period of his rule (1603–25). **2** of or relating to the style of furniture current at this time, characterized by the use of dark brown carved oak. **3** relating to or having the style of architecture used in England during this period. ORIG C18: from NL, from *Jacōbus* James

Jacobi ★ *n* **1** ('dʒækəbɪ). Sir **Derek** (**George**). born 1938, British actor. **2** (*German* ja'koːbi). **Karl Gustav Jacob** (karl 'gʊstaf 'jaːkɔp). 1804–51, German mathematician.

Jacobin ('dʒækəbɪn) *n* **1** a member of the most radical club founded during the French Revolution, which instituted the Reign of Terror. **2** an extreme political radical. **3** a French Dominican friar. ◆ *adj* **4** of or relating to the Jacobins or their policies. ORIG C14: from OF, from Med. L *Jacōbīnus,* from LL *Jacōbus* James; the political club orig. met in the convent near the church of *St Jacques* in 1789
▸ ,**Jaco'binic** *or* ,**Jaco'binical** *adj* ▸ '**Jacobinism** *n*

Jacobite ('dʒækə,baɪt) *n Brit. history.* an adherent of James II after his overthrow in 1688, or of his descendants in their attempts to regain the throne. ORIG C17: from LL *Jacōbus* James + -ITE[1]
▸ **Jacobitic** (,dʒækə'bɪtɪk) *adj*

Jacobsen ★ (*Danish* 'jakɔbsən) *n* **Arne** ('arnə). 1902–71, Danish architect and designer. His buildings include the Town Hall at Rodovre (1955).

Jacob's ladder *n* **1** *Old Testament.* the ladder reaching up to heaven that Jacob saw in a dream (Genesis 28:12–17). **2** a ladder made of wooden or metal steps supported by ropes or chains. **3** a North American plant with blue flowers and a ladder-like arrangement of leaves.

Jacob's staff *n* a medieval instrument for measuring heights and distances.

jaconet ('dʒækənɪt) *n* a light cotton fabric used for clothing, etc. ORIG C18: from Urdu *jagannāthī,* from *Jagannāthpūrī,* India, where orig. made

Jacquard ('dʒækɑːd, dʒə'kɑːd) *n* **1** Also called: **Jacquard weave.** a fabric in which the design is incorporated into the weave. **2** Also called: **Jacquard loom.** the loom that produces this fabric. ORIG C19: after Joseph M. *Jacquard* (1752–1834), F inventor

jactation (dʒæk'teɪʃən) *n* **1** *Rare.* the act of boasting. **2** *Pathol.* another word for **jactitation.** ORIG C16: from L *jactātiō* bragging, from *jactāre* to flourish, from *jacere* to throw

jactitation (,dʒæktɪ'teɪʃən) *n* **1** the act of boasting. **2** a false assertion that one is married to another, formerly actionable at law. **3** *Pathol.* restless tossing in bed, characteristic of severe fevers. ORIG C17: from Med. L, from L *jacitāre* to utter publicly, from *jactitāre* to toss about; see JACTATION

Jacuzzi (dʒə'kuːzɪ) *n Trademark.* **1** a device which swirls water in a bath. **2** a bath containing such a device. ORIG C20: from *Candido* and *Roy Jacuzzi,* who developed and marketed it

jade[1] (dʒeɪd) *n* **1** a semiprecious stone which varies in colour from white to green and is used for making ornaments and jewellery. **2a** the green colour of jade. **2b** (*as adj*): *a jade skirt.* ORIG C18: from F, from It. *giada,* from obs. Sp. *piedra de ijada* colic stone (lit.: stone of the flank, because it was believed to cure renal colic)

jade[2] (dʒeɪd) *n* **1** an old overworked horse. **2** *Derog., facetious.* a woman considered to be disreputable. ◆ *vb* **jades, jading, jaded. 3** to exhaust or make exhausted from work or use. ORIG C14: from ?
▸ '**jadish** *adj*

jaded ('dʒeɪdɪd) *adj* **1** exhausted or dissipated. **2** satiated.
▸ '**jadedly** *adv* ▸ '**jadedness** *n*

jadeite ('dʒeɪdaɪt) *n* a green or white mineral, a variety of jade, consisting of sodium aluminium silicate in monoclinic crystalline form.

Jadotville ★ (*French* ʒadovil) *n* the former name of **Likasi.**

j'adoube *French.* (ʒadub) *interj Chess.* an expression of an intention to touch a piece in order to adjust its placement rather than to make a move. ORIG lit.: I adjust

Jael ★ ('dʒeɪəl) *n Old Testament.* the woman who killed Sisera when he took refuge in her tent (Judges 4:17–21).

Jaén ★ (xa'en) *n* a city in S Spain. Pop.: 112 772 (1994 est.).

Jaffa ★ ('dʒæfə, 'dʒɑː-) *n* **1** a port in W Israel, on the Mediterranean: incorporated into Tel Aviv in 1950; an old Canaanite city. Biblical name: **Joppa.** Hebrew name: **Yafo. 2** a large variety of orange, grown esp. in Israel, having a thick skin.

Jaffna ★ ('dʒæfnə) *n* a port in N Sri Lanka: for many centuries the capital of a Tamil kingdom. Pop.: 129 000 (1990 est.).

jag[1] (dʒæg) *vb* **jags, jagging, jagged. 1** (*tr*) to cut unevenly. **2** *Austral.* to catch (fish) by impaling them on an unbaited hook. ◆ *n* **3** *Scot.* an informal word for **jab** (senses 3, 5). **4** a jagged notch or projection. ORIG C14: from ?

jag² (dʒæg) *n Sl.* **1a** intoxication from drugs or alcohol. **1b** a bout of drinking or drug taking. **2** a period of uncontrolled activity: *a crying jag.* ORIG of unknown origin

jagged ('dʒægɪd) *adj* having sharp projecting notches.
▸ **'jaggedly** *adv*

Jagger ★ ('dʒægə) *n* **Mick,** full name *Michael Philip Jagger.* born 1943, British rock singer and songwriter: lead vocalist with the Rolling Stones.

jaggy ('dʒægɪ) *adj* **jaggier, jaggiest. 1** a less common word for **jagged. 2** *Scot.* prickly.

jaguar ('dʒægjʊə) *n* a large feline mammal of S North America, Central America, and N South America, similar to the leopard but with larger spots on its coat. ORIG C17: from Port., from Guarani *yaguara*

Jahwism ('jɑːˌwɪzᵊm) *or* **Jahvism** ('jɑːˌvɪzəm) *n* a variant of **Yahwism** *or* **Yahvism.**
▸ **Jah'wistic** *or* **Jah'vistic** *adj*

jai alai ('haɪ 'laɪ, 'haɪ əˌlaɪ) *n* a version of pelota played by two or four players. ORIG via Sp. from Basque, from *jai* game + *alai* merry

jail *or* **gaol** (dʒeɪl) *n* **1** a place for the confinement of persons convicted and sentenced to imprisonment or of persons awaiting trial. ◆ *vb* **2** (*tr*) to confine in prison. ORIG C13: from OF *jaiole* cage, from Vulgar L *caveola* (unattested), from L *cavea* enclosure

jailbait ('dʒeɪlˌbeɪt) *n Inf.* a young person, or young persons collectively, considered sexually attractive but below the age of consent.

jailbird *or* **gaolbird** ('dʒeɪlˌbɜːd) *n* a person who is or has been confined to jail, esp. repeatedly; convict.

jailbreak *or* **gaolbreak** ('dʒeɪlˌbreɪk) *n* an escape from jail.

jailer, jailor, *or* **gaoler** ('dʒeɪlə) *n* a person in charge of prisoners in a jail.

Jain (dʒaɪn) *or* **Jaina** ('dʒaɪnə) *n* **1** an adherent of Jainism. ◆ *adj* **2** of or relating to Jainism. ORIG C19: from Hindi *jaina* saint, lit.: overcomer, from Sansk.

Jainism ('dʒaɪˌnɪzəm) *n* an ancient Hindu religion, characterized by the belief that the material world is progressing endlessly in a series of cycles.
▸ **'Jainist** *n, adj*

Jaipur ★ (dʒaɪ'pʊə) *n* a city of great beauty in N India, capital of Rajasthan state: University of Rajasthan (1947). Pop.: 1 458 183 (1991).

Jakarta *or* **Djakarta ★** (dʒə'kɑːtə) *n* the capital of Indonesia, in N West Java: founded in 1619 and ruled by the Dutch until 1945; the chief trading centre of the East in the 17th century; University of Indonesia (1947). Pop.: 9 160 500 (1995 est.). Former name (until 1949): **Batavia.**

jake (dʒeɪk) *adj Austral. & NZ sl.* all right; fine: *she's jake.* ORIG from ?

Jalandhar ★ ('dʒæləndə) *n* a city in NW India, in central Punjab. Pop.: 509 510 (1991).

jalap *or* **jalop** ('dʒæləp) *n* **1** a Mexican climbing plant. **2** the dried and powdered root of any of these plants, used as a purgative. ORIG C17: from F, from Mexican Sp. *jalapa*
▸ **jalapic** (dʒə'læpɪk) *adj*

Jalapa ★ (*Spanish* xa'lapa) *n* a city in E central Mexico, capital of Veracruz State, at an altitude of 1427 m (4681 ft): resort. Pop.: 288 331 (1990).

jalapeño (dʒælə'piːnəʊ; *Spanish* xala'peɲo) *n, pl* **jalapeñoños.** a type of red capsicum with a hot taste used in Mexican cookery. ORIG Mexican Sp.

Jalisco ★ (*Spanish* xa'lisko) *n* a state of W Mexico, on the Pacific: crossed by the Sierra Madre; valuable mineral resources. Capital: Guadalajara. Pop.: 6 161 437 (1997 est.). Area: 80 137 sq. km (30 934 sq. miles).

jalopy *or* **jaloppy** (dʒə'lɒpɪ) *n, pl* **jalopies** *or* **jaloppies.** *Inf.* a dilapidated old car. ORIG C20: from ?

jalousie ('ʒæluˌziː) *n* **1** a window blind or shutter constructed from angled slats of wood, etc. **2** a window made of angled slats of glass. ORIG C19: from OF *gelosie* latticework screen

jam¹ (dʒæm) *vb* **jams, jamming, jammed. 1** (*tr*) to cram or wedge into or against something: *to jam paper into an incinerator.* **2** (*tr*) to crowd or pack: *cars jammed the roads.* **3** to make or become stuck or locked. **4** (*tr;* often foll. by *on*) to activate suddenly (esp. in **jam on the brakes**). **5** (*tr*) to block; congest. **6** (*tr*) to crush or squeeze. **7** *Radio.* to prevent the clear reception of (radio communications) by transmitting other signals on the same frequency. **8** (*intr*) *Sl.* to play in a jam session. ◆ *n* **9** a crowd or congestion in a confined space: *a traffic jam.* **10** the act of jamming or the state of being jammed. **11** *Inf.* a predicament: *to help a friend out of a jam.* **12** See **jam session.** ORIG C18: prob. imit.
▸ **'jammer** *n*

jam² (dʒæm) *n* **1** a preserve containing fruit, which has been boiled with sugar until the mixture sets. **2** *Sl.* something desirable: *you want jam on it.* ORIG C18: ?from JAM¹ (the act of squeezing)

Jam. *abbrev. for:* **1** Jamaica. **2** *Bible.* James.

Jamaica ★ (dʒə'meɪkə) *n* an island and state of the Caribbean: colonized by the Spanish from 1494 onwards, large numbers of Black slaves being imported; captured by the British in 1655 and established as a colony in 1866; gained full independence in 1962; a member of the Commonwealth. Exports: chiefly bauxite and alumina, sugar, and bananas. Official language: English. Religion: Protestant majority. Currency: Jamaican dollar. Capital: Kingston. Pop.: 2 592 000 (1999 est.). Area: 10 992 sq. km (4244 sq. miles).
▸ **Ja'maican** *n, adj*

jamb *or* **jambe** (dʒæm) *n* a vertical side member of a doorframe, window frame, or lining. ORIG C14: from OF *jambe* leg, jamb, from LL *gamba* hoof, from Gk *kampē* joint

Jambi *or* **Djambi ★** ('dʒæmbɪ) *n* a port in W Indonesia, in SE Sumatra on the Hari River. Pop.: 410 400 (1995 est.). Also called: **Telanaipura.**

jamboree (ˌdʒæmbə'riː) *n* **1** a large and often international gathering of Scouts. **2** a party or celebration. ORIG C19: from ?

James ★ (dʒeɪmz) *n* **1** *New Testament.* **1a** known as *James the Great.* one of the twelve apostles, a son of Zebedee and brother to John the apostle (Matthew 4:21). **1b** known as *James the Less.* one of the twelve apostles, son of Alphaeus (Matthew 10:3). Feast day: May 3 or Oct. 9. **1c** known as *James the brother of the Lord.* a brother or close relative of Jesus (Mark 6:3; Galatians 1:19). Feast day: Oct. 23. **1d** the book ascribed to his authorship (in full **The Epistle of James**). **2 Henry.** 1843–1916, British writer and critic, born in the US. Among his novels are *Washington Square* (1880), *The Ambassadors* (1903), and *The Golden Bowl* (1904). **3 Jesse (Woodson).** 1847–82, US outlaw. **4 P(hyllis) D(orothy),** Baroness James of Holland Park. born 1920, British detective novelist. Her books include *Death of an Expert Witness* (1977), *A Certain Justice* (1997), and an autobiography *Time to Be in Earnest* (2001). **5 William,** brother of Henry James. 1842–1910, US philosopher and psychologist, whose books include *Essays in Radical Empiricism* (1912) and *The Varieties of Religious Experience* (1902).

James I ★ *n* **1** 1394–1437, king of Scotland (1406–37), second son of Robert III. **2** 1566–1625, king of England and Ireland (1603–25) and, as James VI, king of Scotland (1567–1625), in succession to Elizabeth I of England and his mother, Mary Queen of Scots, respectively. He alienated Parliament by his assertion of the divine right of kings and his subservience to Spain.

James II ★ *n* **1** 1430–60, king of Scotland (1437–60), son of James I. **2** 1633–1701, king of England, Ireland, and, as James VII, of Scotland (1685–88); son of Charles I. His pro-Catholic sympathies and arbitrary rule caused the Whigs and Tories to unite in inviting his eldest surviving daughter, Mary, and her husband, William of Orange, to take the throne. James was defeated at the Boyne (1690) when he attempted to regain the throne.

James III ★ *n* 1451–88, king of Scotland (1460–88), son of James II.

James IV ★ *n* 1473–1513, king of Scotland (1488–1513), son of James III; he invaded England (1496) in support of Perkin Warbeck; he was killed at Flodden.

James V ★ *n* 1512–42, king of Scotland (1513–42), son of James IV.

James VI ★ *n* title as king of Scotland of **James I** of England and Ireland.

James VII ★ *n* title as king of Scotland of **James II** of England and Ireland.

James Bay ★ *n* the S arm of Hudson Bay, in central Canada. Area: 108 780 sq. km (42 000 sq. miles).

Jameson ★ ('dʒeɪms°n) *n* Sir **Leander Starr.** 1853–1917, British administrator in South Africa, who led an expedition into the Transvaal in 1895 in an unsuccessful attempt to topple its Boer regime (the **Jameson Raid**); prime minister of Cape Colony (1904–08).

Jamestown ★ ('dʒeɪmz,taʊn) *n* a ruined village in E Virginia, on **Jamestown Island** (a peninsula in the James River): the first permanent settlement by the English in America (1607); capital of Virginia (1607–98); abandoned in 1699.

Jammu ★ ('dʒʌmu:) *n* a city in N India, winter capital of the state of Jammu and Kashmir. Pop.: 207 000 (latest est.).

Jammu and Kashmir ★ *n* the official name for the part of **Kashmir** under Indian control.

jammy ('dʒæmɪ) *adj* **jammier, jammiest.** *Brit. sl.* **1** pleasant; desirable. **2** lucky.

Jamnagar ★ ('dʒæmnəgə) *n* a city in India, in Gujarat: noted for its palaces and temples: cement, pottery, textiles. Pop.: 294 344 (1989).

jam-packed *adj* packed or filled to capacity.

jam session *n Sl.* an unrehearsed or improvised performance by jazz or rock musicians. ORIG C20: prob. from JAM[1]

Jamshedpur ★ (,dʒʌmʃɛd'pʊə) *n* a city in NE India, in SE Bihar: large iron and steel works (1907–11); a major industrial centre. Pop.: 461 000 (1991).

Jamshid *or* **Jamshyd** ★ (dʒæm'ʃi:d) *n Persian myth.* a ruler of the peris who was punished for bragging that he was immortal by being changed into human form. He then became a great king of Persia. See also **peri.**

Jan. *abbrev. for* January.

Janáček ★ (*Czech* 'jana:tʃɛk) *n* **Leoš** ('lɛɔʃ). 1854–1928, Czech composer. His music is influenced by Czech folksong and speech rhythms. His works include the operas *Jenufa* (1904) and *The Cunning Little Vixen* (1924) as well as orchestral and chamber music and songs.

Jandal ('dʒænd°l) *n NZ trademark.* a kind of sandal with a strip of material between the big toe and the other toes and over the foot.

Janet ★ (*French* ʒanɛ) *n* **Pierre Marie Félix** (pjɛr mari feliks). 1859–1947, French psychologist and neurologist, noted particularly for his work on the origins of hysteria.

jangle ('dʒæŋg°l) *vb* **jangles, jangling, jangled. 1** to sound or cause to sound discordantly, harshly, or unpleasantly. **2** (*tr*) to produce a jarring effect on: *the accident jangled his nerves.* **3** *Arch.* to wrangle. ◆ *n* **4** a harsh unpleasant ringing noise. **5** an argument or quarrel. ORIG C13: from OF *jangler,* of Gmc origin
▸ **'jangler** *n*

Janiculum ★ (dʒə'nɪkjʊləm) *n* a hill in Rome across the River Tiber from the Seven Hills.

Janina ★ ('jani:na) *n* the Serbian name for **Ioánnina.**

janissary ('dʒænɪsərɪ) *or* **janizary** ('dʒænɪzərɪ) *n, pl* **janissaries** *or* **janizaries.** an infantryman in the Turkish army, originally a member of the sovereign's guard, from the 14th to the 19th century. ORIG C16: from F, from It., from Turkish *yeniçeri,* from *yeni* new + *çeri* soldiery

janitor ('dʒænɪtə) *n* **1** *Scot., US, & Canad.* the caretaker of a building, esp. a school. **2** *Chiefly US & Canad.* a person employed to clean and maintain a building. ORIG C17: L: doorkeeper, from *jānua* door, from *jānus* covered way
▸ **janitorial** (,dʒænɪ'tɔ:rɪəl) *adj*

Jan Mayen ★ ('jæn 'maɪən) *n* an island in the Arctic Ocean, between Greenland and N Norway: volcanic, with large glaciers; former site of Dutch whaling stations; annexed to Norway in 1929. Area: 373 sq. km (144 sq. miles).

Jansen ★ ('dʒæns°n) *n* **Cornelis** (kɔ:'ni:lɪs). Latin name *Cornelius Jansenius.* 1585–1638, Dutch Roman Catholic theologian. In *Augustinus* (1640) he defended the teachings of St Augustine.

Jansenism ('dʒænsə,nɪzəm) *n RC Church.* the doctrine of Cornelis Jansen and his disciples, who believed in predestination and denied free will.
▸ **'Jansenist** *n, adj* ▸ **,Jansen'istic** *adj*

jansky ('dʒænskɪ) *n, pl* **janskys.** (in radio astronomy) a unit used to measure the intensity of radio waves. Also called: **flux unit.** ORIG C20: after Karl G. *Jansky* (1905–50), US electrical engineer

January ('dʒænjʊərɪ) *n, pl* **Januaries.** the first month of the year, consisting of 31 days. ORIG C14: from L *Jānuārius*

Janus ★ ('dʒeɪnəs) *n* the Roman god of doorways, passages, and bridges. In art he is depicted with two heads facing opposite ways. ORIG C16: from L, from *jānus* archway

Jap. *abbrev. for* Japan(ese).

japan (dʒə'pæn) *n* **1** a glossy black lacquer originally from the Orient, used on wood, metal, etc. **2** work decorated and varnished in the Japanese manner. ◆ *vb* **japans, japanning, japanned. 3** (*tr*) to lacquer with japan or any similar varnish.

Japan ★ (dʒə'pæn) *n* an archipelago and empire in E Asia, extending for 3200 km (2000 miles) between the Sea of Japan and the Pacific and consisting of the main islands of Hokkaido, Honshu, Shikoku, and Kyushu and over 3000 smaller islands: feudalism abolished in 1871, followed by industrialization and expansion of territories, esp. during World Wars I and II, when most of SE Asia came under Japanese control; dogma of the emperor's divinity abolished in 1946 under a new democratic constitution; rapid economic growth has made Japan the most industrialized nation in the Far East. Official language: Japanese. Religion: Shintoist majority, large Buddhist minority. Currency: yen. Capital: Tokyo. Pop.: 126 680 000 (1999 est.). Area: 369 660 sq. km (142 726 sq. miles). Japanese names: **Nippon, Nihon.**

Japan Current ★ *n* a warm ocean current flowing northeastwards off the E coast of Japan towards the North Pacific. Also called: **Kuroshio.**

Japanese (,dʒæpə'ni:z) *adj* **1** of or characteristic of Japan, its people, or their language. ◆ *n* **2** (*pl* **Japanese**) a native or inhabitant of Japan. **3** the official language of Japan.

Japanese stranglehold *n* a wrestling hold in which an opponent's arms exert pressure on his own windpipe.

jape (dʒeɪp) *n* **1** a jest or joke. ◆ *vb* **japes, japing, japed. 2** to joke or jest (about). ORIG C14: ?from OF *japper* to yap, imit.
▸ **'japer** *n* ▸ **'japery** *n*

Japheth ★ ('dʒeɪfɛθ) *n Old Testament.* the second son of Noah, traditionally regarded as the ancestor of a number of non-Semitic nations (Genesis 10:1–5).

Japlish ('dʒæplɪʃ) *n* the adoption and adaptation of English words into the Japanese language. ORIG C20: from a blend of JAPANESE + ENGLISH

japonica (dʒə'pɒnɪkə) *n* **1** Also called: **Japanese quince.** a Japanese shrub cultivated for its red flowers and yellowish fruit. **2** another name for the **camellia.** ORIG C19: from NL, fem of *japonicus* Japanese, from *Japonia* JAPAN

Japurá ★ (*Portuguese* ʒapu'ra) *n* a river in NW South America, rising in SW Colombia and flowing southeast across Colombia and Brazil to join the Amazon near Tefé: known as the Caquetá in Colombia. Length: about 2800 km (1750 miles). Spanish name: **Yapurá.**

Jaques-Dalcroze ★ (*French* ʒakdalkroz) *n* **Émile** (emil). 1865–1950, Swiss composer and teacher: invented eurythmics.

jar[1] (dʒɑ:) *n* **1** a wide-mouthed container that is usually cylindrical, made of glass or earthenware, and without handles. **2** Also: **jarful.** the contents or quantity contained in a jar. **3** *Brit. inf.* a glass of beer. ORIG C16: from OF *jarre, jarra,* from Ar. *jarrah* large earthen vessel

jar² (dʒɑː) *vb* **jars, jarring, jarred. 1** to vibrate or cause to vibrate. **2** to make or cause to make a harsh discordant sound. **3** (often foll. by *on*) to have a disturbing or painful effect (on the nerves, mind, etc.). **4** (*intr*) to disagree; clash. ◆ *n* **5** a jolt or shock. **6** a harsh discordant sound. ORIG C16: prob. imit.
▸ **ˈjarring** *adj* ▸ **ˈjarringly** *adv*

jar³ (dʒɑː) *n* **on a** (*or* **the**) **jar.** (of a door) slightly open; ajar. ORIG C17 (in the sense: turn): from earlier *char,* from OE *cierran* to turn

jardinière (ˌʒɑːdɪˈnjɛə) *n* **1** an ornamental pot or trough for plants. **2** a garnish of fresh vegetables for a dish of meat. ORIG C19: from F, fem of *jardinier* gardener, from *jardin* GARDEN

jargon (ˈdʒɑːgən) *n* **1** specialized language concerned with a particular subject, culture, or profession. **2** language characterized by pretentious vocabulary or meaning. **3** gibberish. ORIG C14: from OF, ? imit.

jarl (jɑːl) *n Medieval history.* a Scandinavian chieftain or noble. ORIG C19: from ON
▸ **ˈjarldom** *n*

jarrah (ˈdʒærə) *n* an Australian eucalyptus tree that yields a valuable timber. ORIG from Abor.

Jarrett ★ (ˈdʒærɪt) *n* **Keith.** born 1945, US jazz pianist and composer.

Jarrow ★ (ˈdʒærəʊ) *n* a port in NE England, in South Tyneside: ruined monastery where the Venerable Bede lived and died; its unemployed marched on London in the 1930s; shipyards, oil installations, iron and steel works. Pop.: 29 325 (1991 est.).

Jarry ★ (*French* ʒari) *n* **Alfred** (alfrɛd). 1873–1907, French dramatist and poet, who initiated the theatre of the absurd with his play *Ubu Roi* (1896).

Jaruzelski ★ (*Polish* jaruːˈʒɛlski) *n* **Wojciech** (ˈvɔɪtʃɛk). born 1923, Polish statesman and soldier; prime minister (1981–85); head of state (1985–90; as president from 1989).

Jas. *abbrev. for* James.

jasmine (ˈdʒæsmɪn, ˈdʒæz-) *n* **1** Also called: **jessamine.** any tropical or subtropical oleaceous shrub or climbing plant widely cultivated for their white, yellow, or red fragrant flowers. **2** any of several other shrubs with fragrant flowers, such as the Cape jasmine, yellow jasmine, and frangipani (**red jasmine**). ORIG C16: from OF *jasmin,* from Ar., from Persian *yāsmīn*

Jason ★ (ˈdʒeɪsᵊn) *n Greek myth.* the hero who led the Argonauts in quest of the Golden Fleece. He became the husband of Medea, whom he later abandoned for Glauce.

jaspé (ˈdʒæspeɪ) *adj* resembling jasper; variegated. ORIG C19: from F, from *jasper* to marble

jasper (ˈdʒæspə) *n* **1** an opaque impure form of quartz, red, yellow, brown, or dark green in colour, used as a gemstone and for ornamental decoration. **2** Also called: **jasper ware.** a dense hard stoneware. ORIG C14: from OF *jaspe,* from L *jaspis,* from Gk *iaspis,* of Semitic origin

Jasper National Park (ˈdʒæspə) ★ *n* a national park in SW Canada, in W Alberta in the Rockies: wildlife sanctuary. Area: 10 900 sq. km (4200 sq. miles).

Jaspers ★ (*German* ˈjaspərs) *n* **Karl** (karl). 1883–1969, German existentialist philosopher.

Jassy ★ (ˈjasi) *n* the German name for **Iaşi.**

jato (ˈdʒeɪtəʊ) *n, pl* **jatos.** *Aeronautics.* jet-assisted takeoff. ORIG C20: from *j(et-)a(ssisted) t(ake)o(ff)*

jaundice (ˈdʒɔːndɪs) *n* **1** Also called: **icterus.** yellowing of the skin due to the abnormal presence of bile pigments in the blood, as in hepatitis. **2** jealousy, envy, and ill humour. ◆ *vb* **jaundices, jaundicing, jaundiced. 3** to distort (the judgment, etc.) adversely: *jealousy had jaundiced his mind.* **4** (*tr*) to affect with or as if with jaundice. ORIG C14: from OF *jaunisse,* from *jaune* yellow, from L *galbinus* yellowish

jaunt (dʒɔːnt) *n* **1** a short pleasurable excursion; outing. ◆ *vb* **2** (*intr*) to go on such an excursion. ORIG C16: from ?

jaunting car *n* a light two-wheeled one-horse car, formerly widely used in Ireland.

jaunty (ˈdʒɔːntɪ) *adj* **jauntier, jauntiest. 1** sprightly and cheerful: *a jaunty step.* **2** smart; trim: *a jaunty hat.* ORIG C17: from F *gentil* noble; see GENTEEL
▸ **ˈjauntily** *adv* ▸ **ˈjauntiness** *n*

Jaurès ★ (*French* ʒɔrɛs) *n* **Jean Léon** (ʒɑ̃ leɔ̃). 1859–1914, French politician and writer, who founded the socialist paper *l'Humanité* (1904), and united the French socialist movement into a single party (1905); assassinated.

Java¹ ★ (ˈdʒɑːvə) *n* an island of Indonesia, south of Borneo, from which it is separated by the **Java Sea:** politically the most important island of Indonesia; it consists chiefly of active volcanic mountains and is densely forested. It came under Dutch control in 1596 and became part of Indonesia in 1949. It is one of the most densely populated areas in the world. Capital: Jakarta. Pop. (with Madura): 102 910 500 (1995 est.). Area: 132 174 sq. km (51 032 sq. miles).
▸ **ˈJavan** *n, adj*

Java² (ˈdʒɑːvə) *n Trademark.* a programming language especially applicable to the World Wide Web. ORIG C20: named after *Java* coffee, said to have been consumed in large quantities by the language's creators

Java man *n* a type of primitive man, *Homo erectus,* that lived in the middle Palaeolithic Age in Java.

Javanese (ˌdʒɑːvəˈniːz) *adj* **1** of or relating to the island of Java. ◆ *n* **2** (*pl* **Javanese**) a native or inhabitant of Java. **3** the Malayo-Polynesian language of Java.

Javari *or* **Javary** ★ (*Portuguese* ʒavaˈri) *n* a river in South America, flowing northeast as part of the border between Peru and Brazil to join the Amazon. Length: about 1050 km (650 miles). Spanish name: **Yavarí.**

javelin (ˈdʒævlɪn) *n* **1** a long pointed spear thrown as a weapon or in competitive field events. **2 the javelin.** the event or sport of throwing the javelin. ORIG C16: from OF *javeline,* var. of *javelot,* of Celtic origin

jaw (dʒɔː) *n* **1** the part of the skull of a vertebrate that frames the mouth and holds the teeth. **2** the corresponding part of an invertebrate, esp. an insect. **3** a pair or either of a pair of hinged or sliding components of a machine or tool designed to grip an object. **4** *Sl.* **4a** impudent talk. **4b** idle conversation. **4c** a lecture. ◆ *vb* **5** (*intr*) *Sl.* **5a** to chat; gossip. **5b** to lecture. ORIG C14: prob. from OF *joue* cheek

Jawara ★ (ˈdʒɑːwərə) *n* Sir **Dawda** (ˈdɔːdə). born 1924, Gambian statesman; president of The Gambia (1970–94).

jawbone (ˈdʒɔːˌbəʊn) *n* a nontechnical name for **mandible** or (less commonly) **maxilla.**

jawbreaker (ˈdʒɔːˌbreɪkə) *n* **1** a device having hinged jaws for crushing rocks and ores. **2** *Inf.* a word that is hard to pronounce.
▸ **ˈjawˌbreaking** *adj*

jaw-dropping *adj Inf.* amazing.
▸ **ˈjaw-ˌdroppingly** *adv*

jaws (dʒɔːz) *pl n* **1** the narrow opening of some confined place such as a gorge. **2 the jaws.** a dangerously close position: *the jaws of death.*

Jaxartes ★ (dʒækˈsɑːtiːz) *n* the ancient name for **Syr Darya.**

jay (dʒeɪ) *n* **1** a passerine bird related to the crow having a pinkish-brown body, blue-and-black wings, and a black-and-white crest. **2** a foolish or gullible person. ORIG C13: from OF *jai,* from LL *gāius,* ?from name *Gāius*

Jay ★ (dʒeɪ) *n* **John.** 1745–1829, American statesman, jurist, and diplomat; first chief justice of the Supreme Court (1789–95). He negotiated the treaty with Great Britain (**Jay's treaty,** 1794), that settled outstanding disputes.

Jaya (ˈdʒɑːjə) *or* **Djaja** ★ *n* **Mount.** a mountain in E Indonesia, in Irian Jaya in the Sudirman Range: the highest mountain in New Guinea. Height: 5039 m (16 532 ft). Former names: (Mount) **Carstensz, Sukarno Peak.**

Jayapura (ˌdʒɑːjɑːˈpʊərə) *or* **Djajapura** ★ *n* a port in NE Indonesia, capital of Irian Jaya, on the N coast. Pop.:

180 400 (1995 est.). Former names: **Sukarnapura, Kotabaru, Hollandia.**

Jayawardene ★ (ˌdʒeɪə'wɑːdɪnə) *n* **Junius Richard.** 1906–96, Sri Lankan statesman; prime minister (1977–78) and first president of Sri Lanka (1978–89).

Jaycee ('dʒeɪ'siː) *n US, Canad., Austral., & NZ.* a young person who belongs to a junior chamber of commerce. ORIG C20: from *J(unior) C(hamber)*

jaywalk ('dʒeɪˌwɔːk) *vb (intr)* to cross or walk in a street recklessly or illegally. ORIG C20: from JAY (sense 2)
▸ **'jayˌwalker** *n* ▸ **'jayˌwalking** *n*

jazz (dʒæz) *n* **1a** music of US Black origin, characterized by syncopated rhythms, solo and group improvisation, and a variety of harmonic idioms and instrumental techniques. **1b** *(as modifier): a jazz band.* **1c** *(in combination): a jazzman.* **2** *Sl.* rigmarole: *legal papers and all that jazz.* ◆ *vb* **3** *(intr)* to play or dance to jazz music. ORIG C20: from ?
▸ **'jazzy** *adj* ▸ **'jazzily** *adv* ▸ **'jazziness** *n*

jazz up *vb (tr, adv) Inf.* **1** to imbue (a piece of music) with jazz qualities, esp. by playing at a quicker tempo. **2** to make more lively or appealing.

JC *abbrev. for:* **1** Jesus Christ. **2** Julius Caesar.

JCB *n Trademark.* a type of construction machine with a hydraulically operated shovel on the front and an excavator arm on the back. ORIG from the initials of *J*(oseph) *C*(yril) *B*(amford) (born 1916), its Brit. manufacturer

jealous ('dʒɛləs) *adj* **1** suspicious or fearful of being displaced by a rival. **2** (often *postpositive* and foll. by *of*) resentful (of) or vindictive (towards). **3** (often *postpositive* and foll. by *of*) possessive and watchful in the protection (of): *jealous of one's reputation.* **4** characterized by or resulting from jealousy. **5** *Obsolete except in Biblical use.* demanding exclusive loyalty: *a jealous God.* ORIG C13: from OF *gelos,* from Med. L, from LL *zēlus* emulation, from Gk *zēlos* ZEAL
▸ **'jealously** *adv*

jealousy ('dʒɛləsɪ) *n, pl* **jealousies.** the state or quality of being jealous.

jean (dʒiːn) *n* a tough twill-weave cotton fabric used for hard-wearing trousers, overalls, etc. ORIG C16: short for *jean fustian,* from *Gene* GENOA

Jean ★ *(French* ʒɑ̃) *n* born 1921, grand duke of Luxembourg from 1964.

Jean Baptiste *(French* ʒɑ̃bɑtist) *n Canad. sl.* a French Canadian. ORIG F: John the Baptist, traditional patron saint of French Canada

Jean de Meung ★ *(French* ʒɑ̃ də mœ̃) *n* real name *Jean Clopinel.* ?1250–?1305, French poet, who continued Guillaume de Lorris' *Roman de la Rose.*

Jeanne d'Arc ★ (ʒɑn dark) *n* the French name of **Joan of Arc.**

Jean Paul ★ *(French* ʒɑ̃ pɔl) *n* real name *Johann Paul Friedrich Richter.* 1763–1825, German novelist.

jeans (dʒiːnz) *pl n* trousers for casual wear, made esp. of denim or corduroy. ORIG pl. of JEAN

Jeans ★ (dʒiːnz) *n* Sir **James Hopwood.** 1877–1946, British astronomer, physicist, and mathematician, best known for his popular books on astronomy.

Jebel Musa ★ ('dʒɛbᵊl 'muːsə) *n* a mountain in NW Morocco, near the Strait of Gibraltar: one of the Pillars of Hercules. Height: 850 m (2790 ft).

Jedda ★ ('dʒɛdə) *n* another name for **Jidda.**

Jeep (dʒiːp) *n Trademark.* a small road vehicle with four-wheel drive. ORIG C20: ?from *GP,* for *general-purpose (vehicle),* infl. by Eugene the *Jeep,* creature in a comic strip by E. C. Segar

jeepers *or* **jeepers creepers** ('dʒiːpəz 'kriːpəz) *interj US sl.* a mild exclamation of surprise. ORIG C20: euphemism for *Jesus*

jeer (dʒɪə) *vb* **1** (often foll. by *at*) to laugh or scoff (at a person or thing). ◆ *n* **2** a remark or cry of derision. ORIG C16: from ?
▸ **'jeerer** *n* ▸ **'jeering** *adj, n* ▸ **'jeeringly** *adv*

Jefferson ★ ('dʒɛfəsᵊn) *n* **Thomas.** 1743–1826, US statesman: secretary of state (1790–93); third president (1801–09). He was the chief drafter of the Declaration of Independence (1776), the chief opponent of the centralizing policies of the Federalists under Hamilton, and effected the Louisiana Purchase (1803).
▸ **Jeffersonian** (ˌdʒɛfə'səʊnɪən) *adj, n*

Jefferson City ★ *n* a city in central Missouri, the state capital, on the Missouri River. Pop.: 35 481 (1990).

Jeffrey ★ ('dʒɛfrɪ) *n* **Francis,** Lord. 1773–1850, Scottish judge and literary critic. As editor of the *Edinburgh Review* (1803–29), he severely criticized the romantic poets, esp. Wordsworth.

Jeffreys ★ ('dʒɛfrɪz) *n* **George,** 1st Baron Jeffreys of Wem. ?1645–89, English judge, notorious for his brutality at the "Bloody Assizes" (1685), where those involved in Monmouth's rebellion were tried.

jehad (dʒɪ'hæd) *n* a variant spelling of **jihad.**

Jehol ★ (dʒə'hɒl) *n* **1** a former province of NE China, north of the Great Wall: divided among Hebei, Liaoning, and Inner Mongolia in 1956. Area: 192 380 sq. km (74 278 sq. miles). **2** a region of NE China, in Hebei and Liaoning provinces: mountainous.

Jehoshaphat ★ (dʒɪ'hɒʃəˌfæt, -'hɒs-) *n Old Testament.* **1** the king of Judah (?873–?849 B.C.) (I Kings 22:41–50). **2** **Valley of Jehoshaphat.** the site of Jehovah's apocalyptic judgment upon the nations (Joel 4:14).

Jehovah ★ (dʒɪ'həʊvə) *n Old Testament.* the personal name of God, revealed to Moses on Mount Horeb (Exodus 3). ORIG C16: from Med. L, from Heb. YHVH YAHWEH

Jehovah's Witness *n* a member of a Christian Church of American origin, the followers of which believe that the end of the present world system of government is near.

Jehu ★ ('dʒiːhjuː) *n* **1** *Old Testament.* the successor to Ahab as king of Israel. **2** *Humorous.* a reckless driver.

jejune (dʒɪ'dʒuːn) *adj* **1** naive; unsophisticated. **2** insipid; dull. **3** lacking nourishment. ORIG C17: from L *jējūnus* hungry, empty
▸ **je'junely** *adv* ▸ **je'juneness** *n*

jejunum (dʒɪ'dʒuːnəm) *n* the part of the small intestine between the duodenum and the ileum. ORIG C16: from L, from *jējūnus* empty; from the belief that the jejunum is empty after death

Jekyll ★ ('dʒɛkᵊl) *n* **Gertrude.** 1843–1932, British landscape gardener: noted for her simplicity of design and use of indigenous plants.

Jekyll and Hyde *n* **a** a person with two distinct personalities, one good, the other evil. **b** *(as modifier): a Jekyll-and-Hyde personality.* ORIG C19: after the principal character of Robert Louis Stevenson's novel *The Strange Case of Dr Jekyll and Mr Hyde* (1886)

jell *or* **gel** (dʒɛl) *vb* **1** to make or become gelatinous; congeal. **2** *(intr)* to assume definite form: *his ideas have jelled.* ORIG C19: back formation from JELLY[1]

jellaba *or* **jellabah** ('dʒɛləbə) *n* variant spellings of **djellaba.**

Jellicoe ★ ('dʒɛlɪˌkəʊ) *n* **John Rushworth,** 1st Earl Jellicoe. 1859–1935, British admiral, who commanded the Grand Fleet at the Battle of Jutland (1916), which incapacitated the German fleet for the rest of World War I.

jellies ('dʒɛlɪz) *pl n Brit. sl.* **1** gelatine capsules of temazepam, dissolved and injected as a recreational drug. **2** Also called: **jelly shoes.** shoes made from brightly coloured transparent plastic. ORIG C20: shortened from GELATINE

jellify ('dʒɛlɪˌfaɪ) *vb* **jellifies, jellifying, jellified.** to make into or become jelly.
▸ **ˌjellifi'cation** *n*

jelly[1] ('dʒɛlɪ) *n, pl* **jellies.** **1** a fruit-flavoured clear dessert set with gelatine. **2** a preserve made from the juice of fruit boiled with sugar and used as jam. **3** a savoury food preparation set with gelatine or with gelatinous stock: *calf's-foot jelly.* ◆ *vb* **jellies, jellying, jellied.** **4** to jellify. ORIG C14: from OF *gelee* frost, jelly, from *geler* to set hard, from L, from *gelu* frost
▸ **'jellied** *adj* ▸ **'jelly-ˌlike** *adj*

jelly[2] ('dʒɛlɪ) *n Brit.* a slang name for **gelignite.**

jelly baby *n Brit.* a small sweet made from a gelatinous substance formed to resemble a baby.

jellyfish ('dʒɛlɪˌfɪʃ) *n, pl* **jellyfish** *or* **jellyfishes. 1** any marine coelenterate having a gelatinous umbrella-shaped body with trailing tentacles. **2** *Inf.* a weak indecisive person.

jelly fungus *n* a fungus that grows on trees and has a jelly-like consistency when wet.

Jemappes ★ (*French* ʒəmap) *n* a town in SW Belgium, in Hainaut province west of Mons: scene of a battle (1792) during the French Revolutionary Wars, in which the French defeated the Austrians. Pop.: 18 100 (latest est.).

jemmy ('dʒɛmɪ) *or US* **jimmy** *n, pl* **jemmies** *or US* **jimmies. 1** a short steel crowbar used, esp. by burglars, for forcing doors and windows. ◆ *vb* **jemmies, jemmying, jemmied** *or US* **jimmies, jimmying, jimmied. 2** (*tr*) to prise (something) open with a jemmy. ORIG C19: from the pet name for *James*

Jena ★ (*German* 'jeːna) *n* a city in S East Germany, in Thuringia: university (1558), at which Hegel and Schiller taught; site of the battle (1806) in which Napoleon Bonaparte defeated the Prussians; optical and precision instrument industry. Pop.: 101 061 (1996 est.).

Jenghis Khan ★ ('dʒɛŋgɪs 'kɑːn) *n* See **Genghis Khan.**

Jenkins ★ ('dʒɛŋkɪnz) *n* **Roy** (**Harris**), Baron Jenkins of Hillhead. born 1920, British Social Democrat politician; president of the Common Market Commission (1977–80); originally a Labour politician; cofounder of the Social Democratic Party (1981); leader of party (1982–83); Chancellor of Oxford University from 1987.

Jenner ★ ('dʒɛnə) *n* **1 Edward.** 1749–1823, British physician, who discovered vaccination by showing that injections of cowpox virus produce immunity against smallpox (1796). **2** Sir **William.** 1815–98, British physician and pathologist, who distinguished between typhus and typhoid fevers (1849).

jennet, genet, *or* **gennet** ('dʒɛnɪt) *n* a small Spanish riding horse. ORIG C15: from OF *genet,* from Catalan *ginet,* horse used by the *Zenete,* from Ar. *Zanātah* the Zenete, a Moorish people renowned for their horsemanship

jenny ('dʒɛnɪ) *n, pl* **jennies. 1** a machine for turning up the edge of a piece of sheet metal in preparation for making a joint. **2** the female of certain animals or birds, esp. a donkey, ass, or wren. **3** short for **spinning jenny. 4** *Billiards, etc.* an in-off. ORIG C17: from name *Jenny,* dim. of *Jane*

Jensen ★ (*Danish* 'jɛnsən) *n* **Johannes Vilhelm** (jo'hanəs 'vɪlhelm). 1873–1950, Danish novelist, poet, and essayist: best known for his novel sequence *The Long Journey* (1908–22). Nobel prize for literature 1944.

jeopardize *or* **jeopardise** ('dʒɛpəˌdaɪz) *vb* **jeopardizes, jeopardizing, jeopardized** *or* **jeopardises, jeopardising, jeopardised.** (*tr*) **1** to risk; hazard: *he jeopardized his job by being persistently unpunctual.* **2** to put in danger.

jeopardy ('dʒɛpədɪ) *n* (usually preceded by *in*) **1** danger of injury, loss, death, etc.: *his health was in jeopardy.* **2** *Law.* danger of being convicted and punished for a criminal offence. ORIG C14: from OF *jeu parti,* lit.: divided game, hence uncertain issue, from *jeu* game, from L *jocus* joke, game + *partir* to divide

Jephthah ★ ('dʒɛfθə) *n Old Testament.* a judge of Israel, who sacrificed his daughter in fulfilment of a vow (Judges 11:12–40). Douay spelling: **Jephte** ('dʒɛftə).

jequirity (dʒɪ'kwɪrɪtɪ) *n, pl* **jequirities.** a tropical climbing plant with scarlet black-spotted seeds used as beads, and roots used as a substitute for liquorice. Also called: **Indian liquorice.** ORIG C19: from Port. *jequiriti,* of Amerind origin, from *jekiriti*

Jer. *Bible. abbrev. for* Jeremiah.

jerbil ('dʒɜːbɪl) *n* a variant spelling of **gerbil.**

jerboa (dʒɜː'bəʊə) *n* any small nocturnal burrowing rodent inhabiting dry regions of Asia and N Africa, having long hind legs specialized for jumping. ORIG C17: from NL, from Ar. *yarbū'*

jeremiad (ˌdʒɛrɪ'maɪəd) *n* a long mournful lamentation or complaint. ORIG C18: from F *jérémiade,* referring to the Lamentations of Jeremiah in the Old Testament

Jeremiah ★ (ˌdʒɛrɪ'maɪə) *n* **1** *Old Testament.* **1a** a major prophet of Judah from about 626 to 587 B.C. **1b** the book containing his oracles. **2** a person who habitually prophesies doom or denounces contemporary society.

jerepigo (ˌdʒɛrɪ'pɪgəʊ) *n S. African.* a sweet white or red sherry-type wine. ORIG from Port. *cheripiga* an adulterant of port wine

Jerez ★ (*Spanish* xe'reθ) *n* a town in SW Spain: famous for the making of sherry. Pop.: 190 390 (1994 est.). Official name: **Jerez de la Frontera** (xe'rɛð ðe la frɔn'tera). Former name: **Xeres.**

Jericho ★ ('dʒɛrɪˌkəʊ) *n* a village in the West Bank near the N end of the Dead Sea, 251 m (825 ft) below sea level: on the site of an ancient city, the first place to be taken by the Israelites under Joshua after entering the Promised Land in the 14th century B.C. (Joshua 6).

jerk[1] (dʒɜːk) *vb* **1** to move or cause to move with an irregular or spasmodic motion. **2** to throw, twist, pull, or push (something) abruptly or spasmodically. **3** (*tr; often foll. by out*) to utter (words, etc.) in a spasmodic or breathless manner. ◆ *n* **4** an abrupt or spasmodic movement. **5** an irregular jolting motion: *the car moved with a jerk.* **6** (*pl*) Also called: **physical jerks.** *Brit. inf.* physical exercises. **7** *Sl., chiefly US & Canad.* a stupid or ignorant person. ORIG C16: prob. var. of *yerk* to pull stitches tight ▸ **'jerker** *n*

jerk[2] (dʒɜːk) *vb* (*tr*) **1** to preserve beef, etc., by cutting into thin strips and drying in the sun. ◆ *n* **2** Also called: **jerky.** jerked meat. ORIG C18: back formation from *jerky,* from Sp. *charqui,* from Quechuan

jerkin ('dʒɜːkɪn) *n* **1** a sleeveless short jacket worn by men or women. **2** a man's sleeveless fitted jacket, often made of leather, worn in the 16th and 17th centuries. ORIG C16: from ?

jerk off *or US* **jack off** *vb* (*adv often reflexive*) *Taboo sl.* (of a male) to masturbate.

jerky ('dʒɜːkɪ) *adj* **jerkier, jerkiest.** characterized by jerks. ▸ **'jerkily** *adv* ▸ **'jerkiness** *n*

jeroboam (ˌdʒɛrə'bəʊəm) *n* a wine bottle holding the equivalent of four normal bottles. ORIG C19: allusion to JEROBOAM, a "mighty man of valour" (I Kings 11:28) who "made Israel to sin" (I Kings 14:16)

Jeroboam ★ (ˌdʒɛrə'bəʊəm) *n Old Testament.* **1** the first king of the northern kingdom of Israel (?922–?901 B.C.). **2** king of the northern kingdom of Israel (?786–?746 B.C.).

Jerome ★ (dʒə'rəʊm) *n* **1 Saint.** Latin name *Eusebius Hieronymus.* ?347–?420 A.D., Christian monk and scholar, whose outstanding work was the production of the Vulgate. Feast day: Sept. 30. **2 Jerome K**(**lapka**). 1859–1927, English humorous writer; author of *Three Men in a Boat* (1889).

jerry ('dʒɛrɪ) *n, pl* **jerries.** *Brit.* an informal word for **chamber pot.**

Jerry ('dʒɛrɪ) *n, pl* **Jerries.** *Brit. sl.* **1** a German, esp. a German soldier. **2** the Germans collectively.

jerry-build *vb* **jerry-builds, jerry-building, jerry-built.** (*tr*) to build (houses, flats, etc.) badly using cheap materials. ▸ **'jerry-ˌbuilder** *n*

jerry can *n* a flat-sided can with a capacity of between 4.5 and 5 gallons used for storing or transporting liquids, esp. motor fuel. ORIG C20: from JERRY

jersey ('dʒɜːzɪ) *n* **1** a knitted garment covering the upper part of the body. **2a** a machine-knitted slightly elastic cloth of wool, silk, nylon, etc., used for clothing. **2b** (*as modifier*): *a jersey suit.* **3** a football shirt. ORIG C16: from JERSEY, from the woollen sweaters worn by the fishermen

Jersey ★ ('dʒɜːzɪ) *n* **1** an island in the English Channel, the largest of the Channel Islands: forms, with two other islands, the bailiwick of Jersey; colonized from Normandy in the 11th century and still officially French-speaking; noted for finance, market gardening, dairy farming, and tourism. Capital: St Helier. Pop.: 84 082 (1991). Area: 116 sq. km (45 sq. miles). **2** a breed of dairy cattle producing milk with a high butterfat content, originating from the island of Jersey.

Jersey City ★ *n* an industrial city in NE New Jersey, opposite Manhattan on a peninsula between the Hudson and Hackensack Rivers: part of the Port of New York; site of one of the greatest railway terminals in the world. Pop.: 226 022 (1994 est.).

Jerusalem ★ (dʒəˈruːsələm) *n* **1** the capital of Israel (recognition of this has been withheld by a number of countries pending completion of negotiations on Palestinian autonomy), situated in the Judaean hills: became capital of the Hebrew kingdom after its capture by David around 1000 B.C.; destroyed by Nebuchadnezzar of Babylon in 586 B.C.; taken by the Romans in 63 B.C.; devastated in 70 A.D. and 135 A.D. during the Jewish rebellions against Rome; fell to the Arabs in 637 and to the Seljuk Turks in 1071; ruled by Crusaders from 1099 to 1187 and by the Egyptians and Turks until conquered by the British (1917); centre of the British mandate of Palestine from 1920 to 1948, when the Arabs took the old city and the Jews held the new city; unified after the Six Day War (1967) under the Israelis; the holy city of Jews, Christians, and Muslims. Pop.: 591 400 (1996 est.). **2 the New Jerusalem.** *Christianity.* **2a** Heaven. **2b** any ideal city.

Jerusalem artichoke *n* **1** a North American sunflower widely cultivated for its underground edible tubers. **2** the tuber of this plant, which is eaten as a vegetable. ORIG C17: by folk etymology from It. *girasole articiocco;* see GIRASOL

Jervis Bay ★ (ˈdʒɑːvɪs) *n* an inlet of the Pacific in SE Australia, on the coast of S New South Wales: part of the Australian Capital Territory: site of the Royal Australian Naval College.

Jespersen ★ (ˈjɛspəsᵊn, ˈdʒɛs-) *n* **(Jens) Otto (Harry).** 1860–1943, Danish philologist: author of *Modern English Grammar* (1909–31).

jess (dʒɛs) *n Falconry.* a short leather strap, one end of which is permanently attached to the leg of a hawk or falcon. ORIG C14: from OF *ges,* from L *jactus* a throw, from *jacere* to throw
▸ **jessed** *adj*

jessamine (ˈdʒɛsəmɪn) *n* another name for **jasmine** (sense 1).

Jesse ★ (ˈdʒɛsɪ) *n Old Testament.* the father of David (I Samuel 16).

Jesselton ★ (ˈdʒɛsəltən) *n* the former name of **Kota Kinabalu.**

jessie (ˈdʒɛsɪ) *n Sl.* an effeminate, weak, or cowardly boy or man.

jest (dʒɛst) *n* **1** something done or said for amusement; joke. **2** playfulness; fun: *to act in jest.* **3** a jeer or taunt. **4** an object of derision. ◆ *vb* **5** to act or speak in an amusing or frivolous way. **6** to make fun of (a person or thing). ORIG C13: var. of GEST
▸ **ˈjesting** *adj, n* ▸ **ˈjestingly** *adv*

jester (ˈdʒɛstə) *n* a professional clown employed by a king or nobleman during the Middle Ages.

Jesu ★ (ˈdʒiːzjuː) *n* a poetic name for or vocative form of **Jesus.** ORIG C17: from LL, vocative of JESUS

Jesuit (ˈdʒɛzjʊɪt) *n* **1** a member of a Roman Catholic religious order (the **Society of Jesus**) founded by Ignatius Loyola in 1534 with the aim of defending Catholicism against the Reformation. **2** (*sometimes not cap.*) *Inf., offens.* a person given to subtle and equivocating arguments. ORIG C16: from NL *Jēsuita,* from LL *Jēsus* + *-ita* -ITE[1]
▸ **ˌJesuˈitical** *adj*

Jesus ★ (ˈdʒiːzəs) *n* **1** Also called: **Jesus Christ, Jesus of Nazareth.** ?4 B.C.–?29 A.D., founder of Christianity, born in Bethlehem and brought up in Nazareth as a Jew. He is believed by Christians to be the Son of God and to have been miraculously conceived by the Virgin Mary. After the Last Supper with his disciples, he was betrayed by Judas and crucified. Christians believe that he rose from his tomb after three days, appeared to his disciples several times, and ascended to Heaven after 40 days. **2** *Son of Sirach.* 3rd century B.C., author of the Apocryphal book of Ecclesiasticus. ◆ *interj also* **Jesus wept. 3** *Taboo sl.* used to express intense surprise, dismay, etc. ORIG via L from Gk *Iēsous,* from Heb. *Yeshūaʻ,* shortened from *Yehōshūaʻ* God is help, JOSHUA

Jesus freak *n Inf.* a vociferous Christian, esp. one who is evangelical and belongs to a community.

jet[1] (dʒɛt) *n* **1** a thin stream of liquid or gas forced out of a small aperture. **2** an outlet or nozzle for emitting such a stream. **3** a jet-propelled aircraft. ◆ *vb* **jets, jetting, jetted. 4** to issue or cause to issue in a jet: *water jetted from the hose.* **5** to transport or be transported by jet aircraft. ORIG C16: from OF *jeter* to throw, from L *jactāre* to toss about

jet[2] (dʒɛt) *n* **a** a hard black variety of lignite that takes a brilliant polish and is used for jewellery, etc. **b** (*as modifier*): *jet earrings.* ORIG C14: from OF *jaiet,* from L, from Gk *lithos gagatēs* stone of *Gagai,* a town in Lycia, Asia Minor

jet black *n* **a** a deep black colour. **b** (*as adj*): *jet-black hair.*

jet-boat *n NZ.* a power boat that is powered and steered by a jet of water under pressure.

jeté (ʒəˈteɪ) *n Ballet.* a step in which the dancer springs from one leg and lands on the other. ORIG F, lit.: thrown, from *jeter;* see JET[1]

jet engine *n* a gas turbine, esp. one fitted to an aircraft.

Jethro ★ (ˈdʒɛθrəʊ) *n Old Testament.* a Midianite priest, the father-in-law of Moses (Exodus 3:1; 4:18).

jet lag *n* a general feeling of fatigue, disorientation, or nausea often experienced by air travellers after long journeys.

jet-propelled *adj* **1** driven by jet propulsion. **2** *Inf.* very fast.

jet propulsion *n* **1** propulsion by means of a jet of fluid. **2** propulsion by means of a gas turbine, esp. when the exhaust gases provide the propulsive thrust.

jetsam (ˈdʒɛtsəm) *n* **1** that portion of the cargo of a vessel thrown overboard to lighten her, as during a storm. Cf. **flotsam** (sense 1). **2** another word for **flotsam** (sense 2). ORIG C16: shortened from JETTISON

jet set *n* **a** a rich and fashionable social set, the members of which travel widely for pleasure. **b** (*as modifier*): *jet-set travellers.*
▸ **ˈjet-ˌsetter** *n* ▸ **ˈjet-ˌsetting** *n, adj*

jet ski *Trademark. n* **1** a small self-propelled vehicle for one person resembling a scooter, which skims across water on a flat keel, and is steered by means of handlebars. ◆ *vb* **jet-ski, jet-skis, jet-skiing, jet-skied** *or* **jet ski'd.** (*intr*) **2** to ride a jet ski.
▸ **jet skier** *n* ▸ **jet skiing** *n*

jet stream *n* **1** *Meteorol.* a narrow belt of high-altitude winds moving east at high speeds. **2** the jet of exhaust gases produced by a gas turbine, etc.

jettison (ˈdʒɛtɪsᵊn, -zᵊn) *vb* **jettisons, jettisoning, jettisoned.** (*tr*) **1** to abandon: *to jettison old clothes.* **2** to throw overboard. ◆ *n* **3** another word for **jetsam** (sense 1). ORIG C15: from OF, ult. from L *jactātiō* a tossing about

jetton (ˈdʒɛtᵊn) *n* a counter or token, esp. a chip used in such gambling games as roulette. ORIG C18: from F *jeton,* from *jeter* to cast up (accounts); see JET[1]

jetty (ˈdʒɛtɪ) *n, pl* **jetties. 1** a structure built from a shore out into the water to direct currents or protect a harbour. **2** a landing pier; dock. ORIG C15: from OF *jetee* projecting part, lit.: something thrown out, from *jeter* to throw

jeu d'esprit *French.* (ʒø dɛspri) *n, pl* **jeux d'esprit** (ʒø dɛspri). a light-hearted display of wit or cleverness, esp. in literature. ORIG lit.: play of spirit

Jevons ★ (ˈdʒɛvᵊnz) *n* **William Stanley.** 1835–82, British economist and logician: author of *The Theory of Political Economy* (1871).

Jew (dʒuː) *n* **1** a member of the Semitic people who are descended from the ancient Israelites. **2** a person whose religion is Judaism. ORIG C12: from OF *juiu,* from L *jūdaeus,* from Gk *ioudaios,* from Heb., from *yehūdāh* JUDAH

jewel (ˈdʒuːəl) *n* **1** a precious or semiprecious stone; gem. **2** a person or thing resembling a jewel in preciousness, brilliance, etc. **3** a gemstone used as a bearing in a watch. **4** a piece of jewellery. ◆ *vb* **jewels, jewelling, jewelled** *or US* **jewels, jeweling, jeweled. 5** (*tr*) to fit or decorate with a jewel or jewels. ORIG C13: from OF *jouel,* ?from *jeu* game, from L *jocus*

jewelfish (ˈdʒuːəlˌfɪʃ) *n, pl* **jewelfish** *or* **jewelfishes.** a beautifully coloured and popular aquarium fish native to Africa.

jeweller *or US* **jeweler** (ˈdʒuːələ) *n* a person whose business is the cutting or setting of gemstones or the making or selling of jewellery.

jeweller's rouge *n* a finely powdered form of ferric oxide used as a metal polish.

jewellery *or US* **jewelry** (ˈdʒuːəlrɪ) *n* objects that are worn for personal adornment, such as rings, necklaces, etc., considered collectively.

Jewess (ˈdʒuːɪs) *n Offens.* a Jewish girl or woman.

jewfish (ˈdʒuːˌfɪʃ) *n, pl* **jewfish** *or* **jewfishes. 1** any of various large dark fishes of warm or tropical seas. **2** *Austral.* a freshwater catfish. ORIG C17: from ?

Jewish (ˈdʒuːɪʃ) *adj* of or characteristic of Jews.
▸ **ˈJewishly** *adv* ▸ **ˈJewishness** *n*

Jewish Autonomous Region ★ *n* an administrative division of SE Russia, in E Siberia: colonized by Jews in 1928; largely agricultural. Capital: Birobidzhan. Pop.: 216 000 (1995 est.). Area: 36 000 sq. km (13 895 sq. miles). Also called: **Birobidzhan, Birobijan.**

Jew lizard *n* a large Australian lizard with spiny scales round its neck.

Jewry (ˈdʒʊərɪ) *n, pl* **Jewries. 1a** Jews collectively. **1b** the Jewish religion or culture. **2** a quarter of a town inhabited by Jews.

jew's-ear *n* a pinky-red fungus.

jew's-harp *n* a musical instrument consisting of a small lyre-shaped metal frame held between the teeth, with a steel tongue plucked with the finger.

Jezebel ★ (ˈdʒɛzəˌbɛl) *n* **1** *Old Testament.* the wife of Ahab, king of Israel. **2** (*sometimes not cap.*) a shameless or scheming woman.

Jezreel ★ (ˈdʒɛzrɪəl) *n* **Plain of.** another name for **Esdraelon.**
▸ **ˈJezreelˌite** *n*

JFK *abbrev. for* John Fitzgerald Kennedy.

Jhabvala ★ (dʒæbˈvɑːlə) *n* **Ruth Prawer**, original name *Ruth Prawer.* born 1927, British writer living in India and the US, born in Germany to Polish parents: author of the Booker-prizewinning novel *Heat and Dust* (1975).

Jhansi ★ (ˈdʒɑːnsɪ) *n* a city in central India, in SW Uttar Pradesh: scene of a mutiny against the British in 1857. Pop.: 300 850 (1991).

Jhelum ★ (ˈdʒiːləm) *n* a river in Pakistan and Kashmir, rising in W central Kashmir and flowing northwest through the Vale of Kashmir, then southwest into N West Punjab to join the Chenab River: important for irrigation, having the Mangla Dam (Pakistan), completed in 1967. Length: about 720 km (450 miles).

JHVH *or* **JHWH** *Old Testament.* a variant of **YHVH.**

Jiang Qing (ˈdʒæŋ ˈtʃɪŋ) *or* **Chiang Ch'ing** ★ *n* c. 1913–91, Chinese Communist actress and politician; widow of Mao Tse-tung and a leading member of the Gang of Four.

Jiangsu (ˈdʒæŋˈsuː) *or* **Kiangsu** ★ *n* a province of E China, on the Yellow Sea: consists mostly of the marshy delta of the Yangtze River, with some of China's largest cities and most densely populated areas. Capital: Nanjing. Pop.: 71 480 000 (1997 est.). Area: 102 200 sq. km (39 860 sq. miles).

Jiangxi (ˈdʒæŋˈʃiː) *or* **Kiangsi** ★ *n* a province of SE central China, in the basins of the Kan River and the Poyang Lake: mineral resources include coal and tungsten. Capital: Nanchang. Pop.: 41 500 000 (1997 est.). Area: 164 800 sq. km (64 300 sq. miles).

Jiang Zemin ★ (ˈdʒjæŋ ʒeɪˈmɪn) *n* born 1926, Chinese Communist politician: president of China from 1993.

Jiazhou (ˈdʒjæˈdʒəʊ) *or* **Kiaochow** ★ *n* a territory of NE China, in SE Shandong province, surrounding **Jiazhou Bay** (an inlet of the Yellow Sea): leased to Germany from 1898 to 1914. Area: about 520 sq. km (200 sq. miles).

jib[1] (dʒɪb) *n* **1** *Naut.* any triangular sail set forward of the foremast of a vessel. **2** **cut of someone's jib.** someone's manner, style, etc. ORIG C17: from ?

jib[2] (dʒɪb) *vb* **jibs, jibbing, jibbed.** (*intr*) *Chiefly Brit.* **1** (often foll. by *at*) to be reluctant (to). **2** (of an animal) to stop short and refuse to go forwards. **3** *Naut.* a variant of **gybe.** ORIG C19: from ?
▸ **ˈjibber** *n*

jib[3] (dʒɪb) *n* the projecting arm of a crane or the boom of a derrick. ORIG C18: prob. based on GIBBET

jib boom *n Naut.* a spar forming an extension of the bowsprit.

jibe[1] (dʒaɪb) *or* **jib** (dʒɪb) *vb* **jibes, jibing, jibed** *or* **jibs, jibbing, jibbed.** *n Naut.* a variant of **gybe.**

jibe[2] (dʒaɪb) *vb* **jibes, jibing, jibed.** a variant spelling of **gibe**[1].

jibe[3] (dʒaɪb) *vb* **jibes, jibing, jibed.** (*intr*) *Inf.* to agree; accord; harmonize. ORIG C19: from ?

Jibouti *or* **Jibuti** ★ (dʒɪˈbuːtɪ) *n* variant spellings of **Djibouti.**

Jidda (ˈdʒɪdə) *or* **Jedda** ★ *n* a port in W Saudi Arabia on the Red Sea: the diplomatic capital of the country; the port of entry for Mecca, 80 km (50 miles) east. Pop.: 1 500 000 (1991 est.).

jiffy (ˈdʒɪfɪ) *or* **jiff** *n, pl* **jiffies** *or* **jiffs.** *Inf.* a very short time: *wait a jiffy.* ORIG C18: from ?

Jiffy bag *n Trademark.* a large padded envelope.

jig (dʒɪg) *n* **1** any of several old rustic kicking and leaping dances. **2** a piece of music composed for or in the rhythm of this dance. **3** a mechanical device designed to hold and locate a component during machining. **4** *Angling.* any of various spinning lures that wobble when drawn through the water. **5** Also called: **jigger.** *Mining.* a device for separating ore or coal from waste material by agitation in water. ◆ *vb* **jigs, jigging, jigged. 6** to dance (a jig). **7** to jerk or cause to jerk up and down rapidly. **8** (often foll. by *up*) to fit or be fitted in a jig. **9** (*tr*) to drill or cut (a workpiece) in a jig. **10** (*tr*) *Mining.* to separate ore or coal from waste material using a jig. ORIG C16: from ?

Jigawa ★ (ˌdʒɪˈgɑːwə) *n* a state of N Nigeria. Capital: Dutse. Pop.: 3 164 134 (1995 est.). Area (including Kano state): 43 285 sq. km (16 712 sq. miles).

jigger[1] (ˈdʒɪgə) *n* **1** a person or thing that jigs. **2** *Golf.* (formerly) a club, an iron, usually No. 4. **3** any of a number of mechanical devices having a vibratory motion. **4** a light lifting tackle used on ships. **5** a small glass, esp. for whisky. **6** *Billiards.* another word for **bridge**[1] (sense 11). **7** *NZ.* a light hand- or power-propelled vehicle used on railway lines.

jigger[2] *or* **jigger flea** (ˈdʒɪgə) *n* another name for the **chigoe** (sense 1).

jiggered (ˈdʒɪgəd) *adj* (*postpositive*) *Inf.* damned; blowed: *I'm jiggered if he'll get away with it.* ORIG C19: prob. euphemism for *buggered;* see BUGGER

jiggermast (ˈdʒɪgəˌmɑːst) *n Naut.* any small mast on a sailing vessel.

jiggery-pokery (ˈdʒɪgərɪˈpəʊkərɪ) *n Inf., chiefly Brit.* dishonest or deceitful behaviour. ORIG C19: from Scot. dialect *joukery-pawkery*

jiggle (ˈdʒɪgᵊl) *vb* **jiggles, jiggling, jiggled. 1** to move or cause to move up and down or to and fro with a short jerky motion. ◆ *n* **2** a short jerky motion. ORIG C19: frequentative of JIG
▸ **ˈjiggly** *adj*

jigsaw (ˈdʒɪgˌsɔː) *n* **1** a mechanical saw with a fine steel blade for cutting intricate curves in sheets of material. **2** See **jigsaw puzzle.** ORIG C19: from JIG (to jerk up and down rapidly) + SAW[1]

jigsaw puzzle *n* a puzzle in which the player has to reassemble a picture that has been cut into irregularly shaped interlocking pieces.

jihad *or* **jehad** (dʒɪˈhæd) *n Islam.* a holy war against infidels undertaken by Muslims. ORIG C19: from Ar. *jihād* a conflict

Jilin (ˈdʒiːˈlɪn) *or* **Kirin** ★ *n* **1** a province of NE China, in central Manchuria. Capital: Changchun. Pop.: 26 280 000 (1997 est.). Area: 187 000 sq. km (72 930 sq. miles). **2** Also called: **Chi-lin** (ˈtʃiːˈlɪn). a river port in NE

China, in N central Jilin province on the Songhua River. Pop.: 1 270 000 (1991 est.).

Jilong ★ ('dʒiːˈlʊŋ) *n* the Pinyin transliteration of the Chinese name for **Chilung.**

jilt (dʒɪlt) *vb* **1** (*tr*) to leave or reject (a lover), esp. without previous warning. ◆ *n* **2** a woman who jilts a lover. ORIG C17: from dialect *jillet* flighty girl, dim. of name *Gill*

jim crow ('dʒɪm 'krəʊ) *n* (*often caps.*) *US.* **1a** the policy or practice of segregating Blacks. **1b** (*as modifier*): *jim-crow laws.* **2** a derogatory term for **Black**[1]. **3** an implement for bending iron bars or rails. ORIG C19: from *Jim Crow,* name of song used as the basis of an act by Thomas Rice (1808–60), US entertainer
▸ **'jim-'crowism** *n*

Jiménez ★ (*Spanish* xiˈmenεθ) *n* **Juan Ramón** (xwan raˈmɔn). 1881–1958, Spanish lyric poet. His most famous work is *Platero y yo* (1917), a prose poem: Nobel prize for literature 1956.

Jiménez de Cisneros ★ (*Spanish* xiˈmeneð ðe θizˈnerɔs) *n* **Francisco** (franˈθisko). 1436–1517, Spanish cardinal and statesman; regent of Castile (1506–07) and Spain (1516–17) and grand inquisitor for Castile and León (1507–17). Also called: **Ximenes de Cisneros, Ximenez de Cisneros.**

jimjams ('dʒɪmˌdʒæmz) *pl n* **1** *Sl.* delirium tremens. **2** a state of nervous tension or anxiety. **3** *Inf.* pyjamas. ORIG C19: whimsical formation based on JAM[1]

jimmy ('dʒɪmɪ) *n, pl* **jimmies,** *vb* **jimmies, jimmying, jimmied.** a US variant of **jemmy.**

Jinan ('dʒiːˈnæn), **Chinan,** *or* **Tsinan** ★ *n* an industrial city in NE China, capital of Shandong province; probably over 3000 years old. Pop.: 2 320 000 (1991 est.).

Jingdezhen ('dʒɪŋˈdεdʒεn), **Fowliang,** *or* **Fou-liang** ★ *n* a city in SE China, in NE Jiangxi province east of Lake Poyang: famous for its porcelain industry, established in the sixth century. Pop.: 281 183 (1990 est.).

Jinghis Khan ★ ('dʒɪŋgɪs 'kɑːn) *n* See **Genghis Khan.**

jingle ('dʒɪŋgᵊl) *vb* **jingles, jingling, jingled. 1** to ring or cause to ring lightly and repeatedly. **2** (*intr*) to sound in a manner suggestive of jingling: *a jingling verse.* ◆ *n* **3** a sound of metal jingling. **4** a rhythmic verse, etc., esp. one used in advertising. ORIG C16: prob. imit.
▸ **'jingly** *adj*

jingo ('dʒɪŋgəʊ) *n, pl* **jingoes. 1** a loud and bellicose patriot. **2** jingoism. **3 by jingo.** an exclamation of surprise. ORIG C17: orig. ? euphemism for *Jesus;* applied to bellicose patriots after the use of *by Jingo!* in a 19th-cent. song

jingoism ('dʒɪŋgəʊˌɪzəm) *n* the belligerent spirit or foreign policy of jingoes.
▸ **'jingoist** *n, adj* ▸ **ˌjingo'istic** *adj*

Jinja ★ ('dʒɪndʒə) *n* a town in Uganda, on the N shore of Lake Victoria. Pop.: 60 979 (1991).

Jinjiang ('dʒɪnˈdʒjæŋ), **Chinkiang,** *or* **Cheng-chiang** ★ *n* a port in E China, in S Jiangsu at the confluence of the Yangtze River and the Grand Canal. Pop.: 368 316 (1990 est.).

jink (dʒɪŋk) *vb* **1** (*intr*) to move swiftly or turn in order to dodge. ◆ *n* **2** a jinking movement. ORIG C18: of Scot. origin, imit. of swift movement

jinker ('dʒɪŋkə) *n Austral.* a vehicle for transporting timber, consisting of a tractor and two sets of wheels for supporting the logs. ORIG from ?

jinks (dʒɪŋks) *pl n* boisterous or mischievous play (esp. in **high jinks**). ORIG C18: from ?

jinn (dʒɪn) *n* (*often functioning as sing*) the plural of **jinni.**

Jinnah ★ ('dʒɪnə) *n* **Mohammed Ali.** 1876–1948, Indian Muslim statesman. He campaigned for the partition of India into separate Hindu and Muslim states, becoming first governor general of Pakistan (1947–48).

jinni, jinnee, *or* **djinni** (dʒɪˈniː) *n, pl* **jinn** *or* **djinn** (dʒɪn). a being or spirit in Muslim belief who could assume human or animal form and influence man by supernatural powers. ORIG C17: from Ar.

jinrikisha, jinricksha, *or* **jinrickshaw** (dʒɪnˈrɪkʃɔː) *n* another name for **rickshaw.** ORIG C19: from Japanese, from *jin* man + *riki* power + *sha* carriage

jinx (dʒɪŋks) *n* **1** an unlucky force, person, or thing. ◆ *vb* **2** (*tr*) to be or put a jinx on. ORIG C20: ?from NL *Jynx,* genus name of the wryneck, from Gk *iunx* wryneck, a bird used in magic

Jinzhou ('dʒɪnˈdʒəʊ), **Chin-Chou,** *or* **Chin-chow** ★ *n* a city in NE China, in SW Liaoning province. Pop.: 569 518 (1990 est.). Former name (1913–47): **Chin-hsien.**

JIT *abbrev. for* just-in-time.

jitter ('dʒɪtə) *Inf.* ◆ *vb* **1** (*intr*) to be anxious or nervous. ◆ *n* **2 the jitters.** nervousness and anxiety. ORIG C20: from ?
▸ **'jittery** *adj* ▸ **'jitteriness** *n*

jitterbug ('dʒɪtəˌbʌg) *n* **1** a fast jerky American dance, usually to a jazz accompaniment, that was popular in the 1940s. **2** a person who dances the jitterbug. ◆ *vb* **jitterbugs, jitterbugging, jitterbugged. 3** (*intr*) to perform such a dance.

jiujitsu *or* **jiujutsu** (dʒuːˈdʒɪtsuː) *n* a variant spelling of **jujitsu.**

jive (dʒaɪv) *n* **1** a style of lively and jerky dance, popular esp. in the 1940s and 1950s. **2** *Sl., chiefly US.* **2a** misleading or deceptive talk. **2b** (*as modifier*): *jive talk.* ◆ *vb* **jives, jiving, jived. 3** (*intr*) to dance the jive. **4** *Sl., chiefly US.* to mislead; tell lies (to). ORIG C20: from ?
▸ **'jiver** *n*

Joab ★ ('dʒəʊæb) *n Old Testament.* the successful commander of King David's forces and the slayer of Abner and Absalom (II Samuel 2:18–23; 3:24–27; 18:14–15).

Joachim ★ *n* **1** ('joːaxɪm). **Joseph** ('joːzεf). 1831–1907, Hungarian violinist and composer. **2** ('dʒəʊəkɪm). **Saint.** 1st century B.C., traditionally the father of the Virgin Mary; feast day: July 25 or Sept. 9.

Joan ★ (dʒəʊn) *n* **1** known as *the Fair Maid of Kent.* 1328–85, wife of Edward the Black Prince; mother of Richard II. **2 Pope.** legendary female pope, first mentioned in the 13th century: said to have disguised herself as a man and to have died in childbirth.

Joan of Arc ★ *n* **Saint,** known as *the Maid of Orléans;* French name *Jeanne d'Arc.* ?1412–31, French national heroine, who led the army that relieved Orléans in the Hundred Years' War, enabling Charles VII to be crowned at Reims (1429). After being captured (1430), she was burnt at the stake as a heretic. She was canonized in 1920. Feast day: May 30.

João Pessoa ★ (*Portuguese* 'ʒuãum peˈsoa) *n* a port in NE Brazil, capital of Paraíba state. Pop.: 497 306 (1991).

job (dʒɒb) *n* **1** an individual piece of work or task. **2** an occupation. **3** an object worked on or a result produced from working. **4** a duty or responsibility: *his job was to cook the dinner.* **5** *Inf.* a difficult task or problem: *I had a job to contact him.* **6** a state of affairs: *make the best of a bad job.* **7** *Inf.* a particular type of something: *a four-wheel drive job.* **8** *Inf.* a crime, esp. a robbery. **9** *Computing.* a unit of work for a computer. **10 jobs for the boys.** jobs given to or created for allies or favourites. **11 just the job.** exactly what was required. **12 on the job.** actively engaged in one's employment. ◆ *vb* **jobs, jobbing, jobbed. 13** (*intr*) to work by the piece or at casual jobs. **14** to make a private profit out of (a public office, etc.). **15** (*intr; usually foll. by in*) **15a** to buy and sell (goods or services) as a middleman: *she jobs in government surplus.* **15b** *Brit.* to buy and sell stocks and shares as a stockjobber. **16** *Austral. sl.* to punch. ORIG C16: from ?
▸ **'jobless** *adj*

Job ★ (dʒəʊb) *n* **1** *Old Testament.* **1a** a Jewish patriarch, who maintained his faith in spite of the afflictions sent by God to test him. **1b** the book containing Job's pleas to God under these afflictions, attempted explanations of them by his friends, and God's reply to him. **2** any person who withstands great suffering without despairing.

jobber ('dʒɒbə) *n* **1** *Brit.* short for **stockjobber** (sense 1). See also **market maker. 2** a person who jobs.

jobbery ('dʒɒbərɪ) *n* the practice of making private profit out of a public office.

jobbing ('dʒɒbɪŋ) *adj* working by the piece, not regularly employed: *a jobbing gardener.*

Jobcentre ('dʒɒbˌsɛntə) *n Brit.* any of a number of government offices usually having premises situated in or near the main shopping area of a town in which people seeking jobs can consult displayed advertisements.

Jobclub ('dʒɒbˌklʌb) *n* a group of unemployed people organized through a Jobcentre, which meets every weekday and is given advice on job seeking to increase its members' chances of finding employment.

job description *n* a formal description of the duties and responsibilities involved in a job, esp. as given to applicants for the job.

job lot *n* **1** a miscellaneous collection of articles sold as a lot. **2** a collection of cheap or trivial items.

job satisfaction *n* the extent to which the desires and hopes of a worker are fulfilled as a result of his or her work.

Job's comforter *n* a person who, while purporting to give sympathy, succeeds only in adding to distress.

jobseeker's allowance ('dʒɒbˌsiːkəz) *n* (in Britain) a National Insurance or social security payment for unemployed people; replaced unemployment benefit in 1996. Abbrev.: **JSA.**

job sharing *n* the division of a job between two or more people such that each covers the same job for complementary parts of the day or week.
▸ **job share** *n*

jobsworth ('dʒɒbzˌwɜːθ) *n Inf.* a person in a position of minor authority who invokes the letter of the law in order to avoid any action requiring initiative, cooperation, etc. ORIG C20: from *it's more than my job's worth to…*

Jocasta ★ (dʒəʊ'kæstə) *n Greek myth.* a queen of Thebes, the wife of Laius, who married Oedipus without either of them knowing he was her son.

Jochum ★ (*German* 'jɔxʊm) *n* **Eugen** ('ɔygeːn). 1902–87, German orchestral conductor.

jock (dʒɒk) *n Inf.* **1** short for **disc jockey. 2** short for **jockey. 3** short for **jockstrap.**

Jock (dʒɒk) *n* a slang word or term of address for a **Scot.**

jockey ('dʒɒkɪ) *n* **1** a person who rides horses in races, esp. as a profession. ◆ *vb* **2a** (*tr*) to ride (a horse) in a race. **2b** (*intr*) to ride as a jockey. **3** (*intr:* often foll. by *for*) to try to obtain an advantage by manoeuvring (esp. in **jockey for position**). **4** to trick or cheat (a person). ORIG C16 (in the sense: lad): from name *Jock* + -EY

jockstrap ('dʒɒkˌstræp) *n* an elasticated belt with a pouch worn by men, esp. athletes, to support the genitals. Also called: **athletic support.** ORIG C20: from sl. *jock* penis + STRAP

jocose (dʒə'kəʊs) *adj* characterized by humour. ORIG C17: from L *jocōsus* given to jesting, from *jocus* joke
▸ **jo'cosely** *adv* ▸ **jocosity** (dʒə'kɒsɪtɪ) *n*

jocular ('dʒɒkjʊlə) *adj* **1** characterized by joking and good humour. **2** meant lightly or humorously. ORIG C17: from L *joculāris,* from *joculus* little JOKE
▸ **jocularity** (ˌdʒɒkjʊ'lærɪtɪ) *n* ▸ **'jocularly** *adv*

jocund ('dʒɒkənd) *adj* of a humorous temperament; merry. ORIG C14: from LL *jocundus,* from L *jūcundus* pleasant, from *juvāre* to please
▸ **jocundity** (dʒəʊ'kʌndɪtɪ) *n* ▸ **'jocundly** *adv*

Jodhpur ★ (ˌdʒɒd'pʊə) *n* **1** a former state of NW India, one of the W Rajputana states: now part of Rajasthan. **2** a walled city in NW India, in W Rajasthan: university (1962). Pop.: 666 279 (1991).
▸ **Jodhpuri** (ˌdʒɒd'pʊərɪ) *adj*

jodhpurs ('dʒɒdpəz) *pl n* riding breeches, loose-fitting around the thighs and tight-fitting from the knees to the ankles. ORIG C19: from JODHPUR

Jodl ★ (*German* 'joːdəl) *n* **Alfred** ('alfreːt). 1890–1946, German general, largely responsible for German strategy during World War II: executed as a war criminal.

Joe Blake (ˌdʒəʊ 'bleɪk) *n Austral. sl.* **1** a snake. **2 the Joe Blakes.** the DT's.

Joe Bloggs ('blɒgz) *n Brit. sl.* an average or typical man. US, Canad., and Austral. equivalent: **Joe Blow.** See also **Joe Six-Pack.**

Joel ★ ('dʒəʊəl) *n Old Testament.* **1** a Hebrew prophet. **2** the book containing his oracles.

Joe Public *n Sl.* the general public.

joes (dʒəʊz) *pl n* **the.** *Austral. inf.* a fit of depression. ORIG short for *the Joe Blakes*

Joe Six-Pack *n US sl.* an average or typical man.

joey ('dʒəʊɪ) *n Austral. inf.* **1** a young kangaroo. **2** a young animal or child. ORIG C19: from Abor.

Joffre ★ (*French* ʒɔfrə) *n* **Joseph Jacques Césaire** (ʒozɛf ʒak sezɛr). 1852–1931, French marshal. He commanded the French army (1914–16) and was largely responsible for the Allies' victory at the Marne (1914), which halted the German advance on Paris.

jog (dʒɒg) *vb* **jogs, jogging, jogged. 1** (*intr*) to run or move slowly or at a jog trot, esp. for physical exercise. **2** (*intr;* foll. by *on* or *along*) to continue in a plodding way. **3** (*tr*) to jar or nudge slightly. **4** (*tr*) to remind: *jog my memory.* ◆ *n* **5** the act of jogging. **6** a slight jar or nudge. **7** a jogging motion; trot. ORIG C14: prob. var. of *shog* to shake

jogger ('dʒɒgə) *n* **1** a person who runs at a jog trot over some distance for exercise. **2** *NZ.* a cart with rubber tyres used on farms.

jogger's nipple *n Inf.* painful inflammation of the nipple, caused by friction with a garment when running for long distances.

jogging ('dʒɒgɪŋ) *n* a slow run or trot, esp. as a keep-fit exercise.

joggle ('dʒɒgᵊl) *vb* **joggles, joggling, joggled. 1** to shake or move (someone or something) with a slightly jolting motion. **2** (*tr*) to join or fasten (two pieces of building material) by means of a joggle. ◆ *n* **3** the act of joggling. **4** a slight irregular shake. **5** a joint between two pieces of building material by means of a projection on one piece that fits into a notch in the other. ORIG C16: frequentative of JOG
▸ **'joggler** *n*

Jogjakarta ★ (ˌdʒəʊgjɑː'kɑːtɑː, ˌdʒɒg-) *n* a variant spelling of **Yogyakarta.**

jog trot *n* **1** an easy bouncy gait, esp. of a horse, midway between a walk and a trot. **2** a regular way of living or doing something.

Johannesburg ★ (dʒəʊ'hænɪsˌbɜːg) *n* a city in NE South Africa, in Gauteng province: South Africa's largest city and chief industrial centre; grew with the establishment of the gold-mining industry in 1886; University of Witwatersrand (1922). Pop.: 1 712 507 (1991).

john (dʒɒn) *n* **1** *Chiefly US & Canad.* a slang word for **lavatory. 2** *Sl., chiefly US.* a prostitute's client. ORIG C20: special use of the name

John ★ (dʒɒn) *n* **1** *New Testament.* **1a** the apostle John, the son of Zebedee, identified with the author of the fourth Gospel, three epistles, and the book of Revelation. Feast day: Sept. 26 or Dec. 27. **1b** the fourth Gospel. **1c** any of three epistles (in full **The First, Second,** and **Third Epistles of John**). **2** See **John the Baptist. 3** known as *John Lackland.* 1167–1216, king of England (1199–1216); son of Henry II. He succeeded to the throne on the death of his brother Richard I, having previously tried to usurp the throne. In 1215 he signed the Magna Carta. **4 Augustus (Edwin).** 1878–1961, British painter, esp. of portraits. **5 Barry.** born 1945, Welsh Rugby Union footballer: halfback for Wales (1966–72) and the British Lions (1968–71). **6** Sir **Elton (Hercules).** original name *Reginald Dwight.* born 1947, British singer, composer, and pianist.

John I ★ *n* called *the Great.* 1357–1433, king of Portugal (1385–1433). He secured independence for Portugal by his victory over Castile (1385) and initiated Portuguese overseas expansion.

John II ★ *n* called *the Good.* 1319–64, king of France (1350–64): captured by the English at Poitiers (1356) and forced to sign treaties (1360) surrendering SW France to England.

John III ★ *n* surnamed *Sobieski.* 1624–96, king of Poland (1674–96). He raised the Turkish siege of Vienna (1683).

John IV ★ *n* called *the Fortunate.* 1604–56, king of Portugal (1640–56). As duke of Braganza he led a revolt against Spanish rule and became king: lost most of Portugal's Asian possessions to the Dutch.

John XXII ★ *n* original name *Jacques Duèse.* ?1244–1334, pope (1316–34), residing at Avignon; involved in a long conflict with the Holy Roman Emperor Louis IV and opposed the Franciscan Spirituals.

John XXIII ★ *n* original name *Angelo Giuseppe Roncalli.* 1881–1963, pope (1958–63). He summoned the second Vatican Council (1962–65).

John Barleycorn *n Usually humorous.* the personification of alcoholic drink.

John Bull *n* **1** a personification of England or the English people. **2** a typical Englishman. ORIG C18: name of a character intended to be representative of the English nation in *The History of John Bull* (1712) by John Arbuthnot

John Chrysostom ★ ('krɪsəstəm) *n* **Saint.** ?345–407 A.D., Greek bishop and theologian; one of the Fathers of the Greek Church, noted for his eloquence. Feast day: Sept. 13.

John Doe *n* See **Doe.**

John Dory ('dɔːrɪ) *n* a European dory (the fish), having a deep compressed body and massive mobile jaws. ORIG C18: from name *John* + DORY[1]; on the model of DOE

John Hop *n Austral. sl.* a policeman. ORIG rhyming sl. for COP[1]

johnny ('dʒɒnɪ) *n, pl* **johnnies.** *Brit. inf.* (*often cap.*) a man or boy; chap.

Johnny Canuck ('dʒɒnɪ kə'nʌk) *n Canad.* **1** an informal name for a **Canadian. 2** a personification of Canada.

Johnny-come-lately *n, pl* **Johnny-come-latelies** *or* **Johnnies-come-lately.** *Sl.* a brash newcomer, novice, or recruit.

John of Austria ★ *n* called *Don John.* 1547–78, Spanish general: defeated the Turks at Lepanto (1571).

John of Damascus ★ *n* **Saint.** ?675–749 A.D., Syrian theologian, who defended the veneration of icons and images against the iconoclasts. Feast day: Dec. 4.

John of Gaunt ★ (gɔːnt) *n* Duke of Lancaster. 1340–99, son of Edward III: virtual ruler of England during the last years of his father's reign and during Richard II's minority. ORIG *Gaunt,* variant of GHENT, where he was born

John of Leyden ★ ('laɪdᵊn) *n* original name *Jan Bockelson.* ?1509–36, Dutch Anabaptist leader. He established a theocracy in Münster (1534) but was tortured to death after the city was recaptured (1535) by its prince bishop.

John of Salisbury ★ *n* died 1180, English ecclesiastic and scholar; bishop of Chartres (1176–80). He supported Thomas à Becket against Henry II.

John of the Cross ★ *n* **Saint.** original name *Juan de Yepis y Alvarez.* 1542–91, Spanish Carmelite monk, poet, and mystic. He founded the Discalced Carmelites with Saint Teresa (1568). Feast day: Dec. 14.

John o'Groats ★ (ə'grəuts) *n* a village at the northeasternmost tip of the Scottish mainland: considered to be the northernmost point of the mainland of Great Britain although Dunnet Head, slightly to the west, lies further north. See also **Land's End.**

John Paul I ★ *n* original name *Albino Luciani.* 1912–78, pope (1978); reigned only 33 days.

John Paul II ★ *n* original name *Karol Wojtyla.* born 1920, pope from 1978, born in Poland: the first non-Italian to be elected since 1522.

Johns ★ (dʒɒnz) *n* **Jasper.** born 1930, US artist, noted for his collages and constructions.

Johnson ★ ('dʒɒnsᵊn) *n* **1 Amy.** 1903–41, British flyer, whose record flights included those to Australia (1930) and to Cape Town and back (1936). **2 Andrew.** 1808–75, US Democrat statesman; 17th president of the US (1865–69): he was elected vice president under the Republican Abraham Lincoln and took office following Lincoln's assassination. **3 Jack.** 1878–1946, US boxer; world heavyweight champion (1908–15). **4 Lyndon Baines,** known as *LBJ.* 1908–73, US Democrat statesman; 36th president of the US (1963–69). He lost popularity by increasing US involvement in the Vietnam War. **5 Michael (Duane).** born 1967, US sprinter. **6 Robert.** ?1898–1937, US blues singer and guitarist. **7 Samuel,** known as *Dr Johnson.* 1709–84, British lexicographer and critic. His fame rests on his *Dictionary* (1755) and Boswell's biography of him.

Johnsonian (dʒɒn'səunɪən) *adj* of, relating to, or characteristic of Samuel Johnson, his works, or his style of writing.

John the Baptist ★ *n* **Saint.** *New Testament.* the son of Zacharias and Elizabeth and the cousin and forerunner of Jesus, whom he baptized. He was beheaded by Herod (Matthew 14:1–2). Feast day: June 24.

John Thomas *n Sl.* a euphemistic name for **penis.**

Johore ★ (dʒəu'hɔː) *n* a state of Malaysia, on the S Malay Peninsula: mostly forested, with large swamps; bauxite- and iron-mining. Capital: Johore Bahru. Pop.: 2 106 700 (1993 est.). Area: 18 984 sq. km (7330 sq. miles).

Johore Bahru ★ ('bɑːruː) *n* a city in S Malaysia, capital of Johore state: important trading centre, situated at the sole crossing point of **Johore Strait** (between Malaya and Singapore Island). Pop.: 328 646 (1991).

joie de vivre *French.* (ʒwa də vivrə) *n* joy of living; enjoyment of life; ebullience.

join (dʒɔɪn) *vb* **1** to come or bring together. **2** to become a member of (a club, etc.). **3** (*intr; often foll. by with*) to become associated or allied. **4** (*intr; usually foll. by in*) to take part. **5** (*tr*) to meet (someone) as a companion. **6** (*tr*) to become part of. **7** (*tr*) to unite (two people) in marriage. **8** (*tr*) *Geom.* to connect with a straight line or a curve. **9 join hands. 9a** to hold one's own hands together. **9b** (of two people) to hold each other's hands. **9c** (usually foll. by *with*) to work together in an enterprise. ◆ *n* **10** a joint; seam. **11** the act of joining. ◆ See also **join up.** ORIG C13: from OF, from L *jungere* to yoke

joinder ('dʒɔɪndə) *n* **1** the act of joining, esp. in legal contexts. **2** *Law.* **2a** (in pleading) the stage at which the parties join issue (**joinder of issue**). **2b** the joining of two or more persons as coplaintiffs or codefendants (**joinder of parties**). ORIG C17: from F *joindre* to JOIN

joined-up *adj* integrated by an overall strategy: *joined-up government.*

joiner ('dʒɔɪnə) *n* **1** *Chiefly Brit.* a person skilled in making finished woodwork, such as windows and stairs. **2** a person or thing that joins. **3** *Inf.* a person who joins many clubs, etc.

joinery ('dʒɔɪnərɪ) *n* **1** the skill or craft of a joiner. **2** work made by a joiner.

joint (dʒɔɪnt) *n* **1** a junction of two or more parts or objects. **2** *Anat.* the junction between two or more bones. **3** the point of connection between movable parts in invertebrates. **4** the part of a plant stem from which a branch or leaf grows. **5** one of the parts into which a carcass of meat is cut by the butcher, esp. for roasting. **6** *Geol.* a crack in a rock along which no displacement has occurred. **7** *Sl.* **7a** a bar or nightclub. **7b** *Often facetious.* a dwelling or meeting place. **8** *Sl.* a cannabis cigarette. **9 out of joint. 9a** dislocated. **9b** out of order. ◆ *adj* **10** shared by or belonging to two or more: *joint property.* **11** created by combined effort. **12** sharing with others or with one another: *joint rulers.* ◆ *vb* (*tr*) **13** to provide with or fasten by a joint or joints. **14** to plane the edge of (a board, etc.) into the correct shape for a joint. **15** to cut or divide (meat, etc.) into joints.
▸ **'jointed** *adj* ▸ **'jointly** *adv*

joint account *n* a bank account registered in the name of two or more persons, any of whom may make deposits and withdrawals.

joint stock *n* capital funds held in common and usually divided into shares.

joint-stock company *n* **1** *Brit.* a business enterprise characterized by the sharing of ownership between shareholders, whose liability is limited. **2** *US.* a business enterprise whose owners are issued shares of transferable stock but do not enjoy limited liability.

jointure ('dʒɔɪntʃə) *n Law.* **a** provision made by a husband for his wife by settling property upon her at marriage for her use after his death. **b** the property so settled. ORIG C14: from OF, from L *junctūra* a joining

join up *vb (adv)* **1** *(intr)* to become a member of a military or other organization; enlist. **2** (often foll. by *with*) to unite or connect.

Joinville ★ (*French* ʒwɛ̃vil) *n* **Jean de** (ʒɑ̃ də). ?1224–1317, French chronicler, noted for his *Histoire de Saint Louis* (1309).

joist (dʒɔɪst) *n* a beam made of timber, steel, or reinforced concrete, used in the construction of floors, roofs, etc. ORIG C14: from OF *giste* beam supporting a bridge, from Vulgar L *jacitum* (unattested) support, from *jacēre* to lie

jojoba (həʊˈhəʊbə) *n* a shrub or small tree of SW North America having edible seeds containing a valuable oil that is used in cosmetics.

joke (dʒəʊk) *n* **1** a humorous anecdote. **2** something that is said or done for fun. **3** a ridiculous or humorous circumstance. **4** a person or thing inspiring ridicule or amusement. **5 no joke.** something very serious. ◆ *vb* **jokes, joking, joked. 6** *(intr)* to tell jokes. **7** *(intr)* to speak or act facetiously. **8** to make fun of (someone). **9 joking apart.** seriously: said after there has been joking in a discussion. ORIG C17: from L *jocus* a jest
▸ **ˈjokey** *or* **ˈjoky** *adj* ▸ **ˈjokingly** *adv*

joker (ˈdʒəʊkə) *n* **1** a person who jokes, esp. in an obnoxious manner. **2** *Sl., often derog.* a person: *who does that joker think he is?* **3** an extra playing card in a pack, which in many card games can rank above any other card.

Jokjakarta ★ (ˌdʒəʊkjɑːˈkɑːtɑː, ˌdʒɒk-) *n* a variant spelling of **Yogyakarta.**

jol (dʒɒl) *S. African sl.* ◆ *n* **1** a party. ◆ *vb* **jolls, jolling, jolled. 2** *(intr)* to have a good time. ORIG from Du.

Joliot-Curie ★ (*French* ʒɔljokyri) *n* **Jean-Frédéric** (ʒɑ̃frederik), 1900–58, and his wife, **Irène** (irɛn), 1897–1956, French physicists: shared the Nobel prize for chemistry in 1935 for discovering artificial radioactivity.

jollify (ˈdʒɒlɪˌfaɪ) *vb* **jollifies, jollifying, jollified.** to be or cause to be jolly.
▸ **ˌjollifiˈcation** *n*

jollity (ˈdʒɒlɪtɪ) *n, pl* **jollities.** the condition of being jolly.

jolly (ˈdʒɒlɪ) *adj* **jollier, jolliest. 1** full of good humour. **2** having or provoking gaiety and merrymaking. **3** pleasing. ◆ *adv* **4** *Brit.* (intensifier): *you're jolly nice.* ◆ *vb* **jollies, jollying, jollied.** *(tr) Inf.* **5** (often foll. by *up* or *along*) to try to make or keep (someone) cheerful. **6** to make good-natured fun of. ORIG C14: from OF *jolif,* prob. from ON *jōl* YULE
▸ **ˈjolliness** *n*

jolly boat *n* a small boat used as a utility tender for a vessel. ORIG C18 *jolly* prob. from Danish *jolle* YAWL

Jolly Roger *n* the traditional pirate flag, consisting of a white skull and crossbones on a black field.

Jolo ★ (həʊˈləʊ) *n* an island in the SW Philippines: the main island of the Sulu Archipelago. Pop.: 360 588 (1980). Area: 893 sq. km (345 sq. miles).

Jolson ★ (ˈdʒəʊlsən) *n* **Al,** real name *Asa Yoelson.* 1886–1950, US singer and film actor, born in Russia; star of the first talking picture *The Jazz Singer* (1927).

jolt (dʒəʊlt) *vb* **1** *(tr)* to bump against with a jarring blow. **2** to move in a jolting manner. **3** *(tr)* to surprise or shock. ◆ *n* **4** a sudden jar or blow. **5** an emotional shock. ORIG C16: prob. blend of dialect *jot* to jerk & dialect *joll* to bump

Jon. *Bible. abbrev. for* Jonah.

Jonah (ˈdʒəʊnə) *or* **Jonas** ★ (ˈdʒəʊnəs) *n* **1** *Old Testament.* a Hebrew prophet who, having been thrown overboard from a ship was swallowed by a great fish and vomited onto dry land. **2** a person believed to bring bad luck to those around him.

Jonathan ★ *n Old Testament.* the son of Saul and David's close friend, who was killed in battle (I Samuel 31; II Samuel 1:19–26).

Jones ★ (dʒəʊnz) *n* **1 Daniel.** 1881–1967, British phonetician. **2 Daniel.** 1912–93, Welsh composer. He wrote nine symphonies and much chamber music. **3 David.** 1895–1974, British artist and writer: his literary works include the novel *In Parenthesis* (1937) and the poem *The Anathemata* (1952). **4 Inigo** (ˈɪnɪgəʊ). 1573–1652, English architect, who introduced Palladianism to England. **5 John Paul.** 1747–92, US naval commander in the War of Independence. **7 Robert Tyre,** known as *Bobby Jones.* 1902–71, US golfer. **8 Tom,** original name *Thomas Jones Woodward.* born 1940, Welsh popular singer noted for a number of hit records, including "It's Not Unusual" (1965) and "Delilah" (1968).

Jongkind ★ (*Dutch* ˈjɔŋkɪnt) *n* **Johann Barthold** (joːˈhɑn ˈbartɔlt). 1819–91, Dutch landscape painter and etcher.

jongleur (*French* ʒɔ̃glœr) *n* (in medieval France) an itinerant minstrel. ORIG C18: from OF *jogleour,* from L *joculātor* jester

Jönköping ★ (*Swedish* ˈjœntʃøːpiŋ) *n* a city in S Sweden, on the S shore of Lake Vättern: scene of the conclusion of peace between Sweden and Denmark in 1809. Pop.: 115 429 (1996 est.).

jonquil (ˈdʒɒŋkwɪl) *n* a Eurasian variety of narcissus with long fragrant yellow or white short-tubed flowers. ORIG C17: from F *jonquille,* from Sp. *junquillo,* dim. of *junco* reed

Jonson ★ (ˈdʒɒnsᵊn) *n* **Ben.** 1572–1637, English dramatist and poet. His plays include *Volpone* (1606) and *Bartholomew Fair* (1614); he also wrote court masques.

jook (dʒʊk) *Caribbean inf. vb* **1** *(tr)* to poke or puncture. ◆ *n* **2** a jab or the resulting wound. ORIG C20: of W African origin

Joplin ★ (ˈdʒɒplɪn) *n* **1 Janis.** 1943–70, US rock singer. **2 Scott.** 1868–1917, US pianist and composer: creator of ragtime.

Joppa ★ (ˈdʒɒpə) *n* the biblical name of **Jaffa,** the port from which Jonah embarked (Jonah 1:3).

Jordaens ★ (*Flemish* jɔrˈdaːns) *n* **Jacob** (ˈjaːkɔp). 1593–1678, Flemish painter.

Jordan[1] ★ (ˈdʒɔːdᵊn) *n* **1** a kingdom in SW Asia: coextensive with the biblical Moab, Gilead, and Edom; made a League of Nations mandate and emirate under British control in 1922 and became an independent kingdom in 1946; territories west of the River Jordan and the Jordanian part of Jerusalem were occupied by Israel after the war of 1967. It contains part of the Great Rift Valley and consists mostly of desert. Official language: Arabic. Official religion: (Sunni) Muslim. Currency: dinar. Capital: Amman. Pop.: 4 839 000 (1999 est.). Area: 89 185 sq. km (34 434 sq. miles). Official name: **Hashemite Kingdom of Jordan.** Former name (1922–49): **Trans-Jordan. 2** the chief and only perennial river of Israel and Jordan, rising in several headstreams in Syria and Lebanon, and flowing south through the Sea of Galilee to the Dead Sea: occupies the N end of the Great Rift Valley system and lies mostly below sea level. Length: over 320 km (200 miles).
▸ **Jordanian** (dʒɔːˈdeɪnɪən) *adj, n*

Jordan[2] ★ (ˈdʒɔːdᵊn) *n* **Michael Jeffrey.** born 1963, US basketball and baseball player.

jorum (ˈdʒɔːrəm) *n* a large drinking bowl or vessel or its contents. ORIG C18: prob. after *Jorum,* who brought vessels of silver, gold, and brass to King David (II Samuel 8:10)

Jos ★ (dʒɒs) *n* a city in central Nigeria, capital of Plateau state on the **Jos Plateau:** major centre of the tin-mining industry. Pop.: 201 200 (1995 est.).

Joseph ★ (ˈdʒəʊzɪf) *n* **1** *Old Testament.* **1a** the eleventh son of Jacob and one of the 12 patriarchs of Israel (Genesis 30:2–24). **1b** either or both of two tribes descended from his sons Ephraim and Manasseh. **2 Saint.** *New Testament.* the husband of Mary the mother of Jesus (Matthew 1:16–25). Feast day: Mar. 19.

Joseph II ★ *n* 1741–90, Holy Roman emperor (1765–90); son of Francis I. He ruled Austria jointly with his mother, Maria Theresa, until her death (1780). He abolished serfdom and asserted his independence from the pope.

Joseph Bonaparte Gulf ★ *n* an inlet of the Timor Sea in N Australia. Width: 360 km (225 miles).

Josephine ★ (ˈdʒəʊzəˌfiːn) *n* **Empress,** previous name *Joséphine de Beauharnais;* real name *Marie Joséphine Tascher de la Pagerie.* 1763–1814, empress of France as wife (1796–1809) of Napoleon Bonaparte.

Joseph of Arimathea ★ (ˌærɪmə'θiːə) *n* **Saint.** *New Testament.* a wealthy member of the Sanhedrin, who obtained the body of Jesus after the Crucifixion and laid it in his own tomb (Matthew 27:57–60). Feast day: Mar. 17 or July 31.

Josephus ★ (dʒəʊ'siːfəs) *n* **Flavius** ('fleɪvɪəs). real name *Joseph ben Matthias.* ?37–?100 A.D., Jewish historian and general; author of *Antiquities of the Jews.*

josh (dʒɒʃ) *Sl., chiefly US & Canad.* ◆ *vb* **1** to tease (someone) in a bantering way. ◆ *n* **2** a teasing joke. ORIG C19: ?from JOKE, infl. by BOSH
▸ **'josher** *n*

Josh. *Bible. abbrev. for* Joshua.

Joshua ★ ('dʒɒʃʊə) *n Old Testament.* **1** Moses' successor, who led the Israelites in the conquest of Canaan. **2** the book recounting his deeds. Douay spelling: **Josue** ('dʒɒsjuː).

Josiah ★ (dʒəʊ'saɪə) *n* died ?609 B.C., king of Judah (?640–?609). After the discovery of a book of law (probably Deuteronomy) in the Temple he began a programme of religious reform. Douay spelling: **Josias** (dʒəʊ'saɪəs).

Josquin des Prés ★ (*French* ʒɔskɛ̃ de pre) *n* See **des Prés.**

joss (dʒɒs) *n* a Chinese deity worshipped in the form of an idol. ORIG C18: from pidgin E, from Port. *deos* god, from L *deus*

joss house *n* a Chinese temple or shrine where an idol or idols are worshipped.

joss stick *n* a stick of dried perfumed paste, giving off a fragrant odour when burnt as incense.

jostle ('dʒɒsᵊl) *vb* **jostles, jostling, jostled. 1** to bump or push (someone) roughly. **2** to come or bring into contact. **3** to force (one's way) by pushing. ◆ *n* **4** the act of jostling. **5** a rough bump or push. ORIG C14: see JOUST

jot (dʒɒt) *vb* **jots, jotting, jotted. 1** (*tr;* usually foll. by *down*) to write a brief note of. ◆ *n* **2** (*used with a negative*) a little bit (in **not care** (*or* **give**) **a jot**). ORIG C16: from L *jota,* from Gk *iōta,* of Semitic origin

jota (*Spanish* 'xɔta) *n* a Spanish dance in fast triple time. ORIG Sp., prob. from OSp. *sota,* from *sotar* to dance, from L *saltāre*

jotter ('dʒɒtə) *n* a small notebook.

jotting ('dʒɒtɪŋ) *n* something jotted down.

Jotun *or* **Jotunn** ★ ('jɔːtʊn) *n Norse myth.* any of a race of giants. ORIG from ON *jötunn* giant; related to EAT

Jotunheim *or* **Jotunnheim** ★ ('jɔːtʊnˌheɪm) *n Norse myth.* the home of the giants in the northeast of Asgard. ORIG from ON, from *jötunn* giant + *heimr* world, HOME

joual (ʒwɑːl) *n* nonstandard Canadian French dialect, esp. as associated with ill-educated speakers. ORIG from the pronunciation in this dialect of F *cheval* horse

joule (dʒuːl) *n* the derived SI unit of work or energy; the work done when the point of application of a force of 1 newton is displaced through a distance of 1 metre in the direction of the force. Symbol: J ORIG C19: after J. P. JOULE

Joule ★ (dʒuːl) *n* **James Prescott.** 1818–89, British physicist, who contributed to the study of heat and electricity.

jounce (dʒaʊns) *vb* **jounces, jouncing, jounced. 1** to shake or jolt or cause to shake or jolt. ◆ *n* **2** a shake; bump. ORIG C15: prob. from dialect *joll* to bump + BOUNCE

journal ('dʒɜːnᵊl) *n* **1** a newspaper or periodical. **2** a book in which a daily record of happenings, etc., is kept. **3** an official record of the proceedings of a legislative body. **4** *Book-keeping.* one of several books in which transactions are initially recorded to facilitate subsequent entry in the ledger. **5** *Machinery.* the part of a shaft or axle in contact with or enclosed by a bearing. ORIG C14: from OF: daily, from L *diurnālis;* see DIURNAL

journal box *n Machinery.* a case enclosing or supporting a journal.

journalese (ˌdʒɜːnᵊ'liːz) *n Derog.* a superficial style of writing regarded as typical of newspapers, etc.

journalism ('dʒɜːnᵊˌlɪzəm) *n* **1** the profession or practice of reporting about, photographing, or editing news stories for one of the mass media. **2** newspapers and magazines collectively.

journalist ('dʒɜːnᵊlɪst) *n* **1** a person whose occupation is journalism. **2** a person who keeps a journal.
▸ **ˌjourna'listic** *adj* ▸ **ˌjourna'listically** *adv*

journalize *or* **journalise** ('dʒɜːnᵊˌlaɪz) *vb* **journalizes, journalizing, journalized** *or* **journalises, journalising, journalised.** to record (daily events) in a journal.
▸ **ˌjournali'zation** *or* **ˌjournali'sation** *n*

journey ('dʒɜːnɪ) *n* **1** a travelling from one place to another. **2a** the distance travelled in a journey. **2b** the time taken to make a journey. ◆ *vb* **3** (*intr*) to make a journey. ORIG C13: from OF *journee* a day, a day's travelling, from L *diurnum* day's portion
▸ **'journeyer** *n*

journeyman ('dʒɜːnɪmən) *n, pl* **journeymen. 1** a worker trained in a particular trade who is qualified to work at this trade in the employment of someone else. **2** a competent workman. ORIG C15: from JOURNEY (in obs. sense: a day's work) + MAN

joust (dʒaʊst) *History.* ◆ *n* **1** a combat between two mounted knights tilting against each other with lances. ◆ *vb* **2** (*intr;* often foll. by *against* or *with*) to encounter or engage in such a tournament: *he jousted with five opponents.* ORIG C13: from OF, from *jouster* to fight on horseback, from Vulgar L *juxtāre* (unattested) to come together, from L *juxtā* close
▸ **'jouster** *n*

Jove ★ (dʒəʊv) *n* **1** another name for **Jupiter**[1]. **2 by Jove.** an exclamation of surprise or excitement. ORIG C14: from OL *Jovis* Jupiter
▸ **'Jovian** *n*

jovial ('dʒəʊvɪəl) *adj* having or expressing convivial humour. ORIG C16: from L *joviālis* of (the planet) Jupiter, considered by astrologers to foster good humour
▸ **joviality** (ˌdʒəʊvɪ'ælɪtɪ) *n* ▸ **'jovially** *adv*

Jovian ★ ('dʒəʊvɪən) *n* full name *Flavius Claudius Jovianus.* ?331–364 A.D., Roman emperor (363–64): he made peace with Persia, relinquishing Roman provinces beyond the Tigris, and restored privileges to the Christians.

Jowett ★ ('dʒaʊɪt) *n* **Benjamin.** 1817–93, British classical scholar and educator: translated the works of Plato.

jowl[1] (dʒaʊl) *n* **1** the jaw, esp. the lower one. **2** (*often pl*) a cheek. **3 cheek by jowl.** See **cheek.** ORIG OE *ceafl* jaw
▸ **jowled** *adj*

jowl[2] (dʒaʊl) *n* **1** fatty flesh hanging from the lower jaw. **2** a similar fleshy part in animals, such as the dewlap of a bull. ORIG OE *ceole* throat

joy (dʒɔɪ) *n* **1** a deep feeling or condition of happiness or contentment. **2** something causing such a feeling. **3** an outward show of pleasure or delight. **4** *Brit. inf.* success; satisfaction: *I went for a loan, but got no joy.* ◆ *vb Chiefly poetic.* **5** (*intr*) to feel joy. **6** (*tr*) to gladden. ORIG C13: from OF, from L *gaudium* joy, from *gaudēre* to be glad

Joyce ★ (dʒɔɪs) *n* **1 James** (**Augustine Aloysius**). 1882–1941, Irish writer. He influenced the development of the novel, esp. by his stream of consciousness technique and coined words. His works include the novels *Ulysses* (1922) and *Finnegans Wake* (1939) and the short stories *Dubliners* (1914). **2 William,** known as *Lord Haw-Haw.* 1906–46, British broadcaster of Nazi propaganda to Britain; executed for treason.

Joycean ('dʒɔɪsɪən) *adj* **1** of, relating to, or like, James Joyce or his works. ◆ *n* **2** a student or admirer of Joyce or his works.

joyful ('dʒɔɪfʊl) *adj* **1** full of joy; elated. **2** expressing or producing joy: *a joyful look; a joyful occasion.*
▸ **'joyfully** *adv* ▸ **'joyfulness** *n*

joyless ('dʒɔɪlɪs) *adj* having or producing no joy or pleasure.
▸ **'joylessly** *adv* ▸ **'joylessness** *n*

joyous ('dʒɔɪəs) *adj* **1** having a happy nature or mood. **2** joyful.
▸ **'joyously** *adv*

joyride ('dʒɔɪˌraɪd) *n* **1** a ride taken for pleasure in a car, esp. in a stolen car driven recklessly. ◆ *vb* **joy-ride, joy-**

rides, joy-riding, joy-rode, joy-ridden. 2 (*intr*) to take such a ride.
▸ **'joy,rider** *n* ▸ **'joyriding** *n*

joystick ('dʒɔɪ,stɪk) *n* **1** *Inf.* the control stick of an aircraft, machine, etc. **2** *Computing.* a lever for controlling the movement of a cursor on a screen.

JP *abbrev. for* Justice of the Peace.

JPEG ('dʒeɪ,pɛg) *n Computing.* **a** a standard compressed file format used for pictures. **b** a picture held in this file format. **c** (*as modifier*): *a JPEG image.* ORIG C20: technique devised by the *J(oint) P(hotographic) E(xperts) G(roup)*

J/psi particle *n* a type of elementary particle thought to be formed from charmed quarks.

Jr *or* **jr** *abbrev. for* junior.

JSA (in Britain) *abbrev. for* jobseeker's allowance.

Juan Carlos ★ (*Spanish* xwan 'karlɔs) *n* born 1938, king of Spain from 1975. He was nominated by Franco as the first king of the restored monarchy to follow Franco's death.

Juan de Fuca ★ ('dʒu:ən dɪ 'fju:kə; *Spanish* xwan de 'fuka) *n* **Strait of.** a strait between Vancouver Island (Canada) and NW Washington (US). Length: about 129 km (80 miles). Width: about 24 km (15 miles).

Juan Fernández Islands ★ ('dʒu:ən fə'nændɛz; *Spanish* xwan fɛr'nandɛθ) *pl n* a group of three islands in the S Pacific Ocean, administered by Chile: volcanic and wooded. Area: about 180 sq. km (70 sq. miles).

Juantorena ★ (*Spanish* xwanto'rena) *n* **Alberto** (al'βɛrto). born 1951, Cuban runner: won the 400 metres and the 800 metres in the 1976 Olympic Games.

Juárez[1] ★ (*Spanish* 'xwarɛθ) *n* short for **Ciudad Juárez.**

Juárez[2] ★ (Spanish 'xwarɛθ) *n* **Benito Pablo** (be'nito 'paβlo). 1806–72, Mexican statesman. As president (1861–65; 1867–72) he thwarted Napoleon III's attempt to impose an empire under Maximilian.

Juba ★ ('dʒu:bə) *n* a river in NE Africa, rising in S central Ethiopia and flowing south across Somalia to the Indian Ocean: the chief river of Somalia. Length: about 1660 km (1030 miles).

Jubal ★ ('dʒu:bᵊl) *n Old Testament.* the alleged inventor of musical instruments (Genesis 4:21).

jubbah ('dʒʊbə) *n* a long loose outer garment with wide sleeves, worn by Muslim men and women, esp. in India. ORIG C16: from Ar.

Jubbulpore ★ (,dʒʌbᵊl'pʊə) *n* a variant spelling of **Jabalpur.**

jube (dʒu:b) *n Austral. & NZ inf.* any jelly-like sweet. ORIG C20: shortened from JUJUBE

jubilant ('dʒu:bɪlənt) *adj* feeling or expressing great joy. ORIG C17: from L, from *jūbilāre* to give a joyful cry, from *jūbilum* a shout
▸ **'jubilance** *n* ▸ **'jubilantly** *adv*

jubilate ('dʒu:bɪ,leɪt) *vb* **jubilates, jubilating, jubilated.** (*intr*) **1** to have or express great joy; rejoice. **2** to celebrate a jubilee. ORIG C17: from L *jūbilāre;* see JUBILANT

jubilation (,dʒu:bɪ'leɪʃən) *n* a feeling of great joy and celebration.

jubilee ('dʒu:bɪ,li:) *n* **1** a time or season for rejoicing. **2** a special anniversary, esp. a 25th or 50th one. **3** *RC Church.* a specially appointed period in which special indulgences are granted. **4** *Old Testament.* a year that was to be observed every 50th year, during which Hebrew slaves were to be liberated, etc. **5** a less common word for **jubilation.** ORIG C14: from OF *jubile,* from LL *jubilaeus,* from LGk, from Heb. *yōbhēl* ram's horn, used for the proclamation of the year of jubilee

Jud. *Bible. abbrev. for:* **1** Also: **Judg.** Judges. **2** Judith.

Judaea *or* **Judea** ★ (dʒu:'dɪə) *n* the S division of ancient Palestine, succeeding the kingdom of Judah: a Roman province during the time of Christ.
▸ **Ju'daean** *or* **Ju'dean** *adj, n*

Judah ★ ('dʒu:də) *n Old Testament.* **1** the fourth son of Jacob, one of whose descendants was to be the Messiah (Genesis 29:35; 49:8–12). **2** the tribe descended from him. **3** the tribal territory of his descendants which became the nucleus of David's kingdom and, after the kingdom had been divided into Israel and Judah, the southern kingdom of Judah, with Jerusalem as its centre. Douay spelling: **Juda.**

Judah ha-Levi ★ (hɑ:'li:vaɪ) *n* ?1075–1141, Jewish poet and philosopher, born in Spain; his works include the *Sefer ha-Kuzari.*

Judah ha-Nasi ★ (hɑ:nɑ:'si:) *n* ?135–?220 A.D., rabbi and patriarch of the Sanhedrin, who compiled the Mishnah.

Judaic (dʒu:'deɪɪk) *adj* of or relating to the Jews or Judaism.
▸ **Ju'daically** *adv*

Judaism ('dʒu:deɪ,ɪzəm) *n* **1** the religion of the Jews, based on the Old Testament and the Talmud and having as its central point a belief in one God. **2** the religious and cultural traditions of the Jews.
▸ **,Juda'istic** *adj*

Judaize *or* **Judaise** ('dʒʊdeɪ,aɪz) *vb* **Judaizes, Judaizing, Judaized** *or* **Judaises, Judaising, Judaised. 1** to conform or bring into conformity with Judaism. **2** (*tr*) to convert to Judaism.
▸ **,Judai'zation** *or* **,Judai'sation** *n*

Judas ★ ('dʒu:dəs) *n* **1** *New Testament.* the apostle who betrayed Jesus to his enemies for 30 pieces of silver (Luke 22:3–6, 47–48). Full name: **Judas Iscariot. 2** a person who betrays a friend; traitor. **3** a brother or relative of James and also of Jesus (Matthew 13:55).

Judas Maccabaeus ★ (,mækə'bi:əs) *n* Jewish leader, whose revolt (166–161 B.C.) against the Seleucid kingdom of Antiochus IV (Epiphanes) enabled him to recapture Jerusalem and rededicate the Temple.

Judas tree *n* small Eurasian leguminous tree with pinkish-purple flowers that bloom before the leaves appear.

judder ('dʒʌdə) *Inf., chiefly Brit.* ◆ *vb* **1** (*intr*) to shake or vibrate. ◆ *n* **2** abnormal vibration in a mechanical system. **3** a juddering motion. ORIG prob. blend of JAR[2] + SHUDDER

Jude ★ (dʒu:d) *n* **1** a book of the New Testament (in full **The Epistle of Jude**). **2 Saint.** Also called: **Judas.** the author of this, stated to be the brother of James (Jude 1) and almost certainly identical with Thaddaeus (Matthew 10:2–4). Feast day: June 19 or Oct. 28.

Judea ★ (dʒu:'dɪə) *n* a variant spelling of **Judaea.**

judge (dʒʌdʒ) *n* **1** a public official with authority to hear cases in a court of law and pronounce judgment upon them. **2** a person who is appointed to determine the result of contests or competitions. **3** a person qualified to comment critically: *a good judge of antiques.* **4** a leader of the peoples of Israel from Joshua's death to the accession of Saul. ◆ *vb* **judges, judging, judged. 5** to hear and decide upon (a case at law). **6** (*tr*) to pass judgment on. **7** (when *tr, may take a clause as object or an infinitive*) to decide (something) after inquiry. **8** to determine the result of (a contest or competition). **9** to appraise (something) critically. **10** (*tr; takes a clause as object*) to believe something to be the case. ORIG C14: from OF, from L *jūdicāre* to pass judgment, from *jūdex* a judge
▸ **'judge,like** *adj* ▸ **'judger** *n* ▸ **'judgeship** *n*

judge advocate *n, pl* **judge advocates.** an officer who superintends proceedings at a military court martial.

judges' rules *pl n* (in English law) a set of rules, not legally binding, governing the behaviour of police towards suspects.

judgment *or* **judgement** ('dʒʌdʒmənt) *n* **1** the faculty of being able to make critical distinctions and achieve a balanced viewpoint. **2a** the verdict pronounced by a court of law. **2b** an obligation arising as a result of such a verdict, such as a debt. **2c** (*as modifier*): *a judgment debtor.* **3** the formal decision of one or more judges at a contest or competition. **4** a particular decision formed in a case in dispute or doubt. **5** an estimation: *a good judgment of distance.* **6** criticism or censure. **7 against one's better judgment.** contrary to a preferred course of action. **8 in someone's judgment.** in someone's opinion. **9 sit in judgment. 9a** to preside as judge. **9b** to assume the position of critic.

Judgment ('dʒʌdʒmənt) *n* **1** the estimate by God of the ultimate worthiness or unworthiness of the individual or of all mankind. **2** God's subsequent decision determining the final destinies of all individuals.

judgmental *or* **judgemental** (dʒʌdʒ'mɛntᵊl) *adj* of or denoting an attitude in which judgments about other people's conduct are made.

Judgment Day *n* the occasion of the Last Judgment by God at the end of the world. Also called: **Day of Judgment.** See **Last Judgment.**

judicatory ('dʒuːdɪkətərɪ) *adj* **1** of or relating to the administration of justice. ◆ *n* **2** a court of law. **3** the administration of justice.

judicature ('dʒuːdɪkətʃə) *n* **1** the administration of justice. **2** the office, function, or power of a judge. **3** the extent of authority of a court or judge. **4** a body of judges; judiciary. **5** a court of justice or such courts collectively.

judicial (dʒuː'dɪʃəl) *adj* **1** of or relating to the administration of justice. **2** of or relating to judgment in a court of law or to a judge exercising this function. **3** allowed or enforced by a court of law: *judicial separation.* **4** having qualities appropriate to a judge. **5** giving or seeking judgment. ORIG C14: from L *jūdiciālis* belonging to the law courts, from *jūdicium* judgment, from *jūdex* a judge
▸ **ju'dicially** *adv*

judiciary (dʒuː'dɪʃɪərɪ) *adj* **1** of or relating to courts of law, judgment, or judges. ◆ *n, pl* **judiciaries. 2** the branch of the central authority in a state concerned with the administration of justice. **3** the system of courts in a country. **4** the judges collectively.

judicious (dʒuː'dɪʃəs) *adj* having or proceeding from good judgment.
▸ **ju'diciously** *adv* ▸ **ju'diciousness** *n*

Judith ★ ('dʒuːdɪθ) *n* **1** the heroine of one of the books of the Apocrypha, who saved her native town by decapitating Holofernes. **2** the book recounting this episode.

judo ('dʒuːdəʊ) *n* **a** the modern sport derived from jujitsu, in which the object is to force an opponent to submit using the minimum of physical effort. **b** (*as modifier*)*: a judo throw.* ORIG Japanese, from *jū* gentleness + *dō* way
▸ **'judoist** *n*

Judy ('dʒuːdɪ) *n, pl* **Judies. 1** the wife of Punch in the children's puppet show *Punch and Judy*. See **Punch. 2** (*often not cap.*) *Brit. sl.* a girl.

jug (dʒʌg) *n* **1** a vessel for holding or pouring liquids, usually having a handle and a lip. US equivalent: **pitcher. 2** *Austral. & NZ.* a container in which water is boiled, esp. an electric kettle. **3** *US.* a large vessel with a narrow mouth. **4** Also called: **jugful.** the amount of liquid held by a jug. **5** *Brit. inf.* a glass of beer. **6** *Sl.* jail. ◆ *vb* **jugs, jugging, jugged. 7** to stew or boil (meat, esp. hare) in an earthenware container. **8** (*tr*) *Sl.* to put in jail. ORIG C16: prob. from *Jug,* nickname from name *Joan*

jugate ('dʒuːgeɪt, -gɪt) *adj* (esp. of compound leaves) having parts arranged in pairs. ORIG C19: from NL *jugātus* (unattested), from L *jugum* a yoke

juggernaut ('dʒʌgəˌnɔːt) *n* **1** any terrible force, esp. one that demands complete self-sacrifice. **2** *Brit.* a very large heavy lorry. ORIG C17: from Hindi, from Sansk. *Jagannātha* lord of the world: devotees supposedly threw themselves under a cart carrying *Juggernaut,* an idol of Krishna

juggins ('dʒʌgɪnz) *n* (*functioning as sing*) *Brit. inf.* a silly person. ORIG C19: special use of the surname *Juggins*

juggle ('dʒʌgᵊl) *vb* **juggles, juggling, juggled. 1** to throw and catch (several objects) continuously so that most are in the air all the time. **2** to manipulate (facts, etc.) so as to give a false picture. **3** (*tr*) to keep (several activities) in progress, esp. with difficulty. ◆ *n* **4** an act of juggling. ORIG C14: from OF *jogler* to perform as a jester, from L, from *jocus* a jest
▸ **'juggler** *n*

Jugoslavia ★ (ˌjuːgəʊ'slɑːvɪə) *n* a variant spelling of **Yugoslavia.**
▸ **'Jugoˌslav** *or* **ˌJugo'slavian** *adj, n*

jugular ('dʒʌgjʊlə) *adj* **1** of, relating to, or situated near the throat or neck. ◆ *n* **2** Also called: **jugular vein.** any of the large veins in the neck carrying blood to the heart from the head. ORIG C16: from LL, from L *jugulum* throat

Jugurtha ★ (dʒuː'gɜːθə) *n* died 104 B.C., king of Numidia (?112–104), who waged war against the Romans (the **Jugurthine War,** 112–105) and was defeated and executed.

juice (dʒuːs) *n* **1** any liquid that occurs naturally in or is secreted by plant or animal tissue: *the juice of an orange.* **2** *Inf.* **2a** petrol. **2b** electricity. **2c** alcoholic drink. **3** vigour or vitality. ORIG C13: from OF *jus,* from L
▸ **'juiceless** *adj*

juice up *vb* (*tr, adv*) *US sl.* to make lively: *to juice up a party.*

juicy ('dʒuːsɪ) *adj* **juicier, juiciest. 1** full of juice. **2** provocatively interesting; spicy: *juicy gossip.* **3** profitable: *a juicy contract.*
▸ **'juicily** *adv* ▸ **'juiciness** *n*

Juiz de Fora ★ (*Portuguese* ʒu'iʃ di 'fɔra) *n* a city in SE Brazil, in Minas Gerais state on the Rio de Janeiro–Belo Horizonte railway: textiles. Pop.: 377 538 (1991).

jujitsu, jujutsu, *or* **jiujutsu** (dʒuː'dʒɪtsuː) *n* the traditional Japanese system of unarmed self-defence perfected by the samurai. See also **judo.** ORIG C19: from Japanese, from *jū* gentleness + *jutsu* art

juju ('dʒuːdʒuː) *n* **1** an object superstitiously revered by certain West African peoples and used as a charm or fetish. **2** the power associated with a juju. ORIG C19: prob. from Hausa *djudju* evil spirit, fetish

jujube ('dʒuːdʒuːb) *n* **1** any of several Old World spiny trees that have small yellowish flowers and dark red edible fruits. **2** the fruit of any of these trees. **3** a chewy sweet made of flavoured gelatine and sometimes medicated to soothe sore throats. ORIG C14: from Med. L *jujuba,* modification of L *zīzyphum,* from Gk *zizuphon*

jukebox ('dʒuːkˌbɒks) *n* a coin-operated machine, usually found in pubs, clubs, etc., that contains records, CDs, or videos, which are played when selected by a customer. ORIG C20: from Gullah (an African-American language) *juke* bawdy (as in *juke house* brothel) + BOX[1]

jukskei ('jʊkˌskeɪ) *n* a South African game in which a peg is thrown over a fixed distance at a stake driven into the ground. ORIG from Afrik. *juk* yoke + *skei* pin

julep ('dʒuːlɪp) *n* **1** a sweet drink, variously prepared and sometimes medicated. **2** *Chiefly US.* short for **mint julep.** ORIG C14: from OF, from Ar. *julāb,* from Persian, from *gul* rose + *āb* water

Julian ★ ('dʒuːljən, -lɪən) *n* known as *Julian the Apostate;* Latin name *Flavius Claudius Julianus.* 331–363 A.D., Roman emperor (361–363), who attempted to revive paganism while remaining tolerant to Christians and Jews.

Juliana ★ (ˌdʒuːlɪ'ɑːnə; *Dutch* jyːliː'aːnaː) *n* full name *Juliana Louise Emma Marie Wilhelmina.* born 1909, queen of the Netherlands (1948–80). She abdicated in favour of her eldest daughter Beatrix.

Julian Alps ★ *pl n* a mountain range in Slovenia: an E range of the Alps.

Julian calendar *n* the calendar introduced by Julius Caesar in 46 B.C., in which leap years occurred every fourth year and in every centenary year. Cf. **Gregorian calendar.**

Julian of Norwich ★ *n* ?1342–?1413, English mystic and anchoress: best known for the *Revelations of Divine Love* describing her visions.

julienne (ˌdʒuːlɪ'ɛn) *adj* **1** (of vegetables) cut into thin shreds. ◆ *n* **2** a clear consommé to which such vegetables have been added. ORIG F, from name *Jules, Julien,* or *Julienne*

Julius II ★ ('dʒuːljəs, -lɪəs) *n* original name *Guiliano della Rovere.* 1443–1513, pope (1503–13). He completed the restoration of the Papal States to the Church, began the building of St Peter's, Rome (1506), and patronized Michelangelo and Raphael.

Julius Caesar ★ *n* See **Caesar.**

Jullundur ★ ('dʒʌləndə) *n* the former name of **Jalandhar.**

July (dʒuː'laɪ) *n, pl* **Julies.** the seventh month of the year, consisting of 31 days. ORIG C13: from Anglo-F *julie,* from L *Jūlius,* after Gaius *Julius* CAESAR, in whose honour it was named

jumble ('dʒʌmbᵊl) *vb* **jumbles, jumbling, jumbled. 1** to mingle (objects, etc.) in a state of disorder. **2** (*tr; usually pas-*

sive) to remember in a confused form. ◆ *n* **3** a disordered mass, state, etc. **4** *Brit.* articles donated for a jumble sale. ORIG C16: from ?
▸ **'jumbly** *adj*

jumble sale *n* a sale of miscellaneous articles, usually second-hand, in aid of charity. US and Canad. equivalent: **rummage sale.**

jumbo ('dʒʌmbəʊ) *n, pl* **jumbos. 1** *Inf.* **1a** a very large person or thing. **1b** (*as modifier*): *a jumbo box of detergent.* **2** See **jumbo jet.** ORIG C19: after a famous elephant exhibited by P. T. Barnum, from Swahili *jumbe* chief

jumbo jet *n Inf.* a type of large jet-propelled airliner that carries several hundred passengers.

jumbo pack *n* **1** the promotion of bulk sales of small unit items, such as confectionery, by packing several in one wrapping, usually with a unit price reduction. **2** such a package of items.

jumbuck ('dʒʌmˌbʌk) *n Austral.* an informal word for **sheep.** ORIG C19: from Abor.

Jumna ★ ('dʒʌmnə) *n* a river in N India, rising in Uttar Pradesh in the Himalayas and flowing south and south-east to join the Ganges just below Allahabad (a confluence held sacred by Hindus). Length: 1385 km (860 miles).

jump (dʒʌmp) *vb* **1** (*intr*) to leap or spring clear of the ground or other surface by using the muscles in the legs and feet. **2** (*tr*) to leap over or clear (an obstacle): *to jump a gap.* **3** (*tr*) to cause to leap over an obstacle: *to jump a horse over a hedge.* **4** (*intr*) to move or proceed hastily (into, onto, out of, etc.): *she jumped into a taxi.* **5** (*tr*) *Inf.* to board so as to travel illegally on: *he jumped the train as it was leaving.* **6** (*intr*) to parachute from an aircraft. **7** (*intr*) to jerk or start, as with astonishment, surprise, etc. **8** to rise or cause to rise suddenly or abruptly. **9** to pass or skip over (intervening objects or matter): *she jumped a few lines and then continued reading.* **10** (*intr*) to change from one thing to another, esp. from one subject to another. **11** *Draughts.* to capture (an opponent's piece) by moving one of one's own pieces over it to an unoccupied square. **12** (*intr*) *Bridge.* to bid in response to one's partner at a higher level than is necessary, to indicate a strong hand. **13** (*tr*) to come off (a track, etc.): *the locomotive jumped the rails.* **14** (*intr*) (of the stylus of a record player) to be jerked out of the groove. **15** (*intr*) *Sl.* to be lively: *the party was jumping.* **16** (*tr*) *Inf.* to attack without warning: *thieves jumped the old man.* **17** (*tr*) *Inf.* (of a driver or a motor vehicle) to pass through (a red traffic light) or move away from (traffic lights) before they change to green. **18 jump down someone's throat.** *Inf.* to address or reply to someone sharply. **19 jump ship.** to desert, esp. to leave a ship in which one is legally bound to serve. **20 jump the queue.** *Inf.* to obtain some advantage out of turn or unfairly. **21 jump to it.** *Inf.* to begin something quickly and efficiently. ◆ *n* **22** an act or instance of jumping. **23** a space, distance, or obstacle to be jumped or that has been jumped. **24** a descent by parachute from an aircraft. **25** *Sport.* any of several contests involving a jump: *the high jump.* **26** a sudden rise: *the jump in prices last month.* **27** a sudden or abrupt transition. **28** a sudden jerk or involuntary muscular spasm, esp. as a reaction of surprise. **29** a step or degree: *one jump ahead.* **30** *Draughts.* a move that captures an opponent's piece by jumping over it. **31** *Films.* **31a** a break in continuity in the normal sequence of shots. **31b** (*as modifier*): *a jump cut.* **32 on the jump.** *Inf., chiefly US & Canad.* **32a** in a hurry. **32b** busy. **33 take a running jump.** *Brit. inf.* a contemptuous expression of dismissal. ◆ See also **jump at, jump-off,** etc. ORIG C16: prob. imit.

jump at *vb* (*intr, prep*) to be glad to accept: *I would jump at the chance of going.*

jumped-up *adj Inf.* suddenly risen in significance, esp. when appearing arrogant.

jumper[1] ('dʒʌmpə) *n* **1** *Chiefly Brit.* a knitted or crocheted garment covering the upper part of the body. **2** the US and Canad. term for **pinafore dress.** ORIG C19: from obs. *jump* man's loose jacket, var. of *jupe,* from OF, from Ar. *jubbah* long cloth coat

jumper[2] ('dʒʌmpə) *n* **1** a boring tool that works by repeated impact, such as a steel bit in a drill used in boring rock. **2** Also called: **jumper cable, jumper lead.** a short length of wire used to make a connection, usually temporarily. **3** a person or animal that jumps.

jumping bean *n* a seed of any of several Mexican plants that contains a moth caterpillar whose movements cause it to jerk about.

jumping jack *n* a toy figure of a man with jointed limbs that can be moved by pulling attached strings.

jump jet *n Inf.* a fixed-wing jet aircraft that is capable of landing and taking off vertically.

jump jockey *n Brit. inf.* a jockey riding in a steeplechase, as opposed to racing on the flat.

jump leads (liːdz) *pl n* two heavy cables fitted with crocodile clips used to start a motor vehicle with a discharged battery by connecting the battery to an external battery.

jump-off *n* **1** an extra round in a showjumping contest when two or more horses are equal first, deciding the winner. ◆ *vb* **jump off. 2** (*intr, adv*) to engage in a jump-off.

jump on *vb* (*intr, prep*) *Inf.* to reprimand or attack suddenly and forcefully.

jump seat *n* **1** a folding seat on some aircraft for an additional crew member. **2** *Brit.* a folding seat in a motor vehicle.

jump-start *vb* **1** to start the engine of (a car) by pushing or rolling it and then engaging the gears or (of a car) to start in this way. ◆ *n* **2** the act of starting a car in this way. ◆ Also called (Brit.): **bump-start.**

jump suit *n* a one-piece garment of combined trousers and jacket or shirt.

jumpy ('dʒʌmpɪ) *adj* **jumpier, jumpiest. 1** nervous or apprehensive. **2** moving jerkily or fitfully.
▸ **'jumpily** *adv* ▸ **'jumpiness** *n*

Jun. *abbrev. for:* **1** June. **2** Also: **jun.** junior.

Junagadh ★ (ˌdʒuːnə'gæd) *n* a town in India, in Gujarat: noted for its Buddhist caves and temples. Pop.: 130 484 (1991).

junco ('dʒʌŋkəʊ) *n, pl* **juncos** *or* **juncoes.** a North American bunting having a greyish plumage. ORIG C18: from Sp.: a rush, from L *juncus* rush

junction ('dʒʌŋkʃən) *n* **1** a place where several routes, lines, or roads meet, link, or cross each other: *a railway junction.* **2** a point on a motorway where traffic may leave or join it. **3** *Electronics.* **3a** a contact between two different metals or other materials: *a thermocouple junction.* **3b** a transition region in a semiconductor. **4** the act of joining or the state of being joined. ORIG C18: from L *junctiō* a joining, from *jungere* to join

junction box *n* an earthed enclosure within which wires or cables can be safely connected.

junction transistor *n* a bipolar transistor consisting of two p-n junctions combined to form either an n-p-n or a p-n-p transistor.

juncture ('dʒʌŋktʃə) *n* **1** a point in time, esp. a critical one (often in **at this juncture**). **2** *Linguistics.* the set of phonological features signalling a division between words, such as those that distinguish *a name* from *an aim.* **3** a less common word for **junction.**

Jundiaí ★ (*Portuguese* ʒundia'i) *n* an industrial city in SE Brazil, in São Paulo state. Pop.: 253 177 (1991).

June (dʒuːn) *n* the sixth month of the year, consisting of 30 days. ORIG OE *iunius,* from L *junius,* prob. from *Junius* name of Roman gens

Juneau ★ ('dʒuːnəʊ) *n* a port in SE Alaska: state capital. Pop.: 26 751 (1990).

Jung ★ (jʊŋ) *n* **Carl Gustav** (*German* karl 'gʊstaf). 1875–1961, Swiss psychologist who developed the concepts of the collective unconscious and of the extrovert and introvert types.
▸ **'Jungian** *adj*

Jungfrau ★ (*German* 'jʊŋfrau) *n* a mountain in S Switzerland, in the Bernese Alps south of Interlaken. Height: 4158 m (13 642 ft).

Junggar Pendi ('dʒʊŋ'gɑːr 'pɛn'diː), **Dzungaria,** *or* **Zungaria** ★ *n* an arid region of W China, in N

Xinjiang Uygur between the Altai Mountains and the Tian Shan.

jungle ('dʒʌŋgᵊl) *n* **1** an equatorial forest area with luxuriant vegetation. **2** any dense or tangled thicket or growth. **3** a place of intense or ruthless struggle for survival: *the concrete jungle.* **4** a type of fast electronic dance music, originating in the early 1990s, which combines elements of techno and ragga. ORIG C18: from Hindi, from Sansk. *jāngala* wilderness
▸ **'jungly** *adj*

jungle fever *n* a serious malarial fever occurring in the East Indies.

jungle fowl *n* **1** any small gallinaceous bird of S and SE Asia, the males of which (**junglecock**) have an arched tail and a combed and wattled head. **2** *Austral.* any of several megapodes.

jungle juice *n Sl.* alcoholic liquor.

junior ('dʒu:njə) *adj* **1** lower in rank or length of service; subordinate. **2** younger in years. **3** of or relating to youth or childhood. **4** *Brit.* of schoolchildren between the ages of 7 and 11 approximately. **5** *US.* of or designating the third year of a four-year course at college or high school. ◆ *n* **6** *Law.* (in England) any barrister below the rank of Queen's Counsel. **7** a junior person. **8** *Brit.* a junior schoolchild. **9** *US.* a junior student. ORIG C17: from L: younger, from *juvenis* young

Junior ('dʒu:njə) *adj* being the younger: usually used after a name to distinguish the son from the father: *Charles Parker, Junior.* Abbrev.: **Jnr, Jr, Jun., Junr.**

junior common room *n* (in certain universities and colleges) a common room for the use of students.

junior lightweight *n* **a** a professional boxer weighing 126–130 pounds (57–59 kg). **b** (*as modifier*): *a junior-lightweight bout.*

junior middleweight *n* **a** a professional boxer weighing 147–154 pounds (66.5–70 kg). **b** (*as modifier*): *the junior-middleweight championship.*

junior school *n* (in England and Wales) a school for children aged between 7 and 11.

junior technician *n* a rank in the Royal Air Force comparable to that of private in the army.

junior welterweight *n* **a** a professional boxer weighing 135–140 pounds (61–63.5 kg). **b** (*as modifier*): *a junior-welterweight fight.*

juniper ('dʒu:nɪpə) *n* a coniferous shrub or small tree of the N hemisphere having purple berry-like cones. The cones of the **common** or **dwarf juniper** are used as a flavouring in making gin. ORIG C14: from L *jūniperus,* from ?

junk[1] (dʒʌŋk) *n* **1** discarded objects, etc., collectively. **2** *Inf.* **2a** rubbish generally. **2b** nonsense: *the play was absolute junk.* **3** *Sl.* any narcotic drug, esp. heroin. ◆ *vb* **4** (*tr*) *Inf.* to discard as junk. ORIG C15 *jonke* old useless rope

junk[2] (dʒʌŋk) *n* a sailing vessel used in Chinese waters and characterized by a very high poop, flat bottom, and square sails supported by battens. ORIG C17: from Port. *junco,* from Javanese *jon*

junk bond *n Finance.* a security that offers a high yield but often involves a high risk of default.

Junker ('jʊŋkə) *n* **1** *History.* any of the aristocratic landowners of Prussia. **2** an arrogant German army officer or official. **3** (formerly) a young German nobleman. ORIG C16: from G, from OHG *junchērro* young lord
▸ **'Junkerdom** *n*

Junkers ★ ('jʊŋkəz) *n* **Hugo.** 1859–1935, German aircraft designer; his aircraft were used in both World Wars.

junket ('dʒʌŋkɪt) *n* **1** a sweet dessert made of flavoured milk set to a curd with rennet. **2** a feast. **3** an excursion, esp. one made for pleasure at public expense. ◆ *vb* **4** to have or entertain with a feast. **5** (*intr*) (of a public official, etc.) to go on a junket. ORIG C14 (in the sense: rush basket, hence custard served on rushes): from OF (dialect) *jonquette,* from *jonc* rush, from L *juncus* reed
▸ **'junketing** *n*

junk food *n* food which is eaten in addition to or instead of regular meals, and which often has a low nutritional value.

junkie *or* **junky** ('dʒʌŋkɪ) *n, pl* **junkies.** an informal word for **drug addict.**

junk mail *n* unsolicited mail advertising goods or services.

junk shop *n* a shop selling miscellaneous second-hand goods and sometimes antiques.

Juno ★ ('dʒu:nəʊ) *n* **1** (in Roman tradition) the queen of the Olympian gods. Greek counterpart: **Hera. 2** a woman of stately bearing and regal beauty.

junta ('dʒʌntə, 'hʊntə) *n* (*functioning as sing or pl*) **1** a group of military officers holding the power in a country, esp. after a coup d'état. **2** Also called: **junto.** a small group of men. **3** a legislative or executive council in some parts of Latin America. ORIG C17: from Sp.: council, from L, from *jungere* to join

junto ('dʒʊntəʊ) *n, pl* **juntos.** a variant of **junta** (sense 2). ORIG C17

Jupiter[1] ★ ('dʒu:pɪtə) *n* (in Roman tradition) the king and ruler of the Olympian gods. Also called: **Jove.**

Jupiter[2] ('dʒu:pɪtə) *n* the largest of the planets and the fifth from the sun.

Jura ★ ('dʒʊərə) *n* **1** a department of E France, in Franche-Comté region. Capital: Lons-le-Saunier. Pop.: 251 853 (1994 est.). Area: 5055 sq. km (1971 sq. miles). **2** a canton of Switzerland, bordering the French frontier: formed in 1979 from part of Bern. Capital: Delémont. Pop.: 68 979 (1995 est.). Area: 838 sq. km (323 sq. miles). **3** an island off the W coast of Scotland, in the Inner Hebrides, separated from the mainland by the **Sound of Jura.** Pop. (with Colonsay): 250 (latest est.). Area: 381 sq. km (147 sq. miles). **4** a mountain range in W central Europe, between the Rivers Rhine and Rhône: mostly in E France, extending into W Switzerland. **5** a range of mountains in the NE quadrant of the moon lying on the N border of the Mare Imbrium.

Jurassic (dʒʊ'ræsɪk) *adj* **1** of or formed in the second period of the Mesozoic era, during which dinosaurs and ammonites flourished. ◆ *n* **2 the.** the Jurassic period or rock system. ORIG C19: from F *jurassique,* after the JURA (Mountains)

jurat ('dʒʊəræt) *n* **1** *Law.* a statement at the foot of an affidavit, naming the parties, stating when, where, and before whom it was sworn, etc. **2** (in England) a municipal officer of the Cinque Ports. **3** (in France and the Channel Islands) a magistrate. ORIG C16: from Med. L *jūrātus* one who has been sworn, from L *jūrāre* to swear

juridical (dʒʊ'rɪdɪkᵊl) *adj* of or relating to law or to the administration of justice; legal. ORIG C16: from L, from *iūs* law + *dicere* to say
▸ **ju'ridically** *adv*

jurisdiction (ˌdʒʊərɪs'dɪkʃən) *n* **1** the right or power to administer justice and to apply laws. **2** the exercise or extent of such right or power. **3** authority in general. ORIG C13: from L *jūrisdictiō* administration of justice, from *jus* law + DICTION
▸ **ˌjuris'dictional** *adj*

jurisprudence (ˌdʒʊərɪs'pru:dᵊns) *n* **1** the science or philosophy of law. **2** a system or body of law. **3** a branch of law: *medical jurisprudence.* ORIG C17: from L *jūris prūdentia,* from *jus* law + PRUDENCE
▸ **jurisprudential** (ˌdʒʊərɪspru:'denʃəl) *adj*

jurist ('dʒʊərɪst) *n* a person versed in the science of law, esp. Roman or civil law. ORIG C15: from F *juriste,* from Med. L *jūrista*

juristic (dʒʊ'rɪstɪk) *or* **juristical** *adj* **1** of or relating to jurists. **2** of or characteristic of the study of law or the legal profession.

juror ('dʒʊərə) *n* **1** a member of a jury. **2** a person who takes an oath. ORIG C14: from Anglo-F *jurour,* from OF *jurer* to take an oath, from L *jūrāre*

Juruá ★ (*Portuguese* ʒu'rua) *n* a river in South America, rising in E central Peru and flowing northeast across NW Brazil to join the Amazon. Length: 1900 km (1200 miles).

jury[1] ('dʒʊərɪ) *n, pl* **juries. 1** a group of, usually, twelve people sworn to deliver a true verdict according to the evidence upon a case presented in a court of law. **2** a body of persons appointed to judge a competition and award prizes. ORIG C14: from OF *juree,* from *jurer* to swear

jury[2] ('dʒʊərɪ) *adj Chiefly naut.* (*in combination*) makeshift: *jury-rigged.* ORIG C17: from ?

jury box *n* an enclosure where the jury sits in court.

juryman ('dʒʊərɪmən) *or* (*fem*) **jurywoman** *n, pl* **jurymen** *or* **jurywomen.** a member of a jury.

jury-rigged *adj Chiefly naut.* set up in a makeshift manner.

just *adj* (dʒʌst). **1a** fair or impartial in action or judgment. **1b** (*as collective n;* preceded by *the*): *the just.* **2** conforming to high moral standards; honest. **3** consistent with justice: *a just action.* **4** rightly applied or given: *a just reward.* **5** legally valid; lawful: *a just inheritance.* **6** well-founded: *just criticism.* **7** correct or true: *a just account.* ◆ *adv* (dʒʌst; *unstressed* dʒəst). **8** used with forms of *have* to indicate an action performed in the very recent past: *I have just closed the door.* **9** at this very instant: *he's just coming in to land.* **10** no more than; only: *just an ordinary car.* **11** exactly: *that's just what I mean.* **12** barely: *he just got there in time.* **13 just about. 13a** at the point of starting (to do something). **13b** almost: *I've just about had enough.* **14 just a moment, second,** *or* **minute.** an expression requesting the hearer to wait or pause for a brief period of time. **15 just now. 15a** a very short time ago. **15b** at this moment. **15c** *S. African inf.* in a little while. **16 just so.** arranged with precision. ORIG C14: from L *jūstus* righteous, from *jūs* justice
▸ **'justly** *adv* ▸ **'justness** *n*

> **USAGE NOTE** The use of *just* with *exactly* (*it's just exactly what they want*) is redundant and should be avoided: *it's exactly what they want.*

justice ('dʒʌstɪs) *n* **1** the quality or fact of being just. **2** *Ethics.* the principle of fairness that like cases should be treated alike. **3** the administration of law according to prescribed and accepted principles. **4** conformity to the law. **5** a judge of the Supreme Court of Judicature. **6** short for **justice of the peace. 7** good reason (esp. in **with justice**). **8 bring to justice.** to capture, try, and usually punish (a criminal, etc.). **9 do justice to. 9a** to show to full advantage. **9b** to show full appreciation of by action. **9c** to treat or judge fairly. **10 do oneself justice.** to make full use of one's abilities. ORIG C12: from OF, from L *jūstitia,* from *justus* JUST
▸ **'justice,ship** *n*

justice of the peace *n* a lay magistrate whose function is to preserve the peace in his area and try summarily such cases as are within his jurisdiction.

justiciar (dʒʌ'stɪʃɪ,ɑː) *n English legal history.* the chief political and legal officer from the time of William I to that of Henry III, who deputized for the king in his absence. Also called: **justiciary.**
▸ **jus'ticiar,ship** *n*

justiciary (dʒʌ'stɪʃɪərɪ) *adj* **1** of or relating to the administration of justice. ◆ *n, pl* **justiciaries. 2** an officer or administrator of justice; judge.

justifiable ('dʒʌstɪ,faɪəbᵊl) *adj* capable of being justified.
▸ **,justi,fia'bility** *n* ▸ **'justi,fiably** *adv*

justifiable homicide *n* lawful killing, as in the execution of a death sentence.

justification (,dʒʌstɪfɪ'keɪʃən) *n* **1** reasonable grounds for complaint, defence, etc. **2** proof, vindication, or exculpation. **3** *Christian theol.* **3a** the act of justifying. **3b** the process of being justified or the condition of having been justified.
▸ **'justifi,catory** *adj*

justify ('dʒʌstɪ,faɪ) *vb* **justifies, justifying, justified.** (*mainly tr*) **1** (*often passive*) to prove or see to be just or valid; vindicate. **2** to show to be reasonable: *his behaviour justifies our suspicion.* **3** to declare or show to be free from blame or guilt. **4** *Law.* to show good reason in court for (some action taken). **5** (*also intr*) *Printing, computing.* to adjust the spaces between words in (a line of type or data) so that it is of the required length or (of a line of type or data) to fit exactly. **6a** *Protestant theol.* to declare righteous by the imputation of Christ's merits to the sinner. **6b** *RC theol.* to change from sinfulness to righteousness by the transforming effects of grace. **7** (*also intr*) *Law.* to prove (a person) to have sufficient means to act as surety, etc., or (of a person) to qualify to provide bail or surety. ORIG C14: from OF *justifier,* from L *justificāre,* from *jūstus* JUST + *facere* to make
▸ **'justi,fier** *n*

Justinian I ★ (dʒʌ'stɪnɪən) *n* called *the Great;* Latin name *Flavius Anicius Justinianus.* 483–565 A.D., Byzantine emperor (527–565). He recovered North Africa, SE Spain, and Italy, largely owing to his generals, such as Belisarius. He sponsored the Justinian Code.

Justinian Code *n* a compilation of Roman imperial law made by order of Justinian I (483–565 A.D.), Byzantine emperor. *n* a compilation of Roman imperial law made by order of Justinian I.

Justin Martyr ★ ('dʒʌstɪn) *n* **Saint.** ?100–?165 A.D., Christian apologist and philosopher. Feast day: June 1.

just-in-time *adj* denoting or relating to an industrial method in which waste, queues, bottlenecks, etc., are eliminated or reduced by producing production-line components, etc., and by delivering materials just before they are needed. Abbrev.: **JIT.**

justle ('dʒʌsᵊl) *vb* **justles, justling, justled.** a less common word for **jostle.**

jut (dʒʌt) *vb* **juts, jutting, jutted. 1** (*intr;* often foll. by *out*) to stick out or overhang beyond the surface or main part. ◆ *n* **2** something that juts out. ORIG C16: var. of JET[1]
▸ **'jutting** *adj*

jute (dʒuːt) *n* **1** either of two Old World tropical yellow-flowered herbaceous plants, cultivated for their strong fibre. **2** this fibre, used in making sacks, rope, etc. ORIG C18: from Bengali *jhuto,* from Sansk. *jūta* braid of hair

Jutland ★ ('dʒʌtlənd) *n* a peninsula of N Europe: forms the continental portion of Denmark and geographically includes the N part of the German province of Schleswig-Holstein, while politically it includes only the mainland of Denmark and the islands north of Limfjorden; a major but inconclusive naval battle was fought off its NW coast in 1916 between the British and German fleets. Danish name: **Jylland.**
▸ **'Jutlander** *n*

juv. *abbrev. for* juvenile.

Juvenal ★ ('dʒuːvɪnᵊl) *n* Latin name *Decimus Junius Juvenalis.* ?60–?140 A.D., Roman satirist, who denounced the vices of imperial Rome.

juvenescence (,dʒuːvɪ'nɛsəns) *n* **1** youth or immaturity. **2** the act or process of growing from childhood to youth.
▸ **,juve'nescent** *adj*

juvenile ('dʒuːvɪ,naɪl) *adj* **1** young, youthful, or immature. **2** suitable or designed for young people: *juvenile pastimes.* ◆ *n* **3** a juvenile person, animal, or plant. **4** an actor who performs youthful roles. **5** a book intended for young readers. ORIG C17: from L *juvenīlis* youthful, from *juvenis* young
▸ **'juve,nilely** *adv*

juvenile court *n* a court that deals with juvenile offenders and children beyond parental control or in need of care.

juvenile delinquency *n* antisocial or criminal conduct by juvenile delinquents.

juvenile delinquent *n* a child or young person guilty of some offence, act of vandalism, or antisocial behaviour and who may be brought before a juvenile court.

juvenilia (,dʒuːvɪ'nɪlɪə) *n* works of art, literature, or music produced in youth, before the artist, author, or composer has formed a mature style. ORIG C17: from L, lit.: youthful things

juxtapose (,dʒʌkstə'pəʊz) *vb* **juxtaposes, juxtaposing, juxtaposed.** (*tr*) to place close together or side by side. ORIG C19: back formation from *juxtaposition,* from L *juxta* next to + POSITION
▸ **,juxtapo'sition** *n* ▸ **,juxtapo'sitional** *adj*

Jylland ★ ('jylan) *n* the Danish name for **Jutland.**

★ people and places

Kk

k *or* **K** (keɪ) *n, pl* **k's, K's,** *or* **Ks. 1** the 11th letter and 8th consonant of the English alphabet. **2** a speech sound represented by this letter, usually a voiceless velar stop, as in *kitten.*

k *symbol for:* **1** kilo(s). **2** *Maths.* the unit vector along the *z*-axis.

K *symbol for:* **1** kelvin(s). **2** *Chess.* king. **3** *Chem.* potassium. ORIG from NL *kalium* **4** *Physics.* kaon. **5** *Currency.* **5a** kina. **5b** kip. **5c** kopeck. **5d** kwacha. **5e** kyat. **6** one thousand. ORIG from KILO- **7** *Computing.* **7a** a unit of 1024 words, bits, or bytes. **7b** (not in technical usage) 1000.

K *or* **K.** *abbrev. for* Köchel: indicating the serial number in the catalogue of the works of Mozart made by Ludwig von Köchel, 1800–77.

k. *abbrev. for:* **1** karat. **2** Also: **K.** king.

K2 ★ *n* a mountain in the Karakoram Range on the Kashmir-Xinjiang Uygur AR border: the second highest mountain in the world. Height: 8611 m (28 250 ft). Also called: **Godwin Austen, Dapsang.**

Kaaba *or* **Caaba** ★ ('kɑːbə) *n* a cube-shaped building in Mecca, the most sacred Muslim pilgrim shrine, into which is built the black stone believed to have been given by Gabriel to Abraham. ORIG from Ar. *ka'bah,* from *ka'b* cube

kabaddi (kə'bɑːdɪ) *n* a game played between two teams of seven players, in which individuals take turns to chase and try to touch members of the opposing team without being captured by them. ORIG Tamil

Kabalega Falls ★ (ˌkɑːbə'leɪgə) *pl n* rapids on the lower Victoria Nile, about 35 km (22 miles) east of Lake Albert, where the Nile drops 120 m (400 ft).

Kabardino-Balkar Republic ★ ('kæbəˌdiːnəʊ-'bælkə) *n* a constituent republic of S Russia, on the N side of the Caucasus Mountains. Capital: Nalchik. Pop.: 790 000 (1996 est.). Area: 12 500 sq. km (4825 sq. miles). Also called: **Kabardino-Balkaria** (kæbəˌdiːnəubæl'kɑːrɪə).

kabbala *or* **kabala** (kə'bɑːlə) *n* variant spellings of **cabbala.**

Kabila ★ (kæ'biːlə) *n* **Laurent** (*French* lorɑ̃). 1940–2001, Congolese politician and guerrilla leader; president of the Democratic Republic of Congo (1997–2001); assassinated.

kabuki (kæ'buːkɪ) *n* a form of Japanese drama based on legends and characterized by elaborate costumes and the use of male actors. ORIG Japanese, from *ka* singing + *bu* dancing + *ki* art

Kabul ★ (kə'bʊl, 'kɑːbᵊl) *n* **1** the capital of Afghanistan, in the northeast of the country at an altitude of 1800 m (5900 ft) on the **Kabul River**: over 3000 years old, with a strategic position commanding passes through the Hindu Kush and main routes to the Khyber Pass; destroyed and rebuilt many times; capital of the Mogul Empire from 1504 until 1738 and of Afghanistan from 1773; university (1932). Pop.: 700 000 (1993 est.). **2** a river in Afghanistan and Pakistan, rising in the Hindu Kush and flowing east into the Indus at Attock, Pakistan. Length: 700 km (435 miles).

Kabyle (kə'baɪl) *n* **1** (*pl* **Kabyles** *or* **Kabyle**) a member of a Berber people in Tunisia and Algeria. **2** the dialect of Berber spoken by this people. ORIG C19: from Ar. *qabā'il,* pl. of *qabīlah* tribe

Kádár ★ (*Hungarian* 'kaːdaːr) *n* **János** ('jaːnoʃ). 1912–89, Hungarian statesman; Communist prime minister of Hungary (1956–58; 1961–65) and first secretary of the Communist Party (1956–88).

kadi ('kɑːdɪ, 'keɪdɪ) *n, pl* **kadis.** a variant spelling of **cadi.**

Kaduna ★ (kə'duːnə) *n* **1** a state of N Nigeria. Capital: Kaduna. Pop.: 4 438 007 (1995 est.). Area: 46 053 sq. km (17 781 sq. miles). Former name (until 1976): **North-Central State. 2** a city in N central Nigeria, capital of Kaduna state on the **Kaduna River** (a principal tributary of the Niger). Pop.: 333 600 (1995 est.).

Kaesŏng ★ ('kæˌsʌŋ) *n* a city in SW North Korea: former capital of Korea (938–1392). Pop.: 120 000 (1987 est.).

Kaffir *or* **Kafir** ('kæfə) *n, pl* **Kaffirs** *or* **Kaffir, Kafirs** *or* **Kafir. 1** *Offens.* **1a** (in southern Africa) any Black African. **1b** (*as modifier*): *Kaffir farming.* **2** a former name for the **Xhosa** language. ORIG C19: from Ar. *kāfir* infidel, from *kafara* to deny

> **USAGE NOTE** This word is considered deeply offensive in South Africa and using it can be grounds for prosecution for crimen injuria.

kaffir beer *n S. African.* beer made from sorghum (kaffir corn) or millet.

kaffirboom ('kæfəˌbʊəm) *n* a S. African deciduous flowering tree. ORIG from KAFFIR + Afrik. *boom* tree

kaffir corn *n* a southern African variety of sorghum, cultivated in dry regions for its grain and as fodder. Sometimes shortened to **kaffir.**

Kaffraria ★ (kæ'freərɪə) *n* a former region of central South Africa: inhabited chiefly by the Kaffirs; British Kaffraria was a crown colony established in 1853 in the southwest of the region and annexed to Cape Colony in 1865.
▸ **Kaf'frarian** *adj, n*

Kafir ('kæfə) *n, pl* **Kafirs** *or* **Kafir. 1** a member of a people inhabiting E Afghanistan. **2** a variant spelling of **Kaffir.** ORIG C19: from Ar.; see KAFFIR

Kafiristan ★ (ˌkæfɪrɪ'stɑːn) *n* the former name of **Nuristan.**

Kafka ★ ('kæfkə; *Czech* 'kafka) *n* **Franz** (frants). 1883–1924, Czech writer, born in Prague (then in Bohemia) of German Jewish parents, writing in German. His nightmarish novels *The Trial* (1925) and *The Castle* (1926), were published posthumously against his wishes.
▸ **Kafkaesque** (ˌkæfkə'ɛsk) *adj*

kaftan *or* **caftan** ('kæftæn) *n* **1** a long coatlike garment, usually with a belt, worn in the East. **2** an imitation of this, worn esp. by women, consisting of a loose dress with long wide sleeves. ORIG C16: from Turkish *qaftān*

Kagera ★ (kæ'gɛrə) *n* a river in E Africa, rising in headstreams on the border between Tanzania and Rwanda and flowing east to Lake Victoria: the most remote headstream of the Nile and largest tributary of Lake Victoria. Length: about 480 km (300 miles).

Kagoshima ★ (ˌkægɒ'ʃiːmə) *n* a port in SW Japan, on S Kyushu. Pop.: 546 294 (1995).

kagoul (kə'guːl) *n* a variant spelling of **cagoule.**

kahawai ('kɑːhəwaɪ, 'kɑːwaɪ) *n* a New Zealand food and game fish. ORIG from Maori

Kahn ★ (kɑːn) *n* **1 Herman.** 1922–83, US mathematician and futurologist; director of the Hudson Institute (1961–83). **2 Louis I(sadore).** 1901–74, US architect, noted for his art museums at Yale (1951–53) and New Haven (1969–74).

kai (kaɪ) *n NZ inf.* food. ORIG from Maori

kaiak ('kaɪæk) *n* a variant spelling of **kayak.**

Kaieteur Falls ★ (ˌkaɪə'tʊə) *pl n* a waterfall in Guyana, on the Potaro River. Height: 226 m (741 ft). Width: about 107 m (350 ft).

Kaifeng ★ ('kaɪ'fɛŋ) *n* a city in E China, in N Henan on the Yellow River: one of the oldest cities in China and its capital (as Pien-liang) from 907 to 1126. Pop.: 507 763 (1990 est.).

kail (keɪl) *n* a variant spelling of **kale.**

kai moana (məʊ'ænə) *n NZ.* seafood. ORIG Maori

kainite ('kaɪnaɪt) *n* a white mineral consisting of potassium chloride and magnesium sulphate: a fertilizer and source of potassium salts. ORIG C19: from G *Kainit*, from Gk *kainos* new + -ITE[1]

Kairouan (*French* kɛrwɑ̃), **Kairwan,** *or* **Qairwan** ★ (kaɪə'wɑːn) *n* a city in NE Tunisia: one of the holy cities of Islam; pilgrimage and trading centre. Pop.: 102 600 (1994).

Kaiser[1] ('kaɪzə) *n* (*sometimes not cap.*) *History.* **1** any of the three German emperors. **2** *Obs.* any Austro-Hungarian emperor. ORIG C16: from G, ult. from L *Caesar* emperor

Kaiser[2] ★ (*German* 'kaizər) *n* **Georg** ('geːɔrk). 1878–1945, German expressionist dramatist.

Kaiserslautern ★ (*German* kaizərs'lautərn) *n* a city in W Germany, in S Rhineland-Palatinate. Pop.: 102 002 (1996 est.).

kaizen *Japanese.* (kaɪ'zɛn) *n* a philosophy of continuous improvement of working practices that underlies total quality management and just-in-time business techniques. ORIG lit.: improvement

kak (kʌk) *n S. African taboo sl.* **1** faeces. **2** rubbish. ORIG Afrik.

kaka ('kɑːkə) *n* a New Zealand parrot with a long compressed bill. ORIG C18: from Maori, ? imit. of its call

kaka beak *n* a New Zealand shrub with beaklike red flowers. ORIG from KAKA

kakapo ('kɑːkəˌpəʊ) *n, pl* **kakapos.** a ground-living nocturnal parrot of New Zealand, resembling an owl. ORIG C19: from Maori, lit.: night kaka

kakemono (ˌkækɪ'məʊnəʊ) *n, pl* **kakemonos.** a Japanese paper or silk wall hanging, usually long and narrow, with a picture or inscription on it. ORIG C19: from Japanese, from *kake* hanging + *mono* thing

Kalaallit Nunaat ★ (kə'lɑːlɪt 'nuːnɑːt) *n* the Greenlandic name for **Greenland.**

kala-azar (ˌkɑːləə'zɑː) *n* a tropical infectious disease caused by a protozoan in the liver, spleen, etc. ORIG C19: from Assamese *kālā* black + *āzār* disease

Kalahari ★ (ˌkælə'hɑːrɪ) *n* **the.** an extensive arid plateau of South Africa, Namibia, and Botswana: inhabited by Bushmen. Also called: **Kalahari Desert.**

Kalamazoo ★ (ˌkæləmə'zuː) *n* a city in SW Michigan, midway between Detroit and Chicago. Pop.: 81 644 (1994 est.).

Kalashnikov (kə'læʃnɪˌkɒf) *n* a Russian-made automatic rifle. See also **AK-47.** ORIG C20: after Mikhail *Kalashnikov* (born 1919), its designer

Kalat *or* **Khelat** ★ (kə'lɑːt) *n* a region of SW Pakistan, in S Baluchistan: formerly a princely state ruled by the Khan of Kalat, which joined Pakistan in 1948.

kale *or* **kail** (keɪl) *n* **1** a cultivated variety of cabbage with crinkled leaves. **2** *Scot.* a cabbage. ◆ Cf. **sea kale.** ORIG OE *cāl*

kaleidoscope (kə'laɪdəˌskəʊp) *n* **1** an optical toy for producing symmetrical patterns by multiple reflections in inclined mirrors enclosed in a tube. Loose pieces of coloured glass, paper, etc., are placed between transparent plates at the far end of the tube, which is rotated to change the pattern. **2** any complex pattern of frequently changing shapes and colours. ORIG C19: from Gk *kalos* beautiful + *eidos* form + -SCOPE
▸ **kaleidoscopic** (kəˌlaɪdə'skɒpɪk) *adj*

kalends ('kælɪndz) *pl n* a variant spelling of **calends.**

Kalevala (ˌkɑːlə'vɑːlə) *n Finnish legend.* **1** the land of the hero Kaleva, who performed legendary exploits. **2** the Finnish national epic in which these exploits are recounted. ORIG Finnish, from *kaleva* of a hero + *-la* home

kaleyard *or* **kailyard** ('keɪlˌjɑːd; *Scot.* -ˌjard) *n Scot.* a vegetable garden. ORIG C19: lit.: cabbage garden

kaleyard school *or* **kailyard school** *n* a group of writers who depicted the homely aspects of life in the Scottish Lowlands. The best-known contributor was J. M. Barrie.

Kalgan ★ ('kɑːl'gɑːn) *n* a former name of **Zhangjiakou.**

Kalgoorlie ★ (kæl'gʊəlɪ) *n* a city in Western Australia, adjoining the town of Boulder: a centre of the Coolgardie gold rushes of the early 1890s; declining gold resources superseded by the discovery of nickel ore in 1966. Pop.: 26 079 (including Boulder) (1991).

Kali ★ ('kɑːlɪ) *n* the Hindu goddess of destruction, consort of Siva. Her cult was characterized by savagery and cannibalism.

Kalidasa ★ (ˌkælɪ'dɑːsə) *n* ?5th century A.D., Indian dramatist, noted for his verse drama *Sakuntala.*

kalied ('keɪlaɪd) *adj N English dialect.* drunk.

Kalimantan ★ (ˌkælɪ'mæntən) *n* the Indonesian name for Borneo: applied to the Indonesian part of the island only, excluding the Malaysian states of Sabah and Sarawak and the sultanate of Brunei. Pop.: 6 723 086 (1980).

Kalinin[1] ★ (*Russian* ka'linin) *n* the former name (1932–91) of **Tver.**

Kalinin[2] ★ (*Russian* ka'linin) *n* **Mikhail Ivanovich** (mixa'il i'vanəvitʃ). 1875–1946, Soviet statesman: titular head of state (1919–46); a founder of *Pravda* (1912).

Kaliningrad ★ (*Russian* kəlinin'grat) *n* a port in W Russia, on the Pregolya River: an exclave of Russian territory between Poland and Lithuania: severely damaged in World War II as the chief German naval base on the Baltic; ceded to the Soviet Union in 1945 and now Russia's chief Baltic naval base. Pop.: 419 000 (1995 est.). Former name (until 1946): **Königsberg.**

Kalisz ★ (*Polish* 'kaliʃ) *n* a town in central Poland, on an island in the Prosna River: textile industry. Pop.: 106 800 (1995 est.). Ancient name: **Calissia** (kə'lɪsɪə).

Kalmar ★ (*Swedish* 'kalmar) *n* a port in SE Sweden, partly on the mainland and partly on a small island in the **Sound of Kalmar,** opposite Öland: scene of the signing of the Union of Kalmar, which united Sweden, Denmark, and Norway into a single monarchy (1397–1523). Pop.: 58 070 (1994).

kalmia ('kælmɪə) *n* an evergreen North American ericaceous shrub having showy clusters of white or pink flowers. ORIG C18: after Peter *Kalm* (1715–79), Swedish botanist and pupil of Linnaeus

Kalmuck ('kælmʌk) *or* **Kalmyk** ('kælmɪk) *n* **1** (*pl* **Kalmucks, Kalmuck** *or* **Kalmyks, Kalmyk**) a member of a Mongoloid people of Buddhist tradition, who migrated from W China to Russia in the 17th century. **2** the language of this people.

Kalmuck *or* **Kalmyk Republic** ★ *n* a constituent republic of Russia, on the Caspian Sea: became subject to Russia in 1646. Capital: Elista. Pop.: 319 000 (1996 est.). Area: 76 100 sq. km (29 382 sq. miles). Also called: **Kalmykia** (ˌkæl'mɪkɪə).

kalong ('kɑːlɒŋ) *n* a fruit bat of the Malay Archipelago; a flying fox. ORIG Javanese

kalpa ('kælpə) *n* (in Hindu cosmology) a period in which the universe experiences a cycle of creation and destruction. ORIG C18: Sansk.

Kaluga ★ (*Russian* ka'lugə) *n* a city in central Russia, on the Oka River. Pop.: 347 000 (1995 est.).

Kama[1] ★ (*Russian* 'kamə) *n* a river in central Russia, rising in the Ural Mountains and flowing to the River Volga, of which it is the largest tributary. Length: 2030 km (1260 miles).

Kama[2] ★ ('kɑːmə) *n* the Hindu god of love. ORIG from Sansk.

Kamakura ★ (ˌkæmə'kʊərə) *n* a city in central Japan, on S Honshu: famous for its Great Buddha (Daibutsu), a 13th-century bronze, 15 m (49 ft) high. Pop.: 170 319 (1995).

Kamasutra (ˌkɑːmə'suːtrə) *n* **the.** an ancient Hindu text on erotic pleasure. ORIG Sansk.: book on love, from *kāma* love + *sūtra* thread

Kamchatka ★ (*Russian* kam'tʃatkə) *n* a peninsula in E Russia, between the Sea of Okhotsk and the Bering Sea. Length: about 1200 km (750 miles).
▸ **Kam'chatkan** *adj, n*

kame (keɪm) *n* an irregular mound or ridge of gravel, sand, etc., deposited by water derived from melting glaciers. ORIG C19: Scot. & N English var. of COMB

kameez (kə'mi:z) *n, pl* **kameez** *or* **kameezes**. a long tunic worn in the Indian subcontinent, often with a shalwar. ORIG Urdu *kamis*, from Ar. *gamīs*

Kamensk-Uralski ★ (*Russian* 'kamınsku'raljskij) *n* an industrial city in S Russia. Pop.: 197 000 (1995 est.).

Kamerlingh-Onnes ★ (*Dutch* 'ka:mərlıŋ'ɔnəs) *n* **Heike** ('hɛikə). 1853–1926, Dutch physicist: a discoverer (1911) of superconductivity. Nobel prize for physics 1913.

Kamerun ★ ('kaməru:n) *n* the German name for **Cameroon**.

Kamet ★ ('ka:mɛt, 'kʌmeıt) *n* a mountain in N India, in Uttar Pradesh in the Himalayas. Height: 7756 m (25 447 ft).

kamikaze (ˌkæmı'ka:zı) *n* **1** (*often cap.*) (in World War II) one of a group of Japanese pilots who performed suicidal missions. **2** (*modifier*) (of an action) undertaken or (of a person) undertaking an action in the knowledge that it will result in the death of the person performing it in order to inflict maximum damage on an enemy: *a kamikaze attack.* **3** (*modifier*) extremely foolhardy and possibly self-defeating: *kamikaze prices.* ORIG C20: from Japanese, from *kami* divine + *kaze* wind

kamilaroi ('kæmələˌrɔı) *n* an Australian Aboriginal language formerly used in NW New South Wales.

Kamloops trout ('kæmlu:ps) *n* a variety of rainbow trout common in British Columbia.

Kampala ★ (kæm'pa:lə) *n* the capital and largest city of Uganda, on Lake Victoria: Makerere University (1961). Pop.: 773 500 (1991).

kampong ('kæmpɒŋ) *n* (in Malaysia) a village. ORIG C19: from Malay

Kampuchea ★ (ˌkæmpʊ'tʃıə) *n* the name from 1976 until 1989 of Cambodia, chosen by the Khmer Rouge (communist) government in 1976. During the Vietnamese occupation of Cambodia (1976–89) exiled Cambodian factions, including the Khmer Rouge, formed the Coalition Government of Democratic Kampuchea (CGDK). The pro-Vietnamese government reverted to the name Cambodia in 1989, and all factions of the CGDK except the Khmer Rouge participated in democratic elections in Cambodia in 1993. See also **Cambodia**.
▸ **ˌKampu'chean** *adj, n*

Kan. *abbrev. for* Kansas.

Kanak (kə'næk) *n* a native or inhabitant of New Caledonia who seeks independence from France. ORIG C20: from Hawaiian: man

Kanaka (kə'nækə) *n* **1** a native Hawaiian. **2** (*often not cap.*) *Austral.* any native of the South Pacific islands, esp. (formerly) one abducted to work in Australia. ORIG C19: from Hawaiian: man

Kananga ★ (kə'næŋgə) *n* a city in SW Democratic Republic of Congo: a commercial centre on the railway from Lubumbashi to Port Francqui. Pop.: 393 030 (1994 est.). Former name (until 1966): **Luluabourg**.

Kanara *or* **Canara** ★ (kə'na:rə) *n* a region of SW India, in Karnataka on the Deccan Plateau and the W Coast. Area: about 155 000 sq. km (60 000 sq. miles).

Kanarese *or* **Canarese** (ˌkænə'ri:z) *n* **1** (*pl* **Kanarese** *or* **Canarese**) a member of a people of S India living chiefly in Kanara. **2** the language of this people.

Kanazawa ★ (ˌkænə'za:wə) *n* a port in Japan, on W Honshu: textile and porcelain industries. Pop.: 453 977 (1995).

kanban *Japanese.* ('kænbæn) *n* **1** a just-in-time manufacturing process in which the movements of materials through a process are recorded on specially designed cards. **2** any of the cards used for ordering materials in such a system. ORIG lit.: advertisement hoarding

Kanchenjunga ★ (ˌkæntʃən'dʒʌŋgə) *n* a variant spelling of **Kangchenjunga**.

Kanchipuram ★ (ka:n'tʃi:pərəm) *n* a city in SE India, in Tamil Nadu: a sacred Hindu town known as "the Benares of the South"; textile industries. Pop.: 144 955 (1991).

Kandahar ★ (ˌkændə'ha:) *n* a city in S Afghanistan: an important trading centre, built by Ahmad Shah Durrani (1724–73) as his capital on the site of several former cities. Pop.: 237 500 (1990 est.).

Kandinsky ★ (*Russian* kan'dinskij) *n* **Vasili** (va'silij). 1866–1944, Russian expressionist painter and theorist; a founder of *der Blaue Reiter* (a group of German expressionist painters).

Kandy ★ ('kændı) *n* a city in central Sri Lanka: capital of the kingdom of Kandy from 1480 until 1815, when occupied by the British; sacred Buddhist temple; University of Sri Lanka. Pop.: 104 000 (1990 est.).

kanga *or* **khanga** ('kæŋgə) *n* a piece of gaily decorated thin cotton cloth used as a woman's garment, originally in E Africa. ORIG from Swahili

kangaroo (ˌkæŋgə'ru:) *n, pl* **kangaroos. 1** a large herbivorous marsupial of Australia and New Guinea, having large powerful hind legs used for leaping, and a long thick tail. **2** (*usually pl*) *Stock Exchange.* an Australian share, esp. in mining, land, or a tobacco company. ORIG C18: prob. from Abor.
▸ **ˌkanga'roo-ˌlike** *adj*

kangaroo closure *n Parliamentary procedure.* a form of closure in which the chairman or speaker selects certain amendments for discussion and excludes others.

kangaroo court *n* an irregular court, esp. one set up by strikers to judge strikebreakers.

Kangaroo Island ★ *n* an island in the Indian Ocean, off South Australia. Area: 4350 sq. km (1680 sq. miles).

kangaroo paw *n* any of various Australian plants having green-and-red hairy flowers.

kangaroo rat *n* **1** a small leaping rodent related to the squirrels and inhabiting desert regions of North America, having a stocky body and very long hind legs and tail. **2** Also called: **kangaroo mouse.** any of several leaping Australian rodents.

Kangchenjunga, Kanchenjunga (ˌkæntʃən'dʒʌŋgə), *or* **Kinchinjunga** ★ *n* a mountain on the border between Nepal and Sikkim, in the Himalayas: the third highest mountain in the world. Height: 8598 m (28 208 ft).

kanji ('kændʒı) *n, pl* **kanji** *or* **kanjis. 1** a Japanese writing system using characters mainly derived from Chinese ideograms. **2** a character in this system. ORIG Japanese, from Chinese *han* Chinese + *zi* character

Kano ★ ('ka:nəʊ, 'keınəʊ) *n* **1** a state of N Nigeria: consists of wooded savanna in the south and scrub vegetation in the north. Capital: Kano. Pop.: 6 297 165 (1995 est.). Area: 20 131 sq. km (7773 sq. miles). **2** a city in N Nigeria, capital of Kano state: transport and market centre. Pop.: 594 800 (1991 est.).

Kanpur ★ (ka:n'pʊə) *n* an industrial city in NE India, in S Uttar Pradesh on the River Ganges: scene of the massacre by Nana Sahib of British soldiers and European families and his later defeat by British forces in 1857. Pop.: 1 874 409 (1991). Former name: **Cawnpore.**

Kans. *abbrev. for* Kansas.

Kansas ★ ('kænzəs) *n* a state of the central US: consists of undulating prairie, drained chiefly by the Arkansas, Kansas, and Missouri Rivers; mainly agricultural. Capital: Topeka. Pop.: 2 629 067 (1998 est.). Area: 213 096 sq. km (82 277 sq. miles). Abbrevs.: **Kan., Kans.,** or (with zip code) **KS**

Kansas City ★ *n* **1** a city in W Missouri, at the confluence of the Missouri and Kansas Rivers: important centre of livestock and meat-packing industry. Pop.: 443 878 (1994 est.). **2** a city in NE Kansas, adjacent to Kansas City, Missouri. Pop.: 142 630 (1994 est.).

Kansu ★ ('kæn'su:) *n* a variant transliteration of the Chinese name for **Gansu.**

Kant ★ (kænt; *German* kant) *n* **Immanuel** (ı'ma:nue:l). 1724–1804, German idealist philosopher. His main works are the *Critique of Pure Reason* (1781) and the *Critique of Practical Reason* (1788).
▸ **'Kantian** *adj* ▸ **'Kantianˌism** *or* **'Kantism** *n*

KANU ('ka:nu:) *n acronym for* Kenya African National Union.

Kaohsiung *or* **Kao-hsiung** ★ ('kaʊ'ʃjʊŋ) *n* a variant transliteration of the Chinese name for **Gaoxiong.**

Kaolack ★ ('kɑːəʊˌlæk, 'kaʊlæk) *n* a port in SW Senegal, on the Saloum River. Pop.: 193 115 (1994 est.).

kaolin ('keɪəlɪn) *n* a fine white clay used for the manufacture of hard-paste porcelain and bone china and in medicine as a poultice. Also called: **china clay.** ORIG C18: from F, from Chinese *Kaoling* Chinese mountain where supplies for Europe were first obtained
▸ ˌ**kao'linic** *adj* ▸ '**kaolinˌize** *or* '**kaolinˌise** *vb*

kaon ('keɪɒn) *n* a meson that has a rest mass of about 996 or 964 electron masses. Also called: **K-meson.** ORIG C20 *ka* representing the letter *k* + (MES)ON

kapellmeister (kæ'pɛlˌmaɪstə) *n* a variant spelling of **capellmeister.**

Kapfenberg ★ (*German* 'kapfənbɛrk) *n* an industrial town in E Austria, in Styria. Pop.: 23 490 (1991).

Kapil Dev ★ ('kæpɪl 'dɛv) *n* (**Ramlal**) **Nikhanj** (nɪ'kændʒ). born 1959, Indian cricketer: captain of India (1983–84).

Kapitza ★ (kə'pitsa) *n* **Piotr Leonidovich** ('pjɔtᵊr liɔ'nidovitʃ). 1894–1984, Russian physicist. He worked in England and the Soviet Union, mainly in cryogenics; Nobel prize for physics in 1978.

kapok ('keɪpɒk) *n* a silky fibre obtained from the hairs covering the seeds of a tropical tree (**kapok tree**): used for stuffing pillows, etc. ORIG C18: from Malay

Kaposi's sarcoma (kæ'pəʊsɪz) *n* a form of skin cancer found in Africans and more recently in victims of AIDS. ORIG C20: after Moritz Kohn *Kaposi* (1837–1902), Austrian dermatologist who first described the sores that characterize the disease

kappa ('kæpə) *n* the tenth letter in the Greek alphabet (Κ, κ). ORIG Gk, of Semitic origin

kaput (kæ'pʊt) *adj* (*postpositive*) *Inf.* ruined, broken, or not functioning. ORIG C20: from G *kaputt* done for

karabiner (ˌkærə'biːnə) *n Mountaineering.* a metal clip with a spring for attaching to a piton, belay, etc. Also called: **snaplink, krab.** ORIG shortened from G *Karabinerhaken,* lit.: carbine hook

Karachai-Cherkess Republic ★ (kərʌ'tʃaɪtʃeə'kɛs) *n* a constituent republic of W Russia, on the N side of the Caucasus Mountains. Capital: Cherkessk. Pop.: 436 000 (1996 est.). Area: 14 100 sq. km (5440 sq. miles). Also called: **Karachayevo-Cherkess Republic** (kərʌ'tʃaɪɛvəʊtʃeə'kɛs), **Karachai-Cherkessia** (kærəˌtʃaɪtʃeə'kɛsɪə).

Karachi ★ (kə'rɑːtʃɪ) *n* a port in S Pakistan, on the Arabian Sea: capital of Pakistan (1947–60); university (1950); chief port: commercial and industrial centre. Pop.: 9 863 000 (1995 est.).

Karafuto ★ (ˌkɑːrɑː'fuːtɔ) *n* transliteration of the Japanese name for **Sakhalin.**

Karaganda ★ (*Russian* kərəgan'da) *n* a city in E central Kazakhstan: a major coal-mining and industrial centre. Pop.: 573 700 (1995 est.). Also called: **Qaraghandy.**

Karajan ★ (*German* 'kaːrajan) *n* **Herbert von** ('hɛrbɛrt fɔn). 1908–89, Austrian conductor

Kara-Kalpak Autonomous Republic ★ (kə'rɑːkəl'pɑːk) *n* an administrative division of NW Uzbekistan, on the Aral Sea: came under Russian rule by stages from 1873 onwards until Uzbekistan became independent. Capital: Nukus. Pop.: 1 343 000 (1993 est.). Area: 165 600 sq. km (63 900 sq. miles). Also called: **Kara-Kalpakia** (kə'rɑːkəl'pɑːkɪə), **Kara-Kalpakstan** (kə'rɑːkəlˌpɑːk'stæn, -'stɑːn).

Karakoram *or* **Karakorum** ★ (ˌkærə'kɔːrəm) *n* a mountain system in N Kashmir, extending for about 480 km (300 miles) from northwest to southeast: contains the second highest peak in the world (K2); the range is crossed by several high passes, notably the **Karakoram Pass,** 5575 m (18 290 ft).

Karakorum ★ (ˌkærə'kɔːrəm) *n* a ruined city in Mongolia; ancient capital (1220–67), founded by Ghenghis Khan, of the Mongolian empire: destroyed in 1388.

karakul *or* **caracul** ('kærəkᵊl) *n* **1** a breed of sheep of central Asia having coarse black, grey, or brown hair: the lambs have soft curled hair. **2** the fur prepared from these lambs. ◆ See also **Persian lamb.** ORIG C19: from Russian, from the name of a region in Bukhara where the sheep originated

Kara Kum ★ (*Russian* kəra 'kum) *n* a desert in Turkmenistan, covering most of the country: extensive areas now irrigated. Area: about 300 000 sq. km (120 000 sq. miles).

Karamanlis ★ (*Greek* karaman'lis) *n* **Konstantinos** (kɔnstan'tinɔs). 1907–98, Greek statesman; prime minister of Greece (1955–58; 1958–61; 1961–63; 1974–80): president of Greece (1980–85; 1990–95).

karaoke (ˌkɑːrə'əʊkɪ) *n* **a** an entertainment of Japanese origin in which people take it in turns to sing well-known songs over a prerecorded backing tape. **b** (*as modifier*): *a karaoke bar.* ORIG from Japanese, from *kara* empty + *ōkesutora* orchestra

Kara Sea ★ ('kɑːrə) *n* a shallow arm of the Arctic Ocean off the N coast of Russia: ice-free for about three months of the year.

karat ('kærət) *n* the usual US and Canad. spelling of **carat** (sense 2).

karate (kə'rɑːtɪ) *n* **a** a traditional Japanese system of unarmed combat, employing smashes, chops, kicks, etc., made with the hands, feet, elbows, or legs. **b** (*as modifier*): *karate chop.* ORIG Japanese, lit.: empty hand

karateka (kə'rɑːtɪˌkɑː) *n* a competitor or expert in karate. ORIG Japanese; see KARATE

Karbala ('kɑːbələ) *or* **Kerbela** ★ *n* a town in central Iraq: the chief holy city of Iraq and centre of Shiah Muslim pilgrimage; burial place of Mohammed's grandson Husain. Pop.: 296 705 (1987).

Karelia ★ (kə'riːlɪə; *Russian* ka'reljə) *n* **1** a region of NE Europe, formerly in Finland but annexed in several stages by the former Soviet Union: corresponds roughly to the Karelian Republic in Russia. **2** another name for the **Karelian Republic.**
▸ **Ka'relian** *adj, n*

Karelian Republic ★ (kə'riːlɪən) *n* a constituent republic of NW Russia between the White Sea and Lakes Onega and Ladoga. Capital: Petrozavodsk. Pop.: 785 000 (1996 est.). Area: 172 400 sq. km (66 560 sq. miles). Also called: **Karelia.**

Karelian Isthmus ★ *n* a strip of land, now in Russia, between the Gulf of Finland and Lake Ladoga: annexed by the former Soviet Union after the Russo-Finnish War (1939–40).

Kariba ★ (kə'riːbə) *n* **Lake.** a lake on the Zambia-Zimbabwe border, created by the building of the **Kariba Dam** across the Zambezi for hydroelectric power. Length: 282 km (175 miles).

Karitane (ˌkærɪ'tɑːnɛ) *n NZ.* a nurse for babies; nanny. ORIG from former child-care hospital at *Karitane,* New Zealand

Karl-Marx-Stadt ★ (*German* karl'marksʃtat) *n* the former name (1953–90) of **Chemnitz.**

Karloff ★ ('kɑːlɒf) *n* **Boris,** real name *William Pratt.* 1887–1969, British film actor, known for his roles in horror films.

Karlovy Vary ★ (*Czech* 'karlɔvi 'vari) *n* a city in the W Czech Republic, at the confluence of the Tepla and Ohře Rivers: warm mineral springs. Pop.: 56 290 (1991). German name: **Karlsbad** *or* **Carlsbad** ('karlsbaːt).

Karlskrona ★ (*Swedish* kɑːrls'kruːnə) *n* a port in S Sweden: Sweden's main naval base since 1680. Pop.: 60 642 (1994).

Karlsruhe ★ (*German* 'karlsruːə) *n* a city in SW Germany, in Baden-Württemberg: capital of the former Baden state. Pop.: 275 690 (1996 est.).

karma ('kɑːmə) *n* **1** *Hinduism, Buddhism.* the principle of retributive justice determining a person's state of life and the state of his reincarnations as the effect of his past deeds. **2** destiny or fate. **3** *Inf.* an aura or quality that a person, place, or thing is felt to have. ORIG C19: from Sansk.: action, effect, from *karoti* he does
▸ '**karmic** *adj*

Karnak ★ ('kɑːnæk) *n* a village in E Egypt, on the Nile: site of the N part of the ruins of ancient Thebes.

Karnataka ★ (kə'nɑːtəkə) *n* a state of S India, on the Arabian Sea: consists of a narrow coastal plain rising to the South Deccan plateau; mainly agricultural. Capital:

Bangalore. Pop.: 44 977 201 (1991). Area: 191 791 sq. km (74 051 sq. miles). Former name (1956–73): **Mysore.**

Kärnten ★ ('kɛrntən) *n* the German name for **Carinthia.**

Karoo *or* **Karroo** ★ (kə'ruː) *n, pl* **Karoos** *or* **Karroos.** (*often not cap.*) **1** any of several high arid plateaus in South Africa, esp. the **Central Karoo** and the **Little Karoo.** The highveld, north of the Great Karoo, is sometimes called the **Northern Karoo. 2** a period or rock system in S Africa equivalent to the period or system extending from the Upper Carboniferous to the Lower Jurassic: divided into **Lower** and **Upper Karoo.** ◆ *adj* **3** of, denoting or formed in the Karoo period. ORIG C18: from Afrik. *karo,* probably from Khoikhoi *garo* desert

kaross (kə'rɒs) *n* a garment of skins worn by indigenous peoples in southern Africa. ORIG C18: from Afrik. *karos,* ?from Du., from F *cuirasse* CUIRASS

Karpov ★ (*Russian* 'karpəf) *n* **Anatoly** (ana'tɔlij). born 1951, Russian chess player: world champion (1975–85; 1993).

karri ('kɑːrɪ) *n, pl* **karris. 1** an Australian eucalyptus tree. **2** the durable dark red wood of this tree, used for construction, etc. ORIG from Abor.

karst (kɑːst) *n* (*modifier*) denoting the characteristic scenery of a limestone region, including underground streams, gorges, etc. ORIG C19: G, from *Karst,* limestone plateau near Trieste

kart (kɑːt) *n* a light low-framed vehicle with small wheels and engine used for recreational racing (**karting**). Also called: **go-cart, go-kart.**

karyo- *or* **caryo-** *combining form.* indicating the nucleus of a cell. ORIG from NL, from Gk *karuon* kernel

karyotype ('kærɪəˌtaɪp) *n* **1** the appearance of the chromosomes in a somatic cell of an individual or species, with reference to their number, size, shape, etc. ◆ *vb* **karyotypes, karyotyping, karyotyped.** (*tr*) **2** to determine the karyotype of (a cell).
▸ **karyotypic** (ˌkærɪə'tɪpɪk) *or* ˌ**karyo'typical** *adj*

Kasai ★ (kɑː'saɪ) *n* a river in SW Africa, rising in central Angola and flowing east then north as part of the border between Angola and the Democratic Republic of Congo, continuing northwest to the River Congo. Length: 2154 km (1338 miles).

kasbah *or* **casbah** ('kæzbɑː) *n* (*sometimes cap.*) **1** the citadel of any of various North African cities. **2** the quarter in which a kasbah is located. ORIG from Ar. *kaṣbạ* citadel

kasha ('kɑːʃə) *n* a dish originating in Eastern Europe, consisting of boiled or baked buckwheat. ORIG from Russian

Kashi ('kɑː'ʃiː) *or* **Kashgar** ★ ('kɑːʃ'gɑː) *n* an oasis city in W China, in W Xinjiang Uygur AR. Pop.: 174 570 (1990 est.).

Kashmir ★ (kæʃ'mɪə) *n* a region of SW central Asia: from the 16th century ruled by the Moguls, Afghanis, Sikhs, and British successively; since 1947 disputed between India, Pakistan, and China; 84 000 sq. km (33 000 sq. miles) in the northwest are held by Pakistan and known as Azad Kashmir (Free Kashmir); 42 735 sq. km (16 496 sq. miles) in the east are held by China; the remainder was in 1956 officially incorporated into India as the state of Jammu and Kashmir; traversed by the Himalaya and Karakoram mountain ranges and the Rivers Jhelum and Indus; a fruit-growing and cattle-grazing region, with a woollen industry. Capitals: (Azad Kashmir) Muzaffarabad; (Jammu and Kashmir) Srinagar (summer), Jammu (winter).
▸ **Kash'miri** *adj, n* ▸ **Kash'mirian** *adj, n*

kashruth *or* ***kashrut*** *Hebrew.* (kaʃ'ruːt) *n* **1** the condition of being fit for ritual use in general. **2** the system of dietary laws that requires ritual slaughter, the complete separation of milk and meat, and the prohibition of such foods as pig meat and shell fish. ◆ See also **kosher** (sense 1). ORIG lit.: appropriateness

Kasparov ★ ('kæspərɒf) *n* **Garri** (**Kimovich**) ('gærɪ), real name *Harry Weinstein.* born 1963, Russian chess player, born in Azerbaijan: FIDE world champion (1985–93).

Kassa ★ ('kɔʃʃɔ) *n* the Hungarian name for **Košice.**

Kassala ★ (kə'sɑːlə) *n* a city in the E Sudan: founded as a fort by the Egyptians in 1834. Pop.: 234 270 (1993).

Kassel *or* **Cassel** ★ (*German* 'kasəl) *n* a city in central Germany, in Hesse: capital of Westphalia (1807–13) and of the Prussian province of Hesse-Nassau (1866–1945). Pop.: 201 573 (1996 est.).

kata ('kætə) *n* an exercise consisting of a sequence of the specific movements of a martial art, used in training and designed to show skill in technique. ORIG C20: Japanese, lit.: shape, pattern

kata- *prefix* a variant spelling of **cata-.**

katabatic (ˌkætə'bætɪk) *adj* (of winds) blowing downhill through having become denser with cooling.

Katanga ★ (kə'tæŋgə) *n* the former name (until 1972) of **Shaba.**

Katar ★ (kæ'tɑː) *n* a variant spelling of **Qatar.**

Kathiawar ★ (ˌkætɪə'wɑː) *n* a large peninsula of W India, in Gujarat between the Gulf of Kutch and the Gulf of Cambay. Area: about 60 690 sq. km (23 430 sq. miles).

katipo ('kætɪˌpəʊ, 'kɑːdɪ-) *n, pl* **katipos.** a small venomous spider of New Zealand, commonly black with a red or orange stripe on the abdomen. ORIG Maori

Katmai ★ ('kætmaɪ) *n* **Mount.** a volcano in SW Alaska, in the Aleutian Range: erupted in 1912 forming the Valley of Ten Thousand Smokes, a region with numerous fumaroles; established as **Katmai National Monument,** 10 917 sq. km (4215 sq. miles), in 1918. Height: 2100 m (7000 ft). Depth of crater: 1130 m (3700 ft). Width of crater: about 4 km (2.5 miles).

Katmandu *or* **Kathmandu** ★ (ˌkætmæn'duː) *n* the capital of Nepal, in the east at the confluence of the Baghmati and Vishnumati Rivers. Pop.: 535 000 (1993 est.).

Katowice ★ (*Polish* katɔ'vitsɛ) *n* an industrial city in S Poland. Pop.: 355 100 (1995 est.). Former name (1953–56): **Stalinogrod.**

Katrine ★ ('kætrɪn) *n* **Loch.** a lake in central Scotland, east of Loch Lomond: noted for its associations with Sir Walter Scott's *Lady of the Lake.* Length: about 13 km (8 miles).

Katsina ★ (kæt'siːnə) *n* **1** a state of N central Nigeria. Capital: Katsina. Pop.: 4 336 363 (1995 est.). Area: 24 192 sq. km (9340 sq. miles). **2** a city in N Nigeria, capital of Katsina state: a major intellectual and cultural centre of the Hausa people (16th–18th centuries). Pop.: 201 500 (1995 est.).

Kattegat *or* **Cattegat** ★ ('kætɪˌgæt) *n* a strait between Denmark and Sweden: linked by the Sound, the Great Belt, and the Little Belt with the Baltic Sea and by the Skagerrak with the North Sea.

katydid ('keɪtɪˌdɪd) *n* a green long-horned grasshopper living on the foliage of trees in North America. ORIG C18: imit.

Katz ★ (kæts) *n* Sir **Bernard.** born 1911, British neurophysiologist, born in Germany. Shared the Nobel prize for physiology or medicine (1970) with Julius Axelrod and Ulf von Euler.

Kauai ★ (kɑː'wɑːiː) *n* a volcanic island in NW Hawaii, northwest of Oahu. Chief town: Lihue. Pop.: 50 947 (1990). Area: 1433 sq. km (553 sq. miles).

Kauffmann ★ (*German* 'kaufman) *n* **Angelica** (aŋ'geːlika). 1741–1807, Swiss painter, who worked chiefly in England.

Kaufman ★ ('kɔːfmən) *n* **1 George S(imon).** 1889–1961, US dramatist who, with Moss Hart, wrote many Broadway comedy hits.

kaumatua (kaʊ'mɑːtuːə) *n NZ.* a senior member of a tribe; elder. ORIG Maori

Kaunas ★ ('kaʊnəs) *n* a city in S central Lithuania at the confluence of the Neman and Viliya Rivers: ceded by Poland to Russia in 1795; the provisional capital of Lithuania (1920–40); part of the Soviet Union (1944–91); university (1922). Pop.: 429 000 (1993 est.). Russian name: **Kovno.**

Kaunda ★ (kɑː'ʊndə) *n* **Kenneth** (**David**). born 1924, Zam-

★ people and places

bian statesman. He led his country into independence and became its first president (1964–91).

kauri ('kaurɪ) *n, pl* **kauris. 1** a New Zealand coniferous tree with oval leaves and round cones. **2** the wood or resin of this tree. ORIG C19: from Maori

kauri gum *n* the fossil resin of the kauri tree.

kava ('kɑːvə) *n* **1** a Polynesian shrub. **2** a drink prepared from the aromatic roots of this shrub. ORIG C18: from Polynesian: bitter

Kaválla ★ (kə'vælə; *Greek* ka'vala) *n* a port in E Greece, on the **Bay of Kaválla:** an important Macedonian fortress of the Byzantine empire; ceded to Greece by Turkey after the Balkan War (1912–13). Pop.: 58 576 (1991). Ancient name: **Neapolis** (ˌnɪ'æpɒlɪs).

Kavir Desert ★ (kæ'vɪə) *n* another name for the **Dasht-i-Kavir.**

Kawasaki ★ (ˌkɑːwə'sɑːkɪ) *n* a port in central Japan, on SE Honshu: heavy industries. Pop.: 1 202 811 (1995).

Kawasaki's disease *n* a disease of children that causes a rash, fever, and swelling of the lymph nodes and often damages the heart muscle. ORIG C20: after T. *Kawasaki*, Japanese physician who first described it

Kay ★ (keɪ) *n* **Sir.** (in Arthurian legend) the braggart foster brother and steward of King Arthur.

kayak *or* **kaiak** ('kaɪæk) *n* **1** a canoe-like boat used by Eskimos, consisting of a frame covered with animal skins. **2** a fibreglass or canvas-covered canoe of similar design. ORIG C18: from Eskimo

kayo *or* **KO** ('keɪ'əu) *n, pl* **kayos,** *vb* **kayos, kayoing, kayoed.** *Boxing, sl.* another term for **knockout** or **knock out.** ORIG C20: from the initial letters of *knock out*

Kayseri ★ (ˌkaɪsɛ'riː; *Turkish* 'kaiseri) *n* a city in central Turkey: in ancient times the chief city of Cappadocia. Pop.: 454 000 (1994 est.). Ancient name: **Caesarea Mazaca** (ˌmə'zækə).

Kazakh *or* **Kazak** (kə'zɑːk, kɑː-) *n* **1** (*pl* **Kazakhs** *or* **Kazaks**) a member of a Mongoloid people of Kazakhstan. **2** the official language of Kazakhstan.

Kazakhstan *or* **Kazakstan** ★ (ˌkɑːzɑːk'stæn, -'stɑːn) *n* a republic in central Asia: conquered by Mongols in the 13th century; came under Russian control in the 18th and 19th centuries; a Soviet republic from 1936 until it gained independence in 1991. It is agricultural, but has rich mineral deposits. Official language: Kazakh. Religion: believers are mostly Muslim or Christian. Official currency: tenge. Capital: Astana. Pop.: 15 348 000 (1999 est.). Area: 2 715 100 sq. km (1 048 030 sq. miles).

Kazan[1] ★ (kə'zæn, -'zɑːn; *Russian* ka'zanj) *n* a city in W Russia, capital of the Tatar Autonomous Republic on the River Volga: capital of an independent khanate in the 15th century; university (1804); an industrial centre. Pop.: 1 085 000 (1995 est.).

Kazan[2] ★ (kə'zɑːn) *n* **Elia** ('iːljə), real name *Elia Kazanjoglous.* born 1909, US film director and writer, born in Turkey. His films include *Gentleman's Agreement* (1947), *On the Waterfront* (1954), and *East of Eden* (1955).

Kazan Retto ★ (kɑː'zɑːn 'rɛtəu) *n* transliteration of the Japanese name for the **Volcano Islands.**

Kazantzakis ★ (*Greek* kazan'dzakis) *n* **Nikos** ('nikɔs). 1885–1957, Greek writer, noted particularly for his novels *Zorba the Greek* (1946) and *Christ Recrucified* (1954).

Kazbek ★ (kɑːz'bɛk) *n* **Mount.** an extinct volcano in N Georgia, in the Caucasus Mountains. Height: 5047 m (16 558 ft).

Kaz Daği ★ ('kɑz 'dɑj) *n* the Turkish name for (Mount) **Ida** (sense 2).

kazoo (kə'zuː) *n, pl* **kazoos.** a cigar-shaped musical instrument of metal or plastic with a membranous diaphragm of thin paper that vibrates with a nasal sound when the player hums into it. ORIG C20: prob. imit.

KB (in Britain) *abbrev. for:* **1** King's Bench. **2** *Computing.* kilobyte.

KBE *abbrev. for* Knight (Commander of the Order) of the British Empire.

kbyte *Computing. abbrev. for* kilobyte.

kc *abbrev. for* kilocycle.

KC (in Britain) *abbrev. for:* **1** King's Counsel. **2** Kennel Club.

kcal *abbrev. for* kilocalorie.

KCB *abbrev. for* Knight Commander of the Bath (a Brit. title).

KCMG *abbrev. for* Knight Commander (of the Order) of St Michael and St George (a Brit. title).

KE *abbrev. for* kinetic energy.

kea ('keɪə) *n* a large New Zealand parrot with a brownish-green plumage. ORIG C19: from Maori, imit. of its call

Kéa ★ ('kɛa) *n* transliteration of the Modern Greek name for **Keos.**

Kean ★ (kiːn) *n* **Edmund.** ?1789–1833, British actor, noted for his Shakespearean roles.

Keating ★ ('kiːtɪŋ) *n* **Paul** (**John**). born 1944, Australian statesman; prime minister (1991–96).

Keaton ★ ('kiːtᵊn) *n* **Buster,** real name *Joseph Francis Keaton.* 1895–1966, US film comedian known for his role in *The Navigator* (1924) and *Steamboat Bill Junior* (1927).

Keats ★ (kiːts) *n* **John.** 1795–1821, British poet. His best known poetry is contained in *Lamia and other Poems* (1820), which includes "The Eve of St Agnes" and the odes "On a Grecian Urn", "To a Nightingale", and "To Psyche".

kebab (kə'bæb) *n* a dish consisting of small pieces of meat, tomatoes, onions, etc., grilled on skewers. Also called: **shish kebab.** ORIG C17: from Ar. *kabāb* roast meat

Keble ★ ('kiːbᵊl) *n* **John.** 1792–1866, British clergyman, who helped to inspire the Oxford Movement.

kecks *or* **keks** (kɛks) *pl n N English dialect.* trousers. ORIG C19: from obs. *kicks* breeches

Kecskemét ★ (*Hungarian* 'kɛtʃkɛmeːt) *n* a city in central Hungary: vineyards and fruit farms. Pop.: 105 000 (1996 est.).

Kedah ★ ('kɛdə) *n* a state of NW Malaysia; the chief exports are rice, tin, and rubber. Capital: Alor Star. Pop.: 1 412 000 (1993 est.). Area: 9425 sq. km (3639 sq. miles).

kedge (kɛdʒ) *Naut.* ◆ *vb* **kedges, kedging, kedged. 1** to draw (a vessel) along by hauling in on the cable of a light anchor, or (of a vessel) to be drawn in this fashion. ◆ *n* **2** a light anchor, used esp. for kedging. ORIG C15: from *caggen* to fasten

kedgeree (ˌkɛdʒə'riː) *n Chiefly Brit.* a dish consisting of rice, cooked flaked fish, and hard-boiled eggs. ORIG C17: from Hindi, from Sansk. *khiccā*

Kediri ★ (kɪ'dɪərɪ) *n* a city in Indonesia, in E Java: commercial centre. Pop.: 261 300 (1995 est.).

Kedron ('kɛdrɒn) *or* **Kidron** ★ *n Bible.* a ravine under the eastern wall of Jerusalem.

Keegan ★ ('kiːgən) *n* **Kevin.** born 1951, English footballer; manager of Newcastle United (1992–97); England national coach (1999–2000).

keek (kiːk) *n, vb* a Scot. word for **peep**[1]. ORIG C18: prob. from MDu. *kīken* to look

keel[1] (kiːl) *n* **1** one of the main longitudinal structural members of a vessel to which the frames are fastened. **2 on an even keel.** well-balanced; steady. **3** any structure corresponding to or resembling the keel of a ship. **4** *Biol.* a ridgelike part; carina. ◆ *vb* **5** to capsize. ◆ See also **keel over.** ORIG C14: from ON *kjölr*

keel[2] (kiːl) *n Eastern English dialect.* **1** a flat-bottomed vessel, esp. one used for carrying coal. **2** a measure of coal. ORIG C14 *kele,* from MDu. *kiel*

keelage ('kiːlɪdʒ) *n* a fee charged by certain ports to allow a ship to dock.

keelhaul ('kiːlˌhɔːl) *vb* (*tr*) **1** to drag (a person) by a rope from one side of a vessel to the other through the water under the keel. **2** to rebuke harshly. ORIG C17: from Du. *kielhalen;* see KEEL[1], HAUL

Keeling Islands ★ ('kiːlɪŋ) *pl n* another name for the **Cocos Islands.**

keel over *vb* (*adv*) **1** to turn upside down; capsize. **2** (*intr*) *Inf.* to collapse suddenly.

keelson ('kɛlsən, 'kiːl-) *or* **kelson** *n* a longitudinal beam fastened to the keel of a vessel for strength and stiffness. ORIG C17: prob. from Low G *kielswin* keel swine, ult. of Scand. origin

Keelung ★ ('ki:'lʊŋ) *n* another name for **Chilung.**

keen[1] (ki:n) *adj* **1** eager or enthusiastic. **2** (*postpositive;* foll. by *on*) fond (of); devoted (to): *keen on golf.* **3** intellectually acute: *a keen wit.* **4** (of sight, smell, hearing, etc.) capable of recognizing fine distinctions. **5** having a sharp cutting edge or point. **6** extremely cold and penetrating: *a keen wind.* **7** intense or strong: *a keen desire.* **8** *Chiefly Brit.* extremely low so as to be competitive: *keen prices.* ORIG OE *cēne*
▸ **'keenly** *adv* ▸ **'keenness** *n*

keen[2] (ki:n) *vb* (*intr*) **1** to lament the dead. ◆ *n* **2** a dirge or lament for the dead. ORIG C19: from Irish Gaelic *caoine,* from OIrish *coīnim* I wail
▸ **'keener** *n*

keep (ki:p) *vb* **keeps, keeping, kept. 1** (*tr*) to have or retain possession of. **2** (*tr*) to have temporary possession or charge of: *keep my watch for me.* **3** (*tr*) to store in a customary place: *I keep my books in the desk.* **4** to remain or cause to remain in a specified state or condition: *keep ready.* **5** to continue or cause to continue: *keep in step.* **6** (*tr*) to have or take charge or care of: *keep the shop for me till I return.* **7** (*tr*) to look after or maintain for use, pleasure, etc.: *to keep chickens.* **8** (*tr*) to provide for the upkeep or livelihood of. **9** (*tr*) to support financially, esp. in return for sexual favours. **10** to confine or detain or be confined or detained. **11** to withhold or reserve or admit of withholding or reserving: *your news will keep.* **12** (*tr*) to refrain from divulging or violating: *to keep a secret.* **13** to preserve or admit of preservation. **14** (*tr;* sometimes foll. by *up*) to observe with due rites or ceremonies. **15** (*tr*) to maintain by writing regular records in: *to keep a diary.* **16** (when *intr,* foll. by *in, on, to,* etc.) to stay in, on, or at (a place or position): *keep to the path.* **17** (*tr*) to associate with (esp. in **keep bad company**). **18** (*tr*) to maintain in existence: *to keep court in the palace.* **19** (*tr*) *Chiefly Brit.* to have habitually in stock: *this shop keeps all kinds of wool.* **20 how are you keeping?** how are you? ◆ *n* **21** living or support. **22** *Arch.* charge or care. **23** Also called: **dungeon, donjon.** the main tower within the walls of a medieval castle or fortress. **24 for keeps.** *Inf.* **24a** permanently. **24b** for the winner or possessor to keep permanently. ◆ See also **keep at, keep away,** etc. ORIG OE *cēpan* to observe

keep at *vb* (*prep*) **1** (*intr*) to persist in. **2** (*tr*) to constrain (a person) to continue doing (a task).

keep away *vb* (*adv;* often foll. by *from*) to refrain or prevent from coming (near).

keep back *vb* (*adv;* often foll. by *from*) **1** (*tr*) to refuse to reveal or disclose. **2** to prevent or be prevented from advancing, entering, etc.

keep down *vb* (*adv, mainly tr*) **1** to repress. **2** to restrain or control: *he had difficulty keeping his anger down.* **3** to cause not to increase or rise. **4** (*intr*) to lie low. **5** not to vomit.

keeper ('ki:pə) *n* **1** a person in charge of animals, esp. in a zoo. **2** a person in charge of a museum, collection, or section of a museum. **3** a person in charge of other people, such as a warder in a jail. **4** See **goalkeeper, wicketkeeper, gamekeeper, park keeper. 5** a person who keeps something. **6** a bar placed across the poles of a permanent magnet to close the magnetic circuit when it is not in use.

keep fit *n* exercises designed to promote physical fitness if performed regularly.

keep from *vb* (*prep*) **1** (foll. by a gerund) to prevent or restrain (oneself or another); refrain or cause to refrain. **2** (*tr*) to protect or preserve from.

keeping ('ki:pɪŋ) *n* **1** conformity or harmony (esp. in **in** *or* **out of keeping**). **2** charge or care: *valuables in the keeping of a bank.*

keepnet ('ki:pˌnɛt) *n* a net strung on wire hoops and sealed at one end, suspended in water by anglers to keep alive the fish they have caught.

keep off *vb* **1** to stay or cause to stay at a distance (from). **2** (*prep*) not to eat or drink or to prevent from eating or drinking. **3** (*prep*) to avoid or cause to avoid (a topic).

keep on *vb* (*adv*) **1** to continue or persist in (doing something): *keep on running.* **2** (*tr*) to continue to wear. **3** (*tr*) to continue to employ: *the firm kept on only ten men.* **4** (*intr;* foll. by *about*) to persist in talking (about). **5** (*intr;* foll. by *at*) to nag (a person).

keep out *vb* (*adv*) **1** to remain or cause to remain outside. **2 keep out of. 2a** to remain or cause to remain unexposed to. **2b** to avoid or cause to avoid: *keep out of his way.*

keepsake ('ki:pˌseɪk) *n* a gift that evokes memories of a person or event.

keep to *vb* (*prep*) **1** to adhere to or stand by or cause to adhere to or stand by. **2** to confine or be confined to. **3 keep oneself to oneself.** to avoid the society of others. **4 keep to oneself. 4a** (*intr*) to avoid the society of others. **4b** (*tr*) to refrain from sharing or disclosing.

keep up *vb* (*adv*) **1** (*tr*) to maintain (prices, one's morale) at the present level. **2** (*intr;* often foll. by *with*) to maintain a pace or rate set by another. **3** (*intr;* often foll. by *with*) to remain informed: *to keep up with developments.* **4** (*tr*) to maintain in good condition. **5** (*tr*) to hinder (a person) from going to bed at night. **6 keep it up.** to continue a good performance. **7 keep up with.** to remain in contact with, esp. by letter. **8 keep up with (the Joneses).** *Inf.* to compete with (one's neighbours) in material possessions, etc.

Keewatin ★ (ki:'weɪtɪn) *n* a former administrative district of the Northwest Territories of Canada stretching from the district of Mackenzie to Hudson Bay: mostly tundra: became part of Nunavut in 1999. Area: 590 930 sq. km (228 160 sq. miles).

kef (kɛf) *n* a variant spelling of **kif.**

keffiyeh (kɛ'fi:jə), **kaffiyeh,** *or* **kufiyah** *n* a cotton headdress worn by Arabs. ORIG C19: from Ar., ?from LL *cofea* COIF

Keflavík ★ ('kɛfləvɪk) *n* a port in SW Iceland: NATO airbase, fishing. Pop.: 7627 (1994).

keg (kɛg) *n* **1** a small barrel with a capacity of between five and ten gallons. **2** *Brit., Austral., & NZ.* an aluminium container in which beer is transported and stored. ORIG C17: var. of ME *kag,* of Scand. origin

Keighley ★ ('ki:θlɪ) *n* a town in N England, in Bradford unitary authority, West Yorkshire on the River Aire: textile industry. Pop.: 49 567 (1991).

Keijo ★ (ˌkeɪ'dʒəʊ) *n* transliteration of the Japanese name for **Seoul.**

Keitel ★ (*German* 'kaɪtəl) *n* **Wilhelm** ('vɪlhɛlm). 1882–1946, German field marshal; chief of the armed forces (1938–45); convicted at the Nuremberg trials and executed.

Kekkonen ★ (*Finnish* 'kɛkkɔnɛn) *n* **Urho** ('urhɔ). (1900–86), Finnish statesman; president (1956–81).

keks (kɛks) *pl n* a variant spelling of **kecks.**

Kekulé von Stradonitz ★ (*German* 'ke:kule fɔn 'ʃtra:donɪts) *n* **(Friedrich) August** ('aʊgʊst). 1829–96, German chemist. He elucidated valence and the structure of benzene (**Kekulé structure**).

Kelantan ★ (kɛ'læntən, kɪˌlæn'tæn) *n* a state of NE Malaysia: under Thai control until it came under the British in 1909; produces rice and rubber. Capital: Kota Bharu. Pop.: 1 221 700 (1993 est.). Area: 14 930 sq. km (5765 sq. miles).

Keller ★ ('kɛlə) *n* **Helen (Adams).** 1880–1968, US author and lecturer. Blind and deaf from infancy, she learned to read, write, and speak and worked for the handicapped.

Kells ★ (kɛlz) *n* a town in the Republic of Ireland, in Co. Meath: *The Book of Kells,* an illuminated manuscript of the Gospels, was produced at the monastery here in the 8th century. Pop.: 2187 (1991).

Kelly ★ ('kɛlɪ) *n* **1 Gene,** full name *Eugene Curran Kelly.* 1912–96, US dancer and film actor. His many films include *An American in Paris* (1951) and *Singin' in the Rain* (1952). **2 Grace.** 1929–82, US film actress, whose films included *High Noon* (1952) and *High Society* (1956). She married Prince Rainier III of Monaco in 1956 and died following a car crash. **3 Ned.** 1855–80, Australian horse thief and bushranger: captured by the police and hanged.

Kelman ★ ('kɛlmən) *n* **James.** born 1946, Scottish novelist; his novels include the Booker prizewinner *How Late It Was, How Late* (1994).

keloid ('ki:lɔɪd) *n Pathol.* a hard raised growth of scar tissue at the site of an injury. ORIG C19: from Gk *khēlē* claw

kelp (kɛlp) *n* **1** any large brown seaweed. **2** the ash of such seaweed, used as a source of iodine and potash. ORIG C14: from ?

kelpie[1] *or* **kelpy** ('kɛlpɪ) *n, pl* **kelpies.** an Australian breed of sheepdog having a coat of various colours and erect ears. ORIG named after a particular specimen of the breed, c. 1870

kelpie[2] ('kɛlpɪ) *n* (in Scottish folklore) a water spirit in the form of a horse. ORIG C18: prob. rel. to Scot. Gaelic *cailpeach* heifer, from ?

kelson ('kɛlsən) *n* a variant spelling of **keelson.**

kelt (kɛlt) *n* a salmon that has recently spawned. ORIG C14: from ?

Kelt (kɛlt) *n* a variant spelling of **Celt.**

kelter ('kɛltə) *n* a variant of **kilter.**

kelvin ('kɛlvɪn) *n* the basic SI unit of thermodynamic temperature; the fraction 1/273.16 of the thermodynamic temperature of the triple point of water. Symbol: K

Kelvin ★ ('kɛlvɪn) *n* **William Thomson,** 1st Baron Kelvin. 1824–1907, British physicist, noted for his work in thermodynamics and pioneering undersea telegraphy.

Kelvin scale *n* a thermodynamic temperature scale in which the zero is absolute zero. Originally the degree was equal to that on the Celsius scale but it is now defined so that the triple point of water is exactly 273.16 kelvins.

Kemal Atatürk ★ (kɛ'mɑ:l 'ætə,tɜ:k) *n* See **Atatürk.**
▸ **Ke'malism** *n* ▸ **Ke'malist** *n, adj*

Kemerovo ★ (*Russian* 'kjemɪrəvə) *n* a city in S Russia: a coal-mining centre with chemical plants. Pop.: 503 000 (1995 est.). Former name (until 1932): **Shcheglovsk.**

Kempe ★ (*German* 'kɛmpə) *n* **Rudolf** ('ru:dɔlf). 1910–76, German conductor.

Kempis ★ ('kɛmpɪs) *n* **Thomas à.** ?1380–1471, German Augustinian monk, thought to be the author of *The Imitation of Christ.*

kempt (kɛmpt) *adj* (of hair) tidy; combed. See also **unkempt.** ORIG C20: back formation from *unkempt;* orig. p.p. of dialect *kemb* to COMB

ken (kɛn) *n* **1** range of knowledge (esp. in **beyond** *or* **in one's ken**). ♦ *vb* **kens, kenning, kenned** *or* **kent. 2** *Scot. & northern English dialect.* to know. **3** *Scot. & northern English dialect.* to understand. ORIG OE *cennan*

Ken. *abbrev. for* Kentucky.

Kendal ★ ('kɛnd^əl) *n* a town in NW England, in Cumbria: a gateway town to the Lake District, with an ancient woollen industry. Pop.: 25 461 (1991).

Kendall ★ ('kɛnd^əl) *n* **Edward Calvin.** 1886–1972, US biochemist, who isolated the hormone thyroxine (1916). He shared the Nobel prize for physiology or medicine (1950).

kendo ('kɛndəʊ) *n* the Japanese art of fencing with pliable bamboo staves or, sometimes, real swords. ORIG Japanese, lit.: way of the sword, from *ken* sword + *do* way

Kendrew ★ ('kɛndru:) *n* Sir **John Cowdery.** 1917–97, British biochemist. He discovered the structure of myoglobin, for which he shared a Nobel Prize (1962) with Max Perutz.

Keneally ★ (kə'nɪəlɪ) *n* **Thomas (Michael).** born 1935, Australian writer. His novels include the Booker prizewinner *Schindler's Ark* (1982), *The Playmaker* (1987), and *Bettany's Book* (2000).

Kenilworth ★ ('kɛnɪl,wɜ:θ) *n* a town in central England, in Warwickshire: ruined 12th-century castle, subject of Sir Walter Scott's novel *Kenilworth.* Pop.: 21 623 (1991).

Kénitra ★ (*French* kenitra) *n* another name for **Mina Hassan Tani.**

Kennedy[1] ★ ('kɛnɪdɪ) *n* **Cape.** a former name (1963–73) of (Cape) **Canaveral.**

Kennedy[2] ★ ('kɛnɪdɪ) *n* **1 Charles (Peter).** born 1959, British politician; leader of the Liberal Democrats from 1999. **2 Edward (Moore),** known as *Ted.* born 1932, US Democrat politician: brother of J. F. Kennedy; senator since 1962. **3 John Fitzgerald,** known as *JFK.* 1917–63, US Democrat statesman; 35th president of the US (1961–63), the first Roman Catholic and the youngest man to be president; assassinated. **4 Nigel (Paul).** born 1956, British violinist. **5 Robert (Francis).** 1925–68, US Democrat statesman: brother of J. F. Kennedy; attorney general (1961–64) and senator for New York (1965–68); assassinated.

kennel ('kɛn^əl) *n* **1** a hutlike shelter for a dog. US name: **doghouse. 2** (*usually pl*) an establishment where dogs are bred, trained, boarded, etc. **3** a hovel. **4** a pack of hounds. ♦ *vb* **kennels, kennelling, kennelled** *or US* **kennels, kenneling, kenneled. 5** to keep or stay in a kennel. ORIG C14: from OF, from Vulgar L *canīle* (unattested), from L *canis* dog

Kennelly ★ ('kɛnəlɪ) *n* **Arthur Edwin.** 1861–1939, US electrical engineer: he predicted the existence of an ionized layer in the upper atmosphere, known as the Kennelly-Heaviside layer.

Kenneth I ★ ('kɛnɪθ) *n* surnamed *MacAlpine.* died 858, king of the Scots of Dalriada and of the Picts (?844–858): considered the first Scottish king.

kenning ('kɛnɪŋ) *n* a conventional metaphoric name for something, esp. in Old Norse and Old English poetry. ORIG C14: from ON, from *kenna;* see KEN

Kenny ★ ('kɛnɪ) *n* **Yvonne.** born 1950, Australian opera singer.

Kensington and Chelsea ★ ('kɛnzɪŋtən) *n* a borough of Greater London, on the River Thames: **Kensington Palace** (17th century) and gardens. Pop.: 151 500 (1994 est.). Area: 12 sq. km (5 sq. miles).

kenspeckle ('kɛn,spɛk^əl) *adj Scot.* easily seen or recognized. ORIG C18: from dialect *kenspeck,* of Scand. origin

Kent[1] ★ (kɛnt) *n* a county of SE England, on the English Channel: the first part of Great Britain to be colonized by the Romans; one of the seven kingdoms of Anglo-Saxon England until absorbed by Wessex in the 9th century A.D. Apart from the Downs it is mostly low-lying and agricultural, specializing in fruit and hops. In 1998 Gillingham and Rochester became an independent unitary authority, Medway. Administrative centre: Maidstone. Pop. (excluding Medway): 1 317 800 (1996 est.). Area (excluding Medway): 3526 sq. km (1361 sq. miles).
▸ **'Kentish** *adj*

Kent[2] ★ (kɛnt) *n* **William.** ?1685–1748, English architect and landscape gardener.

Kentucky ★ (kɛn'tʌkɪ) *n* **1** a state of the S central US: consists of an undulating plain in the west, the Bluegrass region in the centre, the Tennessee and Ohio River basins in the southwest, and the Appalachians in the east. Capital: Frankfort. Pop.: 3 936 499 (1998 est.). Area: 102 693 sq. km (39 650 sq. miles). Abbrevs.: **Ken., Ky.** or (with zip code) **KY 2** a river in central Kentucky, rising in the Cumberland Mountains and flowing northwest to the Ohio River. Length: 417 km (259 miles).
▸ **Ken'tuckian** *adj, n*

Kenya ★ ('kɛnjə, 'ki:njə) *n* **1** a republic in E Africa, on the Indian Ocean: became a British protectorate in 1895 and a colony in 1920; gained independence in 1963 and is a member of the Commonwealth. Coffee constitutes about a third of the total export. Official languages: Swahili and English. Religions: animist and Christian. Currency: shilling. Capital: Nairobi. Pop.: 28 809 000 (1999 est.). Area: 582 647 sq. km (224 960 sq. miles). **2 Mount.** an extinct volcano in central Kenya: the second highest mountain in Africa; girth at 2400 m (8000 ft) is about 150 km (95 miles). The regions above 3200 m (10 500 ft) constitute **Mount Kenya National Park.** Height: 5200 m (17 058 ft).
▸ **'Kenyan** *adj, n*

Kenyatta ★ (kɛn'jætə) *n* **Jomo** ('dʒəuməu). ?1891–1978, Kenyan statesman: imprisoned as a suspected leader of the Mau Mau revolt (1953–59); elected president of the Kenya African National Union (1961); prime minister of independent Kenya (1963) and president (1964–78).

Keos ★ ('keɪɒs) *n* an island in the Aegean Sea, in the NW Cyclades. Pop.: 1700 (latest est.). Area: 174 sq. km (67 sq. miles). Italian name: **Zea**. Modern Greek name: **Kéa**.

Kephallinía ★ (ˌkɛfali'nia; *English* ˌkɛfə'liːnɪə) *n* transliteration of the Modern Greek name for **Cephalonia**.

kepi ('keɪpiː) *n, pl* **kepis**. a military cap with a circular top and a horizontal peak. ORIG C19: from F *képi*, from G (Swiss dialect) *käppi* a little cap, from *kappe* CAP

Kepler ★ ('kɛplə) *n* **Johannes** (jo'hanəs). 1571–1630, German astronomer. As discoverer of Kepler's laws he is regarded as one of the founders of modern astronomy.

Kepler's laws *pl n* three laws of planetary motion published by Johan Kepler between 1609 and 1619. They deal with the shape of a planet's orbit, the constant velocity of the planet in orbit, and the relationship between the length of a planetary year and the distance from the sun.

kept (kɛpt) *vb* **1** the past tense and past participle of **keep**. **2 kept woman.** *Derog.* a woman maintained by a man as his mistress.

Kerala ★ ('kɛrələ, kə'rɑːlə) *n* a state of SW India, on the Arabian Sea: formed in 1956, it includes the former state of Travancore-Cochin; has the highest population density of any Indian state. Capital: Trivandrum. Pop.: 30 555 000 (1994 est.). Area: 38 863 sq. km (15 005 sq. miles).

keratin ('kɛrətɪn) *n* a fibrous protein that occurs in the outer layer of the skin and in hair, nails, hooves, etc.

keratose ('kɛrəˌtəus, -ˌtəuz) *adj* (esp. of certain sponges) having a horny skeleton. ORIG C19: from Gk *keras* horn + -OSE[1]

kerb *or US & Canad.* **curb** (kɜːb) *n* a line of stone or concrete forming an edge between a pavement and a roadway. ORIG C17: from OF *courbe* bent, from L *curvus;* see CURVE
▸ **'kerbing** *n*

kerb crawling *n* the act of driving slowly beside the pavement seeking to entice someone into the car for sexual purposes.
▸ **kerb crawler** *n*

kerb drill *n* a pedestrian's procedure for crossing a road safely, esp. as taught to children.

Kerbela ★ ('kɜːbələ) *n* a variant of **Karbala**.

kerbstone *or US & Canad.* **curbstone** ('kɜːbˌstəun) *n* one of a series of stones that form a kerb.

Kerch ★ (*Russian* kjertʃ) *n* a port in S Ukraine, on the **Kerch Peninsula** and the **Strait of Kerch** (linking the Black Sea with the Sea of Azov): founded as a Greek colony in the 6th century B.C.; ceded to Russia in 1774; iron-mining, steel production, and fishing. Pop.: 175 000 (1996 est.).

kerchief ('kɜːtʃɪf) *n* a piece of cloth worn over the head. ORIG C13: from OF, from *covrir* to COVER + *chef* head
▸ **'kerchiefed** *adj*

kerel ('kɛərəl) *n S. African.* a young man. ORIG from Afrik. *kêrel;* cf. OE *ceorl*

Kerenski *or* **Kerensky** ★ (kə'rɛnskɪ; *Russian* 'kjerɪnskij) *n* **Aleksandr Fyodorovich** (alɪk'sandr 'fjɔdərəvitʃ). 1881–1970, Russian liberal revolutionary leader; prime minister (July–October 1917): overthrown by the Bolsheviks.

kerf (kɜːf) *n* the cut made by a saw, an axe, etc. ORIG OE *cyrf* a cutting

kerfuffle (kə'fʌfᵊl) *n Inf., chiefly Brit.* commotion; disorder. ORIG from Scot. *curfuffle, carfuffle,* from Scot. Gaelic *car* twist, turn + *fuffle* to disarrange

Kerguelen ★ ('kɜːgɪlɪn) *n* an archipelago in the S Indian Ocean: consists of one large volcanic island (Kerguelen or Desolation Island) and 300 small islands; part of the French Southern and Antarctic Territories.

Kerkrade ★ (*Dutch* 'kɛrkraːdə) *n* a town in the SE Netherlands, in Limburg: one of the oldest coal-mining centres in Europe. Pop.: 52 848 (1994).

Kérkyra ★ ('kɛrkira) *n* transliteration of the Modern Greek name for **Corfu**.

Kerman ★ (kə'mɑːn) *n* a city in SE Iran: carpet-making centre. Pop.: 349 626 (1994 est.).

Kermanshah ★ (ˌkɜːmæn'ʃɑː) *n* the former name (until 1987) of **Bakhtaran**.

kermes ('kɜːmɪz) *n* **1** the dried bodies of female scale insects used as a red dyestuff. **2** a small evergreen Eurasian oak tree: the host plant of kermes scale insects. ORIG C16: from F, from Ar. *qirmiz,* from Sansk. *krmija-* red dye, lit.: produced by a worm

kermis *or* **kirmess** ('kɜːmɪs) *n* **1** (formerly, esp. in Holland and northern Germany) an annual country festival. **2** *US & Canad.* a similar event held to collect money for charity. ORIG C16: from MDu., from *kerc* church + *misse* MASS; orig. a festival held to celebrate the dedication of a church

kern[1] *or* **kerne** (kɜːn) *n* the part of the character on a piece of printer's type that projects beyond the body. ORIG C17: from F *carne* corner of type, ult. from L *cardō* hinge

kern[2] (kɜːn) *n* **1** a lightly armed foot soldier in medieval Ireland or Scotland. **2** *Arch.* a loutish peasant. ORIG C14: from MIrish *cethern* band of foot soldiers, from *cath* battle

Kern ★ (kɜːn) *n* **Jerome (David)**. 1885–1945, US songwriter and composer of musicals, including *Show Boat* (1927).

kernel ('kɜːnᵊl) *n* **1** the edible seed of a nut or fruit within the shell or stone. **2** the grain of a cereal, esp. wheat, consisting of the seed in a hard husk. **3** the central or essential part of something. ORIG OE *cyrnel* a little seed, from *corn* seed
▸ **'kernel-less** *adj*

kerosene *or* **kerosine** ('kɛrəˌsiːn) *n* **1** another name (esp. US, Canad., Austral., & NZ) for **paraffin** (sense 1). **2** the general name for paraffin as a fuel for jet aircraft. ORIG C19: from Gk *kēros* wax + -ENE

> **USAGE NOTE** The spelling *kerosine* is now the preferred form in technical and industrial usage.

Kerouac ★ ('kɛruˌæk) *n* **Jack**, real name *Jean-Louis Lebris de Kérouac*. 1922–69, US novelist and poet of the Beat Generation. His works include *On the Road* (1957) and *Big Sur* (1962).

Kerr ★ (kɜː) *n* Sir **John Robert**. 1914–91, Australian public servant. As governor general of Australia (1974–77), he dismissed the Labor prime minister Gough Whitlam (1975).

Kerry ★ ('kɛrɪ) *n* a county of SW Republic of Ireland, in W Munster province: mostly mountainous (including the highest peaks in Ireland), with a deeply indented coast and many offshore islands. County town: Tralee. Pop.: 126 000 (1996). Area: 4701 sq. km (1815 sq. miles).

kersey ('kɜːzɪ) *n* a twilled woollen cloth with a cotton warp. ORIG C14: prob. from *Kersey,* village in Suffolk

kerseymere ('kɜːzɪˌmɪə) *n* a fine soft woollen cloth of twill weave. ORIG C18: from KERSEY + *(cassi)mere,* var. of CASHMERE

Kesey ★ ('kiːzɪ) *n* **Ken**. born 1935, US novelist, best known for *One Flew Over the Cuckoo's Nest* (1962).

Kesselring ★ ('kɛsᵊlrɪŋ) *n* **Albert** ('albɛrt). 1885–1960, German field marshal. He commanded the Luftwaffe (1939–40), and was supreme commander in Italy (1943–45) and on the western front (1945).

Kesteven ★ ('kɛstɪvᵊn, kɛ'stiːvᵊn) *n* **Parts of.** an area in E England constituting a former administrative division of Lincolnshire.

kestrel ('kɛstrəl) *n* any of several small falcons that feed on small mammals and tend to hover against the wind. ORIG C15: changed from OF *cresserele,* from *cressele* rattle, from Vulgar L *crepicella* (unattested), from L, from *crepāre* to rustle

Keswick ★ (ˈkɛzɪk) *n* a market town in NW England, in Cumbria in the Lake District: tourist centre. Pop.: 4836 (1991).

ketch (kɛtʃ) *n* a two-masted sailing vessel, fore-and-aft rigged, with a tall mainmast. ORIG C15 *cache,* prob. from *cacchen* to hunt; see CATCH

ketchup (ˈkɛtʃəp), **catchup,** *or* **catsup** *n* any of various sauces containing vinegar: *tomato ketchup.* ORIG C18: from Chinese *kōetsiap* brine of pickled fish, from *kōe* seafood + *tsiap* sauce

ketone (ˈkiːtəʊn) *n* any of a class of compounds with the general formula R′COR, where R and R′ are alkyl or aryl groups. ORIG C19: from G, from *Aketon* ACETONE
▸ **ketonic** (kɪˈtɒnɪk) *adj*

ketone body *n Biochem.* any of three compounds produced when fatty acids are broken down in the liver to provide a source of energy. Excess ketone bodies are present in the blood and urine of people unable to use glucose as an energy source, as in diabetes.

Kettering ★ (ˈkɛtərɪŋ) *n* a town in central England, in Northamptonshire: footwear industry. Pop.: 47 186 (1991).

kettle (ˈkɛtᵊl) *n* **1** a metal container with a handle and spout for boiling water. **2** any of various metal containers for heating liquids, cooking fish, etc. **3** a large metal vessel designed to withstand high temperatures, used in various industrial processes such as refining and brewing. ORIG C13: from ON *ketill,* ult. from L *catillus* a little pot, from *catīnus* pot

kettledrum (ˈkɛtᵊlˌdrʌm) *n* a percussion instrument of definite pitch, consisting of a hollow bowl-like hemisphere covered with a skin or membrane, supported on a tripod. The pitch may be adjusted by means of screws, which alter the tension of the skin.
▸ **ˈkettleˌdrummer** *n*

kettle hole *n* a round hollow formed by the melting of a mass of buried ice.

kettle of fish *n* **1** a situation; state of affairs (often used ironically in **a pretty** *or* **fine kettle of fish**). **2** case; matter for consideration: *that's quite a different kettle of fish.*

Kevlar (ˈkɛvˌlɑː) *n Trademark.* a synthetic fibre, consisting of long-chain polyamides, having high tensile strength and temperature resistance.

Kew ★ (kjuː) *n* part of the Greater London borough of Richmond-upon-Thames, on the River Thames: famous for **Kew Gardens** (the Royal Botanic Gardens), established in 1759 and given to the nation in 1841.

key¹ (kiː) *n* **1** a metal instrument, usually of a specifically contoured shape, that is made to fit a lock and, when rotated, operates the lock's mechanism. **2** any instrument that is rotated to operate a valve, clock winding mechanism, etc. **3** a small metal peg or wedge inserted to prevent relative motion. **4** any of a set of buttons operating a typewriter, computer, etc. **5** any of the visible parts of the lever mechanism of a musical keyboard instrument that when depressed cause the instrument to sound. **6a** Also called: **tonality.** any of the 24 major and minor diatonic scales considered as a corpus of notes upon which a piece of music draws for its tonal framework. **6b** the main tonal centre in an extended composition: *a symphony in the key of F major.* **7** something that is crucial in providing an explanation or interpretation. **8** (*modifier*) of great importance: *a key issue.* **9** a means of achieving a desired end: *the key to happiness.* **10** a means of access or control: *Gibraltar is the key to the Mediterranean.* **11** a list of explanations of symbols, codes, etc. **12** a text that explains or gives information about a work of literature, art, or music. **13** *Electrical engineering.* a hand-operated switch that is pressed to transmit coded signals, esp. Morse code. **14** the grooving or scratching of a surface or the application of a rough coat of plaster, etc., to provide a bond for a subsequent finish. **15** pitch: *he spoke in a low key.* **16** a mood or style: *a poem in a melancholic key.* **17** short for **keystone** (sense 1). **18** *Bot.* any dry winged fruit, esp. that of the ash. ◆ *vb* (*mainly tr*) **19** (foll. by *to*) to harmonize (with): *to key one's actions to the prevailing mood.* **20** to adjust or fasten with a key or some similar device. **21** to provide with a key or keys. **22** (*also intr*) another word for **keyboard** (sense 3). **23** to include a distinguishing device in (an advertisement, etc.), so that responses to it can be identified. **24** (*also intr*) to groove, scratch, or apply a rough coat of plaster, etc., to (a surface) to provide a bond for a subsequent finish. ◆ See also **key in, key up.** ORIG OE *cǣg*
▸ **ˈkeyless** *adj*

key² (kiː) *n* a variant spelling of **cay.**

keyboard (ˈkiːˌbɔːd) *n* **1a** a set of keys, usually hand-operated, as on a piano, typewriter, or typesetting machine. **1b** (*as modifier*): *a keyboard instrument.* **2** (*pl*) electronic keyboard instruments: *John plays keyboards for the band.* ◆ *vb* **3** (*tr*) to set (a text) in type by using a keyboard machine.
▸ **ˈkeyˌboarder** *n*

key grip *n* the person in charge of moving and setting up camera tracks and scenery in a film or television studio.

keyhole (ˈkiːˌhəʊl) *n* an aperture in a door or a lock case through which a key may be passed to engage the lock mechanism.

keyhole surgery *n* surgery carried out through a very small incision.

key in *vb* (*tr, adv*) to enter (information or instructions) in a computer or other device by means of a keyboard or keypad.

key-man assurance *n* an assurance policy taken out, esp. by a small company, on the life of a senior executive whose death would create a serious loss.

key money *n* a fee payment required from a new tenant of a house or flat before he moves in.

Keynes ★ (keɪnz) *n* **John Maynard,** 1st Baron Keynes. 1883–1946, British economist. His most influential work was *The General Theory of Employment, Interest and Money* (1936). He helped to found the International Monetary Fund and the World Bank.
▸ **ˈKeynesian** *adj, n* ▸ **ˈKeynesianˌism** *n*

keynote (ˈkiːˌnəʊt) *n* **1a** a central or determining principle in a speech, literary work, etc. **1b** (*as modifier*): *a keynote speech.* **2** the note upon which a scale or key is based; tonic. ◆ *vb* **keynotes, keynoting, keynoted.** (*tr*) **3** to deliver a keynote address to (a political convention, etc.).

keypad (ˈkiːˌpæd) *n* a small panel with a set of buttons for operating a teletext system, electronic calculator, etc.

key punch *n* **1** Also called: **card punch.** a device having a keyboard that is operated manually to transfer data onto punched cards, paper tape, etc. ◆ *vb* **key-punch. 2** to transfer (data) by using a key punch.

key signature *n Music.* a group of sharps or flats appearing at the beginning of each stave line to indicate the key in which a piece, section, etc., is to be performed.

key stage *n Brit. education.* any one of four broad age-group divisions (5–7; 7–11; 11–14; 14–16) to which each level of the National Curriculum applies.

keystone (ˈkiːˌstəʊn) *n* **1** the central stone at the top of an arch or the top stone of a dome or vault. **2** something that is necessary to connect other related things.

key up *vb* (*tr, adv*) to raise the intensity, excitement, tension, etc., of.

kg 1 *abbrev. for* keg. ◆ **2** *symbol for* kilogram.

KG *abbrev. for* Knight of the Order of the Garter (a Brit. title).

KGB *abbrev. for* the former Soviet secret police, founded in 1954. ORIG from Russian *Komitet gosudarstvennoi bezopasnosti* State Security Committee

Khabarovsk ★ (*Russian* xaˈbarəfsk) *n* a port in E Russia, on the Amur River: the administrative centre of the whole Soviet Far Eastern territory until 1938; a major industrial centre. Pop.: 618 000 (1995 est.).

Khachaturian ★ (ˌkɑːtʃəˈtʊərɪən; *Russian* xətʃətuˈrjan) *n* **Aram Ilich** (ˈarəm iljˈjitʃ). 1903–78, Russian composer. His works include a piano concerto and the ballets *Gayaneh* (1942) and *Spartacus* (1954).

khaddar (ˈkɑːdə) *or* **khadi** (ˈkɑːdɪ) *n* a cotton cloth of plain weave, produced in India. ORIG from Hindi *khādar*

Khakass Republic ★ (kəˈkæs) *n* a constituent republic of S central Russia, in the Krasnoyarsk Territory: formed in 1930. Capital: Abakan. Pop.: 586 000 (1996 est.). Area: 61 900 sq. km (23 855 sq. miles). Also called: **Khakassia** (kəˈkæsɪə; *Russian* xəˈkasɪjə).

khaki (ˈkɑːkɪ) *n, pl* **khakis.** **1** a dull yellowish-brown colour. **2a** a hard-wearing fabric of this colour, used esp. for military uniforms. **2b** (*as modifier*): *a khaki jacket.* ORIG C19: from Urdu, from Persian: dusty, from *khāk* dust

Khalid ibn Abdul Aziz ★ (ˈkɑːlɪd ˈɪbᵊn ˈæbdʊl əˈziːz) *n* 1913–82, king and President of the Council of Ministers of Saudi Arabia (1975–82).

khalif (ˈkeɪlɪf) *n* a variant spelling of **caliph.**

Khalkidíki ★ (xalkiðiˈki) *n* transliteration of the Modern Greek name for **Chalcidice.**

Khalkís ★ (xalˈkis) *n* transliteration of the Modern Greek name for **Chalcis.**

Khalsa (ˈkælsə) *n* an order of the Sikh religion, founded (1699) by Guru Gobind Singh.

Khama ★ (ˈkɑːmə) *n* Sir **Seretse** (səˈrɛtsɪ). 1921–80, Botswanan statesman; first president of Botswana (1966–80).

khan[1] (kɑːn) *n* **1a** (formerly) a title borne by medieval Chinese emperors and Mongol and Turkic rulers. **1b** such a ruler. **2** a title of respect borne by important personages in Afghanistan and central Asia. ORIG C14: from OF, from Med. L, from Turkish *khān,* contraction of *khāqān* ruler
▸ **ˈkhanate** *n*

khan[2] (kɑːn) *n* an inn in Turkey, etc.; caravanserai. ORIG C14: via Ar. from Persian

Khan ★ (kɑːn) *n* **Imran.** See **Imran Khan.**

Khaniá ★ (xaˈnja) *n* transliteration of the Modern Greek name for **Canea.**

Kharkov ★ (*Russian* ˈxarjkəf) *n* a city in E Ukraine: capital of the Ukrainian Soviet Socialist Republic from 1917 until 1934; university (1805). Pop.: 1 555 000 (1996 est.).

Khartoum *or* **Khartum** ★ (kɑːˈtuːm) *n* the capital of the Sudan, at the junction of the Blue and the White Nile: with adjoining Khartoum North and Omdurman, the largest conurbation in the country; destroyed by the Mahdists in 1885 when General Gordon was killed; seat of the Anglo-Egyptian government of the Sudan until 1954, then capital of the new republic. Pop.: 924 505 (1993).

Khayyám ★ (kaɪˈɑːm) *n* **Omar.** See **Omar Khayyám.**

khedive (kɪˈdiːv) *n* the viceroy of Egypt under Ottoman suzerainty (1867–1914). ORIG C19: from F, from Turkish, from Persian *khidīw* prince
▸ **kheˈdival** *or* **kheˈdivial** *adj*

Khelat ★ (kəˈlɑːt) *n* a variant spelling of **Kalat.**

Kherson ★ (*Russian* xɪrˈsɔn) *n* a port in S Ukraine, on the Dnieper River near the Black Sea: shipyards. Pop.: 363 000 (1996 est.).

Khingan Mountains ★ (ˈʃɪŋˈɑːn) *pl n* a mountain system of NE China, in W Manchuria. Highest peak: 2034 m (6673 ft).

Khíos ★ (ˈçiɔs) *n* transliteration of the Modern Greek name for **Chios.**

Khirbet Qumran ★ (ˈkɪəbɛt ˈkʊmrɑːn) *n* an archaeological site in NW Jordan, near the NW shore of the Dead Sea: includes the caves where the Dead Sea Scrolls were found.

Khmer (kmɛə) *n* **1** a member of a people of Cambodia, noted for a civilization that flourished from about 800 A.D. to about 1370. **2** the language of this people: the official language of Cambodia. ◆ *adj* **3** of or relating to this people or their language.
▸ **ˈKhmerian** *adj*

Khmer Republic ★ *n* the former official name (1970–76) of **Cambodia.**

Khoikhoi (kɔɪˈkɔɪ *or* xɔɪˈxɔɪ) *n* **1** a member of a Southern African people who formerly occupied the region around the Cape of Good Hope and are now almost extinct. **2** any of the languages of this people.

Khojent, Khodzhent (*Russian* xadˈʒɛnt), *or* **Khujand** ★ (*Russian* xuˈʃænd) *n* a town in Tajikistan, on the Syr Darya River: one of the oldest towns in central Asia; textile industries. Pop.: 164 500 (1991 est.). Former name (1936–91) **Leninabad.**

Khomeini ★ (ˈxɔmeɪˈniː) *n* **Ruholla** (ˈruhɒˈlɑː), known as *Ayatollah Khomeini.* 1900–89, Iranian Shiite Muslim religious leader. Following the overthrow of the shah of Iran (1979) he returned from exile and instituted an Islamic republic. His rule saw deteriorating relations with the West and war (1980–88) with Iraq.

Khotan ★ (ˈkəʊˈtɑːn) *n* another name for **Hotan.**

Khrushchev ★ (kruːsˈtʃɒf, ˈkrʊstʃɒf; *Russian* xruˈʃtʃɔf) *n* **Nikita Sergeyevich** (niˈkitə sɪrˈgjejɪvitʃ). 1894–1971, Soviet statesman; premier of the Soviet Union (1958–64), when he pursued a policy of peaceful coexistence with the West, but alienated Communist China. He was removed from office in 1964.

Khufu ★ (ˈkuːfuː) *n* the original name of **Cheops.**

Khulna ★ (ˈkʊlnɑː) *n* a city in S Bangladesh. Pop.: 731 000 (1991).

Khyber Pass ★ (ˈkaɪbə) *n* a narrow pass over the Safed Koh Range between Afghanistan and Pakistan, over which came the Persian, Greek, Tatar, Mogul, and Afghan invasions of India; scene of bitter fighting between the British and Afghans (1838–42, 1878–80). Length: about 53 km (33 miles). Highest point: 1072 m (3518 ft).

kHz *symbol for* kilohertz.

kiang (kɪˈæŋ) *n* a variety of the wild ass that occurs in Tibet and surrounding regions. ORIG C19: from Tibetan *rkyan*

Kiangsi ★ (ˈkjæŋˈsiː) *n* a variant transliteration of the Chinese name for **Jiangxi.**

Kiangsu ★ (ˈkjæŋˈsuː) *n* a variant transliteration of the Chinese name for **Jiangsu.**

Kiaochow ★ (ˈkjaʊˈtʃaʊ) *n* a variant transliteration of the Chinese name for **Jiazhou.**

kia ora (ˌkɪə ˈɔːrə) *sentence substitute. NZ.* greetings! good luck! ORIG Maori, lit.: be well!

kibble[1] (ˈkɪbᵊl) *n Brit.* a bucket used in wells or in mining for hoisting. ORIG C17: from G *kübel,* ult. from Med. L *cuppa* CUP

kibble[2] (ˈkɪbᵊl) *vb* **kibbles, kibbling, kibbled.** (*tr*) to grind into small pieces. ORIG C18: from ?

kibbutz (kɪˈbʊts) *n, pl* **kibbutzim** (ˌkɪbʊtˈsiːm). a collective agricultural settlement in modern Israel, owned and administered communally by its members. ORIG C20: from Mod. Heb. *qibbūs* gathering, from Heb. *qibbūtz*

kibe (kaɪb) *n* a chilblain, esp. an ulcerated one on the heel. ORIG C14: prob. from Welsh *cibi,* from ?

kibi- (ˈkɪbɪ) *prefix Computing.* denoting 2^{10}: *kibibyte.* Symbol: Ki ORIG C20: from KI(LO-) + BI(NARY)

> **USAGE NOTE** See at **kilo-.**

kiblah (ˈkɪblɑː) *n Islam.* the direction of Mecca, to which Muslims turn in prayer. ORIG C18: from Ar. *qiblah* that which is placed opposite

kibosh (ˈkaɪˌbɒʃ) *n* **put the kibosh on.** *Sl.* to put a stop to; prevent from continuing; halt. ORIG C19: from ?

kick (kɪk) *vb* **1** (*tr*) to drive or impel with the foot. **2** (*tr*) to hit with the foot or feet. **3** (*intr*) to strike out or thrash about with the feet, as in fighting or swimming. **4** (*intr*) to raise a leg high, as in dancing. **5** (of a gun, etc.) to recoil or strike in recoiling when fired. **6** (*tr*) *Rugby.* to make (a conversion or a drop goal) by means of a kick. **7** (*tr*) *Soccer.* to score (a goal) by a kick. **8** (*intr*) *Athletics.* to put on a sudden spurt. **9** (*intr*) to make a sudden violent movement. **10** (*intr;* sometimes foll. by *against*) *Inf.* to object or resist. **11** (*intr*) *Inf.* to be active and in good health (esp. in **alive and kicking**). **12** *Inf.* to change gear in (a car): *he kicked into third.* **13** (*tr*) *Inf.* to free oneself of (an addiction, etc.): *he tried to kick the habit.* **14 kick up one's heels.** *Inf.* to enjoy oneself without inhibition. ◆ *n* **15** a thrust or blow with the foot. **16** any of certain rhythmic leg movements used in swimming. **17** the recoil of a gun or

other firearm. **18** *Inf.* exciting quality or effect (esp. in **get a kick out of, for kicks**). **19** *Athletics.* a sudden spurt, acceleration, or boost. **20** a sudden violent movement. **21** *Inf.* the sudden stimulating effect of strong alcoholic drink or certain drugs. **22** *Inf.* power or force. **23 kick in the teeth.** *Sl.* a humiliating rebuff. ◆ See also **kick about, kickback,** etc. ORIG C14 *kiken,* ?from ON
▸ **'kickable** *adj*

kick about *or* **around** *vb (mainly adv) Inf.* **1** *(tr)* to treat harshly. **2** *(tr)* to discuss (ideas, etc.) informally. **3** *(intr)* to wander aimlessly. **4** *(intr)* to lie neglected or forgotten.

kickback ('kɪk,bæk) *n* **1** a strong reaction. **2** part of an income paid to a person in return for an opportunity to make a profit, often by some illegal arrangement. ◆ *vb* **kick back.** *(adv)* **3** *(intr)* to have a strong reaction. **4** *(intr)* (esp. of a gun) to recoil. **5** to pay a kickback to (someone).

kick boxing *n* a martial art that resembles boxing but permits blows with the feet as well as punches.

kickdown ('kɪk,daʊn) *n* a method of changing gear in a car with automatic transmission, by fully depressing the accelerator.

kicker ('kɪkə) *n* **1** a person or thing that kicks. **2** *US & Canad. sl.* a hidden and disadvantageous factor.

kick in *vb (adv)* **1** *(intr)* to start or become activated. **2** *(tr) Chiefly Austral. & NZ inf.* to contribute.

kick off *vb (intr, adv)* **1** to start play in a game of football by kicking the ball from the centre of the field. **2** *Inf.* to commence (a discussion, job, etc.). ◆ *n* **kickoff. 3a** a place kick from the centre of the field in a game of football. **3b** the time at which the first such kick is due to take place.

kick on *vb (adv) Inf.* to continue.

kick out *vb (tr, adv) Inf.* to eject or dismiss.

kickshaw ('kɪk,ʃɔː) *or* **kickshaws** *n* **1** a valueless trinket. **2** *Arch.* a small exotic delicacy. ORIG C16: back formation from *kickshaws,* by folk etymology from F *quelque chose* something

kickstand ('kɪk,stænd) *n* a short metal bar attached to the frame of a motorcycle or bicycle, which when kicked into a vertical position holds the stationary vehicle upright.

kick-start ('kɪk,stɑːt) *vb (tr)* **1** to start (an engine, esp. of a motorcycle) by means of a pedal that is kicked downwards. **2** *Inf.* to make (something) active, functional, or productive again. ◆ *n* **3** an action or event resulting in the reactivation of something.
▸ **'kick-,starter** *n*

kick up *vb (adv) Inf.* to cause (trouble, etc.).

kick upstairs *vb (tr, adv) Inf.* to promote to a higher but effectively powerless position.

kid[1] (kɪd) *n* **1** the young of a goat or of a related animal, such as an antelope. **2** soft smooth leather made from the hide of a kid. **3** *Inf.* **3a** a young person; child. **3b** *(modifier)* younger or being still a child: *kid brother.* ◆ *vb* **kids, kidding, kidded. 4** (of a goat) to give birth to (young). ORIG C12: from ON
▸ **'kiddishness** *n* ▸ **'kid,like** *adj*

kid[2] (kɪd) *vb* **kids, kidding, kidded.** *Inf.* (sometimes foll. by *on* or *along*) **1** *(tr)* to tease or deceive for fun. **2** *(intr)* to behave or speak deceptively for fun. **3** *(tr)* to fool (oneself) into believing (something): *don't kid yourself that no-one else knows.* ORIG C19: prob. from KID[1]
▸ **'kidder** *n* ▸ **'kiddingly** *adv*

Kid ★ (kɪd) *n* **Thomas.** a variant spelling of (Thomas) **Kyd.**

Kidd ★ (kɪd) *n* **William,** known as *Captain Kidd.* 1645–1701, Scottish pirate and murderer; hanged.

Kidderminster ★ ('kɪdə,mɪnstə) *n* **1** a town in W central England, in NE Hereford and Worcester on the River Stour: carpet industry. Pop.: 54 644 (1991). **2** a type of ingrain reversible carpet originally made at Kidderminster.

kiddy *or* **kiddie** ('kɪdɪ) *n, pl* **kiddies.** *Inf.* an affectionate word for **child.**

kid glove *n* **1** a glove made of kidskin. **2 handle with kid gloves.** to treat with great tact or caution. ◆ *adj* **kidglove. 3** overdelicate. **4** diplomatic; tactful: *a kidglove approach.*

Kidman ★ ('kɪdmən) *n* **Nicole (Mary)** (nɪ'kɒl). born 1967, Australian actress; her films include *To Die For* (1995), *The Portrait of a Lady* (1996), and *Eyes Wide Shut* (1999); she was married to Tom Cruise.

kidnap ('kɪdnæp) *vb* **kidnaps, kidnapping, kidnapped** *or US* **kidnaps, kidnaping, kidnaped.** *(tr)* to carry off and hold (a person), usually for ransom. ORIG C17: KID[1] + obs. *nap* to steal; see NAB
▸ **'kidnapper** *n*

kidney ('kɪdnɪ) *n* **1** either of two bean-shaped organs at the back of the abdominal cavity in man. They filter waste products from the blood, which are excreted as urine. Related adj: **renal. 2** the corresponding organ in other animals. **3** the kidneys of certain animals used as food. **4** class, type, or disposition (esp. in **of the same** *or* **a different kidney**). ORIG C14: from ?

kidney bean *n* **1** any of certain bean plants having kidney-shaped seeds, esp. the scarlet runner. **2** the seed of any of these beans.

kidney machine *n* a machine carrying out the functions of a kidney, esp. used in haemodialysis.

kidney stone *n* **1** *Pathol.* a hard mass formed in the kidney, usually composed of oxalates, phosphates, and carbonates. **2** *Mineralogy.* another name for **nephrite.**

kidology (kɪ'dɒlədʒɪ) *n Brit. inf.* the practice of bluffing or deception. ORIG C20: from KID[2] + *ology* a science

Kidron ★ ('kiːdrən) *n* a variant of **Kedron.**

kidskin ('kɪd,skɪn) *n* a soft smooth leather made from the hide of a young goat. Often shortened to **kid.**

kids' stuff *n Sl.* **1** something considered fit only for children. **2** something considered easy.

kidstakes ('kɪd,steɪks) *pl n Austral. inf.* pretence; nonsense: *cut the kidstakes!*

kie kie ('kiːɛ kiːɛ) *n* a New Zealand climbing plant with edible bracts. ORIG from Maori

Kiel ★ (kiːl) *n* a port in N Germany, capital of Schleswig-Holstein state, on the **Kiel Canal** (connecting the North Sea with the Baltic): joined the Hanseatic League in 1284; became part of Denmark in 1773 and passed to Prussia in 1866; an important naval base in World Wars I and II; shipbuilding and engineering industries. Pop.: 246 033 (1996 est.).

Kielce ★ (*Polish* 'kjɛltsɛ) *n* an industrial city in S Poland. Pop.: 213 800 (1995 est.).

Kierkegaard ★ ('kɪəkə,gɑːd; *Danish* 'kirgəgɔːr) *n* **Søren Aabye** ('søːrən 'ɔːby). 1813–55, Danish philosopher, who rejected organized Christianity and anticipated the existentialists. His works include *Either/Or* (1843) and *The Sickness unto Death* (1849).
▸ **,Kierke'gaardian** *adj*

kieselguhr ('kiːzᵊl,gʊə) *n* an unconsolidated form of diatomite. ORIG C19: from G *Kieselgur,* from *Kiesel* flint + *Gur* loose earthy deposit

Kiev ★ ('kiːɛf; *Russian* 'kijɪf) *n* the capital of Ukraine, on the Dnieper River: formed the first Russian state by the late 9th century; university (1834). Pop.: 2 630 000 (1996 est.).

kif (kɪf, kiːf), **kef,** *or* **kief** (kiːf) *n* **1** another name for **marijuana. 2** any drug that when smoked is capable of producing a euphoric condition. **3** the euphoric condition produced by smoking marijuana. ORIG C20: from Ar. *kayf* pleasure

Kigali ★ (kɪ'gɑːlɪ) *n* the capital of Rwanda, in the central part. Pop.: 232 733 (1991).

kike (kaɪk) *n US & Canad. sl.* an offensive word for **Jew.** ORIG C20: prob. var. of *kiki,* reduplication of *-ki,* common name-ending among Jews from Slavic countries

Kikládhes ★ (ki'klaðɛs) *n* transliteration of the Modern Greek name for **Cyclades.**

Kilauea ★ (,kiːlɑːuː'eɪə) *n* a crater on the E side of Mauna Loa volcano, on SE Hawaii Island: the world's largest active crater. Height: 1247 m (4090 ft). Width: 3 km (2 miles).

Kildare ★ (kɪl'dɛə) *n* a county of E Republic of Ireland, in Leinster province: mostly low-lying and fertile. County town: Naas. Pop.: 135 000 (1996). Area: 1694 sq. km (654 sq. miles).

kilderkin ('kɪldəkɪn) *n* **1** an obsolete unit of liquid capacity equal to 16 or 18 Imperial gallons or of dry capacity equal to 16 or 18 wine gallons. **2** a cask capable of holding a kilderkin. ORIG C14: from MDu. *kindekijn,* from *kintal* hundredweight, from Med. L *quintale*

kilim (kɪ'liːm, 'kiːlɪm) *n* a pileless woven rug of intricate design made in the Middle East. ORIG C19: from Turkish, from Persian *kilīm*

Kilimanjaro ★ (ˌkɪlɪmən'dʒɑːrəʊ) *n* a volcanic massif in N Tanzania: the highest peak in Africa; extends from east to west for 80 km (50 miles). Height: 5895 m (19 340 ft).

Kilkenny ★ (kɪl'kɛnɪ) *n* **1** a county of SE Republic of Ireland, in Leinster province: mostly agricultural. County town: Kilkenny. Pop.: 75 000 (1996). Area: 2062 sq. km (796 sq. miles). **2** a market town in SE Republic of Ireland, county town of Co. Kilkenny: capital of the ancient kingdom of Ossory. Pop.: 9500 (latest est.).

kill (kɪl) *vb (mainly tr)* **1** *(also intr;* when *tr,* sometimes foll. by *off)* to cause the death of (a person or animal). **2** to put an end to: *to kill someone's interest.* **3** to occupy (time) by doing something unimportant, esp. while waiting for something. **4** to deaden (sound). **5** *Inf.* to tire out: *the effort killed him.* **6** *Inf.* to cause to suffer pain or discomfort: *my shoes are killing me.* **7** *Inf.* to quash or veto: *the bill was killed in the House of Lords.* **8** *Inf.* to switch off; stop. **9** *(also intr) Inf.* to overcome with attraction, laughter, surprise, etc.: *she was dressed to kill.* **10** *Tennis, squash, etc.* to hit (a ball) so hard or so accurately that the opponent cannot return it. **11** *Soccer.* to bring (a moving ball) under control. **12 kill oneself.** *Inf.* to overexert oneself: *don't kill yourself.* **13 kill two birds with one stone.** to achieve two results with one action. ◆ *n* **14** the act of causing death, esp. at the end of a hunt, bullfight, etc. **15** the animal or animals killed during a hunt. **16** *NZ.* a seasonal tally of the number of stock killed at a meatworks. **17** the destruction of a battleship, tank, etc. **18 in at the kill.** present at the end of some undertaking. ORIG C13 *cullen;* see QUELL

Killarney ★ (kɪ'lɑːnɪ) *n* a town in SW Republic of Ireland, in Co. Kerry: a tourist centre near the **Lakes of Killarney.** Pop.: 7250 (1991).

killdeer ('kɪlˌdɪə) *n, pl* **killdeer** *or* **killdeers.** a large brown-and-white North American plover with two black breast bands. ORIG C18: imit.

killer ('kɪlə) *n* **1a** a person or animal that kills, esp. habitually. **1b** *(as modifier): a killer shark.* **2** something, esp. a task or activity, that is particularly taxing or exhausting. **3** *Austral. & NZ.* a farm animal selected to be killed for food.

killer bee *n* an African honeybee, or one of its hybrids originating in Brazil, that is extremely aggressive when disturbed.

killer cell *n* a type of white blood cell that is able to kill cells, such as cancer cells and cells infected with viruses.

killer whale *n* a predatory black-and-white toothed whale most common in cold seas.

killick ('kɪlɪk) *or* **killock** ('kɪlək) *n Naut.* a small anchor, esp. one made of a heavy stone. ORIG C17: from ?

Killiecrankie ★ (ˌkɪlɪ'kræŋkɪ) *n* a pass in central Scotland, in the Grampians: scene of a battle (1689) in which the Jacobites defeated William III's forces but lost their leader, Viscount Dundee.

killifish ('kɪlɪˌfɪʃ) *n, pl* **killifish** *or* **killifishes.** any of various chiefly American minnow-like fishes of fresh and brackish waters: used to control mosquitoes and as anglers' bait. ORIG C19: from MDu. *kille* river + FISH

killing ('kɪlɪŋ) *adj* **1** *Inf.* very tiring: *a killing pace.* **2** *Inf.* extremely funny. **3** causing death; fatal. ◆ *n* **4** the act of causing death; slaying. **5** *Inf.* a sudden stroke of success, usually financial, as in speculations on the stock market (esp. in **make a killing**).

killjoy ('kɪlˌdʒɔɪ) *n* a person who spoils other people's pleasure.

Kilmarnock ★ (kɪl'mɑːnək) *n* a town in SW Scotland, the administrative centre of East Ayrshire: associations with Robert Burns; engineering and textile industries; whisky blending. Pop.: 44 307 (1991).

kiln (kɪln) *n* a large oven for burning, drying, or processing something, such as porcelain or bricks. ORIG OE *cylen,* from LL *culīna* kitchen, from L *coquere* to COOK

kilo ('kiːləʊ) *n, pl* **kilos.** short for **kilogram** or **kilometre.**

kilo- *prefix* **1** denoting 10^3 (1000): *kilometre.* Symbol: k **2** Also: **kibi-.** *Computing.* denoting 2^{10} (1024): *kilobyte.* Symbol Ki ORIG from F, from Gk *khilioi* thousand

> **USAGE NOTE** In general and scientific use *kilo-* means 10^3 (i.e. 1000). However, in computing it denotes 2^{10} (1024) but only for words connected with amounts of data (e.g. *kilobit*). In other computer contexts it retains its common meaning of 1000 (e.g. *kilohertz*). A recommended new prefix *kibi-* has been introduced to denote the specific computing use of 2^{10}. Other metric prefixes, *mega-, giga-, tera-, peta-,* and *exa-,* behave in a similar way and the equivalent prefixes for binary multiples are *mebi-, gibi-, tebi-, pebi-,* and *exbi-.*

kilobyte ('kɪləˌbaɪt) *n Computing.* 1024 bytes. Abbrev.: **KB, kbyte.** See also **kilo-** (sense 2).

kilocalorie ('kɪləʊˌkælərɪ) *n* another name for **Calorie.**

kilocycle ('kɪləʊˌsaɪkᵊl) *n* short for kilocycle per second: a former unit of frequency equal to 1 kilohertz.

kilogram ('kɪləʊˌgræm) *n* **1** one thousand grams. **2** the basic SI unit of mass, equal to the mass of the international prototype held by the *Bureau International des Poids et Mesures.* Symbol: kg

kilohertz ('kɪləʊˌhɜːts) *n* one thousand hertz; one thousand cycles per second. Symbol: kHz

kilolitre ('kɪləˌliːtə) *n* one thousand litres. Symbol: kl

kilometre *or US* **kilometer** ('kɪləˌmiːtə, kɪ'lɒmɪtə) *n* one thousand metres. Symbol: km
▸ **kilometric** (ˌkɪləʊ'mɛtrɪk) *adj*

kiloton ('kɪləʊˌtʌn) *n* **1** one thousand tons. **2** an explosive power, esp. of a nuclear weapon, equal to the power of 1000 tons of TNT. Abbrev.: **kt.**

kilovolt ('kɪləʊˌvəʊlt) *n* one thousand volts. Symbol: kV

kilowatt ('kɪləʊˌwɒt) *n* one thousand watts. Symbol: kW

kilowatt-hour *n* a unit of energy equal to the work done by a power of 1000 watts in one hour. Symbol: kWh

kilt (kɪlt) *n* **1** a knee-length pleated skirt, esp. one in tartan, as worn by men in Highland dress. ◆ *vb (tr)* **2** to tuck (the skirt) up around one's body. **3** to put pleats in (cloth, etc.). ORIG C18: of Scand. origin
▸ **'kilted** *adj*

kilter ('kɪltə) *or* **kelter** *n* working order (esp. in **out of kilter**). ORIG C17: from ?

Kilung ★ ('kiː'lʊŋ) *n* another name for **Chilung.**

Kilvert ★ ('kɪlvət) *n* **Francis.** 1840–79, British clergyman and diarist. His diary (published 1938–40) gives a vivid account of life in the Welsh Marches in the 1870s.

Kimberley ★ ('kɪmbəlɪ) *n* **1** a city in central South Africa: besieged (1899–1900) for 126 days during the Boer War; diamond-mining and -marketing centre, with heavy engineering works. Pop.: 183 000 (1995 est.). **2** Also called: **the Kimberleys.** a plateau region of NW Australia, in N Western Australia: consists of rugged mountains surrounded by grassland. Area: about 360 000 sq. km (140 000 sq. miles).

kimberlite ('kɪmbəˌlaɪt) *n* an intrusive igneous rock consisting largely of peridotite and often containing diamonds. ORIG C19: from KIMBERLEY + -ITE[1]

Kim Il Sung ★ (ˌkim il 'sʌŋ) *n* 1912–94, North Korean statesman and marshal; prime minister (1948–72) and president (1972–94) of North Korea.

kimono (kɪ'məʊnəʊ) *n, pl* **kimonos.** a loose sashed ankle-length garment with wide sleeves, worn in Japan. ORIG C19: from Japanese: clothing, from *kiru* to wear + *mono* thing
▸ **ki'monoed** *adj*

kin (kɪn) *n* **1** a person's relatives collectively. **2** a class or group with similar characteristics. **3** See **next of kin.** ◆ *adj* **4** *(postpositive)* related by blood. ORIG OE *cyn*

-kin *suffix forming nouns.* small: *lambkin.* ORIG from MDu., of West Gmc origin

Kinabalu ★ (ˌkɪnəbəˈluː) *n* a mountain in Malaysia, on N Borneo in central Sabah: the highest peak in Borneo. Height: 4125 m (13 533 ft).

kinaesthesia (ˌkɪnɪsˈθiːzɪə) *or US* **kinesthesia** *n* the sensation by which bodily position, weight, muscle tension, and movement are perceived. ORIG C19: from NL, from Gk *kinein* to move + AESTHESIA
▸ **kinaesthetic** *or US* **kinesthetic** (ˌkɪnɪsˈθɛtɪk) *adj*

Kincardineshire ★ (kɪnˈkɑːdɪnˌʃɪə, -ʃə) *n* a historic county of E Scotland, now part of Aberdeenshire. Also called: **the Mearns.**

Kinchinjunga ★ (ˌkɪntʃɪnˈdʒʌŋgə) *n* a variant of **Kangchenjunga.**

kincob (ˈkɪŋkɒb) *n* a fine silk fabric embroidered with threads of gold or silver, of a kind made in India. ORIG C18: from Urdu *kimkhāb*

kind[1] (kaɪnd) *adj* **1** having a friendly nature or attitude. **2** helpful to others or to another: *a kind deed.* **3** considerate or humane. **4** cordial; courteous (esp. in **kind regards**). **5** pleasant; mild: *a kind climate.* **6** *Inf.* beneficial or not harmful. ORIG OE *gecynde* natural, native

kind[2] (kaɪnd) *n* **1** a class or group having characteristics in common; sort; type: *two of a kind.* **2** an instance or example of a class or group, esp. a rudimentary one: *heating of a kind.* **3** essential nature or character: *the difference is one of kind rather than degree.* **4** *Arch.* nature; the natural order. **5 in kind. 5a** (of payment) in goods or produce rather than in money. **5b** with something of the same sort: *to return an insult in kind.* ORIG OE *gecynd* nature

> **USAGE NOTE** The mixture of plural and singular, although often used informally with *kind* and *sort*, should be avoided in serious writing: *children enjoy those kinds* (not *those kind*) *of stories; these sorts* (not *these sort*) *of distinctions are becoming blurred.*

kindergarten (ˈkɪndəˌgɑːtᵊn) *n* a class or small school for young children, usually between the ages of four and six. ORIG C19: from G, lit.: children's garden

kind-hearted *adj* kindly, readily sympathetic.
▸ ˌ**kind-ˈheartedly** *adv* ▸ ˌ**kind-ˈheartedness** *n*

kindle (ˈkɪndᵊl) *vb* **kindles, kindling, kindled. 1** to set alight or start to burn. **2** to arouse or be aroused: *the project kindled his interest.* **3** to make or become bright. ORIG C12: from ON *kynda,* infl. by ON *kyndill* candle
▸ ˈ**kindler** *n*

kindling (ˈkɪndlɪŋ) *n* material for starting a fire, such as dry wood, straw, etc.

kindly (ˈkaɪndlɪ) *adj* **kindlier, kindliest. 1** having a sympathetic or warm-hearted nature. **2** motivated by warm and sympathetic feelings. **3** pleasant: *a kindly climate.* **4** *Arch.* natural; normal. ◆ *adv* **5** in a considerate or humane way. **6** with tolerance: *he kindly forgave my rudeness.* **7** cordially: *he greeted us kindly.* **8** please (often used to express impatience or formality): *will you kindly behave yourself!* **9** *Arch.* appropriately. **10 not take kindly to.** to react unfavourably towards.
▸ ˈ**kindliness** *n*

kindness (ˈkaɪndnɪs) *n* **1** the practice or quality of being kind. **2** a kind or helpful act.

kindred (ˈkɪndrɪd) *adj* **1** having similar or common qualities, origin, etc. **2** related by blood or marriage. **3 kindred spirit.** a person with whom one has something in common. ◆ *n* **4** relationship by blood. **5** similarity in character. **6** a person's relatives collectively. ORIG C12 *kinred,* from KIN + *-red,* from OE *rǣden* rule, from *rǣdan* to rule

kine (kaɪn) *n* (*functioning as pl*) an archaic word for cows or cattle. ORIG OE *cȳna* of cows, from *cū* COW[1]

kinematics (ˌkɪnɪˈmætɪks) *n* (*functioning as sing*) the study of the motion of bodies without reference to mass or force. ORIG C19: from Gk *kinēma* movement; see CINEMA, -ICS
▸ ˌ**kineˈmatic** *adj* ▸ ˌ**kineˈmatically** *adv*

kinematograph (ˌkɪnɪˈmætəˌgrɑːf) *n* a variant spelling of **cinematograph.**

kinesics (kɪˈniːsɪks) *n* (*functioning as sing*) the study of the role of body movements, such as winking, shrugging, etc., in communication.

kinesis (kɪˈniːsɪs, kaɪ-) *n Biol.* the nondirectional movement of an organism or cell in response to a stimulus, the rate of movement being dependent on the strength of the stimulus.

kinesthesia (ˌkɪnɪsˈθiːzɪə) *n* the usual US spelling of **kinaesthesia.**

kinetic (kɪˈnɛtɪk) *adj* relating to or caused by motion. ORIG C19: from Gk *kinētikos,* from *kinein* to move
▸ **kiˈnetically** *adv*

kinetic art *n* art, esp. sculpture, that moves or has moving parts.

kinetic energy *n* the energy of motion of a body equal to the work it would do if it were brought to rest. It is equal to the product of the increase of mass caused by motion times the square of the speed of light.

kinetics (kɪˈnɛtɪks, kaɪ-) *n* (*functioning as sing*) **1** another name for **dynamics** (sense 2). **2** the branch of mechanics, including both dynamics and kinematics, concerned with the study of bodies in motion. **3** the branch of dynamics that excludes the study of bodies at rest.

kinetic theory (**of gases**) *n* **the.** a theory of gases postulating that they consist of particles moving at random and undergoing elastic collisions.

kinfolk (ˈkɪnˌfəʊk) *pl n Chiefly US & Canad.* another word for **kinsfolk.**

king (kɪŋ) *n* **1** a male sovereign prince who is the official ruler of an independent state; monarch. Related adjs.: **royal, regal. 2a** a ruler or chief: *king of the fairies.* **2b** (*in combination*): *the pirate king.* **3** a person, animal, or thing considered as the best or most important of its kind. **4** any of four playing cards in a pack, one for each suit, bearing the picture of a king. **5** the most important chess piece. **6** *Draughts.* a piece that has moved entirely across the board and has been crowned, after which it may move backwards as well as forwards. **7** (*cap.*) *Caribbean.* a man who wins a nationally recognized festive or costume competition. **8 king of kings. 8a** God. **8b** a title of any of various oriental monarchs. ◆ *vb* (*tr*) **9** to make (someone) a king. **10 king it.** to act in a superior fashion. ORIG OE *cyning*
▸ ˈ**kingˌhood** *n* ▸ ˈ**kingˌlike** *adj*

King ★ (kɪŋ) *n* **1 B.B.,** real name *Riley B. King.* born 1925, US blues singer and guitarist. **2 Billie Jean** (née *Moffitt*). born 1943, US tennis player: Wimbledon champion 1966–68, 1972–73, and 1975; US champion 1967, 1971–72, and 1974. **3 Martin Luther.** 1929–68, US Baptist minister and civil-rights leader. He advocated nonviolence in his campaigns against the segregation of Black people in the South: assassinated: Nobel Peace Prize 1964. **4 Stephen.** born 1947, US writer of horror novels: his books, many of which have been adapted for the screen, include *Carrie* (1974), *The Shining* (1977), and *Hearts in Atlantis* (1999). **5 William Lyon Mackenzie.** 1874–1950, Canadian Liberal statesman; prime minister (1921–26; 1926–30; 1935–48).

kingbird (ˈkɪŋˌbɜːd) *n* any of several large American flycatchers.

kingbolt (ˈkɪŋˌbəʊlt) *or* **king rod** *n* **a** the pivot bolt that connects the body of a horse-drawn carriage to the front axle and provides the steering joint. **b** a similar bolt placed between a railway carriage and the bogies.

King Charles spaniel *n* a toy breed of spaniel with a short turned-up nose and a domed skull. ORIG C17: after Charles II of England, who popularized the breed

king cobra *n* a very large venomous tropical Asian snake that extends its neck into a hood when alarmed. Also called: **hamadryad.**

King Country ★ *n* **the.** an area in the centre of the North Island, New Zealand: home of the King Movement, a nineteenth-century Maori separatist movement.

king crab *n* another name for the **horseshoe crab.**

kingcup (ˈkɪŋˌkʌp) *n Brit.* any of several yellow-flowered plants, esp. the marsh marigold.

kingdom (ˈkɪŋdəm) *n* **1** a territory, state, people, or community ruled or reigned over by a king or queen. **2** any of the three groups into which natural objects may be divided: the animal, plant, and mineral kingdoms. **3** *Biol.* any of the major categories into which living organisms are classified. Modern systems recognize five kingdoms: *Prokaryotae* (bacteria), *Protoctista* (algae, protozoans, etc.), *Fungi, Plantae,* and *Animalia.* **4** *Theol.* the eternal sovereignty of God. **5** an area of activity: *the kingdom of the mind.*

kingdom come *n* **1** the next world. **2** *Inf.* the end of the world (esp. in **until kingdom come**). **3** *Inf.* unconsciousness.

kingfish (ˈkɪŋˌfɪʃ) *n, pl* **kingfish** *or* **kingfishes. 1** a marine food and game fish occurring in warm American Atlantic coastal waters. **2** *Austral.* any of various types of trevally, mulloway, and barracouta. **3** any of various other large food fishes, esp. the Spanish mackerel.

kingfisher (ˈkɪŋˌfɪʃə) *n* a bird which has a greenish-blue and orange plumage, a large head, short tail, and long sharp bill, and feeds on fish. ORIG C15: orig. *king's fisher*

King James Version *or* **Bible** *n* **the.** another name for the **Authorized Version.**

kingklip (ˈkɪŋˌklɪp) *n* an edible eel-like marine fish. ORIG from Afrik., from Du. *koning* king + *klip* rock

kinglet (ˈkɪŋlɪt) *n* **1** *Often derog.* the king of a small or insignificant territory. **2** *US & Canad.* any of various small warblers having a black-edged yellow crown.

kingly (ˈkɪŋlɪ) *adj* **kinglier, kingliest. 1** appropriate to a king. **2** royal. ◆ *adv* **3** *Poetic or arch.* in a manner appropriate to a king.
▸ **ˈkingliness** *n*

kingmaker (ˈkɪŋˌmeɪkə) *n* a person who has control over appointments to positions of authority.

king-of-arms *n, pl* **kings-of-arms. 1** the highest rank of heraldic officer. **2** a person holding this rank.

king of the castle *n Chiefly Brit.* a children's game in which each child attempts to stand alone on a mound by pushing other children off it.

king penguin *n* a large New Zealand subantarctic penguin.

kingpin (ˈkɪŋˌpɪn) *n* **1** the most important person in an organization. **2** Also called (Brit.): **swivel pin.** a pivot pin that provides a steering joint in a motor vehicle by securing the stub axle to the axle beam. **3** *Tenpin bowling.* the front pin in the triangular arrangement of the ten pins. **4** (in ninepins) the central pin in the diamond pattern of the nine pins.

king post *n* a vertical post connecting the apex of a triangular roof truss to the tie beam.

King's Bench *n* (when the sovereign is male) another name for **Queen's Bench.**

King's Counsel *n* (when the sovereign is male) another name for **Queen's Counsel.**

King's English *n* (esp. when the British sovereign is male) standard Southern British English.

king's evidence *n* (when the sovereign is male) another name for **queen's evidence.**

king's evil *n* **the.** *Pathol.* a former name for **scrofula.** ORIG C14: from the belief that the king's touch would heal scrofula

Kingsford-Smith ★ (ˈkɪŋzfədˈsmɪθ) *n* Sir **Charles (Edward).** 1897–1935, Australian aviator and pioneer (with Charles Ulm) of trans-Pacific and trans-Tasman flights.

king's highway *n* (in Britain, esp. when the sovereign is male) any public road or right of way.

kingship (ˈkɪŋʃɪp) *n* **1** the position or authority of a king. **2** the skill of ruling as a king.

king-size *or* **king-sized** *adj* larger or longer than a standard size.

Kingsley ★ (ˈkɪŋzlɪ) *n* **1 Ben.** born 1943, British actor, whose films include *Gandhi* (1982). **2 Charles.** 1819–75, British clergyman and author. His works include the novels *Westward Ho!* (1855), *Hereward the Wake* (1866), and *The Water Babies* (1863). **3** his brother, **Henry.** 1830–76, British novelist and journalist, who spent some time in Australia. His works include the Anglo-Australian novel *The Recollections of Geoffrey Hamlyn* (1859).

King's Lynn ★ (ˈkɪŋz ˈlɪn) *n* a market town in E England, in Norfolk on the estuary of the Great Ouse near the Wash: a leading port in the Middle Ages. Pop.: 41 281 (1991). Also called: **Lynn, Lynn Regis.**

Kingston ★ (ˈkɪŋstən) *n* **1** the capital and chief port of Jamaica, on the SE coast: University of the West Indies. Pop.: 103 771 (1991). **2** a port in SE Canada, in SE Ontario: the chief naval base of Lake Ontario and a large industrial centre; university (1841). Pop.: 56 597 (1991). **3** short for **Kingston upon Thames.**

Kingston upon Hull ★ *n* **1** the official name of **Hull**[1]. **2** a unitary authority in NE England, in the East Riding of Yorkshire. Pop.: 266 800 (1996 est.). Area: 71 sq. km (27 sq. miles).

Kingston upon Thames ★ *n* a borough of SW Greater London, on the River Thames: formed in 1965 by the amalgamation of several former boroughs of Surrey; seat of Kingston University (1992). Pop.: 138 500 (1994 est.). Area: 38 sq. km (15 sq. miles).

Kingstown ★ (ˈkɪŋzˌtaʊn) *n* the capital of St Vincent and the Grenadines: a port and resort. Pop.: 15 466 (1991).

kinin (ˈkaɪnɪn) *n* **1** any of a group of polypeptides in the blood that cause dilation of the blood vessels. **2** *Bot.* another name for **cytokinin.** ORIG C20: from Gk *kin(ēma)* motion + -IN

kink (kɪŋk) *n* **1** a sharp twist or bend in a wire, rope, hair, etc. **2** a crick in the neck or similar muscular spasm. **3** a flaw or minor difficulty in some undertaking. **4** a flaw or idiosyncrasy of personality. ORIG C17: from Du.: a curl in a rope

kinkajou (ˈkɪŋkəˌdʒuː) *n* an arboreal fruit-eating mammal of Central and South America, with a long prehensile tail. Also called: **honey bear.** ORIG C18: from F *quincajou,* from Algonquian

kinky (ˈkɪŋkɪ) *adj* **kinkier, kinkiest. 1** *Sl.* given to unusual, abnormal, or deviant sexual practices. **2** *Inf.* exhibiting unusual idiosyncrasies of personality. **3** *Inf.* attractive or provocative in a bizarre way: *kinky clothes.* **4** tightly looped, as a wire or rope. **5** tightly curled, as hair.
▸ **ˈkinkily** *adv* ▸ **ˈkinkiness** *n*

Kinnock ★ (ˈkɪnək) *n* **Neil (Gordon).** born 1942, British Labour politician, born in Wales; leader of the Labour Party (1983–92); European Commissioner (1994–99); vice president of the European Commission from 1999.

kino (ˈkiːnəʊ) *n* a dark red resin obtained from various tropical plants, esp. an Indian leguminous tree, used as an astringent and in tanning. ORIG C18: of West African origin

Kinross-shire ★ (kɪnˈrɒsˌʃɪə, -ʃə) *n* a historic county of E central Scotland, now part of Perth and Kinross.

kin selection *n Biol.* natural selection resulting from altruistic behaviour by animals towards members of the same species, esp. their offspring or other relatives.

Kinsey ★ (ˈkɪnzɪ) *n* **Alfred Charles.** 1894–1956, US zoologist, who directed a survey of human sexual behaviour.

kinsfolk (ˈkɪnzˌfəʊk) *pl n* one's family or relatives.

Kinshasa ★ (kɪnˈʃɑːzə, -ˈʃɑːsə) *n* the capital of the Democratic Republic of Congo, on the River Congo opposite Brazzaville: became capital of the Belgian Congo in 1929 and of Zaïre in 1960; university (1954). Pop.: 4 655 313 (1994 est.). Former name (until 1966): **Léopoldville.**

kinship (ˈkɪnʃɪp) *n* **1** blood relationship. **2** the state of having common characteristics.

kinsman (ˈkɪnzmən) *n, pl* **kinsmen.** a blood relation or a relation by marriage.
▸ **ˈkinsˌwoman** *fem n*

kiosk (ˈkiːɒsk) *n* **1** a small sometimes movable booth from which cigarettes, newspapers, sweets, etc., are sold. **2** *Chiefly Brit.* a telephone box. **3** (in Turkey, Iran, etc.) a light open-sided pavilion. ORIG C17: from F *kiosque* bandstand, from Turkish, from Persian *kūshk* pavilion

Kioto ★ (kɪˈəʊtəʊ, ˈkjəʊ-) *n* a variant spelling of **Kyoto.**

kip[1] (kɪp) *Brit. sl.* ◆ *n* **1** sleep or slumber: *to get some kip.* **2** a bed or lodging. ◆ *vb* **kips, kipping, kipped.** (*intr*) **3** to sleep or take a nap. **4** (foll. by *down*) to prepare for sleep. ORIG C18: from ?

kip[2] (kɪp) *or* **kipskin** *n* the hide of a young animal, esp. a calf or lamb. ORIG C16: from MDu. *kipp*

kip[3] (kɪp) *n Austral.* a small board used to spin the coins in two-up. ORIG C19: from Brit. dialect *kep* to catch

Kipling ★ ('kɪplɪŋ) *n* **(Joseph) Rudyard** ('rʌdjəd). 1865–1936, British poet, short-story writer, and novelist, born in India. His works include *Barrack-Room Ballads* (1892), the two *Jungle Books* (1894, 1895), *Stalky and Co.* (1899), *Kim* (1901), and the *Just So Stories* (1902): Nobel prize for literature 1907.

kipper ('kɪpə) *n* **1** a fish, esp. a herring, that has been cleaned, salted, and smoked. **2** a male salmon during the spawning season. ◆ *vb* **3** (*tr*) to cure (herrings or other fish) by salting and smoking. ORIG OE *cypera,* ?from *coper* COPPER[1], referring to its colour

kir (kɜː; *French* kir) *n* a drink made from dry white wine and cassis. ORIG after Canon F. *Kir* (1876–1968), mayor of Dijon, who is said to have invented it

kirby grip ('kɜːbɪ) *n Trademark.* a type of hairgrip with one straight and one wavy side.

Kirchhoff ★ (*German* 'kɪrçhɔf) *n* **Gustav Robert** ('gʊstaf 'roːbɛrt). 1824–87, German physicist. With Bunsen he developed spectrum analysis and discovered caesium (1860) and rubidium (1861): also worked on electrical networks.

Kirghiz *or* **Kirgiz** ('kɜːgɪz) *n* variant spellings of **Kyrgyz.**

Kirghizia *or* **Kirgizia** ★ (kɜː'gɪzɪə) *n* another name for **Kyrgyzstan.**

Kiribati ★ (ˌkɪrɪ'bætɪ) *n* an independent republic in the W Pacific: comprises 33 islands including Banaba (Ocean Island), the Gilbert and Phoenix Islands, and eight of the Line Islands; part of the British colony of the Gilbert and Ellice Islands until 1975; became self-governing in 1977 and gained full independence in 1979; a member of the Commonwealth. Official language: English; I-Kiribati (Gilbertese) is widely spoken. Religion: Christian majority. Currency: Australian dollar. Capital: Bairiki islet, in Tarawa atoll. Pop.: 85 500 (1999 est.). Area: 684 sq. km (264 sq. miles).

Kirin ★ ('kiː'rɪn) *n* a variant transliteration of the Chinese name for **Jilin.**

Kiritimati ★ ('kɪrɪtɪ'mɑːtɪ) *n* an island in the central Pacific, in Kiribati: one of the Line Islands; the largest atoll in the world. Pop.: 2537 (1990). Former name: **Christmas Island.**

kirk (kɜːk) *n* **1** a Scottish word for **church. 2** a Scottish church. ORIG C12: from ON *kirkja,* from OE *cirice* CHURCH

Kirk ★ (kɜːk) *n* **Norman.** 1923–74, prime minister of New Zealand (1972–74).

Kirkby ★ ('kɜːbɪ) *n* a town in NW England, in Knowsley, in Merseyside. Pop.: 43 017 (1991).

Kirkcaldy ★ (kɜː'kɔːdɪ) *n* a port in E Scotland, in SE Fife on the Firth of Forth. Pop.: 47 155 (1991).

Kirkcudbrightshire ★ (kɜː'kuːbrɪˌʃɪə, -ʃə) *n* a historic county of SW Scotland, now part of Dumfries and Galloway region.

Kirklees ★ (ˌkɜːk'liːz) *n* a unitary authority in N England, in West Yorkshire. Pop.: 388 800 (1996 est.). Area: 410 sq. km (158 sq. miles).

Kirkpatrick ★ (kɜːk'pætrɪk) *n* **Mount.** a mountain in Antarctica, in S Victoria Land in the Queen Alexandra Range. Height: 4528 m (14 856 ft).

kirk session *n* the lowest court of the Presbyterian Church.

Kirkuk ★ (kɜː'kuk, 'kɜːkuk) *n* a city in NE Iraq: centre of a rich oilfield with pipelines to the Mediterranean. Pop.: 418 624 (1987).

Kirkwall ★ ('kɜːkˌwɔːl) *n* a town on the N coast of Mainland in the Orkney Islands: administrative centre of the island authority of Orkney: cathedral built by Norsemen (begun in 1137). Pop.: 6469 (1991).

kirmess ('kɜːmɪs) *n* a variant spelling of **kermis.**

Kirov[1] ★ ('kɪərɒf; *Russian* 'kirəf) *n* a city in NW Russia, on the Vyatka River: an early trading centre; engineering industries. Pop.: 464 000 (1995 est.). Former name (1780–1934): **Vyatka.**

Kirov[2] ★ ('kɪərɒf; *Russian* 'kirəf) *n* **Sergei Mironovich** (sɪr'gjej mi'rɔnəvitʃ). 1888–1934, Soviet politician. His assassination was the start for Stalin's purge of the Communist Party (1934–38).

Kirovabad ★ (*Russian* kirəva'bat) *n* the former name (1935–91) of **Gandzha.**

Kirovograd ★ (*Russian* kirəva'grat) *n* a city in S central Ukraine, on the Ingul River: manufacturing centre of a rich agricultural area. Pop.: 276 000 (1996 est.). Former names: **Yelisavetgrad** (until 1924), **Zinovievsk** (1924–36).

Kirsch (kɪəʃ) *or* **Kirschwasser** ('kɪəʃˌvɑːsə) *n* a brandy distilled from cherries, made chiefly in the Black Forest in Germany. ORIG G *Kirschwasser* cherry water

kirtle ('kɜːtᵊl) *n Arch.* **1** a woman's skirt or dress. **2** a man's coat. ORIG OE *cyrtel,* prob. from *cyrtan* to shorten, ult. from L *curtus* cut short

Kiruna ★ (*Swedish* 'kiːruna) *n* a town in N Sweden: iron-mining centre. Pop.: 26 150 (1990).

Kisangani ★ (ˌkɪsæŋ'gɑːnɪ) *n* a city in N Democratic Republic of Congo, at the head of navigation of the River Congo below Stanley Falls: Université Libre du Congo (1963). Pop.: 417 517 (1994 est.). Former name (until 1966): **Stanleyville.**

Kishinev ★ (*Russian* kiʃi'njɔf) *n* the capital of Moldova, on the Byk River: manufacturing centre of a rich agricultural region; university (1945). Pop.: 662 000 (1994 est.). Romanian name: **Chişinău.**

Kismayu ★ (kɪs'mɑːjuː) *n* another name for **Chisimaio.**

kismet ('kɪzmɛt, 'kɪs-) *n* **1** *Islam.* the will of Allah. **2** fate or destiny. ORIG C19: from Turkish, from Persian *qismat,* from Ar. *qasama* he divided

kiss (kɪs) *vb* **1** (*tr*) to touch with the lips or press the lips against as an expression of love, greeting, respect, etc. **2** (*intr*) to join lips with another person in an act of love or desire. **3** to touch (each other) lightly. **4** *Billiards.* (of balls) to touch (each other) lightly while moving. ◆ *n* **5** a caress with the lips. **6** a light touch. ORIG OE *cyssan,* from *coss*
▸ **'kissable** *adj*

kissagram ('kɪsəˌgræm) *n* a greetings service in which a person is employed to present greetings by kissing the person celebrating. ORIG C20: blend of *kiss* and *telegram*

kiss-and-tell *n* (*modifier*) denoting the practice of publicizing one's former sexual relationship with a celebrity, esp. in the tabloid press: *a kiss-and-tell interview.*

kiss curl *n Brit.* a circular curl of hair pressed flat against the cheek or forehead.

kisser ('kɪsə) *n* **1** a person who kisses, esp. in a way specified. **2** a slang word for **mouth** or **face.**

Kissinger ★ ('kɪsɪndʒə) *n* **Henry (Alfred).** born 1923, US academic and diplomat, born in Germany; assistant to President Nixon for national security affairs (1969–75); Secretary of State (1973–77): shared the Nobel peace prize 1973.

kissing gate *n* a gate set in a U- or V-shaped enclosure, allowing only one person to pass through at a time.

kiss of life *n* **the.** mouth-to-mouth resuscitation in which a person blows gently into the mouth of an unconscious person, allowing the lungs to deflate after each blow.

kist (kɪst) *n S. African.* a large wooden chest in which linen is stored, esp. one used to store a bride's trousseau. ORIG from Afrik., from Du.: CHEST

Kistna ★ ('kɪstnə) *n* another name for the (River) **Krishna.**

Kisumu ★ (kɪ'suːmuː) *n* a port in W Kenya, in Nyanza province on the NE shore of Lake Victoria: fishing and trading centre. Pop.: 201 100 (1991 est.).

kit[1] (kɪt) *n* **1** a set of tools, supplies, etc., for use together or for a purpose: *a first-aid kit.* **2** the case or container for such a set. **3** a set of pieces of equipment sold ready to be assembled. **4a** clothing and other personal effects, esp. those of a traveller or soldier: *safari kit.* **4b** *Inf.* clothing in general (esp. in the phrase **get one's kit off**). ◆ See also **kit out.** ORIG C14: from MDu. *kitte* tankard

kit[2] (kɪt) *n NZ old-fashioned.* a string bag for shopping. ORIG from Maori *kete* flax basket

Kitaj ★ (ˈkaɪtæʒ) *n* **R. B.** born 1932, US painter working in Britain, noted for such large figurative works as *If Not, Not* (1976).

Kitakyushu ★ (ˌkiːtəˈkjuːʃuː) *n* a port in Japan, on N Kyushu: formed in 1963 by the amalgamation of the cities of Wakamatsu, Yahata, Tobata, Kokura, and Moji; one of Japan's largest industrial centres. Pop.: 1 019 562 (1995).

kitbag (ˈkɪtˌbæg) *n* a canvas or other bag for a serviceman's kit.

kitchen (ˈkɪtʃɪn) *n* **a** a room or part of a building equipped for preparing and cooking food. **b** (*as modifier*): *a kitchen table.* ORIG OE *cycene,* ult. from LL *coquīna,* from L *coquere* to COOK

kitchen cabinet *n* a group of unofficial advisers to a political leader, esp. when considered to be more influential than the offical cabinet.

Kitchener[1] ★ (ˈkɪtʃɪnə) *n* an industrial town in SE Canada, in S Ontario: founded in 1806 as Dutch Sand Hills, it was renamed Berlin in 1830 and Kitchener in 1916. Pop.: 168 282 (1991).

Kitchener[2] ★ (ˈkɪtʃɪnə) *n* **Horatio Herbert,** 1st Earl Kitchener of Khartoum. 1850–1916, British field marshal. As head of the Egyptian army (1892–98), he expelled the Mahdi from the Sudan (1898) and commanded British forces (1900–02) in the Boer War and later (1902–09) in India. He became war minister (1914–16) but drowned on his way to Russia.

kitchenette (ˌkɪtʃɪˈnɛt) *n* a small kitchen or part of a room equipped for use as a kitchen.

kitchen garden *n* a garden where vegetables and sometimes also fruit are grown.

kitchen midden *n Archaeol.* the site of a large mound of domestic refuse marking a prehistoric settlement.

kitchen police *pl n US* soldiers who have been detailed to work in the kitchen, esp. as a punishment.

kitchen sink *n* **1** a sink in a kitchen for washing dishes, vegetables, etc. **2** (*modifier*) denoting a type of drama or painting of the 1950s depicting sordid reality.

kitchen tea *n Austral. & NZ old-fashioned.* a party held before a wedding to which guests bring items of kitchen equipment as wedding presents.

kitchenware (ˈkɪtʃɪnˌwɛə) *n* pots and pans, knives, forks, spoons, etc., used in the kitchen.

kite (kaɪt) *n* **1** a light frame covered with a thin material flown in the wind at the end of a length of string. **2** *Brit. sl.* an aeroplane. **3** (*pl*) *Naut.* any of various light sails set in addition to the working sails of a vessel. **4** a bird of prey having a long forked tail and long broad wings and usually preying on small mammals and insects. **5** *Arch.* a person who preys on others. **6** *Commerce.* a negotiable paper drawn without any actual transaction or assets and designed to obtain money on credit, give an impression of affluence, etc. ◆ *vb* **kites, kiting, kited. 7** to issue (fictitious papers) to obtain credit or money. **8** (*intr*) to soar and glide. ORIG OE *cȳta*

Kite mark *n Brit.* the official mark of quality and reliability, in the form of a kite, on articles approved by the British Standards Institution.

kith (kɪθ) *n* **kith and kin.** one's friends and relations. ORIG OE *cȳthth,* from *cūth;* see UNCOUTH

Kíthira ★ (ˈkiθira) *n* transliteration of the Modern Greek name for **Cythera.**

kit out *or* **up** *vb* **kits, kitting, kitted.** (*tr, adv*) *Chiefly Brit.* to provide with (a kit of personal effects and necessities).

kitsch (kɪtʃ) *n* tawdry, vulgarized, or pretentious art, literature, etc., usually with popular appeal. ORIG C20: from G

▸ ˈ**kitschy** *adj*

kitten (ˈkɪtᵊn) *n* **1** a young cat. **2 have kittens.** *Brit. inf.* to react with disapproval, anxiety, etc.: *she had kittens when she got the bill.* ◆ *vb* **3** (of cats) to give birth to (young). ORIG C14: from OF *caton,* from CAT; prob. infl. by ME *kiteling*

kittenish (ˈkɪtᵊnɪʃ) *adj* **1** like a kitten; lively. **2** (of a woman) flirtatious, esp. coyly flirtatious.

kittiwake (ˈkɪtɪˌweɪk) *n* either of two oceanic gulls having pale grey black-tipped wings and a square-cut tail. ORIG C17: imit.

kitty[1] (ˈkɪtɪ) *n, pl* **kitties.** a diminutive or affectionate name for a **kitten** or **cat.** ORIG C18

kitty[2] (ˈkɪtɪ) *n, pl* **kitties. 1** the pool of bets in certain gambling games. **2** any shared fund of money. **3** (in bowls) the jack. ORIG C19: see KIT[1]

kitty-cornered *adj* a variant of **cater-cornered.**

Kitty Hawk ★ (ˈkɪtɪ ˌhɔːk) *n* a village in NE North Carolina, near Kill Devil Hill, where the Wright brothers made the first aeroplane flight in the US (1903).

Kitwe ★ (ˈkɪtweɪ) *n* a city in N Zambia: commercial centre of the Copper Belt. Pop.: 338 207 (1990).

Kitzbühel ★ (ˈkɪtsˌbuːəl) *n* a town in W Austria, in the Tirol: centre for winter sports. Pop.: 8223 (1991).

Kiushu ★ (ˈkjuːʃuː) *n* a variant spelling of **Kyushu.**

Kivu ★ (ˈkiːvuː) *n* **Lake.** a lake in central Africa, between the Democratic Republic of Congo and Rwanda at an altitude of 1460 m (4790 ft). Area: 2698 sq. km (1042 sq. miles). Depth: (maximum) 475 m (1558 ft).

Kiwano (kɪˈwɑːnəʊ) *n, pl* **Kiwanos.** *Trademark.* an edible oval fruit of the passionflower family, having a golden spiky skin, juicy green pulp and many seeds.

kiwi (ˈkiːwiː) *n, pl* **kiwis. 1** a nocturnal flightless New Zealand bird having a long beak, stout legs, and weakly barbed feathers. **2** *Inf. except in NZ.* a New Zealander. **3** *NZ inf.* a lottery. ORIG C19: from Maori, imit.: NZ sense from the *Golden Kiwi Lottery*

kiwi fruit *n* the fuzzy edible fruit of an Asian climbing plant. Also called: **Chinese gooseberry.**

Kizil Irmak ★ (kɪˈzɪl ɪəˈmɑːk) *n* a river in Turkey, rising in the Kizil Dag and flowing southwest, northwest, and northeast to the Black Sea: the longest river in Asia Minor. Length: about 1150 km (715 miles). Ancient name: **Halys** (ˈheɪlɪs).

KKK *abbrev. for* Ku Klux Klan.

Klagenfurt ★ (*German* ˈklaːgənfʊrt) *n* a city in S Austria, capital of Carinthia province: tourist centre. Pop.: 89 415 (1991).

Klaipeda ★ (*Russian* ˈklajpɪdə) *n* a port in Lithuania on the Baltic: shipbuilding. Pop.: 206 400 (1993 est.). German name: **Memel.**

Klan (klæn) *n* (usually preceded by *the*) short for **Ku Klux Klan.**

▸ ˈ**Klanism** *n*

klaxon (ˈklæksᵊn) *n* a type of loud horn formerly used on motor vehicles. ORIG C20: former trademark

Kléber ★ (*French* klebɛr) *n* **Jean Baptiste** (ʒɑ̃ batist). 1753–1800, French general, who succeeded Napoleon as commander in Egypt (1799); assassinated.

Klee ★ (*German* kleː) *n* **Paul** (paul). 1879–1940, Swiss painter and etcher. A founder member of *der Blaue Reiter* (a group of German expressionist painters), he subsequently evolved an intensely personal style of unusual fantasy and wit.

Kleenex (ˈkliːnɛks) *n, pl* **Kleenex** *or* **Kleenexes.** *Trademark.* a kind of soft paper tissue, used esp. as a handkerchief.

Klein ★ (klaɪn) *n* **1 Calvin** (**Richard**). born 1942, US fashion designer. **2 Melanie.** 1882–1960, Austrian psychoanalyst resident in England (from 1926).

Klein bottle (klaɪn) *n Maths.* a three-dimensional surface formed by inserting the smaller end of an open tapered tube through the surface of the tube and making this end stretch to fit the other end. ORIG after Felix *Klein* (1849–1925), G mathematician

kleinhuisie (ˈkleɪnˌheɪsɪ) *n S. African.* an outside lavatory. ORIG C20: Afrik. lit.: little house

Kleist ★ (klaɪst) *n* (**Bernd**) **Heinrich** (**Wilhelm**) **von** (ˈhainrɪç fɔn). 1777–1811, German writer. His plays include *The Broken Pitcher* (1808).

Klemperer ★ (ˈklɛmpərə) *n* **Otto.** 1885–1973, Israeli conductor, born in Germany.

★ people and places

kleptomania (ˌklɛptəʊˈmeɪnɪə) *n Psychol.* a strong impulse to steal, esp. when there is no obvious motivation. ORIG C19: *klepto-* from Gk, from *kleptein* to steal + -MANIA
▸ ˌ**kleptoˈmaniˌac** *n*

klieg light (kliːg) *n* an intense carbon-arc light used in producing films. ORIG C20: after John H. *Kliegl* (1869–1959) & his brother Anton (1872–1927), German-born American inventors

Kline ★ (klaɪn) *n* **Franz** (frænts). 1910–62, US abstract expressionist painter.

klipspringer (ˈklɪpˌsprɪŋə) *n* a small agile antelope inhabiting rocky regions of Africa south of the Sahara. ORIG C18: from Afrik., from Du. *klip* rock + *springer,* from *springen* to SPRING

Klondike ★ (ˈklɒndaɪk) *n* **1** a region of NW Canada, in the Yukon in the basin of the Klondike River: site of rich gold deposits, discovered in 1896 but largely exhausted by 1910. Area: about 2100 sq. km (800 sq. miles). **2** a river in NW Canada, rising in the Yukon and flowing west to the Yukon River. Length: about 145 km (90 miles).

kloof (kluːf) *n* a mountain pass or gorge in southern Africa. ORIG C18: from Afrik., from MDu. *clove* a cleft

klystron (ˈklɪstrɒn) *n* an electron tube for the amplification or generation of microwaves. ORIG C20: *klys-,* from Gk *kluzein* to wash over + -TRON

km *symbol for* kilometre.

K-meson *n* another name for **kaon.**

knack (næk) *n* **1** a skilful, ingenious, or resourceful way of doing something. **2** a particular talent or aptitude, esp. an intuitive one. ORIG C14: prob. var. of *knak* sharp knock, imit.

knacker (ˈnækə) *Brit.* ◆ *n* **1** a person who buys up old horses for slaughter. **2** a person who buys up old buildings and breaks them up for scrap. **3** *Irish sl.* a despicable person. ◆ *vb* **4** (*tr; usually passive*) *Sl.* to tire. ORIG C16: prob. from *nacker* saddler, prob. of Scand. origin
▸ ˈ**knackery** *n*

knacker's yard *n Brit.* **1** a slaughterhouse for horses. **2** *Inf.* destruction because of being beyond all usefulness (esp. in the phrase **ready for the knacker's yard**).

knag (næg) *n* **1** a knot in wood. **2** a wooden peg. ORIG C15: ?from Low G *knagge*

knap (næp) *vb* **knaps, knapping, knapped.** (*tr*) *Dialect.* to hit or chip. ORIG C15 (in the sense: to strike with a sharp sound): imit.
▸ ˈ**knapper** *n*

knapping hammer *n* a hammer used for breaking and shaping stones.

knapsack (ˈnæpˌsæk) *n* a canvas or leather bag carried strapped on the back or shoulder. ORIG C17: from Low G, prob. from *knappen* to bite + *sack* bag

knapweed (ˈnæpˌwiːd) *n* any of several plants having purplish thistle-like flowers. ORIG C15 *knopwed,* from *knop* of Gmc origin + WEED

knar (nɑː) *n* a variant of **knur.** ORIG C14 *knarre* rough stone, knot on a tree

knave (neɪv) *n* **1** *Arch.* a dishonest man. **2** another word for **jack** (the playing card). **3** *Obs.* a male servant. ORIG OE *cnafa*
▸ ˈ**knavish** *adj*

knavery (ˈneɪvərɪ) *n, pl* **knaveries. 1** a deceitful or dishonest act. **2** dishonest conduct; trickery.

knead (niːd) *vb* (*tr*) **1** to work and press (a soft substance, such as bread dough) into a uniform mixture with the hands. **2** to squeeze or press with the hands. **3** to make by kneading. ORIG OE *cnedan*
▸ ˈ**kneader** *n*

knee (niː) *n* **1** the joint of the human leg connecting the tibia and fibula with the femur and protected in front by the patella. Technical name: **genu. 2a** the area surrounding and above this joint. **2b** (*modifier*) reaching or covering the knee: *knee socks.* **3** the upper surface of a sitting person's thigh: *the child sat on her mother's knee.* **4** a corresponding or similar part in other vertebrates. **5** the part of a garment that covers the knee. **6** anything resembling a knee in action or shape. **7** any of the hollow rounded protuberances that project upwards from the roots of the swamp cypress. **8 bend** *or* **bow the knee.** to kneel or submit. **9 bring someone to his** (*or* **her**) **knees.** to force someone into submission. ◆ *vb* **knees, kneeing, kneed. 10** (*tr*) to strike, nudge, or push with the knee. ORIG OE *cnēow*

kneecap (ˈniːˌkæp) *n* **1** *Anat.* a nontechnical name for **patella.** ◆ *vb* **kneecaps, kneecapping, kneecapped.** (*tr*) **2** (esp. of certain terrorist groups) to shoot (a person) in the kneecap.

knee-deep *adj* **1** so deep as to reach or cover the knees. **2** (*postpositive; often foll. by in*) **2a** sunk or covered to the knees: *knee-deep in sand.* **2b** deeply involved: *knee-deep in work.*

knee-high *adj* another word for **knee-deep** (sense 1).

kneehole (ˈniːˌhəʊl) *n* a space for the knees, esp. under a desk.

knee jerk *n* **1** *Physiol.* an outward reflex kick of the lower leg caused by a sharp tap on the tendon just below the kneecap. ◆ *modifier.* **kneejerk. 2** made or occurring as a predictable and automatic response, without thought: *a kneejerk reaction.*

kneel (niːl) *vb* **kneels, kneeling, knelt** *or* **kneeled. 1** (*intr*) to rest, fall, or support oneself on one's knees. ◆ *n* **2** the act or position of kneeling. ORIG OE *cnēowlian;* see KNEE
▸ ˈ**kneeler** *n*

knees-up *n, pl* **knees-ups.** *Brit. inf.* a lively party. ORIG C20: after popular song *Knees-up, Mother Brown!*

knell (nɛl) *n* **1** the sound of a bell rung to announce a death or a funeral. **2** something that precipitates or indicates death or destruction. ◆ *vb* **3** (*intr*) to ring a knell. **4** (*tr*) to proclaim by or as if by a tolling bell. ORIG OE *cnyll*

Kneller ★ (ˈnɛlə) *n* Sir **Godfrey.** ?1646–1723, portrait painter at the English court, born in Germany.

knelt (nɛlt) *vb* a past tense and past participle of **kneel.**

Knesset (ˈknɛsɪt) *n* the representative assembly of Israel. ORIG C20: Heb., lit.: gathering

knew (njuː) *vb* the past tense of **know.**

knickerbocker glory (ˈnɪkəˌbɒkə) *n* a rich confection consisting of layers of ice cream, jelly, cream, and fruit, served in a tall glass.

knickerbockers (ˈnɪkəˌbɒkəz) *pl n* baggy breeches fastened with a band at the knee or above the ankle. Also called (US): **knickers.** ORIG C19: regarded as the traditional dress of the Du. settlers in America; after Diedrich *Knickerbocker,* fictitious author of Washington Irving's *History of New York* (1809)

knickers (ˈnɪkəz) *pl n* an undergarment for women covering the lower trunk and sometimes the thighs and having separate legs or leg-holes. ORIG C19: contraction of KNICKERBOCKERS

knick-knack *or* **nick-nack** (ˈnɪkˌnæk) *n* **1** a cheap ornament. **2** an ornamental article of furniture, dress, etc. ORIG C17: by reduplication from *knack,* in obs. sense: toy

knife (naɪf) *n, pl* **knives** (naɪvz). **1** a cutting instrument consisting of a sharp-edged blade of metal fitted into a handle or onto a machine. **2** a similar instrument used as a weapon. **3 have one's knife in someone.** to have a grudge against someone. **4 under the knife.** undergoing a surgical operation. ◆ *vb* **knifes, knifing, knifed.** (*tr*) **5** to stab or kill with a knife. **6** to betray or depose in an underhand way. ORIG OE *cnīf*
▸ ˈ**knifeˌlike** *adj*

knife edge *n* **1** the sharp cutting edge of a knife. **2** any sharp edge, esp. an arête. **3** a sharp-edged wedge of hard material on which the beam of a balance pivots. **4** a critical point.

knight (naɪt) *n* **1** (in medieval Europe) **1a** (originally) a person who served his lord as a mounted and heavily armed soldier. **1b** (later) a gentleman with the military and social standing of this rank. **2** (in modern times) a person invested by a sovereign with a nonhereditary rank and dignity usually in recognition of personal services, achievements, etc. **3** a chess piece, usually shaped like a horse's head. **4** a heroic champion of a lady or of a cause or principle. **5** a member of the Roman class below the senators. ◆ *vb* **6** (*tr*) to make (a person) a knight. ORIG OE *cniht* servant

Knight ★ (naɪt) *n* Dame **Laura.** 1887–1970, British painter.

knight errant *n, pl* **knights errant.** (esp. in medieval romance) a knight who wanders in search of deeds of courage, chivalry, etc.
▸ **knight errantry** *n*

knighthood ('naɪthʊd) *n* **1** the order, dignity, or rank of a knight. **2** the qualities of a knight.

knightly ('naɪtlɪ) *adj* of, relating to, resembling, or befitting a knight.
▸ **'knightliness** *n*

knight of the road *n Inf. or facetious.* **1** a tramp. **2** a commercial traveller. **3** a lorry driver.

Knights Hospitallers *pl n* a military Christian religious order founded about the time of the first crusade (1096–99).

Knight Templar *n, pl* **Knights Templars** *or* **Knights Templar.** another term for **Templar.**

kniphofia (nɪf'əʊfɪə) *n* the Latin name for **red-hot poker.** ORIG C19: after Johann Hieronymus *Kniphof* (1704–63), G professor of medicine

knit (nɪt) *vb* **knits, knitting, knitted** *or* **knit. 1** to make (a garment, etc.) by looping and entwining (wool) by hand by means of long eyeless needles (**knitting needles**) or by machine (**knitting machine**). **2** to join or be joined together closely. **3** to draw (the brows) together or (of the brows) to come together, as in frowning or concentrating. **4** (of a broken bone) to join together; heal. ◆ *n* **5a** a fabric made by knitting. **5b** (*in combination*): *a heavy knit.* ORIG OE *cnyttan* to tie in
▸ **'knitter** *n*

knitting ('nɪtɪŋ) *n* knitted work or the process of producing it.

knitwear ('nɪt,wɛə) *n* knitted clothes, esp. sweaters.

knives (naɪvz) *n* the plural of **knife.**

knob (nɒb) *n* **1** a rounded projection from a surface, such as a lump on a tree trunk. **2** a handle of a door, drawer, etc., esp. one that is rounded. **3** a round hill or knoll. ◆ *vb* **knobs, knobbing, knobbed. 4** (*tr*) to supply or ornament with knobs. **5** (*intr*) to bulge. ORIG C14: from MLow G *knobbe* knot in wood
▸ **'knobbly** *adj* ▸ **'knobby** *adj* ▸ **'knob,like** *adj*

knobkerrie ('nɒb,kɛrɪ), **knobkierie,** *or* **knobstick** *n* a stick with a round knob at the end, used as a club or missile by South African tribesmen. ORIG C19: from Afrik., from *knop* knob, from MDu. *cnoppe* + *kierie* stick, from Khoikhoi *kīrri*

knock (nɒk) *vb* **1** (*tr*) to give a blow or push to. **2** (*intr*) to rap sharply with the knuckles, a hard object, etc.: *to knock at the door.* **3** (*tr*) to make or force by striking: *to knock a hole in the wall.* **4** (*intr;* usually foll. by *against*) to collide (with). **5** (*tr*) to bring into a certain condition by hitting: *to knock someone unconscious.* **6** (*tr*) *Inf.* to criticize adversely. **7** (*intr*) Also: **pink.** (of an internal-combustion engine) to emit a metallic noise as a result of faulty combustion. **8** (*intr*) (of a bearing, esp. one in an engine) to emit a regular characteristic sound as a result of wear. **9** *Brit. sl.* to have sexual intercourse with (a person). **10 knock (a person) into the middle of next week.** *Inf.* to hit (a person) with a very heavy blow. **11 knock on the head. 11a** to daze or kill (a person) by striking on the head. **11b** to prevent the further development of (a plan). ◆ *n* **12a** a blow, push, or rap: *he gave the table a knock.* **12b** the sound so caused. **13** the sound of knocking in an engine or bearing. **14** *Inf.* a misfortune, rebuff, or setback. **15** *Inf.* criticism. ◆ See also **knock about, knock back,** etc. ORIG OE *cnocian,* imit.

knock about *or* **around** *vb* **1** (*intr, adv*) to wander about aimlessly. **2** (*intr, prep*) to travel about, esp. as resulting in varied experience: *he's knocked about the world.* **3** (*intr, adv;* foll. by *with*) to associate. **4** (*tr, adv*) to treat brutally: *he knocks his wife about.* **5** (*tr, adv*) to consider or discuss informally. ◆ *adj* **knockabout. 6** tough; boisterous: *knockabout farce.*

knock back *vb* (*tr, adv*) *Inf.* **1** to drink, esp. quickly. **2** to cost. **3** to reject or refuse. **4** to shock; disconcert. ◆ *n* **knock-back. 5** *Sl.* a refusal or rejection. **6** *Prison sl.* failure to obtain parole.

knock down *vb* (*tr, adv*) **1** to strike to the ground with a blow, as in boxing. **2** (in auctions) to declare (an article) sold. **3** to demolish. **4** to dismantle for ease of transport. **5** *Inf.* to reduce (a price, etc.). **6** *Austral. sl.* to spend (a cheque). **7** *Austral. sl.* to drink. ◆ *adj* **knockdown.** (*prenominal*) **8** powerful: *a knockdown blow.* **9** *Chiefly Brit.* cheap: *a knockdown price.* **10** easily dismantled: *knockdown furniture.*

knocker ('nɒkə) *n* **1** an object, usually made of metal, attached to a door by a hinge and used for knocking. **2** *Inf.* a person who finds fault or disparages. **3** (*usually pl*) *Sl.* a female breast. **4** a person or thing that knocks. **5 on the knocker.** *Inf.* promptly: *you pay on the knocker here.*

knocking copy *n* publicity material designed to denigrate a competing product.

knocking-shop *n Brit.* a slang word for **brothel.**

knock-knee *n* a condition in which the legs are bent inwards causing the knees to touch when standing.
▸ **,knock-'kneed** *adj*

knock off *vb* (*mainly adv*) **1** (*intr, also prep*) *Inf.* to finish work: *we knocked off an hour early.* **2** (*tr*) *Inf.* to make or do hastily or easily: *to knock off a novel in a week.* **3** (*tr; also prep*) *Inf.* to reduce the price of (an article). **4** (*tr*) *Sl.* to kill. **5** (*tr*) *Sl.* to rob or steal: *to knock off a bank.* **6** (*tr*) *Sl.* to stop doing something, used as a command: *knock it off!* ◆ *n* **knockoff. 7** *Inf.* **7a** an illegal imitation of a well-known product. **7b** (*as modifier*): *knockoff merchandise.*

knock-on *Rugby.* ◆ *n* **1** the infringement of playing the ball forward with the hand or arm. ◆ *vb* **knock on.** (*adv*) **2** to play (the ball) forward with the hand or arm.

knock-on effect *n* the indirect result of an action: *the number of redundancies was not great but there were as many again from the knock-on effect.*

knockout ('nɒk,aʊt) *n* **1** the act of rendering unconscious. **2** a blow that renders an opponent unconscious. **3a** a competition in which competitors are eliminated progressively. **3b** (*as modifier*): *a knockout contest.* **4** *Inf.* a person or thing that is overwhelmingly impressive or attractive: *she's a knockout.* ◆ *vb* **knock out.** (*tr, adv*) **5** to render unconscious, esp. by a blow. **6** *Boxing.* to defeat (an opponent) by a knockout. **7** to destroy or injure badly. **8** to eliminate, esp. in a knockout competition. **9** *Inf.* to overwhelm or amaze: *I was knocked out by that new song.* **10 knock the bottom out of.** *Inf.* to invalidate (an argument).

knockout drops *pl n Sl.* a drug secretly put into someone's drink to cause stupefaction. ◆ See also **Mickey Finn.**

knock up *vb* (*adv, mainly tr*) **1** Also: **knock together.** *Inf.* to assemble quickly: *to knock up a set of shelves.* **2** *Brit. inf.* to waken; rouse: *to knock someone up early.* **3** *Sl.* to make pregnant. **4** *Brit. inf.* to exhaust. **5** *Cricket.* to score (runs). **6** (*intr*) *Tennis, squash, etc.* to practise, esp. before a match. ◆ *n* **knock-up. 7** a practice session at tennis, squash, etc.

knoll (nəʊl) *n* a small rounded hill. ORIG OE *cnoll*
▸ **'knolly** *adj*

Knossos *or* **Cnossus** ★ ('nɒsəs, 'knɒs-) *n* a ruined city in N central Crete: remains of the Minoan Bronze Age civilization.

knot[1] (nɒt) *n* **1** any of various fastenings formed by looping and tying a piece of rope, cord, etc., in upon itself or to another piece of rope. **2** a prescribed method of tying a particular knot. **3** a tangle, as in hair or string. **4** a decorative bow, as of ribbon. **5** a small cluster or huddled group. **6** a tie or bond: *the marriage knot.* **7** a difficult problem. **8a** a hard mass of wood where a branch joins the trunk of a tree. **8b** a cross section of this visible on a piece of timber. **9** a sensation of constriction, caused by tension or nervousness: *his stomach was tying itself in knots.* **10** *Pathol.* a lump of vessels or fibres formed in a part, as in a muscle. **11** a unit of velocity used by ships and aircraft, being one nautical mile (about 1.15 statute miles or 1.85 km) per hour. **12 at a rate of knots.** very fast. **13 tie (someone) in knots.** to completely perplex (someone). ◆ *vb* **knots, knotting, knotted. 14** (*tr*) to tie or fasten in a knot. **15** to form or cause to form into a knot. **16** (*tr*) to entangle or become entangled. **17** (*tr*) to make (an article

★ people and places

or design) by tying thread in ornamental knots. ORIG OE *cnotta*
▸ **ˈknotted** *adj* ▸ **ˈknotter** *n* ▸ **ˈknotless** *adj*

knot² (nɒt) *n* a small northern sandpiper with a short bill and grey plumage. ORIG C15: from ?

knot garden *n* (esp. formerly) a formal garden of intricate design.

knotgrass (ˈnɒtˌgrɑːs) *n* **1** Also called: **allseed.** a weed whose small green flowers produce numerous seeds. **2** any of several related plants.

knothole (ˈnɒtˌhəʊl) *n* a hole in a piece of wood where a knot has been.

knotty (ˈnɒtɪ) *adj* **knottier, knottiest. 1** (of wood, rope, etc.) full of or characterized by knots. **2** extremely difficult or intricate.

knout (naʊt) *n* a stout whip used formerly in Russia as an instrument of punishment. ORIG C17: from Russian *knut,* of Scand. origin

know (nəʊ) *vb* **knows, knowing, knew, known.** (*mainly tr*) **1** (*also intr; may take a clause as object*) to be or feel certain of the truth or accuracy of (a fact, etc.). **2** to be acquainted or familiar with: *she's known him five years.* **3** to have a familiarity or grasp of: *he knows French.* **4** (*also intr; may take a clause as object*) to understand, be aware of, or perceive (facts, etc.): *he knows the answer now.* **5** (foll. by *how*) to be sure or aware of (how to be or do something). **6** to experience, esp. deeply: *to know poverty.* **7** to be intelligent, informed, or sensible enough (to do something). **8** (*may take a clause as object*) to be able to distinguish or discriminate. **9** *Arch.* to have sexual intercourse with. **10 know what's what.** to know how one thing or things in general work. **11 you never know.** things are uncertain. ◆ *n* **12 in the know.** *Inf.* aware or informed. ORIG OE *gecnāwan*
▸ **ˈknowable** *adj* ▸ **ˈknower** *n*

know-all *n Inf., disparaging.* a person who pretends or appears to know a great deal.

know-how *n Inf.* **1** ingenuity, aptitude, or skill. **2** commercial and saleable knowledge of how to do a particular thing.

knowing (ˈnəʊɪŋ) *adj* **1** suggesting secret knowledge. **2** wise, shrewd, or clever. **3** deliberate. ◆ *n* **4 there is no knowing.** one cannot tell.
▸ **ˈknowingly** *adv* ▸ **ˈknowingness** *n*

knowledge (ˈnɒlɪdʒ) *n* **1** the facts or experiences known by a person or group of people. **2** the state of knowing. **3** consciousness or familiarity gained by experience or learning. **4** erudition or informed learning. **5** specific information about a subject. **6 to my knowledge. 6a** as I understand it. **6b** as I know.

knowledgeable *or* **knowledgable** (ˈnɒlɪdʒəbᵊl) *adj* possessing or indicating much knowledge.
▸ **ˈknowledgeably** *or* **ˈknowledgably** *adv*

knowledge worker *n* a person employed to produce or analyse ideas and information.

known (nəʊn) *vb* **1** the past participle of **know.** ◆ *adj* **2** identified: *a known criminal.*

Knowsley ★ (ˈnəʊzlɪ) *n* a unitary authority in NW England, in Merseyside. Pop.: 154 000 (1994 est.). Area: 97 sq. km (38 sq. miles).

Knox ★ (nɒks) *n* **John.** ?1514–72, Scottish theologian and historian. After exile in England and on the Continent (1547–59), he returned to Scotland in 1559 and established the Presbyterian Church of Scotland (1560). His chief historical work was the *History of the Reformation in Scotland* (1586).

Knox-Johnston ★ (ˌnɒksˈdʒɒnstən) *n* Sir **Robin (William Robert Patrick).** born 1939, British yachtsman. He was the first to sail round the world alone nonstop (1968–69).

Knoxville ★ (ˈnɒksvɪl) *n* an industrial city in E Tennessee, on the Tennessee River: state capital (1796–1812; 1817–19). Pop.: 169 311 (1994 est.).

knuckle (ˈnʌkᵊl) *n* **1** a joint of a finger, esp. that connecting a finger to the hand. **2** a joint of veal, pork, etc., consisting of the part of the leg below the knee joint. **3 near the knuckle.** *Inf.* approaching indecency. ◆ *vb* **knuckles, knuckling, knuckled. 4** (*tr*) to rub or press with the knuckles. **5** (*intr*) to keep the knuckles on the ground while shooting a marble. ◆ See also **knuckle down, knuckle under.** ORIG C14
▸ **ˈknuckly** *adj*

knucklebones (ˈnʌkᵊlˌbəʊnz) *n* (*functioning as sing*) a less common name for **jacks** (the game).

knuckle down *vb* (*intr, adv*) *Inf.* to apply oneself diligently: *to knuckle down to some work.*

knuckle-duster *n* (*often pl*) a metal bar fitted over the knuckles, often with holes for the fingers, for inflicting injury by a blow with the fist.

knucklehead (ˈnʌkᵊlˌhɛd) *n Inf.* a fool; idiot.
▸ **ˈknuckleˌheaded** *adj*

knuckle under *vb* (*intr, adv*) to give way under pressure or authority; yield.

knur, knurr (nɜː), *or* **knar** *n* a knot or protuberance in a tree trunk or in wood. ORIG C16 *knor;* cf. KNAR

knurl *or* **nurl** (nɜːl) *vb* (*tr*) **1** to impress with a series of fine ridges or serrations. ◆ *n* **2** a small ridge, esp. one of a series. ORIG C17: prob. from KNUR

Knut ★ (kəˈnjuːt) *n* a variant spelling of **Canute.**

KO *or* **k.o.** (ˈkeɪˈəʊ) *vb* **KO's, KO'ing, KO'd** *or* **k.o.'s, k.o.'ing, k.o.'d,** *n, pl* **KO's** *or* **k.o.'s.** a slang term for **knockout** or **knock out.**

koala *or* **koala bear** (kəʊˈɑːlə) *n* a slow-moving Australian arboreal marsupial, having dense greyish fur and feeding on eucalyptus leaves. Also called (Austral.): **native bear.** ORIG from Abor.

koan (ˈkəʊæn) *n* (in Zen Buddhism) a problem that admits no logical solution. ORIG from Japanese

Kobarid ★ (ˈkəʊbəˌriːd; *Serbo-Croat* ˈkɔbaˌrid) *n* a village in Slovenia, on the Isonzo River: part of Italy until 1947; scene of the defeat of the Italians by Austro-German forces (1917). Italian name: **Caporetto.**

Kobe ★ (ˈkəʊbɪ) *n* a port in S Japan, on S Honshu on Osaka Bay: formed in 1889 by the amalgamation of Hyogo and Kobe; a major industrial complex, producing ships, steel, and rubber goods. Pop.: 1 423 830 (1995).

København ★ (købənˈhaun) *n* the Danish name for **Copenhagen.**

Koblenz *or* **Coblenz** ★ (kəʊˈblɛnts; *German* ˈkoːblɛnts) *n* a city in W central Germany, in the Rhineland-Palatinate at the confluence of the Rivers Moselle and Rhine: ruled by the archbishop-electors of Trier from 1018 until occupied by the French in 1794; passed to Prussia in 1815, becoming capital of the Rhine Province (1824–1945) and of the Rhineland-Palatinate (1946–50); wine trade centre. Pop.: 109 219 (1996 est.). Latin name: **Confluentes** (ˌkɒnfluˈɛntiːz).

kobold (ˈkɒbəʊld) *n German myth.* **1** a mischievous household sprite. **2** a spirit that haunts mines. ORIG C19: from G; see COBALT

Koch ★ (*German* kɔx) *n* **Robert** (ˈroːbɛrt). 1843–1910, German bacteriologist, who isolated the anthrax bacillus (1876), the tubercle bacillus (1882), and the cholera bacillus (1883): Nobel prize for physiology or medicine 1905.

Kochi ★ (kəʊˈtʃiː) *n* a port in SW Japan, on central Shikoku on Urado Bay. Pop.: 322 077 (1995 est.).

kochia (ˈkɒˈʃiːə) *n* an annual plant with ornamental foliage that turns purple-red in late summer. ORIG C19: after W.D.J. *Koch,* G botanist

Kodály ★ (*Hungarian* ˈkodaːj) *n* **Zoltán** (ˈzoltaːn). 1882–1967, Hungarian composer. His works include the comic opera *Háry János* (1926) and *Psalmus Hungaricus* (1923) for chorus and orchestra.

Kodiak ★ (ˈkəʊdɪˌæk) *n* an island in S Alaska, in the Gulf of Alaska: site of the first European settlement in Alaska, made by Russians in 1784. Pop.: 13 309 (1990). Area: 8974 sq. km (3465 sq. miles).

Kodiak bear *or* **Kodiak** *n* a large variety of the brown bear inhabiting the W coast of Alaska and neighbouring islands, esp. Kodiak.

koeksister (ˈkʊkˌsɪstə) *n S. African.* a plaited doughnut deep-fried and soaked in syrup. ORIG Afrik. but possibly of Malay origin

koel (ˈkəʊəl) *n* any of several parasitic cuckoos of S and SE

Asia and Australia. ORIG C19: from Hindi, from Sansk. *kokila*

Koestler ★ ('kɜːstlə) *n* **Arthur.** 1905–83, British writer, born in Hungary. His works include the novel *Darkness at Noon* (1940) and the nonfiction *The Sleepwalkers* (1959) and *The Ghost in the Machine* (1967), which reflect his interest in science and philosophy.

Kofu ★ ('kəʊfuː) *n* a city in central Japan, on S Honshu. Pop.: 201 123 (1995 est.).

Kogi ★ ('kəʊgɪ) *n* a state of W Nigeria. Capital: Lokoja: Pop.: 2 346 936 (1995 est.).

koha ('kəʊhə) *n NZ.* a gift or donation. ORIG Maori

kohanga reo ('kɔːhɑːŋɑː 'reɪɔː) *n NZ.* an infant class in which the lessons are conducted in Maori. ORIG Maori, lit.: language nest

Kohima ★ ('kəʊhɪˌmɑː) *n* a city in NE India, capital of Nagaland, near the Burmese border: centre of fierce fighting in World War II, when it was surrounded by the Japanese but not captured (1944). Pop.: 53 122 (1991).

kohl (kəʊl) *n* a cosmetic powder used, originally esp. in Muslim and Asian countries, to darken the area around the eyes. ORIG C18: from Ar. *kohl;* see ALCOHOL

Kohl ★ (kəʊl) *n* **Helmut** ('hɛlmuːt). born 1930, German statesman: chancellor of West Germany (1982–90) and of Germany (1990–98).

Köhler ★ (*German* 'køːlər) *n* **Wolfgang** ('vɔlfgaŋ). 1887–1967, German psychologist; exponent of Gestalt psychology.

kohlrabi (kəʊl'rɑːbɪ) *n, pl* **kohlrabies.** a cultivated variety of cabbage whose thickened stem is eaten as a vegetable. Also called: **turnip cabbage.** ORIG C19: from G, from It. *cavoli rape* (pl), from *cavolo* cabbage (from L *caulis*) + *rapa* turnip (from L)

koi (kɔɪ) *n* any of various ornamental forms of the common carp. ORIG Japanese

koine ('kɔɪniː) *n* a common language among speakers of different languages; lingua franca. ORIG from Gk *koinē dialektos* common language

Koine ('kɔɪniː) *n* (*sometimes not cap.*) **the.** the ancient Greek dialect that was the lingua franca of the empire of Alexander the Great and in Roman times.

Kokand ★ (*Russian* ka'kant) *n* a city in NE Uzbekistan, in the Fergana valley. Pop.: 184 000 (1996).

kokanee (kəʊ'kænɪ) *n* a landlocked salmon of lakes in W North America: a variety of sockeye. ORIG prob. from *Kokanee* Creek, in SE British Columbia

Koko Nor ('kəʊ'kəʊ 'nɔː) *or* **Kuku Nor** ★ *n* a lake in W China, in Qinghai province in the NE Tibetan Highlands at an altitude of about 3000 m (10 000 ft): the largest lake in China. Area: about 4100 sq. km (1600 sq. miles). Chinese name: **Qinghai.**

Kokoschka ★ (*German* ko'kɔʃka, 'kɔkɔʃka) *n* **Oskar** ('ɔskar). 1886–1980, Austrian expressionist painter.

Kokura ★ (ˌkəʊkə'rɑː) *n* a former city in SW Japan, on N Kyushu: merged with adjacent townships in 1963 to form the new city of **Kitakyushu.**

kola ('kəʊlə) *n* a variant spelling of **cola.**

kola nut *n* a variant spelling of **cola nut.**

Kola Peninsula ★ ('kəʊlə) *n* a peninsula of NW Russia, between the Barents and White Seas: forms most of the Murmansk Region. Area: about 130 000 sq. km (50 000 sq. miles).

Kolar Gold Fields ★ (kəʊ'lɑː) *n* a city in S India, in SE Karnataka: a major gold-mining centre since 1881. Pop.: 83 219 (1991 est.).

Kolding ★ (*Danish* 'kɔleŋ) *n* a port in Denmark, in E Jutland at the head of **Kolding Fjord** (an inlet of the Little Belt). Pop.: 59 558 (1995).

Kolhapur ★ (ˌkəʊlhɑː'pʊə) *n* a city in W India, in S Maharashtra: university (1963). Pop.: 406 370 (1991).

kolinsky (kə'lɪnskɪ) *n, pl* **kolinskies. 1** any of various Asian minks. **2** the rich tawny fur of this animal. ORIG C19: from Russian *kolinski* of Kola: see KOLA PENINSULA

kolkhoz (kɒl'hɔːz) *n* a Russian collective farm. ORIG C20: from Russian, short for *kollektivnoe khozyaistvo* collective farm

Kolmar ★ ('kɔlmar) *n* the German name for **Colmar.**

Kolmogorov ★ (ˌkɒlmɒ'gɔːrɒf) *n* **Andrei Nikolaevich** (an-'drjej nika'lajəvitʃ). 1903–87, Soviet mathematician, who made important contributions to the theoretical foundations of probability.

Köln ★ (kœln) *n* the German name for **Cologne.**

Kol Nidre (kɔːl 'nɪdreɪ) *n Judaism.* **1** the evening service with which Yom Kippur begins. **2** the opening prayer of that service. ORIG Aramaic *kōl nidhrē* all the vows; the prayer's opening words

Kolomna ★ (*Russian* ka'lɔmnə) *n* a city in W central Russia, at the confluence of the Moskva and Oka Rivers: railway engineering centre. Pop.: 154 000 (1995 est.).

Kolyma ★ (*Russian* kəli'ma) *n* a river in NE Russia, rising in the Kolyma Mountains north of the Sea of Okhotsk and flowing generally north to the East Siberian Sea. Length: 2600 km (1615 miles).

Kolyma Range ★ *n* a mountain range in NE Russia, in NE Siberia, extending about 1100 km (700 miles) between the Kolyma River and the Sea of Okhotsk. Highest peak: 1862 m (6109 ft).

Komati ★ (kə'mɑːtɪ, 'kəʊmətɪ) *n* a river in southern Africa, rising in E South Africa and flowing east through Swaziland and Mozambique to the Indian Ocean at Delagoa Bay. Length: about 800 km (500 miles).

komatik ('kəʊmætɪk) *n* a sledge having wooden runners and crossbars bound with rawhide, used by Eskimos. ORIG C20: from Eskimo

Komi Republic ★ ('kəʊmɪ) *n* a constituent republic of NW Russia: annexed by the princes of Moscow in the 14th century. Capital: Syktyvkar. Pop.: 1 185 000 (1996 est.). Area: 415 900 sq. km (160 540 sq. miles).

Kommunarsk ★ (*Russian* kəmu'narsk) *n* the former (until 1992) name of **Alchevsk.**

Kommunizma Peak ★ (*Russian* kəmu'njizmə) *n* a mountain in SE Tajikistan, in the Pamirs: the highest mountain in the former Soviet Union. Height: 7495 m (24 590 ft). Former name: **Stalin Peak.**

Komsomolsk ★ (*Russian* kəmsa'mɔljsk) *n* an industrial city in W Russia, on the Amur River: built by members of the Komsomol (Communist youth league) in 1932. Pop.: 309 000 (1995 est.).

Konakry *or* **Konakri** ★ (*French* kɔnakri) *n* variant spellings of **Conakry.**

Kongur Shan ('kʊŋgʊə 'ʃæn), **Kungur,** *or* **Qungur** ★ *n* a mountain in China, in W Xinjiang Uygur: the highest peak in the Pamirs. Height: 7719 m (25 325 ft).

Kong Zi ★ ('kʊŋ ziː) *n* the Pinyin transliteration of the Chinese name for **Confucius.**

Königgrätz ★ (køːnɪç'grɛːts) *n* the German name for **Hradec Králové.**

Königsberg ★ ('kɜːnɪgzˌbɜːg; *German* 'køːnɪçsbɛrk) *n* the former name (until 1946) of **Kaliningrad.**

Königshütte ★ ('køːnɪçshytə) *n* the German name for **Chorzów.**

Konstanz ★ ('kɔnstants) *n* the German name for **Constance.**

Konya *or* **Konia** ★ ('kɔːnjɑː) *n* a city in SW central Turkey: in ancient times a Phrygian city and capital of Lycaonia. Pop.: 576 000 (1994 est.). Ancient name: **Iconium.**

koodoo ('kuːduː) *n* a variant spelling of **kudu.**

kook (kuːk) *n US & Canad. inf.* an eccentric or foolish person. ORIG C20: prob. from CUCKOO
▸ **'kooky** *or* **'kookie** *adj*

kookaburra ('kʊkəˌbʌrə) *n* a large Australian kingfisher with a cackling cry. Also called: **laughing jackass.** ORIG C19: from Abor.

Kooning ★ ('kuːnɪŋ) *n* **Willem de** ('wɪləm də). 1904–97, US abstract expressionist painter, born in Holland.

Kootenay *or* **Kootenai** ★ ('kuːtᵊniː, 'kuːtneɪ) *n* a river in W North America, rising in SE British Columbia and flowing south into NW Montana, then north into Idaho before re-entering British Columbia, broadening into **Kootenay Lake,** then flowing to the Columbia River. Length: 655 km (407 miles).

kopeck *or* **copeck** ('kəupɛk) *n* a monetary unit of Russia and Belarus worth one hundredth of a rouble: coins are still used as tokens for coin-operated machinery although the kopeck itself is virtually valueless. ORIG Russian *kopeika,* from *kopye* lance

Kopeisk *or* **Kopeysk** ★ (*Russian* ka'pjejsk) *n* a city in SW central Russia, in Chelyabinsk province: lignite mining. Pop.: 78 300 (1991 est.). Former name: **Kopi** ('kɔpi).

koppie *or* **kopje** ('kɒpɪ) *n* (in southern Africa) a small isolated hill. ORIG C19: from Afrik., from Du. *kopje,* lit.: a little head, from *kop* head

kora ('kɔːrə) *n* a West African instrument with twenty-one strings, combining features of the harp and the lute.

Koran (kɔː'rɑːn) *n* the sacred book of Islam, believed by Muslims to be the infallible word of God dictated to Mohammed. Also: **Qur'an.** ORIG C17: from Ar. *qur'ān* reading, book
▸ **Ko'ranic** *adj*

Korbut ★ (*Russian* 'kɔrbʊt) *n* **Olga** ('ɔljgə). born 1955, Soviet gymnast.

Korçë ★ (*Albanian* 'kortʃə) *n* a market town in SE Albania. Pop.: 67 100 (1991 est.).

Korchnoi ★ ('kɔːtʃˌnɔɪ) *n* **Victor.** born 1931, Soviet-born chess player: Soviet champion 1960, 1962, and 1964: defected to the West in 1976.

Korda ★ ('kɔːdə) *n* Sir **Alexander,** real name *Sandor Kellner.* 1893–1956, British film producer and director, born in Hungary: his films include *The Scarlet Pimpernel* (1934) and *The Third Man* (1949).

Kordofan ★ (ˌkɔːdəʊ'fæn) *n* a region of the central Sudan: consists of a plateau with rugged uplands (the Nuba Mountains). Area: 380 548 sq. km (146 930 sq. miles).

Korea ★ (kə'riːə) *n* a former country in E Asia, now divided into two separate countries, North Korea and South Korea. Korea occupied the peninsula between the Sea of Japan and the Yellow Sea: an isolated vassal of China for three centuries until the opening of ports to foreign trade in 1876; annexed to Japan in 1910 and divided in 1945 into two occupation zones (Russian in the north, American in the south), which became North Korea and South Korea in 1948: the Korean War (1950–53), in which US-led UN forces backed the South and China backed the North, ended with the country still divided. See **North Korea, South Korea.**
▸ **Ko'rean** *adj, n*

Korea Strait ★ *n* a strait between South Korea and SW Japan, linking the Sea of Japan with the East China Sea.

korfball ('kɔːfˌbɔːl) *n* a game similar to basketball, in which each team consists of six men and six women. ORIG C20: from Du. *korfbal* basketball

Kórinthos ★ ('kɔrinθɔs) *n* transliteration of the Modern Greek name for **Corinth.**

korma ('kɔːmə) *n* an Indian dish consisting of meat or vegetables braised with stock, yogurt, or cream. ORIG from Urdu

Korsakoffian (ˌkɔːsə'kɒfɪən) *adj* **1** relating to or suffering from **Korsakoff's psychosis**, a mental illness involving severe confusion and inability to retain recent memories, usually caused by alcoholism. ◆ *n* **2** a person suffering from Korsakoff's psychosis. ORIG C19: after Sergei *Korsakoff* (1854–1900), Russian neuropsychiatrist

Korzybski ★ (kɔː'zɪbskɪ) *n* **Alfred (Habdank Skarbek).** 1879–1950, US originator of the theory and study of general semantics, born in Poland.

Kos *or* **Cos** ★ (kɒs) *n* an island in the SE Aegean Sea, in the Greek Dodecanese Islands: separated from SW Turkey by the **Kos Channel;** settled in ancient times by Dorians and became famous for literature and medicine. Pop.: 21 000 (latest est.). Area: 282 sq. km (109 sq. miles).

Kosciusko ★ (ˌkɒsɪ'ʌskəʊ) *n* **Mount.** a mountain in Australia, in SE New South Wales in the Australian Alps: the highest peak in Australia. Height: 2230 m (7316 ft).

kosher ('kəʊʃə) *adj* **1** *Judaism.* conforming to religious law; fit for use: esp. (of food) prepared in accordance with the dietary laws. **2** *Inf.* **2a** genuine or authentic. **2b** legitimate. ORIG C19: from Yiddish, from Heb. *kāshēr* proper

Košice ★ (*Czech* 'kɔʃitsɛ) *n* a city in E Slovakia: passed from Hungary to Czechoslovakia in 1920 and to Slovakia in 1993. Pop.: 239 927 (1995 est.). Hungarian name: **Kassa.**

Kosovo ★ (*Serbo-Croat* 'kɔsɔvɔ) *n* a region in S central Yugoslavia, in SW Serbia: became an autonomous region in 1946; chiefly Albanian in population, it was deprived of its autonomous status by Serbia after declaring independence in 1990: mainly a plateau. Capital: **Priština.** Pop.: 1 989 000 (1995 est.). Area: 10 887 sq. km (4203 sq. miles).
▸ **'Kosovar** *or* **'Kosovan** *adj, n*

Kossoff ★ ('kɒsɒf) *n* **Leon.** born 1926, British painter, esp. of London scenes.

Kossuth ★ (*Hungarian* 'koʃuːt) *n* **Lajos** ('lɔjoʃ). 1802–94, Hungarian statesman. He led the revolution against Austria (1848) and was provisional governor (1849), but he fled when the revolt was suppressed (1849).

Kostroma ★ (*Russian* kəstra'ma) *n* a city in W central Russia, on the River Volga: fought over bitterly by Novgorod, Tver, and Moscow, until annexed by Moscow in 1329; textile centre. Pop.: 285 000 (1995 est.).

Kostunica ★ (kɒs'tuːnɪkə) *n* **Vojislav** (*Serbo-Croat* 'vɔjɪslaːv) Serbian politician; president of the Federal Republic of Yugoslavia from 2000.

Kosygin ★ (*Russian* ka'sigin) *n* **Aleksei Nikolayevich** (alɪk'sjej nika'lajɪvitʃ). 1904–80, Soviet statesman; premier of the Soviet Union (1964–80).

Kota *or* **Kotah** ★ ('kəʊtə) *n* a city in NW India, in Rajasthan on the Chambal River: textile industry. Pop.: 537 371 (1991).

Kotabaru ★ ('kəʊtə'bɑːruː) *n* a former name of **Jayapura.**

Kota Bharu *or* **Bahru** ★ ('kəʊtə 'bɑːruː) *n* a port in NE Peninsular Malaysia: capital of Kelantan state on the delta of the Kelantan River. Pop.: 219 713 (1991).

Kota Kinabalu ★ ('kəʊtə ˌkɪnəbə'luː) *n* a port in Malaysia, capital of Sabah state on the South China Sea: exports timber and rubber. Pop.: 208 484 (1991). Former name: **Jesselton.**

koto ('kəʊtəʊ) *n, pl* **kotos.** a Japanese stringed instrument. ORIG Japanese

kotuku ('kəʊtʊkuː) *n, pl* **kotuku.** *NZ.* a white heron having brilliant white plumage, black legs and yellow eyes and bill. ORIG Maori

kouprey ('kuːpreɪ) *n* a large wild member of the cattle tribe, of SE Asia, having a blackish-brown body and white legs: an endangered species. ORIG C20: from F, from Cambodian, from Pali *gō* cow + Khmer *brai* forest

Kovno ★ ('kɔvnɔ) *n* transliteration of the Russian name for **Kaunas.**

Kovrov ★ (*Russian* kav'rɔf) *n* a city in W central Russia, on the Klyazma River: textiles and heavy engineering. Pop.: 162 000 (1995 est.).

Koweit ★ (kəʊ'weɪt) *n* a variant of **Kuwait.**

kowhai ('koːwaɪ) *n, pl* **kowhais.** *NZ.* a small leguminous tree of New Zealand and Chile with clusters of yellow flowers. ORIG C19: from Maori

Kowloon ★ ('kaʊ'luːn) *n* **1** a peninsula of SE China, opposite Hong Kong Island: part of the former British colony of Hong Kong. Area: 10 sq. km (3.75 sq. miles). **2** a port in Hong Kong, on Kowloon Peninsula. Pop.: 1 990 000 (1994 est.).

kowtow (ˌkaʊ'taʊ) *vb* (*intr*) **1** to touch the forehead to the ground as a sign of deference: a former Chinese custom. **2** (often foll. by *to*) to be servile (towards). ◆ *n* **3** the act of kowtowing. ORIG C19: from Chinese, from *k'o* to strike, knock + *t'ou* head

Kozhikode ★ (ˌkəʊʒɪ'kəʊd) *n* a port in SW India, in W Kerala on the Malabar coast: important European trading post (1511–1765): formerly calico-manufacturing. Pop.: 420 000 (1991). Former name: **Calicut.**

Kr 1 *Currency. symbol for:* **1a** krona. **1b** krone. **2** *the chemical symbol for* krypton.

kr. *abbrev. for:* **1** krona. **2** krone.

Kra ★ (krɑː) *n* **Isthmus of.** an isthmus of SW Thailand, between the Bay of Bengal and the Gulf of Siam: the narrowest part of the Malay Peninsula. Width: about 56 km (35 miles).

kraal (krɑːl) *n S. African.* **1** a hut village in southern Africa, esp. one surrounded by a stockade. **2** an enclosure for livestock. ORIG C18: from Afrik., from Port. *curral* pen

Krafft-Ebing ★ (*German* 'kraft'eːbɪŋ) *n* **Richard** ('rɪçart), Baron von Krafft-Ebing. 1840–1902, German neurologist, who pioneered the study of sexual behaviour in *Psychopathia Sexualis* (1886).

kraft (krɑːft) *n* strong wrapping paper. ORIG G: force

Kragujevac ★ (*Serbo-Croat* 'kragujɛvats) *n* a town in E central Yugoslavia, in Serbia; capital of Serbia (1818–39); automobile industry. Pop.: 147 305 (1991).

krait (kraɪt) *n* any nonaggressive brightly coloured venomous snake of S and SE Asia. ORIG C19: from Hindi *karait,* from ?

Krakatoa (ˌkrɑːkə'təʊə, ˌkrækə'təʊə) *or* **Krakatau** ★ (ˌkrɑːkə'taʊ, ˌkrækə'taʊ) *n* a volcanic island in Indonesia, in the Sunda Strait between Java and Sumatra: partially destroyed by its eruption in 1883, the greatest in recorded history. Further eruptions 44 years later formed a new island, **Anak Krakatau** ("Child of Krakatau"). Also called: **Rakata.**

Krakau ★ ('kraːkau) *n* the German name for **Cracow.**

kraken ('krɑːkən) *n* a legendary sea monster of gigantic size believed to dwell off the coast of Norway. ORIG C18: from Norwegian, from ?

Kraków ★ ('krakuf) *n* the Polish name for **Cracow.**

Kramatorsk ★ (*Russian* krəma'tɔrsk) *n* a city in E Ukraine: a major industrial centre of the Donets Basin. Pop.: 197 000 (1996 est.).

Kranj ★ (kraːnj) *n* the Slovene name for **Carniola.**

krans (krɑːns) *n S. African.* a sheer rock face; precipice. ORIG C18: from Afrik.

Krasnodar ★ (*Russian* krəsna'dar) *n* an industrial city in SW Russia, on the Kuban River. Pop.: 646 000 (1995 est.). Former name (until 1920): **Yekaterinodar.**

Krasnoyarsk ★ (*Russian* krəsna'jarsk) *n* a city in E central Russia, on the Yenisei River: the country's largest hydroelectric power station is nearby. Pop.: 869 000 (1995 est.).

Krebs ★ (krɛbz) *n* Sir **Hans Adolf.** 1900–81, British biochemist, born in Germany, who shared a Nobel prize for physiology or medicine (1953) for the discovery of the **Krebs cycle**, a cycle of metabolic reactions.

Krefeld ★ ('kreɪfɛld; *German* 'kreːfɛlt) *n* a city in W Germany, in W North Rhine-Westphalia: textile industries. Pop.: 249 606 (1996 est.).

Kreisler ★ (*German* 'kraislər) *n* **Fritz** (frɪts). 1875–1962, US violinist, born in Austria.

Kremenchug ★ (*Russian* krɪmɪn'tʃuk) *n* an industrial city in E central Ukraine, on the Dnieper River. Pop.: 246 000 (1996 est.).

kremlin ('krɛmlɪn) *n* the citadel of any Russian city. ORIG C17: from obs. G *Kremelin,* from Russian *kreml*

Kremlin ★ ('krɛmlɪn) *n* **1** the 12th-century citadel in Moscow, containing the offices of the Russian government. **2** (formerly) the central government of the Soviet Union.

Krems ★ (*German* krɛms) *n* a town in NE Austria, in Lower Austria on the River Danube. Pop.: 22 830 (1991).

Kriemhild ('kriːmhɪlt) *or* **Kriemhilde** ★ ('kriːmˌhɪldə) *n* (in the *Nibelungenlied*) the wife of Siegfried. She corresponds to Gudrun in Norse mythology.

krill (krɪl) *n, pl* **krill.** any small shrimplike marine crustacean: the principal food of whalebone whales. ORIG C20: from Norwegian *kril* young fish

krimmer ('krɪmə) *n* a tightly curled light grey fur obtained from the skins of lambs from Crimea in Ukraine. ORIG C20: from G, from *Krim* Crimea

Kriol ('kriːɒl) *n* a creole language used by Aboriginal communities in the northern regions of Australia, developed from Northern Territory pidgin.

kris (krɪs) *n* a Malayan and Indonesian stabbing or slashing knife with a scalloped edge. Also called: **crease, creese.** ORIG C16: from Malay

Krishna[1] ★ ('krɪʃnə) *n* a river in S India, rising in the Western Ghats and flowing generally southeast to the Bay of Bengal. Length: 1300 km (800 miles). Also called: **Kistna.**

Krishna[2] ★ ('krɪʃnə) *n Hinduism.* the most celebrated of the Hindu deities, whose life story is told in the *Mahabharata.* ORIG via Hindi from Sansk., lit.: dark, black

▸ **'Krishnaism** *n*

Krishna Menon ★ ('kriːʃnə 'mɛnən) *n* **Vengalil Krishnan** ('vɛŋgəlɪl 'kriːʃnən). See (Vengalil Krishnan Krishna) **Menon.**

Kristiania ★ (ˌkrɪstɪ'ɑːnɪə) *n* a former name (1877–1924) of **Oslo.**

Kristiansand *or* **Christiansand** ★ ('krɪstʃənˌsænd; *Norwegian* kristian'san) *n* a port in S Norway, on the Skagerrak: shipbuilding. Pop.: 65 543 (1990).

Kristiansen ★ ('krɪstʃənsən) *n* **Ingrid.** born 1956, Norwegian long-distance runner.

Kristianstad ★ ('krɪstʃənˌstɑːd; *Swedish* kri'ʃanstɑːd) *n* a town in S Sweden: founded in 1614 as a Danish fortress, it was acquired by Sweden in 1678. Pop.: 73 543 (1994).

Kríti ★ ('kriti) *n* transliteration of the Modern Greek name for **Crete.**

Krivoy Rog ★ (*Russian* kri'vɔj 'rɔk) *n* a city in SE Ukraine: founded in the 17th century by Cossacks; iron-mining centre; iron- and steelworks. Pop.: 720 000 (1996 est.).

krona ('krəʊnə) *n, pl* **kronor** (-nə). the standard monetary unit of Sweden.

króna ('krəʊnə) *n, pl* **krónur** (-nə). the standard monetary unit of Iceland.

krone ('krəʊnə) *n, pl* **kroner** (-nə). **1** the standard monetary unit of Denmark. **2** the standard monetary unit of Norway. ORIG C19: from Danish or Norwegian, ult. from L *corōna* CROWN

Kronos ★ ('krəʊnɒs) *n* a variant of **Cronus.**

Kronstadt ★ *n* **1** (*Russian* kran'ʃtat). a port in NW Russia, on Kotlin island in the Gulf of Finland: naval base. Pop.: 44 400 (1994 est.). **2** ('kroːnʃtat). the German name for **Braşov.**

Kropotkin ★ (*Russian* kra'pɔtkin) *n* Prince **Peter,** Russian name *Pyotr Alexeyevich.* 1842–1921, Russian anarchist: his books include *Modern Science and Anarchism* (1903).

Kroto ★ ('krəʊtəʊ) *n* Sir **Harold (Walter)**. born 1939, British chemist who discovered buckminsterfullerene; Nobel prize for chemistry 1996.

Kruger ★ ('kruːgə) *n* **Stephanus Johannes Paulus** ('stɛfənʊs jəʊ'hænɪs 'pɔːlʊs), known as *Oom Paul.* 1825–1904, Boer statesman; president of the Transvaal (1883–1900). His denial of civil rights to the Uitlanders led to the Boer War (1899–1902).

Kruger National Park ★ *n* a wildlife sanctuary in NE South Africa: the world's largest game reserve. Area: over 21 700 sq. km (8400 sq. miles).

Krugerrand ('kruːgəˌrænd) *n* a one-ounce gold coin minted in South Africa for investment only. ORIG C20: from Paul KRUGER + RAND[1]

Krugersdorp ★ ('kruːgəzˌdɔːp) *n* a city in NE South Africa, on the Witwatersrand, at an altitude of 1722 m (5650 ft): a gold-, manganese-, and uranium-mining centre. Pop.: 74 000 (latest est.).

krummhorn ('krʌmˌhɔːn) *or* **crumhorn** *n* a medieval wind instrument consisting of an upward-curving tube blown through a double reed.

Krupp ★ (krʊp, krʌp) *n* a German family of steel and armaments manufacturers, including **Alfred,** 1812–87, his son **Friedrich Alfred,** 1854–1902, and the latter's son-in-law, **Gustav Krupp von Bohlen und Halbach,** 1870–1950.

Krušné Hory ★ (ˈkruʃne ˈhɔrɪ) *n* the Czech name for the **Erzgebirge.**

Krym *or* **Krim** ★ (krɪm) *n* transliteration of the Russian name for **Crimea.**

krypton (ˈkrɪptɒn) *n* an inert gaseous element occurring in trace amounts in air and used in fluorescent lights and lasers. Symbol: Kr; atomic no.: 36; atomic wt.: 83.80. ORIG C19: from Gk, from *kruptos* hidden

krytron (ˈkraɪtrɒn) *n Electronics.* a type of fast electronic gas-discharge switch, used as a trigger in nuclear weapons.

KS *abbrev. for* Kansas.

Kshatriya (ˈkʃætrɪə) *n* a member of the second of the four main Hindu castes, the warrior caste. ORIG C18: from Sansk., from *kshatra* rule

kt *abbrev. for:* **1** karat. **2** *Naut.* knot.

Kt 1 Also: **knt.** *abbrev. for* Knight. **2** Also: **N.** *Chess. symbol for* knight.

Kuala Lumpur ★ (ˈkwɑːlə ˈlʊmpʊə, -pə) *n* the capital of Malaysia, in the SW Malay Peninsula: became capital of the Federated Malay States in 1895, and of Malaysia in 1963; capital of Selangor state from 1880 to 1973, when it was made a federal territory. Pop.: 1 145 342 (1991).

Kuban ★ (*Russian* kuˈbanj) *n* a river in SW Russia, rising in the Caucasus Mountains and flowing north and northwest to the Sea of Azov. Length: 906 km (563 miles).

Kubelik ★ (*Czech* ˈkubeliːk) *n* **Raphael** (ˈraːfaɛl). 1914–96, Czech conductor and composer.

Kublai Khan ★ (ˈkuːblaɪ ˈkɑːn) *n* ?1216–94, Mongol emperor of China: grandson of Genghis Khan. He completed his grandfather's conquest of China and founded the Yuan dynasty (1279–1368).

Kubrick ★ (ˈkjuːbrɪk) *n* **Stanley.** 1928–99, US film writer and director. His films include *2001: A Space Odyssey* (1968), *A Clockwork Orange* (1971), *Full Metal Jacket* (1987), and *Eyes Wide Shut* (1999).

Kuch Bihar ★ (ˈkuːtʃ bɪˈhɑː) *n* a variant spelling of **Cooch Behar.**

Kuching ★ (ˈkuːtʃɪŋ) *n* a port in E Malaysia, capital of Sarawak state, on the Sarawak River 24 km (15 miles) from its mouth. Pop.: 147 729 (1991).

kudos (ˈkjuːdɒs) *n* (*functioning as sing*) acclaim, glory, or prestige. ORIG C18: from Gk

kudu *or* **koodoo** (ˈkuːduː) *n* either of two spiral-horned antelopes (**greater kudu** or **lesser kudu**), which inhabit the bush of Africa. ORIG C18: from Afrik. *koedoe,* prob. from Khoi

Kuenlun ★ (ˈkʊnˈlʊn) *n* a variant spelling of **Kunlun.**

Kuibyshev *or* **Kuybyshev** ★ (*Russian* ˈkujbɪʃəf) *n* former name (1935–91) of **Samara.**

Ku Klux Klan (ˌkuː klʌks ˈklæn) *n* **1** a secret organization of White Southerners formed after the US Civil War to fight Black emancipation. **2** a secret organization of White Protestant Americans, mainly in the South, who use violence against Blacks, Jews, etc. ORIG C19 *Ku Klux,* prob. based on Gk *kuklos* CIRCLE + *Klan* CLAN
▸ **Ku Klux Klanner** (ˈklænə) *n*

kukri (ˈkʊkrɪ) *n, pl* **kukris.** a knife with a curved blade that broadens towards the point, esp. as used by Gurkhas. ORIG from Hindi

Kuku Nor ★ (ˈkuːˈkuː ˈnɔː) *n* a variant of **Koko Nor.**

kulak (ˈkuːlæk) *n* (in Russia after 1906) a member of the class of peasants who became proprietors of their own farms. In 1929 Stalin initiated their liquidation. ORIG C19: from Russian: fist, hence, tightfisted person

kulfi (ˈkʊlfɪ) *n* an Indian dessert that resembles ice cream flavoured with nuts and cardamom seeds.

Kulun ★ (ˈkuːˈluːn) *n* the Chinese name for **Ulan Bator.**

Kum ★ (kʊm) *n* a variant spelling of **Qom.**

Kumamoto ★ (ˌkʊməˈməʊtəʊ) *n* a city in SW Japan, on W central Kyushu: Kumamoto Medical University (1949). Pop.: 650 322 (1995).

Kumaratunge ★ (ˌkʊməˈrætʊŋgə) *n* **Chandrika** (ˈtʃʊnˌdrɪkə) **Bandaranaike.** born 1945, Sri Lankan politician: president from 1994.

Kumasi ★ (kuːˈmæsɪ) *n* a city in S Ghana: seat of Ashanti kings since 1663; university (1961); market town for a cocoa-producing region. Pop.: 385 192 (1988 est.).

Kumayri ★ (ˌkʊmaɪˈrɪ) *n* a city in NW Armenia. Pop.: 120 000 (1989). Former names: **Aleksandropol** (1840–1924), **Leninakan** (1924–91).

Kumbh Mela (kʊm ˈmɛlə) *n* a Hindu religious festival held every 12 years at Allahabad, India.

kumera *or* **kumara** (ˈkuːmərə) *n NZ.* the sweet potato. ORIG from Maori

kumiss *or* **koumiss** (ˈkuːmɪs) *n* a drink made from fermented mare's or other milk, drunk by certain Asian tribes. ORIG C17: from Russian *kumys*

kumite (ˈkuːmɪˌteɪ) *n Karate, etc.* freestyle sparring or fighting. ORIG C20: Japanese, lit.: sparring

kümmel (ˈkʊməl) *n* a German liqueur flavoured with aniseed and cumin. ORIG C19: from G, from OHG *kumil,* prob. var. of *kumin* CUMIN

kumquat *or* **cumquat** (ˈkʌmkwɒt) *n* **1** a small Chinese citrus tree. **2** the small round orange fruit of such a tree, with a sweet rind, used in preserves and confections. ORIG C17: from Mandarin Chinese *chin chü* golden orange

Kun ★ (kuːn) *n* **Béla** (ˈbeːlɔ). 1886–?1937, Hungarian Communist, president of the Communist republic in Hungary (1919). Forced into exile, he died in a Stalinist purge.

Kundera ★ (ˈkʌndərə) *n* **Milan.** born 1929, Czech novelist living in France. His novels include *The Book of Laughter and Forgetting* (1979) and *Slowness* (1996).

Küng ★ (*German* kyŋ) *n* **Hans** (hans). born 1928, Swiss Roman Catholic theologian. His books include *On Being a Christian* (1976) and *Does God Exist?* (1980); his licence to teach was withdrawn (1979).

kung fu (ˈkʌŋ ˈfuː) *n* a Chinese martial art combining principles of karate and judo. ORIG from Chinese: martial art

K'ung Fu-tse ★ (ˈkʊŋ ˈfuːˈtseɪ) *n* the Chinese name of **Confucius.**

Kungur ★ (ˈkʊngʊə) *n* a variant transliteration of the Chinese name for **Kongur Shan.**

Kunlun, Kuenlun, *or* **Kwenlun** ★ (ˈkʊnˈlʊn) *n* a mountain range in China, between the Tibetan plateau and the Tarim Basin, extending over 1600 km (1000 miles) east from the Pamirs: the largest mountain system of Asia. Highest peak: Ulugh Muztagh, 7723 m (25 338 ft).

Kunming *or* **K'un-ming** ★ (ˈkʊnˈmɪŋ) *n* a city in SW China, capital of Yunnan province, near Lake Tien: important during World War II as a Chinese military centre, American air base, and transport terminus for the Burma Road; Yunnan University (1934). Pop.: 1 520 000 (1991 est.).

Kuopio ★ (*Finnish* ˈkwɔpjɔ) *n* a city in S central Finland. Pop.: 83 955 (1994).

Kura ★ (kʊˈrɑː) *n* a river in W Asia, rising in NE Turkey and flowing across Georgia and Azerbaijan to the Caspian Sea. Length: 1515 km (941 miles).

kura kaupapa Maori (ˈkuːrɑː ˈkɑːuːpɑːpɑː) *n NZ.* a primary school in which the lessons are conducted in Maori and the teaching is based on Maori culture. ORIG from Maori *kura* school + *kaupapa* scheme

kurchatovium (ˌkɜːtʃəˈtəʊvɪəm) *n* another name for **rutherfordium,** esp. as used in the former Soviet Union. ORIG C20: from Russian, after I. V. *Kurchatov* (1903–60), Soviet physicist

Kurd (kɜːd) *n* a member of a nomadic people living chiefly in E Turkey, N Iraq, and W Iran.

Kurdish (ˈkɜːdɪʃ) *n* **1** the language of the Kurds. ◆ *adj* **2** of or relating to the Kurds or their language.

Kurdistan, Kurdestan, *or* **Kordestan** ★ (ˌkɜːdɪˈstɑːn) *n* a large plateau and mountainous region, between the Caspian Sea and the Black Sea, south of the Caucasus. Area: over 29 000 sq. km (74 000 sq. miles).

Kure ★ (kuː'reɪ) *n* a port in SW Japan, on SW Honshu: a naval base; shipyards. Pop.: 209 477 (1995 est.).

Kurgan ★ (*Russian* kur'gan) *n* a city in W central Russia, on the Tobol River: industrial centre for an agricultural region. Pop.: 363 000 (1995 est.).

kuri ('kuːrɪ) *n, pl* **kuris.** *NZ.* a mongrel dog. Also called: **goorie.** ORIG Maori

Kuril Islands *or* **Kurile Islands** ★ (kʊ'riːl) *pl n* a chain of 56 volcanic islands off the NE coast of Asia, extending for 1200 km (750 miles) from the S tip of the Kamchatka Peninsula to NE Hokkaido. Area: 14 990 sq. km (6020 sq. miles). Japanese name: **Chishima.**

Kurosawa ★ (ˌkʊərə'sɑːwə) *n* **Akira** (ə'kɪərə). 1910–98, Japanese film director. His works include *Rashomon* (1950), *The Seven Samurai* (1954), *Ran* (1985), and *Madadayo* (1993).

Kuroshio ★ (kə'rəʊʃɪˌəʊ) *n* another name for **Japan Current.**

kurrajong *or* **currajong** ('kʌrəˌdʒɒŋ) *n* any of various Australian trees or shrubs, esp. one that yields a tough durable fibre. ORIG C19: from Abor.

kursaal ('kɜːzᵊl) *n* a public room at a health resort. ORIG from G, lit.: cure room

Kursk ★ (*Russian* kursk) *n* a city in W Russia: industrial centre of an agricultural region: scene of a major Soviet victory (1943). Pop.: 442 000 (1995 est.).

kurtosis (kə'təʊsɪs) *n Statistics.* a measure of the concentration of a distribution around its mean. ORIG from Gk, from *kurtos* arched

kuru ('kʊruː) *n* a degenerative disease of the nervous system, restricted to certain tribes in New Guinea, marked by loss of muscular control and thought to be caused by a slow virus. ORIG C20: from a native name

Kush ★ (kʌʃ, kʊʃ) *n* a variant spelling of **Cush.**

Kuskokwim ★ ('kʌskəˌkwɪm) *n* a river in SW Alaska, rising in the Alaska Range and flowing generally southwest to **Kuskokwim Bay,** an inlet of the Bering Sea. Length: about 970 km (600 miles).

Kutaisi ★ (*Russian* kuta'isi) *n* an industrial city in W Georgia, on the Rioni River: one of the oldest towns of the Caucasus. Pop.: 240 600 (1994 est.).

Kutch *or* **Cutch** ★ (kʌtʃ) *n* **1** a former state of W India, on the **Gulf of Kutch** (an inlet of the Arabian Sea): part of Gujarat state since 1960. **2 Rann of.** an extensive salt waste in W central India, and S Pakistan: consists of the Great Rann in the north and the Little Rann in the southeast; seasonal alternation between marsh and desert; some saltworks. In 1968 an international tribunal awarded about 10 per cent of the border area to Pakistan. Area: 23 000 sq. km (9000 sq. miles).

Kutuzov ★ (*Russian* ku'tuzəf) *n* Prince **Mikhail Ilarionovich** (mixa'il ilərɪ'ɔnəvitʃ). 1745–1813, Russian field marshal, who harried Napoleon's army on their retreat from Moscow (1812–13).

Kuwait (kʊ'weɪt) *or* **Koweit** ★ *n* **1** a state on the NW coast of the Persian Gulf: came under British protection in 1899 and gained independence in 1961; invaded by Iraq in 1990 and liberated by US-led forces in 1991 following the Gulf War: mainly desert. The economy is dependent on oil. Official language: Arabic. Official religion: Muslim. Currency: dinar. Capital: Kuwait. Pop.: 1 924 000 (1999 est.). Area: 24 280 sq. km (9375 sq. miles). **2** the capital of Kuwait: a port on the Persian Gulf. Pop.: 31 241 (1993 est.).
▸ **Ku'waiti** *or* **Ko'weiti** *adj, n*

Kuznets ★ ('kuznɪts) *n* **Simon.** 1901–85, US economist born in Russia. His books include *Economic Growth of Nations* (1971): Nobel Prize for economics (1971).

Kuznetsk Basin (*Russian* kuz'njɛtsk) *or* **Kuzbass** ★ (*Russian* kuz'bas) *n* a region of S Russia, in the Kemerovo Region of W Siberia: the richest coalfield in the country, with important reserves of iron ore. Chief industrial centre: Novokuznetsk. Area: about 69 900 sq. km (27 000 sq. miles).

Kvaløy ★ (*Norwegian* 'kvaːlœj) *n* two islands in the Arctic Ocean, off the N coast of Norway: **North Kvaløy,** 329 sq. km (127 sq. miles), and **South Kvaløy,** 735 sq. km (284 sq. miles).

kvass (kvɑːs) *n* an alcoholic drink of low strength made in Russia and E Europe from cereals and stale bread. ORIG C16: from Russian *kvas*

kvetch (kvɛtʃ) *vb (intr) Sl., chiefly US.* to complain or grumble, esp. incessantly. ORIG C20: from Yiddish *kvetshn*, lit.: to squeeze, press

kW *abbrev. for* kilowatt.

kwacha ('kwɑːtʃɑː) *n* **1** the standard monetary unit of Zambia. **2** the standard monetary unit of Malawi. ORIG from a native word in Zambia

Kwajalein ★ ('kwɑːdʒəˌleɪn) *n* an atoll in the W Pacific, in the W Marshall Islands, in the central part of the Ralik Chain. Length: about 125 km (78 miles).

Kwangchow ★ ('kwæŋ'tʃaʊ) *n* a variant transliteration of the Chinese name for **Canton.**

Kwangchowan ★ ('kwæŋ'tʃaʊ'wɑːn) *n* a territory of SE China, in SW Kwantung province: leased to France as part of French Indochina from 1898 to 1945. Area: 842 sq. km (325 sq. miles).

Kwangju ★ ('kwæŋ'dʒuː) *n* a city in SW South Korea: an important military base during the Korean War; cotton textile industry. Pop.: 1 257 504 (1995).

Kwangsi-Chuang Autonomous Region ★ ('kwæŋ'siː'tʃwæŋ) *n* a variant transliteration of the Chinese name for **Guangxi Zhuang Autonomous Region.**

Kwangtung ★ ('kwæŋ'tʊŋ) *n* a variant transliteration of the Chinese name for **Guangdong.**

Kwantung Leased Territory ★ ('kwæn'tʊŋ) *n* a strategic territory of NE China, at the S tip of the Liaotung Peninsula of Manchuria: leased forcibly by Russia in 1898; taken over by Japan in 1905; occupied by the Soviet Union in 1945 and subsequently returned to China on the condition of shared administration; made part of Liaoning province by China in 1954. Area: about 3400 sq. km (1300 sq. miles). Also called: **Kuan-tung.**

Kwara ★ ('kwɑːrə) *n* a state of W Nigeria: mainly wooded savanna. Capital: Ilorin. Pop.: 1 751 464 (1995 est.). Area: 36 825 sq. km (14 218 sq. miles).

kwashiorkor (ˌkwæʃɪ'ɔːkə) *n* severe malnutrition of infants and young children, resulting from dietary deficiency of protein. ORIG C20: from native word in Ghana

Kwazulu ★ (kwɑː'zuːlʊ) *n* (formerly) a Bantu homeland in South Africa, replaced in 1994 by KwaZulu/Natal.

KwaZulu/Natal ★ (kwɑːˌzuːluːnə'tæl, -'tɑːl) *n* a province of NE South Africa. Capital: Ulundi. Pop.: 8 713 100 (1995 est.). Area: 92 180 sq. km (35 591 sq. miles).

Kweichow *or* **Kueichou** ★ ('kweɪ'tʃaʊ) *n* a variant transliteration of the Chinese name for **Guizhou.**

Kweilin *or* **Kuei-lin** ★ ('kweɪ'lɪn) *n* a variant transliteration of the Chinese name for **Guilin.**

Kweisui ★ ('kweɪ'sweɪ) *n* the former name of **Hohhot.**

Kweiyang *or* **Kuei-yang** ★ ('kweɪ'jæŋ) *n* a variant transliteration of the Chinese name for **Guiyang.**

kWh *abbrev. for* kilowatt-hour.

KWIC (kwɪk) *n acronym for* key word in context (esp. in **KWIC index**).

KWOC (kwɒk) *n acronym for* key word out of context.

Ky ★ (kiː) *n* **Nguyen Kao** (ᵊŋ'guːjɛn 'kaʊ). born 1930, Vietnamese military and political leader: premier of South Vietnam (1965–67); vice president (1967–69).

Ky. *or* **KY** *abbrev. for* Kentucky.

kyanite ('kaɪəˌnaɪt) *n* a variant spelling of **cyanite.**
▸ **kyanitic** (ˌkaɪə'nɪtɪk) *adj*

kyanize *or* **kyanise** ('kaɪəˌnaɪz) *vb* **kyanizes, kyanizing, kyanized** *or* **kyanises, kyanising, kyanised.** *(tr)* to treat (timber) with corrosive sublimate to make it resistant to decay. ORIG C19: after J.H. *Kyan* (died 1850), Brit. inventor of the process
▸ ˌ**kyani'zation** *or* ˌ**kyani'sation** *n*

Kyd *or* **Kid** ★ (kɪd) *n* **Thomas.** 1558–94, English dramatist, noted for his play *The Spanish Tragedy* (1586).

kyle (kaɪl) *n Scot.* (esp. in place names) a narrow strait or channel: *Kyle of Lochalsh.* ORIG C16: from Gaelic *caol* narrow

kylie *or* **kiley** ('kaɪlɪ) *n Austral.* a boomerang that is flat on one side and convex on the other. ORIG C19: from Abor.

kyloe ('kaɪləʊ) *n* a breed of small long-horned long-haired beef cattle from NW Scotland. ORIG C19: from ?

kymograph ('kaɪmə,grɑːf) *n* a rotatable drum for holding paper on which a tracking stylus continuously records variations in sound waves, blood pressure, respiratory movements, etc. ORIG C20: from Gk *kuma* wave + -GRAPH

► ,**kymo'graphic** *adj*

Kymric ('kɪmrɪk) *n, adj* a variant spelling of **Cymric**.

Kymry ('kɪmrɪ) *pl n* a variant spelling of **Cymry**.

Kynewulf ★ ('kɪnə,wʊlf) *n* a variant spelling of **Cynewulf**.

Kyongsong ★ ('kjɔːŋ'sɔːŋ) *n* another name for **Seoul**.

Kyoto *or* **Kioto** ★ (kɪ'əʊtəʊ, 'kjəʊ-) *n* a city in central Japan, on S Honshu: the capital of Japan from 794 to 1868; cultural centre, with two universities (1875, 1897). Pop.: 1 463 601 (1995).

kyphosis (kaɪ'fəʊsɪs) *n Pathol.* backward curvature of the thoracic spine, of congenital origin or resulting from injury or disease. ORIG C19: from NL, from Gk *kuphōsis*, from *kuphos* humpbacked

► **kyphotic** (kaɪ'fɒtɪk) *adj*

Kyrgyz ('kɪəgɪz) *n* **1** (*pl* **Kyrgyz**) a member of a Mongoloid people of central Asia, inhabiting Kyrgyzstan and a vast area of central Siberia. **2** the language of this people, belonging to the Turkic branch of the Altaic family. Also: **Kirghiz, Kirgiz.**

Kyrgyzstan, Kirghizstan, *or* **Kirgizstan** ★ ('kɜːgiz,stɑːn, -,stæn) *n* a republic in central Asia: came under Russian rule in the 19th century, became a Soviet republic in 1936 and gained independence in 1991; it has deposits of minerals, oil, and gas. Official languages: Kirghiz and Russian. Religion: nonreligious, Muslim. Currency: som. Capital: Bishkek. Pop.: 4 761 000 (1999 est.). Area: 198 500 sq. km (76 460 sq. miles). Also called: **Kirghizia, Kirgizia.**

Kyrgyz Steppe ★ *n* a vast steppe region in central Kazakhstan. Also called: (the) **Steppes.**

Kyrie eleison ('kɪrɪɪ ə'leɪsᵊn) *n* **1** a formal invocation used in the liturgies of the Roman Catholic, Greek Orthodox, and Anglican Churches. **2** a musical setting of this. Often shortened to **Kyrie.** ORIG C14: via LL from LGk *kurie, eleēson* Lord, have mercy

Kythera ★ ('kɪθɪrə) *n* a variant spelling of **Cythera**.

kyu (kjuː) *n Judo.* one of the student grades for inexperienced competitors. ORIG from Japanese

Kyushu *or* **Kiushu** ★ ('kjuːʃuː) *n* an island of SW Japan: the southernmost of Japan's four main islands, with over 300 surrounding small islands; coalfield and chemical industries. Chief cities: Fukuoka, Kitakyushu, and Nagasaki. Pop.: 13 424 000 (1995). Area: 35 659 sq. km (13 768 sq. miles).

Kyzyl Kum ★ (*Russian* ki'zil 'kum) *n* a desert in Kazakhstan and Uzbekistan.

★ people and places

Ll

l *or* **L** (ɛl) *n, pl* **l's, L's,** *or* **Ls. 1** the 12th letter of the English alphabet. **2** a speech sound represented by this letter. **3a** something shaped like an L. **3b** (*in combination*): *an L-shaped room.*

l *symbol for* litre.

L *symbol for:* **1** lambert(s). **2** large. **3** Latin. **4** (on British motor vehicles) learner driver. **5** *Physics.* length. **6** live. **7** Usually written: £, pound. ORIG L *libra.* **8** lire. **9** *Electronics.* inductor (in circuit diagrams). **10** *Physics.* **10a** latent heat. **10b** self-inductance. **11** the Roman numeral for 50. See **Roman numerals.**

L. *or* **l.** *abbrev. for:* **1** lake. **2** law. **3** leaf. **4** league. **5** left. **6** length. **7** (*pl* **LL** *or* **ll.**) line. **8** link. **9** low.

L. *abbrev. for:* **1** *Politics.* Liberal. **2** (in titles) Licentiate. **3** Linnaeus.

L8R (ˈleɪtə) later; an abbreviation used in text messages, e-mails, etc. ORIG C20

la[1] (lɑː) *n Music.* the syllable used in the fixed system of solmization for the note A. ORIG C14: see GAMUT

la[2] (lɔː) *interj* an exclamation of surprise or emphasis. ORIG OE *lā* lo

La *the chemical symbol for* lanthanum.

laager (ˈlɑːgə) *n* **1** (in Africa) a camp, esp. one defended by a circular formation of wagons. **2** *Mil.* a place where armoured vehicles are parked. ◆ *vb* **3** to form (wagons) into a laager. **4** (*tr*) to park (armoured vehicles) in a laager. ORIG C19: from Afrik. *lager,* via G from OHG *legar* bed, lair

Laaland ★ (*Danish* ˈlɔlan) *n* a variant spelling of **Lolland.**

lab (læb) *n Inf.* short for **laboratory.**

lab. *abbrev. for:* **1** laboratory. **2** labour.

Lab. *abbrev. for:* **1** *Politics.* Labour. **2** Labrador.

Laban ★ (ˈleɪbᵊn) *n Old Testament.* the father-in-law of Jacob, father of Leah and Rachel (Genesis 29:16).

Labe ★ (ˈlabɛ) *n* the Czech name for the (River) **Elbe.**

label (ˈleɪbᵊl) *n* **1** a piece of paper, card, or other material attached to an object to identify it or give instructions or details concerning its ownership, use, nature, destination, etc.; tag. **2** a brief descriptive phrase or term given to a person, group, school of thought, etc.: *the label "Romantic" is applied to many kinds of poetry.* **3** a word or phrase heading a piece of text to indicate or summarize its contents. **4** a trademark or company or brand name on certain goods, esp. on records. **5** *Computing.* a group of characters appended to a statement in a program to allow it to be identified. **6** *Chem.* a radioactive element used in a compound to trace the mechanism of a chemical reaction. ◆ *vb* **labels, labelling, labelled** *or US* **labels, labeling, labeled.** (*tr*) **7** to fasten a label to. **8** to mark with a label. **9** to describe or classify in a word or phrase: *to label someone a liar.* **10** to make (one or more atoms in a compound) radioactive, for use in determining the mechanism of a reaction. ORIG C14: from OF, from Gmc
▸ **ˈlabeller** *n*

labia (ˈleɪbɪə) *n* the plural of **labium.**

labial (ˈleɪbɪəl) *adj* **1** of, relating to, or near lips or labia. **2** *Music.* producing sounds by the action of an air stream over a narrow liplike fissure, as in a flue pipe of an organ. **3** *Phonetics.* relating to a speech sound whose articulation involves movement or use of the lips. ◆ *n* **4** Also called: **labial pipe.** *Music.* an organ pipe with a liplike fissure. **5** *Phonetics.* a speech sound such as English *p* or *m,* whose articulation involves movement or use of the lips. ORIG C16: from Med. L *labiālis,* from L *labium* lip
▸ **ˈlabially** *adv*

labiate (ˈleɪbɪˌeɪt, -ɪt) *n* **1** any plant of the family *Labiatae,* having square stems, aromatic leaves, and a two-lipped corolla: includes mint, thyme, sage, rosemary, etc. ◆ *adj* **2** of, relating to, or belonging to the family *Labiatae.* ORIG C18: from NL *labiātus,* from L *labium* lip

Labiche ★ (*French* labiʃ) *n* **Eugène Marin** (øʒɛn marɛ̃). 1815–88, French dramatist, noted for his farces, which include *Le Chapeau de paille d'Italie* (1851) and *Le Voyage de Monsieur Perrichon* (1860).

labile (ˈleɪbɪl) *adj Chem.* (of a compound) prone to chemical change. ORIG C15: via LL *lābilis,* from L *lābī* to slide
▸ **lability** (ləˈbɪlɪtɪ) *n*

labiodental (ˌleɪbɪəʊˈdɛntᵊl) *Phonetics.* ◆ *adj* **1** pronounced by bringing the bottom lip into contact with the upper teeth, as for *f* in *fat, puff.* ◆ *n* **2** a labiodental consonant. ORIG C17: from L LABIUM + DENTAL

labium (ˈleɪbɪəm) *n, pl* **labia** (-bɪə). **1** a lip or liplike structure. **2** any one of the four lip-shaped folds of the female vulva, comprising an outer pair (**labia majora**) and an inner pair (**labia minora**). ORIG C16: NL, from L.: lip

laboratory (ləˈbɒrətərɪ, -trɪ; *US.* ˈlæbrəˌtɔːrɪ) *n, pl* **laboratories. 1a** a building or room equipped for conducting scientific research or for teaching practical science. **1b** (*as modifier*): *laboratory equipment.* **2** a place where chemicals or medicines are manufactured. ◆ Often shortened to **lab.** ORIG C17: from Med. L *labōrātōrium* workshop, from L *labōrāre* to LABOUR

Labor Day *n* **1** a public holiday in the US and Canada in honour of labour, held on the first Monday in September. **2** a public holiday in Australia, observed on different days in different states.

laborious (ləˈbɔːrɪəs) *adj* **1** involving great exertion or long effort. **2** given to working hard. **3** (of literary style, etc.) not fluent.
▸ **laˈboriously** *adv* ▸ **laˈboriousness** *n*

Labor Party *n* one of the chief political parties of Australia, generally supporting the interests of organized labour.

labour *or US & sometimes Canad.* **labor** (ˈleɪbə) *n* **1** productive work, esp. physical toil done for wages. **2a** the people, class, or workers involved in this, esp. in contrast to management, capital, etc. **2b** (*as modifier*): *labour relations.* **3a** difficult or arduous work or effort. **3b** (*in combination*): *labour-saving.* **4** a particular job or task, esp. of a difficult nature. **5a** the process or effort of childbirth or the time during which this takes place. **5b** (*as modifier*): *labour pain; labour ward.* ◆ *vb* **6** (*intr*) to perform labour; work. **7** (*intr;* foll. by *for,* etc.) to strive or work hard (for something). **8** (*intr;* usually foll. by *under*) to be burdened (by) or be at a disadvantage (because of): *to labour under a misapprehension.* **9** (*intr*) to make one's way with difficulty. **10** (*tr*) to deal with too persistently: *to labour a point.* **11** (*intr*) (of a woman) to be in labour. **12** (*intr*) (of a ship) to pitch and toss. ORIG C13: via OF from L *labor*

labour camp *n* **1** a penal colony involving forced labour. **2** a camp for migratory labourers.

Labour Day *n* a public holiday in many countries in honour of labour, usually held on May 1.

laboured *or US & sometimes Canad.* **labored** (ˈleɪbəd) *adj* **1** (of breathing) performed with difficulty. **2** showing effort; contrived; lacking grace or fluency.

labourer *or US & sometimes Canad.* **laborer** (ˈleɪbərə) *n* a person engaged in physical work, esp. unskilled work.

labour exchange *n Brit.* a former name for the **employment office.**

labour-intensive *adj* of or denoting a task, organization, industry, etc., in which a high proportion of the costs are due to wages, salaries, etc.

Labourite (ˈleɪbəˌraɪt) *n* an adherent of the Labour Party.

Labour Party *n* **1** a British political party, formed in 1900 as an amalgam of various trade unions and socialist groups, generally supporting the interests of organized labour and advocating democratic socialism and social equality. **2** any similar party in any of various other countries.

★ people and places

Labrador ★ (ˈlæbrəˌdɔː) *n* **1** Also called: **Labrador-Ungava.** a large peninsula of NE Canada, on the Atlantic, the Gulf of St Lawrence, Hudson Strait, and Hudson Bay: contains most of the province of Quebec and the mainland part of Newfoundland; geologically part of the Canadian Shield. Area: 1 619 000 sq. km (625 000 sq. miles). **2** Also called: **Coast of Labrador.** a region of NE Canada, on the Atlantic and consisting of the mainland part of Newfoundland province. **3** (*often not cap.*) short for **Labrador retriever.**

Labrador retriever *n* a powerfully-built variety of retriever with a short dense usually black or golden-brown coat. Often shortened to **Labrador.**

labret (ˈleɪbrɛt) *n* a piece of bone, shell, etc., inserted into the lip as an ornament by certain peoples. ORIG C19: from L *labrum* lip

labrum (ˈleɪbrəm, ˈlæb-) *n, pl* **labra** (-brə). a lip or liplike part, such as the cuticular plate forming the upper lip of insects. ORIG C19: NL, from L

La Bruyère ★ (*French* la bryjɛr) *n* **Jean de** (ʒɑ̃ də). 1645–96, French moralist, noted for his *Caractères* (1688), satirical studies of contemporary figures.

Labuan ★ (ləˈbuːən) *n* an island in Malaysia, off the NW coast of Borneo: part of the Straits Settlements until 1946, when transferred to North Borneo. Chief town: Victoria. Pop.: 54 241 (1991). Area: 98 sq. km (38 sq. miles).

laburnum (ləˈbɜːnəm) *n* any tree or shrub of a Eurasian genus having clusters of yellow drooping flowers: all parts of the plant are poisonous. ORIG C16: NL, from L

labyrinth (ˈlæbərɪnθ) *n* **1** a mazelike network of tunnels, chambers, or paths, either natural or man-made. **2** any complex or confusing system of streets, passages, etc. **3** a complex or intricate situation. **4** any system of interconnecting cavities, esp. those comprising the internal ear. **5** *Electronics.* an enclosure behind a high-performance loudspeaker, consisting of a series of air chambers designed to absorb unwanted sound waves. ORIG C16: via L from Gk *laburinthos,* from ?

labyrinthine (ˌlæbəˈrɪnθaɪn) *adj* **1** of or relating to a labyrinth. **2** resembling a labyrinth in complexity.

lac[1] (læk) *n* a resinous substance secreted by certain insects (**lac insects**), used in the manufacture of shellac. ORIG C16: from Du. *lak* or F *laque,* from Hindi *lākh* resin, ult. from Sansk. *lākshā*

lac[2] (lɑːk) *n* a variant spelling of **lakh.**

Lacan ★ (*French* lakɑ̃) *n* **Jacques** (ʒak). 1901–81, French psychoanalyst, who reinterpreted Freud in terms of structural linguistics: an important influence on structuralist thought.

Laccadive, Minicoy, and Amindivi Islands ★ (ˈlækədɪv, ˈmɪnɪˌkɔɪ; ˌʌmənˈdiːviː) *pl n* the former name (until 1973) of the **Lakshadweep Islands.**

laccolith (ˈlækəlɪθ) *or* **laccolite** (ˈlækəˌlaɪt) *n* a dome of igneous rock between two layers of older sedimentary rock. ORIG C19: from Gk *lakkos* cistern + -LITH

lace (leɪs) *n* **1** a delicate decorative fabric made from cotton, silk, etc., woven in an open web of different symmetrical patterns and figures. **2** a cord or string drawn through eyelets or around hooks to fasten a shoe or garment. **3** ornamental braid often used on military uniforms, etc. ◆ *vb* **laces, lacing, laced.** (*tr*) **4** to fasten (shoes, etc.) with a lace. **5** to draw (a cord or thread) through holes, eyes, etc., as when tying shoes. **6** to compress the waist of (someone), as with a corset. **7** to add a small amount of alcohol or drugs to (food or drink). **8** (*usually passive* and foll. by *with*) to streak or mark with lines or colours: *the sky was laced with red.* **9** to intertwine; interlace. **10** *Inf.* to give a sound beating to. ORIG C13 *las,* from OF *laz,* from L *laqueus* noose

lacebark (ˈleɪsbɑːk) *n* another name for **ribbonwood.**

Lacedaemon ★ (ˌlæsɪˈdiːmən) *n* another name for **Sparta** or **Laconia.**
▸ **Lacedaeˈmonian** *adj, n*

lacerate *vb* (ˈlæsəˌreɪt), **lacerates, lacerating, lacerated.** (*tr*) **1** to tear (the flesh, etc.) jaggedly. **2** to hurt or harrow (the feelings, etc.). ◆ *adj* (ˈlæsəˌreɪt, -rɪt). **3** having edges that are jagged: *lacerate leaves.* ORIG C16: from L *lacerāre* to tear, from *lacer* mangled
▸ **ˌlaceˈration** *n*

lace up *vb* **1** (*tr, adv*) to tighten or fasten (clothes or footwear) with laces. ◆ *adj* **lace-up. 2** (of footwear) to be fastened with laces. ◆ *n* **lace-up. 3** a lace-up shoe or boot.

lacewing (ˈleɪsˌwɪŋ) *n* any of various insects, esp. the green lacewings and brown lacewings, having lacy wings and preying on aphids and similar pests.

laches (ˈlætʃɪz) *n Law.* negligence or unreasonable delay in pursuing a legal remedy. ORIG C14 *lachesse,* via OF *lasche* slack, from L *laxus* LAX

Lachesis ★ (ˈlækɪsɪs) *n Greek myth.* one of the three Fates. ORIG via L from Gk, from *lakhesis* destiny, from *lakhein* to befall by lot

Lachlan ★ (ˈlɒklən) *n* a river in SE Australia, rising in central New South Wales and flowing northwest then southwest to the Murrumbidgee River. Length: about 1450 km (900 miles). ORIG named after *Lachlan* Macquarie, governor of New South Wales (1809–21)

lachrymal (ˈlækrɪməl) *adj* a variant spelling of **lacrimal.**

lachrymatory (ˈlækrɪmətərɪ, -trɪ) *n, pl* **lachrymatories. 1** a small vessel found in ancient tombs, formerly thought to hold the tears of mourners. ◆ *adj* **2** a variant spelling of **lacrimatory.**

lachrymose (ˈlækrɪˌməʊs) *adj* **1** given to weeping; tearful. **2** mournful; sad. ORIG C17: from L, from *lacrima* a tear
▸ **ˈlachryˌmosely** *adv*

lacing (ˈleɪsɪŋ) *n* **1** *Chiefly Brit.* a course of bricks, stone, etc., for strengthening a rubble or flint wall. **2** another word for **lace** (senses 2, 3). **3** *Inf.* a severe beating.

laciniate (ləˈsɪnɪˌeɪt, -ɪt) *or* **laciniated** *adj* **1** *Biol.* jagged: *a laciniate leaf.* **2** having a fringe. ORIG C17: from L *lacinia* flap
▸ **laˌciniˈation** *n*

lack (læk) *n* **1** an insufficiency, shortage, or absence of something required or desired. **2** something that is required but is absent or in short supply. ◆ *vb* **3** (when *intr,* often foll. by *in* or *for*) to be deficient (in) or have need (of). ORIG C12: rel. to MDu. *laken* to be wanting

lackadaisical (ˌlækəˈdeɪzɪkəl) *adj* **1** lacking vitality and purpose. **2** lazy, esp. in a dreamy way. ORIG C18: from earlier *lackadaisy*
▸ **ˌlackaˈdaisically** *adv*

lackey (ˈlækɪ) *n* **1** a servile follower; hanger-on. **2** a liveried male servant or valet. **3** a person who is treated like a servant. ◆ *vb* **4** (when *intr,* often foll. by *for*) to act as a lackey (to). ORIG C16: via F *laquais,* from OF, ?from Catalan *lacayo, alacayo*

lacklustre *or US* **lackluster** (ˈlækˌlʌstə) *adj* lacking force, brilliance, or vitality.

Laclos ★ (*French* laklo) *n* **Pierre Choderlos de** (pjɛr ʃodɛrlo də). 1741–1803, French soldier and writer, noted for his novel in epistolary form *Les Liaisons dangereuses* (1782).

Laconia ★ (ləˈkəʊnɪə) *n* an ancient country of S Greece, in the SE Peloponnese, of which Sparta was the capital: corresponds to the present-day department of Lakonia.
▸ **Laˈconian** *n, adj*

laconic (ləˈkɒnɪk) *adj* (of a person's speech) using few words; terse. ORIG C16: via L from Gk *Lakōnikos,* from *Lakōn* Laconian, Spartan; referring to the Spartans' terseness of speech
▸ **laˈconically** *adv*

La Coruña ★ (*Spanish* la koˈruɲa) *n* a port in NW Spain, on the Atlantic: point of departure for the Spanish Armada (1588); site of the defeat of the French by the English under Sir John Moore in the Peninsular War (1809). Pop.: 255 087 (1994 est.). English name: **Corunna.**

lacquer (ˈlækə) *n* **1** a hard glossy coating made by dissolving cellulose derivatives or natural resins in a volatile solvent. **2** a black resinous substance, obtained from certain trees (**lacquer trees**), used to give a hard glossy finish to wooden furniture. **3** Also called: **hair lacquer.** a mixture of shellac and alcohol for spraying onto the hair to hold a style in place. **4** *Art.* decorative objects coated with such lacquer, often inlaid. ◆ *vb* (*tr*) **5** to apply lac-

quer to. ORIG C16: from obs. F *lacre* sealing wax, from Port. *laca* LAC[1]
▸ 'lacquerer *n*

lacrimal, lachrymal, *or* **lacrymal** ('lækrɪməl) *adj* of or relating to tears or to the glands that secrete tears. ORIG C16: from Med. L, from L *lacrima* a tear

lacrimation (ˌlækrɪ'meɪʃən) *n* the secretion of tears.

lacrimatory, lachrymatory, *or* **lacrymatory** ('lækrɪmətərɪ, -trɪ) *adj* of, causing, or producing tears.

lacrosse (lə'krɒs) *n* a ball game invented by American Indians, now played by two teams who try to propel a ball into each other's goal by means of long-handled pouched sticks (**lacrosse sticks**). ORIG C19: Canad. F: the hooked stick, crosier

lactam ('læktæm) *n Chem.* any of a group of cyclic amides, derived from amino acids, having the characteristic group -CONH-. ORIG C20: from LACTO- + AM(IDE)

lactate[1] ('lækteɪt) *n* an ester or salt of lactic acid. ORIG C18

lactate[2] (læk'teɪt) *vb* **lactates, lactating, lactated.** (*intr*) (of mammals) to produce or secrete milk.

lactation (læk'teɪʃən) *n* **1** the secretion of milk from the mammary glands after parturition. **2** the period during which milk is secreted.

lacteal ('læktɪəl) *adj* **1** of, relating to, or resembling milk. **2** (of lymphatic vessels) conveying or containing chyle. ◆ *n* **3** any of the lymphatic vessels conveying chyle from the small intestine to the thoracic duct. ORIG C17: from L *lacteus* of milk, from *lac* milk

lactescent (læk'tɛsᵊnt) *adj* **1** (of plants and certain insects) secreting a milky fluid. **2** milky or becoming milky. ORIG C18: from L, from *lactescēre* to become milky, from *lact-, lac* milk
▸ lac'tescence *n*

lactic ('læktɪk) *adj* relating to or derived from milk. ORIG C18: from L *lact-, lac* milk

lactic acid *n* a colourless syrupy carboxylic acid found in sour milk and many fruits and used as a preservative (**E270**) for foodstuffs. Formula: $CH_3CH(OH)COOH$. Systematic name: **2-hydroxypropanoic acid.**

lactiferous (læk'tɪfərəs) *adj* producing, conveying, or secreting milk or a milky fluid. ORIG C17: from L *lactifer*, from *lact-, lac* milk

lacto- ('læktəʊ) *or before a vowel* **lact-** *combining form.* indicating milk: *lactobacillus.* ORIG from L *lact-, lac* milk

lactose ('læktəʊs, -təʊz) *n* a white crystalline sugar occurring in milk and used in pharmaceuticals and baby foods. Formula: $C_{12}H_{22}O_{11}$.

lacto-vegetarian *n* a vegetarian whose diet includes dairy produce.

La Cumbre ★ (lə 'kuːmbreɪ) *n* another name for the **Uspallata Pass.**

lacuna (lə'kjuːnə) *n, pl* **lacunae** (-niː) *or* **lacunas. 1** a gap or space, esp. in a book or manuscript. **2** *Biol.* a cavity or depression, such as any of the spaces in the matrix of bone. ORIG C17: from L *lacūna* pool, cavity, from *lacus* lake
▸ la'cunose, la'cunal, la'cunar, *or* la'cunary *adj*

lacustrine (lə'kʌstraɪn) *adj* **1** of or relating to lakes. **2** living or growing in or on the shores of a lake. ORIG C19: from It. *lacustre*, from L *lacus* lake

lacy ('leɪsɪ) *adj* **lacier, laciest.** made of or resembling lace.
▸ 'lacily *adv* ▸ 'laciness *n*

lad (læd) *n* **1** a boy or young man. **2** *Inf.* a familiar form of address for any male. **3** a lively or dashing man or youth (esp. in **a bit of a lad**). **4** a young man whose behaviour is characteristic of male adolescents, esp. in being rowdy, macho, or immature. **5** *Brit.* a boy or man who looks after horses. ORIG C13 *ladde;* ?from ON

ladanum ('lædənəm) *n* a dark resinous juice obtained from various rockroses: used in perfumery. ORIG C16: L from Gk, from *lēdon* rockrose

ladder ('lædə) *n* **1** a portable framework of wood, metal, rope, etc., in the form of two long parallel members connected by rungs or steps fixed to them at right angles, for climbing up or down. **2** any hierarchy conceived of as having a series of ascending stages, levels, etc.: *the social ladder.* **3** Also called: **run.** *Chiefly Brit.* a line of connected stitches that have come undone in knitted material, esp. stockings. ◆ *vb* **4** *Chiefly Brit.* to cause a line of interconnected stitches in (stockings, etc.) to undo, as by snagging, or (of a stocking) to come undone in this way. ORIG OE *hlǣdder*

ladder back *n* a type of chair in which the back is constructed of horizontal slats between two uprights.

ladette (ˌlæd'ɛt) *n Inf.* a young woman whose social behaviour is similar to that of laddish males.

laddie ('lædɪ) *n Chiefly Scot.* a familiar term for a male, esp. a boy; lad.

laddish ('lædɪʃ) *adj Inf., usually derog.* characteristic of male adolescents or young men, esp. by being rowdy, macho, or immature: *laddish behaviour.*

lade (leɪd) *vb* **lades, lading, laded; laden** *or* **laded. 1** to put cargo or freight on board (a ship, etc.) or (of a ship, etc.) to take on cargo or freight. **2** (*tr; usually passive* and foll. by *with*) to burden or oppress. **3** (*tr; usually passive* and foll. by *with*) to fill or load. **4** to remove (liquid) with or as if with a ladle. ORIG OE *hladen* to load

laden ('leɪdᵊn) *vb* **1** a past participle of **lade.** ◆ *adj* **2** weighed down with a load; loaded. **3** encumbered; burdened.

la-di-da, lah-di-dah, *or* **la-de-da** (ˌlɑːdiː'dɑː) *adj Inf.* affecting exaggeratedly genteel manners or speech. ORIG C19: mockingly imit. of affected speech

ladies *or* **ladies' room** *n* (*functioning as sing*) *Inf.* a women's public lavatory.

lading ('leɪdɪŋ) *n* a load; cargo; freight.

Ladislaus I ('lædɪsˌlɔːs) *or* **Ladislas** ★ ('lædɪsˌlæs) *n* **Saint.** 1040–95, king of Hungary (1077–95). He extended his country's boundaries and suppressed paganism. Feast day: June 27.

ladle ('leɪdᵊl) *n* **1** a long-handled spoon having a deep bowl for serving or transferring liquids. **2** a large bucket-shaped container for transferring molten metal. ◆ *vb* **ladles, ladling, ladled. 3** (*tr*) to serve out as with a ladle. ORIG OE *hlædel*, from *hladan* to draw out
▸ 'ladleful *n*

ladle out *vb* (*tr, adv*) *Inf.* to distribute (money, gifts, etc.) generously.

Ladoga ★ (*Russian* 'ladəgə) *n* **Lake.** a lake in NW Russia, in the SW Karelian Republic: the largest lake in Europe; it drains through the River Neva into the Gulf of Finland. Area: about 18 000 sq. km (7000 sq. miles). Russian name: **Ladozhskoye Ozero** ('ladəʃskəjə 'ɔzɪrə).

Ladrone Islands ★ (lə'drəʊn) *pl n* the former name (1521–1668) of the **Mariana Islands.**

lady ('leɪdɪ) *n, pl* **ladies. 1** a woman regarded as having the characteristics of a good family and high social position. **2a** a polite name for a woman. **2b** (*as modifier*): *a lady doctor.* **3** an informal name for **wife. 4 lady of the house.** the female head of the household. **5** *History.* a woman with proprietary rights and authority, as over a manor. ORIG OE *hlǣfdīge*, from *hlāf* bread + *dīge* kneader, rel. to *dāh* dough

Lady ('leɪdɪ) *n, pl* **Ladies. 1** (in Britain) a title of honour borne by various classes of women of the peerage. **2 my lady.** a term of address to holders of the title Lady. **3 Our Lady.** a title of the Virgin Mary.

ladybird ('leɪdɪˌbɜːd) *n* any of various small brightly coloured beetles, esp. one having red elytra with black spots. ORIG C18: after Our *Lady*, the Virgin Mary

lady bountiful *n* an ostentatiously charitable woman. ORIG C19: after a character in George Farquhar's play *The Beaux' Stratagem* (1707)

Lady Chapel *n* a chapel within a church or cathedral, dedicated to the Virgin Mary.

Lady Day *n* March 25, the feast of the Annunciation of the Virgin Mary. Also called: **Annunciation Day.**

lady-in-waiting *n, pl* **ladies-in-waiting.** a lady who attends a queen or princess.

lady-killer *n Inf.* a man who is, or believes he is, irresistibly fascinating to women.

ladylike (ˈleɪdɪˌlaɪk) *adj* like or befitting a lady in manners and bearing; refined and fastidious.

ladylove (ˈleɪdɪˌlʌv) *n Now rare.* a beloved woman.

Lady Macbeth strategy *n* a strategy in a takeover battle in which a third party makes a bid acceptable to the target company, appearing to act as a white knight but subsequently joining forces with the original (unwelcome) bidder. ORIG C20: after *Lady Macbeth* in Shakespeare's *Macbeth* (1605)

lady mayoress *n Brit.* the wife of a lord mayor.

Lady of the Lake ★ *n* (in Arthurian legend) a mysterious supernatural being sometimes identified with **Vivian.**

lady's bedstraw *n* a Eurasian plant with clusters of small yellow flowers.

lady's finger *n* another name for **bhindi.**

Ladyship (ˈleɪdɪʃɪp) *n* (preceded by *your* or *her*) a title used to address or refer to any peeress except a duchess.

Ladysmith ★ (ˈleɪdɪˌsmɪθ) *n* a city in E South Africa: besieged by Boers for four months (1899–1900) during the Boer War. Pop.: 56 599 (1989).

lady's-slipper *n* any of various orchids having reddish or purple flowers.

lady's-smock *n* a N temperate plant with white or rose-pink flowers. Also called: **cuckooflower.**

Laënnec ★ (*French* laɛnɛk) *n* **René Théophile Hyacinthe** (rəne teɔfil jasɛ̃t). 1781–1826, French physician, who invented the stethoscope.

Laertes ★ (leɪˈɜːtiːz) *n Greek myth.* the father of Odysseus.

laevo- *or US* **levo-** *combining form.* **1** on or towards the left: *laevorotatory.* **2** (in chemistry) denoting a laevorotatory compound. ORIG from L *laevus* left

laevorotation (ˌliːvəʊrəʊˈteɪʃən) *n* **1** a rotation to the left. **2** an anticlockwise rotation of the plane of polarization of plane-polarized light as a result of its passage through a crystal, liquid, or solution. ◆ Cf. **dextrorotation.**
▸ **laevorotatory** (ˌliːvəʊˈrəʊtətərɪ) *adj*

Lafayette *or* **La Fayette** ★ (*French* lafajɛt) *n* **1 Marie Joseph Paul Yves Roch Gilbert du Motier** (mari ʒozɛf pɔl iv rɔk ʒilbɛr dy mɔtje), Marquis de Lafayette. 1757–1834, French general and statesman. He fought on the side of the colonists in the War of American Independence and played a leading part in the French Revolution and the revolution of 1830. **2 Marie-Madeleine** (marimadlɛn), Comtesse de Lafayette. 1634–93, French novelist.

Laffer curve (ˈlæfə) *n Econ.* a graph showing government tax revenue plotted against percentage tax rates; it illustrates that a cut in a high tax rate can increase government revenue. ORIG C20: after Arthur *Laffer* (born 1940), US economist

La Fontaine ★ (*French* la fɔ̃tɛn) *n* **Jean de** (ʒɑ̃ də). 1621–95, French poet, famous for his *Fables* (1668–94).

Laforgue ★ (*French* lafɔrg) *n* **Jules** (ʒyl). 1860–87, French symbolist poet and an originator of free verse.

LAFTA (ˈlæftə) *n acronym for* Latin American Free Trade Area, the name before 1981 of the Latin American Integration Association. See **LAIA.**

lag[1] (læg) *vb* **lags, lagging, lagged.** (*intr*) **1** (often foll. by *behind*) to hang (back) or fall (behind) in movement, progress, development, etc. **2** to fall away in strength or intensity. ◆ *n* **3** the act or state of slowing down or falling behind. **4** the interval of time between two events, esp. between an action and its effect. ORIG C16: from ?

lag[2] (læg) *Sl.* ◆ *n* **1** a convict or ex-convict (esp. in **old lag**). **2** a term of imprisonment. ◆ *vb* **lags, lagging, lagged. 3** (*tr*) to arrest or put in prison. ORIG C19: from ?

lag[3] (læg) *vb* **lags, lagging, lagged. 1** (*tr*) to cover (a pipe, cylinder, etc.) with lagging to prevent loss of heat. ◆ *n* **2** the insulating casing of a steam cylinder, boiler, etc. **3** a stave. ORIG C17: of Scand. origin

lagan (ˈlægᵊn) *n* goods or wreckage on the sea bed, sometimes attached to a buoy to permit recovery. ORIG C16: from OF *lagan,* prob. of Gmc origin

lager (ˈlɑːgə) *n* a light-bodied effervescent beer, fermented in a closed vessel using yeasts that sink to the bottom of the brew. ORIG C19: from G *Lagerbier* beer for storing, from *Lager* storehouse

Lagerkvist ★ (*Swedish* ˈlɑːgərkvist) *n* **Pär** (**Fabian**) (pæːr). 1891–1974, Swedish novelist and dramatist. His novels include *Barabbas* (1950): Nobel prize for literature 1951.

Lagerlöf ★ (*Swedish* ˈlɑːgərløːv) *n* **Selma** (ˈsɛlma). 1858–1940, Swedish novelist, noted esp. for her children's classic *The Wonderful Adventures of Nils* (1906–07): Nobel prize for literature 1909.

lager lout *n* a rowdy or aggressive young drunk male.

laggard (ˈlægəd) *n* **1** a person who lags behind. ◆ *adj* **2** *Rare.* sluggish, slow, or dawdling.
▸ ˈ**laggardly** *adj, adv* ▸ ˈ**laggardness** *n*

lagging (ˈlægɪŋ) *n* **1** insulating material wrapped around pipes, boilers, etc., or laid in a roof loft, to prevent loss of heat. **2** the act or process of applying lagging.

lagomorph (ˈlægəʊˌmɔːf) *n* any placental mammal having two pairs of upper incisors specialized for gnawing, such as rabbits and hares. ORIG C19: via NL from Gk *lagōs* hare; see -MORPH

lagoon (ləˈguːn) *n* **1** a body of water cut off from the open sea by coral reefs or sand bars. **2** any small body of water, esp. one adjoining a larger one. ORIG C17: from It. *laguna,* from L *lacūna* pool; see LACUNA

Lagoon Islands ★ *pl n* a former name of **Tuvalu.**

Lagos ★ (ˈleɪgɒs) *n* **1** the former capital and chief port of Nigeria, on the Bight of Benin: first settled in the sixteenth century; a slave market until the nineteenth century; ceded to Britain (1861); university (1962). Pop.: 1 484 000 (1995 est.). **2** a state of SW Nigeria. Capital: Ikeja. Pop.: 6 357 253 (1995 est.). Area: 3345 sq. km (1292 sq. miles).

Lagrange ★ (*French* lagrɑ̃ʒ) *n* Comte **Joseph Louis** (ʒozɛf lwi). 1736–1813, French mathematician and astronomer.
▸ **Lagrangian** (ləˈgreɪndʒɪən) *adj*

Lagrangian point *n Astron.* one of five points in the plane of revolution of two bodies in orbit around their common centre of gravity, at which a third body of negligible mass can remain in equilibrium with respect to the other two bodies. ORIG after J. L. LAGRANGE

La Granja ★ (*Spanish* la ˈgraŋxa) *n* another name for **San Ildefonso.**

La Guaira *or* **La Guayra** ★ (*Spanish* la ˈgwaira) *n* the chief seaport of Venezuela, on the Caribbean. Pop.: 26 669 (1990 est.).

La Guardia ★ (lə ˈgwɑːdɪə) *n* **Fiorello H(enry)** (ˌfɪəˈrɛləʊ). 1882–1947, US politician and mayor of New York (1933–45).

lah (lɑː) *n Music.* (in tonic sol-fa) the sixth note of any major scale; submediant. ORIG C14: later variant of *la;* see GAMUT

lahar (ˈlɑːhɑː) *n* a landslide of volcanic debris mixed with water down the sides of a volcano, usually precipitated by heavy rainfall. ORIG C20: from Javanese: lava

lah-di-dah (ˌlɑːdiːˈdɑː) *adj, n Inf.* a variant spelling of **la-di-da.**

Lahore ★ (ləˈhɔː) *n* a city in NE Pakistan: capital of the former province of West Pakistan (1955–70); University of the Punjab (1882). Pop.: 5 085 000 (1995 est.).

Lahti ★ (*Finnish* ˈlɑhti) *n* a town in S Finland: site of the main Finnish radio and television stations; furniture industry. Pop.: 94 706 (1994).

LAIA *abbrev. for* Latin American Integration Association (before 1981, known as the Latin American Free Trade Area). An economic group, its members are Argentina, Bolivia, Brazil, Chile, Colombia, Ecuador, Mexico, Paraguay, Peru, Uruguay, and Venezuela.

Laibach ★ (ˈlaibax) *n* the German name for **Ljubljana.**

laic (ˈleɪɪk) *adj also* **laical. 1** of or involving the laity; secular. ◆ *n* **2** a rare word for **layman.** ORIG C15: from LL *lāicus* LAY[3]
▸ ˈ**laically** *adv*

laicize *or* **laicise** (ˈleɪɪˌsaɪz) *vb* **laicizes, laicizing, laicized** *or* **laicises, laicising, laicised.** (*tr*) to withdraw clerical or ec-

clesiastical character or status from (an institution, building, etc.).
▸ **ˌlaiciˈzation** *or* **ˌlaiciˈsation** *n*

laid (leɪd) *vb* the past tense and past participle of **lay**[1].

laid-back *adj* relaxed in style or character; easy-going and unhurried.

laid paper *n* paper with a regular mesh impressed upon it.

Lailat-ul-Qadr (ˌleɪlætʊlˈkɑːdə) *n* a night of study and prayer observed annually by Muslims to mark the communication of the Koran: it usually follows the 27th day of Ramadan. ORIG from Ar.: night of determination

lain (leɪn) *vb* the past participle of **lie**[2].

Laine ★ (leɪn) *n* **Cleo,** full name *Clementina Dinah Laine.* born 1927, British jazz singer, noted esp. for her recordings with her husband John Dankworth.

Laing ★ (læŋ) *n* **R(onald) D(avid).** 1927–89, Scottish psychiatrist; his books include *The Divided Self* (1960) and the poems *Knots* (1970).

Laingian (ˈlæŋɪən) *adj* **1** of or based on R. D. Laing's theory that mental illnesses can be responses to stress in family and social situations. ◆ *n* **2** a follower or adherent of Laing's teaching.

lair[1] (lɛə) *n* **1** the resting place of a wild animal. **2** *Inf.* a place of seclusion or hiding. ◆ *vb* **3** (*intr*) (esp. of a wild animal) to retreat to or rest in a lair. **4** (*tr*) to drive or place (an animal) in a lair. ORIG OE *leger*

lair[2] (lɛə) *Austral. sl.* ◆ *n* **1** a flashy man who shows off. ◆ *vb* **2** (*intr;* foll. by *up* or *around*) to behave or dress like a lair. ORIG ?from LEER

laird (lɛəd) *n Scot.* a landowner, esp. of a large estate. ORIG C15: Scot. var. of LORD

laissez faire *or* **laisser faire** *French.* (ˌlɛseɪ ˈfɛə) *n* **1a** Also called: **individualism.** the doctrine of unrestricted freedom in commerce, esp. for private interests. **1b** (*as modifier*): *a laissez-faire economy.* **2** indifference or noninterference, esp. in the affairs of others. ORIG F, lit.: let (them) act

laissez passer (ˌlɛseɪ ˈpæseɪ) *n* a permit allowing someone to pass, cross a frontier, etc. ORIG F, lit.: let (them) pass

laity (ˈleɪɪtɪ) *n* **1** laymen, as distinguished from clergymen. **2** all people not of a specific occupation. ORIG C16: from LAY[3]

Laius ★ (ˈlaɪəs) *n Greek myth.* a king of Thebes, killed by his son Oedipus, who did not know of their relationship.

lake[1] (leɪk) *n* **1** an expanse of water entirely surrounded by land and unconnected to the sea except by rivers or streams. Related adj: **lacustrine. 2** anything resembling this. **3** a surplus of a liquid commodity: *a wine lake.* ORIG C13: *lac,* via OF from L *lacus* basin

lake[2] (leɪk) *n* **1** a bright pigment produced by the combination of an organic colouring matter with an inorganic compound, usually a metallic salt, oxide, or hydroxide. **2** a red dye obtained by combining a metallic compound with cochineal. ORIG C17: var. of LAC[1]

Lake District ★ *n* a region of lakes and mountains in NW England, in Cumbria: includes England's largest lake (Windermere) and highest mountain (Scafell Pike); national park; literary associations (the Lake Poets); tourist region. Also called: **Lakeland, the Lakes.**

lake dwelling *n* a dwelling, esp. in prehistoric villages, constructed on platforms supported by wooden piles driven into the bottom of a lake.
▸ **lake dweller** *n*

Lakeland ★ (ˈleɪkˌlænd) *n* **1** another name for the **Lake District.** ◆ *adj* **2** of or relating to the Lake District.

Lakeland terrier *n* a wire-haired breed of terrier, originally from the Lake District.

Lake of the Woods ★ *n* a lake in N central North America, mostly in W Northern Ontario, Canada: fed chiefly by the Rainy River; drains into Lake Winnipeg by the Winnipeg River; many islands; tourist region. Area: 3846 sq. km (1485 sq. miles).

Lake Poets *pl n* the English poets Wordsworth, Coleridge, and Southey, who lived in and drew inspiration from the Lake District at the beginning of the 19th century.

Lake Success ★ *n* a village in SE New York State, on W Long Island: headquarters of the United Nations Security Council from 1946 to 1951. Pop.: 2450 (1990 est.).

lake trout *n* a yellow-spotted char of the Great Lakes region of Canada.

lakh *or* **lac** (lɑːk) *n* (in India) the number 100 000, esp. referring to this sum of rupees. ORIG C17: from Hindi *lākh,* ult. from Sansk. *lakshā* a sign

Lakshadweep Islands ★ (lækˈʃædwiːp) *pl n* a group of 26 coral islands and reefs in the Arabian Sea, off the SW coast of India: a union territory of India since 1956. Administrative centre: Kavaratti Island. Pop.: 56 000 (1994 est.). Area: 28 sq. km (11 sq. miles). Former name (until 1973): **Laccadive, Minicoy, and Amindivi Islands.**

-lalia *n combining form.* indicating a speech defect or abnormality: *echolalia.* ORIG NL, from Gk *lalia* chatter, from *lalein* to babble

La Línea ★ (*Spanish* la ˈlinea) *n* a town in SW Spain, on the Bay of Gibraltar. Pop.: 57 000 (latest est.). Official name: **La Línea de la Concepción** (ðe la ˌkonθepˈθjon).

Lalique ★ (*French* lalik) *n* **René** (**Jules**) (rəne). 1860–1945, French Art-Nouveau jeweller, glass-maker, and designer: noted esp. for his frosted glassware.

Lallans (ˈlælənz) *or* **Lallan** (ˈlælən) *n* **1** a literary version of the variety of English spoken and written in the Lowlands of Scotland. **2** (*modifier*) of or relating to the Lowlands of Scotland or their dialects. ORIG Scot. var. of *Lowlands*

lallation (læˈleɪʃən) *n Phonetics.* a defect of speech consisting of the pronunciation of (r) as (l). ORIG C17: from L *lallāre* to sing lullaby, imit.

Lalo ★ (ˈlɑːləʊ) *n* (**Victor-Antoine-**)**Édouard** (edwar). 1823–92, French composer of Spanish descent. His works include the *Symphonie espagnole* (1873).

lam[1] (læm) *vb* **lams, lamming, lammed.** *Sl.* **1** (*tr*) to thrash or beat. **2** (*intr;* usually foll. by *into* or *out*) to make a sweeping stroke or blow. ORIG C16: from Scand.

lam[2] (læm) *n US & Canad. sl.* **1** a sudden flight or escape, esp. to avoid arrest. **2 on the lam.** making an escape. ORIG C19: ? from LAM[1] (hence, to be off)

Lam. *Bible. abbrev. for* Lamentations.

lama (ˈlɑːmə) *n* a priest or monk of Lamaism. ORIG C17: from Tibetan *blama*

Lamaism (ˈlɑːməˌɪzəm) *n* the Mahayana form of Buddhism of Tibet and Mongolia.
▸ **ˈLamaist** *n, adj* ▸ **ˌLamaˈistic** *adj*

La Mancha ★ (*Spanish* la ˈmantʃa) *n* a plateau of central Spain, between the mountains of Toledo and the hills of Cuenca: traditionally associated with episodes in *Don Quixote.* Average height: 600 m (2000 ft).

La Manche ★ (*French* la mɑ̃ʃ) *n* See **Manche** (sense 2).

Lamarck ★ (*French* lamark) *n* **Jean Baptiste Pierre Antoine de Monet** (ʒɑ̃ batist pjɛr ɑ̃twan də mɔnɛ), Chevalier de Lamarck. 1744–1829, French naturalist. He outlined his theory of organic evolution (Lamarckism) in *Philosophie zoologique* (1809).
▸ **Laˈmarckian** *adj, n*

Lamarckism (lɑːˈmɑːkɪzəm) *n* the theory of organic evolution proposed by Lamarck, based on the principle that characteristics of an organism modified during its lifetime are inheritable.

Lamartine ★ (*French* lamartin) *n* **Alphonse Marie Louis de Prat de** (alfɔ̃s mari lwi də pra də). 1790–1869, French romantic poet, historian, and statesman: his works include *Méditations poétiques* (1820) and *Histoire des Girondins* (1847).

lamasery (ˈlɑːməsərɪ) *n, pl* **lamaseries.** a monastery of lamas. ORIG C19: from F *lamaserie,* from LAMA + F *-serie,* from Persian *serāī* palace

lamb (læm) *n* **1** the young of a sheep. **2** the meat of a young sheep. **3** a person, esp. a child, who is innocent, meek, good, etc. **4** a person easily deceived. ◆ *vb* **5** (*intr*) (of a ewe) to give birth. **6** (*intr*) (of a shepherd) to tend

the ewes and newborn lambs at lambing time. ORIG OE *lamb,* from Gmc
▸ **'lamb,like** *adj*

Lamb[1] ★ (læm) *n* **the.** a title given to Christ in the New Testament.

Lamb[2] ★ (læm) *n* **1 Charles,** pen name *Elia.* 1775–1834, British essayist and critic. He collaborated with his sister Mary on *Tales from Shakespeare* (1807). His other works include the largely autobiographical *Essays of Elia* (1823; 1833). **2 William.** See (2nd Viscount) **Melbourne. 3 Willis Eugene.** born 1913, US physicist. He detected the small difference in energy between two states of the hydrogen atom (**Lamb shift**). Nobel prize for physics 1955.

lambada (læm'bɑːdə) *n* **1** an erotic dance, originating in Brazil, performed by two people who hold each other closely and gyrate their hips in synchronized movements. **2** the music that accompanies the lambada, combining salsa, calypso, and reggae. ORIG C20: from Port., lit.: the snapping of a whip

Lambaréné ★ (*French* lɑ̃barene) *n* a town in W Gabon on the Ogooué River: site of the hospital built by Albert Schweitzer, who died and was buried there (1965). Pop.: 50 000 (1985 est.).

lambast (læm'bæst) *or* **lambaste** (læm'beɪst) *vb* **lambasts, lambasting, lambasted** *or* **lambastes, lambasting, lambasted.** (*tr*) **1** to beat or whip severely. **2** to reprimand or scold. ORIG C17: ?from LAM[1] + BASTE[3]

lambda ('læmdə) *n* the 11th letter of the Greek alphabet (Λ, λ). ORIG C14: from Gk, from Semitic

lambent ('læmbənt) *adj* **1** (esp. of a flame) flickering softly over a surface. **2** glowing with soft radiance. **3** (of wit or humour) light or brilliant. ORIG C17: from the present participle of L *lambere* to lick
▸ **'lambency** *n* ▸ **'lambently** *adv*

lambert ('læmbət) *n* the cgs unit of illumination, equal to 1 lumen per square centimetre. Symbol: L ORIG C20: after J. H. *Lambert* (1728–77), G mathematician & physicist

Lambert ★ ('læmbət) *n* **Constant.** 1905–51, British composer and conductor. His works include much ballet music and the choral *The Rio Grande* (1929).

Lambeth ★ ('læmbəθ) *n* a borough of S Greater London, on the Thames: contains **Lambeth Palace** (the London residence of the Archbishop of Canterbury). Pop.: 260 700 (1994 est.). Area: 27 sq. km (11 sq. miles).

lambing ('læmɪŋ) *n* **1** the birth of lambs. **2** the shepherd's work of tending the ewes and newborn lambs at this time.

lambkin ('læmkɪn) *n* **1** a small lamb. **2** a term of affection for a small endearing child.

Lamb of God *n* a title given to Christ in the New Testament, probably with reference to his sacrificial death.

lambrequin ('læmbrɪkɪn, 'læmbə-) *n* **1** an ornamental hanging covering the edge of a shelf or the upper part of a window or door. **2** (*often pl*) a scarf worn over a helmet. ORIG C18: from F, from Du. *lamperkin* (unattested), dim. of *lamper* veil

Lambrusco (læm'bruskəu) *n* **1** a red grape grown in Italy. **2** a sparkling red wine made in Italy from this grape. **3** a much less common white variety of this grape or wine.

lambskin ('læm,skɪn) *n* **1** the skin of a lamb, esp. with the wool still on. **2** a material or garment prepared from this skin.

lamb's lettuce *n* another name for **corn salad.**

lamb's tails *pl n* the pendulous catkins of the hazel tree.

lame (leɪm) *adj* **1** disabled or crippled in the legs or feet. **2** painful or weak: *a lame back.* **3** weak; unconvincing: *a lame excuse.* **4** not effective or enthusiastic: *a lame try.* **5** *US sl.* conventional or uninspiring. ◆ *vb* **lames, laming, lamed. 6** (*tr*) to make lame. ORIG OE *lama*
▸ **'lamely** *adv* ▸ **'lameness** *n*

lamé ('lɑːmeɪ) *n* a fabric of silk, cotton, or wool interwoven with threads of metal. ORIG C20: from F, from OF *lame* gold or silver thread, thin plate, from L *lāmina* thin plate

lame duck *n* **1** a person or thing that is disabled or ineffectual. **2** *Stock Exchange.* a speculator who cannot discharge his liabilities. **3** *US.* an elected official or body of officials remaining in office in the interval between the election and inauguration of a successor.

lamella (lə'mɛlə) *n, pl* **lamellae** (-liː) *or* **lamellas.** a thin layer, plate, or membrane, esp. any of the calcified layers of which bone is formed. ORIG C17: NL, from L, dim. of *lāmina* thin plate
▸ **la'mellar, lamellate** ('læmɪ,leɪt, -lɪt), *or* **lamellose** (lə'mɛləus, 'læmɪ,ləus) *adj*

lamellibranch (lə'mɛlɪ,bræŋk) *n, adj* another word for **bivalve.** ORIG C19: from NL *lamellibranchia* plate-gilled (animals)

lamellicorn (lə'mɛlɪ,kɔːn) *n* **1** any beetle having flattened terminal plates to the antennae, such as the scarabs and stag beetles. ◆ *adj* **2** designating antennae with platelike terminal segments. ORIG C19: from NL *Lamellicornia* plate-horned (animals)

lament (lə'mɛnt) *vb* **1** to feel or express sorrow, remorse, or regret (for or over). ◆ *n* **2** an expression of sorrow. **3** a poem or song in which a death is lamented. ORIG C16: from L *lāmentum*
▸ **la'menter** *n* ▸ **la'mentingly** *adv*

lamentable ('læməntəbᵊl) *adj* **1** wretched, deplorable, or distressing. **2** an archaic word for **mournful.**
▸ **'lamentably** *adv*

lamentation (,læmɛn'teɪʃən) *n* **1** a lament; expression of sorrow. **2** the act of lamenting.

lamented (lə'mɛntɪd) *adj* grieved for or regretted (often in **late lamented**): *our late lamented employer.*
▸ **la'mentedly** *adv*

lamina ('læmɪnə) *n, pl* **laminae** (-,niː) *or* **laminas. 1** a thin plate, esp. of bone or mineral. **2** *Bot.* the flat blade of a leaf. ORIG C17: NL, from L: thin plate
▸ **'laminar** *or* **laminose** ('læmɪ,nəus, -,nəuz) *adj*

laminar flow *n* nonturbulent motion of a fluid in which parallel layers have different velocities relative to each other.

laminate *vb* ('læmɪ,neɪt), **laminates, laminating, laminated. 1** (*tr*) to make (material in sheet form) by bonding together two or more thin sheets. **2** to split or be split into thin sheets. **3** (*tr*) to beat, form, or press (material, esp. metal) into thin sheets. **4** (*tr*) to cover or overlay with a thin sheet of material. ◆ *n* ('læmɪ,neɪt, -nɪt). **5** a material made by bonding together two or more sheets. ◆ *adj* ('læmɪ,neɪt, -nɪt). **6** having or composed of lamina; laminated. ORIG C17: from NL *lāminātus* plated
▸ **'laminable** *adj* ▸ **,lami'nation** *n* ▸ **'lami,nator** *n*

laminated ('læmɪ,neɪtɪd) *adj* **1** composed of many layers of plastic, wood, etc., bonded together. **2** covered with a thin protective layer of plastic, etc.

lamington ('læmɪŋtən) *n Austral. & NZ.* a cube of sponge cake coated in chocolate or red jelly and dried coconut. ORIG C20 (in the earlier sense: a homburg hat): after Lady *Lamington,* wife of Baron Lamington, governor of Queensland (1896–1901)

Lammas ('læməs) *n* **1** *RC Church.* Aug. 1, held as a feast, commemorating St Peter's miraculous deliverance from prison. **2** Also called: **Lammas Day.** the same day formerly observed in England as a harvest festival. ORIG OE *hlāfmæsse* loaf mass

lammergeier *or* **lammergeyer** ('læmə,gaɪə) *n* a rare vulture of S Europe, Africa, and Asia, with dark wings, a pale breast, and black feathers around the bill. ORIG C19: from G *Lämmergeier,* from *Lämmer* lambs + *Geier* vulture

lamp (læmp) *n* **1a** any of a number of devices that produce illumination: *an electric lamp; a gas lamp; an oil lamp.* **1b** (*in combination*): *lampshade.* **2** a device for holding one or more electric light bulbs: *a table lamp.* **3** a vessel in which a liquid fuel is burned to supply illumination. **4** any of a variety of devices that produce radiation, esp. for therapeutic purposes: *an ultraviolet lamp.* ORIG C13 *lampe,* via OF from L *lampas,* from Gk, from *lampein* to shine

lampblack ('læmp,blæk) *n* a finely divided form of almost pure carbon produced by the incomplete combustion of organic compounds, such as natural gas, used in

★ people and places

making carbon electrodes and dynamo brushes and as a pigment.

lamp chimney *n* a glass tube that surrounds the wick in an oil lamp.

Lampedusa[1] ★ (ˌlæmpɪˈdjuːzə) *n* an island in the Mediterranean, between Malta and Tunisia. Area: about 21 sq. km (8 sq. miles).

Lampedusa[2] ★ (ˌlæmpɪˈdjuːzə) *n* **Giuseppe Tomasi di.** 1896–1957, Italian novelist: author of the historical novel *The Leopard* (1958).

lamplight (ˈlæmpˌlaɪt) *n* the light produced by a lamp or lamps.

lamplighter (ˈlæmpˌlaɪtə) *n* **1** (formerly) a person who lit and extinguished street lamps, esp. gas ones. **2** *Chiefly US & Canad.* any of various devices used to light lamps.

lampoon (læmˈpuːn) *n* **1** a satire in prose or verse ridiculing a person, literary work, etc. ◆ *vb* **2** (*tr*) to attack or satirize in a lampoon. ORIG C17: from F *lampon,* ?from *lampons* let us drink (frequently used as a refrain in poems)
▸ **lamˈpooner** *or* **lamˈpoonist** *n* ▸ **lamˈpoonery** *n*

lamppost (ˈlæmpˌpəʊst) *n* a post supporting a lamp, esp. in a street.

lamprey (ˈlæmprɪ) *n* any eel-like vertebrate having a round sucking mouth for clinging to and feeding on the blood of other animals. Also called: **lamper eel.** ORIG C13: from OF *lamproie,* from LL *lamprēda,* from ?

Lanai ★ (lɑːˈnɑːɪ, ləˈnaɪ) *n* an island in central Hawaii, west of Maui Island. Pop.: 2426 (1990). Area: 363 sq. km. (140 sq. miles).

Lanarkshire ★ (ˈlænəkˌʃɪə, -ʃə) *n* a historic county of S Scotland, now administered by North Lanarkshire, South Lanarkshire, and Glasgow.

Lancashire ★ (ˈlæŋkəˌʃɪə, -ʃə) *n* **1** a county of NW England, on the Irish Sea: became a county palatine in 1351 and a duchy attached to the Crown; much reduced in size after the 1974 boundary changes, losing the Furness district to Cumbria and much of the south to Greater Manchester, Merseyside, and Cheshire; in 1998 Blackburn with Darwen and Blackpool became independent unitary authorities. It was traditionally a cotton textiles manufacturing region. Administrative centre: Preston. Pop. (excluding Blackburn with Darwen and Blackpool): 1 134 000 (1996 est.). Area (excluding Blackburn with Darwen and Blackpool): 2889 sq. km (1115 sq. miles). Abbrev.: **Lancs. 2** a mild whitish-coloured cheese with a crumbly texture.

Lancaster[1] (ˈlæŋkəstə, ˈlæŋˌkæstə) *n* the English royal house that reigned from 1399 to 1461.

Lancaster[2] ★ (ˈlæŋkəstə) *n* a city in NW England, former county town of Lancashire, on the River Lune: castle (built on the site of a Roman camp); seat of The University of Lancaster (1964). Pop.: 44 497 (1991).

Lancastrian (læŋˈkæstrɪən) *n* **1** a native or resident of Lancashire or Lancaster. **2** an adherent of the house of Lancaster in the Wars of the Roses. ◆ *adj* **3** of or relating to Lancashire or Lancaster. **4** of or relating to the house of Lancaster.

lance (lɑːns) *n* **1** a long weapon with a pointed head used by horsemen. **2** a similar weapon used for hunting, whaling, etc. **3** *Surgery.* another name for **lancet.** ◆ *vb* **lances, lancing, lanced.** (*tr*) **4** to pierce (an abscess or boil) with a lancet. **5** to pierce with or as with a lance. ORIG C13 *launce,* from OF *lance,* from L *lancea*

lance corporal *n* a noncommissioned army officer of the lowest rank.

lancelet (ˈlɑːnslɪt) *n* any of several marine animals closely related to the vertebrates: they burrow in sand. Also called: **amphioxus.** ORIG C19: referring to the slender shape

Lancelot ★ (ˈlɑːnslət) *n* (in Arthurian legend) one of the Knights of the Round Table; the lover of Queen Guinevere.

lanceolate (ˈlɑːnsɪəˌleɪt, -lɪt) *adj* narrow and tapering to a point at each end: *lanceolate leaves.* ORIG C18: from LL *lanceolātus,* from *lanceola* small LANCE

lancer (ˈlɑːnsə) *n* **1** (formerly) a cavalryman armed with a lance. **2** a member of a regiment retaining such a title.

lancers (ˈlɑːnsəz) *n* (*functioning as sing*) **1** a quadrille for eight or sixteen couples. **2** a piece of music composed for or in the rhythm of this dance.

lancet (ˈlɑːnsɪt) *n* **1** Also called: **lance.** a pointed surgical knife with two sharp edges. **2** short for **lancet arch** or **lancet window.** ORIG C15 *lancette,* from OF: small LANCE

lancet arch *n* a narrow acutely pointed arch.

lancet window *n* a narrow window having a lancet arch.

lancewood (ˈlɑːnsˌwʊd) *n* a New Zealand tree with slender leaves showing different configurations in youth and maturity.

Lanchow *or* **Lan-chou** ★ (ˈlænˈtʃaʊ) *n* a variant transliteration of the Chinese name for **Lanzhou.**

Lancs (læŋks) *abbrev. for* Lancashire.

land (lænd) *n* **1** the solid part of the surface of the earth as distinct from seas, lakes, etc. Related adj: **terrestrial. 2** ground, esp. with reference to its use, quality, etc. **3** rural or agricultural areas as contrasted with urban ones. **4** farming as an occupation or way of life. **5** *Law.* any tract of ground capable of being owned as property. **6a** a country, region, or area. **6b** the people of a country, etc. **7** *Econ.* the factor of production consisting of all natural resources. ◆ *vb* **8** to transfer (something) or go from a ship or boat to the shore: *land the cargo.* **9** (*intr*) to come to or touch shore. **10** (*intr*) (in Canada) to be legally admitted to the country, as an immigrant or **landed immigrant. 11** to come down or bring (something) down to earth after a flight or jump. **12** to come or bring to some point, condition, or state. **13** (*tr*) *Angling.* to retrieve (a hooked fish) from the water. **14** (*tr*) *Inf.* to win or obtain: *to land a job.* **15** (*tr*) *Inf.* to deliver (a blow). ◆ See also **land up.** ORIG OE
▸ **ˈlandless** *adj*

Land ★ (lænd) *n* **Edwin Herbert.** 1909–91, US inventor of the Polaroid Land camera.

Land *German.* (lant) *n, pl* **Länder** (ˈlɛndər). **1** any of the federal states of Germany. **2** any of the provinces of Austria.

land agent *n* **1** a person who administers a landed estate and its tenancies. **2** a person who acts as an agent for the sale of land.
▸ **land agency** *n*

landau (ˈlændɔː) *n* a four-wheeled carriage, usually horse-drawn, with two folding hoods over the passenger compartment. ORIG C18: after *Landau* (a town in Germany), where first made

Landau ★ (*Russian* lanˈdau) *n* **Lev Davidovich** (ljɛf daˈvidəvitʃ). 1908–68, Soviet physicist, noted for his researches on quantum theory: Nobel prize for physics 1962.

landaulet (ˌlændɔːˈlɛt) *n* **1** a small landau. **2** *US.* an early type of car with a folding hood over the passenger seats.

landed (ˈlændɪd) *adj* **1** owning land: *landed gentry.* **2** consisting of or including land: *a landed estate.* **3** *Canad.* having been formally admitted into Canada as an immigrant.

Landes ★ (*French* lɑ̃d) *n* **1** a department of SW France, in Aquitaine region. Capital: Mont-de-Marsan. Pop.: 317 828 (1994 est.). Area: 9364 sq. km (3652 sq. miles). **2** a region of SW France, on the Bay of Biscay: occupies most of the Landes department and parts of Gironde and Lot-et-Garonne; consists chiefly of the most extensive forest in France. Area: 14 000 sq. km (5400 sq. miles).

landfall (ˈlændˌfɔːl) *n* **1** the act of sighting or nearing land, esp. from the sea. **2** the land sighted or neared.

landfill (ˈlændˌfɪl) *adj* of or denoting low-lying sites or tips being filled up with alternate layers of rubbish and earth.

landform (ˈlændˌfɔːm) *n Geol.* any natural feature of the earth's surface.

land girl *n* a girl or woman who does farm work, esp. in wartime.

landgrave (ˈlændˌgreɪv) *n German history.* **1** (from the 13th century to 1806) a count who ruled over a specified territory. **2** (after 1806) the title of any of various sovereign princes. ORIG C16: via G, from MHG *lantgrāve,* from *lant* land + *grāve* count

land-holder *n* a person who owns or occupies land.
▸ **'land-ˌholding** *adj, n*

landing ('lændɪŋ) *n* **1a** the act of coming to land, esp. after a flight or a sea voyage. **1b** (*as modifier*): *landing place.* **2** a place of disembarkation. **3** the floor area at the top of a flight of stairs.

landing craft *n Mil.* any small vessel designed for the landing of troops and equipment on beaches.

landing field *n* an area of land on which aircraft land and from which they take off.

landing gear *n* another name for **undercarriage.**

landing net *n Angling.* a loose long-handled net for lifting hooked fish from the water.

landing stage *n* a platform used for landing goods and passengers from a vessel.

landing strip *n* another name for **airstrip.**

landlady ('lændˌleɪdɪ) *n, pl* **landladies. 1** a woman who owns and leases property. **2** a woman who owns or runs a lodging house, pub, etc.

ländler (*German* 'lɛntlər) *n* **1** an Austrian country dance in which couples spin and clap. **2** a piece of music composed for or in the rhythm of this dance, in three-four time. ORIG G, from dialect *Landl* Upper Austria

land line *n* a telecommunications wire or cable laid over land.

landlocked ('lændˌlɒkt) *adj* **1** (esp. of lakes) completely surrounded by land. **2** (esp. of certain salmon) living in fresh water that is permanently isolated from the sea.

landlord ('lændˌlɔːd) *n* **1** a man who owns and leases property. **2** a man who owns or runs a lodging house, pub, etc.

landlubber ('lændˌlʌbə) *n Naut.* any person having no experience at sea.

landmark ('lændˌmɑːk) *n* **1** a prominent or well-known object in or feature of a particular landscape. **2** an important or unique decision, event, fact, discovery, etc. **3** a boundary marker.

landmass ('lændˌmæs) *n* a large continuous area of land, as opposed to seas or islands.

land mine *n Mil.* an explosive charge placed in the ground, usually detonated by stepping or driving on it.

land of milk and honey *n* **1** *Old Testament.* the fertile land promised to the Israelites by God (Ezekiel 20:6). **2** any fertile land, state, etc.

land of Nod ★ *n* **1** *Old Testament.* a region to the east of Eden to which Cain went after he had killed Abel (Genesis 4:14). **2** an imaginary land of sleep.

Landor ★ ('lændɔː) *n* **Walter Savage.** 1775–1864, British poet, noted also for his prose works, including *Imaginary Conversations* (1824–29).

landowner ('lændˌəʊnə) *n* a person who owns land.
▸ **'landˌownerˌship** *n* ▸ **'landˌowning** *n, adj*

Landowska ★ (*Polish* lan'dɔfska) *n* **Wanda** ('vanda). 1877–1959, US harpsichordist, born in Poland.

land rail *n* another name for **corncrake.**

land reform *n* the redistributing of large agricultural holdings among the landless.

landscape ('lændˌskeɪp) *n* **1** an extensive area of land regarded as being visually distinct. **2** a painting, drawing, photograph, etc., depicting natural scenery. **3** the genre including such pictures. **4** the distinctive features of a given area of intellectual activity, regarded as an integrated whole. ◆ *adj* **5** *Printing.* **5a** (of an illustration in a book, magazine, etc.) of greater width than depth. Cf. **portrait** (sense 3). **5b** (of a page) carrying an illustration or table printed at right angles to the normal text. ◆ *vb* **landscapes, landscaping, landscaped. 6** (*tr*) to improve the natural features of (a garden, park, etc.), as by creating contoured features and planting trees. **7** (*intr*) to work as a landscape gardener. ORIG C16 *landskip* (orig. a term in painting), from MDu. *lantscap* region

landscape gardening *n* the art of laying out grounds in imitation of natural scenery. Also called: **landscape architecture.**
▸ **landscape gardener** *n*

landscapist ('lændˌskeɪpɪst) *n* a painter of landscapes.

Landseer ★ ('lænsɪə) *n* Sir **Edwin Henry.** 1802–73, British painter, noted for his studies of animals.

Land's End ★ *n* a granite headland in SW England, on the SW coast of Cornwall: the westernmost point of England.

Landshut ★ (*German* 'lantshuːt) *n* a city in SE Germany, in Bavaria: Trausnitz castle (13th century); manufacturing centre for machinery and chemicals. Pop.: 59 670 (1991).

landside ('lændˌsaɪd) *n* **1** the part of an airport farthest from the aircraft, the boundary of which is the security check, customs, passport control, etc. Cf. **airside. 2** the part of a plough that slides along the face of the furrow wall on the opposite side to the mouldboard.

landslide ('lændˌslaɪd) *n* **1** Also called: **landslip. 1a** the sliding of a large mass of rock material, soil, etc., down the side of a mountain or cliff. **1b** the material dislodged in this way. **2** an overwhelming electoral victory.

landsman ('lændzmən) *n, pl* **landsmen.** a person who works or lives on land, as distinguished from a seaman.

Landsteiner ★ (*German* 'lantˌʃtaɪnər) *n* **Karl** (karl). 1868–1943, Austrian immunologist, who discovered (1900) human blood groups and introduced the ABO classification system. He also discovered (1940) the Rhesus (Rh) factor in blood. Nobel prize for physiology or medicine (1930).

land up *vb* (*adv, usually intr*) to arrive or cause to arrive at a final point or condition.

landward ('lændwəd) *adj* **1** lying, facing, or moving towards land. **2** in the direction of the land. ◆ *adv* **3** a variant of **landwards.**

landwards ('lændwədz) *or* **landward** *adv* towards land.

lane (leɪn) *n* **1** a narrow road or way between buildings, hedges, fences, etc. **2a** any of the parallel strips into which the carriageway of a major road or motorway is divided. **2b** any narrow well-defined route or course for ships or aircraft. **3** one of the parallel strips into which a running track or swimming bath is divided for races. **4** the long strip of wooden flooring down which balls are bowled in a bowling alley. ORIG OE *lane, lanu*

Lanfranc ★ ('lænfræŋk) *n* ?1005–89, Italian ecclesiastic and scholar; archbishop of Canterbury (1070–89) and adviser to William the Conqueror.

Lang ★ (læŋ) *n* **1 Cosmo Gordon,** 1st Baron Lang of Lambeth. 1864–1945, British churchman; archbishop of Canterbury (1928–42). **2 Fritz.** 1890–1976, Austrian film director, later in the US, notable for such silent films as *Metropolis* (1926) and *The Testament of Dr. Mabuse* (1932). **3 Jack (John Thomas).** 1876–1975, Australian Labor politician; premier of New South Wales (1925–27; 1930–32): dismissed (1932) by the governor, Sir Philip Game, for acting unconstitutionally.

lang. *abbrev. for* language.

Lange ★ ('lɒŋɪ) *n* **David.** born 1942, New Zealand statesman: Labour prime minister (1984–89).

Langer ★ ('læŋə; *German* 'laŋər) *n* **Bernhard** ('bernhart). born 1957, German professional golfer: won the US Masters Championship (1985, 1993).

Langerhans islets *or* **islands** ('læŋəˌhæns) *pl n Anat.* See **islets of Langerhans.**

Langland ★ ('læŋlənd) *n* **William.** ?1332–?1400, English poet. The allegorical religious poem in alliterative verse, *The Vision of William concerning Piers the Plowman,* is attributed to him.

langlauf ('læŋˌlaʊf) *n* cross-country skiing. ORIG G, lit.: long run
▸ **langläufer** ('læŋˌlɔɪfə) *n* ▸ **langläufing** ('læŋˌlɔɪfɪŋ) *n*

Langley ★ ('læŋlɪ) *n* **Samuel Pierpont.** 1834–1906, US astronomer and physicist: invented the bolometer (1878) and pioneered powered flight.

Langmuir ★ ('læŋmjʊə) *n* **Irving.** 1881–1957, US chemist. He developed the gas-filled tungsten lamp and the atomic hydrogen welding process: Nobel prize for chemistry 1932.

langouste ('lɒŋguːst, lɒŋ'guːst) *n* another name for the **spiny lobster.** ORIG F, from OProvençal *langosta,* ? from L *lōcusta* lobster, locust

langoustine (ˌlɒŋguːs'tiːn) *n* a large prawn or small lobster. ORIG from F, dim. of LANGOUSTE

Langres Plateau ★ (*French* lɑ̃grə) *n* a calcareous plateau of E France north of Dijon between the Seine and the Saône, reaching over 580 m (1900 ft): forms a watershed between rivers flowing to the Mediterranean and to the English Channel.

langsam ('læŋzæm) *adj Music.* slow. ORIG G

langsyne (ˌlæŋ'saɪn) *Scot.* ◆ *adv* **1** long ago; long since. ◆ *n* **2** times long past, esp. those fondly remembered. ORIG C16: Scot.: long since

Langton ★ ('læŋtən) *n* **Stephen.** ?1150–1228, English cardinal; archbishop of Canterbury (1213–28). He was consecrated archbishop by Pope Innocent III in 1207 but was kept out of his see by King John until 1213. He was partly responsible for the Magna Carta (1215).

Langtry ★ ('læŋtrɪ) *n* **Lillie,** known as *the Jersey Lily,* real name *Émilie Charlotte le Breton.* 1852–1929, British actress, noted for her friendship with Edward VII.

language ('læŋgwɪdʒ) *n* **1** a system for the expression of thoughts, feelings, etc., by the use of spoken sounds or conventional symbols. **2** the faculty for the use of such systems, which is a distinguishing characteristic of man as compared with other animals. **3** the language of a particular nation or people. **4** any other means of communicating, such as gesture or animal sounds: *the language of love.* **5** the specialized vocabulary used by a particular group: *medical language.* **6** a particular manner or style of verbal expression: *your language is disgusting.* **7** *Computing.* See **programming language.** ORIG C13: from OF *language,* ult. from L *lingua* tongue

language laboratory *n* a room equipped with tape recorders, etc., for learning foreign languages.

langue (lɑːŋg) *n Linguistics.* language considered as an abstract system or a social institution, being the common possession of a speech community. ORIG C19: from F: language

Languedoc ★ (*French* lɑ̃gdɔk) *n* **1** a former province of S France, lying between the foothills of the Pyrenees and the River Rhône: formed around the countship of Toulouse in the 13th century. **2** a wine from this region.

langue d'oc *French.* (lɑ̃g dɔk) *n* the group of medieval French dialects spoken in S France: often regarded as including Provençal. ORIG lit.: language of *oc* (form for the Provençal *yes*), ult. from L *hoc* this

Languedoc-Roussillon ★ (*French* lɑ̃gdɔkrusijɔ̃) *n* a region of S France, on the Gulf of Lions: consists of the departments of Lozère, Gard, Hérault, Aude, and Pyrénées-Orientales; mainly mountainous with a coastal plain.

langue d'oïl *French.* (lɑ̃g dɔj) *n* the group of medieval French dialects spoken in France north of the Loire; the medieval basis of modern French. ORIG lit.: language of *oïl* (the northern form for *yes*), ult. from L *hoc ille* (*fecit*) this he (did)

languid ('læŋgwɪd) *adj* **1** without energy or spirit. **2** without interest or enthusiasm. **3** sluggish; inactive. ORIG C16: from L *languidus,* from *languēre* to languish
▸ **'languidly** *adv* ▸ **'languidness** *n*

languish ('læŋgwɪʃ) *vb* (*intr*) **1** to lose or diminish in strength or energy. **2** (often foll. by *for*) to be listless with desire; pine. **3** to suffer deprivation, hardship, or neglect: *to languish in prison.* **4** to put on a tender, nostalgic, or melancholic expression. ORIG C14 *languishen,* from OF *languiss-,* stem of *languir,* ult. from L *languēre*
▸ **'languishing** *adj* ▸ **'languishingly** *adv* ▸ **'languishment** *n*

languor ('læŋgə) *n* **1** physical or mental laziness or weariness. **2** a feeling of dreaminess and relaxation. **3** oppressive silence or stillness. ORIG C14 *langour,* via OF from L *languor,* from *languēre* to languish; the modern spelling is directly from L
▸ **'languorous** *adj*

langur (lʌŋ'gʊə) *n* any of various agile arboreal Old World monkeys of S and SE Asia having a long tail and long hair surrounding the face. ORIG Hindi

laniard ('lænjəd) *n* a variant spelling of **lanyard.**

laniary ('lænɪərɪ) *adj* **1** (esp. of canine teeth) adapted for tearing. ◆ *n, pl* **laniaries. 2** a tooth adapted for tearing. ORIG C19: from L *lanius* butcher, from *laniāre* to tear

laniferous (lə'nɪfərəs) *or* **lanigerous** (lə'nɪdʒərəs) *adj Biol.* bearing wool or fleecy hairs resembling wool. ORIG C17: from L *lānifer,* from *lāna* wool

La Niña (læ 'niːnjə) *n Meteorol.* a cooling of the eastern tropical Pacific, occurring in certain years. ORIG from Sp.: The Little Girl, to distinguish it from EL NIÑO

lank (læŋk) *adj* **1** long and limp. **2** thin or gaunt. ORIG OE *hlanc* loose
▸ **'lankly** *adv* ▸ **'lankness** *n*

Lankester ★ ('læŋkɪstə) *n* Sir **Edwin Ray.** 1847–1929, British zoologist, noted particularly for his study of protozoans.

lanky ('læŋkɪ) *adj* **lankier, lankiest.** tall, thin, and loose-jointed.
▸ **'lankily** *adv* ▸ **'lankiness** *n*

lanner ('lænə) *n* **1** a large falcon of Mediterranean regions, N Africa, and S Asia. **2** *Falconry.* the female of this falcon. The male is called **lanneret.** ORIG C15: from OF (*faucon*) *lanier* cowardly (falcon), from L *lanārius* wool worker, coward; referring to its sluggish flight and timid nature

lanolin ('lænəlɪn) *or* **lanoline** ('lænəlɪn, -ˌliːn) *n* a yellowish viscous substance extracted from wool: used in some ointments. ORIG C19: via G from L *lāna* wool + *oleum* oil; see -IN

Lansbury ★ ('lænzbərɪ) *n* **George.** 1859–1940, British Labour politician, who led the Labour Party in opposition (1931–35). A committed pacifist, he resigned over the party's reaction to Mussolini's seizure of Ethiopia.

Lansing ★ ('lænsɪŋ) *n* a city in S Michigan, on the Grand River: the state capital. Pop.: 119 590 (1994 est.).

lantern ('læntən) *n* **1** a light with a transparent protective case. **2** a structure on top of a dome or roof having openings or windows to admit light or air. **3** the upper part of a lighthouse that houses the light. ORIG C13: from L *lanterna,* from Gk *lamptēr* lamp, from *lampein* to shine

lantern jaw *n* (when *pl,* refers to upper and lower jaw; when *sing,* usually to lower jaw) a long hollow jaw that gives the face a drawn appearance.
▸ **'lantern-ˌjawed** *adj*

lantern slide *n* (formerly) a photographic slide for projection, used in a magic lantern.

lanthanide ('lænθəˌnaɪd) *or* **lanthanoid** ('lænθəˌnɔɪd) *n* any of a class of 15 chemically related elements with atomic numbers from 57 (lanthanum) to 71 (lutetium).

lanthanum ('lænθənəm) *n* a silvery-white ductile metallic element of the lanthanide series: used in pyrophoric alloys, electronic devices, and in glass manufacture. Symbol: La; atomic no.: 57; atomic wt.: 138.91. ORIG C19: NL, from Gk *lanthanein* to lie unseen

lanthorn ('læntˌhɔːn, 'læntən) *n* an archaic word for **lantern.**

lanugo (lə'njuːgəʊ) *n, pl* **lanugos.** a layer of fine hairs, esp. the covering of the human fetus before birth. ORIG C17: from L: down, from *lāna* wool

Lanús ★ (*Spanish* la'nus) *n* a city in E Argentina: a S suburb of Buenos Aires. Pop.: 466 755 (1991).

lanyard *or* **laniard** ('lænjəd) *n* **1** a cord, esp. one worn around the neck, to hold a whistle, knife, etc. **2** a cord used in firing certain types of cannon. **3** *Naut.* a line for extending or tightening standing rigging. ORIG C15 *lanyer,* from F *lanière,* from *lasne* strap, prob. of Gmc origin

Lanzhou, Lanchow, *or* **Lan-chou** ★ ('læn'dʒəʊ) *n* a city in N China, capital of Gansu province, on the Yellow River: situated on the main route between China and the West. Pop.: 1 510 000 (1991 est.).

Laoag ★ (lɑːˈwɑːɡ) *n* a city in the N Philippines, on NW Luzon: trade centre for an agricultural region. Pop.: 84 000 (1990 est.).

Laocoon ★ (leɪˈɒkəʊˌɒn) *n Greek myth.* a priest of Apollo at Troy who warned the Trojans against the wooden horse left by the Greeks; killed with his twin sons by two sea serpents.

Laodicea ★ (ˌleɪəʊdɪˈsɪə) *n* the ancient name of several Greek cities in W Asia, notably of **Latakia.**

laodicean (ˌleɪəʊdɪˈsɪən) *adj* **1** lukewarm and indifferent, esp. in religious matters. ◆ *n* **2** a person having a lukewarm attitude towards religious matters. ORIG C17: referring to the early Christians of Laodicea (Revelation 3:14–16)

Laoighis ★ (ˈleɪɪʃ) *n* a variant spelling of **Laois.**

Laois ★ (ˈleɪɪʃ) *n* a county of central Republic of Ireland, in Leinster province: formerly boggy but largely reclaimed for agriculture. County town: Portlaoise. Pop.: 53 000 (1996). Area: 1719 sq. km (664 sq. miles). Also called: **Laoighis, Leix.** Former name: **Queen's County.**

Laomedon ★ (leɪˈɒmɪˌdɒn) *n Greek myth.* the founder and ruler of Troy, who cheated Apollo and Poseidon of their wage for constructing the city's walls; the father of Priam.

Laos ★ (laʊz, laʊs) *n* a republic in SE Asia: first united as the kingdom of Lan Xang ("million elephants") in 1353, after being a province of the Khmer Empire for about four centuries; made part of French Indochina in 1893 and gained independence in 1949; became a republic in 1975. It is generally forested and mountainous, with the Mekong River running almost the whole length of the W border. Official language: Lao. Religion: Buddhist majority, tribal religions. Currency: kip. Capital: Vientiane. Pop.: 5 407 000 (1999 est.). Area: 236 800 sq. km (91 429 sq. miles). Official name: **People's Democratic Republic of Laos.**
▸ **Laotian** (ˈlaʊʃɪən) *adj, n*

Lao Zi (ˈlaʊ ˈzɪə) *or* **Lao-tzu** ★ (ˈlaʊˈtsuː) *n* ?604–?531 B.C., Chinese philosopher, traditionally regarded as the founder of Taoism and the author of the *Tao-te Ching.*

lap[1] (læp) *n* **1** the area formed by the upper surface of the thighs of a seated person. **2** Also called: **lapful.** the amount held in one's lap. **3** a protected place or environment: *in the lap of luxury.* **4** the part of one's clothing that covers the lap. **5 drop in someone's lap.** give someone the responsibility of. ORIG OE *læppa* flap

lap[2] (læp) *n* **1** one circuit of a racecourse or track. **2** a stage or part of a journey, race, etc. **3a** an overlapping part or projection. **3b** the extent of overlap. **4** the length of material needed to go around an object. **5** a rotating disc coated with fine abrasive for polishing gemstones. ◆ *vb* **laps, lapping, lapped. 6** (*tr*) to wrap or fold (around or over): *he lapped a bandage around his wrist.* **7** (*tr*) to enclose or envelop in: *he lapped his wrist in a bandage.* **8** to place or lie partly or completely over or project beyond. **9** (*tr; usually passive*) to envelop or surround with comfort, love, etc.: *lapped in luxury.* **10** (*intr*) to be folded. **11** (*tr*) to overtake (an opponent) in a race so as to be one or more circuits ahead. **12** (*tr*) to polish or cut (a workpiece, gemstone, etc.) with a fine abrasive. ORIG C13 (in the sense: to wrap): prob. from LAP[1]
▸ **ˈlapper** *n*

lap[3] (læp) *vb* **laps, lapping, lapped. 1** (of small waves) to wash against (a shore, boat, etc.), usually with light splashing sounds. **2** (often foll. by *up*) (esp. of animals) to scoop (a liquid) into the mouth with the tongue. ◆ *n* **3** the act or sound of lapping. **4** a thin food for dogs or other animals. ◆ See also **lap up.** ORIG OE *lapian*
▸ **ˈlapper** *n*

La Palma ★ (*Spanish* la ˈpalma) *n* an island in the N Atlantic, in the NW Canary Islands: administratively part of Spain. Chief town: Santa Cruz de la Palma. Pop.: 77 000 (latest est.). Area: 725 sq. km (280 sq. miles).

laparoscope (ˈlæpərəˌskəʊp) *n* a medical instrument consisting of a tube that is inserted through the abdominal wall and illuminated to enable a doctor to view the internal organs. ORIG C19 (applied to various instruments used to examine the abdomen) and C20 (in the specific modern sense): from Gk *lapara* (see LAPAROTOMY) + -SCOPE
▸ **ˌlapaˈroscopy** *n*

laparotomy (ˌlæpəˈrɒtəmɪ) *n, pl* **laparotomies.** surgical incision through the abdominal wall. ORIG C19: from Gk *lapara* flank, from *laparos* soft + -TOMY

La Paz ★ (læ ˈpæz; *Spanish* la ˈpaθ) *n* a city in W Bolivia, at an altitude of 3600 m (12 000 ft): seat of government since 1898 (though Sucre is still the official capital); the country's largest city; founded in 1548 by the Spaniards; university (1830). Pop.: 784 976 (1993 est.).

lap dancing *n* a form of entertainment in which scantily dressed women dance erotically for individual members of the audience.

lap dissolve *n Films.* the technique of allowing the end of one scene to overlap the beginning of the next scene by fading out the former while fading in the latter.

lapdog (ˈlæpˌdɒɡ) *n* a pet dog small and docile enough to be cuddled in the lap.

lapel (ləˈpɛl) *n* the continuation of the turned or folded back collar on a suit, coat, jacket, etc. ORIG C18: from LAP[1]
▸ **laˈpelled** *adj*

lapheld (ˈlæpˌhɛld) *adj* (esp. of a personal computer) small enough to be used on one's lap; portable.

lapidary (ˈlæpɪdərɪ) *n, pl* **lapidaries. 1** a person whose business is to cut, polish, set, or deal in gemstones. ◆ *adj* **2** of or relating to gemstones or the work of a lapidary. **3** Also: **lapidarian** (ˌlæpɪˈdɛərɪən). engraved, cut, or inscribed in a stone or gemstone. **4** of sufficiently high quality to be engraved on a stone: *a lapidary inscription.* ORIG C14: from L *lapidārius,* from *lapid-, lapis* stone

lapillus (ləˈpɪləs) *n, pl* **lapilli** (-laɪ). a small piece of lava thrown from a volcano. ORIG C18: L: little stone

lapis lazuli (ˈlæpɪs ˈlæzjʊˌlaɪ) *n* **1** a brilliant blue mineral used as a gemstone. **2** the deep blue colour of lapis lazuli. ORIG C14: from L *lapis* stone + Med. L *lazulī,* from Ar. *lāzaward,* from Persian *lāzhuward,* from ?

Lapith ★ (ˈlæpɪθ) *n, pl* **Lapithae** (ˈlæpɪˌθiː) *or* **Lapiths.** *Greek myth.* a member of a people in Thessaly who at the wedding of their king, Pirithoüs, fought the drunken centaurs.

lap joint *n* a joint made by placing one member over another and fastening them together. Also called: **lapped joint.**
▸ **ˈlap-ˌjointed** *adj*

Laplace ★ (*French* laplas) *n* **Pierre Simon** (pjɛr simɔ̃), Marquis de Laplace. 1749–1827, French mathematician, physicist, and astronomer. He formulated the nebular hypothesis (1796). He also developed the theory of probability.

Laplace operator *n Maths.* the operator $\partial^2/\partial x^2 + \partial^2/\partial y^2 + \partial^2/\partial z^2$, used in differential analysis. Symbol: ∇^2

Lapland ★ (ˈlæpˌlænd) *n* an extensive region of N Europe, mainly within the Arctic Circle: consists of the N parts of Norway, Sweden, Finland, and the Kola Peninsula of the extreme NW of Russia. Also called (informal): **Land of the Midnight Sun.**
▸ **ˈLapˌlander** *n*

La Plata ★ (*Spanish* la ˈplata) *n* **1** a port in E Argentina, near the Río de la Plata estuary: founded in 1882 and modelled on Washington DC; university (1897). Pop.: 642 979 (1991). **2** See (Río de la) **Plata.**

lap of honour *n* a ceremonial circuit of a racing track, etc., by the winner of a race.

Lapp (læp) *n* **1** Also **Laplander.** a member of a nomadic people living chiefly in N Scandinavia and the Kola Peninsula of Russia. **2** the language of this people. ◆ *adj* **3** of or relating to this people or their language.
▸ **ˈLappish** *adj, n*

USAGE NOTE The indigenous people of Lapland prefer to be called *Sami,* although *Lapp* is still in widespread use.

lappet (ˈlæpɪt) *n* **1** a small hanging flap or piece of lace, etc. **2** *Zool.* a lobelike hanging structure, such as the wattle on a bird's head. ORIG C16: from LAP[1] + -ET

lapse (læps) *n* **1** a drop in standard of an isolated or temporary nature: *a lapse of justice.* **2** a break in occurrence, usage, etc.: *a lapse of five weeks between letters.* **3** a gradual decline or a drop to a lower degree, condition, or state: *a lapse from high office.* **4** a moral fall. **5** *Law.* the termination of some right, interest, or privilege, as by neglecting to exercise it or through failure of some contingency. **6** *Insurance.* the termination of coverage following a failure to pay the premiums. ◆ *vb* **lapses, lapsing, lapsed.** (*intr*) **7** to drop in standard or fail to maintain a norm. **8** to decline gradually or fall in status, condition, etc. **9** to be discontinued, esp. through negligence or other failure. **10** (usually foll. by *into*) to drift or slide (into a condition): *to lapse into sleep.* **11** (often foll. by *from*) to turn away (from beliefs or norms). **12** (of time) to slip away. ORIG C15: from L *lāpsus* error, from *lābī* to glide
▸ **ˈlapsable** *or* **ˈlapsible** *adj* ▸ **lapsed** *adj* ▸ **ˈlapser** *n*

lapse rate *n* the rate of change of any meteorological factor with altitude, esp. atmospheric temperature.

Laptev Sea ★ (ˈlæptɪf) *n* a shallow arm of the Arctic Ocean, along the N coast of Russia between the Taimyr Peninsula and the New Siberian Islands. Former name: **Nordenskjöld Sea.**

laptop (ˈlæpˌtɒp) *or* **laptop computer** *n* a personal computer that is small and light enough to be operated on the user's lap. Cf. **palmtop computer.**

lap up *vb* (*tr, adv*) **1** to eat or drink. **2** to relish or delight in: *he laps up horror films.* **3** to believe or accept eagerly and uncritically: *he laps up stories.*

lapwing (ˈlæpˌwɪŋ) *n* any of several plovers, typically having a crested head, wattles, and spurs. Also called: **green plover, peewit.** ORIG C17: altered form of OE *hlēapewince* plover

Lara ★ (ˈlɑːrə) *n* **Brian.** born 1970, Trinidadian cricketer; holder of records for highest individual score in first-class cricket and for highest Test innings score.

larboard (ˈlɑːbəd) *n, adj Naut.* a former word for **port**[2]. ORIG C14 *laddeborde* (changed to *larboard* by association with *starboard*), from *laden* to load + *borde* BOARD

larceny (ˈlɑːsɪnɪ) *n, pl* **larcenies.** *Law.* (formerly) a technical word for **theft.** ORIG C15: from OF *larcin,* from L *lātrocinium* robbery, from *latrō* robber
▸ **ˈlarcenist** *or* **ˈlarcener** *n* ▸ **ˈlarcenous** *adj*

larch (lɑːtʃ) *n* **1** any coniferous tree having deciduous needle-like leaves and egg-shaped cones. **2** the wood of any of these trees. ORIG C16: from G *Lärche,* ult. from L *larix*

lard (lɑːd) *n* **1** the rendered fat from a pig, used in cooking. ◆ *vb* (*tr*) **2** to prepare (lean meat, poultry, etc.) by inserting small strips of bacon or fat before cooking. **3** to cover or smear (foods) with lard. **4** to add extra material to (speech or writing); embellish. ORIG C15: via OF from L *lāridum* bacon fat
▸ **ˈlardy** *adj*

larder (ˈlɑːdə) *n* a room or cupboard, used as a store for food. ORIG C14: from OF *lardier,* from LARD

Lardner ★ (ˈlɑːdnə) *n* **Ring(old Wilmer).** 1885–1933, US short-story writer and journalist, whose best-known works are collected in *How to Write Short Stories* (1924) and *The Love Nest* (1926).

lardon (ˈlɑːdᵊn) *or* **lardoon** (lɑːˈduːn) *n* a strip of fat or piece of bacon used in larding meat. ORIG C15: from OF, from LARD

lardy cake (ˈlɑːdɪ) *n Brit.* a rich sweet cake made of bread dough, lard, sugar, and dried fruit.

Laredo ★ (ləˈreɪdəʊ) *n* a city in the US, in Texas, on the Mexican border: founded by the Spanish in 1755 on the Rio Grande. Pop.: 149 914 (1994 est.).

lares and penates (ˈlɛəriːz, ˈlɑː-) *pl n* **1** *Roman myth.* **1a** household gods. **1b** statues of these gods kept in the home. **2** the valued possessions of a household. ORIG from L

large (lɑːdʒ) *adj* **1** having a relatively great size, quantity, extent, etc.; big. **2** of wide or broad scope, capacity, or range; comprehensive. **3** having or showing great breadth of understanding. ◆ *n* **4 at large. 4a** (esp. of a dangerous criminal or wild animal) free; not confined. **4b** roaming freely, as in a foreign country. **4c** as a whole; in general. **4d** in full detail; exhaustively. **4e ambassador at large.** See **ambassador** (sense 4). ◆ *vb* **larges, larging, larged. 5 large it.** *Brit. sl.* to enjoy oneself or celebrate in an extravagant way. ORIG C12 (orig.: generous): via OF from L *largus* ample
▸ **ˈlargeness** *n*

large intestine *n* the part of the alimentary canal consisting of the caecum, colon, and rectum.

largely (ˈlɑːdʒlɪ) *adv* **1** principally; to a great extent. **2** on a large scale or in a large manner.

larger-than-life *adj* exceptionally striking or colourful.

large-scale *adj* **1** wide-ranging or extensive. **2** (of maps and models) constructed or drawn to a big scale.

largesse *or* **largess** (lɑːˈdʒɛs) *n* **1** the generous bestowal of gifts, favours, or money. **2** the things so bestowed. **3** generosity of spirit or attitude. ORIG C13: from OF, from LARGE

larghetto (lɑːˈgɛtəʊ) *Music.* ◆ *adj, adv* **1** to be performed moderately slowly. ◆ *n, pl* **larghettos. 2** a piece or passage to be performed in this way. ORIG It.: dim. of LARGO

largish (ˈlɑːdʒɪʃ) *adj* fairly large.

largo (ˈlɑːgəʊ) *Music.* ◆ *adj, adv* **1** to be performed slowly and broadly. ◆ *n, pl* **largos. 2** a piece or passage to be performed in this way. ORIG C17: from It., from L *largus* large

Lariam (ˈlærɪəm) *n Trademark.* a preparation of the drug mefloquine, used in the treatment and prevention of malaria.

lariat (ˈlærɪət) *n US & Canad.* **1** another word for **lasso. 2** a rope for tethering animals. ORIG C19: from Sp. *la reata* the LASSO

Larisa *or* **Larissa** ★ (ləˈrɪsə; *Greek* ˈlarisa) *n* a city in E Greece, in E Thessaly: fortified by Justinian; annexed to Greece in 1881. Pop.: 113 426 (1991).

lark[1] (lɑːk) *n* **1** any brown bird of a predominantly Old World family of songbirds, esp. the skylark: noted for their singing. **2** short for **titlark.** ORIG OE *lāwerce, lǣwerce,* of Gmc origin

lark[2] (lɑːk) *Inf.* ◆ *n* **1** a carefree adventure or frolic. **2** a harmless piece of mischief. ◆ *vb* (*intr*) **3** (often foll. by *about*) to have a good time by frolicking. **4** to play a prank. ORIG C19: orig. sl.
▸ **ˈlarkish** *or* **ˈlarky** *adj*

Larkin ★ (ˈlɑːkɪn) *n* **Philip.** 1922–85, British poet: his verse collections include *The Whitsun Weddings* (1964).

larkspur (ˈlɑːkˌspɜː) *n* any of various plants related to the delphinium, with spikes of blue, pink, or white irregular spurred flowers. ORIG C16: LARK[1] + SPUR

larn (lɑːn) *vb Not standard.* **1** *Facetious.* to learn. **2** (*tr*) to teach (someone) a lesson: *that'll larn you!* ORIG C18: from a dialect form of LEARN

Larne ★ (lɑːn) *n* a district of E Northern Ireland, on the Irish Sea N of Belfast: harbour services. Administrative centre: Larne. Pop.: 29 419 (1991). Area: 340 sq. km (131 sq. miles).

larney (ˈlɑːnɪ) *adj S. African.* (of clothes) smart. ORIG C20: prob. from an Indian language

La Rochefoucauld ★ (*French* la rɔʃfuko) *n* **François** (frɑ̃swa), Duc de La Rochefoucauld. 1613–80, French writer, best known for his *Réflexions ou sentences et maximes morales* (1665), a collection of cynical epigrams on human nature.

La Rochelle ★ (*French* la rɔʃɛl) *n* a port in W France, on the Bay of Biscay: a Huguenot stronghold until its submission through famine to Richelieu's forces after a long siege (1627–28). Pop.: 71 094 (1990).

Larousse ★ (*French* larus) *n* **Pierre Athanase** (pjɛr atanɑz). 1817–75, French grammarian, lexicographer, and encyclopedist. He edited and helped to compile the *Grand Dictionnaire universel du XIX siècle* (1866–76).

larrigan (ˈlærɪgən) *n* a knee-high oiled leather moccasin boot worn by trappers, etc. ORIG C19: from ?

larrikin (ˈlærɪkɪn) *Austral. & NZ sl.* ◆ *n* **1** a mischievous person. **2** a hooligan. ◆ *adj* **3** mischievous: *larrikin wit.* ORIG C19: from E dialect: a mischievous youth

larrup ('lærəp) *vb* (*tr*) *Dialect.* to beat or flog. ORIG C19: from ?
▸ **'larruper** *n*

Larry ('lærɪ) *n* **happy as Larry.** *Inf.* very happy.

larva ('lɑːvə) *n, pl* **larvae** (-viː). an immature free-living form of many animals that develops into a different adult form by metamorphosis. ORIG C18: (C17 in the orig. L sense: ghost): NL
▸ **'larval** *adj*

Larwood ★ ('lɑːwʊd) *n* **Harold.** 1904–95, English cricketer. An outstanding fast bowler, he played 21 times for England between 1926 and 1932.

laryngeal (ˌlærɪn'dʒiːəl, lə'rɪndʒɪəl) *or* **laryngal** (lə'rɪŋgᵊl) *adj* **1** of or relating to the larynx. **2** *Phonetics.* articulated at the larynx; glottal. ORIG C18: from NL *laryngeus* of the LARYNX

laryngitis (ˌlærɪn'dʒaɪtɪs) *n* inflammation of the larynx.
▸ **laryngitic** (ˌlærɪn'dʒɪtɪk) *adj*

laryngo- *or before a vowel* **laryng-** *combining form.* indicating the larynx: *laryngoscope.*

laryngoscope (lə'rɪŋgəˌskəʊp) *n* a medical instrument for examining the larynx.
▸ **ˌlaryn'goscopy** *n*

laryngotomy (ˌlærɪŋ'gɒtəmɪ) *n, pl* **laryngotomies.** surgical incision into the larynx to facilitate breathing.

larynx ('lærɪŋks) *n, pl* **larynges** (lə'rɪndʒiːz) *or* **larynxes.** a cartilaginous and muscular hollow organ forming part of the air passage to the lungs: in higher vertebrates it contains the vocal cords. ORIG C16: from NL, from Gk *larunx*

lasagne *or* **lasagna** (lə'zænjə, -'sæn-) *n* **1** a form of pasta consisting of wide flat sheets. **2** any of several dishes made from layers of lasagne and meat, cheese, etc. ORIG from It. *lasagna,* from L *lasanum* cooking pot

La Salle[1] ★ (lə 'sæl) *n* a city in SE Canada, in Quebec: a S suburb of Montreal. Pop.: 73 804 (1991).

La Salle[2] ★ (*French* la sal) *n* Sieur **Robert Cavelier de** (rɔbɛr kavəlje də). 1643–87, French explorer and fur trader in North America; founder of Louisiana (1682).

La Scala ★ (læ 'skɑːlə) *n* the chief opera house in Italy, in Milan (opened 1776).

lascar ('læskə) *n* a sailor from the East Indies. ORIG C17: from Urdu *lashkar* soldier, from Persian: the army

Lascaux ★ (*French* lasko) *n* site of a cave in SW France, in the Dordogne: contains Palaeolithic wall drawings and paintings.

lascivious (lə'sɪvɪəs) *adj* **1** lustful; lecherous. **2** exciting sexual desire. ORIG C15: from LL *lascīviōsus,* from L *lascīvia* wantonness, from *lascīvus*
▸ **las'civiously** *adv* ▸ **las'civiousness** *n*

Lasdun ★ ('læzdᵊn) *n* Sir **Denys.** 1914–2001, British architect. He was best known for the University of East Anglia (1968) and the National Theatre in London (1976).

lase (leɪz) *vb* **lases, lasing, lased.** (*intr*) (of a substance, such as carbon dioxide or ruby) to be capable of acting as a laser.

laser ('leɪzə) *n* **1** a source of high-intensity optical, infrared, or ultraviolet radiation produced as a result of stimulated emission maintained within a solid, liquid, or gaseous medium. The photons involved in the emission process all have the same energy and phase so that the laser beam is monochromatic and coherent, allowing it to be brought to a fine focus. **2** any similar source producing a beam of any electromagnetic radiation, such as infrared or microwave radiation. ORIG C20: from *l*ight *a*mplification by *s*timulated *e*mission of *r*adiation

laserdisc *or* (*esp. US*) **laserdisk** ('leizəˌdɪsk) *n* a disk similar in size to a long-playing record, on which data is stored in pits in a similar way to data storage on a compact disk, used esp. for storing high-quality video.

laser printer *n* a quiet high-quality computer printer that uses a laser beam shining on a photoconductive drum to produce characters, which are then transferred to paper.

lash[1] (læʃ) *n* **1** a sharp cutting blow from a whip or other flexible object. **2** the flexible end or ends of a whip. **3** a cutting or hurtful blow to the feelings, as one caused by ridicule or scolding. **4** a forceful beating or impact, as of wind, rain, or waves against something. **5 have a lash at.** *Austral. & NZ inf.* to make an attempt at or take part in (something). **6** See **eyelash.** ◆ *vb* (*tr*) **7** to hit (a person or thing) sharply with a whip, rope, etc., esp. as punishment. **8** (of rain, waves, etc.) to beat forcefully against. **9** to attack with words, ridicule, etc. **10** to flick or wave sharply to and fro: *the panther lashed his tail.* **11** to urge or drive as with a whip: *to lash the audience into a violent mood.* ◆ See also **lash out.** ORIG C14: ? imit.
▸ **'lasher** *n*

lash[2] (læʃ) *vb* (*tr*) to bind or secure with rope, string, etc. ORIG C15: from OF *lachier,* ult. from L *laqueāre* to ensnare, from *laqueus* noose

-lashed *adj* having eyelashes as specified: *long-lashed.*

lashing[1] ('læʃɪŋ) *n* **1** a whipping; flogging. **2** a scolding. **3** (*pl; usually foll. by of*) *Brit. inf.* large amounts; lots.

lashing[2] ('læʃɪŋ) *n* rope, cord, etc., used for binding or securing.

Lashio ★ ('læʃɪˌəʊ) *n* a town in NE central Myanmar: starting point of the Burma Road to Chongqing, China.

Lashkar ★ ('lʌʃkə) *n* a former city in N India, in Madhya Pradesh: capital of the former states of Gwalior and Madhya Bharat; now part of the city of Gwalior.

lash out *vb* (*intr, adv*) **1** to burst into or resort to verbal or physical attack. **2** *Brit. inf.* to be extravagant, as in spending.

lash-up *n* a temporary connection of equipment for experimental or emergency use.

Lasker ★ ('læskə) *n* **Emanuel.** 1868–1941, German chess player: world champion (1894–1921).

Laski ★ ('læskɪ) *n* **Harold (Joseph).** 1893–1950, British political scientist and socialist leader.

Las Palmas ★ (*Spanish* las 'palmas) *n* a port in the central Canary Islands, on NE Grand Canary: a major fuelling port on the main shipping route between Europe and South America. Pop.: 373 772 (1995 est.).

La Spezia ★ (*Italian* la 'spɛttsia) *n* a port in NW Italy, in Liguria, on the **Gulf of Spezia:** the chief naval base in Italy. Pop.: 100 458 (1992).

lass (læs) *n* **1** a girl or young woman. **2** *Inf.* a familiar form of address for any female. ORIG C13: from ?

Lassa ★ ('lɑːsə) *n* a variant spelling of **Lhasa.**

Lassa fever ('læsə) *n* a serious viral disease of Central West Africa, characterized by high fever and muscular pains. ORIG from *Lassa,* the Nigerian village where it was first identified

Lassalle ★ (*German* la'sal) *n* **Ferdinand** ('fɛrdinant). 1825–64, German socialist and writer: a founder of the first German workers' political party (1863), which later became the Social Democratic Party.

Lassen Peak ★ ('læsᵊn) *n* a volcano in S California, in the S Cascade Range. An area of 416 sq. km (161 sq. miles) was established as **Lassen Volcanic National Park** in 1916. Height: 3187 m (10 457 ft).

lassie ('læsɪ) *n Inf.* a little lass; girl.

lassitude ('læsɪˌtjuːd) *n* physical or mental weariness. ORIG C16: from L *lassitūdō,* from *lassus* tired

lasso (læ'suː, 'læsəʊ) *n, pl* **lassos** *or* **lassoes. 1** a long rope or thong with a running noose at one end, used (esp. in America) for roping horses, cattle, etc.; lariat. ◆ *vb* **lassos, lassoing, lassoed. 2** (*tr*) to catch as with a lasso. ORIG C19: from Sp. *lazo,* ult. from L *laqueus* noose
▸ **las'soer** *n*

Lassus ★ ('læsəs) *n* **Roland de.** Italian name *Orlando di Lasso.* ?1532–94, Flemish composer.

last[1] (lɑːst) *adj* (*often prenominal*) **1** being, happening, or coming at the end or after all others: *the last horse in the race.* **2** being or occurring just before the present; most recent: *last Thursday.* **3** only remaining: *one's last cigarette.* **4** most extreme; utmost. **5** least suitable, appropriate, or likely: *he was the last person I would have chosen.* **6** (esp. relating to the end of a person's life or of the world) final or ultimate: *last rites.* ◆ *adv* **7** after all others; at or in the end: *he came last.* **8** most recently: *he was last seen in the mountains.* **9** (*sentence modifier*) as the last or latest item. ◆ *n* **10 the last. 10a** a person or thing that is last. **10b** the final moment; end. **11** one's last moments before death. **12** the final appearance, mention, or occurrence: *we've seen the last of him.* **13 at last.** in the end; finally. **14 at long last.** finally, after difficulty, delay, or irritation. ORIG var. of OE *latest, lætest,* sup. of LATE

> **USAGE NOTE** Since *last* can mean either *after all others* or *most recent,* it is better to avoid using this word where ambiguity might arise, as in *her last novel. Final* or *latest* should be used in such contexts to avoid any possible confusion.

last[2] (lɑːst) *vb* **1** (when *intr,* often foll. by *for*) to remain in being (for a length of time); continue: *his hatred lasted for several years.* **2** to be sufficient for the needs of (a person) for (a length of time): *it will last us until Friday.* **3** (when *intr,* often foll. by *for*) to remain fresh, uninjured, or unaltered (for a certain time). ◆ See also **last out.** ORIG OE *lǣstan*
▸ **'laster** *n*

last[3] (lɑːst) *n* **1** the wooden or metal form on which a shoe or boot is fashioned or repaired. ◆ *vb* **2** (*tr*) to fit (a shoe or boot) on a last. ORIG OE *lǣste,* from *lāst* footprint
▸ **'laster** *n*

last-ditch *n* **a** a last resort or place of last defence. **b** (*as modifier*): *a last-ditch effort.*

last-gasp *n* (*modifier*) done in desperation at the last minute: *a last-gasp attempt to save the talks.*

lasting ('lɑːstɪŋ) *adj* permanent or enduring.
▸ **'lastingly** *adv* ▸ **'lastingness** *n*

Last Judgment *n* **the.** the occasion, after the resurrection of the dead at the end of the world, when, according to biblical tradition, God will decree the final destinies of all men according to the good and evil in their earthly lives. Also called: **the Last Day, Doomsday, Judgment Day.**

lastly ('lɑːstlɪ) *adv* **1** at the end or at the last point. ◆ *sentence connector.* **2** finally.

last name *n* another term for **surname.**

last out *vb* (*intr, adv*) **1** to be sufficient for one's needs: *how long will our supplies last out?* **2** to endure or survive: *some old people don't last out the winter.*

last post *n* (in the British military services) **1** a bugle call that orders men to retire for sleep. **2** a similar call sounded at military funerals.

last rites *pl n Christianity.* religious rites prescribed for those close to death.

Last Supper *n* **the.** the meal eaten by Christ with his disciples on the night before his Crucifixion.

Las Vegas ★ (læs 'veɪgəs) *n* a city in SE Nevada: famous for luxury hotels and casinos. Pop.: 368 360 (1995 est.).

lat. *abbrev. for* latitude.

Lat. *abbrev. for* Latin.

latah ('lɑːtə) *n* a psychological condition, observed esp. in Malaysian cultures, in which an individual, after experiencing a shock, becomes anxious and suggestible, often imitating the actions of another person. ORIG C19: from Malay

Latakia *or* **Lattakia** ★ (ˌlætə'kiːə) *n* the chief port of Syria, in the northwest: tobacco industry. Pop.: 306 535 (1994 est.). Latin name: **Laodicea ad Mare.**

latch (lætʃ) *n* **1** a fastening for a gate or door that consists of a bar that may be slid or lowered into a groove, hole, etc. **2** a spring-loaded door lock that can be opened by a key from outside. **3** Also called: **latch circuit.** *Electronics.* a logic circuit that transfers the input states to the output states when signalled. ◆ *vb* **4** to fasten, fit, or be fitted as with a latch. ORIG OE *læccan* to seize, of Gmc origin

latchkey ('lætʃˌkiː) *n* **1** a key for an outside door or gate, esp. one that lifts a latch. **2** a supposed freedom from restrictions.

latchkey child *n* a child who has to let himself or herself in at home on returning from school, as his or her parents are out at work.

latch on *vb* (*intr, adv;* often foll. by *to*) *Inf.* **1** to attach oneself (to). **2** to understand.

latchstring ('lætʃˌstrɪŋ) *n* a length of string fastened to a latch and passed through a hole in the door so that it can be opened from the other side.

late (leɪt) *adj* **1** occurring or arriving after the correct or expected time: *the train was late.* **2** (*prenominal*) occurring at, scheduled for, or being at a relatively advanced time: *a late marriage.* **3** (*prenominal*) towards or near the end: *the late evening.* **4** at an advanced time in the evening or at night: *it was late.* **5** (*prenominal*) occurring or being just previous to the present time: *his late remarks on industry.* **6** (*prenominal*) having died, esp. recently: *my late grandfather.* **7** (*prenominal*) just preceding the present or existing person or thing; former: *the late manager of this firm.* **8 of late.** recently; lately. ◆ *adv* **9** after the correct or expected time: *he arrived late.* **10** at a relatively advanced age: *she married late.* **11** recently; lately: *as late as yesterday he was selling books.* **12 late in the day. 12a** at a late or advanced stage. **12b** too late. ORIG OE *læt*
▸ **'lateness** *n*

lateen (lə'tiːn) *adj Naut.* denoting a rig with a triangular sail (**lateen sail**) bent to a yard hoisted to the head of a low mast, used esp. in the Mediterranean. ORIG C18: from F *voile latine* Latin sail

Late Greek *n* the Greek language from about the 3rd to the 8th centuries A.D.

Late Latin *n* the form of written Latin used from the 3rd to the 7th centuries A.D.

lately ('leɪtlɪ) *adv* in recent times; of late.

La Tène (læ 'tɛn) *adj* of or relating to a Celtic culture in Europe from about the 5th to the 1st centuries B.C., characterized by a distinctive type of curvilinear decoration. ORIG C20: from *La Tène,* a part of Lake Neuchâtel, Switzerland, where remains of this culture were first discovered

latent ('leɪtᵊnt) *adj* **1** potential but not obvious or explicit. **2** (of buds, spores, etc.) dormant. **3** *Pathol.* (esp. of an infectious disease) not yet revealed or manifest. **4** (of a virus) inactive in the host cell. **5** *Psychoanal.* relating to that part of a dream expressive of repressed desires: *latent content.* Cf. **manifest** (sense 2). ORIG C17: from L *latēnt-,* from *latēre* to lie hidden
▸ **'latency** *n* ▸ **'latently** *adv*

latent heat *n* (*no longer in technical usage*) the heat evolved or absorbed by unit mass (**specific latent heat**) or unit amount of substance (**molar latent heat**) when it changes phase without change of temperature.

latent image *n Photog.* the invisible image produced by the action of light, etc., on silver halide crystals suspended in the emulsion of a photographic material. It becomes visible after development.

later ('leɪtə) *adj, adv* **1** the comparative of **late.** ◆ *adv* **2** afterwards; subsequently.

lateral ('lætərəl) *adj* **1** of or relating to the side or sides: *a lateral blow.* ◆ *n* **2** a lateral object, part, passage, or movement. ORIG C17: from L *laterālis,* from *latus* side
▸ **'laterally** *adv*

lateral thinking *n* a way of solving problems by employing unorthodox and apparently illogical means.

laterite ('lætəˌraɪt) *n* any of a group of residual insoluble deposits of ferric and aluminium oxides: formed by weathering of rocks in tropical regions. ORIG C19: from L *later* brick

latest ('leɪtɪst) *adj, adv* **1** the superlative of **late.** ◆ *adj* **2** most recent, modern, or new: *the latest fashions.* ◆ *n* **3 at the latest.** no later than the time specified. **4 the latest.** *Inf.* the most recent fashion or development.

latex ('leɪtɛks) *n, pl* **latexes** *or* **latices** ('lætɪˌsiːz). **1** a whitish milky fluid containing protein, starch, alkaloids, etc., that is produced by many plants. Latex from the rubber tree is used in the manufacture of rubber. **2** a suspension of synthetic rubber or plastic in water, used in the manufacture of synthetic rubber products, etc. ORIG C19: NL, from L: liquid

lath (lɑːθ) *n, pl* **laths** (lɑːðz, lɑːθs). **1** one of several thin narrow strips of wood used to provide a supporting framework for plaster, tiles, etc. **2** expanded sheet metal, wire mesh, etc., used to provide backing for plaster or rendering. **3** any thin strip of wood. ◆ *vb* **4** (*tr*) to attach laths to (a ceiling, roof, floor, etc.). ORIG OE *lætt*

lathe (leɪð) *n* **1** a machine for shaping or boring metal, wood, etc., in which the workpiece is turned about a horizontal axis against a fixed tool. ◆ *vb* **lathes, lathing, lathed. 2** (*tr*) to shape or bore (a workpiece) on a lathe. ORIG ? C15 *lath* a support, from ON

lather (ˈlɑːðə) *n* **1** foam formed by the action of soap or a detergent in water. **2** foam formed by other liquid, such as the sweat of a horse. **3** *Inf.* a state of agitation. ◆ *vb* **4** to coat or become coated with lather. **5** (*intr*) to form a lather. ORIG OE *lēathor* soap
▸ **ˈlathery** *adj*

lathi (ˈlɑːtɪ) *n, pl* **lathis.** a long heavy wooden stick used as a weapon in India, esp. by the police. ORIG Hindi

Latimer ★ (ˈlætəmə) *n* **Hugh.** ?1485–1555, English Protestant bishop: burnt at the stake for refusing to disavow his Protestant beliefs when Mary I assumed the throne.

Latin (ˈlætɪn) *n* **1** the language of ancient Rome and the Roman Empire and of the educated in medieval Europe. Having originally been the language of Latium in W central Italy, belonging to the Italic branch of the Indo-European family, it later formed the basis of the Romance group. **2** a member of any of those peoples whose languages are derived from Latin. **3** an inhabitant of ancient Latium. ◆ *adj* **4** of or relating to the Latin language, the ancient Latins, or Latium. **5** characteristic of or relating to those peoples in Europe and Latin America whose languages are derived from Latin. **6** of or relating to the Roman Catholic Church. ORIG OE *latin* and *læden* Latin, language, from L *Latīnus* of Latium

Latina ★ (*Italian* laˈtiːna) *n* a city in W central Italy, in Lazio: built as a planned town in 1932 on reclaimed land of the Pontine Marshes. Pop.: 110 233 (1996 est.). Former name (until 1947): **Littoria.**

Latin America ★ *n* those areas of America whose official languages are Spanish and Portuguese, derived from Latin: South America, Central America, Mexico, and certain islands in the Caribbean.
▸ **Latin American** *n, adj*

Latinate (ˈlætɪˌneɪt) *adj* (of writing, vocabulary, etc.) imitative of or derived from Latin.

Latinism (ˈlætɪˌnɪzəm) *n* a word, idiom, or phrase borrowed from Latin.

Latinist (ˈlætɪnɪst) *n* a person who studies or is proficient in Latin.

Latinize *or* **Latinise** (ˈlætɪˌnaɪz) *vb* **Latinizes, Latinizing, Latinized** *or* **Latinises, Latinising, Latinised.** (*tr*) **1** to translate into Latin or Latinisms. **2** to cause to acquire Latin style or customs. **3** to bring Roman Catholic influence to bear upon (the form of religious ceremonies, etc.).
▸ **ˌLatiniˈzation** *or* **ˌLatiniˈsation** *n* ▸ **ˈLatinˌizer** *or* **ˈLatinˌiser** *n*

Latin Quarter ★ *n* an area of Paris, on the S bank of the River Seine: contains the city's main educational establishments; centre for students and artists.

latish (ˈleɪtɪʃ) *adj, adv* rather late.

latitude (ˈlætɪˌtjuːd) *n* **1a** an angular distance measured in degrees north or south of the equator (latitude 0°). **1b** (*often pl*) a region considered with regard to its distance from the equator. **2** scope for freedom of action, thought, etc.; freedom from restriction: *his parents gave him a great deal of latitude.* ORIG C14: from L *lātitūdō*, from *lātus* broad
▸ **ˌlatiˈtudinal** *adj* ▸ **ˌlatiˈtudinally** *adv*

latitudinarian (ˌlætɪˌtjuːdɪˈnɛərɪən) *adj* **1** permitting or marked by freedom of attitude or behaviour, esp. in religious matters. ◆ *n* **2** a person with latitudinarian views. ORIG C17: from L *lātitūdō* breadth, infl. in form by TRINITARIAN
▸ **ˌlatiˌtudiˈnarianism** *n*

Latium ★ (ˈleɪʃɪəm) *n* an ancient territory in W central Italy, in modern Lazio, on the Tyrrhenian Sea: inhabited by the Latin people from the 10th century B.C. until dominated by Rome (4th century B.C.).

Latona ★ (ləˈtəʊnə) *n* the Roman name of **Leto.**

Latour ★ (*French* latur) *n* **Maurice Quentin de** (mɔris kɑ̃tɛ̃ də) 1704–88, French pastelist noted for his portraits.

La Tour ★ (*French* la tur) *n* **Georges de** (ʒɔrʒ də). ?1593–1652, French painter, esp. of candlelit religious scenes.

latria (ləˈtraɪə) *n RC Church, theol.* the adoration that may be offered to God alone. ORIG C16: via L from Gk *latreia* worship

latrine (ləˈtriːn) *n* a lavatory, as in a barracks, camp, etc. ORIG C17: from F, from L *lātrīna,* shortened form of *lavātrīna* bath, from *lavāre* to wash

-latry *n combining form.* indicating worship of or excessive veneration of: *idolatry; Mariolatry.* ORIG from Gk *-latria,* from *latreia* worship
▸ **-latrous** *adj combining form.*

latter (ˈlætə) *adj* (*prenominal*) **1a** denoting the second or second mentioned of two: distinguished from *former.* **1b** (*as n; functioning as sing or pl*): *the latter is not important.* **2** near or nearer the end: *the latter part of a film.* **3** more advanced in time or sequence; later. ORIG OE *lætra*

> **USAGE NOTE** *The latter* should only be used to refer to the second of two items: *many people choose to go by hovercraft rather than use the ferry, but I prefer the latter.* The last of three or more items can be referred to as *the last-named.*

latter-day *adj* present-day; modern.

Latter-day Saint *n* a more formal name for a **Mormon.**

latterly (ˈlætəlɪ) *adv* recently; lately.

lattice (ˈlætɪs) *n* **1** Also called: **latticework.** an open framework of strips of wood, metal, etc., arranged to form an ornamental pattern. **2a** a gate, screen, etc., formed of such a framework. **2b** (*as modifier*): *a lattice window.* **3** something, such as a decorative or heraldic device, resembling such a framework. **4** an array of objects or points in a periodic pattern in two or three dimensions, esp. an array of atoms, ions, etc., in a crystal or an array of points indicating their positions in space. ◆ *vb* **lattices, latticing, latticed. 5** to make, adorn, or supply with a lattice or lattices. ORIG C14: from OF *lattis,* from *latte* LATH
▸ **ˈlatticed** *adj*

Latvia ★ (ˈlætvɪə) *n* a republic in central Europe, on the Gulf of Riga and the Baltic Sea. It was successively under Teutonic, Polish, Swedish, and Russian rule from the 13th century to 1918, when it became an independent republic: annexed (1940) by the Soviet Union as the Latvian Soviet Socialist Republic: regained independence in 1991. Official language: Latvian. Religion: believers are mostly Christian. Currency: lats. Capital: Riga. Pop.: 2 428 000 (1999 est.). Area: 63 700 sq. km (25 590 sq. miles).

Latvian (ˈlætvɪən) *adj* **1** of or relating to Latvia, its people, or their language. ◆ *n* **2** Also called: **Lettish.** the official language of Latvia. **3** a native or inhabitant of Latvia.

laud (lɔːd) *Literary.* ◆ *vb* **1** (*tr*) to praise or glorify. ◆ *n* **2** praise or glorification. ORIG C14: vb from L *laudāre;* n from *laudēs,* pl. of L *laus* praise

Laud ★ (lɔːd) *n* **William.** 1573–1645, English prelate; archbishop of Canterbury (1633–45). His persecution of Puritans and his High Church policies in England and Scotland were a cause of the Civil War; he was impeached by the Long Parliament (1640) and executed.
▸ **ˈLaudian** *adj*

laudable (ˈlɔːdəbᵊl) *adj* deserving or worthy of praise; admirable; commendable.
▸ **ˈlaudableness** *or* **ˌlaudaˈbility** *n* ▸ **ˈlaudably** *adv*

laudanum (ˈlɔːdᵊnəm) *n* **1** a tincture of opium. **2** (formerly) any medicine of which opium was the main ingredient. ORIG C16: NL, name chosen by Paracelsus for a preparation prob. containing opium

laudation (lɔːˈdeɪʃən) *n* a formal word for **praise.**

laudatory (ˈlɔːdətərɪ, -trɪ) *or* **laudative** *adj* expressing or containing praise; eulogistic.

Lauder ★ (ˈlɔːdə) *n* Sir **Harry.** real name *Hugh MacLennan.* 1870–1950, Scottish ballad singer and music-hall comedian.

lauds (lɔːdz) *n (functioning as sing or pl) Chiefly RC Church.* the traditional morning prayer, constituting with matins the first of the seven canonical hours. ORIG C14: see LAUD

Laue ★ (*German* ˈlauə) *n* **Max Theodor Felix von** (maks ˈteːodoːr ˈfeːlɪks fɔn). 1879–1960, German physicist. He pioneered studies of X-ray diffraction by crystals and contributed to the theory of relativity: Nobel prize for physics 1914.

laugh (lɑːf) *vb* **1** (*intr*) to express or manifest emotion, esp. mirth or amusement, typically by expelling air from the lungs in short bursts to produce an inarticulate voiced noise, with the mouth open. **2** (*intr*) (esp. of certain mammals or birds) to make a noise resembling a laugh. **3** (*tr*) to utter or express with laughter: *he laughed his derision at the play.* **4** (*tr*) to bring or force (someone, esp. oneself) into a certain condition by laughter: *he laughed himself sick.* **5** (*intr;* foll. by *at*) to make fun (of); jeer (at). **6 laugh up one's sleeve.** to laugh or have grounds for amusement, self-satisfaction, etc., secretly. **7 laugh on the other side of one's face.** to show sudden disappointment or shame after appearing cheerful or confident. ◆ *n* **8** the act or an instance of laughing. **9** a manner of laughter. **10** *Inf.* a person or thing that causes laughter: *that holiday was a laugh.* **11 the last laugh.** the final success in an argument, situation, etc., after previous defeat. ◆ See also **laugh off.** ORIG OE *læhan, hliehhen*
▸ **ˈlaugher** *n* ▸ **ˈlaughing** *n, adj* ▸ **ˈlaughingly** *adv*

laughable (ˈlɑːfəbᵊl) *adj* **1** producing scorn; ludicrous: *he offered me a laughable sum for the picture.* **2** arousing laughter.
▸ **ˈlaughableness** *n* ▸ **ˈlaughably** *adv*

laughing gas *n* another name for **nitrous oxide.**

laughing jackass *n* another name for the **kookaburra.**

laughing stock *n* an object of humiliating ridicule.

laugh off *vb* (*tr, adv*) to treat or dismiss lightly, esp. with stoicism.

laughter (ˈlɑːftə) *n* **1** the action of or noise produced by laughing. **2** the experience or manifestation of mirth, amusement, scorn, or joy. ORIG OE *hleahtor*

Laughton ★ (ˈlɔːtᵊn) *n* **Charles.** 1899–1962, US actor, born in England: noted esp. for such films as *The Private Life of Henry VIII* (1933) and *Mutiny on the Bounty* (1935).

Launceston ★ (ˈlɔːnsəstᵊn) *n* a city in Australia, the chief port of the island state of Tasmania on the Tamar River, 64 km (40 miles) from Bass Strait. Pop.: 93 347 (1991).

launch¹ (lɔːntʃ) *vb* **1** to move (a vessel) into the water. **2** to move (a newly built vessel) into the water for the first time. **3** (*tr*) **3a** to start off or set in motion: *to launch a scheme.* **3b** to put (a new product) on the market. **4** (*tr*) to propel with force. **5** to involve (oneself) totally and enthusiastically: *to launch oneself into work.* **6** (*tr*) to set (a missile, spacecraft, etc.) into motion. **7** (*intr;* foll. by *into*) to start talking or writing (about): *he launched into a story.* **8** (*intr;* usually foll. by *out*) to start (out) on a fresh course. ◆ *n* **9** an act or instance of launching. ORIG C14: from Anglo-F *lancher,* from LL *lanceāre* to use a lance, hence, to set in motion. See LANCE
▸ **ˈlauncher** *n*

launch² (lɔːntʃ) *n* **1** a motor driven boat used chiefly as a transport boat. **2** the largest of the boats of a man-of-war. ORIG C17: via Sp. *lancha* and Port. from Malay *lancharan* boat, from *lanchar* speed

launch pad *or* **launching pad** *n* **1** a platform from which a spacecraft, rocket, etc., is launched. **2** an effective starting point for a career, enterprise, or campaign.

launch window *n* the limited period during which a spacecraft can be launched on a particular mission.

launder (ˈlɔːndə) *vb* **1** to wash and often also iron (clothes, linen, etc.). **2** (*intr*) to be capable of being laundered without shrinking, fading, etc. **3** (*tr*) to make (money illegally obtained) appear to be legally gained by passing it through foreign banks or legitimate enterprises. ORIG C14 (n, meaning: a person who washes linen): changed from *lavender* washerwoman, from OF *lavandiere,* ult. from L *lavāre* to wash
▸ **ˈlaunderer** *n*

Launderette (ˌlɔːndəˈrɛt, lɔːnˈdrɛt) *Brit. & NZ trademark.* a commercial establishment where clothes can be washed and dried, using coin-operated machines. Also called (US, Canad., and NZ): **Laundromat.**

laundress (ˈlɔːndrɪs) *n* a woman who launders clothes, sheets, etc., for a living.

laundry (ˈlɔːndrɪ) *n, pl* **laundries. 1** a place where clothes and linen are washed and ironed. **2** the clothes or linen washed and ironed. **3** the act of laundering. ORIG C16: changed from C14 *lavendry;* see LAUNDER

laundryman (ˈlɔːndrɪmən) *or* (*fem*) **laundrywoman** *n, pl* **laundrymen** *or* **laundrywomen. 1** a person who collects or delivers laundry. **2** a person who works in a laundry.

Laurasia ★ (lɔːˈreɪʃə) *n* one of the two ancient supercontinents comprising what are now North America, Greenland, Europe, and Asia (excluding India). ORIG C20: from NL *Laur(entia)* (referring to the ancient N American landmass, from *Laurentian* strata of the Canadian Shield) + *(Eur)asia*

laureate (ˈlɔːrɪɪt) *adj* (*usually immediately postpositive*) **1** *Literary.* crowned with laurel leaves as a sign of honour. ◆ *n* **2** short for **poet laureate. 3** a person honoured with an award for art or science: *a Nobel laureate.* **4** *Rare.* a person honoured with the laurel crown or wreath. ORIG C14: from L *laureātus,* from *laurea* LAUREL
▸ **ˈlaureateˌship** *n*

laurel (ˈlɒrəl) *n* **1** Also called: **bay, bay laurel, sweet bay, true laurel.** a small Mediterranean evergreen tree with glossy aromatic leaves, used for flavouring in cooking, and small blackish berries. **2** a similar and related tree of the Canary Islands and Azores. **3** short for **mountain laurel. 4 spurge laurel.** a European evergreen shrub, *Daphne laureola,* with glossy leaves and small green flowers. **5** (*pl*) a wreath of true laurel, worn on the head as an emblem of victory or honour in classical times. **6** (*pl*) honour, distinction, or fame. **7 look to one's laurels.** to be on guard against one's rivals. **8 rest on one's laurels.** to be satisfied with distinction won by past achievements and cease to strive for further achievements. ◆ *vb* **laurels, laurelling, laurelled** *or US* **laurels, laureling, laureled. 9** (*tr*) to crown with laurels. ORIG C13 *lorer,* from OF *lorier* laurel tree, ult. from L *laurus*

Laurel and Hardy ★ (ˈlɒrəl; ˈhɑːdɪ) *n* a team of US film comedians, **Stan Laurel,** 1890–1965, born in Britain, the thin one, and his partner, **Oliver Hardy,** 1892–1957, the fat one.

Laurentian (lɔːˈrɛnʃən) *adj* **1** Also: **Lawrentian.** of or resembling the style of D. H. or T. E. Lawrence. **2** of, relating to, or situated near the St Lawrence River.

Laurentian Mountains ★ *pl n* a range of low mountains in E Canada, in Quebec between the St Lawrence River and Hudson Bay. Highest point: 1191 m (3905 ft). Also called: **Laurentides** (ˈlɔːrənˌtaɪdz).

Laurentian Shield *n* another name for the **Canadian Shield.** Also: **Laurentian Plateau.**

Laurier ★ (ˈlɒrɪə) *n* Sir **Wilfrid.** 1841–1919, Canadian Liberal statesman; the first French-Canadian prime minister (1896–1911).

laurustinus (ˌlɔːrəˈstaɪnəs) *n* a Mediterranean shrub with glossy evergreen leaves and white or pink fragrant flowers. ORIG C17: from NL, from L *laurus* laurel

Lausanne ★ (ləʊˈzæn; *French* lozan) *n* a city in W Switzerland, capital of Vaud canton, on Lake Geneva; cultural and commercial centre; university (1537). Pop.: 116 795 (1995 est.).

Lautrec ★ (*French* lotrɛk) *n* See (Henri de) **Toulouse-Lautrec.**

lav (læv) *n Brit. inf.* short for **lavatory.**

lava (ˈlɑːvə) *n* **1** magma emanating from volcanoes. **2** any extrusive igneous rock formed by the solidification of lava. ORIG C18: from It., from L *lavāre* to wash

lavabo (lə'veɪbəʊ) *n, pl* **lavaboes** *or* **lavabos.** *Chiefly RC Church.* **1a** the ritual washing of the celebrant's hands after the offertory at Mass. **1b** *(as modifier): lavabo basin; lavabo towel.* **2** another name for **washbasin. 3** a trough for washing in a convent or monastery. ORIG C19: from L: I shall wash, the opening of Psalm 26:6

lavage ('lævɪdʒ, læ'vɑːʒ) *n Med.* the washing out of a hollow organ by flushing with water. ORIG C19: via F, from L *lavāre* to wash

Laval[1] ★ (lə'væl) *n* a city in SE Canada, in Quebec: a NW suburb of Montreal. Pop.: 314 398 (1991).

Laval[2] ★ (*French* laval) *n* **Pierre** (pjɛr). 1883–1945, French statesman. He was premier of France (1931–32; 1935–36) and premier of the Vichy government (1942–44). He was executed for collaboration with Germany.

lavatorial (ˌlævə'tɔːrɪəl) *adj* characterized by excessive mention of the excretory functions; vulgar or scatological: *lavatorial humour.*

lavatory ('lævətərɪ, -trɪ) *n, pl* **lavatories. a** a sanitary installation for receiving and disposing of urine and faeces, consisting of a bowl fitted with a water-flushing device and connected to a drain. **b** a room containing such an installation. Also called: **toilet, water closet, WC.** ORIG C14: from LL *lavātōrium,* from L *lavāre* to wash

lavatory paper *n Brit.* another name for **toilet paper.**

lave (leɪv) *vb* **laves, laving, laved.** an archaic word for **wash.** ORIG OE *lafian,* ?from L *lavāre* to wash

lavender ('lævəndə) *n* **1** any of various perennial shrubs or herbaceous plants of the labiate family, esp. *Lavandula vera,* cultivated for its mauve or blue flowers and as the source of a fragrant oil (**oil of lavender**). **2** the dried parts of *L. vera,* used to perfume clothes. **3** a pale or light bluish-purple colour. **4** perfume scented with lavender. ORIG C13 *lavendre,* via F from Med. L *lavendula,* from ?

laver ('leɪvə) *n Old Testament.* a large basin of water used by the priests for ritual ablutions. ORIG C14: from OF *laveoir,* from LL *lavātōrium* washing place

Laver ★ ('leɪvə) *n* **Rod(ney George).** born 1938, Australian tennis player: Wimbledon champion 1961, 1962, 1968, 1969; US champion 1962, 1969.

lavish ('lævɪʃ) *adj* **1** prolific, abundant, or profuse. **2** generous; unstinting; liberal. **3** extravagant; prodigal; wasteful: *lavish expenditure.* ◆ *vb* **4** *(tr)* to give, expend, or apply abundantly, generously, or in profusion. ORIG C15: adj use of *lavas* profusion, from OF *lavasse* torrent, from L *lavāre* to wash
▸ **'lavisher** *n* ▸ **'lavishly** *adv* ▸ **'lavishness** *n*

Lavoisier ★ (*French* lavwazje) *n* **Antoine Laurent** (ɑ̃twan lɔrɑ̃). 1743–94, French chemist; one of the founders of modern chemistry. He named oxygen and discovered its importance in respiration and combustion.

law (lɔː) *n* **1** a rule or set of rules, enforceable by the courts regulating the relationship between the state and its subjects, and the conduct of subjects towards one another. **2a** a rule or body of rules made by the legislature. See **statute law. 2b** a rule or body of rules made by a municipal or other authority. See **bylaw. 3a** the condition and control enforced by such rules. **3b** *(in combination): lawcourt.* **4 law and order. 4a** the policy of strict enforcement of the law, esp. against crime and violence. **4b** *(as modifier): law-and-order candidate.* **5** a rule of conduct: *a law of etiquette.* **6** one of a set of rules governing a particular field of activity: *the laws of tennis.* **7 the law. 7a** the legal or judicial system. **7b** the profession or practice of law. **7c** *Inf.* the police or a policeman. **8** Also called: **law of nature.** a generalization based on a recurring fact or event. **9** the science or knowledge of law; jurisprudence. **10** the principles originating and formerly applied only in courts of common law. Cf. **equity** (sense 3). **11** a general principle, formula, or rule describing a phenomenon in mathematics, science, philosophy, etc.: *the laws of thermodynamics.* **12** Also called: **Law of Moses.** *(often cap.; preceded by the)* the body of laws contained in the first five books of the Old Testament. **13 go to law.** to resort to legal proceedings on some matter. **14 lay down the law.** to speak in an authoritative or dogmatic manner. ◆ Related adjs.: **judicial, juridical, legal.** ORIG OE *lagu,* from ON

Law ★ (lɔː) *n* **1 Andrew Bonar** ('bɒnə). 1858–1923, British Conservative statesman, born in Canada; prime minister (1922–23). **2 John.** 1671–1729, Scottish financier. He founded the Mississippi Scheme for the development of Louisiana (1717), which collapsed due to excessive speculation.

law-abiding *adj* adhering more or less strictly to the laws: *a law-abiding citizen.*

law agent *n* (in Scotland) a solicitor entitled to appear for a client in any Sheriff Court.

lawbreaker ('lɔːˌbreɪkə) *n* a person who breaks the law.
▸ **'lawˌbreaking** *n, adj*

law centre *n Brit.* an independent service financed by a local authority, which provides free legal advice and information to the general public.

Lawes ★ (lɔːz) *n* **1 Henry.** 1596–1662, English composer, noted for his music for Milton's masque *Comus* (1634) and for his settings of some of Robert Herrick's poems. **2** his brother, **William.** 1602–45, English composer, noted for his instrumental music.

lawful ('lɔːfʊl) *adj* allowed, recognized, or sanctioned by law; legal.
▸ **'lawfully** *adv* ▸ **'lawfulness** *n*

lawgiver ('lɔːˌgɪvə) *n* **1** the giver of a code of laws. **2** Also called: **lawmaker.** a maker of laws.
▸ **'lawˌgiving** *n, adj*

lawks (lɔːks) *interj Brit.* an expression of surprise or dismay. ORIG C18: var. of *Lord!,* prob. infl. in form by ALACK

lawless ('lɔːlɪs) *adj* **1** without law. **2** disobedient to the law. **3** contrary to or heedless of the law. **4** uncontrolled; unbridled: *lawless rage.*
▸ **'lawlessly** *adv* ▸ **'lawlessness** *n*

Law Lords *pl n* (in Britain) members of the House of Lords who sit as the highest court of appeal.

lawn[1] (lɔːn) *n* a flat and usually level area of mown and cultivated grass. ORIG C16: changed form of C14 *launde,* from OF *lande,* of Celtic origin
▸ **'lawny** *adj*

lawn[2] (lɔːn) *n* a fine linen or cotton fabric, used for clothing. ORIG C15: prob. from *Laon,* town in France where made
▸ **'lawny** *adj*

lawn mower *n* a hand-operated or power-operated machine for cutting grass on lawns.

lawn tennis *n* **1** tennis played on a grass court. **2** the formal name for **tennis.**

law of averages *n* (popularly) the expectation that a possible event is bound to occur regularly with a frequency approximating to its probability.

law of supply and demand *n* the theory that the price of an article or service is determined by the interaction of supply and demand.

law of the jungle *n* a state of ruthless competition or self-interest.

law of thermodynamics *n* any of three principles governing the relationships between different forms of energy. The **first law** (conservation of energy) states that energy can be transformed but not destroyed. The **second law** states that in any irreversible process entropy always increases. The **third law** states that it is impossible to reduce the temperature of a system to absolute zero in a finite number of steps.

Lawrence ★ ('lɒrəns) *n* **1 D(avid) H(erbert).** 1885–1930, British writer. His novels include *Sons and Lovers* (1913), *Women in Love* (1920), and *Lady Chatterley's Lover* (1928). **2 Ernest Orlando.** 1901–58, US physicist, who invented the cyclotron (1931): Nobel prize for physics 1939. **3 Gertrude.** 1898–1952, British actress, noted esp. for her roles in comedies. **4** Sir **Thomas.** 1769–1830, British portrait painter. **5 T(homas) E(dward),** known as *Lawrence of Arabia.* 1888–1935, British soldier and writer. He took a major part in the Arab revolt against the Turks (1916–18), describing his experiences in *The Seven Pillars of Wisdom* (1926).

lawrencium (lɒ'rensɪəm) *n* an element artificially produced from californium. Symbol: Lr; atomic no.: 103; half-life of most stable isotope, ^{256}Lr: 35 seconds. ORIG C20: after Ernest O. LAWRENCE

Lawrentian (lɔːˈrɛnʃən) *adj* a variant spelling of **Laurentian** (sense 1).

Lawson ★ (ˈlɔːsən) *n* **1 Henry Archibald.** 1867–1922, Australian poet and short-story writer, whose work is taken as being most representative of the Australian outback, esp. in *While the Billy Boils* (1896) and *Joe Wilson and his Mates* (1901). **2 Nigel**, Baron. born 1932, British Conservative politician; Chancellor of the Exchequer (1983–89). **3** his daughter **Nigella** (naɪˈdʒɛlə). born 1959, British journalist, broadcaster, and cookery writer.

lawsuit (ˈlɔːˌsuːt) *n* a proceeding in a court of law brought by one party against another, esp. a civil action.

law term *n* **1** an expression or word used in law. **2** a period of time appointed for the sitting of law courts.

lawyer (ˈlɔːjə, ˈlɔɪə) *n* a member of the legal profession, esp. a solicitor. ORIG C14: from LAW

lax (læks) *adj* **1** lacking firmness; not strict. **2** lacking precision or definition. **3** not taut. **4** *Phonetics.* (of a speech sound) pronounced with little muscular effort. ORIG C14 (orig. used with reference to the bowels): from L *laxus* loose
▸ **ˈlaxly** *adv* ▸ **ˈlaxity** *or* **ˈlaxness** *n*

laxative (ˈlæksətɪv) *n* **1** an agent stimulating evacuation of faeces. ◆ *adj* **2** stimulating evacuation of faeces. ORIG C14 (orig.: relaxing): from Med. L *laxātīvus*, from L *laxāre* to loosen

Laxness ★ (*Icelandic* ˈlaxsnɛs) *n* **Halldór (Kiljan)** (ˈhaldɔur). 1902–98, Icelandic novelist, noted for his treatment of rural working life in Iceland. His works include *Salka Valka* (1932) and *Independent People* (1935). Nobel prize for literature 1955.

lay[1] (leɪ) *vb* **lays, laying, laid.** (*mainly tr*) **1** to put in a low or horizontal position; cause to lie: *to lay a cover on a bed.* **2** to place, put, or be in a particular state or position: *he laid his finger on his lips.* **3** (*intr*) *Dialect or not standard.* to be in a horizontal position; lie: *he often lays in bed all the morning.* **4** (sometimes foll. by *down*) to establish as a basis. **5** to place or dispose in the proper position: *to lay a carpet.* **6** to arrange (a table) for eating a meal. **7** to prepare (a fire) for lighting by arranging fuel in the grate. **8** (*also intr*) (of birds, esp. the domestic hen) to produce (eggs). **9** to present or put forward: *he laid his case before the magistrate.* **10** to impute or attribute: *all the blame was laid on him.* **11** to arrange, devise, or prepare: *to lay a trap.* **12** to place, set, or locate: *the scene is laid in London.* **13** to make (a bet) with (someone): *I lay you five to one on Prince.* **14** to cause to settle: *to lay the dust.* **15** to allay; suppress: *to lay a rumour.* **16** to bring down forcefully: *to lay a whip on someone's back.* **17** *Taboo sl.* to have sexual intercourse with. **18** to press down or make smooth: *to lay the nap of cloth.* **19** (*intr*) *Naut.* to move or go, esp. into a specified position or direction: *to lay close to the wind.* **20 lay bare.** to reveal or explain: *he laid bare his plans.* **21 lay hold of.** to seize or grasp. **22 lay oneself open.** to make oneself vulnerable (to criticism, attack, etc.). **23 lay open.** to reveal or disclose. ◆ *n* **24** the manner or position in which something lies or is placed. **25** *Taboo sl.* **25a** an act of sexual intercourse. **25b** a sexual partner. ◆ See also **lay aside, lay-by,** etc. ORIG OE *lecgan*

> **USAGE NOTE** In standard English, the verb *lay* can only be used with an object, and *lie* can only be used without one: *the Queen laid a wreath; he was lying on the floor.*

lay[2] (leɪ) *vb* the past tense of **lie**[2].

lay[3] (leɪ) *adj* **1** of, involving, or belonging to people who are not clergy. **2** nonprofessional or nonspecialist; amateur. ORIG C14: from OF *lai*, from LL *lāicus*, ult. from Gk *laos* people

lay[4] (leɪ) *n* **1** a ballad or short narrative poem, esp. one intended to be sung. **2** a song or melody. ORIG C13: from OF *lai*, ? of Gmc origin

layabout (ˈleɪəˌbaʊt) *n* a lazy person; loafer.

Layamon (ˈlaɪəmən) *or* **Lawman** ★ (ˈlɔːmən) *n* 12th-century English poet and priest; author of the *Brut*, a chronicle providing the earliest English version of the Arthurian story.

lay analyst *n* a person without medical qualifications who practises psychoanalysis.

Layard ★ (lɛəd) *n* Sir **Austen Henry.** 1817–94, British archaeologist, noted for his excavations at Nimrud and Nineveh.

lay aside *vb* (*tr, adv*) **1** to abandon or reject. **2** to store or reserve for future use.

lay brother *or* (*fem*) **lay sister** *n* a person who has taken the vows of a religious order but is not ordained and not bound to divine office.

lay-by *n* **1** *Brit.* a place for drivers to stop at the side of a main road. **2** *Naut.* an anchorage in a narrow waterway, away from the channel. **3** a small railway siding where rolling stock may be stored or parked. **4** *Austral. & NZ.* a system of payment whereby a buyer pays a deposit on an article, which is reserved until the full price has been paid. ◆ *vb* **lay by.** (*tr, adv*) **5** to set aside or save for future needs.

lay days *pl n* **1** *Commerce.* the number of days permitted for the loading or unloading of a ship without payment of demurrage. **2** *Naut.* the time during which a ship is kept from sailing because of loading, bad weather, etc.

lay down *vb* (*tr, adv*) **1** to place on the ground, etc. **2** to relinquish or discard: *to lay down one's life.* **3** to formulate (a rule, principle, etc.). **4** to build or begin to build: *the railway was laid down as far as Chester.* **5** to record (plans) on paper. **6** to convert (land) into pasture. **7** to store or stock: *to lay down wine.* **8** *Inf.* to wager or bet. **9** *Inf.* to record (tracks) in a studio.

layer (ˈleɪə) *n* **1** a thickness of some homogeneous substance, such as a stratum or a coating on a surface. **2** a laying hen. **3** *Horticulture.* a shoot or branch rooted during layering. ◆ *vb* **4** to form or make a layer of (something). **5** to take root or cause to take root by layering. ORIG C14 *leyer, legger,* from LAY[1] + -ER[1]

layering (ˈleɪərɪŋ) *n* **1** *Horticulture.* a method of propagation that induces a shoot to take root while it is still attached to the parent plant. **2** *Geol.* the banded appearance of certain igneous rocks, each band being of a different mineral composition.

layette (leɪˈɛt) *n* a complete set of articles, including clothing, bedclothes, and other accessories, for a newborn baby. ORIG C19: from F, from OF, from *laie*, from MDu. *laege* box

lay figure *n* **1** an artist's jointed dummy, used in place of a live model, esp. for studying effects of drapery. **2** a person considered to be subservient or unimportant. ORIG C18: from obs. *layman*, from Du. *leeman*, lit.: joint-man

lay in *vb* (*tr, adv*) to accumulate and store: *we must lay in food for the party.*

lay into *vb* (*intr, prep*) *Inf.* **1** to attack forcefully. **2** to berate severely.

layman (ˈleɪmən) *or* (*fem*) **laywoman** *n, pl* **laymen** *or* **laywomen. 1** a person who is not a clergyman. **2** a person who does not have specialized or professional knowledge of a subject: *science for the layman.*

lay off *vb* **1** (*tr, adv*) to suspend from work with the intention of re-employing later: *the firm had to lay off 100 men.* **2** (*intr*) *Inf.* to leave (a person, thing, or activity) alone: *lay off me, will you!* **3** (*tr, adv*) to mark off the boundaries of. ◆ *n* **lay-off. 4** the act of suspending employees. **5** a period of imposed unemployment.

lay on *vb* (*tr, adv*) **1** to provide or supply: *to lay on entertainment.* **2** *Brit.* to install: *to lay on electricity.* **3 lay it on.** *Sl.* **3a** to exaggerate, esp. when flattering. **3b** to charge an exorbitant price. **3c** to punish or strike harshly.

lay out *vb* (*tr, adv*) **1** to arrange or spread out. **2** to prepare (a corpse) for burial or cremation. **3** to plan or contrive. **4** *Inf.* to spend (money), esp. lavishly. **5** *Inf.* to knock unconscious. ◆ *n* **layout. 6** the arrangement or plan of something, such as a building. **7** the arrangement of written material, photographs, or other artwork on an advertisement or page in a book, newspaper, etc. **8** a preliminary plan indicating this. **9** a drawing showing the relative disposition of parts in a machine, etc. **10** the act of laying out. **11** something laid out.

lay over *US.* ◆ *vb* (*adv*) **1** (*tr*) to postpone for future action. **2** (*intr*) to make a temporary stop in a journey. ◆ *n* **layover. 3** a break in a journey, esp. in waiting for a connection.

lay reader *n* **1** *Church of England.* a person licensed by a bishop to conduct religious services other than the Eucharist. **2** *RC Church.* a layman chosen from among the congregation to read the epistle at Mass.

lay up *vb* (*tr, adv*) **1** to store or reserve for future use. **2** (*usually passive*) *Inf.* to incapacitate or confine through illness.

lazar ('læzə) *n* an archaic word for **leper.** ORIG C14: via OF and Med. L, after LAZARUS

lazaretto (ˌlæzə'rɛtəʊ), **lazaret,** *or* **lazarette** (ˌlæzə'rɛt) *n, pl* **lazarettos, lazarets,** *or* **lazarettes. 1** Also called: **glory hole.** *Naut.* a small locker at the stern of a boat or a storeroom between decks of a ship. **2** Also called: **lazar house, pesthouse.** (formerly) a hospital for persons with infectious diseases, esp. leprosy. ORIG C16: It., from *lazzaro* LAZAR

Lazarus ★ ('læzərəs) *n New Testament.* **1** the brother of Mary and Martha, whom Jesus restored to life (John 11–12). **2** the beggar who lay at the gate of the rich man Dives in Jesus' parable (Luke 16:19–31).

laze (leɪz) *vb* **lazes, lazing, lazed. 1** (*intr*) to be indolent or lazy. **2** (*tr;* often foll. by *away*) to spend (time) in indolence. ◆ *n* **3** the act or an instance of idling. ORIG C16: back formation from LAZY

Lazio ★ ('lattsjo) *n* **1** a region of W central Italy, on the Tyrrhenian Sea: includes the plain of the lower Tiber, the reclaimed Pontine Marshes, and Campagne. Capital: Rome. Pop.: 5 202 098 (1996 est.). **2** the Italian name for **Latium.**

lazy ('leɪzɪ) *adj* **lazier, laziest. 1** not inclined to work or exertion. **2** conducive to or causing indolence. **3** moving in a languid or sluggish manner: *a lazy river.* ORIG C16: from ?
▸ **'lazily** *adv* ▸ **'laziness** *n*

lazybones ('leɪzɪˌbəʊnz) *n Inf.* a lazy person.

lazy Susan *n* a revolving tray, often divided into sections, for holding condiments, etc.

lb *abbrev. for:* **1** pound (weight). ORIG L *libra* **2** *Cricket.* leg bye.

LBJ *abbrev. for* Lyndon Baines Johnson.

LBO *abbrev. for* leveraged buyout.

lbw *Cricket. abbrev. for* leg before wicket.

lc *abbrev. for:* **1** left centre (of a stage, etc.). **2** loco citato. ORIG L: in the place cited **3** *Printing.* lower case.

L/C, l/c, *or* **lc** *abbrev. for* letter of credit.

LCD *abbrev. for:* **1** liquid-crystal display. **2** Also: **lcd.** lowest common denominator.

LCJ (in Britain) *abbrev. for* Lord Chief Justice.

lcm *or* **LCM** *abbrev. for* lowest common multiple.

L/Cpl *abbrev. for* lance corporal.

LD *abbrev. for* lethal dose (esp. in LD_{50}). See **median lethal dose.**

LDL *abbrev. for* low-density lipoprotein.

L-dopa (ˌɛl'dəʊpə) *n* a substance occurring naturally in the body and used to treat Parkinson's disease. Also called: **levodopa.** ORIG C20: from *L-d(ihydr)o(xy)p(henyl)-a(lanine)*

LDS *abbrev. for:* **1** Latter-day Saints. **2** laus Deo semper. ORIG L: praise be to God forever **3** (in Britain) Licentiate in Dental Surgery.

lea (liː) *n* **1** *Poetic.* a meadow or field. **2** land that has been sown with grass seed. ORIG OE *lēah*

LEA (in Britain) *abbrev. for* Local Education Authority.

leach (liːtʃ) *vb* **1** to remove or be removed from a substance by a percolating liquid. **2** to lose or cause to lose soluble substances by the action of a percolating liquid. ◆ *n* **3** the act or process of leaching. **4** a substance that is leached or the constituents removed by leaching. **5** a porous vessel for leaching. ORIG C17: var. of obs. *letch* to wet, ?from OE *leccan* to water
▸ **'leacher** *n*

Leach ★ (liːtʃ) *n* **Bernard (Howell).** 1887–1979, British potter, born in Hong Kong.

Leacock ★ ('liːˌkɒk) *n* **Stephen Butler.** 1869–1944, Canadian humorist and economist: his comic works include *Literary Lapses* (1910) and *Frenzied Fiction* (1917).

lead[1] (liːd) *vb* **leads, leading, led. 1** to show the way to (an individual or a group) by going with or ahead: *lead the party into the garden.* **2** to guide or be guided by holding, pulling, etc.: *he led the horse by its reins.* **3** (*tr*) to cause to act, feel, think, or behave in a certain way; induce; influence: *he led me to believe that he would go.* **4** (when *intr,* foll. by *to*) (of a road, route, etc.) to serve as the means of reaching a place. **5** (*tr*) to go ahead so as to indicate (esp. in **lead the way**). **6** to guide, control, or direct: *to lead an army.* **7** (*tr*) to direct the course of or conduct (water, a rope, or wire, etc.) along or as if along a channel. **8** to initiate the action of (something); have the principal part in (something): *to lead a discussion.* **9** to go at the head of or have the top position in (something): *he leads his class in geography.* **10** (*intr;* foll. by *with*) to have as the first or principal item: *the newspaper led with the royal birth.* **11** *Music, Brit.* to play first violin in (an orchestra). **12** to direct and guide (one's partner) in a dance. **13** (*tr*) **13a** to pass or spend: *I lead a miserable life.* **13b** to cause to pass a life of a particular kind: *to lead a person a dog's life.* **14** (*intr;* foll. by *to*) to tend (to) or result (in): *this will only lead to misery.* **15** to initiate a round of cards by putting down (the first card) or to have the right to do this: *she led a diamond.* **16** (*intr*) *Boxing.* to make an offensive blow, esp. as one's habitual attacking punch. ◆ *n* **17a** the first, foremost, or most prominent place. **17b** (*as modifier*): *lead singer.* **18** example, precedence, or leadership: *the class followed the teacher's lead.* **19** an advance or advantage held over others: *the runner had a lead of twenty yards.* **20** anything that guides or directs; indication; clue. **21** another name for **leash. 22** the act or prerogative of playing the first card in a round of cards or the card so played. **23** the principal role in a play, film, etc., or the person playing such a role. **24a** the principal news story in a newspaper: *the scandal was the lead in the papers.* **24b** (*as modifier*): *lead story.* **25** *Music.* an important entry assigned to one part. **26** a wire, cable, or other conductor for making an electrical connection. **27** *Boxing.* **27a** one's habitual attacking punch. **27b** a blow made with this. **28** a deposit of metal or ore; lode. ◆ See also **lead off, lead on,** etc. ORIG OE *lǣdan;* rel. to *līthan* to travel

lead[2] (lɛd) *n* **1** a heavy toxic bluish-white metallic element that is highly malleable: used in alloys, accumulators, cable sheaths, paints, and as a radiation shield. Symbol: Pb; atomic no.: 82; atomic wt.: 207.2. **2** a lead weight suspended on a line used to take soundings of the depth of water. **3** lead weights or shot, as used in cartridges, fishing lines, etc. **4** a thin grooved strip of lead for holding small panes of glass or pieces of stained glass. **5** (*pl*) **5a** thin sheets or strips of lead used as a roof covering. **5b** a flat or low-pitched roof covered with such sheets. **6** Also called: **leading.** *Printing.* a thin strip of type metal used for spacing between lines. **7a** graphite used for drawing. **7b** a thin stick of this material, esp. the core of a pencil. **8** (*modifier*) of, consisting of, relating to, or containing lead. ◆ *vb* (*tr*) **9** to fill or treat with lead. **10** to surround, cover, or secure with lead or leads. **11** *Printing.* to space (type) by use of leads. ORIG OE

lead acetate (lɛd) *n* a white crystalline toxic solid used in dyeing cotton and in making varnishes and enamels. Formula: $Pb(CH_3COOH)_2$. Systematic name: **lead ethanoate.**

Leadbelly ★ ('lɛdˌbɛlɪ) *n,* real name *Huddie Ledbetter.* 1888–1949, US blues singer and guitarist.

lead chromate (lɛd) *n Chem.* a yellow solid used as a pigment, as in chrome yellow. Formula: $PbCrO_4$.

leaded ('lɛdɪd) *adj* (of windows) composed of small panes of glass held in place by thin grooved strips of lead: *leaded lights.*

leaden ('lɛdᵊn) *adj* **1** heavy and inert. **2** laboured or sluggish: *leaden steps.* **3** gloomy, spiritless, or lifeless. **4** made partly or wholly of lead. **5** of a dull greyish colour: *a leaden sky.*
▸ **'leadenly** *adv* ▸ **'leadenness** *n*

leader ('li:də) *n* **1** a person who rules, guides, or inspires others; head. **2** *Music.* **2a** Also called (esp. US and Canad.): **concertmaster.** the principal first violinist of an orchestra, who plays solo parts, and acts as the conductor's deputy and spokesman for the orchestra. **2b** *US.* a conductor or director of an orchestra or chorus. **3a** the leading horse or dog in a team. **3b** the first man on a climbing rope. **4** *Chiefly Brit.* the leading editorial in a newspaper. Also: **leading article. 5** *Angling.* another word for **trace**[2] (sense 2). **6** a strip of blank film or tape used to facilitate threading a projector, developing machine, etc. **7** (*pl*) *Printing.* rows of dots or hyphens used to guide the reader's eye across a page, as in a table of contents. **8** *Bot.* any of the long slender shoots that grow from the stem or branch of a tree. **9** *Brit.* a member of the Government having primary authority in initiating legislative business (esp. in **Leader of the House of Commons** and **Leader of the House of Lords**).
▸ **'leaderless** *adj*

leaderboard ('li:də,bɔ:d) *n* a board displaying the names and current scores of the leading competitors, esp. in a golf tournament.

leadership ('li:dəʃɪp) *n* **1** the position or function of a leader. **2** the period during which a person occupies the position of leader: *during her leadership very little was achieved.* **3a** the ability to lead. **3b** (*as modifier*): *leadership qualities.* **4** the leaders as a group of a party, union, etc.: *the union leadership is now very reactionary.*

lead-free (,lɛd'fri:) *adj* See **unleaded.**

lead glass (lɛd) *n* glass that contains lead oxide as a flux.

lead-in ('li:d,ɪn) *n* **1** an introduction to a subject. **2** the connection between a radio transmitter, receiver, etc., and the aerial or transmission line.

leading[1] ('li:dɪŋ) *adj* **1** guiding, directing, or influencing. **2** (*prenominal*) principal or primary. **3** in the first position.

leading[2] ('lɛdɪŋ) *n Printing.* **1** the spacing between lines of photocomposed or digitized type. **2** another name for **lead**[2] (sense 6). ◆ Also called: **interlinear spacing.**

leading aircraftman ('li:dɪŋ) *n Brit. airforce.* the rank above aircraftman.
▸ **leading aircraftwoman** *fem n*

leading edge ('li:dɪŋ) *n* **1** the forward edge of a propeller blade, wing, or aerofoil. Cf. **trailing edge. 2** *Electrical engineering.* the part of a pulse signal that has an increasing amplitude. **3a** the leading position in any field. **3b** (*as modifier*): *leading-edge technology.*

leading light ('li:dɪŋ) *n* an important or outstanding person, esp. in an organization.

leading note ('li:dɪŋ) *n Music.* **1** another word for **subtonic. 2** (esp. in cadences) a note that tends most naturally to resolve to the note lying one semitone above it.

leading question ('li:dɪŋ) *n* a question phrased in a manner that tends to suggest the desired answer, such as *What do you think of the horrible effects of pollution?*

leading rating ('li:dɪŋ) *n* a rank in the Royal Navy comparable but junior to that of a corporal in the army.

leading reins *or US & Canad.* **leading strings** ('li:dɪŋ) *pl n* **1** straps or a harness and strap used to assist and control a child who is learning to walk. **2** excessive guidance or restraint.

lead monoxide (lɛd) *n* a poisonous insoluble oxide of lead existing in red and yellow forms: used in making glass, glazes, and cements, and as a pigment. Formula: PbO. Systematic name: **lead(II) oxide.**

lead off (li:d) *vb* (*adv*) **1** to initiate the action of (something); begin. ◆ *n* **lead-off. 2** an initial move or action.

lead on (li:d) *vb* (*tr, adv*) to lure or entice, esp. into trouble or wrongdoing.

lead pencil (lɛd) *n* a pencil containing a thin stick of a graphite compound.

lead poisoning (lɛd) *n* **1** acute or chronic poisoning by lead, characterized by abdominal pain, vomiting, convulsions, and coma. **2** *US sl.* death or injury resulting from being shot with bullets.

lead screw (li:d) *n* a threaded rod that drives the tool carriage in a lathe.

lead tetraethyl (lɛd) *n* another name for **tetraethyl lead.**

lead time (li:d) *n* **1** *Manufacturing, chiefly US.* the time between the design of a product and its production. **2** *Commerce.* the time from the placing of an order to the delivery of the goods.

lead up to (li:d) *vb* (*intr, adv + prep*) **1** to act as a preliminary or introduction to. **2** to approach (a topic) gradually or cautiously.

leaf (li:f) *n, pl* **leaves** (li:vz). **1** the main organ of photosynthesis and transpiration in higher plants, usually consisting of a flat green blade attached to the stem directly or by a stalk. **2** foliage collectively. **3 in leaf.** (of shrubs, trees, etc.) having a full complement of foliage leaves. **4** one of the sheets of paper in a book. **5** a hinged, sliding, or detachable part, such as an extension to a table. **6** metal in the form of a very thin flexible sheet: *gold leaf.* **7 take a leaf out of** (*or* **from**) **someone's book.** to imitate someone, esp. in one particular course of action. **8 turn over a new leaf.** to begin a new and improved course of behaviour. ◆ *vb* **9** (when *intr,* usually foll. by *through*) to turn (through pages, sheets, etc.) cursorily. **10** (*intr*) (of plants) to produce leaves. ORIG OE
▸ **'leafless** *adj* ▸ **'leaf,like** *adj*

leafage ('li:fɪdʒ) *n* a less common word for **foliage.**

leaflet ('li:flɪt) *n* **1** a printed and usually folded sheet of paper for distribution, usually free, esp. for advertising, giving information about a charity, etc. **2** any of the subdivisions of a compound leaf such as a fern leaf. **3** any small leaf or leaflike part. ◆ *vb* **leaflets, leafleting, leafleted. 4** to distribute leaflets (to).

leaf miner *n* **1** any of various insect larvae that bore into and feed on leaf tissue. **2** the adult insect of any of these larvae.

leaf mould *n* **1** a nitrogen-rich material consisting of decayed leaves, etc., used as a fertilizer. **2** any of various fungus diseases affecting the leaves of certain plants.

leaf spring *n* **1** one of a number of metal strips bracketed together in length to form a spring. **2** the compound spring so formed.

leafstalk ('li:f,stɔ:k) *n* the stalk attaching a leaf to a stem or branch. Technical name: **petiole.**

leafy ('li:fɪ) *adj* **leafier, leafiest. 1** covered with or having leaves. **2** resembling a leaf or leaves.
▸ **'leafiness** *n*

league[1] (li:g) *n* **1** an association or union of persons, nations, etc., formed to promote the interests of its members. **2** an association of sporting clubs that organizes matches between member teams. **3** a class, category, or level: *he is not in the same league.* **4 in league** (**with**). working or planning together with. **5** (*modifier*) of, involving, or belonging to a league: *a league game; a league table.* ◆ *vb* **leagues, leaguing, leagued. 6** to form or be formed into a league. ORIG C15: from OF *ligue,* from It. *liga,* ult. from L *ligāre* to bind

league[2] (li:g) *n* an obsolete unit of distance of varying length. It is commonly equal to 3 miles. ORIG C14 *leuge,* from LL *leuga, leuca,* of Celtic origin

league football *n* **1** Also called: **league.** *Chiefly Austral.* rugby league football. Cf. **rugby union. 2** *Austral.* an Australian Rules competition conducted within a league.

leaguer ('li:gə) *n Chiefly US & Canad.* a member of a league.

league table *n* **1** a list of sports clubs ranked in order according to their performance. **2** a comparison of performance in any sphere.

Leah ★ ('lɪə) *n Old Testament.* the first wife of Jacob and elder sister of Rachel, his second wife (Genesis 29).

leak (li:k) *n* **1a** a crack, hole, etc., that allows the accidental escape or entrance of fluid, light, etc. **1b** such escaping or entering fluid, light, etc. **2 spring a leak.** to develop a leak. **3** something resembling this in effect: *a leak in the defence system.* **4** the loss of current from an electrical conductor because of faulty insulation, etc. **5** a disclosure of secret information. **6** the act or an instance of leaking. **7** a slang word for **urination.** ◆ *vb* **8** to enter or escape or allow to enter or escape through a crack, hole, etc. **9** (when *intr,* often foll. by *out*) to disclose (secret in-

formation) or (of secret information) to be disclosed. **10** (*intr*) a slang word for **urinate**. ORIG C15: from ON
▸ **'leaker** *n*

leakage ('liːkɪdʒ) *n* **1** the act or an instance of leaking. **2** something that escapes or enters by a leak. **3** *Physics.* an undesired flow of electric current, neutrons, etc.

Leakey ★ ('liːkɪ) *n* **1** **Louis Seymour Bazett** ('bæzɪt). 1903–72, British anthropologist and archaeologist, settled in Kenya; discovered remains of manlike apes. **2** his son, **Richard.** born 1944, Kenyan anthropologist; discovered the remains of primitive man over 2 million years old.

leaky ('liːkɪ) *adj* **leakier, leakiest.** leaking or tending to leak.
▸ **'leakiness** *n*

leal (liːl) *adj Arch. or Scot.* loyal; faithful. ORIG C13: from OF *leial,* from L *lēgālis* LEGAL; rel. to LOYAL
▸ **'leally** *adv* ▸ **lealty** ('liːəltɪ) *n*

Leamington Spa ★ ('lɛmɪŋtən) *n* a town in central England, in central Warwickshire: saline springs. Pop.: 55 396 (1991). Official name: **Royal Leamington Spa.**

lean[1] (liːn) *vb* **leans, leaning, leaned** *or* **leant. 1** (foll. by *against, on,* or *upon*) to rest or cause to rest against a support. **2** to incline or cause to incline from a vertical position. **3** (*intr;* foll. by *to* or *towards*) to have or express a tendency or leaning. ◆ *n* **4** the condition of inclining from a vertical position. ORIG OE *hleonian, hlinian*

lean[2] (liːn) *adj* **1** (esp. of a person or animal) having no surplus flesh or bulk; not fat. **2** not bulky or full. **3** (of meat) having little or no fat. **4** not rich, abundant, or satisfying. **5** (of mixture of fuel and air) containing insufficient fuel and too much air. ◆ *n* **6** the part of meat that contains little or no fat. ORIG OE *hlǣne,* of Gmc origin
▸ **'leanly** *adv* ▸ **'leanness** *n*

Lean ★ (liːn) *n* Sir **David.** 1908–91, British film director. His films include *Brief Encounter* (1946), *Oliver Twist* (1948), *The Bridge on the River Kwai* (1957), *Lawrence of Arabia* (1962), *Dr Zhivago* (1965), and *A Passage to India* (1984).

lean-burn *adj* (esp. of an internal-combustion engine) designed to use a lean mixture of fuel and air in order to reduce petrol consumption and exhaust emissions.

Leander ★ (lɪ'ændə) *n* (in Greek legend) a youth of Abydos, who drowned in the Hellespont in a storm on one of his nightly visits to Hero, his beloved. See also **Hero**[1].

leaning ('liːnɪŋ) *n* a tendency or inclination.

leant (lɛnt) *vb* a past tense and past participle of **lean**[1].

lean-to *n, pl* **lean-tos. 1** a roof that has a single slope adjoining a wall or building. **2** a shed or outbuilding with such a roof.

leap (liːp) *vb* **leaps, leaping, leapt** *or* **leaped. 1** (*intr*) to jump suddenly from one place to another. **2** (*intr;* often foll. by *at*) to move or react quickly. **3** (*tr*) to jump over. **4** to come into prominence rapidly: *the thought leapt into his mind.* **5** (*tr*) to cause (an animal, esp. a horse) to jump a barrier. ◆ *n* **6** the act of jumping. **7** a spot from which a leap was or may be made. **8** an abrupt change or increase. **9 a leap in the dark.** an action performed without knowledge of the consequences. **10 by leaps and bounds.** with unexpectedly rapid progress. ORIG OE *hlēapan*
▸ **'leaper** *n*

leapfrog ('liːpˌfrɒg) *n* **1** a children's game in which each player in turn leaps over the others' bent backs. ◆ *vb* **leapfrogs, leapfrogging, leapfrogged. 2a** (*intr*) to play leapfrog. **2b** (*tr*) to leap in this way over (something). **3** to advance or cause to advance by jumps or stages.

leap second *n* a second added to or removed from a scale for reckoning time on one particular occasion, to synchronize it with another scale.

leapt (lɛpt, liːpt) *vb* a past tense and past participle of **leap**.

leap year *n* a calendar year of 366 days, February 29 (**leap day**) being the additional day, that occurs every four years (those whose number is divisible by four) except for century years whose number is not divisible by 400.

Lear ★ (lɪə) *n* **Edward.** 1812–88, British humorist and painter, noted for his illustrated nonsense poems and limericks.

learn (lɜːn) *vb* **learns, learning, learned** (lɜːnd) *or* **learnt. 1** (when *tr, may take a clause as object*) to gain knowledge of (something) or acquire skill in (some art or practice). **2** (*tr*) to commit to memory. **3** (*tr*) to gain by experience, example, etc. **4** (*intr;* often foll. by *of* or *about*) to become informed; know. **5** *Not standard.* to teach. ORIG OE *leornian*
▸ **'learnable** *adj* ▸ **'learner** *n*

learned ('lɜːnɪd) *adj* **1** having great knowledge or erudition. **2** involving or characterized by scholarship. **3** (*prenominal*) a title applied in referring to a member of the legal profession, esp. to a barrister: *my learned friend.*
▸ **'learnedly** *adv* ▸ **'learnedness** *n*

learning ('lɜːnɪŋ) *n* **1** knowledge gained by study; instruction or scholarship. **2** the act of gaining knowledge.

learning curve *n* a graphical representation of progress in learning: *I'm still only halfway up the learning curve.*

learnt (lɜːnt) *vb* a past tense and past participle of **learn**.

lease (liːs) *n* **1** a contract by which property is conveyed to a person for a specified period, usually for rent. **2** the instrument by which such property is conveyed. **3** the period of time for which it is conveyed. **4** a prospect of renewed health, happiness, etc.: *a new lease of life.* ◆ *vb* **leases, leasing, leased.** (*tr*) **5** to grant possession of (land, buildings, etc.) by lease. **6** to take a lease of (property); hold under a lease. ORIG C15: via Anglo-F from OF *lais* (n), from *laissier* to let go, from L *laxāre* to loosen
▸ **'leasable** *adj* ▸ **'leaser** *n*

leaseback ('liːsˌbæk) *n* a transaction in which the buyer leases the property to the seller.

leasehold ('liːsˌhəʊld) *n* **1** land or property held under a lease. **2** the tenure by which such property is held. **3** (*modifier*) held under a lease.
▸ **'leaseˌholder** *n*

leash (liːʃ) *n* **1** a line or rope used to walk or control a dog or other animal; lead. **2** something resembling this in function: *he kept a tight leash on his emotions.* **3 straining at the leash.** eagerly impatient to begin something. ◆ *vb* **4** (*tr*) to control or secure as by a leash. ORIG C13: from OF *laisse,* from *laissier* to loose (hence, to let a dog run on a leash), ult. from L *laxus* lax

least (liːst) *determiner* **1a the.** the superlative of **little:** *you have the least talent of anyone.* **1b** (*as pronoun; functioning as sing*): *least isn't necessarily worst.* **2 at least. 2a** if nothing else: *you should at least try.* **2b** at the least. **3 at the least.** Also: **at least.** at the minimum: *at the least you should earn a hundred pounds.* **4 in the least.** (*usually used with a negative*) in the slightest degree; at all: *I don't mind in the least.* ◆ *adv* **5 the least.** superlative of **little:** *they travel the least.* ◆ *adj* **6** of very little importance. ORIG OE *lǣst,* sup. of *lǣssa* less

least common denominator *n* another name for **lowest common denominator.**

least common multiple *n* another name for **lowest common multiple.**

least squares *n* a method for determining the best value of an unknown quantity relating one or more sets of observations or measurements, esp. to find a curve that best fits a set of data.

leastways ('liːstˌweɪz) *or US & Canad.* **leastwise** *adv Inf.* at least; anyway; at any rate.

least-worst *adj Inf.* bad but better than any available alternative: *a least-worst scenario.*

leather ('lɛðə) *n* **1a** a material consisting of the skin of an animal made smooth and flexible by tanning, removing the hair, etc. **1b** (*as modifier*): *leather goods.* **2** (*pl*) leather clothes, esp. as worn by motorcyclists. ◆ *vb* (*tr*) **3** to cover with leather. **4** to whip as with a leather strap. ORIG OE *lether-* (in compound words)

Leatherhead ★ ('lɛðəˌhɛd) *n* a town in S England, in Surrey. Pop.: 42 903 (1991).

leatherjacket ('lɛðəˌdʒækɪt) *n* **1** any of various tropical fishes having a leathery skin. **2** the greyish-brown tough-skinned larva of certain craneflies, which destroy the roots of grasses, etc.

leathern ('lɛðən) *adj Arch.* made of or resembling leather.

leatherneck ('lɛðəˌnɛk) *n Sl.* a member of the US Marine

Corps. ORIG from the custom of facing the neckband of their uniform with leather

leathery (ˈlɛðərɪ) *adj* having the appearance or texture of leather, esp. in toughness.
▸ **ˈleatheriness** *n*

leave[1] (liːv) *vb* **leaves, leaving, left.** (*mainly tr*) **1** (*also intr*) to go or depart (from a person or place). **2** to cause to remain behind, often by mistake, in a place: *he often leaves his keys in his coat.* **3** to cause to be or remain in a specified state: *paying the bill left him penniless.* **4** to renounce or abandon: *to leave a political movement.* **5** to refrain from consuming or doing something: *the things we have left undone.* **6** to result in; cause: *childhood problems often leave emotional scars.* **7** to entrust or commit: *leave the shopping to her.* **8** to pass in a specified direction: *flying out of the country, we left the cliffs on our left.* **9** to be survived by (members of one's family): *he leaves a wife and two children.* **10** to bequeath: *he left his investments to his children.* **11** (*tr*) to have as a remainder: *37 – 14 leaves 23.* **12** *Not standard.* to permit; let. **13 leave (someone) alone. 13a** Also: **let alone.** See **let**[1] (sense 6). **13b** to permit to stay or be alone. ORIG OE *lǣfan;* rel. to *belīfan* to be left as a remainder ◆ See also **leave off, leave out.**
▸ **ˈleaver** *n*

leave[2] (liːv) *n* **1** permission to do something: *he was granted leave to speak.* **2 by** *or* **with your leave.** with your permission. **3** permission to be absent, as from a place of work: *leave of absence.* **4** the duration of such absence: *ten days' leave.* **5** a farewell or departure (esp. in **take (one's) leave**). **6 on leave.** officially excused from work or duty. **7 take leave (of).** to say farewell (to). ORIG OE *lēaf;* rel. to *alȳfan* to permit

leave[3] (liːv) *vb* **leaves, leaving, leaved.** (*intr*) to produce or grow leaves.

leaved (liːvd) *adj* **a** having a leaf or leaves; leafed. **b** (*in combination*): *a five-leaved stem.*

leaven (ˈlɛvᵊn) *n also* **leavening. 1** any substance that produces fermentation in dough or batter, such as yeast, and causes it to rise. **2** a piece of such a substance kept to ferment a new batch of dough. **3** an agency or influence that produces a gradual change. ◆ *vb* (*tr*) **4** to cause fermentation in (dough or batter). **5** to pervade, causing a gradual change, esp. with some moderating or enlivening influence. ORIG C14: via OF ult. from L *levāmen* relief, (hence, raising agent), from *levāre* to raise

Leavenworth ★ (ˈlɛvᵊnˌwɜːθ, -wəθ) *n* a city in NE Kansas, on the Missouri River: the state's oldest city, founded in 1854 by proslavery settlers from Missouri. Pop.: 38 495 (1990).

leave off *vb* **1** (*intr*) to stop; cease. **2** (*tr, adv*) to stop wearing or using.

leave out *vb* (*tr, adv*) **1** to cause to remain in the open. **2** to omit or exclude.

leaves (liːvz) *n* the plural of **leaf.**

leave-taking *n* the act of departing; a farewell.

leavings (ˈliːvɪŋz) *pl n* something remaining, such as food on a plate, residue, refuse, etc.

Leavis ★ (ˈliːvɪs) *n* **F(rank) R(aymond).** 1895–1978, British literary critic. He edited *Scrutiny* (1932–53) and his books include *The Great Tradition* (1948).
▸ **ˈLeavisˌite** *adj, n*

Lebanon ★ (ˈlɛbənən) *n* (sometimes preceded by *the*) a republic in W Asia, on the Mediterranean: an important centre of the Phoenician civilization in the third millennium B.C.; part of the Ottoman Empire from 1516 until 1919; gained independence in 1941 (effective by 1945). Official language: Arabic; French and English are also widely spoken. Religion: Muslim and Christian. Currency: Lebanese pound. Capital: Beirut. Pop.: 3 563 000 (1999 est.). Area: 10 400 sq. km (4015 sq. miles).
▸ **Lebanese** (ˌlɛbəˈniːz) *adj, n*

Lebanon Mountains ★ *pl n* a mountain range in central Lebanon, extending across the whole country parallel with the Mediterranean coast. Highest peak: 3104 m (10 184 ft). Arabic name: **Jebel Liban** (ˈdʒɛbᵊl ˈliːbɑːn).

Lebensraum (ˈleɪbənzˌraʊm) *n* territory claimed by a nation or state as necessary for survival or growth. ORIG G, lit.: living space

Leblanc ★ (*French* ləblɑ̃) *n* **Nicolas** (nikɔlɑ). ?1742–1806, French chemist, who invented a process for the manufacture of soda from common salt.

Lebrun ★ (*French* ləbrœ̃) *n* **1 Albert** (albɛr). 1871–1950, French statesman; president (1932–40). **2** Also: **Le Brun. Charles** (ʃarl). 1619–90, French historical painter.

LEC (lɛk) *n acronym for* Local Enterprise Company. See **Training Agency.**

Le Carré (lə ˈkæreɪ) ★ *n* **John,** real name *David John Cornwell.* born 1931, British novelist, esp. of such spy thrillers as *The Spy who came in from the Cold* (1963), *Tinker, Tailor, Soldier, Spy* (1974), and *The Tailor of Panama* (1996).

Lecce ★ (*Italian* ˈlettʃe) *n* a walled city in SE Italy, in Puglia: Greek and Roman remains. Pop.: 100 046 (1996 est.).

lech (lɛtʃ) *Inf.* ◆ *vb* **1** (*intr;* usually foll. by *after*) to behave lecherously (towards); lust (after). ◆ *n* **2** a lecherous act or indulgence. ORIG C19: back formation from LECHER

Lech ★ (lɛk; *German* lɛç) *n* a river in central Europe, rising in SW Austria and flowing generally north through S Germany to the River Danube. Length: 285 km (177 miles).

lecher (ˈlɛtʃə) *n* a promiscuous or lewd man. ORIG C12: from OF *lecheor,* from *lechier* to lick, of Gmc origin

lecherous (ˈlɛtʃərəs) *adj* characterized by or inciting lechery.
▸ **ˈlecherously** *adv*

lechery (ˈlɛtʃərɪ) *n, pl* **lecheries.** unrestrained and promiscuous sexuality.

lecithin (ˈlɛsɪθɪn) *n Biochem.* any of a group of phospholipids that are found in many plant and animal tissues, esp. egg yolk: used in making candles, cosmetics, and inks, and as an emulsifier and stabilizer (**E322**) in foods. Systematic name: **phosphatidycholine.** ORIG C19: from Gk *lekithos* egg yolk

lecky (ˈlɛkɪ) *n Brit. sl.* short for **electricity.**

Lecky ★ (ˈlɛkɪ) *n* **William Edward Hartpole.** 1838–1903, Irish historian; author of *The History of England in the 18th Century* (1878–90).

Leclanché cell (ləˈklɑːnʃeɪ) *n Electrical engineering.* a primary cell with a carbon anode, surrounded by crushed carbon and manganese dioxide in a porous container in an electrolyte of aqueous ammonium chloride into which a zinc cathode dips. ORIG C19: after Georges *Leclanché* (1839–82), F engineer

Leconte de Lisle ★ (*French* ləkɔ̃t də lil) *n* **Charles Marie René** (ʃarl mari rəne). 1818–94, French Parnassian poet.

Le Corbusier ★ (*French* lə kɔrbyzje) *n* real name *Charles Édouard Jeanneret.* 1887–1965, French architect and town planner, born in Switzerland. He is noted for his modular system. His works include Unité d'Habitation at Marseilles (1946–52) and the city of Chandigarh, India (1954).

Le Creusot ★ (*French* lə krøzo) *n* a town in E central France: metal, machinery, and armaments industries. Pop.: 33 274 (1983 est.).

lectern (ˈlɛktən) *n* **1** a reading desk in a church. **2** any similar desk or support. ORIG C14: from OF *lettrun,* from LL *lectrum,* ult. from *legere* to read

lectionary (ˈlɛkʃənərɪ) *n, pl* **lectionaries.** a book containing readings appointed to be read at divine services. ORIG C15: from Church L *lectiōnārium,* from *lectio* a reading, from *legere* to read

lector (ˈlɛktɔː) *n* **1** a lecturer or reader in certain universities. **2** *RC Church.* **2a** a person appointed to read lessons at certain services. **2b** (in convents or monastic establishments) a member of the community appointed to read aloud during meals. ORIG C15: from L, from *legere* to read

lecture (ˈlɛktʃə) *n* **1** a discourse on a particular subject given or read to an audience. **2** the text of such a discourse. **3** a method of teaching by formal discourse. **4** a lengthy reprimand or scolding. ◆ *vb* **lectures, lecturing, lectured. 5** to give or read a lecture (to an audience or class). **6** (*tr*) to reprimand at length. ORIG C14: from Med. L *lectūra* reading, from *legere* to read
▸ **ˈlecturer** *n* ▸ **ˈlectureship** *n*

led (lɛd) *vb* the past tense and past participle of **lead**[1].

LED *Electronics. abbrev. for* light-emitting diode.

Leda ★ (ˈliːdə) *n Greek myth.* a queen of Sparta who was the mother of Helen and Pollux by Zeus, who visited her in the form of a swan.

Lederberg ★ (ˈlɛdəˌbɜːg) *n* **Joshua.** born 1925, US geneticist, who discovered genetic recombination in bacteria. Nobel prize for physiology or medicine 1958 with George Beadle and Edward Tatum.

lederhosen (ˈleɪdəˌhəʊzᵊn) *pl n* leather shorts with H-shaped braces, worn by men in Austria, Bavaria, etc. ORIG G

ledge (lɛdʒ) *n* **1** a narrow horizontal surface resembling a shelf and projecting from a wall, window, etc. **2** a layer of rock that contains an ore; vein. **3** a ridge of rock that lies beneath the surface of the sea. **4** a narrow shelflike projection on a cliff or mountain. ORIG C14 *legge,* ?from *leggen* to LAY[1]
▸ ˈ**ledgy** *or* **ledged** *adj*

ledger (ˈlɛdʒə) *n* **1** *Book-keeping.* the principal book in which the commercial transactions of a company are recorded. **2** *Angling.* a wire trace that allows the weight to rest on the bottom and the bait to float freely. ◆ *vb* **3** (*intr*) *Angling.* to fish using a ledger. ORIG C15 *legger* book retained in a specific place, prob. from *leggen* to LAY[1]

ledger line *n Music.* a short line placed above or below the staff to accommodate notes representing pitches above or below the staff.

lee (liː) *n* **1** a sheltered part or side; the side away from the direction from which the wind is blowing. ◆ *adj* **2** (*prenominal*) *Naut.* on, at, or towards the side or part away from the wind: *on a lee shore.* Cf. **weather** (sense 4). ORIG OE *hlēow* shelter

Lee[1] ★ (liː) *n* a river in SW Republic of Ireland, flowing east into Cork Harbour. Length: about 80 km (50 miles).

Lee[2] ★ (liː) *n* **1 Ang** (æŋ). born 1954, Taiwanese film director; his films include *Sense and Sensibility* (1995), *The Ice Storm* (1997), and *Crouching Tiger, Hidden Dragon* (2000). **2 Laurie** (ˈlɒrɪ). 1914–97, British writer, best known for the autobiographical novel *Cider with Rosie* (1959) and several volumes of poetry. **3 Richard Henry.** 1732–94, American Revolutionary statesman, who moved the resolution in favour of American independence (1776). **4 Robert E(dward).** 1807–70, American general; commander-in-chief of the Confederate armies in the Civil War. **5 Spike**, real name *Shelton Jackson Lee.* born 1957, US film director: his films include *Malcolm X* (1992) and *He Got Game* (1998). **6 T(sung)-D(ao)** (ˈtsuːŋˈdaʊ). born 1926, US physicist, born in China. With Yang he disproved the principle that parity is always conserved and shared the Nobel prize for physics in 1957.

leech[1] (liːtʃ) *n* **1** an annelid worm which has a sucker at each end of the body and feeds on the blood or tissues of other animals. **2** a person who clings to or preys on another person. **3a** an archaic word for **physician. 3b** (*in combination*): *leechcraft.* ◆ *vb* (*tr*) **4** to use leeches to suck the blood of (a person), as a method of medical treatment. ORIG OE *lǣce, lœce*

leech[2] (liːtʃ) *n Naut.* the after edge of a fore-and-aft sail or either of the vertical edges of a squaresail. ORIG C15: of Gmc origin

Leeds ★ (liːdz) *n* **1** a city in N England, in Leeds unitary authority, West Yorkshire, on the River Aire: linked with Liverpool and Goole by canals; a former centre of the clothing industry; seat of The University of Leeds (1904) and Leeds Metropolitan University (1992). Pop.: 424 194 (1991). **2** a unitary authority in N England, in West Yorkshire. Pop.: 726 900 (1996 est.). Area: 562 sq. km (217 sq. miles).

leek (liːk) *n* **1** a vegetable with a slender white bulb, cylindrical stem, and broad flat overlapping leaves. **2** a leek, or a representation of one, as a national emblem of Wales. ORIG OE *lēac*

leer (lɪə) *vb* **1** (*intr*) to give an oblique, sneering, or suggestive look or grin. ◆ *n* **2** such a look. ORIG C16: ? verbal use of obs. *leer* cheek, from OE *hlēor*
▸ ˈ**leering** *adj, n* ▸ ˈ**leeringly** *adv*

leery (ˈlɪərɪ) *adj* **leerier, leeriest. 1** *Now chiefly dialect.* knowing or sly. **2** *Sl.* (foll. by *of*) suspicious or wary. ORIG C18: ?from obs. sense (to look askance) of LEER
▸ ˈ**leeriness** *n*

lees (liːz) *pl n* the sediment from an alcoholic drink. ORIG C14: pl of obs. *lee,* from OF, prob. from Celtic

leet (liːt) *n Scot.* a list of candidates for an office. ORIG C15: ?from Anglo-F *litte,* var. of LIST[1]

Leeuwarden ★ (*Dutch* ˈleːwɑrdə) *n* a city in the N Netherlands, capital of Friesland province. Pop.: 87 464 (1994).

Leeuwenhoek ★ (ˈleɪvᵊnˌhuːk; *Dutch* ˈleːwənhuːk) *n* **Anton van** (ˈɑntɔn vɑn). 1632–1723, Dutch microscopist, who provided the first accurate description of blood corpuscles, spermatozoa, and microbes.

leeward (ˈliːwəd; *Naut.* ˈluːəd) *Chiefly naut.* ◆ *adj* **1** of, in, or moving to the quarter towards which the wind blows. ◆ *n* **2** the point or quarter towards which the wind blows. **3** the side towards the lee. ◆ *adv* **4** towards the lee. ◆ Cf. **windward.**

Leeward Islands ★ (ˈliːwəd) *pl n* **1** a group of islands in the Caribbean, in the N Lesser Antilles between Puerto Rico and Martinique. **2** a former British colony in the E West Indies (1871–1956), consisting of Antigua, Barbuda, Redonda, Saint Kitts, Nevis, Anguilla, Montserrat, and the British Virgin Islands. **3** a group of islands in the S Pacific, in French Polynesia in the W Society Archipelago: Huahiné, Raiatéa, Tahaa, Bora-Bora, and Maupiti. Pop.: 22 232 (1988). French name: **Îles sous le Vent.**

lee wave *n Meteorol.* a stationary wave sometimes formed in an air stream on the leeward side of a hill or mountain range.

leeway (ˈliːˌweɪ) *n* **1** room for free movement within limits, as in action or expenditure. **2** sideways drift of a boat or aircraft.

Le Fanu ★ (ˈlɛfəˌnjuː) *n* (**Joseph**) **Sheridan.** 1814–73, Irish writer, best known for his stories of mystery and the supernatural, esp. *Uncle Silas* (1864) and the collection *In a Glass Darkly* (1872).

Lefkoşa ★ (lɛfˈkoʃə) *n* the Turkish name for **Nicosia.**

left[1] (lɛft) *adj* **1** (*usually prenominal*) of or designating the side of something or someone that faces west when the front is turned towards the north. **2** (*usually prenominal*) worn on a left hand, foot, etc. **3** (*sometimes cap.*) of or relating to the political left. **4** (*sometimes cap.*) radical or progressive. ◆ *adv* **5** on or in the direction of the left. ◆ *n* **6** a left side, direction, position, area, or part. Related adjs.: **sinister, sinistral. 7** (*often cap.*) the supporters or advocates of varying degrees of social, political, or economic change, reform, or revolution. **8** *Boxing.* **8a** a blow with the left hand. **8b** the left hand. ORIG OE *left* idle, weak, var. of *lyft-* (in *lyftādl* palsy, lit.: left-disease)

left[2] (lɛft) *vb* the past tense and past participle of **leave**[1].

Left Bank ★ *n* a district of Paris, on the S bank of the River Seine; frequented by artists, students, etc.

left-hand *adj* (*prenominal*) **1** of, relating to, located on, or moving towards the left. **2** for use by the left hand; left-handed.

left-handed *adj* **1** using the left hand with greater ease than the right. **2** performed with the left hand. **3** designed or adapted for use by the left hand. **4** awkward or clumsy. **5** ironically ambiguous: *a left-handed compliment.* **6** turning from right to left; anticlockwise. ◆ *adv* **7** with the left hand.
▸ ˌ**left-**ˈ**handedly** *adv* ▸ ˌ**left-**ˈ**handedness** *n* ▸ ˌ**left-**ˈ**hander** *n*

leftist (ˈlɛftɪst) *adj* **1** of, tending towards, or relating to the political left or its principles. ◆ *n* **2** a person who supports or belongs to the political left.
▸ ˈ**leftism** *n*

left-luggage office *n Brit.* a place at a railway station, etc., where luggage may be left for a small charge. US and Canad. name: **checkroom.**

leftover (ˈlɛftˌəʊvə) *n* **1** (*often pl*) an unused portion or remnant, as of material or of cooked food. ◆ *adj* **2** left as an unused portion.

leftward ('lɛftwəd) *adj* **1** on or towards the left. ◆ *adv* **2** a variant of **leftwards.**

leftwards ('lɛftwədz) *or* **leftward** *adv* towards or on the left.

left wing *n* **1** (*often cap.*) the leftist faction of an assembly, party, group, etc.; the radical or progressive wing. **2** *Sport.* **2a** the left-hand side of the field of play from the point of view of either team facing its opponents' goal. **2b** a player positioned in this area in certain games. ◆ *adj* **left-wing. 3** of, belonging to, or relating to the political left wing.
▸ ˌ**left-'winger** *n*

lefty ('lɛftɪ) *n, pl* **lefties.** *Inf.* **1** a left-winger. **2** *Chiefly US & Canad.* a left-handed person.

leg (lɛg) *n* **1** either of the two lower limbs in humans, or any similar or analogous structure in animals that is used for locomotion or support. **2** this part of an animal, esp. the thigh, used for food: *leg of lamb.* **3** something similar to a leg in appearance or function, such as one of the four supporting members of a chair. **4** a branch, limb, or part of a forked or jointed object. **5** the part of a garment that covers the leg. **6** a section or part of a journey or course. **7** a single stage, lap, length, etc., in a relay race. **8** either the opposite or adjacent side of a right-angled triangle. **9** one of a series of games, matches, or parts of games. **10** either one of two races on which a cumulative bet has been placed. **11** *Cricket.* **11a** the side of the field to the left of a right-handed batsman as he or she faces the bowler. **11b** (*as modifier*): *a leg slip; leg stump.* **12 have legs.** *Inf.* to be successful or show the potential to succeed. **13 not have a leg to stand on.** *Inf.* to have no reasonable or logical basis for an opinion or argument. **14 on his, its,** etc., **last legs.** (of a person or thing) worn out; exhausted. **15 pull (someone's) leg.** *Inf.* to tease, fool, or make fun of (someone). **16 shake a leg.** *Inf.* to hurry up: usually used in the imperative. **17 stretch one's legs.** to stand up or walk around, esp. after sitting for some time. ◆ *vb* **legs, legging, legged. 18 leg it.** *Inf.* to walk, run, or hurry. ORIG C13: from ON *leggr,* from ?

leg. *abbrev. for:* **1** legal. **2** legate. **3** legato. **4** legislation. **5** legislative. **6** legislature.

legacy ('lɛgəsɪ) *n, pl* **legacies. 1** a gift by will, esp. of money or personal property. **2** something handed down or received from an ancestor or predecessor. ORIG C14 (meaning: office of a legate), C15 (meaning: bequest): from Med. L *lēgātia* commission; see LEGATE

legal ('liːgᵊl) *adj* **1** established by or founded upon law; lawful. **2** of or relating to law. **3** recognized, enforceable, or having a remedy at law rather than in equity. **4** relating to or characteristic of the profession of law. ORIG C16: from L *lēgālis,* from *lēx* law
▸ '**legally** *adv*

legal aid *n* financial assistance available to persons unable to meet the full cost of legal proceedings.

legalese (ˌliːgə'liːz) *n* the conventional language in which legal documents are written.

legalism ('liːgəˌlɪzəm) *n* strict adherence to the law, esp. the letter of the law rather than its spirit.
▸ '**legalist** *n, adj* ▸ ˌ**legal'istic** *adj*

legality (lɪ'gælɪtɪ) *n, pl* **legalities. 1** the state or quality of being legal or lawful. **2** adherence to legal principles.

legalize *or* **legalise** ('liːgəˌlaɪz) *vb* **legalizes, legalizing, legalized** *or* **legalises, legalising, legalised.** (*tr*) to make lawful or legal.
▸ ˌ**legali'zation** *or* ˌ**legali'sation** *n*

legal tender *n* currency that a creditor must by law accept in redemption of a debt.

Legaspi ★ (lɛ'gæspɪ) *n* a port in the Philippines, on SE Luzon on the Gulf of Albay. Pop.: 125 128 (1994 est.).

legate ('lɛgɪt) *n* **1** a messenger, envoy, or delegate. **2** *RC Church.* an emissary representing the Pope. ORIG OE, via OF from L *lēgātus* deputy, from *lēgāre* to delegate; rel. to *lēx* law
▸ '**legateˌship** *n*

legatee (ˌlɛgə'tiː) *n* a person to whom a legacy is bequeathed.

legation (lɪ'geɪʃən) *n* **1** a diplomatic mission headed by a minister. **2** the official residence and office of a diplomatic minister. **3** the act of sending forth a diplomatic envoy. **4** the mission of a diplomatic envoy. **5** the rank or office of a legate. ORIG C15: from L *lēgātiō,* from *lēgātus* LEGATE

legato (lɪ'gɑːtəʊ) *Music.* ◆ *adj, adv* **1** to be performed smoothly and connectedly. ◆ *n, pl* **legatos. 2a** a style of playing with no perceptible gaps between notes. **2b** (*as modifier*): *a legato passage.* ORIG C19: from It., lit.: bound

leg before wicket *n Cricket.* a manner of dismissal on the grounds that a batsman has been struck on the leg by a bowled ball that otherwise would have hit the wicket. Abbrev.: **lbw.**

leg break *n Cricket.* a bowled ball that spins from leg to off on pitching.

legend ('lɛdʒənd) *n* **1** a popular story handed down from earlier times whose truth has not been ascertained. **2** a group of such stories: *the Arthurian legend.* **3** a modern story that has the characteristics of a traditional tale. **4** a person whose fame or notoriety makes him or her a source of exaggerated or romanticized tales. **5** an inscription or title, as on a coin or beneath a coat of arms. **6** explanatory matter accompanying a table, map, chart, etc. ORIG C14 (in the sense: a saint's life): from Med. L *legenda* passages to be read, from L *legere* to read

legendary ('lɛdʒəndərɪ, -drɪ) *adj* **1** of or relating to legend. **2** celebrated or described in a legend or legends. **3** very famous or notorious.

Legendre ★ (*French* ləʒɑ̃drə) *n* **Adrien Marie** (adriɛ̃ mari). 1752–1833, French mathematician, noted for his work on the theory of numbers, the theory of elliptical functions, and the method of least squares.

Léger ★ (*French* leʒe) *n* **Fernand** (fɛrnɑ̃). 1881–1955, French cubist painter, influenced by industrial technology.

legerdemain (ˌlɛdʒədə'meɪn) *n* **1** another name for **sleight of hand. 2** cunning deception or trickery. ORIG C15: from OF: light of hand

leger line ('lɛdʒə) *n* a variant spelling of **ledger line.**

legged ('lɛgɪd, lɛgd) *adj* **a** having a leg or legs. **b** (*in combination*): *three-legged; long-legged.*

leggiero (lɛdʒ'ɛərəʊ) *adj, adv Music.* to be performed lightly and nimbly. ORIG It.

leggings ('lɛgɪŋz) *pl n* **1** an extra outer covering for the lower legs. **2** children's closefitting trousers, usually with a strap under the instep, worn for warmth in winter. **3** a fashion garment for women consiting of closefitting trousers.

leggy ('lɛgɪ) *adj* **leggier, leggiest. 1** having unusually long legs. **2** (of a woman) having long and shapely legs. **3** (of a plant) having an unusually long and weak stem.
▸ '**legginess** *n*

leghorn ('lɛgˌhɔːn) *n* **1** a type of Italian wheat straw that is woven into hats. **2** any hat made from this straw. ORIG C19: after LEGHORN (Livorno)

Leghorn ★ *n* **1** ('lɛgˌhɔːn). the English name for **Livorno. 2** (lɛ'gɔːn). a breed of domestic fowl.

legible ('lɛdʒəbᵊl) *adj* (of handwriting, print, etc.) able to be read or deciphered. ORIG C14: from LL *legibilis,* from L *legere* to read
▸ ˌ**legi'bility** *n* ▸ '**legibly** *adv*

legion ('liːdʒən) *n* **1** a unit in the ancient Roman army of infantry with supporting cavalry of three to six thousand men. **2** any large military force: *the French Foreign Legion.* **3** (*usually cap.*) an association of ex-servicemen: *the British Legion.* **4** (*often pl*) any very large number. ◆ *adj* **5** (*usually postpositive*) very numerous. ORIG C13: from OF, from L *legio,* from *legere* to choose

legionary ('liːdʒənərɪ) *adj* **1** of a legion. ◆ *n, pl* **legionaries. 2** a soldier belonging to a legion.

legionnaire (ˌliːdʒə'nɛə) *n* (*often cap.*) a member of certain military forces or associations.

legionnaire's *or* **legionnaires' disease** *n* a serious, sometimes fatal, infection, caused by a bacterium (**legionella**), which has symptoms similar to those of pneumonia. ORIG C20: after the outbreak at a meeting of the American Legion in Philadelphia in 1976

legislate ('lɛdʒɪsˌleɪt) *vb* **legislates, legislating, legislated. 1** (*intr*) to make or pass laws. **2** (*tr*) to bring into effect by legislation. ORIG C18: back formation from LEGISLATOR

legislation (ˌlɛdʒɪs'leɪʃən) *n* **1** the act or process of making laws. **2** the laws so made.

legislative ('lɛdʒɪslətɪv) *adj* **1** of or relating to legislation. **2** having the power or function of legislating: *a legislative assembly.* **3** of or relating to a legislature.
▸ **'legislatively** *adv*

legislative assembly *n* (*often caps.*) **1** the bicameral legislature in 28 states of the US. **2** the chamber of the bicameral state legislatures in several Commonwealth countries, such as Australia. **3** the unicameral legislature in most Canadian provinces. **4** any assembly with legislative powers.

legislative council *n* (*often caps.*) **1** the upper chamber of certain bicameral legislatures, such as those of the Indian and Australian states (except Queensland). **2** the unicameral legislature of certain colonies or dependent territories. **3** (in the US) a committee of members of both chambers of a state legislature that discusses problems, constructs a legislative programme, etc.

legislator ('lɛdʒɪsˌleɪtə) *n* **1** a person concerned with the making of laws. **2** a member of a legislature. ORIG C17: from L *lēgis lātor,* from *lēx* law + *lātor* from *lātus,* p.p. of *ferre* to bring

legislature ('lɛdʒɪsˌleɪtʃə) *n* a body of persons vested with power to make and repeal laws.

legit (lɪ'dʒɪt) *Sl.* ◆ *adj* **1** short for **legitimate.** ◆ *n* **2** legitimate drama.

legitimate *adj* (lɪ'dʒɪtɪmɪt). **1** born in lawful wedlock. **2** conforming to established standards of usage, behaviour, etc. **3** based on correct or acceptable principles of reasoning. **4** authorized by or in accordance with law. **5** of, relating to, or ruling by hereditary right: *a legitimate monarch.* **6** of or relating to a body of famous long-established plays as distinct from films, television, vaudeville, etc. ◆ *vb* (lɪ'dʒɪtɪˌmeɪt), **legitimates, legitimating, legitimated. 7** (*tr*) to make, pronounce, or show to be legitimate. ORIG C15: from Med. L *lēgitimātus* made legal, from *lēx* law
▸ **le'gitimacy** *n* ▸ **le'gitimately** *adv* ▸ **leˌgiti'mation** *n*

legitimist (lɪ'dʒɪtɪmɪst) *n* a monarchist who supports the rule of a legitimate dynasty or of its senior branch.
▸ **le'gitimism** *n*

legitimize, legitimise (lɪ'dʒɪtɪˌmaɪz) *or* **legitimatize, legitimatise** (lɪ'dʒɪtɪməˌtaɪz) *vb* **legitimizes, legitimizing, legitimized; legitimises, legitimising, legitimised** *or* **legitimatizes, legitimatizing, legitimatized; legitimatises, legitimatising, legitimatised.** (*tr*) to make legitimate; legalize.
▸ **leˌgitimi'zation, leˌgitimi'sation** *or* **leˌgitimatiˌzation, leˌgitimati'sation** *n*

legless ('lɛglɪs) *adj* **1** without legs. **2** *Inf.* very drunk.

Legnica ★ (*Polish* lɛg'nitsa) *n* an industrial town in SW Poland. Pop.: 107 800 (1995 est.). German name: **Liegnitz.**

Lego ('lɛgəʊ) *n Trademark.* a construction toy consisting of plastic bricks and other components that fit together. ORIG C20: from Danish *leg godt* play well

leg-of-mutton *or* **leg-o'-mutton** *n* (*modifier*) (of a sail, sleeve, etc.) tapering sharply.

leg-pull *n Brit. inf.* a practical joke or mild deception.

legroom ('lɛgˌruːm) *n* room to move one's legs comfortably, as in a car.

leg rope *n Austral. & NZ.* a rope used to secure an animal by its hind leg.

leguan ('lɛgʊˌɑːn) *n* a large amphibious S African lizard. ORIG C19: Du., from F *l'iguane* the iguana

legume ('lɛgjuːm, lɪ'gjuːm) *n* **1** the long dry fruit produced by leguminous plants; a pod. **2** any of various table vegetables, esp. beans or peas. **3** any leguminous plant. ORIG C17: from F *légume,* from L *legūmen* bean, from *legere* to pick (a crop)

leguminous (lɪ'gjuːmɪnəs) *adj* of, relating to, or belonging to any family of flowering plants having pods (or legumes) as fruits and root nodules enabling storage of nitrogen-rich material. ORIG C17: from L *legūmen;* see LEGUME

legwarmer ('lɛgˌwɔːmə) *n* one of a pair of garments resembling stockings without feet, often worn over jeans, tights, etc., or during exercise.

legwork ('lɛgˌwɜːk) *n Inf.* work that involves travelling on foot or as if on foot.

Lehár ★ ('leɪhɑː, lɪ'hɑː) *n* **Franz** (frants). 1870–1948, Hungarian composer of operettas, esp. *The Merry Widow* (1905).

Le Havre ★ (lə 'hɑːvrə; *French* lə ɑvrə) *n* a port in N France, on the English Channel at the mouth of the River Seine: transatlantic trade; oil refining. Pop.: 197 219 (1990).

Lehmann ★ ('leɪmən) *n* **1 Lilli** ('lɪlɪ). 1848–1929, German soprano. **2 Lotte** ('lɒtə). 1888–1976, US soprano, born in Germany. **3 Rosamond** (**Nina**). 1903–90, British novelist. Her books include *The Weather in the Streets* (1936) and *The Echoing Grove* (1953).

Lehmbruck ★ (*German* 'leːmbrʊk) *n* **Wilhelm** ('vɪlhɛlm). 1881–1919, German sculptor and graphic artist.

lei (leɪ) *n* (in Hawaii) a garland of flowers, worn around the neck. ORIG from Hawaiian

Leibnitz *or* **Leibniz** ★ ('laɪbnɪts) *n* Baron **Gottfried Wilhelm von** ('gɔtfriːt 'vɪlhɛlm fɔn). 1646–1716, German rationalist philosopher and mathematician. His works include *Théodicée* (1710) and *Monadologia* (1714). He devised the calculus, independently of Newton.
▸ **Leib'nitzian** *adj*

Leicester[1] ★ ('lɛstə) *n* **1** a city in central England, on the River Soar: Roman remains and a ruined Norman castle; seat of The University of Leicester (1957) and De Montfort University (1992); light engineering, hosiery, and footwear industries. Pop.: 293 400 (1994 est.). **2** a unitary authority in central England, in Leicestershire. Pop.: 294 800 (1996 est.). Area: 73 sq. km (28 sq. miles). **3** a fairly mild dark orange whole-milk cheese, similar to Cheddar.

Leicester[2] ★ ('lɛstə) *n* **Earl of.** title of *Robert Dudley.* ?1532–88, English courtier; favourite of Elizabeth I. He led an unsuccessful expedition to the Netherlands (1585–87).

Leicestershire ★ ('lɛstəˌʃɪə, -ʃə) *n* a county of central England, formerly (1974–97) including Rutland; in 1997 Rutland and Leicester city became independent unitary authorities; largely agricultural. Administrative centre: Leicester. Pop. (excluding Rutland and Leicester city): 597 400 (1996 est.). Area (excluding Rutland and Leicester city): 2084 sq. km (806 sq. miles). Shortened form: **Leicester.** Abbrev.: **Leics.**

Leichhardt ★ ('laɪkˌhɑːt; *German* 'laiçhart) *n* **Friedrich Wilhelm Ludwig** ('friːdrɪç 'vɪlhɛlm 'luːtvɪç). 1813–48, Australian explorer, born in Prussia. He disappeared during an attempt to cross Australia from East to West.

Leics *abbrev. for* Leicestershire.

Leiden *or* **Leyden** ★ ('laɪdᵊn; *Dutch* 'lɛidə) *n* a city in the W Netherlands, in South Holland province: residence of the Pilgrim Fathers for 11 years before they sailed for America in 1620; university (1575). Pop.: 115 473 (1995 est.).

Leif Ericson ★ ('liːf 'ɛrɪksən) *n* See **Ericson.**

Leigh[1] ★ (liː) *n* a town in NW England, in Wigan, in Greater Manchester: engineering industries. Pop.: 43 150 (1991).

Leigh[2] ★ (liː) *n* **1 Mike.** born 1943, British film director: his films include *Secrets and Lies* (1996) and *Topsy-Turvey* (2000). **2 Vivien,** real name *Vivian Hartley.* 1913–67, British stage and film actress. Her films include *Gone with the Wind* (1939) and *A Streetcar Named Desire* (1951).

Leighton ★ ('leɪtᵊn) *n* **Frederic,** 1st Baron Leighton of Stretton. 1830–96, British painter and sculptor of classical subjects: president of the Royal Academy (1878).

Leinster ★ ('lɛnstə) *n* a province of E and SE Republic of Ireland: it consists of the counties of Carlow, Dublin, Kildare, Kilkenny, Laois, Longford, Louth, Meath, Offaly, Westmeath, Wexford, and Wicklow. Pop.: 1 922 000 (1996). Area: 19 632 sq. km (7580 sq. miles).

Leipzig ★ ('laɪpsɪg; *German* 'laiptsɪç) *n* a city in E central Germany, in Saxony: famous fairs, begun about 1170; publishing and music centre; university (1409); scene of a decisive defeat for Napoleon Bonaparte in 1813. Pop.: 470 778 (1996 est.).

Leiria ★ (*Portuguese* lei'riə) *n* a city in central Portugal: site of the first printing press in Portugal (1466). Pop.: 96 583 (1981).

leishmaniasis (ˌliːʃmə'naɪəsɪs) *or* **leishmaniosis** (liːʃˌmeɪnɪ'əʊsɪs, -ˌmæn-) *n* any disease, such as kala-azar, caused by protozoa of the genus *Leishmania*. ORIG C20: NL, after Sir W. B. *Leishman* (1865–1926), Scot. bacteriologist

leister ('liːstə) *n* **1** a spear with three or more prongs for spearing fish, esp. salmon. ◆ *vb* **2** (*tr*) to spear (a fish) with a leister. ORIG C16: from Scand.

leisure ('lɛʒə) *n* **1a** time or opportunity for ease, relaxation, etc. **1b** (*as modifier*): *leisure activities*. **2** ease or leisureliness. **3 at leisure. 3a** having free time. **3b** not occupied or engaged. **3c** without hurrying. **4 at one's leisure.** when one has free time. ORIG C14: from OF *leisir;* ult. from L *licēre* to be allowed
▸ **'leisured** *adj*

leisure centre *n* a building designed to provide such leisure facilities as a library, sports hall, café, and rooms for meetings.

leisurely ('lɛʒəlɪ) *adj* **1** unhurried; relaxed. ◆ *adv* **2** without haste; in a relaxed way.
▸ **'leisureliness** *n*

Leith ★ (liːθ) *n* a port in SE Scotland, on the Firth of Forth: part of Edinburgh since 1920.

leitmotif *or* **leitmotiv** ('laɪtməʊˌtiːf) *n* **1** *Music.* a recurring short melodic phrase used, esp. in Wagnerian music dramas, to suggest a character, thing, etc. **2** an often repeated image or theme in a literary work. ORIG C19: from G: leading motif

Leitrim ★ ('liːtrɪm) *n* a county of north Republic of Ireland in Connacht province, on Donegal Bay: agricultural. County town: Carrick-on-Shannon. Pop.: 25 000 (1996). Area: 1525 sq. km (589 sq. miles).

Leix ★ (liːʃ) *n* another name for **Laois.**

Leizhou ('leɪ'dʒəʊ) *or* **Luichow Peninsula** ★ *n* a peninsula of SE China, in SW Guangdong province, separated from Hainan Island by Hainan Strait.

lek (lɛk) *n* a small area in which birds of certain species, notably the black grouse, gather for sexual display and courtship. ORIG C19: ?from dialect *lake* (vb) from OE *lácan* to frolic, fight, or ?from Swedish *leka* to play

lekker ('lɛkə) *adj S. African sl.* **1** pleasing, enjoyable, or likeable. **2** tasty. ORIG from Afrik., from Du.

Lely ★ ('liːlɪ) *n* Sir **Peter,** Dutch name *Pieter van der Faes.* 1618–80, Dutch portrait painter in England.

LEM (lɛm) *n acronym for* lunar excursion module.

Lemaître ★ (*French* ləmɛtrə) *n* Abbé **Georges (Édouard)** (ʒɔrʒ). 1894–1966, Belgian astronomer and priest, who first proposed the big-bang theory of the universe (1927).

Léman ★ (lemɑ̃) *n* **Lac.** the French name for (Lake) **Geneva.**

Le Mans ★ (*French* lə mɑ̃) *n* a city in NW France: scene of the first experiments in motoring and flying; annual motor race. Pop.: 148 465 (1990).

Lemberg ★ ('lɛmbɛrk) *n* the German name for **Lviv.**

lemma ('lɛmə) *n, pl* **lemmas** *or* **lemmata** (-mətə). **1** a subsidiary proposition, assumed to be valid, that is used in the proof of another proposition. **2** an argument or theme, esp. when used as the subject or title of a composition. **3** *Linguistics.* a word considered as its citation form together with all the inflected forms. ORIG C16 (meaning: proposition), C17 (meaning: title, theme): via L from Gk: premise, from *lambanein* to take (for granted)

lemming ('lɛmɪŋ) *n* **1** any of various volelike rodents of northern and arctic regions of Europe, Asia, and North America. **2** a member of any group following an unthinking course towards destruction. ORIG C17: from Norwegian
▸ **'lemming-ˌlike** *adj*

Lemnos ★ ('lɛmnɒs) *n* a Greek island in the N Aegean Sea: famous for its medicinal earth (**Lemnian seal**). Chief town: Kastron. Pop.: 16 000 (latest est.). Area: 477 sq. km (184 sq. miles). Modern Greek name: **Límnos.**
▸ **Lemnian** ('lɛmnɪən) *adj, n*

lemon ('lɛmən) *n* **1** a small Asian evergreen tree widely cultivated in warm and tropical regions for its edible fruits. Related adjs.: **citric, citrine, citrous. 2a** the yellow oval fruit of this tree, having juicy acidic flesh. **2b** (*as modifier*): *a lemon jelly.* **3** Also called: **lemon yellow. 3a** a greenish-yellow or pale yellow colour. **3b** (*as adj*): *lemon wallpaper.* **4** a distinctive tart flavour made from or in imitation of the lemon. **5** *Sl.* a person or thing considered to be useless or defective. ORIG C14: from Med. L *lemōn-,* from Ar. *laymūn*
▸ **'lemony** *adj*

lemonade (ˌlɛmə'neɪd) *n* a drink made from lemon juice, sugar, and water or from carbonated water, citric acid, etc.

lemon balm *n* the full name of **balm.**

lemon cheese *or* **curd** *n* a soft spread made from lemons, sugar, eggs, and butter.

lemon grass *n* a perennial grass with a large flower spike: used in cooking and grown in tropical regions as the source of an aromatic oil (**lemon grass oil**).

lemon sole *n* a European flatfish with a variegated brown body: highly valued as a food fish.

lemon squash *n Brit.* a drink made from a sweetened lemon concentrate and water.

lemur ('liːmə) *n* **1** any of a family of Madagascan prosimian primates such as the ring-tailed lemur. They are typically arboreal, having foxy faces and long tails. **2** any similar or closely related animal, such as a loris or indris. ORIG C18: NL, adapted from L *lemurēs* ghosts; so named for its ghost-like face and nocturnal habits
▸ **lemuroid** ('lɛmjuˌrɔɪd) *n, adj*

Lena ★ ('liːnə; *Russian* 'ljɛnə) *n* a river in Russia, rising in S Siberia and flowing generally north through the Sakha Republic to the Laptev Sea by an extensive delta: the longest river in Russia. Length: 4271 km (2653 miles).

lend (lɛnd) *vb* **lends, lending, lent. 1** (*tr*) to permit the use of (something) with the expectation of its return. **2** to provide (money) temporarily, often at interest. **3** (*intr*) to provide loans, esp. as a profession. **4** (*tr*) to impart or contribute (something, esp. some abstract quality): *her presence lent beauty.* **5 lend an ear.** to listen. **6 lend oneself** *or* **itself.** to possess the right characteristics or qualities for: *the novel lends itself to serialization.* ORIG C15 *lende* (orig. the past tense), from OE *lǣnan,* from *lǣn* loan
▸ **'lender** *n*

lending library *n* **1** Also called (esp. US): **circulating library.** the department of a public library providing books for use outside the building. **2** a small commercial library.

Lendl ★ ('lɛndᵊl) *n* **Ivan** (iː'væn, -'vɑːn). born 1960, Czech tennis player; US Open champion (1985–87).

lend-lease *n* (during World War II) the system organized by the US in 1941 by which equipment and services were provided for countries fighting Germany.

Lenglen ★ (*French* lɑ̃glɑ̃) *n* **Suzanne** (syzan). 1899–1938, French tennis player: Wimbledon champion (1919-25).

length (lɛŋkθ, lɛŋθ) *n* **1** the linear extent or measurement of something from end to end, usually being the longest dimension. **2** the extent of something from beginning to end, measured in some more or less regular units or intervals: *the book was 600 pages in length.* **3** a specified distance, esp. between two positions: *the length of a race.* **4** a period of time, as between specified limits or moments. **5** a piece or section of something narrow and long: *a length of tubing.* **6** the quality, state, or fact of being long rather than short. **7** (*usually pl*) the amount of trouble taken in pursuing or achieving something (esp. in **to great lengths**). **8** (*often pl*) the extreme or limit of action (esp. in **to any length(s)**). **9** *Prosody, phonetics.* the metrical quantity or temporal duration of a vowel or syllable. **10** the distance from one end of a rectangular swimming bath to the other. **11 at length. 11a** in depth; fully. **11b** eventually. **11c** interminably. ORIG OE *lengthu*

★ people and places

lengthen (ˈlɛŋkθən, ˈlɛŋθən) *vb* to make or become longer.
▸ ˈ**lengthener** *n*

lengthways (ˈlɛŋkθˌweɪz, ˈlɛŋθ-) *or* **lengthwise** *adv, adj* in, according to, or along the direction of length.

lengthy (ˈlɛŋkθɪ, ˈlɛŋθɪ) *adj* **lengthier, lengthiest.** of relatively great or tiresome extent or duration.
▸ ˈ**lengthily** *adv* ▸ ˈ**lengthiness** *n*

lenient (ˈliːnɪənt) *adj* showing or characterized by mercy or tolerance. ORIG C17: from L *lēnīre* to soothe, from *lēnis* soft
▸ ˈ**leniency** *or* ˈ**lenience** *n* ▸ ˈ**leniently** *adv*

Lenin ★ (ˈlɛnɪn) *n* **Vladimir Ilyich** (vlaˈdimir iljˈjitʃ), original surname *Ulyanov.* 1870–1924, Russian statesman; first premier of the Soviet Union. He formed the Bolsheviks (1903) and led them in the October Revolution (1917), which established the Soviet Government. He adopted the New Economic Policy (1921), formed the Comintern (1919), and was the originator of the doctrine of Marxism-Leninism. After the Soviet Union broke up in 1991, many statues of Lenin were demolished.

Leninabad ★ (*Russian* lɪninaˈbat) *n* the former name (1936–91) of **Khojent.**

Leninakan ★ (*Russian* lɪninaˈkan) *n* the former name (1925–91) of **Kumayri.**

Leningrad ★ (ˈlɛnɪnˌgræd; *Russian* lɪninˈgrat) *n* the former name (1924–91) of **Saint Petersburg.**

Leninism (ˈlɛnɪˌnɪzəm) *n* the political and economic theories of Lenin.
▸ ˈ**Leninist** *n, adj*

Lenin Peak ★ *n* a mountain in NE Tajikistan; the highest peak in the Trans Alai Range and the second highest in the former Soviet Union. Height: 7134 m (23 406 ft).

lenitive (ˈlɛnɪtɪv) *adj* **1** soothing or alleviating pain or distress. ◆ *n* **2** a lenitive drug. ORIG C16: from Med. L *lēnītīvus,* from L *lēnīre* to soothe

lenity (ˈlɛnɪtɪ) *n, pl* **lenities.** the state or quality of being lenient. ORIG C16: from L *lēnitās* gentleness, from *lēnis* soft

Lennon ★ (ˈlɛnən) *n* **John** (**Ono**), original name *John Winston Lennon.* 1940–80, British songwriter, singer, and guitarist: member of the Beatles (1962–70). Subsequent recordings, many in collaboration with his wife Yoko Ono, include *Imagine* (1971) and *Double Fantasy* (1980). He was murdered by a demented fan.

leno (ˈliːnəʊ) *n, pl* **lenos. 1** (in textiles) a weave in which the warp yarns are twisted together in pairs between the weft or filling yarns. **2** a fabric of this weave. ORIG C19: prob. from F *linon* lawn, from *lin* flax, from L *līnum*

Leno ★ (ˈliːnəʊ) *n* **Dan**, original name *George Galvin.* 1860–1904, British music-hall entertainer, noted esp. for his pantomime performances: he died insane.

lens (lɛnz) *n* **1** a piece of glass or other transparent material, used to converge or diverge transmitted light and form optical images. **2** Also called: **compound lens.** a combination of such lenses for forming images or concentrating a beam of light. **3** a device that diverges or converges a beam of electromagnetic radiation, sound, or particles. **4** *Anat.* See **crystalline lens.** ORIG C17: from L *lēns* lentil, referring to the similarity of a lens to the shape of a lentil

lent (lɛnt) *vb* the past tense and past participle of **lend.**

Lent (lɛnt) *n Christianity.* the period of forty weekdays lasting from Ash Wednesday to Holy Saturday, observed as a time of penance and fasting commemorating Jesus' fasting in the wilderness. ORIG OE *lencten, lengten* spring, lit.: lengthening (of hours of daylight)

lentamente (ˌlɛntəˈmɛnteɪ) *adv Music.* slowly. ORIG It.

lenten (ˈlɛntən) *adj* **1** (*often cap.*) of or relating to Lent. **2** *Arch. or literary.* spare, plain, or meagre: *lenten fare.*

lenticel (ˈlɛntɪˌsɛl) *n* any of numerous pores in the stem of a woody plant allowing exchange of gases between the plant and the exterior. ORIG C19: from NL *lenticella,* from L *lenticula* dim. of *lēns* lentil

lenticular (lɛnˈtɪkjʊlə) *adj* **1** shaped like a biconvex lens. **2** of or concerned with a lens or lenses. **3** shaped like a lentil seed. ORIG C17: from L *lenticulāris* like a LENTIL

lentil (ˈlɛntɪl) *n* **1** a small annual leguminous plant of the Mediterranean region and W Asia, having edible convex seeds. **2** any of the seeds of this plant, which are cooked and eaten in soups, etc. ORIG C13: from OF *lentille,* from L *lenticula,* dim. of *lēns* lentil

lentivirus (ˈlɛntɪˌvaɪrəs) *n* another name for **slow virus.** ORIG C20: NL, from L *lentus* slow + VIRUS

lent lily *n* another name for the **daffodil.**

lento (ˈlɛntəʊ) *Music.* ◆ *adj, adv* **1** to be performed slowly. ◆ *n, pl* **lentos. 2** a movement or passage performed in this way. ORIG C18: It., from L *lentus* slow

Lent term *n* the spring term at Cambridge University and some other educational establishments.

Lenya ★ (ˈleɪnjə) *n* **Lotte** (ˈlɒtə; *German* ˈlɔtə), original name *Caroline Blamauer.* 1900–81, Austrian singer and actress, associated esp. with the songs of her husband Kurt Weill.

Leo (ˈliːəʊ) *n, Latin genitive* **Leonis** (liːˈəʊnɪs). **1** *Astron.* a zodiacal constellation in the N hemisphere, lying between Cancer and Virgo. **2** *Astrol.* Also called: the **Lion.** the fifth sign of the zodiac. The sun is in this sign between about July 23 and Aug. 22.

Leo I ★ (ˈliːəʊ) *n* **Saint,** known as *Leo the Great.* ?390–461 A.D., pope (440–461). He persuaded Attila not to attack Rome (452). Feast day: Nov. 10 or Feb. 18.

Leo III ★ *n* **Saint.** ?750–816 A.D., pope (795–816). He crowned Charlemagne emperor of the Romans (800). Feast day: June 12.

Leo X ★ *n* original name *Giovanni de' Medici.* 1475–1521, pope (1513–21): noted for his patronage of Renaissance art; excommunicated Luther (1521).

Leo XIII ★ *n* original name *Gioacchino Pecci.* 1810–1903, pope (1878–1903). His encyclicals include *Rerum novarum* (1891) on social problems.

Leoben ★ (*German* leˈoːbən) *n* a city in E central Austria, in Styria on the Mur River: lignite mining. Pop.: 28 504 (1991).

León ★ (*Spanish* leˈɔn) *n* **1** a region and former kingdom of NW Spain, which united with Castile in 1230. **2** a city of NW Spain: capital of the kingdom of León (10th century). Pop.: 147 311 (1994 est.). **3** a city in central Mexico, in W Guanajuato state: commercial centre of a rich agricultural region. Pop.: 867 920 (1990). Official name **León de los Aldamas** (de los ˈaldamas). **4** a city in W Nicaragua: one of the oldest towns of Central America, founded in 1524; capital of Nicaragua until 1855; university (1812). Pop.: 171 375 (1994 est.).

Leonard ★ (ˈlɛnəd) *n* **Sugar Ray**, real name *Ray Charles Leonard.* born 1956, US boxer: the first man to have won world titles at five officially recognized weights.

Leonardo da Vinci ★ (ˌliːəˈnɑːdəʊ də ˈvɪntʃɪ) *n* 1452–1519, Italian painter, sculptor, architect, and engineer: the most versatile talent of the Italian Renaissance. His paintings include the *Mona Lisa* (or *La Gioconda,* 1503) and the *Last Supper* (?1495–97). His numerous drawings ranged over biology, physiology, hydraulics, and aeronautics. He foresaw the invention of aircraft and submarines.
▸ **Leonardesque** (ˌliːənɑːˈdɛsk) *adj*

Leonardo of Pisa ★ *n* See (Leonardo) **Fibonacci.**

Leoncavallo ★ (*Italian* leoŋkaˈvallo) *n* **Ruggiero** (rudˈdʒɛːro). 1858–1919, Italian composer of operas, notably *I Pagliacci* (1892).

Leonid (ˈliːənɪd) *n, pl* **Leonids** *or* **Leonides** (lɪˈɒnɪˌdiːz). any member of a meteor shower appearing to radiate from the constellation Leo. ORIG C19: from NL *Leōnidēs,* from *leō* lion

Leonidas ★ (lɪˈɒnɪˌdæs) *n* died 480 B.C., king of Sparta (?490–480), hero of the Battle of Thermopylae, in which he was killed by the Persians under Xerxes.

leonine (ˈliːəˌnaɪn) *adj* of, characteristic of, or resembling a lion. ORIG C14: from L *leōnīnus,* from *leō* lion

Leonine (ˈliːəˌnaɪn) *adj* **1** connected with one of the popes called Leo: an epithet applied to a district of Rome fortified by Pope Leo IV (**Leonine City**). **2 Leonine verse. 2a** a type of medieval hexameter or elegiac verse having internal rhyme. **2b** a type of English verse with internal rhyme.

leopard ('lɛpəd) *n* **1** Also called: **panther.** a large feline mammal of forests of Africa and Asia, usually having a tawny yellow coat with black rosette-like spots. **2** any of several similar felines, such as the snow leopard and cheetah. **3** *Heraldry.* a stylized leopard, painted as a lion with the face turned towards the front. ORIG C13: from OF *lepart,* from LL, from LGk *leópardos,* from *leōn* lion + *pardos* PARD (the leopard was thought to be the result of cross-breeding)
▸ **'leopardess** *fem n*

Leopardi ★ (*Italian* leo'pardi) *n* Count **Giacomo** ('dʒaːkomo). 1798–1837, Italian poet and philosopher, noted esp. for his lyrics, collected in *I Canti* (1831).

Leopold I ★ ('lɪəˌpəʊld) *n* **1** 1640–1705, Holy Roman Emperor (1658–1705). His reign was marked by wars with Louis XIV of France and with the Turks. **2** 1790–1865, first king of the Belgians (1831–65).

Leopold II ★ *n* **1** 1747–92, Holy Roman Emperor (1790–92). He formed an alliance with Prussia against France (1792) after the downfall of his brother-in-law Louis XVI. **2** 1835–1909, king of the Belgians (1865–1909); son of Leopold I. He became the first sovereign of the Congo Free State (1885).

Leopold III ★ *n* 1901–83, king of the Belgians (1934–51); son of Albert I. His surrender to the Nazis (1940) forced his abdication in favour of his son, Baudouin.

Léopoldville ★ ('lɪəpəʊldˌvɪl; *French* leɔpɔlvil) *n* the former name (until 1966) of **Kinshasa.**

leotard ('lɪəˌtɑːd) *n* **1** a tight-fitting garment covering the body from the shoulders down to the thighs and worn by acrobats, ballet dancers, etc. **2** (*pl*) *US & Canad.* another name for **tights** (sense 1b). ORIG C19: after Jules *Léotard,* F acrobat

Lepanto ★ *n* **1** (*Italian* 'lɛːpanto) a port in W Greece, between the Gulfs of Corinth and Patras: scene of a naval battle (1571) in which the Turkish fleet was defeated by the fleets of the Holy League. Pop.: 8200 (latest est.). Greek name: **Návpaktos. 2** (lɪ'pæntəʊ). **Gulf of.** another name for the (Gulf of) **Corinth.**

Lepaya ★ (lɪ'pɑːjə) *n* a variant spelling of **Liepāja.**

leper ('lɛpə) *n* **1** a person who has leprosy. **2** a person who is ignored or despised. ORIG C14: via LL from Gk *lepra,* n. use of *lepros* scaly, from *lepein* to peel

lepido- *or before a vowel* **lepid-** *combining form.* scale or scaly: *lepidopterous.* ORIG from Gk *lepis* scale; see LEPER

lepidopteran (ˌlɛpɪ'dɒptərən) *n, pl* **lepidopterans** *or* **lepidoptera** (-tərə). **1** any of a large order of insects typically having two pairs of wings covered with fragile scales: comprises the butterflies and moths. ◆ *adj also* **lepidopterous. 2** of, relating to, or belonging to this order. ORIG C19: from NL, from LEPIDO- + Gk *pteron* wing

lepidopterist (ˌlɛpɪ'dɒptərɪst) *n* a person who studies or collects moths and butterflies.

Lepidus ★ ('lɛpɪdəs) *n* **Marcus Aemilius** ('mɑːkəs iː'mɪlɪəs). died ?13 B.C., Roman statesman: formed the Second Triumvirate with Octavian (later Augustus) and Mark Antony.

Lepontine Alps ★ (lɪ'pɒntaɪn) *pl n* a range of the S central Alps, in S Switzerland and N Italy. Highest peak: Monte Leone, 3553 m (11 657 ft).

leprechaun ('lɛprəˌkɔːn) *n* (in Irish folklore) a mischievous elf, often believed to have a treasure hoard. ORIG C17: from Irish Gaelic *leipreachān,* from MIrish *lūchorpān,* from *lū* small + *corp* body, from L *corpus* body

leprosy ('lɛprəsɪ) *n Pathol.* a chronic infectious disease occurring mainly in tropical and subtropical regions, characterized by the formation of painful inflamed nodules beneath the skin and disfigurement and wasting of affected parts. ORIG C16: from LEPROUS + -Y[3]

leprous ('lɛprəs) *adj* **1** having leprosy. **2** relating to or resembling leprosy. ORIG C13: from OF, from LL *leprosus,* from *lepra* LEPER

-lepsy *or sometimes* **-lepsia** *n combining form.* indicating a seizure: *catalepsy.* ORIG from NL *-lepsia,* from Gk, from *lēpsis* a seizure, from *lambanein* to seize
▸ **-leptic** *adj combining form.*

★ people and places

leptodactylous (ˌlɛptəʊ'dæktɪləs) *adj Zool.* having slender digits.

lepton[1] ('lɛptɒn) *n, pl* **lepta** (-tə). **1** a Greek monetary unit worth one hundredth of a drachma. **2** a small coin of ancient Greece. ORIG from Gk *lepton* (*nomisma*) small (coin)

lepton[2] ('lɛptɒn) *n Physics.* any of a group of elementary particles and their antiparticles, such as an electron, muon, or neutrino, that participate in electromagnetic and weak interactions. ORIG C20: from Gk *leptos* thin, from *lepein* to peel + -ON

lepton number *n Physics.* a quantum number describing the behaviour of elementary particles, equal to the number of leptons present minus the number of antileptons. It is thought to be conserved in all processes.

leptospirosis (ˌlɛptəʊspaɪ'rəʊsɪs) *n* any of several infectious diseases caused by bacteria, transmitted to man by animals and characterized by jaundice, meningitis, and kidney failure. Also called: **Weil's disease.** ORIG C20: from NL *Leptospira* (from Gk *leptos* thin + *speira* coil + -OSIS)

Lérida ★ (*Spanish* 'leriða) *n* a city in NE Spain, in Catalonia: commercial centre of an agricultural region. Pop.: 114 234 (1994 est.).

Lermontov ★ (*Russian* 'ljɛrməntəf) *n* **Mikhail Yurievich** (mixa'il 'jurjɪvitʃ). 1814–41, Russian novelist and poet: noted for the novel *A Hero of Our Time* (1840).

Lerner ★ ('lɜːnə) *n* **Alan Jay.** 1914–86, US songwriter and librettist. With Frederick Loewe he wrote *My Fair Lady* (1956) and *Camelot* (1960), as well as a number of film scripts, including *Gigi* (1958).

Lerwick ★ ('lɜːwɪk) *n* a town in Shetland, administrative centre of the island authority of Shetland, on the island of Mainland: the most northerly town in the British Isles; knitwear, oil refining. Pop.: 7500 (1987 est.).

Le Sage *or* **Lesage** ★ (*French* lə saʒ) *n* **Alain-René** (alɛ̃rəne). 1668–1747, French novelist and dramatist, author of the novel *Gil Blas* (1715–35).

lesbian ('lɛzbɪən) *n* **1** a female homosexual. ◆ *adj* **2** of or characteristic of lesbians. ORIG C19: from the homosexuality attributed to SAPPHO
▸ **'lesbianism** *n*

Lesbos ★ ('lɛzbɒs) *n* an island in the E Aegean, off the NW coast of Turkey: a centre of lyric poetry, led by Alcaeus and Sappho (6th century B.C.); annexed to Greece in 1913. Chief town: Mytilene. Pop.: 105 082 (1991). Area: 1630 sq. km (630 sq. miles). Modern Greek name: **Lésvos.** Former name: **Mytilene.**

Les Cayes ★ (leɪ 'keɪ; *French* le kaj) *n* a port in SW Haiti, on the S Tiburon Peninsula. Pop.: 45 904 (1992). Also called: **Cayes.** Former name: **Aux Cayes.**

lese-majesty ('liːz'mædʒɪstɪ) *n* **1** any of various offences committed against the sovereign power in a state; treason. **2** an attack on authority or position. ORIG C16: from F *lèse majesté,* from L *laesa mājestās* wounded majesty

lesion ('liːʒən) *n* **1** any structural change in a bodily part resulting from injury or disease. **2** an injury or wound. ORIG C15: via OF from LL *laesiō* injury, from L *laedere* to hurt

Lesotho ★ (lɪ'suːtuː, lə'səʊtəʊ) *n* a kingdom in southern Africa, forming an enclave in the Republic of South Africa: annexed to British Cape Colony in 1871; made a protectorate in 1884; gained independence in 1966; a member of the Commonwealth. It is generally mountainous, with temperate grasslands throughout. Languages: Sesotho and English. Religion: Christian majority. Currency: loti. Capital: Maseru. Pop.: 2 129 000 (1999 est.). Area: 30 344 sq. km (11 716 sq. miles). Former name (1884–1966): **Basutoland.**

less (lɛs) *determiner* **1a** the comparative of **little** (sense 1): *less sugar; less spirit than before.* **1b** (*as pronoun; functioning as sing or pl*): *she has less than she needs; the less you eat, the less you want.* **2** (usually preceded by *no*) lower in rank or importance: *no less a man than the president.* **3 less of.** to a smaller extent or degree: *we see less of John these days; less* *of a success than I'd hoped.* ◆ *adv* **4** the comparative of **little** (sense 10): *she walks less than she should; less quickly; less beautiful.* ◆ *prep* **5** subtracting; minus: *three weeks less a day.* ORIG OE *lǣssa* (adj), *lǣs* (adv, n)

> **USAGE NOTE** *Less* should not be confused with *fewer. Less* refers strictly only to quantity and not to number: *there is less water than before. Fewer* means smaller in number: *there are fewer people than before.*

-less *suffix forming adjectives.* **1** without; lacking: *speechless.* **2** not able to (do something) or not able to be (done, performed, etc.): *countless.* ORIG OE *-lās,* from *lēas* lacking

lessee (lɛ'siː) *n* a person to whom a lease is granted; a tenant under a lease. ORIG C15: via Anglo-F from OF *lessé,* from *lesser* to LEASE

lessen ('lɛsᵊn) *vb* **1** to make or become less. **2** (*tr*) to make little of.

Lesseps ★ ('lɛsəps; *French* lɛsɛps) *n* Vicomte **Ferdinand Marie de** (fɛrdinɑ̃ mari də). 1805–94, French diplomat: directed the construction of the Suez Canal (1859–69) and the unsuccessful first attempt to build the Panama Canal (1881–89).

lesser ('lɛsə) *adj* not as great in quantity, size, or worth.

Lesser Antilles ★ *pl n* **the.** a group of islands in the Caribbean, including the Leeward Islands, the Windward Islands, Barbados, and the Netherlands Antilles. Also called: **Caribbees.**

lesser celandine *n* a Eurasian plant, related to the buttercup, having yellow flowers and heart-shaped leaves.

lesser panda *n* See **panda** (sense 2).

Lesser Sunda Islands ★ *pl n* the former name of **Nusa Tenggara.**

Lessing ★ ('lɛsɪŋ) *n* **1 Doris** (**May**). born 1919, British writer, brought up in Rhodesia: her work includes the five-novel sequence *Children of Violence* (1952–69), *The Golden Notebook* (1962), and a series of science-fiction works (1979–83). **2 Gotthold Ephraim** ('gɔthɔlt 'eːfrˌaɪm). 1729–81, German dramatist and critic. His plays include *Miss Sara Sampson* (1755) and *Nathan der Weise* (1779).

lesson ('lɛsᵊn) *n* **1a** a unit, or single period of instruction in a subject; class: *an hour-long music lesson.* **1b** the content of such a unit. **2** material assigned for individual study. **3** something from which useful knowledge or principles can be learned; example. **4** the principles, knowledge, etc., gained. **5** a reprimand or punishment intended to correct. **6** a portion of Scripture appointed to be read at divine service. ORIG C13: from OF *leçon,* from L *lēctiō,* from *legere* to read

lessor ('lɛsɔː, lɛ'sɔː) *n* a person who grants a lease of property.

lest (lɛst) *conj* (*subordinating; takes a subjunctive vb*) **1** so as to prevent any possibility that: *keep down lest anyone see us.* **2** (*after vbs. or phrases expressing fear, worry, anxiety, etc.*) for fear that; in case: *he was alarmed lest she should find out.* ORIG OE *thē lǣste,* earlier *thȳ lǣs the,* lit.: whereby less that

Lésvos ★ ('lɛzvɔs) *n* transliteration of the Modern Greek name for **Lesbos.**

let¹ (lɛt) *vb* **lets, letting, let.** (*tr;* usually takes an infinitive without *to* or an implied infinitive) **1** to permit; allow: *she lets him roam around.* **2** (*imperative or dependent imperative*) **2a** used as an auxiliary to express a request, proposal, or command, or to convey a warning or threat: *let's get on; just let me catch you here again!* **2b** (in mathematical or philosophical discourse) used as an auxiliary to express an assumption or hypothesis: *let "a" equal "b".* **2c** used as an auxiliary to express resigned acceptance of the inevitable: *let the worst happen.* **3a** to allow the occupation of (accommodation) in return for rent. **3b** to assign (a contract for work). **4** to allow or cause the movement of (something) in a specified direction: *to let air out of a tyre.* **5 let alone.** (*conj*) much less; not to mention: *I can't afford wine, let alone champagne.* **6 let** *or* **leave alone** *or* **be.** refrain from annoying or interfering with: *let the poor cat alone.* **7 let go.** See **go** (sense 45). **8 let loose. 8a** to set free. **8b** *Inf.* to make (a sound or remark) suddenly: *he let loose a hollow laugh.* **8c** *Inf.* to discharge (rounds) from a gun or guns: *they let loose a couple of rounds of ammunition.* ◆ *n* **9** *Brit.* the act of letting property or accommodation. ◆ See also **let down, let off,** etc. ORIG OE *lǣtan* to permit

let² (lɛt) *n* **1** an impediment or obstruction (esp. in **without let or hindrance**). **2** *Tennis, squash, etc.* **2a** a minor infringement or obstruction of the ball, requiring a point to be replayed. **2b** the point so replayed. ◆ *vb* **lets, letting, letted** *or* **let. 3** (*tr*) *Arch.* to hinder; impede. ORIG OE *lettan* to hinder, from *læt* late

-let *suffix forming nouns.* **1** small or lesser: *booklet.* **2** an article of attire or ornament worn on a specified part of the body: *anklet.* ORIG from OF *-elet,* from L *-āle,* from L *-ellus,* dim. suffix

Letchworth ★ ('lɛtʃwəθ, -ˌwɜːθ) *n* a town in SE England, in N Hertfordshire: the first garden city in Great Britain (founded in 1903). Pop.: 31 418 (1991).

let down *vb* (*tr, mainly adv*) **1** (*also prep*) to lower. **2** to fail to fulfil the expectations of (a person); disappoint. **3** to undo, shorten, and resew (the hem) so as to lengthen (a dress, skirt, etc.). **4** to untie (long hair that is bound up) and allow to fall loose. **5** to deflate: *to let down a tyre.* ◆ *n* **letdown. 6** a disappointment.

lethal ('liːθəl) *adj* **1** able to cause or causing death. **2** of or suggestive of death. ORIG C16: from L *lēthālis,* from *lētum* death
▸ **lethality** (liː'θælɪtɪ) *n* ▸ **'lethally** *adv*

lethargy ('lɛθədʒɪ) *n, pl* **lethargies. 1** sluggishness, slowness, or dullness. **2** an abnormal lack of energy. ORIG C14: from LL *lēthargīa,* from Gk *lēthargos* drowsy, from *lēthē* forgetfulness
▸ **lethargic** (lɪ'θɑːdʒɪk) *adj* ▸ **le'thargically** *adv*

Lethbridge ★ ('lɛθbrɪdʒ) *n* a city in Canada, in S Alberta: coal-mining. Pop.: 60 974 (1991).

Lethe ★ ('liːθɪ) *n* **1** *Greek myth.* a river in Hades that caused forgetfulness in those who drank its waters. **2** forgetfulness. ORIG C16: via L from Gk, from *lēthē* oblivion
▸ **Lethean** (lɪ'θiːən) *adj*

Leto ★ ('liːtəʊ) *n* the mother by Zeus of Apollo and Artemis. Roman name: **Latona.**

let off *vb* (*tr, mainly adv*) **1** (*also prep*) to allow to disembark or leave. **2** to explode or fire (a bomb, gun, etc.). **3** (*also prep*) to excuse from (work or other responsibilities): *I'll let you off for a week.* **4** *Inf.* to allow to get away without the expected punishment, work, etc. **5** to let (accommodation) in portions. **6** to release (liquid, air, etc.).

let on *vb* (*adv; when tr, takes a clause as object*) *Inf.* **1** to allow (something, such as a secret) to be known; reveal: *he never let on that he was married.* **2** (*tr*) to cause or encourage to be believed; pretend.

let out *vb* (*adv, mainly tr*) **1** to give vent to; emit: *to let out a howl.* **2** to allow to go or run free; release. **3** (*may take a clause as object*) to reveal (a secret). **4** to make available to tenants, hirers, or contractors. **5** to permit to flow out: *to let air out of the tyres.* **6** to make (a garment) larger, as by unpicking (the seams) and sewing nearer the outer edge. ◆ *n* **let-out. 7** a chance to escape.

let's (lɛts) *contraction of* let us: used to express a suggestion, command, etc., by the speaker to himself and his hearers.

Lett (lɛt) *n* a former name for a **Latvian.**

letter ('lɛtə) *n* **1** any of a set of conventional symbols used in writing or printing a language, each symbol being associated with a group of phonetic values; character of the alphabet. **2** a written or printed communication addressed to a person, company, etc., usually sent by post. **3** (often preceded by *the*) the strict legalistic or pedantic interpretation of the meaning of an agreement, document, etc.; exact wording as distinct from actual intention (esp. in **the letter of the law**). **4 to the letter. 4a** following the literal interpretation or wording exactly. **4b** attending to every detail. ◆ *vb* **5** to write or mark letters on (a sign, etc.), esp. by hand. **6** (*tr*) to set down or print using letters. ORIG C13: from OF *lettre,* from L *littera* letter of the alphabet
▸ **'letterer** *n*

letter bomb *n* an explosive device in an envelope, detonated when the envelope is opened.

letter box *n Chiefly Brit.* **1a** a slot through which letters, etc., are delivered to a building. **1b** a private box into which letters, etc., are delivered. **2** Also: **postbox.** a public box into which letters, etc., are put for collection.

lettered ('lɛtəd) *adj* **1** well educated in literature, the arts, etc. **2** literate. **3** of or characterized by learning or culture. **4** printed or marked with letters.

letterhead ('lɛtəˌhɛd) *n* a sheet of writing paper printed with one's address, name, etc.

lettering ('lɛtərɪŋ) *n* **1** the act, art, or technique of inscribing letters on to something. **2** the letters so inscribed.

letter of credit *n* a letter issued by a bank entitling the bearer to draw funds up to a specified maximum from that bank or its agencies.

letter of intent *n* a letter indicating that the writer has the serious intention of doing something, such as signing a contract, in the circumstances specified. It does not constitute either a promise or a contract.

letter of marque *or* **letters of marque** *n* (formerly) a licence granted by a state to a private citizen to arm a ship and seize merchant vessels of another nation. Also called: **letter of marque and reprisal.**

letter-perfect *adj* another term (esp. US) for **word-perfect.**

letterpress ('lɛtəˌprɛs) *n* **1a** a method of printing in which ink is transferred from raised surfaces to paper by pressure. **1b** matter so printed. **2** text matter as distinct from illustrations.

letters ('lɛtəz) *n* (*functioning as sing or pl*) **1** literary knowledge, ability, or learning: *a man of letters.* **2** literary culture in general. **3** an official title, degree, etc., indicated by an abbreviation: *letters after one's name.*

letters patent *pl n* See **patent** (senses 1, 4).

Lettish ('lɛtɪʃ) *n* another name for **Latvian** (sense 2).

lettuce ('lɛtɪs) *n* **1** any of various plants of the composite family cultivated in many varieties for their large edible leaves. **2** the leaves of any of these varieties, which are eaten in salads. **3** any of various plants that resemble true lettuce, such as lamb's lettuce. ORIG C13: prob. from OF *laitues,* from L *lactūca,* from *lac-* milk, because of its milky juice

let up *vb* (*intr, adv*) **1** to diminish, slacken, or stop. **2** (foll. by *on*) *Inf.* to be less harsh (towards someone). ◆ *n* **let-up. 3** *Inf.* a lessening or abatement.

Leucas ★ ('lu:kəs) *n* a variant spelling of **Leukas.**

Leucippus ★ (lu:'sɪpəs) *n* 5th century B.C. Greek philosopher, who originated the atomic theory of matter, developed by his disciple, Democritus.

leuco-, leuko- *or before a vowel* **leuc-, leuk-** *combining form.* white or lacking colour: *leucocyte; leukaemia.* ORIG from Gk *leukos* white

leucoblast *or esp. US* **leukoblast** ('lu:kəʊˌblæst) *n* an immature leucocyte.

leucocyte *or esp. US* **leukocyte** ('lu:kəˌsaɪt) *n* any of the various large unpigmented cells in the blood of vertebrates. Also called: **white blood cell, white (blood) corpuscle.**
▸ **leucocytic** *or esp. US* **leukocytic** (ˌlu:kə'sɪtɪk) *adj*

leucoma (lu:'kəʊmə) *n Pathol.* a white opaque scar of the cornea.

leucotomy (lu:'kɒtəmɪ) *n, pl* **leucotomies.** the surgical operation of cutting some of the nerve fibres in the frontal lobes of the brain for treating intractable mental disorders.

Leuctra ★ ('lu:ktrə) *n* an ancient town in Greece southwest of Thebes in Boeotia: site of a victory of Thebes over Sparta (371 B.C.), which marked the end of Spartan military supremacy in Greece.

leukaemia *or esp. US* **leukemia** (lu:'ki:mɪə) *n* an acute or chronic disease characterized by a gross proliferation of leucocytes, which crowd into the bone marrow, spleen, lymph nodes, etc., and suppress the blood-forming apparatus. ORIG C19: from LEUCO- + Gk *haima* blood

Leukas *or* **Leucas** ★ ('lu:kəs) *n* another name for **Levkás.**

Leuven ★ ('lø:və) *n* the Flemish name for **Louvain.**

Lev. *Bible. abbrev. for* Leviticus.

levant (lɪ'vænt) *n* a type of leather made from the skins of goats, sheep, or seals, having a pattern of irregular creases. ORIG C19: shortened from *Levant morocco* (type of leather)

Levant ★ (lɪ'vænt) *n* **the.** a former name for the area of the E Mediterranean now occupied by Lebanon, Syria, and Israel. ORIG C15: from OF, from *lever* to raise (referring to the rising of the sun in the east), from L *levāre*
▸ **Levantine** ('lɛvənˌtaɪn) *adj, n*

levanter (lɪ'væntə) *n* (*sometimes cap.*) **1** an easterly wind in the W Mediterranean area. **2** an inhabitant of the Levant.

levator (lɪ'veɪtə, -tɔ:) *n Anat.* any of various muscles that raise a part of the body. ORIG C17: NL, from L *levāre* to raise

levee[1] ('lɛvɪ) *n US.* **1** an embankment alongside a river, produced naturally by sedimentation or constructed by man to prevent flooding. **2** an embankment that surrounds a field that is to be irrigated. **3** a landing place on a river; quay. ORIG C18: from F, from Med. L *levāta* from L *levāre* to raise

levee[2] ('lɛvɪ, 'lɛveɪ) *n* **1** a formal reception held by a sovereign just after rising from bed. **2** (in Britain) a public court reception for men. **3** *Canad.* a reception held on New Year's Day. ORIG C17: from F, var. of *lever* a rising, from L *levāre* to raise

level ('lɛvᵊl) *adj* **1** on a horizontal plane. **2** having a surface of completely equal height. **3** being of the same height as something else. **4** (of quantities to be measured, as in recipes) even with the top of the cup, spoon, etc. **5** equal to or even with (something or someone else). **6** not having or showing inconsistency or irregularities. **7** Also: **level-headed.** even-tempered; steady. **8 one's level best.** the best one can do. ◆ *vb* **levels, levelling, levelled** *or US* **levels, leveling, leveled. 9** (*tr;* sometimes foll. by *off*) to make (a surface) horizontal, level, or even. **10** to make (two or more people or things) equal, as in position or status. **11** (*tr*) to raze to the ground. **12** (*tr*) to knock (a person) down as by a blow. **13** (*tr*) to direct (a gaze, criticism, etc.) emphatically at someone. **14** (*intr;* often foll. by *with*) *Inf.* to be straightforward and frank. **15** (*intr;* foll. by *off* or *out*) to manoeuvre an aircraft into a horizontal flight path after a dive, climb, or glide. **16** (often foll. by *at*) to aim (a weapon) horizontally. ◆ *n* **17** a horizontal datum line or plane. **18** a device, such as a spirit level, for determining whether a surface is horizontal. **19** a surveying instrument used for measuring relative heights of land. **20** position or status in a scale of values. **21** amount or degree of progress; stage. **22** a specified vertical position; altitude. **23** a horizontal line or plane with respect to which measurement of elevation is based: *sea level.* **24** a flat even surface or area of land. **25** *Physics.* the ratio of the magnitude of a physical quantity to an arbitrary magnitude: *sound-pressure level.* **26 on the level.** *Inf.* sincere or genuine. ORIG C14: from OF *livel,* from Vulgar L *lībellum* (unattested), from L *lībella,* dim. of *lībra* scales
▸ **'leveller** *or US* **'leveler** *n* ▸ **'levelly** *adv* ▸ **'levelness** *n*

level crossing *n Brit., Canad., Austral., & NZ.* a point at which a railway and a road cross, esp. one with barriers that close the road when a train is due to pass.

level-headed *adj* even-tempered, balanced, and reliable; steady.
▸ **ˌlevel-'headedly** *adv* ▸ **ˌlevel-'headedness** *n*

level of attainment *n Brit. education.* one of ten groupings, each with its own attainment criteria based on pupil age and ability, within which a pupil is assessed.

level pegging *Brit. inf.* ◆ *n* **1** equality between two contestants. ◆ *adj* **2** (of two contestants) equal.

level playing field *n* a situation in which none of the competing parties has an advantage at the outset of a competitive activity.

Leven ★ (ˈliːvᵊn) *n* **Loch. 1** a lake in E central Scotland: one of the shallowest of Scottish lochs, with seven islands, on one of which Mary Queen of Scots was imprisoned (1567–8). Length: 6 km (3·7 miles). Width: 4 km (2·5 miles). **2** a sea loch in W Scotland, extending for about 14 km (9 miles) east from Loch Linnhe.

lever (ˈliːvə) *n* **1** a rigid bar pivoted about a fulcrum, used to transfer a force to a load and usually to provide a mechanical advantage. **2** any of a number of mechanical devices employing this principle. **3** a means of exerting pressure in order to accomplish something. ◆ *vb* **4** to prise or move (an object) with a lever. ORIG C13: from OF *leveour,* from *lever* to raise, from L *levāre* from *levis* light

leverage (ˈliːvərɪdʒ, -vrɪdʒ) *n* **1** the action of a lever. **2** the mechanical advantage gained by employing a lever. **3** strategic advantage. **4** power or influence: *the supermarket chains have greater leverage than single-outlet enterprises.* **5** the US word for **gearing** (sense 3). **6** the use made by a company of its limited assets to guarantee the substantial loans required to finance its business.

leveraged buyout (ˈliːvərɪdʒd, -vrɪdʒd) *n* a takeover bid in which a small company makes use of its limited assets, and those of the usually larger target company, to raise the loans required to finance the takeover. Abbrev.: **LBO**.

leveret (ˈlɛvərɪt, -vrɪt) *n* a young hare, esp. one less than one year old. ORIG C15: from Norman F *levrete,* dim. of *levre,* from L *lepus* hare

Leverhulme ★ (ˈliːvəˌhjuːm) *n* **William Hesketh,** 1st Viscount. 1851–1925, British soap manufacturer and philanthropist, who founded (1881) the model industrial town Port Sunlight.

Leverkusen ★ (*German* ˈleːvərˌkuːzən) *n* a town in NW Germany, in North Rhine-Westphalia on the Rhine: chemical industries. Pop.: 162 252 (1996 est.).

Leverrier ★ (*French* ləvɛrje) *n* **Urbain Jean Joseph** (yrbɛ̃ ʒɑ̃ ʒozɛf). 1811–77, French astronomer: calculated the existence and position of the planet Neptune.

Levi[1] ★ (ˈliːvaɪ) *n* **1** *Old Testament.* **1a** the third son of Jacob and Leah and the ancestor of the tribe of Levi (Genesis 29:34). **1b** the priestly tribe descended from this patriarch (Numbers 18:21–24). **2** *New Testament.* another name for **Matthew** (the apostle).

Levi[2] ★ (*Italian* ˈlɛːvi) *n* **1 Carlo** (ˈkarlo). 1902–75, Italian physician, painter, and writer, best known for his novel *Christ Stopped at Eboli* (1947). **2 Primo** (ˈpriːmo). 1919–87, Italian novelist. His book *If This is a Man* (1947) relates his experiences in Auschwitz. Other books include *The Drowned and the Saved* (1988), published after his suicide.

leviable (ˈlɛvɪəbᵊl) *adj* **1** (of taxes, etc.) liable to be levied. **2** (of goods, etc.) liable to bear a levy; taxable.

leviathan (lɪˈvaɪəθən) *n* **1** *Bible.* a monstrous beast, esp. a sea monster. **2** any huge or powerful thing. ORIG C14: from LL, ult. from Heb. *liwyāthān,* from ?

levigate (ˈlɛvɪˌgeɪt) *vb* **levigates, levigating, levigated.** *Chem.* **1** (*tr*) to grind into a fine powder or a smooth paste. **2** to form or cause to form a homogeneous mixture, as in the production of gels. **3** (*tr*) to suspend (fine particles) by grinding in a liquid, esp. as a method of separating fine from coarse particles. ORIG C17: from L *lēvigāre,* from *lēvis* smooth
▸ **ˌleviˈgation** *n*

Levis (ˈliːvaɪz) *pl n Trademark.* jeans, usually blue and made of denim.

Lévi-Strauss ★ (ˈlɛvɪˈstraʊs; *French* levistros) *n* **Claude** (klod). born 1908, French anthropologist, leading exponent of structuralism. His books include *The Elementary Structures of Kinship* (1969), *Mythologies* (1964–71), and *Saudades do Brazil* (Memories of Brazil; 1994).

levitate (ˈlɛvɪˌteɪt) *vb* **levitates, levitating, levitated.** to rise or cause to rise and float in the air, without visible agency, usually attributed, esp. formerly, to supernatural intervention. ORIG C17: from L *levis* light + *-tate,* as in *gravitate*
▸ **ˌleviˈtation** *n* ▸ **ˈleviˌtator** *n*

levity (ˈlɛvɪtɪ) *n, pl* **levities. 1** inappropriate lack of seriousness. **2** fickleness or instability. **3** *Arch.* lightness in weight. ORIG C16: from L *levitās* lightness, from *levis* light

Levkás (lɛfˈkæs), **Leukas** *or* **Leucas** ★ *n* a Greek island in the Ionian Sea, in the Ionian Islands. Pop.: 22 000 (latest est.). Area: 295 sq. km (114 sq. miles). Italian name: **Santa Maura.**

Levkosia (lɛfˈkəʊsɪə) *or* **Leukosia** ★ *n* the Greek name for **Nicosia.**

levodopa (ˌliːvəʊˈdəʊpə) *n* another name for **L-dopa.**

levy (ˈlɛvɪ) *vb* **levies, levying, levied.** (*tr*) **1** to impose and collect (a tax, tariff, fine, etc.). **2** to conscript troops for service. **3** to seize or attach (property) in accordance with the judgment of a court. ◆ *n, pl* **levies. 4a** the act of imposing and collecting a tax, tariff, etc. **4b** the money so raised. **5a** the conscription of troops for service. **5b** a person conscripted in this way. ORIG C15: from OF *levée* a raising, from *lever,* from L *levāre* to raise

Lévy-Bruhl ★ (*French* levibryl) *n* **Lucien** (lysjɛ̃). 1857–1939, French anthropologist and philosopher, noted for his study of the psychology of primitive peoples.

lewd (luːd) *adj* characterized by or intended to excite crude sexual desire; obscene. ORIG C14: from OE *lǣwde* ignorant
▸ **ˈlewdly** *adv* ▸ **ˈlewdness** *n*

Lewes ★ (ˈluːɪs) *n* a market town in S England, administrative centre of East Sussex, on the River Ouse: site of a battle (1264) in which Henry III was defeated by Simon de Montfort. Pop.: 15 376 (1991).

lewis (ˈluːɪs) *n* a lifting device for heavy stone blocks consisting of a number of curved pieces of metal fitting into a dovetailed recess cut into the stone. ORIG C18: ?from the name of the inventor

Lewis[1] ★ (ˈluːɪs) *n* the N part of the island of Lewis with Harris, in the Outer Hebrides. Area: 1634 sq. km (631 sq. miles).

Lewis[2] ★ (ˈluːɪs) *n* **1 Carl.** full name *Frederick Carleton Lewis.* born 1961, US athlete: won four gold medals at the Los Angeles Olympics (1984) and single gold medals at the 1988, 1992, and 1996 Olympics; for sprinting, relay, and long jump events. **2** See (Cecil) **Day-Lewis. 3 C(live) S(taples).** 1898–1963, British writer, noted for his theological study *The Screwtape Letters* (1942) and his children's books chronicling the land of Narnia. **4 Denise.** born 1977, British heptathlete; gold medallist in the 2000 Olympics. **5 Lennox.** born 1965, British heavyweight boxer: undisputed world champion 2000–2001. **6 Matthew Gregory,** known as *Monk Lewis.* 1775–1818, British writer, noted for his Gothic horror story *The Monk* (1796). **7 Meriwether.** 1774–1807, American explorer who led an overland expedition from St Louis to the Pacific Ocean (1804–06). **8 (Harry) Sinclair.** 1885–1951, US writer, whose novels include *Main Street* (1920) and *Babbit* (1922): Nobel prize for literature 1930. **9 (Percy) Wyndham.** 1884–1957, British painter and writer, born in the US. A founder of vorticism, his writings include *The Apes of God* (1930) and the trilogy *The Human Age* (1928–55).

Lewis acid *n* a substance capable of accepting a pair of electrons from a base to form a covalent bond. Cf. **Lewis base.** ORIG C20: after G. N. *Lewis* (1875–1946), US chemist

Lewis base *n* a substance capable of donating a pair of electrons to an acid to form a covalent bond. Cf. **Lewis acid.** ORIG C20: after G. N. *Lewis;* see LEWIS ACID

Lewis gun *n* a light air-cooled gas-operated machine gun used chiefly in World Wars I and II. ORIG C20: after I. N. *Lewis* (1858–1931), US soldier

Lewisham ★ (ˈluːɪʃəm) *n* a borough of S Greater London, on the River Thames. Pop.: 242 400 (1994 est.). Area: 35 sq. km (13 sq. miles).

lewisite (ˈluːɪˌsaɪt) *n* a colourless oily poisonous liquid having a powerful blistering action and used as a war gas. Formula: $ClCH{:}CHAsCl_2$. Systematic name: **1-chloro-2-dichloroarsinoethene.** ORIG C20: after W. L. *Lewis* (1878–1943), US chemist

Lewis with Harris *or* **Lewis and Harris** ★ *n* an island in the Outer Hebrides, separated from the NW coast of Scotland by the Minch: consists of Lewis in the north and Harris in the south; many lakes and peat moors; economy based chiefly on the Harris tweed industry, with some fishing. Chief town: Stornoway. Pop.: 23 500 (latest est.). Area: 2134 sq. km (824 sq. miles).

lexeme ('lɛksiːm) *n Linguistics.* a minimal meaningful unit that cannot be understood from the meanings of its component morphemes. ORIG C20: from LEX(ICON) + -EME

lexical ('lɛksɪk(ə)l) *adj* **1** of or relating to items of vocabulary in a language. **2** of or relating to a lexicon.
▸ **'lexically** *adv*

lexicography (ˌlɛksɪ'kɒgrəfɪ) *n* the process or profession of writing or compiling dictionaries.
▸ **ˌlexi'cographer** *n* ▸ **lexicographic** (ˌlɛksɪkə'græfɪk) *or* **ˌlexico'graphical** *adj*

lexicon ('lɛksɪkən) *n* **1** a dictionary, esp. one of an ancient language such as Greek or Hebrew. **2** a list of terms relating to a particular subject. **3** the vocabulary of a language or of an individual. **4** *Linguistics.* the set of all the morphemes of a language. ORIG C17: NL, from Gk *lexikon*, n use of *lexikos* relating to words, from Gk *lexis* word, from *legein* to speak

lexigraphy (lɛk'sɪgrəfɪ) *n* a system of writing in which each word is represented by a sign. ORIG C19: from Gk *lexis* word + -GRAPHY

Lexington ★ ('lɛksɪŋtən) *n* **1** a city in NE central Kentucky, in the bluegrass region: major centre for horse-breeding. Pop.: 237 612 (1995 est.). **2** a city in Massachusetts, northwest of Boston: site of the first action (1775) of the War of American Independence. Pop.: 28 974 (1990).

lexis ('lɛksɪs) *n* the totality of vocabulary items in a language. ORIG C20: from Gk *lexis* word

ley (leɪ, liː) *n* **1** arable land temporarily under grass. **2** Also: **ley line.** a line joining two prominent points in the landscape, thought to be the line of a prehistoric track. ORIG C14: var. of LEA

Leyden[1] ★ ('laɪd(ə)n; *Dutch* 'lɛidə) *n* a variant of **Leiden.**

Leyden[2] ★ ('laɪd(ə)n) *n* See **Lucas van Leyden.**

Leyden jar *n Physics.* an early type of capacitor consisting of a glass jar with the lower part of the inside and outside coated with tin foil. ORIG C18: first made in Leiden

Leyland cypress ('leɪlənd) *n* a hybrid coniferous tree that is widely grown for hedging because it grows quickly. Also called: **Leylandii** (leɪ'lændɪˌaɪ). ORIG C20: named after C. J. *Leyland* (1849–1926), Brit. horticulturalist

Leyte ★ ('leɪteɪ) *n* an island in the central Philippines, in the Visayan Islands. Chief town: Tacloban. Pop.: 1 362 050 (1990). Area: 7215 sq. km (2786 sq. miles).

Leyte Gulf ★ *n* an inlet of the Pacific in the E Philippines, east of Leyte and south of Samar: scene of a battle (Oct. 23–26, 1944) during World War II, in which the Americans defeated almost the entire Japanese navy, thereby ensuring ultimate Allied victory.

lf *Printing. abbrev. for* light face.

LF *Radio. abbrev. for* low frequency.

LG *abbrev. for* Low German.

LGV (in Britain) *abbrev. for* large goods vehicle.

lh *or* **LH** *abbrev. for* left hand.

Lhasa *or* **Lassa** ★ ('lɑːsə) *n* a city in SW China, capital of Tibet AR, at an altitude of 3606 m (11 830 ft): for centuries the sacred city of Lamaism and residence of the Dalai Lamas from the 17th century until 1950; known as the Forbidden City because it was closed to Westerners until the beginning of the 20th century; annexed by China in 1951. The Dalai Lama fled after an unsuccessful revolt against Chinese rule in 1959. Pop.: 106 885 (1990 est.).

Li *the chemical symbol for* lithium.

LI *abbrev. for:* **1** Long Island. **2** Light Infantry.

liabilities (ˌlaɪə'bɪlɪtɪz) *pl n Accounting.* business obligations not discharged and shown as balanced against assets on the balance sheet.

liability (ˌlaɪə'bɪlɪtɪ) *n, pl* **liabilities. 1** the state of being liable. **2** a financial obligation. **3** a hindrance or disadvantage.

liable ('laɪəb(ə)l) *adj* (*postpositive*) **1** legally obliged or responsible; answerable. **2** susceptible or exposed; subject. **3** probable or likely: *it's liable to happen soon.* ORIG C15: ? via Anglo-F, from OF *lier* to bind, from L *ligāre*

> **USAGE NOTE** The use of *liable* to mean *probable* or *likely* was formerly considered incorrect, but is now acceptable.

liaise (lɪ'eɪz) *vb* **liaises, liaising, liaised.** (*intr;* usually foll. by *with*) to communicate and maintain contact (with). ORIG C20: back formation from LIAISON

liaison (lɪ'eɪzɒn) *n* **1** communication and contact between groups or units. **2** a secretive or adulterous sexual relationship. **3** the relationship between military units necessary to ensure unity of purpose. **4** (esp. in French) the pronunciation of a normally silent consonant at the end of a word immediately before another word commencing with a vowel, in such a way that the consonant is taken over as the initial sound of the following word, as in *ils ont* (ilzɔ̃). **5** any thickening for soups, sauces, etc., such as egg yolks or cream. ORIG C17: via F from OF, from *lier* to bind, from L *ligāre*

Liákoura ★ ('ljakura) *n* transliteration of the Modern Greek name for (Mount) **Parnassus.**

liana (lɪ'ɑːnə) *or* **liane** (lɪ'ɑːn) *n* any of various woody climbing plants of tropical forests. ORIG C19: changed from earlier *liane* (through infl. of F *lier* to bind), from F, from ?

Lianyungang ('ljæn'jʊŋ'gæŋ), **Sinhailien,** *or* **Hsinhai-lien** ★ *n* a city in E China, near the coast of Jiangsu. Pop.: 354 139 (1990 est.).

Liao ★ (ljaʊ) *n* a river in NE China, rising in SE Inner Mongolia and flowing northeast then southwest to the Gulf of Liaodong. Length: about 1100 km (700 miles).

Liaodong ('ljɑʊ'dʊŋ) *or* **Liaotung** ★ ('ljaʊ'tʊŋ) *n* **1** a peninsula of NE China, in S Manchuria extending south into the Yellow Sea: forms the S part of Liaoning province. **2 Gulf of.** the N part of the Gulf of Chihli, west of the peninsula of Liaodong.

Liaoning ★ ('ljaʊ'nɪŋ) *n* a province of NE China, in S Manchuria. Capital: Shenyang. Pop.: 41 380 000 (1997 est.). Area: 150 000 sq. km (58 500 sq. miles).

Liaoyang ★ ('ljaʊ'jæŋ) *n* a city in NE China, in S Manchuria, in Liaoning province: a regional capital in the early dynasties. Pop.: 492 559 (1990 est.).

liar ('laɪə) *n* a person who tells lies.

Liard ★ ('liːɑːd, liː'ɑːd, -'ɑː) *n* a river in W Canada, rising in the SE Yukon and flowing east and then northwest to the Mackenzie River. Length: 885 km (550 miles).

Lias ('laɪəs) *n* the lowest series of rocks of the Jurassic system. ORIG C15 (referring to a kind of limestone), C19 (geological sense): from OF *liois,* ?from *lie* dregs, so called from its appearance
▸ **Liassic** (laɪ'æsɪk) *adj*

lib (lɪb) *n Inf., sometimes derog.* short for **liberation.**

lib. *abbrev. for:* **1** liber. ORIG L: book **2** librarian. **3** library.

Lib. *abbrev. for* Liberal.

libation (laɪ'beɪʃən) *n* **1a** the pouring-out of wine, etc., in honour of a deity. **1b** the liquid so poured out. **2** *Usually facetious.* an alcoholic drink. ORIG C14: from L *lībātiō*, from *lībāre* to pour an offering of drink

Libau ★ ('liːbaʊ) *n* the German name for **Liepāja.**

Libava ★ (lɪ'bavə) *n* transliteration of the Russian name for **Liepāja.**

Libby ★ ('lɪbɪ) *n* **Willard Frank.** 1908–80, US chemist, who devised the technique of radiocarbon dating: Nobel prize for chemistry 1960.

libel ('laɪb(ə)l) *n* **1** *Law.* **1a** the publication of defamatory matter in permanent form, as by a written or printed statement, picture, etc. **1b** the act of publishing such matter. **2** any defamatory or unflattering representation or statement. **3** *Scots Law.* the formal statement of a charge. ◆ *vb* **libels, libelling, libelled** *or US* **libels, libeling,**

libeled. (*tr*) **4** *Law.* to make or publish a defamatory statement or representation about (a person). **5** to misrepresent injuriously. ORIG C13 (in the sense: written statement), hence C14 legal sense: a plaintiff's statement, via OF from L *libellus* a little book
▸ **'libeller** *or* **'libelist** *n* ▸ **'libellous** *or* **'libelous** *adj*

liberal ('lɪbərəl, 'lɪbrəl) *adj* **1** relating to or having social and political views that favour progress and reform. **2** relating to or having policies or views advocating individual freedom. **3** giving and generous in temperament or behaviour. **4** tolerant of other people. **5** abundant; lavish: *a liberal helping of cream.* **6** not strict; free: *a liberal translation.* **7** of or relating to an education that aims to develop general cultural interests and intellectual ability. ◆ *n* **8** a person who has liberal ideas or opinions. ORIG C14: from L *līberālis* of freedom, from *līber* free
▸ **'liberally** *adv* ▸ **'liberalness** *n*

Liberal ('lɪbərəl, 'lɪbrəl) *n* **1** a member or supporter of a Liberal Party or Liberal Democrat party. ◆ *adj* **2** of or relating to a Liberal Party.

liberal arts *pl n* the fine arts, humanities, sociology, languages, and literature. Often shortened to **arts.**

Liberal Democrat *n* a member or supporter of the Liberal Democrats.

Liberal Democrats *pl n* (in Britain) a political party with centrist policies; established in 1988 as the Social and Liberal Democrats when the Liberal Party merged with the Social Democratic Party; renamed Liberal Democrats in 1989.

liberalism ('lɪbərəˌlɪzəm, 'lɪbrə-) *n* liberal opinions, practices, or politics.

liberality (ˌlɪbə'rælɪtɪ) *n, pl* **liberalities. 1** generosity; bounty. **2** the quality or condition of being liberal.

liberalize *or* **liberalise** ('lɪbərəˌlaɪz, 'lɪbrə-) *vb* **liberalizes, liberalizing, liberalized** *or* **liberalises, liberalising, liberalised.** to make or become liberal.
▸ **ˌliberali'zation** *or* **ˌliberali'sation** *n* ▸ **'liberalˌizer** *or* **'liberalˌiser** *n*

Liberal Party *n* **1** one of the former major political parties in Britain; in 1988 it merged with the Social Democratic Party to form the Social and Liberal Democrats; renamed the Liberal Democrats in 1989. **2** one of the major political parties in Australia, a conservative party, generally opposed to the Labor Party. **3** any other party supporting liberal policies.

liberal studies *n* (*functioning as sing*) *Brit.* a supplementary arts course for those specializing in scientific, technical, or professional studies.

liberate ('lɪbəˌreɪt) *vb* **liberates, liberating, liberated.** (*tr*) **1** to give liberty to; make free. **2** to release (something, esp. a gas) from chemical combination. **3** to release from occupation or subjugation by a foreign power. **4** to free from social prejudices or injustices. **5** *Euphemistic or facetious.* to steal.
▸ **'liberˌator** *n*

liberated ('lɪbəˌreɪtɪd) *adj* **1** given liberty; freed; released. **2** released from occupation or subjugation by a foreign power. **3** (esp. in feminist theory) not bound by traditional sexual and social roles.

liberation (ˌlɪbə'reɪʃən) *n* **1** a liberating or being liberated. **2** the seeking of equal status or just treatment for or on behalf of any group believed to be discriminated against: *women's liberation; animal liberation.*
▸ **ˌliber'ationist** *n, adj*

liberation theology *n* the belief that Christianity involves not only faith in the Church but a commitment to change social and political conditions where it is considered exploitation and oppression exist: applied esp. to South America.

Liberec ★ (*Czech* 'libɛrɛts) *n* a city in the NW Czech Republic, on the Neisse River: a centre of the German Sudeten movement in 1938. Pop.: 100 698 (1995 est.). German name: **Reichenberg.**

Liberia ★ (laɪ'bɪərɪə) *n* a republic in W Africa, on the Atlantic: originated in 1822 as a home for freed Afro-American slaves, with land purchased by the American Colonization Society; republic declared in 1847; exports are predominantly rubber and iron ore. Official language: English. Religion: Christian majority, also animist. Currency: dollar. Capital: Monrovia. Pop.: 2 924 000 (1999 est.). Area: 111 400 sq. km (43 000 sq. miles).
▸ **Li'berian** *adj, n*

libertarian (ˌlɪbə'tɛərɪən) *n* **1** a believer in freedom of thought, expression, etc. **2** a believer in the doctrine of free will. Cf. **determinism.** ◆ *adj* **3** of, relating to, or characteristic of a libertarian. ORIG C18: from LIBERTY
▸ **ˌliber'tarianism** *n*

libertine ('lɪbəˌtiːn, -ˌtaɪn) *n* **1** a morally dissolute person. ◆ *adj* **2** morally dissolute. ORIG C14 (in the sense: freedman, dissolute person): from L *lībertīnus* freedman, from *lībertus* freed, from *līber* free
▸ **'liberˌtinage** *or* **'libertinˌism** *n*

liberty ('lɪbətɪ) *n, pl* **liberties. 1** the power of choosing, thinking, and acting for oneself; freedom from control or restriction. **2** the right or privilege of access to a particular place; freedom. **3** (*often pl*) a social action regarded as being familiar, forward, or improper. **4** (*often pl*) an action that is unauthorized: *he took liberties with the translation.* **5a** authorized leave granted to a sailor. **5b** (*as modifier*): *liberty man; liberty boat.* **6 at liberty.** free, unoccupied, or unrestricted. **7 take liberties (with).** to be overfamiliar or overpresumptuous. ORIG C14: from OF *liberté,* from L *lībertās,* from *līber* free

liberty bodice *n* a sleeveless vestlike undergarment covering the upper part of the body, formerly worn esp. by young children.

liberty hall *n* (*sometimes caps.*) *Inf.* a place or condition of complete liberty.

Liberty Island ★ *n* a small island in upper New York Bay: site of the Statue of Liberty. Area: 5 hectares (12 acres). Former name (until 1956): **Bedloe's Island.**

Libia ★ ('liːbja) *n* the Italian name for **Libya.**

libidinous (lɪ'bɪdɪnəs) *adj* characterized by excessive sexual desire.
▸ **li'bidinously** *adv* ▸ **li'bidinousness** *n*

libido (lɪ'biːdəʊ) *n, pl* **libidos. 1** *Psychoanal.* psychic energy emanating from the id. **2** sexual urge or desire. ORIG C20 (in psychoanalysis): from L: desire
▸ **libidinal** (lɪ'bɪdɪnᵊl) *adj* ▸ **li'bidinally** *adv*

libra ('laɪbrə) *n, pl* **librae** (-briː). an ancient Roman unit of weight corresponding to 1 pound. ORIG C14: from L, lit.: scales

Libra ('liːbrə) *n, Latin genitive* **Librae** ('liːbriː). **1** *Astron.* a small faint zodiacal constellation in the S hemisphere, lying between Virgo and Scorpius. **2** Also called: the **Scales,** the **Balance.** *Astrol.* the seventh sign of the zodiac. The sun is in this sign between about Sept. 23 and Oct. 22.

librarian (laɪ'brɛərɪən) *n* a person in charge of or assisting in a library.
▸ **li'brarianˌship** *n*

library ('laɪbrərɪ) *n, pl* **libraries. 1** a room or set of rooms where books and other literary materials are kept. **2** a collection of literary materials, films, CDs, etc., kept for borrowing or reference. **3** the building or institution that houses such a collection: *a public library.* **4** a set of books published as a series, often in a similar format. **5** *Computing.* a collection of standard programs and subroutines, usually stored on disk. **6** a collection of specific items for reference or checking against: *a library of genetic material.* ORIG C14: from OF *librairie,* from Med. L *librāris,* n. use of L *librārius* relating to books, from *liber* book

libration (laɪ'breɪʃən) *n* **1** the act of oscillating. **2** a real or apparent oscillation of the moon enabling approximately nine per cent of the surface facing away from earth to be seen. ORIG C17: from L, from *librāre* to balance

librettist (lɪ'brɛtɪst) *n* the author of a libretto.

libretto (lɪ'brɛtəʊ) *n, pl* **librettos** *or* **libretti** (-tiː). a text written for and set to music in an opera, etc. ORIG C18: from It., dim. of *libro* book

Libreville ★ (*French* librəvil) *n* the capital of Gabon, in the west on the estuary of the Gabon River: founded as a French trading post in 1843 and expanded with the settlement of freed slaves in 1848. Pop.: 362 386 (1993).

Librium (ˈlɪbrɪəm) *n Trademark.* a preparation of the drug chlordiazepoxide used as a tranquillizer. See also **benzodiazepine.**

Libya ★ (ˈlɪbɪə) *n* a republic in N Africa, on the Mediterranean: became an Italian colony in 1912; divided after World War II into Tripolitania and Cyrenaica (under British administration) and Fezzan (under French); gained independence in 1951; monarchy overthrown by a military junta in 1969. It consists almost wholly of desert and is a major exporter of oil. Official language: Arabic. Official religion: (Sunni) Muslim. Currency: Libyan dinar. Capital: Tripoli. Pop.: 4 993 000 (1999 est.). Area: 1 760 000 sq. km (680 000 sq. miles). Official name: **Al-Jumhuria al-Arabia allibya** (-ˌdʒæməˈhɪriːjθ).
▸ ˈ**Libyan** *adj, n*

Libyan Desert ★ *n* a desert in N Africa, in E Libya, W Egypt, and the NW Sudan: the NE part of the Sahara.

lice (laɪs) *n* the plural of **louse.**

licence *or US* **license** (ˈlaɪsəns) *n* **1** a certificate, tag, document, etc., giving official permission to do something. **2** formal permission or exemption. **3** liberty of action or thought; freedom. **4** intentional disregard of conventional rules to achieve a certain effect: *poetic licence.* **5** excessive freedom. ORIG C14: via OF and Med. L *licentia* permission, from L: freedom, from *licet* it is allowed

license (ˈlaɪsəns) *vb* **licenses, licensing, licensed.** (*tr*) **1** to grant or give a licence for (something, such as the sale of alcohol). **2** to give permission to or for.
▸ ˈ**licensable** *adj* ▸ ˈ**licenser** *or* ˈ**licensor** *n*

licensee (ˌlaɪsənˈsiː) *n* a person who holds a licence, esp. one to sell alcoholic drink.

licentiate (laɪˈsɛnʃɪɪt) *n* **1** a person who holds a formal attestation of competence to practise a certain profession. **2** a higher degree awarded by certain, chiefly European, universities. **3** a person who holds this degree. **4** *Chiefly Presbyterian Church.* a person holding a licence to preach. ORIG C15: from Med. L *licentiātus,* from *licentiāre* to permit
▸ **liˈcentiateˌship** *n*

licentious (laɪˈsɛnʃəs) *adj* **1** sexually unrestrained or promiscuous. **2** *Now rare.* showing disregard for convention. ORIG C16: from L *licentiōsus* capricious, from *licentia* LICENCE
▸ **liˈcentiously** *adv* ▸ **liˈcentiousness** *n*

lichee (ˌlaɪˈtʃiː) *n* a variant spelling of **litchi.**

lichen (ˈlaɪkən, ˈlɪtʃən) *n* an organism that is formed by the symbiotic association of a fungus and an alga or cyanobacterium and occurs as crusty patches or bushy growths on tree trunks, bare ground, etc. Lichens are now classified as a phylum of fungi. ORIG C17: via L from Gk *leikhēn,* from *leikhein* to lick
▸ ˈ**lichened** *adj* ▸ ˈ**lichenous** *adj*

Lichfield ★ (ˈlɪtʃˌfiːld) *n* a city in central England, in SE Staffordshire: cathedral with three spires (13th-14th century); birthplace of Samuel Johnson, during whose lifetime the **Lichfield Group** (a literary circle) flourished. Pop.: 28 666 (1991).

lich gate (lɪtʃ) *n* a variant spelling of **lych gate.**

Lichtenstein ★ (ˈlɪktənˌstaɪn) *n* **Roy.** 1923–97, US pop artist.

licit (ˈlɪsɪt) *adj* a less common word for **lawful.** ORIG C15: from L *licitus,* from *licēre* to be permitted
▸ ˈ**licitly** *adv* ▸ ˈ**licitness** *n*

lick (lɪk) *vb* **1** (*tr*) to pass the tongue over, esp. in order to taste or consume. **2** to flicker or move lightly over or round (something): *the flames licked around the door.* **3** (*tr*) *Inf.* **3a** to defeat or vanquish. **3b** to flog or thrash. **3c** to be or do much better than. **4 lick into shape.** to put into a satisfactory condition. **5 lick one's wounds.** to retire after a defeat. ◆ *n* **6** an instance of passing the tongue over something. **7** a small amount: *a lick of paint.* **8** short for **salt lick. 9** *Inf.* a hit; blow. **10** *Sl.* a short musical phrase, usually on one instrument. **11** *Inf.* rate of movement; speed. **12 a lick and a promise.** something hastily done, esp. a hurried wash. ORIG OE *liccian*
▸ ˈ**licker** *n*

lickerish *or* **liquorish** (ˈlɪkərɪʃ) *adj Arch.* **1** lecherous or lustful. **2** greedy; gluttonous. **3** appetizing or tempting. ORIG C16: changed from C13 *lickerous,* from OF *lechereus* lecherous; see LECHER

lickety-split (ˈlɪkɪtɪˈsplɪt) *adv US & Canad. inf.* very quickly; speedily. ORIG C19: from LICK + SPLIT

licking (ˈlɪkɪŋ) *n Inf.* **1** a beating. **2** a defeat.

lickspittle (ˈlɪkˌspɪtᵊl) *n* a flattering or servile person.

licorice (ˈlɪkərɪs) *n* the usual US and Canad. spelling of **liquorice.**

lictor (ˈlɪktə) *n* one of a group of ancient Roman officials, usually bearing fasces, who attended magistrates, etc. ORIG C16 *lictor,* C14 *littour,* from L *ligāre* to bind

lid (lɪd) *n* **1** a cover, usually removable or hinged, for a receptacle: *a saucepan lid; a desk lid.* **2** short for **eyelid. 3 put the lid on.** *Inf.* **3a** *Brit.* to be the final blow to. **3b** to curb, prevent, or discourage. ORIG OE *hlid*
▸ ˈ**lidded** *adj* ▸ ˈ**lidless** *adj*

Liddell Hart ★ (ˈlɪdᵊl ˈhɑːt) *n* Sir **Basil Henry.** 1895–1970, British military strategist and advocate of mechanized warfare.

Lidice ★ (*Czech* ˈlidjtsɛ) *n* a mining village in the Czech Republic: destroyed by the Germans in 1942 in reprisal for the assassination of Reinhard Heydrich; rebuilt as a national memorial.

lido (ˈliːdəʊ) *n, pl* **lidos.** *Brit.* a public place of recreation, including a swimming pool. ORIG C20: after the *Lido,* island bathing beach near Venice, from L *litus* shore

lie[1] (laɪ) *vb* **lies, lying, lied. 1** (*intr*) to speak untruthfully with intent to mislead or deceive. **2** (*intr*) to convey a false impression or practise deception: *the camera does not lie.* ◆ *n* **3** an untrue or deceptive statement deliberately used to mislead. **4** something that is deliberately intended to deceive. **5 give the lie to. 5a** to disprove. **5b** to accuse of lying. ◆ Related adj: **mendacious.** ORIG OE *lyge* (n), *lēogan* (vb)

lie[2] (laɪ) *vb* **lies, lying, lay, lain.** (*intr*) **1** (often foll. by *down*) to place oneself or be in a prostrate position, horizontal to the ground. **2** to be situated, esp. on a horizontal surface: *the pencil is lying on the desk; India lies to the south of Russia.* **3** to be buried: *here lies Jane Brown.* **4** (*copula*) to be and remain (in a particular state or condition): *to lie dormant.* **5** to stretch or extend: *the city lies before us.* **6** (usually foll. by *on* or *upon*) to rest or weigh: *my sins lie heavily on my mind.* **7** (usually foll. by *in*) to exist or consist inherently: *strength lies in unity.* **8** (foll. by *with*) **8a** to be or rest (with): *the ultimate decision lies with you.* **8b** *Arch.* to have sexual intercourse (with). **9** (of an action, claim, appeal, etc.) to subsist; be maintainable or admissible. **10** *Arch.* to stay temporarily. ◆ *n* **11** the manner, place, or style in which something is situated. **12** the hiding place or lair of an animal. **13 lie of the land. 13a** the topography of the land. **13b** the way in which a situation is developing. ◆ See also **lie down, lie in,** etc. ORIG OE *licgan* akin to OHG *ligen* to lie, L *lectus* bed

USAGE NOTE See at **lay**[1].

Lie ★ (liː) *n* **Trygve Halvdan** (ˈtrygvə ˈhalðan). 1896–1968, Norwegian statesman; first secretary-general of the United Nations (1946–52).

Liebig ★ (*German* ˈliːbɪç) *n* **Justus** (ˈjʊstʊs), Baron von Liebig. 1803–73, German chemist, who founded agricultural chemistry and discovered chloroform.

Liebig condenser (ˈliːbɪg) *n Chem.* a laboratory condenser consisting of a glass tube surrounded by a glass envelope through which cooling water flows.

Liebknecht ★ (*German* ˈliːpknɛçt) *n* **1 Karl** (karl). 1871–1919, German socialist leader: with Rosa Luxemburg he led an unsuccessful Communist revolt (1919) and was assassinated. **2** his father, **Wilhelm** (ˈvɪlhɛlm). 1826–1900, German socialist leader and founder (1869) of what became (1891) the German Social Democratic Party.

Liechtenstein ★ (ˈlɪktənˌstaɪn; *German* ˈlɪçtənʃtain) *n* a small mountainous principality in central Europe on the Rhine: formed in 1719 by the uniting of the lordships of Schellenburg and Vaduz, which had been purchased by the Austrian family of Liechtenstein; customs union formed with Switzerland in 1924. Official language: German. Religion: mostly Roman Catholic. Currency: Swiss franc. Capital: Vaduz. Pop.: 31 700 (1999 est.). Area: 160 sq. km (62 sq. miles).

lied (li:d; *German* li:t) *n, pl* **lieder** (ˈli:də; *German* ˈli:dər). *Music.* any of various musical settings for solo voice and piano of a romantic or lyrical poem. ORIG from G: song

lie detector *n Inf.* a polygraph used esp. by a police interrogator to detect false or devious answers to questions, a sudden change in one or more involuntary physiological responses being considered a manifestation of guilt, fear, etc.

lie down *vb (intr, adv)* **1** to place oneself or be in a prostrate position in order to rest. **2** to accept without protest or opposition (esp. in **take something lying down**). ◆ *n* **lie-down. 3** a rest.

lief (li:f) *adv* **1** *Now rare.* gladly; willingly: *I'd as lief go today as tomorrow.* ◆ *adj* **2** *Arch.* **2a** ready; glad. **2b** dear; beloved. ORIG OE *leof;* rel. to *lufu* love

liege (li:dʒ) *adj* **1** (of a lord) owed feudal allegiance (esp. in **liege lord**). **2** (of a vassal or servant) owing feudal allegiance: *a liege subject.* **3** faithful; loyal. ◆ *n* **4** a liege lord. **5** a liegeman or true subject. ORIG C13: from OF *lige,* from Med. L *līticus,* from *lītus, laetus* serf, of Gmc origin

Liège ★ (lɪˈeɪʒ; *French* ljɛʒ) *n* **1** a province of E Belgium: formerly a principality of the Holy Roman Empire, much larger than the present-day province. Pop.: 1 016 762 (1998 est.). Area: 3877 sq. km (1497 sq. miles). **2** a city in E Belgium, capital of Liège province: the largest French-speaking city in Belgium; river port and industrial centre. Pop.: 190 525 (1996 est.). ◆ Flemish name: **Luik.**

liegeman (ˈli:dʒˌmæn) *n, pl* **liegemen. 1** (formerly) a vassal. **2** a loyal follower.

Liegnitz ★ (ˈli:gnɪts) *n* the German name for **Legnica.**

lie in *vb (intr, adv)* **1** to remain in bed late in the morning. **2** to be confined in childbirth. ◆ *n* **lie-in. 3** a long stay in bed in the morning.

lien (ˈli:ən, li:n) *n Law.* a right to retain possession of another's property pending discharge of a debt. ORIG C16: via OF from L *ligāmen* bond, from *ligāre* to bind

Liepāja *or* **Lepaya** ★ (lɪˈpɑ:jə) *n* a port in Latvia on the Baltic Sea: a naval and industrial centre, with a fishing fleet. Pop.: 100 271 (1995 est.). Russian name: **Libava.** German name: **Libau.**

lierne (lɪˈɜ:n) *n Archit.* a short rib that connects the intersections of the primary ribs, esp. in Gothic vaulting. ORIG C19: from F, ? rel. to *lier* to bind

Liestal ★ (*German* ˈli:sta:l) *n* a city in NW Switzerland, capital of Basel-Land demicanton. Pop.: 12 161 (1987 est.).

lie to *vb (intr, adv) Naut.* (of a vessel) to be hove to with little or no swinging.

Lietuva ★ (lɪəˈtu:və) *n* the Lithuanian name for **Lithuania.**

lieu (lju:, lu:) *n* stead; place (esp. in **in lieu, in lieu of**). ORIG C13: from OF, ult. from L *locus* place

lieutenant (lɛfˈtɛnənt; *US* lu:ˈtɛnənt) *n* **1** a military officer holding commissioned rank immediately junior to a captain. **2** a naval officer holding commissioned rank immediately junior to a lieutenant commander. **3** *US.* an officer in a police or fire department ranking immediately junior to a captain. **4** a person who holds an office in subordination to or in place of a superior. ORIG C14: from OF, lit.: place-holding
▸ **lieuˈtenancy** *n*

lieutenant colonel *n* an officer holding commissioned rank immediately junior to a colonel in certain armies, air forces, and marine corps.

lieutenant commander *n* an officer holding commissioned rank in certain navies immediately junior to a commander.

lieutenant general *n* an officer holding commissioned rank in certain armies, air forces, and marine corps immediately junior to a general.

lieutenant governor *n* **1** a deputy governor. **2** (in the US) an elected official who acts as deputy to a state governor. **3** (in Canada) the representative of the Crown in a province: appointed by the federal government.

Lifar ★ (*French* lifar) *n* **Serge** (sɛrʒ). 1905–86, Russian ballet dancer and choreographer: ballet master at the Paris Opera Ballet (1932–58). His ballets include *Prométhée* (1929) and *Phèdre* (1950).

life (laɪf) *n, pl* **lives** (laɪvz). **1** the state or quality that distinguishes living beings or organisms from dead ones and from inorganic matter, characterized chiefly by metabolism, growth, and the ability to reproduce and respond to stimuli. Related adj: **animate. 2** the period between birth and death. **3** a living person or being: *to save a life.* **4** the time between birth and the present time. **5a** the remainder or extent of one's life. **5b** *(as modifier): a life sentence; life membership; life work.* **6** *Inf.* short for **life imprisonment. 7** the amount of time that something is active or functioning: *the life of a battery.* **8** a present condition, state, or mode of existence: *my life is very dull here.* **9a** a biography. **9b** *(as modifier): a life story.* **10** a characteristic state or mode of existence: *town life.* **11** the sum or course of human events and activities. **12** liveliness or high spirits: *full of life.* **13** a source of strength, animation, or vitality: *he was the life of the show.* **14** all living things, taken as a whole: *there is no life on Mars; plant life.* **15** *(modifier) Arts.* drawn or taken from a living model: *life drawing.* **16** (in certain games) one of a number of opportunities for participation. **17 a matter of life and death.** a matter of extreme urgency. **18 as large as life.** *Inf.* real and living. **19 for the life of me (him, her,** etc.) though trying desperately. **20 not on your life.** *Inf.* certainly not. **21 the life and soul.** *Inf.* a person regarded as the main source of merriment and liveliness: *the life and soul of the party.* **22 to the life.** (of a copy or image) resembling the original exactly. **23 true to life.** faithful to reality. ORIG OE *līf*

life assurance *n* a form of insurance providing for the payment of a specified sum to a named beneficiary on the death of the policyholder. Also called: **life insurance.**

life belt *n* a buoyant ring used to keep a person afloat when in danger of drowning.

lifeblood (ˈlaɪfˌblʌd) *n* **1** the blood, considered as vital to life. **2** the essential or animating force.

lifeboat (ˈlaɪfˌbəʊt) *n* **1** a boat used for rescuing people at sea, escaping from a sinking ship, etc. **2** *Inf.* a fund set up by the dealers in a market to rescue any member who may become insolvent as a result of a collapse in market prices.

life buoy *n* any of various kinds of buoyant device for keeping people afloat in an emergency.

life cycle *n* the series of changes occurring in an animal or plant between one stage and the identical stage in the next generation.

life expectancy *n* the statistically determined average number of years of life remaining after a specified age.

lifeguard (ˈlaɪfˌgɑ:d) *n* a person at a beach or pool to guard people against the risk of drowning.

life imprisonment *n* an indeterminate sentence always given for murder and as a maximum sentence in several other crimes. There is no remission, although the Home Secretary may order the prisoner's release on licence.

life jacket *n* an inflatable sleeveless jacket worn to keep a person afloat when in danger of drowning.

lifeless (ˈlaɪflɪs) *adj* **1** without life; inanimate; dead. **2** not sustaining living organisms. **3** having no vitality or animation. **4** unconscious.
▸ **ˈlifelessly** *adv* ▸ **ˈlifelessness** *n*

lifelike (ˈlaɪfˌlaɪk) *adj* closely resembling or representing life.
▸ **ˈlifeˌlikeness** *n*

lifeline (ˈlaɪfˌlaɪn) *n* **1** a line thrown or fired aboard a vessel for hauling in a hawser for a breeches buoy. **2** a line by which a deep-sea diver is raised or lowered. **3** a single means of contact, communication, or support on which a person or an area, etc., relies.

lifelong (ˈlaɪfˌlɒŋ) *adj* lasting for or as if for a lifetime.

life peer *n Brit.* a peer whose title lapses at his or her death.

life preserver *n* **1** *Brit.* a club or bludgeon, esp. one kept for self-defence. **2** *US & Canad.* a life belt or life jacket.

lifer ('laɪfə) *n Inf.* a prisoner sentenced to imprisonment for life.

life raft *n* a raft for emergency use at sea.

life-saver *n* **1** the saver of a person's life. **2** *Austral.* an expert swimmer, esp. a member of a surf life-saving club at a surfing beach, who rescues surfers or swimmers from drowning. **3** *Inf.* a person or thing that gives help in time of need.
▸ **'life-ˌsaving** *adj, n*

life science *n* any one of the branches of science concerned with the structure and behaviour of living organisms, such as biology, botany, zoology, physiology, or biochemistry.

life-size *or* **life-sized** *adj* representing actual size.

life span *n* the period of time during which a human being, animal, machine, etc., may be expected to live or function.

lifestyle ('laɪfˌstaɪl) *n* **1** a set of attitudes, habits, or possessions associated with a particular person or group. **2** such attitudes, etc., regarded as fashionable or desirable. **3** *NZ.* **3a** a luxurious semirural manner of living. **3b** (*as modifier*): *a lifestyle property.* **4** (*modifier*) suggestive of a fashionable or desirable lifestyle: *a lifestyle café.* **5** (*modifier*) (of a drug) designed to treat problems, such as impotence, that affect a person's quality of life rather than his or her health.

lifestyle business *n* a small business in which the owners are more anxious to pursue interests that reflect their lifestyle than to make more than a comfortable living.

life-support *adj* of, providing, or relating to the equipment or treatment necessary to keep a person alive.

lifetime ('laɪfˌtaɪm) *n* **1a** the length of time a person or animal is alive. **1b** (*as modifier*): *a lifetime supply.* **2** the length of time that something functions, is useful, etc. **3** Also called: **life.** *Physics.* the average time of existence of an unstable or reactive entity.

Liffey ★ ('lɪfɪ) *n* a river in E Republic of Ireland, rising in the Wicklow Mountains and flowing west, then northeast through Dublin into Dublin Bay. Length: 80 km (50 miles).

Lifford ★ ('lɪfəd) *n* the county town of Donegal, Republic of Ireland; market town. Pop.: 1461 (1986).

LIFO ('laɪfəʊ) *n acronym for* last in, first out (as an accounting principle in sorting stock). Cf. **FIFO.**

lift (lɪft) *vb* **1** to rise or cause to rise upwards from the ground or another support to a higher place: *to lift a sack.* **2** to move or cause to move upwards: *to lift one's eyes.* **3** (*tr*) to take hold of in order to carry or remove: *to lift something down from a shelf.* **4** (*tr*) to raise in status, spirituality, estimation, etc.: *his position lifted him from the common crowd.* **5** (*tr*) to revoke or rescind: *to lift tax restrictions.* **6** (*tr*) to take (plants or underground crops) out of the ground for transplanting or harvesting. **7** (*intr*) to disappear by lifting or as if by lifting: *the fog lifted.* **8** (*tr*) *Inf.* to take unlawfully or dishonourably; steal. **9** (*tr*) *Inf.* to plagiarize. **10** (*tr*) *Sl.* to arrest. **11** (*tr*) to perform a face-lift on. ◆ *n* **12** the act or an instance of lifting. **13** the power or force available or used for lifting. **14a** *Brit.* a platform, compartment, or cage raised or lowered in a vertical shaft to transport persons or goods in a building. US and Canad. word: **elevator. 14b** See **chairlift, ski lift. 15** the distance or degree to which something is lifted. **16** a ride in a car or other vehicle for part or all of a passenger's journey. **17** a rise in the height of the ground. **18** a rise in morale or feeling of cheerfulness usually caused by some specific thing or event. **19** the force required to lift an object. **20** a layer inserted in the heel of a shoe, etc., to give the wearer added height. **21** aid; help. **22** the component of the aerodynamic forces acting on a wing, etc., at right angles to the airflow and opposing gravity. ORIG C13: from ON
▸ **'lifter** *n*

liftoff ('lɪftˌɒf) *n* **1** the initial movement of a rocket from its launch pad. **2** the instant at which this occurs. ◆ *vb* **lift off. 3** (*intr, adv*) (of a rocket) to leave its launch pad.

lift pump *n* a pump that raises a fluid to a higher level. Cf. **force pump.**

lig (lɪg) *Brit. sl.* ◆ *n* **1** (esp. in the media) a function at which free entertainment and refreshments are available. ◆ *vb* **ligs, ligging, ligged. 2** (*intr*) to attend such a function; freeload. ORIG C20: from ?
▸ **'ligger** *n* ▸ **'ligging** *n*

ligament ('lɪgəmənt) *n* **1** *Anat.* any one of the bands of tough fibrous connective tissue that restrict movement in joints, connect various bones or cartilages, support muscles, etc. **2** any physical or abstract bond. ORIG C14: from Med. L *ligāmentum,* from L (in the sense: bandage), from *ligāre* to bind

ligand ('lɪgənd, 'laɪ-) *n Chem.* an atom, molecule, radical, or ion forming a complex with a central atom. ORIG C20: from L *ligandum,* from *ligāre* to bind

ligate ('laɪgeɪt) *vb* **ligates, ligating, ligated.** (*tr*) to tie up or constrict (something) with a ligature. ORIG C16: from L *ligātus,* from *ligāre* to bind
▸ **li'gation** *n*

ligature ('lɪgətʃə, -ˌtʃʊə) *n* **1** the act of binding or tying up. **2** something used to bind. **3** a link, bond, or tie. **4** *Surgery.* a thread or wire for tying around a vessel, duct, etc., as for constricting the flow of blood. **5** *Printing.* a character of two or more joined letters, such as ff, fi, fl, ffi. **6** *Music.* a slur or the group of notes connected by it. ◆ *vb* **ligatures, ligaturing, ligatured. 7** (*tr*) to bind with a ligature; ligate. ORIG C14: from LL *ligātūra,* ult. from L *ligāre* to bind

liger ('laɪgə) *n* the hybrid offspring of a female tiger and a male lion.

Ligeti ★ (*Hungarian* 'ligeti) *n* **György** (djørdj). born 1923, Hungarian composer, resident in Vienna. His works include *Atmospheres* (1961), *Volumina* (1962), and a requiem mass (1965).

light[1] (laɪt) *n* **1** the medium of illumination that makes sight possible. **2** Also called: **visible radiation.** electromagnetic radiation that is capable of causing a visual sensation. See also **speed of light. 3** (*not in technical usage*) electromagnetic radiation that has a wavelength outside this range, esp. ultraviolet radiation: *ultraviolet light.* **4** the sensation experienced when electromagnetic radiation within the visible spectrum falls on the retina of the eye. **5** anything that illuminates, such as a lamp or candle. **6** See **traffic light. 7** a particular quality or type of light: *a good light for reading.* **8a** illumination from the sun during the day; daylight. **8b** the time this appears; daybreak; dawn. **9** anything that allows the entrance of light, such as a window or compartment of a window. **10** the condition of being visible or known (esp. in **bring** *or* **come to light**). **11** an aspect or view: *he saw it in a different light.* **12** mental understanding or spiritual insight. **13** a person considered to be an authority or leader. **14** brightness of countenance, esp. a sparkle in the eyes. **15a** the act of igniting or kindling something, such as a cigarette. **15b** something that ignites or kindles, esp. in a specified manner, such as a spark or flame. **15c** something used for igniting or kindling, such as a match. **16** See **lighthouse. 17 in (the) light of.** in view of; taking into account; considering. **18 see the light.** to acquire insight. **19 see the light (of day).** **19a** to come into being. **19b** to come to public notice. **20 strike a light. 20a** (*vb*) to ignite something, esp. a match, by friction. **20b** (*interj*) *Brit.* an exclamation of surprise. ◆ *adj* **21** full of light; well-lighted. **22** (of a colour) reflecting or transmitting a large amount of light: *light yellow.* ◆ *vb* **lights, lighting, lighted** *or* **lit. 23** to ignite or cause to ignite. **24** (often foll. by *up*) to illuminate or cause to illuminate. **25** to make or become cheerful or animated. **26** (*tr*) to guide or lead by light. ◆ See also **lights**[1], **light up.** ORIG OE *lēoht*
▸ **'lightish** *adj* ▸ **'lightless** *adj*

light[2] (laɪt) *adj* **1** not heavy; weighing relatively little. **2** having relatively low density: *magnesium is a light metal.* **3** lacking sufficient weight; not agreeing with standard or official weights. **4** not great in degree, intensity, or number: *light rain.* **5** without burdens, difficulties, or problems; easily borne or done: *a light heart; light work.* **6** graceful, agile, or deft: *light fingers.* **7** not bulky or clumsy. **8** not serious or profound; entertaining: *light music; light*

verse. **9** without importance or consequence; insignificant: *no light matter.* **10** frivolous or capricious. **11** loose in morals. **12** dizzy or unclear: *a light head.* **13** (of bread, cake, etc.) spongy or well leavened. **14** easily digested: *a light meal.* **15** relatively low in alcoholic content: *a light wine.* **16** (of a soil) having a crumbly texture. **17** (of a vessel, lorry, etc.) **17a** designed to carry light loads. **17b** not loaded. **18** carrying light arms or equipment: *light infantry.* **19** (of an industry) engaged in the production of small consumer goods using light machinery. **20** *Aeronautics.* (of an aircraft) having a maximum take-off weight less than 5670 kilograms (12 500 pounds). **21** *Chem.* (of an oil fraction obtained from coal tar) having a boiling range between about 100° and 210°C. **22** (of a railway) having a narrow gauge, or in some cases a standard gauge with speed or load restrictions not applied to a main line. **23** *Phonetics, prosody.* (of a syllable, vowel, etc.) unaccented or weakly stressed; short. **24 light on.** *Inf.* lacking a sufficient quantity of (something). **25 make light of.** to treat as insignificant or trifling. ◆ *adv* **26** a less common word for lightly. **27** with little equipment, baggage, etc.: *to travel light.* ◆ *vb* **lights, lighting, lighted** *or* **lit.** (*intr*) **28** (esp. of birds) to settle or land after flight. **29** to get down from a horse, vehicle, etc. **30** (foll. by *on* or *upon*) to come upon unexpectedly. **31** to strike or fall on: *the choice lighted on me.* ◆ See also **light into, light out, lights**[2]. ORIG OE *lēoht*
▸ **'lightish** *adj* ▸ **'lightly** *adv* ▸ **'lightness** *n*

light air *n* very light air movement of force one (1–3 mph) on the Beaufort scale.

light box *n* a light source contained in a box and covered with a diffuser, used for viewing photographic transparencies, negatives, etc.

light breeze *n* a very light wind of force two (4–7 mph) on the Beaufort scale.

light bulb *n* a glass bulb containing a gas at low pressure and enclosing a thin metal filament that emits light when an electric current is passed through it. Sometimes shortened to **bulb.**

light-emitting diode *n* a semiconductor that emits light when an electric current is applied to it: used in electronic calculators, digital watches, etc.

lighten[1] ('laɪtᵊn) *vb* **1** to become or make light. **2** (*intr*) to shine; glow. **3** (*intr*) (of lightning) to flash. **4** (*tr*) *Arch.* to cause to flash.

lighten[2] ('laɪtᵊn) *vb* **1** to make or become less heavy. **2** to make or become less burdensome or oppressive; mitigate. **3** to make or become more cheerful or lively.

lightening ('laɪtᵊnɪŋ) *n Obstetrics.* the sensation, experienced by many women late in pregnancy when the head of the fetus enters the pelvis, of a reduction in pressure on the diaphragm.

lighter[1] ('laɪtə) *n* **1** a small portable device for providing a naked flame to light cigarettes, etc. **2** a person or thing that ignites something.

lighter[2] ('laɪtə) *n* a flat-bottomed barge used for transporting cargo, esp. in loading or unloading a ship. ORIG C15: prob. from MDu.

lighterage ('laɪtərɪdʒ) *n* **1** the conveyance or loading and unloading of cargo by means of a lighter. **2** the charge for this service.

light face *n* **1** *Printing.* a weight of type characterized by light thin lines. ◆ *adj also* **light-faced. 2** (of type) having this weight.

light-fingered *adj* having nimble or agile fingers, esp. for thieving or picking pockets.

light flyweight *n* **1** an amateur boxer weighing not more than 48 kg (106 pounds). **2** an amateur wrestler weighing not more than 48 kg (106 pounds).

light-footed *adj* having a light or nimble tread.
▸ **,light-'footedly** *adv*

light-headed *adj* **1** frivolous. **2** giddy; feeling faint or slightly delirious.
▸ **,light-'headedly** *adv* ▸ **,light-'headedness** *n*

light-hearted *adj* cheerful or carefree in mood or disposition.
▸ **,light-'heartedly** *adv* ▸ **,light-'heartedness** *n*

light heavyweight *n* **1** Also (in Britain): **cruiserweight. 1a** a professional boxer weighing 160–175 pounds (72.5–79.5 kg). **1b** an amateur boxer weighing 75–81 kg (165–179 pounds). **2a** a professional wrestler weighing not more than 198 pounds (90 kg). **2b** an amateur wrestler weighing not more than 90 kg (198 pounds).

lighthouse ('laɪt,haʊs) *n* a fixed structure in the form of a tower equipped with a light visible to mariners for warning them of obstructions, etc.

lighting ('laɪtɪŋ) *n* **1** the act or quality of illumination or ignition. **2** the apparatus for supplying artificial light effects to a stage, film, or television set. **3** the distribution of light on an object or figure, as in painting, photography, etc.

lighting cameraman *n Films.* the person who designs and supervises the lighting of scenes to be filmed.

lighting-up time *n* the time when vehicles are required by law to have their lights on.

light into *vb* (*tr, prep*) *Inf.* to assail physically or verbally.

light middleweight *n* an amateur boxer weighing 67–71 kg (148–157 pounds).

lightness ('laɪtnɪs) *n* the attribute of an object or colour that enables an observer to judge the extent to which the object or colour reflects or transmits incident light.

lightning ('laɪtnɪŋ) *n* **1** a flash of light in the sky, occurring during a thunderstorm and caused by a discharge of electricity, either between clouds or between a cloud and the earth. **2** (*modifier*) fast and sudden: *a lightning raid.* ORIG C14: var. of *lightening*

lightning conductor *or* **rod** *n* a metal strip terminating in sharp points, attached to the highest part of a building, etc., to discharge the electric field before it can reach a dangerous level and cause a lightning strike.

light opera *n* another term for **operetta.**

light out *vb* (*intr, adv*) *Inf.* to depart quickly, as if being chased.

light pen *n Computer technol.* **a** a rodlike device which, when applied to the screen of a cathode-ray tube, can detect the time of passage of the illuminated spot across that point thus enabling a computer to determine the position on the screen being pointed at. **b** a penlike device, used to read bar codes, that emits light and determines the intensity of that light as reflected from a small area of an adjacent surface.

light pollution *n* the glow from street and domestic lighting that obscures the night sky and hinders the observation of faint stars.

light rail *n* a transport system using small trains or trams, often serving parts of a large metropolitan area.

lights[1] (laɪts) *pl n* a person's ideas, knowledge, or understanding: *he did it according to his lights.*

lights[2] (laɪts) *pl n* the lungs, esp. of sheep, bullocks, and pigs, used esp. for feeding pets ORIG C13: pl n use of LIGHT[2], referring to the light weight of the lungs

light-sensitive *adj Physics.* (of a surface) having a photoelectric property, such as the ability to generate a current, change its electrical resistance, etc., when exposed to light.

lightship ('laɪt,ʃɪp) *n* a ship equipped as a lighthouse and moored where a fixed structure would prove impracticable.

light show *n* a kaleidoscopic display of moving lights, etc., projected onto a screen, esp. during pop concerts.

lightsome ('laɪtsəm) *adj Arch. or poetic.* **1** light-hearted or gay. **2** airy or buoyant. **3** not serious; frivolous.

lights out *n* **1** the time when those resident at an institution, such as soldiers in barracks or children at a boarding school, are expected to retire to bed. **2** a signal indicating this.

light table *n Printing.* a translucent surface of ground glass or a similar substance, illuminated from below and used for the examination of film, pages, etc.

light trap *n* any mechanical arrangement that allows some form of movement to take place while excluding light, such as a light-proof door or the lips of a film cassette.

light up *vb* (*adv*) **1** to light a cigarette, pipe, etc. **2** to illuminate or cause to illuminate. **3** to make or become cheerful or animated.

lightweight (ˈlaɪtˌweɪt) *adj* **1** of a relatively light weight. **2** not serious; trivial. ◆ *n* **3** a person or animal of a relatively light weight. **4a** a professional boxer weighing 130–135 pounds (59–61 kg). **4b** an amateur boxer weighing 57–60 kg (126–132 pounds). **5a** a professional wrestler weighing not more than 154 pounds (70 kg). **5b** an amateur wrestler weighing not more than 68 kg (150 pounds). **6** *Inf.* a person of little importance or influence.

light welterweight *n* an amateur boxer weighing 60–63.5 kg (132–140 pounds).

light year *n* a unit of distance used in astronomy, equal to the distance travelled by light in one year, i.e. 9.4607×10^{12} kilometres or 0.3066 parsecs.

ligneous (ˈlɪgnɪəs) *adj* of or resembling wood. ORIG C17: from L *ligneus,* from *lignum* wood

lignin (ˈlɪgnɪn) *n* a complex polymer occurring in certain plant cell walls making the plant rigid. ORIG C19: from L *lignum* wood + -IN

lignite (ˈlɪgnaɪt) *n* a brown carbonaceous sedimentary rock with woody texture that consists of accumulated layers of partially decomposed vegetation: used as a fuel. Also called: **brown coal.**
▸ **lignitic** (lɪgˈnɪtɪk) *adj*

lignum vitae (ˈlɪgnəm ˈvaɪtɪ) *n* **1** either of two tropical American trees having blue or purple flowers. **2** the heavy resinous wood of either of these trees. ◆ See also **guaiacum.** ORIG NL, from LL, lit.: wood of life

ligroin (ˈlɪgrəʊɪn) *n* a volatile fraction of petroleum: used as a solvent. ORIG from ?

Liguria ★ (lɪˈgjʊərɪə) *n* a region of NW Italy, on the **Ligurian Sea** (an arm of the Mediterranean): the third smallest of the regions of Italy. Pop.: 1 658 513 (1996 est.). Area: 5410 sq. km (2089 sq. miles).
▸ **Liˈgurian** *adj, n*

likable *or* **likeable** (ˈlaɪkəbᵊl) *adj* easy to like; pleasing.
▸ **ˈlikableness** *or* **ˈlikeableness** *n*

Likasi ★ (lɪˈkɑːsɪ) *n* a city in S Democratic Republic of Congo, in Shaba province: a centre of copper and cobalt production. Pop.: 299 118 (1994 est.). Former name: **Jadotville.**

like[1] (laɪk) *adj* **1** (*prenominal*) similar; resembling. ◆ *prep* **2** similar to; similarly to; in the manner of: *acting like a maniac; he's so like his father.* **3** used correlatively to express similarity: *like mother, like daughter.* **4** such as: *there are lots of games — like draughts, for instance.* ◆ *adv* **5** a dialect word for **likely.** ◆ *conj* **6** *Not standard.* as though; as if: *you look like you've just seen a ghost.* **7** in the same way as; in the same way that: *she doesn't dance like you do.* ◆ *n* **8** the equal or counterpart of a person or thing. **9 the like.** similar things: *dogs, foxes, and the like.* **10 the likes** (*or* **like**) **of.** people or things similar to (someone or something specified): *we don't want the likes of you around here.* ORIG shortened from OE *gelīc*

> **USAGE NOTE** The use of *like* to mean *such as* was formerly thought to be undesirable in formal writing, but has now become acceptable. It was also thought that *as* rather than *like* should be used to mean *in the same way that,* but now both *as* and *like* are acceptable: *they hunt and catch fish as/like their ancestors used to.* The use of *look like* and *seem like* before a clause, although very common, is thought by many people to be incorrect or nonstandard: *it looks as though he won't come* (not *it looks like he won't come*).

like[2] (laɪk) *vb* **likes, liking, liked. 1** (*tr*) to find (something) enjoyable or agreeable or find it enjoyable or agreeable (to do something): *he likes boxing; he likes to hear music.* **2** (*tr*) to be fond of. **3** (*tr*) to prefer or wish (to do something): *we would like you to go.* **4** (*tr*) to feel towards; consider; regard: *how did she like it?* **5** (*intr*) to feel disposed or inclined; choose; wish. ◆ *n* **6** (*usually pl*) a favourable feeling, desire, preference, etc. (esp. in **likes and dislikes**). ORIG OE *līcian*

-like *suffix forming adjectives.* **1** resembling or similar to: *lifelike.* **2** having the characteristics of: *childlike.* ORIG from LIKE[1] (prep)

likelihood (ˈlaɪklɪˌhʊd) *or* **likeliness** *n* **1** the condition of being likely or probable; probability. **2** something that is probable.

likely (ˈlaɪklɪ) *adj* **1** (usually foll. by an infinitive) tending or inclined; apt: *likely to rain.* **2** probable: *a likely result.* **3** believable or feasible; plausible. **4** appropriate for a purpose or activity. **5** having good possibilities of success: *a likely candidate.* ◆ *adv* **6** probably or presumably. **7 as likely as not.** very probably. ORIG C14: from ON *līkligr*

> **USAGE NOTE** *Likely* as an adverb is preceded by another, intensifying, adverb, as in *it will very likely rain* or *it will most likely rain.* Its use without an intensifier, as in *it will likely rain,* is regarded as nonstandard by most users of British English, though it is common in colloquial US English.

like-minded *adj* agreeing in opinions, goals, etc.
▸ **ˌlike-ˈmindedly** *adv* ▸ **ˌlike-ˈmindedness** *n*

liken (ˈlaɪkən) *vb* (*tr*) to see or represent as the same or similar; compare. ORIG C14: from LIKE[1] (adj)

likeness (ˈlaɪknɪs) *n* **1** the condition of being alike; similarity. **2** a painted, carved, moulded, or graphic image of a person or thing. **3** an imitative appearance; semblance.

likewise (ˈlaɪkˌwaɪz) *adv* **1** in addition; moreover; also. **2** in like manner; similarly.

liking (ˈlaɪkɪŋ) *n* **1** the feeling of a person who likes; fondness. **2** a preference, inclination, or pleasure.

lilac (ˈlaɪlək) *n* **1** any of various Eurasian shrubs or small trees of the olive family which have large sprays of purple or white fragrant flowers. **2a** a light or moderate purple colour. **2b** (*as adj*): *a lilac carpet.* ORIG C17: via F from Sp., from Ar. *līlak,* changed from Persian *nīlak* bluish, from *nīl* blue

Lilburne ★ (ˈlɪlˌbɜːn) *n* **John.** ?1614-57, English Puritan pamphleteer and leader of the Levellers, a radical group prominent during the Civil War.

liliaceous (ˌlɪlɪˈeɪʃəs) *adj* of, relating to, or belonging to a family of plants having showy flowers and a bulb or bulblike organ: includes the lily, tulip, bluebell, and onion. ORIG C18: from LL *līliăceus,* from *līlium* lily

Lilienthal ★ (*German* ˈliːliəntaːl) *n* **Otto** (ˈɔto). 1848–96, German aeronautical engineer, a pioneer of glider design.

Lilith ★ (ˈlɪlɪθ) *n* **1** (in the Old Testament and in Jewish folklore) a female demon, who attacks children. **2** (in Talmudic literature) Adam's first wife. **3** a witch notorious in medieval demonology.

Liliuokalani ★ (liːˌliːʊəʊkɑːˈlɑːniː) *n* **Lydia Kamekeha** (ˌkɑːmeɪˈkeɪhɑː). 1838–1917, queen and last sovereign of the Hawaiian Islands (1891–95).

Lille ★ (*French* lil) *n* an industrial city in N France: the medieval capital of Flanders; forms with Roubaix and Tourcoing one of the largest conurbations in France. Pop.: 178 301 (1990).

Lille Bælt ★ (ˈlilə ˈbɛld) *n* the Danish name for the **Little Belt.**

Lillee ★ (ˈlɪlɪ) *n* **Dennis** (**Keith**). born 1949, Australian cricketer who, by the end of the 1982–83 season, had taken a total of 355 wickets in 65 tests.

Lilliputian (ˌlɪlɪˈpjuːʃɪən) *n* **1** a tiny person or being. ◆ *adj* **2** tiny; very small. **3** petty or trivial. ORIG C18: from *Lilliput,* an imaginary country of tiny inhabitants in Swift's *Gulliver's Travels* (1726)

Lilo (ˈlaɪˌləʊ) *n, pl* **Lilos.** *Trademark.* a type of inflatable plastic or rubber mattress.

Lilongwe ★ (lɪˈlɒŋwɪ) *n* the capital of Malawi, in the central part west of Lake Malawi. Pop.: 395 500 (1994 est.).

lilt (lɪlt) *n* **1** (in music) a jaunty rhythm. **2** a buoyant motion. ◆ *vb* (*intr*) **3** (of a melody) to have a lilt. **4** to move in a buoyant manner. ORIG C14 *lulten,* from ?
▸ **ˈlilting** *adj*

lily (ˈlɪlɪ) *n, pl* **lilies. 1** any perennial plant of a N temperate genus, such as the tiger lily, having scaly bulbs and showy typically pendulous flowers. **2** the bulb or flower of any of these plants. **3** any of various similar or related plants, such as the water lily. ORIG OE, from L *līlium;* rel. to Gk *leirion* lily
▸ **ˈlily-ˌlike** *adj*

lily-livered *adj* cowardly; timid.

lily of the valley *n, pl* **lilies of the valley.** a small liliaceous plant of Eurasia and North America cultivated for its spikes of fragrant white bell-shaped flowers.

lily-white *adj* **1** of a pure white: *lily-white skin.* **2** *Inf.* pure; irreproachable.

Lima ★ (ˈliːmə) *n* **1** the capital of Peru, near the Pacific coast on the Rímac River: the centre of Spanish colonization in South America; university founded in 1551 (the oldest in South America); an industrial centre with a port at nearby Callao. Pop. (city): 421 570 (1995 est.); (conurbation): 6 022 213 (1995). **2** *Communications.* a code word for the letter *L.*

lima bean (ˈlaɪmə, ˈliː-) *n* **1** any of several varieties of the bean plant native to tropical America, cultivated for its flat pods containing pale green edible seeds. **2** the seed of such a plant. ORIG C19: after LIMA

Limassol ★ (ˈlɪməˌsɒl) *n* a port in S Cyprus: trading centre. Pop.: 143 400 (1994 est.). Ancient name: **Lemessus** (ləˈmɛsəs).

Limavady ★ (ˌlɪməˈvædɪ) *n* a district of N Northern Ireland, on Lough Foyle: mainly agricultural. Administrative centre: Limavady. Pop.: 29 567 (1991). Area: 622 sq. km (240 sq. miles).

limb[1] (lɪm) *n* **1** an arm or leg, or the analogous part on an animal, such as a wing. **2** any of the main branches of a tree. **3** a branching or projecting section or member; extension. **4** a person or thing considered to be a member, part, or agent of a larger group or thing. **5** *Chiefly Brit.* a mischievous child (esp. in **limb of Satan,** etc.). **6 out on a limb. 6a** in a precarious or questionable position. **6b** *Brit.* isolated, esp. because of unpopular opinions. ORIG OE *lim*
▸ **ˈlimbless** *adj*

limb[2] (lɪm) *n* **1** the edge of the apparent disc of the sun, a moon, or a planet. **2** a graduated arc attached to instruments, such as the sextant, used for measuring angles. **3** *Bot.* the expanded part of a leaf, petal, or sepal. **4** Also called: **fold limb.** either of the sides of a geological fold. ORIG C15: from L *limbus* edge

limbed (lɪmd) *adj* **a** having limbs. **b** (*in combination*): *short-limbed; strong-limbed.*

limber[1] (ˈlɪmbə) *adj* **1** capable of being easily bent or flexed; pliant. **2** able to move or bend freely; agile. ORIG C16: from ?
▸ **ˈlimberness** *n*

limber[2] (ˈlɪmbə) *n* **1** part of a gun carriage, consisting of an axle, pole, and two wheels. ◆ *vb* **2** (usually foll. by *up*) to attach the limber (to a gun, etc.). ORIG C15 *lymour* shaft of a gun carriage, from ?

limber up *vb* (*intr, adv*) (esp. in sports) to exercise in order to be limber and agile.

limbic system (ˈlɪmbɪk) *n* the part of the brain concerned with basic emotion, hunger, and sex. ORIG C19 *limbic,* from F, from *limbe,* from NL *limbus,* from L: border

limbo[1] (ˈlɪmbəʊ) *n, pl* **limbos. 1** (*often cap.*) *Christianity.* the supposed abode of infants dying without baptism and the just who died before Christ. **2** an imaginary place for lost, forgotten, or unwanted persons or things. **3** an unknown intermediate place or condition between two extremes: *in limbo.* ORIG C14: from Med. L *in limbo* on the border (of hell)

limbo[2] (ˈlɪmbəʊ) *n, pl* **limbos.** a Caribbean dance in which dancers pass, while leaning backwards, under a bar. ORIG C20: from ?

Limburg ★ (ˈlɪmbɜːg; *Dutch* ˈlɪmbyrx) *n* **1** a medieval duchy of W Europe: divided between the Netherlands and Belgium in 1839. **2** a province of the SE Netherlands: contains a coalfield and industrial centres. Capital: Maastricht. Pop.: 1 136 200 (1997 est.). Area: 2253 sq. km (809 sq. miles). **3** a province of NE Belgium: contains the industrial regions of the Kempen coalfield. Capital: Hassett. Pop.: 783 927 (1998 est.). Area: 2422 sq. km (935 sq. miles). French name: **Limbourg** (lɛ̃bur).

Limburger (ˈlɪmˌbɜːgə) *n* a semihard white cheese of very strong smell and flavour. Also called: **Limburg cheese.**

lime[1] (laɪm) *n* **1** short for **quicklime, birdlime, slaked lime. 2** *Agriculture.* any of certain calcium compounds, esp. calcium hydroxide, spread as a dressing on lime-deficient land. ◆ *vb* **limes, liming, limed.** (*tr*) **3** to spread (twigs, etc.) with birdlime. **4** to spread a calcium compound upon (land) to improve plant growth. **5** to catch (animals, esp. birds) as with birdlime. **6** to whitewash (a wall, ceiling, etc.) with a mixture of lime and water (**limewash**). ORIG OE *līm*

lime[2] (laɪm) *n* **1** a small Asian citrus tree with stiff sharp spines and small round or oval greenish fruits. **2a** the fruit of this tree, having acid fleshy pulp rich in vitamin C. **2b** (*as modifier*): *lime juice.* ◆ *adj* **3** having the flavour of lime fruit. ORIG C17: from F, from Ar. *līmah*

lime[3] (laɪm) *n* a European linden tree planted in many varieties for ornament. ORIG C17: changed from obs. *line,* from OE *lind* LINDEN

limeade (ˌlaɪmˈeɪd) *n* a drink made from sweetened lime juice and plain or carbonated water.

lime green *n* **a** a moderate greenish-yellow colour. **b** (*as adj*): *a lime-green dress.*

limekiln (ˈlaɪmˌkɪln) *n* a kiln in which calcium carbonate is calcined to produce quicklime.

limelight (ˈlaɪmˌlaɪt) *n* **1 the.** a position of public attention or notice (esp. in **in the limelight**). **2a** a type of lamp, formerly used in stage lighting, in which light is produced by heating lime to white heat. **2b** Also called: **calcium light.** brilliant white light produced in this way.

limerick (ˈlɪmərɪk) *n* a form of comic verse consisting of five anapaestic lines. ORIG C19: allegedly from *will you come up to Limerick?,* a refrain sung between nonsense verses at a party

Limerick ★ (ˈlɪmərɪk) *n* **1** a county of SW Republic of Ireland, in N Munster province: consists chiefly of an undulating plain with rich pasture and mountains in the south. County town: Limerick. Pop.: 165 000 (1996). Area: 2686 sq. km (1037 sq. miles). **2** a port in SW Republic of Ireland, county town of Limerick, at the head of the Shannon estuary. Pop.: 74 900 (1995 est.).

limescale (ˈlaɪmˌskeɪl) *n* a flaky deposit left in containers such as kettles by the precipitation of calcium salts from water. Often shortened to **scale.**

limestone (ˈlaɪmˌstəʊn) *n* a sedimentary rock consisting mainly of calcium carbonate: used as a building stone and in making cement, lime, etc.

limewater (ˈlaɪmˌwɔːtə) *n* **1** a clear colourless solution of calcium hydroxide in water, sometimes used in medicine as an antacid. **2** water that contains dissolved lime or calcium salts, esp. calcium carbonate or calcium sulphate.

limey (ˈlaɪmɪ) *US, Canad., & Austral. sl.* ◆ *n* **1** a British person. **2** a British sailor or ship. ◆ *adj* **3** British. ORIG abbrev. from C19 *lime-juicer,* because British sailors drank lime juice as a protection against scurvy

limit (ˈlɪmɪt) *n* **1** (*sometimes pl*) the ultimate extent, degree, or amount of something: *the limit of endurance.* **2** (*often pl*) the boundary or edge of a specific area: *the city limits.* **3** (*often pl*) the area of premises within specific boundaries. **4** the largest quantity or amount allowed. **5** *Maths.* **5a** a value to which a function approaches as the independent variable approaches a specified value or infinity. **5b** a value to which a sequence a_n approaches as n approaches infinity. **5c** the limit of a sequence of partial sums of a convergent infinite series. **6** *Maths.* one of the two specified values between which a definite integral is evaluated. **7 the limit.** *Inf.* a person or thing that is intolerably exasperating. ◆ *vb* **limits, limiting, limited.** (*tr*) **8** to restrict or confine, as to area, extent, time, etc. ORIG C14: from L *līmes* boundary
▸ **ˈlimitable** *adj* ▸ **ˈlimitless** *adj* ▸ **ˈlimitlessly** *adv* ▸ **ˈlimitlessness** *n*

★ people and places

limitary (ˈlɪmɪtərɪ, -trɪ) *adj* **1** of, involving, or serving as a limit. **2** restricted or limited.

limitation (ˌlɪmɪˈteɪʃən) *n* **1** something that limits a quality or achievement. **2** the act of limiting or the condition of being limited. **3** *Law.* a certain period of time, legally defined, within which an action, claim, etc., must be commenced.

limited (ˈlɪmɪtɪd) *adj* **1** having a limit; restricted; confined. **2** without fullness or scope; narrow. **3** (of governing powers, sovereignty, etc.) restricted or checked, by or as if by a constitution, laws, or an assembly: *limited government.* **4** *Chiefly Brit.* (of a business enterprise) owned by shareholders whose liability for the enterprise's debts is restricted.
▸ **ˈlimitedly** *adv* ▸ **ˈlimitedness** *n*

limited liability *n Brit.* liability restricted to the unpaid portion (if any) of the par value of the shares of a limited company.

limiter (ˈlɪmɪtə) *n* an electronic circuit that produces an output signal whose positive or negative amplitude, or both, is limited to some predetermined value above which the peaks become flattened. Also called: **clipper.**

limn (lɪm) *vb (tr)* **1** to represent in drawing or painting. **2** *Arch.* to describe in words. ORIG C15: from OF *enluminer* to illumine (a manuscript) from L *inlūmināre* to brighten, from *lūmen* light
▸ **limner** (ˈlɪmnə) *n*

limnology (lɪmˈnɒlədʒɪ) *n* the study of bodies of fresh water with reference to their plant and animal life, physical properties, geographical features, etc. ORIG C20: from Gk *limnē* lake
▸ **limnological** (ˌlɪmnəˈlɒdʒɪkᵊl) *adj* ▸ **limˈnologist** *n*

Límnos ★ (ˈlimnɔs) *n* transliteration of the Modern Greek name for **Lemnos.**

Limoges ★ (lɪˈməʊʒ; *French* limɔʒ) *n* a city in S central France, on the Vienne River: a centre of the porcelain industry since the 18th century. Pop.: 175 646 (1990).

Limousin ★ (*French* limuzɛ̃) *n* a region and former province of W central France, in the W part of the Massif Central.

limousine (ˈlɪməˌziːn, ˌlɪməˈziːn) *n* any large and luxurious car, esp. one that has a glass division between the driver and passengers. ORIG C20: from F, lit.: cloak (orig. one worn by shepherds in *Limousin*), hence later applied to the car

limp[1] (lɪmp) *vb (intr)* **1** to walk with an uneven step, esp. with a weak or injured leg. **2** to advance in a labouring or faltering manner. ◆ *n* **3** an uneven walk or progress. ORIG C16: prob. a back formation from obs. *limphalt* lame, from OE *lempheallt*
▸ **ˈlimper** *n* ▸ **ˈlimping** *adj, n*

limp[2] (lɪmp) *adj* **1** not firm or stiff. **2** not energetic or vital. **3** (of the binding of a book) not stiffened with boards. ORIG C18: prob. of Scand. origin
▸ **ˈlimply** *adv* ▸ **ˈlimpness** *n*

limpet (ˈlɪmpɪt) *n* **1** any of numerous marine gastropods, such as the common limpet and keyhole limpet, that have a conical shell and are found clinging to rocks. **2** (*modifier*) relating to or denoting certain weapons that are attached to their targets by magnetic or adhesive properties and resist removal: *limpet mines.* ORIG OE *lempedu,* from L *lepas,* from Gk

limpid (ˈlɪmpɪd) *adj* **1** clear or transparent. **2** (esp. of writings, style, etc.) free from obscurity. **3** calm; peaceful. ORIG C17: from F *limpide,* from L *limpidus* clear
▸ **limˈpidity** *or* **ˈlimpidness** *n* ▸ **ˈlimpidly** *adv*

Limpopo ★ (lɪmˈpəʊpəʊ) *n* a river in SE Africa, rising in E South Africa and flowing northeast, then southeast as the border between South Africa and Zimbabwe and through Mozambique to the Indian Ocean. Length: 1770 km (1100 miles).

limp-wristed *adj* ineffectual; effete.

limy[1] (ˈlaɪmɪ) *adj* **limier, limiest.** of, like, or smeared with birdlime.
▸ **ˈliminess** *n*

limy[2] (ˈlaɪmɪ) *adj* **limier, limiest.** of or tasting of lime (the fruit).

Linacre ★ (ˈlɪnəkə) *n* **Thomas.** ?1460–1524, English humanist and physician: founded the Royal College of Physicians (1518).

linage (ˈlaɪnɪdʒ) *n* **1** the number of lines in a piece of written or printed matter. **2** payment for written material calculated according to the number of lines.

Linares ★ (*Spanish* liˈnares) *n* a city in S Spain: site of Scipio Africanus' defeat of the Carthaginians (208 B.C.); lead mines. Pop.: 57 210 (1991).

Lin Biao ★ (ˈlɪn ˈbjaʊ) *n* See **Lin Piao.**

linchpin *or* **lynchpin** (ˈlɪntʃˌpɪn) *n* **1** a pin placed transversely through an axle to keep a wheel in position. **2** a person or thing regarded as an essential or coordinating element: *the linchpin of the company.* ORIG C14 *lynspin,* from OE *lynis*

Lincoln[1] ★ (ˈlɪŋkən) *n* **1** a city in E central England, administrative centre of Lincolnshire: an important ecclesiastical and commercial centre in the Middle Ages; Roman ruins, a castle (founded by William the Conqueror) and a famous cathedral (begun in 1086). Pop.: 80 281 (1991). Latin name: **Lindum** (ˈlɪndəm). **2** a city in SE Nebraska: state capital; University of Nebraska (1869). Pop.: 203 076 (1994 est.).

Lincoln[2] ★ (ˈlɪŋkən) *n* **Abraham.** 1809–65, US Republican statesman; 16th president of the US. He saved the Union in the Civil War (1861–65) and emancipated slaves (1863); assassinated by Booth.

Lincoln green *n* **1a** a yellowish-green or brownish-green colour. **1b** (*as adj*): *a Lincoln-green suit.* **2** a cloth of this colour. ORIG C16: after a green fabric formerly made at LINCOLN in England

Lincolnshire ★ (ˈlɪŋkənˌʃɪə, -ʃə) *n* a county of E England, on the North Sea and the Wash; includes the unitary authorities of North Lincolnshire and North East Lincolnshire: mostly low-lying and fertile, with fenland around the Wash and hills (the **Lincoln Wolds**) in the east; one of the main agricultural counties of Great Britain. Administrative centre: Lincoln. Pop. (excluding North Lincolnshire and North East Lincolnshire): 615 900 (1996 est.). Area (excluding North Lincolnshire and North East Lincolnshire): 5918 sq. km (2284 sq. miles). Abbrev.: **Lincs.**

Lincs (lɪŋks) *abbrev. for* Lincolnshire.

linctus (ˈlɪŋktəs) *n, pl* **linctuses.** a syrupy medicinal preparation, taken to relieve coughs and sore throats. ORIG C17 (in the sense: medicine to be licked with the tongue): from L, p.p. of *lingere* to lick

Lind ★ (lɪnd) *n* **Jenny.** Swedish name *Johanna Maria Lind Goldschmidt.* 1820–87, Swedish coloratura soprano.

lindane (ˈlɪndeɪn) *n* a white poisonous crystalline powder: used as an insecticide and weedkiller. ORIG C20: after T. van der *Linden,* Du. chemist

Lindbergh ★ (ˈlɪndbɜːg, ˈlɪnbɜːg) *n* **Charles Augustus.** 1902–74, US aviator, who made the first solo nonstop flight across the Atlantic (1927).

Lindemann ★ (ˈlɪndəmən) *n* **Frederick Alexander,** 1st Viscount Cherwell. 1886–1957, British physicist, born in Germany; Churchill's scientific adviser during World War II.

linden (ˈlɪndən) *n* any of various deciduous trees of a N temperate genus having heart-shaped leaves and small fragrant yellowish flowers: cultivated for timber and as shade trees. See also **lime**[3]. ORIG C16: n use of obs. adj *linden,* from OE *linde* lime tree

Lindesnes ★ (ˈlɪndɪsˌnes) *n* a cape at the S tip of Norway, projecting into the North Sea. Also called: (the) **Naze.**

Lindisfarne ★ (ˈlɪndɪsˌfɑːn) *n* another name for **Holy Island.**

Lindsay ★ (ˈlɪndzɪ) *n* **1 Norman Alfred William.** 1879–1969, Australian artist and writer. **2 (Nicholas) Vachel** (ˈveɪtʃəl). 1879–1931, US poet; best known for *General William Booth Enters into Heaven* (1913) and *The Congo* (1914).

Lindsey ★ (ˈlɪndzɪ) *n* **Parts of.** an area in E England constituting a former administrative division of Lincolnshire.

Lindwall ★ (ˈlɪndˌwɔːl) *n* **Ray(mond Russell).** 1921–96,

Australian cricketer. A fast bowler, he played for Australia 61 times.

line[1] (laɪn) *n* **1** a narrow continuous mark, as one made by a pencil, pen, or brush across a surface. **2** such a mark cut into or raised from a surface. **3** a thin indented mark or wrinkle. **4** a straight or curved continuous trace having no breadth that is produced by a moving point. **5** *Maths.* **5a** any straight one-dimensional geometrical element whose identity is determined by two points. A **line segment** lies between any two points on a line. **5b** a set of points (x, y) that satisfies the equation $y = mx + c$, where m is the gradient and c is the intercept with the y-axis. **6** a border or boundary: *the county line.* **7** *Sport.* **7a** a white or coloured band indicating a boundary or division on a field, track, etc. **7b** a mark or imaginary mark at which a race begins or ends. **8** *American football.* **8a** See **line of scrimmage. 8b** the players arranged in a row on either side of the line of scrimmage at the start of each play. **9** a specified point of change or limit: *the dividing line between sanity and madness.* **10a** the edge or contour of a shape. **10b** the sum or type of such contours, characteristic of a style or design: *the line of a building.* **11** anything long, flexible, and thin, such as a wire or string: *a washing line; a fishing line.* **12** a telephone connection: *a direct line to New York.* **13** a conducting wire, cable, or circuit for making connections between pieces of electrical apparatus, such as a cable for electric-power transmission, telecommunications, etc. **14** a system of travel or transportation, esp. over agreed routes: *a shipping line.* **15** a company operating such a system. **16** a route between two points on a railway. **17** *Chiefly Brit.* a railway track, including the roadbed, sleepers, etc. **18** a course or direction of movement or advance: *the line of flight of a bullet.* **19** a course or method of action, behaviour, etc.: *take a new line with him.* **20** a policy or prescribed course of action or way of thinking (often in **bring** *or* **come into line**). **21** a field of study, interest, occupation, trade, or profession: *this book is in your line.* **22** alignment; true (esp. in **in line, out of line**). **23** one kind of product or article: *a nice line in hats.* **24** a row of persons or things: *a line of cakes on the conveyor belt.* **25** a chronological or ancestral series, esp. of people: *a line of prime ministers.* **26** a row of words printed or written across a page or column. **27** a unit of verse consisting of the number of feet appropriate to the metre being used and written or printed with the words in a single row. **28** a short letter; note: *just a line to say thank you.* **29** a piece of useful information or hint about something: *give me a line on his work.* **30** one of a number of narrow horizontal bands forming a television picture. **31** *Physics.* a narrow band in an electromagnetic spectrum, resulting from a transition in an atom of a gas. **32** *Music.* **32a** any of the five horizontal marks that make up the stave. **32b** the musical part or melody notated on one such set. **32c** a discernible shape formed by sequences of notes or musical sounds: *a meandering melodic line.* **32d** (in polyphonic music) a set of staves that are held together with a bracket or brace. **33** a defensive or fortified position, esp. one that marks the most forward position in war or a national boundary: *the front line.* **34** a formation adopted by a body or a number of military units when drawn up abreast. **35** the combatant forces of certain armies and navies, excluding supporting arms. **36a** the equator (esp. in **crossing the line**). **36b** any circle or arc on the terrestrial or celestial sphere. **37** a US and Canad. word for **queue. 38** *Sl.* a portion of a powdered drug for snorting. **39** *Sl.* something said for effect, esp. to solicit for money, sex, etc. **40 all along the line. 40a** at every stage in a series. **40b** in every detail. **41 draw the line (at).** to object (to) or set a limit (on): *her father draws the line at her coming in after midnight.* **42 get a line on.** *Inf.* to obtain information about. **43 hold the line. 43a** to keep a telephone line open. **43b** *Football.* to prevent the opponents from taking the ball forward. **43c** (of soldiers) to keep formation, as when under fire. **44 in line for.** in the running for; a candidate for: *he's in line for a directorship.* **45 in line with.** conforming to. **46 lay** *or* **put on the line. 46a** to pay money. **46b** to speak frankly and directly. **46c** to risk (one's career, reputation, etc.) on something. ◆ *vb* **lines, lining, lined. 47** *(tr)* to mark with a line or lines. **48** *(tr)* to draw or represent with a line or lines. **49** *(tr)* to be or put as a border to: *tulips lined the lawns.* **50** to place in or form a row, series, or alignment. ◆ See also **lines, line-up.** ORIG C13: partly from OF *ligne,* ult. from L *līnea,* n. use of *līneus* flaxen, from *līnum* flax; partly from OE *līn,* ult. also from L *līnum* flax
▸ **ˈlinable** *or* **ˈlineable** *adj* ▸ **lined** *adj*

line[2] (laɪn) *vb* **lines, lining, lined.** *(tr)* **1** to attach an inside covering to (a garment, curtain, etc.), as for protection, to hide the seaming, or so that it should hang well. **2** to cover or fit the inside of: *to line the walls with books.* **3** to fill plentifully: *a purse lined with money.* ORIG C14: ult. from L *līnum* flax, since linings were often of linen

lineage[1] (ˈlɪnɪɪdʒ) *n* direct descent from an ancestor, esp. a line of descendants from one ancestor. ORIG C14: from OF *lignage,* from L *līnea* LINE[1]

lineage[2] (ˈlaɪnɪdʒ) *n* a variant spelling of **linage.**

lineal (ˈlɪnɪəl) *adj* **1** being in a direct line of descent from an ancestor. **2** of, involving, or derived from direct descent. **3** a less common word for **linear.** ORIG C14: via OF from LL *līneālis,* from L *līnea* LINE[1]
▸ **ˈlineally** *adv*

lineament (ˈlɪnɪəmənt) *n (often pl)* **1** a facial outline or feature. **2** a distinctive feature. ORIG C15: from L: line, from *līneāre* to draw a line

linear (ˈlɪnɪə) *adj* **1** of, in, along, or relating to a line. **2** of or relating to length. **3** resembling, represented by, or consisting of a line or lines. **4** having one dimension. **5** designating a style in the arts, esp. painting, that obtains its effects through line rather than colour or light. **6** *Maths.* of or relating to the first degree: *a linear equation.* **7** narrow and having parallel edges: *a linear leaf.* **8** *Electronics.* **8a** (of a circuit, etc.) having an output that is directly proportional to input: *linear amplifier.* **8b** having components arranged in a line. ORIG C17: from L *līneāris* of lines
▸ **linearity** (ˌlɪnɪˈærɪtɪ) *n* ▸ **ˈlinearly** *adv*

linear accelerator *n* an accelerator in which charged particles are accelerated along a linear path by potential differences applied to a number of electrodes along their path.

Linear B *n* an ancient system of writing found on clay tablets and jars of the second millennium B.C. excavated in Crete and on the Greek mainland. The script is apparently a modified form of the earlier and hitherto undeciphered **Linear A** and is generally accepted as being an early representation of Mycenaean Greek.

linear measure *n* a unit or system of units for the measurement of length.

linear motor *n* a form of electric motor in which the stator and the rotor are linear and parallel. It can be used to drive a train, one part of the motor being in the locomotive, the other in the track.

linear programming *n Maths.* a technique used in economics, etc., for determining the maximum or minimum of a linear function of non-negative variables subject to constraints expressed as linear equalities or inequalities.

lineation (ˌlɪnɪˈeɪʃən) *n* **1** the act of marking with lines. **2** an arrangement of or division into lines.

line dancing *n* a form of dancing performed by rows of people to country and western music.

line drawing *n* a drawing made with lines only.

Line Islands ★ *pl n* a group of coral islands in the central Pacific, including Tabuaeran, Teraina, and Kiritimati: part of Kiribati, with Palmyra and Jarvis administered by the US.

lineman (ˈlaɪnmən) *n, pl* **linemen. 1** another name for **platelayer. 2** a person who does the chaining, taping, or marking of points for a surveyor. **3** *Austral. & NZ.* (formerly) the member of a beach life-saving team who controlled the line used to help drowning swimmers and surfers. **4** *American football.* a member of the row of players who start each down, positioned on either side of the line of scrimmage. **5** *US & Canad.* another word for **linesman** (sense 2).

line management *n* the managers in charge of specific functions and concerned in the day-to-day operations of a company.
▸ **ˈline manager** *n*

★ people and places

linen ('lɪnɪn) *n* **1a** a hard-wearing fabric woven from the spun fibres of flax. **1b** (*as modifier*): *a linen tablecloth.* **2** yarn or thread spun from flax fibre. **3** clothes, sheets, tablecloths, etc., made from linen cloth or from cotton. ORIG OE *linnen,* ult. from L *līnum* flax

line of battle *n* a formation adopted by a military or naval force when preparing for action.

line of fire *n* the flight path of a missile discharged or to be discharged from a firearm.

line of force *n* a line in a field of force, such as an electric or magnetic field, for which the tangent at any point is the direction of the force at that point.

line of scrimmage *n American football.* an imaginary line, parallel to the goal lines, on which the ball is placed at the start of a down and on either side of which the offense and defense line up.

line-out *n Rugby Union.* the method of restarting play when the ball goes into touch, the forwards forming two parallel lines at right angles to the touchline and jumping for the ball when it is thrown in.

line printer *n* an electromechanical device that prints a line of characters at a time: used in printing and in computer systems.

liner[1] ('laɪnə) *n* **1** a passenger ship or aircraft, esp. one that is part of a commercial fleet. **2** See **freightliner. 3** Also called: **eyeliner.** a cosmetic used to outline the eyes. **4** a person or thing that uses lines, esp. in drawing or copying.

liner[2] ('laɪnə) *n* **1** a material used as a lining. **2** a person who supplies or fits linings.

lines (laɪnz) *pl n* **1** general appearance or outline: *a car with fine lines.* **2** a plan of procedure or construction: *built on traditional lines.* **3a** the spoken words of a theatrical presentation. **3b** the words of a particular role: *he forgot his lines.* **4** *Inf., chiefly Brit.* a marriage certificate: *marriage lines.* **5** a defensive position, row of trenches, or other fortification: *we broke through the enemy lines.* **6** a school punishment of writing the same sentence or phrase out a specified number of times. **7 read between the lines.** to understand or find an implicit meaning in addition to the obvious one.

linesman ('laɪnzmən) *n, pl* **linesmen. 1** an official who helps the referee or umpire in various sports, esp. by indicating when the ball has gone out of play. **2** *Chiefly Brit.* a person who installs, maintains, or repairs telephone or electric-power lines. US and Canad. name: **lineman.**

line-up *n* **1** a row or arrangement of people or things assembled for a particular purpose: *the line-up for the football match.* **2** the members of such a row or arrangement. **3** *US.* an identity parade. ◆ *vb* **line up.** (*adv*) **4** to form, put into, or organize a line-up. **5** (*tr*) to produce, organize, and assemble: *they lined up some questions.* **6** (*tr*) to align.

ling[1] (lɪŋ) *n, pl* **ling** *or* **lings. 1** any of several northern coastal food fishes having an elongated body with long fins. **2** another name for **burbot** (a fish). ORIG C13: prob. from Low G

ling[2] (lɪŋ) *n* another name for **heather.** ORIG C14: from ON *lyng*

ling. *abbrev. for* linguistics.

-ling[1] *suffix forming nouns.* **1** *Often disparaging.* a person or thing belonging to or associated with the group, activity, or quality specified: *nestling; underling.* **2** used as a diminutive: *duckling.* ORIG OE *-ling,* of Gmc origin

-ling[2] *suffix forming adverbs.* in a specified condition, manner, or direction: *darkling.* ORIG OE *-ling,* adv. suffix

lingam ('lɪŋgəm) *or* **linga** ('lɪŋgə) *n* the Hindu phallic image of the god Siva. ORIG C18: from Sansk.

Lingayen Gulf ★ (ˌlɪŋgɑː'jen) *n* a large inlet of the South China Sea in the Philippines, on the NW coast of Luzon: site of Japanese landing in 1941 invasion.

linger ('lɪŋgə) *vb* (*mainly intr*) **1** to delay or prolong departure. **2** to go in a slow or leisurely manner; saunter. **3** to remain just alive for some time prior to death. **4** to persist or continue, esp. in the mind. **5** to be slow to act; dither. ORIG C13 (northern dialect) *lengeren* to dwell, from *lengen* to prolong, from OE *lengan*
▸ **'lingerer** *n* ▸ **'lingering** *adj* ▸ **'lingeringly** *adv*

lingerie ('lænʒərɪ) *n* women's underwear and nightwear. ORIG C19: from F, from *linge,* from L *līneus* linen, from *līnum* flax

lingo ('lɪŋgəʊ) *n, pl* **lingoes.** *Inf.* any foreign or unfamiliar language, jargon, etc. ORIG C17: ?from LINGUA FRANCA

lingua franca ('lɪŋgwə 'fræŋkə) *n, pl* **lingua francas** *or* **linguae francae** ('lɪŋgwiː 'frænsiː). **1** a language used for communication among people of different mother tongues. **2** a hybrid language containing elements from several different languages used in this way. **3** any system of communication providing mutual understanding. ORIG C17: It., lit.: Frankish tongue

Lingua Franca *n* a particular lingua franca spoken from the Crusades to the 18th century in the ports of the Mediterranean, based on Italian, Spanish, French, Arabic, Greek, and Turkish.

lingual ('lɪŋgwəl) *adj* **1** *Anat.* of or relating to the tongue. **2a** *Rare.* of or relating to language or languages. **2b** (*in combination*): *polylingual.* **3** articulated with the tongue. ◆ *n* **4** a lingual consonant, such as Scots (r).
▸ **'lingually** *adv*

linguiform ('lɪŋgwɪˌfɔːm) *adj* shaped like a tongue.

linguist ('lɪŋgwɪst) *n* **1** a person who is skilled in foreign languages. **2** a person who studies linguistics. ORIG C16: from L *lingua* tongue

linguistic (lɪŋ'gwɪstɪk) *adj* **1** of or relating to language. **2** of or relating to linguistics.
▸ **lin'guistically** *adv*

linguistic atlas *n* an atlas showing the distribution of distinctive linguistic features.

linguistics (lɪŋ'gwɪstɪks) *n* (*functioning as sing*) the scientific study of language.

liniment ('lɪnɪmənt) *n* a medicated liquid, usually containing alcohol, camphor, and an oil, applied to the skin to relieve pain, stiffness, etc. ORIG C15: from LL *linīmentum,* from *linere* to smear

lining ('laɪnɪŋ) *n* **1** material used to line a garment, curtain, etc. **2** any material used as an interior covering.

link[1] (lɪŋk) *n* **1** any of the separate rings, loops, or pieces that connect or make up a chain. **2** something that resembles such a ring, loop, or piece. **3** a road, rail, air, or sea connection, as between two main routes. **4** a connecting part or episode. **5** a connecting piece in a mechanism. **6** Also called: **radio link.** a system of transmitters and receivers that connect two locations by means of radio and television signals. **7** a unit of length equal to one hundredth of a chain. 1 link of a Gunter's chain is equal to 7.92 inches, and of an engineer's chain to 1 foot. **8** *Computing.* short for **hyperlink.** ◆ *vb* **9** (often foll. by *up*) to connect or be connected with or as if with links. **10** (*tr*) to connect by association, etc. ORIG C14: from ON

link[2] (lɪŋk) *n* (formerly) a torch used to light dark streets. ORIG C16: ?from L *lychnus,* from Gk *lukhnos* lamp

linkage ('lɪŋkɪdʒ) *n* **1** the act of linking or the state of being linked. **2** a system of interconnected levers or rods for transmitting or regulating the motion of a mechanism. **3** *Electronics.* the product of the total number of lines of magnetic flux and the number of turns in a coil or circuit through which they pass. **4** *Genetics.* the occurrence of two genes close together on the same chromosome so that they tend to be inherited as a single unit.

linkman ('lɪŋkmən) *n, pl* **linkmen.** a presenter of a television or radio programme, esp. a sports transmission, consisting of a number of outside broadcasts from different locations.

Linköping ★ (*Swedish* 'lintçøːpiŋ) *n* a city in S Sweden: a political and ecclesiastical centre in the Middle Ages; engineering industry. Pop.: 131 370 (1996 est.).

links (lɪŋks) *pl n* **1a** short for **golf links. 1b** (*as modifier*): *a links course.* See **golf course. 2** *Chiefly Scot.* undulating sandy ground near the shore. ORIG OE *hlincas* pl. of *hlinc* ridge

link-up *n* a joining or linking together of two factions, objects, etc.

Linlithgow ★ (lɪn'lɪθgəʊ) *n* **1** a town in SE Scotland, in West Lothian: ruined palace, residence of Scottish kings and birthplace of Mary, Queen of Scots. Pop.: 11 866 (1991). **2** the former name of **West Lothian.**

linn (lɪn) *n Chiefly Scot.* **1** a waterfall or a pool at the foot of it. **2** a ravine or precipice. ORIG C16: prob. from a confusion of two words, Scot. Gaelic *linne* pool and OE *hlynn* torrent

Linnaeus ★ (lɪ'niːəs, -'neɪ-) *n* **Carolus** ('kærələs), original name *Carl von Linné.* 1707–78, Swedish botanist, who established the binomial system of biological nomenclature.
▸ **Lin'nean** *or* **Lin'naean** *adj*

linnet ('lɪnɪt) *n* a brownish Old World finch: the male has a red breast and forehead. ORIG C16: from OF *linotte,* ult. from L *līnum* flax (because the bird feeds on flaxseeds)

Linnhe ★ ('lɪnɪ) *n* **Loch.** a sea loch of W Scotland, at the SW end of the Great Glen. Length: about 32 km (20 miles).

lino ('laɪnəʊ) *n* short for **linoleum.**

linocut ('laɪnəʊˌkʌt) *n* **1** a design cut in relief on linoleum mounted on a wooden block. **2** a print made from such a design.

linoleum (lɪ'nəʊlɪəm) *n* a sheet material made of hessian, jute, etc., coated with a mixture of powdered cork, linseed oil, rosin, and pigment, used as a floor covering. Often shortened to **lino.** ORIG C19: from L *līnum* flax + *oleum* oil

Linotype ('laɪnəʊˌtaɪp) *n* **1** *Trademark.* a typesetting machine, operated by a keyboard, that casts an entire line on one solid slug of metal. **2** type produced by such a machine.

Lin Piao ('lɪn 'pjaʊ) *or* **Lin Biao** ★ *n* 1908–71, Chinese Communist general and statesman. He became minister of defence (1959) and second in rank to Mao Tse-tung (1966). He fell from grace and is reported to have died in an air crash while attempting to flee to the Soviet Union.

linseed ('lɪnˌsiːd) *n* another name for **flaxseed.** ORIG OE *līnsǣd,* from *līn* flax + *sǣd* seed

linseed oil *n* a yellow oil extracted from seeds of the flax plant. It is used in making oil paints, printer's ink, linoleum, etc.

linsey-woolsey ('lɪnzɪ'wʊlzɪ) *n* **1** a thin rough fabric of linen warp and coarse wool or cotton filling. **2** a strange nonsensical mixture or confusion. ORIG C15: prob. from *Lindsey,* village in Suffolk where first made + WOOL (with rhyming suffix *-sey*)

lint (lɪnt) *n* **1** an absorbent cotton or linen fabric with the nap raised on one side, used to dress wounds, etc. **2** shreds of fibre, yarn, etc. ORIG C14: prob. from L *linteus* made of linen, from *līnum* flax
▸ **'linty** *adj*

lintel ('lɪntᵊl) *n* a horizontal beam, as over a door or window. ORIG C14: via OF prob. from LL *līmitāris* (unattested) of the boundary, infl. by *līminaris* of the threshold

linter ('lɪntə) *n* **1** a machine for stripping the short fibres of ginned cotton seeds. **2** (*pl*) the fibres so removed.

Linz ★ (lɪnts) *n* a port in N Austria, capital of Upper Austria, on the River Danube: cultural centre; steelworks. Pop.: 203 044 (1991). Latin name: **Lentia** ('lɛntɪə, 'lɛnsɪə).

lion ('laɪən) *n* **1** a large gregarious predatory feline mammal of open country in parts of Africa and India, having a tawny yellow coat and, in the male, a shaggy mane. Related adj: **leonine. 2** a conventionalized lion, the principal beast used as an emblem in heraldry. **3** a courageous, strong, or bellicose person. **4** a celebrity or idol who attracts much publicity and a large following. **5 the lion's share.** the largest portion. ORIG OE *līo, lēo* (ME *lioun,* from Anglo-F *liun*), both from L *leo,* Gk *leōn*
▸ **'lioness** *fem n*

Lion ('laɪən) *n* **the.** the constellation Leo, the fifth sign of the zodiac.

lion-hearted *adj* very brave; courageous.

lionize *or* **lionise** ('laɪəˌnaɪz) *vb* **lionizes, lionizing, lionized** *or* **lionises, lionising, lionised.** (*tr*) to treat as or make into a celebrity.
▸ **ˌlioni'zation** *or* **ˌlioni'sation** *n* ▸ **'lionˌizer** *or* **'lionˌiser** *n*

Lions ★ ('laɪənz) *n* **Gulf of.** a wide bay of the Mediterranean off the S coast of France, between the Spanish border and Toulon. French name: **Golfe du Lion** (gɔlf dy ljɔ̃).

lip (lɪp) *n* **1** *Anat.* **1a** either of the two fleshy folds surrounding the mouth. Related adj: **labial. 1b** (*as modifier*): *lip salve.* **2** the corresponding part in animals, esp. mammals. **3** any structure resembling a lip, such as the rim of a crater, the margin of a gastropod shell, etc. **4** a nontechnical word for **labium. 5** *Sl.* impudent talk or backchat. **6 bite one's lip. 6a** to stifle one's feelings. **6b** to be annoyed or irritated. **7 keep a stiff upper lip.** to maintain one's courage or composure during a time of trouble. **8 lick** *or* **smack one's lips.** to anticipate or recall something with glee or relish. ◆ *vb* **lips, lipping, lipped. 9** (*tr*) to touch with the lip or lips. **10** (*tr*) to form or be a lip or lips for. **11** (*tr*) *Rare.* to murmur or whisper. **12** (*intr*) to use the lips in playing a wind instrument. ORIG OE *lippa*
▸ **'lipless** *adj* ▸ **'lipˌlike** *adj*

Lipari Islands ★ ('lɪpərɪ) *pl n* a group of volcanic islands under Italian administration off the N coast of Sicily: remains that form a continuous record from Neolithic times. Chief town: Lipari. Pop.: 10 300 (1987 est.). Area: 114 sq. km (44 sq. miles). Also called: **Aeolian Islands.** Italian name: **Isole Eolie** ('iːzole e'ɔːlje).

lipase ('laɪpeɪs, 'lɪpeɪs) *n* any of a group of fat-digesting enzymes produced in the stomach, pancreas, and liver. ORIG C19: from Gk *lipos* fat + -ASE

Lipchitz ★ ('lɪpʃɪts) *n* **Jacques** (ʒɑːk). 1891–1973, US sculptor, born in Lithuania: he pioneered cubist sculpture.

Li Peng ★ ('liː 'pɛŋ) *n* born 1928, Chinese Communist politician: premier of China from 1988.

Lipetsk ★ (*Russian* 'lipɪtsk) *n* a city in central Russia, on the Voronezh River: steelworks. Pop.: 474 000 (1995 est.).

lip gloss *n* a cosmetic applied to the lips to give a sheen.

lipid *or* **lipide** ('laɪpɪd, 'lɪpɪd) *n Biochem.* any of a large group of organic compounds that are esters of fatty acids or closely related substances. They are important structural materials in living organisms. Former name: **lipoid.** ORIG C20: from F *lipide,* from Gk *lipos* fat

Lipizzaner *or* **Lippizaner** (ˌlɪpɪt'sɑːnə) *n* a breed of riding and carriage horse used by the Spanish Riding School in Vienna and nearly always grey in colour. ORIG G, after *Lipizza,* near Trieste, where these horses were bred

Li Po *or* **Li T'ai-po** ★ ('liː 'taɪ 'pəʊ) *n* ?700–762 A.D., Chinese poet.

lipo- *or before a vowel* **lip-** *combining form.* fat or fatty: *lipoprotein.* ORIG from Gk *lipos* fat

lipogram ('lɪpəʊˌgræm) *n* a piece of writing from which all words containing a particular letter have been deliberately omitted.

lipography (lɪ'pɒgrəfɪ) *n* the accidental omission of words or letters in writing. ORIG C19: from Gk *lip-,* stem of *leipein* to omit + -GRAPHY

lipoid ('lɪpɔɪd, 'laɪ-) *adj also* **lipoidal. 1** resembling fat; fatty. ◆ *n* **2** a fatlike substance, such as wax. **3** *Biochem.* a former name for **lipid.**

lipoprotein (ˌlɪpəʊ'prəʊtiːn, ˌlaɪ-) *n* any of a group of proteins to which a lipid molecule is attached, important in the transport of lipids in the bloodstream. See also **low-density lipoprotein.**

liposuction ('lɪpəʊˌsʌkʃən) *n* a cosmetic surgical operation in which subcutaneous fat is removed from the body by suction.

Lippe ★ ('lɪpə) *n* **1** a former state of NW Germany: now part of the German state of North Rhine-Westphalia; part of West Germany until 1990. **2** a river in NW Germany, flowing west to the Rhine. Length: about 240 km (150 miles).

-lipped *adj* having a lip or lips as specified: *tight-lipped.*

Lippi ★ (*Italian* 'lippi) *n* **1 Filippino** (filip'piːno). ?1457–1504, Italian painter of the Florentine school. **2** his father, **Fra Filippo** (fra fi'lippo). ?1406–69, Italian painter of the Florentine school, noted for his frescoes at Prato Cathedral (1452–64).

Lippizaner (ˌlɪpɪt'sɑːnə) *n* a variant spelling of **Lipizzaner**.

Lippmann ★ ('lɪpmən; *French* lipman) *n* **Gabriel** (gabriɛl). 1845–1921, French physicist. He devised the earliest process of colour photography: Nobel prize for physics 1908.

lip-read ('lɪpˌriːd) *vb* **lip-reads, lip-reading, lip-read** (-ˈrɛd). to interpret (words) by lip-reading.

lip-reading *n* a method used by deaf people to comprehend spoken words by interpreting movements of the speaker's lips. Also called: **speech-reading**.
▸ **'lip-ˌreader** *n*

lip service *n* insincere support or respect expressed but not practised.

lipstick ('lɪpˌstɪk) *n* a cosmetic for colouring the lips, usually in the form of a stick.

lip-synch *or* **lip-sync** ('lɪpˌsɪŋk) *vb* to mouth (prerecorded words) on television or film.

liq. *abbrev. for:* **1** liquid. **2** liquor.

liquefacient (ˌlɪkwɪ'feɪʃənt) *n* **1** a substance that liquefies or that causes liquefaction. ◆ *adj* **2** becoming or causing to become liquid. ORIG C19: from L *liquefacere* to make LIQUID

liquefied natural gas *n* a mixture of various gases, esp. methane, liquefied under pressure for transportation and used as an engine fuel. Abbrev.: **LNG**.

liquefied petroleum gas *n* a mixture of various petroleum gases, esp. propane and butane, stored as a liquid under pressure and used as an engine fuel. Abbrev.: **LPG** *or* **LP gas**.

liquefy ('lɪkwɪˌfaɪ) *vb* **liquefies, liquefying, liquefied.** (esp. of a gas) to become or cause to become liquid. ORIG C15: via OF from L *liquefacere* to make liquid
▸ **liquefaction** (ˌlɪkwɪ'fækʃən) *n* ▸ **'liqueˌfiable** *adj* ▸ **'liqueˌfier** *n*

liquescent (lɪ'kwɛsᵊnt) *adj* (of a solid or gas) becoming or tending to become liquid. ORIG C18: from L *liquescere*
▸ **li'quescence** *or* **li'quescency** *n*

liqueur (lɪ'kjʊə; *French* likœr) *n* **1a** any of several highly flavoured sweetened spirits, such as Kirsch or Cointreau, intended to be drunk after a meal. **1b** (*as modifier*): *liqueur glass*. **2** a small hollow chocolate sweet containing liqueur. ORIG C18: from F; see LIQUOR

liquid ('lɪkwɪd) *n* **1** a substance in a physical state in which it does not resist change of shape but does resist change of size. Cf. **gas** (sense 1), **solid** (sense 1). **2** a substance that is a liquid at room temperature and atmospheric pressure. **3** *Phonetics*. a frictionless continuant, esp. (l) or (r). ◆ *adj* **4** of, concerned with, or being a liquid or having the characteristic state of liquids: *liquid wax*. **5** shining, transparent, or brilliant. **6** flowing, fluent, or smooth. **7** (of assets) in the form of money or easily convertible into money. ORIG C14: via OF from L *liquidus*, from *liquēre* to be fluid
▸ **li'quidity** *or* **'liquidness** *n* ▸ **'liquidly** *adv*

liquid air *n* air that has been liquefied by cooling: used in the production of pure oxygen, nitrogen, and as a refrigerant.

liquidambar (ˌlɪkwɪd'æmbə) *n* **1** a deciduous tree of Asia and North and Central America, with star-shaped leaves, and exuding a yellow aromatic balsam. **2** the balsam of this tree, used in medicine. ORIG C16: NL, from L *liquidus* liquid + Med. L *ambar* AMBER

liquidate ('lɪkwɪˌdeɪt) *vb* **liquidates, liquidating, liquidated. 1** to settle or pay off (a debt, claim, etc.). **2a** to terminate the operations of (a commercial firm, bankrupt estate, etc.) by assessment of liabilities and appropriation of assets for their settlement. **2b** (of a commercial firm, etc.) to terminate operations in this manner. **3** (*tr*) to convert (assets) into cash. **4** (*tr*) to eliminate or kill.
▸ **'liquiˌdator** *n*

liquidation (ˌlɪkwɪ'deɪʃən) *n* **1a** the process of terminating the affairs of a business firm, etc., by realizing its assets to discharge its liabilities. **1b** the state of a business firm, etc., having its affairs so terminated (esp. in **to go into liquidation**). **2** destruction; elimination.

liquid-crystal display *n* a flat-screen display used, for example, in portable computers, digital watches, and calculators, in which an array of liquid-crystal elements can be selectively activated to generate an image, by means of an electric field, which when applied to an element alters its optical properties.

liquidize *or* **liquidise** ('lɪkwɪˌdaɪz) *vb* **liquidizes, liquidizing, liquidized** *or* **liquidises, liquidising, liquidised. 1** to make or become liquid; liquefy. **2** (*tr*) to pulverize (food) in a liquidizer so as to produce a fluid.

liquidizer *or* **liquidiser** ('lɪkwɪˌdaɪzə) *n* a kitchen appliance with blades for puréeing vegetables, blending liquids, etc. Also called: **blender**.

liquid measure *n* a unit or system of units for measuring volumes of liquids or their containers.

liquid oxygen *n* the clear pale blue liquid state of oxygen produced by liquefying air and allowing the nitrogen to evaporate: used in rocket fuels. Also called: **lox**.

liquid paraffin *n* an oily liquid obtained by petroleum distillation and used as a laxative. Also called (esp. US and Canad.): **mineral oil**.

liquor ('lɪkə) *n* **1** any alcoholic drink, esp. spirits, or such drinks collectively. **2** any liquid substance, esp. that in which food has been cooked. **3** *Pharmacol*. a solution of a pure substance in water. **4 in liquor.** drunk. ORIG C13: via OF from L, from *liquēre* to be liquid

liquorice *or US & Canad.* **licorice** ('lɪkərɪs, -ərɪʃ) *n* **1** a perennial Mediterranean leguminous shrub. **2** the dried root of this plant, used as a laxative and in confectionery. **3** a sweet having a liquorice flavour. ORIG C13: via Anglo-Norman and OF from LL *liquirītia*, from L *glycyrrhīza*, from Gk *glukurrhiza*, from *glukus* sweet + *rhiza* root

lira ('lɪərə; *Italian* 'liːra) *n, pl* **lire** ('lɪərɪ; *Italian* 'liːre) *or* **liras. 1** the standard monetary unit of Italy and San Marino. **2** Also called: **pound**. the standard monetary unit of Turkey. **3** the standard monetary unit of Malta. ORIG It., from L *lībra* pound

liriodendron (ˌlɪrɪəʊ'dɛndrən) *n, pl* **liriodendrons** *or* **liriodendra** (-drə). a deciduous tulip tree of North America or a similar Chinese tree. ORIG C18: NL, from Gk *leiron* lily + *dendron* tree

Lisbon ★ ('lɪzbən) *n* the capital and chief port of Portugal, in the southwest on the Tagus estuary: became capital in 1256; subject to earthquakes and severely damaged in 1755; university (1911). Pop.: 677 790 (1991). Portuguese name: **Lisboa** (liʒ'boə).

Lisburn ★ ('lɪzbɜːn) *n* **1** a town in Northern Ireland in Co. Antrim, noted for its linen industry: headquarters of the British Army in Northern Ireland. Pop.: 42 110 (1991). **2** a district of E Northern Ireland, S of Belfast. Administrative centre: Lisburn. Pop.: 99 458 (1991). Area: 447 sq. km (172 sq. miles).

Lisieux ★ (*French* lizjø) *n* a town in NW France: Roman Catholic pilgrimage centre, for its shrine of St Thérèse, who lived there. Pop.: 24 506 (1990).

lisle (laɪl) *n* **a** a strong fine cotton thread or fabric. **b** (*as modifier*): *lisle stockings*. ORIG C19: after *Lisle* (now Lille), town in France where this thread was orig. manufactured

lisp (lɪsp) *n* **1** the articulation of *s* and *z* like or nearly like the *th* sounds in English *thin* and *then* respectively. **2** the habit or speech defect of pronouncing *s* and *z* in this manner. **3** the sound of a lisp in pronunciation. ◆ *vb* **4** to use a lisp in the pronunciation of (speech). **5** to speak or pronounce imperfectly or haltingly. ORIG OE *āwlispian*, from *wlisp* lisping (adj), imit.
▸ **'lisper** *n* ▸ **'lisping** *adj, n* ▸ **'lispingly** *adv*

lissom *or* **lissome** ('lɪsəm) *adj* **1** supple in the limbs or body; lithe; flexible. **2** agile; nimble. ORIG C19: var. of *lithesome*, LITHE + -SOME[1]
▸ **'lissomly** *or* **'lissomely** *adv* ▸ **'lissomness** *or* **'lissomeness** *n*

list[1] (lɪst) *n* **1** an item-by-item record of names or things, usually written or printed one under the other. **2** *Computing*. a linearly ordered data structure. ◆ *vb* **3** (*tr*) to make a list of. **4** (*tr*) to include in a list. **5** (*tr*) *Brit*. to declare to be a listed building. **6** (*tr*) *Stock Exchange*. to obtain an official quotation for (a security) so that it may

be traded on the recognized market. **7** an archaic word for **enlist.** ORIG C17: from F, ult. rel. to LIST[2]
▸ **ˈlistable** *adj* ▸ **ˈlisting** *n*

list² (lɪst) *n* **1** a border or edging strip, esp. of cloth. **2** a less common word for **selvage.** ◆ *vb* (*tr*) **3** to border with or as if with a list or lists. ◆ See also **lists.** ORIG OE *līst*

list³ (lɪst) *vb* **1** (esp. of ships) to lean over or cause to lean over to one side. ◆ *n* **2** the act or an instance of leaning to one side. ORIG C17: from ?

list⁴ (lɪst) *Arch.* ◆ *vb* **1** to be pleasing to (a person). **2** (*tr*) to desire or choose. ◆ *n* **3** a liking or desire. ORIG OE *lystan*

list⁵ (lɪst) *vb* an archaic or poetic word for **listen.** ORIG OE *hlystan*

listed building *n* (in Britain) a building officially recognized as having special historical or architectural interest and therefore protected from demolition or alteration.

listed company *n Stock Exchange.* a company whose shares are quoted on the main market of the London stock exchange.

listed security *n Stock Exchange.* a security that is quoted on the main market of the London stock exchange and appears in its *Official List of Securities.* Cf. **Third Market, Unlisted Securities Market.**

listen (ˈlɪsᵊn) *vb* (*intr*) **1** to concentrate on hearing something. **2** to take heed; pay attention: *I warned you but you wouldn't listen.* ORIG OE *hlysnan*
▸ **ˈlistener** *n*

listen in *vb* (*intr, adv;* often foll. by *to*) **1** to listen to the radio. **2** to intercept radio communications. **3** to listen but not contribute (to a discussion), esp. surreptitiously.

listening post *n* **1** *Mil.* a forward position set up to obtain early warning of enemy movement. **2** any strategic position for obtaining information about another country or area.

lister (ˈlɪstə) *n US & Canad. agriculture.* a plough with a double mouldboard designed to throw soil to either side of a central furrow. ORIG C19: from LIST[2]

Lister ★ (ˈlɪstə) *n* **Joseph,** 1st Baron Lister. 1827–1912, British surgeon, who introduced the use of antiseptics.

listeriosis (lɪˌstɪərɪˈəʊsɪs) *n* a serious form of food poisoning, caused by a bacterium (**listeria**). Its symptoms can include meningitis and in pregnant women it may cause damage to the fetus. ORIG after Joseph LISTER

listless (ˈlɪstlɪs) *adj* having or showing no interest; lacking vigour or energy. ORIG C15: from *list* desire + -LESS
▸ **ˈlistlessly** *adv* ▸ **ˈlistlessness** *n*

Liston ★ (ˈlɪstən) *n* **Sonny,** real name *Charles.* 1922–70, US boxer: former world heavyweight champion.

list price *n* the selling price of merchandise as quoted in a catalogue or advertisement.

list renting *n* the practice of renting a list of potential customers to a direct-mail seller of goods or to the fundraisers of a charity.

lists (lɪsts) *pl n* **1** *History.* **1a** the enclosed field of combat at a tournament. **1b** the barriers enclosing the field at a tournament. **2** any arena or scene of conflict, controversy, etc. **3 enter the lists.** to engage in a conflict, controversy, etc. ORIG C14: pl of LIST[2] (border)

listserv (ˈlɪstˌsɜːv) *n* a service on the Internet that provides an electronic mailing to subscribers with similar interests.

Liszt ★ (lɪst) *n* **Franz** (frants). 1811–86, Hungarian composer and pianist. The greatest piano virtuoso of the 19th century, he originated the symphonic poem, pioneered the one-movement sonata form, and developed new harmonic combinations. His works include the symphonies *Faust* (1861) and *Dante* (1867), piano compositions and transcriptions, songs, and church music.

lit (lɪt) *vb* **1** a past tense and past participle of **light**[1] (senses 23–26). **2** a past tense and past participle of **light**[2] (senses 28–31).

lit. *abbrev. for:* **1** literal(ly). **2** literary. **3** literature. **4** litre.

Li T'ai-po ★ (ˈliː ˈtaɪˈpəʊ) *n* See **Li Po.**

litany (ˈlɪtənɪ) *n, pl* **litanies. 1** *Christianity.* **1a** a form of prayer consisting of a series of invocations, each followed by an unvarying response. **1b the Litany.** the general supplication in this form in the Book of Common Prayer. **2** any tedious recital. ORIG C13: via OF from Med. L *litanīa* from LGk *litaneia* prayer, ult. from Gk *litē* entreaty

litchi, lichee, *or* **lychee** (ˌlaɪˈtʃiː) *n* **1** a Chinese tree cultivated for its round edible fruits. **2** the fruit of this tree, which has whitish juicy pulp. ORIG C16: from Cantonese *lai chi*

lite (ˈlaɪt) *adj* **1** (of food and drink) containing few calories or little alcohol or fat. **2** denoting a more restrained or less extreme version of a person or thing: *reggae lite.* ORIG C20: var. spelling of LIGHT[2]

-lite *n combining form.* (in names of minerals) stone: *chrysolite.* ORIG from F *-lite* or *-lithe,* from Gk *lithos* stone

liter (ˈliːtə) *n* the US spelling of **litre.**

literacy (ˈlɪtərəsɪ) *n* **1** the ability to read and write. **2** the ability to use language proficiently.

literal (ˈlɪtərəl) *adj* **1** in exact accordance with or limited to the primary or explicit meaning of a word or text. **2** word for word. **3** dull, factual, or prosaic. **4** consisting of, concerning, or indicated by letters. **5** true; actual. ◆ *n* **6** Also called: **literal error.** a misprint or misspelling in a text. ORIG C14: from LL *litterālis* concerning letters, from L *littera* letter
▸ **ˈliteralness** *or* **literality** (ˌlɪtəˈrælɪtɪ) *n*

literalism (ˈlɪtərəˌlɪzəm) *n* **1** the disposition to take words and statements in their literal sense. **2** literal or realistic portrayal in art or literature.
▸ **ˈliteralist** *n* ▸ **ˌliteralˈistic** *adj*

literally (ˈlɪtərəlɪ) *adv* **1** in a literal manner. **2** (*intensifier*): *there were literally thousands of people.*

> **USAGE NOTE** The use of *literally* as an intensifier is common, esp. in informal contexts. In some cases, it provides emphasis without adding to the meaning: *the house was literally only five minutes walk away.* Often, however, its use results in absurdity: *the news was literally an eye-opener to me.* It is therefore best avoided in formal contexts.

literary (ˈlɪtərərɪ, ˈlɪtrərɪ) *adj* **1** of, relating to, concerned with, or characteristic of literature or scholarly writing: *a literary style.* **2** versed in or knowledgeable about literature. **3** (of a word) formal; not colloquial. ORIG C17: from L *litterārius* concerning reading & writing. See LETTER
▸ **ˈliterarily** *adv* ▸ **ˈliterariness** *n*

literate (ˈlɪtərɪt) *adj* **1** able to read and write. **2** educated; learned. ◆ *n* **3** a literate person. ORIG C15: from L *litterātus* learned. See LETTER
▸ **ˈliterately** *adv*

literati (ˌlɪtəˈrɑːtiː) *pl n* literary or scholarly people. ORIG C17: from L

literature (ˈlɪtərɪtʃə, ˈlɪtrɪ-) *n* **1** written material such as poetry, novels, essays, etc. **2** the body of written work of a particular culture or people: *Scandinavian literature.* **3** written or printed matter of a particular type or genre: *scientific literature.* **4** the art or profession of a writer. **5** *Inf.* printed matter on any subject. ORIG C14: from L *litterātūra* writing; see LETTER

lith. *abbrev. for:* **1** lithograph. **2** lithography.

Lith. *abbrev. for* Lithuania(n).

-lith *n combining form.* indicating stone or rock: *megalith.* ORIG from Gk *lithos* stone

litharge (ˈlɪθɑːdʒ) *n* another name for **lead monoxide.** ORIG C14: via OF from L *lithargyrus,* from Gk, from *lithos* stone + *arguros* silver

lithe (laɪð) *adj* flexible or supple. ORIG OE (in the sense: gentle; C15: supple)
▸ **ˈlithely** *adv* ▸ **ˈlitheness** *n*

lithia (ˈlɪθɪə) *n* **1** another name for **lithium oxide. 2** lithium present in mineral waters as lithium salts. ORIG C19: NL, ult. from Gk *lithos* stone

lithic (ˈlɪθɪk) *adj* **1** of, relating to, or composed of stone. **2**

Pathol. of or relating to a calculus or calculi. **3** of or containing lithium. ORIG C18: from Gk *lithikos* stony

-lithic *n and adj combining form.* relating to the use of stone implements in a specified cultural period: *Neolithic.* ORIG from Gk *lithikos,* from *lithos* stone

lithium ('lɪθɪəm) *n* a soft silvery element of the alkali metal series: the lightest known metal, used as an alloy hardener, as a reducing agent, and in batteries. Symbol: Li; atomic no.: 3; atomic wt.: 6.941. ORIG C19: NL, from LITHO- + -IUM

lithium carbonate *n* a white crystalline solid used in the treatment of manic-depressive illness and mania. Formula: Li_2CO_3.

lithium oxide *n* a white crystalline compound. It absorbs carbon dioxide and water vapour. Formula: Li_2O.

litho ('laɪθəʊ) *n, pl* **lithos,** *adj, adv* short for **lithography, lithograph, lithographic,** or **lithographically.**

litho- *or before a vowel* **lith-** *combining form.* stone: *lithograph.* ORIG from L, from Gk, from *lithos* stone

lithograph ('lɪθəˌgrɑːf) *n* **1** a print made by lithography. ◆ *vb* **2** (*tr*) to reproduce (pictures, text, etc.) by lithography.
▸ **lithographic** (ˌlɪθə'græfɪk) *adj* ▸ ˌ**litho'graphically** *adv*

lithography (lɪ'θɒgrəfɪ) *n* a method of printing from a metal or stone surface on which the printing areas are not raised but made ink-receptive as opposed to ink-repellent. ORIG C18: from NL *lithographia*
▸ **li'thographer** *n*

lithology (lɪ'θɒlədʒɪ) *n* **1** the physical characteristics of a rock, including colour, composition, and texture. **2** the study of rocks.

lithophyte ('lɪθəˌfaɪt) *n* **1** a plant that grows on stony ground. **2** an organism, such as a coral, that is partly composed of stony material.

lithosphere ('lɪθəˌsfɪə) *n* the rigid outer layer of the earth, comprising the earth's crust and the solid upper part of the mantle.

lithotomy (lɪ'θɒtəmɪ) *n, pl* **lithotomies.** the surgical removal of a calculus, esp. one in the urinary bladder. ORIG C18: via LL from Gk

lithotripsy ('lɪθəʊˌtrɪpsɪ) *n, pl* **-sies.** the use of ultrasound to pulverize kidney stones and gallstones *in situ.* ORIG C20: from LITHO- + Gk *thruptein* to crush

Lithuania ★ (ˌlɪθjʊ'eɪnɪə) *n* a republic in central Europe, on the Baltic Sea: a grand duchy in medieval times, it came under Russian rule in the 18th century: became an independent republic in 1918: annexed (1940) by the Soviet Union as the Lithuanian Soviet Socialist Republic: declared independence in 1990, which was recognized in 1991. Official language: Lithuanian. Religion: chiefly Roman Catholic. Currency: litas. Capital: Vilnius. Pop.: 3 699 000 (1999 est.). Area: 65 200 sq. km (25 174 sq. miles). Lithuanian name: **Lietuva.**

Lithuanian (ˌlɪθjʊ'eɪnɪən) *adj* **1** of, relating to, or characteristic of Lithuania, its people, or their language. ◆ *n* **2** the official language of Lithuania. **3** a native or inhabitant of Lithuania.

litigable ('lɪtɪgəbᵊl) *adj Law.* that may be the subject of litigation.

litigant ('lɪtɪgənt) *n* **1** a party to a lawsuit. ◆ *adj* **2** engaged in litigation.

litigate ('lɪtɪˌgeɪt) *vb* **litigates, litigating, litigated. 1** to bring or contest (a claim, action, etc.) in a lawsuit. **2** (*intr*) to engage in legal proceedings. ORIG C17: from L *lītigāre,* from *līt-,* stem of *līs* lawsuit + *agere* to carry on
▸ **'litiˌgator** *n*

litigation (ˌlɪtɪ'geɪʃən) *n* **1** the act or process of bringing or contesting a lawsuit. **2** a judicial proceeding or contest.

litigious (lɪ'tɪdʒəs) *adj* **1** excessively ready to go to law. **2** of or relating to litigation. **3** inclined to dispute or disagree. ORIG C14: from L *lītigiōsus* quarrelsome, from *lītigium* strife
▸ **li'tigiously** *adv* ▸ **li'tigiousness** *n*

litmus ('lɪtməs) *n* a soluble powder obtained from certain lichens. It turns red under acid conditions and blue under basic conditions. Absorbent paper treated with it (**litmus paper**) is used as an indicator. ORIG C16: ?from Scand.

litotes ('laɪtəʊˌtiːz) *n, pl* **litotes.** understatement for rhetorical effect, esp. using negation with a term in place of using an antonym of that term, as in "She was not a little upset" for "She was extremely upset". ORIG C17: from Gk, from *litos* small

litre *or US* **liter** ('liːtə) *n* **1** one cubic decimetre. **2** (formerly) the volume occupied by 1 kilogram of pure water. This is equivalent to 1.000 028 cubic decimetres or about 1.76 pints. ORIG C19: from F, from Med. L *litra,* from Gk: a unit of weight

LittD *or* **LitD** *abbrev. for* Doctor of Letters *or* Doctor of Literature. ORIG L: *Litterarum Doctor*

litter ('lɪtə) *n* **1a** small refuse or waste materials carelessly dropped, esp. in public places. **1b** (*as modifier*): *litter bin.* **2** a disordered or untidy condition or a collection of objects in this condition. **3** a group of offspring produced at one birth by a mammal such as a sow. **4** a layer of partly decomposed leaves, twigs, etc., on the ground in a wood or forest. **5** straw, hay, or similar material used as bedding, protection, etc., by animals or plants. **6** a means of conveying people, esp. sick or wounded people, consisting of a light bed or seat held between parallel sticks. **7** see **cat litter.** ◆ *vb* **8** to make (a place) untidy by strewing (refuse). **9** to scatter (objects, etc.) about or (of objects) to lie around or upon (anything) in an untidy fashion. **10** (of pigs, cats, etc.) to give birth to (offspring). **11** (*tr*) to provide (an animal or plant) with straw or hay for bedding, protection, etc. ORIG C13 (in the sense: bed): via Anglo-F, ult. from L *lectus* bed

littérateur (ˌlɪtərə'tɜː; *French* literatœr) *n* an author, esp. a professional writer. ORIG C19: from F from L *litterātor* a grammarian

litter lout *or US & Canad.* **litterbug** ('lɪtəˌbʌg) *n Sl.* a person who tends to drop refuse in public places.

little ('lɪtᵊl) *determiner* **1** (often preceded by *a*) **1a** a small quantity, extent, or duration of: *the little hope there is left; very little milk.* **1b** (*as pronoun*): *save a little for me.* **2** not much: *little damage was done.* **3 make little of.** to regard or treat as insignificant; dismiss. **4 not a little. 4a** very. **4b** a lot. **5 think little of.** to have a low opinion of. ◆ *adj* **6** of small or less than average size. **7** young: *a little boy.* **8** endearingly familiar; dear: *my husband's little ways.* **9** contemptible, mean, or disagreeable: *your filthy little mind.* ◆ *adv* **10** (usually preceded by *a*) in a small amount; to a small extent or degree; not a lot: *to laugh a little.* **11** (*used preceding a verb*) not at all, or hardly: *he little realized his fate.* **12** not much or often: *we go there very little now.* **13 little by little.** by small degrees. ◆ See also **less, lesser, least.** ORIG OE *lӯtel*

Little Bear *n* **the.** the English name for **Ursa Minor.**

Little Belt ★ *n* a strait in Denmark, between Jutland and Funen Island, linking the Kattegat with the Baltic. Length: about 48 km (30 miles). Width: up to 29 km (18 miles). Danish name: **Lille Bælt.**

Little Bighorn ★ *n* a river in the W central US, rising in N Wyoming and flowing north to the Bighorn River. Its banks were the scene of the defeat (1876) and killing of General Custer and his command by Indians.

Little Diomede ★ *n* the smaller of the two Diomede Islands in the Bering Strait: administered by the US. Area: about 10 sq. km (4 sq. miles).

Little Dipper *n* **the.** a US name for **Ursa Minor.**

Little John ★ *n* one of Robin Hood's companions, noted for his great size and strength.

little people *pl n Folklore.* small supernatural beings, such as elves or leprechauns.

Little Rock ★ *n* a city in central Arkansas, on the Arkansas River: state capital. Pop.: 178 136 (1994 est.).

Little Russia ★ *n* (formerly) a region of the SW Soviet Union, consisting chiefly of Ukraine.

little slam *n Bridge, etc.* the winning of all tricks except one. Cf. **grand slam.** Also called: **small slam.**

Little St Bernard Pass ★ *n* a pass over the Savoy Alps, between Bourg-Saint-Maurice, France, and La

Thuile, Italy: 11th-century hospice. Height: 2187 m (7177 ft).

Littlewood ★ (ˈlɪtᵊlˌwʊd) *n* **(Maud) Joan.** born 1914, British theatre director, who founded the Theatre Workshop Company (1945) with the aim of bringing theatre to the working classes: noted esp. for her production of *Oh, What a Lovely War!* (1963).

littlie (ˈlɪtlɪ) *n Austral. inf.* a young child.

littoral (ˈlɪtərəl) *adj* **1** of or relating to the shore of a sea, lake, or ocean. ◆ *n* **2** a coastal or shore region. ORIG C17: from LL *littorālis,* from *lītus* shore

Littoria ★ (*Italian* litˈtɔːrja) *n* the former name (until 1947) of **Latina.**

liturgical (lɪˈtɜːdʒɪkᵊl) *adj* **1** of or relating to public worship. **2** of or relating to the liturgy.
▸ **liˈturgically** *adv*

liturgy (ˈlɪtədʒɪ) *n, pl* **liturgies. 1** the forms of public services officially prescribed by a Church. **2** (*often cap.*) Also called: **Divine Liturgy.** *Chiefly Eastern Churches.* the Eucharistic celebration. **3** a particular order or form of public service laid down by a Church. ORIG C16: via Med. L, from Gk *leitourgia,* from *leitourgos* minister, from *leit-* people + *ergon* work

Liturgy of the Hours *n Christianity.* another name for **divine office.**

Liu Shao Qi *or* **Liu Shao-ch'i** ★ (ˈljuː ˈʃauˈtʃiː) *n* 1898–1974, Chinese Communist statesman; chairman of the People's Republic of China (1959–68); deposed during the Cultural Revolution.

livable *or* **liveable** (ˈlɪvəbᵊl) *adj* **1** (of a room, house, etc.) suitable for living in. **2** worth living; tolerable. **3** (foll. by *with*) pleasant to live (with).
▸ **ˈlivableness, ˈliveableness** *or* **ˌlivaˈbility, ˌliveaˈbility** *n*

live[1] (lɪv) *vb* **lives, living, lived.** (*mainly intr*) **1** to show the characteristics of life; be alive. **2** to remain alive or in existence. **3** to exist in a specified way: *to live poorly.* **4** (usually foll. by *in* or *at*) to reside or dwell: *to live in London.* **5** (often foll. by *on*) to continue or last: *the pain still lives in her memory.* **6** (usually foll. by *by*) to order one's life (according to a certain philosophy, religion, etc.). **7** (foll. by *on, upon,* or *by*) to support one's style of life; subsist: *to live by writing.* **8** (foll. by *with*) to endure the effects (of a crime, mistake, etc.). **9** (foll. by *through*) to experience and survive: *he lived through the war.* **10** (*tr*) to pass or spend (one's life, etc.). **11** to enjoy life to the full: *he knows how to live.* **12** (*tr*) to put into practice in one's daily life; express: *he lives religion every day.* **13 live and let live.** to refrain from interfering in others' lives; be tolerant. ◆ See also **live down, live in,** etc. ORIG OE *libban, lifian*

live[2] (laɪv) *adj* **1** (*prenominal*) showing the characteristics of life. **2** (*usually prenominal*) of, relating to, or abounding in life: *the live weight of an animal.* **3** (*usually prenominal*) of current interest; controversial: *a live issue.* **4** actual: *a real live cowboy.* **5** *Inf.* full of life and energy. **6** (of a coal, ember, etc.) glowing or burning. **7** (esp. of a volcano) not extinct. **8** loaded or capable of exploding: *a live bomb.* **9** *Radio, television, etc.* transmitted or present at the time of performance, rather than being a recording: *a live show.* **10** (of a record) **10a** recorded in concert. **10b** recorded in one studio take. **11** connected to a source of electric power: *a live circuit.* **12** being in a state of motion or transmitting power. **13** acoustically reverberant. ◆ *adv* **14** during, at, or in the form of a live performance. ORIG C16: from *on live* ALIVE

-lived (-lɪvd) *adj* having or having had a life as specified: *short-lived.*

lived-in *adj* having a comfortable, natural, or homely appearance.

live down (lɪv) *vb* (*tr, adv*) to withstand the effects of (a crime, mistake, etc.) by waiting until others forget or forgive it.

live in (lɪv) *vb* (*intr, adv*) **1** (of an employee) to dwell at one's place of employment, as in a hotel, etc. ◆ *adj* **live-in. 2** resident: *a live-in nanny; a live-in lover.*

livelihood (ˈlaɪvlɪˌhʊd) *n* occupation or employment.

livelong (ˈlɪvˌlɒŋ) *adj Chiefly poetic.* **1** (of time) long or seemingly long (esp. in **all the livelong day**). **2** whole; entire.

lively (ˈlaɪvlɪ) *adj* **livelier, liveliest. 1** full of life or vigour. **2** vivacious or animated, esp. when in company. **3** busy; eventful. **4** characterized by mental or emotional intensity; vivid. **5** having a striking effect on the mind or senses. **6** refreshing or invigorating: *a lively breeze.* **7** springy or bouncy or encouraging springiness: *a lively ball.* ◆ *adv* also **livelily. 8** in a brisk or lively manner: *step lively.*
▸ **ˈliveliness** *n*

liven (ˈlaɪvᵊn) *vb* (usually foll. by *up*) to make or become lively; enliven.
▸ **ˈlivener** *n*

live oak (laɪv) *n* a hard-wooded evergreen oak of S North America: used for shipbuilding.

live out (lɪv) *vb* (*intr, adv*) (of an employee, as in a hospital or hotel) to dwell away from one's place of employment.

liver[1] (ˈlɪvə) *n* **1** a large highly vascular reddish-brown glandular organ in the human abdominal cavity. Its main function is the metabolic transformation of nutrients. It also secretes bile, stores glycogen, and detoxifies certain poisons. Related adj: **hepatic. 2** the corresponding organ in animals. **3** the liver of certain animals used as food. **4** a reddish-brown colour. ORIG OE *lifer*

liver[2] (ˈlɪvə) *n* a person who lives in a specified way: *a fast liver.*

liveried (ˈlɪvərɪd) *adj* (esp. of servants or footmen) wearing livery.

liverish (ˈlɪvərɪʃ) *adj* **1** *Inf.* having a disorder of the liver. **2** disagreeable; peevish.
▸ **ˈliverishness** *n*

liver opal *n* a form of opal having a reddish-brown coloration.

Liverpool[1] ★ (ˈlɪvəˌpuːl) *n* **1** a city in NW England, on the Mersey estuary: second largest seaport in Great Britain; developed chiefly in the 17th century with the industrialization of S Lancashire; seat of The University of Liverpool (1881) and Liverpool John Moores University (1992). Pop.: 474 000 (1994 est.). **2** a unitary authority in NW England, in Merseyside. Pop.: 468 000 (1996 est.). Area: 113 sq. km (44 sq. miles).

Liverpool[2] ★ (ˈlɪvəˌpuːl) *n* **Robert Banks Jenkinson,** 2nd Earl of Liverpool. 1770–1828, British Tory statesman; prime minister (1812–27).

Liverpudlian (ˌlɪvəˈpʌdlɪən) *n* **1** a native or inhabitant of Liverpool. ◆ *adj* **2** of or relating to Liverpool. ORIG C19: from LIVERPOOL, with humorous alteration of *pool* to *puddle*

liver salts *pl n* a preparation of mineral salts used to treat indigestion.

liver sausage *or esp. US* **liverwurst** (ˈlɪvəˌwɜːst) *n* a sausage containing liver.

liverwort (ˈlɪvəˌwɜːt) *n* any of a class of bryophyte plants growing in wet places and resembling green seaweeds or leafy mosses. ORIG late OE *liferwyrt*

livery (ˈlɪvərɪ) *n, pl* **liveries. 1** the identifying uniform, badge, etc., of a member of a guild or one of the servants of a feudal lord. **2** a uniform worn by some menservants. **3** an individual or group that wears such a uniform. **4** distinctive dress or outward appearance. **5a** the stabling, keeping, or hiring out of horses for money. **5b** (*as modifier*): *a livery horse.* **6 at livery.** being kept in a livery stable. ORIG C14: via Anglo-F from OF *livrée* allocation, from *livrer* to hand over, from L *līberāre* to set free

livery company *n Brit.* one of the chartered companies of the City of London originating from the craft guilds.

liveryman (ˈlɪvərɪmən) *n, pl* **liverymen. 1** *Brit.* a member of a livery company. **2** a worker in a livery stable.

livery stable *n* a stable where horses are accommodated and from which they may be hired out.

lives (laɪvz) *n* the plural of **life.**

livestock (ˈlaɪvˌstɒk) *n* (*functioning as sing or pl*) cattle, horses, and similar animals kept for domestic use but not as pets, esp. on a farm.

live together (lɪv) *vb* (*intr, adv*) (esp. of an unmarried couple) to dwell in the same house or flat; cohabit.

live up (lɪv) *vb* **1** (*intr, adv;* foll. by *to*) to fulfil (an expectation, obligation, principle, etc.). **2 live it up.** *Inf.* to enjoy oneself, esp. flamboyantly.

live wire (laɪv) *n* **1** *Inf.* an energetic or enterprising person. **2** a wire carrying an electric current.

live with (lɪv) *vb* (*tr, prep*) to dwell with (a person to whom one is not married).

Livia Drusilla ★ ('lɪvɪə druː'sɪlə) *n* 58 B.C.–29 A.D., Roman noblewoman: wife (from 39 B.C.) of Emperor Augustus and mother of Emperor Tiberius.

livid ('lɪvɪd) *adj* **1** (of the skin) discoloured, as from a bruise or contusion. **2** of a greyish tinge or colour. **3** *Inf.* angry or furious. ORIG C17: via F from L *līvidus,* from *līvēre* to be black and blue
▸ **'lividly** *adv* ▸ **'lividness** *or* **li'vidity** *n*

living ('lɪvɪŋ) *adj* **1a** possessing life; not dead. **1b** (*as collective n* preceded by *the*): *the living.* **2** having the characteristics of life (used esp. to distinguish organisms from nonliving matter). **3** currently in use or valid: *living language.* **4** seeming to be real: *a living image.* **5** (of animals or plants) existing in the present age. **6** presented by actors before a live audience: *living theatre.* **7** (*prenominal*) (intensifier): *the living daylights.* ◆ *n* **8** the condition of being alive. **9** the manner in which one conducts one's life: *fast living.* **10** the means, esp. the financial means, whereby one lives. **11** *Church of England.* another term for **benefice. 12** (*modifier*) of, involving, or characteristic of everyday life: *living area.* **13** (*modifier*) of or involving those now alive (esp. in **living memory**).

living death *n* a life or lengthy experience of constant misery.

living room *n* a room in a private house or flat used for relaxation and entertainment.

Livingston ★ ('lɪvɪŋstən) *n* a town in SE Scotland, the administrative centre of West Lothian: founded as a new town in 1962. Pop.: 41 647 (1991).

Livingstone ★ ('lɪvɪŋstən) *n* **1 David.** 1813–73, Scottish missionary and explorer in Africa, who was the first European to see Lake Ngami (1849), the Zambezi River (1851), the Victoria Falls (1855), and Lake Malawi (1859). Searching for the source of the Nile, he was rescued (1871) by the journalist H. M. Stanley. **2 Ken(neth Robert).** born 1945, British politician; formerly a member of the Labour Party,
he became the first elected mayor of London (2000).

living wage *n* a wage adequate to maintain a person and his family in reasonable comfort.

living will *n* a document that states that a person who becomes terminally ill does not wish his or her life to be prolonged by artificial means such as a life-support machine.

Livonia ★ (lɪ'vəunɪə) *n* **1** a former Russian province on the Baltic, north of Lithuania: became Russian in 1721; divided between Estonia and Latvia in 1918. **2** a city in SE Michigan, west of Detroit. Pop.: 100 415 (1994 est.).
▸ **Li'vonian** *adj, n*

Livorno ★ (*Italian* li'vorno) *n* a port in W central Italy, in Tuscany on the Ligurian Sea: shipyards; oil-refining. Pop.: 164 569 (1996 est.). English name: **Leghorn.**

Livy ★ ('lɪvɪ) *n* Latin name *Titus Livius.* 59 B.C.–17 A.D., Roman historian, famous for his history of Rome in 142 books of which only 35 survive.

lizard ('lɪzəd) *n* any of a group of reptiles typically having an elongated body, four limbs, and a long tail: includes the geckos, iguanas, chameleons, monitors, and slowworms. ORIG C14: via OF from L *lacerta*

Lizard ★ ('lɪzəd) *n* **the.** a promontory in SW England, in SW Cornwall: the southernmost point in Great Britain. Also called: **Lizard Head, Lizard Peninsula.**

LJ (in Britain) *abbrev. for* Lord Justice.

Ljubljana ★ (luː'bljɑːnə) *n* the capital of Slovenia: capital of Illyria (1816–49); university (1595). Pop.: 276 119 (1995 est.). German name: **Laibach.**

LL *abbrev. for:* **1** Late Latin. **2** Low Latin. **3** Lord Lieutenant.

ll. *abbrev. for* lines (of written matter).

llama ('lɑːmə) *n* **1** a domesticated South American cud-chewing mammal of the camel family, that is used as a beast of burden and is valued for its hair, flesh, and hide. **2** the cloth made from the wool of this animal. ORIG C17: via Sp. from Amerind

Llandaff ('lændəf, -dæf) *or* **Llandaf** ★ (*Welsh* hlan'dav) *n* a town in SE Wales, now a suburb of Cardiff; the oldest bishopric in Wales (6th century).

Llandudno ★ (læn'dɪdnəu; *Welsh* hlan'dɪdnɔ) *n* a town and resort in NW Wales, in Conwy county borough on the Irish Sea. Pop.: 14 576 (1991).

Llanelli *or* **Llanelly** ★ (θlæ'nɛθlɪ; *Welsh* hla'nɛhliː) *n* an industrial town in S Wales, in SE Carmarthenshire on an inlet of Carmarthen Bay. Pop.: 44 953 (1991).

Llanfairpwllgwyngyll (*Welsh* hlan,vaɪrpuhl'gwɪngɪhl), **Llanfairpwll,** *or* **Llanfair P. G.** ★ *n* a village in NW Wales, in SE Anglesey: reputed to be the longest place name in Great Britain when unabbreviated; means: St Mary's Church in the hollow of the white hazel near the rapid whirlpool of Llandysilio of the red cave. Full name: **Llanfairpwllgwyngyllgogerychwyrndrobwllllantysiliogogogoch** (*Welsh* hlan'vaɪrpuhl'gwɪngɪhlgɔ'gɛrəxwɪrn'drɔbuhl'hlantə'sɪljɔ'gɔgɔ'gɔx).

Llangollen ★ (*Welsh* hlan'gɒhlɛn) *n* a town in NE Wales, in Denbighshire on the River Dee: International Musical Eisteddfod held annually since 1946. Pop.: 3267 (1991).

llano ('lɑːnəu; *Spanish* 'ʎano) *n, pl* **llanos** (-nəuz; *Spanish* -nɔs). an extensive grassy treeless plain, esp. in South America. ORIG C17: Sp., from L *plānum* level ground

Llano Estacado ★ ('lɑːnəu ˌɛstə'kɑːdəu) *n* the S part of the Great Plains of the US, extending over W Texas and E New Mexico: oil and natural gas resources. Chief towns: Lubbock and Amarillo. Area: 83 700 sq. km (30 000 sq. miles). Also called: **Staked Plain.**

LLB *abbrev. for* Bachelor of Laws. ORIG L: *Legum Baccalaureus*

LLD *abbrev. for* Doctor of Laws. ORIG L: *Legum Doctor*

Llewelyn II ★ (hlə'wɛlɪn) *n* See **Llywelyn ap Gruffudd.**

Lleyn Peninsula ★ (*Welsh* hliːn) *n* a peninsula in NW Wales between Cardigan Bay and Caernarvon Bay.

LLM *abbrev. for* Master of Laws. ORIG L: *Legum Magister*

Lloyd ★ (lɔɪd) *n* **1 Clive (Hubert).** born 1944, West Indian cricketer; captained West Indies (1974–88). **2 Harold (Clayton).** 1893–1971, US comic film actor. **3 Marie,** real name *Matilda Alice Victoria Wood.* 1870–1922, British music-hall entertainer.

Lloyd George ★ *n* **David,** 1st Earl Lloyd George of Dwyfor. 1863–1945, British Liberal statesman: prime minister (1916–22). As chancellor of the exchequer (1908–15) he introduced old age pensions (1908), a radical budget (1909), and an insurance scheme (1911).

Lloyd's (lɔɪdz) *n* an association of London underwriters, set up in the late 17th century. Originally concerned with marine insurance, it now underwrites a variety of insurance policies and publishes a daily list (**Lloyd's List**) of shipping information. ORIG C17: after Edward *Lloyd* (died ?1726) at whose coffee house in London the underwriters orig. carried on their business

Lloyd Webber ★ ('wɛbə) *n* **Andrew,** Baron Lloyd-Webber. born 1948, British composer. His musicals include *Jesus Christ Superstar* (1970) and *Evita* (1978) (with lyrics by Tim Rice), *Cats* (1981), *The Phantom of the Opera* (1986), and *The Beautiful Game* (2000).

Llywelyn ap Gruffudd ★ (hlə'wɛlɪn æp 'grɪfɪð) *n* died 1282, prince of Wales (1258–82): the only Welsh ruler to be recognized as such by the English.

lm *symbol for* lumen.

LMS (in Britain) *abbrev. for* local management of schools: the system of making each school responsible for controlling its total budget, after the budget has been calculated by the Local Education Authority.

LNG *abbrev. for* liquefied natural gas.

lo (ləu) *interj* look! see! (now often in **lo and behold**). ORIG OE *lā*

loach (ləutʃ) *n* a carplike freshwater fish of Eurasia and Af-

★ people and places

rica, having a long narrow body with barbels around the mouth. ORIG C14: from OF *loche,* from ?

Loach ★ (ləutʃ) *n* **Ken(neth).** born 1936, British television and film director: his films include *Kes* (1970) and *My Name is Joe* (1998).

load (ləud) *n* **1** something to be borne or conveyed; weight. **2a** the usual amount borne or conveyed. **2b** (*in combination*): *a carload.* **3** something that weighs down, oppresses, or burdens: *that's a load off my mind.* **4** a single charge of a firearm. **5** the weight that is carried by a structure. **6** *Electrical engineering, electronics.* **6a** a device that receives or dissipates the power from an amplifier, oscillator, generator, or some other source of signals. **6b** the power delivered by a machine, generator, circuit, etc. **7** the resistance overcome by an engine or motor when it is driving a machine, etc. **8** an external force applied to a component or mechanism. **9 a load of.** *Inf.* a quantity of: *a load of nonsense.* **10 get a load of.** *Inf.* pay attention to. **11 have a load on.** *US & Canad. sl.* to be intoxicated. ◆ *vb* (*mainly tr*) **12** (*also intr*) to place or receive (cargo, goods, etc.) upon (a ship, lorry, etc.). **13** to burden or oppress. **14** to supply in abundance: *load with gifts.* **15** to cause to be biased: *to load a question.* **16** (*also intr*) to put an ammunition charge into (a firearm). **17** *Photog.* to position (a film, cartridge, or plate) in (a camera). **18** to weight or bias (a roulette wheel, dice, etc.). **19** *Insurance.* to increase (a premium) to cover expenses, etc. **20** *Computing.* to transfer (a program) to a memory. **21 load the dice. 21a** to add weights to dice in order to bias them. **21b** to arrange to have a favourable or unfavourable position. ◆ See also **loads.** ORIG OE *lād* course; in meaning, infl. by LADE
▸ **'loader** *n*

loaded ('ləudɪd) *adj* **1** carrying a load. **2** (of dice, a roulette wheel, etc.) weighted or otherwise biased. **3** (of a question or statement) containing a hidden trap or implication. **4** charged with ammunition. **5** (of concrete) containing heavy metals, esp. iron or lead, for use in making radiation shields. **6** *Sl.* wealthy. **7** (*postpositive*) *Sl., chiefly US & Canad.* **7a** drunk. **7b** drugged.

loading ('ləudɪŋ) *n* **1** a load or burden; weight. **2** the addition of an inductance to electrical equipment, such as a transmission line or aerial, to improve its performance. **3** *Austral. & NZ.* a payment made in addition to a basic wage or salary to reward special skills, compensate for unfavourable conditions, etc.

load line *n* a pattern of lines painted on the hull of a ship, approximately midway between the bow and the stern, indicating the various levels that the water line should reach if the ship is properly loaded in different conditions.

loads (ləudz) *Inf.* ◆ *pl n* **1** (often foll. by *of*) a lot. ◆ *adv* **2** (intensifier): *loads better.*

loadstar ('ləudˌstɑː) *n* a variant spelling of **lodestar.**

loadstone ('ləudˌstəun) *n* a variant spelling of **lodestone.**

loaf[1] (ləuf) *n, pl* **loaves** (ləuvz). **1** a shaped mass of baked bread. **2** any shaped or moulded mass of food, such as sugar, cooked meat, etc. **3** *Sl.* the head; sense: *use your loaf!* ORIG OE *hlāf*

loaf[2] (ləuf) *vb* **1** (*intr*) to loiter or lounge around in an idle way. **2** (*tr;* foll. by *away*) to spend (time) idly: *he loafed away his life.* ORIG C19: ? back formation from LOAFER

loafer ('ləufə) *n* **1** a person who avoids work; idler. **2** *Chiefly US & Canad.* a moccasin-like shoe. ORIG C19: ?from G *Landläufer* vagabond

loam (ləum) *n* **1** rich soil consisting of a mixture of sand, clay, and decaying organic material. **2** a paste of clay and sand used for making moulds in a foundry, plastering walls, etc. ◆ *vb* **3** (*tr*) to cover, treat, or fill with loam. ORIG OE *lām*
▸ **'loamy** *adj* ▸ **'loaminess** *n*

loan (ləun) *n* **1** the act of lending: *the loan of a car.* **2** property lent, esp. money lent at interest for a period of time. **3** the adoption by speakers of one language of a form current in another language. **4** short for **loan word. 5 on loan.** lent out; borrowed. ◆ *vb* **6** to lend (something, esp. money). ORIG C13 *loon, lan,* from ON *lān*
▸ **'loaner** *n*

loanback ('ləunˌbæk) *n* **1** a facility offered by some life-assurance companies in which an individual can borrow from his pension fund. ◆ *vb* **loan back. 2** to make use of this facility.

Loan Council *n* (in Australia) a statutory body that controls borrowing by the states.

Loanda ★ (ləu'ændə) *n* a variant of **Luanda.**

loan shark *n Inf.* a person who lends funds at illegal or exorbitant rates of interest.

loan translation *n* the adoption by one language of a phrase or compound word whose components are literal translations of the components of a corresponding phrase or compound in a foreign language: *English "superman" from German "Übermensch".* Also called: **calque.**

loan word *n* a word adopted, often in a modified form, from one language into another.

loath *or* **loth** (ləuθ) *adj* **1** (usually foll. by *to*) reluctant or unwilling. **2 nothing loath.** willing. ORIG OE *lāth* (in the sense: hostile)

loathe (ləuð) *vb* **loathes, loathing, loathed.** (*tr*) to feel strong hatred or disgust for. ORIG OE *lāthiān,* from LOATH
▸ **'loather** *n*

loathing ('ləuðɪŋ) *n* abhorrence; disgust.

loathly[1] ('ləuθlɪ) *adv* with reluctance; unwillingly.

loathly[2] ('ləuðlɪ) *adj* an archaic word for **loathsome.**

loathsome ('ləuðsəm) *adj* causing loathing; abhorrent.
▸ **'loathsomely** *adv* ▸ **'loathsomeness** *n*

loaves (ləuvz) *n* the plural of **loaf**[1].

lob (lɒb) *Sport.* ◆ *n* **1** a ball struck in a high arc. **2** *Cricket.* a ball bowled in a slow high arc. ◆ *vb* **lobs, lobbing, lobbed. 3** to hit or kick (a ball) in a high arc. **4** to throw, esp. in a high arc. ORIG C14: prob. from Low G, orig. in the sense: something dangling

Lobachevsky ★ (*Russian* ləba'tʃɛfskij) *n* **Nikolai Ivanovich** (nika'laj i'vanəvitʃ). 1793–1856, Russian mathematician; a founder of non-Euclidean geometry.

lobar ('ləubə) *adj* of, relating to, or affecting a lobe.

lobate ('ləubeɪt) *adj* **1** having or resembling lobes. **2** (of birds) having separate toes that are each fringed with a weblike lobe.
▸ **'lobately** *adv* ▸ **lo'bation** *n*

lobby ('lɒbɪ) *n, pl* **lobbies. 1** a room or corridor used as an entrance hall, vestibule, etc. **2** *Chiefly Brit.* a hall in a legislative building used for meetings between the legislators and members of the public. **3** Also called: **division lobby.** *Chiefly Brit.* one of two corridors in a legislative building in which members vote. **4** a group of persons who attempt to influence legislators on behalf of a particular interest. ◆ *vb* **lobbies, lobbying, lobbied. 5** to attempt to influence (legislators, etc.) in the formulation of policy. **6** (*intr*) to act in the manner of a lobbyist. **7** (*tr*) to apply pressure for the passage of (a bill, etc.). ORIG C16: from Med. L *lobia* portico, from OHG *lauba* arbor, from *laub* leaf
▸ **'lobbyer** *n*

lobbyist ('lɒbɪɪst) *n* a person employed by a particular interest to lobby.
▸ **'lobbyˌism** *n*

lobe (ləub) *n* **1** any rounded projection forming part of a larger structure. **2** any of the subdivisions of a bodily organ or part, delineated by shape or connective tissue. **3** Also called: **ear lobe.** the fleshy lower part of the external ear. **4** any of the parts, not entirely separate from each other, into which a flattened plant part, such as a leaf, is divided. ORIG C16: from LL *lobus,* from Gk *lobos* lobe of the ear or of the liver

lobectomy (ləu'bɛktəmɪ) *n, pl* **lobectomies.** surgical removal of a lobe from any organ or gland in the body.

lobelia (ləu'biːlɪə) *n* any of a genus of plants having red, blue, white, or yellow five-lobed flowers with the three lower lobes forming a lip. ORIG C18: from NL, after Matthias de *Lobel* (1538–1616), Flemish botanist

Lobengula ★ (ˌləubən'gjuːlə) *n* ?1836–94, last Matabele king (1870–93); his kingdom was destroyed by the British.

Lobito ★ (*Portuguese* lu'βitu) *n* the chief port in Angola, in the west on **Lobito Bay**: terminus of the railway through Benguela to Mozambique. Pop.: 70 000 (latest est.).

loblolly ('lɒb,lɒlɪ) *n, pl* **loblollies.** a southern US pine tree with bright reddish-brown bark, green needle-like leaves, and reddish-brown cones. ORIG C16: ?from dialect *lob* to boil + obs. dialect *lolly* thick soup

lobola *or* **lobolo** (lɔ:'bɔ:lə, lə'bəʊ-) *n* (in southern Africa) an African custom by which a bridegroom's family makes a payment in cattle or cash to the bride's family shortly before the marriage. ORIG from Nguni *ukulobola* to give the bride price

lobotomy (ləʊ'bɒtəmɪ) *n, pl* **lobotomies. 1** surgical incision into a lobe of any organ. **2** Also called: **prefrontal leucotomy.** surgical interruption of one or more nerve tracts in the frontal lobe of the brain: used in the treatment of intractable mental disorders. ORIG C20: from LOBE + -TOMY

lobscouse ('lɒb,skaʊs) *n* a sailor's stew of meat, vegetables, and hardtack. ORIG C18: ?from dialect *lob* to boil + *scouse* broth

lobster ('lɒbstə) *n, pl* **lobsters** *or* **lobster. 1** any of several large marine decapod crustaceans occurring on rocky shores and having the first pair of limbs modified as large pincers. **2** any of several similar crustaceans, esp. the spiny lobster. **3** the flesh of any of these crustaceans, eaten as a delicacy. ORIG OE *loppestre,* from *loppe* spider

lobster pot *or* **trap** *n* a round basket or trap made of open slats used to catch lobsters.

lobule ('lɒbju:l) *n* a small lobe or a subdivision of a lobe. ORIG C17: from NL *lobulus,* from LL *lobus* LOBE
▸ **lobular** ('lɒbjʊlə) *or* **lobulate** ('lɒbjʊlɪt) *adj*

lobworm ('lɒb,wɜ:m) *n* **1** another name for **lugworm. 2** a large earthworm used as bait in fishing. ORIG C17: from obs. *lob* lump + WORM

local ('ləʊkᵊl) *adj* **1** characteristic of or associated with a particular locality or area. **2** of, concerned with, or relating to a particular place or point in space. **3** *Med.* of, affecting, or confined to a limited area or part. **4** (of a train, bus, etc.) stopping at all stations or stops. ◆ *n* **5** a train, bus, etc., that stops at all stations or stops. **6** an inhabitant of a specified locality. **7** *Brit. inf.* a pub close to one's home or place of work. **8** *Med.* short for **local anaesthetic** (see **anaesthesia**). **9** *US & Canad.* an item of local interest in a newspaper. ORIG C15: via OF from LL *locālis,* from L *locus* place
▸ **'locally** *adv* ▸ **'localness** *n*

local anaesthetic *n Med.* See **anaesthesia.**

local authority *n Brit. & NZ.* the governing body of a county, district, etc. US equivalent: **local government.**

locale (ləʊ'kɑ:l) *n* a place or area, esp. with reference to events connected with it. ORIG C18: from F *local* (n use of adj); see LOCAL

local government *n* **1** government of the affairs of counties, towns, etc., by locally elected political bodies. **2** the US equivalent of **local authority.**

Local Group *n Astron.* the cluster of galaxies to which the Galaxy and the Andromeda Galaxy belong.

localism ('ləʊkə,lɪzəm) *n* **1** a pronunciation, phrase, etc., peculiar to a particular locality. **2** another word for **provincialism.**

locality (ləʊ'kælɪtɪ) *n, pl* **localities. 1** a neighbourhood or area. **2** the site or scene of an event. **3** the fact or condition of having a location or position in space.

localize *or* **localise** ('ləʊkə,laɪz) *vb* **localizes, localizing, localized** *or* **localises, localising, localised. 1** to make or become local in attitude, behaviour, etc. **2** (*tr*) to restrict or confine (something) to a particular area or part. **3** (*tr*) to assign or ascribe to a particular region.
▸ **'local,izable** *or* **'local,isable** *adj* ▸ **,locali'zation** *or* **,locali'sation** *n*

local loan *n* (in Britain) a loan issued by a local government authority.

local option *n* (esp. in Scotland, New Zealand, and the US) the privilege of a municipality, county, etc., to determine by referendum whether a particular activity, esp. the sale of liquor, shall be permitted there.

Locarno ★ (*Italian* lo'karno) *n* a town in S Switzerland, in Ticino canton at the N end of Lake Maggiore: tourist resort. Pop.: 14 150 (1990 est.).

locate (ləʊ'keɪt) *vb* **locates, locating, located. 1** (*tr*) to discover the position, situation, or whereabouts of; find. **2** (*tr; often passive*) to situate or place: *located on the edge of the city.* **3** (*intr*) to become established or settled.
▸ **lo'cater** *n*

location (ləʊ'keɪʃən) *n* **1** a site or position; situation. **2** the act or process of locating or the state of being located. **3** a place outside a studio where filming is done: *shot on location.* **4** (in South Africa) **4a** a Black African or Coloured township, usually located near a small town. **4b** (formerly) a Black African tribal reserve. **5** *Computing.* a position in a memory capable of holding a unit of information, such as a word, and identified by its address. ORIG C16: from L *locātiō,* from *locāre* to place

locative ('lɒkətɪv) *Grammar.* ◆ *adj* **1** (of a word or phrase) indicating place or direction. **2** denoting a case of nouns, etc., that refers to the place at which the action described by the verb occurs. ◆ *n* **3a** the locative case. **3b** a word or speech element in this case. ORIG C19: LOCATE + -IVE, on the model of *vocative*

loc. cit. (in textual annotation) *abbrev. for* loco citato. ORIG L: in the place cited

loch (lɒx, lɒk) *n* **1** a Scot. word for **lake**[1] (senses 1 and 2). **2** Also: **sea loch.** a long narrow bay or arm of the sea in Scotland. ORIG C14: from Gaelic

lochia ('lɒkɪə) *n* a vaginal discharge of cellular debris, mucus, and blood following childbirth. ORIG C17: NL from Gk *lokhia,* from *lokhos* childbirth
▸ **'lochial** *adj*

loci ('ləʊsaɪ) *n* the plural of **locus.**

lock[1] (lɒk) *n* **1** a device fitted to a gate, door, drawer, lid, etc., to keep it firmly closed. **2** a similar device attached to a machine, vehicle, etc. **3a** a section of a canal or river that may be closed off by gates to control the water level and the raising and lowering of vessels that pass through it. **3b** (*as modifier*): *a lock gate; a lock keeper.* **4** the jamming, fastening, or locking together of parts. **5** *Brit.* the extent to which a vehicle's front wheels will turn to the right or left: *this car has a good lock.* **6** a mechanism that detonates the charge of a gun. **7 lock, stock, and barrel.** completely; entirely. **8** any wrestling hold in which a wrestler seizes a part of his opponent's body. **9** Also called: **lock forward.** *Rugby.* **9a** a player in the second row of the scrum. **9b** this position. **10** a gas bubble in a hydraulic system or a liquid bubble in a pneumatic system that stops the fluid flow in a pipe, capillary, etc.: *an air lock.* ◆ *vb* **11** to fasten (a door, gate, etc.) or (of a door, etc.) to become fastened with a lock, bolt, etc., so as to prevent entry or exit. **12** (*tr*) to secure (a building) by locking all doors, windows, etc. **13** to fix or become fixed together securely or inextricably. **14** to become or cause to become rigid or immovable: *the front wheels of the car locked.* **15** (when *tr, often passive*) to clasp or entangle (someone or each other) in a struggle or embrace. **16** (*tr*) to furnish (a canal) with locks. **17** (*tr*) to move (a vessel) through a system of locks. ◆ See also **lock out, lock up.** ORIG OE *loc*
▸ **'lockable** *adj*

lock[2] (lɒk) *n* **1** a strand, curl, or cluster of hair. **2** a tuft or wisp of wool, cotton, etc. **3** (*pl*) *Chiefly literary.* hair, esp. when curly or fine. ORIG OE *loc*

Locke ★ (lɒk) *n* **1 John.** 1632–1704, English empiricist philosopher; his main works were *An Essay Concerning Human Understanding* (1690) and *Two Treatises on Government* (1690). **2 Matthew.** ?1630–77, English composer, esp. of works for the stage.

locked-in syndrome *n* a condition in which a person is conscious but unable to move any part of the body except the eyes: results from damage to the brainstem.

locker ('lɒkə) *n* **1a** a small compartment or drawer that may be locked, as one of several in a gymnasium, etc., for clothes and valuables. **1b** (*as modifier*): *a locker room.* **2** a person or thing that locks.

Lockerbie ★ ('lɒkəbɪ) *n* a town in SW Scotland, in

Dumfries and Galloway: scene (1988) of the UK's worst air disaster when a jumbo jet was brought down by a terrorist bomb, killing 270 people, including eleven residents of the town.

locket ('lɒkɪt) *n* a small ornamental case, usually on a necklace or chain, that holds a picture, keepsake, etc. ORIG C17: from F *loquet* latch, dim. of *loc* LOCK[1]

lockjaw ('lɒk,dʒɔː) *n Pathol.* a nontechnical name for **trismus** and (often) **tetanus.**

lock out *vb (tr, adv)* **1** to prevent from entering by locking a door. **2** to prevent (employees) from working during an industrial dispute, as by closing a factory. ◆ *n* **lockout. 3** the closing of a place of employment by an employer, in order to bring pressure on employees to agree to terms.

locksmith ('lɒk,smɪθ) *n* a person who makes or repairs locks.

lock step *n* a method of marching such that the men follow one another as closely as possible.

lock up *vb (adv)* **1** *(tr)* Also: **lock in, lock away.** to imprison or confine. **2** to lock or secure the doors, windows, etc., of (a building). **3** *(tr)* to keep or store securely: *secrets locked up in history.* **4** *(tr)* to invest (funds) so that conversion into cash is difficult. ◆ *n* **lockup. 5** the action or time of locking up. **6** a jail or block of cells. **7** *Brit.* a small shop with no attached quarters for the owner. **8** *Brit.* a garage or storage place separate from the main premises. **9** *Stock Exchange.* an investment that is intended to be held for a relatively long period. ◆ *adj* **lock-up. 10** *Brit. & NZ.* (of premises) without living quarters: *a lock-up shop.*

Lockyer ★ ('lɒkjə) *n* Sir **Joseph Norman.** 1836–1920, British astronomer: a pioneer in solar spectroscopy.

loco[1] ('ləukəu) *n, pl* **locos.** *Inf.* short for **locomotive.**

loco[2] ('ləukəu) *adj* **1** *Sl., chiefly US.* insane. **2** (of an animal) affected with loco disease. ◆ *n, pl* **locos. 3** *US.* short for **locoweed.** ◆ *vb* **locos, locoing, locoed.** *(tr)* **4** to poison with locoweed. **5** *US sl.* to make insane. ORIG C19: via Mexican Sp. from Sp.: crazy

loco[3] ('ləukəu) *adj* denoting a price for goods, esp. goods to be exported, that are in a place specified or known, the buyer being responsible for all transport charges from that place: *loco Bristol; a loco price.* ORIG C20: from L *locō* from a place

loco disease *n* a disease of cattle, sheep, and horses characterized by paralysis and faulty vision, caused by ingestion of locoweed.

locomotion (,ləukə'məuʃən) *n* the act, fact, ability, or power of moving. ORIG C17: from L *locō* from a place, ablative of *locus* place + MOTION

locomotive (,ləukə'məutɪv) *n* **1a** Also called: **locomotive engine.** a self-propelled engine driven by steam, electricity, or diesel power and used for drawing trains along railway tracks. **1b** *(as modifier): a locomotive shed; a locomotive works.* ◆ *adj* **2** of or relating to locomotion. **3** moving or able to move, as by self-propulsion.

locomotor (,ləukə'məutə) *adj* of or relating to locomotion. ORIG C19: from L *locō* from a place + MOTOR (mover)

locomotor ataxia *n Pathol.* another name for **tabes dorsalis.**

locoweed ('ləukəu,wiːd) *n* any of several perennial leguminous plants of W North America that cause loco disease in horses, cattle, and sheep.

Locris *or* **Lokris** ★ ('ləukrɪs, 'lɒk-) *n* an ancient region of central Greece.
▸ **'Locrian** *or* **'Lokrian** *adj, n*

loculus ('lɒkjʊləs) *n, pl* **loculi** ('lɒkjʊ,laɪ). **1** *Bot.* any of the chambers of an ovary or anther. **2** *Biol.* any small cavity or chamber. ORIG C19: NL, from L: compartment, from *locus* place
▸ **'locular** *adj*

locum tenens ('ləukəm 'tiːnɛnz) *n, pl* **locum tenentes** (tə'nɛntiːz). *Chiefly Brit.* a person who stands in temporarily for another member of the same profession, esp. for a physician, chemist, or clergyman. Often shortened to **locum.** ORIG C17: Med. L: (someone) holding the place (of another)

locus ('ləukəs) *n, pl* **loci. 1** (in many legal phrases) a place or area, esp. the place where something occurred. **2** *Maths.* a set of points or lines whose location satisfies or is determined by one or more specified conditions: *the locus of points equidistant from a given point is a circle.* **3** *Genetics.* the position of a particular gene on a chromosome. ORIG C18: L

locust ('ləukəst) *n* **1** any of numerous insects, related to the grasshopper, of warm and tropical regions of the Old World, which travel in vast swarms, stripping large areas of vegetation. **2** Also called: **locust tree.** a North American leguminous tree having prickly branches, hanging clusters of white fragrant flowers, and reddish-brown seed pods. **3** the yellowish durable wood of this tree. **4** any of several similar trees, such as the honey locust and carob. ORIG C13 (the insect): from L *locusta;* applied to the tree (C17) because the pods resemble locusts

locution (ləu'kjuːʃən) *n* **1** a word, phrase, or expression. **2** manner or style of speech. ORIG C15: from L *locūtiō* an utterance, from *loquī* to speak

Lod ★ (lɒd) *n* a town in central Israel, southeast of Tel Aviv: Israel's chief airport. Pop.: 42 000 (1989 est.). Also called: **Lydda.**

lode (ləud) *n* **1** a deposit of valuable ore occurring between definite limits in the surrounding rock; vein. **2** a deposit of metallic ore filling a fissure in the surrounding rock. ORIG OE *lād* course

loden ('ləudᵊn) *n* **1** a thick heavy waterproof woollen cloth with a short pile, used for coats. **2** a dark bluish-green colour, in which the cloth is often made. ORIG G, from OHG *lodo* thick cloth

lodestar *or* **loadstar** ('ləud,stɑː) *n* **1** a star, esp. the North Star, used in navigation or astronomy as a point of reference. **2** something that serves as a guide or model. ORIG C14: lit.: guiding star

lodestone *or* **loadstone** ('ləud,stəun) *n* **1a** magnetite that is naturally magnetic. **1b** a piece of this, which can be used as a magnet. **2** a person or thing regarded as a focus of attraction. ORIG C16: lit.: guiding stone

lodge (lɒdʒ) *n* **1** *Chiefly Brit.* a small house at the entrance to the grounds of a country mansion, usually occupied by a gatekeeper or gardener. **2** a house or cabin used occasionally, as for some seasonal activity. **3** *(cap. when part of a name)* a large house or hotel. **4** a room for the use of porters in a university, college, etc. **5** a local branch or chapter of certain societies. **6** the building used as the meeting place of such a society. **7** the dwelling place of certain animals, esp. beavers. **8** a hut or tent of certain North American Indian peoples. ◆ *vb* **lodges, lodging, lodged. 9** to provide or be provided with accommodation or shelter, esp. rented accommodation. **10** *(intr)* to live temporarily, esp. in rented accommodation. **11** to implant, embed, or fix or be implanted, embedded, or fixed. **12** *(tr)* to deposit or leave for safety, storage, etc. **13** *(tr)* to bring (a charge or accusation) against someone. **14** *(tr;* often foll. by *in* or *with)* to place (authority, power, etc.) in the control (of someone). ORIG C15: from OF *loge,* ?from OHG *louba* porch

Lodge ★ (lɒdʒ) *n* **1 David (John).** born 1935, British novelist. His books include *Changing Places* (1975), *Nice Work* (1988), and *Therapy* (1995). **2** Sir **Oliver (Joseph).** 1851–1940, British physicist. **3 Thomas.** ?1558–1625, English writer. His romance *Rosalynde* (1590) supplied the plot for Shakespeare's *As You Like It.*

lodger ('lɒdʒə) *n* a person who pays rent in return for accommodation in someone else's house.

lodging ('lɒdʒɪŋ) *n* **1** a temporary residence. **2** *(sometimes pl)* sleeping accommodation.

lodging house *n* a private home providing accommodation and meals for lodgers.

lodgings ('lɒdʒɪŋz) *pl n* a rented room or rooms, esp. in another person's house.

lodgment *or* **lodgement** ('lɒdʒmənt) *n* **1** the act of lodging or the state of being lodged. **2** a blockage or accumulation. **3** a small area gained and held in enemy territory.

Lodi ★ (*Italian* 'lɔːdi) *n* a town in N Italy, in Lombardy:

scene of Napoleon's defeat of the Austrians in 1796. Pop.: 42 277 (1993 est.).

Łódź ★ (*Polish* wutʃ) *n* a city in central Poland: the country's second largest city; major centre of the textile industry; university (1945). Pop.: 828 500 (1995 est.).

loess (ˈləʊɪs) *n* a light-coloured fine-grained accumulation of clay and silt deposited by the wind. ORIG C19: from G *Löss,* from Swiss G dialect *lösch* loose
▸ **loessial** (ləʊˈɛsɪəl) *adj*

Loewe ★ *n* **1** (ləʊ). **Frederick.** 1904–88, US composer of such musicals as *My Fair Lady* (1956) and *Camelot* (1960), with librettos by Alan Jay Lerner. **2** Also: **Löwe** (*German* ˈløːvə). **(Johann) Karl (Gottfried).** 1796–1869, German composer, esp. of songs.

Loewi ★ (ˈləʊɪ) *n* **Otto.** 1873–1961, US pharmacologist, born in Germany. He shared a Nobel prize for physiology or medicine (1936) for work on the transmission of nerve impulses.

Lofoten and Vesterålen ★ (*Norwegian* ˈluːfutən; ˈvɛstəroːlən) *pl n* a group of islands off the NW coast of Norway, within the Arctic Circle. Largest island: Hinny. Pop.: 66 600 (1985 est.). Area: about 5130 sq. km (1980 sq. miles).

loft (lɒft) *n* **1** the space inside a roof, used for storage or converted into living space. **2** a gallery, esp. one for the choir in a church. **3** a room over a stable used to store hay. **4** an upper storey of a warehouse or factory, esp. when converted into living space. **5** a raised house or coop in which pigeons are kept. **6** *Sport.* **6a** (in golf) the angle from the vertical made by the club face to give elevation to a ball. **6b** elevation imparted to a ball. **6c** a lofting stroke or shot. ◆ *vb* (*tr*) **7** *Sport.* to strike or kick (a ball) high in the air. **8** to store or place in a loft. **9** *Golf.* to slant (the face of a golf club). ORIG OE, from ON *lopt* air, ceiling

lofty (ˈlɒftɪ) *adj* **loftier, loftiest. 1** of majestic or imposing height. **2** exalted or noble in character or nature. **3** haughty or supercilious. **4** elevated, eminent, or superior.
▸ **ˈloftily** *adv* ▸ **ˈloftiness** *n*

log[1] (lɒg) *n* **1a** a section of the trunk or a main branch of a tree, when stripped of branches. **1b** (*modifier*) constructed out of logs: *a log cabin.* **2a** a detailed record of a voyage of a ship or aircraft. **2b** a record of the hours flown by pilots and aircrews. **2c** a book in which these records are made; logbook. **3** a written record of information about transmissions kept by radio stations, amateur radio operators, etc. **4** Also called: **chip log.** a device consisting of a float with an attached line, formerly used to measure the speed of a ship. **5 like a log.** without stirring or being disturbed (in **sleep like a log**). ◆ *vb* **logs, logging, logged. 6** (*tr*) to fell the trees of (a forest, area, etc.) for timber. **7** (*tr*) to saw logs from (trees). **8** (*intr*) to work at the felling of timber. **9** (*tr*) to enter (a distance, event, etc.) in a logbook or log. **10** (*tr*) to travel (a specified distance or time) or move at (a specified speed). ORIG C14: from ?

log[2] (lɒg) *n* short for **logarithm.**

-log *n combining form.* a US variant of **-logue.**

logan (ˈləʊgən) *n Canad.* another name for **bogan** (a backwater).

Logan ★ (ˈləʊgən) *n* **Mount.** a mountain in NW Canada, in SW Yukon in the St Elias Range: the highest peak in Canada and the second highest in North America. Height: 6050 m (19 850 ft).

loganberry (ˈləʊgənbərɪ, -brɪ) *n, pl* **loganberries. 1** a trailing prickly hybrid plant of the rose family, cultivated for its edible fruit. **2** the purplish-red acid fruit of this plant. ORIG C19: after James H. *Logan* (1841–1928), American judge and horticulturalist who first grew it (1881)

logarithm (ˈlɒgəˌrɪðəm) *n* the exponent indicating the power to which a fixed number, the base, must be raised to obtain a given number or variable. It is used esp. to simplify multiplication and division. Often shortened to **log.** ORIG C17: from NL *logarithmus,* coined 1614 by John NAPIER, from Gk *logos* ratio + *arithmos* number
▸ **logarithmic** (ˌlɒgəˈrɪðmɪk) *adj*

logarithmic function *n* **a** the mathematical function $y = \log x$. **b** a function that can be expressed in terms of this function.

logbook (ˈlɒgˌbʊk) *n* **1** a book containing the official record of trips made by a ship or aircraft. **2** *Brit.* a former name for **registration document.**

log chip *n Naut.* the wooden chip or float of a chip log. See **log**[1] (sense 4).

loge (ləʊʒ) *n* a small enclosure or box in a theatre or opera house. ORIG C18: F; see LODGE

logger (ˈlɒgə) *n* another word for **lumberjack.**

loggerhead (ˈlɒgəˌhɛd) *n* **1** Also called: **loggerhead turtle.** a large-headed turtle occurring in most seas. **2** a tool consisting of a large metal sphere attached to a long handle, used for warming liquids, melting tar, etc. **3** *Arch. or dialect.* a blockhead; dunce. **4 at loggerheads.** engaged in dispute or confrontation. ORIG C16: prob. from dialect *logger* wooden block + HEAD

loggia (ˈlɒdʒə, ˈlɒdʒɪə) *n, pl* **loggias** *or* **loggie** (-dʒɛ). a covered area on the side of a building. ORIG C17: It., from F *loge.* See LODGE

logging (ˈlɒgɪŋ) *n* the work of felling, trimming, and transporting timber.

logic (ˈlɒdʒɪk) *n* **1** the branch of philosophy concerned with analysing the patterns of reasoning by which a conclusion is properly drawn from a set of premises, without reference to meaning or context. **2** any formal system in which are defined axioms and rules of inference. **3** the system and principles of reasoning used in a specific field of study. **4** a particular method of argument or reasoning. **5** force or effectiveness in argument or dispute. **6** reasoned thought or argument, as distinguished from irrationality. **7** the relationship and interdependence of a series of events, facts, etc. **8** *Electronics, computing.* the principles underlying the units in a computer system that perform arithmetical and logical operations. See also **logic circuit.** ORIG C14: from OF *logique* from Med. L *logica,* from Gk *logikos* concerning speech or reasoning

logical (ˈlɒdʒɪkəl) *adj* **1** relating to, used in, or characteristic of logic: *logical connective.* **2** using, according to, or deduced from the principles of logic: *a logical conclusion.* **3** capable of or characterized by clear or valid reasoning. **4** reasonable or necessary because of facts, events, etc.: *the logical candidate.* **5** *Computing.* of, performed by, used in, or relating to the logic circuits in a computer.
▸ **ˌlogiˈcality** *or* **ˈlogicalness** *n* ▸ **ˈlogically** *adv*

logical form *n* the structure of an argument by virtue of which it can be shown to be formally valid.

logical positivism *or* **empiricism** *n* a philosophical theory holding that the only meaningful statements are those that are analytic or can be tested empirically. It therefore rejects theology, metaphysics, etc., as meaningless.

logic bomb *n Computing.* an unauthorized program that is inserted into a computer system; when activated it interferes with the operation of the computer.

logic cell *n* a logic circuit forming part of a chip.

logic circuit *n* an electronic circuit used in computers to perform a logical operation on its two or more input signals.

logician (lɒˈdʒɪʃən) *n* a person who specializes in or is skilled at logic.

logic programming *n* the study or implementation of computer programs capable of discovering or checking proofs of formal expressions or segments.

log in *Computing.* ◆ *vb* **1** Also: **log on.** to enter (an identification number, password, etc.) from a remote terminal to gain access to a multiaccess system. ◆ *n* **login. 2** the process by which a computer user logs in.

logistics (lɒˈdʒɪstɪks) *n* (*functioning as sing or pl*) **1** the science of the movement and maintenance of military forces. **2** the management of materials flow through an organization. **3** the detailed planning and organization of any large complex operation. ORIG C19: from F *logistique,* from *loger* to LODGE
▸ **loˈgistical** *adj*

log jam *n Chiefly US & Canad.* **1** blockage caused by the

★ people and places

crowding together of a number of logs floating in a river. **2** a deadlock; standstill.

loglog (ˈlɒɡlɒɡ) *n* the logarithm of a logarithm (in equations, etc.).

logo (ˈləʊɡəʊ, ˈlɒɡ-) *n, pl* **logos.** short for **logotype** (sense 2).

logo- *combining form.* indicating word or speech: *logogram.* ORIG from Gk *logos* word, from *legein* to speak

logogram (ˈlɒɡəˌɡræm) *n* single symbol representing an entire morpheme, word, or phrase, as for example the symbol (%) meaning *per cent.*

logorrhoea *or esp. US* **logorrhea** (ˌlɒɡəˈrɪə) *n* uncontrollable or incoherent talkativeness.

logos (lɒɡɒs) *n* **1** *Philosophy.* reason, regarded as the controlling principle of the universe. **2** (*cap.*) the divine Word; the second person of the Trinity. ORIG C16: Gk: word, reason

logotype (ˈlɒɡəʊˌtaɪp) *n* **1** *Printing.* a piece of type with several uncombined characters cast on it. **2** Also called: **logo.** a trademark, company emblem, or similar device.

log out *Computing.* ◆ *vb* **1** Also: **log off.** to disconnect a remote terminal from a multiaccess system by entering (an identification number, password, etc.). ◆ *n* **2** Also: **logout.** the process by which a computer user logs out.

logroll (ˈlɒɡˌrəʊl) *vb Chiefly US.* to use logrolling in order to procure the passage of (legislation).
▸ ˈ**logˌroller** *n*

logrolling (ˈlɒɡˌrəʊlɪŋ) *n* **1** *US.* the practice of undemocratic agreements between politicians involving mutual favours, the trading of votes, etc. **2** another name for **birling.** See **birl.**

Logroño ★ (*Spanish* loˈɣroɲo) *n* a walled city in N Spain, on the Ebro River: trading centre of an agricultural region noted for its wine. Pop.: 124 823 (1994 est.).

-logue *or US* **-log** *n combining form.* indicating speech or discourse of a particular kind: *travelogue; monologue.* ORIG from F, from Gk *-logos*

logwood (ˈlɒɡˌwʊd) *n* **1** a leguminous tree of the Caribbean and Central America. **2** the heavy reddish-brown wood of this tree, yielding a dye.

-logy *n combining form.* **1** indicating the science or study of: *musicology.* **2** indicating writing, discourse, or body of writings: *trilogy; phraseology; martyrology.* ORIG from L *-logia,* from Gk, from *logos* word
▸ **-logical** *or* **-logic** *adj combining form.* ▸ **-logist** *n combining form.*

Lohengrin ★ (ˈləʊɪŋɡrɪn) *n* (in German legend) a son of Parzival and knight of the Holy Grail.

loin (lɔɪn) *n* **1** *Anat.* the lower back and sides between the pelvis and the ribs. Related adj: **lumbar. 2** a cut of meat from this part of an animal. ◆ See also **loins.** ORIG C14: from OF *loigne,* ?from Vulgar L *lumbra* (unattested), from L *lumbus* loin

loincloth (ˈlɔɪnˌklɒθ) *n* a piece of cloth worn round the loins. Also called: **breechcloth.**

loins (lɔɪnz) *pl n* **1** the hips and the inner surface of the legs where they join the trunk of the body; crotch. **2** *Euphemistic.* the reproductive organs.

Loire ★ (*French* lwar) *n* **1** a department of E central France, in Rhône-Alpes region. Capital: St Étienne. Pop.: 748 881 (1994 est.). Area: 4799 sq. km (1872 sq. miles). **2** a river in France, rising in the Massif Central and flowing north and west in a wide curve to the Bay of Biscay: the longest river in France. Its valley is famous for its wines and châteaux. Length: 1020 km (634 miles). Ancient name: **Liger.**

Loire-Atlantique ★ (*French* lwaratlɑ̃tik) *n* a department of W France, in Pays de la Loire region. Capital: Nantes. Pop.: 1 085 912 (1994 est.). Area: 6980 sq. km (2722 sq. miles).

Loiret ★ (*French* lwarɛ) *n* a department of central France, in Centre region. Capital: Orléans. Pop.: 606 652 (1994 est.). Area: 6812 sq. km (2657 sq. miles).

Loir-et-Cher ★ (*French* lwareʃɛr) *n* a department of N central France, in Centre region. Capital: Blois. Pop.: 311 779 (1994 est.). Area: 6422 sq. km (2505 sq. miles).

loiter (ˈlɔɪtə) *vb* (*intr*) to stand or act aimlessly or idly. ORIG C14: ?from MDu. *löteren* to wobble
▸ ˈ**loiterer** *n* ▸ ˈ**loitering** *n, adj*

Loki ★ (ˈləʊkɪ) *n Norse myth.* the god of mischief and destruction.

loll (lɒl) *vb* **1** (*intr*) to lie, lean, or lounge in a lazy or relaxed manner. **2** to hang or allow to hang loosely. ◆ *n* **3** an act or instance of lolling. ORIG C14: ? imit.
▸ ˈ**loller** *n* ▸ ˈ**lolling** *adj*

Lolland *or* **Laaland** ★ (*Danish* ˈlɔlan) *n* an island of Denmark in the Baltic Sea, south of Sjælland. Pop.: 80 500 (1988 est.). Area: 1240 sq. km (480 sq. miles).

Lollard (ˈlɒləd) *n English history.* a follower of John Wycliffe during the 14th, 15th, and 16th centuries. ORIG C14: from MDu.; mutterer, from *lollen* to mumble (prayers)
▸ ˈ**Lollardism** *n*

lollipop (ˈlɒlɪˌpɒp) *n* **1** a boiled sweet or toffee stuck on a small wooden stick. **2** *Brit.* another word for **ice lolly.** ORIG C18: ?from N. English dialect *lolly* the tongue + POP[1]

lollipop man *or* **lady** *n Brit. inf.* a person who stops traffic by holding up a circular sign on a pole, to enable children to cross the road safely.

lollop (ˈlɒləp) *vb* **lollops, lolloping, lolloped.** (*intr*) *Chiefly Brit.* **1** to walk or run with a clumsy or relaxed bouncing movement. **2** a less common word for **lounge.** ORIG C18: prob. from LOLL + *-op* as in GALLOP, to emphasize the contrast in meaning

lollo rosso (ˈlɒləʊ ˈrɒsəʊ) *n* a variety of lettuce originating in Italy, having curly red-tipped leaves and a slightly bitter taste.

lolly (ˈlɒlɪ) *n, pl* **lollies. 1** an informal word for **lollipop. 2** *Brit.* short for **ice lolly. 3** *Brit., Austral. & NZ.* a slang word for **money. 4** *Austral. & NZ inf.* a sweet, esp. a boiled one. **5 do the** (*or* **one's**) **lolly.** *Austral. inf.* to lose one's temper. ORIG shortened from LOLLIPOP

Lomax ★ (ˈləʊmæks) *n* **Alan.** born 1915, and his father **John Avery** (ˈeɪvərɪ) (1867–1948), US folklorists.

Lombard[1] (ˈlɒmbəd, -bɑːd, ˈlʌm-) *n* **1** a native or inhabitant of Lombardy. **2** a member of an ancient Germanic people who settled in N Italy after 568 A.D. ◆ *adj also* **Lombardic. 3** of or relating to Lombardy or the Lombards.

Lombard[2] ★ (ˈlɒmbəd, -bɑːd, ˈlʌm-) *n* **Peter.** ?1100–?60, Italian theologian, noted for his *Sententiarum libri quatuor.*

Lombard Street *n* the British financial and banking world. ORIG C16: from a street in London once occupied by Lombard bankers

Lombardy ★ (ˈlɒmbədɪ, ˈlʌm-) *n* a region of N central Italy, bordering on the Alps: dominated by prosperous lordships and city-states during the Middle Ages; later ruled by Spain and then by Austria before becoming part of Italy in 1859; intensively cultivated and in parts highly industrialized. Pop.: 8 924 870 (1996 est.). Area: 23 804 sq. km (9284 sq. miles). Italian name: **Lombardia** (ˌlombarˈdiːa).

Lombardy poplar *n* an Italian poplar tree with upwardly pointing branches giving it a columnar shape.

Lombok ★ (ˈlɒmbɒk) *n* an island of Indonesia, in the Nusa Tenggara Islands east of Java: came under Dutch rule in 1894; important biologically as being transitional between Asian and Australian in flora and fauna, the line of demarcation beginning at **Lombok Strait** (a channel between Lombok and Bali, connecting the Flores Sea with the Indian Ocean). Chief town: Mataram. Pop.: 2 500 000 (1991). Area: 4730 sq. km (1826 sq. miles).

Lomé ★ (*French* lɔme) *n* the capital and chief port of Togo, on the Bight of Benin. Pop.: 513 000 (1990 est.).

Lomond ★ (ˈləʊmənd) *n* **1 Loch.** a lake in W Scotland, north of Glasgow: the largest Scottish lake. Length: about 38 km (24 miles). Width: up to 8 km (5 miles). **2** See **Ben Lomond.**

London[1] ★ (ˈlʌndən) *n* **1** the capital of the United Kingdom, a port in S England on the River Thames near its estuary on the North Sea: consists of the **City** (the financial quarter), the **West End** (the entertainment and major shopping centre), the **East End** (the industrial and dock

area), and extensive suburbs. Latin name: **Londinium.** See also **City. 2 Greater.** the administrative area of London, consisting of the City of London and 32 boroughs (13 Inner London boroughs and 19 Outer London boroughs): formed in 1965 from the City, parts of Surrey, Kent, Essex, and Hertfordshire, and almost all of Middlesex. Pop.: 6 964 400 (1994 est.). Area: 1579 sq. km (610 sq. miles). **3** a city in SE Canada, in SE Ontario on the Thames River: University of Western Ontario (1878). Pop.: 303 165 (1991).
▸ **'Londoner** *n*

London[2] ★ ('lʌndən) *n* **Jack,** full name *John Griffith London.* 1876–1916, US writer and adventurer. His works include *Call of the Wild* (1903) and *White Fang* (1906).

Londonderry ★ ('lʌndən,dɛrɪ) *n* **1** Also called: **Derry.** a historic county of Northern Ireland, on the Atlantic. Area: 2075 sq. km (801 sq. miles). **2** Also called: **Derry.** a port in N Northern Ireland, second city of Northern Ireland: given to the City of London in 1613 to be colonized by Londoners; besieged by James II's forces (1688–89). Pop.: 72 334 (1991). **3** another name for **Derry** (sense 1).

London Eye *n* the world's largest Ferris wheel (diameter 132 m), opened on London's South Bank in 2000 and providing passengers with unique views of London. Also called: **Millennium Wheel.**

London pride *n* a type of saxifrage plant having a basal rosette of leaves and pinkish-white flowers.

Londrina ★ (*Portuguese* lon'drina) *n* a city in S Brazil, in Paraná: centre of a coffee-growing area. Pop.: 355 062 (1991).

lone (ləʊn) *adj* (*prenominal*) **1** unaccompanied; solitary. **2** single or isolated: *a lone house.* **3** a literary word for **lonely. 4** unmarried or widowed. ORIG C14: from the mistaken division of ALONE into *a lone*
▸ **'loneness** *n*

lonely ('ləʊnlɪ) *adj* **lonelier, loneliest. 1** unhappy as a result of being without companions. **2** causing or resulting from the state of being alone. **3** isolated, unfrequented, or desolate. **4** without companions; solitary.
▸ **'loneliness** *n*

lonely hearts *adj* (*often caps.*) of or for people who wish to meet a congenial companion or marriage partner: *a lonely hearts advertisement.*

loner ('ləʊnə) *n Inf.* a person who avoids the company of others or prefers to be alone.

lonesome ('ləʊnsəm) *adj* **1** *Chiefly US & Canad.* another word for **lonely.** ◆ *n* **2 on** *or US* **by one's lonesome.** *Inf.* on one's own.
▸ **'lonesomely** *adv* ▸ **'lonesomeness** *n*

long[1] (lɒŋ) *adj* **1** having relatively great extent in space or duration in time. **2a** (*postpositive*) of a specified number of units in extent or duration: *three hours long.* **2b** (*in combination*): *a two-foot-long line.* **3** having or consisting of a relatively large number of items or parts: *a long list.* **4** having greater than the average or expected range, extent, or duration: *a long match.* **5** seeming to occupy a greater time than is really so: *she spent a long afternoon waiting.* **6** (of drinks) containing a large quantity of nonalcoholic beverage. **7** (of a garment) reaching to the wearer's ankles. **8** *Inf.* (foll. by *on*) plentifully supplied or endowed (with): *long on good ideas.* **9** *Phonetics.* (of a speech sound, esp. a vowel) **9a** of relatively considerable duration. **9b** (in popular usage) denoting the qualities of the five English vowels in such words as *mate, mete, mite, moat, moot,* and *mute.* **10** from end to end; lengthwise. **11** unlikely to win, happen, succeed, etc.: *a long chance.* **12** *Prosody.* **12a** denoting a vowel of relatively great duration. **12b** denoting a syllable containing such a vowel. **12c** carrying the emphasis. **13** *Finance.* having or characterized by large holdings of securities or commodities in anticipation of rising prices. **14** *Cricket.* (of a fielding position) near the boundary: *long leg.* **15 in the long run.** ultimately; after or over a period of time. ◆ *adv* **16** for a certain time or period: *how long will it last?* **17** for or during an extensive period of time: *long into the next year.* **18** at a distant time; quite a bit of time: *long before I met you.* **19** *Finance.* into a position with more security or commodity holdings than are required by sale contracts and therefore dependent on rising prices for profit: *to go long.* **20 as** (*or* **so**) **long as. 20a** for or during just the length of time that. **20b** inasmuch as; since. **20c** provided that; if. **21 no longer.** not any more; formerly but not now. ◆ *n* **22** a long time (esp. in **for long**). **23** a relatively long thing, such as a dash in Morse code. **24** *Phonetics.* a long vowel or syllable. **25** *Finance.* a person with large holdings of a security or commodity in expectation of a rise in its price; bull. **26 before long.** soon. **27 the long and the short of it.** the essential points or facts. ◆ See also **longs.** ORIG OE *lang*

long[2] (lɒŋ) *vb* (*intr;* foll. by *for* or an infinitive) to have a strong desire. ORIG OE *langian*

Long ★ (lɒŋ) *n* **Crawford Williamson.** 1815–78, US surgeon. He was the first to use ether as an anaesthetic.

long. *abbrev. for* longitude.

long- *adv* (*in combination*) for or lasting a long time: *long-awaited; long-established; long-lasting.*

long-acting *adj* (of a drug) slowly effective after initial dosage, but maintaining its effects over a long period of time. Cf. **intermediate-acting, short-acting.**

Long Beach ★ *n* a city in SW California, on San Pedro Bay: resort and naval base; oil-refining. Pop.: 433 852 (1994 est.).

Longbenton ★ (,lɒŋ'bɛntən) *n* a town in N England, in North Tyneside. Pop.: 34 630 (1991).

longboat ('lɒŋ,bəʊt) *n* the largest boat carried aboard a commercial sailing vessel.

longbow ('lɒŋ,bəʊ) *n* a large powerful hand-drawn bow, esp. as used in medieval England.

longcase clock ('lɒŋ,keɪs) *n* another name for **grandfather clock.**

longcloth ('lɒŋ,klɒθ) *n* a fine plain-weave cotton cloth made in long strips.

long-dated *adj* (of a gilt-edged security) having more than 15 years to run before redemption. Cf. **medium-dated, short-dated.**

long-day *adj* (of certain plants) able to mature and flower only if exposed to long periods of daylight. Cf. **short-day.**

long-distance *n* **1** (*modifier*) covering relatively long distances. **2** (*modifier*) (of telephone calls, lines, etc.) connecting points a relatively long way apart. **3** *Chiefly US & Canad.* a long-distance telephone call. **4** a long-distance telephone system or its operator. ◆ *adv* **5** by a long-distance telephone line: *he phoned long-distance.*

long-drawn-out *adj* overprolonged or extended.

Long Eaton ★ ('iːtᵊn) *n* a town in N central England, in SE Derbyshire. Pop.: 44 826 (1991).

longeron ('lɒndʒərən) *n* a main longitudinal structural member of an aircraft. ORIG C20: from F: side support, ult. from L *longus* LONG[1]

longevity (lɒn'dʒɛvɪtɪ) *n* **1** long life. **2** relatively long duration of employment, service, etc. ORIG C17: from LL *longaevitās,* from L *longaevus* long-lived, from *longus* LONG[1] + *aevum* age

long face *n* a disappointed, solemn, or miserable facial expression.
▸ **,long-'faced** *adj*

Longfellow ★ ('lɒŋ,fɛləʊ) *n* **Henry Wadsworth.** 1807–82, US poet, noted for his long poems *Evangeline* (1847) and *The Song of Hiawatha* (1855).

Longford ★ ('lɒŋfəd) *n* **1** a county of north Republic of Ireland, in Leinster province. County town: Longford. Pop.: 30 000 (1996). Area: 1043 sq. km (403 sq. miles). **2** a town in north Republic of Ireland, county town of Co. Longford. Pop.: 6800 (1995 est.).

longhand ('lɒŋ,hænd) *n* ordinary handwriting in which letters, words, etc., are set down in full, as opposed to typing or to shorthand.

long haul *n* **1** a journey over a long distance, esp. one involving the transport of goods. **2** a lengthy job.

long-headed *adj* astute; shrewd; sagacious.
▸ **,long-'headedly** *adv* ▸ **,long-'headedness** *n*

longhorn ('lɒŋ,hɔːn) *n* **1** a long-horned breed of beef cattle, formerly common in the southwestern US. **2** a British breed of beef cattle with long curved horns.

longing ('lɒŋɪŋ) *n* **1** a prolonged unfulfilled desire or

need. ◆ *adj* **2** having or showing desire or need: *a longing look.*
▸ **'longingly** *adv*

Longinus ★ (lɒn'dʒaɪnəs) *n* **Dionysius** (ˌdaɪə'nɪsɪəs). ?2nd century A.D., supposed author of the famous Greek treatise on literary criticism, *On the Sublime.*
▸ **Longinean** (lɒn'dʒɪnɪən) *adj*

longish ('lɒŋɪʃ) *adj* rather long.

Long Island ★ *n* an island in SE New York State, separated from the S shore of Connecticut by **Long Island Sound** (an arm of the Atlantic): contains the New York City boroughs of Brooklyn and Queens in the west, many resorts (notably Coney Island), and two large airports (La Guardia and John F. Kennedy). Area: 4462 sq. km (1723 sq. miles).

longitude ('lɒndʒɪˌtjuːd, 'lɒŋgɪ-) *n* distance in degrees east or west of the prime meridian at 0° measured by the angle between the plane of the prime meridian and that of the meridian through the point in question, or by the time difference. ORIG C14: from L *longitūdō* length, from *longus* LONG[1]

longitudinal (ˌlɒndʒɪ'tjuːdɪnᵊl, ˌlɒŋgɪ-) *adj* **1** of or relating to longitude or length. **2** placed or extended lengthways.
▸ **ˌlongi'tudinally** *adv*

longitudinal wave *n* a wave that is propagated in the same direction as the displacement of the transmitting medium.

long johns *pl n Inf.* underpants with long legs.

long jump *n* an athletic contest in which competitors try to cover the farthest distance possible with a running jump from a fixed board or mark. US and Canad. equivalent: **broad jump.**

long leg *n Cricket.* **a** a fielding position on the leg side near the boundary almost directly behind the batsman's wicket. **b** a fielder in this position.

long list *Chiefly Brit.* ◆ *n* **1** a list of suitable applicants for a job, post, etc., from which a short list will be selected. ◆ *vb* **long-list.** (*tr*) **2** to put (someone) on a long list.

long-lived *adj* having long life, existence, or currency.
▸ **ˌlong-'livedness** *n*

long-off *n Cricket.* **a** a fielding position on the off side near the boundary almost directly behind the bowler. **b** a fielder in this position.

long-on *n Cricket.* **a** a fielding position on the leg side near the boundary almost directly behind the bowler. **b** a fielder in this position.

long-playing *adj* of or relating to an LP (long player).

long-range *adj* **1** of or extending into the future: *a long-range weather forecast.* **2** (of vehicles, aircraft, etc.) capable of covering great distances without refuelling. **3** (of weapons) made to be fired at a distant target.

longs (lɒŋz) *pl n* **1** full-length trousers. **2** long-dated gilt-edged securities. **3** unsold securities or commodities held in anticipation of rising prices.

longship ('lɒŋˌʃɪp) *n* a narrow open vessel with oars and a square sail, used esp. by the Vikings.

longshore ('lɒŋˌʃɔː) *adj* situated on, relating to, or along the shore. ORIG C19: short form of *alongshore*

longshore drift *n* the process whereby beach material is gradually shifted laterally.

longshoreman ('lɒŋˌʃɔːmən) *n, pl* **longshoremen.** a US and Canad. word for **docker.**

long shot *n* **1** a competitor, as in a race, considered to be unlikely to win. **2** a bet against heavy odds. **3** an undertaking, guess, or possibility with little chance of success. **4** *Films, television.* a shot where the camera is or appears to be distant from the object to be photographed. **5 by a long shot.** by any means: *he still hasn't finished by a long shot.*

long-sighted *adj* **1** related to or suffering from hyperopia. **2** able to see distant objects in focus. **3** another term for **far-sighted.**
▸ **ˌlong-'sightedly** *adv* ▸ **ˌlong-'sightedness** *n*

Longs Peak ★ *n* a mountain in N Colorado, in the Front Range of the Rockies: the highest peak in the Rocky Mountain National Park. Height: 4345 m (14 255 ft).

long-standing *adj* existing for a long time.

long-suffering *adj* **1** enduring pain, unhappiness, etc., without complaint. ◆ *n* **2** long and patient endurance.
▸ **ˌlong-'sufferingly** *adv*

long suit *n* **1a** the longest suit in a hand of cards. **1b** a holding of four or more cards of a suit. **2** *Inf.* an outstanding advantage, personal quality, or talent.

long-term *adj* **1** lasting or extending over a long time: *long-term prospects.* **2** *Finance.* maturing after a long period: *a long-term bond.*

long-termism *n* the tendency to focus attention on long-term gains.

longtime ('lɒŋˌtaɪm) *adj* of long standing.

long ton *n* the full name for **ton**[1] (sense 1).

Longueuil ★ (lɒŋ'geɪl; *French* lɔ̃gœj) *n* a city in SE Canada, in S Quebec: a suburb of Montreal. Pop.: 129 874 (1991).

longueur (*French* lɔ̃gœr) *n* a period of boredom or dullness. ORIG lit.: length

Longus ★ ('lɒŋgəs) *n* ?3rd century A.D., Greek author of the prose romance *Daphnis and Chloe.*

long vacation *n* the long period of holiday in the summer during which universities, law courts, etc., are closed.

long wave *n* **a** a radio wave with a wavelength greater than 1000 metres. **b** (*as modifier*): *a long-wave broadcast.*

longways ('lɒŋˌweɪz) *or US & Canad.* **longwise** *adv* another word for **lengthways.**

long weekend *n* a weekend holiday extended by a day or days on either side.

long-winded (ˌlɒŋ'wɪndɪd) *adj* **1** tiresomely long. **2** capable of energetic activity without becoming short of breath.
▸ **ˌlong-'windedly** *adv* ▸ **ˌlong-'windedness** *n*

Longyearbyen ★ ('lɒŋjɪəˌbjɛn) *n* a village on Spitsbergen island, administrative centre of the Svalbard archipelago: coal-mining.

lonicera (lɒ'nɪsərə) *n* See **honeysuckle.**

Lons-le-Saunier ★ (*French* lɔ̃ləsonje) *n* a town in E France: saline springs; manufactures sparkling wines. Pop. (urban area): 210 140 (1990).

loo[1] (luː) *n, pl* **loos.** *Brit.* an informal word for **lavatory.** ORIG C20: ?from F *lieux d'aisance* water closet

loo[2] (luː) *n, pl* **loos. 1** a gambling card game. **2** a stake used in this game. ORIG C17: shortened from *lanterloo,* via Du. from F *lanterelu,* orig. a nonsense word from the refrain of a popular song

loofah ('luːfə) *n* the fibrous interior of the fruit of a type of gourd, which is dried and used as a bath sponge or for scrubbing. Also (esp. US). **loofa, luffa.** ORIG C19: from NL *luffa,* from Ar. *lūf*

look (lʊk) *vb* (*mainly intr*) **1** (often foll. by *at*) to direct the eyes (towards): *to look at the sea.* **2** (often foll. by *at*) to direct one's attention (towards): *let's look at the circumstances.* **3** (often foll. by *to*) to turn one's interests or expectations (towards): *to look to the future.* **4** (*copula*) to give the impression of being by appearance to the eye or mind; seem: *that looks interesting.* **5** to face in a particular direction: *the house looks north.* **6** to expect, hope, or plan (to do something): *I look to hear from you soon; he's looking to get rich.* **7** (foll. by *for*) **7a** to search or seek: *I looked for you everywhere.* **7b** to cherish the expectation (of); hope (for): *I look for success.* **8** (foll. by *to*) **8a** to be mindful (of): *to look to the promise one has made.* **8b** to have recourse (to): *look to your swords, men!* **9** (foll. by *into*) to carry out an investigation. **10** (*tr*) to direct a look at (someone) in a specified way: *she looked her rival up and down.* **11** (*tr*) to accord in appearance with (something): *to look one's age.* **12 look alive, lively, sharp,** *or* **smart.** to hurry up; get busy. **13 look here.** an expression used to attract someone's attention, add emphasis to a statement, etc. ◆ *n* **14** the act or an instance of looking: *a look of despair.* **15** a view or sight (of something): *let's have a look.* **16** (*often pl*) appearance to the eye or mind; aspect: *the look of innocence; I don't like*

the looks of this place. **17** style; fashion: *the new look for spring.* ◆ *sentence connector.* **18** an expression demanding attention or showing annoyance, determination, etc.: *look, I've had enough of this.* ◆ See also **look after, look back,** etc. ORIG OE *lōcian*
▸ **'looker** *n*

USAGE NOTE See at **like**[1].

look after *vb (intr, prep)* **1** to take care of; be responsible for. **2** to follow with the eyes.

lookalike ('lʊkəˌlaɪk) *n* **a** a person or thing that is the double of another, often well-known, person or thing. **b** *(as modifier)*: *a lookalike Minister; a lookalike newspaper.*

look back *vb (intr, adv)* **1** to cast one's mind to the past. **2 never look back**: to become increasingly successful: *after his first book was published, he never looked back.*

look down *vb (intr, adv;* foll. by *on* or *upon)* to express or show contempt or disdain (for).

look forward to *vb (intr, adv + prep)* to wait or hope for, esp. with pleasure.

look-in *Inf.* ◆ *n* **1** a chance to be chosen, participate, etc. **2** a short visit. ◆ *vb* **look in. 3** *(intr, adv;* often foll. by *on)* to pay a short visit.

looking glass *n* a mirror.

look on *vb (intr)* **1** *(adv)* to be a spectator at an event or incident. **2** *(prep)* Also: **look upon.** to consider or regard: *she looked on the whole affair as a joke.*
▸ **ˌlooker-'on** *n*

lookout ('lʊkˌaʊt) *n* **1** the act of keeping watch against danger, etc. **2** a person or persons instructed or employed to keep such a watch, esp. on a ship. **3** a strategic point from which a watch is kept. **4** *Inf.* worry or concern: *that's his lookout.* **5** *Chiefly Brit.* outlook, chances, or view. ◆ *vb* **look out.** *(adv, mainly intr)* **6** to heed one's behaviour; be careful. **7** to be on the watch: *look out for my mother at the station.* **8** *(tr)* to search for and find. **9** (foll. by *on* or *over)* to face in a particular direction: *the house looks out over the moor.*

look over *vb* **1** *(intr, prep)* to inspect by making a tour of (a factory, house, etc.). **2** *(tr, adv)* to examine (a document, letter, etc.). ◆ *n* **look-over. 3** an inspection.

look-see *n Sl.* a brief inspection or look.

look up *vb (adv)* **1** *(tr)* to discover (something required to be known) by resorting to a work of reference, such as a dictionary. **2** *(intr)* to increase, as in quality or value: *things are looking up.* **3** *(intr;* foll. by *to)* to have respect (for): *I've always wanted a girlfriend I could look up to.* **4** *(tr)* to visit or make contact with (a person): *I'll look you up when I'm in town.*

loom[1] (luːm) *n* an apparatus, worked by hand or mechanically (**power loom**), for weaving yarn into a textile. ORIG C13 (meaning any kind of tool): var. of OE *gelōma* tool

loom[2] (luːm) *vb (intr)* **1** to come into view indistinctly with an enlarged and often threatening aspect. **2** (of an event) to seem ominously close. **3** (often foll. by *over)* (of large objects) to dominate or overhang. ◆ *n* **4** a rising appearance, as of something far away. ORIG C16: ?from East Frisian *lomen* to move slowly

loon[1] (luːn) *n* the US and Canad. name for **diver** (the bird). ORIG C17: of Scand. origin

loon[2] (luːn) *n* **1** *Inf.* a simple-minded or stupid person. **2** *Arch.* a person of low rank or occupation. ORIG C15: from ?

loony *or* **looney** ('luːnɪ) *Sl.* ◆ *adj* **loonier, looniest. 1** lunatic; insane. **2** foolish or ridiculous. ◆ *n, pl* **loonies** *or* **looneys. 3** a foolish or insane person. **4** Also: **loonie.** *Canad. inf.* a Canadian dollar coin with a loon bird on one of its faces.
▸ **'looniness** *n*

loony bin *n Sl.* a mental hospital or asylum.

loop (luːp) *n* **1** the round or oval shape formed by a line, string, etc., that curves around to cross itself. **2** any round or oval-shaped thing that is closed or nearly closed. **3** an intrauterine contraceptive device in the shape of a loop. **4** *Electronics.* a closed electric or magnetic circuit through which a signal can circulate, as in a feedback control system. **5** a flight manoeuvre in which an aircraft flies one complete circle in the vertical plane. **6** Also called: **loop line.** *Chiefly Brit.* a railway branch line which leaves the main line and rejoins it after a short distance. **7** *Maths, physics.* a closed curve on a graph: *hysteresis loop.* **8** a continuous strip of cinematographic film. **9** *Computing.* a series of instructions in a program, performed repeatedly until some specified condition is satisfied. **10** a group of people to whom information is circulated (esp. in **in** *or* **out of the loop**). ◆ *vb* **11** *(tr)* to make a loop in or of (a line, string, etc.). **12** *(tr)* to fasten or encircle with a loop or something like a loop. **13** Also: **loop the loop.** to cause (an aircraft) to perform a loop or (of an aircraft) to perform a loop. **14** *(intr)* to move in loops or in a path like a loop. ORIG C14 *loupe*, from ?
▸ **'looper** *n*

loophole ('luːpˌhəʊl) *n* **1** an ambiguity, omission, etc., as in a law, by which one can avoid a penalty or responsibility. **2** a small gap or hole in a wall, esp. one in a fortified wall. ◆ *vb* **loopholes, loopholing, loopholed. 3** *(tr)* to provide with loopholes.

loopy ('luːpɪ) *adj* **loopier, loopiest. 1** full of loops; curly or twisted. **2** *Inf.* slightly mad, crazy.

Loos ★ (*German* loːs) *n* **Adolf** ('aːdɔlf). 1870–1933, Austrian architect: a pioneer of modern architecture, noted for his plain austere style in such buildings as Steiner House, Vienna (1910).

loose (luːs) *adj* **1** free or released from confinement or restraint. **2** not close, compact, or tight in structure or arrangement. **3** not fitted or fitting closely: *loose clothing.* **4** not bundled, packaged, fastened, or put in a container: *loose nails.* **5** inexact; imprecise: *a loose translation.* **6** (of funds, cash, etc.) not allocated or locked away; readily available: *loose change.* **7a** (esp. of women) promiscuous or easy. **7b** (of attitudes, ways of life, etc.) immoral or dissolute. **8a** lacking a sense of responsibility or propriety: *loose talk.* **8b** *(in combination): loosetongued.* **9a** (of the bowels) emptying easily, esp. excessively. **9b** (of a cough) accompanied by phlegm, mucus, etc. **10** *Inf., chiefly US & Canad.* very relaxed; easy. ◆ *n* **11 the loose.** *Rugby.* the part of play when the forwards close round the ball in a ruck or loose scrum. **12 on the loose. 12a** free from confinement or restraint. **12b** *Inf.* on a spree. ◆ *adv* **13a** in a loose manner; loosely. **13b** *(in combination): loose-fitting.* ◆ *vb* **looses, loosing, loosed. 14** *(tr)* to set free or release, as from confinement, restraint, or obligation. **15** *(tr)* to unfasten or untie. **16** to make or become less strict, tight, firmly attached, compact, etc. **17** (when *intr,* often foll. by *off)* to let fly (a bullet, arrow, or other missile). ORIG C13 (in the sense: not bound): from ON *lauss* free
▸ **'loosely** *adv* ▸ **'looseness** *n*

loosebox ('luːsˌbɒks) *n* an enclosed stall with a door in which an animal can be confined.

loose cannon *n* a person or thing that appears to be beyond control and is potentially a source of unintentional damage.

loose cover *n* a fitted but easily removable cloth cover for a chair, sofa, etc.

loose end *n* **1** a detail that is left unsettled, unexplained, or incomplete. **2 at a loose end.** without purpose or occupation.

loose head *n Rugby.* the prop on the hooker's left in the front row of a scrum. Cf. **tight head.**

loose-jointed *adj* **1** supple and easy in movement. **2** loosely built; with ill-fitting joints.
▸ **ˌloose-'jointedness** *n*

loose-leaf *adj* (of a binder, album, etc.) capable of being opened to allow removal and addition of pages.

loosen ('luːsᵊn) *vb* **1** to make or become less tight, fixed, etc. **2** (often foll. by *up)* to make or become less firm, compact, or rigid. **3** *(tr)* to untie. **4** *(tr)* to let loose; set free. **5** (often foll. by *up)* to make or become less strict, severe, etc. **6** *(tr)* to rid or relieve (the bowels) of constipation. ORIG C14: from LOOSE
▸ **'loosener** *n*

loosestrife ('luːsˌstraɪf) *n* **1** any of a genus of plants, esp. the yellow-flowered yellow loosestrife. **2 purple loose-**

strife. a purple-flowered marsh plant. ORIG C16: LOOSE + STRIFE, an erroneous translation of L *lysimachia,* as if from Gk *lusimakhos* ending strife, instead of the name of the supposed discoverer, *Lusimakhos*

loot (lu:t) *n* **1** goods stolen during pillaging, as in wartime, during riots, etc. **2** goods, money, etc., obtained illegally. **3** *Inf.* money or wealth. ◆ *vb* **4** to pillage (a city, etc.) during war or riots. **5** to steal (money or goods), esp. during pillaging. ORIG C19: from Hindi *lūt*
▸ **'looter** *n*

lop[1] (lɒp) *vb* **lops, lopping, lopped.** (*tr;* usually foll. by *off*) **1** to sever (parts) from a tree, body, etc., esp. with swift strokes. **2** to cut out or eliminate from as excessive. ◆ *n* **3** a part or parts lopped off, as from a tree. ORIG C15 *loppe* branches cut off
▸ **'lopper** *n*

lop[2] (lɒp) *vb* **lops, lopping, lopped. 1** to hang or allow to hang loosely. **2** (*intr*) to slouch about or move awkwardly. ORIG C16: ? rel. to LOP[1]

lope (ləʊp) *vb* **lopes, loping, loped. 1** (*intr*) (of a person) to move or run with a long swinging stride. **2** (*intr*) (of four-legged animals) to run with a regular bounding movement. **3** to cause (a horse) to canter with a long easy stride or (of a horse) to canter in this manner. ◆ *n* **4** a long steady gait or stride. ORIG C15: from ON *hlaupa* to LEAP

lop-eared *adj* (of animals) having ears that droop.

Lope de Vega ★ (*Spanish* 'lope ðe 'βeγa) *n* full name *Lope Felix de Vega Carpio.* 1562–1635, Spanish dramatist, novelist, and poet. He established the classic form of Spanish drama and was a major influence on European literature. Some 500 of his 1800 plays are extant.

Lopez ★ ('ləʊpɛz) *n* **Jennifer.** born 1970, Puerto Rican film actress and singer; her films include *Selena* (1997) and *The Wedding Planner* (2001) and her records include *On the 6* (1999) and *J. Lo* (2001).

lopsided (ˌlɒp'saɪdɪd) *adj* **1** leaning to one side. **2** greater in weight, height, or size on one side.
▸ **ˌlop'sidedly** *adv* ▸ **ˌlop'sidedness** *n*

loquacious (lɒ'kweɪʃəs) *adj* characterized by or showing a tendency to talk a great deal. ORIG C17: from L *loquāx* from *loquī* to speak
▸ **lo'quaciously** *adv* ▸ **loquacity** (lɒ'kwæsɪtɪ) *or* **lo'quaciousness** *n*

loquat ('ləʊkwɒt, -kwət) *n* **1** an ornamental evergreen tree of China and Japan, having reddish woolly branches, white flowers, and small yellow edible plum-like fruits. **2** the fruit of this tree. ORIG C19: from Chinese (Cantonese) *lō kwat,* lit.: rush orange

lor (lɔ:) *interj Not standard.* an exclamation of surprise or dismay. ORIG from LORD (interj.)

loran ('lɔ:rən) *n* a radio navigation system operating over long distances. Synchronized pulses are transmitted from widely spaced radio stations to aircraft or shipping, the time of arrival of the pulses being used to determine position. ORIG C20: *lo(ng-)ra(nge) n(avigation)*

Lorca[1] ★ (*Spanish* 'lɔrka) *n* a town in SE Spain, on the Guadalentín River. Pop.: 66 940 (1991).

Lorca[2] ★ (*Spanish* 'lɔrka) *n* **Federico García** (feðe'riko gar'θia). 1898–1936, Spanish poet and dramatist. His plays include the trilogy *Bodas de sangre* (1933), *Yerma* (1934), and *La Casa de Bernarda Alba* (1936).

lord (lɔ:d) *n* **1** a person who has power or authority over others, such as a monarch or master. **2** a male member of the nobility, esp. in Britain. **3** (in medieval Europe) a feudal superior, esp. the master of a manor. **4** a husband considered as head of the household (archaic except in the facetious phrase **lord and master**). **5 my lord.** a respectful form of address used to a judge, bishop, or nobleman. ◆ *vb* **6** (*tr*) *Now rare.* to make a lord of (a person). **7** to act in a superior manner towards (esp. in **lord it over**). ORIG OE *hlāford* bread keeper
▸ **'lordless** *adj* ▸ **'lordˌlike** *adj*

Lord (lɔ:d) *n* **1** a title given to God or Jesus Christ. **2** *Brit.* **2a** a title given to men of high birth, specifically to an earl, marquess, baron, or viscount. **2b** a courtesy title given to the younger sons of a duke or marquess. **2c** the ceremonial title of certain high officials or of a bishop or archbishop: *Lord Mayor.* ◆ *interj* **3** (*sometimes not cap.*) an exclamation of dismay, surprise, etc.: *Good Lord!*

Lord Chancellor *n Brit. government.* the cabinet minister who is head of the judiciary in England and Wales, and Speaker of the House of Lords.

Lord Chief Justice *n* the judge who is second only to the Lord Chancellor in the English legal hierarchy; president of one division of the High Court of Justice.

Lord High Chancellor *n* another name for the **Lord Chancellor.**

Lord Howe Island ★ *n* an island in the Tasman Sea, southeast of Australia: part of New South Wales. Area: 17 sq. km (6 sq. miles). Pop.: 300 (1981 est.).

Lord Lieutenant *n* **1** (in Britain) the representative of the Crown in a county. **2** (formerly) the British viceroy in Ireland.

lordly ('lɔ:dlɪ) *adj* **lordlier, lordliest. 1** haughty; proud. **2** of or befitting a lord. ◆ *adv* **3** *Arch.* in the manner of a lord.
▸ **'lordliness** *n*

Lord Mayor *n* the mayor in the City of London and in certain other important boroughs and large cities.

Lord of Misrule *n* (formerly, in England) a person appointed master of revels at a Christmas celebration.

Lord of the Flies ★ *n* a name for **Beelzebub.** ORIG translation of Heb.: see BEELZEBUB

lordosis (lɔ:'dəʊsɪs) *n Pathol.* forward curvature of the lumbar spine. ORIG C18: NL from Gk, from *lordos* bent backwards
▸ **lordotic** (lɔ:'dɒtɪk) *adj*

Lord President of the Council *n* (in Britain) the cabinet minister who presides at meetings of the Privy Council.

Lord Privy Seal *n* (in Britain) the senior cabinet minister without official duties.

Lord Protector *n* See **Protector.**

Lord Provost *n* the provost of one of the five major Scottish cities.

Lords (lɔ:dz) *n* **the.** short for **House of Lords.**

Lord's ★ (lɔ:dz) *n* a cricket ground in N London; headquarters of the MCC.

lords-and-ladies *n* (*functioning as sing*) another name for **cuckoopint.**

Lord's Day *n* **the.** the Christian Sabbath; Sunday.

lordship ('lɔ:dʃɪp) *n* the position or authority of a lord.

Lordship ('lɔ:dʃɪp) *n* (preceded by *Your* or *His*) *Brit.* a title used to address or refer to a bishop, a judge of the high court, or any peer except a duke.

Lord's Prayer *n* **the.** the prayer taught by Jesus Christ to his disciples, as in Matthew 6:9–13, Luke 11:2–4. Also called: **Our Father, Paternoster** (esp. Latin version).

Lords Spiritual *pl n* the Anglican archbishops and senior bishops of England and Wales who are members of the House of Lords.

Lord's Supper *n* **the.** another term for **Holy Communion** (I Corinthians 11:20).

Lords Temporal *pl n* **the.** (in Britain) peers other than bishops as members of the House of Lords.

lore (lɔ:) *n* **1** collective knowledge or wisdom on a particular subject, esp. of a traditional nature. **2** knowledge or learning. ORIG OE *lār;* rel. to *leornian* to LEARN

Lorelei ★ ('lɒrəˌlaɪ) *n* (in German legend) a siren, said to dwell on a rock at the edge of the Rhine south of Koblenz, who lures boatmen to destruction. ORIG C19: from G *Lurlei* name of the rock; from a poem by Clemens Brentano (1778–1842)

Loren ★ (lə'rɛn, *Italian* 'lɔ:ren) *n* **Sophia** (səʊ'fi:ə, *Italian* so'fi:a), real name *Sophia Scicolone.* born 1934, Italian film actress. Her films include *The Millionairess* (1961), *The Cassandra Crossing* (1977), and *Prêt à Porter* (1994).

Lorentz ★ (*Dutch* 'lo:rənts) *n* **Hendrik Antoon** ('hɛndrɪk 'anto:n). 1853–1928, Dutch physicist: shared the Nobel prize for physics (1902) for his work on electromagnetic theory.

Lorenz ★ (*German* 'lo:rɛnts) *n* **Konrad Zacharias** ('kɔnra:t tsaxa'ri:as) 1903–89, Austrian zoologist, who founded ethology. His works include *On Aggression* (1966): shared the Nobel prize for physiology or medicine 1973.

lorgnette (lɔːˈnjɛt) *n* a pair of spectacles or opera glasses mounted on a handle. ORIG C19: from F, from *lorgner* to squint, from OF *lorgne* squinting

Lorient ★ (*French* lɔrjɑ̃) *n* a port in W France, on the Bay of Biscay. Pop.: 59 437 (1990).

lorikeet (ˈlɒrɪˌkiːt, ˌlɒrɪˈkiːt) *n* any of various small lories, such as the varied lorikeet or rainbow lorikeet. ORIG C18: from LORY + *-keet,* as in PARAKEET

loris (ˈlɔːrɪs) *n, pl* **loris.** any of several omnivorous nocturnal slow-moving prosimian primates of S and SE Asia, esp. the slow loris and slender loris, having vestigial digits and no tails. ORIG C18: from F; from ?

lorn (lɔːn) *adj Poetic.* forsaken or wretched. ORIG OE *loren,* p.p. of *-lēosan* to lose

Lorrain ★ (*French* lɔrɛ̃) *n* See **Claude Lorrain.**

Lorraine ★ (lɒˈreɪn; *French* lɔrɛn) *n* **1** a region and former province of E France; ceded to Germany in 1871 after the Franco-Prussian war and regained by France in 1919; rich iron-ore deposits. German name: **Lothringen. 2 Kingdom of.** an early medieval kingdom on the Meuse, Moselle, and Rhine rivers: later a duchy. **3** a former duchy in E France, once the S half of this kingdom.

Lorris ★ (*French* lɔris) *n* See **Guillaume de Lorris.**

lorry (ˈlɒrɪ) *n, pl* **lorries. 1** a large motor vehicle designed to carry heavy loads, esp. one with a flat platform. US and Canad. name: **truck. 2 off the back of a lorry.** *Brit. inf.* a phrase used humorously to indicate that something has been dishonestly acquired. **3** any of various vehicles with a flat load-carrying surface, esp. one designed to run on rails. ORIG C19: ? rel. to northern English dialect *lurry* to pull

lory (ˈlɔːrɪ), **lowry,** *or* **lowrie** (ˈlaʊrɪ) *n, pl* **lories** *or* **lowries.** any of various small brightly coloured parrots of Australia and Indonesia, having a brush-tipped tongue with which to feed on nectar and pollen. ORIG C17: via Du. from Malay *lūrī,* var. of *nūrī*

Los Alamos ★ (lɒs ˈæləmɒs) *n* a town in the US, in New Mexico: the first atomic bomb was developed here. Pop.: 11 455 (1990).

Los Angeles ★ (lɒs ˈændʒɪˌliːz) *n* a city in SW California, on the Pacific: the second largest city in the US, having absorbed many adjacent townships; industrial centre and port, with several universities. Pop.: 3 488 613 (1994 est.). Abbrev.: **LA.**

lose (luːz) *vb* **loses, losing, lost.** (*mainly tr*) **1** to part with or come to be without, as through theft, accident, negligence, etc. **2** to fail to keep or maintain: *to lose one's balance.* **3** to suffer the loss or deprivation of: *to lose a parent.* **4** to cease to have or possess. **5** to fail to get or make use of: *to lose a chance.* **6** (*also intr*) to fail to gain or win (a contest, game, etc.): *to lose the match.* **7** to fail to see, hear, perceive, or understand: *I lost the gist of his speech.* **8** to waste: *to lose money gambling.* **9** to wander from so as to be unable to find: *to lose one's way.* **10** to cause the loss of: *his delay lost him the battle.* **11** to allow to go astray or out of sight: *we lost him in the crowd.* **12** (*usually passive*) to absorb or engross: *he was lost in contemplation.* **13** (*usually passive*) to cause the death or destruction of: *two men were lost in the attack.* **14** to outdistance or elude: *he soon lost his pursuers.* **15** (*intr*) to decrease or depreciate in value or effectiveness: *poetry always loses in translation.* **16** (*also intr*) (of a timepiece) to run slow (by a specified amount). **17** (of a woman) to fail to give birth to (a viable baby), esp. as the result of a miscarriage. **18 lose it.** *Sl.* to lose control of oneself or one's temper. ORIG OE *losian* to perish
▸ **ˈlosable** *adj*

lose out *vb Inf.* **1** (*intr, adv*) to be defeated or unsuccessful. **2 lose out on.** to fail to secure or make use of: *we lost out on the sale.*

loser (ˈluːzə) *n* **1** a person or thing that loses. **2** *Inf.* a person or thing that seems destined to be taken advantage of, fail, etc.: *a born loser.*

Losey ★ (ˈləʊsɪ) *n* **Joseph.** 1909–84, US film director, in Britain from 1952. His films include *The Servant* (1963) and *The Go-Between* (1971).

losing (ˈluːzɪŋ) *adj* unprofitable; failing: *the business was a losing concern.*

losings (ˈluːzɪŋz) *pl n* losses, esp. in gambling.

loss (lɒs) *n* **1** the act or an instance of losing. **2** the disadvantage or deprivation resulting from losing: *a loss of reputation.* **3** the person, thing, or amount lost: *a large loss.* **4** (*pl*) military personnel lost by death or capture. **5** (*sometimes pl*) the amount by which the costs of a business transaction or operation exceed its revenue. **6** *Insurance.* **6a** an occurrence of something that has been insured against, thus giving rise to a claim by a policyholder. **6b** the amount of the resulting claim. **7 at a loss. 7a** uncertain what to do; bewildered. **7b** rendered helpless (for lack of something): *at a loss for words.* **7c** with income less than outlay: *the firm was running at a loss.* ORIG C14: n prob. formed from *lost,* p.p. of *losen* to perish, from OE *lōsian* to be destroyed, from *los* destruction

loss adjuster *n Insurance.* a person qualified to adjust losses incurred through fire, theft, natural disaster, etc., to agree the loss and the compensation to be paid.

loss leader *n* an article offered below cost to attract customers.

lost (lɒst) *adj* **1** unable to be found or recovered. **2** unable to find one's way or ascertain one's whereabouts. **3** confused, bewildered, or helpless: *he is lost in discussions of theory.* **4** (sometimes foll. by *on*) not utilized, noticed, or taken advantage of (by): *rational arguments are lost on her.* **5** no longer possessed or existing because of defeat, misfortune, or the passage of time: *a lost art.* **6** destroyed physically: *the lost platoon.* **7** (foll. by *to*) no longer available or open (to). **8** (foll. by *to*) insensible or impervious (to a sense of shame, justice, etc.). **9** (foll. by *in*) engrossed (in): *he was lost in his book.* **10** morally fallen: *a lost woman.* **11** damned: *a lost soul.*

Lost Generation *n* (*sometimes not cap.*) **1** the large number of talented young men killed in World War I. **2** the generation of writers, esp. American authors, active after World War I.

lot (lɒt) *pron* **1** (*functioning as sing or pl;* preceded by *a*) a great number or quantity: *a lot to do; a lot of people.* ◆ *n* **2** a collection of objects, items, or people: *a nice lot of youngsters.* **3** portion in life; destiny; fortune: *it falls to my lot to be poor.* **4** any object, such as a straw or slip of paper, drawn from others at random to make a selection or choice (esp. in **draw** *or* **cast lots**). **5** the use of lots in making a selection or choice (esp. in **by lot**). **6** an assigned or apportioned share. **7** an item or set of items for sale in an auction. **8** *Chiefly US & Canad.* an area of land: *a parking lot.* **9** *Chiefly US & Canad.* a film studio. **10 a bad lot.** an unpleasant or disreputable person. **11 cast** *or* **throw in one's lot with.** to join with voluntarily and share the fortunes of. **12 the lot.** the entire amount or number. ◆ *adv* (preceded by *a*) *Inf.* **13** to a considerable extent, degree, or amount; very much: *to delay a lot.* **14** a great deal of the time or often: *to sing madrigals a lot.* ◆ *vb* **lots, lotting, lotted. 15** to draw lots for (something). **16** (*tr*) to divide (land, etc.) into lots. **17** (*tr*) another word for **allot.** ◆ See also **lots.** ORIG OE *hlot*

Lot[1] ★ (lɒt) *n* **1** a department of S central France, in Midi-Pyrénées region. Capital: Cahors. Pop.: 156 881 (1994 est.). Area: 5226 sq. km (2038 sq. miles). **2** a river in S France, rising in the Cevennes and flowing west into the Garonne River. Length: about 483 km (300 miles).

Lot[2] ★ (lɒt) *n Old Testament.* Abraham's nephew: he escaped the destruction of Sodom, but his wife was changed into a pillar of salt for looking back as they fled (Genesis 19).

Lot-et-Garonne ★ (*French* lɔtegarɔn) *n* a department of SW France, in Aquitaine. Capital: Agen. Pop.: 303 496 (1994 est.). Area: 5385 sq. km (2100 sq. miles).

loth (ləʊθ) *adj* a variant spelling of **loath.**

Lothair I ★ (ləʊˈθɛə) *n* ?795–855 A.D., Frankish ruler and Holy Roman Emperor (823–30, 833–34, 840–55); son of Louis I.

Lothair II ★ *n* called *the Saxon.* ?1070–1137, German king (1125–37) and Holy Roman Emperor (1133–37).

Lothario (ləʊˈθɑːrɪˌəʊ) *n, pl* **Lotharios.** (*sometimes not cap.*) a rake, libertine, or seducer. ORIG C18: after a seducer in Nicholas Rowe's tragedy *The Fair Penitent* (1703)

Lothian Region ★ ('ləʊðɪən) *n* a former local government region in SE central Scotland, replaced in 1996.

Lothians ★ ('ləʊðɪənz) *pl n* **the.** three historical counties of SE central Scotland: East Lothian, West Lothian, and Midlothian.

Lothringen ★ ('loːtrɪŋən) *n* the German name for **Lorraine.**

lotion ('ləʊʃən) *n* a liquid preparation having a soothing, cleansing, or antiseptic action, applied to the skin, eyes, etc. ORIG C14: via OF from L *lōtiō* a washing, from *lōtus* p.p. of *lavāre* to wash

lots (lɒts) *Inf.* ◆ *pl n* **1** (often foll. by *of*) great numbers or quantities: *lots of people; to eat lots.* ◆ *adv* **2** a great deal. **3** (intensifier): *the journey is lots quicker by train.*

lottery ('lɒtərɪ) *n, pl* **lotteries. 1** a game of chance in which tickets are sold, which may later qualify the holder for a prize. **2** an endeavour, the success of which is regarded as a matter of luck. ORIG C16: from OF *loterie,* from MDu. *loterije*

lotto ('lɒtəʊ) *n* **1** Also called: **housey-housey.** a children's game in which numbered discs are drawn at random and called out, while the players cover the corresponding numbers on cards, the winner being the first to cover all the numbers, a particular row, etc. Cf. **bingo. 2** *Austral.* a lottery with cash prizes based on this principle. ORIG C18: from It., from OF *lot,* from Gmc

lotus ('ləʊtəs) *n* **1** (in Greek mythology) a fruit that induces forgetfulness and a dreamy languor in those who eat it. **2** any of several water lilies of tropical Africa and Asia, esp. the **white lotus,** which was regarded as sacred in ancient Egypt. **3** a related plant which is the sacred lotus of India, China, and Tibet. **4** a representation of such a plant, common in Hindu, Buddhist, and ancient Egyptian art. **5** any of a genus of leguminous plants of the legume family of the Old World and North America, having yellow, pink, or white pealike flowers. ◆ Also (rare): **lotos.** ORIG C16: via L from Gk *lōtos,* from Semitic

lotus-eater *n Greek myth.* one of a people encountered by Odysseus in North Africa who lived in indolent forgetfulness, drugged by the fruit of the legendary lotus.

lotus position *n* a seated cross-legged position used in yoga, meditation, etc.

loud (laud) *adj* **1** (of sound) relatively great in volume: *a loud shout.* **2** making or able to make sounds of relatively great volume: *a loud voice.* **3** clamorous, insistent, and emphatic: *loud protests.* **4** (of colours, designs, etc.) offensive or obtrusive to look at. **5** characterized by noisy, vulgar, and offensive behaviour. ◆ *adv* **6** in a loud manner. **7 out loud.** audibly, as distinct from silently. ORIG OE *hlud*
▸ **'loudish** *adj* ▸ **'loudly** *adv* ▸ **'loudness** *n*

louden ('laudᵊn) *vb* to make or become louder.

loud-hailer *n* a portable loudspeaker having a built-in amplifier and microphone. Also (US and Canad.): **bullhorn.**

loudmouth ('laud,mauθ) *n Inf.* a person who brags or talks too loudly.
▸ **loudmouthed** ('laud,mauðd, -,mauθt) *adj*

loudspeaker (,laud'spiːkə) *n* a device for converting audio-frequency signals into sound waves. Often shortened to **speaker.**

Lou Gehrig's disease (luː 'gerɪg) *n* another name for **amyotrophic lateral sclerosis.** ORIG C20: named after *Lou Gehrig* (1903–41), US baseball player who suffered from it

lough (lɒx, lɒk) *n* **1** an Irish word for **lake**[1] (senses 1 and 2). **2** a long narrow bay or arm of the sea in Ireland. ORIG C14: from Irish *loch* lake

Loughborough ★ ('lʌfbərə, -brə) *n* a town in central England, in N Leicestershire: seat of Loughborough University (1966). Pop.: 46 867 (1991).

Louis ★ ('luːɪs) *n* **Joe,** real name *Joseph Louis Barrow,* nicknamed *the Brown Bomber.* 1914–81, US boxer; world heavyweight champion (1937–49).

Louis I ★ ('luːɪ; *French* lwi) *n* known as *Louis the Pious* or *Louis the Debonair.* 778–840 A.D., king of France and Holy Roman Emperor (814–23, 830–33, 834–40).

Louis II ★ *n* **1** known as *Louis the German.* ?804–876 A.D., king of Germany (843–76); son of Louis I. **2 de Bourbon.** See (Prince de) **Condé.**

Louis IV ★ *n* known as *Louis the Bavarian.* ?1287–1347, king of Germany (1314–47) and Holy Roman Emperor (1328–47).

Louis V ★ *n* known as *Louis le Fainéant.* ?967–987 A.D., last Carolingian king of France (986–87).

Louis VIII ★ *n* known as *Cœur-de-Lion.* 1187–1226, king of France (1223–26). He was offered the English throne by opponents of King John but his invasion failed (1216).

Louis IX ★ *n* known as *Saint Louis.* 1214–70, king of France (1226–70): led the Sixth Crusade (1248–54) and was held to ransom (1250); died at Tunis while on another crusade.

Louis XI ★ *n* 1423–83, king of France (1461–83); involved in a struggle with his vassals, esp. the duke of Burgundy, in his attempt to unite France.

Louis XII ★ *n* 1462–1515, king of France (1498–1515).

Louis XIII ★ *n* 1601–43, king of France (1610–43). His mother (Marie de Médicis) was regent until 1617.

Louis XIV ★ *n* known as *le roi soleil* (the Sun King). 1638–1715, king of France (1643–1715). Effective ruler from 1661, he failed to establish French supremacy in Europe but his reign was regarded as a golden age of French arts.

Louis XV ★ *n* 1710–74, king of France (1715–74); great-grandson of Louis XIV. He engaged France in the disastrous Seven Years' War (1756–63).

Louis XVI ★ *n* 1754–93, king of France (1774–92); grandson of Louis XV. He and his wife, Marie Antoinette, were guillotined during the Revolution.

Louis XVII ★ *n* 1785–95, titular king of France (1793–95) during the Revolution; he died in prison.

Louis XVIII ★ *n* 1755–1824, king of France (1814–24). He became titular king after the death of Louis XVII (1795) and ascended the throne at the Bourbon restoration. He was forced to flee during the Hundred Days.

Louisburg *or* **Louisbourg** ★ ('luːɪs,bɜːg) *n* a fortress in Canada, in Nova Scotia on SE Cape Breton Island: founded in 1713 by the French and strongly fortified (1720–40); captured by the British (1758) and demolished; reconstructed as a historic site.

louis d'or (,luːɪ 'dɔː) *n, pl* **louis d'or** (,luːɪz 'dɔː). **1** a former French gold coin worth 20 francs. **2** an old French coin minted in the reign of Louis XIII. ◆ Often shortened to **louis.** ORIG C17: from F: golden louis, after Louis XIII

Louisiana ★ (luː,iːzɪ'ænə) *n* a state of the southern US, on the Gulf of Mexico: originally a French colony; bought by the US in 1803 as part of the Louisiana Purchase; chiefly low-lying. Capital: Baton Rouge. Pop.: 4 368 967 (1998 est.). Area: 116 368 sq. km (44 930 sq. miles). Abbrevs.: **La.** or (with zip code) **LA**

Louis Napoleon ★ *n* the original name of **Napoleon III.**

Louis Philippe ★ (*French* filip) *n* known as the *Citizen King.* 1773–1850, king of the French (1830–48). His régime became excessively identified with the bourgeoisie and he was forced to abdicate by the revolution of 1848.

Louisville ★ ('luːɪ,vɪl) *n* a port in N Kentucky, on the Ohio River: site of the annual Kentucky Derby; university (1837). Pop.: 270 308 (1994 est.).

lounge (laundʒ) *vb* **lounges, lounging, lounged. 1** (*intr;* often foll. by *about* or *around*) to sit, lie, walk, or stand in a relaxed manner. **2** to pass (time) lazily or idly. ◆ *n* **3** a communal room in a hotel, ship, etc., used for waiting or relaxing in. **4** *Chiefly Brit.* a living room in a private house. **5** Also called: **lounge bar, saloon.** *Brit.* a more expensive bar in a pub or hotel. **6** a sofa or couch. **7** the act or an instance of lounging. ORIG C16: from ?

lounger ('laundʒə) *n* **1** a comfortable couch or extending chair designed for someone to relax on. **2** a loose comfortable leisure garment. **3** a person who lounges.

lounge suit *n* a man's suit of matching jacket and trousers worn for the normal business day.

loupe (lu:p) *n* a small magnifying glass used by jewellers, horologists, etc., worn in the eye socket. ORIG C20: from F (formerly an imperfect precious stone), from OF, from ?

lour *or* **lower** ('lauə) *vb* (*intr*) **1** (esp. of the sky, weather, etc.) to be overcast, dark, and menacing. **2** to scowl or frown. ◆ *n* **3** a menacing scowl or appearance. ORIG C13 *louren* to scowl
▸ **'louring** *or* **'lowering** *adj*

Lourdes ★ (*French* lurd) *n* a town in SW France: a place of pilgrimage for Roman Catholics after a peasant girl, Bernadette Soubirous, claimed to have seen visions of the Virgin Mary in 1858. Pop.: 17 100 (1995 est.).

Lourenço Marques ★ (lə'rεnsəu 'mɑ:k, 'mɑ:ks; *Portuguese* lo'rẽsu 'markɪʃ) *n* the former name (until 1975) of **Maputo.**

lourie *or* **loerie** ('laurɪ) *n* a type of African bird with bright plumage. ORIG from Malay *luri*

louse (laus) *n, pl* **lice. 1** a wingless bloodsucking insect, such as the head louse, body louse, and crab louse, all of which infest man. **2 biting** *or* **bird louse.** a wingless insect, such as the chicken louse: external parasites of birds and mammals, with biting mouthparts. **3** any of various similar but unrelated insects. **4** (*pl* **louses**) *Sl.* an unpleasant or mean person. ◆ *vb* **louses, lousing, loused.** (*tr*) **5** to remove lice from. **6** (foll. by *up*) *Sl.* to ruin or spoil. ORIG OE *lūs*

lousewort ('laus,wɜ:t) *n* any of various N temperate plants having spikes of white, yellow, or mauve flowers.

lousy ('lauzɪ) *adj* **lousier, lousiest. 1** *Sl.* very mean or unpleasant. **2** *Sl.* inferior or bad. **3** infested with lice. **4** (foll. by *with*) *Sl.* provided with an excessive amount (of): *he's lousy with money.*
▸ **'lousily** *adv* ▸ **'lousiness** *n*

lout (laut) *n* a crude or oafish person; boor. ORIG C16: ? from OE *lūtan* to stoop
▸ **'loutish** *adj*

Louth ★ (lauθ) *n* a county of NE Republic of Ireland, in Leinster province on the Irish Sea: the smallest of the counties. County town: Dundalk. Pop.: 92 000 (1996). Area: 821 sq. km (317 sq. miles).

Louvain ★ (*French* luvɛ̃) *n* a town in central Belgium, in Flemish Brabant province: capital of the duchy of Brabant (11th–15th centuries) and centre of the cloth trade; university (1426). Pop.: 87 165 (1995 est.). Flemish name: **Leuven.**

louvre *or US* **louver** ('lu:və) *n* **1a** any of a set of horizontal parallel slats in a door or window, sloping outwards to throw off rain and admit air. **1b** Also called: **louvre boards.** the slats and frame supporting them. **2** *Archit.* a turret that allows smoke to escape. ORIG C14: from OF *lovier,* from ?
▸ **'louvred** *or US* **'louvered** *adj*

Louvre ★ (*French* luvrə) *n* the national museum and art gallery of France, in Paris: formerly a royal palace, begun in 1546; used for its present purpose since 1793.

lovable *or* **loveable** ('lʌvəbᵊl) *adj* attracting or deserving affection.
▸ **,lova'bility, ,lovea'bility** *or* **'lovableness, 'loveableness** *n*
▸ **'lovably** *or* **'loveably** *adv*

lovage ('lʌvɪdʒ) *n* a European umbelliferous plant with greenish-white flowers and aromatic fruits, which are used for flavouring food. ORIG C14 *loveache,* from OF *luvesche,* from LL *levisticum,* from L *ligusticum,* lit.: Ligurian (plant)

love (lʌv) *vb* **loves, loving, loved. 1** (*tr*) to have a great attachment to and affection for. **2** (*tr*) to have passionate desire, longing, and feelings for. **3** (*tr*) to like or desire (to do something) very much. **4** (*tr*) to make love to. **5** (*intr*) to be in love. ◆ *n* **6a** an intense emotion of affection, warmth, fondness, and regard towards a person or thing. **6b** (*as modifier*): *love story.* **7** a deep feeling of sexual attraction and desire. **8** wholehearted liking for or pleasure in something. **9** *Christianity.* God's benevolent attitude towards man. **10** Also: **my love.** a beloved person: used esp. as an endearment. **11** *Brit. inf.* a term of address, not necessarily for a person regarded as likable. **12** (in tennis, squash, etc.) a score of zero. **13 fall in love.** to become in love. **14 for love.** without payment. **15 for love or money.** (*used with a negative*) in any circumstances: *I would not eat a snail for love or money.* **16 for the love of.** for the sake of. **17 in love.** in a state of strong emotional attachment and usually sexual attraction. **18 make love (to). 18a** to have sexual intercourse (with). **18b** *Now arch.* to court. ORIG OE *lufu*

love affair *n* a romantic or sexual relationship, esp. temporary, between two people.

love apple *n* an archaic name for **tomato.**

lovebird ('lʌv,bɜ:d) *n* any of several small African parrots often kept as cagebirds.

lovebite ('lʌv,baɪt) *n* a temporary red mark left on a person's skin by a partner's biting or sucking it during lovemaking.

love child *n Euphemistic.* an illegitimate child; bastard.

love-in-a-mist *n* an erect S European plant, cultivated as a garden plant, having finely cut leaves and white or pale blue flowers.

Lovelace ★ ('lʌv,leɪs) *n* **1 Countess of,** title of *Ada Augusta King.* 1815–52, British mathematician and assistant to Charles Babbage: daughter of Lord Byron. She wrote the first computer program. **2 Richard.** 1618–58, English Cavalier poet, noted for *To Althea from Prison* (1642) and *Lucasta* (1649).

loveless ('lʌvlɪs) *adj* **1** without love: *a loveless marriage.* **2** receiving or giving no love.
▸ **'lovelessly** *adv* ▸ **'lovelessness** *n*

love-lies-bleeding *n* any of several plants having drooping spikes of small red flowers.

Lovell ★ ('lʌvᵊl) *n* Sir **Bernard.** born 1913, British radio astronomer; founder (1951) and director of Jodrell Bank.

lovelock ('lʌv,lɒk) *n* a long lock of hair worn on the forehead.

lovelorn ('lʌv,lɔ:n) *adj* miserable because of unrequited love or unhappiness in love.

lovely ('lʌvlɪ) *adj* **lovelier, loveliest. 1** very attractive or beautiful. **2** highly pleasing or enjoyable: *a lovely time.* **3** inspiring love; lovable. ◆ *n, pl* **lovelies. 4** *Sl.* a lovely woman.
▸ **'loveliness** *n*

lovemaking ('lʌv,meɪkɪŋ) *n* **1** sexual play and activity between lovers, esp. including sexual intercourse. **2** an archaic word for **courtship.**

love potion *n* any drink supposed to arouse sexual love in the one who drinks it.

lover ('lʌvə) *n* **1** a person, now esp. a man, who has an extramarital or premarital sexual relationship with another person. **2** (*often pl*) either of the two people involved in a love affair. **3a** someone who loves a specified person or thing: *a lover of music.* **3b** (*in combination*): *a music-lover; a cat-lover.*

love seat *n* a small upholstered sofa for two people.

lovesick ('lʌv,sɪk) *adj* pining or languishing because of love.
▸ **'love,sickness** *n*

lovey-dovey (,lʌvɪ'dʌvɪ) *adj* making an excessive or ostentatious display of affection.

loving ('lʌvɪŋ) *adj* feeling or showing love and affection.
▸ **'lovingly** *adv* ▸ **'lovingness** *n*

loving cup *n* **1** a large vessel, usually two-handled, out of which people drink in turn at a banquet. **2** a similar cup awarded to the winner of a competition.

low[1] (ləu) *adj* **1** having a relatively small distance from base to top; not tall or high: *a low hill; a low building.* **2a** situated at a relatively short distance above the ground, sea level, the horizon, or other reference position: *low cloud.* **2b** (*in combination*): *low-lying.* **3** of less than usual height, depth, or degree: *low temperature.* **4a** (of numbers) small. **4b** (of measurements) expressed in small numbers. **5a** involving or containing a relatively small amount of something: *a low supply.* **5b** (*in combination*): *low-pressure.* **6a** having little value or quality. **6b** (*in combination*): *low-grade.* **7** coarse or vulgar: *a low conversation.*

8a inferior in culture or status. **8b** (*in combination*): *low-class.* **9** in a physically or mentally depressed or weakened state. **10** low-necked: *a low dress.* **11** with a hushed tone; quiet or soft: *a low whisper.* **12** of relatively small price or monetary value: *low cost.* **13** *Music.* relating to or characterized by a relatively low pitch. **14** (of latitudes) situated not far north or south of the equator. **15** having little or no money. **16** abject or servile. **17** unfavourable: *a low opinion.* **18** not advanced in evolution: *a low form of plant life.* **19** deep: *a low bow.* **20** *Phonetics.* of, relating to, or denoting a vowel whose articulation is produced by moving the back of the tongue away from the soft palate, such as for the *a* in English *father.* **21** (of a gear) providing a relatively low forward speed for a given engine speed. **22** (*usually cap.*) of or relating to the Low Church. ◆ *adv* **23** in a low position, level, degree, intensity, etc.: *to bring someone low.* **24** at a low pitch; deep: *to sing low.* **25** at a low price; cheaply: *to buy low.* **26 lay low. 26a** to cause to fall by a blow. **26b** to overcome, defeat, or destroy. **27 lie low. 27a** to keep or be concealed or quiet. **27b** to wait for a favourable opportunity. ◆ *n* **28** a low position, level, or degree: *an all-time low.* **29** an area of relatively low atmospheric pressure, esp. a depression. ORIG C12 *lāh,* from ON *lāgr*
▸ **'lowness** *n*

low[2] (ləʊ) *n also* **lowing. 1** the sound uttered by cattle; moo. ◆ *vb* **2** to make or express by a low or moo. ORIG OE *hlōwan*

Low ★ (ləʊ) *n* Sir **David.** 1891–1963, British political cartoonist, born in New Zealand: created Colonel Blimp. See **blimp**[2].

low-alcohol *adj* (of beer or wine) containing only a small amount of alcohol. Cf. **alcohol-free.**

lowan ('ləʊən) *n* another name for **mallee fowl.** ORIG from Abor.

Low Archipelago ★ *n* another name for the **Tuamotu Archipelago.**

lowborn (ˌləʊ'bɔːn) *or* **lowbred** (ˌləʊ'brɛd) *adj Now rare.* of ignoble or common parentage.

lowbrow ('ləʊˌbraʊ) *Disparaging.* ◆ *n* **1** a person who has uncultivated or nonintellectual tastes. ◆ *adj also* **lowbrowed. 2** of or characteristic of such a person.

Low Church *n* **1** the school of thought in the Church of England stressing evangelical beliefs and practices. ◆ *adj* **Low-Church. 2** of or relating to this school.

low comedy *n* comedy characterized by slapstick and physical action.

Low Countries ★ *pl n* the lowland region of W Europe, on the North Sea: consists of Belgium, Luxembourg, and the Netherlands.

low-density lipoprotein *n* a lipoprotein that is the form in which cholesterol is transported in the bloodstream. High levels in the blood are associated with atheroma. Abbrev.: **LDL.**

low-down *Inf.* ◆ *adj* **1** mean, underhand, or despicable. ◆ *n* **lowdown. 2 the.** information.

Löwe ★ (*German* 'løːvə) *n* See (Karl) **Loewe.**

Lowell ★ ('ləʊəl) *n* **1 Amy (Lawrence).** 1874–1925, US imagist poet and critic. **2 James Russell.** 1819–91, US poet, essayist, and diplomat, noted for his poems in Yankee dialect, *Biglow Papers* (1848; 1867). **3 Robert.** 1917–77, US poet. His books include *Lord Weary's Castle* (1946), *Life Studies* (1959), and the verse drama *The Old Glory* (1968).

lower[1] ('ləʊə) *adj* **1** being below one or more other things: *the lower shelf.* **2** reduced in amount or value: *a lower price.* **3** *Maths.* (of a limit or bound) less than or equal to one or more numbers or variables. **4** (*sometimes cap.*) *Geol.* denoting the early part of a period, formation, etc.: *Lower Silurian.* ◆ *vb* **5** (*tr*) to cause to become low or on a lower level; bring, put, or cause to move down. **6** (*tr*) to reduce or bring down in estimation, dignity, value, etc.: *to lower oneself.* **7** to reduce or be reduced: *to lower one's confidence.* **8** (*tr*) to make quieter: *to lower the radio.* **9** (*tr*) to reduce the pitch of. **10** (*intr*) to diminish or become less. ORIG C12 (comp. of LOW[1]); C17 (vb)

lower[2] ('laʊə) *vb* a variant of **lour.**

Lower Austria ★ *n* a state of NE Austria: the largest Austrian province, containing most of the Vienna basin. Capital: Sankt Pölten. Pop.: 1 534 001 (1998 est.). Area: 19 170 sq. km (7476 sq. miles). German name: **Niederösterreich.**

Lower California ★ *n* a mountainous peninsula of NW Mexico, between the Pacific and the Gulf of California: administratively divided into the states of Baja California and Baja California Sur. Spanish name: **Baja California.**

Lower Canada ★ *n* (from 1791 to 1841) the official name of the S region of the present-day province of Quebec. Cf. **Upper Canada.**

lower case *n* **1** the bottom half of a compositor's type case, in which the small letters are kept. ◆ *adj* **lower-case. 2** of or relating to small letters. ◆ *vb* **lower-case, lower-cases, lower-casing, lower-cased. 3** (*tr*) to print with lower-case letters.

lower chamber *n* another name for a **lower house.**

lower class *n* **1** the social stratum having the lowest position in the social hierarchy. ◆ *adj* **lower-class. 2** of or relating to the lower class. **3** inferior or vulgar.

lowerclassman (ˌləʊ'klɑːsmən) *n, pl* **lowerclassmen.** *US.* a freshman or sophomore. Also called: **underclassman.**

lower deck *n* **1** the deck of a ship situated immediately above the hold. **2** *Inf.* the petty officers and seamen of a ship collectively.

Lower Egypt ★ *n* one of the two main administrative districts of Egypt: consists of the Nile Delta.

lower house *n* one of the houses of a bicameral legislature: usually the larger and more representative. Also called: **lower chamber.**

Lower Hutt ★ (hʌt) *n* an industrial town in New Zealand on the S coast of the North Island. Pop.: 62 900 (1983).

Lower Lakes ★ *pl n Chiefly Canadian.* Lakes Erie and Ontario.

lowermost ('ləʊəˌməʊst) *adj* lowest.

lower regions *pl n* (usually preceded by *the*) hell.

Lower Saxony ★ *n* a state of N Germany, on the North Sea and including the E Frisian Islands; formerly in West Germany: a leading European producer of petroleum. Capital: Hanover. Pop.: 7 795 100 (1996 est.). Area: 47 408 sq. km (18 489 sq. miles). German name: **Niedersachsen.**

lower world *n* **1** the earth as opposed to heaven. **2** another name for **hell.**

lowest common denominator *n* the smallest integer or polynomial that is exactly divisible by each denominator of a set of fractions. Abbrevs.: **lcd, LCD.** Also called: **least common denominator.**

lowest common multiple *n* the smallest number or quantity that is exactly divisible by each member of a set of numbers or quantities. Abbrevs.: **lcm, LCM.** Also called: **least common multiple.**

Lowestoft ★ ('ləʊstɒft) *n* a fishing port and resort in E England, in NE Suffolk on the North Sea. Pop.: 62 907 (1991).

low frequency *n* a radio-frequency band or a frequency lying between 300 and 30 kilohertz.

Low German *n* a language of N Germany, spoken esp. in rural areas: more closely related to Dutch than to standard High German. Abbrev.: **LG.** Also called: **Plattdeutsch.**

low-key *or* **low-keyed** *adj* **1** having a low intensity or tone. **2** restrained or subdued. **3** (of a photograph, painting, etc.) having a predominance of dark grey tones or dark colours with few highlights. Cf. **high-key.**

lowland ('ləʊlənd) *n* **1** relatively low ground. **2** (*often pl*) a low generally flat region. ◆ *adj* **3** of or relating to a lowland or lowlands.
▸ **'lowlander** *n*

Lowland ('ləʊlənd) *adj* of or relating to the Lowlands of Scotland or the dialects of English spoken there.

Lowlands ★ ('ləʊləndz) *pl n* **the.** a low, generally flat region of S central Scotland.
▸ **'Lowlander** *n*

★ people and places

Low Latin *n* any form of Latin other than the classical, such as Medieval Latin.

low-level language *n* a computer programming language that is closer to machine language than to human language.

low-level waste *n* waste material contaminated by traces of radioactivity that can be disposed of in steel drums in concrete-lined trenches. Cf. **high-level waste, intermediate-level waste.**

lowlife (ˈləʊˌlaɪf) *n, pl* **lowlifes.** *Sl.* a member or members of the criminal underworld.

low-loader *n* a road or rail vehicle with a low platform for ease of access.

lowly (ˈləʊlɪ) *adj* **lowlier, lowliest. 1** humble or low in position, rank, status, etc. **2** full of humility; meek. **3** simple, unpretentious, or plain. ◆ *adv* **4** in a low or lowly manner.
▸ ˈ**lowliness** *n*

Low Mass *n* a Mass that has a simplified ceremonial form and is spoken rather than sung.

low-minded *adj* having a vulgar or crude mind and character.
▸ ˌ**low-ˈmindedly** *adv* ▸ ˌ**low-ˈmindedness** *n*

low-pass filter *n Electronics.* a filter that transmits all frequencies below a specified value, attenuating frequencies above this value.

low-pitched *adj* **1** pitched low in tone. **2** (of a roof) having sides with a shallow slope.

low-pressure *adj* **1** having, using, or involving a pressure below normal: *a low-pressure gas.* **2** relaxed or calm.

low profile *n* **1** a position or attitude characterized by a deliberate avoidance of prominence or publicity. ◆ *adj* **low-profile. 2** (of a tyre) wide in relation to its height.

low-rise *adj* **1** of or relating to a building having only a few storeys. ◆ *n* **2** such a building.

lowry *or* **lowrie** (ˈlaʊrɪ) *n* variant spellings of **lory.**

Lowry ★ (ˈlaʊrɪ) *n* **1 L**(**awrence**) **S**(**tephen**). 1887–1976, British painter, noted for his bleak northern industrial scenes. **2** (**Clarence**) **Malcolm.** 1909–57. British novelist, best known for his semiautobiographical *Under the Volcano* (1947).

low-spirited *adj* depressed or dejected.
▸ ˌ**low-ˈspiritedly** *adv* ▸ ˌ**low-ˈspiritedness** *n*

low tech *n* **1** short for **low technology. 2** a style of interior design using items associated with low technology. ◆ *adj* **low-tech. 3** of or using low technology. **4** of or in the interior design style. ◆ Cf. **hi tech.**

low technology *n* simple unsophisticated technology that is limited to the production of basic necessities.

low-tension *adj* subjected to, carrying, or operating at a low voltage. Abbrev.: **LT.**

low tide *n* **1** the tide when it is at its lowest level or the time at which it reaches this. **2** a lowest point.

Lowveld ★ (ˈləʊˌfɛlt, -ˌvɛlt) *n* **the.** another name for **Bushveld.**

low water *n* **1** another name for **low tide. 2** the state of any stretch of water at its lowest level.

low-water mark *n* **1** the level reached at low tide. **2** the lowest point or level; nadir.

lox[1] (lɒks) *n* a kind of smoked salmon. ORIG C19: from Yiddish *laks,* from MHG *lahs* salmon

lox[2] (lɒks) *n* short for **liquid oxygen,** esp. when used as an oxidizer for rocket fuels.

loyal (ˈlɔɪəl) *adj* **1** showing allegiance. **2** faithful to one's country, government, etc. **3** of or expressing loyalty. ORIG C16: from OF *loial, leial,* from L *lēgālis* LEGAL
▸ ˈ**loyally** *adv*

loyalist (ˈlɔɪəlɪst) *n* a patriotic supporter of his or her sovereign or government.
▸ ˈ**loyalism** *n*

Loyalist (ˈlɔɪəlɪst) *n* **1** (in Northern Ireland) any of the Protestants wishing to retain Ulster's link with Britain. **2** (in North America) an American colonist who supported Britain during the War of American Independence. **3** (in Canada) short for **United Empire Loyalist. 4** (during the Spanish Civil War) a supporter of the republican government.

loyalty (ˈlɔɪəltɪ) *n, pl* **loyalties. 1** the state or quality of being loyal. **2** (*often pl*) allegiance.

loyalty card *n* a swipe card issued by a supermarket or chain store to a customer, used to record credit points awarded for money spent in the store.

Loyang ★ (ˈləʊˈjæŋ) *n* a variant transliteration of the Chinese name for **Luoyang.**

Loyola ★ (lɔɪˈəʊlə) *n* See (Saint) **Ignatius Loyola.**

lozenge (ˈlɒzɪndʒ) *n* **1** *Med.* a medicated tablet held in the mouth until it has dissolved. **2** *Geom.* another name for **rhombus. 3** *Heraldry.* a diamond-shaped charge. ORIG C14: from OF *losange* of Gaulish origin
▸ ˈ**lozenged** *or* ˈ**lozengy** *adj*

Lozère ★ (*French* lɔzɛr) *n* a department of S central France, in Languedoc-Roussillon region. Capital: Mende. Pop.: 72 859 (1994 est.). Area: 5180 sq. km (2020 sq. miles).

LP[1] *n* **1a** a long-playing gramophone record, usually 12 inches (30 cm) in diameter, designed to rotate at 33⅓ revolutions per minute. **1b** (*as modifier*): *an LP sleeve.* **2** long play: a slow-recording facility on a VCR which allows twice the length of material to be recorded on a tape from that of standard play.

LP[2] *abbrev. for:* **1** (in Britain) Lord Provost. **2** Also: **lp.** low pressure.

L/P *Printing abbrev. for* letterpress.

LPG *or* **LP gas** *abbrev. for* liquefied petroleum gas.

L-plate *n Brit.* a white rectangle with an "L" sign fixed to the back and front of a motor vehicle; a red "L" sign shows that the driver has not passed the driving test; a green "L" sign may be displayed by new drivers for up to a year after passing the driving test.

Lr *the chemical symbol for* lawrencium.

LSD *n* lysergic acid diethylamide; a crystalline compound prepared from lysergic acid, used in experimental medicine and taken illegally as a hallucinogenic drug. Informal name: **acid.**

L.S.D., £.s.d., *or* **l.s.d.** (in Britain, esp. formerly) *abbrev. for* librae, solidi, denarii. ORIG L: pounds, shillings, pence

LSE *abbrev. for* London School of Economics.

LSO *abbrev. for* London Symphony Orchestra.

Lt *abbrev. for* Lieutenant.

Ltd *or* **ltd** *abbrev. for* limited (liability). US equivalent: **Inc.**

Lu *the chemical symbol for* lutetium.

Lualaba ★ (ˌluːəˈlɑːbə) *n* a river in SE Democratic Republic of Congo, rising in Shaba province and flowing north as the W headstream of the River Congo. Length: about 1800 km (1100 miles).

Luanda (luˈændə) *or* **Loanda** ★ *n* the capital of Angola, a port in the west, on the Atlantic: founded in 1576, it became a centre of the slave trade to Brazil in the 17th and 18th centuries; oil refining. Pop.: 2 250 000 (1995 est.). Official name: **São Paulo de Loanda.**

Luang Prabang ★ (luːˈæŋ prɑːˈbæŋ) *n* a market town in N Laos, on the Mekong River: residence of the monarch of Laos (1946–75). Pop.: 44 244 (1984 est.).

luau (luːˈaʊ, ˈluːaʊ) *n* a feast of Hawaiian food. ORIG from Hawaiian *lu'au*

lubber (ˈlʌbə) *n* **1** a big, awkward, or stupid person. **2** short for **landlubber.** ORIG C14 *lobre,* prob. from ON
▸ ˈ**lubberly** *adj, adv* ▸ ˈ**lubberliness** *n*

lubber line *n* a mark on a ship's compass that designates the fore-and-aft axis of the vessel. Also called: **lubber's line.**

Lubbock ★ (ˈlʌbək) *n* a city in NW Texas: cotton market. Pop.: 194 467 (1994 est.).

Lübeck ★ (*German* ˈlyːbɛk) *n* a port in N Germany, in Schleswig-Holstein: the leading member of the Hanseatic League, and a major European commercial centre until the 15th century. Pop.: 216 986 (1996 est.).

Lublin ★ (*Polish* ˈlublin) *n* an industrial city in E Poland:

provisional seat of the government in 1918 and 1944. Pop.: 352 500 (1995 est.). Russian name: **Lyublin.**

lubra ('lu:brə) *n Austral.* an Aboriginal woman. ORIG C19: from Abor.

lubricant ('lu:brɪkənt) *n* **1** a lubricating substance, such as oil. ◆ *adj* **2** serving to lubricate. ORIG C19: from L *lūbricāns,* present participle of *lūbricāre*

lubricate ('lu:brɪˌkeɪt) *vb* **lubricates, lubricating, lubricated. 1** (*tr*) to cover or treat with an oily substance so as to lessen friction. **2** (*tr*) to make greasy, slippery, or smooth. **3** (*intr*) to act as a lubricant. ORIG C17: from L *lūbricāre,* from *lūbricus* slippery
▸ **ˌlubri'cation** *n* ▸ **'lubriˌcative** *adj* ▸ **'lubriˌcator** *n*

lubricity (lu:'brɪsɪtɪ) *n* **1** *Formal or literary.* lewdness or salaciousness. **2** *Rare.* smoothness or slipperiness. ORIG C15 (lewdness), C17 (slipperiness): from OF *lubricité,* from Med. L *lubricitās,* from L, from *lūbricus* slippery
▸ **lubricious** (lu:'brɪʃəs) *or* **lubricous** ('lu:brɪkəs) *adj*

Lubumbashi ★ (ˌlu:bum'bæʃɪ) *n* a city in S Democratic Republic of Congo: founded in 1910 as a copper-mining centre; university (1955). Pop.: 851 381 (1994 est.). Former name (until 1966): **Elisabethville.**

Lucan ★ ('lu:kən) *n* Latin name *Marcus Annaeus Lucanus.* 39–65 A.D., Roman poet. His epic poem *Pharsalia* describes the civil war between Caesar and Pompey.

Lucania ★ (lu:'keɪnɪə) *n* the Latin name for **Basilicata.**

Lucas ★ ('lu:kəs) *n* **George.** born 1944, US film director, producer, and writer of screenplays. Films include *American Graffiti* (1973) and *Star Wars* (1977).

Lucas van Leyden ★ ('lu:kəs væn 'laɪdᵊn) *n* ?1494–1533, Dutch painter and engraver.

Lucca ★ (*Italian* 'lukka) *n* a city in NW Italy, in Tuscany: centre of a rich agricultural region, noted for the production of olive oil. Pop.: 86 676 (1990). Ancient name: **Luca** ('lu:kə).

luce (lu:s) *n* another name for the **pike** (the fish). ORIG C14: from OF *lus,* from LL *lūcius* pike

lucent ('lu:sᵊnt) *adj* brilliant, shining, or translucent. ORIG C16: from L *lūcēns,* present participle of *lūcēre* to shine
▸ **'lucency** *n* ▸ **'lucently** *adv*

lucerne (lu:'sɜ:n) *n Brit.* another name for **alfalfa.**

Lucerne ★ (lu:'sɜ:n; *French* lysɛrn) *n* **1** a canton in central Switzerland, northwest of Lake Lucerne: joined the Swiss Confederacy in 1332. Pop.: 337 941 (1995 est.). Area: 1494 sq. km (577 sq. miles). **2** a city in central Switzerland, capital of Lucerne canton, on Lake Lucerne: tourist centre. Pop.: 60 600 (1987). **3 Lake.** a lake in central Switzerland: fed and drained chiefly by the River Reuss. Area: 115 sq. km (44 sq. miles). German name: **Vierwaldstättersee.** ◆ German name (for senses 1 and 2): **Luzern.**

Lucian ★ ('lu:sɪən) *n* 2nd century A.D., Greek writer, noted for his satirical *Dialogues of the Gods* and *Dialogues of the Dead.*

lucid ('lu:sɪd) *adj* **1** readily understood; clear. **2** shining or glowing. **3** of or relating to a period of normality between periods of insane behaviour. ORIG C16: from L *lūcidus* full of light, from *lūx* light
▸ **lu'cidity** *or* **'lucidness** *n* ▸ **'lucidly** *adv*

lucifer ('lu:sɪfə) *n* a friction match: originally a trade name.

Lucifer ★ ('lu:sɪfə) *n* **1** the leader of the rebellion of the angels; Satan. **2** the planet Venus when it rises as the morning star. ORIG OE, from L *Lūcifer* light-bearer, from *lūx* light + *ferre* to bear

Lucilius ★ (lu:'sɪlɪəs) *n* **Gaius** ('gaɪəs). ?180–102 B.C., Roman satirist, originated poetical satire.

Lucina ★ (lu:'saɪnə) *n Roman myth.* a title or name given to Juno as goddess of childbirth. ORIG C14: from L *lūcīnus* bringing to the light, from *lūx* light

luck (lʌk) *n* **1** events that are beyond control and seem subject to chance; fortune. **2** success or good fortune. **3** something considered to bring good luck. **4 down on one's luck.** having little or no good luck to the point of suffering hardships. **5 no such luck.** *Inf.* unfortunately not. **6 try one's luck.** to attempt something that is uncertain. ORIG C15: from MDu. *luc*

luckless ('lʌklɪs) *adj* having no luck; unlucky.
▸ **'lucklessly** *adv* ▸ **'lucklessness** *n*

Lucknow ★ ('lʌknau) *n* a city in N India, capital of Uttar Pradesh: capital of Oudh (1775–1856); the British residency was besieged (1857) during the Indian Mutiny. Pop.: 1 619 115 (1991).

lucky ('lʌkɪ) *adj* **luckier, luckiest. 1** having or bringing good fortune. **2** happening by chance, esp. as desired.
▸ **'luckily** *adv* ▸ **'luckiness** *n*

lucky dip *n Brit., Austral., & NZ.* **1** a box filled with sawdust containing small prizes for which children search. **2** *Inf.* an undertaking of uncertain outcome.

lucrative ('lu:krətɪv) *adj* producing a profit; profitable. ORIG C15: from OF *lucratif;* see LUCRE
▸ **'lucratively** *adv* ▸ **'lucrativeness** *n*

lucre ('lu:kə) *n Usually facetious.* money or wealth (esp. in **filthy lucre**). ORIG C14: from L *lūcrum* gain

Lucretia ★ (lu:'kri:ʃɪə) *n* (in Roman legend) a Roman woman who killed herself after being raped by a son of Tarquin the Proud.

Lucretius ★ (lu:'kri:ʃɪəs) *n* full name *Titus Lucretius Carus.* ?96–55 B.C., Roman poet and philosopher. In his *De rerum natura,* he expounds Epicurus's atomist theory.
▸ **Lu'cretian** *adj*

lucubrate ('lu:kjuˌbreɪt) *vb* **lucubrates, lucubrating, lucubrated.** (*intr*) to write or study, esp. at night. ORIG C17: from L *lūcubrāre* to work by lamplight
▸ **'lucuˌbrator** *n*

lucubration (ˌlu:kju'breɪʃən) *n* **1** laborious study, esp. at night. **2** (*often pl*) a solemn literary work.

Lucullus ★ (lu:'kʌləs) *n* **Lucius Licinius** ('lu:sɪəs lɪ'sɪnɪəs). ?110–56 B.C., Roman general and consul, famous for his banquets.
▸ **Lu'cullan, Lucullean** (ˌlu:kʌ'lɪən), *or* **ˌLucul'lian** *adj*

Lucy ★ ('lu:sɪ) *n* **Saint.** died ?303 A.D., a virgin martyred by Diocletian in Syracuse. Feast day: Dec 13.

lud (lʌd) *n Brit.* lord (in **my lud, m'lud**): used when addressing a judge in court.

Lüda ('lu:'dɑ:) *or* **Lü-ta** ★ *n* a port complex in NE China, in S Liaoning province at the S end of the Liaodong peninsula, comprising the two cities of Lüshun and Dalian: the chief northern port. Pop.: 2 400 000 (1991 est.).

Luddite ('lʌdaɪt) *n Brit. history.* **1** any of the textile workers opposed to mechanization, believing that its use led to unemployment, who organized machine-breaking between 1811 and 1816. **2** any opponent of industrial change or innovation. ◆ *adj* **3** of or relating to the Luddites. ORIG C19: alleged to be after Ned *Ludd,* an 18th-century Leicestershire workman, who destroyed industrial machinery

Ludendorff ★ (*German* 'lu:dəndɔrf) *n* **Erich Friedrich Wilhelm von** ('e:rɪç 'fri:drɪç 'vɪlhɛlm fɔn). 1865–1937, German general, Hindenburg's aide in World War I.

Lüdenscheid ★ (*German* 'ly:dənʃait) *n* a city in W Germany, in North Rhine-Westphalia: manufacturing of aluminium and plastics. Pop.: 76 110 (1989 est.).

Lüderitz ★ (*German* 'ly:dərɪts) *n* a port in Namibia: diamond-mining centre. Pop.: 6000 (1990).

Ludhiana ★ (ˌlʊdɪ'ɑ:nə) *n* a city in N India, in the central Punjab: Punjab Agricultural University (1962). Pop.: 1 042 740 (1991).

ludicrous ('lu:dɪkrəs) *adj* absurd or incongruous to the point of provoking laughter. ORIG C17: from L *lūdicrus* done in sport, from *lūdus* game
▸ **'ludicrously** *adv* ▸ **'ludicrousness** *n*

Ludlow ★ ('lʌdləu) *n* a market town in W central England, in Shropshire: castle (11th–16th century). Pop.: 9040 (1991).

ludo ('lu:dəu) *n Brit.* a simple board game in which players advance their counters by throwing dice. ORIG C19: from L: I play

Ludwigsburg ★ (*German* 'lu:tvɪçsbʊrk) *n* a city in SW Germany, in Baden-Württemberg northeast of Stuttgart:

expanded in the 18th century around the palace of the dukes of Württemberg. Pop.: 79 340 (1989 est.).

Ludwigshafen ★ (*German* 'lu:tvɪçsha:fən) *n* a city in SW Germany, in the Rhineland-Palatinate, on the Rhine: chemical industry. Pop.: 167 369 (1996 est.).

luff (lʌf) *n* **1** *Naut.* the leading edge of a fore-and-aft sail. ◆ *vb* **2** *Naut.* to head (a sailing vessel) into the wind so that her sails flap. **3** (*intr*) *Naut.* (of a sail) to flap when the wind is blowing equally on both sides. **4** to move the jib of (a crane) in order to shift a load. ORIG C13 (in the sense: steering gear): from OF *lof*, ?from MDu. *loef* peg of a tiller

lug[1] (lʌg) *vb* **lugs, lugging, lugged. 1** to carry or drag (something heavy) with great effort. **2** (*tr*) to introduce (an irrelevant topic) into a conversation or discussion. ◆ *n* **3** the act or an instance of lugging. ORIG C14: prob. from ON

lug[2] (lʌg) *n* **1** a projecting piece by which something is connected, supported, or lifted. **2** a box or basket for vegetables or fruit. **3** *Inf. or Scot.* another word for **ear**[1]. **4** *Sl.* a man, esp. a stupid or awkward one. ORIG C15 (Scots dialect) *lugge* ear

lug[3] (lʌg) *n Naut.* short for **lugsail.**

Lugano ★ (lʊ'gɑ:nəʊ) *n* a town in S Switzerland, on Lake Lugano: a centre for international finance and a tourist resort noted for the beauty of its setting. Pop.: 26 800 (1995).

Lugansk ★ (*Russian* lu'gansk) *n* an industrial city in E Ukraine, in the Donbass mining region: established in 1795 as an iron-founding centre. Pop.: 487 000 (1996 est.). Former name (1935–91): **Voroshilovgrad.**

luge (lu:ʒ) *n* **1** a racing toboggan on which riders lie on their backs, descending feet first. ◆ *vb* **luges, luging, luged. 2** (*intr*) to ride or race on a luge. ORIG C20: from F

Luger ('lu:gə) *n Trademark.* a German 9 mm calibre automatic pistol.

luggage ('lʌgɪdʒ) *n* suitcases, trunks, etc. ORIG C16: ? from LUG[1], infl. in form by BAGGAGE

luggage van *n Brit.* a railway carriage used to transport passengers' luggage, bicycles, etc.

lugger ('lʌgə) *n Naut.* a small working boat rigged with a lugsail. ORIG C18: from LUGSAIL

lughole ('lʌg,həʊl) *n Brit.* an informal word for **ear**[1]. See also **lug**[2] (sense 3).

Lugo ★ (*Spanish* 'luɣo) *n* a city in NW Spain: Roman walls; Romanesque cathedral. Pop.: 86 658 (1991). Latin name: **Lucus Augusti** ('lu:kəs aʊ'gu:sti:, ɔ:'gʌsti:).

lugsail ('lʌgsəl) *n Naut.* a four-sided sail bent and hoisted on a yard. ORIG C17: ?from ME (now dialect) *lugge* pole, or from *lugge* ear

lug screw *n* a small screw without a head.

lugubrious (lʊ'gu:brɪəs) *adj* excessively mournful; doleful. ORIG C17: from L *lūgubris* mournful, from *lūgēre* to grieve
▸ **lu'gubriously** *adv* ▸ **lu'gubriousness** *n*

lugworm ('lʌg,wɜ:m) *n* a worm living in burrows on sandy shores and having tufted gills: much used as bait. Sometimes shortened to **lug.** ORIG C17: from ?

Luichow Peninsula ★ ('lu:'tʃaʊ) *n* a variant transliteration of the Chinese name for **Leizhou Peninsula.**

Luik ★ (lœik) *n* the Flemish name for **Liège.**

Lukács ★ ('lu:kætʃ) *n* **Georg** ('geɪɔ:k), original name *György.* 1885–1971, Hungarian Marxist philosopher and literary critic, whose works include *History and Class Consciousness* (1923) and *The Historical Novel* (1955).

Luke ★ (lu:k) *n New Testament.* **1 Saint.** a fellow worker of Paul and a physician (Colossians 4:14). Feast day: Oct. 18. **2** the third Gospel, traditionally ascribed to Luke. Related adj: **Lucan.**

lukewarm (,lu:k'wɔ:m) *adj* **1** (esp. of water) moderately warm; tepid. **2** having or expressing little enthusiasm or conviction. ORIG C14 *luke* prob. from OE *hlēow* warm
▸ **,luke'warmly** *adv* ▸ **,luke'warmness** *n*

Luleå ★ (*Swedish* 'lu:ləo:) *n* a port in N Sweden, on the Gulf of Bothnia: industrial and shipbuilding centre; icebound in winter. Pop.: 70 694 (1994).

★ people and places

lull (lʌl) *vb* (*tr*) **1** to soothe (a person or animal) by soft sounds or motions (esp. in **lull to sleep**). **2** to calm (someone or someone's fears, suspicions, etc.), esp. by deception. ◆ *n* **3** a short period of calm or diminished activity. ORIG C14: ? imit. of crooning sounds; rel. to MLow G *lollen* to soothe, MDu. *lollen* to talk drowsily, mumble

lullaby ('lʌlə,baɪ) *n, pl* **lullabies. 1** a quiet song to lull a child to sleep. ◆ *vb* **lullabies, lullabying, lullabied. 2** (*tr*) to quiet or soothe as with a lullaby. ORIG C16: ? a blend of LULL + GOODBYE

Lully ★ *n* **1** (*French* lyli). **Jean Baptiste** (ʒɑ̃ batist), Italian name *Giovanni Battista Lulli.* 1632–87, French composer, born in Italy; founder of French opera, writing such operas as *Alceste* (1674) and *Armide* (1686). **2** ('lʌlɪ). Also: **Lull** (*Spanish* lul). **Raymond** *or* **Ramón** (ra'mɔn). ?1235–1315, Spanish philosopher, mystic, and missionary. His chief works are *Ars generalis sive magna* and the Utopian novel *Blaquerna.*

Luluabourg ★ (lu:'lu:ə,bʊə) *n* the former name (until 1966) of **Kananga.**

lumbago (lʌm'beɪgəʊ) *n* pain in the lower back; backache. ORIG C17: from LL, from L *lumbus* loin

lumbar ('lʌmbə) *adj* of, near, or relating to the part of the body between the lowest ribs and the hipbones. ORIG C17: from NL *lumbāris,* from L *lumbus* loin

lumbar puncture *n Med.* insertion of a hollow needle into the lower spinal cord to withdraw cerebrospinal fluid, introduce drugs, etc.

lumber[1] ('lʌmbə) *n* **1** *Chiefly US & Canad.* **1a** logs; sawn timber. **1b** (*as modifier*): *the lumber trade.* **2** *Brit.* **2a** useless household articles that are stored away. **2b** (*as modifier*): *lumber room.* ◆ *vb* **3** (*tr*) to pile together in a disorderly manner. **4** (*tr*) to fill up or encumber with useless household articles. **5** *Chiefly US & Canad.* to convert (the trees) of (a forest) into marketable timber. **6** (*tr*) *Brit. inf.* to burden with something unpleasant, tedious, etc. ORIG C17: ?from a n use of LUMBER[2]
▸ **'lumberer** *n* ▸ **'lumbering** *n*

lumber[2] ('lʌmbə) *vb* (*intr*) **1** to move or proceed in an awkward heavy manner. **2** an obsolete word for **rumble.** ORIG C14 *lomeren*
▸ **'lumbering** *adj*

lumberjack ('lʌmbə,dʒæk) *n* (esp. in North America) a person whose work involves felling trees, transporting the timber, etc. ORIG C19: from LUMBER[1] + JACK (man)

lumberjacket ('lʌmbə,dʒækɪt) *n* a boldly coloured, usually checked jacket in warm cloth.

lumberyard ('lʌmbə,jɑ:d) *n* the US and Canad word for **timberyard.**

lumen ('lu:mɪn) *n, pl* **lumens** *or* **lumina** (-mɪnə). **1** the derived SI unit of luminous flux; the flux emitted in a solid angle of 1 steradian by a point source having a uniform intensity of 1 candela. Symbol: lm **2** *Anat.* a passage, duct, or cavity in a tubular organ. **3** a cavity within a plant cell. ORIG C19: NL, from L: light, aperture
▸ **'luminal** *adj*

Lumière ★ (*French* lymjɛr) *n* **Auguste Marie Louis Nicolas** (ogyst mari lwi nikɔla). 1862–1954, and his brother, **Louis Jean** (lwi ʒɑ̃), 1864–1948, French chemists and cinema pioneers, who invented a cinematograph and a process of colour photography.

luminance ('lu:mɪnəns) *n* **1** a state or quality of radiating or reflecting light. **2** a measure (in candelas per square metre) of the brightness of a point on a surface that is radiating or reflecting light. Symbol: *L* ORIG C19: from L *lūmen* light

luminary ('lu:mɪnərɪ) *n, pl* **luminaries. 1** a person who enlightens or influences others. **2** a famous person. **3** *Literary.* something, such as the sun or moon, that gives off light. ORIG C15: via OF, from L *lūmināre* lamp, from *lūmen* light

luminesce (,lu:mɪ'nɛs) *vb* **luminesces, luminescing, luminesced.** (*intr*) to exhibit luminescence. ORIG back formation from LUMINESCENT

luminescence (,lu:mɪ'nɛsəns) *n Physics.* the emission of

light at low temperatures by any process other than incandescence. ORIG C19: from L *lūmen* light
▸ ˌ**lumiˈnescent** *adj*

luminous (ˈluːmɪnəs) *adj* **1** radiating or reflecting light; shining; glowing: *luminous colours.* **2** (*not in technical use*) exhibiting luminescence: *luminous paint.* **3** full of light; well-lit. **4** (of a physical quantity in photometry) evaluated according to the visual sensation produced in an observer rather than by absolute energy measurements: *luminous intensity.* **5** easily understood; lucid; clear. **6** enlightening or wise. ORIG C15: from L *lūminōsus* full of light, from *lūmen* light
▸ **luminosity** (ˌluːmɪˈnɒsɪtɪ) *n* ▸ ˈ**luminously** *adv* ▸ ˈ**luminousness** *n*

luminous flux *n* a measure of the rate of flow of luminous energy, evaluated according to its ability to produce a visual sensation. It is measured in lumens.

luminous intensity *n* a measure of the amount of light that a point source radiates in a given direction.

lumme *or* **lummy** (ˈlʌmɪ) *interj Brit.* an exclamation of surprise or dismay. ORIG C19: alteration of *Lord love me*

lummox (ˈlʌməks) *n Inf.* a clumsy or stupid person. ORIG C19: from ?

lump[1] (lʌmp) *n* **1** a small solid mass without definite shape. **2** *Pathol.* any small swelling or tumour. **3** a collection of things; aggregate. **4** *Inf.* an awkward, heavy, or stupid person. **5 the lump.** *Brit.* self-employed workers in the building trade considered collectively. **6** (*modifier*) in the form of a lump or lumps: *lump sugar.* **7 a lump in one's throat.** a tight dry feeling in one's throat, usually caused by great emotion. **8 in the lump.** collectively; en masse. ◆ *vb* **9** (*tr; often foll. by together*) to collect into a mass or group. **10** (*intr*) to grow into lumps or become lumpy. **11** (*tr*) to consider as a single group, often without justification. **12** (*tr*) to make or cause lumps in or on. **13** (*intr; often foll. by along*) to move in a heavy manner. ORIG C13: prob. rel. to early Du. *lompe* piece, Scand. dialect *lump* block, MHG *lumpe* rag

lump[2] (lʌmp) *vb* (*tr*) *Inf.* to tolerate or put up with; endure (in **lump it**). ORIG C16: from ?

lumpectomy (lʌmˈpɛktəmɪ) *n, pl* **lumpectomies.** the surgical removal of a tumour in a breast. ORIG C20: from LUMP[1] + -ECTOMY

lumpen (ˈlʌmpᵊn) *adj Inf.* stupid or unthinking. ORIG from G *Lump* vagabond, infl. by *Lumpen* rags, as in LUMPENPROLETARIAT

lumpenproletariat (ˌlʌmpənˌprəʊlɪˈtɛərɪət) *n* (esp. in Marxist theory) the urban social group below the proletariat, consisting of criminals, tramps, etc. ORIG G, lit.: ragged proletariat

lumpfish (ˈlʌmpˌfɪʃ) *n, pl* **lumpfish** *or* **lumpfishes.** a North Atlantic fish having a globular body covered with tubercles, pelvic fins fused into a sucker, and an edible roe. Also called: **lumpsucker.** ORIG C16 *lump* (now obs.) lumpfish, from MDu. *lumpe,* ? rel. to LUMP[1]

lumpish (ˈlʌmpɪʃ) *adj* **1** resembling a lump. **2** stupid, clumsy, or heavy.
▸ ˈ**lumpishly** *adv* ▸ ˈ**lumpishness** *n*

lump sum *n* a relatively large sum of money, paid at one time, esp. in cash.

lumpy (ˈlʌmpɪ) *adj* **lumpier, lumpiest. 1** full of or having lumps. **2** (esp. of the sea) rough. **3** (of a person) heavy or bulky.
▸ ˈ**lumpily** *adv* ▸ ˈ**lumpiness** *n*

Lumumba ★ (lʊˈmʊmbə) *n* **Patrice** (pəˈtriːs). 1925–61, Congolese statesman; first prime minister of the Democratic Republic of Congo (1960); assassinated.

Luna ★ (ˈluːnə) *n* the Roman goddess of the moon. ORIG from L: moon

lunacy (ˈluːnəsɪ) *n, pl* **lunacies. 1** (formerly) any severe mental illness. **2** foolishness.

luna moth *n* a large American moth having light green wings with a yellow crescent-shaped marking on each forewing. ORIG C19: from the markings on its wings

lunar (ˈluːnə) *adj* **1** of or relating to the moon. **2** occuring on or used on the moon: *lunar module.* **3** relating to, caused by, or measured by the position or orbital motion of the moon. ORIG C17: from L *lūnāris,* from *lūna* the moon

lunar eclipse *n* See **eclipse.**

lunar module *n* the module used to carry astronauts on a spacecraft to the surface of the moon and back to the spacecraft.

lunar month *n* See **month** (sense 6).

lunar year *n* See **year** (sense 6).

lunate (ˈluːneɪt) *or* **lunated** *adj Anat., bot.* shaped like a crescent. ORIG C18: from L *lūnātus* crescent-shaped, from *lūna* moon

lunatic (ˈluːnətɪk) *adj* **1** an archaic word for **insane. 2** foolish; eccentric. ◆ *n* **3** a person who is insane. ORIG C13 (adj): via OF from LL *lūnāticus* crazy, moonstruck, from L *lūna* moon

lunatic asylum *n Offens.* an institution for the mentally ill.

lunatic fringe *n* the members of a society who adopt views regarded as fanatical.

lunch (lʌntʃ) *n* **1** a meal eaten during the middle of the day. ◆ *vb* **2** (*intr*) to eat lunch. **3** (*tr*) to provide or buy lunch for. ORIG C16: prob. short form of LUNCHEON
▸ ˈ**luncher** *n*

luncheon (ˈlʌntʃən) *n* a lunch, esp. a formal one. ORIG C16: prob. var. of *nuncheon,* from ME *noneschench,* from *none* NOON + *schench* drink

luncheon meat *n* a ground mixture of meat (often pork) and cereal, usually tinned.

luncheon voucher *n* a voucher worth a specified amount issued to employees and redeemable at a restaurant for food. Abbrev.: **LV.**

lunchroom (ˈlʌntʃˌruːm, -ˌrʊm) *n US & Canad.* a room where lunch is served or where students, employees, etc., may eat lunches they bring.

Lund ★ (lʊnd) *n* a city in SE Sweden, northeast of Malmö: founded in about 1020 by the Danish King Canute; the archbishopric for all Scandinavia in the Middle Ages; university (1668). Pop.: 95 895 (1994).

Lundy ★ (ˈlʌndɪ) *n* an island in SW England, in Devon, in the Bristol Channel: now a bird sanctuary. Pop.: 52 (1981).

Lüneburg ★ (*German* ˈlyːnəbʊrk) *n* a city in N Germany, in Lower Saxony: capital of the duchy of Brunswick-Lüneburg from 1235 to 1369; prominent Hanse town; saline springs. Pop.: 61 000 (1990 est.).

lunette (luːˈnɛt) *n* **1** anything that is shaped like a crescent. **2** an oval or circular opening to admit light in a dome. **3** a semicircular panel containing a window, mural, or sculpture. **4** a type of fortification like a detached bastion. **5** Also called: **lune.** *RC Church.* a case fitted with a bracket to hold the consecrated host. ORIG C16: from F: crescent, from *lune* moon, from L *lūna*

Lunéville ★ (*French* lynevil) *n* a city in NE France: scene of the signing of the **Peace of Lunéville** between France and Austria (1801). Pop.: 22 393 (1990).

lung (lʌŋ) *n* **1** either one of a pair of spongy saclike respiratory organs within the thorax of higher vertebrates, which oxygenate the blood and remove its carbon dioxide. **2 at the top of one's lungs.** in one's loudest voice; yelling. ORIG OE *lungen*

lunge[1] (lʌndʒ) *n* **1** a sudden forward motion. **2** *Fencing.* a thrust made by advancing the front foot and straightening the back leg, extending the sword arm forwards. ◆ *vb* **lunges, lunging, lunged. 3** to move or cause to move with a lunge. **4** (*intr*) *Fencing.* to make a lunge. ORIG C18: short form of obs. C17 *allonge,* from F *allonger* to stretch out (one's arm) from LL *ēlongāre* to lengthen
▸ ˈ**lunger** *n*

lunge[2] (lʌndʒ) *n* **1** a rope used in training or exercising a horse. ◆ *vb* **lunges, lunging, lunged. 2** to exercise or train (a horse) on a lunge. ORIG C17: from OF *longe,* shortened from *allonge,* ult. from L *longus* long

lungfish (ˈlʌŋˌfɪʃ) *n, pl* **lungfish** *or* **lungfishes.** a freshwater bony fish having an air-breathing lung, fleshy paired fins, and an elongated body.

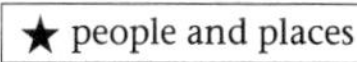

Lungki *or* **Lung-chi** ★ ('lʊŋ'kiː) *n* the former name of **Zhangzhou.**

lungwort ('lʌŋˌwɜːt) *n* **1** any of several Eurasian plants which have spotted leaves and clusters of blue or purple flowers: formerly used to treat lung diseases. **2** See **oyster plant.**

lunula ('luːnjʊlə) *n, pl* **lunulae** (-njʊˌliː). the white crescent-shaped area at the base of the human fingernail. Nontechnical name: **half-moon.** ORIG C16: from L: small moon, from *lūna*

Luoyang *or* **Loyang** ★ ('ləʊ'jæŋ) *n* a city in E China, in N Henan province on the Luo River near its confluence with the Yellow River; an important Buddhist centre in the 5th and 6th centuries; a commercial and industrial centre. Pop.: 1 190 000 (1990 est.).

Lupercalia (ˌluːpɜː'keɪlɪə) *n, pl* **Lupercalia** *or* **Lupercalias.** an ancient Roman festival of fertility, celebrated on Feb. 15. ORIG L, from *Lupercālis* belonging to *Lupercus,* a Roman god of the flocks
▸ **ˌLuper'calian** *adj*

lupin *or US* **lupine** ('luːpɪn) *n* a leguminous plant of North America, Europe, and Africa, with large spikes of brightly coloured flowers and flattened pods. ORIG C14: from L *lupīnus* wolfish (see LUPINE); from the belief that the plant ravenously exhausted the soil

lupine ('luːpaɪn) *adj* of, relating to, or resembling a wolf. ORIG C17: from L *lupīnus,* from *lupus* wolf

lupus ('luːpəs) *n* any of various ulcerative skin diseases. ORIG C16: via Med. L from L: wolf; so called because it rapidly eats away the affected part

lupus vulgaris (vʌl'gɛərɪs) *n* tuberculosis of the skin, esp. of the face. Sometimes shortened to **lupus.**

lurch[1] (lɜːtʃ) *vb (intr)* **1** to lean or pitch suddenly to one side. **2** to stagger. ◆ *n* **3** the act or an instance of lurching. ORIG C19: from ?

lurch[2] (lɜːtʃ) *n* **1 leave (someone) in the lurch.** to desert (someone) in trouble. **2** *Cribbage.* the state of a losing player with less than 30 points at the end of a game. ORIG C16: from F *lourche* a game similar to backgammon, from *lourche* (adj) deceived, prob. of Gmc origin

lurch[3] (lɜːtʃ) *vb (intr) Arch. or dialect.* to prowl suspiciously. ORIG C15: ? a var. of LURK

lurcher ('lɜːtʃə) *n* **1** a crossbred hunting dog, esp. one trained to hunt silently. **2** *Arch.* a person who prowls or lurks. ORIG C16: from LURCH[3]

lure (lʊə) *vb* **lures, luring, lured.** *(tr)* **1** (sometimes foll. by *away* or *into*) to tempt or attract by the promise of some type of reward. **2** *Falconry.* to entice (a hawk or falcon) from the air to the falconer by a lure. ◆ *n* **3** a person or thing that lures. **4** *Angling.* any of various types of brightly coloured artificial spinning baits. **5** *Falconry.* a feathered decoy to which small pieces of meat can be attached. ORIG C14: from OF *loirre* falconer's lure, from Gmc
▸ **'lurer** *n*

Lurex ('lʊərɛks) *n* **1** *Trademark.* a thin metallic thread coated with plastic. **2** fabric containing such thread, which makes it glitter.

lurgy ('lɛːgɪ) *n, pl* **lurgies.** *Facetious.* any undetermined illness. ORIG C20: from ?

lurid ('lʊərɪd) *adj* **1** vivid in shocking detail; sensational. **2** horrible in savagery or violence. **3** pallid in colour; wan. **4** glowing with an unnatural glare. ORIG C17: from L *lūridus* pale yellow
▸ **'luridly** *adv* ▸ **'luridness** *n*

lurk (lɜːk) *vb (intr)* **1** to move stealthily or be concealed, esp. for evil purposes. **2** to be present in an unobtrusive way; be latent. **3** to read messages posted on an electronic network without contributing messages oneself. ◆ *n* **4** *Austral. & NZ sl.* a scheme for success. ORIG C13: prob. frequentative of LOUR
▸ **'lurker** *n*

lurking ('lɜːkɪŋ) *adj* lingering but almost unacknowledged: *a lurking suspicion.*

Lusaka ★ (luː'zɑːkə, -'sɑːkə) *n* the capital of Zambia, in the southeast at an altitude of 1280 m (4200 ft): became capital of Northern Rhodesia in 1932 and of Zambia in 1964; University of Zambia (1966). Pop.: 982 362 (1990).

Lusatia ★ (luː'seɪʃɪə) *n* a region of central Europe, lying between the upper reaches of the Elbe and Oder Rivers: now mostly in E Germany, extending into SW Poland; inhabited chiefly by Sorbs.
▸ **Lu'satian** *adj, n*

luscious ('lʌʃəs) *adj* **1** extremely pleasurable, esp. to the taste or smell. **2** very attractive. **3** *Arch.* cloying. ORIG C15 *lucius, licius,* ? short for DELICIOUS
▸ **'lusciously** *adv* ▸ **'lusciousness** *n*

lush[1] (lʌʃ) *adj* **1** (of vegetation) abounding in lavish growth. **2** (esp. of fruits) succulent and fleshy. **3** luxurious, elaborate, or opulent. ORIG C15: prob. from OF *lasche* lazy, from L *laxus* loose
▸ **'lushly** *adv* ▸ **'lushness** *n*

lush[2] (lʌʃ) *Sl.* ◆ *n* **1** a heavy drinker, esp. an alcoholic. **2** alcoholic drink. ◆ *vb* **3** *US & Canad.* to drink (alcohol) to excess. ORIG C19: from ?

Lüshun ★ ('luː'ʃʊn) *n* a port in NE China, in S Liaoning province, at the S end of the Liaodong peninsula; together with Dalian it comprises the port complex of Lüda: jointly held by China and the Soviet Union (1945–55). Former name: **Port Arthur.**

Lusitania ★ (ˌluːsɪ'teɪnɪə) *n* an ancient region of the W Iberian Peninsula: a Roman province from 27 B.C. to the late 4th century A.D.; corresponds to most of present-day Portugal and the Spanish provinces of Salamanca and Cáceres.

lust (lʌst) *n* **1** a strong desire for sexual gratification. **2** a strong desire or drive. ◆ *vb* **3** *(intr;* often foll. by *after* or *for)* to have a lust (for). ORIG OE
▸ **'lustful** *adj* ▸ **'lustfully** *adv* ▸ **'lustfulness** *n*

lustral ('lʌstrəl) *adj* of or relating to a ceremony of purification. ORIG C16: from L *lūstrālis* (adj) from LUSTRUM

lustrate ('lʌstreɪt) *vb* **lustrates, lustrating, lustrated.** *(tr)* to purify by means of religious rituals or ceremonies. ORIG C17: from L *lūstrāre* to brighten
▸ **lus'tration** *n*

lustre *or US* **luster** ('lʌstə) *n* **1** reflected light; sheen; gloss. **2** radiance or brilliance of light. **3** great splendour of accomplishment, beauty, etc. **4** a dress fabric of cotton and wool with a glossy surface. **5** a vase or chandelier from which hang cut-glass drops. **6** a drop-shaped piece of cut glass or crystal used as such a decoration. **7** a shiny metallic surface on some pottery and porcelain. **8** *Mineralogy.* the way in which light is reflected from the surface of a mineral. ◆ *vb* **lustres, lustring, lustred** *or US* **lusters, lustering, lustered. 9** to make, be, or become lustrous. ORIG C16: from OF, from OIt. *lustro,* from L *lustrāre* to make bright
▸ **'lustreless** *or US* **'lusterless** *adj* ▸ **'lustrous** *adj*

lustreware *or US* **lusterware** ('lʌstəˌwɛə) *n* pottery with lustre decoration.

lustrum ('lʌstrəm) *or* **lustre** *n, pl* **lustrums, lustra** (-trə), *or* **lustres.** *Rare.* a period of five years. ORIG C16: from L: ceremony of purification, from *lustrāre* to brighten, purify

lusty ('lʌstɪ) *adj* **lustier, lustiest. 1** having or characterized by robust health. **2** strong or invigorating.
▸ **'lustily** *adv* ▸ **'lustiness** *n*

Lü-ta ★ ('luː'tɑː) *n* a variant transliteration of the Chinese name for **Lüda.**

lute[1] (luːt) *n* an ancient plucked stringed instrument with a long fretted fingerboard and a body shaped like a sliced pear. ORIG C14: from OF *lut,* from Ar. *al 'ūd,* lit.: the wood

lute[2] (luːt) *n* **1** a mixture of cement and clay used to seal the joints between pipes, etc. **2** *Dentistry.* a thin layer of cement used to fix a crown or inlay in place on a tooth. ◆ *vb* **lutes, luting, luted. 3** *(tr)* to seal (a joint or surface) with lute. ORIG C14: via OF ult. from L *lutum* clay

lutein ('luːtɪɪn) *n* a xanthophyll pigment, occurring in plants, that has a light-absorbing function in photosynthesis. ORIG C20: from L *lūteus* yellow + -IN

luteinizing hormone ('luːtɪɪˌnaɪzɪŋ) *n* a hormone secreted by the anterior lobe of the pituitary gland. In female vertebrates it stimulates ovulation, and in mammals it also induces corpus luteum formation. In male vertebrates it promotes maturation of the interstitial cells of the testes and stimulates androgen secretion. ORIG C19: from L *lūteum* egg yolk, from *lūteus* yellow

lutenist, lutanist, ('lu:tənɪst) *or US & Canad.* (*sometimes*) **lutist** ('lu:tɪst) *n* a person who plays the lute. ORIG C17: from Med. L *lūtānista,* from *lūtāna,* apparently from OF *lut* LUTE[1]

Lutetia *or* **Lutetia Parisiorum** ★ (lu:'ti:ʃə pəˌrɪzɪ'ɔ:rəm) *n* an ancient name for **Paris**[1].

lutetium *or* **lutecium** (lʊ'ti:ʃɪəm) *n* a silvery-white metallic element of the lanthanide series. Symbol: Lu; atomic no.: 71; atomic wt.: 174.97. ORIG C19: NL, from L *Lūtētia* ancient name of Paris, home of G. Urbain (1872–1938), F chemist, who discovered it

Luther ★ ('lu:θə) *n* **Martin.** 1483–1546, German leader of the Protestant Reformation. He began preaching the doctrine of justification by faith rather than by works, and in 1517 nailed 95 theses to the church door at Wittenberg. He was excommunicated by the Diet of Worms (1521) but he was protected in Wartburg Castle by Frederick III of Saxony (1521–22). He translated the Bible into German (1521–34) and approved Melanchthon's Augsburg Confession (1530), defining the tenets of Lutheranism.
▸ **'Lutherism** *n*

Lutheran ('lu:θərən) *n* **1** a follower of Luther or a member of a Lutheran Church. ◆ *adj* **2** of or relating to Luther or his doctrines. **3** of or denoting any of the Churches that follow Luther's doctrines.
▸ **'Lutheranism** *n*

Luthuli *or* **Lutuli** ★ (lu:'tu:lɪ) *n* Chief **Albert John.** 1899–1967, South African political leader and president of the African National Congress (1952–60): Nobel peace prize 1961.

Lutine bell ('lu:ti:n, lu:'ti:n) *n* a bell, taken from the ship *Lutine,* kept at Lloyd's in London and rung before important announcements, esp. the loss of a vessel.

Luton ★ ('lu:tᵊn) *n* **1** a town in SE central England, in S Bedfordshire: airport; motor-vehicle industries; seat of the University of Luton (1993). Pop.: 171 671 (1991). **2** a unitary authority in SE central England, in Bedfordshire. Pop.: 181 700 (1997 est.). Area: 43 sq. km (17 sq. miles).

Lutyens ★ ('lʌtjəns) *n* **1** Sir **Edwin.** 1869–1944, British architect, noted for his neoclassical houses and his planning of New Delhi, India. **2** his daughter, **Elisabeth.** 1906–83, British composer.

Lützen ★ (*German* 'lytsən) *n* a town near Leipzig in E Germany, in Saxony: site of a battle (1632) in the Thirty Years' War in which the army of the Holy Roman Empire was defeated by the Swedes.

Lützow-Holm Bay ★ ('lʊtsəʊ'həʊm) *n* an inlet of the Indian Ocean on the coast of Antarctica, between Enderby Land and Queen Maud Land.

luvvie *or* **luvvy** ('lʌvɪ) *n, pl* **luvvies.** *Facetious.* a person who is involved in the acting profession or the theatre, esp. one with a tendency to affectation.

lux[1] (lʌks) *n, pl* **lux.** the derived SI unit of illumination equal to a luminous flux of 1 lumen per square metre. ORIG C19: from L: light

lux[2] (lʌks) *vb NZ inf.* to clean with a vacuum cleaner. ORIG C20: from *Electrolux,* a vacuum-cleaner manufacturer

Lux. *abbrev. for* Luxembourg.

luxate ('lʌkseɪt) *vb* **luxates, luxating, luxated.** (*tr*) *Pathol.* to dislocate (a shoulder, knee, etc.). ORIG C17: from L *luxāre* to displace, from *luxus* dislocated
▸ **lux'ation** *n*

luxe (lʌks, lʊks; *French* lyks) *n* See **de luxe.** ORIG C16: from F from L *luxus* extravagance

Luxembourg ★ ('lʌksəmˌbɜ:g; *French* lyksɑ̃bur) *n* **1** a grand duchy in W Europe: formed the Benelux customs union with Belgium and the Netherlands in 1948; a founder member of the Common Market (now the European Union). Official languages: French, German, and Luxembourgian. Religion: mostly Roman Catholic. Currency: Luxembourgian franc; euro; Belgian franc is also used. Capital: Luxembourg. Pop.: 434 000 (1999 est.). Area: 2586 sq. km (999 sq. miles). **2** the capital of Luxembourg, on the Alzette River: an industrial centre. Pop.: 76 446 (1995 est.). **3** a province in SE Belgium, in the Ardennes. Capital: Arlon. Pop.: 243 790 (1998 est.). Area: 4416 sq. km (1705 sq. miles).

Luxemburg ★ (*German* 'lʊksəmbʊrk) *n* **Rosa** ('ro:za). 1871–1919, German socialist leader, involved with Karl Liebknecht in an unsuccessful Communist revolt (1919) and assassinated.

Luxor ★ ('lʌksɔ:) *n* a town in S Egypt, on the River Nile: the southern part of the site of ancient Thebes; many ruins and tombs, notably the temple built by Amenhotep III (about 1411–1375 B.C.). Pop.: 155 000 (1994 est.).

luxuriant (lʌg'zjʊərɪənt) *adj* **1** rich and abundant; lush. **2** very elaborate or ornate. **3** extremely productive or fertile. ORIG C16: from L *luxuriāns,* present participle of *luxuriāre* to abound to excess
▸ **lux'uriance** *n* ▸ **lux'uriantly** *adv*

> **USAGE NOTE** See at **luxurious.**

luxuriate (lʌg'zjʊərɪˌeɪt) *vb* **luxuriates, luxuriating, luxuriated.** (*intr*) **1** (foll. by *in*) to take voluptuous pleasure; revel. **2** to flourish profusely. **3** to live in a sumptuous way. ORIG C17: from L *luxuriāre*
▸ **lux,uri'ation** *n*

luxurious (lʌg'zjʊərɪəs) *adj* **1** characterized by luxury. **2** enjoying or devoted to luxury. ORIG C14: via OF from L *luxuriōsus* excessive
▸ **lux'uriously** *adv* ▸ **lux'uriousness** *n*

> **USAGE NOTE** *Luxurious* is sometimes wrongly used where *luxuriant* is meant: *he had a luxuriant (not luxurious) moustache; the walls were covered with a luxuriant growth of wisteria.*

luxury ('lʌkʃərɪ) *n, pl* **luxuries. 1** indulgence in and enjoyment of rich and sumptuous living. **2** (*sometimes pl*) something considered an indulgence rather than a necessity. **3** something pleasant and satisfying: *the luxury of independence.* **4** (*modifier*) relating to, indicating, or supplying luxury: *a luxury liner.* ORIG C14 (in the sense: lechery): via OF from L *luxuria* excess, from *luxus* extravagance

Luzern ★ (lu'tsɛrn) *n* the German name for **Lucerne.**

Luzon ★ (lu:'zɒn) *n* the main and largest island of the Philippines, in the N part of the archipelago, separated from the other islands by the Sibuyan Sea: important agriculturally, producing most of the country's rice, with large forests and rich mineral resources; industrial centres at Manila and Batangas. Capital: Quezon City. Pop.: 32 558 000 (1995 est.). Area: 108 378 sq. km (41 845 sq. miles).

LV *abbrev. for* luncheon voucher.

Lviv ★ (*Ukrainian* lvif) *n* an industrial city in W Ukraine: it had belonged to Poland (1340–1772; 1819–39), Austria (1772–1918), Germany (1939–45), and the Soviet Union (1945–91); cultural centre, with a university (1661). Pop.: 802 000 (1996 est.). Russian name: **Lvov** (ljvəf). Polish name: **Lwów.** German name: **Lemberg.**

LW *abbrev. for:* **1** *Radio.* long wave. **2** low water.

Lwów ★ (lvuf) *n* the Polish name for **Lviv.**

lx *Physics. symbol for* lux.

LXX *symbol for* Septuagint.

-ly[1] *suffix forming adjectives.* **1** having the nature or qualities of: *godly.* **2** occurring at certain intervals; every: *daily.* ORIG OE *-lic*

-ly[2] *suffix forming adverbs.* in a certain manner; to a certain degree: *quickly; recently; chiefly.* ORIG OE *-lice,* from *-lic* -LY[1]

Lyallpur ★ (ˌlaɪəl'pʊə) *n* the former name (until 1979) of **Faisalabad.**

lyase ('laɪeɪz) *n* any enzyme that catalyses the separation of two parts of a molecule by the formation of a double bond between them. ORIG C20: from Gk *lusis* a loosening + -ASE

lycanthropy (laɪ'kænθrəpɪ) *n* **1** the supposed magical transformation of a human being into a wolf. **2** *Psychiatry.* a delusion in which a person believes that he or she is a wolf. ORIG C16: from Gk *lukānthropía,* from *lukos* wolf + *anthrōpos* man
▸ **lycanthrope** ('laɪkən,θrəup) *n* ▸ **lycanthropic** (,laɪkən'θrɒpɪk) *adj*

Lycaon ★ (laɪ'keɪɒn) *n Greek myth.* a king of Arcadia said to have offered Zeus a plate of human flesh to learn whether the god was omniscient.

Lycaonia ★ (,lɪkə'əunɪə) *n* an ancient region of S Asia Minor, north of the Taurus Mountains; corresponds to present-day S central Turkey.

lycée ('li:seɪ) *n, pl* **lycées** (-seɪz). *Chiefly French.* a secondary school. ORIG C19: F, from L: *Lyceum* a school in ancient Athens

lyceum (laɪ'sɪəm) *n* (now chiefly in the names of buildings) **1** a public building for concerts, lectures, etc. **2** *US.* a cultural organization responsible for presenting concerts, lectures, etc.

lychee (,laɪ'tʃi:) *n* a variant spelling of **litchi.**

lych gate *or* **lich gate** (lɪtʃ) *n* a roofed gate to a churchyard, formerly used as a temporary shelter for the bier. ORIG C15: *lich,* from OE *līc* corpse

lychnis ('lɪknɪs) *n* any of a genus of plants having red, pink, or white five-petalled flowers: includes ragged robin. ORIG C17: NL, via L, from Gk *lukhnis* a red flower

Lycia ★ ('lɪsɪə) *n* an ancient region on the coast of SW Asia Minor: a Persian, Rhodian, and Roman province.
▸ **'Lycian** *adj, n*

lycopodium (,laɪkə'pəudɪəm) *n* **1** any of a genus of club moss resembling moss but having woody tissue and spore-bearing cones. **2** a flammable yellow powder from the spores of this plant, used in medicine and in making fireworks. ORIG C18: NL, from Gk, from *lukos* wolf + *pous* foot

Lycra ('laɪkrə) *n Trademark.* a type of synthetic elastic fabric and fibre used for tight-fitting garments, such as swimming costumes.

Lycurgus ★ (laɪ'kɜ:gəs) *n* 9th century B.C., Spartan lawgiver, regarded as the founder of the Spartan constitution.

Lydda ★ ('lɪdə) *n* another name for **Lod.**

lyddite ('lɪdaɪt) *n* an explosive consisting chiefly of fused picric acid. ORIG C19: after *Lydd,* town in Kent near which the first tests were made

Lydgate ★ ('lɪd,geɪt) *n* **John.** ?1370–?1450, English poet and monk. His devotional works and translations include a version of Boccaccio's *The Fall of Princes* (1430–38).

Lydia ★ ('lɪdɪə) *n* an ancient region on the coast of W Asia Minor: a powerful kingdom in the century and a half before the Persian conquest (546 B.C.). Chief town: Sardis.
▸ **'Lydian** *adj, n*

lye (laɪ) *n* **1** any solution obtained by leaching, such as the caustic solution obtained by leaching wood ash. **2** a concentrated solution of sodium hydroxide or potassium hydroxide. ORIG OE *lēag*

Lyell ★ ('laɪəl) *n* Sir **Charles.** 1797–1875, British geologist.

lying[1] ('laɪɪŋ) *vb* the present participle and gerund of **lie**[1].

lying[2] ('laɪɪŋ) *vb* the present participle and gerund of **lie**[2].

lying-in *n, pl* **lyings-in.** confinement in childbirth.

lyke-wake ('laɪk,weɪk) *n Brit.* a watch held over a dead person, often with festivities. ORIG C16: ?from ON

Lyle ★ (laɪl) *n* **Sandy,** full name *Alexander Walter Barr Lyle.* born 1958, British professional golfer: winner of the British Open Championship (1985) and the US Masters (1988).

Lyly ★ ('lɪlɪ) *n* **John.** ?1554–1606, English dramatist and novelist, noted for his romances, *Euphues, or the Anatomy of Wit* (1578) and *Euphues and his England* (1580). See also **euphuism.**

Lyme disease (laɪm) *n* a disease of domestic animals and humans, caused by a spirochaete and transmitted by ticks, and affecting the joints, heart, and brain. ORIG C20: after *Lyme,* Connecticut, the town where it was first identified in humans

Lyme Regis ★ ('ri:dʒɪs) *n* a resort in S England, in Dorset, on the English Channel: noted for finds of prehistoric fossils. Pop.: 3851 (1991).

Lymington ★ ('lɪmɪŋtən) *n* a market town in S England, in SW Hampshire, on the Solent: yachting centre and holiday resort. Pop.: 13 508 (1991).

lymph (lɪmf) *n* the almost colourless fluid, containing chiefly white blood cells, that is collected from the tissues of the body and transported in the lymphatic system. ORIG C17: from L *lympha* water, from earlier *limpa,* infl. in form by Gk *numphē* nymph

lymphatic (lɪm'fætɪk) *adj* **1** of, relating to, or containing lymph. **2** of or relating to the lymphatic system. **3** sluggish or lacking vigour. ◆ *n* **4** a lymphatic vessel. ORIG C17 (meaning: mad): from L *lymphāticus.* Original meaning ?from a confusion between *nymph* and LYMPH

lymphatic system *n* an extensive network of capillary vessels that transports the interstitial fluid of the body as lymph to the venous blood circulation.

lymphatic tissue *n* tissue, such as the lymph nodes, tonsils, spleen, and thymus, that produces lymphocytes.

lymph gland *n* a former name for **lymph node.**

lymph node *n* any of numerous bean-shaped masses of tissue, situated along the course of lymphatic vessels, that help to protect against infection and are a source of lymphocytes.

lympho- *or before a vowel* **lymph-** *combining form.* indicating lymph or the lymphatic system: *lymphocyte.*

lymphocyte ('lɪmfəu,saɪt) *n* a type of white blood cell formed in lymphatic tissue.
▸ **lymphocytic** (,lɪmfəu'sɪtɪk) *adj*

lymphoid ('lɪmfɔɪd) *adj* of or resembling lymph, or relating to the lymphatic system.

lymphoma (lɪm,fəumə) *n* cancer of the lymph nodes. Also called: **lymphosarcoma** (,lɪmfəusɑ:'kəumə).

lynch (lɪntʃ) *vb* (*tr*) (of a mob) to punish (a person) for some supposed offence by hanging without a trial. ORIG orig. *Lynch's law;* ? after Capt. William *Lynch* (1742–1820) of Virginia, USA
▸ **'lyncher** *n* ▸ **'lynching** *n*

Lynch ★ (lɪntʃ) *n* **1 David.** born 1946, US film director; his work includes the films *The Grandmother* (1970), *Eraserhead* (1977), and *Wild at Heart* (1990) and the television series *Twin Peaks* (1990). **2 John,** known as *Jack Lynch.* 1917–99, Irish statesman; prime minister of the Republic of Ireland (1966–73; 1977–79).

lynchet ('lɪntʃɪt) *n* a terrace or ridge formed in prehistoric or medieval times by ploughing a hillside. ORIG OE *hlinc* ridge

lynch law *n* the practice of punishing a person by mob action without a proper trial.

lynchpin ('lɪntʃ,pɪn) *n* a variant spelling of **linchpin.**

Lynn[1] ★ (lɪn) *n* another name for **King's Lynn.** Also called: **Lynn Regis** ('ri:dʒɪs).

Lynn[2] ★ (lɪn) *n* Dame **Vera,** original name *Vera Margaret Lewis.* born 1917, British singer popular during World War II and known as "the forces' sweetheart". Her best-known songs include "We'll Meet Again" and "White Cliffs of Dover".

lynx (lɪŋks) *n, pl* **lynxes** *or* **lynx. 1** a feline mammal of Europe and North America, with grey-brown mottled fur, tufted ears, and a short tail. **2** the fur of this animal. **3 bay lynx.** another name for **bobcat. 4 desert lynx.** another name for **caracal.** ORIG C14: via L from Gk *lunx*
▸ **'lynx,like** *adj*

lynx-eyed *adj* having keen sight.

Lyon ★ (*French* ljɔ̃) *n* a city in SE central France, capital of Rhône department, at the confluence of the Rivers Rhône and Saône: the third largest city in France; a major industrial centre and river port. Pop.: 422 444 (1990). English name: **Lyons** ('laɪənz). Ancient name: **Lugdunum** (lug'du:nəm).

Lyon King of Arms ('laɪən) *n* the chief herald of Scotland. Also called: **Lord Lyon.** ORIG C14: archaic spelling of LION, referring to the figure on the royal shield

Lyonnais ★ (*French* ljɔnɛ) *n* a former province of E central France, on the Rivers Rhône and Saône: occupied by the present-day departments of Rhône and Loire. Chief town: Lyon.

Lyonnesse ★ (ˌlaɪəˈnɛs) *n* (in Arthurian legend) the mythical birthplace of Sir Tristram, situated in SW England and believed to have been submerged by the sea.

Lyons ★ (ˈlaɪənz) *n* **Joseph Aloysius.** 1879–1939, Australian statesman; prime minister of Australia (1931–39).

lyrate (ˈlaɪərɪt) *adj* **1** shaped like a lyre. **2** (of leaves) having a large terminal lobe and smaller lateral lobes. ORIG C18: from NL *lyrātus, from* L *lyra* LYRE

lyre (ˈlaɪə) *n* an ancient Greek stringed instrument consisting of a resonating tortoise shell to which a crossbar was attached by two projecting arms. It was plucked with a plectrum and used for accompanying songs. ORIG C13: via OF from L *lyra,* from Gk *lura*

lyrebird (ˈlaɪəˌbɜːd) *n* either of two pheasant-like Australian birds: during courtship displays, the male spreads its tail into the shape of a lyre.

lyric (ˈlɪrɪk) *adj* **1** (of poetry) **1a** expressing the writer's personal feelings and thoughts. **1b** having the form and manner of a song. **2** of or relating to such poetry. **3** (of music) having songlike qualities. **4** (of a singing voice) having a light quality and tone. **5** intended for singing, esp. (in classical Greece) to the accompaniment of the lyre. ◆ *n* **6** a short poem of songlike quality. **7** (*pl*) the words of a popular song. ◆ Also (for senses 1–4): **lyrical.** ORIG C16: from L *lyricus,* from Gk *lurikos,* from *lura* lyre ▸ **ˈlyrically** *adv* ▸ **ˈlyricalness** *n*

lyrical (ˈlɪrɪkᵊl) *adj* **1** another word for **lyric** (senses 1–4). **2** enthusiastic; effusive.

lyricism (ˈlɪrɪˌsɪzəm) *n* **1** the quality or style of lyric poetry. **2** emotional outpouring.

lyricist (ˈlɪrɪsɪst) *n* **1** a person who writes the words for a song, opera, or musical play. **2** Also called: **lyrist.** a lyric poet.

Lysander ★ (laɪˈsændə) *n* died 395 B.C., Spartan naval commander of the Peloponnesian War.

lyse (laɪs, laɪz) *vb* **lyses, lysing, lysed.** to undergo or cause to undergo lysis.

Lysenko ★ (lɪˈsɛŋkəʊ; *Russian* liˈsjɛnkə) *n* **Trofim Denisovich** (traˈfim dɪˈnisəvitʃ). 1898–1976, Soviet biologist and geneticist.

lysergic acid diethylamide (lɪˈsɜːdʒɪk; daɪˌɛθɪlˈeɪmaɪd) *n* See **LSD.**

Lysias ★ (ˈlɪsɪˌæs) *n* ?450–?380 B.C., Athenian orator.

Lysimachus ★ (laɪˈsɪməkəs) *n* ?360–281 B.C., Macedonian general under Alexander the Great; king of Thrace (323–281); killed in battle.

lysin (ˈlaɪsɪn) *n* any of a group of antibodies that cause dissolution of cells.

Lysippus ★ (laɪˈsɪpəs) *n* 4th century B.C., Greek sculptor.

lysis (ˈlaɪsɪs) *n, pl* **lyses** (-siːz). **1** the destruction of cells by the action of a particular lysin. **2** *Med.* the gradual reduction in the symptoms of a disease. ORIG C19: NL, from Gk, from *luein* to release

-lysis *n combining form.* indicating a loosening, decomposition, or breaking down: *electrolysis; paralysis.* ORIG from Gk, from *lusis* a loosening; see LYSIS

Lysol (ˈlaɪsɒl) *n Trademark.* a solution containing a mixture of cresols in water, used as an antiseptic and disinfectant.

-lyte *n combining form.* indicating a substance that can be decomposed or broken down: *electrolyte.* ORIG from Gk *lutos* soluble, from *luein* to loose

Lytham Saint Anne's ★ (ˈlɪðəm sənt ˈænz) *n, usually abbreviated to* **Lytham St Anne's.** a resort in NW England, in Lancashire on the Irish Sea. Pop.: 40 866 (1991).

-lytic *adj combining form.* indicating a loosening or dissolving: *paralytic.* ORIG from Gk, from *lusis;* see -LYSIS

Lyttelton ★ (ˈlɪtᵊltən) *n* **Humphrey.** born 1921, British jazz trumpeter and band leader who influenced the British revival of New Orleans jazz.

Lytton ★ (ˈlɪtᵊn) *n* **1st Baron,** title of *Edward George Earle Lytton Bulwer-Lytton.* 1803–73, British writer and statesman, noted for his historical romances.

Lyublin ★ (ˈljublɪn) *n* transliteration of the Russian name for **Lublin.**

Mm

m *or* **M** (ɛm) *n, pl* **m's, M's,** *or* **Ms. 1** the 13th letter of the English alphabet. **2** a speech sound represented by this letter, as in *mat.*

m *symbol for:* **1** metre(s). **2** mile(s). **3** milli-. **4** minute(s).

M *symbol for:* **1** mach. **2** *Currency.* mark(s). **3** medium. **4** mega-. **5** million. **6** (in Britain) motorway. **7** *the Roman numeral for* 1000.

m. *abbrev. for:* **1** *Cricket.* maiden (over). **2** male. **3** mare. **4** married. **5** masculine. **6** meridian. **7** month.

M. *abbrev. for:* **1** Majesty. **2** Manitoba. **3** Master. **4** Medieval. **5** (in titles) Member. **6** million. **7** (*pl* **MM.** *or* **MM**) Also: **M** *French.* Monsieur. ORIG F equivalent of *Mr*

m- *prefix* short for **meta-** (sense 4).

M'- *prefix* a variant of **Mac-**.

ma (mɑː) *n* an informal word for **mother.**

MA *abbrev. for:* **1** Massachusetts. **2** Master of Arts. **3** Military Academy.

ma'am (mæm, mɑːm; *unstressed* məm) *n* short for **madam:** used as a title of respect, esp. for female royalty.

Maarianhamina ★ ('mɑːriɑnhɑminɑ) *n* the Finnish name for **Mariehamn.**

maas (mɑːs) *n S. African.* thick soured milk. ORIG from Nguni *amasi* milk

Maas ★ (maːs) *n* the Dutch name for the **Meuse.**

Maastricht *or* **Maestricht** ★ ('mɑːstrɪxt; *Dutch* maː'strɪxt) *n* a city in the SE Netherlands near the Belgian and German borders: capital of Limburg province, on the River Maas (Meuse); a European Union treaty (**Maastricht Treaty**) was signed here in 1992. Pop.: 118 518 (1996 est.).

Mab ★ (mæb) *n* (in English and Irish folklore) a fairy queen said to create and control men's dreams.

Mabuse ★ (mə'bjuːz; *French* mabyz) *n* **Jan** (jɑn). original name *Jan Gossaert.* ?1478–?1533, Flemish painter.

mac *or* **mack** (mæk) *n Brit. inf.* short for **mackintosh.**

Mac (mæk) *n Chiefly US & Canad.* an informal term of address to a man. ORIG C20: abstracted from MAC-

Mac-, Mc-, *or* **M'-** *prefix* (in surnames of Scottish or Irish Gaelic origin) son of: *MacDonald.* ORIG from Goidelic *mac* son of

macabre (mə'kɑːbə, -brə) *adj* gruesome; ghastly; grim. ORIG C15: from OF *danse macabre* dance of death, prob. from *macabé* relating to the Maccabees, who were associated with death because of the doctrines and prayers for the dead in II Macc. (12:43–46)

macadam (mə'kædəm) *n* a road surface made of compressed layers of small broken stones, esp. one that is bound together with tar or asphalt. ORIG C19: after John *McAdam* (1756–1836), Scot. engineer, the inventor

macadamia (ˌmækə'deɪmɪə) *n* **1** an Australian tree having clusters of small white flowers and edible nutlike seeds. **2 macadamia nut.** the seed. ORIG C19: NL, after John *Macadam* (died 1865), Australian chemist

macadamize *or* **macadamise** (mə'kædəˌmaɪz) *vb* **macadamizes, macadamizing, macadamized** *or* **macadamises, macadamising, macadamised.** (*tr*) to construct or surface (a road) with macadam.
▸ **macˌadamiˈzation** *or* **macˌadamiˈsation** *n* ▸ **macˈadamˌizer** *or* **macˈadamˌiser** *n*

Macao ★ (mə'kaʊ) *n* a special administrative region of China, on the S coast, across the estuary of the Zhu Jiang from Hong Kong: formerly Portuguese overseas province; chief centre of European trade with China in the 18th century; attained partial autonomy in 1976; sovereignty passed to China in 1999; commercial and financial centre; tourism. Pop.: 395 304 (1994 est.). Area: 16 sq. km (6 sq. miles). Portuguese name: **Macáu.**

Macapá ★ (*Portuguese* maka'pa) *n* a town in NE Brazil, capital of the federal territory of Amapá, on the Canal do Norte of the Amazon delta. Pop.: 146 523 (1991).

macaque (mə'kɑːk) *n* any of various Old World monkeys of Asia and Africa. Typically the tail is short or absent and cheek pouches are present. ORIG C17: from F, from Port. *macaco,* from W African *makaku,* from *kaku* monkey

macaroni *or* **maccaroni** (ˌmækə'rəʊnɪ) *n, pl* **macaronis, macaronies** *or* **maccaronis, maccaronies. 1** pasta tubes made from wheat flour. **2** (in 18th-century Britain) a dandy who affected foreign manners and style. ORIG C16: from It. (dialect) *maccarone,* prob. from Gk *makaria* food made from barley

macaroon (ˌmækə'ruːn) *n* a kind of sweet biscuit made of ground almonds, sugar, and egg whites. ORIG C17: via F *macaron* from It. *maccarone* MACARONI

Macarthur ★ (mə'kɑːθə) *n* **John.** 1767–1834, Australian military officer and entrepreneur, born in England. He established the breeding of merino sheep in Australia.

MacArthur ★ (mə'kɑːθə) *n* **Douglas.** 1880–1964, US general. During World War II he commanded US forces in the Pacific (1944) and accepted the surrender of Japan. He was commander in chief of United Nations forces in Korea (1950–51) until dismissed by President Truman.

Macassar ★ (mə'kæsə) *n* a variant spelling of **Makasar.**

Macassar oil *n* an oily preparation formerly put on the hair to make it smooth and shiny. ORIG C19: from MAKASAR

Macáu ★ (mə'kaʊ) *n* the Portuguese name for **Macao.**

Macaulay ★ (mə'kɔːlɪ) *n* **1** Dame **Rose.** 1881–1958, British novelist. Her books include *Dangerous Ages* (1921) and *The Towers of Trebizond* (1956). **2 Thomas Babington,** 1st Baron. 1800–59, British historian and statesman, best known for his *History of England from the Accession of James the Second* (1848–61).

macaw (mə'kɔː) *n* a large tropical American parrot having a long tail and brilliant plumage. ORIG C17: from Port. *macau,* from ?

Macbeth ★ (mək'bɛθ, mæk-) *n* died 1057, king of Scotland (1040–57): succeeded Duncan, whom he killed in battle; defeated and killed by Duncan's son Malcolm III.

MacBride ★ (mək'braɪd) *n* **Sean** (ʃɔːn). 1904–88, Irish statesman; minister for external affairs (1948–51); chairman of Amnesty International (1961–75); Nobel Peace Prize 1974; UN commissioner for Namibia (1974–76).

McBride ★ (mək'braɪd) *n* **Willie John.** born 1940, Irish Rugby Union footballer; played for Ireland (1962–75) and the British Lions (1962–74).

Macc. *abbrev. for* Maccabees (books of the Apocrypha).

McCarthy ★ (mə'kɑːθɪ) *n* **1 Joseph R**(**aymond**). 1908–57, US Republican senator, who led (1950–54) the notorious investigations of alleged Communist infiltration into the US government. **2 Mary** (**Therese**). 1912–89, US novelist; her works include *The Group* (1963).

McCarthyism (mə'kɑːθɪˌɪzəm) *n Chiefly US.* **1** the practice of making unsubstantiated accusations of disloyalty or Communist leanings. **2** the use of unsupported accusations for any purpose. ORIG C20: after Senator Joseph MCCARTHY
▸ **McˈCarthyist** *n, adj*

McCartney ★ (mə'kɑːtnɪ) *n* Sir **Paul.** born 1942, British rock musician and songwriter; member of the Beatles (1961–70); leader of Wings (1971–81). His recordings include *Band on the Run* (1973) and "Mull of Kintyre" (1977). See also **Beatles.**

Macclesfield ★ ('mækᵊlzˌfiːld) *n* a market town in NW England, in Cheshire: silk industry. Pop.: 50 270 (1991).

McCormack ★ (mə'kɔːmæk) *n* **John.** 1884–1945, Irish tenor: became a US citizen 1919.

McCoy (məˈkɔɪ) *n Sl.* the genuine person or thing (esp. in **the real McCoy**). ORIG C20: ? after Kid *McCoy*, professional name of Norman Selby (1873–1940), American boxer, who was called "the real McCoy" to distinguish him from another boxer of that name

McCullers ★ (məˈkʌləz) *n* **Carson**. 1917–67, US writer, whose novels include *The Heart is a Lonely Hunter* (1940).

McDiarmid ★ (məkˈdɜːmɪd) *n* **Hugh**, pen name of *Christopher Murray Grieve*. 1892–1978, Scottish poet; a founder of the Scottish National Party. His poems include *A Drunk Man Looks at the Thistle* (1926).

Macdonald ★ (məkˈdɒnəld) *n* **1 Flora**. 1722–90, Scottish heroine, who helped the Young Pretender to escape to Skye after the battle of Culloden (1746). **2** Sir **John Alexander**. 1815–91, Canadian statesman, born in Scotland, who was the first prime minister of the Dominion of Canada (1867–73; 1878–91).

MacDonald ★ (məkˈdɒnəld) *n* **(James) Ramsay**. 1866–1937, British statesman, who led the first and second Labour Governments (1924 and 1929–31). He also led a coalition (1931–35).

McDonald ★ (məkˈdɒnəld) *n* Sir **Trevor**. born 1939, British broadcasting journalist, born in Trinidad; presenter of ITV's *News at Ten* (1990–99).

Macdonnell Ranges ★ (məkˈdɒnəl) *pl n* a mountain system of central Australia, in S central Northern Territory, extending about 160 km (100 miles) east and west of Alice Springs. Highest peak: Mount Ziel, 1510 m (4955 ft).

mace[1] (meɪs) *n* **1** a club, usually having a spiked metal head, used esp. in the Middle Ages. **2** a ceremonial staff carried by certain officials. **3** See **macebearer**. **4** an early form of billiard cue. ORIG C13: from OF, prob. from Vulgar L *mattea* (unattested); apparently rel. to L *mateola* mallet

mace[2] (meɪs) *n* a spice made from the dried aril round the nutmeg seed. ORIG C14: formed as a singular from OF *macis* (wrongly assumed to be pl), from L *macir* a spice

macebearer (ˈmeɪsˌbɛərə) *n* a person who carries a mace in processions or ceremonies.

Maced. *abbrev. for* Macedonia(n).

macedoine (ˌmæsɪˈdwɑːn) *n* **1** a mixture of diced vegetables. **2** a mixture of fruit in a syrup or in jelly. **3** any mixture; medley. ORIG C19: from F, lit.: Macedonian, alluding to the mixture of nationalities in Macedonia

Macedon (ˈmæsɪˌdɒn) *or* **Macedonia** ★ *n* a region of the S Balkans, now divided among Greece, Bulgaria, and the Former Yugoslav Republic of Macedonia. As a kingdom in the ancient world it achieved prominence under Philip II (359–336 B.C.) and his son Alexander the Great.

Macedonia ★ (ˌmæsɪˈdəʊnɪə) *n* **1** a country in SE Europe, comprising part of ancient Macedon: it became part of the kingdom of Serbs, Croats, and Slovenes (subsequently Yugoslavia) in 1913; it declared independence in 1992, but Greece objected to its use of the historical name Macedonia; in 1993 it was recognized by the UN under its current official name. Official language: Macedonian. Religion: Christian majority, Muslim, nonreligious, and Jewish minorities. Currency: denar. Capital: Skopje. Pop.: 2 023 000 (1999 est.). Area: 25 713 sq. km (10 028 sq. miles). Serbian name: **ˌMakedoˈnija**. Official name: **Former Yugoslav Republic of Macedonia**. Abbrev.: **FYROM**. **2** an area of N Greece, comprising the regions of Macedonia Central, Macedonia West, and part of Macedonia East and Thrace. Modern Greek name: **Makedhonia**. **3** a district of SW Bulgaria, now occupied by Blagoevgrad province. Area: 6465 sq. km (2496 sq. miles).
▸ **ˌMaceˈdonian** *adj, n*

Maceió ★ (maseˈjɔ) *n* a port in NE Brazil, capital of Alagôas state, on the Atlantic. Pop.: 554 727 (1991).

McEnroe ★ (ˈmækᵊnˌrəʊ) *n* **John (Patrick Jr)**. born 1959, US tennis player: US singles champion (1979–81; 1984): Wimbledon singles champion (1981; 1983; 1984).

macerate (ˈmæsəˌreɪt) *vb* **macerates, macerating, macerated**. **1** to soften or separate or be softened or separated as a result of soaking. **2** to become or cause to become thin. ORIG C16: from L *mācerāre* to soften
▸ **ˌmacerˈation** *n* ▸ **ˈmacerˌator** *n*

McEwan ★ (məˈkjuːən) *n* **Ian (Russell)**. born 1948, British writer. His books include *The Child in Time* (1987) and *Amsterdam* (1998).

McGonagall ★ (məˈgɒnəgəl) *n* **William**. 1830–?1902, Scottish writer of doggerel.

MacGuffin (məˈgʌfɪn) *n* an object or event in a book or a film that serves as the impetus for the plot. ORIG C20: coined (c. 1935) by Sir Alfred HITCHCOCK

Mach[1] (mæk) *n* short for **Mach number**.

Mach[2] ★ (*German* max) *n* **Ernst** (ɛrnst). 1838–1916, Austrian physicist and philosopher. He devised the Mach number and founded logical positivism.

mach. *abbrev. for:* **1** machine. **2** machinery. **3** machinist.

Machado ★ (*Portuguese* maˈʃadu) *n* **Joaquim Maria** (ʒuaˈkĩ maˈria). 1839–1908, Brazilian writer, whose novels include *Epitaph of a Small Winner* (1881).

machair (ˈmæxər) *n Scot.* (in the western Highlands and islands) a strip of sandy grassy land just above the shore: used for grazing, etc. ORIG C17: from Scot. Gaelic

Machel ★ (məˈʃɛl) *n* **Samora (Moises)** (səˈmɔːrə). 1933–86, Mozambique statesman; president of Mozambique (1975–86).

machete (məˈʃɛtɪ, -ˈtʃeɪ-) *n* a broad heavy knife used for cutting or as a weapon, esp. in parts of Central and South America. ORIG C16 *macheto*, from Sp. *machete*, from *macho* club, ?from Vulgar L *mattea* (unattested) club

Machiavelli ★ (ˌmækɪəˈvɛlɪ) *n* **Niccolò** (nikkoˈlɔ). 1469–1527, Florentine statesman and political philosopher; secretary to the war council of the Florentine republic (1498–1512); author of *Il Principe* (*The Prince*, 1532).

Machiavellian (ˌmækɪəˈvɛlɪən) *adj* **1** of or relating to the alleged political principles of Machiavelli; cunning, amoral, and opportunist. ◆ *n* **2** a cunning, amoral, and opportunist person, esp. a politician.
▸ **ˌMachiaˈvellianˌism** *n*

machicolate (məˈtʃɪkəʊˌleɪt) *vb* **machicolates, machicolating, machicolated**. (*tr*) to construct machicolations at the top of (a wall). ORIG C18: from OF *machicoller*, ult. from Provençal *machacol*, from *macar* to crush + *col* neck

machicolation (məˌtʃɪkəʊˈleɪʃən) *n* **1** (esp. in medieval castles) a projecting gallery or parapet having openings through which missiles could be dropped. **2** any such opening.

machinate (ˈmækɪˌneɪt) *vb* **machinates, machinating, machinated**. (*usually tr*) to contrive, plan, or devise (schemes, plots, etc.). ORIG C17: from L *māchinārī* to plan, from *māchina* MACHINE
▸ **ˈmachiˌnator** *n*

machination (ˌmækɪˈneɪʃən) *n* **1** a plot or scheme. **2** the act of devising plots or schemes.

machine (məˈʃiːn) *n* **1** an assembly of interconnected components arranged to transmit or modify force in order to perform useful work. **2** a device for altering the magnitude or direction of a force, such as a lever or screw. **3** a mechanically operated device or means of transport, such as a car or aircraft. **4** any mechanical or electrical device that automatically performs tasks or assists in performing tasks. **5** any intricate structure or agency. **6** a mechanically efficient, rigid, or obedient person. **7** an organized body of people that controls activities, policies, etc. ◆ *vb* **machines, machining, machined**. **8** (*tr*) to shape, cut, or remove (excess material) from (a workpiece) using a machine tool. **9** to use a machine to carry out a process on (something). ORIG C16: via F from L *māchina* machine, from Doric Gk *makhana* pulley
▸ **maˈchinable** *or* **maˈchineable** *adj* ▸ **maˌchinaˈbility** *n*

machine code *or* **language** *n* instructions for the processing of data in a binary, octal, or hexadecimal code that can be understood and executed by a computer.

machine-down time *n* a period during which a machine, computer, etc., is out of service, because it is out of order or being serviced.

machine gun *n* **1a** a rapid-firing automatic gun, using small-arms ammunition. **1b** (*as modifier*): *machine-gun fire*. ◆ *vb* **machine-gun, machine-guns, machine-gunning, machine-gunned**. **2** (*tr*) to shoot or fire at with a machine gun.
▸ **machine gunner** *n*

machine learning *n* a branch of artificial intelligence in which a computer generates rules underlying or based on raw data that has been fed into it.

machinery (məˈʃiːnərɪ) *n, pl* **machineries. 1** machines, machine parts, or machine systems collectively. **2** a particular machine system or set of machines. **3** a system similar to a machine.

machine shop *n* a workshop in which machine tools are operated.

machine tool *n* a power-driven machine, such as a lathe, for cutting, shaping, and finishing metals, etc. ▸ **maˈchine-ˌtooled** *adj*

machinist (məˈʃiːnɪst) *n* **1** a person who operates machines to cut or process materials. **2** a maker or repairer of machines.

machismo (mæˈkɪzməʊ, -ˈtʃɪz-) *n* strong or exaggerated masculinity. ORIG Mexican Sp., from Sp. *macho* male, from L *masculus* MASCULINE

> **USAGE NOTE** This word is still in the process of being naturalized in English, and consequently pronunciation of the *ch* varies between a *k* and the standard pronunciation of *ch* at the beginning of a word, as in *chief.* The adjective *macho* is nearly always pronounced in the second way in English, and it would be more in keeping with the pronunciation of *ch* in general, and more in line with Spanish pronunciation, to pronounce *machismo* in the same way.

Mach number *n* (*often not cap.*) the ratio of the speed of a body in a particular medium to the speed of sound in that medium. Mach number 1 corresponds to the speed of sound. ORIG C19: after Ernst MACH

macho (ˈmætʃəʊ) *adj* **1** strongly or exaggeratedly masculine. ◆ *n, pl* **machos. 2** a strong virile man.

> **USAGE NOTE** See at **machismo.**

Machu Picchu ★ (ˈmɑːtʃuː ˈpiːktʃuː) *n* a ruined Incan city in S central Peru.

Macías Nguema ★ (məˈsiːəs ᵊŋˈgweɪmə) *n* the former name (until 1979) of **Bioko.**

mack (mæk) *n Brit. inf.* short for **mackintosh.**

Mackay ★ (məˈkaɪ) *n* a port in E Australia, in Queensland: artificial harbour. Pop.: 55 772 (1993).

Mackellar ★ (məˈkɛlə) *n* **Dorothea.** 1885–1968, Australian poet, who wrote "My Country".

McKellen ★ (məˈkɛlən) *n* Sir **Ian** (**Murray**). born 1939, British actor, noted esp. for his Shakespearean roles.

McKenna ★ (məˈkɛnə) *n* **Siobhán** (ʃəˈvɔːn). 1923–86, Irish actress.

Mackenzie[1] ★ (məˈkɛnzɪ) *n* a river in NW Canada, in Nunavut and the Northwest Territories, flowing northwest from Great Slave Lake to the Beaufort Sea: the longest river in Canada; navigable in summer. Length: 1770 km (1100 miles).

Mackenzie[2] ★ (məˈkɛnzɪ) *n* **1** Sir **Alexander.** ?1755–1820, Scottish explorer and fur trader in Canada. He explored the Mackenzie River (1789) and was the first European to cross America north of Mexico (1793). **2 Alexander.** 1822–92, Canadian statesman; first Liberal prime minister (1873–78). **3** Sir **Compton.** 1883–1972, British author. His works include *Sinister Street* (1913–14) and the comic novel *Whisky Galore* (1947). **4** Sir **Thomas.** 1854–1930, New Zealand statesman born in Scotland: prime minister of New Zealand (1912).

mackerel (ˈmækrəl) *n, pl* **mackerel** *or* **mackerels. 1** a spiny-finned food fish occurring in northern coastal regions of the Atlantic and in the Mediterranean. It has a deeply forked tail and a greenish-blue body marked with wavy dark bands on the back. **2** any of various related fishes. ORIG C13: from Anglo-F, from OF *maquerel,* from ?

mackerel sky *n* a sky patterned with cirrocumulus or small altocumulus clouds. ORIG from similarity to pattern on mackerel's back

Mackerras ★ (məˈkɛrəs) *n* **Charles.** born 1925, Australian conductor, esp. of opera; resident in England.

Mackinac ★ (ˈmækɪˌnɔː, -ˌnæk) *n* a wooded island in N Michigan, in the **Straits of Mackinac** (a channel between the lower and upper peninsulas of Michigan): an ancient Indian burial ground; state park. Length: 5 km (3 miles).

McKinley[1] ★ (məˈkɪnlɪ) *n* **Mount.** a mountain in S central Alaska, in the Alaska Range: the highest peak in North America. Height: 6194 m (20 320 ft).

McKinley[2] ★ (məˈkɪnlɪ) *n* **William.** 1843–1901, 25th president of the US (1897–1901): assassinated.

mackintosh *or* **macintosh** (ˈmækɪnˌtɒʃ) *n* **1** a waterproof raincoat made of rubberized cloth. **2** such cloth. **3** any raincoat. ORIG C19: after Charles *Macintosh* (1760–1843), who invented it

Mackintosh ★ (ˈmækɪnˌtɒʃ) *n* **Charles Rennie.** 1868–1928, Scottish architect and artist, exponent of the Art Nouveau style.

Maclean ★ (məˈkleɪn) *n* **1 Donald.** 1913–83, British civil servant, who spied for the Soviet Union, to which he fled (with Guy Burgess) in 1951. **2 Sorley** (ˈsɔːlɪ). 1911–96, Scottish Gaelic poet. His works include *Spring Tide and Neap Tide* (1977).

Macleod ★ (məˈklaʊd) *n* **John James Rickard.** 1876–1935, Scottish physiologist: shared the Nobel prize for physiology or medicine (1923) with Banting for their part in discovering insulin.

McLeish ★ (məˈkliːʃ)*n* **Henry.** born 1948, Scottish Labour politician: first minister of the Scottish parliament from 2000.

McLuhan ★ (məˈkluːən) *n* (**Herbert**) **Marshall.** 1911–80, Canadian author of works analysing the mass media, including *The Medium is the Message* (1967).

Macmahon ★ (*French* makmaõ) *n* **Marie Edme Patrice Maurice** (mari ɛdmə patris mɔris), Comte de Macmahon. 1808–93, French military commander. He commanded the troops that suppressed the Paris Commune (1871) and was elected president of the Third Republic (1873–79).

McMahon ★ (məkˈmɑːən) *n* Sir **William.** 1908–88, Australian statesman; prime minister of Australia (1971–72).

Macmillan ★ (məkˈmɪlən) *n* (**Maurice**) **Harold,** 1st Earl of Stockton. 1894–1986, British statesman; Conservative prime minister (1957–63).

MacMillan ★ (məkˈmɪlən) *n* Sir **Kenneth.** 1929–92, British ballet dancer and choreographer; director (1970–77) and principal choreographer (1977–92) of the Royal Ballet.

McMillan ★ (məkˈmɪlən) *n* **Edwin M(attison).** 1907–91, US physicist; shared Nobel prize for chemistry 1951 for the discovery of transuranic elements.

Mcmurdo Sound ★ (məkˈmɜːdəʊ) *n* an inlet of the Ross Sea in Antarctica, north of Victoria Land.

McNaughten Rules *or* **McNaghten Rules** (məkˈnɔːtᵊn) *pl n* (in English law) a set of rules established by the case of Regina v. McNaughten (1843) by which legal proof of criminal insanity depends on the accused being shown to be incapable of understanding what he has done.

MacNeice ★ (məkˈniːs) *n* **Louis.** 1907–63, British poet, born in Northern Ireland. His works include the poems in *Autumn Journal* (1939) and *Solstices* (1961).

Macon ★ (ˈmeɪkən) *n* a city in the US, in central Georgia, on the Ocmulgee River. Pop.: 113 352 (1996 est.).

Mâcon ★ (*French* mɑkõ) *n* **1** a city in E central France, in the Saône valley: a centre of the wine-producing region of lower Burgundy. Pop.: 39 700 (1995 est.). **2** a red or white wine from the Mâcon area, heavier than other burgundies.

Maconchy ★ (məˈkɒŋkɪ) *n* Dame **Elizabeth,** married name *Elizabeth LeFanu.* 1907–94, British composer of Irish parentage; noted esp. for her chamber music, which includes 13 string quartets and *Romanza* (1980) for viola and ensemble.

Macpherson ★ (məkˈfɜːsᵊn) *n* **James.** 1736–96, Scottish poet and translator. He published supposed translations of the legendary Gaelic poet Ossian, in reality largely his own work.

Macquarie[1] ★ (mə'kwɒrɪ) *n* **1** an Australian island in the Pacific, southeast of Tasmania: noted for its species of albatross and penguin. Area: about 168 sq. km (65 sq. miles). **2** a river in SE Australia, in E central New South Wales, rising in the Blue Mountains and flowing northwest to the Darling. Length: about 1200 km (750 miles).

Macquarie[2] ★ (mə'kwɒrɪ) *n* **Lachlan.** 1762–1824, Australian colonial administrator; governor of New South Wales (1809–21).

McQueen ★ (mə'kwi:n) *n* **Steve.** 1930–80, US film actor.

macramé (mə'krɑ:mɪ) *n* a type of ornamental work made by knotting and weaving coarse thread. ORIG C19: via F & It. from Turkish *makrama* towel, from Ar. *migramah* striped cloth

Macready ★ (mə'kri:dɪ) *n* **William Charles.** 1793–1873, British actor and theatre manager.

macro ('mækrəʊ) *n, pl* **macros. 1** *Photog.* a camera lens used for close-up photography. Also called: **macro lens. 2** *Computing.* a single computer instruction that initiates a set of instructions. Also called: **macro instruction.** ORIG C20: from Gk *makros* large

macro- *or before a vowel* **macr-** *combining form.* **1** large, long, or great in size or duration: *macroscopic.* **2** *Pathol.* indicating abnormal enlargement or overdevelopment: *macrocephaly.* ORIG from Gk *makros* large

macrobiotics (ˌmækrəʊbaɪ'ɒtɪks) *n* (*functioning as sing*) a dietary system which advocates whole grains and vegetables grown without chemical additives. ORIG C20: from MACRO- + Gk *biotos* life + -ICS
▸ **ˌmacrobi'otic** *adj*

macrocarpa (ˌmækrəʊ'kɑ:pə) *n* a large Californian coniferous tree, used in New Zealand and elsewhere to form shelter belts on farms and for rough timber. ORIG C19: from NL, from MACRO- + Gk *karpos* fruit

macrocephaly (ˌmækrəʊ'sefəlɪ) *n* the condition of having an abnormally large head or skull.
▸ **macrocephalic** (ˌmækrəʊsɪ'fælɪk) *or* **ˌmacro'cephalous** *adj*

macroclimate ('mækrəʊˌklaɪmɪt) *n* the predominant climate over a large area.

macrocosm ('mækrəˌkɒzəm) *n* a complex structure, such as the universe or society, regarded as an entirety. Cf. **microcosm.** ORIG C16: via F & L from Gk *makros kosmos* great world
▸ **ˌmacro'cosmic** *adj* ▸ **ˌmacro'cosmically** *adv*

macroeconomics (ˌmækrəʊˌi:kə'nɒmɪks, -ˌɛk-) *n* (*functioning as sing*) the branch of economics concerned with aggregates, such as national income, consumption, and investment.
▸ **ˌmacroˌeco'nomic** *adj*

macromolecule (ˌmækrəʊ'mɒlɪˌkju:l) *n* any very large molecule, such as a protein or synthetic polymer.

macron ('mækrɒn) *n* a diacritical mark (¯) placed over a letter to represent a long vowel. ORIG C19: from Gk *makron* something long, from *makros* long

macropod ('mækrəʊˌpɒd) *n* any member of a family of marsupials consisting of the kangaroos and related animals.

macroscopic (ˌmækrəʊ'skɒpɪk) *adj* **1** large enough to be visible to the naked eye. **2** comprehensive; concerned with large units. ORIG C19: see MACRO-, -SCOPIC
▸ **ˌmacro'scopically** *adv*

macula ('mækjʊlə) *or* **macule** ('mækju:l) *n, pl* **maculae** (-jʊˌli:) *or* **macules.** *Anat.* **1** a small spot or area of distinct colour, esp. the macula lutea. **2** any small discoloured spot or blemish on the skin, such as a freckle. ORIG C14: from L
▸ **'macular** *adj* ▸ **ˌmacu'lation** *n*

macula lutea ('lu:tɪə) *n, pl* **maculae luteae** ('lu:tɪˌi:). a small yellowish oval-shaped spot on the retina of the eye, where vision is especially sharp. ORIG NL, lit.: yellow spot

macular degeneration *n* pathological changes in the macula lutea, resulting in loss of central vision: a common cause of blindness in the elderly.

mad (mæd) *adj* **madder, maddest. 1** mentally deranged; insane. **2** senseless; foolish. **3** (often foll. by *at*) *Inf.* angry; resentful. **4** (foll. by *about, on,* or *over;* often *postpositive*) wildly enthusiastic (about) or fond (of). **5** extremely excited or confused; frantic: *a mad rush.* **6** temporarily overpowered by violent reactions, emotions, etc.: *mad with grief.* **7** (of animals) **7a** unusually ferocious: *a mad buffalo.* **7b** afflicted with rabies. **8 like mad.** *Inf.* with great energy, enthusiasm, or haste. ◆ *vb* **mads, madding, madded. 9** *US or arch.* to make or become mad; act or cause to act as if mad. ORIG OE *gemǣded,* p.p. of *gemǣdan* to render insane

Madag. *abbrev. for* Madagascar.

Madagascar ★ (ˌmædə'gæskə) *n* an island republic in the Indian Ocean, off the E coast of Africa: made a French protectorate in 1895; became autonomous in 1958 and fully independent in 1960; contains unique flora and fauna. Languages: Malagasy and French. Religions: animist and Christian. Currency: franc. Capital: Antananarivo. Pop.: 14 873 000 (1999 est.). Area: 587 041 sq. km (266 657 sq. miles). Official name (since 1975): **Democratic Republic of Madagascar.** Former name (1958–75): **Malagasy Republic.**
▸ **ˌMada'gascan** *n, adj*

madam ('mædəm) *n, pl* **madams** *or* (for sense 1) **mesdames. 1** a polite term of address for a woman, esp. one of relatively high social status. **2** a woman who runs a brothel. **3** *Brit. inf.* a precocious or pompous little girl. ORIG C13: from OF *ma dame* my lady

madame ('mædəm) *n, pl* **mesdames.** a married Frenchwoman: used as a title equivalent to *Mrs,* and sometimes extended to older unmarried women to show respect. ORIG C17: from F; see MADAM

madcap ('mædˌkæp) *adj* **1** impulsive, reckless, or lively. ◆ *n* **2** an impulsive, reckless, or lively person.

mad cow disease *n* an informal name for **BSE.**

madden ('mædᵊn) *vb* to make or become mad or angry.
▸ **'maddening** *adj* ▸ **'maddeningly** *adv*

madder ('mædə) *n* **1** a plant having small yellow flowers and a red fleshy root. **2** this root. **3** a dark reddish-purple dye formerly obtained from this root. **4** a red lake obtained from alizarin and an inorganic base; used as a pigment in inks and paints. ORIG OE *mædere*

madding ('mædɪŋ) *adj Arch.* **1** acting or behaving as if mad: *the madding crowd.* **2** making mad; maddening.
▸ **'maddingly** *adv*

made (meɪd) *vb* **1** the past tense and past participle of **make.** ◆ *adj* **2** artificially produced. **3** (*in combination*) produced or shaped as specified: *handmade.* **4 get** *or* **have it made.** *Inf.* to be assured of success.

Madeira ★ (mə'dɪərə; *Portuguese* mə'ðəirə) *n* **1** a group of volcanic islands in the N Atlantic, west of Morocco: constitutes the Portuguese administrative district of Funchal; consists of the chief island, Madeira, Pôrto Santo, and the uninhabited Deserta and Selvagen Islands; gained partial autonomy in 1976. Capital: Funchal. Pop.: 253 800 (1993 est.). Area: 797 sq. km (311 sq. miles). **2** a river in W Brazil, flowing northeast to the Amazon below Manaus. Length: 3241 km (2013 miles). **3** a rich strong fortified white wine made on Madeira.

madeleine ('mædəlɪn, -ˌleɪn) *n* a small fancy sponge cake. ORIG C19: ? after *Madeleine* Paulmier, F pastry cook

mademoiselle (ˌmædmwə'zɛl) *n, pl* **mesdemoiselles. 1** a young unmarried French girl or woman: used as a title equivalent to *Miss.* **2** a French teacher or governess. ORIG C15: F, from *ma* my + *demoiselle* DAMSEL

made-up *adj* **1** invented; fictional. **2** wearing make-up. **3** put together. **4** (of a road) surfaced with tarmac, concrete, etc.

madhouse ('mædˌhaʊs) *n Inf.* **1** a mental hospital or asylum. **2** a state of uproar or confusion.

Madhya Bharat ★ ('mʌdjə 'bɑ:rət) *n* a former state of central India: part of Madhya Pradesh since 1956.

Madhya Pradesh ★ ('mʌdjə prɑ:'dɛʃ) *n* a state of central India, situated on the Deccan Plateau: the largest Indian state; rich in mineral resources, with several industrial cities. Capital: Bhopal. Pop.: 71 950 000 (1994 est.). Area: 443 446 sq. km (171 215 sq. miles).

★ people and places

Madison[1] ★ ('mædɪsᵊn) *n* a city in the US in S central Wisconsin, on an isthmus between Lakes Mendota and Monona: the state capital. Pop.: 197 630 (1996 est.).

Madison[2] ★ ('mædɪsᵊn) *n* **James.** 1751–1836, US statesman; 4th president of the US (1809–17). He helped to draft the US Constitution and Bill of Rights.

Madison Avenue ★ *n* a street in New York City: a centre of American advertising and public-relations firms and a symbol of their attitudes and methods.

madly ('mædlɪ) *adv* **1** in an insane or foolish manner. **2** with great speed and energy. **3** *Inf.* extremely or excessively: *I love you madly.*

madman ('mædmən) *or (fem)* **madwoman** *n, pl* **madmen** *or* **madwomen.** a person who is insane.

madness ('mædnɪs) *n* **1** insanity; lunacy. **2** extreme anger, excitement, or foolishness. **3** a nontechnical word for **rabies.**

Madonna[1] ★ (mə'dɒnə) *n* **1** *Chiefly RC Church.* a designation of the Virgin Mary. **2** (*sometimes not cap.*) a picture or statue of the Virgin Mary. ORIG C16: It., from *ma* my + *donna* lady

Madonna[2] ★ (mə'dɒnə) *n* full name *Madonna Louise Veronica Ciccone.* born 1958, US rock singer and actress. Her hits include "Like a Virgin" (1985) and "American Pie" (2000). Her films include *Desperately Seeking Susan* (1985) and *Evita* (1996).

Madonna lily *n* a perennial widely cultivated Mediterranean lily plant with white trumpet-shaped flowers.

madras ('mædrəs, mə'dræs) *n* **1** a strong fine cotton or silk fabric, usually with a woven stripe. **2** a medium-hot curry: *chicken madras.* ORIG from MADRAS

Madras ★ (mə'drɑːs, -'dræs) *n* **1** a port in SE India, capital of Tamil Nadu, on the Bay of Bengal: founded in 1639 by the English East India Company as **Fort St George;** traditional burial place of St Thomas; university (1857). Pop. (urban area): 5 421 985 (1991). Official name: **Chennai. 2** the former name (until 1968) for the state of **Tamil Nadu.**

Madre de Dios ★ (*Spanish* 'maðre ðe 'ðiɔs) *n* a river in NE South America, rising in SE Peru and flowing northeast to the Beni River in N Bolivia. Length: about 965 km (600 miles).

madrepore (ˌmædrɪ'pɔː) *n* any coral of the genus *Madrepora,* many of which occur in tropical seas and form large coral reefs. ORIG C18: via F from It. *madrepora* mother-stone
▸ **ˌmadre'poral, madreporic** (ˌmædrɪ'pɒrɪk), *or* **ˌmadre'porian** *adj*

Madrid ★ (mə'drɪd) *n* the capital of Spain, situated centrally in New Castile: the highest European capital, at an altitude of about 700 m (2300 ft); a Moorish fortress in the 10th century, captured by Castile in 1083 and made capital of Spain in 1561; university (1836). Pop.: 3 029 734 (1995 est.).

madrigal ('mædrɪgᵊl) *n* **1** *Music.* a type of 16th- or 17th-century part song for unaccompanied voices, with an amatory or pastoral text. **2** a short love poem. ORIG C16: from It., from Med. L *mātricāle* primitive, apparently from L *mātrīcālis,* from *matrīx* womb
▸ **'madrigalˌesque** *adj* ▸ **madrigalian** (ˌmædrɪ'gælɪən, -'geɪ-) *adj* ▸ **'madrigalist** *n*

Madura ★ (mə'dʊərə) *n* an island in Indonesia, off the NE coast of Java: extensive forests and saline springs. Capital: Pamekasan. Area: 5472 sq. km (2113 sq. miles).
▸ **Madurese** (ˌmædjʊə'riːz) *adj, n*

Madurai ★ ('mædjʊˌraɪ) *n* a city in S India, in S Tamil Nadu: centre of Dravidian culture for over 2000 years; cotton industry. Pop.: 940 989 (1991). Former name: **Madura.**

Maeander ★ (miː'ændə) *n* ancient name of the river **Menderes** (sense 1). Also spelled: **Meander.**

Maebashi ★ ('mɑːɛ'bɑːʃiː) *n* a city in central Japan, on central Honshu: centre of sericulture and silk-spinning; university (1949). Pop.: 284 780 (1995).

Maecenas ★ (miː'siːnæs) *n* **1 Gaius** ('gaɪəs). ?70–8 B.C., Roman statesman; adviser to Augustus and patron of Horace and Virgil. **2** a wealthy patron of the arts.

maelstrom ('meɪlstrəʊm) *n* **1** a large powerful whirlpool. **2** any turbulent confusion. ORIG C17: from obs. Du. *maelstroom,* from *malen* to whirl round + *stroom* STREAM

Maelstrom ★ ('meɪlstrəʊm) *n* a strong tidal current in a restricted channel in the Lofoten Islands off the NW coast of Norway.

maenad ('miːnæd) *n* **1** *Classical history.* a woman participant in the orgiastic rites of Dionysus, Greek god of wine. **2** a frenzied woman. ORIG C16: from L *Maenas,* from Gk *mainas* madwoman
▸ **mae'nadic** *adj*

maestoso (maɪ'stəʊsəʊ) *Music.* ◆ *adj, adv* **1** to be performed majestically. ◆ *n, pl* **maestosos. 2** a piece or passage directed to be played in this way. ORIG C18: It.: majestic, from L *māiestās* MAJESTY

Maestricht ★ ('mɑːstrɪxt; *Dutch* maː'strɪxt) *n* an obsolete spelling of **Maastricht.**

maestro ('maɪstrəʊ) *n, pl* **maestri** (-trɪ) *or* **maestros. 1** a distinguished music teacher, conductor, or musician. **2** any master of an art: often used as a term of address. ORIG C18: It.: master

Maeterlinck ★ ('meɪtəˌlɪŋk; *French* mɛtɛrlɛ̃k) *n* Comte **Maurice** (mɔris). 1862–1949, Belgian poet and dramatist, noted for such plays as *Pelléas et Mélisande* (1892) and *L'Oiseau bleu* (1909). He won the Nobel prize for literature in 1911.

mae west (meɪ) *n Sl.* an inflatable life jacket, esp. as issued to the US armed forces. ORIG C20: after *Mae* WEST (1892–1980), US actress, renowned for her large bust

Maewo ★ (mɑː'eɪwəʊ) *n* an almost uninhabited island in Vanuatu. Also called: **Aurora.**

Mafeking ★ ('mæfɪˌkɪŋ) *n* the former name (until 1980) of **Mafikeng.**

MAFF (in Britain) *abbrev. for* Ministry of Agriculture, Fisheries, and Food.

Mafia ('mæfɪə) *n* **1 the.** an international secret criminal organization founded in Sicily, and carried to the US by Italian immigrants. **2** any group considered to resemble the Mafia. ORIG C19: from Sicilian dialect of It., lit.: hostility to the law, ?from Ar. *mahyah* bragging

Mafikeng ★ ('mæfɪˌkɛŋ) *n* a town in N South Africa: besieged by the Boers for 217 days (1899–1900) during the second Boer War: administrative headquarters of the British protectorate of Bechuanaland until 1965, although outside its borders; capital of North West Province. Pop.: 7000 (latest est.). Also called: **Mmabatho.** Former name (until 1980): **Mafeking.**

mafioso (ˌmæfɪ'əʊsəʊ) *n, pl* **mafiosos** *or* **mafiosi** (-sɪ). a person belonging to the Mafia.

mag. *abbrev. for:* **1** magazine. **2** magnesium. **3** magnetic. **4** magnetism. **5** magnitude.

magainin (mə'geɪnɪn) *n* any of a series of related substances with antibiotic properties, derived from the skins of frogs. ORIG C20: from Heb. *magain* a shield

Magallanes ★ (*Spanish* maɣa'ʎanes) *n* the former name of **Punta Arenas.**

magazine (ˌmægə'ziːn) *n* **1** a periodical paperback publication containing articles, fiction, photographs, etc. **2** a metal case holding several cartridges used in some firearms; it is removed and replaced when empty. **3** a building or compartment for storing weapons, explosives, military provisions, etc. **4** a stock of ammunition. **5** *Photog.* another name for **cartridge** (sense 3). **6** a rack for automatically feeding slides through a projector. **7** a TV or radio programme made up of a series of short nonfiction items. ORIG C16: via F *magasin* from It. *magazzino,* from Ar. *makhāzin,* pl. of *makhzan* storehouse, from *khazana* to store away

magdalen ('mægdəlɪn) *or* **magdalene** ('mægdəˌliːn) *n* **1** *Literary.* a reformed prostitute. **2** *Rare.* a reformatory for prostitutes. ORIG from Mary MAGDALENE

Magdalena ★ (ˌmægdə'leɪnə, -'liː-; *Spanish* maɣða'lena) *n* a river in SW Colombia, rising on the E slopes of the Andes and flowing north to the Caribbean near Barranquilla. Length: 1540 km (956 miles).

Magdalena Bay ★ *n* an inlet of the Pacific on the coast of NW Mexico, in Lower California.

Magdalene ★ (ˈmæɡdəˌliːn, ˌmæɡdəˈliːnɪ) *n* See **Mary Magdalene.**

Magdalenian (ˌmæɡdəˈliːnɪən) *adj* **1** of or relating to the latest Palaeolithic culture in Europe, which ended about 10 000 years ago. ◆ *n* **2 the.** the Magdalenian culture. ORIG C19: from F *magdalénien,* after *La Madeleine,* village in Dordogne, France, near which artefacts of the culture were found

Magdeburg ★ (ˈmæɡdəˌbɜːɡ; *German* ˈmakdəburk) *n* an industrial city and port in central Germany, on the River Elbe, capital of Saxony-Anhalt: a leading member of the Hanseatic League, whose local laws, the **Magdeburg Laws,** were adopted by many European cities. Pop.: 257 656 (1996 est.).

Magellan[1] ★ (məˈɡɛlən) *n* **Strait of.** a strait between the mainland of S South America and Tierra del Fuego, linking the S Pacific with the S Atlantic. Length: 600 km (370 miles). Width: up to 32 km (20 miles).

Magellan[2] ★ (məˈɡɛlən) *n* **Ferdinand.** Portuguese name *Fernão de Magalhães.* ?1480–1521, Portuguese navigator in the service of Spain. He discovered the Strait of Magellan (1520) and crossed the Pacific to the Philippines (1521), where he was killed by natives.

Magellanic cloud (ˌmæɡɪˈlænɪk) *n* either of two small irregular galaxies near the S celestial pole. Distances: 163 000 light years (Large Magellanic Cloud), 196 000 light years (Small Magellanic Cloud).

magenta (məˈdʒɛntə) *n* **1a** a deep purplish red. **1b** (*as adj*): *a magenta filter.* **2** another name for **fuchsin.** ORIG C19: after *Magenta,* Italy, alluding to the blood shed in a battle there (1859)

Maggiore ★ (ˌmædʒɪˈɔːrɪ; *Italian* madˈdʒore) *n* **Lake.** a lake in N Italy and S Switzerland, in the S Lepontine Alps.

maggot (ˈmæɡət) *n* **1** the limbless larva of dipterous insects, esp. the housefly and blowfly. **2** *Rare.* a fancy or whim. ORIG C14: from earlier *mathek;* rel. to ON *mathkr* worm, OE *matha,* OHG *mado* grub

maggoty (ˈmæɡətɪ) *adj* **1** of, like, or ridden with maggots. **2** *Austral. sl.* angry.

Magherafelt ★ (ˌmæxərəˈfɛlt) *n* a district of central Northern Ireland, on the NW shore of Lough Neagh: mainly agricultural. Administrative centre: Magherafelt. Pop.: 36 293 (1991). Area: 635 sq. km (245 sq. miles).

Maghreb *or* **Maghrib** ★ (ˈmʌɡrəb) *n* NW Africa, including Morocco, Algeria, Tunisia, and sometimes Libya. ORIG from Ar., lit.: the West
▸ ˈ**Maghrebi** *or* ˈ**Maghribi** *adj, n*

magi (ˈmeɪdʒaɪ) *pl n, sing* **magus** (ˈmeɪɡəs). **1** See **magus. 2 the three Magi.** the wise men from the East who came to do homage to the infant Jesus (Matthew 2:1–12). ORIG see MAGUS
▸ **magian** (ˈmeɪdʒɪən) *adj*

magic (ˈmædʒɪk) *n* **1** the art that, by use of spells, supposedly invokes supernatural powers to influence events; sorcery. **2** the practice of this art. **3** the practice of illusory tricks to entertain; conjuring. **4** any mysterious or extraordinary quality or power. **5 like magic.** very quickly. ◆ *adj also* **magical. 6** of or relating to magic. **7** possessing or considered to possess mysterious powers. **8** unaccountably enchanting. **9** *Inf.* wonderful; marvellous. ◆ *vb* **magics, magicking, magicked.** (*tr*) **10** to transform or produce by or as if by magic. **11** (foll. by *away*) to cause to disappear as if by magic. ORIG C14: via OF *magique,* from Gk *magikē* witchcraft, from *magos* MAGUS
▸ ˈ**magically** *adv*

magic bullet *n Inf.* any therapeutic agent, esp. one in the early stages of development, reputed to be very effective in treating a condition, such as a malignant tumour, by specifically targeting the diseased tissue.

magic eye *n* a miniature cathode-ray tube in some radio receivers, on the screen of which a pattern is displayed to assist tuning. Also called: **electric eye.**

magician (məˈdʒɪʃən) *n* **1** another term for **conjuror. 2** a person who practises magic. **3** a person with extraordinary skill, influence, etc.

magic lantern *n* an early type of slide projector.

magic mushroom *n Inf.* any of various types of fungi that contain a hallucinogenic substance.

magic realism *or* **magical realism** *n* a style of painting or writing that depicts images or scenes of surreal fantasy in a representational or realistic way.
▸ **magic realist** *or* **magical realist** *n*

magic square *n* a square array of rows of integers arranged so that the sum of the integers is the same when taken vertically, horizontally, or diagonally.

Maginot line (ˈmæʒɪˌnəʊ) *n* **1** a line of fortifications built by France to defend its border with Germany prior to World War II; it proved ineffective. **2** any line of defence in which blind confidence is placed. ORIG after André *Maginot* (1877–1932), F minister of war when the fortifications were begun in 1929

magisterial (ˌmædʒɪˈstɪərɪəl) *adj* **1** commanding; authoritative. **2** domineering; dictatorial. **3** of or relating to a teacher or person of similar status. **4** of or relating to a magistrate. ORIG C17: from LL *magisteriālis,* from *magister* master
▸ ˌ**magisˈterially** *adv*

magistracy (ˈmædʒɪstrəsɪ) *or* **magistrature** (ˈmædʒɪstrəˌtjʊə) *n, pl* **magistracies** *or* **magistratures. 1** the office or function of a magistrate. **2** magistrates collectively. **3** the district under the jurisdiction of a magistrate.

magistral (məˈdʒɪstrəl) *adj* **1** *Pharmacol.* made up according to a special prescription. **2** of a master; masterly. ORIG C16: from L *magistrālis,* from *magister* master
▸ **magistrality** (ˌmædʒɪˈstrælɪtɪ) *n*

magistrate (ˈmædʒɪˌstreɪt, -strɪt) *n* **1** a public officer concerned with the administration of law. **2** another name for **justice of the peace.** ORIG C17: from L *magistrātus,* from *magister* master
▸ ˈ**magisˌtrateship** *n*

magistrates' court *n* (in England) a court held before two or more justices of the peace or a stipendiary magistrate to deal with minor crimes, certain civil actions, and preliminary hearings.

Maglemosian *or* **Maglemosean** (ˌmæɡləˈməʊzɪən) *n* **1** the first Mesolithic culture of N Europe, dating from 8000 B.C. to about 5000 B.C. ◆ *adj* **2** designating or relating to this culture. ORIG C20: after the site at *Maglemose,* Denmark, where the culture was first classified

magma (ˈmæɡmə) *n, pl* **magmas** *or* **magmata** (-mətə). **1** a paste or suspension consisting of a finely divided solid dispersed in a liquid. **2** hot molten rock within the earth's crust which sometimes finds its way to the surface where it solidifies to form igneous rock. ORIG C15: from L: dregs (of an ointment), from Gk: salve made by kneading, from *massein* to knead
▸ **magmatic** (mæɡˈmætɪk) *adj*

Magna Carta *or* **Magna Charta** (ˈmæɡnə ˈkɑːtə) *n English history.* the charter granted by King John at Runnymede in 1215, recognizing the rights and privileges of the barons, church, and freemen. ORIG Med. L. great charter

Magna Graecia ★ (ˈmæɡnə ˈɡriːʃɪə) *n* (in the ancient world) S Italy, where numerous colonies were founded by Greek cities. ORIG L: Great Greece

magnanimity (ˌmæɡnəˈnɪmɪtɪ) *n, pl* **magnanimities.** generosity. ORIG C14: via OF from L *magnanimitās,* from *magnus* great + *animus* soul

magnanimous (mæɡˈnænɪməs) *adj* generous and noble. ORIG C16: from L *magnanimus* great-souled
▸ **magˈnanimously** *adv*

magnate (ˈmæɡneɪt, -nɪt) *n* **1** a person of power and rank, esp. in industry. **2** *History.* a great nobleman. ORIG C15: back formation from earlier *magnates,* from LL: great men, from L *magnus* great
▸ ˈ**magnateˌship** *n*

magnesia (mæɡˈniːʃə) *n* another name for **magnesium oxide.** ORIG C14: via Med. L from Gk *Magnēsia,* of *Magnēs,* ancient mineral-rich region
▸ **magˈnesian** *or* **magnesic** (mæɡˈniːsɪk) *adj*

magnesium (mæɡˈniːzɪəm) *n* a light silvery-white metallic element of the alkaline earth series that burns with an intense white flame: used in light structural alloys, flashbulbs, flares, and fireworks. Symbol: Mg; atomic no.: 12; atomic wt.: 24.305. ORIG C19: NL, from MAGNESIA

magnesium oxide *n* a white tasteless substance used as an antacid and laxative and in refractory materials. Formula: MgO. Also called: **magnesia.**

magnet ('mægnɪt) *n* **1** a body that can attract certain substances, such as iron or steel, as a result of a magnetic field; a piece of ferromagnetic substance. See also **electromagnet. 2** a person or thing that exerts a great attraction. ORIG C15: via L from Gk *magnēs,* shortened from *ho Magnēs lithos* the Magnesian stone. See MAGNESIA

magnetar (mæg'ni:ˌtɑ:) *n* a type of neutron star that has a very intense magnetic field, over 1000 times greater than that of a pulsar. ORIG C20: from MAGNET(IC ST)AR, on the model of QUASAR

magnetic (mæg'nɛtɪk) *adj* **1** of, producing, or operated by means of magnetism. **2** of or concerned with a magnet. **3** of or concerned with the magnetism of the earth: *the magnetic equator.* **4** capable of being magnetized. **5** exerting a powerful attraction: *a magnetic personality.*
▸ **mag'netically** *adv*

magnetic constant *n* the magnetic permeability of free space; it has the value $4\pi \times 10^{-7}$ H m^{-1}.

magnetic declination *n* the angle that a compass needle makes with the direction of the geographical north pole at any given point on the earth's surface.

magnetic dip *or* **inclination** *n* another name for **dip** (sense 24).

magnetic dipole moment *n* a measure of the magnetic strength of a magnet or current-carrying coil, expressed as the torque produced when the magnet or coil is set with its axis perpendicular to unit magnetic field.

magnetic disk *n* another name for **disk** (sense 2).

magnetic equator *n* an imaginary line on the earth's surface, near the equator, at all points on which there is no magnetic dip.

magnetic field *n* a field of force surrounding a permanent magnet or a moving charged particle, in which another permanent magnet or moving charge experiences a force.

magnetic flux *n* a measure of the strength of a magnetic field over a given area, equal to the product of the area and the magnetic flux density through it. Symbol: ϕ

magnetic mine *n* a mine designed to explode when a magnetic field such as that generated by the metal of a ship's hull is detected.

magnetic needle *n* a slender magnetized rod used in certain instruments, such as the magnetic compass, for indicating the direction of a magnetic field.

magnetic north *n* the direction in which a compass needle points, at an angle (the declination) from the direction of true (geographic) north.

magnetic pick-up *n* a type of record-player pick-up in which the stylus moves an iron core in a coil, causing a changing magnetic field that produces the current.

magnetic pole *n* **1** either of two regions in a magnet where the magnetic induction is concentrated. **2** either of two variable points on the earth's surface towards which a magnetic needle points, where the lines of force of the earth's magnetic field are vertical.

magnetic resonance *n* the response by atoms, molecules, or nuclei subjected to a magnetic field to radio waves or other forms of energy: used in medicine for scanning (**magnetic resonance imaging**; abbrev.: **MRI**).

magnetic storm *n* a sudden severe disturbance of the earth's magnetic field, caused by emission of charged particles from the sun.

magnetic stripe *n* (across the back of various types of bank card, credit card, etc.) a dark stripe of magnetic material consisting of several tracks onto which information may be coded and which may be read or written to electronically.

magnetic tape *n* a long narrow plastic or metal strip coated or impregnated with iron oxide, chrome dioxide, etc., used to record sound or video signals or to store information in computing.

magnetism ('mægnɪˌtɪzəm) *n* **1** the property of attraction displayed by magnets. **2** any of a class of phenomena in which a field of force is caused by a moving electric charge. **3** the branch of physics concerned with magnetic phenomena. **4** powerful attraction.

magnetite ('mægnɪˌtaɪt) *n* a black magnetizable mineral that is an important source of iron.

magnetize *or* **magnetise** ('mægnɪˌtaɪz) *vb* **magnetizes, magnetizing, magnetized** *or* **magnetises, magnetising, magnetised.** (*tr*) **1** to make (a substance or object) magnetic. **2** to attract strongly.
▸ **'magnetˌizable** *or* **'magnetˌisable** *adj* ▸ **ˌmagneti'zation** *or* **ˌmagneti'sation** *n* ▸ **'magnetˌizer** *or* **'magnetˌiser** *n*

magneto (mæg'ni:təʊ) *n, pl* **magnetos.** a small electric generator in which the magnetic field is produced by a permanent magnet, esp. one for providing the spark in an internal-combustion engine. ORIG C19: short for *magnetoelectric generator*

magneto- *combining form.* indicating magnetism or magnetic properties: *magnetosphere.*

magnetoelectricity (mægˌni:təʊɪlɛk'trɪsɪtɪ) *n* electricity produced by the action of magnetic fields.
▸ **magˌnetoe'lectric** *or* **magˌnetoe'lectrical** *adj*

magnetometer (ˌmægnɪ'tɒmɪtə) *n* any instrument for measuring the intensity or direction of a magnetic field, esp. the earth's field.
▸ **ˌmagne'tometry** *n*

magnetomotive (mægˌni:təʊ'məʊtɪv) *adj* causing a magnetic flux.

magnetosphere (mæg'ni:təʊˌsfɪə) *n* the region surrounding a planet, such as the earth, in which the behaviour of charged particles is controlled by the planet's magnetic field.

magnetron ('mægnɪˌtrɒn) *n* a two-electrode electronic valve used with an applied magnetic field to generate high-power microwave oscillations, esp. for use in radar. ORIG C20: from MAGNET + ELECTRON

magnet school *n* a school that attracts pupils from outside its immediate vicinity, either because of its high educational standards or because of its concentration on some specialist area.

Magnificat (mæg'nɪfɪˌkæt) *n Christianity.* the hymn of the Virgin Mary (Luke 1:46-55), used as a canticle. ORIG from the opening phrase, *Magnificat anima mea Dominum* (my soul doth magnify the Lord)

magnification (ˌmægnɪfɪ'keɪʃən) *n* **1** the act of magnifying or the state of being magnified. **2** the degree to which something is magnified. **3** a magnified copy, photograph, drawing, etc., of something. **4** a measure of the ability of a lens or other optical instrument to magnify.

magnificence (mæg'nɪfɪsəns) *n* the quality of being magnificent. ORIG C14: via F from L *magnificentia*

magnificent (mæg'nɪfɪsᵊnt) *adj* **1** splendid or impressive in appearance. **2** superb or very fine. **3** (esp. of ideas) noble or elevated. ORIG C16: from L *magnificentior,* irregular comp. of *magnificus* great in deeds, from *magnus* great + *facere* to do
▸ **mag'nificently** *adv*

magnifico (mæg'nɪfɪkəʊ) *n, pl* **magnificoes.** a magnate; grandee. ORIG C16: It. from L *magnificus;* see MAGNIFICENT

magnify ('mægnɪˌfaɪ) *vb* **magnifies, magnifying, magnified. 1** to increase, cause to increase, or be increased in apparent size, as through the action of a lens, microscope, etc. **2** to exaggerate or become exaggerated in importance: *don't magnify your troubles.* **3** (*tr*) *Arch.* to glorify. ORIG C14: via OF from L *magnificāre* to praise
▸ **'magniˌfiable** *adj*

magnifying glass *or* **magnifier** *n* a convex lens used to produce an enlarged image of an object.

magniloquent (mæg'nɪləkwənt) *adj* (of speech) lofty in style; grandiloquent. ORIG C17: from L *magnus* great + *loquī* to speak
▸ **mag'niloquence** *n* ▸ **mag'niloquently** *adv*

Magnitogorsk ★ (*Russian* məgnita'gɔrsk) *n* a city in central Russia, on the Ural River: founded in 1930 to exploit local magnetite ores; site of one of the world's largest (but outdated) metallurgical plants. Pop.: 427 000 (1995 est.).

magnitude ('mægnɪˌtjuːd) *n* **1** relative importance or significance: *a problem of the first magnitude.* **2** relative size or extent. **3** *Maths.* a number assigned to a quantity as a basis of comparison for the measurement of similar quantities. **4** Also called: **apparent magnitude.** *Astron.* the apparent brightness of a celestial body expressed on a numerical scale on which bright stars have a low value. **5** Also called: **earthquake magnitude.** *Geol.* a measure of the size of an earthquake based on the quantity of energy released. ORIG C14: from L *magnitūdō* size, from *magnus* great

magnolia (mæg'nəʊlɪə) *n* **1** any tree or shrub of the genus *Magnolia* of Asia and North America: cultivated for their white, pink, purple, or yellow showy flowers. **2** the flower of any of these plants. **3a** a very pale pinkish-white colour. **3b** (*as adj*): *magnolia walls.* ORIG C18: NL, after Pierre *Magnol* (1638–1715), F botanist

magnox ('mægnɒks) *n* an alloy consisting mostly of magnesium with small amounts of aluminium, used in fuel elements of nuclear reactors. ORIG C20: from *mag(nesium) n(o) ox(idation)*

magnox reactor *n* a nuclear reactor using carbon dioxide as the coolant, graphite as the moderator, and uranium cased in magnox as the fuel.

magnum ('mægnəm) *n, pl* **magnums.** a wine bottle holding the equivalent of two normal bottles (approximately 52 fluid ounces). ORIG C18: from L: a big thing, from *magnus* large

magnum opus *n* a great work of art or literature, esp. the greatest single work of an artist. ORIG L

Magog ★ ('meɪgɒg) *n* See **Gog and Magog.**

magpie ('mægˌpaɪ) *n* **1** any of various birds having a black-and-white plumage, long tail, and a chattering call. **2** any of various similar birds of Australia. **3** *Brit.* a person who hoards small objects. **4** a person who chatters. **5a** the outermost ring but one on a target. **5b** a shot that hits this ring. ORIG C17: from *Mag,* dim. of *Margaret,* used to signify a chatterbox + PIE[2]

Magritte ★ (*French* magrit) *n* **René** (rəne). 1898–1967, Belgian surrealist painter.

maguey ('mægweɪ) *n* **1** any of various tropical American agave plants, esp. one that yields a fibre or is used in making an alcoholic beverage. **2** the fibre from any of these plants, used esp. for rope. ORIG C16: Sp., of Amerind origin

magus ('meɪgəs) *n, pl* **magi. 1** a Zoroastrian priest. **2** an astrologer, sorcerer, or magician of ancient times. ORIG C14: from L, from Gk *magos,* from OPersian *magus* magician

Magus ★ ('meɪgəs) *n* **Simon.** *New Testament.* a sorcerer who tried to buy spiritual powers from the apostles (Acts 8:9-24).

Magyar ('mægjɑː) *n* **1** (*pl* **Magyars**) a member of the predominant ethnic group of Hungary. **2** the Hungarian language. ◆ *adj* **3** of or relating to the Magyars or their language. **4** *Sewing.* of or relating to a style of sleeve cut in one piece with the bodice.

Magyarország ★ ('mɔdjɔrorsaːg) *n* the Hungarian name for **Hungary.**

Mahabharata (ˌmɑːhə'bɑːrətə), **Mahabharatam,** *or* **Mahabharatum** (ˌmɑːhə'bɑːrətəm) *n* an epic Sanskrit poem of India of which the *Bhagavad-Gita* forms a part. ORIG Sansk., from *mahā* great + *bhārata* story

Mahajanga ★ (ˌmæhə'dʒæŋgə) *n* a port in NW Madagascar, on Bombetoka Bay. Pop.: 100 807 (1993). Former name: **Majunga.**

Mahalla el Kubra ★ (mə'hɑːlə ɛl 'kuːbrə) *n* a city in N Egypt, on the Nile delta: one of the largest diversified textile centres in Egypt. Pop.: 408 000 (1992 est.).

Mahanadi ★ (mə'hɑːnədɪ) *n* a river in E India, rising in S Madhya Pradesh and flowing north, then south and east to the Bay of Bengal. Length: 885 km (550 miles).

maharajah *or* **maharaja** (ˌmɑːhə'rɑːdʒə) *n* any of various Indian princes, esp. any of the rulers of the former native states. ORIG C17: Hindi, from *mahā* great + RAJAH

maharani *or* **maharanee** (ˌmɑːhə'rɑːniː) *n* **1** the wife of a maharajah. **2** a woman holding the rank of maharajah. ORIG C19: from Hindi, from *mahā* great + RANI

Maharashtra ★ (ˌmɑːhə'ræʃtrə) *n* a state of W central India, formed in 1960 from the Marathi-speaking S and E parts of former Bombay state: lies mainly on the Deccan plateau; mainly agricultural. Capital: Bombay. Pop.: 85 565 000 (1994 est.). Area: 307 690 sq. km (118 800 sq. miles).

maharishi (ˌmɑːhə'riːʃɪ, mə'hɑːriːʃɪ) *n Hinduism.* a Hindu teacher of religious and mystical knowledge. ORIG from Hindi, from *mahā* great + *rishi* sage

mahatma (mə'hɑːtmə) *n* (*sometimes cap.*) **1** *Hinduism.* a Brahman sage. **2** *Theosophy.* an adept or sage. ORIG C19: from Sansk. *mahātman,* from *mahā* great + *ātman* soul

Mahayana (ˌmɑːhə'jɑːnə) *n* **a** a liberal Buddhist school of Tibet, China, and Japan, whose adherents seek enlightenment for all sentient beings. **b** (*as modifier*): *Mahayana Buddhism.* ORIG from Sansk., from *mahā* great + *yāna* vehicle

Mahdi ★ ('mɑːdɪ) *n* **1** the title assumed by *Mohammed Ahmed.* ?1843–85, Sudanese military leader, who led a revolt against Egypt (1881) and captured Khartoum (1885). **2** *Islam.* any of a number of Muslim messiahs expected to forcibly convert all mankind to Islam. ORIG Ar. *mahdīy* one who is guided, from *madā* to guide aright ▸ **'Mahdism** *n* ▸ **'Mahdist** *n, adj*

Mahé ★ (mɑː'heɪ) *n* an island in the Indian Ocean, the chief island of the Seychelles. Capital: Victoria. Pop.: 59 500 (1987). Area: 147 sq. km (57 sq. miles).

Mahfouz *or* **Mahfuz** ★ (mɑː'fuːz) *n* **Naguib** (nɑː'giːb). born 1911, Egyptian writer, known for his novels, including *The Cairo Trilogy* (1956–57) and *Children of Gebelawi* (1959). Nobel prize for literature 1988.

mah jong *or* **mah-jongg** (ˌmɑː'dʒɒŋ) *n* a game of Chinese origin, usually played by four people, using tiles bearing various designs. ORIG from Chinese, lit.: sparrows

Mahler ★ ('mɑːlə) *n* **Gustav** ('gʊstaf). 1860–1911, Austrian composer and conductor. His works include nine symphonies, the symphonic song cycle *Das Lied von der Erde* (1908), and the song cycle *Kindertotenlieder* (1902).

mahlstick ('mɔːlˌstɪk) *n* a variant spelling of **maulstick.**

mahogany (mə'hɒgənɪ) *n, pl* **mahoganies. 1** any of various tropical American trees valued for their hard reddish-brown wood. **2** any of several trees with similar wood, such as African mahogany and Philippine mahogany. **3a** the wood of any of these trees. **3b** (*as modifier*): *a mahogany table.* **4a** a reddish-brown colour. **4b** (*as adj*): *mahogany skin.* ORIG C17: from ?

Mahomet ★ (mə'hɒmɪt) *n* a variant of **Mohammed.**

Mahometan (mə'hɒmɪt°n) *n, adj* a former word for **Muslim.**

mahonia (mə'həʊnɪə) *n* any evergreen shrub of the Asian and American genus *Mahonia:* cultivated for their ornamental spiny divided leaves and clusters of small yellow flowers. ORIG C19: NL, after Bernard *McMahon* (died 1816), American botanist

Mahound ★ (mə'haʊnd, -'huːnd) *n* an archaic name for **Mohammed.** ORIG C16: from OF *Mahun*

mahout (mə'haʊt) *n* (in India and the East Indies) an elephant driver or keeper. ORIG C17: Hindi *mahāut,* from Sansk. *mahāmātra* of great measure, orig. a title

Mähren ★ ('mɛːrən) *n* the German name for **Moravia**[1].

mahseer ('mɑːsɪə) *n* any of various large freshwater Indian cyprinid fishes. ORIG from Hindi

Maia ★ ('maɪə) *n Greek myth.* the eldest of the seven Pleiades, mother by Zeus of Hermes.

maid (meɪd) *n* **1** *Arch. or literary.* a young unmarried girl; maiden. **2a** a female servant. **2b** (*in combination*): *a housemaid.* **3** a spinster. ORIG C12: form of MAIDEN

maiden ('meɪd°n) *n* **1** *Arch. or literary.* **1a** a young unmarried girl, esp. a virgin. **1b** (*as modifier*): *a maiden blush.* **2** *Horse racing.* **2a** a horse that has never won a race. **2b** (*as modifier*): *a maiden race.* **3** *Cricket.* See **maiden over. 4** (*modifier*) of or relating to an older unmarried woman: *a maiden aunt.* **5** (*modifier*) of or involving an initial experi-

★ people and places

ence or attempt: *a maiden voyage.* **6** (*modifier*) (of a person or thing) untried; unused. **7** (*modifier*) (of a place) never trodden, penetrated, or captured. ORIG OE *mægden*
▸ **'maidenish** *adj* ▸ **'maiden,like** *adj*

maidenhair fern *or* **maidenhair** ('meɪdᵊn,hɛə) *n* any of various ferns of tropical and warm regions, having delicate fan-shaped fronds with small pale green leaflets. ORIG C15: from the hairlike appearance of its fronds

maidenhair tree *n* another name for **ginkgo.**

maidenhead ('meɪdᵊn,hɛd) *n* **1** a nontechnical word for the **hymen. 2** virginity; maidenhood. ORIG C13: from *maiden* + *-hed,* var. of -HOOD

Maidenhead ★ ('meɪdᵊn,hɛd) *n* a town in S England, in Berkshire on the River Thames. Pop.: 59 605 (1991).

maidenhood ('meɪdᵊn,hʊd) *n* **1** the time during which a woman is a maiden or virgin. **2** the condition of being a maiden or virgin.

maidenly ('meɪdᵊnlɪ) *adj* of or befitting a maiden.
▸ **'maidenliness** *n*

maiden name *n* a woman's surname before marriage.

maiden over *n Cricket.* an over in which no runs are scored.

maid of honour *n* **1** *US & Canad.* the principal unmarried attendant of a bride. **2** *Brit.* a small tart with an almond-flavoured filling. **3** an unmarried lady attending a queen or princess.

Maid of Orléans ★ *n* **the.** another name for **Joan of Arc.**

maidservant ('meɪd,sɜːvənt) *n* a female servant.

Maidstone ★ ('meɪdstən, -,stəʊn) *n* a town in SE England, administrative centre of Kent, on the River Medway. Pop.: 90 878 (1991).

Maiduguri ★ (,maɪdʊ'guːrɪ) *n* a city in NE Nigeria, capital of Bornu State; agricultural trade centre. Pop.: 320 000 (1996 est.). Also called: **Yerwa-Maiduguri.**

maihem ('meɪhɛm) *n* a variant spelling of **mayhem.**

Maikop ★ (*Russian* maj'kɔp) *n* a city in SW Russia, capital of the Adygei Republic: extensive oilfields to the southwest; mineral springs. Pop.: 165 000 (1995 est.).

mail[1] (meɪl) *n* **1** Also called (esp. Brit.): **post.** letters, packages, etc., that are transported and delivered by the post office. **2** the postal system. **3** a single collection or delivery of mail. **4** a train, ship, or aircraft that carries mail. **5** short for **electronic mail. 6** (*modifier*) of, involving, or used to convey mail: *a mail train.* ◆ *vb* (*tr*) **7** *Chiefly US & Canad.* to send by mail. **8** to contact (a person) by electronic mail. **9** to send (a message, document, etc.) by electronic mail. ORIG C13: from OF *male* bag, prob. from OHG *malha* wallet
▸ **'mailable** *adj*

mail[2] (meɪl) *n* **1** a type of flexible armour consisting of riveted metal rings or links. **2** the hard protective shell of such animals as the turtle and lobster. ◆ *vb* **3** (*tr*) to clothe or arm with mail. ORIG C14: from OF *maille* mesh, from L *macula* spot

mailbag ('meɪl,bæg) *or* **mailsack** *n* a large bag for transporting or delivering mail.

mailbox ('meɪl,bɒks) *n* another name (esp. US and Canad.) for **letter box.**

Mailer ★ ('meɪlə) *n* **Norman.** born 1923, US author. His works include the war novel *The Naked and the Dead* (1948), *The Armies of the Night* (1968), and *Harlot's Ghost* (1991).

mailing list *n* a register of names and addresses to which advertising matter, etc., is sent by post or electronic mail.

Maillol ★ (*French* majɔl) *n* **Aristide** (aristid). 1861–1944, French sculptor.

maillot (mæ'jəʊ) *n* **1** tights worn for ballet, gymnastics, etc. **2** a woman's swimsuit. **3** a jersey. ORIG from F

mailman ('meɪl,mæn) *n, pl* **mailmen.** *Chiefly US & Canad.* another name for **postman.**

mail merging *n Computing.* a software facility that can produce a large number of personalized letters by combining a file containing a list of names and addresses with one containing a single standard document.

mail order *n* **1** an order for merchandise sent by post. **2a** a system of buying and selling merchandise through the post. **2b** (*as modifier*): *a mail-order firm.*

mailshot ('meɪl,ʃɒt) *n* a circular, leaflet, or other advertising material sent by post, or the posting of such material to a large group of people at one time.

maim (meɪm) *vb* (*tr*) **1** to mutilate, cripple, or disable a part of the body of (a person or animal). **2** to make defective. ORIG C14: from OF *mahaignier* to wound, prob. of Gmc origin

mai mai (maɪ maɪ) *n NZ.* a duck shooter's shelter; hide. ORIG probably from Australian Aboriginal *mia-mia* shelter

Maimonides ★ (maɪ'mɒnɪ,diːz) *n* also called Rabbi *Moses ben Maimon.* 1135–1204, Jewish philosopher and jurist, born in Spain. He codified Jewish law in *Mishneh Torah* (1180).
▸ **Mai,moni'dean** *adj, n*

main[1] (meɪn) *adj* (*prenominal*) **1** chief or principal. **2** sheer or utmost (esp. in **by main force**). **3** *Naut.* of, relating to, or denoting any gear, such as a stay or sail, belonging to the mainmast. ◆ *n* **4** a principal pipe, conduit, duct, or line in a system used to distribute water, electricity, etc. **5** (*pl*) **5a** the main distribution network for water, gas, or electricity. **5b** (*as modifier*): *mains voltage.* **6** the chief or most important part or consideration. **7** great strength or force (now esp. in **might and main**). **8** *Literary.* the open ocean. **9** *Arch.* short for **Spanish Main. 10** *Arch.* short for **mainland. 11 in** (*or* **for**) **the main.** on the whole; for the most part. ORIG C13: from OE *mægen* strength

main[2] (meɪn) *n* **1** a throw of the dice in dice games. **2** a cockfighting contest. **3** a match in archery, boxing, etc. ORIG C16: from ?

Main ★ (meɪn; *German* main) *n* a river in central and W Germany, flowing west through Würzburg and Frankfurt to the Rhine. Length: about 515 km (320 miles).

mainbrace ('meɪn,breɪs) *n Naut.* **1** a brace attached to the main yard. **2 splice the mainbrace.** See **splice.**

main clause *n Grammar.* a clause that can stand alone as a sentence.

Maine ★ (meɪn) *n* a state of the northeastern US, on the Atlantic: chiefly hilly, with many lakes, rivers, and forests. Capital: Augusta. Pop.: 1 244 250 (1998 est.). Area: 86 156 sq. km (33 265 sq. miles). Abbrev. (with zip code): **ME**

Maine-et-Loire ★ (*French* mɛnelwar) *n* a department of W France, in Pays de la Loire region. Capital: Angers. Pop.: 719 172 (1994 est.). Area: 7218 sq. km (2815 sq. miles).

mainframe ('meɪn,freɪm) *Computing.* ◆ *adj* **1** denoting a high-speed general-purpose computer, usually with a large store capacity. ◆ *n* **2** such a computer. **3** the central processing unit of a computer.

mainland ('meɪnlənd) *n* the main part of a landmass as opposed to an island or peninsula.
▸ **'mainlander** *n*

Mainland ★ ('meɪnlənd) *n* **1** an island off N Scotland: the largest of the Shetland Islands. Chief town: Lerwick. Pop.: 17 596 (1991). Area: about 583 sq. km (225 sq. miles). **2** Also called: **Pomona.** an island off N Scotland: the largest of the Orkney Islands. Chief town: Kirkwall. Pop.: 15 128 (1991). Area: 492 sq. km (190 sq. miles). **3 the Mainland.** *NZ.* another name for **South Island.**

main line *n* **1** *Railways.* **1a** the trunk route between two points, usually fed by branch lines. **1b** (*as modifier*): *a main-line station.* **2** *US.* a main road. ◆ *vb* **mainline, mainlines, mainlining, mainlined. 3** (*intr*) *Sl.* to inject a drug into a vein. ◆ *adj* **mainline. 4** having an important position.
▸ **'main,liner** *n*

mainly ('meɪnlɪ) *adv* for the most part; to the greatest extent; principally.

main market *n* the market for trading in the listed securities of companies on the London stock exchange. Cf. **Third Market, Unlisted Securities Market.**

mainmast ('meɪn,mɑːst) *n Naut.* the chief mast of a sailing vessel with two or more masts.

mainsail ('meɪnˌseɪl; *Naut.* 'meɪnsᵊl) *n Naut.* the largest and lowermost sail on the mainmast.

mainsheet ('meɪnˌʃiːt) *n Naut.* the line used to control the angle of the mainsail to the wind.

mainspring ('meɪnˌsprɪŋ) *n* **1** the principal spring of a mechanism, esp. in a watch or clock. **2** the chief cause or motive of something.

mainstay ('meɪnˌsteɪ) *n* **1** *Naut.* the forestay that braces the mainmast. **2** a chief support.

mainstream ('meɪnˌstriːm) *n* **1** the main current (of a river, cultural trend, etc.). ◆ *adj* **2** of or relating to the style of jazz that lies between the traditional and the modern.

mainstream corporation tax *n* (in Britain) the balance of the corporation tax paid by a company for an accounting period after the advance corporation tax has been deducted.

mainstreeting ('meɪnˌstriːtɪŋ) *n Canad.* the practice of a politician walking about the streets of a town or city to gain votes and greet supporters.

maintain (meɪn'teɪn) *vb (tr)* **1** to continue or retain; keep in existence. **2** to keep in proper or good condition. **3** to enable (a person) to support a style of living: *the money maintained us for a month.* **4** (*takes a clause as object*) to state or assert. **5** to defend against contradiction; uphold: *she maintained her innocence.* **6** to defend against physical attack. ORIG C13: from OF *maintenir,* ult. from L *manū tenēre* to hold in the hand
▸ **main'tainable** *adj* ▸ **main'tainer** *n*

maintenance ('meɪntɪnəns) *n* **1** the act of maintaining or the state of being maintained. **2** a means of support; livelihood. **3** (*modifier*) of or relating to the maintaining of buildings, machinery, etc.: *maintenance man.* **4** *Law.* the interference in a legal action by a person having no interest in it, as by providing funds to continue the action. **5** *Law.* a provision ordered to be made by way of periodical payments or a lump sum, as for a spouse after a divorce. ORIG C14: from OF; see MAINTAIN

Maintenon ★ (*French* mɛ̃tnɔ̃) *n* **Marquise de,** title of *Françoise d'Aubigné.* 1635–1719, the mistress and, from about 1685, second wife of Louis XIV.

maintop ('meɪnˌtɒp) *n* a top or platform at the head of the mainmast.

main-topmast *n Naut.* the mast immediately above the mainmast.

maintopsail (ˌmeɪn'tɒpseɪl; *Naut.* ˌmeɪn'tɒpsᵊl) *n Naut.* a topsail on the mainmast.

main yard *n Naut.* a yard for a square mainsail.

Mainz ★ (*German* maints) *n* a port in W Germany, capital of the Rhineland-Palatinate, at the confluence of the Main and Rhine: an archbishopric from about 780 until 1801; important in the 15th century for the development of printing (by Johann Gutenberg). Pop.: 183 720 (1996 est.). French name: **Mayence.**

maiolica (mə'jɒlɪkə) *n* a variant of **majolica.**

maisonette *or* **maisonnette** (ˌmeɪzə'nɛt) *n* self-contained living accommodation often occupying two floors of a larger house and having its own outside entrance. ORIG C19: from F, dim. of *maison* house

mai tai ('maɪ ˌtaɪ) *n* a mixed drink consisting of rum, Curaçao, fruit juice, and grenadine. ORIG C20: from ?

Maitland[1] ★ ('meɪtlənd) *n* a town in SE Australia, in E New South Wales: industrial centre of an agricultural region. Pop.: 38 863 (1981).

Maitland[2] ★ ('meɪtlənd) *n* **Frederic William.** 1850–1906, British legal historian.

maître d'hôtel (ˌmɛtrə dəʊ'tɛl) *n, pl* **maîtres d'hôtel. 1** a head waiter or steward. **2** the manager or owner of a hotel. ORIG C16: from F: master of (the) hotel

maize (meɪz) *n* **1** Also called: **sweet corn, Indian corn. 1a** a tall annual grass cultivated for its yellow edible grains, which develop on a spike. **1b** the grain of this plant, used for food, for fodder, and as a source of oil. **2a** a yellow colour. **2b** (*as adj*): *a maize gown.* ORIG C16: from Sp. *maíz,* from Taino *mahiz*

Maj. *abbrev. for* Major.

majestic (mə'dʒɛstɪk) *adj* having or displaying majesty or great dignity; grand; lofty.
▸ **ma'jestically** *adv*

majesty ('mædʒɪstɪ) *n* **1** great dignity of bearing; loftiness; grandeur. **2** supreme power or authority. ORIG C13: from OF, from L *mājestās;* rel. to L *major,* comp. of *magnus* great

Majesty ('mædʒɪstɪ) *n, pl* **Majesties.** (preceded by *Your, His, Her,* or *Their*) a title used to address or refer to a sovereign or the wife or widow of a sovereign.

majolica (mə'dʒɒlɪkə, mə'jɒl-) *or* **maiolica** *n* a type of porous pottery glazed with bright metallic oxides. It was originally imported into Italy via Majorca and was extensively made in Renaissance Italy. ORIG C16: from It., from LL *Mājorica* Majorca

major ('meɪdʒə) *n* **1** *Mil.* an officer immediately junior to a lieutenant colonel. **2** a person who is superior in a group or class. **3** a large or important company: *the oil majors.* **4** (often preceded by *the*) *Music.* a major key, chord, mode, or scale. **5** *US, Canad., Austral., & NZ.* **5a** the principal field of study of a student. **5b** a student who is studying a particular subject as his or her principal field: *a sociology major.* **6** a person who has reached the age of legal majority. **7** a principal or important record company, film company, etc. **8** *Logic.* a major term or premise. ◆ *adj* **9** larger in extent, number, etc. **10** of greater importance or priority. **11** very serious or significant. **12** main, chief, or principal. **13** of, involving, or making up a majority. **14** *Music.* **14a** (of a scale or mode) having notes separated by a whole tone, except for the third and fourth degrees, and seventh and eighth degrees, which are separated by a semitone. **14b** relating to or employing notes from the major scale: *a major key.* **14c** (*postpositive*) denoting a specified key or scale as being major: *C major.* **14d** denoting a chord or triad having a major third above the root. **14e** (in jazz) denoting a major chord with a major seventh added above the root. **15** *Logic.* constituting the major term or major premise of a syllogism. **16** *Chiefly US, Canad., Austral., & NZ.* of or relating to a student's principal field of study at a university, etc. **17** *Brit.* the elder: used after a schoolboy's surname if he has one or more younger brothers in the same school: *Price major.* **18** of full legal age. ◆ *vb* **19** (*intr; usually foll. by in*) *US, Canad., Austral., & NZ.* to do one's principal study (in a particular subject): *to major in English literature.* **20** (*intr; usually foll. by on*) to take or deal with as the main area of interest: *the book majors on peasant dishes.* ORIG C15 (adj): from L, comp. of *magnus* great; C17 (n, in military sense): from F, short for SERGEANT MAJOR
▸ **'majorship** *n*

Major ★ ('meɪdʒə) *n* **John.** born 1943, British Conservative politician: Chancellor of the Exchequer (1989–90); prime minister (1990–97).

Majorca ★ (mə'jɔːkə, -'dʒɔː-) *n* an island in the W Mediterranean: the largest of the Balearic Islands; tourism. Capital: Palma. Pop.: 605 512 (1987 est.). Area: 3639 sq. km (1465 sq. miles). Spanish name: **Mallorca.**

major-domo (-'dəʊməʊ) *n, pl* **major-domos. 1** the chief steward or butler of a great household. **2** *Facetious.* a steward or butler. ORIG C16: from Sp. *mayordomo,* from Med. L *mājor domūs* head of the household

majorette (ˌmeɪdʒə'rɛt) *n* **1** one of a group of girls who practise formation marching and baton twirling. **2** See **drum majorette.**

major general *n Mil.* an officer immediately junior to a lieutenant general.
▸ **ˌmajor-'generalship** *or* **major-'generalcy** *n*

majority (mə'dʒɒrɪtɪ) *n, pl* **majorities. 1** the greater number or part of something. **2** (in an election) the number of votes or seats by which the strongest party or candidate beats the combined opposition or the runner-up. **3** the largest party or group that votes together in a legislative or deliberative assembly. **4** the time of reaching or state of having reached full legal age. **5** the rank, office, or commission of major. **6** *Euphemistic.* the dead (esp. in **join the majority, go** *or* **pass over to the majority**). **7** (*modifier*) of, involving, or being a majority: *a majority decision.* **8 in the**

majority. forming or part of the greater number of something. ORIG C16: from Med. L *mājoritās,* from MAJOR (adj)

> **USAGE NOTE** *The majority of* can only refer to a number of things or people. When talking about an amount, *most of* should be used: *most of* (not *the majority of*) *the harvest was saved.*

major league *n US & Canad.* a league of highest classification in baseball, football, hockey, etc.

majorly (ˈmeɪdʒəlɪ) *adv Sl., chiefly US & Canad.* very; extremely: *it was majorly important for us to do that.*

major orders *pl n RC Church.* the three higher degrees of holy orders: bishop, priest, and deacon.

major premise *n Logic.* the premise of a syllogism containing the predicate of its conclusion.

major term *n Logic.* the predicate of the conclusion of a syllogism.

Majunga ★ (*French* maʒœ̃ga) *n* the former name of **Mahajanga.**

majuscule (ˈmædʒəˌskjuːl) *n* **1** a large letter, either capital or uncial, used in printing or writing. ◆ *adj* **2** relating to, printed, or written in such letters. ◆ Cf. **minuscule.** ORIG C18: via F from L *mājusculus,* dim. of *mājor* bigger ▸ **majuscular** (məˈdʒʌskjulə) *adj*

Makalu ★ (ˈmʌkəˌluː) *n* a massif in NE Nepal, on the border with Tibet in the Himalayas.

Makarios III ★ (məˈkɑːrɪˌɒs) *n* original name *Mikhail Christodoulou Mouskos.* 1913–77, Cypriot archbishop, patriarch, and statesman; first president of the republic of Cyprus (1960–74; 1974–77).

Makasar, Makassar, *or* **Macassar** ★ (məˈkæsə, -ˈkɑː-) *n* another name for **Ujung Pandang.**

make (meɪk) *vb* **makes, making, made.** (*mainly tr*) **1** to bring into being by shaping, changing, or combining materials, ideas, etc.; form or fashion. **2** to draw up, establish, or form: *to make one's will.* **3** to cause to exist, bring about, or produce: *don't make a noise.* **4** to cause, compel, or induce: *please make him go away.* **5** to appoint or assign: *they made him chairman.* **6** to constitute: *one swallow doesn't make a summer.* **7** (*also intr*) to come or cause to come into a specified state or condition: *to make merry.* **8** (*copula*) to be or become through development: *he will make a good teacher.* **9** to cause or ensure the success of: *your news has made my day.* **10** to amount to: *twelve inches make a foot.* **11** to serve as or be suitable for: *that piece of cloth will make a coat.* **12** to prepare or put into a fit condition for use: *to make a bed.* **13** to be the essential element in or part of: *charm makes a good salesman.* **14** to carry out, effect, or do. **15** (*intr; foll. by* to, as if to, *or* as though to) to act with the intention or with a show of doing something: *he made as if to hit her.* **16** to use for a specified purpose: *I will make this town my base.* **17** to deliver or pronounce: *to make a speech.* **18** to give information or an opinion: *what time do you make it?* **19** to cause to seem or represent as being. **20** to earn, acquire, or win for oneself: *to make friends.* **21** to engage in: *to make war.* **22** to traverse or cover (distance) by travelling: *we can make a hundred miles by nightfall.* **23** to arrive in time for: *he didn't make the first act of the play.* **24** *Cards.* **24a** to win a trick with (a specified card). **24b** to shuffle (the cards). **24c** *Bridge.* to fulfil (a contract) by winning the necessary number of tricks. **25** *Cricket.* to score (runs). **26** *Electronics.* to close (a circuit) permitting a flow of current. **27** (*intr*) to increase in depth: *the water in the hold was making a foot a minute.* **28** *Inf.* to gain a place or position on or in: *to make the headlines.* **29** *Inf., chiefly US.* to achieve the rank of. **30** *Taboo sl.* to seduce. **31 make a book.** to take bets on a race or another contest. **32 make a day, night,** etc., **of it.** to cause an activity to last a day, night, etc. **33 make do.** See **do**[1] (sense 32). **34 make eyes at.** to flirt with or ogle. **35 make it. 35a** *Inf.* to be successful in doing something. **35b** (foll. by *with*) *Taboo sl.* to have sexual intercourse. **36 make like.** *Sl., chiefly US & Canad.* **36a** to imitate. **36b** to pretend. ◆ *n* **37** brand, type, or style. **38** the manner or way in which something is made. **39** disposition or character; make-up. **40** the act or process of making. **41** the amount or number made. **42** *Cards.* a player's turn to shuffle. **43 on the make.** *Sl.* **43a** out for profit or conquest. **43b** in search of a sexual partner. ◆ See also **make away, make for,** etc. ORIG OE *macian* ▸ ˈ**makable** *adj*

make away *vb* (*intr, adv*) **1** to depart in haste. **2 make away with. 2a** to steal or abduct. **2b** to kill, destroy, or get rid of.

make believe *vb* **makes believe, making believe, made believe. 1** to pretend or enact a fantasy. ◆ *n* **make-believe. 2a** a fantasy or pretence. **2b** (*as modifier*): *a make-believe world.*

Makedhonia ★ (ˌmakɛðɔˈnia) *n* transliteration of the Modern Greek name for **Macedonia** (sense 1).

make for *vb* (*intr, prep*) **1** to head towards. **2** to prepare to attack. **3** to help bring about.

make of *vb* (*tr, prep*) **1** to interpret as the meaning of. **2** to produce or construct from: *houses made of brick.* **3 make little, much,** etc., **of. 3a** to gain little, much, etc., benefit from. **3b** to attribute little, much, etc., significance to.

make off *vb* **1** (*intr, adv*) to go or run away in haste. **2 make off with.** to steal or abduct.

make out *vb* (*adv*) **1** (*tr*) to discern or perceive. **2** (*tr*) to understand or comprehend. **3** (*tr*) to write out: *he made out a cheque.* **4** (*tr*) to attempt to establish or prove: *he made me out to be a liar.* **5** (*intr*) to pretend: *he made out that he could cook.* **6** (*intr*) to manage or fare.

make over *vb* (*tr, adv*) **1** to transfer the title or possession of (property, etc.). **2** to renovate or remodel: *she made over the dress to fit her sister.* ◆ *n* **makeover. 3** a complete remodelling. **4** a series of alterations, including beauty treatments and new clothes, intended to make a significant improvement to a person's appearance.

maker (ˈmeɪkə) *n* a person who executes a legal document, esp. one who signs a promissory note.

Maker (ˈmeɪkə) *n* **1** a title given to God (as Creator). **2** (**go to**) **meet one's Maker.** to die.

makeshift (ˈmeɪkˌʃɪft) *adj* **1** serving as a temporary or expedient means. ◆ *n* **2** something serving in this capacity.

make-up *n* **1** cosmetics, such as powder, lipstick, etc., applied to the face. **2a** the cosmetics, false hair, etc., used by an actor to adapt his appearance. **2b** the art or result of applying such cosmetics. **3** the manner of arrangement of the parts or qualities of someone or something. **4** the arrangement of type matter and illustrations on a page or in a book. **5** mental or physical constitution. ◆ *vb* **make up.** (*adv*) **6** (*tr*) to form or constitute: *these arguments make up the case for the defence.* **7** (*tr*) to devise, construct, or compose, sometimes with the intent to deceive: *to make up an excuse.* **8** (*tr*) to supply what is lacking or deficient in; complete: *these extra people will make up our total.* **9** (*tr*) to put in order, arrange, or prepare: *to make up a bed.* **10** (*intr; foll. by* for) to compensate or atone (for). **11** to settle (differences) amicably (often in **make it up**). **12** to apply cosmetics to (the face) to enhance one's appearance or for a theatrical role. **13** to assemble (type and illustrations) into (columns or pages). **14** (*tr*) to surface (a road) with tarmac, concrete, etc. **15 make up to.** *Inf.* **15a** to make friendly overtures to. **15b** to flirt with.

makeweight (ˈmeɪkˌweɪt) *n* **1** something put on a scale to make up a required weight. **2** an unimportant person or thing added to make up a lack.

Makeyevka ★ (*Russian* maˈkjejɪfkə) *n* a city in SE Ukraine: coal-mining centre. Pop.: 409 000 (1996 est.).

Makhachkala ★ (*Russian* məxətʃkaˈla) *n* a port in SW Russia, capital of the Dagestan Republic, on the Caspian Sea: fishing fleet; oil refining. Pop.: 339 000 (1995 est.). Former name (until 1921): **Petrovsk.**

making (ˈmeɪkɪŋ) *n* **1a** the act of a person or thing that makes or the process of being made. **1b** (*in combination*): *watchmaking.* **2 be the making of.** to cause the success of. **3 in the making.** in the process of becoming or being made. **4** something made or the quantity of something made at one time.

makings (ˈmeɪkɪŋz) *pl n* **1** potentials, qualities, or materials: *he had the makings of a leader.* **2** Also called: **rollings.** *Sl.* the tobacco and cigarette paper used for rolling a cigarette. **3** profits; earnings.

Makkah *or* **Makah** ★ ('mækə, -kɑː) *n* transliteration of the Arabic name for **Mecca**.

mako[1] ('mɑːkəʊ) *n, pl* **makos**. a blue-pointer game shark. ORIG from Maori

mako[2] ('mɑːkəʊ) *n, pl* **makos**. a small evergreen New Zealand tree. ORIG from Maori

Makurdi ★ (mə'kɜːdɪ) *n* a port in E central Nigeria, capital of Benue State on the Benue River: agricultural trade centre. Pop.: 123 100 (1996 est.).

Mal. *abbrev. for:* **1** *Bible*. Malachi. **2** Malay(an).

mal- *combining form*. bad or badly; wrong or wrongly; imperfect or defective: *maladjusted; malfunction*. ORIG OF, from L *malus* bad, *male* badly

Malabar Coast *or* **Malabar** ★ ('mælə,bɑː) *n* a region along the SW coast of India, extending from Goa to Cape Comorin: includes most of Kerala state.

Malabo ★ (mə'lɑːbəʊ) *n* the capital and chief port of Equatorial Guinea, on the island of Bioko in the Gulf of Guinea. Pop.: 58 040 (1991 est.). Former name (until 1973): **Santa Isabel**.

malabsorption (mæləb'sɔːpʃən) *n* a failure of absorption, esp. by the small intestine in coeliac disease, cystic fibrosis, etc.

malacca *or* **malacca cane** (mə'lækə) *n* **1** the stem of the rattan palm. **2** a walking stick made from this stem.

Malacca ★ (mə'lækə) *n* a state of SW Peninsular Malaysia: rubber plantations. Capital: Malacca. Pop.: 583 400 (1993 est.). Area: 1650 sq. km (637 sq. miles).

Malachi ★ ('mælə,kaɪ) *n Old Testament*. **1** a Hebrew prophet of the 5th century B.C. **2** the book containing his oracles. Douay spelling: **Malachias** (,mælə'kaɪəs).

malachite ('mælə,kaɪt) *n* a green mineral consisting of hydrated basic copper carbonate: a source of copper, also used for making ornaments. ORIG C16: via OF from L *molochītēs*, from Gk *molokhitis* mallow-green stone, from *molokhē* mallow

maladjustment (,mælə'dʒʌstmənt) *n* **1** *Psychol*. a failure to meet the demands of society, such as coping with problems and social relationships. **2** faulty or bad adjustment.
▸ **,malad'justed** *adj*

maladminister (,mæləd'mɪnɪstə) *vb* (*tr*) to administer badly, inefficiently, or dishonestly.
▸ **,malad,minis'tration** *n*

maladroit (,mælə'drɔɪt) *adj* **1** clumsy; not dexterous. **2** tactless and insensitive. ORIG C17: from F, from *mal* badly + ADROIT
▸ **,mala'droitly** *adv* ▸ **,mala'droitness** *n*

malady ('mælədɪ) *n, pl* **maladies**. **1** any disease or illness. **2** any unhealthy, morbid, or desperate condition. ORIG C13: from OF, from Vulgar L *male habitus* (unattested) in poor condition, from L *male* badly + *habitus*, from *habēre* to have

Málaga ★ ('mæləgə; *Spanish* 'malaɣa) *n* **1** a port and resort in S Spain, in Andalusia on the Mediterranean. Pop.: 532 425 (1995 est.). **2** a sweet fortified dessert wine from Málaga.

Malagasy (,mælə'gæsɪ) *n* **1** (*pl* **Malagasy** *or* **Malagasies**) a native or inhabitant of Madagascar. **2** the official language of Madagascar. ◆ *adj* **3** of or relating to Madagascar, its people, or their language.

Malagasy Republic ★ *n* the former name (1958–75) of **Madagascar**.

malaise (mæ'leɪz) *n* **1** a feeling of unease or depression. **2** a mild sickness, not symptomatic of any disease or ailment. **3** a complex of problems affecting a country, economy, etc.: *Bulgaria's economic malaise*. ORIG C18: from OF, from *mal* bad + *aise* EASE

Malamud ★ ('mæləməd, -mʊd) *n* **Bernard**. 1914–86, US writer. His novels include *The Fixer* (1966) and *Dubin's Lives* (1979).

malamute *or* **malemute** ('mælə,muːt) *n* an Alaskan Eskimo dog of the spitz type. ORIG from the name of an Eskimo tribe

Malang ★ ('mælæŋ) *n* a city in S Indonesia, on E Java: commercial centre. Pop.: 763 400 (1995 est.).

malapropism ('mæləprɒp,ɪzəm) *n* **1** the unintentional misuse of a word by confusion with one of similar sound, esp. when creating a ridiculous effect, as in *under the affluence of alcohol*. **2** the habit of misusing words in this manner. ORIG C18: after Mrs *Malaprop* in Sheridan's play *The Rivals* (1775), a character who misused words, from MALAPROPOS

malapropos (,mælæprə'pəʊ) *adj* **1** inappropriate or misapplied. ◆ *adv* **2** in an inappropriate way or manner. ◆ *n* **3** something inopportune or inappropriate. ORIG C17: from F *mal à propos* not to the purpose

Mälar ★ ('meɪlə) *n* **Lake**. a lake in S Sweden, extending 121 km (75 miles) west from Stockholm, where it joins with an inlet of the Baltic Sea (the **Saltsjön**). Area: 1140 sq. km (440 sq. miles). Swedish name: **Mälaren** ('melaren).

malaria (mə'lɛərɪə) *n* an infectious disease characterized by recurring attacks of chills and fever, caused by the bite of an anopheles mosquito infected with any of certain protozoans. ORIG C18: from It. *mala aria* bad air, from the belief that the disease was caused by the unwholesome air in swampy districts
▸ **ma'larial, ma'larian,** *or* **ma'larious** *adj*

malarkey *or* **malarky** (mə'lɑːkɪ) *n Sl*. nonsense; rubbish. ORIG C20: from ?

Malatesta ★ (*Italian* mala'tɛsta) *n* an Italian family that ruled Rimini from the 13th to the 16th century.

Malathion (,mælə'θaɪɒn) *n Trademark*. an insecticide consisting of an organic phosphate. ORIG C20: from (*diethyl*) MAL(EATE) + THIO- + -ON

Malatya ★ (,mɑːlɑː'tjɑː) *n* a city in E central Turkey: nearby is the ruined Roman and medieval city of Melitene (Old Malatya). Pop.: 314 539 (1995 est.).

Malawi ★ (mə'lɑːwɪ) *n* **1** a republic in E central Africa: established as a British protectorate in 1891; became independent in 1964 and a republic, within the Commonwealth, in 1966; lies along the Great Rift Valley, with Lake Nyasa (Malawi) along the E border, the Nyika Plateau in the northwest, and the Shiré Highlands in the southeast. Official languages: Chichewa; English and Bantu languages are also spoken. Religion: Christian, Muslim, and animist. Currency: kwacha. Capital: Lilongwe. Pop.: 10 000 000 (1999 est.). Area: 118 484 sq. km (45 747 sq. miles). Former name: **Nyasaland**. **2 Lake**. the Malawi name for (Lake) **Nyasa**.

Malay (mə'leɪ) *n* **1** a member of a people living chiefly in Malaysia and Indonesia. **2** the language of this people. ◆ *adj* **3** of or relating to the Malays or their language.

Malaya ★ (mə'leɪə) *n* **1 States of the Federation of.** part of Malaysia, in the S Malay Peninsula, constituting Peninsular Malaysia: consists of the former Federated Malay States, the former Unfederated Malay States, and the former Straits Settlements. Capital: Kuala Lumpur. Pop.: 14 127 556 (1990). Area: 131 587 sq. km (50 806 sq. miles). **2 Federation of.** a federation of the nine Malay States of the Malay Peninsula and two of the Straits Settlements (Malacca and Penang): formed in 1948: became part of the British Commonwealth in 1957 and joined Malaysia in 1963.
▸ **Ma'layan** *adj, n*

Malayalam *or* **Malayalaam** (,mælɪ'ɑːləm) *n* a language of SW India.

Malay Archipelago ★ *n* a group of islands in the Indian and Pacific Oceans, between SE Asia and Australia: the largest group of islands in the world; includes over 3000 Indonesian islands, about 7000 islands of the Philippines, and, sometimes, New Guinea.

Malayo-Polynesian *n* **1** Also called: **Austronesian**. a family of languages extending from Madagascar to the central Pacific. ◆ *adj* **2** of or relating to this family of languages.

Malay Peninsula ★ *n* a peninsula of SE Asia, extending south from the Isthmus of Kra in Thailand to Cape Tanjong Piai in Malaysia: consists of SW Thailand and the states of Malaya (Peninsular Malaysia). Ancient name: **Chersonesus Aurea** (,kɜːsə'niːsəs 'ɔːrɪə).

Malaysia ★ (mə'leɪzɪə) *n* a federation in SE Asia (within the Commonwealth), consisting of **Peninsular Malaysia**,

on the Malay Peninsula, and **East Malaysia** (Sabah and Sarawak), occupying the N part of the island of Borneo: formed in 1963 as a federation of Malaya, Sarawak, Sabah, and Singapore (the latter seceded in 1965); densely forested and mostly mountainous. Official language: Malay; English, various Chinese and Indian minority languages are also spoken. Official religion: Muslim. Currency: ringgit. Capital: Kuala Lumpur (a new administrative capital is under development at Putrajaya). Pop.: 22 710 000 (1999 est.). Area: 333 403 sq. km (128 727 sq. miles).
▸ **Ma'laysian** *adj, n*

Malay States ★ *pl n* the former states of the Malay Peninsula that, together with Penang and Malacca, formed the Union of Malaya (1946) and the Federation of Malaya (1948). Perak, Selangor, Negri Sembilan, and Pahang were established as the **Federated Malay States** by the British in 1895 and Perlis, Kedah, Kelantan, and Trengannu as the **Unfederated Malay States** in 1909 (joined by Johore in 1914).

Malcolm ★ ('mælkəm) *n* **George.** born 1917, British harpsichordist.

Malcolm III ★ *n* died 1093, king of Scotland (1057–93). He became king after Macbeth.

Malcolm X ★ (ɛks) *n* original name *Malcolm Little.* 1925–65, US Black civil-rights leader: assassinated.

malcontent ('mælkən,tɛnt) *adj* **1** disgusted or discontented. ◆ *n* **2** a person who is malcontent. ORIG C16: from OF

mal de mer *French.* (mal də mɛr) *n* seasickness.

Maldives ★ ('mɔːldaɪvz) *pl n* **Republic of.** a republic occupying an archipelago of 1087 coral islands in the Indian Ocean, southwest of Sri Lanka: came under British protection in 1887; became independent in 1965 and a republic in 1968; a member of the Commonwealth. Official language: Divehi. Official religion: (Sunni) Muslim. Currency: rufiyaa. Capital: Malé. Pop.: 278 000 (1999 est.). Area: 298 sq. km (115 sq. miles). Also called: **Maldive Islands.**
▸ **Maldivian** (mɔːl'dɪvɪən) *or* **Maldivan** ('mɔːldaɪvᵊn, -dɪ-) *adj, n*

Maldon ★ ('mɔːldən) *n* a market town in SE England, in Essex; scene of a battle (991) between the East Saxons and the victorious Danes, celebrated in *The Battle of Maldon,* an Old English poem. Pop.: 15 841 (1991).

male (meɪl) *adj* **1** of, relating to, or designating the sex producing gametes (spermatozoa) that can fertilize female gametes (ova). **2** of, relating to, or characteristic of a man. **3** for or composed of men or boys: *a male choir.* **4** (of gametes) capable of fertilizing an egg cell. **5** (of reproductive organs) capable of producing male gametes. **6** (of flowers) bearing stamens but lacking a functional pistil. **7** *Electronics, engineering.* having a projecting part or parts that fit into a female counterpart: *a male plug.* ◆ *n* **8** a male person, animal, or plant. ORIG C14: via OF from L *masculus* MASCULINE
▸ **'maleness** *n*

Malé ★ ('mɑːleɪ) *n* the capital of the Republic of Maldives, on Malé Island in the centre of the island group. Pop.: 62 973 (1995 est.).

maleate ('mælɪ,eɪt) *n* any salt or ester of maleic acid. ORIG C19: from MALE(IC) ACID + -ATE[1]

Malebranche ★ (*French* malbrɑ̃ʃ) *n* **Nicolas** (nikɔlɑ). 1638–1715, French philosopher, whose works include *De la recherche de la vérité* (1674).

male chauvinism *n* the belief, held or alleged to be held by certain men, that men are superior to women.
▸ **male chauvinist** *n, adj*

malediction (,mælɪ'dɪkʃən) *n* **1** the utterance of a curse against someone or something. **2** a slanderous accusation or comment. ORIG C15: from L *maledictiō* a reviling, from *male* ill + *dīcere* to speak
▸ **,male'dictive** *or* **,male'dictory** *adj*

malefactor ('mælɪ,fæktə) *n* a criminal; wrongdoer. ORIG C15: via OF from L, from *malefacere* to do evil
▸ **'male,faction** *n*

maleficent (mə'lɛfɪsənt) *adj* causing evil or mischief; harmful or baleful. ORIG C17: from L, from *maleficus* wicked, from *malum* evil
▸ **ma'lefic** *adj* ▸ **ma'leficence** *n*

maleic acid (mə'leɪɪk) *n* a colourless soluble crystalline substance used to synthesize other compounds, such as polyester resins. Formula: HOOCCH:CHCOOH. Systematic name: **cis-butenedioic acid.** ORIG C19: from F *maléique,* altered form of *malique;* see MALIC ACID

male menopause *n* a period in a man's later middle age in which he may experience an identity crisis as he feels age overtake his sexual powers.

Malenkov ★ (*Russian* məlɪn'kɔf) *n* **Georgi Maksimilianovich** (gɪ'ɔrgij ,məksimil'janəvitʃ). 1902–88, Soviet politician; prime minister (1953–55). He was removed from the presidium (1957) for plotting against Khrushchev; expelled from the Communist Party (1961).

Malevich ★ (*Russian* 'malɪvitʃ) *n* **Kasimir** (kəzi'mir). 1878–1935, Russian painter and founder of Suprematism, an abstract art movement.

malevolent (mə'lɛvələnt) *adj* wishing or appearing to wish evil to others; malicious. ORIG C16: from L *malevolens,* from *male* ill + *volens,* present participle of *velle* to wish
▸ **ma'levolence** *n* ▸ **ma'levolently** *adv*

malfeasance (mæl'fiːzᵊns) *n Law.* the doing of a wrongful or illegal act, esp. by a public official. Cf. **misfeasance, nonfeasance.** ORIG C17: from OF *mal faisant,* from *mal* evil + *faisant,* from *faire* to do, from L *facere*
▸ **mal'feasant** *n, adj*

malformation (,mælfɔː'meɪʃən) *n* **1** the condition of being faulty or abnormal in form or shape. **2** *Pathol.* a deformity, esp. when congenital.
▸ **mal'formed** *adj*

malfunction (mæl'fʌŋkʃən) *vb* **1** (*intr*) to function imperfectly or fail to function. ◆ *n* **2** failure to function or defective functioning.

Malherbe ★ (*French* malɛrb) *n* **François de** (frɑ̃swa də). 1555–1628, French poet and critic.

Mali ★ ('mɑːlɪ) *n* a landlocked republic in West Africa: conquered by the French by 1898 and incorporated (as French Sudan) into French West Africa; became independent in 1960; settled chiefly in the basins of the Rivers Senegal and Niger in the south. Official language: French. Religion: Muslim and animist. Currency: franc. Capital: Bamako. Pop.: 10 429 000 (1999 est.). Area: 1 248 574 sq. km (482 077 sq. miles). Former name (1898–1959): **French Sudan.**

malic acid ('mælɪk, 'meɪ-) *n* a colourless crystalline compound occurring in apples and other fruits. ORIG C18 *malic,* via F *malique* from L *mālum* apple

malice ('mælɪs) *n* **1** the desire to do harm or mischief. **2** evil intent. **3** *Law.* the state of mind with which an act is committed and from which the intent to do wrong may be inferred. ORIG C13: via OF from L *malitia,* from *malus* evil

malice aforethought *n Law.* **1** the predetermination to do an unlawful act, esp. to kill or seriously injure. **2** the intent with which an unlawful killing is effected, which must be proved for the crime to constitute murder.

malicious (mə'lɪʃəs) *adj* **1** characterized by malice. **2** motivated by wrongful, vicious, or mischievous purposes.
▸ **ma'liciously** *adv* ▸ **ma'liciousness** *n*

malign (mə'laɪn) *adj* **1** evil in influence, intention, or effect. ◆ *vb* **2** (*tr*) to slander or defame. ORIG C14: via OF from L *malīgnus* spiteful, from *malus* evil
▸ **ma'ligner** *n* ▸ **ma'lignly** *adv*

malignancy (mə'lɪgnənsɪ) *n, pl* **malignancies. 1** the state or quality of being malignant. **2** *Pathol.* a cancerous growth.

malignant (mə'lɪgnənt) *adj* **1** having or showing desire to harm others. **2** tending to cause great harm; injurious. **3** *Pathol.* (of a tumour) uncontrollable or resistant to therapy. ORIG C16: from LL *malīgnāre* to behave spitefully, from L *malīgnus* MALIGN
▸ **ma'lignantly** *adv*

malignity (mə'lɪgnɪtɪ) *n, pl* **malignities. 1** the condition or quality of being malign or deadly. **2** (*often pl*) a malign or malicious act or feeling.

malines (mə'li:n) *n* **1** a type of silk net used in dressmaking. **2** another name for **Mechlin lace.** ORIG C19: from F *Malines* (Mechelen), where this lace was traditionally made

Malines ★ (malin) *n* the French name for **Mechelen.**

malinger (mə'lɪŋgə) *vb* (*intr*) to pretend or exaggerate illness, esp. to avoid work. ORIG C19: from F *malingre* sickly, ?from *mal* badly + OF *haingre* feeble
▸ **ma'lingerer** *n*

Malinowski ★ (ˌmælɪ'nɒfskɪ) *n* **Bronislaw Kasper** (brɔ'nislaf 'kaspɛr). 1884–1942, Polish anthropologist in Britain and the US.

mall (mɔ:l, mæl) *n* **1** a shaded avenue, esp. one open to the public. **2** short for **shopping mall.** ORIG C17: after *the Mall,* in St James's Park, London

mallard ('mælɑ:d) *n, pl* **mallard** *or* **mallards.** a duck common over most of the N hemisphere, the male of which has a dark green head and reddish-brown breast: the ancestor of all domestic breeds of duck. ORIG C14: from OF *mallart,* ?from *maslart* (unattested); see MALE, -ARD

Mallarmé ★ (*French* malarme) *n* **Stéphane** (stefan). 1842–98, French symbolist poet, whose works include *L'Après-midi d'un Faune* (1876) and *Divagations* (1897).

Malle ★ (*French* mal) *n* **Louis.** 1932–95, French film director: his films include *Au revoir les enfants* (1987) and *Vanya on 42nd Street* (1994).

malleable ('mælɪəbᵊl) *adj* **1** (esp. of metal) able to be worked, hammered, or shaped under pressure or blows without breaking. **2** able to be influenced; pliable or tractable. ORIG C14: via OF from Med. L *malleābilis,* from L *malleus* hammer
▸ ˌ**mallea'bility** *or* (*less commonly*) '**malleableness** *n*
▸ '**malleably** *adv*

mallee ('mæli:) *n* **1** any of several low shrubby eucalyptus trees in desert regions of Australia. **2** (usually preceded by *the*) *Austral. inf.* another name for the **bush** (sense 4). ORIG C19: Abor.

Mallee ★ ('mæli:) *n* a region in NW Victoria, Australia.

mallee fowl *n* an Australian megapode.

malleolus (mə'li:ələs) *n, pl* **malleoli** (-ˌlaɪ). either of two rounded bony projections, one on each side of the ankle. ORIG C17: dim. of L *malleus* hammer

mallet ('mælɪt) *n* **1** a tool resembling a hammer but having a large head of wood, copper, lead, leather, etc., used for driving chisels, beating sheet metal, etc. **2** a long stick with a head like a hammer used to strike the ball in croquet or polo. ORIG C15: from OF *maillet* wooden hammer, dim. of *mail* MAUL (n)

malleus ('mælɪəs) *n, pl* **mallei** (-lɪˌaɪ). the outermost and largest of the three small bones in the middle ear of mammals. See also **incus, stapes.** ORIG C17: from L: hammer

mallie ('mɔ:lɪ) *n Inf., chiefly US.* a teenage girl who spends most of her spare time loitering in shopping malls.

Mallorca ★ (ma'ʎɔrka) *n* the Spanish name for **Majorca.**

mallow ('mæləʊ) *n* **1** any of several malvaceous plants of Europe, having purple, pink, or white flowers. **2** any of various related plants, such as the marsh mallow. ORIG OE *mealuwe,* from L *malva*

malm (mɑ:m) *n* **1** a soft greyish limestone that crumbles easily. **2** a chalky soil formed from this. **3** an artificial mixture of clay and chalk used to make bricks. ORIG OE *mealm-* (in compound words)

Malmédy ★ (*French* malmedi) *n* See **Eupen and Malmédy.**

Malmö ★ ('mælməʊ; *Swedish* 'malmø:) *n* a port in S Sweden, on the Sound: part of Denmark until 1658; industrial centre. Pop.: 248 007 (1997 est.).

malmsey ('mɑ:mzɪ) *n* a sweet Madeira wine. ORIG C15: from Med. L *Malmasia,* corruption of Gk *Monembasia,* Gk port from which the wine was shipped

malnutrition (ˌmælnju:'trɪʃən) *n* lack of adequate nutrition resulting from insufficient food, unbalanced diet, or defective assimilation.

malodorous (mæl'əʊdərəs) *adj* having a bad smell.

Malory ★ ('mælərɪ) *n* Sir **Thomas.** English author of *Le Morte d'Arthur* (?1470), collected Arthurian legends translated from the French.

Malpighi ★ (*Italian* mal'pi:gi) *n* **Marcello** (mar'tʃɛllo). 1628–94, Italian physiologist, who identified the capillary system (1661).
▸ **Malpighian** (mæl'pɪgɪən) *adj*

malpractice (mæl'præktɪs) *n* **1** immoral, illegal, or unethical professional conduct or neglect of professional duty. **2** any instance of improper professional conduct.

Malraux ★ (*French* malro) *n* **André** (ɑ̃dre). 1901–76, French writer and statesman. His novels include *La Condition humaine* (1933) and *L'Espoir* (1937).

malt (mɔ:lt) *n* **1** cereal grain, such as barley, that is kiln-dried after it has germinated by soaking in water. **2** See **malt liquor, malt whisky.** ◆ *vb* **3** to make into or become malt. **4** to make (something, esp. liquor) with malt. ORIG OE *mealt*
▸ '**malty** *adj*

Malta ★ ('mɔ:ltə) *n* a republic occupying the islands of Malta, Gozo, and Comino, in the Mediterranean south of Sicily: governed by the Knights Hospitallers from 1530 until Napoleon's conquest in 1798; French driven out, with British help, 1800; became British dependency 1814; suffered severely in World War II; became independent in 1964 and a republic in 1974; a member of the Commonwealth. Official languages: Maltese and English. Official religion: Roman Catholic. Currency: Maltese lira. Capital: Valletta. Pop.: 380 400 (1999 est.). Area: 316 sq. km (122 sq. miles).

malted milk *n* **1** a soluble powder made from dehydrated milk and malted cereals. **2** a drink made from this powder.

Maltese (mɔ:l'ti:z) *adj* **1** of or relating to Malta, its inhabitants, or their language. ◆ *n* **2** (*pl* **Maltese**) a native or inhabitant of Malta or a descendant of one. **3** the official language of Malta, a form of Arabic with borrowings from Italian, etc.

Maltese cross *n* a cross with triangular arms that taper towards the centre, sometimes having indented outer sides.

malt extract *n* a sticky substance obtained from an infusion of malt.

Malthus ★ ('mælθəs) *n* **Thomas Robert.** 1766–1834, British economist, noted for his population theory in *An Essay on the Principle of Population* (1798).

Malthusian (mæl'θju:zɪən) *adj* **1** of or relating to the theory of Malthus stating that increases in population tend to exceed increases in the means of subsistence and that therefore sexual restraint should be exercised. ◆ *n* **2** a supporter of this theory.
▸ **Mal'thusianism** *n*

malting ('mɔ:ltɪŋ) *n* a building in which malt is made or stored. Also called: **malt house.**

malt liquor *n* any alcoholic drink brewed from malt.

maltose ('mɔ:ltəʊz) *n* a sugar formed by the enzymic hydrolysis of starch. ORIG C19: from MALT + -OSE[2]

maltreat (mæl'tri:t) *vb* (*tr*) to treat badly, cruelly, or inconsiderately. ORIG C18: from F *maltraiter*
▸ **mal'treater** *n* ▸ **mal'treatment** *n*

maltster ('mɔ:ltstə) *n* a person who makes or deals in malt.

malt whisky *n* whisky made from malted barley.

Maluku ★ (mɑ:'lu:ku:) *n* the Indonesian name for the **Moluccas.**

malvaceous (mæl'veɪʃəs) *adj* of, relating to, or belonging to a family of plants that includes mallow, cotton, okra, althaea, and abutilon. ORIG C17: from L *malvāceus,* from *malva* MALLOW

Malvern ★ ('mɔ:lvən) *n* a town and resort in W England, in Hereford and Worcester on the E slopes of the **Malvern Hills:** annual dramatic festival; mineral springs. Pop.: 31 537 (1991).

malversation (ˌmælvɜ:'seɪʃən) *n Rare.* professional or public misconduct. ORIG C16: from F, from *malverser* to behave badly, from L *male versārī*

Malvinas ★ (*Spanish* malˈβinas) *pl n* **Islas** (ˈizlas). the Argentine name for the **Falkland Islands.**

mam (mæm) *n Inf. or dialect.* another word for **mother.**

mama *or esp. US* **mamma** (məˈmɑː) *n Old-fashioned.* an informal word for **mother**[1]. ORIG C16: reduplication of childish syllable *ma*

mamba (ˈmæmbə) *n* any of various partly arboreal tropical African venomous snakes, esp. the **green** and **black mambas.** ORIG from Zulu *im-amba*

mambo (ˈmæmbəʊ) *n, pl* **mambos. 1** a modern Latin American dance, resembling the rumba. ◆ *vb* **2** (*intr*) to perform this dance. ORIG American Sp., prob. from Haitian Creole: voodoo priestess

Mameluke *or* **Mamaluke** (ˈmæmɪˌluːk) *n* **1** a member of a military class, originally of Turkish slaves, ruling in Egypt from about 1250 to 1517 and remaining powerful until 1811. **2** (in Muslim countries) a slave. ORIG C16: via F, ult. from Ar. *mamlūk* slave, from *malaka* to possess

Mamet ★ (ˈmæmɪt) *n* **David.** born 1947, US dramatist and film director. His plays include *Oleanna* (1992) and his films include *House of Games* (1986) and *The Spanish Prisoner* (1998).

mamilla *or US* **mammilla** (mæˈmɪlə) *n, pl* **mamillae** (-liː) *or US* **mammillae. 1** a nipple or teat. **2** any nipple-shaped prominence. ORIG C17: from L, dim. of *mamma* breast
▸ **ˈmamillary** *or US* **ˈmammillary** *adj*

mamma (ˈmæmə) *n, pl* **mammae** (-miː). the milk-secreting organ of female mammals: the breast in women, the udder in cows, sheep, etc. ORIG C17: from L: breast
▸ **ˈmammary** *adj*

mammal (ˈmæməl) *n* any animal of the *Mammalia,* a large class of warm-blooded vertebrates having mammary glands in the female. ORIG C19: via NL from L *mamma* breast
▸ **mammalian** (mæˈmeɪlɪən) *adj, n*

mammary gland *n* any of the milk-producing glands in mammals.

mammogram (ˈmæməʊˌgræm) *n* an X-ray photograph of the breast.

mammography (mæˈmɒgrəfɪ) *n* examination of the breasts by X-ray, esp. to detect early signs of cancer.

mammon (ˈmæmən) *n* riches or wealth regarded as a source of evil and corruption. ORIG C14: via LL from New Testament Gk *mammōnas,* from Aramaic *māmōnā* wealth
▸ **ˈmammonish** *adj* ▸ **ˈmammonism** *n* ▸ **ˈmammonist** *or* **ˈmammonite** *n*

Mammon (ˈmæmən) *n Bible.* the personification of riches and greed in the form of a false god.

mammoth (ˈmæməθ) *n* **1** any large extinct elephant of the Pleistocene epoch, such as the **woolly mammoth,** having a hairy coat and long curved tusks. ◆ *adj* **2** of gigantic size or importance. ORIG C18: from Russian *mamot,* from Tartar *mamont,* ?from *mamma* earth, because of a belief that the animal made burrows

mammy *or* **mammie** (ˈmæmɪ) *n, pl* **mammies. 1** a child's word for **mother**[1] (senses 1–3). **2** *Chiefly southern US.* a Black woman employed as a nurse or servant to a White family.

Mamoré ★ (*Spanish* mamoˈre) *n* a river in central Bolivia, flowing north to the Beni River to form the Madeira River. Length: about 1500 km (930 miles).

man (mæn) *n, pl* **men. 1** an adult male human being, as distinguished from a woman. **2** (*modifier*) male; masculine: *a man child.* **3** a human being, considered as representative of mankind. **4** human beings collectively; mankind. **5** Also called: **modern man. 5a** a member of any of the living races of *Homo sapiens,* characterized by erect bipedal posture, a highly developed brain, and powers of articulate speech, abstract reasoning, and imagination. **5b** any extinct member of the species *Homo sapiens,* such as Cro-Magnon man. **6** a member of any of the extinct species of the genus *Homo,* such as Java man. **7** an adult male human being with qualities associated with the male, such as courage or virility: *be a man.* **8** manly qualities or virtues: *the man in him was outraged.* **9a** a subordinate, servant, or employee. **9b** (*in combination*): *the man-days required to complete a job.* **10** (*usually pl*) a member of the armed forces who does not hold commissioned, warrant, or noncommissioned rank (as in **officers and men**). **11** a member of a group, team, etc. **12** a husband, boyfriend, etc. **13** an expression used parenthetically to indicate an informal relationship between speaker and hearer. **14** a movable piece in various games, such as draughts. **15** a vassal of a feudal lord. **16** *S. African sl.* any person: used as a term of address. **17 as one man.** with unanimous action or response. **18 be one's own man.** to be independent or free. **19 he's your man.** he's the person needed. **20 man and boy.** from childhood. **21 sort out** *or* **separate the men from the boys.** to separate the experienced from the inexperienced. **22 to a man.** without exception. ◆ *interj* **23** *Inf.* an exclamation or expletive, often indicating surprise or pleasure. ◆ *vb* **mans, manning, manned.** (*tr*) **24** to provide with sufficient men for operation, defence, etc. **25** to take one's place at or near in readiness for action. ORIG OE *mann*

Man ★ (mæn) *n* **Isle of.** an island in the British Isles, in the Irish Sea between Cumbria and Northern Ireland: a Crown possession with its own parliament, the Court of Tynwald; a dependency of Norway until 1266, when it came under Scottish rule; its own language, Manx, is now almost extinct. Capital: Douglas. Pop.: 69 788 (1991). Area: 588 sq. km (227 sq. miles).

Man. *abbrev. for:* **1** Manila paper. **2** Manitoba.

-man *n combining form.* indicating a person who has a role, works in a place, or operates equipment as specified: *salesman; barman; cameraman.*

> **USAGE NOTE** The use of words ending in *-man* is avoided as implying a male in job advertisements, where sexual discrimination is illegal, and in many other contexts where a term that is not gender-specific is available, such as *salesperson, barperson, camera operator.* See also at **chairman.**

mana (ˈmɑːnə) *n Anthropol.* **1** (in Polynesia, Melanesia, etc.) a concept of a life force associated with high social status and ritual power. **2** any power achieved by ritual means; prestige; authority. ORIG of Polynesian origin

man about town *n* a fashionable sophisticate, esp. one in a big city.

manacle (ˈmænəkᵊl) *n* **1** (*usually pl*) a shackle, handcuff, or fetter, used to secure the hands of a prisoner, convict, etc. ◆ *vb* **manacles, manacling, manacled.** (*tr*) **2** to put manacles on. **3** to confine or constrain. ORIG C14: via OF from L *manicula,* dim. of *manus* hand

Manado ★ (məˈnɑːdəʊ) *n* a variant of **Menado.**

manage (ˈmænɪdʒ) *vb* **manages, managing, managed.** (*mainly tr*) **1** (*also intr*) to be in charge (of); administer: *to manage a shop.* **2** to succeed in being able (to do something); contrive. **3** to have room, time, etc., for: *can you manage dinner tomorrow?* **4** to exercise control or domination over. **5** (*intr*) to contrive to carry on despite difficulties, esp. financial ones. **6** to wield or handle (a weapon). ORIG C16: from It. *maneggiare* to train (esp. horses), ult. from L *manus* hand

manageable (ˈmænɪdʒəbᵊl) *adj* able to be managed or controlled.
▸ **ˌmanageaˈbility** *or* **ˈmanageableness** *n* ▸ **ˈmanageably** *adv*

managed currency *n* a currency subject to governmental control with respect to the amount in circulation and rate of exchange.

managed fund *n* an investment managed by an insurance company to provide low-risk investments for the small investor.

management (ˈmænɪdʒmənt) *n* **1** the members of the executive or administration of an organization or business. **2** managers or employers collectively. **3** the technique, practice, or science of managing or controlling. **4** the skilful or resourceful use of materials, time, etc. **5** the specific treatment of a disease, etc.

management buyout *n* the purchase of a company by its managers, usually with outside backing from a bank or other institution.

management company *n* a company that manages a unit trust.

manager ('mænɪdʒə) *n* **1** a person who directs or manages an organization, industry, shop, etc. **2** a person who controls the business affairs of an actor, entertainer, etc. **3** a person who controls the training of a sportsman or team. **4** a person who has a talent for managing efficiently. **5** (in Britain) a member of either House of Parliament appointed to arrange a matter in which both Houses are concerned. **6** *Computing.* a computer program that organizes a resource, such as a set of files or a database.
▸ **'managership** *n*

manageress (ˌmænɪdʒə'rɛs) *n* a woman who is in charge of a shop, department, etc.

managerial (ˌmænɪ'dʒɪərɪəl) *adj* of or relating to a manager or management.
▸ **ˌmana'gerially** *adv*

managing ('mænɪdʒɪŋ) *adj* having administrative control or authority: *a managing director.*

Managua ★ (mə'nægwə; *Spanish* ma'naɣwa) *n* **1** the capital of Nicaragua, on the S shore of Lake Managua: chosen as capital in 1857. Pop.: 1 195 000 (1995 est.). **2 Lake.** a lake in W Nicaragua: drains into Lake Nicaragua by the Tipitapa River. Length: 61 km (38 miles). Width: about 26 km (16 miles).

Manama ★ (mə'nɑːmə) *n* the capital of Bahrain, at the N end of Bahrain Island: transit port. Pop.: 140 401 (1992 est.).

mañana *Spanish.* (mə'njɑːnə) *n, adv* **a** tomorrow. **b** some other and later time.

Manáos ★ (*Portuguese* mə'naus) *n* a variant spelling of **Manaus.**

Manassas ★ (mə'næsəs) *n* a town in NE Virginia, west of Alexandria: site of the victory of Confederate forces in the Battles of Bull Run, or First and Second Manassas (1861; 1862), during the American Civil War. Pop.: 27 957 (1990).

Manasseh ★ (mə'næsɪ) *n Old Testament.* **1** the elder son of Joseph (Genesis 41:51). **2** the Israelite tribe descended from him. **3** the territory of this tribe, in the upper Jordan valley. Douay spelling: **Manases** (mə'næsiːz).

man-at-arms *n, pl* **men-at-arms.** a soldier, esp. a heavily armed mounted soldier in medieval times.

manatee (ˌmænə'tiː) *n* a sirenian mammal occurring in tropical coastal waters of America, the Caribbean, and Africa, having a prehensile upper lip and a broad flattened tail. ORIG C16: via Sp. from Carib *Manattouï*

Manaus *or* **Manáos** ★ (*Portuguese* mə'naus) *n* a port in N Brazil, capital of Amazonas state, on the Rio Negro 19 km (12 miles) above its confluence with the Amazon: chief commercial centre of the Amazon basin. Pop. (urban area): 1 189 000 (1995).

Manche ★ (*French* mɑ̃ʃ) *n* **1** a department of NW France, in Basse-Normandie region. Capital: St Lô. Pop.: 483 352 (1994 est.). Area: 6412 sq. km (2501 sq. miles). **2 La.** the French name for the **English Channel.**

manchester ('mæntʃɪstə) *n Austral. & NZ.* **1** goods, such as sheets and pillowcases, which are, or were originally, made of cotton. **2 manchester department.** a section of a store which sells such goods. ORIG from MANCHESTER, England

Manchester ★ ('mæntʃɪstə) *n* **1** a city in NW England, in Manchester unitary authority, Greater Manchester; linked to the Mersey estuary by the **Manchester Ship Canal**: commercial and industrial centre, esp. of the cotton and textile trades; seat of the University of Manchester Institute of Science and Technology (1824), The University of Manchester (1851), and Manchester Metropolitan University (1992). Pop.: 402 889 (1991). Latin name: **Man'cunium. 2** a unitary authority in NW England, in Greater Manchester. Pop.: 430 800 (1996 est.). Area: 116 sq. km (45 sq. miles).

manchineel (ˌmæntʃɪ'niːl) *n* a tropical American tree having fruit and milky highly caustic poisonous sap, which causes skin blisters. ORIG C17: via F from Sp. MANZANILLA

Manchu (mæn'tʃuː) *n* **1** (*pl* **Manchus** *or* **Manchu**) a member of a Mongoloid people of Manchuria, a region of NE China, who conquered China in the 17th century, establishing a dynasty that lasted until 1912. **2** the language of this people. ◆ *adj* **3** Also: **Ching.** of or relating to the dynasty of the Manchus. ORIG from Manchu, lit.: pure

Manchukuo *or* **Manchoukuo** ★ ('mæn'tʃuː'kwəʊ) *n* a former state of E Asia (1932–45), consisting of the three provinces of old Manchuria and Jehol.

Manchuria ★ (mæn'tʃʊərɪə) *n* a region of NE China, historically the home of the Manchus, rulers of China from 1644 to 1912: includes part of the Inner Mongolian AR and the provinces of Heilongjiang, Jilin, and Liaoning. Area: about 1 300 000 sq. km (502 000 sq. miles).
▸ **Man'churian** *adj, n*

manciple ('mænsɪpᵊl) *n* a steward who buys provisions, esp. in an Inn of Court. ORIG C13: via OF from L *mancipium* purchase, from *manceps* purchaser, from *manus* hand + *capere* to take

Mancunian (mæŋ'kjuːnɪən) *n* **1** a native or inhabitant of Manchester. ◆ *adj* **2** of or relating to Manchester. ORIG from Med. L *Mancunium* Manchester

-mancy *n combining form.* indicating divination of a particular kind: *chiromancy.* ORIG from OF *-mancie,* from L *-mantia,* from Gk *manteia* soothsaying
▸ **-mantic** *adj combining form.*

mandala ('mændələ, mæn'dɑːlə) *n Hindu & Buddhist art.* any of various designs symbolizing the universe, usually circular. ORIG Sansk.: circle

Mandalay ★ (ˌmændə'leɪ) *n* a city in central Myanmar, on the Irrawaddy River: the second largest city in the country and former capital of Burma and of Upper Burma; Buddhist religious centre. Pop.: 677 000 (1995 est.).

mandamus (mæn'deɪməs) *n, pl* **mandamuses.** *Law.* (formerly) a writ from (now an order of) a superior court commanding an inferior tribunal, public official, etc., to carry out a public duty. ORIG C16: L, lit.: we command, from *mandāre*

mandarin ('mændərɪn) *n* **1** (in the Chinese Empire) a member of a senior grade of the bureaucracy. **2** a high-ranking official whose powers are extensive and thought to be outside political control. **3** a person of standing and influence, as in literary or intellectual circles, esp. one regarded as conservative or reactionary. **4a** a small citrus tree cultivated for its edible fruit. **4b** the fruit, resembling the tangerine. ORIG C16: from Port. via Malay from Sansk. *mantrin* counsellor, from *mantra* counsel
▸ **'mandarinate** *n*

Mandarin Chinese *or* **Mandarin** *n* the official language of China since 1917.

Mandarin collar *n* a high stiff round collar.

mandarin duck *n* an Asian duck, the male of which has a distinctive brightly coloured and patterned plumage and crest.

mandate *n* ('mændeɪt, -dɪt). **1** an official or authoritative instruction or command. **2** *Politics.* the support or commission given to a government and its policies or an elected representative and his or her policies through an electoral victory. **3** (*often cap.*) Also called: **mandated territory.** (formerly) any of the territories under the trusteeship of the League of Nations administered by one of its member states. **4a** *Roman law.* a contract by which one person commissions another to act for him or her gratuitously. **4b** *Contract law.* a contract under which a party entrusted with goods undertakes to perform gratuitously some service in respect of such goods. **4c** *Scots Law.* a contract by which a person is engaged to act in the management of the affairs of another. ◆ *vb* ('mændeɪt), **mandates, mandating, mandated.** (*tr*) **5** to assign (territory) to a nation under a mandate. **6** to delegate authority to. ORIG C16: from L *mandātum* something commanded, from *mandāre* to command, ?from *manus* hand + *dāre* to give
▸ **'mandator** *n*

mandatory ('mændətərɪ, -trɪ) *adj* **1** having the nature or powers of a mandate. **2** obligatory; compulsory. **3** (of a state) having received a mandate over some territory.

◆ *n, pl* **mandatories.** *also* **mandatary. 4** a person or state holding a mandate.
▸ ˈ**mandatorily** *adv*

Mandela ★ (mænˈdɛlə) *n* **1 Nelson (Rolihlahla).** born 1918, South African statesman: first Black president of South Africa (1994–99); jailed for life (1964), but released (1990) after an international campaign; instrumental in ending apartheid; awarded the Nobel peace prize (1993) jointly with F. W. de Klerk. **2 (Numzano) Winnie.** born 1934, South African politician and political activist: married to Nelson Mandela (1958–96).

Mandelson ★ (ˈmændᵊlsən) *n* **Peter (Benjamin).** born 1953, British Labour politician; secretary of state for Northern Ireland (1999–2001).

Mandelstam *or* **Mandelshtam ★** (ˈmændᵊlˌʃtɑːm) *n* **Osip (Emilyevich)** (ˈɒsiːp). 1891–?1938, Soviet poet and writer, born in Warsaw; persecuted by Stalin, he died in a labour camp. His works include *Tristia* (1922) and the autobiographical *Journey to Armenia* (1933).

Mandeville ★ (ˈmændəvɪl) *n* **1 Bernard de.** ?1670–1733, English author, born in Holland, noted for his satire *The Fable of the Bees* (1723). **2** Sir **John.** 14th century, English author of *The Travels of Sir John Mandeville.*

mandible (ˈmændɪbᵊl) *n* **1** the lower jawbone in vertebrates. **2** either of a pair of mouthparts in insects and other arthropods that are usually used for biting and crushing food. **3** *Ornithol.* either part of the bill, esp. the lower part. ORIG C16: via OF from LL *mandibula* jaw, from *mandere* to chew
▸ **mandibular** (mænˈdɪbjʊlə) *adj* ▸ **mandibulate** (mænˈdɪbjʊlɪt, -ˌleɪt) *n, adj*

mandolin *or* **mandoline** (ˌmændəˈlɪn) *n* a plucked stringed instrument having four pairs of strings stretched over a small light body with a fretted fingerboard: usually played with a plectrum. ORIG C18: via F from It. *mandolino,* dim. of *mandora* lute, ult. from Gk *pandoura* musical instrument with three strings
▸ ˌ**mandoˈlinist** *n*

mandrake (ˈmændreɪk) *or* **mandragora** (mænˈdrægərə) *n* **1** a Eurasian plant with purplish flowers and a forked root. It was formerly thought to have magic powers and a narcotic was prepared from its root. **2** another name for the **May apple.** ORIG C14: prob. via MDu. from L *mandragoras,* from Gk. The form *mandrake* was prob. adopted through folk etymology, because of the allegedly human appearance of the root and because *drake* (dragon) suggested magical powers

mandrel *or* **mandril** (ˈmændrəl) *n* **1** a spindle on which a workpiece is supported during machining operations. **2** a shaft or arbor on which a machining tool is mounted. ORIG C16: ? rel. to F *mandrin* lathe

mandrill (ˈmændrɪl) *n* an Old World monkey of W Africa. It has a short tail and brown hair, and the ridged muzzle, nose, and hindquarters are red and blue. ORIG C18: from MAN + DRILL[4]

mane (meɪn) *n* **1** the long coarse hair that grows from the crest of the neck in such mammals as the lion and horse. **2** long thick human hair. ORIG OE *manu*
▸ **maned** *adj*

manège *or* **manege** (mæˈneɪʒ) *n* **1** the art of training horses and riders. **2** a riding school. ORIG C17: via F from It. *maneggio,* from *maneggiare* to MANAGE

manes (ˈmɑːneɪz) *pl n* (*sometimes cap.*) (in Roman legend) **1** the spirits of the dead, often revered as minor deities. **2** (*functioning as sing*) the shade of a dead person. ORIG C14: from L, prob.: the good ones, from OL *mānus* good

Manes ★ (ˈmeɪniːz) *n* See **Mani.**

Manet ★ (*French* manɛ) *n* **Édouard** (edwar). 1832–83, French painter. His painting *Le Déjeuner sur l'herbe* (1863), which was condemned by the Parisian establishment, was acclaimed by the impressionists, whom he decisively influenced.

maneuver (məˈnuːvə) *n, vb* the usual US spelling of **manoeuvre.**

man Friday *n* **1** a loyal male servant or assistant. **2** Also: **girl Friday, person Friday.** any factotum, esp. in an office. ORIG after the native in Daniel Defoe's novel *Robinson Crusoe* (1719)

manful (ˈmænfʊl) *adj* resolute, strong; manly.
▸ ˈ**manfully** *adv* ▸ ˈ**manfulness** *n*

mangabey (ˈmæŋgəˌbeɪ) *n* any of several large agile arboreal Old World monkeys of central Africa, having long limbs and tail. ORIG C18: after a region in Madagascar

Mangalore ★ (ˌmæŋgəˈlɔː) *n* a port in S India, in Karnataka on the Malabar Coast. Pop.: 273 304 (1991).

manganese (ˈmæŋgəˌniːz) *n* a brittle greyish-white metallic element: used in making steel and other alloys. Symbol: Mn; atomic no.: 25; atomic wt.: 54.938. ORIG C17: via F from It., prob. altered form of Med. L MAGNESIA

mange (meɪndʒ) *n* an infectious disorder mainly affecting domestic animals, characterized by itching and loss of hair: caused by parasitic mites. ORIG C14: from OF *mangeue* itch, from *mangier* to eat

mangelwurzel (ˈmæŋgᵊlˌwɜːzᵊl) *or* **mangoldwurzel** (ˈmæŋgəʊldˌwɜːzᵊl) *n* a Eurasian variety of beet, cultivated as a cattle food, having a large yellowish root. ORIG C18: from G *Mangoldwurzel,* from *Mangold* beet + *Wurzel* root

manger (ˈmeɪndʒə) *n* a trough or box in a stable, barn, etc., from which horses or cattle feed. ORIG C14: from OF *maingeure* food trough, from *mangier* to eat, ult. from L *mandūcāre* to chew

mangetout (ˌmɒnʒˈtuː) *n* a variety of garden pea in which the pod is also edible. Also called: **sugar pea.** ORIG C20: from F lit.: eat all

mangey (ˈmeɪndʒɪ) *adj* **mangier, mangiest.** a variant spelling of **mangy.**

mangle[1] (ˈmæŋgᵊl) *vb* **mangles, mangling, mangled.** (*tr*) **1** to mutilate, disfigure, or destroy by cutting, crushing, or tearing. **2** to ruin, spoil, or mar. ORIG C14: from Norman F *mangler,* prob. from OF *mahaignier* to maim
▸ ˈ**mangled** *adj* ▸ ˈ**mangler** *n*

mangle[2] (ˈmæŋgᵊl) *n* **1** Also called: **wringer.** a machine for pressing or drying textiles, clothes, etc., consisting of two heavy rollers between which the cloth is passed.
◆ *vb* **mangles, mangling, mangled.** (*tr*) **2** to press or dry in a mangle. ORIG C18: from Du. *mangel,* ult. from LL *manganum.* See MANGONEL

mango (ˈmæŋgəʊ) *n, pl* **mangoes** *or* **mangos. 1** a tropical Asian evergreen tree, cultivated in the tropics for its fruit. **2** the ovoid edible fruit of this tree, having a smooth rind and sweet juicy flesh. ORIG C16: via Port. from Malay *mangā,* from Tamil *mānkāy,* from *mān* mango tree + *kāy* fruit

mangonel (ˈmæŋgəˌnɛl) *n History.* a war engine for hurling stones. ORIG C13: via OF from Med. L *manganellus,* ult. from Gk *manganon*

mangrove (ˈmæŋgrəʊv, ˈmæn-) *n* any of various tropical evergreen trees or shrubs, having stiltlike intertwining aerial roots and forming dense thickets along coasts. ORIG C17 *mangrow* (changed through infl. of *grove*), from Port. *mangue,* ult. from Taino

mangy *or* **mangey** (ˈmeɪndʒɪ) *adj* **mangier, mangiest. 1** having or caused by mange. **2** scruffy or shabby.
▸ ˈ**mangily** *adv* ▸ ˈ**manginess** *n*

manhandle (ˈmænˌhændᵊl, ˌmænˈhændᵊl) *vb* **manhandles, manhandling, manhandled.** (*tr*) **1** to handle or push (someone) about roughly. **2** to move or do by manpower rather than by machinery.

Manhattan ★ (mænˈhætᵊn, mən-) *n* **1** an island at the N end of New York Bay, between the Hudson, East, and Harlem Rivers: administratively (with adjacent islets) a borough of New York City; a major financial, commercial, and cultural centre. Pop.: 1 487 536 (1990). Area: 47 sq. km (22 sq. miles). **2** a mixed drink consisting of four parts whisky, one part vermouth, and a dash of bitters.

manhole (ˈmænˌhəʊl) *n* **1** Also called: **inspection chamber.** a shaft with a removable cover that leads down to a sewer or drain. **2** a hole, usually with a detachable cover, through which a man can enter a boiler, tank, etc.

manhood (ˈmænhʊd) *n* **1** the state or quality of being a man or being manly. **2** men collectively. **3** the state of being human.

man-hour *n* a unit of work in industry, equal to the work done by one man in one hour.

★ people and places

manhunt ('mæn,hʌnt) *n* an organized search, usually by police, for a wanted man or fugitive.

Mani ★ ('mɑːnɪ) *n* ?216–?276 A.D., Persian prophet who founded Manichaeism. Also called: **Manes, Manichaeus.**

mania ('meɪnɪə) *n* **1** a mental disorder characterized by great excitement and occasionally violent behaviour. **2** obsessional enthusiasm or partiality. ORIG C14: via LL from Gk: madness

-mania *n combining form.* indicating extreme desire or pleasure of a specified kind or an abnormal excitement aroused by something: *kleptomania; nymphomania; pyromania.* ORIG from MANIA
▸ **-maniac** *n and adj combining form.*

maniac ('meɪnɪ,æk) *n* **1** a wild disorderly person. **2** a person who has a great craving or enthusiasm for something. **3** *Psychiatry, obs.* a person afflicted with mania. ORIG C17: from LL *maniacus* belonging to madness, from Gk

maniacal (mə'naɪək[ə]l) *or* **maniac** *adj* **1** affected with or characteristic of mania. **2** characteristic of or befitting a maniac: *maniacal laughter.*
▸ **ma'niacally** *adv*

manic ('mænɪk) *adj* **1** characterizing, denoting, or affected by mania. ◆ *n* **2** a person afflicted with mania. ORIG C19: from Gk, from MANIA

manic-depressive *Psychiatry.* ◆ *adj* **1** denoting a mental disorder characterized by an alternation between extreme euphoria and deep depression. ◆ *n* **2** a person afflicted with this disorder.

Manichaeism *or* **Manicheism** ('mænɪkiː,ɪzəm) *n* the system of religious doctrines taught by the Persian prophet Mani about the 3rd century A.D. It was based on a supposed primordial conflict between light and darkness or goodness and evil. ORIG C14: from LL *Manichaeus,* from LGk *Manikhaios* of Mani
▸ **,Mani'chaean** *or* **,Mani'chean** *adj, n* ▸ **'Manichee** *n*

Manichaeus *or* **Manicheus** ★ (,mænɪ'kiːəs) *n* See **Mani.**

manicure ('mænɪ,kjʊə) *n* **1** care of the hands and fingernails, involving shaping the nails, removing cuticles, etc. **2** Also called: **manicurist.** a person who gives manicures, esp. as a profession. ◆ *vb* **manicures, manicuring, manicured. 3** to care for (the hands and fingernails) in this way. ORIG C19: from F, from L *manus* hand + *cūra* care

manifest ('mænɪ,fɛst) *adj* **1** easily noticed or perceived; obvious. **2** *Psychoanalysis.* of or relating to the ostensible elements of a dream: *manifest content.* Cf. **latent** (sense 5). ◆ *vb* **3** (*tr*) to show plainly; reveal or display. **4** (*tr*) to prove beyond doubt. **5** (*intr*) (of a disembodied spirit) to appear in visible form. ◆ *n* **6** a customs document containing particulars of a ship, its cargo, and its destination. **7a** a list of cargo, passengers, etc., on an aeroplane. **7b** a list of railway trucks or their cargo. ORIG C14: from L *manifestus* plain, lit.: struck with the hand
▸ **'mani,festable** *adj* ▸ **'mani,festly** *adv*

manifestation (,mænɪfɛ'steɪʃən) *n* **1** the act of demonstrating; display. **2** the state of being manifested. **3** an indication or sign. **4** a public demonstration of feeling. **5** the materialization of a disembodied spirit.
▸ **,mani'festative** *adj*

manifesto (,mænɪ'fɛstəʊ) *n, pl* **manifestos** *or* **manifestoes.** a public declaration of intent, policy, aims, etc., as issued by a political party, government, or movement. ORIG C17: from It., from *manifestare* to MANIFEST

manifold ('mænɪ,fəʊld) *adj Formal.* **1** of several different kinds; multiple. **2** having many different forms, features, or elements. ◆ *n* **3** something having many varied parts, forms, or features. **4** a chamber or pipe with a number of inlets or outlets used to collect or distribute a fluid. In an internal-combustion engine the **inlet manifold** carries the vaporized fuel from the carburettor to the inlet ports and the **exhaust manifold** carries the exhaust gases away. ◆ *vb* (*tr*) **5** to duplicate (a page, book, etc.). **6** to make manifold; multiply. ORIG OE *manigfeald.* See MANY, -FOLD
▸ **'mani,foldly** *adv* ▸ **'mani,foldness** *n*

manikin *or* **mannikin** ('mænɪkɪn) *n* **1** a little man; dwarf or child. **2** an anatomical model of the body or a part of the body, esp. for use in medical or art instruction. **3** a variant of **mannequin.** ORIG C17: from Du. *manneken,* dim. of MAN

Manila ★ (mə'nɪlə) *n* **1** the chief port of the Philippines, on S Luzon on Manila Bay: capital of the republic until 1948 and from 1976; seat of the Far Eastern University and the University of Santo Tomas (1611). Pop. (urban area): 8 594 150 (1994 est.). **2** a type of cigar made in this city. **3** (*often not cap.*) short for **Manila hemp, Manila paper.**

Manila Bay ★ *n* an almost landlocked inlet of the South China Sea in the Philippines, in W Luzon: mostly forms Manila harbour. Area: 1994 sq. km (770 sq. miles).

Manila hemp *or* **Manilla hemp** *n* a fibre obtained from the abaca plant, used for rope, paper, etc.

Manila paper *or* **Manilla paper** *n* a strong usually brown paper made from Manila hemp or similar fibres.

manilla (mə'nɪlə) *n* an early form of currency in W Africa in the pattern of a small bracelet. ORIG from Sp.: bracelet, dim. of *mano* hand, from L *manus*

man in the street *n* the typical or ordinary person.

manioc ('mænɪ,ɒk) *or* **manioca** (,mænɪ'əʊkə) *n* another name for **cassava** (sense 1). ORIG C16: from Tupi *mandioca*

manipulate (mə'nɪpjʊ,leɪt) *vb* **manipulates, manipulating, manipulated. 1** (*tr*) to handle or use, esp. with some skill. **2** to control or influence (something or someone) cleverly, deviously, or skilfully. **3** to falsify (a bill, accounts, etc.) for one's own advantage. **4** (in physiotherapy) to examine or treat manually, as in loosening a joint. ORIG C19: back formation from *manipulation,* from L *manipulus* handful
▸ **manipulability** (mə,nɪpjʊlə'bɪlɪtɪ) *n* ▸ **ma'nipu,latable** *or* **ma'nipulable** *adj* ▸ **ma,nipu'lation** *n* ▸ **ma'nipulative** *adj* ▸ **ma'nipu,lator** *n* ▸ **ma'nipulatory** *adj*

Manipur ★ (,mʌnɪ'pʊə) *n* a state in NE India: largely densely forested mountains. Capital: Imphal. Pop.: 2 010 000 (1994 est.). Area: 22 327 sq. km (8621 sq. miles).

Manisa ★ ('mɑːnɪ,sɑː) *n* a city in W Turkey: the Byzantine seat of government (1204–1313). Pop.: 191 287 (1995 est.).

Manitoba ★ (,mænɪ'təʊbə) *n* **1** a province of W Canada: consists of prairie in the southwest, with extensive forests in the north and tundra near Hudson Bay in the northeast. Capital: Winnipeg. Pop.: 1 143 391 (1999 est.). Area: 650 090 sq. km (251 000 sq. miles). Abbrev.: **MB. 2 Lake.** a lake in W Canada, in S Manitoba: fed by the outflow from Lake Winnipegosis; drains into Lake Winnipeg. Area: 4706 sq. km (1817 sq. miles).
▸ **,Mani'toban** *n, adj*

manitou, manitu ('mænɪ,tuː), *or* **manito** ('mænɪ,təʊ) *n, pl* **manitous, manitus, manitos** *or* **manitou, manitu, manito.** (among the Algonquian Indians) a deified spirit or force. ORIG C17: of Amerind origin

Manitoulin Island ★ (,mænɪ'tuːlɪn) *n* an island in N Lake Huron in Ontario: the largest freshwater island in the world. Length: 129 km (80 miles). Width: up to 48 km (30 miles).

Manizales ★ (,mænɪ'zɑːlɛs; *Spanish* mani'θales) *n* a city in W Colombia, in the Cordillera Central of the Andes at an altitude of 2100 m (7000 ft): commercial centre of a rich coffee-growing area. Pop.: 358 194 (1997 est.).

man jack *n Inf.* a single individual (in **every man jack, no man jack**).

mankind (,mæn'kaɪnd) *n* **1** human beings collectively; humanity. **2** men collectively, as opposed to womankind.

> **USAGE NOTE** Some people object to the use of *mankind* to refer to all human beings and prefer the term *humankind.*

Manley ★ ('mænlɪ) *n* **Michael Norman.** 1924–97, Jamaican statesman; prime minister of Jamaica (1972–80; 1989–92).

manlike ('mæn,laɪk) *adj* resembling or befitting a man.

manly ('mænlɪ) *adj* **manlier, manliest. 1** possessing qualities, such as vigour or courage, generally regarded as ap-

propriate to or typical of a man; masculine. **2** characteristic of or befitting a man.
▸ **'manliness** *n*

man-made *adj* made by man; artificial.

Mann ★ (*German* man) *n* **1** **Heinrich** ('hainrıç). 1871–1950, German novelist: works include *Professor Unrat* (1905), filmed as *The Blue Angel* (1928), and *Man of Straw* (1918). **2** his brother, **Thomas** ('to:mas). 1875–1955, German novelist, in the US after 1937. His works include the short story *Death in Venice* (1913) and the novels *The Magic Mountain* (1924) and *Doctor Faustus* (1947): Nobel prize for literature 1929.

manna ('mænə) *n* **1** *Old Testament.* the miraculous food which sustained the Israelites in the wilderness (Exodus 16:14–36). **2** any spiritual or divine nourishment. **3** a windfall (esp. in **manna from heaven**). **4** a sweet substance obtained from various plants, esp. from the **manna** or **flowering ash** of S Europe, used as a mild laxative. ORIG OE via LL from Gk, from Heb. *mān*

Mannar ★ (mə'nɑ:) *n* **Gulf of.** the part of the Indian Ocean between SE India and the island of Sri Lanka: pearl fishing.

manned (mænd) *adj* **1** supplied or equipped with men, esp. soldiers. **2** (of spacecraft, etc.) having a human crew.

mannequin ('mænıkın) *n* **1** a woman who wears the clothes displayed at a fashion show; model. **2** a life-size dummy of the human body used to fit or display clothes. ORIG C18: via F from Du. *manneken* MANIKIN

manner ('mænə) *n* **1** a way of doing or being. **2** a person's bearing and behaviour. **3** the style or customary way of doing or accomplishing something. **4** type or kind. **5** mannered style, as in art; mannerism. **6** **in a manner of speaking.** in a way; so to speak. **7** **to the manner born.** naturally fitted to a specified role or activity. ORIG C12: via Norman F from OF *maniere,* from Vulgar L *manuāria* (unattested) a way of handling something, noun use of L *manuārius* belonging to the hand, from *manus* hand

mannered ('mænəd) *adj* **1** having idiosyncrasies or mannerisms; affected. **2** (*in combination*) having manners as specified: *ill-mannered.*

Mannerheim ★ ('mænə,heım) *n* Baron **Carl Gustaf Emil.** 1867–1951, Finnish soldier and statesman; president of Finland (1944–46).

mannerism ('mænə,rızəm) *n* **1** a distinctive and individual gesture or trait. **2** (*often cap.*) a principally Italian movement in art and architecture between the High Renaissance and Baroque periods (1520–1600), using distortion and exaggeration of human proportions, perspective, etc. **3** adherence to a distinctive or affected manner, esp. in art or literature.
▸ **'mannerist** *n, adj* ▸ **,manner'istic** *adj* ▸ **,manner'istically** *adv*

mannerless ('mænəlıs) *adj* having bad manners; boorish.
▸ **'mannerlessness** *n*

mannerly ('mænəlı) *adj* **1** well-mannered; polite. ◆ *adv* **2** *Now rare.* with good manners; politely.
▸ **'mannerliness** *n*

manners ('mænəz) *pl n* **1** social conduct. **2** a socially acceptable way of behaving.

Mannheim ★ ('mænhaım; *German* 'manhaım) *n* a city in SW Germany, in Baden-Württemberg at the confluence of the Rhine and Neckar: one of Europe's largest inland harbours; a cultural and musical centre. Pop.: 311 292 (1996 est.).

mannikin ('mænıkın) *n* a variant spelling of **manikin**.

Manning ★ ('mænıŋ) *n* **1** **Henry Edward.** 1808–92, British churchman. An Anglican who converted to Roman Catholicism (1851), he became archbishop of Westminster (1865) and cardinal (1875). **2** **Olivia.** 1908–80, British writer, best known for her novel sequence *Fortunes of War,* comprising the *Balkan Trilogy* (1960–65) and the *Levant Trilogy* (1977–80).

mannish ('mænıʃ) *adj* **1** (of a woman) displaying qualities regarded as typical of a man. **2** of or resembling a man.
▸ **'mannishly** *adv* ▸ **'mannishness** *n*

manoeuvre *or US* **maneuver** (mə'nu:və) *n* **1** a contrived, complicated, and possibly deceptive plan or action. **2** a movement or action requiring dexterity and skill. **3a** a tactic or movement of a military or naval unit. **3b** (*pl*) tactical exercises, usually on a large scale. **4** a planned movement of an aircraft in flight. **5** any change from the straight steady course of a ship. ◆ *vb* **manoeuvres, manoeuvring, manoeuvred** *or US* **manoeuvers, manoeuvering, manoeuvered.** **6** (*tr*) to contrive or accomplish with skill or cunning. **7** (*intr*) to manipulate situations, etc., in order to gain some end. **8** (*intr*) to perform a manoeuvre or manoeuvres. **9** to move or deploy or be moved or deployed, as military units, etc. ORIG C15: from F, from Med. L *manuopera* manual work, from L *manū operāre* to work with the hand
▸ **ma'noeuvrable** *or US* **ma'neuverable** *adj* ▸ **ma,noeuvra'bility** *or US* **ma,neuvera'bility** *n* ▸ **ma'noeuvrer** *or US* **ma'neuverer** *n* ▸ **ma'noeuvring** *or US* **ma'neuvering** *n*

man of God *n* **1** a saint or prophet. **2** a clergyman.

man of straw *n* **1** a man who cannot be relied upon to honour his financial commitments, esp. because of his limited resources. **2** any weak or vulnerable man.

man-of-war *or* **man o' war** *n, pl* **men-of-war** *or* **men o' war.** **1** a warship. **2** See **Portuguese man-of-war.**

man-of-war bird *or* **man-o'-war bird** *n* another name for **frigate bird.**

Manolete ★ (*Spanish* mano'lete) *n* original name *Manuel Rodriguez y Sánchez.* 1917–47, Spanish bullfighter.

manometer (mə'nɒmıtə) *n* an instrument for comparing pressures. ORIG C18: from F *manomètre,* from Gk *manos* sparse + *metron* measure
▸ **manometric** (,mænəʊ'mɛtrık) *or* **,mano'metrical** *adj*

manor ('mænə) *n* **1** (in medieval Europe) the manor house of a lord and the lands attached to it. **2** a manor house. **3** a landed estate. **4** *Brit. sl.* a geographical area of operation, esp. of a local police force. ORIG C13: from OF *manoir* dwelling, from *maneir* to dwell, from L *manēre* to remain
▸ **manorial** (mə'nɔ:rıəl) *adj*

manor house *n* (esp. formerly) the house of the lord of a manor.

manpower ('mæn,paʊə) *n* **1** power supplied by men. **2** a unit of power based on the rate at which a man can work; roughly 75 watts. **3** the number of people needed or available for a job.

manqué *French.* ('mɒŋkeı) *adj* (*postpositive*) unfulfilled; potential; would-be: *the manager is an actor manqué.* ORIG C19: lit.: having missed

Manresa ★ (*Spanish* man'rɛsa) *n* a city in NE Spain: contains a cave used as the spiritual retreat of St Ignatius Loyola. Pop.: 65 607 (1988 est.).

mansard ('mænsɑ:d, -səd) *n* a roof having two slopes on both sides and both ends, the lower slopes being steeper than the upper. Also called: **mansard roof.** ORIG C18: from F *mansarde,* after François MANSART

Mansart ★ (*French* mɑ̃sar) *n* **1** **François** (frɑ̃swa). 1598–1666, French architect, who established the French classical style. **2** his great-nephew, **Jules Hardouin** (ʒyl ardwɛ̃). 1646–1708, French architect and town planner, who completed the Palace of Versailles.

manse (mæns) *n* (in certain religious denominations) the house provided for a minister. ORIG C15: from Med. L *mansus* dwelling, from p.p. of L *manēre* to stay

Mansell ★ ('mænsᵊl) *n* **Nigel.** born 1953, British motor-racing driver; world champion in 1992.

manservant ('mæn,sɜ:vənt) *n, pl* **menservants.** a male servant, esp. a valet.

Mansfield[1] ★ ('mæns,fi:ld) *n* a town in central England, in W Nottinghamshire: former coal-mining and cotton-textiles industries. Pop.: 71 858 (1991).

Mansfield[2] ★ ('mæns,fi:ld) *n* **Katherine,** real name *Kathleen Mansfield Beauchamp.* 1888–1923, British writer, born in New Zealand, noted for such short-story collections as *Bliss* (1920) and *The Garden Party* (1922).

Mansholt ★ (*Dutch* 'mɑnshɔlt) *n* **Sicco Leendert** ('sıko 'le:ndərt). 1908–95, Dutch economist and politician;

vice president (1958–72) and president (1972–73) of the European Commission.

mansion ('mænʃən) *n* **1** Also called: **mansion house.** a large and imposing house. **2** a less common word for **manor house. 3** (*pl*) *Brit.* a block of flats. ORIG C14: via OF from L *mansio* a remaining, from *mansus;* see MANSE

Mansion House ★ *n* **the. 1** the residence of the Lord Mayor of London. **2** the residence of the Lord Mayor of Dublin.

man-sized *adj* **1** of a size appropriate for or convenient for a man. **2** *Inf.* big; large.

manslaughter ('mænˌslɔːtə) *n* **1** *Law.* the unlawful killing of one human being by another without malice aforethought. Cf. **murder. 2** (loosely) the killing of a human being.

Mansûra ★ (mæn'sʊərə) *n* See **El Mansûra.**

manta ('mæntə) *n* **1** Also called: **manta ray, devilfish, devil ray.** any large ray (fish), having very wide winglike pectoral fins and feeding on plankton. **2** a rough cotton cloth made in Spain and Spanish America. **3** a piece of this used as a blanket or shawl. ORIG Sp.: cloak, from Vulgar L; see MANTLE

manteau ('mæntəʊ) *n, pl* **manteaus** (-təuz) *or* **manteaux** (-təʊ). a cloak or mantle. ORIG C17: via F from L *mantellum* MANTLE

Mantegna ★ (*Italian* man'teɲɲa) *n* **Andrea** (an'drɛːa). 1431–1506, Italian painter and engraver.

mantel ('mænt^əl) *n* **1** a wooden, stone, or iron frame around the opening of a fireplace, together with its decorative facing. **2** Also called: **mantel shelf.** a shelf above this frame. ORIG C15: from F, var. of MANTLE

mantelet ('mænt^əˌlɛt) *or* **mantlet** *n* **1** a woman's short mantle, worn in the mid-19th century. **2** a portable bulletproof screen or shelter. ORIG C14: from OF, dim. of *mantel* MANTLE

mantelpiece ('mænt^əlˌpiːs) *n* **1** Also called: **mantel shelf, chimneypiece.** a shelf above a fireplace often forming part of the mantel. **2** another word for **mantel** (sense 1).

mantic ('mæntɪk) *adj* **1** of or relating to divination and prophecy. **2** having divining or prophetic powers. ORIG C19: from Gk *mantikos* prophetic, from *mantis* seer
▸ **'mantically** *adv*

-mantic *adj combining form.* forming adjectives from nouns ending in **-mancy.**

mantilla (mæn'tɪlə) *n* a woman's lace or silk scarf covering the shoulders and head, worn esp. in Spain. ORIG C18: Sp., dim. of *manta* cloak

Mantinea *or* **Mantineia** ★ (ˌmæntɪ'neɪə) *n* (in ancient Greece) a city in E Arcadia; site of several battles.

mantis ('mæntɪs) *n, pl* **mantises** *or* **mantes** (-tiːz). any carnivorous typically green insect of warm and tropical regions, having a long body and large eyes and resting with the first pair of legs raised as if in prayer. Also called: **praying mantis.** ORIG C17: NL, from Gk: prophet, alluding to its praying posture

mantissa (mæn'tɪsə) *n* the fractional part of a common logarithm representing the digits of the associated number but not its magnitude: *the mantissa of 2.4771 is .4771.* ORIG C17: from L: something added

mantle ('mænt^əl) *n* **1** *Arch.* a loose wrap or cloak. **2** such a garment regarded as a symbol of someone's power or authority. **3** anything that covers completely or envelops. **4** a small dome-shaped or cylindrical mesh, used to increase illumination in a gas or oil lamp by becoming incandescent. **5** *Zool.* a protective layer of epidermis in molluscs and brachiopods that secretes a substance forming the shell. **6** *Ornithol.* the feathers of the folded wings and back, esp. when of a different colour from the remaining feathers. **7** *Geol.* the part of the earth between the crust and the core. **8** a less common spelling of **mantel.** ◆ *vb* **mantles, mantling, mantled. 9** (*tr*) to envelop or supply with a mantle. **10** (*tr*) to spread over or become spread over. **11** (*intr*) to blush; flush. ORIG C13: via OF from L *mantellum,* dim. of *mantum* cloak

mantle rock *n* the loose rock material, including glacial drift, soils, etc., that covers the bedrock and forms the land surface.

Mantova ★ ('mantova) *n* the Italian name for **Mantua.**

mantra ('mæntrə, 'mʌn-) *n* **1** *Hinduism.* any of those parts of the Vedic literature which consist of the metrical psalms of praise. **2** *Hinduism, Buddhism.* any sacred word or syllable used as an object of concentration. ORIG C19: from Sansk., lit.: speech, instrument of thought, from *man* to think

mantua ('mæntjʊə) *n* a woman's loose gown of the 17th and 18th centuries. ORIG C17: changed from MANTEAU, through the infl. of MANTUA

Mantua ★ ('mæntjʊə) *n* a city in N Italy, in E Lombardy, surrounded by lakes: birthplace of Virgil. Pop.: 54 808 (1990). Italian name: **Mantova.**

manual ('mænjʊəl) *adj* **1** of or relating to a hand or hands. **2** operated or done by hand. **3** physical, as opposed to mental or mechanical: *manual labour.* **4** by human labour rather than automatic or computer-aided means. ◆ *n* **5** a book, esp. of instructions or information. **6** *Music.* one of the keyboards played by hand on an organ. **7** *Mil.* the prescribed drill with small arms. ORIG C15: via OF from L *manuālis,* from *manus* hand
▸ **'manually** *adv*

manufactory (ˌmænjʊ'fæktərɪ, -trɪ) *n, pl* **manufactories.** an obsolete word for **factory.** ORIG C17: from obs. *manufact;* see MANUFACTURE

manufacture (ˌmænjʊ'fæktʃə) *vb* **manufactures, manufacturing, manufactured. 1** to process or make (a product) from a raw material, esp. as a large-scale operation using machinery. **2** (*tr*) to invent or concoct. ◆ *n* **3** the production of goods, esp. by industrial processes. **4** a manufactured product. **5** the creation or production of anything. ORIG C16: from obs. *manufact* handmade, from LL *manūfactus,* from L *manus* hand + *facere* to make
▸ **ˌmanu'facturing** *n, adj*

manufacturer (ˌmænjʊ'fæktʃərə) *n* a person or business concern that manufactures goods or owns a factory.

manuka ('mɑːnʊkə) *n* a New Zealand tree with strong elastic wood and aromatic leaves. Also called: **tea tree.** ORIG from Maori

Manukau ★ ('mɑːnuˌkaʊ) *n* a city in New Zealand, on **Manukau Harbour** (an inlet of the Tasman Sea) near Auckland on NW North Island. Pop.: 254 577 (1996).

manumit (ˌmænjʊ'mɪt) *vb* **manumits, manumitting, manumitted.** (*tr*) to free from slavery, servitude, etc.; emancipate. ORIG C15: from L *manūmittere* to release, from *manū* from one's hand + *ēmittere* to send away
▸ **manumission** (ˌmænjʊ'mɪʃən) *n*

manure (mə'njʊə) *n* **1** animal excreta, usually with straw, etc., used to fertilize land. **2** *Chiefly Brit.* any material, esp. chemical fertilizer, used to fertilize land. ◆ *vb* **manures, manuring, manured. 3** (*tr*) to spread manure upon (fields or soil). ORIG C14: from Med. L *manuopera* manual work; see MANOEUVRE
▸ **ma'nurer** *n*

manus ('meɪnəs) *n, pl* **manus. 1** *Anat.* the wrist and hand. **2** the corresponding part in other vertebrates. ORIG C19: L: hand

manuscript ('mænjʊˌskrɪpt) *n* **1** a book or other document written by hand. **2** the original handwritten or typed version of a book, article, etc., as submitted by an author for publication. **3** handwriting, as opposed to printing. ORIG C16: from Med. L *manūscriptus,* from L *manus* hand + *scribere* to write

Manutius ★ (mə'njuːʃɪəs) *n* See **Aldus Manutius.**

Manx (mæŋks) *adj* **1** of or relating to the Isle of Man (an island in the Irish Sea), its inhabitants, their language, or their dialect of English. ◆ *n* **2** an almost extinct language of the Isle of Man, closely related to Scottish Gaelic. **3 the Manx.** (*functioning as pl*) the people of the Isle of Man. ORIG C16: earlier *Maniske,* of Scand. origin, from *Mana* Isle of Man + *-iske* -ISH

Manx cat *n* a short-haired tailless variety of cat, believed to originate on the Isle of Man.

Manxman ('mæŋksmən) *or* (*fem*) **Manxwoman** ('mæŋksˌwʊmən) *n, pl* **Manxmen** *or* **Manxwomen.** a native or inhabitant of the Isle of Man.

many ('mɛnɪ) *determiner* **1** (sometimes preceded by *a great* or *a good*) **1a** a large number of: *many times.* **1b** (*as pron; functioning as pl*): *many are seated already.* **2** (foll. by *a, an,* or *another,* and a sing noun) each of a considerable number of: *many a man.* **3** (preceded by *as, too, that,* etc.) **3a** a great number of: *as many apples as you like.* **3b** (*as pron; functioning as pl*): *I have as many as you.* ◆ *n* **4 the many.** the majority of mankind, esp. the common people. ORIG OE *manig*

many-sided *adj* having many sides, aspects, etc.
▸ **ˌmany-ˈsidedness** *n*

many-valued logic *n* any of various logics in which the truth-values that a proposition may have are not restricted to truth and falsity.

manzanilla (ˌmænzəˈnɪlə) *n* a very dry pale sherry. ORIG C19: from Sp.: camomile (referring to its bouquet)

Manzoni ★ (*Italian* manˈdzoːni) *n* **Alessandro** (alesˈsandro). 1785–1873, Italian romantic novelist and poet, famous for his historical novel *I Promessi sposi* (1825–27).

Maoism (ˈmaʊɪzəm) *n* **1** Marxism-Leninism as interpreted by Mao Tse-tung: distinguished by its theory of guerrilla warfare and its emphasis on the revolutionary potential of the peasantry. **2** adherence to or reverence for Mao Tse-tung and his teachings.
▸ **ˈMaoist** *n, adj*

Maori (ˈmaʊrɪ) *n* **1** (*pl* **Maoris** *or* **Maori**) a member of the people of Polynesian origin living in New Zealand and the Cook Islands since before the arrival of European settlers. **2** the language of this people, belonging to the Malayo-Polynesian family. ◆ *adj* **3** of or relating to this people or their language.

Maoriland ★ (ˈmaʊrɪˌlænd) *n* an obsolete name for **New Zealand.**
▸ **ˈMaoriˌlander** *n*

Mao Tse-tung (ˈmaʊ tseɪˈtʊŋ) *or* **Mao Ze Dong** ★ *n* 1893–1976, Chinese Marxist and statesman, who helped to found the Chinese Communist Party (1921) and established a soviet republic in SE China (1931–34). He led the retreat of Communist forces to NW China known as the Long March (1935–36), emerging as leader of the party. He united with the Kuomintang regime in World War II, but defeated them in the ensuing civil war. He founded the People's Republic of China (1949), of which he was chairman until 1959, and as party chairman instigated the Cultural Revolution in 1966.

map (mæp) *n* **1** a diagrammatic representation of the earth's surface or part of it, showing the geographical distributions, positions, etc., of features such as roads, towns, relief, rainfall, etc. **2** a diagrammatic representation of the stars or of the surface of a celestial body. **3** a maplike drawing of anything. **4** *Maths.* another name for **function** (sense 5). **5** a slang word for **face** (sense 1). **6 off the map.** no longer important; out of existence (esp. in **wipe off the map**). **7 put on the map.** to make (a town, company, etc.) well-known. ◆ *vb* **maps, mapping, mapped.** (*tr*) **8** to make a map of. **9** *Maths.* to represent or transform (a function, figure, set, etc.). ◆ See also **map out.** ORIG C16: from Med. L *mappa* (*mundi*) map (of the world), from L *mappa* cloth

Map (mæp) *or* **Mapes** ★ (mæps, ˈmeɪpiːz) *n* **Walter.** ?1140–?1209, Welsh ecclesiastic and satirical writer. His chief work is the miscellany *De Nugis curialium.*

maple (ˈmeɪpᵊl) *n* **1** any tree or shrub of a N temperate genus, having winged seeds borne in pairs and lobed leaves. **2** the hard wood of any of these trees, used for furniture and flooring. **3** the flavour of the sap of the sugar maple. ◆ See also **sugar maple.** ORIG C14: from OE *mapel-,* as in *mapeltrēow* maple tree

maple leaf *n* the leaf of the maple tree, the national emblem of Canada.

maple sugar *n US & Canad.* sugar made from the sap of the sugar maple.

maple syrup *n Chiefly US & Canad.* a very sweet syrup made from the sap of the sugar maple.

map out *vb* (*tr, adv*) to plan or design.

mapping (ˈmæpɪŋ) *n Maths.* another name for **function** (sense 5).

map projection *n* a means of representing or a representation of a globe or celestial sphere or part of it on a flat map.

Maputo ★ (məˈpuːtəʊ) *n* the capital and chief port of Mozambique, in the south on Delagoa Bay: became capital in 1907; the nearest port to the Rand gold-mining and industrial region of South Africa. Pop.: 931 591 (1991 est.). Former name (until 1975): **Lourenço Marques.**

maquette (mæˈkɛt) *n* a sculptor's small preliminary model or sketch. ORIG C20: from F, from It. *macchietta* a little sketch, from *macchiare,* from L *macula* blemish

maquis (mɑːˈkiː) *n, pl* **maquis** (-ˈkiː). **1** shrubby, mostly evergreen, vegetation found in coastal regions of the Mediterranean. **2** (*often cap.*) **2a** the French underground movement that fought against the German occupying forces in World War II. **2b** a member of this movement. ORIG C20: from F, from It. *macchia* thicket, from L *macula* spot

mar (mɑː) *vb* **mars, marring, marred.** (*tr*) to cause harm to; spoil or impair. ORIG OE *merran*
▸ **ˈmarrer** *n*

mar. *abbrev. for:* **1** maritime. **2** married.

Mar. *abbrev. for* March.

marabou (ˈmærəˌbuː) *n* **1** a large black-and-white African carrion-eating stork. **2** a down feather of this bird, used to trim garments. ORIG C19: from F, from Ar. *murābit* MARABOUT: the stork is considered a holy bird in Islam

marabout (ˈmærəˌbuː) *n* **1** a Muslim holy man or hermit of North Africa. **2** a shrine of the grave of a marabout. ORIG C17: via F & Port. *marabuto,* from Ar. *murābit*

maraca (məˈrækə) *n* a percussion instrument, usually one of a pair, consisting of a gourd or plastic shell filled with dried seeds, pebbles, etc. ORIG C20: Brazilian Port., of Amerind origin

Maracaibo ★ (ˌmærəˈkaɪbəʊ; *Spanish* maraˈkaiβo) *n* **1** a port in NW Venezuela, on the channel from Lake Maracaibo to the Gulf of Venezuela: the second largest city in the country; University of Zulia (1891); major oil centre. Pop.: 1 249 670 (1990). **2 Lake.** a lake in NW Venezuela, linked with the Gulf of Venezuela by a dredged channel: centre of the Venezuelan and South American oil industry. Area: about 13 000 sq. km (500 sq. miles).

Maracanda ★ (ˌmærəˈkændə) *n* the ancient name for **Samarkand.**

Maracay ★ (*Spanish* maraˈkai) *n* a city in N central Venezuela: developed greatly as the headquarters of Juan Vicente Gómez during his dictatorship; textile industries. Pop.: 354 196 (1990).

Maradona ★ (ˌmærəˈdɒnə) *n* **Diego Armando** (dɪˈeɪgəʊ). born 1960, Argentinian footballer.

marae (məˈraɪ) *n* **1** *NZ.* the enclosed space in front of a Maori meeting house. **2** *NZ.* a Maori meeting house, with its courtyard and associated buildings. **3** (in Polynesia) an open-air place of worship. ORIG from Maori

Marajó ★ (*Portuguese* maraˈʒɔ) *n* an island in N Brazil, at the mouth of the Amazon. Area: 38 610 sq. km (15 444 sq. miles).

Maranhão ★ (*Portuguese* marəˈɲɐ̃u) *n* a state of NE Brazil, on the Atlantic: forested and humid in the northwest, with high plateaus in the east and south. Capital: São Luís. Pop.: 5 222 183 (1996). Area: 328 666 sq. km (128 179 sq. miles).

Marañón ★ (*Spanish* maraˈɲɔn) *n* a river in NE Peru, rising in the Andes and flowing northwest into the Ucayali River, forming the Amazon. Length: about 1450 km (900 miles).

maranta (mɑːˈræntə) *n* any of various tropical monocotyledons with ornamental leaves. ORIG C19: after B. *Maranta* 16th-century Venetian botanist

Maraş ★ (*Turkish* ˈmɑrɑʃ) *n* a town in S Turkey: noted formerly for the manufacture of weapons but now for carpets and embroidery. Pop.: 228 129 (1985).

marasca (məˈræskə) *n* a European cherry tree with red acid-tasting fruit. ORIG C19: from It., var. of *amarasca,* ult. from L *amārus* bitter

maraschino (ˌmærəˈskiːnəʊ, -ˈʃiːnəʊ) *n* a liqueur made from marasca cherries, having a taste like bitter almonds. ORIG C18: from It.; see MARASCA

maraschino cherry *n* a cherry preserved in maraschino or an imitation of this liqueur.

marasmus (məˈræzməs) *n Pathol.* general emaciation, esp. of infants, thought to be associated with severe malnutrition or impaired utilization of nutrients. ORIG C17: from NL, from Gk *marasmos,* from *marainein* to waste
▸ **maˈrasmic** *adj*

Marat ★ (*French* mara) *n* **Jean Paul** (ʒɑ̃ pɔl). 1743–93, French revolutionary leader and founder of the newspaper *L'Ami du peuple.* Instrumental in overthrowing the Girondists (1793), he was assassinated by Charlotte Corday.

marathon (ˈmærəθən) *n* **1** a race on foot of 26 miles 385 yards (42.195 kilometres). **2a** any long or arduous task, etc. **2b** (*as modifier*): *a marathon effort.* ORIG referring to the feat of the messenger who ran more than 20 miles from Marathon to Athens to bring the news of victory in 490 B.C.

Marathon ★ (ˈmærəθən) *n* a plain in Attica northeast of Athens: site of a victory of the Athenians and Plataeans over the Persians (490 B.C.).

marathon group *n* (in psychotherapy) an encounter group that lasts for many hours or days.

maraud (məˈrɔːd) *vb* to wander or raid in search of plunder. ORIG C18: from F *marauder* to prowl, from *maraud* vagabond
▸ **maˈrauder** *n* ▸ **maˈrauding** *adj*

marble (ˈmɑːbᵊl) *n* **1a** a hard crystalline metamorphic rock resulting from the recrystallization of a limestone. **1b** (*as modifier*): *a marble bust.* **2** a block or work of art of marble. **3** a small round glass or stone ball used in playing marbles. ◆ *vb* **marbles, marbling, marbled. 4** (*tr*) to mottle with variegated streaks in imitation of marble. ORIG C12: via OF from L *marmor,* from Gk *marmaros,* rel. to Gk *marmairein* to gleam
▸ **ˈmarbled** *adj*

marbles (ˈmɑːbᵊlz) *n* **1** (*functioning as sing*) a game in which marbles are rolled at one another, similar to bowls. **2** (*functioning as pl*) *Inf.* wits: *to lose one's marbles.*

marbling (ˈmɑːblɪŋ) *n* **1** a mottled effect or pattern resembling marble. **2** such an effect obtained by transferring floating colours from a gum solution. **3** the streaks of fat in lean meat.

Marburg ★ (ˈmɑːˌbɜːg; *German* ˈmaːrbʊrk) *n* **1** a city in W central Germany, in Hesse: famous for the religious debate between Luther and Zwingli in 1529; Europe's first Protestant university (1527). Pop.: 75 400 (1995 est.). **2** the German name for **Maribor.**

Marburg disease *n* a severe, sometimes fatal, viral disease of vervet (green) monkeys, which may be transmitted to humans. Also called: **green monkey disease.** ORIG C20: after MARBURG, in which the first human cases were recorded

marc (mɑːk) *n* **1** the remains of grapes or other fruit that have been pressed for wine-making. **2** a brandy distilled from these. ORIG C17: from F, from OF *marchier* to trample (grapes)

Marc ★ (*German* mark) *n* **Franz** (frants). 1880–1916, German expressionist painter; cofounder with Kandinsky of the *Blaue Reiter* group (1911). He is noted for his symbolic compositions of animals.

marcasite (ˈmɑːkəˌsaɪt) *n* **1** a metallic pale yellow mineral consisting of iron pyrites in crystalline form used in jewellery. **2** a cut and polished form of steel or any white metal used for making jewellery. ORIG C15: from Med. L *marcasīta,* from Ar. *marqashītā,* ?from Persian

marcato (mɑːˈkɑːtəʊ) *adj, adv Music.* with each note heavily accented. ORIG from It.: marked

Marceau ★ (*French* marso) *n* **Marcel** (marsɛl). born 1923, French mime artist.

Marcellus ★ (mɑːˈsɛləs) *n* **Marcus Claudius** (ˈmɑːkəs ˈklɔːdɪəs). ?268–208 B.C., Roman general and consul, who captured Syracuse (212) in the Second Punic War.

march¹ (mɑːtʃ) *vb* **1** (*intr*) to walk or proceed with stately or regular steps, usually in a procession or military formation. **2** (*tr*) to make (a person or group) proceed. **3** (*tr*) to traverse or cover by marching. ◆ *n* **4** the act or an instance of marching. **5** a regular stride. **6** a long or exhausting walk. **7** advance; progression (of time, etc.). **8** a distance or route covered by marching. **9** a piece of music, as for a march. **10 steal a march on.** to gain an advantage over, esp. by a secret enterprise or trick. ORIG C16: from OF *marchier* to tread, prob. of Gmc origin
▸ **ˈmarcher** *n*

march² (mɑːtʃ) *n* **1** a frontier, border, or boundary or the land lying along it, often of disputed ownership. ◆ *vb* **2** (*intr; often foll. by upon* or *with*) to share a common border (with). ORIG C13: from OF *marche,* of Gmc origin

March¹ (mɑːtʃ) *n* the third month of the year, consisting of 31 days. ORIG from OF, from L *Martius* (month) of Mars

March² ★ (març) *n* the German name for the **Morava** (sense 1).

Marche ★ (*French* marʃ) *n* a former province of central France.

Marches ★ (ˈmɑːtʃɪz) *n* **the. 1** the border area between England and Wales or Scotland, both characterized by continual feuding (13th–16th centuries). **2** a region of central Italy. Capital: Ancona. Pop.: 1 443 172 (1996 est.). Area: 9692 sq. km (3780 sq. miles). Italian name: **Le Marche** (le ˈmarke). **3** any of various other border regions.

March hare *n* a hare during its breeding season in March, noted for its wild and excitable behaviour (esp. in **mad as a March hare**).

marching orders *pl n* **1** military orders, esp. to infantry, giving instructions about a march, its destination, etc. **2** *Inf.* any dismissal, esp. notice of dismissal from employment.

marchioness (ˈmɑːʃənɪs, ˌmɑːʃəˈnɛs) *n* **1** the wife or widow of a marquis. **2** a woman who holds the rank of marquis. ORIG C16: from Med. L *marchionissa,* fem. of *marchiō* MARQUIS

marchpane (ˈmɑːtʃˌpeɪn) *n* an archaic word for **marzipan.** ORIG C15: from F

Marciano ★ (ˌmɑːsɪˈænəʊ, -ˈɑːnəʊ) *n* **Rocky.** original name *Rocco Francis Marchegiano.* 1923–69, US boxer; world heavyweight champion, 1952–56.

Marconi ★ (mɑːˈkəʊnɪ) *n* **Guglielmo** (guʎˈʎɛlmo). 1874–1937, Italian physicist, who transmitted radio signals across the Atlantic (1901), making wireless telegraphy a reality: Nobel prize for physics 1909.

Marco Polo ★ (ˈmɑːkəʊ ˈpəʊləʊ) *n* See (Marco) **Polo.**

Marcos ★ (ˈmɑːkɒs) *n* **Ferdinand** (**Edralin**). 1917–89, Filipino statesman; president of the Philippines (1965–86): deposed and exiled.

Marcus Aurelius Antoninus ★ (ˈmɑːkəs ɔːˈriːlɪəs ˌæntəˈnaɪnəs) *n* original name *Marcus Annius Verus.* 121–180 A.D., Roman emperor (161–180) noted particularly for his *Meditations.*

Marcuse ★ (mɑːˈkuːzə) *n* **Herbert.** 1898–1979, US philosopher, born in Germany. His works include *Eros and Civilization* (1958) and *One Dimensional Man* (1964).

Mar del Plata ★ (*Spanish* ˈmar ðel ˈplata) *n* a city and resort in E Argentina, on the Atlantic: fishing port. Pop.: 512 880 (1991).

Mardi Gras (ˈmɑːdɪ ˈgrɑː) *n* the festival of Shrove Tuesday, celebrated in some cities with great revelry. ORIG F: fat Tuesday

Marduk ★ (ˈmɑːdʊk) *n* the chief god of the Babylonian pantheon.

mare¹ (mɛə) *n* the adult female of a horse or zebra. ORIG C12: from OE, of Gmc origin

mare² (ˈmɑːreɪ, -rɪ) *n, pl* **maria. 1** (*cap. when part of a name*) any of a large number of huge dry plains on the surface of the moon, visible as dark markings and once thought to be seas. **2** a similar area on the surface of Mars. ORIG from L: sea

Marengo ★ (məˈrɛŋgəʊ; *Italian* maˈreŋgo) *n* a village in NW Italy: site of a major battle in which Napoleon decisively defeated the Austrians (1800).

Marenzio ★ (*Italian* maˈrentsjo) *n* **Luca** (ˈluːka). 1553–99, Italian composer of madrigals.

mare's-nest (ˈmɛəzˌnɛst) *n* **1** a discovery imagined to be important but proving worthless. **2** a disordered situation.

mare's-tail ('mɛəz,teɪl) *n* **1** a wisp of trailing cirrus cloud, indicating strong winds at high levels. **2** an erect pond plant with minute flowers and crowded whorls of narrow leaves.

Margaret ★ ('mɑːgrət) *n* **1** called the *Maid of Norway.* ?1282–90, queen of Scotland (1286–90); daughter of Eric II of Norway. Her death while sailing to England to marry the future Edward II led Edward I to declare dominion over Scotland. **2 Princess.** born 1930, younger sister of Queen Elizabeth II.

Margaret of Anjou ★ *n* 1430–82, queen of England. She married the mentally unstable Henry VI of England in 1445 to confirm the truce with France during the Hundred Years' War. She became a leader of the Lancastrians in the Wars of the Roses and was defeated at Tewkesbury (1471) by Edward IV.

Margaret of Navarre ★ *n* 1492–1549, queen of Navarre (1544–49) by marriage to Henry II of Navarre; sister of Francis I of France. She was a poet, a patron of humanism, and author of the *Heptaméron* (1558). Also called: **Margaret of Angoulême.**

Margaret of Scotland ★ *n* **Saint.** 1045–93, queen consort of Malcolm III of Scotland. Her piety led to her canonization (1250). Feast days: June 10, Nov. 16.

Margaret of Valois ★ *n* 1553–1615, daughter of Henry II of France and Catherine de' Medici; queen of Navarre (1572) by marriage to Henry of Navarre. The marriage was dissolved (1599) after his accession as Henry IV of France: noted for her *Mémoires.*

margaric (mɑː'gærɪk) *or* **margaritic** *adj* of or resembling pearl. ORIG C19: from Gk *margaron* pearl

margarine (,mɑːdʒə'riːn, ,mɑːgə-) *n* a substitute for butter, prepared from vegetable and animal fats with added small amounts of milk, salt, vitamins, colouring matter, etc. ORIG C19: from MARGARIC

Margarita ★ (,mɑːgə'riːtə) *n* an island in the Caribbean, off the NE coast of Venezuela: pearl fishing. Capital: La Asunción.

Margate ★ ('mɑːgeɪt) *n* a town and resort in SE England, in E Kent on the Isle of Thanet. Pop.: 56 734 (1991).

marge[1] (mɑːdʒ) *n Brit. inf.* short for **margarine.**

marge[2] (mɑːdʒ) *n Arch.* a margin. ORIG C16: from F

margin ('mɑːdʒɪn) *n* **1** an edge or rim, and the area immediately adjacent to it; border. **2** the blank space surrounding the text on a page. **3** a vertical line on a page delineating this space. **4** an additional amount or one beyond the minimum necessary: *a margin of error.* **5** *Chiefly Austral.* a payment made in addition to a basic wage, esp. for special skill or responsibility. **6** a bound or limit. **7** the amount by which one thing differs from another. **8** *Commerce.* the profit on a transaction. **9** *Econ.* the minimum return below which an enterprise becomes unprofitable. **10** *Finance.* collateral deposited by a client with a broker as security. ◆ Also (archaic): **margent** ('mɑːdʒənt). ◆ *vb* (*tr*) **11** to provide with a margin; border. **12** *Finance.* to deposit a margin upon. ORIG C14: from L *margō* border

marginal ('mɑːdʒɪnᵊl) *adj* **1** of, in, on, or constituting a margin. **2** close to a limit, esp. a lower limit: *marginal legal ability.* **3** not considered central or important; insignificant. **4** *Econ.* relating to goods or services produced and sold at the margin of profitability: *marginal cost.* **5** *Politics, chiefly Brit. & NZ.* of or designating a constituency in which elections tend to be won by small margins: *a marginal seat.* **6** designating agricultural land on the margin of cultivated zones. ◆ *n* **7** *Politics, chiefly Brit. & NZ.* a marginal constituency.
▸ **marginality** (,mɑːdʒɪ'nælɪtɪ) *n* ▸ **'marginally** *adv*

marginalia (,mɑːdʒɪ'neɪlɪə) *pl n* notes in the margin of a book, manuscript, or letter. ORIG C19: NL, noun (neuter pl) from *margināl̄is* marginal

marginate ('mɑːdʒɪ,neɪt) *vb* **marginates, marginating, marginated. 1** (*tr*) to provide with a margin or margins. ◆ *adj* **2** *Biol.* having a margin of a distinct colour or form. ORIG C18: from L *margināre*
▸ **,margin'ation** *n*

margrave ('mɑː,greɪv) *n* a German nobleman ranking above a count. Margraves were originally counts appointed to govern frontier provinces, but all eventually became princes of the Holy Roman Empire. ORIG C16: from MDu. *markgrave,* lit.: count of the MARCH[2]
▸ **margravate** ('mɑːgrəvɪt) *n*

margravine ('mɑːgrə,viːn) *n* **1** the wife or widow of a margrave. **2** a woman who holds the rank of margrave. ORIG C17: from MDu., fem of MARGRAVE

Margrethe II ★ (*Danish* mar'greːdə) *n* born 1940, queen of Denmark from 1972.

marguerite (,mɑːgə'riːt) *n* **1** a cultivated garden plant whose flower heads have white or pale yellow rays around a yellow disc. **2** any of various related plants with daisy-like flowers. ORIG C19: from F: daisy, pearl, from L, from Gk, from *margaron*

maria ('mɑːrɪə) *n* the plural of **mare**[2].

mariachi (,mɑːrɪ'ɑːtʃɪ) *n* a small ensemble of street musicians in Mexico. ORIG C20: from Mexican Sp.

Maria de' Medici ★ (*Italian* ma'riːa de 'mɛːditʃi) *n* French name *Marie de Médicis.* 1573–1642, queen of France (1600–10) by marriage to Henry IV of France. She became regent for her son (later Louis XIII) but was finally exiled from France in 1631 after plotting to undermine Richelieu's influence.

Mariana Islands ★ (,mærɪ'ɑːnə) *pl n* a chain of volcanic and coral islands in the W Pacific, east of the Philippines and north of New Guinea: administered by the US and divided politically into Guam and the islands north of Guam constituting the Commonwealth of the Northern Mariana Islands. Pop.: 187 400 (1995 est.). Area: 958 sq. km (370 sq. miles). Former name (1521–1668): **Ladrone Islands.**

Marianao ★ (*Spanish* marja'nao) *n* a city in NW Cuba, adjacent to W Havana city: the chief Cuban military base. Pop.: 133 016 (1989 est.).

Mariánské Lázně ★ (*Czech* 'marjanskeː 'laːznjɛ) *n* a town in the W Czech Republic: a fashionable spa in the 18th and 19th centuries. Pop.: 15 380 (1991). German name: **Marienbad.**

Maria Theresa ★ (mə'riːə tə'reɪzə) *n* 1717–80, archduchess of Austria and queen of Hungary and Bohemia (1740–80); the daughter and heiress of Emperor Charles VI of Austria and wife of Emperor Francis I. In the War of the Austrian Succession (1740–48) she was confirmed in all her possessions except Silesia, which she attempted unsuccessfully to regain in the Seven Years' War (1756–63).

Mari El Republic ★ ('mɑːrɪ) *n* a constituent republic of W central Russia, in the middle Volga basin. Capital: Yoshkar-Ola. Pop.: 766 000 (1996 est.). Area: 23 200 sq. km (8955 sq. miles).

Maribor ★ ('mærɪbɔː) *n* an industrial city in N Slovenia, on the Drava River: a flourishing Hapsburg trading centre in the 13th century; resort. Pop.: 134 289 (1996 est.). German name: **Marburg.**

Marie Antoinette ★ (*French* mari ɑ̃twanɛt) *n* 1755–93, queen of France (1774–93) by marriage to Louis XVI of France. Her opposition to reform during the Revolution contributed to the overthrow of the monarchy; guillotined.

Marie Byrd Land ★ ('mɑːrɪ 'bɜːd) *n* the former name of **Byrd Land.**

Marie Galante ★ (*French* mari galɑ̃t) *n* an island in the E Caribbean southeast of Guadeloupe, of which it is a dependency. Chief town: Grand Bourg. Pop.: 13 463 (1990). Area: 155 sq. km (60 sq. miles).

Mariehamn ★ (mariə'hamn) *n* a city in SW Finland, chief port of the Åland Islands. Pop.: 10 260 (1990). Finnish name: **Maarianhamina.**

Marie Louise ★ (*French* mari lɥiz) *n* 1791–1847, empress of France (1811–15) as the second wife of Napoleon I; daughter of Francis I of Austria. On Napoleon's abdication (1815) she became Duchess of Parma.

Marienbad ★ ('mærɪən,bæd; *German* ma'riːənbaːt) *n* the German name for **Mariánské Lázně.**

marigold ('mærɪ,gəʊld) *n* **1** any of various tropical American plants cultivated for their yellow or orange flower heads and strongly scented foliage. **2** any of various similar or related plants, such as the marsh marigold. ORIG C14: from *Mary* (the Virgin) + GOLD

marijuana *or* **marihuana** (ˌmærɪˈhwɑːnə) *n* **1** the dried leaves and flowers of the hemp plant, used for its euphoric effects, esp. in cigarettes. See also **cannabis. 2** another name for **hemp** (the plant). ORIG C19: from Mexican Sp.

marimba (məˈrɪmbə) *n* a Latin American percussion instrument consisting of a set of hardwood plates placed over tuned metal resonators, played with two soft-headed sticks in each hand. ORIG C18: of West African origin

Marin ★ (ˈmɑːrɪn) *n* **John.** 1870–1953, US watercolour painter.

marina (məˈriːnə) *n* an elaborate docking facility for yachts and other pleasure boats. ORIG C19: via It. & Sp. from L: MARINE

marinade *n* (ˌmærɪˈneɪd). **1** a spiced liquid mixture of oil, wine, vinegar, etc., in which meat or fish is soaked before cooking. **2** meat or fish soaked in this. ◆ *vb* (ˈmærɪˌneɪd), **marinades, marinading, marinaded. 3** a variant of **marinate.** ORIG C17: from F, from Sp., from *marinar* to MARINATE

marinate (ˈmærɪˌneɪt) *vb* **marinates, marinating, marinated.** to soak in marinade. ORIG C17: prob. from It. *marinato,* from *marinare* to pickle, ult. from L *marīnus* MARINE
▸ **ˌmariˈnation** *n*

Marinduque ★ (ˌmɑːrɪnˈduːkeɪ) *n* an island of the central Philippines, east of Mindoro: forms, with offshore islets, a province of the Philippines. Capital: Boac. Pop.: 173 715 (1980). Area: 960 sq. km (370 sq. miles).

marine (məˈriːn) *adj* (*usually prenominal*) **1** of, found in, or relating to the sea. **2** of or relating to shipping, navigation, etc. **3** of or relating to a body of seagoing troops: *marine corps.* **4** of or relating to a government department concerned with maritime affairs. **5** used or adapted for use at sea. ◆ *n* **6** shipping and navigation in general. **7** (*cap. when part of a name*) a member of a marine corps or similar body. **8** a picture of a ship, seascape, etc. **9 tell it to the marines.** *Inf.* an expression of disbelief. ORIG C15: from OF *marin,* from L *marīnus,* from *mare* sea

mariner (ˈmærɪnə) *n* a formal or literary word for **seaman.** ORIG C13: from Anglo-F, ult. from L *marīnus* MARINE

Marinetti ★ (*Italian* mariˈnetti) *n* **Filippo Tommaso** (fiˈlippo tomˈmaːzo). 1876–1944, Italian poet; founder of futurism (1909).

Mariolatry (ˌmɛərɪˈɒlətrɪ) *n Derog.* devotion to the Virgin Mary, considered as excessive.
▸ **ˌMariˈolater** *n* ▸ **ˌMariˈolatrous** *adj*

marionette (ˌmærɪəˈnɛt) *n* a puppet or doll whose jointed limbs are moved by strings. ORIG C17: from F, from *Marion,* dim. of *Marie* Mary + -ETTE

Marist (ˈmɛərɪst) *n RC Church.* a member of the Society of Mary, a religious congregation founded in 1824. ORIG C19: from F *Mariste,* from *Marie* Mary (the Virgin)

Maritain ★ (*French* maritɛ̃) *n* **Jacques** (ʒak). 1882–1973, French neo-Thomist Roman Catholic philosopher.

marital (ˈmærɪtᵊl) *adj* **1** of or relating to marriage. **2** of or relating to a husband. ORIG C17: from L *marītālis,* from *marītus* married (adj), husband (n)
▸ **ˈmaritally** *adv*

maritime (ˈmærɪˌtaɪm) *adj* **1** of or relating to navigation, shipping, etc. **2** of, relating to, near, or living near the sea. **3** (of a climate) having small temperature differences between summer and winter. ORIG C16: from L *maritimus,* from *mare* sea

Maritime Alps ★ *pl n* a range of the W Alps in SE France and NW Italy. Highest peak: Argentera, 3297 m (10 817 ft).

Maritime Provinces *or* **Maritimes** ★ *pl n* **the.** another name for the **Atlantic Provinces,** but often excluding Newfoundland.

Maritimer (ˈmærɪˌtaɪmə) *n* a native or inhabitant of the Maritime Provinces of Canada.

Maritsa ★ (*Bulgarian* maˈritsa) *n* a river in S Europe, rising in S Bulgaria and flowing east into Turkey, then south from Edirne as part of the border between Turkey and Greece to the Aegean. Length: 483 km (300 miles). Turkish name: **Meriç.** Greek name: **Évros.**

Mariupol ★ (*Russian* məriˈupəlj) *n* a port in SE Ukraine, near the Sea of Azov: industrial centre. Pop.: 529 000 (1987). Former name (1948–91): **Zhdanov.**

Marius ★ (ˈmɛərɪəs, ˈmærɪəs) *n* **Gaius** (ˈgaɪəs). ?155–86 B.C., Roman general and consul. He defeated Jugurtha, the Cimbri, and the Teutons (107–101), but his rivalry with Sulla caused civil war (88). He was exiled but returned (87) and took Rome.

Marivaux ★ (*French* marivo) *n* **Pierre Carlet de Chamblain de** (pjɛr karlɛ də ʃɑ̃blɛ̃ də). 1688–1763, French dramatist and novelist, noted for such comedies as *La Vie de Marianne* (1731–41).

marjoram (ˈmɑːdʒərəm) *n* **1** Also called: **sweet marjoram.** an aromatic Mediterranean plant with sweet-scented leaves, used for seasoning food and in salads. **2** Also called: **wild marjoram, pot marjoram, origan.** a similar and related European plant. See also **oregano.** ORIG C14: via OF *majorane,* from Med. L *marjorana*

mark[1] (mɑːk) *n* **1** a visible impression, stain, etc., on a surface, such as a spot or scratch. **2** a sign, symbol, or other indication that distinguishes something. **3** a cross or other symbol made instead of a signature. **4** a written or printed sign or symbol, as for punctuation. **5** a letter, number, or percentage used to grade academic work. **6** a thing that indicates position or directs; marker. **7** a desired or recognized standard: *up to the mark.* **8** an indication of some quality, feature, or prowess. **9** quality or importance: *a person of little mark.* **10** a target or goal. **11** impression or influence. **12** one of the temperature settings on a gas oven: *gas mark 5.* **13** *Sl.* a suitable victim, esp. for swindling. **14** (*often cap.*) (in trade names) a model, brand, or type. **15** *Naut.* one of the intervals distinctively marked on a sounding lead. **16** *Rugby.* an action in which a player within his or her own 22 m line catches a forward kick by an opponent and shouts "mark", which entitles him or her to a free kick. **17** *Australian Rules football.* **17a** a catch of the ball from a kick of at least 10 yards, after which a free kick is taken. **17b** the spot where this occurs. **18** (in medieval England and Germany) a piece of land held in common by the free men of a community. **19 the mark.** *Boxing.* the middle of the stomach. **20 make one's mark.** to succeed or achieve recognition. **21 on your mark** *or* **marks.** a command given to runners in a race to prepare themselves at the starting line. ◆ *vb* **22** to make or receive (a visible impression, trace, or stain) on (a surface). **23** (*tr*) to characterize or distinguish. **24** (often foll. by *off* or *out*) to set boundaries or limits (on). **25** (*tr*) to select, designate, or doom by or as if by a mark: *a marked man.* **26** (*tr*) to put identifying or designating labels, stamps, etc., on, esp. to indicate price. **27** (*tr*) to pay heed or attention to: *mark my words.* **28** to observe; notice. **29** to grade or evaluate (scholastic work). **30** *Football, etc.* to stay close to (an opponent) to hamper his or her play. **31** to keep (score) in some games. **32 mark time. 32a** to move the feet alternately as in marching but without advancing. **32b** to act in a mechanical and routine way. **32c** to halt progress temporarily. ◆ See also **markdown, mark-up.** ORIG OE *mearc* mark
▸ **ˈmarker** *n*

mark[2] (mɑːk) *n* **1** See **Deutschmark, markka, Reichsmark, Ostmark. 2** a former monetary unit and coin in England and Scotland worth two thirds of a pound sterling. **3** a silver coin of Germany until 1924. ORIG OE *marc* unit of weight of precious metal, ?from the marks on metal bars; apparently of Gmc origin and rel. to MARK[1]

Mark ★ (mɑːk) *n New Testament.* **1** one of the four Evangelists. Feast day: April 25. **2** the second Gospel, traditionally ascribed to him.

Mark Antony ★ *n* See (Mark) **Antony.**

markdown (ˈmɑːkˌdaʊn) *n* **1** a price reduction. ◆ *vb* **mark down. 2** (*tr, adv*) to reduce in price.

marked (mɑːkt) *adj* **1** obvious, evident, or noticeable. **2** singled out, esp. as the target of attack: *a marked man.* **3** *Linguistics.* distinguished by a specific feature, as in phonology. For example, of the two phonemes /t/ and /d/, the /d/ is marked because it exhibits the feature of voice. ▸ **markedly** ('mɑːkɪdlɪ) *adv* ▸ **'markedness** *n*

market ('mɑːkɪt) *n* **1a** an event or occasion, usually held at regular intervals, at which people meet to buy and sell merchandise. **1b** (*as modifier*): *market day.* **2** a place at which a market is held. **3** a shop that sells a particular merchandise: *an antique market.* **4** the trading or selling opportunities provided by a particular group of people: *the foreign market.* **5** demand for a particular product or commodity. **6** See **stock market. 7** See **market price, market value. 8 be in the market for.** to wish to buy or acquire. **9 on the market.** available for purchase. **10 seller's** (*or* **buyer's**) **market.** a market characterized by excess demand (or supply) and thus favourable to sellers (or buyers). **11 the market.** business or trade in a commodity as specified: *the sugar market.* ◆ *vb* **markets, marketing, marketed. 12** (*tr*) to offer or produce for sale. **13** (*intr*) to buy or deal in a market. ORIG C12: from L *mercātus,* from *mercāri* to trade, from *merx* merchandise
▸ **'marketable** *adj* ▸ **'marketer** *n*

marketeer (ˌmɑːkɪ'tɪə) *n* **1** *Brit.* (formerly) a supporter of the Common Market and of Britain's membership of it; a Europhile. **2** a marketer.

market forces *pl n* the effect of supply and demand on trading within a free market.

market garden *n Chiefly Brit.* an establishment where fruit and vegetables are grown for sale.
▸ **market gardener** *n* ▸ **market gardening** *n*

marketing ('mɑːkɪtɪŋ) *n* the provision of goods or services to meet consumer needs.

market maker *n* a dealer in securities on the London stock exchange, who buys and sells as a principal and since 1986 can also deal directly with the public.

marketplace ('mɑːkɪtˌpleɪs) *n* **1** a place where a public market is held. **2** any centre where ideas, etc., are exchanged. **3** the commercial world of buying and selling.

market price *n* the prevailing price, as determined by supply and demand, at which goods, services, etc., may be bought or sold.

market research *n* the study of influences upon customer behaviour and the analysis of market characteristics and trends.

market-test *vb* (*tr*) to put (a section of a public-sector enterprise) out to tender, often as a prelude to full-scale privatization.

market town *n Chiefly Brit.* a town that holds a market, esp. an agricultural centre.

market value *n* the amount obtainable on the open market for the sale of property, financial assets, or goods and services.

Markham ★ ('mɑːkəm) *n* **Mount.** a mountain in Antarctica, in Victoria Land. Height: 4350 m (14 272 ft).

markhor ('mɑːkɔː) *or* **markhoor** ('mɑːkʊə) *n, pl* **markhors, markhor** *or* **markhoors, markhoor.** a large wild Himalayan goat with large spiralled horns. ORIG C19: from Persian, lit.: snake-eater

Markiewicz ★ (mɑː'kjeɪvɪtʃ) *n* **Constance,** Countess, original name *Constance Gore-Booth.* 1868–1927, Irish nationalist, married to a Polish count. She fought in the Easter Rising (1916) and was sentenced to death but reprieved. The first woman elected to the British parliament (1918), she refused to take her seat.

marking ('mɑːkɪŋ) *n* **1** a mark or series of marks. **2** the arrangement of colours on an animal, plant, etc. **3** assessment and correction of pupils' or students' written work by teachers.

markka ('mɑːkɑː, -kə) *n, pl* **markkaa** (-kɑː). the standard monetary unit of Finland. ORIG Finnish; see MARK[2]

Markova ★ (mɑː'kəʊvə) *n* Dame **Alicia,** real name *Lilian Alicia Marks.* born 1910, British ballerina.

marksman ('mɑːksmən) *n, pl* **marksmen. 1** a person skilled in shooting. **2** a serviceman selected for his skill in shooting.
▸ **'marksmanship** *n* ▸ **'marksˌwoman** *fem n*

mark-up *n* **1** an amount added to the cost of a commodity to provide the seller with a profit. **2a** an increase in the price of a commodity. **2b** the amount of this. ◆ *vb* **mark up.** (*tr, adv*) **3** to add a percentage for profit, etc., to the cost of (a commodity). **4** to increase the price of.

marl (mɑːl) *n* **1** a fine-grained sedimentary rock consisting of clay minerals, calcium carbonate, and silt: used as a fertilizer. ◆ *vb* **2** (*tr*) to fertilize (land) with marl. ORIG C14: via OF, from LL *margila,* dim. of L *marga*
▸ **'marly** *adj*

Marlborough[1] ★ ('mɑːlbərə, -brə, 'mɔːl-) *n* a town in S England, in Wiltshire: besieged and captured by Royalists in the Civil War (1642); site of Marlborough College, a public school founded in 1843. Pop.: 6429 (1991).

Marlborough[2] ★ ('mɑːlbərə, -brə, 'mɔːl-) *n* **1st Duke of,** title of *John Churchill.* 1650–1722, English general; commander of British forces in the War of the Spanish Succession (1701–14).

Marley ★ ('mɑːlɪ) *n* **Bob,** full name *Robert Nesta Marley.* 1945–81, Jamaican reggae singer, guitarist, and songwriter.

marlin ('mɑːlɪn) *n, pl* **marlin** *or* **marlins.** any of several large food and game fishes of warm and tropical seas, having a very long upper jaw. ORIG C20: from MARLINESPIKE, from shape of the beak

marline *or* **marlin** ('mɑːlɪn) *n Naut.* a light rope, usually tarred, made of two strands laid left-handed. ORIG C15: from Du. *marlijn,* from *marren* to tie + *lijn* line

marlinespike *or* **marlinspike** ('mɑːlɪnˌspaɪk) *n Naut.* a pointed metal tool used in separating strands of rope, etc.

marlite ('mɑːlaɪt) *or* **marlstone** ('mɑːlˌstəʊn) *n* a type of marl that is resistant to the decomposing action of air.

Marlowe ★ ('mɑːləʊ) *n* **Christopher.** 1564–93, English dramatist. His plays include *Tamburlaine the Great* (1590) and *Dr Faustus* (1604). He was killed in a tavern brawl.

marmalade ('mɑːməˌleɪd) *n* a preserve made by boiling the pulp and rind of citrus fruits, esp. oranges, with sugar. ORIG C16: via F from Port. *marmelada,* from *marmelo* quince, from L, from Gk *melimēlon,* from *meli* honey + *mēlon* apple

Marmara *or* **Marmora** ★ ('mɑːmərə) *n* **Sea of.** a deep inland sea in NW Turkey, linked with the Black Sea by the Bosporus and with the Aegean by the Dardanelles: separates Turkey in Europe from Turkey in Asia. Area: 11 471 sq. km (4429 sq. miles). Ancient name: **Propontis.**

marmite ('mɑːmaɪt) *n* a large cooking pot. ORIG from F: pot

Marmite ('mɑːmaɪt) *n Trademark.* a yeast and vegetable extract used as a spread, flavouring, etc.

Marmolada ★ (*Italian* marmo'laːda) *n* a mountain in NE Italy: highest peak in the Dolomites. Height: 3342 m (10 965 ft).

marmoreal (mɑː'mɔːrɪəl) *adj* of, relating to, or resembling marble. ORIG C18: from L *marmoreus,* from *marmor* marble

marmoset ('mɑːməˌzɛt) *n* **1** any of various small South American monkeys having long hairy tails. **2 pygmy marmoset.** a related form: the smallest monkey, inhabiting tropical forests of the Amazon. ORIG C14: from OF *marmouset* grotesque figure, from ?

marmot ('mɑːmət) *n* **1** any of various burrowing rodents of Europe, Asia, and North America. They are heavily built and have coarse fur. **2 prairie marmot.** another name for **prairie dog.** ORIG C17: from F *marmotte,* ? ult. from L *mūr-* (stem of *mūs*) mouse + *montis* of the mountain

Marne ★ (*French* marn) *n* **1** a department of NE France, in Champagne-Ardenne region. Capital: Châlons-sur-Marne. Pop.: 566 222 (1994 est.). Area: 8205 sq. km (3200 sq. miles). **2** a river in NE France, rising on the plateau of Langres and flowing north, then west to the River Seine, north of Paris: linked by canal with the Rivers Saône, Rhine, and Aisne; scene of two unsuccessful German offensives (1914, 1918) during World War I. Length: 525 km (326 miles).

Maroc ★ (marɔk) *n* the French name for **Morocco.**

marocain ('mærəˌkeɪn) *n* **1** a fabric of ribbed crepe. **2** a garment made from this fabric. ORIG C20: from F *maroquin* Moroccan

maroon[1] (mə'ru:n) *vb* (*tr*) **1** to abandon ashore, esp. on an island. **2** to isolate without resources. ◆ *n* **3** a descendant of a group of runaway slaves living in the remoter areas of the Caribbean or Guyana. ORIG C17 (applied to fugitive slaves): from American Sp. *cimarrón* wild, lit.: dwelling on peaks, from Sp. *cima* summit

maroon[2] (mə'ru:n) *n* **1a** a dark red to purplish-red colour. **1b** (*as adj*): *a maroon carpet.* **2** an exploding firework, esp. one used as a warning signal. ORIG C18: from F, lit.: chestnut

Maros ★ ('mɔrɔʃ) *n* the Hungarian name for the **Mureş**.

Marprelate ★ ('mɑ:prɛlɪt) *n* **Martin,** the pen name of the anonymous author of a series of Puritan tracts (1588–89) attacking the bishops of the Church of England.

Marq. *abbrev. for:* **1** Marquess. **2** Marquis.

Marquand ★ (mɑ:'kwɒnd) *n* **J(ohn) P(hillips).** 1893–1960, US novelist, noted for his fictional Japanese detective Mr Moto and for his comedies, such as *The Late George Apley* (1937).

marque (mɑ:k) *n* **1** a brand of product, esp. of a car. **2** See **letter of marque.** ORIG from F, from *marquer* to MARK[1]

marquee (mɑ:'ki:) *n* **1** a large tent used for entertainment, exhibition, etc. **2** Also called: **marquise.** *Chiefly US & Canad.* a canopy over the entrance to a theatre, hotel, etc. ORIG C17 (orig. an officer's tent): invented sing form of MARQUISE, erroneously taken to be pl

Marquesas Islands ★ (mɑ:'keɪsæs) *pl n* a group of volcanic islands in the S Pacific, in French Polynesia. Pop.: 7538 (1988). Area: 1287 sq. km (497 sq. miles). French name: **Îles Marquises** (il markiz).

marquess ('mɑ:kwɪs) *n* **1** (in the British Isles) a nobleman ranking between a duke and an earl. **2** See **marquis.**

marquetry *or* **marqueterie** ('mɑ:kɪtrɪ) *n, pl* **marquetries** *or* **marqueteries.** a pattern of inlaid veneers of wood, brass, ivory, etc., used chiefly as ornamentation in furniture. ORIG C16: from OF, from *marqueter* to inlay, from *marque* MARK[1]

Marquette ★ (mɑ:'kɛt) *n* **Jacques** (ʒak), known as *Père Marquette.* 1637–75, French Jesuit missionary and explorer of the Mississippi river.

Márquez ★ (*Spanish* 'markeθ) *n* **Gabriel García.** See (Gabriel) **García Márquez.**

marquis ('mɑ:kwɪs, mɑ:'ki:) *n, pl* **marquises** *or* **marquis.** (in various countries) a nobleman ranking above a count, corresponding to a British marquess. The title of marquis is often used in place of that of marquess. ORIG C14: from OF *marchis,* lit.: count of the march, from *marche* MARCH[2]

Marquis ★ ('mɑ:kwɪs) *n* **Don(ald Robert Perry).** 1878–1937, US humorist; author of *archy and mehitabel* (1927).

marquise (mɑ:'ki:z) *n* **1** (in various countries) another word for **marchioness. 2a** a gemstone, esp. a diamond, cut in a pointed oval shape and usually faceted. **2b** a piece of jewellery, esp. a ring, set with such a stone or with an oval cluster of stones. **3** another name for **marquee** (sense 2). ORIG C18: from F, fem of MARQUIS

marquisette (ˌmɑ:kɪ'zɛt, -kwɪ-) *n* a leno-weave fabric of cotton, silk, etc. ORIG C20: from F, dim. of MARQUISE

Marrakech *or* **Marrakesh** ★ (mə'rækɛʃ, ˌmærə'kɛʃ) *n* a city in W central Morocco: several times capital of Morocco; tourist centre. Pop.: 621 914 (1994).

marram grass ('mærəm) *n* any of several grasses that grow on sandy shores: often planted to stabilize sand dunes. ORIG C17 *marram,* from ON *marálmr,* from *marr* sea + *hálmr* HAULM

marri ('mærɪ) *n* a species of eucalyptus of Western Australia, widely cultivated for its coloured flowers. ORIG C19: from Abor.

marriage ('mærɪdʒ) *n* **1** the state or relationship of being husband and wife. **2a** the legal union or contract made by a man and woman to live as husband and wife. **2b** (*as modifier*): *marriage certificate.* **3** the ceremony formalizing this union; wedding. **4** a close or intimate union, relationship, etc. ORIG C13: from OF; see MARRY[1], -AGE

marriageable ('mærɪdʒəb°l) *adj* (esp. of women) suitable for marriage, usually with reference to age.
▸ ˌ**marriagea'bility** *n*

marriage guidance *n* advice given to couples who have problems in their married life.

married ('mærɪd) *adj* **1** having a husband or wife. **2** joined in marriage. **3** of or involving marriage or married persons. **4** closely or intimately united. ◆ *n* **5** (*usually pl*) a married person (esp. in **young marrieds**).

Marriner ★ ('mærɪnə) *n* Sir **Neville.** born 1924, British conductor and violinist; founder (1956) and director of the Academy of St Martin in the Fields.

marrons glacés *French.* (marɔ̃ glase) *pl n* chestnuts cooked in syrup and glazed.

marrow ('mærəʊ) *n* **1** the fatty network of connective tissue that fills the cavities of bones. **2** the vital part; essence. **3** *Brit.* short for **vegetable marrow.** ORIG OE *mærg*
▸ '**marrowy** *adj*

marrowbone ('mærəʊˌbəʊn) *n* **a** a bone containing edible marrow. **b** (*as modifier*): *marrowbone jelly.*

marrowfat ('mærəʊˌfæt) *or* **marrow pea** *n* **1** any of several varieties of pea plant that have large seeds. **2** the seed of such a plant.

marry[1] ('mærɪ) *vb* **marries, marrying, married. 1** to take (someone as one's husband or wife) in marriage. **2** (*tr*) to join or give in marriage. **3** to unite closely or intimately. **4** (*tr; sometimes foll. by up*) to fit together or align (two things); join. **5** (*tr*) *Naut.* to match up (the strands of ropes) before splicing. ORIG C13: from OF *marier,* from L *marītāre,* from *marītus* married (man), ?from *mās* male

marry[2] ('mærɪ) *interj Arch.* an exclamation of surprise, anger, etc. ORIG C14: euphemistic for the Virgin *Mary*

Marryat ★ ('mærɪət) *n* **Frederick,** known as *Captain Marryat.* 1792–1848, British novelist and naval officer; author of novels of sea life, such as *Mr Midshipman Easy* (1836), and children's stories, such as *The Children of the New Forest* (1847).

marry off *vb* (*tr, adv*) to find a husband or wife for (a person, esp. one's son or daughter).

Mars[1] ★ (mɑ:z) *n* the Roman god of war.

Mars[2] ★ (mɑ:z) *n* the fourth planet from the sun.

Marsala ★ (mɑ:'sɑ:lə) *n* **1** a port in W Sicily: landing place of Garibaldi at the start of his Sicilian campaign (1860). Pop.: 80 760 (1990). **2** (*sometimes not caps.*) a dark sweet dessert wine made in Sicily.

Marsalis ★ (mɑ:'sɑ:lɪs) *n* **Wynton.** born 1962, US jazz and classical trumpeter.

Marseillaise (ˌmɑ:seɪ'jeɪz, -sə'leɪz) *n* **the.** the French national anthem. ORIG C18: from F (*chanson*) *marseillaise* song of Marseilles (first sung in Paris by the battalion of Marseilles)

marseille (mɑ:'seɪl) *or* **marseilles** (mɑ:'seɪlz) *n* a strong cotton fabric with a raised pattern, used for bedspreads, etc. ORIG C18: from *Marseille quilting,* made in Marseilles

Marseille ★ (*French* marsɛj) *n* a port in SE France, on the Gulf of Lions: second largest city in the country and a major port; founded in about 600 B.C. by Greeks from Phocaea; oil refining. Pop.: 807 726 (1990). Ancient name: **Mas'silia.** English name: **Marseilles** (mɑ:'seɪ, -'seɪlz).

marsh (mɑ:ʃ) *n* low poorly drained land that is sometimes flooded and often lies at the edge of lakes, etc. Cf. **swamp** (sense 1). ORIG OE *merisc*

Marsh ★ (mɑ:ʃ) *n* **1** Dame **(Edith) Ngaio** ('naɪəʊ). 1899–1981, New Zealand crime writer, living in Britain from 1928. Her novels include *Final Curtain* (1947) and *Last Ditch* (1977). **2 Rodney (William).** born 1947, Australian cricketer.

marshal ('mɑ:ʃəl) *n* **1** (in some armies and air forces) an officer of the highest rank. **2** (in England) an officer who accompanies a judge on circuit and performs secretarial duties. **3** (in the US) **3a** a Federal court officer assigned to a judicial district whose functions are similar to those of a sheriff. **3b** (in some states) the chief police or fire officer. **4** an officer who organizes or conducts ceremonies, parades, etc. **5** Also called: **knight marshal.** (formerly in England) an officer of the royal family or court, esp. one in charge of protocol. ◆ *vb* **marshals, marshalling, marshalled** *or US* **marshals, marshaling, marshaled.** (*tr*) **6** to arrange in order: *to marshal the facts.* **7** to assemble and

organize (troops, vehicles, etc.) prior to onward movement. **8** to guide or lead, esp. in a ceremonious way. **9** to combine (coats of arms) on one shield. ORIG C13: from OF *mareschal;* rel. to OHG *marahscalc,* from *marah* horse + *scalc* servant
▸ **'marshalcy** *or* **'marshalship** *n*

Marshall ★ ('mɑːʃəl) *n* **1 Alfred.** 1842–1924, British economist, author of *Principles of Economics* (1890). **2 George Catlett.** 1880–1959, US general and statesman; chief of staff of the US army (1939–45); as secretary of state (1947–49), he proposed the Marshall Plan (1947): Nobel peace prize 1953. **3 John.** 1755–1835, US jurist and statesman; chief justice of the Supreme Court (1801–35). **4 Sir John Ross.** 1912–88, New Zealand politician; prime minister (1972).

marshalling yard *n Railways.* a place or depot where railway wagons are shunted and made up into trains.

Marshall Islands ★ *pl n* a republic consisting of a group of 34 coral islands in the W central Pacific, in E Micronesia: formerly part of the Trust Territory of the Pacific Islands (1947–87); status of free association with the US from 1986; consists of two parallel chains, Ralik and Ratak. Official languages: Marshallese and English. Religion: Roman Catholic majority. Currency: US dollar. Capital: Majuro. Pop.: 65 400 (1999 est.). Area: (land) 181 sq. km (70 sq. miles); (lagoon) 11 655 sq. km (4500 sq. miles).

Marshal of the Royal Air Force *n* a rank in the Royal Air Force comparable to that of a field marshal in the army.

marsh fever *n* another name for **malaria.**

marsh gas *n* a hydrocarbon gas largely composed of methane formed when organic material decays in the absence of air.

marshmallow (ˌmɑːʃ'mæləʊ) *n* **1** a spongy sweet containing gum arabic or gelatine, sugar, etc. **2** a sweetened paste or confection made from the root of the marsh mallow.

marsh mallow *n* a malvaceous plant that grows in salt marshes and has pale pink flowers. The roots yield a mucilage formerly used to make marshmallows.

marsh marigold *n* a yellow-flowered plant that grows in swampy places.

marshy ('mɑːʃɪ) *adj* **marshier, marshiest.** of, involving, or like a marsh.
▸ **'marshiness** *n*

Marsilius of Padua ★ (mɑː'sɪlɪəs) *n* Italian name *Marsiglio dei Mainardini.* ?1290–?1343, Italian political philosopher, best known as the author of the *Defensor pacis* (1324), which upheld the power of the temporal ruler over that of the church.

Marston ★ ('mɑːstən) *n* **John.** ?1576–1634, English dramatist and satirist. His works include the revenge tragedies *Antonio and Mellida* (1602) and *Antonio's Revenge* (1602) and the satirical comedy *The Malcontent* (1604).

Marston Moor ★ *n* a flat low-lying area in NE England, west of York: scene of a battle (1644) in which the Parliamentarians defeated the Royalists.

marsupial (mɑː'sjuːpɪəl, -'suː-) *n* **1** any mammal of an order in which the young are born in an immature state and continue development in the marsupium. The order occurs mainly in Australia and South and Central America and includes the opossums and kangaroos. ◆ *adj* **2** of, relating to, or belonging to marsupials. **3** of or relating to a marsupium. ORIG C17: see MARSUPIUM

marsupium (mɑː'sjuːpɪəm, -'suː-) *n, pl* **marsupia** (-pɪə). an external pouch in most female marsupials within which the newly born offspring complete their development. ORIG C17: NL, from L: purse, from Gk, dim. of *marsipos*

mart (mɑːt) *n* a market or trading centre. ORIG C15: from MDu.: MARKET

Martaban ★ (ˌmɑːtɑː'bɑːn) *n* **Gulf of.** an inlet of the Bay of Bengal in Myanmar.

martagon *or* **martagon lily** ('mɑːtəgən) *n* a Eurasian lily plant cultivated for its mottled purplish-red flowers with reflexed petals. ORIG C15: from F, from Turkish *martağān* a type of turban

Martel ★ (mɑː'tɛl) *n* See **Charles Martel.**

Martello tower (mɑː'tɛləʊ) *n* a small circular tower for coastal defence. ORIG C18: after Cape *Mortella* in Corsica, where the British navy captured a tower of this type in 1794

marten ('mɑːtɪn) *n, pl* **martens** *or* **marten. 1** any of several agile arboreal mammals of Europe, Asia, and North America, having bushy tails and golden-brown to blackish fur. See also **pine marten. 2** the highly valued fur of these animals. ◆ See also **sable** (sense 1). ORIG C15: from MDu. *martren,* from OF *(peau) martrine* skin of a marten, from *martre,* prob. of Gmc origin

Martha ★ ('mɑːθə) *n* **Saint.** *New Testament.* a sister of Mary and Lazarus, who lived at Bethany and ministered to Jesus (Luke 10:38–42). Feast day: July 29 or June 4.

martial ('mɑːʃəl) *adj* of, relating to, or characteristic of war, soldiers, or the military life. ORIG C14: from L *martiālis* of MARS[1]
▸ **'martialism** *n* ▸ **'martialist** *n* ▸ **'martially** *adv*

Martial ★ ('mɑːʃəl) *n* full name *Marcus Valerius Martialis.* ?40–?104 A.D., Latin epigrammatist and poet, born in Spain.

martial art *n* any of various philosophies of self-defence and techniques of single combat, such as judo or karate, originating in the Far East.

martial law *n* rule of law maintained by the military in the absence of civil law.

Martian ('mɑːʃən) *adj* **1** of, occurring on, or relating to the planet Mars. ◆ *n* **2** an inhabitant of Mars, esp. in science fiction.

martin ('mɑːtɪn) *n* any of various birds of the swallow family, having a square or slightly forked tail. See also **house martin.** ORIG C15: ?from St MARTIN, because the birds were believed to migrate at the time of Martinmas

Martin ★ ('mɑːtɪn) *n* **1 Archer John Porter.** 1910–94, British biochemist; Nobel prize for chemistry 1952 for developing paper chromatography (1944). He subsequently developed gas chromatography (1953). **2** (*French* martɛ̃) **Frank** (frɑ̃k). 1890–1974, Swiss composer. Works include *Petite Symphonie Concertante* (1946) and the oratorio *Golgotha* (1949). **3 John.** 1789–1854, British painter. **4 Michael.** born 1945, British Labour politician; Speaker of the House of Commons from 2000. **5 Saint,** called *Saint Martin of Tours.* ?316–?397 A.D., bishop of Tours (?371–?397); a patron saint of France. Feast day: Nov. 11 or 12.

Martin du Gard ★ (*French* martɛ̃ dy gar) *n* **Roger** (rɔʒe). 1881–1958, French novelist, noted for his series of novels, *Les Thibault* (1922–40): Nobel prize for literature 1937.

martinet (ˌmɑːtɪ'nɛt) *n* a person who maintains strict discipline, esp. in a military force. ORIG C17: from F, from General *Martinet,* drillmaster under Louis XIV

martingale ('mɑːtɪnˌgeɪl) *n* **1** a strap from the reins to the girth of a horse, preventing it from carrying its head too high. **2** any gambling system in which the stakes are raised, usually doubled, after each loss. **3** *Naut.* a chain or cable running from a jib boom to the stern or stem. ORIG C16: from F, from ?

martini (mɑː'tiːnɪ) *n* **1** (*often cap.*) *Trademark.* an Italian vermouth. **2** a cocktail of gin and vermouth. ORIG C19 (sense 2): ?from the name of the inventor

Martini ★ (*Italian* mar'tiːni) *n* **Simone** (si'moːne). ?1284–1344, Sienese painter.

Martinique ★ (ˌmɑːtɪ'niːk) *n* an island in the E Caribbean, in the Windward Islands of the Lesser Antilles: administratively an overseas region of France. Capital: Fort-de-France. Pop.: 382 000 (1999 est.). Area: 1090 sq. km (420 sq. miles).
▸ **ˌMarti'nican** *n, adj*

Martinmas ('mɑːtɪnməs) *n* the feast of St Martin on Nov. 11; a quarter day in Scotland.

Martinů ★ ('mɑːtɪˌnuː; *Czech* 'martjinuː) *n* **Bohuslav** ('bɔhuslaf). 1890–1959, Czech composer.

martyr ('mɑːtə) *n* **1** a person who suffers death rather than renounce his or her religious beliefs. **2** a person who suffers greatly or dies for a cause, belief, etc. **3** a per-

son who suffers from poor health, misfortune, etc.: *a martyr to rheumatism.* ◆ *vb also* **ˈmartyrize** *or* **martyrise.** (*tr*) **4** to kill as a martyr. **5** to make a martyr of. ORIG OE *martir,* from Church L *martyr,* from LGk *martur-, martus* witness
▸ **ˈmartyrdom** *n* ▸ **ˌmartyriˈzation** *or* **ˌmartyriˈsation** *n*

martyrology (ˌmɑːtəˈrɒlədʒɪ) *n, pl* **martyrologies. 1** an official list of martyrs. **2** *Christianity.* the study of the lives of the martyrs. **3** a historical account of the lives of martyrs.
▸ **ˌmartyrˈologist** *n*

marvel (ˈmɑːvᵊl) *vb* **marvels, marvelling, marvelled** *or US* **marvels, marveling, marveled. 1** (when *intr,* often foll. by *at* or *about;* when *tr, takes a clause as object*) to be filled with surprise or wonder. ◆ *n* **2** something that causes wonder. **3** *Arch.* astonishment. ORIG C13: from OF *merveille,* from LL *mīrābilia,* from L *mīrābilis* from *mīrārī* to wonder at

Marvell ★ (ˈmɑːvᵊl) *n* **Andrew.** 1621–78, English poet, noted for his lyrical poems and satires attacking the government after the Restoration.

marvellous *or US* **marvelous** (ˈmɑːvᵊləs) *adj* **1** causing great wonder, surprise, etc.; extraordinary. **2** improbable or incredible. **3** excellent; splendid.
▸ **ˈmarvellously** *or US* **ˈmarvelously** *adv* ▸ **ˈmarvellousness** *or US* **ˈmarvelousness** *n*

marvel-of-Peru *n, pl* **marvels-of-Peru.** another name for **four-o'clock** (the plant). ORIG C16: first found in Peru

Marx ★ (mɑːks) *n* **Karl** (karl). 1818–83, German founder of modern communism, in Britain from 1849. With Engels, he wrote *The Communist Manifesto* (1848). Other works include *Das Kapital* (1867; 1885; 1895). He was a founder of the International Workingmen's Association (First International) (1864).
▸ **ˈMarxian** *adj*

Marx Brothers ★ (mɑːks) *n* **the.** a US family of film comedians, **Arthur Marx,** known as *Harpo* (1888–1964), **Herbert Marx,** known as *Zeppo* (1901–79), **Julius Marx,** known as *Groucho* (1890–1977), and **Leonard Marx,** known as *Chico* (1886–1961). Their films include *Animal Crackers* (1930), *Duck Soup* (1933), and *A Day at the Races* (1937).

Marxism (ˈmɑːksɪzəm) *n* the economic and political theory originated by Karl Marx and Friedrich Engels, holding that human institutions are economically determined, the class struggle is the agency of historical change, and communism will ultimately replace capitalism.
▸ **ˈMarxist** *n, adj*

Marxism-Leninism *n* the modification of Marxism by Lenin stressing that imperialism is the highest form of capitalism.
▸ **ˈMarxist-ˈLeninist** *n, adj*

Mary ★ (ˈmɛərɪ) *n* **1** *New Testament.* **1a Saint.** Also called: the **Virgin Mary.** the mother of Jesus, believed to have conceived and borne him while still a virgin; she was married to Joseph (Matthew 1:18–25). Major feast days: Feb. 2, Mar. 25, May 31, Aug. 15, Sept. 8. **1b** the sister of Martha and Lazarus (Luke 10:38–42, John 11:1–2). **2** original name *Princess Mary of Teck.* 1867–1953, queen of Great Britain and Northern Ireland (1910–36) by marriage to George V. **3** (*pl* **Maries**) *Austral. derog. sl.* an Aboriginal woman or girl.

Mary I ★ *n* family name *Tudor,* known as *Bloody Mary.* 1516–58, queen of England (1553–58). The daughter of Henry VIII and Catherine of Aragon, she married Philip II of Spain in 1554. She restored Roman Catholicism to England and about 300 Protestants were burnt at the stake.

Mary II ★ *n* 1662–94, queen of England, Scotland, and Ireland (1689–94), ruling jointly with her husband William III. They were offered the crown by parliament, which objected to the arbitrary rule of her father James II.

Maryland ★ (ˈmɛərɪˌlænd, ˈmɛrɪlənd) *n* a state of the eastern US, on the Atlantic: divided into two unequal parts by Chesapeake Bay: mostly low-lying, with the Alleghenies in the northwest. Capital: Annapolis. Pop.: 5 134 808 (1998 est.). Area: 31 864 sq. km (12 303 sq. miles). Abbrevs.: **Md.** or (with zip code) **MD**

Mary Magdalene ★ *n New Testament.* **Saint.** a woman of **Magdala** (ˈmægdələ) in Galilee whom Jesus cured of evil spirits (Luke 8:2) and who is often identified with the sinful woman of Luke 7:36–50. In Christian tradition she is usually taken to have been a prostitute. See **magdalen.** Feast day: July 22.

Mary, Queen of Scots ★ *n* family name *Stuart.* 1542–87, queen of Scotland (1542–67); daughter of James V of Scotland and Mary of Guise. She was married to Francis II of France (1558–60), her cousin Lord Darnley (1565–67), and the Earl of Bothwell (1567–71). Forced to abdicate in favour of her son (later James VI of Scotland), she fled to England. Imprisoned by Elizabeth I until 1587, she was beheaded for plotting against the English crown.

marzipan (ˈmɑːzɪˌpæn) *n* **1** a paste made from ground almonds, sugar, and egg whites, used to coat fruit cakes or moulded into sweets. **2** (*modifier*) *Inf.* of or relating to the stratum of middle managers in a financial institution or other business: *marzipan layer job losses.* ORIG C19: via G from It. *marzapane*

-mas *n combining form.* indicating a Christian festival: *Christmas; Michaelmas.* ORIG from MASS

Masaccio ★ (*Italian* maˈzattʃo) *n* original name *Tommaso Guidi.* 1401–28, Florentine painter, who first applied the laws of perspective discovered by Brunelleschi.

Masada ★ (məˈsɑːdə) *n* an ancient mountaintop fortress in Israel, 400 m (1300 ft) above the W shore of the Dead Sea: the last Jewish stronghold during a revolt in Judaea (66–73 A.D.). Besieged by the Romans for a year, almost all of the inhabitants killed themselves rather than surrender. The site is an Israeli national monument.

Masai (ˈmɑːsaɪ, mɑːˈsaɪ) *n* **1** (*pl* **Masais** *or* **Masai**) a member of a Nilotic people, formerly noted as warriors, living chiefly in Kenya and Tanzania. **2** the language of this people.

masala (mɑːˈsɑːlə) *n* a mixture of spices ground into a paste, used in Indian cookery. ORIG from Urdu *masalah,* from Ar. *masalih* ingredients

Masan ★ (ˈmɑːˌsɑːn) *n* a port in SE South Korea, on an inlet of the Korea Strait: first opened to foreign trade in 1899. Pop.: 441 358 (1995).

Masaryk ★ (ˈmæsərɪk; *Czech* ˈmasarik) *n* **1 Jan** (jan). 1886–1948, Czech statesman; foreign minister (1941–48). He died in mysterious circumstances after the Communist coup. **2** his father, **Tomáš Garrigue** (ˈtɔmaːʃ ˈgarik). 1850–1937, Czech statesman; a founder of Czechoslovakia (1918) and its first president (1918–35).

Masbate ★ (mæsˈbɑːtɪ) *n* **1** an island in the central Philippines, between Negros and SE Luzon: agricultural, with resources of gold, copper, and manganese. Pop.: 599 355 (1990). Area: 4045 sq. km (1562 sq. miles). **2** the capital of this island, a port in the northeast. Pop.: 54 000 (latest est.).

masc. *abbrev. for* masculine.

Mascagni ★ (*Italian* masˈkaɲɲi) *n* **Pietro** (ˈpjɛːtro). 1863–1945, Italian composer of operas, including *Cavalleria rusticana* (1890).

mascara (mæˈskɑːrə) *n* a cosmetic for darkening the eyelashes. ORIG C20: from Sp.: mask

Mascarene Islands ★ (ˌmæskəˈriːn) *pl n* a group of volcanic islands in the W Indian Ocean, east of Madagascar: consists of the islands of Réunion, Mauritius, and Rodrigues. French name: **Îles Mascareignes.**

mascarpone (ˌmæskəˈpəʊnɪ) *n* an Italian soft cream cheese. ORIG from It. from dialect *mascherpa* ricotta

mascon (ˈmæskɒn) *n* any of several lunar regions of high gravity. ORIG C20: from MAS(S) + CON(CENTRATION)

mascot (ˈmæskət) *n* a person, animal, or thing considered to bring good luck. ORIG C19: from F *mascotte,* from Provençal *mascotto* charm, from *masco* witch

masculine (ˈmæskjʊlɪn) *adj* **1** possessing qualities or characteristics considered typical of or appropriate to a man; manly. **2** unwomanly. **3** *Grammar.* denoting a gender of nouns that includes all kinds of referents as well as some male animate referents. **4** *Prosody.* denoting an ending consisting of a single stressed syllable. **5** *Prosody.*

denoting a rhyme between pairs of single final stressed syllables. ORIG C14: via F from L *masculīnus,* from *masculus* male, from *mās* a male
▸ **ˈmasculinely** *adv* ▸ **ˌmascuˈlinity** *n*

masculinize *or* **masculinise** (ˈmæskjulɪnˌaɪz) *vb* **masculinizes, masculinizing, masculinized** *or* **masculinises, masculinising, masculinised.** to make or become masculine, esp. to cause (a woman) to show male secondary characteristics as a result of taking steroids.
▸ **ˌmasculiniˈzation** *or* **ˌmasculiniˈsation** *n*

Masefield ★ (ˈmeɪsˌfiːld) *n* **John.** 1878–1967, British poet, novelist, and critic; poet laureate (1930–67).

maser (ˈmeɪzə) *n* a device for amplifying microwaves, working on the same principle as a laser. ORIG C20: *m(icrowave) a(mplification by) s(timulated) e(mission of) r(adiation)*

Maseru ★ (məˈsɛəruː) *n* the capital of Lesotho, in the northwest near the W border with South Africa; established as capital of Basutoland in 1869. Pop.: 297 000 (1995 est.).

mash (mæʃ) *n* **1** a soft pulpy mass or consistency. **2** *Agriculture.* a feed of bran, meal, or malt mixed with water and fed to horses, cattle, or poultry. **3** (esp. in brewing) a mixture of mashed malt grains and hot water, from which malt is extracted. **4** *Brit. inf.* mashed potatoes. ◆ *vb (tr)* **5** to beat or crush into a mash. **6** to steep (malt grains) in hot water in order to extract malt. **7** *Scot. & N English dialect.* to brew (tea). ORIG OE *mǣsc-* (in compound words)
▸ **mashed** *adj* ▸ **ˈmasher** *n*

Masharbrum *or* **Masherbrum** ★ (ˈmʌʃəˌbrum) *n* a mountain in N India, in N Kashmir in the Karakoram Range of the Himalayas. Height: 7822 m (25 660 ft).

Mashhad (mæʃˈhæd) *or* **Meshed** ★ *n* a city in NE Iran: the holy city of Shi'ite Muslims; carpet manufacturing. Pop.: 1 964 489 (1994 est.).

mashie *or* **mashy** (ˈmæʃɪ) *n, pl* **mashies.** *Golf.* (formerly) an iron for lofting shots, usually No. 5. ORIG C19: ?from F *massue* club, ult. from L *mateola* mallet

Masinissa *or* **Massinissa** ★ (ˌmæsɪˈnɪsə) *n* ?238–?149 B.C., king of Numidia (?210–149), who fought as an ally of Rome against Carthage in the Second Punic War.

mask (mɑːsk) *n* **1** any covering for the whole or a part of the face worn for amusement, protection, disguise, etc. **2** a fact, action, etc., that conceals something. **3** another name for **masquerade. 4** a likeness of a face or head, either sculpted or moulded, such as a death mask. **5** an image of a face worn by an actor, esp. in classical drama, in order to symbolize a character. **6** a variant spelling of **masque. 7** *Surgery.* a sterile gauze covering for the nose and mouth worn to minimize the spread of germs. **8** *Sport.* a protective covering for the face worn for fencing, ice hockey, etc. **9** a carving in the form of a face or head, used as an ornament. **10** a device placed over the nose and mouth to facilitate or prevent inhalation of a gas. **11** *Photog.* a shield of paper, paint, etc., placed over an area of unexposed photographic surface to stop light falling on it. **12** the face or head of an animal, such as a fox. **13** *Rare.* a person wearing a mask. ◆ *vb* **14** to cover with or put on a mask. **15** *(tr)* to conceal; disguise: *to mask an odour.* **16** *(tr)* to cover; protect. **17** *(tr) Photog.* to shield a particular area of (an unexposed photographic surface) to prevent or reduce the action of light there. ORIG C16: from It. *maschera,* ult. from Ar. *maskharah* clown, from *sakhira* mockery
▸ **masked** *adj* ▸ **ˈmasker** *n*

masked ball *n* a ball at which masks are worn.

masking tape *n* an adhesive tape used to protect surfaces surrounding an area to be painted.

maskinonge (ˈmæskəˌnɒndʒ) *n* another name for **muskellunge.**

masochism (ˈmæsəˌkɪzəm) *n* **1** *Psychiatry.* an abnormal condition in which pleasure, esp. sexual pleasure, is derived from pain or from humiliation, domination, etc., by another person. **2** a tendency to take pleasure from one's own suffering. Cf. **sadism.** ORIG C19: after Leopold von Sacher *Masoch* (1836–95), Austrian novelist, who described it
▸ **ˈmasochist** *n, adj* ▸ **ˌmasoˈchistic** *adj* ▸ **ˌmasoˈchistically** *adv*

mason (ˈmeɪsᵊn) *n* **1** a person skilled in building with stone. **2** a person who dresses stone. ◆ *vb* **3** *(tr)* to construct or strengthen with masonry. ORIG C13: from OF *masson,* of Frankish origin; ? rel. to OE *macian* to make

Mason (ˈmeɪsᵊn) *n* short for **Freemason.**

Mason-Dixon Line (-ˈdɪksən) *n* in the US, the state boundary between Maryland and Pennsylvania: surveyed between 1763 and 1767 by Charles Mason and Jeremiah Dixon; popularly regarded as the dividing line between North and South.

masonic (məˈsɒnɪk) *adj* **1** *(often cap.)* of or relating to Freemasons or Freemasonry. **2** of or relating to masons or masonry.
▸ **maˈsonically** *adv*

Masonite (ˈmeɪsənaɪt) *n Austral. trademark.* a kind of dark brown hardboard.

masonry (ˈmeɪsənrɪ) *n, pl* **masonries. 1** the craft of a mason. **2** work that is built by a mason; stonework or brickwork. **3** *(often cap.)* short for **Freemasonry.**

Masqat ★ (ˈmʌskət, -kæt) *n* a transliteration of the Arabic name for **Muscat.**

masque *or* **mask** (mɑːsk) *n* **1** a dramatic entertainment of the 16th to 17th centuries, consisting of pantomime, dancing, dialogue, and song. **2** the words and music for this. **3** short for **masquerade.** ORIG C16: var. of MASK

masquerade (ˌmæskəˈreɪd) *n* **1** a party or other gathering at which the guests wear masks and costumes. **2** the disguise worn at such a function. **3** a pretence or disguise. ◆ *vb* **masquerades, masquerading, masqueraded.** *(intr)* **4** to participate in a masquerade; disguise oneself. **5** to dissemble. ORIG C16: from Sp. *mascarada,* from *mascara* MASK
▸ **ˌmasquerˈader** *n*

mass (mæs) *n* **1** a large coherent body of matter without a definite shape. **2** a collection of the component parts of something. **3** a large amount or number, as of people. **4** the main part or majority. **5 in the mass.** in the main; collectively. **6** the size of a body; bulk. **7** *Physics.* a physical quantity expressing the amount of matter in a body. It is a measure of a body's resistance to changes in velocity (**inertial mass**) and also of the force experienced in a gravitational field (**gravitational mass**). **8** (in painting, drawing, etc.) an area of unified colour, shade, or intensity, usually denoting a solid form or plane. ◆ *(modifier)* **9** done or occurring on a large scale: *mass hysteria.* **10** consisting of a mass or large number, esp. of people: *a mass meeting.* ◆ *vb* **11** to form (people or things) or (of people or things) to join together into a mass. ◆ See also **masses.** ORIG C14: from OF *masse,* from L *massa* that which forms a lump, from Gk *maza* barley cake

Mass (mæs, mɑːs) *n* **1** (in the Roman Catholic Church and certain Protestant Churches) the celebration of the Eucharist. See also **High Mass, Low Mass. 2** a musical setting of those parts of the Eucharistic service sung by choir or congregation. ORIG OE *mæsse,* from Church L *missa,* ult. from L *mittere* to send away; ?from the concluding dismissal in the Roman Mass, *Ite, missa est* Go, it is the dismissal

Mass. *abbrev. for* Massachusetts.

Massa ★ (*Italian* ˈmassa) *n* a town in W Italy, in NW Tuscany. Pop.: 67 780 (1990).

Massachusetts ★ (ˌmæsəˈtʃuːsɪts) *n* a state of the northeastern US, on the Atlantic: a centre of resistance to English colonial policy during the War of American Independence; consists of a coastal plain rising to mountains in the west. Capital: Boston. Pop.: 6 147 132 (1998 est.). Area: 20 269 sq. km (7826 sq. miles). Abbrevs.: **Mass.** or (with zip code) **MA**

Massachusetts Bay ★ *n* an inlet of the Atlantic on the E coast of Massachusetts.

massacre (ˈmæsəkə) *n* **1** the wanton or savage killing of large numbers of people, as in battle. **2** *Inf.* an overwhelming defeat, as in a game. ◆ *vb* **massacres, massacring, massacred.** *(tr)* **3** to kill indiscriminately or in large numbers. **4** *Inf.* to defeat overwhelmingly. ORIG C16: from OF

massage (ˈmæsɑːʒ, -sɑːdʒ) *n* **1** the act of kneading, rubbing, etc., parts of the body to promote circulation, suppleness, or relaxation. ◆ *vb* **massages, massaging, massaged.** (*tr*) **2** to give a massage to. **3** to treat (stiffness, etc.) by a massage. **4** to manipulate (statistics, etc.) to produce a desired result; doctor. **5 massage (someone's) ego.** to boost (someone's) sense of self-esteem by flattery. ORIG C19: from F, from *masser* to rub

massasauga (ˌmæsəˈsɔːɡə) *n* a North American venomous snake that has a horny rattle at the end of the tail. ORIG C19: after the *Missisauga* River, Ontario, Canada, where it was first found

Massasoit ★ (ˈmæsəˌsɔɪt) *n* died 1661, Wampanoag Indian chief, who negotiated peace with the Pilgrim Fathers (1621).

Massawa *or* **Massaua** ★ (məˈsɑːwə) *n* a port in E central Eritrea, on the Red Sea: capital of the Italian colony of Eritrea from 1885 until 1900. Pop.: 40 000 (1992).

mass defect *n Physics.* the amount by which the mass of a particular nucleus is less than the total mass of its constituent particles.

massé *or* **massé shot** (ˈmæsɪ) *n Billiards.* a stroke made by hitting the cue ball off centre with the cue held nearly vertically, esp. so as to make the ball move in a curve. ORIG C19: from F, from *masser,* from *masse* sledgehammer, from OF *mace* MACE[1]

Masséna ★ (*French* masena) *n* **André** (ɑ̃dre), Prince d'Essling. 1758–1817, French marshal under Napoleon I: victories at Saorgio (1794), Loano (1795), Rivoli (1797), Zürich (1799), and Caldiero (1805): defeated by Wellington in the Peninsular War (1810–11).

Massenet ★ (ˈmæsəˌneɪ; *French* masnɛ) *n* **Jules Émile Frédéric** (ʒyl emil frederik). 1842–1912, French composer of operas, including *Manon* (1884), *Werther* (1892), and *Thaïs* (1894).

masses (ˈmæsɪz) *pl n* **1** (preceded by *the*) the body of common people. **2** (often foll. by *of*) *Inf., chiefly Brit.* great numbers or quantities: *masses of food.*

masseur (mæˈsɜː) *or* (*fem*) **masseuse** (mæˈsɜːz) *n* a person who gives massages, esp. as a profession. ORIG C19: from F *masser* to MASSAGE

Massey ★ (ˈmæsɪ) *n* **1 Raymond.** 1896–1983, Canadian stage and film actor. **2 Vincent.** 1887–1967, Canadian statesman: first Canadian governor general of Canada (1952–59). **3 William Ferguson.** 1856–1925, New Zealand statesman, born in Ireland: prime minister of New Zealand (1912–25).

massif (ˈmæsiːf) *n* a mass of rock or a series of connected masses forming a mountain range. ORIG C19: from F, noun use of *massif* MASSIVE

Massif Central ★ (*French* masif sɑ̃tral) *n* a mountainous plateau region of S central France, occupying about one sixth of the country: contains several extinct volcanic cones, notably Puy de Dôme, 1465 m (4806 ft). Highest point: Puy de Sancy, 1886 m (6188 ft). Area: about 85 000 sq. km (33 000 sq. miles).

Massine ★ (mɑːˈsiːn) *n* **Léonide** (leɔnid). 1896–1979, US ballet dancer and choreographer, born in Russia.

Massinger ★ (ˈmæsɪndʒə) *n* **Philip.** 1583–?1640, English dramatist, noted esp. for his comedy *A New Way to pay Old Debts* (1633).

Massinissa ★ (ˌmæsɪˈnɪsə) *n* a variant spelling of **Masinissa.**

massive (ˈmæsɪv) *adj* **1** (of objects) large in mass; bulky, heavy, and usually solid. **2** impressive or imposing. **3** relatively intensive or large; considerable: *a massive dose.* **4** *Geol.* **4a** (of igneous rocks) having no stratification, cleavage, etc.; homogeneous. **4b** (of sedimentary rocks) arranged in thick poorly defined strata. **5** *Mineralogy.* without obvious crystalline structure. ORIG C15: from F *massif,* from *masse* MASS
▸ **ˈmassively** *adv* ▸ **ˈmassiveness** *n*

mass-market *adj* of, for, or appealing to a large number of people; popular: *mass-market paperbacks.*

mass media *pl n* the means of communication that reach large numbers of people, such as television, newspapers, magazines, and radio.

mass noun *n* a noun that refers to an extended substance rather than to each of a set of objects, e.g., *water* as opposed to *lake.* In English when used indefinitely they are characteristically preceded by *some* rather than *a* or *an;* they do not have normal plural forms. Cf. **count noun.**

mass number *n* the total number of neutrons and protons in the nucleus of a particular atom.

mass observation *n* (*sometimes cap.*) *Chiefly Brit.* the study of the social habits of people through observation, interviews, etc.

mass-produce *vb* **mass-produces, mass-producing, mass-produced.** (*tr*) to manufacture (goods) to a standardized pattern on a large scale by means of extensive mechanization and division of labour.
▸ **ˌmass-proˈduced** *adj* ▸ **ˌmass-proˈducer** *n* ▸ **mass production** *n*

mass spectrometer *or* **spectroscope** *n* an instrument in which ions, produced from a sample, are separated by electric or magnetic fields according to their ratios of charge to mass. A record is produced (**mass spectrum**) of the types of ion present and their amounts.

mast[1] (mɑːst) *n* **1** *Naut.* any vertical spar for supporting sails, rigging, flags, etc., above the deck of a vessel. **2** any sturdy upright pole used as a support. **3 before the mast.** *Naut.* as an apprentice seaman. ◆ *vb* **4** (*tr*) *Naut.* to equip with a mast or masts. ORIG OE *mæst;* rel. to MDu. *mast* & L *mālus* pole

mast[2] (mɑːst) *n* the fruit of forest trees, such as beech, oak, etc., used as food for pigs. ORIG OE *mæst;* rel. to OHG *mast* food

mastaba *or* **mastabah** (ˈmæstəbə) *n* a mudbrick superstructure above tombs in ancient Egypt. ORIG from Ar.: bench

mast cell *n* any of a number of cells in connective tissue that release heparin, histamine, and serotonin during inflammation and allergic reactions.

mastectomy (mæˈstɛktəmɪ) *n, pl* **mastectomies.** the surgical removal of a breast.

master (ˈmɑːstə) *n* **1** the man in authority, such as the head of a household, the employer of servants, or the owner of slaves or animals. **2a** a person with exceptional skill at a certain thing. **2b** (*as modifier*): *a master thief.* **3** (*often cap.*) a great artist, esp. an anonymous but influential one. **4a** a person who has complete control of a situation, etc. **4b** an abstract thing regarded as having power or influence: *they regarded fate as the master of their lives.* **5a** a workman or craftsman fully qualified to practise his trade and to train others. **5b** (*as modifier*): *master carpenter.* **6a** an original copy, stencil, tape, etc., from which duplicates are made. **6b** (*as modifier*): *master copy.* **7** a player of a game, esp. chess or bridge, who has won a specified number of tournament games. **8** the principal of some colleges. **9** a highly regarded teacher or leader. **10** a graduate holding a master's degree. **11** the chief executive officer aboard a merchant ship. **12** a person presiding over a function, organization, or institution. **13** *Chiefly Brit.* a male teacher. **14** an officer of the Supreme Court of Judicature subordinate to a judge. **15** the superior person or side in a contest. **16** (*often cap.*) the heir apparent of a Scottish viscount or baron. ◆ (*modifier*) **17** overall or controlling: *master plan.* **18** designating a device or mechanism that controls others: *master switch.* **19** main; principal: *master bedroom.* ◆ *vb* (*tr*) **20** to become thoroughly proficient in. **21** to overcome; defeat. **22** to rule or control as master. ORIG OE *magister* teacher, from L

Master (ˈmɑːstə) *n* **1** a title of address for a boy. **2** a term of address, esp. as used by disciples addressing or referring to a religious teacher. **3** an archaic equivalent of **Mr.**

master aircrew *n* a warrant rank in the Royal Air Force, equal to but before a warrant officer.

master-at-arms *n, pl* **masters-at-arms.** the senior rating in a naval unit responsible for discipline and police duties.

master builder *n* **1** a person skilled in the design and construction of buildings, esp. before the foundation of the profession of architecture. **2** a self-employed builder who employs labour.

masterclass (ˈmɑːstəˌklɑːs) *n* a session of tuition by an expert, esp. a musician, for exceptional students, usually given in public or on television.

masterful (ˈmɑːstəful) *adj* **1** having or showing mastery. **2** fond of playing the master; imperious.
▸ **ˈmasterfully** *adv* ▸ **ˈmasterfulness** *n*

USAGE NOTE In current usage there is a lot of overlap between the meanings of *masterful* and *masterly*. According to some, the first should only be used where there is a connotation of power and domination, the second where the connotations are of great skill. Nevertheless, as the Bank of English shows, the majority of uses of *masterful* these days relate to the second meaning, as in *musically, it was a masterful display of the folk singer's art.* Anyone wishing to observe the distinction would use only *masterly* in the context just given, and *masterful* in contexts such as: *...his need to be masterful with women was extreme; Alec was so masterful that he surprised himself.*

master key *n* a key that opens all the locks of a set. Also called: **passkey**.

masterly (ˈmɑːstəlɪ) *adj* of the skill befitting a master.
▸ **ˈmasterliness** *n*

master mason *n* **1** see **master** (sense 5a). **2** a Freemason who has reached the rank of third degree.

mastermind (ˈmɑːstəˌmaɪnd) *vb* **1** (*tr*) to plan and direct (a complex undertaking). ◆ *n* **2** a person of great intelligence or executive talent, esp. one who directs an undertaking.

Master of Arts *n* a degree, usually postgraduate and in a nonscientific subject, or the holder of this degree. Abbrev.: **MA**.

master of ceremonies *n* a person who presides over a public ceremony, formal dinner, or entertainment, introducing the events, performers, etc.

Master of Science *n* a postgraduate degree, usually in science, or the holder of this degree. Abbrev.: **MSc**.

Master of the Rolls *n* (in England) a judge of the court of appeal: the senior civil judge in the country and the Keeper of the Records at the Public Record Office.

masterpiece (ˈmɑːstəˌpiːs) *or* (*less commonly*) **masterwork** (ˈmɑːstəˌwɜːk) *n* **1** an outstanding work or performance. **2** the most outstanding piece of work of a creative artist, craftsman, etc. ORIG C17: cf. Du. *meesterstuk*, G *Meisterstück*, a sample of work submitted to a guild by a craftsman in order to qualify for the rank of master

masterplan (ˈmɑːstəˌplæn) *n* a comprehensive, often long-term, strategy.

masterstroke (ˈmɑːstəˌstrəʊk) *n* an outstanding piece of strategy, skill, talent, etc.

mastery (ˈmɑːstərɪ) *n, pl* **masteries. 1** full command or understanding of a subject. **2** outstanding skill; expertise. **3** the power of command; control. **4** victory or superiority.

masthead (ˈmɑːstˌhɛd) *n* **1** *Naut.* the head of a mast. **2** the name of a newspaper or periodical, its proprietors, staff, etc., printed at the top of the front page. ◆ *vb* (*tr*) **3** to send (a sailor) to the masthead as a punishment. **4** to raise (a sail) to the masthead.

mastic (ˈmæstɪk) *n* **1** an aromatic resin obtained from the mastic tree and used as an astringent and to make varnishes and lacquers. **2 mastic tree.** a small Mediterranean evergreen tree that yields the resin mastic. **3** any of several putty-like substances used as a filler, adhesive, or seal in wood, plaster, or masonry. **4** a liquor flavoured with mastic gum. ORIG C14: via OF from LL *mastichum*, from L from Gk *mastikhē* resin used as chewing gum

masticate (ˈmæstɪˌkeɪt) *vb* **masticates, masticating, masticated. 1** to chew (food). **2** to reduce (materials such as rubber) to a pulp by crushing, grinding, or kneading. ORIG C17: from LL *masticāre*, from Gk *mastikhan* to grind the teeth
▸ **ˌmastiˈcation** *n* ▸ **ˈmastiˌcator** *n*

masticatory (ˈmæstɪkətərɪ, -trɪ) *adj* **1** of, relating to, or adapted to chewing. ◆ *n, pl* **masticatories. 2** a medicinal substance chewed to increase the secretion of saliva.

mastiff (ˈmæstɪf) *n* a breed of large powerful short-haired dog, usually fawn or brindled. ORIG C14: from OF, ult. from L *mansuētus* tame

mastitis (mæˈstaɪtɪs) *n* inflammation of a breast or an udder.

masto- *or before a vowel* **mast-** *combining form.* indicating the breast, mammary glands, or something resembling a breast or nipple: *mastodon; mastoid.* ORIG from Gk *mastos* breast

mastodon (ˈmæstəˌdɒn) *n* an extinct elephant-like mammal common in Pliocene times. ORIG C19: from NL, lit.: breast-tooth, referring to the nipple-shaped projections on the teeth

mastoid (ˈmæstɔɪd) *adj* **1** shaped like a nipple or breast. **2** designating or relating to a nipple-like process of the temporal bone behind the ear. ◆ *n* **3** the mastoid process. **4** *Inf.* mastoiditis.

mastoiditis (ˌmæstɔɪˈdaɪtɪs) *n* inflammation of the mastoid process.

Mastroianni ★ (ˌmæstrɔɪˈjɑːnɪ) *n* **Marcello** (mɑːˈtʃɛləʊ). 1924–96, Italian film actor; his films include *Le Notti Bianche* (1957), *La Dolce Vita* (1960), and *Prêt à Porter* (1995).

masturbate (ˈmæstəˌbeɪt) *vb* **masturbates, masturbating, masturbated.** to stimulate the genital organs of (oneself or another) to achieve sexual pleasure. ORIG C19: from L *masturbārī*, from ?; formerly thought to be derived from *manus* hand + *stuprāre* to defile
▸ **ˌmasturˈbation** *n* ▸ **ˈmasturˌbator** *n* ▸ **masturbatory** (ˈmæstəˌbeɪtərɪ) *adj*

Masuria ★ (məˈsjʊərɪə) *n* a region of NE Poland: until 1945 part of East Prussia: includes the **Masurian Lakes,** scene of Russian defeats by the Germans (1914, 1915) during World War I.
▸ **Maˈsurian** *adj, n*

mat[1] (mæt) *n* **1** a thick flat piece of fabric used as a floor covering, a place to wipe one's shoes, etc. **2** a smaller pad of material used to protect a surface from the heat, scratches, etc., of an object placed upon it. **3** a large piece of thick padded material put on the floor as a surface for wrestling, judo, etc. **4** any surface or mass that is densely interwoven or tangled: *a mat of weeds.* ◆ *vb* **mats, matting, matted. 5** to tangle or weave or become tangled or woven into a dense mass. **6** (*tr*) to cover with a mat or mats. ORIG OE *matte*

mat[2] (mæt) *n* **1** a border of cardboard, cloth, etc., placed around a picture as a frame or between picture and frame. ◆ *adj* **2** having a dull, lustreless, or roughened surface. ◆ *vb* **mats, matting, matted.** (*tr*) **3** to furnish (a picture) with a mat. **4** to give (a surface) a mat finish. ◆ Also (for senses 2 & 4): **matt.** ORIG C17: from F, lit.: dead

mat[3] (mæt) *n Printing, inf.* short for **matrix** (senses 4 and 5).

mat. *abbrev. for* matinée.

Matabeleland ★ (ˌmætəˈbiːlɪˌlænd, -ˈbɛlɪ-) *n* a region of W Zimbabwe, between the Rivers Limpopo and Zambezi: rich gold deposits. Chief town: Bulawayo. Area: 181 605 sq. km (70 118 sq. miles).

Matadi ★ (məˈtɑːdɪ) *n* the chief port of the Democratic Republic of Congo, in the west at the mouth of the River Congo. Pop.: 172 730 (1994 est.).

matador (ˈmætədɔː) *n* **1** the principal bullfighter who kills the bull. **2** (in some card games) one of the highest cards. **3** a game played with dominoes in which the dots on adjacent halves must total seven. ORIG C17: from Sp., from *matar* to kill

matagouri (ˌmætəˈguːrɪ) *n* a New Zealand thorny bush which forms thickets in open country. Also called: **wild Irishman.** ORIG from Maori *tumatakuru*

Mata Hari ★ (ˈmɑːtə ˈhɑːrɪ) *n* real name *Gertrud Margarete Zelle.* 1876–1917, Dutch dancer in France; executed as a German spy in World War I.

matai (ˈmɑːtaɪ) *n* a New Zealand tree, the black pine, the wood of which is used as building timber. Also called: **black pine.** ORIG from Maori

Matamoros ★ (ˌmætə'mɔːrəs; *Spanish* mata'morɔs) *n* a port in NE Mexico, on the Río Grande: scene of bitter fighting during the US-Mexican War; centre of a cotton-growing area. Pop.: 266 055 (1990).

Matanzas ★ (mə'tænzəs; *Spanish* ma'tanθas) *n* a port in W central Cuba: founded in 1693 and developed into the second city of Cuba in the mid-19th century; exports chiefly sugar. Pop.: 123 843 (1994 est.).

Matapan ★ ('mætəˌpæn, ˌmætə'pæn) *n* **Cape.** a cape in S Greece, at the S central tip of the Peloponnese: the southern point of the mainland of Greece. Modern Greek name: **Taínaron.**

match[1] (mætʃ) *n* **1** a formal game or sports event in which people, teams, etc., compete. **2** a person or thing able to provide competition for another: *she's met her match.* **3** a person or thing that resembles, harmonizes with, or is equivalent to another in a specified respect. **4** a person or thing that is an exact copy or equal of another. **5a** a partnership between a man and a woman, as in marriage. **5b** an arrangement for such a partnership. **6** a person regarded as a possible partner, as in marriage. ◆ *vb* (*mainly tr*) **7** to fit (parts) together. **8** (*also intr;* sometimes foll. by *up*) to resemble, harmonize with, or equal (one another or something else). **9** (sometimes foll. by *with* or *against*) to compare in order to determine which is the superior. **10** (often foll. by *to* or *with*) to adapt so as to correspond with: *to match hope with reality.* **11** (often foll. by *with* or *against*) to arrange a competition between. **12** to find a match for. **13** *Electronics.* to connect (two circuits) so that their impedances are equal, to produce a maximum transfer of energy. ORIG OE *gemæcca* spouse
▸ **'matchable** *adj* ▸ **'matching** *adj*

match[2] (mætʃ) *n* **1** a thin strip of wood or cardboard tipped with a chemical that ignites by friction on a rough surface or a surface coated with a suitable chemical (see **safety match**). **2** a length of cord or wick impregnated with a chemical so that it burns slowly. It is used to fire cannons, explosives, etc. ORIG C14: from OF *meiche,* ?from L *myxa* wick, from Gk *muxa* lamp nozzle

matchboard ('mætʃˌbɔːd) *n* a long flimsy board tongued and grooved for lining work.

matchbox ('mætʃˌbɒks) *n* a small box for holding matches.

match-fit *adj Sport.* in good physical condition for competing in a match.

matchless ('mætʃlɪs) *adj* unequalled; incomparable; peerless.
▸ **'matchlessly** *adv*

matchlock ('mætʃˌlɒk) *n* **1** an obsolete type of gunlock igniting the powder by means of a slow match. **2** a gun having such a lock.

matchmaker ('mætʃˌmeɪkə) *n* **1** a person who brings together suitable partners for marriage. **2** a person who arranges competitive matches.
▸ **'matchˌmaking** *n, adj*

match play *n Golf.* scoring according to the number of holes won and lost. Cf. **Stableford, stroke play.**
▸ **match player** *n*

match point *n* **1** *Tennis, squash, etc.* the final point needed to win a match. **2** *Bridge.* the unit used for scoring in tournaments.

matchstick ('mætʃˌstɪk) *n* **1** the wooden part of a match. ◆ *adj* **2** made with or as if with matchsticks. **3** (esp. of drawn figures) thin and straight: *matchstick men.*

matchwood ('mætʃˌwʊd) *n* **1** wood suitable for making matches. **2** splinters or fragments.

mate[1] (meɪt) *n* **1** the sexual partner of an animal. **2** a marriage partner. **3a** *Inf., chiefly Brit., Austral. & NZ.* a friend, usually of the same sex: often used to any male in direct address. **3b** (*in combination*) an associate, colleague, fellow sharer, etc.: *a classmate.* **4** one of a pair of matching items. **5** *Naut.* **5a** short for **first mate. 5b** any officer below the master on a commercial ship. **6** (in some trades) an assistant: *a plumber's mate.* ◆ *vb* **mates, mating, mated. 7** to pair (a male and female animal) or (of animals) to pair for reproduction. **8** to marry or join in marriage. **9** (*tr*) to join as a pair. ORIG C14: from MLow G; rel. to OE *gemetta* table-guest, from *mete* MEAT

mate[2] (meɪt) *n, vb* **mates, mating, mated.** *Chess.* See **checkmate.**

maté *or* **mate** ('mɑːteɪ) *n* **1** an evergreen tree cultivated in South America for its leaves, which contain caffeine. **2** a stimulating milky beverage made from the dried leaves of this tree. ◆ Also called: **Paraguay tea, yerba, yerba maté.** ORIG C18: from American Sp. (orig. referring to the vessel in which the drink was brewed), from Quechua *máti* gourd

matelot, matlo, *or* **matlow** ('mætləʊ) *n Sl., chiefly Brit.* a sailor. ORIG C20: from F

mater ('meɪtə) *n Brit. sl.* a word for **mother**[1]: often used facetiously. ORIG C16: from L

material (mə'tɪərɪəl) *n* **1** the substance of which a thing is made or composed; component or constituent matter. **2** facts, notes, etc., that a finished work may be based on or derived from. **3** cloth or fabric. **4** a person who has qualities suitable for a given occupation, training, etc.: *that boy is university material.* ◆ *adj* **5** of, relating to, or composed of physical substance: *material possessions.* **6** of, relating to, or affecting economic or physical wellbeing: *material ease.* **7** of or concerned with physical rather than spiritual interests. **8** of great import or consequence: *material benefit.* **9** (often foll. by *to*) relevant. **10** *Philosophy.* of or relating to matter as opposed to form. ◆ See also **materials.** ORIG C14: via F from LL *māteriālis,* from L *māteria* MATTER
▸ **maˌteri'ality** *n*

material implication *n Logic.* a form of implication in which the proposition "if A then B" is true except when A is true and B is false.

materialism (mə'tɪərɪəˌlɪzəm) *n* **1** interest in and desire for money, possessions, etc., rather than spiritual or ethical values. **2** *Philosophy.* the doctrine that matter is the only reality and that the mind, the emotions, etc., are merely functions of it. Cf. **idealism, dualism. 3** *Ethics.* the rejection of any religious or supernatural account of things.
▸ **ma'terialist** *n* ▸ **maˌterial'istic** *adj* ▸ **maˌterial'istically** *adv*

materialize *or* **materialise** (mə'tɪərɪəˌlaɪz) *vb* **materializes, materializing, materialized** *or* **materialises, materialising, materialised. 1** (*intr*) to become fact; actually happen. **2** to invest or become invested with a physical shape or form. **3** to cause (a spirit, as of a dead person) to appear in material form or (of a spirit) to appear in such form. **4** (*intr*) to take shape; become tangible.
▸ **maˌteriali'zation** *or* **maˌteriali'sation** *n* ▸ **ma'terialˌizer** *or* **ma'terialˌiser** *n*

materially (mə'tɪərɪəlɪ) *adv* **1** to a significant extent; considerably. **2** with respect to material objects. **3** *Philosophy.* with respect to substance as distinct from form.

materials (mə'tɪərɪəlz) *pl n* the equipment necessary for a particular activity.

materia medica (mə'tɪərɪə 'mɛdɪkə) *n* **1** the branch of medical science concerned with the study of drugs used in the treatment of disease. **2** the drugs used in the treatment of disease. ORIG C17: from Med. L: medical matter

materiel *or* **matériel** (məˌtɪərɪ'ɛl) *n* the materials and equipment of an organization, esp. of a military force. ORIG C19: from F: MATERIAL

maternal (mə'tɜːnᵊl) *adj* **1** of, relating to, or characteristic of a mother. **2** related through the mother's side of the family: *his maternal uncle.* ORIG C15: from Med. L *māternālis,* from L *māternus,* from *māter* mother
▸ **ma'ternalism** *n* ▸ **maˌternal'istic** *adj* ▸ **ma'ternally** *adv*

maternity (mə'tɜːnɪtɪ) *n* **1** motherhood. **2** the characteristics associated with motherhood; motherliness. **3** (*modifier*) relating to pregnant women or women at the time of childbirth: *a maternity ward.*

mateship ('meɪtʃɪp) *n Austral.* friendly egalitarian comradeship.

mate's rates *pl n NZ inf.* discounted or preferential rates of payment offered to a friend or colleague: *he got the job done cheaply by a plumber friend at mate's rates.*

matey *or* **maty** ('meɪtɪ) *Brit. inf.* ◆ *adj* **1** friendly or intimate. ◆ *n* **2** friend or fellow: usually used in direct address.
▸ **'mateyness** *or* **'matiness** *n*

math (mæθ) *n US & Canad. inf.* short for **mathematics.** Brit. equivalent: **maths.**

mathematical (ˌmæθə'mætɪkᵊl) *or* **mathematic** *adj* **1** of, used in, or relating to mathematics. **2** characterized by or using the precision of mathematics. **3** using, determined by, or in accordance with the principles of mathematics.
▸ **ˌmathe'matically** *adv*

mathematical logic *n* symbolic logic, esp. when concerned with the foundations of mathematics.

mathematician (ˌmæθəmə'tɪʃən) *n* an expert or specialist in mathematics.

mathematics (ˌmæθə'mætɪks) *n* **1** (*functioning as sing*) a group of related sciences, including algebra, geometry, and calculus, concerned with the study of number, quantity, shape, and space and their interrelationships by using a specialized notation. **2** (*functioning as sing or pl*) mathematical operations and processes involved in the solution of a problem or study of some scientific field. ORIG C14 *mathematik* (n), via L from Gk (adj), from *mathēma* a science; rel. to *manthanein* to learn

maths (mæθs) *n* (*functioning as sing*) *Brit. inf.* short for **mathematics.** US and Canad. equivalent: **math.**

Mathura ★ ('mʌtʊərə, mʌ'θʊərə) *n* a city in N India, in W Uttar Pradesh on the Jumna River: a place of Hindu pilgrimage, revered as the birthplace of Krishna. Pop.: 226 691 (1991). Former name: **Muttra.**

Matilda[1] (mə'tɪldə) *n Austral. inf.* **1** a bushman's swag. **2 waltz Matilda.** to travel as a bushman carrying one's swag. ORIG C20: from the Christian name

Matilda[2] ★ (mə'tɪldə) *n* known as *the Empress Maud.* 1102–67, wife of Geoffrey of Anjou. After the death (1135) of her father, Henry I of England, she unsuccessfully waged war with Stephen for the English throne; her son succeeded as Henry II.

matin, mattin ('mætɪn), *or* **matinal** *adj* of or relating to matins. ORIG C14: see MATINS

matinée ('mætɪˌneɪ) *n* a daytime, esp. afternoon, performance of a play, concert, etc. ORIG C19: from F; see MATINS

matinée coat *or* **jacket** *n* a short coat for a baby.

matins *or* **mattins** ('mætɪnz) *n* (*functioning as sing or pl*) **1a** *Chiefly RC Church.* the first of the seven canonical hours of prayer. **1b** the service of morning prayer in the Church of England. **2** *Literary.* a morning song, esp. of birds. ORIG C13: from OF, ult. from L *mātūtīnus* of the morning, from *Mātūta* goddess of dawn

Matisse ★ (*French* matis) *n* **Henri** (ɑ̃ri). 1869–1954, French painter and sculptor; leader of Fauvism.

matlo *or* **matlow** ('mætləʊ) *n* variant spellings of **matelot.**

Matlock ★ ('mætˌlɒk) *n* a town in N England, on the River Derwent, administrative centre of Derbyshire: mineral springs. Pop.: 14 680 (1991).

Mato Grosso *or* **Matto Grosso** ★ ('mætəʊ 'grɒsəʊ; *Portuguese* 'matu 'grosu) *n* **1** a high plateau of SW Brazil: forms the watershed separating the Amazon and Plata river systems. **2** a state of W central Brazil: mostly on the Mato Grosso Plateau, with the Amazon basin to the north; valuable mineral resources. Capital: Cuiabá. Pop.: 2 235 832 (1996). Area: 881 001 sq. km (340 083 sq. miles).

Mato Grosso do Sul ★ ('du: sul) *n* a state of W central Brazil: formed in 1979 from part of Mato Grosso state. Capital: Campo Grande. Pop.: 1 927 834 (1996). Area: 350 548 sq. km (135 318 sq. miles).

Matopo Hills (mə'təʊpə) *or* **Matopos** ★ *pl n* the granite hills south of Bulawayo, Zimbabwe, where Cecil Rhodes chose to be buried.

Matozinhos ★ (*Portuguese* mətu'ziɲuʃ) *n* a port in N Portugal, on the estuary of the Leça River north of Oporto: fishing industry. Pop.: 26 500 (latest est.).

matrass ('mætrəs) *n Chem., obs.* a long-necked glass flask, used for distilling, dissolving substances, etc. ORIG C17: from F, ? rel. to L *mētiri* to measure

matri- *combining form.* mother or motherhood: *matriarchy.* ORIG from L *māter* mother

matriarch ('meɪtrɪˌɑ:k) *n* **1** a woman who dominates an organization, community, etc. **2** the female head of a tribe or family. **3** a very old or venerable woman. ORIG C17: from MATRI- + -ARCH, by false analogy with PATRIARCH
▸ **'matriˌarchal** *or* **'matriˌarchic** *adj*

matriarchy ('meɪtrɪˌɑ:kɪ) *n, pl* **matriarchies. 1** a form of social organization in which a female is head of the family or society, and descent and kinship are traced through the female line. **2** any society dominated by women.

matric (mə'trɪk) *n Brit.* short for **matriculation** (see **matriculate**).

matrices ('meɪtrɪˌsi:z, 'mæ-) *n* a plural of **matrix.**

matricide ('mætrɪˌsaɪd, 'meɪ-) *n* **1** the act of killing one's own mother. **2** a person who kills his or her mother. ORIG C16: from L *mātrīcīdium* (the act), *mātrīcīda* (the agent). See MATRI-, -CIDE
▸ **ˌmatri'cidal** *adj*

matriculate (mə'trɪkjʊˌleɪt) *vb* **matriculates, matriculating, matriculated. 1** to enrol or be enrolled in an institution, esp. a college or university. **2** (*intr*) to attain the academic standard required for a course at such an institution. ORIG C16: from Med. L *mātrīculāre* to register, from *mātrīcula,* dim. of *matrix* list
▸ **maˌtricu'lation** *n*

matrilineal (ˌmætrɪ'lɪnɪəl, ˌmeɪ-) *adj* relating to descent or kinship through the female line.

matrimony ('mætrɪmənɪ) *n, pl* **matrimonies. 1** the state or condition of being married. **2** the ceremony of marriage. **3a** a card game in which the king and queen together are a winning combination. **3b** such a combination. ORIG C14: via Norman F from L *mātrimōnium* wedlock, from *māter* mother
▸ **ˌmatri'monial** *adj*

matrix ('meɪtrɪks, 'mæ-) *n, pl* **matrices** *or* **matrixes. 1** a substance, situation, or environment in which something has its origin, takes form, or is enclosed. **2** the intercellular substance of bone, cartilage, connective tissue, etc. **3** the rock in which fossils, pebbles, etc., are embedded. **4** *Printing.* **4a** a metal mould for casting type. **4b** a papier-mâché or plastic mould impressed from the forme and used for stereotyping. **5** a mould used in the production of gramophone records. **6** a bed of perforated material placed beneath a workpiece in a press or stamping machine against which the punch operates. **7** *Maths.* a rectangular array of elements set out in rows and columns, used to facilitate the solution of problems, such as transformation of coordinates. **8** *Obs.* the womb. ORIG C16: from L: womb, female animal used for breeding, from *māter* mother

matron ('meɪtrən) *n* **1** a married woman regarded as staid or dignified. **2** a woman in charge of the domestic or medical arrangements in an institution. **3** *US.* a wardress in a prison. **4** *Brit.* the administrative head of the nursing staff in a hospital. Official name: **nursing officer.** ORIG C14: via OF from L *mātrōna,* from *māter* mother
▸ **'matronal** *or* **'matronly** *adj* ▸ **'matronˌhood** *or* **'matronship** *n*

matron of honour *n, pl* **matrons of honour.** a married woman serving as chief attendant to a bride.

Matsu *or* **Mazu** ★ (mæt'su:) *n* an island group in Formosa Strait, off the SE coast of mainland China: belongs to Taiwan. Pop.: 3145 (1990 est.). Area: 44 sq. km (17 sq. miles).

Matsuo Basho ★ (mɑ:'tsu:əʊ bɑ:'ʃɔ:) *n* See **Basho.**

Matsuyama ★ (ˌmætsʊ'jɑ:mə) *n* a port in SW Japan, on NW Shikoku: textile and chemical industries; Ehime University (1949). Pop.: 460 870 (1995).

matt *or* **matte** (mæt) *adj, vb* **matts, matting, matted** *or* **mattes, matting, matted.** variant spellings of **mat**[2] (senses 2 & 4).

Matt. *Bible. abbrev. for* Matthew.

mattamore ('mætəˌmɔ:) *n* a subterranean storehouse or

★ people and places

dwelling. ORIG C17: from F, from Ar. *matmurā,* from *tamara* to store, bury

matted ('mætɪd) *adj* **1** tangled into a thick mass. **2** covered with or formed of matting.

matter ('mætə) *n* **1** that which makes up something, esp. a physical object; material. **2** substance that occupies space and has mass, as distinguished from substance that is mental, spiritual, etc. **3** substance of a specified type: *vegetable matter.* **4** (sometimes foll. by *of* or *for*) thing; affair; concern; question: *a matter of taste.* **5** a quantity or amount: *a matter of a few pence.* **6** the content of written or verbal material as distinct from its style or form. **7** (*used with a negative*) importance; consequence. **8** *Philosophy.* (in the writings of Aristotle and the Scholastics) that which is itself formless but can receive form and become substance. **9** *Philosophy.* (in the Cartesian tradition) one of two basic modes of existence, the other being mind. **10** *Printing.* **10a** type set up. **10b** copy to be set in type. **11** a secretion or discharge, such as pus. **12** *Law.* **12a** something to be proved. **12b** statements or allegations to be considered by a court. **13 for that matter.** as regards that. **14 no matter. 14a** regardless of; irrespective of: *no matter what the excuse, you must not be late.* **14b** (*sentence substitute*) it is unimportant. **15 the matter.** wrong; the trouble: *there's nothing the matter.* ◆ *vb* (*intr*) **16** to be of consequence or importance. **17** to form and discharge pus. ORIG C13 (n), C16 (vb): from L *māteria* cause, substance, esp. wood, or a substance that produces something else

Matterhorn ★ ('mætəˌhɔːn) *n* a mountain on the border between Italy and Switzerland, in the Pennine Alps. Height: 4477 m (14 688 ft). French name: **Mont Cervin.** Italian name: **Monte Cervino** ('monte tʃer'viːno).

matter of course *n* **1** an event or result that is natural or inevitable. ◆ *adj* **matter-of-course. 2** (*usually postpositive*) occurring as a matter of course. **3** accepting things as inevitable or natural: *a matter-of-course attitude.*

matter of fact *n* **1** a fact that is undeniably true. **2** *Law.* a statement of facts the truth of which the court must determine on the basis of the evidence before it. **3 as a matter of fact.** actually; in fact. ◆ *adj* **matter-of-fact. 4** unimaginative or emotionless: *he gave a matter-of-fact account of the murder.*

Matthew ★ ('mæθjuː) *n New Testament.* **1** Also called: **Levi.** a tax collector of Capernaum called by Christ to be one of the 12 apostles (Matthew 9:9–13; 10:3). Feast day: Sept. 12 or Nov. 16. **2** the first Gospel, traditionally ascribed to him.

Matthew Paris ★ *n* See (Matthew) **Paris**[2] (sense 2).

Matthews ★ ('mæθjuːz) *n* Sir **Stanley.** 1915–2000, English footballer.

Matthias ★ (mə'θaɪəs) *n New Testament.* the disciple chosen by lot to replace Judas as one of the 12 apostles (Acts 1:15–26).

Matthias I Corvinus ★ (kɔː'vaɪnəs) *n* ?1440–90, king of Hungary (1458–90): a patron of Renaissance art, he founded the Corvina library. Hungarian name: **Mátyás Hollós** ('maːtjaːʃ 'hɔloʃ).

matting[1] ('mætɪŋ) *n* **1** a coarsely woven fabric, usually made of a natural fibre such as straw or hemp and used as a floor covering, packing material, etc. **2** the act or process of making mats. **3** material for mats.

matting[2] ('mætɪŋ) *n* **1** another word for **mat**[2] (sense 1). **2** the process of producing a mat finish.

mattins ('mætɪnz) *n* a variant spelling of **matins.**

mattock ('mætək) *n* a type of large pick that has one end of its blade shaped like an adze, used for loosening soil, cutting roots, etc. ORIG OE *mattuc,* from ?; rel. to L *mateola* club, mallet

Matto Grosso ★ ('mætəʊ 'grɒsəʊ) *n* a variant spelling of **Mato Grosso.**

mattress ('mætrɪs) *n* **1** a large flat pad with a strong cover, filled with straw, foam rubber, etc., and often incorporating coiled springs, used as a bed or as part of a bed. **2** a woven mat of brushwood, poles, etc., used to protect an embankment, dyke, etc., from scour. **3** a concrete or steel raft or slab used as a foundation or footing. ORIG C13: via OF from It. *materasso,* from Ar. *almatrah* place where something is thrown

maturate ('mætjʊˌreɪt, 'mætʃʊ-) *vb* **maturates, maturating, maturated. 1** to mature or bring to maturity. **2** a less common word for **suppurate.**
▸ ˌ**matu'ration** *n* ▸ **maturative** (mə'tjʊərətɪv, mə'tʃʊə-) *adj*

mature (mə'tjʊə, -'tʃʊə) *adj* **1** relatively advanced physically, mentally, etc.; grown-up. **2** (of plans, theories, etc.) fully considered; perfected. **3** due or payable: *a mature debenture.* **4** *Biol.* **4a** fully developed or differentiated: *a mature cell.* **4b** fully grown; adult: *a mature animal.* **5** (of fruit, wine, cheese, etc.) ripe or fully aged. ◆ *vb* **matures, maturing, matured. 6** to make or become mature. **7** (*intr*) (of notes, bonds, etc.) to become due for payment or repayment. ORIG C15: from L *mātūrus* early, developed
▸ **ma'turely** *adv* ▸ **ma'tureness** *n*

mature student *n* a student at a college or university who has passed the usual age for formal education.

maturity (mə'tjʊərɪtɪ, -'tʃʊə-) *n* **1** the state or quality of being mature; full development. **2** *Finance.* **2a** the date upon which a bond, note, etc., becomes due for repayment. **2b** the state of a bill, note, etc., when due.

matutinal (ˌmætjʊ'taɪnᵊl) *adj* of, occurring in, or during the morning. ORIG C17: from LL *mātūtīnālis,* from L, from *Mātūta* goddess of the dawn

matzo, matzoh ('mætsəʊ) *or* **matza, matzah** ('mætsə) *n, pl* **matzos, matzohs, matzas, matzahs,** *or* **matzoth** (*Hebrew* ma'tsɔt). a large very thin biscuit of unleavened bread, traditionally eaten during Passover. ORIG from Heb. *matsāh*

Maubeuge ★ (*French* mobøʒ) *n* an industrial town in N France, near the border with Belgium. Pop.: 35 225 (1990).

maudlin ('mɔːdlɪn) *adj* foolishly tearful or sentimental, as when drunk. ORIG C17: from ME *Maudelen* Mary Magdalene, typically portrayed as a tearful penitent

mauger ('mɔːgə) *adj Caribbean.* (of persons or animals) thin or lean. ORIG from Du. *mager* thin, MEAGRE

Maugham ★ ('mɔːm) *n* **W(illiam) Somerset.** 1874–1965, British writer. His works include the novels *Of Human Bondage* (1915) and *Cakes and Ale* (1930), short stories, and comedies.

maugre *or* **mauger** ('mɔːgə) *prep Obs.* in spite of. ORIG C13 (meaning: ill will): from OF *maugre,* lit.: bad pleasure

Maui ★ ('maʊɪ) *n* a volcanic island in S central Hawaii: the second largest of the Hawaiian Islands. Pop.: 91 361 (1990). Area: 1885 sq. km (728 sq. miles).

maul (mɔːl) *vb* (*tr*) **1** to handle clumsily; paw. **2** to batter or lacerate. ◆ *n* **3** a heavy two-handed hammer. **4** *Rugby.* a loose scrum. ORIG C13: from OF *mail,* from L *malleus* hammer
▸ '**mauler** *n*

Maulmain ★ (maʊl'meɪn) *n* a variant spelling of **Moulmein.**

maulstick *or* **mahlstick** ('mɔːlˌstɪk) *n* a long stick used by artists to steady the hand holding the brush. ORIG C17: partial translation of Du. *maalstok,* from obs. *malen* to paint + *stok* STICK[1]

Mauna Kea ★ ('maʊnɑː 'keɪɑː) *n* an extinct volcano in Hawaii, on N central Hawaii Island: the highest island mountain in the world. Height: 4206 m (13 799 ft).

Mauna Loa ★ ('maʊnɑː 'ləʊɑː) *n* an active volcano in Hawaii, on S central Hawaii Island. Height: 4171 m (13 684 ft).

maunder ('mɔːndə) *vb* (*intr*) to move, talk, or act aimlessly or idly. ORIG C17: ?from obs. *maunder* to beg, from L *mendīcāre*

maundy ('mɔːndɪ) *n, pl* **maundies.** *Christianity.* the ceremonial washing of the feet of poor persons in commemoration of Jesus' washing of his disciples' feet. ORIG C13: from OF *mandé* something commanded, from L, ult. from Christ's words: *Mandātum novum dō vōbīs* A new commandment give I unto you

Maundy money *n* specially minted coins distributed by the British sovereign on the Thursday before Easter (**Maundy Thursday**).

Maupassant ★ (*French* mopasɑ̃) *n* (**Henri René Albert**) **Guy de** (gi də). 1850–93, French writer, noted esp. for his short stories, such as *Boule de suif* (1880) and *Mademoiselle Fifi* (1883). His novels include *Bel Ami* (1885).

Maupertuis ★ (*French* mopɛrtɥi) *n* **Pierre Louis Moreau de** (pjɛr lwi mɔro də). 1698–1759, French mathematician, who originated the principle of least action (or Maupertuis principle).

Mauretania ★ (ˌmɒrɪˈteɪnɪə) *n* an ancient region of N Africa, corresponding approximately to the N parts of modern Algeria and Morocco.
▸ **ˌMaureˈtanian** *adj, n*

Mauriac ★ (*French* mɔrjak) *n* **François** (frɑ̃swa). 1885–1970, French novelist. His works include *Le Désert de l'amour* (1925) and *Le Nœud de vipères* (1932): Nobel prize for literature 1952.

Maurice ★ (ˈmɒrɪs) *n* **1** 1521–53, duke of Saxony (1541–53) and elector of Saxony (1547–53); promoted Protestantism in Germany. **2** known as *Maurice of Nassau.* 1567–1625, prince of Orange and count of Nassau; the son of William the Silent, after whose death he led the United Provinces of the Netherlands in their struggle for independence. **3 Frederick Denison.** 1805–72, British Anglican theologian who pioneered Christian socialism.

Mauritania ★ (ˌmɒrɪˈteɪnɪə) *n* a republic in NW Africa, on the Atlantic: established as a French protectorate in 1903 and a colony in 1920; gained full independence in 1960; lies mostly in the Sahara; contains rich resources of iron ore. Official language: Arabic; African languages and French are also spoken. Official religion: Muslim. Currency: ouguiya. Capital: Nouakchott. Pop.: 2 582 000 (1999 est.). Area: 1 030 700 sq. km (398 000 sq. miles). Official name: **Islamic Republic of Mauritania.**
▸ **ˌMauriˈtanian** *adj, n*

Mauritius ★ (məˈrɪʃəs) *n* an island and state in the Indian Ocean, east of Madagascar: originally uninhabited, it was settled by the Dutch (1638–1710) then abandoned; taken by the French in 1715 and the British in 1810; became an independent member of the Commonwealth in 1968. It is economically dependent on sugar. Official language: English; a French creole is widely spoken. Religion: mostly Hindu and Christian. Currency: rupee. Capital: Port Louis. Pop.: 1 171 000 (1999 est.). Area: 1865 sq. km (720 sq. miles). Former name (1715–1810): **Île-de-France.**
▸ **Mauˈritian** *adj, n*

Maurois ★ (*French* mɔrwa) *n* **André** (ɑ̃dre), pen name of *Émile Herzog.* 1885–1967, French writer, known for his biographies of Shelley, Byron, and Proust.

Maury ★ (ˈmɔːrɪ) *n* **Matthew Fontaine.** 1806–73, US pioneer hydrographer and oceanographer.

mausoleum (ˌmɔːsəˈlɪəm) *n, pl* **mausoleums** *or* **mausolea** (-ˈlɪə). a large stately tomb. ORIG C16: via L from Gk *mausōleion,* the tomb of *Mausolus,* king of Caria; built at Halicarnassus in the 4th cent. B.C.

mauve (məʊv) *n* **1a** any of various pale to moderate pinkish-purple or bluish-purple colours. **1b** (*as adj*): *a mauve flower.* **2** a reddish-purple aniline dye. ORIG C19: from F, from L *malva* MALLOW

maven *or* **mavin** (ˈmeɪvən) *n US.* an expert or connoisseur. ORIG C20: from Yiddish, from Heb. *mevin* understanding

maverick (ˈmævərɪk) *n* **1** (in the US and Canada) an unbranded animal, esp. a stray calf. **2a** a person of independent or unorthodox views. **2b** (*as modifier*): *a maverick politician.* ORIG C19: after Samuel A. *Maverick* (1803–70), Texas rancher, who did not brand his cattle

mavis (ˈmeɪvɪs) *n* a popular name for the **song thrush.** ORIG C14: from OF *mauvis* thrush; from ?

maw (mɔː) *n* **1** the mouth, throat, crop, or stomach of an animal, esp. of a voracious animal. **2** *Inf.* the mouth or stomach of a greedy person. ORIG OE *maga*

mawkish (ˈmɔːkɪʃ) *adj* **1** falsely sentimental, esp. in a weak or maudlin way. **2** nauseating or insipid. ORIG C17: from obs. *mawk* MAGGOT + -ISH
▸ **ˈmawkishly** *adv* ▸ **ˈmawkishness** *n*

Mawson ★ (ˈmɔːsən) *n* Sir **Douglas.** 1882–1958, Australian Antarctic explorer, born in England.

max (mæks) *n Inf.* **1** the most significant, highest, furthest, or greatest thing. **2 to the max.** to the ultimate extent.

max. *abbrev. for* maximum.

maxi (ˈmæksɪ) *adj* **1a** (of a garment) reaching the ankle. **1b** (*as n*): *she wore a maxi.* **1c** (*in combination*): *a maxidress.* **2** large or considerable. ORIG C20: from MAXIMUM

maxilla (mækˈsɪlə) *n, pl* **maxillae** (-liː). **1** the upper jawbone in vertebrates. **2** any member of one or two pairs of mouthparts in insects and other arthropods. ORIG C17: NL, from L: jaw
▸ **maxˈillary** *adj*

maxim (ˈmæksɪm) *n* a brief expression of a general truth, principle, or rule of conduct. ORIG C15: via F from Med. L, from *maxima,* in the phrase *maxima prōpositio* basic axiom (lit.: greatest proposition)

Maxim ★ (ˈmæksɪm) *n* Sir **Hiram Stevens.** 1840–1916, British inventor of the first automatic machine gun (1884), born in the US.

maxima (ˈmæksɪmə) *n* a plural of **maximum.**

maximal (ˈmæksɪməl) *adj* of, relating to, or achieving a maximum; being the greatest or best possible.
▸ **ˈmaximally** *adv*

Maximilian ★ (ˌmæksɪˈmɪlɪən) *n* full name *Ferdinand Maximilian Joseph.* 1832–67, archduke of Austria and emperor of Mexico (1864–67). After the French had partially conquered Mexico, he was offered the throne but was defeated and shot by the Mexicans under Juárez.

Maximilian I ★ *n* 1459–1519, king of Germany (1486–1519) and Holy Roman Emperor (1493–1519).

maximin (ˈmæksɪˌmɪn) *n* **1** *Maths.* the highest of a set of minimum values. **2** (in game theory, etc.) the procedure of choosing the strategy that most benefits the least advantaged member of a group. Cf. **minimax.** ORIG C20: from MAXI(MUM) + MIN(IMUM)

maximize *or* **maximise** (ˈmæksɪˌmaɪz) *vb* **maximizes, maximizing, maximized** *or* **maximises, maximising, maximised.** (*tr*) to make as high or great as possible; increase to a maximum.
▸ **ˌmaximiˈzation** *or* **ˌmaximiˈsation** *n* ▸ **ˈmaxiˌmizer** *or* **ˈmaxiˌmiser** *n*

maximum (ˈmæksɪməm) *n, pl* **maximums** *or* **maxima. 1** the greatest possible amount, degree, etc. **2** the highest value of a variable quantity. ◆ *adj* **3** of, being, or showing a maximum or maximums. ◆ Abbrev.: **max.** ORIG C18: from L: greatest (neuter form used as noun), from *magnus* great

Max Müller ★ (*German* maks ˈmylər) *n* See (Friedrich Max) **Müller.**

maxwell (ˈmækswəl) *n* the cgs unit of magnetic flux equal to the flux through one square centimetre normal to a field of one gauss. It is equivalent to 10^{-8} weber. Symbol: Mx ORIG C20: after J. C. MAXWELL

Maxwell ★ (ˈmækswəl) *n* **1 James Clerk.** 1831–79, Scottish physicist. He developed the equations (**Maxwell equations**) upon which classical electromagnetic theory is based and also contributed to the kinetic theory of gases. **2 (Ian) Robert,** original name *Jan Ludvik Hoch.* 1923–91, British publisher, born in Czechoslovakia; chairman (1984–91) of Mirror Group Newspapers Ltd; posthumously disgraced for fraud and theft.

may[1] (meɪ) *vb past* **might.** (takes an infinitive without *to* or an implied infinitive) used as an auxiliary: **1** to indicate that permission is requested by or granted to someone: *he may go.* **2** (often foll. by *well*) to indicate possibility: *the rope may break.* **3** to indicate ability or capacity, esp. in questions: *may I help you?* **4** to express a strong wish: *long may she reign.* **5** to indicate result or purpose: used only in clauses introduced by *that* or *so that*: *he writes so that the average reader may understand.* **6** another word for **might**[1]. **7** to express courtesy in a question: *whose child may this little girl be?* **8 be that as it may.** in spite of that: a sentence connector conceding the possible truth of a previous statement and introducing an adversative clause: *be that as it may, I still think he should come.* **9 come what may.** whatever happens. **10 that's as may be.** (foll. by a clause introduced by *but*) that may be so. ORIG OE *mæg,* from *magan*

may[2] *or* **may tree** (meɪ) *n* a Brit. name for **hawthorn.** ORIG C16: from MAY

May[1] (meɪ) *n* the fifth month of the year, consisting of 31 days. ORIG from OF, from L *Maius* (month) of *Maia,* Roman goddess

May[2] ★ (meɪ) *n* Sir **Robert McCredie.** born 1936, Australian biologist and ecologist.

Maya[1] ('maɪə) *n* **1** (*pl* **Maya** *or* **Mayas**) Also called: **Mayan.** a member of an American Indian people of Yucatán, Belize, and N Guatemala, once having an advanced civilization. **2** the language of this people.

Maya[2] ★ ('maɪə, 'mɑːjə, 'mɑːjɑː) *n* the Hindu goddess of illusion, the personification of the idea that the material world is illusory.
▸ **'Mayan** *adj*

Mayagüez ★ (*Spanish* maja'ɣweθ) *n* a port in W Puerto Rico; needlework industry. Pop.: 101 684 (1995 est.).

Mayakovski *or* **Mayakovsky** ★ (*Russian* məjɪ'kɔfskij) *n* **Vladimir Vladimirovich** (vla'dimir vla'dimirəvitʃ). 1893–1930, Russian Futurist poet and dramatist. His poems include *At the Top of my Voice* (1930); his plays include *The Bedbug* (1929).

May apple *n* **1** an American plant with edible yellowish egg-shaped fruit. **2** the fruit.

maybe ('meɪˌbiː) *adv* **1** perhaps. ◆ *sentence substitute.* **2** possibly; neither yes nor no.

May beetle *or* **bug** *n* another name for **cockchafer.**

Mayday ('meɪˌdeɪ) *n* the international radiotelephone distress signal. ORIG C20: phonetic spelling of F *m'aidez* help me

May Day *n* the first day of May, traditionally a celebration of the coming of spring: in some countries now observed as a holiday in honour of workers.

Mayence ★ (majɑ̃s) *n* the French name for **Mainz.**

Mayenne ★ (*French* majɛn) *n* a department of NW France, in Pays de la Loire region. Capital: Laval. Pop.: 281 301 (1994 est.). Area: 5212 sq. km (2033 sq. miles).

Mayer ★ (*German* 'maiər) *n* **Julius Robert von** ('juːlius 'roːbɛrt fɔn). 1814–78, German physicist who contributed to the discovery of the law of conservation of energy.

mayest ('meɪɪst) *vb* a variant of **mayst.**

Mayfair ★ ('meɪˌfɛə) *n* a fashionable district of London.

mayflower ('meɪˌflaʊə) *n* **1** any of various plants that bloom in May. **2** *Brit.* another name for **hawthorn, cowslip,** or **marsh marigold.**

Mayflower ('meɪˌflaʊə) *n* **the.** the ship in which the Pilgrim Fathers sailed from Plymouth to America in 1620.

mayfly ('meɪˌflaɪ) *n, pl* **mayflies.** any of an order of short-lived insects having large transparent wings.

mayhap ('meɪˌhæp) *adv* an archaic word for **perhaps.** ORIG C16: shortened from *it may hap*

mayhem *or* **maihem** ('meɪhɛm) *n* **1** *Law.* the wilful and unlawful infliction of injury upon a person, esp. (formerly) the injuring or removing of a limb rendering him less capable of defending himself against attack. **2** any violent destruction or confusion. ORIG C15: from Anglo-F *mahem* injury, of Gmc origin

Mayhew ★ ('meɪhjuː) *n* **Henry.** 1812–87, British journalist, and writer; a founder of *Punch* (1841): best known for *London Labour and the London Poor* (1851–62).

Maying ('meɪɪŋ) *n* the traditional celebration of May Day.

mayn't ('meɪənt, meɪnt) *contraction of* may not.

Mayo ★ ('meɪəʊ) *n* a county of NW Republic of Ireland, in NW Connacht province, on the Atlantic: has many offshore islands and several large lakes. County town: Castlebar. Pop.: 111 000 (1996). Area: 5397 sq. km (2084 sq. miles).

Mayon ★ (mɑː'jɔːn) *n* a volcano in the Philippines, on SE Luzon: Height: 2421 m (7943 ft).

mayonnaise (ˌmeɪə'neɪz) *n* a thick creamy sauce made from egg yolks, oil, and vinegar or lemon juice. ORIG C19: from F, ? from *mahonnais* of Mahón, a port in Minorca

mayor (mɛə) *n* the civic head of a municipal corporation in many countries. Scot. equivalent: **provost.** ORIG C13: from OF *maire,* from L *maior* greater
▸ **'mayoral** *adj* ▸ **'mayorship** *n*

mayoralty ('mɛərəltɪ) *n, pl* **mayoralties.** the office or term of office of a mayor. ORIG C14: from OF *mairalté*

mayoress ('mɛərɪs) *n* **1** *Chiefly Brit.* the wife of a mayor. **2** a female mayor.

Mayotte ★ (*French* majɔt) *n* an island in the Indian Ocean, northwest of Madagascar; administered by France. Pop.: 109 600 (1994 est.). Area: 374 sq. km (146 sq. miles).

maypole ('meɪˌpəʊl) *n* a tall pole around which people dance during May-Day celebrations.

May queen *n* a girl chosen, esp. for her beauty, to preside over May-Day celebrations.

mayst (meɪst) *or* **mayest** *vb Arch.* (used with *thou* or its relative equivalent) a singular form of the present tense of **may**[1].

mayweed ('meɪˌwiːd) *n* **1** Also called: **dog fennel, stinking mayweed.** a widespread Eurasian weedy plant having evil-smelling leaves and daisy-like flower heads. **2 scentless mayweed.** a similar and related plant, with scentless leaves. ORIG C16: changed from OE *mægtha* mayweed + WEED

Mazarin ★ ('mæzərɪn; *French* mazarɛ̃) *n* **Jules** (ʒyl), original name *Giulio Mazarini.* 1602–61, French cardinal and statesman, born in Italy. He succeeded Richelieu (1642) as chief minister to Louis XIII.

Mazatlán ★ (*Spanish* maθa'tlan) *n* a port in W Mexico, in S Sinaloa on the Pacific: situated opposite the tip of the peninsula of Lower California, for which it is the chief link with the mainland. Pop.: 262 705 (1990).

maze (meɪz) *n* **1** a complex network of paths or passages, esp. one with high hedges in a garden, designed to puzzle those walking through it. **2** a similar system represented diagrammatically as a pattern of lines. **3** any confusing network of streets, paths, etc. **4** a state of confusion. ◆ *vb* **mazes, mazing, mazed. 5** an archaic or dialect word for **amaze.** ORIG C13: see AMAZE
▸ **'mazement** *n* ▸ **'mazy** *adj*

Mazu ★ ('mæ'zuː) *n* the Pinyin transliteration of the Chinese name for **Matsu.**

mazurka *or* **mazourka** (mə'zɜːkə) *n* **1** a Polish national dance in triple time. **2** a piece of music composed for this dance. ORIG C19: from Polish: (dance) of *Mazur* (Mazovia) province in Poland

Mazzini ★ (*Italian* mat'tsiːni) *n* **Giuseppe** (dʒu'zɛppe). 1805–72, Italian nationalist. In 1831, in exile, he established the Young Italy association which sought to unite Italy. In 1849 he was one of the triumvirate that ruled the short-lived Roman republic.

Mb *Computing. abbrev. for* megabyte.

MB *abbrev. for* Bachelor of Medicine.

MBA *abbrev. for* Master of Business Administration.

Mbabane ★ (ᵊmbɑː'bɑːnɪ) *n* the capital of Swaziland, in the northwest: administrative and financial centre, with a large iron mine nearby. Pop.: 47 000 (1990 est.).

mbaqanga (ᵊmbɑː'kæŋgə) *n* a style of Black popular music of urban South Africa. ORIG C20: ? from Zulu *umbaqanga* mixture

MBE *abbrev. for* Member of the Order of the British Empire (a Brit. title).

Mbeki ★ (ᵊm'bɛkɪ) *n* **Thabo** ('tɑːbəʊ). born 1942, South African politician: president of South Africa from 1999.

mbira (ᵊm'biːrə) *n* an African musical instrument consisting of tuned metal strips attached to a resonating box, which are plucked with the thumbs. Also called: **thumb piano.** ORIG Bantu

Mbujimayi ★ (ᵊm'buːdʒɪˌmaɪiː) *n* a city in S Democratic Republic of Congo: diamond mining. Pop.: 806 475 (1994 est.).

MC *abbrev. for:* **1** Master of Ceremonies. **2** (in the US) Member of Congress. **3** (in Britain) Military Cross.

Mc- *prefix* a variant of **Mac-**. For entries beginning with this prefix, see under **Mac-**.

MCC (in Britain) *abbrev. for* Marylebone Cricket Club.

MCh *abbrev. for* Master of Surgery. ORIG L *Magister Chirurgiae*

MCP *Inf. abbrev. for* male chauvinist pig.

Md *the chemical symbol for* mendelevium.

MD *abbrev. for:* **1** Doctor of Medicine. ORIG from L *Medicinae Doctor* **2** Managing Director. **3** mentally deficient.

Md. *abbrev. for* Maryland.

MDF *abbrev. for* medium density fibreboard: a material made of compressed wood fibres used as a substitute for wood, esp. in interior decoration.

MDMA *abbrev. for* 3,4-methylenedioxymethamphetmine. See **ecstasy** (sense 4).

MDS See **MMDS**.

MDT (in the US and Canada) *abbrev. for* Mountain Daylight Time.

me[1] (miː; *unstressed* mɪ) *pron* (*objective*) **1** refers to the speaker or writer: *that shocks me.* ◆ *n* **2** *Inf.* the personality of the speaker or writer or something that expresses it: *the real me.* ORIG OE *mē* (dative)

> **USAGE NOTE** It was formerly regarded as correct to use *I, he, she,* etc., rather than *me, him, her,* after the verb *to be,* as in: *it is I who told him.* Since both *I* and *me* can sound strange in a sentence like this, it is better to use a different construction altogether: *I am the one who told him.* The use of a possessive before an *-ing* form of a verb was formerly thought to be preferable to using *me,* etc., but now both forms are acceptable: *he didn't like my/me having a job of my own.*

me[2] (miː) *n* a variant spelling of **mi** (sense 2).

ME *abbrev. for:* **1** Marine Engineer. **2** Mechanical Engineer. **3** Methodist Episcopal. **4** Middle English. **5** Mining Engineer. **6** (in titles) Most Excellent. **7** myalgic encephalomyelitis.

Me. *abbrev. for:* **1** Maine. **2** Maître.

mea culpa *Latin.* (ˈmeɪɑː ˈkʊlpɑː) an acknowledgment of guilt. ORIG lit.: my fault

mead[1] (miːd) *n* an alcoholic drink made by fermenting a solution of honey, often with spices added. ORIG OE *meodu*

mead[2] (miːd) *n* an archaic or poetic word for **meadow**. ORIG OE *mæd*

Mead[1] ★ (miːd) *n* **Lake.** a reservoir in NW Arizona and SE Nevada, formed by the Hoover Dam across the Colorado River: one of the largest man-made lakes in the world. Area: 588 sq. km (227 sq. miles).

Mead[2] ★ (miːd) *n* **Margaret.** 1901–78, US anthropologist. Her works include *Male and Female* (1949).

Meade ★ (miːd) *n* **George Gordon.** 1815–72, Union general in the American Civil War. He defeated the Confederates at Gettysburg (1863).

meadow (ˈmɛdəʊ) *n* **1** an area of grassland, often used for hay or for grazing of animals. **2** a low-lying piece of grassland, often boggy and near a river. ORIG OE *mædwe,* from *mǣd* MEAD[2]
▸ ˈ**meadowy** *adj*

meadow grass *n* a perennial grass that grows in meadows and similar places in N temperate regions.

meadow saffron *n* another name for **autumn crocus**.

meadowsweet (ˈmɛdəʊˌswiːt) *n* **1** a Eurasian plant with dense heads of small fragrant cream-coloured flowers. **2** any of several related North American plants. See also **spiraea**.

meagre *or US* **meager** (ˈmiːɡə) *adj* **1** deficient in amount, quality, or extent. **2** thin or emaciated. **3** lacking in richness or strength. ORIG C14: from OF *maigre,* from L *macer* lean, poor
▸ ˈ**meagrely** *adv* ▸ ˈ**meagreness** *n*

meal[1] (miːl) *n* **1a** any of the regular occasions, such as breakfast, lunch, dinner, etc., when food is served and eaten. **1b** (*in combination*): *mealtime.* **2** the food served and eaten. **3 make a meal of.** *Inf.* to perform (a task) with unnecessarily great effort. ORIG OE *mǣl* measure, set time, meal

meal[2] (miːl) *n* **1** the edible part of a grain or pulse (excluding wheat) ground to a coarse powder. **2** *Scot.* oatmeal. **3** *Chiefly US.* maize flour. ORIG OE *melu*

mealie *or* **mielie** (ˈmiːlɪ) *n* (*often pl*) a S. African word for **maize.** ORIG C19: from Afrik. *milie,* from Port. *milho,* from L *milium* millet

mealie-meal *n S. African.* meal made from finely ground maize.

meals-on-wheels *n* (*functioning as sing*) a service taking hot meals to the elderly, infirm, etc., in their own homes.

meal ticket *n Sl.* a person, situation, etc., providing a source of livelihood or income. ORIG from orig. US sense of ticket entitling holder to a meal

mealworm (ˈmiːlˌwɜːm) *n* the larva of various beetles feeding on stored foods, esp. meal and flour.

mealy (ˈmiːlɪ) *adj* **mealier, mealiest. 1** resembling meal; powdery. **2** containing or consisting of meal or grain. **3** sprinkled or covered with meal or similar granules. **4** (esp. of horses) spotted; mottled. **5** pale in complexion. **6** short for **mealy-mouthed.**
▸ ˈ**mealiness** *n*

mealy bug *n* any of various plant-eating insects coated with a powdery waxy secretion: some species are pests of citrus fruits and greenhouse plants.

mealy-mouthed *adj* hesitant or afraid to speak plainly; not outspoken. ORIG C16: from MEALY (in the sense: soft, soft-spoken)

mean[1] (miːn) *vb* **means, meaning, meant.** (*mainly tr*) **1** (*may take a clause as object or an infinitive*) to intend to convey or express. **2** (*may take a clause as object or an infinitive*) to intend: *she didn't mean to hurt it.* **3** (*may take a clause as object*) to say or do in all seriousness: *the boss means what he says.* **4** (*often passive;* often foll. by *for*) to destine or design (for a certain person or purpose): *she was meant for greater things.* **5** (*may take a clause as object*) to denote or connote; signify; represent. **6** (*may take a clause as object*) to produce; cause: *the weather will mean long traffic delays.* **7** (*may take a clause as object*) to foretell; portend: *those dark clouds mean rain.* **8** to have the importance of: *money means nothing to him.* **9** (*intr*) to have the intention of behaving or acting (esp. in **mean well** *or* **mean ill**). ORIG OE *mænan*

> **USAGE NOTE** In standard British English *mean* should not be followed by *for* when expressing intention: *I didn't mean this to happen* (not *I didn't mean for this to happen*).

mean[2] (miːn) *adj* **1** *Chiefly Brit.* miserly, ungenerous, or petty. **2** despicable, ignoble, or callous: *a mean action.* **3** poor or shabby: *a mean abode.* **4** *Inf., chiefly US & Canad.* bad-tempered; vicious. **5** *Inf.* ashamed: *he felt mean about not letting the children stay out late.* **6** *Sl.* excellent; skilful: *he plays a mean trombone.* **7 no mean. 7a** of high quality: *no mean performer.* **7b** difficult: *no mean feat.* ORIG C12: from OE *gemǣne* common
▸ ˈ**meanly** *adv* ▸ ˈ**meanness** *n*

mean[3] (miːn) *n* **1** the middle point, state, or course between limits or extremes. **2** moderation. **3** *Maths.* **3a** the second and third terms of a proportion, as *b* and *c* in $a/b = c/d$. **3b** another name for **average** (sense 2). **4** *Statistics.* a statistic obtained by multiplying each possible value of a variable by its probability and then taking the sum or integral over the range of the variable. ◆ *adj* **5** intermediate or medium in size, quantity, etc. **6** occurring halfway between extremes or limits; average. ORIG C14: via Anglo-Norman from OF *moien,* from LL *mediānus* MEDIAN

meander (mɪˈændə) *vb* (*intr*) **1** to follow a winding course. **2** to wander without definite aim or direction. ◆ *n* **3** (*often pl*) a curve or bend, as in a river. **4** (*often pl*) a winding course or movement. **5** an ornamental pattern, esp. as used in ancient Greek architecture. ORIG C16:

from L *maeander,* from Gk *Maiandros* the River Maeander; see MENDERES (sense 1)
▸ **me'andering** *adj*

Meander ★ (miː'ændə) *n* a variant spelling of **Maeander.**

mean deviation *n Statistics.* **1** the difference between an observed value of a variable and its mean. **2** Also called: **mean deviation from the mean** (*or* **median**), **average deviation.** a measure of dispersion derived by computing the mean of the absolute values of the differences between observed values of a variable and the variable's mean.

meanie *or* **meany** ('miːnɪ) *n Inf.* **1** *Chiefly Brit.* a miserly or stingy person. **2** *Chiefly US.* a nasty ill-tempered person.

meaning ('miːnɪŋ) *n* **1** the sense or significance of a word, sentence, symbol, etc.; import. **2** the purpose behind speech, action, etc. **3** the inner, symbolic, or true interpretation, value, or message. **4** valid content; efficacy. ◆ *adj* **5** expressive of some sense, intention, criticism, etc.: *a meaning look.* ◆ See also **well-meaning.**

meaningful ('miːnɪŋfʊl) *adj* **1** having great meaning or validity. **2** eloquent; expressive: *a meaningful silence.*
▸ **'meaningfully** *adv* ▸ **'meaningfulness** *n*

meaningless ('miːnɪŋlɪs) *adj* futile or empty of meaning.
▸ **'meaninglessly** *adv* ▸ **'meaninglessness** *n*

mean lethal dose *n* another term for **median lethal dose.**

mean life *n Physics.* the average time of existence of an unstable or reactive entity, such as a nucleus, elementary particle, etc.

means (miːnz) *n* **1** (*functioning as sing or pl*) the medium, method, or instrument used to obtain a result or achieve an end: *a means of communication.* **2** (*functioning as pl*) resources or income. **3** (*functioning as pl*) considerable wealth or income: *a man of means.* **4 by all means.** without hesitation or doubt; certainly. **5 by means of.** with the use or help of. **6 by no manner of means.** definitely not. **7 by no** (*or* **not by any**) **means.** on no account; in no way.

means test *n* the checking of a person's income to determine whether he or she qualifies for financial or social aid from a government.

mean sun *n* an imaginary sun moving along the celestial equator at a constant speed and completing its annual course in the same time as the sun takes to move round the ecliptic at a varying speed. It is used in the measurement of mean solar time.

meant (mɛnt) *vb* the past tense and past participle of **mean**[1].

meantime ('miːnˌtaɪm) *or* **meanwhile** ('miːnˌwaɪl) *n* **1** the intervening time or period (esp. in **in the meantime**). ◆ *adv* **2** during the intervening time or period. **3** at the same time, esp. in another place.

mean time *or* **mean solar time** *n* the times, at a particular place, measured in terms of the passage of the mean sun, giving 24-hour days (mean solar days) throughout a year.

meany ('miːnɪ) *n, pl* **meanies.** a variant of **meanie.**

Mearns ★ (mɛənz) *n* **the.** another name for **Kincardineshire.**

measles ('miːzəlz) *n* (*functioning as sing*) **1** a highly contagious viral disease common in children, characterized by fever, profuse nasal discharge of mucus, conjunctivitis, and a rash of small red spots. See also **German measles. 2** a disease of cattle, sheep, and pigs, caused by infestation with tapeworm larvae. ORIG C14: from MLow G *masele* spot on the skin; infl. by ME *mesel* leper, from L *misellus,* dim. of *miser* wretched

measly ('miːzlɪ) *adj* **measlier, measliest. 1** *Inf.* meagre in quality or quantity. **2** (of meat) infested with tapeworm larvae. **3** having or relating to measles. ORIG C17: see MEASLES

measurable ('mɛʒərəbᵊl) *adj* able to be measured; perceptible or significant.
▸ **'measurably** *adv*

measure ('mɛʒə) *n* **1** the extent, quantity, amount, or degree of something, as determined by measurement or calculation. **2** a device for measuring distance, volume, etc., such as a graduated scale or container. **3** a system of measurement: *metric measure.* **4** a standard used in a system of measurements. **5** a specific or standard amount of something: *a measure of grain; full measure.* **6** a basis or standard for comparison. **7** reasonable or permissible limit or bounds: *within measure.* **8** degree or extent (often in **in some measure, in a measure,** etc.): *a measure of freedom.* **9** (*often pl*) a particular action intended to achieve an effect. **10** a legislative bill, act, or resolution. **11** *Music.* another word for **bar**[1] (sense 15). **12** *Prosody.* poetic rhythm or cadence; metre. **13** a metrical foot. **14** *Poetic.* a melody or tune. **15** the act of measuring; measurement. **16** *Arch.* a dance. **17** *Printing.* the width of a page or column of type. **18 for good measure.** as an extra precaution or beyond requirements. **19 made to measure.** (of clothes) made to fit an individual purchaser. ◆ *vb* **measures, measuring, measured. 20** (*tr;* often foll. by *up*) to determine the size, amount, etc., of by measurement. **21** (*intr*) to make a measurement. **22** (*tr*) to estimate or determine. **23** (*tr*) to function as a measurement of: *the ohm measures electrical resistance.* **24** (*tr*) to bring into competition or conflict with: *he measured his strength against that of his opponent.* **25** (*intr*) to be as specified in extent, amount, etc.: *the room measures six feet.* **26** (*tr*) to travel or move over as if measuring. ◆ See also **measure up.** ORIG C13: from OF, from L *mēnsūra,* from *mēnsus,* p.p. of *mētīrī* to measure

measured ('mɛʒəd) *adj* **1** determined by measurement. **2** slow or stately. **3** carefully considered; deliberate.
▸ **'measuredly** *adv*

measureless ('mɛʒəlɪs) *adj* limitless, vast, or infinite.
▸ **'measurelessly** *adv*

measurement ('mɛʒəmənt) *n* **1** the act or process of measuring. **2** an amount, extent, or size determined by measuring. **3** a system of measures based on a particular standard.

measures ('mɛʒəz) *pl n* rock strata that are characterized by a particular type of sediment or deposit: *coal measures.*

measure up *vb* **1** (*adv*) to determine the size of (something) by measurement. **2 measure up to.** to fulfil (expectations, standards, etc.).

measuring jug *n* a graduated jug used in cooking to measure ingredients.

measuring worm *n* the larva of a geometrid moth: it moves in a series of loops. Also called: **inchworm.**

meat (miːt) *n* **1** the flesh of mammals used as food. **2** anything edible, esp. flesh with the texture of meat: *crab meat.* **3** food, as opposed to drink. **4** the essence or gist. **5** an archaic word for **meal**[1] (senses 1 and 2). **6 meat and drink.** a source of pleasure. ORIG OE *mete*
▸ **'meatless** *adj*

meatball ('miːtˌbɔːl) *n* **1** minced beef, shaped into a ball before cooking. **2** *US & Canad. sl.* a stupid or boring person.

Meath ★ (miːð, miːθ) *n* a county of E Republic of Ireland, in Leinster province on the Irish Sea. formerly a kingdom much larger than the present county; livestock farming. County town: Trim. Pop.: 109 000 (1996). Area: 2338 sq. km (903 sq. miles).

meatus (mɪ'eɪtəs) *n, pl* **meatuses** *or* **meatus.** *Anat.* a natural opening or channel, such as the canal leading from the outer ear to the eardrum. ORIG C17: from L: passage, from *meāre* to pass

meaty ('miːtɪ) *adj* **meatier, meatiest. 1** of, relating to, or full of meat. **2** heavily built; fleshy or brawny. **3** full of import or interest: *a meaty discussion.*
▸ **'meatily** *adv* ▸ **'meatiness** *n*

mebi- ('mɛbɪ) *prefix Computing.* denoting 2^{20}: *mebibyte.* Symbol: Mi ORIG C20: from ME(GA-) + BI(NARY)

Mecca *or* **Mekka** ★ ('mɛkə) *n* **1** a city in W Saudi Arabia, joint capital (with Riyadh) of Saudi Arabia: birthplace of Mohammed; the holiest city of Islam, containing the Kaaba. Pop.: 630 000 (1991 est.). Arabic name: **Makkah. 2** (*sometimes not cap.*) a place that attracts many visitors: *Athens is a Mecca for tourists.*

Meccano (mɪ'kɑːnəʊ) *n Trademark.* a construction set of miniature metal parts from which mechanical models can be made.

mech. *abbrev. for:* **1** mechanical. **2** mechanics. **3** mechanism.

mechanic (mɪˈkænɪk) *n* a person skilled in maintaining or operating machinery, motors, etc. ORIG C14: from L *mēchanicus,* from Gk, from *mēkhanē* MACHINE

mechanical (mɪˈkænɪkᵊl) *adj* **1** made, performed, or operated by or as if by a machine or machinery. **2** concerned with machines or machinery. **3** relating to or controlled or operated by physical forces. **4** of or concerned with mechanics. **5** (of a gesture, etc.) automatic; lacking thought, feeling, etc. **6** *Philosophy.* accounting for phenomena by physically determining forces.
▸ **meˈchanicalism** *n* ▸ **meˈchanically** *adv* ▸ **meˈchanicalness** *n*

mechanical advantage *n* the ratio of the working force exerted by a mechanism to the applied effort.

mechanical drawing *n* a drawing to scale of a machine, machine component, architectural plan, etc., from which dimensions can be taken.

mechanical engineering *n* the branch of engineering concerned with the design, construction, and operation of machines.

mechanical equivalent of heat *n Physics.* a factor for converting units of energy into heat units.

mechanician (ˌmɛkəˈnɪʃən) *or* **mechanist** *n* a person skilled in making machinery and tools; technician.

mechanics (mɪˈkænɪks) *n* **1** (*functioning as sing*) the branch of science, divided into statics, dynamics, and kinematics, concerned with the equilibrium or motion of bodies in a particular frame of reference. **2** (*functioning as sing*) the science of designing, constructing, and operating machines. **3** the working parts of a machine. **4** the technical aspects of something.

mechanism (ˈmɛkəˌnɪzəm) *n* **1** a system or structure of moving parts that performs some function, esp. in a machine. **2** something resembling a machine in the arrangement and working of its parts. **3** any mechanical device or part of such a device. **4** a process or technique: *the mechanism of novel writing.* **5** *Philosophy.* the doctrine that human action can be explained in purely physical terms. **6** *Psychoanal.* **6a** the ways in which psychological forces interact and operate. **6b** a structure having an influence on the behaviour of a person, such as a defence mechanism.

mechanistic (ˌmɛkəˈnɪstɪk) *adj* **1** *Philosophy.* of or relating to the theory of mechanism. **2** *Maths.* of or relating to mechanics.
▸ **ˈmechanist** *n* ▸ **ˌmechaˈnistically** *adv*

mechanize *or* **mechanise** (ˈmɛkəˌnaɪz) *vb* **mechanizes, mechanizing, mechanized** *or* **mechanises, mechanising, mechanised.** (*tr*) **1** to equip (a factory, industry, etc.) with machinery. **2** to make mechanical, automatic, or monotonous. **3** to equip (an army, etc.) with motorized or armoured vehicles.
▸ **ˌmechaniˈzation** *or* **ˌmechaniˈsation** *n* ▸ **ˈmechaˌnizer** *or* **ˈmechaˌniser** *n*

mechanoreceptor (ˌmɛkənəʊrɪˈsɛptə) *n Physiol.* a sensory receptor, as in the skin, that is sensitive to a mechanical stimulus, such as pressure.

mechanotherapy (ˌmɛkənəʊˈθɛrəpɪ) *n* the treatment of disorders or injuries by means of mechanical devices, esp. devices that provide exercise for bodily parts.

Mechelen ★ (ˈmɛxələn) *n* a city in N Belgium, in Antwerp province: capital of the Netherlands from 1507 to 1530; formerly famous for lace-making; now has an important vegetable market. Pop.: 75 718 (1995 est.). French name: **Malines.** English name: **Mechlin.**

Mechlin ★ (ˈmɛklɪn) *n* the English name for **Mechelen.**

Mechlin lace *n* bobbin lace made at Mechelin, characterized by patterns outlined by a heavier flat thread. Also called: **malines.**

Mecklenburg ★ (ˈmɛklənˌbɜːg; *German* ˈmeːklənburk) *n* a historic region and former state of NE Germany, along the Baltic coast: now part of Mecklenburg-West Pomerania: formerly in East Germany.

Mecklenburg-West Pomerania ★ *n* a state of NE Germany, along the Baltic coast: consists of the former state of Mecklenburg and those parts of W Pomerania not incorporated into Poland after World War II: part of East Germany until 1990. Pop.: 1 820 600 (1996 est.).

meconium (mɪˈkəʊnɪəm) *n* the first faeces of a newborn infant. ORIG C17: from NL, from L: poppy juice, from Gk, from *mēkōn* poppy

meconopsis (ˌmiːkənˈɒpsɪs) *n* any of various mainly Asiatic poppies. ORIG C19: from Gk *mēkōn* poppy + -OPSIS

Med (mɛd) *n Inf.* the Mediterranean region.

MEd *abbrev. for* Master of Education.

med. *abbrev. for:* **1** medical. **2** medicine. **3** medieval. **4** medium.

médaillons (*French* medajɔ̃) *pl n Cookery.* small round pieces of meat, fish, vegetables, etc. Also called: **medallions.**

medal (ˈmɛdᵊl) *n* a small flat piece of metal bearing an inscription or image, given as an award or commemoration of some outstanding event, etc. ORIG C16: from F *médaille,* prob. from It. *medaglia,* ult. from L *metallum* METAL

medallion (mɪˈdæljən) *n* **1** a large medal. **2** an oval or circular decorative device resembling a medal, usually bearing a portrait or relief moulding, used in architecture and textile design. ORIG C17: from F, from It., from *medaglia* MEDAL

medallist *or US* **medalist** (ˈmɛdᵊlɪst) *n* **1** a designer, maker, or collector of medals. **2** *Chiefly sport.* a recipient of a medal or medals.

medal play *n Golf.* another name for **stroke play.**

Medan ★ (ˈmɛdɑːn) *n* a city in Indonesia, in NE Sumatra: seat of the University of North Sumatra (1952) and the Indonesian Islam University (1952). Pop.: 1 909 700 (1995 est.).

Medawar ★ (ˈmɛdəwə) *n* Sir **Peter Brian.** 1915–87, British zoologist, who shared the Nobel prize for physiology or medicine (1960) for work on immunology.

meddle (ˈmɛdᵊl) *vb* **meddles, meddling, meddled.** (*intr*) **1** (usually foll. by *with*) to interfere officiously or annoyingly. **2** (usually foll. by *in*) to involve oneself unwarrantedly. ORIG C14: from OF *medler,* ult. from L *miscēre* to mix
▸ **ˈmeddler** *n* ▸ **ˈmeddling** *adj*

meddlesome (ˈmɛdᵊlsəm) *adj* intrusive or meddling.
▸ **ˈmeddlesomely** *adv* ▸ **ˈmeddlesomeness** *n*

Mede (miːd) *n* a member of an Indo-European people who established an empire in SW Asia in the 7th and 6th centuries B.C.
▸ **ˈMedian** *n, adj*

Medea ★ (mɪˈdɪə) *n Greek myth.* a princess of Colchis, who assisted Jason in obtaining the Golden Fleece from her father.

Medellín ★ (*Spanish* meðeˈʎin) *n* a city in W Colombia, at an altitude of 1554 m (5100 ft): the second largest city in the country, with three universities; important coffee centre, with large textile mills; dominated by drug cartels in recent years. Pop.: 1 970 691 (1997 est.).

media (ˈmiːdɪə) *n* **1** a plural of **medium. 2a** the means of communication that reach large numbers of people, such as television, newspapers, and radio. **2b** (*as modifier*): *media hype.*

> **USAGE NOTE** When *media* refers to the mass media, it is sometimes treated as a singular, as in: *the media has shown great interest in these events.* Many people think this use is incorrect and that *media* should always be treated as a plural form: *the media have shown great interest in these events.*

Media ★ (ˈmiːdɪə) *n* an ancient country of SW Asia, south of the Caspian Sea: inhabited by the Medes; overthrew the Assyrian Empire in 612 B.C. in alliance with Babylonia; conquered by Cyrus the Great in 550 B.C.; corresponds to present-day NW Iran.

mediaeval (ˌmɛdɪˈiːvᵊl) *adj* a variant spelling of **medieval.**

media event *n* an event that is staged for or exploited by the mass media.

medial ('mi:dɪəl) *adj* **1** of or situated in the middle. **2** ordinary or average in size. **3** *Maths.* relating to an average. **4** another word for **median** (senses 1, 2). ORIG C16: from LL *mediālis,* from *medius* middle
▸ '**medially** *adv*

median ('mi:dɪən) *adj* **1** of, relating to, situated in, or directed towards the middle. **2** *Statistics.* of or relating to the median. ◆ *n* **3** a middle point, plane, or part. **4** *Geom.* **4a** a straight line joining one vertex of a triangle to the midpoint of the opposite side. **4b** a straight line joining the midpoints of the nonparallel sides of a trapezium. **5** *Statistics.* the middle value in a frequency distribution, below and above which lie values with equal total frequencies. **6** *Statistics.* the middle number or average of the two middle numbers in an ordered sequence of numbers. ORIG C16: from L *mediānus,* from *medius* middle
▸ '**medianly** *adv*

median lethal dose *or* **mean lethal dose** *n* **1** the amount of a drug or other substance that, when administered to a group of experimental animals, will kill 50 per cent of the group in a specified time. **2** the amount of ionizing radiation that will kill 50 per cent of a population in a specified time. ◆ Abbrev.: LD_{50}.

mediant ('mi:dɪənt) *n Music.* **a** the third degree of a major or minor scale. **b** (*as modifier*): *a mediant chord.* ORIG C18: from It. *mediante,* from LL *mediāre* to be in the middle

mediastinum (ˌmi:dɪə'staɪnəm) *n, pl* **mediastina** (-nə). *Anat.* **1** a membrane between two parts of an organ or cavity such as the pleural tissue between the two lungs. **2** the part of the thoracic cavity that lies between the lungs, containing the heart, trachea, etc. ORIG C16: from Medical L, neuter of Med. L *mediastīnus* median, from L: low grade of servant, from *medius* mean
▸ ˌ**medias'tinal** *adj*

mediate *vb* ('mi:dɪˌeɪt), **mediates, mediating, mediated. 1** (*intr;* usually foll. by *between* or *in*) to intervene (between parties or in a dispute) in order to bring about agreement. **2** to bring about (an agreement) between parties in a dispute. **3** to resolve (differences) by mediation. **4** (*intr*) to be in an intermediate position. **5** (*tr*) to serve as a medium for causing (a result) or transferring (objects, information, etc.). ◆ *adj* ('mi:dɪɪt). **6** occurring as a result of or dependent upon mediation. ORIG C16: from LL *mediāre* to be in the middle
▸ '**mediately** *adv* ▸ '**mediˌator** *n*

mediation (ˌmi:dɪ'eɪʃən) *n* the act of mediating; intercession between people, states, etc. in an attempt to reconcile disputed matters.

Medibank ('mɛdɪbæŋk) *n* (in Australia), a government-run health insurance scheme.

medic[1] ('mɛdɪk) *n Inf.* a doctor, medical orderly, or medical student. ORIG C17: from MEDICAL

medic[2] ('mɛdɪk) *n* the usual US spelling of **medick.**

medicable ('mɛdɪkəbᵊl) *adj* potentially able to be treated or cured medically.

medical ('mɛdɪkᵊl) *adj* **1** of or relating to the science of medicine or to the treatment of patients by drugs, etc., as opposed to surgery. ◆ *n* **2** *Inf.* a medical examination. ORIG C17: from Med. L *medicālis,* from L *medicus* physician, surgeon, from *medērī* to heal
▸ '**medically** *adv*

medical certificate *n* **1** a document stating the result of a satisfactory medical examination. **2** a doctor's certificate giving evidence of a person's unfitness for work.

medical jurisprudence *n* another name for **forensic medicine.**

medicament (mɪ'dɪkəmənt, 'mɛdɪ-) *n* a medicine or remedy. ORIG C16: via F from L *medicāmentum,* from *medicāre* to cure

medicate ('mɛdɪˌkeɪt) *vb* **medicates, medicating, medicated.** (*tr*) **1** to cover or impregnate (a wound, etc.) with an ointment, etc. **2** to treat (a patient) with a medicine. **3** to add a medication to (a bandage, shampoo, etc.). ORIG C17: from L *medicāre* to heal
▸ '**medicative** *adj*

medication (ˌmɛdɪ'keɪʃən) *n* **1** treatment with drugs or remedies. **2** a drug or remedy.

Medici ★ ('mɛdɪtʃɪ, mə'di:tʃɪ; *Italian* 'mɛ:ditʃi) *n* **1** an Italian family of bankers, art patrons, and rulers of Florence and Tuscany, prominent in the 15th, 16th, and 17th centuries, including: **2 Catherine de'** (ka'tri:n de). See **Catherine de' Medici. 3 Cosimo I** ('kɔ:zimo), known as *Cosimo the Great.* 1519–74, duke of Florence and first grand duke of Tuscany (1569–74). **4 Cosimo de',** known as *Cosimo the Elder.* 1389–1464, who established the political power of the family in Florence (1434). **5 Giovanni de'** (dʒo'vanni de). See **Leo X. 6 Giulio de'** ('dʒu:ljo de). See **Clement VII. 7 Lorenzo de'** (lo'rɛntso de), known as *Lorenzo the Magnificent.* 1449–92, ruler of Florence (1469–92) and first patron of Michelangelo. **8 Maria de'** (ma'ri:a de). See **Maria de' Medici.** ◆ French name: **Médicis** (medisis).
▸ **Medicean** (ˌmɛdɪ'si:ən, -'tʃi:-) *adj*

medicinal (mɛ'dɪsɪnᵊl) *adj* **1** relating to or having therapeutic properties. ◆ *n* **2** a medicinal substance.
▸ **me'dicinally** *adv*

medicine ('mɛdɪsɪn, 'mɛdsɪn) *n* **1** any drug or remedy for use in treating, preventing, or alleviating the symptoms of disease. **2** the science of preventing, diagnosing, alleviating, or curing disease. **3** any nonsurgical branch of medical science. **4** the practice or profession of medicine. **5** something regarded by primitive people as having magical or remedial properties. **6 a taste** (*or* **dose**) **of one's own medicine.** an unpleasant experience in retaliation for a similar unkind or aggressive act. **7 take one's medicine.** to accept a deserved punishment. ORIG C13: via OF from L *medicīna* (*ars*) (art) of healing, from *medicus* doctor, from *medērī* to heal

medicine ball *n* a heavy ball used for physical training.

medicine man *n* (among certain peoples, esp. North American Indians) a person believed to have supernatural powers of healing; a magician or sorcerer.

medick *or US* **medic** ('mɛdɪk) *n* any of various small plants having yellow or purple flowers and trifoliate leaves. ORIG C15: from L *mēdica,* from Gk *mēdikē* (*poa*) Median (grass), a type of clover

medico ('mɛdɪˌkəʊ) *n, pl* **medicos.** *Inf.* a doctor or medical student. ORIG C17: via It. from L *medicus*

medieval *or* **mediaeval** (ˌmɛdɪ'i:vᵊl) *adj* **1** of, relating to, or in the style of the Middle Ages. **2** *Inf.* old-fashioned; primitive. ORIG C19: from NL *medium aevum* the middle age

Medieval Greek *n* the Greek language from the 7th century A.D. to shortly after the sacking of Constantinople in 1204. Also called: **Middle Greek, Byzantine Greek.**

medievalism *or* **mediaevalism** (ˌmɛdɪ'i:vəˌlɪzəm) *n* **1** the beliefs, life, or style of the Middle Ages or devotion to those. **2** a belief, custom, or point of style copied or surviving from the Middle Ages.

medievalist *or* **mediaevalist** (ˌmɛdɪ'i:vəlɪst) *n* a student or devotee of the Middle Ages.

Medieval Latin *n* the Latin language as used throughout Europe in the Middle Ages.

Medina ★ (mɛ'di:nə) *n* a city in W Saudi Arabia: the second most holy city of Islam (after Mecca), with the tomb of Mohammed; university (1960). Pop.: 400 000 (1991 est.). Arabic name: **Al Madinah.** Ancient Arabic name: **Yathrib.**

mediocre (ˌmi:dɪ'əʊkə) *adj Often derog.* average or ordinary in quality. ORIG C16: via F from L *mediocris* moderate, lit.: halfway up the mountain, from *medius* middle + *ocris* stony mountain

mediocrity (ˌmi:dɪ'ɒkrɪtɪ, ˌmɛd-) *n, pl* **mediocrities. 1** the state or quality of being mediocre. **2** a mediocre person or thing.

Medit. *abbrev. for* Mediterranean.

meditate ('mɛdɪˌteɪt) *vb* **meditates, meditating meditated. 1** (*intr;* foll. by *on* or *upon*) to think about something deeply. **2** (*intr*) to reflect deeply on spiritual matters, esp. as a religious act. **3** (*tr*) to plan, consider, or think of doing (something). ORIG C16: from L *meditārī* to reflect upon
▸ '**meditative** *adj* ▸ '**meditatively** *adv* ▸ '**mediˌtator** *n*

meditation (ˌmɛdɪˈteɪʃən) *n* **1** the act of meditating; reflection. **2** contemplation of spiritual matters, esp. as a religious practice.

Mediterranean ★ (ˌmɛdɪtəˈreɪnɪən) *n* **1** short for the **Mediterranean Sea. 2** a native or inhabitant of a Mediterranean country. ◆ *adj* **3** of, relating to, situated or dwelling near the Mediterranean Sea. **4** denoting a postulated subdivision of the Caucasoid race, characterized by slender build and dark complexion. **5** *Meteorol.* (of a climate) characterized by hot summers and relatively warm winters when most of the annual rainfall occurs. **6** (*often not cap.*) *Obs.* situated in the middle of a landmass; inland. ORIG C16: from L *mediterrāneus,* from *medius* middle + *-terrāneus,* from *terra* land

Mediterranean Sea ★ *n* a large inland sea between S Europe, N Africa, and SW Asia: linked with the Atlantic by the Strait of Gibraltar, with the Red Sea by the Suez Canal, and with the Black Sea by the Dardanelles, Sea of Marmara, and Bosporus; many ancient civilizations developed around its shores. Greatest depth: 4770 m (15 900 ft). Length: (west to east) over 3700 km (2300 miles). Greatest width: about 1368 km (850 miles). Area: (excluding the Black Sea) 2 512 300 sq. km (970 000 sq. miles). Ancient name: **Mare Internum** (ˈmɑːreɪ ɪnˈtɜːnəm).

medium (ˈmiːdɪəm) *adj* **1** midway between extremes; average. ◆ *n, pl* **media** *or* **mediums. 2** an intermediate or middle state, degree, or condition; mean: *the happy medium.* **3** an intervening substance or agency for transmitting or producing an effect; vehicle. **4** a means or agency for communicating or diffusing information, news, etc., to the public. **5** a person supposedly used as a spiritual intermediary between the dead and the living. **6** the substance in which specimens of animals and plants are preserved or displayed. **7** *Biol.* Also called: **culture medium.** a nutritive substance in which cultures of bacteria or fungi are grown. **8** the substance or surroundings in which an organism naturally lives or grows. **9** *Art.* **9a** the category of a work of art, as determined by its materials and methods of production. **9b** the materials used in a work of art. **10** any solvent in which pigments are mixed and thinned. ORIG C16: from L: neuter sing of *medius* middle

> **USAGE NOTE** See at **media.**

medium-dated *adj* (of a gilt-edged security) having between five and fifteen years to run before redemption. Cf. **long-dated, short-dated.**

medium frequency *n* a radio-frequency band or radio frequency lying between 3000 and 300 kilohertz. Abbrev: **MF.**

medium wave *n* **a** a radio wave with a wavelength between 100 and 1000 metres. **b** (*as modifier*): *a medium-wave broadcast.*

medlar (ˈmɛdlə) *n* **1** a small Eurasian tree. **2** its fruit, which resembles the crab apple and is not edible until it has begun to decay. ORIG C14: from OF *medlier,* from L *mespilum* medlar fruit, from Gk *mespilon*

medley (ˈmɛdlɪ) *n* **1** a mixture of various types or elements. **2** a musical composition consisting of various tunes arranged as a continuous whole. **3a** *Swimming.* a race in which a different stroke is used for each length: *an individual medley.* **3b** *Athletics.* a relay race in which each leg has a different distance. **3c** (*as modifier*): *a medley relay.* ORIG C14: from OF *medlee,* from *medler* to mix, quarrel

Médoc ★ (meɪˈdɒk, ˈmɛdɒk; *French* medɔk) *n* **1** a district of SW France, on the left bank of the Gironde estuary: famous vineyards. **2** a fine red wine from this district.

medulla (mɪˈdʌlə) *n, pl* **medullas** *or* **medullae** (-liː). **1** *Anat.* **1a** the innermost part of an organ or structure. **1b** short for **medulla oblongata. 2** *Bot.* another name for **pith** (sense 4). ORIG C17: from L: marrow, prob. from *medius* middle
▸ **meˈdullary** *or* **meˈdullar** *adj*

medulla oblongata (ˌɒblɒŋˈɡɑːtə) *n, pl* **medulla oblongatas** *or* **medullae oblongatae** (mɪˈdʌliː ˌɒblɒŋˈɡɑːtiː). the lower stalklike section of the brain, continuous with the spinal cord, containing control centres for the heart and lungs. ORIG C17: NL: oblong-shaped medulla

medusa (mɪˈdjuːzə) *n, pl* **medusas** *or* **medusae** (-ziː). another name for **jellyfish** (sense 1). ORIG C18: from the likeness of its tentacles to the snaky locks of MEDUSA
▸ **meˈdusoid** *adj, n*

Medusa ★ (mɪˈdjuːzə) *n Greek myth.* a mortal woman who was transformed by Athena into one of the three Gorgons. She became so hideous that those who looked at her were turned to stone. Perseus eventually slew her. See also **Pegasus.**
▸ **Meˈdusan** *adj*

Medway ★ (ˈmɛdˌweɪ) *n* **1** a river in SE England, flowing through Kent and the **Medway towns** (Rochester, Chatham, and Gillingham) to the Thames estuary. Length: 110 km (70 miles). **2** a unitary authority in SE England, in Kent. Pop.: 239 500 (1996 est.). Area: 204 sq. km (79 sq. miles).

meed (miːd) *n Arch.* a recompense; reward. ORIG OE: wages

meek (miːk) *adj* **1** patient, long-suffering, or submissive; humble. **2** spineless or spiritless; compliant. ORIG C12: rel. to ON *mjūkr* amenable
▸ **ˈmeekly** *adv* ▸ **ˈmeekness** *n*

meerkat (ˈmɪəˌkæt) *n* any of several South African mongooses, esp. the slender-tailed meerkat or suricate, which has a lemur-like face and four-toed feet. ORIG C19: from Du.: sea-cat

meerschaum (ˈmɪəʃəm) *n* **1** a white, yellowish, or pink compact earthy mineral consisting of hydrated magnesium silicate: used to make tobacco pipes and as a building stone. **2** a tobacco pipe having a bowl made of this mineral. ORIG C18: from G *Meerschaum* lit.: sea foam

Meerut ★ (ˈmɪərət) *n* an industrial city in N India, in W Uttar Pradesh: founded as a military base by the British in 1806 and scene of the first uprising (1857) of the Indian Mutiny. Pop.: 753 778 (1991).

meet[1] (miːt) *vb* **meets, meeting, met. 1** (sometimes foll. by *up* or (US) *with*) to come together (with), either by design or by accident; encounter. **2** to come into or be in conjunction or contact with (something or each other). **3** (*tr*) to come to or be at the place of arrival of: *to meet a train.* **4** to make the acquaintance of or be introduced to (someone or each other). **5** to gather in the company of (someone or each other). **6** to come into the presence of (someone or each other) as opponents. **7** (*tr*) to cope with effectively; satisfy: *to meet someone's demands.* **8** (*tr*) to be apparent to (esp. in **meet the eye**). **9** (*tr*) to return or counter: *to meet a blow with another.* **10** to agree with (someone or each other): *we met him on the price he suggested.* **11** (*tr;* sometimes foll. by *with*) to experience; suffer: *he met his death in a road accident.* **12** (*intr*) to occur together: *courage and kindliness met in him.* ◆ *n* **13** the assembly of hounds, huntsmen, etc., prior to a hunt. **14** a meeting, esp. a sports meeting. ORIG OE *mētan*
▸ **ˈmeeter** *n*

meet[2] (miːt) *adj Arch.* proper, fitting, or correct. ORIG C13: from var. of OE *gemǣte*
▸ **ˈmeetly** *adv*

meeting (ˈmiːtɪŋ) *n* **1** an act of coming together; encounter. **2** an assembly or gathering. **3** a conjunction or union. **4** a sporting competition, as of athletes, or of horse racing.

meeting house *n* the place in which certain religious groups, esp. Quakers, hold their meetings for worship.

mefloquine (ˈmɛfləʊˌkwiːn) *n* a synthetic drug administered orally to prevent or treat malaria. ORIG C20

mega (ˈmɛɡə) *adj Sl.* extremely good, great, or successful. ORIG C20: prob. independent use of MEGA-

mega- *prefix* **1** denoting 10^6: *megawatt.* **2** Also: **mebi-.** *Computing.* denoting 2^{20} (1 048 576): *megabyte.* **3** large or great: *megalith.* ◆ Symbol (for senses 1, 2): M ORIG from Gk *megas* huge, powerful

> **USAGE NOTE** See at **kilo-.**

megabit (ˈmɛɡəˌbɪt) *n Computing.* **1** one million bits. **2** 2^{20} bits.

megabuck (ˈmɛɡəˌbʌk) *n US & Canad. sl.* a million dollars.

★ people and places

megacephaly (ˌmɛgəˈsɛfəlɪ) *or* **megalocephaly** *n* the condition of having an unusually large head or cranial capacity.
▸ **megacephalic** (ˌmɛgəsɪˈfælɪk), ˌ**megaˈcephalous,** ˌ**megaloceˈphalic,** *or* ˌ**megaloˈcephalous** *adj*

megacycle (ˈmɛgəˌsaɪkᵊl) *n* a former unit of frequency equal to one million cycles per second; megahertz.

megadeath (ˈmɛgəˌdɛθ) *n* the death of a million people, esp. in a nuclear war or attack.

Megaera ★ (mɪˈdʒɪərə) *n Greek myth.* one of the three Furies; the others are Alecto and Tisiphone.

megafauna (ˈmɛgəˌfɔːnə) *n* the component of the fauna of a region or period that comprises the larger terrestrial animals.

megaflop (ˈmɛgəˌflɒp) *n Computing.* a measure of processing speed, consisting of a million floating-point operations a second. ORIG C20: from MEGA- + *flo(ating) p(oint)*

megahertz (ˈmɛgəˌhɜːts) *n, pl* **megahertz.** one million hertz. Former name: **megacycle.**

megalith (ˈmɛgəlɪθ) *n* a stone of great size, esp. one forming part of a prehistoric monument.
▸ ˌ**megaˈlithic** *adj*

megalo- *or before a vowel* **megal-** *combining form.* indicating greatness or abnormal size: *megalopolis.* ORIG from Gk *megas* great

megalomania (ˌmɛgələʊˈmeɪnɪə) *n* **1** a mental illness characterized by delusions of grandeur, power, wealth, etc. **2** *Inf.* a lust or craving for power.
▸ ˌ**megaloˈmaniac** *adj, n* ▸ **megalomaniacal** (ˌmɛgələʊməˈnaɪəkᵊl) *adj*

megalopolis (ˌmɛgəˈlɒpəlɪs) *n* an urban complex, usually comprising several large towns. ORIG C20: MEGALO- + Gk *polis* city
▸ **megalopolitan** (ˌmɛgələˈpɒlɪtᵊn) *adj, n*

megalosaur (ˈmɛgələʊˌsɔː) *n* any very large Jurassic or Cretaceous bipedal carnivorous dinosaur. ORIG C19: from NL *megalosaurus,* from MEGALO- + Gk *sauros* lizard

megaphone (ˈmɛgəˌfəʊn) *n* a funnel-shaped instrument used to amplify the voice. See also **loud-hailer.**
▸ **megaphonic** (ˌmɛgəˈfɒnɪk) *adj*

megapode (ˈmɛgəˌpəʊd) *n* any of various ground-living gallinaceous birds of Australia, New Guinea, and adjacent islands. Their eggs incubate in mounds of sand, rotting vegetation, etc., by natural heat.

Megara ★ (ˈmɛgərə) *n* a town in E central Greece: an ancient trading city, founding many colonies in the 7th and 8th centuries B.C. Pop.: 26 562 (1991 est.).

megathere (ˈmɛgəˌθɪə) *n* any of various gigantic extinct American sloths, common in late Cenozoic times. ORIG C19: from NL *megathērium,* from MEGA- + *-there,* from Gk *thērion* wild beast

megaton (ˈmɛgəˌtʌn) *n* **1** one million tons. **2** an explosive power, esp. of a nuclear weapon, equal to the power of one million tons of TNT.

Me generation *n* **the.** the generation, originally in the 1970s, characterized by self-absorption; in the 1980s, characterized by material greed.

Megger (ˈmɛgə) *n Trademark.* an instrument that generates a high voltage in order to test the resistance of insulation, etc.

Meghalaya ★ (ˌmeɪgəˈleɪə) *n* a state of NE India, created in 1969 from part of Assam. Capital: Shillong. Pop.: 1 960 000 (1994 est.). Area: 22 429 sq. km (7800 sq. miles).

Megiddo ★ (məˈgɪdəʊ) *n* an ancient town in N Palestine, strategically located on a route linking Egypt to Mesopotamia: site of many battles, including an important Egyptian victory over rebel chieftains in 1469 or 1468 B.C. See also **Armageddon.**

megilp *or* **magilp** (məˈgɪlp) *n* an oil-painting medium of linseed oil mixed with mastic varnish or turpentine. ORIG C18: from ?

megohm (ˈmɛgˌəʊm) *n* one million ohms.

megrim (ˈmiːgrɪm) *n Arch.* **1** a caprice. **2** a migraine. **3** *(pl) Rare.* a fit of depression. **4** *(pl)* a disease of horses and cattle; staggers. ORIG C14: see MIGRAINE

Mehemet Ali (mɪˈhɛmɪt ˈɑːlɪ) *or* **Mohammed Ali** ★ *n* 1769–1849, Albanian commander in the service of Turkey. He was made viceroy of Egypt (1805) and its hereditary ruler (1841), founding a dynasty that ruled until 1952.

meibomian gland (maɪˈbəʊmɪən) *n* any of the small sebaceous glands in the eyelid, beneath the conjunctiva. ORIG C19: after H. *Meibom* (1638–1700), G anatomist

meiosis (maɪˈəʊsɪs) *n, pl* **meioses** (-ˌsiːz). **1** a type of cell division in which a nucleus divides into four daughter nuclei, each containing half the chromosome number of the parent nucleus. **2** *Rhetoric.* another word for **litotes.** ORIG C16: via NL from Gk, from *meioun* to diminish, from *meiōn* less
▸ **meiotic** (maɪˈɒtɪk) *adj* ▸ **meiˈotically** *adv*

Meir ★ (meɪˈɪə) *n* **Golda** (ˈgəʊldə) 1898–1978, Israeli stateswoman, born in Russia; prime minister (1969–74).

Meissen ★ (*German* ˈmaisən) *n* a town in E Germany, in Saxony, in Dresden district on the River Elbe: famous for its porcelain (Dresden china), first made here in 1710. Pop.: 38 100 (1989 est.).

-meister (ˈmaɪstə) *n combining form.* a person who excels at a particular activity: *spinmeister; horror-meister.* ORIG C20: from G *Meister* master

Meistersinger (ˈmaɪstəˌsɪŋə) *n, pl* **Meistersinger** *or* **Meistersingers.** a member of one of the German guilds organized to compose and perform poetry and music, esp. in the 15th and 16th centuries. ORIG C19: from G *Meistersinger* master singer

Meitner ★ (*German* ˈmaitnər) *n* **Lise** (ˈliːzə). 1878–1968, Austrian physicist. With Hahn, she discovered protactinium (1918), and demonstrated the fission of uranium.

meitnerium (ˌmaɪtˈnɛərɪəm) *n* a synthetic element produced in small quantities by high-energy ion bombardment. Symbol: Mt; atomic no.: 109. ORIG C20: from Lise MEITNER

Méjico ★ (ˈmɛxiko) *n* the Spanish name for **Mexico.**

Mekka ★ (ˈmɛkə) *n* a variant spelling of **Mecca.**

Meknès ★ (mɛkˈnɛs) *n* a city in N central Morocco, in the Middle Atlas Mountains: noted for the making of carpets. Pop.: 188 224 (1994).

Mekong ★ (ˌmiːˈkɒŋ) *n* a river in SE Asia, rising in SW China in Qinghai province: flows southeast forming the border between Laos and Myanmar, and part of the border between Laos and Thailand, then continues south across Cambodia and Vietnam to the South China Sea by an extensive delta, one of the greatest rice-growing areas in Asia. Length: about 4025 km (2500 miles).

melaleuca (ˌmɛləˈluːkə) *n* any shrub or tree of the mostly Australian genus *Melaleuca,* found in sandy or swampy regions. ORIG C19: NL from Gk *melas* black + *leukos* white, from its black trunk and white branches

melamine (ˈmɛləˌmiːn) *n* **1** a colourless crystalline compound used in making synthetic resins. Formula: $C_3N_6H_6$. **2** a resin produced from melamine (**melamine resin**) or a material made from this resin. ORIG C19: from G *Melamin,* from *Melam* distillate of ammonium thiocyanate, with *-am* representing *ammonia*

melancholia (ˌmɛlənˈkəʊlɪə) *n* a former name for **depression** (sense 3).
▸ ˌ**melanˈcholiˌac** *adj, n*

melancholy (ˈmɛlənkəlɪ) *n, pl* **melancholies. 1** a tendency to gloominess or depression. **2** a sad thoughtful state of mind. **3** *Arch.* **3a** a gloomy character. **3b** one of the four bodily humours; black bile. ◆ *adj* **4** characterized by, causing, or expressing sadness, dejection, etc. ORIG C14: via OF from LL *melancholia,* from Gk, from *melas* black + *kholē* bile
▸ ˈ**melanˌcholic** *adj, n*

Melanchthon ★ (məˈlæŋkθən; *German* meˈlançtɔn) *n* **Philipp** (ˈfiːlɪp). original surname *Schwarzerd.* 1497–1560, German Protestant reformer. His *Loci Communes* (1521) was the first presentation of Protestant theology. In the

Augsburg Confession (1530) he stated the Lutheran faith.

Melanesia ★ (ˌmɛləˈniːzɪə) *n* one of the three divisions of islands in the Pacific (the others being Micronesia and Polynesia); the SW division of Oceania: includes Fiji, New Caledonia, Vanuatu, the Bismarck Archipelago, and the Louisiade, Solomon, Santa Cruz, and Loyalty Islands, which all lie northeast of Australia. ORIG C19: from Gk *melas* black + *nēsos* island; with reference to the dark skins of the inhabitants; on the model of *Polynesia*

Melanesian (ˌmɛləˈniːʒən, -zɪən) *adj* **1** of or relating to Melanesia, its people, or their languages. ◆ *n* **2** a native or inhabitant of Melanesia: generally Negroid with frizzy hair and small stature. **3** a group or branch of languages spoken in Melanesia.

melange *or* **mélange** (meɪˈlɑːnʒ) *n* a mixture; confusion. ORIG C17: from F *mêler* to mix

melanin (ˈmɛlənɪn) *n* any of a group of black or dark brown pigments present in the hair, skin, and eyes of man and animals: produced in excess in certain skin diseases and in melanomas.

melanism (ˈmɛləˌnɪzəm) *n* **1** the condition in man and animals of having dark-coloured or black skin, feathers, etc. **2** another name for **melanosis**.
▸ **ˌmelaˈnistic** *adj*

melano- *or before a vowel* **melan-** *combining form.* black or dark: *melanin; melanism; melanoma.* ORIG from Gk *melas* black

melanoma (ˌmɛləˈnəʊmə) *n, pl* **melanomas** *or* **melanomata** (-mətə). *Pathol.* a malignant tumour composed of melanin-containing cells, occurring esp. in the skin, often as a result of excessive exposure to sunlight.

melanosis (ˌmɛləˈnəʊsɪs) *or* **melanism** (ˈmɛləˌnɪzəm) *n Pathol.* a skin condition characterized by excessive deposits of melanin.
▸ **melanotic** (ˌmɛləˈnɒtɪk) *adj*

Melba ★ (ˈmɛlbə) *n* **1** Dame **Nellie,** stage name of *Helen Porter Mitchell.* 1861–1931, Australian soprano. **2 do a Melba.** *Austral. sl.* to make repeated farewell appearances.

Melba toast *n* very thin crisp toast. ORIG C20: after Dame Nellie MELBA

Melbourne[1] ★ (ˈmɛlbən) *n* a port in SE Australia, capital of Victoria, on Port Phillip Bay: the second largest city in the country; settled in 1835 and developed rapidly with the discovery of rich goldfields in 1851; three universities. Pop.: 3 218 100 (1996 est.).
▸ **Melburnian** (melˈbɜːnɪən) *n, adj*

Melbourne[2] ★ (ˈmɛlbən) *n* **William Lamb,** 2nd Viscount. 1779–1848; Whig prime minister (1834; 1835–41) and chief political adviser to the young Queen Victoria.

Melchior ★ (ˈmɛlkɪˌɔː) *n* **1** (in Christian tradition) one of the Magi, the others being Balthazar and Caspar. **2 Lauritz** (ˈlaurɪts). 1890–1973, US operatic tenor, born in Denmark.

Melchizedek ★ (mɛlˈkɪzəˌdɛk) *n Old Testament.* the priest-king of Salem who blessed Abraham (Genesis 14:18-19) and was taken as a prototype of Christ's priesthood (Hebrews 7). Douay spelling: **Melchisedech.**

meld[1] (mɛld) *vb* to blend or become blended; combine. ORIG C20: blend of MELT + WELD[1]

meld[2] (mɛld) *vb* **1** (in some card games) to declare or lay down (cards), which then score points. ◆ *n* **2** the act of melding. **3** a set of cards for melding. ORIG C19: from G *melden* to announce

Meleager ★ (ˌmɛlɪˈeɪgə) *n Greek myth.* one of the Argonauts, slayer of the Calydonian boar.

melee *or* **mêlée** (ˈmɛleɪ) *n* a noisy riotous fight or brawl. ORIG C17: from F *mêlée,* from *mêler* to mix

Méliès ★ (*French* meljɛs) *n* **Georges** (ʒɔrʒ). 1861–1938, French film director.

Melilla ★ (*French* melija) *n* the chief town of a Spanish enclave in Morocco, on the Mediterranean coast: founded by the Phoenicians; exports iron ore. Pop.: 58 052 (1994 est.).

meliorate (ˈmiːlɪəˌreɪt) *vb* **meliorates, meliorating, meliorated.** a variant of **ameliorate.**
▸ **ˌmelioˈration** *n* ▸ **meliorative** (ˈmiːlɪərətɪv) *adj, n*

melisma (mɪˈlɪzmə) *n, pl* **melismata** (-mətə) *or* **melismas.** *Music.* an expressive vocal phrase or passage consisting of several notes sung to one syllable. ORIG C19: from Gk: melody

Melitopol ★ (*Russian* mɪliˈtɔpəlj) *n* a city in SE Ukraine. Pop.: 174 000 (1996 est.).

Melk ★ (mɛlk) *n* a town in N Austria, on the River Danube: noted for its baroque Benedictine abbey. Pop.: 5163 (1991).

melliferous (mɪˈlɪfərəs) *or* **mellific** (mɪˈlɪfɪk) *adj* forming or producing honey. ORIG C17: from L *mellifer,* from *mel* honey + *ferre* to bear

mellifluous (mɪˈlɪflʊəs) *or* **mellifluent** *adj* (of sounds or utterances) smooth or honeyed; sweet. ORIG C15: from LL *mellifluus,* from L *mel* honey + *fluere* to flow
▸ **melˈlifluously** *adv* ▸ **melˈlifluousness** *or* **melˈlifluence** *n*

mellow (ˈmɛləʊ) *adj* **1** (esp. of fruits) full-flavoured; sweet; ripe. **2** (esp. of wines) well-matured. **3** (esp. of colours or sounds) soft or rich. **4** kind-hearted, esp. through maturity or old age. **5** genial, as through the effects of alcohol. **6** (of soil) soft and loamy. ◆ *vb* **7** to make or become mellow. **8** (foll. by *out*) to become calm and relaxed or (esp. of a drug) to have a calming and relaxing effect on (someone). ORIG C15: ?from OE *meru* soft (as through ripeness)
▸ **ˈmellowness** *n*

melodeon *or* **melodion** (mɪˈləʊdɪən) *n Music.* **1** a type of small accordion. **2** a type of keyboard instrument similar to the harmonium. ORIG C19: from G, from *Melodie* melody

melodic (mɪˈlɒdɪk) *adj* **1** of or relating to melody. **2** of or relating to a part in a piece of music. **3** melodious.
▸ **meˈlodically** *adv*

melodic minor scale *n Music.* a minor scale modified from the natural by the sharpening of the sixth and seventh when taken in ascending order and the restoration of their original pitches when taken in descending order.

melodious (mɪˈləʊdɪəs) *adj* **1** having a tune that is pleasant to the ear. **2** of or relating to melody; melodic.
▸ **meˈlodiously** *adv* ▸ **meˈlodiousness** *n*

melodist (ˈmɛlədɪst) *n* **1** a composer of melodies. **2** a singer.

melodize *or* **melodise** (ˈmɛləˌdaɪz) *vb* **melodizes, melodizing, melodized** *or* **melodises, melodising, melodised. 1** (*tr*) to provide with a melody. **2** (*tr*) to make melodious. **3** (*intr*) to sing or play melodies.
▸ **ˈmeloˌdizer** *or* **ˈmeloˌdiser** *n*

melodrama (ˈmɛləˌdrɑːmə) *n* **1** a play, film, etc., characterized by extravagant action and emotion. **2** (formerly) a romantic drama characterized by sensational incident, music, and song. **3** overdramatic emotion or behaviour. ORIG C19: from F *mélodrame,* from Gk *melos* song + *drame* DRAMA
▸ **melodramatist** (ˌmɛləˈdræmətɪst) *n* ▸ **melodramatic** (ˌmɛlədrəˈmætɪk) *adj* ▸ **ˌmelodraˈmatics** *pl n* ▸ **ˌmelodraˈmatically** *adv*

melody (ˈmɛlədɪ) *n, pl* **melodies. 1** *Music.* **1a** a succession of notes forming a distinctive sequence; tune. **1b** the horizontally represented aspect of the structure of a piece of music. Cf. **harmony** (sense 4b). **2** sounds that are pleasant because of tone or arrangement, esp. words of poetry. ORIG C13: from OF, from LL *melōdia,* from Gk *melōidia,* from *melos* song + *aoidein* to sing

melon (ˈmɛlən) *n* **1** any of several varieties of trailing plants (see **muskmelon, watermelon**), cultivated for their edible fruit. **2** the fruit of any of these plants, which has a hard rind and juicy flesh. ORIG C14: via OF from LL *mēlo,* form of *mēlopepō,* from Gk, from *mēlon* apple + *pepōn* gourd

Melos ★ (ˈmiːlɒs) *n* an island in the SW Aegean Sea, in the Cyclades: of volcanic origin, with hot springs; centre of early Aegean civilization, where the Venus de Milo was found. Pop.: 5000 (latest est.). Area: 132 sq. km (51 sq. miles). Modern Greek name: **Mílos.**

Melpomene ★ (mɛlˈpɒmɪnɪ) *n Greek myth.* the Muse of tragedy.

melt (mɛlt) *vb* **melts, melting, melted; melted** *or* **molten. 1** to liquefy (a solid) or (of a solid) to become liquefied, as a result of the action of heat. **2** to become or make liquid; dissolve. **3** (often foll. by *away*) to disappear; fade. **4** (foll. by *down*) to melt (metal scrap) for reuse. **5** (often foll. by *into*) to blend or cause to blend gradually. **6** to make or become emotional or sentimental; soften. ◆ *n* **7** the act or process of melting. **8** something melted or an amount melted. ORIG OE *meltan* to digest
▸ **'meltable** *adj* ▸ **'melter** *n* ▸ **'meltingly** *adv*

meltdown ('mɛlt,daʊn) *n* **1** (in a nuclear reactor) the melting of the fuel rods as a result of a defect in the cooling system, with the possible escape of radiation. **2** *Inf.* a sudden disastrous failure with potential for widespread harm, as a stock-exchange crash. **3** *Inf.* the process or state of irreversible breakdown or decline: *the community is slowly going into meltdown.*

melting point *n* the temperature at which a solid turns into a liquid.

melting pot *n* **1** a pot in which metals or other substances are melted, esp. in order to mix them. **2** an area in which many races, ideas, etc., are mixed.

melton ('mɛltən) *n* a heavy smooth woollen fabric with a short nap. Also called: **melton cloth.** ORIG C19: from MELTON MOWBRAY, a former centre for making this

Melton Mowbray ★ ('mɛltən 'məʊbrɪ) *n* a town in central England, in Leicestershire: pork pies and Stilton cheese. Pop.: 24 348 (1991).

meltwater ('mɛlt,wɔːtə) *n* melted snow or ice.

Melville ★ ('mɛlvɪl) *n* **Herman.** 1819–91, US writer. His works include *Moby Dick* (1851) and *Billy Budd* (written 1891, published 1924).

Melville Island ★ *n* **1** an island in the Arctic Ocean, north of Victoria Island: administratively part of the Northwest Territories of Canada. Area: 41 865 sq. km (16 164 sq. miles). **2** an island in the Arafura Sea, off the N central coast of Australia, separated from the mainland by Clarence Strait. Area: 6216 sq. km (2400 sq. miles).

Melville Peninsula ★ *n* a peninsula of N Canada, in the Northwest Territories, between the Gulf of Boothia and Foxe Basin.

mem. *abbrev. for:* **1** member. **2** memoir. **3** memorandum. **4** memorial.

member ('mɛmbə) *n* **1** a person who belongs to a club, political party, etc. **2** any individual plant or animal in a taxonomic group. **3** any part of an animal body, such as a limb. **4** any part of a plant, such as a petal, root, etc. **5** *Maths, logic.* any individual object belonging to a set or logical class. **6** a component part of a building or construction. ORIG C13: from L *membrum* limb, part
▸ **'memberless** *adj*

Member ('mɛmbə) *n* (*sometimes not cap.*) **1** short for **Member of Parliament. 2** short for **Member of Congress. 3** a member of some other legislative body.

Member of Congress *n* a member of the US Congress, esp. of the House of Representatives.

Member of Parliament *n* a member of the House of Commons or similar legislative body, as in many Commonwealth countries.

membership ('mɛmbəʃɪp) *n* **1** the members of an organization collectively. **2** the state of being a member.

membrane ('mɛmbreɪn) *n* **1** any thin pliable sheet of material. **2** a pliable sheetlike usually fibrous tissue that covers, lines, or connects plant and animal organs or cells. ORIG C16: from L *membrāna* skin covering a part of the body, from *membrum* MEMBER
▸ **membranous** ('mɛmbrənəs) *or* **membraneous** (mɛm'breɪnɪəs) *adj*

meme (miːm) *n* an idea or element of social behaviour passed on through generations in a culture, esp. by imitation. ORIG C20: ? from MIMIC, on the model of GENE

Memel ★ ('meːməl) *n* **1** the German name for **Klaipeda. 2** the lower course of the Neman River.

memento (mɪ'mɛntəʊ) *n, pl* **mementos** *or* **mementoes.** something that reminds one of past events; a souvenir. ORIG C15: from L, imperative of *meminisse* to remember

memento mori ('mɔːriː) *n, pl* **memento mori.** an object, such as a skull, intended to remind people of death. ORIG C16: L: remember you must die

Memling ('mɛmlɪŋ) *or* **Memlinc** ★ ('mɛmlɪŋk) *n* **Hans** (hɑns). ?1430–94, Flemish painter.

Memnon ★ ('mɛmnɒn) *n* **1** *Greek myth.* a king of Ethiopia, son of Eos: slain by Achilles in the Trojan War. **2** a colossal statue of Amenhotep III at Thebes in ancient Egypt, which emitted a sound thought by the Greeks to be the voice of Memnon.
▸ **Memnonian** (mɛm'nəʊnɪən) *adj*

memo ('mɛməʊ, 'miːməʊ) *n, pl* **memos.** short for **memorandum.**

memoir ('mɛmwɑː) *n* **1** a biography or historical account, esp. one based on personal knowledge. **2** an essay, as on a specialized topic. ORIG C16: from F, from L *memoria* MEMORY
▸ **'memoirist** *n*

memoirs ('mɛmwɑːz) *pl n* **1** a collection of reminiscences about a period, series of events, etc., written from personal experience or special sources. **2** an autobiographical record. **3** a record, as of transactions of a society, etc.

memorabilia (,mɛmərə'bɪlɪə) *pl n, sing* **memorabile** (-'ræbɪlɪ). **1** memorable events or things. **2** objects connected with famous people or events. ORIG C17: from L, from *memorābilis* MEMORABLE

memorable ('mɛmərəbᵊl) *adj* worth remembering or easily remembered. ORIG C15: from L *memorābilis,* from *memorāre* to recall, from *memor* mindful
▸ **,memora'bility** *n* ▸ **'memorably** *adv*

memorandum (,mɛmə'rændəm) *n, pl* **memorandums** *or* **memoranda** (-də). **1** a written statement, record, or communication. **2** a note of things to be remembered. **3** an informal diplomatic communication. **4** *Law.* a short written summary of the terms of a transaction. ◆ Often (esp. for senses 1, 2) shortened to **memo.** ORIG C15: from L: (something) to be remembered

memorial (mɪ'mɔːrɪəl) *adj* **1** serving to preserve the memory of the dead or a past event. **2** of or involving memory. ◆ *n* **3** something serving as a remembrance. **4** a written statement of facts submitted to a government, authority, etc., in conjunction with a petition. **5** an informal diplomatic paper. ORIG C14: from LL *memoriāle* a reminder, neuter of *memoriālis*
▸ **me'morially** *adv*

memorialize *or* **memorialise** (mɪ'mɔːrɪə,laɪz) *vb* **memorializes, memorializing, memorialized** *or* **memorialises, memorialising, memorialised.** (*tr*) **1** to honour or commemorate. **2** to present or address a memorial to.

memorize *or* **memorise** ('mɛmə,raɪz) *vb* **memorizes, memorizing, memorized** *or* **memorises, memorising, memorised.** (*tr*) to commit to memory; learn so as to remember.

memory ('mɛmərɪ) *n, pl* **memories. 1a** the ability of the mind to store and recall past sensations, thoughts, knowledge, etc.: *he can do it from memory.* **1b** the part of the brain that appears to have this function. **2** the sum of everything retained by the mind. **3** a particular recollection of an event, person, etc. **4** the time over which recollection extends: *within his memory.* **5** commemoration or remembrance: *in memory of our leader.* **6** the state of being remembered, as after death. **7** a part of a computer in which information is stored for immediate use by the central processing unit. Cf. **RAM**[1]. ORIG C14: from OF *memorie,* from L *memoria,* from *memor* mindful

Memphis ★ ('mɛmfɪs) *n* **1** a port in SW Tennessee, on the Mississippi River: the largest city in the state; a major cotton and timber market; Memphis State University (1909). Pop.: 596 725 (1996 est.). **2** a ruined city in N Egypt, the ancient centre of Lower Egypt, on the Nile: administrative and artistic centre, sacred to the worship of Ptah.
▸ **'Memphian** *adj, n*

Memphremagog ★ (,mɛmfriː'meɪgɒg) *n* **Lake.** a lake on the border between the US and Canada, in N Vermont and S Quebec. Length: about 43 km (27 miles). Width: up to 6 km (4 miles).

memsahib ('mɛm,sɑːɪb, -hɪb) *n* (formerly, in India) a term of respect used for a European married woman. ORIG C19: from MA'AM + SAHIB

men (mɛn) *n* the plural of **man**.

menace ('mɛnɪs) *vb* **menaces, menacing, menaced. 1** to threaten with violence, danger, etc. ◆ *n* **2** *Literary.* a threat. **3** something menacing; a source of danger. **4** *Inf.* a nuisance. ORIG C13: ult. rel. to L *minax* threatening, from *minārī* to threaten
▸ **'menacer** *n* ▸ **'menacing** *adj* ▸ **'menacingly** *adv*

menad ('miːnæd) *n* a variant spelling of **maenad**.

Menado (mɛ'nɑːdəʊ) *or* **Manado** ★ *n* a port in NE Indonesia, on NE Sulawesi: founded by the Dutch in 1657. Pop.: 398 900 (1995 est.).

ménage (meɪ'nɑːʒ) *n* the persons of a household. ORIG C17: from F, from Vulgar L (unattested) *mansiōnāticum* household

ménage à trois *French.* (menaʒ a trwɑ) *n, pl* ***ménages à trois*** (menaʒ a trwɑ). a sexual arrangement involving a married couple and the lover of one of them. ORIG lit.: household of three

menagerie (mɪ'nædʒərɪ) *n* **1** a collection of wild animals kept for exhibition. **2** the place where such animals are housed. ORIG C18: from F: household management, which formerly included care of domestic animals

Menai Strait ★ ('mɛnaɪ) *n* a channel of the Irish Sea between the island of Anglesey and the mainland of NW Wales: famous suspension bridge (1819–26) designed by Thomas Telford and tubular bridge (1846–50) designed by Robert Stephenson. Length: 24 km (15 miles). Width: up to 3 km (2 miles).

Menander ★ (mə'nændə) *n* ?342–?292 B.C., Greek comic dramatist. The *Dyskolos* is his only complete extant comedy but others survive in adaptations by Terence and Plautus.

Mencius ★ ('mɛnʃɪəs, -ʃəs) *n* Chinese name *Mengzi* or *Meng-tze.* ?372–?289 B.C., Chinese philosopher, who propounded the ethical system of Confucius.

Mencken ★ ('mɛŋkən) *n* **H(enry) L(ouis).** 1880–1956, US journalist and critic, noted for *The American Language* (1919): editor of the *American Mercury,* which he founded (1924).

mend (mɛnd) *vb* **1** (*tr*) to repair (something broken or unserviceable). **2** to improve or undergo improvement; reform (often in **mend one's ways**). **3** (*intr*) to heal or recover. **4** (*intr*) (of conditions) to improve; become better. ◆ *n* **5** the act of repairing. **6** a mended area, esp. on a garment. **7 on the mend.** becoming better, esp. in health. ORIG C12: from AMEND
▸ **'mendable** *adj* ▸ **'mender** *n*

mendacity (mɛn'dæsɪtɪ) *n, pl* **mendacities. 1** the tendency to be untruthful. **2** a falsehood. ORIG C17: from LL *mendācitās,* from L *mendāx* untruthful
▸ **mendacious** (mɛn'deɪʃəs) *adj* ▸ **men'daciously** *adv*

Mendel ★ ('mɛndᵊl) *n* **Gregor Johann** ('greːgɔr jo'han). 1822–84, Austrian monk and botanist; founder of genetics, with his experiments on the hybridization of green peas. His findings were published (1865) but unrecognized until 1900. See **Mendel's laws.**

mendelevium (,mɛndɪ'liːvɪəm) *n* a transuranic element artificially produced by bombardment of einsteinium. Symbol: Md; atomic no.: 101; half-life of most stable isotope, ^{258}Md: 60 days (approx.). ORIG C20: after D. I. MENDELEYEV

Mendeleyev *or* **Mendeleev** ★ (*Russian* mɪndɪ'ljejɪf) *n* **Dmitri Ivanovich** ('dmitrij i'vanəvitʃ). 1834–1907, Russian chemist. He devised the first form of the periodic table (1869).

Mendelian (mɛn'diːlɪən) *adj* of or relating to Mendel's laws.

Mendel's laws *pl n* the principles of heredity proposed by Gregor Mendel. The **Law of Segregation** states that each hereditary character is determined by a pair of units in the reproductive cells: the pairs separate during meiosis so that each gamete carries only one unit of each pair. The **Law of Independent Assortment** states that the separation of the units of each pair is not influenced by that of any other pair.

Mendelssohn ★ ('mɛndᵊlsən; *German* 'mɛndəlzoːn) *n* **1 Felix** ('feːlɪks), full name *Jacob Ludwig Felix Mendelssohn-Bartholdy.* 1809–47, German composer. His works include the overtures *A Midsummer Night's Dream* (1826) and *Fingal's Cave* (1832), five symphonies, the oratorio *Elijah* (1846), and many songs. **2** his grandfather, **Moses** ('moːzəs). 1729–86, German Jewish philosopher, noted for his book *Jerusalem* (1783).

Menderes ★ (,mɛnde'rɛs) *n* **1** a river in SW Turkey flowing southwest, then west to the Aegean. Length: about 386 km (240 miles). Ancient name: **Maeander. 2** a river in NW Turkey flowing west and northwest to the Dardanelles. Length: 104 km (65 miles). Ancient name: **Scamander.**

Mendès-France ★ (*French* mɛ̃dɛsfrɑ̃s) *n* **Pierre** (pjɛr). 1907–82, French statesman; prime minister (1954–55).

mendicant ('mɛndɪkənt) *adj* **1** begging. **2** (of a member of a religious order) dependent on alms for sustenance. ◆ *n* **3** a mendicant friar. **4** a less common word for **beggar.** ORIG C16: from L *mendīcāre,* from *mendīcus* beggar, from *mendus* flaw
▸ **'mendicancy** *or* **mendicity** (mɛn'dɪsɪtɪ) *n*

Mendips ★ ('mɛndɪps) *pl n* a range of limestone hills in SW England, in N Somerset: includes the Cheddar Gorge and numerous caves. Highest point: 325 m (1068 ft). Also called: **Mendip Hills.**

Mendoza[1] ★ (mɛn'dəʊzə; *Spanish* men'doθa) *n* a city in W central Argentina, in the foothills of the Sierra de los Paramillos: largely destroyed by an earthquake in 1861; commercial centre of an intensively cultivated irrigated region; University of Cuyo (1939). Pop.: 773 113 (1991).

Mendoza[2] ★ (*Spanish* men'doθa) *n* **Pedro de** ('peðro de). died 1537, Spanish soldier and explorer; founder of Buenos Aires (1536).

meneer (mə'nɪə) *n* a S. African title of address equivalent to *sir* when used alone or *Mr* when placed before a name. ORIG Afrik.

Menelaus ★ (,mɛnɪ'leɪəs) *n Greek myth.* a king of Sparta and the brother of Agamemnon. He was the husband of Helen, whose abduction led to the Trojan War.

Menelik II ★ ('mɛnɪlɪk) *n* 1844–1913, emperor of Abyssinia (1889–1910). He defeated the Italians at Aduwa (1896), maintaining the independence of Abyssinia.

Menes ★ ('miːniːz) *n* the first king of the first dynasty of Egypt (?3100 B.C.). He is said to have united Upper and Lower Egypt and founded Memphis.

menfolk ('mɛn,fəʊk) *pl n* men collectively, esp. the men of a particular family.

Mengelberg ★ ('mɛŋgᵊl,bɜːg; *Dutch* 'mɛŋəlbɛrx) *n* **(Josef) Willem** ('wɪləm). 1871–1951, Dutch conductor.

Mengistu Haile Mariam ★ (mɛŋ'gɪstuː 'haɪlɪ 'mɑːrɪəm) *n* born 1937, Ethiopian soldier and statesman; head of state from 1977 until overthrown and forced into exile in 1991.

Mengzi *or* **Meng-tze** ★ ('mɛŋ'tseɪ) *n* the Chinese name for **Mencius.**

menhaden (mɛn'heɪdᵊn) *n, pl* **menhaden.** a marine North American fish: source of fishmeal, fertilizer, and oil. ORIG C18: from Algonquian; prob. rel. to another Amerind word, *munnawhatteaúg* fertilizer

menhir ('mɛnhɪə) *n* a single standing stone, dating from prehistoric times. ORIG C19: from Breton *men* stone + *hir* long

menial ('miːnɪəl) *adj* **1** consisting of or occupied with work requiring little skill, esp. domestic duties. **2** of, involving, or befitting servants. **3** servile. ◆ *n* **4** a domestic servant. **5** a servile person. ORIG C14: from Anglo-Norman *meignial,* from OF *meinie* household

Meninga ★ (mɪn'ɪŋgə) *n* **Mal.** born 1960, Australian rugby league player.

meninges (mɪ'nɪndʒiːz) *pl n, sing* **meninx** ('miːnɪŋks). the three membranes (**dura mater, arachnoid, pia mater**) that envelop the brain and spinal cord. ORIG C17: from Gk, pl of *meninx* membrane
▸ **meningeal** (mɪ'nɪndʒɪəl) *adj*

meningitis (ˌmɛnɪnˈdʒaɪtɪs) *n* inflammation of the membranes that surround the brain or spinal cord, caused by infection.
▸ **meningitic** (ˌmɛnɪnˈdʒɪtɪk) *adj*

meningococcus (mɛˌnɪŋgəʊˈkɒkəs) *n, pl* **meningococci** (-ˈkɒkaɪ, -ˈkɒkiː). the bacterium that causes cerebrospinal meningitis.
▸ **meˌningoˈcoccal** *adj*

meniscus (mɪˈnɪskəs) *n, pl* **menisci** (-ˈnɪsaɪ) *or* **meniscuses.** **1** the curved upper surface of a liquid standing in a tube, produced by the surface tension. **2** a crescent-shaped lens; a concavo-convex or convexo-concave lens. ORIG C17: from NL, from Gk *mēniskos* crescent, dim. of *mēnē* moon
▸ **meˈniscoid** *adj*

Mennonite (ˈmɛnəˌnaɪt) *n* a member of a Protestant sect that rejects infant baptism and Church organization, and in most cases refuses military service, public office, and the taking of oaths. ORIG C16: from G *Mennonit,* after *Menno* Simons (1496–1561), Frisian religious leader
▸ **ˈMennonitism** *n*

meno (ˈmɛnəʊ) *adv Music.* to be played less quickly, less softly, etc. ORIG from It., from L *minus* less

meno- *combining form.* menstruation. ORIG from Gk *mēn* month

Menon ★ (ˈmɛnən) *n* **Vengalil Krishnan Krishna** (ˈvɛŋgəlɪl ˈkriːʃnən ˈkriːʃnə). 1897–1974, Indian diplomat and close associate of Nehru.

menopause (ˈmɛnəʊˌpɔːz) *n* the period during which a woman's menstrual cycle ceases, normally at an age of 45 to 50. ORIG C19: from F, from Gk *mēn* month + *pausis* halt
▸ **ˌmenoˈpausal** *adj*

menorah (mɪˈnɔːrə) *n Judaism.* **1** a seven-branched candelabrum used in the Temple and now an emblem of Judaism and the badge of the state of Israel. **2** a similar lamp lit during the Chanukah festival. ORIG from Heb.: candlestick

Menorca ★ (meˈnɔrka) *n* the Spanish name for **Minorca.**

menorrhagia (ˌmɛnɔːˈreɪdʒɪə) *n* excessive bleeding during menstruation.

menorrhoea (ˌmɛnəˈrɪə) *n* normal bleeding in menstruation.

Menotti ★ (məˈnɒtɪ; *Italian* meˈnɔtti) *n* **Gian Carlo** (dʒan ˈkarlo). born 1911, Italian composer, in the US from 1928. His operas include *The Consul* (1950) and *Amahl and the Night Visitors* (1951).

menses (ˈmɛnsiːz) *n* (*functioning as sing or pl*) **1** another name for **menstruation. 2** the period of time during which one menstruation occurs. **3** the matter discharged during menstruation. ORIG C16: from L, pl of *mensis* month

Menshevik (ˈmɛnʃɪvɪk) *or* **Menshevist** *n* a member of the moderate wing of the Russian Social Democratic Party. Cf. **Bolshevik.** ORIG C20: from Russian, lit.: minority, from *menshe* less, from *malo* few
▸ **ˈMensheˌvism** *n*

menstruate (ˈmɛnstrʊˌeɪt) *vb* **menstruates, menstruating, menstruated.** (*intr*) to undergo menstruation. ORIG C17: from L *menstruāre,* from *mensis* month

menstruation (ˌmɛnstrʊˈeɪʃən) *n* the approximately monthly discharge of blood and cellular debris from the uterus by nonpregnant women from puberty to the menopause.
▸ **ˈmenstrual** *or* **ˈmenstruous** *adj*

menstruum (ˈmɛnstrʊəm) *n, pl* **menstruums** *or* **menstrua** (-strʊə). a solvent, esp. one used in the preparation of a drug. ORIG C17 (meaning: solvent), C14 (menstrual discharge): from Med. L, from L *mēnstruus* monthly, from *mēnsis* month; from alchemical comparison between a base metal being transmuted into gold and the supposed action of the menses

mensurable (ˈmɛnsjʊrəbᵊl, -ʃə-) *adj* a less common word for **measurable.** ORIG C17: from LL *mēnsūrābilis,* from *mēnsūra* MEASURE
▸ **ˌmensuraˈbility** *n*

mensural (ˈmɛnʃərəl) *adj* **1** of or involving measure. **2** *Music.* of or relating to music in which notes have fixed values. ORIG C17: from LL *mēnsūrālis,* from *mēnsūra* MEASURE

mensuration (ˌmɛnʃəˈreɪʃən) *n* **1** the study of the measurement of geometric magnitudes such as length. **2** the act or process of measuring.
▸ **mensurative** (ˈmɛnʃərətɪv) *adj*

-ment *suffix forming nouns, esp. from verbs.* **1** indicating state, condition, or quality: *enjoyment.* **2** indicating the result or product of an action: *embankment.* **3** indicating process or action: *management.* ORIG from F, from L *-mentum*

mental (ˈmɛntᵊl) *adj* **1** of or involving the mind. **2** occurring only in the mind: *mental arithmetic.* **3** affected by mental illness: *a mental patient.* **4** concerned with mental illness: *a mental hospital.* **5** *Sl.* insane. ORIG C15: from LL *mentālis,* from L *mēns* mind
▸ **ˈmentally** *adv*

mental deficiency *n Psychiatry.* a less common term for **mental retardation.**

mental handicap *n* any intellectual disability resulting from injury to the brain or from abnormal neurological development.
▸ **mentally handicapped** *adj*

mental healing *n* the healing of a disorder by mental concentration or suggestion.

mental illness *n* any of various disorders in which a person's thoughts, emotions, or behaviour are so abnormal as to cause suffering to himself, herself, or other people.

mentalism (ˈmɛntᵊˌlɪzəm) *n Philosophy.* the doctrine that mind is the fundamental reality and that objects of knowledge exist only as aspects of the subject's consciousness.
▸ **ˌmentalˈistic** *adj*

mentality (mɛnˈtælɪtɪ) *n, pl* **mentalities. 1** the state or quality of mental or intellectual ability. **2** a way of thinking; mental inclination or character.

mental lexicon *n* the store of words in a person's mind.

mental reservation *n* a tacit withholding of full assent or an unexpressed qualification made when taking an oath, making a statement, etc.

mental retardation *n Psychiatry.* the condition of having a low intelligence quotient (below 70).

menthol (ˈmɛnθɒl) *n* an organic compound found in peppermint oil and used as an antiseptic, in inhalants, and as an analgesic. Formula: $C_{10}H_{19}OH$. ORIG C19: from G, from L *mentha* MINT[1]

mentholated (ˈmɛnθəˌleɪtɪd) *adj* containing, treated with, or impregnated with menthol.

mention (ˈmɛnʃən) *vb* (*tr*) **1** to refer to or speak about briefly or incidentally. **2** to acknowledge or honour. **3 not to mention (something).** to say nothing of (something too obvious to mention). ♦ *n* **4** a recognition or acknowledgment. **5** a slight reference or allusion. **6** the act of mentioning. ORIG C14: via OF from L *mentiō* a calling to mind, from *mēns* mind
▸ **ˈmentionable** *adj*

Menton ★ (mɛnˈtəʊn; *French* mɑ̃tɔ̃) *n* a town and resort in SE France, on the Mediterranean: belonged to Monaco from the 14th century until 1848, then an independent republic until purchased by France in 1860. Pop.: 25 500 (latest est.).

mentor (ˈmɛntɔː) *n* a wise or trusted adviser or guide. ORIG C18: from MENTOR

Mentor ★ (ˈmɛntɔː) *n* the friend whom Odysseus put in charge of his household when he left for Troy. He was the adviser of the young Telemachus.

mentoring (ˈmɛntərɪŋ) *n* (in business) the practice of assigning a junior member of staff to the care of a more experienced person who assists him in his career.

menu (ˈmɛnjuː) *n* **1** a list of dishes served at a meal or that can be ordered in a restaurant. **2** a list of options displayed on a visual display unit from which the operator selects an action to be carried out. ORIG C19: from F *menu* small, detailed (list), from L *minūtus* MINUTE[2]

menuetto (mɛnjuˈɛtəʊ) *n, pl* **menuettos**. *Music*. another term for **minuet**. ORIG from It.

Menuhin ★ (ˈmɛnjʊɪn) *n* **Yehudi**, Baron. (jɛˈhuːdɪ) 1916–99, British violinist, born in the US.

Menzies ★ (ˈmɛnzɪz) *n* Sir **Robert Gordon**. 1894–1978, Australian statesman; prime minister (1939–41; 1949–66).

meow, miaou, miaow (mɪˈaʊ, mjaʊ), *or* **miaul** (mɪˈaʊl, mjaʊl) *vb* **1** (*intr*) (of a cat) to make a characteristic crying sound. ◆ *interj* **2** an imitation of this sound.

MEP (in Britain) *abbrev. for* Member of the European Parliament.

mepacrine (ˈmɛpəkrɪn) *n Brit.* a drug formerly widely used to treat malaria. ORIG C20: from ME(THYL) + PA(LUDISM + A)CR(ID)INE

meperidine (məˈpɛrɪˌdiːn, -dɪn) *n* the US name for **pethidine**. ORIG C20: from METHYL + PIPERIDINE

Mephistopheles (ˌmɛfɪˈstɒfɪˌliːz) *or* **Mephisto** ★ (məˈfɪstəʊ) *n* a devil in medieval mythology and the one to whom Faust sold his soul in German legend.
▸ **Mephistophelean** *or* **Mephistophelian** (ˌmɛfɪstəˈfiːlɪən) *adj*

mephitic (mɪˈfɪtɪk) *or* **mephitical** *adj* **1** poisonous; foul. **2** foul-smelling; putrid. ORIG C17: from LL *mephīticus* pestilential

meprobamate (məˈprəʊbəˌmeɪt, ˌmɛprəʊˈbæmeɪt) *n* a white bitter powder used as a tranquillizer. ORIG C20: from ME(THYL) + PRO(PYL + *car*)*bamate* a salt or ester of an amide of carbonic acid

-mer *suffix forming nouns. Chem.* denoting a substance of a particular class: *monomer; polymer.* ORIG from Gk *meros* part

Merano ★ (məˈrɑːnəʊ; *Italian* meˈraːno) *n* a town and resort in NE Italy, in the foothills of the central Alps: capital of the Tyrol (12th–15th century); under Austrian rule until 1919. Pop.: 33 638 (1993 est.). German name: **Meran** (meˈraːn).

Merca ★ (ˈmɛəkə) *n* a port in S Somalia on the Indian Ocean. Pop.: 100 000 (1987 est.).

mercantile (ˈmɜːkənˌtaɪl) *adj* **1** of, relating to, or characteristic of trade or traders; commercial. **2** of or relating to mercantilism. ORIG C17: from F, from It., from *mercante* MERCHANT

mercantilism (ˈmɜːkəntɪˌlɪzəm) *n Econ.* a theory prevalent in Europe during the 17th and 18th centuries asserting that the wealth of a nation depends on possession of precious metals and therefore that a government must maximize foreign trade surplus and foster national commercial interests, a merchant marine, the establishment of colonies, etc.
▸ **ˈmercantilist** *n, adj*

mercaptan (mɜːˈkæptæn) *n* another name (not in technical use) for **thiol**. ORIG C19: from G, from Med. L *mercurium captans*, lit.: seizing quicksilver

Mercator ★ (mɜːˈkeɪtə) *n* **Gerardus** (dʒəˈrɑːdəs). Latinized name of *Gerhard Kremer*. 1512–94, Flemish cartographer and mathematician.

Mercator projection *n* a conformal map projection on which parallels and meridians form a rectangular grid, scale being exaggerated with increasing distance from the equator. Also called: **Mercator's projection**. ORIG C17: after G. MERCATOR

mercenary (ˈmɜːsɪnərɪ, -sɪnrɪ) *adj* **1** influenced by greed or desire for gain. **2** of or relating to a mercenary or mercenaries. ◆ *n, pl* **mercenaries**. **3** a man hired to fight for a foreign army, etc. **4** *Rare.* any person who works solely for pay. ORIG C16: from L *mercēnārius*, from *mercēs* wages

mercer (ˈmɜːsə) *n Brit.* a dealer in textile fabrics and fine cloth. ORIG C13: from OF *mercier* dealer, from Vulgar L, from L *merx* wares
▸ **ˈmercery** *n*

mercerize *or* **mercerise** (ˈmɜːsəˌraɪz) *vb* **mercerizes, mercerizing, mercerized** *or* **mercerises, mercerising, mercerised**. (*tr*) to treat (cotton yarn) with an alkali to increase its strength and reception to dye and impart a lustrous silky appearance. ORIG C19: after John *Mercer* (1791–1866), E maker of textiles

merchandise *n* (ˈmɜːtʃənˌdaɪs, -ˌdaɪz). **1** commercial goods; commodities. ◆ *vb* (ˈmɜːtʃənˌdaɪz), **merchandises, merchandising, merchandised**. **2** to engage in the commercial purchase and sale of (goods or services); trade. ORIG C13: from OF; see MERCHANT

merchandising (ˈmɜːtʃənˌdaɪzɪŋ) *n* **1** the selection and display of goods in a retail outlet. **2** commercial goods, esp. ones issued to exploit the popularity of a pop group, sporting event, etc.

merchant (ˈmɜːtʃənt) *n* **1** a person engaged in the purchase and sale of commodities for profit; trader. **2** *Chiefly Scot., US, & Canad.* a person engaged in retail trade. **3** (esp. in historical contexts) any trader. **4** *Derog.* a person dealing or involved in something undesirable: *a gossip merchant.* **5** (*modifier*) **5a** of the merchant navy: *a merchant sailor.* **5b** of or concerned with trade: *a merchant ship.* ◆ *vb* **6** (*tr*) to conduct trade in; deal in. ORIG C13: from OF, prob. from Vulgar L, from L *mercārī* to trade, from *merx* wares

Merchant ★ (ˈmɜːtʃənt) *n* **Ismail** (ˈɪzmeɪəl). born 1936, Indian film producer, noted for his collaboration with James Ivory on such films as *Shakespeare Wallah* (1965), *A Room with a View* (1986), and *A Soldier's Daughter Never Cries* (1998).

merchantable (ˈmɜːtʃəntəbᵊl) *adj* suitable for trading.

merchant bank *n Brit.* a financial institution engaged primarily in accepting foreign bills, advising companies on flotations and takeovers, underwriting new issues, hire-purchase finance, making long-term loans to companies, and managing investment portfolios, funds, and trusts.
▸ **merchant banker** *n*

merchantman (ˈmɜːtʃəntmən) *n, pl* **merchantmen**. a merchant ship.

merchant navy *or* **marine** *n* the ships or crew engaged in a nation's commercial shipping.

Mercia ★ (ˈmɜːʃɪə) *n* a kingdom and earldom of central and S England during the Anglo-Saxon period that reached its height under King Offa (757–96).

Mercian (ˈmɜːʃɪən) *adj* **1** of or relating to Mercia, or its dialect. ◆ *n* **2** the dialect of Old and Middle English spoken in Mercia. **3** a native or inhabitant of Mercia.

merciful (ˈmɜːsɪfʊl) *adj* showing or giving mercy; compassionate.
▸ **ˈmercifully** *adv* ▸ **ˈmercifulness** *n*

merciless (ˈmɜːsɪlɪs) *adj* without mercy; pitiless, cruel, or heartless.
▸ **ˈmercilessly** *adv* ▸ **ˈmercilessness** *n*

Merckx ★ (mɜːks) *n* **Eddy**. born 1945, Belgian professional cyclist: five times winner of the Tour de France.

Mercouri ★ (mɜːˈkuːrɪ) *n* **Melina** (məˈliːnə). 1925–94, Greek actress and politician: her films include *Never on Sunday* (1960); minister of culture and science (1981–85), minister of culture (1985–89; 1993–94).

mercurial (mɜːˈkjʊərɪəl) *adj* **1** of, like, containing, or relating to mercury. **2** volatile; lively: *a mercurial temperament.* **3** (*sometimes cap.*) of, like, or relating to the god or the planet Mercury. ◆ *n* **4** *Med.* any salt of mercury for use as a medicine. ORIG C14: from L *mercuriālis*
▸ **merˌcuriˈality** *n* ▸ **merˈcurially** *adv*

mercuric (mɜːˈkjʊərɪk) *adj* of or containing mercury in the divalent state; denoting a mercury(II) compound.

mercuric chloride *n* a white poisonous crystalline substance used as a pesticide, antiseptic, and preservative for wood. Formula: $HgCl_2$. Systematic name: **mercury(II) chloride**.

Mercurochrome (məˈkjʊərəˌkrəʊm) *n Trademark.* a solution of a crystalline compound, used as topical antibacterial agent.

mercurous (ˈmɜːkjʊrəs) *adj* of or containing mercury in the monovalent state; denoting a mercury(I) compound.

mercury (ˈmɜːkjʊrɪ) *n, pl* **mercuries**. **1** Also called: **quicksilver**. a heavy silvery-white toxic liquid metallic element: used in thermometers, barometers, mercury-vapour lamps, and dental amalgams. Symbol: Hg; atomic no.: 80; atomic wt.: 200.59. **2** any plant of the genus *Mercurialis*. **3** *Arch.* a messenger or courier. ORIG C14:

from L *Mercurius,* messenger of Jupiter, god of commerce; rel. to *merx* merchandise

Mercury[1] ★ (ˈmɜːkjʊrɪ) *n Roman myth.* the messenger of the gods.

Mercury[2] (ˈmɜːkjʊrɪ) *n* the second smallest planet and the nearest to the sun.

mercury-vapour lamp *n* a lamp in which an electric discharge through mercury vapour is used to produce a greenish-blue light.

mercy (ˈmɜːsɪ) *n, pl* **mercies. 1** compassionate treatment of or attitude towards an offender, adversary, etc., who is in one's power or care; clemency; pity. **2** the power to show mercy. **3** a relieving or welcome occurrence or state of affairs. **4 at the mercy of.** in the power of. ORIG C12: from OF, from L *mercēs* recompense, from *merx* goods

mercy flight *n* an aircraft flight to bring a seriously ill or injured person to hospital from an isolated community.

mercy killing *n* another term for **euthanasia.**

mere[1] (mɪə) *adj* being nothing more than something specified: *a mere child.* ORIG C15: from L *merus* pure
▸ **ˈmerely** *adv*

mere[2] (mɪə) *n* **1** *Dialect or arch.* a lake or marsh. **2** *Obs.* the sea or an inlet of it. ORIG OE *mere* sea, lake

mere[3] (ˈmɛrɪ) *n* a short flat Maori striking weapon. ORIG from Maori

-mere *n combining form.* indicating a part or division. ORIG from Gk *meros* part
▸ **meric** *adj combining form.*

Meredith ★ (ˈmɛrɪdɪθ) *n* **George.** 1828–1909, British novelist and poet. His works include the novel *The Egoist* (1879) and the poem *Modern Love* (1862).

meretricious (ˌmɛrɪˈtrɪʃəs) *adj* **1** superficially or garishly attractive. **2** insincere. **3** *Arch.* of, like, or relating to a prostitute. ORIG C17: from L *merētrīcius,* from *merētrix* prostitute, from *merēre* to earn money
▸ **ˌmereˈtriciously** *adv* ▸ **ˌmereˈtriciousness** *n*

merganser (mɜːˈgænsə) *n, pl* **mergansers** *or* **merganser.** any of several typically crested large marine diving ducks, having a long slender hooked bill with serrated edges. ORIG C18: from NL, from L *mergus* waterfowl, from *mergere* to plunge + *anser* goose

merge (mɜːdʒ) *vb* **merges, merging, merged. 1** to meet and join or cause to meet and join. **2** to blend or cause to blend; fuse. ORIG C17: from L *mergere* to plunge
▸ **ˈmergence** *n*

merger (ˈmɜːdʒə) *n* **1** *Commerce.* the combination of two or more companies. **2** *Law.* the absorption of an estate, interest, offence, etc., into a greater one. **3** the act of merging or the state of being merged.

Mergui Archipelago ★ (mɜːˈgwiː) *n* a group of over 200 islands in the Andaman Sea, off the Tenasserim coast of S Myanmar: mountainous and forested.

Meriç ★ (məˈriːtʃ) *n* the Turkish name for the **Maritsa.**

Mérida ★ (*Spanish* ˈmeriða) *n* **1** a city in SE Mexico, capital of Yucatán state: founded in 1542 on the site of the ancient Mayan city of T'ho; centre of the henequen industry; university. Pop.: 523 422 (1990). **2** a city in W Venezuela: founded in 1558 by Spanish conquistadores; University of Los Andes (1785). Pop.: 167 990 (1991). **3** a market town in W Spain, in Estremadura, on the Guadiana River: founded in 25 B.C.; became the capital of Lusitania and one of the chief cities of Iberia. Pop.: 49 830 (1991). Latin name: **Auˈgusta Eˈmerita.**

meridian (məˈrɪdɪən) *n* **1a** one of the imaginary lines joining the north and south poles at right angles to the equator, designated by degrees of longitude from 0° at Greenwich to 180°. **1b** the great circle running through both poles. **2** *Astron.* the great circle on the celestial sphere passing through the north and south celestial poles and the zenith and nadir of the observer. **3** the peak; zenith: *the meridian of his achievements.* **4** (in acupuncture, etc.) any of the channels through which vital energy is believed to circulate round the body. **5** *Obs.* noon. ◆ *adj* **6** along or relating to a meridian. **7** of or happening at noon. **8** relating to the peak of something. ORIG C14: from L *merīdiānus* of midday, from *merīdiēs* midday, from *medius* MID[1] + *diēs* day

meridional (məˈrɪdɪənᵊl) *adj* **1** along, relating to, or resembling a meridian. **2** characteristic of or located in the south, esp. of Europe. ◆ *n* **3** an inhabitant of the south, esp. of France. ORIG C14: from LL *merīdiōnālis* southern; see MERIDIAN

Mérimée ★ (*French* merime) *n* **Prosper** (prɔspɛr). 1803–70, French writer, noted for his short novel *Carmen* (1845), on which Bizet's opera was based.

meringue (məˈræŋ) *n* **1** stiffly beaten egg whites mixed with sugar and baked. **2** a small cake or shell of this mixture, often filled with cream. ORIG C18: from F, from ?

merino (məˈriːnəʊ) *n, pl* **merinos. 1** a breed of sheep originating in Spain. **2** the long fine wool of this sheep. **3** the yarn made from this wool. ◆ *adj* **4** made from merino wool. ORIG C18: from Sp., from ?

Merionethshire ★ (ˌmɛrɪˈɒnɪθˌʃɪə, -ʃə) *n* (until 1974) a county of N Wales, now part of Gwynedd.

meristem (ˈmɛrɪˌstɛm) *n* a plant tissue responsible for growth, whose cells divide and differentiate to form the tissues and organs of the plant. ORIG C19: from Gk *meristos* divided, from *merizein,* from *meris* portion
▸ **meristematic** (ˌmɛrɪstɪˈmætɪk) *adj*

merit (ˈmɛrɪt) *n* **1** worth or superior quality; excellence. **2** (*often pl*) a deserving or commendable quality or act. **3** *Christianity.* spiritual credit granted or received for good works. **4** the fact or state of deserving; desert. ◆ *vb* **merits, meriting, merited. 5** (*tr*) to be worthy of; deserve. ORIG C13: via OF from L *meritum* reward, from *merēre* to deserve
▸ **ˈmerited** *adj* ▸ **ˈmeritless** *adj*

meritocracy (ˌmɛrɪˈtɒkrəsɪ) *n, pl* **meritocracies. 1** rule by persons chosen for their superior talents or intellect. **2** the persons constituting such a group. **3** a social system formed on such a basis.
▸ **meritocratic** (ˌmɛrɪtəˈkrætɪk) *adj*

meritorious (ˌmɛrɪˈtɔːrɪəs) *adj* praiseworthy; showing merit. ORIG C15: from L *meritōrius* earning money
▸ **ˌmeriˈtoriously** *adv* ▸ **ˌmeriˈtoriousness** *n*

merits (ˈmɛrɪts) *pl n* **1** the actual and intrinsic rights and wrongs of an issue, esp. in a law case. **2 on its (his, her,** etc.) **merits.** on the intrinsic qualities or virtues.

merle *or* **merl** (mɜːl) *n Scot.* another name for the (European) **blackbird.** ORIG C15: via OF from L *merula*

merlin (ˈmɜːlɪn) *n* a small falcon that has a dark plumage with a black-barred tail. ORIG C14: from OF *esmerillon,* from *esmeril,* of Gmc origin

Merlin ★ (ˈmɜːlɪn) *n* (in Arthurian legend) a wizard and counsellor to King Arthur eternally imprisoned in a tree by a woman to whom he revealed his secret craft.

Merlot (ˈmɜːləʊ) *n* (*sometimes not cap.*) **1** a black grape grown in France, Hungary, Bulgaria, etc., used, often in a blend, for making wine. **2** any of various wines made from this grape. ORIG from F *merlot,* lit.: young blackbird, dim. of *merle* MERLE, prob. alluding to the colour of the grape

mermaid (ˈmɜːˌmeɪd) *n* an imaginary sea creature fabled to have a woman's head and upper body and a fish's tail. ORIG C14: from MERE[2] + MAID

merman (ˈmɜːˌmæn) *n, pl* **mermen.** a male counterpart of the mermaid. ORIG C17: see MERMAID

Meroë ★ (ˈmɛrəʊˌiː) *n* an ancient city in N Sudan, on the Nile; capital of a kingdom that flourished from about 700 B.C. to about 350 A.D.

-merous *adj combining form.* (in biology) having a certain number or kind of parts. ORIG from Gk *meros* part

Merovingian (ˌmɛrəʊˈvɪndʒɪən) *adj* **1** of or relating to a Frankish dynasty which ruled Gaul and W Germany from about 500 to 751 A.D. ◆ *n* **2** a member or supporter of this dynasty. ORIG C17: from F, from Med. L *Merovingi* offspring of *Merovaeus,* L form of *Merowig,* traditional founder of the line

merriment (ˈmɛrɪmənt) *n* gaiety, fun, or mirth.

merry (ˈmɛrɪ) *adj* **merrier, merriest. 1** cheerful; jolly. **2** very funny; hilarious. **3** *Brit. inf.* slightly drunk. **4 make merry.** to revel; be festive. **5 play merry hell with.** *Inf.* to disturb greatly; disrupt. ORIG OE *merige* agreeable
▸ **ˈmerrily** *adv* ▸ **ˈmerriness** *n*

merry-andrew (-'ændru:) *n* a joker, clown, or buffoon. ORIG C17: from ?

merry-go-round *n* **1** another name for **roundabout** (sense 1). **2** a whirl of activity.

merrymaking ('mɛrɪˌmeɪkɪŋ) *n* fun, revelry, or festivity. ▸ **'merryˌmaker** *n*

merrythought ('mɛrɪˌθɔ:t) *n Brit.* a less common word for **wishbone.**

Merse ★ (mɜ:s; *Scot.* mɛrs) *n* **the.** a fertile lowland area of SE Scotland, in the Scottish Borders, north of the Tweed.

Merseburg ★ (*German* 'mɛrzəburk) *n* a city in E Germany, on the Saale River, in Saxony-Anhalt: residence of the dukes of Saxe-Merseburg (1656–1738); chemical industry. Pop.: 46 250 (1989 est.).

Mersey ★ ('mɜ:zɪ) *n* a river in W England, rising in N Derbyshire and flowing northwest and west to the Irish Sea through a large estuary on which is situated the port of Liverpool. Length: about 112 km (70 miles).

Merseyside ★ ('mɜ:zɪˌsaɪd) *n* a metropolitan county of NW England, administered by the unitary authorities of Sefton, Liverpool, St Helens, Knowsley, and Wirral. Area: 652 sq. km (252 sq. miles).

Mersin ★ (mɛə'si:n) *n* a port in S Turkey, on the Mediterranean: oil refinery. Pop.: 523 000 (1995 est.). Also called: **Içel.**

Merthyr Tydfil ★ ('mɜ:θə 'tɪdvɪl) *n* **1** a town in SE Wales, a former mining town. Pop.: 39 482 (1991). **2** a county borough in SE Wales. Pop.: 59 500 (1996 est.). Area: 111 sq. km (43 sq. miles).

Merton[1] ★ ('mɜ:tᵊn) *n* a borough in SW Greater London. Pop.: 177 200 (1994 est.). Area: 38 sq. km (15 sq. miles).

Merton[2] ★ ('mɜ:tᵊn) *n* **Thomas** (**Feverel**). 1915–68, US monk and mystic; noted for his autobiography *The Seven Storey Mountain* (1948).

mesa ('meɪsə) *n* a flat tableland with steep edges, common in the southwestern US. ORIG from Sp.: table

mésalliance (mɛ'zælɪəns) *n* a marriage with a person of lower social status. ORIG C18: from F: MISALLIANCE

Mesa Verde ★ ('meɪsə 'vɜ:d) *n* a high plateau in SW Colorado: remains of numerous prehistoric cliff dwellings, inhabited by the Pueblo Indians.

mescal (mɛ'skæl) *n* **1** Also called: **peyote.** a spineless globe-shaped cactus of Mexico and the southwestern US. Its button-like tubercles (**mescal buttons**) are chewed by certain Indian tribes for their hallucinogenic effects. **2** a colourless alcoholic spirit distilled from the fermented juice of certain agave plants. ORIG C19: from American Sp., from Nahuatl *mexcalli* the liquor, from *metl* MAGUEY + *ixcalli* stew

mescaline *or* **mescalin** ('mɛskəˌli:n, -lɪn) *n* a hallucinogenic drug derived from mescal buttons.

mesdames ('meɪˌdæm) *n* the plural of **madame** and **madam** (sense 1).

mesdemoiselles (ˌmeɪdmwə'zɛl) *n* the plural of **mademoiselle.**

meseems (mɪ'si:mz) *vb* (*tr; takes a clause as object*) *Arch.* it seems to me.

mesembryanthemum (mɪzˌɛmbrɪ'ænθɪməm) *n* any of a genus of plants with succulent leaves and bright flowers with rayed petals which typically open at midday. ORIG C18: NL, from Gk *mesēmbria* noon + *anthemon* flower

mesencephalon (ˌmɛsɛn'sɛfəˌlɒn) *n* the part of the brain that develops from the middle portion of the embryonic neural tube. Nontechnical name: **midbrain.**

mesentery ('mɛsəntərɪ, 'mɛz-) *n, pl* **mesenteries.** the double layer of peritoneum that is attached to the back wall of the abdominal cavity and supports most of the small intestine. ORIG C16: from NL *mesenterium, from* MESO- + Gk *enteron* intestine
▸ **ˌmesen'teric** *adj* ▸ **mesenteritis** (mɛsˌɛntə'raɪtɪs) *n*

mesh (mɛʃ) *n* **1** a network; net. **2** an open space between the strands of a network. **3** (*often pl*) the strands surrounding these spaces. **4** anything that ensnares, or holds like a net. **5** the engagement of teeth on interacting gearwheels: *the gears are in mesh.* ◆ *vb* **6** to entangle or become entangled. **7** (of gear teeth) to engage or cause to engage. **8** (*intr; often* foll. by *with*) to coordinate (with). **9** to work or cause to work in harmony. ORIG C16: prob. from Du. *maesche*

Meshach ★ ('mi:ʃæk) *n Old Testament.* one of Daniel's three companions who, together with Shadrach and Abednego, was miraculously saved from destruction in Nebuchadnezzar's fiery furnace (Daniel 3:12-30).

Meshed ★ (mɛ'ʃɛd) *n* a variant of **Mashhad.**

mesial ('mi:zɪəl) *adj Anat.* another word for **medial** (sense 1). ORIG C19: from MESO- + -IAL

mesmerism ('mɛzməˌrɪzəm) *n Psychol.* **1** a hypnotic state induced by the operator's imposition of his or her will on that of the patient. **2** an early doctrine concerning this. ORIG C19: after F. A. *Mesmer* (1734–1815), Austrian physician
▸ **mesmeric** (mɛz'mɛrɪk) *adj* ▸ **'mesmerist** *n*

mesmerize *or* **mesmerise** ('mɛzməˌraɪz) *vb* **mesmerizes, mesmerizing, mesmerized** *or* **mesmerises, mesmerising, mesmerised.** (*tr*) **1** to hold (someone) as if spellbound. **2** a former word for **hypnotize.**
▸ **ˌmesmeri'zation** *or* **ˌmesmeri'sation** *n* ▸ **'mesmerˌizer** *or* **'mesmerˌiser** *n*

mesne (mi:n) *adj Law.* **1** intermediate or intervening: *a mesne assignment of property.* **2 mesne profits.** rents or profits accruing during the rightful owner's exclusion from his land. ORIG C15: from legal F *meien* in the middle

meso- *or before a vowel* **mes-** *combining form.* middle or intermediate: *mesomorph.* ORIG from Gk *misos* middle

mesoblast ('mɛsəʊˌblæst) *n* another name for **mesoderm.** ▸ **ˌmeso'blastic** *adj*

mesocarp ('mɛsəʊˌkɑ:p) *n* the middle layer of the pericarp of a fruit, such as the flesh of a peach.

mesocephalic (ˌmɛsəʊsɪ'fælɪk) *Anat.* ◆ *adj* **1** having a medium-sized head. ◆ *n* **2** an individual with such a head.
▸ **mesocephaly** (ˌmɛsəʊ'sɛfəlɪ) *n*

mesoderm ('mɛsəʊˌdɜ:m) *n* the middle germ layer of an animal embryo, giving rise to muscle, blood, bone, connective tissue, etc.
▸ **ˌmeso'dermal** *or* **ˌmeso'dermic** *adj*

Mesolithic (ˌmɛsəʊ'lɪθɪk) *n* **1** the period between the Palaeolithic and the Neolithic, in Europe from about 12 000 to 3000 B.C. ◆ *adj* **2** of or relating to the Mesolithic.

Mesolonghi ★ (ˌmɛsə'lɔ:ŋgɪ) *n* a variant of **Missolonghi.**

Mesolóngion ★ (ˌmɛsə'lɒŋgɪˌɒn) *n* transliteration of the Modern Greek name for **Missolonghi.**

mesomorph ('mɛsəʊˌmɔ:f) *n* a type of person having a muscular body build with a relatively prominent underlying bone structure.

mesomorphic (ˌmɛsəʊ'mɔ:fɪk) *adj* **1** *Chem.* existing in or concerned with an intermediate state of matter between a true liquid and a true solid. **2** relating to or being a mesomorph. ◆ Also: **mesomorphous.**
▸ **ˌmeso'morphism** *n*

meson ('mi:zɒn) *n* any of a group of elementary particles that has a rest mass between those of an electron and a proton, and an integral spin. ORIG C20: from MESO- + -ON
▸ **me'sonic** *or* **'mesic** *adj*

mesophyte ('mɛsəʊˌfaɪt) *n* any plant that grows in surroundings receiving an average supply of water.

Mesopotamia ★ (ˌmɛsəpə'teɪmɪə) *n* a region of SW Asia between the lower and middle reaches of the Tigris and Euphrates rivers: site of several ancient civilizations. ORIG L, from Gk *mesopotamia* (*khora*) (the land) between rivers
▸ **ˌMesopo'tamian** *n, adj*

mesosphere ('mɛsəʊˌsfɪə) *n* the atmospheric layer lying between the stratosphere and the thermosphere.

Mesozoic (ˌmɛsəʊ'zəʊɪk) *adj* **1** of, denoting, or relating to an era of geological time that began 225 000 000 years ago and lasted about 155 000 000 years. ◆ *n* **2 the.** the Mesozoic era.

mesquite *or* **mesquit** (mɛ'ski:t, 'mɛski:t) *n* any of various small trees, esp. a tropical American variety, whose sugary pods (**mesquite beans**) are used as animal fodder. ORIG C19: from Mexican Sp., from Nahautl *mizquitl*

mess (mɛs) *n* **1** a state of confusion or untidiness, esp. if dirty or unpleasant. **2** a chaotic or troublesome state of affairs; muddle. **3** *Inf.* a dirty or untidy person or thing. **4** *Arch.* a portion of food, esp. soft or semiliquid food. **5** a place where service personnel eat or take recreation. **6** a group of people, usually servicemen, who eat together. **7** the meal so taken. ◆ *vb* **8** (*tr;* often foll. by *up*) to muddle or dirty. **9** (*intr*) to make a mess. **10** (*intr;* often foll. by *with*) to interfere; meddle. **11** (*intr;* often foll. by *with* or *together*) *Mil.* to group together, esp. for eating. ORIG C13: from OF *mes* dish of food, from LL *missus* course (at table), from L *mittere* to send forth

mess about *or* **around** *vb* (*adv*) **1** (*intr*) to occupy oneself trivially; potter. **2** (when *intr,* often foll. by *with*) to interfere or meddle (with). **3** (*intr;* sometimes foll. by *with*) *Chiefly US.* to engage in adultery.

message (ˈmɛsɪdʒ) *n* **1** a communication, usually brief, from one person or group to another. **2** an implicit meaning, as in a work of art. **3** a formal communiqué. **4** an inspired communication of a prophet or religious leader. **5** a mission; errand. **6** **get the message.** *Inf.* to understand. ◆ *vb* **messages, messaging, messaged. 7** (*tr*) to send as a message. ORIG C13: from OF, from Vulgar L *missāticum* (unattested) something sent, from L *missus,* p.p. of *mittere*

Messager ★ (*French* mɛsaʒe) *n* **André** (**Charles Prosper**) (ɑ̃dre). 1853–1929, French composer and conductor.

messages (ˈmɛsɪdʒɪz) *pl n Scot. & NE English dialect.* household shopping.

message stick *n* a stick bearing carved symbols, carried by a native Australian as identification.

messaging (ˈmɛsidʒɪŋ) *n* the sending and processing of a message by any form of electronic communication.

Messalina ★ (ˌmɛsəˈliːnə) *n* **Valeria** (vəˈlɪərɪə). died 48 A.D., wife of the Roman emperor Claudius, notorious for her debauchery.

Messene ★ (mɛˈsiːnɪ) *n* an ancient Greek city in the SW Peloponnese: founded in 369 B.C. as the capital of Messenia.

messenger (ˈmɛsɪndʒə) *n* **1** a person who takes messages from one person or group to another. **2** a person who runs errands. **3** a carrier of official dispatches; courier. ORIG C13: from OF *messagier,* from MESSAGE

messenger RNA *n Biochem.* a form of RNA, transcribed from a single strand of DNA, that carries genetic information required for protein synthesis from DNA to the ribosomes.

Messenia ★ (məˈsiːnɪə) *n* the southwestern area of the Peloponnese in S Greece.

Messerschmitt ★ (*German* ˈmɛsərʃmɪt) *n* **Willy** (ˈvɪli). 1898–1978, German aeronautical engineer. His planes figured in World War II, including the Me 262, the first jet fighter.

mess hall *n* a military dining room.

Messiaen ★ (*French* mɛsjɑ̃) *n* **Olivier** (ɔlivje). 1908–92, French composer and organist. His music is distinguished by its rhythmic intricacy; he was influenced by Hindu and Greek rhythms and bird song.

Messiah (mɪˈsaɪə) *n* **1** *Judaism.* the awaited king of the Jews, to be sent by God to free them. **2** Jesus Christ, when regarded in this role. **3** an exceptional or hoped-for liberator of a country or people. ORIG C14: from OF *Messie,* ult. from Heb. *māshīah* anointed
▸ **Mesˈsiahship** *n* ▸ **Messianic** *or* **messianic** (ˌmɛsɪˈænɪk) *adj*

Messier catalogue (ˈmɛsɪˌeɪ) *n Astronomy.* a catalogue of 103 nonstellar objects, such as nebulae and galaxies, prepared in 1781–86. An object is referred to by its number in this catalogue, for example the Andromeda Galaxy is referred to as *M31.* ORIG C18: after Charles *Messier* (1730–1817), F astronomer

messieurs (ˈmɛsəz) *n* the plural of **monsieur.**

Messina ★ (mɛˈsiːnə) *n* a port in NE Sicily, on the **Strait of Messina**: colonized by Greeks around 730 B.C.; under Spanish rule (1282–1676 and 1678–1713); university (1549). Pop.: 263 092 (1996 est.).

mess jacket *n* a waist-length jacket, worn by officers in the mess for formal dinners.

mess kit *n Mil.* **1** *Brit.* formal evening wear for officers. **2** Also called: **mess gear.** eating utensils used esp. in the field.

messmate (ˈmɛsˌmeɪt) *n* a person with whom one shares meals in a mess, esp. in the army.

Messrs (ˈmɛsəz) *n* the plural of **Mr.** ORIG C18: abbrev. from F *messieurs,* pl. of MONSIEUR

messy (ˈmɛsɪ) *adj* **messier, messiest.** dirty, confused, or untidy.
▸ **ˈmessily** *adv* ▸ **ˈmessiness** *n*

mestizo (mɛˈstiːzəʊ, mɪ-) *n, pl* **mestizos** *or* **mestizoes.** a person of mixed parentage, esp. the offspring of a Spanish American and an American Indian. ORIG C16: from Sp., ult. from L *miscēre* to mix
▸ **mestiza** (mɛˈstiːzə) *fem n*

mestranol (ˈmɛstrəˌnɒl, -ˌnəʊl) *n* a synthetic oestrogen used in combination with progesterones as an oral contraceptive. ORIG C20: from M(ETHYL) + (O)ESTR(OGEN) + (*pregn*)*an*(*e*) + -OL

Meštrović ★ (*Serbo-Croat* ˈmɛʃtrɔvitʃ) *n* **Ivan** (ˈivan). 1883–1962, US sculptor, born in Austria.

met (mɛt) *vb* the past tense and past participle of **meet**[1].

met. *abbrev. for:* **1** meteorological. **2** meteorology. **3** metropolitan.

Meta ★ (ˈmeɪtə; *Spanish* ˈmeta) *n* a river in Colombia, rising in the Andes and flowing northeast and east, forming part of the border between Colombia and Venezuela, to join the Orinoco River. Length: about 1000 km (620 miles).

meta- *or sometimes before a vowel* **met-** *prefix* **1** indicating change or alternation: *metabolism; metamorphosis.* **2** (of an academic discipline) concerned with the concepts and results of that discipline: *metamathematics.* **3** occurring or situated behind or after: *metaphysics.* **4** (*often in italics*) denoting that an organic compound contains a benzene ring with substituents in the 1,3-positions: *meta*-cresol. Abbrev.: *m*-. **5** denoting an isomer, polymer, or compound related to a specified compound: *metaldehyde.* **6** denoting an oxyacid that is the least hydrated form of the anhydride or a salt of such an acid: *metaphosphoric acid.* ORIG from Gk (prep)

metabolism (mɪˈtæbəˌlɪzəm) *n* **1** the sum total of the chemical processes that occur in living organisms, resulting in growth, production of energy, elimination of waste, etc. **2** the sum total of the chemical processes affecting a particular substance in the body: *carbohydrate metabolism.* ORIG C19: from Gk *metabolē* change, from *metaballein,* from META- + *ballein* to throw
▸ **metabolic** (ˌmɛtəˈbɒlɪk) *adj* ▸ **ˌmetaˈbolically** *adv*

metabolize *or* **metabolise** (mɪˈtæbəˌlaɪz) *vb* **metabolizes, metabolizing, metabolized** *or* **metabolises, metabolising, metabolised.** to produce or be produced by metabolism.

metacarpus (ˌmɛtəˈkɑːpəs) *n, pl* **metacarpi** (-paɪ). **1** the skeleton of the hand between the wrist and the fingers, consisting of five long bones. **2** the corresponding bones in other vertebrates.
▸ **ˌmetaˈcarpal** *adj, n*

metacentre *or US* **metacenter** (ˈmɛtəˌsɛntə) *n* the intersection of a vertical line through the centre of buoyancy of a floating body at equilibrium with a vertical line through the centre of buoyancy when the body is tilted.
▸ **ˌmetaˈcentric** *adj*

metage (ˈmiːtɪdʒ) *n* **1** the official measuring of weight or contents. **2** a charge for this. ORIG C16: from METE[1]

metal (ˈmɛtᵊl) *n* **1a** any of a number of chemical elements, such as iron or copper, that are often lustrous ductile solids, have basic oxides, form positive ions, and are good conductors of heat and electricity. **1b** an alloy, such as brass or steel, containing one or more of these elements. **2** the substance of glass in a molten state or as the finished product. **3** short for **road metal. 4** *Inf.* short for **heavy metal. 5** *Heraldry.* gold or silver. **6** the basic quality of

a person or thing; stuff. **7** (*pl*) the rails of a railway. ◆ *adj* **8** made of metal. ◆ *vb* **metals, metalling, metalled** *or US* **metals, metaling, metaled.** (*tr*) **9** to fit or cover with metal. **10** to make or mend (a road) with road metal. ORIG C13: from L *metallum* mine, product of a mine, from Gk *metallon*
▸ **'metalled** *adj*

> **USAGE NOTE** *Metal* is sometimes mistakenly used instead of *mettle: this is a real test of the club's mettle* (not *metal*).

metal. *or* **metall.** *abbrev. for:* **1** metallurgical. **2** metallurgy.

metalanguage ('mɛtəˌlæŋgwɪdʒ) *n* a language or system of symbols used to discuss another language or system. Cf. **object language.**

metal detector *n* a device that gives an audible or visual signal when its search head comes close to a metallic object embedded in food, buried in the ground, etc.

metallic (mɪ'tælɪk) *adj* **1** of, concerned with, or consisting of metal or a metal. **2** suggestive of a metal: *a metallic click; metallic lustre.* **3** *Chem.* (of a metal element) existing in the free state rather than in combination: *metallic copper.*

metallic soap *n* any one of a number of salts or esters containing a metal, such as aluminium, calcium, magnesium, iron, and zinc. They are used as bases for ointments, fungicides, fireproofing and waterproofing agents, and dryers for paints and varnishes.

metalliferous (ˌmɛtᵊ'lɪfərəs) *adj* containing a metallic element. ORIG C17: from L *metallifer* yielding metal, from *metallum* metal + *ferre* to bear

metallize, metallise, *or US* **metalize** ('mɛtəˌlaɪz) *vb* **metallizes, metallizing, metallized; metallises, metallising, metallised** *or US* **metalizes, metalizing, metalized.** (*tr*) to make metallic or to coat or treat with metal.
▸ **ˌmetalliˈzation, metalliˈsation,** *or US* **ˌmetaliˈzation** *n*

metallography (ˌmɛtə'lɒgrəfɪ) *n* the branch of metallurgy concerned with the composition and structure of metals and alloys.
▸ **metallographic** (mɪˌtælə'græfɪk) *adj*

metalloid ('mɛtəˌlɔɪd) *n* **1** a nonmetallic element, such as arsenic or silicon, that has some of the properties of a metal. ◆ *adj also* **ˌmetal'loidal. 2** of or being a metalloid. **3** resembling a metal.

metallurgy (mɛ'tælədʒɪ) *n* the scientific study of the extraction, refining, alloying, and fabrication of metals and of their structure and properties.
▸ **metallurgic** (ˌmɛtə'lɜːdʒɪk) *or* **ˌmetal'lurgical** *adj* ▸ **metallurgist** (mɛ'tælədʒɪst, 'mɛtəˌlɜːdʒɪst) *n*

metal road *n Austral. & NZ.* an unsealed road covered in gravel or shingle.

metal tape *n* a magnetic recording tape coated with pure iron: it gives enhanced recording quality.

metalwork ('mɛtᵊlˌwɜːk) *n* **1** the craft of working in metal. **2** work in metal or articles made from metal.

metalworking ('mɛtᵊlˌwɜːkɪŋ) *n* the processing of metal to change its shape, size, etc.
▸ **'metalˌworker** *n*

metamere ('mɛtəˌmɪə) *n* one of the similar body segments into which earthworms, crayfish, and similar animals are divided longitudinally.
▸ **metameral** (mɪ'tæmərəl) *adj*

metamerism (mɪ'tæməˌrɪzəm) *n* **1** Also called: (**metameric**) **segmentation.** the division of an animal into metameres. **2** *Chem.* a type of isomerism in which molecular structures differ by the attachment of different groups to the same atom.
▸ **metameric** (ˌmɛtə'mɛrɪk) *adj*

metamict ('mɛtəˌmɪkt) *adj* of or denoting the amorphous state of a substance that has lost its crystalline structure as a result of the radioactivity of uranium or thorium within it.
▸ **ˌmetaˌmictiˈzation** *or* **ˌmetaˌmictiˈsation** *n*

metamorphic (ˌmɛtə'mɔːfɪk) *or* **metamorphous** *adj* **1** relating to or resulting from metamorphosis or metamorphism. **2** (of rocks) altered considerably from the original structure and composition by pressure and heat.

metamorphism (ˌmɛtə'mɔːfɪzəm) *n* **1** the process by which metamorphic rocks are formed. **2** a variant of **metamorphosis.**

metamorphose (ˌmɛtə'mɔːfəʊz) *vb* **metamorphoses, metamorphosing, metamorphosed.** to undergo or cause to undergo metamorphosis or metamorphism.

metamorphosis (ˌmɛtə'mɔːfəsɪs) *n, pl* **metamorphoses** (-ˌsiːz). **1** a complete change of physical form or substance. **2** a complete change of character, appearance, etc. **3** a person or thing that has undergone metamorphosis. **4** *Zool.* the rapid transformation of a larva into an adult that occurs in certain animals, for example the stage between chrysalis and butterfly. ORIG C16: via L from Gk: transformation, from META- + *morphē* form

metaphor ('mɛtəfə, -ˌfɔː) *n* a figure of speech in which a word or phrase is applied to an object or action that it does not literally denote in order to imply a resemblance, for example *he is a lion in battle.* Cf. **simile.** ORIG C16: from L, from Gk *metaphora,* from *metapherein* to transfer, from META- + *pherein* to bear
▸ **metaphoric** (ˌmɛtə'fɒrɪk) *or* **ˌmeta'phorical** *adj* ▸ **ˌmeta'phorically** *adv*

metaphrase ('mɛtəˌfreɪz) *n* **1** a literal translation. ◆ *vb* **metaphrases, metaphrasing, metaphrased.** (*tr*) **2** to alter or manipulate the wording of. **3** to translate literally. ORIG C17: from Gk *metaphrazein* to translate

metaphrast ('mɛtəˌfræst) *n* a person who metaphrases, esp. one who changes the form of a text, as by rendering verse into prose. ORIG C17: from Med. Gk *metaphrastēs* translator
▸ **ˌmeta'phrastic** *or* **ˌmeta'phrastical** *adj* ▸ **ˌmeta'phrastically** *adv*

metaphysic (ˌmɛtə'fɪzɪk) *n* the system of first principles and assumptions underlying an inquiry or philosophical theory.

metaphysical (ˌmɛtə'fɪzɪkᵊl) *adj* **1** of or relating to metaphysics. **2** (of a statement or theory) having an empirical form but in fact immune from empirical testing. **3** (popularly) abstract, abstruse, or unduly theoretical. **4** incorporeal; supernatural.
▸ **ˌmeta'physically** *adv*

Metaphysical (ˌmɛtə'fɪzɪkᵊl) *adj* **1** denoting or relating to certain 17th-century poets who combined intense feeling with elaborate imagery. ◆ *n* **2** a poet of this group.

metaphysics (ˌmɛtə'fɪzɪks) *n* (*functioning as sing*) **1** the branch of philosophy that deals with first principles, esp. of being and knowing. **2** the philosophical study of the nature of reality. **3** (popularly) abstract or subtle discussion or reasoning. ORIG C16: from Med. L, from Gk *ta meta ta phusika* the things after the physics, from the arrangement of subjects treated in the works of Aristotle
▸ **metaphysician** (ˌmɛtəfɪ'zɪʃən) *or* **metaphysicist** (ˌmɛtə'fɪzɪsɪst) *n*

metapsychology (ˌmɛtəsaɪ'kɒlədʒɪ) *n Psychol.* **1** the study of philosophical questions, such as the relation between mind and body, that go beyond the laws of experimental psychology. **2** any attempt to state the general laws of psychology. **3** another word for **parapsychology.**
▸ **metapsychological** (ˌmɛtəˌsaɪkə'lɒdʒɪkᵊl) *adj*

metastable (ˌmɛtə'steɪbᵊl) *adj Physics.* (of a body or system) having a state of apparent equilibrium although capable of changing to a more stable state.
▸ **ˌmetasta'bility** *n*

metastasis (mɪ'tæstəsɪs) *n, pl* **metastases** (-ˌsiːz). *Pathol.* the spreading of a disease organism, esp. cancer cells, from one part of the body to another. ORIG C16: via L from Gk: transition
▸ **metastatic** (ˌmɛtə'stætɪk) *adj* ▸ **ˌmeta'statically** *adv*

metastasize *or* **metastasise** (mɪ'tæstəˌsaɪz) *vb* **metastasizes, metastasizing, metastasized** *or* **metastasises, metastasising, metastasised.** (*intr*) *Pathol.* (esp. of cancer cells) to spread to a new site in the body via blood or lymph vessels.

metatarsus (ˌmɛtə'tɑːsəs) *n, pl* **metatarsi** (-saɪ). **1** the skel-

eton of the human foot between the toes and the tarsus, consisting of five long bones. **2** the corresponding skeletal part in other vertebrates.
▸ **ˌmetaˈtarsal** *adj, n*

metathesis (mɪˈtæθəsɪs) *n, pl* **metatheses** (-ˌsiːz). the transposition of two sounds or letters in a word. ORIG C16: from LL, from Gk, from *metatithenai* to transpose
▸ **metathetic** (ˌmɛtəˈθɛtɪk) *or* **ˌmetaˈthetical** *adj*

metazoan (ˌmɛtəˈzəʊən) *n* **1** any multicellular animal: includes all animals except sponges. ◆ *adj also* **metazoic.** **2** of or relating to the metazoans. ORIG C19: from NL *Metazoa;* see META-, -ZOA

Metchnikoff ★ (*French* mɛtʃnikɔf; *Russian* ˈmjetʃnikəf) *n* **Élie** (eli). 1845–1916, Russian bacteriologist in France. He shared the Nobel prize for physiology or medicine (1908) for his theory of phagocytosis.

mete[1] (miːt) *vb* **metes, meting, meted.** (*tr*) **1** (usually foll. by *out*) *Formal.* to distribute or allot (something, often unpleasant). **2** *Poetic, dialect.* to measure. ORIG OE *metan*

mete[2] (miːt) *n Rare.* a mark, limit, or boundary (esp. in **metes and bounds**). ORIG C15: from OF, from L *mēta* goal, turning post (in race)

metempsychosis (ˌmɛtəmsaɪˈkəʊsɪs) *n, pl* **metempsychoses** (-siːz). the migration of a soul from one body to another. ORIG C16: via LL from Gk, from *metempsukhousthai,* from META- + *-em-* in + *psukhē* soul
▸ **ˌmetempsyˈchosist** *n*

meteor (ˈmiːtɪə) *n* **1** a very small meteoroid that has entered the earth's atmosphere. **2** Also called: **shooting star, falling star.** the bright streak of light appearing in the sky due to the incandescence of such a body heated by friction at its surface. ORIG C15: from Med. L *meteōrum,* from Gk *meteōron,* from *meteōros* lofty, from *meta-* (intensifier) + *aeirein* to raise

meteoric (ˌmiːtɪˈɒrɪk) *adj* **1** of, formed by, or relating to meteors. **2** like a meteor in brilliance, speed, or transience. **3** *Rare.* of weather; meteorological.
▸ **ˌmeteˈorically** *adv*

meteorism (ˈmiːtɪəˌrɪzəm) *n Med.* another name for **tympanites.**

meteorite (ˈmiːtɪəˌraɪt) *n* a rocklike object consisting of the remains of a meteoroid that has fallen on earth.
▸ **meteoritic** (ˌmiːtɪəˈrɪtɪk) *adj*

meteoroid (ˈmiːtɪəˌrɔɪd) *n* any of the small celestial bodies that are thought to orbit the sun. When they enter the earth's atmosphere, they become visible as meteors.
▸ **ˌmeteorˈoidal** *adj*

meteorol. *or* **meteor.** *abbrev for:* **1** meteorological. **2** meteorology.

meteorology (ˌmiːtɪəˈrɒlədʒɪ) *n* the study of the earth's atmosphere, esp. of weather-forming processes and weather forecasting. ORIG C17: from Gk; see METEOR, -LOGY
▸ **meteorological** (ˌmiːtɪərəˈlɒdʒɪkᵊl) *or* **ˌmeteoroˈlogic** *adj*
▸ **ˌmeteoroˈlogically** *adv* ▸ **ˌmeteorˈologist** *n*

meteor shower *n* a transient rain of meteors occurring at regular intervals and coming from a particular region in the sky.

meter[1] (ˈmiːtə) *n* **1** any device that measures and records a quantity, such as of gas, current, voltage, etc., that has passed through it during a specified period. **2** See **parking meter.** ◆ *vb* (*tr*) **3** to measure (a rate of flow) with a meter. ORIG C19: see METE[1]

meter[2] (ˈmiːtə) *n* the US spelling of **metre**[1].

meter[3] (ˈmiːtə) *n* the US spelling of **metre**[2].

-meter *n combining form.* **1** indicating an instrument for measuring: *barometer.* **2** *Prosody.* indicating a verse having a specified number of feet: *pentameter.* ORIG from Gk *metron* measure

Meth. *abbrev. for* Methodist.

meth- *combining form.* indicating a chemical compound derived from methane or containing methyl groups: *methacrylic acid.*

methacrylic acid (ˌmɛθəˈkrɪlɪk) *n* a colourless crystalline water-soluble substance used in the manufacture of acrylic resins.

methadone (ˈmɛθəˌdəʊn) *or* **methadon** (ˈmɛθəˌdɒn) *n* a narcotic analgesic drug similar to morphine and formerly thought to be less habit-forming. ORIG C20: from *(di)meth(yl)* + A(MINO) + *d(iphenyl)* + -ONE

methamphetamine (ˌmɛθæmˈfɛtəmiːn, -mɪn) *n* a variety of amphetamine used for its stimulant action. ORIG C20: from METH- + AMPHETAMINE

methanal (ˈmɛθəˌnæl) *n* the systematic name for **formaldehyde.**

methane (ˈmiːθeɪn) *n* a colourless odourless flammable gas, the main constituent of natural gas: used as a fuel. Formula: CH_4.

methane series *n* another name for **alkane series.**

methanoic acid (ˈmɛθəˌnəʊɪk) *n* the systematic name for **formic acid.**

methanol (ˈmɛθəˌnɒl) *n* a colourless volatile poisonous liquid compound used as a solvent and fuel. Formula: CH_3OH. Also called: **methyl alcohol, wood alcohol.** ORIG C20: from METHANE + -OL[1]

methinks (mɪˈθɪŋks) *vb past* **methought.** (*tr; takes a clause as object*) *Arch.* it seems to me.

metho (ˈmɛθəʊ) *n Austral. inf.* **1** another name for **methylated spirits.** **2** (*pl* **methos**) a drinker of methylated spirits.

method (ˈmɛθəd) *n* **1** a way of proceeding or doing something, esp. a systematic or regular one. **2** orderliness of thought, action, etc. **3** (*often pl*) the techniques or arrangement of work for a particular field or subject. ORIG C16: via F from L, from Gk *methodos,* lit.: a going after, from *meta-* after + *hodos* way

Method (ˈmɛθəd) *n* (*sometimes not cap.*) **a** a technique of acting in which the actor bases his role on the inner motivation of the character played. **b** (*as modifier*): *a Method actor.*

methodical (mɪˈθɒdɪkᵊl) *or* (*less commonly*) **methodic** *adj* characterized by method or orderliness; systematic.
▸ **meˈthodically** *adv*

Methodism (ˈmɛθəˌdɪzəm) *n* the system and practices of the Methodist Church.

Methodist (ˈmɛθədɪst) *n* **1** a member of any of the Nonconformist denominations that derive from the system of faith and practice initiated by John Wesley and his followers. ◆ *adj also* **ˌMethodˈistic** *or* **ˌMethodˈistical.** **2** of or relating to Methodism or the Church embodying it (the **Methodist Church**).

Methodius ★ (mɛˈθəʊdɪəs) *n* **Saint,** with his younger brother Saint Cyril called *the Apostles of the Slavs.* 815–885 A.D., Greek theologian sent as a missionary to the Moravians. Feast day: Feb. 14 or May 11.

methodize *or* **methodise** (ˈmɛθəˌdaɪz) *vb* **methodizes, methodizing, methodized** *or* **methodises, methodising, methodised.** (*tr*) to organize according to a method; systematize
▸ **ˈmethodˌizer** *or* **ˈmethodˌiser** *n*

methodology (ˌmɛθəˈdɒlədʒɪ) *n, pl* **methodologies. 1** the system of methods and principles used in a particular discipline. **2** the branch of philosophy concerned with the science of method.
▸ **methodological** (ˌmɛθədəˈlɒdʒɪkᵊl) *adj* ▸ **ˌmethodoˈlogically** *adv* ▸ **ˌmethodˈologist** *n*

methought (mɪˈθɔːt) *vb Arch.* the past tense of **methinks.**

meths (mɛθs) *n Chiefly Brit., Austral., & NZ.* an informal name for **methylated spirits.**

Methuselah ★ (mɪˈθjuːzələ) *n Old Testament.* a patriarch reputed to have lived 969 years (Genesis 5:21–27), regarded as epitomizing longevity. Douay spelling: **Mathusala.**

methyl (ˈmiːθaɪl, ˈmɛθɪl) *n* **1** (*modifier*) of, consisting of, or containing the monovalent group of atoms CH_3. **2** a compound in which methyl groups are bound directly to a metal atom. ORIG C19: from F *méthyle,* back formation from METHYLENE
▸ **methylic** (məˈθɪlɪk) *adj*

methyl acetate *n* a colourless volatile flammable liquid ester used as a solvent, esp. in paint removers. Formula: CH_3COOCH_3. Systematic name: **methyl ethanoate.**

methyl alcohol *n* another name for **methanol.**

methylate ('mɛθɪˌleɪt) *vb* **methylates, methylating, methylated.** (*tr*) to mix with methanol.

methylated spirits *n* (*functioning as sing or pl*) alcohol that has been denatured by the addition of methanol and pyridine and a violet dye. Also: **methylated spirit.**

methyl chloride *n* a colourless gas with an ether-like odour, used as a refrigerant and anaesthetic. Formula: CH_3Cl. Systematic name: **chloromethane.**

methylene ('mɛθɪˌliːn) *n* (*modifier*) of, consisting of, or containing the divalent group of atoms $=CH_2$: *a methylene group or radical.* ORIG C19: from F *méthylène*, from Gk *methu* wine + *hulē* wood + -ENE: orig. referring to a substance distilled from wood

methylene dichloride *n* the traditional name for **dichloromethane.**

methylphenol (ˌmiːθaɪl'fiːnɒl) *n* the systematic name for **cresol.**

meticulous (mɪ'tɪkjʊləs) *adj* very precise about details; painstaking. ORIG C16 (meaning: timid): from L *meticulōsus* fearful, from *metus* fear
▸ **me'ticulously** *adv* ▸ **me'ticulousness** *n*

métier ('mɛtɪeɪ) *n* **1** a profession or trade. **2** a person's strong point or speciality. ORIG C18: from F, ult. from L *ministerium* service

Métis (me'tiːs) *n, pl* **Métis** (-'tiːs, -'tiːz). a person of mixed parentage, esp. the offspring of a French Canadian and a North American Indian. ORIG C19: from F, from Vulgar L *mixtīcius* (unattested) of mixed race
▸ **Métisse** (mɛ'tiːs) *fem n*

metol ('miːtɒl) *n* a colourless soluble organic substance used, in the form of its sulphate, as a photographic developer. ORIG C20: from G, arbitrary coinage

Metonic cycle (mɪ'tɒnɪk) *n* a cycle of 235 synodic months after which the phases of the moon recur on the same day of the month. ORIG C17: after *Meton*, 5th-cent. B.C. Athenian astronomer

metonymy (mɪ'tɒnɪmɪ) *n, pl* **metonymies.** the substitution of a word referring to an attribute for the thing that is meant, e.g. *the crown*, used to refer to a monarch. Cf. **synecdoche.** ORIG C16: from LL, from Gk, from *meta-* (indicating change) + *onoma* name
▸ **metonymical** (ˌmɛtə'nɪmɪkᵊl) *or* ˌ**meto'nymic** *adj*

metope ('mɛtəʊp, 'mɛtəpɪ) *n Archit.* a square space between triglyphs in a Doric frieze. ORIG C16: via L from Gk, from *meta* between + *opē* one of the holes for the beam-ends

metre[1] *or US* **meter** ('miːtə) *n* **1** a metric unit of length equal to approximately 1.094 yards. **2** the basic SI unit of length; the length of the path travelled by light in free space during a time interval of 1/299 792 458 of a second. Symbol: m ORIG C18: from F; see METRE[2]

metre[2] *or US* **meter** ('miːtə) *n* **1** *Prosody.* the rhythmic arrangement of syllables in verse, usually according to the number and kind of feet in a line. **2** *Music.* another word (esp. US) for **time** (sense 22). ORIG C14: from L *metrum*, from Gk *metron* measure

metre-kilogram-second *n* See **mks units.**

metric ('mɛtrɪk) *adj* of or relating to the metre or metric system.

metrical ('mɛtrɪkᵊl) *or* **metric** *adj* **1** of or relating to measurement. **2** of or in poetic metre.
▸ **'metrically** *adv*

metricate ('mɛtrɪˌkeɪt) *vb* **metricates, metricating, metricated.** to convert (a measuring system, instrument, etc.) from nonmetric to metric units.
▸ ˌ**metri'cation** *n*

metric system *n* any decimal system of units based on the metre. For scientific purposes SI units are used.

metric ton *n* another name (not in technical use) for **tonne.**

metro ('mɛtrəʊ) *or* **métro** *French.* (metro) *n, pl* **metros.** an underground, or largely underground, railway system in certain cities, such as that in Paris. ORIG C20: from F, *chemin de fer métropolitain* metropolitan railway

Metro ('mɛtrəʊ) *n Canad.* a metropolitan city administration, esp. Metropolitan Toronto.

metronome ('mɛtrəˌnəʊm) *n* a device which indicates the tempo of music by producing a clicking sound from a pendulum with an adjustable period of swing. ORIG C19: from Gk *metron* measure + *nomos* law
▸ **metronomic** (ˌmɛtrə'nɒmɪk) *adj*

metronymic (ˌmɛtrəʊ'nɪmɪk) *adj* **1** (of a name) derived from the name of the mother or other female ancestor. ◆ *n* **2** a metronymic name. ORIG C19: from Gk *mētronumikos*, from *mētēr* mother + *onoma* name

metropolis (mɪ'trɒpəlɪs) *n, pl* **metropolises. 1** the main city, esp. of a country or region. **2** a centre of activity. **3** the chief see in an ecclesiastical province. ORIG C16: from LL from Gk, from *mētēr* mother + *polis* city

metropolitan (ˌmɛtrə'pɒlɪtən) *adj* **1** of or characteristic of a metropolis. **2** constituting a city and its suburbs. **3** of, relating to, or designating an ecclesiastical metropolis. **4** of or belonging to the home territories of a country, as opposed to overseas territories: *metropolitan France.* ◆ *n* **5a** *Eastern Churches.* the head of an ecclesiastical province, ranking between archbishop and patriarch. **5b** *Church of England.* an archbishop. **5c** *RC Church.* an archbishop or bishop having authority over the dioceses in his province.
▸ ˌ**metro'politanism** *n*

metropolitan county *n* (in England) any of the six conurbations established as units in the new local government system in 1974; the metropolitan county councils were abolished in 1986.

metropolitan district *n* (in England since 1974) any of the districts that make up the metropolitan counties of England: since 1986 they have functioned as unitary authorities.

Metropolitan Museum of Art ★ *n* the principal museum in New York City: founded in 1870 and housed in its present premises on the edge of Central Park since 1880.

metrorrhagia (ˌmiːtrɔː'reɪdʒɪə, ˌmɛt-) *n* abnormal bleeding from the uterus. ORIG C19: NL, from Gk *mētra* womb + *-rrhagia* a breaking forth

-metry *n combining form.* indicating the process or science of measuring: *geometry.* ORIG from OF *-metrie*, from L, ult. from Gk *metron* measure
▸ **-metric** *adj combining form.*

Metternich ★ (*German* 'mɛtərnɪç) *n* **Klemens** ('kleːməns). 1773–1859, Austrian statesman. Foreign minister (1809–48) and chancellor of Austria (1821–48).

mettle ('mɛtᵊl) *n* **1** courage; spirit. **2** character. **3 on one's mettle.** roused to making one's best efforts. ORIG C16: orig. var. of METAL

USAGE NOTE See at **metal.**

mettled ('mɛtᵊld) *or* **mettlesome** ('mɛtᵊlsəm) *adj* courageous, spirited, or valiant.

Metz ★ (mɛts; *French* mɛs) *n* a city in NE France on the River Moselle: a free imperial city in the 13th century; annexed by France in 1552; part of Germany (1871–1918); centre of the Lorraine iron-mining region. Pop.: 123 920 (1990).

Meung ★ (*French* mœ̃) *n* See **Jean de Meung.**

Meurthe-et-Moselle ★ (*French* mœrtemozɛl) *n* a department of NE France, in Lorraine region. Capital: Nancy. Pop.: 715 907 (1994 est.). Area: 5280 sq. km (2059 sq. miles).

Meuse ★ (mɜːz; *French* møz) *n* **1** a department of N France, in Lorraine region: heavy fighting occurred here in World War I. Capital: Bar-le-Duc. Pop.: 194 384 (1994 est.). Area: 6241 sq. km (2434 sq. miles). **2** a river in W Europe, rising in NE France and flowing north across E Belgium and the S Netherlands to join the Waal River before entering the North Sea. Length: 926 km (575 miles). Dutch name: **Maas.**

MeV *symbol for* million electronvolts (10^6 electronvolts).

mevrou (mə'frəʊ) *n* a S. African title of address equivalent to *Mrs* when placed before a surname or *madam* when used alone. ORIG Afrik.

mew[1] (mjuː) *vb* **1** (*intr*) (esp. of a cat) to make a characteristic high-pitched cry. ◆ *n* **2** such a sound. ORIG C14: imit.

mew[2] (mjuː) *n* any seagull, esp. the common gull. ORIG OE *mǣw*

mew[3] (mjuː) *n* **1** a room or cage for hawks, esp. while moulting. ◆ *vb* (*tr*) **2** (often foll. by *up*) to confine (hawks or falcons) in a shelter, cage, etc. **3** to confine; conceal. ORIG C14: from OF *mue*, from *muer* to moult, from L *mūtāre* to change

Mewar ★ (mɛ'wɑː) *n* another name for **Udaipur** (sense 1).

mewl (mjuːl) *vb* **1** (*intr*) (esp. of a baby) to cry weakly; whimper. ◆ *n* **2** such a cry. ORIG C17: imit.

mews (mjuːz) *n* (*functioning as sing or pl*) *Chiefly Brit.* **1** a yard or street lined by buildings originally used as stables but now often converted into dwellings. **2** the buildings around a mews. ORIG C14: pl of MEW[3], orig. referring to royal stables built on the site of hawks' mews at Charing Cross in London

Mex. *abbrev. for:* **1** Mexican. **2** Mexico.

Mexicali ★ (ˌmɛksɪ'kɑːlɪ; *Spanish* mexi'kali) *n* a city in NW Mexico, capital of Baja California Norte state, on the border with the US adjoining Calexico, California: centre of a rich irrigated agricultural region. Pop.: 438 377 (1990).

Mexican wave *n* the rippling effect produced when the spectators in successive sections of a sports stadium stand up while raising their arms and then sit down. ORIG C20: first seen at the World Cup in Mexico in 1986

Mexico ★ ('mɛksɪˌkəʊ) *n* **1** a republic in North America, on the Gulf of Mexico and the Pacific: early Mexican history includes the Maya, Toltec, and Aztec civilizations; conquered by the Spanish between 1519 and 1525 and achieved independence in 1821; lost Texas to the US in 1836 and California and New Mexico in 1848. It is generally mountainous with three ranges of the Sierra Madre (east, west, and south) and a large central plateau. Official language: Spanish. Religion: chiefly Roman Catholic. Currency: peso. Capital: Mexico City. Pop.: 97 367 000 (1999 est.). Area: 1 967 183 sq. km (761 530 sq. miles). Official name: **United Mexican States.** Spanish name: **Méjico. 2** a state of Mexico, on the central plateau surrounding Mexico City, which is not administratively part of the state. Capital: Toluca. Pop.: 12 222 841 (1997 est.). Area: 21 460 sq. km (8287 sq. miles). **3 Gulf of.** an arm of the Atlantic, bordered by the US, Cuba, and Mexico: linked with the Atlantic by the Straits of Florida and with the Caribbean by the Yucatán Channel. Area: about 1 600 000 sq. km (618 000 sq. miles).
▸ **Mexican** ('mɛksɪkən) *adj, n*

Mexico City ★ *n* the capital of Mexico, on the central plateau at an altitude of 2240 m (7350 ft): founded as the Aztec capital (Tenochtitlán) in about 1300; conquered and rebuilt by the Spanish in 1521; forms, with its suburbs, the federal district of Mexico; the largest industrial complex in the country. Pop.: 9 815 795 (1990).

Meyerbeer ★ (*German* 'maiərbeːr) *n* **Giacomo** ('dʒaːkomo), real name *Jakob Liebmann Beer.* 1791–1864, German composer, esp. of operas, such as *Les Huguenots* (1836) and *L'Africaine* (1864).

Meyerhof ★ (*German* 'maiərhoːf) *n* **Otto** (**Fritz**) ('ɔto). 1884–1951, German physiologist, noted for his work on the metabolism of muscles. He shared the Nobel prize for physiology or medicine 1922.

Meyerhold ★ ('miːəˌhəʊlt) *n* **Vsevolod** (**Emilievich**) ('fsjɛvələt), original name *Karl Theodor Kasimir.* 1874–?1940, Russian theatre director; died in custody.

MEZ *abbrev. for* Central European Time. ORIG from G *Mitteleuropäische Zeit*

mezcal (mɛ'skæl) *n* a variant spelling of **mescal.**

mezcaline ('mɛskəˌliːn) *n* a variant spelling of **mescaline.**

Mézières ★ (*French* mezjɛr) *n* a town in NE France, on the River Meuse opposite Charleville. See **Charleville-Mézières.**

mezuzah (mə'zuzə) *n, pl* **mezuzahs** *or* **mezuzoth** (*Hebrew* məzu'zɔt). *Judaism.* **1** a piece of parchment inscribed with biblical passages and fixed to the doorpost of a Jewish house. **2** a metal case for such a parchment, sometimes worn as an ornament. ORIG from Heb., lit.: doorpost

mezzanine ('mɛzəˌniːn, 'mɛtsəˌniːn) *n* **1** Also called: **mezzanine floor.** an intermediate storey, esp. a low one between the ground and first floor of a building. **2** *Theatre, US & Canad.* the first balcony. **3** *Theatre, Brit.* a room or floor beneath the stage. ◆ *adj* **4** often shortened to **mezz.** of or relating to an intermediate stage in a financial process: *mezzanine funding.* ORIG C18: from F, from It., dim. of *mezzano* middle, from L *mediānus* MEDIAN

mezzo ('mɛtsəʊ) *adv Music.* moderately; quite: *mezzo piano.* ORIG C19: from It., lit.: half, from L *medius* middle

mezzo-soprano *n, pl* **mezzo-sopranos. 1** a female voice intermediate between a soprano and contralto. **2** a singer with such a voice.

mezzotint ('mɛtsəʊˌtɪnt) *n* **1** a method of engraving a copper plate by scraping and burnishing the roughened surface. **2** a print made from a plate so treated. ◆ *vb* **3** (*tr*) to engrave (a copper plate) in this fashion. ORIG C18: from It. *mezzotinto* half tint

mf *Music. symbol for* mezzo forte. ORIG It.: moderately loud

MF *abbrev. for:* **1** *Radio.* medium frequency. **2** Middle French.

mfd *abbrev. for* manufactured.

mfg *abbrev. for* manufacturing.

MFH *Hunting. abbrev. for* Master of Foxhounds.

mfr *abbrev. for:* **1** manufacture. **2** manufacturer.

mg *symbol for* milligram.

Mg *the chemical symbol for* magnesium.

M. Glam *abbrev. for* Mid Glamorgan.

Mgr *abbrev. for:* **1** manager. **2** Monseigneur. **3** Monsignor.

MHA (in Australia) *abbrev. for* Member of the House of Assembly.

MHG *abbrev. for* Middle High German.

mho (məʊ) *n, pl* **mhos.** the former name for **siemens.** ORIG C19: formed by reversing the letters of OHM (first used by Lord Kelvin)

MHR (in the US and Australia) *abbrev. for* Member of the House of Representatives.

MHz *symbol for* megahertz.

mi (miː) *n Music.* **1** the syllable used in the fixed system of solmization for the note E. **2** Also: **me.** (in tonic sol-fa) the third degree of any major scale; a mediant. ORIG C14: see GAMUT

MI *abbrev. for:* **1** Michigan. **2** Military Intelligence.

mi. *abbrev. for* mile.

MI5 *abbrev. for* Military Intelligence, section five; a former official and current popular name for the counterintelligence agency of the British Government.

MI6 *abbrev. for* Military Intelligence, section six; a former official and current popular name for the intelligence and espionage agency of the British Government.

Miami ★ (maɪ'æmɪ) *n* a city and resort in SE Florida, on Biscayne Bay: developed chiefly after 1896, esp. with the Florida land boom of the 1920s; centre of an extensive tourist area. Pop.: 365 127 (1996 est.).

Miami Beach ★ *n* a resort in SE Florida, on an island separated from Miami by Biscayne Bay. Pop.: 94 540 (1996 est.).

miaou *or* **miaow** (mɪ'aʊ, mjaʊ) *vb, interj* variant spellings of **meow.**

miasma (mɪ'æzmə) *n, pl* **miasmata** (-mətə) *or* **miasmas. 1** an unwholesome or foreboding atmosphere. **2** pollution in the atmosphere, esp. noxious vapours from decomposing organic matter. ORIG C17: NL, from Gk: defilement, from *miainein* to defile
▸ **mi'asmal** *or* **miasmatic** (ˌmiːəz'mætɪk) *adj*

Mic. *Bible. abbrev. for* Micah.

mica ('maɪkə) *n* any of a group of minerals consisting of hydrous silicates of aluminium, potassium, etc., in monoclinic crystalline form, occurring in igneous and metamorphic rock. Because of their resistance to electricity and heat they are used as dielectrics, in heating el-

ements, etc. Also called: **isinglass**. ORIG C18: from L: crumb
▸ **micaceous** (maɪˈkeɪʃəs) *adj*

Micah ★ (ˈmaɪkə) *n Old Testament*. **1** a Hebrew prophet of the late 8th century B.C. **2** the book containing his prophecies. Douay spelling: **Micheas** (maɪˈkiːəs).

mice (maɪs) *n* the plural of **mouse**.

micelle, micell (mɪˈsɛl), *or* **micella** (mɪˈsɛlə) *n Chem*. **a** a charged aggregate of molecules of colloidal size in a solution. **b** any molecular aggregate of colloidal size. ORIG C19: from NL *micella*, dim. of L *mīca* crumb

Mich. *abbrev. for*: **1** Michaelmas. **2** Michigan.

Michael ★ (ˈmaɪkᵊl) *n* **1** 1596–1645, tsar of Russia (1613–45); founder of the Romanov dynasty. **2** born 1921, king of Romania (1927–30 as part of a three-part regency, 1940–47), who relinquished the throne (1930–40) in favour of his father, Carol II. He led the coup d'état that overthrew Antonescu (1944) but was forced to abdicate (1947) by the Communists. **3 Saint**. *Bible*. one of the archangels. Feast day: Sept. 29 or Nov. 8.

Michaelmas (ˈmɪkᵊlməs) *n* Sept. 29, the feast of St Michael the archangel; in England, Ireland, and Wales, one of the four quarter days.

Michaelmas daisy *n Brit*. any of various composite plants that have small autumn-blooming purple, pink, or white flowers.

Michaelmas term *n* the autumn term at Oxford and Cambridge Universities, the Inns of Court, and some other educational establishments.

Michelangelo ★ (ˌmaɪkᵊlˈændʒɪˌləʊ) *n* full name *Michelangelo Buonarroti*. 1475–1564, Florentine sculptor, architect, and painter. His works include the sculptures of *David* (1504) and of *Moses*, the painted ceiling of the Sistine Chapel (1508–12), the painting *The Last Judgment* (1533–41), the design of the Laurentian Library (1523–29) and of the dome of St Peter's, Rome.

Michelet ★ (*French* miʃlɛ) *n* **Jules** (ʒyl). 1798–1874, French historian, noted for his *Histoire de France* (1833–67).

Michelin ★ (*French* miʃlɛ̃) *n* **André** (ɑ̃dre). 1853–1931, French industrialist; founder, with his brother **Édouard Michelin** (1859–1940), of the Michelin Tyre Company (1888).

Michelozzo ★ (*Italian* mikeˈlɔttso) *n* full name *Michelozzo di Bartolommeo*. 1396–1472, Italian architect and sculptor.

Michelson ★ (ˈmaɪkᵊlsᵊn) *n* **Albert Abraham**. 1852–1931, US physicist, born in Germany: noted for his part in the Michelson-Morley experiment: Nobel prize for physics 1907.

Michigan ★ (ˈmɪʃɪgən) *n* **1** a state of the N central US, occupying two peninsulas between Lakes Superior, Huron, Michigan, and Erie: generally low-lying. Capital: Lansing. Pop.: 9 817 242 (1998 est.). Area: 147 156 sq. km (56 817 sq. miles). Abbrevs.: **Mich.** or (with zip code) **MI** **2 Lake**. a lake in the N central US between Wisconsin and Michigan: the third largest of the five Great Lakes and the only one wholly in the US; linked with Lake Huron by the Straits of Mackinac. Area: 58 000 sq. km (22 400 sq. miles).
▸ **Michigander** (ˌmɪʃɪˈgændə) *n* ▸ **ˈMichiganˌite** *adj, n*

Michoacán ★ (*Spanish* mitʃoaˈkan) *n* a state of SW Mexico, on the Pacific: rich mineral resources. Capital: Morelia. Pop.: 3 925 450 (1997 est.). Area: 59 864 sq. km (23 114 sq. miles).

Mick (mɪk) *n* (*sometimes not cap.*) **1** Also: **Mickey**. *Derog*. a slang name for an **Irishman** or a **Roman Catholic**. **2** *Austral*. the tails side of a coin. ORIG C19: from nickname for *Michael*

mickey *or* **micky** (ˈmɪkɪ) *n Inf*. **take the mickey (out of)**. to tease. ORIG C20: from ?

Mickey Finn *n Sl*. **a** a drink containing a drug to make the drinker unconscious. **b** the drug itself. ◆ Often shortened to **Mickey**. ORIG C20: from ?

Mickiewicz ★ (*Polish* mitsˈkjɛvitʃ) *n* **Adam** (ˈadam). 1798–1855, Polish poet, whose epic *Thaddeus* (1834) is highly regarded.

★ people and places

mickle (ˈmɪkᵊl) *or* **muckle** (ˈmʌkᵊl) *Arch. or Scot. & N English dialect*. ◆ *adj* **1** great or abundant. ◆ *adv* **2** much; greatly. ◆ *n* **3** a great amount, esp. in the proverb, *many a little makes a mickle*. **4** *Scot*. a small amount, esp. in the proverb *mony a mickle makes a muckle*. ORIG C13 *mikel*, from ON *mikell*, replacing OE *micel* MUCH

micro (ˈmaɪkrəʊ) *adj* **1** very small. ◆ *n, pl* **micros**. **2** short for **microcomputer, microprocessor, microwave oven**.

micro- *or* **micr-** *combining form*. **1** small or minute: *microdot*. **2** involving the use of a microscope: *microscopy*. **3** indicating a method or instrument for dealing with small quantities: *micrometer*. **4** (in pathology) indicating abnormal smallness or underdevelopment: *microcephaly*. **5** denoting 10^{-6}: *microsecond*. Symbol: μ ORIG from Gk *mikros* small

microbe (ˈmaɪkrəʊb) *n* any microscopic organism, esp. a disease-causing bacterium. ORIG C19: from F, from MICRO- + Gk *bios* life
▸ **miˈcrobial** *or* **miˈcrobic** *adj*

microbiology (ˌmaɪkrəʊbaɪˈɒlədʒɪ) *n* the branch of biology involving the study of microorganisms.
▸ **microbiological** (ˌmaɪkrəʊˌbaɪəˈlɒdʒɪkᵊl) *or* **ˌmicroˌbioˈlogic** *adj* ▸ **ˌmicroˌbioˈlogically** *adv* ▸ **ˌmicrobiˈologist** *n*

microcephaly (ˌmaɪkrəʊˈsɛfəlɪ) *n* the condition of having an abnormally small head or cranial capacity.
▸ **microcephalic** (ˌmaɪkrəʊsɪˈfælɪk) *adj, n* ▸ **ˌmicroˈcephalous** *adj*

microchemistry (ˌmaɪkrəʊˈkɛmɪstrɪ) *n* chemical experimentation with minute quantities of material.
▸ **ˌmicroˈchemical** *adj*

microchip (ˈmaɪkrəʊˌtʃɪp) *n* another word for **chip** (sense 7).

microcircuit (ˈmaɪkrəʊˌsɜːkɪt) *n* a miniature electronic circuit, esp. one in which a number of permanently connected components are contained in one small chip of semiconducting material. See **integrated circuit**.
▸ **ˌmicroˈcircuitry** *n*

microclimate (ˈmaɪkrəʊˌklaɪmɪt) *n Ecology*. the atmospheric conditions affecting an individual or a small group of organisms, esp. when they differ from the climate of the rest of the community.
▸ **microclimatic** (ˌmaɪkrəʊklaɪˈmætɪk) *adj* ▸ **ˌmicroˌclimaˈtology** *n*

microcomputer (ˌmaɪkrəʊkəmˈpjuːtə) *n* a computer in which the central processing unit is contained in one or more silicon chips.

microcosm (ˈmaɪkrəʊˌkɒzəm) *or* **microcosmos** (ˌmaɪkrəʊˈkɒzmɒs) *n* **1** a miniature representation of something. **2** man regarded as epitomizing the universe. ◆ Cf. **macrocosm**. ORIG C15: via Med. L from Gk *mikros kosmos* little world
▸ **ˌmicroˈcosmic** *or* **ˌmicroˈcosmical** *adj*

microdot (ˈmaɪkrəʊˌdɒt) *n* **1** a greatly reduced photographic copy (about the size of a pinhead) of a document, etc., used esp. in espionage. **2** a tiny tablet containing LSD.

microeconomics (ˌmaɪkrəʊˌiːkəˈnɒmɪks, -ˌɛkə-) *n* (*functioning as sing*) the branch of economics concerned with particular commodities, firms, or individuals and the economic relationships between them.
▸ **ˌmicroˌecoˈnomic** *adj*

microelectronics (ˌmaɪkrəʊɪlɛkˈtrɒnɪks) *n* (*functioning as sing*) the branch of electronics concerned with microcircuits.

microfibre (ˈmaɪkrəʊˌfaɪbə) *n* a very fine synthetic fibre used for textiles.

microfiche (ˈmaɪkrəʊˌfiːʃ) *n* a sheet of film, usually the size of a filing card, on which books, newspapers, documents, etc., can be recorded in miniaturized form. ORIG C20: from F, from MICRO- + *fiche* small card

microfilm (ˈmaɪkrəʊˌfɪlm) *n* **1** a strip of film on which books, documents, etc., can be recorded in miniaturized form. ◆ *vb* **2** to photograph (a page, document, etc.) on microfilm.

microgravity (ˈmaɪkrəʊˌgrævɪtɪ) *n* gravitational effects operating, or apparently operating, in a localized region, as in a spacecraft under conditions of weightlessness.

microhabitat (ˌmaɪkrəʊˈhæbɪtæt) *n Ecology.* the smallest part of the environment that supports a distinct flora and fauna, such as a fallen log in a forest.

microlight *or* **microlite** (ˈmaɪkrəʊˌlaɪt) *n* a small private aircraft carrying no more than two people, with a wing area not less than 10 square metres: used in pleasure flying and racing.

microlith (ˈmaɪkrəʊˌlɪθ) *n Archaeol.* a small Mesolithic flint tool which formed part of a hafted tool.
▸ **ˌmicroˈlithic** *adj*

micrometer (maɪˈkrɒmɪtə) *n* **1** any of various instruments or devices for the accurate measurement of distances or angles. **2** Also called: **micrometer gauge, micrometer calliper.** a type of gauge for the accurate measurement of small distances, thicknesses, etc. The gap between its measuring faces is adjusted by a fine screw (**micrometer screw**).
▸ **micrometric** (ˌmaɪkrəʊˈmɛtrɪk) *or* **ˌmicroˈmetrical** *adj*
▸ **miˈcrometry** *n*

microminiaturization *or* **microminiaturisation** (ˌmaɪkrəʊˌmɪnɪtʃəraɪˈzeɪʃən) *n* the production and application of very small components and the circuits and equipment in which they are used.

micron (ˈmaɪkrɒn) *n, pl* **microns** *or* **micra** (-krə). a unit of length equal to 10^{-6} metre. It is being replaced by the micrometre, the equivalent SI unit. ORIG C19: NL, from Gk *mikros* small

Micronesia ★ (ˌmaɪkrəʊˈniːzɪə) *n* **1** one of the three divisions of islands in the Pacific (the others being Melanesia and Polynesia); the NW division of Oceania: includes the Mariana, Caroline, Marshall, and Kiribati island groups, and Nauru Island. **2 Federated States of.** an island group in the W Pacific, formerly within the United States Trust Territory of the Pacific Islands: comprises the islands of Truk, Yap, Ponape, and Kosrae: formed in 1979 when the islands became self-governing: status of free association with the US from 1982. Languages: English and Micronesian languages. Religion: Christian majority. Currency: US dollar. Capital: Palikir. Pop.: 109 000 (1999 est.). ORIG C19: from MICRO- + Gk *nēsos* island; so called from the small size of many of the islands; on the model of *Polynesia*

Micronesian (ˌmaɪkrəʊˈniːʒən, -ʒɪən) *adj* **1** of or relating to Micronesia, its inhabitants, or their languages. ◆ *n* **2** a native or inhabitant of Micronesia or a descendant of one. **3** a group of languages spoken in Micronesia.

microorganism (ˌmaɪkrəʊˈɔːgəˌnɪzəm) *n* any organism, such as a bacterium, of microscopic size.

micropayment (ˌmaɪkrəʊˈpeɪmənt) *n* a system whereby a user pays a small fee to access a specific area of a website.

microphone (ˈmaɪkrəˌfəʊn) *n* a device used in sound-reproduction systems for converting sound into electrical energy.
▸ **microphonic** (ˌmaɪkrəˈfɒnɪk) *adj*

microprint (ˈmaɪkrəʊˌprɪnt) *n* a greatly reduced photographic copy of print, read by a magnifying device. It is used in order to reduce the size of large books, etc.

microprocessor (ˌmaɪkrəʊˈprəʊsɛsə) *n Computing.* a single integrated circuit performing the basic functions of the central processing unit in a small computer.

micro-scooter *n* a foldable lightweight aluminium foot-propelled scooter, used by both children and adults.

microscope (ˈmaɪkrəˌskəʊp) *n* **1** an optical instrument that uses a lens or combination of lenses to produce a magnified image of a small, close object. **2** any instrument, such as the electron microscope, for producing a magnified visual image of a small object.

microscopic (ˌmaɪkrəˈskɒpɪk) *or (less commonly)* **microscopical** *adj* **1** not large enough to be seen with the naked eye but visible under a microscope. **2** very small; minute. **3** of, concerned with, or using a microscope.
▸ **ˌmicroˈscopically** *adv*

microscopy (maɪˈkrɒskəpɪ) *n* **1** the study, design, and manufacture of microscopes. **2** investigation by use of a microscope.
▸ **microscopist** (maɪˈkrɒskəpɪst) *n*

microsecond (ˈmaɪkrəʊˌsɛkənd) *n* one millionth of a second.

microstructure (ˈmaɪkrəʊˌstrʌktʃə) *n* structure on a microscopic scale, esp. the structure of an alloy as observed by etching, polishing, and observation under a microscope.

microsurgery (ˌmaɪkrəʊˈsɜːdʒərɪ) *n* intricate surgery performed on cells, tissues, etc., using a specially designed operating microscope and miniature precision instruments.

microswitch (ˈmaɪkrəʊˌswɪtʃ) *n Electrical engineering.* a switch that operates by small movements of a lever.

microtome (ˈmaɪkrəʊˌtəʊm) *n* an instrument used for cutting thin sections for microscopical examination.
▸ **microtomy** (maɪˈkrɒtəmɪ) *n*

microwave (ˈmaɪkrəʊˌweɪv) *n* **1a** electromagnetic radiation in the wavelength range 0.3 to 0.001 metres: used in radar, cooking, etc. **1b** *(as modifier): microwave oven.* **2** short for **microwave oven.** ◆ *vb* **microwaves, microwaving, microwaved.** *(tr)* **3** to cook in a microwave oven.

microwave background *n* a background of microwave electromagnetic radiation discovered in space in 1965, believed to have emanated from the big bang with which the universe began.

microwave detector *n NZ.* a device for recording the speed of a motorist.

microwave oven *n* an oven in which food is cooked by microwaves. Often shortened to **micro, microwave.**

microwave spectroscopy *n* a type of spectroscopy in which information is obtained on the structure and chemical bonding of molecules and crystals by measurements of the wavelengths of microwaves emitted or absorbed by the sample.
▸ **microwave spectroscope** *n*

micturate (ˈmɪktjʊˌreɪt) *vb* **micturates, micturating, micturated.** *(intr)* a less common word for **urinate.** ORIG C19: from L *micturīre* to desire to urinate, from *mingere* to urinate
▸ **micturition** (ˌmɪktjʊˈrɪʃən) *n*

mid[1] (mɪd) *adj* **1** *Phonetics.* of, relating to, or denoting a vowel whose articulation lies approximately halfway between high and low, such as *e* in English *bet.* ◆ *n* **2** an archaic word for **middle.** ORIG C12 *midre* (inflected form of *midd,* unattested)

mid[2] *or* **'mid** (mɪd) *prep* a poetic word for **amid.**

mid- *combining form.* indicating a middle part, point, time, or position: *midday; mid-April; mid-Victorian.* ORIG OE; see MIDDLE, MID[1]

midair (ˌmɪdˈɛə) *n* **a** some point above ground level, in the air. **b** *(as modifier): a midair collision of aircraft.*

Midas ★ (ˈmaɪdəs) *n* **1** *Greek legend.* a king of Phrygia given the power by Dionysus of turning everything he touched to gold. **2 the Midas touch.** ability to make money.

mid-Atlantic *adj* characterized by a blend of British and American styles, elements, etc.: *a mid-Atlantic accent.*

midbrain (ˈmɪdˌbreɪn) *n* the nontechnical name for **mesencephalon.**

midday (ˈmɪdˈdeɪ) *n* **a** the middle of the day; noon. **b** *(as modifier): a midday meal.*

Middelburg ★ (ˈmɪdᵊlˌbɜːg; *Dutch* ˈmɪdəlbyrx) *n* a city in the SW Netherlands, capital of Zeeland province, on Walcheren Island: an important trading centre in the Middle Ages and member of the Hanseatic League; 12th-century abbey; market town. Pop.: 40 118 (1994).

middelmannetjie (ˌmɪdᵊlˈmænɪkɪ) *n S. African.* a continuous hump between wheel ruts on a dirt road. ORIG Afrik.

middelskot (ˈmɪdᵊlˌskɒt) *n* (in South Africa) an intermediate payment to a farmers' cooperative for a crop or wool clip. ORIG from Afrik. *middel* middle + *skot* payment

midden (ˈmɪdᵊn) *n* **1a** *Arch. or dialect.* a dunghill or pile of refuse. **1b** *Dialect.* a dustbin. **2** See **kitchen midden.** ORIG C14: from ON

middle (ˈmɪdᵊl) *adj* **1** equally distant from the ends or periphery of something; central. **2** intermediate in status, situation, etc. **3** located between the early and late parts of a series, time sequence, etc. **4** not extreme, esp. in size;

medium. **5** (esp. in Greek and Sanskrit grammar) denoting a voice of verbs expressing reciprocal or reflexive action. **6** (*usually cap.*) (of a language) intermediate between the earliest and the modern forms. ◆ *n* **7** an area or point equal in distance from the ends or periphery or in time between the early and late parts. **8** an intermediate part or section, such as the waist. **9** *Grammar.* the middle voice. **10** *Logic.* See **middle term. 11** *Cricket.* a position on the batting crease in alignment with the middle stumps on which a batsman may take guard. ◆ *vb* **middles, middling, middled.** (*tr*) **12** to place in the middle. **13** *Naut.* to fold in two. **14** *Cricket.* to hit (the ball) with the middle of the bat. ORIG OE *middel*

middle age *n* the period of life between youth and old age, usually (in man) considered to occur approximately between the ages of 40 and 60.
▸ **ˌmiddle-ˈaged** *adj*

Middle Ages *n* **the.** *European history.* **1** (broadly) the period from the deposition of the last W Roman emperor in 476 A.D. to the Italian Renaissance (or the fall of Constantinople in 1453). **2** (narrowly) the period from about 1000 A.D. to the 15th century. Cf. **Dark Ages.**

Middle America ★ *n* **1** the territories between the US and South America: Mexico, Central America, and the Antilles. **2** the US middle class, esp. those groups that are politically conservative.
▸ **Middle American** *adj, n*

middle-and-leg *n Cricket.* a position on the batting crease in alignment with the space between the middle and leg stumps on which a batsman may take guard.

middle-and-off *n Cricket.* a position on the batting crease in alignment with the space between the middle and off stumps on which a batsman may take guard.

Middle Atlantic States *or* **Middle States** ★ *pl n* the states of New York, Pennsylvania, and New Jersey.

middlebrow (ˈmɪdᵊlˌbraʊ) *Disparaging.* ◆ *n* **1** a person with conventional tastes and limited cultural appreciation. ◆ *adj also* **middlebrowed. 2** of or appealing to middlebrows.

middle C *n Music.* the note written on the first ledger line below the treble staff or the first ledger line above the bass staff.

middle class *n* **1** Also called: **bourgeoisie.** a social stratum between the lower and upper classes. It consists of businessmen, professional people, etc., along with their families, and is marked by bourgeois values. ◆ *adj* **middle-class. 2** of, relating to, or characteristic of the middle class.

Middle Congo ★ *n* one of the four territories of former French Equatorial Africa, in W central Africa: became an autonomous member of the French Community, as the Republic of the Congo (now Congo-Brazzaville), in 1958.

middle ear *n* the sound-conducting part of the ear, containing the malleus, incus, and stapes.

Middle East ★ *n* **1** (loosely) the area around the E Mediterranean, esp. Israel and the Arab countries from Turkey to North Africa and eastwards to Iran. **2** (formerly) the area extending from the Tigris and Euphrates to Myanmar.
▸ **Middle Eastern** *adj*

Middle England *n* a characterization of a predominantly middle-class, middle-income section of British society living mainly in suburban and rural England.

Middle English *n* the English language from about 1100 to about 1450.

middle game *n Chess.* the central phase between the opening and the endgame.

Middle High German *n* High German from about 1200 to about 1500.

Middle Low German *n* Low German from about 1200 to about 1500.

middleman (ˈmɪdᵊlˌmæn) *n, pl* **middlemen. 1** a trader engaged in the distribution of goods from producer to consumer. **2** an intermediary.

middlemost (ˈmɪdᵊlˌməʊst) *adj* another word for **midmost.**

middle name *n* **1** a name between a person's first name and surname. **2** a characteristic quality for which a person is known: *caution is my middle name.*

middle-of-the-road *adj* **1** not extreme, esp. in political views; moderate. **2** of, denoting, or relating to popular music having a wide general appeal.

middle passage *n* **the.** *History.* the journey across the Atlantic Ocean from the W coast of Africa to the Caribbean: the longest part of the journey of the slave ships.

Middlesbrough ★ (ˈmɪdᵊlzbrə) *n* **1** an industrial town in NE England, on the Tees estuary, administrative centre of Cleveland; seat of the University of Teeside (1992). Pop.: 145 800 (1994 est.). **2** a unitary authority in NE England, in North Yorkshire. Pop.: 146 800 (1996 est.). Area: 54 sq. km (21 sq. miles).

middle school *n* (in England and Wales) a school for children aged between 8 or 9 and 12 or 13.

Middlesex ★ (ˈmɪdᵊlˌsɛks) *n* a former county of SE England: became mostly part of N and W Greater London in 1965. Abbrev.: **Middx.**

Middle States ★ *pl n* another name for the **Middle Atlantic States.**

middle term *n Logic.* the term that appears in both minor and major premises but not in the conclusion of a syllogism.

Middleton[1] ★ (ˈmɪdᵊltən) *n* a town in NW England, in Rochdale unitary authority, in Greater Manchester. Pop.: 45 621 (1991).

Middleton[2] ★ (ˈmɪdᵊltən) *n* **Thomas.** ?1570–1627, English dramatist. His plays include *Women beware Women* (1621) and the satire *A Game at Chess* (1624).

middle watch *n Naut.* the watch between midnight and 4 a.m.

middleweight (ˈmɪdᵊlˌweɪt) *n* **1a** a professional boxer weighing 154–160 pounds (70–72.5 kg). **1b** an amateur boxer weighing 71–75 kg (157–165 pounds). **2a** a professional wrestler weighing 166–176 pounds (76–80 kg). **2b** an amateur wrestler weighing 75–82 kg (162–180 pounds).

Middle West ★ *n* another name for the **Midwest.**
▸ **Middle Western** *adj* ▸ **Middle Westerner** *n*

middling (ˈmɪdlɪŋ) *adj* **1** mediocre in quality, size, etc.; neither good nor bad, esp. in health (often in **fair to middling**). ◆ *adv* **2** *Inf.* moderately: *middling well.* ORIG C15 (N English & Scot.): from MID[1] + -LING[2]
▸ **ˈmiddlingly** *adv*

Middx. *abbrev. for* Middlesex.

middy (ˈmɪdɪ) *n, pl* **middies. 1** *Inf.* short for **midshipman. 2** *Austral.* **2a** a glass of middling size, used for beer. **2b** the measure of beer it contains.

Mideast ★ (ˌmɪdˈiːst) *n Chiefly US.* another name for **Middle East.**

midfield (ˌmɪdˈfiːld) *n Soccer.* **a** the general area between the two opposing defences. **b** (*as modifier*): *a midfield player.*

Midgard (ˈmɪdgɑːd), **Midgarth** (ˈmɪdgɑːð), *or* **Mithgarthr** ★ (ˈmɪðgɑːðə) *n Norse myth.* the dwelling place of mankind, formed from the body of the giant Ymir and linked by the bridge Bifrost to Asgard, home of the gods. ORIG C19: from Old Norse *mithgarthr;* see MID[1], YARD[2]

midge (mɪdʒ) *n* **1** a mosquito-like dipterous insect occurring in dancing swarms, esp. near water. **2** a small or diminutive person or animal. ORIG OE *mycge*
▸ **ˈmidgy** *adj*

midget (ˈmɪdʒɪt) *n* **1** a dwarf whose skeleton and features are of normal proportions. **2a** something small of its kind. **2b** (*as modifier*): *a midget car.* ORIG C19: from MIDGE + -ET

Mid Glamorgan ★ *n* (from 1974 to 1996) a county of S Wales, formed from three historic counties and replaced by four county boroughs.

midgut (ˈmɪdˌgʌt) *n* **1** the middle part of the digestive tract of vertebrates, including the small intestine. **2** the middle part of the digestive tract of arthropods.

mid-heavyweight *n* **a** a professional wrestler weighing 199–209 pounds (91–95 kg). **b** an amateur wrestler weighing 91–100 kg (199–220 pounds).

midi ('mɪdɪ) *adj* (formerly) **a** (of a skirt, coat, etc.) reaching to below the knee or midcalf. **b** (*as n*): *she wore her new midi.* ORIG C20: from MID-, on the model of MINI

Midi ★ (*French* midi) *n* **1** the south of France. **2 Canal du.** a canal in S France, extending from the River Garonne at Toulouse to the Mediterranean at Sète and providing a link between the Mediterranean and Atlantic coasts: built between 1666 and 1681. Length: 181 km (150 miles).

MIDI ('mɪdɪ) *n* (*modifier*) a generally accepted specification for the external control of electronic musical instruments: *a MIDI synthesizer; a MIDI system.* ORIG C20: from *m(usical) i(nstrument) d(igital) i(nterface)*

midi- *combining form.* of medium or middle size, length, etc.: *midibus; midi system.*

Midian ★ ('mɪdɪən) *n Old Testament.* **1** a son of Abraham (Genesis 25:1–2). **2** a nomadic nation claiming descent from him.
▸ **'Midian,ite** *n, adj* ▸ **'Midian,itish** *adj*

midinette (,mɪdɪ'nɛt) *n* a Parisian seamstress or salesgirl in a clothes shop. ORIG C20: from F, from *midi* noon + *dinette* light meal; the girls had time for only a snack at midday

Midi-Pyrénées ★ (*French* midipirene) *n* a region of SW France: consists of N slopes of the Pyrenees in the south, a fertile lowland area in the west crossed by the River Garonne, and the edge of the Massif Central in the north and east.

midiron ('mɪd,aɪən) *n Golf.* a club, usually a No. 5, 6, or 7 iron, used for medium-length approach shots.

midi system *n* a complete set of hi-fi sound equipment designed as a single unit that is more compact than the standard equipment.

midland ('mɪdlənd) *n* **a** the central or inland part of a country. **b** (*as modifier*): *a midland region.*

Midlands ★ ('mɪdləndz) *n* (*functioning as pl or sing*) **the.** the central counties of England: characterized by manufacturing industries.
▸ **'Midlander** *n*

midlife crisis *n* a crisis that may be experienced in middle age involving frustration, panic, and feelings of pointlessness, sometimes resulting in radical and often ill-advised changes of lifestyle.

Midlothian ★ (mɪd'ləʊðɪən) *n* a council area of SE central Scotland, roughly corresponding to the historic county of Midlothian. Administrative centre: Dalkeith. Pop.: 79 910 (1996 est.). Area: 356 sq. km (137 sq. miles).

midmost ('mɪd,məʊst) *adj, adv* in the middle or midst.

midnight ('mɪd,naɪt) *n* **1a** the middle of the night; 12 o'clock at night. **1b** (*as modifier*): *the midnight hour.* **2 burn the midnight oil.** to work or study late into the night.

midnight sun *n* the sun visible at midnight during the summer inside the Arctic and Antarctic circles.

mid-off *n Cricket.* the fielding position on the off side closest to the bowler.

mid-on *n Cricket.* the fielding position on the on side closest to the bowler.

midpoint ('mɪd,pɔɪnt) *n* **1** the point on a line that is at an equal distance from either end. **2** a point in time halfway between the beginning and end of an event.

midrib ('mɪd,rɪb) *n* the main vein of a leaf, running down the centre of the blade.

midriff ('mɪdrɪf) *n* **1a** the middle part of the human body, esp. between waist and bust. **1b** (*as modifier*): *midriff bulge.* **2** *Anat.* another name for the **diaphragm** (sense 1). **3** the part of a woman's garment covering the midriff. ORIG OE *midhrif,* from MID[1] + *hrif* belly

midship ('mɪd,ʃɪp) *Naut.* ◆ *adj* **1** in, of, or relating to the middle of a vessel. ◆ *n* **2** the middle of a vessel.

midshipman ('mɪd,ʃɪpmən) *n, pl* **midshipmen.** a probationary rank held by young naval officers under training, or an officer holding such a rank.

midships ('mɪd,ʃɪps) *adv, adj Naut.* See **amidships.**

midst[1] (mɪdst) *n* **1 in our midst.** among us. **2 in the midst of.** surrounded or enveloped by; at a point during. ORIG C14: back formation from *amiddes* AMID

midst[2] (mɪdst) *prep Poetic.* See **amid.**

midsummer ('mɪd'sʌmə) *n* **1a** the middle or height of the summer. **1b** (*as modifier*): *a midsummer carnival.* **2** another name for **summer solstice.**

Midsummer's Day *or* **Midsummer Day** *n* June 24, the feast of St John the Baptist; in England, Ireland, and Wales, one of the four quarter days. See also **summer solstice.**

midterm ('mɪd'tɜːm) *n* **1a** the middle of a term in a school, university, etc. **1b** (*as modifier*): *midterm exam.* **2** *US politics.* **2a** the middle of a term of office, esp. of a presidential term, when congressional and local elections are held. **2b** (*as modifier*): *midterm elections.* **3a** the middle of the gestation period. **3b** (*as modifier*): *midterm pregnancy.* See **term** (sense 6).

mid-Victorian *adj* **1** *Brit. history.* of or relating to the middle period of the reign of Queen Victoria (1837–1901). ◆ *n* **2** a person of the mid-Victorian era.

midway ('mɪd,weɪ *or, for adv, n* ,mɪd'weɪ) *adj* **1** in or at the middle of the distance; halfway. ◆ *adv* **2** to the middle of the distance. ◆ *n* **3** *Obs.* a middle place, way, etc.

Midway Islands ★ *pl n* an atoll in the central Pacific, about 2100 km (1300 miles) northwest of Honolulu: annexed by the US in 1867: scene of a decisive battle (June, 1942), in which the US combined fleets destroyed Japan's carrier fleet. Pop.: 450 (1995 est.). Area: 5 sq. km (2 sq. miles).

midweek ('mɪd'wiːk) *n* **a** the middle of the week. **b** (*as modifier*): *a midweek holiday.*

Midwest ('mɪd'wɛst) *or* **Middle West** ★ *n* the N central part of the US; the states from Ohio westwards that border on the Great Lakes, and often the upper Mississippi and Missouri valleys.
▸ **'Mid'western** *adj* ▸ **'Mid'westerner** *n*

mid-wicket *n Cricket.* the fielding position on the on side, midway between square leg and mid-on.

midwife ('mɪd,waɪf) *n, pl* **midwives** (-,waɪvz). a person qualified to deliver babies and to care for women before, during, and after childbirth. ORIG C14: from OE *mid* with + *wif* woman

midwifery ('mɪd,wɪfərɪ) *n* the training, art, or practice of a midwife; obstetrics.

midwinter ('mɪd'wɪntə) *n* **1a** the middle or depth of the winter. **1b** (*as modifier*): *a midwinter festival.* **2** another name for **winter solstice.**

midyear ('mɪd'jɪə) *n* the middle of the year.

mien (miːn) *n Literary.* a person's manner, bearing, or appearance. ORIG C16: prob. var. of obs. *demean* appearance; rel. to F *mine* aspect

Mieres ★ (*Spanish* 'mjeres) *n* a city in N Spain, south of Oviedo: steel and chemical industries; iron and coal mines. Pop.: 26 500 (1987 est.).

Mies van der Rohe ★ ('miːz væn də 'rəʊə) *n* **Ludwig.** 1886–1969, US architect, born in Germany, who directed the Bauhaus (1929–33); his works include the Seagram building, New York (1958).

mifepristone (mɪ'fɛprɪ,stəʊn) *n* See **abortion pill.**

miff (mɪf) *Inf.* ◆ *vb* **1** to take offence or to offend. ◆ *n* **2** a petulant mood. **3** a petty quarrel. ORIG C17: ? an imitative expression of bad temper
▸ **'miffy** *adj*

MIG (mɪg) *n acronym for* minimum income guarantee: a minimum assured weekly income in retirement.

might[1] (maɪt) *vb* (takes an implied infinitive or an infinitive without *to*) used as an auxiliary: **1** making the past tense or subjunctive mood of **may**[1]: *he might have come.* **2** (often foll. by *well*) expressing possibility: *he might well come.* In this sense *might* looks to the future and functions as a weak form of *may.* See **may**[1] (sense 2). ORIG OE *miht*

might[2] (maɪt) *n* **1** power, force, or vigour, esp. of a great or supreme kind. **2** physical strength. **3** (**with**) **might and main.** See **main**[1] (sense 7). ORIG OE *miht*

mighty ('maɪtɪ) *adj* **mightier, mightiest. 1a** having or indicating might; powerful or strong. **1b** (*as collective n; preceded by the*): *the mighty.* **2** very large; vast. **3** very great in

extent, importance, etc. ◆ *adv* **4** *Inf., chiefly US & Canad.* (intensifier): *mighty tired.*
▸ **'mightily** *adv* ▸ **'mightiness** *n*

mignon ('mɪnjɒn) *adj* small and pretty; dainty. ORIG C16: from F, from OF *mignot* dainty
▸ **mignonne** ('mɪnjɒn) *fem n*

mignonette (ˌmɪnjəˈnɛt) *n* **1** any of various mainly Mediterranean plants, such as **garden mignonette**, that have spikes of small greenish-white flowers. **2** a type of fine pillow lace. **3a** a greyish-green colour. **3b** (*as adj*): *mignonette ribbons.* ORIG C18: from F, dim. of MIGNON

migraine ('mi:greɪn, 'maɪ-) *n* a throbbing headache usually affecting only one side of the head and commonly accompanied by nausea and visual disturbances. ORIG C18: (earlier form, C14 *mygrame* MEGRIM): from F, from LL *hēmicrānia* pain in half of the head, from Gk, from HEMI- + *kranion* CRANIUM
▸ **'migrainous** *adj*

migrant ('maɪgrənt) *n* **1** a person or animal that moves from one region, place, or country to another. **2** an itinerant agricultural worker. ◆ *adj* **3** moving from one region, place, or country to another; migratory.

migrate (maɪˈgreɪt) *vb* **migrates, migrating, migrated.** (*intr*) **1** to go from one place to settle in another, esp. in a foreign country. **2** (of birds, fishes, etc.) to journey between different habitats at specific times of the year. ORIG C17: from L *migrāre* to change one's abode
▸ **miˈgrator** *n*

migration (maɪˈgreɪʃən) *n* **1** the act or an instance of migrating. **2** a group of people, birds, etc., migrating in a body. **3** *Chem.* a movement of atoms, ions, or molecules, such as the motion of ions in solution under the influence of electric fields.
▸ **miˈgrational** *adj*

migratory ('maɪgrətərɪ, -trɪ) *adj* **1** of or characterized by migration. **2** nomadic; itinerant.

mihrab ('mi:ræb, -rəb) *n Islam.* the niche in a mosque showing the direction of Mecca. ORIG from Ar.

mikado (mɪˈkɑ:dəʊ) *n, pl* **mikados.** (*often cap.*) *Arch.* the Japanese emperor. ORIG C18: from Japanese, from *mi-* honourable + *kado* gate

mike (maɪk) *n Inf.* short for **microphone.**

Míkonos ★ ('mikɔnɔs) *n* transliteration of the Modern Greek name for **Mykonos.**

mil (mɪl) *n* **1** a unit of length equal to one thousandth of an inch. **2** a unit of angular measure, used in gunnery, equal to one six-thousand-four-hundredth of a circumference. **3** *Photog.* short for millimetre: *35-mil film.* ORIG C18: from L *millēsimus* thousandth

mil. *abbrev. for:* **1** military. **2** militia.

milady *or* **miladi** (mɪˈleɪdɪ) *n, pl* **miladies.** (formerly) a continental title used for an English gentlewoman.

Milan ★ (mɪˈlæn) *n* a city in N Italy, in central Lombardy: Italy's second largest city and chief financial and industrial centre; a centre of the Renaissance under the Visconti and Sforza families. Pop.: 1 306 494 (1996 est.). Italian name: **Milano** (miˈla:no).
▸ ˌ**Milaˈnese** *adj, n*

Milazzo ★ (*Italian* miˈlattso) *n* a port in NE Sicily: founded in the 8th century B.C.; scene of a battle (1860), in which Garibaldi defeated the Bourbon forces. Pop.: 32 000 (1987 est.). Ancient name: **Mylae** ('maɪˌli:).

milch (mɪltʃ) *n* **1** (*modifier*) (esp. of cattle) yielding milk. **2** **milch cow.** *Inf.* a source of easy income, esp. a person. ORIG C13: from OE *-milce* (in compounds); rel. to OE *melcan* to milk

mild (maɪld) *adj* **1** (of a taste, sensation, etc.) not powerful or strong; bland. **2** gentle or temperate in character, climate, behaviour, etc. **3** not extreme; moderate. **4** feeble; unassertive. ◆ *n* **5** *Brit.* draught beer, of darker colour than bitter and flavoured with fewer hops. ORIG OE *milde*
▸ **'mildly** *adv* ▸ **'mildness** *n*

mildew ('mɪlˌdju:) *n* **1** any of various diseases of plants that affect mainly the leaves and are caused by parasitic fungi. **2** any fungus causing this. **3** another name for **mould**[2]. ◆ *vb* **4** to affect or become affected with mildew. ORIG OE *mildēaw,* from *mil-* honey + *dēaw* DEW
▸ **'milˌdewy** *adj*

mild steel *n* any of a class of strong tough steels that contain a low quantity of carbon.

mile (maɪl) *n* **1** Also called: **statute mile.** a unit of length used in the UK, the US, and certain other countries, equal to 1760 yards. 1 mile is equivalent to 1.60934 kilometres. **2** See **nautical mile. 3** the Roman mile, equivalent to 1620 yards. **4** (*often pl*) *Inf.* a great distance; great deal: *he missed by a mile.* **5** a race extending over a mile. ◆ *adv* **6 miles.** (intensifier): *that's miles better.* ORIG OE *mīl,* from L *mīlia* (*passuum*) a thousand (paces)

mileage *or* **milage** ('maɪlɪdʒ) *n* **1** a distance expressed in miles. **2** the total number of miles that a motor vehicle has travelled. **3** allowance for travelling expenses, esp. as a fixed rate per mile. **4** the number of miles a motor vehicle will travel on one gallon of fuel. **5** *Inf.* use, benefit, or service provided by something. **6** *Inf.* grounds, substance, or weight: *some mileage in their arguments.*

mileometer *or* **milometer** (maɪˈlɒmɪtə) *n* a device that records the number of miles that a bicycle or motor vehicle has travelled.

milepost ('maɪlˌpəʊst) *n* **1** *Horse racing.* a marking post on a racecourse a mile before the finishing line. **2** *Chiefly US & Canad.* a signpost that shows the distance in miles to or from a place.

miler ('maɪlə) *n* an athlete, horse, etc., that runs or specializes in races of one mile.

Miles ★ (maɪlz) *n* **Bernard,** Baron Miles of Blackfriars. 1907–91, British actor and theatre manager. He founded the Mermaid Theatre in Blackfriars, London, and was known as a character actor.

milestone ('maɪlˌstəʊn) *n* **1** a stone pillar that shows the distance in miles to or from a place. **2** a significant event in life, history, etc.

Miletus ★ (mɪˈli:təs) *n* an ancient city on the W coast of Asia Minor: a major Ionian centre of trade and learning in the ancient world.
▸ **Miˈlesian** *adj, n*

milfoil ('mɪlˌfɔɪl) *n* **1** another name for **yarrow. 2** See **water milfoil.** ORIG C13: from OF, from L *milifolium,* from *mille* thousand + *folium* leaf

Milford Haven ★ ('mɪlfəd) *n* a port in SW Wales, in Pembrokeshire, on **Milford Haven** (a large inlet of St George's Channel): major oil port. Pop.: 13 194 (1991).

Milhaud ★ (*French* mijo) *n* **Darius** (darjys). 1892–1974, French composer; member of Les Six. His works include operas, symphonies, ballets, string quartets, and songs.

miliaria (ˌmɪlɪˈɛərɪə) *n* an acute itching eruption of the skin, caused by blockage of the sweat glands. ORIG C19: from NL, from L *miliārius* MILIARY

miliary ('mɪljərɪ) *adj* **1** resembling or relating to millet seeds. **2** (of a disease or skin eruption) characterized by small lesions resembling millet seeds: *miliary fever.* ORIG C17: from L *miliārius,* from *milium* MILLET

milieu ('mi:ljɜ:; *French* miljø) *n, pl* **milieux** (-ljɜ:, -ljɜ:z; *French* -ljø) *or* **milieus.** (miljø). surroundings, location, or setting. ORIG C19: from F, from *mi-* MID[1] + *lieu* place

militant ('mɪlɪtənt) *adj* **1** aggressive or vigorous, esp. in the support of a cause. **2** warring; engaged in warfare. ◆ *n* **3** a militant person. ORIG C15: from L *mīlitāre* to be a soldier, from *mīles* soldier
▸ **'militancy** *n* ▸ **'militantly** *adv*

militarism ('mɪlɪtəˌrɪzəm) *n* **1** military spirit; pursuit of military ideals. **2** domination by the military, esp. on a political level. **3** a policy of maintaining a strong military organization in aggressive preparedness for war.
▸ **'militarist** *n*

militarize *or* **militarise** ('mɪlɪtəˌraɪz) *vb* **militarizes, militarizing, militarized** *or* **militarises, militarising, militarised.** (*tr*) **1** to convert to military use. **2** to imbue with militarism.
▸ ˌ**militariˈzation** *or* ˌ**militariˈsation** *n*

military ('mɪlɪtərɪ, -trɪ) *adj* **1** of or relating to the armed forces, warlike matters, etc. **2** of or characteristic of soldiers. ◆ *n, pl* **militaries** *or* **military. 3** (preceded by *the*) the

armed services, esp. the army. ORIG C16: via F from L *mīlitāris,* from *mīles* soldier
▸ **mili'tarily** *adv*

military police *n* a corps within an army that performs police and disciplinary duties.
▸ **military policeman** *n*

militate ('mɪlɪˌteɪt) *vb* **militates, militating, militated.** (*intr; usually foll. by against* or *for*) (of facts, etc.) to have influence or effect: *the evidence militated against his release.* ORIG C17: from L *mīlitātus,* from *mīlitāre* to be a soldier

USAGE NOTE See at **mitigate.**

militia (mɪ'lɪʃə) *n* **1** a body of citizen (as opposed to professional) soldiers. **2** an organization containing men enlisted for service in emergency only. ORIG C16: from L: soldiery, from *mīles* soldier
▸ **mi'litiaman** *n*

milk (mɪlk) *n* **1a** a whitish fluid secreted by the mammary glands of mature female mammals and used for feeding their young until weaned. **1b** the milk of cows, goats, etc., used by man as a food or in the production of butter, cheese, etc. **2** any similar fluid in plants, such as the juice of a coconut. **3** a milklike pharmaceutical preparation, such as milk of magnesia. **4 cry over spilt milk.** to lament something that cannot be altered. ◆ *vb* **5** to draw milk from the udder of (an animal). **6** (*intr*) (of animals) to yield milk. **7** (*tr*) to draw off or tap in small quantities: *to milk the petty cash.* **8** (*tr*) to extract as much money, help, etc., as possible from: *to milk a situation of its news value.* **9** (*tr*) to extract venom, sap, etc., from. ORIG OE *milc*
▸ **'milker** *n*

milk-and-water *adj* (**milk and water** *when postpositive*). weak, feeble, or insipid.

milk bar *n* **1** a snack bar at which milk drinks and light refreshments are served. **2** (in Australia) a shop selling, in addition to milk, basic provisions and other items.

milk chocolate *n* chocolate that has been made with milk, having a creamy taste.

milk float *n Brit.* a small motor vehicle used to deliver milk to houses.

milk leg *n* inflammation and thrombosis of the femoral vein following childbirth, characterized by painful swelling of the leg.

milkmaid ('mɪlkˌmeɪd) *n* a girl or woman who milks cows.

milkman ('mɪlkmən) *n, pl* **milkmen.** a man who delivers or sells milk.

milk of magnesia *n* a suspension of magnesium hydroxide in water, used as an antacid and laxative.

milk pudding *n Chiefly Brit.* a pudding made by boiling or baking milk with a grain, esp. rice.

milk round *n Brit.* **1** a route along which a milkman regularly delivers milk. **2** a regular series of visits, esp. as made by recruitment officers from industry to universities.

milk run *n Aeronautics, inf.* a routine and uneventful flight. ORIG C20: from a milkman's safe and regular routine

milk shake *n* a cold frothy drink made of milk, flavouring, and sometimes ice cream, whisked or beaten together.

milksop ('mɪlkˌsɒp) *n* a feeble or ineffectual man or youth.

milk sugar *n* another name for **lactose.**

milk tooth *n* any of the first teeth to erupt; a deciduous tooth. Also called: **baby tooth.**

milkwort ('mɪlkˌwɜːt) *n* any of several plants having small blue, pink, or white flowers. They were formerly believed to increase milk production in nursing women.

milky ('mɪlkɪ) *adj* **milkier, milkiest. 1** resembling milk, esp. in colour or cloudiness. **2** of or containing milk. **3** spiritless or spineless.
▸ **'milkily** *adv* ▸ **'milkiness** *n*

Milky Way *n* **the.** the diffuse band of light stretching across the night sky that consists of millions of faint stars, nebulae, etc., and forms part of the Galaxy. ORIG C14: translation of L *via lactea*

mill (mɪl) *n* **1** a building in which grain is crushed and ground to make flour. **2** a building fitted with machinery for processing materials, manufacturing goods, etc.; factory. **3** a machine that processes materials, manufactures goods, etc., by performing a continuous or repetitive operation, such as a machine to grind flour, pulverize solids, or press fruit. **4** a machine that tools or polishes metal. **5** a small machine for grinding solids: *a pepper mill.* **6** a system, institution, etc., that influences people or things in the manner of a factory: *the educational mill.* **7** an unpleasant experience; ordeal (esp. in **go** *or* **be put through the mill**). **8** a fist fight. ◆ *vb* **9** (*tr*) to grind, press, or pulverize in or as if in a mill. **10** (*tr*) to process or produce in or with a mill. **11** to cut or roll (metal) with or as if with a milling machine. **12** (*tr*) to groove or flute the edge of (a coin). **13** (*intr;* often foll. by *about* or *around*) to move about in a confused manner. **14** *Arch. sl.* to fight, esp. with the fists. ORIG OE *mylen* from LL *molīna* a mill, from L *mola* mill, from *molere* to grind
▸ **'millable** *adj* ▸ **milled** *adj*

Mill ★ (mɪl) *n* **1 James.** 1773–1836, Scottish philosopher, historian, and economist. He expounded Bentham's utilitarian philosophy in *Elements of Political Economy* (1821) and *Analysis of the Phenomena of the Human Mind* (1829) and also wrote a *History of British India* (1817–18). **2** his son, **John Stuart.** 1806–73, British philosopher and economist. He modified Bentham's utilitarian philosophy in *Utilitarianism* (1861) and in his treatise *On Liberty* (1859) he defended the rights and freedom of the individual. Other works include *A System of Logic* (1843) and *Principles of Political Economy* (1848).

Millais ★ ('mɪleɪ) *n* Sir **John Everett.** 1829–96, British painter, who was a founder of the Pre-Raphaelite Brotherhood. His works include *The Order of Release* (1853) and *The Blind Girl* (1856).

Millay ★ (mɪ'leɪ) *n* **Edna St Vincent.** 1892–1950, US poet, noted esp. for her sonnets; her collections include *The Buck in the Snow* (1928) and *Fatal Interview* (1931).

millboard ('mɪlˌbɔːd) *n* strong pasteboard, used esp. in book covers. ORIG C18: from *milled board*

milldam ('mɪlˌdæm) *n* a dam built in a stream to raise the water level sufficiently for it to turn a millwheel.

millefeuille *French.* (milfœj) *n Brit.* a small iced cake made of puff pastry filled with jam and cream. ORIG lit.: thousand leaves

millefleurs ('miːlˌflɜː) *n* (*functioning as sing*) a design of stylized floral patterns, used in textiles, paperweights, etc. ORIG F: thousand flowers

millenarian (ˌmɪlɪ'nɛərɪən) *adj* **1** of or relating to a thousand or to a thousand years. **2** of or relating to the millennium or millenarianism. ◆ *n* **3** an adherent of millenarianism.

millenarianism (ˌmɪlɪ'nɛərɪəˌnɪzəm) *n* **1** *Christianity.* the belief in a future millennium during which Christ will reign on earth: based on Revelation 20:1–5. **2** any belief in a future period of ideal peace and happiness.

millenary (mɪ'lɛnərɪ) *n, pl* **millenaries. 1** a sum or aggregate of one thousand. **2** another word for a **millennium.** ◆ *adj, n* **3** another word for **millenarian.** ORIG C16: from LL *millēnārius* containing a thousand, from L *mille* thousand

millennium (mɪ'lɛnɪəm) *n, pl* **millennia** (-nɪə) *or* **millenniums. 1 the.** *Christianity.* the period of a thousand years of Christ's awaited reign upon earth. **2** a period or cycle of one thousand years. **3** a time of peace and happiness, esp. in the distant future. ORIG C17: from NL, from L *mille* thousand + *annus* year
▸ **mil'lennial** *adj* ▸ **mil'lennialist** *n*

millennium bug *n Computing.* any software problem arising from the change in date at the start of the 21st century.

millepede ('mɪlɪˌpiːd) *or* **milleped** *n* variants of **millipede.**

millepore ('mɪlɪˌpɔː) *n* any of a genus of tropical colonial coral-like hydrozoans, having a calcareous skeleton. ORIG C18: from NL, from L *mille* thousand + *porus* hole

miller (ˈmɪlə) *n* **1** a person who keeps, operates, or works in a mill, esp. a corn mill. **2** another name for **milling machine.** **3** a person who operates a milling machine.

Miller ★ (ˈmɪlə) *n* **1 Arthur.** born 1915, US dramatist. His plays include *Death of a Salesman* (1949), *The Crucible* (1953), *A View from the Bridge* (1955), and *Mr Peters' Connections* (1998). **2 (Alton) Glenn.** 1904–44, US band leader. His compositions include "Moonlight Serenade". He died when his aeroplane disappeared on a flight between England and France. **3 Henry (Valentine).** 1891–1980, US novelist, author of *Tropic of Cancer* (1934) and *Tropic of Capricorn* (1938). **4 Jonathan (Wolfe).** born 1934, British doctor, theatre director, and television broadcaster.

miller's thumb *n* any of several small freshwater European fishes having a flattened body. ORIG C15: from the alleged likeness of the fish's head to a thumb

millesimal (mɪˈlɛsɪməl) *adj* **1a** denoting a thousandth. **1b** *(as n): a millesimal.* **2** of, consisting of, or relating to a thousandth. ORIG C18: from L *mīllēsimus*

millet (ˈmɪlɪt) *n* **1** a cereal grass cultivated for grain and animal fodder. **2a** an Indian annual grass cultivated for grain and forage, having pale round shiny seeds. **2b** the seed of this plant. **3** any of various similar or related grasses. ORIG C14: via OF from L *milium*

Millet ★ (*French* milɛ) *n* **Jean François** (ʒɑ̃ frɑ̃swa). 1814–75, French painter of the Barbizon school.

milli- *prefix* denoting 10^{-3}: *millimetre.* Symbol: m ORIG from F, from L *mille* thousand

milliard (ˈmɪlɪˌɑːd, ˈmɪljɑːd) *n Brit.* (no longer in technical use) a thousand million. US & Canad. equivalent: **billion.** ORIG C19: from F

millibar (ˈmɪlɪˌbɑː) *n* a cgs unit of atmospheric pressure equal to 10^{-3} bar, 100 newtons per square metre or 0.7500617 millimetre of mercury.

Milligan ★ (ˈmɪlɪgən) *n* **Spike,** real name *Terence Alan Milligan.* born 1918, British comedian and author, born in India, who appeared in *The Goon Show* (1952–60): noted also for the wartime memoir *Adolf Hitler, My Part in his Downfall* (1971) and its sequels. He received an honorary knighthood in 2000.

milligram *or* **milligramme** (ˈmɪlɪˌgræm) *n* one thousandth of a gram. ORIG C19: from F

Millikan ★ (ˈmɪlɪkən) *n* **Robert Andrews.** 1868–1953, US physicist. He measured electronic charge (1910) and studied cosmic rays; Nobel prize for physics 1923.

millilitre *or US* **milliliter** (ˈmɪlɪˌliːtə) *n* one thousandth of a litre.

millimetre *or US* **millimeter** (ˈmɪlɪˌmiːtə) *n* one thousandth of a metre.

millimicron (ˈmɪlɪˌmaɪkrɒn) *n Obs.* one thousand-millionth of a metre; nanometre.

milliner (ˈmɪlɪnə) *n* a person who makes or sells women's hats. ORIG C16: orig. *Milaner,* a native of *Milan,* at that time famous for its fancy goods

millinery (ˈmɪlɪnərɪ, -ɪnrɪ) *n* **1** hats, trimmings, etc., sold by a milliner. **2** the business or shop of a milliner.

milling (ˈmɪlɪŋ) *n* **1** the act or process of grinding, pressing, or crushing in a mill. **2** the grooves or fluting on the edge of a coin, etc.

milling machine *n* a machine tool in which a horizontal arbor or vertical spindle rotates a cutting tool above a horizontal table.

million (ˈmɪljən) *n, pl* **millions** *or* **million.** **1** the cardinal number that is the product of 1000 multiplied by 1000. **2** a numeral, 1 000 000, 10^6, $\bar{M}$, etc., representing this number. **3** *(often pl) Inf.* an extremely large but unspecified number or amount: *I have millions of things to do.* ◆ *determiner* **4** (preceded by *a* or by a numeral) **4a** amounting to a million: *a million light years.* **4b** *(as pron): I can see a million.* ORIG C17: via OF from early It. *millione,* from *mille* thousand, from L

millionaire (ˌmɪljəˈnɛə) *n* a person whose assets are worth at least a million of the standard monetary units of his or her country.
▸ ˌ**millionˈairess** *fem n*

millionth (ˈmɪljənθ) *n* **1a** one of 1 000 000 equal parts of something. **1b** *(as modifier): a millionth part.* **2** one of 1 000 000 equal divisions of a scientific quantity. **3** the fraction one divided by 1 000 000. ◆ *adj* **4** *(usually prenominal)* **4a** being the ordinal number of 1 000 000 in numbering or counting order, etc. **4b** *(as n): the millionth to be manufactured.*

millipede, millepede (ˈmɪlɪˌpiːd), *or* **milleped** (ˈmɪlɪˌpɛd) *n* any of various terrestrial herbivorous arthropods, having a cylindrical segmented body, each segment of which bears two pairs of legs. ORIG C17: from L, from *mille* thousand + *pēs* foot

millisecond (ˈmɪlɪˌsɛkənd) *n* one thousandth of a second.

millpond (ˈmɪlˌpɒnd) *n* **1** a pool formed by damming a stream to provide water to turn a mill-wheel. **2** any expanse of calm water.

millrace (ˈmɪlˌreɪs) *or* **millrun** *n* **1** the current of water that turns a millwheel. **2** the channel for this water.

Mills ★ (mɪlz) *n* Sir **John.** born 1908, British actor. His films include *This Happy Breed* (1944) and *Ryan's Daughter* (1971).

Mills bomb (mɪlz) *n* a type of high-explosive hand grenade. ORIG C20: after Sir William *Mills* (1856–1932), Brit. inventor

millstone (ˈmɪlˌstəʊn) *n* **1** one of a pair of heavy flat disc-shaped stones that are rotated one against the other to grind grain. **2** a heavy burden, such as a responsibility or obligation.

millstream (ˈmɪlˌstriːm) *n* a stream of water used to turn a millwheel.

millwheel (ˈmɪlˌwiːl) *n* a wheel, esp. a waterwheel, that drives a mill.

millwork (ˈmɪlˌwɜːk) *n* work done in a mill.

millwright (ˈmɪlˌraɪt) *n* a person who designs, builds, or repairs grain mills or mill machinery.

Milne ★ (mɪln) *n* **A(lan) A(lexander).** 1882–1956, British writer, noted for his children's books, including *When We Were Very Young* (1924) and *Winnie the Pooh* (1926).

milometer (maɪˈlɒmɪtə) *n* a variant spelling of **mileometer.**

milord (mɪˈlɔːd) *n* (formerly) a continental title used for an English gentleman. ORIG C19: via F from E *my lord*

Mílos ★ (ˈmilɔs) *n* transliteration of the Modern Greek name for **Melos.**

Milošević ★ (mɪˈlɒsəvɪtʃ) *n* **Slobodan** (slɒbədæn). born 1941, Serbian politician: president of Serbia (1989–97) and of the Federal Republic of Yugoslavia (1997–2000).

Miłosz ★ (ˈmiːlɒʃ; *Polish* ˈmiwɔʃ) *n* **Czeslaw** (ˈtʃɛslɔː; ˈtʃɛswaf). born 1911, US poet and writer, born in Lithuania, writing in Polish; author of *The Captive Mind* (1953). Nobel prize for literature 1980.

milt (mɪlt) *n* **1** the testis of a fish. **2** the spermatozoa and seminal fluid produced by a fish. **3** *Rare.* the spleen, esp. of fowls and pigs. ◆ *vb* **4** to fertilize (fish roe) with milt, esp. artificially. ORIG OE *milte* spleen; in the sense: fish sperm, prob. from MDu. *milte*
▸ ˈ**milter** *n*

Miltiades ★ (mɪlˈtaɪəˌdiːz) *n* ?540–?489 B.C., Athenian general, who defeated the Persians at Marathon (490).

Milton ★ (ˈmɪltən) *n* **John.** 1608–74, English poet. His early works include *L'Allegro* and *Il Penseroso* (1632), the masque *Comus* (1634), and the elegy *Lycidas* (1637). He also published pamphlets during the Civil War, including *Areopagitica* (1644). His later works included the poems *Paradise Lost* (1667; 1674) and *Paradise Regained* (1671).
▸ **Milˈtonic** *or* **Milˈtonian** *adj*

Milton Keynes ★ (ˈmɪltən ˈkiːnz) *n* **1** a new town in central England, in Milton Keynes unitary authority, N Buckinghamshire, founded in 1967: electronics, clothing, machinery; seat of The Open University (1969). Pop.: 156 148 (1991). **2** a unitary authority in central England, Buckinghamshire. Pop.: 197 100 (1996 est). Area: 310 sq. km (119 sq. miles).

Milwaukee ★ (mɪlˈwɔːkiː) *n* a port in SE Wisconsin, on Lake Michigan: the largest city in the state; established

as a trading post in the 18th century; an important industrial centre. Pop.: 590 503 (1996 est.).
▸ **Mil'waukeean** *adj, n*

mim (mɪm) *adj Dialect.* prim, modest, or demure. ORIG C17: ? imit. of lip-pursing

mime (maɪm) *n* **1** the theatrical technique of expressing an idea or mood or portraying a character entirely by gesture and bodily movement without the use of words. **2** Also called: **mime artist.** a performer specializing in this. **3** a dramatic presentation using such a technique. **4** (in the classical theatre) **4a** a comic performance with exaggerated gesture and physical action. **4b** an actor in such a performance. ◆ *vb* **mimes, miming, mimed. 5** to express (an idea, etc.) in actions or gestures without speech. **6** (of singers or musicians) to perform as if singing a song or playing a piece of music that is actually prerecorded. ORIG OE *mīma,* from L *mīmus* mimic actor, from Gk *mimos* imitator
▸ **'mimer** *n*

Mimeograph ('mɪmɪəˌgrɑːf) *n* **1** *Trademark.* an office machine for printing multiple copies of text or line drawings from a stencil. **2** a copy produced by this. ◆ *vb* **3** to print copies from (a prepared stencil) using this machine.

mimesis (mɪ'miːsɪs) *n* **1** *Art, literature.* the imitative representation of nature or human behaviour. **2** *Biol.* another name for **mimicry** (sense 2). **3** *Rhetoric.* representation of another person's alleged words in a speech. ORIG C16: from Gk, from *mimeisthai* to imitate

mimetic (mɪ'mɛtɪk) *adj* **1** of, resembling, or relating to mimesis or imitation, as in art, etc. **2** *Biol.* of or exhibiting mimicry.
▸ **mi'metically** *adv*

mimic ('mɪmɪk) *vb* **mimics, mimicking, mimicked.** (*tr*) **1** to imitate (a person, a manner, etc.), esp. for satirical effect; ape. **2** to take on the appearance of: *certain flies mimic wasps.* **3** to copy closely or in a servile manner. ◆ *n* **4** a person or an animal, such as a parrot, that is clever at mimicking. **5** an animal that displays mimicry. ◆ *adj* **6** of, relating to, or using mimicry. **7** simulated, make-believe, or mock. ORIG C16: from L *mīmicus,* from Gk *mimikos,* from *mimos* MIME
▸ **'mimicker** *n*

mimicry ('mɪmɪkrɪ) *n, pl* **mimicries. 1** the act or art of copying or imitating closely; mimicking. **2** the resemblance shown by one animal species to another, which protects it from predators.

MIMinE *abbrev. for* Member of the Institute of Mining Engineers.

Mimir ★ ('miːmɪə) *n Norse myth.* a giant who guarded the well of wisdom near the roots of Yggdrasil.

mimosa (mɪ'məʊsə, -zə) *n* any of various tropical shrubs or trees having ball-like clusters of typically yellow flowers and leaves that are often sensitive to touch or light. See also **sensitive plant.** ORIG C18: from NL, prob. from L *mīmus* MIME, because the plant's sensitivity to touch imitates the similar reaction of animals

mimulus ('mɪmjʊləs) *n* any of a genus of flowering plants of temperate regions. See **monkey flower.** ORIG C19: Med. L, from L *mimus* MIME, alluding to masklike flowers

min. *abbrev. for:* **1** mineralogy. **2** minimum. **3** mining. **4** minute *or* minutes.

Min. *abbrev. for:* **1** Minister. **2** Ministry.

Mina Hassan Tani ★ ('miːnə hɑː'sɑːn 'tɑːnɪ) *n* a port in NW Morocco, on the Sebou River 16 km (10 miles) from the Atlantic. Pop.: 234 000 (1993 est.). Also called: **Kénitra.** Former name (1932–56): **Port Lyautey.**

minaret (ˌmɪnə'rɛt, 'mɪnəˌrɛt) *n* a slender tower of a mosque having one or more balconies. ORIG C17: from F, from Turkish, from Ar. *manārat* lamp, from *nār* fire
▸ **ˌmina'reted** *adj*

Minas Basin ★ ('maɪnəs) *n* a bay in E Canada, in central Nova Scotia: the NE arm of the Bay of Fundy, with which it is linked by **Minas Channel.**

Minas Gerais ★ (*Portuguese* 'minaʒ ʒə'rais) *n* an inland state of E Brazil: situated on the high plateau of the Brazilian Highlands; large reserves of iron ore and manganese. Capital: Belo Horizonte. Pop.: 16 672 613 (1996). Area: 587 172 sq. km (226 707 sq. miles).

minatory ('mɪnətərɪ, -trɪ) *or* **minatorial** *adj* threatening or menacing. ORIG C16: from LL *minātōrius,* from L *minārī* to threaten

mince (mɪns) *vb* **minces, mincing, minced. 1** (*tr*) to chop, grind, or cut into very small pieces. **2** (*tr*) to soften or moderate: *I didn't mince my words.* **3** (*intr*) to walk or speak in an affected dainty manner. ◆ *n* **4** *Chiefly Brit.* minced meat. ORIG C14: from OF *mincier,* ult. from LL *minūtia;* see MINUTIAE
▸ **'mincer** *n*

mincemeat ('mɪnsˌmiːt) *n* **1** a mixture of dried fruit, spices, etc., used esp. for filling pies. **2 make mincemeat of.** *Inf.* to defeat completely.

mince pie *n* a small round pastry tart filled with mincemeat.

Minch ★ (mɪntʃ) *n* **the.** a channel of the Atlantic divided into the **North Minch,** between the mainland of Scotland and the Isle of Lewis, and the **Little Minch,** between the Isle of Skye and Harris and North Uist.

mincing ('mɪnsɪŋ) *adj* (of a person) affectedly elegant in gait, manner, or speech.
▸ **'mincingly** *adv*

mind (maɪnd) *n* **1** the human faculty to which are ascribed thought, feelings, intention, etc. **2** intelligence or the intellect, esp. as opposed to feelings or wishes. **3** recollection or remembrance: *it comes to mind.* **4** the faculty of original or creative thought; imagination: *it's all in the mind.* **5** a person considered as an intellectual being: *great minds.* **6** condition, state, or manner of feeling or thought: *his state of mind.* **7** an inclination, desire, or purpose: *I have a mind to go.* **8** attention or thoughts: *keep your mind on your work.* **9** a sound mental state; sanity (esp. in **out of one's mind**). **10** (in Cartesian philosophy) one of two basic modes of existence, the other being matter. **11 blow someone's mind.** *Sl.* **11a** (of a drug) to alter someone's mental state. **11b** to astound or surprise someone. **12 change one's mind.** to alter one's decision or opinion. **13 in** *or* **of two minds.** undecided; wavering. **14 give (someone) a piece of one's mind.** to criticize or censure (someone) frankly or vehemently. **15 make up one's mind.** to decide (something or to do something). **16 on one's mind.** in one's thoughts. ◆ *vb* **17** (when *tr, may take a clause as object*) to take offence at: *do you mind if I smoke?* **18** to pay attention to (something); heed; notice: *to mind one's own business.* **19** (*tr; takes a clause as object*) to make certain; ensure: *mind you tell her.* **20** (*tr*) to take care of; have charge of: *to mind the shop.* **21** (when *tr, may take a clause as object*) to be cautious or careful about (something): *mind how you go.* **22** (*tr*) to obey (someone or something); heed: *mind your father!* **23** to be concerned (about); be troubled (about): *never mind about your hat.* **24** (*tr; passive; takes an infinitive*) to be intending or inclined (to do something): *clearly he was not minded to finish the story.* **25 mind you.** an expression qualifying a previous statement: *Dogs are nice. Mind you, I don't like all dogs.* ◆ Related adj: **mental.** ◆ See also **mind out.** ORIG OE *gemynd* mind

Mindanao ★ (ˌmɪndə'naʊ) *n* the second largest island of the Philippines, in the S part of the archipelago: mountainous and volcanic. Chief towns: Davao, Zamboanga. Pop.: 14 298 000 (1990). Area: (including offshore islands) 94 631 sq. km (36 537 sq. miles).

mind-bending *adj Inf.* **1** Also: **mind-blowing.** altering one's state of consciousness, esp. as a result of taking drugs. **2** reaching the limit of credibility: *they offered a mind-bending salary.* ◆ *n* **3** the process of brainwashing.

mind-boggling *adj Inf.* astonishing; bewildering.

minded ('maɪndɪd) *adj* **1** having a mind, inclination, intention, etc., as specified: *politically minded.* **2** (*in combination*): *money-minded.*

minder ('maɪndə) *n* **1** someone who looks after someone or something. **2** short for **childminder. 3** *Sl.* an aide to someone in public life who keeps control of press and public relations. **4** *Sl.* someone acting as a bodyguard or assistant, esp. in the criminal underworld.

★ people and places

mindful ('maɪndfʊl) *adj* (usually *postpositive* and foll. by *of*) keeping aware; heedful: *mindful of your duty.*
▸ 'mindfully *adv* ▸ 'mindfulness *n*

mindless ('maɪndlɪs) *adj* **1** stupid or careless. **2** requiring little or no intellectual effort.
▸ 'mindlessly *adv* ▸ 'mindlessness *n*

mind-numbing *adj* extremely boring and uninspiring.
▸ 'mind-ˌnumbingly *adv*

Mindoro ★ (mɪn'dɔːrəʊ) *n* a mountainous island in the central Philippines, south of Luzon. Pop.: 912 000 (1995 est.). Area: 9736 sq. km (3759 sq. miles).

mind out *vb* (*intr, adv*) *Brit.* to be careful or pay attention.

mind-reader *n* a person seemingly able to discern the thoughts of another.
▸ 'mind-ˌreading *n*

mind-set *n* the ideas and attitudes with which a person approaches a situation, esp. when these are seen as being difficult to alter.

mind's eye *n* the visual memory or the imagination.

Mindszenty ★ ('mɪndsɛntɪ) *n* **Joseph.** 1892–1975, Hungarian cardinal. Sentenced to life imprisonment for treason (1949), he was released during the 1956 Revolution.

mine[1] (maɪn) *pron* **1** something or someone belonging to or associated with me: *mine is best.* **2 of mine.** belonging to or associated with me. ◆ *determiner* **3** (*preceding a vowel*) an archaic word for **my**: *mine eyes; mine host.* ORIG OE *mīn*

mine[2] (maɪn) *n* **1** a system of excavations made for the extraction of minerals, esp. coal, ores, or precious stones. **2** any deposit of ore or minerals. **3** a lucrative source or abundant supply: *a mine of information.* **4** a device containing explosive designed to destroy ships, vehicles, or personnel, usually laid beneath the ground or in water. **5** a tunnel dug to undermine a fortification, etc. ◆ *vb* **mines, mining, mined. 6** to dig into (the earth) for (minerals). **7** to make (a hole, tunnel, etc.) by digging or boring. **8** to place explosive mines in position below the surface of (the sea or land). **9** to undermine (a fortification, etc.) by digging mines. **10** another word for **undermine.** ORIG C13: from OF, prob. of Celtic origin

mine detector *n* an instrument designed to detect explosive mines.
▸ mine detection *n*

mine dump *n S. African.* a large mound of residue esp. from gold-mining operations.

minefield ('maɪnˌfiːld) *n* **1** an area of ground or water containing explosive mines. **2** a subject, situation, etc., beset with hidden problems.

minelayer ('maɪnˌleɪə) *n* a warship or aircraft designed for the carrying and laying of mines.

miner ('maɪnə) *n* **1** a person who works in a mine. **2** any of various insects or insect larvae that bore into and feed on plant tissues. See also **leaf miner. 3** *Austral.* any of several honeyeaters.

mineral ('mɪnərəl, 'mɪnrəl) *n* **1** any of a class of naturally occurring solid inorganic substances with a characteristic crystalline form and a homogeneous chemical composition. **2** any inorganic matter. **3** any substance obtained by mining, esp. a metal ore. **4** (*often pl*) *Brit.* short for **mineral water. 5** *Brit.* a soft drink containing carbonated water and flavourings. ◆ *adj* **6** of, relating to, containing, or resembling minerals. ORIG C15: from Med. L *minerāle* (n), from *minerālis* (adj); rel. to *minera* mine, ore, from ?

mineral. *abbrev. for* mineralogy *or* mineralogical.

mineralize *or* **mineralise** ('mɪnərəˌlaɪz) *vb* **mineralizes, mineralizing, mineralized** *or* **mineralises, mineralising, mineralised.** (*tr*) **1a** to impregnate (organic matter, water, etc.) with a mineral substance. **1b** to convert (such matter) into a mineral; petrify. **2** (of gases, vapours, etc., in magma) to transform (a metal) into an ore.
▸ ˌminerali'zation *or* ˌminerali'sation *n* ▸ 'mineralˌizer *or* 'mineralˌiser *n*

mineralogy (ˌmɪnə'rælədʒɪ) *n* the branch of geology concerned with the study of minerals.
▸ mineralogical (ˌmɪnərə'lɒdʒɪkᵊl) *or* ˌminera'logic *adj*
▸ ˌminer'alogist *n*

mineral oil *n Brit.* any oil of mineral origin, esp. petroleum.

mineral water *n* water containing dissolved mineral salts or gases, usually having medicinal properties.

mineral wool *n* a fibrous material made by blowing steam or air through molten slag and used for packing and insulation.

miner's right *n Austral.* a licence to prospect for and mine gold, etc.

Minerva ★ (mɪ'nɜːvə) *n* the Roman goddess of wisdom. Greek counterpart: **Athena.**

minestrone (ˌmɪnɪ'strəʊnɪ) *n* a soup made from a variety of vegetables and pasta. ORIG from It., from *minestrare* to serve

minesweeper ('maɪnˌswiːpə) *n* a naval vessel equipped to clear mines.
▸ 'mineˌsweeping *n*

Ming (mɪŋ) *n* **1** the imperial dynasty of China from 1368 to 1644. ◆ *adj* **2** of or relating to Chinese porcelain from the Ming dynasty.

mingle ('mɪŋgᵊl) *vb* **mingles, mingling, mingled. 1** to mix or cause to mix. **2** (*intr;* often foll. by *with*) to come into close association. ORIG C15: from OE *mengan* to mix
▸ 'mingler *n*

Mingus ★ ('mɪŋgəs) *n* **Charles,** known as *Charlie Mingus.* 1922–79, US jazz bass player, composer, and band leader.

mingy ('mɪndʒɪ) *adj* **mingier, mingiest.** *Brit. inf.* miserly, stingy, or niggardly. ORIG C20: prob. a blend of MEAN[2] + STINGY[1]

Minho ★ ('miɲu) *n* the Portuguese name for the **Miño.**

mini ('mɪnɪ) *adj* **1** (of a woman's dress, skirt, etc.) very short; thigh-length. **2** (*prenominal*) small; miniature. ◆ *n, pl* **minis. 3** something very small of its kind, esp. a small car or a miniskirt.

mini- *combining form.* smaller or shorter than the standard size: *minibus; miniskirt.* ORIG C20: from MINIATURE & MINIMUM

miniature ('mɪnɪtʃə) *n* **1** a model, copy, or representation on a very small scale. **2** anything that is very small of its kind. **3** a very small painting, esp. a portrait. **4** an illuminated decoration in a manuscript. **5 in miniature.** on a small scale. ◆ *adj* **6** greatly reduced in size, etc. **7** on a small scale; minute. ORIG C16: from It., from Med. L, from *miniāre* to paint red (in illuminating manuscripts), from *minium* red lead
▸ 'miniaturist *n*

miniaturize *or* **miniaturise** ('mɪnɪtʃəˌraɪz) *vb* **miniaturizes, miniaturizing, miniaturized** *or* **miniaturises, miniaturising, miniaturised.** (*tr*) to make or construct (something, esp. electronic equipment) on a very small scale; reduce in size.
▸ ˌminiaturi'zation *or* ˌminiaturi'sation *n*

minibar ('mɪnɪˌbɑː) *n* a selection of drinks and confectionery provided in a hotel room and charged to the guest's bill if used.

minibus ('mɪnɪˌbʌs) *n* a small bus able to carry approximately ten passengers.

minicab ('mɪnɪˌkæb) *n Brit.* a small saloon car used as a taxi.

minicomputer (ˌmɪnɪkəm'pjuːtə) *n* a small comparatively cheap digital computer.

minidisc ('mɪnɪˌdɪsk) *n* a small recordable disc similar to a compact disc, used mainly for sound recording.

minidish ('mɪnɪˌdɪʃ) *n* a small parabolic aerial for reception or transmission to a communications satellite.

minim ('mɪnɪm) *n* **1** a unit of fluid measure equal to one sixtieth of a drachm. It is approximately equal to one drop. Symbol: **M** **2** *Music.* a note having the time value of half a semibreve. **3** a small or insignificant thing. **4** a downward stroke in calligraphy. ORIG C15 (*Music.*): from L *minimus* smallest

minimal art *n* abstract painting or sculpture in which expressiveness and illusion are minimized by the use of simple geometric shapes, flat colour, and arrangements of ordinary objects.
▸ minimal artist *n*

minimalism ('mɪnɪməˌlɪzəm) *n* **1** another name for **mini-**

mal art. 2 a type of music based on simple elements and avoiding elaboration or embellishment. **3** design or style in which the simplest and fewest elements are used to create the maximum effect.
▸ **'minimalist** *adj, n*

minimax ('mɪnɪˌmæks) *n* **1** *Maths.* the lowest of a set of maximum values. **2** (in game theory, etc.) the procedure of choosing the strategy that least benefits the most advantaged member of a group. Cf. **maximin.** ORIG C20: from MINI(MUM) + MAX(IMUM)

minimize *or* **minimise** ('mɪnɪˌmaɪz) *vb* **minimizes, minimizing, minimized** *or* **minimises, minimising, minimised.** (*tr*) **1** to reduce to or estimate at the least possible degree or amount. **2** to rank or treat at less than the true worth; belittle.
▸ **ˌminimi'zation** *or* **ˌminimi'sation** *n* ▸ **'miniˌmizer** *or* **'miniˌmiser** *n*

minimum ('mɪnɪməm) *n, pl* **minimums** *or* **minima** (-mə). **1** the least possible amount, degree, or quantity. **2** the least amount recorded, allowed, or reached. **3** (*modifier*) being the least possible, recorded, allowed, etc.: *minimum age.* ◆ *adj* **4** of or relating to a minimum or minimums. ORIG C17: from L: smallest thing, from *minimus* least
▸ **'minimal** *adj* ▸ **'minimally** *adv*

minimum lending rate *n* (in Britain) the minimum rate at which the Bank of England would lend to discount houses between 1971 and 1981, after which it was replaced by the less formal base rate.

minimum wage *n* the lowest wage that an employer is permitted to pay by law or union contract.

mining ('maɪnɪŋ) *n* **1** the act, process, or industry of extracting coal, ores, etc., from the earth. **2** *Mil.* the process of laying mines.

minion ('mɪnjən) *n* **1** a favourite or dependant, esp. a servile or fawning one. **2** a servile agent. ORIG C16: from F *mignon,* from OF *mignot,* of Gaulish origin

minipill ('mɪnɪˌpɪl) *n* a low-dose oral contraceptive containing progesterone only.

miniseries ('mɪnɪˌsɪəriːz) *n, pl* **miniseries.** a television programme in several parts that is shown on consecutive days for a short period.

miniskirt ('mɪnɪˌskɜːt) *n* a very short skirt, originally in the 1960s, one at least four inches above the knee. Often shortened to **mini.**

minister ('mɪnɪstə) *n* **1** (esp. in Presbyterian and some Nonconformist Churches) a member of the clergy. **2** a head of a government department. **3** any diplomatic agent accredited to a foreign government or head of state. **4** Also called: **minister plenipotentiary.** another term for **envoy**[1] (sense 1). **5** Also called: **minister resident.** a diplomat ranking after an envoy. **6** a person who attends to the needs of others, esp. in religious matters. **7** a person who acts as the agent or servant of a person or thing. ◆ *vb* **8** (*intr;* often foll. by *to*) to attend to the needs (of); take care (of). **9** (*tr*) *Arch.* to provide; supply. ORIG C13: via OF from L: servant; rel. to *minus* less

ministerial (ˌmɪnɪ'stɪərɪəl) *adj* **1** of or relating to a minister of religion or his or her office. **2** of or relating to a government minister or ministry. **3** (*often cap.*) of or supporting the ministry against the opposition. **4** *Law.* relating to or possessing delegated executive authority. **5** acting as an agent or cause; instrumental.
▸ **ˌminis'terially** *adv*

minister of state *n* **1** (in the British Parliament) a minister, usually below cabinet rank, appointed to assist a senior minister. **2** any government minister.

Minister of the Crown *n Brit.* any Government minister of cabinet rank.

minister plenipotentiary *n, pl* **ministers plenipotentiary.** another term for **envoy**[1] (sense 1).

ministrant ('mɪnɪstrənt) *adj* **1** ministering or serving as a minister. ◆ *n* **2** a person who ministers. ORIG C17: from L *ministrans,* from *ministrāre* to wait upon

ministration (ˌmɪnɪ'streɪʃən) *n* **1** the act or an instance of serving or giving aid. **2** the act or an instance of ministering religiously. ORIG C14: from L *ministrātiō,* from *ministrāre* to wait upon
▸ **ministrative** ('mɪnɪstrətɪv) *adj*

ministry ('mɪnɪstrɪ) *n, pl* **ministries. 1a** the profession or duties of a minister of religion. **1b** the performance of these duties. **2** ministers of religion or government ministers considered collectively. **3** the tenure of a minister. **4a** a government department headed by a minister. **4b** the buildings of such a department. ORIG C14: from L *ministerium* service; see MINISTER

miniver ('mɪnɪvə) *n* white fur, used in ceremonial costumes. ORIG C13: from OF *menu vair,* from *menu* small + *vair* variegated fur

mink (mɪŋk) *n, pl* **mink** *or* **minks. 1** any of several mammals of Europe, Asia, and North America, having slightly webbed feet. **2** their highly valued fur, esp. that of the American mink. **3** a garment made of this, esp. a woman's coat or stole. ORIG C15: from ON

Minkowski ★ (mɪŋ'kɒfskɪ) *n* **Hermann** ('hɜːmən). 1864–1909, German mathematician, born in Russia. His four-dimensional space-time continuum (1907) was used by Einstein in his general theory of relativity.

Minn. *abbrev. for* Minnesota.

Minna ★ ('mɪnə) *n* a city in W central Nigeria, capital of Niger state. Pop.: 136 900 (1996 est.).

Minneapolis ★ (ˌmɪnɪ'æpəlɪs) *n* a city in SE Minnesota, on the Mississippi River adjacent to St Paul: the largest city in the state; important centre for the grain trade. Pop.: 358 785 (1996 est.).

Minnelli ★ (mɪ'nɛlɪ) *n* **Liza** ('laɪzə). born 1946, US actress, daughter of Judy Garland. Her films include *Cabaret* (1972).

minneola (ˌmɪnɪ'əʊlə) *n* a juicy citrus fruit that is a cross between a tangerine and a grapefruit. ORIG C20: ?from *Mineola,* Texas

minnesinger ('mɪnɪˌsɪŋə) *n* one of the German lyric poets and musicians of the 12th to 14th centuries. ORIG C19: from G *Minnesinger* love-singer

Minnesota ★ (ˌmɪnɪ'səʊtə) *n* **1** a state of the N central US: chief US producer of iron ore. Capital: St Paul. Pop.: 4 725 419 (1998 est.). Area: 218 600 sq. km (84 402 sq. miles). Abbrevs.: **Minn.** or (with zip code) **MN** **2** a river in S Minnesota, flowing southeast and northeast to the Mississippi River near St Paul. Length: 534 km (332 miles).
▸ **ˌMinne'sotan** *adj, n*

minnow ('mɪnəʊ) *n, pl* **minnows** *or* **minnow. 1** a small slender European freshwater cyprinid fish. **2** a small or insignificant person. ORIG C15: rel. to OE *myne* minnow

Miño ★ (*Spanish* 'miɲo) *n* a river in SW Europe, rising in NW Spain and flowing southwest (as part of the border between Spain and Portugal) to the Atlantic. Length: 338 km (210 miles). Portuguese name: **Minho.**

Minoan (mɪ'nəʊən) *adj* **1** of or denoting the Bronze Age culture of Crete from about 3000 B.C. to about 1100 B.C. ◆ *n* **2** a Cretan belonging to the Minoan culture. ORIG C19: after MINOS from the excavations at his supposed palace at Knossos

minor ('maɪnə) *adj* **1** lesser or secondary in amount, importance, etc. **2** of or relating to the minority. **3** below the age of legal majority. **4** *Music.* **4a** (of a scale) having a semitone between the second and third and fifth and sixth degrees (**natural minor**). **4b** (of a key) based on the minor scale. **4c** (*postpositive*) denoting a specified key based on the minor scale: *C minor.* **4d** (of an interval) reduced by a semitone from the major. **4e** (of a chord, esp. a triad) having a minor third above the root. **4f** (esp. in jazz) of or relating to a chord built upon a minor triad and containing a minor seventh: *a minor ninth.* **5** *Logic.* (of a term or premise) having less generality or scope than another term or proposition. **6** *US education.* of or relating to an additional secondary subject taken by a student. **7** (*immediately postpositive*) *Brit.* the younger or junior: sometimes used after the surname of a schoolboy if he has an older brother in the same school. ◆ *n* **8** a person or thing that is lesser or secondary. **9** a person below the age of legal majority. **10** *US & Canad. education.* a subsidiary subject. **11** *Music.* a minor key, chord, mode, or scale. **12** *Logic.* a minor term or premise. ◆ *vb* **13** (*intr;* usually foll. by *in*) *US education.* to take a minor. ORIG C13: from L: less, smaller

minor axis *n* the shorter or shortest axis of an ellipse or ellipsoid.

Minorca ★ (mɪ'nɔːkə) *n* an island in the W Mediterranean, northeast of Majorca: the second largest of the Balearic Islands. Chief town: Mahón. Pop.: 55 500 (1985). Area: 702 sq. km (271 sq. miles). Spanish name: **Menorca.**
▸ **Mi'norcan** *adj, n*

minority (maɪ'nɒrɪtɪ, mɪ-) *n, pl* **minorities.** **1** the smaller of two parts, factions, or groups. **2** a group that is different racially, politically, etc., from a larger group of which it is a part. **3a** the state of being a minor. **3b** the period during which a person is below legal age. **4** (*modifier*) relating to or being a minority: *a minority opinion.* ORIG C16: from Med. L *minōritās,* from L MINOR

minor league *n US & Canad.* any professional league in baseball other than a major league.

minor orders *pl n RC Church.* the four lower degrees of holy orders, namely porter, exorcist, lector, and acolyte.

minor premise *n Logic.* the premise of a syllogism containing the subject of its conclusion.

minor term *n Logic.* the subject of the conclusion of a syllogism.

Minos ★ ('maɪnɒs) *n Greek myth.* a king of Crete for whom Daedalus built the Labyrinth to contain the Minotaur.

Minotaur ★ ('maɪnətɔː) *n Greek myth.* a monster with the head of a bull and the body of a man. It was kept in the Labyrinth in Crete, feeding on human flesh, until destroyed by Theseus. ORIG C14: via L from Gk *Minōtauros,* from MINOS + *tauros* bull

Minsk ★ (mɪnsk) *n* the capital of Belarus: an industrial city and an educational and cultural centre, with a university (1921). Pop.: 1 700 000 (1996 est.).

minster ('mɪnstə) *n Brit.* any of certain cathedrals and large churches, usually originally connected to a monastery. ORIG OE *mynster,* prob. from Vulgar L *monisterium* (unattested), var. of Church L *monastērium* MONASTERY

minstrel ('mɪnstrəl) *n* **1** a medieval musician who performed songs or recited poetry with instrumental accompaniment. **2** a performer in a minstrel show. **3** *Arch. or poetic.* any poet, musician, or singer. ORIG C13: from OF *menestral,* from LL *ministeriālis* an official, from L MINISTER

minstrel show *n* a theatrical entertainment consisting of songs, dances, etc., performed by actors wearing black face make-up.

minstrelsy ('mɪnstrəlsɪ) *n, pl* **minstrelsies.** **1** the art of a minstrel. **2** the poems, music, or songs of a minstrel. **3** a troupe of minstrels.

mint[1] (mɪnt) *n* **1** any N temperate plant of a genus having aromatic leaves. The leaves of some species are used for seasoning and flavouring. See also **peppermint, spearmint.** **2** a sweet flavoured with mint. ORIG OE *minte,* from L *mentha,* from Gk *minthē*
▸ **'minty** *adj*

mint[2] (mɪnt) *n* **1** a place where money is coined by governmental authority. **2** a very large amount of money. ◆ *adj* **3** (of coins, postage stamps, etc.) in perfect condition as issued. **4 in mint condition.** in perfect condition; as if new. ◆ *vb* **5** to make (coins) by stamping metal. **6** (*tr*) to invent (esp. phrases or words). ORIG OE *mynet* coin, from L *monēta* money, mint, from the temple of Juno *Monēta,* used as a mint in ancient Rome
▸ **'minter** *n*

mintage ('mɪntɪdʒ) *n* **1** the process of minting. **2** the money minted. **3** a fee paid for minting a coin. **4** an official impression stamped on a coin.

mint julep *n Chiefly US.* a long drink consisting of bourbon whiskey, crushed ice, sugar, and sprigs of mint.

minuend ('mɪnjʊˌɛnd) *n* the number from which another number, the **subtrahend,** is to be subtracted. ORIG C18: from L *minuendus* (*numerus*) (the number) to be diminished

minuet (ˌmɪnjʊ'ɛt) *n* **1** a stately court dance of the 17th and 18th centuries in triple time. **2** a piece of music composed for or in the rhythm of this dance. ORIG C17: from F *menuet* dainty, from *menu* small

minus ('maɪnəs) *prep* **1** reduced by the subtraction of: *four minus two* (written 4 – 2). **2** *Inf.* deprived of; lacking: *minus the trimmings.* ◆ *adj* **3a** indicating or involving subtraction: *a minus sign.* **3b** Also: **negative.** having a value or designating a quantity less than zero: *a minus number.* **4** involving a disadvantage, harm, etc.: *a minus factor.* **5** (*postpositive*) *Education.* slightly below the standard of a particular grade: *a B minus.* **6** denoting a negative electric charge. ◆ *n* **7** short for **minus sign.** **8** a negative quantity. **9** a disadvantage, loss, or deficit. **10** *Inf.* something detrimental or negative. ◆ Mathematical symbol: – ORIG C15: from L, neuter of MINOR

minuscule ('mɪnəˌskjuːl) *n* **1** a lower-case letter. **2** writing using such letters. **3** a small cursive 7th-century style of lettering. ◆ *adj* **4** relating to, printed in, or written in small letters. Cf. **majuscule.** **5** very small. **6** (of letters) lower-case. ORIG C18: from F, from L (*littera*) *minuscula* very small (letter), dim. of MINOR
▸ **minuscular** (mɪ'nʌskjʊlə) *adj*

minus sign *n* the symbol –, indicating subtraction or a negative quantity.

minute[1] ('mɪnɪt) *n* **1** a period of time equal to 60 seconds; one sixtieth of an hour. **2** Also called: **minute of arc.** a unit of angular measure equal to one sixtieth of a degree. Symbol: ′. **3** any very short period of time; moment. **4** a short note or memorandum. **5** the distance that can be travelled in a minute: *it's only two minutes away.* **6 up to the minute** (**up-to-the-minute** *when prenominal*). the very latest or newest. ◆ *vb* **minutes, minuting, minuted.** (*tr*) **7** to record in minutes: *to minute a meeting.* **8** to time in terms of minutes. ◆ See also **minutes.** ORIG C14: from OF, from Med. L *minūta,* n. use of L *minūtus* MINUTE[2]
▸ **minutely** ('mɪnɪtlɪ) *adv*

minute[2] (maɪ'njuːt) *adj* **1** very small; diminutive; tiny. **2** unimportant; petty. **3** precise or detailed. ORIG C15: from L *minūtus,* p.p. of *minuere* to diminish
▸ **mi'nuteness** *n* ▸ **mi'nutely** *adv*

minute gun ('mɪnɪt) *n* a gun fired at one-minute intervals as a sign of distress or mourning.

minute hand ('mɪnɪt) *n* the pointer on a timepiece that indicates minutes.

Minuteman ('mɪnɪtˌmæn) *n, pl* **Minutemen.** **1** (*sometimes not cap.*) (in the War of American Independence) a colonial militiaman who promised to be ready to fight at one minute's notice. **2** a US three-stage intercontinental ballistic missile.

minutes ('mɪnɪts) *pl n* an official record of the proceedings of a meeting, conference, etc.

minute steak ('mɪnɪt) *n* a small piece of steak that can be cooked quickly.

minutiae (mɪ'njuːʃɪˌiː) *pl n, sing* **minutia** (-ʃɪə). small, precise, or trifling details. ORIG C18: pl of LL *minūtia* smallness, from L *minūtus* MINUTE[2]

minx (mɪŋks) *n* a bold, flirtatious, or scheming woman. ORIG C16: from ?

Minya ★ ('mɪnjə) *n* See **El Minya.**

Miocene ('maɪəˌsiːn) *adj* **1** of or denoting the fourth epoch of the Tertiary period. ◆ *n* **2 the.** this epoch or rock series. ORIG C19: Gk *meiōn* less + -CENE

miosis *or* **myosis** (maɪ'əʊsɪs) *n, pl* **mioses** (-siːz) *or* **myoses.** **1** excessive contraction of the pupil of the eye. **2** a variant spelling of **meiosis** (sense 1). ORIG C20: from Gk *muein* to shut the eyes + -OSIS
▸ **miotic** *or* **myotic** (maɪ'ɒtɪk) *adj, n*

MIP *abbrev. for:* **1** monthly investment plan. **2** maximum investment plan: an endowment assurance policy designed to produce maximum profits.

Miquelon ★ ('miːkəˌlɒn; *French* miklɔ̃) *n* a group of islands in the French territory of **Saint Pierre and Miquelon.**

Mir (mɪə) *n* the Russian (formerly Soviet) orbiting space station launched in 1986: it was destroyed in 2001. ORIG Russian

Mirabeau ★ (*French* mirabo) *n* **Comte de,** title of *Honoré-*

Gabriel Riqueti. 1749–91, French Revolutionary politician.

mirabelle (ˌmɪrəˈbɛl) *n* **1** a small sweet yellow-orange variety of greengage. **2** a liqueur produced from this. ORIG C18: from F

miracle (ˈmɪrəkᵊl) *n* **1** an event contrary to the laws of nature and attributed to a supernatural cause. **2** any amazing or wonderful event. **3** a marvellous example of something: *a miracle of engineering.* **4** short for **miracle play. 5** (*modifier*) being or seeming a miracle: *a miracle cure.* ORIG C12: from L *mīrāculum,* from *mīrārī* to wonder at

miracle play *n* a medieval play based on a biblical story or the life of a saint. Cf. **mystery play.**

miraculous (mɪˈrækjʊləs) *adj* **1** of, like, or caused by a miracle; marvellous. **2** surprising. **3** having the power to work miracles.
▸ **miˈraculously** *adv* ▸ **miˈraculousness** *n*

Miraflores ★ (ˌmɪrəˈflɔːrəs; *Spanish* miraˈflores) *n* **Lake.** an artificial lake in Panama, in the S Canal Zone of the Panama Canal.

mirage (mɪˈrɑːʒ) *n* **1** an image of a distant object or sheet of water, often inverted or distorted, caused by atmospheric refraction by hot air. **2** something illusory. ORIG C19: from F, from (*se*) *mirer* to be reflected

mire (ˈmaɪə) *n* **1** a boggy or marshy area. **2** mud, muck, or dirt. ◆ *vb* **mires, miring, mired. 3** to sink or cause to sink in a mire. **4** (*tr*) to make dirty or muddy. **5** (*tr*) to involve, esp. in difficulties. ORIG C14: from ON *mýrr*

mirepoix (mɪəˈpwɑː) *n* a mixture of sautéed root vegetables used as a base for braising meat or for various sauces. ORIG F, prob. after Duke of *Mirepoix,* 18th-cent. F general

Miriam ★ (ˈmɪrɪəm) *n Old Testament.* the sister of Moses and Aaron. (Numbers 12:1–15). Douay name: **Mary.**

mirk (mɜːk) *n* a variant spelling of **murk.**
▸ **ˈmirky** *adj* ▸ **ˈmirkily** *adv* ▸ **ˈmirkiness** *n*

Miró ★ (*Spanish* miˈro) *n* **Joan** (xwan). 1893–1983, Spanish surrealist painter.

mirror (ˈmɪrə) *n* **1** a surface, such as polished metal or glass coated with a metal film, that reflects an image of an object placed in front of it. **2** such a reflecting surface mounted in a frame. **3** any reflecting surface. **4** a thing that reflects or depicts something else. ◆ *vb* **5** (*tr*) to reflect, represent, or depict faithfully: *he mirrors his teacher's ideals.* ORIG C13: from OF from *mirer* to look at, from L *mīrārī* to wonder at

mirror ball *n* a large revolving ball covered with small pieces of mirror glass so that it reflects light in changing patterns: used in discos and ballrooms.

mirror carp *n* a variety of carp with a smooth shiny body surface.

mirror image *n* **1** an image as observed in a mirror. **2** an object that corresponds to another but has left and right reversed as if seen in a mirror.

mirror writing *n* backward writing that forms a mirror image of normal writing.

mirth (mɜːθ) *n* laughter, gaiety, or merriment. ORIG OE *myrgth*
▸ **ˈmirthful** *adj* ▸ **ˈmirthfulness** *n* ▸ **ˈmirthless** *adj* ▸ **ˈmirthlessness** *n*

MIRV (mɜːv) *n acronym for* multiple independently targeted re-entry vehicle: a missile that has several warheads, each one being directed to a different enemy target.

mis- *prefix* **1** wrong or bad; wrongly or badly: *misunderstanding; misfortune; mistreat; mislead.* **2** lack of; not: *mistrust.* ORIG OE *mis(se)-*

misadventure (ˌmɪsədˈvɛntʃə) *n* **1** an unlucky event; misfortune. **2** *Law.* accidental death not due to crime or negligence.

misalliance (ˌmɪsəˈlaɪəns) *n* an unsuitable alliance or marriage.
▸ **ˌmisalˈly** *vb*

misanthrope (ˈmɪzənˌθrəʊp) *or* **misanthropist** (mɪˈzænθrəpɪst) *n* a person who dislikes or distrusts other people or mankind in general. ORIG C17: from Gk *mīsanthrōpos,* from *misos* hatred + *anthrōpos* man
▸ **misanthropic** (ˌmɪzənˈθrɒpɪk) *or* **ˌmisanˈthropical** *adj*
▸ **misanthropy** (mɪˈzænθrəpɪ) *n*

misapply (ˌmɪsəˈplaɪ) *vb* **misapplies, misapplying, misapplied.** (*tr*) **1** to apply wrongly or badly. **2** another word for **misappropriate.**
▸ **misapplication** (ˌmɪsæplɪˈkeɪʃən) *n*

misapprehend (ˌmɪsæprɪˈhɛnd) *vb* (*tr*) to misunderstand.
▸ **misapprehension** (ˌmɪsæprɪˈhɛnʃən) *n* ▸ **ˌmisappreˈhensive** *adj* ▸ **ˌmisappreˈhensiveness** *n*

misappropriate (ˌmɪsəˈprəʊprɪˌeɪt) *vb* **misappropriates, misappropriating, misappropriated.** (*tr*) to appropriate for a wrong or dishonest use; embezzle or steal.
▸ **ˌmisapˌpropriˈation** *n*

misbecome (ˌmɪsbɪˈkʌm) *vb* **misbecomes, misbecoming, misbecame, misbecome.** (*tr*) to be unbecoming to or unsuitable for.

misbegotten (ˌmɪsbɪˈgɒtᵊn) *adj* **1** unlawfully obtained. **2** badly conceived, planned, or designed. **3** *Literary and dialect.* illegitimate; bastard.

misbehave (ˌmɪsbɪˈheɪv) *vb* **misbehaves, misbehaving, misbehaved.** to behave (oneself) badly.
▸ **ˌmisbeˈhaver** *n* ▸ **misbehaviour** *or US* **misbehavior** (ˌmɪsbɪˈheɪvjə) *n*

misbelief (ˌmɪsbɪˈliːf) *n* a false or unorthodox belief.
▸ **ˌmisbeˈliever** *n*

misc. *abbrev. for:* **1** miscellaneous. **2** miscellany.

miscalculate (ˌmɪsˈkælkjʊˌleɪt) *vb* **miscalculates, miscalculating, miscalculated.** (*tr*) to calculate wrongly.
▸ **ˌmiscalcuˈlation** *n*

miscall (ˌmɪsˈkɔːl) *vb* (*tr*) **1** to call by the wrong name. **2** *Dialect.* to abuse or malign.
▸ **ˌmisˈcaller** *n*

miscarriage (mɪsˈkærɪdʒ) *n* **1** (*also* ˈmɪskær-). spontaneous expulsion of a fetus from the womb, esp. prior to the 20th week of pregnancy. **2** an act of mismanagement or failure: *a miscarriage of justice.* **3** *Brit.* the failure of freight to reach its destination.

miscarry (mɪsˈkærɪ) *vb* **miscarries, miscarrying, miscarried.** (*intr*) **1** to expel a fetus prematurely from the womb; abort. **2** to fail. **3** *Brit.* (of freight, mail, etc.) to fail to reach a destination.

miscast (ˌmɪsˈkɑːst) *vb* **miscasts, miscasting, miscast.** (*tr*) **1** to cast badly. **2** (*often passive*) **2a** to cast (a role) in (a play, film, etc.) inappropriately: *Falstaff was miscast.* **2b** to assign an inappropriate role to: *he was miscast as Othello.*

miscegenation (ˌmɪsɪdʒɪˈneɪʃən) *n* interbreeding of races, esp. where differences of pigmentation are involved. ORIG C19: from L *miscēre* to mingle + *genus* race

miscellanea (ˌmɪsəˈleɪnɪə) *pl n* a collection of miscellaneous items, esp. literary works. ORIG C16: from L: neuter pl of *miscellāneus* MISCELLANEOUS

miscellaneous (ˌmɪsəˈleɪnɪəs) *adj* **1** composed of or containing a variety of things; mixed. **2** having varied capabilities, sides, etc. ORIG C17: from L *miscellāneus,* from *miscellus* mixed, from *miscēre* to mix
▸ **ˌmiscelˈlaneously** *adv* ▸ **ˌmiscelˈlaneousness** *n*

miscellany (mɪˈsɛlənɪ; *US* ˈmɪsəˌleɪnɪ) *n, pl* **miscellanies. 1** a mixed assortment of items. **2** (*sometimes pl*) a miscellaneous collection of items, esp. essays, poems, etc. ORIG C16: from F *miscellanées* (pl) MISCELLANEA
▸ **miscellanist** (mɪˈsɛlənɪst) *n*

mischance (mɪsˈtʃɑːns) *n* **1** bad luck. **2** a stroke of bad luck.

mischief (ˈmɪstʃɪf) *n* **1** wayward but not malicious behaviour, usually of children, that causes trouble, irritation, etc. **2** a playful inclination to behave in this way or to tease or disturb. **3** injury or harm caused by a person or thing. **4** a person, esp. a child, who is mischievous. **5** a source of trouble, difficulty, etc. ORIG C13: from OF *meschief,* from *meschever* to meet with calamity; from *mes-* MIS- + *chever,* from *chef* end

mischievous (ˈmɪstʃɪvəs) *adj* **1** inclined to acts of mischief. **2** teasing; slightly malicious. **3** causing or intended to cause harm.
▸ **ˈmischievously** *adv* ▸ **ˈmischievousness** *n*

miscible (ˈmɪsɪbᵊl) *adj* capable of mixing: *miscible with water.* ORIG C16: from Med. L *miscibilis,* from L *miscēre* to mix
▸ ˌ**misciˈbility** *n*

misconceive (ˌmɪskənˈsiːv) *vb* **misconceives, misconceiving, misconceived.** to have the wrong idea; fail to understand.
▸ ˌ**misconˈceiver** *n*

misconception (ˌmɪskənˈsɛpʃən) *n* a false or mistaken view, opinion, or attitude.

misconduct *n* (mɪsˈkɒndʌkt). **1** behaviour, such as adultery or professional negligence, that is regarded as immoral or unethical. ◆ *vb* (ˌmɪskənˈdʌkt). (*tr*) **2** to conduct (oneself) in such a way. **3** to manage (something) badly.

misconstrue (ˌmɪskənˈstruː) *vb* **misconstrues, misconstruing, misconstrued.** (*tr*) to interpret mistakenly.
▸ ˌ**misconˈstruction** *n*

miscreant (ˈmɪskrɪənt) *n* **1** a wrongdoer or villain. **2** *Arch.* an unbeliever or heretic. ◆ *adj* **3** evil or villainous. **4** *Arch.* unbelieving or heretical. ORIG C14: from OF *mescreant* unbelieving, from *mes-* MIS- + *creant,* ult. from L *credere* to believe

miscue (ˌmɪsˈkjuː) *n* **1** *Billiards, etc.* a faulty stroke in which the cue tip slips off the cue ball or misses it. **2** *Inf.* a blunder or mistake. ◆ *vb* **miscues, miscuing, miscued.** (*intr*) **3** *Billiards.* to make a miscue. **4** *Theatre.* to fail to answer one's cue.

miscue analysis *n Brit. education.* analysis of the errors a pupil makes while reading.

misdate (mɪsˈdeɪt) *vb* **misdates, misdating, misdated.** (*tr*) to date (a letter, event, etc.) wrongly.

misdeal (ˌmɪsˈdiːl) *vb* **misdeals, misdealing, misdealt. 1** (*intr*) to deal out cards incorrectly. ◆ *n* **2** a faulty deal.
▸ ˌ**misˈdealer** *n*

misdeed (ˌmɪsˈdiːd) *n* an evil or illegal action.

misdemean (ˌmɪsdɪˈmiːn) *vb* a rare word for **misbehave.**

misdemeanour *or US* **misdemeanor** (ˌmɪsdɪˈmiːnə) *n* **1** *Criminal law.* (formerly) an offence generally less heinous than a felony. **2** any minor offence or transgression.

misdirect (ˌmɪsdɪˈrɛkt) *vb* (*tr*) **1** to give (a person) wrong directions or instructions. **2** to address (a letter, parcel, etc.) wrongly.
▸ ˌ**misdiˈrection** *n*

misdoubt (mɪsˈdaʊt) *vb* an archaic word for **doubt** or **suspect.**

mise en scène *French.* (miz ɑ̃ sɛn) *n* **1a** the arrangement of properties, scenery, etc., in a play. **1b** the objects so arranged; stage setting. **2** the environment of an event.

Miseno ★ (*Italian* miˈzɛːno) *n* a cape in SW Italy, on the N shore of the Bay of Naples: remains of the town of **Misenum,** a naval base constructed by Agrippa in 31 B.C.

miser (ˈmaɪzə) *n* **1** a person who hoards money or possessions, often living miserably. **2** a selfish person. ORIG C16: from L: wretched

miserable (ˈmɪzərəbᵊl) *adj* **1** unhappy or depressed; wretched. **2** causing misery, discomfort, etc.: *a miserable life.* **3** contemptible: *a miserable villain.* **4** sordid or squalid: *miserable living conditions.* **5** mean; stingy. ORIG C16: from OF, from L *miserābilis,* from *miserārī* to pity, from *miser* wretched
▸ ˈ**miserableness** *n* ▸ ˈ**miserably** *adv*

misère (mɪˈzɛə) *n* **1** a call in solo whist, etc. declaring a hand that will win no tricks. **2** a hand that will win no tricks. ORIG C19: from F: misery

Miserere (ˌmɪzəˈrɛərɪ, -ˈrɪərɪ) *n* the 51st psalm, the Latin version of which begins "Miserere mei, Deus" ("Have mercy on me, O God").

misericord *or* **misericorde** (mɪˈzɛrɪˌkɔːd) *n* **1** a ledge projecting from the underside of the hinged seat of a choir stall in a church, on which the occupant can support himself while standing. **2** *Christianity.* **2a** a relaxation of certain monastic rules for infirm or aged monks or nuns. **2b** a monastery or room where this can be enjoyed. **3** a medieval dagger used to give the death stroke to a wounded foe. ORIG C14: from OF, from L *misericordia* compassion, from *miserēre* to pity + *cor* heart

miserly (ˈmaɪzəlɪ) *adj* of or resembling a miser; avaricious.
▸ ˈ**miserliness** *n*

misery (ˈmɪzərɪ) *n, pl* **miseries. 1** intense unhappiness, suffering, etc. **2** a cause of such unhappiness, etc. **3** squalid or poverty-stricken conditions. **4** *Brit. inf.* a person who is habitually depressed: *he is such a misery.* ORIG C14: via Anglo-Norman from L *miseria,* from *miser* wretched

misfeasance (mɪsˈfiːzəns) *n Law.* the improper performance of an act that is lawful in itself. Cf. **malfeasance, nonfeasance.** ORIG C16: from OF *mesfaisance,* from *mesfaire* to perform misdeeds

misfile (ˌmɪsˈfaɪl) *vb* **misfiles, misfiling, misfiled.** to file (papers, records, etc.) wrongly.

misfire (ˌmɪsˈfaɪə) *vb* **misfires, misfiring, misfired.** (*intr*) **1** (of a firearm or its projectile) to fail to fire or explode as expected. **2** (of a motor engine or vehicle, etc.) to fail to fire at the appropriate time. **3** to fail to operate or occur as intended. ◆ *n* **4** the act or an instance of misfiring.

misfit *n* (ˈmɪsˌfɪt). **1** a person not suited to a particular social environment. **2** something that does not fit or fits badly. ◆ *vb* (ˌmɪsˈfɪt), **misfits, misfitting, misfitted.** (*intr*) **3** to fail to fit or be fitted.

misfortune (mɪsˈfɔːtʃən) *n* **1** evil fortune; bad luck. **2** an unfortunate or disastrous event.

misgive (mɪsˈgɪv) *vb* **misgives, misgiving, misgave, misgiven.** to make or be apprehensive or suspicious.

misgiving (mɪsˈgɪvɪŋ) *n* (*often pl*) a feeling of uncertainty, apprehension, or doubt.

misguide (ˌmɪsˈgaɪd) *vb* **misguides, misguiding, misguided.** (*tr*) to guide or direct wrongly or badly.

misguided (ˌmɪsˈgaɪdɪd) *adj* foolish or unreasonable, esp. in action or behaviour.
▸ ˌ**misˈguidedly** *adv*

mishandle (ˌmɪsˈhændᵊl) *vb* **mishandles, mishandling, mishandled.** (*tr*) to handle or treat badly or inefficiently.

mishap (ˈmɪshæp) *n* **1** an unfortunate accident. **2** bad luck.

Mishima ★ (ˈmɪʃɪmə) *n* **Yukio** (ˈjuːkɪəʊ). 1925–70, Japanese writer. He committed harakiri in protest at the decline of traditional Japanese values.

mishit *Sport.* ◆ *n* (ˈmɪsˌhɪt). **1** a faulty shot or stroke. ◆ *vb* (ˌmɪsˈhɪt), **mishits, mishitting, mishit. 2** to hit (a ball) with a faulty stroke.

mishmash (ˈmɪʃˌmæʃ) *n* a confused collection or mixture. ORIG C15: reduplication of MASH

Mishna (ˈmɪʃnə) *n, pl* **Mishnayoth** (mɪʃˈnɑːjəʊt). *Judaism.* a compilation of precepts collected in the late second century A.D. It forms the earlier part of the Talmud. ORIG C17: from Heb., from *shānāh* to repeat
▸ **Mishnaic** (mɪʃˈneɪɪk) *or* ˈ**Mishnic** *adj*

misinform (ˌmɪsɪnˈfɔːm) *vb* (*tr*) to give incorrect information to.
▸ **misinformation** (ˌmɪsɪnfəˈmeɪʃən) *n*

misinterpret (ˌmɪsɪnˈtɜːprɪt) *vb* (*tr*) to interpret badly, misleadingly, or incorrectly.
▸ ˌ**misinˌterpreˈtation** *n* ▸ ˌ**misinˈterpreter** *n*

misjudge (mɪsˈdʒʌdʒ) *vb* **misjudges, misjudging, misjudged.** to judge (a person or persons) wrongly or unfairly.
▸ **misˈjudger** *n* ▸ **misˈjudgment** *or* **misˈjudgement** *n*

Miskolc ★ (*Hungarian* ˈmiʃkolts) *n* a city in NE Hungary: the second most important industrial centre in Hungary; iron and steel industries. Pop.: 178 000 (1997 est.).

mislay (mɪsˈleɪ) *vb* **mislays, mislaying, mislaid.** (*tr*) **1** to lose (something) temporarily, esp. by forgetting where it is. **2** to lay (something) badly.

mislead (mɪsˈliːd) *vb* **misleads, misleading, misled.** (*tr*) **1** to give false or confusing information to. **2** to lead or guide in the wrong direction.
▸ **misˈleader** *n* ▸ **misˈleading** *adj*

mismarriage (mɪsˈmærɪdʒ) *n* a marriage to an unsuitable partner.

★ people and places

mismatch (ˌmɪs'mætʃ) *vb* **1** to match badly, esp. in marriage. ◆ *n* **2** a bad match.

misname (mɪs'neɪm) *vb* **misnames, misnaming, misnamed.** (*tr*) to call by a wrong or inappropriate name.

misnomer (ˌmɪs'nəʊmə) *n* **1** an incorrect or unsuitable name for a person or thing. **2** the act of referring to a person by the wrong name. ORIG C15: via Anglo-Norman from OF *mesnommer* to misname, from L *nōmināre* to call by name

miso- *or before a vowel* **mis-** *combining form.* indicating hatred: *misogyny.* ORIG from Gk *misos* hatred

misogamy (mɪ'sɒgəmɪ, maɪ-) *n* hatred of marriage.
▸ **mi'sogamist** *n*

misogyny (mɪ'sɒdʒɪnɪ, maɪ-) *n* hatred of women. ORIG C17: from Gk, from MISO- + *gunē* woman
▸ **mi'sogynist** *n* ▸ **mi'sogynous** *or* **miˌsogy'nistic** *adj*

misplace (ˌmɪs'pleɪs) *vb* **misplaces, misplacing, misplaced.** (*tr*) **1** to put (something) in the wrong place, esp. to lose (something) temporarily by forgetting where it was placed. **2** (*often passive*) to bestow (trust, affection, etc.) unadvisedly.
▸ **ˌmis'placement** *n*

misplaced modifier *n Grammar.* a participle intended to modify a noun but having the wrong grammatical relationship to it, for example *having left* in the sentence *Having left Europe for good, Peter's future seemed bleak.*

misplay (ˌmɪs'pleɪ) *vb* **1** (*tr*) to play badly or wrongly in games or sports. ◆ *n* **2** a wrong or unskilful play.

misprint *n* ('mɪsˌprɪnt). **1** an error in printing, made through damaged type, careless reading, etc. ◆ *vb* (ˌmɪs'prɪnt). **2** (*tr*) to print (a letter) incorrectly.

misprision[1] (mɪs'prɪʒən) *n* **a** a failure to inform the authorities of the commission of an act of treason. **b** the deliberate concealment of the commission of a felony. ORIG C15: via Anglo-F from OF *mesprision* error, from *mesprendre* to mistake, from *mes-* MIS- + *prendre* to take

misprision[2] (mɪs'prɪʒən) *n Arch.* **1** contempt. **2** failure to appreciate the value of something. ORIG C16: from MISPRIZE

misprize *or* **misprise** (mɪs'praɪz) *vb* **misprizes, misprizing, misprized** *or* **misprises, misprising, misprised.** to fail to appreciate the value of; disparage. ORIG C15: from OF *mesprisier,* from *mes-* MIS- + *prisier* to PRIZE[2]

mispronounce (ˌmɪsprə'naʊns) *vb* **mispronounces, mispronouncing, mispronounced.** to pronounce (a word) wrongly.
▸ **mispronunciation** (ˌmɪsprəˌnʌnsɪ'eɪʃən) *n*

misproportion (ˌmɪsprə'pɔːʃən) *n* a lack of due proportion.

misquote (ˌmɪs'kwəʊt) *vb* **misquotes, misquoting, misquoted.** to quote (a text, speech, etc.) inaccurately.
▸ **ˌmisquo'tation** *n*

misread (ˌmɪs'riːd) *vb* **misreads, misreading, misread** (-'rɛd). (*tr*) **1** to read incorrectly. **2** to misinterpret.

misrepresent (ˌmɪsrɛprɪ'zɛnt) *vb* (*tr*) to represent wrongly or inaccurately.
▸ **ˌmisrepresen'tation** *n* ▸ **ˌmisrepre'sentative** *adj*

misrule (ˌmɪs'ruːl) *vb* **misrules, misruling, misruled. 1** (*tr*) to govern inefficiently or without justice. ◆ *n* **2** inefficient or unjust government. **3** disorder.

miss[1] (mɪs) *vb* **1** to fail to reach, hit, meet, find, or attain (some aim, target, etc.). **2** (*tr*) to fail to attend or be present for: *to miss an appointment.* **3** (*tr*) to fail to see, hear, understand, or perceive. **4** (*tr*) to lose, overlook, or fail to take advantage of: *to miss an opportunity.* **5** (*tr*) to leave out; omit: *to miss an entry in a list.* **6** (*tr*) to discover or regret the loss or absence of: *she missed him.* **7** (*tr*) to escape or avoid (something, esp. a danger), usually narrowly: *he missed death by inches.* ◆ *n* **8** a failure to reach, hit, etc. **9 give (something) a miss.** *Inf.* to avoid (something): *give the pudding a miss.* ◆ See also **miss out.** ORIG OE *missan* (meaning: to fail to hit)

miss[2] (mɪs) *n Inf.* an unmarried woman or girl. ORIG C17: from MISTRESS

Miss (mɪs) *n* a title of an unmarried woman or girl, usually used before the surname or sometimes alone in direct address. ORIG C17: shortened from MISTRESS

Miss. *abbrev. for* Mississippi.

missal ('mɪsᵊl) *n RC Church.* a book containing the prayers, rites, etc., of the Masses for a complete year. ORIG C14: from Church L *missale* (n), from *missālis* concerning the MASS

mis-sell *vb* **mis-sells, mis-selling, mis-sold.** to sell (a financial product) that is inappropriate for the needs of the customer.

misshape *vb* (ˌmɪs'ʃeɪp), **misshapes, misshaping, misshaped; misshaped** *or* **misshapen. 1** (*tr*) to shape badly; deform. ◆ *n* ('mɪsˌʃeɪp). **2** something that is badly shaped.

misshapen (ˌmɪs'ʃeɪpᵊn) *adj* badly shaped; deformed.
▸ **ˌmis'shapenness** *n*

missile ('mɪsaɪl) *n* **1** any object or weapon that is thrown at a target or shot from an engine, gun, etc. **2** a rocket-propelled weapon that flies either in a fixed trajectory (**ballistic missile**) or in a trajectory controlled during flight (**guided missile**). ORIG C17: from L *missilis,* from *mittere* to send

missilery *or* **missilry** ('mɪsaɪlrɪ) *n* **1** missiles collectively. **2** the design, operation, or study of missiles.

missing ('mɪsɪŋ) *adj* **1** not present; absent or lost. **2** not able to be traced and not known to be dead: *nine men were missing after the attack.* **3 go missing.** to become lost or disappear.

missing link *n* **1** (*sometimes cap.;* usually preceded by *the*) a hypothetical extinct animal, formerly thought to be intermediate between the anthropoid apes and man. **2** any missing section or part in a series.

mission ('mɪʃən) *n* **1** a specific task or duty assigned to a person or group of people. **2** a person's vocation (often in **mission in life**). **3** a group of persons representing or working for a particular country, business, etc., in a foreign country. **4** a special embassy sent to a foreign country for a specific purpose. **5a** a group of people sent by a religious body, esp. a Christian church, to a foreign country to do religious and social work. **5b** the campaign undertaken by such a group. **6a** a building in which missionary work is performed. **6b** the area assigned to a particular missionary. **7** the dispatch of aircraft or spacecraft to achieve a particular task. **8** a charitable centre that offers shelter or aid to the destitute or underprivileged. **9** (*modifier*) of or relating to an ecclesiastical mission: *a mission station.* ◆ *vb* **10** (*tr*) to direct a mission to or establish a mission in (a given region). ORIG C16: from L *missiō,* from *mittere* to send

missionary ('mɪʃənərɪ) *n, pl* **missionaries. 1** a member of a religious mission. ◆ *adj* **2** of or relating to missionaries: *missionary work.* **3** resulting from a desire to convert people to one's own beliefs: *missionary zeal.*

missionary position *n Inf.* a position for sexual intercourse in which the man lies on top of the woman and they are face to face. ORIG C20: from the belief that missionaries advocated this as the proper position to primitive peoples among whom it was unknown

Missionary Ridge ★ *n* a ridge in NW Georgia and SE Tennessee: site of a battle (1863) during the Civil War: Northern victory leading to the campaign in Georgia.

mission statement *n* an official statement of the aims and objectives of a business or other organization.

Mississauga ★ (ˌmɪsə'sɔːgə) *n* a town in SE Ontario: a SW suburb of Toronto. Pop.: 463 388 (1991).

Mississippi ★ (ˌmɪsɪ'sɪpɪ) *n* **1** a state of the southeastern US, on the Gulf of Mexico: consists of a largely forested undulating plain, with swampy regions in the northwest and on the coast, the Mississippi river forming the W border; cotton, rice, and oil. Capital: Jackson. Pop.: 2 752 092 (1998 est.). Area: 122 496 sq. km (47 296 sq. miles). Abbrevs.: **Miss.** or (with zip code) **MS** **2** a river in the central US, rising in NW Minnesota and flowing generally south to the Gulf of Mexico through several mouths, known as the Passes: the second longest river in North America (after its tributary, the Missouri), with the third largest drainage basin in the world (after the Amazon and the Congo). Length: 3780 km (2348 miles).

Mississippian (ˌmɪsɪ'sɪpɪən) *adj* **1** of or relating to the state of Mississippi, or the Mississippi river. **2** (in North America) of or denoting the lower of two subdivisions of the Carboniferous period (see also **Pennsylvanian** (sense 2)). ◆ *n* **3** an inhabitant or native of the state of Mississippi. **4 the.** the Mississippian period or rock system.

missive ('mɪsɪv) *n* **1** a formal or official letter. **2** a formal word for **letter.** ORIG C15: from Med. L *missivus*, from *mittere* to send

Missolonghi (ˌmɪsəˈlɒŋgɪ) *or* **Mesolonghi** ★ *n* a town in W Greece, near the Gulf of Patras: famous for its defence against the Turks in 1822–23 and 1825–26 and for its association with Lord Byron, who died here in 1824. Pop.: 11 275 (1981). Modern Greek name: **Mesolóngion.**

Missouri ★ (mɪˈzʊərɪ) *n* **1** a state of the central US: consists of rolling prairies in the north, the Ozark Mountains in the south, and part of the Mississippi flood plain in the southeast, with the Mississippi forming the E border; chief US producer of lead and barytes. Capital: Jefferson City. Pop.: 5 438 559 (1998 est.). Area: 178 699 sq. km (68 995 sq. miles). Abbrevs.: **Mo.** or (with zip code) **MO** **2** a river in the W and central US, rising in SW Montana: flows north, east, and southeast to join the Mississippi above St Louis; the longest river in North America; chief tributary of the Mississippi. Length: 3970 km (2466 miles).
▸ **Misˈsourian** *n, adj*

miss out *vb* (*adv*) **1** (*tr*) to leave out; overlook. **2** (*intr;* often foll. by *on*) to fail to experience: *you missed out on the celebrations.*

misspell (ˌmɪsˈspɛl) *vb* **misspells, misspelling, misspelt** *or* **misspelled.** to spell (a word or words) wrongly.

misspelling (ˌmɪsˈspɛlɪŋ) *n* a wrong spelling.

misspend (ˌmɪsˈspɛnd) *vb* **misspends, misspending, misspent.** to spend thoughtlessly or wastefully.

misstep (ˌmɪsˈstɛp) *n* **1** a false step. **2** an error.

missus *or* **missis** ('mɪsɪz, -ɪs) *n* **1** (usually preceded by *the*) *Inf.* one's wife or the wife of the person addressed or referred to. **2** an informal term of address for a woman. ORIG C19: spoken version of MISTRESS

missy ('mɪsɪ) *n, pl* **missies.** *Inf.* an affectionate or disparaging form of address to a young girl.

mist (mɪst) *n* **1** a thin fog resulting from condensation in the air near the earth's surface. **2** *Meteorol.* such an atmospheric condition with a horizontal visibility of 1–2 kilometres. **3** a fine spray of liquid, such as that produced by an aerosol container. **4** condensed water vapour on a surface. **5** something that causes haziness or lack of clarity, such as a film of tears. ◆ *vb* **6** to cover or be covered with or as if with mist. ORIG OE

mistake (mɪˈsteɪk) *n* **1** an error or blunder in action, opinion, or judgment. **2** a misconception or misunderstanding. ◆ *vb* **mistakes, mistaking, mistook, mistaken. 3** (*tr*) to misunderstand; misinterpret: *she mistook his meaning.* **4** (*tr;* foll. by *for*) to take (for), interpret (as), or confuse (with): *she mistook his directness for honesty.* **5** (*tr*) to choose badly or incorrectly: *he mistook his path.* **6** (*intr*) to make a mistake. ORIG C13 (meaning: to do wrong, err): from ON *mistaka* to take erroneously
▸ **misˈtakable** *adj*

mistaken (mɪˈsteɪkən) *adj* **1** (*usually predicative*) wrong in opinion, judgment, etc.: *a mistaken viewpoint.* **2** arising from error in opinion, judgment, etc.
▸ **misˈtakenly** *adv* ▸ **misˈtakenness** *n*

Mistassini ★ (ˌmɪstəˈsiːnɪ) *n* **Lake.** a lake in E Canada, in N Quebec: the largest lake in the province; drains through the Rupert River into James Bay. Area: 2175 sq. km (840 sq. miles). Length: about 160 km (100 miles).

mister ('mɪstə) (*sometimes cap.*) ◆ *n* **1** an informal form of address for a man. **2** *Mil.* the official form of address for subordinate or senior warrant officers. **3** *Naval.* the official form of address for all officers in a merchant ship, other than the captain. **4** *Brit.* the form of address for a surgeon. **5** the form of address for officials holding certain positions: *mister chairman.* ◆ *vb* **6** (*tr*) *Inf.* to call (someone) mister. ORIG C16: var. of MASTER

Mister ('mɪstə) *n* the full form of **Mr.**

misterioso (mɪˌstɛrɪˈəʊsəʊ) *adv Music.* in a mysterious manner; mysteriously. ORIG It.

Misti ★ (*Spanish* 'misti) *n* See **El Misti.**

mistigris ('mɪstɪgriː) *n* **1** the joker or a blank card used as a wild card in a variety of draw poker. **2** the game. ORIG C19: from F: jack of clubs, game in which this card was wild

mistime (ˌmɪsˈtaɪm) *vb* **mistimes, mistiming, mistimed.** (*tr*) to time (an action, utterance, etc.) wrongly.

mistle thrush *or* **missel thrush** ('mɪsᵊl) *n* a large European thrush with a brown back and spotted breast, noted for feeding on mistletoe berries. ORIG C18: from OE *mistel* MISTLETOE

mistletoe ('mɪsᵊlˌtəʊ) *n* **1** a Eurasian evergreen shrub with waxy white berries: grows as a partial parasite on various trees: used as a Christmas decoration. **2** any of several similar and related American plants. ORIG OE *misteltān*, from *mistel* mistletoe + *tān* twig; rel. to ON *mistilteinn*

mistook (mɪˈstʊk) *vb* the past tense of **mistake.**

mistral ('mɪstrəl, mɪˈstrɑːl) *n* a strong cold dry wind that blows through the Rhône valley and S France to the Mediterranean coast, mainly in the winter. ORIG C17: via F from Provençal, from L *magistrālis* MAGISTRAL

Mistral ★ *n* **1** (*French* mistral). **Frédéric** (frederik). 1830–1914, French Provençal poet, who shared the Nobel prize for literature 1904. **2** (*Spanish* misˈtral). **Gabriela** (gaˈβrjela), pen name of *Lucila Godoy de Alcayaga.* 1889–1957, Chilean poet, educationalist, and diplomatist. Her poetry includes the collection *Desolación* (1922): Nobel prize for literature 1945.

mistreat (ˌmɪsˈtriːt) *vb* (*tr*) to treat badly.
▸ **ˌmisˈtreatment** *n*

mistress ('mɪstrɪs) *n* **1** a woman who has a continuing extramarital sexual relationship with a man, esp. a married man. **2** a woman in a position of authority, ownership, or control. **3** a woman having control over something specified: *mistress of her own destiny.* **4** *Chiefly Brit.* short for **schoolmistress. 5** an archaic or dialect word for **sweetheart.** ORIG C14: from OF; see MASTER, -ESS

Mistress ('mɪstrɪs) *n* an archaic or dialect title equivalent to **Mrs.**

Mistress of the Robes *n* (in Britain) a lady of high rank in charge of the Queen's wardrobe.

mistrial (mɪsˈtraɪəl) *n* **1** a trial made void because of some error. **2** *US.* an inconclusive trial, as when a jury cannot agree on a verdict.

mistrust (ˌmɪsˈtrʌst) *vb* **1** to have doubts or suspicions about (someone or something). ◆ *n* **2** distrust.
▸ **ˌmisˈtrustful** *adj* ▸ **ˌmisˈtrustfully** *adv* ▸ **ˌmisˈtrustfulness** *n*

misty ('mɪstɪ) *adj* **mistier, mistiest. 1** consisting of or resembling mist. **2** obscured as by mist. **3** indistinct; blurred.
▸ **ˈmistily** *adv* ▸ **ˈmistiness** *n*

misunderstand (ˌmɪsʌndəˈstænd) *vb* **misunderstands, misunderstanding, misunderstood.** to fail to understand properly.

misunderstanding (ˌmɪsʌndəˈstændɪŋ) *n* **1** a failure to understand properly. **2** a disagreement.

misunderstood (ˌmɪsʌndəˈstʊd) *adj* not properly or sympathetically understood: *a misunderstood adolescent.*

misuse *n* (ˌmɪsˈjuːs), *also* **misusage. 1** erroneous, improper, or unorthodox use: *misuse of words.* **2** cruel or inhumane treatment. ◆ *vb* (ˌmɪsˈjuːz), **misuses, misusing, misused.** (*tr*) **3** to use wrongly. **4** to treat badly or harshly.
▸ **ˌmisˈuser** *n*

Mitchell ★ ('mɪtʃəl) *n* **1 Joni,** original name *Roberta Joan Anderson.* born 1943, Canadian singer and songwriter. Her albums include *Blue* (1971) and *Turbulent Indigo* (1994). **2 Margaret.** 1900–49, US novelist; author of *Gone with the Wind* (1936). **3 Reginald Joseph.** 1895–1937, British aeronautical engineer; designer of the Spitfire fighter. **4** Sir **Thomas Livingstone**, known as *Major Mitchell.* 1792–1855, Australian explorer born in Scotland.

Mitchum ★ ('mɪtʃəm) *n* **Robert.** 1917–97, US film actor. His films include *Night of the Hunter* (1955) and *Farewell my Lovely* (1975).

mite[1] (maɪt) *n* any of numerous small terrestrial or aquatic free-living or parasitic arachnids. ORIG OE *mīte*

mite[2] (maɪt) *n* **1** a very small particle, creature, or object. **2** a very small contribution or sum of money. See also **widow's mite. 3** a former Flemish coin of small value. **4 a mite.** *Inf.* somewhat: *he's a mite foolish.* ORIG C14: from MLow G, MDu. *mīte*

Mithgarthr ★ ('mɪð,gɑːðə) *n* a variant of **Midgard.**

Mithraism ('mɪθreɪ,ɪzəm) *or* **Mithraicism** (mɪθ'reɪɪ,sɪzəm) *n* the ancient religion of Mithras.
▸ **Mithraic** (mɪθ'reɪɪk) *adj* ▸ **'Mithraist** *n, adj*

Mithras ('mɪθræs) *or* **Mithra** ★ ('mɪθrə) *n Persian myth.* the god of light, identified with the sun, who slew a primordial bull and fertilized the world with its blood.

Mithridates VI *or* **Mithradates VI** ★ (,mɪθrɪ'deɪtiːz) *n* called *the Great.* ?132–63 B.C., king of Pontus (?120–63). He waged three wars against Rome (88–84; 83–81; 74–64) and was finally defeated by Pompey: committed suicide.

mithridatism ('mɪθrɪdeɪ,tɪzəm) *n* immunity to large doses of poison by prior ingestion of gradually increased doses.
▸ **mithridatic** (,mɪθrɪ'dætɪk, -'deɪ-) *adj*

mitigate ('mɪtɪ,geɪt) *vb* **mitigates, mitigating, mitigated.** to make or become less severe or harsh; moderate. ORIG C15: from L *mītigāre,* from *mītis* mild + *agere* to make
▸ **'mitigable** *adj* ▸ **,miti'gation** *n* ▸ **'miti,gative** *or* **'miti,gatory** *adj* ▸ **'miti,gator** *n*

> **USAGE NOTE** *Mitigate* is sometimes wrongly used where *militate* is meant: *his behaviour militates* (not *mitigates*) *against his chances of promotion.*

Mitilíni ★ (miti'lini) *n* transliteration of the Modern Greek name for **Mytilene** (sense 1).

mitochondrion (,maɪtəʊ'kɒndrɪən) *n, pl* **mitochondria** (-drɪə). a small spherical or rodlike body, in the cytoplasm of most cells: contains enzymes responsible for energy production. ORIG C19: NL, from Gk *mitos* thread + *khondrion* small grain

mitosis (maɪ'təʊsɪs, mɪ-) *n* a method of cell division, in which the nucleus divides into daughter nuclei, each containing the same number of chromosomes as the parent nucleus. ORIG C19: from NL, from Gk *mitos* thread
▸ **mitotic** (maɪ'tɒtɪk, mɪ-) *adj*

mitral ('maɪtrəl) *adj* **1** of or like a mitre. **2** *Anat.* of or relating to the mitral valve.

mitral valve *n* the valve between the left atrium and the left ventricle of the heart.

mitre *or US* **miter** ('maɪtə) *n* **1** *Christianity.* the liturgical headdress of a bishop or abbot, consisting of a tall pointed cleft cap with two bands hanging down at the back. **2** Also called: **mitre joint.** a corner joint formed by cutting bevels of equal angles at the ends of each piece of material. **3** a bevelled surface of a mitre joint. ◆ *vb* **mitres, mitring, mitred** *or US* **miters, mitering, mitered.** (*tr*) **4** to make a mitre joint between (two pieces of material). **5** to confer a mitre upon: *a mitred abbot.* ORIG C14: from OF, from L *mitra,* from Gk: turban

mitre box *n* an open-ended box with sides slotted to guide a saw in cutting mitre joints.

mitt (mɪt) *n* **1** any of various glovelike hand coverings, such as one that does not cover the fingers. **2** short for **mitten** (sense 1). **3** *Baseball.* a large round thickly padded leather mitten worn by the catcher. **4** (*often pl*) a slang word for **hand. 5** *Sl.* a boxing glove. ORIG C18: from MITTEN

Mittelland Canal ★ (*German* 'mɪtəllant) *n* a canal in Germany, linking the Rivers Rhine and Elbe. Length: 325 km (202 miles).

mitten ('mɪtᵊn) *n* **1** a glove having one section for the thumb and a single section for the other fingers. Sometimes shortened to **mitt. 2** *Sl.* a boxing glove. ORIG C14: from OF *mitaine,* from ?

Mitterrand ★ (*French* mitɛrɑ̃) *n* **François Maurice Marie** (frɑ̃swa mɔris mari). 1916–96, French statesman; first secretary of the socialist party (1971–81); president of France (1981–95).

mittimus ('mɪtɪməs) *n, pl* **mittimuses.** *Law.* a warrant of commitment to prison or a command to a jailer to hold someone in prison. ORIG C15: from L: we send, the first word of such a command

mix (mɪks) *vb* **1** (*tr*) to combine or blend (ingredients, liquids, objects, etc.) together into one mass. **2** (*intr*) to become or have the capacity to become combined, joined, etc.: *some chemicals do not mix.* **3** (*tr*) to form (something) by combining constituents: *to mix cement.* **4** (*tr; often* foll. by *in* or *into*) to add as an additional element (to a mass or compound): *to mix flour into a batter.* **5** (*tr*) to do at the same time: *to mix study and pleasure.* **6** (*tr*) to consume (different alcoholic drinks) in close succession. **7** to come or cause to come into association socially: *Pauline mixed well.* **8** (*intr; often* foll. by *with*) to go together; complement. **9** (*tr*) to crossbreed (differing strains of plants or breeds of livestock), esp. more or less at random. **10** *Music.* to balance and adjust (individual performers' parts) to make an overall sound by electronic means. **11 mix it.** *Inf.* to cause mischief or trouble, often for a person named: *she tried to mix it for John.* ◆ *n* **12** the act or an instance of mixing. **13** the result of mixing; mixture. **14** a mixture of ingredients, esp. one commercially prepared for making a cake, bread, etc. **15** *Inf.* a state of confusion. **16** *Music.* the sound produced by mixing. ◆ See also **mix-up.** ORIG C15: back formation from *mixt* mixed, via OF from L *mixtus,* from *miscēre* to mix
▸ **'mixable** *adj*

mixed (mɪkst) *adj* **1** formed or blended together by mixing. **2** composed of different elements, races, sexes, etc.: *a mixed school.* **3** consisting of conflicting elements, thoughts, attitudes, etc.: *mixed feelings.* **4** *Maths.* (of a number) consisting of the sum of an integer and a fraction or a decimal fraction, as 5½ or 17.43.
▸ **mixedness** ('mɪksɪdnɪs) *n*

mixed bag *n Inf.* something composed of diverse elements, characteristics, people, etc.

mixed blessing *n* an event, situation, etc., having both advantages and disadvantages.

mixed doubles *pl n Tennis.* a doubles game with a man and a woman as partners on each side.

mixed economy *n* an economic system in which the public and private sectors coexist.

mixed farming *n* combined arable and livestock farming (on **mixed farms**).

mixed marriage *n* a marriage between persons of different races or religions.

mixed metaphor *n* a combination of incongruous metaphors, as *when the Nazi jackboots sing their swan song.*

mixed-up *adj* in a state of mental confusion.

mixer ('mɪksə) *n* **1** a person or thing that mixes. **2** *Inf.* **2a** a person considered in relation to his or her ability to mix socially. **2b** a person who creates trouble for others. **3** a kitchen appliance, usually electrical, used for mixing foods, etc. **4** a drink such as ginger ale, fruit juice, etc., used in preparing cocktails. **5** *Electronics.* a device in which two or more input signals are combined to give a single output signal.

mixer tap *n* a tap in which hot and cold water supplies have a joint outlet but are controlled separately.

mixture ('mɪkstʃə) *n* **1** the act of mixing or state of being mixed. **2** something mixed; a result of mixing. **3** *Chem.* a substance consisting of two or more substances mixed together without any chemical bonding between them. **4** *Pharmacol.* a liquid medicine in which an insoluble compound is suspended in the liquid. **5** *Music.* an organ stop that controls several ranks of pipes. **6** the mixture of petrol vapour and air in an internal-combustion engine. ORIG C16: from L *mixtūra,* from *mixtus,* p.p. of *miscere* to mix

mix-up *n* **1** a confused condition or situation. **2** *Inf.* a fight. ◆ *vb* **mix up.** (*tr, adv*) **3** to make into a mixture. **4** to confuse or confound: *Tom mixes John up with Bill.* **5** (*often passive*) to put (someone) into a state of confusion: *I'm all mixed up.* **6** (foll. by *in* or *with; usually passive*) to involve (in an activity or group, esp. one that is illegal): *mixed up in the drugs racket.*

Mizoguchi ★ (ˌmiːtsəˈguːtʃɪ) *n* **Kenji** (ˈkɛndʒɪ). 1898–1956, Japanese film director. His films include *A Paper Doll's Whisper of Spring* (1925) and *Ugetsu Monogatari* (1952).

Mizoram ★ (mɪˈzɔːrəm) *n* a state (since 1986) in NE India, created in 1972 from the former Mizo Hills District of Assam. Capital: Aijal. Pop.: 775 000 (1994 est.). Area: about 21 081 sq. km (8140 sq. miles).

mizzen *or* **mizen** (ˈmɪzᵊn) *Naut.* ◆ *n* **1** a sail set on a mizzenmast. **2** short for **mizzenmast.** ◆ *adj* **3** of or relating to a mizzenmast: *a mizzen staysail.* ORIG C15: from F *misaine,* from It. *mezzana, mezzano* middle

mizzenmast *or* **mizenmast** (ˈmɪzᵊnˌmɑːst; *Naut.* ˈmɪzᵊnməst) *n Naut.* (on a vessel with three or more masts) the third mast from the bow.

mizzle[1] (ˈmɪzᵊl) *vb* **mizzles, mizzling, mizzled,** *n* a dialect word for **drizzle.** ORIG C15: ?from Low G *miseln* to drizzle
▸ **ˈmizzly** *adj*

mizzle[2] (ˈmɪzᵊl) *vb* **mizzles, mizzling, mizzled.** (*intr*) *Brit. sl.* to decamp. ORIG C18: from ?

mk *Currency. symbol for:* **1** mark. **2** markka.

mks units *pl n* a metric system of units based on the metre, kilogram, and second as the units of length, mass, and time; it forms the basis of the SI units.

mkt *abbrev. for* market.

ml *symbol for:* **1** mile. **2** millilitre.

ML *abbrev. for* Medieval Latin.

MLA *abbrev. for:* **1** Member of the Legislative Assembly. **2** Modern Language Association (of America).

MLC (in Australia and India) *abbrev. for* Member of the Legislative Council.

MLitt *abbrev. for* Master of Letters. ORIG L *Magister Litterarum*

Mlle *or* **Mlle.** *pl* **Mlles** *or* **Mlles.** the French equivalent of **Miss.** ORIG from F *Mademoiselle*

MLR *abbrev. for* minimum lending rate.

mm *symbol for* millimetre.

MM **1** the French equivalent of **Messrs.** ORIG from F *Messieurs* **2** *abbrev. for* Military Medal.

Mmabatho ★ (məˈbæθəʊ) *n* another name for **Mafikeng.**

MMC (formerly, in Britain) *abbrev. for* Monopolies and Mergers Commission.

MMDS *abbrev. for* multipoint microwave distribution system: a radio alternative to cable television. Sometimes shortened to **MDS.**

Mme *pl* **Mmes** the French equivalent of **Mrs.** ORIG from F *Madame, Mesdames*

MMP *abbrev. for* mixed member proportional: a system of proportional representation, used in Germany and New Zealand.

MMR *n* a combined vaccine against measles, mumps, and rubella, given to very young children.

MMus *abbrev. for* Master of Music.

Mn *the chemical symbol for* manganese.

MN *abbrev. for:* **1** (in Britain) Merchant Navy. **2** Minnesota.

MNA (in Canada) *abbrev. for* Member of the National Assembly (of Quebec).

mnemonic (nɪˈmɒnɪk) *adj* **1** aiding or meant to aid one's memory. **2** of or relating to memory or mnemonics. ◆ *n* **3** something, such as a verse, to assist memory. ORIG C18: from Gk *mnēmonikos,* from *mnēmōn* mindful, from *mnasthai* to remember
▸ **mneˈmonically** *adv*

mnemonics (nɪˈmɒnɪks) *n* (*usually functioning as sing*) **1** the art or practice of improving or of aiding the memory. **2** a system of rules to aid the memory.

Mnemosyne ★ (niːˈmɒzɪˌniː, -ˈmɒs-) *n Greek myth.* the goddess of memory and mother by Zeus of the Muses.

mo (məʊ) *n Inf.* **1** *Chiefly Brit.* short for **moment** (sense 1) (esp. in **half a mo**). **2** *Austral.* short for **moustache** (sense 1).

Mo *the chemical symbol for* molybdenum.

MO *abbrev. for:* **1** Missouri. **2** Medical Officer. **3** modus operandi.

Mo. *abbrev. for* Missouri.

m.o. *or* **MO** *abbrev. for:* **1** mail order. **2** money order.

-mo *suffix forming nouns.* (in bookbinding) indicating book size by specifying the number of leaves formed by folding one sheet of paper: *16mo* or *sixteenmo.* ORIG abstracted from DUODECIMO

moa (ˈməʊə) *n* any of various recently extinct large flightless birds of New Zealand (see **ratite**). ORIG C19: from Maori

Moab ★ (ˈməʊæb) *n Old Testament.* an ancient kingdom east of the Dead Sea, in what is now the SW part of Jordan: flourished mainly from the 9th to the 6th centuries B.C.
▸ **Moabite** (ˈməʊəˌbaɪt) *adj, n*

moa hunter *n NZ obs.* an anthropologists' term for an early Maori.

moan (məʊn) *n* **1** a low prolonged mournful sound expressive of suffering or pleading. **2** any similar mournful sound, esp. that made by the wind. **3** *Inf.* a grumble or complaint. ◆ *vb* **4** to utter (words, etc.) in a low mournful manner. **5** (*intr*) to make a sound like a moan. **6** (*usually intr*) *Inf.* to grumble or complain. ORIG C13: rel. to OE *mǣnan* to grieve over
▸ **ˈmoaner** *n* ▸ **ˈmoanful** *adj* ▸ **ˈmoaning** *n, adj*

moat (məʊt) *n* **1** a wide water-filled ditch surrounding a fortified place, such as a castle. ◆ *vb* **2** (*tr*) to surround with or as if with a moat. ORIG C14: from OF *motte* mound

mob (mɒb) *n* **1a** a riotous or disorderly crowd of people; rabble. **1b** (*as modifier*): *mob law.* **2** *Often derog.* a group or class of people, animals, or things. **3** *Often derog.* the masses. **4** *Sl.* a gang of criminals. **5** *Austral. & NZ.* a large number of anything. **6** *Austral. & NZ.* a flock or herd of animals. **7** **mobs of.** *Austral. & NZ inf.* lots of. ◆ *vb* **mobs, mobbing, mobbed.** (*tr*) **8** to attack in a group resembling a mob. **9** (of a group of animals of a prey species) to harass (a predator). **10** to surround, esp. in order to acclaim. **11** to crowd into (a building, etc.). ORIG C17: shortened from L *mōbile vulgus* the fickle populace

mobcap (ˈmɒbˌkæp) *n* a woman's large cotton cap with a pouched crown, worn esp. during the 18th century. ORIG C18: from obs. *mob* woman, esp. loose-living, + CAP

mobile (ˈməʊbaɪl) *adj* **1** having freedom of movement; movable. **2** changing quickly in expression: *a mobile face.* **3** *Sociol.* (of individuals or social groups) moving within and between classes, occupations, and localities. **4** (of military forces) able to move freely and quickly. **5** (*postpositive*) *Inf.* having transport available: *are you mobile?* ◆ *n* **6a** a sculpture suspended in midair with delicately balanced parts that are set in motion by air currents. **6b** (*as modifier*): *mobile sculpture.* **7** short for **mobile phone.** ORIG C15: via OF from L *mōbilis,* from *movēre* to move
▸ **mobility** (məʊˈbɪlɪtɪ) *n*

Mobile ★ (ˈməʊbiːl, məʊˈbiːl) *n* a port in SW Alabama, on **Mobile Bay** (an inlet of the Gulf of Mexico): the state's only port and its first permanent settlement, made by French colonists in 1711. Pop.: 202 581 (1996 est.).

-mobile (məʊˌbiːl) *suffix forming nouns.* indicating a vehicle designed for a particular person or purpose: *Popemobile.*

mobile home *n* living quarters mounted on wheels and capable of being towed by a motor vehicle.

mobile phone *n* a portable telephone that works by means of a cellular radio system.

mobilize *or* **mobilise** (ˈməʊbɪˌlaɪz) *vb* **mobilizes, mobilizing, mobilized** *or* **mobilises, mobilising, mobilised.** **1** to prepare for war or another emergency by organizing (national resources, the armed services, etc.). **2** (*tr*) to organize for a purpose. **3** (*tr*) to put into motion or use.
▸ **ˈmobiˌlizable** *or* **ˈmobiˌlisable** *adj* ▸ **ˌmobiliˈzation** *or* **ˌmobiliˈsation** *n*

Möbius strip (ˈmɜːbɪəs) *n Maths.* a one-sided continuous surface, formed by twisting a long narrow rectangular strip of material through 180° and joining the ends.

★ people and places

ORIG C19: after August *Möbius* (1790–1868), G mathematician

mobocracy (mɒ'bɒkrəsɪ) *n, pl* **mobocracies. 1** rule or domination by a mob. **2** the mob that rules.

mobster ('mɒbstə) *n* a US slang word for **gangster.**

Mobutu ★ (mə'bu:tu:) *n* **Lake.** the former name (1970–97) of (Lake) **Albert.**

Mobutu Sese Seko ★ ('sɛsɛ 'sɛkəʊ) *n* original name *Joseph Mobutu.* 1930–97, Zaïrese statesman; president of Zaïre (1970–97): accused of corruption and overthrown; died in exile.

Moçambique ★ (musəm'bikə) *n* the Portuguese name for **Mozambique.**

moccasin ('mɒkəsɪn) *n* **1** a shoe of soft leather, esp. deerskin, worn by North American Indians. **2** any soft shoe resembling this. **3** short for **water moccasin.** ORIG C17: of Amerind origin

moccasin flower *n* any of several North American orchids with a pink solitary flower. See also **lady's-slipper, cypripedium.**

mocha ('mɒkə) *n* **1** a dark brown coffee originally imported from the port of Mocha in Arabia. **2** a flavouring made from coffee and chocolate. **3** a soft glove leather, made from goatskin or sheepskin. **4a** a dark brown colour. **4b** (*as adj*): *mocha shoes.*

Mocha *or* **Mokha** ★ ('mɒkə) *n* a port in Yemen, on the Red Sea; in North Yemen until 1990: formerly important for the export of Arabian coffee. Pop.: 2000 (1990 est.).

mock (mɒk) *vb* **1** (when *intr,* often foll. by *at*) to behave with scorn or contempt (towards); show ridicule (for). **2** (*tr*) to imitate, esp. in fun; mimic. **3** (*tr*) to deceive, disappoint, or delude. **4** (*tr*) to defy or frustrate. ◆ *n* **5** the act of mocking. **6** a person or thing mocked. **7** a counterfeit; imitation. **8** (*often pl*) *Inf.* (in England and Wales) school exams taken as practice before public exams. ◆ *adj* (*prenominal*) **9** sham or counterfeit. **10** serving as an imitation or substitute, esp. for practice purposes: *a mock battle.* ◆ See also **mock-up.** ORIG C15: from OF *mocquer* ▸ **'mocker** *n* ▸ **'mocking** *n, adj* ▸ **'mockingly** *adv*

mockers ('mɒkəz) *pl n Inf.* **put the mockers on.** to ruin the chances of success of. ORIG C20: ?from MOCK

mockery ('mɒkərɪ) *n, pl* **mockeries. 1** ridicule, contempt, or derision. **2** a derisive action or comment. **3** an imitation or pretence. **4** a person or thing that is mocked. **5** a person, thing, or action that is inadequate.

mock-heroic *adj* **1** (of a literary work, esp. a poem) imitating the style of heroic poetry in order to satirize an unheroic subject. ◆ *n* **2** burlesque imitation of the heroic style.

mockingbird ('mɒkɪŋˌbɜ:d) *n* any of various American songbirds, noted for their ability to mimic the song of other birds.

mockney ('mɒknɪ) *n* **1** (*often cap.*) a person who affects a cockney accent. **2** an affected cockney accent. ◆ *adj* **3** denoting an affected cockney accent or a person who has one. ORIG C20: MOCK + COCKNEY

mock orange *n* **1** Also called: **syringa, philadelphus.** a shrub with white fragrant flowers resembling those of the orange. **2** an Australian shrub with white flowers and dark shiny leaves.

mock turtle soup *n* an imitation turtle soup made from a calf's head.

mock-up *n* **1** a working full-scale model of a machine, etc., for testing, research, etc. **2** a layout of printed matter. ◆ *vb* **mock up. 3** (*tr, adv*) to build or make a mock-up of.

mod[1] (mɒd) *n Brit.* **a** a member of a group of teenagers, originally in the mid-1960s, noted for their clothes-consciousness. **b** a member of a revived group of this type in the late 1970s and early 1980s. ORIG C20: from MODERNIST

mod[2] (mɒd) *n* an annual Highland Gaelic meeting with musical and literary competitions. ORIG C19: from Gaelic *mōd* assembly, from ON

MOD (in Britain) *abbrev. for* Ministry of Defence.

mod. *abbrev. for:* **1** moderate. **2** moderato. **3** modern.

modal ('məʊdᵊl) *adj* **1** of or relating to mode or manner. **2** *Grammar.* (of a verb form or auxiliary verb) expressing a distinction of mood, such as that between possibility and actuality. **3** qualifying, or expressing a qualification of, the truth of some statement. **4** *Metaphysics.* of or relating to the form of a thing as opposed to its attributes, substance, etc. **5** *Music.* of or relating to a mode. **6** of or relating to a statistical mode.
▸ **mo'dality** *n* ▸ **'modally** *adv*

modal logic *n* **1** the logical study of such philosophical concepts as necessity, possibility, etc. **2** the logical study of concepts whose formal properties resemble certain moral, epistemological, and psychological concepts.

mod cons *pl n Inf.* modern conveniences; the usual installations of a modern house, such as hot water, heating, etc.

mode (məʊd) *n* **1** a manner or way of doing, acting, or existing. **2** the current fashion or style. **3** *Music.* **3a** any of the various scales of notes within one octave, esp. any of the twelve natural diatonic scales taken in ascending order used in plainsong, folk song, and art music until 1600. **3b** (in the music of classical Greece) any of the descending diatonic scales from which the liturgical modes evolved. **3c** either of the two main scale systems in music since 1600: *major mode; minor mode.* **4** *Logic, linguistics.* another name for **mood**[2]. **5** *Philosophy.* a complex combination of ideas which is not simply the sum of its component ideas. **6** that one of a range of values that has the highest frequency as determined statistically. ORIG C14: from L *modus* manner

model ('mɒdᵊl) *n* **1a** a representation, usually on a smaller scale, of a device, structure, etc. **1b** (*as modifier*): *a model train.* **2a** a standard to be imitated. **2b** (*as modifier*): *a model wife.* **3** a representative form, style, or pattern. **4** a person who poses for a sculptor, painter, or photographer. **5** a person who wears clothes to display them to prospective buyers; mannequin. **6** a preparatory sculpture in clay, wax, etc., from which the finished work is copied. **7** a design or style of a particular product. ◆ *vb* **models, modelling, modelled** *or US* **models, modeling, modeled. 8** to make a model of (something or someone). **9** to form in clay, wax, etc.; mould. **10** to display (clothing and accessories) as a mannequin. **11** to plan or create according to a model or models. ORIG C16: from OF *modelle,* from It., from L *modulus,* dim. of *modus* MODE
▸ **'modeller** *or US* **'modeler** *n*

modelling *or US* **modeling** ('mɒdᵊlɪŋ) *n* **1** the act or an instance of making a model. **2** the practice or occupation of a person who models clothes. **3** a technique in psychotherapy in which the therapist encourages the patient to model his behaviour on his own.

modem ('məʊdɛm) *n Computing.* a device for connecting two computers by a telephone line, consisting of a modulator that converts computer signals into audio signals and a corresponding demodulator. ORIG C20: from *mo*(*dulator*) *dem*(*odulator*)

Modena ★ (*Italian* 'mɔ:dena) *n* a city in N Italy, in Emilia-Romagna: ruled by the Este family (18th–19th century); university (1678). Pop.: 174 518 (1996 est.). Ancient name: **Mutina.**

moderate *adj* ('mɒdərɪt). **1** not extreme or excessive. **2** not violent; mild or temperate. **3** of average quality or extent: *moderate success.* ◆ *n* ('mɒdərɪt). **4** a person who holds moderate views, esp. in politics. ◆ *vb* ('mɒdəˌreɪt). **moderates, moderating, moderated. 5** to become or cause to become less extreme or violent. **6** (when *intr,* often foll. by *over*) to preside over a meeting, discussion, etc. **7** *Physics.* to slow down (neutrons), esp. by using a moderator. ORIG C14: from L *moderātus,* from *moderārī* to restrain

moderate breeze *n* a wind of force 4 on the Beaufort scale, reaching speeds of 13 to 18 mph.

moderation (ˌmɒdə'reɪʃən) *n* **1** the state or an instance of being moderate. **2** the act of moderating. **3 in moderation.** within moderate or reasonable limits.

moderato (ˌmɒdə'rɑ:təʊ) *adv Music.* **1** at a moderate tempo. **2** a direction indicating that the tempo specified is to be used with restraint: *allegro moderato.* ORIG It.

moderator ('mɒdəˌreɪtə) *n* **1** a person or thing that moderates. **2** *Presbyterian Church.* a minister appointed to preside over a Church court, synod, or general assembly. **3** a

presiding officer at a public or legislative assembly. **4** a material, such as heavy water, used for slowing down neutrons in nuclear reactors. **5** an examiner at Oxford or Cambridge Universities in first public examinations. **6** (in Britain and New Zealand) one who is responsible for consistency of standards in the grading of some public examinations.
▸ **'moder,atorship** *n*

modern ('mɒdən) *adj* **1** of, involving, or befitting the present or a recent time; contemporary. **2** of, relating to, or characteristic of contemporary styles or schools of art, literature, music, etc., esp. those of an experimental kind. **3** belonging or relating to the period in history from the end of the Middle Ages to the present. ◆ *n* **4** a contemporary person. ORIG C16: from OF, from LL *modernus,* from *modō* (adv) just recently, from *modus* MODE
▸ **mo'dernity** *or* **'modernness** *n*

modern apprenticeship *n* an arrangement that allows a school-leaver to gain vocational qualifications while being trained in a job.

Modern English *n* the English language since about 1450.

Modern Hebrew *n* the official language of Israel; a revived form of ancient Hebrew.

modernism ('mɒdə,nɪzəm) *n* **1** modern tendencies, thoughts, etc., or the support of these. **2** something typical of contemporary life or thought. **3** a 20th-century divergence in the arts from previous traditions, esp. in architecture. See **International Style. 4** (*cap.*) *RC Church.* the movement at the end of the 19th and beginning of the 20th centuries that sought to adapt doctrine to modern thought.
▸ **'modernist** *n, adj* ▸ **,modern'istic** *adj* ▸ **,modern'istically** *adv*

modernize *or* **modernise** ('mɒdə,naɪz) *vb* **modernizes, modernizing, modernized** *or* **modernises, modernising, modernised. 1** (*tr*) to make modern in appearance or style. **2** (*intr*) to adopt modern ways, ideas, etc.
▸ **,moderni'zation** *or* **,moderni'sation** *n* ▸ **'modern,izer** *or* **'modern,iser** *n*

modern pentathlon *n* an athletic contest consisting of five different events: horse riding with jumps, fencing with electric épée, freestyle swimming, pistol shooting, and cross-country running.

modest ('mɒdɪst) *adj* **1** having or expressing a humble opinion of oneself or one's accomplishments or abilities. **2** reserved or shy. **3** not ostentatious or pretentious. **4** not extreme or excessive. **5** decorous or decent. ORIG C16: via OF from L *modestus* moderate, from *modus* MODE
▸ **'modestly** *adv*

modesty ('mɒdɪstɪ) *n, pl* **modesties.** the quality or condition of being modest.

modicum ('mɒdɪkəm) *n* a small amount or portion. ORIG C15: from L: a little way, from *modicus* moderate

modification (,mɒdɪfɪ'keɪʃən) *n* **1** the act of modifying or the condition of being modified. **2** something modified. **3** a small change or adjustment. **4** *Grammar.* the relation between a modifier and the word or phrase that it modifies.
▸ **'modifi,catory** *or* **'modifi,cative** *adj*

modifier ('mɒdɪ,faɪə) *n* **1** Also called: **qualifier.** *Grammar.* a word or phrase that qualifies the sense of another word; for example, the noun *alarm* is a modifier of *clock* in *alarm clock* and the phrase *every day* is an adverbial modifier of *walks* in *he walks every day.* **2** a person or thing that modifies.

modify ('mɒdɪ,faɪ) *vb* **modifies, modifying, modified.** (*mainly tr*) **1** to change the structure, character, intent, etc., of. **2** to make less extreme or uncompromising. **3** *Grammar.* (of a word or phrase) to bear the relation of modifier to (another word or phrase). **4** *Linguistics.* to change (a vowel) by umlaut. **5** (*intr*) to be or become modified. ORIG C14: from OF *modifier,* from L *modificāre* to limit, from *modus* measure + *facere* to make
▸ **'modi,fiable** *adj*

Modigliani ★ (*Italian* modiʎ'ʎa:ni) *n* **Amedeo** (ame'dɛ:o). 1884–1920, Italian painter and sculptor, noted for the elongated forms of his portraits.

modish ('məʊdɪʃ) *adj* in the current fashion or style.
▸ **'modishly** *adv* ▸ **'modishness** *n*

modiste (məʊ'di:st) *n* a fashionable dressmaker or milliner. ORIG C19: from F, from *mode* fashion

Modred ('məʊdrɪd) *or* **Mordred** ★ *n* (in Arthurian legend) a knight of the Round Table who rebelled against and killed his uncle King Arthur.

modular ('mɒdjʊlə) *adj* of, consisting of, or resembling a module or modulus.

modulate ('mɒdjʊ,leɪt) *vb* **modulates, modulating, modulated. 1** (*tr*) to change the tone, pitch, or volume of. **2** (*tr*) to adjust or regulate the degree of. **3** *Music.* **3a** to change or cause to change from one key to another. **3b** (often foll. by *to*) to make or become in tune (with a pitch, key, etc.). **4** *Physics, electronics.* to superimpose the amplitude, frequency, phase, etc., of a wave or signal onto another wave or signal or onto an electron beam. ORIG C16: from L *modulātus* in due measure, melodious, from *modulārī,* from *modus* measure
▸ **,modu'lation** *n* ▸ **'modu,lator** *n*

module ('mɒdju:l) *n* **1** a standard unit of measure, esp. one used to coordinate the dimensions of buildings and components. **2** a standard self-contained unit or item, such as an assembly of electronic components, or a standardized piece of furniture, that can be used in combination with other units. **3** *Astronautics.* any of several self-contained separable units making up a spacecraft or launch vehicle, each of which has one or more specified tasks. **4** *Education.* a short course of study that together with other such courses counts towards a qualification. ORIG C16: from L *modulus,* dim. of *modus* MODE

modulus ('mɒdjʊləs) *n, pl* **moduli** (-,laɪ). **1** *Physics.* a coefficient expressing a specified property of a specified substance. See **modulus of elasticity. 2** *Maths.* another name for the **absolute value** of a complex number. **3** *Maths.* the number by which a logarithm to one base is multiplied to give the corresponding logarithm to another base. **4** *Maths.* an integer that can be divided exactly into the difference between two other integers: *7 is a modulus of 25 and 11.* ORIG C16: from L, dim. of *modus* measure

modulus of elasticity *n* the ratio of the stress applied to a body or substance to the resulting strain within the elastic limit. Also called: **elastic modulus.**

modus operandi ('məʊdəs ,ɒpə'rændi:, -'rændaɪ) *n, pl* **modi operandi** ('məʊdi: ,ɒpə'rændi:, 'məʊdaɪ ,ɒpə'rændaɪ). procedure; method of operating. ORIG C17: from L

modus vivendi ('məʊdəs vɪ'vɛndi:, -'vɛndaɪ) *n, pl* **modi vivendi** ('məʊdi: vɪ'vɛndi:, 'məʊdaɪ vɪ'vɛndaɪ). a working arrangement between conflicting interests; practical compromise. ORIG C19: from L: way of living

Moers ★ (*German* mø:rs) *n* a city in W Germany, in North Rhine-Westphalia: coalmining centre. Pop.: 107 095 (1996 est.).

moffie ('mɒfɪ) *S. African sl.* ◆ *n* **1** a homosexual. ◆ *adj* **2** homosexual. ORIG C18: from *mophradite* var. of HERMAPHRODITE

mog (mɒg) *or* **moggy** *n, pl* **mogs** *or* **moggies.** *Brit.* a slang name for **cat**[1]. ORIG C20: dialect, orig. a pet name for a cow

Mogadishu (,mɒgə'dɪʃu:) *or* **Mogadiscio** ★ (,mɒgə'dɪʃɪ,əʊ, -'dɪʃəʊ) *n* the capital and chief port of Somalia, on the Indian Ocean: founded by Arabs around the 10th century; taken by the Sultan of Zanzibar in 1871 and sold to Italy in 1905. Pop.: 900 000 (1995 est.).

Mogadon ('mɒgə,dɒn) *n Trademark.* a minor tranquillizer used to treat insomnia.

Mogador ★ (,mɒgə'dɔ:; *French* mɔgadɔr) *n* the former name (until 1956) of **Essaouira.**

Mogilev (*Russian* məgi'ljɔf) *or* **Mohilev** ★ *n* an industrial city in E Belarus, on the Dnieper River: passed to Russia in 1772 after Polish rule. Pop.: 367 000 (1996 est.).

mogul ('məʊgʌl, məʊ'gʌl) *n* an important or powerful person. ORIG C18: from MOGUL

Mogul ('məʊgʌl, məʊ'gʌl) *n* **1** a member of the Muslim dynasty of Indian emperors established in 1526. **2** a Muslim Indian, Mongol, or Mongolian. ◆ *adj* **3** of or relating to the Moguls or their empire. ORIG C16: from Persian *mughul* Mongolian

mogul skiing *n* an event in which skiers descend a slope covered in mounds of snow, making two jumps during their descent. ORIG C20: *mogul* ? from G dialect *Mugl* hillock or hummock

MOH (in Britain) *abbrev. for* Medical Officer of Health.

mohair ('məʊˌhɛə) *n* **1** Also called: **angora.** the long soft silky hair of the Angora goat. **2a** a fabric made from the yarn of this hair and cotton or wool. **2b** (*as modifier*): *a mohair suit.* ORIG C16: (infl. by *hair*), ult. from Ar. *mukhayyar*, lit.: choice

Moham. *abbrev. for* Mohammedan.

Mohammed (məʊ'hæmɪd) *or* **Muhammad** ★ *n* ?570–632 A.D., the prophet and founder of Islam. He began to teach in Mecca in 610 but persecution forced him to flee with his followers to Medina in 622. After several battles, he conquered Mecca (630), establishing the principles of Islam (embodied in the Koran) over all Arabia. Other names: **Mahomet,** (*archaic*) **Mahound.**

Mohammed II ★ *n* ?1430–81, Ottoman sultan of Turkey (1451–81). He captured Constantinople (1453) and conquered large areas of the Balkans.

Mohammed Ahmed ★ (məʊ'hæmɪd 'ɑːmɛd) *n* the original name of the **Mahdi.**

Mohammed Ali ★ *n* **1** See **Mehemet Ali. 2** See **Muhammad Ali.**

Mohammedan (məʊ'hæmɪdᵊn) *n, adj* another word (not in Muslim use) for **Muslim.**

Mohammedanism (məʊ'hæmɪdᵊˌnɪzəm) *n* another word (not in Muslim use) for **Islam.**

Mohammed Reza Pahlavi ★ (məʊ'hæmɪd 'riːzə) *n* See **Pahlavi** (sense 1).

Mohave Desert *n* a variant spelling of **Mojave Desert.**

Mohawk[1] ★ ('məʊhɔːk) *n* **1** (*pl* **Mohawks** *or* **Mohawk**) a member of a North American Indian people formerly living along the Mohawk River. **2** the Iroquoian language of this people.

Mohawk[2] ★ ('məʊhɔːk) *n* a river in E central New York State, flowing south and east to the Hudson River at Cohoes: the largest tributary of the Hudson. Length: 238 km (148 miles).

Mohenjo-Daro ★ (mə'hɛndʒəʊ'dɑːrəʊ) *n* an excavated city in SE Pakistan, southwest of Sukkur near the River Indus: flourished during the third millennium B.C.

mohican (məʊ'hiːkən) *n* a punk hairstyle in which the head is shaved at the sides and the remaining strip of hair is worn stiffly erect and sometimes brightly coloured.

Moholy-Nagy ★ (mə'həʊlɪ'nɒdʒ) *n* **Laszlo** ('læzləʊ) *or* **Ladislaus** ('lɑːdɪsˌlaʊs). 1895–1946, US painter and teacher, born in Hungary. He worked at the Bauhaus (1923–29).

moidore ('mɔɪdɔː) *n* a former Portuguese gold coin. ORIG C18: from Port. *moeda de ouro* money of gold

moiety ('mɔɪɪtɪ) *n, pl* **moieties.** one of two parts or divisions of something: *the sugar moiety of a molecule.* ORIG C15: from OF *moitié*, from L *mediētās* middle, from *medius*

moil (mɔɪl) *Arch. or dialect.* ◆ *vb* **1** to moisten or soil or become moist, soiled, etc. **2** (*intr*) to toil or drudge (esp. in **toil and moil**). ◆ *n* **3** toil; drudgery. **4** confusion. ORIG C14 (to moisten; later: to work hard in unpleasantly wet conditions) from OF *moillier*, ult. from L *mollis* soft

Moirai ★ ('mɔɪraɪ) *pl n, sing* **Moira** ('mɔɪrə), **the.** the Greek goddesses of fate. Roman counterparts: the **Parcae.** See **Fates.**

moire (mwɑː) *n* a fabric, usually silk, having a watered effect. ORIG C17: from F, earlier *mouaire*, from MOHAIR

moiré ('mwɑːreɪ) *adj* **1** having a watered or wavelike pattern. ◆ *n* **2** such a pattern, impressed on fabrics by means of engraved rollers. **3** any fabric having such a pattern; moire. **4** Also: **moiré pattern.** a pattern seen when two geometrical patterns, such as grids, are visually superimposed. ORIG C17: from F, from *moire* MOHAIR

Moism ('məʊˌɪzəm) *n* the religious and ethical teaching of Mo-Zi (?470–?391 B.C.), Chinese philosopher, and his followers, emphasizing universal love, ascetic self-discipline, and obedience to the will of Heaven.

moist (mɔɪst) *adj* **1** slightly damp or wet. **2** saturated with or suggestive of moisture. ORIG C14: from OF, ult. rel. to L *mūcidus* musty
▸ **'moistly** *adv* ▸ **'moistness** *n*

moisten ('mɔɪsᵊn) *vb* to make or become moist.

moisture ('mɔɪstʃə) *n* water or other liquid diffused as vapour or condensed on or in objects.

moisturize *or* **moisturise** ('mɔɪstʃəˌraɪz) *vb* **moisturizes, moisturizing, moisturized** *or* **moisturises, moisturising, moisturised.** (*tr*) to add moisture to (the air, the skin, etc.).
▸ **'moisturˌizer** *or* **'moisturˌiser** *n*

Mojave Desert *or* **Mohave Desert** ★ (məʊ'hɑːvɪ) *n* a desert in S California, south of the Sierra Nevada: part of the Great Basin. Area: 38 850 sq. km (15 000 sq. miles).

mojo ('məʊdʒəʊ) *n, pl* **mojos** *or* **mojoes.** *US sl.* **1** an amulet, charm, or magic spell. **2** the art of casting magic spells. ORIG C20: of W African origin

moke (məʊk) *n Brit. sl.* a donkey. ORIG C19: from ?

Mokha ★ ('məʊkə, 'mɒk-) *n* a variant of **Mocha.**

Mokpo ★ (ˌməʊk'pəʊ) *n* a port in SW South Korea, on the Yellow Sea. Pop.: 247 524 (1995).

mol *Chem. symbol for* mole[3].

mol. *abbrev. for:* **1** molecular. **2** molecule.

molal ('məʊləl) *adj Chem.* of or consisting of a solution containing one mole of solute per thousand grams of solvent. ORIG C20: from MOLE[3] + -AL[1]

molar[1] ('məʊlə) *n* **1** any of the 12 grinding teeth in man. **2** a corresponding tooth in other mammals. ◆ *adj* **3** of or relating to any of these teeth. **4** used for or capable of grinding. ORIG C16: from L *molāris*, from *mola* millstone

molar[2] ('məʊlə) *adj* **1** (of a physical quantity) per unit amount of substance: *molar volume.* **2** (not recommended in technical usage) (of a solution) containing one mole of solute per litre of solution. ORIG C19: from L *mōlēs* a mass

molasses (mə'læsɪz) *n* (*functioning as sing*) **1** the thick brown uncrystallized bitter syrup obtained from sugar during refining. **2** the US and Canad. name for **treacle** (sense 1). ORIG C16: from Port. *melaço*, from LL *mellāceum* must, from L *mel* honey

mold (məʊld) *n, vb* the US spelling of **mould.**

Moldau ★ ('mɔldaʊ) *n* **1** the German name for **Moldavia. 2** the German name for the **Vltava.**

Moldavia ★ (mɒl'deɪvɪə) *n* **1** another name for **Moldova. 2** a former principality of E Europe, consisting of the basins of the Rivers Prut and Dniester: the E part (Bessarabia) formed part of the Soviet Union from 1940 until 1991, when it became the republic of Moldavia; the W part remains a province of Romania. Romanian name: **Moldova** (mol'dova). German name: **Moldau.**
▸ **Mol'davian** *adj, n*

moldboard ('məʊldˌbɔːd) *n* the US spelling of **mouldboard.**

molder ('məʊldə) *vb* the US spelling of **moulder.**

molding ('məʊldɪŋ) *n* the US spelling of **moulding.**

Moldova ★ (mɒl'dəʊvə) *n* a republic in SE Europe, comprising part of the former principality of Moldavia: as the Moldavian Soviet Socialist Republic, it was part of the Soviet Union from 1940 until gaining independence in 1991; an agricultural region. Official language: Romanian. Religion: nonreligious and Christian. Currency: leu. Capital: Kishinev. Pop.: 4 301 000 (1999 est.). Area: 37 670 sq. km (13 000 sq. miles). Also called: **Moldavia.**
▸ **Mol'dovan** *adj, n*

moldy ('məʊldɪ) *adj* the US spelling of **mouldy.**

mole[1] (məʊl) *n Pathol.* a nontechnical name for **naevus.** ORIG OE *māl*

mole[2] (məʊl) *n* **1** any small burrowing mammal of a family of Europe, Asia, and North and Central America. They have velvety, typically dark fur and forearms specialized for digging. **2** *Inf.* a spy who has infiltrated an organization and become a trusted member of it. ORIG C14: from MDu. *mol,* of Gmc origin

mole[3] (məʊl) *n* the basic SI unit of amount of substance; the amount that contains as many elementary entities as there are atoms in 0.012 kilogram of carbon-12. The entity may be an atom, a molecule, an ion, a radical, etc. Symbol: mol. See **gram molecule**. ORIG C20: from G *Mol,* short for *Molekül* MOLECULE

mole[4] (məʊl) *n* **1** a breakwater. **2** a harbour protected by a breakwater. ORIG C16: from F *môle,* from L *mōlēs* mass

Molech ★ ('məʊlɛk) *n Old Testament.* a variant of **Moloch**.

molecular (məʊ'lɛkjʊlə, mə-) *adj* of or relating to molecules.
▸ **mo'lecularly** *adv*

molecular biology *n* the study of the structure and function of biological molecules, esp. nucleic acids and proteins.

molecular formula *n* a chemical formula indicating the numbers and types of atoms in a molecule: *H_2SO_4 is the molecular formula of sulphuric acid.*

molecular genetics *n* (*functioning as sing*) the study of the molecular constitution of genes and chromosomes.

molecular weight *n* the former name for **relative molecular mass**.

molecule ('mɒlɪˌkjuːl) *n* **1** the simplest unit of a chemical compound that can exist, consisting of two or more atoms held together by chemical bonds. **2** a very small particle. ORIG C18: via F from NL *mōlēcula,* dim. of L *mōlēs* mass

molehill ('məʊlˌhɪl) *n* **1** the small mound of earth thrown up by a burrowing mole. **2 make a mountain out of a molehill.** to exaggerate an unimportant matter out of all proportion.

moleskin ('məʊlˌskɪn) *n* **1** the dark grey dense velvety pelt of a mole, used as a fur. **2** a hard-wearing cotton fabric of twill weave. **3** (*modifier*)*: a moleskin waistcoat.*

molest (mə'lɛst) *vb* (*tr*) **1** to disturb or annoy by malevolent interference. **2** to accost or attack, esp. with the intention of assaulting sexually. ORIG C14: from L *molestāre* to annoy, from *molestus* troublesome, from *mōlēs* mass
▸ **molestation** (ˌməʊlɛ'steɪʃən) *n* ▸ **mo'lester** *n*

Molière ★ (*French* mɔljɛr) *n* real name *Jean-Baptiste Poquelin.* 1622–73, French dramatist. His works include *Tartuffe* (1664), *Le Misanthrope* (1666), *L'Avare* (1668), and *Le Malade imaginaire* (1673).

Molise ★ (*Italian* mo'liːze) *n* a region of S central Italy, the second smallest of the regions: separated from **Abruzzi e Molise** in 1965. Capital: Campobasso. Pop.: 331 446 (1996 est.). Area: 4438 sq. km (1731 sq. miles).

moll (mɒl) *n Sl.* **1** the female accomplice of a gangster. **2** a prostitute. ORIG C17: from *Moll,* familiar form of *Mary*

mollify ('mɒlɪˌfaɪ) *vb* **mollifies, mollifying, mollified.** (*tr*) **1** to pacify; soothe. **2** to lessen the harshness or severity of. ORIG C15: from OF *mollifier,* via LL, from L *mollis* soft + *facere* to make
▸ **'molliˌfiable** *adj* ▸ **ˌmollifi'cation** *n* ▸ **'molliˌfier** *n*

mollusc *or US* **mollusk** ('mɒləsk) *n* any of various invertebrates having a soft unsegmented body and often a shell, secreted by a fold of skin (the mantle). The group includes the gastropods (snails, slugs, etc.), bivalves (clams, mussels, etc.), and cephalopods (squid, octopuses, etc.). ORIG C18: via NL from L *molluscus,* from *mollis* soft
▸ **molluscan** *or US* **molluskan** (mɒ'lʌskən) *adj, n* ▸ **mollusc-like** *or US* **mollusk-like** *adj*

molly[1] ('mɒlɪ) *n, pl* **mollies.** any of various brightly coloured tropical or subtropical American freshwater fishes. ORIG C19: from NL *Mollienisia,* from Comte F. N. *Mollien* (1758–1850), F statesman

molly[2] ('mɒlɪ) *n, pl* **mollies.** *Irish inf.* an effeminate, weak, or cowardly boy or man. ORIG C18: perhaps from *Molly,* pet name for *Mary*

mollycoddle ('mɒlɪˌkɒdᵊl) *vb* **mollycoddles, mollycoddling, mollycoddled. 1** (*tr*) to treat with indulgent care; pamper. ◆ *n* **2** a pampered person. ORIG C19: from MOLLY[2] + CODDLE

Molnár ★ (*Hungarian* 'molnaːr) *n* **Ferenc** ('fɛrɛnts). 1878–1952, Hungarian dramatist and novelist. His works include the play *Liliom* (1909).

Moloch ('məʊlɒk) *or* **Molech** ★ ('məʊlɛk) *n Old Testament.* a Semitic deity to whom parents sacrificed their children.

Molokai ★ (ˌməʊləʊ'kɑːɪ) *n* an island in central Hawaii. Pop.: 6717 (1990). Area: 676 sq. km (261 sq. miles).

Molopo ★ (mə'ləʊpəʊ) *n* a seasonal river rising in N central South Africa and flowing west and southwest to the Orange river. Length: about 1000 km (600 miles).

Molotov[1] ★ ('mɒləˌtɒf; *Russian* 'mɔlətəf) *n* the former name (1940–62) for **Perm**.

Molotov[2] ★ ('mɒləˌtɒf; *Russian* 'mɔlətəf) *n* **Vyacheslav Mikhailovich** (vɪtʃɪ'slaf mi'xajləvitʃ), original surname *Skriabin.* 1890–1986, Soviet statesman. As commissar and later minister for foreign affairs (1939–49; 1953–56) he negotiated the nonaggression pact with Nazi Germany.

Molotov cocktail *n* an elementary incendiary weapon, usually a bottle of petrol with a short delay fuse or wick; petrol bomb. ORIG C20: after V. M. MOLOTOV

molt (məʊlt) *vb, n* the usual US spelling of **moult**.
▸ **'molter** *n*

molten ('məʊltən) *adj* **1** liquefied; melted. **2** made by having been melted: *molten casts.* ◆ *vb* **3** the past participle of **melt**.

Moltke ★ (*German* 'mɔltkə) *n* **1** Count **Helmuth Johannes Ludwig von** ('hɛlmuːt jo'hanəs 'luːtvɪç fɔn). 1848–1916, German general; chief of the German general staff (1906–14). **2** his uncle Count **Helmuth Karl Bernhard von** ('hɛlmuːt karl 'bɛrnhart fɔn). 1800–91, German field marshal; chief of the Prussian general staff (1858–88).

molto ('mɒltəʊ) *adv Music.* very: *allegro molto; molto adagio.* ORIG from It., from L *multum* (adv) much

Moluccas (məʊ'lʌkəz, mə-) *or* **Molucca Islands** ★ *pl n* a group of islands in the Malay Archipelago, between Sulawesi (Celebes) and New Guinea. Capital: Amboina. Pop.: 2 094 700 (1995 est.). Area: about 74 505 sq. km (28 766 sq. miles). Indonesian name: **Maluku**. Former name: **Spice Islands**.

mol. wt. *abbrev. for* molecular weight.

moly ('məʊlɪ) *n, pl* **molies. 1** *Greek myth.* a magic herb given by Hermes to Odysseus to nullify the spells of Circe. **2** a variety of wild garlic of S Europe having yellow flowers. ORIG C16: from L *mōly,* from Gk *mōlu*

molybdenite (mɒ'lɪbdɪˌnaɪt) *n* a soft grey mineral consisting of molybdenum sulphide in hexagonal crystalline form with rhenium as an impurity. Formula: MoS_2.

molybdenum (mɒ'lɪbdɪnəm) *n* a very hard silvery-white metallic element occurring principally in molybdenite: used in alloys, esp. to harden and strengthen steels. Symbol: Mo; atomic no.: 42; atomic wt.: 95.94. ORIG C19: from NL, from L *molybdaena* galena, from Gk, from *molubdos* lead

mom (mɒm) *n Chiefly US & Canad.* an informal word for **mother**[1].

Mombasa ★ (mɒm'bæsə) *n* a port in S Kenya, on a coral island in a bay of the Indian Ocean: the chief port for Kenya, Uganda, and NE Tanzania; became British in 1887, capital of the East African Protectorate until 1907. Pop.: 600 000 (1991 est.).

moment ('məʊmənt) *n* **1** a short indefinite period of time. **2** a specific instant or point in time: *at that moment the phone rang.* **3 the moment.** the present point of time: *at the moment it's fine.* **4** import, significance, or value: *a man of moment.* **5** *Physics.* **5a** a tendency to produce motion, esp. rotation about a point or axis. **5b** the product of a physical quantity, such as force or mass, and its distance from a fixed reference point. See also **moment of inertia**. ORIG C14: from OF, from L *mōmentum,* from *movēre* to move

momentarily ('məʊməntərɪlɪ, -trɪlɪ, ˌməʊmən'tærɪlɪ) *adv* **1** for an instant; temporarily. **2** from moment to moment; every instant. **3** *US & Canad.* very soon. ◆ Also (for senses 1, 2): **momently**.

momentary ('məʊməntərɪ, -trɪ) *adj* **1** lasting for only a

moment; temporary. **2** *Rare.* occurring or present at each moment.
▸ **'momentariness** *n*

moment of inertia *n* the tendency of a body to resist angular acceleration, expressed as the sum of the products of the mass of each particle in the body and the square of its perpendicular distance from the axis of rotation.

moment of truth *n* **1** a moment when a person or thing is put to the test. **2** the point in a bullfight when the matador is about to kill the bull.

momentous (məʊ'mɛntəs) *adj* of great significance.
▸ **mo'mentously** *adv* ▸ **mo'mentousness** *n*

momentum (məʊ'mɛntəm) *n, pl* **momenta** (-tə) *or* **momentums. 1** *Physics.* the product of a body's mass and its velocity. **2** the impetus of a body resulting from its motion. **3** driving power or strength. ORIG C17: from L: movement; see MOMENT

momma ('mɒmə) *n Chiefly US.* **1** an informal or childish word for **mother**[1]. **2** *Inf.* a buxom and voluptuous woman.

Mommsen ★ (*German* 'mɔmzən) *n* **Theodor** ('teːodoːr). 1817–1903, German historian, noted esp. for *The History of Rome* (1854–56): Nobel prize for literature 1902.

Momus ★ ('məʊməs) *n, pl* **Momuses** *or* **Momi** (-maɪ). **1** *Greek myth.* the god of blame and mockery. **2** a cavilling critic.

mon. *abbrev. for* monetary.

Mon. *abbrev. for* Monday.

mon- *combining form.* a variant of **mono-** before a vowel.

Monaco ★ ('mɒnəˌkəʊ, mə'nɑːkəʊ; *French* mɔnako) *n* a principality in SW Europe, on the Mediterranean and forming an enclave in SE France: the second smallest sovereign state in the world (after the Vatican); consists of **Monaco-Ville** (the capital) on a rocky headland, **La Condamine** (a business area and port), **Monte Carlo** (the resort centre), and **Fontvieille,** a light industrial area. Language: French. Religion: Roman Catholic. Currency: franc. Pop.: 31 900 (1997 est.). Area: 189 hectares (476 acres). Related adj: **Monegasque.**
▸ **Monacan** ('mɒnəkən, mə'nɑː-) *n, adj*

monad ('mɒnæd, 'məʊ-) *n* **1** (*pl* **monads** *or* **monades** (-əˌdiːz)). *Philosophy.* any fundamental singular metaphysical entity, esp. if autonomous. **2** a single-celled organism. **3** an atom, ion, or radical with a valency of one. ◆ Also (for senses 1, 2): **monas.** ORIG C17: from LL *monas,* from Gk: unit, from *monos* alone
▸ **monadic** (mɒ'nædɪk) *adj*

monadelphous (ˌmɒnə'dɛlfəs) *adj* **1** (of stamens) having united filaments forming a tube around the style. **2** (of flowers) having monadelphous stamens. ORIG C19: from MONO- + Gk *adelphos* brother

monadnock (mə'nædnɒk) *n* a residual hill of hard rock in an otherwise eroded area. ORIG C19: after Mount *Monadnock,* New Hampshire, US

Monaghan ★ ('mɒnəhən) *n* **1** a county of NE Republic of Ireland, in Ulster province: many small lakes. County town: Monaghan. Pop.: 51 000 (1996). Area: 1292 sq. km (499 sq. miles). **2** a town in NE Republic of Ireland, county town of Co. Monaghan. Pop.: 6200 (1995 est.).

monandrous (mɒ'nændrəs) *adj* **1** having only one male sexual partner over a period of time. **2** (of plants) having flowers with only one stamen. **3** (of flowers) having only one stamen. ORIG C19: from MONO- + -ANDROUS
▸ **mo'nandry** *n*

Mona Passage ★ ('məʊnə) *n* a strait between Puerto Rico and the Dominican Republic, linking the Atlantic with the Caribbean.

monarch ('mɒnək) *n* **1** a sovereign head of state, esp. a king, queen, or emperor, who rules usually by hereditary right. **2** a supremely powerful or pre-eminent person or thing. **3** Also called: **milkweed.** a large migratory orange-and-black butterfly that feeds on the milkweed plant. ORIG C15: from LL *monarcha,* from Gk; see MONO-, -ARCH
▸ **monarchal** (mɒ'nɑːkᵊl) *or* **mo'narchial** *adj* ▸ **mo'narchical** *or* **mo'narchic** *adj* ▸ **'monarchism** *n* ▸ **'monarchist** *n, adj* ▸ **ˌmonar'chistic** *adj*

monarchy ('mɒnəkɪ) *n, pl* **monarchies. 1** a form of government in which supreme authority is vested in a single and usually hereditary figure, such as a king. **2** a country reigned over by a monarch.

monarda (mɒ'nɑːdə) *n* any of various mintlike North American plants. ORIG C19: from NL, after N. *Monardés* (1493–1588), Sp. botanist

monastery ('mɒnəstərɪ) *n, pl* **monasteries.** the residence of a religious community, esp. of monks, living in seclusion from secular society and bound by religious vows. ORIG C15: from Church L *monastērium,* ult. from Gk *monazein* to live alone, from *monos* alone
▸ **monasterial** (ˌmɒnə'stɪərɪəl) *adj*

monastic (mə'næstɪk) *adj* **1** of or relating to monasteries or monks, nuns, etc. **2** resembling this sort of life. ◆ *n* **3** a person committed to this way of life, esp. a monk.

monasticism (mə'næstɪˌsɪzəm) *n* the monastic system, movement, or way of life.

monatomic (ˌmɒnə'tɒmɪk) *or* **monoatomic** (ˌmɒnəʊə'tɒmɪk) *adj Chem.* **1** (of an element) having or consisting of single atoms. **2** (of a compound or molecule) having only one atom or group that can be replaced in a chemical reaction.

monaural (mɒ'nɔːrəl) *adj* **1** relating to, having, or hearing with only one ear. **2** another word for **monophonic.**
▸ **mon'aurally** *adv*

monazite ('mɒnəˌzaɪt) *n* a yellow to reddish-brown mineral consisting of a phosphate of thorium, cerium, and lanthanum in monoclinic crystalline form. ORIG C19: from G, from Gk *monazein* to live alone, so called because of its rarity

Mönchengladbach ★ (*German* mœnçən'glatbax) *n* a city in W Germany, in W North Rhine-Westphalia: headquarters of NATO forces in N central Europe; textile industry. Pop.: 266 702 (1996 est.). Former name: **München-Gladbach.**

Monck ★ (mʌŋk) *n* **George.** 1st Duke of Albemarle. 1608–70, English general. A Royalist until captured (1644) in the Civil War and persuaded to support the Commonwealth. After Cromwell's death he was instrumental in the restoration of Charles II (1660).

Moncton ★ ('mɒŋktən) *n* a city in E Canada, in SE New Brunswick. Pop.: 80 744 (1991).

Monday ('mʌndɪ) *n* the second day of the week; first day of the working week. ORIG OE *mōnandæg* moon's day, translation of LL *lūnae diēs*

Mondrian ★ (*Dutch* 'mɔndriːaːn) *n* **Piet** (piːt). 1872–1944, Dutch painter, noted as an exponent of De Stijl.

monecious (mɒ'niːʃəs) *adj* a variant spelling of **monoecious.**

Monel metal *or* **Monell metal** (mɒ'nɛl) *n Trademark.* any of various silvery corrosion-resistant alloys. ORIG C20: after A. *Monell* (died 1921), president of the International Nickel Co., New York, which introduced the alloys

Monet ★ (*French* mɔnɛ) *n* **Claude** (klod). 1840–1926, French impressionist painter, whose works include the series *Haystacks* (1889–93), *Rouen Cathedral* (1892–94), and the *Thames* (1899–1904).

monetarism ('mʌnɪtəˌrɪzəm) *n* **1** the theory that inflation is caused by an excess quantity of money in an economy. **2** an economic policy based on this theory and on a belief in the efficiency of free market forces.
▸ **'monetarist** *n, adj*

monetary ('mʌnɪtərɪ, -trɪ) *adj* **1** of or relating to money or currency. **2** of or relating to monetarism. ORIG C19: from LL *monētārius,* from L *monēta* MONEY
▸ **'monetarily** *adv*

monetize *or* **monetise** ('mʌnɪˌtaɪz) *vb* **monetizes, monetizing, monetized** *or* **monetises, monetising, monetised.** (*tr*) **1** to establish as legal tender. **2** to give a legal value to (a coin).
▸ **ˌmoneti'zation** *or* **ˌmoneti'sation** *n*

money ('mʌnɪ) *n* **1** a medium of exchange that functions as legal tender. **2** the official currency, in the form of banknotes, coins, etc., issued by a government or other authority. **3** a particular denomination or form of currency: *silver money.* **4** (*Law or arch. pl* **moneys** *or* **monies**) a pecuniary sum or income. **5** an unspecified amount of paper currency or coins: *money to lend.* **6 for one's money.** in one's opinion. **7 in the money.** *Inf.* well-off; rich. **8 one's money's worth.** full value for the money one has paid for something. **9 put money on.** to place a bet on. ◆ Related adj: **pecuniary.** ORIG C13: from OF *moneie,* from L *monēta;* see MINT[2]

moneybags (ˈmʌnɪˌbæɡz) *n* (*functioning as sing*) *Inf.* a very rich person.

moneychanger (ˈmʌnɪˌtʃeɪndʒə) *n* **1** a person engaged in the business of exchanging currencies or money. **2** *Chiefly US.* a machine for dispensing coins.

moneyed *or* **monied** (ˈmʌnɪd) *adj* **1** having a great deal of money; rich. **2** arising from or characterized by money.

money-grubbing *adj Inf.* seeking greedily to obtain money.
▸ **ˈmoney-ˌgrubber** *n*

moneylender (ˈmʌnɪˌlɛndə) *n* a person who lends money at interest as a living.
▸ **ˈmoneyˌlending** *adj, n*

moneymaker (ˈmʌnɪˌmeɪkə) *n* **1** a person who is intent on accumulating money. **2** a person or thing that is or might be profitable.
▸ **ˈmoneyˌmaking** *adj, n*

money of account *n* another name (esp. US and Canad.) for **unit of account.**

money-spinner *n Inf.* an enterprise, idea, person, or thing that is a source of wealth.

money supply *n* the total amount of money in a country's economy at a given time, which can be calculated in various ways.

monger (ˈmʌŋɡə) *n* **1** (*in combination except in archaic use*) a trader or dealer: *ironmonger.* **2** (*in combination*) a promoter of something: *warmonger.* ORIG OE *mangere,* ult. from L *mangō* dealer
▸ **ˈmongering** *n, adj*

mongol (ˈmɒŋɡəl) *n* (not in technical use) a person affected by Down's syndrome.

> **USAGE NOTE** This term is nowadays considered offensive and should be replaced by reference to Down's syndrome.

Mongol (ˈmɒŋɡɒl, -ɡəl) *n* another word for **Mongolian.**

Mongolia ★ (mɒŋˈɡəʊlɪə) *n* **1** a republic in E central Asia: made a Chinese province in 1691; became autonomous in 1911 and a republic in 1924; multiparty democracy introduced in 1990. It consists chiefly of a high plateau, with the Gobi Desert in the south, a large lake district in the northwest, and the Altai and Khangai Mountains in the west. Official language: Khalkha. Religion: nonreligious majority. Currency: tugrik. Capital: Ulan Bator. Pop.: 2 334 000 (1996). Area: 1 565 000 sq. km (604 095 sq. miles). Former names: **Outer Mongolia** (until 1924), **Mongolian People's Republic** (1924–92). **2** a vast region of central Asia, inhabited chiefly by Mongols: now divided into Mongolia, the Inner Mongolian Autonomous Region of China, and the Tuva Autonomous Republic of Russia; at its height during the 13th century under Genghis Khan.

mongolian (mɒŋˈɡəʊlɪən) *adj* (not in technical use) of, relating to, or affected by Down's syndrome.

Mongolian (mɒŋˈɡəʊlɪən) *adj* **1** of or relating to Mongolia, its people, or their language. ◆ *n* **2** a native or inhabitant of Mongolia. **3** the language of Mongolia.

Mongolic (mɒŋˈɡɒlɪk) *n* **1** a branch or subfamily of the Altaic family of languages, including Mongolian and Kalmuck. **2** another word for **Mongoloid.**

mongolism (ˈmɒŋɡəˌlɪzəm) *n Pathol.* a former name (not in technical use) for **Down's syndrome.** ORIG C20: the condition produces facial features similar to those of the Mongoloid peoples

mongoloid (ˈmɒŋɡəˌlɔɪd) *adj* (not in technical use) **1** relating to or characterized by Down's syndrome. ◆ *n* **2** a person affected by Down's syndrome.

Mongoloid (ˈmɒŋɡəˌlɔɪd) *adj* **1** of or relating to a major racial group of mankind, characterized by yellowish complexion, straight black hair, slanting eyes, short nose, and scanty facial hair, including most of the peoples of Asia, the Eskimos, and the North American Indians. ◆ *n* **2** a member of this group.

mongoose (ˈmɒŋˌɡuːs) *n, pl* **mongooses.** any of various small predatory mammals occurring in Africa and from S Europe to SE Asia, typically having a long tail and brindled coat. ORIG C17: from Marathi (a language of India) *mangūs*

mongrel (ˈmʌŋɡrəl) *n* **1** a plant or animal, esp. a dog, of mixed or unknown breeding. **2** *Derog.* a person of mixed race. ◆ *adj* **3** of mixed origin, breeding, character, etc. ORIG C15: from obs. *mong* mixture
▸ **ˈmongrelism** *n* ▸ **ˈmongreˌlize** *or* **ˈmongreˌlise** *vb*
▸ **ˌmongreliˈzation** *or* **ˌmongreliˈsation** *n* ▸ **ˈmongrelly** *adj*

ˈmongst (mʌŋst) *prep Poetic.* short for **amongst.**

monied (ˈmʌnɪd) *adj* a less common spelling of **moneyed.**

monies (ˈmʌnɪz) *n Law, arch.* a plural of **money.**

moniker *or* **monicker** (ˈmɒnɪkə) *n Sl.* a person's name or nickname. ORIG C19: from Shelta *munnik,* altered from Irish Gaelic *ainm* name

monism (ˈmɒnɪzəm) *n* **1** *Philosophy.* the doctrine that reality consists of only one basic substance or element, such as mind or matter. Cf. **dualism** (sense 2), **pluralism** (sense 4). **2** the attempt to explain anything in terms of one principle only.
▸ **ˈmonist** *n, adj* ▸ **moˈnistic** *adj*

monition (məʊˈnɪʃən) *n* **1** a warning or caution; admonition. **2** *Christianity.* a formal notice from a bishop or ecclesiastical court requiring a person to refrain from committing a specific offence. ORIG C14: via OF from L *monitiō,* from *monēre* to warn

monitor (ˈmɒnɪtə) *n* **1** a person or piece of equipment that warns, checks, controls, or keeps a continuous record of something. **2** *Education.* **2a** a senior pupil with various supervisory duties, etc. **2b** a pupil assisting a teacher in classroom organization, etc. **3** a television set used to display certain kinds of information in a television studio, airport, etc. **4a** a loudspeaker used in a recording studio to determine quality or balance. **4b** a loudspeaker used on stage to enable musicians to hear themselves. **5** any of various large predatory lizards inhabiting warm regions of Africa, Asia, and Australia. **6** (formerly) a small heavily armoured warship used for coastal assault. ◆ *vb* **7** to act as a monitor of. **8** (*tr*) to observe or record (the activity or performance of) (an engine or other device). **9** (*tr*) to check (the technical quality of) (a radio or television broadcast). ORIG C16: from L, from *monēre* to advise
▸ **monitorial** (ˌmɒnɪˈtɔːrɪəl) *adj* ▸ **ˈmonitorship** *n*
▸ **ˈmonitress** *fem n*

monitory (ˈmɒnɪtərɪ, -trɪ) *adj also* **monitorial. 1** warning or admonishing. ◆ *n, pl* **monitories. 2** *Rare.* a letter containing a monition.

monk (mʌŋk) *n* a male member of a religious community bound by vows of poverty, chastity, and obedience. Related adj: **monastic.** ORIG OE *munuc,* from LL *monachus,* from LGk: solitary (man), from Gk *monos* alone
▸ **ˈmonkish** *adj*

Monk ★ (mʌŋk) *n* **1 Thelonious** (**Sphere**) (θəˈləʊnɪəs). 1920–82, US jazz pianist and composer. **2** a variant spelling of (George) **Monck.**

monkey (ˈmʌŋkɪ) *n* **1** any of numerous long-tailed primates excluding lemurs, tarsiers, etc.: see **Old World monkey, New World monkey. 2** any primate except man. **3** a naughty or mischievous person, esp. a child. **4** the head of a pile-driver (**monkey engine**) or of some similar mechanical device. **5** *US & Canad. sl.* an addict's dependence on a drug (esp. in **have a monkey on one's back**). **6** *Sl.* a butt of derision; someone made to look a fool (esp. in **make a monkey of**). **7** *Sl.* (esp. in bookmaking) £500. **8** *US & Canad. sl.* $500. ◆ *vb* **9** (*intr;* usually foll. by *around, with,* etc.) to meddle, fool, or tinker. **10** (*tr*) *Rare.* to imitate; ape. ORIG C16: ?from Low G; cf. MLow G *Moneke,* name of the ape's son in the tale of Reynard the Fox

monkey business *n Inf.* mischievous, suspect, or dishonest behaviour or acts.

monkey flower *n* any of various plants of the genus *Mimulus,* cultivated for their yellow or red flowers.

monkey jacket *n* a short close-fitting jacket, esp. a waist-length jacket similar to a mess jacket.

monkey nut *n Brit.* another name for a **peanut.**

monkey puzzle *n* a South American coniferous tree having branches shaped like a candelabrum and stiff sharp leaves. Also called: **Chile pine.**

monkey's wedding *n S. African inf.* a combination of rain and sunshine. ORIG from ?

monkey tricks *or US* **monkey shines** *pl n Inf.* mischievous behaviour or acts.

monkey wrench *n* a wrench with adjustable jaws.

monkfish (ˈmʌŋkˌfɪʃ) *n, pl* **monkfish** *or* **monkfishes. 1** any of various angler fishes. **2** another name for **angelfish** (sense 3).

monk's cloth *n* a heavy cotton fabric of basket weave, used mainly for bedspreads.

monkshood (ˈmʌŋkshʊd) *n* any of several poisonous N temperate plants that have hooded blue-purple flowers.

Monmouth[1] ★ (ˈmɒnməθ) *n* a market town in E Wales, in Monmouthshire: Norman castle, where Henry V was born in 1387. Pop.: 7246 (1991).

Monmouth[2] ★ (ˈmɒnməθ) *n* **James Scott,** Duke of Monmouth. 1649–85, the illegitimate son of Charles II of England, he led a rebellion against James II in support of his own claim to the Crown; captured and beheaded.

Monmouthshire ★ (ˈmɒnməθˌʃɪə, -ʃə) *n* a county of E Wales: administratively part of England for three centuries (until 1830): mainly absorbed into Gwent in 1974; reinstated with reduced boundaries in 1996. Administrative centre: Cwmbran. Pop.: 85 600 (1996 est.). Area: 851 sq. km (329 sq. miles).

Monnet ★ (*French* mɔnɛ) *n* **Jean** (ʒɑ̃). 1888–1979, French economist, regarded as founding father of the European Economic Community. He was first president (1952–55) of the European Coal and Steel Community.

mono (ˈmɒnəʊ) *adj* **1** short for **monophonic.** ◆ *n* **2** monophonic sound.

mono- *or before a vowel* **mon-** *combining form.* **1** one; single: *monorail.* **2** indicating that a chemical compound contains a single specified atom or group: *monoxide.* ORIG from Gk *monos*

monoacid (ˌmɒnəʊˈæsɪd), **monacid, monoacidic** (ˌmɒnəʊəˈsɪdɪk), *or* **monacidic** *adj Chem.* (of a base) capable of reacting with only one molecule of a monobasic acid; having only one hydroxide ion per molecule.

monobasic (ˌmɒnəʊˈbeɪsɪk) *adj Chem.* (of an acid, such as hydrogen chloride) having only one replaceable hydrogen atom per molecule.

monocarpic (ˌmɒnəʊˈkɑːpɪk) *or* **monocarpous** *adj* (of some flowering plants) producing fruit only once before dying.

monochromatic (ˌmɒnəʊkrəʊˈmætɪk) *or* **monochroic** (ˌmɒnəʊˈkrəʊɪk) *adj* (of light or other electromagnetic radiation) having only one wavelength.

monochromator (ˌmɒnəʊˈkrəʊmˌeɪtə) *n Physics.* a device that isolates a single wavelength of radiation.

monochrome (ˈmɒnəˌkrəʊm) *n* **1** a black-and-white photograph or transparency. **2** *Photog.* black-and-white. **3a** a painting, drawing, etc., done in a range of tones of a single colour. **3b** the technique or art of this. **4** (*modifier*) executed in or resembling monochrome: *a monochrome print.* ◆ *adj* **5** devoid of any distinctive or stimulating characteristics. ◆ Also called (for senses 3, 4): **monotint.** ORIG C17: via Med. L from Gk *monokhrōmos* of one colour
▸ ˌ**monoˈchromic** *adj* ▸ ˈ**monoˌchromist** *n*

monocle (ˈmɒnək^əl) *n* a lens for correcting defective vision of one eye, held in position by the facial muscles. ORIG C19: from F, from LL, from MONO- + *oculus* eye
▸ ˈ**monocled** *adj*

monocline (ˈmɒnəʊˌklaɪn) *n* a fold in stratified rocks in which the strata are inclined in the same direction from the horizontal. ORIG C19: from MONO- + Gk *klīnein* to lean
▸ ˌ**monoˈclinal** *adj, n*

monoclinic (ˌmɒnəʊˈklɪnɪk) *adj Crystallog.* relating to or belonging to the crystal system characterized by three unequal axes, one pair of which are not at right angles to each other. ORIG C19: from MONO- + Gk *klīnein* to lean

monoclinous (ˌmɒnəʊˈklaɪnəs, ˈmɒnəʊˌklaɪnəs) *adj* (of flowering plants) having the male and female reproductive organs on the same flower. Cf. **diclinous.** ORIG C19: from MONO- + Gk *klīne* bed
▸ ˈ**monoˌclinism** *n*

monoclonal antibody (ˌmɒnəʊˈkləʊn^əl) *n* an antibody, produced by a single clone of cells grown in culture, that is both pure and specific and capable of proliferating indefinitely: used in diagnosis, therapy, and biotechnology.

monocotyledon (ˌmɒnəʊˌkɒtɪˈliːd^ən) *n* any of various flowering plants having a single embryonic seed leaf, leaves with parallel veins, and flowers with parts in threes: includes grasses, lilies, palms, and orchids. Cf. **dicotyledon.**
▸ ˌ**monoˌcotyˈledonous** *adj*

monocracy (mɒˈnɒkrəsɪ) *n, pl* **monocracies.** government by one person.
▸ **monocrat** (ˈmɒnəˌkræt) *n* ▸ ˌ**monoˈcratic** *adj*

monocular (mɒˈnɒkjʊlə) *adj* having or intended for the use of only one eye. ORIG C17: from LL *monoculus* one-eyed
▸ **moˈnocularly** *adv*

monoculture (ˈmɒnəʊˌkʌltʃə) *n* the continuous growing of one type of crop.

monocycle (ˈmɒnəˌsaɪk^əl) *n* another name for **unicycle.**

monocyte (ˈmɒnəʊˌsaɪt) *n* the largest type of white blood cell that acts as part of the immune system by engulfing particles, such as invading microorganisms.

monody (ˈmɒnədɪ) *n, pl* **monodies. 1** (in Greek tragedy) an ode sung by a single actor. **2** any poem of lament for someone's death. **3** *Music.* a style of composition consisting of a single vocal part, usually with accompaniment. ORIG C17: via LL from Gk *monōidia,* from MONO- + *aeidein* to sing
▸ **monodic** (mɒˈnɒdɪk) *adj* ▸ ˈ**monodist** *n*

monoecious (mɒˈniːʃəs) *adj* **1** (of some flowering plants) having the male and female reproductive organs in separate flowers on the same plant. **2** (of some animals and lower plants) hermaphrodite. ORIG C18: from NL *monoecia,* from MONO- + Gk *oikos* house

monofilament (ˌmɒnəˈfɪləmənt) *or* **monofil** (ˈmɒnəfɪl) *n* synthetic thread or yarn composed of a single strand rather than twisted fibres.

monogamy (mɒˈnɒgəmɪ) *n* **1** the state or practice of having only one husband or wife over a period of time. **2** *Zool.* the practice of having only one mate. ORIG C17: via F from LL *monogamia,* from Gk; see MONO- + -GAMY
▸ **moˈnogamist** *n* ▸ **moˈnogamous** *adj*

monogenesis (ˌmɒnəʊˈdʒɛnɪsɪs) *or* **monogeny** (mɒˈnɒdʒɪnɪ) *n* **1** the hypothetical descent of all organisms from a single cell. **2** asexual reproduction in animals. **3** the direct development of an ovum into an organism resembling the adult. **4** the hypothetical descent of all human beings from a single pair of ancestors.

monogram (ˈmɒnəˌgræm) *n* a design of one or more letters, esp. initials, on clothing, stationery, etc. ORIG C17: from LL *monogramma,* from Gk; see MONO-, -GRAM
▸ **monogrammatic** (ˌmɒnəgrəˈmætɪk) *adj*

monograph (ˈmɒnəˌgrɑːf) *n* **1** a paper, book, or other work concerned with a single subject or aspect of a subject. ◆ *vb* **monographs, monographing, monographed.** (*tr*) **2** to write a monograph on.
▸ **monographer** (mɒˈnɒgrəfə) *or* **moˈnographist** *n* ▸ ˌ**monoˈgraphic** *adj*

monogyny (mɒˈnɒdʒɪnɪ) *n* the custom of having only one female sexual partner over a period of time.
▸ **moˈnogynous** *adj*

monohull (ˈmɒnəʊˌhʌl) *n* a sailing vessel with a single hull.

monokini (ˈmɒnəʊˌkiːnɪ) *n* a woman's one-piece bathing garment usually equivalent to the bottom half of a bikini. ORIG C20: from MONO- + BIKINI (as if *bikini* were from BI-)

monolayer (ˈmɒnəʊˌleɪə) *n* a single layer of atoms or molecules adsorbed on a surface. Also called: **molecular film.**

monolingual (ˌmɒnəʊˈlɪŋgwəl) *adj* knowing or expressed in only one language.

monolith (ˈmɒnəlɪθ) *n* **1** a large block of stone or anything that resembles one in appearance, intractability, etc. **2** a statue, obelisk, column, etc., cut from one block of stone. **3** a large hollow foundation piece sunk as a caisson and filled with concrete. ORIG C19: via F from Gk *monolithos* made from a single stone
▸ ˌ**monoˈlithic** *adj*

monologue (ˈmɒnəˌlɒg) *n* **1** a long speech made by one actor in a play, film, etc., esp. when alone. **2** a dramatic piece for a single performer. **3** any long speech by one person, esp. when interfering with conversation. ORIG C17: via F from Gk *monologos* speaking alone
▸ **monologic** (ˌmɒnəˈlɒdʒɪk) *or* ˌ**monoˈlogical** *adj* ▸ **monologist** (ˈmɒnəˌlɒgɪst) *n* ▸ **monologize** *or* **monologise** (mɒˈnɒlədʒaɪz) *vb*

USAGE NOTE See at **soliloquy.**

monomania (ˌmɒnəʊˈmeɪnɪə) *n* an excessive mental preoccupation with one thing, idea, etc.
▸ ˌ**monoˈmaniˌac** *n, adj* ▸ **monomaniacal** (ˌmɒnəʊməˈnaɪəkᵊl) *adj*

monomark (ˈmɒnəmɑːk) *n Brit.* a series of letters or figures to identify goods, personal articles, etc.

monomer (ˈmɒnəmə) *n Chem.* a compound whose molecules can join together to form a polymer.
▸ **monomeric** (ˌmɒnəˈmɛrɪk) *adj*

monometallism (ˌmɒnəʊˈmɛtᵊˌlɪzəm) *n* **1** the use of one metal, esp. gold or silver, as the sole standard of value and currency. **2** the economic policies supporting a monometallic standard.
▸ **monometallic** (ˌmɒnəʊmɪˈtælɪk) *adj* ▸ ˌ**monoˈmetallist** *n*

monomial (mɒˈnəʊmɪəl) *n* **1** *Maths.* an expression consisting of a single term, such as *5ax*. ◆ *adj* **2** consisting of a single algebraic term. ORIG C18: MONO- + (BIN)OMIAL

monomorphic (ˌmɒnəʊˈmɔːfɪk) *or* **monomorphous** *adj* **1** (of an individual organism) showing little or no change in structure during the entire life history. **2** (of a species) existing or having parts that exist in only one form. **3** (of a chemical compound) having only one crystalline form.

Monongahela ★ (məˌnɒŋgəˈhiːlə) *n* a river in the northeastern US, flowing generally north to the Allegheny River at Pittsburgh, Pennsylvania, forming the Ohio River. Length: 206 km (128 miles).

mononucleosis (ˌmɒnəʊˌnjuːklɪˈəʊsɪs) *n* **1** *Pathol.* the presence of a large number of monocytes in the blood. **2** See **infectious mononucleosis.**

monophonic (ˌmɒnəʊˈfɒnɪk) *adj* **1** Also: **monaural.** (of a system of broadcasting, recording, or reproducing sound) using only one channel between source and loudspeaker. Sometimes shortened to **mono.** Cf. **stereophonic. 2** *Music.* of or relating to a style of musical composition consisting of a single melodic line.

monophthong (ˈmɒnəfˌθɒŋ) *n* a simple or pure vowel. ORIG C17: from Gk *monophthongos,* from MONO- + *thongos* sound

Monophysite (mɒˈnɒfɪˌsaɪt) *n Christianity.* a person who holds that there is only one nature in the person of Christ, which is primarily divine with human attributes. ORIG C17: via Church L from LGk, from MONO- + *phusis* nature
▸ **Monophysitic** (ˌmɒnəʊfɪˈsɪtɪk) *adj*

monoplane (ˈmɒnəʊˌpleɪn) *n* an aeroplane with only one pair of wings. Cf. **biplane.**

monopole (ˈmɒnəˌpəʊl) *n Physics.* **1** an electric charge or magnetic pole considered in isolation. **2** Also called: **magnetic monopole.** a hypothetical elementary particle postulated in certain theories of particle physics to exist as an isolated north or south magnetic pole.

monopolize *or* **monopolise** (məˈnɒpəˌlaɪz) *vb* **monopolizes, monopolizing, monopolized** *or* **monopolises, monopolising, monopolised.** (*tr*) **1** to have, control, or make use of fully, excluding others. **2** to obtain, maintain, or exploit a monopoly of (a market, commodity, etc.).
▸ **moˌnopoliˈzation** *or* **moˌnopoliˈsation** *n* ▸ **moˈnopoˌlizer** *or* **moˈnopoˌliser** *n*

monopoly (məˈnɒpəlɪ) *n, pl* **monopolies. 1** exclusive control of the market supply of a product or service. **2a** an enterprise exercising this control. **2b** the product or service so controlled. **3** *Law.* the exclusive right granted to a person, company, etc., by the state to purchase, manufacture, use, or sell some commodity or to trade in a specified area. **4** exclusive control, possession, or use of something. ORIG C16: from LL, from Gk *monopōlion,* from MONO- + *pōlein* to sell
▸ **moˈnopolist** *n* ▸ **moˌnopoˈlistic** *adj*

Monopoly (məˈnɒpəlɪ) *n Trademark.* a board game for two to six players who throw dice to advance their tokens, the object being to acquire the property on which their tokens land.

monorail (ˈmɒnəʊˌreɪl) *n* a single-rail railway, often elevated and with suspended cars.

monosaccharide (ˌmɒnəʊˈsækəˌraɪd) *n* a simple sugar, such as glucose or fructose, that does not hydrolyse to yield other sugars.

monoski (ˈmɒnəʊˌskiː) *n* a wide ski on which the skier stands with both feet.
▸ ˈ**monoˌskier** *n* ▸ ˈ**monoˌskiing** *n*

monosodium glutamate (ˌmɒnəʊˈsəʊdɪəm ˈgluːtəˌmeɪt) *n* a white crystalline substance that has little flavour itself but enhances protein flavours: used as a food additive.

monostable (ˌmɒnəʊˈsteɪbᵊl) *adj Physics.* (of an electronic circuit) having only one stable state but able to pass into a second state in response to an input pulse.

monosyllabic (ˌmɒnəsɪˈlæbɪk) *adj* **1** (of a word) containing only one syllable. **2** characterized by monosyllables; curt.
▸ ˌ**monosylˈlabically** *adv*

monosyllable (ˈmɒnəˌsɪləbᵊl) *n* a word of one syllable, esp. one used as a sentence.

monoterpene (ˈmɒnəˌtɜːpiːn) *n Chem.* an isoprene unit, C_5H_8, forming a terpene.

monotheism (ˈmɒnəʊθɪˌɪzəm) *n* the belief or doctrine that there is only one God.
▸ ˈ**monoˌtheist** *n, adj* ▸ ˌ**monotheˈistic** *adj* ▸ ˌ**monotheˈistically** *adv*

monotint (ˈmɒnəˌtɪnt) *n* another word for **monochrome** (senses 3, 4).

monotone (ˈmɒnəˌtəʊn) *n* **1** a single unvaried pitch level in speech, sound, etc. **2** utterance, etc., without change of pitch. **3** lack of variety in style, expression, etc. ◆ *adj* **4** unvarying.

monotonous (məˈnɒtənəs) *adj* **1** tedious, esp. because of repetition. **2** in unvarying tone.
▸ **moˈnotonously** *adv* ▸ **moˈnotonousness** *n*

monotony (məˈnɒtənɪ) *n, pl* **monotonies. 1** wearisome routine; dullness. **2** lack of variety in pitch or cadence.

monotreme (ˈmɒnəʊˌtriːm) *n* any mammal of a primitive order of Australia and New Guinea, having a single opening (cloaca) for the passage of eggs or sperm, faeces, and urine. The group contains only the echidnas and the platypus. ORIG C19: via NL from MONO- + Gk *trēma* hole
▸ **monotrematous** (ˌmɒnəʊˈtriːmətəs) *adj*

monotype (ˈmɒnəˌtaɪp) *n* **1** a single print made from a metal or glass plate on which a picture has been painted. **2** *Biol.* a monotypic genus or species.

Monotype (ˈmɒnəˌtaɪp) *n* **1** *Trademark.* any of various typesetting systems, esp. originally one in which each character was cast individually from hot metal. **2** type produced by such a system.

monotypic (ˌmɒnəʊˈtɪpɪk) *adj* **1** (of a genus or species) consisting of only one type of animal or plant. **2** of or relating to a monotype.

monounsaturated (ˌmɒnəʊʌn'sætʃəˌreɪtɪd) *adj* of or relating to a class of vegetable oils, such as olive oil, the molecules of which have long chains of carbon atoms containing only one double bond. See also **polyunsaturated.**

monovalent (ˌmɒnəʊ'veɪlənt) *adj Chem.* **a** having a valency of one. **b** having only one valency. ◆ Also: **univalent.**
▸ **ˌmonoˈvalence** *or* **ˌmonoˈvalency** *n*

monoxide (mɒ'nɒksaɪd) *n* an oxide that contains one oxygen atom per molecule.

Monroe ★ (mən'rəʊ) *n* **1 James.** 1758–1831, US statesman; fifth president of the US (1817–25). He promulgated the Monroe Doctrine (1823). **2 Marilyn,** real name *Norma Jean Baker* or *Mortenson.* 1926–62, US actress, whose films include *Gentlemen Prefer Blondes* (1953) and *Some Like It Hot* (1959).

Monrovia ★ (mɒn'rəʊvɪə) *n* the capital and chief port of Liberia, on the Atlantic: founded in 1822 as a home for freed American slaves; University of Liberia (1862). Pop.: 962 000 (1995 est.).

Mons ★ (*French* mɔ̃s) *n* a town in SW Belgium, capital of Hainaut province: scene of the first battle (1914) of the British Expeditionary Force during World War I. Pop.: 92 666 (1995 est.). Flemish name: **Bergen.**

Monseigneur *French.* (mɔ̃sɛɲœr) *n, pl* ***Messeigneurs*** (mesɛɲœr). a title given to French bishops, prelates, and princes. ORIG lit.: my lord

monsieur (məs'jɜː) *n, pl* **messieurs.** a French title of address equivalent to *sir* when used alone or *Mr* before a name. ORIG lit.: my lord

Monsignor (mɒn'siːnjə) *n, pl* **Monsignors** *or* **Monsignori** (*Italian* monsiɲ'ɲoːri). *RC Church.* an ecclesiastical title attached to certain offices. ORIG C17: from It., from F MONSEIGNEUR

monsoon (mɒn'suːn) *n* **1** a seasonal wind of S Asia from the southwest in summer and from the northeast in winter. **2** the rainy season when the SW monsoon blows, from about April to October. **3** any wind that changes direction with the seasons. ORIG C16: from obs. Du. *monssoen,* from Port., from Ar. *mawsim* season
▸ **monˈsoonal** *adj*

mons pubis ('mɒnz 'pjuːbɪs) *n, pl* **montes pubis** ('mɒntiːz). the fatty flesh in human males over the junction of the pubic bones. Cf. **mons veneris.** ORIG C17: NL: hill of the pubes

monster ('mɒnstə) *n* **1** an imaginary beast, usually made up of various animal or human parts. **2** a person, animal, or plant with a marked deformity. **3** a cruel, wicked, or inhuman person. **4a** a very large person, animal, or thing. **4b** (*as modifier*): *a monster cake.* ORIG C13: from OF *monstre,* from L *monstrum* portent, from *monēre* to warn

monstera (mɒn'stɪərə) *n* any of various tropical evergreen climbing plants. ORIG from ?

monstrance ('mɒnstrəns) *n RC Church.* a receptacle in which the consecrated Host is exposed for adoration. ORIG C16: from Med. L *mōnstrantia,* from L *mōnstrāre* to show

monstrosity (mɒn'strɒsɪtɪ) *n, pl* **monstrosities. 1** an outrageous or ugly person or thing; monster. **2** the state or quality of being monstrous.

monstrous ('mɒnstrəs) *adj* **1** abnormal, hideous, or unnatural in size, character, etc. **2** (of plants and animals) abnormal in structure. **3** outrageous, atrocious, or shocking. **4** huge. **5** of, relating to, or resembling a monster.
▸ **ˈmonstrously** *adv* ▸ **ˈmonstrousness** *n*

mons veneris ('mɒnz 'vɛnərɪs) *n, pl* **montes veneris** ('mɒntiːz). the fatty flesh in human females over the junction of the pubic bones. Cf. **mons pubis.** ORIG C17: NL: hill of Venus

Mont. *abbrev. for* Montana.

montage (mɒn'tɑːʒ) *n* **1** the art or process of composing pictures of miscellaneous elements, such as other pictures or photographs. **2** such a composition. **3** a method of film editing by juxtaposition or partial superimposition of several shots to form a single image. **4** a film sequence of this kind. ORIG C20: from F, from *monter* to MOUNT[1]

Montagu ★ ('mɒntəˌgjuː) *n* **1 Charles.** See (Earl of) **Halifax. 2** Lady **Mary Wortley.** 1689–1762, British writer, noted for her *Letters from the East* (1763).

Montaigne ★ (*French* mɔ̃tɛɲ) *n* **Michel Eyquem de** (miʃɛl ikɛm də). 1533–92, French writer. His *Essays* (begun in 1571), established the essay as a literary genre.

Montale ★ (*Italian* mon'taːle) *n* **Eugenio** (eu'dʒɛːnjo). 1896–1981, Italian poet: Nobel prize for literature 1975.

Montana[1] ★ (mɒn'tænə) *n* a state of the western US: consists of the Great Plains in the east and the Rocky Mountains in the west. Capital: Helena. Pop.: 880 453 (1998 est.). Area: 377 070 sq. km (145 587 sq. miles). Abbrevs.: **Mont.** or (with zip code) **MT**
▸ **Monˈtanan** *adj, n*

Montana[2] ★ (mɒn'tænə) *n* **Joe.** born 1958, American footballer.

montane ('mɒnteɪn) *adj* of or inhabiting mountainous regions. ORIG C19: from L *montānus,* from *mons* MOUNTAIN

Montauban ★ (*French* mɔ̃tobɑ̃) *n* a city in SW France: a Huguenot stronghold in the 16th and 17th centuries, taken by Richelieu in 1629. Pop.: 53 280 (1990).

Montbéliard ★ (*French* mɔ̃beljar) *n* an industrial town in E France: former capital of the duchy of Burgundy. Pop.: 30 639 (1990).

Mont Blanc ★ (*French* mɔ̃ blɑ̃) *n* a massif in SW Europe, mainly between France and Italy: the highest mountain in the Alps; beneath it is **Mont Blanc Tunnel,** 12 km (7.5 miles) long. Highest peak (in France): 4807 m (15 771 ft). Italian name: **Monte Bianco** ('monte 'bjaŋko).

montbretia (mɒn'briːʃə) *n* any plant of an African genus related to the iris with ornamental orange or yellow flowers. ORIG C19: NL, after A. F. E. Coquebert de *Montbret* (1780–1801), F botanist

Montcalm ★ (mɒnt'kɑːm; *French* mɔ̃kalm) *n* **Louis Joseph** (lwi ʒozɛf), Marquis de Montcalm de Saint-Véran. 1712–59, French general in Canada (1756); killed in Quebec by British forces under General Wolfe.

Mont Cenis ★ (*French* mɔ̃səni) *n* See (Mont) **Cenis.**

Mont Cervin ★ (mɔ̃ sɛrvɛ̃) *n* the French name for the **Matterhorn.**

monte ('mɒntɪ) *n* a gambling card game of Spanish origin. ORIG C19: from Sp.: mountain, hence pile of cards

Monte Carlo ★ ('mɒntɪ 'kɑːləʊ; *French* mɔ̃te karlo) *n* a town and resort forming part of the principality of Monaco, on the Riviera: famous casino and the destination of an annual car rally (the **Monte Carlo Rally**). Pop.: 12 000 (1985).

Monte Cassino ★ ('mɒntɪ kə'siːnəʊ; *Italian* 'monte kas'siːno) *n* a hill above Cassino in central Italy: site of Benedictine monastery (530 A.D.); in 1944 mistaken for German observation post and destroyed by the Allies.

Monte Corno ★ (*Italian* 'monte 'korno) *n* See (Monte) **Corno.**

Montego Bay ★ (mɒn'tiːgəʊ) *n* a port and resort in NW Jamaica. Pop.: 83 446 (1991).

Montenegro ★ (ˌmɒntɪ'niːgrəʊ) *n* a constituent republic of Yugoslavia, bordering on the Adriatic: declared a kingdom in 1910 and united with Serbia, Croatia, and other territories in 1918 to form Yugoslavia; remained united with Serbia as the Federal Republic of Yugoslavia when the other former Yugoslav republics became independent in 1991–92. Capital: Podgorica. Pop.: 635 000 (1995 est.). Area: 13 812 sq. km (5387 sq. miles).
▸ **ˌMonteˈnegrin** *adj, n*

Monterey ★ (ˌmɒntə'reɪ) *n* a city in W California: capital of Spain's Pacific empire from 1774 to 1825; taken by the US (1846). Pop.: 31 954 (1990).

Monterrey ★ (ˌmɒntə'reɪ; *Spanish* monte'rrei) *n* a city in NE Mexico, capital of Nuevo Léon state: a major industrial centre, esp. for metals. Pop.: 1 068 996 (1990).

Montespan ★ (*French* mɔ̃tɛspɑ̃) *n* **Marquise de,** title of

Françoise Athénaïs de Rochechouart. 1641–1707, French noblewoman; mistress of Louis XIV of France.

Montesquieu ★ (*French* mɔ̃tɛskjø) *n* **Baron de la Brède et de** (barɔ̃ də la brɛd e də), title of *Charles Louis de Secondat.* 1689–1755, French political philosopher. His chief works are the satirical *Lettres persanes* (1721) and *L'Esprit des lois* (1748).

Montessori ★ (ˌmɒntɪˈsɔːrɪ; *Italian* monteˈsɔːri) *n* **Maria** (maˈriːa). 1870–1952, Italian educational reformer, who evolved the **Montessori method** of teaching children, providing them with facilities for practical play and allowing them to develop at their own pace.

Monteux ★ (*French* mɔ̃tø) *n* **Pierre** (pjɛr). 1875–1964, US conductor, born in France.

Monteverdi ★ (ˌmɒntɪˈvɛədɪ) *n* **Claudio** (ˈklaudɪˌəʊ). ?1567–1643, Italian composer. His operas include *Orfeo* (1607) and he also wrote many motets and madrigals.

Montevideo ★ (ˌmɒntɪvɪˈdeɪəʊ; *Spanish* monteβiˈðeo) *n* the capital and chief port of Uruguay, in the south on the Río de la Plata estuary: the largest city in the country: University of the Republic (1849); resort. Pop.: 1 378 707 (1996).

Montezuma II ★ (ˌmɒntɪˈzuːmə) *n* 1466–1520, Aztec emperor of Mexico (?1502–20). He was overthrown and killed by the Spanish conquistador Cortés.

Montfort ★ (ˈmɒntfət) *n* **Simon de,** Earl of Leicester. ?1208–65, English soldier, born in Normandy. He led the baronial rebellion against Henry III and ruled England from 1264 to 1265; he was killed at Evesham.

Montgolfier ★ (*French* mɔ̃gɔlfje) *n* **Jacques Étienne** (ʒak etjɛn), 1745–99, and his brother **Joseph Michel** (ʒozɛf miʃɛl), 1740–1810, French inventors, who made the first hot-air balloon ascent (1783).

Montgomery[1] ★ (məntˈgʌmərɪ) *n* a city in central Alabama, on the Alabama River: state capital; capital of the Confederacy (1861). Pop.: 193 363 (1996 est.).

Montgomery[2] ★ (məntˈgʌmərɪ) *n* **Bernard Law,** 1st Viscount Montgomery of Alamein, nicknamed *Monty.* 1887–1976, British field marshal. As commander of the 8th Army in North Africa, he launched the offensive that drove Rommel's forces back to Tunis. He also commanded the ground forces in Normandy (1944) and accepted Germany's surrender (May 7, 1945).

Montgomeryshire ★ (məntˈgʌmərɪˌʃɪə, -ʃə) *n* (until 1974) a county of central Wales, now part of Powys.

month (mʌnθ) *n* **1** one of the twelve divisions (**calendar months**) of the calendar year. **2** a period of time extending from one date to a corresponding date in the next calendar month. **3** a period of four weeks or of 30 days. **4** the period of time (**solar month**) taken by the moon to return to the same longitude after one complete revolution around the earth; 27.321 58 days (approximately 27 days, 7 hours, 43 minutes, 4.5 seconds). **5** the period of time (**sidereal month**) taken by the moon to make one complete revolution around the earth, measured between two successive conjunctions with a particular star; 27.321 66 days (approximately 27 days, 7 hours, 43 minutes, 11 seconds). **6** Also called: **lunation.** the period of time (**lunar** or **synodic month**) taken by the moon to make one complete revolution around the earth, measured between two successive new moons; 29.530 59 days (approximately 29 days, 12 hours, 44 minutes, 3 seconds). ORIG OE *mōnath*

Montherlant ★ (*French* mɔ̃tɛrlɑ̃) *n* **Henri (Millon) de** (ɑ̃ri də). 1896–1972, French novelist and dramatist: his novels include *Les Jeunes Filles* (1935–39) and *Le Chaos et la nuit* (1963).

monthly (ˈmʌnθlɪ) *adj* **1** occurring, done, appearing, payable, etc., once every month. **2** lasting or valid for a month. ◆ *adv* **3** once a month. ◆ *n, pl* **monthlies. 4** a book, periodical, magazine, etc., published once a month. **5** *Inf.* a menstrual period.

Montluçon ★ (*French* mɔ̃lysɔ̃) *n* an industrial city in central France, on the Cher River. Pop.: 56 434 (1983 est.).

Montmartre ★ (*French* mɔ̃martrə) *n* a district of N Paris: the highest point in the city and famous for its association with artists.

Montparnasse ★ (*French* mɔ̃parnas) *n* a district of S Paris, on the left bank of the Seine, frequented by artists, writers, and students.

Montpelier ★ (mɒntˈpiːljə) *n* a city in N central Vermont, on the Winooski River: the state capital. Pop.: 8254 (1990).

Montpellier ★ (*French* mɔ̃pəlje) *n* a city in S France, the chief town of Languedoc: its university was founded by Pope Nicholas IV in 1289; wine trade. Pop.: 210 866 (1990).

Montreal ★ (ˌmɒntrɪˈɔːl) *n* a city and major port in central Canada, in S Quebec on **Montreal Island** at the junction of the Ottawa and St Lawrence Rivers. Pop.: 1 017 666 (1991), with a conurbation of 3 127 242 (1991). French name: **Montréal** (mɔ̃real).

Montreuil ★ (*French* mɔ̃trœj) *n* an E suburb of Paris: formerly famous for peaches, but now increasingly industrialized. Pop.: 94 754 (1990).

Montreux ★ (*French* mɔ̃trø) *n* a town and resort in W Switzerland, in Vaud canton on Lake Geneva: annual television festival. Pop.: 19 850 (1990).

Montrose ★ (mɒnˈtrəʊz) *n* **James Graham,** 1st Marquess and 5th Earl of Montrose. 1612–50, Scottish general, noted for his victories in Scotland for Charles I in the Civil War. He was later captured and hanged.

Mont-Saint-Michel ★ (*French* mɔ̃sɛ̃miʃɛl) *n* a rocky islet off the coast of NW France, accessible at low tide by a causeway: Benedictine abbey (966), used as a prison from the Revolution until 1863; reoccupied by Benedictine monks since 1966. Area: 1 hectare (3 acres).

Montserrat ★ *n* **1** (ˌmɒntsəˈræt). a volcanic island in the Caribbean, in the Leeward Islands of the West Indies: a UK overseas territory: devastated by volcanic eruptions in 1997. Capital: Plymouth. Pop.: 11 957 (1991). Area: 103 sq. km (40 sq. miles). **2** (*Spanish* monsɛˈrrat). a mountain in NE Spain, northwest of Barcelona: famous Benedictine monastery. Height: 1235 m (4054 ft). Ancient name: **Mons Serratus** (mɒnz səˈrætəs).

monument (ˈmɒnjʊmənt) *n* **1** an obelisk, statue, building, etc., erected in commemoration of a person or event. **2** a notable building or site, esp. one preserved as public property. **3** a tomb or tombstone. **4** a literary or artistic work regarded as commemorative of its creator or a particular period. **5** *US.* a boundary marker. **6** an exceptional example: *his lecture was a monument of tedium.* ORIG C13: from L *monumentum,* from *monēre* to remind

Monument ★ (ˈmɒnjʊmənt) *n* **the.** a tall columnar building designed (1671) by Sir Christopher Wren to commemorate the Fire of London (1666), which destroyed a large part of the medieval city.

monumental (ˌmɒnjʊˈmɛntᵊl) *adj* **1** like a monument, esp. in large size, endurance, or importance. **2** of, relating to, or being a monument. **3** *Inf.* (intensifier): *monumental stupidity.*

▸ **ˌmonuˈmentally** *adv*

Monza ★ (*Italian* ˈmontsa) *n* a city in N Italy, northeast of Milan: the ancient capital of Lombardy; scene of the assassination of King Umberto I in 1900; motor-racing circuit. Pop.: 119 658 (1996 est.).

moo (muː) *vb* **1** (*intr*) (of a cow, bull, etc.) to make a characteristic deep long sound; low. ◆ *interj* **2** an instance or imitation of this sound.

mooch (muːtʃ) *vb Sl.* **1** (*intr;* often with *around*) to loiter or walk aimlessly. **2** (*intr*) to lurk; skulk. **3** (*tr*) to cadge. **4** (*tr*) *Chiefly US & Canad.* to steal. ORIG C17: ?from OF *muchier* to skulk

▸ **ˈmoocher** *n*

mood[1] (muːd) *n* **1** a temporary state of mind or temper: *a cheerful mood.* **2** a sullen or gloomy state of mind, esp. when temporary: *she's in a mood.* **3** a prevailing atmosphere or feeling. **4 in the mood.** in a favourable state of mind. ORIG OE *mōd* mind, feeling

mood[2] (muːd) *n* **1** *Grammar.* a category of the verb or verbal inflections that expresses semantic and grammatical differences, including such forms as the indicative, subjunctive, and imperative. **2** *Logic.* one of the possible arrangements of the syllogism, classified by whether the component propositions are universal or particular and affirmative or negative. ◆ Also called: **mode.** ORIG C16: from MOOD[1], infl. in meaning by MODE

moody ('muːdɪ) *adj* **moodier, moodiest. 1** sullen, sulky, or gloomy. **2** temperamental or changeable.
▸ **'moodily** *adv* ▸ **'moodiness** *n*

Moody ★ ('muːdɪ) *n* **Dwight Lyman.** 1837–99, US evangelist and hymnodist, noted for his revivalist campaigns in Britain and the US with I. D. Sankey.

Moog (muːg, məʊg) *n Music, trademark.* a type of synthesizer. ORIG C20: after Robert *Moog* (born 1934), US engineer

mooi (mɔɪ) *adj S. African sl.* pleasing; nice. ORIG from Afrik.

mooli ('muːlɪ) *n* a type of large white radish. ORIG E African native name

moolvie *or* **moolvi** ('muːlviː) *n* (esp. in India) a Muslim doctor of the law, teacher, or learned man: also used as a title of respect. ORIG C17: from Urdu, from Ar. *mawlawīy;* cf. MULLAH

Moomba ('muːmbə) *n* an annual carnival that takes place in Melbourne, Australia, in March. ORIG from Abor. *moom* buttocks, anus; *moomba* orig. thought to be Abor. word meaning "Let's get together and have fun"

moon (muːn) *n* **1** the natural satellite of the earth. **2** the face of the moon as it is seen during its revolution around the earth, esp. at one of its phases: *new moon; full moon.* **3** any natural satellite of a planet. **4** moonlight. **5** something resembling a moon. **6** a month, esp. a lunar one. **7 over the moon.** *Inf.* extremely happy; ecstatic. ◆ *vb* **8** (when *tr,* often foll. by *away;* when *intr,* often foll. by *around*) to be idle in a listless way, as if in love, or to idle (time) away. **9** (*intr*) *Sl.* to expose one's buttocks to passers-by. ORIG OE *mōna*
▸ **'moonless** *adj*

Moon ★ (muːn) *n* **William.** 1818–94, blind British inventor of the Moon writing system (1847) for blind children.

moonbeam ('muːnˌbiːm) *n* a ray of moonlight.

mooncalf ('muːnˌkɑːf) *n, pl* **mooncalves** (-ˌkɑːvz). **1** a born fool; dolt. **2** a person who idles time away.

moon-faced *adj* having a round face.

moonlight ('muːnˌlaɪt) *n* **1** light from the sun received on earth after reflection by the moon. **2** (*modifier*) illuminated by the moon: *a moonlight walk.* ◆ *vb* **moonlights, moonlighting, moonlighted. 3** (*intr*) *Inf.* to work at a secondary job, esp. at night and illegally.
▸ **'moonˌlighter** *n*

moonlight flit *n Brit. inf.* a hurried departure at night, esp. from rented accommodation to avoid payments of rent owed. Often shortened to **moonlight.**

moonlit ('muːnlɪt) *adj* illuminated by the moon.

moonquake ('muːnˌkweɪk) *n* a light tremor of the moon, detected on the moon's surface.

moonscape ('muːnˌskeɪp) *n* the general surface of the moon or a representation of it.

moonshine ('muːnˌʃaɪn) *n* **1** another word for **moonlight** (sense 1). **2** *US & Canad.* illegally distilled or smuggled whisky. **3** foolish talk or thought.

moonshot ('muːnˌʃɒt) *n* the launching of a spacecraft, rocket, etc., to the moon.

moonstone ('muːnˌstəʊn) *n* a gem variety of orthoclase or albite that is white and translucent.

moonstruck ('muːnˌstrʌk) *or* **moonstricken** ('muːnˌstrɪkən) *adj* deranged or mad.

moony ('muːnɪ) *adj* **moonier, mooniest. 1** *Inf.* dreamy or listless. **2** of or like the moon.

moor[1] (mʊə, mɔː) *n* a tract of unenclosed ground, usually covered with heather, coarse grass, bracken, and moss. ORIG OE *mōr*

moor[2] (mʊə, mɔː) *vb* **1** to secure (a ship, boat, etc.) with cables or ropes. **2** (of a ship, boat, etc.) to be secured in this way. **3** (not in technical usage) a less common word for **anchor** (senses 7 and 8). ORIG C15: of Gmc origin; rel. to OE *mǣrelsrāp* rope for mooring
▸ **moorage** ('mʊərɪdʒ) *n*

Moor (mʊə, mɔː) *n* a member of a Muslim people of North Africa, of mixed Arab and Berber descent. ORIG C14: via OF from L *Maurus,* from Gk *Mauros,* ?from Berber
▸ **'Moorish** *adj*

moorcock ('mʊəˌkɒk, 'mɔː-) *n* the male of the red grouse.

Moore ★ (mʊə, mɔː) *n* **1 Bobby,** full name *Robert Frederick Moore.* 1941–93, British footballer: captain of England team that won the World Cup in 1966. **2 George.** 1852–1933, Irish novelist. His works include *Esther Waters* (1894). **3 G(eorge) E(dward).** 1873–1958, British philosopher, noted esp. for his *Principia Ethica* (1903). **4 Henry.** 1898–1986, British sculptor. His many works include the *Madonna and Child* (1943) at St Matthew's Church, Northampton. **5** Sir **John.** 1761–1809, British general; commander of the British army (1808–09) in the Peninsular War: killed at Corunna. **6 Marianne.** 1887–1972, US poet. **7 Thomas.** 1779–1852, Irish poet, best known for *Irish Melodies* (1807–34).

moorhen ('mʊəˌhɛn, 'mɔː-) *n* **1** a bird of the rail family, inhabiting ponds, lakes, etc., having a black plumage, red bill, and a red shield above the bill. **2** the female of the red grouse.

mooring ('mʊərɪŋ, 'mɔː-) *n* **1** a place for mooring a vessel. **2** a permanent anchor with a floating buoy, to which vessels can moor.

moorings ('mʊərɪŋz, 'mɔː-) *pl n* **1** *Naut.* the ropes, anchors, etc., used in mooring a vessel. **2** (*sometimes sing*) something that provides security or stability.

Moorish idol *n* a tropical marine spiny-finned fish that is common around coral reefs. It has a deeply compressed body with yellow and black stripes.

moorland ('mʊələnd) *n Brit.* an area of moor.

moose (muːs) *n, pl* **moose.** a large North American deer having large flattened palmate antlers: also occurs in Europe and Asia where it is called an elk. ORIG C17: of Amerind origin

Moose Jaw ★ *n* a city in W Canada, in S Saskatchewan. Pop.: 33 593 (1991).

moot (muːt) *adj* **1** subject or open to debate: *a moot point.* ◆ *vb* **2** (*tr*) to suggest or bring up for debate. **3** (*intr*) to plead or argue hypothetical cases, as an academic exercise or as training for law students. ◆ *n* **4** a discussion or debate of a hypothetical case or point, held as an academic activity. **5** (in Anglo-Saxon England) an assembly dealing with local legal and administrative affairs. ORIG OE *gemōt*

USAGE NOTE See at **mute.**

moot court *n* a mock court trying hypothetical legal cases.

mop (mɒp) *n* **1** an implement with a wooden handle and a head made of twists of cotton or a piece of synthetic sponge, used for polishing or washing floors, or washing dishes. **2** something resembling this, such as a tangle of hair. ◆ *vb* **mops, mopping, mopped.** (*tr*) **3** (often foll. by *up*) to clean or soak up as with a mop. ◆ See also **mop up.** ORIG C15 *mappe,* ult. from L *mappa* napkin

mopani *or* **mopane** (mɒ'pɑːnɪ) *n* **1** a leguminous tree, native to southern Africa, that is highly resistant to drought and produces very hard wood. **2** Also called: **mopani worm.** an edible caterpillar that feeds on mopani leaves. ORIG C19: from Bantu

mope (məʊp) *vb* **mopes, moping, moped.** (*intr*) **1** to be gloomy or apathetic. **2** to move or act in an aimless way. ◆ *n* **3** a gloomy person. ORIG C16: ?from obs. *mope* fool & rel. to *mop* grimace
▸ **'moper** *n* ▸ **'mopy** *adj*

moped ('məʊpɛd) *n* a light motorcycle not over 50cc. ORIG C20: from MOTOR + PEDAL[1]

mopes (məʊps) *pl n* **the.** low spirits.

mopoke ('məʊˌpəʊk) *n* **1** a small spotted owl of Australia and New Zealand. In Australia the tawny frogmouth is often wrongly identified as the mopoke. **2** *Austral. & NZ sl.* a slow or lugubrious person. ◆ Also called: **morepork.** ORIG C19: imit. of the bird's cry

moppet (ˈmɒpɪt) *n* a less common word for **poppet** (sense 1). ORIG C17: from obs. *mop* rag doll; from ?

mop up *vb* (*tr, adv*) **1** to clean with a mop. **2** *Inf.* to complete (a task, etc.). **3** *Mil.* to clear (remaining enemy forces) after a battle, as by killing, taking prisoner, etc.

moquette (mɒˈkɛt) *n* a thick velvety fabric used for carpets, upholstery, etc. ORIG C18: from F; from ?

MOR *abbrev. for* middle-of-the-road: used esp. in radio programming.

Mor. *abbrev. for* Morocco.

mora *or* **morra** (ˈmɔːrə) *n* a guessing game played with the fingers, esp. in Italy and China. ORIG C18: from It. *mora*

Moradabad ★ (ˌmɔːrədəˈbæd) *n* a city in N India, in N Uttar Pradesh. Pop.: 429 214 (1991).

moraine (mɒˈreɪn) *n* a mass of debris, carried by glaciers and forming ridges and mounds when deposited. ORIG C18: from F, from Savoy dialect *morena,* from ?
▸ **moˈrainal** *or* **moˈrainic** *adj*

moral (ˈmɒrəl) *adj* **1** concerned with or relating to human behaviour, esp. the distinction between good and bad or right and wrong behaviour: *moral sense.* **2** adhering to conventionally accepted standards of conduct. **3** based on a sense of right and wrong according to conscience: *moral courage; moral law.* **4** having psychological rather than tangible effects: *moral support.* **5** having the effects but not the appearance of (victory or defeat): *a moral victory.* **6** having a strong probability: *a moral certainty.* ◆ *n* **7** the lesson to be obtained from a fable or event. **8** a concise truth; maxim. **9** (*pl*) principles of behaviour in accordance with standards of right and wrong. **10** *Austral. sl.* a certainty: *a moral to win.* ORIG C14: from L *mōrālis* relating to morals or customs, from *mōs* custom
▸ **ˈmorally** *adv*

morale (mɒˈrɑːl) *n* the degree of mental or moral confidence of a person or group. ORIG C18: morals, from F, n use of MORAL (adj)

moralist (ˈmɒrəlɪst) *n* **1** a person who seeks to regulate the morals of others. **2** a person who lives in accordance with moral principles.
▸ **ˌmoralˈistic** *adj* ▸ **ˌmoralˈistically** *adv*

morality (məˈrælɪtɪ) *n, pl* **moralities. 1** the quality of being moral. **2** conformity, or degree of conformity, to conventional standards of moral conduct. **3** a system of moral principles. **4** an instruction or lesson in morals. **5** short for **morality play.**

morality play *n* a type of drama between the 14th and 16th centuries concerned with the conflict between personified virtues and vices.

moralize *or* **moralise** (ˈmɒrəˌlaɪz) *vb* **moralizes, moralizing, moralized** *or* **moralises, moralising, moralised. 1** (*intr*) to make moral pronouncements. **2** (*tr*) to interpret or explain in a moral sense. **3** (*tr*) to improve the morals of.
▸ **ˌmoraliˈzation** *or* **ˌmoraliˈsation** *n* ▸ **ˈmoralˌizer** *or* **ˈmoralˌiser** *n*

moral majority *n* a presumed majority of people believed to be in favour of a stricter code of public morals. ORIG C20: after *Moral Majority,* a right-wing US religious organization, based on SILENT MAJORITY

moral philosophy *n* the branch of philosophy dealing with ethics.

Moral Rearmament *n* a worldwide movement for moral and spiritual renewal founded by Frank Buchman in 1938. Also called: **Buchmanism.** Former name: **Oxford Group.**

moral theology *n* the branch of theology dealing with ethics.

Morar ★ (ˈmɔːrə) *n* **Loch.** a lake in W Scotland, in the SW Highlands: the deepest in Scotland. Length: 18 km (11 miles). Depth: 296 m (987 ft).

morass (məˈræs) *n* **1** a tract of swampy low-lying land. **2** a disordered or muddled situation or circumstance, esp. one that impedes progress. ORIG C17: from Du. *moeras,* ult. from OF *marais* MARSH

moratorium (ˌmɒrəˈtɔːrɪəm) *n, pl* **moratoria** (-rɪə) *or* **moratoriums. 1** a legally authorized postponement of the fulfilment of an obligation. **2** an agreed suspension of activity. ORIG C19: NL, from LL *morātōrius* dilatory, from *mora* delay

Morava ★ (məˈrɑːvə) *n* **1** a river in central Europe, rising in the Sudeten Mountains, in the Czech Republic, and flowing south to the Danube: forms part of the border between the Czech Republic, Slovakia, and Austria. Length: 370 km (230 miles). German name: **March. 2** a river in E Yugoslavia, formed by the confluence of the Southern Morava and the Western Morava near Stalac: flows north to the Danube. Length: 209 km (130 miles). **3** (ˈmɔrava). the Czech name for **Moravia**[1].

Moravia[1] ★ (məˈreɪvɪə, mɒ-) *n* a region of the Czech Republic, around the Morava River, bounded by the Bohemian-Moravian Highlands, the Sudeten Mountains, and the W Carpathians: became a separate Austrian crownland in 1848; part of Czechoslovakia (1918–92); valuable mineral resources. Czech name: **Morava.** German name: **Mähren.**

Moravia[2] ★ (*Italian* moˈraːvja) *n* **Alberto** (alˈbɛrto), pen name of *Alberto Pincherle.* 1907–90, Italian writer: his works include *The Woman of Rome* (1949) and *Erotic Tales* (1985).

Moravian (məˈreɪvɪən, mɒ-) *adj* **1** of or relating to Moravia, its people, or their dialect of Czech. **2** of or relating to the Moravian Church. ◆ *n* **3** the Moravian dialect. **4** a native or inhabitant of Moravia. **5** a member of the Moravian Church.
▸ **Moˈravianism** *n*

moray (mɒˈreɪ) *n, pl* **morays.** a voracious marine coastal eel marked with brilliant colours. ORIG C17: from Port. *moréia,* from L *mūrēna,* from Gk *muraina*

Moray[1] ★ (ˈmʌrɪ) *n* **1** a council area of NE Scotland. Administrative centre: Elgin. Pop.: 86 250 (1996 est.). Area: 2238 sq. km (874 sq miles). **2** another name for **Morayshire.**

Moray[2] *or* **Murray** ★ (ˈmʌrɪ) *n* **1st Earl of,** title of *James Stuart.* ?1531–70, regent of Scotland (1567–70) following the abdication of Mary, Queen of Scots, his half-sister. He defeated Mary and Bothwell at Langside (1568); assassinated by a follower of Mary.

Moray Firth ★ *n* an inlet of the North Sea on the NE coast of Scotland. Length: about 56 km (35 miles).

Morayshire ★ (ˈmʌrɪˌʃɪə, -ʃə) *n* a historic county of NE Scotland. Former name: **Elgin.**

morbid (ˈmɔːbɪd) *adj* **1** having an unusual interest in death or unpleasant events. **2** gruesome. **3** relating to or characterized by disease. ORIG C17: from L *morbidus* sickly, from *morbus* illness
▸ **morˈbidity** *n* ▸ **ˈmorbidly** *adv* ▸ **ˈmorbidness** *n*

morbid anatomy *n* the branch of medical science concerned with the study of the structure of diseased organs and tissues.

morbific (mɔːˈbɪfɪk) *adj* causing disease.

Morbihan ★ (*French* mɔrbiɑ̃) *n* a department of NW France, in S Brittany. Capital: Vannes. Pop.: 631 290 (1994 est.). Area: 7092 sq. km (2766 sq. miles).

mordant (ˈmɔːdᵊnt) *adj* **1** sarcastic or caustic. **2** having the properties of a mordant. **3** pungent. ◆ *n* **4** a substance used before the application of a dye, possessing the ability to fix colours. **5** an acid or other corrosive fluid used to etch lines on a printing plate. ORIG C15: from OF: biting, from *mordre* to bite, from L *mordēre*
▸ **ˈmordancy** *n* ▸ **ˈmordantly** *adv*

Mordecai ★ (ˌmɔːdəˈkaɪ, ˈmɔːdəˌkaɪ) *n Old Testament.* the cousin of Esther who averted a threatened massacre of the Jews (Esther 2–9).

mordent (ˈmɔːdᵊnt) *n Music.* a melodic ornament consisting of the rapid alternation of a note with a note one degree lower than it. ORIG C19: from G, from It. *mordente,* from *mordere* to bite

Mordred ★ (ˈmɔːdrɪd) *n* a variant of **Modred.**

Mordvinian Republic ★ (mɔːˈdvɪnɪən) *n* a constituent republic of W central Russia, in the middle Volga basin. Capital: Saransk. Pop.: 956 000 (1996 est.). Area: 26 200 sq. km (10 110 sq. miles). Also called: **Mordovian Republic** (mɔːˈdəuvɪən), **Mordovia** (mɔːˈdəuvɪə).

more (mɔː) *determiner* **1a** the comparative of **much** or **many:**

more joy than you know; more sausages. **1b** (*as pron; functioning as sing or pl*): *he has more than she has; even more are dying.* **2a** additional; further: *no more bananas.* **2b** (*as pron; functioning as sing or pl*): *I can't take any more; more than expected.* **3 more of.** to a greater extent or degree: *we see more of Sue; more of a nuisance.* ◆ *adv* **4** used to form the comparative of some adjectives and adverbs: *a more believable story; more quickly.* **5** the comparative of **much:** *people listen to the radio more now.* **6 more or less. 6a** as an estimate; approximately. **6b** to an unspecified extent or degree: *the party was ruined, more or less.* ORIG OE *māra*

USAGE NOTE See at **most.**

More ★ (mɔː) *n* **1 Hannah.** 1745–1833, British writer, noted for her religious tracts, esp. *The Shepherd of Salisbury Plain.* **2** Sir **Thomas.** 1478–1535, English statesman and Roman Catholic Saint; Lord Chancellor (1529–32) to Henry VIII. He opposed the annulment of Henry's marriage to Catherine of Aragon and refused to recognize the Act of Supremacy; executed on a charge of treason. In *Utopia* (1516), he set forth his concept of the ideal state. Feast day: June 22 or July 6.

Morea ★ (mɔːˈrɪə) *n* the medieval name for the **Peloponnese.**

Moreau ★ (*French* mɔro) *n* **1 Gustave** (gystav) 1826–98, French symbolist painter. **2 Jeanne** (ʒan). born 1928, French actress. Her films include *Jules et Jim* (1961) and *Viva Maria* (1965). **3 Jean Victor** (ʒɑ̃ viktɔr). 1763–1813, French general in the Revolutionary and Napoleonic Wars.

Morecambe ★ (ˈmɔːkəm) *n* a port and resort in NW England, in NW Lancashire on **Morecambe Bay** (an inlet of the Irish Sea). Pop. (with Heysham): 46 657 (1991).

Morecambe and Wise ★ (ˈmɔːkəm; waɪz) *n* a team of British comedians, **Eric Morecambe**, real name *John Eric Bartholomew*, 1926–84, and **Ernie Wise**, real name *Ernest Wiseman*, 1925–99.

moreish *or* **morish** (ˈmɔːrɪʃ) *adj Inf.* (of food) causing a desire for more.

morel (mɒˈrɛl) *n* an edible fungus in which the mushroom has a pitted cap. ORIG C17: from F *morille,* prob. of Gmc origin

Morelia ★ (*Spanish* moˈrelia) *n* a city in central Mexico, capital of Michoacán state: a cultural centre during colonial times; two universities. Pop.: 428 486 (1990). Former name (until 1828): **Valladolid.**

morello (məˈrɛləʊ) *n, pl* **morellos.** a variety of small very dark sour cherry. ORIG C17: ?from Med. L *amārellum,* dim. of L *amārus* bitter, but also infl. by It. *morello* blackish

Morelos ★ (*Spanish* moˈrelɔs) *n* an inland state of S central Mexico, on the S slope of the great plateau. Capital: Cuernavaca. Pop.: 1 496 030 (1997 est.). Area: 4988 sq. km (1926 sq. miles)

morendo (mɒrˈɛndəʊ) *adv Music.* gradually dying away. ORIG It.: dying

moreover (mɔːˈrəʊvə) *sentence connector.* in addition to what has already been said.

morepork (ˈmɔːˌpɔːk) *n* another name, esp. in New Zealand, for **mopoke.**

mores (ˈmɔːreɪz) *pl n* the customs and conventions embodying the fundamental values of a group or society. ORIG C20: from L, pl of *mōs* custom

Morgan ★ (ˈmɔːgən) *n* **1** Sir **Henry.** 1635–88, Welsh buccaneer, who raided Spanish colonies in the West Indies. **2 John Pierpont.** 1837–1913, US financier, philanthropist, and art collector. **3** (**Hywel**) **Rhodri** (ˈrɒdrɪ). born 1939, Welsh Labour politician: first secretary of Wales from 2000. **4 Thomas Hunt.** 1866–1945, US biologist, who formulated the chromosome theory of heredity. Nobel prize for physiology or medicine 1933.

morganatic (ˌmɔːgəˈnætɪk) *adj* of or designating a marriage between a person of high rank and a person of low rank, by which the latter is not elevated to the higher rank and any issue have no rights to the succession of the higher party's titles, property, etc. ORIG C18: from Med. L *mātrimōnium ad morganāticum* marriage based on the morning-gift (a token present after consummation representing the husband's only liability); *morganātica,* ult. from OHG *morgan* morning
▸ ˌ**morgaˈnatically** *adv*

Morgan le Fay (ˈmɔːgən lə ˈfeɪ) *or* **Morgain le Fay** ★ (ˈmɔːgaɪn, -gən) *n* a wicked sorceress of Arthurian legend, the half-sister of King Arthur.

morgen (ˈmɔːgən) *n* **1** a South African unit of area, equal to about two acres or 0.8 hectare. **2** a unit of area, formerly used in Prussia and Scandinavia, equal to about two thirds of an acre. ORIG C17: from Du.: morning, a morning's ploughing

morgue (mɔːg) *n* **1** another word for **mortuary. 2** *Inf.* a room or file containing clippings, etc., used for reference in a newspaper. ORIG C19: from F *le Morgue,* a Paris mortuary

moribund (ˈmɒrɪˌbʌnd) *adj* **1** near death. **2** without force or vitality. ORIG C18: from L, from *morī* to die
▸ ˌ**moriˈbundity** *n* ▸ ˈ**moriˌbundly** *adv*

Mörike ★ (*German* ˈmøːrɪkə) *n* **Eduard** (ˈeːduart). 1804–75, German poet, noted for his lyrics, such as *On a Winter's Morning before Sunrise* and *At Midnight.*

Morisco (məˈrɪskəʊ) *or* **Moresco** (məˈrɛskəʊ) *n, pl* **Moriscos** *or* **Moriscoes. 1** a Spanish Moor. **2** a morris dance. ◆ *adj* **3** another word for **Moorish;** see **Moor.** ORIG C16: from Sp., from *Moro* MOOR

morish (ˈmɔːrɪʃ) *adj* a variant spelling of **moreish.**

Morisot ★ (*French* mɔrizo) *n* **Berthe** (bɛrt). 1841–95, French impressionist painter.

Morley[1] ★ (ˈmɔːlɪ) *n* an industrial town in N England, in Leeds unitary authority West Yorkshire. Pop.: 47 579 (1991).

Morley[2] ★ (ˈmɔːlɪ) *n* **1 Edward Williams.** 1838–1923, US chemist who collaborated with A. A. Michelson in the Michelson-Morley experiment. **2 John,** Viscount Morley of Blackburn. 1838–1923, British Liberal statesman and writer; secretary of state for India (1905–10). **3 Robert.** 1908–92, British actor. His many films include *Oscar Wilde* (1960) and *The Blue Bird* (1976). **4 Thomas.** ?1557–?1603, English composer, noted for his madrigals and his textbook on music.

Mormon (ˈmɔːmən) *n* **1** a member of the Church of Jesus Christ of Latter-day Saints, founded in 1830 in New York by Joseph Smith. **2** a prophet whose supposed revelations were recorded by Joseph Smith in the Book of Mormon. ◆ *adj* **3** of or relating to the Mormons, their Church, or their beliefs.
▸ ˈ**Mormonism** *n*

morn (mɔːn) *n* a poetic word for **morning.** ORIG OE *morgen*

mornay (ˈmɔːneɪ) *adj* (*often immediately postpositive*) denoting a cheese sauce: *eggs mornay.* ORIG ? after Philippe de MORNAY

Mornay ★ (*French* mɔrnɛ) *n* **Philippe de** (filip də), Seigneur du Plessis-Marly. 1549–1623, French Huguenot leader. Also called: **Duplessis-Mornay** (dyplɛsimɔrnɛ).

morning (ˈmɔːnɪŋ) *n* **1** the first part of the day, ending at noon. **2** sunrise; daybreak; dawn. **3** the beginning or early period. **4 the morning after.** *Inf.* the aftereffects of excess, esp. a hangover. **5** (*modifier*) of, used in, or occurring in the morning: *morning coffee.* ORIG C13 *morwening,* from MORN, on the model of EVENING

morning-after pill *n* an oral contraceptive effective if taken within 72 hours after unprotected intercourse.

morning dress *n* formal day dress for men, comprising a cutaway frock coat (**morning coat**), usually with grey trousers and top hat.

morning-glory *n, pl* **morning-glories.** any of various mainly tropical plants of the convolvulus family, with trumpet-shaped blue, pink, or white flowers, which close in late afternoon.

mornings (ˈmɔːnɪŋz) *adv Inf.* in the morning, esp. regularly, or during every morning.

morning sickness *n* nausea occurring shortly after rising: a symptom of pregnancy.

morning star *n* a planet, usually Venus, seen just before sunrise. Also called: **daystar.**

Moro[1] ('mɔːrəʊ) *n* **1** (*pl* **Moros** *or* **Moro**) a member of a group of predominantly Muslim peoples of the S Philippines. **2** the language of these peoples. ORIG C19: via Sp. from L *Maurus* MOOR

Moro[2] ★ (*Italian* 'mɔːro) *n* **Aldo** ('aldo). 1916–78, Italian Christian Democrat statesman; prime minister of Italy (1963–68; 1974–76) and minister of foreign affairs (1965–66; 1969–72; 1973–74); kidnapped by the Red Brigades in 1978 and murdered.

morocco (mə'rɒkəʊ) *n* a fine soft leather made from goatskins, used for bookbinding, shoes, etc. ORIG C17: after MOROCCO, where it was orig. made

Morocco ★ (mə'rɒkəʊ) *n* a kingdom in NW Africa, on the Mediterranean and the Atlantic: conquered by the Arabs in about 683, who introduced Islam; at its height under Berber dynasties (11th–13th centuries); became a French protectorate in 1912 and gained independence in 1956. It is mostly mountainous, with the Atlas Mountains in the centre and the Rif range along the Mediterranean coast, with the Sahara in the south and southeast; an important exporter of phosphates. Official languages: Arabic; Berber and French are also widely spoken. Official religion: (Sunni) Muslim. Currency: dirham. Capital: Rabat. Pop.: 26 736 000 (1996). Area: 458 730 sq. km (177 117 sq. miles). French name: **Maroc.**
▸ **Moroccan** (mə'rɒkən) *adj, n*

moron ('mɔːrɒn) *n* **1** a foolish or stupid person. **2** a person having an intelligence quotient of between 50 and 70. ORIG C20: from Gk *mōros* foolish
▸ **moronic** (mə'rɒnɪk) *adj* ▸ **mo'ronically** *adv* ▸ **'moronism** *or* **mo'ronity** *n*

Moroni ★ (mə'rəʊnɪ; *French* mɔrɔni) *n* the capital of Comoros, on the island of Njazídja (Grande Comore). Pop.: 30 000 (1991).

morose (mə'rəʊs) *adj* ill-tempered or gloomy. ORIG C16: from L *mōrōsus* peevish, from *mōs* custom, will
▸ **mo'rosely** *adv* ▸ **mo'roseness** *n*

-morph *n combining form.* indicating shape, form, or structure of a specified kind: *ectomorph.* ORIG from Gk *-morphos,* from *morphē* shape
▸ **-morphic** *or* **-morphous** *adj combining form.* ▸ **-morphy** *n combining form.*

morpheme ('mɔːfiːm) *n Linguistics.* a speech element having a meaning or grammatical function that cannot be subdivided into further such elements. ORIG C20: from F, from Gk *morphē* form, on the model of PHONEME
▸ **mor'phemic** *adj* ▸ **mor'phemically** *adv*

Morpheus ★ ('mɔːfɪəs, -fjuːs) *n Greek myth.* the god of sleep and dreams.
▸ **'Morphean** *adj*

morphine ('mɔːfiːn) *or* **morphia** ('mɔːfɪə) *n* an alkaloid extracted from opium: used in medicine as an anaesthetic and sedative. ORIG C19: from F, from MORPHEUS

morphing ('mɔːfɪŋ) *n* a computer technique used for graphics and in films, in which one image is gradually transformed into another. ORIG C20: from METAMORPHOSIS

morphogenesis (ˌmɔːfəʊ'dʒɛnɪsɪs) *n* **1** the development of form in an organism during its growth. **2** the evolutionary development of form in an organism or part of an organism.
▸ **morphogenetic** (ˌmɔːfəʊdʒɪ'nɛtɪk) *adj*

morphology (mɔː'fɒlədʒɪ) *n* **1** the branch of biology concerned with the form and structure of organisms. **2** the form and structure of words in a language. **3** the form and structure of anything.
▸ **morphologic** (ˌmɔːfə'lɒdʒɪk) *or* **ˌmorpho'logical** *adj* ▸ **ˌmorpho'logically** *adv* ▸ **mor'phologist** *n*

Morphy ★ ('mɔːfɪ) *n* **Paul.** 1837–84, US chess player, widely considered to have been the world's greatest player.

Morris ★ ('mɒrɪs) *n* **William.** 1834–96, British Pre-Raphaelite painter, craftsman, and writer.

Morris chair *n* an armchair with an adjustable back. ORIG C19: after William MORRIS

morris dance *n* any of various old English folk dances usually performed by men (**morris men**) adorned with bells and often representing characters from folk tales. Often shortened to **morris.** ORIG C15 *moreys daunce* Moorish dance
▸ **morris dancing** *n*

Morrison ★ ('mɒrɪsᵊn) *n* **1 Herbert Stanley,** Baron Morrison of Lambeth. 1888–1965, British Labour statesman, Home Secretary and Minister for Home Security (1942–45). **2 Jim,** full name *James Douglas Morrison.* 1943–71, US rock singer and songwriter, lead vocalist with the Doors. **3 Toni.** full name *Chloe Anthony Morrison.* born 1931, US novelist: her works include *Sula* (1974) and *Jazz* (1992): Nobel prize for literature 1993. **4 Van,** full name *George Ivan Morrison.* born 1945, Northern Irish rock singer and songwriter: his albums include *Moondance* (1970) and *Too Long in Exile* (1993).

morro ('mɒrəʊ) *n, pl* **morros** (-rəʊz). a rounded hill or promontory. ORIG from Sp.

morrow ('mɒrəʊ) *n* (usually preceded by *the*) *Arch. or poetic.* **1** the next day. **2** the period following a specified event. **3** the morning. ORIG C13 *morwe,* from OE *morgen* morning

Mors ★ (mɔːz) *n* the Roman god of death. Greek counterpart: **Thanatos.**

Morse ★ (mɔːs) *n* **Samuel Finley Breese** ('fɪnlɪ briːz). 1791–1872, US inventor and painter. He invented the first electric telegraph and the Morse code.

Morse code *n* a telegraph code formerly used internationally for transmitting messages. Letters, numbers, etc., are represented by groups of shorter dots and longer dashes, or by groups of the corresponding sounds.

morsel ('mɔːsᵊl) *n* **1** a small slice or mouthful of food. **2** a small piece; bit. **3** *Irish inf.* a term of endearment for a child. ORIG C13: from OF, from *mors* a bite, from L *morsus,* from *mordēre* to bite

mortal ('mɔːtᵊl) *adj* **1** (of living beings, esp. human beings) subject to death. **2** of or involving life or the world. **3** ending in or causing death; fatal: *a mortal blow.* **4** deadly or unrelenting: *a mortal enemy.* **5** of or like the fear of death: *mortal terror.* **6** great or very intense: *mortal pain.* **7** conceivable or possible: *there was no mortal reason to go.* **8** *Sl.* long and tedious: *for three mortal hours.* ◆ *n* **9** a mortal being. **10** *Inf.* a person: *a mean mortal.* ORIG C14: from L *mortālis,* from *mors* death
▸ **'mortally** *adv*

mortality (mɔː'tælɪtɪ) *n, pl* **mortalities. 1** the condition of being mortal. **2** great loss of life, as in war or disaster. **3** the number of deaths in a given period. **4** mankind; humanity.

mortal sin *n Christianity.* a sin regarded as involving total loss of grace.

mortar ('mɔːtə) *n* **1** a mixture of cement or lime or both with sand and water, used as a bond between bricks or stones or as a covering on a wall. **2** a cannon having a short barrel and relatively wide bore that fires low-velocity shells in high trajectories. **3** a vessel, usually bowl-shaped, in which substances are pulverized with a pestle. ◆ *vb* (*tr*) **4** to join (bricks or stones) or cover (a wall) with mortar. **5** to fire on with mortars. ORIG C13: from L *mortārium* basin in which mortar is mixed; in some senses, via OF *mortier* substance mixed inside such a vessel

mortarboard ('mɔːtəˌbɔːd) *n* **1** a black tasselled academic cap with a flat square top. **2** a small square board with a handle on the underside for carrying mortar.

mortgage ('mɔːgɪdʒ) *n* **1** an agreement under which a person borrows money to buy property, esp. a house, and the lender may take possession of the property if the borrower fails to repay the money. **2** the deed affecting such an agreement. **3** the loan obtained under such an agreement: *a mortgage of £48,000.* **4** a regular payment of money borrowed under such an agreement: *a mortgage of £347 per month.* ◆ *vb* **mortgages, mortgaging, mortgaged.** (*tr*) **4** to convey (property) by mortgage. **5** *Inf.* to pledge. ORIG C14: from OF, lit.: dead pledge
▸ **'mortgageable** *adj*

mortgagee (ˌmɔːgɪ'dʒiː) *n Law.* the party to a mortgage who makes the loan.

mortgagor (ˌmɔːgɪ'dʒɔː) *or* **mortgager** *n Property law.* a

★ people and places

person who borrows money by mortgaging his or her property to the lender as security.

mortician (mɔːˈtɪʃən) *n Chiefly US.* another word for **undertaker.** ORIG C19: from MORTUARY + *-ician,* as in *physician*

mortification (ˌmɔːtɪfɪˈkeɪʃən) *n* **1** a feeling of humiliation. **2** something causing this. **3** *Christianity.* the practice of mortifying the senses. **4** another word for **gangrene.**

mortify (ˈmɔːtɪˌfaɪ) *vb* **mortifies, mortifying, mortified. 1** (*tr*) to humiliate or cause to feel shame. **2** (*tr*) *Christianity.* to subdue and bring under control by self-denial, disciplinary exercises, etc. **3** (*intr*) to undergo tissue death or become gangrenous. ORIG C14: via OF from Church L *mortificāre* to put to death, from L *mors* death + *facere* to do

▸ **ˈmortiˌfier** *n* ▸ **ˈmortiˌfying** *adj*

Mortimer ★ (ˈmɔːtɪmə) *n* **1** Sir **John (Clifford).** born 1923, British barrister and writer. His works include *The Dock Brief* (1958) and *The Sound of Trumpets* (1998); best known for the television series featuring the barrister Horace Rumpole. **2 Roger de,** 8th Baron of Wigmore and 1st Earl of March. 1287–1330, lover of Isabella, the wife of Edward II of England: they invaded England in 1326 and compelled the king to abdicate in favour of his son, Edward III; executed.

mortise *or* **mortice** (ˈmɔːtɪs) *n* **1** a slot or recess cut into a piece of wood, stone, etc., to receive a matching projection (tenon) of another piece, or a mortise lock. ◆ *vb* **mortises, mortising, mortised** *or* **mortices, morticing, morticed.** (*tr*) **2** to cut a slot or recess in (a piece of wood, stone, etc.). **3** to join (two pieces of wood, stone, etc.) by means of a mortise and tenon. ORIG C14: from OF *mortoise,* ?from Ar. *murtazza* fastened in position

mortise lock *n* a lock set into a mortise in a door so that the mechanism of the lock is enclosed by the door.

mortmain (ˈmɔːtˌmeɪn) *n Law.* the state or condition of lands, buildings, etc., held inalienably, as by an ecclesiastical or other corporation. ORIG C15: from OF *mortemain,* from Med. L *mortua manus* dead hand, inalienable ownership

Morton ★ (ˈmɔːtᵊn) *n* **Jelly Roll,** real name *Ferdinand Joseph La Menthe Morton.* 1885–1941, US jazz pianist and songwriter; one of the creators of New Orleans jazz.

mortuary (ˈmɔːtʃuərɪ) *n, pl* **mortuaries. 1** Also called: **morgue.** a building where dead bodies are kept before cremation or burial. ◆ *adj* **2** of or relating to death or burial. ORIG C14 (as n, a funeral gift to a parish priest): via Med. L *mortuārium* (n) from L *mortuārius* of the dead

morwong (ˈmɔːˌwɒŋ) *n* a food fish of Australasian coastal waters. ORIG from Abor.

moryah (mɒrˈjæ) *interj Irish.* an exclamation of annoyance, disbelief, etc. ORIG from Irish Gaelic *Mar dhea* forsooth

mosaic (məˈzeɪɪk) *n* **1** a design or decoration made up of small pieces of coloured glass, stone, etc. **2** the process of making a mosaic. **3a** a mottled yellowing that occurs in the leaves of plants affected with any of various virus diseases. **3b** Also called: **mosaic disease.** any of the diseases, such as **tobacco mosaic,** that produce this discoloration. **4** a light-sensitive surface on a television camera tube, consisting of a large number of granules of photoemissive material. ORIG C16: via F & It. from Med. L, from LGk: mosaic work, from Gk: of the Muses, from *mousa* MUSE

▸ **mosaicist** (məˈzeɪɪsɪst) *n*

Mosaic (məʊˈzeɪɪk) *adj* of or relating to Moses or the laws and traditions ascribed to him.

Mosaic law *n Bible.* the laws ascribed to Moses and contained in the Pentateuch.

moschatel (ˌmɒskəˈtɛl) *n* a small N temperate plant with greenish-white musk-scented flowers. Also called: **townhall clock, five-faced bishop.** ORIG C18: via F from It. *moscatella,* dim. of *moscato* MUSK

Moscow ★ (ˈmɒskəʊ) *n* the capital of Russia, on the Moskva River: dates from the 11th century; capital of the grand duchy of Russia from 1547 to 1712; capital of the Soviet Union (1918–91); centres on the medieval Kremlin; chief political, cultural, and industrial centre of Russia, with two universities. Pop.: 8 717 000 (1995 est.). Russian name: **Moskva.**

Moseley ★ (ˈməʊzlɪ) *n* **Henry Gwyn-Jeffreys.** 1887–1915, British physicist. He showed that the wavelengths of X-rays emitted from the elements are related to their atomic numbers.

Moselle ★ (məʊˈzɛl) *n* **1** a department of NE France, in Lorraine region. Capital: Metz. Pop.: 1 015 593 (1994 est.). Area: 6253 sq. km (2439 sq. miles). **2** a river in W Europe, rising in NE France and flowing northwest, forming part of the border between Luxembourg and Germany, then northeast to the Rhine: many vineyards along its lower course. Length: 547 km (340 miles). German name: **Mosel** (ˈmoːzᵊl). **3** (*sometimes not cap.*) a German white wine from the Moselle valley.

Moses ★ (ˈməʊzɪz) *n* **1** *Old Testament.* the Hebrew prophet who led the Israelites out of Egypt to the Promised Land and gave them divinely revealed laws. **2 Ed.** born 1956, US hurdler; winner of the 400 m hurdles in the 1976 and 1984 Olympic Games. **3 Grandma,** real name *Anna Mary Robertson Moses.* 1860–1961, US painter of primitives, who began to paint at the age of 75.

mosey (ˈməʊzɪ) *vb* (*intr*) *Inf.* (often foll. by *along* or *on*) to amble. ORIG C19: from ?

Moshesh (mɒˈʃɛʃ) *or* **Moshoeshoe** ★ (mɒˈʃuʃu) *n* died 1870, African chief, who founded the Basotho nation, now Lesotho.

Moskva ★ (*Russian* masˈkva) *n* **1** transliteration of the Russian name for **Moscow. 2** a river in W central Russia, rising in the Smolensk-Moscow upland, and flowing southeast through Moscow to the Oka River: linked with the River Volga by the Moscow Canal. Length: about 500 km (310 miles).

Moslem (ˈmɒzləm) *n, pl* **Moslems** *or* **Moslem.** *adj* a variant of **Muslim.**

▸ **Moslemic** (mɒzˈlɛmɪk) *adj* ▸ **ˈMoslemism** *n*

Mosley ★ (ˈməʊzlɪ) *n* Sir **Oswald Ernald.** 1896–1980, British politician; founder of the British Union of Fascists (1932).

mosque (mɒsk) *n* a Muslim place of worship. ORIG C14: earlier *mosquee,* from OF via It. *moschea,* ult. from Ar. *masjid* temple

mosquito (məˈskiːtəʊ) *n, pl* **mosquitoes** *or* **mosquitos.** any dipterous insect of the family Culicidae: the females have a long proboscis adapted for piercing the skin of man and animals to suck their blood. See also **aedes, anopheles, culex.** ORIG C16: from Sp., dim. of *mosca* fly, from L *musca*

mosquito net *or* **netting** *n* a fine curtain or net to keep mosquitoes out.

moss (mɒs) *n* **1** any of a class of plants, typically growing in dense mats on trees, rocks, moist ground, etc. **2** a clump or growth of any of these plants. **3** any of various similar but unrelated plants, such as Spanish moss and reindeer moss. **4** *Scot. & N English.* a peat bog or marsh. ORIG OE *mos* swamp

▸ **ˈmossˌlike** *adj* ▸ **ˈmossy** *adj* ▸ **ˈmossiness** *n*

Moss ★ (mɒs) *n* Sir **Stirling.** born 1929, British racing driver.

moss agate *n* a variety of chalcedony with dark greenish mossy markings.

mossie (ˈmɒsɪ) *n* another name for the **Cape sparrow.** ORIG Afrik.

mosso (ˈmɒsəʊ) *adv Music.* to be performed with rapidity. ORIG It., p.p. of *muovere* to MOVE

moss rose *n* a variety of rose that has a mossy stem and calyx and fragrant pink flowers.

moss stitch *n* a knitting stitch made up of alternate plain and purl stitches.

mosstrooper (ˈmɒsˌtruːpə) *n* a raider in the Borders of England and Scotland in the mid-17th century. ORIG C17 *moss,* in dialect sense: bog

most (məʊst) *determiner* **1a** a great majority of; nearly all: *most people like eggs.* **1b** (*as pron; functioning as sing or pl*): *most of them don't know; most of it is finished.* **2 the most. 2a** the superlative of **many** and **much:** *you have the most money; the most apples.* **2b** (*as pron*): *the most he can afford is two* *pounds.* **3 at (the) most.** at the maximum: *that girl is four at the most.* **4 make the most of.** to use to the best advantage: *she makes the most of her accent.* ◆ *adv* **5 the most.** used to form the superlative of some adjectives and adverbs: *he suffered the most terribly of all.* **6** the superlative of **much**: *people welcome a drink most after work.* **7** (intensifier): *a most absurd story.* ORIG OE *māst* or *mǣst,* whence ME *moste, mēst*

> **USAGE NOTE** *More* and *most* should be distinguished when used in comparisons. *More* applies to cases involving two people, objects, etc., *most* to cases involving three or more: *John is the more intelligent of the two; he is the most intelligent of the students.*

-most *suffix. forming the superlative degree of some adjectives and adverbs: hindmost; uppermost.* ORIG OE *-mǣst, -mest,* orig. a sup. suffix, later mistakenly taken as from *mǣst* (adv) most

Mostaganem ★ (mə͵stæɡəˈnɛm) *n* a port in NW Algeria, on the Mediterranean Sea: exports wine, fruit, and vegetables. Pop.: 107 000 (1987 est.).

mostly (ˈməʊstlɪ) *adv* **1** almost entirely; chiefly. **2** on many or most occasions; usually.

Most Reverend *n* (in Britain) a courtesy title applied to Anglican and Roman Catholic archbishops.

Mosul ★ (ˈməʊsᵊl) *n* a city in N Iraq, on the River Tigris opposite the ruins of Nineveh: an important commercial centre with nearby Ayn Zalah oilfield; university. Pop.: 664 221 (1987).

mot (məʊ) *n* short for **bon mot.** ORIG C16: via F from Vulgar L *mottum* (unattested) utterance, from L *muttum,* from *muttīre* to mutter

MOT *abbrev. for:* **1** (in New Zealand and formerly in Britain) Ministry of Transport (in Britain, now Department of Transport). **2** *Brit.* MOT test: a compulsory annual test for road vehicles over a certain age, which require a valid **MOT certificate.**

mote (məʊt) *n* a tiny speck. ORIG OE *mot*

motel (məʊˈtɛl) *n* a roadside hotel for motorists. ORIG C20: from *motor* + *hotel*

motet (məʊˈtɛt) *n* a polyphonic choral composition used as an anthem in the Roman Catholic service. ORIG C14: from OF, dim. of *mot* word; see MOT

moth (mɒθ) *n* any of numerous insects that typically have stout bodies with antennae of various shapes (but not clubbed), including large brightly coloured species, such as hawk moths, and small inconspicuous types, such as the clothes moths. Cf. **butterfly** (sense 1). ORIG OE *moththe*

mothball (ˈmɒθ͵bɔːl) *n* **1** a small ball of camphor or naphthalene used to repel clothes moths in stored clothing, etc. **2 put in mothballs.** to postpone work on (a project, activity, etc.). ◆ *vb* (*tr*) **3** to prepare (a ship) for a long period of storage by sealing with plastic. **4** to take (a factory, etc.) out of operation but maintain it for future use. **5** to postpone work on (a project, activity, etc.).

moth-eaten *adj* **1** decayed, decrepit, or outdated. **2** eaten away by or as if by moths.

mother[1] (ˈmʌðə) *n* **1a** a female who has given birth to offspring. **1b** (*as modifier*): *a mother bird.* **2** (*often cap., esp. as a term of address*) a person's own mother. **3** a female substituting in the function of a mother. **4** (*often cap.*) *Chiefly arch.* a term of address for an old woman. **5a** motherly qualities, such as maternal affection: *it appealed to the mother in her.* **5b** (*as modifier*): *mother love.* **5c** (*in combination*): *mothercraft.* **6a** a female or thing that creates, nurtures, protects, etc., something. **6b** (*as modifier*): *mother church; mother earth.* **7** a title given to certain members of female religious orders. **8** (*modifier*) native or innate: *mother wit.* **9 the mother of all...** *Inf.* the greatest example of its kind: *the mother of all parties.* ◆ *vb* (*tr*) **10** to give birth to or produce. **11** to nurture, protect, etc. as a mother. ORIG OE *mōdor*
▸ **ˈmotherless** *adj*

mother[2] (ˈmʌðə) *n* a stringy slime containing various bacteria that forms on the surface of liquids undergoing fermentation. Also called: **mother of vinegar.** ORIG C16: ?from MOTHER[1], but cf. Sp. *madre* scum, Du. *modder* dregs, MLow G *modder* decaying object, *mudde* sludge

Mother Carey's chicken (ˈkɛərɪz) *n* another name for **stormy petrel.** ORIG from ?

mother country *n* **1** the original country of colonists or settlers. **2** a person's native country.

Mother Goose *n* the imaginary author of a collection of nursery rhymes. ORIG C18: translated from F *Contes de ma mère l'Oye* (1697), a collection of tales by Charles PERRAULT

motherhood (ˈmʌðə͵hʊd) *n* **1** the state of being a mother. **2** the qualities characteristic of a mother.

Mothering Sunday (ˈmʌðərɪŋ) *n* another name for **Mother's Day** (sense 1).

mother-in-law *n, pl* **mothers-in-law.** the mother of one's wife or husband.

motherland (ˈmʌðə͵lænd) *n* a person's native country.

mother lode *n Mining.* the principal lode in a system.

motherly (ˈmʌðəlɪ) *adj* of or resembling a mother, esp. in warmth or protectiveness.
▸ **ˈmotherliness** *n*

mother-of-pearl *n* a hard iridescent substance that forms the inner layer of the shells of certain molluscs, such as the oyster. It is used to make buttons, etc. Also called: **nacre.**

Mother's Day *n* **1** Also called: **Mothering Sunday.** *Brit.* the fourth Sunday in Lent, when mothers traditionally receive presents from their children. **2** *US & Canad.* the second Sunday in May, observed as a day in honour of mothers.

mother ship *n* a ship providing facilities and supplies for a number of small vessels.

mother superior *n, pl* **mother superiors** *or* **mothers superior.** the head of a community of nuns.

mother tongue *n* **1** the language first learned by a child. **2** a language from which another has evolved.

Motherwell ★ (ˈmʌðəwəl) *n* a town in S central Scotland, the administrative centre of North Lanarkshire on the River Clyde: industrial centre. Pop.: 30 717 (1991).

mother wit *n* native practical intelligence; common sense.

mothproof (ˈmɒθ͵pruːf) *adj* **1** (esp. of clothes) chemically treated so as to repel clothes moths. ◆ *vb* **2** (*tr*) to make (clothes, etc.) mothproof.

mothy (ˈmɒθɪ) *adj* **mothier, mothiest. 1** moth-eaten. **2** containing moths; full of moths.

motif (məʊˈtiːf) *n* **1** a distinctive idea, esp. a theme elaborated on in a piece of music, literature, etc. **2** Also called: **motive.** a recurring shape in a design. **3** a single decoration, such as a symbol or name on a jumper, sweatshirt, etc. ORIG C19: from F; see MOTIVE

motile (ˈməʊtaɪl) *adj* capable of moving spontaneously and independently. ORIG C19: from L *mōtus* moved, from *movēre* to move
▸ **motility** (məʊˈtɪlɪtɪ) *n*

motion (ˈməʊʃən) *n* **1** the process of continual change in the physical position of an object; movement. **2** a movement or action, esp. of part of the human body; a gesture. **3a** the capacity for movement. **3b** a manner of movement, esp. walking; gait. **4** a mental impulse. **5** a formal proposal to be discussed and voted on in a debate, meeting, etc. **6** *Law.* an application made to a judge or court for an order or ruling necessary to the conduct of legal proceedings. **7** *Brit.* **7a** the evacuation of the bowels. **7b** excrement. **8a** part of a moving mechanism. **8b** the action of such a part. **9 go through the motions. 9a** to act or perform the task (of doing something) mechanically or without sincerity. **9b** to mimic the action (of something) by gesture. **10 in motion.** operational or functioning (often in **set in motion, set the wheels in motion**). ◆ *vb* **11** (when *tr, may take a clause as object or an infinitive*) to signal or direct (a person) by a movement or gesture. ORIG C15: from L *mōtiō* a moving, from *movēre* to move
▸ **ˈmotionless** *adj*

Motion ('məʊʃən) *n* **Andrew.** born 1952, British biographer and poet; his publications include *Pleasure Steamers* (1978) and *Of Salt Water* (1997); poet laureate from 1999.

motion picture *n* a US and Canad. term for **film** (sense 1).

motivate ('məʊtɪˌveɪt) *vb* **motivates, motivating, motivated.** (*tr*) to give incentive to.
▸ ˌ**moti'vation** *n* ▸ '**motiˌvator** *n*

motivational research (ˌməʊtɪ'veɪʃənᵊl) *n* the application of psychology to the study of consumer behaviour, esp. the planning of advertising and sales campaigns. Also called: **motivation research.**

motive ('məʊtɪv) *n* **1** the reason for a certain course of action, whether conscious or unconscious. **2** a variant of **motif** (sense 2). ◆ *adj* **3** of or causing motion: *a motive force.* **4** of or acting as a motive; motivating. ◆ *vb* **motives, motiving, motived.** (*tr*) **5** to motivate. ORIG C14: from OF *motif,* from LL *mōtīvus* (adj) moving, from L *mōtus,* p.p. of *movēre* to move
▸ '**motiveless** *adj*

motive power *n* **1** any source of energy used to produce motion. **2** the means of supplying power to an engine, vehicle, etc.

mot juste *French.* (mo ʒyst) *n, pl* ***mots justes*** (mo ʒyst). the appropriate word or expression.

motley ('mɒtlɪ) *adj* **1** made up of elements of varying type, quality, etc. **2** multicoloured. ◆ *n* **3** a motley collection. **4** the particoloured attire of a jester. ORIG C14: ?from *mot* speck

moto ('məʊtəʊ) *n Music.* movement. ORIG It.

motocross ('məʊtəˌkrɒs) *n* **1** cross-country motorcycle racing across rough ground. **2** another name for **rallycross.** ORIG C20: from MOTO(R) + CROSS(-COUNTRY)

motor ('məʊtə) *n* **1a** the engine, esp. an internal-combustion engine, of a vehicle. **1b** (*as modifier*): *a motor scooter.* **2** Also called: **electric motor.** a machine that converts electrical energy into mechanical energy. **3** any device that converts another form of energy into mechanical energy to produce motion. **4a** *Chiefly Brit.* a car. **4b** (*as modifier*): *motor spares.* ◆ *adj* **5** producing or causing motion. **6** *Physiol.* **6a** of or relating to nerves or neurons that carry impulses that cause muscles to contract. **6b** of or relating to movement or to muscles that induce movement. ◆ *vb* **7** (*intr*) to travel by car. **8** (*tr*) *Brit.* to transport by car. **9** (*intr*) *Inf.* to move fast; make good progress. ORIG C16: from L *mōtor* a mover, from *movēre* to move

motorbicycle ('məʊtəˌbaɪsɪkᵊl) *n* **1** a motorcycle. **2** a moped.

motorbike ('məʊtəˌbaɪk) *n* a less formal name for **motorcycle.**

motorboat ('məʊtəˌbəʊt) *n* any boat powered by a motor.

motorbus ('məʊtəˌbʌs) *n* a bus driven by an internal-combustion engine.

motorcade ('məʊtəˌkeɪd) *n* a parade of cars. ORIG C20: from MOTOR + CAVALCADE

motorcar ('məʊtəˌkɑː) *n* **1** a more formal word for **car. 2** a self-propelled electric railway car.

motorcycle ('məʊtəˌsaɪkᵊl) *n* **1** Also called: **motorbike.** a two-wheeled vehicle that is driven by a petrol engine. ◆ *vb* **motorcycles, motorcycling, motorcycled.** (*intr*) **2** to ride on a motorcycle.
▸ '**motorˌcyclist** *n*

motorist ('məʊtərɪst) *n* a driver of a car.

motorize *or* **motorise** ('məʊtəˌraɪz) *vb* **motorizes, motorizing, motorized** *or* **motorises, motorising, motorised.** (*tr*) **1** to equip with a motor. **2** to provide (military units) with motor vehicles.
▸ ˌ**motori'zation** *or* ˌ**motori'sation** *n*

motorman ('məʊtəmən) *n, pl* **motormen. 1** the driver of an electric train. **2** the operator of a motor.

motormouth ('məʊtəˌmaʊθ) *n Sl.* a garrulous person.

motor scooter *n* a light motorcycle with small wheels and an enclosed engine. Often shortened to **scooter.**

motor vehicle *n* a road vehicle driven esp. by an internal-combustion engine.

motorway ('məʊtəˌweɪ) *n Brit., Austral., & NZ.* a main road for fast-moving traffic, having separate carriageways for vehicles travelling in opposite directions.

Motown ('məʊˌtaʊn) *n Trademark.* music combining rhythm and blues and pop, or gospel rhythms and modern ballad harmony. ORIG C20: from *Motown Records* of Detroit, from *Mo(tor) Town,* nickname for Detroit, centre of the US car industry

motte (mɒt) *n History.* a mound on which a castle was erected. ORIG C14: see MOAT

MOT test *n* (in Britain) See **MOT** (sense 2).

mottle ('mɒtᵊl) *vb* **mottles, mottling, mottled. 1** (*tr*) to colour with streaks or blotches of different shades. ◆ *n* **2** a mottled appearance, as of the surface of marble. ORIG C17: back formation from MOTLEY
▸ '**mottled** *adj*

motto ('mɒtəʊ) *n, pl* **mottoes** *or* **mottos. 1** a short saying expressing the guiding maxim or ideal of a family, organization, etc., esp. when part of a coat of arms. **2** a verse or maxim contained in a paper cracker. **3** a quotation prefacing a book or chapter of a book. ORIG C16: via It. from L *muttum* utterance

moue *French.* (mu) *n* a pouting look.

moufflon ('muːflɒn) *n* a wild short-fleeced mountain sheep of Corsica and Sardinia. ORIG C18: via F from Romance *mufrone,* from LL *mufrō*

mouillé ('mwiːeɪ) *adj Phonetics.* palatalized, as in the sounds represented by Spanish *ll* or *ñ,* (pronounced as (ʎ) and (ɲ)), or French *ll* (representing a (j) sound). ORIG C19: from F, p.p. of *mouiller* to moisten, from L *mollis* soft

moujik ('muːʒɪk) *n* a variant spelling of **muzhik.**

mould[1] *or US* **mold** (məʊld) *n* **1** a shaped cavity used to give a definite form to fluid or plastic material. **2** a frame on which something may be constructed. **3** something shaped in or made on a mould. **4** a shape, form, design, or pattern. **5** a specific nature, character, or type. ◆ *vb* (*tr*) **6** to make in a mould. **7** to shape or form, as by using a mould. **8** to influence or direct: *to mould opinion.* **9** to cling to: *the skirt moulds her figure.* **10** *Metallurgy.* to make (a material) into a mould used in casting. ORIG C13 (n): from OF *modle,* from L *modulus* a small measure
▸ '**mouldable** *or US* '**moldable** *adj* ▸ '**moulder** *or US* '**molder** *n*

mould[2] *or US* **mold** (məʊld) *n* **1** a coating or discoloration caused by various fungi that develop in a damp atmosphere on the surface of food, fabrics, etc. **2** any of the fungi that cause this growth. ◆ *vb* **3** to become or cause to become covered with this growth. ◆ Also called: **mildew.** ORIG C15: dialect (N English) *mowlde* mouldy, from p.p. of *moulen* to become mouldy, prob. from ON

mould[3] *or US* **mold** (məʊld) *n* loose soil, esp. when rich in organic matter. ORIG OE *molde*

mouldboard *or US* **moldboard** ('məʊldˌbɔːd) *n* the curved blade of a plough, which turns over the furrow.

moulder *or US* **molder** ('məʊldə) *vb* (often foll. by *away*) to crumble or cause to crumble, as through decay. ORIG C16: verbal use of MOULD[3]

moulding *or US* **molding** ('məʊldɪŋ) *n* **1** *Archit.* **1a** a shaped outline, esp. one used on cornices, etc. **1b** a shaped strip made of wood, stone, etc. **2** something moulded.

mouldy *or US* **moldy** ('məʊldɪ) *adj* **mouldier, mouldiest** *or US* **moldier, moldiest. 1** covered with mould. **2** stale or musty, esp. from age or lack of use. **3** *Sl.* boring; dull.
▸ '**mouldiness** *or US* '**moldiness** *n*

Moulin ★ (*French* mulɛ̃) *n* **Jean** (ʒɑ̃). 1899–1943, French lawyer and Resistance hero; Chairman of the National Council of the Resistance (1943): tortured to death by the Nazis.

Moulins ★ (*French* mulɛ̃) *n* a market town in central France, on the Allier River. Pop.: 25 548 (1982).

Moulmein *or* **Maulmain** ★ (maʊl'meɪn) *n* a port in S Myanmar, near the mouth of the Salween River: exports teak and rice. Pop.: 23 350 (1990).

moult *or US* **molt** (məʊlt) *vb* **1** (of birds, mammals, arthropods, etc.) to shed (feathers, hair, or cuticle) in order that new growth can take place. ◆ *n* **2** the periodic process of moulting. ORIG C14 *mouten,* from OE *mūtian,* as in *bimūtian* to exchange for, from L *mūtāre* to change
▸ **'moulter** *or US* **'molter** *n*

mound (maʊnd) *n* **1** a raised mass of earth, debris, etc. **2** any heap or pile. **3** a small natural hill. **4** an artificial ridge of earth, stone, etc., as used for defence. ◆ *vb* **5** (often foll. by *up*) to gather into a mound; heap. **6** (*tr*) to cover or surround with a mound: *to mound a grave.* ORIG C16: earthwork, ?from OE *mund* hand, hence defence

Mound Builder *n* a member of a group of prehistoric inhabitants of the Mississippi region of the US, who built altar mounds, barrows, etc.

mound-builder *n* another name for **megapode.**

mount[1] (maʊnt) *vb* **1** to go up (a hill, stairs, etc.); climb. **2** to get up on (a horse, a platform, etc.). **3** (*intr;* often foll. by *up*) to increase; accumulate: *excitement mounted.* **4** (*tr*) to fix onto a backing, setting, or support: *to mount a photograph; to mount a slide.* **5** (*tr*) to provide with a horse for riding, or to place on a horse. **6** (of male animals) to climb onto (a female animal) for copulation. **7** (*tr*) to prepare (a play, etc.) for production. **8** (*tr*) to plan and organize (a campaign, etc.). **9** (*tr*) to prepare (a skeleton, etc.) for exhibition as a specimen. **10** (*tr*) to place or carry (weapons) in such a position that they can be fired. **11** **mount guard.** See **guard.** ◆ *n* **12** a backing, setting, or support onto which something is fixed. **13** the act or manner of mounting. **14** a horse for riding. **15** a slide used in microscopy. ORIG C16: from OF *munter,* from Vulgar L *montāre* (unattested) from L *mons* MOUNT[2]
▸ **'mountable** *adj* ▸ **'mounter** *n*

mount[2] (maʊnt) *n* a mountain or hill: used in literature and (when cap.) in proper names: *Mount Everest.* ORIG OE *munt,* from L *mons* mountain, but infl. in ME by OF *mont*

mountain ('maʊntɪn) *n* **1a** a natural upward projection of the earth's surface, higher and steeper than a hill. **1b** (*as modifier*): *mountain scenery.* **1c** (*in combination*): *a mountaintop.* **2** a huge heap or mass: *a mountain of papers.* **3** anything of great quantity or size. **4** a surplus of a commodity, esp. in the European Union: *a butter mountain.* ORIG C13: from OF *montaigne,* ult. from L *montānus,* from *mons* mountain

mountain ash *n* **1** any of various trees, such as the European mountain ash or rowan, having clusters of small white flowers and bright red berries. **2** any of several Australian eucalyptus trees, such as *Eucalyptus regnans.*

mountain avens *n* See **avens** (sense 2).

mountain bike *n* a type of sturdy bicycle with at least 16 gears, straight handlebars, and heavy-duty tyres.

mountain cat *n* any of various wild feline mammals, such as the bobcat, lynx, or puma.

mountaineer (ˌmaʊntɪ'nɪə) *n* **1** a person who climbs mountains. **2** a person living in a mountainous area. ◆ *vb* **3** (*intr*) to climb mountains.
▸ **ˌmountain'eering** *n*

mountain goat *n* any wild goat inhabiting mountainous regions.

mountain laurel *n* any of various ericaceous shrubs or trees of E North America having leathery poisonous leaves and clusters of pink or white flowers. Also called: **calico bush.**

mountain lion *n* another name for **puma.**

mountainous ('maʊntɪnəs) *adj* **1** of or relating to mountains: *a mountainous region.* **2** like a mountain, esp. in size or impressiveness.

mountain sickness *n* nausea, headache, and shortness of breath caused by climbing to high altitudes. Also called: **altitude sickness.**

Mountbatten ★ (maʊnt'bæt^ən) *n* **Louis (Francis Albert Victor Nicholas)**, 1st Earl Mountbatten of Burma. 1900–79, British naval commander; great-grandson of Queen Victoria. During World War II he was supreme allied commander in SE Asia (1943–46). He was the last viceroy of India (1947) and governor general (1947–48); killed by an IRA bomb.

Mount Desert Island ★ *n* an island off the coast of Maine: lakes and granite peaks. Area: 279 sq. km (108 sq. miles).

mountebank ('maʊntɪˌbæŋk) *n* **1** (formerly) a person who sold quack medicines in public places. **2** a charlatan; fake. ◆ *vb* **3** (*intr*) to play the mountebank. ORIG C16: from It. *montambanco* a climber on a bench, from *montare* to MOUNT[1] + *banco* BENCH
▸ **ˌmounte'bankery** *n*

mounted ('maʊntɪd) *adj* **1** riding horses: *mounted police.* **2** provided with a support, backing, etc.

Mountie *or* **Mounty** ('maʊntɪ) *n, pl* **Mounties.** *Inf.* a member of the Royal Canadian Mounted Police. ORIG from MOUNTED

mounting ('maʊntɪŋ) *n* another word for **mount**[1] (sense 12).

mounting-block *n* a block of stone formerly used to aid a person when mounting a horse.

Mount Isa ★ ('aɪzə) *n* a city in NE Australia in NW Queensland: mining of copper and other minerals. Pop.: 24 104 (1988 est.).

Mount McKinley National Park ★ *n* a national park in S central Alaska: contains part of the Alaska Range. Area: 7847 sq. km (3030 sq. miles).

Mount Rainier National Park ★ *n* a national park in W Washington, in the Cascade Range. Area: 976 sq. km (377 sq. miles).

mourn (mɔːn) *vb* **1** to feel or express sadness for the death or loss of (someone or something). **2** (*intr*) to observe the customs of mourning, as by wearing black. ORIG OE *murnan*
▸ **'mourner** *n*

mournful ('mɔːnfʊl) *adj* **1** evoking grief; sorrowful. **2** gloomy; sad.
▸ **'mournfully** *adv* ▸ **'mournfulness** *n*

mourning ('mɔːnɪŋ) *n* **1** the act or feelings of one who mourns; grief. **2** the conventional symbols of grief, such as the wearing of black. **3** the period of time during which a death is officially mourned. ◆ *adj* **4** of or relating to mourning.
▸ **'mourningly** *adv*

mourning band *n* a piece of black material, esp. an armband, worn to indicate mourning.

mourning dove *n* a brown North American dove with a plaintive song.

mouse *n* (maʊs), *pl* **mice** (maɪs). **1** any of numerous small long-tailed rodents that are similar to but smaller than rats. See also **fieldmouse, harvest mouse, house mouse.** **2** any of various related rodents, such as the jumping mouse. **3** a quiet, timid, or cowardly person. **4** *Computing.* a hand-held device used to control cursor movements and computing functions without keying. **5** *Sl.* a black eye. ◆ *vb* (maʊz), **mouses, mousing, moused.** **6** to stalk and catch (mice, etc.). **7** (*intr*) to go about stealthily. ORIG OE *mūs*
▸ **'mouseˌlike** *adj*

mouser ('maʊzə, 'maʊsə) *n* a cat or other animal that is used to catch mice.

mousetrap ('maʊsˌtræp) *n* **1** any trap for catching mice, esp. one with a spring-loaded metal bar that is released by the taking of the bait. **2** *Brit. inf.* cheese of indifferent quality.

moussaka *or* **mousaka** (mʊ'sɑːkə) *n* a dish originating in the Balkan States, consisting of meat, aubergines, and tomatoes, topped with cheese sauce. ORIG C20: from Mod. Gk

mousse (muːs) *n* **1** a light creamy dessert made with eggs, cream, fruit, etc., set with gelatine. **2** a similar dish made from fish or meat. **3** short for **styling mousse.** ORIG C19: from F: froth

mousseline (*French* muslin) *n* **1** a fine fabric made of rayon or silk. **2** a type of fine glass. ORIG C17: F: MUSLIN

Moussorgsky ★ (mʊ'sɔːgskɪ; *Russian* 'musərkskij) *n* a variant spelling of (Modest Petrovich) **Mussorgsky.**

moustache *or US* **mustache** (mə'stɑːʃ) *n* **1** the

unshaved growth of hair on the upper lip. **2** a similar growth of hair or bristles (in animals). **3** a mark like a moustache. ORIG C16: via F from It. *mostaccio*, ult. from Doric Gk *mustax* upper lip
▸ **mous'tached** *or US* **mus'tached** *adj*

moustache cup *n* a cup with a partial cover to protect a drinker's moustache.

Mousterian (mu:'stɪərɪən) *n* **1** a culture characterized by flint flake tools and associated with Neanderthal man, dating from before 70 000–32 000 B.C. ◆ *adj* **2** of or relating to this culture. ORIG C20: from F *moustérien*, from archaeological finds of the same period in the cave of *Le Moustier*, Dordogne, France

mousy *or* **mousey** ('maʊsɪ) *adj* **mousier, mousiest. 1** resembling a mouse, esp. in hair colour. **2** shy or ineffectual. **3** infested with mice.
▸ **'mousily** *adv* ▸ **'mousiness** *n*

mouth *n* (maʊθ), *pl* **mouths** (maʊðz). **1** the opening through which many animals take in food and issue vocal sounds. **2** the system of organs surrounding this opening, including the lips, tongue, teeth, etc. **3** the visible part of the lips on the face. **4** a person regarded as a consumer of food: *four mouths to feed*. **5** a particular manner of speaking: *a foul mouth*. **6** *Inf.* boastful, rude, or excessive talk: *he is all mouth*. **7** the point where a river issues into a sea or lake. **8** the opening of a container, such as a jar. **9** the opening of a cave, tunnel, volcano, etc. **10** that part of the inner lip of a horse on which the bit acts. **11** a pout; grimace. **12 down in** *or* **at the mouth.** in low spirits. ◆ *vb* (maʊð). **13** to speak or say (something) insincerely, esp. in public. **14** (*tr*) to form (words) with movements of the lips but without speaking. **15** (*tr*) to take (something) into the mouth or to move (something) around inside the mouth. **16** (*intr*; usually foll. by *at*) to make a grimace. ORIG OE *mūth*
▸ **mouther** ('maʊðə) *n*

mouthful ('maʊθ,fʊl) *n, pl* **mouthfuls. 1** as much as is held in the mouth at one time. **2** a small quantity, as of food. **3** a long word or phrase that is difficult to say. **4** *Brit. inf.* an abusive response.

mouth organ *n* another name for **harmonica.**

mouthpart ('maʊθ,pɑ:t) *n* any of the paired appendages in arthropods that surround the mouth and are specialized for feeding.

mouthpiece ('maʊθ,pi:s) *n* **1** the part of a wind instrument into which the player blows. **2** the part of a telephone receiver into which a person speaks. **3** the part of a container forming its mouth. **4** a person who acts as a spokesman, as for an organization. **5** a publication expressing the official views of an organization.

mouthwash ('maʊθ,wɒʃ) *n* a medicated solution for gargling and cleansing the mouth.

mouthy ('maʊðɪ) *adj* **mouthier, mouthiest.** bombastic; excessively talkative.

mouton ('mu:tɒn) *n* sheepskin processed to resemble the fur of another animal, esp. beaver or seal. ORIG from F: sheep

movable *or* **moveable** ('mu:vəbᵊl) *adj* **1** able to be moved; not fixed. **2** (esp. of Easter) varying in date from year to year. **3** (usually spelt **moveable**) *Law.* denoting or relating to personal property as opposed to realty. ◆ *n* **4** (*often pl*) a movable article, esp. a piece of furniture.
▸ **,mova'bility** *or* **'movableness** *n* ▸ **'movably** *adv*

move (mu:v) *vb* **moves, moving, moved. 1** to go or take from one place to another; change in position. **2** (*usually intr*) to change (one's dwelling, place of business, etc.). **3** to be or cause to be in motion; stir. **4** (*intr*) (of machines, etc.) to work or operate. **5** (*tr*) to cause (to do something); prompt. **6** (*intr*) to begin to act: *move soon or we'll lose the order*. **7** (*intr*) to associate oneself with a specified social circle: *to move in exalted spheres*. **8** (*intr*) to make progress. **9** (*tr*) to arouse affection, pity, or compassion in; touch. **10** (in board games) to change the position of (a piece) or (of a piece) to change position. **11** (*intr*) (of merchandise) to be disposed of by being bought. **12** (when *tr, often takes a clause as object;* when *intr*, often foll. by *for*) to suggest (a proposal) formally, as in debating or parliamentary procedure. **13** (*intr;* usually foll. by *on* or *along*) to go away or to another place; leave. **14** to cause (the bowels) to evacuate or (of the bowels) to be evacuated. ◆ *n* **15** the act of moving; movement. **16** one of a sequence of actions, usually part of a plan; manoeuvre. **17** the act of moving one's residence, place of business, etc. **18** (in board games) **18a** a player's turn to move his or her piece. **18b** a manoeuvre of a piece. **19 get a move on.** *Inf.* **19a** to get started. **19b** to hurry up. **20 on the move. 20a** travelling from place to place. **20b** advancing; succeeding. **20c** very active; busy. ORIG C13: from Anglo-F *mover*, from L *movēre*

move in *vb* (*mainly adv*) **1** (*also prep*) Also (when *prep*): **move into.** to occupy or take possession of (a new residence, place of business, etc.). **2** (*intr;* often foll. by *on*) *Inf.* to creep close (to), as in preparing to capture. **3** (*intr;* often foll. by *on*) *Inf.* to try to gain power or influence (over).

movement ('mu:vmənt) *n* **1a** the act, process, or result of moving. **1b** an instance of moving. **2** the manner of moving. **3a** a group of people with a common ideology. **3b** the organized action of such a group. **4** a trend or tendency. **5** the driving and regulating mechanism of a watch or clock. **6** (*often pl*) a person's location and activities during a specific time. **7a** the evacuation of the bowels. **7b** the matter evacuated. **8** *Music.* a principal self-contained section of a symphony, sonata, etc. **9** tempo or pace, as in music or literature. **10** *Fine arts.* the appearance of motion in painting, sculpture, etc. **11** *Prosody.* the rhythmic structure of verse. **12** a positional change by one or a number of military units. **13** a change in the market price of a security or commodity.

mover ('mu:və) *n* **1** *Inf.* a person, business, idea, etc., that is advancing or progressing. **2** a person or thing that moves. **3** a person who moves a proposal, as in a debate. **4** *US & Canad.* a removal firm or a person who works for one.

movers and shakers *pl n Inf.* the people with power and influence in a particular field of activity. ORIG C20: ? from the line "We are the movers and shakers of the world for ever" in 'Ode' by Arthur O'Shaughnessy (1844–81), Brit. poet

movie ('mu:vɪ) *n* **a** an informal word for **film** (sense 1). **b** (*as modifier*): *movie ticket.*

moving ('mu:vɪŋ) *adj* **1** arousing or touching the emotions. **2** changing or capable of changing position. **3** causing motion.
▸ **'movingly** *adv*

moving staircase *or* **stairway** *n* less common terms for **escalator** (sense 1).

mow (məʊ) *vb* **mows, mowing, mowed; mowed** *or* **mown. 1** to cut down (grass, crops, etc.), with a hand implement or machine. **2** (*tr*) to cut the growing vegetation of (a field, lawn, etc.). ORIG OE *māwan*
▸ **'mower** *n*

mow down *vb* (*tr, adv*) to kill in large numbers, esp. by gunfire.

Mowlam ★ ('məʊlæm) *n* **Mo**, full name *Marjorie Mowlam.* born 1949, British Labour politician; secretary of state for Northern Ireland (1997–99).

mown (məʊn) *vb* the past participle of **mow.**

Moya ★ ('mɔɪjə) *n* (**John**) **Hidalgo.** 1920–94, British architect.

Moyle ★ (mɔɪl) *n* a district of N Northern Ireland, on the North Channel and including Rathlin Island: tourism, agriculture. Administrative centre: Ballycastle. Pop.: 14 789 (1991). Area: 494 sq. km (191 sq. miles).

Mozambique ★ (,məʊzəm'bi:k) *n* a republic in SE Africa: colonized by the Portuguese from 1505 onwards and a slave-trade centre until 1878; made an overseas province of Portugal in 1951; became an independent republic in 1975; joined the Commonwealth in 1995. Official language: Portuguese. Religion: animist majority. Currency: metical. Capital: Maputo. Pop.: 19 124 000 (1999 est.). Area: 812 379 sq. km (313 661 sq. miles). Portuguese name: **Moçambique.** Also called (until 1975): **Portuguese East Africa.**

Mozambique Channel ★ *n* a strait between Mozambique and Madagascar. Length: about 1600 km (1000 miles). Width: 400 km (250 miles).

Mozart ★ (ˈməʊtsɑːt) *n* **Wolfgang Amadeus** (ˈvɔlfgaŋ amaˈdeːʊs). 1756–91, composer born in Salzburg. A child prodigy, his works include operas, such as *The Marriage of Figaro* (1786) and *The Magic Flute* (1791), symphonies, concertos, chamber music, sonatas, songs, and Masses, such as the unfinished *Requiem* (1791).
▸ **Moˈzartean** *or* **Moˈzartian** *adj*

mozzarella (ˌmɒtsəˈrɛlə) *n* a moist white curd cheese originally made in Italy from buffalo milk. ORIG from It., dim. of *mozza* a type of cheese, from *mozzare* to cut off

mp **1** *abbrev. for* melting point. **2** *Music. symbol for* mezzo piano. ORIG It.: moderately soft

MP *abbrev. for:* **1** (in Britain, Canada, etc.) Member of Parliament. **2** (in Britain) Metropolitan Police. **3** Military Police. **4** Mounted Police.

MP3 (ˈɛmˈpiːˈθriː) *n Computing.* **a** a format used for the digital compression of audio files without loss of sound quality, used extensively on the World Wide Web. **b** an audio file held in this format. ORIG C20: from MP(EG, *Audio Layer-)3*

MPEG (ˈɛmˌpɛg) *n Computing.* **a** a standard compressed file format used for audio and video files. **b** a file in this format. **c** (*as modifier*): *an MPEG video.* ORIG C20: technique devised by the *M(otion) P(icture) E(xperts) G(roup)*

mpg *abbrev. for* miles per gallon.

mph *abbrev. for* miles per hour.

MPhil *or* **MPh** *abbrev. for* Master of Philosophy.

MPP (in Canada) *abbrev. for* Member of Provincial Parliament.

Mpumalanga ★ (ᵊmˈpʌmɑːˌlɑːngə) *n* a province of E South Africa. Capital: Nelspruit. Pop.: 3 007 100 (1995 est.). Area: 78 370 sq. km (30 259 sq. miles).

MPV *abbrev. for* multipurpose vehicle.

Mr (ˈmɪstə) *n, pl* **Messrs.** a title used before a man's name or before some office that he holds: *Mr Jones; Mr President.* ORIG C17: abbrev. of MISTER

MR *abbrev. for:* **1** (in Britain) Master of the Rolls. **2** motivation(al) research.

MRC (in Britain) *abbrev. for* Medical Research Council.

MRI *abbrev. for* magnetic resonance imaging.

m-RNA *abbrev. for* messenger RNA.

MRP *abbrev. for* manufacturers' recommended price.

Mrs (ˈmɪsɪz) *n, pl* **Mrs** *or* **Mesdames.** a title used before the name or names of a married woman. ORIG C17: orig. abbrev. of MISTRESS

MRSA *abbrev. for* methicillin-resistant *Staphylococcus aureus*: a bacterium that enters the skin through open wounds to cause septicaemia and is extremely resistant to most antibiotics. It has been responsible for outbreaks of untreatable infections among patients in hospitals.

Ms (mɪz, məs) *n* a title substituted for **Mrs** or **Miss** to avoid making a distinction between married and unmarried women.

MS *abbrev. for:* **1** Master of Surgery. **2** (on gravestones, etc.) memoriae sacrum. ORIG L: sacred to the memory of **3** multiple sclerosis.

MS. *or* **ms.** *pl* **MSS.** *or* **mss.** *abbrev. for* manuscript.

MSc *abbrev. for* Master of Science.

MS-DOS (ɛmˈɛsˈdɒs) *n Trademark, computing.* a type of disk operating system. ORIG C20: from *M(icro)s(oft)*, the company that developed it, + DOS

MSF (in Britain) *abbrev. for* Manufacturing, Science, and Finance Union.

MSG *abbrev. for* monosodium glutamate.

Msgr *abbrev. for* Monsignor.

MSP *abbrev. for* Member of the Scottish Parliament.

MST *abbrev. for* Mountain Standard Time.

Mt *or* **mt** *abbrev. for:* **1** mount: *Mt Everest.* **2** Also: **mtn.** mountain.

MT *abbrev. for* Montana.

MTech *abbrev. for* Master of Technology.

mtg *abbrev. for:* **1** meeting. **2** Also: **mtge.** mortgage.

MTV *abbrev. for* music television: a US music channel that operates 24 hours a day.

mu (mjuː) *n* the 12th letter in the Greek alphabet (Μ, μ).

Mubarak ★ (mʊˈbɑːrək) *n* (**Muhammad**) **Hosni** (ˈhʊsnɪ). born 1928, Egyptian statesman; president of Egypt from 1981.

much (mʌtʃ) *determiner* **1a** (*usually used with a negative*) a great quantity or degree of: *there isn't much honey left.* **1b** (*as pron*): *much has been learned from this.* **2 a bit much.** *Inf.* rather excessive. **3 make much of. 3a** (*used with a negative*) to make sense of: *he couldn't make much of her babble.* **3b** to give importance to: *she made much of this fact.* **3c** to pay flattering attention to: *the reporters made much of the film star.* **4 not much of.** not to any appreciable degree or extent: *he's not much of an actor really.* **5 not up to much.** *Inf.* of a low standard: *this beer is not up to much.* ◆ *adv* **6** considerably: *they're much better now.* **7** practically; nearly (esp. in **much the same**). **8** (*usually used with a negative*) often; a great deal: *it doesn't happen much in this country.* **9** (**as**) **much as.** even though; although: *much as I'd like to, I can't come.* ◆ See also **more, most.** ORIG OE *mycel*

muchness (ˈmʌtʃnɪs) *n* **1** *Arch. or inf.* magnitude. **2 much of a muchness.** *Brit.* very similar.

mucilage (ˈmjuːsɪlɪdʒ) *n* **1** a sticky preparation, such as gum or glue, used as an adhesive. **2** a complex glutinous carbohydrate secreted by certain plants. ORIG C14: via OF from LL *mūcilāgo* mouldy juice, from L, from *mucēre* to be mouldy
▸ **mucilaginous** (ˌmjuːsɪˈlædʒɪnəs) *adj*

muck (mʌk) *n* **1** farmyard dung or decaying vegetable matter. **2** an organic soil rich in humus and used as a fertilizer. **3** dirt or filth. **4** *Sl., chiefly Brit.* rubbish. **5 make a muck of.** *Sl., chiefly Brit.* to ruin or spoil. ◆ *vb* (*tr*) **6** to spread manure upon (fields, etc.). **7** to soil or pollute. **8** (usually foll. by *up*) *Brit. sl.* to ruin or spoil. **9** (often foll. by *out*) to clear muck from. ORIG C13: prob. from ON
▸ **ˈmucky** *adj*

muck about *vb Brit. sl.* **1** (*intr*) to waste time; misbehave. **2** (when *intr,* foll. by *with*) to interfere (with), annoy, or waste the time (of).

mucker (ˈmʌkə) *n Brit. sl.* **a** a friend; mate. **b** a coarse person.
▸ **ˈmuckerish** *adj*

muck in *vb* (*intr, adv*) *Brit. sl.* to share duties, work, etc. (with other people).

muckrake (ˈmʌkˌreɪk) *vb* **muckrakes, muckraking, muckraked.** (*intr*) to seek out and expose scandal, esp. concerning public figures.
▸ **ˈmuckˌraker** *n* ▸ **ˈmuckˌraking** *n*

mucksweat (ˈmʌkˌswɛt) *n Brit. inf.* profuse sweat or a state of profuse sweating.

mucous (ˈmjuːkəs) *adj* of, resembling, or secreting mucus. ORIG C17: from L *mūcōsus* slimy, from MUCUS
▸ **mucosity** (mjuːˈkɒsɪtɪ) *n*

> **USAGE NOTE** The noun *mucus* is often misspelt *mucous. Mucous* can only be correctly used as an adjective.

mucous membrane *n* a mucus-secreting membrane that lines body cavities or passages that are open to the external environment.

mucus (ˈmjuːkəs) *n* the slimy protective secretion of the mucous membranes. ORIG C17: from L: nasal secretions; cf. *mungere* to blow the nose

> **USAGE NOTE** See at **mucous.**

mud (mʌd) *n* **1** a fine-grained soft wet deposit that occurs on the ground after rain, at the bottom of ponds, etc. **2** *Inf.* slander or defamation. **3 clear as mud.** *Inf.* not at all clear. **4 here's mud in your eye.** *Inf.* a humorous drinking toast. **5** (**someone's**) **name is mud.** *Inf.* (someone) is disgraced. **6 throw** (*or* **sling**) **mud at.** *Inf.* to slander; vilify. ◆ *vb* **muds, mudding, mudded. 7** (*tr*) to soil or cover with mud. ORIG C14: prob. from MLow G *mudde*

★ people and places

mud bath *n* **1** a medicinal bath in heated mud. **2** a dirty or muddy occasion, state, etc.

mudbrick (ˈmʌdˌbrɪk) *n* a brick made with mud.

muddle (ˈmʌdᵊl) *vb* **muddles, muddling, muddled.** (*tr*) **1** (often foll. by *up*) to mix up (objects, items, etc.). **2** to confuse. **3** *US.* to mix or stir (alcoholic drinks, etc.). ◆ *n* **4** a state of physical or mental confusion. ORIG C16: ?from MDu. *moddelen* to make muddy
▸ ˈ**muddled** *adj* ▸ ˈ**muddler** *n* ▸ ˈ**muddling** *adj, n*

muddleheaded (ˌmʌdᵊlˈhɛdɪd) *adj* mentally confused or vague.
▸ ˌ**muddleˈheadedness** *n*

muddle through *vb* (*intr, adv*) *Chiefly Brit.* to succeed in spite of lack of organization.

muddy (ˈmʌdɪ) *adj* **muddier, muddiest. 1** covered or filled with mud. **2** not clear or bright: *muddy colours.* **3** cloudy: *a muddy liquid.* **4** (esp. of thoughts) confused or vague. ◆ *vb* **muddies, muddying, muddied. 5** to become or cause to become muddy.
▸ ˈ**muddily** *adv* ▸ ˈ**muddiness** *n*

mudfish (ˈmʌdˌfɪʃ) *n, pl* **mudfish** *or* **mudfishes.** any of various fishes, such as the bowfin, that live at the muddy bottoms of rivers, lakes, etc.

mud flat *n* a tract of low muddy land that is covered at high tide and exposed at low tide.

mudflow (ˈmʌdˌfləʊ) *n Geol.* a flow of soil mixed with water down a steep unstable slope.

mudguard (ˈmʌdˌgɑːd) *n* a curved part of a motorcycle, bicycle, etc., attached above the wheels to reduce the amount of water or mud thrown up by them. US and Canad. name: **fender.**

mud hen *n* any of various birds that frequent marshes, esp. the coots, rails, etc.

mudlark (ˈmʌdˌlɑːk) *n* **1** (formerly) a person who made a living by picking up odds and ends in the mud of tidal rivers. **2** *Sl., now rare.* a street urchin. **3** *Austral. sl.* a racehorse that runs well on a wet or muddy course.

mud map *n Austral.* **1** a rough map drawn on the ground with a stick. **2** any rough sketch map.

mudpack (ˈmʌdˌpæk) *n* a cosmetic astringent paste containing fuller's earth.

mud puppy *n* an aquatic North American salamander having persistent larval features.

mudskipper (ˈmʌdˌskɪpə) *n* any of various gobies that occur in tropical coastal regions of Africa and Asia and can move on land by means of their strong pectoral fins.

mudslinging (ˈmʌdˌslɪŋɪŋ) *n* casting malicious slurs on an opponent, esp. in politics.
▸ ˈ**mudˌslinger** *n*

mudstone (ˈmʌdˌstəʊn) *n* a dark grey clay rock similar to shale.

mud turtle *n* any of various small turtles that inhabit muddy rivers in North and Central America.

muesli (ˈmjuːzlɪ) *n* a mixture of rolled oats, nuts, fruit, etc., usually eaten with milk. ORIG Swiss G, from G *Mus* mush, purée + *-li,* dim. suffix

muezzin (muːˈɛzɪn) *n Islam.* the official of a mosque who calls the faithful to prayer from the minaret. ORIG C16: from Ar. *mu'adhdhin*

muff[1] (mʌf) *n* an open-ended cylinder of fur or cloth into which the hands are placed for warmth. ORIG C16: prob. from Du. *mof,* ult. from F *mouffle* MUFFLE[1]

muff[2] (mʌf) *vb* **1** to perform (an action) awkwardly. **2** (*tr*) to bungle (a shot, catch, etc.). ◆ *n* **3** any unskilful play, esp. a dropped catch. **4** any bungled action. **5** a bungler. ORIG C19: from ?

muffin (ˈmʌfɪn) *n* **1** *Brit.* a thick round baked yeast roll, usually toasted and served with butter. **2** *US & Canad.* a small cup-shaped sweet bread roll, usually eaten hot with butter. ORIG C18: ?from Low G *muffen* cakes

muffin man *n Brit.* (formerly) an itinerant seller of muffins.

muffle[1] (ˈmʌfᵊl) *vb* **muffles, muffling, muffled.** (*mainly tr*) **1** (*also intr;* often foll. by *up*) to wrap up (the head) in a scarf, cloak, etc., esp. for warmth. **2** (*also intr*) to deaden (a sound or noise), esp. by wrapping. **3** to prevent (the expression of something) by (someone). ◆ *n* **4** something that muffles. **5** a kiln with an inner chamber for firing porcelain, enamel, etc. ORIG C15: prob. from OF; cf. OF *moufle* mitten, *emmouflé* wrapped up

muffle[2] (ˈmʌfᵊl) *n* the fleshy hairless part of the upper lip and nose in ruminants and some rodents. ORIG C17: from F *mufle,* from ?

muffler (ˈmʌflə) *n* **1** a thick scarf, collar, etc. **2** the US and Canad. name for **silencer** (sense 1).

mufti (ˈmʌftɪ) *n* civilian dress, esp. as worn by a person who normally wears a military uniform. ORIG C19: ? from MUFTI

Mufti (ˈmʌftɪ) *n, pl* **Muftis.** a Muslim legal expert and adviser on the law of the Koran. ORIG C16: from Ar. *muftī,* from *aftā* to give a (legal) decision

Mufulira ★ (ˌmuːfuːˈlɪərə) *n* a mining town in the Copper Belt of Zambia. Pop.: 152 944 (1990).

mug[1] (mʌg) *n* **1** a drinking vessel with a handle, usually cylindrical and made of earthenware. **2** Also called: **mugful.** the quantity held by a mug or its contents. ORIG C16: prob. of Scand. origin

mug[2] (mʌg) *n* **1** *Sl.* a person's face or mouth. **2** *Brit. sl.* a gullible person, esp. one who is swindled easily. **3 a mug's game.** a worthless activity. ◆ *vb* **mugs, mugging, mugged. 4** (*tr*) *Inf.* to attack or rob (someone) violently. ORIG C18: ?from MUG[1], since drinking vessels were sometimes modelled into the likeness of a face
▸ ˈ**mugger** *n*

Mugabe ★ (muˈgɑːbɪ) *n* **Robert.** born 1925, Zimbabwean politician; leader of one wing of the Patriotic Front and the Zanu party; prime minister (1980–87); president from 1988.

muggins (ˈmʌgɪnz) *n* (*functioning as sing*) **1** *Brit. sl.* **1a** a simpleton. **1b** a title used humorously to refer to oneself as a dupe or victim. **2** a card game. ORIG C19: prob. from the surname *Muggins*

muggy (ˈmʌgɪ) *adj* **muggier, muggiest.** (of weather, air, etc.) unpleasantly warm and humid. ORIG C18: dialect *mug* drizzle, prob. of Scand. origin
▸ ˈ**mugginess** *n*

mug shot *n Inf.* a photograph of a person's face, esp. one resembling a police-file picture.

mug up *vb* (*adv*) *Brit. sl.* to study (a subject) hard, esp. for an exam. ORIG C19: from ?

Muhammad ★ (muˈhæməd) *n* a variant of **Mohammed.**

Muhammad Ali *or* **Mohammad Ali** ★ (ˈɑːlɪ, ɑːˈliː, ˈælɪ) *n* original name *Cassius* (*Marcellus*) *Clay.* born 1942, US boxer; world heavyweight champion (1964–67; 1974–78; 1978).

Muhammadan *or* **Muhammedan** (muˈhæmədᵊn) *n, adj* another word (not in Muslim use) for **Muslim.**

Mühlhausen ★ (myːlˈhauzən) *n* the German name for **Mulhouse.**

Muir ★ (mjʊə) *n* **Edwin.** 1887–1959, Scottish poet and novelist.

Muir Glacier ★ *n* a glacier in SE Alaska, in the St Elias Mountains, flowing southeast from Mount Fairweather. Area: about 900 sq. km (350 sq. miles).

mujaheddin *or* **mujahedeen** (ˌmuːdʒəhəˈdiːn) *pl n* (preceded by *the; sometimes cap.*) (in Afghanistan and Iran) fundamentalist Muslim guerrillas. In Afghanistan in 1992 the mujaheddin overthrew the government but were unable to agree on a new constitution and were themselves overthrown by the Taliban militia in 1996. ORIG C20: from Ar. *mujāhidīn* fighters, ult. from JIHAD

Mukden ★ (ˈmʊkdən) *n* a former name of **Shenyang.**

mukluk (ˈmʌklʌk) *n* a soft boot, usually of sealskin, worn by Eskimos. ORIG from Eskimo *muklok* large seal

mulatto (mjuːˈlætəʊ) *n, pl* **mulattos** *or* **mulattoes. 1** a person having one Black and one White parent. ◆ *adj* **2** of a light brown colour; tawny. ORIG C16: from Sp. *mulato* young mule, var. of *mulo* MULE[1]

mulberry (ˈmʌlbərɪ, -brɪ) *n, pl* **mulberries. 1** a tree having edible blackberry-like fruit, such as the white mulberry, the leaves of which are used to feed silkworms. **2** the fruit of any of these trees. **3** any of several similar or related trees. **4a** a dark purple colour. **4b** (*as adj*): *a mulberry dress.* ORIG C14: from L *mōrum,* from Gk *moron;* rel. to OE *mōrberie*

mulch (mʌltʃ) *n* **1** half-rotten vegetable matter, peat, etc., used to prevent soil erosion or enrich the soil. ◆ *vb* **2** (*tr*) to cover (the surface of land) with mulch. ORIG C17: from obs. *mulch* soft; rel. to OE *mylisc* mellow

Mulciber ★ (ˈmʌlsɪbə) *n* another name for **Vulcan.**

mulct (mʌlkt) *vb* (*tr*) **1** to cheat or defraud. **2** to fine (a person). ◆ *n* **3** a fine or penalty. ORIG C15: via F from L *multa* a fine

Muldoon ★ (mʌlˈduːn) *n* Sir **Robert David.** 1921–92, New Zealand statesman; prime minister (1975–84).

mule[1] (mjuːl) *n* **1** the sterile offspring of a male donkey and a female horse, used as a beast of burden. **2** any hybrid animal: *a mule canary.* **3** Also called: **spinning mule.** a machine that spins cotton into yarn and winds the yarn on spindles. **4** *Inf.* an obstinate or stubborn person. ORIG C13: from OF *mul,* from L *mūlus* ass, mule

mule[2] (mjuːl) *n* a backless shoe or slipper. ORIG C16: from OF from L *mulleus* a magistrate's shoe

muleta (mjuːˈlɛtə) *n* the small cape attached to a stick used by the matador during a bullfight. ORIG Sp.: small mule, crutch, from *mula* MULE[1]

muleteer (ˌmjuːlɪˈtɪə) *n* a person who drives mules.

mulga (ˈmʌlgə) *n Austral.* **1** any of various Australian acacia shrubs. **2** scrub comprised of a dense growth of acacia. **3** *Inf.* the outback; bush. ORIG from Abor.

Mulhacén ★ (*Spanish* mulaˈθen) *n* a mountain in S Spain, in the Sierra Nevada: the highest peak in Spain. Height: 3478 m (11 410 ft).

Mülheim an der Ruhr (*German* ˈmyːlhaim an der ˈruːr) *or* **Mülheim** ★ *n* an industrial city in W Germany, in North Rhine-Westphalia on the River Ruhr: river port. Pop.: 176 530 (1996 est.).

Mulhouse ★ (*French* myluz) *n* a city in E France, on the Rhône–Rhine canal: under German rule (1871–1918); textiles. Pop.: 109 905 (1990). German name: **Mühlhausen.**

muliebrity (ˌmjuːlɪˈɛbrɪtɪ) *n* **1** the condition of being a woman. **2** femininity. ORIG C16: via LL from L *muliēbris* womanly, from *mulier* woman

mulish (ˈmjuːlɪʃ) *adj* stubborn; obstinate.
▸ **ˈmulishly** *adv* ▸ **ˈmulishness** *n*

mull[1] (mʌl) *vb* (*tr*) (often foll. by *over*) to study or ponder. ORIG C19: prob. from MUDDLE

mull[2] (mʌl) *vb* (*tr*) to heat (wine, ale, etc.) with sugar and spices. ORIG C17: from ?
▸ **mulled** *adj*

mull[3] (mʌl) *n* a light muslin fabric of soft texture. ORIG C18: earlier *mulmull,* from Hindi *malmal*

mull[4] (mʌl) *n Scot.* a promontory. ORIG C14: rel. to Gaelic *maol,* Icelandic *múli*

Mull ★ (mʌl) *n* a mountainous island off the west coast of Scotland, in the Inner Hebrides, separated from the mainland by the **Sound of Mull.** Chief town: Tobermory. Pop.: 2605 (latest est.). Area: 909 sq. km (351 sq. miles).

mullah *or* **mulla** (ˈmʌlə, ˈmʊlə) *n* (formerly) a Muslim scholar, teacher, or religious leader: also used as a title of respect. ORIG C17: from Turkish *molla,* Persian & Hindi *mulla,* from Ar. *mawlā* master

mullein (ˈmʌlɪn) *n* any of various Mediterranean herbaceous plants such as the common mullein or Aaron's rod, typically having tall spikes of yellow flowers and broad hairy leaves. ORIG C15: from OF *moleine,* prob. from OF *mol* soft, from L *mollis*

muller (ˈmʌlə) *n* a flat heavy implement of stone or iron used to grind material against a slab of stone, etc. ORIG C15: prob. from *mullen* to grind to powder

Muller ★ (ˈmʌlə) *n* **Hermann Joseph.** 1890–1967, US geneticist, noted for his work on the transmutation of genes by X-rays: Nobel prize for physiology or medicine 1946.

Müller ★ (*German* ˈmylər) *n* **1 Friedrich Max** (ˈfriːdrɪç maks). 1823–1900, British Sanskrit scholar born in Germany. **2 Johann** (joˈhan). See **Regiomontanus. 3 Johannes Peter** (joˈhanəs ˈpeːtər). 1801–58, German physiologist, anatomist, and experimental psychologist. **4 Paul Hermann** (paul ˈhɛrman). 1899–1965, Swiss chemist. He synthesized DDT (1939) and discovered its use as an insecticide: Nobel prize for physiology or medicine 1948.

mullet (ˈmʌlɪt) *n* any of various teleost food fishes such as the grey mullet or red mullet. ORIG C15: via OF from L *mullus,* from Gk *mullos*

mulligatawny (ˌmʌlɪgəˈtɔːnɪ) *n* a curry-flavoured soup of Anglo-Indian origin, made with meat stock. ORIG C18: from Tamil *milakutanni,* from *milaku* pepper + *tanni* water

Mulliken ★ (ˈmʌlɪkən) *n* **Robert Sanderson.** 1896–1986, US physicist and chemist; Nobel prize for chemistry (1966) for his work on chemical bonding.

Mullingar ★ (ˌmʌlɪnˈgɑː) *n* a town in N central Republic of Ireland, the county town of Co. Westmeath; site of cathedral; cattle raised. Pop.: 11 800 (1995 est.).

mullion (ˈmʌlɪən) *n* **1** a vertical member between the casements or panes of a window. ◆ *vb* **2** (*tr*) to furnish (a window, screen, etc.) with mullions. ORIG C16: var. of ME *munial,* from OF *moinel,* from ?

mullock (ˈmʌlək) *n Austral.* **1** waste material from a mine. **2 poke mullock at.** *Inf.* to ridicule. ORIG C14: rel. to OE *myl* dust, ON *mylja* to crush

mulloway (ˈmʌləˌweɪ) *n* a large Australian marine food fish. ORIG C19: from ?

Mulroney ★ (mʌlˈrəunɪ) *n* (**Martin**) **Brian.** born 1939, Canadian statesman; Conservative prime minister (1984–93).

Multan ★ (ˌmulˈtɑːn) *n* a city in central Pakistan, near the Chenab River. Pop.: 1 257 000 (1995 est.).

multangular (mʌlˈtæŋgjulə) *or* **multiangular** *adj* having many angles.

multi- *combining form.* **1** many or much: *multimillion.* **2** more than one: *multistorey.* ORIG from L *multus* much, many

multicultural (ˌmʌltɪˈkʌltʃərəl) *adj* consisting of, relating to, or designed for the cultures of several different races.
▸ **ˌmultiˈculturalˌism** *n*

multifactorial (ˌmʌltɪfækˈtɔːrɪəl) *adj* having many separate factors, causes, components, etc.: *multifactorial disease; multifactorial inheritance.*

multifarious (ˌmʌltɪˈfɛərɪəs) *adj* having many parts of great variety. ORIG C16: from LL *multifārius* manifold, from L *multifāriam* on many sides
▸ **ˌmultiˈfariously** *adv* ▸ **ˌmultiˈfariousness** *n*

multiflora rose (ˌmʌltɪˈflɔːrə) *n* an Asian climbing shrubby rose having clusters of small fragrant flowers.

multiform (ˈmʌltɪˌfɔːm) *adj* having many forms.
▸ **ˌmultiˈformity** *n*

multigym (ˈmʌltɪˌdʒɪm) *n* an exercise apparatus incorporating a variety of weights, used for toning the muscles.

multilateral (ˌmʌltɪˈlætərəl, -ˈlætrəl) *adj* **1** of or involving more than two nations or parties: *a multilateral pact.* **2** having many sides.
▸ **ˌmultiˈlaterally** *adv*

multilingual (ˌmʌltɪˈlɪŋgwəl) *adj* **1** able to speak more than two languages. **2** written or expressed in more than two languages.

multimedia (ˌmʌltɪˈmiːdɪə) *adj* **1** of or relating to the combined use of such media as television, slides, etc. **2** *Computing.* of or relating to any of various systems that can manipulate data in a variety of forms, such as sound, graphics, or text.

multimillionaire (ˌmʌltɪˌmɪljəˈnɛə) *n* a person with a fortune of several million pounds, dollars, etc.

multinational (ˌmʌltɪˈnæʃənᵊl) *adj* **1** (of a large business company) operating in several countries. ◆ *n* **2** such a company.

multipack (ˈmʌltɪˌpæk) *n* a form of packaging of foodstuffs, etc., that contains several units and is offered at a price below that of the equivalent number of units.

multiparous (mʌlˈtɪpərəs) *adj* (of certain species of

★ people and places

mammal) producing many offspring at one birth. ORIG C17: from NL *multiparus*

multipartite (ˌmʌltɪˈpɑːtaɪt) *adj* **1** divided into many parts or sections. **2** *Government.* a less common word for **multilateral.**

multiparty (ˌmʌltɪˈpɑːtɪ) *adj* of or relating to a state, political system, etc., in which more than one political party is permitted: *multiparty democracy.*

multiple (ˈmʌltɪpᵊl) *adj* **1** having or involving more than one part, individual, etc. **2** *Electronics, US & Canad.* (of a circuit) having a number of conductors in parallel. ◆ *n* **3** the product of a given number or polynomial and any other one: *6 is a multiple of 2.* **4** short for **multiple store.** ORIG C17: via F from LL *multiplus,* from L MULTIPLEX
▸ **ˈmultiply** *adv*

multiple-choice *adj* having a number of possible given answers out of which the correct one must be chosen.

multiple personality *n Psychiatry.* a mental disorder in which an individual's personality appears to have become separated into two or more distinct personalities. Nontechnical name: **split personality.**

multiple sclerosis *n* a chronic progressive disease of the central nervous system, resulting in speech and visual disorders, tremor, muscular incoordination, partial paralysis, etc.

multiple store *n* one of several retail enterprises under the same ownership and management. Also called: **multiple shop.**

multiplex (ˈmʌltɪˌplɛks) *n* **1** *Telecomm.* **1a** the use of a common communications channel for sending two or more messages or signals. **1b** (*as modifier*): *a multiplex transmitter.* **2a** a purpose-built complex containing a number of cinemas and usually a restaurant or bar. **2b** (*as modifier*): *a multiplex cinema.* ◆ *adj* **3** a less common word for **multiple.** ◆ *vb* **4** to send (messages or signals) or (of messages and signals) to be sent by multiplex. ORIG C16: from L: having many folds, from MULTI- + *plicāre* to fold

multiplicand (ˌmʌltɪplɪˈkænd) *n* a number to be multiplied by another number, the **multiplier.** ORIG C16: from L *multiplicandus,* gerund of *multiplicāre* to MULTIPLY

multiplication (ˌmʌltɪplɪˈkeɪʃən) *n* **1** a mathematical operation, the inverse of division, in which the product of two or more numbers or quantities is calculated. Usually written $a \times b$, $a.b$, ab. **2** the act of multiplying or state of being multiplied. **3** the act or process in animals, plants, or people, of reproducing or breeding.

multiplication sign *n* the symbol ×, placed between numbers to be multiplied.

multiplication table *n* one of a group of tables giving the results of multiplying two numbers together.

multiplicity (ˌmʌltɪˈplɪsɪtɪ) *n, pl* **multiplicities. 1** a large number or great variety. **2** the state of being multiple.

multiplier (ˈmʌltɪˌplaɪə) *n* **1** a person or thing that multiplies. **2** the number by which another number, the **multiplicand,** is multiplied. **3** *Physics.* any instrument, such as a photomultiplier, for increasing an effect. **4** *Econ.* the ratio of the total change in income (resulting from successive rounds of spending) to an initial autonomous change in expenditure.

multiply (ˈmʌltɪˌplaɪ) *vb* **multiplies, multiplying, multiplied. 1** to increase or cause to increase in number, quantity, or degree. **2** (*tr*) to combine (two numbers or quantities) by multiplication. **3** (*intr*) to increase in number by reproduction. ORIG C13: from OF *multiplier,* from L *multiplicāre* to multiply, from *multus* much, many + *plicāre* to fold
▸ **ˈmultiˌpliable** *or* **multiplicable** (ˈmʌltɪˌplɪkəbᵊl) *adj*

multiprocessor (ˌmʌltɪˈprəusɛsə) *n Computing.* a number of central processing units linked together to enable parallel processing to take place.

multipurpose vehicle *n* a large car, similar to a van, designed to carry up to eight passengers. Abbrev.: **MPV.**

multiskilling (ˈmʌltɪˌskɪlɪŋ) *n* the practice of training employees to do a number of different tasks.

multistage (ˈmʌltɪˌsteɪdʒ) *adj* **1** (of a rocket or missile) having several stages, each of which can be jettisoned after it has burnt out. **2** (of a turbine, compressor, or supercharger) having more than one rotor. **3** (of any process or device) having more than one stage.

multistorey (ˌmʌltɪˈstɔːrɪ) *adj* **1** (of a building) having many storeys. ◆ *n* **2** a multistorey car park.

multitasking (ˌmʌltɪˈtɑːskɪŋ) *n* **1** *Computing.* the execution of various diverse tasks simultaneously. **2** the carrying out of two or more tasks at the same time by one person.

multitrack (ˈmʌltɪˌtræk) *adj* (in sound recording) using tape containing two or more tracks, usually four to twenty-four.

multitude (ˈmʌltɪˌtjuːd) *n* **1** a large gathering of people. **2 the.** the common people. **3** a large number. **4** the state or quality of being numerous. ORIG C14: via OF from L *multitūdō*

multitudinous (ˌmʌltɪˈtjuːdɪnəs) *adj* **1** very numerous. **2** *Rare.* great in extent, variety, etc. **3** *Poetic.* crowded.
▸ **ˌmultiˈtudinously** *adv* ▸ **ˌmultiˈtudinousness** *n*

multi-user *adj* (of a computer) capable of being used by several people at once.

multivalent (ˌmʌltɪˈveɪlənt) *adj* another word for **polyvalent.**
▸ **ˌmultiˈvalency** *n*

mum[1] (mʌm) *n Chiefly Brit.* an informal word for **mother.** ORIG C19: a child's word

mum[2] (mʌm) *adj* **1** keeping information, etc., to oneself; silent. ◆ *n* **2 mum's the word.** (*interj*) silence or secrecy is to be observed. ORIG C14: suggestive of closed lips

mum[3] (mʌm) *vb* **mums, mumming, mummed.** (*intr*) to act in a mummer's play. ORIG C16: verbal use of MUM[2]

Mumbai ★ (mʊmˈbaɪ) *n* the Hindi name for **Bombay.**

mumble (ˈmʌmbᵊl) *vb* **mumbles, mumbling, mumbled. 1** to utter indistinctly, as with the mouth partly closed. **2** *Rare.* to chew (food) ineffectually. ◆ *n* **3** an indistinct or low utterance or sound. ORIG C14 *momelen,* from MUM[2]
▸ **ˈmumbler** *n* ▸ **ˈmumbling** *adj* ▸ **ˈmumblingly** *adv*

mumbo jumbo (ˈmʌmbəʊ) *n, pl* **mumbo jumbos. 1** foolish religious reverence, ritual, or incantation. **2** meaningless or unnecessarily complicated language. **3** an object of superstitious awe or reverence. ORIG C18: prob. from W African *mama dyumbo,* name of a tribal god

mu meson (mjuː) *n* a former name for **muon.**

Mumford ★ (ˈmʌmfəd) *n* **Lewis.** 1895–1990, US sociologist, whose works include *The City in History* (1962) and *Roots of Contemporary Architecture* (1972).

mummer (ˈmʌmə) *n* **1** one of a group of masked performers in a folk play or mime. **2** *Humorous or derog.* an actor. ORIG C15: from OF *momeur,* from *momer* to mime

Mummerset (ˈmʌməsɪt, -ˌsɛt) *n* an imitation West Country accent used in drama. ORIG C20: from MUMMER + (SOMER)SET

mummery (ˈmʌmərɪ) *n, pl* **mummeries. 1** a performance by mummers. **2** hypocritical or ostentatious ceremony.

mummify (ˈmʌmɪˌfaɪ) *vb* **mummifies, mummifying, mummified. 1** (*tr*) to preserve (a body) as a mummy. **2** (*intr*) to dry up; shrivel.
▸ **ˌmummifiˈcation** *n*

mummy[1] (ˈmʌmɪ) *n, pl* **mummies. 1** an embalmed or preserved body, esp. as prepared for burial in ancient Egypt. **2** a mass of pulp. **3** a dark brown pigment. ORIG C14: from OF *momie,* from Med. L, from Ar.: asphalt, from Persian *mūm* wax

mummy[2] (ˈmʌmɪ) *n, pl* **mummies.** *Chiefly Brit.* a child's word for **mother**[1] (senses 1–3). ORIG C19: var. of MUM[1]

mumps (mʌmps) *n* (*functioning as sing or pl*) **1** an acute contagious viral disease of the parotid salivary glands, characterized by swelling of the affected parts, fever, and pain beneath the ear. **2** sulks. ORIG C16: from *mump* to grimace
▸ **ˈmumpish** *adj*

mumsy (ˈmʌmzɪ) *adj* **mumsier, mumsiest.** homely or drab.
▸ **ˈmumsiness** *n*

mun. *abbrev. for* municipal.

munch (mʌntʃ) *vb* to chew (food) steadily, esp. with a crunching noise. ORIG C14 *monche,* imit.

★ people and places

Munch ★ (mʊŋk) *n* **Edvard** ('ɛdvard). 1863–1944, Norwegian painter and engraver; works include *The Cry* (1893).

München ★ ('mynçən) *n* the German name for **Munich**.

München-Gladbach ★ (mynçən'glatbax) *n* the former name of **Mönchengladbach**.

mundane (mʌn'deɪn, 'mʌndeɪn) *adj* **1** everyday, ordinary, or banal. **2** relating to the world or worldly matters. ORIG C15: from F *mondain,* via LL, from L *mundus* world
▸ **mun'danely** *adv* ▸ **mun'daneness** *n*

mung bean (mʌŋ) *n* **1** an E Asian bean plant grown for forage and as the source of bean sprouts for cookery. **2** the seed of this plant. ORIG C20: from *mung,* changed from *mungo,* from Tamil *mūngu,* from Sansk. *mudga*

Munich ★ ('mju:nɪk) *n* a city in SE Germany, capital of the state of Bavaria, on the Isar River: became capital of Bavaria in 1508; headquarters of the Nazi movement in the 1920s; a major financial, commercial, and manufacturing centre. Pop.: 1 236 370 (1996 est.). German name: **München**.

municipal (mju:'nɪsɪpᵊl) *adj* of or relating to a town, city, or borough or its local government. ORIG C16: from L *mūnicipium* a free town, from *mūniceps* citizen, from *mūnia* responsibilities + *capere* to take
▸ **mu'nicipally** *adv*

municipality (mju:ˌnɪsɪ'pælɪtɪ) *n, pl* **municipalities. 1** a city, town, or district enjoying local self-government. **2** the governing body of such a unit.

municipalize *or* **municipalise** (mju:'nɪsɪpəˌlaɪz) *vb* **municipalizes, municipalizing, municipalized** *or* **municipalises, municipalising, municipalised.** (*tr*) **1** to bring under municipal ownership or control. **2** to make a municipality of.
▸ **muˌnicipali'zation** *or* **muˌnicipali'sation** *n*

munificent (mju:'nɪfɪsənt) *adj* **1** (of a person) generous; bountiful. **2** (of a gift) liberal. ORIG C16: back formation from L *mūnificentia* liberality, from *mūnificus,* from *mūnus* gift + *facere* to make
▸ **mu'nificence** *n* ▸ **mu'nificently** *adv*

muniments ('mju:nɪmənts) *pl n Law.* the title deeds and other documentary evidence relating to the title to land. ORIG C15: via OF from L *munire* to defend

munition (mju:'nɪʃən) *vb* (*tr*) to supply with munitions. ORIG C16: via F from L *mūnītiō* fortification, from *mūnīre* to fortify

munitions (mju:'nɪʃənz) *pl n* (*sometimes sing*) military equipment and stores, esp. ammunition.

Munro[1] (mʌn'rəʊ) *n, pl* **Munros.** *Mountaineering.* any separate mountain peak over 3000 feet high: originally used of Scotland only but now sometimes extended to other parts of the British Isles. ORIG C20: after Hugh Thomas *Munro* (1856–1919), who listed these in 1891

Munro[2] ★ (mʌn'rəʊ) *n* **H(ector) H(ugh)**, pen name *Saki.* 1870–1916, Scottish author, born in Burma, noted for his satirical short stories.

Munster ★ ('mʌnstə) *n* a province of SW Republic of Ireland: the largest of the four provinces and historically a kingdom; consists of the counties of Clare, Cork, Kerry, Limerick, Tipperary, and Waterford. Capital: Cork. Pop.: 1 033 000 (1996). Area: 24 125 sq. km (9315 sq. miles).

Münster ★ (*German* 'mynstər) *n* a city in NW Germany in North Rhine-Westphalia, on the Dortmund–Ems Canal: one of the treaties comprising the Peace of Westphalia (1648) was signed here; became capital of Prussian Westphalia in 1815. Pop.: 265 061 (1996 est.).

munted ('mʌntɪd) *adj NZ sl.* **1** (of an object) destroyed or ruined. **2** (of a person) abnormal or peculiar. ORIG C20: from ?

muntjac *or* **muntjak** ('mʌntˌdʒæk) *n* any small Asian deer typically having a chestnut-brown coat and small antlers. ORIG C18: prob. from Javanese *mindjangan* deer

Müntzer ★ ('mʊntzə; *German* 'myntzər) *n* **Thomas.** ?1490–1525, German religious and political reformer; executed for organizing the Peasants' War (1524–25).

muon ('mju:ɒn) *n* a positive or negative elementary particle with a mass 207 times that of an electron. It was originally called the **mu meson.** ORIG C20: short for MU MESON
▸ **mu'onic** *adj*

mural ('mjʊərəl) *n* **1** a large painting on a wall. ◆ *adj* **2** of or relating to a wall. ORIG C15: from L *mūrālis,* from *mūrus* wall
▸ **'muralist** *n*

Murasaki Shikibu ★ (ˌmjʊərə'sɑ:ki: 'ʃi:ki:ˌbu:) *n* 11th-century Japanese court lady, author of *The Tale of Genji,* perhaps the world's first novel.

Murat ★ (*French* myra) *n* **Joachim** (ʒɔaʃɛ̃). 1767?–1815, French marshal, during the Napoleonic Wars; king of Naples (1808–15).

Murchison ★ ('mɜ:tʃɪsᵊn) *n* Sir **Roderick Impey.** 1792–1871, Scottish geologist: established parts of the geological time scale.

Murcia ★ (*Spanish* 'murθja) *n* **1** a region and ancient kingdom of SE Spain, on the Mediterranean: taken by the Moors in the 8th century; an independent Muslim kingdom in the 11th and 12th centuries. **2** a city in SE Spain, capital of Murcia province: trading centre for a rich agricultural region; silk industry; university (1915). Pop.: 344 904 (1995 est.).

murder ('mɜ:də) *n* **1** the unlawful premeditated killing of one human being by another. Cf. **manslaughter. 2** *Inf.* something dangerous, difficult, or unpleasant: *driving around London is murder.* **3 cry blue murder.** *Inf.* to make an outcry. **4 get away with murder.** *Inf.* to escape censure; do as one pleases. ◆ *vb* (*mainly tr*) **5** (*also intr*) to kill (someone) unlawfully with premeditation or during the commission of a crime. **6** to kill brutally. **7** *Inf.* to destroy; ruin. **8** *Inf.* to defeat completely; beat decisively: *the home team murdered their opponents.* ORIG OE *morthor*
▸ **'murderer** *n* ▸ **'murderess** *fem n*

murderous ('mɜ:dərəs) *adj* **1** intending, capable of, or guilty of murder. **2** *Inf.* very dangerous or difficult: *a murderous road.*
▸ **'murderously** *adv* ▸ **'murderousness** *n*

Murdoch ★ ('mɜ:dɒk) *n* **1** Dame **(Jean) Iris.** 1919–99, British novelist. Her novels include *The Bell* (1958), *The Sea, The Sea* (1978), and *Jackson's Dilemma* (1995). **2 (Keith) Rupert.** born 1931, US entrepreneur, born in Australia; chairman of News International Ltd and Times Newspapers Ltd.

Mureş ★ ('mʊərɛʃ) *n* a river in SE central Europe, rising in central Romania in the Carpathian Mountains and flowing west to the Tisza River at Szeged, Hungary. Length: 885 km (550 miles). Hungarian name: **Maros.**

murex ('mjʊərɛks) *n, pl* **murices** ('mjʊərɪˌsi:z). any of a genus of spiny-shelled marine gastropods: formerly used as a source of the dye Tyrian purple. ORIG C16: from L *mūrex* purple fish

muriatic acid (ˌmjʊərɪ'ætɪk) *n* a former name for **hydrochloric acid.** ORIG C17: from L *muriāticus* pickled, from *muria* brine

Murillo ★ (mjʊə'rɪləʊ; *Spanish* mu'riʎo) *n* **Bartolomé Esteban** (bartolo'me es'teβan). 1618–82, Spanish painter.

murk *or* **mirk** (mɜ:k) *n* **1** gloomy darkness. ◆ *adj* **2** an archaic variant of **murky.** ORIG C13: prob. from ON *myrkr* darkness

murky *or* **mirky** ('mɜ:kɪ) *adj* **murkier, murkiest** *or* **mirkier, mirkiest. 1** gloomy or dark. **2** cloudy or impenetrable, as with smoke or fog. **3** *Inf.* obscure and suspicious; shady: *she had a murky past.*
▸ **'murkily** *or* **'mirkily** *adv* ▸ **'murkiness** *or* **'mirkiness** *n*

Murman Coast ('mʊəmən) *or* **Murmansk Coast** ★ *n* a coastal region of NW Russia, in the north of the Kola Peninsula: within the Arctic Circle, but ice-free.

Murmansk ★ (*Russian* 'murmənsk) *n* a port in NW Russia, on the Kola Inlet of the Barents Sea: founded in 1915; the world's largest town north of the Arctic Circle, with a large fishing fleet. Pop.: 407 000 (1995 est.).

murmur ('mɜ:mə) *n* **1** a continuous low indistinct sound, as of distant voices. **2** an indistinct utterance: *a murmur of satisfaction.* **3** a complaint; grumble: *he made no murmur at my suggestion.* **4** *Med.* any abnormal soft blowing sound heard usually over the chest (**heart murmur**). ◆ *vb* **murmurs, murmuring, murmured. 5** to utter (something) in a murmur. **6** (*intr*) to complain. ORIG C14: as n, from L *murmur;* vb. via OF *murmurer* from L *murmurāre* to rumble

▸ 'murmurer *n* ▸ 'murmuring *n, adj* ▸ 'murmuringly *adv* ▸ 'murmurous *adj*

murphy ('mɜːfɪ) *n, pl* **murphies.** a dialect or informal word for **potato.** ORIG C19: from the common Irish surname *Murphy*

Murphy-O'Connor ★ ('mɜːfɪ əʊ'kɒnə) *n* **Cormac.** born 1932, British Roman Catholic cardinal; archbishop of Westminster from 2000.

murrain ('mʌrɪn) *n* **1** any plaguelike disease in cattle. **2** *Arch.* a plague. ORIG C14: from OF *morine,* from *morir* to die, from L *morī*

Murray[1] ★ ('mʌrɪ) *n* a river in SE Australia, rising in New South Wales and flowing northwest into SE South Australia, then south into the sea at Encounter Bay: the main river of Australia, important for irrigation and power. Length: 2590 km (1609 miles).

Murray[2] ★ ('mʌrɪ) *n* **1 1st Earl of.** See (1st Earl of) **Moray. 2** Sir **(George) Gilbert (Aimé).** 1866–1957, British classical scholar, born in Australia. **3** Sir **James Augustus Henry.** 1837–1915, British lexicographer; one of the original editors (1879–1915) of what became the *Oxford English Dictionary.*

Murray cod *n* a large greenish Australian freshwater food fish. ORIG after MURRAY River

Murrumbidgee ★ (ˌmʌrəm'bɪdʒɪ) *n* a river in SE Australia, rising in S New South Wales and flowing north and west to the Murray River: important for irrigation. Length: 1690 km (1050 miles).

murther ('mɜːðə) *n, vb* an archaic word for **murder.**
▸ 'murtherer *n*

mus. *abbrev. for:* **1** museum. **2** music. **3** musical.

MusB *or* **MusBac** *abbrev. for* Bachelor of Music.

muscadine ('mʌskədɪn, -ˌdaɪn) *n* **1** a woody climbing plant of the southeastern US. **2** the musk-scented purple grape produced by this plant: used to make wine. ORIG C16: from MUSCATEL

muscae volitantes ('mʌsiː vɒlɪ'tæntiːz) *pl n Pathol.* moving black specks or threads seen before the eyes, caused by opaque fragments floating in the vitreous humour or a defect in the lens. ORIG C18: NL: flying flies

muscat ('mʌskət, -kæt) *n* **1** any of various grapevines that produce sweet white grapes used for making wine or raisins. **2** another name for **muscatel** (sense 1). ORIG C16: via OF from Provençal, from *musc* MUSK

Muscat ★ ('mʌskət, -kæt) *n* the capital of the Sultanate of Oman, a port on the Gulf of Oman: a Portuguese port from the early 16th century; controlled by Persia (1650–1741). Pop.: 51 969 (1993). Arabic name: **Masqat.**

Muscat and Oman ★ *n* the former name (until 1970) of (the Sultanate of) **Oman.**

muscatel (ˌmʌskə'tɛl) *or* **muscadel** *n* **1** Also called: **muscat.** a rich sweet wine made from muscat grapes. **2** the grape or raisin from a muscat vine. ORIG C14: from OF *muscadel,* from OProvençal, from *moscadel,* from *muscat* musky

muscle ('mʌsᵊl) *n* **1** a tissue composed of bundles of elongated cells capable of contraction and relaxation to produce movement in an organ or part. **2** an organ composed of muscle tissue. **3** strength or force. ◆ *vb* **muscles, muscling, muscled. 4** (*intr;* often foll. by *in, on,* etc.) *Inf.* to force one's way (in). ORIG C16: from Medical L *musculus* little mouse, from the imagined resemblance of some muscles to mice
▸ 'muscly *adj*

muscle-bound *adj* **1** having overdeveloped and inelastic muscles. **2** lacking flexibility.

muscleman ('mʌsᵊlˌmæn) *n, pl* **musclemen. 1** a man with highly developed muscles. **2** a henchman employed by a gangster to intimidate or use violence upon victims.

Muscovite ('mʌskəˌvaɪt) *n* **1** a native or inhabitant of Moscow. ◆ *adj* **2** an archaic word for **Russian.**

Muscovy ★ ('mʌskəvɪ) *n* **1** a Russian principality (13th to 16th centuries), of which Moscow was the capital. **2** an archaic name for **Russia** and **Moscow.**

Muscovy duck *or* **musk duck** *n* a large crested widely domesticated South American duck, having a greenish-black plumage with white markings and a large red caruncle on the bill. ORIG C17: orig. *musk duck,* a name later mistakenly associated with MUSCOVY

muscular ('mʌskjʊlə) *adj* **1** having well-developed muscles; brawny. **2** of, relating to, or consisting of muscle. ORIG C17: from NL *muscularis,* from *musculus* MUSCLE
▸ **muscularity** (ˌmʌskjʊ'lærɪtɪ) *n* ▸ 'muscularly *adv*

muscular dystrophy *n* a genetic disease characterized by progressive deterioration and wasting of muscle fibres.

musculature ('mʌskjʊlətʃə) *n* **1** the arrangement of muscles in an organ or part. **2** the total muscular system of an organism.

MusD *or* **MusDoc** *abbrev. for* Doctor of Music.

muse[1] (mjuːz) *vb* **muses, musing, mused. 1** (when *intr,* often foll. by *on* or *about*) to reflect (about) or ponder (on), usually in silence. **2** (*intr*) to gaze thoughtfully. ◆ *n* **3** a state of abstraction. ORIG C14: from OF *muser,* ?from *mus* snout, from Med. L *mūsus*

muse[2] (mjuːz) *n* a goddess or woman who inspires a poet or other creative artist. ORIG C14: from OF, from L *Mūsa,* from Gk *Mousa* a Muse

Muse (mjuːz) *n Greek myth.* any of nine sister goddesses, each of whom was regarded as the protectress of a different art or science.

musette (mjuː'zɛt) *n* **1** a type of bagpipe popular in France during the 17th and 18th centuries. **2** a dance, originally accompanied by a musette. ORIG C14: from OF, dim. of *muse* bagpipe

museum (mjuː'zɪəm) *n* a building where objects of historical, artistic, or scientific interest are exhibited and preserved. ORIG C17: via L from Gk *Mouseion* home of the Muses, from *Mousa* MUSE

museum piece *n* **1** an object of sufficient age or interest to be kept in a museum. **2** *Inf.* a person or thing regarded as antiquated.

Museveni ★ (mʊsə'veɪnɪ) *n* **Yoweri.** born 1944, Ugandan politician; president of Uganda from 1986.

mush[1] (mʌʃ) *n* **1** a soft pulpy mass or consistency. **2** *US.* a thick porridge made from corn meal. **3** *Inf.* cloying sentimentality. ◆ *vb* **4** (*tr*) to reduce (a substance) to a soft pulpy mass. ORIG C17: from obs. *moose* porridge; prob. rel. to MASH

mush[2] (mʌʃ) *Canad.* ◆ *interj* **1** an order to dogs in a sled team to start up or go faster. ◆ *vb* **2** to travel by or drive a dogsled. ◆ *n* **3** a journey with a dogsled. ORIG C19: ?from imperative of F *marcher* to advance

mushroom ('mʌʃruːm, -rʊm) *n* **1a** the fleshy spore-producing body of any of various fungi, typically consisting of a cap at the end of a stem. Some species, such as the field mushroom, are edible. Cf. **toadstool. 1b** (*as modifier*): *mushroom soup.* **2a** something resembling a mushroom in shape or rapid growth. **2b** (*as modifier*): *mushroom expansion.* ◆ *vb* (*intr*) **3** to grow rapidly: *demand mushroomed overnight.* **4** to assume a mushroom-like shape. ORIG C15: from OF *mousseron,* from LL *mussiriō,* from ?

mushroom cloud *n* the large mushroom-shaped cloud produced by a nuclear explosion.

mushy ('mʌʃɪ) *adj* **mushier, mushiest. 1** soft and pulpy. **2** *Inf.* excessively sentimental or emotional.
▸ 'mushily *adv* ▸ 'mushiness *n*

music ('mjuːzɪk) *n* **1** an art form consisting of sequences of sounds in time, esp. tones of definite pitch organized melodically, harmonically and rhythmically. **2** the sounds so produced, esp. by singing or musical instruments. **3** written or printed music, such as a score or set of parts. **4** any sequence of sounds perceived as pleasing or harmonious. **5 face the music.** *Inf.* to confront the consequences of one's actions. ORIG C13: via OF from L *mūsica,* from Gk *mousikē* (*tekhnē*) (art) belonging to the Muses, from *Mousa* MUSE

musical ('mjuːzɪkᵊl) *adj* **1** of, relating to, or used in music. **2** harmonious; melodious: *musical laughter.* **3** talented in or fond of music. **4** involving or set to music. ◆ *n* **5** Also called: **musical comedy.** a light romantic play or

film having dialogue interspersed with songs and dances.
▸ ˌmusiˈcality *n* ▸ ˈmusically *adv*

musical box *or* **music box** *n* a mechanical instrument that plays tunes by means of pins on a revolving cylinder striking the tuned teeth of a comblike metal plate, contained in a box.

musical chairs *n* (*functioning as sing*) **1** a party game in which players walk around chairs while music is played, there being one more player than chairs. Whenever the music stops, the player who fails to find a chair is eliminated. **2** any situation involving several people in a series of interrelated changes.

music centre *n* a single hi-fi unit containing a turntable, amplifier, radio, cassette player, and compact disc player.

music drama *n* **1** an opera in which the musical and dramatic elements are of equal importance and strongly interfused. **2** the genre of such operas. ORIG C19: from G *Musikdrama,* coined by Wagner to describe his later operas

music hall *n Chiefly Brit.* **1** a variety entertainment consisting of songs, comic turns, etc. US and Canad. name: **vaudeville. 2** a theatre at which such entertainments are staged.

musician (mjuːˈzɪʃən) *n* a person who plays or composes music, esp. as a profession.
▸ **muˈsicianly** *adj* ▸ **muˈsicianship** *n*

musicology (ˌmjuːzɪˈkɒlədʒɪ) *n* the scholarly study of music.
▸ **musicological** (ˌmjuːzɪkəˈlɒdʒɪkᵊl) *adj* ▸ **ˌmusiˈcologist** *n*

music paper *n* paper ruled or printed with a stave for writing music.

Musil ★ (*German* ˈmuːzɪl) *n* **Robert** (ˈroːbɛrt). 1880–1942, Austrian novelist, best known for *The Man Without Qualities* (1930–42).

musique concrète *French.* (myzik kɔ̃krɛt) *n* another term for **concrete music.**

musk (mʌsk) *n* **1** a strong-smelling glandular secretion of the male musk deer, used in perfumery. **2** a similar substance produced by certain other animals, such as the civet and otter, or manufactured synthetically. **3** a North American plant which has yellow flowers and was formerly cultivated for its musky scent. **4** the smell of musk or a similar heady smell. **5** (*modifier*) containing or resembling musk: *musk oil.* ORIG C14: from LL *muscus,* from Gk, from Persian, prob. from Sansk. *mushká* scrotum (from the appearance of the musk deer's musk bag), dim. of *mūsh* MOUSE

musk deer *n* a small central Asian mountain deer. The male secretes musk.

musk duck *n* **1** another name for **Muscovy duck. 2** a duck inhabiting swamps, lakes, and streams in Australia. The male emits a musky odour.

muskeg (ˈmʌsˌkɛg) *n Chiefly Canad.* **1** undrained boggy land. **2** a bog or swamp of this nature. ORIG C19: of Amerind origin: grassy swamp

muskellunge (ˈmʌskəˌlʌndʒ) *or* **maskinonge** (ˈmæskɪˌnɒndʒ) *n, pl* **muskellunges** *or* **muskellunge, maskinonges** *or* **maskinonge.** a large North American freshwater game fish, related to the pike. Often shortened (informally) to **musky** or **muskie.** ORIG C18 *maskinunga,* of Amerind origin

musket (ˈmʌskɪt) *n* a long-barrelled muzzle-loading shoulder gun used between the 16th and 18th centuries by infantry soldiers. ORIG C16: from F *mousquet,* from It. *moschetto* arrow, earlier: sparrow hawk, from *moscha* a fly, from L *musca*

musketeer (ˌmʌskɪˈtɪə) *n* (formerly) a soldier armed with a musket.

musketry (ˈmʌskɪtrɪ) *n* **1** muskets or musketeers collectively. **2** the technique of using small arms.

Muskie ★ (ˈmʌskɪ) *n* **Edmund (Sixtus).** 1914–96, US Democratic politician: Governor of Maine (1955–59): senator for Maine (1959–80): Secretary of State (1980–81).

muskmelon (ˈmʌskˌmɛlən) *n* **1** any of several varieties of the melon, such as the cantaloupe and honeydew. **2** the fruit of any of these melons, having ribbed or warty rind and sweet yellow, white, orange, or green flesh with a musky aroma.

musk ox *n* a large bovid mammal, which has a dark shaggy coat, short legs, and widely spaced downward-curving horns, and emits a musky smell: now confined to the tundras of Canada and Greenland.

muskrat (ˈmʌskˌræt) *n, pl* **muskrats** *or* **muskrat. 1** a North American beaver-like amphibious rodent, closely related to but larger than the voles. **2** the brown fur of this animal. ◆ Also called: **musquash.**

musk rose *n* a Mediterranean rose, cultivated for its white musk-scented flowers.

musky (ˈmʌskɪ) *adj* **muskier, muskiest.** resembling the smell of musk; having a heady or pungent sweet aroma.
▸ **ˈmuskiness** *n*

Muslim (ˈmʊzlɪm, ˈmʌz-) *or* **Moslem** *n, pl* **Muslims** *or* **Muslim, Moslems** *or* **Moslem. 1** a follower of the religion of Islam. ◆ *adj* **2** of or relating to Islam, its doctrines, culture, etc. ◆ Also (but not in Muslim use): **Mohammedan, Muhammadan.** ORIG C17: from Ar., lit.: one who surrenders
▸ **ˈMuslimism** *or* **ˈMoslemism** *n*

muslin (ˈmʌzlɪn) *n* a fine plain-weave cotton fabric. ORIG C17: from F *mousseline,* from It., from Ar. *mawṣilīy* of Mosul (Iraq), where it was first produced

muso (ˈmjuːzəʊ) *n, pl* **musos.** *Sl.* **1** *Brit. derog.* a musician, esp. a pop musician, regarded as being overconcerned with technique rather than musical content or expression. **2** *Austral.* any musician, esp. a professional one.

musquash (ˈmʌskwɒʃ) *n* another name for **muskrat,** esp. the fur. ORIG C17: of Amerind origin

muss (mʌs) *US & Canad. inf.* ◆ *vb* **1** (*tr;* often foll. by *up*) to make untidy; rumple. ◆ *n* **2** a state of disorder; muddle. ORIG C19: prob. a blend of MESS + FUSS
▸ **ˈmussy** *adj*

mussel (ˈmʌsᵊl) *n* **1** any of various marine bivalves, esp. the edible mussel, having a dark slightly elongated shell and living attached to rocks, etc. **2** any of various freshwater bivalves, attached to rocks, sand, etc., having a flattened oval shell (a source of mother-of-pearl). ORIG OE *muscle,* from Vulgar L *muscula* (unattested), from L *musculus,* dim. of *mūs* mouse

Musset ★ (*French* mysɛ) *n* **Alfred de** (alfrɛd də). 1810–57, French romantic poet and dramatist: his works include the play *Lorenzaccio* (1834) and the lyrics *Les Nuits* (1835–37).

Mussolini ★ (ˌmʊsəˈliːnɪ; *Italian* mussoˈliːni) *n* **Benito** (beˈniːto) known as *il Duce.* 1883–1945, Italian Fascist dictator. He was appointed prime minister by King Victor Emmanuel III (1922) and assumed dictatorial powers. He annexed Abyssinia and allied Italy with Germany (1936), entering World War II in 1940. Forced to resign following the Allied invasion of Sicily (1943), he was shot by Italian partisans.

Mussorgsky *or* **Moussorgsky** ★ (mʊˈsɔːgskɪ; *Russian* ˈmusərkskij) *n* **Modest Petrovich** (maˈdɛst pɪˈtrɔvitʃ). 1839–81, Russian composer. His works include the song cycle *Songs and Dances of Death* (1875–77), the opera *Boris Godunov* (1874), and *Pictures at an Exhibition* (1874) for piano.

Mussulman (ˈmʌsᵊlmən) *n pl* **Mussulmans.** an archaic word for **Muslim.** ORIG C16: from Persian *Musulmān* (pl) from Ar. *Muslimūn,* pl. of MUSLIM

must[1] (mʌst; *unstressed* məst, məs) *vb* (takes an infinitive without *to* or an implied infinitive) used as an auxiliary: **1** to express obligation or compulsion: *you must pay your dues.* In this sense, *must* does not form a negative. If used with a negative infinitive it indicates obligatory prohibition. **2** to indicate necessity: *I must go to the bank tomorrow.* **3** to indicate the probable correctness of a statement: *he must be there by now.* **4** to indicate inevitability: *all good things must come to an end.* **5** to express resolution: **5a** on the part of the speaker: *I must finish this.* **5b** on the part of another or others: *let him get drunk if he must.* **6** (used emphatically) to express conviction or certainty on the part of the speaker: *you must be joking.* **7**

(foll. by *away*) used with an implied verb of motion to express compelling haste: *I must away.* ◆ *n* **8** an essential or necessary thing: *strong shoes are a must for hill walking.* ORIG OE *mōste,* p.t. of *mōtan* to be allowed, be obliged to

must[2] (mʌst) *n* the pressed juice of grapes or other fruit ready for fermentation. ORIG OE, from L *mustum* new wine, from *mustus* newborn

must[3] (mʌst) *n* mustiness or mould. ORIG C17: back formation from MUSTY

must- *combining form.* indicating that something is highly recommended or desirable: *a must-see film; this season's must-haves.*

mustache (mə'stɑːʃ) *n* the US spelling of **moustache.**
▸ **mus'tached** *adj*

mustachio (mə'stɑːʃɪˌəʊ) *n, pl* **mustachios.** (*often pl*) *Often humorous.* a moustache, esp. when bushy or elaborately shaped. ORIG C16: from Sp. *mostacho* & It. *mostaccio*
▸ **mus'tachioed** *adj*

Mustafa Kemal ★ ('mʊstəfə kə'mɑːl) *n* See (Kemal) **Atatürk.**

mustang ('mʌstæŋ) *n* a small breed of horse, often wild or half wild, found in the southwestern US. ORIG C19: from Mexican Sp. *mestengo,* from *mesta* a group of stray animals

mustard ('mʌstəd) *n* **1** any of several Eurasian plants, esp. black mustard and white mustard, having yellow flowers and slender pods: cultivated for their pungent seeds. **2** a paste made from the powdered seeds of any of these plants and used as a condiment. **3a** a brownish-yellow colour. **3b** (*as adj*): *a mustard carpet.* **4** *Sl., chiefly US.* zest or enthusiasm. ORIG C13: from OF *moustarde,* from L *mustum* MUST[2], since the original was made by adding must

mustard and cress *n* seedlings of white mustard and garden cress, used in salads, etc.

mustard gas *n* an oily liquid vesicant compound used in chemical warfare. Its vapour causes blindness and burns.

mustard plaster *n Med.* a mixture of powdered black mustard seeds applied to the skin for its counterirritant effects.

musteline ('mʌstɪˌlaɪn, -lɪn) *adj* of or belonging to a family of typically predatory mammals, including weasels, ferrets, badgers, skunks, and otters. ORIG C17: from L *mustēlīnus,* from *mustēla* weasel

muster ('mʌstə) *vb* **1** to call together (numbers of men) for duty, inspection, etc., or (of men) to assemble in this way. **2 muster in** *or* **out.** *US.* to enlist into or discharge from military service. **3** (*tr;* sometimes foll. by *up*) to summon or gather: *to muster one's arguments; to muster up courage.* **4** (*tr*) *Austral. & NZ.* to round up (stock). ◆ *n* **5** an assembly of military personnel for duty, etc. **6** a collection, assembly, or gathering. **7** *Austral. & NZ.* the act of rounding up stock. **8 pass muster.** to be acceptable. ORIG C14: from OF *moustrer,* from L *monstrāre* to show, from *monstrum* portent

musth *or* **must** (mʌst) *n* (often preceded by *in*) a state of frenzied sexual excitement in the males of certain large mammals, esp. elephants. ORIG C19: from Urdu *mast,* from Persian: drunk

musty ('mʌstɪ) *adj* **mustier, mustiest. 1** smelling or tasting old, stale, or mouldy. **2** old-fashioned, dull, or hackneyed: *musty ideas.* ORIG C16: ? var. of obs. *moisty*
▸ **'mustily** *adv* ▸ **'mustiness** *n*

mutable ('mjuːtəbᵊl) *adj* able to or tending to change. ORIG C14: from L *mūtābilis* fickle, from *mūtāre* to change
▸ **ˌmuta'bility** *or* (*less commonly*) **'mutableness** *n* ▸ **'mutably** *adv*

mutagen ('mjuːtədʒən) *n* a substance that can induce genetic mutation. ORIG C20: from MUTATION + -GEN
▸ **mutagenic** (ˌmjuːtə'dʒɛnɪk) *adj*

mutagenesis (ˌmjuːtə'dʒɛnɪsɪs) *n Genetics.* the origin and development of a mutation. ORIG C20: from MUTA(TION) + -GENESIS

mutant ('mjuːtᵊnt) *n* **1** Also called: **mutation.** an animal, organism, or gene that has undergone mutation. ◆ *adj* **2** of, undergoing, or resulting from mutation. ORIG C20: from L *mutāre* to change

Mutare ★ (muː'tɑːrɪ) *n* a city in E Zimbabwe, near the Mozambique border: rail and trade centre in a mining and tobacco-growing region. Pop.: 131 808 (1992). Former name (until 1982): **Umtali.**

mutate (mjuː'teɪt) *vb* **mutates, mutating, mutated.** to undergo or cause to undergo mutation. ORIG C19: from L *mūtātus,* p.p. of *mūtāre* to change

mutation (mjuː'teɪʃən) *n* **1** the act or process of mutating; change; alteration. **2** a change or alteration. **3** a change in the chromosomes or genes of a cell which may affect the structure and development of the resultant offspring. **4** another word for **mutant** (sense 1). **5** a physical characteristic of an individual resulting from this type of chromosomal change. **6** *Phonetics.* **6a** (in Germanic languages) another name for **umlaut. 6b** (in Celtic languages) a phonetic change in certain initial consonants caused by a preceding word.
▸ **mu'tational** *adj* ▸ **mu'tationally** *adv*

mutatis mutandis *Latin.* (muː'tɑːtɪs muː'tændɪs) the necessary changes having been made.

mutch (mʌtʃ) *n* a close-fitting linen cap formerly worn by women and children in Scotland. ORIG C15: from MDu. *mutse* cap, from Med. L *almucia* AMICE

mute (mjuːt) *adj* **1** not giving out sound or speech; silent. **2** unable to speak; dumb. **3** unspoken or unexpressed. **4** *Law.* (of a person arraigned on indictment) refusing to answer a charge. **5** *Phonetics.* another word for **plosive. 6** (of a letter in a word) silent. ◆ *n* **7** a person who is unable to speak. **8** *Law.* a person who refuses to plead. **9** any of various devices used to soften the tone of stringed or brass instruments. **10** *Phonetics.* a plosive consonant. **11** a silent letter. **12** an actor in a dumb show. **13** a hired mourner. ◆ *vb* **mutes, muting, muted.** (*tr*) **14** to reduce the volume of (a musical instrument) by means of a mute, soft pedal, etc. **15** to subdue the strength of (a colour, tone, lighting, etc.). ORIG C14 *muwet* from OF *mu,* from L *mūtus* silent
▸ **'mutely** *adv* ▸ **'muteness** *n*

> **USAGE NOTE** *Mute* is occasionally wrongly used in the phrase *moot* (not *mute*) *point.*

mute swan *n* a Eurasian swan with a pure white plumage and an orange-red bill.

muti ('muːtɪ) *n S. African inf.* medicine, esp. herbal. ORIG from Zulu *umuthi* tree, medicine

mutilate ('mjuːtɪˌleɪt) *vb* **mutilates, mutilating, mutilated.** (*tr*) **1** to deprive of a limb, essential part, etc.; maim. **2** to expurgate, damage, etc. (a text, book, etc.). ORIG C16: from L *mutilāre* to cut off; rel. to *mutilus* maimed
▸ **ˌmuti'lation** *n* ▸ **'mutiˌlative** *adj* ▸ **'mutiˌlator** *n*

mutineer (ˌmjuːtɪ'nɪə) *n* a person who mutinies.

mutinous ('mjuːtɪnəs) *adj* **1** openly rebellious. **2** characteristic or indicative of mutiny.
▸ **'mutinously** *adv* ▸ **'mutinousness** *n*

mutiny ('mjuːtɪnɪ) *n, pl* **mutinies. 1** open rebellion against constituted authority, esp. by seamen or soldiers against their officers. ◆ *vb* **mutinies, mutinying, mutinied. 2** (*intr*) to engage in mutiny. ORIG C16: from obs. *mutine,* from OF *mutin* rebellious, from *meute* mutiny, ult. from L *movēre* to move

mutism ('mjuːˌtɪzəm) *n* **1** the state of being mute. **2** *Psychiatry.* **2a** a refusal to speak. **2b** the lack of development of speech.

mutt (mʌt) *n Sl.* **1** an inept, ignorant, or stupid person. **2** a mongrel dog; cur. ORIG C20: from MUTTONHEAD

mutter ('mʌtə) *vb* **1** to utter (something) in a low and indistinct tone. **2** (*intr*) to grumble or complain. **3** (*intr*) to make a low continuous murmuring sound. ◆ *n* **4** a muttered sound or complaint. ORIG C14 *moteren*
▸ **'muttering** *n, adj*

Mutter ★ ('mʊtə) *n* **Anne-Sophie.** born 1963, German violinist.

mutton ('mʌtᵊn) *n* **1** the flesh of sheep, esp. of mature sheep, used as food. **2 mutton dressed as lamb.** an older

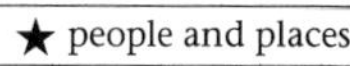
★ people and places

woman dressed up to look young. ORIG C13 *moton* sheep, from OF, from Med. L *multō*, of Celtic origin
▸ **'muttony** *adj*

mutton bird *n* any of several shearwaters, having a dark plumage with greyish underparts. In New Zealand, applied to one collected for food, esp. by Maoris. ORIG C19: from the taste of its flesh

mutton chop *n* a piece of mutton from the loin.

muttonchops ('mʌtᵊn,tʃɒps) *pl n* side whiskers trimmed in the shape of chops.

muttonhead ('mʌtᵊn,hɛd) *n Sl.* a stupid or ignorant person; fool.
▸ **'mutton,headed** *adj*

Muttra ★ ('mʌtrə) *n* the former name of **Mathura.**

mutual ('mju:tʃʊəl) *adj* **1** experienced or expressed by each of two or more people about the other; reciprocal: *mutual distrust.* **2** *Inf.* common to or shared by both: *a mutual friend.* **3** denoting an insurance company, etc., in which the policyholders share the profits and expenses and there are no shareholders. See also **mutual insurance.** ORIG C15: from OF *mutuel*, from L *mūtuus* reciprocal (orig.: borrowed); rel. to *mūtāre* to change
▸ **mutuality** (,mju:tʃʊ'ælɪtɪ) *n* ▸ **'mutually** *adv*

> **USAGE NOTE** The use of *mutual* to mean 'common to or shared by two or more people' was formerly considered incorrect by some people, on the grounds of its original meaning in Latin, but usage has now made it generally acceptable.

mutual induction *n* the production of an electromotive force in a circuit by a current change in a second circuit magnetically linked to the first.

mutual insurance *n* a system of insurance by which all policyholders become company members under contract to pay premiums into a common fund out of which claims are paid. See also **mutual** (sense 3).

mutuel ('mju:tʃʊəl) *n* short for **pari-mutuel.**

muu-muu ('mu:,mu:) *n* a loose brightly coloured dress worn by women in Hawaii. ORIG from Hawaiian

Muzak ('mju:zæk) *n Trademark.* recorded light music played in shops, restaurants, factories, etc.

muzhik *or* **moujik** ('mu:ʒɪk) *n* a Russian peasant, esp. under the tsars. ORIG C16: from Russian: peasant

Muzorewa ★ (,mʊzə'reɪwə) *n* **Abel** (**Tendekayi**) ('eɪbᵊl). born 1925, Zimbabwean Methodist bishop and politician; president of the African National Council (1971–85); prime minister of Rhodesia (1979).

muzzle ('mʌzᵊl) *n* **1** the projecting part of the face, usually the jaws and nose, of animals such as the dog and horse. **2** a guard or strap fitted over an animal's nose and jaws to prevent it biting or eating. **3** the front end of a gun barrel. ◆ *vb* **muzzles, muzzling, muzzled.** (*tr*) **4** to prevent from being heard or noticed. **5** to put a muzzle on (an animal). ORIG C15 *mosel*, from OF *musel*, dim. of *muse* snout, from Med. L *mūsus*, from ?
▸ **'muzzler** *n*

muzzle-loader *n* a firearm receiving its ammunition through the muzzle.
▸ **'muzzle-,loading** *adj*

muzzle velocity *n* the velocity of a projectile as it leaves a firearm's muzzle.

muzzy ('mʌzɪ) *adj* **muzzier, muzziest. 1** blurred or hazy. **2** confused or befuddled. ORIG C18: from ?
▸ **'muzzily** *adv* ▸ **'muzziness** *n*

MVO (in Britain) *abbrev. for* Member of the Royal Victorian Order.

MW 1 *symbol for* megawatt. **2** *Radio. abbrev. for* medium wave.

Mweru ★ ('mwɛəru:) *n* a lake in central Africa, on the border between Zambia and the Democratic Republic of Congo. Area: 4196 sq. km (1620 sq. miles).

Mx *Physics. symbol for* maxwell.

my (maɪ) *determiner* **1** of, belonging to, or associated with the speaker or writer (me): *my own ideas.* **2** used in various forms of address: *my lord.* ◆ *interj* **3** an exclamation of surprise, awe, etc.: *my, how you've grown!* ORIG C12 *mī*, var. of OE *mīn* when preceding a word beginning with a consonant

> **USAGE NOTE** See at **me**[1].

myalgia (maɪ'ældʒɪə) *n* pain in a muscle or a group of muscles. ORIG C19: from MYO- + -ALGIA

myalgic encephalomyelitis (maɪ'ældʒɪk ɛn,sɛfələʊ-,maɪɪ'laɪtɪs) *n* a former name for **chronic fatigue syndrome.** Abbrev.: **ME.**

myalism ('maɪə,lɪzəm) *n* a kind of witchcraft practised esp. in the Caribbean. ORIG C19: from *myal*, prob. West African

myall ('maɪəl) *n* **1** any of several Australian acacias having hard scented wood. **2** a native Australian living independently of society. ORIG C19: Abor. name

Myanmar *or* **Myanma** ★ ('maɪæn,mɑ:, 'mjænmɑ:) *n* a republic in SE Asia, on the Bay of Bengal and the Andaman Sea: unified from small states in 1752; annexed by Britain (1823–85) and made a province of India in 1886; became independent in 1948. It is generally mountainous, with the basins of the Chindwin and Irrawaddy Rivers in the central part and the Irrawaddy delta in the south. Official language: Burmese. Religion: chiefly Buddhist. Currency: kyat. Capital: Yangon. Pop.: 48 081 000 (1999 est.). Area: 676 577 sq. km (261 228 sq. miles). Official name: **the Union of Myanmar.** Former name (until 1989): **Burma.**

mycelium (maɪ'si:lɪəm) *n, pl* **mycelia** (-lɪə). the vegetative body of fungi: a mass of branching filaments (hyphae). ORIG C19 (lit.: nail of fungus): from MYCO- + Gk *hēlos* nail
▸ **my'celial** *adj*

Mycenae ★ (maɪ'si:ni:) *n* an ancient Greek city in the NE Peloponnesus on the plain of Argos.

Mycenaean (,maɪsɪ'ni:ən) *adj* **1** of or relating to ancient Mycenae, or its inhabitants. **2** of or relating to the Aegean civilization of Mycenae (1400 to 1100 B.C.).

-mycete *n combining form.* indicating a member of a class of fungi: *myxomycete.* ORIG from NL *-mycetes*, from Gk *mukētes*, pl. of *mukēs* fungus

myco- *or before a vowel* **myc-** *combining form.* indicating fungus: *mycology.* ORIG from Gk *mukēs* fungus

mycology (maɪ'kɒlədʒɪ) *n* the branch of biology concerned with the study of fungi.
▸ **mycological** (,maɪkə'lɒdʒɪkᵊl) *or* **,myco'logic** *adj* ▸ **my'cologist** *n*

mycoplasma (,maɪkəʊ'plæzmə) *n* any one of a genus of prokaryotic microorganisms some species of which cause disease (**mycoplasmosis**) in animals and humans.

mycorrhiza *or* **mycorhiza** (,maɪkə'raɪzə) *n, pl* **mycorrhizae** (-zi:) *or* **mycorrhizas, mycorhizae** *or* **mycorhizas.** an association of a fungus and a plant in which the fungus lives within or on the outside of the plant's roots forming a symbiotic or parasitic relationship. ORIG C19: from MYCO- + Gk *rhiza* root
▸ **,mycor'rhizal** *or* **,myco'rhizal** *adj*

mycosis (maɪ'kəʊsɪs) *n* any infection or disease caused by fungus.
▸ **mycotic** (maɪ'kɒtɪk) *adj*

mycotoxin (,maɪkə'tɒksɪn) *n* any of various toxic substances produced by fungi, some of which may affect food.
▸ **,mycotox'ology** *n*

mycotrophic (,maɪkəʊ'trɒfɪk) *adj Bot.* (of a plant) symbiotic with a fungus, esp. a mycorrhizal fungus.
▸ **mycotrophy** (maɪ'kɒtrəfɪ) *n*

myelin ('maɪɪlɪn) *or* **myeline** ('maɪɪ,li:n) *n* a white tissue forming an insulating sheath (**myelin sheath**) around certain nerve fibres. Damage to the myelin sheath causes neurological disease, as in multiple sclerosis.

myelitis (,maɪɪ'laɪtɪs) *n* inflammation of the spinal cord or of the bone marrow.

myeloma (,maɪə'ləʊmə) *n, pl* **myelomas** *or* **myelomata** (-mətə). a usually malignant tumour of the bone marrow.

Myers ★ ('maɪəz) *n* **L**(**eopold**) **H**(**amilton**). 1881–1944, British novelist, best known for his novel sequence *The Near and the Far* (1929–40).

Mykonos ★ ('mɪkənɒs, -nəʊs, 'miːkə-) *n* a Greek island in the S Aegean Sea, one of the Cyclades: a popular tourist resort with many churches. Pop.: 5500 (latest est.). Greek name: **Míkonos.**

My Lai ★ ('maɪ 'laɪ, 'miː) *n* a village in S Vietnam where in 1968 US troops massacred over 400 civilians.

mynah *or* **myna** ('maɪnə) *n* any of various tropical Asian starlings, some of which can mimic human speech. ORIG C18: from Hindi *mainā*, from Sansk. *madana*

Mynheer (mə'nɪə) *n* a Dutch title of address equivalent to *Sir* when used alone or to *Mr* before a name. ORIG C17: from Du. *mijnheer* my lord

myo- *or before a vowel* **my-** *combining form.* muscle: *myocardium.* ORIG from Gk *mus* MUSCLE

myocardium (ˌmaɪəʊ'kɑːdɪəm) *n, pl* **myocardia** (-dɪə). the muscular tissue of the heart. ORIG C19: *myo-* + *cardium*, from Gk *kardia* heart
▸ ˌ**myo'cardial** *adj*

myology (maɪ'ɒlədʒɪ) *n* the branch of medical science concerned with muscles.

myope ('maɪəʊp) *n* any person afflicted with myopia. ORIG C18: via F from Gk *muōps*; see MYOPIA

myopia (maɪ'əʊpɪə) *n* inability to see distant objects clearly because the images are focused in front of the retina; short-sightedness. ORIG C18: via NL from Gk *muōps* short-sighted, from *mūein* to close (the eyes), + *ōps* eye
▸ **myopic** (maɪ'ɒpɪk) *adj* ▸ **my'opically** *adv*

myosin ('maɪəsɪn) *n* the chief protein of muscle. ORIG C19: from MYO- + -OSE[2] + -IN

myosotis (ˌmaɪə'səʊtɪs) *n* any plant of the genus *Myosotis*. See **forget-me-not.** ORIG C18: NL from Gk *muosōtis* mouse-ear (referring to its furry leaves), from *mus* mouse + *ous* ear

myriad ('mɪrɪəd) *adj* **1** innumerable. ◆ *n* (*also used in pl*) **2** a large indefinite number. **3** *Arch.* ten thousand. ORIG C16: via LL from Gk *murias* ten thousand

myriapod ('mɪrɪəˌpɒd) *n* **1** any of a group of terrestrial arthropods having a long segmented body and many walking limbs, such as the centipedes and millipedes. ◆ *adj* **2** of, relating to, or belonging to this group. ORIG C19: from NL *Myriapoda*. See MYRIAD, -POD

Myrmidon ('mɜːmɪˌdɒn, -dᵊn) *n* **1** *Greek myth.* one of a race of people who were led against Troy by Achilles. **2** (*often not cap.*) a follower or henchman.

myrobalan (maɪ'rɒbələn, mɪ-) *n* **1** the dried plumlike fruit of various tropical trees used in dyeing, tanning, ink, and medicine. **2** a dye extracted from this fruit. ORIG C16: via L from Gk *murobalanos*, from *muron* ointment + *balanos* acorn

Myron ★ ('maɪərən) *n* 5th century B.C., Greek sculptor.

myrrh (mɜː) *n* **1** any of several trees and shrubs of Africa and S Asia that exude an aromatic resin. **2** the resin obtained from such a plant, used in perfume, incense, and medicine. ORIG OE *myrre*, via L from Gk *murrha*, ult. from Akkadian *murrū*

myrtle ('mɜːtᵊl) *n* an evergreen shrub or tree, esp. a S European shrub with pink or white flowers and aromatic blue-black berries. ORIG C16: from Med. L *myrtilla*, from L *myrtus*, from Gk *murtos*

myself (maɪ'sɛlf) *pron* **1a** the reflexive form of *I* or *me*. **1b** (intensifier): *I myself know of no answer.* **2** (*preceded by a copula*) my usual self: *I'm not myself today.* **3** *Not standard.* used instead of *I* or *me* in compound noun phrases: *John and myself are voting together.*

Mysia ★ ('mɪsɪə) *n* an ancient region in the NW corner of Asia Minor.
▸ '**Mysian** *adj, n*

Mysore ★ (maɪ'sɔː) *n* **1** a city in S India, in S Karnataka state: former capital of the state of Mysore; manufacturing and trading centre; university (1916). Pop.: 480 692 (1991). **2** the former name (until 1973) of **Karnataka.**

mysterious (mɪ'stɪərɪəs) *adj* **1** characterized by or indicative of mystery. **2** puzzling, curious.
▸ **mys'teriously** *adv* ▸ **mys'teriousness** *n*

mystery[1] ('mɪstərɪ, -trɪ) *n, pl* **mysteries. 1** an unexplained or inexplicable event, phenomenon, etc. **2** a person or thing that arouses curiosity or suspense because of an unknown, obscure, or enigmatic quality. **3** the state or quality of being obscure, inexplicable, or enigmatic. **4** a story, film, etc., which arouses suspense and curiosity because of facts concealed. **5** *Christianity.* any truth that is divinely revealed but otherwise unknowable. **6** *Christianity.* a sacramental rite, such as the Eucharist, or (*when pl*) the consecrated elements of the Eucharist. **7** (*often pl*) any rites of certain ancient Mediterranean religions. **8** short for **mystery play.** ORIG C14: via L from Gk *mustērion* secret rites

mystery[2] ('mɪstərɪ) *n, pl* **mysteries.** *Arch.* **1** a trade, occupation, or craft. **2** a guild of craftsmen. ORIG C14: from Med. L *mistērium*, from L *ministerium* occupation, from *minister* official

mystery play *n* (in the Middle Ages) a type of drama based on the life of Christ. Cf. **miracle play.**

mystery tour *n* an excursion to an unspecified destination.

mystic ('mɪstɪk) *n* **1** a person who achieves mystical experience or an apprehension of divine mysteries. ◆ *adj* **2** another word for **mystical.** ORIG C14: via L from Gk *mustikos*, from *mustēs* mystery initiate; rel. to *muein* to initiate into sacred rites

mystical ('mɪstɪkᵊl) *adj* **1** relating to or characteristic of mysticism. **2** *Christianity.* having a divine or sacred significance that surpasses human apprehension. **3** having occult or metaphysical significance.
▸ '**mystically** *adv*

mysticism ('mɪstɪˌsɪzəm) *n* **1** belief in or experience of a reality surpassing normal human understanding or experience. **2** a system of contemplative prayer and spirituality aimed at achieving direct intuitive experience of the divine. **3** obscure or confused belief or thought.

mystify ('mɪstɪˌfaɪ) *vb* **mystifies, mystifying, mystified.** (*tr*) **1** to confuse, bewilder, or puzzle. **2** to make obscure. ORIG C19: from F *mystifier*, from *mystère* MYSTERY[1] or *mystique* MYSTIC
▸ ˌ**mystifi'cation** *n* ▸ '**mystiˌfying** *adj*

mystique (mɪ'stiːk) *n* an aura of mystery, power, and awe that surrounds a person or thing. ORIG C20: from F (adj): MYSTIC

myth (mɪθ) *n* **1a** a story about superhuman beings of an earlier age, usually of how natural phenomena, social customs, etc., came into existence. **1b** another word for **mythology** (senses 1, 3). **2** a person or thing whose existence is fictional or unproven. ORIG C19: via LL from Gk *muthos* fable

myth. *abbrev. for:* **1** mythological. **2** mythology.

mythical ('mɪθɪkᵊl) *or* **mythic** *adj* **1** of or relating to myth. **2** imaginary or fictitious.
▸ '**mythically** *adv*

mythicize *or* **mythicise** ('mɪθɪˌsaɪz) *vb* **mythicizes, mythicizing, mythicized** *or* **mythicises, mythicising, mythicised.** (*tr*) to make into or treat as a myth.
▸ '**mythicist** *n*

mytho- *combining form.* myth: *mythopoeia.*

mythologize *or* **mythologise** (mɪ'θɒləˌdʒaɪz) *vb* **mythologizes, mythologizing, mythologized** *or* **mythologises, mythologising, mythologised. 1** to tell, study, or explain (myths). **2** (*intr*) to create or make up myths. **3** (*tr*) to convert into a myth.
▸ **my'tholoˌgizer** *or* **my'tholoˌgiser** *n*

mythology (mɪ'θɒlədʒɪ) *n, pl* **mythologies. 1** a body of myths, esp. one associated with a particular culture, person, etc. **2** a body of stories about a person, institution, etc. **3** myths collectively. **4** the study of myths.
▸ **mythological** (ˌmɪθə'lɒdʒɪkᵊl) *adj* ▸ **my'thologist** *n*

mythomania (ˌmɪθəʊ'meɪnɪə) *n Psychiatry.* the tendency to lie or exaggerate, occurring in some mental disorders.
▸ ˌ**mytho'maniˌac** *n, adj*

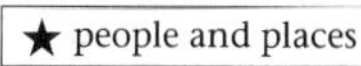

mythopoeia (ˌmɪθəʊˈpiːə) *n* the composition or making of myths. ORIG C19: from Gk, ult. from *muthos* myth + *poiein* to make
► ˌ**mythoˈpoeic** *adj*

mythos (ˈmaɪθɒs, ˈmɪθɒs) *n, pl* **mythoi** (-θɔɪ). **1** the complex of beliefs, values, attitudes, etc., characteristic of a specific group or society. **2** another word for **myth** or **mythology**.

Mytilene ★ (ˌmɪtɪˈliːnɪ) *n* **1** a port on the Greek island of Lesbos: Roman remains; Byzantine fortress. Pop.: 25 000 (latest est.). Modern Greek name: **Mitilíni**. **2** a former name for **Lesbos**.

myxo (ˈmɪksəʊ) *n Austral. sl.* myxomatosis.

myxo- *or before a vowel* **myx-** *combining form.* mucus or slime: *myxomatosis.* ORIG from Gk *muxa*

myxoedema *or US* **myxedema** (ˌmɪksɪˈdiːmə) *n* a disease resulting from underactivity of the thyroid gland characterized by puffy eyes, face, and hands and mental sluggishness. See also **cretinism**.

myxoma (mɪkˈsəʊmə) *n, pl* **myxomas** *or* **myxomata** (-mətə). a tumour composed of mucous connective tissue, usually situated in subcutaneous tissue.
► **myxomatous** (mɪkˈsɒmətəs) *adj*

myxomatosis (ˌmɪksəməˈtəʊsɪs) *n* an infectious and usually fatal viral disease of rabbits characterized by swelling of the mucous membranes and formation of skin tumours.

myxomycete (ˌmɪksəʊmaɪˈsiːt) *n* a slime mould, esp. a slime mould of the phylum *Myxomycota* (division *Myxomycetes* in traditional classifications).

myxovirus (ˈmɪksəʊˌvaɪrəs) *n* any of a group of viruses that cause influenza, mumps, etc.

★ people and places

Nn

n *or* **N** (ɛn) *n, pl* **n's, N's,** *or* **Ns. 1** the 14th letter of the English alphabet. **2** a speech sound represented by this letter.

n[1] *symbol for:* **1** neutron. **2** *Optics.* index of refraction. **3** nano-.

n[2] (ɛn) *determiner* an indefinite number (of): *there are n objects in a box.*

N *symbol for:* **1** Also: **kt.** *Chess.* knight. **2** newton(s). **3** *Chem.* nitrogen. **4** North. **5** noun. **6** (*in combination*) nuclear: *N-power; N-plant.*

n. *abbrev. for:* **1** neuter. **2** new. **3** nominative. **4** noon. **5** note. **6** noun. **7** number.

N. *abbrev. for:* **1** National(ist). **2** Navy. **3** New. **4** Norse.

Na *the chemical symbol for* sodium. ORIG L *natrium*

NA *abbrev. for* North America.

NAAFI *or* **Naafi** ('næfɪ) *n* **1** *acronym for* Navy, Army, and Air Force Institutes: an organization providing canteens, shops, etc., for British military personnel at home or overseas. **2** a canteen, shop, etc., run by this organization.

naartjie ('nɑːtʃɪ) *n S. African.* a tangerine. ORIG from Afrik., from Tamil

nab (næb) *vb* **nabs, nabbing, nabbed.** (*tr*) *Inf.* **1** to arrest (a criminal, etc.). **2** to seize suddenly; snatch. ORIG C17: ? of Scand. origin

nabla ('næblə) *n Maths.* another name for **del.** ORIG C19: from Gk: stringed instrument, because it is shaped like a harp

Nablus ★ ('nɑːbləs) *n* a town west of the River Jordan: near the site of ancient Shechem. Pop.: 98 000 (1989 est.).

nabob ('neɪbɒb) *n* **1** *Inf.* a rich or important man. **2** (formerly) a European who made a fortune in India. **3** another name for a **nawab.** ORIG C17: from Port. *nababo,* from Hindi *nawwāb;* see NAWAB

Nabokov ★ (nə'bɒkɒf, 'næbəˌkɒf) *n* **Vladimir Vladimirovich** (vla'dimir vla'dimirəvitʃ). 1899–1977, US novelist, born in Russia. His works include *Lolita* (1955), *Pnin* (1957), and *Ada* (1969).
▸ **Nabokovian** (ˌnæbə'kəʊvɪən) *adj*

Naboth ★ ('neɪbɒθ) *n Old Testament.* an inhabitant of Jezreel, murdered by King Ahab at the instigation of his wife Jezebel for refusing to sell his vineyard (I Kings 21).

NAC *abbrev. for* National Advisory Council.

nacelle (nə'sɛl) *n* a streamlined enclosure on an aircraft, not part of the fuselage, to accommodate an engine, passengers, crew, etc. ORIG C20: from F: small boat, from LL *nāvicella,* a dim. of L *nāvis* ship

nacho ('nɑːtʃəʊ) *n, pl* **nachos.** a Mexican snack consisting of a piece of tortilla topped with melted cheese.

NACODS ('neɪkɒdz) *n* (in Britain) *acronym for* National Association of Colliery Overmen, Deputies, and Shotfirers.

nacre ('neɪkə) *n* the technical name for **mother-of-pearl.** ORIG C16: via F from OIt. *naccara,* from Ar. *naqqārah* shell, drum
▸ **'nacred** *adj*

nacreous ('neɪkrɪəs) *adj* relating to, consisting of, or having the lustre of mother-of-pearl.

NACRO *or* **Nacro** ('nækrəʊ) *n* (in Britain) *acronym for* National Association for the Care and Resettlement of Offenders.

Nader ★ ('neɪdə) *n* **Ralph.** born 1934, US lawyer and campaigner for consumer rights.

nadir ('neɪdɪə, 'næ-) *n* **1** the point on the celestial sphere directly below an observer and diametrically opposite the zenith. **2** the lowest point; depths. ORIG C14: from OF, from Ar. *nazīr as-samt,* lit.: opposite the zenith

nadors ('nɑːˌdɔːz) *n S. African.* a thirst brought on by excessive consumption of alcohol. ORIG from Afrik. *na* after + *dors* thirst

nae (neɪ) *or* **na** (nɑː) a Scot. word for **no[2]** or **not.**

naevus *or US* **nevus** ('niːvəs) *n, pl* **naevi** *or US* **nevi** (-vaɪ). any pigmented blemish on the skin; birthmark or mole. ORIG C19: from L; rel. to (*g*)*natus* born, produced by nature
▸ **'naevoid** *or US* **'nevoid** *adj*

naff (næf) *adj Brit. sl.* inferior; in poor taste. ORIG C19: ?from back slang on *fan,* short for FANNY
▸ **'naffness** *n*

naff off *sentence substitute. Brit sl.* a forceful expression of dismissal or contempt.

NAFTA ('næftə) *n acronym for* North American Free Trade Agreement.

nag[1] (næg) *vb* **nags, nagging, nagged. 1** to scold or annoy constantly. **2** (when *intr,* often foll. by *at*) to be a constant source of discomfort or worry (to). ◆ *n* **3** a person, esp. a woman, who nags. ORIG C19: of Scand. origin
▸ **'nagger** *n*

nag[2] (næg) *n* **1** *Often derog.* a horse. **2** a small riding horse. ORIG C14: of Gmc origin

Nagaland ★ ('nɑːgəˌlænd) *n* a state of NE India: formed in 1962 from parts of Assam and the North-East Frontier Agency; inhabited chiefly by Naga tribes; consists of almost inaccessible forested hills and mountains (the **Naga Hills**); shifting cultivation predominates. Capital: Kohima. Pop.: 1 410 000 (1994 est.). Area: 16 579 sq. km (6401 sq. miles).

nagana (nə'gɑːnə) *n* a disease of hoofed animals of central and southern Africa, transmitted by tsetse flies. ORIG from Zulu *u-nakane*

Nagano ★ (nə'gɑːnəʊ) *n* a city in central Japan, on central Honshu: Buddhist shrine; two universities. Pop.: 358 512 (1995).

Nagasaki ★ (ˌnɑːgə'sɑːkɪ) *n* a port in SW Japan, on W Kyushu: almost completely destroyed in 1945 by the second atomic bomb dropped on Japan by the US; shipbuilding industry. Pop.: 438 724 (1995).

Nagorno-Karabakh Autonomous Region ★ (nə'gɔːnəʊkərʌ'bɑːk) *n* an administrative division of S Azerbaijan: acquired by Russia in 1813. In 1991 Armenian claims to the region culminated in its unilateral declaration as an independent Armenian republic and armed conflict broke out. Capital: Stepanakert. Pop.: 193 300 (1991 est.). Area: 4400 sq. km (1700 sq. miles).

Nagoya ★ ('nɑːgəʊjə) *n* a city in central Japan, on S Honshu on Ise Bay: a major industrial centre. Pop.: 2 152 258 (1995).

Nagpur ★ (næg'pʊə) *n* a city in central India, in NE Maharashtra state: became capital of the kingdom of Nagpur (1743); capital of the Central Provinces (later Madhya Pradesh) from 1861 to 1956. Pop.: 1 624 752 (1991).

Nagy ★ (*Hungarian* nɔdj) *n* **Imre** ('imrɛ). 1896–1958, Hungarian statesman; prime minister (1953–55; 1956): removed from office when Soviet forces suppressed the revolution of 1956: executed; reburied with honours in 1989.

Nagyszeben ★ ('nɔdjseːˌbɛn) *n* the Hungarian name for **Sibiu.**

Nagyvárad ★ ('nɔdjvaːrɔd) *n* the Hungarian name for **Oradea.**

Nah. *Bible. abbrev. for* Nahum.

Naha ★ ('nɑːhə) *n* a port in S Japan, on the SW coast of Okinawa Island: chief city of the Ryukyu Islands. Pop.: 301 928 (1995).

★ people and places

NAHT (in Britain) *abbrev. for* National Association of Head Teachers.

Nahuatl ('nɑːwɑːtᵊl, nɑː'wɑːtᵊl) *n* **1** (*pl* **Nahuatl** *or* **Nahuatls**) a member of one of a group of Central American and Mexican Indian peoples including the Aztecs. **2** the language of these peoples.

Nahum ★ ('neɪhəm) *n Old Testament.* **1** a Hebrew prophet of the 7th century B.C. **2** the book containing his oracles.

naiad ('naɪæd) *n, pl* **naiads** *or* **naiades** (-əˌdiːz). **1** *Greek myth.* a nymph dwelling in a lake, river, or spring. **2** the aquatic larva of the dragonfly, mayfly, and related insects. **3** Also called: **water nymph.** a submerged aquatic plant, with narrow leaves and small flowers. ORIG C17: via L from Gk *nāias* water nymph; rel. to *náein* to flow

naïf (nɑː'iːf) *adj, n* a less common word for **naive.**

nail (neɪl) *n* **1** a fastening device, usually made of metal, having a point at one end and a head at the other. **2** anything resembling such a device in function or shape. **3** the horny plate covering part of the dorsal surface of the fingers or toes. Related adj: **ungual. 4** the claw of a mammal, bird, or reptile. **5** a unit of length, formerly used for measuring cloth, equal to two and a quarter inches. **6 hit the nail on the head.** to do or say something correct or telling. **7 on the nail.** (of payments) at once. ◆ *vb* (*tr*) **8** to attach with or as if with nails. **9** *Inf.* to arrest, catch, or seize. **10** *Inf.* to hit or bring down, as with a shot. **11** *Inf.* to expose or detect (a lie or liar). **12** to fix (one's eyes, attention, etc.) on. **13** to stud with nails. ORIG OE *nægl*
▸ **'nailer** *n*

nail bar *n* a type of beauty salon specializing in manicure and the decoration of, esp. women's, fingernails.

nail-biting *n* **1** the act or habit of biting one's fingernails. **2a** anxiety or tension. **2b** (*as modifier*): *nail-biting suspense.*

nail bomb *n* an explosive device containing nails, used by terrorists to cause serious injuries in crowded situations.

nailbrush ('neɪlˌbrʌʃ) *n* a small stiff-bristled brush for cleaning the fingernails.

nailfile ('neɪlˌfaɪl) *n* a small file of metal or of board coated with emery, used to trim the nails.

nail polish *or* **varnish** *or esp. US* **enamel** *n* a quick-drying cosmetic lacquer applied to colour the nails or make them shiny or esp. both.

nail set *or* **punch** *n* a punch for driving the head of a nail below or flush with the surrounding surface.

nainsook ('neɪnsʊk, 'næn-) *n* a light soft plain-weave cotton fabric. ORIG C19: from Hindi, from *nain* eye + *sukh* delight

Naipaul ★ (naɪ'pɔːl) *n* Sir **V(idiadhar) S(urajprasad).** born 1932, Trinidadian novelist of Indian descent, living in Britain. His books include *A House for Mr Biswas* (1961), *A Way in the World* (1994), and *Letters Between a Father and Son* (1999).

naira ('naɪrə) *n* the standard monetary unit of Nigeria. ORIG C20: altered from *Nigeria*

Nairnshire ★ ('nɛənˌʃɪə, -ʃə) *n* a historic county of NE Scotland, now part of Highland.

Nairobi ★ (naɪ'rəʊbɪ) *n* the capital of Kenya, in the southwest at an altitude of 1650 m (5500 ft): founded in 1899; became capital in 1905; commercial and industrial centre; the **Nairobi National Park** (a game reserve) is nearby. Pop.: 2 000 000 (1991 est.).

naive, naïve (nɑː'iːv, naɪ'iːv), *or* **naïf** *adj* **1** having or expressing innocence and credulity; ingenuous. **2** lacking developed powers of reasoning or criticism: *a naive argument.* **3** another word for **primitive** (sense 5). ◆ *n* **4** a person who is naive, esp. in artistic style. See **primitive** (sense 10). ORIG C17: from F fem of *naïf,* from OF: native, spontaneous, from L *nātīvus* NATIVE
▸ **na'ively, na'ïvely,** *or* **na'ïfly** *adv* ▸ **na'iveness, na'ïveness,** *or* **na'ïfness** *n*

naivety (naɪ'iːvtɪ), **naiveté,** *or* **naïveté** (ˌnɑːiːv'teɪ) *n, pl* **naiveties, naivetés** *or* **naïvetés. 1** the state or quality of being naive. **2** a naive act or statement.

naked ('neɪkɪd) *adj* **1** having the body unclothed; undressed. **2** having no covering; exposed: *a naked flame.* **3** with no qualification or concealment: *the naked facts.* **4** unaided by any optical instrument (esp. in **the naked eye**). **5** (usually foll. by *of*) destitute: *naked of weapons.* **6** (of animals) lacking hair, feathers, scales, etc. **7** *Law.* **7a** unsupported by authority: *a naked contract.* **7b** lacking some essential condition to render valid; incomplete. ORIG OE *nacod*
▸ **'nakedly** *adv* ▸ **'nakedness** *n*

naked ladies *n* (*functioning as sing*) another name for **autumn crocus.**

naked lady *n* a pink orchid found in Australia and New Zealand.

Nakhichevan ★ (*Russian* nəxitʃɪ'vanj) *n* a city in W Azerbaijan, capital of the Nakhichevan Autonomous Republic: an ancient trading town. Pop.: 66 800 (1994). Ancient name: **Naxuana** (ˌnæk'swɑːnə).

Nakhichevan Autonomous Republic ★ (nəˌkɪtʃɛ'vɑːn) *n* an administrative division of Azerbaijan, from which it is separated by part of Armenia; annexed by Russia in 1828; unilaterally declared secession from the Soviet Union in 1990. Capital: Nakhichevan. Pop.: 315 000 (1994). Area: 5500 sq. km (2120 sq. miles).

Nakuru ★ (nə'kuːruː) *n* a town in W Kenya, on Lake Nakuru: commercial centre of an agricultural region. Pop.: 124 200 (1991 est.).

Nalchik ★ (*Russian* 'naljtʃik) *n* a city in SW Russia, capital of the Kabardino-Balkar Autonomous Republic, in a valley of the Caucasus: health resort. Pop.: 239 000 (1995 est.).

NALGO ('nælgəʊ) *n* (formerly, in Britain) *acronym for* National and Local Government Officers' Association.

naltrexone (næl'trɛksəʊn) *n* a drug that blocks opioid receptors in the brain and is used in treatments for opioid addiction.

Nam *or* **'Nam** (næm) *n US inf.* short for Vietnam (referring to the Vietnam War).

Namangan ★ (*Russian* nəman'gan) *n* a city in E Uzbekistan. Pop.: 341 000 (1996).

Namaqualand ★ (nə'mɑːkwəˌlænd) *n* a semiarid coastal region of SW Africa, extending from near Windhoek, in Namibia, into W South Africa: divided by the Orange River into **Little Namaqualand** in South Africa, and **Great Namaqualand** in Namibia; rich mineral resources. Area: 47 961 sq. km (18 518 sq. miles). Also called: **Namaland** ('nɑːməˌlænd).

namby-pamby (ˌnæmbɪ'pæmbɪ) *adj* **1** sentimental or prim in a weak insipid way. **2** clinging, feeble, or spineless. ◆ *n, pl* **namby-pambies. 3** a person who is namby-pamby. ORIG C18: a nickname of Ambrose Phillips (died 1749), whose pastoral verse was ridiculed for being insipid

Nam Co ('nɑːm 'kɔː) *or* **Nam Tso** ★ *n* a salt lake in SW China, in SE Tibet at an altitude of 4629 m (15 186 ft). Area: about 1800 sq. km (700 sq. miles). Also called: **Tengri Nor.**

name (neɪm) *n* **1** a word or term by which a person or thing is commonly and distinctively known. **2** mere outward appearance as opposed to fact: *he was ruler in name only.* **3** a word or phrase descriptive of character, usually abusive: *to call a person names.* **4** reputation, esp., if unspecified, good reputation: *he's made quite a name for himself.* **5a** a famous person or thing: *a name in the advertising world.* **5b** *Chiefly US & Canad.* (*as modifier*): *a name product.* **6** a member of Lloyd's who provides part of the capital of a syndicate and shares in its profits or losses but does not arrange its business. **7 in the name of. 7a** for the sake of. **7b** by the authority of. **8 name of the game. 8a** anything that is significant or important. **8b** normal conditions, circumstances, etc.: *in gambling, losing money's the name of the game.* **9 to one's name.** belonging to one: *I haven't a penny to my name.* ◆ *vb* **names, naming, named.** (*tr*) **10** to give a name to. **11** to refer to by name; cite: *he named three French poets.* **12** to fix or specify: *they have named a date for the meeting.* **13** to appoint or nominate: *he was named Journalist of the Year.* **14** (*tr*) to ban (an MP) from the House of Commons by mentioning him or her formally by name as being guilty of disorderly

conduct. **15 name and shame.** to reveal the identity of (a person or organization guilty of illegal or unacceptable behaviour) in order to embarrass them into not repeating the offence. **16 name names.** to cite people, esp. in order to blame or accuse them. **17 name the day.** to choose the day for an event, esp. one's wedding. ORIG OE *nama,* rel. to L *nomen,* Gk *noma*
▸ **'namable** *or* **'nameable** *adj*

name-calling *n* verbal abuse.

namecheck ('neɪmˌtʃɛk) *vb (tr)* **1** to mention (someone) specifically by name. ◆ *n* **2** a specific mention of someone's name, for example on a radio programme.

name day *n* **1** *RC Church.* the feast day of a saint whose name one bears. **2** another name for **ticket day.**

name-dropping *n Inf.* the practice of referring frequently to famous people, esp. as though they were intimate friends, in order to impress others.
▸ **'name-ˌdropper** *n*

nameless ('neɪmlɪs) *adj* **1** without a name. **2** indescribable: *a nameless horror seized him.* **3** too unpleasant or disturbing to be mentioned: *nameless atrocities.*
▸ **'namelessness** *n*

namely ('neɪmlɪ) *adv* that is to say.

Namen ★ ('na:mə) *n* the Flemish name for **Namur.**

nameplate ('neɪmˌpleɪt) *n* a small panel on or next to the door of a room or building, bearing the occupant's name and profession.

namesake ('neɪmˌseɪk) *n* a person or thing named after another, or with the same name as another. ORIG C17: prob. describing people connected *for the name's sake*

nametape ('neɪmˌteɪp) *n* a tape bearing the owner's name and attached to an article.

Namhoi ★ ('nɑ:m'hɔɪ) *n* another name for **Foshan.**

Namibe ★ (nə'mi:b) *n* a port in SW Angola: fishing industry. Pop.: 77 000 (1987).

Namibia ★ (nə'mɪbɪə) *n* a country in southern Africa bordering on South Africa: annexed by Germany in 1884 and mandated by the League of Nations to South Africa in 1920. The mandate was terminated by the UN in 1966 but this was ignored by South Africa; achieved independence in 1990 and joined the Commonwealth. Official language: English; Afrikaans and German also spoken. Religion: mostly animist, with some Christians. Currency: dollar. Capital: Windhoek. Pop.: 1 648 000 (1999 est.). Area: 823 328 sq. km (317 887 sq. miles). Also called: **South West Africa.** Former name (1885–1919): **German Southwest Africa.**
▸ **Na'mibian** *adj, n*

Namier ★ ('neɪmɪə) *n* Sir **Lewis Bernstein,** original name *Ludwik Bernsztajn vel Niemirowski.* 1888–1960, British political historian, born in Poland.

Nam Tso ★ ('nɑ:m 'tsɔ:) *n* a variant transliteration of the Chinese name for **Nam Co.**

Namur ★ (næ'mʊə; *French* namyr) *n* **1** a province of S Belgium. Capital: Namur. Pop.: 438 864 (1998 est.). Area: 3660 sq. km (1413 sq. miles). **2** a town in S Belgium, capital of Namur province: strategically situated on a promontory between the Sambre and Meuse Rivers, besieged and captured many times. Pop.: 105 059 (1996 est.). Flemish name: **Namen.**

nan (næn), **nana,** *or* **nanna** ('nænə) *n* a child's word for **grandmother.**

nana ('nɑ:nə) *n* **1** *Sl.* a fool. **2 do one's nana.** *Austral. sl.* to become very angry. **3 off one's nana.** *Austral. sl.* mad; insane. ORIG C19: prob. from BANANA

nan bread *or* **naan** (nɑ:n) *n* (in Indian cookery) a slightly leavened bread in a large flat leaf shape. ORIG from Hindi

Nanchang *or* **Nan-ch'ang** ★ ('næn'tʃæŋ) *n* a walled city in SE China, capital of Jiangxi province, on the Kan River: largest city in the Poyang basin. Pop.: 1 350 000 (1991 est.).

Nan-ching ★ ('næn'tʃɪŋ) *n* a variant spelling of **Nanjing.**

nancy ('nænsɪ) *n, pl* **nancies.** an effeminate or homosexual boy or man. Also called: **nance, nancy boy.** ORIG C20: from the girl's name *Nancy*

Nancy ★ ('nænsɪ; *French* nɑ̃si) *n* a city in NE France: became the capital of the dukes of Lorraine in the 12th century, becoming French in 1766; administrative and financial centre. Pop.: 102 410 (1990).

Nanda Devi ★ ('nʌndə 'di:vɪ) *n* a mountain in N India, in N Uttar Pradesh in the Himalayas. Height: 7817 m (25 645 ft).

NAND circuit *or* **gate** (nænd) *n Electronics.* a computer logic circuit having two or more input wires and one output wire that has an output signal if one or more of the input signals are at a low voltage. Cf. **OR circuit.** ORIG C20: from *not* + AND; see NOT CIRCUIT, AND CIRCUIT

nandrolone ('nændrəˌləʊn) *n* an anabolic steroid present in the body in small amounts but also produced by metabolism of other steroids, sometimes taken as performance-enhancing drugs by athletes and bodybuilders.

Nanga Parbat ★ ('nʌŋgə 'pɑ:bʌt) *n* a mountain in N India, in NW Kashmir in the W Himalayas. Height: 8126 m (26 660 ft).

Nanhai ★ ('nɑ:n'haɪ) *n* the Chinese name for the **South China Sea.**

Nanjing ('næn'dʒɪŋ), **Nanking** ('næn'kɪŋ) *or* **Nanching** ★ *n* a port in E central China, capital of Jiangsu province, on the Yangtze River: capital of the Chinese empire and a literary centre from the 14th to 17th centuries; capital of Nationalist China (1928–37); site of a massacre of about 300 000 civilians by the invading Japanese army in 1937; university (1928). Pop.: 2 500 000 (1991 est.).

nankeen (næŋ'ki:n) *or* **nankin** ('nænkɪn) *n* **1** a hardwearing buff-coloured cotton fabric. **2a** a pale greyish-yellow colour. **2b** *(as adj)*: *a nankeen carpet.* ORIG C18: after *Nanking,* China, where it originated

Nanning *or* **Nan-ning** ★ ('næn'nɪŋ) *n* a port in S China, capital of Guanxi Zhuang AR, on the Xiang River: rail links with North Vietnam. Pop.: 1 070 000 (1991 est.).

nanny ('nænɪ) *n, pl* **nannies. 1** a nurse or nursemaid for children. **2a** any person or thing regarded as treating people like children, esp. by being overprotective. **2b** *(as modifier)*: *the nanny state.* **3** a child's word for **grandmother.** ◆ *vb* **nannies, nannying, nannied. 4** *(intr)* to nurse or look after someone else's children. **5** *(tr)* to be overprotective towards. ORIG C19: child's name for a nurse

nannygai ('nænɪˌgaɪ) *n, pl* **nannygais.** an edible red Australian sea fish. ORIG from Abor.

nanny goat *n* a female goat.

nano- *combining form.* denoting 10^{-9}: *nanometre; nanosecond.* Symbol: n ORIG from L *nānus* dwarf, from Gk *nanos*

nanotechnology (ˌnænəʊtɛk'nɒlədʒɪ) *n* a branch of technology dealing with the manufacture of objects with dimensions of less than 100 thousand-millionths of a metre and the manipulation of individual molecules and atoms.

Nansen ★ ('nænsən) *n* **Fridtjof** ('fridjɔf). 1861–1930, Norwegian arctic explorer. He attempted to reach the North Pole (1893–96), and became League of Nations' high commissioner for refugees (1920–22): Nobel peace prize 1922.

Nansen bottle *n* an instrument used by oceanographers for obtaining samples of sea water from a desired depth. ORIG C19: after F. NANSEN

Nan Shan ★ ('næn 'ʃæn) *pl n* a mountain range in N central China, mainly in Qinghai province, with peaks over 6000 m (20 000 ft).

Nanterre ★ (*French* nɑ̃tɛr) *n* a town in N France, on the Seine: an industrial suburb of Paris. Pop.: 84 565 (1990).

Nantes ★ (*French* nɑ̃t) *n* a port in W France, at the head of the Loire estuary: scene of the signing of the Edict of Nantes and of the Noyades (drownings) during the French Revolution; extensive shipyards, and large metallurgical and food processing industries. Pop.: 264 857 (1990).

Nantong *or* **Nantung** ★ ('næn'tʌŋ) *n* a city in E China, in Jiangsu province on the Yangtze estuary. Pop.: 343 341 (1990 est.).

Nantucket ★ (næn'tʌkɪt) *n* an island off SE Massachusetts: formerly a centre of the whaling industry; now a resort. Length: nearly 24 km (15 miles). Width: 5 km (3 miles). Pop.: 6012 (1990).

Naoise ★ ('ni:ʃə) *n Irish myth.* the husband of Deirdre, killed by his uncle Conchobar. See also **Deirdre.**

Naomi ★ ('neɪəmɪ) *n Old Testament.* the mother-in-law of Ruth (Ruth 1:2). Douay spelling: **Noemi.**

nap[1] (næp) *vb* **naps, napping, napped.** (*intr*) **1** to sleep for a short while; doze. **2** to be inattentive or off guard (esp. in **catch someone napping**). ◆ *n* **3** a short light sleep; doze. ORIG OE *hnappian*

nap[2] (næp) *n* **1a** the raised fibres of velvet or similar cloth. **1b** the direction in which these fibres lie. **2** any similar downy coating. **3** *Austral. inf.* blankets; bedding. ◆ *vb* **naps, napping, napped. 4** (*tr*) to raise the nap of (velvet, etc.) by brushing. ORIG C15: prob. from MDu. *noppe*

nap[3] (næp) *n* **1** Also called: **napoleon.** a card game similar to whist, usually played for stakes. **2** a call in this game, undertaking to win all five tricks. **3** *Horse racing.* a tipster's choice for a certain winner. **4 nap hand.** a position in which there is a very good chance of success if a risk is taken. ◆ *vb* **naps, napping, napped.** (*tr*) **5** *Horse racing.* to name (a horse) as likely to win a race. ORIG C19: from NAPOLEON, the card game

napalm ('neɪpɑ:m, 'næ-) *n* **1** a thick and highly incendiary liquid, usually consisting of petrol gelled with aluminium soaps, used in firebombs, flame-throwers, etc. ◆ *vb* **2** (*tr*) to attack with napalm. ORIG C20: from NA(PHTHENE) + *palm(itate)* salt of PALMITIC ACID

nape (neɪp) *n* the back of the neck. ORIG C13: from ?

napery ('neɪpərɪ) *n Scot. & Arch.* household linen, esp. table linen. ORIG C14: from OF *naperie,* from *nape* tablecloth, from L *mappa*

Naphtali ★ ('næftəˌlaɪ) *n Old Testament.* **1** Jacob's sixth son, whose mother was Rachel's handmaid (Genesis 30:7–8). **2** the tribe descended from him. **3** the territory of this tribe, between the Sea of Galilee and the mountains of central Galilee. Douay spelling: **Nephtali.**

naphtha ('næfθə, 'næp-) *n* a distillation product from coal tar or petroleum: used as a solvent and in petrol. ORIG C16: via L from Gk, from Iranian

naphthalene ('næfθəˌli:n, 'næp-) *n* a white crystalline hydrocarbon with a characteristic penetrating odour, used in mothballs and in dyes, explosives, etc. Formula: $C_{10}H_8$. ORIG C19: from NAPHTHA + ALCOHOL + -ENE
▸ **naphthalic** (næf'θælɪk, næp-) *adj*

naphthene ('næfθi:n, 'næp-) *n* any of various cyclic methylene hydrocarbons found in petroleum. ORIG C20: from NAPHTHA + -ENE

naphthol ('næfθɒl, 'næp-) *n* a white crystalline solid having two isomeric forms, used in dyes and as an antioxidant. Formula: $C_{10}H_7OH$. ORIG C19: from NAPHTHA + -OL[1]

Napier[1] ★ ('neɪpɪə) *n* a port in New Zealand, on E North Island on Hawke Bay: wool trade centre. Pop.: 53 500 (1995 est.).

Napier[2] ★ ('neɪpɪə) *n* **1** Sir **Charles James.** 1782–1853, British general: conquered Sind (1843): governor of Sind (1843–47). **2 John.** 1550–1617, Scottish mathematician: invented logarithms and pioneered the decimal notation.

Napierian logarithm (nə'pɪərɪən, neɪ-) *n* another name for **natural logarithm.**

Napier's bones *pl n* a set of graduated rods formerly used for multiplication and division. ORIG C17: based on a method invented by John NAPIER

napkin ('næpkɪn) *n* **1** Also called: **table napkin.** a usually square piece of cloth or paper used while eating to protect the clothes, wipe the mouth, etc.; serviette. **2** *Rare.* a small piece of cloth. **3** a more formal name for **nappy**[1]. **4** a less common term for **sanitary towel.** ORIG C15: from OF, from *nape* tablecloth, from L *mappa* cloth

Naples ★ ('neɪpᵊlz) *n* **1** a port in SW Italy, capital of Campania region, on the Bay of Naples: the third largest city in the country; founded by Greeks in the 6th century B.C.; incorporated into the Kingdom of the Two Sicilies in 1140 and its capital (1282–1503); university (1224). Pop.: 1 050 234 (1996 est.). Ancient name: **Ne'apolis.** Italian name: **Napoli.** Related adj: **Neapolitan. 2 Bay of.** an inlet of the Tyrrhenian Sea in the SW coast of Italy.

napoleon (nə'pəʊlɪən) *n* **1** a former French gold coin worth 20 francs. **2** *Cards.* the full name for **nap**[3] (sense 1). ORIG C19: from F *napoléon,* after NAPOLEON I

Napoleon I ★ (nə'pəʊlɪən) *n* full name *Napoleon Bonaparte.* 1769–1821, Emperor of the French (1804–15). Coming to power after a coup in 1799, he defeated every European coalition against him until, weakened by the Peninsular War and the Russian campaign (1812), he was defeated at Leipzig (1813) and, finally, at Waterloo (1815). The *Code Napoléon* remains the basis of French law.

Napoleon II ★ *n* Duke of Reichstadt. 1811–32, son of Napoleon Bonaparte and Marie Louise. Known as the *King of Rome* during the first French empire, he was entitled Napoleon II by Bonapartists after his father's death (1821).

Napoleon III ★ *n* full name *Charles Louis Napoleon Bonaparte,* known as *Louis-Napoleon.* 1808–73, Emperor of the French (1852–70); nephew of Napoleon I. He was elected president of the Second Republic (1848), establishing the Second Empire in 1852. He was deposed after the disastrous Franco-Prussian War.

Napoleonic (nəˌpəʊlɪ'ɒnɪk) *adj* relating to or characteristic of Napoleon I or his era.

Napoli ★ ('na:poli) *n* the Italian name for **Naples.**

nappe (næp) *n* **1** a large sheet or mass of rock, originally a recumbent fold, that has been thrust from its original position by earth movements. **2** the sheet of water that flows over a dam or weir. **3** *Geom.* either of the two parts into which a cone is divided by the vertex. ORIG C20: from F: tablecloth

nappy[1] ('næpɪ) *n, pl* **nappies.** *Brit.* a piece of soft towelling or a disposable material wrapped around a baby in order to absorb its urine or excrement. Also called: **napkin.** US and Canad. name: **diaper.** ORIG C20: changed from NAPKIN

nappy[2] ('næpɪ) *adj* **nappier, nappiest. 1** having a nap; downy; fuzzy. **2** (of beer) **2a** having a head; frothy. **2b** strong or heady.

nappy rash *n Brit.* (in babies) any irritation to the skin around the genitals, anus, or buttocks, usually caused by contact with urine or excrement. Formal name: **napkin rash.** US and Canad. name: **diaper rash.**

Nara ★ ('nɑ:rə) *n* a city in central Japan, on S Honshu: the first permanent capital of Japan (710–784). Pop.: 359 234 (1995).

Narayan ★ (nə'raɪjən) *n* **R(asipuram) K(rishnaswamy).** born 1906, Indian novelist writing in English. His books include *Swami and Friends* (1938) and *Under the Banyan Tree* (1985).

Narayanganj ★ (nə'rɑ:jənˌgʌndʒ) *n* a city in central Bangladesh, on the Ganges delta just southeast of Dhaka. Pop.: 296 000 (1991).

Narbada ★ (nə'bʌdə) *n* another name for the **Narmada.**

Narbonne ★ (*French* narbɔn) *n* a city in S France: capital of the Roman province of **Gallia Narbonensis**; harbour silted up in the 14th century. Pop.: 47 090 (1990).

narc (nɑ:k) *n US sl.* a narcotics agent.

narcissism ('nɑ:sɪˌsɪzəm) *or* **narcism** ('nɑ:sɪzəm) *n* **1** an exceptional interest in or admiration for oneself, esp. one's physical appearance. **2** sexual satisfaction derived from contemplation of one's own physical endowments. ORIG C19: after NARCISSUS
▸ **'narcissist** *n* ▸ **ˌnarcis'sistic** *adj*

narcissus (nɑ:'sɪsəs) *n, pl* **narcissuses** *or* **narcissi** (-'sɪsaɪ). a plant of a Eurasian genus whose yellow, orange, or white flowers have a crown surrounded by spreading segments. ORIG C16: via L from Gk *nárkissos,* ?from *narkē* numbness, because of narcotic properties attributed to the plant

Narcissus ★ (nɑ:'sɪsəs) *n Greek myth.* a beautiful youth who fell in love with his reflection in a pool and pined away, becoming the flower that bears his name.

narco- *or sometimes before a vowel* **narc-** *combining form.* **1** indicating numbness or torpor: *narcolepsy.* **2** connected with or derived from illicit drug production: *narcoeconomies.* ORIG from Gk *narkē* numbness

narcoanalysis (ˌnɑːkəʊəˈnælɪsɪs) *n* psychoanalysis of a patient in a trance induced by a narcotic drug.

narcolepsy (ˈnɑːkəˌlɛpsɪ) *n Pathol.* a rare condition characterized by sudden episodes of deep sleep.
▸ **ˌnarcoˈleptic** *adj*

narcosis (nɑːˈkəʊsɪs) *n* unconsciousness induced by narcotics or general anaesthetics.

narcosynthesis (ˌnɑːkəʊˈsɪnθɪsɪs) *n* a method of treating severe personality disorders by working with the patient while he is under the influence of a barbiturate drug.

narcotic (nɑːˈkɒtɪk) *n* **1** any of a group of drugs, such as opium and morphine, that produce numbness and stupor. **2** anything that relieves pain or induces sleep, mental numbness, etc. **3** any illegal drug. ◆ *adj* **4** of or relating to narcotics or narcotics addicts. **5** of or relating to narcosis. ORIG C14: via Med. L from Gk *narkōtikós*, from *narkoūn* to numb, from *narkē* numbness
▸ **narˈcotically** *adv*

narcotism (ˈnɑːkəˌtɪzəm) *n* stupor or addiction induced by narcotic drugs.

narcotize *or* **narcotise** (ˈnɑːkəˌtaɪz) *vb* **narcotizes, narcotizing, narcotized** *or* **narcotises, narcotising, narcotised.** (*tr*) to place under the influence of a narcotic drug.
▸ **ˌnarcotiˈzation** *or* **ˌnarcotiˈsation** *n*

nard (nɑːd) *n* **1** another name for **spikenard. 2** any of several plants whose aromatic roots were formerly used in medicine. ORIG C14: via L from Gk *nárdos*, ? ult. from Sansk. *nalada* Indian spikenard

nardoo (ˈnɑːduː) *n* (in Australia) **1** any of certain cloverlike ferns that grow in swampy areas. **2** the spores of such a plant, used as food. ORIG C19: from Abor.

nares (ˈnɛəriːz) *pl n, sing* **naris** (ˈnɛərɪs). *Anat.* the technical name for the nostrils. ORIG C17: from L; rel. to OE *nasu*, L *nāsus* nose
▸ **ˈnarial** *adj*

narghile, nargile, *or* **nargileh** (ˈnɑːgɪlɪ, -ˌleɪ) *n* another name for **hookah.** ORIG C19: from F *narguilé*, from Persian *nārgīleh* a pipe having a bowl made of coconut shell, from *nārgīl* coconut

nark (nɑːk) *Sl.* ◆ *n* **1** *Brit., Austral., & NZ.* an informer or spy: *copper's nark.* **2** *Brit., Austral., & NZ.* someone who complains in an irritating or whining manner. ◆ *vb* **3** *Brit., Austral., & NZ.* to annoy, upset, or irritate. **4** (*intr*) *Brit., Austral., & NZ.* to inform or spy, esp. for the police. **5** (*intr*) *Brit.* to complain irritatingly. ORIG C19: prob. from Romany *nāk* nose

narky (ˈnɑːkɪ) *adj* **narkier, narkiest.** *Sl.* irritable, complaining, or sarcastic.

Narmada (nəˈmʌdə) *or* **Narbada** ★ *n* a river in central India, rising in Madhya Pradesh and flowing generally west to the Gulf of Cambay in a wide estuary: the second most sacred river in India. Length: 1290 km (801 miles).

Narraganset (ˌnærəˈgænsɪt) *n* **1** (*pl* **Narraganset** *or* **Narragansets**) a member of a North American Indian people formerly living in Rhode Island. **2** the language of this people, belonging to the Algonquian family.

Narragansett Bay ★ *n* an inlet of the Atlantic in SE Rhode Island: contains several islands, including Rhode Island, Prudence Island, and Conanicut Island.

narrate (nəˈreɪt) *vb* **narrates, narrating, narrated. 1** to tell (a story); relate. **2** to speak in accompaniment of (a film, etc.). ORIG C17: from L *narrāre* to recount, from *gnārus* knowing
▸ **narˈratable** *adj* ▸ **narˈrator** *n*

narration (nəˈreɪʃən) *n* **1** the act or process of narrating. **2** a narrated account or story.

narrative (ˈnærətɪv) *n* **1** an account or story, as of events, experiences, etc. **2** the part of a literary work, etc., that relates events. **3** the process or technique of narrating. ◆ *adj* **4** telling a story: *a narrative poem.* **5** of or relating to narration: *narrative art.*

narrow (ˈnærəʊ) *adj* **1** small in breadth, esp. in comparison to length. **2** limited in range or extent. **3** limited in outlook. **4** limited in means or resources. **5** barely adequate or successful (esp. in **a narrow escape**). **6** painstakingly thorough: *a narrow scrutiny.* **7** *Finance.* denoting an assessment of liquidity as including notes and coins in circulation with the public, banks' till money, and banks' balances: *narrow money.* Cf. **broad** (sense 12). **8** *Phonetics.* another word for **tense**[1] (sense 4). ◆ *vb* **9** to make or become narrow. **10** (often foll. by *down*) to limit or restrict. ◆ *n* **11** a narrow place, esp. a pass or strait. ◆ See also **narrows.** ORIG OE *nearu*
▸ **ˈnarrowly** *adv* ▸ **ˈnarrowness** *n*

narrowboat (ˈnærəʊˌbəʊt) *n* a long bargelike boat with a beam of 2.1 metres (7 feet), used on canals.

narrow gauge *n* **1** a railway track with a smaller distance between the lines than the standard gauge of 56½ inches. ◆ *adj* **narrow-gauge. 2** of or denoting a railway with a narrow gauge.

narrow-minded *adj* having a biased or illiberal viewpoint; bigoted, intolerant, or prejudiced.
▸ **ˌnarrow-ˈmindedness** *n*

narrows (ˈnærəʊz) *pl n* a narrow part of a strait, river, current, etc.

narthex (ˈnɑːθɛks) *n* **1** a portico at the west end of a church, esp. one at right angles to the nave. **2** a rectangular entrance hall between the porch and nave of a church. ORIG C17: via L from Med. Gk: enclosed porch (earlier: box), from Gk *narthēx* giant fennel, the stems of which were used to make boxes

Narva ★ (*Russian* ˈnarvə) *n* a port in Estonia on the Narva River near the Gulf of Finland: developed around a Danish fortress in the 13th century; textile centre. Pop.: 77 770 (1995).

Narvik ★ (ˈnɑːvɪk; *Norwegian* ˈnarvik) *n* a port in N Norway: scene of two naval battles in 1940; exports iron ore from Kiruna and Gällivare (Sweden). Pop.: 18 500 (1990).

narwhal, narwal (ˈnɑːwəl), *or* **narwhale** (ˈnɑːˌweɪl) *n* an arctic toothed whale having a black-spotted whitish skin and, in the male, a long spiral tusk. ORIG C17: of Scand. origin; cf. Danish, Norwegian *narhval*, from ON *nāhvalr*, from *nār* corpse + *hvalr* whale

nary (ˈnɛərɪ) *adv Dialect or inf.* not; never: *nary a man was left.* ORIG C19: var. of *ne'er a* never a

NASA (ˈnæsə) *n* (in the US) *acronym for* National Aeronautics and Space Administration.

nasal (ˈneɪzᵊl) *adj* **1** of the nose. **2** *Phonetics.* pronounced with the soft palate lowered allowing air to escape via the nasal cavity. ◆ *n* **3** a nasal speech sound, such as English *m, n,* or *ng.* ORIG C17: from F from LL *nāsālis*, from L *nāsus* nose
▸ **nasality** (neɪˈzælɪtɪ) *n* ▸ **ˈnasally** *adv*

nasalize *or* **nasalise** (ˈneɪzᵊˌlaɪz) *vb* **nasalizes, nasalizing, nasalized** *or* **nasalises, nasalising, nasalised.** (*tr*) to pronounce nasally.
▸ **ˌnasaliˈzation** *or* **ˌnasaliˈsation** *n*

nascent (ˈnæsᵊnt, ˈneɪ-) *adj* starting to grow or develop; being born. ORIG C17: from L *nascēns*, present participle of *nāscī* to be born
▸ **ˈnascency** *n*

nascent hydrogen *n Chem.* hydrogen produced in a reactive form within the reaction mixture.

Nasdaq *or* **NASDAQ** (ˈnæzˌdæk) *n acronym for* National Association of Securities Dealers Automated Quotation System: a computerized system for trading in over-the-counter securities. It is the second largest stock market in the United States.

Naseby ★ (ˈneɪzbɪ) *n* a village in Northamptonshire: site of a major Parliamentarian victory (1645) in the Civil War.

Nash ★ (næʃ) *n* **1 John.** 1752–1835, British town planner and architect. He designed Regent's Park, Regent Street, and the Marble Arch in London. **2 Ogden.** 1902–71, US humorous poet. **3 Paul.** 1889–1946, British painter, noted as a war artist in both World Wars. **4 Richard,** known as *Beau Nash.* 1674–1762, English dandy. **5 Thomas.** See (Thomas) **Nashe. 6** Sir **Walter.** 1882–1968, New Zealand Labour statesman, born in England: prime minister (1957–60).

Nashe *or* **Nash** ★ (næʃ) *n* **Thomas.** 1567–1601, English pamphleteer and novelist.

Nashville ★ ('næʃvɪl) *n* a city in central Tennessee, the state capital, on the Cumberland River: an industrial and commercial centre, noted for its recording industry. Pop.: 511 263 (1996 est.).

Nasik ★ ('nɑːsɪk) *n* a city in W India, in Maharashtra: a centre for Hindu pilgrims. Pop.: 656 925 (1991).

naso- *combining form.* nose: *nasopharynx.* ORIG from L *nāsus* nose

nasogastric (ˌneɪzəʊ'gæstrɪk) *adj Anat.* of or relating to the nose and stomach: *a nasogastric tube.*

Nassau ★ *n* **1** (*German* 'nasaʊ). a region of W central Germany: formerly a duchy (1816–66), from which a branch of the House of Orange arose (represented by the present rulers of the Netherlands and Luxembourg); annexed to the Prussian province of Hesse-Nassau in 1866; corresponds to present-day W Hesse and NE Rhineland-Palatinate states; formerly (1949–90) part of West Germany. **2** ('næsɔː). the capital and chief port of the Bahamas, on the NE coast of New Providence Island: resort. Pop.: 172 196 (1990).

Nasser ★ ('nɑːsə, 'næsə) *n* **Gamal Abdel** (gə'mɑːl 'æbdɛl). 1918–70, Egyptian soldier and statesman; president (1956–70). A leader of the coup that deposed King Farouk (1952), he became premier (1954). His nationalization of the Suez Canal (1956) led to an international crisis.

nastic movement ('næstɪk) *n* a response of plant parts that is independent of the direction of the external stimulus, such as the opening of buds caused by an alteration in light intensity. ORIG C19 *nastic,* from Gk *nastos* close-packed, from *nassein* to press down

nasturtium (nə'stɜːʃəm) *n* a plant having round leaves and yellow, red, or orange trumpet-shaped spurred flowers. ORIG C17: from L: kind of cress, from *nāsus* nose + *tortus* twisted; because the pungent smell causes one to wrinkle one's nose

nasty ('nɑːstɪ) *adj* **nastier, nastiest. 1** unpleasant or repugnant. **2** dangerous or painful. **3** spiteful or ill-natured. **4** obscene or indecent. ◆ *n, pl* **nasties. 5** an offensive or unpleasant person or thing: *a video nasty.* ORIG C14: from ?; prob. rel. to Swedish dialect *nasket* & Du. *nestig* dirty
▸ **'nastily** *adv* ▸ **'nastiness** *n*

Nasty Nick *n* someone who seeks to advance his or her own position by pretending to be congenial and co-operative while, at the same time, undermining the others in the group. ORIG C20: from one of the participants in the first series of UK television programme *Big Brother,* who behaved in this way

NAS/UWT (in Britain) *abbrev. for* National Association of Schoolmasters/Union of Women Teachers.

nat. *abbrev. for:* **1** national. **2** native. **3** natural.

natal ('neɪtᵊl) *adj* of or relating to birth. ORIG C14: from L *nātālis* of one's birth, from *nātus,* from *nascī* to be born

Natal ★ *n* **1** (nə'tæl). a former province of E South Africa, in 1994 it was replaced by the Kwazulu/Natal region. **2** (*Portuguese* na'tal). a port in NE Brazil, capital of Rio Grande do Norte state, near the mouth of the Potengi River. Pop.: 459 827 (1991).

natant ('neɪtᵊnt) *adj* floating or swimming. ORIG C18: from L *natāns,* present participle of *natāre* to swim

natation (nə'teɪʃən) *n* a literary word for **swimming.** ORIG C16: from L *natātiō* a swimming, from *natāre* to swim

natatory (nə'teɪtərɪ) *or* **natatorial** (ˌnætə'tɔːrɪəl) *adj* of or relating to swimming. ORIG C18: from LL *natātōrius,* from L *natāre* to swim

natch (nætʃ) *sentence substitute. Inf.* short for **naturally.**

nates ('neɪtiːz) *pl n, sing* **natis** (-tɪs). a technical word for the **buttocks.** ORIG C17: from L

NATFHE (in Britain) *abbrev. for* National Association of Teachers in Further and Higher Education.

Nathan ★ ('neɪθən) *n Old Testament.* a prophet at David's court (II Samuel 7:1–17; 12:1–15).

Nathanael ★ (nə'θænjəl) *n New Testament.* a Galilean who is perhaps to be identified with Bartholomew among the apostles (John 1:45–51; 21:1).

natheless ('neɪθlɪs) *or* **nathless** ('næθlɪs) *Arch. sentence connector.* nonetheless. ORIG OE *nāthylǣs,* from *nā* never + *thȳ* for that + *lǣs* less

nation ('neɪʃən) *n* **1** an aggregation of people or peoples of one or more cultures, races, etc., organized into a single state: *the Australian nation.* **2** a community of persons not constituting a state but of common descent, language, history, etc.: *the French-Canadian nation.* ORIG C13: via OF from L *nātiō* birth, tribe, from *nascī* to be born
▸ **'nationˌhood** *n*

national ('næʃənᵊl) *adj* **1** of or relating to a nation as a whole. **2** characteristic of a particular nation: *the national dress of Poland.* ◆ *n* **3** a citizen or subject. **4** a national newspaper.
▸ **'nationally** *adv*

national anthem *n* a patriotic song adopted by a nation for use on public occasions.

national assistance *n* (formerly, in Britain) a weekly allowance paid to individuals of various groups by the state to bring their incomes up to minimum levels established by law. Now replaced by income support.

national bank *n* **1** (in the US) a commercial bank incorporated under a Federal charter and legally required to be a member of the Federal Reserve System. **2** a bank operated by a government.

national call *n Brit.* a telephone call made to a number within the country but outside the local area.

National Curriculum *n* (in England and Wales) the curriculum of subjects taught in state schools from 1989. The ten foundation subjects are: English, maths, and science (the core subjects); art, design and technology, geography, history, music, physical education, and a foreign language. Pupils are assessed at four stages. Abbrev.: **NC.**

national debt *n* the total outstanding borrowings of a nation's central government.

National Economic Development Council *n* a former advisory body on economic policy in Britain: abolished in 1992. Abbrevs.: **NEDC,** (inf.) **Neddy.**

National Enterprise Board *n* a public corporation established in 1975 to help the economy of the UK. In 1981 it merged with the National Research and Development Council to form the British Technology Group. Abbrev.: **NEB.**

National Football *n* (in Australia) another name for **Australian Rules.**

National Front *n* an extreme right-wing British political party founded in 1967.

National Gallery ★ *n* a major art gallery in London, in Trafalgar Square. Founded in 1824, it contains the largest collection of paintings in Britain.

national grid *n Brit.* **1** a network of high-voltage electric power lines linking major electric power stations. **2** the metric coordinate system used in ordnance survey maps.

National Guard *n* **1** (*sometimes not cap.*) the armed force that was established in France in 1789 and existed intermittently until 1871. **2** (in the US) a state military force that can be called into federal service by the president.

National Health Service *n* (in Britain) the system of national medical services since 1948, financed mainly by taxation. Abbrev.: **NHS.**

national hunt *n Brit.* (*often caps.*) **a** the racing of horses on racecourses with jumps. **b** (*as modifier*): *a National Hunt jockey.*

national income *n Econ.* the total of all incomes accruing over a specified period to residents of a country.

national insurance *n* (in Britain) state insurance based on weekly contributions from employees and employers and providing payments to the unemployed, the sick, the retired, etc., as well as medical services.

nationalism ('næʃənəˌlɪzəm) *n* **1** a sentiment based on

common cultural characteristics that binds a population and often produces a policy of national independence. **2** loyalty to one's country; patriotism. **3** exaggerated or fanatical devotion to a national community.
▸ **'nationalist** *n, adj* ▸ **,national'istic** *adj*

nationality (,næʃə'nælɪtɪ) *n, pl* **nationalities. 1** the fact of being a citizen of a particular nation. **2** a body of people sharing common descent, history, language, etc.; a nation. **3** a national group: *30 different nationalities are found in this city.* **4** national character. **5** the fact of being a nation; national status.

nationalize *or* **nationalise** ('næʃənə,laɪz) *vb* **nationalizes, nationalizing, nationalized** *or* **nationalises, nationalising, nationalised.** (*tr*) **1** to put (an industry, resources, etc.) under state control. **2** to make national in character or status. **3** a less common word for **naturalize.**
▸ **,nationali'zation** *or* **,nationali'sation** *n*

national park *n* an area of countryside for public use designated by a national government as being of notable scenic, environmental, or historical importance.

National Park ★ *n NZ.* a mountainous volcanic region in the North Island.

National Party *n* **1** (in New Zealand) the more conservative of the two main political parties. **2** (in Australia) a political party drawing its main support from rural areas. Former name: **National Country Party. 3** (in South Africa) a political party composed mainly of centre-to-right-wing Afrikaners. It ruled from 1948 until 1994, when South Africa's first multiracial elections were won by the African National Congress.

National Savings Bank *n* (in Britain) a government savings bank, run through the Post Office.

national service *n* compulsory military service.

National Socialism *n German history.* the doctrines and practices of the Nazis, involving the supremacy of Hitler as Führer, anti-Semitism, state control of the economy, and national expansion.
▸ **National Socialist** *n, adj*

national superannuation *n NZ.* a government pension given on the attainment of a specified age; old age pension. Often shortened to **national super.**

National Theatre ★ *n* the former name of the **Royal National Theatre.**

National Trust *n* **1** (in Britain) an organization concerned with the preservation of historic buildings and areas of the countryside of great beauty. **2** (in Australia) a similar organization in each of the states.

nation-building *n S. African.* the advocacy of national solidarity in South Africa in the post-apartheid era.

nationwide ('neɪʃən,waɪd) *adj* covering or available to the whole of a nation; national.

native ('neɪtɪv) *adj* **1** relating or belonging to a person by virtue of conditions existing at birth: *a native language.* **2** natural or innate: *a native strength.* **3** born in a specified place: *a native Indian.* **4** (when *postpositive,* foll. by *to*) originating in: *kangaroos are native to Australia.* **5** relating to the indigenous inhabitants of a country: *the native art of the New Guinea Highlands.* **6** (of metals) found naturally in the elemental form; not chemically combined as in an ore. **7** unadulterated by civilization, artifice, or adornment; natural. **8** *Arch.* related by birth or race. **9 go native.** (of a settler) to adopt the lifestyle of the local population, esp. when it appears less civilized. ◆ *n* **10** (usually foll. by *of*) a person born in a particular place: *a native of Geneva.* **11** (usually foll. by *of*) a species of animal or plant originating in a particular place. **12** a member of an indigenous people of a country, esp. a non-White people, as opposed to colonial immigrants. ORIG C14: from L *nātīvus* innate, natural, from *nascī* to be born
▸ **'natively** *adv* ▸ **'nativeness** *n*

Native American *n* another name for an **American Indian.**

native bear *n* an Australian name for **koala.**

native-born *adj* born in the country or area indicated.

native companion *n* (in Australia) another name for **brolga.**

native dog *n Austral.* a dingo.

Native States ★ *pl n* the former 562 semi-independent states of India, ruled by Indians but subject to varying degrees of British authority: merged with provinces by 1948; largest states were Hyderabad, Gwalior, Baroda, Mysore, Cochin, Jammu and Kashmir, Travancore, Sikkim, and Indore. Also called: **Indian States and Agencies.**

nativity (nə'tɪvɪtɪ) *n, pl* **nativities.** birth or origin. ORIG C14: from LL *nātīvitas* birth; see NATIVE

Nativity (nə'tɪvɪtɪ) *n* **1** the birth of Christ. **2** the feast of Christmas as a commemoration of this. **3a** an artistic representation of the circumstances of the birth of Christ. **3b** (*as modifier*): *a Nativity play.*

NATO *or* **Nato** ('neɪtəʊ) *n acronym for* North Atlantic Treaty Organization: an international organization established (1949) for purposes of collective security.

natron ('neɪtrən) *n* a whitish or yellow mineral that consists of hydrated sodium carbonate and occurs in saline deposits and salt lakes. ORIG C17: via F & Sp. from Ar. *natrūn,* from Gk *nitron* NITRE

NATSOPA (næt'səʊpə) *n* (formerly, in Britain) *acronym for* National Society of Operative Printers, Graphical and Media Personnel.

natter ('nætə) *Chiefly Brit. inf.* ◆ *vb* **1** (*intr*) to talk idly and at length; chatter. ◆ *n* **2** prolonged idle chatter. ORIG C19: from *gnatter* to grumble, imit.

natterjack ('nætə,dʒæk) *n* a European toad having a greyish-brown body marked with reddish warty processes. ORIG C18: from ?

natty ('nætɪ) *adj* **nattier, nattiest.** *Inf.* smart; spruce; dapper. ORIG C18: from obs. *netty,* from *net* NEAT[1]
▸ **'nattily** *adv* ▸ **'nattiness** *n*

natural ('nætʃrəl) *adj* **1** of, existing in, or produced by nature: *natural science; natural cliffs.* **2** in accordance with human nature. **3** as is normal or to be expected: *the natural course of events.* **4** not acquired; innate: *a natural gift for sport.* **5** being so through innate qualities: *a natural leader.* **6** not supernatural or strange: *natural phenomena.* **7** genuine or spontaneous. **8** lifelike: *she looked more natural without make-up.* **9** not affected by man; wild: *in the natural state this animal is not ferocious.* **10** being or made from organic material; not synthetic: *a natural fibre like cotton.* **11** born out of wedlock. **12** not adopted but rather related by blood: *her natural parents.* **13** *Music.* **13a** not sharp or flat. **13b** (*postpositive*) denoting a note that is neither sharp nor flat. **13c** (of a key or scale) containing no sharps or flats. **14** based on the principles and findings of human reason rather than on revelation: *natural religion.* ◆ *n* **15** *Inf.* a person or thing regarded as certain to qualify for success, selection, etc.: *the horse was a natural for first place.* **16** *Music.* **16a** Also called (US): **cancel.** an accidental cancelling a previous sharp or flat. Usual symbol: ♮ **16b** a note affected by this accidental. **17** *Obs.* an imbecile; idiot.
▸ **'naturalness** *n*

natural childbirth *n* a method of childbirth characterized by the absence of anaesthetics, in which the expectant mother is given special breathing and relaxing exercises.

natural gas *n* a gaseous mixture, consisting mainly of methane, trapped below ground; used extensively as a fuel.

natural history *n* **1** the study of animals and plants in the wild state. **2** the sum of these phenomena in a given place or at a given time.
▸ **natural historian** *n*

natural immunity *n* immunity with which an individual is born, which has a genetic basis.

naturalism ('nætʃrə,lɪzəm) *n* **1** a movement, esp. in art and literature, advocating detailed realistic and factual description. **2** the belief that all religious truth is based not on revelation but rather on the study of natural causes and processes. **3** *Philosophy.* a scientific account of the world in terms of causes and natural forces. **4** action or thought caused by natural instincts.

naturalist ('nætʃrəlɪst) *n* **1** a person who is versed in or interested in botany or zoology. **2** a person who advocates or practises naturalism.

naturalistic (ˌnætʃrəˈlɪstɪk) *adj* **1** of or reproducing nature in effect or characteristics. **2** of or characteristic of naturalism. **3** of naturalists.
▸ ˌ**naturalˈistically** *adv*

naturalize *or* **naturalise** (ˈnætʃrəˌlaɪz) *vb* **naturalizes, naturalizing, naturalized** *or* **naturalises, naturalising, naturalised. 1** (*tr*) to give citizenship to (a person of foreign birth). **2** to be or cause to be adopted in another place, as a word, custom, etc. **3** (*tr*) to introduce (a plant or animal from another region) and cause it to adapt to local conditions. **4** (*intr*) (of a plant or animal) to adapt successfully to a foreign environment. **5** (*tr*) to make natural or more lifelike.
▸ ˌ**naturaliˈzation** *or* ˌ**naturaliˈsation** *n*

natural language *n* a language that has evolved naturally as a means of communication among people, as opposed to an invented language or a code.

natural logarithm *n* a logarithm to the base e. Usually written $\log_e$ or ln. Also called: **Napierian logarithm.**

naturally (ˈnætʃrəlɪ) *adv* **1** in a natural way. **2** instinctively. ◆ *adv, sentence substitute.* **3** of course; surely.

natural number *n* any of the numbers 0 ,1, 2, 3, 4,... that can be used to count the members of a set; the non-negative integers.

natural philosophy *n* physical science, esp. physics.
▸ **natural philosopher** *n*

natural resources *pl n* naturally occurring materials such as coal, fertile land, etc.

natural science *n* the sciences that are involved in the study of the physical world and its phenomena, including biology, physics, chemistry, and geology.

natural selection *n* a process resulting in the survival of those individuals from a population of animals or plants that are best adapted to the prevailing environmental conditions.

natural theology *n* the attempt to derive theological truth, and esp. the existence of God, from empirical facts by reasoned argument. Cf. **revealed religion.**

natural wastage *n* the loss of employees, etc., through not replacing those who retire or resign rather than dismissal or redundancy.

nature (ˈneɪtʃə) *n* **1** fundamental qualities; identity or essential character. **2** (*often cap.*) the whole system of the existence, forces, and events of all physical life that are not controlled by man. **3** plant and animal life, as distinct from man. **4** a wild primitive state untouched by man. **5** natural unspoilt countryside. **6** disposition or temperament. **7** desires or instincts governing behaviour. **8** the normal biological needs of the body. **9** sort; character. **10 against nature.** unnatural or immoral. **11 by nature.** essentially or innately. **12 call of nature.** *Inf.* the need to urinate or defecate. **13 from nature.** using natural models in drawing, painting, etc. **14 in** (*or* **of**) **the nature of.** essentially the same as; by way of. ORIG C13: via OF from L *nātūra,* from *nātus,* p.p. of *nascī* to be born

nature reserve *n* an area of land that is protected and managed in order to preserve its flora and fauna.

nature study *n* the study of the natural world, esp. animals and plants, by direct observation at an elementary level.

nature trail *n* a path through countryside designed and usually signposted to draw attention to natural features of interest.

naturism (ˈneɪtʃəˌrɪzəm) *n* another name for **nudism.**
▸ ˈ**naturist** *n, adj*

naturopathy (ˌnætʃəˈrɒpæθɪ) *n* the treatment of illness by stimulating natural healing, esp. by herbal remedies, manipulation, etc.
▸ ˈ**naturoˌpath** *n* ▸ ˌ**naturoˈpathic** *adj*

Naucratis ★ (ˈnɔːkrətɪs) *n* an ancient Greek city in N Egypt, in the Nile delta: founded in the 7th century B.C.

naught (nɔːt) *n* **1** *Arch. or literary.* nothing; ruin or failure. **2** a variant spelling (esp. US) of **nought. 3 set at naught.** to disregard or scorn; disdain. ◆ *adv* **4** *Arch. or literary.* not at all: *it matters naught.* ◆ *adj* **5** *Obs.* worthless, ruined, or wicked. ORIG OE *nāwiht,* from *nā* NO[1] + *wiht* thing, person

naughty (ˈnɔːtɪ) *adj* **naughtier, naughtiest. 1** (esp. of children) mischievous or disobedient. **2** mildly indecent; titillating. ORIG C14: (orig.: needy, poor): from NAUGHT
▸ ˈ**naughtily** *adv* ▸ ˈ**naughtiness** *n*

nauplius (ˈnɔːplɪəs) *n, pl* **nauplii** (-plɪˌaɪ). the larva of many crustaceans, having a rounded unsegmented body with three pairs of limbs. ORIG C19: from L: type of shellfish, from Gk *Nauplios,* one of the sons of the Greek god Poseidon

Nauru ★ (nɑːˈuːruː) *n* an island republic in the SW Pacific, west of Kiribati: administered jointly by Australia, New Zealand, and Britain as a UN trust territory before becoming independent and a special member of the Commonwealth in 1968. The economy is based on export of phosphates. Languages: Nauruan (a Malayo-Polynesian language) and English. Religion: Christian. Currency: Australian dollar. Pop.: 8100 (1990). Area: 2130 hectares (5263 acres). Former name: **Pleasant Island.**
▸ **Naˈuruan** *adj, n*

nausea (ˈnɔːzɪə, -sɪə) *n* **1** the sensation that precedes vomiting. **2** a feeling of revulsion. ORIG C16: via L from Gk: seasickness, from *naus* ship

nauseate (ˈnɔːzɪˌeɪt, -sɪ-) *vb* **nauseates, nauseating, nauseated. 1** (*tr*) to arouse feelings of disgust or revulsion in. **2** to feel or cause to feel sick.
▸ ˈ**nauseˌating** *adj*

nauseous (ˈnɔːzɪəs, -sɪəs) *adj* **1** causing nausea. **2** distasteful; repulsive.
▸ ˈ**nauseously** *adv* ▸ ˈ**nauseousness** *n*

Nausicaä ★ (nɔːˈsɪkɪə) *n Greek myth.* a daughter of Alcinous, king of the Phaeacians, who assisted the shipwrecked Odysseus after discovering him on a beach.

nautch *or* **nauch** (nɔːtʃ) *n* an intricate traditional Indian dance performed by professional dancing girls. ORIG C18: from Hindi *nāc,* from Sansk., from *nṛtyati* he acts or dances

nautical (ˈnɔːtɪkəl) *adj* of or involving ships, navigation, or seamen. ORIG C16: from L *nauticus,* from Gk *nautikos,* from *naus* ship
▸ ˈ**nautically** *adv*

nautical mile *n* **1** Also called **international nautical mile, air mile.** a unit of length, used esp. in navigation, equivalent to the average length of a minute of latitude, and corresponding to a latitude of 45°, i.e. 1852 m (6076.12 ft). **2** a former British unit of length equal to 1853.18 m (6080 ft), which was replaced by the international nautical mile in 1970. Former name: **geographical mile.** Cf. **sea mile.**

nautilus (ˈnɔːtɪləs) *n, pl* **nautiluses** *or* **nautili** (-ˌlaɪ). **1** any of a genus of cephalopod molluscs, esp. the pearly nautilus. **2** short for **paper nautilus.** ORIG C17: via L from Gk *nautilos* sailor, from *naus* ship

NAV *abbrev. for* net asset value.

Navaho *or* **Navajo** (ˈnævəˌhəʊ) *n* **1** (*pl* **Navaho, Navahos, Navahoes** *or* **Navajo, Navajos, Navajoes**) a member of a North American Indian people of Arizona, New Mexico, and Utah. **2** the language of this people. ORIG C18: from Sp. *Navajó* pueblo, from Tena *Navahu* large planted field

naval (ˈneɪvəl) *adj* **1** of, characteristic of, or having a navy. **2** of or relating to ships; nautical. ORIG C16: from L *nāvālis,* from *nāvis* ship

naval architecture *n* the designing of ships.
▸ **naval architect** *n*

Navaratri (ˌnævəˈrɑːtrɪ) *n* an annual Hindu festival celebrated over nine days in September–October. It commemorates the slaying of demons by Rama and the goddess Durga. Also called: **Durga Puja.** ORIG from Sansk. *navaratri* nine nights

navarin (ˈnævərɪn) *n* a stew of mutton or lamb with root vegetables. ORIG from F

Navarino ★ (navaˈriːno) *n* the Italian name for **Pylos.**

Navarre ★ (nəˈvɑː) *n* a former kingdom of SW Europe: established in the 9th century by the Basques; the parts south of the Pyrenees joined Spain in 1515 and the N parts passed to France in 1589. Capital: Pamplona. Spanish name: **Navarra** (naˈβarra).

nave[1] (neɪv) *n* the central space in a church, extending from the narthex to the chancel and often flanked by aisles. ORIG C17: via Med. L from L *nāvis* ship, from the similarity of shape

nave[2] (neɪv) *n* the central block or hub of a wheel. ORIG OE *nafu, nafa*

navel ('neɪvᵊl) *n* **1** the scar in the centre of the abdomen, usually forming a slight depression, where the umbilical cord was attached. Technical name: **umbilicus.** Related adj: **umbilical. 2** a central part or point. ORIG OE *nafela*

navel orange *n* a sweet orange that has at its apex a navel-like depression enclosing an underdeveloped secondary fruit.

navelwort ('neɪvᵊl,wɜːt) *n* another name for **pennywort** (sense 1).

navicular (nə'vɪkjʊlə) *Anat.* ◆ *adj* **1** shaped like a boat. ◆ *n* **2** a small boat-shaped bone of the wrist or foot. ORIG C16: from LL *nāviculāris,* from L *nāvicula,* dim. of *nāvis* ship

navigable ('nævɪgəbᵊl) *adj* **1** wide, deep, or safe enough to be sailed through: *a navigable channel.* **2** capable of being steered: *a navigable raft.*
▸ **,naviga'bility** *n* ▸ **'navigably** *adv*

navigate ('nævɪ,geɪt) *vb* **navigates, navigating, navigated. 1** to direct or plot the path or position of (a ship, an aircraft, etc.). **2** (*tr*) to travel over, through, or on in a boat, aircraft, etc. **3** *Inf.* to direct (oneself) carefully or safely: *he navigated his way to the bar.* **4** (*intr*) (of a passenger in a motor vehicle) to give directions to the driver; point out the route. ORIG C16: from L *nāvigāre* to sail, from *nāvis* ship + *agere* to drive

navigation (,nævɪ'geɪʃən) *n* **1** the skill or process of plotting a route and directing a ship, aircraft, etc., along it. **2** the act or practice of navigating: *dredging made navigation of the river possible.*
▸ **,navi'gational** *adj*

navigator ('nævɪ,geɪtə) *n* **1** a person who performs navigation. **2** (esp. formerly) a person who explores by ship. **3** an instrument for assisting a pilot to navigate an aircraft.

Návpaktos ★ (*Greek* 'nafpaktos) *n* the Greek name for **Lepanto.**

Navratilova ★ (næ,vrætɪ'ləʊvə) *n* **Martina.** born 1956, Czech-born US tennis player: Wimbledon champion 1978–79, 1982–87, 1990; US Open champion 1983, 1984, 1986, 1987; world champion 1980.

navvy ('nævɪ) *n, pl* **navvies.** *Brit. inf.* a labourer on a building site, etc. ORIG C19: from *navigator* builder of a *navigation* (in the sense: canal)

navy ('neɪvɪ) *n, pl* **navies. 1** the warships and auxiliary vessels of a nation or ruler. **2** (*often cap.*) the branch of a country's armed services comprising such ships, their crews, and all their supporting services. **3** short for **navy blue. 4** *Arch. or literary.* a fleet of ships. ORIG C14: via OF from Vulgar L *nāvia* (unattested) ship, from L *nāvis* ship

navy blue *n* **a** a dark greyish-blue colour. **b** (*as adj*): *a navy-blue suit.* ORIG C19: from the colour of the British naval uniform

Navy List *n* (in Britain) an official list of all commissioned officers of the Royal Navy.

navy yard *n* a naval shipyard, esp. in the US.

nawab (nə'wɑːb) *n* (formerly) a Muslim ruling prince or powerful landowner in India. ORIG C18: from Hindi *nawwāb,* from Ar. *nuwwāb,* pl. of *na'ib* viceroy

Naxos ★ ('næksɒs) *n* a Greek island in the S Aegean, the largest of the Cyclades: ancient centre of the worship of Dionysius. Pop.: 14 000 (latest est.). Area: 438 sq. km (169 sq. miles).

nay (neɪ) *sentence substitute.* **1** a word for **no**[1]: archaic or dialectal except in voting by voice. ◆ *n* **2** a person who votes in the negative. ◆ *adv* **3** (*sentence modifier*) *Arch.* an emphatic form of **no**[1]. ORIG C12: from ON *nei,* from *ne* not + *ei* ever

Nayarit ★ (*Spanish* naja'rit) *n* a state of W Mexico, on the Pacific: includes the offshore Tres Marías Islands. Capital: Tepic. Pop.: 903 886 (1997 est.). Area: 27 621 sq. km (10 772 sq. miles).

Nazarene (,næzə'riːn) *n* **1** an early name for a **Christian** (Acts 24:5) or (when preceded by *the*) for **Jesus Christ. 2** a member of one of several groups of Jewish-Christians found principally in Syria. ◆ *adj* **3** of Nazareth in N Israel, or the Nazarenes.

Nazareth ★ ('næzərɪθ) *n* a town in N Israel, in Lower Galilee: the home of Jesus in his youth. Pop.: 51 000 (1989).

Nazarite ('næzə,raɪt) *or* **Nazirite** *n* a religious ascetic of ancient Israel. ORIG C16: from L *Nazaraeus,* from Heb. *nāzar* to consecrate + -ITE[1]

Naze ★ (neɪz) *n* **the. 1** a flat marshy headland in SE England, in Essex on the North Sea coast. **2** another name for **Lindesnes.**

Nazi ('nɑːtsɪ) *n, pl* **Nazis. 1** a member of the fascist National Socialist German Workers' Party, which seized political control in Germany in 1933. ◆ *adj* **2** characteristic of or relating to the Nazis. ORIG C20: from G, phonetic spelling of the first two syllables of *Nationalsozialist* National Socialist
▸ **Nazism** ('nɑːt,sɪzəm) *or* **Naziism** ('nɑːtsɪ,ɪzəm) *n*

Nb *the chemical symbol for* niobium.

NB *abbrev. for* New Brunswick.

NB, N.B., nb, *or* **n.b.** *abbrev. for* nota bene. ORIG L: note well

NBA *abbrev. for:* **1** (in the US) National Basketball Association. **2** (the former) Net Book Agreement.

NC *or* **N.C.** *abbrev. for:* **1** North Carolina. **2** *Brit. education.* National Curriculum.

NCB (in Britain) *abbrev. for* National Coal Board: now British Coal.

NCC (in Britain) *abbrev. for:* **1** Nature Conservancy Council. **2** *Brit. education.* National Curriculum Council: a statutory organization responsible for the content of the National Curriculum.

NCO *abbrev. for* noncommissioned officer.

NCU (in Britain) *abbrev. for* National Communications Union.

nd *abbrev. for* no date.

Nd *the chemical symbol for* neodymium.

ND, N.D., *or* **N. Dak.** *abbrev. for* North Dakota.

Ndjamena *or* **N'djamena** ★ (ᵊndʒɑː'meɪnə) *n* the capital of Chad, in the southwest, at the confluence of the Shari and Logone Rivers: trading centre for livestock. Pop.: 530 965 (1993). Former name (until 1973): **Fort Lamy.**

Ndola ★ (ᵊn'dəʊlə) *n* a city in N Zambia: copper, cobalt, and sugar refineries. Pop.: 376 311 (1990).

NDP *abbrev. for:* **1** net domestic product. **2** (in Canada) New Democratic Party.

NDT (in Canada) *abbrev. for* Newfoundland Daylight Time.

Ne *the chemical symbol for* neon.

NE 1 *symbol for* northeast(ern). **2** *abbrev. for* Nebraska. **3** Also: **N.E.** *abbrev. for* New England.

ne- *combining form.* a variant of **neo-,** esp. before a vowel: *Nearctic.*

Neagh ★ (neɪ) *n* **Lough.** a lake in Northern Ireland, in SW Co. Antrim: the largest lake in the British Isles. Area: 388 sq. km (150 sq. miles).

Neanderthal man (nɪ'ændə,tɑːl) *n* a type of primitive man occurring throughout much of Europe in late Palaeolithic times. They are not thought to be ancestors of modern humans. ORIG C19: from the anthropological findings (1857) in the Neandertal, a valley near Düsseldorf, Germany

neap (niːp) *adj* **1** of, relating to, or constituting a neap tide. ◆ *n* **2** short for **neap tide.** ORIG OE, as in *nēpflōd* neap tide, from ?

Neapolitan (,nɪə'pɒlɪtᵊn) *n* **1** a native or inhabitant of Naples. ◆ *adj* **2** of or relating to Naples. ORIG C15: from L *Neāpolītānus,* ult. from Gk *Neapolis* new town

Neapolitan ice cream *n* ice cream with several layers of different colours and flavours.

neap tide *n* either of the tides that occur at the first or last quarter of the moon when the tide-generating forces of the sun and moon oppose each other and produce the smallest rise and fall in tidal level. Cf. **spring tide** (sense 1).

near (nɪə) *prep* **1** at or to a place or time not far away from; close to. ◆ *adv* **2** at or to a place or time not far away; close by. **3** short for **nearly** (sense 1): *I was damn near killed.* ◆ *adj* **4** (*postpositive*) at or in a place not far away. **5** (*prenominal*) only just successful or only just failing: *a near thing.* **6** (*postpositive*) *Inf.* miserly, mean. **7** (*prenominal*) closely connected or intimate: *a near relation.* ◆ *vb* **8** to come or draw close (to). ◆ *n* **9** Also called: **nearside. 9a** the left side of a horse, vehicle, etc. **9b** (*as modifier*): *the near foreleg.* ORIG OE *nēar* (adv), comp. of *nēah* close
▸ **'nearness** *n*

nearby *adj* ('nɪəˌbaɪ), *adv* (ˌnɪə'baɪ). not far away; close at hand.

Nearctic (nɪ'ɑːktɪk) *adj* of a zoogeographical region consisting of North America, north of the tropic of Cancer, and Greenland.

Near East ★ *n* **1** another term for the **Middle East. 2** (formerly) the Balkan States and the area of the Ottoman Empire.

near gale *n Meteorol.* a wind of force seven on the Beaufort scale or from 32-38 mph.

nearly ('nɪəlɪ) *adv* **1** almost. **2 not nearly.** nowhere near: *not nearly enough.* **3** closely: *the person most nearly concerned.*

near-market *n* (*modifier*) (of scientific research, etc.) very close to being commercially exploitable.

near miss *n* **1** a bomb, shell, etc., that does not exactly hit the target. **2** any attempt or shot that just fails to be successful. **3** an incident in which two aircraft, etc., narrowly avoid collision.

near point *n Optics.* the nearest point to the eye at which an object remains in focus.

nearside ('nɪəˌsaɪd) *n* **1** (usually preceded by *the*) *Chiefly Brit.* **1a** the side of a vehicle, etc., nearer the kerb. **1b** (*as modifier*): *the nearside door.* **2a** the left side of an animal, etc. **2b** (*as modifier*): *the nearside flank.*

near-sighted (ˌnɪə'saɪtɪd) *adj* relating to or suffering from myopia.
▸ **ˌnear-'sightedly** *adv*

near thing *n Inf.* an event or action whose outcome is nearly a failure, success, disaster, etc.

neat[1] (niːt) *adj* **1** clean, tidy, and orderly. **2** liking or insisting on order and cleanliness. **3** smoothly or competently done; efficient: *a neat job.* **4** pat or slick: *his excuse was suspiciously neat.* **5** (of alcoholic drinks, etc.) undiluted. **6** (of language) concise and well-phrased. **7** *Sl., chiefly US & Canad.* pleasing; admirable; excellent. ORIG C16: from OF *net,* from L *nitidus* clean, from *nitēre* to shine
▸ **'neatly** *adv* ▸ **'neatness** *n*

neat[2] (niːt) *n, pl* **neat.** *Arch. or dialect.* a domestic bovine animal. ORIG OE *neat*

neaten ('niːtᵊn) *vb* (*tr*) to make neat; tidy.

neath *or* **'neath** (niːθ) *prep Arch.* short for **beneath.**

Neath Port Talbot ★ ('niːθ 'pɔːt 'tɔːlbət, 'tæl-) *n* a county borough in S Wales. Administrative centre: Port Talbot. Pop.: 106 307 (1996 est.). Area: 439 sq. km (169 sq. miles).

neat's-foot oil *n* a yellow oil obtained by boiling the feet and shinbones of cattle.

neb (nɛb) *n Arch. or dialect.* **1** the peak of a cap. **2** the beak of a bird or the nose or snout of an animal. **3** the projecting end of anything. ORIG OE *nebb*

NEB *abbrev. for:* **1** New English Bible. **2** National Enterprise Board.

Nebo ★ ('niːbəʊ) *n* **Mount.** a mountain in Jordan, northeast of the Dead Sea: the highest point of a ridge known as Pisgah, from which Moses viewed the Promised Land just before his death (Deuteronomy 34:1). Height: 802 m (2631 ft).

Nebr. *abbrev. for* Nebraska.

Nebraska ★ (nɪ'bræskə) *n* a state of the western US: consists of an undulating plain. Capital: Lincoln. Pop.: 1 662 719 (1998 est.). Area: 197 974 sq. km (76 483 sq. miles). Abbrevs.: **Nebr.** or (with zip code) **NE**
▸ **Ne'braskan** *adj, n*

Nebuchadnezzar *or* **Nebuchadrezzar** ★ (ˌnɛbjʊkəd'nɛzə, -'drɛzə) *n Old Testament.* a king of Babylon, 605–562 B.C., who conquered and destroyed Jerusalem and exiled the Jews to Babylon (II Kings 24–25).

nebula ('nɛbjʊlə) *n, pl* **nebulae** (-ˌliː) *or* **nebulas. 1** *Astron.* a diffuse cloud of particles and gases visible either as a hazy patch of light (either an **emission** or **reflection nebula**) or an irregular dark region (**dark nebula**). **2** *Pathol.* opacity of the cornea. ORIG C17: from L: mist, cloud
▸ **'nebular** *adj*

nebular hypothesis *n* the theory that the solar system evolved from nebular matter.

nebulize *or* **nebulise** ('nɛbjʊˌlaɪz) *vb* **nebulizes, nebulizing, nebulized** *or* **nebulises, nebulising, nebulized.** (*tr*) to convert (a liquid) into a fine mist or spray; atomize.
▸ **ˌnebuli'zation** *or* **ˌnebuli'sation** *n*

nebulizer *or* **nebuliser** ('nɛbjʊˌlaɪzə) *n* a device for converting a drug in liquid form into a mist or fine spray which is inhaled through a mask to provide medication for the respiratory system.

nebulosity (ˌnɛbjʊ'lɒsɪtɪ) *n, pl* **nebulosities. 1** the state of being nebulous. **2** *Astron.* a nebula.

nebulous ('nɛbjʊləs) *adj* **1** lacking definite form, shape, or content; vague or amorphous. **2** of a nebula. **3** *Rare.* misty or hazy.
▸ **'nebulousness** *n*

NEC *abbrev. for* National Executive Committee.

necessaries ('nɛsɪsərɪz) *pl n* (*sometimes sing*) what is needed; essential items: *the necessaries of life.*

necessarily ('nɛsɪsərɪlɪ, ˌnɛsɪ'sɛrɪlɪ) *adv* **1** as an inevitable or natural consequence. **2** as a certainty: *he won't necessarily come.*

necessary ('nɛsɪsərɪ) *adj* **1** needed to achieve a certain desired result; required. **2** inevitable: *the necessary consequences of your action.* **3** *Logic.* **3a** (of a statement, formula, etc.) true under all interpretations. **3b** (of a proposition) determined to be true by its meaning, so that its denial would be self-contradictory. Cf. **sufficient** (sense 2). **4** *Rare.* compelled, as by necessity or law; not free. ◆ *n* **5** (preceded by *the*) *Inf.* the money required for a particular purpose. **6 do the necessary.** *Inf.* to do something that is necessary in a particular situation. ◆ See also **necessaries.** ORIG C14: from L *necessārius* indispensable, from *necesse* unavoidable

necessitarianism (nɪˌsɛsɪ'tɛərɪəˌnɪzəm) *n Philosophy.* another word for **determinism.**
▸ **neˌcessi'tarian** *n, adj*

necessitate (nɪ'sɛsɪˌteɪt) *vb* **necessitates, necessitating, necessitated.** (*tr*) **1** to cause as an unavoidable result. **2** (*usually passive*) to compel or require (someone to do something).

necessitous (nɪ'sɛsɪtəs) *adj* very needy; destitute; poverty-stricken.

necessity (nɪ'sɛsɪtɪ) *n, pl* **necessities. 1** (*sometimes pl*) something needed; prerequisite: *necessities of life.* **2** a condition or set of circumstances that inevitably requires a certain result: *it is a matter of necessity to wear formal clothes when meeting the Queen.* **3** the state or quality of being obligatory or unavoidable. **4** urgent requirement, as in an emergency. **5** poverty or want. **6** *Rare.* compulsion through laws of nature; fate. **7** *Logic.* the property of being necessary. **8 of necessity.** inevitably.

neck (nɛk) *n* **1** the part of an organism connecting the head with the body. **2** the part of a garment around the neck. **3** something resembling a neck in shape or position: *the neck of a bottle.* **4** *Anat.* a constricted portion of an organ or part. **5** a narrow strip of land; peninsula or isthmus. **6** a strait or channel. **7** the part of a violin, cello, etc., that extends from the body to the tuning pegs and supports the fingerboard. **8** a solid block of lava from an extinct volcano, exposed after erosion of the surrounding rock. **9** the length of a horse's head and neck taken as an approximate distance by which one horse beats another in a race: *to win by a neck.* **10** *Archit.* the narrow band at the top of the shaft of a column. **11** *Inf.* impudence or cheek. **12 get it in the neck.** *Inf.* to be reprimanded or punished severely. **13 neck and neck.** absolutely level in a race or competition. **14 neck of the woods.** *Inf.* a particular area: *what brings you to this neck of the woods?* **15 neck or nothing.** at any cost. **16 save one's** *or* **someone's neck.** *Inf.* to escape from or help someone else to escape from a difficult or dangerous situation. **17 stick one's neck out.** *Inf.* to risk criticism, ridicule, etc., by speaking one's mind. ◆ *vb* **18** (*intr*) *Inf.* to kiss or fondle someone or one another passionately. ORIG OE *hnecca*

Neckar ★ ('nɛkɑː) *n* a river in SW Germany, rising in the Black Forest and flowing generally north into the Rhine at Mannheim. Length: 394 km (245 miles).

neckband ('nɛkˌbænd) *n* a band around the neck of a garment as finishing, decoration, or a base for a collar.

neckcloth ('nɛkˌklɒθ) *n* a large ornamental usually white cravat worn formerly by men.

neckerchief ('nɛkətʃɪf, -ˌtʃiːf) *n* a piece of ornamental cloth, often square, worn round the neck. ORIG C14: from NECK + KERCHIEF

necking ('nɛkɪŋ) *n Inf.* the activity of kissing and embracing lovingly.

necklace ('nɛklɪs) *n* **1** a chain, band, or cord, often bearing beads, pearls, jewels, etc., worn around the neck as an ornament, esp. by women. **2** (in South Africa) **2a** a tyre soaked in petrol, placed round a person's neck, and set on fire in order to burn the person to death. **2b** (*as modifier*): *necklace victims.* ◆ *vb* **necklaces, necklacing, necklaced.** (*tr*) **3** (in South Africa) to kill (a person) by means of a necklace.

neckline ('nɛkˌlaɪn) *n* the shape or position of the upper edge of a dress, blouse, etc.

necktie ('nɛkˌtaɪ) *n* the US name for **tie** (sense 10).

neckwear ('nɛkˌwɛə) *n* articles of clothing, such as ties, scarves, etc., worn round the neck.

necro- *or before a vowel* **necr-** *combining form.* indicating death, a dead body, or dead tissue: *necrosis.* ORIG from Gk *nekros* corpse

necrobiosis (ˌnɛkrəʊbaɪ'əʊsɪs) *n Physiol.* the normal degeneration and death of cells.

necrolatry (nɛ'krɒlətrɪ) *n* the worship of the dead.

necrology (nɛ'krɒlədʒɪ) *n, pl* **necrologies. 1** a list of people recently dead. **2** a less common word for **obituary.**
▸ **necrological** (ˌnɛkrə'lɒdʒɪkᵊl) *adj*

necromancy ('nɛkrəʊˌmænsɪ) *n* **1** the art of supposedly conjuring up the dead, esp. in order to obtain from them knowledge of the future. **2** black magic; sorcery. ORIG C13: (sense 1) ult. from Gk *nekromanteia,* from *nekros* corpse; (sense 2) from Med. L *nigromantia,* from L *niger* black, which replaced *necro-* through folk etymology
▸ **'necroˌmancer** *n* ▸ **ˌnecro'mantic** *adj*

necrophilia (ˌnɛkrəʊ'fɪlɪə) *n* sexual attraction for or sexual intercourse with dead bodies. Also called: **necromania, necrophilism.**
▸ **necrophile** ('nɛkrəʊˌfaɪl) *n* ▸ **ˌnecro'philic** *adj*

necropolis (nɛ'krɒpəlɪs) *n, pl* **necropolises** *or* **necropoleis** (-ˌleɪs). a burial site or cemetery. ORIG C19: from Gk, from *nekros* dead + *polis* city

necropsy ('nɛkrɒpsɪ) *or* **necroscopy** (nɛ'krɒskəpɪ) *n, pl* **necropsies** *or* **necroscopies.** another name for **autopsy.** ORIG C19: from Gk *nekros* dead body + *opsis* sight

necrosis (nɛ'krəʊsɪs) *n* **1** the death of one or more cells in the body, usually within a localized area, as from an interruption of the blood supply. **2** death of plant tissue due to disease, frost, etc. ORIG C17: NL, from Gk *nekrōsis,* from *nekroun* to kill, from *nekros* corpse
▸ **necrotic** (nɛ'krɒtɪk) *adj*

nectar ('nɛktə) *n* **1** a sugary fluid produced in the nectaries of flowers and collected by bees. **2** *Classical myth.* the drink of the gods. Cf. **ambrosia** (sense 1). **3** any delicious drink. ORIG C16: via L from Gk *néktar*
▸ **'nectarous** *adj*

nectarine ('nɛktərɪn) *n* **1** a variety of peach tree. **2** the smooth-skinned fruit of this tree. ORIG C17: apparently from NECTAR

nectary ('nɛktərɪ) *n, pl* **nectaries.** any of various structures secreting nectar that occur in the flowers, leaves, stipules, etc., of a plant. ORIG C18: from NL *nectarium,* from NECTAR

ned (nɛd) *n Scot. sl.* a hooligan. ORIG from ?

NEDC *abbrev. for* National Economic Development Council. Also (inf.): **Neddy** ('nɛdɪ).

neddy ('nɛdɪ) *n, pl* **neddies.** a child's word for a **donkey.** ORIG C18: from *Ned,* pet form of *Edward*

Nederland ★ ('neːdərlɑnt) *n* the Dutch name for the **Netherlands.**

née *or* **nee** (neɪ) *adj* indicating the maiden name of a married woman: *Mrs Bloggs née Blandish.* ORIG C19: from F: p.p. (fem) of *naître* to be born, from L *nascī*

need (niːd) *vb* **1** (*tr*) to be in want of: *to need money.* **2** (*tr*) to be obliged: *to need to do more work.* **3** (takes an infinitive without *to*) used as an auxiliary to express necessity or obligation and does not add *-s* when used with *he, she, it,* and singular nouns: *need he go?* **4** (*intr*) *Arch.* to be essential to: *there needs no reason for this.* ◆ *n* **5** the fact or an instance of feeling the lack of something: *he has need of a new coat.* **6** a requirement: *the need for vengeance.* **7** necessity or obligation: *no need to be frightened.* **8** distress: *a friend in need.* **9** poverty or destitution. ◆ See also **needs.** ORIG OE *nēad, nied*

needful ('niːdfʊl) *adj* **1** necessary; required. **2** *Arch.* poverty-stricken. ◆ *n* **3 the needful.** *Inf.* what is necessary, esp. money.
▸ **'needfulness** *n*

needle ('niːdᵊl) *n* **1** a pointed slender piece of metal with a hole in it through which thread is passed for sewing. **2** a somewhat larger rod with a point at one end, used in knitting. **3** a similar instrument with a hook at one end for crocheting. **4** a small thin pointed device, esp. one made of stainless steel, used to transmit the vibrations from a gramophone record to the pick-up. Cf. **stylus** (sense 3). **5** *Med.* the long hollow pointed part of a hypodermic syringe, which is inserted into the body. **6** *Surgery.* a pointed instrument, often curved, for suturing, puncturing, or ligating. **7** a long narrow stiff leaf in which water loss is greatly reduced: *pine needles.* **8** any slender sharp spine. **9** a pointer on the scale of a measuring instrument. **10** short for **magnetic needle. 11** a sharp pointed instrument used in engraving. **12** anything long and pointed, such as an obelisk. **13** *Inf.* **13a** anger or intense rivalry, esp. in a sporting encounter. **13b** (*as modifier*): *a needle match.* **14 have** *or* **get the needle.** *Brit. inf.* to feel dislike, nervousness, or annoyance: *she got the needle after he had refused her invitation.* ◆ *vb* **needles, needling, needled.** (*tr*) **15** *Inf.* to goad or provoke, as by constant criticism. **16** to sew, embroider, or prick (fabric) with a needle. ORIG OE *nǣdl*

needlecord ('niːdᵊlˌkɔːd) *n* a corduroy fabric with narrow ribs.

needlepoint ('niːdᵊlˌpɔɪnt) *n* **1** embroidery done on canvas with various stitches so as to resemble tapestry. **2** another name for **point lace.**

needless ('niːdlɪs) *adj* not required; unnecessary.
▸ **'needlessly** *adv* ▸ **'needlessness** *n*

needlestick injury ('niːdᵊlˌstɪk) *n* an injury caused by accidentally pricking the skin with a hypodermic needle.

needle time *n* the limited time allocated by a radio channel to the broadcasting of music from records.

needlewoman ('niːdᵊlˌwʊmən) *n, pl* **needlewomen.** a woman who does needlework; seamstress.

needlework ('niːdᵊlˌwɜːk) *n* sewing and embroidery.

needs (niːdz) *adv* **1** (preceded or foll. by *must*) of necessity: *we must needs go.* ◆ *pl n* **2** what is required; necessities: *his needs are modest.*

needy ('niːdɪ) *adj* **needier, neediest. a** in need of practical or emotional support; distressed. **b** (*as collective n;* preceded by *the*): *the needy.*

Néel ★ (*French* neɛl) *n* **Louis** (lwi). born 1904, French physicist, noted for his research on magnetism; shared the Nobel prize for physics in 1970.

ne'er (nɛə) *adv* a poetic contraction of **never.**

ne'er-do-well *n* **1** an improvident, irresponsible, or lazy person. ◆ *adj* **2** useless; worthless: *your ne'er-do-well schemes.*

nefarious (nɪˈfɛərɪəs) *adj* evil; wicked; sinful. ORIG C17: from L *nefārius,* from *nefās* unlawful deed, from *nē* not + *fās* divine law
▸ **neˈfariously** *adv* ▸ **neˈfariousness** *n*

Nefertiti (ˌnɛfəˈtiːtɪ) *or* **Nofretete** ★ *n* 14th century B.C., Egyptian queen; wife of Akhenaton.

neg. *abbrev. for* negative(ly).

negate (nɪˈgeɪt) *vb* **negates, negating, negated.** (*tr*) **1** to nullify; invalidate. **2** to contradict. ORIG C17: from L *negāre,* from *neg-,* var. of *nec* not + *aio* I say
▸ **neˈgator** *or* **neˈgater** *n*

negation (nɪˈgeɪʃən) *n* **1** the opposite or absence of something. **2** a negative thing or condition. **3** the act of negating. **4** *Logic.* a proposition that is the denial of another proposition and is true only if the original proposition is false.

negative (ˈnɛgətɪv) *adj* **1** expressing a refusal or denial: *a negative answer.* **2** lacking positive qualities, such as enthusiasm or optimism. **3** showing opposition or resistance. **4** measured in a direction opposite to that regarded as positive. **5** *Biol.* indicating movement or growth away from a stimulus: *negative geotropism.* **6** *Med.* indicating absence of the disease or condition for which a test was made. **7** another word for **minus** (senses 3b, 4). **8** *Physics.* **8a** (of an electric charge) having the same polarity as the charge of an electron. **8b** (of a body, system, ion, etc.) having a negative electric charge; having an excess of electrons. **9** short for **electronegative. 10** of or relating to a photographic negative. **11** *Logic.* (of a categorial proposition) denying the satisfaction by the subject of the predicate, as in *some men are irrational; no pigs have wings.* ◆ *n* **12** a statement or act of denial or refusal. **13** a negative thing. **14** *Photog.* a piece of photographic film or a plate, previously exposed and developed, showing an image that, in black-and-white photography, has a reversal of tones. **15** *Physics.* a negative object, such as a terminal or a plate in a voltaic cell. **16** a sentence or other linguistic element with a negative meaning, as the English word *not.* **17** a quantity less than zero. **18** *Logic.* a negative proposition. **19 in the negative.** indicating denial or refusal. ◆ *vb* **negatives, negativing, negatived.** (*tr*) **20** to deny; negate. **21** to show to be false; disprove. **22** to refuse consent to or approval of: *the proposal was negatived.*
▸ **ˈnegatively** *adv* ▸ **ˈnegativeness** *or* **ˌnegaˈtivity** *n*

negative equity *n* the state of holding a property the value of which is less than the amount of mortgage still unpaid.

negative feedback *n* See **feedback.**

negative resistance *n* a characteristic of certain electronic components in which an increase in the applied voltage increases the resistance, producing a proportional decrease in current.

negative sign *n* the symbol (–) used to indicate a negative quantity or a subtraction.

negativism (ˈnɛgətɪvˌɪzəm) *n* **1** a tendency to be unconstructively critical. **2** any sceptical or derisive system of thought.
▸ **ˈnegativist** *n, adj*

Negev (ˈnɛgɛv) *or* **Negeb** ★ (ˈnɛgɛb) *n* the S part of Israel, on the Gulf of Aqaba: a triangular-shaped semidesert region, with large areas under irrigation; scene of fighting between Israeli and Egyptian forces in 1948. Chief town: Beersheba. Area: 12 820 sq. km (4950 sq. miles).

neglect (nɪˈglɛkt) *vb* (*tr*) **1** to fail to give due care, attention, or time to: *to neglect a child.* **2** to fail (to do something) through carelessness: *he neglected to tell her.* **3** to disregard. ◆ *n* **4** lack of due care or attention; negligence: *the child starved through neglect.* **5** the act or an instance of neglecting or the state of being neglected. ORIG C16: from L *neglegere,* from *nec* not + *legere* to select

neglectful (nɪˈglɛktfʊl) *adj* (when *postpositive,* foll. by *of*) careless; heedless.

negligee *or* **negligée** (ˈnɛglɪˌʒeɪ) *n* **1** a woman's light dressing gown, esp. one that is lace-trimmed. **2** a thin and revealing woman's nightdress. **3** (formerly) any informal women's attire. ORIG C18: from F *négligée,* p.p. (fem) of *négliger* to NEGLECT

negligence (ˈnɛglɪdʒəns) *n* **1** the state of being negligent. **2** a negligent act. **3** *Law.* a civil wrong whereby the defendant is in breach of a legal duty of care, resulting in injury to the plaintiff.

negligent (ˈnɛglɪdʒənt) *adj* **1** lacking attention, care, or concern; neglectful. **2** careless or nonchalant.
▸ **ˈnegligently** *adv*

negligible (ˈnɛglɪdʒəb^{ə}l) *adj* so small, unimportant, etc., as to be not worth considering.
▸ **ˈnegligibly** *adv*

negotiable (nɪˈgəʊʃəb^{ə}l) *adj* **1** able to be negotiated. **2** (of a bill of exchange, promissory note, etc.) legally transferable in title from one party to another.
▸ **neˌgotiaˈbility** *n*

negotiable instrument *n* a legal document, such as a cheque or bill of exchange, that is freely negotiable.

negotiate (nɪˈgəʊʃɪˌeɪt) *vb* **negotiates, negotiating, negotiated. 1** to talk (with others) to achieve (an agreement, etc.). **2** (*tr*) to succeed in passing round or over. **3** (*tr*) *Finance.* **3a** to transfer (a negotiable commercial paper) to another in return for value received. **3b** to sell (financial assets). **3c** to arrange for (a loan). ORIG C16: from L *negōtiārī* to do business, from *negōtium* business, from *nec* not + *ōtium* leisure
▸ **neˌgotiˈation** *n* ▸ **neˈgotiˌator** *n*

Negress (ˈniːgrɪs) *n* a female Black person.

Negrillo (nɪˈgrɪləʊ) *n, pl* **Negrillos** *or* **Negrilloes.** a member of a dwarfish Negroid race of central and southern Africa. ORIG C19: from Sp., dim. of *negro* black

Negri Sembilan ★ (ˈnɛgrɪ sɛmˈbiːlən) *n* a state of S Peninsular Malaysia: mostly mountainous, with large areas under paddy and rubber. Capital: Seremban. Pop.: 723 900 (1993 est.). Area: 6643 sq. km (2565 sq. miles).

Negrito (nɪˈgriːtəʊ) *n, pl* **Negritos** *or* **Negritoes.** a member of any of various dwarfish Negroid peoples of SE Asia and Melanesia. ORIG C19: from Sp., dim. of *negro* black

negritude (ˈniːgrɪˌtjuːd, ˈnɛg-) *n* **1** the fact of being a Negro. **2** awareness and cultivation of the Negro heritage, values, and culture. ORIG C20: from F, from *nègre* NEGRO[1]

Negro[1] (ˈniːgrəʊ) *Old-fashioned.* ◆ *n, pl* **Negroes. 1** a member of any of the dark-skinned indigenous peoples of Africa and their descendants elsewhere. ◆ *adj* **2** relating to or characteristic of Negroes. ORIG C16: from Sp. or Port.: black, from L *niger*
▸ **ˈNegroˌism** *n*

Negro[2] ★ (ˈneɪgrəʊ, ˈnɛg-) *n* **Río. 1** a river in NW South America, rising in E Colombia (as the Guainía) and flowing east, then south as part of the border between Colombia and Venezuela, entering Brazil and continuing southeast to join the Amazon at Manáus. Length: about 2250 km (1400 miles). **2** a river in S central Argentina, formed by the confluence of the Neuquén and Limay Rivers and flowing east and southeast to the Atlantic. Length: about 1014 km (630 miles). **3** a river in central Uruguay, rising in S Brazil and flowing southwest into the Uruguay River. Length: about 467 km (290 miles).

Negroid (ˈniːgrɔɪd) *adj* **1** denoting, relating to, or belonging to one of the major racial groups of mankind, characterized by brown-black skin, tightly curled hair, a short nose, and full lips. ◆ *n* **2** a member of this racial group.

Negropont ★ (ˈnɛgrəʊˌpɒnt) *n* **1** the former English name for **Euboea. 2** the medieval English name for **Chalcis.**

Negros ★ (ˈneɪgrəʊs; *Spanish* ˈneɣrɔs) *n* an island of the central Philippines, one of the Visayan Islands. Capital: Bacolod. Pop.: 3 168 000 (1990 est.). Area: 13 670 sq. km (5278 sq. miles).

negus (ˈniːgəs) *n, pl* **neguses.** a hot drink of port and lemon juice, usually spiced and sweetened. ORIG C18: after Col. Francis *Negus* (died 1732), its E inventor

Negus (ˈniːgəs) *n, pl* **Neguses.** *History.* a title of the emperor of Ethiopia. ORIG from Amharic: king

Neh. *Bible. abbrev. for* Nehemiah.

Nehemiah ★ (ˌniːɪˈmaɪə) *n Old Testament.* **1** a Jewish official at the court of Artaxerxes, king of Persia, who in 444 B.C. became a leader in the rebuilding of Jerusalem after the Babylonian captivity. **2** the book recounting the acts of Nehemiah.

Nehru ★ (ˈnɛəruː) *n* **1 Jawaharlal** (dʒəwəhəˈlɑːl). 1889–1964, Indian statesman and first premier of the republic; imprisoned several times (1921–45) for noncooperation with Britain. **2** his father, **Motilal** (məʊtɪˈlɑːl), known as *Pandit Nehru.* 1861–1931, Indian nationalist; first president of the reconstructed Indian National Congress.

neigh (neɪ) *n* **1** the high-pitched cry of a horse. ◆ *vb* **2** to make a neigh or utter with a sound like a neigh. ORIG OE *hnǣgan*

neighbour *or US* **neighbor** (ˈneɪbə) *n* **1** a person who lives near or next to another. **2a** a person or thing near or next to another. **2b** (*as modifier*): *neighbour states.* ◆ *vb* **3** (when *intr*, often foll. by *on*) to be or live close to. ORIG OE *nēahbūr*, from *nēah* NIGH + *būr, gebūr* dweller; see BOOR
▸ **ˈneighbouring** *or US* **ˈneighboring** *adj*

neighbourhood *or US* **neighborhood** (ˈneɪbəˌhʊd) *n* **1** the immediate environment; surroundings. **2** a district where people live. **3** the people in a particular area. **4** *Maths.* the set of all points whose distance from a given point is less than a specified value. **5** (*modifier*) living or situated in and serving the needs of a local area: *a neighbourhood community worker.* **6 in the neighbourhood of.** approximately.

neighbourhood watch *n* a scheme in which members of a community agree to take joint responsibility for keeping a watch on each other's property, as a way of preventing crime.

neighbourly *or US* **neighborly** (ˈneɪbəlɪ) *adj* kind, friendly, or sociable, as befits a neighbour.
▸ **ˈneighbourliness** *or US* **ˈneighborliness** *n*

Neill ★ (niːl) *n* **A(lexander) S(utherland).** 1883–1973, Scottish progressive educationalist; founder (1921) of Summerhill school.

Neisse ★ (ˈnaɪsə) *n* **1** Also called: **Glatzer Neisse** (ˈglɑːtsə). Polish name: **Nysa.** a river in SW Poland, rising on the northern Czech border and flowing northeast to join the Oder near Brzeg. Length: about 193 km (120 miles). **2** Also called: **Lusatian Neisse.** a river in E Europe, rising near Liberec, in the Czech Republic, and flowing north to join the Oder: forms part of the German-Polish border. Length: 225 km (140 miles).

neither (ˈnaɪðə, ˈniːðə) *determiner* **1a** not one nor the other (of two). **1b** (*as pronoun*): *neither can win.* ◆ *conj* **2** (*coordinating*) **2a** (used preceding alternatives joined by *nor*) not: *neither John nor Mary nor Joe went.* **2b** another word for **nor** (sense 2). ◆ *adv* (*sentence modifier*) **3** *Not standard.* another word for **either** (sense 4). ORIG C13 (lit.: *ne either* not either): changed from OE *nāwther*, from *nāhwæther*, from *nā* not + *hwæther* which of two

> **USAGE NOTE** A verb following a compound subject that uses *neither...(nor)* should be in the singular if both subjects are in the singular: *neither Jack nor John has done the work.*

Nejd ★ (nɛʒd, neɪd) *n* a region of central Saudi Arabia: formerly an independent sultanate of Arabia; it was united with Hejaz to form the kingdom of Saudi Arabia (1932).

nekton (ˈnɛktɒn) *n* the population of free-swimming animals that inhabits the middle depths of a sea or lake. ORIG C19: via G from Gk *nēkton* a swimming thing, from *nēkhein* to swim

nelly (ˈnɛlɪ) *n* **not on your nelly.** (*sentence substitute*). *Brit. sl.* certainly not.

nelson (ˈnɛlsən) *n* any wrestling hold in which a wrestler places an arm or arms under the opponent's arm or arms from behind and exerts pressure with the palms of the hands on the back of the opponent's neck. ORIG C19: from a proper name

Nelson[1] ★ (ˈnɛlsən) *n* **1** a town in NW England, in E Lancashire: textile industry. Pop.: 29 120 (1991). **2** a port in New Zealand, on N South Island on Tasman Bay. Pop.: 51 200 (1995 est.). **3 River.** a river in central Canada, in N central Manitoba, flowing from Lake Winnipeg northeast to Hudson Bay. Length: about 650 km (400 miles).

Nelson[2] ★ (ˈnɛlsən) *n* **Horatio,** Viscount Nelson. 1758–1805, British naval commander during the Revolutionary and Napoleonic Wars. He destroyed French naval power at the battle of the Nile (1798); killed at Trafalgar (1805) after defeating Villeneuve's fleet.

Neman *or* **Nyeman** ★ (*Russian* ˈnjɛmən) *n* a river in central Europe, rising in Belarus and flowing generally northwest through Lithuania to the Baltic. Length: 937 km (582 miles). Polish name: **Niemen.**

nematic (nɪˈmætɪk) *adj Chem.* (of a substance) existing in or having a mesomorphic state in which a linear orientation of the molecules causes anisotropic properties. ORIG C20: NEMAT(O)- (referring to the threadlike chains of molecules in liquid) + -IC

nemato- *or before a vowel* **nemat-** *combining form.* indicating a threadlike form: *nematocyst.* ORIG from Gk *nēma* thread

nematocyst (ˈnɛmətəˌsɪst, nɪˈmætə-) *n* a structure in coelenterates, such as jellyfish, consisting of a capsule containing a hollow coiled thread that can sting or paralyse.

nematode (ˈnɛməˌtəʊd) *n* any of a class of unsegmented worms having a tough outer cuticle, including the hookworm and filaria. Also called: **nematode worm, roundworm.**

Nembutal (ˈnɛmbjʊˌtɑːl) *n* a trademark for **pentobarbitone sodium.**

Nemea ★ (nɪˈmiːə) *n* (in ancient Greece) a valley in N Argolis in the NE Peloponnese; site of the **Nemean Games,** a Panhellenic festival and athletic competition held every other year.
▸ **Neˈmean** *adj*

Nemean lion *n Greek myth.* an enormous lion that was strangled by Hercules as his first labour.

nemertean (nɪˈmɜːtɪən) *or* **nemertine** (ˈnɛməˌtaɪn) *n* **1** any of a class of soft flattened ribbon-like marine worms having an eversible threadlike proboscis. ◆ *adj* **2** of or belonging to the *Nemertea.* ORIG C19: via NL from Gk *Nēmertēs* a NEREID

nemesia (nɪˈmiːʒə) *n* any plant of a southern African genus cultivated for their brightly coloured flowers. ORIG C19: NL, from Gk *nemesion,* name of a plant resembling this

Nemesis ★ (ˈnɛmɪsɪs) *n* **1** *Greek myth.* the goddess of retribution and vengeance. **2** (*pl* **Nemeses** (-ˌsiːz)). (*sometimes not cap.*) any agency of retribution and vengeance. ORIG C16: via L from Gk: righteous wrath, from *nemein* to distribute what is due

nemophila (nɛˈmɒfɪlə) *n* an annual trailing plant with blue flowers. ORIG from Gk *nemos* grove + *philos* loving

neo- *or sometimes before a vowel* **ne-** *combining form.* **1** (*sometimes cap.*) new, recent, or a modern form: *neoclassicism; neocolonialism.* **2** (*usually cap.*) the most recent subdivision of a geological period: *Neogene.* ORIG from Gk *neos* new

neoclassicism (ˌniːəʊˈklæsɪˌsɪzəm) *n* **1** a late 18th- and early 19th-century style in architecture and art, based on classical models. **2** *Music.* a movement of the 1920s that sought to avoid the emotionalism of late romantic music.
▸ **neoclassical** (ˌniːəʊˈklæsɪkəl) *or* **ˌneoˈclassic** *adj*

neocolonialism (ˌniːəʊkəˈləʊnɪəˌlɪzəm) *n* (in the modern world) political control by an outside power of a country that is in theory independent, esp. through the domination of its economy.
▸ **ˌneocoˈlonialist** *n, adj*

Neo-Darwinism (ˌniːəʊˈdɑːwɪnˌɪzəm) *n* a modern theory of evolution that relates Darwinism to the occurrence of inheritable variation by genetic mutation.

neodymium (ˌniːəʊˈdɪmɪəm) *n* a toxic silvery-white metallic element of the lanthanide series. Symbol: Nd;

atomic no.: 60; atomic wt.: 144.24. ORIG C19: NL; see NEO- + DIDYMIUM

neogothic (ˌniːəʊ'gɒθɪk) *n* another name for **Gothic Revival.**

Neolithic (ˌniːə'lɪθɪk) *n* **1** the cultural period that was characterized by primitive farming and the use of polished stone and flint tools and weapons. ◆ *adj* **2** relating to this period.

neologism (nɪ'ɒləˌdʒɪzəm) *or* **neology** *n, pl* **neologisms** *or* **neologies. 1** a newly coined word, or a phrase or familiar word used in a new sense. **2** the practice of using or introducing neologisms. ORIG C18: via F from NEO- + *-logism,* from Gk *logos* word
▸ **ne'ologist** *n*

neologize *or* **neologise** (nɪ'ɒləˌdʒaɪz) *vb* **neologizes, neologizing, neologized** *or* **neologises, neologising, neologised.** (*intr*) to invent or use neologisms.

neomycin (ˌniːəʊ'maɪsɪn) *n* an antibiotic obtained from the bacterium *Streptomyces fradiae,* administered in the treatment of skin and eye infections. ORIG C20: from NEO- + Gk *mukēs* fungus + -IN

neon ('niːɒn) *n* **1** a colourless odourless rare gaseous element occurring in trace amounts in the atmosphere: used in illuminated signs and lights. Symbol: Ne; atomic no.: 10; atomic wt.: 20.179. **2** (*modifier*) of or illuminated by neon: *neon sign.* ORIG C19: via NL from Gk *neon* new

neonatal (ˌniːəʊ'neɪtᵊl) *adj* occurring in or relating to the first few weeks of life in human babies.
▸ **'neoˌnate** *n*

neon light *n* a glass bulb or tube containing neon at low pressure that gives a pink or red glow when a voltage is applied.

neophyte ('niːəʊˌfaɪt) *n* **1** a person newly converted to a religious faith. **2** a novice in a religious order. **3** a beginner. ORIG C16: via Church L from New Testament Gk *neophutos* recently planted, from *neos* new + *phuton* a plant

neoplasm ('niːəʊˌplæzəm) *n Pathol.* any abnormal new growth of tissue; tumour.

Neo-Platonism (ˌniːəʊ'pleɪtəˌnɪzəm) *n* a philosophical system which was developed in the 3rd century A.D. as a synthesis of Platonic, Pythagorean, and Aristotelian elements.
▸ **Neo-Platonic** (ˌniːəʊplə'tɒnɪk) *adj* ▸ **ˌNeo-'Platonist** *n, adj*

neoprene ('niːəʊˌpriːn) *n* a synthetic rubber obtained by the polymerization of chloroprene, a colourless liquid derivative of butadiene, resistant to oil and ageing and used in waterproof products. ORIG C20: from NEO- + PR(OPYL) + -ENE

Neoptolemus (ˌniːɒp'tɒləməs) ★ *n Greek myth.* a son of Achilles and slayer of King Priam of Troy. Also called: **Pyrrhus.**

neoteny (nɪ'ɒtənɪ) *n* the persistence of larval or fetal features in the adult form of an animal. ORIG C19: from NL *neotenia,* from Gk NEO- + *teinein* to stretch

neoteric (ˌniːəʊ'tɛrɪk) *Rare.* ◆ *adj* **1** belonging to a new fashion or trend; modern. ◆ *n* **2** a new writer or philosopher. ORIG C16: via LL from Gk *neōterikos* young, fresh, from *neoteros* younger, more recent, from *neos* new, recent

Nepal ★ (nɪ'pɔːl) *n* a kingdom in S Asia: the world's only Hindu kingdom; united in 1768 by the Gurkhas; consists of swampy jungle in the south and great massifs, valleys, and gorges of the Himalayas over the rest of the country, with many peaks over 8000 m (26 000 ft) (notably Everest and Kangchenjunga). A multiparty democracy was instituted in 1990. Official language: Nepali. Official religion: Hindu and Mahayana Buddhist. Currency: rupee. Capital: Katmandu. Pop.: 22 499 000 (1999 est.). Area: 147 181 sq. km (56 815 sq. miles).
▸ **Nepalese** (ˌnɛpə'liːz) *adj, n*

Nepali (nɪ'pɔːlɪ) *n* **1** the official language of Nepal, also spoken in Sikkim and parts of India. **2** (*pl* **Nepali** *or* **Nepalis**) a native or inhabitant of Nepal; a Nepalese. ◆ *adj* **3** of or relating to Nepal, its inhabitants, or their language; Nepalese.

nepenthe (nɪ'pɛnθɪ) *or* **nepenthes** (nɪ'pɛnθiːz) *n* a drug that ancient writers referred to as a means of forgetting grief or trouble. ORIG C16: via L from Gk *nēpenthes* sedative made from a herb, from *nē-* not + *penthos* grief

nepeta ('nɛpɛtə, nə'pɛtə) *n* any of a genus of plants found in N temperate regions. It includes catmint. ORIG from L

nephew ('nɛvjuː, 'nɛf-) *n* a son of one's sister or brother. ORIG C13: from OF *neveu,* from L *nepōs*

nephology (nɪ'fɒlədʒɪ) *n* the study of clouds. ORIG C19: from Gk *nephos* cloud + -LOGY

nephridium (nɪ'frɪdɪəm) *n, pl* **nephridia** (-ɪə). a simple excretory organ of many invertebrates, consisting of a tube through which waste products pass to the exterior. ORIG C19: NL: little kidney

nephrite ('nɛfraɪt) *n* a tough fibrous mineral: a variety of jade. Also called: **kidney stone.** ORIG C18: via G from Gk *nephros* kidney; it was thought to help in kidney disorders

nephritic (nɪ'frɪtɪk) *adj* **1** of or relating to the kidneys. **2** relating to or affected with nephritis.

nephritis (nɪ'fraɪtɪs) *n* inflammation of a kidney.

nephro- *or before a vowel* **nephr-** *combining form.* kidney or kidneys: *nephritis.* ORIG from Gk *nephros*

nephrology (nɪ'frɒlədʒɪ) *n* the branch of medicine concerned with diseases of the kidney.
▸ **ne'phrologist** *n*

nephron ('nɛfrɒn) *n* one of the units of the kidney that secretes urine, via ducts, into the ureter.

nephroscope ('nɛfrəˌskəʊp) *n* a tubular medical instrument inserted through an incision in the skin to enable examination of a kidney.
▸ **nephroscopy** (nɪ'frɒskəpɪ) *n*

ne plus ultra *Latin.* ('neɪ 'plʊs 'ʊltrɑː) *n* the extreme or perfect point or state. ORIG lit.: not more beyond (that is, go no further), allegedly a warning to sailors inscribed on the Pillars of Hercules at Gibraltar

nepotism ('nɛpəˌtɪzəm) *n* favouritism shown to relatives or close friends by those with power. ORIG C17: from It. *nepotismo,* from *nepote* NEPHEW, from the former papal practice of granting favours to nephews or other relatives
▸ **'nepotist** *n*

Neptune[1] ★ ('nɛptjuːn) *n* the Roman god of the sea. Greek counterpart: **Poseidon.**

Neptune[2] ('nɛptjuːn) *n* the eighth planet from the sun, having two satellites, Triton and Nereid.

neptunium (nɛp'tjuːnɪəm) *n* a silvery metallic element synthesized in the production of plutonium and occurring in trace amounts in uranium ores. Symbol: Np; atomic no.: 93; half-life of most stable isotope, ^{237}Np: 2.14×10^6 years. ORIG C20: from NEPTUNE[2], the planet beyond Uranus, because neptunium is beyond uranium in the periodic table

NERC *abbrev. for* Natural Environment Research Council.

nerd *or* **nurd** (nɜːd) *n Sl.* **1** a boring or unpopular person, esp. one obsessed with something specified: *a computer nerd.* **2** a stupid and feeble person. ORIG C20: from ?
▸ **'nerdish** *or* **'nurdish** *adj* ▸ **'nerdy** *or* **'nurdy** *adj*

Nereid ('nɪərɪɪd) *n, pl* **Nereides** (nə'riːədiːz). *Greek myth.* any of 50 sea nymphs who were the daughters of the sea god Nereus. ORIG C17: via L from Gk

Nereus ★ ('nɪərɪˌuːs) *n Greek myth.* a sea god who lived in the depths of the sea with his wife Doris and their daughters the Nereides.

Neri ★ ('nɪərɪ) *n* **Saint Philip.** Italian name *Filippo de' Neri.* 1515–95, Italian priest; founder of the Congregation of the Oratory (1564). Feast day: May 26.

nerine (nɪ'raɪnɪ; *S. African* nə'riːn) *n* any of a genus of bulbous plants native to South Africa and grown elsewhere as greenhouse plants for their pink, red, or orange flowers: includes the Guernsey lily. ORIG after the water nymph *Nerine* in Roman myth

Nernst ★ (*German* nɛrnst) *n* **Walther Hermann** ('valtər 'hɛrman). 1864–1941, German physical chemist who formulated the third law of thermodynamics: Nobel prize for chemistry 1920.

Nero ★ ('nɪərəʊ) *n* full name *Nero Claudius Caesar Drusus Germanicus;* original name *Lucius Domitius Ahenobarbus.* 37–68 A.D., Roman emperor (54–68). Notorious for his cruelty, he was alleged to have started the fire (64) that largely destroyed Rome.

neroli oil *or* **neroli** ('nɪərəlɪ) *n* a brown oil distilled from the flowers of various orange trees: used in perfumery. ORIG C17: after Anne Marie de la Tremoïlle of *Neroli,* French-born It. princess believed to have discovered it

Neruda ★ (*Spanish* ne'ruða) *n* **Pablo** ('paβlo), real name *Neftali Ricardo Reyes.* 1904–73, Chilean poet. His works include *Canto general* (1950): Nobel prize for literature 1971.

Nerva ★ ('nɜːvə) *n* full name *Marcus Cocceius Nerva.* ?30–98 A.D., Roman emperor (96–98); adopted Trajan as his son and successor.

Nerval ★ (*French* nɛrval) *n* **Gérard de** (ʒerar də), real name *Gérard Labrunie.* 1808–55, French poet.

nervate ('nɜːveɪt) *adj* (of leaves) having veins.

nervation (nɜː'veɪʃən) *or* **nervature** ('nɜːvətʃə) *n* a less common word for **venation.**

nerve (nɜːv) *n* **1** any of the cordlike bundles of fibres that conduct impulses between the brain or spinal cord and another part of the body. **2** bravery or steadfastness. **3** **lose one's nerve.** to become timid, esp. failing to perform some audacious act. **4** *Inf.* effrontery; impudence. **5** muscle or sinew (often in **strain every nerve**). **6** a vein in a leaf or an insect's wing. ◆ *vb* **nerves, nerving, nerved.** (*tr*) **7** to give courage to (oneself); steel (oneself). **8** to provide with nerve or nerves. ◆ See also **nerves.** ORIG C16: from L *nervus;* rel. to Gk *neuron*

nerve block *n* induction of anaesthesia in a specific part of the body by injecting a local anaesthetic close to the sensory nerves that supply it.

nerve cell *n* another name for **neurone.**

nerve centre *n* **1** a group of nerve cells associated with a specific function. **2** a principal source of control over any complex activity.

nerve fibre *n* a threadlike extension of a nerve cell; axon.

nerve gas *n* any of various poisonous gases that have a paralysing effect on the central nervous system that can be fatal.

nerve impulse *n* the electrical wave transmitted along a nerve fibre, usually following stimulation of the nerve-cell body.

nerveless ('nɜːvlɪs) *adj* **1** calm and collected. **2** listless or feeble.
▸ **'nervelessly** *adv*

nerve-racking *or* **nerve-wracking** *adj* very distressing, exhausting, or harrowing.

nerves (nɜːvz) *pl n Inf.* **1** the imagined source of emotional control: *my nerves won't stand it.* **2** anxiety, tension, or imbalance: *she's all nerves.* **3** **get on one's nerves.** to irritate or upset one.

nervine ('nɜːviːn) *adj* **1** having a soothing effect upon the nerves. ◆ *n* **2** a nervine agent. ORIG C17: from NL *nervīnus,* from L *nervus* NERVE

nervous ('nɜːvəs) *adj* **1** very excitable or sensitive; highly strung. **2** (often foll. by *of*) apprehensive or worried. **3** of or containing nerves: *nervous tissue.* **4** affecting the nerves or nervous tissue: *a nervous disease.* **5** *Arch.* vigorous or forceful.
▸ **'nervously** *adv* ▸ **'nervousness** *n*

nervous breakdown *n* any mental illness not primarily of organic origin, in which the patient ceases to function properly, often accompanied by severely impaired concentration, anxiety, insomnia, and lack of self-esteem.

nervous system *n* the sensory and control apparatus of animals, consisting of a network of neurones.

nervure ('nɜːvjʊə) *n* **1** *Entomol.* any of the chitinous rods that form the framework of an insect's wing; vein. **2** *Bot.* any of the veins of a leaf. ORIG C19: from F; see NERVE, -URE

nervy ('nɜːvɪ) *adj* **nervier, nerviest. 1** *Brit. inf.* tense or apprehensive. **2** having or needing bravery or endurance. **3** *US & Canad. inf.* brash or cheeky. **4** *Arch.* muscular; sinewy.

nescience ('nɛsɪəns) *n* a formal or literary word for **ignorance.** ORIG C17: from LL *nescientia,* from L *nescīre* to be ignorant of, from *ne* not + *scīre* to know
▸ **'nescient** *adj*

ness (nɛs) *n Arch.* a promontory or headland. ORIG OE *næs* headland

Ness ★ (nɛs) *n* **Loch.** a lake in NW Scotland, in the Great Glen: said to be inhabited by a legendary aquatic monster. Length: 36 km (22.5 miles). Depth: 229 m (754 ft).

-ness *suffix forming nouns chiefly from adjectives and participles.* indicating state, condition, or quality: *greatness; selfishness.* ORIG OE *-nes,* of Gmc origin

Nessus ★ ('nɛsəs) *n Greek myth.* a centaur that killed Hercules. A garment dipped in its blood fatally poisoned Hercules, who had been given it by Deianira who thought it was a love charm.

nest (nɛst) *n* **1** a place or structure in which birds, fishes, etc., lay eggs or give birth to young. **2** a number of animals of the same species occupying a common habitat: *an ants' nest.* **3** a place fostering something undesirable: *a nest of thievery.* **4** a cosy or secluded place. **5** a set of things, usually of graduated sizes, designed to fit together: *a nest of tables.* ◆ *vb* **6** (*intr*) to make or inhabit a nest. **7** (*intr*) to hunt for birds' nests. **8** (*tr*) to place in a nest. **9** *Computing.* to position data within other data at different ranks or levels so that the different levels of data can be used or accessed recursively. ORIG OE

nest egg *n* **1** a fund of money kept in reserve; savings. **2** a natural or artificial egg left in a nest to induce hens to lay their eggs in it.

nestle ('nɛs^{ə}l) *vb* **nestles, nestling, nestled. 1** (*intr;* often foll. by *up* or *down*) to snuggle, settle, or cuddle closely. **2** (*intr*) to be in a sheltered position; lie snugly. **3** (*tr*) to shelter or place snugly or partly concealed, as in a nest. ORIG OE *nestlian*

nestling ('nɛstlɪŋ, 'nɛslɪŋ) *n* **a** a young bird not yet fledged. **b** (*as modifier*): *a nestling thrush.* ORIG C14: from NEST + -LING[1]

Nestor ★ ('nɛstɔː) *n Greek myth.* the oldest and wisest of the Greeks in the Trojan War.

Nestorius ★ (nɛ'stɔːrɪəs) *n* died ?451 A.D., Syrian patriarch of Constantinople (428–431); deposed by the Council of Ephesus.

net[1] (nɛt) *n* **1** an openwork fabric of string, wire, etc.; mesh. **2** a device made of net, used to protect or enclose things or to trap animals. **3** a thin light mesh fabric used for curtains, etc. **4** a plan, strategy, etc., intended to trap or ensnare: *the murderer slipped through the police net.* **5** *Tennis, badminton, etc.* **5a** a strip of net that divides the playing area into two equal parts. **5b** a shot that hits the net. **6** the goal in soccer, hockey, etc. **7** (*often pl*) *Cricket.* **7a** a pitch surrounded by netting, used for practice. **7b** a practice session in a net. **8** *Inf.* short for **Internet. 9** another word for **network** (sense 2). ◆ *vb* **nets, netting, netted. 10** (*tr*) to ensnare. **11** (*tr*) to shelter or surround with a net. **12** (*intr*) *Tennis, badminton, etc.* to hit a shot into the net. **13** to make a net out of (rope, string, etc.). ORIG OE *net;* rel. to Gothic *nati,* Du. *net*

net[2] *or* **nett** (nɛt) *adj* **1** remaining after all deductions, as for taxes, expenses, losses, etc.: *net profit.* Cf. **gross** (sense 2). **2** (of weight) after deducting tare. **3** final; conclusive (esp. in **net result**). ◆ *n* **4** net income, profits, weight, etc. ◆ *vb* **nets, netting, netted. 5** (*tr*) to yield or earn as clear profit. ORIG C14: clean, neat, from F *net* NEAT[1]

Netaji ★ ('neɪtɑːdʒɪ) *n* the title for (Subhash Chandra) **Bose.** ORIG Hindi, from *neta* leader + *-ji,* suffix denoting respect

Netanyahu ★ (nɛt^{ə}n'jɑːhuː) *n* **Benjamin** ('benjə,miːn). born 1949, Israeli politician: prime minister (1996–99).

net asset value *n* the total value of the assets of an organization less its liabilities and capital charges. Abbrev.: **NAV.**

★ people and places

netball (ˈnɛtˌbɔːl) *n* a game for two teams of seven players (usually women) played on a hard court. Points are scored by shooting the ball through a net hanging from a ring at the top of a pole.

Net Book Agreement *n* a former (until 1995) agreement between UK publishers and booksellers that prohibited booksellers from reducing the price of books. Abbrev.: **NBA**.

net domestic product *n Econ.* the gross domestic product minus an allowance for the depreciation of capital goods. Abbrev.: **NDP**.

Neth. *abbrev. for* Netherlands.

nether (ˈnɛðə) *adj* below, beneath, or underground: *nether regions.* ORIG OE *niothera, nithera,* lit.: further down, from *nither* down

Netherlands ★ (ˈnɛðələndz) *n* (*functioning as sing or pl*) **the. 1** Also called: **Holland**. a kingdom in NW Europe, on the North Sea: declared independence from Spain in 1581 as the United Provinces; became a major maritime and commercial power in the 17th century, gaining many overseas possessions; a member of the European Union. It is mostly flat and low-lying, with about 40 per cent of the land being below sea level, much of it on polders protected by dykes. Official language: Dutch. Religion: Christian majority with both Protestant and Roman Catholic Churches. Currency: guilder and euro. Capital: Amsterdam, with the seat of government at The Hague. Pop.: 15 777 000 (1999 est.). Area: 41 526 sq. km (16 033 sq. miles). Dutch name: **Nederland**. **2** the kingdom of the Netherlands together with the Flemish-speaking part of Belgium, esp. as ruled by Spain and Austria before 1581; the Low Countries.
▸ **Netherlander** (ˈnɛðəˌlændə) *n*

Netherlands Antilles ★ *pl n* **the.** two groups of islands in the Caribbean, in the Lesser Antilles: overseas division of the Netherlands, consisting of the S group of Curaçao, Aruba, and Bonaire, and the N group of St Eustatius, Saba, and the S part of St Martin; economy based on refining oil from Venezuela. Capital: Willemstad (on Curaçao). Pop.: 202 244 (1994 est.). Area: 996 sq. km (390 sq. miles). Former names: **Curaçao** (until 1949), **Dutch West Indies, Netherlands West Indies.**

Netherlands East Indies ★ *pl n* **the.** a former name (1798–1945) for **Indonesia.**

Netherlands Guiana ★ *n* a former name for **Surinam.**

Netherlands West Indies ★ *pl n* **the.** a former name for the **Netherlands Antilles.**

nethermost (ˈnɛðəˌməʊst) *adj* **the.** farthest down; lowest.

netherworld (ˈnɛðəˌwɜːld) *n* **1** the world after death; the underworld. **2** hell. **3** a criminal underworld. ◆ Also called (for senses 1, 2): **nether regions.**

netiquette (ˈnɛtɪˌkɛt) *n* the informal code of behaviour on the Internet. ORIG C20: from NET(WORK) + (ET)IQUETTE

netizen (ˈnɛtɪzən) *n* someone who can be found on the Internet, esp. via a website. ORIG C20: from *Internet* + *denizen*

net national product *n* gross national product minus an allowance for the depreciation of capital goods. Abbrev.: **NNP**.

net present value *n Accounting.* an assessment of the long-term profitability of a project made by adding up all the revenue it can be expected to achieve over its whole life and deducting all the costs involved. Abbrev.: **NPV**.

net profit *n* gross profit minus all operating costs not included in the calculation of gross profit, esp. wages, overheads, and depreciation.

net realizable value *n* the net value of an asset if it were to be sold. Abbrev.: **NRV**.

net statutory income *n* (in Britain) the total taxable income of a person for the tax assessment year, after the deduction of personal allowances.

netsuke (ˈnɛtsʊkɪ) *n* (in Japan) a carved toggle, esp. of wood or ivory, originally used to tether a medicine box, purse, etc., worn dangling from the waist. ORIG C19: from Japanese

nett (nɛt) *adj, n, vb* a variant spelling of **net**[2].

netting (ˈnɛtɪŋ) *n* any netted fabric or structure.

nettle (ˈnɛtᵊl) *n* **1** a plant having serrated leaves with stinging hairs and greenish flowers. **2** any of various other plants with stinging hairs or spines. **3** any of various plants that resemble nettles, such as the dead-nettle. **4 grasp the nettle.** to attempt something with boldness and courage. ◆ *vb* **nettles, nettling, nettled.** (*tr*) **5** to bother; irritate. **6** to sting as a nettle does. ORIG OE *netele*

nettle rash *n* a nontechnical name for **urticaria.**

network (ˈnɛtˌwɜːk) *n* **1** an interconnected group or system: *a network of shops.* **2** a system of intersecting lines, roads, veins, etc. **3** another name for **net**[1] (sense 1) or **netting. 4** *Radio & TV.* a group of broadcasting stations that all transmit the same programme simultaneously. **5** *Computing.* a system of interconnected computer systems, terminals, and other equipment. **6** *Electronics.* a system of interconnected components or circuits. ◆ *vb* **7** *Radio & TV.* to broadcast over a network. **8** (of computers, terminals, etc.) to connect or be connected. **9** (*intr*) to form business contacts through informal social meetings.

Neubrandenburg ★ (*German* nɔyˈbrandənburk) *n* a city in NE Germany, in Mecklenburg-West Pomerania: 14th-century city walls. Pop.: 87 880 (1991).

Neuchâtel ★ (*French* nøʃatɛl) *n* **1** a canton in the Jura Mountains of W Switzerland. Capital: Neuchâtel. Pop.: 164 176 (1995 est.). Area: 798 sq. km (308 sq. miles). **2** a town in W Switzerland, capital of Neuchâtel canton, on Lake Neuchâtel. Pop.: 32 509 (1990). **3 Lake.** a lake in W Switzerland: the largest lake wholly in Switzerland. Area: 216 sq. km (83 sq. miles). ◆ German name (for senses 1, 2): **Neuenburg** (ˈnɔyənburk).

Neuilly-sur-Seine ★ (*French* nœjisyrsɛn) *n* a town in N France, on the Seine: a suburb of NW Paris. Pop.: 61 768 (1990).

Neumann ★ *n* **1** (*German* ˈnɔyman). **Johann Balthasar** (joˈhan ˈbaltazar). 1687–1753, German rococo architect. **2** (ˈnjuːmən). See (John) **von Neumann.**

neume *or* **neum** (njuːm) *n Music.* one of a series of notational symbols used before the 14th century. ORIG C15: from Med. L *neuma* group of notes sung on one breath, from Gk *pneuma* breath

Neumünster ★ (*German* nɔyˈmynstər) *n* a town in N Germany, in Schleswig-Holstein: manufacturing of textiles and machinery. Pop.: 81 175 (1991).

neural (ˈnjʊərəl) *adj* of or relating to a nerve or the nervous system.
▸ **ˈneurally** *adv*

neural chip *n* another name for **neurochip.**

neural computer *n* another name for **neurocomputer.**

neuralgia (njʊˈrældʒə) *n* severe spasmodic pain caused by damage to or malfunctioning of a nerve and often following the course of the nerve.
▸ **neuˈralgic** *adj*

neural tube *n* the embryonic brain and spinal cord in mammals. Incomplete development results in **neural-tube defects,** such as spina bifida, in a newborn baby.

neurasthenia (ˌnjʊərəsˈθiːnɪə) *n* (no longer in technical use) a neurosis characterized by extreme lassitude and inability to cope with any but the most trivial tasks.

neuritis (njʊˈraɪtɪs) *n* inflammation of a nerve or nerves, often accompanied by pain and loss of function in the affected part.
▸ **neuritic** (njʊˈrɪtɪk) *adj*

neuro- *or before a vowel* **neur-** *combining form.* indicating a nerve or the nervous system: *neurology.* ORIG from Gk *neuron* nerve; rel. to L *nervus*

neurobiology (ˌnjʊərəʊbaɪˈɒlədʒɪ) *n* the study of the anatomy, physiology, and biochemistry of the nervous system.
▸ **ˌneurobiˈologist** *n*

neurochip (ˈnjʊərəʊˌtʃɪp) *n Computing.* a semiconductor chip designed for use in an electronic neural network. Also called: **neural chip.**

neurocomputer (ˈnjʊərəʊkəmˌpjuːtə) *n* a type of computer designed to mimic the action of the human brain by use of an electronic neural network. Also called: **neural computer.**

neuroendocrine (ˌnjʊərəʊˈɛndəʊˌkraɪn) *adj* of, relating to, or denoting the dual control of certain body functions by both nervous and hormonal stimulation: *neuroendocrine system.*

neuroglia (njʊ'rɒglɪə) *n* another name for **glia**.

neurohormone ('njʊərəʊˌhɔːməʊn) *n* a hormone, such as noradrenaline, that is produced by specialized nervous tissue rather than by endocrine glands.

neurolemma (ˌnjʊərəʊ'lɛmə) *n* the thin membrane that forms a sheath around nerve fibres. ORIG C19: NL, from NEURO- + Gk *eilēma* covering

neurology (njʊ'rɒlədʒɪ) *n* the study of the anatomy, physiology, and diseases of the nervous system.
▸ **neurological** (ˌnʊərə'lɒdʒɪkᵊl) *adj*

neuromuscular (ˌnjʊərəʊ'mʌskjʊlə) *adj* of, relating to, or affecting nerves and muscles.

neurone ('njʊərəʊn) *or* **neuron** ('njʊərɒn) *n* a cell specialized to conduct nerve impulses: consists of a cell body, axon, and dendrites. Also called: **nerve cell.**
▸ **neu'ronal** *adj* ▸ **neuronic** (njʊ'rɒnɪk) *adj*

neuropathology (ˌnjʊərəʊpə'θɒlədʒɪ) *n* the study of diseases of the nervous system.

neuropathy (njʊ'rɒpəθɪ) *n* any disease of the nervous system.
▸ **neuropathic** (ˌnjʊərəʊ'pæθɪk) *adj* ▸ **ˌneuro'pathically** *adv*

neurophysiology (ˌnjʊərəʊˌfɪzɪ'ɒlədʒɪ) *n* the study of the functions of the nervous system.
▸ **neurophysiological** (ˌnjʊərəʊˌfɪzɪə'lɒdʒɪkᵊl) *adj*

neuropterous (njʊ'rɒptərəs) *or* **neuropteran** *adj* of or belonging to an order of insects having two pairs of large much-veined wings and biting mouthparts. ORIG C18: from NL *Neuroptera,* from NEURO- + Gk *pteron* wing

neuroscience ('njʊərəʊsaɪəns) *n* the study of the anatomy, physiology, and biochemistry of the nervous system.

neurosis (njʊ'rəʊsɪs) *n, pl* **neuroses** (-siːz). a relatively mild mental disorder, characterized by hysteria, anxiety, depression, or obsessive behaviour.

neurosurgery (ˌnjʊərəʊ'sɜːdʒərɪ) *n* the branch of surgery concerned with the nervous system.
▸ **ˌneuro'surgical** *adj*

neurotic (njʊ'rɒtɪk) *adj* **1** of or afflicted by neurosis. ◆ *n* **2** a person who is afflicted with a neurosis or who tends to be emotionally unstable.
▸ **neu'rotically** *adv* ▸ **neu'rotiˌcism** *n*

neurotomy (njʊ'rɒtəmɪ) *n, pl* **neurotomies**. the surgical cutting of a nerve.

neurotransmitter (ˌnjʊərəʊtrænz'mɪtə) *n* a chemical by which a nerve cell communicates with another nerve cell or with a muscle.

Neusatz ★ ('nɔyzats) *n* the German name for **Novi Sad.**

Neuss ★ (*German* nɔys) *n* an industrial city in W Germany, in North Rhine-Westphalia west of Düsseldorf: founded as a Roman fortress in the 1st century A.D. Pop.: 148 796 (1996 est.). Latin name: **No'vaesium.**

Neustria ★ ('njuːstrɪə) *n* the western part of the kingdom of the Merovingian Franks formed in 561 A.D. in what is now N France.
▸ **'Neustrian** *adj*

neuter ('njuːtə) *adj* **1** *Grammar.* **1a** denoting or belonging to a gender of nouns which do not specify the sex of their referents. **1b** (*as n*): *German "Mädchen" (meaning "girl") is a neuter.* **2** (of animals and plants) having nonfunctional, underdeveloped, or absent reproductive organs. **3** giving no indication of sex. ◆ *n* **4** a sexually underdeveloped female insect, such as a worker bee. **5** a castrated animal. ◆ *vb* **6** (*tr*) to castrate (an animal). ORIG C14: from L, from *ne* not + *uter* either (of two)

neutral ('njuːtrəl) *adj* **1** not siding with any party to a war or dispute. **2** of or belonging to a neutral party, country, etc. **3** of no distinctive quality or type. **4** (of a colour) **4a** having no hue; achromatic. **4b** dull, but harmonizing with most other colours. **5** a less common term for **neuter** (sense 2). **6** *Chem.* neither acidic nor alkaline. **7** *Physics.* having zero charge or potential. **8** *Phonetics.* (of a vowel) articulated with the tongue relaxed in mid-central position: *"about" begins with a neutral vowel.* ◆ *n* **9** a neutral person, nation, etc. **10** a citizen of a neutral state. **11** the position of the controls of a gearbox that leaves the transmission disengaged. ORIG C16: from L *neutrālis;* see NEUTER
▸ **'neutrally** *adv*

neutralism ('njuːtrəˌlɪzəm) *n* (in international affairs) the policy of noninvolvement or nonalignment with power blocs.
▸ **'neutralist** *n*

neutrality (njuː'trælɪtɪ) *n* **1** the state of being neutral. **2** the condition of being chemically or electrically neutral.

neutralize *or* **neutralise** ('njuːtrəˌlaɪz) *vb* **neutralizes, neutralizing, neutralized** *or* **neutralises, neutralising, neutralised.** (*mainly tr*) **1** (*also intr*) to render or become neutral by counteracting, mixing, etc. **2** (*also intr*) to make or become electrically or chemically neutral. **3** to exclude (a country) from warfare or alliances by international agreement: *the great powers neutralized Belgium in the 19th century.*
▸ **ˌneutrali'zation** *or* **ˌneutrali'sation** *n* ▸ **'neutralˌizer** *or* **'neutralˌiser** *n*

neutretto (njuː'trɛtəʊ) *n, pl* **neutrettos.** *Physics.* **1** the neutrino associated with the muon. **2** (formerly) any of various hypothetical neutral particles. ORIG C20: from NEUTR(INO) + diminutive suffix *-etto*

neutrino (njuː'triːnəʊ) *n, pl* **neutrinos.** *Physics.* a stable elementary particle with zero rest mass and spin ½ that travels at the speed of light. ORIG C20: from It., dim. of *neutrone* NEUTRON

neutron ('njuːtrɒn) *n Physics.* a neutral elementary particle with approximately the same mass as a proton. In the nucleus of an atom it is stable but when free it decays. ORIG C20: from NEUTRAL, on the model of ELECTRON

neutron bomb *n* a type of nuclear weapon designed to cause little blast or long-lived radioactive contamination. The neutrons destroy all life in the target area. Technical name: **enhanced radiation weapon.**

neutron gun *n Physics.* a device used for producing a beam of fast neutrons.

neutron number *n* the number of neutrons in the nucleus of an atom. Symbol: *N*

neutron star *n* a star, composed solely of neutrons, that has collapsed under its own gravity.

Nev. *abbrev. for* Nevada.

Neva ★ ('niːvə; *Russian* nɪ'va) *n* a river in NW Russia, flowing west to the Gulf of Finland by the delta on which Saint Petersburg stands. Length: 74 km (46 miles).

Nevada ★ (nɪ'vɑːdə) *n* a state of the western US: lies almost wholly within the Great Basin, a vast desert plateau; noted for production of gold and copper and as a gambling centre. Capital: Carson City. Pop.: 1 746 898 (1998 est.). Area: 284 612 sq. km (109 889 sq. miles). Abbrevs.: **Nev.** or (with zip code) **NV**

névé ('nɛveɪ) *n* a mass of porous ice, formed from snow, that has not yet become frozen into glacier ice. ORIG C19: from Swiss F *névé* glacier, from LL *nivātus* snow-cooled, from *nix* snow

never ('nɛvə) *adv, sentence substitute.* **1** at no time; not ever. **2** certainly not; by no means; in no case. ◆ *sentence substitute.* **3** Also: **well I never!** surely not! ORIG OE *nǣfre,* from *ne* not + *ǣfre* EVER

USAGE NOTE In informal speech and writing, *never* can be used for emphasis instead of *not* with the simple past tenses of certain verbs (*I never said that; I never realized how clever he was*), but this usage should be avoided in careful writing.

nevermore (ˌnɛvə'mɔː) *adv Literary.* never again.

never-never *Inf.* ◆ *n* **1** *Brit.* the hire-purchase system of buying. **2** *Austral.* remote desert country. ◆ *adj* **3** imaginary; idyllic (esp. in **never-never land**).

Nevers ★ (*French* nəvɛr) *n* a city in central France: capital of the former duchy of Nivernais; engineering industry. Pop.: 43 890 (1990).

nevertheless (ˌnɛvəðəˈlɛs) *sentence connector.* in spite of that; however; yet.

Nevis ★ *n* **1** (ˈniːvɪs, ˈnɛvɪs). an island in the Caribbean: part of St Kitts-Nevis; the volcanic cone of **Nevis Peak,** which rises to 1002 m (3287 ft), lies in the centre of the island. Capital: Charlestown. Pop.: 8794 (1991). Area: 129 sq. km (50 sq. miles). **2** (ˈnɛvɪs). See **Ben Nevis.**

Nevski ★ (ˈnɛfskɪ; *Russian* ˈnjɛfskij) *n* See **Alexander Nevski.**

new (njuː) *adj* **1a** recently made or brought into being. **1b** (*as collective n;* preceded by *the*): *the new.* **2** of a kind never before existing; novel: *a new concept in marketing.* **3** recently discovered: *a new comet.* **4** markedly different from what was before: *the new liberalism.* **5** (often foll. by *to* or *at*) recently introduced (to); inexperienced (in) or unaccustomed (to): *new to this neighbourhood.* **6** (*cap. in names or titles*) more or most recent of things with the same name: *the New Testament.* **7** (*prenominal*) fresh; additional: *send some new troops.* **8** (often foll. by *to*) unknown: *this is new to me.* **9** (of a cycle) beginning or occurring again: *a new year.* **10** (*prenominal*) (of crops) harvested early. **11** changed, esp. for the better: *she returned a new woman.* **12** up-to-date; fashionable. **13 the new** set to replace the current vogue: *comedy is the new rock 'n' roll.* ◆ *adv* (*usually in combination*) **14** recently, freshly: *new-laid eggs.* **15** anew; again. ◆ See also **news.** ORIG OE *nīowe*
▸ ˈ**newness** *n*

New Age *n* **1a** a philosophy, originating in the late 1980s, characterized by a belief in alternative medicine, astrology, spiritualism, etc. **1b** (*as modifier*): *New Age therapies.* **2** short for **New Age music.**

New Age music *or* **New Age** *n* a type of gentle melodic popular music originating in the US in the late 1980s, which takes in elements of jazz, folk, and classical music and is played largely on synthesizers and acoustic instruments.

New Amsterdam ★ *n* the Dutch settlement established on Manhattan (1624–26); capital of New Netherlands; captured by the English and renamed New York in 1664.

Newark ★ (ˈnjuːək) *n* **1** a town in N central England, in Nottinghamshire. Pop.: 35 129 (1991). Official name: **Newark-on-Trent. 2** a port in NE New Jersey, just west of New York City, on Newark Bay and the Passaic River: the largest city in the state; founded in 1666 by Puritans from Connecticut; industrial and commercial centre. Pop.: 268 510 (1996 est.).

New Australia ★ *n* the colony on socialist principles founded by William Lane in Paraguay in 1893.

New Australian *n* an Australian name for a recent immigrant, esp. one from Europe.

New Bedford ★ *n* a port and resort in SE Massachusetts, near Buzzards Bay: settled by Plymouth colonists in 1652; a leading whaling port (18th–19th centuries). Pop.: 96 903 (1996 est.).

newbie (ˈnjuːbɪ) *n Sl.* a newcomer, esp. in computing or on the Internet. ORIG C20: ?from *new boy*

newborn (ˈnjuːˌbɔːn) *adj* **1** recently or just born. **2** (of hope, faith, etc.) reborn.

New Britain ★ *n* an island in the S Pacific, northeast of New Guinea: the largest island of the Bismarck Archipelago; part of Papua New Guinea; mountainous, with several active volcanoes. Capital: Rabaul. Pop.: 312 955 (1990). Area: 36 519 sq. km (14 100 sq. miles).

New Brunswick ★ *n* a province of SE Canada on the Gulf of St Lawrence and the Bay of Fundy: extensively forested. Capital: Fredericton. Pop.: 754 741 (1999 est.). Area: 72 092 sq. km (27 835 sq. miles). Abbrev.: **NB.**
▸ **New Brunswicker** (ˈbrʌnzwɪkə) *n*

new brutalism *n* another name for **brutalism.**

Newbury ★ (ˈnjuːbərɪ) *n* a market town in S England, in Berkshire: scene of a Parliamentarian victory (1643) and a Royalist victory (1644) during the Civil War; racecourse. Pop.: 33 273 (1991).

New Caledonia ★ *n* an island in the SW Pacific, east of Australia: forms, with its dependencies, an overseas territory of France; discovered by Captain Cook in 1774; rich mineral resources. Capital: Nouméa. Pop.: 183 200 (1994 est.). Area: 19 103 sq. km (7374 miles). French name: **Nouvelle-Calédonie.**

New Canadian *n Canad.* a recent immigrant to Canada.

New Castile ★ *n* a region and former province of central Spain. Chief town: Toledo.

Newcastle[1] ★ (ˈnjuːˌkɑːsᵊl) *n* a port in SE Australia, in E New South Wales near the mouth of the Hunter River: important industrial centre, with extensive steel, metalworking, engineering, shipbuilding, and chemical industries: site of Australia's first fatal earthquake (1989). Pop.: 466 000 (1995 est.).

Newcastle[2] ★ (ˈnjuːˌkɑːsᵊl) *n* **Duke of,** the title of *Thomas Pelham Holles.* 1693–1768, English Whig prime minister (1754–56; 1757–62).

Newcastle-under-Lyme ★ *n* a town in W central England, in Staffordshire: seat of Keele University (1962). Pop.: 73 731 (1991). Often shortened to **Newcastle.**

Newcastle upon Tyne ★ *n* **1** a port in NE England, in Newcastle upon Tyne unitary authority, Tyne and Wear, near the mouth of the River Tyne opposite Gateshead: Roman remains; engineering industries; seat of The University of Newcastle upon Tyne (1937) and the University of Northumbria at Newcastle (1992). Pop.: 189 150 (1991). Often shortened to **Newcastle. 2** a unitary authority in NE England, in Tyne and Wear. Pop.: 283 100 (1995 est.). Area: 112 sq. km (43 sq. miles).

new chum *n* **1** *Austral.* a novice in any activity. **2** *Austral. & NZ inf.* (formerly) a recent British immigrant.

Newcomen ★ (ˈnjuːˌkʌmən) *n* **Thomas.** 1663–1729, English engineer who invented a steam engine.

newcomer (ˈnjuːˌkʌmə) *n* a person who has recently arrived or started to participate in something.

New Country *n* a style of country music of the late 1980s characterized by down-to-earth lyrics.

New Delhi ★ *n* See **Delhi.**

newel (ˈnjuːəl) *n* **1** the central pillar of a winding staircase, esp. one that is made of stone. **2** Also called: **newel post.** the post at the top or bottom of a flight of stairs that supports the handrail. ORIG C14: from OF *nouel* knob, from Med. L *nōdellus,* dim. of *nōdus* NODE

New England ★ *n* **1** the NE part of the US, consisting of the states of Maine, New Hampshire, Vermont, Massachusetts, Rhode Island, and Connecticut: settled originally chiefly by Puritans in the mid-17th century. **2** a region in SE Australia, in the northern tablelands of New South Wales.
▸ **New Englander** *n*

New England Range ★ *n* a mountain range in SE Australia, in NE New South Wales: part of the Great Dividing Range. Highest peak: Ben Lomond, 1520 m (4986 ft).

New English Bible *n* a new translation of the Bible made between 1962 and 1970.

newfangled (ˈnjuːˈfæŋgᵊld) *adj* newly come into existence or fashion, esp. excessively modern. ORIG C14 *newefangel* liking new things, from *new* + *-fangel,* from OE *fōn* to take

New Forest ★ *n* a region of woodland and heath in S England, in SW Hampshire: a hunting ground of the West Saxon kings; tourist area and national park, noted for its ponies. Area: 336 sq. km (130 sq. miles).

new-found *adj* newly or recently discovered: *new-found confidence.*

Newfoundland ★ (ˈnjuːfəndlənd, -fənlənd, -ˌlænd; njuːˈfaʊndlənd) *n* **1** an island of E Canada, separated from the mainland by the Strait of Belle Isle: with the Coast of Labrador forms the province of Newfoundland; consists of a rugged plateau with the Long Range Mountains in the west. Area: 110 681 sq. km (42 734 sq. miles). **2** a province of E Canada, consisting of the island of Newfoundland and Labrador. Capital: St John's. Pop.: 541 164 (1999 est.). Area: 404 519 sq. km (156 185 sq.

miles). Abbrevs.: **Nfld** *or* **NF.** **3** a large heavy breed of dog with a flat coarse usually black coat.
▸ **New'foundlander** *n*

New France ★ *n* the former French colonies and possessions in North America, most of which were lost to England and Spain by 1763: often restricted to the French possessions in Canada.

Newgate ★ ('nju:gɪt, -ˌgeɪt) *n* a famous London prison, demolished in 1902.

New Georgia ★ *n* **1** a group of islands in the SW Pacific, in the Solomon Islands. **2** the largest island in this group. Area: about 1300 sq. km (500 sq. miles).

New Granada ★ *n* **1** a former Spanish presidency and later viceroyalty in South America. At its greatest extent it consisted of present-day Panama, Colombia, Venezuela, and Ecuador. **2** the name of Colombia when it formed, with Panama, part of Great Colombia (1819–30).

New Guinea ★ *n* **1** an island in the W Pacific, north of Australia: divided politically into Irian Jaya (a province of Indonesia) in the west and Papua New Guinea in the east. There is a central chain of mountains and a lowland area of swamps in the south and along the Sepik River in the north. Area: 775 213 sq. km (299 310 sq. miles). **2 Trust Territory of.** (until 1975) an administrative division of the former Territory of Papua and New Guinea, consisting of the NE part of the island of New Guinea together with the Bismarck Archipelago; now part of Papua New Guinea.

Newham ★ ('nju:əm) *n* a borough of E Greater London, on the River Thames: established in 1965. Pop.: 226 800 (1994 est.). Area: 36 sq. km (14 sq. miles).

New Hampshire ★ *n* a state of the northeastern US: generally hilly. Capital: Concord. Pop.: 1 185 048 (1998 est.). Area: 23 379 sq. km (9027 sq. miles). Abbrevs.: **N.H.** or (with zip code) **NH**

New Harmony ★ *n* a village in SW Indiana, on the Wabash River: scene of two experimental cooperative communities, the first founded in 1815 by George Rapp, a German religious leader, and the second by Robert Owen in 1825.

Newhaven ★ ('nju:ˌheɪvᵊn) *n* a ferry port and resort on the S coast of England, in East Sussex. Pop.: 11 208 (1991).

New Haven ★ *n* an industrial city and port in S Connecticut, on Long Island Sound: settled in 1638 by English Puritans, who established it as a colony in 1643; seat of Yale University (1701). Pop.: 124 665 (1996 est.).

New Hebrides ★ *pl n* the former name (until 1980) of **Vanuatu.**

Ne Win ★ ('neɪ 'wɪn) *n* **U** (u:). born 1911, Burmese statesman; prime minister (1958–60) and president (1974–81).

New Ireland ★ *n* an island in the S Pacific, in the Bismarck Archipelago, separated from New Britain by St George's Channel: part of Papua New Guinea. Chief town and port: Kavieng. Pop.: 87 194 (1990). Area (including adjacent islands): 9850 sq. km (3800 sq. miles).

newish ('nju:ɪʃ) *adj* fairly new.

new issue *n Stock Exchange.* an issue of shares being offered to the public for the first time.

New Jersey ★ *n* a state of the eastern US, on the Atlantic and Delaware Bay: mostly low-lying, with a heavy industrial area in the northeast and many coastal resorts. Capital: Trenton. Pop.: 8 115 011 (1998 est.). Area: 19 479 sq. km (7521 sq. miles). Abbrevs.: **N.J.** or (with zip code) **NJ**

New Jerusalem *n Christianity.* heaven.

New Journalism *n* a style of journalism using techniques borrowed from fiction to portray a situation or event as vividly as possible.

Newlands ★ ('nju:ləndz) *n* **John Alexander.** 1838–98, British chemist: discovered the law of octaves.

New Latin *n* the form of Latin used since the Renaissance, esp. for scientific nomenclature.

New Look *n* **the.** a fashion in women's clothes introduced in 1947, characterized by long full skirts.

newly ('nju:lɪ) *adv* **1** recently. **2** again; anew: *newly raised hopes.* **3** in a new manner; differently: *a newly arranged hairdo.*

newlywed ('nju:lɪˌwɛd) *n* (*often pl*) a recently married person.

Newman ★ ('nju:mən) *n* **1 John Henry.** 1801–90, British theologian. Originally an Anglican minister, he was prominent in the Oxford Movement before becoming a Roman Catholic priest (1847) and a cardinal (1879). **2 Paul.** born 1925, US actor, whose films include *Cat on a Hot Tin Roof* (1958), *Butch Cassidy and the Sundance Kid* (1969), and *Twilight* (1998).

New Man *n* **the.** a type of modern man who allows the caring side of his nature to show by being supportive and by sharing child care and housework.

Newmarket ★ ('nju:ˌmɑ:kɪt) *n* a town in SE England, in W Suffolk: a famous horse-racing centre since the reign of James I. Pop.: 18 430 (1991).

new maths *n* (*functioning as sing*) *Brit.* an approach to mathematics in which the basic principles of set theory are introduced at an elementary level.

New Mexico ★ *n* a state of the southwestern US: consists of high semiarid plateaus and mountains, crossed by the Rio Grande and the Pecos River; large Spanish-American and Indian populations; contains over two-thirds of US uranium reserves. Capital: Santa Fé. Pop.: 1 736 431 (1998 est.). Area: 314 451 sq. km (121 412 sq. miles). Abbrevs.: **N. Mex, N.M.,** or (with zip code) **NM**
▸ **New Mexican** *adj, n*

new moon *n* the moon when it appears as a narrow waxing crescent.

New Netherland ★ ('nɛðələnd) *n* a Dutch North American colony of the early 17th century, centred on the Hudson valley. Captured by the English in 1664, it was divided into New York and New Jersey.

New Orleans ★ ('ɔ:li:ənz, -lənz; ɔ:'li:nz) *n* a port in SE Louisiana, on the Mississippi River about 172 km (107 miles) from the sea: the largest city in the state and the second most important port in the US; founded by the French in 1718; belonged to Spain (1763–1803). It is largely below sea level, built around the Vieux Carré (French quarter); famous for its annual Mardi Gras festival and for its part in the history of jazz; a major commercial, industrial, and transportation centre. Pop.: 476 625 (1996 est.).

New Plymouth ★ *n* a port in New Zealand, on W North Island: founded in 1841. Pop.: 49 800 (1995 est.).

Newport ★ ('nju:ˌpɔ:t) *n* **1** a port in SE Wales on the River Usk. Pop.: 129 900 (1991). **2** a county borough in SE Wales. Pop.: 133 318 (1996 est.). Area: 190 sq. km (73 sq. miles). **3** a port in SE Rhode Island: founded in 1639, it became one of the richest towns of colonial America; centre of a large number of US naval establishments. Pop.: 28 227 (1990). **4** a town in S England, administrative centre of the Isle of Wight. Pop.: 20 574 (1991).

Newport News ★ *n* (*functioning as sing*) a port in SE Virginia, at the mouth of the James River: an industrial centre, with one of the world's largest shipyards. Pop.: 176 122 (1996 est.).

New Providence ★ *n* an island in the Atlantic, in the Bahamas. Chief town: Nassau. Pop.: 172 196 (1990). Area: 150 sq. km (58 sq. miles).

New Quebec ★ *n* a region of E Canada, formerly the Ungava district of Northwest Territories (1895–1912), extending from the line of the Eastmain and Hamilton Rivers north between Hudson Bay and Labrador: absorbed by Quebec in 1912: contains extensive iron deposits. Area: about 777 000 sq. km (300 000 sq. miles).

New Romney ★ *n* a market town in SE England, in Kent on Romney Marsh: of early importance as one of the Cinque Ports, but is now over 1.6 km (1 mile) inland. Pop.: 5000 (latest est.). Former name (until 1563): **Romney.**

Newry ★ ('njʊərɪ) *n* a port in Northern Ireland, in Co. Down: close to the border with the Republic of Ireland, it has been the scene of sectarian violence. Pop.: 22 975 (1991).

Newry and Mourne ★ (mɔːn) *n* a district of SE Northern Ireland, on the Irish Sea and bordering the Irish Republic: agriculture, textiles. Administrative centre: Newry. Pop.: 82 943 (1991). Area: 890 sq. km (344 sq. miles).

news (njuːz) *n* (*functioning as sing*) **1** important or interesting recent happenings. **2** information about such events, as in the mass media. **3 the news.** a presentation, such as a radio broadcast, of information of this type. **4** interesting or important information not previously known. **5** a person, fashion, etc., widely reported in the mass media: *she is news in the film world.* ORIG C15: from ME *newes,* pl. of *newe* new (adj), a model of OF *noveles* or Med. L *nova* new things
▸ **'newsless** *adj*

news agency *n* an organization that collects news reports for newspapers, etc. Also called: **press agency.**

newsagent ('njuːzˌeɪdʒənt) *or US* **newsdealer** *n* a shopkeeper who sells newspapers, stationery, etc.

newscast ('njuːzˌkɑːst) *n* a radio or television broadcast of the news. ORIG C20: from NEWS + (BROAD)CAST
▸ **'newsˌcaster** *n*

news conference *n* another term for **press conference.**

newsflash ('njuːzˌflæʃ) *n* a brief item of important news, often interrupting a radio or television programme.

newsgroup ('njuːzˌgruːp) *n Computing.* a forum where subscribers exchange information about a specific subject by electronic mail.

New Siberian Islands ★ *pl n* an archipelago in the Arctic Ocean, off the N mainland of Russia, in the Sakha Republic. Area: about 37 555 sq. km (14 500 sq. miles).

newsletter ('njuːzˌlɛtə) *n* **1** Also called: **news-sheet.** a printed periodical bulletin circulated to members of a group. **2** *History.* a written or printed account of the news.

newsmonger ('njuːzˌmʌŋgə) *n Old-fashioned.* a gossip.

New South ★ *n Austral. inf.* short for **New South Wales.**

New South Wales ★ *n* a state of SE Australia: originally contained over half the continent, but was reduced by the formation of other states (1825–1911); consists of a narrow coastal plain, separated from extensive inland plains by the Great Dividing Range; the most populous state; mineral resources. Capital: Sydney. Pop.: 6 038 696 (1996). Area: 801 428 sq. km (309 433 sq. miles).

New Spain ★ *n* a Spanish viceroyalty of the 16th to 19th centuries, composed of Mexico, Central America north of Panama, the Spanish West Indies, the southwestern US, and the Philippines.

newspaper ('njuːzˌpeɪpə) *n* a weekly or daily publication consisting of folded sheets and containing articles on the news, features, reviews, and advertisements. Often shortened to **paper.**

newspaperman ('njuːzˌpeɪpəˌmæn) *n, pl* **newspapermen. 1** a person who works for a newspaper as a reporter or editor. **2** the owner or proprietor of a newspaper. **3** a person who sells newspapers in the street.

newspeak ('njuːˌspiːk) *n* the language of bureaucrats and politicians, regarded as deliberately ambiguous and misleading. ORIG C20: from *1984,* a novel by George Orwell

newsprint ('njuːzˌprɪnt) *n* an inexpensive wood-pulp paper used for newspapers.

newsreader ('njuːzˌriːdə) *n* a news announcer on radio or television.

newsreel ('njuːzˌriːl) *n* a short film with a commentary presenting current events.

newsroom ('njuːzˌruːm, -ˌrʊm) *n* a room in a newspaper office, television station, etc., where news is received and prepared for publication or broadcasting.

newsstand ('njuːzˌstænd) *n* a portable stand or stall from which newspapers are sold.

New Style *n* the present method of reckoning dates using the Gregorian calendar.

news vendor *n* a person who sells newspapers.

newsworthy ('njuːzˌwɜːðɪ) *adj* sufficiently interesting to be reported in a news bulletin, etc.

newsy ('njuːzɪ) *adj* **newsier, newsiest.** full of news, esp. gossipy or personal news.

newt (njuːt) *n* any of various small semiaquatic amphibians having a long slender body and tail and short feeble legs. ORIG C15: from *a newt,* a mistaken division of *an ewt; ewt,* from OE *eveta* EFT

New Testament *n* a collection of writings composed soon after Christ's death and added to the Jewish writings of the Old Testament to make up the Christian Bible.

newton ('njuːtᵊn) *n* the derived SI unit of force that imparts an acceleration of 1 metre per second per second to a mass of 1 kilogram. Symbol: N ORIG C20: after Sir Isaac NEWTON

Newton ★ ('njuːtᵊn) *n* Sir **Isaac.** 1642–1727, English mathematician and physicist, noted for his law of gravitation, laws of motion, and theory of light and for developing calculus independently of Leibnitz. His works include *Principia Mathematica* (1687) and *Opticks* (1704).
▸ **Newtonian** (njuː'təʊnɪən) *adj*

Newtonian telescope *n* a type of astronomical reflecting telescope in which light is reflected from a large concave mirror onto a plane mirror, and through a hole in the side of the body of the telescope to form an image.

Newton's law of gravitation *n* the principle that two particles attract each other with forces directly proportional to the product of their masses divided by the square of the distance between them.

Newton's laws of motion *pl n* three laws of mechanics describing the motion of a body. **The first law** states that a body remains at rest or in uniform motion unless acted upon by a force. **The second law** states that a body's rate of change of momentum is proportional to the force causing it. **The third law** states that when a force acts on a body an equal and opposite force acts simultaneously on another body.

new town *n* (in Britain) a town planned as a complete unit and built with government sponsorship, esp. to accommodate overspill population.

Newtown ★ ('njuːtaʊn) *n* a new town in central Wales, in Powys. Pop.: 10 548 (1991).

Newtownabbey ★ (ˌnjuːtᵊn'æbɪ) *n* **1** a town in Northern Ireland, in Co. Antrim on Belfast Lough: the third largest town in Northern Ireland, formed in 1958 by the amalgamation of seven villages; light industrial centre, esp. for textiles. Pop.: 57 103 (1991). **2** a district of E Northern Ireland, on Belfast Lough: residential area for Belfast, light industry. Administrative centre: Ballyclare. Pop.: 74 035 (1991). Area: 150 sq. km (58 sq. miles).

Newtown St Boswells ★ ('njuːtaʊn sənt 'bɒzwəlz) *n* a village in SE Scotland, administrative centre of Scottish Borders: agricultural centre. Pop.: 1108 (1991).

new-variant Creutzfeldt-Jakob disease *or* **variant Creutzfeldt-Jakob disease** *n* a form of Creutzfeldt-Jakob disease thought to be transmitted by eating beef or beef products infected with BSE. Often shortened to **new-variant** (*or* **variant**) **CJD.** Abbrevs.: **nvCJD; vCJD.**

new wave *n* a movement in art, politics, etc., that consciously breaks with traditional ideas, esp. **the New Wave,** a movement in the French cinema of the 1960s, characterized by a fluid use of the camera.

New Windsor ★ *n* the official name of **Windsor**[1] (sense 1).

New World ★ *n* **the.** the Americas; the western hemisphere.

New World monkey *n* any of a family of monkeys of Central and South America, many of which are arboreal and have a prehensile tail.

New Year *n* the first day or days of the year in various calendars, usually a holiday.

New Year's Day *n* January 1, celebrated as a holiday in many countries. Often shortened to (US and Canad. inf.) **New Year's.**

New Year's Eve *n* the evening of Dec. 31. See also **Hogmanay.**

★ people and places

New York ★ *n* **1** Also called: **New York City.** a city in SE New York State, at the mouth of the Hudson River: the largest city and chief port of the US; settled by the Dutch as New Amsterdam in 1624 and captured by the British in 1664; the country's leading commercial and industrial city. Pop.: 7 380 906 (1996 est.). Abbrevs.: **N.Y.C., NYC. 2** a state of the northeastern US: consists chiefly of a plateau with the Finger Lakes in the centre, the Adirondack Mountains in the northeast, the Catskill Mountains in the southeast, and Niagara Falls in the west. Capital: Albany. Pop.: 18 175 301 (1998 est.). Area: 123 882 sq. km (47 831 sq. miles). Abbrevs.: **N.Y.** or (with zip code) **NY**
▸ **New Yorker** *n*

New York Bay ★ *n* an inlet of the Atlantic at the mouth of the Hudson River: forms the harbour of the port of New York.

New York State Barge Canal ★ *n* a system of inland waterways in New York State, connecting the Hudson River with Lakes Erie and Ontario and, via Lake Champlain, with the St Lawrence. Length: 845 km (525 miles).

New Zealand ★ ('ziːlənd) *n* an independent dominion within the Commonwealth, occupying two main islands (the North Island and the South Island), Stewart Island, the Chatham Islands, and a number of minor islands in the SE Pacific: original Maori inhabitants surrendered sovereignty in 1840 and were finally subdued by 1870; became a dominion in 1907; a major world exporter of dairy products, wool, and meat. Official languages: English and Maori. Religion: Christian majority, nonreligious and Maori minorities. Currency: New Zealand dollar. Capital: Wellington. Pop.: 3 841 000 (1999 est.). Area: 270 534 sq. km (104 454 sq. miles).
▸ **New Zealander** *n*

Nexø ★ (*Danish* 'nɛgsøː) *n* **Martin Andersen** ('marten). 1869–1954, Danish novelist. His chief works are the novels *Pelle the Conqueror* (1906–10), which deals with the labour movement, and *Ditte, Daughter of Man* (1917–21).

next (nɛkst) *adj* **1** immediately following: *the next patient to be examined.* **2** immediately adjoining: *the next room.* **3** closest to in degree: *the next-best thing.* **4 the next (Sunday) but one.** the (Sunday) after the next. ◆ *adv* **5** at a time immediately to follow: *the patient to be examined next.* **6 next to. 6a** adjacent to: *the house next to ours.* **6b** following in degree: *next to your mother, who do you love most?* **6c** almost: *next to impossible.* ◆ *prep* **7** *Arch.* next to. ORIG OE *nēhst,* sup. of *nēah* NIGH

next door *adj* (**next-door** *when prenominal*), *adv* at or to the adjacent house, flat, etc.

next of kin *n* a person's closest relative.

nexus ('nɛksəs) *n, pl* **nexus. 1** a means of connection; link; bond. **2** a connected group or series. ORIG C17: from L, from *nectere* to bind

Ney ★ (neɪ; *French* nɛ) *n* **Michel** (miʃɛl), Duc d'Elchingen. 1769–1815, French marshal, who earned the epithet *Bravest of the Brave* at the battle of Borodino (1812); executed for treason (1815).

Nez Percé ('nɛz 'pɜːs) *n* **1** (*pl* **Nez Percés** ('pɜːsɪz) *or* **Nez Percé**) a member of a North American Indian people of the Pacific coast. **2** the language of this people. ORIG F, lit. pierced nose

NF (in Britain) *abbrev. for* National Front.

Nfld. *or* **NF.** *abbrev. for* Newfoundland.

NFU (in Britain) *abbrev. for* National Farmers' Union.

NG *abbrev. for:* **1** (in the US) National Guard. **2** New Guinea. **3** Also: **ng.** no good.

NGA (formerly, in Britain) *abbrev. for* National Graphical Association.

ngaio ('naɪəʊ) *n, pl* **ngaios.** a small evergreen New Zealand tree. ORIG from Maori

Ngaliema Mountain ★ (ᵊŋgɑː'ljeɪmə) *n* the Congolese name for (Mount) **Stanley.**

ngati ('nɑːtiː) *n, pl* **ngati.** *NZ.* a tribe or clan. ORIG from Maori

Nguyen Kao Ky ★ (ᵊŋ'guːjɛn 'kaʊ 'kiː) *n* See (Nguyen Kao) **Ky.**

Nha Trang ★ ('njɑː 'træŋ) *n* a port in SE Vietnam, on the South China Sea: nearby temples of the Cham civilization; fishing industry. Pop.: 221 331 (1992 est.).

NHI (in Britain) *abbrev. for* National Health Insurance.

NHS (in Britain) *abbrev. for* National Health Service.

Ni *the chemical symbol for* nickel.

NI *abbrev. for:* **1** (in Britain) National Insurance. **2** Northern Ireland. **3** (in New Zealand) North Island.

niacin ('naɪəsɪn) *n* another name for **nicotinic acid.** ORIG C20: from NI(COTINIC) AC(ID) + -IN

Niagara ★ (naɪ'ægrə, -'ægərə) *n* **1** a river in NE North America, on the border between W New York State and Ontario, Canada, flowing from Lake Erie to Lake Ontario. Length: 45 km (28 miles). **2** a torrent.

Niagara Falls ★ *n* **1** (*functioning as pl*) the falls of the Niagara River, on the border between the US and Canada: divided by Goat Island into the American Falls, 50 m (167 ft) high, and the Horseshoe or Canadian Falls, 47 m (158 ft) high. **2** (*functioning as sing*) a city in W New York State, situated at the falls of the Niagara River. Pop.: 61 840 (1990). **3** (*functioning as sing*) a city in S Canada, in SE Ontario on the Niagara River just below the falls: linked to the city of Niagara Falls in the US by three bridges. Pop.: 75 399 (1991).

Niamey ★ (njɑː'meɪ) *n* the capital of Niger, in the southwest on the River Niger: became capital in 1926; airport and land route centre. Pop.: 495 000 (1995 est.).

Niarchos ★ (nɪ'ɑːkɒs) *n* **Stavros Spyro** ('stævrɒs 'spɪərəʊ). 1909–96, Greek shipowner.

nib (nɪb) *n* **1** the writing point of a pen, esp. an insertable tapered metal part. **2** a point, tip, or beak. **3** (*pl*) crushed cocoa beans. ◆ *vb* **nibs, nibbing, nibbed.** (*tr*) **4** to provide with a nib. **5** to sharpen the nib of. ORIG C16 (in the sense: beak): from ?

nibble ('nɪbᵊl) *vb* **nibbles, nibbling, nibbled.** (when *intr,* often foll. by *at*) **1** (esp. of animals) to take small repeated bites (of). **2** to take dainty or tentative bites: *to nibble at a cake.* **3** to bite (at) gently. ◆ *n* **4** a small mouthful. **5** an instance of nibbling. ORIG C15: rel. to Low G *nibbelen*
▸ **'nibbler** *n*

Nibelung ★ ('niːbəˌlʊŋ) *n, pl* **Nibelungs** *or* **Nibelungen** (-ˌlʊŋən). *German myth.* **1** any of the race of dwarfs who possessed a treasure hoard subsequently stolen by Siegfried. **2** one of Siegfried's companions or followers. **3** (in the *Nibelungenlied*) a member of the family of Gunther, king of Burgundy.

niblick ('nɪblɪk) *n Golf.* (formerly) a club giving a great deal of lift. ORIG C19: from ?

nibs (nɪbz) *n* **his nibs.** *Sl.* a mock title used of someone in authority. ORIG C19: from ?

Nicaea ★ (naɪ'siːə) *n* an ancient city in NW Asia Minor, in Bithynia: site of the **first council of Nicaea** (325 A.D.), which composed the Nicene Creed. Modern Turkish name: **Iznik.**
▸ **Nicene** ('naɪsiːn) *or* **Ni'caean** *adj*

NICAM ('naɪkæm) *n acronym for* near-instantaneous companded audio multiplex: a technique for coding audio signals into digital form.

Nicaragua ★ (ˌnɪkə'rægjʊə, -gwə; *Spanish* nika'raɣwa) *n* **1** a republic in Central America, on the Caribbean and the Pacific: colonized by the Spanish from the 1520s; gained independence in 1821 and was annexed by Mexico, becoming a republic in 1838. Official language: Spanish. Religion: Roman Catholic. Currency: córdoba. Capital: Managua. Pop.: 4 923 000 (1999 est.). Area: 131 812 sq. km (50 893 sq. miles). **2 Lake.** a lake in SW Nicaragua, separated from the Pacific by an isthmus 19 km (12 miles) wide: the largest lake in Central America. Area: 8264 sq. km (3191 sq. miles).
▸ **ˌNica'raguan** *adj, n*

nice (naɪs) *adj* **1** pleasant: *a nice day.* **2** kind or friendly: *a nice gesture of help.* **3** good or satisfactory: *they made a nice job of it.* **4** subtle or discriminating: *a nice point in the argument.* **5** precise; skilful: *a nice fit.* **6** *Now rare.* fastidious; respectable: *he was not too nice about his methods.* **7** *Obs.* **7a**

foolish or ignorant. **7b** delicate. **7c** shy; modest. **7d** wanton. ORIG C13 (orig.: foolish): from OF *nice* simple, silly, from L *nescius,* from *nescīre* to be ignorant
▸ **'nicely** *adv* ▸ **'niceness** *n* ▸ **'nicish** *adj*

Nice ★ (*French* nis) *n* a city in SE France, on the Mediterranean: a leading resort of the French Riviera; founded by Phocaeans from Marseille in about the 3rd century B.C. Pop.: 345 674 (1990).

NICE (in Britain) acronym for National Institute for Clinical Excellence.

nice-looking *adj Inf.* attractive in appearance.

nicety ('naɪsɪtɪ) *n, pl* **niceties. 1** a subtle point: *a nicety of etiquette.* **2** (*usually pl*) a refinement or delicacy: *the niceties of first-class travel.* **3** subtlety, delicacy, or precision. **4 to a nicety.** with precision.

niche (nɪtʃ, niːʃ) *n* **1** a recess in a wall, esp. one that contains a statue, etc. **2** a position particularly suitable for the person occupying it: *he found his niche in politics.* **3** (*modifier*) relating to or aimed at a small specialized group or market: *shampoo shops and other niche retailing ventures.* **4** *Ecology.* the status of a plant or animal within its community, which determines its activities, relationships with other organisms, etc. ◆ *vb* **niches, niching, niched. 5** (*tr*) to place (a statue) in a niche; ensconce (oneself). ORIG C17: from F, from OF *nichier* to nest, from Vulgar L *nīdicāre* (unattested), from L *nīdus* NEST

Nicholas ★ ('nɪkələs) *n* **Saint.** 4th-century A.D. bishop of Myra, in Asia Minor; patron saint of Russia and of children. Feast day: Dec. 6. See also **Santa Claus.**

Nicholas I ★ *n* **1 Saint,** called *the Great.* died 867 A.D., Italian ecclesiastic; pope (858–867). Feast day: Nov. 13. **2** 1796–1855, tsar of Russia (1825–55): notorious for his autocracy.

Nicholas II ★ *n* 1868–1918, tsar of Russia (1894–1917). His autocracy precipitated the Russian Revolution (1917): he abdicated and was shot.

Nicholas V ★ *n* original name *Tommaso Parentucelli.* 1397–1455, Italian ecclesiastic; pope (1447–55).

Nicholas of Cusa ★ ('kjuːzə) *n* 1401–64, German cardinal and mathematician: asserted that the earth revolves around the sun.

Nicholson ★ ('nɪkᵊlsən) *n* **1 Ben.** 1894–1982, British abstract painter. **2 Jack.** born 1937, US actor. His films include *Easy Rider* (1969), *One Flew Over the Cuckoo's Nest* (1974), and *As Good As It Gets* (1998).

Nichrome ('naɪˌkrəʊm) *n Trademark.* any of various alloys containing nickel, iron, and chromium, used in electrical heating elements, furnaces, etc.

Nicias ★ ('nɪsɪəs) *n* died 414 B.C., Athenian statesman and general. Made peace with Sparta (421), ending the first part of the Peloponnesian War.

nick (nɪk) *n* **1** a small notch or indentation. **2** *Brit. sl.* a prison or police station. **3 in good nick.** *Inf.* in good condition. **4 in the nick of time.** just in time. ◆ *vb* **5** (*tr*) to chip or cut. **6** *Sl., chiefly Brit.* **6a** to steal. **6b** to arrest. **7** (*intr; often foll. by off*) *Inf.* to depart rapidly. **8 nick (someone) for.** *US & Canad. sl.* to defraud (someone) to the extent of. **9** to divide and reset (the tail muscles of a horse) to give the tail a high carriage. **10** (*tr*) to guess, catch, etc., exactly. ORIG C15: ? changed from C14 *nocke* NOCK

nickel ('nɪkᵊl) *n* **1** a malleable silvery-white metallic element that is corrosion-resistant: used in alloys, in electroplating, and as a catalyst in organic synthesis. Symbol: Ni; atomic no.: 28; atomic wt.: 58.71. **2** a US or Canadian coin worth five cents. ◆ *vb* **nickels, nickelling, nickelled** *or US* **nickels, nickeling, nickeled. 3** (*tr*) to plate with nickel. ORIG C18: from G *Kupfernickel* niccolite, lit.: copper demon; it was mistakenly thought to contain copper

nickelodeon (ˌnɪkə'ləʊdɪən) *n US.* **1** an early form of jukebox. **2** (formerly) a Pianola, esp. one operated by a five-cent piece. ORIG C20: from NICKEL + (MEL)ODEON

nickel plate *n* a thin layer of nickel deposited on a surface, usually by electrolysis.

nickel silver *n* any of various white alloys containing copper, zinc, and nickel: used in making tableware, etc. Also called: **German silver.**

nickel steel *n Engineering.* steel containing between 0.5 and 6.0 per cent nickel to increase its strength.

nicker[1] ('nɪkə) *vb* (*intr*) **1** (of a horse) to neigh softly. **2** to snigger. ORIG C18: ?from NEIGH

nicker[2] ('nɪkə) *n, pl* **nicker.** *Brit. sl.* a pound sterling. ORIG C20: from ?

Nicklaus ★ ('nɪklaʊs) *n* **Jack.** born 1940, US golfer: won the British Open Championship (1966; 1970; 1978) and the US Open Championship (1962; 1967; 1972; 1980).

nick-nack ('nɪkˌnæk) *n* a variant spelling of **knick-knack.**

nickname ('nɪkˌneɪm) *n* **1** a familiar, pet, or derisory name given to a person, animal, or place. **2** a shortened or familiar form of a person's name: *Joe is a nickname for Joseph.* ◆ *vb* **nicknames, nicknaming, nicknamed. 3** (*tr*) to call by a nickname. ORIG C15 *a nekename,* mistaken division of *an ekename* an additional name

Nicobar Islands ★ ('nɪkəˌbɑː) *pl n* a group of 19 islands in the Indian Ocean, south of the Andaman Islands, with which they form a territory of India. Area: 1645 sq. km (635 sq. miles).

Nicodemus ★ (ˌnɪkə'diːməs) *n New Testament.* a Pharisee and a member of the Sanhedrin, who supported Jesus against the other Pharisees (John 8:50–52).

Nicolai ★ (*German* nikoˈlaɪ) *n* **Carl Otto Ehrenfried** (karl 'ɔto 'eːrənfriːt). 1810–49, German composer: noted for his opera *The Merry Wives of Windsor* (1849).

Nicol prism ('nɪkᵊl) *n* two prisms of Iceland spar or calcite cut at specified angles and cemented together, to produce plane-polarized light. ORIG C19: after William *Nicol* (?1768–1851), Scot. physicist, its inventor

Nicosia ★ (ˌnɪkə'siːə, -'sɪə) *n* the capital of Cyprus, in the central part on the Pedieos River: capital since the 10th century. Pop.: 228 215 (1994 est.). Greek name: **Levkosia** *or* **Leukosia.** Turkish name: **Lefkoşa.**

nicotiana (nɪˌkəʊʃɪ'ɑːnə) *n* a plant of an American and Australian genus, having white, yellow, or purple fragrant flowers. Also called: **tobacco plant.** ORIG C16: see NICOTINE

nicotinamide (ˌnɪkə'tɪnəˌmaɪd) *n* the amide of nicotinic acid: a component of the vitamin B complex. Formula: $C_6H_6ON_2$.

nicotine ('nɪkəˌtiːn) *n* a colourless oily acrid toxic liquid that turns yellowish-brown in air and light: the principal alkaloid in tobacco. ORIG C19: from F, from NL *herba nicotiana* Nicot's plant, after J. *Nicot* (1530-1600), F diplomat who introduced tobacco into France
▸ **'nicoˌtined** *adj* ▸ **nicotinic** (ˌnɪkə'tɪnɪk) *adj*

nicotinic acid *n* a vitamin of the B complex that occurs in milk, liver, yeast, etc. Lack of it in the diet leads to the disease pellagra.

nicotinism ('nɪkətiːˌnɪzəm) *n Pathol.* a toxic condition of the body caused by nicotine.

Nictheroy ★ (*Portuguese* nite'rɔi) *n* another name for **Niterói.**

nictitate ('nɪktɪˌteɪt) *or* **nictate** ('nɪkteɪt) *vb* **nictitates, nictitating, nictitated** *or* **nictates, nictating, nictated.** a technical word for **blink.** ORIG C19: from Med. L *nictitāre* to wink repeatedly, from L *nictāre* to blink
▸ **ˌnicti'tation** *or* **nic'tation** *n*

nictitating membrane *n* (in reptiles, birds, and some mammals) a thin fold of skin beneath the eyelid that can be drawn across the eye.

Nidaros ★ (*Norwegian* 'niːdaroːs) *n* the former name (1930–31) of **Trondheim.**

nidicolous (nɪ'dɪkələs) *adj* (of young birds) remaining in the nest some time after hatching. ORIG C19: from L *nīdus* nest + *colere* to inhabit

nidifugous (nɪ'dɪfjʊgəs) *adj* (of young birds) leaving the nest very soon after hatching. ORIG C19: from L *nīdus* nest + *fugere* to flee

nidify ('nɪdɪˌfaɪ) *or* **nidificate** ('nɪdɪfɪˌkeɪt) *vb* **nidifies, nidifying, nidified** *or* **nidificates, nidificating, nidificated.** (*intr*) (of birds) to make or build a nest. ORIG C17: from L *nīdificāre,* from *nīdus* a nest + *facere* to make
▸ **ˌnidifi'cation** *n*

niece (niːs) *n* a daughter of one's sister or brother. ORIG

C13: from OF: niece, granddaughter, ult. from L *neptis* granddaughter

Niederösterreich ★ ('ni:dərø:stəraɪç) *n* the German name for **Lower Austria**.

Niedersachsen ★ ('ni:dərzaksən) *n* the German name for **Lower Saxony**.

niello (nɪ'ɛləʊ) *n, pl* **nielli** (-lɪ) *or* **niellos**. **1** a black compound of sulphur and silver, lead, or copper used to incise a design on a metal surface. **2** this process. **3** an object decorated with niello. ORIG C19: from It. from L *nigellus* blackish, from *niger* black

Nielsen ★ ('ni:lsən; *Danish* 'nelsən) *n* **Carl (August)** (karl). 1865–1931, Danish composer. His works include six symphonies and the opera *Masquerade* (1906).

Niemen ★ ('njɛmɛn) *n* the Polish name for the **Neman**.

Niemeyer ★ ('ni:ˌmaɪə) *n* **Oscar**. born 1907, Brazilian architect. His work includes many buildings in Brasília.

Niemöller ★ (*German* 'ni:mœlər) *n* **Martin** ('marti:n). 1892–1984, German Protestant theologian; imprisoned (1938–45) for opposing Hitler.

Niepce ★ (*French* njɛps) *n* **Joseph-Nicéphore** (ʒozɛf-nisefɔr). 1765–1833, French inventor. He produced the first permanent camera photograph (1826).

Nietzsche ★ ('ni:tʃə) *n* **Friedrich Wilhelm** ('fri:drɪç 'vɪlhɛlm). 1844–1900, German philosopher. His works include *Thus Spake Zarathustra* (1883–91) and *Beyond Good and Evil* (1886).
▸ **Nietzschean** ('ni:tʃɪən) *n, adj* ▸ **'Nietzscheˌism** *or* **'Nietzscheanˌism** *n*

Nièvre ★ (*French* njɛvrə) *n* a department of central France, in Burgundy region. Capital: Nevers. Pop.: 230 529 (1994 est.). Area: 6888 sq. km (2686 sq. miles).

niff (nɪf) *Brit. sl.* ◆ *n* **1** a bad smell. ◆ *vb* (*intr*) **2** to stink. ORIG C20: ?from SNIFF
▸ **'niffy** *adj*

Niflheim ★ ('nɪvəlˌheɪm) *n Norse myth.* the abode of the dead. ORIG ON, lit.: mist home

nifty ('nɪftɪ) *adj* **niftier, niftiest**. *Inf.* **1** pleasing, apt, or stylish. **2** quick; agile. ORIG C19: from ?
▸ **'niftily** *adv* ▸ **'niftiness** *n*

nigella (naɪ'dʒɛlə) *n* another name for **love-in-a-mist**.

Niger ★ *n* **1** (ni:'ʒɛə, 'naɪdʒə) a landlocked republic in West Africa: important since earliest times for its trans-Saharan trade routes; made a French colony in 1922 and became fully independent in 1960; exports peanuts and livestock. Official language: French. Religion: mostly Muslim. Currency: franc. Capital: Niamey. Pop.: 9 962 000 (1999 est.). Area: 1 267 000 sq. km (489 000 sq. miles). **2** ('naɪdʒə) a river in West Africa, rising in S Guinea and flowing in a great northward curve through Mali, then southwest through Niger and Nigeria to the Gulf of Guinea: the third longest river in Africa, with the largest delta, covering an area of 36 260 sq. km (14 000 sq. miles). Length: 4184 km (2600 miles). **3** ('naɪdʒə) a state of W central Nigeria, formed in 1976 from part of North-Western State. Capital: Minna. Pop.: 2 775 526 (1995 est.). Area: 65 037 sq. km (25 105 sq. miles).

Nigeria ★ (naɪ'dʒɪərɪə) *n* a republic in West Africa, on the Gulf of Guinea: Lagos annexed by the British in 1861; protectorates of Northern and Southern Nigeria formed in 1900 and united as a colony in 1914; gained independence as a member of the Commonwealth in 1960 (membership suspended in 1995 following human rights violations); Eastern Region seceded as the Republic of Biafra for the duration of the severe civil war (1967–70); ruled by military governments from 1966; in 1993 the annulment of democratic elections by the military government precipitated a political and social crisis. It consists of a belt of tropical rain forest in the south, with semidesert in the extreme north and highlands in the east; the main export is petroleum. Official language: English; Hausa, Ibo, and Yoruba are the chief regional languages. Religion: animist, Muslim, and Christian. Currency: naira. Capital: Abuja. Pop.: 113 829 000 (1999 est.). Area: 923 773 sq. km (356 669 sq. miles).
▸ **Ni'gerian** *adj, n*

niggard ('nɪgəd) *n* **1** a stingy person. ◆ *adj* **2** *Arch.* miserly. ORIG C14: ?from ON

niggardly ('nɪgədlɪ) *adj* **1** stingy. **2** meagre: *a niggardly salary*. ◆ *adv* **3** stingily; grudgingly.
▸ **'niggardliness** *n*

nigger ('nɪgə) *n Derog.* **1** another name for a Negro. **2** a member of any dark-skinned race. **3 nigger in the woodpile**. a hidden cause of trouble. ORIG C18: from C16 dialect *neeger*, from F *nègre*, from Sp. NEGRO[1]

niggle ('nɪgəl) *vb* **niggles, niggling, niggled**. **1** (*intr*) to find fault continually. **2** (*intr*) to be preoccupied with details; fuss. **3** (*tr*) to irritate; worry. ◆ *n* **4** a trivial objection or complaint. **5** a slight feeling as of misgiving, uncertainty, etc. ORIG C16: from Scand.
▸ **'niggler** *n* ▸ **'niggly** *adj*

niggling ('nɪglɪŋ) *adj* **1** petty. **2** fussy. **3** irritating. **4** requiring painstaking work. **5** persistently troubling.

nigh (naɪ) *adj, adv, prep* an archaic, poetic, or dialect word for **near**. ORIG OE *nēah, nēh*

night (naɪt) *n* **1** the period of darkness that occurs each 24 hours, as distinct from day. **2** (*modifier*) of, occurring, working, etc., at night: *a night nurse*. **3** this period considered as a unit: *four nights later they left*. **4** the period between sunset and retiring to bed; evening. **5** the time between bedtime and morning. **6** the weather at night: *a clear night*. **7** the activity or experience of a person during a night. **8** (*sometimes cap.*) any evening designated for a special observance or function. **9** nightfall or dusk. **10** a state or period of gloom, ignorance, etc. **11 make a night of it**. to celebrate for most of the night. ◆ Related adj: **nocturnal**. ◆ See also **nights**. ORIG OE *niht*

night blindness *n Pathol.* a nontechnical term for **nyctalopia**.
▸ **'night-ˌblind** *adj*

nightcap ('naɪtˌkæp) *n* **1** a bedtime drink. **2** a soft cap formerly worn in bed.

nightclothes ('naɪtˌkləʊðz) *pl n* clothes worn in bed.

nightclub ('naɪtˌklʌb) *n* a place of entertainment open in the evening until the early hours of the morning, usually having a bar and music for dancing and sometimes food and a floorshow.

nightdress ('naɪtˌdrɛs) *n Brit.* a loose dress worn in bed by women. Also called: **nightgown, nightie**.

nightfall ('naɪtˌfɔ:l) *n* the approach of darkness; dusk.

night fighter *n* an interceptor aircraft used for operations at night.

nightgown ('naɪtˌgaʊn) *n* **1** another name for **nightdress**. **2** a man's nightshirt.

nighthawk ('naɪtˌhɔ:k) *n* **1** any of various nocturnal American birds. **2** *Inf.* another name for **night owl**.

nightie *or* **nighty** ('naɪtɪ) *n, pl* **nighties**. *Inf.* short for **nightdress**.

nightingale ('naɪtɪnˌgeɪl) *n* a brownish European songbird with a broad reddish-brown tail: well known for its musical song, usually heard at night. ORIG OE *nihtegale*, from NIGHT + *galan* to sing

Nightingale ★ ('naɪtɪŋˌgeɪl) *n* **Florence**, known as *the Lady with the Lamp*. 1820–1910, British nurse, noted for her work during the Crimean War.

nightjar ('naɪtˌdʒɑ:) *n* any of a family of nocturnal birds which have large eyes and feed on insects. ORIG C17: NIGHT + JAR[2], so called from its discordant cry

night latch *n* a door lock operated by means of a knob on the inside and a key on the outside.

nightlife ('naɪtˌlaɪf) *n* social life or entertainment taking place at night.

night-light *n* a dim light burning at night, esp. for children.

nightlong ('naɪtˌlɒŋ) *adj, adv* throughout the night.

nightly ('naɪtlɪ) *adj* **1** happening or relating to each night. **2** happening at night. ◆ *adv* **3** at night or each night.

nightmare ('naɪtˌmɛə) *n* **1** a terrifying or deeply distressing dream. **2a** an event or condition resembling a terrifying dream. **2b** (*as modifier*): *a nightmare drive*. **3** a thing that is feared. **4** (formerly) an evil spirit supposed to suf-

focate sleeping people. ORIG C13 (meaning: incubus; C16: bad dream): from NIGHT + OE *mare, mære* evil spirit, from Gmc
▸ **'night,marish** *adj*

night owl *or* **nighthawk** *n Inf.* a person who is or prefers to be up and about late at night.

nights (naɪts) *adv Inf.* at night, esp. regularly: *he works nights.*

night safe *n* a safe built into the outside wall of a bank, in which customers can deposit money at times when the bank is closed.

night school *n* an educational institution that holds classes in the evening.

nightshade ('naɪt,ʃeɪd) *n* any of various solanaceous plants, such as deadly nightshade and black nightshade. ORIG OE *nihtscada,* apparently NIGHT + SHADE, referring to the poisonous or soporific qualities of these plants

night shift *n* **1** a group of workers who work a shift during the night. **2** the period worked.

nightshirt ('naɪt,ʃɜːt) *n* a loose knee-length or longer shirtlike garment worn in bed.

nightspot ('naɪt,spɒt) *n* an informal word for **nightclub.**

night-time *n* the time from sunset to sunrise; night as distinct from day.

night watch *n* **1** a watch or guard kept at night, esp. for security. **2** the period of time the watch is kept. **3** a night watchman.

night watchman *n* **1** Also called: **night watch.** a person who keeps guard at night on a factory, public building, etc. **2** *Cricket.* a batsman sent in to bat to play out time when a wicket has fallen near the end of a day's play.

nightwear ('naɪt,wɛə) *n* apparel worn in bed or before retiring to bed; pyjamas, etc.

nigrescent (naɪ'grɛsᵊnt) *adj* blackish; dark. ORIG C18: from L *nigrescere* to grow black, from *niger* black
▸ **ni'grescence** *n*

nihilism ('naɪɪ,lɪzəm) *n* **1** a complete denial of all established authority and institutions. **2** *Philosophy.* an extreme form of scepticism that systematically rejects all values, belief in existence, etc. **3** a revolutionary doctrine of destruction for its own sake. **4** the practice of terrorism. ORIG C19: from L *nihil* nothing
▸ **'nihilist** *n, adj* ▸ **,nihil'istic** *adj* ▸ **nihility** (naɪ'hɪlɪtɪ) *n*

nihil obstat ('naɪhɪl 'ɒbstæt) the phrase used by a Roman Catholic censor to declare publication inoffensive to faith or morals. ORIG L, lit.: nothing hinders

Nihon ★ ('niː'hɒn) *n* transliteration of a Japanese name for **Japan.**

Niigata ★ ('niːɪ,gɑːtə) *n* a port in central Japan, on NW Honshu at the mouth of the Shinano River: the chief port on the Sea of Japan. Pop.: 494 785 (1995).

Nijinsky ★ (nɪ'dʒɪnskɪ) *n* **Waslaw** *or* **Vaslaw** (*Russian* vats'laf). 1890–1950, Russian ballet dancer and choreographer.

Nijmegen ★ ('naɪ,meɪgən; *Dutch* 'nɛimeːxə) *n* an industrial town in the E Netherlands, in Gelderland province on the Waal River: the oldest town in the country; scene of the signing (1678) of the peace treaty between Louis XIV, the Netherlands, Spain, and the Holy Roman Empire. Pop.: 147 600 (1996 est.). Latin name: **,Novio'magus.** German name: **Nimwegen.**

-nik *suffix forming nouns.* denoting a person associated with a specified state or quality: *beatnik.* ORIG C20: from Russian *-nik,* as in SPUTNIK, and infl. by Yiddish *-nik* (agent suffix)

Nikaria ★ (nɪ'kɛərɪə, naɪ-) *n* another name for **Icaria.**

Nike ★ ('naɪkiː) *n Greek myth.* the winged goddess of victory. Roman counterpart: **Victoria.** ORIG from Gk: victory

Nikkei Stock Average ('nɪkeɪ) *n* an index of share prices based on an average of 225 equities quoted on the Tokyo Stock Exchange. ORIG C20: from *Nik(on) Kei(zai Shimbun),* a Japanese newspaper group

Nikko ★ ('niːkəʊ) *n* a town in central Japan, on NE Honshu: a major pilgrimage centre, with a 4th-century Shinto shrine, a Buddhist temple (767), and the shrines and mausoleums of the Tokugawa shoguns. Pop.: 20 128 (1990).

Nikolainkaupunki ★ (*Finnish* ,nikəlaɪn'kaupuŋki) *n* the former name of **Vaasa.**

Nikolayev ★ (*Russian* nika'lajɪf) *n* a city in S Ukraine, on the Southern Bug about 64 km (40 miles) from the Black Sea: founded as a naval base in 1788; one of the leading Black Sea ports. Pop.: 508 000 (1996 est.). Former name: **Vernoleninsk.**

nil (nɪl) *n* nothing: used esp. in the scoring of certain games. ORIG C19: from L

Nile ★ (naɪl) *n* a river in Africa, rising in S central Burundi in its remotest headstream, the **Luvironza:** flows into Lake Victoria and leaves the lake as the **Victoria Nile,** flowing to Lake Albert, which is drained by the **Albert Nile,** becoming the White Nile on the border between Uganda and the Sudan; joined by its chief tributary, the **Blue Nile** (which rises near Lake Tana, Ethiopia) at Khartoum, and flows north to its delta on the Mediterranean; the longest river in the world. Length: (from the source of the Luvironza to the Mediterranean) 6741 km (4187 miles).

Nile green *n* **a** a pale bluish-green colour. **b** (*as adj*): *a Nile-green dress.*

nilgai ('nɪlgaɪ) *or* **nilghau** ('nɪlgɔː) *n, pl* **nilgai, nilgais** *or* **nilghau, nilghaus.** a large Indian antelope, the male of which has small horns. ORIG C19: from Hindi *nīlgāw,* from Sansk. *nīla* blue + *go* bull

Nilgiri Hills ('nɪlgɪrɪ) *or* **Nilgiris** ★ *pl n* a plateau in S India, in Tamil Nadu. Average height: 2000 m (6500 ft), reaching 2635 m (8647 ft) in Doda Betta.

Nilotic (naɪ'lɒtɪk) *adj* **1** of the Nile. **2** of or belonging to a Negroid pastoral people inhabiting the S Sudan, parts of Kenya and Uganda, and neighbouring countries. **3** relating to the group of languages spoken by the Nilotic peoples. ORIG C17: via L from Gk *Neilotikós,* from *Neilos* the NILE

Nilsson ★ (*Swedish* 'nilsɔn) *n* **Birgit** ('birgit). born 1918, Swedish soprano.

nimble ('nɪmbᵊl) *adj* **1** agile, quick, and neat in movement. **2** alert; acute. ORIG OE *næmel* quick to grasp, & *numol* quick at seizing, both from *niman* to take
▸ **'nimbleness** *n* ▸ **'nimbly** *adv*

nimbostratus (,nɪmbəʊ'streɪtəs, -'strɑːtəs) *n, pl* **nimbostrati** (-taɪ). a dark rain-bearing stratus cloud.

nimbus ('nɪmbəs) *n, pl* **nimbi** (-baɪ) *or* **nimbuses. 1a** a dark grey rain-bearing cloud. **1b** (*in combination*): *cumulonimbus clouds.* **2a** an emanation of light surrounding a saint or deity. **2b** a representation of this emanation. **3** a surrounding aura. ORIG C17: from L: cloud

NIMBY ('nɪmbɪ) *n acronym for* not in my back yard: a person who objects to the occurrence of something if it will affect them or take place in their locality.

Nîmes ★ (*French* nim) *n* a city in S France: Roman remains including an amphitheatre and the Pont du Gard aqueduct. Pop.: 133 607 (1990).

Nimrod ★ ('nɪmrɒd) *n* **1** a hunter famous for his prowess (Genesis 10:8–9). **2** a person dedicated to or skilled in hunting.

Nimrud ★ (nɪm'ruːd) *n* an ancient city in Assyria, near the present-day city of Mosul (Iraq): founded in about 1250 B.C. and destroyed by the Medes in 612 B.C.; excavated by Sir Austen Henry Layard.

Nimwegen ★ ('nɪmveːgən) *n* the German name for **Nijmegen.**

nincompoop ('nɪnkəm,puːp, 'nɪŋ-) *n* a stupid person; fool; idiot. ORIG C17: from ?

nine (naɪn) *n* **1** the cardinal number that is the sum of one and eight. **2** a numeral, 9, IX, etc., representing this number. **3** something representing, represented by, or consisting of nine units, such as a playing card with nine symbols on it. **4** Also: **nine o'clock.** nine hours after noon or midnight: *the play starts at nine.* **5 dressed** (**up**) **to the nines.** *Inf.* elaborately dressed. **6 999** (in Britain) the telephone number of the emergency services. **7 nine to five.** normal office hours: *a nine-to-five job.* ◆ *determiner* **8a**

amounting to nine: *nine days.* **5b** (*as pronoun*): *nine are ready.* ORIG OE *nigon*

nine-days wonder *n* something that arouses great interest but only for a short period.

ninefold ('naɪn,fəʊld) *adj* **1** equal to or having nine times as many or as much. **2** composed of nine parts. ◆ *adv* **3** by nine times as much.

ninepins ('naɪn,pɪnz) *n* **1** (*functioning as sing*) another name for **skittles. 2** (*sing*) one of the pins used in this game.

nineteen ('naɪn'tiːn) *n* **1** the cardinal number that is the sum of ten and nine. **2** a numeral, 19, XIX, etc., representing this number. **3** something represented by, representing, or consisting of 19 units. **4 talk nineteen to the dozen.** to talk incessantly. ◆ *determiner* **5a** amounting to nineteen: *nineteen pictures.* **5b** (*as pronoun*): *only nineteen voted.* ORIG OE *nigontīne*

nineteenth (,naɪn'tiːnθ) *adj* **1** (*usually prenominal*) **1a** coming after the eighteenth in numbering, position, etc.; being the ordinal number of *nineteen.* Often written: 19th. **1b** (*as n*): *the nineteenth was rainy.* ◆ *n* **2a** one of 19 equal parts of something. **2b** (*as modifier*): *a nineteenth part.* **3** the fraction equal to one divided by 19 (1/19).

nineteenth hole *n Golf, sl.* the bar in a golf clubhouse. ORIG C20: from its being the next objective after a standard 18-hole round

ninetieth ('naɪntɪɪθ) *adj* **1** (*usually prenominal*) **1a** being the ordinal number of *ninety* in numbering, position, etc. Often written: 90th. **1b** (*as n*): *ninetieth in succession.* ◆ *n* **2a** one of 90 equal parts of something. **2b** (*as modifier*): *a ninetieth part.* **3** the fraction one divided by 90 (1/90).

ninety ('naɪntɪ) *n, pl* **nineties. 1** the cardinal number that is the product of ten and nine. **2** a numeral, 90, XC, etc., representing this number. **3** something represented by, representing, or consisting of 90 units. ◆ *determiner* **4a** amounting to ninety: *ninety times.* **4b** (*as pronoun*): *at least ninety are missing.* ORIG OE *nigontig*
▸ **'ninetieth** *adj, n*

Nineveh ★ ('nɪnɪvə) *n* the ancient capital of Assyria, on the River Tigris opposite the present-day city of Mosul (N Iraq): at its height in the 8th and 7th centuries B.C.; destroyed in 612 B.C. by the Medes and Babylonians.
▸ **'Ninevite** *n*

Ningbo *or* **Ningpo** ★ ('nɪŋ'pəʊ) *n* a port in E China, in NE Zhejiang, on the Yung River, about 20 km (12 miles) from its mouth at Hangzhou Bay: one of the first sites of European settlement in China. Pop.: 1 090 000 (1991 est.).

Ningsia *or* **Ninghsia** ★ ('nɪŋ'ʃjɑː) *n* **1** a former province of NW China: mostly included in the Inner Mongolian AR in 1956, with the smaller part constituted as the Ningxia Hui AR in 1958. **2** the former name of **Yinchuan.**

Ningxia Hui Autonomous Region ★ ('nɪŋ'ʃjɑː 'huːɪ) *n* an administrative division of NW China, south of the Inner Mongolian AR. Capital: Yinchuan. Pop.: 5 300 000 (1997 est.). Area: 66 400 sq. km (25 896 sq. miles).

Ninian ★ ('nɪnjən) *n* **Saint.** ?360–?432 A.D., the first apostle of Scotland; built a stone church at his native Whithorn. Feast day: Sept. 16.

ninja ('nɪndʒə) *n, pl* **ninja** *or* **ninjas.** (*sometimes cap.*) a person skilled in **ninjutsu,** a Japanese martial art characterized by stealthy movement and camouflage. ORIG Japanese

ninny ('nɪnɪ) *n, pl* **ninnies.** a dull-witted person. ORIG C16: ?from *an innocent* simpleton

ninth (naɪnθ) *adj* **1** (*usually prenominal*) **1a** coming after the eighth in order, position, etc.; being the ordinal number of *nine.* Often written: 9th. **1b** (*as n*): *ninth in line.* ◆ *n* **2a** one of nine equal parts. **2b** (*as modifier*): *a ninth part.* **3** the fraction one divided by nine (1/9). **4** *Music.* an interval of one octave plus a second. ◆ *adv* **5** Also: **ninthly.** after the eighth person, position, event, etc. ORIG OE *nigotha*

Ninus ★ ('naɪnəs) *n* a king of Assyria and the legendary founder of Nineveh, husband of Semiramis.

Niobe ★ ('naɪəbɪ) *n Greek myth.* a daughter of Tantalus, whose children were slain after she boasted of them: although turned into stone, she continued to weep.
▸ **Niobean** (naɪ'əʊbɪən) *adj*

niobium (naɪ'əʊbɪəm) *n* a ductile white superconductive metallic element that occurs principally in the black mineral columbite and tantalite. Symbol: Nb; atomic no.: 41; atomic wt.: 92.906. Former name: **columbium.** ORIG C19: from NL, from NIOBE; because it occurred in TANTALITE

nip[1] (nɪp) *vb* **nips, nipping, nipped.** (*mainly tr*) **1** to compress, as between a finger and the thumb; pinch. **2** (often foll. by *off*) to remove by clipping, biting, etc. **3** (when *intr,* often foll. by *at*) to give a small sharp bite (to): *the dog nipped at his heels.* **4** (esp. of the cold) to affect with a stinging sensation. **5** to harm through cold: *the frost nipped the young plants.* **6** to check or destroy the growth of (esp. in **nip in the bud**). **7** (*intr;* foll. by *along, up, out,* etc.) *Brit. inf.* to hurry; dart. **8** *Sl., chiefly US & Canad.* to snatch. ◆ *n* **9** a pinch, snip, etc. **10** severe frost or cold: *the first nip of winter.* **11 put the nips in.** *Austral. & NZ sl.* to exert pressure on someone, esp. in order to extort money. **12** *Arch.* a taunting remark. **13 nip and tuck.** *US & Canad.* neck and neck. ORIG C14: from ON

nip[2] (nɪp) *n* **1** a small drink of spirits; dram. ◆ *vb* **nips, nipping, nipped. 2** to drink spirits, esp. habitually in small amounts. ORIG C18: from *nipperkin* a vessel holding a half-pint or less, from ?

Nipigon ★ ('nɪpəgɒn) *n* **Lake.** a lake in central Canada, in NW Ontario, draining into Lake Superior via the **Nipigon River.** Area: 4843 sq. km (1870 sq. miles).

Nipissing ★ ('nɪpɪsɪŋ) *n* **Lake.** a lake in central Canada, in E Ontario between the Ottawa River and Georgian Bay. Area: 855 sq. km (330 sq. miles).

nipper ('nɪpə) *n* **1** a person or thing that nips. **2** the large pincer-like claw of a lobster, crab, etc. **3** *Inf., chiefly Brit. & Austral.* a small child. **4** *Austral.* a type of small prawn used as bait.

nippers ('nɪpəz) *pl n* an instrument or tool, such as a pair of pliers, for snipping or squeezing.

nipple ('nɪpᵊl) *n* **1** the small conical projection in the centre of each breast, which in women contains the outlet of the milk ducts. **2** something resembling a nipple in shape or function. **3** Also called: **grease nipple.** a small drilled bush, usually screwed into a bearing, through which grease is introduced. ORIG C16: from earlier *neble, nible,* ?from NEB, NIB

nipplewort ('nɪpᵊl,wɜːt) *n* an annual Eurasian plant with pointed oval leaves and small yellow flower heads.

Nippon ★ ('nɪpɒn) *n* transliteration of a Japanese name for **Japan.**
▸ **Nipponese** (,nɪpə'niːz) *adj, n*

Nippur ★ (nɪ'pʊə) *n* an ancient Sumerian and Babylonian city, the excavated site of which is in SE Iraq: an important religious centre, abandoned in the 12th or 13th century.

nippy ('nɪpɪ) *adj* **nippier, nippiest. 1** (of weather) frosty or chilly. **2** *Brit. inf.* **2a** quick; nimble; active. **2b** (of a motor vehicle) small and relatively powerful. **3** (of dogs) inclined to bite.
▸ **'nippily** *adv*

Nirenberg ★ ('naɪrən,bɜːg) *n* **Marshall Warren.** born 1927, US biochemist; shared the Nobel prize for physiology or medicine (1968) for helping to decipher the genetic code.

NIREX ('naɪrɛks) *n acronym for* Nuclear Industry Radioactive Waste Executive.

nirvana (nɪə'vɑːnə, nɜː-) *n Buddhism & Hinduism.* final release from the cycle of reincarnation attained by extinction of all desires and individual existence, culminating (in Buddhism) in absolute blessedness, or (in Hinduism) in absorption into Brahman. ORIG C19: from Sansk.: extinction, from *nir-* out + *vāti* it blows

Niš *or* **Nish** ★ (niːʃ) *n* an industrial town in E Yugoslavia, in SE Serbia: situated on routes between central Europe and the Aegean. Pop.: 175 391 (1991).

Nisei ('niːseɪ) *n* a native-born citizen of the United States or Canada whose parents were Japanese immigrants. ORIG Japanese, lit.: second generation

Nishapur ★ (ˌniːʃɑːˈpʊə) *n* a town in NE Iran, at an altitude of 1195 m (3920 ft): birthplace and burial place of Omar Khayyám. Pop.: 135 681 (1991).

Nishinomiya ★ (ˌniːʃɪˈnɒmɪjə) *n* an industrial city in central Japan, on S Honshu, northwest of Osaka. Pop.: 390 388 (1995).

nisi (ˈnaɪsaɪ) *adj* (*postpositive*) *Law.* (of a court order) coming into effect on a specified date unless cause is shown why it should not: *a decree nisi.* ORIG C19: from: unless, if not

Nissen hut (ˈnɪsᵊn) *n* a military shelter of semicircular cross section, made of corrugated steel sheet. ORIG C20: after Lt Col. Peter *Nissen* (1871–1930), British mining engineer, its inventor

nit[1] (nɪt) *n* **1** the egg of a louse, esp. adhering to human hair. **2** the larva of a louse. ORIG OE *hnitu*

nit[2] (nɪt) *n* a unit of luminance equal to 1 candela per square metre. ORIG C20: from L *nitor* brightness

nit[3] (nɪt) *n Inf., chiefly Brit.* short for **nitwit.**

nit[4] (nɪt) *n* a unit of information equal to 1.44 bits. Also called: **nepit.** ORIG C20: from *N(apierian dig)it*

nit[5] (nɪt) *n* **keep nit.** *Austral. inf.* to keep watch, esp. during illegal activity. ORIG C19: from *nix!* a shout of warning
▸ **ˈnit-ˌkeeper** *n*

Niterói ★ (*Portuguese* niteˈrɔi) *n* a port in SE Brazil, on Guanabara Bay opposite Rio de Janeiro: contains Brazil's chief shipyards. Pop.: 400 586 (1991). Also called: **Nictheroy.**

nit-picking *Inf.* ◆ *n* **1** a concern with insignificant details, esp. with the intention of finding fault. ◆ *adj* **2** showing such a concern; fussy. ORIG C20: from NIT[1] + PICK[1]
▸ **ˈnit-ˌpicker** *n*

nitrate (ˈnaɪtreɪt) *n* **1** any salt or ester of nitric acid. **2** a fertilizer containing nitrate salts. ◆ *vb* **nitrates, nitrating, nitrated. 3** (*tr*) to treat with nitric acid or a nitrate. **4** to convert or be converted into a nitrate.
▸ **niˈtration** *n*

nitre *or US* **niter** (ˈnaɪtə) *n* another name for **potassium nitrate** or **sodium nitrate.** ORIG C14: via OF from L *nitrum,* prob. from Gk *nitron*

nitric (ˈnaɪtrɪk) *adj* of or containing nitrogen.

nitric acid *n* a colourless corrosive liquid important in the manufacture of fertilizers, explosives, and many other chemicals. Formula: HNO_3. Former name: **aqua fortis.**

nitric oxide *n* a colourless reactive gas. Formula: NO. Systematic name: **nitrogen monoxide.**

nitride (ˈnaɪtraɪd) *n* a compound of nitrogen with a more electropositive element.

nitrification (ˌnaɪtrɪfɪˈkeɪʃən) *n* **1** the oxidation of the ammonium compounds in dead organic material into nitrites and nitrates by soil nitrobacteria, making nitrogen available to plants. **2** the addition of a nitro group to an organic compound.

nitrify (ˈnaɪtrɪˌfaɪ) *vb* **nitrifies, nitrifying, nitrified.** (*tr*) **1** to treat or cause to react with nitrogen. **2** to treat (soil) with nitrates. **3** (of nitrobacteria) to convert (ammonium compounds) into nitrates by oxidation.
▸ **ˈnitriˌfiable** *adj*

nitrite (ˈnaɪtraɪt) *n* any salt or ester of nitrous acid.

nitro- *or before a vowel* **nitr-** *combining form.* **1** indicating that a chemical compound contains a nitro group, $-NO_2$: *nitrobenzene.* **2** indicating that a chemical compound is a nitrate ester: *nitrocellulose.* ORIG from Gk *nitron* NATRON

nitrobacteria (ˌnaɪtrəʊbækˈtɪərɪə) *pl n, sing* **nitrobacterium** (-ˈtɪərɪəm). soil bacteria that are involved in nitrification.

nitrobenzene (ˌnaɪtrəʊˈbɛnziːn) *n* a yellow oily liquid compound, used as a solvent and in the manufacture of aniline. Formula: $C_6H_5NO_2$.

nitrocellulose (ˌnaɪtrəʊˈsɛljʊˌləʊs) *n* another name (not in chemical usage) for **cellulose nitrate.**

nitrogen (ˈnaɪtrədʒən) *n* a colourless odourless relatively unreactive gaseous element that forms 78 per cent of the air and is an essential constituent of proteins and nucleic acids. Symbol: N; atomic no.: 7; atomic wt.: 14.0067.

nitrogen cycle *n* the natural circulation of nitrogen by living organisms. Nitrates in the soil, derived from dead organic matter by bacterial action, are absorbed and synthesized into complex organic compounds by plants and reduced to nitrates again when the plants and the animals feeding on them die and decay.

nitrogen dioxide *n* a red-brown poisonous gas that is an intermediate in the manufacture of nitric acid, a nitrating agent, and an oxidizer for rocket fuels. Formula: NO_2.

nitrogen fixation *n* **1** the conversion of atmospheric nitrogen into nitrogen compounds by certain bacteria in the root nodules of legumes. **2** a process in which atmospheric nitrogen is converted into a nitrogen compound, used esp. for fertilizer.

nitrogenize *or* **nitrogenise** (naɪˈtrɒdʒɪˌnaɪz) *vb* **nitrogenizes, nitrogenizing, nitrogenized** *or* **nitrogenises, nitrogenising, nitrogenised.** to combine or treat with nitrogen or a nitrogen compound.
▸ **niˌtrogeniˈzation** *or* **niˌtrogeniˈsation** *n*

nitrogen monoxide *n* the systematic name for **nitric oxide.**

nitrogen mustard *n* any of a class of organic compounds resembling mustard gas in their molecular structure: important in the treatment of cancer.

nitrogenous (naɪˈtrɒdʒɪnəs) *adj* containing nitrogen or a nitrogen compound.

nitroglycerine (ˌnaɪtrəʊˈglɪsəriːn) *or* **nitroglycerin** (ˌnaɪtrəʊˈglɪsəˌrɪn) *n* a pale yellow viscous explosive liquid made from glycerol and nitric and sulphuric acids. Formula: $CH_2NO_3CHNO_3CH_2NO_3$. Also called: **trinitroglycerine.**

nitromethane (ˌnaɪtrəʊˈmiːθeɪn) *n* an oily colourless liquid obtained from methane and used as a solvent and rocket fuel.

nitrous (ˈnaɪtrəs) *adj* of, derived from, or containing nitrogen, esp. in a low valency state. ORIG C17: from L *nitrōsus* full of natron

nitrous acid *n* a weak monobasic acid known only in solution and in the form of nitrite salts. Formula: HNO_2. Systematic name: **dioxonitric(III) acid.**

nitrous oxide *n* a colourless gas with a sweet smell: used as an anaesthetic in dentistry. Formula: N_2O. Also called: **laughing gas.** Systematic name: **dinitrogen oxide.**

nitty (ˈnɪtɪ) *adj* **nittier, nittiest.** infested with nits.

nitty-gritty (ˈnɪtɪˈgrɪtɪ) *n* **the.** *Inf.* the basic facts of a matter, situation, etc.; the core. ORIG C20: ? rhyming compound from GRIT

nitwit (ˈnɪtˌwɪt) *n Inf.* a foolish or dull person. ORIG C20: ?from NIT[1] + WIT[1]

Niue ★ (ˈnjuːeɪ) *n* an island in the S Pacific, between Tonga and the Cook Islands: annexed by New Zealand (1901); achieved full internal self-government in 1974. Chief town and port: Alofi. Pop.: 1977 (1993 est.). Area: 260 sq. km (100 sq. miles). Also called: **Savage Island.**
▸ **Niuean** (njuːˈɪən) *n, adj*

Niven ★ (ˈnɪvᵊn) *n* **David.** 1909–83, British film actor. His films include *The Prisoner of Zenda* (1937), *Around the World in 80 Days* (1956), and *Paper Tiger* (1975). His autobiographical books include *The Moon's a Balloon* (1972).

Nivernais ★ (*French* nivɛrnɛ) *n* a former province of central France, around Nevers.

nix[1] (nɪks) *Inf.* ◆ *sentence substitute.* **1** another word for **no**[1]. ◆ *n* **2** a refusal. **3** nothing. ORIG C18: from G, inf. form of *nichts* nothing

nix[2] (nɪks) *or* (*fem*) **nixie** (ˈnɪksɪ) *n Germanic myth.* a water sprite, usually unfriendly to humans. ORIG C19: from G *Nixe,* from OHG *nihhus*

Nixon ★ (ˈnɪksən) *n* **Richard M(ilhous).** 1913–94, US Republican politician; 37th president from 1969 until he resigned in 1974.

Nizam ★ (nɪˈzɑːm) *n* the title of the ruler of Hyderabad, India, from 1724 to 1948.

Nizhni Novgorod ★ (*Russian* ˈniʒnij ˈnɔvgərət) *n* industrial city and port in central Russia, at the confluence of the Volga and Oka Rivers: situated on the Volga route from the Baltic to central Asia; birthplace of Maxim Gorki. Pop.: 1 383 000 (1995 est.). Former name (1932–91): **Gorki.**

Nizhni Tagil ★ (*Russian* ˈniʒnij taˈgil) *n* a city in central Russia, on the E slopes of the Ural Mountains: a major metallurgical centre. Pop.: 409 000 (1995 est.).

NJ *or* **N.J.** *abbrev. for* New Jersey.

Njord (njɔːd) *or* **Njorth** ★ (njɔːθ) *n Norse myth.* the god of the sea, fishing, and prosperity.

Nkomo ★ (əŋˈkəʊməʊ) *n* **Joshua.** 1917–99, Zimbabwean politician; co-leader, with Robert Mugabe, of the Patriotic Front (1976–80); vice-president of Zimbabwe (1990–99).

nkosi (əŋˈkɔːsɪ) *n S. African.* a term of address to a superior; master. ORIG Nguni *inkosi* chief, lord

Nkrumah ★ (əŋˈkruːmə) *n* **Kwame** (ˈkwɑːmɪ). 1909–72, Ghanaian statesman; prime minister (1957–60) and president (1960–66).

NM *or* **N. Mex.** *abbrev. for* New Mexico.

NMR *abbrev. for* nuclear magnetic resonance.

NNE *symbol for* north-northeast.

NNP *abbrev. for* net national product.

NNW *symbol for* north-northwest.

no[1] (nəʊ) *sentence substitute.* **1** used to express denial, disagreement, refusal, etc. ◆ *n, pl* **noes** *or* **nos. 2** an answer or vote of *no.* **3 not take no for an answer.** to continue in a course of action, etc., despite refusals. **4** (*often pl*) a person who votes in the negative. **5 the noes have it.** there is a majority of votes in the negative. ORIG OE *nā,* from *ne* not, no + *ā* ever

no[2] (nəʊ) *determiner* **1** not any, not a, or not one: *there's no money left.* **2** not at all: *she's no youngster.* **3** (foll. by comparative adjectives and adverbs) not: *no less than forty; no taller than a child.* ORIG OE *nā,* from *nān* NONE

No[1] *or* **Noh** (nəʊ) *n, pl* **No** *or* **Noh.** the stylized classic drama of Japan, developed in the 15th century or earlier, using music, dancing, and themes from religious stories or myths. ORIG from Japanese *nō* talent, from Chinese *neng*

No[2] *the chemical symbol for* nobelium.

No[3] ★ (nəʊ) *n* **Lake.** a lake in the S central Sudan, where the Bahr el Jebel (White Nile) is joined by the Bahr el Ghazal. Area: about 103 sq. km (40 sq. miles).

no' (no, nəʊ) *adv Scot.* not.

No. *abbrev. for:* **1** north(ern). **2** Also: **no.** (*pl* **Nos.** *or* **nos.**) number. ORIG from L *numero* the ablative of *numerus* number

n.o. *Cricket. abbrev. for* not out.

no-account *adj* **1** worthless; good-for-nothing. ◆ *n* **2** a worthless person.

Noah ★ (ˈnəʊə) *n Old Testament.* a Hebrew patriarch, who saved himself, his family, and specimens of every animal and bird from the Flood by building a ship (**Noah's Ark**) in which they all survived (Genesis 6–8).

nob[1] (nɒb) *n Cribbage.* **1** the jack of the suit turned up. **2 one for his nob.** the call made with this jack, scoring one point. ORIG C19: from ?

nob[2] (nɒb) *n Sl., chiefly Brit.* a person of wealth or social distinction. ORIG C19: from ?

no-ball *n* **1** *Cricket.* an illegal ball, as for overstepping the crease, for which the batting side scores a run, and from which the batsman can only be out by being run out. **2** *Rounders.* an illegal ball, esp. one bowled too high or too low. ◆ *interj* **3** *Cricket, rounders.* a call by the umpire indicating a no-ball. ◆ *vb* (*tr*) **4** *Cricket.* (of an umpire) **4a** to declare (a bowler) to have bowled a no-ball. **4b** to declare (a delivery) to be a no-ball.

nobble (ˈnɒbəl) *vb* **nobbles, nobbling, nobbled.** (*tr*) *Brit. sl.* **1** to disable (a racehorse), esp. with drugs. **2** to win over or outwit (a person) by underhand means. **3** to suborn (a person, esp. a juror) by threats, bribery, etc. **4** to steal. **5** to grab. **6** to kidnap. ORIG C19: from *nobbler,* from a false division of *an hobbler* (one who hobbles horses) as *a nobbler*

Nobel ★ (nəʊˈbɛl) *n* **Alfred Bernhard** (ˈalfreːd ˈbærnhard). 1833–96, Swedish chemist and philanthropist, noted for his invention of dynamite (1866) and his bequest for the Nobel prizes.

nobelium (nəʊˈbiːlɪəm) *n* a transuranic element produced artificially from curium. Symbol: No; atomic no.: 102; half-life of most stable isotope, ^{255}No: 180 seconds (approx.). ORIG C20: NL, after *Nobel* Institute, Stockholm, where it was discovered

Nobel prize *n* a prize for outstanding contributions to chemistry, physics, physiology or medicine, literature, economics, and peace that may be awarded annually; established 1901. ORIG C20: after Alfred NOBEL

nobility (nəʊˈbɪlɪtɪ) *n, pl* **nobilities. 1** a privileged class whose titles are conferred by descent or royal decree. **2** the quality of being good; dignity: *nobility of mind.* **3** (in the British Isles) the class of people holding the title of dukes, marquesses, earls, viscounts, or barons and their feminine equivalents; peerage.

nobilmente (ˌnəʊbɪlˈmɛnteɪ) *adj, adv Music.* to be performed in a noble manner. ORIG It.

noble (ˈnəʊbəl) *adj* **1** of or relating to a hereditary class with special status, often derived from a feudal period. **2** of or characterized by high moral qualities; magnanimous: *a noble deed.* **3** having dignity or eminence; illustrious. **4** imposing; magnificent: *a noble avenue of trees.* **5** superior; excellent: *a noble strain of horses.* **6** *Chem.* **6a** (of certain elements) chemically unreactive. **6b** (of certain metals, esp. copper, silver, and gold) resisting oxidation. ◆ *n* **7** a person belonging to a privileged class whose status is usually indicated by a title. **8** (in the British Isles) a person holding the title of duke, marquess, earl, viscount, or baron, or a feminine equivalent. **9** a former British gold coin having the value of one third of a pound. ORIG C13: via OF from L *nōbilis,* orig., capable of being known, hence well-known, from *noscere* to know ► **ˈnobleness** *n* ► **ˈnobly** *adv*

nobleman (ˈnəʊbəlmən) *or* (*fem*) **noblewoman** *n, pl* **noblemen** *or* **noblewomen.** a person of noble rank, title, or status; peer; aristocrat.

noble savage *n* (in romanticism) an idealized view of primitive man.

noblesse oblige (nəʊˈblɛs əʊˈbliːʒ) *n Often ironic.* the supposed obligation of nobility to be honourable and generous. ORIG F, lit.: nobility obliges

nobody (ˈnəʊbədɪ) *pron* **1** no person; no-one. ◆ *n, pl* **nobodies. 2** an insignificant person.

> **USAGE NOTE** See at **everyone.**

no brainer *n Inf., derog.* a stupid or foolish person.

nock (nɒk) *n* **1** a notch on an arrow that fits on the bowstring. **2** either of the grooves at each end of a bow that hold the bowstring. ◆ *vb* (*tr*) **3** to fit (an arrow) on a bowstring. ORIG C14: rel. to Swedish *nock* tip

no-claims bonus *n* a reduction on an insurance premium, esp. one covering a motor vehicle, if no claims have been made within a specified period. Also called: **no-claim bonus.**

noctambulism (nɒkˈtæmbjʊˌlɪzəm) *or* **noctambulation** *n* another word for **somnambulism.** ORIG C19: from L *nox* night + *ambulāre* to walk

noctilucent (ˌnɒktɪˈluːsənt) *adj* shining at night, usually of very thin high altitude clouds observable in the summer twilight sky. ORIG from L, from *nox* night + *lūcēre* to shine

noctuid (ˈnɒktjʊɪd) *n* any of a large family of nocturnal moths that includes the underwings. ORIG C19: via NL from L *noctua* night owl, from *nox* night

noctule (ˈnɒktjuːl) *n* any of several large Old World insectivorous bats. ORIG C18: prob. from LL *noctula* small owl, from L *noctua* night owl

nocturnal (nɒkˈtɜːnəl) *adj* **1** of, used during, occurring in, or relating to the night. **2** (of animals) active at night.

3 (of plants) having flowers that open at night and close by day. ORIG C15: from LL *nocturnālis*, from L *nox* night
▸ ˌ**noctur'nality** *n* ▸ **noc'turnally** *adv*

nocturne ('nɒktɜːn) *n* **1** a short, dreamy, and melodic piece of music, esp. one for the piano. **2** a painting of a night scene.

nod (nɒd) *vb* **nods, nodding, nodded. 1** to lower and raise (the head) briefly, as to indicate agreement, etc. **2** (*tr*) to express by nodding: *she nodded approval*. **3** (*intr*) (of flowers, trees, etc.) to sway or bend forwards and back. **4** (*intr*) to let the head fall forwards through drowsiness; be almost asleep. **5** (*intr*) to be momentarily careless: *even Homer sometimes nods*. **6 nodding acquaintance.** a slight, casual, or superficial knowledge (of a subject or person). ◆ *n* **7** a quick down-and-up movement of the head, as in assent, command, etc. **8 on the nod.** *Inf.* agreed, as in committee, without formal procedure. **9** See **land of Nod.** ◆ See also **nod off.** ORIG C14 *nodde*, from ?
▸ '**nodding** *adj, n*

noddle[1] ('nɒdᵊl) *n Inf., chiefly Brit.* the head or brains: *use your noddle!* ORIG C15: from ?

noddle[2] ('nɒdᵊl) *vb* **noddles, noddling, noddled.** *Inf., chiefly Brit.* to nod (the head), as through drowsiness. ORIG C18: from NOD

noddy[1] ('nɒdɪ) *n, pl* **noddies. 1** any of several tropical terns, typically having a dark plumage. **2** a fool or dunce. ORIG C16: ? n use of obs. *noddy* foolish, drowsy, ?from NOD (vb); the bird is so called because it allows itself to be caught by hand

noddy[2] ('nɒdɪ) *n, pl* **noddies.** (*usually pl*) *Television.* film footage of an interviewer's reactions to comments made by an interviewee, used in editing the interview after it has been recorded. ORIG C20: from NOD

node (nəʊd) *n* **1** a knot, swelling, or knob. **2** the point on a plant stem from which the leaves or lateral branches grow. **3** *Physics.* a point at which the amplitude of one of the two kinds of displacement in a standing wave has zero or minimum value. **4** Also called: **crunode.** *Maths.* a point at which two branches of a curve intersect. **5** *Maths., linguistics.* one of the objects of which a graph or a tree consists. **6** *Astron.* either of the two points at which the orbit of a body intersects the plane of the ecliptic. **7** *Anat.* any natural bulge or swelling, such as those along the course of a lymphatic vessel (**lymph node**). **8** *Computing.* an interconnection point on a computer network. ORIG C16: from L *nōdus* knot
▸ '**nodal** *adj*

nod off *vb* (*intr, adv*) *Inf.* to fall asleep.

nodule ('nɒdjuːl) *n* **1** a small knot, lump, or node. **2** any of the knoblike outgrowths on the roots of clover and other legumes that contain bacteria involved in nitrogen fixation. **3** a small rounded lump of rock or mineral substance, esp. in a matrix of different rock material. ORIG C17: from L *nōdulus*, from *nōdus* knot
▸ '**nodular,** '**nodulose,** *or* '**nodulous** *adj*

Noel *or* **Noël** (nəʊ'ɛl) *n* (in carols, etc.) another word for **Christmas.** ORIG C19: from F, from L *nātālis* a birthday

noetic (nəʊ'ɛtɪk) *adj* of or relating to the mind. ORIG C17: from Gk *noētikos*, from *noein* to think

Nofretete ★ (ˌnɒfrɛ'tiːtɪ) *n* a variant of **Nefertiti.**

nog *or* **nogg** (nɒg) *n* **1** Also called: **flip.** a drink, esp. an alcoholic one, containing beaten egg. **2** *East Anglian dialect.* strong local beer. ORIG C17 (orig.: a strong beer): from ?

noggin ('nɒgɪn) *n* **1** a small quantity of spirits. **2** a small mug. **3** *Inf.* the head. ORIG C17: from ?

no-go area *n* a district in a town that is barricaded off, usually by a paramilitary organization, which the police, army, etc., can only enter by force.

Noh (nəʊ) *n* a variant spelling of **No**[1].

noir (nwɑː) *adj* (of a film) showing characteristics of a *film noir*, in plot or style. ORIG C20: from French, lit.: black

noise (nɔɪz) *n* **1** a sound, esp. one that is loud or disturbing. **2** loud shouting; clamour; din. **3** any undesired electrical disturbance in a circuit, etc. **4** undesired or irrelevant elements in a visual image: *removing noise from pictures*. **5** (*pl*) conventional comments or sounds conveying a reaction: *sympathetic noises*. **6 make a noise.** to talk a great deal or complain (about). ◆ *vb* **noises, noising, noised. 7** (*tr*; usually foll. by *abroad* or *about*) to spread (news, gossip, etc.). ORIG C13: from OF, from L: NAUSEA

noiseless ('nɔɪzlɪs) *adj* making little or no sound.
▸ '**noiselessly** *adv* ▸ '**noiselessness** *n*

noise pollution *n* annoying or harmful noise in an environment.

noisette (nwɑː'zɛt) *adj* **1** flavoured with hazelnuts. **2** nutbrown, as butter browned over heat. ◆ *n* **3** a small round or oval piece of meat. **4** a hazelnut chocolate. ORIG from F: hazelnut

noisome ('nɔɪsəm) *adj* **1** (esp. of smells) offensive. **2** harmful or noxious. ORIG C14: from obs. *noy*, var. of ANNOY + -SOME[1]
▸ '**noisomeness** *n*

noisy ('nɔɪzɪ) *adj* **noisier, noisiest. 1** making a loud or constant noise. **2** full of or characterized by noise.
▸ '**noisily** *adv* ▸ '**noisiness** *n*

Nolan ★ ('nəʊlən) *n* Sir **Sidney.** 1917–92, Australian painter.

nolens volens *Latin.* ('nəʊlɛnz 'vəʊlɛnz) *adv* whether willing or unwilling.

nolle prosequi ('nɒlɪ 'prɒsɪˌkwaɪ) *n Law.* an entry made on the court record when the plaintiff or prosecutor undertakes not to continue the action or prosecution. ORIG L: do not pursue

nomad ('nəʊmæd) *n* **1** a member of a people or tribe who move from place to place to find pasture and food. **2** a wanderer. ORIG C16: via F from L *nomas* wandering shepherd, from Gk
▸ **no'madic** *adj* ▸ '**nomadism** *n*

no-man's-land *n* **1** land between boundaries, esp. an unoccupied zone between opposing forces. **2** an unowned or unclaimed piece of land. **3** an ambiguous area of activity.

nom de guerre ('nɒm də 'gɛə) *n, pl* **noms de guerre** ('nɒm də 'gɛə). an assumed name. ORIG F, lit.: war name

nom de plume ('nɒm də 'pluːm) *n, pl* **noms de plume** ('nɒm də 'pluːm). another term for **pen name.** ORIG F

nomenclature (nəʊ'mɛnklətʃə; *US.* 'nəʊmənˌkleɪtʃər) *n* the terminology used in a particular science, art, activity, etc. ORIG C17: from L *nōmenclātūra* list of names

nominal ('nɒmɪnᵊl) *adj* **1** in name only; theoretical: *the nominal leader*. **2** minimal in comparison with real worth; token: *a nominal fee*. **3** of, constituting, or giving a name. **4** *Grammar.* of or relating to a noun or noun phrase. ◆ *n* **5** *Grammar.* a noun, noun phrase, or syntactically similar structure. ORIG C15: from L *nōminālis*, from *nōmen* name
▸ '**nominally** *adv*

nominalism ('nɒmɪnᵊˌlɪzəm) *n* the philosophical theory that the variety of objects to which a single general name, such as *dog*, applies have nothing in common other than that name.
▸ '**nominalist** *n*

nominal value *n* another name for **par value.**

nominate ('nɒmɪˌneɪt) *vb* **nominates, nominating, nominated.** (*mainly tr*) **1** to propose as a candidate, esp. for an elective office. **2** to appoint to an office or position. **3** to name (someone) to act on one's behalf, esp. to conceal one's identity. **4** (*intr*) *Austral.* to stand as a candidate in an election. ORIG C16: from L *nōmināre* to call by name, from *nōmen* name
▸ ˌ**nomi'nation** *n* ▸ '**nomiˌnator** *n*

nominative ('nɒmɪnətɪv) *adj* **1** *Grammar.* denoting a case of nouns and pronouns in inflected languages that is used esp. to identify the subject of a finite verb. **2** appointed rather than elected to a position, office, etc. ◆ *n* **3** *Grammar.* **3a** the nominative case. **3b** a word or speech element in the nominative case. ORIG C14: from L *nōminātīvus* belonging to naming, from *nōmen* name
▸ **nominatival** (ˌnɒmɪnə'taɪvᵊl) *adj*

nominee (ˌnɒmɪ'niː) *n* **1** a person who is nominated to an office or as a candidate. **2a** a person or organization named to act on behalf of someone else, esp. to conceal the identity of the nominator. **2b** (*as modifier*): *nominee shareholder.* ORIG C17: from NOMINATE + -EE

nomogram ('nɒmə,græm, 'nəʊmə-) *or* **nomograph** *n* an arrangement of two linear or logarithmic scales such that an intersecting straight line enables intermediate values or values on a third scale to be read off. ORIG C20: from Gk *nomos* law + -GRAM

-nomy *n combining form.* indicating a science or the laws governing a certain field of knowledge: *agronomy; economy.* ORIG from Gk *-nomia* law
▸ **-nomic** *adj combining form.*

non- *prefix* **1** indicating negation: *nonexistent.* **2** indicating refusal or failure: *noncooperation.* **3** indicating exclusion from a specified class: *nonfiction.* **4** indicating lack or absence: *nonobjective; nonevent.* ORIG from L *nōn* not

nonaddictive (,nɒnə'dɪktɪv) *adj* (of a drug, etc.) not causing addiction.

nonage ('nəʊnɪdʒ) *n* **1** *Law.* the state of being under any of various ages at which a person may legally enter into certain transactions, such as marrying, etc. **2** any period of immaturity.

nonagenarian (,nəʊnədʒɪ'nɛərɪən) *n* **1** a person who is from 90 to 99 years old. ◆ *adj* **2** of, relating to, or denoting a nonagenarian. ORIG C19: from L *nōnāgēnārius,* from *nōnāginta* ninety

nonaggression (,nɒnə'grɛʃən) *n* **a** restraint of aggression, esp. between states. **b** (*as modifier*): *a nonaggression pact.*

nonagon ('nɒnə,gɒn) *n* a polygon having nine sides.
▸ **nonagonal** (nɒn'ægən^{ə}l) *adj*

nonalcoholic (,nɒn,ælkə'hɒl'ɪk) *adj* (of a drink, etc.) not containing alcohol.

nonaligned (,nɒnə'laɪnd) *adj* (of states, etc.) not part of a major alliance or power bloc.
▸ **,nona'lignment** *n*

non-A, non-B hepatitis *n* the former name for **hepatitis C.**

nonce (nɒns) *n* the present time or occasion (now only in **for the nonce**). ORIG C12: from *for the nonce,* a mistaken division of *for then anes,* from *then* dative singular of *the* + *anes* ONCE

nonce word *n* a word coined for a single occasion.

nonchalant ('nɒnʃələnt) *adj* casually unconcerned or indifferent; uninvolved. ORIG C18: from F, from *nonchaloir* to lack warmth, from NON- + *chaloir* from L *calēre* to be warm
▸ **'nonchalance** *n*

non-com ('nɒn,kɒm) *n* short for **noncommissioned officer.**

noncombatant (nɒn'kɒmbətənt) *n* **1** a civilian in time of war. **2** a member of the armed forces whose duties do not include fighting, such as a chaplain or surgeon.

noncommissioned officer (,nɒnkə'mɪʃənd) *n* (in the armed forces) a person, such as a sergeant or corporal, who is appointed from the ranks as a subordinate officer.

noncommittal (,nɒnkə'mɪt^{ə}l) *adj* not involving or revealing commitment to any particular opinion or action.

non compos mentis *Latin.* ('nɒn 'kɒmpəs 'mɛntɪs) *adj* mentally incapable of managing one's own affairs; of unsound mind. ORIG L: not in control of one's mind

nonconformist (,nɒnkən'fɔːmɪst) *n* **1** a person who does not conform to generally accepted patterns of behaviour or thought. ◆ *adj* **2** of or characterized by behaviour that does not conform to accepted patterns.
▸ **,noncon'formity** *or* **,noncon'formism** *n*

Nonconformist (,nɒnkən'fɔːmɪst) *n* **1** a member of a Protestant denomination that dissents from an Established Church, esp. the Church of England. ◆ *adj* **2** of, relating to, or denoting Nonconformists.
▸ **,Noncon'formity** *or* **,Noncon'formism** *n*

noncontributory (,nɒnkən'trɪbjʊtərɪ) *adj* **1** denoting an insurance or pension scheme for employees, the premiums of which are paid by the employer. **2** (of a state benefit) not dependent on national insurance contributions.

nondenominational (,nɒndɪ,nɒmɪ'neɪʃən^{ə}l) *adj* not restricted with regard to religious denomination.

nondescript ('nɒndɪ,skrɪpt) *adj* **1** having no outstanding features. ◆ *n* **2** a nondescript person or thing. ORIG C17: from NON- + L *dēscriptus,* p.p. of *dēscribere* to copy

nondomiciled (nɒn'dɒmɪ,saɪld) *adj* of, relating to, or denoting a person who is not domiciled in his country of origin.

none[1] (nʌn) *pron* **1** not any of a particular class: *none of my letters has arrived.* **2** no-one; nobody: *there was none to tell the tale.* **3** not any (of): *none of it looks edible.* **4 none other.** no other person: *none other than the Queen herself.* **5 none the.** (*foll. by a comparative adj*) in no degree: *she was none the worse for her ordeal.* **6 none too.** not very: *he was none too pleased.* ORIG OE *nān,* lit.: not one

none[2] (nəʊn) *n* another word for **nones.**

nonentity (nɒn'ɛntɪtɪ) *n, pl* **nonentities.** **1** an insignificant person or thing. **2** a nonexistent thing. **3** the state of not existing; nonexistence.

nones (nəʊnz) *n* (*functioning as sing or pl*) **1** (in the Roman calendar) the ninth day before the ides of each month: the seventh day of March, May, July, and October, and the fifth of each other month. **2** *Chiefly RC Church.* the fifth of the seven canonical hours of the divine office, originally fixed at the ninth hour of the day, about 3 p.m. ORIG OE *nōn,* from L *nōna hora* ninth hour, from *nōnus* ninth

nonesuch *or* **nonsuch** ('nʌn,sʌtʃ) *n Arch.* a matchless person or thing; nonpareil.

nonet (nəʊ'nɛt) *n* **1** a piece of music for nine instruments or voices. **2** a group of nine singers or instrumentalists.

nonetheless (,nʌnðə'lɛs) *sentence connector.* despite that; however; nevertheless.

non-Euclidean geometry *n* the branch of modern geometry in which certain axioms of Euclidean geometry are denied.

nonevent (,nɒnɪ'vɛnt) *n* a disappointing or insignificant occurrence, esp. one predicted to be important.

nonexecutive director (,nɒnɪg'zɛkjʊtɪv) *n* a director of a commercial company who is not a full-time employee of the company.

nonexistent (,nɒnɪg'zɪstənt) *adj* **1** not having being or reality. **2** not present under specified conditions or in a specified place.
▸ **nonex'istence** *n*

nonfeasance (nɒn'fiːz^{ə}ns) *n Law.* a failure to act when under an obligation to do so. Cf. **malfeasance, misfeasance.** ORIG C16: from NON- + *feasance* (obs.) doing, from F *faisance,* from *faire* to do, L *facere*

nonferrous (nɒn'fɛrəs) *adj* **1** denoting any metal other than iron. **2** not containing iron.

nonflammable (nɒn'flæməb^{ə}l) *adj* incapable of burning or not easily set on fire.

nonfunctional (,nɒn'fʌŋkʃən^{ə}l) *adj* not having a function.

nong (nɒŋ) *n Austral. sl.* a stupid or incompetent person. ORIG C19: ?from obs. E dialect *nigmenog* silly fellow, from ?

non-Hodgkin's lymphoma *n* any form of lymphoma other than Hodgkin's disease.

nonillion (nəʊ'nɪljən) *n* **1** (in Britain, France, and Germany) the number represented as one followed by 54 zeros (10^{54}). **2** (in the US and Canada) the number represented as one followed by 30 zeros (10^{30}). Brit. word: **quintillion.** ORIG C17: from F, from L *nōnus* ninth, on the model of MILLION

nonintervention (,nɒnɪntə'vɛnʃən) *n* refusal to intervene, esp. the abstention by a state from intervening in the affairs of other states or in its own internal disputes.

noninvasive (,nɒnɪn'veɪsɪv) *adj* (of medical treatment) not involving the making of a relatively large incision in the body or the insertion of instruments, etc., into the patient.

nonjudgmental (,nɒndʒʌdʒ'mɛnt^{ə}l) *adj* avoiding moral judgments, esp. relating to the conduct of others.

nonjuror (nɒnˈdʒʊərə) *n* a person who refuses to take an oath, as of allegiance.

Nonjuror (nɒnˈdʒʊərə) *n* any of a group of clergy in England and Scotland who declined to take the oath of allegiance to William and Mary in 1689.

nonlinear (ˌnɒnˈlɪnɪə) *adj* not linear, esp. with regard to dimension.

nonmetal (nɒnˈmɛtᵊl) *n* any of a number of chemical elements that have acidic oxides and are poor conductors of heat and electricity.
▸ **ˌnonmeˈtallic** *adj*

nonmoral (nɒnˈmɒrəl) *adj* not involving morality or ethics; neither moral nor immoral.

Nono ★ (*Italian* ˈnɔːno) *n* **Luigi** (luˈiːdʒi). 1924–90, Italian composer of 12-tone music.

nonobjective (ˌnɒnəbˈdʒɛktɪv) *adj* of or designating an art movement in which things are depicted in an abstract or purely formalized way.

no-nonsense (ˌnəʊˈnɒnsəns) *adj* sensible, practical, and straightforward: *a severe no-nonsense look.*

nonpareil (ˈnɒnpərəl, ˌnɒnpəˈreɪl) *n* a person or thing that is unsurpassed; peerless example. ORIG C15: from F, from NON- + *pareil* similar

nonpersistent (ˌnɒnpəˈsɪstənt) *adj* (of pesticides) breaking down rapidly after application; not persisting in the environment.

non-person *n* a person regarded as nonexistent or unimportant; a nonentity.

nonplus (nɒnˈplʌs) *vb* **nonplusses, nonplussing, nonplussed** *or US* **nonpluses, nonplusing, nonplused. 1** (*tr*) to put at a loss; confound. ◆ *n, pl* **nonpluses. 2** a state of utter perplexity prohibiting action or speech. ORIG C16: from L *nōn plūs* no further

nonprofessional (ˌnɒnprəˈfɛʃənᵊl) *adj* **1** not professional in status. ◆ *n* **2** a person who is not a professional.

non-profit-making *adj* not yielding a profit, esp. because organized or established for some other reason: *a non-profit-making organization.*

nonproliferation (ˌnɒnprəˌlɪfəˈreɪʃən) *n* **a** limitation of the production or spread of something, esp. nuclear or chemical weapons. **b** (*as modifier*): *a nonproliferation treaty.*

non-pros (ˌnɒnˈprɒs) *n* **1** short for **non prosequitur.** ◆ *vb* **non-prosses, non-prossing, non-prossed. 2** (*tr*) to enter a judgment of non prosequitur against (a plaintiff).

non prosequitur (ˈnɒn prəʊˈsɛkwɪtə) *n Law.* (formerly) a judgment in favour of a defendant when the plaintiff failed to take the necessary steps in an action within the time allowed. ORIG L, lit.: he does not prosecute

nonracial (ˌnɒnˈreɪʃəl) *adj* not involving race or racial factors.

nonrepresentational (ˌnɒnrɛprɪzɛnˈteɪʃənᵊl) *adj Art.* another word for **abstract.**

nonresident (nɒnˈrɛzɪdənt) *n* **1** a person who is not residing in the place implied or specified. **2** a British person employed abroad for a minimum of one year, who is exempt from UK income tax provided that he does not spend more than 90 days in the UK during that tax year. ◆ *adj* **3** not residing in the place specified.
▸ **nonˈresidence** *or* **nonˈresidency** *n* ▸ **ˌnonresiˈdential** *adj*

nonresistant (ˌnɒnrɪˈzɪstənt) *adj* **1** incapable of resisting something, such as a disease; susceptible. **2** *History.* (esp. in 17th-century England) practising passive obedience to royal authority even when its commands were unjust.

nonrestrictive (ˌnɒnrɪˈstrɪktɪv) *adj* **1** not limiting. **2** *Grammar.* denoting a relative clause that is not restrictive. Cf. **restrictive** (sense 2).

nonsense (ˈnɒnsəns) *n* **1** something that has or makes no sense; unintelligible language; drivel. **2** conduct or action that is absurd. **3** foolish behaviour: *she'll stand no nonsense.* **4** things of little or no value; trash. ◆ *interj* **5** an exclamation of disagreement.
▸ **nonsensical** (nɒnˈsɛnsɪkᵊl) *adj* ▸ **nonˈsensically** *adv*
▸ **nonˈsensicalness** *or* **nonˌsensiˈcality** *n*

nonsense verse *n* verse in which the sense is nonexistent or absurd.

non sequitur (ˈnɒn ˈsɛkwɪtə) *n* **1** a statement having little or no relevance to what preceded it. **2** *Logic.* a conclusion that does not follow from the premises. ORIG L, lit.: it does not follow

nonsmoker (nɒnˈsməʊkə) *n* **1** a person who does not smoke. **2** a train compartment in which smoking is forbidden.
▸ **nonˈsmoking** *adj*

nonspecific urethritis *n* inflammation of the urethra as a result of a sexually transmitted infection that cannot be traced to a specific cause. Abbrev.: **NSU.**

nonstandard (nɒnˈstændəd) *adj* **1** denoting or characterized by idiom, vocabulary, etc., that is not regarded as correct and acceptable by educated native speakers of a language; not standard. **2** deviating from a given standard.

nonstarter (nɒnˈstɑːtə) *n* **1** a horse that fails to run in a race for which it has been entered. **2** a person or thing that has little chance of success.

nonstick (ˈnɒnˈstɪk) *adj* (of saucepans, etc.) coated with a substance that prevents food sticking to them.

nonstop (ˈnɒnˈstɒp) *adj, adv* done without pause or interruption: *a nonstop flight.*

nonsuch (ˈnʌnˌsʌtʃ) *n* a variant spelling of **nonesuch.**

nonsuit (nɒnˈsuːt) *Law.* ◆ *n* **1** an order of a judge dismissing a suit when the plaintiff fails to show he has a good cause of action or fails to produce any evidence. ◆ *vb* **2** (*tr*) to order the dismissal of the suit of (a person).

nontechnical (ˌnɒnˈtɛknɪkᵊl) *adj* **1** not technical in nature. **2** (of a person) not having technical knowledge or aptitude.

non troppo (ˈnɒn ˈtrɒpəʊ) *adv Music.* (preceded by a direction, esp. a tempo marking) not to be observed too strictly (esp. in **allegro ma non troppo, adagio ma non troppo**). ORIG It.

non-U (nɒnˈjuː) *adj Brit. inf.* (esp. of language) not characteristic of or used by the upper class.

nonunion (nɒnˈjuːnjən) *adj* **1** not belonging or related to a trade union: *nonunion workers.* **2** not favouring or employing union labour: *a nonunion shop.* **3** not produced by union labour.

nonvoter (nɒnˈvəʊtə) *n* **1** a person who does not vote. **2** a person not eligible to vote.

nonvoting (nɒnˈvəʊtɪŋ) *adj* **1** of or relating to a nonvoter. **2** *Finance.* (of shares, etc.) not entitling the holder to vote at company meetings.

noodle[1] (ˈnuːdᵊl) *n* (*often pl*) pasta in the form of ribbons or fine strands. ORIG C18: from G *Nudel* from ?

noodle[2] (ˈnuːdᵊl) *n* **1** *US & Canad. sl.* the head. **2** a simpleton. ORIG C18: ? a blend of NODDLE[1] & NOODLE[1]

nook (nʊk) *n* **1** a corner or narrow recess. **2** a secluded or sheltered place. ORIG C13: from ?

nooky *or* **nookie** (ˈnʊkɪ) *n Sl.* lovemaking.

noon (nuːn) *n* **1** the middle of the day; 12 o'clock. **2** *Poetic.* the most important part; culmination. ORIG OE *nōn,* from L *nōna* (*hōra*) ninth hour (orig. 3 p.m., the ninth hour from sunrise)

noonday (ˈnuːnˌdeɪ) *n* the middle of the day; noon.

no-one *or* **no one** *pron* no person; nobody.

USAGE NOTE See at **everyone.**

noontime (ˈnuːnˌtaɪm) *or* **noontide** *n* the middle of the day; noon.

Noordbrabant ★ (noːrdˈbraːbɑnt) *n* the Dutch name for **North Brabant.**

Noordholland ★ (noːrtˈhɔlɑnt) *n* the Dutch name for **North Holland.**

noose (nuːs) *n* **1** a loop in the end of a rope, such as a lasso or hangman's halter, usually tied with a slipknot. **2** something that restrains or traps. **3 put one's head in a noose.** to bring about one's own downfall. ◆ *vb* **nooses, noosing, noosed.** (*tr*) **4** to secure as in a noose. **5** to make a noose of or in. ORIG C15: ?from Provençal *nous,* from L *nōdus* NODE

no-par *adj* (of securities) without a par value.

nor (nɔː; *unstressed* nə) *conj* (*coordinating*) **1** (used to join alternatives, the first of which is preceded by *neither*) and not: *neither measles nor mumps.* **2** (foll. by a verb) (and) not...either: *they weren't talented — nor were they particularly funny.* **3** *Poetic.* neither: *nor wind nor rain.* ORIG C13: contraction of OE *nōther,* from *nāhwæther* NEITHER

Nor. *abbrev. for:* **1** Norman. **2** north. **3** Norway. **4** Norwegian.

noradrenaline (ˌnɔːrəˈdrɛnəlɪn, -liːn) *or* **noradrenalin** *n* a hormone secreted by the adrenal medulla, increasing blood pressure and heart rate. US name: **norepinephrine.**

NOR circuit *or* **gate** (nɔː) *n Computing.* a logic circuit having two or more input wires and one output wire that has a high-voltage output signal only if all input signals are at a low voltage. Cf. **AND circuit.** ORIG C20: from NOR; the action performed is similar to the operation of the conjunction *nor* in logic

Nord ★ (*French* nɔr) *n* a department of N France, in Nord-Pas-de-Calais region. Capital: Lille. Pop.: 2 553 939 (1994 est.). Area: 5774 sq. km (2252 sq. miles).

Nordenskjöld ★ (*Swedish* ˈnuːrdənʃœld) *n* Baron **Nils Adolf Erik** (nils ˈɑːdɔlf ˈeːrik). 1832–1901, Swedish Arctic explorer and geologist, born in Finland. He was the first to navigate the Northeast Passage (1878–79).

Nordenskjöld Sea ★ *n* the former name of the **Laptev Sea.** ORIG named after N. A. E. NORDENSKJÖLD

nordic (ˈnɔːdɪk) *adj Skiing.* of competitions in cross-country racing and ski-jumping. Cf. **alpine** (sense 4).

Nordic (ˈnɔːdɪk) *adj* of or belonging to a subdivision of the Caucasoid race typified by the tall blond blue-eyed long-headed inhabitants of Scandinavia. ORIG C19: from F *nordique,* from *nord* NORTH

Nordkyn Cape ★ (*Norwegian* ˈnuːrçyːn) *n* a cape in N Norway: the northernmost point of the European mainland.

Nord-Pas-de-Calais ★ (*French* nɔrpɑdəkalɛ) *n* a region of N France, on the Straits of Dover (the **Pas de Calais**): coal-mining, textile, and metallurgical industries.

Nordrhein-Westfalen ★ (ˈnɔrtrainvɛstˈfaːlən) *n* the German name for **North Rhine-Westphalia.**

norepinephrine (ˌnɔːrɛpɪˈnɛfrɪn, -riːn) *n* the US name for **noradrenaline.**

Norfolk ★ (ˈnɔːfək) *n* **1** a county of E England, on the North Sea and the Wash: low-lying, with large areas of fens in the west and the Broads in the east; rich agriculturally. Administrative centre: Norwich. Pop.: 768 500 (1994 est.). Area: 5368 sq. km (2072 sq. miles). **2** a port in SE Virginia, on the Elizabeth River and Hampton Roads: headquarters of the US Atlantic fleet; shipbuilding. Pop.: 233 430 (1996 est.).

Norfolk Island ★ *n* an island in the S Pacific, between New Caledonia and N New Zealand: an Australian external territory; discovered by Captain Cook in 1774; a penal settlement in early years. Pop.: 2665 (1993). Area: 36 sq. km (14 sq. miles).

Norfolk jacket *n* a man's single-breasted belted jacket with one or two chest pockets and a box pleat down the back. ORIG C19: worn in NORFOLK for duck shooting

Norge ★ (ˈnɔrgə) *n* the Norwegian name for **Norway.**

noria (ˈnɔːrɪə) *n* a water wheel with buckets attached to its rim for raising water from a stream into irrigation canals, etc. ORIG C18: via Sp. from Ar. *nā'ūra,* from *na'ara* to creak

Noricum ★ (ˈnɒrɪkəm) *n* an Alpine kingdom of the Celts, south of the Danube: comprises present-day central Austria and parts of Bavaria; a Roman province from about 16 B.C.

nork (nɔːk) *n* (*usually pl*) *Austral. taboo sl.* a female breast. ORIG C20: from ?

norm (nɔːm) *n* **1** an average level of achievement or performance, as of a group. **2** a standard of achievement or behaviour that is required, desired, or designated as normal. ORIG C19: from L *norma* carpenter's square

normal (ˈnɔːmᵊl) *adj* **1** usual; regular; common; typical: *the normal level.* **2** constituting a standard: *if we take this as normal.* **3** *Psychol.* **3a** being within certain limits of intelligence, ability, etc. **3b** conforming to the conventions of one's group. **4** (of laboratory animals) maintained in a natural state for purposes of comparison with animals treated with drugs, etc. **5** *Chem.* (of a solution) containing a number of grams equal to the equivalent weight of the solute in each litre of solvent. **6** *Geom.* another word for **perpendicular** (sense 1). ◆ *n* **7** the usual, average, or typical state, degree, form, etc. **8** anything that is normal. **9** *Geom.* a perpendicular line or plane. ORIG C16: from L *normālis* conforming to the carpenter's square, from *norma* NORM

▸ **normality** (nɔːˈmælɪtɪ) *or esp. US* ˈ**normalcy** *n*

normal curve *n Statistics.* a symmetrical bell-shaped curve representing the probability density function of a normal distribution.

normal distribution *n Statistics.* a continuous distribution of a random variable with its mean, median, and mode equal.

normalize *or* **normalise** (ˈnɔːməˌlaɪz) *vb* **normalizes, normalizing, normalized** *or* **normalises, normalising, normalised.** (*tr*) **1** to bring or make into the normal state. **2** to bring into conformity with a standard. **3** to heat (steel) above a critical temperature and allow it to cool in air to relieve internal stresses; anneal.

▸ ˌ**normaliˈzation** *or* ˌ**normaliˈsation** *n*

normally (ˈnɔːməlɪ) *adv* **1** as a rule; usually; ordinarily. **2** in a normal manner.

Norman[1] (ˈnɔːmən) *n* **1** (in the Middle Ages) a member of the people of Normandy in N France, descended from the 10th-century Scandinavian conquerors of the country and the native French. **2** a native or inhabitant of Normandy. **3** another name for **Norman French.** ◆ *adj* **4** of or characteristic of the Normans, esp. the Norman kings of England and the Norman people living in England, or their dialect of French. **5** of or characteristic of Normandy. **6** denoting or having the style of Romanesque architecture used in Britain from the Norman Conquest until the 12th century, characterized by the rounded arch, massive masonry walls, etc.

Norman[2] ★ (ˈnɔːmən) *n* **1 Greg.** born 1955, Australian golfer. **2 Jessye** (ˈdʒɛsɪ). born 1945, US soprano.

Norman Conquest *n* the invasion and settlement of England by the Normans, following the Battle of Hastings (1066).

Normandy ★ (ˈnɔːməndɪ) *n* a former province of N France, on the English Channel: settled by Vikings under Rollo in the 10th century; scene of the Allied landings in 1944. Chief town: Rouen. French name: **Normandie** (nɔrmɑ̃di).

Norman French *n* the medieval Norman and English dialect of Old French.

normative (ˈnɔːmətɪv) *adj* **1** implying, creating, or prescribing a norm or standard, as in language: *normative grammar.* **2** expressing value judgments as contrasted with stating facts.

Norn[1] ★ (nɔːn) *n Norse myth.* any of the three virgin goddesses of fate. ORIG C18: ON

Norn[2] (nɔːn) *n* the medieval Norse language of the Orkneys, Shetlands, and parts of N Scotland. ORIG C17: from ON *norrœna* Norwegian, from *northr* north

Norodom Sihanouk ★ (ˌnɒrəˈdɒm ˈsiːənuk) *n* See (Norodom) **Sihanouk.**

Norrköping ★ (*Swedish* ˈnɔrtçøːpiŋ) *n* a port in SE Sweden, near the Baltic. Pop.: 123 531 (1997 est.).

Norse (nɔːs) *adj* **1** of ancient and medieval Scandinavia or its inhabitants. **2** of or characteristic of Norway. ◆ *n* **3a** the N group of Germanic languages, spoken in Scandinavia. **3b** any one of these languages, esp. in their ancient or medieval forms. **4 the Norse.** (*functioning as pl*) **4a** the Norwegians. **4b** the Vikings.

Norseman (ˈnɔːsmən) *n, pl* **Norsemen.** another name for a **Viking.**

north (nɔːθ) *n* **1** one of the four cardinal points of the compass, at 0° or 360°, that is 90° from east and west and 180° from south. **2** the direction along a meridian towards the North Pole. **3** the direction in which a compass needle points; magnetic north. **4** **the north.** (*often cap.*) any area lying in or towards the north. **5** (*usually cap.*) *Cards.* the player or position at the table corresponding to north on the compass. ◆ *adj* **6** in, towards, or facing the north. **7** (esp. of the wind) from the north. ◆ *adv* **8** in, to, or towards the north. ORIG OE

North[1] (nɔːθ) *n* **the.** **1** the northern area of England, generally regarded as reaching the southern boundaries of Yorkshire, Derbyshire, and Cheshire. **2** (in the US) the states north of the Mason-Dixon Line that were known as the Free States during the Civil War. **3** the northern part of North America, esp. Alaska, the Yukon, Nunavut, and the Northwest Territories. **4** the countries of the world that are economically and technically advanced. ◆ *adj* **5** of or denoting the northern part of a specified country, area, etc.

North[2] ★ (nɔːθ) *n* **1** **Frederick,** 2nd Earl of Guildford, called *Lord North.* 1732–92, British statesman; prime minister (1770–82), dominated by George III. He was held responsible for the loss of the American colonies. **2** Sir **Thomas.** ?1535–?1601, English translator of Plutarch's *Lives* (1579), which was the chief source of Shakespeare's Roman plays.

North Africa ★ *n* the part of Africa between the Mediterranean and the Sahara: consists chiefly of Morocco, Algeria, Tunisia, Libya, and N Egypt.
▸ **North African** *adj, n*

Northallerton ★ (nɔːˈθæləteⁿ) *n* a market town in N England, administrative centre of North Yorkshire. Pop.: 13 774 (1991).

North America ★ *n* the third largest continent, linked with South America by the Isthmus of Panama and bordering on the Arctic Ocean, the N Pacific, the N Atlantic, the Gulf of Mexico, and the Caribbean. It consists generally of a great mountain system (the Western Cordillera) extending along the entire W coast, actively volcanic in the extreme north and south, with the Great Plains to the east and the Appalachians still further east, separated from the Canadian Shield by an arc of large lakes (Great Bear, Great Slave, Winnipeg, Superior, Michigan, Huron, Erie, Ontario); reaches its greatest height of 6194 m (20 320 ft) in Mount McKinley, Alaska, and its lowest point of 85 m (280 ft) below sea level in Death Valley, California, and ranges from snowfields, tundra, and taiga in the north to deserts in the southwest and tropical forests in the extreme south. Pop.: 421 006 000 (1996 est.). Area: over 24 000 000 sq. km (9 500 000 sq. miles).
▸ **North American** *adj, n*

Northampton ★ (nɔːˈθæmptən, nɔːθˈhæmp-) *n* **1** a town in central England, administrative centre of Northamptonshire, on the River Nene: footwear and engineering industries. Pop.: 179 596 (1991). **2** short for **Northamptonshire.**

Northamptonshire ★ (nɔːˈθæmptənˌʃɪə, -ʃə, nɔːθˈhæmp-) *n* a county of central England: agriculture, food processing, engineering. Administrative centre: Northampton. Pop.: 604 400 (1996 est.). Area: 2367 sq. km (914 sq. miles). Abbrev.: **Northants.**

Northants (nɔːˈθænts) *abbrev. for* Northamptonshire.

North Atlantic Drift *or* **Current** *n* the warm ocean current flowing northeast, under the influence of prevailing winds, from the Gulf of Mexico towards NW Europe and warming its climate. Also called: **Gulf Stream.**

North Ayrshire ★ *n* a council area of W central Scotland, on the Firth of Clyde. Administrative centre: Irvine. Pop.: 139 020 (1996 est.). Area: 884 sq. km (341 sq. miles).

North Borneo ★ *n* the former name (until 1963) of **Sabah.**

northbound (ˈnɔːθˌbaʊnd) *adj* going or leading towards the north.

North Brabant ★ *n* a province of the S Netherlands: formed part of the medieval duchy of Brabant. Capital: 's Hertogenbosch. Pop.: 2 304 100 (1997 est.). Area: 4965 sq. km (1917 sq. miles). Dutch name: **Noordbrabant.**

north by east *n* one point on the compass east of north.

north by west *n* one point on the compass west of north.

North Cape ★ *n* **1** a cape on N Magerøy Island, in the Arctic Ocean off the N coast of Norway. **2** a cape on N North Island, New Zealand.

North Carolina ★ *n* a state of the southeastern US, on the Atlantic: consists of a coastal plain rising to the Piedmont Plateau and the Appalachian Mountains in the west. Capital: Raleigh. Pop.: 7 546 493 (1998 est.). Area: 126 387 sq. km (48 798 sq. miles). Abbrevs.: **N.C.** or (with zip code) **NC**
▸ **North Carolinian** *adj, n*

North Channel ★ *n* a strait between NE Ireland and SW Scotland, linking the North Atlantic with the Irish Sea.

Northcliffe ★ (ˈnɔːθklɪf) *n* **Viscount.** title of *Alfred Charles William Harmsworth.* 1865–1922, British newspaper proprietor. With his brother, 1st Viscount Rothermere, he built up a chain of newspapers.

North Country *n* (usually preceded by *the*) **1** another name for **North**[1] (sense 1). **2** another name for **North**[1] (sense 3).

Northd *abbrev. for* Northumberland.

North Dakota ★ *n* a state of the western US: mostly undulating prairies and plains, rising from the Red River valley in the east to the Missouri plateau in the west, with the infertile Bad Lands in the extreme west. Capital: Bismarck. Pop.: 638 244 (1998 est.). Area: 183 019 sq. km (70 664 sq. miles). Abbrevs.: **N.Dak., N.D.,** or (with zip code) **ND**
▸ **North Dakotan** *adj, n*

North Down ★ *n* a district of E Northern Ireland, on Belfast Lough E of Belfast: residential area for Belfast, tourism. Administrative centre: Bangor. Area: 74 sq. km (28 sq. miles). Pop.: 71 832 (1991).

northeast (ˌnɔːθˈiːst; *Naut.* ˌnɔːrˈiːst) *n* **1** the point of the compass or direction midway between north and east. **2** (*often cap.;* usually preceded by *the*) any area lying in or towards this direction. ◆ *adj also* **northeastern. 3** (*sometimes cap.*) of or denoting the northeastern part of a specified country, area, etc.: *northeast Lincolnshire.* **4** in, towards, or facing the northeast. **5** (esp. of the wind) from the northeast. ◆ *adv* **6** in, to, or towards the northeast.
▸ ˌ**north'easternmost** *adj*

Northeast (ˌnɔːθˈiːst) *n* (usually preceded by *the*) the northeastern part of England, esp. Northumberland, Durham, and the Tyneside area.

northeast by east *n* one point on the compass east of northeast.

northeast by north *n* one point on the compass north of northeast.

northeaster (ˌnɔːθˈiːstə; *Naut.* ˌnɔːrˈiːstə) *n* a strong wind or storm from the northeast.

northeasterly (ˌnɔːθˈiːstəlɪ; *Naut.* ˌnɔːrˈiːstəlɪ) *adj, adv* **1** in, towards, or (esp. of a wind) from the northeast. ◆ *n, pl* **northeasterlies. 2** a wind or storm from the northeast.

North East Frontier Agency ★ *n* the former name (until 1972) of **Arunachal Pradesh.**

North East Lincolnshire ★ *n* a unitary authority in E England, in Lincolnshire. Pop.: 164 000 (1996 est.). Area: 192 sq. km (74 sq. miles).

Northeast Passage ★ *n* a shipping route along the Arctic coasts of Europe and Asia, between the Atlantic and Pacific: first navigated by Nordenskjöld (1878–79).

northeastward (ˌnɔːθˈiːstwəd; *Naut.* ˌnɔːrˈiːstwəd) *adj* **1** towards or (esp. of a wind) from the northeast. ◆ *n* **2** a direction towards or area in the northeast.
▸ ˌ**north'eastwardly** *adj, adv*

norther (ˈnɔːðə) *n Chiefly southern US.* a wind or storm from the north.

northerly (ˈnɔːðəlɪ) *adj* **1** of or situated in the north.

◆ *adv, adj* **2** towards the north. **3** from the north: *a northerly wind.* ◆ *n, pl* **northerlies. 4** a wind from the north.
▸ **'northerliness** *n*

northern ('nɔːðən) *adj* **1** in or towards the north. **2** (esp. of winds) proceeding from the north. **3** (*sometimes cap.*) of or characteristic of the north or North.

Northern Cape ★ *n* a province of South Africa: a subdivision of the former Cape Province. Capital: Kimberly. Pop.: 840 321 (1996). Area: 361 830 sq. km (139 703 sq. miles).

Northern Dvina ★ *n* See **Dvina** (sense 1).

Northerner ('nɔːðənə) *n* (*sometimes not cap.*) a native or inhabitant of the north of any specified region, esp. England, the US, or the far north of Canada.

northern hemisphere *n* (*often caps.*) that half of the globe lying north of the equator.

Northern Ireland ★ *n* that part of the United Kingdom occupying the NE part of Ireland: separated from the rest of Ireland, which became officially independent in 1920, remaining part of the United Kingdom, with a separate Parliament (Stormont), which was inaugurated in 1921, and limited self-government: scene of severe conflict between Catholics and Protestants, including terrorist bombing from 1969; peace agreement reached in 1998: direct administration from Westminster from 1972; separate Northern Irish assembly established in 1998. Capital: Belfast. Pop.: 1 641 700 (1994 est.). Area: 14 121 sq. km (5452 sq. miles).

Northern Isles ★ *pl n* the Orkneys and Shetland.

northern lights *pl n* another name for **aurora borealis.**

northernmost ('nɔːðən,məʊst) *adj* situated or occurring farthest north.

Northern Province ★ *n* a province of South Africa incorporating part of the former Transvaal. Capital: Pietersburg. Pop.: 4 929 368 (1996). Area: 123 910 sq. km (47 842 sq. miles).

Northern Rhodesia ★ *n* the former name (until 1964) of **Zambia.**

Northern Territories ★ *pl n* a former British protectorate in W Africa, established in 1897; attached to the Gold Coast in 1901; now constitutes the Northern Region of Ghana (since 1957).

Northern Territory ★ *n* an administrative division of N central Australia, on the Timor and Arafura Seas: includes Ashmore and Cartier Islands; the Arunta Desert lies in the east, the Macdonnell Ranges in the south, and Arnhem Land in the north (containing Australia's largest Aboriginal reservation). Capital: Darwin. Pop.: 195 101 (1996). Area: 1 347 525 sq. km (520 280 sq. miles).

North Holland ★ *n* a province of the NW Netherlands, on the peninsula between the North Sea and IJsselmeer: includes the West Frisian Island of Texel. Capital: Haarlem. Pop.: 2 474 800 (1997 est.). Area: 2663 sq. km (1029 sq. miles). Dutch name: **Noordholland.**

northing ('nɔːθɪŋ, -ðɪŋ) *n* **1** *Navigation.* movement or distance covered in a northerly direction, esp. as expressed in the resulting difference in latitude. **2** *Astron.* a north or positive declination.

North Island ★ *n* **the.** the northernmost of the two main islands of New Zealand. Pop.: 2 733 083 (1996). Area: 114 729 sq. km (44 297 sq. miles).

North Korea ★ *n* a republic in NE Asia, on the Sea of Japan and the Yellow Sea: established in 1948 as a people's republic; invaded South Korea in 1950 but division remained unchanged at the end of the war (1953): mostly rugged and mountainous, with fertile lowlands in the west. Language: Korean. Currency: won. Capital: Pyongyang. Pop.: 21 386 000 (1999 est.). Area: 122 313 sq. km (47 225 sq. miles). Official name: **Democratic People's Republic of Korea.** Korean name: **Chosŏn.**
▸ **North Korean** *adj, n*

North Lanarkshire ★ *n* a council area of central Scotland. Administrative centre: Motherwell. Pop.: 307 100 (1996 est.). Area: 1771 sq. km (684 sq. miles).

Northland ★ ('nɔːθlənd) *n* **1** the peninsula containing Norway and Sweden. **2** (in Canada) the far north.
▸ **'Northlander** *n*

North Lincolnshire ★ *n* a unitary authority of E England, in Lincolnshire. Pop.: 153 000 (1996 est.). Area: 1497 sq. km (578 sq. miles).

Northman ('nɔːθmən) *n, pl* **Northmen.** another name for a **Viking.**

north-northeast *n* **1** the point on the compass or the direction midway between north and northeast. ◆ *adj, adv* **2** in, from, or towards this direction.

north-northwest *n* **1** the point on the compass or the direction midway between northwest and north. ◆ *adj, adv* **2** in, from, or towards this direction.

North Ossetian Republic ★ (ə'siːʃən) *n* a constituent republic of S Russia, on the N slopes of the central Caucasus Mountains. Capital: Vladikavkaz. Pop.: 658 000 (1995 est.). Area: 8000 sq. km (3088 sq. miles). Also called: **North Ossetia** (ə'siːʃə), **Alania.**

North Pole ★ *n* **1** the northernmost point on the earth's axis, at a latitude of 90°N, characterized by very low temperatures. **2** Also called: **north celestial pole.** *Astron.* the point of intersection of the earth's extended axis and the northern half of the celestial sphere. **3** (*usually not cap.*) the pole of a freely suspended magnet, which is attracted to the earth's magnetic North Pole.

North Rhine-Westphalia ★ *n* a state of W Germany: formed in 1946 by the amalgamation of the Prussian province of Westphalia with the N part of the Prussian Rhine province and later with the state of Lippe; part of West Germany until 1990: highly industrialized. Capital: Düsseldorf. Pop.: 17 908 500 (1996 est.). Area: 34 039 sq. km (13 142 sq. miles). German name: **Nordrhein-Westfalen.**

North Riding ★ *n* (until 1974) an administrative division of Yorkshire, now constituting most of North Yorkshire.

North Saskatchewan ★ *n* a river in W Canada, rising in W Alberta and flowing northeast, east, and southeast to join the South Saskatchewan River and form the Saskatchewan River. Length: 1223 km (760 miles).

North Sea ★ *n* an arm of the Atlantic between Great Britain and the N European mainland. Area: about 569 800 sq. km (220 000 sq. miles). Former name: **German Ocean.**

North-Sea gas *n* (in Britain) natural gas obtained from deposits below the North Sea.

North Somerset ★ *n* a unitary authority of SW England, in Somerset. Pop.: 177 000 (1996 est.). Area: 375 sq. km (145 sq. miles).

North Star *n* **the.** another name for **Polaris.**

North Tyneside ★ *n* a unitary authority of NE England, in Tyne and Wear. Pop.: 191 000 (1996 est.). Area: 84 sq. km (32 sq. miles).

Northumberland[1] ★ (nɔː'θʌmbələnd) *n* the northernmost county of England, on the North Sea: hilly in the north (the Cheviots) and west (the Pennines), with many Roman remains, notably Hadrian's Wall; shipbuilding, coal-mining. Administrative centre: Morpeth. Pop.: 307 700 (1996 est.). Area: 5032 sq. km (1943 sq. miles). Also called: **Northumbria.** Abbrev.: **Northd**

Northumberland[2] ★ (nɔː'θʌmbələnd) *n* **1st Duke of,** title of *John Dudley.* 1502–53, English statesman and soldier, who governed England (1549–53) during the minority of Edward VI. His attempt (1553) to gain the throne for his daughter-in-law, Lady Jane Grey, led to his execution.

Northumbria ★ (nɔː'θʌmbrɪə) *n* **1** (in Anglo-Saxon Britain) a region that stretched from the Humber to the Firth of Forth: formed in the 7th century A.D., it became an important intellectual centre; a separate kingdom until 876 A.D. **2** another name for **Northumberland**[1].
▸ **Nor'thumbrian** *adj*

North Vietnam ★ *n* a region of N Vietnam, on the Gulf of Tonkin: an independent Communist state from 1954 until 1976. Area: 164 061 sq. km (63 344 sq. miles).

northward ('nɔːθwəd; *Naut.* 'nɔːðəd) *adj* **1** moving, facing, or situated towards the north. ◆ *n* **2** the northward part, direction, etc. ◆ *adv also* **northwards. 3** towards the north.

northwest (ˌnɔːθˈwɛst; *Naut.* ˌnɔːˈwɛst) *n* **1** the point of the compass or direction midway between north and west. **2** (*often cap.;* usually preceded by *the*) any area lying in or towards this direction. ◆ *adj also* **northwestern. 3** (*sometimes cap.*) of or denoting the northwestern part of a specified country, area, etc.: *northwest Greenland.* ◆ *adj, adv* **4** in, to, or towards the northwest.
▸ ˌ**north**ˈ**westernmost** *adj*

Northwest (ˌnɔːθˈwɛst) *n* (usually preceded by *the*) the northwestern part of England, esp. Merseyside, Greater Manchester, Lancashire, and the Lake District.

northwest by north *n* one point on the compass north of northwest.

northwest by west *n* one point on the compass south of northwest.

northwester (ˌnɔːθˈwɛstə; *Naut.* ˌnɔːˈwɛstə) *n* a strong wind or storm from the northwest.

northwesterly (ˌnɔːθˈwɛstəlɪ; *Naut.* ˌnɔːˈwɛstəlɪ) *adj, adv* **1** in, towards, or (esp. of a wind) from the northwest. ◆ *n, pl* **northwesterlies. 2** a wind or storm from the northwest.

North-West Frontier Province ★ *n* a province in N Pakistan between Afghanistan and Jammu and Kashmir: part of British India (1901–47); of strategic importance, esp. for the Khyber Pass. Capital: Peshawar. Pop.: 12 287 000 (1985 est.). Area: 74 522 sq. km (28 773 sq. miles).

Northwest Passage ★ *n* the passage by sea from the Atlantic to the Pacific along the N coast of America: attempted for over 300 years by Europeans seeking a short route to the Far East, before being successfully navigated by Amundsen (1903–06).

North West Province ★ *n* a province of South Africa incorporating part of the former Transvaal. Capital: Mmbatho. Pop.: 3 354 825 (1996). Area: 116 320 sq. km (44 911 sq. miles).

Northwest Territories ★ *pl n* the part of Canada north of the provinces and east of the Yukon Territory, including the islands of the Arctic, Hudson Bay, James Bay, and Ungava Bay; comprised over a third of Canada's total area until Nunavut became a separate territory in 1999: rich mineral resources. Pop.: 41 668 (1999 est.). Area: 2 011 204 sq. km (481 438 sq. miles). Abbrev.: **NWT.**

Northwest Territory ★ *n* See **Old Northwest.**

northwestward (ˌnɔːθˈwɛstwəd; *Naut.* ˌnɔːˈwɛstwəd) *adj* **1** towards or (esp. of a wind) from the northwest. ◆ *n* **2** a direction towards or area in the northwest.
▸ ˌ**north**ˈ**westwardly** *adj, adv*

Northwich ★ (ˈnɔːθwɪtʃ) *n* a town in NW England, in Cheshire: salt and chemical industries. Pop.: 34 520 (1991).

North Yemen ★ *n* a former republic (1962–90) in SW Arabia, on the Red Sea; now part of Yemen. Official name: **Yemen Arab Republic.** See also **Yemen, South Yemen.**

North Yorkshire ★ *n* a county in N England, formed in 1974 from most of the North Riding of Yorkshire and parts of the East and West Ridings; includes four unitary authorities (Langbaurgh, Middlesbrough, Stockton-on-Tees, and York). Administrative centre: Northallerton. Pop. (excluding unitary authorities): 559 600 (1996 est.). Area (excluding unitary authorities): 8037 sq. km (3102 sq. miles).

Norw. *abbrev. for:* **1** Norway. **2** Norwegian.

Norway ★ (ˈnɔːˌweɪ) *n* a kingdom in NW Europe, occupying the W part of the Scandinavian peninsula: first united in the Viking age (800–1050); under the rule of Denmark (1523–1814) and Sweden (1814–1905); became an independent monarchy in 1905. Its coastline is deeply indented by fjords and fringed with islands, rising inland to plateaus and mountains. Norway has a large fishing fleet and its merchant navy is among the world's largest. Official language: Norwegian. Official religion: Lutheran. Currency: krone. Capital: Oslo. Pop.: 4 452 000 (1999 est.). Area: 323 878 sq. km (125 050 sq. miles). Norwegian name: **Norge.**

Norway lobster *n* a European lobster fished for food.

Norway maple *n* a large Eurasian maple tree.

Norway spruce *n* a European spruce tree having drooping branches and dark green needle-like leaves.

Norwegian (nɔːˈwiːdʒən) *adj* **1** of or characteristic of Norway, its language, or its people. ◆ *n* **2** any of the various North Germanic languages of Norway. **3** a native or inhabitant of Norway.

Norwegian Sea ★ *n* part of the Arctic Ocean between Greenland and Norway.

Norwich ★ (ˈnɒrɪdʒ) *n* a city in E England, administrative centre of Norfolk: cathedral (founded 1096); seat of The University of East Anglia (1963). Pop.: 171 304 (1991).

Nos. *or* **nos.** *abbrev. for* numbers.

nose (nəuz) *n* **1** the organ of smell and entrance to the respiratory tract, consisting of a prominent structure divided into two hair-lined air passages. Related adj: **nasal. 2** the sense of smell itself: in animals, the ability to follow trails by scent (esp. in **a good nose**). **3** the scent, aroma, bouquet of something, esp. wine. **4** instinctive skill in discovering things (sometimes in **follow one's nose**): *he had a nose for good news stories.* **5** any part resembling a nose in form or function, such as a nozzle or spout. **6** the forward part of a vehicle, aircraft, etc. **7** narrow margin of victory (in **(win) by a nose**). **8 cut off one's nose to spite one's face.** to carry out a vengeful action that hurts oneself more than another. **9 get up (someone's) nose.** *Inf.* to annoy or irritate (someone). **10 keep one's nose clean.** to stay out of trouble. **11 lead by the nose.** to make (someone) do unquestioningly all one wishes; dominate. **12 look down one's nose at.** *Inf.* to be disdainful of. **13 nose to tail.** (of vehicles) moving or standing very close behind one another. **14 on the nose.** *Sl.* **14a** (in horse-race betting) to win only: *I bet twenty pounds on the nose on that horse.* **14b** *Chiefly US & Canad.* precisely; exactly. **14c** *Austral.* bad or bad-smelling. **15 pay through the nose.** *Inf.* to pay an exorbitant price. **16 put someone's nose out of joint.** *Inf.* to thwart or offend someone. **17 rub someone's nose in it.** *Inf.* to remind someone unkindly of a failing or error. **18 turn up one's nose (at).** *Inf.* to behave disdainfully (towards). **19 with one's nose in the air.** haughtily. ◆ *vb* **noses, nosing, nosed. 20** (*tr*) (esp. of horses, dogs, etc.) to rub, touch, or sniff with the nose; nuzzle. **21** to smell or sniff (wine, etc.). **22** (*intr;* usually foll. by *after* or *for*) to search (for) by or as if by scent. **23** to move or cause to move forwards slowly and carefully: *we nosed the car into the garage.* **24** (*intr;* foll. by *into, around, about,* etc.) to pry or snoop (into) or meddle (in). ORIG OE *nosu*
▸ ˈ**noseless** *adj* ▸ ˈ**nose**ˌ**like** *adj*

nosebag (ˈnəuzˌbæg) *n* a bag, fastened around the head of a horse and covering the nose, in which feed is placed.

noseband (ˈnəuzˌbænd) *n* the detachable part of a horse's bridle that goes around the nose.

nosebleed (ˈnəuzˌbliːd) *n* bleeding from the nose as the result of injury, etc.

nose cone *n* the conical forward section of a missile, spacecraft, etc., designed to withstand high temperatures, esp. during re-entry into the earth's atmosphere.

nose dive *n* **1** a sudden plunge with the nose or front pointing downwards, esp. of an aircraft. **2** *Inf.* a sudden drop or sharp decline: *prices took a nose dive.* ◆ *vb* **nose-dive, nose-dives, nose-diving, nose-dived.** (*intr*) **3** to perform a nose dive.

nose flute *n* (esp. in the South Sea Islands) a type of flute blown through the nose.

nosegay (ˈnəuzˌgeɪ) *n* a small bunch of flowers; posy. ORIG C15: from NOSE + *gay* (arch.) toy

nose job *n Sl.* a surgical remodelling of the nose for cosmetic reasons.

nosepiece (ˈnəuzˌpiːs) *n* **1** a piece of armour to protect the nose. **2** the connecting part of a pair of spectacles that rests on the nose; bridge. **3** the part of a microscope to which one or more objective lenses are attached. **4** a less common word for **noseband.**

nose rag *n Sl.* a handkerchief.

nose ring *n* a ring fixed through the nose, as for leading a bull.

nose wheel *n* a wheel fitted to the forward end of a vehicle, esp. the landing wheel under an aircraft's nose.

nosey ('nəʊzɪ) *adj* a variant spelling of **nosy.**

nosh (nɒʃ) *Sl.* ◆ *n* **1** food or a meal. ◆ *vb* **2** to eat. ORIG C20: from Yiddish; cf. G *naschen* to nibble

no-show *n* a person who fails to take up a reserved seat, place, etc., without having cancelled it.

nosh-up *n Brit. sl.* a large and satisfying meal.

no-side *n Rugby.* the end of a match, signalled by the referee's whistle.

nosocomial (ˌnɒsə'kəʊmɪəl) *adj* of or denoting an infection that originates in a hospital. ORIG C19: from Gk *nosokomos* one that tends the sick

nosology (nɒ'sɒlədʒɪ) *n* the branch of medicine concerned with the classification of diseases. ORIG C18: from Gk *nosos* disease
▸ **nosological** (ˌnɒsə'lɒdʒɪkᵊl) *adj*

nostalgia (nɒ'stældʒə, -dʒɪə) *n* **1** a yearning for past circumstances, events, etc. **2** the evocation of this emotion, as in a book, film, etc. **3** homesickness. ORIG C18: NL, from Gk *nostos a* return home + -ALGIA
▸ **nos'talgic** *adj* ▸ **nos'talgically** *adv*

nostoc ('nɒstɒk) *n* a gelatinous cyanobacterium occurring in moist places. ORIG C17: NL, coined by Paracelsus (1493–1541) Swiss physician

Nostradamus ★ (ˌnɒstrə'dɑːməs) *n* Latinized name of *Michel de Notredame.* 1503–66, French physician and astrologer; author of a book of prophecies in rhymed quatrains, *Centuries* (1555).

nostril ('nɒstrɪl) *n* either of the two external openings of the nose. See **nares.** ORIG OE *nosthyrl,* from *nosu* NOSE + *thyrel* hole

nostro account ('nɒstrəʊ) *n* a bank account conducted by a British bank with a foreign bank, usually in the foreign currency. Cf. **vostro account.**

nostrum ('nɒstrəm) *n* **1** a patent or quack medicine. **2** a favourite remedy. ORIG C17: from L: our own (make), from *noster* our

nosy *or* **nosey** ('nəʊzɪ) *adj* **nosier, nosiest.** *Inf.* prying or inquisitive.
▸ **'nosily** *adv* ▸ **'nosiness** *n*

nosy parker *n Inf.* a prying person. ORIG C20: arbitrary use of surname *Parker*

not (nɒt) *adv* **1a** used to negate the sentence, phrase, or word that it modifies: *I will not stand for it.* **1b** (*in combination*): *they cannot go.* **2 not that.** (*conj*) Also (arch.): **not but what.** which is not to say or suppose that: *I expect to lose the game — not that I mind.* ◆ *sentence substitute.* **3** used to indicate denial or refusal: *certainly not.* **4** *Inf., humorous.* used to emphatically negate the previous statement: *Oh, yes, he'll be absolutely thrilled at that news – not!* ORIG C14 *not,* var. of *nought* nothing, from OE *nāwiht,* from *nā* no + *wiht* creature, thing

nota bene *Latin.* ('nəʊtə 'biːnɪ) note well; take note. Abbrevs.: **NB, N.B., nb, n.b.**

notability (ˌnəʊtə'bɪlɪtɪ) *n, pl* **notabilities. 1** the quality of being notable. **2** a distinguished person.

notable ('nəʊtəbᵊl) *adj* **1** worthy of being noted or remembered; remarkable; distinguished. ◆ *n* **2** a notable person. ORIG C14: via OF from L *notābilis,* from *notāre* to NOTE
▸ **'notably** *adv*

notarize *or* **notarise** ('nəʊtəˌraɪz) *vb* **notarizes, notarizing, notarized** *or* **notarises, notarising, notarised.** (*tr*) *US.* to attest to (a document, etc.), as a notary.

notary ('nəʊtərɪ) *n, pl* **notaries. 1** a notary public. **2** (formerly) a clerk licensed to prepare legal documents. **3** *Arch.* a clerk or secretary. ORIG C14: from L *notārius* clerk, from *nota* a mark, note
▸ **notarial** (nəʊ'tɛərɪəl) *adj* ▸ **'notaryship** *n*

notary public *n, pl* **notaries public.** a public official, usually a solicitor, who is legally authorized to administer oaths, attest and certify certain documents, etc.

notation (nəʊ'teɪʃən) *n* **1** any series of signs or symbols used to represent quantities or elements in a specialized system, such as music or mathematics. **2** the act or process of notating. **3** a note or record. ORIG C16: from L *notātiō,* from *notāre* to NOTE
▸ **no'tational** *adj*

notch (nɒtʃ) *n* **1** a V-shaped cut or indentation; nick. **2** a nick made in a tally stick. **3** *US & Canad.* a narrow gorge. **4** *Inf.* a step or level (esp. in **a notch above**). ◆ *vb* (*tr*) **5** to cut or make a notch in. **6** to record with or as if with a notch. **7** (usually foll. by *up*) *Inf.* to score or achieve: *the team notched up its fourth win.* ORIG C16: from incorrect division of *an otch* (as *a notch*), from OF *oche* notch, from L *obsecāre,* from *secāre* to cut

NOT circuit *or* **gate** (nɒt) *n Computing.* a logic circuit that has a high-voltage output signal if the input signal is low, and vice versa: used extensively in computing. Also called: **inverter, negator.** ORIG C20: the action performed on electrical signals is similar to the operation of *not* in logical constructions

note (nəʊt) *n* **1** a brief record in writing, esp. a jotting for future reference. **2** a brief informal letter. **3** a formal written communication, esp. from one government to another. **4** a short written statement giving any kind of information. **5** a critical comment, explanatory statement, or reference in a book. **6** short for **banknote. 7** a characteristic atmosphere: *a note of sarcasm.* **8** a distinctive vocal sound, as of a species of bird or animal. **9** any of a series of graphic signs representing the pitch and duration of a musical sound. **10** Also called (esp. US and Canad.): **tone.** a musical sound of definite fundamental frequency or pitch. **11** a key on a piano, organ, etc. **12** a sound used as a signal or warning: *the note to retreat was sounded.* **13** short for **promissory note. 14** *Arch. or poetic.* a melody. **15 of note. 15a** distinguished or famous. **15b** important: *nothing of note.* **16 strike the right** (*or* **a false**) **note.** to behave appropriately (or inappropriately). **17 take note.** (often foll. by *of*) to pay attention (to). ◆ *vb* **notes, noting, noted.** (*tr; may take a clause as object*) **18** to notice; perceive. **19** to pay close attention to: *they noted every movement.* **20** to make a written note of: *she noted the date in her diary.* **21** to remark upon: *I note that you do not wear shoes.* **22** to write down (music, a melody, etc.) in notes. **23** to take (an unpaid or dishonoured bill of exchange) to a notary public to re-present the bill and if it is still unaccepted or unpaid to note the circumstances in a register. See **protest** (sense 9). **24** a less common word for **annotate.** ORIG C13: via OF from L *nota* sign
▸ **'noteless** *adj*

notebook ('nəʊtˌbʊk) *n* a book for recording notes or memoranda.

notebook computer *n* a portable computer smaller than a laptop model, often approximately the size of a sheet of A4 paper.

notecase ('nəʊtˌkeɪs) *n* a less common word for **wallet** (sense 1).

noted ('nəʊtɪd) *adj* **1** celebrated; famous. **2** of special significance; noticeable.
▸ **'notedly** *adv*

notelet ('nəʊtlɪt) *n* a folded card with a printed design on the front, for writing a short letter.

notepaper ('nəʊtˌpeɪpə) *n* paper for writing letters; writing paper.

noteworthy ('nəʊtˌwɜːðɪ) *adj* worthy of notice; notable.
▸ **'noteˌworthiness** *n*

nothing ('nʌθɪŋ) *pron* **1** (*indefinite*) no thing; not anything: *I can give you nothing.* **2** no part or share: *to have nothing to do with this crime.* **3** a matter of no importance: *it doesn't matter, it's nothing.* **4** indicating the absence of anything perceptible; nothingness. **5** indicating the absence of meaning, value, worth, etc.: *to amount to nothing.* **6** zero quantity; nought. **7 be nothing to. 7a** not to concern or be significant to (someone). **7b** to be not nearly as good, etc., as. **8 have** *or* **be nothing to do with.** to have no connection with. **9 nothing but.** not something other than; only. **10 nothing doing.** *Inf.* an expression of dismissal, refusal, etc. **11 nothing if not.** at the very least; certainly. **12 nothing less than** *or* **nothing short of.** downright; truly. **13 there's nothing to it.** it is very simple, easy, etc. **14 think nothing of. 14a** to regard as easy or natural. **14b** to have no compunction about. **14c** to have a very low opinion of. ◆ *adv* **15** in no way; not at all: *he looked nothing like his brother.* ◆ *n* **16** *Inf.* a person or thing of no importance or significance. **17 sweet nothings.** words of endearment or affection. ORIG OE *nāthing, nān thing,* from *nān* NONE[1] + THING

nothingness ('nʌθɪŋnɪs) *n* **1** the state of being nothing; nonexistence. **2** absence of consciousness or life. **3** complete insignificance. **4** something that is worthless.

notice ('nəʊtɪs) *n* **1** observation; attention: *to escape notice.* **2 take notice.** to pay attention. **3 take no notice of.** to ignore or disregard. **4** a warning; announcement. **5** a displayed placard or announcement giving information. **6** advance notification of intention to end an arrangement, contract, etc., as of employment (esp. in **give notice**). **7 at short notice.** with notification only a little in advance. **8** *Chiefly Brit.* dismissal from employment. **9** favourable, interested, or polite attention: *she was beneath his notice.* **10** a theatrical or literary review: *the play received very good notices.* ◆ *vb* **notices, noticing, noticed. 11** to become aware (of); perceive; note. **12** (*tr*) to point out or remark upon. **13** (*tr*) to pay polite or interested attention to. **14** (*tr*) to acknowledge (an acquaintance, etc.). ORIG C15: via OF from L *notitia* fame, from *nōtus* known

noticeable ('nəʊtɪsəbᵊl) *adj* easily seen or detected; perceptible.
▸ '**noticeably** *adv*

notice board *n* a board on which notices, advertisements, bulletins, etc., are displayed. US and Canad. name: **bulletin board.**

notifiable ('nəʊtɪˌfaɪəbᵊl) *adj* **1** denoting certain infectious diseases of humans, such as tuberculosis, outbreaks of which must be reported to the public health authorities. **2** denoting certain infectious diseases of animals, such as BSE and rabies, outbreaks of which must be reported to the appropriate veterinary authority.

notification (ˌnəʊtɪfɪ'keɪʃən) *n* **1** the act of notifying. **2** a formal announcement. **3** something that notifies; a notice.

notify ('nəʊtɪˌfaɪ) *vb* **notifies, notifying, notified.** (*tr*) **1** to tell. **2** *Chiefly Brit.* to make known; announce. ORIG C14: from OF *notifier,* from L *notificāre,* from *nōtus* known + *facere* to make
▸ '**notiˌfier** *n*

notion ('nəʊʃən) *n* **1** a vague idea; impression. **2** an idea, concept, or opinion. **3** an inclination or whim. ◆ See also **notions.** ORIG C16: from L *nōtiō* a becoming acquainted (with), examination (of), from *noscere* to know

notional ('nəʊʃənᵊl) *adj* **1** expressing or consisting of ideas. **2** not evident in reality; hypothetical or imaginary: *a notional tax credit.* **3** characteristic of a notion, esp. in being speculative or abstract. **4** *Grammar.* **4a** (of a word) having lexical meaning. **4b** another word for **semantic.**
▸ '**notionally** *adv*

notions ('nəʊʃənz) *pl n Chiefly US & Canad.* pins, cotton, ribbon, etc., used for sewing; haberdashery.

notochord ('nəʊtəˌkɔːd) *n* a fibrous longitudinal rod in all embryo and some adult chordate animals, immediately above the gut, that supports the body. ORIG C19: from Gk *nōton* the back + CHORD[1]

notorious (nəʊ'tɔːrɪəs) *adj* **1** well-known for some bad or unfavourable quality, deed, etc.; infamous. **2** *Rare.* generally known or widely acknowledged. ORIG C16: from Med. L *notōrius* well-known, from *nōtus* known
▸ **notoriety** (ˌnəʊtə'raɪɪtɪ) *n* ▸ **no'toriously** *adv*

notornis (nəʊ'tɔːnɪs) *n* a rare flightless rail of New Zealand. ORIG C19: NL, from Gk *notos* south + *ornis* bird

not proven ('prəʊvᵊn) *adj* (*postpositive*) a third verdict available to Scottish courts, returned when there is insufficient evidence against the accused to convict.

Notre Dame ★ ('nəʊtrə 'dɑːm, 'nɒtrə; *French* nɔtrə dam) *n* the early Gothic cathedral of Paris, on the Île de la Cité: built between 1163 and 1257.

no-trump *Cards.* ◆ *n also* **no-trumps. 1** a bid or contract to play without trumps. ◆ *adj also* **no-trumper. 2** (of a hand) suitable for playing without trumps.

Nottingham ★ ('nɒtɪŋəm) *n* **1** a city in N central England, administrative centre of Nottinghamshire, on the River Trent: scene of the outbreak of the Civil War (1642); famous for its associations with the Robin Hood legend; seat of The University of Nottingham (1948) and Nottingham Trent University (1992). Pop.: 270 222 (1991). **2** a unitary authority in N central England. Pop.: 283 800 (1995 est.). Area: 78 sq. km (30 sq. miles).

Nottinghamshire ★ ('nɒtɪŋəmˌʃɪə, -ʃə) *n* an inland county of central England: generally low-lying, with part of the S Pennines and the remnant of Sherwood Forest in the east. Nottingham became an independent unitary authority in 1998. Administrative centre: Nottingham. Pop. (excluding Nottingham): 747 800 (1996 est.). Area (excluding Nottingham): 2086 sq. km (805 sq. miles). Abbrev.: **Notts.**

Nottm *abbrev. for* Nottingham.

Notts (nɒts) *abbrev. for* Nottinghamshire.

Notus ★ ('nəʊtəs) *n Classical myth.* a personification of the south or southwest wind.

notwithstanding (ˌnɒtwɪθ'stændɪŋ) *prep* **1** (*often immediately postpositive*) in spite of; despite. ◆ *conj* **2** (*subordinating*) although. ◆ *sentence connector.* **3** nevertheless.

Nouakchott ★ (*French* nwakʃɔt) *n* the capital of Mauritania, near the Atlantic coast: replaced St Louis as capital in 1957; situated on important caravan routes. Pop.: 735 000 (1995 est.).

nougat ('nuːgɑː) *n* a hard chewy pink or white sweet containing chopped nuts, cherries, etc. ORIG C19: via F from Provençal *nogat,* from *noga* nut, from L *nux* nut

nought (nɔːt) *n also* **naught, ought, aught. 1** another name for **zero:** used esp. in numbering. ◆ *n, adj, adv* **2** a variant spelling of **naught.** ORIG OE *nōwiht,* from *ne* not, no + *ōwiht* something

noughts and crosses *n* (*functioning as sing*) a game in which two players, one using a nought, "O", the other a cross, "X", alternately mark squares formed by two pairs of crossed lines, the winner being the first to get three of his symbols in a row. US and Canad. term: **tick-tack-toe,** (US) **crisscross.**

Nouméa ★ (ˌnuː'meɪə; *French* numea) *n* the capital and chief port of the French Overseas Territory of New Caledonia. Pop.: 65 000 (1994 est.).

noun (naʊn) *n* **a** a word or group of words that refers to a person, place, or thing. **b** (*as modifier*): *a noun phrase.* Abbrev.: **N, n.** Related adj: **nominal.** ORIG C14: via Anglo-F from L *nōmen* NAME
▸ '**nounal** *adj*

nourish ('nʌrɪʃ) *vb* (*tr*) **1** to provide with the materials necessary for life and growth. **2** to encourage (an idea, etc.); foster: *to nourish resentment.* ORIG C14: from OF *norir,* from L *nūtrīre* to feed
▸ '**nourisher** *n* ▸ '**nourishing** *adj*

nourishment ('nʌrɪʃmənt) *n* **1** the act or state of nourishing. **2** a substance that nourishes; food.

nous (naʊs) *n* **1** *Metaphysics.* mind or reason, esp. regarded as the principle governing all things. **2** *Brit. sl.* common sense. ORIG C17: from Gk: mind

nouveau *or before a plural noun* **nouveaux** ('nuːvəʊ) *adj* (*prenominal*) *Facetious or derog.* having recently become the thing specified: *a nouveau hippy.* ORIG C20: F, lit.: new; on the model of NOUVEAU RICHE

nouveau riche (riːʃ) *n, pl* **nouveaux riches** (riːʃ). (often preceded by *the*) a person who has acquired wealth recently and is regarded as vulgarly ostentatious or lacking in social graces. ORIG C19: from F lit.: new rich

Nouvelle-Calédonie ★ (*French* nuvɛlkaledɔni) *n* the French name for **New Caledonia.**

nouvelle cuisine ('nuːvɛl kwiː'ziːn; *French* nuvɛl kɥizin) *n* a style of cooking based on presenting small attractively arranged helpings of lightly cooked fresh ingredients. ORIG C20: F, lit.: new cookery

Nov. *abbrev. for* November.

nova ('nəʊvə) *n, pl* **novae** (-viː) *or* **novas.** a variable star that undergoes a cataclysmic eruption, observed as a sudden large increase in brightness with a subsequent decline over months or years; it is a close binary system with one component a white dwarf. ORIG C19: NL *nova (stella)* new (star), from L *novus* new

Novalis ★ (*German* no'va:lɪs) *n* real name *Friedrich von Hardenberg*. 1772–1801, German romantic poet. His works include the mystical *Hymnen an die Nacht* (1797; published 1800) and *Geistliche Lieder* (1799).

Nova Lisboa ★ (*Portuguese* 'nɔvə liʒ'βoə) *n* the former name (1928–73) of **Huambo**.

Novara ★ (*Italian* no'va:ra) *n* a city in NW Italy, in NE Piedmont: scene of the Austrian defeat of the Piedmontese in 1849. Pop.: 102 219 (1996 est.).

Nova Scotia ★ ('nəʊvə 'skəʊʃə) *n* **1** a peninsula in E Canada, between the Gulf of St Lawrence and the Bay of Fundy. **2** a province of E Canada, consisting of the Nova Scotia peninsula and Cape Breton Island: first settled by the French as Acadia. Capital: Halifax. Pop.: 940 825 (1999 est.). Area: 52 841 sq. km (20 402 sq. miles). Abbrev.: **NS.**
▸ ˌ**Nova 'Scotian** *n, adj*

Novaya Zemlya ★ (*Russian* 'nɔvəjə zɪm'lja) *n* an archipelago in the Arctic Ocean, off the NE coast of Russia: consists of two large islands and many islets. Area: about 81 279 sq. km (31 382 sq. miles).

novel[1] ('nɒvᵊl) *n* **1** an extended fictional work in prose dealing with character, action, thought, etc., esp. in the form of a story. **2 the novel.** the literary genre represented by novels. ORIG C15: from OF *novelle*, from L *novella (narrātiō)* new (story); see NOVEL[2]

novel[2] ('nɒvᵊl) *adj* of a kind not seen before; fresh; new; original: *a novel suggestion.* ORIG C15: from L *novellus*, dim. of *novus* new

novelette (ˌnɒvə'lɛt) *n* **1** an extended prose narrative or short novel. **2** a novel that is regarded as slight, trivial, or sentimental. **3** a short piece of lyrical music, esp. for piano.

novelettish (ˌnɒvə'lɛtɪʃ) *adj* characteristic of a novelette; trite or sentimental.

novelist ('nɒvəlɪst) *n* a writer of novels.

novelistic (ˌnɒvə'lɪstɪk) *adj* of or characteristic of novels, esp. in style or method of treatment.

novella (nəʊ'vɛlə) *n, pl* **novellas** *or* **novelle** (-leɪ). **1** a short narrative tale, esp. one having a satirical point, such as those in Boccaccio's *Decameron*. **2** a short novel. ORIG C20: from It.; see NOVEL[1]

Novello ★ (nə'vɛləʊ) *n* **Ivor,** real name *Ivor Novello Davies*. 1893–1951, Welsh actor and composer of musicals.

novelty ('nɒvᵊltɪ) *n, pl* **novelties. 1a** the quality of being new and interesting. **1b** (*as modifier*): *novelty value.* **2** a new or unusual experience. **3** (*often pl*) a small usually cheap new ornament or trinket. ORIG C14: from OF *novelté*; see NOVEL[2]

November (nəʊ'vɛmbə) *n* the eleventh month of the year, consisting of 30 days. ORIG C13: via OF from L: ninth month (the Roman year orig. began in March), from *novem* nine

novena (nəʊ'vi:nə) *n, pl* **novenas** *or* **novenae** (-ni:). *RC Church.* a devotion consisting of prayers or services on nine consecutive days. ORIG C19: from Med. L, from L *novem* nine

Novgorod ★ (*Russian* 'nɔvgərət) *n* a city in NW Russia, on the Volkhov River. Novgorod became a principality in 862 under Rurik, an event regarded as the founding of the Russian state; a major trading centre in the Middle Ages; destroyed by Ivan the Terrible in 1570. Pop.: 233 000 (1995 est.).

novice ('nɒvɪs) *n* **1a** a person who is new to or inexperienced in a certain task, situation, etc.; beginner; tyro. **1b** (*as modifier*): *novice driver.* **2** a probationer in a religious order. **3** a racehorse that has not won a specified number of races. ORIG C14: via OF from L *novīcius*, from *novus* new

Novi Sad ★ (*Serbo-Croat* 'nɔvi: 'sa:d) *n* a port in NE Yugoslavia, in Serbia, on the River Danube: founded in 1690 as the seat of the Serbian patriarch; university (1960). Pop.: 179 626 (1991). German name: **Neusatz.**

novitiate *or* **noviciate** (nəʊ'vɪʃɪɪt, -ˌeɪt) *n* **1** the state of being a novice, esp. in a religious order, or the period for which this lasts. **2** the part of a religious house where the novices live. ORIG C17: from F *noviciat*, from L *novīcius* NOVICE

Novocaine ('nəʊvəˌkeɪn) *n* a trademark for **procaine hydrochloride.** See **procaine.**

Novokuznetsk ★ (*Russian* nɔvəkuz'njɛtsk) *n* a city in S central Russia: iron and steel works. Pop.: 572 000 (1995 est.). Former name (1932–61): **Stalinsk.**

Novosibirsk ★ (*Russian* nəvəsi'birsk) *n* a city in W central Russia, on the River Ob: the largest town in Siberia; developed with the coming of the Trans-Siberian railway in 1893. Pop.: 1 369 000 (1995 est.).

now (naʊ) *adv* **1** at or for the present time. **2** immediately. **3** in these times; nowadays. **4** given the present circumstances: *now we'll have to stay to the end.* **5** (preceded by *just*) very recently: *he left just now.* **6** (often preceded by *just*) very soon: *he is leaving just now.* **7** (**every**) **now and again** *or* **then.** occasionally; on and off. **8 now now!** an exclamation used to rebuke or pacify someone. ◆ *conj* **9** (*subordinating; often foll. by that*) seeing that: *now you're in charge, things will be better.* ◆ *sentence connector.* **10a** used as a hesitation word: *now, I can't really say.* **10b** used for emphasis: *now listen to this.* **10c** used at the end of a command: *run along, now.* ◆ *n* **11** the present time: *now is the time to go.* ◆ *adj* **12** *Inf.* of the moment; fashionable: *the now look.* ORIG OE *nū*

nowadays ('naʊəˌdeɪz) *adv* in these times. ORIG C14: from NOW + *adays* from OE *a* on + *daeges* genitive of DAY

noway ('nəʊˌweɪ) *adv* **1** not at all. ◆ *sentence substitute.* **no way. 2** used to make an emphatic refusal, denial, etc.

Nowel *or* **Nowell** (nəʊ'ɛl) *n* archaic spellings of **Noel.**

nowhere ('nəʊwɛə) *adv* **1** in, at, or to no place; not anywhere. **2 get nowhere (fast).** *Inf.* to fail completely to make any progress. **3 nowhere near.** far from; not nearly. ◆ *n* **4** a nonexistent or insignificant place. **5 middle of nowhere.** a completely isolated place.

no-win *adj* offering no possibility of a favourable outcome (esp. in **a no-win situation**).

nowise ('nəʊˌwaɪz) *adv* in no manner; not at all.

nowt (naʊt) *n N English.* a dialect word for **nothing.** ORIG from NAUGHT

Nox ★ (nɒks) *n* the Roman goddess of the night. Greek counterpart: **Nyx.**

noxious ('nɒkʃəs) *adj* poisonous or harmful. ORIG C17: from L *noxius* harmful, from *noxa* injury
▸ **'noxiously** *adv* ▸ **'noxiousness** *n*

Noyon ★ (*French* nwajɔ̃) *n* a town in N France: scene of the coronations of Charlemagne (768) and Hugh Capet (987); birthplace of John Calvin. Pop.: 14 426 (1990).

nozzle ('nɒzᵊl) *n* a projecting pipe or spout from which fluid is discharged. ORIG C17 *nosle, nosel*, dim. of NOSE

Np *the chemical symbol for* neptunium.

NP *or* **np.** *abbrev. for* Notary Public.

NPA *abbrev. for* Newspaper Publishers' Association.

NPD *Commerce. abbrev. for* new product development.

NPL *abbrev. for* National Physical Laboratory.

NPV *abbrev. for:* **1** net present value. **2** no par value.

NRV *abbrev. for* net realizable value.

NS *abbrev. for:* **1** New Style (method of reckoning dates). **2** Nova Scotia. **3** Nuclear Ship.

NSAID *abbrev. for* nonsteroidal anti-inflammatory drug: any of a class of drugs, including aspirin and ibuprofen, used for treating rheumatic diseases.

NSB (in Britain) *abbrev. for* National Savings Bank.

NSC (in Britain) *abbrev. for* National Safety Council.

NSG *Brit. education. abbrev. for* nonstatutory guidelines: practical nonmandatory advice and information on the implementation of the National Curriculum.

NSPCC (in Britain) *abbrev. for* National Society for the Prevention of Cruelty to Children.

NST (in Canada) abbrev. for Newfoundland Standard Time.

NSU *abbrev. for* nonspecific urethritis.

NSW *abbrev. for* New South Wales.

★ people and places

NT *abbrev. for:* **1** (in Britain) National Trust. **2** New Testament. **3** Northern Territory. **4** no-trump.

-n't *contraction of* not: used as an enclitic after *be* and *have* when they function as main verbs and after auxiliary verbs or verbs operating syntactically as auxiliaries: *can't; don't; isn't.*

nth (ɛnθ) *adj* **1** *Maths.* of or representing an unspecified ordinal number, usually the greatest in a series: *the nth power.* **2** *Inf.* being the last or most extreme of a long series: *for the nth time.* **3 to the nth degree.** *Inf.* to the utmost extreme.

NTP *abbrev. for* normal temperature and pressure. Also: **STP.**

nt. wt. *or* **nt wt** *abbrev. for* net weight.

n-type *adj* **1** (of a semiconductor) having more conduction electrons than mobile holes. **2** associated with or resulting from the movement of electrons in a semiconductor.

nu (nju:) *n* the 13th letter in the Greek alphabet (Ν, ν), a consonant. ORIG from Gk, of Semitic origin

Nu ★ (nju:) *n* **U** (u:), original name *Thakin Nu.* 1907–99, Burmese statesman; prime minister (1948–56, 1957–58, 1960–62).

nuance (nju:'ɑ:ns, 'nju:ɑ:ns) *n* a subtle difference in colour, meaning, tone, etc. ORIG C18: from F, from *nuer* to show light and shade, ult. from L *nūbēs* a cloud

nub (nʌb) *n* **1** a small lump or protuberance. **2** a small piece or chunk. **3** the point or gist: *the nub of a story.* ORIG C16: var. of *knub,* from MLow G *knubbe* KNOB
▸ **'nubbly** *or* **'nubby** *adj*

nubble ('nʌbᵊl) *n* a small lump. ORIG C19: dim. of NUB

Nubia ★ ('nju:bɪə) *n* an ancient region of NE Africa, on the Nile, extending from Aswan to Khartoum.

Nubian ('nju:bɪən) *n* **1** a native or inhabitant of Nubia. **2** the language spoken by the people of Nubia. ◆ *adj* **3** of or relating to Nubia. **4** *Inf.* of or relating to Black culture.

Nubian Desert ★ *n* a desert in the NE Sudan, between the Nile valley and the Red Sea: mainly a sandstone plateau.

nubile ('nju:baɪl) *adj* (of a girl) **1** ready or suitable for marriage by virtue of age or maturity. **2** sexually attractive. ORIG C17: from L *nūbilis,* from *nūbere* to marry
▸ **nubility** (nju:'bɪlɪtɪ) *n*

Nubuck ('nju:ˌbʌk) *n* (*sometimes not cap.*) leather that has been rubbed on the flesh side of the skin to give it a fine velvet-like finish.

nucha ('nju:kə) *n, pl* **nuchae** (-ki:). *Zool., anat.* the back or nape of the neck. ORIG C14: from Med. L, from Ar.: spinal marrow
▸ **'nuchal** *adj*

nuclear ('nju:klɪə) *adj* **1** of or involving the nucleus of an atom: *nuclear fission.* **2** *Biol.* of, relating to, or contained within the nucleus of a cell: *a nuclear membrane.* **3** of, forming, or resembling any other kind of nucleus. **4** of or operated by energy from fission or fusion of atomic nuclei: *a nuclear weapon.* **5** involving or possessing nuclear weapons: *nuclear war.*

nuclear bomb *n* a bomb whose force is due to uncontrolled nuclear fusion or nuclear fission.

nuclear chemistry *n* the branch of chemistry concerned with nuclear reactions.

nuclear energy *n* energy released during a nuclear reaction as a result of fission or fusion. Also called: **atomic energy.**

nuclear family *n Sociol., anthropol.* a primary social unit consisting of parents and their offspring.

nuclear fission *n* the splitting of an atomic nucleus into approximately equal parts, either spontaneously or as a result of the impact of a particle usually with an associated release of energy. Sometimes shortened to **fission.**

nuclear fuel *n* a fuel that provides nuclear energy, used in nuclear submarines, etc.

nuclear fusion *n* a reaction in which two nuclei combine to form a nucleus with the release of energy. Sometimes shortened to **fusion.**

nuclear magnetic resonance *n* a technique for determining the magnetic moments of nuclei by subjecting a substance to high-frequency radiation and a large magnetic field. It is used for determining structure, esp. in body scanning. Abbrev.: **NMR.**

nuclear medicine *n* the branch of medicine concerned with the use of radionuclides in the diagnosis and treatment of disease.

nuclear physics *n* (*functioning as sing*) the branch of physics concerned with the structure and behaviour of the nucleus and the particles of which it consists.

nuclear power *n* power, esp. electrical or motive, produced by a nuclear reactor. Also called: **atomic power.**

nuclear reaction *n* a process in which the structure and energy content of an atomic nucleus is changed by interaction with another nucleus or particle.

nuclear reactor *n* a device in which a nuclear reaction is maintained and controlled for the production of nuclear energy. Sometimes shortened to **reactor.**

nuclear waste *n* another name for **radioactive waste.**

nuclear winter *n* a period of low temperatures and little light that has been suggested would occur after a nuclear war.

nuclease ('nju:klɪˌeɪz) *n* any of a group of enzymes that hydrolyse nucleic acids to simple nucleotides.

nucleate *adj* ('nju:klɪɪt, -ˌeɪt). **1** having a nucleus. ◆ *vb* ('nju:klɪˌeɪt), **nucleates, nucleating, nucleated.** (*intr*) **2** to form a nucleus.

nuclei ('nju:klɪˌaɪ) *n* a plural of **nucleus.**

nucleic acid (nju:'kli:ɪk, -'kleɪ-) *n Biochem.* any of a group of complex compounds with a high molecular weight that are vital constituents of all living cells. See also **RNA, DNA.**

nucleo- *or before a vowel* **nucle-** *combining form.* **1** nucleus or nuclear. **2** nucleic acid. ORIG from Latin *nucleus* kernel, from *nux* nut

nucleolus (ˌnju:klɪ'əʊləs) *n, pl* **nucleoli** (-laɪ). a small rounded body within a resting cell nucleus that contains RNA and proteins and is involved in protein synthesis. Also called: **nucleole.** ORIG C19: from L, dim. of NUCLEUS
▸ **ˌnucle'olar** *adj*

nucleon ('nju:klɪˌɒn) *n* a proton or neutron, esp. one present in an atomic nucleus.

nucleonics (ˌnju:klɪ'ɒnɪks) *n* (*functioning as sing*) the branch of physics concerned with the applications of nuclear energy.
▸ **ˌnucle'onic** *adj* ▸ **ˌnucle'onically** *adv*

nucleon number *n* the number of nucleons in an atomic nucleus; mass number.

nucleophile ('nju:klɪəˌfaɪl) *n* a molecule or ion that can donate electrons.
▸ **nucleophilic** (ˌnju:klɪə'fɪlɪk) *adj*

nucleoside ('nju:klɪəˌsaɪd) *n Biochem.* a compound containing a purine or pyrimidine base linked to a sugar (usually ribose or deoxyribose).

nucleotide ('nju:klɪəˌtaɪd) *n Biochem.* a compound consisting of a nucleoside linked to phosphoric acid.

nucleus ('nju:klɪəs) *n, pl* **nuclei** *or* **nucleuses. 1** a central or fundamental thing around which others are grouped; core. **2** a centre of growth or development; basis: *the nucleus of an idea.* **3** *Biol.* the spherical or ovoid compartment of a cell that contains the chromosomes and associated molecules that control the characteristics and growth of the cell. **4** *Astron.* the central portion in the head of a comet, consisting of small solid particles of ice and frozen gases. **5** *Physics.* the positively charged dense region at the centre of an atom, composed of protons and neutrons, about which electrons orbit. **6** *Chem.* a fundamental group of atoms in a molecule serving as the base structure for related compounds. ORIG C18: from L: kernel, from *nux* nut

nuclide ('nju:klaɪd) *n* a species of atom characterized by its atomic number and its mass number. ORIG C20: from NUCLEO- + *-ide,* from Gk *eidos* shape

nude (nju:d) *adj* **1** completely undressed. **2** having no covering; bare; exposed. **3** *Law.* **3a** lacking some essential

legal requirement. **3b** (of a contract, etc.) made without consideration and void unless under seal. ◆ *n* **4** the state of being naked (esp. in **in the nude**). **5** a naked figure, esp. in painting, sculpture, etc. ORIG C16: from L *nūdus*
▸ **'nudely** *adv*

nudge (nʌdʒ) *vb* **nudges, nudging, nudged.** (*tr*) **1** to push (someone) gently, esp. with the elbow, to get attention; jog. **2** to push slowly or lightly: *as I drove out, I just nudged the gatepost.* ◆ *n* **3** a gentle poke or push. ORIG C17: ?from Scand.
▸ **'nudger** *n*

nudibranch ('nju:dɪˌbræŋk) *n* a marine gastropod of an order characterized by a shell-less, often beautifully coloured, body bearing external gills. Also called: **sea slug.** ORIG C19: from L *nudus* naked + *branche,* from L *branchia* gills

nudism ('nju:dɪzəm) *n* the practice of nudity, esp. for reasons of health, etc.
▸ **'nudist** *n, adj*

nudity ('nju:dɪtɪ) *n, pl* **nudities.** the state or fact of being nude; nakedness.

Nuevo Laredo ★ (*Spanish* 'nweβo la'reðo) *n* a city and port of entry in NE Mexico, in Tamaulipas state on the Rio Grande opposite Laredo, Texas: oil industries. Pop.: 218 413 (1990).

Nuevo León ★ ('nweɪvəʊ leɪ'əʊn, nu:'eɪ-; *Spanish* 'nweβo le'ɔn) *n* a state of NE Mexico: the first centre of heavy industry in Latin America. Capital: Monterrey. Pop.: 3 684 845 (1997 est.). Area: 64 555 sq. km (24 925 sq. miles).

Nuffield ★ ('nʌfi:ld) *n* **William Richard Morris,** 1st Viscount Nuffield. 1877–1963, British car manufacturer and philanthropist. He endowed Nuffield College at Oxford (1937) and the Nuffield Foundation (1943).

nugatory ('nju:gətərɪ, -trɪ) *adj* **1** of little value; trifling. **2** not valid: *a nugatory law.* ORIG C17: from L *nūgātōrius,* from *nūgārī* to jest, from *nūgae* trifles

nugget ('nʌgɪt) *n* **1** a small piece or lump, esp. of gold in its natural state. **2** something small but valuable or excellent. ORIG C19: from ?

nuggety ('nʌgɪtɪ) *adj* **1** of or resembling a nugget. **2** *Austral. & NZ inf.* (of a person) thickset; stocky.

nuisance ('nju:səns) *n* **1a** a person or thing that causes annoyance or bother. **1b** (*as modifier*): *nuisance calls.* **2** *Law.* something unauthorized that is obnoxious or injurious to the community at large or to an individual, esp. in relation to his ownership of property. **3 nuisance value.** the usefulness of a person's or thing's capacity to cause difficulties or irritation. ORIG C15: via OF from *nuire* to injure, from L *nocēre*

NUJ (in Britain) *abbrev. for* National Union of Journalists.

Nu Jiang ★ ('nu: 'dʒjæŋ) *n* the Chinese name for the **Salween.**

nuke (nju:k) *Sl., chiefly US.* ◆ *vb* **nukes, nuking, nuked.** (*tr*) **1** to attack or destroy with nuclear weapons. ◆ *n* **2** a nuclear bomb.

Nuku'alofa ★ (ˌnu:ku:ə'lɔ:fə) *n* the capital of Tonga, a port on the N coast of Tongatapu Island. Pop.: 34 000 (1990 est.).

Nukus ★ (*Russian* nu'kus) *n* a city in Uzbekistan, capital of the Kara-Kalpak Autonomous Republic, on the Amu Darya River. Pop.: 185 000 (1993 est.).

null (nʌl) *adj* **1** without legal force; invalid; (esp. in **null and void**). **2** without value or consequence; useless. **3** lacking distinction; characterless. **4** nonexistent; amounting to nothing. **5** *Maths.* **5a** quantitatively zero. **5b** relating to zero. **5c** (of a set) having no members. **6** *Physics.* involving measurement in which conditions are adjusted so that an instrument has a zero reading, as with a Wheatstone bridge. ORIG C16: from L *nullus* none, from *ne* not + *ullus* any

nullah ('nʌlɑ:) *n* a stream or drain. ORIG C18: from Hindi *nālā*

Nullarbor Plain ★ ('nʌləˌbɔ:) *n* a vast low plateau of S Australia: extends north from the Great Australian Bight to the Great Victoria Desert; has no surface water or trees. Area: 260 000 sq. km (100 000 sq. miles).

null hypothesis *n Statistics.* the residual hypothesis if the alternative hypothesis tested against it fails to achieve a predetermined significance level.

nullify ('nʌlɪˌfaɪ) *vb* **nullifies, nullifying, nullified.** (*tr*) **1** to render legally void or of no effect. **2** to render ineffective or useless; cancel out. ORIG C16: from LL *nullificāre* to despise, from L *nullus* of no account + *facere* to make
▸ **ˌnullifi'cation** *n*

nullity ('nʌlɪtɪ) *n, pl* **nullities. 1** the state of being null. **2** a null or legally invalid act or instrument. **3** something null, ineffective, characterless, etc. ORIG C16: from Med. L *nullitās,* from L *nullus* no, not any

NUM (in Britain) *abbrev. for* National Union of Mineworkers.

num. *abbrev. for:* **1** number. **2** numeral.

Num. *Bible. abbrev. for* Numbers.

Numantia ★ (nju:'mæntɪə) *n* an ancient city in N Spain: a centre of Celtic resistance to Rome in N Spain: captured by Scipio the Younger in 133 B.C.
▸ **Nu'mantian** *adj, n*

Numa Pompilius ★ ('nju:mə pɒm'pɪlɪəs) *n* the legendary second king of Rome (?715–?673 B.C.).

numb (nʌm) *adj* **1** deprived of feeling through cold, shock, etc. **2** unable to move; paralysed. ◆ *vb* **3** (*tr*) to make numb; deaden, shock, or paralyse. ORIG C15 *nomen,* lit.: taken (with paralysis), from OE *niman* to take
▸ **'numbly** *adv* ▸ **'numbness** *n*

numbat ('nʌmˌbæt) *n* a small Australian marsupial having a long snout and tongue and strong claws for hunting and feeding on termites. ORIG C20: from Abor.

number ('nʌmbə) *n* **1** a concept of quantity that is or can be derived from a single unit, the sum of a collection of units, or zero. Every number occupies a unique position in a sequence, enabling it to be used in counting. See also **cardinal number, ordinal number. 2** the symbol used to represent a number; numeral. **3** a numeral or string of numerals used to identify a person or thing: *a telephone number.* **4** the person or thing so identified or designated: *she was number seven in the race.* **5** sum or quantity: *a large number of people.* **6** one of a series, as of a magazine; issue. **7a** a self-contained piece of pop or jazz music. **7b** a self-contained part of an opera or other musical score. **8** a group of people, esp. an exclusive group: *he was not one of our number.* **9** *Sl.* a person, esp. a sexually attractive girl: *who's that nice little number?* **10** *Inf.* an admired article: *that little number is by Dior.* **11** a grammatical category for the variation in form of nouns, pronouns, and any words agreeing with them, depending on how many persons or things are referred to. **12 any number of.** several or many. **13 by numbers.** *Mil.* (of a drill procedure, etc.) performed step by step, each move being made on the call of a number. **14 get** *or* **have someone's number.** *Inf.* to discover a person's true character or intentions. **15 one's number is up.** *Brit. inf.* one is finished; one is ruined or about to die. **16 without** *or* **beyond number.** innumerable. ◆ *vb* (*mainly tr*) **17** to assign a number to. **18** to add up to; total. **19** (*also intr*) to list (items) one by one; enumerate. **20** (*also intr*) to put or be put into a group, category, etc.: *they were numbered among the worst hit.* **21** to limit the number of: *his days were numbered.* ORIG C13: from OF *nombre,* from L *numerus*

number crunching *n Computing.* the large-scale processing of numerical data.

numbered account *n Banking.* an account identified only by a number, esp. one in a Swiss bank that could contain funds illegally obtained.

numberless ('nʌmbəlɪs) *adj* **1** too many to be counted; countless. **2** not containing numbers.

number one *n* **1** the first in a series or sequence. **2** an informal phrase for **oneself, myself,** etc.: *to look after number one.* **3** *Inf.* the most important person; chief: *he's number one in the organization.* **4** *Inf.* the bestselling pop record in any one week. ◆ *adj* **5** first in importance, urgency, quality, etc.: *number one priority.*

numberplate ('nʌmbəˌpleɪt) *n* a plate mounted on the front and back of a motor vehicle bearing the registration number. Usual US term: **license plate,** (Canad.) **licence plate.**

numbers game *or* **racket** *n US.* an illegal lottery in which money is wagered on a certain combination of digits appearing at the beginning of a series of numbers published in a newspaper, as in share prices or sports results. Often shortened to **numbers.**

Number Ten *n* 10 Downing Street, the British prime minister's official London residence.

number theory *n* the study of integers, their properties, and the relationship between integers.

numbfish ('nʌm,fɪʃ) *n, pl* **numbfish** *or* **numbfishes.** any of several electric rays. ORIG C18: so called because it numbs its victims

numbles ('nʌmbᵊlz) *pl n Arch.* the heart, lungs, liver, etc., of a deer or other animal. ORIG C14: from OF *nombles,* pl. of *nomble* thigh muscle of a deer, changed from L *lumbulus,* dim. of *lumbus* loin

numbskull *or* **numskull** ('nʌm,skʌl) *n* a stupid person; dolt; blockhead.

numen ('nju:mɛn) *n, pl* **numina** (-mɪnə). **1** (esp. in ancient Roman religion) a deity or spirit presiding over a thing or place. **2** a guiding principle, force, or spirit. ORIG C17: from L: a nod (indicating a command), divine power

numerable ('nju:mərəbᵊl) *adj* able to be numbered or counted.
▸ **'numerably** *adv*

numeral ('nju:mərəl) *n* **1** a symbol or group of symbols used to express a number: for example, *6* (*Arabic*), *VI* (*Roman*), *110* (*binary*). ◆ *adj* **2** of, consisting of, or denoting a number. ORIG C16: from LL *numerālis* belonging to number, from L *numerus*

numerate *adj* ('nju:mərɪt). **1** able to use numbers, esp. in arithmetical operations. ◆ *vb* ('nju:mə,reɪt), **numerates, numerating, numerated.** (*tr*) **2** to read (a numerical expression). **3** a less common word for **enumerate.** ORIG C18 (vb): from L *numerus* number + -ATE[1], by analogy with *literate*
▸ **numeracy** ('nju:mərəsɪ) *n*

numeration (,nju:mə'reɪʃən) *n* **1** the writing, reading, or naming of numbers. **2** a system of numbering.
▸ **'numerative** *adj*

numerator ('nju:mə,reɪtə) *n* **1** *Maths.* the dividend of a fraction: the numerator of 7/8 is 7. Cf. **denominator. 2** a person or thing that numbers; enumerator.

numerical (nju:'mɛrɪkᵊl) *or* **numeric** *adj* **1** of, relating to, or denoting a number or numbers. **2** measured or expressed in numbers: *numerical value.*
▸ **nu'merically** *adv*

numerology (,nju:mə'rɒlədʒɪ) *n* the study of numbers, such as the figures in a birth date, and of their supposed influence on human affairs.
▸ **numerological** (,nju:mərə'lɒdʒɪkᵊl) *adj*

numerous ('nju:mərəs) *adj* **1** being many. **2** consisting of many parts: *a numerous collection.*
▸ **'numerously** *adv* ▸ **'numerousness** *n*

Numidia ★ (nju:'mɪdɪə) *n* an ancient country of N Africa, corresponding roughly to present-day Algeria: flourished until its invasion by Vandals in 429; chief towns were Cirta and Hippo Regius.
▸ **Nu'midian** *n, adj*

numinous ('nju:mɪnəs) *adj* **1** denoting, being, or relating to a numen; divine. **2** arousing spiritual or religious emotions. **3** mysterious or awe-inspiring. ORIG C17: from L *numin-,* NUMEN + -OUS

numismatics (,nju:mɪz'mætɪks) *n* (*functioning as sing*) the study or collection of coins, medals, etc. Also called: **,numisma'tology.** ORIG C18: from F *numismatique,* from L *nomisma,* from Gk: piece of currency, from *nomizein* to have in use, from *nōmos* use
▸ **,numis'matic** *adj* ▸ **,numis'matically** *adv*

nummulite ('nʌmjʊ,laɪt) *n* any of a family of large fossil protozoans common in Tertiary times. ORIG C19: from NL, from L *nummulus,* from *nummus* coin

numpty ('nʌmptɪ) *n, pl* **numpties.** *Scot. inf.* a foolish or ignorant person.

numskull ('nʌm,skʌl) *n* a variant spelling of **numbskull.**

nun (nʌn) *n* a female member of a religious order. ORIG OE *nunne,* from Church L *nonna,* from LL: form of address used for an elderly woman
▸ **'nunhood** *n* ▸ **'nunlike** *adj*

Nunavut ★ ('nu:nəvʊt) *n* a territory of N Canada, created in 1999 from part of Northwest Territories as an autonomous region for the Inuit people. Capital: Iqaluit. Pop.: 27 146 (1999 est.). Area: 1 235 200 sq. km (772 000 sq. miles)

nun buoy *n Naut.* a buoy, conical at the top, marking the right side of a channel leading into a harbour: green in British waters but red in US waters. ORIG C18: from obs. *nun* child's spinning top + BUOY

Nunc Dimittis ('nʌŋk dɪ'mɪtɪs, 'nʊŋk) *n* **1** the Latin name for the Canticle of Simeon (Luke 2:29–32). **2** a musical setting of this. ORIG from the opening words (Vulgate): now let depart

nunciature ('nʌnsɪətʃə) *n* the office or term of office of a nuncio. ORIG C17: from It. *nunziatura;* see NUNCIO

nuncio ('nʌnʃɪ,əʊ, -sɪ-) *n, pl* **nuncios.** *RC Church.* a diplomatic representative of the Holy See. ORIG C16: via It. from L *nuntius* messenger

Nuneaton ★ (nʌn'i:tᵊn) *n* a town in central England, in Warwickshire. Pop.: 66 715 (1991).

Nunn ★ (nʌn) *n* **Trevor** (**Robert**). born 1940, British theatre director; chief executive (1978–86) of the Royal Shakespeare Company; artistic director of the Royal National Theatre from 1997.

nunnery ('nʌnərɪ) *n, pl* **nunneries.** the convent or religious house of a community of nuns.

NUPE ('nju:pɪ) *n* (formerly, in Britain) *acronym for* National Union of Public Employees.

nuptial ('nʌpʃəl, -tʃəl) *adj* **1** relating to marriage; conjugal: *nuptial vows.* **2** *Zool.* of or relating to mating: *the nuptial flight of a queen bee.* ORIG C15: from L *nuptiālis,* from *nuptiae* marriage, from *nubere* to marry
▸ **'nuptially** *adv*

nuptials ('nʌpʃəlz, -tʃəlz) *pl n* (*sometimes sing*) a marriage ceremony; wedding.

NUR (formerly, in Britain) *abbrev. for* National Union of Railwaymen.

nurd a variant spelling of **nerd.**

Nuremberg ★ ('njʊərəm,bɜ:g) *n* a city in S Germany, in N Bavaria: scene of annual Nazi rallies (1933–38), the anti-Semitic Nuremberg decrees (1935), and the trials of Nazi leaders for their war crimes (1945–46); important metalworking and electrical industries. Pop.: 492 425 (1996 est.). German name: **Nürnberg.**

Nureyev ★ ('njʊərɪɛf, nju'reɪ-) *n* **Rudolf.** 1938–93, Austrian ballet dancer, born in the Soviet Union: joined the Royal Ballet in 1962; artistic director of the Paris Opéra Ballet (1983–89).

Nuristan ★ (,nʊərɪ'stɑ:n) *n* a region of E Afghanistan: consists mainly of high mountains (including part of the Hindu Kush), steep narrow valleys, and extensive forests. Area: about 13 000 sq. km (5000 sq. miles). Former name: **Kafiristan.**

Nürnberg ★ ('nyrnbɛrk) *n* the German name for **Nuremberg.**

nurse (nɜ:s) *n* **1** a person, often a woman, who is trained to tend the sick and infirm, assist doctors, etc. **2** short for **nursemaid. 3** a woman employed to breast-feed another woman's child; wet nurse. **4** a worker in a colony of social insects that takes care of the larvae. ◆ *vb* **nurses, nursing, nursed.** (*mainly tr*) **5** (*also intr*) to tend (the sick). **6** (*also intr*) to feed (a baby) at the breast. **7** to try to cure (an ailment). **8** to clasp fondly: *she nursed the child in her arms.* **9** to look after (a child) as one's employment. **10** to harbour; preserve: *to nurse a grudge.* **11** to give special attention to, esp. in order to promote goodwill: *to nurse a difficult constituency.* **12** *Billiards.* to keep (the balls) together for a series of cannons. ORIG C16: from earlier *norice,* OF *nourice,* from LL *nūtrīcia,* from L *nūtrīcius* nourishing, from *nūtrīre* to nourish

nursemaid ('nɜ:s,meɪd) *or* **nurserymaid** *n* a woman employed to look after someone else's children. Often shortened to **nurse.**

nursery ('nɜ:srɪ) *n, pl* **nurseries. 1** a room in a house set

★ people and places

apart for children. **2** a place where plants, young trees, etc., are grown commercially. **3** an establishment providing daycare for babies and young children; crèche. **4** anywhere serving to foster or nourish new ideas, etc. **5** Also called: **nursery cannon.** *Billiards.* **5a** a series of cannons with the three balls adjacent to a cushion, esp. near a corner pocket. **5b** a cannon in such a series.

nurseryman ('nɜːsrɪmən) *n, pl* **nurserymen.** a person who owns or works in a nursery in which plants are grown.

nursery rhyme *n* a short traditional verse or song for children, such as *Little Jack Horner.*

nursery school *n* a school for young children, usually from three to five years old.

nursery slopes *pl n* gentle slopes used by beginners in skiing.

nursery stakes *pl n* a race for two-year-old horses.

nurse shark *n* any of various sharks having an external groove on each side of the head between the mouth and nostril. ORIG C15 *nusse fisshe* (later infl. in spelling by NURSE), ?from a division of obs. *an huss* shark, dogfish (from ?) as *a nuss*

nursing ('nɜːsɪŋ) *n* **a** the practice or profession of caring for the sick and injured. **b** (*as modifier*): *a nursing home.*

nursing home *n* a private hospital or residence for aged or infirm persons.

nursing officer *n* (in Britain) the official name for **matron** (sense 4).

nursling *or* **nurseling** ('nɜːslɪŋ) *n* a child or young animal that is being suckled, nursed, or fostered.

nurture ('nɜːtʃə) *n* **1** the act or process of promoting the development, etc., of a child. **2** something that nourishes. ◆ *vb* **nurtures, nurturing, nurtured.** (*tr*) **3** to feed or support. **4** to educate or train. ORIG C14: from OF *norriture,* from L *nūtrīre* to nourish
▸ **'nurtural** *adj* ▸ **'nurturer** *n*

NUS (in Britain) *abbrev. for:* **1** (formerly) National Union of Seamen. **2** National Union of Students.

Nusa Tenggara ★ ('nuːsə tɛŋ'gɑːrə) *n* an island chain of Indonesia, east of Java: the main islands are Bali, Lombok, Sumbawa, Sumba, Flores, Alor, and Timor. Pop.: 7 237 600 (1995 est.). Area: 73 144 sq. km (28 241 sq. miles). Former name: **Lesser Sunda Islands.**

nut (nʌt) *n* **1** a dry one-seeded indehiscent fruit that usually possesses a woody wall. **2** (*not in technical use*) any similar fruit, such as the walnut, having a hard shell and an edible kernel. **3** the edible kernel of such a fruit. **4** *Sl.* an eccentric or mad person. **5** *Sl.* the head. **6 do one's nut.** *Brit. sl.* to be extremely angry. **7 off one's nut.** *Sl.* mad or foolish. **8** a person or thing that presents difficulties (esp. in **a tough nut to crack**). **9** a small square hexagonal block, usually metal, with a threaded hole through the middle for screwing on the end of a bolt. **10** Also called (US and Canad.): **frog.** *Music.* **10a** the ridge at the upper end of the fingerboard of a violin, cello, etc., over which the strings pass to the tuning pegs. **10b** the end of a violin bow that is held by the player. **11** a small usually gingery biscuit. **12** *Brit.* a small piece of coal. ◆ *vb* **nuts, nutting, nutted. 13** (*intr*) to gather nuts. ◆ See also **nuts.** ORIG OE *hnutu*

NUT (in Britain) *abbrev. for* National Union of Teachers.

nutant ('njuːt^{ə}nt) *adj Bot.* having the apex hanging down. ORIG C18: from L *nūtāre* to nod

nutation (njuː'teɪʃən) *n* **1** *Astron.* a periodic variation in the precession of the earth's axis causing the earth's poles to oscillate about their mean position. **2** the spiral growth of a shoot or similar plant organ, caused by variation in the growth rate in different parts. **3** the act of nodding. ORIG C17: from L *nutātiō,* from *nūtāre* to nod

nutbrown ('nʌt'braʊn) *adj* reddish-brown.

nutcase ('nʌtˌkeɪs) *n Sl.* an insane or very foolish person.

nutcracker ('nʌtˌkrækə) *n* **1** (*often pl*) a device for cracking the shells of nuts. **2** either an Old World bird or a North American bird (**Clark's nutcracker**) having speckled plumage and feeding on nuts, seeds, etc.

nutgall ('nʌtˌgɔːl) *n* a nut-shaped gall caused by gall wasps on the oak and other trees.

nuthatch ('nʌtˌhætʃ) *n* a songbird having strong feet and bill, and feeding on insects, seeds, and nuts. ORIG C14 *notehache,* from *note* nut + *hache* hatchet, from its habit of splitting nuts

nuthouse ('nʌtˌhaʊs) *n Sl.* a mental hospital.

nutmeg ('nʌtˌmɛg) *n* **1** an East Indian evergreen tree cultivated in the tropics for its hard aromatic seed. See also **mace**[2]. **2** the seed of this tree, used as a spice. ◆ *vb* **nutmegs, nutmegging, nutmegged.** (*tr*) **3** *Brit. sport inf.* to kick or hit the ball between the legs of (an opposing player). ORIG C13: from OF *nois muguede,* from OProvençal *noz muscada* musk-scented nut, from L *nux* NUT + *muscus* MUSK

nutraceutical (ˌnjuːtrə'sjuːtɪk^{ə}l) *n* another name for **functional food.**

nutria ('njuːtrɪə) *n* another name for **coypu,** esp. the fur. ORIG C19: from Sp., var. of *lutria,* ult. from L *lūtra* otter

nutrient ('njuːtrɪənt) *n* **1** any of the mineral substances that are absorbed by the roots of plants. **2** any substance that nourishes an animal. ◆ *adj* **3** providing or contributing to nourishment. ORIG C17: from L *nūtrīre* to nourish

nutriment ('njuːtrɪmənt) *n* any material providing nourishment. ORIG C16: from L *nūtrīmentum,* from *nūtrīre* to nourish
▸ **nutrimental** (ˌnjuːtrɪ'mɛnt^{ə}l) *adj*

nutrition (njuː'trɪʃən) *n* **1** a process in animals and plants involving the intake and assimilation of nutrient materials. **2** the act or process of nourishing. **3** the study of nutrition, esp. in humans. ORIG C16: from LL *nūtrītiō,* from *nūtrīre* to nourish
▸ **nu'tritional** *adj* ▸ **nu'tritionist** *n*

nutritious (njuː'trɪʃəs) *adj* nourishing. ORIG C17: from L *nūtrīcius,* from *nūtrix* NURSE
▸ **nu'tritiously** *adv* ▸ **nu'tritiousness** *n*

nutritive ('njuːtrɪtɪv) *adj* **1** providing nourishment. **2** of, concerning, or promoting nutrition. ◆ *n* **3** a nutritious food.

nuts (nʌts) *adj* **1** a slang word for **insane. 2** (foll. by *about* or *on*) *Sl.* extremely fond (of) or enthusiastic (about). ◆ *interj* **3** *Sl.* an expression of contempt, refusal, or defiance.

nuts and bolts *pl n Inf.* the essential or practical details.

nutshell ('nʌtˌʃɛl) *n* **1** the shell around the kernel of a nut. **2 in a nutshell.** in essence; briefly.

nutter ('nʌtə) *n Brit. sl.* a mad or eccentric person.

nutty ('nʌtɪ) *adj* **nuttier, nuttiest. 1** containing nuts. **2** resembling nuts. **3** a slang word for **insane. 4** (foll. by *over* or *about*) *Inf.* extremely enthusiastic (about).
▸ **'nuttiness** *n*

Nuuk ★ (nuːk) *n* the capital of Greenland, in the southwest: the oldest Danish settlement in Greenland, founded in 1721. Pop.: 12 882 (1996 est.). Former name (until 1979): **Godthaab.**

nux vomica ('nʌks 'vɒmɪkə) *n* **1** an Indian tree with orange-red berries containing poisonous seeds. **2** any of the seeds of this tree, which contain strychnine and other poisonous alkaloids. **3** a medicine manufactured from the seeds of this tree, formerly used as a heart stimulant. ORIG C16: from Med. L: vomiting nut

nuzzle ('nʌz^{ə}l) *vb* **nuzzles, nuzzling, nuzzled. 1** to push or rub gently with the nose or snout. **2** (*intr*) to nestle; lie close. **3** (*tr*) to dig out with the snout. ORIG C15 *nosele,* from NOSE (n)

NV *abbrev. for* Nevada.

nvCJD *abbrev. for* new-variant Creutzfeldt-Jakob disease.

NVQ *abbrev. for* National Vocational Qualification.

NW *symbol for* northwest(ern).

NWMP (in Canada) *abbrev. for* North West Mounted Police.

NWT *abbrev. for* Northwest Territories (of Canada).

NY *or* **N.Y.** *abbrev. for* New York (city or state).

nyala ('njɑːlə) *n, pl* **nyala** *or* **nyalas. 1** a spiral-horned southern African antelope with a fringe of white hairs along the length of the back and neck. **2 mountain nyala.** a similar Ethiopian animal lacking the white crest. ORIG from Zulu

Nyasa *or* **Nyassa** ★ (nɪ'æsə, naɪ'æsə) *n* **Lake.** a lake in central Africa at the S end of the Great Rift Valley: the third largest lake in Africa, drained by the Shiré River into the Zambezi. Area: about 28 500 sq. km (11 000 sq. miles). Malawi name: **Lake Malawi.**

Nyasaland ★ (nɪ'æsə,lænd, naɪ'æsə-) *n* the former name (until 1964) of **Malawi.**

NYC *abbrev. for* New York City.

nyctalopia (,nɪktə'ləʊpɪə) *n* inability to see normally in dim light. Nontechnical name: **night blindness.** ORIG C17: via LL from Gk *nuktálōps,* from *nux* night + *alaos* blind + *ōps* eye

nyctitropism (nɪk'tɪtrə,pɪzəm) *n* a tendency of some plant parts to assume positions at night that are different from their daytime positions. ORIG C19: *nyct-,* from Gk *nukt-, nux* night + -TROPISM

nye (naɪ) *n* a flock of pheasants. Also called: **nide, eye.** ORIG C15: from OF *ni,* from L *nīdus* nest

Nyeman ★ (*Russian* 'njɛmən) *n* a variant spelling of **Neman.**

Nyerere ★ (njə'rɛrɪ, nɪ-) *n* **Julius Kambarage** (kæm'ba:ra:gə). 1922–99, Tanzanian statesman; president (1964–85). He became prime minister of Tanganyika (1961) and president (1962), negotiating the union of Tanganyika and Zanzibar to form Tanzania (1964).

Nyíregyháza ★ (*Hungarian* 'nji:rɛtjha:zɔ) *n* a market town in NE Hungary. Pop.: 113 000 (1997 est.).

Nykøbing ★ (*Danish* 'nykø:beŋ) *n* a port in Denmark, on the W coast of Falster Island. Pop.: 64 428 (1987).

nylon ('naɪlɒn) *n* **1** a class of synthetic polyamide materials of which monofilaments are used for bristles, etc., and fibres can be spun into yarn. **2** yarn or cloth made of nylon, used for clothing, stockings, etc. ORIG C20: orig. a trademark

nylons ('naɪlɒnz) *pl n* stockings made of nylon.

nymph (nɪmf) *n* **1** *Myth.* a spirit of nature envisaged as a beautiful maiden. **2** *Chiefly poetic.* a beautiful young woman. **3** the larva of insects such as the dragonfly. It resembles the adult, apart from having underdeveloped wings, and develops without a pupal stage. ORIG C14: via OF from L, from Gk *numphē*
▸ **'nymphal** *or* **nymphean** ('nɪmfɪən) *adj* ▸ **'nymphlike** *adj*

nympha ('nɪmfə) *n, pl* **nymphae** (-fi:). *Anat.* either one of the labia minora. ORIG C17: from L: bride

nymphet ('nɪmfɪt) *n* a young girl who is sexually precocious and desirable. ORIG C17 (meaning: a young nymph): dim. of NYMPH

nympho ('nɪmfəʊ) *n, pl* **nymphos.** *Inf.* short for **nymphomaniac.**

nympholepsy ('nɪmfə,lɛpsɪ) *n, pl* **nympholepsies.** a state of violent emotion, esp. when associated with a desire for something that one cannot have. ORIG C18: from Gk *numpholēptos* caught by nymphs, from *numphē* nymph + *lambanein* to seize
▸ **'nympho,lept** *n* ▸ **,nympho'leptic** *adj*

nymphomania (,nɪmfə'meɪnɪə) *n* a neurotic compulsion in women to have sexual intercourse with many men without being able to have lasting relationships with them. ORIG C18: NL, from Gk *numphē* nymph + -MANIA
▸ **,nympho'maniac** *n, adj*

Nysa ★ ('naɪsə) *n* the Polish name for the **Neisse** (sense 1).

nystagmus (nɪ'stægməs) *n* involuntary movement of the eye comprising a smooth drift followed by a flick back. ORIG C19: NL, from Gk *nustagmos*
▸ **nys'tagmic** *adj*

Nyx ★ (nɪks) *n Greek myth.* the goddess of the night, daughter of Chaos. Roman counterpart: **Nox.**

NZ *or* **N. Zeal.** *abbrev. for* New Zealand.

NZBC (formerly) *abbrev. for* New Zealand Broadcasting Commission.

NZEF (in New Zealand) *abbrev. for* New Zealand Expeditionary Force, the New Zealand army that served in 1914–18. **2NZEF** refers to the Second New Zealand Expeditionary Force, in World War II.

Oo

o *or* **O** (əʊ) *n, pl* **o's, O's,** *or* **Os. 1** the 15th letter and fourth vowel of the English alphabet. **2** any of several speech sounds represented by this letter, as in *code, pot, cow,* or *form.* **3** another name for **nought.**

O¹ *symbol for:* **1** *Chem.* oxygen. **2** a human blood type of the ABO group. **3** Old.

O² (əʊ) *interj* **1** a variant of **oh. 2** an exclamation introducing an invocation, entreaty, wish, etc.: *O God! O for the wings of a dove!*

o. *abbrev. for:* **1** octavo. **2** old. **3** only. **4** order. **5** *Pharmacol.* pint. ORIG from L *octarius*

O. *abbrev. for:* **1** Ocean. **2** octavo. **3** old.

o' (ə) *prep Inf. or arch.* shortened form of **of:** *a cup o' tea.*

O'- *prefix* (in surnames of Irish Gaelic origin) descendant of: *O'Corrigan.* ORIG from Irish Gaelic *ó, ua* descendant

-o *suffix forming nouns.* indicating a diminutive or slang abbreviation: *wino.*

oaf (əʊf) *n* a stupid or loutish person. ORIG C17: var. of OE *ælf* ELF
▸ **'oafish** *adj* ▸ **'oafishness** *n*

Oahu ★ (əʊ'ɑːhuː) *n* an island in central Hawaii: the third largest of the Hawaiian Islands. Chief town: Honolulu. Pop.: 836 231 (1990). Area: 1574 sq. km (608 sq. miles).

oak (əʊk) *n* **1** any deciduous or evergreen tree or shrub having acorns as fruits and lobed leaves. **2a** the wood of any of these trees, used esp. as building timber and for making furniture. **2b** (*as modifier*): *an oak table.* **3** any of various trees that resemble the oak, such as the poison oak. **4** the leaves of an oak tree, worn as a garland. ORIG OE *āc*

oak apple *or* **gall** *n* any of various brownish round galls on oak trees, containing the larvae of certain wasps.

oaken ('əʊkən) *adj* made of the wood of the oak.

Oakham ★ ('əʊkəm) *n* a market town in E central England, administrative centre of Rutland. Pop.: 8691 (1991).

Oakland ★ ('əʊklənd) *n* a port and industrial centre in W California, on San Francisco Bay; damaged by earthquake in 1989. Pop.: 367 230 (1996 est.).

Oakley ★ ('əʊklɪ) *n* **Annie,** real name *Phoebe Anne Oakley Mozee.* 1860–1926, US markswoman.

Oaks (əʊks) *n* (*functioning as sing*) **the.** a horse race for fillies held annually at Epsom since 1779: one of the classics of English flat racing. ORIG named after an estate near Epsom

oakum ('əʊkəm) *n* loose fibre obtained by unravelling old rope, used esp. for caulking seams in wooden ships. ORIG OE *ācuma,* var. of *ācumba,* lit.: off-combings, from *ā-* off + *-cumba,* from *cemban* to COMB

Oakville ★ ('əʊkvɪl) *n* a city in SE Canada, in SE Ontario on Lake Ontario southwest of Toronto: motor-vehicle industry. Pop.: 114 670 (1991).

O & M *abbrev. for* organization and method (in studies of working methods).

OAP (in Britain) *abbrev. for* old age pension *or* pensioner.

oar (ɔː) *n* **1** a long shaft of wood for propelling a boat by rowing, having a broad blade that is dipped into and pulled against the water. **2** short for **oarsman. 3 stick** *or* **put one's oar in.** to interfere or interrupt. ◆ *vb* **4** to row or propel with or as if with oars. ORIG OE *ār,* of Gmc origin
▸ **'oarless** *adj* ▸ **'oar,like** *adj*

oarfish ('ɔːˌfɪʃ) *n, pl* **oarfish** *or* **oarfishes.** a very long ribbonfish with long slender ventral fins. ORIG C19: referring to the flattened oarlike body

oarlock ('ɔːˌlɒk) *n* the usual US and Canad. word for **rowlock.**

oarsman ('ɔːzmən) *n, pl* **oarsmen.** a man who rows, esp. one who rows in a racing boat.
▸ **'oarsmanship** *n*

OAS *abbrev. for:* **1** Organization of American States. **2** Organisation de l'Armée Secrète; an organization which opposed Algerian independence by acts of terrorism.

oasis (əʊ'eɪsɪs) *n, pl* **oases** (-iːz). **1** a fertile patch in a desert occurring where the water table approaches or reaches the ground surface. **2** a place of peace, safety, or happiness. ORIG C17: via L from Gk, prob. from Egyptian

oast (əʊst) *n Chiefly Brit.* **1** a kiln for drying hops. **2** Also called: **oast house.** a building containing such kilns, usually having a conical or pyramidal roof. ORIG OE *āst*

oat (əʊt) *n* **1** an erect annual grass grown in temperate regions for its edible seed. **2** (*usually pl*) the seeds or fruits of this grass. **3** any of various other grasses such as the wild oat. **4** *Poetic.* a flute made from an oat straw. **5 feel one's oats.** *US & Canad. inf.* **5a** to feel exuberant. **5b** to feel self-important. **6 sow one's (wild) oats.** to indulge in adventure or promiscuity during youth. ORIG OE *āte,* from ?

oatcake ('əʊtˌkeɪk) *n* a crisp brittle unleavened biscuit made of oatmeal.

oaten ('əʊtᵊn) *adj* made of oats or oat straw.

Oates ★ (əʊts) *n* **1** Captain **Lawrence Edward Grace.** 1880–1912, British explorer; died on Scott's second Antarctic expedition. **2 Titus** ('taɪtəs). 1649–1705, English conspirator. He fabricated the Popish Plot (1678), a supposed Catholic conspiracy to kill Charles II.

oath (əʊθ) *n, pl* **oaths** (əʊðz). **1** a solemn pronouncement to affirm the truth of a statement or to pledge a person to some course of action. **2** the form of such a pronouncement. **3** an irreverent or blasphemous expression, esp. one involving the name of a deity; curse. **4 my oath.** *Austral. sl.* certainly; yes indeed. **5 on, upon,** *or* **under oath. 5a** under the obligation of an oath. **5b** *Law.* having sworn to tell the truth, usually with one's hand on the Bible. **6 take an oath.** to declare formally with a pledge, esp. before giving evidence. ORIG OE *āth*

oatmeal ('əʊtˌmiːl) *n* **1** meal ground from oats, used for making porridge, oatcakes, etc. **2a** a greyish-yellow colour. **2b** (*as adj*): *an oatmeal coat.*

OAU *abbrev. for* Organization of African Unity.

Oaxaca ★ (wə'hɑːkə; *Spanish* oa'xaka) *n* **1** a state of S Mexico, on the Pacific: includes most of the Isthmus of Tehuantepec; inhabited chiefly by Indians. Capital: Oaxaca de Juárez. Pop.: 3 286 175 (1997 est.). Area: 95 363 sq. km (36 820 sq. miles). **2** a city in S Mexico, capital of Oaxaca state: founded in 1486 by the Aztecs and conquered by Spain in 1521. Pop.: 212 818 (1990). Official name: **Oaxaca de Juárez** (de 'xwareθ).

Ob ★ (*Russian* ɔpj) *n* a river in N central Russia, formed at Bisk by the confluence of the Biya and Katun Rivers and flowing generally north to the **Gulf of Ob** (an inlet of the Arctic Ocean): one of the largest rivers in the world, with a drainage basin of about 2 930 000 sq. km (1 131 000 sq. miles). Length: 3682 km (2287 miles).

OB *Brit. abbrev. for:* **1** Old Boy. **2** outside broadcast.

ob. *abbrev. for:* **1** (on tombstones, etc.) obiit. ORIG L: he (or she) died **2** obiter. ORIG L: incidentally; in passing **3** oboe.

ob- *prefix* inverse or inversely: *obovate.* ORIG from OF, from L *ob.* In compound words from L, *ob-* (and *oc-, of-, op-*) indicates: to, towards (*object*); against (*oppose*); away from (*obsolete*); before (*obstetric*); and is used as an intensifier (*oblong*)

Obad. *Bible. abbrev. for* Obadiah.

Obadiah ★ (ˌəʊbə'daɪə) *n Old Testament.* **1** a Hebrew prophet. **2** the book containing his oracles, chiefly directed against Edom. ◆ Douay spelling: **Abdias** (æb'daɪəs).

Oban ★ ('əʊbᵊn) *n* a small port and resort in W Scotland, in Argyll and Bute on the Firth of Lorne. Pop.: 8203 (1991).

obbligato *or* **obligato** (ˌɒblɪ'gɑːtəʊ) *Music.* ◆ *adj* **1** not to be omitted in performance ◆ *n, pl* **obbligatos, obbligati** (-tiː) *or* **obligatos, obligati** (-tiː). **2** an essential part in a score: *with oboe obbligato.* ORIG C18: from It., from *obbligare* to OBLIGE

obconic (ɒb'kɒnɪk) *or* **obconical** *adj Bot.* (of a fruit) shaped like a cone and attached at the pointed end.

obcordate (ɒb'kɔːdeɪt) *adj Bot.* heart-shaped and attached at the pointed end: *obcordate leaves.*

obdurate ('ɒbdjurɪt) *adj* **1** not easily moved by feelings or supplication; hardhearted. **2** impervious to persuasion. ORIG C15: from L *obdūrāre* to make hard, from *ob-* (intensive) + *dūrus* hard
▸ **'obduracy** *or* **'obdurateness** *n* ▸ **'obdurately** *adv*

OBE *abbrev. for* Officer of the Order of the British Empire (a Brit. title).

obeah ('əubɪə) *n* **1** a kind of witchcraft practised by some West Indians. **2** a charm used in this. ORIG of W African origin

obedience (ə'biːdɪəns) *n* **1** the condition or quality of being obedient. **2** the act or an instance of obeying; dutiful or submissive behaviour. **3** the authority vested in a Church or similar body. **4** the collective group of persons submitting to this authority.

obedient (ə'biːdɪənt) *adj* obeying or willing to obey. ORIG C13: from OF, from L *oboediens,* present participle of *oboedīre* to OBEY
▸ **o'bediently** *adv*

obeisance (əu'beɪsəns) *n* **1** an attitude of deference or homage. **2** a gesture expressing obeisance. ORIG C14: from OF *obéissant,* present participle of *obéir* to OBEY
▸ **o'beisant** *adj*

obelisk ('ɒbɪlɪsk) *n* **1** a stone pillar having a square or rectangular cross section and sides that taper towards a pyramidal top. **2** *Printing.* another name for **dagger** (sense 2). ORIG C16: via L from Gk *obeliskos* a little spit, from *obelos* spit
▸ **ˌobe'liscal** *adj* ▸ **ˌobe'liskoid** *adj*

obelus ('ɒbɪləs) *n, pl* **obeli** (-laɪ). **1** a mark (— or ÷) used in ancient documents to indicate spurious words or passages. **2** another name for **dagger** (sense 2). ORIG C14: via LL from Gk *obelos* spit

Oberammergau ★ (*German* oːbər'amərgau) *n* a village in S Germany, in Bavaria in the foothills of the Alps: famous for its Passion Play, performed by the villagers every ten years (except during the World Wars) since 1634, in thanksgiving for the end of the Black Death. Pop.: 4740 (1989 est.).

Oberhausen ★ (*German* 'oːbərhauzən) *n* an industrial city in W Germany, in North Rhine-Westphalia on the Rhine-Herne Canal: site of the first ironworks in the Ruhr. Pop.: 224 397 (1996 est.).

Oberland ★ ('əubəˌlænd) *n* the lower parts of the Bernese Alps in central Switzerland, mostly in S Bern canton.

Oberon ★ ('əubəˌrɒn) *n* (in medieval folklore) the king of the fairies, husband of Titania.

Oberösterreich ★ ('oːbərˌøːstəraiç) *n* the German name for **Upper Austria.**

obese (əu'biːs) *adj* excessively fat or fleshy; corpulent. ORIG C17: from L *obēsus,* from *ob-* (intensive) + *edere* to eat
▸ **o'besity** *or* **o'beseness** *n*

obey (ə'beɪ) *vb* **1** to carry out (instructions or orders); comply with (demands). **2** to behave or act in accordance with (one's feelings, whims, etc.). ORIG C13: from OF *obéir,* from L *oboedīre,* from *ob-* towards + *audīre* to hear
▸ **o'beyer** *n*

obfuscate ('ɒbfʌsˌkeɪt) *vb* **obfuscates, obfuscating, obfuscated.** (*tr*) **1** to obscure or darken. **2** to perplex or bewilder. ORIG C16: from L *ob-* (intensive) + *fuscāre* to blacken, from *fuscus* dark
▸ **ˌobfus'cation** *n* ▸ **'obfusˌcatory** *adj*

obi ('əubɪ) *n, pl* **obis** *or* **obi.** a broad sash tied in a large flat bow at the back, worn as part of the Japanese national costume. ORIG C19: from Japanese

obit ('ɒbɪt, 'əubɪt) *n Inf.* **1** short for **obituary. 2** a memorial service.

obiter dictum ('ɒbɪtə 'dɪktəm, 'əu-) *n, pl* **obiter dicta** ('dɪktə). **1** *Law.* an observation by a judge on some point of law not directly in issue in the case before him. **2** any comment or remark made in passing. ORIG L: something said in passing

obituary (ə'bɪtjuərɪ) *n, pl* **obituaries.** a published announcement of a death, often accompanied by a short biography of the dead person. ORIG C18: from Med. L *obituārius,* from L *obīre* to fall
▸ **o'bituarist** *n*

obj. *abbrev. for:* **1** objection. **2** *Grammar.* object(ive).

object[1] ('ɒbdʒɪkt) *n* **1** a tangible and visible thing. **2** a person or thing seen as a focus for feelings, thought, etc. **3** an aim or objective. **4** *Inf.* a ridiculous or pitiable person, spectacle, etc. **5** *Philosophy.* that towards which cognition is directed as contrasted with the thinking subject. **6** *Grammar.* a noun, pronoun, or noun phrase whose referent is the recipient of the action of a verb. See also **direct object, indirect object. 7** *Grammar.* a noun, pronoun, or noun phrase that is governed by a preposition. **8** *Computing.* a self-contained identifiable component of a software system or design. **9 no object.** not a hindrance or obstacle: *money is no object.* ORIG C14: from LL *objectus* something thrown before (the mind), from L *obicere;* see OBJECT[2]

object[2] (əb'dʒɛkt) *vb* **1** (*tr; takes a clause as object*) to state as an objection. **2** (*intr;* often foll. by *to*) to raise or state an objection (to); present an argument (against). ORIG C15: from L *obicere,* from *ob-* against + *jacere* to throw
▸ **ob'jector** *n*

object glass *n Optics.* another name for **objective** (sense 10).

objectify (əb'dʒɛktɪˌfaɪ) *vb* **objectifies, objectifying, objectified.** (*tr*) to represent concretely; present as an object.
▸ **obˌjectifi'cation** *n*

objection (əb'dʒɛkʃən) *n* **1** an expression or feeling of opposition or dislike. **2** a cause for such an expression or feeling. **3** the act of objecting.

objectionable (əb'dʒɛkʃənəbᵊl) *adj* unpleasant, offensive, or repugnant.
▸ **obˌjectiona'bility** *or* **ob'jectionableness** *n* ▸ **ob'jectionably** *adv*

objective (əb'dʒɛktɪv) *adj* **1** existing independently of perception or an individual's conceptions. **2** undistorted by emotion or personal bias. **3** of or relating to actual and external phenomena as opposed to thoughts, feelings, etc. **4** *Med.* (of disease symptoms) perceptible to persons other than the individual affected. **5** *Grammar.* denoting a case of nouns and pronouns, esp. in languages having only two cases, that is used to identify the direct object of a finite verb or preposition. See also **accusative. 6** of or relating to a goal or aim. ◆ *n* **7** the object of one's endeavours; goal; aim. **8** an actual phenomenon; reality. **9** *Grammar.* the objective case. **10** Also called: **object glass.** *Optics.* the lens or combination of lenses nearest to the object in an optical instrument. ◆ Abbrev.: **obj.** Cf. **subjective.**
▸ **objectival** (ˌɒbdʒɛk'taɪvəl) *adj* ▸ **ob'jectively** *adv*
▸ **ˌobjec'tivity** *or* (*less commonly*) **ob'jectiveness** *n*

objectivism (əb'dʒɛktɪˌvɪzəm) *n* **1** the tendency to stress what is objective. **2** the philosophical doctrine that reality is objective, and that sense data correspond with it.
▸ **ob'jectivist** *n, adj* ▸ **obˌjectiv'istic** *adj*

object language *n* a language described by another language. Cf. **metalanguage.**

object lesson *n* a convincing demonstration of some principle or ideal.

object program *n* a computer program translated from the equivalent source program into machine language by the compiler or assembler.

object relations theory *n* a form of psychoanalytic theory postulating that people relate to others in order to develop themselves.

objet d'art *French.* (ɔbʒɛ dar) *n, pl* **objets d'art** (ɔbʒɛ dar). a small object considered to be of artistic worth. ORIG lit.: object of art

objurgate ('ɒbdʒəˌgeɪt) *vb* **objurgates, objurgating, objur-**

gated. (*tr*) to scold or reprimand. ORIG C17: from L *objurgāre*, from *ob-* against + *jurgāre* to scold
▸ **ˌobjurˈgation** *n* ▸ **ˈobjurˌgator** *n* ▸ **objurgatory** (ɒbˈdʒɜːɡətərɪ, -trɪ) *adj*

obl. *abbrev. for:* **1** oblique. **2** oblong.

oblate[1] (ˈɒbleɪt) *adj* having an equatorial diameter of greater length than the polar diameter: *the earth is an oblate sphere.* Cf. **prolate.** ORIG C18: from NL *oblātus* lengthened, from L *ob-* towards + *lātus*, p.p. of *ferre* to bring

oblate[2] (ˈɒbleɪt) *n* a person dedicated to a monastic or religious life. ORIG C19: from F *oblat*, from Med. L *oblātus*, from L *offerre* to OFFER

oblation (ɒˈbleɪʃən) *n* **1** *Christianity.* the offering of the Eucharist to God. **2** any offering made for religious or charitable purposes. ORIG C15: from Church L *oblātiō*; see OBLATE[2]
▸ **oblatory** (ˈɒblətərɪ, -trɪ) *or* **obˈlational** *adj*

obligate (ˈɒblɪˌɡeɪt) *vb* **obligates, obligating, obligated. 1** to compel, constrain, or oblige morally or legally. **2** (in the US) to bind (property, funds, etc.) as security. ◆ *adj* **3** compelled, bound, or restricted. **4** *Biol.* able to exist under only one set of environmental conditions. ORIG C16: from L *obligāre* to OBLIGE
▸ **ˈobligable** *adj* ▸ **obˈligative** *adj* ▸ **ˈobliˌgator** *n*

obligation (ˌɒblɪˈɡeɪʃən) *n* **1** a moral or legal requirement; duty. **2** the act of obligating or the state of being obligated. **3** *Law.* **3a** a written contract containing a penalty. **3b** an instrument acknowledging indebtedness to secure the repayment of money borrowed. **4** a person or thing to which one is bound morally or legally. **5** a service or favour for which one is indebted.

obligato (ˌɒblɪˈɡɑːtəʊ) *adj, n Music.* a variant spelling of **obbligato.**

obligatory (ɒˈblɪɡətərɪ, -trɪ) *adj* **1** required to be done, obtained, possessed, etc. **2** of the nature of or constituting an obligation.
▸ **obˈligatorily** *adv*

oblige (əˈblaɪdʒ) *vb* **obliges, obliging, obliged. 1** (*tr; often passive*) to bind or constrain (someone to do something) by legal, moral, or physical means. **2** (*tr; usually passive*) to make indebted or grateful (to someone) by doing a favour. **3** to do a service or favour to (someone): *she obliged the guests with a song.* ORIG C13: from OF *obliger*, from L *obligāre*, from *ob-* towards + *ligāre* to bind
▸ **oˈbliger** *n*

obligee (ˌɒblɪˈdʒiː) *n* a person in whose favour an obligation, contract, or bond is created; creditor.

obliging (əˈblaɪdʒɪŋ) *adj* ready to do favours; agreeable; kindly.
▸ **oˈbligingly** *adv* ▸ **oˈbligingness** *n*

obligor (ˌɒblɪˈɡɔː) *n* a person who binds himself or herself by contract to perform some obligation; debtor.

oblique (əˈbliːk) *adj* **1** at an angle; slanting; sloping. **2** *Geom.* **2a** (of lines, planes, etc.) neither perpendicular nor parallel to one another or to another line, plane, etc. **2b** not related to or containing a right angle. **3** indirect or evasive. **4** *Grammar.* denoting any case of nouns, pronouns, etc., other than the nominative and vocative. **5** *Biol.* having asymmetrical sides or planes: *an oblique leaf.* ◆ *n* **6** something oblique, esp. a line. **7** another name for **solidus** (sense 1). ◆ *vb* **obliques, obliquing, obliqued.** (*intr*) **8** to take or have an oblique direction. **9** (of a military formation) to move forward at an angle. ORIG C15: from OF, from L *oblīquus*, from ?
▸ **oˈbliquely** *adv* ▸ **oˈbliqueness** *n* ▸ **obliquity** (əˈblɪkwɪtɪ) *n*

oblique angle *n* an angle that is not a right angle or any multiple of a right angle.

obliterate (əˈblɪtəˌreɪt) *vb* **obliterates, obliterating, obliterated.** (*tr*) to destroy every trace of; wipe out completely. ORIG C16: from L *oblitterāre* to erase, from *ob-* out + *littera* letter
▸ **oˌbliteˈration** *n* ▸ **oˈbliterative** *adj* ▸ **oˈbliterˌator** *n*

oblivion (əˈblɪvɪən) *n* **1** the condition of being forgotten or disregarded. **2** *Law.* amnesty; pardon. ORIG C14: via OF from L *oblīviō* forgetfulness, from *oblīviscī* to forget

oblivious (əˈblɪvɪəs) *adj* (foll. by *of* or *to*) unaware or forgetful.
▸ **obˈliviously** *adv* ▸ **obˈliviousness** *n*

> **USAGE NOTE** It was formerly considered incorrect to use *oblivious* to mean *unaware*, but this use is now acceptable. When employed with this meaning, it is followed either by *to* or *of*, *to* being much the commoner.

oblong (ˈɒbˌlɒŋ) *adj* **1** having an elongated, esp. rectangular, shape. ◆ *n* **2** a figure or object having this shape. ORIG C15: from L *oblongus*, from *ob-* (intensive) + *longus* LONG[1]

obloquy (ˈɒbləkwɪ) *n, pl* **obloquies. 1** defamatory or censorious statements, esp. when directed against one person. **2** disgrace brought about by public abuse. ORIG C15: from L *obloquium* contradiction, from *ob-* against + *loquī* to speak

obnoxious (əbˈnɒkʃəs) *adj* **1** extremely unpleasant. **2** *Obs.* exposed to harm, injury, etc. ORIG C16: from L *obnoxius*, from *ob-* to + *noxa* injury, from *nocēre* to harm
▸ **obˈnoxiously** *adv* ▸ **obˈnoxiousness** *n*

oboe (ˈəʊbəʊ) *n* **1** a woodwind instrument consisting of a conical tube fitted with a mouthpiece having a double reed. It has a penetrating nasal tone. **2** a person who plays this instrument in an orchestra. ◆ Arch. form: **hautboy.** ORIG C18: via It. *oboe*, phonetic approximation to F *haut bois*, lit.: high wood (referring to its pitch)
▸ **ˈoboist** *n*

oboe d'amore (dɑːˈmɔːreɪ) *n* a type of oboe pitched a minor third lower than the oboe itself: used chiefly in baroque music.

Obote ★ (ɒˈbəʊteɪ, -tɪ) *n* (**Apollo**) **Milton.** born 1924, Ugandan politician; prime minister of Uganda (1962–66) and president (1966–71; 1980–85). He was deposed by Amin in 1971 and remained in exile until 1980; deposed again in 1985.

O'Brien ★ (əˈbraɪən) *n* **1 Edna.** born 1936, Irish writer. Her novels include *The Country Girls* (1960) and *Down by the River* (1997). **2 Flann**, real name *Brian O'Nolan.* 1911–66, Irish novelist. His novels include *At Swim-Two-Birds* (1939).

obs. *abbrev. for:* **1** observation. **2** obsolete.

obscene (əbˈsiːn) *adj* **1** offensive or outrageous to accepted standards of decency or modesty. **2** *Law.* (of publications, etc.) having a tendency to deprave or corrupt. **3** disgusting; repellent. ORIG C16: from L *obscēnus* inauspicious
▸ **obˈscenely** *adv*

obscenity (əbˈsɛnɪtɪ) *n, pl* **obscenities. 1** the state or quality of being obscene. **2** an obscene act, statement, word, etc.

obscurant (əbˈskjʊərənt) *n* an opposer of reform and enlightenment.
▸ **obscurantism** (ˌɒbskjʊəˈrænˌtɪzəm) *n* ▸ **ˌobscuˈrantist** *n, adj*

obscure (əbˈskjʊə) *adj* **1** unclear. **2** indistinct, vague, or indefinite. **3** inconspicuous or unimportant. **4** hidden, secret, or remote. **5** (of a vowel) reduced to a neutral vowel (ə). **6** gloomy, dark, clouded, or dim. ◆ *vb* **obscures, obscuring, obscured.** (*tr*) **7** to make unclear, vague, or hidden. **8** to cover or cloud over. **9** *Phonetics.* to pronounce (a vowel) so that it becomes a neutral sound represented by (ə). ORIG C14: via OF from L *obscūrus* dark
▸ **obscuration** (ˌɒbskjʊˈreɪʃən) *n* ▸ **obˈscurely** *adv* ▸ **obˈscureness** *n*

obscurity (əbˈskjʊərɪtɪ) *n, pl* **obscurities. 1** the state or quality of being obscure. **2** an obscure person or thing.

obsequies (ˈɒbsɪkwɪz) *pl n, sing* **obsequy.** funeral rites. ORIG C14: via Anglo-Norman from Med. L *obsequiae* (infl. by L *exsequiae*), from *obsequium* compliance

obsequious (əbˈsiːkwɪəs) *adj* **1** obedient or attentive in an ingratiating or servile manner. **2** *Now rare.* submissive or compliant. ORIG C15: from L *obsequiōsus* compliant, from *obsequī* to follow
▸ **obˈsequiously** *adv* ▸ **obˈsequiousness** *n*

★ people and places

observance (əb'zɜːvəns) *n* **1** recognition of or compliance with a law, custom, practice, etc. **2** a ritual, ceremony, or practice, esp. of a religion. **3** observation or attention. **4** the degree of strictness of a religious order in following its rule. **5** *Arch.* respectful or deferential attention.

observant (əb'zɜːvənt) *adj* **1** paying close attention to detail; watchful or heedful. **2** adhering strictly to rituals, ceremonies, laws, etc.
▸ **ob'servantly** *adv*

observation (ˌɒbzə'veɪʃən) *n* **1** the act of observing or the state of being observed. **2** a comment or remark. **3** detailed examination of phenomena prior to analysis, diagnosis, or interpretation: *the patient was under observation.* **4** the facts learned from observing. **5** *Navigation.* **5a** a sight taken with an instrument to determine the position of an observer relative to that of a given heavenly body. **5b** the data so taken.
▸ **ˌobser'vational** *adj* ▸ **ˌobser'vationally** *adv*

observatory (əb'zɜːvətərɪ, -trɪ) *n, pl* **observatories. 1** an institution or building specially designed and equipped for observing meteorological and astronomical phenomena. **2** any building or structure providing an extensive view of its surroundings.

observe (əb'zɜːv) *vb* **observes, observing, observed. 1** (*tr; may take a clause as object*) to see; perceive; notice: *we have observed that you steal.* **2** (when *tr, may take a clause as object*) to watch (something) carefully; pay attention to (something). **3** to make observations of (something), esp. scientific ones. **4** (when *intr,* usually foll. by *on* or *upon;* when *tr, may take a clause as object*) to make a comment or remark: *the speaker observed that times had changed.* **5** (*tr*) to abide by, keep, or follow (a custom, tradition, etc.). ORIG C14: via OF from L *observāre,* from *ob-* to + *servāre* to watch
▸ **ob'servable** *adj* ▸ **ob'server** *n*

obsess (əb'sɛs) *vb* **1** (*tr;* when passive, foll. by *with* or *by*) to preoccupy completely; haunt. **2** (*intr,* usually foll. by *on* or *over*) to brood in an obsessional way. ORIG C16: from L *obsessus* besieged, p.p. of *obsidēre,* from *ob-* in front of + *sedēre* to sit
▸ **ob'sessive** *adj, n* ▸ **ob'sessively** *adv* ▸ **ob'sessiveness** *n*

obsession (əb'sɛʃən) *n* **1** *Psychiatry.* a persistent idea or impulse, often associated with anxiety and mental illness. **2** a persistent preoccupation, idea, or feeling. **3** the act of obsessing or the state of being obsessed.
▸ **ob'sessional** *adj* ▸ **ob'sessionally** *adv*

obsidian (ɒb'sɪdɪən) *n* a dark glassy volcanic rock formed by very rapid solidification of lava. Also called: **Iceland agate.** ORIG C17: from L *obsidiānus,* erroneous transcription of *obsiānus* (*lapis*) (stone of) *Obsius,* (in Pliny) the discoverer of a stone resembling obsidian

obsolesce (ˌɒbsə'lɛs) *vb* **obsolesces, obsolescing, obsolesced.** (*intr*) to become obsolete.

obsolescent (ˌɒbsə'lɛsᵊnt) *adj* becoming obsolete or out of date. ORIG C18: from L *obsolescere;* see OBSOLETE
▸ **ˌobso'lescence** *n*

obsolete ('ɒbsəˌliːt, ˌɒbsə'liːt) *adj* **1** out of use or practice; not current. **2** out of date; unfashionable or outmoded. **3** *Biol.* (of parts, organs, etc.) vestigial; rudimentary. ORIG C16: from L *obsolētus* worn out, p.p. of *obsolēre* (unattested), from *ob-* opposite to + *solēre* to be used
▸ **'obsoˌletely** *adv* ▸ **'obsoˌleteness** *n*

obstacle ('ɒbstəkᵊl) *n* **1** a person or thing that opposes or hinders something. **2** *Brit.* a fence or hedge used in showjumping. ORIG C14: via OF from L *obstāculum,* from *obstāre,* from *ob-* against + *stāre* to stand

obstacle race *n* a race in which competitors have to negotiate various obstacles.

obstetric (ɒb'stɛtrɪk) *or* **obstetrical** *adj* of or relating to childbirth or obstetrics. ORIG C18: via NL from L *obstetrīcius,* from *obstetrix* a midwife, lit.: woman who stands opposite, from *obstāre* to stand in front of; see OBSTACLE
▸ **ob'stetrically** *adv*

obstetrician (ˌɒbstɪ'trɪʃən) *n* a physician who specializes in obstetrics.

obstetrics (ɒb'stɛtrɪks) *n* (*functioning as sing*) the branch of medicine concerned with childbirth and the treatment of women before and after childbirth.

obstinacy ('ɒbstɪnəsɪ) *n, pl* **obstinacies. 1** the state or quality of being obstinate. **2** an obstinate act, attitude, etc.

obstinate ('ɒbstɪnɪt) *adj* **1** adhering fixedly to a particular opinion, attitude, course of action, etc. **2** self-willed or headstrong. **3** difficult to subdue or alleviate; persistent: *an obstinate fever.* ORIG C14: from L *obstinātus,* p.p. of *obstināre* to persist in, from *ob-* (intensive) + *stin-,* var. of *stare* to stand
▸ **'obstinately** *adv*

obstreperous (əb'strɛpərəs) *adj* noisy or rough, esp. in resisting restraint or control. ORIG C16: from L, from *obstrepere,* from *ob-* against + *strepere* to roar
▸ **ob'streperously** *adv* ▸ **ob'streperousness** *n*

obstruct (əb'strʌkt) *vb* (*tr*) **1** to block (a road, passageway, etc.) with an obstacle. **2** to make (progress or activity) difficult. **3** to impede or block a clear view of. ORIG C17: L *obstructus* built against, p.p. of *obstruere,* from *ob-* against + *struere* to build
▸ **ob'structive** *adj, n* ▸ **ob'structively** *adv* ▸ **ob'structiveness** *n* ▸ **ob'structor** *n*

obstruction (əb'strʌkʃən) *n* **1** a person or thing that obstructs. **2** the act or an instance of obstructing. **3** delay of business, esp. in a legislature by means of procedural devices. **4** *Sport.* the act of unfairly impeding an opposing player.
▸ **ob'structional** *adj*

obstructionist (əb'strʌkʃənɪst) *n* a person who deliberately obstructs business, etc., esp. in a legislature.
▸ **ob'structionism** *n*

obtain (əb'teɪn) *vb* **1** (*tr*) to gain possession of; acquire; get. **2** (*intr*) to be customary, valid, or accepted: *a new law obtains in this case.* ORIG C15: via OF from L *obtinēre* to take hold of
▸ **ob'tainable** *adj* ▸ **obˌtaina'bility** *n* ▸ **ob'tainer** *n* ▸ **ob'tainment** *n*

obtrude (əb'truːd) *vb* **obtrudes, obtruding, obtruded. 1** to push (oneself, one's opinions, etc.) on others in an unwelcome way. **2** (*tr*) to push out or forward. ORIG C16: from L *obtrūdere,* from *ob-* against + *trūdere* to push forward
▸ **ob'truder** *n* ▸ **obtrusion** (əb'truːʒən) *n*

obtrusive (əb'truːsɪv) *adj* **1** obtruding or tending to obtrude. **2** sticking out; protruding; noticeable.
▸ **ob'trusively** *adv* ▸ **ob'trusiveness** *n*

obtuse (əb'tjuːs) *adj* **1** mentally slow or emotionally insensitive. **2** *Maths.* (of an angle) lying between 90° and 180°. **3** not sharp or pointed. **4** indistinctly felt, heard, etc.; dull: *obtuse pain.* **5** (of a leaf or similar flat part) having a rounded or blunt tip. ORIG C16: from L *obtūsus* dulled, p.p. of *obtundere* to beat down
▸ **ob'tusely** *adv* ▸ **ob'tuseness** *n*

obverse ('ɒbvɜːs) *adj* **1** facing or turned towards the observer. **2** forming or serving as a counterpart. **3** (of leaves) narrower at the base than at the top. ◆ *n* **4** a counterpart or complement. **5** *Logic.* a proposition derived from another by replacing the original predicate by its negation and changing the proposition from affirmative to negative or vice versa, as *no sum is correct* from *every sum is incorrect.* **6** the side of a coin that bears the main design or device. ORIG C17: from L *obversus* turned towards, p.p. of *obvertere*
▸ **ob'versely** *adv*

obvert (ɒb'vɜːt) *vb* (*tr*) **1** *Logic.* to deduce the obverse of (a proposition). **2** *Rare.* to turn so as to show the main or other side. ORIG C17: from L *obvertere* to turn towards
▸ **ob'version** *n*

obviate ('ɒbvɪˌeɪt) *vb* **obviates, obviating, obviated.** (*tr*) to avoid or prevent (a need or difficulty). ORIG C16: from LL *obviātus* prevented, p.p. of *obviāre;* see OBVIOUS
▸ **ˌobvi'ation** *n*

obvious ('ɒbvɪəs) *adj* **1** easy to see or understand; evident. **2** exhibiting motives, feelings, intentions, etc., clearly or without subtlety. **3** naive or unsubtle: *the play was rather obvious.* ORIG C16: from L *obvius,* from *obviam* in the way
▸ **'obviously** *adv* ▸ **'obviousness** *n*

OC *abbrev. for* Officer Commanding.

Oc. *abbrev. for* Ocean.

o/c *abbrev. for* overcharge.

ocarina (ˌɒkəˈriːnə) *n* an egg-shaped wind instrument with a protruding mouthpiece and six to eight finger holes, producing an almost pure tone. ORIG C19: from It.: little goose, from *oca* goose, ult. from L *avis* bird

O'Casey ★ (əʊˈkeɪsɪ) *n* **Sean** (ʃɔːn). 1880–1964, Irish dramatist. His plays include *Juno and the Paycock* (1924).

Occam ★ (ˈɒkəm) *n* a variant spelling of (William of) **Ockham.**

Occam's razor *n* a variant spelling of **Ockham's razor.**

occas. *abbrev. for* occasional(ly).

occasion (əˈkeɪʒən) *n* **1** (sometimes foll. by *of*) the time of a particular happening or event. **2** (sometimes foll. by *for*) a reason or cause (to do or be something); grounds: *there was no occasion to complain.* **3** an opportunity (to do something); chance. **4** a special event, time, or celebration: *the party was quite an occasion.* **5 on occasion.** every so often. **6 rise to the occasion.** to have the courage, wit, etc., to meet the special demands of a situation. **7 take occasion.** to avail oneself of an opportunity (to do something). ◆ *vb* **8** (*tr*) to bring about, esp. incidentally or by chance. ORIG C14: from L *occāsiō* a falling down, from *occidere* to fall

occasional (əˈkeɪʒənᵊl) *adj* **1** taking place from time to time; not frequent or regular. **2** of, for, or happening on special occasions. **3** serving as an occasion (for something).
▸ **ocˈcasionally** *adv*

occasional table *n* a small table with no regular use.

occident (ˈɒksɪdənt) *n* a literary or formal word for **west.** Cf. **orient.** ORIG C14: via OF from L *occidere* to fall (with reference to the setting sun)
▸ **ˌocciˈdental** *adj*

Occident (ˈɒksɪdənt) *n* (usually preceded by *the*) **1** the countries of Europe and America. **2** the western hemisphere.
▸ **ˌOcciˈdental** *adj, n*

occipital (ɒkˈsɪpɪtᵊl) *adj* **1** of or relating to the back of the head or skull. ◆ *n* **2** short for **occipital bone.** ORIG See OCCIPUT

occipital bone *n* the bone that forms the back part of the skull and part of its base.

occipital lobe *n* the posterior portion of each cerebral hemisphere, concerned with the interpretation of visual sensory impulses.

occiput (ˈɒksɪˌpʌt) *n, pl* **occiputs** *or* **occipita** (ɒkˈsɪpɪtə). the back part of the head or skull. ORIG C14: from L, from *ob-* at the back of + *caput* head

occlude (əˈkluːd) *vb* **occludes, occluding, occluded. 1** (*tr*) to block or stop up (a passage or opening); obstruct. **2** (*tr*) to prevent the passage of. **3** (*tr*) *Chem.* (of a solid) to incorporate (a substance) by absorption or adsorption. **4** *Meteorol.* to form or cause to form an occluded front. **5** *Dentistry.* to produce or cause to produce occlusion, as in chewing. ORIG C16: from L *occlūdere,* from *ob-* (intensive) + *claudere* to close
▸ **ocˈcludent** *adj*

occluded front *n Meteorol.* the line or plane occurring where the cold front of a depression has overtaken the warm front, raising the warm sector from ground level. Also called: **occlusion.**

occlusion (əˈkluːʒən) *n* **1** the act of occluding or the state of being occluded. **2** *Meteorol.* another term for **occluded front. 3** *Dentistry.* the normal position of the teeth when the jaws are closed.
▸ **ocˈclusive** *adj*

occult *adj* (ɒˈkʌlt, ˈɒkʌlt). **1a** of or characteristic of mystical or supernatural phenomena or influences. **1b** (*as n*): *the occult.* **2** beyond ordinary human understanding. **3** secret or esoteric. ◆ *vb* (ɒˈkʌlt). **4** *Astron.* (of a celestial body) to hide (another celestial body) from view by occultation or (of a celestial body) to become hidden by occultation. **5** to hide or become hidden or shut off from view. **6** (*intr*) (of lights, esp. in lighthouses) to shut off at regular intervals. ORIG C16: from L *occultus,* p.p. of *occulere,* from *ob-* over, up + *-culere,* rel. to *celāre* to conceal
▸ **ˈoccultˌtism** *n* ▸ **ˈoccultist** *n* ▸ **ocˈcultness** *n*

occultation (ˌɒkʌlˈteɪʃən) *n* the temporary disappearance of one celestial body as it moves out of sight behind another body.

occupancy (ˈɒkjʊpənsɪ) *n, pl* **occupancies. 1** the act of occupying; possession of a property. **2** *Law.* the possession and use of property by or without agreement and without any claim to ownership. **3** *Law.* the act of taking possession of unowned property, esp. land, with the intent of thus acquiring ownership. **4** the condition or fact of being an occupant, esp. a tenant. **5** the period of time during which one is an occupant, esp. of property.

occupant (ˈɒkjʊpənt) *n* **1** a person, thing, etc., holding a position or place. **2** *Law.* a person who has possession of something, esp. an estate, house, etc.; tenant. **3** *Law.* a person who acquires by occupancy the title to something previously without an owner.

occupation (ˌɒkjʊˈpeɪʃən) *n* **1** a person's regular work or profession; job. **2** any activity on which time is spent by a person. **3** the act of occupying or the state of being occupied. **4** the control of a country by a foreign military power. **5** the period of time that a nation, place, or position is occupied. **6** (*modifier*) for the use of the occupier of a particular property: *occupation road.*
▸ **ˌoccuˈpational** *adj*

occupational psychology *n* the scientific study of mental or emotional problems associated with the working environment.

occupational therapy *n Med.* treatment of people with physical, emotional, or social problems, using purposeful activity to help them overcome or learn to deal with their problems.

occupation groupings *pl n* a system of classifying people according to occupation, based originally on information obtained by government census and subsequently developed by market research. The classifications are used by the advertising industry to identify potential markets. The groups are **A, B, C1, C2, D,** and **E.**

occupier (ˈɒkjʊˌpaɪə) *n* **1** *Brit.* a person who is in possession or occupation of a house or land. **2** a person or thing that occupies.

occupy (ˈɒkjʊˌpaɪ) *vb* **occupies, occupying, occupied.** (*tr*) **1** to live or be established in (a house, flat, office, etc.). **2** (*often passive*) to keep (a person) busy or engrossed. **3** (*often passive*) to take up (time or space). **4** to take and hold possession of, esp. as a demonstration: *students occupied the college buildings.* **5** to fill or hold (a position or rank). ORIG C14: from OF *occuper,* from L *occupāre* to seize hold of

occur (əˈkɜː) *vb* **occurs, occurring, occurred.** (*intr*) **1** to happen; take place; come about. **2** to be found or be present; exist. **3** (foll. by *to*) to be realized or thought of (by); suggest itself (to). ORIG C16: from L *occurrere* to run up to

> **USAGE NOTE** It is usually regarded as incorrect to talk of pre-arranged events *occurring* or *happening*: *the wedding took place* (not *occurred* or *happened*) *in the afternoon.*

occurrence (əˈkʌrəns) *n* **1** something that occurs; a happening; event. **2** the act or an instance of occurring: *a crime of frequent occurrence.*
▸ **ocˈcurrent** *adj*

ocean (ˈəʊʃən) *n* **1** a very large stretch of sea, esp. one of the five oceans of the world, the Atlantic, Pacific, Indian, Arctic, and Antarctic. **2** the body of salt water covering approximately 70 per cent of the earth's surface. **3** a huge quantity or expanse: *an ocean of replies.* **4** *Literary.* the sea. ORIG C13: via OF from L *ōceanus,* from OCEANUS

oceanarium (ˌəʊʃəˈnɛərɪəm) *n, pl* **oceanariums** *or* **oceanaria** (-ɪə). a large saltwater aquarium for marine life.

ocean-going *adj* (of a ship, boat, etc.) suited for travel on the open ocean.

Oceania ★ (ˌəʊʃɪˈɑːnɪə) *n* the islands of the central and S

★ people and places

Pacific, including Melanesia, Micronesia, and Polynesia: sometimes also including Australasia and the Malay Archipelago.
▸ **ˌOceˈanian** *adj, n*

oceanic (ˌəʊʃɪˈænɪk) *adj* **1** of or relating to the ocean. **2** living in the depths of the ocean beyond the continental shelf at a depth exceeding 200 metres: *oceanic fauna.* **3** huge or overwhelming.

Oceanid (əʊˈsɪənɪd) *n, pl* **Oceanids** *or* **Oceanides** (ˌəʊsɪˈænɪˌdiːz). *Greek myth.* an ocean nymph.

oceanography (ˌəʊʃəˈnɒgrəfɪ, ˌəʊʃɪə-) *n* the branch of science dealing with the physical, chemical, geological, and biological features of the oceans.
▸ **ˌoceanˈographer** *n* ▸ **oceanographic** (ˌəʊʃənəˈgræfɪk, ˌəʊʃɪə-) *or* **ˌoceanoˈgraphical** *adj*

oceanology (ˌəʊʃəˈnɒlədʒɪ, ˌəʊʃɪə-) *n* the study of the sea, esp. of its economic geography.

Oceanus ★ (əʊˈsɪənəs) *n Greek myth.* a Titan, divinity of the stream believed to flow around the earth.

ocellus (ɒˈsɛləs) *n, pl* **ocelli** (-laɪ). **1** the simple eye of insects and some other invertebrates, consisting basically of light-sensitive cells. **2** any eyelike marking in animals, such as the eyespot on the tail feather of a peacock. ORIG C19: via NL from L: small eye, from *oculus* eye
▸ **oˈcellar** *adj* ▸ **ocellate** (ˈɒsɪˌleɪt) *or* **ˈocelˌlated** *adj* ▸ **ˌocelˈlation** *n*

ocelot (ˈɒsɪˌlɒt, ˈəʊ-) *n* a feline mammal inhabiting Central and South America and having a dark-spotted buff-brown coat. ORIG C18: via F from Nahuatl *ocelotl* jaguar

och (ɒx) *interj Scot. & Irish.* an expression of surprise, contempt, disagreement, etc.

oche (ˈɒkɪ) *n Darts.* the mark or ridge on the floor behind which a player must stand to throw. ORIG from ?

ochlocracy (ɒkˈlɒkrəsɪ) *n, pl* **ochlocracies.** rule by the mob; mobocracy. ORIG C16: via F, from Gk *okhlokratia,* from *okhlos* mob + *kratos* power
▸ **ochlocrat** (ˈɒkləˌkræt) *n* ▸ **ˌochloˈcratic** *adj*

ochone (ɒˈxəʊn) *interj Scot. & Irish.* an expression of sorrow or regret. ORIG from Gaelic *ochóin*

ochre *or US* **ocher** (ˈəʊkə) *n* **1** any of various natural earths containing ferric oxide, silica, and alumina: used as yellow or red pigments. **2a** a moderate yellow-orange to orange colour. **2b** (*as adj*): *an ochre dress.* ◆ *vb* **ochres, ochring, ochred** *or US* **ochers, ochering, ochered. 3** (*tr*) to colour with ochre. ORIG C15: from OF *ocre,* from L *ōchra,* from Gk *ōkhros* pale yellow
▸ **ochreous** (ˈəʊkrɪəs, ˈəʊkərəs), **ochrous** (ˈəʊkrəs), **ochry** (ˈəʊkərɪ, ˈəʊkrɪ) *or US* **ˈocherous, ˈochery** *adj*

-ock *suffix forming nouns.* indicating smallness: *hillock.* ORIG OE *-oc, -uc*

ocker (ˈɒkə) *Austral. sl.* ◆ *n* **1** (*often cap.*) an uncultivated or boorish Australian. ◆ *adj* **2** typical of such a person. ORIG C20: after an Australian TV character

Ockham *or* **Occam** ★ (ˈɒkəm) *n* **William of.** died ?1349, English philosopher. See **Ockham's razor.**

Ockham's razor *or* **Occam's razor** *n* a maxim, attributed to William of Ockham, stating that in explaining something assumptions must not be needlessly multiplied. Also called: **the principle of economy.**

o'clock (əˈklɒk) *adv* **1** used after a number from one to twelve to indicate the hour of the day or night. **2** used after a number to indicate direction or position relative to the observer, twelve o'clock being directly ahead and other positions being obtained by comparisons with a clock face. ORIG C18: abbrev. for *of the clock*

O'Connell ★ (əʊˈkɒnᵊl) *n* **Daniel.** 1775–1847, Irish nationalist leader; his election to the British House of Commons (1828) forced the acceptance of Catholic emancipation (1829).

OCR *abbrev. for* optical character reader *or* recognition.

oct. *abbrev. for* octavo.

Oct. *abbrev. for* October.

oct- *combining form.* a variant of **octo-** before a vowel.

octa- *combining form.* a variant of **octo-**.

octad (ˈɒktæd) *n* **1** a group or series of eight. **2** *Chem.* an element with a valency of eight. ORIG C19: from Gk *oktās,* from *oktō* eight
▸ **ocˈtadic** *adj*

octagon (ˈɒktəgən) *n* a polygon having eight sides. ORIG C17: via L from Gk *oktagōnos* having eight angles
▸ **octagonal** (ɒkˈtægənᵊl) *adj*

octahedron (ˌɒktəˈhiːdrən) *n, pl* **octahedrons** *or* **octahedra** (-drə). a solid figure having eight plane faces.

octal notation *or* **octal** (ˈɒktəl) *n Computing.* a number system having a base 8, one octal digit being equivalent to a group of three bits.

octane (ˈɒkteɪn) *n* a liquid hydrocarbon found in petroleum. Formula: C_8H_{18}.

octane number *or* **rating** *n* a measure of the antiknock quality of a petrol expressed as a percentage.

octant (ˈɒktənt) *n* **1** *Maths.* **1a** any of the eight parts into which the three planes containing the Cartesian coordinate axes divide space. **1b** an eighth part of a circle. **2** *Astron.* the position of a celestial body when it is at an angular distance of 45° from another body. **3** an instrument used for measuring angles, similar to a sextant but having a graduated arc of 45°. ORIG C17: from L *octans* half quadrant, from *octo* eight

octavalent (ˌɒktəˈveɪlənt) *adj Chem.* having a valency of eight.

octave (ˈɒktɪv) *n* **1a** the interval between two musical notes one of which has twice the pitch of the other and lies eight notes away from it counting inclusively along the diatonic scale. **1b** one of these two notes, esp. the one of higher pitch. **1c** (*as modifier*): *an octave leap.* **2** *Prosody.* a rhythmic group of eight lines of verse. **3** (ˈɒkteɪv). **3a** a feast day and the seven days following. **3b** the final day of this period. **4** the eighth of eight basic positions in fencing. **5** any set or series of eight. ◆ *adj* **6** consisting of eight parts. ORIG C14: (orig.: eighth day) via OF from Med. L *octāva diēs* eighth day (after a festival), from L *octo* eight

Octavian ★ (ɒkˈteɪvɪən) *n* the name of **Augustus** before he became emperor (27 B.C.).

octavo (ɒkˈteɪvəʊ) *n, pl* **octavos. 1** a book size resulting from folding a sheet of paper of a specified size to form eight leaves: *demi-octavo.* Often written: **8vo, 8°. 2** a book of this size. ORIG C16: from NL *in octavo* in an eighth (of a sheet)

octennial (ɒkˈtɛnɪəl) *adj* **1** occurring every eight years. **2** lasting for eight years. ORIG C17: from L *octennium,* from *octo* eight + *annus* year
▸ **ocˈtennially** *adv*

octet (ɒkˈtɛt) *n* **1** any group of eight, esp. singers or musicians. **2** a piece of music composed for such a group. **3** *Prosody.* another word for **octave** (sense 2). **4** *Chem.* a stable group of eight electrons. ◆ Also (for senses 1, 2, 3): **octette.** ORIG C19: from L *octo* eight, on the model of DUET

octillion (ɒkˈtɪljən) *n* **1** (in Britain and Germany) the number represented as one followed by 48 zeros (10^{48}). **2** (in the US, Canada, and France) the number represented as one followed by 27 zeros (10^{27}). ORIG C17: from F, on the model of MILLION
▸ **ocˈtillionth** *adj, n*

octo-, octa-, *or before a vowel* **oct-** *combining form.* eight: *octosyllabic; octagon.* ORIG from L *octo,* Gk *oktō*

October (ɒkˈtəʊbə) *n* the tenth month of the year, consisting of 31 days. ORIG OE, from L, from *octo* eight, since it was orig. the eighth month in Roman reckoning

Octobrist (ɒkˈtəʊbrɪst) *n* a member of a Russian political party favouring the constitutional reforms granted in a manifesto issued by Nicholas II in Oct. 1905.

octocentenary (ˌɒktəʊsɛnˈtiːnərɪ) *n, pl* **octocentenaries.** an 800th anniversary.

octogenarian (ˌɒktəʊdʒɪˈnɛərɪən) *n* **1** a person who is from 80 to 89 years old. ◆ *adj* **2** of or relating to an octogenarian. ORIG C19: from L *octōgēnārius* containing eighty, from *octōgēnī* eighty each

octopus (ˈɒktəpəs) *n, pl* **octopuses. 1** a cephalopod mollusc having a soft oval body with eight long suckered tentacles and occurring at the sea bottom. **2** a powerful influential organization, etc., with far-reaching effects, esp. harmful ones. ORIG C18: via NL from Gk *oktōpous* having eight feet

octoroon *or* **octaroon** (ˌɒktəˈruːn) *n* a person having one quadroon and one White parent and therefore having one-eighth Black blood. Cf. **quadroon**. ORIG C19: OCTO- + *-roon* as in QUADROON

octosyllable (ˈɒktəˌsɪləbᵊl) *n* **1** a line of verse composed of eight syllables. **2** a word of eight syllables.
▸ **octosyllabic** (ˌɒktəʊsɪˈlæbɪk) *adj*

octroi (ˈɒktrwɑː) *n* **1** (in some European countries, esp. France) a duty on goods brought into certain towns. **2** the place where it is collected. **3** the officers responsible for its collection. ORIG C17: from F *octroyer* to concede, from Med. L *auctorizāre* to AUTHORIZE

octuple (ˈɒktjʊpᵊl) *n* **1** a quantity or number eight times as great as another. ◆ *adj* **2** eight times as much or as many. **3** consisting of eight parts. ◆ *vb* **octuples, octupling, octupled. 4** (*tr*) to multiply by eight. ORIG C17: from L *octuplus,* from *octo* eight + *-plus* as in *duplus* double

ocular (ˈɒkjʊlə) *adj* **1** of or relating to the eye. ◆ *n* **2** another name for **eyepiece**. ORIG C16: from L *oculāris* from *oculus* eye
▸ **ˈocularly** *adv*

ocularist (ˈɒkjʊlərɪst) *n* a person who makes artificial eyes.

oculate (ˈɒkjʊlɪt) *adj Zool.* **1** having eyes. **2** relating to or resembling eyes: *oculate markings.*

oculist (ˈɒkjʊlɪst) *n Med.* a former term for **ophthalmologist**. ORIG C17: via F from L *oculus* eye

od (ɒd, əʊd), **odyl,** *or* **odyle** (ˈɒdɪl) *n Arch.* a hypothetical force formerly thought to be responsible for many natural phenomena, such as magnetism, light, and hypnotism. ORIG C19: coined by Baron Karl von Reichenbach (1788–1869), G scientist
▸ **ˈodic** *adj*

OD[1] (ˌəʊˈdiː) *Inf.* ◆ *n* **1** an overdose of a drug. ◆ *vb* **OD's, OD'ing, OD'd.** (*intr*) **2** to take an overdose of a drug. ORIG C20: from *o(ver)d(ose)*

OD[2] *abbrev. for:* **1** Officer of the Day. **2** Also: **o.d.** *Mil.* olive drab. **3** Also: **O/D** *Banking.* **3a** on demand. **3b** overdrawn. **4** ordnance datum. **5** outside diameter.

ODA (in Britain) *abbrev. for* Overseas Development Administration.

odalisque *or* **odalisk** (ˈəʊdəlɪsk) *n* a female slave or concubine. ORIG C17: via F, changed from Turkish *ōdalik,* from *ōdah* room + *-lik,* n. suffix

odd (ɒd) *adj* **1** unusual or peculiar in appearance, character, etc. **2** occasional, incidental, or random: *odd jobs.* **3** leftover or additional: *odd bits of wool.* **4a** not divisible by two. **4b** represented or indicated by a number that is not divisible by two: *graphs are on odd pages.* Cf. **even**[1] (sense 7). **5** being part of a matched pair or set when the other or others are missing: *an odd sock.* **6** (*in combination*) used to designate an indefinite quantity more than the quantity specified in round numbers: *fifty-odd pounds.* **7** out-of-the-way or secluded: *odd corners.* **8 odd man out.** a person or thing excluded from others forming a group, unit, etc. ◆ *n* **9** *Golf.* **9a** one stroke more than the score of one's opponent. **9b** a handicap of one stroke. **10** a thing or person that is odd in sequence or number. ◆ See also **odds.** ORIG from ON *oddi* triangle, point
▸ **ˈoddly** *adv* ▸ **ˈoddness** *n*

oddball (ˈɒdˌbɔːl) *Inf.* ◆ *n* **1** Also: **odd bod, odd fish.** a strange or eccentric person or thing. ◆ *adj* **2** strange or peculiar.

Oddfellow (ˈɒdˌfɛləʊ) *n* a member of a secret benevolent and fraternal association founded in England in the 18th century.

oddity (ˈɒdɪtɪ) *n, pl* **oddities. 1** an odd person or thing. **2** an odd quality or characteristic. **3** the condition of being odd.

odd-jobman *or* **odd-jobber** *n* a person who does casual work, esp. domestic repairs.

oddment (ˈɒdmənt) *n* **1** (*often pl*) an odd piece or thing; leftover. **2** *Printing.* **2a** pages that do not make a complete signature. **2b** any individual part of a book excluding the main text.

odd pricing *n* pricing goods in such a way as to imply that a bargain is being offered, as £5.99 instead of £6.

odds (ɒdz) *pl n* **1** (foll. by *on* or *against*) the probability, expressed as a ratio, that a certain event will take place: *the odds against the outsider are a hundred to one.* **2** the amount, expressed as a ratio, by which the wager of one better is greater than that of another: *he was offering odds of five to one.* **3** the likelihood that a certain state of affairs will be so: *the odds are that he is drunk.* **4** an equalizing allowance, esp. one given to a weaker side in a contest. **5** the advantage that one contender is judged to have over another. **6** *Brit.* a significant difference (esp. in **it makes no odds**). **7 at odds.** on bad terms. **8 give** *or* **lay odds.** to offer a bet with favourable odds. **9 over the odds. 9a** more than is expected, necessary, etc. **9b** unfair or excessive. **10 take odds.** to accept a bet with favourable odds. **11 what's the odds?** *Brit. inf.* what difference does it make?

odds and ends *pl n* miscellaneous items or articles.

odds-on *adj* **1** (of a horse, etc.) rated at even money or less to win. **2** regarded as more or most likely to win, succeed, happen, etc.

ode (əʊd) *n* **1** a lyric poem, typically addressed to a particular subject, with lines of varying lengths and complex rhythms. **2** (formerly) a poem meant to be sung. ORIG C16: via F from LL *ōda,* from Gk *ōidē,* from *aeidein* to sing

-ode[1] *n combining form.* denoting resemblance: *nematode.* ORIG from Gk *-ōdēs,* from *eidos* shape

-ode[2] *n combining form.* denoting a path or way: *electrode.* ORIG from Gk *-odos,* from *hodos* a way

Odense ★ (*Danish* ˈoːðənsə) *n* a port in S Denmark, on Funen Island: cathedral founded by King Canute in the 11th century. Pop.: 183 564 (1996 est.).

Oder ★ (ˈəʊdə) *n* a river in central Europe, rising in the N Czech Republic and flowing north and west to the Baltic, forming part of the border between Germany and Poland. Length: 913 km (567 miles). Czech and Polish name: **Odra.**

Oder-Neisse Line ★ (-ˈnaɪsə) *n* the present-day boundary between Germany and Poland along the Rivers Oder and Neisse. Established in 1945, it originally separated the Soviet Zone of Germany from the regions of Germany under Polish administration.

Odessa ★ (əʊˈdɛsə; *Russian* aˈdjɛsə) *n* a port in S Ukraine, on the Black Sea: the chief Russian grain port in the 19th century; university (1865); industrial centre, major port, and naval base. Pop.: 1 046 000 (1996 est.).

odeum (ˈəʊdɪəm) *n, pl* **odea** (ˈəʊdɪə). (esp. in ancient Greece and Rome) a building for musical performances. Also called: **odeon.** ORIG C17: from L, from Gk *ōideion,* from *ōidē* ODE

Odin (ˈəʊdɪn) *or* **Othin** ★ *n Norse myth.* the supreme creator; the divinity of wisdom, culture, war, and the dead. Germanic counterpart. **Wotan, Woden.**

odious (ˈəʊdɪəs) *adj* offensive; repugnant. ORIG C17: from L; see ODIUM
▸ **ˈodiousness** *n*

odium (ˈəʊdɪəm) *n* **1** the dislike accorded to a hated person or thing. **2** hatred; repugnance. ORIG C17: from L; rel. to *ōdī* I hate, Gk *odussasthai* to be angry

Odoacer (ˌɒdəˈeɪsə) *or* **Odovacar** ★ (ˌəʊdəˈvɑːkə) *n* ?434–493 A.D., barbarian ruler of Italy (476–493); assassinated by Theodoric.

odometer (ɒˈdɒmɪtə, əʊ-) *n* the usual US and Canad. name for **mileometer.** ORIG C18 *hodometer,* from Gk *hodos* way + -METER
▸ **oˈdometry** *n*

-odont *adj and n combining form.* -toothed: *acrodont.* ORIG from Gk *odōn* tooth

odonto- *or before a vowel* **odont-** *combining form.* indicating a tooth or teeth: *odontology.* ORIG from Gk *odōn* tooth

odontoglossum (ɒˌdɒntəˈglɒsəm) *n* a tropical American epiphytic orchid having clusters of brightly coloured flowers.

odontology (ˌɒdɒnˈtɒlədʒɪ) *n* the branch of science

concerned with the anatomy, development, and diseases of teeth.
▸ **odontological** (ɒˌdɒntəˈlɒdʒɪkᵊl) *adj* ▸ **ˌodonˈtologist** *n*

odoriferous (ˌəʊdəˈrɪfərəs) *adj* having or emitting an odour, esp. a fragrant one.
▸ **ˌodorˈiferously** *adv* ▸ **ˌodorˈiferousness** *n*

odoriphore (əʊˈdɒrɪˌfɔː) *n Chem.* the group of atoms in an odorous molecule responsible for its odour.

odorous (ˈəʊdərəs) *adj* having or emitting a characteristic smell or odour.
▸ **ˈodorously** *adv* ▸ **ˈodorousness** *n*

odour *or US* **odor** (ˈəʊdə) *n* **1** the property of a substance that gives it a characteristic scent or smell. **2** a pervasive quality about something: *an odour of dishonesty.* **3** repute or regard (in **in good odour, in bad odour**). **4** *Arch.* a sweet-smelling fragrance. ORIG C13: from OF *odur,* from L *odor*
▸ **ˈodourless** *or US* **ˈodorless** *adj*

Odovacar ★ (ˌəʊdəˈvɑːkə) *n* a variant of **Odoacer.**

Odra ★ (ˈɔdra) *n* the Czech and Polish name for the **Oder.**

Odysseus ★ (əˈdiːsɪəs) *n Greek myth.* one of the foremost of the Greek heroes at the siege of Troy, noted for his courage and ingenuity. His return to his kingdom of Ithaca was fraught with adventures in which he lost all his companions. Roman name: **Ulysses.**

Odyssey (ˈɒdɪsɪ) *n* **1** a Greek epic poem, attributed to Homer, describing the ten-year homeward wanderings of Odysseus after the fall of Troy. **2** (*often not cap.*) any long eventful journey.
▸ **Odyssean** (ˌɒdɪˈsiːən) *adj*

Oe *symbol for* oersted.

OE *abbrev. for* Old English (language).

OECD *abbrev. for* Organization for Economic Cooperation and Development.

OECS *abbrev. for* Organization of Eastern Caribbean States.

OED *abbrev. for* Oxford English Dictionary.

oedema *or US* **edema** (ɪˈdiːmə) *n, pl* **oedemata** *or US* **edemata** (-mətə). **1** *Pathol.* an excessive accumulation of serous fluid in the intercellular spaces of tissue. **2** *Bot.* an abnormal swelling in a plant caused by parenchyma or an accumulation of water in the tissues. ORIG C16: via NL from Gk *oidēma,* from *oidein* to swell
▸ **oedematous** (ɪˈdɛmətəs), **oeˈdemaˌtose** *or US* **eˈdematous, eˈdemaˌtose** *adj*

Oedipus ★ (ˈiːdɪpəs) *n Greek myth.* the son of Laius and Jocasta. He killed his father, unaware of his identity, and unwittingly married his mother. When the truth was revealed, he put out his eyes and Jocasta killed herself.

Oedipus complex *n Psychoanal.* the repressed sexual feeling of a child, esp. male, for its parent of the opposite sex combined with a rivalry with the parent of the same sex.
▸ **ˈoedipal** *or* **ˌoediˈpean** *adj*

OEEC *abbrev. for* Organization for European Economic Cooperation. It was superseded by the OECD in 1961.

Oehlenschläger *or* **Öhlenschläger** ★ (*Danish* ˈøːlənslɛːgər) *n* **Adam Gottlob** (ˈadam ˈgɔtlɔp). 1779–1850, Danish romantic poet and dramatist.

OEM *abbrev. for* original equipment manufacturer: a computer company whose products are made by combining basic parts supplied by others to meet a customer's needs.

oenology *or* **enology** (iːˈnɒlədʒɪ) *n* the study of wine. ORIG C19: from Gk *oinos* wine + -LOGY
▸ **oenological** *or* **enological** (ˌiːnəˈlɒdʒɪkᵊl) *adj* ▸ **oeˈnologist** *or* **eˈnologist** *n*

Oenone ★ (iːˈnəʊnɪ) *n Greek myth.* a nymph of Mount Ida, whose lover Paris left her for Helen.

oenothera (iːˈnɒθərə) *n* any of various hardy biennial or herbaceous perennial plants having yellow flowers. Also called: **evening primrose.** ORIG from Gk *oinothēras,* ?from *onothēras* a plant whose roots smell of wine

o'er (ɔː, əʊə) *prep, adv* a poetic contraction of **over.**

oersted (ˈɜːstɛd) *n* the cgs unit of magnetic field strength; the field strength that would cause a unit magnetic pole to experience a force of 1 dyne in free space. It is equivalent to 79.58 amperes per metre. Symbol. Oe ORIG C20: after H. C. *Oersted* (1777–1851), Danish physicist who discovered electromagnetism

★ people and places

oesophagus *or US* **esophagus** (iːˈsɒfəgəs) *n, pl* **oesophagi** *or US* **esophagi** (-ˌgaɪ). the part of the alimentary canal between the pharynx and the stomach; gullet. ORIG C16: via NL from Gk *oisophagos,* from *oisein,* future infinitive of *pherein* to carry + *-phagos,* from *phagein* to eat
▸ **oesophageal** *or US* **esophageal** (iːˌsɒfəˈdʒiːəl) *adj*

oestradiol (ˌiːstrəˈdaɪɒl, ˌɛstrə-) *or US* **estradiol** *n* the most potent oestrogenic horome secreted by the mammalian ovary: synthesized and used to treat oestrogen deficiency and cancer of the breast. ORIG C20: from NL, from OESTRIN + DI-[1] + -OL[1]

oestrin (ˈiːstrɪn) *n* an obsolete term for **oestrogen.** ORIG C20: from OESTR(US) + -IN

oestrogen (ˈiːstrədʒən, ˈɛstrə-) *or US* **estrogen** *n* any of several hormones that induce oestrus, stimulate changes in the female reproductive organs, and promote development of female secondary sexual characteristics. ORIG C20: from OESTRUS + -GEN
▸ **oestrogenic** (ˌiːstrəˈdʒɛnɪk, ˌɛstrə-) *or US* **estrogenic** (ˌɛstrəˈdʒɛnɪk, ˌiːstrə-) *adj* ▸ **ˌoestroˈgenically** *or US* **ˌestroˈgenically** *adv*

oestrous cycle (ˈiːstrəs) *n* a hormonally controlled cycle of activity of the reproductive organs in many female mammals.

oestrus (ˈiːstrəs, ˈɛstrəs) *or US* **estrus, estrum** (ˈɛstrəm, ˈiːstrəm) *n* a regularly occurring period of sexual receptivity in most female mammals, except humans, during which ovulation occurs and copulation can take place; heat. ORIG C17: from L *oestrus* gadfly, hence frenzy, from Gk *oistros*
▸ **ˈoestrous, ˈoestral** *or US* **ˈestrous, ˈestral** *adj*

oeuvre *French.* (œvrə) *n* **1** a work of art, literature, music, etc. **2** the total output of a writer, painter, etc. ORIG ult. from L *opera,* pl. of *opus* work

of (ɒv; *unstressed* əv) *prep* **1** used with a verbal noun or gerund to link it with a following noun that is either the subject or the object of the verb embedded in the gerund: *the breathing of a fine swimmer* (subject); *the breathing of clean air* (object). **2** used to indicate possession, origin, or association: *the house of my sister; to die of hunger.* **3** used after words or phrases expressing quantities. **4** constituted by, containing, or characterized by: *a family of idiots; a rod of iron.* **5** used to indicate separation, as in time or space: *within a mile of the town; within ten minutes of the beginning of the concert.* **6** used to mark apposition: *the city of Naples; a speech on the subject of archaeology.* **7** about; concerning: *speak to me of love.* **8** used in passive constructions to indicate the agent: *he was beloved of all.* **9** *Inf.* used to indicate a day or part of a period of time when some activity habitually occurs: *I go to the pub of an evening.* **10** *US.* before the hour of: *a quarter of nine.* ORIG OE (as prep & adv); rel. to L *ab*

USAGE NOTE See at **off.**

OF *abbrev. for* Old French (language).

Ofcom (ˈɒfˌkɒm) *n* (in Britain) *acronym for* Office of Communications: a government body regulating the telecommunications industries; a super-regulator merging the Radio Authority, Independent Television Commission, and Oftel.

off (ɒf) *prep* **1** used to indicate actions in which contact is absent, as between an object and a surface: *to lift a cup off the table.* **2** used to indicate the removal of something that is appended to or in association with something else: *to take the tax off potatoes.* **3** out of alignment with: *we are off course.* **4** situated near to or leading away from: *just off the High Street.* **5** not inclined towards: *I've gone off you.* ◆ *adv* **6** (*particle*) so as to be deactivated or disengaged: *turn off the radio.* **7** (*particle*) **7a** so as to get rid of: *sleep off a hangover.* **7b** so as to be removed from, esp. as a reduction: *he took ten per cent off.* **8** spent away from work or other duties: *take the afternoon off.* **9a** on a trip, journey, or race: *I saw her off at the station.* **9b** (*particle*) so as to be completely absent, used up, or exhausted: *this stuff kills off all vermin.* **10** out from the shore or land: *the ship stood off.* **11a** out of contact; at a distance: *the ship was 10 miles off.* **11b** out of the present location: *the girl ran off.* **12** away in the future: *August is less than a week off.* **13** (*particle*) so as to be no longer taking place: *the match has been* rained off. **14** (*particle*) removed from contact with something, as clothing from the body: *the girl took all her clothes off.* **15** offstage: *noises off.* **16 off and on.** intermittently; from time to time: *he comes here off and on.* **17 off with.** (*interj*) a command or an exhortation to remove or cut off (something specified): *off with his head; off with that coat.* ◆ *adj* **18** not on; no longer operative: *the off position on the dial.* **19** (*postpositive*) not taking place; cancelled or postponed: *the meeting is off.* **20** in a specified condition regarding money, provisions, etc.: *well off; how are you off for bread?* **21** unsatisfactory or disappointing: *his performance was rather off; an off year for good tennis.* **22** (*postpositive*) in a condition as specified: *I'd be better off without this job.* **23** (*postpositive*) no longer on the menu: *haddock is off.* **24** (*postpositive*) (of food or drink) having gone bad, sour, etc.: *this milk is off.* ◆ *n* **25** *Cricket.* **25a** the part of the field on that side of the pitch to which the batsman presents his bat when taking strike. **25b** (*in combination*) a fielding position in this part of the field: *mid-off.* **25c** (*as modifier*): *the off stump.* ORIG orig. var. of OF; fully distinguished from it in the 17th cent.

USAGE NOTE In standard English, *off* is not followed by *of*: *he stepped off* (not *off of*) *the platform.* The use of *off* after verbs such as *borrow, buy, get,* as in *I got this chair off an antique dealer,* is acceptable in conversation, but should be replaced in formal writing by *from.*

off. *abbrev. for:* **1** offer. **2** office. **3** officer. **4** official.

Offa ★ ('ɒfə) *n* died 796 A.D., king of Mercia (757–796), who constructed an earthwork (**Offa's Dyke**) between Wales and Mercia.

offal ('ɒfᵊl) *n* **1** the edible internal parts of an animal, such as the heart, liver, and tongue. **2** dead or decomposing organic matter. **3** refuse; rubbish. ORIG C14: from OFF + FALL, referring to parts fallen or cut off

Offaly ★ ('ɒfəlɪ) *n* an inland county of E central Republic of Ireland, in Leinster province: formerly an ancient kingdom, which also included parts of Tipperary, Leix, and Kildare. County town: Tullamore. Pop.: 59 000 (1996). Area: 2000 sq. km (770 sq. miles).

off-balance-sheet reserve *n Accounting.* a sum of money or an asset that should appear on a company's balance but does not; hidden reserve.

offbeat ('ɒfˌbiːt) *n* **1** *Music.* any of the normally unaccented beats in a bar, such as the second and fourth beats in a bar of four-four time. ◆ *adj* **2a** unusual, unconventional, or eccentric. **2b** (*as n*): *he liked the offbeat in fashion.*

off break *n Cricket.* a bowled ball that spins from off to leg on pitching.

off-Broadway *adj* **1** designating the kind of experimental, low-budget, or noncommercial productions associated with theatre outside the Broadway area in New York. **2** (of theatres) not located on Broadway.

off colour *adj* (**off-colour** *when prenominal*). **1** *Chiefly Brit.* slightly ill; unwell. **2** indecent or indelicate; risqué.

offcut ('ɒfˌkʌt) *n* a piece of paper, wood, fabric, etc., remaining after the main pieces have been cut; remnant.

Offenbach[1] ★ (*German* 'ɔfənbax) *n* a city in central Germany, on the River Main in Hesse opposite Frankfurt am Main: leather-goods industry. Pop.: 116 533 (1996 est.).

Offenbach[2] ★ ('ɒfənˌbɑːk; *French* ɔfɛnbak) *n* **Jacques** (ʒak). 1819–80, German-born French composer of operettas, including *Orpheus in the Underworld* (1858), and of the opera *The Tales of Hoffmann* (1881).

offence *or US* **offense** (ə'fɛns) *n* **1** a violation or breach of a law, rule, etc. **2** any public wrong or crime. **3** annoyance, displeasure, or resentment. **4 give offence (to).** to cause annoyance or displeasure (to). **5 take offence.** to feel injured, humiliated, or offended. **6** a source of annoyance, displeasure, or anger. **7** attack; assault. **8** *Arch.* injury or harm.

offend (ə'fɛnd) *vb* **1** to hurt the feelings, sense of dignity, etc., of (a person, etc.). **2** (*tr*) to be disagreeable to; disgust: *the smell offended him.* **3** (*intr except in archaic uses*) to break (a law). ORIG C14: via OF *offendre* to strike against, from L *offendere*
▸ **of'fender** *n* ▸ **of'fending** *adj*

offensive (ə'fɛnsɪv) *adj* **1** unpleasant or disgusting, as to the senses. **2** causing anger or annoyance; insulting. **3** for the purpose of attack rather than defence. ◆ *n* **4** (usually preceded by *the*) an attitude or position of aggression. **5** an assault, attack, or military initiative, esp. a strategic one.
▸ **of'fensively** *adv* ▸ **of'fensiveness** *n*

offer ('ɒfə) *vb* **1** to present (something, someone, oneself, etc.) for acceptance or rejection. **2** (*tr*) to present as part of a requirement: *she offered English as a second subject.* **3** (*tr*) to provide or make accessible: *this stream offers the best fishing.* **4** (*intr*) to present itself: *if an opportunity should offer.* **5** (*tr*) to show or express willingness or the intention (to do something). **6** (*tr*) to put forward (a proposal, opinion, etc.) for consideration. **7** (*tr*) to present for sale. **8** (*tr*) to propose as payment; bid or tender. **9** (when *tr,* often foll. by *up*) to present (a prayer, sacrifice, etc.) as or during an act of worship. **10** (*tr*) to show readiness for: *to offer battle.* **11** (*intr*) *Arch.* to make a proposal of marriage. ◆ *n* **12** something, such as a proposal or bid, that is offered. **13** the act of offering or the condition of being offered. **14** a proposal of marriage. **15 on offer.** for sale at a reduced price. ORIG OE, from L *offerre* to present, from *ob-* to + *ferre* to bring

offer document *n* a document sent by a person or firm making a takeover bid to the shareholders of the target company, giving details of the offer that has been made and, usually, reasons for accepting it.

offering ('ɒfərɪŋ) *n* **1** something that is offered. **2** a contribution to the funds of a religious organization. **3** a sacrifice, as of an animal, to a deity.

offertory ('ɒfətərɪ) *n, pl* **offertories.** *Christianity.* **1** the oblation of the bread and wine at the Eucharist. **2** the offerings of the worshippers at this service. **3** the prayers said or sung while the worshippers' offerings are being brought to the altar during the **offertory procession.** ORIG C14: from Church L *offertōrium* place appointed for offerings, from L *offerre* to OFFER

offhand (ˌɒf'hænd) *adj also* **offhanded,** *adv* **1** without care, thought, attention, or consideration; sometimes, brusque or ungracious: *an offhand manner.* **2** without preparation or warning; impromptu.
▸ ˌ**off'handedly** *adv* ▸ ˌ**off'handedness** *n*

office ('ɒfɪs) *n* **1a** a room or rooms in which business, professional duties, clerical work, etc., are carried out. **1b** (*as modifier*): *office furniture; an office boy.* **2** (*often pl*) the building or buildings in which the work of an organization, such as a business, is carried out. **3** a commercial or professional business: *the architect's office approved the plans.* **4** the group of persons working in an office: *it was a happy office until she came.* **5** (*cap. when part of a name*) a department of the national government: *the Home Office.* **6** (*cap. when part of a name*) **6a** a governmental agency, esp. of the Federal government in the US. **6b** a subdivision of such an agency: *Office of Science and Technology.* **7a** a position of trust, responsibility, or duty, esp. in a government or organization: *to seek office.* **7b** (*in combination*): *an office-holder.* **8** duty or function: *the office of an administrator.* **9** (*often pl*) a minor task or service: *domestic offices.* **10** (*often pl*) an action performed for another, usually a beneficial action: *through his good offices.* **11** a place where tickets, information, etc., can be obtained: *a ticket office.* **12** *Christianity.* **12a** (*often pl*) a ceremony or service, prescribed by ecclesiastical authorities, esp. one for the dead. **12b** *RC Church.* the official daily service. **12c** short for **divine office.** **13** (*pl*) the parts of a house or estate where work is done, goods are stored, etc. **14** (*usually pl*) *Brit., euphemistic.* a lavatory (esp. in **usual offices**). **15 in** (*or* **out of**) **office.** (of a government) in (*or* out of) power. **16 the office.** a hint or signal. ORIG C13: via OF from L *officium* service, duty, from *opus* work, service + *facere* to do

office block *n* a large building designed to provide office accommodation.

office boy *n* a male office junior.

office junior *n* a young person, esp. a school-leaver,

employed in an office for running errands and doing other minor jobs.

officer ('ɒfɪsə) *n* **1** a person in the armed services who holds a position of responsibility, authority, and duty. **2** See **police officer**. **3** (on a non-naval ship) any person, including the captain and mate, who holds a position of authority and responsibility: *radio officer; engineer officer.* **4** a person appointed or elected to a position of responsibility or authority in a government, society, etc. **5** a government official: *a customs officer.* **6** (in the Order of the British Empire) a member of the grade below commander. ◆ *vb (tr)* **7** to furnish with officers. **8** to act as an officer over (some section, group, organization, etc.).

officer of the day *n* a military officer whose duty is to take charge of the security of the unit or camp for a day. Also called: **orderly officer**.

official (ə'fɪʃəl) *adj* **1** of or relating to an office, its administration, or its duration. **2** sanctioned by, recognized by, or derived from authority: *an official statement.* **3** having a formal ceremonial character: *an official dinner.* ◆ *n* **4** a person who holds a position in an organization, government department, etc., esp. a subordinate position.
▸ **of'ficially** *adv*

officialdom (ə'fɪʃəldəm) *n* **1** the outlook or behaviour of officials, esp. those rigidly adhering to regulations; bureaucracy. **2** officials or bureaucrats collectively.

officialese (əˌfɪʃə'li:z) *n* language characteristic of official documents, esp. when verbose or pedantic.

Official Receiver *n* an officer appointed by the Department of Trade and Industry to receive the income and manage the estate of a bankrupt. See also **receiver** (sense 2).

officiant (ə'fɪʃɪənt) *n* a person who presides and officiates at a religious ceremony.

officiate (ə'fɪʃɪˌeɪt) *vb* **officiates, officiating, officiated.** *(intr)* **1** to hold the position, responsibility, or function of an official. **2** to conduct a religious or other ceremony. ORIG C17: from Med. L *officiāre*, from L *officium*; see OFFICE
▸ **ofˌfici'ation** *n* ▸ **of'ficiˌator** *n*

officious (ə'fɪʃəs) *adj* **1** unnecessarily or obtrusively ready to offer advice or services. **2** *Diplomacy.* informal or unofficial. ORIG C16: from L *officiōsus* kindly, from *officium* service; see OFFICE
▸ **of'ficiously** *adv* ▸ **of'ficiousness** *n*

offing ('ɒfɪŋ) *n* **1** the part of the sea that can be seen from the shore. **2** **in the offing.** likely to occur soon.

offish ('ɒfɪʃ) *adj Inf.* aloof or distant in manner.
▸ **'offishly** *adv* ▸ **'offishness** *n*

off key *adj* (**off-key** *when prenominal*), *adv* **1** *Music.* **1a** not in the correct key. **1b** out of tune. **2** out of keeping; discordant.

off-licence *n Brit.* **1** a shop or a counter in a pub or hotel where alcoholic drinks are sold for consumption elsewhere. US equivalents: **package store, liquor store.** **2** a licence permitting such sales.

off limits *adj* (**off-limits** *when prenominal*). **1** *US, chiefly mil.* not to be entered; out of bounds. ◆ *adv* **2** in or into an area forbidden by regulations.

off line *adj* (**off-line** *when prenominal*). **1** of or concerned with a part of a computer system not connected to the central processing unit but controlled by a computer storage device. **2** disconnected from a computer; switched off. ◆ *adv* **3** while not connected to a computer or the Internet. ◆ Cf. **on line**.

off-load *vb (tr)* to get rid of (something unpleasant), as by delegation to another.

off message *adj* (**off-message** *when prenominal*) (esp. of a politician) not following the official line of his or her party.

off-peak *adj* of or relating to services as used outside periods of intensive use.

off-piste *adj* of or relating to skiing on virgin snow off the regular runs.

off-putting *adj Brit. inf.* arousing reluctance or aversion.

off-road *adj* **1** denoting the use of a vehicle away from public roads, esp. on rough terrain: *off-road motorcycling.* **2** (of a vehicle) designed or built for off-road use.

off-roader *n* a motor vehicle designed for use away from public roads, esp. on rough terrain.

off-sales *pl n Brit.* sales of alcoholic drink for consumption off the premises by a pub or an off-licence attached to a pub.

off season *adj* (**off-season** *when prenominal*). **1** denoting or occurring during a period of little activity in a trade or business. ◆ *n* **2** such a period. ◆ *adv* **3** in an off-season period.

offset *n* ('ɒfˌsɛt). **1** something that counterbalances or compensates for something else. **2a** a printing method in which the impression is made onto an intermediate surface, such as a rubber blanket, which transfers it to the paper. **2b** *(modifier)* relating to, involving, or printed by offset: *offset letterpress.* **3** another name for **set off**. **4** *Bot.* a short runner in certain plants that produces roots and shoots at the tip. **5** a ridge projecting from a range of hills or mountains. **6** a narrow horizontal or sloping surface formed where a wall is reduced in thickness towards the top. **7** *Surveying.* a measurement of distance to a point at right angles to a survey line. ◆ *vb* (ˌɒf'sɛt), **offsets, offsetting, offset.** **8** *(tr)* to counterbalance or compensate for. **9** *(tr)* to print (text, etc.) using the offset process. **10** *(tr)* to construct an offset in (a wall). **11** *(intr)* to project or develop as an offset.

offshoot ('ɒfˌʃu:t) *n* **1** a shoot or branch growing from the main stem of a plant. **2** something that develops or derives from a principal source or origin.

offshore (ˌɒf'ʃɔ:) *adj, adv* **1** from, away from, or at some distance from the shore. ◆ *adj* **2** sited or conducted at sea: *offshore industries.* **3** based or operating abroad: *offshore banking; offshore fund.*

offside *adj, adv* (ˌɒf'saɪd). **1** *Sport.* (in football, etc.) in a position illegally ahead of the ball when it is played. Cf. **onside**. ◆ *n* ('ɒfˌsaɪd). **2** (usually preceded by *the*) *Chiefly Brit.* **2a** the side of a vehicle, etc., nearest the centre of the road. **2b** *(as modifier): the offside passenger door.*

off-sider (ˌɒf'saɪdə) *n Austral. & NZ.* a partner or assistant.

offspring ('ɒfˌsprɪŋ) *n* **1** the immediate descendant or descendants of a person, animal, etc.; progeny. **2** a product, outcome, or result.

offstage ('ɒf'steɪdʒ) *adj, adv* out of the view of the audience; off the stage.

off-the-peg *adj* (of clothing) ready to wear; not produced especially for the person buying.

off the shelf *adv* **1** from stock and readily available: *you can have this model off the shelf.* ◆ *adj* (**off-the-shelf** *when prenominal*). **2** of or relating to a product that is readily available: *an off-the-shelf model.* **3** of or denoting a company that has been registered with the Registrar of Companies for the sole purpose of being sold.

off-the-wall *adj* (**off the wall** *when postpositive*). *Sl.* new or unexpected in an unconventional or eccentric way. ORIG C20: ?from the use of the phrase in handball and squash to describe a shot that is unexpected

off-white *n* **1** a colour consisting of white with a tinge of grey or yellow. ◆ *adj* **2** of such a colour: *an off-white coat.*

OFS *abbrev. for* Orange Free State.

oft (ɒft) *adv* short for **often** (archaic or poetic except in combinations such as **oft-repeated** and **oft-recurring**). ORIG OE *oft;* rel. to OHG *ofto*

OFT (in Britain) *abbrev. for* Office of Fair Trading.

often ('ɒfᵊn) *adv* **1** frequently or repeatedly; much of the time. Arch. equivalents: **'oftenˌtimes, 'oftˌtimes.** **2** **as often as not.** quite frequently. **3** **every so often.** at intervals. **4** **more often than not.** in more than half the instances. ◆ *adj* **5** *Arch.* repeated; frequent. ORIG C14: var. of OFT before vowels and *h*

Ogaden ★ (ˌɒgə'dɛn) *n* **the.** an autonomous region of SE Ethiopia, bordering on Somalia: consists of a desert plateau, inhabited by Somali nomads; a secessionist movement, supported by Somalia, has existed within the region since the early 1960s and led to bitter fighting between Ethiopia and Somalia (1977–78).

Ogasawara Gunto ★ (ˌɒgəsə'wɑ:rə 'gu:ntəʊ) *n* transliteration of the Japanese name for the **Bonin Islands**.

★ people and places

Ogbomosho ★ (ˌɒgbəˈməʊʃəʊ) *n* a city in SW Nigeria: the third largest town in Nigeria; trading centre for an agricultural region. Pop.: 730 000 (1996 est.).

Ogden ★ (ˈɒgdən) *n* **C(harles) K(ay).** 1889–1957, British linguist, who, with I. A. Richards, devised Basic English.

ogee (ˈəʊdʒiː) *n Archit.* **1** Also called: **talon.** a moulding having a cross section in the form of a letter S. **2** short for **ogee arch.** ORIG C15: prob. var. of OGIVE

ogee arch *n Archit.* a pointed arch having an S-shaped curve on both sides. Sometimes shortened to **ogee.**

Ogen melon (ˈəʊgen) *n* a variety of small melon with sweet pale orange flesh. ORIG C20: after a kibbutz in Israel where it was first developed

ogham *or* **ogam** (ˈɒgəm) *n* an ancient alphabetical writing system used by the Celts in Britain, consisting of straight lines drawn or carved perpendicular to or at an angle to another long straight line. ORIG C17: from OIrish *ogom,* from ?, but associated with the name *Ogma,* legendary inventor of this alphabet

ogive (ˈəʊdʒaɪv, əʊˈdʒaɪv) *n* **1** a diagonal rib or groin of a Gothic vault. **2** another name for **lancet arch.** ORIG C17: from OF, from ?
▸ **oˈgival** *adj*

ogle (ˈəʊgᵊl) *vb* **ogles, ogling, ogled. 1** to look at (someone) amorously or lustfully. **2** (*tr*) to stare or gape at. ◆ *n* **3** a flirtatious or lewd look. ORIG C17: prob. from Low G *oegeln,* from *oegen* to look at
▸ **ˈogler** *n*

Oglethorpe ★ (ˈəʊgᵊlˌθɔːp) *n* **James Edward.** 1696–1785, British general; founder of the colony of Georgia (1733).

Ogooué *or* **Ogowe** ★ (ɒˈgəʊweɪ) *n* a river in W central Africa, rising in SW Congo-Brazzaville and flowing generally northwest and north through Gabon to the Atlantic. Length: about 970 km (683 miles).

O grade *n* (formerly, in Scotland). **1a** the basic level of the Scottish Certificate of Education, now replaced by **Standard Grade. 1b** (*as modifier*): *O-grade history.* **2** a pass in a subject at O grade: *she has ten O grades.*

ogre (ˈəʊgə) *n* **1** (in folklore) a giant, usually given to eating human flesh. **2** any monstrous or cruel person. ORIG C18: from F, ?from L *Orcus,* god of the infernal regions
▸ **ˈogreish** *adj* ▸ **ˈogress** *fem n*

Ogun ★ (əʊˈgʊn) *n* a state of SW Nigeria, formed in 1976 from part of Western State. Capital: Abeokuta. Pop.: 2 614 747 (1995 est.). Area: 16 762 sq. km (6472 sq. miles).

oh (əʊ) *interj* an exclamation expressive of surprise, pain, pleasure, etc.

OH *abbrev. for* Ohio.

OHG *abbrev. for* Old High German.

O'Higgins ★ (əʊˈhɪgɪnz; *Spanish* oˈiɣins) *n* **1 Ambrosio** (æmˈbrəʊzɪˌəʊ). ?1720–1801, Irish soldier, who became viceroy of Chile (1789–96) and of Peru (1796–1801). **2** his son, **Bernardo** (bɛrˈnarðo). 1778–1842, Chilean revolutionary; became Chile's first president (1817–23).

Ohio ★ (əʊˈhaɪəʊ) *n* **1** a state of the central US, in the Midwest on Lake Erie: consists of prairies in the W and the Allegheny plateau in the E, the Ohio River forming the S and most of the E borders. Capital: Columbus. Pop.: 11 209 493 (1998 est.). Area: 107 044 sq. km (41 330 sq. miles). Abbrev. (with zip code): **OH** **2** a river in the eastern US, formed by the confluence of the Allegheny and Monongahela Rivers at Pittsburgh: flows generally W and SW to join the Mississippi at Cairo, Illinois, as its chief E tributary. Length: 1570 km (975 miles).

Öhlenschläger *Danish.* ★ (ˈøːlənslɛːyər) *n* a variant spelling of **Oehlenschläger.**

ohm (əʊm) *n* the derived SI unit of electrical resistance; the resistance between two points on a conductor when a constant potential difference of 1 volt between them produces a current of 1 ampere. Symbol: Ω ORIG C19: after Georg Simon OHM
▸ **ˈohmage** *n*

Ohm ★ (əʊm) *n* **Georg Simon** (ˈgeːɔrk ˈziːmɔn). 1787–1854, German physicist. See **Ohm's law.**

ohmmeter (ˈəʊmˌmiːtə) *n* an instrument for measuring electrical resistance.

OHMS (in Britain and the Commonwealth) *abbrev. for* On Her (*or* His) Majesty's Service.

Ohm's law *n* the principle that the electric current passing through a conductor is directly proportional to the potential difference across it. The constant of proportionality is the resistance of the conductor.

oho (əʊˈhəʊ) *interj* an exclamation expressing surprise, exultation, or derision.

-oic *suffix forming adjectives.* indicating that a chemical compound is a carboxylic acid: *ethanoic acid.*

-oid *suffix forming adjectives and associated nouns.* indicating likeness, resemblance, or similarity: *anthropoid.* ORIG from Gk *-oeidēs* resembling, from *eidos* form

-oidea *suffix forming plural proper nouns.* forming the names of zoological classes or superfamilies: *Canoidea.* ORIG from NL, from L *-oīdēs* -OID

oil (ɔɪl) *n* **1** any of a number of viscous liquids with a smooth sticky feel. They are usually flammable, insoluble in water, soluble in organic solvents, and are obtained from plants and animals, from mineral deposits, and by synthesis. See also **essential oil. 2a** another name for **petroleum. 2b** (*as modifier*): *an oil engine; an oil rig.* **3a** any of a number of substances usually derived from petroleum and used for lubrication. **3b** (*in combination*): *an oilcan.* **3c** (*as modifier*): *an oil pump.* **4** Also called: **fuel oil.** a petroleum product used as a fuel in domestic heating, marine engines, etc. **5** *Brit.* **5a** paraffin, esp. when used as a domestic fuel. **5b** (*as modifier*): *an oil lamp.* **6** any substance of a consistency resembling that of oil: *oil of vitriol.* **7** the solvent, usually linseed oil, with which pigments are mixed to make artists' paints. **8a** (*often pl*) oil colour or paint. **8b** (*as modifier*): *an oil painting.* **9** an oil painting. **10** *Austral. & NZ sl.* facts or news: *he gave me the dinkum oil.* **11 strike oil. 11a** to discover petroleum while drilling for it. **11b** *Inf.* to become very rich or successful. ◆ *vb* (*tr*) **12** to lubricate, smear, polish, etc., with oil or an oily substance. **13 oil one's tongue.** *Inf.* to speak flatteringly or glibly. **14 oil someone's palm.** *Inf.* to bribe someone. **15 oil the wheels.** to make things run smoothly. ORIG C12: from OF *oile,* from L *oleum* (olive) oil, from *olea* olive tree, from Gk *elaia* OLIVE
▸ **ˈoiler** *n* ▸ **ˈoil-ˌlike** *adj*

oil cake *n* stock feed consisting of compressed cubes made from the residue of the crushed seeds of oil-bearing crops such as linseed.

oilcan (ˈɔɪlˌkæn) *n* a container with a long nozzle for applying lubricating oil to machinery.

oilcloth (ˈɔɪlˌklɒθ) *n* **1** waterproof material made by treating one side of a cotton fabric with a drying oil or a synthetic resin. **2** another name for **linoleum.**

oil drum *n* a metal drum used to contain or transport oil.

oilfield (ˈɔɪlˌfiːld) *n* an area containing reserves of petroleum, esp. one that is already being exploited.

oilfired (ˈɔɪlˌfaɪəd) *adj* (of central heating, etc.) using oil as fuel.

oilgas (ˈɔɪlˌgæs) *n* a gaseous mixture of hydrocarbons used as a fuel, obtained by the destructive distillation of mineral oils.

oilman (ˈɔɪlmən) *n, pl* **oilmen. 1** a person who owns or operates oil wells. **2** a person who sells oil.

oil minister *n* a government official in charge of or representing the interests of an oil-producing country.

oil of cloves *n* another name for **clove oil.**

oil of vitriol *n* another name for **sulphuric acid.**

oil paint *n* paint made of pigment ground in oil, usually linseed oil.

oil painting *n* **1** a picture painted with oil paints. **2** the art or process of painting with oil paints. **3 he's** *or* **she's no oil painting.** *Inf.* he *or* she is not good-looking.

oil palm *n* a tropical African palm tree, the fruits of which yield palm oil.

oil rig *n* See **rig** (sense 6).

Oil Rivers ★ *pl n* the delta of the Niger River in S Nigeria.

oil sand *n* a sandstone impregnated with hydrocarbons, esp. such deposits in Alberta, Canada.

oil-seed rape *n* another name for **rape**[2].

oil shale *n* a carbonaceous rock from which oil can be extracted.

oilskin ('ɔɪlˌskɪn) *n* **1a** a cotton fabric treated with oil and pigment to make it waterproof. **1b** (*as modifier*): *an oilskin hat.* **2** (*often pl*) a protective outer garment of this fabric.

oil slick *n* a mass of floating oil covering an area of water.

oilstone ('ɔɪlˌstəʊn) *n* a stone with a fine grain lubricated with oil and used for sharpening cutting tools. See also **whetstone.**

oil well *n* a boring into the earth or sea bed for the extraction of petroleum.

oily ('ɔɪlɪ) *adj* **oilier, oiliest. 1** soaked in or smeared with oil or grease. **2** consisting of, containing, or resembling oil. **3** flatteringly servile or obsequious.
▸ **'oilily** *adv* ▸ **'oiliness** *n*

oink (ɔɪŋk) *interj* an imitation or representation of the grunt of a pig.

ointment ('ɔɪntmənt) *n* **1** a fatty or oily medicated preparation applied to the skin to heal or protect. **2** a similar substance used as a cosmetic. ORIG C14: from OF *oignement,* from L *unguentum* UNGUENT

Oireachtas ('ɛrəkθəs) *n* the parliament of the Republic of Ireland. ORIG Irish Gaelic: assembly, from OIrish *airech* nobleman

Oise ★ (*French* waz) *n* **1** a department of N France, in Picardy region. Capital: Beauvais. Pop.: 760 070 (1994 est.). Area: 5887 sq. km (2296 sq. miles). **2** a river in N France, rising in Belgium, in the Ardennes, and flowing southwest to join the Seine at Conflans. Length: 302 km (188 miles).

Oistrakh ★ ('ɔɪstrɑːk; *Russian* 'ɔjstrəx) *n* **1 David** (da'vit). 1908–74, Russian violinist. **2** his son, **Igor** ('igərj). born 1931, Russian violinist.

Oita ★ ('ɔɪtə) *n* an industrial city in SW Japan, on NE Kyushu: dominated most of Kyushu in the 16th century. Pop.: 426 981 (1995).

Ojibwa (əʊ'dʒɪbwə) *n* **1** (*pl* **Ojibwas** *or* **Ojibwa**) a member of a North American Indian people living west of Lake Superior. **2** the language of this people.

OK *abbrev. for* Oklahoma.

O.K. (ˌəʊ'keɪ) *Inf.* ◆ *sentence substitute.* **1** an expression of approval or agreement. ◆ *adj* (*usually postpositive*), *adv* **2** in good or satisfactory condition. ◆ *vb* **O.K.s, O.K.ing** (ˌəʊ'keɪɪŋ), **O.K.ed** (ˌəʊ'keɪd). **3** (*tr*) to approve or endorse. ◆ *n, pl* **O.K.s. 4** approval or agreement. ◆ Also: **okay.** ORIG C19: ?from *o(ll) k(orrect)*, jocular alteration of *all correct*

Okanagan ★ (ˌəʊkə'nɑːgən) *n* a river in North America that flows south from Okanagan Lake in Canada into the Columbia River in NE Washington, US. Length: about 483 km (300 miles). Also (US): **ˌOka'nogan.**

Okanagan Lake ★ *n* a lake in SW Canada, in S British Columbia: drained by the Okanagan River into the Columbia River. Length: about 111 km (69 miles). Width: from 3.2–6.4 km (2–4 miles).

okapi (əʊ'kɑːpɪ) *n, pl* **okapis** *or* **okapi.** a ruminant mammal of the forests of central Africa, having a reddish-brown coat with horizontal white stripes on the legs, and small horns. ORIG C20: from a Central African word

Okavango *or* **Okovango** ★ (ˌəʊkə'vɑːŋgəʊ) *n* a river in SW central Africa, rising in central Angola and flowing southeast, then east as part of the border between Angola and Namibia, then southeast across the Caprivi Strip into Botswana to form a great marsh known as the **Okavango Basin.** Length: about 1600 km (1000 miles).

okay (ˌəʊ'keɪ) *sentence substitute, adj, adv, vb, n* a variant spelling of **O.K.**

Okayama ★ (ˌɒkə'jɑːmə) *n* a city in SW Japan, on W Honshu on the Inland Sea. Pop.: 616 056 (1995).

Okeechobee ★ (ˌəʊkɪ'tʃəʊbɪ) *n* **Lake.** a lake in S Florida, in the Everglades: second largest freshwater lake wholly within the US. Area: 1813 sq. km (700 sq. miles).

O'Keeffe ★ (əʊ'kiːf) *n* **Georgia.** 1887–1986, US painter, best known for her semiabstract still lifes.

Okefenokee Swamp ★ (ˌəʊkɪfɪ'nəʊkɪ) *n* a swamp in the US, in SE Georgia and N Florida: protected flora and fauna. Area: 1554 sq. km (600 sq. miles).

Okhotsk ★ ('əʊkɒtsk; *Russian* a'xɔtsk) *n* **Sea of.** part of the NW Pacific, surrounded by the Kamchatka Peninsula, the Kurile Islands, Sakhalin Island, and the E coast of Siberia. Area: 1 589 840 sq. km (613 838 sq. miles).

Okinawa ★ (ˌəʊkɪ'nɑːwə) *n* a coral island of SW Japan, the largest of the Ryukyu Islands in the N Pacific: scene of heavy fighting in World War II; administered by the US (1945–72); agricultural. Chief town: Naha City. Pop.: 1 273 508 (1995). Area: 1176 sq. km (454 sq. miles).

Okla. *abbrev. for* Oklahoma.

Oklahoma ★ (ˌəʊklə'həʊmə) *n* a state in the S central US: consists of plains in the west, rising to mountains in the southwest and east; important for oil. Capital: Oklahoma City. Pop.: 3 346 713 (1998 est.). Area: 181 185 sq. km (69 956 sq. miles). Abbrevs.: **Okla.** or (with zip code) **OK**
▸ **ˌOkla'homan** *adj, n*

Oklahoma City ★ *n* a city in central Oklahoma: the state capital and a major agricultural and industrial centre. Pop.: 469 852 (1996 est.).

Okovango ★ (ˌəʊkə'vɑːŋgəʊ) *n* a variant spelling of **Okavango.**

okra ('əʊkrə) *n* **1** an annual plant of the Old World tropics, with yellow-and-red flowers and edible oblong green pods. **2** the pod of this plant, eaten in soups, stews, etc. See also **gumbo** (sense 1). ORIG C18: of West African origin

-ol[1] *suffix forming nouns.* denoting a chemical compound containing a hydroxyl group, esp. alcohols and phenols: *ethanol; quinol.* ORIG from ALCOHOL

-ol[2] *n combining form.* (not used systematically) a variant of **-ole**[1].

Olaf I ('əʊləf) *or* **Olav I** ★ ('əʊləv) *n* known as *Olaf Tryggvesson.* ?965–?1000 A.D., king of Norway (995–?1000). He began the conversion of Norway to Christianity.

Olaf II *or* **Olav II** ★ *n* **Saint.** 995–1030 A.D., king of Norway (1015–28); deposed by Canute: patron saint of Norway. Feast day: July 29.

Olaf V *or* **Olav V** ★ *n* 1903–91, king of Norway (1957–91).

Öland ★ (*Swedish* 'øːland) *n* an island in the Baltic Sea, separated from the mainland of SE Sweden by Kalmar Sound: the second largest Swedish island. Chief town: Borgholm. Pop.: 24 100 (1988 est.). Area: 1347 sq. km (520 sq. miles).

old (əʊld) *adj* **1** having lived or existed for a relatively long time: *an old man; an old tradition; an old house.* **2a** of or relating to advanced years or a long life: *old age.* **2b** (*as collective n;* preceded by *the*): *the old.* **2c old and young.** people of all ages. **3** decrepit or senile. **4** worn with age or use: *old clothes; an old car.* **5a** (*postpositive*) having lived or existed for a specified period: *a child who is six years old.* **5b** (*in combination*): *a six-year-old child.* **5c** (*as n in combination*): *a six-year-old.* **6** (*cap. when part of a name or title*) earlier or earliest of two or more things with the same name: *the old edition; the Old Testament.* **7** (*cap. when part of a name*) designating the form of a language in which the earliest known records are written: *Old English.* **8** (*prenominal*) familiar through long acquaintance or repetition: *an old friend; an old excuse.* **9** practised; hardened: *old in cunning.* **10** (*prenominal;* often preceded by *good*) cherished; dear: used as a term of affection or familiarity: *good old George.* **11** *Inf.* (with any of several nouns) used as a familiar form of address to a person: *old thing; old bean; old stick.* **12** skilled through long experience (esp. in **an old hand**). **13** out of date; unfashionable. **14** remote or distant in origin or time of origin: *an old culture.* **15** (*prenominal*) former; previous: *my old house was small.* **16a** (*prenominal*) established for a relatively long time: *an old member.* **16b** (*in combination*): *old-established.* **17** sensible, wise, or mature: *old beyond one's years.* **18** (intensifier) (esp. in **a high old time, any old thing, any old how,** etc.). **19**

good old days. an earlier period of time regarded as better than the present. **20 little old.** *Inf.* indicating affection, esp. humorous affection. **21 the old one** (*or* **gentleman**). *Inf.* a jocular name for **Satan.** ◆ *n* **22** an earlier or past time: *in days of old.* ORIG OE *eald*
▸ **'oldish** *adj* ▸ **'oldness** *n*

old age pension *n* a former name for **retirement pension.**
▸ **old age pensioner** *n*

Old Bailey ★ ('beɪlɪ) *n* the Central Criminal Court of England.

Old Bill (bɪl) *n* (*functioning as pl*, preceded by *the*) *Brit. sl.* policemen collectively. ORIG C20: ?from the World War I cartoon of a soldier with a drooping moustache

old boy *n* **1** (*sometimes caps.*) *Brit. & Canad.* a male ex-pupil of a school. **2** *Inf., chiefly Brit.* **2a** a familiar name used to refer to a man. **2b** an old man.

old boy network *n Brit. & Canad. inf.* the appointment to power of former pupils of the same small group of public schools or universities.

Old Castile ★ *n* a region of N Spain, on the Bay of Biscay: formerly a province. Spanish name: **Castilla la Vieja.**

Oldcastle ★ ('əʊldˌkɑːsᵊl) *n* Sir **John,** Baron Cobham. ?1378–1417, Lollard leader; hanged as a heretic. He is thought to have been a model for Shakespeare's Falstaff.

Old Contemptibles *pl n* the British expeditionary force to France in 1914. ORIG from the Kaiser's alleged reference to them as a "contemptible little army"

old country *n* the country of origin of an immigrant or an immigrant's ancestors.

Old Dart ★ *n* **the.** *Austral. sl.* Britain, esp. England. ORIG C19: from ?

Old Delhi ★ *n* See **Delhi.**

olden ('əʊldᵊn) *adj* an archaic or poetic word for **old** (often in **in olden days** and **in olden times**).

Oldenbarneveldt ★ (*Dutch* ɔldən'bɑrnəvɛlt) *n* **Johan van** (joː'hɑn vɑn). 1547–1619, Dutch statesman, regarded as a founder of Dutch independence: executed by Maurice of Nassau.

Oldenburg[1] ★ ('əʊldᵊnˌbɜːg; *German* 'ɔldənburk) *n* **1** a city in NW Germany, in Lower Saxony: former capital of Oldenburg state. Pop.: 157 382 (1996 est.). **2** a former state of NW Germany: became part of Lower Saxony in 1946.

Oldenburg[2] ★ ('əʊldᵊnˌbɜːg) *n* **Claes** (klɔːs). born 1929, US pop sculptor and artist, born in Sweden.

Old English *n* **1** Also called: **Anglo-Saxon.** the English language from the time of the earliest Saxon settlements in the fifth century A.D. to about 1100. Abbrev.: **OE. 2** *Printing.* a Gothic typeface commonly used in England up to the 18th century.

Old English sheepdog *n* a breed of large bobtailed sheepdog with a profuse shaggy coat.

older ('əʊldə) *adj* **1** the comparative of **old. 2** Also (of people): **elder.** of greater age.

old-fashioned *adj* **1** belonging to, characteristic of, or favoured by former times; outdated: *old-fashioned ideas.* **2** favouring or adopting the dress, manners, fashions, etc., of a former time. **3** *Scot. & N English dialect.* old for one's age: *an old-fashioned child.* ◆ *n* **4** a cocktail containing spirit, bitters, fruit, etc.

Old French *n* the French language in its earliest forms, from about the 9th century up to about 1400. Abbrev.: **OF.**

old girl *n* **1** (*sometimes caps.*) *Brit. & Canad.* a female ex-pupil of a school. **2** *Inf., chiefly Brit.* **2a** a familiar name used to refer to a woman. **2b** an old woman.

Old Glory *n* a nickname for the flag of the United States of America.

old gold *n* **a** a dark yellow colour, sometimes with a brownish tinge. **b** (*as adj*): *an old-gold carpet.*

old guard *n* **1** a group that works for a long-established or old-fashioned cause or principle. **2** the conservative element in a political party or other group. ORIG C19: after Napoleon's imperial guard

Oldham ★ ('əʊldəm) *n* **1** a town in NW England, in Greater Manchester. Pop.: 103 931 (1991). **2** a unitary authority in NW England, in Greater Manchester. Pop.: 220 400 (1996 est.). Area: 141 sq. km (54 sq. miles).

old hat *adj* (*postpositive*) old-fashioned or trite.

Old High German *n* a group of West Germanic dialects that eventually developed into modern German; High German up to about 1200. Abbrev.: **OHG.**

oldie ('əʊldɪ) *n Inf.* an old joke, song, film, person, etc.

Old Irish *n* the Celtic language of Ireland up to about 900 A.D.

old lady *n* an informal term for **mother** or **wife.**

Old Latin *n* the Latin language before the classical period, up to about 100 B.C.

Old Low German *n* the Saxon and Low Franconian dialects of German up to about 1200; the old form of modern Low German and Dutch. Abbrev.: **OLG.**

old maid *n* **1** a woman regarded as unlikely ever to marry; spinster. **2** *Inf.* a prim, fastidious, or excessively cautious person. **3** a card game in which players try to avoid holding the unpaired card at the end of the game.
▸ **ˌold-'maidish** *adj*

old man *n* **1** an informal term for **father** or **husband. 2** (*sometimes caps.*) *Inf.* a man in command, such as an employer, foreman, or captain of a ship. **3** *Sometimes facetious.* an affectionate term used in addressing a man. **4** Also called: **southernwood.** an aromatic shrubby wormwood of S Europe, having drooping yellow flowers. **5** *Christianity.* the unregenerate aspect of human nature.

old man's beard *n* any of various plants having white feathery seed heads, esp. traveller's joy and Spanish moss.

old master *n* **1** one of the great European painters of the period 1500 to 1800. **2** a painting by one of these.

old moon *n* a phase of the moon lying between last quarter and new moon, when it appears as a waning crescent.

Old Nick *n Inf.* a jocular name for **Satan.**

Old Norse *n* the language or group of dialects of medieval Scandinavia and Iceland from about 700 to about 1350. Abbrev.: **ON.**

Old Northwest ★ *n* (in the early US) the land between the Great Lakes, the Mississippi, and the Ohio River. Awarded to the US in 1783, it was organized into the **Northwest Territory** in 1787 and now forms the states of Ohio, Indiana, Illinois, Wisconsin, Michigan, and part of Minnesota.

Old Pretender ★ *n* See (James Francis Edward) **Stuart.**

Old Prussian *n* the former language of the non-German Prussians, belonging to the Baltic branch of the Indo-European family: extinct by 1700.

old rose *n* **a** a greyish-pink colour. **b** (*as adj*): *old-rose gloves.*

Old Saxon *n* the Saxon dialect of Low German up to about 1200, from which modern Low German is derived. Abbrev.: **OS.**

old school *n* **1** *Chiefly Brit.* one's former school. **2** a group of people favouring traditional ideas or conservative practices.

old school tie *n* **1** *Brit.* a distinctive tie that indicates which school the wearer attended. **2** the attitudes, loyalties, values, etc., associated with British public schools.

Old South *n* the American South before the Civil War.

oldster ('əʊldstə) *n Inf.* an older person.

old style *n Printing.* a type style reviving the characteristics of **old face,** a type style that originated in the 18th century and was characterized by having little contrast between thick and thin strokes.

Old Style *n* the former method of reckoning dates using the Julian calendar. Cf. **New Style.**

Old Testament *n* the collection of books comprising the sacred Scriptures of the Hebrews; the first part of the Christian Bible.

old-time *adj* (*prenominal*) of or relating to a former time; old-fashioned: *old-time dancing.*

old-timer *n* **1** a person who has been in a certain place, occupation, etc., for a long time. **2** *US.* an old man.

Olduvai Gorge ★ ('ɒldʊˌvaɪ) *n* a gorge in N Tanzania, north of the Ngorongoro Crater: fossil evidence of early man and other closely related species, together with artefacts.

old wives' tale *n* a belief, usually superstitious or erroneous, passed on by word of mouth as a piece of traditional wisdom.

old woman *n* **1** an informal term for **mother** or **wife. 2** a timid, fussy, or cautious person.
▸ **ˌold-'womanish** *adj*

Old World *n* that part of the world that was known before the discovery of the Americas; the eastern hemisphere.

old-world *adj* of or characteristic of former times, esp., in Europe, quaint or traditional.

Old World monkey *n* any monkey such as a macaque, baboon, or mandrill, which has nostrils that are close together and a nonprehensile tail.

-ole[1] *or* **-ol** *n combining form.* **1** denoting an organic unsaturated compound containing a 5-membered ring: *thiazole.* **2** denoting an aromatic organic ether: *anisole.* ORIG from L *oleum* oil, from Gk *elaion,* from *elaia* olive

-ole[2] *suffix of nouns.* indicating something small: *arteriole.* ORIG from L *-olus,* dim. suffix

oleaceous (ˌəʊlɪ'eɪʃəs) *adj* of, relating to, or belonging to a family of trees and shrubs which includes the ash, jasmine, privet, lilac, and olive. ORIG C19: via NL from L *olea* OLIVE; see also OIL

oleaginous (ˌəʊlɪ'ædʒɪnəs) *adj* **1** resembling or having the properties of oil. **2** containing or producing oil. ORIG C17: from L *oleāginus,* from *olea* OLIVE; see also OIL

oleander (ˌəʊlɪ'ændə) *n* a poisonous evergreen Mediterranean shrub or tree with fragrant white, pink, or purple flowers. Also called: **rosebay.** ORIG C16: from Med. L, var. of *arodandrum,* ?from L RHODODENDRON

oleate ('əʊlɪˌeɪt) *n* any salt or ester of oleic acid.

oleic acid (əʊ'liːɪk) *n* a colourless oily liquid unsaturated acid occurring, as the glyceride, in almost all natural fats; used in making soaps, ointments, cosmetics, and lubricating oils. Formula: $CH_3(CH_2)_7CH{:}CH(CH_2)_7COOH$. Systematic name: ***cis*-9-octadecenoic acid.** ORIG C19 *oleic,* from L *oleum* oil + -IC

olein ('əʊlɪɪn) *n* another name for **triolein.** ORIG C19: from F *oléine,* from L *oleum* oil + -IN

oleo- *combining form.* oil: *oleomargarine.* ORIG from L *oleum* OIL

oleomargarine (ˌəʊlɪəʊˌmɑːdʒə'riːn) *or* **oleomargarin** (ˌəʊlɪəʊ'mɑːdʒərɪn) *n* another name (esp. US) for **margarine.**

oleoresin (ˌəʊlɪəʊ'rɛzɪn) *n* **1** a semisolid mixture of a resin and essential oil, obtained from certain plants. **2** *Pharmacol.* a liquid preparation of resins and oils, obtained by extraction from plants.
▸ **ˌoleo'resinous** *adj*

oleum ('əʊlɪəm) *n, pl* **olea** ('əʊlɪə) *or* **oleums.** another name for **fuming sulphuric acid.** ORIG from L: oil, referring to its oily consistency

O level *n Brit.* **1a** the former basic (ordinary) level of the General Certificate of Education. **1b** (*as modifier*): *O-level maths.* **2** a pass in a particular subject at O level: *he has eight O levels.*

olfaction (ɒl'fækʃən) *n* **1** the sense of smell. **2** the act or function of smelling.

olfactory (ɒl'fæktərɪ, -trɪ) *adj* **1** of or relating to the sense of smell. ◆ *n, pl* **olfactories. 2** (*usually pl*) an organ or nerve concerned with the sense of smell. ORIG C17: from L *olfactus,* p.p. of *olfacere,* from *olere* to smell + *facere* to make

OLG *abbrev. for* Old Low German.

oligarch ('ɒlɪˌgɑːk) *n* a member of an oligarchy.

oligarchy ('ɒlɪˌgɑːkɪ) *n, pl* **oligarchies. 1** government by a small group of people. **2** a state or organization so governed. **3** a small body of individuals ruling such a state. **4** *Chiefly US.* a small clique of private citizens who exert a strong influence on government. ORIG C16: via Med. L from Gk *oligarkhia,* from *oligos* few + -ARCHY
▸ **ˌoli'garchic** *or* **ˌoli'garchical** *adj*

oligo- *or before a vowel* **olig-** *combining form.* indicating a few or little: *oligopoly.* ORIG from Gk *oligos* little, few

Oligocene ('ɒlɪgəʊˌsiːn, ɒ'lɪg-) *adj* **1** of, denoting, or formed in the third epoch of the Tertiary period. ◆ *n* **2 the.** the Oligocene epoch or rock series. ORIG C19: OLIGO- + -CENE

oligochaete ('ɒlɪgəʊˌkiːt) *n* **1** any freshwater or terrestrial annelid worm having bristles borne singly along the length of the body: includes the earthworms. ◆ *adj* **2** of or relating to this type of worm. ORIG C19: from NL from OLIGO- + Gk *khaitē* long hair

oligopoly (ˌɒlɪ'gɒpəlɪ) *n, pl* **oligopolies.** *Econ.* a market situation in which control over the supply of a commodity is held by a small number of producers. ORIG C20: from OLIGO- + Gk *pōlein* to sell
▸ **ˌoliˌgopo'listic** *adj*

oligospermia (ˌɒlɪgəʊ'spɜːmɪə) *n* the condition of having less than the normal number of spermatozoa in the semen: a cause of infertility in men.

oligotrophic (ˌɒlɪgəʊ'trɒfɪk) *adj* (of lakes and similar habitats) poor in nutrients and plant life and rich in oxygen. ORIG C20: from OLIGO- + Gk *trophein* to nourish + -IC
▸ **oligotrophy** (ˌɒlɪ'gɒtrəfɪ) *n*

Ólimbos ★ ('ɔlimbɔs) *n* transliteration of the Modern Greek name for (Mount) **Olympus** (sense 1).

olio ('əʊlɪˌəʊ) *n, pl* **olios. 1** a dish of many different ingredients. **2** a miscellany or potpourri. ORIG C17: from Sp. *olla* stew, from L: jar

Oliphant ★ ('ɒlɪfənt) *n* Sir **Marcus Laurence Elwin.** 1901–2000, British nuclear physicist, born in Australia.

olivaceous (ˌɒlɪ'veɪʃəs) *adj* of an olive colour.

olive ('ɒlɪv) *n* **1** an evergreen oleaceous tree of the Mediterranean region having white fragrant flowers and edible fruits that are black when ripe. **2** the fruit of this plant, eaten as a relish and used as a source of olive oil. **3** the wood of the olive tree, used for ornamental work. **4a** a yellow-green colour like that of an unripe olive. **4b** (*as adj*): *an olive coat.* ◆ *adj* **5** of, relating to, or made of the olive tree, its wood, or its fruit. ORIG C13: via OF from L *oliva,* rel. to Gk *elaia* olive tree

olive branch *n* **1** a branch of an olive tree used to symbolize peace. **2** any offering of peace or conciliation.

olive crown *n* (esp. in ancient Greece and Rome) a garland of olive leaves awarded as a token of victory.

olive drab *n US.* **1a** a dull but fairly strong greyish-olive colour. **1b** (*as adj*): *an olive-drab jacket.* **2** cloth or clothes in this colour, esp. the uniform of the US Army.

olive green *n* **a** a colour that is greener, stronger, and brighter than olive; deep yellowish-green. **b** (*as adj*): *an olive-green coat.*

olive oil *n* a yellow to yellowish-green oil pressed from ripe olive fruits and used in cooking, medicines, etc.

Oliver ★ ('ɒlɪvə) *n* **1** one of Charlemagne's 12 paladins. See also **Roland. 2 Jamie** (**Trevor**). born 1975, British chef and presenter of television cookery programmes. **3 Joseph,** known as *King Oliver.* 1885–1938, US jazz cornettist.

Olives ★ ('ɒlɪvz) *n* **Mount of.** a hill to the east of Jerusalem: in New Testament times the village Bethany (Mark 11:11) was on its eastern slope and Gethsemane on its western slope.

Olivier ★ (ə'lɪvɪˌeɪ) *n* **Laurence** (**Kerr**), Baron Olivier of Brighton. 1907–89, British actor: his films include *Henry V* (1944) and *Richard III* (1956); director National Theatre Company (1961–73).

olivine ('ɒlɪˌviːn, ˌɒlɪ'viːn) *n* any of a group of glassy olive-green minerals consisting of magnesium iron silicate in crystalline form. ORIG C18: from G, after its colour

olla ('ɒlə) *n* **1** a cooking pot. **2** short for **olla podrida.** ORIG Sp., from L *olla,* var. of *aulla* pot

olla podrida ('ɒlə pɒ'driːdə) *n* **1** a Spanish dish, consisting of a stew with beans, sausages, etc. **2** an assortment; miscellany. ORIG Sp., lit.: rotten pot

Olmec ('ɒlmɛk) *n, pl* **Olmecs** *or* **Olmec. 1** a member of an ancient Central American Indian people who inhabited the S Gulf Coast of Mexico. ◆ *adj* **2** of or relating to this people.

Olmütz ★ ('ɔlmyts) *n* the German name for **Olomouc.**

ology ('ɒlədʒɪ) *n, pl* **ologies.** *Inf.* a science or other branch of knowledge. ORIG C19: abstracted from words such as *theology, biology,* etc.; see -LOGY

-ology *n combining form.* See **-logy.**

Olomouc ★ (*Czech* 'ɔlɔmɔuts) *n* a city in the Czech Republic, in North Moravia on the Morava River: capital of Moravia until 1640; university (1576). Pop.: 104 845 (1996 est.). German name: **Olmütz.**

oloroso (ˌɒlə'rəʊsəʊ) *n, pl* **olorosos.** a full-bodied golden-coloured sweet sherry. ORIG from Sp.: fragrant

Olsztyn ★ (*Polish* 'ɔlʃtin) *n* a town in NE Poland: founded in 1334 by the Teutonic Knights; communications centre. Pop.: 167 400 (1996 est.).

Olympia ★ (ə'lɪmpɪə) *n* **1** a plain in Greece, in the NW Peloponnese: in ancient times a major sanctuary of Zeus and site of the original Olympic Games. **2** a port in W Washington, the state capital, on Puget Sound. Pop.: 33 840 (1990).

Olympiad (ə'lɪmpɪˌæd) *n* **1** a staging of the modern Olympic Games. **2** the four-year period between consecutive celebrations of the Olympic Games; a unit of ancient Greek chronology dating back to 776 B.C. **3** an international contest in chess, bridge, etc.

Olympian (ə'lɪmpɪən) *adj* **1** of or relating to Mount Olympus or to the classical Greek gods. **2** majestic or godlike in manner or bearing. **3** of or relating to ancient Olympia, a plain in Greece, or its inhabitants. ◆ *n* **4** a god of Mount Olympus. **5** an inhabitant of ancient Olympia. **6** *Chiefly US.* a competitor in the Olympic Games.

Olympic (ə'lɪmpɪk) *adj* **1** of or relating to the Olympic Games. **2** of or relating to ancient Olympia.

Olympic Games *n* (*functioning as sing or pl*) **1** the greatest Panhellenic festival, held every fourth year in honour of Zeus at ancient Olympia, consisting of games and festivities. **2** Also called: **the Olympics.** the modern revival of these games, consisting of international athletic and sporting contests held every four years in a selected country.

Olympic Mountains ★ *pl n* a mountain range in NW Washington: part of the Coast Range. Highest peak: Mount Olympus, 2427 m (7965 ft).

Olympic Peninsula ★ *n* a large peninsula of W Washington.

Olympus ★ (əʊ'lɪmpəs) *n* **1 Mount.** a mountain in NE Greece: the highest mountain in Greece, believed in Greek mythology to be the dwelling place of the greater gods. Height: 2911 m (9550 ft). Modern Greek name: **Ólimbos. 2 Mount.** a mountain in NW Washington: highest peak of the Olympic Mountains. Height: 2427 m (7965 ft).

Olynthus ★ (əʊ'lɪnθəs) *n* an ancient city in N Greece: the centre of Chalcidice.

OM *abbrev. for* Order of Merit (a Brit. title).

-oma *n combining form.* indicating a tumour: *carcinoma.* ORIG from Gk *-ōma*

Omagh ★ (əʊ'mɑː, 'əʊmə) *n* **1** a market town in Northern Ireland: scene of a disaster in 1998 when a Republican car bomb exploded killing 28 people. Pop.: 17 280 (1991). **2** a district of W central Northern Ireland: cattle and sheep. Administrative centre: Omagh. Pop.: 45 809 (1991). Area: 1125 sq. km (434 sq. miles).

Omaha ★ ('əʊməˌhɑː) *n* a city in E Nebraska, on the Missouri River opposite Council Bluffs, Iowa: the largest city in the state; the country's largest livestock market and meat-packing centre. Pop.: 364 253 (1996 est.).

Oman ★ (əʊ'mɑːn) *n* a sultanate in SE Arabia, on the **Gulf of Oman** and the Arabian Sea: the most powerful state in Arabia in the 19th century, ruling Zanzibar, much of the Persian coast, and part of Pakistan. Official language: Arabic. Official religion: Muslim. Currency: rial. Capital: Muscat. Pop.: 2 447 000 (1999 est.). Area: 306 000 sq. km (118 150 sq. miles). Former name (until 1970): **Muscat and Oman.**
▸ **O'mani** *adj, n*

Omar ('əʊmɑː) *or* **Umar** ★ *n* died 644 A.D., the second caliph of Islam (634–44).

Omar Khayyám ★ ('əʊmɑː kaɪ'ɑːm) *n* ?1050–?1123, Persian poet and astronomer, noted for the *Rubáiyát,* a collection of quatrains.

omasum (əʊ'meɪsəm) *n, pl* **omasa** (-sə). another name for **psalterium.** ORIG C18: from L: bullock's tripe

Omayyad *or* **Ommiad** ★ (əʊ'maɪæd) *n, pl* **Omayyads, Omayyades** (-əˌdiːz) *or* **Ommiads, Ommiades** (-əˌdiːz). **1** a caliph of the dynasty ruling (661–750 A.D.) from its capital at Damascus. **2** an emir (756–929 A.D.) or caliph (929–1031 A.D.) of the Omayyad dynasty in Spain.

ombre *or US* **omber** ('ɒmbə) *n* an 18th-century card game. ORIG C17: from Sp. *hombre* man, referring to the player who attempts to win the stakes

ombudsman ('ɒmbʊdzmən) *n, pl* **ombudsmen.** an official who investigates citizens' complaints against the government or its servants. Also called (Brit.): **Parliamentary Commissioner.** See also **Financial Ombudsman.** ORIG C20: from Swedish: commissioner

Omdurman ★ (ˌɒmdɜː'mɑːn) *n* a city in the central Sudan, on the White Nile, opposite Khartoum: the largest town in the Sudan; scene of the **Battle of Omdurman** (1898), in which the Mahdi's successor was defeated by Lord Kitchener's forces. Pop.: 1 267 077 (1993).

-ome *n combining form.* denoting a mass or part of a specified kind: *rhizome.* ORIG var. of -OMA

omega ('əʊmɪgə) *n* **1** the 24th and last letter of the Greek alphabet (Ω, ω). **2** the ending or last of a series. ORIG C16: from Gk *ō mega* big o

omega-3 *n* a type of unsaturated fatty acid present in some foodstuffs, esp. fish oils, the consumption of which may reduce the risk of heart disease.

omega minus *n* an unstable negatively charged elementary particle, classified as a baryon, that has a mass 3276 times that of the electron.

omelette *or esp. US* **omelet** ('ɒmlɪt) *n* a savoury or sweet dish of beaten eggs cooked in fat. ORIG C17: from F *omelette,* changed from *alumette,* from *alumelle* sword blade, changed by mistaken division from *la lemelle,* from L (see LAMELLA); apparently from the flat shape of the omelette

omen ('əʊmən) *n* **1** a phenomenon or occurrence regarded as a sign of future happiness or disaster. **2** prophetic significance. ◆ *vb* **3** (*tr*) to portend. ORIG C16: from L

omentum (əʊ'mɛntəm) *n, pl* **omenta** (-tə). *Anat.* a double fold of peritoneum connecting the stomach with other abdominal organs. ORIG C16: from L: membrane, esp. a caul, from ?

omertà *Italian.* (omer'ta) *n* a conspiracy of silence.

omicron (əʊ'maɪkrɒn, 'ɒmɪkrɒn) *n* the 15th letter in the Greek alphabet (Ο, ο). ORIG from Gk *ō mikron* small o

ominous ('ɒmɪnəs) *adj* **1** foreboding evil. **2** serving as or having significance as an omen. ORIG C16: from L *ōminōsus,* from OMEN
▸ **'ominously** *adv* ▸ **'ominousness** *n*

omission (əʊ'mɪʃən) *n* **1** something that has been omitted or neglected. **2** the act of omitting or the state of having been omitted. ORIG C14: from L *omissiō,* from *omittere* to OMIT
▸ **o'missive** *adj*

omit (əʊ'mɪt) *vb* **omits, omitting, omitted.** (*tr*) **1** to neglect to do or include. **2** to fail (to do something). ORIG C15: from L *omittere,* from *ob-* away + *mittere* to send
▸ **omissible** (əʊ'mɪsɪbᵊl) *adj* ▸ **o'mitter** *n*

omni- *combining form.* all or everywhere: *omnipresent.* ORIG from L *omnis* all

omnibus ('ɒmnɪˌbʌs, -bəs) *n, pl* **omnibuses. 1** a formal word for **bus** (sense 1). **2** Also called: **omnibus volume.** a collection of works by one author or several works on a similar topic, reprinted in one volume. **3** Also called: **omnibus edition.** a television or radio programme consisting of two or more episodes of a serial broadcast earlier in the week. ◆ *adj* **4** (*prenominal*) of, dealing with, or providing for many different things or cases. ORIG C19: from L, lit.: for all, dative pl of *omnis* all

omnicompetent (ˌɒmnɪˈkɒmpɪtənt) *adj* able to judge or deal with all matters.
▸ **ˌomniˈcompetence** *n*

omnidirectional (ˌɒmnɪdɪˈrɛkʃənᵊl, -daɪ-) *adj* (of an antenna) capable of transmitting and receiving radio signals equally in any direction of the horizontal plane.

omnifarious (ˌɒmnɪˈfɛərɪəs) *adj* of many or all varieties or forms. ORIG C17: from LL *omnifārius*, from L *omnis* all + *-farius* doing
▸ **ˌomniˈfariously** *adv* ▸ **ˌomniˈfariousness** *n*

omnific (ɒmˈnɪfɪk) *or* **omnificent** (ɒmˈnɪfɪsənt) *adj Rare.* creating all things. ORIG C17: via Med. L from L *omni-* + *-ficus*, from *facere* to do
▸ **omˈnificence** *n*

omnipotent (ɒmˈnɪpətənt) *adj* **1** having very great or unlimited power. ◆ *n* **2 the Omnipotent.** an epithet for God. ORIG C14: via OF from L *omnipotens* all-powerful, from OMNI- + *potens*, from *posse* to be able
▸ **omˈnipotence** *n* ▸ **omˈnipotently** *adv*

omnipresent (ˌɒmnɪˈprɛzᵊnt) *adj* (esp. of a deity) present in all places at the same time.
▸ **ˌomniˈpresence** *n*

omniscient (ɒmˈnɪsɪənt) *adj* **1** having infinite knowledge or understanding. **2** having very great or seemingly unlimited knowledge. ORIG C17: from Med. L *omnisciens*, from L OMNI- + *scīre* to know
▸ **omˈniscience** *n* ▸ **omˈnisciently** *adv*

omnium-gatherum (ˈɒmnɪəmˈgæðərəm) *n Often facetious.* a miscellaneous collection. ORIG C16: from L *omnium* of all, + Latinized form of E *gather*

omnivorous (ɒmˈnɪvərəs) *adj* **1** eating any type of food indiscriminately. **2** taking in or assimilating everything, esp. with the mind. ORIG C17: from L *omnivorus* all-devouring, from OMNI- + *vorāre* to eat greedily
▸ **ˈomniˌvore** *n* ▸ **omˈnivorously** *adv* ▸ **omˈnivorousness** *n*

omov (ˈəʊmɒv) *n acronym for* one member one vote.

Omphale ★ (ˈɒmfəˌliː) *n Greek myth.* a queen of Lydia, whom Hercules was required to serve as a slave to atone for the murder of Iphitus.

omphalos (ˈɒmfəˌlɒs) *n* **1** (in the ancient world) a sacred conical object, esp. a stone. The famous omphalos at Delphi was assumed to mark the centre of the earth. **2** the central point. **3** *Literary.* another word for **navel.** ORIG Gk: navel

Omsk ★ (ɒmsk) *n* a city in W central Russia, at the confluence of the Irtysh and Om Rivers: a major industrial centre, with pipelines from the second Baku oilfield. Pop.: 1 163 000 (1995 est.).

Omuta ★ (ˈəʊmuːˌtɑː) *n* a city in SW Japan, on W Kyushu on Ariake Bay: chemical industries. Pop.: 146 691 (1996).

on (ɒn) *prep* **1** in contact or connection with the surface of; at the upper surface of: *an apple on the ground; a mark on the tablecloth.* **2** attached to: *a puppet on a string.* **3** carried with: *I've no money on me.* **4** in the immediate vicinity of; close to or along the side of: *a house on the sea.* **5** within the time limits of (a day or date): *he arrived on Thursday.* **6** being performed upon or relayed through the medium of: *what's on the television?* **7** at the occasion of: *on his retirement.* **8** used to indicate support, subsistence, contingency, etc.: *he lives on bread.* **9a** regularly taking (a drug): *she's on the pill.* **9b** addicted to: *he's on heroin.* **10** by means of (something considered as a mode of transport) (esp. in **on foot, on horseback,** etc.). **11** in the process or course of: *on a journey; on strike.* **12** concerned with or relating to: *a programme on archaeology.* **13** used to indicate the basis or grounds, as of a statement or action: *I have it on good authority.* **14** against: used to indicate opposition: *they marched on the city at dawn.* **15** used to indicate a meeting or encounter: *he crept up on her.* **16** (used with an adj preceded by *the*) indicating the manner or way in which an action is carried out: *on the sly; on the cheap.* **17** staked or wagered as a bet upon: *ten pounds on that horse.* **18** *Inf.* charged to: *the drinks are on me.* ◆ *adv* (*often used as a particle*) **19** in the position or state required for the commencement or sustained continuation, as of a mechanical operation: *the radio's been on all night.* **20** attached to, surrounding, or placed in contact with something: *the child had nothing on.* **21** arranged: *we've nothing on for tonight.* **22** in a manner indicating continuity, persistence, etc.: *don't keep on about it; the play went on all afternoon.* **23** in a direction towards something, esp. forward: *we drove on towards London; march on!* **24 on and off.** intermittently; from time to time. **25 on and on.** without ceasing; continually. ◆ *adj* **26** functioning; operating: *put the switch into the on position.* **27** (*postpositive*) *Inf.* performing, as on stage, etc.: *I'm on in five minutes.* **28** definitely taking place: *the match is on for Friday.* **29** tolerable or practicable, acceptable, etc.: *your plan just isn't on.* **30** *Cricket.* (of a bowler) bowling. **31 on at.** *Inf.* nagging: *she was always on at her husband.* ◆ *n* **32** *Cricket.* **32a** (*modifier*) relating to or denoting the leg side of a cricket field or pitch: *an on drive.* **32b** (*in combination*) used to designate certain fielding positions on the leg side: *mid-on.* ORIG OE *an, on*

On ★ (ɒn) *n* the ancient Egyptian and biblical name for **Heliopolis.**

ON *abbrev. for:* **1** Old Norse. **2** Ontario.

-on *suffix forming nouns.* **1** indicating a chemical substance: *interferon.* **2** (in physics) indicating an elementary particle or quantum: *electron; photon.* **3** (in chemistry) indicating an inert gas: *neon; radon.* **4** (in biochemistry) a molecular unit: *codon; operon.* ORIG from ION

onager (ˈɒnədʒə) *n, pl* **onagri** (-ˌgraɪ) *or* **onagers. 1** a Persian variety of the wild ass. **2** an ancient war engine for hurling stones, etc. ORIG C14: from LL: military engine for stone throwing, from L: wild ass, from Gk *onagros*, from *onos* ass + *agros* field

onanism (ˈəʊnəˌnɪzəm) *n* **1** the withdrawal of the penis from the vagina before ejaculation. **2** masturbation. ORIG C18: after *Onan*, son of Judah; see Genesis 38:9
▸ **ˈonanist** *n, adj* ▸ **ˌonanˈistic** *adj*

Onassis ★ (əʊˈnæsɪs) *n* **Aristotle** (**Socrates**). 1906–75, Argentinian (formerly Greek) shipowner, born in Turkey.

ONC (in Britain) *abbrev. for* Ordinary National Certificate.

once (wʌns) *adv* **1** one time; on one occasion or in one case. **2** at some past time: *I could speak French once.* **3** by one step or degree (of relationship): *a cousin once removed.* **4** (*in conditional clauses, negatives, etc.*) ever; at all: *if you once forget it.* **5** multiplied by one. **6 once and away. 6a** conclusively. **6b** occasionally. **7 once and for all.** conclusively; for the last time. **8 once in a while.** occasionally; now and then. **9 once or twice** *or* **once and again.** a few times. **10 once upon a time.** used to begin fairy tales and children's stories. ◆ *conj* **11** (*subordinating*) as soon as; if ever: *once you begin, you'll enjoy it.* ◆ *n* **12** one occasion or case: *you may do it, this once.* **13 all at once. 13a** suddenly. **13b** simultaneously. **14 at once. 14a** immediately. **14b** simultaneously. **15 for once.** this time, if (or but) at no other time. ORIG C12 *ones, anes*, adverbial genitive of *on, an* ONE

once-over *n Inf.* **1** a quick examination or appraisal. **2** a quick but comprehensive piece of work. **3** a violent beating or thrashing (esp. in **give** (**a person** or **thing**) **the** (or **a**) **once-over**).

oncer (ˈwʌnsə) *n* **1** *Brit. sl.* (formerly) a one-pound note. **2** *Austral. sl.* a person elected to Parliament who can only expect to serve one term. **3** *Austral. & NZ.* something which happens only once. ORIG C20: from ONCE

oncogene (ˈɒŋkəʊˌdʒiːn) *n* any of several genes, present in all cells, that when abnormally activated can cause cancer. ORIG C20: from Gk *onkos* mass, tumour + GENE
▸ **oncogenic** (ˌɒŋkəʊˈdʒɛnɪk) *adj*

oncoming (ˈɒnˌkʌmɪŋ) *adj* **1** coming nearer in space or time; approaching. ◆ *n* **2** the approach or onset: *the oncoming of winter.*

oncost (ˈɒnˌkɒst) *n Brit.* **1** another word for **overhead** (sense 5). **2** (*sometimes pl*) another word for **overheads.**

OND (in Britain) *abbrev. for* Ordinary National Diploma.

Ondaatje ★ (ɒnˈdɑːtʃɪ) *n* **Michael.** born 1943, Sri Lankan-born Canadian writer: his novels include *The English Patient* (1992) and *Anil's Ghost* (2000).

on dit *French.* (ɔ̃ di) *n, pl* **on dits** (ɔ̃ di). a rumour; piece of gossip. ORIG lit.: it is said, they say

Ondo ★ ('ɒndəʊ) *n* a state of SW Nigeria, on the Bight of Benin: formed in 1976 from part of Western State. Capital: Akure. Pop.: 4 343 230 (1995 est.). Area: 20 959 sq. km (8092 sq. miles).

one (wʌn) *determiner* **1a** single; lone; not two or more. **1b** (*as pron*): *one is enough for now; one at a time.* **1c** (*in combination*): *one-eyed.* **2a** distinct from all others; only; unique: *one girl in a million.* **2b** (*as pron*): *one of a kind.* **3a** a specified (person, item, etc.) as distinct from another or others of its kind: *raise one hand and then the other.* **3b** (*as pron*): *which one is correct?* **4** a certain, indefinite, or unspecified (time); some: *one day you'll be sorry.* **5** *Inf.* an emphatic word for **a** or **an**[1]: *it was one hell of a fight.* **6** a certain (person): *one Miss Jones was named.* **7** (**all**) **in one.** combined; united. **8 all one. 8a** all the same. **8b** of no consequence: *it's all one to me.* **9 at one.** (often foll. by *with*) in a state of agreement or harmony. **10 be made one.** to become married. **11 many a one.** many people. **12 neither one thing nor the other.** indefinite, undecided, or mixed. **13 never a one.** none. **14 one and all.** everyone, without exception. **15 one by one.** one at a time; individually. **16 one or two.** a few. **17 one way and another.** on balance. **18 one with another.** on average. ◆ *pron* **19** an indefinite person regarded as typical of every person: *one can't say any more than that.* **20** any indefinite person: used as the subject of a sentence to form an alternative grammatical construction to that of the passive voice: *one can catch fine trout in this stream.* **21** *Arch.* an unspecified person: *one came to him.* ◆ *n* **22** the smallest natural number and the first cardinal number; unity. **23** a numeral (1, I, i, etc.) representing this number. **24** *Inf.* a joke or story (esp. in **the one about**). **25** something representing, represented by, or consisting of one unit. **26** Also: **one o'clock.** one hour after noon or midnight. **27** a blow or setback (esp. in **one in the eye for**). **28 the Evil one.** Satan. **29 the Holy One** *or* **the One above.** God. ◆ Related prefixes: **mono-, uni-.** ORIG OE *ān*

-one *suffix forming nouns.* indicating that a chemical compound is a ketone: *acetone.* ORIG arbitrarily from Gk *-ōnē*, fem. patronymic suffix, but ? infl. by *-one* in OZONE

one another *pron* the reflexive form of plural pronouns when the action, attribution, etc., is reciprocal: *they kissed one another; knowing one another.* Also: **each other.**

one-armed bandit *n Inf.* a fruit machine operated by pulling down a lever at one side.

Onega ★ (*Russian* a'njɛgə) *n* a lake in NW Russia, mostly in the Karelian Republic: the second largest lake in Europe and fourth largest in the former Soviet Union. Area: 9891 sq. km (3819 sq. miles).

one-horse *adj* **1** drawn by or using one horse. **2** (*prenominal*) *Inf.* small or obscure: *a one-horse town.*

Oneida ★ (əʊ'naɪdə) *n* **Lake.** a lake in central New York State: part of the New York State Barge Canal system. Length: about 35 km (22 miles). Greatest width: 9 km (6 miles).

O'Neill ★ (əʊ'ni:l) *n* **Eugene** (**Gladstone**). 1888–1953, US dramatist. His works include *Desire under the Elms* (1924), *Mourning Becomes Elektra* (1931), and *The Iceman Cometh* (1946): Nobel prize for literature 1936.

one-liner *n Inf.* a short joke or witty remark.

one-man *adj* consisting of or done by or for one man: *a one-man band; a one-man show.*

oneness ('wʌnnɪs) *n* **1** the state or quality of being one; singleness. **2** the state of being united; agreement. **3** uniqueness. **4** sameness.

one-night stand *n* **1** a performance given only once at any one place. **2** *Inf.* a sexual encounter lasting only one evening or night.

one-off *n Brit.* **a** something that is carried out or made only once. **b** (*as modifier*): *a one-off job.*

one-on-one *adj* another term for **one-to-one** (sense 2).

one-parent family *n* another name for **single-parent family.**

one-piece *adj* **1** (of a garment, esp. a bathing costume) consisting of one piece. ◆ *n* **2** a garment, esp. a bathing costume, consisting of one piece.

onerous ('ɒnərəs, 'əʊ-) *adj* **1** laborious or oppressive. **2** *Law.* (of a contract, etc.) having or involving burdens or obligations. ORIG C14: from L *onerōsus* burdensome, from *onus* load
▸ **'onerously** *adv* ▸ **'onerousness** *n*

oneself (wʌn'sɛlf) *pron* **1a** the reflexive form of **one** (sense 19). **1b** (intensifier): *one doesn't do that oneself.* **2** (*preceded by a copula*) one's normal or usual self: *one doesn't feel oneself after such an experience.*

one-sided *adj* **1** considering or favouring only one side of a matter, problem, etc. **2** having all the advantage on one side: *a one-sided boxing match.* **3** larger or more developed on one side. **4** having, existing on, or occurring on one side only.
▸ ˌ**one-'sidedly** *adv* ▸ ˌ**one-'sidedness** *n*

one-step *n* an early 20th-century ballroom dance with long quick steps, the precursor of the foxtrot.

one-stop *adj* having or providing a range of related services or goods in one place: *a one-stop shop.*

One Thousand Guineas *n* See **Thousand Guineas.**

one-time *adj* (*prenominal*) at some time in the past; former.

one-to-one *adj* **1** (of two or more things) corresponding exactly. **2** denoting a relationship or encounter in which someone is involved with only one other person: *one-to-one tuition.* **3** *Maths.* involving the pairing of each member of one set with only one member of another set, without remainder.

one-track *adj* **1** *Inf.* obsessed with one idea, subject, etc. **2** having or consisting of a single track.

one-up *adj Inf.* having an advantage or lead over someone or something.
▸ ˌ**one-'upmanship** *n*

one-way *adj* **1** moving or allowing travel in one direction only: *one-way traffic; a one-way bus ticket.* **2** entailing no reciprocal obligation, action, etc.: *a one-way agreement.*

ongoing ('ɒnˌgəʊɪŋ) *adj* **1** actually in progress: *ongoing projects.* **2** continually moving forward; developing. **3** remaining in existence; continuing.

onion ('ʌnjən) *n* **1** an alliaceous plant having greenish-white flowers: cultivated for its rounded edible bulb. **2** the bulb of this plant, consisting of concentric layers of white succulent leaf bases with a pungent odour and taste. **3 know one's onions.** *Brit. sl.* to be fully acquainted with a subject. ORIG C14: via Anglo-Norman from OF *oignon*, from L *unio* onion
▸ **'oniony** *adj*

onionskin ('ʌnjənˌskɪn) *n* a glazed translucent paper.

Onitsha ★ (ə'nɪtʃə) *n* a port in S Nigeria, in Anambra State on the Niger River: industrial centre. Pop.: 371 900 (1996 est.).

on line *or* **online** *adj* (**on-line** *or* **online** *when prenominal*). **1** of or concerned with a peripheral device that is directly connected to and controlled by the central processing unit of a computer. **2** of or relating to the Internet: *online shopping.* **3** occurring as part of, or involving, a continuous sequence of operations, such as a production line. ◆ *adv* **4** while connected to a computer or the Internet. ◆ Cf. **off line.**

onlooker ('ɒnˌlʊkə) *n* a person who observes without taking part.
▸ **'onˌlooking** *adj*

only ('əʊnlɪ) *adj* (*prenominal*) **1 the.** being single or very few in number: *the only men left in town were too old to bear arms.* **2** (of a child) having no siblings. **3** unique by virtue of being superior to anything else; peerless. **4 one and only. 4a** (*adj*) incomparable; unique. **4b** (*as n*) the object of all one's love: *you are my one and only.* ◆ *adv* **5** without anyone or anything else being included; alone: *you have one choice only; only a genius can do that.* **6** merely or just: *it's only Henry.* **7** no more or no greater than: *we met only an hour ago.* **8** used in conditional clauses introduced by *if* to emphasize the impossibility of the condition ever being fulfilled: *if I had only known, this would never have happened.* **9** not earlier than; not...until: *I only found out yesterday.* **10 if only** *or* **if...only.** an expression used to introduce a wish, esp. one felt to be unrealizable. **11 only if.** never...except when. **12 only too. 12a** (intensifier): *he was only too pleased to help.* **12b** most regrettably (esp. in **only too true**). ◆ *sentence connector.* **13** but; however: used to introduce an exception or condition: *you may play outside: only don't go into the street.* ORIG OE *ānlīc,* from *ān* ONE + *-līc* -LY[1]

> **USAGE NOTE** In informal English, *only* is often used as a sentence connector: *I would have phoned you, only I didn't know your number.* This use should be avoided in formal writing: *I would have phoned you, but I didn't know your number.*

on message *adj* (**on-message** *when prenominal*) (esp. of a politician) following the official line of his or her party.

o.n.o. *abbrev. for* or near(est) offer.

onomastics (ˌɒnəˈmæstɪks) *n* (*functioning as sing*) the study of proper names, esp. of their origins. ORIG from Gk *onomastikos,* from *onomazein* to name, from *onoma* NAME

onomatopoeia (ˌɒnəˌmætəˈpiːə) *n* **1** the formation of words whose sound is imitative of the sound of the noise or action designated, such as *hiss.* **2** the use of such words for poetic or rhetorical effect. ORIG C16: via LL from Gk *onoma* name + *poiein* to make
▸ **ˌonoˌmatoˈpoeic** *or* **onomatopoetic** (ˌɒnəˌmætəpəʊˈɛtɪk) *adj* ▸ **ˌonoˌmatoˈpoeically** *or* **ˌonoˌmatopoˈetically** *adv*

Onondaga ★ (ˌɒnənˈdɑːgə) *n* **Lake.** a salt lake in central New York State. Area: about 13 sq. km (5 sq. miles).

onrush (ˈɒnˌrʌʃ) *n* a forceful forward rush or flow.

onset (ˈɒnˌsɛt) *n* **1** an attack; assault. **2** a start; beginning.

onshore (ˈɒnˈʃɔː) *adj, adv* **1** towards the land: *an onshore gale.* **2** on land; not at sea.

onside (ˌɒnˈsaɪd) *adj, adv* **1** *Football, etc.* (of a player) in a legal position, as when behind the ball or with a required number of opponents between oneself and the opposing team's goal line. Cf. **offside.** ◆ *adj* **2** taking one's part or side; working towards the same goal (esp. in **get someone onside**).

onslaught (ˈɒnˌslɔːt) *n* a violent attack. ORIG C17: from MDu. *aenslag,* from *aan* ON + *slag* a blow

Ont. *abbrev. for* Ontario.

Ontario ★ (ɒnˈtɛərɪəʊ) *n* **1** a province of central Canada: lies mostly on the Canadian Shield and contains the fertile plain of the lower Great Lakes and the St Lawrence River, one of the world's leading industrial areas; the second largest and the most populous province. Capital: Toronto. Pop.: 11 560 899 (1999 est.). Area: 891 198 sq. km (344 092 sq. miles). Abbrevs.: **Ont.** *or* **ON. 2 Lake.** a lake between the US and Canada, bordering on New York State and Ontario province: the smallest of the Great Lakes; linked with Lake Erie by the Niagara River and Welland Canal; drained by the St Lawrence. Area: 19 684 sq. km (7600 sq. miles).
▸ **Onˈtarian** *or* **Ontarioan** (ɒnˈtɛərɪˌəʊən) *n, adj*

onto *or* **on to** (ˈɒntu; *unstressed* ˈɒntə) *prep* **1** to a position that is on: *step onto the train.* **2** having become aware of (something illicit or secret): *the police are onto us.* **3** into contact with: *get onto the factory.*

> **USAGE NOTE** *Onto* is now generally accepted as a word in its own right. *On to* is still used, however, where *on* is considered to be part of the verb: *he moved on to a different town* as contrasted with *he jumped onto the stage.*

onto- *combining form.* existence or being: *ontogeny; ontology.* ORIG from LGk, from *ōn* (stem *ont-*) being, present participle of *einai* to be

ontogeny (ɒnˈtɒdʒənɪ) *or* **ontogenesis** (ˌɒntəˈdʒɛnɪsɪs) *n* the entire sequence of events involved in the development of an individual organism. Cf. **phylogeny.**
▸ **ontogenic** (ˌɒntəˈdʒɛnɪk) *or* **ontogenetic** (ˌɒntədʒɪˈnɛtɪk) *adj* ▸ **ˌontoˈgenically** *or* **ˌontogeˈnetically** *adv*

ontology (ɒnˈtɒlədʒɪ) *n* **1** *Philosophy.* the branch of metaphysics that deals with the nature of being. **2** *Logic.* the set of entities presupposed by a theory.
▸ **ˌontoˈlogical** *adj* ▸ **ˌontoˈlogically** *adv*

onus (ˈəʊnəs) *n, pl* **onuses.** a responsibility, task, or burden. ORIG C17: L: burden

onward (ˈɒnwəd) *adj* **1** directed or moving forwards, onwards, etc. ◆ *adv* **2** a variant of **onwards.**

onwards (ˈɒnwədz) *or* **onward** *adv* at or towards a point or position ahead, in advance, etc.

onychophoran (ˌɒnɪˈkɒfərən) *n* a wormlike invertebrate having a segmented body and short unjointed limbs, and breathing by means of tracheae. ORIG from NL *Onychophora,* from Gk *onukh-* claw + -PHORE

-onym *n combining form.* indicating a name or word: *pseudonym.* ORIG from Gk *-onumon,* from var. of *onoma* name

onyx (ˈɒnɪks) *n* **1** a variety of chalcedony with alternating black-and-white parallel bands, used as a gemstone. **2** a variety of calcite used as an ornamental stone; onyx marble. ORIG C13: from L, from Gk: fingernail (so called from its veined appearance)

ONZ *abbrev. for* Order of New Zealand.

oo- *or* **oö-** *combining form.* egg or ovum: *oosperm.* ORIG from Gk *ōion* EGG[1]

oocyte (ˈəʊəˌsaɪt) *n* an immature female germ cell that gives rise to an ovum after two meiotic divisions.

oodles (ˈuːdᵊlz) *pl n Inf.* great quantities: *oodles of money.* ORIG C20: from ?

oogamy (əʊˈɒgəmɪ) *n* sexual reproduction involving a small motile male gamete and a large much less motile female gamete.
▸ **oˈogamous** *adj*

Ookpik (ˈuːkpɪk) *n Canad. trademark.* a sealskin doll resembling an owl, first made in 1963 by an Inuit and used abroad as a symbol of Canadian handicrafts. ORIG from Eskimo *ukpik* a snowy owl

oolite (ˈəʊəˌlaɪt) *n* any sedimentary rock, esp. limestone, consisting of tiny spherical concentric grains within a fine matrix. ORIG C18: from F, from NL *oolitēs,* lit.: egg stone; prob. a translation of G *Rogenstein* roe stone
▸ **oolitic** (ˌəʊəˈlɪtɪk) *adj*

oolith (ˈəʊəˌlɪθ) *n* any of the tiny spherical grains of sedimentary rock of which oolite is composed.

oology (əʊˈɒlədʒɪ) *n* the branch of ornithology concerned with the study of birds' eggs.
▸ **oological** (ˌəʊəˈlɒdʒɪkᵊl) *adj* ▸ **oˈologist** *n*

oolong (ˈuːˌlɒŋ) *n* a kind of dark tea, grown in China, that is partly fermented before being dried. ORIG C19: from Chinese *wu lung,* from *wu* black + *lung* dragon

oom (ˈuːəm) *n S. African.* a title of respect used to address an elderly man. ORIG Afrik., lit.: uncle

oomiak *or* **oomiac** (ˈuːmɪˌæk) *n* a variant of **umiak.**

oompah (ˈuːmˌpɑː) *n* a representation of the sound made by a deep brass instrument, esp. in military band music.

oomph (umf) *n Inf.* **1** enthusiasm, vigour, or energy. **2** sex appeal. ORIG C20: from ?

oops (ups, uːps) *interj* an exclamation of surprise or of apology as when someone drops something or makes a mistake.

Oostende ★ (oːstˈɛndə) *n* the Flemish name for **Ostend.**

ooze[1] (uːz) *vb* **oozes, oozing, oozed. 1** (*intr*) to flow or leak out slowly, as through small holes. **2** to emit (moisture, etc.). **3** (*tr*) to overflow with: *to ooze charm.* **4** (*intr;* often foll. by *away*) to disappear or escape gradually. ◆ *n* **5** a slow flowing or leaking. **6** an infusion of vegetable matter, such as oak bark, used in tanning. ORIG OE *wōs* juice

ooze[2] (uːz) *n* **1** a soft thin mud found at the bottom of lakes and rivers. **2** a fine-grained marine deposit consisting of the hard parts of planktonic organisms. **3** muddy ground, esp. of bogs. ORIG OE *wāse* mud

oozy[1] (ˈuːzɪ) *adj* **oozier, ooziest.** moist or dripping.

oozy[2] (ˈuːzɪ) *adj* **oozier, ooziest.** of, resembling, or containing mud; slimy.
▸ **ˈoozily** *adv* ▸ **ˈooziness** *n*

OP *abbrev. for:* **1** Ordo Praedictatorum (the Dominicans). [ORIG] L: Order of Preachers **2** organophosphate.

op. *abbrev. for:* **1** opera. **2** operation. **3** operator. **4** optical. **5** opposite. **6** opus.

o.p. *or* **O.P.** *abbrev. for* out of print.

opacity (əʊ'pæsɪtɪ) *n, pl* **opacities. 1** the state or quality of being opaque. **2** the degree to which something is opaque. **3** an opaque object or substance. **4** obscurity of meaning; unintelligibility.

opah ('əʊpə) *n* a large soft-finned deep-sea teleost fish having a deep, brilliantly coloured body. Also called: **moonfish, kingfish.** [ORIG] C18: of West African origin

opal ('əʊpəl) *n* an amorphous form of hydrated silicon dioxide that can be of almost any colour. It is used as a gemstone. [ORIG] C16: from L *opalus,* from Gk *opallios,* from Sansk. *upala* precious stone
▸ **'opal-ˌlike** *adj*

opalescent (ˌəʊpə'lɛsənt) *adj* having or emitting an iridescence like that of an opal.
▸ **ˌopa'lesce** *vb* ▸ **ˌopal'escence** *n*

opal glass *n* glass that is opalescent or white, made by the addition of fluorides.

opaline ('əʊpəˌlaɪn) *adj* **1** opalescent. ◆ *n* **2** an opaque or semiopaque whitish glass.

opaque (əʊ'peɪk) *adj* **1** not transmitting light; not transparent or translucent. **2** not reflecting light; lacking lustre or shine; dull. **3** hard to understand; unintelligible. **4** unintelligent; dense. ◆ *n* **5** *Photog.* an opaque pigment used to block out areas on a negative. ◆ *vb* **opaques, opaquing, opaqued.** (*tr*) **6** to make opaque. **7** *Photog.* to block out areas on (a negative), using an opaque. [ORIG] C15: from L *opācus* shady
▸ **o'paquely** *adv* ▸ **o'paqueness** *n*

op art (ɒp) *n* a style of abstract art chiefly concerned with the exploitation of optical effects such as the illusion of movement. [ORIG] C20 *op,* short for *optical*

op. cit. (in textual annotations) *abbrev. for* opere citato. [ORIG] L: in the work cited

ope (əʊp) *vb* **opes, oping, oped,** *adj* an archaic or poetic word for **open.**

OPEC ('əʊpɛk) *n acronym for* Organization of Petroleum-Exporting Countries.

open ('əʊpən) *adj* **1** not closed or barred. **2** affording free passage, access, view, etc.; not blocked or obstructed. **3** not sealed, fastened, or wrapped. **4** having the interior part accessible: *an open drawer.* **5** extended, expanded, or unfolded: *an open flower.* **6** ready for business. **7** able to be obtained; available: *the position is no longer open.* **8** unobstructed by buildings, trees, etc.: *open countryside.* **9** free to all to join, enter, use, visit, etc.: *an open competition.* **10** unengaged or unoccupied: *the doctor has an hour open for you to call.* **11** See **open season. 12** not decided or finalized: *an open question.* **13** ready to entertain new ideas; not biased or prejudiced. **14** unreserved or candid. **15** liberal or generous: *an open hand.* **16** extended or eager to receive (esp. in **with open arms**). **17** exposed to view; blatant: *open disregard of the law.* **18** liable or susceptible: *you will leave yourself open to attack.* **19** (of climate or seasons) free from frost; mild. **20** free from navigational hazards, such as ice, sunken ships, etc. **21** having large or numerous spacing or apertures: *open ranks.* **22** full of small openings or gaps; porous: *an open texture.* **23** *Music.* **23a** (of a string) not stopped with the finger. **23b** (of a pipe, such as an organ pipe) not closed at either end. **23c** (of a note) played on such a string or pipe. **24** *Commerce.* **24a** in operation; active: *an open account.* **24b** unrestricted; unlimited: *open credit; open insurance cover.* **25** See **open cheque. 26** (of a return ticket) not specifying a date for travel. **27** *Sport.* (of a goal, court, etc.) unguarded or relatively unprotected. **28** (of a wound) exposed to the air. **29** (esp. of the large intestine) free from obstruction. **30** undefended and of no military significance: *an open city.* **31** *Phonetics.* **31a** denoting a vowel pronounced with the lips relatively wide apart. **31b** denoting a syllable that does not end in a consonant, as in *pa.* **32** *Maths.* (of a set) containing points whose neighbourhood consists of other points of the same set. **33** *Computing.* designed to an internationally agreed standard in order to allow communication between computers, irrespective of size, manufacturer, etc. ◆ *vb* **34** to move from a closed or fastened position: *to open a window.* **35** (when *intr,* foll. by *on* or *onto*) to render, be, or become accessible or unobstructed: *to open a road; to open a parcel.* **36** (*intr*) to come into or appear in view: *the lake opened before us.* **37** to extend or unfold or cause to extend or unfold: *to open a newspaper.* **38** to disclose or uncover or be disclosed or uncovered: *to open one's heart.* **39** to cause (the mind) to become receptive or (of the mind) to become receptive. **40** to operate or cause to operate: *to open a shop.* **41** (when *intr,* sometimes foll. by *out*) to make or become less compact or dense in structure: *to open ranks.* **42** to set or be set in action; start: *to open the batting.* **43** (*tr*) to arrange for (a bank account, etc.), usually by making an initial deposit. **44** to turn to a specified point in (a book, etc.): *open at page one.* **45** *Law.* to make the opening statement in (a case before a court of law). **46** (*intr*) *Cards.* to bet, bid, or lead first on a hand. ◆ *n* **47** (often preceded by *the*) any wide or unobstructed space or expanse, esp. of land or water. **48** See **open air. 49** *Sport.* a competition which anyone may enter. **50 bring** (*or* **come**) **into the open.** to make (*or* become) evident or public. ◆ See also **open up.** [ORIG] OE
▸ **'openable** *adj* ▸ **'opener** *n* ▸ **'openly** *adv* ▸ **'openness** *n*

open air *n* **a** the place or space where the air is unenclosed; the outdoors. **b** (*as modifier*): *an open-air concert.*

open-and-shut *adj* easily decided or solved; obvious: *an open-and-shut case.*

opencast mining ('əʊpənˌkɑːst) *n Brit.* mining by excavating from the surface. Also called: (esp. US) **strip mining,** (Austral. and NZ) **open cut mining.** [ORIG] C18: from OPEN + arch. *cast* ditch, cutting

open chain *n* a chain of atoms in a molecule that is not joined at its ends into the form of a ring.

open cheque *n* an uncrossed cheque that can be cashed at the drawee bank.

open circuit *n* an incomplete electrical circuit in which no current flows.

Open College *n* **the.** (in Britain) a college of art founded in 1987 for mature students studying foundation courses in arts and crafts by television programmes, written material, and tutorials.

open day *n* an occasion on which an institution, such as a school, is open for inspection by the public.

open door *n* **1** a policy or practice by which a nation grants opportunities for trade to all other nations equally. **2** free and unrestricted admission. ◆ *adj* **open-door. 3** open to all; accessible.

open-ended *adj* **1** without definite limits, as of duration or amount: *an open-ended contract.* **2** denoting a question, esp. one on a questionnaire, that cannot be answered "yes", "no", or "don't know".

open-eyed *adj* **1** with the eyes wide open, as in amazement. **2** watchful; alert.

open-faced *adj* **1** having an ingenuous expression. **2** (of a watch) having no lid or cover other than the glass.

open-handed *adj* generous.
▸ **ˌopen-'handedly** *adv* ▸ **ˌopen-'handedness** *n*

open-hearted *adj* **1** kindly and warm. **2** disclosing intentions and thoughts clearly; candid.
▸ **ˌopen-'heartedness** *n*

open-hearth furnace *n* (esp. formerly) a steel-making reverbatory furnace in which pig iron and scrap are contained in a shallow hearth and heated by producer gas.

open-heart surgery *n* surgical repair of the heart during which the blood circulation is often maintained mechanically.

open house *n* **1** a US and Canad. name for **at-home. 2 keep open house.** to be always ready to receive guests.

opening ('əʊpənɪŋ) *n* **1** the act of making or becoming open. **2** a vacant or unobstructed space, esp. one that will serve as a passageway; gap. **3** *Chiefly US.* a tract in a forest in which trees are scattered or absent. **4** the first part or stage of something. **5a** the first performance of something, esp. a theatrical production. **5b** (*as modifier*): *the opening night.* **6** a specific or formal sequence of moves at the start of any of certain games, esp. chess or draughts. **7** an opportunity or chance. **8** *Law.* the preliminary statement made by counsel to the court or jury.

opening batsman *n Cricket.* one of the two batsmen beginning an innings.

opening time *n Brit.* the time at which public houses can legally start selling alcoholic drinks.

open learning *n* a system of further education on a flexible part-time basis.

open letter *n* a letter, esp. one of protest, addressed to a person but also made public, as through the press.

open market *n* **a** a market in which prices are determined by supply and demand, there are no barriers to entry, and trading is not restricted to a specific area. **b** (*as modifier*): *open-market value.*

open marriage *n* a marriage in which the partners agree to pursue separate social and sexual lives.

open-minded *adj* having a mind receptive to new ideas, arguments, etc.; unprejudiced.
▸ **ˌopen-ˈmindedness** *n*

open-mouthed *adj* **1** having an open mouth, esp. in surprise. **2** greedy or ravenous. **3** clamorous or vociferous.

open-plan *adj* having no or few dividing walls between areas: *an open-plan office floor.*

open position *n Commerce.* a situation in which a dealer in commodities, securities, or currencies has either unsold stock or uncovered sales.

open prison *n* a penal establishment in which the prisoners are trusted to serve their sentences and so do not need to be locked up.

open punctuation *n* punctuation which has relatively few semicolons, commas, etc. Cf. **close punctuation.**

open question *n* **1** a matter which is undecided. **2** a question that cannot be answered with "yes" or "no" but requires a developed answer.

open-reel *adj* another term for **reel-to-reel.**

open season *n* a specified period of time in the year when it is legal to hunt or kill game or fish protected at other times by law.

open secret *n* something that is supposed to be secret but is widely known.

open sesame *n* a very successful means of achieving a result. ORIG from the magical words used in the *Arabian Nights' Entertainments* to open the robbers' den

open shop *n* an establishment in which persons are employed irrespective of their membership or nonmembership of a trade union.

open slather *n* See **slather.**

Open University *n* **the.** (in Britain) a university founded in 1969 for mature students studying by television and radio lectures, correspondence courses, local counselling, and summer schools.

open up *vb* (*adv*) **1** (*intr*) to start firing a gun or guns. **2** (*intr*) to speak freely or without restraint. **3** (*intr*) *Inf.* (of a motor vehicle) to accelerate. **4** (*tr*) to render accessible: *the motorway opened up the remoter areas.* **5** (*intr*) to make or become more exciting or lively: *the game opened up after half-time.*

open verdict *n* a finding by a coroner's jury of death without stating the cause.

openwork (ˈəupᵊnˌwɜːk) *n* ornamental work, as of metal or embroidery, having a pattern of openings or holes.

opera¹ (ˈɒpərə, ˈɒprə) *n* **1** an extended dramatic work in which music constitutes a dominating feature. **2** the branch of music or drama represented by such works. **3** the score, libretto, etc., of an opera. **4** a theatre where opera is performed. ORIG C17: via It. from L: work, a work, pl of *opus* work

opera² (ˈɒpərə) *n* a plural of **opus.**

operable (ˈɒpərəbᵊl, ˈɒprə-) *adj* **1** capable of being treated by a surgical operation. **2** capable of being operated. **3** capable of being put into practice.
▸ **ˌoperaˈbility** *n* ▸ **ˈoperably** *adv*

opéra bouffe (ˈɒpərə ˈbuːf) *n, pl* **opéras bouffes** (ˈɒpərə ˈbuːf). a type of light or satirical opera common in France during the 19th century. ORIG F: comic opera

opera buffa (ˈbuːfə) *n, pl* **opera buffas.** comic opera, esp. that originating in Italy during the 18th century. ORIG It.: comic opera

opéra comique (kɒˈmiːk) *n, pl* **opéras comiques.** (ˈɒpərə kɒˈmiːk). a type of opera current in France during the 19th century and characterized by spoken dialogue. ORIG F: comic opera: it originated in satirical parodies of grand opera

opera glasses *pl n* small low-powered binoculars used by audiences in theatres, etc.

opera hat *n* a collapsible top hat operated by a spring.

opera house *n* a theatre designed for opera.

operand (ˈɒpəˌrænd) *n* a quantity or function upon which a mathematical or logical operation is performed. ORIG C19: from L *operandum* (something) to be worked upon, from *operārī* to work

operant (ˈɒpərənt) *adj* **1** producing effects; operating. ◆ *n* **2** a person or thing that operates. **3** *Psychol.* any response by an organism that is not directly caused by stimulus.

opera seria (ˈsɪərɪə) *n, pl* **opera serias.** a type of opera current in 18th-century Italy based on a serious plot, esp. a mythological tale. ORIG It.: serious opera

operate (ˈɒpəˌreɪt) *vb* **operates, operating, operated. 1** to function or cause to function. **2** (*tr*) to control the functioning of. **3** to manage, direct, run, or pursue (a business, system, etc.). **4** (*intr*) to perform a surgical operation (upon a person or animal). **5** (*intr*) to produce a desired effect. **6** (*tr*; usually foll. by *on*) to treat or process in a particular or specific way. **7** (*intr*) to conduct military or naval operations. **8** (*intr*) to deal in securities on a stock exchange. ORIG C17: from L *operārī* to work

operatic (ˌɒpəˈrætɪk) *adj* **1** of or relating to opera. **2** histrionic or exaggerated.
▸ **ˌoperˈatically** *adv*

operating budget *n Accounting.* a forecast of the sales revenue, production costs, overheads, cash flow, etc., of an organization, used to monitor its trading activities, usually for one year.

operating cycle *n* the time taken by a firm to convert its raw materials into finished goods and thereafter sell them and collect payment.

operating system *n* the set of software controlling a computer.

operating theatre *n* a room in which surgical operations are performed.

operation (ˌɒpəˈreɪʃən) *n* **1** the act, process, or manner of operating. **2** the state of being in effect, in action, or operative (esp. in **in** *or* **into operation**). **3** a process, method, or series of acts, esp. of a practical or mechanical nature. **4** *Surgery.* any manipulation of the body or one of its organs or parts to repair damage, arrest the progress of a disease, remove foreign matter, etc. **5a** a military or naval action, such as a campaign, manoeuvre, etc. **5b** (*cap. and prenominal when part of a name*): *Operation Crossbow.* **6** *Maths.* any procedure, such as addition, in which one or more numbers or quantities are operated upon according to specific rules. **7** a commercial or financial transaction.

operational (ˌɒpəˈreɪʃənᵊl) *adj* **1** of or relating to an operation. **2** in working order and ready for use. **3** *Mil.* capable of, needed in, or actually involved in operations.
▸ **ˌoperˈationally** *adv*

operationalism (ˌɒpəˈreɪʃənəˌlɪzəm) *or* **operationism** (ˌɒpəˈreɪʃəˌnɪzəm) *n Philosophy.* the theory that scientific terms are defined by the experimental operations which determine their applicability.
▸ **ˌoperˌationalˈistic** *adj*

operations research *n* the analysis of problems in business and industry involving quantitative techniques. Also called: **operational research.**

operative (ˈɒpərətɪv) *adj* **1** in force, effect, or operation. **2** exerting force or influence. **3** producing a desired effect; significant: *the operative word.* **4** of or relating to a

surgical procedure. ◆ *n* **5** a worker, esp. one with a special skill. **6** *US.* a private detective.
▸ **'operatively** *adv* ▸ **'operativeness** *or* **ˌopera'tivity** *n*

operator ('ɒpəˌreɪtə) *n* **1** a person who operates a machine, instrument, etc., esp. a telephone switchboard. **2** a person who owns or operates an industrial or commercial establishment. **3** a speculator, esp. one who operates on currency or stock markets. **4** *Inf.* a person who manipulates affairs and other people. **5** *Maths.* any symbol, term, letter, etc., used to indicate or express a specific operation or process, such as ∫ (the integral operator).

operculum (əʊ'pɜːkjʊləm) *n, pl* **opercula** (-lə) *or* **operculums. 1** *Zool.* **1a** the hard bony flap covering the gill slits in fishes. **1b** the bony plate in certain gastropods covering the opening of the shell when the body is withdrawn. **2** *Biol. & Bot.* any other covering or lid in various organisms. ORIG C18: via NL from L: lid, from *operīre* to cover
▸ **o'percular** *or* **operculate** (əʊ'pɜːkjʊlɪt, -ˌleɪt) *adj*

operetta (ˌɒpə'rɛtə) *n* a type of comic or light-hearted opera. ORIG C18: from It.: a small OPERA[1]
▸ **ˌoper'ettist** *n*

ophicleide ('ɒfɪˌklaɪd) *n Music.* an obsolete keyed wind instrument of bass pitch. ORIG C19: from F *ophicléide,* from Gk *ophis* snake + *kleis* key

ophidian (əʊ'fɪdɪən) *adj* **1** snakelike. **2** of, relating to, or belonging to the suborder of reptiles that comprises the snakes. ◆ *n* **3** any reptile of this suborder; a snake. ORIG C19: from NL *Ophidia,* name of suborder, from Gk *ophidion,* from *ophis* snake

Ophir ★ ('əʊfə) *n Bible.* a region, probably situated on the SW coast of Arabia on the Red Sea, renowned, esp. in King Solomon's reign, for its gold and precious stones (I Kings 9:28; 10:10).

ophthalmia (ɒf'θælmɪə) *n* inflammation of the eye, often including the conjunctiva. ORIG C16: via LL from Gk, from *ophthalmos* eye; see OPTIC

ophthalmic (ɒf'θælmɪk) *adj* of or relating to the eye.

ophthalmic optician *n* See **optician.**

ophthalmo- *or before a vowel* **ophthalm-** *combining form.* indicating the eye or the eyeball. ORIG from Gk *ophthalmos* EYE

ophthalmology (ˌɒfθæl'mɒlədʒɪ) *n* the branch of medicine concerned with the eye and its diseases.
▸ **ophthalmological** (ɒfˌθælmə'lɒdʒɪk°l) *adj* ▸ **ˌophthal'mologist** *n*

ophthalmoscope (ɒf'θælməˌskəʊp) *n* an instrument for examining the interior of the eye.
▸ **ophthalmoscopic** (ɒfˌθælmə'skɒpɪk) *adj*

-opia *n combining form.* indicating a visual defect or condition: *myopia.* ORIG from Gk, from *ōps* eye
▸ **-opic** *adj combining form.*

opiate *n* ('əʊpɪɪt). **1** any of various narcotic drugs containing opium. **2** any other narcotic or sedative drug. **3** something that soothes, deadens, or induces sleep. ◆ *adj* ('əʊpɪɪt). **4** containing or consisting of opium. **5** inducing relaxation; soporific. ◆ *vb* ('əʊpɪˌeɪt), **opiates, opiating, opiated.** (*tr*) *Rare.* **6** to treat with an opiate. **7** to dull or deaden. ORIG C16: from Med. L *opiātus,* from L *opium* OPIUM

opine (əʊ'paɪn) *vb* **opines, opining, opined.** (when *tr, usually takes a clause as object*) to hold or express an opinion: *he opined that it was a mistake.* ORIG C16: from L *opīnārī*

opinion (ə'pɪnjən) *n* **1** judgment or belief not founded on certainty or proof. **2** the prevailing or popular feeling or view: *public opinion.* **3** evaluation, impression, or estimation of the value or worth of a person or thing. **4** an evaluation or judgment given by an expert: *a medical opinion.* **5** the advice given by counsel on a case submitted to him or her for his or her view on the legal points involved. **6 a matter of opinion.** a point open to question. **7 be of the opinion (that).** to believe (that). ORIG C13: via OF from L *opīniō* belief, from *opīnārī* to think

opinionated (ə'pɪnjəˌneɪtɪd) *adj* holding obstinately and unreasonably to one's own opinions; dogmatic.
▸ **o'pinionˌatedly** *adv* ▸ **o'pinionˌatedness** *n*

opinionative (ə'pɪnjənətɪv) *adj Rare.* **1** of or relating to opinion. **2** another word for **opinionated.**
▸ **o'pinionatively** *adv* ▸ **o'pinionativeness** *n*

opinion poll *n* another term for a **poll** (sense 3).

opioid ('əʊpɪˌɔɪd) *n* any of a group of substances that resemble morphine in their physiological or pharmacological effects, esp. in their pain-relieving properties.

opium ('əʊpɪəm) *n* **1** an addictive narcotic drug extracted from the seed capsules of the opium poppy: used in medicine as an analgesic and hypnotic. **2** something having a tranquillizing or stupefying effect. ORIG C14: from L: poppy juice, from Gk *opion,* dim. of *opos,* juice of a plant

opium poppy *n* a poppy of SW Asia, with greyish-green leaves and typically white or reddish flowers: widely cultivated as a source of opium.

Oporto ★ (ə'pɔːtəʊ) *n* a port in NW Portugal, near the mouth of the Douro River: the second largest city in Portugal, famous for port wine (begun in 1678). Pop.: 309 485 (1991). Portuguese name: **Pôrto.**

opossum (ə'pɒsəm) *n, pl* **opossums** *or* **opossum. 1** a thick-furred marsupial, esp. the **common opossum** of North and South America, having an elongated snout and a hairless prehensile tail. **2** *Austral. & NZ.* any of various similar animals, esp. a phalanger. ◆ Often shortened to **possum.** ORIG C17: from Algonquian *aposoum*

opp. *abbrev. for:* **1** opposed. **2** opposite.

Oppenheimer ★ ('ɒpənˌhaɪmə) *n* **J(ulius) Robert.** 1904–67, US nuclear physicist. Director of the Los Alamos laboratory (1943–45), which produced the first atomic bomb, he opposed the development of the hydrogen bomb (1949); declared a security risk (1953), he was later exonerated.

opponent (ə'pəʊnənt) *n* **1** a person who opposes another in a contest, battle, etc. **2** *Anat.* an opponent muscle. ◆ *adj* **3** opposite, as in position. **4** *Anat.* (of a muscle) bringing two parts into opposition. **5** opposing; contrary. ORIG C16: from L *oppōnere* to oppose
▸ **op'ponency** *n*

opportune ('ɒpəˌtjuːn) *adj* **1** occurring at a time that is suitable or advantageous. **2** fit or suitable for a particular purpose or occurrence. ORIG C15: via OF from L *opportūnus,* from *ob-* to + *portus* harbour (orig.: coming to the harbour, obtaining timely protection)
▸ **'opporˌtunely** *adv* ▸ **'opporˌtuneness** *n*

opportunist (ˌɒpə'tjuːnɪst) *n* **1** a person who adapts his or her actions, responses, etc., to take advantage of opportunities, circumstances, etc. ◆ *adj* **2** taking advantage of opportunities and circumstances in this way.
▸ **ˌoppor'tunism** *n*

opportunistic (ˌɒpətjʊ'nɪstɪk) *adj* **1** of or characterized by opportunism. **2** *Med.* (of an infection) caused by any microorganism that is harmless to a healthy person but debilitates a person whose immune system has been weakened.

opportunity (ˌɒpə'tjuːnɪtɪ) *n, pl* **opportunities. 1** a favourable, appropriate, or advantageous combination of circumstances. **2** a chance or prospect.

opportunity shop *n Austral. & NZ.* a shop selling used goods for charitable funds. Often shortened to **op shop.**

opposable (ə'pəʊzəb°l) *adj* **1** capable of being opposed. **2** Also: **apposable.** (of the thumb of primates, esp. man) capable of being moved into a position facing the other digits so as to be able to touch the ends of each. **3** capable of being placed opposite something else.
▸ **opˌposa'bility** *n* ▸ **op'posably** *adv*

oppose (ə'pəʊz) *vb* **opposes, opposing, opposed. 1** (*tr*) to fight against, counter, or resist strongly. **2** (*tr*) to be hostile or antagonistic to; be against. **3** (*tr*) to place or set in opposition; contrast or counterbalance. **4** (*tr*) to place opposite or facing. **5** (*intr*) to be or act in opposition. ORIG C14: via OF from L *oppōnere,* from *ob-* against + *pōnere* to place
▸ **op'poser** *n* ▸ **op'posing** *adj* ▸ **oppositive** (ə'pɒzɪtɪv) *adj*

opposite ('ɒpəzɪt, -sɪt) *adj* **1** situated or being on the other side or at each side of something between. **2** facing or going in contrary directions: *opposite ways.* **3** diametri-

cally different in character, tendency, belief, etc. **4** *Bot.* **4a** (of leaves) arranged in pairs on either side of the stem. **4b** (of parts of a flower) arranged opposite the middle of another part. **5** *Maths.* (of a side in a triangle) facing a specified angle. Abbrev.: **opp.** ◆ *n* **6** a person or thing that is opposite; antithesis. ◆ *prep* **7** Also: **opposite to.** facing; corresponding to (something on the other side of a division). **8** as a co-star with: *she played opposite Olivier.* ◆ *adv* **9** on opposite sides: *she lives opposite.*
▸ **'oppositely** *adv* ▸ **'oppositeness** *n*

opposite number *n* a person holding an equivalent and corresponding position on another side or situation.

opposition (ˌɒpəˈzɪʃən) *n* **1** the act of opposing or the state of being opposed. **2** hostility, unfriendliness, or antagonism. **3** a person or group antagonistic or opposite in aims to another. **4a** (usually preceded by *the*) a political party or group opposed to the ruling party or government. **4b** (*cap. as part of a name, esp. in Britain and Commonwealth countries*): *Her Majesty's Loyal Opposition.* **4c in opposition.** (of a political party) opposing the government. **5** a position facing or opposite another. **6** something that acts as an obstacle to some course or progress. **7** *Astron.* the position of an outer planet or the moon when it is in line with the earth as seen from the sun and is approximately at its nearest to the earth. **8** *Astrol.* an exact aspect of 180° between two planets, etc., an orb of 8° being allowed. **9** *Logic.* the relation between propositions having the same subject and predicate but differing in quality, quantity, or both, as with *all men are wicked; no men are wicked; some men are not wicked.*
▸ **ˌoppoˈsitional** *adj* ▸ **ˌoppoˈsitionist** *n* ▸ **ˌoppoˈsitionless** *adj*

oppress (əˈprɛs) *vb* (*tr*) **1** to subjugate by cruelty, force, etc. **2** to afflict or torment. **3** to lie heavy on (the mind, etc.). ORIG C14: via OF from Med. L *oppressāre*, from L *opprimere*, from *ob-* against + *premere* to press
▸ **opˈpressing** *adj* ▸ **opˈpression** *n* ▸ **opˈpressor** *n*

oppressive (əˈprɛsɪv) *adj* **1** cruel, harsh, or tyrannical. **2** heavy, constricting, or depressing.
▸ **opˈpressively** *adv* ▸ **opˈpressiveness** *n*

opprobrious (əˈprəʊbrɪəs) *adj* **1** expressing scorn, disgrace, or contempt. **2** shameful or infamous.
▸ **opˈprobriously** *adv* ▸ **opˈprobriousness** *n*

opprobrium (əˈprəʊbrɪəm) *n* **1** the state of being abused or scornfully criticized. **2** reproach or censure. **3** a cause of disgrace or ignominy. ORIG C17: from L *ob-* against + *probrum* a shameful act

oppugn (əˈpjuːn) *vb* (*tr*) to call into question; dispute. ORIG C15: from L *oppugnāre*, from *ob-* against + *pugnāre* to fight, from *pugnus* clenched fist
▸ **opˈpugner** *n*

Ops ★ (ɒps) *n* the Roman goddess of abundance and fertility, wife of Saturn. Greek counterpart: **Rhea.**

op shop (ɒp) *n Austral. & NZ.* short for **opportunity shop.**

opsin (ˈɒpsɪn) *n* the protein that together with retinene makes up the purple visual pigment rhodopsin. ORIG C20: back formation from RHODOPSIN

-opsis *n combining form.* indicating a specified appearance or resemblance: *meconopsis.* ORIG from Gk *opsis* sight

opsonin (ˈɒpsənɪn) *n* a constituent of blood serum that renders bacteria more susceptible to ingestion by phagocytes. ORIG C20: from Gk *opsōnion* victuals
▸ **opsonic** (ɒpˈsɒnɪk) *adj*

opt (ɒpt) *vb* (when *intr*, foll. by *for*) to show preference (for) or choose (to do something). See also **opt in, opt out.** ORIG C19: from F *opter*, from L *optāre* to choose

opt. *abbrev. for:* **1** *Grammar.* optative. **2** optical. **3** optician. **4** optimum. **5** optional.

optative (ˈɒptətɪv) *adj* **1** indicating or expressing choice or wish. **2** *Grammar.* denoting a mood of verbs in Greek and Sanskrit expressing a wish. ◆ *n* **3** *Grammar.* **3a** the optative mood. **3b** a verb in this mood. ORIG C16: via F *optatif*, from LL *optātīvus*, from L *optāre* to desire

optic (ˈɒptɪk) *adj* **1** of or relating to the eye or vision. **2** a less common word for **optical.** ◆ *n* **3** an informal word for **eye**[1]. **4** *Brit., trademark.* a device attached to an inverted bottle for dispensing measured quantities of liquid. ORIG C16: from Med. L *opticus*, from Gk *optikos*, from *optos* visible; rel. to *ōps* eye

optical (ˈɒptɪkᵊl) *adj* **1** of, relating to, producing, or involving light. **2** of or relating to the eye or to the sense of sight; optic. **3** (esp. of a lens) aiding vision or correcting a visual disorder.
▸ **ˈoptically** *adv*

optical activity *n* the ability of substances that are optical isomers to rotate the plane of polarization of a transmitted beam of plane-polarized light.

optical character reader *n* a computer peripheral device enabling letters, numbers, or other characters usually printed on paper to be optically scanned and input to a storage device, such as magnetic tape. The device uses the process of **optical character recognition.** Abbrev. (for both *reader* and *recognition*): **OCR.**

optical crown *n* an optical glass of low dispersion and relatively low refractive index.

optical disc *n Computing.* an inflexible disc on which information is stored in digital form by laser technology. Also called: **video disc.**

optical fibre *n* a communications cable consisting of a thin glass fibre in a protective sheath. Light transmitted along the fibre may be modulated with vision, sound, or data signals. See also **fibre optics.**

optical flint *n* an optical glass of high dispersion and high refractive index containing lead oxide, used in the manufacture of lenses, artificial gems, and cut glass.

optical glass *n* any of several types of clear homogeneous glass of known refractive index used in the construction of lenses, etc.

optical isomerism *n* isomerism of chemical compounds in which the two isomers differ only in that their molecules are mirror images of each other.
▸ **optical isomer** *n*

optical scanner *n* a computer peripheral device enabling printed material, including characters and diagrams, to be scanned and converted into a form that can be stored in a computer. See also **optical character reader.**

optician (ɒpˈtɪʃən) *n* a general name used to refer to: **a** an **ophthalmic optician.** one qualified to examine the eyes and prescribe and supply spectacles and contact lenses. **b** a **dispensing optician.** one who supplies and fits spectacle frames and lenses, but is not qualified to prescribe lenses.

optics (ˈɒptɪks) *n* (*functioning as sing*) the branch of science concerned with vision and the generation, nature, propagation, and behaviour of electromagnetic light.

optimal (ˈɒptɪməl) *adj* another word for **optimum** (sense 2).

optimism (ˈɒptɪˌmɪzəm) *n* **1** the tendency to expect the best in all things. **2** hopefulness; confidence. **3** the doctrine of the ultimate triumph of good over evil. **4** the philosophical doctrine that this is the best of all possible worlds. ◆ Cf. **pessimism.** ORIG C18: from F *optimisme*, from L *optimus* best, sup. of *bonus* good
▸ **ˈoptimist** *n* ▸ **ˌoptiˈmistic** *adj* ▸ **ˌoptiˈmistically** *adv*

optimize *or* **optimise** (ˈɒptɪˌmaɪz) *vb* **optimizes, optimizing, optimized** *or* **optimises, optimising, optimised. 1** (*tr*) to take full advantage of. **2** (*tr*) to plan or carry out (an economic activity) with maximum efficiency. **3** (*intr*) to be optimistic. **4** (*tr*) to write or modify (a computer program) to achieve maximum efficiency.
▸ **ˌoptimiˈzation** *or* **ˌoptimiˈsation** *n*

optimum (ˈɒptɪməm) *n, pl* **optima** (-mə) *or* **optimums. 1** a condition, degree, amount, or compromise that produces the best possible result. ◆ *adj* **2** most favourable or advantageous; best: *optimum conditions.* ORIG C19: from L: the best (thing), from *optimus* best; see OPTIMISM

optimum population *n Econ.* a population that is sufficiently large to provide an adequate workforce with minimal unemployment.

opt in *vb* (*intr, adv*) to choose to be involved in or part of a scheme, etc.

option (ˈɒpʃən) *n* **1** the act or an instance of choosing or deciding. **2** the power or liberty to choose. **3** an exclusive opportunity, usually for a limited period, to buy something at a future date: *a six-month option on the Canadian rights to this book.* **4** *Commerce.* the right to buy (**call option**) or sell (**put option**) a fixed quantity of a commodity, security, foreign exchange, etc., at a fixed price at a specified date in the future. See also **traded option. 5** something chosen; choice. **6 keep** (*or* **leave**) **one's options open.** not to commit oneself. **7 soft option.** an easy alternative. ◆ *vb* **8** (*tr*) to obtain or grant an option on: *the BBC have optioned her latest novel.* ORIG C17: from L *optiō* free choice, from *optāre* to choose

optional ('ɒpʃənᵊl) *adj* possible but not compulsory; left to personal choice.
▸ **'optionally** *adv*

option money *n Commerce.* the price paid for buying an option.

optometrist (ɒp'tɒmɪtrɪst) *n* a person who is qualified to examine the eyes and prescribe and supply spectacles and contact lenses. Also called (esp. Brit.): **ophthalmic optician.**

optometry (ɒp'tɒmɪtrɪ) *n* the science or practice of testing visual acuity and prescribing corrective lenses.
▸ **optometric** (ˌɒptə'mɛtrɪk) *adj*

optophone ('ɒptəˌfəʊn) *n* a device for blind people that converts printed words into sounds.

opt out *vb* **1** (*intr, adv;* often foll. by *of*) to choose not to be involved (in) or part (of). ◆ *n* **opt-out. 2** the act of opting out, esp. of a local-authority administration: *opt-outs by hospitals and schools.*

opulent ('ɒpjulənt) *adj* **1** having or indicating wealth. **2** abundant or plentiful. ORIG C17: from L *opulens,* from *opēs* (pl) wealth
▸ **'opulence** *or* (*less commonly*) **'opulency** *n* ▸ **'opulently** *adv*

opuntia (ɒ'pʌnʃɪə) *n* a cactus, esp. the prickly pear, having fleshy branched stems and green, red, or yellow flowers. ORIG C17: NL, from L *Opuntia* (*herba*) the Opuntian (plant), from *Opus,* ancient town of Locris, Greece

opus ('əupəs) *n, pl* **opuses** *or* **opera. 1** an artistic composition, esp. a musical work. **2** (*often cap.*) (usually followed by a number) a musical composition by a particular composer, generally catalogued in order of publication: *Beethoven's opus 61.* Abbrev.: **op.** ORIG C18: from L: a work

Opus Dei ('əupəs 'deiː) *n* **1** another name for **divine office. 2** an international Roman Catholic organization founded in Spain in 1928 by Josemaria Escrivá de Balaguer (1902–75), to spread Christian principles.

or[1] (ɔː; *unstressed* ə) *conj* (*coordinating*) **1** used to join alternatives. **2** used to join rephrasings of the same thing: *twelve, or a dozen.* **3** used to join two alternatives when the first is preceded by *either* or *whether: either yes or no.* **4 one or two, four or five,** etc. a few. **5** a poetic word for **either** or **whether,** as the first element in correlatives, with *or* also preceding the second alternative. ORIG C13: contraction of *other,* changed (through infl. of EITHER) from OE *oththe*

or[2] (ɔː) *adj* (*usually postpositive*) *Heraldry.* of the metal gold. ORIG C16: via F from L *aurum* gold

OR *abbrev. for:* **1** operational research. **2** Oregon. **3** *Mil.* other ranks.

-or[1] *suffix forming nouns from verbs.* a person or thing that does what is expressed by the verb: *actor; conductor; generator; sailor.* ORIG via OF *-eur, -eor,* from L *-or* or *-ātor*

-or[2] *suffix forming nouns.* **1** indicating state, condition, or activity: *terror; error.* **2** the US spelling of **-our.**

ora ('ɔːrə) *n* the plural of **os**[2].

orache *or esp. US* **orach** ('ɒrɪtʃ) *n* any of several herbaceous plants or small shrubs of the goosefoot family, esp. **garden orache,** which is cultivated as a vegetable. They have typically greyish-green lobed leaves and inconspicuous flowers. ORIG C15: from OF *arache,* from L *atriplex,* from Gk *atraphaxus,* from ?

oracle ('ɒrəkᵊl) *n* **1** a prophecy revealed through the medium of a priest or priestess at the shrine of a god. **2** a shrine at which an oracular god is consulted. **3** an agency through which a prophecy is transmitted. **4** any person or thing believed to indicate future action with infallible authority. ORIG C14: via OF from L *ōrāculum,* from *ōrāre* to request

Oracle ('ɒrəkᵊl) *n Trademark.* the Teletext system operated by ITV. See **Teletext.** ORIG C20: acronym of *o*(*ptional*) *r*(*eception of*) *a*(*nnouncements by*) *c*(*oded*) *l*(*ine*) *e*(*lectronics*)

oracular (ɒ'rækjulə) *adj* **1** of or relating to an oracle. **2** wise and prophetic. **3** mysterious or ambiguous.
▸ **o'racularly** *adv*

oracy ('ɔːrəsɪ) *n* the capacity to express oneself in and understand speech. ORIG C20: from L *or-, os* mouth, by analogy with *literacy*

Oradea ★ (*Romanian* o'radea) *n* an industrial city in NW Romania, in Transylvania: ceded by Hungary (1919). Pop.: 221 885 (1994 est.). German name: **Grosswardein.** Hungarian name: **Nagyvárad.**

oral ('ɔːrəl, 'ɒrəl) *adj* **1** spoken or verbal. **2** relating to, affecting, or for use in the mouth: *an oral thermometer.* **3** denoting a drug to be taken by mouth: *an oral contraceptive.* **4** of, relating to, or using spoken words. **5** *Psychoanal.* relating to a stage of psychosexual development during which the child's interest is concentrated on the mouth. ◆ *n* **6** an examination in which the questions and answers are spoken rather than written. ORIG C17: from LL *orālis,* from L *ōs* face
▸ **'orally** *adv*

oral history *n* the memories of living people about events or social conditions in their earlier lives taped and preserved as historical evidence.

oral hygiene *n* the maintenance of healthy teeth and gums by brushing, etc. Also called: **dental hygiene.**

oral society *n* a society that has not developed literacy.

Oran ★ (ə'ræn, ə'rɑːn; *French* ɔrɑ̃) *n* a port in NW Algeria: the second largest city in the country; scene of the destruction by the British of most of the French fleet in the harbour in 1940 to prevent its capture by the Germans. Pop.: 609 823 (1987).

orange ('ɒrɪndʒ) *n* **1** any of several citrus trees, esp. **sweet orange** and the Seville orange, cultivated in warm regions for their round edible fruit. **2a** the fruit of any of these trees, having a yellowish-red bitter rind and segmented juicy flesh. **2b** (*as modifier*): *orange peel.* **3** the hard wood of any of these trees. **4** any of a group of colours, such as that of the skin of an orange, that lie between red and yellow in the visible spectrum. **5** a dye or pigment producing these colours. **6** orange cloth or clothing: *dressed in orange.* **7** any of several trees or herbaceous plants that resemble the orange, such as mock orange. ◆ *adj* **8** of the colour orange. ORIG C14: via OF *auranja,* from Ar. *nāranj,* from Persian, from Sansk. *nāranga*

Orange[1] ★ *n* **1** ('ɒrɪndʒ) a river in S Africa, rising in NE Lesotho and flowing generally west across the South African plateau to the Atlantic: the longest river in South Africa. Length: 2093 km (1300 miles). **2** (*French* ɔrɑ̃ʒ). a town in SE France: a small principality in the Middle Ages, the descendants of which formed the House of Orange. Pop.: 28 136 (1990). Ancient name: **Arausio** (ə'rausɪəu).

Orange[2] ★ ('ɒrɪndʒ) *n* **1** a princely family of Europe. Its possessions, originally centred in S France, passed in 1544 to the count of Nassau, who became William I of Orange and helped to found the United Provinces of the Netherlands. Since 1815 it has been the name of the reigning house of the Netherlands. It was the ruling house of Great Britain and Ireland under William III and Mary (1689–94) and under William III as sole monarch (1694–1702). **2** (*modifier*) of or relating to the Orangemen. **3** (*modifier*) of or relating to the royal dynasty of Orange.

orangeade (ˌɒrɪndʒ'eɪd) *n* an effervescent or still orange-flavoured drink.

orange blossom *n* the flowers of the orange tree, traditionally worn by brides.

Orange Free State ★ *n* a former province of central South Africa, between the Orange and Vaal rivers: settled by Boers in 1836 after the Great Trek; annexed by

Britain in 1848; became a province of South Africa in 1910; in 1994 it was replaced by Free State region. Capital: Bloemfontein. Area: 29 152 sq. km (49 866 sq. miles).

Orangeman ('ɒrɪndʒmən) *n, pl* **Orangemen.** a member of a society founded in Ireland (1795) to uphold Protestantism. ORIG C18: after William, prince of *Orange,* later William III

Orangeman's Day *n* the 12th of July, celebrated by Protestants in Northern Ireland and elsewhere, to commemorate the anniversary of the Battle of the Boyne (1690).

orange pekoe *n* a superior grade of black tea growing in India and Sri Lanka.

orange roughy ('rʌfɪ) *n* a marine food fish of S Pacific waters.

orangery ('ɒrɪndʒərɪ, -dʒrɪ) *n, pl* **orangeries.** a building, such as a greenhouse, in which orange trees are grown.

orange stick *n* a small stick used to clean the fingernails and cuticles.

orangewood ('ɒrɪndʒˌwʊd) *n* **a** the hard fine-grained yellowish wood of the orange tree. **b** (*as modifier*): *an orangewood table.*

orang-utan (ɔːˌræŋuː'tæn, ˌɔːræŋ'uːtæn) *or* **orang-utang** (ɔːˌræŋuː'tæŋ, ˌɔːræŋ'uːtæŋ) *n* a large anthropoid ape of the forests of Sumatra and Borneo, with shaggy reddish-brown hair and strong arms. Sometimes shortened to **orang.** ORIG C17: from Malay *orang hutan,* from *ōrang* man + *hūtan* forest

orate (ɔː'reɪt) *vb* **orates, orating, orated.** (*intr*) **1** to make or give an oration. **2** to speak pompously and lengthily.

oration (ɔː'reɪʃən) *n* **1** a formal public declaration or speech. **2** any rhetorical, lengthy, or pompous speech. ORIG C14: from L *ōrātiō* speech, harangue, from *ōrāre* to plead, pray

orator ('ɒrətə) *n* **1** a public speaker, esp. one versed in rhetoric. **2** a person given to lengthy or pompous speeches. **3** *Obs.* the plaintiff in a cause of action in chancery.

oratorio (ˌɒrə'tɔːrɪəʊ) *n, pl* **oratorios.** a dramatic but unstaged musical composition for soloists, chorus, and orchestra, based on a religious theme. ORIG C18: from It., lit.: ORATORY[2], referring to the Church of the Oratory at Rome where musical services were held

oratory[1] ('ɒrətərɪ, -trɪ) *n* **1** the art of public speaking. **2** rhetorical skill or style. ORIG C16: from L (*ars*) *ōrātōria* (the art of) public speaking
▸ **ˌora'torical** *adj* ▸ **ˌora'torically** *adv*

oratory[2] ('ɒrətərɪ, -trɪ) *n, pl* **oratories.** a small room or secluded place, set apart for private prayer. ORIG C14: from Anglo-Norman, from Church L *ōrātōrium* place of prayer, from *ōrāre* to plead, pray

orb (ɔːb) *n* **1** (in regalia) an ornamental sphere surmounted by a cross. **2** a sphere; globe. **3** *Poetic.* another word for **eye**[1] (sense 1). **4** *Obs. or poetic.* **4a** a celestial body, esp. the earth or sun. **4b** the orbit of a celestial body. ◆ *vb* **5** to make or become circular or spherical. **6** (*tr*) an archaic word for **encircle.** ORIG C16: from L *orbis* circle, disc

orbicular (ɔː'bɪkjʊlə), **orbiculate,** *or* **orbiculated** *adj* **1** circular or spherical. **2** (of a leaf or similar flat part) circular or nearly circular.
▸ **orbicularity** (ɔːˌbɪkjʊ'lærɪtɪ) *n* ▸ **or'bicularly** *adv*

orbit ('ɔːbɪt) *n* **1** *Astron.* the curved path followed by a planet, satellite, etc., in its motion around another celestial body. **2** a range or field of action or influence; sphere. **3** the bony cavity containing the eyeball; eye socket. **4** *Zool.* **4a** the skin surrounding the eye of a bird. **4b** the hollow in which lies the eye or eyestalk of an insect. **5** *Physics.* the path of an electron around the nucleus of an atom. **6 go into orbit.** *Inf.* to reach an extreme and often uncontrolled state: *when he realized the price he nearly went into orbit.* ◆ *vb* **7** to move around (a body) in a curved path. **8** (*tr*) to send (a satellite, spacecraft, etc.) into orbit. **9** (*intr*) to move in or as if in an orbit. ORIG C16: from L *orbita* course, from *orbis* circle

orbital ('ɔːbɪtəl) *adj* **1** of or denoting an orbit. **2** (of a motorway or major road) circling a large city. ◆ *n* **3** the region around an atomic nucleus, or around two nuclei in a molecule, within which an electron moves. **4** an orbital road.
▸ **'orbitally** *adv*

orbital velocity *n* the velocity required by a spacecraft to enter and maintain a given orbit.

orc (ɔːk) *n* **1** any of various whales, such as the killer and grampus. **2** a mythical monster. ORIG C16: via L *orca,* ?from Gk *orux* whale

Orcadian (ɔː'keɪdɪən) *n* **1** a native or inhabitant of the Orkneys. ◆ *adj* **2** of or relating to the Orkneys. ORIG from L *Orcades* the Orkney Islands

Orcagna ★ (*Italian* or'caɲɲa) *n* **Andrea** (an'drɛːa), original name *Andrea di Cione.* ?1308–68, Florentine painter, sculptor, and architect.

orchard ('ɔːtʃəd) *n* **1** an area of land devoted to the cultivation of fruit trees. **2** a collection of fruit trees especially cultivated. ORIG OE *orceard, ortigeard,* from *ort-,* from L *hortus* garden + *geard* YARD[2]

orchestra ('ɔːkɪstrə) *n* **1** a large group of musicians, esp. one whose members play a variety of different instruments. **2** a group of musicians, each playing the same type of instrument. **3** Also called: **orchestra pit.** the space reserved for musicians in a theatre, immediately in front of or under the stage. **4** *Chiefly US & Canad.* the stalls in a theatre. **5** (in ancient Greek theatre) the semicircular space in front of the stage. ORIG C17: via L from Gk: the space in the theatre for the chorus, from *orkheisthai* to dance
▸ **orchestral** (ɔː'kɛstrəl) *adj* ▸ **or'chestrally** *adv*

orchestrate ('ɔːkɪˌstreɪt) *vb* **orchestrates, orchestrating, orchestrated.** (*tr*) **1** to score or arrange (a piece of music) for orchestra. **2** to arrange, organize, or build up for special or maximum effect.
▸ **ˌorches'tration** *n* ▸ **'orchesˌtrator** *n*

orchid ('ɔːkɪd) *n* a terrestrial or epiphytic plant having flowers of unusual shapes and beautiful colours, usually with one petal larger than the other two. The flowers are specialized for pollination by certain insects. ORIG C19: from NL *Orchideae;* see ORCHIS

orchidectomy (ˌɔːkɪ'dɛktəmɪ) *n, pl* **orchidectomies.** the surgical removal of one or both testes. ORIG C19: from Gk *orkhis* testicle + -ECTOMY

orchil ('ɔːkɪl, -tʃɪl) *or* **archil** *n* **1** a purplish dye obtained by treating various lichens with aqueous ammonia. **2** the lichens yielding this dye. ORIG C15: from OF *orcheil,* from ?

orchis ('ɔːkɪs) *n* **1** a N temperate terrestrial orchid having fleshy tubers and spikes of typically pink flowers. **2** any of various temperate or tropical orchids such as the fringed orchis. ORIG C16: via L from Gk *orkhis* testicle; so called from the shape of its roots

OR circuit *or* **gate** (ɔː) *n Computing.* a logic circuit having two or more input wires and one output wire that gives a high-voltage output signal if one or more input signals are at a high voltage: used extensively as a basic circuit in computing. ORIG C20: from its similarity to the function of *or* in logical constructions

Orcus ★ ('ɔːkəs) *n* another name for **Dis** (sense 1).

Orczy ★ ('ɔːtsɪ) *n* Baroness **Emmuska** ('ɛmʊʃkə). 1865–1947, British novelist, born in Hungary; author of *The Scarlet Pimpernel* (1905).

Ord ★ (ɔːd) *n* a river in NE Western Australia, rising on the Kimberley Plateau and flowing generally north to the Timor Sea: subject of a major irrigation scheme. Length: about 500 km (300 miles).

ord. *abbrev. for:* **1** order. **2** ordinal. **3** ordinance. **4** ordinary.

ordain (ɔː'deɪn) *vb* (*tr*) **1** to consecrate (someone) as a priest; confer holy orders upon. **2** (*may take a clause as object*) to decree, appoint, or predestine irrevocably. **3** (*may take a clause as object*) to order, establish, or enact with authority. ORIG C13: from Anglo-Norman *ordeiner,* from LL *ordināre,* from L *ordo* ORDER
▸ **or'dainer** *n* ▸ **or'dainment** *n*

ordeal (ɔː'diːl) *n* **1** a severe or trying experience. **2** *History.*

a method of trial in which the innocence of an accused person was determined by subjecting him to physical danger, esp. by fire or water. ORIG OE *ordāl, ordēl* verdict

order ('ɔːdə) *n* **1** a state in which all components or elements are arranged logically, comprehensibly, or naturally. **2** an arrangement or disposition of things in succession; sequence: *alphabetical order.* **3** an established or customary method or state, esp. of society. **4** a peaceful or harmonious condition of society: *order reigned in the streets.* **5** (*often pl*) a class, rank, or hierarchy: *the lower orders.* **6** *Biol.* any of the taxonomic groups into which a class is divided and which contains one or more families. **7** an instruction that must be obeyed; command. **8a** a commission or instruction to produce or supply something in return for payment. **8b** the commodity produced or supplied. **8c** (*as modifier*): *order form.* **9** a procedure followed by an assembly, meeting, etc. **10** (*cap. when part of a name*) a body of people united in a particular aim or purpose. **11** (*usually cap.*) Also called: **religious order.** a group of persons who bind themselves by vows in order to devote themselves to the pursuit of religious aims. **12** (*often pl*) another name for **holy orders, major orders,** or **minor orders. 13** *History.* a society of knights constituted as a fraternity, such as the Knights Templars. **14a** a group of people holding a specific honour for service or merit, conferred on them by a sovereign or state. **14b** the insignia of such a group. **15a** any of the five major classical styles of architecture classified by the style of columns and entablatures used. **15b** any style of architecture. **16** *Christianity.* **16a** the sacrament by which bishops, priests, etc., have their offices conferred upon them. **16b** any of the degrees into which the ministry is divided. **16c** the office of an ordained Christian minister. **17** *Maths.* **17a** the number of times a function must be differentiated to obtain a given derivative. **17b** the order of the highest derivative in a differential equation. **17c** the number of rows or columns in a determinant or square matrix. **17d** the number of members of a finite group. **18** *Mil.* (often preceded by *the*) the dress, equipment, or formation directed for a particular purpose or undertaking: *battle order.* **19 a tall order.** something difficult, demanding, or exacting. **20 in order. 20a** in sequence. **20b** properly arranged. **20c** appropriate or fitting. **21 in order that.** (*conj*) with the purpose that; so that. **22 in order to.** (*prep*; foll. by an infinitive) so that it is possible to: *to eat in order to live.* **23 keep order.** to maintain or enforce order. **24 of** *or* **in the order of.** having an approximately specified size or quantity. **25 on order.** having been ordered but not having been delivered. **26 out of order. 26a** not in sequence. **26b** not working. **26c** not following the rules or customary procedure. **27 to order. 27a** according to a buyer's specifications. **27b** on request or demand. ◆ *vb* **28** (*tr*) to give a command to (a person or animal to do or be something). **29** to request (something) to be supplied or made, esp. in return for payment. **30** (*tr*) to instruct or command to move, go, etc. (to a specified place): *they ordered her into the house.* **31** (*tr; may take a clause as object*) to authorize; prescribe: *the doctor ordered a strict diet.* **32** (*tr*) to arrange, regulate, or dispose (articles, etc.) in their proper places. **33** (*tr*) (of fate) to will; ordain. ◆ *interj* **34** an exclamation demanding that orderly behaviour be restored. ORIG C13: from OF *ordre,* from L *ordō*
▸ **'orderer** *n*

order-driven *adj* denoting an electronic market system, esp. for stock exchanges, in which prices are determined by the publication of orders to buy or sell. Cf. **quote-driven.**

order in council *n* (in Britain and Canada) a decree of the Cabinet, usually made under the authority of a statute: in theory a decree of the sovereign and Privy Council.

orderly ('ɔːdəlɪ) *adj* **1** in order, properly arranged, or tidy. **2** obeying or appreciating method, system, and arrangement. **3** *Mil.* of or relating to orders: *an orderly book.* ◆ *n, pl* **orderlies. 4** *Med.* a male hospital attendant. **5** *Mil.* a junior rank detailed to carry orders or perform minor tasks for a more senior officer.
▸ **'orderliness** *n*

orderly room *n Mil.* a room in the barracks of a battalion or company used for general administrative purposes.

Order of Canada *n* an order awarded to Canadians for outstanding achievement.

order of magnitude *n* a numerical value expressed to the nearest power of ten.

Order of Merit *n Brit.* an order conferred on civilians and servicemen for eminence in any field.

order of the day *n* **1** the general directive of a commander in chief or the specific instructions of a commanding officer. **2** *Inf.* the prescribed or only thing offered or available. **3** (in Parliament) any item of public business ordered to be considered on a specific day. **4** an agenda or programme.

Order of the Garter *n* See **Garter.**

order paper *n* a list indicating the order in which business is to be conducted, esp. in Parliament.

ordinal ('ɔːdɪnᵊl) *adj* **1** denoting a certain position in a sequence of numbers. **2** of, relating to, or characteristic of an order in biological classification. ◆ *n* **3** short for **ordinal number. 4** a book containing the forms of services for the ordination of ministers. **5** *RC Church.* a service book.

ordinal number *n* a number denoting relative position in a sequence, such as *first, second, third.* Sometimes shortened to **ordinal.**

ordinance ('ɔːdɪnəns) *n* an authoritative regulation, decree, law, or practice. ORIG C14: from OF *ordenance,* from L *ordināre* to set in order

ordinarily ('ɔːdᵊnrɪlɪ) *adv* in ordinary, normal, or usual practice; usually; normally.

ordinary ('ɔːdᵊnrɪ) *adj* **1** of common or established type or occurrence. **2** familiar, everyday, or unexceptional. **3** uninteresting or commonplace. **4** having regular or ex officio jurisdiction: *an ordinary judge.* **5** *Maths.* (of a differential equation) containing two variables only and derivatives of one of the variables with respect to the other. ◆ *n, pl* **ordinaries. 6** a common or average situation, amount, or degree (esp. in **out of the ordinary**). **7** a normal or commonplace person or thing. **8** *Civil law.* a judge who exercises jurisdiction in his or her own right. **9** (*usually cap.*) an ecclesiastic, esp. a bishop, holding an office to which certain jurisdictional powers are attached. **10** *RC Church.* **10a** the parts of the Mass that do not vary from day to day. **10b** a prescribed form of divine service, esp. the Mass. **11** the US name for **penny-farthing. 12** *Heraldry.* any of several conventional figures, such as the bend, and the cross, commonly charged upon shields. **13** *History.* a clergyman who visited condemned prisoners. **14** *Brit. obs.* **14a** a meal provided regularly at a fixed price. **14b** the inn, etc., providing such meals. **15 in ordinary.** *Brit.* (used esp. in titles) in regular service or attendance: *physician in ordinary to the sovereign.* ORIG C16 (adj) & C13 (some n senses): ult. from L *ordinārius* orderly, from *ordō* order

Ordinary level *n* a formal name for **O level.**

ordinary rating *n* a rank in the Royal Navy comparable to that of a private in the army.

ordinary seaman *n* a seaman of the lowest rank, being insufficiently experienced to be an able-bodied seaman.

ordinary shares *pl n Brit.* shares representing part of the capital issued by a company, entitling their holders to a share in the profits and the net assets. US equivalent: **common stock.** Cf. **preference shares.**

ordinate ('ɔːdɪnɪt) *n* the vertical or *y*-coordinate of a point in a two-dimensional system of Cartesian coordinates. Cf. **abscissa.** ORIG C16: from NL (*linea*) *ordināte* (*applicāta*) (line applied) in an orderly manner, from *ordināre* to arrange in order

ordination (ˌɔːdɪ'neɪʃən) *n* **1a** the act of conferring holy orders. **1b** the reception of holy orders. **2** the condition of being ordained or regulated. **3** an arrangement or order.

ordnance ('ɔːdnəns) *n* **1** cannon or artillery. **2** military supplies; munitions. **3 the.** a department of an army or government dealing with military supplies. ORIG C14: var. of ORDINANCE

ordnance datum *n* mean sea level calculated from observation taken at Newlyn, Cornwall, and used as the official basis for height calculation on British maps. Abbrev.: **OD**.

Ordnance Survey *n* the official map-making body of the British or Irish government.

Ordovician (ˌɔːdəʊˈvɪʃɪən) *adj* **1** of, denoting, or formed in the second period of the Palaeozoic era, between the Cambrian and Silurian periods. ◆ *n* **2 the.** the Ordovician period or rock system. ORIG C19: from L *Ordovices,* ancient Celtic tribe in N Wales

ordure (ˈɔːdjʊə) *n* excrement; dung. ORIG C14: via OF, from *ord* dirty, from L *horridus* shaggy

Ordzhonikidze *or* **Orjonikidze** ★ (*Russian* ardʒəniˈkidzɪ) *n* the former name (1944–91) of **Vladikavkaz.**

ore (ɔː) *n* any naturally occurring mineral or aggregate of minerals from which economically important constituents, esp. metals, can be extracted. ORIG OE *ār, ōra*

öre (ˈørə) *n, pl* **öre.** a Scandinavian monetary unit worth one hundredth of a Swedish krona and (**øre**) one hundredth of a Danish and Norwegian krone.

oread (ˈɔːrɪˌæd) *n Greek myth.* a mountain nymph. ORIG C16: via L from Gk *Oreias,* from *oros* mountain

Örebro ★ (*Swedish* œːrəˈbruː) *n* a town in S Sweden: one of Sweden's oldest towns. Pop.: 120 774 (1997 est.).

Oreg. *abbrev. for* Oregon.

oregano (ˌɒrɪˈɡɑːnəʊ) *n* **1** a Mediterranean variety of wild marjoram (*Origanum vulgare*), with pungent leaves. **2** the dried powdered leaves of this plant, used to season food. ORIG C18: American Sp., from Sp., from L *orīganum,* from Gk *origanon* an aromatic herb, ? marjoram

Oregon ★ (ˈɒrɪɡən) *n* a state of the northwestern US, on the Pacific: consists of the Coast and Cascade Ranges in the west and a plateau in the east; important timber production. Capital: Salem. Pop.: 3 281 974 (1998 est.). Area: 251 418 sq. km (97 073 sq. miles). Abbrevs.: **Oreg.** or (with zip code) **OR**

Oregon trail ★ *n* an early pioneering route across the central US, from Independence, W Missouri, to the Columbia River country of N Oregon: used chiefly between 1804 and 1860. Length: about 3220 km (2000 miles).

Orel *or* **Oryol** ★ (*Russian* aˈrjɔl) *n* a city in W Russia. Pop.: 348 000 (1995 est.).

Ore Mountains ★ (ɔː) *pl n* another name for the **Erzgebirge.**

Orenburg ★ (ˈɒrənˌbɜːɡ; *Russian* arɪnˈburk) *n* a city in W Russia, on the Ural River. Pop.: 532 000 (1995 est.). Former name (1938–57): **Chkalov.**

Orense ★ (*Spanish* oˈrense) *n* a city in NW Spain, in Galicia on the Miño River: warm springs. Pop.: 110 796 (1995 st.).

Orestes ★ (ɒˈrɛstiːz) *n Greek myth.* the son of Agamemnon and Clytemnestra, who killed his mother and her lover Aegisthus in revenge for their murder of his father.

Øresund ★ (œːrəˈsʊnd) *n* the Swedish and Danish name for the **Sound.**

orfe (ɔːf) *n* a small slender European cyprinoid fish, occurring in two colour varieties, namely the **silver orfe** and the **golden orfe,** popular aquarium fishes. ORIG C17: from G; rel. to L *orphus,* Gk *orphos* the sea perch

Orff ★ (ɔːf; *German* ɔrf) *n* **Carl** (karl). 1895–1982, German composer. His works include the oratorio *Carmina Burana* (1937).

organ (ˈɔːɡən) *n* **1a** Also called: **pipe organ.** a large complex musical keyboard instrument in which sound is produced by means of a number of pipes arranged in sets or stops, supplied with air from a bellows. **1b** (*as modifier*): *organ stop; organ loft.* **2** any instrument, such as a harmonium, in which sound is produced in this way. **3** a fully differentiated structural and functional unit, such as a kidney or a root, in an animal or plant. **4** an agency or medium of communication, esp. a periodical issued by a specialist group or party. **5** an instrument with which something is done or accomplished. **6** a euphemistic word for **penis.** ORIG C13: from OF *organe,* from L *organum* implement, from Gk *organon* tool

organdie *or esp. US* **organdy** (ˈɔːɡəndɪ) *n, pl* **organdies.** a fine and slightly stiff cotton fabric used for dresses, etc. ORIG C19: from F *organdi,* from ?

organelle (ˌɔːɡəˈnɛl) *n* a structural and functional unit in a cell or unicellular organism. ORIG C20: from NL *organella,* from L *organum;* see ORGAN

organ-grinder *n* a street musician playing a hand organ for money.

organic (ɔːˈɡænɪk) *adj* **1** of, relating to, or derived from living plants and animals. **2** of or relating to animal or plant constituents or products having a carbon basis. **3** of or relating to one or more organs of an animal or plant. **4** of, relating to, or belonging to the class of chemical compounds that are formed from carbon: *an organic compound.* **5** constitutional in the structure of something; fundamental; integral. **6** of or characterized by the coordination of integral parts; organized. **7** of or relating to the essential constitutional laws regulating the government of a state: *organic law.* **8** of, relating to, or grown with the use of fertilizers or pesticides deriving from animal or vegetable matter, rather than from chemicals. ◆ *n* **9** any substance, such as a fertilizer or pesticide, that is derived from animal or vegetable matter rather than from chemicals.
▸ **orˈganically** *adv*

organic chemistry *n* the branch of chemistry concerned with the compounds of carbon.

organism (ˈɔːɡəˌnɪzəm) *n* **1** any living animal or plant, including any bacterium or virus. **2** anything resembling a living creature in structure, behaviour, etc.
▸ **ˌorganˈismal** *or* **ˌorganˈismic** *adj* ▸ **ˌorganˈismally** *adv*

organist (ˈɔːɡənɪst) *n* a person who plays the organ.

organization *or* **organisation** (ˌɔːɡənaɪˈzeɪʃən) *n* **1** the act of organizing or the state of being organized. **2** an organized structure or whole. **3** a business or administrative concern united and constructed for a particular end. **4** a body of administrative officials, as of a government department, etc. **5** order, tidiness, or system; method.
▸ **ˌorganiˈzational** *or* **ˌorganiˈsational** *adj*

organizational psychology *n* the study of the structure of an organization and of the ways in which the people in it interact, usually undertaken in order to improve the organization.

organize *or* **organise** (ˈɔːɡəˌnaɪz) *vb* **organizes, organizing, organized** *or* **organises, organising, organised.** **1** to form (parts or elements of something) into a structured whole; coordinate. **2** (*tr*) to arrange methodically or in order. **3** (*tr*) to provide with an organic structure. **4** (*tr*) to enlist (the workers) of (a factory, etc.) in a trade union. **5** (*intr*) to join or form an organization or trade union. **6** (*tr*) *Inf.* to put (oneself) in an alert and responsible frame of mind. ORIG C15: from Med. L *organizare,* from L *organum* ORGAN
▸ **ˈorganˌizer** *or* **ˈorganˌiser** *n*

organometallic (ɔːˌɡænəʊmɪˈtælɪk) *adj* of, concerned with, or being an organic compound with one or more metal atoms in its molecules.

organon (ˈɔːɡəˌnɒn) *or* **organum** *n, pl* **organa** (-nə), **organons** *or* **organa, organums.** **1** *Epistemology.* a system of logical or scientific rules, esp. that of Aristotle. **2** *Arch.* a sense organ, regarded as an instrument for acquiring knowledge. ORIG C16: from Gk: implement; see ORGAN

organophosphate (ɔːˌɡænəʊˈfɒsfeɪt) *n* any of a group of organic compounds containing phosphorus and used as a pesticide.

organotin (ɔːɡænəʊˈtɪn) *adj* **1** of, concerned with, or being an organic compound with one or more tin atoms in its molecules. ◆ *n* **2** such a compound used as a pesticide, formerly believed to decompose safely, now found to be toxic in the food chain.

organza (ɔːˈɡænzə) *n* a thin stiff fabric of silk, cotton, nylon, rayon, etc. ORIG C20: from ?

orgasm (ˈɔːɡæzəm) *n* **1** the most intense point during sexual excitement. **2** *Rare.* intense or violent excitement. ORIG C17: from NL *orgasmus,* from Gk *orgasmos,* from *organ* to mature, swell
▸ **orˈgasmic** *or* **orˈgastic** *adj*

orgeat (ˈɔːʒɑː) *n* a drink made from barley or almonds, and orangeflower water. ORIG C18: via F, from *orge* barley, from L *hordeum*

orgy (ˈɔːdʒɪ) *n, pl* **orgies. 1** a wild gathering marked by promiscuous sexual activity, excessive drinking, etc. **2** an act of immoderate or frenzied indulgence. **3** (*often pl*) secret religious rites of Dionysus, Bacchus, etc., marked by drinking, dancing, and songs. ORIG C16: from F *orgies,* from L *orgia,* from Gk: nocturnal festival
▸ **ˌorgiˈastic** *adj*

oribi (ˈɒrɪbɪ) *n, pl* **oribi** *or* **oribis.** a small African antelope of the grasslands and bush south of the Sahara, with fawn-coloured coat and, in the male, ridged spikelike horns. ORIG C18: from Afrik., prob. from Khoikhoi *arab*

oriel window (ˈɔːrɪəl) *n* a bay window, esp. one that is supported by one or more brackets or corbels. Sometimes shortened to **oriel.** ORIG C14: from OF *oriol* gallery, ?from Med. L *auleolum* niche

orient *n* (ˈɔːrɪənt). **1** *Poetic.* another word for **east.** Cf. **occident. 2** *Arch.* the eastern sky or the dawn. **3a** the iridescent lustre of a pearl. **3b** (*as modifier*): *orient pearls.* **4** a pearl of high quality. ◆ *adj* (ˈɔːrɪənt). **5** *Now chiefly poetic.* oriental. **6** *Arch.* (of the sun, stars, etc.) rising. ◆ *vb* (ˈɔːrɪˌɛnt). **7** to adjust or align (oneself or something else) according to surroundings or circumstances. **8** (*tr*) to position or set (a map, etc.) with reference to the compass or other specific directions. **9** (*tr*) to build (a church) with the chancel end facing in an easterly direction. ORIG C18: via F from L *oriēns* rising (sun), from *orīrī* to rise

Orient (ˈɔːrɪənt) *n* (usually preceded by *the*) **1** the countries east of the Mediterranean. **2** the eastern hemisphere.

oriental (ˌɔːrɪˈɛntᵊl) *adj* another word for **eastern.**

Oriental (ˌɔːrɪˈɛntᵊl) *adj* **1** (*sometimes not cap.*) of or relating to the Orient. **2** of or denoting a region consisting of southeastern Asia from India to Borneo, Java, and the Philippines. ◆ *n* **3** (*sometimes not cap.*) an inhabitant, esp. a native, of the Orient.

Orientalism (ˌɔːrɪˈɛntəˌlɪzəm) *n* **1** knowledge of or devotion to the Orient. **2** an Oriental quality, style, or trait.
▸ **ˌOriˈentalist** *n* ▸ **ˌOriˌentalˈistic** *adj*

orientate (ˈɔːrɪɛnˌteɪt) *vb* **orientates, orientating, orientated.** another word for **orient** (senses 7, 8, 9).

orientation (ˌɔːrɪɛnˈteɪʃən) *n* **1** the act or process of orienting or the state of being oriented. **2** positioning with relation to the compass or other specific directions. **3** the adjustment or alignment of oneself or one's ideas to surroundings or circumstances. **4** Also called: **orientation course.** *Chiefly US & Canad.* **4a** a course, lecture, etc., introducing a new situation or environment. **4b** (*as modifier*): *an orientation talk.* **5** *Psychol.* the knowledge of one's own temporal, social, and practical circumstances. **6** the siting of a church on an east-west axis.
▸ **ˌorienˈtational** *adj*

-oriented *suffix forming adjectives.* geared or directed towards: *sports-oriented.*

orienteer (ˌɔːrɪənˈtɪə) *vb* (*intr*) **1** to take part in orienteering. ◆ *n* **2** a person who takes part in orienteering.

orienteering (ˌɔːrɪɛnˈtɪərɪŋ) *n* a sport in which contestants race on foot over a course consisting of checkpoints found with the aid of a map and a compass. ORIG C20: from Swedish *orientering*

orifice (ˈɒrɪfɪs) *n Chiefly technical.* an opening or mouth into a cavity; vent; aperture. ORIG C16: via F from LL *ōrificium,* from L *ōs* mouth + *facere* to make

oriflamme (ˈɒrɪˌflæm) *n* a scarlet flag adopted as the national banner of France in the Middle Ages. ORIG C15: via OF, from L *aurum* gold + *flamma* flame

orig. *abbrev. for:* **1** origin. **2** original(ly).

origami (ˌɒrɪˈgɑːmɪ) *n* the art or process, originally Japanese, of paper folding. ORIG from Japanese, from *ori* a fold + *kami* paper

origan (ˈɒrɪgən) *n* another name for **marjoram** (sense 2). ORIG C16: from L *orīganum,* from Gk *origanon* an aromatic herb

origanum (ˌɒrɪˈgɑːnəm) *n* See **oregano.**

Origen ★ (ˈɒrɪˌdʒɛn) *n* ?185–?254 A.D., Christian theologian, born in Alexandria. His writings include *Contra Celsum* and *De principiis.*

origin (ˈɒrɪdʒɪn) *n* **1** a primary source; derivation. **2** the beginning of something; first part. **3** (*often pl*) ancestry or parentage; birth; extraction. **4** *Anat.* **4a** the end of a muscle, opposite its point of insertion. **4b** the beginning of a nerve or blood vessel or the site where it first starts to branch out. **5** *Maths.* **5a** the point of intersection of coordinate axes or planes. **5b** the point whose coordinates are all zero. **6** *Commerce.* the country from which a commodity or product originates: *shipment from origin.* ORIG C16: from F *origine,* from L *orīgō* beginning, from *orīrī* to spring from

original (əˈrɪdʒɪnᵊl) *adj* **1** of or relating to an origin or beginning. **2** fresh and unusual; novel. **3** able to think of or carry out new ideas or concepts. **4** being that from which a copy, translation, etc., is made. ◆ *n* **5** the first and genuine form of something, from which others are derived. **6** a person or thing used as a model in art or literature. **7** a person whose way of thinking is unusual or creative. **8** the first form or occurrence of something.
▸ **oˈriginally** *adv*

originality (əˌrɪdʒɪˈnælɪtɪ) *n, pl* **originalities. 1** the quality or condition of being original. **2** the ability to create or innovate.

original sin *n* a state of sin held to be innate in mankind as the descendants of Adam.

originate (əˈrɪdʒɪˌneɪt) *vb* **originates, originating, originated. 1** to come or bring into being. **2** (*intr*) *US & Canad.* (of a bus, train, etc.) to begin its journey at a specified point.
▸ **oˌrigiˈnation** *n* ▸ **oˈrigiˌnator** *n*

O-ring *n* a rubber ring used in machinery as a seal against oil, air, etc.

Orinoco ★ (ˌɒrɪˈnəʊkəʊ) *n* a river in N South America, rising in S Venezuela and flowing west, then north as part of the border between Colombia and Venezuela, then east to the Atlantic by a great delta: the third largest river system in South America, draining an area of 945 000 sq. km (365 000 sq. miles); reaches a width of 22 km (14 miles) during the rainy season. Length: about 2575 km (1600 miles).

oriole (ˈɔːrɪˌəʊl) *n* **1** a tropical Old World songbird, such as the **golden oriole,** having a long pointed bill and a mostly yellow-and-black plumage. **2** an American songbird, esp. the Baltimore oriole, with a typical male plumage of black with either orange or yellow. ORIG C18: from Med. L *oryolus,* from L *aureolus,* dim. of *aureus,* from *aurum* gold

Orion[1] ★ (əˈraɪən) *n Greek myth.* a Boeotian giant famed as a great hunter, who figures in several tales.

Orion[2] (əˈraɪən) *n* a conspicuous constellation containing two first-magnitude stars (Betelgeuse and Rigel) and a distant bright emission nebula (the **Orion Nebula**).

orison (ˈɒrɪzᵊn) *n Literary.* another word for **prayer**[1] (senses 1 and 2). ORIG C12: from OF *oreison,* from LL *ōrātiō,* from L: speech, from *ōrāre* to speak

Orissa ★ (ɒˈrɪsə) *n* a state of E India, on the Bay of Bengal: part of the province of Bihar and Orissa (1912–36); enlarged by the addition of 25 native states in 1949. Capital: Bhubaneswar. Pop.: 33 795 000 (1994 est.). Area: 155 707 sq. km (60 119 sq. miles).

Oriya (ɒˈriːə) *n* **1** (*pl* **Oriya**) a member of a people of India living chiefly in Orissa. **2** the state language of Orissa, belonging to the Indo-European family.

Orizaba ★ (ˌɔːrɪˈzɑːbə; *Spanish* oriˈθaβa) *n* **1** a city and resort in SE Mexico, in Veracruz state. Pop.: 114 216 (1990). **2 Pico de.** the Spanish name for **Citlaltépetl.**

Orjonikidze ★ (*Russian* ardʒəniˈkidzɪ) *n* a variant spelling of **Ordzhonikidze.**

Orkneys (ˈɔːknɪz), **Orkney** (ˈɔːknɪ), *or* **Orkney Islands** ★ *pl n* a group of over 70 islands off the N coast of Scotland, separated from the mainland by the Pentland Firth: constitutes an island authority of Scotland; low-lying and treeless; prehistoric remains. Administrative centre: Kirkwall. Pop.: 19 800 (1996 est.). Area: 974 sq. km (376 sq. miles). Related adj: **Orcadian.**
▸ **ˈOrkneyman** *or fem* **ˈOrkneyˌwoman** *n*

★ people and places

Orlando ★ (ɔːˈlændəʊ) *n* a city in the US, in Florida: site of Walt Disney World. Pop.: 173 902 (1996 est.).

Orléans[1] ★ (ɔːˈlɪənz; *French* ɔrleɑ̃) *n* a city in N central France, on the River Loire: famous for its deliverance by Joan of Arc from the long English siege in 1429; university (1305); an important rail and road junction. Pop.: 107 965 (1990).

Orléans[2] ★ (*French* ɔrleɑ̃) *n* **Louis Philippe Joseph** (lwi filip ʒozɛf), Duc d'Orléans, known as *Philippe Égalité.* 1747–93, French nobleman, who supported the French Revolution; executed after his son, the future king Louis-Philippe, defected to the Austrians.

Orlon (ˈɔːlɒn) *n Trademark.* a crease-resistant acrylic fibre or fabric used for clothing, etc.

orlop *or* **orlop deck** (ˈɔːlɒp) *n Naut.* (in a vessel with four or more decks) the lowest deck. ORIG C15: from Du. *overloopen* to spill

Orly ★ (ˈɔːliː; *French* ɔrli) *n* a suburb of SE Paris, France, with an international airport.

Ormandy ★ (ˈɔːməndɪ) *n* **Eugene.** 1899–1985, US conductor, born in Hungary.

Ormazd ★ (ˈɔːməzd) *n Zoroastrianism.* the creative diety, embodiment of good and opponent of Ahriman. Also called: **Ahura Mazda.** ORIG from Persian

ormer (ˈɔːmə) *n* **1** Also called: **sea-ear.** an edible marine gastropod mollusc that has an ear-shaped shell perforated with holes and occurs near the Channel Islands. **2** any other abalone. ORIG C17: from F, apparently from L *auris* ear + *mare* sea

ormolu (ˈɔːməˌluː) *n* **1a** a gold-coloured alloy of copper, tin, or zinc used to decorate furniture, etc. **1b** (*as modifier): an ormolu clock.* **2** gold prepared for gilding. ORIG C18: from F *or moulu* ground gold

Ormuz ★ (ˈɔːmʌz) *n* a variant spelling of **Hormuz.**

ornament *n* (ˈɔːnəmənt). **1** anything that enhances the appearance of a person or thing. **2** decorations collectively: *she was totally without ornament.* **3** a small decorative object. **4** something regarded as a source of pride or beauty. **5** *Music.* any of several decorations, such as the trill, etc. ◆ *vb* (ˈɔːnəˌmɛnt). (*tr*) **6** to decorate with or as if with ornaments. **7** to serve as an ornament to. ORIG C14: from L *ornāmentum,* from *ornāre* to adorn
▸ **ˌornamenˈtation** *n*

ornamental (ˌɔːnəˈmɛntᵊl) *adj* **1** of value as an ornament; decorative. **2** (of a plant) used to decorate houses, gardens, etc. ◆ *n* **3** a plant cultivated for show or decoration.
▸ **ˌornaˈmentally** *adv*

ornate (ɔːˈneɪt) *adj* **1** heavily or elaborately decorated. **2** (of style in writing, etc.) over-embellished; flowery. ORIG C15: from L *ornāre* to decorate
▸ **orˈnately** *adv* ▸ **orˈnateness** *n*

Orne ★ (*French* ɔrn) *n* a department of NW France, in Basse-Normandie. Capital: Alençon. Pop.: 294 596 (1994 est.). Area: 6144 sq. km (2396 sq. miles).

ornery (ˈɔːnərɪ) *adj US & Canad. dialect or inf.* **1** stubborn or vile-tempered. **2** low; treacherous: *an ornery trick.* **3** ordinary. ORIG C19: alteration of ORDINARY
▸ **ˈorneriness** *n*

ornitho- *or before a vowel* **ornith-** *combining form.* bird or birds. ORIG from Gk *ornis, ornith-* bird

ornithology (ˌɔːnɪˈθɒlədʒɪ) *n* the study of birds.
▸ **ornithological** (ˌɔːnɪθəˈlɒdʒɪkᵊl) *adj* ▸ **ˌornithoˈlogically** *adv* ▸ **ˌorniˈthologist** *n*

ornithorhynchus (ˌɔːnɪθəʊˈrɪŋkəs) *n* the technical name for **duck-billed platypus.** ORIG C19: NL, from ORNITHO- + Gk *rhunkhos* bill

oro-[1] *combining form.* mountain: *orogeny.* ORIG from Gk *oros*

oro-[2] *combining form.* oral; mouth: *oromaxillary.* ORIG from L, from *ōs*

orogeny (ɒˈrɒdʒɪnɪ) *or* **orogenesis** (ˌɒrəʊˈdʒɛnɪsɪs) *n* the formation of mountain ranges.
▸ **orogenic** (ˌɒrəʊˈdʒɛnɪk) *or* **orogenetic** (ˌɒrəʊdʒɪˈnɛtɪk) *adj*

Orontes ★ (ɒˈrɒntiːz) *n* a river in SW Asia, rising in Lebanon and flowing north through Syria into Turkey, where it turns west to the Mediterranean. Length: 571 km (355 miles). Arabic name: **'Asi.**

orotund (ˈɒrəʊˌtʌnd) *adj* **1** (of the voice) resonant; booming. **2** (of speech or writing) bombastic; pompous. ORIG C18: from L *ore rotundo* with rounded mouth

Orozco ★ (*Spanish* oˈrɔθko) *n* **José Clemente** (xoˈse kleˈmente). 1883–1949, Mexican mural painter.

orphan (ˈɔːfən) *n* **1a** a child, one or both of whose parents are dead. **1b** (*as modifier): an orphan child.* ◆ *vb* **2** (*tr*) to deprive of one or both parents. ORIG C15: from LL *orphanus,* from Gk *orphanos*

orphanage (ˈɔːfənɪdʒ) *n* **1** an institution for orphans and abandoned children. **2** the state of being an orphan.

Orphean (ˈɔːfɪən) *adj* **1** of or relating to Orpheus. **2** melodious or enchanting.

Orpheus ★ (ˈɔːfɪəs, -fjuːs) *n Greek myth.* a poet and lyre-player credited with the authorship of the poems forming the basis of Orphism. He married Eurydice and sought her in Hades after her death. He failed to win her back and was killed by a band of bacchantes.

Orphic (ˈɔːfɪk) *adj* **1** of or relating to Orpheus or Orphism, a mystery religion of ancient Greece. **2** (*sometimes not cap.*) mystical or occult.
▸ **ˈOrphically** *adv*

orpine (ˈɔːpaɪn) *or* **orpin** (ˈɔːpɪn) *n* a succulent perennial N temperate plant with toothed leaves and heads of small purplish-white flowers. ORIG C14: from OF, apparently from *orpiment,* a yellow mineral (? referring to the yellow flowers of a related species)

Orpington ★ (ˈɔːpɪŋtən) *n* a district of SE London, part of the Greater London borough of Bromley from 1965.

orrery (ˈɒrərɪ) *n, pl* **orreries.** a mechanical model of the solar system in which the planets can be moved at the correct relative velocities around the sun. ORIG C18: orig. made for Charles Boyle, Earl of *Orrery*

orris[1] *or* **orrice** (ˈɒrɪs) *n* **1** any of various irises that have fragrant rhizomes. **2** Also: **orrisroot.** the rhizome of such a plant, prepared and used as perfume. ORIG C16: var. of IRIS

orris[2] (ˈɒrɪs) *n* a kind of lace made of gold or silver, used esp. in the 18th century. ORIG from Old French *orfreis,* from L *auriphrygium* Phrygian gold

Orsini ★ (*Italian* orˈsiːni) *n* an Italian aristocratic family that was prominent in Rome from the 12th to the 18th century.

Orsk ★ (*Russian* ɔrsk) *n* a city in W Russia, on the Ural River: a major railway and industrial centre, with an oil refinery linked by pipeline with the Emba field (on the Caspian). Pop.: 275 000 (1995 est.).

Ortega ★ (ɔːˈteɪgə) *n* **Daniel,** full surname *Ortega Saavedra.* born 1945, Nicaraguan politician and former guerrilla leader; president of Nicaragua (1985–90).

Ortegal ★ (*Spanish* ɔrteˈɣal) *n* **Cape.** a cape in NW Spain, projecting into the Bay of Biscay.

Ortega y Gasset ★ (*Spanish* ɔrˈteɣa i gaˈsɛt) *n* **José** (xoˈse). 1883–1955, Spanish philosopher, noted for his *The Revolt of the Masses* (1930).

orthicon (ˈɔːθɪˌkɒn) *n* a television camera tube in which an optical image produces a corresponding electrical charge pattern on a mosaic surface that is scanned from behind by an electron beam. The resulting discharge of the mosaic provides the output signal current. See also **image orthicon.** ORIG C20: from ORTHO- + ICON(OSCOPE)

ortho- *or before a vowel* **orth-** *combining form.* **1** straight or upright: *orthorhombic.* **2** perpendicular or at right angles: *orthogonal.* **3** correct or right: *orthodontics.* **4** (*often in italics*) denoting an organic compound containing a benzene ring with substituents attached to adjacent carbon atoms (the 1,2- positions). **5** denoting an oxyacid regarded as the highest hydrated form of the anhydride or a salt of such an acid: *orthophosphoric acid.* **6** denoting a diatomic substance in which the spins of the two atoms are parallel: *orthohydrogen.* ORIG from Gk *orthos* straight, upright

orthochromatic (ˌɔːθəʊkrəʊˈmætɪk) *adj Photog.* of or relating to an emulsion giving a rendering of relative light

intensities of different colours that corresponds approximately to the colour sensitivity of the eye, esp. one that is insensitive to red light. Sometimes shortened to **ortho**.
▸ **orthochromatism** (ˌɔːθəʊˈkrəʊməˌtɪzəm) *n*

orthoclase (ˈɔːθəʊˌkleɪs, -ˌkleɪz) *n* a white or coloured feldspar mineral consisting of an aluminium silicate of potassium in monoclinic crystalline form.

orthodontics (ˌɔːθəʊˈdɒntɪks) *or* **orthodontia** (ˌɔːθəʊˈdɒntɪə) *n* (*functioning as sing*) the branch of dentistry concerned with preventing or correcting irregularities of the teeth.
▸ **ˌorthoˈdontic** *adj* ▸ **ˌorthoˈdontist** *n*

orthodox (ˈɔːθəˌdɒks) *adj* **1** conforming with established standards, as in religion, behaviour, or attitudes. **2** conforming to the Christian faith as established by the early Church. ORIG C16: via Church L from Gk *orthodoxos*, from *orthos* correct + *doxa* belief
▸ **ˈorthoˌdoxy** *n*

Orthodox (ˈɔːθəˌdɒks) *adj* **1** of or relating to the Orthodox Church of the East. **2** (*sometimes not cap.*) of or relating to Orthodox Judaism.

Orthodox Church *n* **1** the collective body of those Eastern Churches that were separated from the western Church in the 11th century and are in communion with the Greek patriarch of Constantinople. **2** any of these Churches.

Orthodox Judaism *n* a form of Judaism characterized by traditional interpretation and strict observance of the Mosaic Law.

orthoepy (ˈɔːθəʊˌɛpɪ) *n* the study of correct or standard pronunciation. ORIG C17: from Gk *orthoepeia*, from ORTHO- straight + *epos* word
▸ **orthoepic** (ˌɔːθəʊˈɛpɪk) *adj* ▸ **ˌorthoˈepically** *adv*

orthogenesis (ˌɔːθəʊˈdʒɛnɪsɪs) *n* **1** *Biol.* **1a** evolution of a group of organisms in a particular direction, which is generally predetermined. **1b** the theory that proposes such a development. **2** the theory that there is a series of stages through which all cultures pass in the same order.
▸ **orthogenetic** (ˌɔːθəʊdʒɪˈnɛtɪk) *adj* ▸ **ˌorthogeˈnetically** *adv*

orthogonal (ɔːˈθɒgənᵊl) *adj* relating to, consisting of, or involving right angles; perpendicular.
▸ **orˈthogonally** *adv*

orthographic (ˌɔːθəˈgræfɪk) *or* **orthographical** *adj* of or relating to spelling.
▸ **ˌorthoˈgraphically** *adv*

orthography (ɔːˈθɒgrəfɪ) *n, pl* **orthographies. 1** a writing system. **2a** spelling considered to be correct. **2b** the principles underlying spelling. **3** the study of spelling.
▸ **orˈthographer** *or* **orˈthographist** *n*

orthopaedics *or US* **orthopedics** (ˌɔːθəʊˈpiːdɪks) *n* (*functioning as sing*) **1** the branch of surgery concerned with disorders of the spine and joints and the repair of deformities of these parts. **2 dental orthopaedics.** another name for **orthodontics.**
▸ **ˌorthoˈpaedic** *or US* **ˌorthoˈpedic** *adj* ▸ **ˌorthoˈpaedist** *or US* **ˌorthoˈpedist** *n*

orthopteran (ɔːˈθɒptərən) *n, pl* **orthoptera** (-tərə). **1** Also: **orthopteron** (*pl* **orthoptera**). any orthopterous insect. ◆ *adj* **2** another word for **orthopterous.**

orthopterous (ɔːˈθɒptərəs) *adj* of, relating to, or belonging to a large order of insects, including crickets, locusts, and grasshoppers, having leathery forewings and membranous hind wings.

orthoptic (ɔːˈθɒptɪk) *adj* relating to normal binocular vision.

orthoptics (ɔːˈθɒptɪks) *n* (*functioning as sing*) the science or practice of correcting defective vision, as by exercises to strengthen weak eye muscles.
▸ **orˈthoptist** *n*

orthorhombic (ˌɔːθəʊˈrɒmbɪk) *adj Crystallog.* relating to the crystal system characterized by three mutually perpendicular unequal axes.

Ortles ★ (*Italian* ˈɔrtles) *pl n* a range of the Alps in N Italy. Highest peak: 3899 m (12 792 ft). Also called: **Ortler** (ˈɔːtlə).

ortolan (ˈɔːtələn) *n* **1** a brownish Old World bunting regarded as a delicacy. **2** any of various other small birds eaten as delicacies, esp. the bobolink. ORIG C17: via F from L *hortulānus*, from *hortulus*, dim. of *hortus* garden

Orton ★ (ˈɔːtən) *n* **Joe.** 1933–67, British dramatist, his black comedies include *Loot* (1965) and *What the Butler Saw* (1969).

Oruro ★ (*Spanish* oˈruro) *n* a city in W Bolivia: a former silver-mining centre; university (1892); tin, copper, and tungsten. Pop.: 201 831 (1993 est.).

Orvieto ★ (*Italian* orˈvjɛːto) *n* **1** a market town in central Italy, in Umbria: Etruscan remains. Pop.: 21 575 (1990). Latin name: **Urbs Vetus** (uəbz ˈviːtəs). **2** a light white wine from this region.

Orwell ★ (ˈɔːwəl, -wɛl) *n* **George,** real name *Eric Arthur Blair.* 1903–50, British novelist, born in India. His works include *The Road to Wigan Pier* (1932), *Animal Farm* (1945), and *1984* (1949).
▸ **Orwellian** (ɔːˈwɛlɪən) *adj*

-ory[1] *suffix forming nouns.* **1** indicating a place for: *observatory.* **2** something having a specified use: *directory.* ORIG via OF *-orie*, from L *-ōrium, -ōria*

-ory[2] *suffix forming adjectives.* of or relating to; characterized by; having the effect of: *contributory.* ORIG via OF *-orie*, from L *-ōrius*

Oryol ★ (*Russian* aˈrjɔl) *n* a variant spelling of **Orel.**

oryx (ˈɒrɪks) *n, pl* **oryxes** *or* **oryx.** any large African antelope of the genus *Oryx*, typically having long straight nearly upright horns. ORIG C14: via L from Gk *orux* stonemason's axe, used also of the pointed horns of an antelope

os[1] (ɒs) *n, pl* **ossa** (ˈɒsə). *Anat.* the technical name for **bone.** ORIG C16: from L: bone

os[2] (ɒs) *n, pl* **ora.** *Anat., zool.* a mouth or mouthlike part or opening. ORIG C18: from L

Os *the chemical symbol for* osmium.

OS *abbrev. for:* **1** Old Saxon (language). **2** Old Style. **3** Ordinary Seaman. **4** (in Britain) Ordnance Survey. **5** outsize.

Osage orange (əʊˈseɪdʒ) *n* **1** a North American thorny tree, grown for hedges and ornament. **2** the warty orange-like fruit of this plant. ORIG from *Osage* Amerind tribe

Osaka ★ (əʊˈsɑːkə) *n* a port in S Japan, on S Honshu on **Osaka Bay** (an inlet of the Pacific): the third largest city in Japan (the chief commercial city during feudal times); university (1931); an industrial and commercial centre. Pop.: 2 602 352 (1995).

Osborne ★ (ˈɒzbən, -ˌbɔːn) *n* **John (James).** 1929–94, British dramatist. His plays include *Look Back in Anger* (1956), *The Entertainer* (1957), *Luther* (1960), and *Déjà Vu* (1992).

Oscar (ˈɒskə) *n* any of several small gold statuettes awarded annually in the US for outstanding achievements in films. Official name: **Academy Award.** ORIG C20: said to have been named after a remark made by a secretary that it reminded her of her uncle Oscar

Oscar II ★ *n* 1829–1907, king of Sweden (1872–1907) and of Norway (1872–1905).

oscillate (ˈɒsɪˌleɪt) *vb* **oscillates, oscillating, oscillated. 1** (*intr*) to move or swing from side to side regularly. **2** (*intr*) to waver between opinions, courses of action, etc. **3** *Physics.* to undergo or produce or cause to undergo or produce oscillation. ORIG C18: from L *oscillāre* to swing

oscillating universe theory *n* the theory that the universe is oscillating between periods of expansion and contraction.

oscillation (ˌɒsɪˈleɪʃən) *n* **1** *Statistics, physics.* **1a** regular fluctuation in value, position, or state about a mean value, such as the variation in an alternating current. **1b** a single cycle of such a fluctuation. **2** the act or process of oscillating.
▸ **oscillatory** (ˈɒsɪlətərɪ, -trɪ) *adj*

oscillator (ˈɒsɪˌleɪtə) *n* **1** a circuit or instrument for producing an alternating current or voltage of a required frequency. **2** any instrument for producing oscillations. **3** a person or thing that oscillates.

oscillogram (ɒˈsɪləˌgræm) *n* the recording obtained

from an oscillograph or the trace on an oscilloscope screen.

oscillograph (ɒ'sɪləˌgrɑːf) *n* a device for producing a graphical record of the variation of an oscillating quantity, such as an electric current.
▸ **oscillographic** (ɒˌsɪlə'græfɪk) *adj* ▸ **oscillography** (ˌɒsɪ'lɒgrəfɪ) *n*

oscilloscope (ɒ'sɪləˌskəʊp) *n* an instrument for producing a representation of a rapidly changing quantity on the screen of a cathode-ray tube.

oscine ('ɒsaɪn, 'ɒsɪn) *adj* of, relating to, or belonging to the suborder of passerine birds that includes most of the songbirds. ORIG C17: via NL from L *oscen* singing bird

oscitancy ('ɒsɪtənsɪ) *or* **oscitance** *n, pl* **oscitancies** *or* **oscitances. 1** the state of being drowsy, lazy, or inattentive. **2** the act of yawning. ◆ Also called: **oscitation.** ORIG C17: from L *oscitāre* to yawn
▸ **'oscitant** *adj*

oscular ('ɒskjʊlə) *adj* **1** *Zool.* of or relating to a mouthlike aperture, esp. of a sponge. **2** of or relating to the mouth or to kissing.

osculate ('ɒskjʊˌleɪt) *vb* **osculates, osculating, osculated. 1** *Usually humorous.* to kiss. **2** (*intr*) (of an organism) to be intermediate between two taxonomic groups. **3** *Geom.* to touch in osculation. ORIG C17: from L *ōsculārī* to kiss

osculation (ˌɒskjʊ'leɪʃən) *n* **1** *Maths.* Also called: **tacnode.** a point at which two branches of a curve have a common tangent, each branch extending in both directions of the tangent. **2** *Rare.* the act of kissing.
▸ **osculatory** ('ɒskjʊlətərɪ, -trɪ) *adj*

-ose[1] *suffix forming adjectives.* possessing; resembling: *grandiose.* ORIG from L *-ōsus;* see -OUS

-ose[2] *suffix forming nouns.* **1** indicating a carbohydrate, esp. a sugar: *lactose.* **2** indicating a decomposition product of protein: *albumose.* ORIG from GLUCOSE

Oshawa ★ ('ɒʃəwə) *n* a city in central Canada, in SE Ontario on Lake Ontario: motor-vehicle industry. Pop.: 129 344 (1991).

Oshogbo ★ (ə'ʃɒgbəʊ) *n* a city in SW Nigeria: trade centre. Pop.: 476 800 (1996 est.).

osier ('əʊzɪə) *n* **1** any of various willow trees, whose flexible branches or twigs are used for making baskets, etc. **2** a twig or branch from such a tree. **3** any of several North American dogwoods, esp. the red osier. ORIG C14: from OF, prob. from Med. L *ausēria,* ? of Gaulish origin

Osijek ★ (*Serbo-Croat* 'ɔsijɛk) *n* a town in NE Croatia, on the Drava River: under Turkish rule from 1526 to 1687. Pop.: 129 792 (1991). Ancient name: **Mursa** ('mʊəsə).

Osiris ★ (əʊ'saɪrɪs) *n* an ancient Egyptian god, ruler of the underworld and judge of the dead.
▸ **O'sirian** *adj*

-osis *suffix forming nouns.* **1** indicating a process or state: *metamorphosis.* **2** indicating a diseased condition: *tuberculosis.* Cf. **-iasis. 3** indicating the formation or development of something: *fibrosis.* ORIG from Gk, suffix used to form nouns from verbs with infinitives in *-oein* or *-oun*

Oslo ★ ('ɒzləʊ; *Norwegian* 'uslu) *n* the capital and chief port of Norway, in the southeast at the head of **Oslo Fjord** (an inlet of the Skagerrak): founded in about 1050; university (1811); a major commercial and industrial centre, producing about a quarter of Norway's total output. Pop.: 493 973 (1997 est.). Former names: **Christiania** (1624–1877), **Kristiania** (1877–1924).

Osman I ('ɒzmən, ɒz'mɑːn) *or* **Othman I** ★ *n* 1259–1326, Turkish sultan; founder of the Ottoman Empire.

Osmanli (ɒz'mænlɪ) *adj* **1** of or relating to the Ottoman Empire. ◆ *n* **2** (formerly) a subject of the Ottoman Empire. ORIG C19: from Turkish, from OSMAN I

osmiridium (ˌɒzmɪ'rɪdɪəm) *n* a very hard corrosion-resistant white or grey natural alloy of osmium and iridium: used in pen nibs, etc. ORIG C19: from OSM(IUM) + IRIDIUM

osmium ('ɒzmɪəm) *n* a very hard brittle bluish-white metal, the heaviest known element, occurring with platinum and alloyed with iridium in osmiridium. Symbol: Os; atomic no.: 76; atomic wt.: 190.2. ORIG C19: from Gk *osmē* smell, from its penetrating odour

osmoregulation (ˌɒzməʊˌrɛgjʊ'leɪʃən) *n Zool.* the adjustment of the osmotic pressure of a cell or organism in relation to the surrounding fluid.

osmose ('ɒzməʊs, -məʊz, 'ɒs-) *vb* **osmoses, osmosing, osmosed.** to undergo or cause to undergo osmosis. ORIG C19 (n): abstracted from the earlier terms *endosmose* and *exosmose;* rel. to Gk *ōsmos* push

osmosis (ɒz'məʊsɪs, ɒs-) *n* **1** the tendency of the solvent of a less concentrated solution of dissolved molecules to pass through a semipermeable membrane into a more concentrated solution until both solutions are of the same concentration. **2** diffusion through any membrane or porous barrier, as in dialysis. **3** gradual or unconscious assimilation or adoption, as of ideas. ORIG C19: Latinized form from OSMOSE, from Gk *ōsmos* push
▸ **osmotic** (ɒz'mɒtɪk, ɒs-) *adj* ▸ **os'motically** *adv*

osmotic pressure *n* the pressure necessary to prevent osmosis into a given solution when the solution is separated from the pure solvent by a semipermeable membrane.

osmunda (ɒz'mʌndə) *or* **osmund** ('ɒzmənd) *n* any of a genus of ferns having large spreading fronds. ORIG C13: from OF *osmonde,* from ?

Osnabrück ★ (*German* ɔsna'bryk) *n* an industrial city in NW Germany, in Lower Saxony: a member of the Hanseatic League in the Middle Ages. Pop.: 168 618 (1996 est.).

osprey ('ɒsprɪ, -preɪ) *n* **1** a large broad-winged fish-eating diurnal bird of prey, with a dark back and whitish head and underparts. Often called (US and Canad.): **fish hawk. 2** any of the feathers of various other birds, used esp. as trimming for hats. ORIG C15: from OF *ospres,* apparently from L *ossifraga,* lit.: bone-breaker, from *os* bone + *frangere* to break

Ossa ★ ('ɒsə) *n* a mountain in NE Greece, in E Thessaly: famous in mythology for the attempt of the twin giants, Otus and Ephialtes, to reach heaven by piling Ossa on Olympus and Pelion on Ossa. Height: 1978 m (6489 ft).

ossein ('ɒsɪɪn) *n* a protein that forms the organic matrix of bone. ORIG C19: from L *osseus* bony, from *os* bone

osseous ('ɒsɪəs) *adj* consisting of or containing bone, bony. ORIG C17: from L *osseus,* from *os* bone
▸ **'osseously** *adv*

Ossetia ★ (ɒ'siːʃə) *n* a region of central Asia, in the Caucasus: consists administratively of the North Ossetian Republic of Russia and the South Ossetian Autonomous Region of Georgia.
▸ **Os'setic** *or* **Os'setian** *adj*

Ossian ★ ('ɒsɪən) *n* a legendary Irish hero and bard of the 3rd century A.D. See also (James) **Macpherson.**
▸ **ˌOssi'anic** *adj*

Ossietzky ★ (ˌɒsɪ'ɛtskɪ) *n* **Carl von** (karl fɔn). 1889–1938, German pacifist; imprisoned for revealing Germany's secret rearmament (1931–32) and again under Hitler (1933–36): Nobel peace prize 1935.

ossify ('ɒsɪˌfaɪ) *vb* **ossifies, ossifying, ossified. 1** to convert or be converted into bone. **2** (*intr*) (of habits, attitudes, etc.) to become inflexible. ORIG C18: from F *ossifier,* from L *os* bone + *facere* to make
▸ **ˌossifi'cation** *n* ▸ **'ossiˌfier** *n*

ossuary ('ɒsjʊərɪ) *n, pl* **ossuaries.** any container for the burial of human bones, such as an urn or vault. ORIG C17: from LL *ossuārium,* from L *os* bone

osteal ('ɒstɪəl) *adj* **1** of or relating to bone or to the skeleton. **2** composed of bone; osseous. ORIG C19: from Gk *osteon* bone

osteitis (ˌɒstɪ'aɪtɪs) *n* inflammation of a bone.
▸ **osteitic** (ˌɒstɪ'ɪtɪk) *adj*

Ostend ★ (ɒs'tɛnd) *n* a port and resort in NW Belgium, in West Flanders on the North Sea. Pop.: 68 858 (1995 est.). French name: **Ostende** (ɔstɑ̃d). Flemish name: **Oostende.**

ostensible (ɒ'stɛnsɪbᵊl) *adj* **1** apparent; seeming. **2** pretended. ORIG C18: via F from Med. L *ostensibilis,* from L *ostendere* to show, from *ob-* before + *tendere* to extend
▸ **osˌtensi'bility** *n* ▸ **os'tensibly** *adv*

ostensive (ɒ'stɛnsɪv) *adj* **1** obviously or manifestly de-

monstrative. **2** (of a definition) giving examples of objects to which a word or phrase is properly applied. **3** a less common word for **ostensible.** ORIG C17: from LL *ostentīvus,* from L *ostendere* to show; see OSTENSIBLE
▸ **os'tensively** *adv*

ostentation (ˌɒstɛn'teɪʃən) *n* pretentious, showy, or vulgar display.
▸ **ˌosten'tatious** *adj* ▸ **ˌosten'tatiously** *adv* ▸ **ˌosten'tatiousness** *n*

osteo- *or before a vowel* **oste-** *combining form.* indicating bone or bones. ORIG from Gk *osteon*

osteoarthritis (ˌɒstɪəʊɑː'θraɪtɪs) *n* chronic inflammation of the joints, esp. those that bear weight, with pain and stiffness.
▸ **osteoarthritic** (ˌɒstɪəʊɑː'θrɪtɪk) *adj, n*

osteology (ˌɒstɪ'ɒlədʒɪ) *n* the study of the structure and function of bones.
▸ **osteological** (ˌɒstɪə'lɒdʒɪkᵊl) *adj* ▸ **ˌosteo'logically** *adv* ▸ **ˌoste'ologist** *n*

osteoma (ˌɒstɪ'əʊmə) *n, pl* **osteomata** (-mətə) *or* **osteomas.** a benign tumour composed of bone or bonelike tissue.

osteomalacia (ˌɒstɪəʊmə'leɪʃɪə) *n* a disease characterized by softening of the bones, resulting from a deficiency of vitamin D and of calcium and phosphorus. ORIG C19: from NL, from OSTEO- + Gk *malakia* softness
▸ **ˌosteoma'lacial** *or* **osteomalacic** (ˌɒstɪəʊmə'læsɪk) *adj*

osteomyelitis (ˌɒstɪəʊˌmaɪɪ'laɪtɪs) *n* inflammation of bone marrow, caused by infection.

osteopathy (ˌɒstɪ'ɒpəθɪ) *n* a system of healing based on the manipulation of bones or other parts of the body.
▸ **'osteoˌpath** *n* ▸ **osteopathic** (ˌɒstɪə'pæθɪk) *adj* ▸ **ˌosteo'pathically** *adv*

osteoplasty ('ɒstɪəˌplæstɪ) *n, pl* **osteoplasties.** the branch of surgery concerned with bone repair or bone grafting.

osteoporosis (ˌɒstɪəʊpɔː'rəʊsɪs) *n* porosity and brittleness of the bones caused by loss of calcium from the bone matrix. ORIG C19: from OSTEO- + PORE[2] + -OSIS
▸ **osteoporotic** (ˌɒstɪəʊpɔː'rɒtɪk) *adj*

Österreich ★ ('øːstəraiç) *n* the German name for **Austria.**

Ostia ★ ('ɒstɪə) *n* an ancient town in W central Italy, originally at the mouth of the Tiber but now about 6 km (4 miles) inland: served as the port of ancient Rome; harbours built by Claudius and Trajan; ruins excavated since 1854.

ostinato (ˌɒstɪ'nɑːtəʊ) *n, pl* **ostinatos. a** a continuously reiterated musical phrase. **b** (*as modifier*): *an ostinato passage.* ORIG It.: from L *obstinātus* OBSTINATE

ostler *or* **hostler** ('ɒslə) *n Arch.* a stableman, esp. one at an inn. ORIG C15: var. of *hostler,* from HOSTEL

Ostmark ('ɒstmɑːk; *German* 'ɔstmark) *n* (formerly) the standard monetary unit of East Germany, divided into 100 pfennigs. ORIG G, lit.: east mark

Ostpreussen ★ ('ɔstprɔysən) *n* the German name for **East Prussia.**

ostracize *or* **ostracise** ('ɒstrəˌsaɪz) *vb* **ostracizes, ostracizing, ostracized** *or* **ostracises, ostracising, ostracised.** (*tr*) **1** to exclude or banish (a person) from a particular group, society, etc. **2** (in ancient Greece) to punish by temporary exile. ORIG C17: from Gk *ostrakizein* to select someone for banishment by voting on potsherds, from *ostrakon* potsherd
▸ **'ostracism** *n* ▸ **'ostraˌcizable** *or* **'ostraˌcisable** *adj* ▸ **'ostraˌcizer** *or* **'ostraˌciser** *n*

Ostrava ★ (*Czech* 'ɔstrava) *n* an industrial city in the E Czech Republic, on the River Oder: the chief coal-mining area in the Czech Republic, in Upper Silesia. Pop.: 324 813 (1996 est.).

ostrich ('ɒstrɪtʃ) *n, pl* **ostriches** *or* **ostrich. 1** a fast-running flightless African bird that is the largest living bird with stout two-toed feet and dark feathers, except on the naked head, neck, and legs. **2 American ostrich.** another name for **rhea. 3** a person who refuses to recognize the truth, reality, etc. ORIG C13: from OF *ostrice,* from L *avis* bird + LL *struthio* ostrich, from Gk *strouthion*

Ostwald ★ (*German* 'ɔstvalt) *n* **Wilhelm** ('vɪlhɛlm). 1853–1932, German chemist, noted for his pioneering work in catalysis: Nobel prize for chemistry 1909.

Osun ★ (əʊ'sʌn) *n* a state of SW Nigeria. Capital: Oshogbo. Pop.: 2 463 185 (1995 est.). Area: 9251 sq. km (3572 sq. miles).

Oswald ★ ('ɒzwəld) *n* **1 Saint.** ?605–41 A.D., king of Northumbria (634–41); with St Aidan he restored Christianity to the region. Feast day: Aug. 5. **2 Lee Harvey.** 1939–63, presumed assassin (1963) of US president John F. Kennedy; murdered by Jack Ruby two days later.

Oświęcim ★ (*Polish* ɔʃ'fjɛntʃim) *n* the Polish name for **Auschwitz.**

OT *abbrev. for:* **1** occupational therapy. **2** Old Testament. **3** overtime.

Otago ★ (ɒ'tɑːgəʊ) *n* a council region of New Zealand, formerly a province, founded by Scottish settlers in the south of South Island. The University of Otago (1869) in Dunedin is the oldest university in New Zealand. Chief town: Dunedin. Pop.: 191 684 (1996).

otalgia (əʊ'tældʒɪə, -dʒə) *n* the technical name for **earache.**

OTC (in Britain) *abbrev. for:* **1** Officers' Training Corps. **2** over-the-counter.

OTE *abbrev. for* on target earnings: referring to the salary a salesman should be able to achieve.

other ('ʌðə) *determiner* **1a** (when used before a singular noun, usually preceded by *the*) the remaining (one or ones in a group of which one or some have been specified): *I'll read the other sections of the paper later.* **1b the other.** (*as pron; functioning as sing*): *one walks while the other rides.* **2** (a) different (one or ones from that or those already specified or understood): *no other man but you.* **3** additional; further: *there are no other possibilities.* **4** (preceded by *every*) alternate; two: *it buzzes every other minute.* **5 other than. 5a** apart from; besides: *a lady other than his wife.* **5b** different from: *he couldn't be other than what he is.* Archaic form: **other from. 6 no other.** *Arch.* nothing else: *I can do no other.* **7 or other.** (preceded by a phrase or word with *some*) used to add vagueness to the preceding pronoun, noun, or noun phrase: *he's somewhere or other.* **8 other things being equal.** conditions being the same or unchanged. **9 the other day, night,** etc. a few days, nights, etc., ago. **10 the other thing.** an unexpressed alternative. ◆ *pron* **11** another: *show me one other.* **12** (*pl*) additional or further ones. **13** (*pl*) other people or things. **14 the others.** the remaining ones (of a group). ◆ *adv* **15** (usually used with a negative and foll. by *than*) otherwise; differently: *they couldn't behave other than they do.* ORIG OE *ōther*
▸ **'otherness** *n*

other-directed *adj* guided by values derived from external influences.

other ranks *pl n* (*rarely sing*) *Chiefly Brit.* (in the armed forces) all those who do not hold a commissioned rank.

otherwise ('ʌðəˌwaɪz) *sentence connector.* **1** or else; if not, then: *go home — otherwise your mother will worry.* ◆ *adv* **2** differently: *I wouldn't have thought otherwise.* **3** in other respects: *an otherwise hopeless situation.* ◆ *adj* **4** (*predicative*) of an unexpected nature; different: *the facts are otherwise.* ◆ *pron* **5** something different in outcome: *success or otherwise.* ORIG C14: from OE *on ōthre wīsan* in other manner

other world *n* the spirit world or afterlife.

otherworldly (ˌʌðə'wɜːldlɪ) *adj* **1** of or relating to the spiritual or imaginative world. **2** impractical or unworldly.
▸ **ˌother'worldliness** *n*

Othin ★ ('əʊðɪn) *n* a variant of **Odin.**

Othman ('ɒθmən, ɒθ'mɑːn) *adj, n* a variant of **Ottoman.**

Othman I ★ *n* a variant of **Osman I.**

Otho I ★ ('əʊθəʊ) *n* a variant of **Otto I.**

otic ('əʊtɪk, 'ɒtɪk) *adj* of or relating to the ear. ORIG C17: from Gk *ōtikos,* from *ous* ear

-otic *suffix forming adjectives.* **1** relating to or affected by: *sclerotic.* **2** causing: *narcotic.* ORIG from Gk *-ōtikos*

otiose ('əʊtɪˌəʊs, -ˌəʊz) *adj* **1** serving no useful purpose: *otiose language.* **2** *Rare.* indolent; lazy. ORIG C18: from L *ōtiōsus* leisured, from *ōtium* leisure
▸ **otiosity** (ˌəʊtɪ'ɒsɪtɪ) *or* **'otiˌoseness** *n*

★ people and places

otitis (əʊ'taɪtɪs) *n* inflammation of the ear.

oto- *or before a vowel* **ot-** *combining form.* indicating the ear. ORIG from Gk *ous, ōt-* ear

otolaryngology (ˌəʊtəʊˌlærɪŋ'gɒlədʒɪ) *n* another name for **otorhinolaryngology.**
▸ **otolaryngological** (ˌəʊtəʊləˌrɪŋgə'lɒdʒɪkᵊl) *adj* ▸ **ˌoto-ˌlaryn'gologist** *n*

otolith ('əʊtəʊˌlɪθ) *n* any of the granules of calcium carbonate in the inner ear of vertebrates. Movement of otoliths, caused by a change in the animal's position, stimulates sensory hair cells, which convey information to the brain.
▸ **ˌoto'lithic** *adj*

otology (əʊ'tɒlədʒɪ) *n* the branch of medicine concerned with the ear.
▸ **otological** (ˌəʊtə'lɒdʒɪkᵊl) *adj* ▸ **o'tologist** *n*

O'Toole ★ (əʊ'tu:l) *n* **(Seamus)** ('ʃeɪməs) **Peter.** born 1932, British actor, born in Ireland. His films include *Lawrence of Arabia* (1962), *The Lion in Winter* (1968), and *Fairytale* (1998).

otorhinolaryngology (ˌəʊtəʊˌraɪnəʊˌlærɪŋ'gɒlədʒɪ) *n* the branch of medicine concerned with the ear, nose, and throat. Sometimes called **otolaryngology.**

otoscope ('əʊtəʊˌskəʊp) *n* a medical instrument for examining the external ear.
▸ **otoscopic** (ˌəʊtəʊ'skɒpɪk) *adj*

Otranto ★ (*Italian* 'ɔ:tranto) *n* a small port in SE Italy, in Apulia on the **Strait of Otranto:** the most easterly town in Italy; an important Roman port. Pop.: 5075 (1987 est.).

OTT *Sl. abbrev. for* over the top: see **top**[1] (sense 16b).

ottava rima (əʊ'tɑ:və 'ri:mə) *n Prosody.* a stanza form consisting of eight iambic pentameter lines, rhyming a b a b a b c c. ORIG It.: eighth rhyme

Ottawa ★ ('ɒtəwə) *n* **1** the capital of Canada, in E Ontario on the Ottawa River: name changed from Bytown to Ottawa in 1854. Pop.: 313 987 (1991). **2** a river in central Canada, rising in W Quebec and flowing west, then southeast to join the St Lawrence River as its chief tributary at Montreal; forms the border between Quebec and Ontario for most of its length. Length: 1120 km (696 miles).

otter ('ɒtə) *n, pl* **otters** *or* **otter. 1** a freshwater carnivorous mammal, esp. the **Eurasian otter,** typically having smooth fur, a streamlined body, and webbed feet. **2** the fur of this animal. **3** a type of fishing tackle consisting of a weighted board to which hooked and baited lines are attached. ORIG OE *otor*

Otterburn ★ ('ɒtəˌbɜ:n) *n* a village in NE England, in central Northumberland: scene of a battle (1388) in which the Scots, led by the Earl of Douglas, defeated the English, led by Hotspur.

otter hound *n* a large rough-coated dog of a breed formerly used for otter hunting.

Otto ★ ('ɒtəʊ) *n* **Nikolaus August.** 1832–91, German engineer; invented the four-stroke engine.

Otto I *or* **Otho I** ★ *n* called *the Great.* 912–73 A.D., king of Germany (936–73); Holy Roman Emperor (962–73).

ottoman ('ɒtəmən) *n, pl* **ottomans. 1a** a low padded seat, usually armless, sometimes in the form of a chest. **1b** a cushioned footstool. **2** a corded fabric. ORIG C17: from F *ottomane,* fem. of OTTOMAN

Ottoman ('ɒtəmən) *or* **Othman** ('ɒθmən) *adj* **1** *History.* of or relating to the Ottomans or the Ottoman Empire. **2** denoting or relating to the Turkish language. ◆ *n, pl* **Ottomans** *or* **Othmans. 3** a member of a Turkish people who invaded the Near East in the late 13th century. ORIG C17: from F, via Med. L, from Ar. *Othmānī* Turkish, from Turkish *Othman* OSMAN I

Ottoman Empire *n* the former Turkish empire in Europe, Asia, and Africa, which lasted from the late 13th century until the end of World War I.

Otway ★ ('ɒtweɪ) *n* **Thomas.** 1652–85, English dramatist, noted for *Venice Preserv'd* (1682).

ou (əʊ) *n S. African. sl.* a man, bloke, or chap. ORIG from Afrik., ?from Du.

OU *abbrev. for:* **1** the Open University. **2** Oxford University.

Ouachita *or* **Washita** ★ ('wɒʃɪˌtɔ:) *n* a river in the S central US, rising in the **Ouachita Mountains** and flowing east, south, and southeast into the Red River in E Louisiana. Length: 974 km (605 miles).

Ouagadougou ★ (ˌwɑ:gə'du:gu:) *n* the capital of Burkina-Faso, on the central plateau: terminus of the railway from Abidjan (Côte d'Ivoire). Pop.: 690 000 (1993 est.).

ouananiche (ˌwɑ:nə'ni:ʃ) *n* a landlocked variety of the Atlantic salmon found in lakes in SE Canada. ORIG from Canad. F, of Amerind origin, from *wananish,* dim. of *wanans* salmon

oubaas ('əʊˌbɑ:s) *n S. African.* a man in authority. ORIG from Afrik., from Du. *oud* old + *baas* boss

Oubangui ★ (u:'bɑ:ŋgi:, ju:'bæŋgɪ) *n* the French name for **Ubangi.**

oubliette (ˌu:blɪ'et) *n* a dungeon, the only entrance to which is through the top. ORIG C19: from F, from *oublier* to forget

ouch (aʊtʃ) *interj* an exclamation of sharp sudden pain.

Oudh ★ (aʊd) *n* **1** a region of N India, in central Uttar Pradesh: annexed by Britain in 1856 and a centre of the Indian Mutiny (1857–58); joined with Agra in 1877, becoming the United Provinces of Agra and Oudh in 1902, which were renamed Uttar Pradesh in 1950. **2** another name for **Ayodha.**

Ouessant ★ (wɛsɑ̃) *n* the French name for **Ushant.**

ought[1] (ɔ:t) *vb* (foll. by *to; takes an infinitive or implied infinitive*) used as an auxiliary: **1** to indicate duty or obligation: *you ought to pay.* **2** to express prudent expediency: *you ought to be more careful with your money.* **3** (usually with reference to future time) to express probability or expectation: *you ought to finish this by Friday.* **4** to express a desire or wish on the part of the speaker: *you ought to come next week.* ORIG OE *āhte,* p.t. of *āgan* to OWE

> **USAGE NOTE** In correct English, *ought* is not used with *did* or *had. I ought not to do it,* not *I didn't ought to do it; I ought not to have done it,* not *I hadn't ought to have done it.*

ought[2] (ɔ:t) *pron, adv* a variant spelling of **aught.**

ought[3] (ɔ:t) *n* a less common word for **nought** (zero). ORIG C19: mistaken division of *a nought* as *an ought;* see NOUGHT

Ouija board ('wi:dʒə) *n Trademark.* a board on which are marked the letters of the alphabet. Answers to questions are spelt out by a pointer and are supposedly formed by spirits. ORIG C19: from F *oui* yes + G *ja* yes

Oujda ★ (u:dʒ'dɑ:) *n* a city in NE Morocco, near the border with Algeria: frontier post. Pop.: 146 142 (1994).

Oulu ★ ('ɔulu) *n* an industrial city and port in W Finland, on the Gulf of Bothnia: university (1959). Pop.: 111 556 (1997 est.). Swedish name: **Uleåborg.**

ouma ('əʊmɑ:) *n S. African.* **1** grandmother, esp. in titular use with her surname. **2** *Sl.* any elderly woman. ORIG from Afrik., from Du. *oma* grandmother

ounce[1] (aʊns) *n* **1** a unit of weight equal to one sixteenth of a pound (avoirdupois). Abbrev.: **oz. 2** a unit of weight equal to one twelfth of a Troy or Apothecaries' pound; 1 ounce is equal to 480 grains. **3** short for **fluid ounce. 4** a small portion or amount. ORIG C14: from OF *unce,* from L *uncia* a twelfth

ounce[2] (aʊns) *n* another name for **snow leopard.** ORIG C18: from OF *once,* by mistaken division of *lonce* as if *l'once,* from L LYNX

oupa ('əʊpɑ:) *n S. African.* **1** grandfather, esp. in titular use with surname. **2** *Sl.* any elderly man. ORIG Afrik.

our ('aʊə) *determiner* **1** of, belonging to, or associated in some way with us: *our best vodka; our parents are good to us.* **2** belonging to or associated with all people or people in general: *our nearest planet is Venus.* **3** a formal word for *my* used by editors or other writers, and monarchs. ORIG OE *ūre* (genitive pl), from US

-our *suffix forming nouns.* indicating state, condition, or activity: *behaviour; labour.* ORIG in OF *-eur*, from L *-or*, n. suffix

Our Father *n* another name for the **Lord's Prayer**, taken from its opening words.

ours ('auəz) *pron* **1** something or someone belonging to or associated with us: *ours have blue tags.* **2 of ours.** belonging to or associated with us.

ourself (auə'sɛlf) *pron Arch.* a variant of **myself**, formerly used by monarchs or editors.

ourselves (auə'sɛlvz) *pron* **1a** the reflexive form of *we* or *us.* **1b** (intensifier): *we ourselves will finish it.* **2** (*preceded by a copula*) our usual selves: *we are ourselves when we're together.* **3** *Not standard.* used instead of *we* or *us* in compound noun phrases: *other people and ourselves.*

-ous *suffix forming adjectives.* **1** having or full of: *dangerous; spacious.* **2** (in chemistry) indicating that an element is chemically combined in the lower of two possible valency states: *ferrous.* Cf. **-ic** (sense 2). ORIG from OF, from L *-ōsus* or *-us*, Gk *-os*, adj. suffixes

Ouse ★ (u:z) *n* **1** Also called: **Great Ouse.** a river in E England, rising in Northamptonshire and flowing northeast to the Wash near King's Lynn; for the last 56 km (35 miles) follows mainly artificial channels. Length: 257 km (160 miles). **2** a river in NE England, in Yorkshire, formed by the confluence of the Swale and Ure Rivers: flows southeast to the Humber. Length: 92 km (57 miles). **3** a river in S England, rising in Sussex and flowing south to the English Channel. Length: 48 km (30 miles).

ousel ('u:zᵊl) *n* a variant spelling of **ouzel**.

oust (aust) *vb* (*tr*) **1** to force out of a position or place; supplant or expel. **2** *Property law.* to deprive (a person) of the possession of land, etc. ORIG C16: from Anglo-Norman *ouster*, from L *obstāre* to withstand

ouster ('austə) *n Property law.* the act of dispossessing of freehold property; eviction.

out (aut) *adv* (*when predicative, can in some senses be regarded as adj*) **1** (*often used as a particle*) at or to a point beyond the limits of some location; outside: *get out at once.* **2** (*particle*) used to indicate exhaustion or extinction: *the sugar's run out; put the light out.* **3** not in a particular place, esp., not at home. **4** public; revealed: *the secret is out.* **5** on sale or on view to the public: *the book is being brought out next May.* **6** (of the sun, stars, etc.) visible. **7** in flower: *the roses are out now.* **8** not in fashion, favour, or current usage. **9** not or not any longer worth considering: *that plan is out.* **10** not allowed: *smoking on duty is out.* **11** (of a fire or light) no longer burning or providing illumination. **12** not working: *the radio's out.* **13** Also: **out on strike.** on strike. **14** (of a jury) withdrawn to consider a verdict in private. **15** (*particle*) out of consciousness: *she passed out.* **16** (*particle*) used to indicate a burst of activity as indicated by the verb: *fever broke out.* **17** (*particle*) used to indicate obliteration of an object: *the graffiti was painted out.* **18** (*particle*) used to indicate an approximate drawing or description: *chalk out.* **19** at or to the fullest length or extent: *spread out.* **20** loudly; clearly: *calling out.* **21** desirous of or intent on (something or doing something): *I'm out for as much money as I can get.* **22** (*particle*) used to indicate a goal or object achieved at the end of the action specified by the verb: *he worked it out.* **23** (*preceded by a superlative*) existing: *the friendliest dog out.* **24** an expression in signalling, radio, etc., to indicate the end of a transmission. **25** used up; exhausted: *our supplies are completely out.* **26** worn into holes: *out at the elbows.* **27** inaccurate, deficient, or discrepant: *out by six pence.* **28** not in office or authority. **29** completed or concluded, as of time: *before the year is out.* **30** *Obs.* (of a young woman) in or into society: *Lucinda had a large party when she came out.* **31** *Sport.* denoting the state in which a player is caused to discontinue active participation, esp. in some specified role. **32 out of. 32a** at or to a point outside: *out of his reach.* **32b** away from; not in: *stepping out of line; out of focus.* **32c** because of; motivated by: *out of jealousy.* **32d** from (a material or source): *made out of plastic.* **32e** not or no longer having any of (a substance, material, etc.): *we're out of sugar.* **32f** no longer in a specified state or condition: *out of work; out of practice.* **32g** (of a horse) born of. ◆ *adj* **33** directed or indicating direction outwards: *the out tray.* **34** (of an island) remote from the mainland. **35** *Inf.* not concealing one's homosexuality. ◆ *prep* **36** *Nonstandard or US.* out of; out through: *he ran out the door.* ◆ *interj* **37a** an exclamation of dismissal, reproach, etc. **37b** (in wireless telegraphy) an expression used to signal that the speaker is signing off. **38 out with it.** a command to make something known immediately, without missing any details. ◆ *n* **39** *Chiefly US.* a method of escape from a place, difficult situation, etc. **40** *Baseball.* an instance of causing a batter to be out by fielding. ◆ *vb* **41** (*tr*) to put or throw out. **42** (*intr*) to be made known or effective despite efforts to the contrary (esp. in **the truth will out**). **43** (*tr*) *Inf.* (of homosexuals) to expose (a public figure) as being a fellow homosexual. **44** *Inf.* to expose something secret, embarrassing, or unknown about (a person): *he was eventually outed as a talented goal scorer.* ORIG OE *ūt*

> **USAGE NOTE** The use of *out* as a preposition, though common in American English, is regarded as incorrect in British English: *he climbed out of* (not *out*) *a window; he went out through the door.*

out- *prefix* **1** excelling or surpassing in a particular action: *outlast; outlive.* **2** indicating an external location or situation away from the centre: *outpost; outpatient.* **3** indicating emergence, an issuing forth, etc.: *outcrop; outgrowth.* **4** indicating the result of an action: *outcome.*

outage ('autɪdʒ) *n* **1** a quantity of goods missing or lost after storage or shipment. **2** a period of power failure, machine stoppage, etc.

out and away *adv* by far.

out-and-out *adj* (*prenominal*) thoroughgoing; complete.

outback ('aut,bæk) *n* **a** the remote bush country of Australia. **b** (*as modifier*): *outback life.*

outbalance (,aut'bæləns) *vb* **outbalances, outbalancing, outbalanced.** another word for **outweigh**.

outboard ('aut,bɔ:d) *adj* **1** (of a boat's engine) portable, with its own propeller, and designed to be attached externally to the stern. **2** in a position away from, or further away from, the centre line of a vessel or aircraft, esp. outside the hull or fuselage. ◆ *adv* **3** away from the centre line of a vessel or aircraft, esp. outside the hull or fuselage. ◆ *n* **4** an outboard motor.

outbound ('aut,baund) *adj* going out; outward bound.

outbrave (,aut'breɪv) *vb* **outbraves, outbraving, outbraved.** (*tr*) **1** to surpass in bravery. **2** to confront defiantly.

outbreak ('aut,breɪk) *n* a sudden, violent, or spontaneous occurrence, esp. of disease or strife.

outbuilding ('aut,bɪldɪŋ) *n* a building separate from a main building; outhouse.

outburst ('aut,bɜ:st) *n* **1** a sudden and violent expression of emotion. **2** an explosion or eruption.

outcast ('aut,kɑ:st) *n* **1** a person who is rejected or excluded from a social group. **2** a vagabond or wanderer. **3** anything thrown out or rejected. ◆ *adj* **4** rejected, abandoned, or discarded; cast out.

outcaste ('aut,kɑ:st) *n* **1** a person who has been expelled from a caste. **2** a person having no caste. ◆ *vb* **outcastes, outcasting, outcasted. 3** (*tr*) to cause (someone) to lose his or her caste.

outclass (,aut'klɑ:s) *vb* (*tr*) **1** to surpass in class, quality, etc. **2** to defeat easily.

outcome ('aut,kʌm) *n* something that follows from an action or situation; result; consequence.

outcrop *n* ('aut,krɒp). **1** part of a rock formation or mineral vein that appears at the surface of the earth. **2** an emergence; appearance. ◆ *vb* (,aut'krɒp), **outcrops, outcropping, outcropped. 3** (*intr*) (of rock strata, mineral veins, etc.) to protrude through the surface of the earth.

outcry *n* ('aut,kraɪ), *pl* **outcries. 1** a widespread or vehement protest. **2** clamour; uproar. **3** *Commerce.* a method of trading in which dealers shout out bids and offers at a prearranged meeting: *sale by open outcry.* ◆ *vb* (,aut'kraɪ),

★ people and places

outcries, outcrying, outcried. (*tr*) **4** to cry louder or make more noise than (someone or something).

outdated (ˌaʊtˈdeɪtɪd) *adj* old-fashioned or obsolete.

outdo (ˌaʊtˈduː) *vb* **outdoes, outdoing, outdid, outdone.** (*tr*) to surpass or exceed in performance.

outdoor (ˈaʊtˈdɔː) *adj* (*prenominal*) taking place, existing, or intended for use in the open air: *outdoor games; outdoor clothes.* Also: **out-of-door.**

outdoors (ˌaʊtˈdɔːz) *adv* **1** Also: **out-of-doors.** in the open air; outside. ◆ *n* **2** the world outside or far away from human habitation.

outer (ˈaʊtə) *adj* (*prenominal*) **1** being or located on the outside; external. **2** further from the middle or central part. ◆ *n* **3** *Archery.* **3a** the white outermost ring on a target. **3b** a shot that hits this ring. **4** *Austral. & NZ.* the unsheltered part of the spectator area at a sports ground. **5** **on the outer.** *Austral. & NZ.* excluded or neglected.

outer bar *n* (in England) a collective name for junior barristers who plead from outside the bar of the court.

Outer Hebrides ★ *pl n* See **Hebrides.**

Outer Mongolia ★ *n* the former name (until 1924) of (the republic of) **Mongolia.**

outermost (ˈaʊtəˌməʊst) *adj* furthest from the centre or middle; outmost.

outer space *n* any region of space beyond the atmosphere of the earth.

outfall (ˈaʊtˌfɔːl) *n* the end of a river, sewer, drain, etc., from which it discharges.

outfield (ˈaʊtˌfiːld) *n* **1** *Cricket.* the area of the field relatively far from the pitch; the deep. Cf. **infield** (sense 1). **2** *Baseball.* **2a** the area of the playing field beyond the lines connecting first, second, and third bases. **2b** the positions of the left fielder, centre fielder, and right fielder taken collectively. **3** *Agriculture.* farmland most distant from the farmstead.
▸ **ˈoutˌfielder** *n*

outfit (ˈaʊtˌfɪt) *n* **1** a set of articles or equipment for a particular task, etc. **2** a set of clothes, esp. a carefully selected one. **3** *Inf.* any group or association regarded as a cohesive unit, such as a military company, etc. ◆ *vb* **outfits, outfitting, outfitted.** **4** to furnish or be furnished with an outfit, equipment, etc.
▸ **ˈoutˌfitter** *n*

outflank (ˌaʊtˈflæŋk) *vb* (*tr*) **1** to go around the flank of (an opposing army, etc.). **2** to get the better of.

outflow (ˈaʊtˌfləʊ) *n* **1** anything that flows out, such as liquid, money, etc. **2** the amount that flows out. **3** the act or process of flowing out.

outfox (ˌaʊtˈfɒks) *vb* (*tr*) to surpass in guile or cunning.

outgeneral (ˌaʊtˈdʒenərəl) *vb* **outgenerals, outgeneralling, outgeneralled** *or US* **outgenerals, outgeneraling, outgeneraled.** (*tr*) to surpass in generalship.

outgo *vb* (ˌaʊtˈgəʊ), **outgoes, outgoing, outwent, outgone. 1** (*tr*) to exceed or outstrip. ◆ *n* (ˈaʊtˌgəʊ). **2** cost; outgoings; outlay. **3** something that goes out; outflow.

outgoing (ˈaʊtˌgəʊɪŋ) *adj* **1** departing; leaving. **2** retiring from office. **3** friendly and sociable. ◆ *n* **4** the act of going out.

outgoings (ˈaʊtˌgəʊɪŋz) *pl n* expenditure.

outgrow (ˌaʊtˈgrəʊ) *vb* **outgrows, outgrowing, outgrew, outgrown.** (*tr*) **1** to grow too large for (clothes, shoes, etc.). **2** to lose (a habit, idea, reputation, etc.) in the course of development or time. **3** to grow larger or faster than.

outgrowth (ˈaʊtˌgrəʊθ) *n* **1** a thing growing out of a main body. **2** a development, result, or consequence. **3** the act of growing out.

outgun (ˌaʊtˈgʌn) *vb* **outguns, outgunning, outgunned.** (*tr*) **1** to surpass in fire power. **2** to surpass in shooting. **3** *Inf.* to surpass or excel.

outhouse (ˈaʊtˌhaʊs) *n* a building near to, but separate from, a main building; outbuilding.

outing (ˈaʊtɪŋ) *n* **1** a short outward and return journey; trip; excursion. **2** *Inf.* the naming by homosexuals of other prominent homosexuals, often against their will.

outjockey (ˌaʊtˈdʒɒkɪ) *vb* (*tr*) to outwit by deception.

outlandish (aʊtˈlændɪʃ) *adj* **1** grotesquely unconventional in appearance, habits, etc. **2** *Arch.* foreign.
▸ **outˈlandishly** *adv* ▸ **outˈlandishness** *n*

outlast (ˌaʊtˈlɑːst) *vb* (*tr*) to last longer than.

outlaw (ˈaʊtˌlɔː) *n* **1** (formerly) a person excluded from the law and deprived of its protection. **2** any fugitive from the law, esp. a habitual transgressor. ◆ *vb* (*tr*) **3** to put (a person) outside the law and deprive of its protection. **4** to ban.
▸ **ˈoutˌlawry** *n*

outlay *n* (ˈaʊtˌleɪ). **1** an expenditure of money, effort, etc. ◆ *vb* (ˌaʊtˈleɪ), **outlays, outlaying, outlaid. 2** (*tr*) to spend (money, etc.).

outlet (ˈaʊtlɛt, -lɪt) *n* **1** an opening or vent permitting escape or release. **2a** a market for a product or service. **2b** a commercial establishment retailing the goods of a particular producer or wholesaler. **3** a channel that drains a body of water. **4** a point in a wiring system from which current can be taken to supply electrical devices.

outlier (ˈaʊtˌlaɪə) *n* **1** an outcrop of rocks that is entirely surrounded by older rocks. **2** a person, thing, or part situated away from a main or related body. **3** a person who lives away from his or her place of work, duty, etc.

outline (ˈaʊtˌlaɪn) *n* **1** a preliminary or schematic plan, draft, etc. **2** (*usually pl*) the important features of a theory, work, etc. **3** the line by which an object or figure is or appears to be bounded. **4a** a drawing or manner of drawing consisting only of external lines. **4b** (*as modifier*): *an outline map.* ◆ *vb* **outlines, outlining, outlined.** (*tr*) **5** to draw or display the outline of. **6** to give the main features or general idea of.

outlive (ˌaʊtˈlɪv) *vb* **outlives, outliving, outlived.** (*tr*) **1** to live longer than (someone). **2** to live beyond (a date or period): *he outlived the century.* **3** to live through (an experience).

outlook (ˈaʊtˌlʊk) *n* **1** a mental attitude or point of view. **2** the probable or expected condition or outcome of something: *the weather outlook.* **3** the view from a place. **4** view or prospect. **5** the act or state of looking out.

outlying (ˈaʊtˌlaɪɪŋ) *adj* distant or remote from the main body or centre, as of a town or region.

outmanoeuvre *or US* **outmaneuver** (ˌaʊtməˈnuːvə) *vb* **outmanoeuvres, outmanoeuvring, outmanoeuvred** *or US* **outmaneuvers, outmaneuvering, outmaneuvered.** (*tr*) to secure a strategic advantage over by skilful manoeuvre.

outmoded (ˌaʊtˈməʊdɪd) *adj* no longer fashionable or widely accepted.
▸ **ˌoutˈmodedly** *adv* ▸ **ˌoutˈmodedness** *n*

outmost (ˈaʊtˌməʊst) *adj* another word for **outermost.**

out of bounds *adj* (*postpositive*), *adv* **1** (often foll. by *to*) not to be entered (by); barred (to). **2** outside specified or prescribed limits.

out of date *adj* (**out-of-date** *when prenominal*), *adv* no longer valid, current, or fashionable; outmoded.

out-of-door *adj* (*prenominal*) another term for **outdoor.**

out-of-doors *adv, adj* (*postpositive*) in the open air; outside. Also: **outdoors.**

out of pocket *adj* (**out-of-pocket** *when prenominal*). **1** (*postpositive*) having lost money, as in a commercial enterprise. **2** without money to spend. **3** (*prenominal*) (of expenses) unbudgeted and paid for in cash.

out of the way *adj* (**out-of-the-way** *when prenominal*). **1** distant from more populous areas. **2** uncommon or unusual.

outpace (ˌaʊtˈpeɪs) *vb* **outpaces, outpacing, outpaced.** (*tr*) **1** to go faster than (someone). **2** to surpass or outdo (something or someone) in growth, development. etc.

outpatient (ˈaʊtˌpeɪʃənt) *n* a nonresident hospital patient. Cf. **inpatient.**

outperform (ˌaʊtpəˈfɔːm) *vb* (*tr*) to outdo or surpass in a specified field or activity.

outplacement (ˈaʊtˌpleɪsmənt) *n* a service that offers counselling and careers advice, esp. to redundant executives, which is paid for by their previous employer.

outpoint (ˌaʊtˈpɔɪnt) *vb* (*tr*) to score more points than.

outport (ˈaʊtˌpɔːt) *n* **1** *Chiefly Brit.* a subsidiary port built in deeper water than the original port. **2** *Canad.* a small fishing village of Newfoundland.

outpost ('aʊtˌpəʊst) *n* **1** *Mil.* **1a** a position stationed at a distance from the area occupied by a major formation. **1b** the troops assigned to such a position. **2** an outlying settlement or position.

outpour *n* ('aʊtˌpɔː). **1** the act of flowing or pouring out. **2** something that pours out. ◆ *vb* (ˌaʊt'pɔː). **3** to pour or cause to pour out freely or rapidly.

outpouring ('aʊtˌpɔːrɪŋ) *n* **1** a passionate or exaggerated outburst; effusion. **2** another word for **outpour** (senses 1, 2).

output ('aʊtˌpʊt) *n* **1** the act of production or manufacture. **2** the amount produced, as in a given period: *a weekly output.* **3** the material produced, manufactured, etc. **4** *Electronics.* **4a** the power, voltage, or current delivered by a circuit or component. **4b** the point at which the signal is delivered. **5** the power, energy, or work produced by an engine or a system. **6** *Computing.* **6a** the information produced by a computer. **6b** the operations and devices involved in producing this information. **7** (*modifier*) of or relating to electronic or computer output: *output signal.* ◆ *vb* **outputs, outputting, outputted** *or* **output. 8** (*tr*) *Computing.* to cause (data) to be emitted as output.

outrage ('aʊtˌreɪdʒ) *n* **1** a wantonly vicious or cruel act. **2** a gross violation of decency, morality, honour, etc. **3** profound indignation, anger, or hurt, caused by such an act. ◆ *vb* **outrages, outraging, outraged.** (*tr*) **4** to cause profound indignation, anger, or resentment in. **5** to offend grossly. **6** to commit an act of wanton viciousness, cruelty, or indecency on. **7** a euphemistic word for **rape**[1]. ORIG C13 (meaning: excess): via F from *outré* beyond, from L *ultrā*

outrageous (aʊt'reɪdʒəs) *adj* **1** being or having the nature of an outrage. **2** grossly offensive to decency, authority, etc. **3** violent or unrestrained in behaviour or temperament. **4** extravagant or immoderate.
▸ **out'rageously** *adv* ▸ **out'rageousness** *n*

outrank (ˌaʊt'ræŋk) *vb* (*tr*) **1** to be of higher rank than. **2** to take priority over.

outré ('uːtreɪ) *adj* deviating from what is usual or proper. ORIG C18: from F, p.p. of *outrer* to pass beyond

outride (ˌaʊt'raɪd) *vb* **outrides, outriding, outrode, outridden.** (*tr*) **1** to outdo by riding faster, farther, or better than. **2** (of a vessel) to ride out (a storm).

outrider ('aʊtˌraɪdə) *n* **1** a person who goes in advance to investigate, discover a way, etc.; scout. **2** a person who rides in front of or beside a carriage, esp. as an attendant or guard. **3** *US.* a mounted herdsman.

outrigger ('aʊtˌrɪgə) *n* **1** a framework for supporting a pontoon outside and parallel to the hull of a boat to provide stability. **2** a boat equipped with such a framework, esp. one of the canoes of the South Pacific. **3** any projecting framework attached to a boat, aircraft, building, etc., to act as a support. **4** *Rowing.* another name for **rigger** (sense 2). ORIG C18: from OUT- + RIG + -ER[1]

outright *adj* ('aʊtˌraɪt). (*prenominal*) **1** without qualifications or limitations: *outright ownership.* **2** complete; total. **3** straightforward; direct. ◆ *adv* (ˌaʊt'raɪt). **4** without restrictions. **5** without reservation or concealment: *ask outright.* **6** instantly: *he was killed outright.*

outrush ('aʊtˌrʌʃ) *n* a flowing or rushing out.

outset ('aʊtˌsɛt) *n* a start; beginning (esp. in **from** (*or* **at**) **the outset**).

outside *prep* (ˌaʊt'saɪd). **1** (sometimes foll. by *of*) on or to the exterior of: *outside the house.* **2** beyond the limits of. **3** apart from; other than: *no-one knows outside you.* ◆ *adj* ('aʊtˌsaɪd). **4** (*prenominal*) situated on the exterior: *an outside lavatory.* **5** remote; unlikely. **6** not a member of. **7** the greatest possible or probable (prices, odds, etc.). **8** (of a road lane, esp. in a dual carriageway or motorway) situated nearer or nearest to the central reservation, for use by faster or overtaking vehicles. ◆ *adv* (ˌaʊt'saɪd). **9** outside a specified thing or place; out of doors. **10** *Sl.* not in prison. ◆ *n* ('aʊt'saɪd). **11** the external side or surface. **12** the external appearance or aspect. **13** (of a pavement, etc.) the side nearest the road or away from a wall. **14** *Sport.* an outside player, as in football. **15** (*pl*) the outer sheets of a ream of paper. **16** *Canad.* (in the north) the settled parts of Canada. **17 at the outside.** *Inf.* at the most or at the greatest extent: *two days at the outside.*

> **USAGE NOTE** The use of *outside of* and *inside of*, although fairly common, is generally thought to be incorrect or nonstandard: *She waits outside* (not *outside of*) *the school.*

outside broadcast *n Radio, television.* a broadcast not made from a studio.

outside director *n* a director of a company who is not employed by that company but is often employed by a holding or associated company.

outsider (ˌaʊt'saɪdə) *n* **1** a person or thing excluded from or not a member of a set, group, etc. **2** a contestant, esp. a horse, thought unlikely to win in a race. **3** *Canad.* a person who does not live in the Arctic regions.

outsize ('aʊtˌsaɪz) *adj* **1** Also: **outsized.** very large or larger than normal. ◆ *n* **2** something outsize, such as a garment or person. **3** (*modifier*) relating to or dealing in outsize clothes: *an outsize shop.*

outskirts ('aʊtˌskɜːts) *pl n* (*sometimes sing*) outlying or bordering areas, districts, etc., as of a city.

outsmart (ˌaʊt'smɑːt) *vb* (*tr*) *Inf.* to get the better of; outwit.

outspan *S. African.* ◆ *n* ('aʊtˌspæn). **1** an area on a farm kept available for travellers to rest and refresh animals, etc. **2** the act of unharnessing or unyoking. ◆ *vb* (ˌaʊt'spæn), **outspans, outspanning, outspanned. 3** to unharness or unyoke (animals). ORIG C19: partial translation of Afrik. *uitspan,* from *uit* out + *spannen* to stretch

outspoken (ˌaʊt'spəʊkən) *adj* **1** candid or bold in speech. **2** said or expressed with candour or boldness.

outspread *vb* (ˌaʊt'sprɛd), **outspreads, outspreading, outspread. 1** to spread out. ◆ *adj* ('aʊt'sprɛd). **2** spread or stretched out. **3** scattered or diffused widely. ◆ *n* ('aʊtˌsprɛd). **4** a spreading out.

outstanding (ˌaʊt'stændɪŋ) *adj* **1** superior; excellent. **2** prominent, remarkable, or striking. **3** unsettled, unpaid, or unresolved. **4** (of shares, bonds, etc.) issued and sold. **5** projecting or jutting upwards or outwards.
▸ ˌ**out'standingly** *adv*

outstare (ˌaʊt'stɛə) *vb* **outstares, outstaring, outstared.** (*tr*) **1** to outdo in staring. **2** to disconcert by staring.

outstation ('aʊtˌsteɪʃən) *n* a station or post at a distance from the base station or in a remote region.

outstay (ˌaʊt'steɪ) *vb* (*tr*) **1** to stay longer than. **2** to stay beyond (a limit). **3 outstay one's welcome.** See **overstay** (sense 2).

outstretch (ˌaʊt'strɛtʃ) *vb* (*tr*) **1** to extend or expand; stretch out. **2** to stretch or extend beyond.

outstrip (ˌaʊt'strɪp) *vb* **outstrips, outstripping, outstripped.** (*tr*) **1** to surpass in a sphere of activity, competition, etc. **2** to be or grow greater than. **3** to go faster than and leave behind.

outtake ('aʊtˌteɪk) *n* an unreleased take from a recording session, film, or television programme.

out there *adj* (**out-there** *when prenominal*) *Sl.* unconventional or eccentric: *he blends sublime pop moments with some real out-there stuff.*

out-tray *n* (in an office, etc.) a tray for outgoing correspondence, documents, etc.

outturn ('aʊtˌtɜːn) *n* another word for **output** (sense 2).

outvote (ˌaʊt'vəʊt) *vb* **outvotes, outvoting, outvoted.** (*tr*) to defeat by a majority of votes.

outward ('aʊtwəd) *adj* **1** of or relating to what is apparent or superficial. **2** of or relating to the outside of the body. **3** belonging or relating to the external, as opposed to the mental, spiritual, or inherent. **4** of, relating to, or directed towards the outside or exterior. **5 the outward man. 5a** *Theol.* the body as opposed to the soul. **5b** *Facetious.* clothing. ◆ *adv* **6** (of a ship) away from port. **7** a variant of **outwards.** ◆ *n* **8** the outward part; exterior.
▸ **'outwardness** *n*

Outward Bound movement *n Trademark.* (in Britain) a scheme to provide adventure training for young people.

outwardly (ˈaʊtwədlɪ) *adv* **1** in outward appearance. **2** with reference to the outside or outer surface; externally.

outwards (ˈaʊtwədz) *or* **outward** *adv* towards the outside; out.

outwear (ˌaʊtˈwɛə) *vb* **outwears, outwearing, outwore, outworn.** (*tr*) **1** to use up or destroy by wearing. **2** to last or wear longer than. **3** to outlive, outgrow, or develop beyond. **4** to deplete or exhaust in strength, determination, etc.

outweigh (ˌaʊtˈweɪ) *vb* (*tr*) **1** to prevail over; overcome. **2** to be more important or significant than. **3** to be heavier than.

outwit (ˌaʊtˈwɪt) *vb* **outwits, outwitting, outwitted.** (*tr*) to get the better of by cunning or ingenuity.

outwith (ˌaʊtˈwɪθ) *prep Scot.* outside; beyond.

outwork *n* (ˈaʊtˌwɜːk). **1** (*often pl*) defences which lie outside main defensive works. **2** work done away from the factory, etc., by which it has been commissioned. ◆ *vb* (ˌaʊtˈwɜːk). (*tr*) **3** to work better, harder, etc., than. **4** to work out to completion.
▸ **ˈoutˌworker** *n*

ouzel *or* **ousel** (ˈuːzᵊl) *n* **1** short for **water ouzel.** See **dipper** (sense 2). **2** an archaic name for the (European) **blackbird.** ORIG OE *ōsle*

ouzo (ˈuːzəʊ) *n, pl* **ouzos.** a strong aniseed-flavoured spirit from Greece. ORIG Mod. Gk *ouzon,* from ?

ova (ˈəʊvə) *n* the plural of **ovum.**

oval (ˈəʊvᵊl) *adj* **1** having the shape of an ellipse or ellipsoid. ◆ *n* **2** anything that is oval in shape, such as a sports ground. **3** *Austral.* **3a** an Australian Rules ground. **3b** any sports field. ORIG C16: from Med. L *ōvālis,* from L *ōvum* egg
▸ **ˈovally** *adv* ▸ **ˈovalness** *or* **ovality** (əʊˈvælɪtɪ) *n*

Oval ★ (ˈəʊvᵊl) *n* **the.** a cricket ground in the S London borough of Lambeth.

ovariectomy (əʊˌvɛərɪˈɛktəmɪ) *n, pl* **ovariectomies.** *Surgery.* surgical removal of an ovary or ovarian tumour.

ovary (ˈəʊvərɪ) *n, pl* **ovaries. 1** either of the two female reproductive organs, which produce ova and secrete oestrogen hormones. **2** the corresponding organ in vertebrate and invertebrate animals. **3** *Bot.* the hollow basal region of a carpel containing one or more ovules. ORIG C17: from NL *ōvārium,* from L *ōvum* egg
▸ **ovarian** (əʊˈvɛərɪən) *adj*

ovate (ˈəʊveɪt) *adj* **1** shaped like an egg. **2** (esp. of a leaf) shaped like the longitudinal section of an egg, with the broader end at the base. ORIG C18: from L *ōvātus* egg-shaped
▸ **ˈovately** *adv*

ovation (əʊˈveɪʃən) *n* **1** an enthusiastic reception, esp. one of prolonged applause. **2** a victory procession less glorious than a triumph awarded to a Roman general. ORIG C16: from L *ovātiō* rejoicing, from *ovāre* to exult
▸ **oˈvational** *adj*

oven (ˈʌvᵊn) *n* **1** an enclosed heated compartment or receptacle for baking or roasting food. **2** a similar device, usually lined with a refractory material, used for drying substances, firing ceramics, heat-treating, etc. ◆ *vb* **3** (*tr*) to cook in an oven. ORIG OE *ofen*
▸ **ˈoven-ˌlike** *adj*

ovenable (ˈʌvᵊnəbᵊl) *adj* suitable for cooking in or using in an oven.

ovenbird (ˈʌvᵊnˌbɜːd) *n* **1** any of numerous small brownish South American passerine birds that build oven-shaped clay nests. **2** a common North American warbler that has an olive-brown striped plumage with an orange crown and builds a cup-shaped nest on the ground.

oven-ready *adj* (of various foods) bought already prepared so that they are ready to be cooked in the oven.

ovenware (ˈʌvᵊnˌwɛə) *n* heat-resistant dishes in which food can be both cooked and served.

over (ˈəʊvə) *prep* **1** directly above; on the top of; via the top or upper surface of: *over one's head.* **2** on or to the other side of: *over the river.* **3** during; through or throughout (a period of time). **4** in or throughout all parts of: *to travel over England.* **5** throughout the whole extent of: *over the racecourse.* **6** above; in preference to. **7** by the agency of (an instrument of telecommunication): *over the radio.* **8** more than: *over a century ago.* **9** on the subject of; about: *an argument over nothing.* **10** while occupied in: *discussing business over golf.* **11** having recovered from the effects of. **12 over and above.** added to; in addition to. ◆ *adv* **13** in a state, condition, situation, or position that is placed or put over something: *to climb over.* **14** (*particle*) so as to cause to fall: *knocking over a policeman.* **15** at or to a point across intervening space, water, etc. **16** throughout a whole area: *the world over.* **17** (*particle*) from beginning to end, usually cursorily: *to read a document over.* **18** throughout a period of time: *stay over for this week.* **19** (esp. in signalling and radio) it is now your turn to speak, act, etc. **20** more than is expected or usual: *not over well.* **21 over again.** once more. **22 over against. 22a** opposite to. **22b** contrasting with. **23 over and over.** (often foll. by *again*) repeatedly. ◆ *adj* **24** (*postpositive*) finished; no longer in progress. ◆ *adv, adj* **25** remaining; surplus (often in **left over**). ◆ *n* **26** *Cricket.* **26a** a series of six balls bowled by a bowler from the same end of the pitch. **26b** the play during this. ORIG OE *ofer*

over- *prefix* **1** excessive or excessively; beyond an agreed or desirable limit: *overcharge; overdue.* **2** indicating superior rank: *overseer.* **3** indicating location or movement above: *overhang.* **4** indicating movement downwards: *overthrow.*

overage (ˌəʊvərˈeɪdʒ) *adj* beyond a specified age.

overall *adj* (ˈəʊvərˌɔːl). (*prenominal*) **1** from one end to the other. **2** including or covering everything: *the overall cost.* ◆ *adv* (ˌəʊvərˈɔːl). **3** in general; on the whole. ◆ *n* (ˈəʊvərˌɔːl). **4** *Brit.* a protective work garment usually worn over ordinary clothes. **5** (*pl*) hard-wearing work trousers with a bib and shoulder straps or jacket attached.

overarch (ˌəʊvərˈɑːtʃ) *vb* (*tr*) to form an arch over.

overarching (ˌəʊvərˈɑːtʃɪŋ) *adj* overall; all-encompassing: *an overarching concept.*

overarm (ˈəʊvərˌɑːm) *adj* **1** *Sport, esp. cricket.* bowled, thrown, or performed with the arm raised above the shoulder. ◆ *adv* **2** with the arm raised above the shoulder.

overawe (ˌəʊvərˈɔː) *vb* **overawes, overawing, overawed.** (*tr*) to subdue, restrain, or overcome by affecting with a feeling of awe.

overbalance *vb* (ˌəʊvəˈbæləns), **overbalances, overbalancing, overbalanced. 1** to lose or cause to lose balance. **2** (*tr*) another word for **outweigh.** ◆ *n* (ˈəʊvəˌbæləns). **3** excess of weight, value, etc.

overbear (ˌəʊvəˈbɛə) *vb* **overbears, overbearing, overbore, overborne. 1** (*tr*) to dominate or overcome. **2** (*tr*) to press or bear down with weight or physical force. **3** to produce (fruit, etc.) excessively.

overbearing (ˌəʊvəˈbɛərɪŋ) *adj* **1** domineering or dictatorial in manner or action. **2** of particular or overriding importance or significance.
▸ **ˌoverˈbearingly** *adv*

overblown (ˌəʊvəˈbləʊn) *adj* **1** overdone or excessive. **2** bombastic; turgid: *overblown prose.* **3** (of flowers) past the stage of full bloom.

overboard (ˈəʊvəˌbɔːd) *adv* **1** from on board a vessel into the water. **2 go overboard.** *Inf.* **2a** to be extremely enthusiastic. **2b** to go to extremes. **3 throw overboard.** to reject or abandon.

overbook (ˌəʊvəˈbʊk) *vb* (*tr, also absol.*) to make more reservations than there are places, tickets, etc., available.

overbuild (ˌəʊvəˈbɪld) *vb* **overbuilds, overbuilding, overbuilt.** (*tr*) **1** to build over or on top of. **2** to erect too many buildings in (an area). **3** to build too large or elaborately.

overburden *vb* (ˌəʊvəˈbɜːdᵊn). **1** (*tr*) to load with excessive weight, work, etc. ◆ *n* (ˈəʊvəˌbɜːdᵊn). **2** an excessive burden or load. **3** *Geol.* the sedimentary rock material that covers coal seams, mineral veins, etc.
▸ **ˌoverˈburdensome** *adj*

overcast *adj* (ˈəʊvəˌkɑːst). **1** covered over or obscured, esp. by clouds. **2** *Meteorol.* (of the sky) cloud-covered. **3**

★ people and places

gloomy or melancholy. **4** sewn over by overcasting. ◆ *vb* (ˌəʊvəˈkɑːst), **overcasts, overcasting, overcast. 5** to sew (an edge, as of a hem) with long stitches passing successively over the edge. ◆ *n* (ˈəʊvəˌkɑːst). **6** *Meteorol.* the state of the sky when it is cloud-covered.

overcharge *vb* (ˌəʊvəˈtʃɑːdʒ), **overcharges, overcharging, overcharged. 1** to charge too much. **2** (*tr*) to fill or load beyond capacity. **3** *Literary.* another word for **exaggerate.** ◆ *n* (ˈəʊvəˌtʃɑːdʒ). **4** an excessive price or charge. **5** an excessive load.

overcloud (ˌəʊvəˈklaʊd) *vb* **1** to make or become covered with clouds. **2** to make or become dark or dim.

overcoat (ˈəʊvəˌkəʊt) *n* a warm heavy coat worn over the outer clothes in cold weather.

overcome (ˌəʊvəˈkʌm) *vb* **overcomes, overcoming, overcame, overcome. 1** (*tr*) to get the better of in a conflict. **2** (*tr; often passive*) to render incapable or powerless by laughter, sorrow, exhaustion, etc. **3** (*tr*) to surmount obstacles, objections, etc. **4** (*intr*) to be victorious.

overcrop (ˌəʊvəˈkrɒp) *vb* **overcrops, overcropping, overcropped.** (*tr*) to exhaust (land) by excessive cultivation.

overdo (ˌəʊvəˈduː) *vb* **overdoes, overdoing, overdid, overdone.** (*tr*) **1** to take or carry too far; do to excess. **2** to exaggerate, overelaborate, or overplay. **3** to cook or bake too long. **4 overdo it** *or* **things.** to overtax one's strength, capacity, etc.

overdose *n* (ˈəʊvəˌdəʊs). **1** (esp. of drugs) an excessive dose. ◆ *vb* (ˌəʊvəˈdəʊs), **overdoses, overdosing, overdosed. 2** to take an excessive dose or give an excessive dose to.
▸ **ˌoverˈdosage** *n*

overdraft (ˈəʊvəˌdrɑːft) *n* **1** a deficit in a bank or building-society cheque account caused by withdrawing more money than is credited to it. **2** the amount of this deficit.

overdraw (ˌəʊvəˈdrɔː) *vb* **overdraws, overdrawing, overdrew, overdrawn. 1** to draw on (a bank account) in excess of the credit balance. **2** (*tr*) to exaggerate in describing or telling.

overdress *vb* (ˌəʊvəˈdrɛs). **1** to dress (oneself or another) too elaborately or finely. ◆ *n* (ˈəʊvəˌdrɛs). **2** a dress that may be worn over a jumper, blouse, etc.

overdrive *n* (ˈəʊvəˌdraɪv). **1** a very high gear in a motor vehicle used at high speeds to reduce wear. ◆ *vb* (ˌəʊvəˈdraɪv), **overdrives, overdriving, overdrove, overdriven. 2** (*tr*) to drive too hard or too far; overwork or overuse.

overdub (in multitrack recording) ◆ *vb* (ˌəʊvəˈdʌb), **overdubs, overdubbing, overdubbed. 1** to add (new sound) on a spare track or tracks. ◆ *n* (ˈəʊvəˌdʌb). **2** the blending of various layers of sound in one recording by this method.

overdue (ˌəʊvəˈdjuː) *adj* past the time specified, required, or preferred for arrival, occurrence, payment, etc.

overestimate *vb* (ˌəʊvərˈɛstɪˌmeɪt), **overestimates, overestimating, overestimated. 1** (*tr*) to estimate too highly. ◆ *n* (ˌəʊvərˈɛstɪmɪt). **2** an estimate that is too high.
▸ **ˌoverˌestiˈmation** *n*

overexpose (ˌəʊvərɪksˈpəʊz) *vb* **overexposes, overexposing, overexposed.** (*tr*) **1** to expose too much or for too long. **2** *Photog.* to expose (a film, etc.) for too long or with too bright a light.
▸ **ˌoverexˈposure** *n*

overflow *vb* (ˌəʊvəˈfləʊ), **overflows, overflowing, overflowed** *or* (*formerly*) **overflown. 1** to flow or run over (a limit, brim, etc.). **2** to fill or be filled beyond capacity so as to spill or run over. **3** (*intr;* usually foll. by *with*) to be filled with happiness, tears, etc. **4** (*tr*) to spread or cover over; flood or inundate. ◆ *n* (ˈəʊvəˌfləʊ). **5** overflowing matter, esp. liquid. **6** any outlet that enables surplus liquid to be discharged or drained off. **7** the amount by which a limit, capacity, etc., is exceeded.

overfold (ˈəʊvəˌfəʊld) *n Geol.* a fold in the form of an anticline in which one limb is more steeply inclined than the other.

overfunding (ˈəʊvəˌfʌndɪŋ) *n* (in Britain) a government policy in which it sells more of its securities than would be required to finance public spending, with the object of absorbing surplus funds to curb inflation.

overgrow (ˌəʊvəˈgrəʊ) *vb* **overgrows, overgrowing, overgrew, overgrown. 1** (*tr*) to grow over or across (an area, path, etc.). **2** (*tr*) to choke or supplant by a stronger growth. **3** (*tr*) to grow too large for. **4** (*intr*) to grow beyond normal size.
▸ **ˈoverˌgrowth** *n*

overhand (ˈəʊvəˌhænd) *adj* **1** thrown or performed with the hand raised above the shoulder. **2** sewn with thread passing over two edges in one direction. ◆ *adv* **3** with the hand above the shoulder; overarm. **4** with shallow stitches passing over two edges. ◆ *vb* **5** to sew (two edges) overhand.

overhang *vb* (ˌəʊvəˈhæŋ), **overhangs, overhanging, overhung. 1** to project or extend beyond (a surface, building, etc.). **2** (*tr*) to hang or be suspended over. **3** (*tr*) to menace, threaten, or dominate. ◆ *n* (ˈəʊvəˌhæŋ). **4** a formation, object, etc., that extends beyond or hangs over something, such as an outcrop of rock overhanging a mountain face. **5** the amount or extent of projection.

overhaul *vb* (ˌəʊvəˈhɔːl). (*tr*) **1** to examine carefully for faults, necessary repairs, etc. **2** to make repairs or adjustments to (a car, machine, etc.). **3** to overtake. ◆ *n* (ˈəʊvəˌhɔːl). **4** a thorough examination and repair.

overhead *adj* (ˈəʊvəˌhɛd). **1** situated or operating above head height or some other reference level. **2** (*prenominal*) inclusive: *the overhead price included meals.* ◆ *adv* (ˌəʊvəˈhɛd). **3** over or above head height, esp. in the sky. ◆ *n* (ˈəʊvəˌhɛd). **4a** a stroke in racket games played from above head height. **4b** (*as modifier*): *an overhead smash.* **5** (*modifier*) of, concerned with, or resulting from overheads: *overhead costs.*

overhead camshaft *n* a type of camshaft situated above the cylinder head in an internal-combustion engine.

overhead projector *n* a projector that throws an enlarged image of a transparency onto a surface above and behind the person using it.

overheads (ˈəʊvəˌhɛdz) *pl n* business expenses, such as rent, that are not directly attributable to any department or product and can therefore be assigned only arbitrarily.

overhead-valve engine *n* a type of internal-combustion engine in which the inlet and exhaust valves are in the cylinder head above the pistons. US name: **valve-in-head engine.**

overhear (ˌəʊvəˈhɪə) *vb* **overhears, overhearing, overheard.** (*tr*) to hear (a person, remark, etc.) without the knowledge of the speaker.

overheat (ˌəʊvəˈhiːt) *vb* **1** to make or become excessively hot. **2** (*tr; often passive*) to make very agitated, irritated, etc. **3** (*intr*) (of an economy) to tend towards inflation, often as a result of excessive growth in demand. **4** (*tr*) to cause (an economy) to tend towards inflation. ◆ *n* **5** the condition of being overheated.

Overijssel ★ (*Dutch* oːvərˈɛisəl) *n* a province of the E Netherlands: generally low-lying. Capital: Zwolle. Pop.: 1 057 700 (1997 est.). Area: 3929 sq. km (1517 sq. miles).

overjoy (ˌəʊvəˈdʒɔɪ) *vb* (*tr*) to give great delight to.
▸ **ˌoverˈjoyed** *adj*

overkill (ˈəʊvəˌkɪl) *n* **1** the capability to deploy more weapons, esp. nuclear weapons, than is necessary to ensure military advantage. **2** any capacity or treatment that is greater than that required or appropriate.

overland (ˈəʊvəˌlænd) *adj* (*prenominal*), *adv* **1** over or across land. ◆ *vb* **2** *Austral.* (formerly) to drive (cattle or sheep) overland.
▸ **ˈoverˌlander** *n*

overlap *vb* (ˌəʊvəˈlæp), **overlaps, overlapping, overlapped. 1** (of two things) to extend or lie partly over (each other). **2** to cover and extend beyond (something). **3** (*intr*) to coincide partly in time, subject, etc. ◆ *n* (ˈəʊvəˌlæp). **4** a part that overlaps or is overlapped. **5** the amount, length, etc., overlapping. **6** *Geol.* the horizontal extension of the lower beds in a series of rock strata beyond the upper beds.

overlay *vb* (ˌəʊvəˈleɪ), **overlays, overlaying, overlaid.** (*tr*) **1** to lay or place over or upon (something else). **2** (often foll. by *with*) to cover, overspread, or conceal (with). **3** (foll. by *with*) to cover (a surface) with an applied decoration:

ebony overlaid with silver. **4** to achieve the correct printing pressure all over (a forme or plate) by adding to the appropriate areas of the packing. ◆ *n* ('əʊvəˌleɪ). **5** something that is laid over something else; covering. **6** an applied decoration or layer, as of gold leaf. **7** a transparent sheet giving extra details to a map or diagram over which it is designed to be placed. **8** *Printing.* material, such as paper, used to overlay a forme or plate.

overleaf (ˌəʊvə'li:f) *adv* on the other side of the page.

overlie (ˌəʊvə'laɪ) *vb* **overlies, overlying, overlay, overlain.** (*tr*) **1** to lie or rest upon. Cf. **overlay. 2** to kill (a baby or newborn animal) by lying upon it.

overlong (ˌəʊvə'lɒŋ) *adj, adv* too or excessively long.

overlook *vb* (ˌəʊvə'lʊk). (*tr*) **1** to fail to notice or take into account. **2** to disregard deliberately or indulgently. **3** to afford a view of from above: *the house overlooks the bay.* **4** to rise above. **5** to look at carefully. **6** to cast the evil eye upon (someone). ◆ *n* ('əʊvəˌlʊk). *US.* **7** a high place affording a view. **8** an act of overlooking.

overlord ('əʊvəˌlɔ:d) *n* a supreme lord or master.
▸ **'overˌlordship** *n*

overly ('əʊvəlɪ) *adv* too; excessively.

overman *vb* (ˌəʊvə'mæn), **overmans, overmanning, overmanned. 1** (*tr*) to supply with an excessive number of men. ◆ *n* ('əʊvəˌmæn), *pl* **overmen. 2** a man who oversees others. **3** a superman.

overmaster (ˌəʊvə'mɑ:stə) *vb* (*tr*) to overpower.

overmatch *Chiefly US.* ◆ *vb* (ˌəʊvə'mætʃ). (*tr*) **1** to be more than a match for. **2** to match with a superior opponent. ◆ *n* ('əʊvəˌmætʃ). **3** a person superior in ability. **4** a match in which one contestant is superior.

overmuch (ˌəʊvə'mʌtʃ) *adv, adj* **1** too much; very much. ◆ *n* **2** an excessive amount.

overnice (ˌəʊvə'naɪs) *adj* too fastidious, precise, etc.

overnight *adv* (ˌəʊvə'naɪt). **1** for the duration of the night. **2** in or as if in the course of one night; suddenly: *the situation changed overnight.* ◆ *adj* ('əʊvəˌnaɪt). (*usually prenominal*) **3** done in, occurring in, or lasting the night: *an overnight stop.* **4** staying for one night. **5** for use during a single night. **6** occurring in or as if in the course of one night; sudden: *an overnight victory.*

overpass *n* ('əʊvəˌpɑ:s). **1** another name for **flyover** (sense 1). ◆ *vb* (ˌəʊvə'pɑ:s). (*tr*) *Now rare.* **2** to pass over, through, or across. **3** to exceed. **4** to ignore.

overplay (ˌəʊvə'pleɪ) *vb* **1** (*tr*) to exaggerate the importance of. **2** to act or behave in an exaggerated manner. **3 overplay one's hand.** to overestimate the worth or strength of one's position.

overpower (ˌəʊvə'paʊə) *vb* (*tr*) **1** to conquer or subdue by superior force. **2** to have such a strong effect on as to make helpless or ineffective. **3** to supply with more power than necessary.
▸ **ˌover'powering** *adj*

overprice (ˌəʊvə'praɪs) *vb* **overprices, overpricing, overpriced.** (*tr*) to ask too high a price for.

overprint *vb* (ˌəʊvə'prɪnt). **1** (*tr*) to print (additional matter or another colour) on a sheet of paper. ◆ *n* ('əʊvəˌprɪnt). **2** additional matter or another colour printed onto a previously printed sheet. **3** additional matter applied to a finished postage stamp by printing, stamping, etc.

overqualified (ˌəʊvə'kwɒlɪfaɪd) *adj* having more managerial experience or academic qualifications than required for a particular job.

overrate (ˌəʊvə'reɪt) *vb* **overrates, overrating, overrated.** (*tr*) to assess too highly.

overreach (ˌəʊvə'ri:tʃ) *vb* **1** (*tr*) to defeat or thwart (oneself) by attempting to do or gain too much. **2** (*tr*) to aim for but miss by going too far. **3** to get the better of (a person) by trickery. **4** (*tr*) to reach beyond or over. **5** (*intr*) to reach or go too far. **6** (*intr*) (of a horse) to strike the back of a forefoot with the edge of the opposite hind foot.

overreact (ˌəʊvərɪ'ækt) *vb* (*intr*) to react excessively to something.
▸ **ˌoverre'action** *n*

override *vb* (ˌəʊvə'raɪd), **overrides, overriding, overrode, overridden.** (*tr*) **1** to set aside or disregard with superior authority or power. **2** to supersede or annul. **3** to dominate or vanquish by or as if by trampling down. **4** to take manual control of (a system that is usually under automatic control). **5** to extend or pass over, esp. to overlap. **6** to ride (a horse, etc.) too hard. **7** to ride over. ◆ *n* ('əʊvəˌraɪd). **8** a device that can override an automatic control.

overrider ('əʊvəˌraɪdə) *n* either of two attachments fitted to the bumper of a motor vehicle to prevent it interlocking with that of another vehicle.

overriding (ˌəʊvə'raɪdɪŋ) *adj* taking precedence.

overrule (ˌəʊvə'ru:l) *vb* **overrules, overruling, overruled.** (*tr*) **1** to disallow the arguments of (a person) by the use of authority. **2** to rule or decide against (an argument, decision, etc.). **3** to prevail over, dominate, or influence. **4** to exercise rule over.

overrun *vb* (ˌəʊvə'rʌn), **overruns, overrunning, overran, overrun. 1** (*tr*) to swarm or spread over rapidly. **2** to run over (something); overflow. **3** to extend or run beyond a limit. **4** (*intr*) (of an engine) to run with a closed throttle at a speed dictated by that of the vehicle it drives. **5** (*tr*) to print (a book, journal, etc.) in a greater quantity than ordered. **6** (*tr*) *Printing.* to transfer (set type) from one column, line, or page, to another. **7** (*tr*) *Arch.* to run faster than. ◆ *n* ('əʊvəˌrʌn). **8** the act or an instance of overrunning. **9** the amount or extent of overrunning. **10** the number of copies of a publication in excess of the quantity ordered.

overseas *adv* (ˌəʊvə'si:z). **1** beyond the sea; abroad. ◆ *adj* ('əʊvə'si:z). **2** of, to, in, from, or situated in countries beyond the sea. **3** Also: **oversea.** of or relating to passage over the sea. ◆ *n* (ˌəʊvə'si:z). **4** (*functioning as sing*) *Inf.* a foreign country or foreign countries collectively.

overseas territory *n* See **United Kingdom overseas territory.**

oversee (ˌəʊvə'si:) *vb* **oversees, overseeing, oversaw, overseen.** (*tr*) **1** to watch over and direct; supervise. **2** to watch secretly or accidentally. **3** *Arch.* to scrutinize; inspect.

overseer ('əʊvəˌsi:ə) *n* **1** a person who oversees others, esp. workmen. **2** *Brit. history.* a minor official of a parish attached to the poorhouse.

oversell (ˌəʊvə'sɛl) *vb* **oversells, overselling, oversold. 1** (*tr*) to sell more of (a commodity, etc.) than can be supplied. **2** to use excessively aggressive methods in selling (commodities). **3** (*tr*) to exaggerate the merits of.

overset (ˌəʊvə'sɛt) *vb* **oversets, oversetting, overset.** (*tr*) **1** to disturb or upset. **2** *Printing.* to set (type or copy) in excess of the space available.

oversew ('əʊvəˌsəʊ, ˌəʊvə'səʊ) *vb* **oversews, oversewing, oversewed; oversewn** *or* **oversewed.** to sew (two edges) with close stitches that pass over them both.

oversexed (ˌəʊvə'sɛkst) *adj* having an excessive preoccupation with sexual activity.

overshadow (ˌəʊvə'ʃædəʊ) *vb* (*tr*) **1** to render insignificant or less important in comparison. **2** to cast a shadow or gloom over.

overshoe ('əʊvəˌʃu:) *n* a protective shoe worn over an ordinary shoe.

overshoot *vb* (ˌəʊvə'ʃu:t), **overshoots, overshooting, overshot. 1** to shoot or go beyond (a mark or target). **2** (of an aircraft) to fly or taxi too far along a runway. **3** (*tr*) to pass swiftly over or down over, as water over a wheel. ◆ *n* ('əʊvəˌʃu:t). **4** an act or instance of overshooting. **5** the extent of such overshooting.

overshot ('əʊvəˌʃɒt) *adj* **1** having or designating an upper jaw that projects beyond the lower jaw. **2** (of a water wheel) driven by a flow of water that passes over the wheel.

oversight ('əʊvəˌsaɪt) *n* **1** an omission or mistake, esp. one made through failure to notice something. **2** supervision.

oversize *adj* (ˌəʊvə'saɪz). **1** Also: **oversized.** larger than the usual size. ◆ *n* ('əʊvəˌsaɪz). **2** a size larger than the usual or proper size. **3** something that is oversize.

overskirt ('əʊvəˌskɜ:t) *n* an outer skirt, esp. one that reveals a decorative underskirt.

overspend *vb* (ˌəʊvəˈspɛnd), **overspends, overspending, overspent.** **1** to spend in excess of (one's desires or what one can afford or is allocated). **2** (*tr; usually passive*) to wear out; exhaust. ◆ *n* (ˈəʊvəˌspɛnd). **3** the amount by which someone or something is overspent.

overspill *n* (ˈəʊvəˌspɪl). **1a** something that spills over or is in excess. **1b** (*as modifier*): *overspill population.* ◆ *vb* (ˌəʊvəˈspɪl), **overspills, overspilling, overspilt** *or* **overspilled. 2** (*intr*) to overflow.

overspread (ˌəʊvəˈsprɛd) *vb* (*tr*) **overspreads, overspreading, overspread.** to extend or spread over.

overstate (ˌəʊvəˈsteɪt) *vb* **overstates, overstating, overstated.** (*tr*) to state too strongly; exaggerate or overemphasize.
▸ **ˌoverˈstatement** *n*

overstay (ˌəʊvəˈsteɪ) *vb* (*tr*) **1** to stay beyond the time, limit, or duration of. **2 overstay** *or* **outstay one's welcome.** to stay (at a party, etc.), longer than pleases the host or hostess.

overstayer (ˈəʊvəˌsteɪə) *n* a person who remains illegally in a country after the period of the permitted visit has expired.

overstep (ˌəʊvəˈstɛp) *vb* **oversteps, overstepping, overstepped.** (*tr*) to go beyond (a certain or proper limit).

overstrung (ˌəʊvəˈstrʌŋ) *adj* **1** too highly strung; tense. **2** (of a piano) having two sets of strings crossing each other at an oblique angle.

overstuff (ˌəʊvəˈstʌf) *vb* (*tr*) **1** to force too much into. **2** to cover (furniture, etc.) entirely with upholstery.

oversubscribe (ˌəʊvəsəbˈskraɪb) *vb* **oversubscribes, oversubscribing, oversubscribed.** (*tr; often passive*) to subscribe or apply for in excess of available supply.
▸ **ˌoversubˈscription** *n*

overt (ˈəʊvɜːt, əʊˈvɜːt) *adj* **1** open to view; observable. **2** *Law.* open; deliberate. ORIG C14: via OF, from *ovrir* to open, from L *aperīre*
▸ **ˈovertly** *adv*

overtake (ˌəʊvəˈteɪk) *vb* **overtakes, overtaking, overtook, overtaken. 1** *Chiefly Brit.* to move past (another vehicle or person) travelling in the same direction. **2** (*tr*) to pass or do better than, after catching up with. **3** (*tr*) to come upon suddenly or unexpectedly: *night overtook him.* **4** (*tr*) to catch up with; draw level with.

overtax (ˌəʊvəˈtæks) *vb* (*tr*) **1** to tax too heavily. **2** to impose too great a strain on.

over-the-counter *adj* **1a** (of securities) not listed or quoted on a stock exchange. **1b** (of a security market) dealing in such securities. **1c** (of security transactions) conducted through a broker's office directly between purchaser and seller and not on a stock exchange. **2** (of a medicinal drug) able to be sold without prescription. Cf. **POM.** ◆ Abbrev.: **OTC.**

overthrow *vb* (ˌəʊvəˈθrəʊ), **overthrows, overthrowing, overthrew, overthrown. 1** (*tr*) to effect the downfall or destruction of (a ruler, institution, etc.), esp. by force. **2** (*tr*) to throw or turn over. **3** to throw (something, esp. a ball) too far. ◆ *n* (ˈəʊvəˌθrəʊ). **4** downfall; destruction. **5** *Cricket.* **5a** a ball thrown back too far by a fielder. **5b** a run scored because of this.

overthrust (ˈəʊvəˌθrʌst) *n Geol.* a reverse fault in which the rocks on the upper surface of a fault plane have moved over the rocks on the lower surface.

overtime *n* (ˈəʊvəˌtaɪm). **1a** work at a regular job done in addition to regular working hours. **1b** (*as modifier*): *overtime pay.* **2** the rate of pay established for such work. **3** time in excess of a set period. **4** *Sport, US & Canad.* extra time. ◆ *adv* (ˈəʊvəˌtaɪm). **5** beyond the regular or stipulated time. ◆ *vb* (ˌəʊvəˈtaɪm), **overtimes, overtiming, overtimed. 6** (*tr*) to exceed the required time for (a photographic exposure, etc.).

overtone (ˈəʊvəˌtəʊn) *n* **1** (*often pl*) additional meaning or nuance: *overtones of despair.* **2** *Music, acoustics.* any of the tones, with the exception of the fundamental, that constitute a musical sound and contribute to its quality.

overture (ˈəʊvəˌtjʊə) *n* **1** *Music.* **1a** a piece of orchestral music that is played at the beginning of an opera or oratorio, often containing the main musical themes of the work. **1b** a one-movement orchestral piece, usually having a descriptive or evocative title. **2** (*often pl*) a proposal, act, or gesture initiating a relationship, negotiation, etc. **3** something that introduces what follows. ◆ *vb* **overtures, overturing, overtured.** (*tr*) **4** to make or present an overture to. **5** to introduce with an overture. ORIG C14: via OF from LL *apertūra* opening, from L *aperīre* to open

overturn *vb* (ˌəʊvəˈtɜːn). **1** to turn or cause to turn from an upright or normal position. **2** (*tr*) to overthrow or destroy. **3** (*tr*) to invalidate; reverse. ◆ *n* (ˈəʊvəˌtɜːn). **4** the act of overturning or the state of being overturned.

overuse *vb* (ˌəʊvəˈjuːz), **overuses, overusing, overused. 1** (*tr*) to use excessively. ◆ *n* (ˌəʊvəˈjuːs) **2** excessive use.

overview (ˈəʊvəˌvjuː) *n* a general survey.

overweening (ˌəʊvəˈwiːnɪŋ) *adj* **1** (of a person) excessively arrogant or presumptuous. **2** (of opinions, appetites, etc.) excessive; immoderate. ORIG C14: from OVER + *weening* from OE *wēnan* WEEN
▸ **ˌoverˈweeningness** *n*

overweight *adj* (ˌəʊvəˈweɪt). **1** weighing more than is usual, allowed, or healthy. ◆ *n* (ˈəʊvəˌweɪt). **2** extra or excess weight. ◆ *vb* (ˌəʊvəˈweɪt). (*tr*) **3** to give too much emphasis or consideration to. **4** to add too much weight to. **5** to weigh down.

overwhelm (ˌəʊvəˈwɛlm) *vb* (*tr*) **1** to overpower the thoughts, emotions, or senses of. **2** to overcome with irresistible force. **3** to cover over or bury completely. **4** to weigh or rest upon overpoweringly.
▸ **ˌoverˈwhelming** *adj*

overwind (ˌəʊvəˈwaɪnd) *vb* **overwinds, overwinding, overwound.** (*tr*) to wind (a watch, etc.) beyond the proper limit.

overwork *vb* (ˌəʊvəˈwɜːk). (*mainly tr*) **1** (*also intr*) to work too hard or too long. **2** to use too much: *to overwork an excuse.* **3** to decorate the surface of. ◆ *n* (ˈəʊvəˌwɜːk). **4** excessive or excessively tiring work.

overwrite (ˌəʊvəˈraɪt) *vb* **overwrites, overwriting, overwrote, overwritten. 1** to write (something) in an excessively ornate style. **2** to write too much about (someone or something). **3** to write on top of (other writing). **4** to record on a storage medium, such as a magnetic disk, thus destroying what was originally recorded there.

overwrought (ˌəʊvəˈrɔːt) *adj* **1** full of nervous tension; agitated. **2** too elaborate; fussy: *an overwrought style.* **3** (*often postpositive* and foll. by *with*) with the surface decorated or adorned.

Ovett ★ (ˈəʊvɛt) *n* **Steve.** born 1955, British middle-distance runner.

ovi- *or* **ovo-** *combining form.* egg or ovum: *oviform; ovoviviparous.* ORIG from L *ōvum*

Ovid ★ (ˈɒvɪd) *n* Latin name *Publius Ovidius Naso.* 43 B.C.–?17 A.D., Roman poet.
▸ **Ovidian** (ɒˈvɪdɪən) *adj*

oviduct (ˈɒvɪˌdʌkt, ˈəʊ-) *n* the tube through which ova are conveyed from an ovary. Also called (in mammals): **Fallopian tube.**
▸ **oviducal** (ˌɒvɪˈdjuːkəl, ˌəʊ-) *or* **ˌoviˈductal** *adj*

Oviedo ★ (*Spanish* oˈβjeðo) *n* a city in NW Spain: capital of Asturias from 810 until 1002; centre of a coal- and iron-mining area. Pop.: 202 421 (1995 est.).

oviform (ˈəʊvɪˌfɔːm) *adj Biol.* shaped like an egg.

ovine (ˈəʊvaɪn) *adj* of, relating to, or resembling a sheep. ORIG C19: from LL *ovīnus,* from L *ovis* sheep

oviparous (əʊˈvɪpərəs) *adj* (of fishes, reptiles, birds, etc.) producing eggs that hatch outside the body of the mother. Cf. **ovoviviparous, viviparous** (sense 1).
▸ **oviparity** (ˌəʊvɪˈpærɪtɪ) *n* ▸ **oˈviparously** *adv*

ovipositor (ˌəʊvɪˈpɒzɪtə) *n* **1** the egg-laying organ of most female insects, consisting of a pair of specialized appendages at the end of the abdomen. **2** a similar organ in certain female fishes, formed by an extension of the edges of the genital opening. ORIG C19:from OVI- + L *positor,* from *ponere* to place
▸ **ˌoviˈposit** *vb* (*intr*)

ovoid (ˈəʊvɔɪd) *adj* **1** egg-shaped. ◆ *n* **2** something that is ovoid.

ovoviviparous (ˌəʊvəʊvaɪˈvɪpərəs) *adj* (of certain rep-

tiles, fishes, etc.) producing eggs that hatch within the body of the mother. Cf. **oviparous, viviparous** (sense 1).
▸ **ovoviviparity** (ˌəʊvəʊˌvaɪvɪˈpærɪtɪ) *n*

ovulate (ˈɒvjʊˌleɪt) *vb* **ovulates, ovulating, ovulated.** (*intr*) to produce or discharge eggs from an ovary. ORIG C19: from OVULE
▸ ˌ**ovuˈlation** *n*

ovulation method *n* another name for **Billings method.**

ovule (ˈɒvjuːl) *n* **1** a small body in seed-bearing plants that contains the egg cell and develops into the seed after fertilization. **2** *Zool.* an immature ovum. ORIG C19: via F from Med. L *ōvulum* a little egg, from L *ōvum* egg
▸ ˈ**ovular** *adj*

ovum (ˈəʊvəm) *n, pl* **ova.** an unfertilized female gamete; egg cell. ORIG from L: egg

ow (aʊ) *interj* an exclamation of pain.

owe (əʊ) *vb* **owes, owing, owed.** (*mainly tr*) **1** to be under an obligation to pay (someone) to the amount of. **2** (*intr*) to be in debt: *he still owes for his house.* **3** (often foll. by *to*) to have as a result (of). **4** to feel the need or obligation to do, give, etc. **5** to hold or maintain in the mind or heart (esp. in **owe a grudge**). ORIG OE *āgan* to have (C12: to have to)

Owen ★ (ˈəʊɪn) *n* **1 David (Anthony Llewellyn)** Baron. born 1938, British politician: Labour foreign secretary (1977–79); cofounder (1981) and leader (1983–87) of the Social Democratic Party; peace envoy to Bosnia-Herzegovina (1992–94). **2 Michael (James).** born 1979, British footballer; plays for Liverpool and England. **3** Sir **Richard.** 1804–92, British comparative anatomist and palaeontologist. **4 Robert.** 1771–1858, Welsh industrialist and social reformer. He formed a model industrial community at New Lanark, Scotland. **5 Wilfred.** 1893–1918, British poet of World War I; killed in action.

Owen gun *n* a simple recoil-operated submachine-gun first used by Australian forces in World War II. ORIG after E. E. *Owen* (1915–49), its Austral. inventor

Owens ★ (ˈəʊɪnz) *n* **Jesse,** real name *John Cleveland Owens.* 1913–80, US Black athlete: won four gold medals at the Berlin Olympics (1936).

Owen Stanley Range ★ *n* a mountain range in SE New Guinea. Highest peak: Mount Victoria, 4073 m (13 363 ft).

Owerri ★ (əˈwɛrɪ) *n* a market town in S Nigeria, capital of Imo state. Pop.: 35 010 (latest est.).

owing (ˈəʊɪŋ) *adj* **1** (*postpositive*) owed; due. **2 owing to.** because of or on account of.

owl (aʊl) *n* **1** a nocturnal bird of prey having large front-facing eyes, a small hooked bill, soft feathers, and a short neck. **2** any of various breeds of owl-like fancy domestic pigeon. **3** a person who looks or behaves like an owl, esp. in having a solemn manner. ORIG OE *ūle*
▸ ˈ**owlish** *adj* ▸ ˈ**owl-ˌlike** *adj*

owlet (ˈaʊlɪt) *n* a young or nestling owl.

own (əʊn) *determiner* (*preceded by a possessive*) **1a** (intensifier): *John's own idea.* **1b** (*as pron*): *I'll use my own.* **2** on behalf of oneself or in relation to oneself: *he is his own worst enemy.* **3 come into one's own. 3a** to become fulfilled: *she really came into her own when she got divorced.* **3b** to receive what is due to one. **4 hold one's own.** to maintain one's situation or position, esp. in spite of opposition or difficulty. **5 on one's own. 5a** without help. **5b** by oneself; alone. ◆ *vb* **6** (*tr*) to have as one's possession. **7** (when *intr*, often foll. by *up, to,* or *up to*) to confess or admit; acknowledge. **8** (*tr; takes a clause as object*) *Now rare.* to concede: *I own that you are right.* ORIG OE *āgen*, orig. p.p. of *āgan* to have. See OWE
▸ ˈ**owner** *n* ▸ ˈ**ownership** *n*

own brand *n* a product which displays the name of the retailer rather than the producer.

owner-occupier *n* someone who has bought or is buying the house in which he lives.

own goal *n* **1** *Soccer.* a goal scored by a player accidentally playing the ball into his or her own team's net. **2** *Inf.* any action that results in disadvantage to the person who took it or to his associates.

ox (ɒks) *n, pl* **oxen. 1** an adult castrated male of any domesticated species of cattle used for draught work and meat. **2** any bovine mammal, esp. any of the domestic cattle. ORIG OE *oxa*

oxalic acid (ɒkˈsælɪk) *n* a colourless poisonous crystalline acid found in many plants: used as a bleach and a cleansing agent for metals. Formula: $(COOH)_2$. Recommended name: **ethanedioic acid.** ORIG C18: from F *oxalique,* from L *oxalis* garden sorrel; see OXALIS

oxalis (ˈɒksəlɪs, ɒkˈsælɪs) *n* a plant having clover-like leaves which contain oxalic acid and white, pink, red, or yellow flowers. See also **wood sorrel.** ORIG C18: via L from Gk: sorrel, sour wine, from *oxus* acid, sharp

oxblood (ˈɒksˌblʌd) *or* **oxblood red** *adj* of a dark reddish-brown colour.

oxbow (ˈɒksˌbəʊ) *n* **1** a U-shaped piece of wood fitted under and around the neck of a harnessed ox and attached to the yoke. **2** Also called: **oxbow lake.** a small curved lake lying on the flood plain of a river and constituting the remnant of a former meander.

Oxbridge (ˈɒksˌbrɪdʒ) *n* **a** the British universities of Oxford and Cambridge, esp. considered as ancient and prestigious academic institutions, bastions of privilege and superiority, etc. **b** (*as modifier*): *Oxbridge graduates.*

oxen (ˈɒksən) *n* the plural of **ox.**

oxeye (ˈɒksˌaɪ) *n* **1** a Eurasian composite plant having daisy-like flower heads with yellow rays and dark centres. **2** any of various North American plants having daisy-like flowers. **3 oxeye daisy.** a type of hardy perennial chrysanthemum.

ox-eyed *adj* having large round eyes, like those of an ox.

Oxfam (ˈɒksˌfæm) *n acronym for* Oxford Committee for Famine Relief.

Oxford[1] ★ (ˈɒksfəd) *n* **1** a city in S England, administrative centre of Oxfordshire, at the confluence of the Rivers Thames and Cherwell: Royalist headquarters during the Civil War; seat of The University of Oxford (consisting of 40 separate colleges, the oldest being University College, 1249) and Oxford Brookes University (1993). Pop.: 118 795 (1991). **2** a type of stout laced shoe with a low heel. **3** a lightweight fabric of plain or twill weave used esp. for men's shirts.

Oxford[2] ★ (ˈɒksfəd) *n* **1st Earl of.** title of (Robert) **Harley.**

Oxford bags *pl n* trousers with very wide baggy legs.

Oxford blue *n* **1a** a dark blue colour. **1b** (*as adj*): *an Oxford-blue scarf.* **2** a person who has been awarded a blue from Oxford University.

Oxford Movement *n* a movement within the Church of England that began at Oxford in 1833. It affirmed the continuity of the Church with early Christianity and strove to restore the High-Church ideals of the 17th century. Also called: **Tractarianism.**

Oxfordshire ★ (ˈɒksfədˌʃɪə, -ʃə) *n* an inland county of S central England: situated mostly in the basin of the Upper Thames, with the Cotswolds in the west and the Chilterns in the southeast. Administrative centre: Oxford. Pop.: 603 200 (1996 est.). Area: 2608 sq. km (1007 sq. miles). Abbrev.: **Oxon.**

oxidant (ˈɒksɪdənt) *n* a substance that acts or is used as an oxidizing agent. Also called (esp. in rocketry): **oxidizer.**

oxidation (ˌɒksɪˈdeɪʃən) *n* **a** the act or process of oxidizing. **b** (*as modifier*): *an oxidation state.*
▸ ˈ**oxiˌdate** *vb* ▸ ˌ**oxiˈdational** *adj* ▸ ˈ**oxiˌdative** *adj*

oxidation-reduction *n* **a** a reversible chemical process usually involving the transfer of electrons, in which one reaction is an oxidation and the reverse reaction is a reduction. **b** (*as modifier*): *an oxidation-reduction reaction.* ◆ Also: **redox.**

oxide (ˈɒksaɪd) *n* **1** any compound of oxygen with another element. **2** any organic compound in which an oxygen atom is bound to two alkyl groups; an ether. ORIG C18: from F, from *ox(ygène)* + *(ac)ide*

oxidize *or* **oxidise** (ˈɒksɪˌdaɪz) *vb* **oxidizes, oxidizing, oxidized** *or* **oxidises, oxidising, oxidised. 1** to undergo or cause to undergo a chemical reaction with oxygen, as in formation of an oxide. **2** to form or cause to form a layer of metal oxide, as in rusting. **3** to lose or cause to lose hy-

drogen atoms. **4** to undergo or cause to undergo a decrease in the number of electrons.
▸ **,oxidi'zation** *or* **,oxidi'sation** *n*

oxidizing agent *n Chem.* a substance that oxidizes another substance, being itself reduced in the process.

oxlip ('ɒks,lɪp) *n* **1** a Eurasian woodland plant, with small drooping pale yellow flowers. **2** a similar and related plant that is a natural hybrid between the cowslip and primrose. ORIG OE *oxanslyppe,* lit.: ox's slippery dropping; see SLIP[3]

oxo acid ('ɒksəʊ) *n* another name for **oxyacid.**

Oxon *abbrev. for* Oxfordshire. ORIG from L *Oxonia*

Oxon. *abbrev. for* (in degree titles, etc.) of Oxford. ORIG from L *Oxoniensis*

Oxonian (ɒk'səʊnɪən) *adj* **1** of or relating to Oxford or Oxford University. ◆ *n* **2** a member of Oxford University. **3** an inhabitant or native of Oxford.

oxpecker ('ɒks,pɛkə) *n* either of two African starlings, having flattened bills with which they obtain food from the hides of cattle. Also called: **tick-bird.**

oxtail ('ɒks,teɪl) *n* the skinned tail of an ox, used esp. in soups and stews.

oxter ('əʊkstə) *n Scot., Irish, & N English dialect.* the armpit. ORIG C16: from OE *oxta*

oxtongue ('ɒks,tʌŋ) *n* **1** any of various Eurasian composite plants having oblong bristly leaves and clusters of dandelion-like flowers. **2** any of various other plants having bristly tongue-shaped leaves. **3** the tongue of an ox, braised or boiled as food.

Oxus ★ ('ɒksəs) *n* the ancient name for the **Amu Darya.**

oxy-[1] *combining form.* denoting something sharp; acute: *oxytone.* ORIG from Gk, from *oxus*

oxy-[2] *combining form.* containing or using oxygen: *oxyacetylene.*

oxyacetylene (,ɒksɪə'sɛtɪ,li:n) *n* **a** a mixture of oxygen and acetylene; used in torches for cutting or welding metals at high temperatures. **b** (*as modifier*): *an oxyacetylene burner.*

oxyacid (,ɒksɪ'æsɪd) *n* any acid that contains oxygen with the acidic hydrogen atoms bound to oxygen atoms. Also called: **oxo acid.**

oxygen ('ɒksɪdʒən) *n* **a** a colourless odourless highly reactive gaseous element: the most abundant element in the earth's crust. Symbol: O; atomic no.: 8; atomic wt.: 15.9994. **b** (*as modifier*): *an oxygen mask.*
▸ **oxygenic** (,ɒksɪ'dʒɛnɪk) *or* **oxygenous** (ɒk'sɪdʒɪnəs) *adj*

oxygenate ('ɒksɪdʒɪ,neɪt) *or* **oxygenize, oxygenise** *vb* **oxygenates, oxygenating, oxygenated** *or* **oxygenizes, oxygenizing, oxygenized; oxygenises, oxygenising, oxygenised.** to enrich or be enriched with oxygen: *to oxygenate blood.*
▸ **,oxygen'ation** *n* ▸ **'oxygen,izer** *or* **'oxygen,iser** *n*

oxygen bar *n* a place where customers pay to inhale high-purity oxygen, which is thought to have beneficial effects.

oxygen tent *n Med.* a transparent enclosure covering a bedridden patient, into which oxygen is released to help maintain respiration.

oxyhaemoglobin (,ɒksɪ,hi:məʊ'gləʊbɪn) *n Biochem.* the bright red product formed when oxygen from the lungs combines with haemoglobin in the blood.

oxyhydrogen (,ɒksɪ'haɪdrɪdʒən) *n* **a** a mixture of hydrogen and oxygen used to provide an intense flame for welding. **b** (*as modifier*): *an oxyhydrogen blowpipe.*

oxymoron (,ɒksɪ'mɔ:rɒn) *n, pl* **oxymora** (-'mɔ:rə). *Rhetoric.* an epigrammatic effect, by which contradictory terms are used in conjunction: *living death.* ORIG C17: via NL from Gk *oxumōron,* from *oxus* sharp + *mōros* stupid

oxytetracycline (,ɒksi,tɛtrə'saɪklɪn) *n* a broad-spectrum antibiotic obtained from *Streptomyces rimosus.*

oyer and terminer ('ɔɪə; 'tɜ:mɪnə) *n* **1** *English law.* (formerly) a commission issued to judges to try cases on assize. **2** the court in which such a hearing was held. ORIG C15: from Anglo-Norman, from *oyer* to hear + *terminer* to judge

oyez *or* **oyes** ('əʊ'jɛs, -'jɛz) *sentence substitute.* **1** a cry, usually uttered three times, by a public crier or court official for silence and attention before making a proclamation. ◆ *n* **2** such a cry. ORIG C15: via Anglo-Norman from OF *oiez!* hear!

-oyl *suffix of nouns* (in chemistry) indicating an acyl group or radical: *ethanoyl, methanoyl.* ORIG C20: from O(XYGEN) + -YL

Oyo ★ ('əʊjəʊ) *n* a state of SW Nigeria, formed in 1976 from part of Western State. Capital: Ibadan. Pop.: 3 900 803 (1995 est.). Area: 28 454 sq. km (10 986 sq. miles).

oyster ('ɔɪstə) *n* **1a** an edible marine bivalve mollusc having a rough irregularly shaped shell and occurring on the sea bed, mostly in coastal waters. **1b** (*as modifier*): *oyster farm; oyster knife.* **2** any of various similar and related molluscs, such as the pearl oyster and the saddle oyster. **3** the oyster-shaped piece of dark meat in the hollow of the pelvic bone of a fowl. **4** something from which advantage, delight, profit, etc., may be derived: *the world is his oyster.* **5** *Inf.* a very uncommunicative person. ◆ *vb* **6** (*intr*) to dredge for, gather, or raise oysters. ORIG C14 *oistre,* from OF *uistre,* from L *ostrea,* from Gk *ostreon;* rel. to Gk *osteon* bone, *ostrakon* shell

oyster bed *n* a place, esp. on the sea bed, where oysters breed and grow naturally or are cultivated for food or pearls. Also called: **oyster bank, oyster park.**

oystercatcher ('ɔɪstə,kætʃə) *n* a shore bird having a black or black-and-white plumage and a long stout laterally compressed red bill.

oyster crab *n* any of several small soft-bodied crabs that live as commensals in the mantles of oysters.

oyster plant *n* **1** another name for **salsify** (sense 1). **2** Also called: **sea lungwort.** a prostrate coastal plant with clusters of blue flowers.

oz *or* **oz.** *abbrev. for* ounce. ORIG from It. *onza*

Oz (ɒz) *n Austral. sl.* Australia.

Özal ★ (əʊ'zɑ:l) *n* **Turgut** ('tɜ:gʊt). 1927–93, Turkish statesman: prime minister (1983–89); president (1989–93).

Ozalid ('ɒzəlɪd) *n* **1** *Trademark.* a method of duplicating type matter, illustrations, etc., when printed on translucent paper. **2** a reproduction produced by this method.

Ozark Plateau ★ ('əʊzɑ:k) *n,* **Ozark Mountains,** *or* **Ozarks** *pl n* an eroded plateau in S Missouri, N Arkansas, and NE Oklahoma. Area: about 130 000 sq. km (50 000 sq. miles).

ozocerite *or* **ozokerite** (əʊ'zəʊkə,raɪt) *n* a brown or greyish wax that occurs associated with petroleum and is used for making candles and waxed paper. ORIG C19: from G *Ozokerit,* from Gk *ozein* to smell + *kēros* beeswax

ozone ('əʊzəʊn, əʊ'zəʊn) *n* **1** a colourless gas with a chlorine-like odour, formed by an electric discharge in oxygen: a strong oxidizing agent, used in bleaching, sterilizing water, purifying air, etc. Formula: O_3. Technical name: **trioxygen. 2** *Inf.* clean bracing air, as found at the seaside. ORIG C19: from G *Ozon,* from Gk: smell
▸ **ozonic** (əʊ'zɒnɪk) *or* **'ozonous** *adj*

ozone-friendly *adj* not harmful to the ozone layer; using substances that do not produce gases harmful to the ozone layer: *an ozone-friendly refrigerator.*

ozone layer *n* the region of the stratosphere with the highest concentration of ozone molecules, which by absorbing high-energy solar ultraviolet radiation protects organisms on earth. Also called: **ozonosphere.**

ozonize *or* **ozonise** ('əʊzəʊ,naɪz) *vb* **ozonizes, ozonizing, ozonized** *or* **ozonises, ozonising, ozonised.** (*tr*) **1** to convert (oxygen) into ozone. **2** to treat (a substance) with ozone.
▸ **,ozoni'zation** *or* **,ozoni'sation** *n* ▸ **'ozo,nizer** *or* **'ozo,niser** *n*

ozonosphere (əʊ'zəʊnə,sfɪə, -'zɒnə-) *n* another name for **ozone layer.**

Pp

p *or* **P** (piː) *n, pl* **p's, P's,** *or* **Ps. 1** the 16th letter of the English alphabet. **2** a speech sound represented by this letter. **3 mind one's p's and q's.** to be careful to behave correctly and use polite or suitable language.

p *symbol for:* **1** (in Britain) penny *or* pence. **2** *Music.* piano: an instruction to play quietly. **3** *Physics.* pico-. **4** *Physics.* **4a** momentum. **4b** proton. **4c** pressure.

P *symbol for:* **1** *Chem.* phosphorus. **2** *Physics.* **2a** parity. **2b** poise. **2c** power. **2d** pressure. **3** (on road signs) parking. **4** *Chess.* pawn. **5** *Currency.* **5a** peseta. **5b** peso. **6** (of a medicine or drug) available only from a chemist's shop, but not requiring a prescription to obtain it.

p. *abbrev. for:* **1** (*pl* **pp.**) page. **2** part. **3** participle. **4** past. **5** per. **6** pint. **7** pipe. **8** population. **9** post. ORIG L: after **10** pro. ORIG L: in favour of; for

p- *prefix* short for **para-**[1] (sense 6).

P45 *n* (in Britain) **1** a severance form issued by the Inland Revenue via an employer to a person leaving employment. **2 get one's P45** *Inf.* to be dismissed from one's employment.

pa[1] (pɑː) *n* an informal word for **father.**

pa[2] or **pah** (pɑː) *n NZ.* **1** a Maori village or settlement. **2** *History.* a Maori defensive position and settlement on a hilltop.

Pa 1 *the chemical symbol for* protactinium. **2** *symbol for* pascal.

PA *abbrev. for:* **1** personal assistant. **2** *Mil.* Post Adjutant. **3** power of attorney. **4** press agent. **5** Press Association. **6** private account. **7** public-address system. **8** publicity agent. **9** Publishers Association. **10** purchasing agent. **11** *Insurance.* particular average.

Pa. *abbrev. for* Pennsylvania.

p.a. *abbrev. for* per annum. ORIG L: yearly

Pabst ★ (*German* paːpst) *n* **G(eorge) W(ilhelm).** 1885–1967, German film director, whose films include *Joyless Street* (1925), *Pandora's Box* (1929), and *The Last Act* (1954).

pabulum (ˈpæbjʊləm) *n Rare.* **1** food. **2** food for thought, esp. when bland or dull. ORIG C17: from L, from *pascere* to feed

PABX (in Britain) *abbrev. for* private automatic branch exchange. See also **PBX.**

Pac. *abbrev. for* Pacific.

paca (ˈpɑːkə, ˈpækə) *n* a large burrowing rodent of Central and South America, having white-spotted brown fur. ORIG C17: from Sp., from Amerind

pace[1] (peɪs) *n* **1a** a single step in walking. **1b** the distance covered by a step. **2** a measure of length equal to the average length of a stride, approximately 3 feet. **3** speed of movement, esp. of walking or running. **4** rate or style of proceeding at some activity: *to live at a fast pace.* **5** manner or action of stepping, walking, etc.; gait. **6** any of the manners in which a horse or other quadruped walks or runs. **7** a manner of moving, sometimes developed in the horse, in which the two legs on the same side are moved at the same time. **8 keep pace with.** to proceed at the same speed as. **9 put (someone) through his** *or* **her paces.** to test the ability of (someone). **10 set the pace.** to determine the rate at which a group runs or walks or proceeds at some other activity. ◆ *vb* **paces, pacing, paced. 11** (*tr*) to set or determine the pace for, as in a race. **12** (often foll. by *about, up and down,* etc.) to walk with regular slow or fast paces, as in boredom, agitation, etc.: *to pace the room.* **13** (*tr;* often foll. by *out*) to measure by paces: *to pace out the distance.* **14** (*intr*) to walk with slow regular strides. **15** (*intr*) (of a horse) to move at the pace (the specially developed gait). ORIG C13: via OF from L *passūs* step, from *pandere* to extend (the legs as in walking)

pace[2] (ˈpeɪsɪ; *Latin* ˈpɑːkɛ) *prep* with due deference to: used to acknowledge politely someone who disagrees. ORIG C19: from L, from *pāx* peace

PACE (peɪs) *n* (in England and Wales) *acronym for* Police and Criminal Evidence Act.

pace bowler *n Cricket.* a bowler who characteristically delivers the ball rapidly.

pacemaker (ˈpeɪsˌmeɪkə) *n* **1** a person, horse, vehicle, etc., used in a race or speed trial to set the pace. **2** a person, organization, etc., regarded as being the leader in a particular activity. **3** Also called: **cardiac pacemaker.** a small area of specialized tissue within the wall of the heart whose spontaneous electrical activity initiates and controls the heartbeat. **4** Also called: **artificial pacemaker.** an electronic device to assume the functions of the natural cardiac pacemaker.

pacer (ˈpeɪsə) *n* **1** a horse trained to move at a special gait. **2** another word for **pacemaker** (sense 1).

pacesetter (ˈpeɪsˌsɛtə) *n* another word for **pacemaker** (senses 1, 2).

paceway (ˈpeɪsˌweɪ) *n Austral.* a racecourse for trotting and pacing.

Pachelbel ★ (*German* ˈpaxɛlbəl) *n* **Johann** (ˈjoːhan). 1653–1706, German organist and composer, noted esp. for his popular *Canon in D Major.*

pachisi (pəˈtʃiːzɪ) *n* an Indian game somewhat resembling backgammon, played on a cruciform board using six cowries as dice. ORIG C18: from Hindi, from *pacīs* twenty-five (the highest throw)

Pachuca ★ (*Spanish* paˈtʃuka) *n* a city in central Mexico, capital of Hidalgo state, in the Sierra Madre Oriental: silver mines; university (1961). Pop.: 174 013 (1990).

pachyderm (ˈpækɪˌdɜːm) *n* any very large thick-skinned mammal, such as an elephant, rhinoceros, or hippopotamus. ORIG C19: from F *pachyderme,* from Gk *pakhudermos,* from *pakhus* thick + *derma* skin
▸ **ˌpachyˈdermatous** *adj*

pacific (pəˈsɪfɪk) *adj* **1** tending or conducive to peace; conciliatory. **2** not aggressive. **3** free from conflict; peaceful. ORIG C16: from OF, from L *pācificus,* from *pāx* peace + *facere* to make
▸ **paˈcifically** *adv*

Pacific ★ (pəˈsɪfɪk) *n* **1 the.** short for **Pacific Ocean.** ◆ *adj* **2** of or relating to the Pacific Ocean or its islands.

Pacific Islands ★ *pl n* a former Trust Territory; an island group in the W Pacific Ocean, mandated to Japan after World War I and assigned to the US by the United Nations in 1947: comprised 2141 islands (96 inhabited) of the Caroline, Marshall, and Mariana groups (excluding Guam). In 1978 the Northern Marianas became a commonwealth in union with the US. The three remaining entities consisting of the Marshall Islands, the Republic of Belau (formerly Palau), and the Federated States of Micronesia became self-governing during the period 1979–80. In 1982 they signed agreements of free association with the US. Administrative centre: Saipan (Mariana Islands). Land area: about 1800 sq. km (700 sq. miles), scattered over about 7 500 000 sq. km (3 000 000 sq. miles) of ocean.

Pacific Northwest ★ *n* the region of North America lying north of the Columbia River and west of the Rockies.

Pacific Ocean ★ *n* the world's largest and deepest ocean, lying between Asia and Australia and North and South America. Area: about 165 760 000 sq. km (64 000 000 sq. miles). Average depth: 4215 m (14 050 ft). Greatest depth: Challenger Deep (in the Marianas Trench), 11 033 m (37 073 ft). Greatest width: (between

Panama and Mindanao, Philippines) 17 066 km (10 600 miles).

Pacific rim *n* the regions, countries, etc. that lie on the western shores of the Pacific Ocean, esp. in the context of their developing manufacturing capacity and consumer markets.

pacifier ('pæsɪˌfaɪə) *n* **1** a person or thing that pacifies. **2** *US & Canad.* a baby's dummy or teething ring.

pacifism ('pæsɪˌfɪzəm) *n* **1** the belief that violence of any kind is unjustifiable and that one should not participate in war, etc. **2** the belief that international disputes can be settled by arbitration rather than war.
▸ **'pacifist** *n, adj*

pacify ('pæsɪˌfaɪ) *vb* **pacifies, pacifying, pacified.** (*tr*) **1** to calm the anger or agitation of; mollify. **2** to restore to peace or order. ORIG C15: from OF *pacifier;* see PACIFIC
▸ **'paciˌfiable** *adj* ▸ **pacification** (ˌpæsɪfɪ'keɪʃən) *n*

Pacino ★ (pə'tʃiːnəʊ) *n* **Al,** full name *Alfredo James Pacino.* born 1940, US film actor; his films include *The Godfather* (1972), *Scent of a Woman* (1992), and *Heat* (1995).

pack[1] (pæk) *n* **1a** a bundle or load, esp. one carried on the back. **1b** (*as modifier*): *a pack animal.* **2** a collected amount of anything. **3** a complete set of similar things, esp. a set of 52 playing cards. **4** a group of animals of the same kind, esp. hunting animals: *a pack of hounds.* **5** any group or band that associates together, esp. for criminal purposes. **6** any group or set regarded dismissively: *a pack of fools; a pack of lies.* **7** *Rugby.* the forwards of a team. **8** the basic organizational unit of Cub Scouts and Brownie Guides. **9** *US & Canad.* same as **packet** (sense 1). **10** short for **pack ice.** **11** the quantity of something, such as food, packaged for preservation. **12** *Med.* a sheet or blanket, either damp or dry, for wrapping about the body, esp. for its soothing effect. **13** another name for **rucksack** *or* **backpack.** **14** Also called: **face pack.** a cream treatment that cleanses and tones the skin. **15** a parachute folded and ready for use. **16 go to the pack.** *Austral. & NZ inf.* to fall into a worse state or condition. **17** *Computing.* another name for **deck** (sense 4). ◆ *vb* **18** to place or arrange (articles) in (a container), such as clothes in a suitcase. **19** (*tr*) to roll up into a bundle. **20** (when *passive,* often foll. by *out*) to press tightly together; cram: *the audience packed into the foyer; the hall was packed out.* **21** to form (snow, ice, etc.) into a hard compact mass or (of snow, etc.) to become compacted. **22** (*tr*) to press in or cover tightly. **23** (*tr*) to load (a horse, donkey, etc.) with a burden. **24** (often foll. by *off* or *away*) to send away or go away, esp. hastily. **25** (*tr*) to seal (a joint) by inserting a layer of compressible material between the faces. **26** (*tr*) *Med.* to treat with a pack. **27** (*tr*) *Sl.* to be capable of inflicting (a blow, etc.): *he packs a mean punch.* **28** (*tr*) *US inf.* to carry or wear habitually: *he packs a gun.* **29** (*tr;* often foll. by *in, into, to,* etc.) *US, Canad., & NZ.* to carry (goods, etc.), esp. on the back. **30 send packing.** *Inf.* to dismiss peremptorily. ◆ See also **pack in, pack up.** ORIG C13: from ?
▸ **'packable** *adj*

pack[2] (pæk) *vb* (*tr*) to fill (a legislative body, committee, etc.) with one's own supporters: *to pack a jury.* ORIG C16: ? changed from PACT

package ('pækɪdʒ) *n* **1** any wrapped or boxed object or group of objects. **2a** a proposition, offer, or thing for sale in which separate items are offered together as a unit. **2b** (*as modifier*): *a package holiday; a package deal.* **3** the act or process of packing or packaging. **4** *Computing.* a set of programs designed for a specific type of problem. **5** the usual US and Canad. word for **packet** (sense 1). ◆ *vb* **packages, packaging, packaged.** (*tr*) **6** to wrap in or put into a package. **7** to design and produce a package for (retail goods). **8** to group (separate items) together as a single unit. **9** to compile (complete books) for a publisher to market.
▸ **'packager** *n*

packaging ('pækɪdʒɪŋ) *n* **1** the box or wrapping in which a product is offered for sale. **2** the presentation of a person, product, etc., to the public in a way designed to build up a favourable image.

pack drill *n* a military punishment of marching about carrying a full pack of equipment.

packer ('pækə) *n* **1** a person or company whose business is to pack goods, esp. food: *a meat packer.* **2** a person or machine that packs.

packet ('pækɪt) *n* **1** a small or medium-sized container of cardboard, paper, etc., often together with its contents: *a packet of biscuits.* Usual US and Canad. word: **package, pack.** **2** a small package; parcel. **3** Also called: **packet boat.** a boat that transports mail, passengers, goods, etc., on a fixed short route. **4** *Sl.* a large sum of money: *to cost a packet.* **5** *Computing.* a unit into which a larger piece of data is broken down for more efficient transmission. ◆ *vb* **6** (*tr*) to wrap up in a packet or as a packet. ORIG C16: from OF *pacquet,* from *pacquer* to pack, from ODu. *pak* a pack

packhorse ('pækˌhɔːs) *n* a horse used to transport goods, equipment, etc.

pack ice *n* a large area of floating ice, consisting of pieces that have become massed together.

pack in *vb* (*tr, adv*) *Brit. & NZ inf.* to stop doing (something) (esp. in **pack it in**).

packing ('pækɪŋ) *n* **1a** material used to cushion packed goods. **1b** (*as modifier*): *a packing needle.* **2** the packaging of foodstuffs. **3** any substance or material used to make joints watertight or gastight.

pack rat *n* a rat of W North America, having a long tail that is furry in some species.

packsaddle ('pækˌsædᵊl) *n* a saddle hung with packs, equipment, etc., used on a pack animal.

packthread ('pækˌθrɛd) *n* a strong twine for sewing or tying up packages.

pack up *vb* (*adv*) **1** to put (things) away in a proper or suitable place. **2** *Inf.* to give up (an attempt) or stop doing (something). **3** (*intr*) (of an engine, etc.) to fail to operate; break down.

pact (pækt) *n* an agreement or compact between two or more parties, nations, etc. ORIG C15: from OF *pacte,* from L *pactum,* from *pacīscī* to agree

pad[1] (pæd) *n* **1** a thick piece of soft material used to make something comfortable, give it shape, or protect it. **2** Also called: **stamp pad, ink pad.** a block of firm absorbent material soaked with ink for transferring to a rubber stamp. **3** Also called: **notepad, writing pad.** a number of sheets of paper fastened together along one edge. **4** a flat piece of stiff material used to back a piece of blotting paper. **5a** the fleshy cushion-like underpart of the foot of a cat, dog, etc. **5b** any of the parts constituting such a structure. **6** any of various level surfaces or flat-topped structures, such as a launch pad. **7** the large flat floating leaf of the water lily. **8** *Sl.* a person's residence. ◆ *vb* **pads, padding, padded.** (*tr*) **9** to line, stuff, or fill out with soft material, esp. in order to protect or shape. **10** (often foll. by *out*) to inflate with irrelevant or false information: *to pad out a story.* ORIG C16: from ?

pad[2] (pæd) *vb* **pads, padding, padded.** **1** (*intr;* often foll. by *along, up,* etc.) to walk with a soft or muffled tread. **2** (when *intr,* often foll. by *around*) to travel (a route, etc.) on foot, esp. at a slow pace; tramp: *to pad around the country.* ◆ *n* **3** a dull soft sound, esp. of footsteps. ORIG C16: ?from MDu. *paden,* from *pad* PATH

Padang ★ ('pɑːdɑːŋ) *n* a port in W Indonesia, in W Sumatra at the foot of the **Padang Highlands** on the Indian Ocean. Pop.: 721 500 (1995 est.).

padded cell *n* a room, esp. one in a mental hospital, with padded surfaces in which violent inmates are placed.

padding ('pædɪŋ) *n* **1** any soft material used to pad clothes, etc. **2** superfluous material put into a speech or written work to pad it out; waffle. **3** inflated or false entries in a financial account, esp. an expense account.

paddle[1] ('pædᵊl) *n* **1** a short light oar with a flat blade at one or both ends, used without a rowlock. **2** Also called: **float.** a blade of a water wheel or paddle wheel. **3** a period of paddling: *to go for a paddle upstream.* **4a** a paddle wheel used to propel a boat. **4b** (*as modifier*): *a paddle steamer.* **5** any of various instruments shaped like a paddle and used for beating, mixing, etc. **6** a table-tennis bat. **7** the flattened limb of a seal, turtle, etc., specialized for swimming. ◆ *vb* **paddles, paddling, paddled.** **8** to propel (a canoe, etc.) with a paddle. **9 paddle one's own canoe.** **9a** to

be self-sufficient. **9b** to mind one's own business. **10** (*tr*) to stir or mix with or as if with a paddle. **11** to row (a boat) steadily, but not at full pressure. **12** (*intr*) to swim with short rapid strokes, like a dog. **13** (*tr*) *US & Canad. inf.* to spank. ORIG C15: from ?
▸ **'paddler** *n*

paddle² ('pædᵊl) *vb* **paddles, paddling, paddled.** (*mainly intr*) **1** to walk or play barefoot in shallow water, mud, etc. **2** to dabble the fingers, hands, or feet in water. **3** to walk unsteadily, like a baby. **4** (*tr*) *Arch.* to fondle with the fingers. ◆ *n* **5** the act of paddling in water. ORIG C16: from ?
▸ **'paddler** *n*

paddle wheel *n* a large wheel fitted with paddles, turned by an engine to propel a vessel.

paddock ('pædək) *n* **1** a small enclosed field, often for grazing or training horses. **2** (in horse racing) the enclosure in which horses are paraded and mounted before a race. **3** *Austral. & NZ.* any area of fenced land. ORIG C17: var. of dialect *parrock,* from OE *pearruc* enclosure, of Gmc origin. See PARK

paddy¹ ('pædɪ) *n, pl* **paddies. 1** Also called: **paddy field.** a field planted with rice. **2** rice as a growing crop or when harvested but not yet milled. ORIG from Malay *pādī*

paddy² ('pædɪ) *n, pl* **paddies.** *Brit. inf.* a fit of temper. ORIG C19: from *Paddy* inf. name for an Irishman

pademelon *or* **paddymelon** ('pædɪˌmɛlən) *n* a small wallaby of coastal scrubby regions of Australia. ORIG C19: of Abor. origin

Paderborn ★ (*German* pa:dər'bɔrn) *n* a market town in NW Germany in North Rhine-Westphalia: scene of the meeting between Charlemagne and Pope Leo III (799 A.D.) that led to the foundation of the Holy Roman Empire. Pop.: 133 717 (1996 est.).

Paderewski ★ (*Polish* padɛ'rɛfski) *n* **Ignace Jan** (iɲas jan). 1860–1941, Polish pianist, composer, and statesman; prime minister (1919).

padkos ('pætˌkɒs) *pl n S. African.* snacks and provisions for a journey. ORIG Afrik., lit.: road food

padlock ('pædˌlɒk) *n* **1** a detachable lock having a hinged or sliding shackle, which can be used to secure a door, lid, etc., by passing the shackle through rings or staples. ◆ *vb* **2** (*tr*) to fasten as with a padlock. ORIG C15 *pad,* from ?

Padova ★ ('pa:dova) *n* the Italian name for **Padua.**

padre ('pɑ:drɪ) *n Inf.* (*sometimes cap.*) **1** father: used to address or refer to a priest. **2** a chaplain to the armed forces. ORIG via Sp. or It. from L *pater* father

padsaw ('pædˌsɔ:) *n* a small narrow saw used for cutting curves. ORIG C19: from PAD¹ (in the sense: a handle that can be fitted to various tools) + SAW¹

Padua ★ ('pædʒuə, 'pædjuə) *n* a city in NE Italy, in Veneto: important in Roman and Renaissance times; university (1222); botanical garden (1545). Pop.: 212 731 (1996 est.). Latin name: **Patavium** (pə'teɪvɪəm). Italian name: **Padova.**

Padus ★ ('peɪdəs) *n* the Latin name for the **Po²**.

paean *or US* (*sometimes*) **pean** ('pi:ən) *n* **1** a hymn sung in ancient Greece in thanksgiving to a deity. **2** any song of praise. **3** enthusiastic praise: *the film received a paean from the critics.* ORIG C16: via L from Gk *paiān* hymn to Apollo, from his title *Paiān,* the physician of the gods

paediatrician *or esp. US* **pediatrician** (ˌpi:dɪə'trɪʃən) *n* a medical practitioner who specializes in paediatrics.

paediatrics *or esp. US* **pediatrics** (ˌpi:dɪ'ætrɪks) *n* (*functioning as sing*) the branch of medical science concerned with children and their diseases.
▸ **ˌpaedi'atric** *or esp. US* **ˌpedi'atric** *adj*

paedo-, *before a vowel* **paed-,** *or esp. US* **pedo-, ped-** *combining form.* indicating a child or children: *paedophilia.* ORIG from Gk *pais, paid-* child

paedomorphosis (ˌpi:də'mɔ:fəsɪs) *n* the resemblance of adult animals to the young of their ancestors.

paedophilia *or esp. US* **pedophilia** (ˌpi:dəʊ'fɪlɪə) *n* the condition of being sexually attracted to children.
▸ **paedophile** *or esp. US* **pedophile** ('pi:dəʊˌfaɪl) *or* **ˌpaedo'philiˌac** *or esp. US* **ˌpedo'philiˌac** *n, adj*

paella (paɪ'ɛlə) *n, pl* **paellas** (-ləz). **1** a Spanish dish made from rice, shellfish, chicken, and vegetables. **2** the pan in which a paella is cooked. ORIG from Catalan, from OF *paelle,* from L *patella* small pan

paeony ('pi:ənɪ) *n, pl* **paeonies.** a variant spelling of **peony.**

Paestum ★ ('pɛstəm) *n* an ancient Greek colony on the coast of Lucania in S Italy.

pagan ('peɪgən) *n* **1** a member of a group professing any religion other than Christianity, Judaism, or Islam. **2** a person without any religion; heathen. ◆ *adj* **3** of or relating to pagans. **4** heathen; irreligious. ORIG C14: from Church L *pāgānus* civilian (hence, not a soldier of Christ), from L: villager, from *pāgus* village
▸ **'pagandom** *n* ▸ **'paganish** *adj* ▸ **'paganism** *n*

Paganini ★ (*Italian* paga'ni:ni) *n* **Niccolò** (nikko'lɔ). 1782–1840, Italian violinist and composer.

paganize *or* **paganise** ('peɪgəˌnaɪz) *vb* **paganizes, paganizing, paganized** *or* **paganises, paganising, paganised.** to become pagan or convert to paganism.

page¹ (peɪdʒ) *n* **1** one side of one of the leaves of a book, newspaper, etc., or the written or printed matter it bears. **2** such a leaf considered as a unit. **3** an episode, phase, or period: *a glorious page in the revolution.* **4** a screenful of information from a website, teletext service, etc., displayed on a television monitor or visual display unit. ◆ *vb* **pages, paging, paged. 5** another word for **paginate.** ORIG C15: via OF from L *pāgina*

page² (peɪdʒ) *n* **1** a boy employed to run errands, carry messages, etc., for the guests in a hotel, club, etc. **2** a youth in attendance at official functions or ceremonies, esp. weddings. **3** *Medieval history.* **3a** a boy in training for knighthood in personal attendance on a knight. **3b** a youth in the personal service of a person of rank. ◆ *vb* **pages, paging, paged.** (*tr*) **4** to call out the name of (a person), esp. by a loudspeaker system, so as to give him a message. **5** to call (a person) by an electronic device, such as a bleeper. **6** to act as a page to or attend as a page. ORIG C13: via OF from It. *paggio,* prob. from Gk *paidion* boy, from *pais* child

Page ★ (peɪdʒ) *n* **1** Sir **Earle** (**Christmas Grafton**). 1880–1961, Australian statesman; co-leader, with S. M. Bruce, of the federal government of Australia (1923–29). **2** Sir **Frederick Handley.** 1885–1962, British pioneer in the design and manufacture of aircraft.

pageant ('pædʒənt) *n* **1** an elaborate colourful display portraying scenes from history, etc. **2** any magnificent or showy display, procession, etc. ORIG C14: from Med. L *pāgina* scene of a play, from L: PAGE¹

pageantry ('pædʒəntrɪ) *n, pl* **pageantries. 1** spectacular display or ceremony. **2** *Arch.* pageants collectively.

pageboy ('peɪdʒˌbɔɪ) *n* **1** a smooth medium-length hairstyle with the ends of the hair curled under. **2** a less common word for **page²**.

pager ('peɪdʒə) *n* an electronic device, capable of receiving short messages, used by people who need to be contacted urgently.

page-three *n modifier Brit.* denoting a scantily dressed attractive girl, as photographed on page three of some tabloid newspapers.

page-turner *n* a very exciting or interesting book. ORIG C20: from the notion that a reader cannot stop turning the pages

paginate ('pædʒɪˌneɪt) *vb* **paginates, paginating, paginated.** (*tr*) to number the pages of (a book, manuscript, etc.) in sequence. Cf. **foliate.**
▸ **ˌpagi'nation** *n*

Pagnol ★ (*French* paɲɔl) *n* **Marcel** (**Paul**) (marsɛl). 1895–1974, French dramatist, film director, and novelist, noted for his depiction of Provençal life in such films as *Manon des Sources* (1952; remade 1986).

pagoda (pə'gəʊdə) *n* an Indian or Far Eastern temple, esp. a tower, usually pyramidal and having many storeys. ORIG C17: from Port. *pagode,* ult. from Sansk. *bhagavatī* divine

pagoda tree *n* a Chinese leguminous tree with ornamental white flowers.

Pago Pago ★ ('pɑ:ŋgəʊ 'pɑ:ŋgəʊ) *n* a port in American

Samoa, on SE Tutuila Island. Pop.: 4000 (1990). Former name: **Pango Pango.**

Pahang ★ (pəˈhʌŋ) *n* a state of Peninsular Malaysia, on the South China Sea: the largest Malayan state; mountainous and heavily forested. Capital: Kuala Lipis. Pop.: 1 056 100 (1993 est.). Area: 35 964 sq. km (13 886 sq. miles).

Pahlavi ★ (ˈpɑːləvɪ) *n* **1** **Mohammed Reza** (ˈriːzə). 1919–80, shah of Iran (1941–79); forced into exile (1979). **2** his father, **Reza.** 1877–1944, shah of Iran (1925–41). Originally an army officer, he gained power by a coup d'état (1921) and was chosen shah by the National Assembly.

Pahsien ★ (ˈpɑːˈʃjɛn) *n* another name for **Chongqing.**

paid (peɪd) *vb* **1** the past tense and past participle of **pay**[1]. **2** **put paid to.** *Chiefly Brit. & NZ.* to end or destroy: *breaking his leg put paid to his hopes of running in the Olympics.*

paid-up *adj* **1** having paid the required fee to be a member of an organization, etc. **2** denoting a security in which all the instalments have been paid; fully paid: *a paid-up share.* **3** denoting all the money that a company has received from its shareholders: *the paid-up capital.* **4** denoting an endowment assurance policy on which the payment of premiums has stopped and the surrender value has been used to purchase a new single-premium policy.

Paignton ★ (ˈpeɪntən) *n* a town and resort in SW England, in Devon: administratively part of Torbay since 1968.

pail (peɪl) *n* **1** a bucket, esp. one made of wood or metal. **2** Also called: **pailful.** the quantity that fills a pail. ORIG OE *pægel*

paillasse (ˈpælɪˌæs, ˌpælɪˈæs) *n* a variant spelling (esp. US) of **palliasse.**

pain (peɪn) *n* **1** the sensation of acute physical hurt or discomfort caused by injury, illness, etc. **2** emotional suffering or mental distress. **3** **on pain of.** subject to the penalty of. **4** Also called: **pain in the neck.** *Inf.* a person or thing that is a nuisance. ◆ *vb* (*tr*) **5** to cause (a person) hurt, grief, anxiety, etc. **6** *Inf.* to annoy; irritate. ◆ See also **pains.** ORIG C13: from OF *peine,* from L *poena* punishment, grief, from Gk *poinē* penalty
▸ **ˈpainless** *adj*

Paine ★ (peɪn) *n* **Thomas.** 1737–1809, US political pamphleteer, born in England. His works include *Common Sense* (1776), supporting the American colonists' fight for independence; and *The Rights of Man* (1791–92), a justification of the French Revolution.

pained (peɪnd) *adj* having or expressing pain or distress, esp. mental or emotional distress.

painful (ˈpeɪnfʊl) *adj* **1** causing pain; distressing: *a painful duty.* **2** affected with pain. **3** tedious or difficult. **4** *Inf.* extremely bad.
▸ **ˈpainfully** *adv* ▸ **ˈpainfulness** *n*

painkiller (ˈpeɪnˌkɪlə) *n* **1** an analgesic drug or agent. **2** anything that relieves pain.

pains (peɪnz) *pl n* **1** care or trouble (esp. in **take pains, be at pains to**). **2** painful sensations experienced during contractions in childbirth; labour pains.

painstaking (ˈpeɪnzˌteɪkɪŋ) *adj* extremely careful, esp. as to fine detail.
▸ **ˈpainsˌtakingly** *adv* ▸ **ˈpainsˌtakingness** *n*

paint (peɪnt) *n* **1** a substance used for decorating or protecting a surface, esp. a mixture consisting of a solid pigment suspended in a liquid that dries to form a hard coating. **2** a dry film of paint on a surface. **3** *Inf.* face make-up, such as rouge. **4** short for **greasepaint.** ◆ *vb* **5** to make (a picture) of (a figure, landscape, etc.) with paint applied to a surface such as canvas. **6** to coat (a surface, etc.) with paint, as in decorating. **7** (*tr*) to apply (liquid, etc.) onto (a surface): *she painted the cut with antiseptic.* **8** (*tr*) to apply make-up onto (the face, lips, etc.). **9** (*tr*) to describe vividly in words. **10** **paint the town red.** *Inf.* to celebrate uninhibitedly. ORIG C13: from OF *peint* painted, from *peindre* to paint, from L *pingere* to paint
▸ **ˈpainty** *adj*

paintball game (ˈpeɪntˌbɔːl) *n* a game in which teams of players simulate a military skirmish, shooting each other with paint pellets that explode on impact.

paintbox (ˈpeɪntˌbɒks) *n* a box containing a tray of dry watercolour paints.

paintbrush (ˈpeɪntˌbrʌʃ) *n* a brush used to apply paint.

Painted Desert ★ *n* a section of the high plateau country of N central Arizona, along the N side of the Little Colorado River Valley: brilliant-coloured rocks; occupied largely by Navaho and Hopi Indians. Area: about 20 000 sq. km (7500 sq. miles).

painted lady *n* a migratory butterfly with pale brownish-red mottled wings.

painter[1] (ˈpeɪntə) *n* **1** a person who paints surfaces as a trade. **2** an artist who paints pictures.
▸ **ˈpainterly** *adj*

painter[2] (ˈpeɪntə) *n* a line attached to the bow of a boat for tying it up. ORIG C15: prob. from OF *penteur* strong rope

painting (ˈpeɪntɪŋ) *n* **1** the art of applying paints to canvas, etc. **2** a picture made in this way. **3** the act of applying paint to a surface.

paint stripper *or* **remover** *n* a liquid, often caustic, used to remove paint from a surface.

paintwork (ˈpeɪntˌwɜːk) *n* a surface, such as wood or a car body, that is painted.

pair (pɛə) *n, pl* **pairs** *or* (*functioning as sing or pl*) **pair.** **1** two identical or similar things matched for use together: *a pair of socks.* **2** two persons, animals, things, etc., used or grouped together: *a pair of horses; a pair of scoundrels.* **3** an object considered to be two identical or similar things joined together: *a pair of trousers.* **4** two people joined in love or marriage. **5** a male and a female animal of the same species kept for breeding purposes. **6** *Parliament.* **6a** two opposed members who both agree not to vote on a specified motion. **6b** the agreement so made. **7** two playing cards of the same rank or denomination. **8** one member of a matching pair: *I can't find the pair to this glove.* ◆ *vb* **9** (often foll. by *off*) to arrange or fall into groups of twos. **10** to group or be grouped in matching pairs. **11** to join or be joined in marriage; mate or couple. **12** (when *tr, usually passive*) *Parliament.* to form or cause to form a pair. ORIG C13: from OF *paire,* from L *paria* equal (things), from *pār* equal

> **USAGE NOTE** Like other collective nouns, *pair* takes a singular or a plural verb according to whether it is seen as a unit or as a collection of two things: *the pair are said to dislike each other; a pair of good shoes is essential.*

paisley (ˈpeɪzlɪ) *n* **1** a pattern of small curving shapes with intricate detailing. **2** a soft fine wool fabric traditionally printed with this pattern. **3** a shawl made of this fabric, popular in the late 19th century. **4** (*modifier*) of or decorated with this pattern: *a paisley scarf.* ORIG C19: after PAISLEY[1]

Paisley[1] ★ (ˈpeɪzlɪ) *n* an industrial town in SW Scotland, the administrative centre of Renfrewshire: one of the world's chief centres for the manufacture of thread, linen, and gauze in the 19th century. Pop.: 75 526 (1991).

Paisley[2] ★ (ˈpeɪzlɪ) *n* **Ian** (**Richard Kyle**). born 1926, Northern Ireland politician and Presbyterian minister; cofounder and leader of the Ulster Democratic Unionist Party.
▸ **ˈPaisleyˌite** *n*

pajamas (pəˈdʒɑːməz) *pl n* the US spelling of **pyjamas.**

Pakeha (ˈpɑːkɪˌhɑː) *n NZ.* a European, as distinct from a Maori: *Maori and Pakeha.* ORIG from Maori

Paki (ˈpækɪ) *Brit. sl., offens.* ◆ *n, pl* **Pakis.** **1** a Pakistani or person of Pakistani descent. ◆ *adj* **2** Pakistani or of Pakistani descent.

Pakistan ★ (ˌpɑːkɪˈstɑːn) *n* **1** a republic in S Asia, on the Arabian Sea: the Union of Pakistan, formed in 1947, comprised West and East Pakistan; East Pakistan gained independence as Bangladesh in 1971 and West Pakistan became Pakistan; a member of the Commonwealth from 1947, it withdrew from 1972 until 1989 and was

suspended in 1999: contains the fertile plains of the Indus valley rising to mountains in the north and west. Official language: Urdu. Official religion: Muslim. Currency: rupee. Capital: Islamabad. Pop.: 152 231 000 (1999 est.). Area: 801 508 sq. km (309 463 sq. miles). **2** a former republic in S Asia consisting of the provinces of West Pakistan and East Pakistan (now Bangladesh), 1500 km (900 miles) apart: formed in 1947 from the predominantly Muslim parts of India.
► **ˌPakiˈstani** *n, adj*

pakora (pəˈkɔːrə) *n* an Indian dish consisting of pieces of vegetable, chicken, etc., dipped in spiced batter and deep-fried. ORIG C20: from Hindi

pal (pæl) *Inf.* ◆ *n* **1** a close friend; comrade. ◆ *vb* **pals, palling, palled. 2** (*intr;* usually foll. by *with*) to associate as friends. ORIG C17: from E Gypsy: brother, ult. from Sansk. *bhrātar* BROTHER

PAL (pæl) *n acronym for* phase alternation line: a colour-television broadcasting system used generally in Europe.

Pal. *abbrev. for* Palestine.

palace (ˈpælɪs) *n* (*cap. when part of a name*) **1** the official residence of a reigning monarch. **2** the official residence of various high-ranking people, as of an archbishop. **3** a large and richly furnished building resembling a royal palace. ORIG C13: from OF *palais,* from L *Palātium* PALATINE

Palacio Valdés ★ (*Spanish* paˈlaθjo balˈdes) *n* **Armando** (arˈmando). 1853–1938, Spanish novelist and critic.

paladin (ˈpælədɪn) *n* **1** one of the legendary twelve peers of Charlemagne's court. **2** a knightly champion. ORIG C16: via F from It. *paladino,* from L *palātīnus* imperial official

palaeo-, *before a vowel* **palae-** *or esp. US* **paleo-, pale-** *combining form.* old, ancient, or prehistoric: *palaeography.* ORIG from Gk *palaios* old

palaeobotany *or US* **paleobotany** (ˌpælɪəʊˈbɒtənɪ) *n* the study of fossil plants.
► **ˌpalaeoˈbotanist** *or US* **ˌpaleoˈbotanist** *n*

Palaeocene *or US* **Paleocene** (ˈpælɪəʊˌsiːn) *adj* **1** of, denoting, or formed in the first epoch of the Tertiary period. ◆ *n* **2 the.** the Palaeocene epoch or rock series. ORIG C19: from F, from *paléo* PALAEO- + Gk *kainos* new

palaeoclimatology *or US* **paleoclimatology** (ˌpælɪəʊˌklaɪməˈtɒlədʒɪ) *n* the study of climates of the geological past.
► **ˌpalaeoˌclimaˈtologist** *or US* **ˌpaleoˌclimaˈtologist** *n*

palaeoecology *or US* **paleoecology** (ˌpælɪəʊɪˈkɒlədʒɪ) *n* the study of fossil animals and plants in order to deduce their ecology and the environment conditions in which they lived.
► **ˌpalaeoˌecoˈlogical** *or US* **ˌpaleoˌecoˈlogical** *adj*
► **ˌpalaeoeˈcologist** *or US* **ˌpaleoeˈcologist** *n*

palaeography *or US* **paleography** (ˌpælɪˈɒgrəfɪ) *n* **1** the study of the handwritings of the past, and often the manuscripts, etc., so that they may be dated, read, etc. **2** a handwriting of the past.
► **ˌpalaeˈographer** *or US* **ˌpaleˈographer** *n* ► **palaeographic** (ˌpælɪəʊˈgræfɪk), **ˌpalaeoˈgraphical** *or US* **ˌpaleoˈgraphic, ˌpaleoˈgraphical** *adj*

Palaeolithic *or US* **Paleolithic** (ˌpælɪəʊˈlɪθɪk) *n* **1** the period of the emergence of primitive man and the manufacture of unpolished chipped stone tools, about 2.5 million to 3 million years ago. ◆ *adj* **2** (*sometimes not cap.*) of or relating to this period.

palaeomagnetism *or US* **paleomagnetism** (ˌpælɪəʊˈmægnɪtɪzəm) *n* the study of the fossil magnetism in rocks, used to determine the past configuration of the earth's constituents.

palaeontology *or US* **paleontology** (ˌpælɪɒnˈtɒlədʒɪ) *n* the study of fossils to determine the structure and evolution of extinct animals and plants and the age and conditions of deposition of the rock strata in which they are found. ORIG C19: from PALAEO- + ONTO- + -LOGY
► **palaeontological** *or US* **paleontological** (ˌpælɪˌɒntəˈlɒdʒɪkᵊl) *adj* ► **ˌpalaeonˈtologist** *or US* **ˌpaleonˈtologist** *n*

Palaeozoic (ˌpælɪəʊˈzəʊɪk) *adj* **1** of, denoting, or relating to an era of geological time that began 600 million years ago with the Cambrian period and lasted about 375 million years until the end of the Permian period. ◆ *n* **2 the.** the Palaeozoic era. ORIG C19: from PALAEO- + Gk *zōē* life + -IC

Palagi (pɑːˈlʌŋiː) *n, pl* **Palagis** *NZ.* a Samoan word for a **European.**

palanquin *or* **palankeen** (ˌpælənˈkiːn) *n* a covered litter, formerly used in the Orient, carried on the shoulders of four men. ORIG C16: from Port. *palanquim,* from Prakrit *pallanka,* from Sansk. *paryanka* couch

palatable (ˈpælətəbᵊl) *adj* **1** pleasant to taste. **2** acceptable or satisfactory.
► **ˌpalataˈbility** *or* **ˈpalatableness** *n* ► **ˈpalatably** *adv*

palatal (ˈpælətᵊl) *adj* **1** Also: **palatine.** of or relating to the palate. **2** *Phonetics.* of, relating to, or denoting a speech sound articulated with the blade of the tongue touching the hard palate. ◆ *n* **3** Also called: **palatine.** the bony plate that forms the palate. **4** *Phonetics.* a palatal speech sound, such as (j).
► **ˈpalatally** *adv*

palatalize *or* **palatalise** (ˈpælətəˌlaɪz) *vb* **palatalizes, palatalizing, palatalized** *or* **palatalises, palatalising, palatalised.** (*tr*) to pronounce (a speech sound) with the blade of the tongue touching the palate.
► **ˌpalataliˈzation** *or* **ˌpalataliˈsation** *n*

palate (ˈpælɪt) *n* **1** the roof of the mouth, separating the oral and nasal cavities. See **hard palate, soft palate. 2** the sense of taste: *she had no palate for the wine.* **3** relish or enjoyment. ORIG C14: from L *palātum,* ? of Etruscan origin

> **USAGE NOTE** See at **palette.**

palatial (pəˈleɪʃəl) *adj* of, resembling, or suitable for a palace; sumptuous.
► **paˈlatially** *adv*

palatinate (pəˈlætɪnɪt) *n* a territory ruled by a palatine prince or noble or count palatine.

Palatinate ★ (pəˈlætɪnɪt) *n* **1 the.** either of two territories in SW Germany, once ruled by the counts palatine. **Upper Palatinate** is now in Bavaria; **Lower** or **Rhine Palatinate** is now in Rhineland-Palatinate, Baden-Württemberg, and Hesse. German name: **Pfalz. 2** a native or inhabitant of the Palatinate.
► **ˈPalaˌtine** *adj, n*

palatine[1] (ˈpæləˌtaɪn) *adj* **1** (of an individual) possessing royal prerogatives in a territory. **2** of or relating to a count palatine, county palatine, palatinate, or palatine. **3** of or relating to a palace. ◆ *n* **4** *Feudal history.* the lord of a palatinate. **5** any of various important officials at the late Roman, Merovingian, or Carolingian courts. ORIG C15: via F from L *palātīnus* belonging to the palace, from *palātium;* see PALACE

palatine[2] (ˈpæləˌtaɪn) *adj* **1** of the palate. ◆ *n* **2** either of two bones forming the hard palate. ORIG C17: from F *palatin,* from L *palātum* palate

Palatine ★ (ˈpæləˌtaɪn) *n* **1** one of the Seven Hills of Rome: traditionally the site of the first settlement of Rome. ◆ *adj* **2** of, relating to, or designating this hill.

Palau Islands ★ (pɑːˈlaʊ) *pl n* a former name (until 1981) of the (Republic of) **Belau.**

palaver (pəˈlɑːvə) *n* **1** tedious or time-consuming business, esp. when of a formal nature: *all the palaver of filling in forms.* **2** confused talk and activity; hubbub. **3** (often used humorously) a conference. **4** *Now rare.* talk intended to flatter or persuade. ◆ *vb* **5** (*intr*) (often used humorously) to have a conference. **6** (*intr*) to talk confusedly. **7** (*tr*) to flatter or cajole. ORIG C18: from Port. *palavra* talk, from L *parabola* PARABLE

Palawan ★ (*Spanish* paˈlavan) *n* an island of the SW Philippines between the South China Sea and the Sulu Sea: the westernmost island in the country; mountainous and forested. Capital: Puerto Princesa. Pop.: 311 548 (1980). Area: 11 785 sq. km (4550 sq. miles).

palazzo pants (pəˈlætsəʊ) *pl n* women's trousers with very wide legs. ORIG C20: *palazzo* from It., lit.: PALACE

pale[1] (peɪl) *adj* **1** lacking brightness or colour: *pale morning light.* **2** (of a colour) whitish. **3** dim or wan: *the pale stars.* **4** feeble: *a pale effort.* ◆ *vb* **pales, paling, paled. 5** to make or become pale or paler; blanch. **6** (*intr;* often foll.

by *before*) to lose superiority (in comparison to): *her beauty paled before that of her hostess.* ORIG C13: from OF *palle,* from L *pallidus,* from *pallēre* to look wan
▸ **'palely** *adv* ▸ **'paleness** *n* ▸ **'palish** *adj*

pale² (peɪl) *n* **1** a wooden post or strip used as an upright member in a fence. **2** an enclosing barrier, esp. a fence made of pales. **3** an area enclosed by a pale. **4** *Heraldry.* a vertical stripe, usually in the centre of a shield. **5 beyond the pale.** outside the limits of social convention. ORIG C14: from OF *pal,* from L *pālus* stake

paleface ('peɪlˌfeɪs) *n* a derogatory term for a White person, said to have been used by North American Indians.

Palembang ★ (pɑːˈlɛmbɑːŋ) *n* a port in W Indonesia, in S Sumatra; oil refineries; university (1955). Pop.: 1 352 300 (1995 est.).

Palencia ★ (*Spanish* paˈlenθia) *n* a city in N central Spain: earliest university in Spain (1208); seat of Castilian kings (12th–13th centuries); communications centre. Pop.: 77 752 (1991).

Palenque ★ (*Spanish* paˈleŋke) *n* the site of an ancient Mayan city in S Mexico famous for its architectural ruins.

paleo- *or before a vowel* **pale-** *combining form.* variants (esp. US) of **palaeo-**.

Palermo ★ (pəˈlɛəməʊ, -ˈlɜː-; *Italian* paˈlɛrmo) *n* the capital of Sicily, on the NW coast: founded by the Phoenicians in the 8th century B.C. Pop.: 689 301 (1996 est.).

Palestine ★ ('pælɪˌstaɪn) *n* **1** Also called: the **Holy Land, Canaan.** the area between the Jordan River and the Mediterranean Sea in which most of the biblical narrative is located. **2** the province of the Roman Empire in this region. **3** the former British mandatory territory created by the League of Nations in 1922 (but effective from 1920), and including all of the present territories of Israel, which was created following the British withdrawal in 1948. In 1993 Israel offered Palestinians autonomy in the Gaza Strip and parts of the West Bank (implemented in 1994).

Palestine Liberation Organization *n* an organization founded in 1964 with the aim of creating a state for Palestinian Arabs. In 1993 it signed a peace agreement with Israel, which granted Palestinian autonomy in the Gaza Strip and parts of the West Bank. Abbrev.: **PLO.**

Palestinian (ˌpælɪˈstɪnɪən) *adj* **1** of or relating to Palestine, its native Arab population, or their descendants. ◆ *n* **2** a Palestinian Arab, esp. one now living in the Palestinian Administered Territories, Israel, Jordan, Lebanon, or as a refugee from Israeli-occupied territory.

Palestinian Administered Territories ★ *n* the Gaza Strip and parts of the West Bank in Israel: these areas were granted autonomous status under the control of the Palestinian National Authority following the 1993 peace agreement between Israel and the Palestine Liberation Organization. Also called: **Palestinian Autonomous Areas.**

Palestinian National Authority *n* the authority formed in 1994 to govern the Palestinian Administered Territories. Abbrev.: **PNA.**

Palestrina ★ (ˌpælɛˈstriːnə) *n* **Giovanni Pierluigi da** (dʒoˈvanni pierˈluiːdʒi da). ?1525–94, Italian composer and master of counterpoint. His works, nearly all for unaccompanied choir and religious in nature, include the *Missa Papae Marcelli* (1555).

palette ('pælɪt) *n* **1** Also: **pallet.** a flat piece of wood, plastic, etc., used by artists as a surface on which to mix their paints. **2** the range of colours characteristic of a particular artist, painting, or school of painting: *a restricted palette.* **3** the available range of colours or patterns that can be displayed by a computer on a visual display unit. ORIG C17: from F, dim. of *pale* shovel, from L *pala* spade

> **USAGE NOTE** This word is occasionally used when *palate* is meant: *I have a sweet palate* (not *palette*).

palette *or* **pallet knife** *n* a spatula with a thin flexible blade used in painting and cookery.

Paley ★ ('peɪlɪ) *n* **William.** 1743–1805, British theologian and utilitarian philosopher. His works include *Horae Paulinae* (1790) and *Natural Theology* (1802).

palfrey ('pɔːlfrɪ) *n Arch.* a light saddle horse, esp. ridden by women. ORIG C12: from OF *palefrei,* from Med. L, from LL *paraverēdus,* from Gk *para* beside + L *verēdus* light fleet horse, of Celtic origin

Pali ('pɑːlɪ) *n* an ancient language of India derived from Sanskrit; the language of the Buddhist scriptures. ORIG C19: from Sansk. *pāli-bhāsa,* from *pāli* canon + *bhāsa* language, of Dravidian origin

palimony ('pælɪmənɪ) *n US.* alimony awarded to a nonmarried partner after the break-up of a long-term relationship. ORIG C20: from PAL + ALIMONY

palimpsest ('pælɪmpˌsɛst) *n* **1** a manuscript on which two or more texts have been written, each one being erased to make room for the next. ◆ *adj* **2** (of a text) written on a palimpsest. **3** (of a document, etc.) used as a palimpsest. ORIG C17: from L *palimpsestus,* from Gk *palimpsēstos,* from *palin* again + *psēstos* rubbed smooth

palindrome ('pælɪnˌdrəʊm) *n* a word or phrase the letters of which, when taken in reverse order, read the same: *able was I ere I saw Elba.* ORIG C17: from Gk *palindromos* running back again
▸ **palindromic** (ˌpælɪnˈdrɒmɪk) *adj*

paling ('peɪlɪŋ) *n* **1** a fence made of pales. **2** pales collectively. **3** a single pale. **4** the act of erecting pales.

palisade (ˌpælɪˈseɪd) *n* **1** a strong fence made of stakes driven into the ground, esp. for defence. **2** one of the stakes used in such a fence. ◆ *vb* **palisades, palisading, palisaded. 3** (*tr*) to enclose with a palisade. ORIG C17: via F from OProvençal *palissada,* ult. from L *pālus* stake

Palk Strait ★ (pɔːk, pɔːlk) *n* a channel between SE India and N Ceylon. Width: about 64 km (40 miles).

pall¹ (pɔːl) *n* **1** a cloth covering, usually black, spread over a coffin or tomb. **2** a coffin, esp. during the funeral ceremony. **3** a dark heavy covering; shroud: *the clouds formed a pall over the sky.* **4** a depressing or oppressive atmosphere: *her bereavement cast a pall on the party.* **5** *Heraldry.* a Y-shaped bearing. **6** *Christianity.* a small square linen cloth with which the chalice is covered at the Eucharist. ◆ *vb* **7** (*tr*) to cover or depress with a pall. ORIG OE *pæll,* from L *pallium* cloak

pall² (pɔːl) *vb* **1** (*intr;* often foll. by *on*) to become boring, insipid, or tiresome (to): *history classes palled on me.* **2** to cloy or satiate, or become cloyed or satiated. ORIG C14: var. of APPAL

Palladian (pəˈleɪdɪən) *adj* denoting, relating to, or having the style of architecture created by Andrea Palladio. ORIG C18: after Andrea PALLADIO
▸ **Pal'ladian,ism** *n*

Palladio ★ (*Italian* palˈlaːdio) *n* **Andrea** (anˈdrɛːa). 1508–80, Italian architect who revived and developed classical architecture, esp. the ancient Roman ideals of symmetrical planning and harmonic proportions. His treatise *Four Books on Architecture* (1570) and his designs for villas and palaces influenced architecture in England and the US.

palladium¹ (pəˈleɪdɪəm) *n* a ductile malleable silvery-white element of the platinum metal group: used as a catalyst and, alloyed with gold, in jewellery, etc. Symbol: Pd; atomic no.: 46; atomic wt.: 106.4. ORIG C19: after the asteroid *Pallas,* at the time (1803) a recent discovery

palladium² (pəˈleɪdɪəm) *n* something believed to ensure protection; safeguard. ORIG C17: after the *Palladium,* a statue of Pallas Athena, Gk goddess of wisdom

Pallas Athena *or* **Pallas** ★ *n* another name for **Athena.**

pallbearer ('pɔːlˌbɛərə) *n* a person who carries or escorts the coffin at a funeral.

pallet¹ ('pælɪt) *n* a straw-filled mattress or bed. ORIG C14: from Anglo-Norman *paillet,* from OF *paille* straw, from L *palea* straw

pallet² ('pælɪt) *n* **1** an instrument with a handle and a flat, sometimes flexible, blade used by potters for shaping. **2** a portable platform for storing and moving goods. **3** *Horology.* the locking lever that engages and disengages to give impulses to the balance. **4** a variant spelling of

palette (sense 1). **5** *Music.* a flap valve that opens to allow air from the wind chest to enter an organ pipe, causing it to sound. ORIG C16: from OF *palette* a little shovel, from L *pala* spade

palletize *or* **palletise** ('pælətaɪz) *vb* **palletizes, palletizing, palletized** *or* **palletises, palletising, palletised.** (*tr*) to store or transport (goods) on pallets.
▸ ˌ**palletiˈzation** *or* ˌ**palletiˈsation** *n*

palliasse *or esp. US* **paillasse** ('pælɪˌæs, ˌpælɪ'æs) *n* a straw-filled mattress; pallet. ORIG C18: from F *paillasse,* from It. *pagliaccio,* ult. from L *palea* PALLET[1]

palliate ('pælɪˌeɪt) *vb* **palliates, palliating, palliated.** (*tr*) **1** to lessen the severity of (pain, disease, etc.) without curing; alleviate. **2** to cause (an offence, etc.) to seem less serious; extenuate. ORIG C16: from LL *palliāre* to cover up, from L *pallium* a cloak
▸ ˌ**palliˈation** *n*

palliative ('pælɪətɪv) *adj* **1** relieving without curing. ◆ *n* **2** something that palliates, such as a sedative drug.
▸ ˈ**palliatively** *adv*

pallid ('pælɪd) *adj* lacking colour, brightness, or vigour: *a pallid complexion; a pallid performance.* ORIG C17: from L *pallidus,* from *pallēre* to be PALE[1]
▸ ˈ**pallidly** *adv* ▸ ˈ**pallidness** *or* **palˈlidity** *n*

pall-mall ('pæl'mæl) *n Obs.* **1** a game in which a ball is driven by a mallet along an alley and through an iron ring. **2** the alley itself. ORIG C17: from obs. F, from It. *pallamaglio,* from *palla* ball + *maglio* mallet

Pall Mall ★ ('pæl 'mæl) *n* a street in London, noted for its many clubs.

pallor ('pælə) *n* a pale condition, esp. when unnatural: *fear gave his face a deathly pallor.* ORIG C17: from L: whiteness (of the skin), from *pallēre* to be PALE[1]

pally ('pælɪ) *adj* **pallier, palliest.** *Inf.* on friendly terms.

palm[1] (pɑːm) *n* **1** the inner part of the hand from the wrist to the base of the fingers. **2** a linear measure based on the breadth or length of a hand, equal to three to four inches (7.5 to 10 centimetres) or seven to ten inches (17.5 to 25 centimetres) respectively. **3** the part of a glove that covers the palm. **4a** one side of the blade of an oar. **4b** the face of the fluke of an anchor. **5** a flattened part of the antlers of certain deer. **6 in the palm of one's hand.** at one's mercy or command. ◆ *vb* (*tr*) **7** to conceal in or about the hand, as in sleight-of-hand tricks, etc. ◆ See also **palm off.** ORIG C14 *paume,* via OF from L *palma*
▸ **palmar** ('pælmə) *adj*

palm[2] (pɑːm) *n* **1** any treelike plant of a tropical and subtropical family having a straight unbranched trunk crowned with large pinnate or palmate leaves. **2** a leaf or branch of any of these trees, a symbol of victory, success, etc. **3** merit or victory. ORIG OE, from L *palma,* from the likeness of its spreading fronds to a hand; see PALM[1]
▸ **palmaceous** (pæl'meɪʃəs) *adj*

Palma[1] ★ (*Spanish* 'palma) *n* the capital of the Balearic Islands, on the SW coast of Majorca: a tourist centre. Pop.: 318 030 (1995 est.). Official name: **Palma de Mallorca.**

Palma[2] ★ (*Italian* 'palma) *n* **Jacopo** ('jaːkopo), known as *Palma Vecchio,* original name *Jacopo Negretti.* ?1480–1528, Venetian painter, noted esp. for his portraits of women.

palmate ('pælmeɪt, -mɪt) *or* **palmated** *adj* **1** shaped like an open hand: *palmate antlers.* **2** *Bot.* having five lobes that spread out from a common point: *palmate leaves.* **3** (of most water birds) having three toes connected by a web.

Palm Beach ★ *n* a town in SE Florida, on an island between Lake Worth (a lagoon) and the Atlantic: major resort and tourist centre. Pop.: 9814 (1990).

Palme ★ (*Swedish* 'palmə) *n* (**Sven**) **Olof** (**Joachim**) ('uːlɔf). 1927–86, Swedish Social Democratic statesman; prime minister (1969–76, 1982–86); assassinated.

palmer ('pɑːmə) *n* (in medieval Europe) **1** a pilgrim bearing a palm branch as a sign of his visit to the Holy Land. **2** any pilgrim. ORIG C13: from OF *palmier,* from Med. L, from L *palma* PALM[2]

Palmer ★ ('pɑːmə) *n* **1 Arnold.** born 1929, US professional golfer: won the US Open Championship (1960) and the British Open Championship (1961; 1962). **2 Samuel.** 1805–81, British painter of visionary landscapes, influenced by William Blake.

Palmer Archipelago ★ *n* a group of islands between South America and Antarctica: part of the British colony of Falkland Islands and Dependencies. Former name: **Antarctic Archipelago.**

Palmer Land ★ *n* the S part of the Antarctic Peninsula.

Palmer Peninsula ★ *n* the former name (until 1964) for the **Antarctic Peninsula.**

Palmerston[1] ★ ('pɑːməstən) *n* the former name (1869–1911) of **Darwin**[1].

Palmerston[2] ★ ('pɑːməstən) *n* **Henry John Temple,** 3rd Viscount Palmerston. 1784–1865, British statesman; foreign secretary (1830–34; 1835–41; 1846–51); prime minister (1855–58; 1859–65). His talent was for foreign affairs, in which he earned a reputation as a British nationalist and for high-handedness and gunboat diplomacy.

Palmerston North ★ *n* a city in New Zealand, in the S North Island on the Manawatu River. Pop. (urban area): 76 300 (1995 est.).

palmetto (pæl'mɛtəʊ) *n, pl* **palmettos** *or* **palmettoes.** any of several small chiefly tropical palms with fan-shaped leaves. ORIG C16: from Sp. *palmito* a little PALM[2]

Palmira ★ (*Spanish* pal'mira) *n* a city in W Colombia: agricultural trading centre. Pop.: 256 823 (1997 est.).

palmistry ('pɑːmɪstrɪ) *n* the process or art of telling fortunes, etc., by the configuration of lines and bumps on a person's hand. Also called: **chiromancy.** ORIG C15 *pawmestry,* from *paume* PALM[1]; the second element is unexplained
▸ ˈ**palmist** *n*

palmitic acid (pæl'mɪtɪk) *n* a white crystalline solid that is a saturated fatty acid: used in the manufacture of soap and candles. Formula: $C_{15}H_{31}COOH$. Systematic name: **hexadecanoic acid.** ORIG C19: from F

palm off *vb* (*tr, adv;* often foll. by *on*) **1** to offer, sell, or spend fraudulently: *to palm off a counterfeit coin.* **2** to divert in order to be rid of: *I palmed the unwelcome visitor off on John.*

palm oil *n* an oil obtained from the fruit of certain palms, used as an edible fat and in soap, etc.

Palm Springs ★ *n* a city in the US, in California: a popular tourist resort. Pop.: 40 181 (1990).

Palm Sunday *n* the Sunday before Easter commemorating Christ's triumphal entry into Jerusalem.

palmtop computer ('pɑːmˌtɒp) *n* a computer that is small enough to be held in the hand; a hand-held computer. Often shortened to **palmtop.** Cf. **laptop computer.**

palmy ('pɑːmɪ) *adj* **palmier, palmiest. 1** prosperous, flourishing, or luxurious: *a palmy life.* **2** covered with, relating to, or resembling palms.

palmyra (pæl'maɪrə) *n* a tall tropical Asian palm with large fan-shaped leaves used for thatching and weaving. ORIG C17: from Port. *palmeira* palm tree; ? infl. by PALMYRA, in Syria

Palmyra ★ (pæl'maɪrə) *n* **1** an ancient city in central Syria: said to have been built by Solomon. Biblical name: **Tadmor. 2** an island in the central Pacific, in the Line Islands: under US administration.

Palo Alto ★ *n* **1** ('pæləʊ 'æltəʊ). a city in W California, southeast of San Francisco: founded in 1891 as the seat of Stanford University. Pop.: 55 900 (1990). **2** (*Spanish* 'palo 'alto). a battlefield in E Mexico, northwest of Monterrey, where the first battle (1846) of the Mexican War took place, in which the Mexicans under General Mariano Arista were defeated by the Americans under General Zachary Taylor.

palo cortado ('pæləʊ kɔː'tɑːdəʊ) *n* a rich dry sherry. ORIG from Sp., lit.: crossed stick (referring to the classification system in which butts of palo cortado are marked with a vertical line and one or more horizontal lines)

Palomar ★ ('pæləˌmɑː) *n* **Mount.** a mountain in S California, northeast of San Diego: site of **Mount Palomar Observatory,** which has a large (200-inch) reflecting telescope. Height: 1871 m (6140 ft).

palomino (ˌpæləˈmiːnəʊ) *n, pl* **palominos.** a golden horse with a white mane and tail. ORIG American Sp., from Sp.: dovelike, from L, from *palumbēs* ring dove

Palos ★ (*Spanish* ˈpalɔs) *n* a village and former port in SW Spain: starting point of Columbus' voyage of discovery to America (1492).

palp (pælp) *or* **palpus** (ˈpælpəs) *n, pl* **palps** *or* **palpi** (ˈpælpaɪ). either of a pair of sensory appendages that arise from the mouthparts of crustaceans and insects. ORIG C19: from F, from L *palpus* a touching

palpable (ˈpælpəbᵊl) *adj* **1** (*usually prenominal*) easily perceived by the senses or the mind; obvious: *a palpable lie.* **2** capable of being touched; tangible. ORIG C14: from LL *palpābilis* that may be touched, from L *palpāre* to touch
▸ ˌ**palpaˈbility** *n* ▸ ˈ**palpably** *adv*

palpate (ˈpælpeɪt) *vb* **palpates, palpating, palpated.** (*tr*) *Med.* to examine (an area of the body) by the sense of touch. ORIG C19: from L *palpāre* to stroke
▸ **palˈpation** *n*

palpebral (ˈpælpɪbrəl) *adj* of or relating to the eyelid. ORIG C19: from LL, from L *palpebra* eyelid

palpitate (ˈpælpɪˌteɪt) *vb* **palpitates, palpitating, palpitated.** (*intr*) **1** (of the heart) to beat rapidly. **2** to flutter or tremble. ORIG C17: from L *palpitāre* to throb, from *palpāre* to stroke
▸ ˈ**palpitant** *adj* ▸ ˌ**palpiˈtation** *n*

palsy (ˈpɔːlzɪ) *Pathol.* ◆ *n, pl* **palsies. 1** paralysis, esp. of a specified type: *cerebral palsy.* ◆ *vb* **palsies, palsying, palsied.** (*tr*) **2** to paralyse. ORIG C13 *palesi,* from OF *paralisie,* from L PARALYSIS
▸ ˈ**palsied** *adj*

palter (ˈpɔːltə) *vb* (*intr*) **1** to act or talk insincerely. **2** to haggle. ORIG C16: from ?

paltry (ˈpɔːltrɪ) *adj* **paltrier, paltriest. 1** insignificant; meagre. **2** worthless or petty. ORIG C16: from Low Gmc *palter, paltrig* ragged
▸ ˈ**paltrily** *adv* ▸ ˈ**paltriness** *n*

paludal (pəˈljuːdᵊl) *adj Rare.* **1** of or relating to marshes. **2** malarial. ORIG C19: from L *palus* marsh

paludism (ˈpæljuˌdɪzəm) *n* a less common word for **malaria.** ORIG C19: from L *palus* marsh

palynology (ˌpælɪˈnɒlədʒɪ) *n* the study of living and fossil pollen grains and plant spores. ORIG C20: from Gk *palunein* to scatter + -LOGY
▸ **palynological** (ˌpælɪnəˈlɒdʒɪkᵊl) *adj* ▸ ˌ**palyˈnologist** *n*

Pamirs ★ (pəˈmɪəz) *pl n* **the.** a mountainous area of central Asia, mainly in Tajikistan and partly in Kyrgyzstan, extending into China and Afghanistan: consists of a complex of high ranges, from which the Tian Shan projects to the north, the Kunlun and Karakoram to the east, and the Hindu Kush to the west. Highest peak: Kongur Shan, 7719 m (25 326 ft). Also called: **Paˈmir.**

Pamlico Sound ★ (ˈpæmlɪkəʊ) *n* an inlet of the Atlantic between the E coast of North Carolina and its chain of offshore islands. Length: 130 km (80 miles).

pampas (ˈpæmpəz) *n* (*functioning as sing or more often pl*) **a** the extensive grassy plains of temperate South America, esp. in Argentina. **b** (*as modifier*): *pampas dwellers.* ORIG C18: from American Sp. *pampa* (sing), from Amerind *bamba* plain
▸ **pampean** (ˈpæmpɪən, pæmˈpiːən) *adj*

pampas grass (ˈpæmpəs, -pəz) *n* any of various large South American grasses, widely cultivated for their large feathery silver-coloured flower branches.

Pampeluna ★ (ˌpæmpəˈluːnə) *n* the former name of **Pamplona.**

pamper (ˈpæmpə) *vb* (*tr*) **1** to treat with affectionate and usually excessive indulgence; coddle; spoil. **2** *Arch.* to feed to excess. ORIG C14: of Gmc origin
▸ ˈ**pamperer** *n*

pamphlet (ˈpæmflɪt) *n* **1** a brief publication generally having a paper cover; booklet. **2** a brief treatise, often on a subject of current interest, in pamphlet form. ORIG C14 *pamflet,* from Med. L *Pamphilus* title of a 12th-century amatory poem from Gk *Pamphilos* proper name

pamphleteer (ˌpæmflɪˈtɪə) *n* **1** a person who writes or issues pamphlets. ◆ *vb* **2** (*intr*) to write or issue pamphlets.

Pamphylia ★ (pæmˈfɪlɪə) *n* an area on the S coast of ancient Asia Minor.

Pamplona ★ (pæmˈpləʊnə; *Spanish* pamˈplona) *n* a city in N Spain in the foothills of the Pyrenees: capital of the kingdom of Navarre from the 11th century until 1841. Pop.: 181 776 (1995 est.). Former name: **Pampeluna.**

pan[1] (pæn) *n* **1a** a wide metal vessel used in cooking. **1b** (*in combination*): *saucepan.* **2** Also called: **panful.** the amount such a vessel will hold. **3** any of various similar vessels used in industry, etc. **4** a dish used esp. by gold prospectors for separating gold from gravel by washing and agitating. **5** either of the two dishlike receptacles on a balance. **6** Also called: **lavatory pan.** *Brit.* the bowl of a lavatory. **7a** a natural or artificial depression in the ground where salt can be obtained by the evaporation of brine. **7b** a natural depression containing water or mud. **8** See **hardpan, brainpan. 9** a small cavity containing priming powder in the locks of old guns. **10** a hard substratum of soil. ◆ *vb* **pans, panning, panned. 11** (when *tr,* often foll. by *off* or *out*) to wash (gravel) in a pan to separate particles of (valuable minerals) from it. **12** (*intr;* often foll. by *out*) (of gravel, etc.) to yield valuable minerals by this process. **13** (*tr*) *Inf.* to criticize harshly: *the critics panned his new play.* ◆ See also **pan out.** ORIG OE *panne*

pan[2] (pæn) *vb* **pans, panning, panned. 1** to move (a film camera) or (of a film camera) to be moved so as to follow a moving object or obtain a panoramic effect. ◆ *n* **2** the act of panning. ORIG C20: shortened from PANORAMIC

Pan ★ (pæn) *n Greek myth.* the god of fields, woods, shepherds, and flocks, represented as a man with a goat's legs, horns, and ears. Related adjs.: **Pandean, Panic.**

Pan. *abbrev. for* Panama.

pan- *combining form.* **1** all or every: *panchromatic.* **2** including or relating to all parts or members: *Pan-American; pantheistic.* ORIG from Gk *pan,* neuter of *pas* all

panacea (ˌpænəˈsɪə) *n* a remedy for all diseases or ills. ORIG C16: via L from Gk *panakeia,* from *pan* all + *akēs* remedy
▸ ˌ**panaˈcean** *adj*

panache (pəˈnæʃ, -ˈnɑːʃ) *n* **1** a dashing manner; swagger: *he rides with panache.* **2** a plume on a helmet. ORIG C16: via F from OIt. *pennacchio,* from LL *pinnāculum* feather, from L *pinna* feather

panada (pəˈnɑːdə) *n* a mixture of flour, water, etc., or of breadcrumbs soaked in milk, used as a thickening. ORIG C16: from Sp., from *pan* bread, from L *pānis*

Panaji ★ (pɑːˈnɑːdʒiː) *n* a variant of **Panjim.**

Panama ★ (ˌpænəˈmɑː, ˈpænəˌmɑː) *n* **1** a republic in Central America, occupying the Isthmus of Panama: gained independence from Spain in 1821 and joined Greater Colombia; became independent in 1903, with the immediate area around the canal forming the Canal Zone under US jurisdiction; in 1979 Panama assumed sovereignty over the Canal Zone. Official language: Spanish; English is also widely spoken. Religion: chiefly Roman Catholic. Currency: balboa. Capital: Panama City. Pop.: 2 809 000 (1999 est.). Area: 75 650 sq. km (29 201 sq. miles). **2 Isthmus of.** an isthmus linking North and South America, between the Pacific and the Caribbean. Length: 676 km (420 miles). Width (at its narrowest point): 50 km (31 miles). Former name: (Isthmus of) **Darien. 3 Gulf of.** a wide inlet of the Pacific in Panama.
▸ **Panamanian** (ˌpænəˈmeɪnɪən) *adj, n*

Panama Canal ★ *n* a canal across the Isthmus of Panama, linking the Atlantic and Pacific Oceans: extends from Colón on the Caribbean Sea southeast to Balboa on the Gulf of Panama; built by the US (1904–14), after an unsuccessful previous attempt (1880–89) by the French under de Lesseps. Length: 64 km (40 miles).

Panama Canal Zone ★ *n* See **Canal Zone.**

Panama City ★ *n* the capital of Panama, near the Pacific entrance of the Panama Canal: developed rapidly with the building of the Panama Canal; seat of the University of Panama (1935). Pop.: 452 041 (1995 est.).

Panama hat *n* (*sometimes not cap.*) a hat made of the plaited leaves of a palmlike plant of Central and South America. Often shortened to **panama** or **Panama.**

Pan-American *adj* of, relating to, or concerning North,

South, and Central America collectively or the advocacy of political or economic unity among American countries.
▸ **'Pan-A'merican,ism** *n*

panatella (ˌpænəˈtɛlə) *n* a long slender cigar. ORIG American Sp. *panetela* long slim biscuit, from It. *panatella* small loaf, from *pane* bread, from L *pānis*

Panay ★ (pɑːˈnaɪ) *n* an island in the central Philippines, the westernmost of the Visayan Islands. Pop.: 2 595 314 (1980). Area: 12 300 sq. km (4750 sq. miles).

pancake (ˈpænˌkeɪk) *n* **1** a thin flat cake made from batter and fried on both sides. **2** a stick or flat cake of compressed make-up. **3** Also called: **pancake landing.** an aircraft landing made by levelling out a few feet from the ground and then dropping onto it. ◆ *vb* **pancakes, pancaking, pancaked. 4** to cause (an aircraft) to make a pancake landing or (of an aircraft) to make a pancake landing.

Pancake Day *n* another name for **Shrove Tuesday**. See **Shrovetide.**

panchromatic (ˌpænkrəʊˈmætɪk) *adj Photog.* (of an emulsion or film) made sensitive to all colours.
▸ **panchromatism** (pænˈkrəʊməˌtɪzəm) *n*

pancosmism (pænˈkɒzˌmɪzəm) *n* the philosophical doctrine that the material universe is all that exists.

pancreas (ˈpæŋkrɪəs) *n* a large elongated glandular organ, situated behind the stomach, that secretes insulin and pancreatic juice. ORIG C16: via NL from Gk *pankreas,* from PAN- + *kreas* flesh
▸ **pancreatic** (ˌpæŋkrɪˈætɪk) *adj*

pancreatic juice *n* the clear alkaline secretion of the pancreas that is released into the duodenum and contains digestive enzymes.

pancreatin (ˈpæŋkrɪətɪn) *n* the powdered extract of the pancreas of certain animals, used in medicine as an aid to the digestion.

panda (ˈpændə) *n* **1** Also called: **giant panda.** a large black-and-white herbivorous bearlike mammal, related to the raccoons and inhabiting the high mountain bamboo forests of China. **2 lesser** *or* **red panda.** a closely related smaller animal resembling a raccoon, of the mountain forests of S Asia, having a reddish-brown coat and ringed tail. ORIG C19: via F from a native Nepalese word

panda car *n Brit.* a police patrol car. ORIG C20: so called because its blue-and-white markings resemble the black-and-white markings of the giant panda

pandanus (pænˈdeɪnəs) *n, pl* **pandanuses.** any of various Old World tropical palmlike plants having leaves and roots yielding a fibre used for making mats, etc. ORIG C19: via NL from Malay *pandan*

Pandarus ★ (ˈpændərəs) *n* **1** *Greek myth.* the leader of the Lycians, allies of the Trojans in their war with the Greeks. He broke the truce by shooting Menelaus with an arrow and was killed in the ensuing battle by Diomedes. **2** (in medieval legend) the procurer of Cressida on behalf of Troilus.

Pandean (pænˈdiːən) *adj* of or relating to the god Pan.

pandect (ˈpændɛkt) *n* **1** a treatise covering all aspects of a particular subject. **2** (*often pl*) the complete body of laws of a country; legal code, esp. the digest of Roman civil law made in the 6th century by order of Justinian. ORIG C16: via LL from Gk *pandektēs* containing everything, from PAN- + *dektēs* receiver

pandemic (pænˈdɛmɪk) *adj* **1** (of a disease) affecting persons over a wide geographical area; extensively epidemic. ◆ *n* **2** a pandemic disease. ORIG C17: from LL *pandēmus,* from Gk *pandēmos* general, from PAN- + *demos* the people

pandemonium (ˌpændɪˈməʊnɪəm) *n* **1** wild confusion; uproar. **2** a place of uproar and chaos. ORIG C17: coined by Milton for the capital of hell in *Paradise Lost,* from PAN- + Gk *daimōn* DEMON

pander (ˈpændə) *vb* **1** (*intr;* foll. by *to*) to give gratification (to weaknesses or desires). **2** (*arch.* when tr) to act as a go-between in a sexual intrigue (for). ◆ *n also* **panderer. 3** a person who caters for vulgar desires. **4** a person who procures a sexual partner for another; pimp. ORIG C16 (n): from *Pandare* Pandarus, in legend, the procurer of Cressida for Troilus

pandit (ˈpʌndɪt; *spelling pron* ˈpændɪt) *n Hinduism.* a variant of **pundit** (sense 3).

P & L *abbrev. for* profit and loss.

P & O *abbrev. for* the Peninsular and Oriental Steam Navigation Company.

Pandora (pænˈdɔːrə) *or* **Pandore** ★ (pænˈdɔː, ˈpændɔː) *n Greek myth.* the first woman, made out of earth as the gods' revenge on man for obtaining fire from Prometheus. Given a box (**Pandora's box**) that she was forbidden to open, she disobeyed out of curiosity and released from it all the ills that beset man, leaving only hope within. ORIG from Gk, lit.: all-gifted

p & p *Brit. abbrev. for* postage and packing.

pane (peɪn) *n* **1** a sheet of glass in a window or door. **2** a panel of a window, door, wall, etc. **3** a flat section or face, as of a cut diamond. ORIG C13: from OF *pan* portion, from L *pannus* rag

panegyric (ˌpænɪˈdʒɪrɪk) *n* a formal public commendation; eulogy. ORIG C17: via F & L from Gk, from *panēguris* public gathering
▸ **ˌpaneˈgyrical** *adj* ▸ **ˌpaneˈgyrically** *adv* ▸ **ˌpaneˈgyrist** *n*
▸ **panegyrize** *or* **panegyrise** (ˈpænɪdʒɪˌraɪz) *vb*

panel (ˈpænᵊl) *n* **1** a flat section of a wall, door, etc. **2** any distinct section of something formed from a sheet of material, esp. of a car body. **3** a piece of material inserted in a skirt, etc. **4a** a group of persons selected to act as a team in a quiz, to discuss a topic before an audience, etc. **4b** (*as modifier*): *a panel game.* **5** *Law.* **5a** a list of persons summoned for jury service. **5b** the persons on a jury. **6** *Scots Law.* a person accused of a crime. **7a** a thin board used as a surface or backing for an oil painting. **7b** a painting done on such a surface. **8** any picture with a length much greater than its breadth. **9** See **instrument panel. 10** *Brit.* (formerly) **10a** a list of patients insured under the National Health Insurance Scheme. **10b** a list of medical practitioners available for consultation by these patients. ◆ *vb* **panels, panelling, panelled** *or US* **panels, paneling, paneled.** (*tr*) **11** to furnish or decorate with panels. **12** *Law.* **12a** to empanel (a jury). **12b** (in Scotland) to bring (a person) to trial; indict. ORIG C13: from OF: portion, from *pan* piece of cloth, from L *pannus*

panel beater *n* a person who beats out the bodywork of motor vehicles, etc.

panelling *or US* **paneling** (ˈpænᵊlɪŋ) *n* **1** panels collectively, as on a wall or ceiling. **2** material used for making panels.

panellist *or US* **panelist** (ˈpænᵊlɪst) *n* a member of a panel, esp. on radio or television.

panel pin *n* a slender nail with a narrow head.

panel saw *n* a saw with a long narrow blade for cutting thin wood.

panel van *n Austral. & NZ.* a small van.

Pan-European *adj* of or relating to all European countries or the advocacy of political or economic unity among European countries.

pang (pæŋ) *n* a sudden brief sharp feeling, as of loneliness, physical pain, or hunger. ORIG C16: var. of earlier *prange,* of Gmc origin

panga (ˈpæŋgə) *n* a broad heavy knife of E Africa. ORIG from a native E African word

Pangaea *or* **Pangea** ★ (pænˈdʒiːə) *n* the ancient supercontinent, comprising all the present continents joined together, which began to break up about 200 million years ago. See also **Laurasia, Gondwanaland.** ORIG C20: from Gk, lit.: all-earth

Pang-fou ★ (ˈpæŋˈfuː) *n* a variant transliteration of the Chinese name for **Bengbu.**

pangolin (pæŋˈgəʊlɪn) *n* a mammal of tropical Africa, S Asia, and Indonesia, having a scaly body and a long snout for feeding on ants and termites. Also called: **scaly anteater.** ORIG C18: from Malay *peng-gōling,* from *gōling* to roll over; from its ability to roll into a ball

Pango Pango ★ (ˈpɑːŋgəʊ ˈpɑːŋgəʊ) *n* the former name of **Pago Pago.**

panhandle[1] ('pæn,hænd°l) *n (sometimes cap.)* (in the US) a narrow strip of land that projects from one state into another.

panhandle[2] ('pæn,hænd°l) *vb* **panhandles, panhandling, panhandled.** *US inf.* to beg from (passers-by). ORIG C19: prob. a back formation from *panhandler* a person who begs with a pan
▸ **'pan,handler** *n*

Panhellenic (,pænhɛ'lɛnɪk) *adj* of or relating to all the Greeks or all Greece.

panic ('pænɪk) *n* **1** a sudden overwhelming feeling of terror or anxiety, esp. one affecting a whole group of people. **2** *(modifier)* of or resulting from such terror: *panic measures.* **3** *(modifier)* for use in an emergency: *panic stations; panic button.* ◆ *vb* **panics, panicking, panicked. 4** to feel or cause to feel panic. ORIG C17: from F *panique,* from NL, from Gk *panikos* emanating from PAN, considered as the source of irrational fear
▸ **'panicky** *adj*

Panic ('pænɪk) *adj* of or relating to the god Pan.

panic attack *n* an episode of acute and disabling anxiety associated with such physical symptoms as hyperventilation and sweating.

panic button *n* a button or switch that operates a safety device or alarm, for use in an emergency.

panic disorder *n Psychiatry.* a condition in which a person experiences recurrent panic attacks.

panic grass *n* any of various grasses, such as millet, grown in warm and tropical regions for fodder and grain. ORIG C15 *panic,* from L *pānicum,* prob. a back formation from *pānicula* PANICLE

panicle ('pænɪk°l) *n* a compound raceme, as in the oat. ORIG C16: from L *pānicula* tuft, dim. of *panus* thread, ult. from Gk *penos* web
▸ **'panicled** *adj* ▸ **paniculate** (pə'nɪkjʊ,leɪt, -lɪt) *adj*

panic-stricken *or* **panic-struck** *adj* affected by panic.

panist ('pænɪst) *n Caribbean.* a player in a steel band, esp. one with considerable skill and experience.

panjandrum (pæn'dʒændrəm) *n* a pompous self-important official or person of rank. ORIG C18: after a character in a nonsense work (1755) by S. Foote, E playwright

Panjim ('pɑ:n,ʒɪm) *or* **Panaji** ★ *n* the capital of the Indian union territory of Goa, Daman, and Diu: a port on the Arabian Sea on the coast of Goa. Pop.: 85 515 (1991).

Pankhurst ★ ('pæŋkhɜ:st) *n* **1** Dame **Christabel.** 1880–1958, British suffragette. **2** her mother, **Emmeline.** 1858–1928, British suffragette leader, who founded the militant Women's Social and Political Union (1903). **3 Sylvia,** daughter of Emmeline Pankhurst. 1882–1960, British suffragette and pacifist.

pan loaf *n Scot.* a loaf of bread with a light crust all the way round. Often shortened to **pan.**

Panmunjom ★ ('pɑ:n'mʊn'dʒɒm) *n* a village in the demilitarized zone of Korea: site of truce talks leading to the end of the Korean War (1950–53).

pannage ('pænɪdʒ) *n Arch.* **1** the right to pasture pigs in a forest. **2** payment for this. **3** acorns, beech mast, etc., on which pigs feed. ORIG C13: from OF *pasnage,* ult. from L *pastion-, pastiō* feeding, from *pascere* to feed

pannier ('pænɪə) *n* **1** a large basket, esp. one of a pair slung over a beast of burden. **2** one of a pair of bags slung either side of the back wheel of a motorcycle, etc. **3** (esp. in the 18th century) **3a** a hooped framework to distend a woman's skirt. **3b** one of two puffed-out loops of material worn drawn back onto the hips. ORIG C13: from OF *panier,* from L *pānārium* basket for bread, from *pānis* bread

pannikin ('pænɪkɪn) *n Chiefly Brit.* a small metal cup or pan. ORIG C19: from PAN[1] + -KIN

pannikin boss *n Austral. sl.* a minor overseer.

Pannonia ★ (pə'nəʊnɪə) *n* a region of the ancient world south and west of the Danube: made a Roman province in 6 A.D.

panoply ('pænəplɪ) *n, pl* **panoplies. 1** a complete or magnificent array. **2** the entire equipment of a warrior. ORIG C17: via F from Gk, from PAN- + *hopla* armour
▸ **'panoplied** *adj*

panoptic (pæn'ɒptɪk) *adj* taking in all parts, aspects, etc., in a single view; all-embracing. ORIG C19: from Gk *panoptēs* seeing everything

panorama (,pænə'rɑ:mə) *n* **1** an extensive unbroken view in all directions. **2** a wide or comprehensive survey of a subject. **3** a large extended picture of a scene, unrolled before spectators a part at a time so as to appear continuous. **4** another name for **cyclorama.** ORIG C18: from PAN- + Gk *horāma* view
▸ **panoramic** (,pænə'ræmɪk) *adj* ▸ **,pano'ramically** *adv*

pan out *vb (intr, adv) Inf.* to work out; result.

panpipes ('pæn,paɪps) *pl n (often sing; often cap.)* a number of reeds or whistles of graduated lengths bound together to form a musical wind instrument. Also called: **pipes of Pan, syrinx.**

pansy ('pænzɪ) *n, pl* **pansies. 1** a garden plant having flowers with rounded velvety petals, white, yellow, or purple in colour. See also **wild pansy. 2** *Sl.* an effeminate or homosexual man or boy. ORIG C15: from OF *pensée* thought, from *penser* to think, from L *pensāre*

pant (pænt) *vb* **1** to breathe with noisy deep gasps, as when out of breath from exertion. **2** to say (something) while breathing thus. **3** *(intr;* often foll. by *for)* to have a frantic desire (for). **4** *(intr)* to throb rapidly. ◆ *n* **5** the act or an instance of panting. **6** a short deep gasping noise. ORIG C15: from OF *pantaisier,* from Gk *phantasioun* to have visions, from *phantasia* FANTASY

pantalets *or* **pantalettes** (,pæntə'lɛts) *pl n* **1** long drawers extending below the skirts: worn during the 19th century. **2** ruffles for the ends of such drawers. ORIG C19: dim. of PANTALOONS

pantaloon (,pæntə'lu:n) *n* **1** (in pantomime) an absurd old man, the butt of the clown's tricks. **2** *(usually cap.)* (in commedia dell'arte) a lecherous old merchant dressed in pantaloons. ORIG C16: from F *Pantalon,* from It. *Pantalone,* prob. from *San Pantaleone,* a fourth-century Venetian saint

pantaloons (,pæntə'lu:nz) *pl n* **1** *History.* **1a** men's tight-fitting trousers fastened below the calf or under the shoe. **1b** children's trousers resembling these. **2** *Inf.* any trousers, esp. baggy ones.

pantechnicon (pæn'tɛknɪkən) *n Brit.* **1** a large van, esp. one used for furniture removals. **2** a warehouse where furniture is stored. ORIG C19: from PAN- + Gk *tekhnikon* relating to the arts, from *tekhnē* art; orig. a London bazaar, later used as a furniture warehouse

Pantelleria ★ *(Italian* pantelle'ri:a) *n* an Italian island in the Mediterranean, between Sicily and Tunisia: of volcanic origin; used by the Romans as a place of banishment. Pop.: 7316 (1991 est.). Area: 83 sq. km (32 sq. miles). Ancient name: **Cossyra** (kə'saɪrə).

pantheism ('pænθɪ,ɪzəm) *n* **1** the doctrine that regards God as identical with the material universe or the forces of nature. **2** readiness to worship all gods.
▸ **'pantheist** *n* ▸ **,panthe'istic** *or* **,panthe'istical** *adj*
▸ **,panthe'istically** *adv*

pantheon ('pænθɪən) *n* **1** (esp. in ancient Greece or Rome) a temple to all the gods. **2** all the gods of a religion. **3** a building commemorating a nation's dead heroes. ORIG C14: via L from Gk *Pantheion,* from PAN- + *-theios* divine, from *theos* god

Pantheon ★ (pæn'θi:ən, 'pænθɪən) *n* a circular temple in Rome dedicated to all the gods, built by Agrippa in 27 B.C., rebuilt by Hadrian 120–24 A.D., and used since 609 A.D. as a Christian church.

panther ('pænθə) *n, pl* **panthers** *or* **panther. 1** another name for **leopard** (sense 1), esp. the black variety (**black panther**). **2** *US & Canad.* any of various related animals, esp. the puma. ORIG C14: from OF *pantère,* from L *panthēra,* from Gk *panthēr*

panties ('pæntɪz) *pl n* a pair of women's or children's underpants.

pantihose ('pæntɪ,həʊz) *pl n* See **panty hose.**

pantile ('pæn,taɪl) *n* a roofing tile, with an S-shaped cross section, so that the downward curve of one tile overlaps the upward curve of the next. ORIG C17: from PAN[1] + TILE

pantisocracy (ˌpæntɪ'sɒkrəsɪ) *n, pl* **pantisocracies.** a community, social group, etc., in which all have rule and everyone is equal. ORIG C18: (coined by Robert SOUTHEY) from Gk, from PANTO- + *isos* equal + -CRACY

panto ('pæntəʊ) *n, pl* **pantos.** *Brit. inf.* short for **pantomime** (sense 1).

panto- *or before a vowel* **pant-** *combining form.* all: *pantisocracy; pantograph; pantomime.* ORIG from Gk *pant-, pas*

pantograph ('pæntəˌgrɑːf) *n* **1** an instrument consisting of pivoted levers for copying drawings, maps, etc., to any scale. **2** a sliding type of current collector, esp. a diamond-shaped frame mounted on a train roof in contact with an overhead wire. **3** a device used to suspend a studio lamp so that its height can be adjusted.
▸ **pantographic** (ˌpæntə'græfɪk) *adj*

pantomime ('pæntəˌmaɪm) *n* **1** (in Britain) a kind of play performed at Christmas time characterized by farce, music, lavish sets, stock roles, and topical jokes. **2** a theatrical entertainment in which words are replaced by gestures and bodily actions. **3** action without words as a means of expression. **4** *Inf., chiefly Brit.* a confused or farcical situation. ◆ *vb* **pantomimes, pantomiming, pantomimed. 5** another word for **mime.** ORIG C17: via L from Gk *pantomīmos*
▸ **pantomimic** (ˌpæntə'mɪmɪk) *adj* ▸ **pantomimist** ('pæntəˌmaɪmɪst) *n*

pantothenic acid (ˌpæntə'θɛnɪk) *n* an oily acid that is a vitamin of the B complex: occurs widely in animal and vegetable foods. ORIG C20: from Gk *pantothen* from every side

pantry ('pæntrɪ) *n, pl* **pantries.** a small room in which provisions, cooking utensils, etc., are kept; larder. ORIG C13: via Anglo-Norman from OF *paneterie* store for bread, ult. from L *pānis* bread

pants (pænts) *pl n* **1** *Brit.* an undergarment covering the body from the waist to the thighs or knees. **2** the usual US and Canad. name for **trousers. 3** *Sl.* rubbish; nonsense. **4 bore, scare,** etc., **the pants off.** *Inf.* to bore, scare, etc., extremely. ◆ *adj* **5** *Sl.* bad; inferior: *a pants film.* ◆ *interj* **6** *Sl.* an exclamation expressing disgust or disapproval. ORIG C19: shortened from *pantaloons*

panty girdle ('pæntɪ) *n* a foundation garment with a crotch, often of lighter material than a girdle.

panty hose *pl n* the US name for **tights** (sense 1). Also (Canad. and NZ) **pantyhose,** (Austral.) **pantihose.**

Panufnik ★ (pæ'nuːfnɪk) *n* Sir **Andrzej** ('ændreɪ). 1914–91, British composer and conductor, born in Poland. His works include ten symphonies, the cantata *Winter Solstice* (1972), and ballet music.

panyard (ˌpæn'jɑːd) *n Caribbean.* an enclosed area in which a steel band practises.

panzer ('pænzə; *German* 'pantsər) *n* **1** (*modifier*) of or relating to the fast mechanized armoured units employed by the German army in World War II: *a panzer attack.* **2** a vehicle belonging to a panzer unit, esp. a tank. **3** (*pl*) armoured troops. ORIG C20: from G, from MHG, from OF *panciere* coat of mail, from L *pantex* PAUNCH

Pão de Açúcar ★ (pɐ̃un di a'sukar) *n* the Portuguese name for the **Sugar Loaf Mountain.**

Paolozzi ★ (pau'lɒtsɪ) *n* Sir **Eduardo** (**Luigi**) (ɛd'wɑːdəʊ). born 1924, British sculptor and designer, noted esp. for his semiabstract metal figures.

Paoting *or* **Pao-ting** ★ ('pau'tɪŋ) *n* a variant transliteration of the Chinese name for **Baoding.**

Paotow ★ ('pau'tau) *n* a variant transliteration of the Chinese name for **Baotou.**

pap[1] (pæp) *n* **1** any soft or semiliquid food, esp. for babies or invalids; mash. **2** worthless or oversimplified ideas, etc.; drivel. **3** *S. African.* maize porridge. ORIG C15: from MLow G *pappe,* via Med. L from L *pappāre* to eat

pap[2] (pæp) *n* **1** *Arch. or Scot. & N English dialect.* a nipple or teat. **2** something resembling a breast, such as one of a pair of rounded hilltops. ORIG C12: from ON, imit. of a sucking sound

papa (pə'pɑː) *n Old-fashioned.* an informal word for **father.** ORIG C17: from F, a children's word for father

papacy ('peɪpəsɪ) *n, pl* **papacies. 1** the office or term of office of a pope. **2** the system of government in the Roman Catholic Church that has the pope as its head. ORIG C14: from Med. L *pāpātia,* from *pāpa* POPE

Papadopoulos ★ (ˌpæpə'dɒpələs; *Greek* papa'ðɔpulɔs) *n* **Georgios.** 1919–99, Greek army officer and statesman; prime minister (1967–73) and president (1973) in Greece's military government.

papain (pə'peɪɪn, -'paɪɪn) *n* an enzyme occurring in the unripe fruit of the papaya tree: used as a meat tenderizer and in medicine as an aid to protein digestion. ORIG C19: from PAPAYA

papal ('peɪpᵊl) *adj* of or relating to the pope or the papacy.
▸ **'papally** *adv*

Papal States ★ *pl n* the temporal domain of the popes in central Italy from 756 A.D. until the unification of Italy in 1870. Also called: **States of the Church.**

Papandreou ★ (ˌpæpən'dreɪuː; *Greek* papan'ðrɛu) *n* **Andreas (George)** (an'dreas). 1919–96, Greek socialist politician; prime minister (1981–89; 1993–96).

paparazzo (ˌpæpə'rætsəʊ) *n, pl* **paparazzi** (-'rætsiː). a freelance photographer who specializes in candid camera shots of famous people. ORIG C20: from It.

papaver (pæ'pɑːvə) *n* any of a genus of hardy annual or perennial plants with showy flowers; poppy. ORIG L: poppy

papaveraceous (pəˌpeɪvə'reɪʃəs) *adj* of or relating to a family of plants having large showy flowers and a cylindrical seed capsule with pores beneath the lid: includes the poppies and greater celandine. ORIG C19: from NL, from L *papāver* poppy

papaverine (pə'peɪvəˌriːn, -rɪn) *n* a white crystalline alkaloid found in opium and used to treat coronary spasms and certain types of colic. ORIG C19: from L *papāver* poppy

papaw (pə'pɔː) *or* **pawpaw** *n* **1** Also called: **custard apple. 1a** a bush or small tree of Central North America, having small fleshy edible fruit. **1b** the fruit of this tree. **2** another name for **papaya.** ORIG C16: from Sp. PAPAYA

papaya (pə'paɪə) *n* **1** a Caribbean evergreen tree with a crown of large dissected leaves and large green hanging fruit. **2** the fruit of this tree, having a yellow sweet edible pulp and small black seeds. ◆ Also called: **papaw, pawpaw.** ORIG C15 *papaye,* from Sp. *papaya,* of Amerind origin

Papeete ★ (ˌpɑːpɪ'iːtɪ) *n* the capital of French Polynesia, on the NW coast of Tahiti: one of the largest towns in the S Pacific. Pop.: 78 814 (1988).

Papen ★ (*German* 'paːpən) *n* **Franz von** (frants fɔn). 1879–1969, German statesman; chancellor (1932) and vice chancellor (1933–34) under Hitler, whom he was instrumental in bringing to power.

paper ('peɪpə) *n* **1** a substance made from cellulose fibres derived from rags, wood, etc., and formed into flat thin sheets suitable for writing on, decorating walls, wrapping, etc. **2** a single piece of such material, esp. if written or printed on. **3** (*usually pl*) documents for establishing the identity of the bearer. **4** (*pl*) Also called: **ship's papers.** official documents relating to a ship. **5** (*pl*) collected diaries, letters, etc. **6** See **newspaper, wallpaper. 7** *Government.* See **white paper, green paper. 8** a lecture or treatise on a specific subject. **9** a short essay. **10a** a set of examination questions. **10b** the student's answers. **11** *Commerce.* See **commercial paper. 12** *Theatre sl.* a free ticket. **13 on paper.** in theory, as opposed to fact. ◆ *adj* **14** made of paper: *paper cups do not last long.* **15** thin like paper: *paper walls.* **16** (*prenominal*) existing only as recorded on paper but not yet in practice: *paper expenditure.* **17** taking place in writing: *paper battles.* ◆ *vb* **18** to cover (walls) with wallpaper. **19** (*tr*) to cover or furnish with paper. **20** (*tr*) *Theatre sl.* to fill (a performance, etc.) by giving away free tickets (esp. in **paper the house**). ◆ See also **paper over.** ORIG C14: from L PAPYRUS
▸ **'paperer** *n* ▸ **'papery** *adj*

paperback ('peɪpəˌbæk) *n* **1** a book or edition with covers made of flexible card. ◆ *adj* **2** of or denoting a paperback or publication of paperbacks. ◆ *vb* **3** (*tr*) to publish a paperback edition of a book.

paperbark ('peɪpəˌbɑːk) *n* any of several Australian trees of swampy regions, having papery bark that can be peeled off in thin layers.

paperboy ('peɪpəˌbɔɪ) *n* a boy employed to deliver newspapers, etc.
▸ **'paperˌgirl** *fem n*

paper chase *n* a former type of cross-country run in which a runner laid a trail of paper for others to follow.

paperclip ('peɪpəˌklɪp) *n* a clip for holding sheets of paper together, esp. one of bent wire.

paper-cutter *n* a machine for cutting paper, usually a blade mounted over a table.

paperhanger ('peɪpəˌhæŋə) *n* a person who hangs wallpaper as an occupation.

paperknife ('peɪpəˌnaɪf) *n, pl* **paperknives.** a knife with a comparatively blunt blade for opening sealed envelopes, etc.

paper money *n* paper currency issued by the government or the central bank as legal tender and which circulates as a substitute for specie.

paper mulberry *n* a small E Asian tree, the inner bark of which was formerly used for making paper in Japan. See also **tapa.**

paper nautilus *n* a cephalopod mollusc of warm and tropical seas, having a papery external spiral shell. Also called: **argonaut.**

paper over *vb* (*tr, adv*) to conceal (something controversial or unpleasant) (esp. in **paper over the cracks**).

paper tape *n* a strip of paper for recording information in the form of rows of either six or eight holes, some or all of which are punched to produce a combination used as a discrete code symbol, formerly used in computers, telex machines, etc. US equivalent: **perforated tape.**

paper tiger *n* a nation, institution, etc., that appears powerful but is in fact weak or insignificant. ORIG C20: translation of a Chinese phrase first applied to the US

paperweight ('peɪpəˌweɪt) *n* a small heavy object to prevent loose papers from scattering.

paperwork ('peɪpəˌwɜːk) *n* clerical work, such as the writing of reports or letters.

Paphian ('peɪfɪən) *adj* **1** of or relating to Paphos. **2** of or relating to Aphrodite. **3** *Literary.* of sexual love.

Paphlagonia ★ (ˌpæfləˈgəʊnɪə) *n* an ancient country and Roman province in N Asia Minor, on the Black Sea.

Paphos[1] ★ ('peɪfɒs) *n* a town in SW Cyprus, near the sites of two ancient cities: famous as the centre of Aphrodite worship and traditionally the place at which she landed after her birth among the waves. Pop.: 32 575 (1992 est.).

Paphos[2] ('peɪfɒs) *or* **Paphus** ★ ('peɪfəs) *n Greek myth.* the son of Pygmalion and Galatea, who succeeded his father on the throne of Cyprus.

papier-mâché (ˌpæpjeɪˈmæʃeɪ) *n* **1** a hard strong substance made of paper pulp or layers of paper mixed with paste, size, etc., and moulded when moist. ◆ *adj* **2** made of papier-mâché. ORIG C18: from F, lit.: chewed paper

papilionaceous (pəˌpɪlɪəˈneɪʃəs) *adj* of, relating to, or belonging to a family of leguminous plants having irregular flowers: includes peas, beans, clover, alfalfa, gorse, and broom. ORIG C17: from NL, from L *pāpiliō* butterfly

papilla (pəˈpɪlə) *n, pl* **papillae** (-liː). **1** the small projection of tissue at the base of a hair, tooth, or feather. **2** any similar protuberance. ORIG C18: from L: nipple
▸ **paˈpillary** *or* **'papillate** *adj*

papilloma (ˌpæpɪˈləʊmə) *n, pl* **papillomata** (-mətə) *or* **papillomas.** *Pathol.* a benign tumour forming a rounded mass. ORIG C19: from PAPILLA + -OMA

papillon ('pæpɪˌlɒn) *n* a breed of toy dog with large ears. ORIG F: butterfly, from L *pāpiliō*

papillote ('pæpɪˌləʊt) *n* **1** a paper frill around cutlets, etc. **2 en papillote** (*French* ɑ̃ papijɔt). (of food) cooked in oiled greaseproof paper or foil. ORIG C18: from F PAPILLON

papist ('peɪpɪst) *n, adj* (*often cap.*) *Usually disparaging.* another term for **Roman Catholic.** ORIG C16: from F *papiste,* from Church L *pāpa* POPE
▸ **paˈpistical** *or* **paˈpistic** *adj* ▸ **'papistry** *n*

papoose (pəˈpuːs) *n* **1** an American Indian baby. **2** a pouchlike bag used for carrying a baby, worn on the back. ORIG C17: from Algonquian *papoos*

pappus ('pæpəs) *n, pl* **pappi** ('pæpaɪ). a ring of fine feathery hairs surrounding the fruit in composite plants, such as the thistle. ORIG C18: via NL from Gk *pappos* old man, old man's beard, hence: pappus, down
▸ **'pappose** *or* **'pappous** *adj*

paprika ('pæprɪkə, pæˈpriː-) *n* **1** a mild powdered seasoning made from a sweet variety of red pepper. **2** the fruit or plant from which this seasoning is obtained. ORIG C19: via Hungarian from Serbian, from *papar* PEPPER

Pap test *or* **smear** (pæp) *n Med.* **1** another name for **cervical smear. 2** a similar test for precancerous cells in organs other than the cervix. ◆ Also called: **Papanicolaou smear.** ORIG C20: after George *Papanicolaou* (1883–1962), US anatomist, who devised it

Papua ★ ('pæpjʊə) *n* **1 Territory of.** a former territory of Australia, consisting of SE New Guinea and adjacent islands: now part of Papua New Guinea. Former name (1888–1906): **British New Guinea. 2 Gulf of.** an inlet of the Coral Sea in the SE coast of New Guinea.
▸ **'Papuan** *adj, n*

Papua New Guinea ★ *n* a country in the SW Pacific; consists of the E half of New Guinea, the Bismarck Archipelago, the W Solomon Islands, Trobriand Islands, D'Entrecasteaux Islands, Woodlark Island, and the Louisiade Archipelago; administered by Australia from 1949 until 1975, when it became an independent member of the Commonwealth. Official language: English; Tok Pisin (English Creole) and Motu are widely spoken. Religion: Christian majority. Currency: kina. Capital: Port Moresby. Pop.: 5 359 000 (1999 est.). Area: 461 693 sq. km (178 260 sq. miles).

papule ('pæpjuːl) *or* **papula** ('pæpjʊlə) *n, pl* **papules** *or* **papulae** (-jʊˌliː). *Pathol.* a small solid usually round elevation of the skin. ORIG C19: from L *papula* pustule
▸ **'papular** *adj*

papyrology (ˌpæpɪˈrɒlədʒɪ) *n* the study of ancient papyri.
▸ **ˌpapyˈrologist** *n*

papyrus (pəˈpaɪrəs) *n, pl* **papyri** (-raɪ) *or* **papyruses. 1** a tall aquatic plant of S Europe and N and central Africa. **2** a kind of paper made from the stem pith of this plant, used by the ancient Egyptians, Greeks, and Romans. **3** an ancient document written on this paper. ORIG C14: via L from Gk *papūros* reed used in making paper

par (pɑː) *n* **1** an accepted standard, such as an average (esp. in **up to par**). **2** a state of equality (esp. in **on a par with**). **3** *Finance.* the established value of the unit of one national currency in terms of the unit of another. **4** *Commerce.* **4a** See **par value. 4b** equality between the current market value of a share, bond, etc., and its face value, indicated by **at par; above** (*or* **below**) **par** indicates that the market value is above (or below) face value. **5** *Golf.* a standard score for a hole or course that a good player should make: *par for the course was 72.* ◆ *adj* **6** average or normal. **7** (*usually prenominal*) of or relating to par: *par value.* ORIG C17: from L *pār* equal

par. *abbrev. for:* **1** paragraph. **2** parallel. **3** parenthesis. **4** parish.

Par. *abbrev. for* Paraguay.

para ('pærə) *n Inf.* **1a** a soldier in an airborne unit. **1b** an airborne unit. **2** a paragraph.

Pará ★ (*Portuguese* paˈra) *n* **1** a state of N Brazil, on the Atlantic: mostly dense tropical rainforest. Capital: Belém. Pop.: 5 510 849 (1996). Area: 1 248 042 sq. km (474 896 sq. miles). **2** another name for **Belém. 3** an estuary in N Brazil into which flow the Tocantins River and a branch of the Amazon. Length: about 320 km (200 miles).

para-[1] *or before a vowel* **par-** *prefix* **1** beside; near: *parameter.* **2** beyond: *parapsychology.* **3** resembling: *paratyphoid fever.* **4** defective; abnormal: *paranoia.* **5** (*usually in italics*) denoting that an organic compound contains a benzene ring with substituents attached to atoms that are directly opposite (the 1,4- positions): *paracresol.* **6** denoting an isomer, polymer, or compound related to a specified compound: *paraldehyde.* **7** denoting the form of a diatomic substance in which the spins of the two constituent atoms are antiparallel: *parahydrogen.* ORIG from Gk *para* (prep) alongside, beyond

para-[2] *combining form.* indicating an object that acts as a protection against something: *parachute; parasol.* ORIG via F from It. *para-,* from *parare* to defend, ult. from L *parāre* to prepare

para-aminobenzoic acid (əˌmaɪnəubɛnˈzəuɪk, -ˌmiː-) *n Biochem.* an acid present in yeast and liver: used in the manufacture of dyes and pharmaceuticals.

parabasis (pəˈræbəsɪs) *n, pl* **parabases** (-ˌsiːz). (in classical Greek comedy) an address by the chorus. ORIG C19: from Gk, from *parabanein* to step forward

parabiosis (ˌpærəbaɪˈəusɪs) *n* **1** the natural union of two individuals, such as Siamese twins. **2** a similar union induced for experimental or therapeutic purposes. ORIG C20: from PARA-[1] + Gk *biōsis* manner of life, from *bios* life
▸ **parabiotic** (ˌpærəbaɪˈɒtɪk) *adj*

parable (ˈpærəbᵊl) *n* **1** a short story that uses familiar events to illustrate a religious or ethical point. **2** any of the stories of this kind told by Jesus Christ. ORIG C14: from OF *parabole,* from L *parabola* comparison, from Gk *parabolē* analogy, from *paraballein* to throw alongside

parabola (pəˈræbələ) *n* a conic section formed by the intersection of a cone by a plane parallel to its side. ORIG C16: via NL from Gk *parabolē* a setting alongside; see PARABLE

parabolic[1] (ˌpærəˈbɒlɪk) *adj* **1** of, relating to, or shaped like a parabola. **2** shaped like a paraboloid: *a parabolic mirror.*

parabolic[2] (ˌpærəˈbɒlɪk) *or* **parabolical** *adj* of or like a parable.
▸ **ˌparaˈbolically** *adv*

parabolic aerial *n* a formal name for **dish aerial.**

paraboloid (pəˈræbəˌlɔɪd) *n* a geometric surface whose sections parallel to two coordinate planes are parabolic and whose sections parallel to the third plane are either elliptical or hyperbolic.
▸ **paˌraboˈloidal** *adj*

Paracelsus ★ (ˌpærəˈsɛlsəs) *n* **Philippus Aureolus** (ˈfɪlɪpəs ˌɔːrɪˈəuləs), real name *Theophrastus Bombastus von Hohenheim.* 1493–1541, Swiss physician and alchemist, who pioneered the use of specific treatment, based on observation and experience, to remedy particular diseases.

paracetamol (ˌpærəˈsiːtəˌmɒl, -ˈsɛtə-) *n* a mild analgesic drug. ORIG C20: from *para-acetamidophenol*

parachronism (pəˈrækrəˌnɪzəm) *n* an error in dating, esp. by giving too late a date. ORIG C17: from PARA-[1] + *-chronism,* as in ANACHRONISM

parachute (ˈpærəˌʃuːt) *n* **1** a device used to retard the fall of a person or package from an aircraft, consisting of a large fabric canopy connected to a harness. ◆ *vb* **parachutes, parachuting, parachuted. 2** (of troops, supplies, etc.) to land or cause to land by parachute from an aircraft. ORIG C18: from F, from PARA-[2] + *chute* fall
▸ **ˈparaˌchutist** *n*

Paraclete (ˈpærəˌkliːt) *n Christianity.* the Holy Ghost as comforter or advocate. ORIG C15: via OF from Church L *Paraclētus,* from LGk *Paraklētos* advocate, from Gk *parakalein* to summon help

parade (pəˈreɪd) *n* **1** an ordered, esp. ceremonial, march or procession, as of troops being reviewed. **2** Also called: **parade ground.** a place where military formations regularly assemble. **3** a visible show or display: *to make a parade of one's grief.* **4** a public promenade or street of shops. **5** a successive display of things or people. **6 on parade. 6a** on display. **6b** showing oneself off. ◆ *vb* **parades, parading, paraded. 7** (when *intr,* often foll. by *through* or *along*) to walk or march, esp. in a procession. **8** (*tr*) to exhibit or flaunt: *he was parading his medals.* **9** (*tr*) to cause to assemble in formation, as for a military parade. **10** (*intr*) to walk about in a public place. ORIG C17: from F: a making ready, a boasting display
▸ **paˈrader** *n*

paradiddle (ˈpærəˌdɪdᵊl) *n* a group of four drumbeats played with alternate sticks in the pattern right-left-right-right or left-right-left-left. ORIG C20: imit.

paradigm (ˈpærəˌdaɪm) *n* **1** the set of all the inflected forms of a word. **2** a pattern or model. **3** (in the philosophy of science) a general conception of the nature of scientific endeavour within which a given enquiry is undertaken. ORIG C15: via F & L from Gk *paradeigma* pattern, from *paradeiknunai* to compare
▸ **paradigmatic** (ˌpærədɪgˈmætɪk) *adj*

paradisal (ˌpærəˈdaɪsᵊl), **paradisiacal** (ˌpærədɪˈsaɪəkᵊl), *or* **paradisiac** (ˌpærəˈdɪsɪˌæk) *adj* of, relating to, or resembling paradise.

paradise (ˈpærəˌdaɪs) *n* **1** heaven as the ultimate abode or state of the righteous. **2** *Islam.* the sensual garden of delights that the Koran promises the faithful after death. **3** Also called: **limbo.** (according to some theologians) the intermediate abode or state of the just prior to the Resurrection of Jesus. **4** the Garden of Eden. **5** any place or condition that fulfils all one's desires or aspirations. **6** a park in which foreign animals are kept. ORIG OE, from Church L *paradīsus,* from Gk *paradeisos* garden, of Persian origin

paradise duck *n* a New Zealand duck with bright plumage.

paradox (ˈpærəˌdɒks) *n* **1** a seemingly absurd or self-contradictory statement that is or may be true: *religious truths are often expressed in paradox.* **2** a self-contradictory proposition, such as *I always tell lies.* **3** a person or thing exhibiting apparently contradictory characteristics. **4** an opinion that conflicts with common belief. ORIG C16: from LL *paradoxum,* from Gk *paradoxos* opposed to existing notions
▸ **ˌparaˈdoxical** *adj* ▸ **ˌparaˈdoxically** *adv*

paradoxical sleep *n Physiol.* sleep that appears deep but is characterized by a brain wave pattern similar to that of wakefulness, rapid eye movements, and heavier breathing.

paraffin (ˈpærəfɪn) *n* **1** Also called: **paraffin oil,** (esp. US, Canad., Austral., & NZ) **kerosene.** a liquid mixture consisting mainly of alkane hydrocarbons, used as an aircraft fuel, in domestic heaters, and as a solvent. **2** another name for **alkane. 3** See **paraffin wax. 4** See **liquid paraffin.** ◆ *vb* (*tr*) **5** to treat with paraffin. ORIG C19: from G, from L *parum* too little + *affinis* adjacent; so called from its chemical inertia

paraffin wax *n* a white insoluble odourless waxlike solid consisting mainly of alkane hydrocarbons, used in candles, waterproof paper, and as a sealant. Also called: **paraffin.**

paragliding (ˈpærəˌglaɪdɪŋ) *n* the sport of cross-country gliding using a specially designed parachute shaped like flexible wings. The parachutist glides from an aeroplane to a predetermined landing area.

paragon (ˈpærəgən) *n* a model of excellence; pattern: *a paragon of virtue.* ORIG C16: via F from OIt. *paragone* comparison, from Med. Gk *parakonē,* from PARA-[1] + *akonē* whetstone

paragraph (ˈpærəˌgrɑːf) *n* **1** (in a piece of writing) one of a series of subsections each usually devoted to one idea and each marked by the beginning of a new line, indention, etc. **2** *Printing.* the character ¶, used to indicate the beginning of a new paragraph. **3** a short article, etc., in a newspaper. ◆ *vb* (*tr*) **4** to form into paragraphs. **5** to express or report in a paragraph. ORIG C16: from Med. L *paragraphus,* from Gk *paragraphos* line drawing attention to part of a text, from *paragraphein* to write beside
▸ **paragraphic** (ˌpærəˈgræfɪk) *adj*

paragraphia (ˌpærəˈgrɑːfɪə) *n Psychiatry.* the habitual writing of a different word or letter from the one intended, often the result of a mental disorder. ORIG C20: from NL; see PARA-[1], -GRAPH

Paraguay ★ (ˈpærəˌgwaɪ) *n* **1** an inland republic in South America: colonized by the Spanish from 1537, gaining independence in 1811; lost 142 500 sq. km (55 000 sq. miles) of territory and over half its population after its defeat in the war against Argentina, Brazil, and Uruguay (1865–70). It is divided by the Paraguay River into a sparsely inhabited semiarid region (Chaco) in the west, and a central region of wooded hills, tropical forests, and rich grasslands, rising to the Paraná plateau in the east. Official languages: Spanish and Guarani. Religion: Roman Catholic majority. Currency: guarani. Capital: Asunción. Pop.: 5 359 000 (1999 est.). Area: 406 750 sq. km (157 047 sq. miles). **2** a river in South America flowing south through Brazil and Paraguay to the Paraná River. Length: about 2400 km (1500 miles). ▸ **ˌPara'guayan** *adj, n*

Paraguay tea *n* another name for **maté**.

parahydrogen (ˌpærə'haɪdrədʒən) *n Chem.* the form of molecular hydrogen in which the nuclei of the two atoms in each molecule spin in opposite directions.

Paraíba ★ (*Portuguese* para'iba) *n* **1** a state of NE Brazil, on the Atlantic: consists of a coastal strip, with hills and plains inland; irrigated agriculture. Capital: João Pessoa. Pop.: 3 305 616 (1996). Area: 56 371 sq. km (21 765 sq. miles). **2** Also called: **Paraíba do Sul** ('du: 'sul). a river in SE Brazil, flowing southwest and then northeast to the Atlantic near Campos. Length: 1060 km (660 miles). **3** Also called: **Paraíba do Norte** ('du: 'nɔrtə). a river in NE Brazil, in Paraíba state, flowing northeast and east to the Atlantic. Length: 386 km (240 miles). **4** the former name (until 1930) of **João Pessoa.**

parakeet *or* **parrakeet** ('pærəˌki:t) *n* any of numerous small long-tailed parrots. ORIG C16: from Sp. *periquito* & OF *paroquet* parrot, from ?

paraldehyde (pə'rældɪˌhaɪd) *n* a colourless liquid that is a cyclic trimer of acetaldehyde: used as a hypnotic.

paralipsis (ˌpaerə'lɪpsɪs) *or* **paraleipsis** (ˌpærə'laɪpsɪs) *n, pl* **paralipses** *or* **paraleipses** (-si:z). a rhetorical device in which an idea is emphasized by the pretence that it is too obvious to discuss, as in *there are many practical drawbacks, not to mention the cost.* ORIG C16: via LL from Gk: neglect, from *paraleipein* to leave aside

parallax ('pærəˌlæks) *n* **1** an apparent change in the position of an object resulting from a change in position of the observer. **2** *Astron.* the angle subtended at a celestial body, esp. a star, by the radius of the earth's orbit. ORIG C17: via F from NL *parallaxis,* from Gk: change, from *parallassein* to change
▸ **parallactic** (ˌpærə'læktɪk) *adj*

parallel ('pærəˌlɛl) *adj* (when *postpositive,* usually foll. by *to*) **1** separated by an equal distance at every point; never touching or intersecting: *parallel walls.* **2** corresponding; similar: *parallel situations.* **3** *Music.* Also: **consecutive.** (of two or more parts or melodies) moving in similar motion but keeping the same interval apart throughout: *parallel fifths.* **4** *Grammar.* denoting syntactic constructions in which the constituents of one construction correspond to those of the other. **5** *Computing.* operating on several items of information, instructions, etc., simultaneously. ◆ *n* **6** *Maths.* one of a set of parallel lines, planes, etc. **7** an exact likeness. **8** a comparison. **9** Also called: **parallel of latitude.** any of the imaginary lines around the earth parallel to the equator, designated by degrees of latitude. **10** *Electronics.* **10a** an arrangement of two or more electrical components connected between two points in a circuit so that the same voltage is applied to each (esp. in **in parallel**). Cf. **series** (sense 6). **10b** (*as modifier*): *a parallel circuit.* **11** *Printing.* the character (‖) used as a reference mark. ◆ *vb* **parallels, paralleling, paralleled.** (*tr*) **12** to make parallel. **13** to supply a parallel to. **14** to be a parallel to or correspond with: *your experience parallels mine.* ORIG C16: via F & L from Gk *parallēlos* alongside one another, from PARA-[1] + *allēlos* one another

parallel bars *pl n Gymnastics.* a pair of wooden bars on uprights used for various exercises.

parallelepiped (ˌpærəˌlɛlɪ'paɪpɛd) *or* **parallelepipedon** (ˌpærəˌlɛlɪ'paɪpɪdən) *n* a geometric solid whose six faces are parallelograms. ORIG C16: from Gk, from *parallēlos* PARALLEL + *epipedon* plane surface, from EPI- + *pedon* ground

parallel importing *n* the importing of certain goods, esp. pharmaceutical drugs, by dealers who undersell local manufacturers.

paralleling ('pærəˌlɛlɪŋ) *n* a form of trading in which companies buy highly priced goods in a market in which the prices are low in order to be able to sell them in a market in which the prices are higher.

parallelism ('pærəˌlɛlɪzəm) *n* **1** the state of being parallel. **2** *Grammar.* the repetition of a syntactic construction in successive sentences for rhetorical effect. **3** *Philosophy.* the doctrine that mental and physical processes are regularly correlated but are not casually connected, so that, for example, pain always accompanies, but is not caused by, a pinprick.

parallelogram (ˌpærə'lɛləˌgræm) *n* a quadrilateral whose opposite sides are parallel and equal in length. ORIG C16: via F from LL, from Gk *parallēlogrammon,* from *parallēlos* PARALLEL + *grammē* line

parallelogram rule *n Maths, physics.* a rule for finding the resultant of two vectors by constructing a parallelogram with two adjacent sides representing the magnitudes and directions of the vectors, the diagonal through the point of intersection of the vectors representing their resultant.

parallel processing *n* the performance by a computer system of two or more simultaneous operations.

parallel ruler *n Engineering.* a drawing instrument in which two parallel edges are connected so that they remain parallel, although the distance between them can be varied.

paralogism (pə'ræləˌdʒɪzəm) *n* **1** *Logic, psychol.* an argument that is unintentionally invalid. Cf. **sophism. 2** any invalid argument or conclusion. ORIG C16: via LL from Gk *paralogismos,* from *paralogizesthai* to argue fallaciously, from PARA-[1] + *-logizesthai,* ult. from *logos* word
▸ **pa'ralogist** *n*

Paralympian (ˌpærə'lɪmpɪən) *n* a competitor in the Paralympics.

Paralympics (ˌpærə'lɪmpɪks) *n* **the.** (*functioning as sing or pl*) a sporting event, modelled on the Olympic Games, held solely for disabled competitors. Also called: **the Parallel Olympics.** ORIG C20: from PARALLEL + OLYMPICS

paralyse *or US* **paralyze** ('pærəˌlaɪz) *vb* **paralyses, paralysing, paralysed** *or US* **paralyzes, paralyzing, paralyzed.** (*tr*) **1** *Pathol.* to affect with paralysis. **2** *Med.* to render (a part of the body) insensitive to pain, touch, etc. **3** to make immobile; transfix. ORIG C19: from F *paralyser,* from *paralysie* PARALYSIS
▸ **ˌparaly'sation** *or US* **ˌparaly'zation** *n* ▸ **'paraˌlyser** *or US* **'paraˌlyzer** *n*

paralysis (pə'rælɪsɪs) *n, pl* **paralyses** (-ˌsi:z). **1** *Pathol.* **1a** impairment or loss of voluntary muscle function or of sensation (**sensory paralysis**) in a part or area of the body. **1b** a disease characterized by such impairment or loss; palsy. **2** cessation or impairment of activity: *paralysis of industry by strikes.* ORIG C16: via L from Gk *paralusis;* see PARA-[1], -LYSIS

paralytic (ˌpærə'lɪtɪk) *adj* **1** of, relating to, or of the nature of paralysis. **2** afflicted with or subject to paralysis. **3** *Brit. inf.* very drunk. ◆ *n* **4** a person afflicted with paralysis.

paramagnetism (ˌpærə'mægnɪˌtɪzəm) *n Physics.* a weakly magnetic condition of substances with a relative permeability just greater than unity: used in some special low temperature techniques.
▸ **paramagnetic** (ˌpærəmæg'nɛtɪk) *adj*

Paramaribo ★ (ˌpærə'mærɪˌbəʊ; *Dutch* pa:ra:'ma:ri:bo:) *n* the capital and chief port of Surinam, 27 km (17 miles) from the Atlantic on the Surinam River: the only large town in the country. Pop.: 200 970 (1993 est.).

paramatta *or* **parramatta** (ˌpærə'mætə) *n* a lightweight twill-weave dress fabric of wool with silk or cotton, now used esp. for rubber-proofed garments. ORIG C19: after *Parramatta,* New South Wales, Australia, where orig. produced

paramecium (ˌpærə'mi:sɪəm) *n, pl* **paramecia** (-sɪə). any of a genus of freshwater protozoa having an oval body covered with cilia and a ventral groove for feeding. ORIG C18: NL, from Gk *paramēkēs* elongated, from PARA-[1] + *mēkos* length

paramedic (ˌpærə'mɛdɪk) *n* **1** a person, such as a laboratory technician, who supplements the work of the medi-

cal profession. **2** a member of an ambulance crew trained in a number of life-saving skills, including infusion and cardiac care.
▸ **ˌparaˈmedical** *adj*

parameter (pəˈræmɪtə) *n* **1** an arbitrary constant that determines the specific form of a mathematical expression, such as a and b in $y = ax^2 + b$. **2** a characteristic constant of a statistical population, such as its variance or mean. **3** *Inf.* any constant or limiting factor: *a designer must work within the parameters of budget and practicality.* ORIG C17: from NL; see PARA-[1], -METER
▸ **parametric** (ˌpærəˈmɛtrɪk) *adj*

parametric amplifier *n* a type of high-frequency amplifier in which energy is transferred to the input signal through a circuit with a varying reactance.

paramilitary (ˌpærəˈmɪlɪtərɪ, -trɪ) *adj* **1** denoting or relating to a group of personnel with military structure functioning either as a civil force or in support of military forces. **2** denoting or relating to a force with military structure conducting armed operations against a ruling power.

paramount (ˈpærəˌmaʊnt) *adj* of the greatest importance or significance. ORIG C16: via Anglo-Norman from OF *paramont,* from *par* by + *-amont* above, from L *ad montem* to the mountain
▸ **ˈparaˌmountcy** *n* ▸ **ˈparaˌmountly** *adv*

paramour (ˈpærəˌmʊə) *n* **1** *Now usually derog.* a lover, esp. adulterous. **2** an archaic word for **beloved.** ORIG C13: from OF, lit.: through love

Paraná ★ *n* **1** (*Portuguese* parəˈna). a state of S Brazil, on the Atlantic: consists of a coastal plain and a large rolling plateau with extensive forests. Capital: Curitiba. Pop.: 9 003 804 (1996). Area: 199 555 sq. km (77 048 sq. miles). **2** (*Portuguese* paraˈna). a city in E Argentina, on the Paraná River opposite Santa Fe: capital of Argentina (1853–1862). Pop.: 211 936 (1991). **3** (*Portuguese* parəˈna; *Spanish* paraˈna). a river in central South America, formed in S Brazil by the confluence of the Rio Grande and the Paranaíba River and flowing generally south to the Atlantic through the Río de la Plata estuary. Length: 2900 km (1800 miles).

parang (ˈpɑːræŋ) *n* a Malay short stout straight-edged knife used in Borneo. ORIG C19: from Malay

paranoia (ˌpærəˈnɔɪə) *n* **1** a mental disorder characterized by any of several types of delusions, as of grandeur or persecution. **2** *Inf.* intense fear or suspicion, esp. when unfounded. ORIG C19: via NL from Gk: frenzy, from *paranoos* distraught, from PARA-[1] + *noos* mind
▸ **ˈparaˌnoid, paranoiac** (ˌpærəˈnɔɪɪk) *or* **paranoic** (ˌpærəˈnəʊɪk) *adj, n*

paranormal (ˌpærəˈnɔːməl) *adj* **1** beyond normal explanation. ◆ *n* **2 the.** paranormal happenings generally.

parapente (ˈpærəˌpɒnt) *n* **1** another name for **paraskiing. 2** the form of parachute used in this sport. ORIG C20: from PARA(CHUTE) + F *pente* slope

parapet (ˈpærəpɪt, -ˌpɛt) *n* **1** a low wall or railing along the edge of a balcony, roof, etc. **2** *Mil.* a rampart, mound of sandbags, etc., in front of a trench giving protection from fire. ORIG C16: from It. *parapetto,* lit.: chest-high wall, from L *pectus* breast

paraph (ˈpærəf) *n* a flourish after a signature, originally to prevent forgery. ORIG C14: via F from Med. L *paraphus,* var. of *paragraphus* PARAGRAPH

paraphernalia (ˌpærəfəˈneɪlɪə) *pl n* (*sometimes functioning as sing*) **1** miscellaneous articles or equipment. **2** *Law.* (formerly) articles of personal property given to a married woman by her husband and regarded in law as her possessions. ORIG C17: via Med. L from L *parapherna* personal property of a married woman, apart from her dowry, from Gk, from PARA-[1] + *phernē* dowry, from *pherein* to carry

paraphrase (ˈpærəˌfreɪz) *n* **1** an expression of a statement or text in other words. ◆ *vb* **paraphrases, paraphrasing, paraphrased. 2** to put into other words; restate. ORIG C16: via F from L *paraphrasis,* from Gk, from *paraphrazein* to recount
▸ **paraphrastic** (ˌpærəˈfræstɪk) *adj*

paraplegia (ˌpærəˈpliːdʒə) *n Pathol.* paralysis of the lower half of the body, usually as the result of disease or injury of the spine. ORIG C17: via NL from Gk: a blow on one side, from PARA-[1] + *plēssein* to strike
▸ **ˌparaˈplegic** *adj, n*

parapraxis (ˌpærəˈpræksɪs) *n, pl* **parapraxes** (-ˈpræksiːz) *Psychoanal.* a minor error in action, such as a slip of the tongue. ORIG C20: from PARA-[1] + Gk *praxis* a deed

parapsychology (ˌpærəsaɪˈkɒlədʒɪ) *n* the study of mental phenomena, such as telepathy, which are beyond the scope of normal physical explanation.
▸ **ˌparapsyˈchologist** *n*

Paraquat (ˈpærəˌkwɒt) *n Trademark.* a yellow extremely poisonous weedkiller.

parascending (ˈpærəˌsɛndɪŋ) *n* a sport in which a parachutist, starting from ground level, is towed by a vehicle until he is airborne and then descends in the normal way.

paraselene (ˌpærəsɪˈliːnɪ) *n, pl* **paraselenae** (-niː). a bright image of the moon on a lunar halo. Also called: **mock moon.** ORIG C17: NL, from PARA-[1] + Gk *selēnē* moon

parasite (ˈpærəˌsaɪt) *n* **1** an animal or plant that lives in or on another (the host) from which it obtains nourishment. **2** a person who habitually lives at the expense of others; sponger. ORIG C16: via L from Gk *parasitos* one who lives at another's expense, from PARA-[1] + *sitos* grain
▸ **parasitic** (ˌpærəˈsɪtɪk) *or* **ˌparaˈsitical** *adj* ▸ **ˌparaˈsitically** *adv* ▸ **ˈparasiˌtism** *n*

parasitize *or* **parasitise** (ˈpærəsɪˌtaɪz) *vb* **parasitizes, parasitizing, parasitized** *or* **parasitises, parasitising, parasitised.** (*tr*) **1** to infest with parasites. **2** to live on (another organism) as a parasite.
▸ **ˌparasitiˈzation** *or* **ˌparasitiˈsation** *n*

parasitoid (ˈpærəsɪˌtɔɪd) *n Zool.* an animal, esp. an insect, that is parasitic as a larva but becomes free-living when adult.

parasitology (ˌpærəsaɪˈtɒlədʒɪ) *n* the branch of biology that is concerned with the study of parasites.
▸ **ˌparasitˈologist** *n*

paraskiing (ˈpærəˌskiːɪŋ) *n* the sport of jumping off high mountains wearing skis and a light parachute composed of inflatable fabric tubes that form a semirigid wing. Also called: **parapente.**

parasol (ˈpærəˌsɒl) *n* an umbrella used for protection against the sun; sunshade. ORIG C17: via F from It. *parasole,* from PARA-[2] + *sole* sun, from L *sōl*

parasuicide (ˌpærəˈsuːɪˌsaɪd) *n* an attempt to inflict an injury on oneself, not motivated by a desire to die.

parasympathetic (ˌpærəˌsɪmpəˈθɛtɪk) *adj Anat., Physiol.* of or relating to the division of the autonomic nervous system that acts by slowing the heartbeat, constricting the bronchi of the lungs, stimulating the smooth muscles of the digestive tract, etc. Cf. **sympathetic** (sense 4).

parasynthesis (ˌpærəˈsɪnθɪsɪs) *n* formation of words by compounding a phrase and adding an affix, as *light-headed, light* + *head* with the affix *-ed.*
▸ **parasynthetic** (ˌpærəsɪnˈθɛtɪk) *adj*

parataxis (ˌpærəˈtæksɪs) *n* the juxtaposition of clauses without the use of a conjunction, as *None of my friends stayed —they all left early.* ORIG C19: NL from Gk, from *paratassein,* lit.: to arrange side by side
▸ **paratactic** (ˌpærəˈtæktɪk) *adj*

parathion (ˌpærəˈθaɪɒn) *n* a toxic oil used as an insecticide. ORIG from PARA-[1] + Gk *theion* sulphur

parathyroid gland (ˌpærəˈθaɪrɔɪd) *n* any one of the small egg-shaped endocrine glands situated near or embedded within the thyroid gland.

paratroops (ˈpærəˌtruːps) *pl n* troops trained and equipped to be dropped by parachute into a battle area. Also called: **paratroopers.**

paratyphoid fever (ˌpærəˈtaɪfɔɪd) *n* a disease resembling but less severe than typhoid fever, caused by bacteria of the genus *Salmonella.*

paravane (ˈpærəˌveɪn) *n* a torpedo-shaped device towed from the bow of a vessel so that the cables will cut the anchors of any moored mines. ORIG C20: from PARA-[2] + VANE

par avion *French.* (par avjɔ̃) *adv* by aeroplane: used in labelling mail sent by air.

parazoan (ˌpærəˈzəʊən) *n, pl* **parazoa** (-ˈzəʊə). any multicellular invertebrate of a division of the animal kingdom, the sponges. ORIG C19: from *parazoa,* on the model of *protozoa* & *metazoa,* from PARA-[1] + Gk *zōon* animal

parboil (ˈpɑːˌbɔɪl) *vb* (*tr*) **1** to boil until partially cooked. **2** to subject to uncomfortable heat. ORIG C15: from OF *parboillir,* from LL *perbullīre* to boil thoroughly (see PER-, BOIL[1]); modern meaning due to confusion of *par-* with *part*

parbuckle (ˈpɑːˌbʌkəl) *n* **1** a rope sling for lifting or lowering a heavy cylindrical object, such as a cask. ◆ *vb* **parbuckles, parbuckling, parbuckled. 2** (*tr*) to raise or lower (an object) with such a sling. ORIG C17 *parbunkel:* from ?

Parcae ★ (ˈpɑːsiː) *pl n, sing* **Parca** (ˈpɑːkə). **the.** the Roman goddesses of fate. Greek counterparts: The **Moirai.**

parcel (ˈpɑːsəl) *n* **1** something wrapped up; package. **2** a group of people or things having some common characteristic. **3** a quantity of some commodity offered for sale; lot. **4** a distinct portion of land. ◆ *vb* **parcels, parcelling, parcelled** *or US* **parcels, parceling, parceled.** (*tr*) **5** (often foll. by *up*) to make a parcel of; wrap up. **6** (often foll. by *out*) to divide (up) into portions. ORIG C14: from OF *parcelle,* from L *particula* PARTICLE

parch (pɑːtʃ) *vb* **1** to deprive or be deprived of water; dry up: *the sun parches the fields.* **2** (*tr; usually passive*) to make very thirsty. **3** (*tr*) to roast (corn, etc.) lightly. ORIG C14: from ?

Parcheesi (pɑːˈtʃiːzɪ) *n Trademark.* a board game derived from the ancient game of pachisi.

parchment (ˈpɑːtʃmənt) *n* **1** the skin of certain animals, such as sheep, treated to form a durable material, as for manuscripts. **2** a manuscript, etc., made of this material. **3** a type of stiff yellowish paper resembling parchment. ORIG C13: from OF *parchemin,* via L from Gk *pergamēnē,* from *Pergamēnos* of Pergamum (where parchment was made); OF *parchemin* was infl. by *parche* leather, from L *Parthica* (*pellis*) Parthian (leather)

pard (pɑːd) *n Arch.* a leopard or panther. ORIG C13: via OF from L *pardus,* from Gk *pardos*

pardon (ˈpɑːdən) *vb* (*tr*) **1** to excuse or forgive (a person) for (an offence, mistake, etc.): *to pardon someone; to pardon a fault.* ◆ *n* **2** forgiveness. **3a** release from punishment for an offence. **3b** the warrant granting such release. **4** a Roman Catholic indulgence. ◆ *sentence substitute.* **5** Also: **pardon me, I beg your pardon. 5a** sorry; excuse me. **5b** what did you say? ORIG C13: from OF, from Med. L *perdōnum,* from *perdōnāre* to forgive freely, from L *per* (intensive) + *dōnāre* to grant
▸ **ˈpardonable** *adj* ▸ **ˈpardonably** *adv*

pardoner (ˈpɑːdənə) *n* (before the Reformation) a person licensed to sell ecclesiastical indulgences.

Pardubice ★ (*Czech* ˈpardubitsɛ) *n* a city in the central Czech Republic, on the Elbe River: 13th-century cathedral; oil refinery. Pop.: 163 000 (1993).

pare (pɛə) *vb* **pares, paring, pared.** (*tr*) **1** to peel (the outer layer) from (something). **2** to cut the edges from (the nails). **3** to decrease bit by bit. ORIG C13: from OF *parer* to adorn, from L *parāre* to make ready
▸ **ˈparer** *n*

Paré ★ (*French* pare) *n* **Ambroise** (ɑ̃brwaz). 1510–90, French surgeon. He reintroduced ligature of arteries following amputation instead of cauterization.

paregoric (ˌpærəˈɡɒrɪk) *n* a medicine consisting of opium, benzoic acid, and camphor, formerly widely used to relieve diarrhoea and coughing. ORIG C17 (meaning: relieving pain): via LL from Gk *parēgoros* relating to soothing speech, from PARA-[1] (beside) + *agora* assembly

pareira (pəˈrɛərə) *n* the root of a South American climbing plant, used as a diuretic, tonic, and as a source of curare. ORIG C18: from Port. *pareira brava,* lit.: wild vine

parenchyma (pəˈrɛŋkɪmə) *n* **1** a soft plant tissue consisting of simple thin-walled cells: constitutes the greater part of fruits, stems, roots, etc. **2** animal tissue that constitutes the essential part of an organ as distinct from the blood vessels, connective tissue, etc. ORIG C17: via NL from Gk *parenkhuma* something poured in beside, from PARA-[1] + *enkhuma* infusion
▸ **parenchymatous** (ˌpærɛŋˈkɪmətəs) *adj*

parent (ˈpɛərənt) *n* **1** a father or mother. **2** a person acting as a father or mother; guardian. **3** *Rare.* an ancestor. **4** a source or cause. **5** an organism or organization that has produced one or more organisms similar to itself. **6** *Physics, chem.* a precursor, such as a nucleus or compound, of a derived entity. ORIG C15: via OF from L *parens* parent, from *parere* to bring forth
▸ **paˈrental** *adj* ▸ **ˈparenthood** *n*

parentage (ˈpɛərəntɪdʒ) *n* **1** ancestry. **2** derivation from a particular origin. **3** the state or condition of being a parent.

parent company *n* a company that owns a number of subsidiary companies.

parenteral (pæˈrɛntərəl) *adj Med.* **1** (esp. of the route by which a drug is administered) by means other than through the digestive tract, esp. by injection. **2** designating a drug to be injected. ORIG C20: from PARA-[1] + ENTERO- + -AL[1]

parenthesis (pəˈrɛnθɪsɪs) *n, pl* **parentheses** (-ˌsiːz). **1** a phrase, often explanatory or qualifying, inserted into a passage with which it is not grammatically connected, and marked off by brackets, dashes, etc. **2** Also called: **bracket.** either of a pair of characters, ( ), used to enclose such a phrase or as a sign of aggregation in mathematical or logical expressions. **3** an interlude; interval. **4 in parenthesis.** inserted as a parenthesis. ORIG C16: via LL from Gk: something placed in besides, from *parentithenai,* from PARA-[1] + EN-[2] + *tithenai* to put
▸ **parenthetic** (ˌpærənˈθɛtɪk) *or* **ˌparenˈthetical** *adj* ▸ **ˌparenˈthetically** *adv*

parenthesize *or* **parenthesise** (pəˈrɛnθɪˌsaɪz) *vb* **parenthesizes, parenthesizing, parenthesized** *or* **parenthesises, parenthesising, parenthesised.** (*tr*) **1** to place in parentheses. **2** to insert as a parenthesis. **3** to intersperse (a speech, writing, etc.) with parentheses.

parenting (ˈpɛərəntɪŋ) *n* all the skills and experience of bringing up children.

parent teacher association *n* a social group of the parents of children at a school and their teachers formed in order to foster better understanding between them and to organize fund-raising activities on behalf of the school.

parergon (pəˈrɛəɡɒn) *n, pl* **parerga** (-ɡə). work that is not one's main employment. ORIG C17: from L, from Gk, from PARA-[1] + *ergon* work

paresis (pəˈriːsɪs, ˈpærɪsɪs) *n, pl* **pareses** (-ˌsiːz). *Pathol.* incomplete or slight paralysis of motor functions. ORIG C17: via NL from Gk: a relaxation, from *parienai* to let go
▸ **paretic** (pəˈrɛtɪk) *adj*

Pareto ★ (*Italian* paˈrɛːto) *n* **Vilfredo** (vilˈfreːdo). 1848–1923, Italian sociologist and economist. He anticipated Fascist principles of government in his *Mind and Society* (1916).

par excellence *French.* (par ɛksɛlɑ̃s; *English* pɑːr ˈɛksələns) *adv* to a degree of excellence; beyond comparison. ORIG lit.: by (way of) excellence

parfait (pɑːˈfeɪ) *n* a rich frozen dessert made from eggs and cream, fruit, etc. ORIG from F: PERFECT

parget (ˈpɑːdʒɪt) *n* **1** Also called: **pargeting. 1a** plaster, mortar, etc., used to line chimney flues or cover walls. **1b** plasterwork that has incised ornamental patterns. ◆ *vb* (*tr*). **2** to cover or decorate with parget. ORIG C14: from OF *pargeter* to throw over, from *par* PER- + *geter* to throw

parhelic circle *n Meteorol.* a luminous band at the same altitude as the sun, parallel to the horizon, caused by reflection of the sun's rays by ice crystals in the atmosphere.

parhelion (pɑːˈhiːlɪən) *n, pl* **parhelia** (-lɪə). one of several bright spots on the parhelic circle or solar halo, caused by the diffraction of light by ice crystals in the atmosphere. Also called: **mock sun.** ORIG C17: via L from Gk *parēlion,* from PARA-[1] (beside) + *hēlios* sun
▸ **parˈhelic** *or* **parheliacal** (ˌpɑːhɪˈlaɪəkəl) *adj*

pariah (pəˈraɪə, ˈpærɪə) *n* **1** a social outcast. **2** (formerly) a member of a low caste in South India. ORIG C17: from Tamil *paraiyan* drummer, from *parai* drum: members were drummers at festivals

pariah dog *n* another term for **pye-dog**.

Paricutín ★ (*Spanish* pariku'tin) *n* a volcano in W central Mexico, in Michoacán state, formed in 1943 after a week of earth tremors; grew to a height of 2500 m (8200 ft) in a year and buried the village of Paricutín.

parietal (pəˈraɪɪtəl) *adj* **1** *Anat., biol.* of or forming the walls of a bodily cavity: *the parietal bones of the skull.* **2** of or relating to the side of the skull. **3** (of plant ovaries) having ovules attached to the walls. **4** *US.* living or having authority within a college. ◆ *n* **5** a parietal bone. ORIG C16: from LL *parietālis,* from L *pariēs* wall

parietal lobe *n* the portion of each cerebral hemisphere concerned with the perception of sensations of touch, temperature, and taste and with muscular movements.

pari-mutuel (ˌpærɪˈmjuːtʃʊəl) *n, pl* **pari-mutuels** *or* **paris-mutuels** (ˌpærɪˈmjuːtʃʊəlz). a system of betting in which those who have bet on the winners of a race share in the total amount wagered less a percentage for the management. ORIG C19: from F, lit.: mutual wager

paring (ˈpɛərɪŋ) *n* (*often pl*) something pared or cut off.

pari passu *Latin.* (ˌpærɪ ˈpæsuː, ˈpɑːrɪ) *adv Usually legal.* with equal speed or progress.

Paris[1] ★ (ˈpærɪs; *French* pari) *n* the capital of France, in the north on the River Seine: constitutes a department; dates from the 3rd century B.C., becoming capital of France in 987; centre of the French Revolution; centres around its original site on an island in the Seine, the **Île de la Cité**, containing Notre Dame; university (1150). Pop.: 2 175 200 (1990). Ancient name: **Lutetia**. ORIG via F and OF, from LL (*Lūtētia*) *Parisiōrum* (marshes) of the *Parisii,* a tribe of Celtic Gaul
▸ **Parisian** (pəˈrɪzɪən) *n, adj*

Paris[2] ★ (ˈpærɪs) *n* **1** *Greek myth.* a prince of Troy, whose abduction of Helen from her husband Menelaus started the Trojan War. **2** **Matthew.** ?1200–59, English chronicler, whose principal work is the *Chronica Majora.*

Paris Club *n* a group of the richest members of the International Monetary Fund, which meets informally in Paris.

Paris Commune *n French history.* the council established in Paris in the spring of 1871 in opposition to the National Assembly and esp. to the peace negotiated with Prussia following the Franco-Prussian War.

Paris green *n* an emerald-green poisonous substance used as a pigment and insecticide.

parish (ˈpærɪʃ) *n* **1** a subdivision of a diocese, having its own church and a clergyman. **2** the churchgoers of such a subdivision. **3** (in England and, formerly, Wales) the smallest unit of local government. **4** (in Louisiana) a county. **5** (in Quebec and New Brunswick, Canada) a subdivision of a county. **6** the people living in a parish. **7** **on the parish.** *History.* receiving parochial relief. ORIG C13: from OF *paroisse,* from Church L, from LGk, from *paroikos* Christian, sojourner, from Gk: neighbour, from PARA-[1] (beside) + *oikos* house

parish clerk *n* a person designated to assist in various church duties.

parish council *n* (in England and, formerly, Wales) the administrative body of a parish. See **parish** (sense 3).

parishioner (pəˈrɪʃənə) *n* a member of a particular parish.

parish pump *adj* of only local interest; parochial.

parish register *n* a book in which the births, baptisms, marriages, and deaths in a parish are recorded.

parity (ˈpærɪtɪ) *n, pl* **parities. 1** equality of rank, pay, etc. **2** close or exact analogy or equivalence. **3** *Finance.* the amount of a foreign currency equivalent to a specific sum of domestic currency. **4** equality between prices of commodities or securities in two separate markets. **5** *Physics.* **5a** a property of a physical system characterized by the behaviour of the sign of its wave function when reflected in space. The wave function either remains unchanged (**even parity**) or changes in sign (**odd parity**). **5b** a quantum number describing this property, equal to +1 for even parity systems and –1 for odd parity systems. Symbol: *P* **6** *Maths.* a relationship between two integers. If both are odd or both even they have the same parity; if one is odd and one even they have different parity. ORIG C16: from LL *pāritās;* see PAR

parity check *n* a check made of computer data to ensure that the total number of bits of value 1 (or 0) in each unit of information remains odd or even after transfer between a peripheral device and the memory or vice versa.

park (pɑːk) *n* **1** a large area of land preserved in a natural state for recreational use by the public. **2** a piece of open land for public recreation in a town. **3** a large area of land forming a private estate. **4** an area designed to accommodate a number of related enterprises: *a business park.* **5** *US & Canad.* a playing field or sports stadium. **6** **the park.** *Brit. inf.* a soccer pitch. **7** a gear selector position on the automatic transmission of a motor vehicle that acts as a parking brake. **8** the area in which the equipment and supplies of a military formation are assembled. ◆ *vb* **9** to stop and leave (a vehicle) temporarily. **10** to manoeuvre (a motor vehicle) into a space for it to be left: *try to park without hitting the kerb.* **11** *Stock Exchange.* to register (securities) in the name of another or of nominees in order to conceal their real ownership. **12** (*tr*) *Inf.* to leave or put somewhere: *park yourself in front of the fire.* **13** (*intr*) *Mil.* to arrange equipment in a park. **14** (*tr*) to enclose in or as a park. ORIG C13: from OF *parc,* from Med. L *parricus* enclosure, from Gmc

Park ★ (pɑːk) *n* **1** **Mungo** (ˈmʌŋgəʊ). 1771–1806, Scottish explorer. He led two expeditions (1795–97; 1805–06) to trace the course of the Niger in Africa. He was drowned during the second expedition. **2** **Chung Hee** (ˈtʃʊŋ ˈhiː). 1917–79, South Korean politician; president of the Republic of Korea (1963–79); assassinated.

parka (ˈpɑːkə) *n* a warm weatherproof coat with a hood, originally worn by Eskimos. ORIG C19: from Aleutian: skin

Parker ★ (ˈpɑːkə) *n* **1** **Charlie.** nickname *Bird* or *Yardbird.* 1920–55, US jazz alto saxophonist and composer; the leading exponent of early bop. **2** **Dorothy** (**Rothschild**). 1893–1967, US writer, noted esp. for the ironical humour of her short stories. **3** **Matthew.** 1504–75, English prelate. As archbishop of Canterbury (1559–75), he supervised Elizabeth I's religious settlement.

Parkes ★ (pɑːks) *n* Sir **Henry.** 1815–96, Australian journalist and politician born in England, five times premier of New South Wales.

parkin (ˈpɑːkɪn) *n* (in Britain and New Zealand) moist spicy ginger cake usually containing oatmeal. ORIG C19: from ?

parking lot *n* the US and Canad. term for **car park**.

parking meter *n* a timing device, usually coin-operated, that indicates how long a vehicle may be left parked.

parking orbit *n* an orbit around the earth or moon in which a spacecraft can be placed temporarily in order to prepare for the next step in its programme.

parking ticket *n* a summons served for a parking offence.

Parkinson's disease (ˈpɑːkɪnsənz) *n* a progressive chronic disorder of the central nervous system characterized by impaired muscular coordination and tremor. Often shortened to **Parkinson's**. Also called: **Parkinsonism.** ORIG C19: after James *Parkinson* (1755–1824), Brit. surgeon, who first described it

Parkinson's law *n* the notion, expressed facetiously as a law of economics, that work expands to fill the time available for its completion. ORIG C20: after C. N. *Parkinson* (1909–93), Brit. historian and writer, who formulated it

park keeper *n* (in Britain) an official who patrols and supervises a public park.

parkland (ˈpɑːkˌlænd) *n* grassland with scattered trees.

parky (ˈpɑːkɪ) *adj* **parkier, parkiest.** (*usually postpositive*) *Brit. inf.* (of the weather) chilly; cold. ORIG C19: ?from PERKY

Parl. *abbrev. for:* **1** Parliament. **2** Also: **parl.** parliamentary.

parlance ('pɑːləns) *n* a particular manner of speaking, esp. when specialized; idiom: *political parlance.* ORIG C16: from OF, from *parler* to talk, via Med. L from LL *parabola* speech

parlando (pɑː'lændəʊ) *adj, adv Music.* to be performed as though speaking. ORIG It.: speaking

parley ('pɑːlɪ) *n* **1** a discussion, esp. between enemies under a truce to decide terms of surrender, etc. ◆ *vb* **2** (*intr*) to discuss, esp. with an enemy. ORIG C16: from F, from *parler* to talk, from Med. L *parabolāre,* from LL *parabola* speech

parliament ('pɑːləmənt) *n* **1** an assembly of the representatives of a political nation or people, often the supreme legislative authority. **2** any legislative or deliberative assembly, conference, etc. ORIG C13: from Anglo-L *parliamentum,* from OF *parlement,* from *parler* to speak; see PARLEY

Parliament ('pɑːləmənt) *n* **1** the highest legislative authority in Britain, consisting of the House of Commons, which exercises effective power, the House of Lords, and the sovereign. **2** a similar legislature in another country or state. **3** any of the assemblies of such a body created by a general election and royal summons and dissolved before the next election.

parliamentarian (ˌpɑːləmɛn'tɛərɪən) *n* **1** an expert in parliamentary procedures. ◆ *adj* **2** of or relating to a parliament.

parliamentary (ˌpɑːlə'mɛntərɪ) *adj* (*sometimes cap.*) **1** of or proceeding from a parliament or Parliament: *a parliamentary decree.* **2** conforming to the procedures of a parliament or Parliament: *parliamentary conduct.* **3** having a parliament or Parliament.

Parliamentary Commissioner *or in full* **Parliamentary Commissioner for Administration** *n* (in Britain) the official name for **ombudsman** (sense 2).

parliamentary private secretary *n* (in Britain) a backbencher in Parliament who assists a minister. Abbrev.: **PPS.**

parliamentary secretary *n* a member of Parliament appointed to assist a minister of the Crown with his departmental responsibilities.

parlour *or US* **parlor** ('pɑːlə) *n* **1** *Old-fashioned.* a living room, esp. one kept tidy for the reception of visitors. **2** a small room for guests away from the public rooms in an inn, club, etc. **3** *Chiefly US, Canad., & NZ.* a room or shop equipped as a place of business: *a billiard parlor; a beauty parlour.* **4** a building equipped for the milking of cows. ORIG C13: from Anglo-Norman *parlur,* from OF *parleur* room in convent for receiving guests, from *parler* to speak; see PARLEY

parlous ('pɑːləs) *Arch. or humorous.* ◆ *adj* **1** dangerous or difficult. **2** cunning. ◆ *adv* **3** extremely. ORIG C14 *perlous,* var. of PERILOUS
▸ **'parlously** *adv*

Parma ★ *n* **1** (*Italian* 'parma). a city in N Italy, in Emilia-Romagna: capital of the duchy of Parma and Piacenza from 1545 until it became part of Italy in 1860; important food industry (esp. Parmesan cheese). Pop.: 167 516 (1996 est.). **2** ('pɑːmə). a city in NE Ohio, south of Cleveland. Pop.: 85 006 (1996 est.).
▸ **Parmesan** (ˌpɑːmɪ'zæn, 'pɑːmɪˌzæn) *adj, n*

Parmenides ★ (pɑː'mɛnɪˌdiːz) *n* 5th century B.C., Greek philosopher, born in Italy. He held that the universe is single and unchanging and denied the existence of change and motion. His doctrines are expounded in his poem *On Nature,* of which only fragments are extant.

Parmesan cheese *n* a hard dry cheese used grated, esp. on pasta dishes and soups.

Parmigianino ★ (*Italian* parmidʒa'nino) *n* real name *Girolamo Francesco Maria Mazzola.* 1503–40, Italian painter, one of the originators of mannerism. Also called: **Parmigiano** (parmi'dʒano).

Parnaíba *or* **Parnahiba** ★ (*Portuguese* parna'iba) *n* a river in NE Brazil, rising in the Serra das Mangabeiras and flowing generally northeast, to the Atlantic. Length: about 1450 km (900 miles).

Parnassus ★ (pɑː'næsəs) *n* **1 Mount.** a mountain in central Greece: in ancient times sacred to Apollo and the Muses. **2a** the world of poetry. **2b** a centre of poetic or other creative activity.
▸ **Par'nassian** *adj*

Parnell ★ ('pɑːnᵊl, pɑː'nɛl) *n* **Charles Stewart.** 1846–91, Irish nationalist, who led the Irish Home Rule movement in Parliament (1880–90) with a calculated policy of obstruction. Although Gladstone was converted to Home Rule (1886), Parnell's career was ruined by the scandal over his adultery with Mrs Katherine O'Shea.
▸ **'Parnelˌlism** *n* ▸ **'Parnellite** *n, adj*

parochial (pə'rəʊkɪəl) *adj* **1** narrow in outlook or scope; provincial. **2** of or relating to a parish. ORIG C14: via OF from Church L *parochiālis;* see PARISH
▸ **pa'rochialˌism** *n* ▸ **pa'rochially** *adv*

parody ('pærədɪ) *n, pl* **parodies. 1** a musical, literary, or other composition that mimics the style of another composer, author, etc., in a humorous or satirical way. **2** something so badly done as to seem an intentional mockery; travesty. ◆ *vb* **parodies, parodying, parodied. 3** (*tr*) to make a parody of. ORIG C16: via L from Gk *paroidiā* satirical poem, from PARA-[1] + *ōidē* song
▸ **parodic** (pə'rɒdɪk) *or* **pa'rodical** *adj* ▸ **'parodist** *n*

parol ('pærəl, pə'rəʊl) *Law.* ◆ *n* **1** an oral statement; word of mouth (now only in **by parol**). ◆ *adj* **2a** (of a contract, lease, etc.) made orally or in writing but not under seal. **2b** expressed or given by word of mouth: *parol evidence.* ORIG C15: from OF *parole* speech; see PAROLE

parole (pə'rəʊl) *n* **1a** the freeing of a prisoner before his or her sentence has expired, on the condition that he or she is of good behaviour. **1b** the duration of such conditional release. **2** a promise given by a prisoner, as to be of good behaviour if granted liberty or partial liberty. **3** *Linguistics.* language as manifested in the individual speech acts of particular speakers. **4 on parole.** conditionally released from detention. ◆ *vb* **paroles, paroling, paroled.** (*tr*) **5** to place (a person) on parole. ORIG C17: from OF, from *parole d'honneur* word of honour; *parole* from LL *parabola* speech
▸ **parolee** (pəˌrəʊ'liː) *n*

paronomasia (ˌpærənəʊ'meɪzɪə) *n Rhetoric.* a play on words, esp. a pun. ORIG C16: via L from Gk, from *paronomazein* to make a change in naming, from PARA-[1] (besides) + *onomazein* to name, from *onoma* a name

Páros ★ ('pærɒs) *n* a Greek island in the S Aegean Sea, in the Cyclades: site of the discovery (1627) of the Parian Chronicle, a marble tablet outlining Greek history from before 1000 B.C. to about 354 B.C. (now at Oxford University). Pop.: 8000 (latest est.). Area: 166 sq. km (64 sq. miles).
▸ **'Parian** *adj, n*

parotid (pə'rɒtɪd) *adj* **1** relating to or situated near the parotid gland. ◆ *n* **2** See **parotid gland.** ORIG C17: via F, via L from Gk *parōtis,* from PARA-[1] (near) + *-ōtis,* from *ous* ear

parotid gland *n* a large salivary gland, in man situated in front of and below each ear.

parotitis (ˌpærə'taɪtɪs) *n* inflammation of the parotid gland. See also **mumps.**

-parous *adj combining form.* giving birth to: *oviparous.* ORIG from L *-parus,* from *parere* to bring forth

paroxysm ('pærəkˌsɪzəm) *n* **1** an uncontrollable outburst: *a paroxysm of giggling.* **2** *Pathol.* **2a** a sudden attack or recurrence of a disease. **2b** any fit or convulsion. ORIG C17: via F from Med. L *paroxysmus* annoyance, from Gk, from *paroxunein* to goad, from PARA-[1] (intensifier) + *oxunein* to sharpen, from *oxus* sharp
▸ **ˌparox'ysmal** *adj*

parquet ('pɑːkeɪ, -kɪ) *n* **1** a floor covering of pieces of hardwood fitted in a decorative pattern; parquetry. **2** Also called: **parquet floor.** a floor so covered. **3** *US.* the stalls of a theatre. ◆ *vb* (*tr*) **4** to cover a floor with parquet. ORIG C19: from OF: small enclosure, from *parc* enclosure; see PARK

parquetry ('pɑːkɪtrɪ) *n* a geometric pattern of inlaid pieces of wood, esp. as used to cover a floor.

parr (pɑː) *n, pl* **parrs** *or* **parr.** a salmon up to two years of age. ORIG C18: from ?

Parr ★ (pɑː) *n* **Catherine.** 1512–48, sixth wife of Henry VIII of England.

parrakeet (ˈpærəˌkiːt) *n* a variant spelling of **parakeet.**

parramatta (ˌpærəˈmætə) *n* a variant spelling of **paramatta.**

parricide (ˈpærɪˌsaɪd) *n* **1** the act of killing either of one's parents. **2** a person who kills his or her parent. ORIG C16: from L *parricīdium* murder of a parent or relative, & from *parricīda* one who murders a relative, from *parri-* (rel. to Gk *pēos* kinsman) + -CIDE
▸ ˌ**parriˈcidal** *adj*

parrot (ˈpærət) *n* **1** any of several related tropical and subtropical birds having a short hooked bill, bright plumage, and an ability to mimic sounds. **2** a person who repeats or imitates the words or actions of another. **3 sick as a parrot.** *Usually facetious.* extremely disappointed. ◆ *vb* **parrots, parroting, parroted. 4** (*tr*) to repeat or imitate without understanding. ORIG C16: prob. from F *paroquet*, from ?

parrot-fashion *adv Inf.* without regard for meaning; by rote: *she learned it parrot-fashion.*

parrot fever *or* **disease** *n* another name for **psittacosis.**

parrotfish (ˈpærətˌfɪʃ) *n, pl* **parrotfish** *or* **parrotfishes.** a brightly coloured tropical marine percoid fish having parrot-like jaws.

Parrott ★ (ˈpærət) *n* **John.** born 1964, British snooker player.

parry (ˈpærɪ) *vb* **parries, parrying, parried. 1** to ward off (an attack, etc.) by blocking or deflecting, as in fencing. **2** (*tr*) to evade (questions, etc.), esp. adroitly. ◆ *n, pl* **parries. 3** an act of parrying. **4** a skilful evasion, as of a question. ORIG C17: from F *parer* to ward off, from L *parāre* to prepare

Parry ★ (ˈpærɪ) *n* **1** Sir (**Charles**) **Hubert** (**Hastings**). 1848–1918, British composer, noted esp. for his choral works. **2** Sir **William Edward.** 1790–1855, British arctic explorer, who searched for the Northwest Passage (1819–25) and attempted to reach the North Pole (1827).

parse (pɑːz) *vb* **parses, parsing, parsed.** *Grammar.* to assign constituent structure to (a sentence or the words in a sentence). ORIG C16: from L *pars* (*ōrātionis*) part (of speech)

parsec (ˈpɑːˌsɛk) *n* a unit of astronomical distance equivalent to 3.0857×10^{16} metres or 3.262 light years. ORIG C20: from PARALLAX + SECOND[2]

Parsee *or* **Parsi** (ˌpɑːˈsiː, ˈpɑːˌsiː) *n* an adherent of a Zoroastrian religion, the practitioners of which were driven out of Persia by the Muslims in the eighth century A.D. It is now found chiefly in western India. ORIG C17: from Persian *Pārsī* a Persian, from OPersian *Pārsa* PERSIA
▸ ˈ**Parseeˌism** *or* ˈ**Parsiˌism** *n*

parser (ˈpɑːzə) *n Computing.* a program that interprets ordinary language typed into a computer by recognizing key words or analysing sentence structure and then translating it into the appropriate machine language.

Parsifal *or* **Parzival** ★ (ˈpɑːsɪfᵊl, -ˌfɑːl) *n German myth.* the hero of a medieval cycle of legends about the Holy Grail. English equivalent: **Percival.**

parsimony (ˈpɑːsɪmənɪ) *n* extreme care in spending; niggardliness. ORIG C15: from L *parcimōnia*, from *parcere* to spare
▸ **parsimonious** (ˌpɑːsɪˈməʊnɪəs) *adj* ▸ ˌ**parsiˈmoniously** *adv*

parsley (ˈpɑːslɪ) *n* **1** a S European umbelliferous plant, widely cultivated for its curled aromatic leaves, which are used in cooking. **2** any of various similar and related plants, such as fool's-parsley and cow parsley. ORIG C14 *persely*, from OE *petersilie* + OF *persil, peresil*, both ult. from L *petroselīnum* rock parsley, from Gk, from *petra* rock + *selinon* parsley

parsnip (ˈpɑːsnɪp) *n* **1** an umbelliferous plant cultivated for its long whitish root. **2** the root of this plant, eaten as a vegetable. ORIG C14: from OF *pasnaie*, from L *pastināca*, from *pastināre* to dig, from *pastinum* two-pronged tool for digging

parson (ˈpɑːsᵊn) *n* **1** a parish priest in the Church of England. **2** any clergyman. ORIG C13: from Med. L *persōna* parish priest, from L: personage; see PERSON

parsonage (ˈpɑːsᵊnɪdʒ) *n* the residence of a parson, as provided by the parish.

parson bird *n* another name for **tui.**

Parsons ★ (ˈpɑːsənz) *n* Sir **Charles Algernon.** 1854–1931, British engineer, who developed the steam turbine.

parson's nose *n* the fatty extreme end portion of the tail of a fowl when cooked.

part (pɑːt) *n* **1** a piece or portion of a whole. **2** an integral constituent of something: *dancing is part of what we teach.* **3** an amount less than the whole; bit: *they only recovered part of the money.* **4** one of several equal divisions: *mix two parts flour to one part water.* **5** an actor's role in a play. **6** a person's proper role or duty: *everyone must do his part.* **7** (*often pl*) region; area: *you're well known in these parts.* **8** *Anat.* any portion of a larger structure. **9** a component that can be replaced in a machine, etc. **10** the US, Canad., and Austral. word for **parting** (sense 1). **11** *Music.* one of a number of separate melodic lines which is assigned to one or more instrumentalists or singers. **12 for one's part.** as far as one is concerned. **13 for the most part.** generally. **14 in part.** to some degree; partly. **15 of many parts.** having many different abilities. **16 on the part of.** on behalf of. **17 part and parcel.** an essential ingredient. **18 play a part. 18a** to pretend to be what one is not. **18b** to have something to do with; be instrumental. **19 take in good part.** to respond to (teasing, etc.) with good humour. **20 take part in.** to participate in. **21 take someone's part.** to support one person in an argument, etc. ◆ *vb* **22** to divide or separate from one another; take or come apart: *to part the curtains; the seams parted when I washed the dress.* **23** to go away or cause to go away from one another: *the couple parted amicably.* **24** (*intr;* foll. by *from*) to leave; say goodbye to. **25** (*intr;* foll. by *with*) to relinquish, esp. reluctantly: *I couldn't part with my teddy bear.* **26** (*tr;* foll. by *from*) to cause to relinquish, esp. reluctantly: *he's not easily parted from his cash.* **27** (*intr*) to split; separate: *the path parts here.* **28** (*tr*) to arrange (the hair) in such a way that a line of scalp is left showing. **29** (*intr*) *Euphemistic.* to die. **30** (*intr*) *Arch.* to depart. ◆ *adv* **31** to some extent; partly. ◆ See also **parts.** ORIG C13: via OF from L *partīre* to divide, from *pars* a part

part. *abbrev. for:* **1** participle. **2** particular.

partake (pɑːˈteɪk) *vb* **partakes, partaking, partook, partaken.** (*mainly intr*) **1** (foll. by *in*) to have a share; participate. **2** (foll. by *of*) to take or receive a portion, esp. of food or drink. **3** (foll. by *of*) to suggest or have some of the quality (of): *music partaking of sadness.* ORIG C16: back formation from *partaker*, earlier *part taker*, based on L *particeps* participant
▸ **parˈtaker** *n*

> **USAGE NOTE** *Partake of* is sometimes inappropriately used as if it were a synonym of *eat* or *drink.* Strictly speaking, you can only *partake of* food or drink which is available for several people to share.

parterre (pɑːˈtɛə) *n* **1** a formally patterned flower garden. **2** the pit of a theatre. ORIG C17: from F, from *par* along + *terre* ground

parthenogenesis (ˌpɑːθɪnəʊˈdʒɛnɪsɪs) *n* a type of reproduction, occurring in some insects and flowers, in which the unfertilized ovum develops directly into a new individual. ORIG C19: from Gk *parthenos* virgin + *genesis* birth
▸ **parthenogenetic** (ˌpɑːθɪˌnəʊdʒɪˈnɛtɪk) *adj*

Parthenon ★ (ˈpɑːθəˌnɒn, -nən) *n* the temple on the Acropolis in Athens built in the 5th century B.C. and regarded as the finest example of the Greek Doric order.

Parthenopaeus ★ (ˌpɑːθənəʊˈpiːəs) *n Greek myth.* one of the Seven against Thebes, son of Atalanta.

Parthenope ★ (pɑːˈθɛnəpɪ) *n Greek myth.* a siren, who drowned herself when Odysseus evaded the lure of the sirens' singing. Her body was said to have been cast ashore at what became Naples.

Parthia ★ (ˈpɑːθɪə) *n* a country in ancient Asia, south-

east of the Caspian Sea, that expanded into a great empire dominating SW Asia in the 2nd century B.C. It was destroyed in the 3rd century A.D.
▸ **'Parthian** *n, adj*

Parthian shot *n* a hostile remark or gesture delivered while departing. ORIG alluding to the custom of Parthian archers who shot their arrows backwards while retreating

partial ('pɑːʃəl) *adj* **1** relating to only a part; not general or complete: *a partial eclipse.* **2** biased: *a partial judge.* **3** (*postpositive;* foll. by *to*) having a particular liking (for). **4** *Maths.* designating or relating to an operation in which only one of a set of independent variables is considered at a time. ◆ *n* **5** Also called: **partial tone.** *Music, acoustics.* any of the component tones of a single musical sound. **6** *Maths.* a partial derivative. ORIG C15: from OF *parcial,* from LL *partiālis* incomplete, from L *pars* part
▸ **'partially** *adv* ▸ **'partialness** *n*

USAGE NOTE See at **partly.**

partial derivative *n* the derivative of a function of two or more variables with respect to one of the variables, the other or others being considered constant. Written $\partial f/\partial x$.

partiality (ˌpɑːʃɪ'ælɪtɪ) *n, pl* **partialities. 1** favourable bias. **2** (usually foll. by *for*) liking or fondness. **3** the state of being partial.

partible ('pɑːtəbᵊl) *adj* (esp. of property or an inheritance) divisible; separable. ORIG C16: from LL *partibilis,* from *part-, pars* part

participate (pɑː'tɪsɪˌpeɪt) *vb* **participates, participating, participated.** (*intr;* often foll. by *in*) to take part, be or become actively involved, or share (in). ORIG C16: from L *participāre,* from *pars* part + *capere* to take
▸ **par'ticipant** *adj, n* ▸ **parˌtici'pation** *n* ▸ **par'ticiˌpator** *n*
▸ **par'ticipatory** *adj*

participle ('pɑːtɪsɪpᵊl) *n* a nonfinite form of verbs, in English and other languages, used adjectivally and in the formation of certain compound tenses. See also **present participle, past participle.** ORIG C14: via OF from L *participium,* from *particeps,* from *pars* part + *capere* to take
▸ **participial** (ˌpɑːtɪ'sɪpɪəl) *adj* ▸ **ˌparti'cipially** *adv*

particle ('pɑːtɪkᵊl) *n* **1** an extremely small piece of matter; speck. **2** a very tiny amount; iota: *it doesn't make a particle of difference.* **3** a function word, esp. (in certain languages) a word belonging to an uninflected class having grammatical function: *"up" is sometimes regarded as an adverbial particle.* **4** a common affix, such as *re-, un-,* or *-ness.* **5** *Physics.* a body with finite mass that can be treated as having negligible size, and internal structure. **6** See **elementary particle.** ORIG C14: from L *particula* a small part, from *pars* part

particle accelerator *n* a machine for accelerating charged elementary particles to very high energies, used in nuclear physics.

particle physics *n* the study of fundamental particles and their properties. Also called: **high-energy physics.**

parti-coloured ('pɑːtɪˌkʌləd) *adj* having different colours in different parts; variegated. ORIG C16 *parti,* from (obs.) *party* of more than one colour, from OF: striped, from L *partīre* to divide

particular (pə'tɪkjʊlə) *adj* **1** (*prenominal*) of or belonging to a single or specific person, thing, category, etc.; specific; special: *the particular demands of the job.* **2** (*prenominal*) exceptional or marked: *a matter of particular importance.* **3** (*prenominal*) relating to or providing specific details or circumstances: *a particular account.* **4** exacting or difficult to please, esp. in details; fussy. **5** (of the solution of a differential equation) obtained by giving specific values to the arbitrary constants in a general equation. **6** *Logic.* (of a proposition) affirming or denying something about only some members of a class of objects, as in *some men are not wicked.* Cf. **universal** (sense 9). ◆ *n* **7** a separate distinct item that helps to form a generalization: opposed to *general.* **8** (*often pl*) an item of information; detail: *complete in every particular.* **9 in particular.** especially or exactly. ORIG C14: from OF *particuler,* from LL *particulāris* concerning a part, from L *particula* PARTICLE
▸ **par'ticularly** *adv*

particular average *n Insurance.* partial damage to or loss of a ship or its cargo affecting only the shipowner or one cargo owner. Abbrev.: **PA.** Cf. **general average.**

particularism (pə'tɪkjʊləˌrɪzəm) *n* **1** exclusive attachment to the interests of one group, class, sect, etc. **2** the principle of permitting each state in a federation the right to further its own interests. **3** *Christian theol.* the doctrine that divine grace is restricted to the elect.
▸ **par'ticularist** *n, adj*

particularity (pəˌtɪkjʊ'lærɪtɪ) *n, pl* **particularities. 1** (*often pl*) a specific circumstance: *the particularities of the affair.* **2** great attentiveness to detail; fastidiousness. **3** the quality of being precise: *a description of great particularity.* **4** the state or quality of being particular as opposed to general; individuality.

particularize *or* **particularise** (pə'tɪkjʊləˌraɪz) *vb* **particularizes, particularizing, particularized** *or* **particularises, particularising, particularised. 1** to treat in detail; give details (about). **2** (*intr*) to go into detail.
▸ **parˌticulari'zation** *or* **parˌticulari'sation** *n*

particulate (pɑː'tɪkjʊlɪt, -ˌleɪt) *n* **1** a substance consisting of separate particles. ◆ *adj* **2** of or made up of separate particles.

parting ('pɑːtɪŋ) *n* **1** *Brit.* the line of scalp showing when sections of hair are combed in opposite directions. US, Canad., and Austral. equivalent: **part. 2** the act of separating or the state of being separated. **3a** a departure or leave-taking, esp. one causing a final separation. **3b** (*as modifier*): *a parting embrace.* **4** a place or line of separation or division. **5** a euphemism for **death.** ◆ *adj* (*prenominal*) **6** *Literary.* departing: *the parting day.* **7** serving to divide or separate.

partisan *or* **partizan** (ˌpɑːtɪ'zæn, 'pɑːtɪˌzæn) *n* **1** an adherent or devotee of a cause, party, etc. **2** a member of an armed resistance group within occupied territory. ◆ *adj* **3** of, relating to, or characteristic of a partisan. **4** excessively devoted to one party, faction, etc.; one-sided. ORIG C16: via F from OIt. *partigiano,* from *parte* faction, from L *pars* part
▸ **ˌparti'sanship** *or* **ˌparti'zanship** *n*

partita (pɑː'tiːtə) *n, pl* **partite** (-teɪ) *or* **partitas** *Music.* a type of suite. ORIG It.: divided (piece), from L *partīre* to divide

partite ('pɑːtaɪt) *adj* **1** (*in combination*) composed of or divided into a specified number of parts: *bipartite.* **2** (esp. of plant leaves) divided almost to the base to form two or more parts. ORIG C16: from L *partīre* to divide

partition (pɑː'tɪʃən) *n* **1** a division into parts; separation. **2** something that separates, such as a large screen dividing a room in two. **3** a part or share. **4** *Property law.* a division of property, esp. realty, among joint owners. ◆ *vb* (*tr*) **5** (often foll. by *off*) to separate or apportion into sections: *to partition a room off with a large screen.* **6** *Property law.* to divide (property, esp. realty) among joint owners. ORIG C15: via OF from L *partītiō,* from *partīre* to divide
▸ **par'titioner** *or* **par'titionist** *n*

partitive ('pɑːtɪtɪv) *adj* **1** *Grammar.* indicating that a noun involved in a construction refers only to a part of what it otherwise refers to. The phrase *some of the butter* is a partitive construction. **2** serving to separate or divide into parts. ◆ *n* **3** *Grammar.* a partitive linguistic element or feature. ORIG C16: from Med. L *partītīvus* serving to divide, from L *partīre* to divide
▸ **'partitively** *adv*

partly ('pɑːtlɪ) *adv* not completely.

USAGE NOTE *Partly* and *partially* are to some extent interchangeable, but *partly* should be used when referring to a part or parts of something: *the building is partly* (not *partially*) *of stone,* while *partially* is preferred for the meaning *to some extent: his mother is partially* (not *partly*) *sighted.*

partner ('pɑːtnə) *n* **1** an ally or companion: *a partner in crime.* **2** a member of a partnership. **3** one of a pair of dancers or players on the same side in a game: *my bridge* *partner*. **4** either member of a couple in a relationship. ◆ *vb* **5** to be or cause to be a partner (of). ORIG C14: var. (infl. by PART) of *parcener* one who shares equally with another, from OF *parçonier,* ult. from L *partīre* to divide

partnership ('pɑːtnəʃɪp) *n* **1a** a contractual relationship between two or more persons carrying on a joint business venture. **1b** the deed creating such a relationship. **1c** the persons associated in such a relationship. **2** the state or condition of being a partner.

part of speech *n* a class of words sharing important syntactic or semantic features; a group of words in a language that may occur in similar positions or fulfil similar functions in a sentence. The chief parts of speech in English are noun, pronoun, adjective, determiner, adverb, verb, preposition, conjunction, and interjection.

parton ('pɑːˌtɒn) *n Physics.* a hypothetical elementary particle postulated as a constituent of neutrons and protons. ORIG from PART + -ON

Parton ★ ('pɑːtən) *n* **Dolly.** born 1946, US country and pop singer and songwriter.

partook (pɑː'tʊk) *vb* the past tense of **partake.**

partridge ('pɑːtrɪdʒ) *n, pl* **partridges** *or* **partridge.** any of various small Old World game birds of the pheasant family, esp. the common or European partridge. ORIG C13: from OF *perdriz,* from L *perdix,* from Gk

parts (pɑːts) *pl n* **1** personal abilities or talents: *a man of many parts.* **2** short for **private parts.**

Parts of Holland ★ *n* See **Holland**[1] (sense 3).

Parts of Kesteven ★ *n* See (Parts of) **Kesteven.**

Parts of Lindsey ★ *n* See (Parts of) **Lindsey.**

part song *n* **1** a song composed in harmonized parts. **2** (*in more technical usage*) a piece of homophonic choral music in which the topmost part carries the melody.

part-time *adj* **1** occupying less than the full time normally associated with an activity: *a part-time job.* ◆ *adv* **part time. 2** on a part-time basis: *he works part time.* ◆ Cf. **full-time.**
▸ **ˌpart-'timer** *n*

parturient (pɑː'tjʊərɪənt) *adj* **1** of or relating to childbirth. **2** giving birth. **3** producing a new idea, etc. ORIG C16: via L *parturīre,* from *parere* to bring forth
▸ **par'turiency** *n*

parturition (ˌpɑːtjʊ'rɪʃən) *n* the act or process of giving birth. ORIG C17: from LL *parturītiō,* from *parturīre* to be in labour

part work *n Brit.* a series of magazines issued weekly or monthly, which are designed to be bound together to form a complete book.

party ('pɑːtɪ) *n, pl* **parties. 1a** a social gathering for pleasure, often held as a celebration. **1b** (*as modifier*): *party spirit.* **1c** (*in combination*): *partygoer.* **2** a group of people associated in some activity: *a rescue party.* **3a** (*often cap.*) a group of people organized together to further a common political aim, etc. **3b** (*as modifier*): *party politics.* **4** a person, esp. one entering into a contract. **5** the person or persons taking part in legal proceedings: *a party to the action.* **6** *Inf., humorous.* a person. ◆ *vb* **parties, partying, partied.** (*intr*) **7** *Inf.* to celebrate; revel. ◆ *adj* **8** *Heraldry.* (of a shield) divided vertically into two colours, metals, or furs. ORIG C13: from OF *partie* part, from L *partīre* to divide; see PART

party line *n* **1** a telephone line serving two or more subscribers. **2** the policies or dogma of a political party, etc.

party list *n* (*modifier*) of or relating to a system of voting in which people vote for a party rather than for a candidate. Parties are assigned the number of seats that reflects their share of the vote. See **proportional representation.**

party pooper ('puːpə) *n Inf.* a person whose behaviour or personality spoils other people's enjoyment. ORIG C20: orig. US

party popper *n* a small plastic cylinder that, when a string is pulled, makes a small bang and fires thin paper streamers into the air.

party wall *n Property law.* a wall separating two properties or pieces of land and over which each of the adjoining owners has certain rights.

par value *n* the value imprinted on the face of a share certificate or bond and used to assess dividend, capital ownership, or interest.

parvenu *or* (*fem*) **parvenue** ('pɑːvəˌnjuː) *n* **1** a person who, having risen socially or economically, is considered to be an upstart. ◆ *adj* **2** of or characteristic of a parvenu. ORIG C19: from F, from *parvenir* to attain, from L *pervenīre,* from *per* through + *venīre* to come

parvovirus ('pɑːvəʊˌvaɪrəs) *n* any of a group of viruses characterized by their very small size, each of which is specific to a particular species, as for example canine parvovirus. ORIG C20: NL, from L *parvus* little + VIRUS

Parzival ★ (*German* 'partsifal) *n* a variant of **Parsifal.**

pas (pɑː) *n, pl* **pas.** a dance step or movement, esp. in ballet. ORIG C18: from F, lit.: step

Pasadena ★ (ˌpæsə'diːnə) *n* a city in SW California, east of Los Angeles. Pop.: 134 116 (1996 est.).

Pasargadae ★ (pæ'sɑːgəˌdiː) *n* an ancient city in Persia, northeast of Persepolis in present-day Iran: built by Cyrus the Great.

Pasay ★ ('pɑːsaɪ) *n* a city in the Philippines, on central Luzon just south of Manila, on Manila Bay. Pop.: 374 000 (1990). Also called: **Rizal.**

pascal ('pæskəl) *n* the derived SI unit of pressure; the pressure exerted on an area of 1 square metre by a force of 1 newton; equivalent to 10 dynes per square centimetre or 1.45×10^{-4} pound per square inch. Symbol: Pa ORIG C20: after B. PASCAL

Pascal ★ (*French* paskal) *n* **Blaise** (blɛz). 1623–62, French philosopher, mathematician, and physicist. As a scientist, he made important contributions to hydraulics and the study of atmospheric pressure and, with Fermat, developed the theory of probability. His chief philosophical works are *Lettres provinciales* (1656–57), written in defence of Jansenism and against the Jesuits, and *Pensées* (1670), fragments of a Christian apologia.

PASCAL ('pæsˌkæl) *n* a high-level computer-programming language developed as a teaching language.

Pascal's triangle *n* a triangle consisting of rows of numbers; the apex is 1 and each row starts and ends with 1, other numbers being obtained by adding together the two numbers on either side in the row above: used to calculate probabilities. ORIG C17: after B. PASCAL

paschal ('pæskəl) *adj* **1** of or relating to **Passover** (sense 1). **2** of or relating to **Easter.** ORIG C15: from OF *pascal,* via Church L from Heb. *pesakh* Passover

Paschal Lamb *n* **1** (*sometimes not caps.*) *Old Testament.* the lamb killed and eaten on the first day of the Passover. **2** Christ regarded as this sacrifice.

pas de basque (ˌpɑː də 'bɑː) *n, pl* **pas de basque.** a dance step performed usually on the spot and used esp. in reels and jigs. ORIG from F, lit.: Basque step

Pas-de-Calais ★ (*French* pɒdkalɛ) *n* a department of N France, in Nord-Pas-de-Calais region, on the Straits of Dover (the **Pas de Calais**): the part of France closest to the British Isles. Capital: Arras. Pop.: 1 437 555 (1994 est.). Area: 6752 sq. km (2633 sq. miles).

pas de deux (*French* pɒddø) *n, pl* **pas de deux.** *Ballet.* a sequence for two dancers. ORIG F: step for two

pash (pæʃ) *n Sl.* infatuation. ORIG C20: from PASSION

pasha *or* **pacha** ('pɑːʃə, 'pæʃə) *n* (formerly) a high official of the Ottoman Empire or the modern Egyptian kingdom: placed after a name when used as a title. ORIG C17: from Turkish *paşa*

pashm ('pæʃəm) *n* the underfur of various Tibetan animals, esp. goats, used for Cashmere shawls. ORIG from Persian, lit.: wool

pashmina (pæʃ'miːnə) *n* a scarf or shawl made of pashm. ORIG from Persian *pashmina;* see PASHM

Pashto, Pushto ('pʌʃtəʊ), *or* **Pushtu** *n* **1** a language of Afghanistan and NW Pakistan. **2** (*pl* **Pashto** *or* **Pashtos, Pushto** *or* **Pushtos, Pushtu** *or* **Pushtus**) a speaker of the Pashto language; a Pathan. ◆ *adj* **3** denoting or relating to this language or a speaker of it.

Pasionaria ★ (*Spanish* pasjo'narja) *n* **La** (la), real name

Dolores Ibarruri. 1895–1989, Spanish Communist leader, who lived in exile in the Soviet Union (1939–75).

Pasiphaë ★ (pəˈsɪfiː) *n Greek myth.* the wife of Minos and mother (by a bull) of the Minotaur.

Pasmore ★ (ˈpæsˌmɔː) *n* **Victor.** 1908–98, British artist. Originally influenced by cubism, he devoted himself to abstract paintings and reliefs after 1947.

paso doble (ˈpæsəʊ ˈdəʊbleɪ) *n, pl* **paso dobles** *or* **pasos dobles. 1** a modern ballroom dance in fast duple time. **2** a piece of music composed for or in the rhythm of this dance. ORIG Sp.: double step

Pasolini ★ (*Italian* pazoˈlini) *n* **Pier Paolo** (pjɛr ˈpaːolo). 1922–75, Italian film director. His films include *The Gospel according to St Matthew* (1964), *Oedipus Rex* (1967), *Theorem* (1968), *Pigsty* (1969), and *Decameron* (1970).

pas op (ˈpɑːs ˌɒp) *interj S. African.* beware. ORIG Afrik.

pasqueflower (ˈpɑːskˌflaʊə) *n* **1** a small purple-flowered plant of N and Central Europe and W Asia. **2** any of several related North American plants. ORIG C16: from F *passefleur,* from *passer* to excel + *fleur* flower; changed to *pasqueflower* Easter flower, because it blooms at Easter

pasquinade (ˌpæskwɪˈneɪd) *n* an abusive lampoon or satire, esp. one posted in a public place. ORIG C17: from It. *Pasquino* name given to an ancient Roman statue disinterred in 1501, which was annually posted with satirical verses

pass (pɑːs) *vb* **1** to go onwards or move by or past (a person, thing, etc.). **2** to run, extend, or lead through, over, or across (a place): *the route passes through the city.* **3** to go through or cause to go through (an obstacle or barrier): *to pass a needle through cloth.* **4** to move or cause to move onwards or over: *he passed his hand over her face.* **5** (*tr*) to go beyond or exceed: *this victory passes all expectation.* **6** to gain or cause to gain an adequate mark or grade in (an examination, course, etc.). **7** (often foll. by *away* or *by*) to elapse or allow to elapse: *we passed the time talking.* **8** (*intr*) to take place or happen: *what passed at the meeting?* **9** to speak or exchange or be spoken or exchanged: *angry words passed between them.* **10** to spread or cause to spread: *we passed the news round the class.* **11** to transfer or exchange or be transferred or exchanged: *the bomb passed from hand to hand.* **12** (*intr*) to undergo change or transition: *to pass from joy to despair.* **13** (when *tr,* often foll. by *down*) to transfer or be transferred by inheritance: *the house passed to the younger son.* **14** to agree to or be agreed to by a legislative body, etc.: *the assembly passed 10 resolutions.* **15** (*tr*) (of a legislative measure) to undergo (a procedural stage) and be agreed: *the bill passed the committee stage.* **16** (when *tr,* often foll. by *on* or *upon*) to pronounce (judgment, findings, etc.): *the court passed sentence.* **17** to go or allow to go without comment or censure: *the insult passed unnoticed.* **18** (*intr*) to opt not to exercise a right, as by not answering a question or not making a bid or a play in card games. **19** to discharge (urine, etc.) from the body. **20** (*intr*) to come to an end or disappear: *his anger soon passed.* **21** (*intr;* usually foll. by *for* or *as*) to be likely to be mistaken for (someone or something else): *you could easily pass for your sister.* **22** (*intr;* foll. by *away, on,* or *over*) *Euphemistic.* to die. **23** *Sport.* to hit, kick, or throw (the ball, etc.) to another player. **24 bring to pass.** *Arch.* to cause to happen. **25 come to pass.** *Arch.* to happen. ◆ *n* **26** the act of passing. **27** a route through a range of mountains where there is a gap between peaks. **28** a permit, licence, or authorization to do something without restriction. **29a** a document allowing entry to and exit from a military installation. **29b** a document authorizing leave of absence. **30** *Brit.* **30a** the passing of a college or university examination to a satisfactory standard but not as high as honours. **30b** (*as modifier*): *a pass degree.* **31** a dive, sweep, or bombing or landing run by an aircraft. **32** a motion of the hand or of a wand as part of a conjuring trick. **33** *Inf.* an attempt to invite sexual intimacy (esp. in **make a pass at**). **34** a state of affairs, esp. a bad one (esp. in **a pretty pass**). **35** *Sport.* the transfer of a ball, etc., from one player to another. **36** *Fencing.* a thrust or lunge. **37** *Bridge, etc.* the act of passing (making no bid). ◆ *sentence substitute.* **38** *Bridge, etc.* a call indicating that a player has no bid to make. ◆ See also **pass off, pass out,** etc. ORIG C13: from OF *passer* to pass, surpass, from L *passūs* step

> **USAGE NOTE** The past participle of *pass* is sometimes wrongly spelt *past: the time for recriminations has passed* (not *past*).

pass. *abbrev. for:* **1** passive. **2** passenger. **3** passage.

passable (ˈpɑːsəbᵊl) *adj* **1** adequate, fair, or acceptable. **2** (of an obstacle) capable of being crossed. **3** (of currency) valid for circulation. **4** (of a proposed law) able to be enacted.
▸ **ˈpassableness** *n* ▸ **ˈpassably** *adv*

passacaglia (ˌpæsəˈkɑːljə) *n* **1** an old Spanish dance in slow triple time. **2** a slow instrumental piece characterized by a series of variations on a particular theme played over a repeated bass part. ORIG C17: earlier *passacalle,* from Sp. *pasacalle* street dance, from *paso* step + *calle* street

passage (ˈpæsɪdʒ) *n* **1** a channel, opening, etc., through or by which a person or thing may pass. **2** *Music.* a section or division of a piece, movement, etc. **3** a way, as in a hall or lobby. **4** a section of a written work, speech, etc. **5** a journey, esp. by ship. **6** the act or process of passing from one place, condition, etc., to another: *passage of a gas through a liquid.* **7** the permission, right, or freedom to pass: *to be denied passage through a country.* **8** the enactment of a law by a legislative body. **9** *Rare.* an exchange, as of blows, words, etc. ORIG C13: from OF from *passer* to PASS

passageway (ˈpæsɪdʒˌweɪ) *n* a way, esp. one in or between buildings; passage.

Passamaquoddy Bay ★ (ˌpæsəməˈkwɒdɪ) *n* an inlet of the Bay of Fundy between the province of New Brunswick, in Canada, and the state of Maine, in the US, at the mouth of the St Croix River.

pass band *n* the band of frequencies that is transmitted with maximum efficiency through a circuit, filter, etc.

passbook (ˈpɑːsˌbʊk) *n* **1** a book for keeping a record of withdrawals from and payments into a building society. **2** another name for **bankbook. 3** *S. African.* an official document to identify the bearer, his race, residence, and employment.

Passchendaele ★ (ˈpæʃᵊnˌdeɪᵊl) *n* a village in NW Belgium, in West Flanders province: the scene of heavy fighting during the third battle of Ypres in World War I during which 245 000 British troops were lost.

passé (ˈpɑːseɪ, ˈpæseɪ) *adj* **1** out-of-date: *passé ideas.* **2** past the prime; faded: *a passé society beauty.* ORIG C18: from F, p.p. of *passer* to PASS

passenger (ˈpæsɪndʒə) *n* **1a** a person travelling in a car, train, boat, etc., driven by another person. **1b** (*as modifier*): *a passenger seat.* **2** *Chiefly Brit.* a member of a group or team who is not participating fully in the work. ORIG C14: from OF *passager* passing, from PASSAGE

passenger pigeon *n* a gregarious North American pigeon, now extinct.

passe-partout (ˌpæspɑːˈtuː) *n* **1** a mounting for a picture in which strips of gummed paper bind together the glass, picture, and backing. **2** the gummed paper used for this. **3** a mat on which a photograph, etc., is mounted. **4** something that secures entry everywhere, esp. a master key. ORIG C17: from F, lit.: pass everywhere

passepied (pɑːsˈpjeɪ) *n, pl* **passepieds** (-ˈpjeɪ). **1** a lively minuet in triple time, popular in the 17th century. **2** a piece of music composed for or in the rhythm of this dance. ORIG C17: from F: pass foot

passer-by *n, pl* **passers-by.** a person who is passing or going by, esp. on foot.

passerine (ˈpæsəˌraɪn, -ˌriːn) *adj* **1** of, relating to, or belonging to an order of birds characterized by the perching habit: includes the larks, finches, starlings, etc. ◆ *n* **2** any bird belonging to this order. ORIG C18: from L *passer* sparrow

passim *Latin.* (ˈpæsɪm) *adv* here and there; throughout: used to indicate that what is referred to occurs frequently in the work cited.

passing (ˈpɑːsɪŋ) *adj* **1** transitory or momentary: *a passing fancy.* **2** cursory or casual in action or manner: *a passing* *reference.* ◆ *adv, adj* **3** *Arch.* to an extreme degree: *the events were passing strange.* ◆ *n* **4** a place where or means by which one may pass, cross, ford, etc. **5** a euphemistic word for **death. 6 in passing.** by the way; incidentally.

passing bell *n* a bell rung to announce a death or a funeral. Also called: **death knell.**

passing note *or US* **passing tone** *n* a nonharmonic note through which a melody passes from one harmonic note to the next.

passion ('pæʃən) *n* **1** ardent love or affection. **2** intense sexual love. **3** a strong affection or enthusiasm for an object, concept, etc.: *a passion for poetry.* **4** any strongly felt emotion, such as love, hate, envy, etc. **5** an outburst of anger: *he flew into a passion.* **6** the object of an intense desire, ardent affection, or enthusiasm. **7** an outburst expressing intense emotion: *he burst into a passion of sobs.* **8** the sufferings and death of a Christian martyr. ORIG C12: via F from Church L *passiō* suffering, from L *patī* to suffer
▸ **'passional** *adj* ▸ **'passionless** *adj*

Passion ('pæʃən) *n* **1** the sufferings of Christ from the Last Supper to his death on the cross. **2** any of the four Gospel accounts of this. **3** a musical setting of this: *the St Matthew Passion.*

passionate ('pæʃənɪt) *adj* **1** manifesting or exhibiting intense sexual feeling or desire. **2** capable of, revealing, or characterized by intense emotion. **3** easily roused to anger; quick-tempered.
▸ **'passionately** *adv*

passionflower ('pæʃənˌflauə) *n* any plant of a tropical American genus cultivated for their red, yellow, greenish, or purple showy flowers: some species have edible fruit. ORIG C17: from alleged resemblance betweeen parts of the flower and the instruments of the Crucifixion

passion fruit *n* the edible fruit of any of various passionflowers, esp. granadilla.

Passion play *n* a play depicting the Passion of Christ.

passive ('pæsɪv) *adj* **1** not active or not participating perceptibly in an activity, organization, etc. **2** unresisting and receptive to external forces; submissive. **3** affected or acted upon by an external object or force. **4** *Grammar.* denoting a voice of verbs in sentences in which the grammatical subject is the recipient of the action described by the verb, as *was broken* in the sentence *The glass was broken by a boy.* **5** *Chem.* (of a substance, esp. a metal) apparently chemically unreactive. **6** *Electronics, telecomm.* **6a** capable only of attenuating a signal: *a passive network.* **6b** not capable of amplifying a signal or controlling a function: *a passive communications satellite.* **7** *Finance.* (of a bond, share, debt, etc.) yielding no interest. ◆ *n* **8** *Grammar.* **8a** the passive voice. **8b** a passive verb. ORIG C14: from L *passīvus* susceptible of suffering, from *patī* to undergo
▸ **'passively** *adv* ▸ **pas'sivity** *or* **'passiveness** *n*

passive resistance *n* resistance to a government, law, etc., without violence, as by fasting, demonstrating, or refusing to cooperate.

passive smoking *n* the inhalation of smoke from other people's cigarettes by a nonsmoker.

passkey ('pɑːsˌkiː) *n* **1** any of various keys, esp. a latchkey. **2** another term for **master key** or **skeleton key.**

pass law *n* (formerly, in South Africa) a law restricting the movement of Black Africans.

pass off *vb* (*adv*) **1** to be or cause to be accepted in a false character: *he passed the fake diamonds off as real.* **2** (*intr*) to come to a gradual end; disappear: *eventually the pain passed off.* **3** (*intr*) to take place: *the meeting passed off without disturbance.* **4** (*tr*) to set aside or disregard: *I managed to pass off his insult.*

pass out *vb* (*adv*) **1** (*intr*) *Inf.* to become unconscious; faint. **2** (*intr*) *Brit.* (esp. of an officer cadet) to qualify for a military commission, etc. **3** (*tr*) to distribute.

pass over *vb* **1** (*tr, adv*) to take no notice of; disregard: *they passed me over in the last round of promotions.* **2** (*intr, prep*) to disregard (something bad or embarrassing).

Passover ('pɑːsˌəuvə) *n* **1** an eight-day Jewish festival celebrated in commemoration of the passing over or sparing of the Israelites in Egypt (Exodus 12). **2** another term for the **Paschal Lamb.** ORIG C16: from *pass over,* translation of Heb. *pesah,* from *pāsah* to pass over

passport ('pɑːspɔːt) *n* **1** an official document issued by a government, identifying an individual, granting him permission to travel abroad, and requesting the protection of other governments for him. **2** a quality, asset, etc., that gains a person admission or acceptance. ORIG C15: from F *passeport,* from *passer* to PASS + PORT[1]

pass up *vb* (*tr, adv*) *Inf.* to let go by; ignore: *I won't pass up this opportunity.*

password ('pɑːsˌwɜːd) *n* **1** a secret word, phrase, etc., that ensures admission by proving identity, membership, etc. **2** an action, quality, etc., that gains admission or acceptance. **3** *Computing.* a sequence of characters used to gain access to a computer system.

past (pɑːst) *adj* **1** completed, finished, and no longer in existence: *past happiness.* **2** denoting or belonging to the time that has elapsed at the present moment: *the past history of the world.* **3** denoting a specific unit of time that immediately precedes the present one: *the past month.* **4** (*prenominal*) denoting a person who has held an office or position; former: *a past president.* **5** *Grammar.* denoting any of various tenses of verbs that are used in describing actions, events, or states that have been begun or completed at the time of utterance. ◆ *n* **6 the past.** the period of time that has elapsed: *forget the past.* **7** the history, experience, or background of a nation, person, etc. **8** an earlier period of someone's life, esp. one regarded as disreputable. **9** *Grammar.* **9a** a past tense. **9b** a verb in a past tense. ◆ *adv* **10** at a time before the present; ago: *three years past.* **11** on or onwards: *I greeted him but he just walked past.* ◆ *prep* **12** beyond in time: *it's past midnight.* **13** beyond in place or position: *the library is past the church.* **14** moving beyond: *he walked past me.* **15** beyond or above the reach, limit, or scope of: *his foolishness is past comprehension.* **16 past it.** *Inf.* unable to perform the tasks one could do when one was younger. **17 not put it past someone.** to consider someone capable of (the action specified). ORIG C14: from *passed,* p.p. of PASS

> **USAGE NOTE** The past participle of *pass* is sometimes wrongly spelt *past*: *the time for recrimination has passed* (not *past*).

pasta ('pæstə) *n* any of several variously shaped edible preparations made from a flour and water dough, such as spaghetti. ORIG It., from LL: PASTE

paste (peɪst) *n* **1** a mixture of a soft or malleable consistency, such as toothpaste. **2** an adhesive made from water and flour or starch, used for joining pieces of paper, etc. **3** a preparation of food, such as meat, that has been pounded to a creamy mass, for spreading on bread, etc. **4** any of various sweet doughy confections: *almond paste.* **5** dough, esp. for making pastry. **6a** a hard shiny glass used for making imitation gems. **6b** an imitation gem made of this glass. **7** the combined ingredients of porcelain. See also **hard paste, soft paste.** ◆ *vb* **pastes, pasting, pasted.** (*tr*) **8** (often foll. by *on* or *onto*) to attach as by using paste: *he pasted posters onto the wall.* **9** (usually foll. by *with*) to cover (a surface) with paper, etc.: *he pasted the wall with posters.* **10** *Sl.* to thrash or beat; defeat. ORIG C14: via OF from LL *pasta* dough, from Gk *pastē* barley porridge, from *passein* to sprinkle

pasteboard ('peɪstˌbɔːd) *n* **1** a stiff board formed from layers of paper or pulp pasted together. ◆ *adj* **2** flimsy or fake.

pastel ('pæstᵊl, pæ'stɛl) *n* **1a** a substance made of ground pigment bound with gum. **1b** a crayon of this. **1c** a drawing done in such crayons. **2** the medium or technique of pastel drawing. **3** a pale delicate colour. ◆ *adj* **4** (of a colour) pale; delicate: *pastel blue.* ORIG C17: via F from It. *pastello,* from LL *pastellus* woad, dim. of *pasta* PASTE
▸ **'pastelist** *or* **'pastellist** *n*

pastern ('pæstən) *n* the part of a horse's foot between the fetlock and the hoof. ORIG C14: from OF *pasturon,* from *pasture* a hobble, from L *pāstōrius* of a shepherd, from PASTOR

Pasternak ★ ('pæstəˌnæk; *Russian* pəstɪr'nak) *n* **Boris Leonidovich** (ba'ris lɪa'nidəvitʃ). 1890–1960, Russian poet, novelist, and translator, noted esp. for his novel *Dr. Zhivago* (1957). He was awarded the Nobel prize for literature in 1958, but was forced to decline it.

paste-up *n Printing.* a sheet of paper or board on which are pasted artwork, proofs, etc., for photographing prior to making a plate.

Pasteur ★ (*French* pastœr) *n* **Louis** (lwi). 1822–95, French chemist and bacteriologist. His discovery that the fermentation of milk and alcohol was caused by microorganisms resulted in the process of pasteurization. He also devised methods of immunization against anthrax and rabies and pioneered stereochemistry.

pasteurism ('pæstəˌrɪzəm, -stjə-, 'pɑː-) *n Med.* a method of securing immunity from rabies or of treating patients with other viral infections by the serial injection of progressively more virulent suspensions of the causative virus. Also called: **Pasteur treatment.**

pasteurization *or* **pasteurisation** (ˌpæstəraɪ'zeɪʃən, -stjə-, ˌpɑː-) *n* the process of heating beverages, such as milk, beer, wine, or cider, or solid foods, such as cheese or crab meat, to destroy harmful microorganisms.

pasteurize *or* **pasteurise** ('pæstəˌraɪz, -stjə-, 'pɑː-) *vb* **pasteurizes, pasteurizing, pasteurized** *or* **pasteurises, pasteurising, pasteurised.** (*tr*) to subject (milk, beer, etc.) to pasteurization.
▸ **'pasteurˌizer** *or* **'pasteurˌiser** *n*

pastiche (pæ'stiːʃ) *or* **pasticcio** (pæ'stɪtʃəʊ) *n, pl* **pastiches** *or* **pasticcios. 1** a work of art that mixes styles, materials, etc. **2** a work of art that imitates the style of another artist or period. ORIG C19: F *pastiche,* It. *pasticcio,* lit.: pie-crust (hence, something blended) from LL *pasta* PASTE

pastille *or* **pastil** ('pæstɪl) *n* **1** a small flavoured or medicated lozenge. **2** an aromatic substance burnt to fumigate the air. ORIG C17: via F from L *pastillus* small loaf, from *pānis* bread

pastime ('pɑːsˌtaɪm) *n* an activity or entertainment which makes time pass pleasantly.

past master *n* **1** a person with talent for, or experience in, a particular activity. **2** a person who has held the office of master in a guild, etc.

Pasto ★ (*Spanish* 'pasto) *n* a city in SE Colombia, at an altitude of 2590 m (8500 ft). Pop.: 362 227 (1997 est.).

pastor ('pɑːstə) *n* **1** a clergyman or priest in charge of a congregation. **2** a person who exercises spiritual guidance over a number of people. **3** a S Asian starling having a black head and wings and a pale pink body. ORIG C14: from L: shepherd, from *pascere* to feed
▸ **'pastorship** *n*

pastoral ('pɑːstərəl) *adj* **1** of, characterized by, or depicting rural life, scenery, etc. **2** (of a literary work) dealing with an idealized form of rural existence. **3** (of land) used for pasture. **4** of or relating to a member of the clergy in charge of a congregation or his or her duties as such. **5** of or relating to shepherds, their work, etc. **6** of or relating to a teacher's responsibility for the personal, as distinct from the educational, development of pupils. ◆ *n* **7** a literary work or picture portraying rural life, esp. in an idealizing way. **8** *Music.* a variant spelling of **pastorale. 9a** a letter from a member of the clergy to the people under his or her charge. **9b** the letter of a bishop to the clergy or people of his or her diocese. **9c** Also called: **pastoral staff.** the crosier carried by a bishop. ORIG C15: from L, from PASTOR
▸ **'pastoralism** *n* ▸ **'pastorally** *adv*

pastorale (ˌpæstə'rɑːl) *n, pl* **pastorales.** *Music.* **1** a composition evocative of rural life, sometimes with a droning accompaniment. **2** a musical play based on a rustic story. ORIG C18: It., from L: PASTORAL

pastoralist ('pɑːstərəlɪst) *n Austral.* a grazier raising sheep, cattle, etc., on a large scale.

pastorate ('pɑːstərɪt) *n* **1** the office or term of office of a pastor. **2** a body of pastors.

pastourelle (ˌpɑːstuː'rɛl) *n Music.* **1** a pastoral piece of music. **2** one of the figures in a quadrille. ORIG C19: from F: little shepherdess

past participle *n* a participial form of verbs used to modify a noun that is logically the object of a verb, also used in certain compound tenses and passive forms of the verb.

past perfect *Grammar.* ◆ *adj* **1** denoting a tense of verbs used in relating past events where the action had already occurred at the time of the action of a main verb that is itself in a past tense. In English this is a compound tense formed with *had* plus the past participle. ◆ *n* **2a** the past perfect tense. **2b** a verb in this tense.

pastrami (pə'strɑːmɪ) *n* highly seasoned smoked beef. ORIG from Yiddish, from Romanian *pastramă,* from *păstra* to preserve

pastry ('peɪstrɪ) *n, pl* **pastries. 1** a dough of flour, water, and fat. **2** baked foods, such as tarts, made with this dough. **3** an individual cake or pastry pie. ORIG C16: from PASTE

pasturage ('pɑːstʃərɪdʒ) *n* **1** the business of grazing cattle. **2** another word for **pasture.**

pasture ('pɑːstʃə) *n* **1** land covered with grass or herbage and grazed by or suitable for grazing by livestock. **2** the grass or herbage growing on it. ◆ *vb* **pastures, pasturing, pastured. 3** (*tr*) to cause (livestock) to graze or (of livestock) to graze (a pasture). ORIG C13: via OF from LL *pāstūra,* from *pascere* to feed

pasty[1] ('peɪstɪ) *adj* **pastier, pastiest. 1** of or like the colour, texture, etc., of paste. **2** (esp. of the complexion) pale or unhealthy-looking.
▸ **'pastily** *adv* ▸ **'pastiness** *n*

pasty[2] ('pæstɪ) *n, pl* **pasties.** a round of pastry folded over a filling of meat, vegetables, etc. ORIG C13: from OF *pastée,* from LL *pasta* dough

PA system *n* See **public-address system.**

pat[1] (pæt) *vb* **pats, patting, patted. 1** to hit (something) lightly with the palm of the hand or some other flat surface: *to pat a ball.* **2** to slap (a person or animal) gently, esp. on the back, as an expression of affection, congratulation, etc. **3** (*tr*) to shape, smooth, etc., with a flat instrument or the palm. **4** (*intr*) to walk or run with light footsteps. **5 pat (someone) on the back.** *Inf.* to congratulate. ◆ *n* **6** a light blow with something flat. **7** a gentle slap. **8** a small mass of something: *a pat of butter.* **9** the sound of patting. **10 pat on the back.** *Inf.* a gesture or word indicating approval. ORIG C14: ? imit.

pat[2] (pæt) *adv* **1** Also: **off pat.** exactly or fluently memorized: *he recited it pat.* **2** opportunely or aptly. **3 stand pat. 3a** *Chiefly US & Canad.* to refuse to abandon a belief, decision, etc. **3b** (in poker, etc.) to play without adding new cards to the hand dealt. ◆ *adj* **4** exactly right; apt: *a pat reply.* **5** too exactly fitting; glib: *a pat answer to a difficult problem.* **6** exactly right: *a pat hand in poker.* ORIG C17: ? adv use ("with a light stroke") of PAT[1]

pat[3] (pæt) *n* **on one's pat.** *Austral. inf.* alone. ORIG C20: rhyming slang, from *Pat* Malone

pat. *abbrev. for* patent(ed).

patagium (pə'teɪdʒɪəm) *n, pl* **patagia** (-dʒɪə). **1** a web of skin in bats and gliding mammals that functions as a wing. **2** a membranous fold of skin connecting a bird's wing to the shoulder. ORIG C19: NL, from L, from Gk *patageion* gold border on a tunic

Patagonia ★ (ˌpætə'gəʊnɪə) *n* **1** the southernmost region of South America, in Argentina and Chile extending from the Andes to the Atlantic. **2** an arid tableland in the southernmost part of Argentina, rising towards the Andes in the west.
▸ **ˌPata'gonian** *adj*

patch (pætʃ) *n* **1** a piece of material used to mend a garment, etc., or to make patchwork, a sewn-on pocket, etc. **2a** a small plot of land. **2b** its produce: *a patch of cabbages.* **3** *Med.* **3a** a protective covering for an injured eye. **3b** any protective dressing. **4** an imitation beauty spot made of black silk, etc., worn esp. in the 18th century. **5** an identifying piece of fabric worn on the shoulder of a uniform. **6** a small contrasting section: *a patch of cloud in the blue sky.* **7** a scrap; remnant. **8 a bad patch.** a difficult or troubled time. **9 not a patch on.** not nearly as good as. ◆ *vb* (*tr*) **10** to mend or supply (a garment, etc.) with a patch

or patches. **11** to put together or produce with patches. **12** (of material) to serve as a patch to. **13** (often foll. by *up*) to mend hurriedly or in a makeshift way. **14** (often foll. by *up*) to make (up) or settle (a quarrel, etc.). **15** to connect (electric circuits) together temporarily by means of a patch board. ORIG C16 *pacche,* ?from F *pieche* PIECE
▸ 'patcher *n*

patch board *or* **panel** *n* a device with a large number of sockets into which electrical plugs can be inserted to form many different temporary circuits: used in telephone exchanges, computer systems, etc. Also called: **plugboard.**

patchouli *or* **patchouly** ('pætʃʊlɪ, pə'tʃu:lɪ) *n, pl* **patchoulis** *or* **patchoulies. 1** any of several Asiatic trees, the leaves of which yield a heavy fragrant oil. **2** the perfume made from this oil. ORIG C19: from Tamil *paccilai,* from *paccu* green + *ilai* leaf

patch pocket *n* a pocket on the outside of a garment.

patch test *n Med.* a test to detect an allergic reaction by applying small amounts of a suspected substance to the skin.

patchwork ('pætʃ,wɜ:k) *n* **1** needlework done by sewing pieces of different materials together. **2** something made up of various parts.

patchy ('pætʃɪ) *adj* **patchier, patchiest. 1** irregular in quality, occurrence, intensity, etc.: *a patchy essay.* **2** having or forming patches.
▸ 'patchily *adv* ▸ 'patchiness *n*

pate (peɪt) *n* the head, esp. with reference to baldness or (in facetious use) intelligence. ORIG C14: from ?

pâté ('pæteɪ) *n* **1** a spread of finely minced liver, poultry, etc., served usually as an hors d'oeuvre. **2** a savoury pie. ORIG C18: from F: PASTE

pâté de foie gras (pɑte də fwa grɑ) *n, pl* **pâtés de foie gras** (pɑte). a smooth rich paste made from the liver of a specially fattened goose. ORIG F: pâté of fat liver

patella (pə'telə) *n, pl* **patellae** (-li:). *Anat.* a small flat triangular bone in front of and protecting the knee joint. Nontechnical name: **kneecap.** ORIG C17: from L, from *patina* shallow pan
▸ pa'tellar *adj*

paten ('pætᵊn) *n* a plate, usually made of silver or gold, esp. for the bread in the Eucharist. ORIG C13: from OF *patene,* from Med. L, from L *patina* pan

patency ('peɪtᵊnsɪ) *n* the condition of being obvious.

patent ('peɪtᵊnt, 'pætᵊnt) *n* **1a** a government grant to an inventor assuring him or her the sole right to make, use, and sell his or her invention for a limited period. **1b** a document conveying such a grant. **2** an invention, privilege, etc., protected by a patent. **3a** an official document granting a right. **3b** any right granted by such a document. ◆ *adj* **4** open or available for inspection (esp. in **letters patent, patent writ**). **5** ('peɪtᵊnt). obvious: *their scorn was patent to everyone.* **6** concerning protection, appointment, etc., of or by a patent or patents. **7** proprietary. **8** (esp. of a bodily passage or duct) being open or unobstructed. ◆ *vb (tr)* **9** to obtain a patent for. **10** to grant by a patent. ORIG C14: via OF from L *patēre* to lie open; n use, short for *letters patent,* from Med. L *litterae patentes* letters lying open (to public inspection)
▸ 'patentable *adj* ▸ ,paten'tee *n* ▸ ,paten'tor *n*

> **USAGE NOTE** The pronunciation 'pætᵊnt is heard in *letters patent* and *Patent Office* and is the usual US pronunciation for all senses. In Britain, although 'pætᵊnt is sometimes heard for senses 1–4 and 6–10, 'peɪtᵊnt is commoner.

patent leather ('peɪtᵊnt) *n* leather processed with lacquer to give a hard glossy surface.

patently ('peɪtᵊntlɪ) *adv* obviously.

patent medicine ('peɪtᵊnt) *n* a medicine with a patent, available without a prescription.

Patent Office ('pætᵊnt) *n* a government department that issues patents.

Patent Rolls ('pætᵊnt) *pl n* (in Britain) the register of patents issued.

pater ('peɪtə) *n Brit. sl.* another word for **father:** now chiefly used facetiously. ORIG from L

Pater ★ ('peɪtə) *n* **Walter (Horatio).** 1839–94, British essayist and critic, noted for his prose style and his advocation of the "love of art for its own sake". His works include the philosophical romance *Marius the Epicurean* (1885), *Studies in the History of the Renaissance* (1873), and *Imaginary Portraits* (1887).

paterfamilias (,peɪtəfə'mɪlɪ,æs) *n, pl* **patresfamilias** (,pɑ:treɪzfə'mɪlɪ,æs). the male head of a household. ORIG L: father of the family

paternal (pə'tɜ:nᵊl) *adj* **1** relating to or characteristic of a father; fatherly. **2** (*prenominal*) related through the father: *his paternal grandfather.* **3** inherited or derived from the male parent. ORIG C17: from LL *paternālis,* from L *pater* father
▸ pa'ternally *adv*

paternalism (pə'tɜ:nə,lɪzəm) *n* the attitude or policy of a government or other authority that manages the affairs of a country, company, etc., in the manner of a father, esp. in usurping individual responsibility.
▸ pa'ternalist *n, adj* ▸ pa,ternal'istic *adj* ▸ pa,ternal'istically *adv*

paternity (pə'tɜ:nɪtɪ) *n* **1a** the fact or state of being a father. **1b** (*as modifier*): *a paternity suit; paternity leave.* **2** descent or derivation from a father. **3** authorship or origin. ORIG C15: from LL *paternitās,* from L *pater* father

paternoster (,pætə'nɒstə) *n* **1** *RC Church.* the beads at the ends of each decade of the rosary at which the Paternoster is recited. **2** a type of fishing tackle in which short lines and hooks are attached at intervals to the main line. **3** a type of lift in which platforms are attached to continuous chains: passengers enter while it is moving. ORIG L, lit.: our father (from the opening of the Lord's Prayer)

Paternoster (,pætə'nɒstə) *n* (*sometimes not cap.*) *RC Church.* **1** the Lord's Prayer, esp. in Latin. **2** the recital of this as an act of devotion.

Paterson[1] ★ ('pætəsᵊn) *n* a city in NE New Jersey: settled by the Dutch in the late 17th century. Pop.: 150 270 (1996 est.).

Paterson[2] ★ ('pætəsᵊn) *n* **Andrew Barton,** known as *Banjo Paterson.* 1864–1941, Australian poet. His works include "Waltzing Matilda" and "The Man from Snowy River".

Paterson's curse *n* an Australian name for **viper's bugloss.**

path (pɑ:θ) *n, pl* **paths** (pɑ:ðz). **1** a road or way, esp. a narrow trodden track. **2** a surfaced walk, as through a garden. **3** the course or direction in which something moves: *the path of a whirlwind.* **4** a course of conduct: *the path of virtue.* ORIG OE *pæth*
▸ 'pathless *adj*

path. *abbrev. for:* **1** pathological. **2** pathology.

-path *n combining form.* **1** denoting a person suffering from a specified disease or disorder: *neuropath.* **2** denoting a practitioner of a particular method of treatment: *osteopath.* ORIG back formation from -PATHY

Pathan (pə'tɑ:n) *n* a member of the Pashto-speaking people of Afghanistan, NW Pakistan, and elsewhere. ORIG C17: from Hindi

pathetic (pə'θetɪk) *adj* **1** evoking or expressing pity, sympathy, etc. **2** distressingly inadequate: *the old man sat huddled before a pathetic fire.* **3** *Brit. sl.* ludicrously or contemptibly uninteresting or worthless. **4** *Obs.* of or affecting the feelings. ORIG C16: from F *pathétique,* via LL from Gk *pathetikos* sensitive, from *pathos* suffering
▸ pa'thetically *adv*

pathetic fallacy *n* (in literature) the presentation of inanimate objects in nature as possessing human feelings.

pathfinder ('pɑ:θ,faɪndə) *n* **1** a person who makes or finds a way, esp. through unexplored areas or fields of knowledge. **2** an aircraft or parachutist that indicates a target area by dropping flares, etc. **3** a radar device used for navigation or homing onto a target.

pathfinder prospectus *n* a prospectus regarding the flotation of a new company that contains only sufficient details to test the market reaction.

patho- *or before a vowel* **path-** *combining form.* disease: *pathology.* ORIG from Gk *pathos* suffering

pathogen ('pæθəˌdʒɛn) *n* any agent that can cause disease.
▸ **ˌpatho'genic** *adj*

pathogenesis (ˌpæθə'dʒɛnɪsɪs) *or* **pathogeny** (pə'θɒdʒɪnɪ) *n* the development of a disease.
▸ **pathogenetic** (ˌpæθədʒɪ'nɛtɪk) *adj*

pathological (ˌpæθə'lɒdʒɪkᵊl) *or (less commonly)* **pathologic** *adj* **1** of or relating to pathology. **2** relating to, involving, or caused by disease. **3** *Inf.* compulsively motivated: *a pathological liar.*
▸ **ˌpatho'logically** *adv*

pathology (pə'θɒlədʒɪ) *n, pl* **pathologies. 1** the branch of medicine concerned with the cause, origin, and nature of disease, including the changes occurring as a result of disease. **2** the manifestations of disease, esp. changes occurring in tissues or organs.
▸ **pa'thologist** *n*

pathos ('peɪθɒs) *n* **1** the quality or power, esp. in literature or speech, of arousing feelings of pity, sorrow, etc. **2** a feeling of sympathy or pity. ORIG C17: from Gk: suffering

pathway ('pɑːθˌweɪ) *n* **1** a path. **2** *Biochem.* a chain of reactions associated with a particular metabolic process.

-pathy *n combining form.* **1** indicating feeling or perception: *telepathy.* **2** indicating disease: *psychopathy.* **3** indicating a method of treating disease: *osteopathy.* ORIG from Gk *patheia* suffering; see PATHOS
▸ **-pathic** *adj combining form.*

Patiala ★ (ˌpʌtɪ'ɑːlə) *n* a city in N India, in E Punjab: seat of the Punjabi University (1962). Pop.: 238 368 (1991).

patience ('peɪʃəns) *n* **1** tolerant and even-tempered perseverance. **2** the capacity for calmly enduring pain, trying situations, etc. **3** *Chiefly Brit.* any of various card games for one player only. US word: **solitaire.** ORIG C13: via OF from L *patientia* endurance, from *patī* to suffer

patient ('peɪʃənt) *adj* **1** enduring trying circumstances with even temper. **2** tolerant; understanding. **3** capable of accepting delay with equanimity. **4** persevering or diligent: *a patient worker.* ◆ *n* **5** a person who is receiving medical care. ORIG C14: see PATIENCE
▸ **'patiently** *adv*

patina¹ ('pætɪnə) *n, pl* **patinas. 1** a film formed on the surface of a metal, esp. the green oxidation of bronze or copper. **2** any fine layer on a surface: *a patina of frost.* **3** the sheen on a surface caused by much handling. ORIG C18: from It.: coating, from L: PATINA²

patina² ('pætɪnə) *n, pl* **patinae** (-ˌniː). a broad shallow dish used in ancient Rome. ORIG from L, from Gk *patanē* platter

patio ('pætɪˌəʊ) *n, pl* **patios. 1** an open inner courtyard, esp. one in a Spanish or Spanish-American house. **2** an area adjoining a house, esp. one that is paved. ORIG C19: from Sp.: courtyard

patisserie (pə'tiːsərɪ) *n* **1** a shop where fancy pastries are sold. **2** such pastries. ORIG C18: F, from *pâtissier* pastry cook, ult. from LL *pasta* PASTE

Patmore ★ ('pætmɔː) *n* **Coventry (Kersey Dighton).** 1823–96, British poet. His works, celebrating both conjugal and divine love, include *The Angel in the House* (1854–62) and *The Unknown Eros* (1877).

Patmos ★ ('pætmɒs) *n* a Greek island in the Aegean, in the NW Dodecanese: St John's place of exile (about 95 A.D.), where he wrote the Apocalypse. Pop.: 2650 (1995 est.). Area: 34 sq. km (13 sq. miles).

Patna ★ ('pætnə) *n* a city in NE India, capital of Bihar state, on the River Ganges: founded in the 5th century B.C.; university (1917); centre of a rice-growing region. Pop.: 917 243 (1991).

Patna rice *n* a variety of long-grain rice, used for savoury dishes.

patois ('pætwɑː) *n, pl* **patois** ('pætwɑːz). **1** a regional dialect of a language, usually considered substandard. **2** the jargon of a particular group. ORIG C17: from OF: rustic speech, ?from *patoier* to handle awkwardly, from *patte* paw

Paton ★ ('peɪtᵊn) *n* **Alan (Stewart).** 1903–88, South African writer, noted esp. for his novel dealing with racism and apartheid in South Africa, *Cry, the Beloved Country* (1948).

pat. pend. *abbrev. for* patent pending.

Patras ★ (pə'træs, 'pætrəs) *n* a port in W Greece, in the NW Peloponnese on the **Gulf of Patras** (an inlet of the Ionian Sea): one of the richest cities in Greece until the 3rd century B.C.; under Turkish rule from 1458 to 1687 and from 1715 until the War of Greek Independence, which began here in 1821. Pop.: 155 180 (1991). Modern Greek name: **Pátrai** ('patrɛ).

patri- *combining form.* father: *patricide; patriarch.* ORIG from L *pater,* Gk *patēr* father

patrial ('peɪtrɪəl) *n* (in Britain, formerly) a person having by statute the right of abode in the United Kingdom. ORIG C20: from L *patria* native land

patriarch ('peɪtrɪˌɑːk) *n* **1** the male head of a tribe or family. **2** a very old or venerable man. **3** *Bible.* **3a** any of a number of persons regarded as the fathers of the human race. **3b** any of the three ancestors of the Hebrew people: Abraham, Isaac, or Jacob. **3c** any of Jacob's twelve sons, regarded as the ancestors of the twelve tribes of Israel. **4** *Early Christian Church.* the bishop of one of several principal sees, esp. those of Rome, Antioch, and Alexandria. **5** *Eastern Orthodox Church.* the bishops of the four ancient principal sees of Constantinople, Antioch, Alexandria, and Jerusalem, and also of Russia, Romania, and Serbia. **6** *RC Church.* **6a** a title given to the pope. **6b** a title given to a number of bishops, esp. of the Uniat Churches, indicating their rank as immediately below that of the pope. **7** the oldest or most venerable member of a group, community, etc. **8** a person regarded as the founder of a community, tradition, etc. ORIG C12: via OF from Church L *patriarcha*
▸ **ˌpatri'archal** *adj*

patriarchate ('peɪtrɪˌɑːkɪt) *n* the office, jurisdiction, province, or residence of a patriarch.

patriarchy ('peɪtrɪˌɑːkɪ) *n, pl* **patriarchies. 1** a form of social organization in which a male is the head of the family and descent, kinship, and title are traced through the male line. **2** any society governed by such a system.

patrician (pə'trɪʃən) *n* **1** a member of the hereditary aristocracy of ancient Rome. **2** (in medieval Europe) a member of the upper class in numerous Italian republics and German free cities. **3** an aristocrat. **4** a person of refined conduct, tastes, etc. ◆ *adj* **5** (esp. in ancient Rome) of, relating to, or composed of patricians. **6** aristocratic. ORIG C15: from OF *patricien,* from L *patricius* noble, from *pater* father

patricide ('pætrɪˌsaɪd) *n* **1** the act of killing one's father. **2** a person who kills his or her father.
▸ **ˌpatri'cidal** *adj*

Patrick ★ ('pætrɪk) *n* **Saint.** 5th century A.D., Christian missionary in Ireland, probably born in Britain; patron saint of Ireland. Feast day: March 17.

patrilineal (ˌpætrɪ'lɪnɪəl) *adj* tracing descent, kinship, or title through the male line.

patrimony ('pætrɪmənɪ) *n, pl* **patrimonies. 1** an inheritance from one's father or other ancestor. **2** the endowment of a church. ORIG C14 *patrimoyne,* from OF, from L *patrimonium* paternal inheritance
▸ **patrimonial** (ˌpætrɪ'məʊnɪəl) *adj*

patriot ('peɪtrɪət, 'pæt-) *n* a person who vigorously supports his or her country and its way of life. ORIG C16: via F from LL *patriōta,* from Gk *patriotēs,* from *patris* native land; rel. to Gk *patēr* father; cf. L *pater* father, *patria* fatherland
▸ **patriotic** (ˌpætrɪ'ɒtɪk) *adj* ▸ **ˌpatri'otically** *adv*

Patriot ('peɪtrɪət) *n* a US surface-to-air missile system with multiple launch stations and the capability to track multiple targets by radar.

patriotism ('pætrɪəˌtɪzəm) *n* devotion to one's own country and concern for its defence.

patristic (pəˈtrɪstɪk) *or* **patristical** *adj* of or relating to the Fathers of the Church, their writings, or the study of these.
▸ **paˈtristics** *n (functioning as sing)*

Patroclus ★ (pəˈtrɒkləs) *n Greek myth.* a friend of Achilles, killed in the Trojan War by Hector. His death made Achilles return to the fight after his quarrel with Agamemnon.

patrol (pəˈtrəʊl) *n* **1** the action of going round a town, etc., at regular intervals for purposes of security or observation. **2** a person or group that carries out such an action. **3** a military detachment with the mission of security or combat with enemy forces. **4** a division of a troop of Scouts or Guides. ◆ *vb* **patrols, patrolling, patrolled. 5** to engage in a patrol of (a place). ORIG C17: from F *patrouiller,* from *patouiller* to flounder in mud, from *patte* paw
▸ **paˈtroller** *n*

patrol car *n* a police car used for patrolling streets and motorways.

patrology (pəˈtrɒlədʒɪ) *n* **1** the study of the writings of the Fathers of the Church. **2** a collection of such writings. ORIG C17: from Gk *patr-, patēr* father + -LOGY
▸ **paˈtrologist** *n*

patrol wagon *n* the usual US and Austral. name for **Black Maria.**

patron[1] (ˈpeɪtrən) *n* **1** a person who sponsors or aids artists, charities, etc.; protector or benefactor. **2** a customer of a shop, hotel, etc., esp. a regular one. **3** See **patron saint.** ORIG C14: via OF from L *patrōnus* protector, from *pater* father
▸ **ˈpatroness** *fem n*

patron[2] (patrɔ̃) *n* the owner of a restaurant, hotel. etc., esp. of a French one. ORIG F

patronage (ˈpætrənɪdʒ) *n* **1a** the support given or custom brought by a patron. **1b** the position of a patron. **2** (in politics) **2a** the practice of making appointments to office, granting contracts, etc. **2b** the favours, etc., so distributed. **3a** a condescending manner. **3b** any kindness done in a condescending way.

patronize *or* **patronise** (ˈpætrəˌnaɪz) *vb* **patronizes, patronizing, patronized** *or* **patronises, patronising, patronised. 1** to behave or treat in a condescending way. **2** *(tr)* to act as a patron by sponsoring or bringing trade to.
▸ **ˈpatronˌizer** *or* **ˈpatronˌiser** *n* ▸ **ˈpatronˌizing** *or* **ˈpatronˌising** *adj* ▸ **ˈpatronˌizingly** *or* **ˈpatronˌisingly** *adv*

patron saint *n* a saint regarded as the particular guardian of a country, person, etc.

patronymic (ˌpætrəˈnɪmɪk) *adj* **1** (of a name) derived from the name of its bearer's father or ancestor. ◆ *n* **2** a patronymic name. ORIG C17: via LL from Gk *patronumikos,* from *patēr* father + *onoma* NAME

patroon (pəˈtruːn) *n US.* a Dutch land holder in New Netherland and New York with manorial rights in the colonial era. ORIG C18: from Du.: PATRON[1]

patsy (ˈpætsɪ) *n, pl* **patsies.** *Sl., chiefly US & Canad.* **1** a person who is easily cheated, victimized, etc. **2** a scapegoat. ORIG C20: from ?

patten (ˈpætᵊn) *n* a wooden clog or sandal on a raised wooden platform or metal ring. ORIG C14: from OF *patin,* prob. from *patte* paw

patter[1] (ˈpætə) *vb* **1** *(intr)* to walk or move with quick soft steps. **2** to strike with or make a quick succession of light tapping sounds. ◆ *n* **3** a quick succession of light tapping sounds, as of feet: *the patter of mice.* ORIG C17: from PAT[1]

patter[2] (ˈpætə) *n* **1** the glib rapid speech of comedians, etc. **2** quick idle talk; chatter. **3** the jargon of a particular group, etc.; lingo. ◆ *vb* **4** *(intr)* to speak glibly and rapidly. **5** to repeat (prayers, etc.) in a mechanical or perfunctory manner. ORIG C14: from L *pater* in *Pater Noster* Our Father

pattern (ˈpætᵊn) *n* **1** an arrangement of repeated or corresponding parts, decorative motifs, etc. **2** a decorative design: *a paisley pattern.* **3** a style: *various patterns of cutlery.* **4** a plan or diagram used as a guide in making something: *a paper pattern for a dress.* **5** a standard way of moving, acting, etc.: *traffic patterns.* **6** a model worthy of imitation: *a pattern of kindness.* **7** a representative sample. **8** a wooden or metal shape or model used in a foundry to make a mould. ◆ *vb (tr)* **9** (often foll. by *after* or *on*) to model. **10** to arrange as or decorate with a pattern. ORIG C14 *patron,* from Med. L *patrōnus* example, from L: PATRON[1]

Patti ★ (ˈpætɪ) *n* **Adelina** (adeˈliːna). 1843–1919, Italian operatic coloratura soprano, born in Spain.

Patton ★ (ˈpætᵊn) *n* **George Smith.** 1885–1945, US general, who successfully developed tank warfare as an extension of cavalry tactics in World War II: captured Palermo, Sicily (1942) and much of France (1944).

patty (ˈpætɪ) *n, pl* **patties. 1** a small cake of minced food. **2** a small pie. ORIG C18: from F PÂTÉ

patu (ˈpɑːtuː) *n, pl* **patus.** *NZ.* a short Maori club, now ceremonial only. ORIG from Maori

patulous (ˈpætjʊləs) *adj Bot.* spreading widely or expanded: *patulous branches.* ORIG C17: from L *patulus* open, from *patēre* to lie open

Pau ★ (*French* po) *n* a city in SW France: residence of the French kings of Navarre; tourist centre for the Pyrenees. Pop.: 82 157 (1990).

paua (ˈpɑːʊɑ) *n* an edible abalone of New Zealand, having an iridescent shell used for jewellery, etc. ORIG from Maori

paucity (ˈpɔːsɪtɪ) *n* **1** insufficiency; dearth. **2** smallness of number; fewness. ORIG C15: from L *paucitās* scarcity, from *paucus* few

Paul ★ (pɔːl) *n* **1 Saint.** Also called: **Paul the Apostle, Saul of Tarsus.** original name *Saul.* died ?67 A.D., one of the first Christian missionaries to the Gentiles, who died a martyr in Rome. Until his revelatory conversion he had assisted in persecuting the Christians. He wrote many of the Epistles in the New Testament. Feast day: June 29. **2 Jean.** See **Jean Paul. 3 Les,** real name *Lester Polfuss.* born 1915, US guitarist: creator of the solid-body electric guitar and pioneer in multitrack recording.

Paul III ★ *n* original name *Alessandro Farnese.* 1468–1549, Italian ecclesiastic; pope (1534–49). He excommunicated Henry VIII of England (1538) and inaugurated the Counter-Reformation by approving the establishment of the Jesuits (1540), instituting the Inquisition in Italy, and convening the Council of Trent (1545).

Paul VI ★ *n* original name *Giovanni Battista Montini.* 1897–1978, Italian ecclesiastic; pope (1963–78).

Pauli ★ (ˈpɔːlɪ, ˈpaʊlɪ) *n* **Wolfgang** (ˈvɒlfˌgæŋ). 1900–58, US physicist, born in Austria. He formulated the exclusion principle (1924) and postulated the existence of the neutrino (1931), later confirmed by Fermi: Nobel prize for physics 1945.

Pauli exclusion principle *n Physics.* the principle that two identical fermions cannot occupy the same quantum state in a body, such as an atom; sometimes shortened to **exclusion principle.**

Pauline (ˈpɔːlaɪn) *adj* relating to Saint Paul or his doctrines.

Pauling ★ (ˈpɔːlɪŋ) *n* **Linus Carl** (ˈlaɪnəs). 1901–94, US chemist, noted particularly for his work on the nature of the chemical bond and his opposition to nuclear tests: Nobel prize for chemistry 1954; Nobel peace prize 1962.

Paulinus ★ (pɔːˈlaɪnəs) *n* **Saint.** died 644 A.D., Roman missionary to England; first bishop of York and archbishop of Rochester. Feast day: Oct. 10.

Paul Jones *n* an old-time dance in which partners are exchanged. ORIG C19: after John Paul JONES

paulownia (pɔːˈləʊnɪə) *n* a tree of a Japanese genus, esp. one having large heart-shaped leaves and clusters of purplish or white flowers. ORIG C19: NL, after Anna *Paulovna,* daughter of Paul I of Russia

Paumotu Archipelago ★ (paʊˈməʊtuː) *n* another name for the **Tuamotu Archipelago.**

paunch (pɔːntʃ) *n* **1** the belly or abdomen, esp. when protruding. **2** another name for **rumen.** ◆ *vb (tr)* **3** to stab in the stomach; disembowel. ORIG C14: from Anglo-Norman *paunche,* from OF *pance,* from L *panticēs* (pl) bowels
▸ **ˈpaunchy** *adj* ▸ **ˈpaunchiness** *n*

pauper (ˈpɔːpə) *n* **1** a person who is extremely poor. **2** (formerly) a person supported by public charity. ORIG C16: from L: poor
▸ **ˈpauper,ism** *n*

pauperize *or* **pauperise** (ˈpɔːpə,raɪz) *vb* **pauperizes, pauperizing, pauperized** *or* **pauperises, pauperising, pauperised.** (*tr*) to make a pauper of; impoverish.

Pausanias ★ (pɔːˈseɪnɪəs) *n* 2nd century A.D. Greek geographer and historian. His *Description of Greece* gives a valuable account of the topography of ancient Greece.

pause (pɔːz) *vb* **pauses, pausing, paused.** (*intr*) **1** to cease an action temporarily. **2** to hesitate; delay: *she replied without pausing.* ◆ *n* **3** a temporary stop or rest, esp. in speech or action; short break. **4** *Prosody.* another word for **caesura. 5** Also called: **fermata.** *Music.* a continuation of a note or rest beyond its normal length. Usual symbol: 𝄐 **6 give pause to.** to cause to hesitate. ORIG C15: from L *pausa* pause, from Gk *pausis,* from *pauein* to halt

pav (pæv) *n Austral. & NZ inf.* short for **pavlova.**

pavane *or* **pavan** (pəˈvɑːn, ˈpævᵊn) *n* **1** a slow and stately dance of the 16th and 17th centuries. **2** a piece of music composed for or in the rhythm of this dance. ORIG C16 *pavan,* via F from Sp. *pavana,* from OIt. *padovana* Paduan (dance), from *Padova* Padua

Pavarotti ★ (,pævəˈrɒtɪ, *Italian* pavaˈrɔtti) *n* **Luciano** (luˈtʃaːno). born 1935, Italian operatic tenor.

pave (peɪv) *vb* **paves, paving, paved.** (*tr*) **1** to cover (a road, etc.) with a firm surface suitable for travel, as with paving stones or concrete. **2** to serve as the material for a pavement or other hard layer: *bricks paved the causeway.* **3** (often foll. by *with*) to cover with a hard layer (of). **4** to prepare or make easier (esp. in **pave the way**). ORIG C14: from OF *paver,* from L *pavīre* to ram down
▸ **ˈpaver** *n*

pavement (ˈpeɪvmənt) *n* **1** a hard-surfaced path for pedestrians alongside and a little higher than a road. US and Canad. word: **sidewalk. 2** the material used in paving. ORIG C13: from L *pavīmentum* hard floor, from *pavīre* to beat hard

Pavese ★ (*Italian* paˈveːse) *n* **Cesare** (ˈtʃeːzare). 1908–50, Italian writer and translator. His works include collections of poems, such as *Verrà la morte e avra i tuoi occhi* (1953), short stories, such as the collection *Notte di festa* (1953), and the novel *La Luna e i falò* (1950).

Pavia ★ (pəˈviːə) *n* a town in N Italy, in Lombardy: noted for its Roman and medieval remains, including the tomb of St Augustine. Pop.: 80 650 (1990). Latin name: **Ticinum.**

pavilion (pəˈvɪljən) *n* **1** *Brit.* a building at a sports ground, esp. a cricket pitch, in which players change, etc. **2** a summerhouse or other decorative shelter. **3** a building or temporary structure, esp. one that is open and ornamental, for housing exhibitions, etc. **4** a large ornate tent, esp. one with a peaked top, as used by medieval armies. **5** one of a set of buildings that together form a hospital or other large institution. ◆ *vb* (*tr*) *Literary.* **6** to place as in a pavilion: *pavilioned in splendour.* **7** to provide with a pavilion or pavilions. ORIG C13: from OF *pavillon* canopied structure, from L *pāpiliō* butterfly, tent

paving (ˈpeɪvɪŋ) *n* **1** a paved surface; pavement. **2** material used for a pavement.

Pavlodar ★ (*Russian* pəvlaˈdar) *n* a port in NE Kazakhstan, on the Irtysh River: major industrial centre with an oil refinery. Pop.: 340 700 (1995 est.).

Pavlov ★ (ˈpævlɒv; *Russian* ˈpavləf) *n* **Ivan Petrovich** (iˈvan pɪˈtrɔvitʃ). 1849–1936, Russian physiologist. His study of conditioned reflexes in dogs influenced behaviourism. He also made important contributions to the study of digestion: Nobel prize for physiology or medicine 1904.
▸ **Pavˈlovian** *adj*

pavlova (pævˈləʊvə) *n* a meringue cake topped with whipped cream and fruit. ORIG C20: after Anna PAVLOVA

Pavlova ★ (pævˈləʊvə; *Russian* ˈpavləvə) *n* **Anna** (ˈannə). 1885–1931, Russian ballerina.

paw (pɔː) *n* **1** any of the feet of a four-legged mammal, bearing claws or nails. **2** *Inf.* a hand, esp. one that is large, clumsy, etc. ◆ *vb* **3** to scrape or contaminate with the paws or feet. **4** (*tr*) *Inf.* to touch or caress in a rough or overfamiliar manner. ORIG C13: via OF from Gmc

pawky (ˈpɔːkɪ) *adj* **pawkier, pawkiest.** *Dialect or Scot.* having a dry wit. ORIG C17: from Scot. *pawk* trick, from ?
▸ **ˈpawkily** *adv* ▸ **ˈpawkiness** *n*

pawl (pɔːl) *n* a pivoted lever shaped to engage with a ratchet to prevent motion in a particular direction. ORIG C17: ?from Du. *pal* pawl

pawn[1] (pɔːn) *vb* (*tr*) **1** to deposit (an article) as security for the repayment of a loan, esp. from a pawnbroker. **2** to stake: *to pawn one's honour.* ◆ *n* **3** an article deposited as security. **4** the condition of being so deposited (esp. in **in pawn**). **5** a person or thing that is held as a security. **6** the act of pawning. ORIG C15: from OF *pan* security, from L *pannus* cloth, apparently because clothing was often left as a surety
▸ **ˈpawnage** *n*

pawn[2] (pɔːn) *n* **1** a chess man of the lowest theoretical value. **2** a person, group, etc., manipulated by another. ORIG C14: from Anglo-Norman *poun,* from OF, from Med. L *pedō* infantryman, from L *pēs* foot

pawnbroker (ˈpɔːn,brəʊkə) *n* a dealer licensed to lend money at a specified rate of interest on the security of movable personal property, which can be sold if the loan is not repaid within a specified period.
▸ **ˈpawn,broking** *n*

pawnshop (ˈpɔːn,ʃɒp) *n* the premises of a pawnbroker.

pawn ticket *n* a receipt for goods pawned.

pawpaw (ˈpɔː,pɔː) *n* another name for **papaw** or **papaya.**

pax (pæks) *n* **1** *Chiefly RC Church.* **1a** the kiss of peace. **1b** a small metal or ivory plate, formerly used to convey the kiss of peace from the celebrant at Mass to those attending it. ◆ *interj* **2** *Brit. school sl.* a call signalling an end to hostilities or claiming immunity from the rules of a game. ORIG L: peace

Pax ★ (pæks) *n* the Roman goddess of peace. Greek counterpart: **Irene.** ORIG L: peace

PAX (in Britain) *abbrev. for* private automatic exchange.

Paxman ★ (ˈpæksmən) *n* **Jeremy** (**Dickson**). born 1950, British journalist, broadcaster, and author, noted for his political interviews.

Paxton ★ (ˈpækstən) *n* Sir **Joseph.** 1801–65, British architect, who designed the Crystal Palace (1851), the first large structure of prefabricated glass and iron parts.

pay[1] (peɪ) *vb* **pays, paying, paid. 1** to discharge (a debt, obligation, etc.) by giving or doing something: *he paid his creditors.* **2** (when *intr,* often foll. by *for*) to give (money, etc.) to (a person) in return for goods or services: *they pay their workers well; they pay by the hour.* **3** to give or afford (a person, etc.) a profit or benefit: *it pays one to be honest.* **4** (*tr*) to give or bestow (a compliment, regards, attention, etc.). **5** (*tr*) to make (a visit or call). **6** (*intr;* often foll. by *for*) to give compensation or make amends. **7** (*tr*) to yield a return of: *the shares pay 15 per cent.* **8** *Austral. inf.* to acknowledge or accept (something) as true, just, etc. **9 pay one's way. 9a** to contribute one's share of expenses. **9b** to remain solvent without outside help. ◆ *n* **10a** money given in return for work or services; a salary or wage. **10b** (*as modifier*): *a pay slip; a pay claim.* **11** paid employment (esp. in **in the pay of**). **12** (*modifier*) requiring the insertion of money before or during use: *a pay phone.* **13** (*modifier*) rich enough in minerals to be profitably worked: *pay gravel.* ◆ See also **pay back, pay for,** etc. ORIG C12: from OF *payer,* from L *pācāre* to appease (a creditor), from *pāx* peace
▸ **ˈpayer** *n*

pay[2] (peɪ) *vb* **pays, paying, payed.** (*tr*) *Naut.* to caulk (the seams of a wooden vessel) with pitch or tar. ORIG C17: from OF *peier,* from L *picāre,* from *pix* pitch

payable (ˈpeɪəbᵊl) *adj* **1** (often foll. by *on*) to be paid: *payable on the third of each month.* **2** that is capable of being paid. **3** capable of being profitable. **4** (of a debt, etc.) imposing an obligation on the debtor to pay, esp. at once.

pay-and-display *adj* denoting a car-parking system in which a motorist buys a permit to park for a specified period and displays the permit on the windscreen of his or her car so that it can be seen by a parking attendant.

pay back *vb (tr, adv)* **1** to retaliate against: *to pay someone back for an insult.* **2** to give or do (something equivalent) in return for a favour, insult, etc. **3** to repay (a loan, etc.). ◆ *n* **payback. 4a** the return on an investment. **4b** Also called: **payback period.** the time taken for a project to cover its outlay. **5a** something done in order to gain revenge. **5b** (*as modifier*): *payback killings.*

pay bed *n* an informal name for **private pay bed.**

payday ('peɪˌdeɪ) *n* the day on which wages or salaries are paid.

pay dirt *n Chiefly US.* **1** soil, gravel, ore, etc. that contains sufficient minerals to make it worthwhile mining. **2 hit** (*or* **strike**) **pay dirt.** *Inf.* to become wealthy, successful, etc.

PAYE (in Britain and New Zealand) *abbrev. for* pay as you earn; a system by which income tax levied on wage and salary earners is paid by employers directly to the government.

payee (peɪ'iː) *n* the person to whom a cheque, money order, etc., is made out.

pay for *vb (prep)* **1** to make payment for. **2** (*intr*) to suffer or be punished, as for a mistake, wrong decision, etc.

paying guest *n* a euphemism for **lodger.**

payload ('peɪˌləʊd) *n* **1** that part of a cargo earning revenue. **2a** the passengers, cargo, or bombs carried by an aircraft. **2b** the equipment carried by a rocket, satellite, or spacecraft. **3** the explosive power of a warhead, bomb, etc., carried by a missile or aircraft.

paymaster ('peɪˌmɑːstə) *n* an official of a government, business, etc., responsible for the payment of wages, etc.

payment ('peɪmənt) *n* **1** the act of paying. **2** a sum of money paid. **3** something given in return; punishment or reward.

paynim ('peɪnɪm) *n Arch.* **1** a heathen or pagan. **2** a Muslim. ORIG C13: from OF *paienime,* from LL *pāgānismus* paganism, from *pāgānus* PAGAN

pay off *vb* **1** (*tr, adv*) to pay all that is due in wages, etc., and discharge from employment. **2** (*tr, adv*) to pay the complete amount of (a debt, bill, etc.). **3** (*intr, adv*) to turn out to be profitable, effective, etc.: *the gamble paid off.* **4** (*tr, adv* or *intr, prep*) to take revenge on (a person) or for (a wrong done): *to pay someone off for an insult.* **5** (*tr, adv*) *Inf.* to give a bribe to. ◆ *n* **payoff. 6** the final settlement, esp. in retribution. **7** *Inf.* the climax, consequence, or outcome of events, a story, etc. **8** the final payment of a debt, etc. **9** the time of such a payment. **10** *Inf.* a bribe.

payola (peɪ'əʊlə) *n Inf.* **1** a bribe given to secure special treatment, esp. to a disc jockey to promote a commercial product. **2** the practice of paying or receiving such bribes. ORIG C20: from PAY[1] + *-ola,* as in PIANOLA

pay out *vb (adv)* **1** to distribute (money, etc.); disburse. **2** (*tr*) to release (a rope) gradually, hand over hand. ◆ *n* **payout. 3** a sum of money paid out.

pay-per-click *n* a system of payment used on the Internet in which an advertiser or website pays according to the number of visitors who click on their site.

pay-per-view *n* **a** a system of television broadcasting by which subscribers pay for each programme they wish to receive. **b** (*as modifier*): *a pay-per-view channel.*

payphone ('peɪˌfəʊn) *n* a public telephone operated by coins or a phonecard.

payroll ('peɪˌrəʊl) *n* **1** a list of employees, specifying the salary or wage of each. **2a** the total of these amounts or the actual money equivalent. **2b** (*as modifier*): *a payroll tax.*

Paysandú ★ (*Spanish* paisan'du) *n* a port in W Uruguay, on the Uruguay River: the third largest city in the country. Pop.: 75 200 (1985).

Pays de la Loire ★ (*French* pei də la lwar) *n* a region of W France, on the Bay of Biscay: generally low-lying, drained by the River Loire and its tributaries; agricultural.

payt *abbrev. for* payment.

pay up *vb (adv)* to pay (money) promptly, in full, or on demand.

Paz ★ (*Spanish* pas) *n* **Octavio** (ɔk'taβjo). 1914–98, Mexican poet and essayist. His poems include the cycle *Piedra de Sol* (1957) and *Blanco* (1967). Nobel prize for literature 1990.

Pb *the chemical symbol for* lead. ORIG from NL *plumbum*

PB *Athletics abbrev. for* personal best.

PBS *US abbrev. for* Public Broadcasting Service.

PBX (in Britain) *abbrev. for* private branch exchange; a telephone system that handles the internal and external calls of a building, firm, etc.

pc *abbrev. for:* **1** per cent. **2** postcard. **3** (in prescriptions) post cibum. ORIG L: after meals

PC *abbrev. for:* **1** personal computer. **2** Parish Council(lor). **3** (in Britain) Police Constable. **4** politically correct. **5** (in Britain and Canada) Privy Council(lor). **6** (in Canada) Progressive Conservative.

pc. *abbrev. for:* **1** (*pl* **pcs.**) piece. **2** price.

PCB *abbrev. for* polychlorinated biphenyl; any of a group of compounds in which chlorine atoms replace the hydrogen atoms in biphenyl: used in electrical insulators and in the manufacture of plastics; a toxic pollutant.

PCC (in Britain) *abbrev. for* Press Complaints Commission.

PCP *n Trademark.* phencyclidine; a depressant drug used illegally as a hallucinogen.

PCV (in Britain) *abbrev. for* passenger carrying vehicle.

pd *abbrev. for:* **1** paid. **2** Also: **PD.** per diem. **3** potential difference.

Pd *the chemical symbol for* palladium.

PDA *abbrev. for* personal digital assistant.

PDR *abbrev. for* price-dividend ratio.

P-D ratio *n* short for **price-dividend ratio.**

PDSA (in Britain) *abbrev. for* People's Dispensary for Sick Animals.

PDT (in the US and Canada) *abbrev. for* Pacific Daylight Time.

PE *abbrev. for:* **1** physical education. **2** potential energy. **3** Presiding Elder. **4** Also: **p.e.** printer's error. **5** *Statistics.* probable error. **6** Protestant Episcopal.

pea (piː) *n* **1** an annual climbing plant with small white flowers and long green pods containing edible green seeds: cultivated in temperate regions. **2** the seed of this plant, eaten as a vegetable. **3** any of several other leguminous plants, such as the sweet pea. ORIG C17: from PEASE (incorrectly assumed to be a pl)

Peabody ★ ('piːˌbɒdɪ) *n* **George.** 1795–1869, US merchant, banker, and philanthropist in the US and England.

peace (piːs) *n* **1a** the state existing during the absence of war. **1b** (*as modifier*): *peace negotiations.* **2** (*often cap.*) a treaty marking the end of a war. **3** a state of harmony between people or groups. **4** law and order within a state: *a breach of the peace.* **5** absence of mental anxiety (often in **peace of mind**). **6** a state of stillness, silence, or serenity. **7 at peace. 7a** in a state of harmony or friendship. **7b** in a state of serenity. **7c** dead: *the old lady is at peace now.* **8 hold** *or* **keep one's peace.** to keep silent. **9 keep the peace.** to maintain law and order. ◆ *vb* **peaces, peacing, peaced. 10** (*intr*) *Obs. except as an imperative.* to be or become silent or still. ◆ *modifier* **11** denoting a person or thing symbolizing support for international peace: *peace women.* ORIG C12: from OF *pais,* from L *pāx*

peaceable ('piːsəbᵊl) *adj* **1** inclined towards peace. **2** tranquil; calm.
▸ **'peaceableness** *n* ▸ **'peaceably** *adv*

Peace Corps *n* an agency of the US government that sends volunteers to developing countries to work on educational projects, etc.

peace dividend *n* additional money available to a government from cuts in defence expenditure because of the end of a period of hostilities.

peaceful ('piːsfʊl) *adj* **1** not in a state of war or disagreement. **2** calm; tranquil. **3** not involving violence: *peaceful picketing.* **4** of, relating to, or in accord with a time of peace. **5** inclined towards peace.
▸ **'peacefully** *adv* ▸ **'peacefulness** *n*

peacekeeping ('piːsˌkiːpɪŋ) *n* **a** the maintenance of peace, esp. the prevention of further fighting between hostile forces. **b** (*as modifier*): *a UN peacekeeping force.*

peacemaker ('piːsˌmeɪkə) *n* a person who establishes peace, esp. between others.
▸ **'peaceˌmaking** *n*

peace offering *n* **1** something given to an adversary in the hope of procuring or maintaining peace. **2** *Judaism.* a sacrificial meal shared between the offerer and Jehovah.

peace pipe *n* a long decorated pipe smoked by North American Indians, esp. as a token of peace. Also called: **calumet.**

Peace River ★ *n* a river in W Canada, rising in British Columbia as the Finlay River and flowing northeast into the Slave River. Length: 1715 km (1065 miles).

peace sign *n* a gesture made with the palm of the hand outwards and the index and middle fingers raised in a V.

peacetime ('piːsˌtaɪm) *n* **a** a period without war; time of peace. **b** (*as modifier*): *a peacetime agreement.*

peach[1] (piːtʃ) *n* **1** a small tree with pink flowers and rounded edible fruit: cultivated in temperate regions. **2** the soft juicy fruit of this tree, which has a downy reddish-yellow skin, yellowish-orange sweet flesh, and a single stone. **3a** a pinkish-yellow to orange colour. **3b** (*as adj*): *a peach dress.* **4** *Inf.* a person or thing that is especially pleasing. ORIG C14 *peche,* from OF, from Med. L *persica,* from L *Persicum mālum* Persian apple

peach[2] (piːtʃ) *vb* (*intr*) *Sl.* to inform against an accomplice. ORIG C15: var. of earlier *apeche,* from F, from LL *impedicāre* to entangle; see IMPEACH

peach brandy *n* (esp. in S. Africa) a coarse brandy made from fermented peaches.

peach Melba *n* a dessert made of halved peaches, vanilla ice cream, and raspberries. ORIG C20: after Dame Nellie MELBA

peachy ('piːtʃɪ) *adj* **peachier, peachiest. 1** of or like a peach, esp. in colour or texture. **2** *Inf.* excellent; fine.
▸ **'peachiness** *n*

peacock ('piːˌkɒk) *n, pl* **peacocks** *or* **peacock. 1** a male peafowl, having a crested head and a very large fanlike tail marked with blue and green eyelike spots. **2** another name for **peafowl. 3** a vain strutting person. ◆ *vb* **4** to display (oneself) proudly. ORIG C14 *pecok, pe-* from OE *pāwa* (from L *pāvō* peacock) + COCK[1]
▸ **'peaˌcockish** *adj* ▸ **'peaˌhen** *fem n*

Peacock ★ ('piːˌkɒk) *n* **Thomas Love.** 1785–1866, British novelist and poet, noted for his satirical romances, including *Headlong Hall* (1816) and *Nightmare Abbey* (1818).

peacock blue *n* **a** a greenish-blue colour. **b** (*as adj*): *a peacock-blue car.*

peafowl ('piːˌfaʊl) *n, pl* **peafowls** *or* **peafowl.** either of two large pheasants of India and Ceylon and of SE Asia. The males (see **peacock** (sense 1)) have a characteristic bright plumage.

pea green *n* **a** a yellowish-green colour. **b** (*as adj*): *a pea-green teapot.*

pea jacket *or* **peacoat** ('piːˌkəʊt) *n* a sailor's short heavy woollen overcoat. ORIG C18: from Du. *pijjekker,* from *pij* coat of coarse cloth + *jekker* jacket

peak[1] (piːk) *n* **1** a pointed end, edge, or projection: *the peak of a roof.* **2** the pointed summit of a mountain. **3** a mountain with a pointed summit. **4** the point of greatest development, strength, etc.: *the peak of his career.* **5a** a sharp increase followed by a sharp decrease: *a voltage peak.* **5b** the maximum value of this quantity. **5c** (*as modifier*): *peak voltage.* **6** Also called: **visor.** a projecting piece on the front of some caps. **7** *Naut.* **7a** the extreme forward (**forepeak**) or aft (**afterpeak**) part of the hull. **7b** (of a fore-and-aft quadrilateral sail) the after uppermost corner. **7c** the after end of a gaff. ◆ *vb* **8** to form or reach or cause to form or reach a peak. **9** (*tr*) *Naut.* to set (a gaff) or tilt (oars) vertically. ◆ *adj* **10** of or relating to a period of greatest use or demand: *peak viewing hours.* ORIG C16: ?from PIKE[2], infl. by BEAK[1]

peak[2] (piːk) *vb* (*intr*) to become wan, emaciated, or sickly. ORIG C16: from ?
▸ **'peaky** *or* **'peakish** *adj*

Peak District ★ *n* a region of N central England, mainly in N Derbyshire at the S end of the Pennines: consists of moors in the north and a central limestone plateau; many caves. Highest point: 727 m (2088 ft).

Peake ★ (piːk) *n* **Mervyn.** 1911–68, British novelist, poet, and illustrator. In his trilogy *Gormenghast* (1946–59), he creates, with vivid imagination, a grotesque Gothic world.

peaked (piːkt) *adj* having a peak; pointed.

peak load *n* the maximum load on an electrical power-supply system.

peal (piːl) *n* **1** a loud prolonged usually reverberating sound, as of bells, thunder, or laughter. **2** *Bell-ringing.* a series of changes rung in accordance with specific rules. **3** (*not in technical usage*) the set of bells in a belfry. ◆ *vb* **4** (*intr*) to sound with a peal or peals. **5** (*tr*) to give forth loudly and sonorously. **6** (*tr*) to ring (bells) in peals. ORIG C14 *pele,* var. of *apele* APPEAL

peanut ('piːˌnʌt) *n* **a** a leguminous plant widely cultivated for its edible seeds. **b** the edible nutlike seed of this plant, used for food and as a source of oil. Also called: **groundnut, monkey nut.** ◆ See also **peanuts.**

peanut butter *n* a brownish oily paste made from peanuts.

peanuts ('piːˌnʌts) *n Sl.* a trifling amount of money.

pear (pɛə) *n* **1** a widely cultivated tree, having white flowers and edible fruits. **2** the sweet gritty-textured juicy fruit of this tree, which has a globular base and tapers towards the apex. **3** the wood of this tree, used for making furniture. **4 go pear-shaped.** *Inf.* to go wrong: *the plan started to go pear-shaped.* ORIG OE *pere,* ult. from L *pirum*

pearl[1] (pɜːl) *n* **1** a hard smooth lustrous typically rounded structure occurring on the inner surface of the shell of a clam or oyster around an invading particle such as a sand grain; much valued as a gem. **2** any artificial gem resembling this. **3** See **mother-of-pearl. 4** a person or thing that is like a pearl, esp. in beauty or value. **5** a pale greyish-white colour, often with a bluish tinge. ◆ *adj* **6** of, made of, or set with pearl or mother-of-pearl. **7** having the shape or colour of a pearl. ◆ *vb* **8** (*tr*) to set with or as if with pearls. **9** to shape into or assume a pearl-like form or colour. **10** (*intr*) to dive or search for pearls. ORIG C14: from OF, from Vulgar L *pernula* (unattested), from L *perna* sea mussel

pearl[2] (pɜːl) *n, vb* a variant spelling of **purl**[1] (senses 2, 3, 5).

pearl ash *n* the granular crystalline form of potassium carbonate.

pearl barley *n* barley ground into small round grains, used esp. in soups and stews.

Pearl Harbor ★ *n* an almost landlocked inlet of the Pacific on the S coast of the island of Oahu, Hawaii: site of a US naval base attacked by the Japanese in 1941, resulting in the US entry into World War II.

Pearl River ★ *n* **1** a river in central Mississippi, flowing southwest and south to the Gulf of Mexico. Length: 789 km (490 miles). **2** the English name for the **Zhu Jiang.**

pearly ('pɜːlɪ) *adj* **pearlier, pearliest. 1** resembling a pearl, esp. in lustre. **2** decorated with pearls or mother-of-pearl. ◆ *n, pl* **pearlies.** *Brit.* **3** a London costermonger or his wife who wear on ceremonial occasions a traditional dress of dark clothes covered with pearl buttons. **4** (*pl*) the clothes or the buttons themselves.
▸ **'pearliness** *n*

Pearly Gates *pl n Inf.* the entrance to heaven.

pearly king *or* (*fem*) **pearly queen** *n* the London costermonger whose ceremonial clothes display the most lavish collection of pearl buttons.

pearly nautilus *n* any of several cephalopod molluscs of warm and tropical seas, having a partitioned pale pearly external shell with brown stripes. Also called: **chambered nautilus.**

pearmain ('pɛəˌmeɪn) *n* any of several varieties of apple having a red skin. ORIG C15: from OF *permain* a type of pear, ?from L *Parmēnsis* of Parma

Pears ★ (pɪəz) *n* **Sir Peter.** 1910–86, British operatic tenor.

Pearse ★ (pɪəs) *n* **Patrick (Henry),** Irish name *Pádraic.* 1879–1916, Irish nationalist, who planned and led the Easter Rising (1916): executed by the British.

★ people and places

Pearson ★ (ˈpɪəsᵊn) *n* **1 Karl.** 1857–1936, British mathematician, noted for his work in statistics, esp. as applied to biological problems. **2 Lester B(owles).** 1897–1972, Canadian Liberal statesman; prime minister (1963–68): Nobel peace prize 1957 for helping to resolve the Suez crisis (1956).

peart (pɪət) *adj Dialect.* lively; spirited; brisk. ORIG C15: var. of PERT
▸ **ˈpeartly** *adv*

Peary ★ (ˈpɪərɪ) *n* **Robert Edwin.** 1856–1920, US arctic explorer, generally regarded as the first man to reach the North Pole (1909).

peasant (ˈpɛzᵊnt) *n* **1** a member of a class of low social status that depends on either cottage industry or agricultural labour as a means of subsistence. **2** *Inf.* a person who lives in the country; rustic. **3** *Inf.* an uncouth or uncultured person. ORIG C15: from Anglo-F, from OF *païsant,* from *païs* country, from L *pāgus* rural area

peasantry (ˈpɛzᵊntrɪ) *n* peasants as a class.

pease (pi:z) *n, pl* **pease.** *Arch. or dialect.* another word for **pea.** ORIG OE *peose,* via LL from L *pisa* peas, pl of *pisum,* from Gk *pison*

peasecod *or* **peascod** (ˈpi:zˌkɒd) *n Arch.* the pod of a pea plant. ORIG C14: from PEASE + COD²

pease pudding *n* (esp. in Britain) a dish of split peas that have been soaked and boiled.

peashooter (ˈpi:ˌʃu:tə) *n* a tube through which dried peas are blown, used as a toy weapon.

peasouper (ˌpi:ˈsu:pə) *n* **1** *Inf., chiefly Brit.* dense dirty yellowish fog. **2** *Canad.* a disparaging name for a **French Canadian.**

peat (pi:t) *n* **a** a compact brownish deposit of partially decomposed vegetable matter saturated with water: found in uplands and bogs and used as a fuel (when dried) and as a fertilizer. **b** (*as modifier*): *peat bog.* ORIG C14: from Anglo-L *peta,* ?from Celtic
▸ **ˈpeaty** *adj*

peat moss *n* any of various mosses, esp. sphagnum, that grow in wet places and decay to form peat. See also **sphagnum.**

pebble (ˈpɛbᵊl) *n* **1** a small smooth rounded stone, esp. one worn by the action of water. **2a** a transparent colourless variety of rock crystal, used for making certain lenses. **2b** such a lens. **3** (*modifier*) *Inf.* (of a lens or of spectacles) thick, with a high degree of magnification or distortion. **4a** a grainy irregular surface, esp. on leather. **4b** leather having such a surface. ◆ *vb* **pebbles, pebbling, pebbled.** (*tr*) **5** to cover with pebbles. **6** to impart a grainy surface to (leather). ORIG OE *papolstān,* from *papol-* (? imit.) + *stān* stone
▸ **ˈpebbly** *adj*

pebble dash *n Brit.* a finish for external walls consisting of small stones embedded in plaster.

pebi (ˈpɛbɪ) *prefix Computing.* denoting 2^{50}: *pebibyte.* ORIG C20: from PE(TA-) + BI(NARY)

> **USAGE NOTE** See at **kilo.**

pec (pɛk) *n* (*usually pl*) *Inf.* short for **pectoral muscle.**

pecan (pɪˈkæn, ˈpi:kən) *n* **1** a hickory tree of the southern US having deeply furrowed bark and edible nuts. **2** the smooth oval nut of this tree, which has a sweet oily kernel. ORIG C18: from Algonquian *paccan*

peccable (ˈpɛkəbᵊl) *adj* liable to sin. ORIG C17: via F from Med. L *peccābilis,* from L *peccāre* to sin

peccadillo (ˌpɛkəˈdɪləʊ) *n, pl* **peccadilloes** *or* **peccadillos.** a petty sin or fault. ORIG C16: from Sp., from *pecado* sin, from L *peccātum,* from *peccāre* to transgress

peccant (ˈpɛkənt) *adj Rare.* **1** guilty of an offence; corrupt. **2** violating or disregarding a rule; faulty. **3** producing disease; morbid. ORIG C17: from L *peccans,* from *peccāre* to sin
▸ **ˈpeccancy** *n*

peccary (ˈpɛkərɪ) *n, pl* **peccaries** *or* **peccary.** either of two piglike mammals of forests of southern North America, Central and South America. ORIG C17: from Carib

Pechora ★ (*Russian* pɪˈtʃɔrə) *n* a river in N Russia, rising in the Ural Mountains and flowing north in a great arc to the **Pechora Sea** (the SE part of the Barents Sea). Length: 1814 km (1127 miles).

peck¹ (pɛk) *n* **1** a unit of dry measure equal to 8 quarts or one quarter of a bushel. **2** a container used for measuring this quantity. **3** a large quantity or number. ORIG C13: from Anglo-Norman, from ?

peck² (pɛk) *vb* **1** (when *intr,* sometimes foll. by *at*) to strike with the beak or with a pointed instrument. **2** (*tr;* sometimes foll. by *out*) to dig (a hole, etc.) by pecking. **3** (*tr*) (of birds) to pick up (corn, worms, etc.) by pecking. **4** (*intr;* often foll. by *at*) to nibble or pick (at one's food). **5** *Inf.* to kiss (a person) quickly and lightly. **6** (*intr;* foll. by *at*) to nag. ◆ *n* **7** a quick light blow, esp. from a bird's beak. **8** a mark made by such a blow. **9** *Inf.* a quick light kiss. ORIG C14: from ?

Peck ★ (pɛk) *n* **Gregory.** born 1916, US film actor; his films include *The Gunfighter* (1950), *The Big Country* (1958), *The Omen* (1976), and *Other People's Money* (1991).

pecker (ˈpɛkə) *n Brit. sl.* spirits (esp. in **keep one's pecker up**).

pecking order *n* **1** Also called: **peck order.** a natural hierarchy in a group of gregarious birds, such as domestic fowl. **2** any hierarchical order, as among people in a particular group.

Peckinpah ★ (ˈpɛkɪnˌpɑ:) *n* **Sam(uel David).** 1926–84, US film director, esp. of Westerns, such as *The Wild Bunch* (1969). Among his other films are *Straw Dogs* (1971).

peckish (ˈpɛkɪʃ) *adj Inf., chiefly Brit.* feeling slightly hungry. ORIG C18: from PECK²

Pecos ★ (ˈpeɪkəs; *Spanish* ˈpekɔs) *n* a river in the southwestern US, rising in N central New Mexico and flowing southeast to the Rio Grande. Length: about 1180 km (735 miles).

Pécs ★ (*Hungarian* pe:tʃ) *n* an industrial city in SW Hungary: university (1367). Pop.: 161 000 (1997 est.).

pecten (ˈpɛktɪn) *n, pl* **pectens** *or* **pectines** (-tɪˌni:z). **1** a comblike structure in the eye of birds and reptiles, consisting of a network of blood vessels projecting inwards from the retina. **2** any other comblike part or organ. ORIG C18: from L: a comb, from *pectere* to comb

pectin (ˈpɛktɪn) *n Biochem.* any of the acidic polysaccharides that occur in ripe fruit and vegetables: used in the manufacture of jams because of their ability to solidify to a gel. ORIG C19: from Gk *pēktos* congealed, from *pegnuein* to set
▸ **ˈpectic** *or* **ˈpectinous** *adj*

pectoral (ˈpɛktərəl) *adj* **1** of or relating to the chest, breast, or thorax: *pectoral fins.* **2** worn on the breast or chest: *a pectoral medallion.* ◆ *n* **3** a pectoral organ or part, esp. a muscle or fin. **4** a medicine for disorders of the chest or lungs. **5** anything worn on the chest or breast for decoration or protection. ORIG C15: from L *pectorālis,* from *pectus* breast
▸ **ˈpectorally** *adv*

pectoral fin *n* either of a pair of fins, situated just behind the head in fishes, that help to control the direction of movement during locomotion.

pectoral muscle *n* either of two large chest muscles (**pectoralis major** and **pectoralis minor**), that assist in movements of the shoulder and upper arm.

peculate (ˈpɛkjʊˌleɪt) *vb* **peculates, peculating, peculated.** to appropriate or embezzle (public money, etc.). ORIG C18: from L *pecūlārī,* from *pecūlium* private property (orig., cattle); see PECULIAR
▸ **ˌpecuˈlation** *n* ▸ **ˈpecuˌlator** *n*

peculiar (pɪˈkju:lɪə) *adj* **1** strange or unusual; odd: *a peculiar idea.* **2** distinct from others; special. **3** (*postpositive;* foll. by *to*) belonging characteristically or exclusively (to): *peculiar to North America.* ORIG C15: from L *pecūliāris* concerning private property, from *pecūlium,* lit.: property in cattle, from *pecus* cattle
▸ **peˈculiarly** *adv*

peculiarity (pɪˌkju:lɪˈærɪtɪ) *n, pl* **peculiarities.** **1** a strange or unusual habit or characteristic. **2** a distinguishing trait, etc., that is characteristic of a particular person; idiosyncrasy. **3** the state or quality of being peculiar.

pecuniary (pɪ'kjuːnɪərɪ) *adj* **1** of or relating to money. **2** *Law.* (of an offence) involving a monetary penalty. ORIG C16: from L *pecūniāris,* from *pecūnia* money
▸ **pe'cuniarily** *adv*

pecuniary advantage *n Law.* financial advantage that is dishonestly obtained by deception and that constitutes a criminal offence.

-ped *or* **-pede** *n combining form.* foot or feet: *quadruped; centipede.* ORIG from L *pēs, ped-* foot

pedagogue *or US (sometimes)* **pedagog** ('pɛdəˌgɒg) *n* **1** a teacher or educator. **2** a pedantic or dogmatic teacher. ORIG C14: from L *paedagōgus,* from Gk *paidagōgos* slave who looked after his master's son, from *pais* boy + *agōgos* leader
▸ **ˌpeda'gogic** *or* **ˌpeda'gogical** *adj* ▸ **ˌpeda'gogically** *adv*

pedagogy ('pɛdəˌgɒgɪ, -ˌgɒdʒɪ, -ˌgəʊdʒɪ) *n* the principles, practice, or profession of teaching.

pedal[1] ('pɛdᵊl) *n* **1a** any foot-operated lever, esp. one of the two levers that drive the chainwheel of a bicycle, the foot brake, clutch control, or accelerator of a car, one of the levers on an organ controlling deep bass notes, or one of the levers on a piano used to mute or sustain tone. **1b** *(as modifier): a pedal cycle.* ◆ *vb* **pedals, pedalling, pedalled** *or US* **pedals, pedaling, pedaled. 2** to propel (a bicycle, etc.) by operating the pedals. **3** *(intr)* to operate the pedals of an organ, piano, etc. **4** to work (pedals of any kind). ORIG C17: from L *pedālis;* see PEDAL[2]

pedal[2] ('piːdᵊl) *adj* of or relating to the foot or feet. ORIG C17: from L *pedālis,* from *pēs* foot

pedal point ('pɛdᵊl) *n Music.* a sustained bass note, over which the other parts move bringing changing harmonies. Often shortened to **pedal.**

pedal steel guitar ('pɛdᵊl) *n* a floor-mounted multineck steel guitar with each set of strings tuned to a different open chord and foot pedals to raise or lower the pitch.

pedant ('pɛdᵊnt) *n* **1** a person who relies too much on academic learning or who is concerned chiefly with insignificant detail. **2** *Arch.* a schoolmaster or teacher. ORIG C16: via OF from It. *pedante* teacher
▸ **pedantic** (pɪ'dæntɪk) *adj* ▸ **pe'dantically** *adv*

pedantry ('pɛdᵊntrɪ) *n, pl* **pedantries.** the habit or an instance of being a pedant, esp. in the display of useless knowledge or minute observance of petty rules or details.

pedate ('pɛdeɪt) *adj* **1** (of a plant leaf) deeply divided into several lobes. **2** *Zool.* having or resembling a foot: *a pedate appendage.* ORIG C18: from L *pedātus* equipped with feet, from *pēs* foot

peddle ('pɛdᵊl) *vb* **peddles, peddling, peddled. 1** to go from place to place selling (goods, esp. small articles). **2** *(tr)* to sell (illegal drugs, esp. narcotics). **3** *(tr)* to advocate (ideas, etc.) persistently: *to peddle a new philosophy.* ORIG C16: back formation from PEDLAR

peddler ('pɛdlə) *n* **1** a person who sells illegal drugs, esp. narcotics. **2** the usual US spelling of **pedlar.**

pederasty *or* **paederasty** ('pɛdəˌræstɪ) *n* homosexual relations between men and boys. ORIG C17: from NL *paederastia,* from Gk, from *pais* boy + *erastēs* lover, from *eran* to love
▸ **'pederˌast** *or* **'paederˌast** *n* ▸ **ˌpeder'astic** *or* **ˌpaeder'astic** *adj*

pedestal ('pɛdɪstᵊl) *n* **1** a base that supports a column, statue, etc. **2** a position of eminence or supposed superiority (esp. in **place, put,** *or* **set on a pedestal**). ORIG C16: from F *piédestal,* from OIt. *piedestallo,* from *pie* foot + *di* of + *stallo* a stall

pedestrian (pɪ'dɛstrɪən) *n* **1a** a person travelling on foot; walker. **1b** *(as modifier): a pedestrian precinct.* ◆ *adj* **2** dull; commonplace: *a pedestrian style of writing.* ORIG C18: from L *pedester,* from *pēs* foot

pedestrian crossing *n Brit.* a path across a road marked as a crossing for pedestrians.

pedestrianize *or* **pedestrianise** (pɪ'dɛstrɪəˌnaɪz) *vb* **pedestrianizes, pedestrianizing, pedestrianized** *or* **pedestrianises, pedestrianising, pedestrianised.** *(tr)* to convert (a street, etc.) into an area for the use of pedestrians only.
▸ **peˌdestriani'zation** *or* **peˌdestriani'sation** *n*

pedi- *combining form.* indicating the foot: *pedicure.* ORIG from L *pēs, ped-* foot

pedicab ('pɛdɪˌkæb) *n* a pedal-operated tricycle, available for hire, with an attached seat for one or two passengers.

pedicel ('pɛdɪˌsɛl) *n* **1** the stalk bearing a single flower of an inflorescence. **2** Also called: **peduncle.** *Biol.* any short stalk bearing an organ or organism. ◆ Also called: **pedicle.** ORIG C17: from NL *pedicellus,* from L *pedīculus,* from *pēs* foot
▸ **pedicellate** (pɪ'dɪsɪˌleɪt) *adj*

pediculosis (pɪˌdɪkjʊ'ləʊsɪs) *n Pathol.* the state of being infested with lice. ORIG C19: via NL from L *pedīculus* louse
▸ **pediculous** (pɪ'dɪkjʊləs) *adj*

pedicure ('pɛdɪˌkjʊə) *n* treatment of the feet, either by a medical expert or a cosmetician. ORIG C19: via F from L *pēs* foot + *curāre* to care for

pedigree ('pɛdɪˌgriː) *n* **1a** the line of descent of a purebred animal. **1b** *(as modifier): a pedigree bull.* **2** a document recording this. **3** a genealogical table, esp. one indicating pure ancestry. ORIG C15: from OF *pie de grue* crane's foot, alluding to the spreading lines used in a genealogical chart
▸ **'pediˌgreed** *adj*

pediment ('pɛdɪmənt) *n* a low-pitched gable, esp. one that is triangular as used in classical architecture. ORIG C16: from obs. *periment,* ? workman's corruption of PYRAMID
▸ **ˌpedi'mental** *adj*

pedipalp ('pɛdɪˌpælp) *n* either member of the second pair of head appendages of arachnids: specialized for feeding, locomotion, etc. ORIG C19: from NL *pedipalpi,* from L *pēs* foot + *palpus* palp

pedlar *or esp. US* **peddler** ('pɛdlə) *n* a person who peddles; hawker. ORIG C14: changed from *peder,* from *ped, pedde* basket, from ?

pedo- *or before a vowel* **ped-** a variant (esp. US) of **paedo-.**

pedology (pɪ'dɒlədʒɪ) *n* the study of soils. ORIG C20: from Gk *pedon* ground, earth + -OLOGY

pedometer (pɪ'dɒmɪtə) *n* a device that records the number of steps taken in walking and hence the distance travelled.

peduncle (pɪ'dʌŋkᵊl) *n* **1** the stalk of a plant bearing an inflorescence or solitary flower. **2** *Anat., pathol.* any stalk-like structure. **3** *Biol.* another name for **pedicel** (sense 2). ORIG C18: from NL *pedunculus,* from L *pedīculus* little foot
▸ **peduncular** (pɪ'dʌŋkjʊlə) *or* **pedunculate** (pɪ'dʌŋkjʊlɪt, -ˌleɪt) *adj*

pee (piː) *Inf.* ◆ *vb* **pees, peeing, peed. 1** *(intr)* to urinate. ◆ *n* **2** urine. **3** the act of urinating. ORIG C18: euphemistic for PISS, based on the initial letter

Peebles ★ ('piːbᵊlz) *n* a town in SE Scotland, in Scottish Borders. Pop.: 7065 (1991).

Peeblesshire ★ ('piːbᵊlzˌʃɪə, -ʃə) *n* a historic county of SE Scotland, now part of Scottish Borders. Also called: **Tweeddale.**

peek (piːk) *vb* **1** *(intr)* to glance quickly or furtively. ◆ *n* **2** such a glance. ORIG C14 *pike,* rel. to M Du *kiken* to peek

peekaboo ('piːkəˌbuː) *n* **1** a game for young children, in which one person hides his or her face and suddenly reveals it and cries "peekaboo". ◆ *adj* **2** (of a garment) made of fabric that is sheer or patterned with small holes. ORIG C16: from PEEK + BOO

peel[1] (piːl) *vb* **1** *(tr)* to remove (the skin, rind, etc.) of (a fruit, egg, etc.). **2** *(intr)* (of paint, etc.) to be removed from a surface, esp. by weathering. **3** *(intr)* (of a surface) to lose its outer covering of paint, etc., esp. by weathering. **4** *(intr)* (of a person or part of the body) to shed skin in flakes or (of skin) to be shed in flakes, esp. as a result of sunburn. ◆ *n* **5** the skin or rind of a fruit, etc. ◆ See also **peel off.** ORIG OE *pilian* to strip off the outer layer, from L *pilāre* to make bald, from *pilus* a hair
▸ **'peeler** *n*

★ people and places

peel[2] (piːl) *n* a long-handled shovel used by bakers for moving bread in an oven. ORIG C14 *pele,* from OF, from L *pāla* spade, from *pangere* to drive in

peel[3] (piːl) *n Brit.* a fortified tower of the 16th century on the borders of Scotland. ORIG C14 (fence made of stakes): from OF *piel* stake, from L *pālus*

Peel ★ (piːl) *n* Sir **Robert.** 1788–1850, British statesman; Conservative prime minister (1834–35; 1841–46). As Home Secretary (1828–30) he founded the Metropolitan Police and in his second ministry carried through a series of free-trade budgets culminating in the repeal of the Corn Laws (1846), which split the Tory party.
▸ **'Peelite** *n*

Peele ★ (piːl) *n* **George.** ?1556–?96, English dramatist and poet. His works include the pastoral drama *The Arraignment of Paris* (1584) and the comedy *The Old Wives' Tale* (1595).

peeler ('piːlə) *n Irish & obs. Brit. sl.* another word for **policeman.** ORIG C19: from the founder of the police force, Sir Robert PEEL

peeling ('piːlɪŋ) *n* a strip of skin, rind, bark, etc., that has been peeled off: *a potato peeling.*

peel off *vb* (*adv*) **1** to remove or be removed by peeling. **2** (*intr*) *Sl.* to undress. **3** (*intr*) (of an aircraft) to turn away as by banking, and leave a formation.

peen (piːn) *n* **1** the end of a hammer head opposite the striking face, often rounded or wedge-shaped. ◆ *vb* **2** (*tr*) to strike with the peen of a hammer or a stream of metal shot. ORIG C17: var. of *pane,* ?from F *panne,* ult. from L *pinna* point

Peenemünde ★ (*German* peːnəˈmyndə) *n* a village in N Germany, on the Baltic coast: site of a German rocket-development centre in World War II.

peep[1] (piːp) *vb* (*intr*) **1** to look furtively or secretly, as through a small aperture or from a hidden place. **2** to appear partially or briefly: *the sun peeped through the clouds.* ◆ *n* **3** a quick or furtive look. **4** the first appearance: *the peep of dawn.* ORIG C15: var. of PEEK

peep[2] (piːp) *vb* (*intr*) **1** (esp. of young birds) to utter shrill small noises. **2** to speak in a weak voice. ◆ *n* **3** a peeping sound. ORIG C15: imit.

peeper ('piːpə) *n* **1** a person who peeps. **2** (*often pl*) a slang word for **eye**[1] (sense 1).

peephole ('piːpˌhəʊl) *n* a small aperture, as in a door for observing callers before opening.

Peeping Tom *n* a man who furtively observes women undressing; voyeur. ORIG C19: after the tailor who, according to legend, peeped at Lady Godiva when she rode naked through Coventry

peepshow ('piːpˌʃəʊ) *n* **1** Also called: **raree show.** a box with a peephole through which a series of pictures can be seen. **2** a booth from which a viewer can see a live nude model for a fee.

peepul ('piːpᵊl) *or* **pipal** *n* an Indian tree resembling the banyan: regarded as sacred by Buddhists. Also called: **bo tree.** ORIG C18: from Hindi *pīpal,* from Sansk. *pippala*

peer[1] (pɪə) *n* **1** a member of a nobility; nobleman. **2** a person who holds any of the five grades of the British nobility: duke, marquess, earl, viscount, and baron. See also **life peer. 3** a person who is an equal in social standing, rank, age, etc.: *to be tried by one's peers.* ORIG C14 (in sense 3): from OF *per,* from L *pār* equal

peer[2] (pɪə) *vb* (*intr*) **1** to look intently with or as if with difficulty: *to peer into the distance.* **2** to appear partially or dimly: *the sun peered through the fog.* ORIG C16: from Flemish *pieren* to look with narrowed eyes

peerage ('pɪərɪdʒ) *n* **1** the whole body of peers; aristocracy. **2** the position, rank, or title of a peer. **3** (esp. in the British Isles) a book listing the peers and giving their genealogy.

peeress ('pɪərɪs) *n* **1** the wife or widow of a peer. **2** a woman holding the rank of a peer in her own right.

peer group *n* a social group composed of individuals of approximately the same age.

peerless ('pɪəlɪs) *adj* having no equals; matchless.

peeve (piːv) *Inf.* ◆ *vb* **peeves, peeving, peeved. 1** (*tr*) to irritate; vex; annoy. ◆ *n* **2** something that irritates; vexation. ORIG C20: back formation from PEEVISH
▸ **peeved** *adj*

peevish ('piːvɪʃ) *adj* fretful or irritable. ORIG C14: from ?
▸ **'peevishly** *adv* ▸ **'peevishness** *n*

peewee ('piːwiː) *n* **1** a small black-and-white Australian bird with long thin legs. **2** *Canad.* a small person or thing. **3** *Canad.* (in sports) a player aged 12 or 13. ORIG imit.

peewit *or* **pewit** ('piːwɪt) *n* another name for **lapwing.** ORIG C16: imit. of its call

peg (pɛg) *n* **1** a small cylindrical pin or dowel used to join two parts together. **2** a pin pushed or driven into a surface: used to mark scores, define limits, support coats, etc. **3** any of several pins on a violin, etc., which can be turned so as to tune strings wound around them. **4** Also called: **clothes peg.** *Brit., Austral., & NZ.* a split or hinged pin for fastening wet clothes to a line to dry. US and Canad. equivalent: **clothespin. 5** *Brit.* a small drink of wine or spirits. **6** an opportunity or pretext for doing something: *a peg on which to hang a theory.* **7** *Inf.* a level of self-esteem, importance, etc. (esp. in **bring** *or* **take down a peg**). **8** *Inf.* See **peg leg. 9 off the peg.** *Chiefly Brit.* (of clothes) ready-to-wear, as opposed to tailor-made. ◆ *vb* **pegs, pegging, pegged. 10** (*tr*) to knock or insert a peg into. **11** (*tr*) to secure with pegs: *to peg a tent.* **12** (*tr*) to mark (a score) with pegs, as in some card games. **13** (*tr*) *Inf.* to throw (stones, etc.) at a target. **14** (*intr;* foll. by *away, along,* etc.) *Chiefly Brit.* to work steadily: *he pegged away at his job for years.* **15** (*tr*) to stabilize (the price of a commodity, an exchange rate, etc.). ORIG C15: from Low Gmc *pegge*

Pegasus ★ ('pɛgəsəs) *n Greek myth.* an immortal winged horse, which sprang from the blood of the slain Medusa and enabled Bellerophon to achieve many great deeds as his rider.

pegboard ('pɛgˌbɔːd) *n* **1** a board having a pattern of holes into which small pegs can be fitted, used for playing certain games or keeping a score. **2** another name for **solitaire** (sense 1). **3** hardboard perforated by a pattern of holes in which articles may be hung, as for display.

peg leg *n Inf.* **1** an artificial leg, esp. one made of wood. **2** a person with an artificial leg.

pegmatite ('pɛgməˌtaɪt) *n* any of a class of coarse-grained intrusive igneous rocks consisting chiefly of quartz and feldspar. ORIG C19: from Gk *pegma* something joined together

peg out *vb* (*adv*) **1** (*intr*) *Inf.* to collapse or die. **2** (*intr*) *Cribbage.* to score the point that wins the game. **3** (*tr*) to mark or secure with pegs: *to peg out one's claims to a piece of land.*

peg top *n* a child's spinning top, usually made of wood with a metal centre pin.

peg-top *adj* (of skirts, trousers, etc.) wide at the hips then tapering off towards the ankle.

Pegu ★ (pɛˈguː) *n* a city in S Myanmar: capital of a united Burma (16th century). Pop.: 150 447 (latest est.).

Péguy ★ (*French* pegi) *n* **Charles** (ʃarl). 1873–1914, French poet and essayist, whose works include *Le Mystère de la charité de Jeanne d'Arc* (1910): killed in World War I.

Pei ★ (peɪ) *n* **I(eoh) M(ing).** born 1917, US architect, born in China. His buildings include the E wing of the National Museum of Art, Washington DC (1978), a glass and steel pyramid at the Louvre, Paris (1989), and the Rock and Roll Hall of Fame, Cleveland, in the US (1995).

PEI *abbrev. for* Prince Edward Island.

peignoir ('peɪnwɑː) *n* a woman's dressing gown. ORIG C19: from F, from *peigner* to comb, since the garment was worn while the hair was combed

Peipus ★ ('paɪpəs) *n* a lake in NE Europe, on the boundary between Russia and Estonia: drains into the Gulf of Finland. Area: 3512 sq. km (1356 sq. miles). Russian name: **Chudskoye Ozero.**

Peiraeus ★ (paɪˈriːəs, pɪˈreɪ-) *n* a variant spelling of **Piraeus.**

Peirce ★ (pɪəs) *n* **Charles Sanders.** 1839–1914, US logician, philosopher, and mathematician; pioneer of pragmatism.

pejoration (ˌpiːdʒəˈreɪʃən) *n* **1** semantic change whereby a word acquires unfavourable connotations. **2** the process of worsening.

pejorative (pɪ'dʒɒrətɪv, 'pi:dʒər-) *adj* **1** (of words, expressions, etc.) having an unpleasant or disparaging connotation. ◆ *n* **2** a pejorative word, etc. ORIG C19: from F *péjoratif,* from LL *pējōrātus,* p.p. of *pējōrāre* to make worse, from L *pēior* worse
▸ **pe'joratively** *adv*

pekan ('pɛkən) *n* another name for **fisher** (the animal). ORIG C18: from Canad. F *pékan,* from Amerind

peke (pi:k) *n Inf.* a Pekingese dog.

Peking ★ ('pi:'kɪŋ) *n* the former English name of **Beijing.**

Pekingese (ˌpi:kɪŋ'i:z) *or* **Pekinese** (ˌpi:kə'ni:z) *n* **1** (*pl* **Pekingese** *or* **Pekinese**) a small breed of pet dog with a profuse straight coat, curled plumed tail, and short wrinkled muzzle. **2** the dialect of Mandarin Chinese spoken in Beijing (formerly Peking). **3** (*pl* **Pekingese** *or* **Pekinese**) a native or inhabitant of Beijing (formerly Peking). ◆ *adj* **4** of Beijing (formerly Peking) or its inhabitants.

Peking man (pi:'kɪŋ) *n* an early type of man, of the Lower Palaeolithic age, remains of which were found in a cave near Beijing (formerly Peking).

pekoe ('pi:kəʊ) *n* a high-quality tea made from the downy tips of the young buds of the tea plant. ORIG C18: from Chinese *peh ho,* from *peh* white + *ho* down

pelage ('pɛlɪdʒ) *n* the coat of a mammal, consisting of hair, wool, fur, etc. ORIG C19: via F from OF *pel* animal's coat, from L *pilus* hair

Pelagian Islands ★ (pɛ'leɪdʒɪən) *pl n* a group of Italian islands (Lampedusa, Linosa, and Lampione) in the Mediterranean, between Tunisia and Malta. Pop.: 4500 (latest est.). Area: about 27 sq. km (11 sq. miles). Italian name: **Isole Pelagie** ('i:zole pe'ladʒe).

Pelagianism (pɛ'leɪdʒɪəˌnɪzəm) *n Christianity.* a heretical doctrine, first formulated by Pelagius, that rejected the concept of original sin.
▸ **Pe'lagian** *n, adj*

pelagic (pɛ'lædʒɪk) *adj* **1** of or relating to the open sea: *pelagic whaling.* **2** (of marine life) occurring in the upper waters of open sea. ORIG C17: from L *pelagicus,* from *pelagus,* from Gk *pelagos* sea

Pelagius ★ (pɛ'leɪdʒɪəs) *n* ?360–?420 A.D., British monk, who originated the body of doctrines known as Pelagianism and was condemned for heresy (417).

pelargonium (ˌpɛlə'gəʊnɪəm) *n* any plant of a chiefly southern African genus having circular or lobed leaves and red, pink, or white aromatic flowers: includes many cultivated geraniums. ORIG C19: via NL from Gk *pelargos* stork, on the model of GERANIUM; from the likeness of the seed vessels to a stork's bill

Pelé ★ ('peleɪ) *n* real name *Edson Arantes do Nascimento.* born 1940, Brazilian footballer: awarded an honorary knighthood in 1997.

Pelée ★ (pə'leɪ) *n* **Mount.** a volcano in the Caribbean, in N Martinique: erupted in 1902, killing every person but one in the town of St Pierre. Height: 1463 m (4800 ft).

Peleus ★ ('pɛlɪəs, 'pi:lɪəs) *n Greek myth.* a king of the Myrmidons; father of Achilles.

Pelew Islands ★ (pi:'lu:) *pl n* a former name of (the Republic of) **Belau.**

pelf (pɛlf) *n Contemptuous.* money or wealth; lucre. ORIG C14: from OF *pelfre* booty

pelham ('pɛləm) *n* a horse's bit for a double bridle, less severe than a curb but more severe than a snaffle. ORIG prob. from the name *Pelham*

Pelham ★ ('pɛləm) *n* **Henry.** 1696–1754, British statesman: prime minister (1743–54); brother of Thomas Pelham Holles, 1st Duke of Newcastle.

Pelham Holles ★ ('hɒlɪs) *n* **Thomas.** See (1st Duke of) **Newcastle.**

Pelias ★ ('pi:lɪˌæs) *n Greek myth.* a son of Poseidon and Tyro. He feared his nephew Jason and sent him to recover the Golden Fleece, hoping he would not return.

pelican ('pɛlɪkən) *n* any aquatic bird of a tropical and warm water family. They have a long straight flattened bill, with a distensible pouch for engulfing fish. ORIG OE *pellican,* from LL *pelicānus,* from Gk *pelekān*

pelican crossing *n* a type of road crossing with a pedestrian-operated traffic-light system. ORIG C20: from *pe(destrian) li(ght) con(trolled) crossing,* with *-con* adapted to *-can* of *pelican*

Pelion ★ ('pi:lɪən) *n* a mountain in NE Greece, in E Thessaly. In Greek mythology it was the home of the centaurs. Height: 1548 m (5079 ft). Modern Greek name: **Pílion.**

pelisse (pɛ'li:s) *n* **1** a fur-trimmed cloak. **2** a loose coat, usually fur-trimmed, worn esp. by women in the early 19th century. ORIG C18: via OF from Med. L *pellicia* cloak, from L *pellis* skin

Pella ★ ('pɛlə) *n* an ancient city in N Greece: the capital of Macedonia under Philip II.

pellagra (pə'leɪgrə, -'læ-) *n Pathol.* a disease caused by a dietary deficiency of nicotinic acid, characterized by scaling of the skin, inflammation of the mouth, diarrhoea, mental impairment, etc. ORIG C19: via It. from *pelle* skin + *-agra,* from Gk *agra* paroxysm
▸ **pel'lagrous** *adj*

pellet ('pɛlɪt) *n* **1** a small round ball, esp. of compressed matter. **2a** an imitation bullet used in toy guns. **2b** a piece of small shot. **3** a stone ball formerly used in a catapult. **4** *Ornithol.* a mass of undigested food that is regurgitated by birds of prey. **5** a small pill. ◆ *vb* (*tr*) **6** to strike with pellets. **7** to make or form into pellets. ORIG C14: from OF *pelote,* from Vulgar L *pilota* (unattested), from L *pila* ball

Pelletier ★ (*French* pɛltje) *n* **Pierre Joseph** (pjɛr ʒozɛf). 1788–1842, French chemist, who isolated quinine, chlorophyll, and other chemical substances.

pellitory ('pɛlɪtərɪ, -trɪ) *n, pl* **pellitories. 1** any of various plants of a S and W European genus, esp. wall pellitory, that grow in crevices and have long narrow leaves and small pink flowers. **2 pellitory of Spain.** a small Mediterranean plant, the root of which contains an oil formerly used to relieve toothache. ORIG C16 *peletre,* from OF *piretre,* from L, from Gk *purethron,* from *pur* fire, from the hot pungent taste of the root

pell-mell ('pɛl'mɛl) *adv* **1** in a confused headlong rush: *the hounds ran pell-mell into the yard.* **2** in a disorderly manner: *the things were piled pell-mell in the room.* ◆ *adj* **3** disordered; tumultuous: *a pell-mell rush for the exit.* ◆ *n* **4** disorder; confusion. ORIG C16: from OF *pesle-mesle,* jingle based on *mesler* to MEDDLE

pellucid (pɛ'lu:sɪd) *adj* **1** transparent or translucent. **2** extremely clear in style and meaning. ORIG C17: from L *pellūcidus,* var. of *perlūcidus,* from *perlūcēre* to shine through
▸ **ˌpellu'cidity** *or* **pel'lucidness** *n* ▸ **pel'lucidly** *adv*

pelmet ('pɛlmɪt) *n* an ornamental drapery or board fixed above a window to conceal the curtain rail. ORIG C19: prob. from F *palmette* palm-leaf decoration on cornice moulding

Peloponnese ★ (ˌpɛləpə'ni:s) *n* **the.** the S peninsula of Greece, joined to central Greece by the Isthmus of Corinth: chief cities in ancient times were Sparta and Corinth, now Patras. Pop.: 607 428 (1991). Area: 21 439 sq. km (8361 sq. miles). Medieval name: **Morea.** Modern Greek name: **Peloponnesos.** Also called: **Peloponnesus.**
▸ **Peloponnesian** (ˌpɛləpə'ni:ʃən) *adj*

Pelops ★ ('pi:lɒps) *n Greek myth.* the son of Tantalus, who as a child was killed by his father and served up as a meal for the gods.

pelota (pə'lɒtə) *n* any of various games played in Spain, Spanish America, SW France, etc., by two players who use a basket strapped to their wrists or a wooden racket to propel a ball against a specially marked wall. ORIG C19: from Sp.: ball, from OF *pelote;* see PELLET

Pelotas ★ (*Portuguese* pe'lɔtas) *n* a port in S Brazil, in Rio Grande do Sul on the Canal de São Gonçalo. Pop.: 260 510 (1991).

peloton ('pɛləˌtɒn) *n* the main field of riders in a cycling race. ORIG C20: F, lit.: pack

pelt[1] (pɛlt) *vb* **1** (*tr*) to throw (missiles, etc.) at (a person, etc.). **2** (*tr*) to hurl (insults, etc.) at (a person, etc.). **3** (*intr;* foll. by *along,* etc.) to hurry. **4** (*intr*) to rain heavily. ◆ *n* **5** a blow. **6** speed (esp. in **at full pelt**). ORIG C15: from ?

pelt[2] (pelt) *n* **1** the skin of a fur-bearing animal, esp. when it has been removed from the carcass. **2** the hide of an animal, stripped of hair. ORIG C15: ? back formation from PELTRY

peltate ('pelteɪt) *adj* (of leaves) having the stalk attached to the centre of the lower surface. ORIG C18: from L *peltātus* equipped with a *pelta* small shield

peltry ('peltrɪ) *n, pl* **peltries.** the pelts of animals collectively. ORIG C15: from OF *peleterie* collection of pelts, from L *pilus* hair

pelvic fin *n* either of a pair of fins attached to the pelvic girdle of fishes that help to control the direction of movement during locomotion.

pelvic inflammatory disease *n* inflammation of a woman's womb, Fallopian tubes, or ovaries as a result of infection. Abbrev.: **PID.**

pelvimetry (pel'vɪmɪtrɪ) *n Obstetrics.* measurement of the dimensions of the female pelvis.

pelvis ('pelvɪs) *n, pl* **pelvises** *or* **pelves** (-vi:z). **1** the large funnel-shaped structure at the lower end of the trunk of most vertebrates. **2** Also called: **pelvic girdle.** the bones that form this structure. **3** any anatomical cavity or structure shaped like a funnel or cup. ORIG C17: from L: basin
▸ **'pelvic** *adj*

Pemba ★ ('pembə) *n* an island in the Indian Ocean, off the E coast of Africa north of Zanzibar: part of Tanzania; produces most of the world's cloves. Chief town: Chake Chake. Pop.: 265 039 (1988). Area: 984 sq. km (380 sq. miles).

Pembroke ★ ('pembrʊk) *n* a town in SW Wales, in Pembrokeshire on Milford Haven: 11th-century castle where Henry VII was born. Pop.: 15 424 (1991).

Pembrokeshire ★ ('pembrʊk,ʃɪə, -ʃə) *n* a county of SW Wales, on the Irish Sea and the Bristol Channel; formerly (1974–96) part of Dyfed: hilly with an indented coast. Administrative centre: Haverfordwest. Pop.: 113 500 (1996 est.). Area: 1589 sq. km (614 sq. miles).

pemmican *or* **pemican** ('pemɪkən) *n* a small pressed cake of shredded dried meat, pounded into paste, used originally by Native Americans and now chiefly for emergency rations. ORIG C19: from Amerind *pimikân,* from *pimii* grease

pemphigus ('pemfɪgəs, pem'faɪ-) *n Pathol.* any of a group of blistering skin diseases. ORIG C18: via NL from Gk *pemphix* bubble

pen[1] (pen) *n* **1** an implement for writing or drawing using ink, formerly consisting of a sharpened and split quill, and now of a metal nib attached to a holder. See also **ballpoint, fountain pen. 2** the writing end of such an implement; nib. **3** style of writing. **4 the pen.** writing as an occupation. ◆ *vb* **pens, penning, penned. 5** (*tr*) to write or compose. ORIG OE *pinne,* from LL *penna* (quill) pen, from L: feather

pen[2] (pen) *n* **1** an enclosure in which domestic animals are kept. **2** any place of confinement. **3** a dock for servicing submarines, esp. having a bombproof roof. ◆ *vb* **pens, penning, penned** *or* **pent. 4** (*tr*) to enclose in a pen. ORIG OE *penn*

pen[3] (pen) *n US & Canad. inf.* short for **penitentiary** (sense 1).

pen[4] (pen) *n* a female swan. ORIG C16: from ?

PEN (pen) *n acronym for* International Association of Poets, Playwrights, Editors, Essayists, and Novelists.

Pen. *abbrev. for* Peninsula.

penal ('pi:nᵊl) *adj* **1** of, relating to, constituting, or prescribing punishment. **2** used or designated as a place of punishment: *a penal institution.* ORIG C15: from LL *poenālis* concerning punishment, from L *poena* penalty
▸ **'penally** *adv*

penal code *n* the codified body of the laws that relate to crime and its punishment.

penalize *or* **penalise** ('pi:nə,laɪz) *vb* **penalizes, penalizing, penalized** *or* **penalises, penalising, penalised.** (*tr*) **1** to impose a penalty on (someone), as for breaking a law or rule. **2** to inflict a disadvantage on. **3** *Sport.* to award a free stroke, point, or penalty against (a player or team). **4** to declare (an act) legally punishable.
▸ **,penali'zation** *or* **,penali'sation** *n*

penalty ('penᵊltɪ) *n, pl* **penalties. 1** a legal or official punishment, such as a term of imprisonment. **2** some other form of punishment, such as a fine or forfeit for not fulfilling a contract. **3** loss, suffering, or other misfortune occurring as a result of one's own action, error, etc. **4** *Sport, games, etc.* a handicap awarded against a player or team for illegal play, such as a free shot at goal by the opposing team. ORIG C16: from Med. L *poenālitās* penalty; see PENAL

penalty area *n* another name for **penalty box** (sense 1).

penalty box *n* **1** *Soccer.* a rectangular area in front of the goal, within which a penalty is awarded for a serious foul by the defending team. **2** *Ice hockey.* a bench for players serving time penalties.

penalty corner *n Hockey.* a free hit from the goal line taken by the attacking side. Also called: **short corner.**

penalty rates *pl n Austral. & NZ.* rates of pay for employees working outside normal hours.

penalty shoot-out *n* **1** *Soccer.* a method of deciding the winner of a drawn match, in which players from each team attempt to score with a penalty kick. **2** a similar method of resolving a tie in hockey, ice hockey, polo, etc.

penance ('penəns) *n* **1** voluntary self-punishment to atone for a sin, crime, etc. **2** a feeling of regret for one's wrongdoings. **3** *Christianity.* a punishment usually consisting of prayer, fasting, etc., imposed by church authority as a condition of absolution. **4** *RC Church.* a sacrament in which repentant sinners are absolved on condition of confession of their sins to a priest and of performing a penance. ◆ *vb* **penances, penancing, penanced. 5** (*tr*) (of ecclesiastical authorities) to impose a penance upon (a sinner). ORIG C13: via OF from L *paenitentia* repentance

Penang ★ (pɪ'næŋ) *n* **1** a state of Peninsular Malaysia: consists of the island of Penang and the province Wellesley on the mainland, which first united administratively in 1798 as a British colony. Capital: George Town. Pop.: 1 141 500 (1993 est.). Area: 1031 sq. km (398 sq. miles). Also called: **Pulau Pinang. 2** a forested island off the NW coast of Malaya, in the Strait of Malacca. Area: 293 sq. km (113 sq. miles). Former name (until about 1867): **Prince of Wales Island. 3** another name for **George Town.**

penates (pə'nɑ:ti:z) *pl n* See **lares and penates.**

pence (pens) *n* a plural of **penny.**

> **USAGE NOTE** Since the decimalization of British currency and the introduction of the abbreviation *p,* as in *10p, 85p,* etc., the abbreviation has tended to replace *pence* in speech. To talk about only one unit *a penny* is still more common than *a p,* and the use of *a pence* should be avoided.

penchant ('pɒŋʃɒn) *n* strong inclination or liking; bent or taste. ORIG C17: from F, from *pencher* to incline, from L *pendēre* to be suspended

Penchi ★ ('pen'tʃi:) *n* a variant transliteration of the Chinese name for **Benxi.**

pencil ('pensᵊl) *n* **1** a thin cylindrical instrument used for writing, drawing, etc., consisting of a rod of graphite or other marking substance usually encased in wood and sharpened. **2** something similar in shape or function: *a styptic pencil.* **3** a narrow set of lines or rays, such as light rays, diverging from or converging to a point. **4** *Rare.* an artist's individual style. **5** a type of artist's brush. ◆ *vb* **pencils, pencilling, pencilled** *or US* **pencils, penciling, penciled.** (*tr*) **6** to draw, colour, or write with a pencil. **7** to mark with a pencil. ORIG C14: from OF *pincel,* from L *pēnicillus* painter's brush, from *pēniculus* a little tail
▸ **'penciller** *or US* **'penciler** *n*

pend (pend) *vb* (*intr*) to await judgment or settlement. ORIG C15: from L *pendēre* to hang

pendant ('pɛndənt) *n* **1a** an ornament that hangs from a piece of jewellery. **1b** a necklace with such an ornament. **2** a hanging light, esp. a chandelier. **3** a carved ornament that is suspended from a ceiling or roof. ◆ *adj* **4** a variant spelling of **pendent**. ORIG C14: from OF, from *pendre* to hang, from L *pendēre* to hang down

pendent ('pɛndənt) *adj* **1** dangling. **2** jutting. **3** (of a grammatical construction) incomplete. **4** a less common word for **pending**. ◆ *n* **5** a variant spelling of **pendant**. ORIG C15: from OF *pendant,* from *pendre* to hang; see PENDANT
▸ **'pendency** *n*

pendentive (pɛn'dɛntɪv) *n* any of four triangular sections of vaulting with concave sides, positioned at a corner of a rectangular space to support a dome. ORIG C18: from F *pendentif,* from L *pendens* hanging, from *pendere* to hang

Penderecki ★ (*Polish* pɛndɛ'rɛtski) *n* **Krzystof** ('kʃiʃtɔf). born 1933, Polish composer. His works include *Threnody for the Victims of Hiroshima* for strings (1960), *Polish Requiem* (1983–84), and the opera *Ubu Rex* (1991).

pending ('pɛndɪŋ) *prep* **1** while waiting for. ◆ *adj* (*postpositive*) **2** not yet decided, confirmed, or finished. **3** imminent: *these developments have been pending for some time.*

pendragon (pɛn'drægən) *n* a supreme war chief or leader of the ancient Britons. ORIG Welsh, lit.: head dragon

pendulous ('pɛndjʊləs) *adj* hanging downwards, esp. so as to swing from side to side. ORIG C17: from L *pendulus,* from *pendēre* to hang down
▸ **'pendulously** *adv* ▸ **'pendulousness** *n*

pendulum ('pɛndjʊləm) *n* **1** a body mounted so that it can swing freely under the influence of gravity. **2** such a device used to regulate a clock mechanism. **3** something that changes fairly regularly: *the pendulum of public opinion.* ORIG C17: from L *pendulus* PENDULOUS

Penelope ★ (pə'nɛləpɪ) *n Greek myth.* the wife of Odysseus, who remained true to him during his long absence despite the importunities of many suitors.

peneplain *or* **peneplane** ('pi:nɪˌpleɪn) *n* a relatively flat land surface produced by erosion. ORIG C19: from L *paene* almost + PLAIN[1]

penetrant ('pɛnɪtrənt) *adj* **1** sharp; penetrating. ◆ *n* **2** *Chem.* a substance that lowers the surface tension of a liquid and thus causes it to penetrate or be absorbed more easily. **3** a person or thing that penetrates.

penetrate ('pɛnɪˌtreɪt) *vb* **penetrates, penetrating, penetrated. 1** to find or force a way into or through (something); pierce; enter. **2** to diffuse through (a substance, etc.); permeate. **3** (*tr*) to see through: *their eyes could not penetrate the fog.* **4** (*tr*) (of a man) to insert the penis into the vagina of (a woman). **5** (*tr*) to grasp the meaning of (a principle, etc.). **6** (*intr*) to be understood: *his face lit up as the new idea penetrated.* ORIG C16: from L *penetrāre*
▸ **'penetrable** *adj* ▸ **ˌpenetra'bility** *n* ▸ **'peneˌtrator** *n*

penetrating ('pɛnɪˌtreɪtɪŋ) *adj* tending to or able to penetrate: *a penetrating mind; a penetrating voice.*
▸ **'peneˌtratingly** *adv*

penetration (ˌpɛnɪ'treɪʃən) *n* **1** the act or an instance of penetrating. **2** the ability or power to penetrate. **3** keen insight or perception. **4** *Mil.* an offensive manoeuvre that breaks through an enemy's defensive position. **5** Also called: **market penetration.** the proportion of the total number of potential purchasers of a product or service who either are aware of its existence or actually buy it.

Peneus ★ (pɪ'ni:əs) *n* the ancient name for the **Salambria.**

pen friend *n* a person with whom one exchanges letters, often a person in another country whom one has not met. Also called: **pen pal.**

Penghu *or* **P'eng-hu** ★ ('pɛŋ'hu:) *n* transliteration of the Chinese name for the **Pescadores.**

Pengpu ★ ('pɛŋ'pu:) *n* a variant transliteration of the Chinese name for **Bengbu.**

penguin ('pɛŋgwɪn) *n* a flightless marine bird of cool southern, esp. Antarctic, regions: they have wings modified as flippers, webbed feet, and feathers lacking barbs. ORIG C16: ?from Welsh *pen gwyn,* from *pen* head + *gwyn* white

penicillin (ˌpɛnɪ'sɪlɪn) *n* any of a group of antibiotics with powerful action against bacteria: originally obtained from the fungus *Penicillium.* ORIG C20: from PENICILLIUM

penicillium (ˌpɛnɪ'sɪlɪəm) *n, pl* **penicilliums** *or* **penicillia** (-'sɪlɪə). any saprophytic fungus of the genus *Penicillium,* which commonly grow as a green or blue mould on stale food. ORIG C19: NL, from L *pēnicillus* tuft of hairs; from the appearance of the sporangia of this fungus

penillion *or* **pennillion** (pɪ'nɪlɪən) *pl n, sing* **penill** (pɪ'nɪl). the Welsh art or practice of singing poetry in counterpoint to a traditional melody played on the harp. ORIG from Welsh: verses

peninsula (pɪ'nɪnsjʊlə) *n* a narrow strip of land projecting into a sea or lake from the mainland. ORIG C16: from L, lit.: almost an island, from *paene* almost + *insula* island
▸ **pen'insular** *adj*

> **USAGE NOTE** The noun *peninsula* is sometimes confused with the adjective *peninsular: the Iberian peninsula* (not *peninsular*).

Peninsula ★ (pɪ'nɪnsjʊlə) *n* **the.** short for the **Iberian Peninsula.**

penis ('pi:nɪs) *n, pl* **penises** *or* **penes** (-ni:z). the male organ of copulation in higher vertebrates, also used for urine excretion in many mammals. ORIG C17: from L: penis
▸ **penile** ('pi:naɪl) *adj*

penitent ('pɛnɪtənt) *adj* **1** feeling regret for one's sins; repentant. ◆ *n* **2** a person who is penitent. **3** *Christianity.* **3a** a person who repents his or her sins and seeks forgiveness for them. **3b** *RC Church.* a person who confesses his or her sins and submits to a penance. ORIG C14: from Church L *paenitēns* regretting, from *paenitēre* to repent, from ?
▸ **'penitence** *n* ▸ **'penitently** *adv*

penitential (ˌpɛnɪ'tɛnʃəl) *adj* **1** of, showing, or constituting penance. ◆ *n* **2** *Chiefly RC Church.* a book or compilation of instructions for confessors. **3** a less common word for **penitent** (senses 2, 3).
▸ **ˌpeni'tentially** *adv*

penitentiary (ˌpɛnɪ'tɛnʃərɪ) *n, pl* **penitentiaries. 1** (in the US and Canada) a state or federal prison. Also (US and Canad. inf.): **pen. 2** *RC Church.* **2a** a cardinal who presides over a tribunal that decides all matters affecting the sacrament of penance. **2b** this tribunal itself. ◆ *adj* **3** another word for **penitential** (sense 1). **4** *US & Canad.* (of an offence) punishable by imprisonment in a penitentiary. ORIG C15 (meaning also: an officer dealing with penances): from Med. L *poenitēntiārius,* from L *paenitēns* PENITENT

Penki ★ ('pɛn'tʃi:) *n* a variant transliteration of the Chinese name for **Benxi.**

penknife ('pɛnˌnaɪf) *n, pl* **penknives.** a small knife with one or more blades that fold into the handle; pocketknife.

penman ('pɛnmən) *n, pl* **penmen. 1** a person skilled in handwriting. **2** a person who writes by hand in a specified way: *a bad penman.* **3** an author. **4** *Rare.* a scribe.

penmanship ('pɛnmənʃɪp) *n* style or technique of writing by hand.

Penn ★ (pɛn) *n* **William.** 1644–1718, English Quaker and founder of Pennsylvania.

Penn. *abbrev. for* Pennsylvania.

penna ('pɛnə) *n, pl* **pennae** (-ni:). *Ornithol.* any large feather that has a vane and forms part of the main plumage of a bird. ORIG L: feather

pen name *n* an author's pseudonym. Also called: **nom de plume.**

pennant ('pɛnənt) *n* **1** a type of pennon, esp. one flown from vessels as identification or for signalling. **2** *Chiefly US, Canad., & Austral.* **2a** a flag serving as an emblem of championship in certain sports. **2b** (*as modifier*): *pennant cricket.* ORIG C17: prob. a blend of PENDANT & PENNON

pennate (ˈpɛneɪt) *adj Biol.* **1** having feathers, wings, or winglike structures. **2** another word for **pinnate.** ORIG C19: from L *pennātus,* from *penna* wing

Penney ★ (ˈpɛnɪ) *n* **William George,** Baron Penney of East Hendred. 1909–91, British mathematician. He worked on the first atomic bomb and became chairman of the UK Atomic Energy Authority (1964–67).

penni (ˈpɛnɪ) *n, pl* **penniä** (-nɪə) *or* **pennis.** a Finnish monetary unit worth one hundredth of a markka. ORIG Finnish, from Low G *pennig* PENNY

penniless (ˈpɛnɪlɪs) *adj* very poor; almost totally without money.
▸ ˈ**pennilessly** *adv* ▸ ˈ**pennilessness** *n*

Pennine Alps ★ (ˈpɛnaɪn) *pl n* a range of the Alps between Switzerland and Italy. Highest peak: Monte Rosa, 4634 m (15 204 ft).

Pennines ★ (ˈpɛnaɪnz) *pl n* a system of hills in England, extending from the Cheviot Hills in the north to the River Trent in the south: forms the watershed for the main rivers of N England. Highest peak: Cross Fell, 893 m (2930 ft). Also called: (the) **Pennine Chain.**

Pennine Way ★ *n* a long-distance footpath extending from Edale, Derbyshire, for 402 km (250 miles) to Kirk Yetholm, Scottish Borders.

pennon (ˈpɛnən) *n* **1** a long flag, often tapering and divided at the end, originally a knight's personal flag. **2** a small tapering or triangular flag borne on a ship or boat. **3** a poetic word for **wing.** ORIG C14: via OF ult. from L *penna* feather

Pennsylvania ★ (ˌpɛnsɪlˈveɪnɪə) *n* a state of the northeastern US: almost wholly in the Appalachians, with the Allegheny Plateau to the west and a plain in the southeast; the second most important US state for manufacturing. Capital: Harrisburg. Pop.: 12 001 451 (1998 est.). Area: 116 462 sq. km (44 956 sq. miles). Abbrevs.: **Pa., Penn., Penna.,** or (with zip code) **PA**

Pennsylvania Dutch *n* **1** a dialect of German spoken in E Pennsylvania. **2** (preceded by *the; functioning as pl*) a group of German-speaking people in E Pennsylvania, descended from 18th-century settlers from SW Germany and Switzerland.

Pennsylvanian (ˌpɛnsɪlˈveɪnɪən) *adj* **1** of the state of Pennsylvania. **2** (in North America) of, denoting, or formed in the upper of two divisions of the Carboniferous period. ◆ *n* **3** an inhabitant or native of the state of Pennsylvania. **4** (preceded by *the*) the Pennsylvanian period or rock system.

penny (ˈpɛnɪ) *n, pl* **pennies** *or* **pence** (pɛns). **1** Also called: **new penny.** *Brit.* a bronze coin having a value equal to one hundredth of a pound. Abbrev.: **p. 2** *Brit.* (before 1971) a bronze or copper coin having a value equal to one twelfth of a shilling. Abbrev.: **d. 3** a monetary unit of the Republic of Ireland worth one hundredth of a pound. **4** (*pl* **pennies**) *US & Canad.* a cent. **5** a coin of similar value, as used in several other countries. **6** (*used with a negative*) *Inf., chiefly Brit.* the least amount of money: *I don't have a penny.* **7 a pretty penny.** *Inf.* a considerable sum of money. **8 spend a penny.** *Brit. inf.* to urinate. **9 the penny dropped.** *Inf., chiefly Brit.* the explanation of something was finally realized. ORIG OE *penig, pening*

> **USAGE NOTE** See at **pence.**

penny arcade *n Chiefly US.* a public place with various coin-operated machines for entertainment.

Penny Black *n* the first adhesive postage stamp, issued in Britain in 1840.

penny-dreadful *n, pl* **penny-dreadfuls.** *Brit. inf.* a cheap, often lurid book or magazine.

penny-farthing *n Brit.* an early type of bicycle with a large front wheel and a small rear wheel, the pedals being on the front wheel.

penny-pinching *adj* **1** excessively careful with money; miserly. ◆ *n* **2** miserliness.
▸ ˈ**penny-**ˌ**pincher** *n*

pennyroyal (ˌpɛnɪˈrɔɪəl) *n* **1** a Eurasian plant with hairy leaves and small mauve flowers, yielding an aromatic oil used in medicine. **2** a similar and related plant of E North America. ORIG C16: var. of Anglo-Norman *puliol real,* from OF *pouliol* (from L *pūleium* pennyroyal) + *real* ROYAL

penny shares *pl n Stock Exchange.* securities with a low market price, esp. less than 20p, enabling small investors to purchase a large number for a relatively small outlay.

pennyweight (ˈpɛnɪˌweɪt) *n* a unit of weight equal to 24 grains or one twentieth of an ounce (Troy).

penny whistle *n* a type of flageolet with six finger holes, esp. a cheap metal one. Also called: **tin whistle.**

penny-wise *adj* **1** greatly concerned with saving small sums of money. **2 penny-wise and pound-foolish.** careful about trifles but wasteful in large ventures.

pennywort (ˈpɛnɪˌwɜːt) *n* **1** a Eurasian rock plant with whitish-green tubular flowers and rounded leaves. **2** a marsh plant of Europe and North Africa, having circular leaves and greenish-pink flowers. **3** any of various other plants with rounded penny-like leaves.

pennyworth (ˈpɛnɪˌwɜːθ) *n* **1** the amount that can be bought for a penny. **2** a small amount: *he hasn't got a pennyworth of sense.*

penology (piːˈnɒlədʒɪ) *n* **1** the branch of the social sciences concerned with the punishment of crime. **2** the science of prison management. ORIG C19: from Gk *poinē* punishment
▸ **penological** (ˌpiːnəˈlɒdʒɪk^{ə}l) *adj* ▸ **pe**ˈ**nologist** *n*

pen pal *n* another name for **pen friend.**

penpusher (ˈpɛnˌpʊʃə) *n* a person who writes a lot, esp. a clerk involved with boring paperwork.
▸ ˈ**pen**ˌ**pushing** *adj, n*

Penrith ★ (pɛnˈrɪθ) *n* a market town in NW England, in Cumbria. Pop.: 12 049 (1991).

Penrose ★ (ˈpɛnˌrəʊz) *n* Sir **Roger.** born 1931, British mathematician and theoretical physicist, noted for his investigation of black holes.

pension[1] (ˈpɛnʃən) *n* **1** a regular payment made by the state to people over a certain age to enable them to subsist without having to work. **2** a regular payment made by an employer to former employees after they retire. **3** any regular payment made by way of patronage, or in recognition of merit, service, etc.: *a pension paid to a disabled soldier.* ◆ *vb* **4** (*tr*) to grant a pension to. ORIG C14: via OF from L *pēnsiō* a payment, from *pendere* to pay
▸ ˈ**pensionable** *adj* ▸ ˈ**pensionary** *adj* ▸ ˈ**pensioner** *n*

pension[2] *French.* (pɑ̃sjɔ̃) *n* (in France and some other countries) a relatively cheap boarding house. ORIG C17: from F; extended meaning of *pension* grant; see PENSION[1]

pensioneer trustee (ˌpɛnʃəˈnɪə) *n* (in Britain) a person authorized by the Inland Revenue to oversee the management of a pension fund.

pension off *vb* (*tr, adv*) **1** to cause to retire from a job and pay a pension to. **2** to discard, because of age: *to pension off submarines.*

pensive (ˈpɛnsɪv) *adj* **1** deeply or seriously thoughtful, often with a tinge of sadness. **2** expressing or suggesting pensiveness. ORIG C14: from OF *pensif,* from *penser* to think, from L *pensāre* to consider
▸ ˈ**pensively** *adv* ▸ ˈ**pensiveness** *n*

penstemon (pɛnˈstiːmən) *n* a variant (esp. US) of **pentstemon.**

penstock (ˈpɛnˌstɒk) *n* **1** a conduit that supplies water to a hydroelectric power plant. **2** a channel bringing water from the head gates to a water wheel. **3** a sluice for controlling water flow. ORIG C17: from PEN[2] + STOCK

pent (pɛnt) *vb* a past tense and past participle of **pen**[2] (sense 4).

penta- *or before a vowel* **pent-** *combining form.* five: *pentagon; pentode.* ORIG from Gk *pente*

pentacle (ˈpɛntək^{ə}l) *n* another name for **pentagram.** ORIG C16: from It. *pentacolo* something having five corners

pentad (ˈpɛntæd) *n* **1** a group or series of five. **2** the number or sum of five. **3** a period of five years. **4** *Chem.* a pentavalent element, atom, or radical. **5** *Meteorol.* a period of five days. ORIG C17: from Gk *pentas* group of five

pentadactyl (ˌpɛntəˈdæktɪl) *adj* (of the limbs of amphibians, reptiles, birds, and mammals) having a hand or foot bearing five digits.

pentagon (ˈpɛntəˌgɒn) *n* a polygon having five sides.
▸ **pentagonal** (pɛnˈtægənᵊl) *adj*

Pentagon ★ (ˈpɛntəˌgɒn) *n* **1** the five-sided building in Arlington, Virginia, that houses the headquarters of the US Department of Defense. **2** the military leadership of the US.

pentagram (ˈpɛntəˌgræm) *n* **1** a star-shaped figure with five points. **2** such a figure used by the Pythagoreans, black magicians, etc. ◆ Also called: **pentacle, pentangle.**

pentahedron (ˌpɛntəˈhiːdrən) *n, pl* **pentahedrons** *or* **pentahedra** (-drə). a solid figure having five plane faces.
▸ ˌ**pentaˈhedral** *adj*

pentamerous (pɛnˈtæmərəs) *adj* consisting of five parts, esp. (of flowers) having the petals, sepals, and other parts arranged in groups of five.

pentameter (pɛnˈtæmɪtə) *n* **1** a verse line consisting of five metrical feet. **2** (in classical prosody) a verse line consisting of two dactyls, one stressed syllable, two dactyls, and a final stressed syllable. ◆ *adj* **3** designating a verse line consisting of five metrical feet.

pentamidine (pɛnˈtæmɪˌdiːn, -dɪn) *n* a drug used to treat protozoal infections, esp. pneumonia caused by *Pneumocystis carinii* in AIDS patients.

pentane (ˈpɛnteɪn) *n* an alkane hydrocarbon having three isomers, esp. the isomer with a straight chain of carbon atoms (*n*-pentane) which is a colourless flammable liquid used as a solvent.

pentangle (ˈpɛnˌtæŋgᵊl) *n* another name for **pentagram.**

pentanoic acid (ˌpɛntəˈnəʊɪk) *n* a colourless liquid carboxylic acid used in making perfumes, flavourings, and pharmaceuticals. Formula: $CH_3(CH_2)_3COOH$. Former name: **valeric acid.**

Pentateuch (ˈpɛntəˌtjuːk) *n* the first five books of the Old Testament. ORIG C16: from Church L *pentateuchus,* from Gk PENTA- + *teukhos* tool (in LGk: scroll)
▸ ˌ**Pentaˈteuchal** *adj*

pentathlon (pɛnˈtæθlən) *n* an athletic contest consisting of five different events. ORIG C18: from Gk *pentathlon,* from PENTA- + *athlon* contest

pentatomic (ˌpɛntəˈtɒmɪk) *adj Chem.* having five atoms in the molecule.

pentatonic scale (ˌpɛntəˈtɒnɪk) *n Music.* any of several scales consisting of five notes.

pentavalent (ˌpɛntəˈveɪlənt) *adj Chem.* having a valency of five. Also: **quinquevalent.**

pentazocine (pɛnˈtæzəʊˌsiːn) *n* a powerful synthetic opiate used in medical practice as an analgesic.

Pentecost (ˈpɛntɪˌkɒst) *n* **1** a Christian festival occurring on Whit Sunday commemorating the descent of the Holy Ghost on the apostles. **2** *Judaism.* the harvest festival, celebrated on the fiftieth day after the second day of Passover. Hebrew name: **Shavuot.** ORIG OE, from Church L, from Gk *pentēkostē* fiftieth

Pentecostal (ˌpɛntɪˈkɒstᵊl) *adj* **1** (*usually prenominal*) of or relating to any of various Christian groups that emphasize the charismatic aspects of Christianity and adopt a fundamental attitude to the Bible. **2** of or relating to Pentecost or the influence of the Holy Spirit. ◆ *n* **3** a member of a Pentecostal Church.
▸ ˌ**Penteˈcostalist** *n, adj*

Pentelikon ★ (pɛnˈtɛlɪkɒn) *n* a mountain in SE Greece, near Athens: famous for its white marble, worked regularly from the 6th century B.C., from which the chief buildings and sculptures in Athens are made. Height: 1109 m (3638 ft). Latin name: **Penˈtelicus.**

Penthesileia *or* **Penthesilea** ★ (ˌpɛnθəsɪˈleɪə) *n Greek myth.* the daughter of Ares and queen of the Amazons, whom she led to the aid of Troy. She was slain by Achilles.

Pentheus ★ (ˈpɛnθɪəs) *n Greek myth.* the grandson of Cadmus and his successor as king of Thebes, who resisted the introduction of the cult of Dionysus. In revenge the god drove him mad and he was torn to pieces by a group of bacchantes, one of whom was his mother.

penthouse (ˈpɛntˌhaʊs) *n* **1** a flat or maisonette built onto the top floor or roof of a block of flats. **2** a construction on the roof of a building, esp. one used to house machinery, etc. **3** a shed built against a building, esp. one that has a sloping roof. ORIG C14 *pentis* (later *penthouse*), from OF *apentis,* from LL *appendicium* appendage, from L *appendere* to hang from; see APPEND

Pentland Firth ★ (ˈpɛntlənd) *n* a channel between the mainland of N Scotland and the Orkney Islands: notorious for rough seas. Length: 32 km (20 miles). Width: up to 13 km (8 miles).

pentobarbitone sodium (ˌpɛntəˈbɑːbɪˌtəʊn) *n* a barbiturate drug used in medicine as a sedative and hypnotic.

pentode (ˈpɛntəʊd) *n* **1** an electronic valve having five electrodes: a cathode, anode, and three grids. **2** (*modifier*) (of a transistor) having three terminals at the base or gate. ORIG C20: from PENTA- + Gk *hodos* way

Pentothal sodium (ˈpɛntəˌθæl) *n* a trademark for **thiopentone sodium.**

pentstemon (pɛntˈstiːmən) *or esp. US* **penstemon** *n* any plant of a North American genus having white, pink, red, blue, or purple flowers with five stamens, one of which is sterile. ORIG C18: NL, from PENTA- + Gk *stēmōn* thread (here: stamen)

pent-up *adj* not released; repressed: *pent-up emotions.*

pentyl acetate (ˈpɛntaɪl, -tɪl) *n* a colourless combustible liquid used as a solvent for paints, in the extraction of penicillin, in photographic film, and as a flavouring. Formula: $C_2H_5OOCCH_3$. Also called: **amyl acetate.**

penult (ˈpɛnʌlt, pɪˈnʌlt) *n* the last syllable but one in a word. ORIG C16: L *paenultima syllaba,* from *paene ultima* almost the last

penultimate (pɪˈnʌltɪmɪt) *adj* **1** next to the last. ◆ *n* **2** anything next to last, esp. a penult.

penumbra (pɪˈnʌmbrə) *n, pl* **penumbrae** (-briː) *or* **penumbras. 1** a fringe region of half shadow resulting from the partial obstruction of light by an opaque object. **2** *Astron.* the lighter and outer region of a sunspot. **3** *Painting.* the area in which light and shade blend. ORIG C17: via NL from L *paene* almost + *umbra* shadow
▸ **peˈnumbral** *adj*

penurious (pɪˈnjʊərɪəs) *adj* **1** niggardly with money. **2** lacking money or means. **3** scanty.
▸ **peˈnuriously** *adv* ▸ **peˈnuriousness** *n*

penury (ˈpɛnjʊrɪ) *n* **1** extreme poverty. **2** extreme scarcity. ORIG C15: from L *pēnūria* dearth, from ?

Penza ★ (*Russian* ˈpjɛnzə) *n* a city in W Russia: manufacturing centre. Pop.: 534 000 (1995 est.).

Penzance ★ (pɛnˈzæns) *n* a town in SW England, in SW Cornwall: the westernmost town in England; resort and fishing port. Pop.: 19 709 (1991).

Penzias ★ (ˈpɛntsɪəs, ˈpɛnz-) *n* **Arno Allan.** born 1933, US astrophysicist, who shared the Nobel prize for physics (1978) with Robert W. Wilson for their discovery of cosmic microwave background radiation.

peon[1] (ˈpiːən, ˈpiːɒn) *n* **1** a Spanish-American farm labourer or unskilled worker. **2** (formerly, in Spanish America) a debtor compelled to work off his or her debts. **3** any very poor person. ORIG C19: from Sp. *peón* peasant, from Med. L *pedō* man who goes on foot, from L *pēs* foot
▸ ˈ**peonage** *n*

peon[2] (pjuːn, ˈpiːən, ˈpiːɒn) *n* (in India, Sri Lanka, etc., esp. formerly) **1** a messenger or attendant, esp. in an office. **2** a native policeman. **3** a foot soldier. ORIG C17: from Port. *peão* orderly; see PEON[1]

peony *or* **paeony** (ˈpiːənɪ) *n, pl* **peonies** *or* **paeonies. 1** any of a genus of shrubs and plants of Eurasia and North America, having large pink, red, white, or yellow flowers. **2** the flower of any of these plants. ORIG OE *peonie,* from L *paeōnia,* from Gk *paiōnia;* rel. to *paiōnios* healing, from *paiōn* physician

people (ˈpiːpᵊl) *n* (*usually functioning as pl*) **1** persons collectively or in general. **2** a group of persons considered together: *blind people.* **3** (*pl* **peoples**) the persons living in a country and sharing the same nationality: *the French peo-*

ple. **4** one's family: *he took her home to meet his people.* **5** persons loyal to someone powerful: *the king's people accompanied him in exile.* **6 the people. 6a** the mass of persons without special distinction, privileges, etc. **6b** the body of persons in a country, etc., esp. those entitled to vote. ◆ *vb* **peoples, peopling, peopled. 7** *(tr)* to provide with or as if with people or inhabitants. ORIG C13: from OF *pople,* from L *populus*

people carrier *n* another name for **multipurpose vehicle.**

people mover *n* **1** any of various automated forms of transport for large numbers of passengers over short distances, such as a moving pavement, driverless cars, etc. **2** another name for **multipurpose vehicle.**

people's democracy *n* (in Communist ideology) a country or government in transition from bourgeois democracy to socialism.

people's front *n* a less common term for **popular front.**

Peoria ★ (piː'ɔːrɪə) *n* a port in N central Illinois, on the Illinois River. Pop.: 112 306 (1996 est.).

pep (pɛp) *n* **1** high spirits, energy, or vitality. ◆ *vb* **peps, pepping, pepped. 2** *(tr; usually foll. by up)* to liven by imbuing with new vigour. ORIG C20: short for PEPPER

PEP (pɛp) *n* **1** *acronym for* personal equity plan: a method of saving in the UK with certain tax advantages, in which investments up to a fixed annual value could be purchased; replaced by ISAs in 1999. ◆ **2** *abbrev. for* political and economic planning.

peperomia (ˌpɛpər'əʊmɪə) *n* any of a genus of tropical plants cultivated for their ornamental foliage. ORIG C19: NL from Gk *peperi* pepper + *omoros* similar

Pepin the Short ★ ('pɛpɪn) *n* died 768 A.D., king of the Franks (751–768); son of Charles Martel and father of Charlemagne. He deposed the Merovingian king (751) and founded the Carolingian dynasty.

peplum ('pɛpləm) *n, pl* **peplums** *or* **pepla** (-lə). a flared ruffle attached to the waist of a jacket, bodice, etc. ORIG C17: from L: full upper garment, from Gk *peplos* shawl

pepo ('piːpəʊ) *n, pl* **pepos.** the fruit of any of various plants, such as the melon, cucumber, and pumpkin, having a firm rind, fleshy watery pulp, and numerous seeds. ORIG C19: from L: pumpkin, from Gk *pepōn* edible gourd, from *peptein* to ripen

pepper ('pɛpə) *n* **1** a woody climbing plant, *Piper nigrum,* of the East Indies, having small black berry-like fruits. **2** the dried fruit of this plant, which is ground to produce a sharp hot condiment. See also **black pepper, white pepper. 3** any of various other plants of the genus *Piper.* **4** Also called: **capsicum.** any of various tropical plants, the fruits of which are used as a vegetable and a condiment. See also **sweet pepper, red pepper, cayenne pepper. 5** the fruit of any of these capsicums, which has a mild or pungent taste. **6** the condiment made from the fruits of any of these plants. ◆ *vb (tr)* **7** to season with pepper. **8** to sprinkle liberally; dot: *his prose was peppered with alliteration.* **9** to pelt with small missiles. ORIG OE *piper,* from L, from Gk *peperi*

pepper-and-salt *adj* **1** (of cloth, etc.) marked with a fine mixture of black and white. **2** (of hair) streaked with grey.

peppercorn ('pɛpəˌkɔːn) *n* **1** the small dried berry of the pepper plant. **2** something trifling.

peppercorn rent *n* a rent that is very low or nominal.

pepper mill *n* a small hand mill used to grind peppercorns.

peppermint ('pɛpəˌmɪnt) *n* **1** a temperate mint plant with purple or white flowers and downy leaves, which yield a pungent oil. **2** the oil from this plant, which is used as a flavouring. **3** a sweet flavoured with peppermint.

pepperoni (ˌpɛpə'rəʊnɪ) *n* a highly seasoned dry sausage of pork and beef spiced with pepper, used esp. on pizza. ORIG C20: from It. *peperoni,* pl of *peperone* cayenne pepper

pepper pot *n* **1** a small container with perforations in the top for sprinkling pepper. **2** a West Indian stew of meat, etc., highly seasoned with an extract of bitter cassava.

pepper tree *n* any of several evergreen trees of a chiefly South American genus having yellowish-white flowers and bright red ornamental fruits.

peppery ('pɛpərɪ) *adj* **1** flavoured with or tasting of pepper. **2** quick-tempered; irritable. **3** full of bite and sharpness: *a peppery speech.*
▸ **'pepperiness** *n*

pep pill *n Inf.* a tablet containing a stimulant drug.

peppy ('pɛpɪ) *adj* **peppier, peppiest.** *Inf.* full of vitality; bouncy or energetic.
▸ **'peppily** *adv* ▸ **'peppiness** *n*

pepsin ('pɛpsɪn) *n* an enzyme produced in the stomach, which, when activated by acid, splits proteins into peptones. ORIG C19: via G from Gk *pepsis,* from *peptein* to digest

pep talk *n Inf.* an enthusiastic talk designed to increase confidence, production, cooperation, etc.

peptic ('pɛptɪk) *adj* **1** of, relating to, or promoting digestion. **2** of, relating to, or caused by pepsin or the action of the digestive juices. ORIG C17: from Gk *peptikos* capable of digesting, from *peptein* to digest

peptic ulcer *n Pathol.* an ulcer of the mucous membrane lining those parts of the alimentary tract exposed to digestive juices. It can occur in the oesophagus, the stomach, the duodenum, the jejunum, or in the ileum.

peptide ('pɛptaɪd) *n* any of a group of compounds consisting of two or more amino acids linked by chemical bonding between their respective carboxyl and amino groups.

peptide bond *n Biochem.* a chemical amide linkage, -NH-CO-, formed by the condensation of the amino group of one amino acid with the carboxyl group of another.

peptone ('pɛptəʊn) *n Biochem.* any of a group of compounds that form an intermediary group in the digestion of proteins to amino acids. ORIG C19: from G *Pepton,* from Gk *pepton* something digested, from *peptein* to digest
▸ **peptonic** (pɛp'tɒnɪk) *adj*

Pepys ★ (piːps) *n* **Samuel.** 1633–1703, English diarist and naval administrator. His diary, which covers the period 1660–69, is a vivid account of London life through such disasters as the Great Plague and the Fire of London.

per (pɜː; *unstressed* pə) *determiner* **1** for every: *three pence per pound.* ◆ *prep* **2** (esp. in some Latin phrases) by; through. **3 as per.** according to: *as per specifications.* **4 as per usual.** *Inf.* as usual. ORIG C15: from L: by, for each

per. *abbrev. for:* **1** period. **2** person.

per- *prefix* **1** through: *pervade.* **2** throughout: *perennial.* **3** away, beyond: *perfidy.* **4** *(intensifier): perfervid.* **5** indicating that a chemical compound contains a high proportion of a specified element: *peroxide.* **6** indicating that a chemical element is in a higher than usual state of oxidation: *permanganate.* ORIG from L *per* through

Pera ★ ('pɪərə) *n* the former name of **Beyoğlu.**

peracid (pɜː'ræsɪd) *n* an acid, such as perchloric acid ($HClO_4$), in which the element forming the acid radical exhibits its highest valency.

peradventure (pərəd'vɛntʃə, ˌpɜːr-) *Arch.* ◆ *adv* **1** by chance; perhaps. ◆ *n* **2** chance or doubt. ORIG C13: from OF *par aventure* by chance

Peraea *or* **Perea** ★ (pə'riːə) *n* a region of ancient Palestine, east of the River Jordan and the Dead Sea.

Perak ★ ('pɛərə, 'pɪərə, pɪ'ræk) *n* a state of NW Peninsular Malaysia, on the Strait of Malacca: tin mining. Capital: Ipoh. Pop.: 2 222 400 (1993 est.). Area: 20 680 sq. km (8030 sq. miles).

perambulate (pə'ræmbjʊˌleɪt) *vb* **perambulates, perambulating, perambulated. 1** to walk about (a place). **2** *(tr)* to walk round in order to inspect. ORIG C16: from L *perambulāre* to traverse, from *per-* through + *ambulāre* to walk
▸ **perˌambu'lation** *n* ▸ **perambulatory** (pə'ræmbjʊlətərɪ, -trɪ) *adj*

perambulator (pə'ræmbjʊˌleɪtə) *n* a formal word for **pram**[1].

per annum (pər 'ænəm) *adv* every year or by the year. ORIG L

P-E ratio *abbrev. for* price-earnings ratio.

percale (pəˈkeɪl, -ˈkɑːl) *n* a close-textured woven cotton fabric, used esp. for sheets. ORIG C17: via F from Persian *pargālah* piece of cloth

per capita (pə ˈkæpɪtə) *adj, adv* of or for each person. ORIG L, lit.: according to heads

perceive (pəˈsiːv) *vb* **perceives, perceiving, perceived. 1** to become aware of (something) through the senses; recognize or observe. **2** (*tr; may take a clause as object*) to come to comprehend; grasp. ORIG C13: from OF *perçoivre*, from L *percipere* to seize entirely
▸ **perˈceivable** *adj* ▸ **perˈceivably** *adv*

per cent (pə ˈsɛnt) *adv* **1** Also: **per centum.** in or for every hundred. Symbol: % ◆ *n also* **percent. 2** a percentage or proportion. **3** (*often pl*) securities yielding a rate of interest as specified: *he bought three percents.* ORIG C16: from Med. L *per centum* out of every hundred

percentage (pəˈsɛntɪdʒ) *n* **1** proportion or rate per hundred parts. **2** *Commerce.* the interest, tax, commission, or allowance on a hundred items. **3** any proportion in relation to the whole. **4** *Inf.* profit or advantage.

percentile (pəˈsɛntaɪl) *n* one of 99 actual or notional values of a variable dividing its distribution into 100 groups with equal frequencies. Also called: **centile.**

percept (ˈpɜːsɛpt) *n* **1** a concept that depends on recognition by the senses, such as sight, of some external object or phenomenon. **2** an object or phenomenon that is perceived. ORIG C19: from L *perceptum*, from *percipere* to PERCEIVE

perceptible (pəˈsɛptəbᵊl) *adj* able to be perceived; noticeable or recognizable.
▸ **perˌceptiˈbility** *n* ▸ **perˈceptibly** *adv*

perception (pəˈsɛpʃən) *n* **1** the act or the effect of perceiving. **2** insight or intuition gained by perceiving. **3** the ability or capacity to perceive. **4** way of perceiving; view. **5** the process by which an organism detects and interprets the external world by means of the sensory receptors. ORIG C15: from L *perceptiō* comprehension; see PERCEIVE
▸ **perˈceptional** *adj* ▸ **perceptual** (pəˈsɛptjʊəl) *adj*

perceptive (pəˈsɛptɪv) *adj* **1** quick at perceiving; observant. **2** perceptual. **3** able to perceive.
▸ **perˈceptively** *adv* ▸ **perˈceptiveness** *or* **ˌpercepˈtivity** *n*

Perceval ★ (ˈpɜːsɪvᵊl) *n* **Spencer.** 1762–1812, British statesman; prime minister (1809–12); assassinated.

perch[1] (pɜːtʃ) *n* **1** a pole, branch, or other resting place above ground on which a bird roosts. **2** a similar resting place for a person or thing. **3** another name for **rod** (sense 7). ◆ *vb* **4** (usually foll. by *on*) to alight, rest, or cause to rest on or as if on a perch: *the bird perched on the branch; the cap was perched on his head.* ORIG C13 *perche* stake, from OF, from L *pertica* long staff

perch[2] (pɜːtʃ) *n, pl* **perch** *or* **perches. 1** any of a family of freshwater spiny-finned teleost fishes of Europe and North America: valued as food and game fishes. **2** any of various similar or related fishes. ORIG C13: from OF *perche*, from L *perca*, from Gk *perkē*

perchance (pəˈtʃɑːns) *adv Arch. or poetic.* **1** perhaps; possibly. **2** by chance; accidentally. ORIG C14: from Anglo-F *par chance*

Percheron (ˈpɜːʃəˌrɒn) *n* a compact heavy breed of carthorse. ORIG C19: from F, from *le Perche*, region of NW France, where the breed originated

perchloric acid (pəˈklɔːrɪk) *n* a colourless syrupy oxyacid of chlorine containing a greater proportion of oxygen than chloric acid. It is a powerful oxidizing agent. Formula: $HClO_4$. Systematic name: **chloric(VII) acid.**

percipient (pəˈsɪpɪənt) *adj* **1** able to perceive. **2** perceptive. ◆ *n* **3** a person who perceives. ORIG C17: from L *percipiens* observing, from *percipere* to grasp
▸ **perˈcipience** *n* ▸ **perˈcipiently** *adv*

Percival *or* **Perceval** ★ (ˈpɜːsɪvᵊl) *n* (in Arthurian legend) a knight in King Arthur's court. German equivalent: **Parzival.**

percolate *vb* (ˈpɜːkəˌleɪt), **percolates, percolating, percolated. 1** to cause (a liquid) to pass through a fine mesh, porous substance, etc., or (of a liquid) to pass through a fine mesh, etc.; trickle: *rain percolated through the roof.* **2** to permeate; penetrate gradually: *water percolated the road.* **3** to make (coffee) or (of coffee) to be made in a percolator. ◆ *n* (ˈpɜːkəlɪt, -ˌleɪt). **4** a product of percolation. ORIG C17: from L *percolāre*, from PER- + *cōlāre* to strain, from *cōlum* a strainer; see COLANDER
▸ **percolable** (ˈpɜːkələbᵊl) *adj* ▸ **ˌpercoˈlation** *n*

percolator (ˈpɜːkəˌleɪtə) *n* a kind of coffeepot in which boiling water is forced up through a tube and filters down through the coffee grounds into a container.

per contra (ˈpɜː ˈkɒntrə) *adv* on the contrary. ORIG from L

percuss (pəˈkʌs) *vb* (*tr*) **1** to strike sharply or suddenly. **2** *Med.* to tap on (a body surface) with the fingertips or a special hammer to aid diagnosis. ORIG C16: from L *percutere*, from *per-* through + *quatere* to shake
▸ **perˈcussor** *n*

percussion (pəˈkʌʃən) *n* **1** the act, an instance, or an effect of percussing. **2** *Music.* the family of instruments in which sound arises from the striking of materials with sticks or hammers. **3** *Music.* instruments of this family constituting a section of an orchestra, etc. **4** *Med.* the act of percussing a body surface. **5** the act of exploding a percussion cap. ORIG C16: from L *percussiō*, from *percutere* to hit; see PERCUSS
▸ **perˈcussive** *adj* ▸ **perˈcussively** *adv* ▸ **perˈcussiveness** *n*

percussion cap *n* a detonator consisting of a paper or thin metal cap containing material that explodes when struck.

percussion instrument *n* any of various musical instruments that produce a sound when their resonating surfaces are struck directly, as with a stick or mallet, or by leverage action.

percussionist (pəˈkʌʃənɪst) *n Music.* a person who plays any of several percussion instruments.

percutaneous (ˌpɜːkjʊˈteɪnɪəs) *adj Med.* effected through the skin, as in the absorption of an ointment.

Percy ★ (ˈpɜːsɪ) *n* **1** Sir **Henry,** known as *Harry Hotspur.* 1364–1403, English rebel, who was killed leading an army against Henry IV. **2 Thomas.** 1729–1811, British bishop and antiquary. His *Reliques of Ancient English Poetry* (1765) stimulated the interest of Romantic writers in old English and Scottish ballads.

Perdido ★ (*Spanish* pɛrˈðiðo) *n* **Monte** (ˈmɔnte). a mountain in NE Spain, in the central Pyrenees. Height: 3352 m (10 997 ft). French name: (Mont) **Perdu.**

per diem (ˈpɜː ˈdaɪɛm, ˈdiːɛm) *adv* **1** every day or by the day. ◆ *n* **2** an allowance for daily expenses. ORIG from L

perdition (pəˈdɪʃən) *n* **1** *Christianity.* **1a** final and irrevocable spiritual ruin. **1b** this state as one that the wicked are said to be destined to endure forever. **2** another word for **hell. 3** *Arch.* utter ruin or destruction. ORIG C14: from LL *perditiō* ruin, from L *perdere* to lose, from PER- (away) + *dāre* to give

Perdu ★ (pɛrdy) *n* **Mont.** the French name for (Monte) **Perdido.**

perdurable (pəˈdjʊərəbᵊl) *adj Rare.* extremely durable. ORIG C13: from LL *perdūrābilis*, from L *per-* (intensive) + *dūrābilis* long-lasting, from *dūrus* hard

père *French.* (pɛr; *English* pɛə) *n* an addition to a French surname to specify the father rather than the son of the same name: *Dumas père.*

Perea ★ (pəˈriːə) *n* a variant spelling of **Peraea.**

Père David's deer *n* a large grey deer, surviving only in captivity. ORIG C20: after Father A. *David* (died 1900), F missionary

peregrinate (ˈpɛrɪgrɪˌneɪt) *vb* **peregrinates, peregrinating, peregrinated. 1** (*intr*) to travel or wander about from place to place; voyage. **2** (*tr*) to travel through (a place). ORIG C16: from L, from *peregrīnārī* to travel; see PEREGRINE
▸ **ˌperegriˈnation** *n* ▸ **ˈperegriˌnator** *n*

peregrine (ˈpɛrɪgrɪn) *adj Arch.* **1** coming from abroad. **2** travelling. ORIG C14: from L *peregrīnus* foreign, from *pereger* being abroad, from *per* through + *ager* land (that is, beyond one's own land)

peregrine falcon *n* a falcon occurring in most parts of the world, having a dark plumage on the back and wings and lighter underparts.

Pereira ★ (*Spanish* pe'reira) *n* a town in W central Colombia: cattle trading and coffee processing. Pop.: 434 267 (1997 est.).

Perelman ★ ('pɛrəlmən, 'pɜːl-) *n* **S(idney) J(oseph)**. 1904–79, US humorous writer. After scriptwriting for the Marx Brothers, he published many collections of articles, including *Crazy Like a Fox* (1944).

peremptory (pə'rɛmptərɪ) *adj* **1** urgent or commanding: *a peremptory ring on the bell.* **2** not able to be remitted or debated; decisive. **3** dogmatic. **4** *Law.* **4a** admitting of no denial or contradiction; precluding debate. **4b** obligatory rather than permissive. ORIG C16: from Anglo-Norman *peremptorie*, from L *peremptōrius* decisive, from *perimere* to take away completely
▸ **per'emptorily** *adv* ▸ **per'emptoriness** *n*

perennial (pə'rɛnɪəl) *adj* **1** lasting throughout the year or through many years. **2** everlasting; perpetual. ◆ *n* **3** a woody or herbaceous plant that continues its growth for at least three years. ORIG C17: from L *perennis* continual, from *per* through + *annus* year
▸ **per'ennially** *adv*

Peres ★ ('pɛrɛs) *n* **Shimon** (ʃiː'məʊn). born 1923, Israeli statesman, born in Poland: prime minister (1984–86; 1995–96); foreign minister (1986–88 and from 1992); shared Nobel peace prize 1994.

perestroika (ˌpɛrə'strɔɪkə) *n* the policy of reconstructing the economy, etc., of the former Soviet Union under the leadership of Mikhail Gorbachov. ORIG C20: Russian, lit.: reconstruction

Pérez de Cuéllar ★ ('pɛrɛs də 'kweɪjɑː) *n* **Javier** ('hævɪˌeɪ). born 1920, Peruvian diplomat; UN secretary-general (1982–91).

Pérez Galdós ★ ('pɛrɛs gɑːl'dəʊs) *n* **Benito**. 1843–1920, Spanish novelist. His works include the *Episodios nacionales* (1873–1912), a series of historical novels, and *Fortunata y Jacinta* (1886–87).

perfect *adj* ('pɜːfɪkt). **1** having all essential elements. **2** unblemished; faultless: *a perfect gemstone.* **3** correct or precise: *perfect timing.* **4** utter or absolute: *a perfect stranger.* **5** excellent in all respects: *a perfect day.* **6** *Maths.* exactly divisible into equal integral or polynomial roots: *36 is a perfect square.* **7** *Bot.* **7a** (of flowers) having functional stamens and pistils. **7b** (of plants) having all parts present. **8** *Grammar.* denoting a tense of verbs used in describing an action that has been completed. In English this is formed with *have* or *has* plus the past participle. **9** *Music.* **9a** of or relating to the intervals of the unison, fourth, fifth, and octave. **9b** (of a cadence) ending on the tonic chord, giving a feeling of conclusion. Also: **final.** ◆ *n* ('pɜːfɪkt). **10** *Grammar.* **10a** the perfect tense. **10b** a verb in this tense. ◆ *vb* (pə'fɛkt). (*tr*) **11** to make perfect; improve to one's satisfaction: *he is in Paris to perfect his French.* **12** to make fully accomplished. ORIG C13: from L *perfectus*, from *perficere* to perform, from *per-* through + *facere* to do

> **USAGE NOTE** For most of its meanings, the adjective *perfect* describes an absolute state, i.e. one that cannot be qualified; thus something is either *perfect* or *not perfect*, and cannot be *more perfect* or *less perfect*. However when *perfect* means 'excellent in all respects', *more* and *most* are quite acceptable: *the next day the weather was even more perfect.*

perfect gas *n* another name for **ideal gas.**

perfectible (pə'fɛktəbᵊl) *adj* capable of becoming or being made perfect.
▸ **perˌfecti'bility** *n*

perfection (pə'fɛkʃən) *n* **1** the act of perfecting or the state or quality of being perfect. **2** the highest degree of a quality, etc. **3** an embodiment of perfection. ORIG C13: from L *perfectiō* a completing, from *perficere* to finish

perfectionism (pə'fɛkʃəˌnɪzəm) *n* **1** *Philosophy.* the doctrine that man can attain perfection in this life. **2** the demand for the highest standard of excellence.
▸ **per'fectionist** *n, adj*

perfective (pə'fɛktɪv) *adj* **1** tending to perfect. **2** *Grammar.* denoting an aspect of verbs used to express that the action or event described by the verb is or was completed: *I lived in London for ten years* is perfective; *I have lived in London for ten years* is imperfective, since the implication is that I still live in London.

perfectly ('pɜːfɪktlɪ) *adv* **1** completely, utterly, or absolutely. **2** in a perfect way.

perfect number *n* an integer, such as 28, that is equal to the sum of all its possible factors, excluding itself.

perfect participle *n* another name for **past participle.**

perfect pitch *n* another name (not in technical usage) for **absolute pitch** (sense 1).

perfervid (pɜː'fɜːvɪd) *adj Literary.* extremely ardent or zealous. ORIG C19: from NL *perfervidus*

perfidious (pə'fɪdɪəs) *adj* guilty, treacherous, or faithless; deceitful. ORIG C18: from L, from *perfidus* faithless
▸ **per'fidiously** *adv* ▸ **per'fidiousness** *n* ▸ **'perfidy** *n*

perfoliate (pə'fəʊlɪɪt, -ˌeɪt) *adj* (of a leaf) having a base that completely encloses the stem, so that the stem appears to pass through it. ORIG C17: from NL *perfoliātus*, from L *per-* through + *folium* leaf
▸ **perˌfoli'ation** *n*

perforate *vb* ('pɜːfəˌreɪt), **perforates, perforating, perforated.** **1** to make a hole or holes in (something). **2** (*tr*) to punch rows of holes between (stamps, etc.) for ease of separation. ◆ *adj* ('pɜːfərɪt). **3** *Biol.* pierced by small holes: *perforate shells.* **4** *Philately.* another word for **perforated.** ORIG C16: from L *perforāre*, from *per-* through + *forāre* to pierce
▸ **'perforable** *adj* ▸ **'perfoˌrator** *n*

perforated ('pɜːfəˌreɪtɪd) *adj* **1** pierced with holes. **2** (esp. of stamps) having perforations.

perforation (ˌpɜːfə'reɪʃən) *n* **1** the act of perforating or the state of being perforated. **2** a hole or holes made in something. **3a** a method of making individual stamps, etc. easily separable by punching holes along their margins. **3b** the holes punched in this way. Abbrev.: **perf.**

perforce (pə'fɔːs) *adv* by necessity; unavoidably. ORIG C14: from OF *par force*

perform (pə'fɔːm) *vb* **1** to carry out (an action). **2** (*tr*) to fulfil: *to perform someone's request.* **3** to present or enact (a play, concert, etc.): *the group performed Hamlet.* ORIG C14: from Anglo-Norman *perfourmer* (infl. by *forme* FORM), from OF *parfournir*, from *par-* PER- + *fournir* to provide
▸ **per'formable** *adj* ▸ **per'former** *n*

performance (pə'fɔːməns) *n* **1** the act, process, or art of performing. **2** an artistic or dramatic production: *last night's performance was terrible.* **3** manner or quality of functioning: *a machine's performance.* **4** *Inf.* mode of conduct or behaviour, esp. when distasteful: *what did you mean by that performance at the restaurant?* **5** *Inf.* any tiresome procedure: *the performance of preparing to go out in the snow.*

performance art *n* a theatrical presentation that incorporates various art forms, such as dance, sculpture, etc.

performative (pə'fɔːmətɪv) *adj Linguistics, philosophy.* **1a** denoting an utterance that itself constitutes the act described by the verb. For example, the sentence *I confess that I was there* is itself a confession. **1b** (*as n*): *that sentence is a performative.* **2a** denoting a verb that may be used as the main verb in such an utterance. **2b** (*as n*): *"promise" is a performative.*

performing arts *pl n* the arts, such as a music and drama, that require a public performance.

perfume *n* ('pɜːfjuːm). **1** a mixture of alcohol and fragrant essential oils extracted from flowers, etc., or made synthetically. **2** a scent or odour, esp. a fragrant one. ◆ *vb* (pə'fjuːm), **perfumes, perfuming, perfumed.** **3** (*tr*) to impart a perfume to. ORIG C16: from F *parfum*, prob. from OProvençal *perfum*, from *perfumar* to make scented, from *per* through (from L) + *fumar* to smoke, from L *fumāre* to smoke

perfumer (pə'fju:mə) *or* **perfumier** (pə'fju:mjeɪ) *n* a person who makes or sells perfume.

perfumery (pə'fju:mərɪ) *n, pl* **perfumeries. 1** a place where perfumes are sold. **2** a factory where perfumes are made. **3** the process of making perfumes. **4** perfumes in general.

perfunctory (pə'fʌŋktərɪ) *adj* **1** done superficially, only as a matter of routine. **2** dull or indifferent. ORIG C16: from LL *perfunctōrius* negligent, from *perfunctus* dispatched, from *perfungī* to fulfil
▸ **per'functorily** *adv* ▸ **per'functoriness** *n*

perfuse (pə'fju:z) *vb* **perfuses, perfusing, perfused.** (*tr*) **1** to suffuse or permeate (a liquid, colour, etc.) through or over (something). **2** *Surgery.* to pass (a fluid) through (tissue). ORIG C16: from L *perfūsus* wetted, from *perfundere* to pour over
▸ **per'fused** *adj*

perfusionist (pə'fju:ʒənɪst) *n Surgery.* the person in a surgical team who is responsible for the perfusion of blood through the patient's lung tissue to ensure adequate exchange of oxygen and carbon dioxide.

Pergamum ★ ('pɜ:gəməm) *n* an ancient city in NW Asia Minor, in Mysia: capital of a major Hellenistic monarchy of the same name that later became a Roman province.

pergola ('pɜ:gələ) *n* a horizontal trellis or framework, supported on posts, that carries climbing plants. ORIG C17: via It. from L *pergula* projection from a roof, from *pergere* to go forward

Pergolesi ★ (*Italian* pergo'le:si) *n* **Giovanni Battista** (dʒo-'vanni bat'tista). 1710–36, Italian composer: his works include the *Stabat Mater* (1736) for women's voices.

perhaps (pə'hæps; *informal* præps) *adv* **1a** possibly; maybe. **1b** (*as sentence modifier*): *he'll arrive tomorrow, perhaps.* ◆ *sentence substitute.* **2** it may happen, be so, etc.; maybe. ORIG C16 *perhappes,* from *per* by + *happes* chance

peri ('pɪərɪ) *n, pl* **peris. 1** (in Persian folklore) one of a race of beautiful supernatural beings. **2** any beautiful fairy-like creature. ORIG C18: from Persian: fairy, from Avestan *pairikā* witch

peri- *prefix* **1** enclosing, encircling, or around: *pericardium; pericarp.* **2** near or adjacent: *perihelion.* ORIG from Gk *peri* around

perianth ('pɛrɪ,ænθ) *n* the outer part of a flower, consisting of the calyx and corolla. ORIG C18: from F *périanthe,* from NL, from PERI- + Gk *anthos* flower

periapt ('pɛrɪ,æpt) *n Rare.* a charm or amulet. ORIG C16: via F from Gk *periapton,* from PERI- + *haptos* clasped, from *haptein* to fasten

pericarditis (,pɛrɪkɑ:'daɪtɪs) *n* inflammation of the pericardium.

pericardium (,pɛrɪ'kɑ:dɪəm) *n, pl* **pericardia** (-dɪə). the membranous sac enclosing the heart. ORIG C16: via NL from Gk *perikardion,* from PERI- + *kardia* heart
▸ **,peri'cardial** *or* **,peri'cardi,ac** *adj*

pericarp ('pɛrɪ,kɑ:p) *n* the part of a fruit enclosing the seeds that develops from the wall of the ovary. ORIG C18: via F from NL *pericarpium*
▸ **,peri'carpial** *adj*

perichondrium (,pɛrɪ'kɒndrɪəm) *n, pl* **perichondria** (-drɪə). the fibrous membrane that covers the cartilage. ORIG C18: NL, from PERI- + Gk *chondros* cartilage

periclase ('pɛrɪ,kleɪs) *n* a mineral consisting of magnesium oxide. ORIG C19: from NL *periclasia,* from Gk *peri* very + *klasis* a breaking, referring to its perfect cleavage

Pericles ★ ('pɛrɪ,kli:z) *n* ?495–429 B.C., Athenian statesman, who contributed greatly to Athens' political and cultural supremacy in Greece. In power from about 460 B.C., he was responsible for the construction of the Parthenon. He conducted the Peloponnesian War (431–404 B.C.) successfully until his death.
▸ **,Peri'clean** *adj*

pericline ('pɛrɪ,klaɪn) *n* **1** a white translucent variety of albite in the form of elongated crystals. **2** Also called: **dome.** a dome-shaped formation of stratified rock with its slopes following the direction of folding. ORIG C19: from Gk *periklinēs* sloping on all sides
▸ **,peri'clinal** *adj*

pericranium (,pɛrɪ'kreɪnɪəm) *n, pl* **pericrania** (-nɪə). the fibrous membrane covering the external surface of the skull. ORIG C16: NL, from Gk *perikranion*

peridot ('pɛrɪ,dɒt) *n* a pale green transparent variety of the olivine chrysolite, used as a gemstone. ORIG C14: from OF *peritot,* from ?

perigee ('pɛrɪ,dʒi:) *n* the point in its orbit around the earth when the moon or a satellite is nearest the earth. ORIG C16: via F from Gk *perigeion,* from PERI- + *gea* earth
▸ **,peri'gean** *adj*

periglacial (,pɛrɪ'gleɪʃəl) *adj* relating to a region bordering a glacier: *periglacial climate.*

Périgueux ★ (,pɛrɪ'gɜ:; *French* perigø) *n* a town in SW France, capital of the Dordogne: noted for its Roman remains, medieval cathedral, and pâté de foie gras. Pop.: 32 850 (1990).

perihelion (,pɛrɪ'hi:lɪən) *n, pl* **perihelia** (-lɪə). the point in its orbit when a planet or comet is nearest the sun. ORIG C17: from NL *perihēlium,* from PERI- + Gk *hēlios* sun

peril ('pɛrɪl) *n* exposure to risk or harm; danger or jeopardy. ORIG C13: via OF from L *perīculum*

perilous ('pɛrɪləs) *adj* very hazardous or dangerous: *a perilous journey.*
▸ **'perilously** *adv* ▸ **'perilousness** *n*

perilune ('pɛrɪ,lu:n) *n* the point in a lunar orbit when a spacecraft is nearest the moon. ORIG C20: from PERI- + *-lune,* from L *lūna* moon

perimeter (pə'rɪmɪtə) *n* **1** *Maths.* **1a** the curve or line enclosing a plane area. **1b** the length of this curve or line. **2a** any boundary around something. **2b** (*as modifier*): *a perimeter fence.* **3** a medical instrument for measuring the field of vision. ORIG C16: from F *périmètre,* from L *perimetros*
▸ **perimetric** (,pɛrɪ'mɛtrɪk) *adj*

perinatal (,pɛrɪ'neɪtᵊl) *adj* of or occurring in the period from about three months before to one month after birth.

perineum (,pɛrɪ'ni:əm) *n, pl* **perinea** (-'ni:ə). **1** the region of the body between the anus and the genital organs. **2** the surface of the human trunk between the thighs. ORIG C17: from NL, from Gk *perinaion,* from PERI- + *inein* to empty
▸ **,peri'neal** *adj*

period ('pɪərɪəd) *n* **1** a portion of time of indefinable length: *he spent a period away from home.* **2a** a portion of time specified in some way: *Picasso's blue period.* **2b** (*as modifier*): *period costume.* **3** a nontechnical name for an occurence of menstruation. **4** *Geol.* a unit of geological time during which a system of rocks is formed: *the Jurassic period.* **5** a division of time, esp. of the academic day. **6** *Physics, maths.* the time taken to complete one cycle of a regularly recurring phenomenon; the reciprocal of frequency. Symbol: *T* **7** *Astron.* **7a** the time required by a body to make one complete rotation on its axis. **7b** the time interval between two successive maxima or minima of light variation of a variable star. **8** *Chem.* one of the horizontal rows of elements in the periodic table. Each period starts with an alkali metal and ends with a rare gas. **9** another term (esp. US and Canad.) for **full stop. 10** a complete sentence, esp. one with several clauses. **11** a completion or end. ORIG C14 *peryod,* from L *periodus,* from Gk *periodos* circuit, from PERI- + *hodos* way

periodic (,pɪərɪ'ɒdɪk) *adj* **1** happening or recurring at intervals; intermittent. **2** of, relating to, or resembling a period. **3** having or occurring in a series of repeated periods or cycles.
▸ **,peri'odically** *adv* ▸ **periodicity** (,pɪərɪə'dɪsɪtɪ) *n*

periodical (,pɪərɪ'ɒdɪkᵊl) *n* **1** a publication issued at regular intervals, usually monthly or weekly. ◆ *adj* **2** of or relating to such publications. **3** published at regular intervals. **4** periodic or occasional.

periodic function *n Maths.* a function whose value is repeated at constant intervals.

periodic law *n* the principle that the chemical properties of the elements are periodic functions of their atomic weights or, more accurately, of their atomic numbers.

periodic sentence *n Rhetoric.* a sentence in which the completion of the main clause is left to the end, thus creating an effect of suspense.

periodic table *n* a table of the elements, arranged in order of increasing atomic number, based on the periodic law.

periodontal (ˌpɛrɪəˈdɒntᵊl) *adj* of, denoting, or affecting the gums and other tissues surrounding the teeth: *periodontal disease.*

periodontics (ˌpɛrɪəˈdɒntɪks) *n* (*functioning as sing*) the branch of dentistry concerned with diseases affecting the tissues and structures that surround teeth. Also called: **periodontology.** ORIG C19: from PERI- + *-odontics,* from Gk *odōn* tooth
▸ ˌ**perio**ˈ**dontical** *adj*

periosteum (ˌpɛrɪˈɒstɪəm) *n, pl* **periostea** (-tɪə). a thick fibrous two-layered membrane covering the surface of bones. ORIG C16: NL, from Gk *periosteon,* from PERI- + *osteon* bone
▸ ˌ**peri**ˈ**osteal** *adj*

peripatetic (ˌpɛrɪpəˈtɛtɪk) *adj* **1** itinerant. **2** *Brit.* employed in two or more educational establishments and travelling from one to another: *a peripatetic football coach.* ◆ *n* **3** a peripatetic person. ORIG C16: from L *peripatēticus,* from Gk, from *peripatein* to pace to and fro
▸ ˌ**peripa**ˈ**tetically** *adv*

Peripatetic (ˌpɛrɪpəˈtɛtɪk) *adj* **1** of or relating to the teachings of Aristotle, who used to teach philosophy while walking about the Lyceum in ancient Athens. ◆ *n* **2** a student of Aristotelianism.

peripeteia (ˌpɛrɪpɪˈtaɪə, -ˈtɪə) *n* (esp. in drama) an abrupt turn of events or reversal of circumstances. ORIG C16: from Gk, from PERI- + *piptein* to fall (to change suddenly, lit.: to fall around)

peripheral (pəˈrɪfərəl) *adj* **1** not relating to the most important part of something; incidental. **2** of or relating to a periphery. **3** *Anat.* of, relating to, or situated near the surface of the body: *a peripheral nerve.*
▸ **pe**ˈ**ripherally** *adv*

peripheral device *or* **unit** *n Computing.* any device, such as a disk, printer, modem, or screen, concerned with input/output, storage, etc. Often shortened to **peripheral.**

periphery (pəˈrɪfərɪ) *n, pl* **peripheries. 1** the outermost boundary of an area. **2** the outside surface of something. ORIG C16: from LL *peripherīa,* from Gk, from PERI- + *pherein* to bear

periphrasis (pəˈrɪfrəsɪs) *n, pl* **periphrases** (-rəˌsiːz). **1** a roundabout way of expressing something; circumlocution. **2** an expression of this kind. ORIG C16: via L from Gk, from PERI- + *phrazein* to declare

periphrastic (ˌpɛrɪˈfræstɪk) *adj* **1** employing or involving periphrasis. **2** expressed in two or more words rather than by an inflected form of one: used esp. of a tense of a verb where the alternative word is an auxiliary verb, as in *He does go.*
▸ ˌ**peri**ˈ**phrastically** *adv*

perisarc (ˈpɛrɪˌsɑːk) *n* the outer chitinous layer secreted by colonial hydrozoan coelenterates. ORIG C19: from PERI- + *-sarc,* from Gk *sarx* flesh

periscope (ˈpɛrɪˌskəʊp) *n* any of a number of optical instruments that enable the user to view objects that are not in the direct line of vision, such as one in a submarine for looking above the surface of the water. They have a system of mirrors or prisms to reflect the light. ORIG C19: from Gk *periskopein* to look around
▸ **periscopic** (ˌpɛrɪˈskɒpɪk) *adj*

perish (ˈpɛrɪʃ) *vb* **1** (*intr*) to be destroyed or die, esp. in an untimely way. **2** (*tr* sometimes foll. by *with* or *from*) to cause to suffer: *we were perished with cold.* **3** to rot or cause to rot: *leather perishes if exposed to bad weather.* ◆ *n* **4 do a perish.** *Austral. inf.* to die or come near to dying of thirst or starvation. ORIG C13: from OF *périr,* from L *perīre* to pass away entirely

perishable (ˈpɛrɪʃəbᵊl) *adj* **1** liable to rot. ◆ *n* **2** (*often pl*) a perishable article, esp. food.
▸ ˌ**perisha**ˈ**bility** *or* ˈ**perishableness** *n*

perishing (ˈpɛrɪʃɪŋ) *adj* **1** *Inf.* (of weather, etc.) extremely cold. **2** *Sl.* (intensifier qualifying something undesirable): *it's a perishing nuisance!*
▸ ˈ**perishingly** *adv*

perisperm (ˈpɛrɪˌspɜːm) *n* the nutritive tissue surrounding the embryo in certain seeds.

perissodactyl (pəˌrɪsəʊˈdæktɪl) *n* **1** any of an order of placental mammals having hooves with an odd number of toes: includes horses, tapirs, and rhinoceroses. ◆ *adj* **2** of, relating to, or belonging to this order. ORIG C19: from NL *perissodactylus,* from Gk *perissos* uneven + *daktulos* digit

peristalsis (ˌpɛrɪˈstælsɪs) *n, pl* **peristalses** (-siːz). *Physiol.* the succession of waves of involuntary muscular contraction of various bodily tubes, esp. of the alimentary tract, where it effects transport of food and waste products. ORIG C19: from NL, from PERI- + Gk *stalsis* compression, from *stellein* to press together
▸ ˌ**peri**ˈ**staltic** *adj*

peristome (ˈpɛrɪˌstəʊm) *n* **1** a fringe of pointed teeth surrounding the opening of a moss capsule. **2** any of various parts surrounding the mouth of invertebrates, such as echinoderms and earthworms, and of protozoans. ORIG C18: from NL *peristoma,* from PERI- + Gk *stoma* mouth

peristyle (ˈpɛrɪˌstaɪl) *n* **1** a colonnade round a court or building. **2** an area surrounded by a colonnade. ORIG C17: via F from L *peristȳlum,* from Gk *peristulon,* from PERI- + *stulos* column

peritoneum (ˌpɛrɪtəˈniːəm) *n, pl* **peritonea** (-ˈniːə) *or* **peritoneums.** a serous sac that lines the walls of the abdominal cavity and covers the viscera. ORIG C16: via LL from Gk *peritonaion,* from *peritonos* stretched around
▸ ˌ**perito**ˈ**neal** *adj*

peritonitis (ˌpɛrɪtəˈnaɪtɪs) *n* inflammation of the peritoneum.

periwig (ˈpɛrɪˌwɪg) *n* a wig, such as a peruke. ORIG C16 *perwyke,* changed from F *perruque* wig, PERUKE

periwinkle[1] (ˈpɛrɪˌwɪŋkᵊl) *n* any of various edible marine gastropods having a spirally coiled shell. Often shortened to **winkle.** ORIG C16: from ?

periwinkle[2] (ˈpɛrɪˌwɪŋkᵊl) *n* any of several Eurasian evergreen plants having trailing stems and blue flowers. ORIG C14 *pervenke,* from OE *perwince,* from LL *pervinca*

perjure (ˈpɜːdʒə) *vb* **perjures, perjuring, perjured.** (*tr*) *Criminal law.* to render (oneself) guilty of perjury. ORIG C15: from OF *parjurer,* from L *perjūrāre,* from PER- + *jūrāre* to make an oath, from *jūs* law
▸ ˈ**perjurer** *n*

perjured (ˈpɜːdʒəd) *adj Criminal law.* **1a** having sworn falsely. **1b** having committed perjury. **2** involving or characterized by perjury: *perjured evidence.*

perjury (ˈpɜːdʒərɪ) *n, pl* **perjuries.** *Criminal law.* the offence committed by a witness in judicial proceedings who, having been lawfully sworn, wilfully gives false evidence. ORIG C14: from Anglo-F *parjurie,* from L *perjūrium* a false oath; see PERJURE
▸ **perjurious** (pɜːˈdʒʊərɪəs) *adj*

perk[1] (pɜːk) *adj* **1** pert; brisk; lively. ◆ *vb* **2** See **perk up.** ORIG C16: see PERK UP

perk[2] (pɜːk) *vb Inf.* short for **percolate** (sense 3).

perk[3] (pɜːk) *n Brit. inf.* short for **perquisite.**

perk up *vb* (*adv*) **1** to make or become more cheerful, hopeful, or lively. **2** to rise or cause to rise briskly: *the dog's ears perked up.* **3** (*tr*) to make smarter in appearance: *she perked up her outfit with a bright scarf.* ORIG C14 *perk,* ?from Norman F *perquer;* see PERCH[1]

perky (ˈpɜːkɪ) *adj* **perkier, perkiest. 1** jaunty; lively. **2** confident; spirited.
▸ ˈ**perkily** *adv* ▸ ˈ**perkiness** *n*

Perl (pɜːl) *n* a computer language that is used for text manipulation, esp. on the World Wide Web. ORIG C20: *p(ractical) e(xtraction and) r(eport) l(anguage)*

perlemoen (ˈpɛələˌmun) *n S. African.* another name for **abalone.** ORIG from Afrik., from Du. *paarlemoer* mother of pearl

Perlis ★ (ˈpɛəlɪs, ˈpɜː-) *n* a state of NW Peninsular Malaysia, on the Andaman Sea: a dependency of Thailand until 1909. Capital: Kangar. Pop.: 187 600 (1993 est.). Area: 803 sq. km (310 sq. miles).

perlite ('pɜːlaɪt) *n* a variety of obsidian consisting of masses of globules. ORIG C19: from F, from *perle* PEARL[1]

Perlman ★ ('pɜːlmən) *n* **Itzhak** ('ɪtzæk). born 1945, Israeli violinist; polio victim.

perm[1] (pɜːm) *n* **1** a hairstyle produced by treatment with heat, chemicals, etc. which gives long-lasting waves or curls. Also called (esp. formerly): **permanent wave.** ◆ *vb* **2** (*tr*) to give a perm to (hair).

perm[2] (pɜːm) *vb, n Inf.* short for **permutate, permutation** (sense 4).

Perm ★ (*Russian* pjermj) *n* a port in W Russia, on the Kama River: oil refinery; university (1916). Pop.: 1 032 000 (1995 est.). Former name (1940–62): **Molotov.**

permafrost ('pɜːməˌfrɒst) *n* ground that is permanently frozen. ORIG C20: from PERMA(NENT) + FROST

permalloy (pɜːm'ælɔɪ) *n* any of various alloys containing iron and nickel and sometimes smaller amounts of chromium and molybdenum.

permanence ('pɜːmənəns) *n* the state or quality of being permanent.

permanency ('pɜːmənənsɪ) *n, pl* **permanencies. 1** a person or thing that is permanent. **2** another word for **permanence.**

permanent ('pɜːmənənt) *adj* **1** existing or intended to exist for an indefinite period: *a permanent structure.* **2** not expected to change; not temporary: *a permanent condition.* ORIG C15: from L *permanens* continuing, from *permanēre* to stay to the end
▸ **'permanently** *adv*

permanent health insurance *n* a form of insurance that provides up to 75 per cent of a person's salary, until retirement, in case of prolonged illness or disability.

permanent magnet *n* a magnet, often of steel, that retains its magnetization after the magnetic field producing it has been removed.

permanent press *n* a chemical treatment for clothing that makes the fabric crease-resistant and sometimes provides a garment with a permanent crease or pleats.

permanent wave *n* another name (esp. formerly) for **perm**[1] (sense 1).

permanent way *n Chiefly Brit.* the track of a railway, including the sleepers, rails, etc.

permanganate (pə'mæŋgəˌneɪt, -nɪt) *n* a salt of permanganic acid.

permanganic acid (ˌpɜːmæn'gænɪk) *n* a monobasic acid known only in solution and in the form of permanganate salts. Formula: $HMnO_4$. Systematic name: **manganic(VII) acid.**

permeability (ˌpɜːmɪə'bɪlɪtɪ) *n* **1** the state or quality of being permeable. **2** a measure of the ability of a medium to modify a magnetic field, expressed as the ratio of the magnetic flux density in the medium to the field strength; measured in henries per metre. Symbol: μ

permeable ('pɜːmɪəbəl) *adj* capable of being permeated, esp. by liquids. ORIG C15: from LL *permeābilis,* from L *permeāre* to pervade; see PERMEATE
▸ **'permeably** *adv*

permeance ('pɜːmɪəns) *n* **1** the act of permeating. **2** the reciprocal of the reluctance of a magnetic circuit.
▸ **'permeant** *adj, n*

permeate ('pɜːmɪˌeɪt) *vb* **permeates, permeating, permeated. 1** to penetrate or pervade (a substance, area, etc.): *a lovely smell permeated the room.* **2** to pass through or cause to pass through by osmosis or diffusion: *to permeate a membrane.* ORIG C17: from L *permeāre,* from *per-* through + *meāre* to pass
▸ **ˌperme'ation** *n* ▸ **'permeative** *adj*

Permian ('pɜːmɪən) *adj* **1** of, denoting, or formed in the last period of the Palaeozoic era, between the Carboniferous and Triassic periods. ◆ *n* **2 the.** the Permian period or rock system. ORIG C19: after PERM

permissible (pə'mɪsəbəl) *adj* permitted; allowable.
▸ **perˌmissi'bility** *n* ▸ **per'missibly** *adv*

permission (pə'mɪʃən) *n* authorization to do something.

permissive (pə'mɪsɪv) *adj* **1** tolerant; lenient: *permissive parents.* **2** indulgent in matters of sex: *a permissive society.* **3** granting permission.
▸ **per'missively** *adv* ▸ **per'missiveness** *n*

permit *vb* (pə'mɪt), **permits, permitting, permitted. 1** (*tr*) to grant permission to do something: *you are permitted to smoke.* **2** (*tr*) to consent to or tolerate: *she will not permit him to come.* **3** (when *intr,* often foll. by *of;* when *tr,* often foll. by an infinitive) to allow the possibility (of): *the passage permits of two interpretations; his work permits him to relax nowadays.* ◆ *n* ('pɜːmɪt). **4** an official document granting authorization; licence. **5** permission. ORIG C15: from L *permittere,* from *per-* through + *mittere* to send
▸ **per'mitter** *n*

permittivity (ˌpɜːmɪ'tɪvɪtɪ) *n, pl* **permittivities.** a measure of the ability of a substance to transmit an electric field.

permutate ('pɜːmjuˌteɪt) *vb* **permutates, permutating, permutated.** to alter the sequence or arrangement (of): *endlessly permutating three basic designs.*

permutation (ˌpɜːmju'teɪʃən) *n* **1** *Maths.* **1a** an ordered arrangement of the numbers, terms, etc., of a set into specified groups: *the permutations of a, b, and c, taken two at a time, are ab, ba, ac, ca, bc, cb.* **1b** a group formed in this way. **2** a combination of items, etc., made by reordering. **3** an alteration; transformation. **4** a fixed combination for selections of results on football pools. Usually shortened to **perm.** ORIG C14: from L *permūtātiō,* from *permūtāre* to change thoroughly
▸ **ˌpermu'tational** *adj*

permute (pə'mjuːt) *vb* **permutes, permuting, permuted.** (*tr*) **1** to change the sequence of. **2** *Maths.* to subject to permutation. ORIG C14: from L *permūtāre,* from PER- + *mūtāre* to change

Pernambuco ★ (ˌpɜːnəm'bjuːkəʊ; *Portuguese* pernəm'buku) *n* **1** a state of NE Brazil, on the Atlantic: consists of a humid coastal plain rising to a high inland plateau. Capital: Recife. Pop.: 7 399 071 (1996). Area: 98 280 sq. km (37 946 sq. miles). **2** the former name of **Recife.**

pernicious (pə'nɪʃəs) *adj* **1** wicked or malicious: *pernicious lies.* **2** causing grave harm; deadly. ORIG C16: from L *perniciōsus,* from *perniciēs* ruin, from PER- (intensive) + *nex* death
▸ **per'niciously** *adv* ▸ **per'niciousness** *n*

pernicious anaemia *n* a form of anaemia characterized by lesions of the spinal cord, weakness, sore tongue, diarrhoea, etc.: associated with inadequate absorption of vitamin B_{12}.

pernickety (pə'nɪkɪtɪ) *adj Inf.* **1** excessively precise; fussy. **2** (of a task) requiring close attention. ORIG C19: orig. Scot. from ?

Pernik ★ (*Bulgarian* 'pɛrnik) *n* an industrial town in W Bulgaria, on the Struma River. Pop.: 99 643 (1990). Former name (1949–62): **Dimitrovo** (di'mitrovo).

Perón ★ (*Spanish* pe'rɔn) *n* **1 Juan Domingo** (xwan do'mingo). 1895–1974, Argentinian soldier and statesman; dictator (1946–55). He was deposed in 1955, remaining in exile until 1973, when he was elected president (1973–74). **2** his third wife, **María Estella** (ma'ria es'teʎa), known as *Isabel.* born 1931, president of Argentina (1974–76); deposed. **3** (**María**) **Eva** (**Duarte**) **de Perón** ('eβa), known as *Evita,* second wife of Juan Domingo Perón. 1919–52, Argentinian film actress: active in politics and social welfare (1946–52).
▸ **Pe'ronist** *n, adj*

peroneal (ˌpɛrə'niːəl) *adj Anat.* of or relating to the fibula. ORIG C19: from NL *peronē,* from Gk: fibula

perorate ('pɛrəˌreɪt) *vb* **perorates, perorating, perorated.** (*intr*) **1** to speak at length, esp. in a formal manner. **2** to conclude a speech or sum up.

peroration (ˌpɛrə'reɪʃən) *n* the conclusion of a speech or discourse, in which points made previously are summed up. ORIG C15: from L *perōrātiō,* from PER- (thoroughly) + *ōrāre* to speak

perovskite (pɛ'rɒvskaɪt) *n* a yellow, brown, or greyish-black mineral. ORIG C19: after *Perovski,* Russian mineralogist

peroxide (pəˈrɒksaɪd) *n* **1** short for **hydrogen peroxide,** esp. when used for bleaching hair. **2** any of a class of metallic oxides, such as sodium peroxide, Na_2O_2. **3** (*not in technical usage*) any of certain dioxides, such as manganese(VI) oxide, MnO_2, that resemble peroxides in their formula. **4** any of a class of organic compounds whose molecules contain two oxygen atoms bound together. **5** (*modifier*) of, relating to, bleached with, or resembling peroxide: *a peroxide blonde.* ◆ *vb* **peroxides, peroxiding, peroxided. 6** (*tr*) to bleach (the hair) with peroxide.

perpendicular (ˌpɜːpənˈdɪkjʊlə) *adj* **1** at right angles to a horizontal plane. **2** denoting, relating to, or having the style of Gothic architecture used in England during the 14th and 15th centuries, characterized by tracery having vertical lines. **3** upright; vertical. ◆ *n* **4** *Geom.* a line or plane perpendicular to another. **5** any instrument used for indicating the vertical line through a given point. ORIG C14: from L *perpendiculāris,* from *perpendiculum* a plumb line, from *per-* through + *pendēre* to hang
▸ **perpendicularity** (ˌpɜːpənˌdɪkjʊˈlærɪtɪ) *n* ▸ **ˌperpenˈdicularly** *adv*

perpetrate (ˈpɜːpɪˌtreɪt) *vb* **perpetrates, perpetrating, perpetrated.** (*tr*) to perform or be responsible for (a deception, crime, etc.). ORIG C16: from L *perpetrāre,* from *per-* (thoroughly) + *patrāre* to perform
▸ **ˌperpeˈtration** *n* ▸ **ˈperpeˌtrator** *n*

USAGE NOTE *Perpetrate* and *perpetuate* are sometimes confused: *he must answer for the crimes he has perpetrated* (not *perpetuated*); *the book helped to perpetuate* (not *perpetrate*) *some of the myths surrounding his early life.*

perpetual (pəˈpɛtjʊəl) *adj* **1** (*usually prenominal*) eternal; permanent. **2** (*usually prenominal*) seemingly ceaseless because often repeated: *your perpetual complaints.* ORIG C14: via OF from L *perpetuālis* universal, from *perpes* continuous, from *per-* (thoroughly) + *petere* to go towards
▸ **perˈpetually** *adv*

perpetual debenture *n* a bond or debenture that can either never be redeemed or cannot be redeemed on demand.

perpetual motion *n* motion of a hypothetical mechanism that continues indefinitely without any external source of energy. It is impossible in practice because of friction.

perpetuate (pəˈpɛtjʊˌeɪt) *vb* **perpetuates, perpetuating, perpetuated.** (*tr*) to cause to continue: *to perpetuate misconceptions.* ORIG C16: from L *perpetuāre* to continue without interruption, from *perpetuus* PERPETUAL
▸ **perˌpetuˈation** *n*

USAGE NOTE See at **perpetrate.**

perpetuity (ˌpɜːpɪˈtjuːɪtɪ) *n, pl* **perpetuities. 1** eternity. **2** the state of being perpetual. **3** *Property law.* a limitation preventing the absolute disposal of an estate for longer than the period allowed by law. **4** an annuity that is payable indefinitely. **5 in perpetuity.** forever. ORIG C15: from OF *perpetuite,* from L *perpetuitās* continuity; see PERPETUAL

Perpignan ★ (*French* pɛrpiɲɑ̃) *n* a town in S France: historic capital of Roussillon. Pop.: 108 049 (1990).

perplex (pəˈplɛks) *vb* (*tr*) **1** to puzzle; bewilder; confuse. **2** to complicate: *to perplex an issue.* ORIG C15: from obs. *perplex* (adj) intricate, from L *perplexus* entangled, from *per-* (thoroughly) + *plectere* to entwine
▸ **perplexedly** (pəˈplɛksɪdlɪ, -ˈplɛkstlɪ) *adv* ▸ **perˈplexingly** *adv*

perplexity (pəˈplɛksɪtɪ) *n, pl* **perplexities. 1** the state of being perplexed. **2** the state of being intricate or complicated. **3** something that perplexes.

per pro (ˈpɜː ˈprəʊ) *prep* by delegation to: through the agency of: used when signing documents on behalf of someone else. ORIG L: abbrev. of *per prōcūrātiōnem*

USAGE NOTE See at **pp.**

perquisite (ˈpɜːkwɪzɪt) *n* **1** an incidental benefit gained from a certain type of employment, such as the use of a company car. **2** a customary benefit received in addition to a regular income. **3** a customary tip. **4** something expected or regarded as an exclusive right. ◆ Often shortened (informal) to **perk.** ORIG C15: from Med. L *perquīsītum,* from L *perquīrere* to seek earnestly for something

Perrault ★ (*French* pero) *n* **Charles** (ʃarl). 1628–1703, French author, noted for his *Contes de ma mère l'oye* (1697), which contains the fairy tales *Little Red Riding Hood, Cinderella,* and *The Sleeping Beauty.*

Perrier water *or* **Perrier** (ˈpɛrɪeɪ) *n Trademark.* a sparkling mineral water from the south of France. ORIG C20: after a spring, *Source Perrier,* at Vergèze, France

Perrin ★ (*French* pɛrɛ̃) *n* **Jean Baptiste** (ʒɑ̃ batist). 1870–1942, French physicist. His researches on the distribution and diffusion of particles in colloids (1911) gave evidence for the physical reality of molecules, confirmed the explanation of Brownian movement in terms of kinetic theory, and determined the magnitude of the Avogadro constant. He also studied cathode rays: Nobel prize for physics 1926.

perron (ˈpɛrən) *n* an external flight of steps, esp. one at the front entrance of a building. ORIG C14: from OF, from *pierre* stone, from L *petra*

perry (ˈpɛrɪ) *n, pl* **perries.** an alcoholic drink made of pears, similar in taste to cider. ORIG C14 *pereye,* from OF *peré,* ult. from L *pirum* pear

Perry ★ (ˈpɛrɪ) *n* **1 Fred(erick John).** 1909–95, British tennis and table-tennis player; world singles table-tennis champion (1929); Wimbledon singles champion (1934–36). **2 Matthew Calbraith.** 1794–1858, US naval officer, who led a naval expedition to Japan that obtained a treaty (1854) opening up Japan to western trade. **3** his brother, **Oliver Hazard.** 1785–1819, US naval officer. His defeat of a British squadron on Lake Erie (1813) was the turning point in the War of 1812, leading to the recapture of Detroit.

pers. *abbrev. for:* **1** person. **2** personal.

Pers. *abbrev. for* Persia(n).

perse (pɜːs) *n* **a** a dark greyish-blue colour. **b** (*as adj*): *perse cloth.* ORIG C14: from OF, from Med. L *persus,* ? changed from L *Persicus* Persian

per se (ˈpɜː ˈseɪ) *adv* by or in itself; intrinsically. ORIG L

Perse ★ (pɜːs; *French* pɛrs) *n* **Saint-John** (ˈsɪndʒən), real name *Alexis Saint-Léger.* 1887–1975, French poet, born in Guadeloupe. His works include *Anabase* (1922). Nobel prize for literature 1960.

persecute (ˈpɜːsɪˌkjuːt) *vb* **persecutes, persecuting, persecuted.** (*tr*) **1** to oppress, harass, or maltreat, esp. because of race, religion, etc. **2** to bother persistently. ORIG C15: from OF, from *persecuteur,* from LL *persecūtor* pursuer, from L *persequī* to take vengeance upon
▸ **ˌperseˈcution** *n* ▸ **ˈperseˌcutive** *adj* ▸ **ˈperseˌcutor** *n*

persecution complex *n Psychol.* an acute irrational fear that other people are plotting one's downfall.

Persephone ★ (pəˈsɛfənɪ) *n Greek myth.* a daughter of Zeus and Demeter, abducted by Hades and made his wife and queen of the underworld, but allowed part of each year to leave it. Roman counterpart: **Proserpina.**

Persepolis ★ (pəˈsɛpəlɪs) *n* the capital of ancient Persia in the Persian Empire and under the Seleucids: founded by Darius; sacked by Alexander the Great in 330 B.C.

Perseus ★ (ˈpɜːsɪəs) *n Greek myth.* a son of Zeus and Danaë, who with Athena's help slew the Gorgon Medusa and rescued Andromeda from a sea monster.

perseverance (ˌpɜːsɪˈvɪərəns) *n* **1** continued steady belief or efforts; persistence. **2** *Christian theol.* continuance in a state of grace.

perseveration (pɜːˌsɛvəˈreɪʃən) *n Psychol.* the tendency for an impression, idea, or feeling to dissipate only slowly and to recur during subsequent experiences.

persevere (ˌpɜːsɪˈvɪə) *vb* **perseveres, persevering, per-**

severed. (*intr;* often foll. by *in*) to show perseverance. ORIG C14: from OF *perseverer,* from L, from *perseverus* very strict; see SEVERE

Pershing ★ (ˈpɜːʃɪŋ) *n* **John Joseph,** nickname *Black Jack.* 1860–1948, US general. He was commander in chief of the American Expeditionary Force in Europe (1917–19).

Persia ★ (ˈpɜːʃə) *n* **1** the former name (until 1935) of **Iran. 2** another name for **Persian Empire.**

Persian (ˈpɜːʃən) *adj* **1** of or relating to ancient Persia or modern Iran, their inhabitants, or their languages. ◆ *n* **2** a native, citizen, or inhabitant of modern Iran; an Iranian. **3** the language of Iran or Persia in any of its ancient or modern forms.

Persian carpet *or* **rug** *n* a carpet or rug made in Persia or the Near East by knotting silk or wool yarn by hand onto a woven backing in rich colours and flowing or geometric designs.

Persian cat *n* a long-haired variety of domestic cat.

Persian Empire ★ *n* the S Asian empire established by Cyrus the Great in the 6th century B.C. and overthrown by Alexander the Great in the 4th century B.C. At its height it extended from India to Europe.

Persian Gulf ★ *n* a shallow arm of the Arabian Sea between SW Iran and Arabia: linked with the Arabian Sea by the Strait of Hormuz and the Gulf of Oman; important for the oilfields on its shores. Area: 233 000 sq. km (90 000 sq. miles).

Persian lamb *n* **1** a black loosely curled fur from the karakul lamb. **2** a karakul lamb.

persiennes (ˌpɜːsɪˈɛnz) *pl n* outside window shutters having louvres. ORIG C19: from F, from *persien* Persian

persiflage (ˈpɜːsɪˌflɑːʒ) *n* light frivolous conversation, style, or treatment; friendly teasing. ORIG C18: via F from *persifler* to tease, from *per-* (intensive) + *siffler* to whistle, from L *sībilāre* to whistle

persimmon (pɜːˈsɪmən) *n* **1** any of several tropical trees, typically having hard wood and large orange-red fruit. **2** Also called: **sharon fruit.** the sweet fruit of any of these trees, which is edible when completely ripe. ORIG C17: from Amerind

Persis ★ (ˈpɜːsɪs) *n* an ancient region of SW Iran: homeland of the Achaemenid dynasty.

persist (pəˈsɪst) *vb* (*intr*) **1** (often foll. by *in*) to continue steadfastly or obstinately despite opposition. **2** to continue without interruption: *the rain persisted throughout the night.* ORIG C16: from L *persistere,* from *per-* (intensive) + *sistere* to stand steadfast
▸ **perˈsister** *n*

persistence (pəˈsɪstəns) *or* **persistency** *n* **1** the quality of persisting; tenacity. **2** the act of persisting; continued effort or existence.

persistent (pəˈsɪstənt) *adj* **1** showing persistence. **2** incessantly repeated; unrelenting: *your persistent questioning.* **3** (of plant parts) remaining attached to the plant after the normal time of withering. **4** *Zool.* (of parts normally present only in young stages) present in the adult. **5** (of a chemical, esp. when used as a insecticide) slow to break down.
▸ **perˈsistently** *adv*

persistent vegetative state *n Med.* an irreversible condition, resulting from brain damage, characterized by lack of consciousness, thought, and feeling, although reflex activities (such as breathing) continue. Abbrev.: **PVS.**

person (ˈpɜːsᵊn) *n, pl* **persons. 1** an individual human being. **2** the body of a human being: *guns hidden on his person.* **3** a grammatical category into which pronouns and forms of verbs are subdivided depending on whether they refer to the speaker, the person addressed, or some other individual, thing, etc. **4** a human being or a corporation recognized in law as having certain rights and obligations. **5 in person.** actually present: *the author will be there in person.* ORIG C13: from OF *persone,* from L *persōna* mask, ?from Etruscan *phersu* mask

-person *n combining form.* sometimes used instead of *-man* and *-woman* or *-lady: chairperson.*

> **USAGE NOTE** See at **-man.**

persona (pɜːˈsəʊnə) *n, pl* **personae** (-niː). **1** (*often pl*) a character in a play, novel, etc. **2** (in Jungian psychology) the mechanism that conceals a person's true thoughts and feelings, esp. in adaptation to the outside world. ORIG L: mask

personable (ˈpɜːsənəbᵊl) *adj* pleasant in appearance and personality.
▸ **ˈpersonableness** *n* ▸ **ˈpersonably** *adv*

personage (ˈpɜːsənɪdʒ) *n* **1** an important or distinguished person. **2** another word for **person** (sense 1). **3** *Rare.* a figure in literature, history, etc.

persona grata *Latin.* (pɜːˈsəʊnə ˈgrɑːtə) *n, pl* ***personae gratae*** (pɜːˈsəʊniː ˈgrɑːtiː). an acceptable person, esp. a diplomat.

personal (ˈpɜːsənᵊl) *adj* **1** of or relating to the private aspects of a person's life: *personal letters.* **2** (*prenominal*) of or relating to a person's body, its care, or its appearance: *personal hygiene.* **3** belonging to or intended for a particular person and no-one else: *for your personal use.* **4** (*prenominal*) undertaken by an individual: *a personal appearance by a celebrity.* **5** referring to or involving a person's individual personality, intimate affairs, etc., esp. in an offensive way: *personal remarks; don't be so personal.* **6** having the attributes of an individual conscious being: *a personal God.* **7** of, relating to, or denoting grammatical person. **8** *Law.* of or relating to movable property, as money, etc.

personal column *n* a newspaper column containing personal messages and advertisements.

personal computer *n* a small inexpensive computer used in word processing, computer games, etc.

personal digital assistant *n* a palmtop computer for storing addresses, telephone numbers, memos, and similar information. Abbrev.: **PDA.**

personal equity plan *n* the full name for **PEP.**

personality (ˌpɜːsəˈnælɪtɪ) *n, pl* **personalities. 1** *Psychol.* the sum total of all the behavioural and mental characteristics by means of which an individual is recognized as being unique. **2** the distinctive character of a person that makes him or her socially attractive: *a salesman needs a lot of personality.* **3** a well-known person in a certain field, such as entertainment. **4** a remarkable person. **5** (*often pl*) a personal remark.

personalize *or* **personalise** (ˈpɜːsənəˌlaɪz) *vb* **personalizes, personalizing, personalized** *or* **personalises, personalising, personalised.** (*tr*) **1** to endow with personal or individual qualities. **2** to mark (stationery, clothing, etc.) with a person's initials, name, etc. **3** to take (a remark, etc.) personally. **4** another word for **personify.**
▸ **ˌpersonaliˈzation** *or* **ˌpersonaliˈsation** *n*

personally (ˈpɜːsənəlɪ) *adv* **1** without the help or intervention of others: *I'll attend to it personally.* **2** (*sentence modifier*) in one's own opinion or as regards oneself: *personally, I hate onions.* **3** as if referring to oneself: *to take the insults personally.* **4** as a person: *we like him personally, but professionally he's incompetent.*

personal organizer *n* **1** a diary that stores personal records, appointments, notes, etc. **2** a pocket-sized electronic device that performs the same functions.

personal pronoun *n* a pronoun having a definite person or thing as an antecedent and functioning grammatically in the same way as the noun that it replaces. The personal pronouns include *I, you, he, she, it, we,* and *they.*

personal property *n Law.* movable property, such as furniture or money. Also called: **personalty.** Cf. **real property.**

personal shopper *n* a person employed, esp. by a shop, to accompany and advise customers on shopping trips or to select items for them.

personal stereo *n* a small audio cassette player worn attached to a belt and used with lightweight headphones.

persona non grata *Latin.* (pɜːˈsəʊnə nɒn ˈgrɑːtə) *n, pl* ***personae non gratae*** (pɜːˈsəʊniː nɒn ˈgrɑːtiː). **1** an unacceptable or unwelcome person. **2** a diplomat who is not acceptable to the government to whom he or she is accredited.

personate ('pɜːsəˌneɪt) *vb* **personates, personating, personated.** (*tr*) **1** to act the part of (a character in a play); portray. **2** *Criminal law.* to assume the identity of (another person) with intent to deceive.
▸ **ˌperson'ation** *n* ▸ **'personative** *adj* ▸ **'personˌator** *n*

personification (pɜːˌsɒnɪfɪ'keɪʃən) *n* **1** the attribution of human characteristics to things, abstract ideas, etc. **2** the representation of an abstract quality or idea in the form of a person, creature, etc., as in art and literature. **3** a person or thing that personifies. **4** a person or thing regarded as an embodiment of a quality: *he is the personification of optimism.*

personify (pɜː'sɒnɪˌfaɪ) *vb* **personifies, personifying, personified.** (*tr*) **1** to attribute human characteristics to (a thing or abstraction). **2** to represent (an abstract quality) in human or animal form. **3** (of a person or thing) to represent (an abstract quality), as in art. **4** to be the embodiment of.
▸ **per'soniˌfier** *n*

personnel (ˌpɜːsə'nɛl) *n* **1** the people employed in an organization or for a service. **2** Also called: **human resources. 2a** the department that interviews, appoints, or keeps records of employees. **2b** (*as modifier*)*: a personnel officer.* ORIG C19: from F, ult. from LL *persōnālis* personal (adj); see PERSON

perspective (pə'spɛktɪv) *n* **1** a way of regarding situations, facts, etc., and judging their relative importance. **2** the proper or accurate point of view or the ability to see it; objectivity: *try to get some perspective on your troubles.* **3** a view over some distance in space or time; prospect. **4** the theory or art of suggesting three dimensions on a two-dimensional surface, in order to recreate the appearance and spatial relationships that objects or a scene in recession present to the eye. **5** the appearance of objects, buildings, etc., relative to each other, as determined by their distance from the viewer, or the effects of this distance on their appearance. ORIG C14: from Med. L *perspectīva ars* the science of optics, from L *perspicere* to inspect carefully
▸ **per'spectively** *adv*

Perspex ('pɜːspɛks) *n Trademark.* any of various clear acrylic resins.

perspicacious (ˌpɜːspɪ'keɪʃəs) *adj* acutely perceptive or discerning. ORIG C17: from L *perspicax,* from *perspicere* to look at closely
▸ **ˌperspi'caciously** *adv* ▸ **perspicacity** (ˌpɜːspɪ'kæsɪtɪ) *or* **ˌperspi'caciousness** *n*

perspicuous (pə'spɪkjuəs) *adj* (of speech or writing) easily understood; lucid. ORIG C15: from L *perspicuus* transparent, from *perspicere* to explore thoroughly
▸ **per'spicuously** *adv* ▸ **per'spicuousness** *or* **perspicuity** (ˌpɜːspɪ'kjuːɪtɪ) *n*

perspiration (ˌpɜːspə'reɪʃən) *n* **1** the salty fluid secreted by the sweat glands of the skin. **2** the act of secreting this fluid.
▸ **perspiratory** (pə'spaɪərətərɪ) *adj*

perspire (pə'spaɪə) *vb* **perspires, perspiring, perspired.** to secrete or exude (perspiration) through the pores of the skin. ORIG C17: from L *perspīrāre* to blow, from *per-* (through) + *spīrāre* to breathe
▸ **per'spiringly** *adv*

persuade (pə'sweɪd) *vb* **persuades, persuading, persuaded.** (*tr; may take a clause as object or an infinitive*) **1** to induce, urge, or prevail upon successfully: *he finally persuaded them to buy it.* **2** to cause to believe; convince: *even with the evidence, the police were not persuaded.* ORIG C16: from L *persuādēre,* from *per-* (intensive) + *suādēre* to urge, advise
▸ **per'suadable** *or* **per'suasible** *adj* ▸ **perˌsuada'bility** *or* **perˌsuasi'bility** *n* ▸ **per'suader** *n*

persuasion (pə'sweɪʒən) *n* **1** the act of persuading or of trying to persuade. **2** the power to persuade. **3** a strong belief. **4** an established creed or belief, esp. a religious one. **5** a sect, party, or faction. ORIG C14: from L *persuāsiō*

persuasive (pə'sweɪsɪv) *adj* having the power or tending to persuade: *a persuasive salesman.*
▸ **per'suasively** *adv* ▸ **per'suasiveness** *n*

pert (pɜːt) *adj* **1** saucy, impudent, or forward. **2** jaunty: *a pert little hat.* **3** *Obs.* clever or brisk. ORIG C13: var. of earlier *apert,* from L *apertus* open, from *aperīre* to open
▸ **'pertly** *adv* ▸ **'pertness** *n*

pert. *abbrev. for* pertaining.

pertain (pə'teɪn) *vb* (*intr;* often foll. by *to*) **1** to have reference or relevance: *issues pertaining to women.* **2** to be appropriate: *the product pertains to real user needs.* **3** to belong (to) or be a part (of). ORIG C14: from L *pertinēre,* from *per-* (intensive) + *tenēre* to hold

Perth ★ (pɜːθ) *n* **1** a city in central Scotland, in Perth and Kinross on the River Tay: capital of Scotland from the 12th century until the assassination of James I there in 1437. Pop.: 41 453 (1991). **2** a city in SW Australia, capital of Western Australia, on the Swan River: major industrial centre; University of Western Australia (1911). Pop.: 1 262 600 (1995 est.).

Perth and Kinross ★ (kɪn'rɒs) *n* a council area of N central Scotland, formed in 1996: mountainous. Administrative centre: Perth. Pop.: 132 570 (1996 est.). Area: 5321 sq. km (2019 sq. miles).

Perthshire ★ ('pɜːθˌʃɪə, -ʃə) *n* (until 1975) a county of central Scotland, now part of Perth and Kinross council area.

pertinacious (ˌpɜːtɪ'neɪʃəs) *adj* **1** doggedly resolute in purpose or belief; unyielding. **2** stubbornly persistent. ORIG C17: from L *pertināx,* from *per-* (intensive) + *tenāx* clinging, from *tenēre* to hold
▸ **ˌperti'naciously** *adv* ▸ **pertinacity** (ˌpɜːtɪ'næsɪtɪ) *or* **ˌperti'naciousness** *n*

pertinent ('pɜːtɪnənt) *adj* relating to the matter at hand; relevant. ORIG C14: from L *pertinēns,* from *pertinēre* to PERTAIN
▸ **'pertinence** *or* **'pertinency** *n* ▸ **'pertinently** *adv*

perturb (pə'tɜːb) *vb* (*tr; often passive*) **1** to disturb the composure of; trouble. **2** to throw into disorder. **3** *Physics, astron.* to cause (a planet, electron, etc.) to undergo a perturbation. ORIG C14: from OF *pertourber,* from L *perturbāre* to confuse, from *per-* (intensive) + *turbāre* to agitate
▸ **per'turbable** *adj* ▸ **per'turbing** *adj*

perturbation (ˌpɜːtə'beɪʃən) *n* **1** the act of perturbing or the state of being perturbed. **2** a cause of disturbance. **3** *Physics.* a secondary influence on a system that modifies simple behaviour, such as the effect of the other electrons on one electron in an atom. **4** *Astron.* a small continuous deviation in the orbit of a planet or comet, due to the attraction of neighbouring planets.

pertussis (pə'tʌsɪs) *n* the technical name for **whooping cough.** ORIG C18: NL, from L *per-* (intensive) + *tussis* cough
▸ **per'tussal** *adj*

Peru ★ (pə'ruː) *n* a republic in W South America, on the Pacific: the centre of the great Inca Empire when conquered by the Spanish in 1532; gained independence in 1824 by defeating Spanish forces with armies led by San Martín and Bolívar; consists of a coastal desert, rising to the Andes; an important exporter of minerals and a major fishing nation. Official languages: Spanish, Quechua, and Aymara. Official religion: Roman Catholic. Currency: nuevo sol. Capital: Lima. Pop.: 25 232 000 (1999 est.). Area: 1 285 215 sq. km (496 222 sq. miles).
▸ **Peruvian** (pə'ruːvɪən) *adj, n*

Peru Current *n* a cold ocean current flowing northwards off the Pacific coast of South America. Also called: **Humboldt Current.**

Perugia ★ (pə'ruːdʒə; *Italian* pe'ruːdʒa) *n* **1** a city in central Italy, in Umbria: centre of the Umbrian school of painting (15th century); university (1308); Etruscan and Roman remains. Pop.: 151 118 (1996 est.). Ancient name: **Pe'rusia. 2 Lake.** another name for (Lake) **Trasimene.**

Perugino ★ (*Italian* peru'dʒino) *n* **Il** (il), real name *Pietro Vannucci.* 1446–1523, Italian painter. His works include the fresco *Christ giving the Keys to Peter* in the Sistine Chapel, Rome.

peruke (pə'ruːk) *n* a wig for men in the 17th and 18th centuries. Also called: **periwig.** ORIG C16: from F *perruque,* from It. *perrucca* wig, from ?

★ people and places

peruse (pəˈruːz) *vb* **peruses, perusing, perused.** (*tr*) **1** to read or examine with care; study. **2** to browse or read in a leisurely way. ORIG C15 (meaning: to use up): from PER- (intensive) + USE
▸ **peˈrusal** *n* ▸ **peˈruser** *n*

Perutz ★ (pəˈrʊts) *n* **Max Ferdinand.** born 1914, British biochemist, born in Austria. With J. C. Kendrew, he worked on the structure of haemoglobin and shared the Nobel prize for chemistry 1962.

Peruzzi ★ (*Italian* peˈruttsi) *n* **Baldassare Tommaso** (baldasˈsaːre tomˈmaːzo). 1481–1536, Italian architect and painter of the High Renaissance.

perv (pɜːv) *Sl.* ◆ *n* **1** a pervert. **2** *Austral.* a lascivious look. ◆ *vb also* **perve.** (*intr*) **3** *Austral.* to behave like a voyeur.

pervade (pɜːˈveɪd) *vb* **pervades, pervading, pervaded.** (*tr*) to spread through or throughout, esp. subtly or gradually; permeate. ORIG C17: from L *pervādere,* from *per-* through + *vādere* to go
▸ **pervasion** (pɜːˈveɪʒən) *n* ▸ **pervasive** (pɜːˈveɪsɪv) *adj* ▸ **perˈvasively** *adv* ▸ **perˈvasiveness** *n*

perverse (pəˈvɜːs) *adj* **1** deliberately deviating from what is regarded as normal, good, or proper. **2** persistently holding to what is wrong. **3** wayward or contrary; obstinate. ORIG C14: from OF *pervers,* from L *perversus* turned the wrong way
▸ **perˈversely** *adv* ▸ **perˈverseness** *or* **perˈversity** *n*

perversion (pəˈvɜːʃən) *n* **1** any abnormal means of obtaining sexual satisfaction. **2** the act of perverting or the state of being perverted. **3** a perverted form or usage.

pervert *vb* (pəˈvɜːt). (*tr*) **1** to use wrongly or badly. **2** to interpret wrongly or badly. **3** to lead into deviant or perverted beliefs or behaviour; corrupt. **4** to debase. ◆ *n* (ˈpɜːvɜːt). **5** a person who practises sexual perversion. ORIG C14: from OF *pervertir,* from L *pervertere* to turn the wrong way
▸ **perˈverted** *adj* ▸ **perˈverter** *n* ▸ **perˈvertible** *adj* ▸ **perˈversive** *adj*

pervious (ˈpɜːvɪəs) *adj* **1** able to be penetrated; permeable. **2** receptive to new ideas, etc.; open-minded. ORIG C17: from L *pervius,* from *per-* (through) + *via* a way
▸ **ˈperviously** *adv* ▸ **ˈperviousness** *n*

pes (peɪz, piːz) *n, pl* **pedes** (ˈpɛdiːz). the technical name for the human **foot.** ORIG C19: NL: foot

Pesaro ★ (*Italian* ˈpeːzaro) *n* a port and resort in E central Italy, in the Marches on the Adriatic. Pop.: 90 340 (1990). Ancient name: **Pisaurum** (pɪˈsaʊrəm).

Pescadores ★ (ˌpɛskəˈdɔːrɪz) *pl n* a group of 64 islands in Formosa Strait, separated from Taiwan (to which it belongs) by the **Pescadores Channel.** Pop.: 91 263 (1995). Area: 127 sq. km (49 sq. miles). Chinese names: **Penghu, P'eng-hu.**

Pescara ★ (*Italian* pesˈkaːra) *n* a city and resort in E central Italy, on the Adriatic. Pop.: 118 764 (1996 est.).

peseta (pəˈseɪtə; *Spanish* peˈseta) *n* the standard monetary unit of Spain, divided into 100 céntimos. ORIG C19: from Sp., dim. of PESO

Peshawar ★ (pəˈʃɔːə) *n* a city in N Pakistan, at the E end of the Khyber Pass: one of the oldest cities in Pakistan and capital of the ancient kingdom of Gandhara; university (1950). Pop.: 1 676 000 (1995 est.).

pesky (ˈpɛskɪ) *adj* **peskier, peskiest.** *US & Canad. inf.* troublesome. ORIG C19: prob. changed from *pesty;* see PEST
▸ **ˈpeskily** *adv* ▸ **ˈpeskiness** *n*

peso (ˈpeɪsəʊ; *Spanish* ˈpeso) *n, pl* **pesos** (-səʊz; *Spanish* -sos). the standard monetary unit of Argentina, Chile, Colombia, Cuba, the Dominican Republic, Guinea-Bissau, Mexico, the Philippines, and Uruguay. ORIG C16: from Sp.: weight, from L *pēnsum* something weighed out, from *pendere* to weigh

pessary (ˈpɛsərɪ) *n, pl* **pessaries.** *Med.* **1** a device for inserting into the vagina, either as a support for the uterus or (**diaphragm pessary**) as a contraceptive. **2** a vaginal suppository. ORIG C14: from LL *pessārium,* from L *pessum,* from Gk *pessos* plug

pessimism (ˈpɛsɪˌmɪzəm) *n* **1** the tendency to expect the worst in all things. **2** the doctrine of the ultimate triumph of evil over good. **3** the doctrine that this world is corrupt and that man's sojourn in it is a preparation for some other existence. ORIG C18: from L *pessimus* worst, sup. of *malus* bad
▸ **ˈpessimist** *n* ▸ **ˌpessiˈmistic** *adj* ▸ **ˌpessiˈmistically** *adv*

Pessoa ★ (*Portuguese* pəˈsoə) *n* **Fernando** (fərˈnəndu). 1888–1935, Portuguese poet, who ascribed much of his work to three imaginary poets, Alvaro de Campos, Alberto Caeiro, and Ricardo Reis.

pest (pɛst) *n* **1** a person or thing that annoys, esp. by imposing itself when it is not wanted; nuisance. **2** any organism that damages crops, or injures or irritates livestock or man. **3** *Rare.* an epidemic disease. ORIG C16: from L *pestis* plague, from ?

Pestalozzi ★ (ˌpɛstəˈlɒtsɪ) *n* **Johann Heinrich** (joˈhan ˈhainrɪç). 1746–1827, Swiss educational reformer, who emphasized learning by observation.

pester (ˈpɛstə) *vb* (*tr*) to annoy or nag continually. ORIG C16: from OF *empestrer* to hobble (a horse), from Vulgar L *impāstōriāre* (unattested) to use a hobble, ult. from L *pastor* herdsman

pester power *n Marketing.* a child's ability to pressurize its parents into buying a certain product or brand.

pesticide (ˈpɛstɪˌsaɪd) *n* a chemical used for killing pests, esp. insects.
▸ **ˌpestiˈcidal** *adj*

pestiferous (pɛˈstɪfərəs) *adj* **1** *Inf.* troublesome; irritating. **2** breeding, carrying, or spreading infectious disease. **3** corrupting; pernicious. ORIG C16: from L *pestifer,* from *pestis* contagion + *ferre* to bring

pestilence (ˈpɛstɪləns) *n* **1a** any epidemic of a deadly infectious disease, such as the plague. **1b** such a disease. **2** an evil influence.

pestilent (ˈpɛstɪlənt) *adj* **1** annoying; irritating. **2** highly destructive morally or physically; pernicious. **3** likely to cause epidemic or infectious disease. ORIG C15: from L *pestilens* unwholesome, from *pestis* plague
▸ **ˈpestilently** *adv* ▸ **pestilential** (ˌpɛstɪˈlɛnʃəl) *adj* ▸ **ˌpestiˈlentially** *adv*

pestle (ˈpɛsᵊl) *n* **1** a club-shaped instrument for mixing or grinding substances in a mortar. **2** a tool for pounding or stamping. ◆ *vb* **pestles, pestling, pestled. 3** to pound (a substance or object) with or as if with a pestle. ORIG C14: from OF *pestel,* from L *pistillum*

pesto (ˈpɛstəʊ) *n* a sauce for pasta, consisting of basil leaves, nuts, garlic, oil, and Parmesan cheese, all crushed together. ORIG It., shortened form of *pestato,* p.p. of *pestare* to pound, crush

pet[1] (pɛt) *n* **1** a tame animal kept for companionship, amusement, etc. **2** a person who is fondly indulged; favourite: *teacher's pet.* ◆ *adj* **3** kept as a pet: *a pet dog.* **4** of or for pet animals: *pet food.* **5** particularly cherished: *a pet hatred.* **6** familiar or affectionate: *a pet name.* ◆ *vb* **pets, petting, petted. 7** (*tr*) to treat (a person, animal, etc.) as a pet; pamper. **8** (*tr*) to pat or fondle (an animal, child, etc.). **9** (*intr*) *Inf.* (of two people) to caress each other in an erotic manner. ORIG C16: from ?
▸ **ˈpetter** *n*

pet[2] (pɛt) *n* a fit of sulkiness, esp. at what is felt to be a slight; pique. ORIG C16: from ?

PET (pɛt) *n acronym for* positron emission tomography.

Pet. *Bible. abbrev. for* Peter.

peta- *prefix* **1** denoting 10^{15}: *petametres.* **2** Also: **pebi-** *Computing.* denoting 10^{50}: *petabyte.* ◆ Symbol: P ORIG C20: so named because it is the SI prefix after TERA-; on the model of PENTA-, the prefix after TETRA-

USAGE NOTE See at **kilo-**.

Pétain ★ (*French* petɛ̃) *n* **Henri Philippe Omer** (ɑ̃ri filip ɔmɛr). 1856–1951, French marshal, noted for his victory at Verdun (1916) in World War I and his leadership of the pro-Nazi government of unoccupied France at Vichy (1940–44); imprisoned for treason (1945).

petal (ˈpɛtᵊl) *n* any of the separate parts of the corolla of a flower: often brightly coloured. ORIG C18: from NL *petalum,* from Gk *petalon* leaf
▸ **ˈpetaline** *adj* ▸ **ˈpetalled** *adj* ▸ **ˈpetal-ˌlike** *adj*

-petal *adj combining form.* seeking: *centripetal.* ORIG from NL *-petus,* from L *petere* to seek

petard (pɪ'tɑːd) *n* **1** (formerly) a device containing explosives used to breach a wall, doors, etc. **2 hoist with one's own petard.** being the victim of one's own schemes, etc. ORIG C16: from F: firework, from *péter* to break wind, from L *pēdere*

petaurist (pət'ɒrɪst) *n* another name for **flying phalanger.** ORIG C19: from L, from Gk *petauristēs* performer on the springboard

petcock ('pɛtˌkɒk) *n* a small valve for checking the water content of a steam boiler or draining waste from the cylinder of a steam engine. ORIG C19: from PET[1] or ? F *pet,* from *péter* to break wind + COCK[1]

petechia (pɪ'tiːkɪə) *n, pl* **petechiae** (-kɪˌiː). a minute discoloured spot on the surface of the skin. ORIG C18: via NL from It. *petecchia* freckle, from ?
▸ **pe'techial** *adj*

peter[1] ('piːtə) *vb* (*intr;* foll. by *out* or *away*) to fall (off) in volume, intensity, etc., and finally cease. ORIG C19: from ?

peter[2] ('piːtə) *n Sl.* **1** a safe, till, or cashbox. **2** a prison cell. ORIG C17 (meaning a case): from the name *Peter*

Peter ★ ('piːtə) *n New Testament.* **Saint.** Also called: **Simon Peter.** died ?67 A.D., a fisherman of Bethsaida, who became leader of the apostles and is regarded by Roman Catholics as the first pope; probably martyred at Rome.

Peter I ★ *n* known as *Peter the Great.* 1672–1725, tsar of Russia (1682–1725), who assumed sole power in 1689. He introduced many reforms in government and technology, acquired new territories for Russia in the Baltic, and founded the new capital of St Petersburg (1703).

Peter III ★ *n* 1728–62, grandson of Peter I and tsar of Russia (1762): deposed in a coup d'état led by his wife (later Catherine II); assassinated.

Peterborough ★ ('piːtəbərə, -brə) *n* **1** a city in central England, in N Cambridgeshire on the River Nene: industrial centre; under development as a new town since 1968. Pop.: 134 788 (1991). **2** a unitary authority in central England. Pop.: 158 700 (1996 est.). Area: 402 sq. km (155 sq. miles). **3 Soke of.** a former administrative area in E central England: absorbed into Cambridgeshire in 1974. **4** a city in SE Canada, in SE Ontario: manufacturing centre. Pop.: 62 500 (1990).

Peterlee ★ ('piːtəˌliː) *n* a new town in Co. Durham, founded in 1948. Pop.: 23 500 (1990).

peterman ('piːtəmən) *n, pl* **petermen.** *Sl.* a burglar skilled in safe-breaking. ORIG C19: from PETER[2]

Petermann Peak ★ ('piːtəmən) *n* a mountain in E Greenland. Height: 2932 m (9645 ft).

Peter Pan *n* a youthful, boyish, or immature man. ORIG C20: after the main character in *Peter Pan* (1904), a play by J. M. BARRIE

Peter Principle *n* **the.** the theory, usually taken facetiously, that all members in a hierarchy rise to their own level of incompetence. ORIG C20: from the book *The Peter Principle* (1969) by Dr Lawrence J. *Peter* and Raymond Hull

Petersburg ★ ('piːtəzˌbɜːg) *n* a city in SE Virginia, on the Appomattox River: scene of prolonged fighting (1864–65) during the final months of the American Civil War. Pop.: 38 386 (1990).

petersham ('piːtəʃəm) *n* **1** a thick corded ribbon used to stiffen belts, etc. **2** a heavy woollen fabric used for coats, etc. **3** a kind of overcoat made of such fabric. ORIG C19: after Viscount *Petersham* (died 1851), E army officer

Peterson ★ ('piːtəsᵊn) *n* **Oscar** (**Emmanuel**). born 1925, Canadian jazz pianist and singer.

Peter's pence *or* **Peter pence** *n* **1** an annual tax, originally of one penny, formerly levied for the maintenance of the Papal See: abolished by Henry VIII in 1534. **2** a voluntary contribution made by Roman Catholics in many countries for the same purpose. ORIG C13: referring to St PETER, considered as the first pope

Peters' projection *n* a form of modified Mercator's map projection that gives prominence to Third World countries. ORIG C20: after Arno *Peters,* G historian

Peter the Hermit ★ *n* ?1050–1115, French monk and preacher of the First Crusade.

pethidine ('pɛθɪˌdiːn) *n* a white crystalline water-soluble drug used as an analgesic. ORIG C20: ? a blend of PIPERIDINE + ETHYL

petiole ('pɛtɪˌəʊl) *n* **1** the stalk by which a leaf is attached to the plant. **2** *Zool.* a slender stalk or stem, as between the thorax and abdomen of ants. ORIG C18: via F from L *petiolus* little foot, from *pēs* foot
▸ **petiolate** ('pɛtɪəˌleɪt) *adj*

petit ('pɛtɪ) *adj* (*prenominal*) *Chiefly law.* of lesser importance; small. ORIG C14: from OF: little, from ?

Petit ★ (*French* pəti) *n* **Roland** (rɔlɑ̃). born 1924, French ballet dancer and choreographer. His innovative ballets include *Carmen* (1949) and *Kraanerg* (1969).

petit bourgeois ('buəʒwɑː) *n, pl* **petits bourgeois** ('buəʒwɑːz). **1** Also called: **petite bourgeoisie, petty bourgeoisie.** the section of the middle class with the lowest social status, as shopkeepers, lower clerical staff, etc. **2** a member of this stratum. ◆ *adj* **3** of, relating to, or characteristic of the petit bourgeois, esp. indicating a sense of self-righteousness and conformity to established standards of behaviour.

petite (pə'tiːt) *adj* (of a woman) small, delicate, and dainty. ORIG C18: from F, fem of *petit* small

petit four (fɔː) *n, pl* **petits fours** (fɔːz). any of various very small fancy cakes and biscuits. ORIG F, lit.: little oven

petition (pɪ'tɪʃən) *n* **1** a written document signed by a large number of people demanding some form of action from a government or other authority. **2** any formal request to a higher authority; entreaty. **3** *Law.* a formal application in writing made to a court asking for some specific judicial action: *a petition for divorce.* **4** the action of petitioning. ◆ *vb* **5** (*tr*) to address or present a petition to (a person in authority, government, etc.): *to petition Parliament.* **6** (*intr;* foll. by *for*) to seek by petition: *to petition for a change in the law.* ORIG C14: from L *petītiō,* from *petere* to seek
▸ **pe'titionary** *adj*

petitioner (pɪ'tɪʃənə) *n* **1** a person who presents a petition. **2** *Chiefly Brit.* the plaintiff in a divorce suit.

petitio principii (pɪ'tɪʃɪˌəʊ prɪn'kɪpɪˌaɪ) *n Logic.* a form of fallacious reasoning in which the conclusion has been assumed in the premises; begging the question. ORIG C16: L, translation of Gk *to en arkhei aiteisthai* an assumption at the beginning

petit jury *n* a jury of 12 persons empanelled to determine the facts of a case and decide the issue pursuant to the direction of the court on points of law. Also called: **petty jury.**
▸ **petit juror** *n*

petit larceny *n* (formerly, in England) the stealing of property valued at 12 pence or under. Abolished 1827. Also called: **petty larceny.**

petit mal (mæl) *n* a mild form of epilepsy characterized by periods of impairment or loss of consciousness for up to 30 seconds. Cf. **grand mal.** ORIG C19: F: little illness

petit point ('pɛtɪ 'pɔɪnt; *French* pəti pwɛ̃) *n* **1** a small diagonal needlepoint stitch used for fine detail. **2** work done with such stitches. ORIG F: small point

Petöfi ★ (*Hungarian* 'pɛtøːfi) *n* **Sándor** ('ʃaːndor). 1823–49, Hungarian lyric poet and patriot.

Petra ★ ('pɛtrə, 'piːtrə) *n* an ancient city in the south of present-day Jordan; capital of the Nabataean kingdom.

Petrarch ★ ('pɛtrɑːk) *n* Italian name *Francesco Petrarca.* 1304–74, Italian lyric poet and scholar, who greatly influenced the values of the Renaissance. His collection of poems *Canzoniere,* inspired by his ideal love for Laura, was written in the Tuscan dialect. He also wrote much in Latin.
▸ **Pe'trarchan** *adj*

Petrarchan sonnet *n* a sonnet form associated with the poet Petrarch, having an octave rhyming a b b a a b b a and a sestet rhyming either c d e c d e or c d c d c d.

petrel ('pɛtrəl) *n* any of a family of oceanic birds having a hooked bill and tubular nostrils: includes albatrosses, storm petrels, and shearwaters. ORIG C17: var. of earlier *pitteral,* associated by folk etymology with St *Peter,* because the bird appears to walk on water

Petri dish (ˈpɛtrɪ) *n* a shallow dish, often with a cover, used in laboratories, esp. for producing cultures of microorganisms. ORIG C19: after J. R. *Petri* (1852–1921), G bacteriologist

Petrie ★ (ˈpiːtrɪ) *n* Sir (**William Matthew**) **Flinders.** 1853–1942, British Egyptologist and archaeologist.

petrifaction (ˌpɛtrɪˈfækʃən) *or* **petrification** (ˌpɛtrɪfɪˈkeɪʃən) *n* **1** the act or process of forming petrified organic material. **2** the state of being petrified.

Petrified Forest ★ *n* a national park in E Arizona, containing petrified coniferous trees about 170 000 000 years old.

petrify (ˈpɛtrɪˌfaɪ) *vb* **petrifies, petrifying, petrified. 1** (*tr; often passive*) to convert (organic material) into a fossilized form by impregnation with dissolved minerals so that the original appearance is preserved. **2** to make or become dull, unresponsive, etc.; deaden. **3** (*tr; often passive*) to stun or daze with horror, fear, etc. ORIG C16: from F *pétrifier,* ult. from Gk *petra* stone
▸ **ˈpetriˌfier** *n*

petro- *or before a vowel* **petr-** *combining form.* **1** indicating stone or rock: *petrology.* **2** indicating petroleum, its products, etc.: *petrochemical.* **3** of or relating to the production, export, or sale of petroleum: *petrostate.* ORIG from Gk *petra* rock or *petros* stone

petrochemical (ˌpɛtrəʊˈkɛmɪkəl) *n* **1** any substance, such as acetone or ethanol, obtained from petroleum. ◆ *adj* **2** of, concerned with, or obtained from petrochemicals or related to petrochemistry.
▸ **ˌpetroˈchemistry** *n*

petrodollar (ˈpɛtrəʊˌdɒlə) *n* money earned by a country by the exporting of petroleum.

petroglyph (ˈpɛtrəˌglɪf) *n* a drawing or carving on rock, esp. a prehistoric one. ORIG C19: via F from Gk *petra* stone + *gluphē* carving

Petrograd ★ (ˈpɛtrəʊˌgræd; *Russian* pɪtraˈgrat) *n* a former name (1914–24) of **Saint Petersburg** (sense 1).

petrography (pɛˈtrɒgrəfɪ) *n* the branch of petrology concerned with the description and classification of rocks.
▸ **peˈtrographer** *n* ▸ **petrographic** (ˌpɛtrəˈgræfɪk) *or* **ˌpetroˈgraphical** *adj*

petrol (ˈpɛtrəl) *n* any one of various volatile flammable liquid mixtures of hydrocarbons, obtained from petroleum and used as a solvent and a fuel for internal-combustion engines. US and Canad. name: **gasoline.** ORIG C16: via F from Med. L PETROLEUM

petrolatum (ˌpɛtrəˈleɪtəm) *n* a translucent gelatinous substance obtained from petroleum; used as a lubricant and in medicine as an ointment base. Also called: **petroleum jelly.**

petrol bomb *n* **1** a device filled with petrol that bursts into flames on impact. ◆ *vb* **petrol-bomb.** (*tr*) **2** to attack with petrol bombs.

petrol engine *n* an internal-combustion engine that uses petrol as fuel.

petroleum (pəˈtrəʊlɪəm) *n* a dark-coloured thick flammable crude oil occurring in sedimentary rocks, consisting mainly of hydrocarbons. Fractional distillation separates the crude oil into petrol, paraffin, diesel oil, lubricating oil, etc. Fuel oil, paraffin wax, asphalt, and carbon black are extracted from the residue. ORIG C16: from Med. L, from L *petra* stone + *oleum* oil

petroleum jelly *n* another name for **petrolatum.**

petrology (pɛˈtrɒlədʒɪ) *n, pl* **petrologies.** the study of the composition, origin, structure, and formation of rocks.
▸ **petrological** (ˌpɛtrəˈlɒdʒɪkəl) *adj* ▸ **peˈtrologist** *n*

petrol station *n Brit.* another term for **filling station.**

Petronius ★ (pɪˈtrəʊnɪəs) *n* **Gaius** (ˈgaɪəs), known as *Petronius Arbiter.* died 66 A.D., Roman satirist, supposed author of the *Satyricon,* a picaresque account of the licentiousness of contemporary society.

Petropavlovsk ★ (*Russian* pɪtraˈpavləfsk) *n* a city in N Kazakhstan, on the Ishim River. Pop.: 239 000 (1995 est.).

Petrópolis ★ (*Portuguese* peˈtrɔpulis) *n* a city in SE Brazil, north of Rio de Janeiro: resort. Pop.: 164 849 (1991).

petrous (ˈpɛtrəs, ˈpiː-) *adj Anat.* denoting the dense part of the temporal bone that surrounds the inner ear. ORIG C16: from L *petrōsus* full of rocks
▸ **petrosal** (pɛˈtrəʊsəl) *adj*

Petrovsk ★ (*Russian* pɪˈtrɔfsk) *n* the former name (until 1921) of **Makhachkala.**

Petrozavodsk ★ (*Russian* pɪtrəzaˈvɔtsk) *n* a city in NW Russia, capital of the Karelian Autonomous Republic, on Lake Onega: developed around ironworks established by Peter the Great in 1703; university (1940). Pop.: 280 000 (1995 est.).

Petsamo ★ (*Finnish* ˈpɛtsɑmɔ) *n* a former territory of N Finland ceded by the Soviet Union to Finland in 1920 and taken back in 1940; now in NW Russia.

petticoat (ˈpɛtɪˌkəʊt) *n* **1** a woman's underskirt. **2** *Inf.* **2a** a humorous or mildly disparaging name for a woman. **2b** (*as modifier*): *petticoat politics.* ORIG C15: see PETTY, COAT

pettifogger (ˈpɛtɪˌfɒgə) *n* **1** a lawyer who conducts unimportant cases, esp. one who resorts to trickery. **2** any person who quibbles. ORIG C16: from PETTY + *fogger,* from ?, perhaps from *Fugger,* a family (C15–16) of G financiers
▸ **ˈpettiˌfoggery** *n* ▸ **ˈpettiˌfog** *vb* **ˈpettiˌfogs, ˈpettiˌfogging, ˈpettiˌfogged.** (*intr*) ▸ **ˈpettiˌfogging** *adj*

pettish (ˈpɛtɪʃ) *adj* peevish; petulant. ORIG C16: from PET[2]
▸ **ˈpettishly** *adv* ▸ **ˈpettishness** *n*

petty (ˈpɛtɪ) *adj* **pettier, pettiest. 1** trivial; trifling: *petty details.* **2** narrow-minded, mean: *petty spite.* **3** minor or subordinate in rank: *petty officialdom.* **4** *Law.* a variant of **petit.** ORIG C14: from OF PETIT
▸ **ˈpettily** *adv* ▸ **ˈpettiness** *n*

petty cash *n* a small cash fund for minor incidental expenses.

petty jury *n* a variant of **petit jury.**

petty larceny *n* a variant of **petit larceny.**

petty officer *n* a noncommissioned officer in a naval service comparable in rank to a sergeant in an army or marine corps.

petty sessions *n* (*functioning as sing or pl*) another term for **magistrates' court.**

petulant (ˈpɛtjʊlənt) *adj* irritable, impatient, or sullen in a peevish or capricious way. ORIG C16: via OF from L *petulāns* bold, from *petulāre* (unattested) to attack playfully, from *petere* to assail
▸ **ˈpetulance** *or* **ˈpetulancy** *n* ▸ **ˈpetulantly** *adv*

petunia (pɪˈtjuːnɪə) *n* any plant of a tropical American genus cultivated for their colourful funnel-shaped flowers. ORIG C19: via NL from obs. F *petun* variety of tobacco, from Tupi *petyn*

petuntse (pɪˈtʌntsɪ, -ˈtʊn-) *n* a fusible mineral used in hard-paste porcelain. ORIG C18: from Chinese, from *pe* white + *tun* heap + *tzu* offspring

Pevsner ★ (ˈpɛvznə) *n* **1 Antoine** (ɑ̃twan). 1886–1962, French constructivist sculptor and painter, born in Russia; brother of Naum Gabo. **2** Sir **Nikolaus** (ˈnɪkəlaʊs). 1902–83, British architectural historian, born in Germany: his monumental series *Buildings of England* (1951–74) describes every structure of account in the country.

pew (pjuː) *n* **1** (in a church) **1a** one of several long benchlike seats with backs, used by the congregation. **1b** an enclosed compartment reserved for the use of a family or other small group. **2** *Brit. inf.* a seat (esp. in **take a pew**). ORIG C14 *pywe,* from OF, from L *podium* a balcony, from Gk *podion* supporting structure, from *pous* foot

pewit *or* **peewit** (ˈpiːwɪt) *n* other names for **lapwing.** ORIG C13: imit. of the bird's cry

pewter (ˈpjuːtə) *n* **1a** any of various alloys containing tin, lead, and sometimes copper and antimony. **1b** (*as modifier*): *pewter ware; a pewter tankard.* **2** plate or kitchen utensils made from pewter. ORIG C14: from OF *peaultre,* from ?
▸ **ˈpewterer** *n*

peyote (peɪ'əʊtɪ, pɪ-) *n* another name for **mescal** (the plant). ORIG Mexican Sp., from Nahuatl *peyotl*

pF *abbrev. for* picofarad.

pf. *abbrev for:* **1** perfect. **2** Also: **pfg.** pfennig. **3** preferred.

Pfalz ★ (pfalts) *n* the German name for the **Palatinate.**

pfennig ('fɛnɪg; *German* 'pfɛnɪç) *n, pl* **pfennigs** *or* **pfennige** (*German* -nɪgə). a German monetary unit worth one hundredth of a Deutschmark. ORIG G: PENNY

PFI (in Britain) *abbrev. for* Private Finance Initiative.

Pforzheim ★ (*German* 'pfɔrtshaim) *n* a city in Germany, in W Baden-Württemberg: centre of the German watch and jewellery industry. Pop.: 118 763 (1996 est.).

PG *symbol for* a film certified for viewing by anyone, but which contains scenes that may be unsuitable for children, for whom parental guidance is necessary. ORIG C20: from abbrev. of *parental guidance*

pg. *abbrev. for* page.

Pg. *abbrev. for:* **1** Portugal. **2** Portuguese.

PGR *abbrev. for* psychogalvanic response.

pH *n* potential of hydrogen; a measure of the acidity or alkalinity of a solution. Pure water has a pH of 7, acid solutions have a pH less than 7, and alkaline solutions a pH greater than 7.

phacelia (fæ'si:lɪə) *n* any of a genus of N American plants having clusters of blue flowers. ORIG NL from Gk *phakelos* a cluster

Phaeacian ★ (fi:'eɪʃən) *n Greek myth.* one of a race of people inhabiting the island of Scheria visited by Odysseus on his way home from the Trojan War.

Phaedra ★ ('fi:drə) *n Greek myth.* the wife of Theseus, who falsely accused her stepson Hippolytus of raping her because he spurned her amorous advances.

Phaedrus ★ ('fi:drəs) *n* ?15 B.C.–?50 A.D., Roman author of five books of Latin verse fables, based chiefly on Aesop.

Phaëthon ★ ('feɪəθən) *n Greek myth.* the son of Helios (the sun god) who borrowed his father's chariot and nearly set the earth on fire by approaching too close to it. Zeus averted the catastrophe by striking him down with a thunderbolt.

phaeton ('feɪtᵊn) *n* a light four-wheeled horse-drawn carriage with or without a top. ORIG C18: from PHAËTHON

-phage *n combining form.* indicating something that eats or consumes something specified: *bacteriophage.* ORIG from Gk *-phagos;* see PHAGO-
▸ **-phagous** *adj combining form.*

phago- *or before a vowel* **phag-** *combining form.* eating, consuming, or destroying: *phagocyte.* ORIG from Gk *phagein* to consume

phagocyte ('fægəˌsaɪt) *n* a cell or protozoan that engulfs particles, such as microorganisms.
▸ **phagocytic** (ˌfægə'sɪtɪk) *adj*

phagocytosis (ˌfægəsaɪ'təʊsɪs) *n* the process by which a cell, such as a white blood cell, ingests microorganisms, other cells, etc.

-phagy *or* **-phagia** *n combining form.* indicating an eating or devouring: *anthropophagy.* ORIG from Gk *-phagia;* see PHAGO-

phalange ('fælændʒ) *n, pl* **phalanges** (fæ'lændʒi:z). *Anat.* another name for **phalanx** (sense 4). ORIG C16: via F, ult. from Gk PHALANX

phalangeal (fə'lændʒɪəl) *adj Anat.* of or relating to a phalanx or phalanges.

phalanger (fə'lændʒə) *n* any of various Australasian arboreal marsupials having dense fur and a long tail. Also called (Austral. and NZ): **possum.** See also **flying phalanger.** ORIG C18: via NL from Gk *phalaggion* spider's web, referring to its webbed hind toes

phalanx ('fælæŋks) *n, pl* **phalanxes** *or* **phalanges** (fæ'lændʒi:z). **1** an ancient Greek and Macedonian battle formation of hoplites presenting long spears from behind a wall of overlapping shields. **2** any closely ranked unit or mass of people: *the police formed a phalanx to protect the embassy.* **3** a number of people united for a common purpose. **4** *Anat.* any of the bones of the fingers or toes. **5** *Bot.* a bundle of stamens. ORIG C16: via L from Gk: infantry formation in close ranks, bone of finger or toe

phalarope ('fæləˌrəʊp) *n* any of a family of aquatic shore birds of northern oceans and lakes, having a long slender bill and lobed toes. ORIG C18: via F from NL *Phalaropus,* from Gk *phalaris* coot + *pous* foot

phallic ('fælɪk) *adj* **1** of, relating to, or resembling a phallus: *a phallic symbol.* **2** *Psychoanal.* relating to a stage of psychosexual development during which a male child's interest is concentrated on the genital organs. **3** of or relating to phallicism.

phallicism ('fælɪˌsɪzəm) *or* **phallism** *n* the worship or veneration of the phallus.

phallus ('fæləs) *n, pl* **phalluses** *or* **phalli** (-laɪ). **1** another word for **penis. 2** an image of the male sexual organ, esp. as a symbol of reproductive power. ORIG C17: via LL from Gk *phallos*

-phane *n combining form.* indicating something resembling a specified substance: *cellophane.* ORIG from Gk *phainein* to shine, appear

phanerogam ('fænərəʊˌgæm) *n* any plant of a former major division which included all seed-bearing plants; a former name for **spermatophyte.** ORIG C19: from NL *phanerogamus,* from Gk *phaneros* visible + *gamos* marriage
▸ ˌ**phanero'gamic** *or* **phanerogamous** (ˌfænə'rɒgəməs) *adj*

phantasm ('fæntæzəm) *n* **1** a phantom. **2** an illusory perception of an object, person, etc. ORIG C13: from OF *fantasme,* from L *phantasma,* from Gk
▸ **phan'tasmal** *or* **phan'tasmic** *adj*

phantasmagoria (ˌfæntæzmə'gɔ:rɪə) *or* **phantasmagory** (fæn'tæzməgərɪ) *n* **1** *Psychol.* a shifting medley of real or imagined figures, as in a dream. **2** *Films.* a sequence of pictures made to vary in size rapidly. **3** a shifting scene composed of different elements. ORIG C19: prob. from F, from PHANTASM + *-agorie,* ?from Gk *ageirein* to gather together
▸ **phantasmagoric** (ˌfæntæzmə'gɒrɪk) *or* ˌ**phantasma'gorical** *adj*

phantasy ('fæntəsɪ) *n, pl* **phantasies.** an archaic spelling of **fantasy.**

phantom ('fæntəm) *n* **1a** an apparition or spectre. **1b** (*as modifier*): *a phantom army marching through the sky.* **2** the visible representation of something abstract, esp. as in a dream or hallucination: *phantoms of evil haunted his sleep.* **3** something apparently unpleasant or horrific that has no material form. ORIG C13: from OF *fantosme,* from L *phantasma*

phantom limb *n* the illusion that a limb still exists following its amputation, sometimes with the sensation of pain (**phantom limb pain**).

phantom pregnancy *n* the occurrence of signs of pregnancy, such as enlarged abdomen and absence of menstruation, when no embryo is present, due to hormonal imbalance. Also called: **false pregnancy.**

-phany *n combining form.* indicating a manifestation: *theophany.* ORIG from Gk *-phania,* from *phainein* to show
▸ **-phanous** *adj combining form.*

phar., Phar., pharm., *or* **Pharm.** *abbrev. for:* **1** pharmaceutical. **2** pharmacist. **3** pharmacopoeia. **4** pharmacy.

Pharaoh ('fɛərəʊ) *n* the title of the ancient Egyptian kings. ORIG OE *Pharaon,* via L, Gk, & Heb., ult. from Egyptian *pr-'o* great house
▸ **Pharaonic** (fɛə'rɒnɪk) *adj*

Pharisaic (ˌfærɪ'seɪɪk) *or* **Pharisaical** *adj* **1** *Judaism.* of, relating to, or characteristic of the Pharisees or Pharisaism. **2** (*often not cap.*) righteously hypocritical.
▸ ˌ**Phari'saically** *adv*

Pharisaism ('færɪseɪˌɪzəm) *or* **Phariseeism** ('færɪsi:ˌɪzəm) *n* **1** *Judaism.* the tenets and customs of the Pharisees. **2** (*often not cap.*) observance of the external forms of religion without genuine belief; hypocrisy.

Pharisee ('færɪˌsi:) *n* **1** a member of an ancient Jewish sect teaching strict observance of Jewish traditions. **2** (*often not cap.*) a self-righteous or hypocritical person.

ORIG OE *Farīsēus,* ult. from Aramaic *perīshāiyā,* pl. of *perīsh* separated

pharmaceutical (ˌfɑːməˈsjuːtɪkᵊl) *or* (*less commonly*) **pharmaceutic** *adj* of or relating to drugs or pharmacy. ORIG C17: from LL *pharmaceuticus,* from Gk *pharmakeus* purveyor of drugs; see PHARMACY
▸ **ˌpharmaˈceutically** *adv*

pharmaceutics (ˌfɑːməˈsjuːtɪks) *n* **1** (*functioning as sing*) another term for **pharmacy** (sense 1). **2** (*functioning as pl*) pharmaceutical remedies.

pharmacist (ˈfɑːməsɪst) *n* a person qualified to prepare and dispense drugs.

pharmaco- *combining form.* indicating drugs: *pharmacology.* ORIG from Gk *pharmakon* drug

pharmacognosy (ˌfɑːməˈkɒgnəsɪ) *n* the study of crude drugs of plant and animal origin. ORIG C19: from PHARMACO- + *gnosy,* from Gk *gnosis* knowledge
▸ **ˌpharmaˈcognosist** *n*

pharmacology (ˌfɑːməˈkɒlədʒɪ) *n* the science or study of drugs, including their characteristics, action, and uses.
▸ **pharmacological** (ˌfɑːməkəˈlɒdʒɪkᵊl) *adj* ▸ **ˌpharmacoˈlogically** *adv* ▸ **ˌpharmaˈcologist** *n*

pharmacopoeia *or US* (*sometimes*) **pharmacopeia** (ˌfɑːməkəˈpiːə) *n* an authoritative book containing a list of medicinal drugs with their uses, preparation, dosages, formulas, etc. ORIG C17: via NL from Gk *pharmakopoiia* art of preparing drugs, from PHARMACO- + *-poiia,* from *poiein* to make
▸ **ˌpharmacoˈpoeial** *adj*

pharmacy (ˈfɑːməsɪ) *n, pl* **pharmacies. 1** Also: **pharmaceutics.** the practice or art of preparing and dispensing drugs. **2** a dispensary. ORIG C14: from Med. L *pharmacia,* from Gk *pharmakeia* making of drugs, from *pharmakon* drug

pharos (ˈfɛərɒs) *n* any marine lighthouse or beacon. ORIG C16: after a large Hellenistic lighthouse on an island off Alexandria in Egypt

Pharsalus ★ (fɑːˈseɪləs) *n* an ancient town in Thessaly in N Greece. Several major battles were fought nearby, including Caesar's victory over Pompey (48 B.C.).

pharyngeal (ˌfærɪnˈdʒiːəl) *or* **pharyngal** (fəˈrɪŋgᵊl) *adj* **1** of, relating to, or situated in or near the pharynx. **2** *Phonetics.* pronounced with an articulation in or constriction of the pharynx. ORIG C19: from NL *pharyngeus;* see PHARYNX

pharyngitis (ˌfærɪnˈdʒaɪtɪs) *n* inflammation of the pharynx.

pharynx (ˈfærɪŋks) *n, pl* **pharynges** (fæˈrɪndʒiːz) *or* **pharynxes.** the part of the alimentary canal between the mouth and the oesophagus. ORIG C17: via NL from Gk *pharunx* throat

phase (feɪz) *n* **1** any distinct or characteristic period or stage in a sequence of events: *there were two phases to the resolution.* **2** *Astron.* one of the recurring shapes of the portion of the moon or an inferior planet illuminated by the sun. **3** *Physics.* the fraction of a cycle of a periodic quantity that has been completed at a specific reference time, expressed as an angle. **4** *Physics.* a particular stage in a periodic process or phenomenon. **5 in phase.** (of two waveforms) reaching corresponding phases at the same time. **6 out of phase.** (of two waveforms) not in phase. **7** *Chem.* a distinct state of matter characterized by homogeneous composition and properties and the possession of a clearly defined boundary. **8** *Zool.* a variation in the normal form of an animal, esp. a colour variation, brought about by seasonal or geographical change. ◆ *vb* **phases, phasing, phased.** (*tr*) **9** (*often passive*) to execute, arrange, or introduce gradually or in stages: *the withdrawal was phased over several months.* **10** (sometimes foll. by *with*) to cause (a part, process, etc.) to function or coincide with (another part, etc.): *he tried to phase the intake and output of the machine; he phased the intake with the output.* **11** *Chiefly US.* to arrange (processes, goods, etc.) to be supplied or executed when required. ORIG C19: from NL *phases,* pl. of *phasis,* from Gk: aspect
▸ **ˈphasic** *adj*

phase in *vb* (*tr, adv*) to introduce in a gradual or cautious manner: *the legislation was phased in over two years.*

phase modulation *n* a type of modulation in which the phase of a radio carrier wave is varied by an amount proportional to the instantaneous amplitude of the modulating signal.

phase out *vb* (*tr, adv*) **1** to discontinue or withdraw gradually. ◆ *n* **phase-out. 2** *Chiefly US.* the action or an instance of phasing out: *a phase-out of conventional forces.*

phase rule *n* the principle that in any system in equilibrium the number of degrees of freedom is equal to the number of components less the number of phases plus two.

-phasia *n combining form.* indicating speech disorder of a specified kind: *aphasia.* ORIG from Gk, from *phanai* to speak
▸ **-phasic** *adj and n combining form.*

phatic (ˈfætɪk) *adj* (of speech) used to establish social contact and to express sociability rather than specific meaning. ORIG C20: from Gk *phat(os)* spoken + -IC

PhD *abbrev. for* Doctor of Philosophy. Also: **DPhil.**

pheasant (ˈfɛzᵊnt) *n* **1** any of various long-tailed gallinaceous birds, having a brightly-coloured plumage in the male: native to Asia but introduced elsewhere. **2** any of various other related birds, including the quails and partridges. **3** *US & Canad.* any of several other gallinaceous birds, esp. the ruffed grouse. ORIG C13: from OF *fesan,* from L *phāsiānus,* from Gk *phasianos ornis* Phasian bird, after the River *Phasis,* in Colchis

Phebe ★ (ˈfiːbɪ) *n* a variant spelling of **Phoebe.**

Pheidippides *or* **Phidippides** ★ (faɪˈdɪpɪˌdiːz) *n* Athenian athlete, who ran to Sparta to seek help against the Persians before the Battle of Marathon (490 B.C.).

phellem (ˈfɛləm) *n Bot.* the technical name for **cork** (sense 4). ORIG C20: from Gk *phellos* cork + PHLOEM

phenacetin (fɪˈnæsɪtɪn) *n* a white crystalline solid used in medicine to relieve pain and fever. Also called: **acetophenetidin.** ORIG C19: from PHENO- + ACETYL + -IN

phenix ★ (ˈfiːnɪks) *n* a US spelling of **phoenix.**

pheno- *or before a vowel* **phen-** *combining form.* **1** showing or manifesting: *phenotype.* **2** indicating that a molecule contains benzene rings: *phenobarbitone.* ORIG from Gk *phaino-* shining, from *phainein* to show; its use in a chemical sense is exemplified in *phenol,* so called because orig. prepared from illuminating gas

phenobarbitone (ˌfiːnəʊˈbɑːbɪˌtəʊn) *or* **phenobarbital** (ˌfiːnəʊˈbɑːbɪtᵊl) *n* a white crystalline derivative of barbituric acid used as a sedative for treating insomnia and epilepsy.

phenocryst (ˈfiːnəˌkrɪst, ˈfɛn-) *n* any of several large crystals in igneous rocks such as porphyry. ORIG C19: from PHENO- (shining) + CRYSTAL

phenol (ˈfiːnɒl) *n* **1** Also called: **carbolic acid.** a white crystalline derivative of benzene, used as an antiseptic and disinfectant and in the manufacture of resins, explosives, and pharmaceuticals. Formula: C_6H_5OH. **2** *Chem.* any of a class of organic compounds whose molecules contain one or more hydroxyl groups bound directly to a carbon atom in an aromatic ring.
▸ **pheˈnolic** *adj*

phenolic resin *n* any one of a class of resins derived from phenol, used in paints, adhesives, and as thermosetting plastics.

phenology (fɪˈnɒlədʒɪ) *n* the study of recurring phenomena, such as animal migration, esp. as influenced by climatic conditions. ORIG C19: from PHENO(MENON) + -LOGY
▸ **phenological** (ˌfiːnəˈlɒdʒɪkᵊl) *adj* ▸ **pheˈnologist** *n*

phenolphthalein (ˌfiːnɒlˈθeɪliːn, -lɪɪn, -ˈθæl-) *n* a colourless crystalline compound used in medicine as a laxative and in chemistry as an indicator. ORIG from PHENO- + *phthal-*, short form of NAPHTHALENE + -IN

phenomena (fɪˈnɒmɪnə) *n* a plural of **phenomenon.**

phenomenal (fɪˈnɒmɪnᵊl) *adj* **1** of or relating to a phenomenon. **2** extraordinary; outstanding; remarkable: *a phenomenal achievement.* **3** *Philosophy.* known or perceived by the senses rather than the mind.
▸ **pheˈnomenally** *adv*

★ people and places

phenomenalism (fɪˈnɒmɪnəˌlɪzəm) *n Philosophy.* the doctrine that statements about physical objects and the external world can be analysed in terms of possible or actual experiences, and that entities, such as physical objects, are only mental constructions out of phenomenal appearances.
▸ **pheˈnomenalist** *n, adj*

phenomenology (fɪˌnɒmɪˈnɒlədʒɪ) *n Philosophy.* **1** the movement that concentrates on the detailed description of conscious experience. **2** the science of phenomena as opposed to the science of being.
▸ **phenomenological** (fɪˌnɒmɪnəˈlɒdʒɪkᵊl) *adj*

phenomenon (fɪˈnɒmɪnən) *n, pl* **phenomena** (-ɪnə) *or* **phenomenons. 1** anything that can be perceived as an occurrence or fact by the senses. **2** any remarkable occurrence or person. **3** *Philosophy.* **3a** the object of perception, experience, etc. **3b** (in the writings of Kant) a thing as it appears, as distinguished from its real nature as a thing-in-itself. ORIG C16: via LL from Gk *phainomenon,* from *phainesthai* to appear, from *phainein* to show

> **USAGE NOTE** Although *phenomena* is often treated as a singular, correct usage is to employ *phenomenon* with a singular construction and *phenomena* with a plural: *that is an interesting phenomenon* (not *phenomena*); *several new phenomena were recorded in his notes.*

phenotype (ˈfiːnəʊˌtaɪp) *n* the physical constitution of an organism as determined by the interaction of its genetic constitution and the environment.
▸ **phenotypic** (ˌfiːnəʊˈtɪpɪk) *or* **ˌphenoˈtypical** *adj* ▸ **ˌphenoˈtypically** *adv*

phenyl (ˈfiːnaɪl, ˈfɛnɪl) *n (modifier)* of, containing, or consisting of the monovalent group C_6H_5, derived from benzene: *a phenyl group.*

phenylalanine (ˌfiːnaɪlˈæləˌniːn) *n* an essential amino acid; a component of proteins.

phenylbutazone (ˌfiːnaɪlˈbjuːtəˌzəʊn) *n* an anti-inflammatory drug used in the treatment of rheumatic diseases. ORIG C20: from *(dioxodi)phenylbut(ylpyr)azo(lidi)ne*

phenylketonuria (ˌfiːnaɪlˌkiːtəˈnjʊərɪə) *n* a congenital metabolic disorder characterized by the abnormal accumulation of phenylalanine in the body fluids, resulting in mental deficiency. ORIG C20: NL; see PHENYL, KETONE, -URIA

pheromone (ˈfɛrəˌməʊn) *n* a chemical substance, secreted externally by certain animals, such as insects, affecting the behaviour of other animals of the same species. ORIG C20 *phero-,* from Gk *pherein* to bear + (HOR)MONE

phew (fjuː) *interj* an exclamation of relief, surprise, disbelief, weariness, etc.

phi (faɪ) *n, pl* **phis.** the 21st letter in the Greek alphabet, Φ, ϕ.

phial (ˈfaɪəl) *n* a small bottle for liquids, etc.; vial. ORIG C14: from OF *fiole,* from L *phiola* saucer, from Gk *phialē* wide shallow vessel

Phi Beta Kappa (ˈfaɪ ˈbeɪtə ˈkæpə, ˈbiːtə) *n* (in the US) **1** a national honorary society, founded in 1776, membership of which is based on high academic ability. **2** a member of this society. ORIG from the initials of the Gk motto *philosophia biou kubernētēs* philosophy the guide of life

Phidias ★ (ˈfɪdɪˌæs) *n* 5th century B.C., Greek sculptor, regarded as one of the greatest of sculptors. He executed the sculptures of the Parthenon and the colossal statue of Zeus at Olympia, one of the Seven Wonders of the World: neither survives in the original.
▸ **ˈPhidian** *adj*

Phidippides ★ (faɪˈdɪpɪˌdiːz) *n* a variant spelling of **Pheidippides.**

phil. *abbrev. for:* **1** philharmonic. **2** philosophy.

Phil. *abbrev. for:* **1** Philadelphia. **2** *Bible.* Philippians. **3** Philippines. **4** Philharmonic.

Philadelphia ★ (ˌfɪləˈdɛlfɪə) *n* a city and port in SE Pennsylvania, at the confluence of the Delaware and Schuylkill Rivers: the fourth largest city in the US; founded by Quakers in 1682; cultural and financial centre of the American colonies and the federal capital (1790–1800); scene of the Continental Congresses (1774–83) and the signing of the Declaration of Independence (1776). Pop.: 1 478 002 (1996 est.).

philadelphus (ˌfɪləˈdɛlfəs) *n* any of a N temperate genus of shrubs cultivated for their strongly scented showy flowers. See also **mock orange** (sense 1). ORIG C19: NL, from Gk *philadelphon* mock orange, lit.: loving one's brother

Philae ★ (ˈfaɪliː) *n* an island in Upper Egypt, in the Nile north of the Aswan Dam: of religious importance in ancient times; almost submerged since the raising of the level of the dam.

philander (fɪˈlændə) *vb* (*intr;* often foll. by *with*) (of a man) to flirt with women. ORIG C17: from Gk *philandros* fond of men, used as a name for a lover in literary works
▸ **phiˈlanderer** *n*

philanthropic (ˌfɪlənˈθrɒpɪk) *or* **philanthropical** *adj* showing concern for humanity, esp. by performing charitable actions, donating money, etc.
▸ **ˌphilanˈthropically** *adv*

philanthropy (fɪˈlænθrəpɪ) *n, pl* **philanthropies. 1** the practice of performing charitable or benevolent actions. **2** love of mankind in general. ORIG C17: from LL *philanthrōpia,* from Gk: love of mankind, from *philos* loving + *anthrōpos* man
▸ **phiˈlanthropist** *or* **philanthrope** (ˈfɪlənˌθrəʊp) *n*

philately (fɪˈlætəlɪ) *n* the collection and study of postage stamps. ORIG C19: from F *philatélie,* from PHILO- + Gk *ateleia* exemption from charges (here referring to stamps)
▸ **philatelic** (ˌfɪləˈtɛlɪk) *adj* ▸ **ˌphilaˈtelically** *adv* ▸ **phiˈlatelist** *n*

Philby ★ (ˈfɪlbɪ) *n* **Harold,** known as *Kim.* 1912–88, British double agent; defected to the Soviet Union (1963).

-phile *or* **-phil** *n combining form.* indicating a person or thing having a fondness for something specified: *bibliophile.* ORIG from Gk *philos* loving

Philem. *Bible. abbrev. for* Philemon.

Philemon[1] ★ (faɪˈliːmɒn) *n New Testament.* **1** a Christian of Colossae whose escaped slave came to meet Paul. **2** the book (in full **The Epistle of Paul the Apostle to Philemon**), asking Philemon to forgive the slave for escaping.

Philemon[2] ★ (faɪˈliːmɒn) *n Greek myth.* a poor Phrygian, who with his wife Baucis offered hospitality to the disguised Zeus and Hermes.

philharmonic (ˌfɪlhɑːˈmɒnɪk, ˌfɪlə-) *adj* **1** fond of music. **2** (*cap. when part of a name*) denoting an orchestra, choir, society, etc., devoted to music. ◆ *n* **3** (*cap. when part of a name*) a specific philharmonic choir, orchestra, or society. ORIG C18: from F *philharmonique,* from It. *filarmonico* music-loving

philhellene (fɪlˈhɛliːn) *n* **1** a lover of Greece and Greek culture. **2** *European history.* a supporter of the cause of Greek national independence.
▸ **philhellenic** (ˌfɪlhɛˈliːnɪk) *adj*

-philia *n combining form.* **1** indicating a tendency towards: *haemophilia.* **2** indicating an abnormal liking for: *necrophilia.* ORIG from Gk *philos* loving
▸ **-philiac** *n combining form.* ▸ **-philous** *or* **-philic** *adj combining form.*

philibeg (ˈfɪlɪˌbɛg) *n* a variant spelling of **filibeg.**

Philip ★ (ˈfɪlɪp) *n* **1** *New Testament.* **1a** an apostle from Bethsaida (John 1:43–51; 6:5–7; 12:21; 14:8). **1b** Also called: **Philip the Evangelist.** one of the seven deacons appointed by the early Church. **1c** Also called: **Philip the Tetrarch.** one of the sons of Herod the Great, who was ruler of part of former Judaea (4 B.C.–34 A.D.) (Luke 3:1). **2 King,** American Indian name *Metacomet.* died 1676, American Indian chief, the son of Massasoit. He waged King Philip's War against the colonists of New England (1675–76) and was killed in battle. **3 Prince.** See (Duke of) **Edinburgh.**

Philip II ★ *n* **1** 382–336 B.C., king of Macedonia (359–336); the father of Alexander the Great. **2** known as *Philip Augustus.* 1165–1223, Capetian king of France (1180–1223); set out on the Third Crusade with Richard I of England (1190). **3** 1527–98, king of Spain (1556–98) and king of Portugal (1580–98) as Philip I; the husband of Mary I of England (1554–58). He championed the Counter-Reformation, sending the Armada against England (1588).

Philip IV ★ *n* known as *Philip the Fair.* 1268–1314, king of France (1285–1314): he challenged the power of the papacy, obtaining the elevation of Clement V as pope residing at Avignon (the beginning of the Babylonian captivity of the papacy).

Philip V ★ *n* 1683–1746, king of Spain (1700–46) and founder of the Bourbon dynasty in Spain. His accession began the War of Spanish Succession (1701–13).

Philip VI ★ *n* 1293–1350, first Valois king of France (1328–50). Edward III of England claimed his throne, which with other disputes led to the beginning of the Hundred Years' War (1337).

Philippeville ★ ('fɪlɪpˌvɪl) *n* the former name of **Skikda.**

Philippi ★ (fɪ'lɪpaɪ, 'fɪlɪ-) *n* an ancient city in NE Macedonia: scene of the victory of Antony and Octavian over Brutus and Cassius (42 B.C.).
▸ **Phi'lippian** *adj*

philippic (fɪ'lɪpɪk) *n* a bitter or impassioned speech of denunciation; invective. ORIG C16: after the orations of Demosthenes, against PHILIP of Macedon

Philippine ('fɪlɪˌpiːn) *n, adj* another word for **Filipino.**

Philippines ★ ('fɪlɪˌpiːnz, ˌfɪlɪ'piːnz) *n* (*functioning as sing*) **Republic of the.** a republic in SE Asia, occupying an archipelago of about 7100 islands (including Luzon, Mindanao, Samar, and Negros): became a Spanish colony in 1571 but ceded to the US in 1898 after the Spanish-American War; gained independence in 1946. The islands are generally mountainous and volcanic. Official languages: Filipino, based on Tagalog, and English. Religion: chiefly Roman Catholic. Currency: peso. Capital: Manila. Pop.: 74 723 000 (1999 est.). Area: 300 076 sq. km (115 860 sq. miles).

Philippine Sea ★ *n* part of the NW Pacific Ocean, east and north of the Philippines.

Philippopolis ★ (ˌfɪlɪ'pɒpəlɪs) *n* transliteration of the Greek name for **Plovdiv.**

Philip the Good ★ *n* 1396–1467, duke of Burgundy (1419–67), under whose rule Burgundy was one of the most powerful states in Europe.

Philistia ★ (fɪ'lɪstɪə) *n* an ancient country on the coast of SW Palestine.
▸ **Phi'listian** *adj*

Philistine ('fɪlɪˌstaɪn) *n* **1** a person who is hostile towards culture, the arts, etc.; a smug boorish person. **2** a member of the non-Semitic people who inhabited ancient Philistia. ◆ *adj* **3** (*sometimes not cap.*) boorishly uncultured. **4** of or relating to the ancient Philistines.
▸ **Philistinism** ('fɪlɪstɪˌnɪzəm) *n*

Phillip ★ ('fɪlɪp) *n* **Arthur.** 1738–1814, British naval commander: founded New South Wales.

phillumenist (fɪ'ljuːmənɪst, -'luː-) *n* a person who collects matchbox labels. ORIG C20: from PHILO- + L *lumen* light + -IST

philo- *or before a vowel* **phil-** *combining form.* indicating a love of: *philology; philanthropic.* ORIG from Gk *philos* loving

Philoctetes ★ (ˌfɪlɒk'tiːtiːz, fɪ'lɒktɪˌtiːz) *n Greek myth.* a hero of the Trojan War, in which he killed Paris with the bow and poisoned arrows given to him by Hercules.

philodendron (ˌfɪlə'dɛndrən) *n, pl* **philodendrons** *or* **philodendra** (-drə). an evergreen climbing plant of a tropical American genus: cultivated as a house plant. ORIG C19: NL from Gk: lover of trees

philogyny (fɪ'lɒdʒɪnɪ) *n Rare.* fondness for women. ORIG C17: from Gk *philogunia,* from PHILO- + *gunē* woman
▸ **phi'logynist** *n*

Philo Judaeus ★ ('faɪləʊ dʒuː'diːəs) *n* ?20 B.C.–?50 A.D., Jewish philosopher, born in Alexandria. He sought to reconcile Judaism with Greek philosophy.

philology (fɪ'lɒlədʒɪ) *n* **1** comparative and historical linguistics. **2** the scientific analysis of written records and literary texts. **3** (no longer in scholarly use) the study of literature. ORIG C17: from L *philologia,* from Gk: love of language
▸ **philological** (ˌfɪlə'lɒdʒɪk^əl) *adj* ▸ ˌ**philo'logically** *adv*
▸ **phi'lologist** *or* (*less commonly*) **phi'lologer** *n*

philomel ('fɪləˌmɛl) *or* **philomela** (ˌfɪləʊ'miːlə) *n* poetic names for a **nightingale.** ORIG C14 *philomene,* via Med. L from L *philomēla,* from Gk

Philomela ★ (ˌfɪləʊ'miːlə) *n Greek myth.* an Athenian princess, who was raped and had her tongue cut out by her brother-in-law Tereus, and subsequently was transformed into a nightingale. See **Procne.**

philoprogenitive (ˌfɪləʊprəʊ'dʒɛnɪtɪv) *adj Rare.* **1** fond of children. **2** producing many offspring.

philos. *abbrev. for:* **1** philosopher. **2** philosophical.

philosopher (fɪ'lɒsəfə) *n* **1** a student, teacher, or devotee of philosophy. **2** a person of philosophical temperament, esp. one who is patient, wise, and stoical. **3** (formerly) an alchemist or devotee of occult science.

philosopher's stone *n* a stone or substance thought by alchemists to be capable of transmuting base metals into gold.

philosophical (ˌfɪlə'sɒfɪk^əl) *or* **philosophic** *adj* **1** of or relating to philosophy or philosophers. **2** reasonable, wise, or learned. **3** calm and stoical, esp. in the face of difficulties or disappointments.
▸ ˌ**philo'sophically** *adv*

philosophical analysis *n* a philosophical method in which language and experience are analysed in an attempt to provide new insights into various philosophical problems.

philosophize *or* **philosophise** (fɪ'lɒsəˌfaɪz) *vb* **philosophizes, philosophizing, philosophized** *or* **philosophises, philosophising, philosophised. 1** (*intr*) to make philosophical pronouncements and speculations. **2** (*tr*) to explain philosophically.
▸ **phi'losoˌphizer** *or* **phi'losoˌphiser** *n*

philosophy (fɪ'lɒsəfɪ) *n, pl* **philosophies. 1** the academic discipline concerned with making explicit the nature and significance of ordinary and scientific beliefs and investigating the intelligibility of concepts by means of rational argument concerning their presuppositions, implications, and interrelationships. **2** the particular doctrines relating to these issues of a specific individual or school: *the philosophy of Descartes.* **3** the basic principles of a discipline: *the philosophy of law.* **4** any system of belief, values, or tenets. **5** a personal outlook or viewpoint. **6** serenity of temper. ORIG C13: from OF *filosofie,* from L *philosophia,* from Gk, from *philosophos* lover of wisdom

-philous *or* **-philic** *adj combining form.* indicating love of or fondness for: *heliophilous.* ORIG from L *-philus,* from Gk *-philos*

philtre *or US* **philter** ('fɪltə) *n* a drink supposed to arouse desire. ORIG C16: from L *philtrum,* from Gk *philtron* love potion, from *philos* loving

phimosis (faɪ'məʊsɪs) *n* abnormal tightness of the foreskin, preventing its being retracted. ORIG C17: via NL from Gk: a muzzling

phiz (fɪz) *n Sl., chiefly Brit.* the face or a facial expression. Also called: **phizog** (fɪ'zɒg). ORIG C17: colloquial shortening of PHYSIOGNOMY

Phiz ★ (fɪz) *n* real name *Hablot Knight Browne.* 1815–82, British painter, noted for his illustrations for Dickens' novels.

phlebitis (flɪ'baɪtɪs) *n* inflammation of a vein. ORIG C19: via NL from Gk
▸ **phlebitic** (flɪ'bɪtɪk) *adj*

phlebo- *or before a vowel* **phleb-** *combining form.* indicating a vein: *phlebotomy.* ORIG from Gk *phleps, phleb-* vein

phlebotomy (flɪ'bɒtəmɪ) *n, pl* **phlebotomies.** surgical incision into a vein. ORIG C14: from OF *flebothomie,* from LL *phlebotomia,* from Gk

Phlegethon ★ ('flɛgɪˌθɒn) *n Greek myth.* a river of fire in Hades. ORIG C14: from Gk, lit.: blazing, from *phlegethein* to flame, blaze

phlegm (flɛm) *n* **1** the viscid mucus secreted by the walls of the respiratory tract. **2** *Arch.* one of the four bodily humours. **3** apathy; stolidity. **4** imperturbability; coolness. ORIG C14: from OF *fleume,* from LL *phlegma,* from Gk: inflammation, from *phlegein* to burn
▸ **'phlegmy** *adj*

phlegmatic (flɛg'mætɪk) *or* **phlegmatical** *adj* **1** having a stolid or unemotional disposition. **2** not easily excited.
▸ **phleg'matically** *adv*

phloem ('fləʊɛm) *n* tissue in higher plants that conducts synthesized food substances to all parts of the plant. ORIG C19: via G from Gk *phloos* bark

phlogiston (flɒ'dʒɪstɒn, -tən) *n Chem.* a hypothetical substance formerly thought to be present in all combustible materials. ORIG C18: via NL from Gk, from *phlogizein* to set alight

phlox (flɒks) *n, pl* **phlox** *or* **phloxes.** any of a chiefly North American genus of plants cultivated for their clusters of white, red, or purple flowers. ORIG C18: via L from Gk: a plant of glowing colour, lit.: flame

phlyctena (flɪk'ti:nə) *n, pl* **phlyctenae** (-ni:). *Pathol.* a small blister, vesicle, or pustule. ORIG C17: via NL from Gk *phluktaina,* from *phluzein* to swell

Phnom Penh *or* **Pnom Penh** ★ (ˌnɒm 'pɛn) *n* the capital of Cambodia, a port in the south at the confluence of the Mekong and Tonle Sap Rivers: capital of the country since 1865; university (1960). Pop.: 920 000 (1994 est.).

-phobe *n combining form.* indicating one that fears or hates: *xenophobe.* ORIG from Gk *-phobos* fearing
▸ **-phobic** *adj combining form.*

phobia ('fəʊbɪə) *n Psychiatry.* an abnormal intense and irrational fear of a given situation, organism, or object. ORIG C19: from Gk *phobos* fear
▸ **'phobic** *adj, n*

-phobia *n combining form.* indicating an extreme abnormal fear of or aversion to: *acrophobia; claustrophobia.* ORIG via L from Gk, from *phobos* fear
▸ **-phobic** *adj combining form.*

Phocaea ★ (fəʊ'si:ə) *n* an ancient port in Asia Minor, the northernmost of Ionian cities on the W coast of Asia Minor: an important maritime state (about 1000–600 B.C.).

Phocis ★ ('fəʊsɪs) *n* an ancient district of central Greece, on the Gulf of Corinth: site of the Delphic oracle.

phocomelia (ˌfəʊkəʊ'mi:lɪə) *n* a congenital deformity characterized esp. by short stubby hands or feet attached close to the body. ORIG C19: via NL from Gk *phōkē* a seal + *melos* a limb

phoebe ('fi:bɪ) *n* any of several greyish-brown North American flycatchers. ORIG C19: imit.

Phoebe *or* **Phebe** ★ ('fi:bɪ) *n* **1** *Classical myth.* a Titaness, who later became identified with Artemis (Diana) as goddess of the moon. **2** *Poetic.* a personification of the moon.

Phoebus ★ ('fi:bəs) *n* **1** Also called: **Phoebus Apollo.** *Greek myth.* Apollo as the sun god. **2** *Poetic.* a personification of the sun. ORIG C14: via L from Gk *Phoibos* bright; related to *phaos* light

Phoenicia ★ (fə'nɪʃɪə, -'ni:-) *n* an ancient maritime country extending from the Mediterranean Sea to the Lebanon Mountains, now occupied by the coastal regions of Lebanon and parts of Syria and Israel: consisted of a group of city-states, at their height between about 1200 and 1000 B.C., that were leading traders of the ancient world.

Phoenician (fə'nɪʃən, -'ni:ʃɪən) *n* **1** a member of an ancient Semitic people of NW Syria. **2** the extinct language of this people. ◆ *adj* **3** of Phoenicia, the Phoenicians, or their language.

phoenix *or US* **phenix** ('fi:nɪks) *n* **1** a legendary Arabian bird said to set fire to itself and rise anew from the ashes every 500 years. **2** a person or thing of surpassing beauty or quality. ORIG OE *fenix,* via L from Gk *phoinix*

Phoenix ★ ('fi:nɪks) *n* a city in central Arizona, capital city of the state, on the Salt River. Pop.: 1 159 014 (1996 est.).

Phoenix Islands ★ *pl n* a group of eight coral islands in the central Pacific: administratively part of Kiribati. Area: 28 sq. km (11 sq. miles).

Phomvihane ★ ('pɒmvɪhɑ:n) *n* **Kaysone** ('kaɪsɒn). 1920–92, Laotian Communist statesman; prime minister of Laos (1975–91); president (1991–92).

phon (fɒn) *n* a unit of loudness that measures the intensity of a sound by the number of decibels it is above a reference tone. ORIG C20: via G from Gk *phōnē* sound

phonate (fəʊ'neɪt) *vb* **phonates, phonating, phonated.** (*intr*) to articulate speech sounds, esp. voiced speech sounds. ORIG C19: from Gk *phōnē* voice
▸ **pho'nation** *n*

phone[1] (fəʊn) *n, vb* **phones, phoning, phoned.** short for **telephone.**

phone[2] (fəʊn) *n Phonetics.* a single speech sound. ORIG C19: from Gk *phōnē* sound, voice

-phone *combining form.* **1** (*forming nouns*) indicating a device giving off sound: *telephone.* **2** (*forming nouns and adjectives*) (a person) speaking a particular language: *Francophone.* ORIG from Gk *phōnē* voice, sound
▸ **-phonic** *adj combining form.*

phonecard ('fəʊnˌkɑ:d) *n* a card used instead of coins to operate certain public telephones.

phone-in *n* **a** a radio or television programme in which listeners' or viewers' questions, comments, etc., are telephoned to the studio and broadcast live as part of a discussion. **b** (*as modifier*): *a phone-in programme.*

phoneme ('fəʊni:m) *n Linguistics.* one of the set of speech sounds in any given language that serve to distinguish one word from another. ORIG C20: via F from Gk *phōnēma* sound, speech
▸ **phonemic** (fə'ni:mɪk) *adj*

phonemics (fə'ni:mɪks) *n* (*functioning as sing*) that aspect of linguistics concerned with the classification and analysis of the phonemes of a language.
▸ **pho'nemicist** *n*

phonetic (fə'nɛtɪk) *adj* **1** of or relating to phonetics. **2** denoting any perceptible distinction between one speech sound and another. **3** conforming to pronunciation: *phonetic spelling.* ORIG C19: from NL *phōnēticus,* from Gk, from *phōnein* to make sounds, speak
▸ **pho'netically** *adv*

phonetics (fə'nɛtɪks) *n* (*functioning as sing*) the science concerned with the study of speech processes, including the production, perception, and analysis of speech sounds.
▸ **phonetician** (ˌfəʊnɪ'tɪʃən) *or* **phonetist** ('fəʊnɪtɪst) *n*

phoney *or esp. US* **phony** ('fəʊnɪ) *Inf.* ◆ *adj* **phonier, phoniest. 1** not genuine; fake. **2** (of a person) insincere or pretentious. ◆ *n, pl* **phoneys** *or esp. US* **phonies. 3** an insincere or pretentious person. **4** something that is not genuine; a fake. ORIG C20: from ?
▸ **'phoneyness** *or esp. US* **'phoniness** *n*

phonics ('fɒnɪks) *n* (*functioning as sing*) **1** an obsolete name for **acoustics** (sense 1). **2** a method of teaching people to read by training them to associate letters with their phonetic values.
▸ **'phonic** *adj* ▸ **'phonically** *adv*

phono- *or before a vowel* **phon-** *combining form.* indicating a sound or voice: *phonograph; phonology.* ORIG from Gk *phōnē* sound, voice

phonogram ('fəʊnəˌgræm) *n* any written symbol standing for a sound, syllable, morpheme, or word.
▸ **ˌphono'gramic** *or* **ˌphono'grammic** *adj*

phonograph ('fəʊnəˌgrɑ:f) *n* **1** an early form of gramophone capable of recording and reproducing sound on wax cylinders. **2** another US and Canad. word for **gramophone** or **record player.**

phonography (fəʊ'nɒgrəfɪ) *n* **1** a writing system that represents sounds by individual symbols. **2** the employment of such a writing system.
▸ **phonographic** (ˌfəʊnə'græfɪk) *adj*

phonology (fəˈnɒlədʒɪ) *n, pl* **phonologies. 1** the study of the sound system of a language or of languages in general. **2** such a sound system.
▸ **phonological** (ˌfəʊnəˈlɒdʒɪkᵊl, ˌfɒn-) *adj* ▸ **ˌphonoˈlogically** *adv* ▸ **phoˈnologist** *n*

phonon (ˈfəʊnɒn) *n Physics.* a quantum of vibrational energy in the acoustic vibrations of a crystal lattice. ORIG C20: from PHONO- + -ON

-phony *n combining form.* indicating a specified type of sound: *cacophony; euphony.* ORIG from Gk *-phōnia,* from *phōnē* sound
▸ **-phonic** *adj combining form.*

phooey (ˈfuːɪ) *interj Inf.* an exclamation of scorn, contempt, etc. ORIG C20: prob. var. of PHEW

-phore *n combining form.* indicating one that bears or produces: *semaphore.* ORIG from NL *-phorus,* from Gk *-phoros* bearing, from *pherein* to bear
▸ **-phorous** *adj combining form.*

-phoresis *n combining form.* indicating a transmission: *electrophoresis.* ORIG from Gk *phorēsis* being carried, from *pherein* to bear

phormium (ˈfɔːmɪəm) *n* any of a genus of plants of the lily family with tough leathery evergreen leaves. Also called: **New Zealand flax, flax lily.** ORIG C19: NL from Gk *phormos* basket

phosgene (ˈfɒzdʒiːn) *n* a colourless poisonous gas: used in chemical warfare and in the manufacture of pesticides, dyes, and polyurethane resins. ORIG C19: from Gk *phōs* light + *-gene,* var. of -GEN

phosphate (ˈfɒsfeɪt) *n* **1** any salt or ester of any phosphoric acid. **2** (*often pl*) any of several chemical fertilizers containing phosphorous compounds. ORIG C18: from F *phosphat;* see PHOSPHORUS, -ATE[1]
▸ **phosphatic** (fɒsˈfætɪk) *adj*

phosphatide (ˈfɒsfəˌtaɪd) *n* another name for **phospholipid.**

phosphatidylcholine (ˌfɒsfæˌtaɪdaɪlˈkəʊliːn) *n* the systematic name for **lecithin.**

phosphene (ˈfɒsfiːn) *n* the sensation of light caused by pressure on the eyelid of a closed eye. ORIG C19: from Gk *phōs* light + *phainein* to show
▸ **phosˈphenic** *adj*

phosphide (ˈfɒsfaɪd) *n* any compound of phosphorus with another element, esp. a more electropositive element.

phosphine (ˈfɒsfiːn) *n* a colourless flammable gas that is slightly soluble in water and has a strong fishy odour: used as a pesticide. Formula: PH_3.

phosphite (ˈfɒsfaɪt) *n* any salt or ester of phosphorous acid.

phospho- *or before a vowel* **phosph-** *combining form.* containing phosphorus: *phosphoric.* ORIG from F, from *phosphore* PHOSPHORUS

phospholipid (ˌfɒsfəˈlɪpɪd) *n* any of a group of fatty compounds: important constituents of all membranes. Also called: **phosphatide.**

phosphonic acid (fɒsˈfɒnɪk) *n* the systematic name for **phosphorous acid.**

phosphor (ˈfɒsfə) *n* a substance capable of emitting light when irradiated with particles of electromagnetic radiation. ORIG C17: from F, ult. from Gk *phōsphoros* PHOSPHORUS

phosphorate (ˈfɒsfəˌreɪt) *vb* **phosphorates, phosphorating, phosphorated.** to treat or combine with phosphorus.

phosphor bronze *n* any of various hard corrosion-resistant alloys containing phosphorus: used in gears, bearings, cylinder casings, etc.

phosphoresce (ˌfɒsfəˈrɛs) *vb* **phosphoresces, phosphorescing, phosphoresced.** (*intr*) to exhibit phosphorescence.

phosphorescence (ˌfɒsfəˈrɛsəns) *n* **1** *Physics.* a fluorescence that persists after the bombarding radiation producing it has stopped. **2** the light emitted in phosphorescence. **3** the emission of light in which insufficient heat is evolved to cause fluorescence. Cf. **fluorescence.**
▸ **ˌphosphoˈrescent** *adj*

phosphoric (fɒsˈfɒrɪk) *adj* of or containing phosphorus in the pentavalent state.

phosphoric acid *n* **1** a colourless solid tribasic acid used in the manufacture of fertilizers and soap. Formula: H_3PO_4. Systematic name: **phosphoric(V) acid.** Also called: **orthophosphoric acid. 2** any oxyacid of phosphorus produced by reaction between phosphorus pentoxide and water.

phosphorous (ˈfɒsfərəs) *adj* of or containing phosphorus in the trivalent state.

phosphorous acid *n* **1** a white or yellowish hygroscopic crystalline dibasic acid. Formula: H_3PO_3. Systematic name: **phosphonic acid.** Also called: **orthophosphorous acid. 2** any oxyacid of phosphorus containing less oxygen than the corresponding phosphoric acid.

phosphorus (ˈfɒsfərəs) *n* **1** an allotropic nonmetallic element occurring in phosphates and living matter. Ordinary phosphorus is a toxic flammable phosphorescent white solid; the red form is less reactive and nontoxic: used in matches, pesticides, and alloys. The radioisotope **phosphorus-32 (radiophosphorus),** with a half-life of 14.3 days, is used in radiotherapy and as a tracer. Symbol: P; atomic no.: 15; atomic wt.: 30.974. **2** a less common name for a **phosphor.** ORIG C17: via L from Gk *phōsphoros* light-bringing, from *phōs* light + *pherein* to bring

Phosphorus (ˈfɒsfərəs) *n* a morning star, esp. Venus.

phossy jaw (ˈfɒsɪ) *n* a gangrenous condition of the lower jawbone caused by prolonged exposure to phosphorus fumes. ORIG C19: *phossy,* colloquial shortening of PHOSPHORUS

phot (fɒt, fəʊt) *n* a unit of illumination equal to one lumen per square centimetre. 1 phot is equal to 10 000 lux. ORIG C20: from Gk *phōs* light

phot. *abbrev. for:* **1** photograph. **2** photographic. **3** photography.

photic (ˈfəʊtɪk) *adj* **1** of or concerned with light. **2** designating the zone of the sea where photosynthesis takes place.

photo (ˈfəʊtəʊ) *n, pl* **photos.** short for **photograph.**

photo- *combining form.* **1** of, relating to, or produced by light: *photosynthesis.* **2** indicating a photographic process: *photolithography.* ORIG from Gk *phōs, phōt-* light

photo call *n* a time arranged for photographers, esp. press photographers, to take pictures of a celebrity.

photocell (ˈfəʊtəʊˌsɛl) *n* a device in which the photoelectric or photovoltaic effect or photoconductivity is used to produce a current or voltage when exposed to light or other electromagnetic radiation. They are used in exposure meters, burglar alarms, etc. Also called: **photoelectric cell, electric eye.**

photochemistry (ˌfəʊtəʊˈkɛmɪstrɪ) *n* the branch of chemistry concerned with the chemical effects of light and other electromagnetic radiations.
▸ **photochemical** (ˌfəʊtəʊˈkɛmɪkᵊl) *adj*

photochromic (ˌfəʊtəʊˈkrəʊmɪk) *adj* (of glass) changing colour with the intensity of incident light, used, for example, in sunglasses that darken as the sunlight becomes brighter.

photocomposition (ˌfəʊtəʊˌkɒmpəˈzɪʃən) *n* another name (esp. US and Canad.) for **filmsetting.**

photoconductivity (ˌfəʊtəʊˌkɒndʌkˈtɪvɪtɪ) *n* the change in the electrical conductivity of certain substances, such as selenium, as a result of the absorption of electromagnetic radiation.
▸ **photoconductive** (ˌfəʊtəʊkənˈdʌktɪv) *adj* ▸ **ˌphotoconˈductor** *n*

photocopier (ˈfəʊtəʊˌkɒpɪə) *n* an instrument using light-sensitive photographic materials to reproduce written, printed, or graphic work.

photocopy (ˈfəʊtəʊˌkɒpɪ) *n, pl* **photocopies. 1** a photographic reproduction of written, printed, or graphic work. ◆ *vb* **photocopies, photocopying, photocopied. 2** to reproduce (written, printed, or graphic work) on photographic material.

photodegradable (ˌfəʊtəʊdɪˈgreɪdəbᵊl) *adj* (of plastic) capable of being decomposed by prolonged exposure to light.

photoelectric (ˌfəʊtəʊɪˈlɛktrɪk) *adj* of or concerned with electric or electronic effects caused by light or other electromagnetic radiation.
▸ **photoelectricity** (ˌfəʊtəʊɪlɛkˈtrɪsɪtɪ) *n*

photoelectric cell *n* another name for **photocell**.

photoelectric effect *n* **1** the ejection of electrons from a solid by an incident beam of sufficiently energetic electromagnetic radiation. **2** any phenomenon involving electric current and electromagnetic radiation, such as photoemission.

photoelectron (ˌfəʊtəʊɪˈlɛktrɒn) *n* an electron ejected from an atom, molecule, or solid by an incident photon.

photoemission (ˌfəʊtəʊɪˈmɪʃən) *n* the emission of electrons due to the impact of electromagnetic radiation.

photoengraving (ˌfəʊtəʊɪnˈgreɪvɪŋ) *n* **1** a photomechanical process for producing letterpress printing plates. **2** a plate made by this process. **3** a print made from such a plate.
▸ ˌ**photoenˈgrave** *vb (tr)*

photo finish *n* **1** a finish of a race in which contestants are so close that a photograph is needed to decide the result. **2** any race or competition in which the winners are separated by a very small margin.

Photofit (ˈfəʊtəʊˌfɪt) *n Trademark.* **a** a method of combining photographs of facial features, hair, etc., into a composite picture of a face: formerly used by the police to trace suspects, criminals, etc. **b** *(as modifier): a Photofit picture.*

photoflash (ˈfəʊtəʊˌflæʃ) *n* another name for **flashbulb**.

photoflood (ˈfəʊtəʊˌflʌd) *n* a highly incandescent tungsten lamp used for indoor photography, television, etc.

photog. *abbrev. for:* **1** photograph. **2** photographer. **3** photographic. **4** photography.

photogenic (ˌfəʊtəˈdʒɛnɪk) *adj* **1** (esp. of a person) having a general facial appearance that looks attractive in photographs. **2** *Biol.* producing or emitting light.
▸ ˌ**photoˈgenically** *adv*

photogram (ˈfəʊtəˌgræm) *n* **1** a picture, usually abstract, produced on a photographic material without the use of a camera. **2** *Obs.* a photograph.

photogrammetry (ˌfəʊtəʊˈgræmɪtrɪ) *n* the process of making measurements from photographs, used esp. in the construction of maps from aerial photographs.

photograph (ˈfəʊtəˌgrɑːf) *n* **1** an image of an object, person, scene, etc., in the form of a print or slide recorded by a camera. Often shortened to **photo**. ◆ *vb* **2** to take a photograph of (an object, person, scene, etc.).

photographic (ˌfəʊtəˈgræfɪk) *adj* **1** of or relating to photography. **2** like a photograph in accuracy or detail. **3** (of a person's memory) able to retain facts, appearances, etc., in precise detail.
▸ ˌ**photoˈgraphically** *adv*

photography (fəˈtɒgrəfɪ) *n* **1** the process of recording images on sensitized material by the action of light, X-rays, etc. **2** the art, practice, or occupation of taking photographs.
▸ **phoˈtographer** *n*

photogravure (ˌfəʊtəʊgrəˈvjʊə) *n* **1** any of various methods in which an intaglio plate for printing is produced by the use of photography. **2** matter printed from such a plate. ORIG C19: from PHOTO- + F *gravure* engraving

photojournalism (ˌfəʊtəʊˈdʒɜːnᵊˌlɪzəm) *n* journalism in which photographs are the predominant feature.
▸ ˌ**photoˈjournalist** *n*

photokinesis (ˌfəʊtəʊkɪˈniːsɪs, -kaɪ-) *n Biol.* the movement of an organism in response to the stimulus of light.

photolithography (ˌfəʊtəʊlɪˈθɒgrəfɪ) *n* **1** a lithographic printing process using photographically made plates. Often shortened to **photolitho**. **2** *Electronics.* a process used in the manufacture of semiconductor devices and printed circuits in which a particular pattern is transferred from a photograph onto a substrate.
▸ ˌ**photoliˈthographer** *n*

photoluminescence (ˌfəʊtəʊˌluːmɪˈnɛsəns) *n* luminescence resulting from the absorption of light or infrared or ultraviolet radiation.

photolysis (fəʊˈtɒlɪsɪs) *n* chemical decomposition caused by light or other electromagnetic radiation.
▸ **photolytic** (ˌfəʊtəʊˈlɪtɪk) *adj*

photomechanical (ˌfəʊtəʊmɪˈkænɪkᵊl) *adj* of or relating to any of various methods by which printing plates are made using photography.
▸ ˌ**photomeˈchanically** *adv*

photometer (fəʊˈtɒmɪtə) *n* an instrument used in photometry, usually one that compares the illumination produced by a particular light source with that produced by a standard source.

photometry (fəʊˈtɒmɪtrɪ) *n* **1** the measurement of the intensity of light. **2** the branch of physics concerned with such measurements.
▸ **phoˈtometrist** *n*

photomicrograph (ˌfəʊtəʊˈmaɪkrəˌgrɑːf) *n* a photograph of a microscope image.
▸ **photomicrography** (ˌfəʊtəʊmaɪˈkrɒgrəfɪ) *n*

photomontage (ˌfəʊtəʊmɒnˈtɑːʒ) *n* **1** the technique of producing a composite picture by combining several photographs. **2** the composite picture so produced.

photomultiplier (ˌfəʊtəʊˈmʌltɪˌplaɪə) *n* a device sensitive to electromagnetic radiation which produces a detectable pulse of current.

photon (ˈfəʊtɒn) *n* a quantum of electromagnetic radiation with energy equal to the product of the frequency of the radiation and the Planck constant.

photo-offset *n Printing.* an offset process in which the plates are produced photomechanically.

photo opportunity *n* an opportunity, either preplanned or accidental, for the press to photograph a politician, celebrity, or event.

photoperiodism (ˌfəʊtəʊˈpɪərɪəˌdɪzəm) *n* the response of plants and animals by behaviour, growth, etc., to the period of daylight in every 24 hours (**photoperiod**).
▸ ˌ**photoˌperiˈodic** *adj*

photophobia (ˌfəʊtəʊˈfəʊbɪə) *n* **1** *Pathol.* abnormal sensitivity of the eyes to light. **2** *Psychiatry.* abnormal fear of sunlight or well-lit places.
▸ ˌ**photoˈphobic** *adj*

photopolymer (ˌfəʊtəʊˈpɒlɪmə) *n* a polymeric material that is sensitive to light: used in printing plates, microfilms, etc.

photoreceptor (ˌfəʊtəʊrɪˈsɛptə) *n Zool., physiol.* a light-sensitive cell or organ that conveys impulses through the sensory neuron connected to it.

photosensitive (ˌfəʊtəʊˈsɛnsɪtɪv) *adj* sensitive to electromagnetic radiation, esp. light.
▸ ˌ**photoˌsensiˈtivity** *n* ▸ ˌ**photoˈsensiˌtize** *or* ˌ**photoˈsensiˌtise** *vb (tr)*

photoset (ˈfəʊtəʊˌsɛt) *vb* **photosets, photosetting, photoset.** another word for **filmset**.
▸ ˈ**photoˌsetter** *n*

photosphere (ˈfəʊtəʊˌsfɪə) *n* the visible surface of the sun.
▸ **photospheric** (ˌfəʊtəʊˈsfɛrɪk) *adj*

photostat (ˈfəʊtəʊˌstæt) *n* **1** a machine or process used to make photographic copies of written, printed, or graphic matter. **2** any copy made by such a machine. ◆ *vb* **photostats, photostatting** *or* **photostating, photostatted** *or* **photostated. 3** to make a photostat copy (of).

photosynthesis (ˌfəʊtəʊˈsɪnθɪsɪs) *n* (in plants) the synthesis of organic compounds from carbon dioxide and water using light energy absorbed by chlorophyll.
▸ ˌ**photoˈsynthesize** *or* ˌ**photoˈsynthesise** *vb* ▸ **photosynthetic** (ˌfəʊtəʊsɪnˈθɛtɪk) *adj* ▸ ˌ**photosynˈthetically** *adv*

phototaxis (ˌfəʊtəʊˈtæksɪs) *n* the movement of an entire organism in response to light.

phototropism (ˌfəʊtəʊˈtrəʊpɪzəm) *n* the growth response of plant parts to the stimulus of light, producing a bending towards the light source.
▸ ˌ**photoˈtropic** *adj*

photovoltaic effect (ˌfəʊtəʊvɒlˈteɪɪk) *n* the effect when electromagnetic radiation falls on a thin film of one solid deposited on the surface of a dissimilar solid producing a difference in potential between the two materials.

phrasal verb *n* a phrase that consists of a verb plus an adverbial or prepositional particle, esp. one the meaning of which cannot be deduced from the constituents: *"take in" meaning "deceive" is a phrasal verb.*

phrase (freɪz) *n* **1** a group of words forming a syntactic constituent of a sentence. Cf. **clause** (sense 1). **2** an idiomatic or original expression. **3** manner or style of speech or expression. **4** *Music.* a small group of notes forming a coherent unit of melody. ◆ *vb* **phrases, phrasing, phrased.** (*tr*) **5** *Music.* to divide (a melodic line, part, etc.) into musical phrases, esp. in performance. **6** to express orally or in a phrase. ORIG C16: from L *phrasis,* from Gk: speech, from *phrazein* to tell
▸ **'phrasal** *adj*

phrase book *n* a book containing frequently used expressions and their equivalents in a foreign language.

phrase marker *n Linguistics.* a representation, esp. a tree diagram, of the constituent structure of a sentence.

phraseogram ('freɪzɪəˌgræm) *n* a symbol representing a phrase, as in shorthand.

phraseology (ˌfreɪzɪ'ɒlədʒɪ) *n, pl* **phraseologies. 1** the manner in which words or phrases are used. **2** a set of phrases used by a particular group of people.
▸ **phraseological** (ˌfreɪzɪə'lɒdʒɪkᵊl) *adj*

phrasing ('freɪzɪŋ) *n* **1** the way in which something is expressed, esp. in writing; wording. **2** *Music.* the division of a melodic line, part, etc., into musical phrases.

phreaking ('friːkɪŋ) *n* the act or practice of gaining unauthorized access to telecommunication systems, esp. to obtain free calls. ORIG C20: from *ph(one)* + *(f)reaking*

phrenetic (frɪ'nɛtɪk) *adj* an obsolete spelling of **frenetic.**
▸ **phre'netically** *adv*

phrenic ('frɛnɪk) *adj* **1a** of or relating to the diaphragm. **1b** (*as n*): *the phrenic.* **2** *Obs.* of or relating to the mind. ORIG C18: from NL *phrenicus,* from Gk *phrēn* mind, diaphragm

phrenology (frɪ'nɒlədʒɪ) *n* (formerly) the branch of science concerned with determination of the strength of the faculties by the shape and size of the skull overlying the parts of the brain thought to be responsible for them.
▸ **phrenological** (ˌfrɛnə'lɒdʒɪkᵊl) *adj* ▸ **phre'nologist** *n*

phrensy ('frɛnzɪ) *n, pl* **phrensies** an obsolete spelling of **frenzy.**

Phrixus ★ ('frɪksəs) *n Greek myth.* the son of Athamas and Nephele who escaped the wrath of his father's mistress, Ino, by flying to Colchis on a winged ram with a golden fleece. See also **Helle, Golden Fleece.**

Phrygia ★ ('frɪdʒɪə) *n* an ancient country of W central Asia Minor.

Phrygian ('frɪdʒɪən) *adj* **1** of or relating to ancient Phrygia, its inhabitants, or their extinct language. **2** *Music.* of or relating to an authentic mode represented by the natural diatonic scale from E to E. ◆ *n* **3** a native or inhabitant of ancient Phrygia. **4** an ancient language of Phrygia.

Phrygian cap *n* a conical cap of soft material worn during ancient times, that became a symbol of liberty during the French Revolution.

Phryne ★ ('fraɪnɪ) *n* real name *Muesarete.* 4th century B.C., Greek courtesan; lover of Praxiteles and model for Apelles' painting *Aphrodite Rising from the Waves.*

phthalate ('θæleɪt, 'fθæl-) *n* a salt or ester of phthalic acid. Esters are commonly used as plasticizers in PVC; when ingested they can cause kidney and liver damage.

phthalic acid ('θælɪk, 'fθæl-) *n* a white crystalline carboxylic acid made from naphthalene and used in the synthesis of dyes and perfumes and the manufacture of plastics. ORIG C19: *phthalic* from (NA)PHTHAL(ENE) + -IC

phthisis ('θaɪsɪs, 'fθaɪ-, 'taɪ-) *n* any disease that causes wasting of the body, esp. pulmonary tuberculosis. ORIG C16: via L from Gk, from *phthinein* to waste away

Phuket ★ (ˌpuː'kɛt) *n* an island and province of S Thailand, in the Andaman Sea. Area: 534 sq. km (206 sq. miles).

phut (fʌt) *Inf.* ◆ *n* **1** a representation of a muffled explosive sound. ◆ *adv* **2 go phut.** to break down or collapse. ORIG C19: imit.

phycomycete (ˌfaɪkəʊ'maɪsiːt) *n* any of a primitive group of fungi formerly included in the class *Phycomycetes,* but now classified in different phyla: includes certain mildews and moulds. ORIG from Gk *phukos* seaweed + -MYCETE

Phyfe *or* **Fife** ★ (faɪf) *n* **Duncan.** ?1768–1854, US cabinetmaker, born in Scotland.

phyla ('faɪlə) *n* the plural of **phylum.**

phylactery (fɪ'læktərɪ) *n, pl* **phylacteries. 1** *Judaism.* either of the pair of blackened square cases containing parchments inscribed with biblical passages, bound by leather thongs to the head and left arm, and worn by Jewish men during weekday morning prayers. **2** a reminder. **3** *Arch.* an amulet or charm. ORIG C14: from LL *phylactērium,* from Gk *phulaktērion* outpost, from *phulax* a guard

phyletic (faɪ'lɛtɪk) *adj* of or relating to the evolutionary development of organisms. ORIG C19: from Gk *phuletikos* tribal

-phyll *or* **-phyl** *n combining form.* leaf: *chlorophyll.* ORIG from Gk *phullon*

phyllo- *or before a vowel* **phyll-** *combining form.* leaf: *phyllopod.* ORIG from Gk *phullon* leaf

phyllode ('fɪləʊd) *n* a flattened leafstalk that resembles and functions as a leaf. ORIG C19: from NL *phyllodium,* from Gk *phullōdēs* leaflike

phylloquinone (ˌfɪləʊkwɪ'nəʊn) *n* a viscous fat-soluble liquid occurring in plants: essential for the production of prothrombin, required in blood clotting. Also called: **vitamin K_1.**

phyllotaxis (ˌfɪlə'tæksɪs) *or* **phyllotaxy** *n, pl* **phyllotaxes** (-'tæksiːz) *or* **phyllotaxies. 1** the arrangement of the leaves on a stem. **2** the study of this arrangement.
▸ **ˌphyllo'tactic** *adj*

-phyllous *adj combining form.* having leaves of a specified number or type: *monophyllous.* ORIG from Gk *-phullos* of a leaf

phylloxera (ˌfɪlɒk'sɪərə, fɪ'lɒksərə) *n, pl* **phylloxerae** (-riː) *or* **phylloxeras.** any of a genus of homopterous insects, such as vine phylloxera, typically feeding on plant juices. ORIG C19: NL, from PHYLLO- + Gk *xēros* dry

phylo- *or before a vowel* **phyl-** *combining form.* tribe; race; phylum: *phylogeny.* ORIG from Gk *phulon* race

phylogeny (faɪ'lɒdʒɪnɪ) *or* **phylogenesis** (ˌfaɪləʊ'dʒɛnɪsɪs) *n, pl* **phylogenies** *or* **phylogeneses** (-'dʒɛnɪˌsiːz). *Biol.* the sequence of events involved in the evolution of a species, genus, etc. Cf. **ontogeny.** ORIG C19: from PHYLO- + -GENY
▸ **phylogenic** (ˌfaɪləʊ'dʒɛnɪk) *or* **phylogenetic** (ˌfaɪləʊdʒɪ'nɛtɪk) *adj*

phylum ('faɪləm) *n, pl* **phyla. 1** a major taxonomic division of living organisms that contain one or more classes. **2** a group of related language families or linguistic stocks. ORIG C19: NL, from Gk *phulon* race

phys. *abbrev. for:* **1** physical. **2** physician. **3** physics. **4** physiological. **5** physiology.

physalis (faɪ'seɪlɪs) *n* any of a genus of plants producing inflated orange seed vessels. See **Chinese lantern.** ORIG NL from Gk *physallis* bladder

physic ('fɪzɪk) *n* **1** *Rare.* a medicine, esp. a cathartic. **2** *Arch.* the art or skill of healing. ◆ *vb* **physics, physicking, physicked. 3** (*tr*) *Arch.* to treat (a patient) with medicine. ORIG C13: from OF *fisique,* via L, from Gk *phusikē,* from *phusis* nature

physical ('fɪzɪkᵊl) *adj* **1** of or relating to the body, as distinguished from the mind or spirit. **2** of, relating to, or resembling material things or nature: *the physical universe.* **3** involving or requiring bodily contact: *rugby is a physical sport.* **4** of or concerned with matter and energy. **5** of or relating to physics. **6** perceptible to the senses; apparent: *a physical manifestation.* ◆ See also **physicals.**
▸ **'physically** *adv*

physical anthropology *n* the branch of anthropology dealing with the genetic aspect of human development and its physical variations.

physical chemistry *n* the branch of chemistry concerned with the way in which the physical properties of substances depend on their chemical structure, properties, and reactions.

physical education *n* training and practice in sports, gymnastics, etc. Abbrev.: **PE**.

physical geography *n* the branch of geography that deals with the natural features of the earth's surface.

physical jerks *pl n Brit. inf.* See **jerk**[1] (sense 6).

physicals ('fɪzɪkᵊlz) *pl n Commerce.* commodities that can be purchased and used, as opposed to those bought and sold in a futures market. Also called: **actuals**.

physical science *n* any of the sciences concerned with nonliving matter, such as physics, chemistry, astronomy, and geology.

physical therapy *n Chiefly US.* another term for **physiotherapy**.

physician (fɪ'zɪʃən) *n* **1** a person legally qualified to practise medicine, esp. other than surgery; doctor of medicine. **2** *Arch.* any person who treats diseases; healer. ORIG C13: from OF *fisicien,* from *fisique* PHYSIC

physicist ('fɪzɪsɪst) *n* a person versed in or studying physics.

physics ('fɪzɪks) *n* (*functioning as sing*) **1** the branch of science concerned with the properties of matter and energy and the relationships between them. It is based on mathematics and traditionally includes mechanics, optics, electricity and magnetism, acoustics, and heat. Modern physics, based on quantum theory, includes atomic, nuclear, particle, and solid-state studies. **2** physical properties of behaviour: *the physics of the electron.* **3** *Arch.* natural science. ORIG C16: from L *physica,* translation of Gk *ta phusika* natural things, from *phusis* nature

physio ('fɪzɪəʊ) *n Inf.* **1** short for **physiotherapy**. **2** (*pl* **physios**) short for **physiotherapist**.

physio- *or before a vowel* **phys-** *combining form.* **1** of or relating to nature or natural functions: *physiology.* **2** physical: *physiotherapy.* ORIG from Gk *phusio,* ult. from *phuein* to make grow

physiocrat ('fɪzɪəʊˌkræt) *n* a believer in the 18th-century French economic theory that the inherent natural order governing society was based on land and its natural products as the only true form of wealth. ORIG C18: from F *physiocrate;* see PHYSIO-, -CRAT
▸ **physiocracy** (ˌfɪzɪ'ɒkrəsɪ) *n*

physiognomy (ˌfɪzɪ'ɒnəmɪ) *n* **1** a person's features considered as an indication of personality. **2** the art or practice of judging character from facial features. **3** the outward appearance of something. ORIG C14: from OF *phisonomie,* via Med. L, from LGk *phusiognōmia,* from *phusis* nature + *gnōmōn* judge
▸ **physiognomic** (ˌfɪzɪə'nɒmɪk) *or* **ˌphysiog'nomical** *adj* ▸ **ˌphysiog'nomically** *adv* ▸ **ˌphysi'ognomist** *n*

physiography (ˌfɪzɪ'ɒgrəfɪ) *n* another name for **geomorphology** or **physical geography**.
▸ **ˌphysi'ographer** *n* ▸ **physiographic** (ˌfɪzɪə'græfɪk) *or* **ˌphysio'graphical** *adj*

physiol. *abbrev. for:* **1** physiological. **2** physiology.

physiology (ˌfɪzɪ'ɒlədʒɪ) *n* **1** the branch of science concerned with the functioning of organisms. **2** the processes and functions of all or part of an organism. ORIG C16: from L *physiologia,* from Gk
▸ **ˌphysi'ologist** *n* ▸ **physiological** (ˌfɪzɪə'lɒdʒɪkᵊl) *adj* ▸ **ˌphysio'logically** *adv*

physiotherapy (ˌfɪzɪəʊ'θɛrəpɪ) *n* the treatment of disease, injury, etc., by physical means, such as massage or exercises, rather than by drugs.
▸ **ˌphysio'therapist** *n*

physique (fɪ'zi:k) *n* the general appearance of the body with regard to size, shape, muscular development, etc. ORIG C19: via F from *physique* (adj) natural, from L *physicus* physical

-phyte *n combining form.* indicating a plant of a specified type or habitat: *lithophyte.* ORIG from Gk *phuton* plant
▸ **-phytic** *adj combining form.*

phyto- *or before a vowel* **phyt-** *combining form.* indicating a plant or vegetation: *phytogenesis.* ORIG from Gk *phuton* plant, from *phuein* to make grow

phytochrome ('faɪtəʊˌkrəʊm) *n Bot.* a blue-green pigment, present in most plants, that mediates many light-dependent processes, including photoperiodism and the greening of leaves.

phytogenesis (ˌfaɪtəʊ'dʒɛnɪsɪs) *or* **phytogeny** (faɪ'tɒdʒənɪ) *n* the branch of botany concerned with the origin and evolution of plants.

phyton ('faɪtɒn) *n* a unit of plant structure, usually considered as the smallest part of the plant that is capable of growth when detached from the parent plant. ORIG C20: from Gk; see -PHYTE

phytopathology (ˌfaɪtəʊpə'θɒlədʒɪ) *n* the branch of botany concerned with diseases of plants.

phytoplankton (ˌfaɪtə'plæŋktən) *n* the photosynthesizing constituent of plankton, mainly unicellular algae.

phytotoxin (ˌfaɪtə'tɒksɪn) *n* a toxin, such as strychnine, that is produced by a plant.
▸ **ˌphyto'toxic** *adj*

pi[1] (paɪ) *n, pl* **pis**. **1** the 16th letter in the Greek alphabet (Π, π). **2** *Maths.* a transcendental number, fundamental to mathematics, that is the ratio of the circumference of a circle to its diameter. Approximate value: 3.141 592...; symbol: π ORIG C18 (mathematical use): representing the first letter of Gk *periphereia* PERIPHERY

pi[2] *or* **pie** (paɪ) *n, pl* **pies**. **1** a jumbled pile of printer's type. **2** a jumbled mixture. ◆ *vb* **pies, piing, pied** *or* **pies, pieing, pied**. (*tr*) **3** to spill and mix (set type) indiscriminately. **4** to mix up. ORIG C17: from ?

pi[3] (paɪ) *adj Brit. sl.* short for **pious** (sense 3).

PI *abbrev. for:* **1** Phillipine Islands. **2** private investigator.

Piacenza ★ (*Italian* pja'tʃɛntsa) *n* a town in N Italy, in Emilia-Romagna on the River Po. Pop.: 101 692 (1994 est.). Latin name: **Placentia** (plə'sɛntʃɪə).

piacevole (pi:ætʃ'eɪvəʊleɪ) *adv Music.* in an agreeable, pleasant manner. ORIG It.

piacular (paɪ'ækjʊlə) *adj* **1** making expiation. **2** requiring expiation. ORIG C17: from L *piāculum* propitiatory sacrifice, from *piāre* to appease

Piaf ★ (*French* pjaf) *n* **Edith** (edit), real name *Edith Giovanna Gassion,* nicknamed *the Little Sparrow.* 1915–63, French singer.

piaffe (pɪ'æf) *n Dressage.* a slow trot done on the spot. ORIG C18: from F, from *piaffer* to strut

Piaget ★ (*French* pjaʒɛ) *n* **Jean** (ʒɑ̃). 1896–1980, Swiss psychologist, noted for his work on the development of the cognitive functions in children.

pia mater ('paɪə 'meɪtə) *n* the innermost of the three membranes (see **meninges**) that cover the brain and spinal cord. ORIG C16: from Med. L, lit.: pious mother

pianism ('pi:əˌnɪzəm) *n* technique, skill, or artistry in playing the piano.
▸ **ˌpia'nistic** *adj*

pianissimo (pɪə'nɪsɪˌməʊ) *adj, adv Music.* to be performed very quietly. Symbol: *pp* ORIG C18: from It., sup. of *piano* soft

pianist ('pɪənɪst) *n* a person who plays the piano.

piano[1] (pɪ'ænəʊ) *n, pl* **pianos**. a musical stringed instrument played by depressing keys that cause hammers to strike the strings and produce audible vibrations. ORIG C19: short for PIANOFORTE

piano[2] ('pjɑ:nəʊ) *adj, adv Music.* to be performed softly. ORIG C17: from It., from L *plānus* flat

piano accordion (pɪ'ænəʊ) *n* an accordion in which the right hand plays a piano-like keyboard. See **accordion**.
▸ **piano accordionist** *n*

pianoforte (pɪˌænəʊ'fɔ:tɪ) *n* the full name for **piano**[1]. ORIG C18: from It., orig. (*gravecembalo col*) *piano e forte* (harpsichord with) soft & loud; see PIANO[2], FORTE[2]

Pianola (pɪə'nəʊlə) *n Trademark.* a type of mechanical piano in which the keys are depressed by air pressure, this air flow being regulated by perforations in a paper roll.

★ people and places

piano roll (pɪˈænəʊ) *n* a perforated roll of paper for a Pianola.

piastre *or* **piaster** (pɪˈæstə) *n* **1** (formerly) the standard monetary unit of South Vietnam. **2a** a fractional monetary unit of Egypt, Lebanon, and Syria worth one hundredth of a pound: also used in the Sudan but its use is being phased out. **2b** Also called: **kurus.** a Turkish monetary unit worth one hundredth of a lira. **2c** a Libyan monetary unit worth one hundredth of a dinar. ORIG C17: from F *piastre,* from It. *piastra d'argento* silver plate

Piauí ★ (*Portuguese* pjaˈui) *n* a state of NE Brazil, on the Atlantic: rises to a semiarid plateau, with the more humid Paranaíba valley in the west. Capital: Teresina. Pop.: 2 673 085 (1996). Area: 250 934 sq. km (96 886 sq. miles).

Piave ★ (*Italian* ˈpjaːve) *n* a river in NE Italy, rising near the border with Austria and flowing south and southeast to the Adriatic: the main line of Italian defence during World War I. Length: 220 km (137 miles).

piazza (pɪˈætsə; *Italian* ˈpjattsa) *n* **1** a large open square in an Italian town. **2** *Chiefly Brit.* a covered passageway or gallery. ORIG C16: from It.: marketplace, from L *platēa* courtyard, from Gk *plateia;* see PLACE

pibroch (ˈpiːbrɒk; *Gaelic* ˈpiːbrɒx) *n* a form of music for Scottish bagpipes, consisting of a theme and variations. ORIG C18: from Gaelic *piobaireachd,* from *piobair* piper

pic (pɪk) *n, pl* **pics** *or* **pix.** *Inf.* a photograph or illustration. ORIG C20: shortened from PICTURE

pica[1] (ˈpaɪkə) *n* **1** another word for **em. 2** (formerly) a size of printer's type equal to 12 point. **3** a typewriter type size having 10 characters to the inch. ORIG C15: from Anglo-L *pīca* list of ecclesiastical regulations, apparently from L *pīca* magpie, with reference to its habit of collecting things; the connection between the orig. sense & the typography meanings is obscure

pica[2] (ˈpaɪkə) *n Pathol.* an abnormal craving to ingest substances such as clay, dirt, or hair. ORIG C16: from Medical L, from L: magpie, an allusion to its omnivorous feeding habits

Picabia ★ (pɪˈkɑːbɪə; *French* pikabja) *n* **Francis.** 1879–1953, French painter, designer, and writer, associated with the cubist, Dadaist, and surrealist movements.

picador (ˈpɪkəˌdɔː) *n Bullfighting.* a horseman who pricks the bull with a lance to weaken it. ORIG C18: from Sp., lit.: pricker, from *picar* to prick

Picard ★ (*French* pikar) *n* **Jean** (ʒɑ̃). 1620–82, French astronomer. He was the first to make a precise measurement of a longitude line, enabling him to estimate the earth's radius.

Picardy ★ (ˈpɪkədɪ) *n* a region of N France: mostly low-lying; scene of heavy fighting in World War I. French name: **Picardie** (pikardi).

picaresque (ˌpɪkəˈrɛsk) *adj* of or relating to a type of fiction in which the hero, a rogue, goes through a series of episodic adventures. ORIG C19: via F from Sp. *picaresco,* from *pícaro* a rogue

picaroon (ˌpɪkəˈruːn) *n Arch.* an adventurer or rogue. ORIG C17: from Sp. *picarón,* from *pícaro*

Picasso ★ (pɪˈkæsəʊ) *n* **Pablo** (ˈpæbləʊ). 1881–1973, Spanish painter and sculptor, resident in France: a highly influential figure in 20th-century art and a founder, with Braque, of cubism. A prolific artist, his works include *Les Demoiselles d'Avignon* (1907) and *Guernica* (1937), inspired by an event in the Spanish Civil War.

picayune (ˌpɪkəˈjuːn) *adj also* **picayunish.** *US & Canad. inf.* **1** of small value or importance. **2** mean; petty. ◆ *n* **3** any coin of little value, esp. a five-cent piece. **4** an unimportant person or thing. ORIG C19: from F *picaillon* coin from Piedmont, from Provençal *picaioun,* from ?

Piccadilly ★ (ˌpɪkəˈdɪlɪ) *n* one of the main streets of London, running from Piccadilly Circus to Hyde Park Corner.

piccalilli (ˈpɪkəˌlɪlɪ) *n* a pickle of mixed vegetables in a mustard sauce. ORIG C18 *piccalillo,* ? based on PICKLE

piccanin (ˈpɪkəˌnɪn) *n S. African offens.* a Black African child. ORIG var. of PICCANINNY

piccaninny *or esp. US* **pickaninny** (ˌpɪkəˈnɪnɪ) *n, pl* **piccaninnies** *or esp. US* **pickaninnies.** *Offens.* a small Black child. ORIG C17: ?from Port. *pequenino* tiny one, from *pequeno* small

Piccard ★ (*French* pikar) *n* **1 Auguste** (ogyst). 1884–1962, Swiss physicist, whose study of cosmic rays led to his pioneer balloon ascents in the stratosphere (1931–32). **2** his twin brother, **Jean Félix** (ʒɑ̃ feliks). 1884–1963, US chemist and aeronautical engineer, born in Switzerland, noted for his balloon ascent into the stratosphere (1934).

piccolo (ˈpɪkəˌləʊ) *n, pl* **piccolos.** a woodwind instrument an octave higher than the flute. ORIG C19: from It.: small

pick[1] (pɪk) *vb* **1** to choose (something) deliberately or carefully, as from a number; select. **2** to pluck or gather (fruit, berries, or crops) from (a tree, bush, field, etc.). **3** (*tr*) to remove loose particles from (the teeth, the nose, etc.). **4** (esp. of birds) to nibble or gather (corn, etc.). **5** (when *intr,* foll. by *at*) to nibble (at) fussily or without appetite. **6** to separate (strands, fibres, etc.), as in weaving. **7** (*tr*) to provoke (an argument, fight, etc.) deliberately. **8** (*tr*) to steal (money or valuables) from (a person's pocket). **9** (*tr*) to open (a lock) with an instrument other than a key. **10** to pluck the strings of (a guitar, banjo, etc.). **11** (*tr*) to make (one's way) carefully on foot: *they picked their way through the rubble.* **12 pick and choose.** to select fastidiously, fussily, etc. **13 pick someone's brains.** to obtain information or ideas from someone. ◆ *n* **14** freedom or right of selection (esp. in **take one's pick**). **15** a person, thing, etc., that is chosen first or preferred: *the pick of the bunch.* **16** the act of picking. **17** the amount of a crop picked at one period or from one area. ◆ See also **pick at, pick off,** etc. ORIG C15: from earlier *piken* to pick, infl. by F *piquer* to pierce
▸ **ˈpicker** *n*

pick[2] (pɪk) *n* **1** a tool with a handle carrying a long steel head curved and tapering to a point at one or both ends, used for loosening soil, breaking rocks, etc. **2** any of various tools used for picking, such as an ice pick or toothpick. **3** a plectrum. ◆ *vb* (*tr*) **4** to pierce, dig, or break up (a hard surface) with a pick. **5** to form (a hole, etc.) in this way. ORIG C14: ? a var. of PIKE[2]

pickaback (ˈpɪkəˌbæk) *n, adv* another word for **piggyback.**

pick at *vb* (*intr, prep*) to make criticisms of in a niggling or petty manner.

pickaxe *or US* **pickax** (ˈpɪkˌæks) *n* **1** a large pick or mattock. ◆ *vb* **pickaxes, pickaxing, pickaxed. 2** to use a pickaxe on (earth, rocks, etc.). ORIG C15: from earlier *pikois* (but infl. also by AXE), from OF, from *pic* PICK[2]

pickerel (ˈpɪkərəl, ˈpɪkrəl) *n, pl* **pickerel** *or* **pickerels. 1** a small pike. **2** any of several North American freshwater game fishes of the pike family. ORIG C14: dim. of PIKE[1]

Pickering ★ (ˈpɪkərɪŋ) *n* **1 Edward Charles.** 1846–1919, US astronomer, who invented the meridian photometer. **2** his brother, **William Henry.** 1858–1938, US astronomer, who discovered Phoebe, the ninth satellite of Saturn, and predicted (1919) the existence and position of Pluto.

picket (ˈpɪkɪt) *n* **1** a pointed stake that is driven into the ground to support a fence, etc. **2** an individual or group standing outside an establishment to make a protest, to dissuade or prevent employees or clients from entering, etc. **3** a small detachment of troops positioned to give early warning of attack. ◆ *vb* **4** to post or serve as pickets at (a factory, embassy, etc.). **5** to guard (a main body or place) by using or acting as a picket. **6** (*tr*) to fasten (a horse or other animal) to a picket. **7** (*tr*) to fence (an area, etc.) with pickets. ORIG C18: from F *piquet,* from OF *piquer* to prick; see PIKE[2]
▸ **ˈpicketer** *n*

picket fence *n* a fence consisting of pickets driven into the ground.

picket line *n* a line of people acting as pickets.

Pickford ★ (ˈpɪkfəd) *n* **Mary,** real name *Gladys Mary Smith.* 1893–1979, US actress in silent films, born in Canada.

pickings ('pɪkɪŋz) *pl n* (*sometimes sing*) money, profits, etc., acquired easily; spoils.

pickle ('pɪkᵊl) *n* **1** (*often pl*) vegetables, such as onions, etc., preserved in vinegar, brine, etc. **2** any food preserved in this way. **3** a liquid or marinade, such as spiced vinegar, for preserving vegetables, meat, fish, etc. **4** *Chiefly US & Canad.* a cucumber that has been preserved and flavoured in a pickling solution, as brine or vinegar. **5** *Inf.* an awkward or difficult situation: *to be in a pickle.* **6** *Brit. inf.* a mischievous child. ◆ *vb* **pickles, pickling, pickled.** (*tr*) **7** to preserve in a pickling liquid. **8** to immerse (a metallic object) in a liquid, such as an acid, to remove surface scale. ORIG C14: ?from MDu. *pekel*
▸ **'pickler** *n*

pickled ('pɪkᵊld) *adj* **1** preserved in a pickling liquid. **2** *Inf.* intoxicated; drunk.

picklock ('pɪk,lɒk) *n* **1** a person who picks locks. **2** an instrument for picking locks.

pick-me-up *n Inf.* a tonic or restorative, esp. a special drink taken as a stimulant.

pick off *vb* (*tr, adv*) to aim at and shoot one by one.

pick on *vb* (*intr, prep*) to select for something unpleasant, esp. in order to bully or blame.

pick out *vb* (*tr, adv*) **1** to select for use or special consideration, etc., as from a group. **2** to distinguish (an object from its surroundings), as in painting: *she picked out the woodwork in white.* **3** to recognize (a person or thing): *we picked out his face among the crowd.* **4** to distinguish (sense or meaning) as from a mass of detail or complication. **5** to play (a tune) tentatively, as by ear.

pickpocket ('pɪk,pɒkɪt) *n* a person who steals from the pockets of others in public places.

pick-up *n* **1** Also called: **pick-up truck.** a small truck with an open body used for light deliveries. **2** *Inf., chiefly US.* an ability to accelerate rapidly: *this car has good pick-up.* **3** *Inf.* a casual acquaintance, usually one made with sexual intentions. **4** *Inf.* **4a** a stop to collect passengers, goods, etc. **4b** the people or things collected. **5** *Inf.* an improvement. **6** *Sl.* a pick-me-up. **7** the light balanced arm of a record player that carries the wires from the cartridge to the preamplifier. **8** an electromagnetic transducer that converts vibrations into electric signals. **9** another name for **cartridge** (sense 2). ◆ *adj* **10** *US & Canad.* organized or assembled hastily and without planning: *a pick-up game.* ◆ *vb* **pick up.** (*adv*) **11** (*tr*) to gather up in the hand or hands. **12** (*reflexive*) to raise (oneself) after a fall or setback. **13** (*tr*) to obtain casually, incidentally, etc. **14** (*intr*) to improve in health, condition, activity, etc.: *the market began to pick up.* **15** (*tr*) to learn gradually or as one goes along. **16** to resume; return to. **17** (*tr*) to accept the responsibility for paying (a bill). **18** (*tr*) to collect or give a lift to (passengers, goods, etc.). **19** (*tr*) *Inf.* to become acquainted with, esp. with a view to having sexual relations. **20** (*tr*) *Inf.* to arrest. **21** to increase (speed). **22** (*tr*) to receive (electrical signals, a radio signal, sounds, etc.).

Pickwickian (pɪk'wɪkɪən) *adj* **1** of, relating to, or resembling Mr Pickwick in Charles Dickens' *The Pickwick Papers,* esp. in being naive or benevolent. **2** (of the use or meaning of a word) odd or unusual.

picky ('pɪkɪ) *adj* **pickier, pickiest.** *Inf.* fussy; finicky.
▸ **'pickily** *adv* ▸ **'pickiness** *n*

picnic ('pɪknɪk) *n* **1** a trip or excursion on which people bring food to be eaten in the open air. **2a** any informal meal eaten outside. **2b** (*as modifier*): *a picnic lunch.* **3** *Inf.* an easy or agreeable task. ◆ *vb* **picnics, picnicking, picnicked.** **4** (*intr*) to eat or take part in a picnic. ORIG C18: from F *piquenique,* from ?
▸ **'picnicker** *n*

picnic races *pl n Austral.* horse races for amateur riders held in rural areas.

pico- *prefix* denoting 10^{-12}: *picofarad.* Symbol: p ORIG from Sp. *pico* small quantity, odd number, peak

Pico de Aneto ★ (*Spanish* 'piko de a'neto) *n* See **Aneto.**

Pico della Mirandola ★ (*Italian* 'pi:ko ,dɛlla mi'randola) *n* Count **Giovanni** (dʒo'vanni). 1463–94, Italian Platonist philosopher. His attempt to reconcile the ideas of classical, Christian, and Arabic writers in a collection of theses was condemned by the pope.

Pico de Teide ★ (*Spanish* 'piko de 'teiðe) *n* See **Teide.**

picot ('pi:kəʊ) *n* any of a pattern of small loops, as on lace. ORIG C19: from F: small point, from *pic* point

picotee (,pɪkə'ti:) *n* a type of carnation having pale petals edged with a darker colour. ORIG C18: from F *picoté* marked with points, from *picot* PICOT

picric acid ('pɪkrɪk) *n* a toxic sparingly soluble crystalline yellow acid used as a dye, antiseptic, and explosive. Formula: $C_6H_3(NO_2)_3$. Systematic name: **2,4,6-trinitrophenol.** ORIG C19: from Gk *pikros* bitter + -IC

Pict (pɪkt) *n* a member of any of the peoples who lived in N Britain in the first to the fourth centuries A.D. ORIG OE *Peohtas;* later forms from LL *Pictī* painted men, from *pingere* to paint
▸ **'Pictish** *adj*

pictograph ('pɪktə,grɑ:f) *n* **1** a picture or symbol standing for a word or group of words, as in written Chinese. **2** a chart on which symbols are used to represent values. ◆ Also called: **pictogram.** ORIG C19: from L *pictus,* from *pingere* to paint
▸ **pictographic** (,pɪktə'græfɪk) *adj* ▸ **pictography** (pɪk'tɒgrəfɪ) *n*

pictorial (pɪk'tɔ:rɪəl) *adj* **1** relating to, consisting of, or expressed by pictures. **2** (of language, style, etc.) suggesting a picture; vivid; graphic. ◆ *n* **3** a magazine, newspaper, etc., containing many pictures. ORIG C17: from LL *pictōrius,* from L *pictor* painter, from *pingere* to paint
▸ **pic'torially** *adv*

picture ('pɪktʃə) *n* **1a** a visual representation of something, such as a person or scene, produced on a surface, as in a photograph, painting, etc. **1b** (*as modifier*): *picture gallery; picture postcard.* **2** a mental image: *a clear picture of events.* **3** a verbal description, esp. one that is vivid. **4** a situation considered as an observable scene: *the political picture.* **5** a person or thing resembling another: *he was the picture of his father.* **6** a person, scene, etc., typifying a particular state: *the picture of despair.* **7** the image on a television screen. **8** a motion picture; film. **9 the pictures.** *Chiefly Brit. & NZ.* a cinema or film show. **10** another name for **tableau vivant.** **11 in the picture.** informed about a situation. ◆ *vb* **pictures, picturing, pictured.** (*tr*) **12** to visualize or imagine. **13** to describe or depict, esp. vividly. **14** (*often passive*) to put in a picture or make a picture of: *they were pictured sitting on the rocks.* ORIG C15: from L *pictūra* painting, from *pingere* to paint

picture card *n* another name for **court card.**

picture hat *n* a hat with a very wide brim.

picture moulding *n* **1** the edge around a framed picture. **2** Also called: **picture rail.** the moulding or rail near the top of a wall from which pictures are hung.

picture palace *or* **house** *n Brit., old-fashioned.* another name for **cinema.**

picturesque (,pɪktʃə'rɛsk) *adj* **1** visually pleasing, esp. in being striking or quaint: *a picturesque view.* **2** (of language) graphic; vivid. ORIG C18: from F *pittoresque* (but also infl. by PICTURE), from It., from *pittore* painter, from L *pictor*
▸ **,pictur'esquely** *adv* ▸ **,pictur'esqueness** *n*

picture tube *n* another name for **television tube.**

picture window *n* a large window having a single pane of glass, usually facing a view.

picture writing *n* **1** any writing system that uses pictographs. **2** a system of artistic expression and communication using pictures.

PID *abbrev. for* pelvic inflammatory disease.

piddle ('pɪdᵊl) *vb* **piddles, piddling, piddled.** **1** (*intr*) *Inf.* to urinate. **2** (when *tr,* often foll. by *away*) to spend (one's time) aimlessly; fritter. ORIG C16: from ?
▸ **'piddler** *n*

piddling ('pɪdlɪŋ) *adj Inf.* petty; trifling; trivial.

piddock ('pɪdək) *n* a marine bivalve boring into rock, clay, or wood by means of sawlike shell valves. ORIG C19: from ?

pidgin ('pɪdʒɪn) *n* a language made up of elements of two or more other languages and used for contacts, esp. trading contacts, between the speakers of other languages. ORIG C19: ?from Chinese pronunciation of E *business*

pidgin English *n* a pidgin in which one of the languages involved is English.

pie[1] (paɪ) *n* **1** a baked sweet or savoury filling in a pastry-lined dish, often covered with a pastry crust. **2 pie in the sky.** illusory hope or promise of some future good. ORIG C14: from ?

pie[2] (paɪ) *n* an archaic or dialect name for **magpie.** ORIG C13: via OF from L *pīca* magpie

pie[3] (paɪ) *n, vb* **pies, pieing, pied.** *Printing.* a variant spelling of **pi**[2].

piebald ('paɪˌbɔːld) *adj* **1** marked in two colours, esp. black and white. ◆ *n* **2** a black-and-white horse. ORIG C16: PIE[2] + BALD; see also PIED

pie cart *n NZ.* a mobile van selling warmed-up food and drinks.

piece (piːs) *n* **1** an amount or portion forming a separate mass or structure; bit: *a piece of wood.* **2** a small part, item, or amount forming part of a whole, esp. when broken off or separated: *a piece of bread.* **3** a length by which a commodity is sold, esp. cloth, wallpaper, etc. **4** an instance or occurrence: *a piece of luck.* **5** an example or specimen of a style or type: *a beautiful piece of Dresden.* **6** *Inf.* an opinion or point of view: *to state one's piece.* **7** a literary, musical, or artistic composition. **8** a coin: *a fifty-pence piece.* **9** a small object used in playing certain games: *chess pieces.* **10** a firearm or cannon. **11** any chessman other than a pawn. **12** *Brit. dialect.* a packed lunch taken to work. **13** *NZ.* fragments of fleece wool. **14 go to pieces. 14a** (of a person) to lose control of oneself; have a breakdown. **14b** (of a building, organization, etc.) to disintegrate. **15 nasty piece of work.** *Brit. inf.* a cruel or mean person. **16 of a piece.** of the same kind; alike. ◆ *vb* **pieces, piecing, pieced.** (*tr*) **17** (often foll. by *together*) to fit or assemble piece by piece. **18** (often foll. by *up*) to patch or make up (a garment, etc.) by adding pieces. ORIG C13 *pece,* from OF, of Gaulish origin

pièce de résistance *French.* (pjɛs də rezistɑ̃s) *n* **1** the principal or most outstanding item in a series. **2** the main dish of a meal. ORIG lit.: piece of resistance

piece goods *pl n* goods, esp. fabrics, made in standard widths and lengths.

piecemeal ('piːsˌmiːl) *adv* **1** by degrees; bit by bit; gradually. **2** in or into pieces. ◆ *adj* **3** fragmentary or unsystematic: *a piecemeal approach.* ORIG C13 *pecemele,* from PIECE + *-mele,* from OE *mælum* quantity taken at one time

piece of eight *n, pl* **pieces of eight.** a former Spanish coin worth eight reals; peso.

piecework ('piːsˌwɜːk) *n* work paid for according to the quantity produced.

pie chart *n* a circular graph divided into sectors proportional to the magnitudes of the quantities represented.

piecrust table ('paɪˌkrʌst) *n* a round table, edged with moulding suggestive of a pie crust.

pied (paɪd) *adj* having markings of two or more colours. ORIG C14: from PIE[2]; an allusion to the magpie's colouring

pied-à-terre (ˌpjeɪtɑː'tɛə) *n, pl* **pieds-à-terre** (ˌpjeɪtɑː'tɛə). a flat or other lodging for occasional use. ORIG from F, lit.: foot on (the) ground

piedmont ('piːdmɒnt) *adj* (*prenominal*) (of glaciers, plains, etc.) formed or situated at the foot of a mountain. ORIG via F from It. *piémonte,* from *pié,* var. of *piede* foot + *mont* mountain

Piedmont ★ ('piːdmɒnt) *n* **1** a region of NW Italy: consists of the upper Po Valley; mainly agricultural. Chief town: Turin. Pop.: 4 288 866 (1996 est.). Area: 25 399 sq. km (9807 sq. miles). Italian name: **Piemonte. 2** a low plateau of the eastern US, between the coastal plain and the Appalachian Mountains.

Pied Piper ★ *n* **1** Also called: **the Pied Piper of Hamelin.** (in German legend) a piper who rid the town of Hamelin of rats by luring them away with his music and then, when he was not paid for his services, lured away its children. **2** (*sometimes not caps.*) a person who entices others to follow him or her.

pied wagtail *n* a British songbird with a black throat and back, long black tail, and white underparts and face.

pie-eyed *adj Sl.* drunk.

Piemonte ★ (*Italian* pje'monte) *n* the Italian name for **Piedmont** (sense 1).

pier (pɪə) *n* **1** a structure with a deck that is built out over water, and used as a landing place, promenade, etc. **2** a pillar that bears heavy loads. **3** the part of a wall between two adjacent openings. **4** another name for **buttress** (sense 1). ORIG C12 *per,* from Anglo-L *pera* pier supporting a bridge

pierce (pɪəs) *vb* **pierces, piercing, pierced.** (*mainly tr*) **1** to form or cut (a hole) in (something) as with a sharp instrument. **2** to thrust into sharply or violently: *the thorn pierced his heel.* **3** to force (a way, route, etc.) through (something). **4** (of light, etc.) to shine through or penetrate (darkness). **5** (*also intr*) to discover or realize (something) suddenly or (of an idea, etc.) to become suddenly apparent. **6** (of sounds or cries) to sound sharply through (the silence, etc.). **7** to move or affect deeply or sharply: *the cold pierced their bones.* **8** (*intr*) to penetrate: *piercing cold.* ORIG C13 *percen,* from OF *percer,* ult. from L *pertundere,* from *per* through + *tundere* to strike
▸ **'piercing** *adj* ▸ **'piercingly** *adv*

Pierce ★ (pɪəs) *n* **Franklin.** 1804–69, US statesman; 14th president of the US (1853–57).

pier glass *n* a tall narrow mirror, designed to hang on the wall between windows.

Pieria ★ (paɪ'ɪərɪə) *n* a region of ancient Macedonia, west of the Gulf of Salonika: site of the Pierian Spring.

Pierian Spring ★ (paɪ'ɪərɪən) *n* a sacred fountain in Pieria, in Greece, fabled to inspire those who drank from it.

Pierides ★ (paɪ'ɪərɪˌdiːz) *pl n Greek myth.* **1** another name for the Muses (see **Muse**). **2** nine maidens of Thessaly, who were defeated in a singing contest by the Muses and turned into magpies for their effrontery.

pieris ('paɪrɪs) *n* an evergreen shrub with white flowers like lily of the valley in spring. ORIG C19: from L, from Gk *Pīeris,* a Muse

Piero della Francesca ★ (*Italian* 'pjɛːro ˌdɛlla fran'tʃeska) *n* ?1420–92, Italian painter, noted particularly for his frescoes of the *Legend of the True Cross* in San Francesco, Arezzo.

Piero di Cosimo ★ (*Italian* 'pjɛːro di 'kɔːzimo) *n* 1462–1521, Italian painter, noted for his mythological works.

Pierre ★ (pɪə) *n* a city in central South Dakota, capital of the state, on the Missouri River. Pop.: 12 906 (1990).

Pierrot ('pɪərəʊ; *French* pjɛro) *n* **1** a male character from French pantomime with a whitened face, white costume, and pointed hat. **2** (*usually not cap.*) a clown so made up.

pier table *n* a side table designed to stand against a wall between windows.

pietà (pɪɛ'tɑː) *n* a sculpture, painting, or drawing of the dead Christ, supported by the Virgin Mary. ORIG It.: pity, from L *pietās* PIETY

Pietermaritzburg ★ (ˌpiːtə'mærɪtsˌbɜːg) *n* a city in E South Africa: founded in 1839 by the Boers: gateway to mountain resorts; major industrial centre. Pop.: 156 473 (1991).

pietism ('paɪɪˌtɪzəm) *n* exaggerated or affected piety.
▸ **'pietist** *n* ▸ **ˌpie'tistic** *or* **ˌpie'tistical** *adj*

piet-my-vrou ('pɪtˌmeɪ'frəʊ) *n S. African.* a red-breasted cuckoo. ORIG imit.

Pietro da Cortona ★ (*Italian* 'pjɛːtro da kor'toːna) *n* real name *Pietro Berrettini.* 1596–1669, Italian baroque painter and architect.

piety ('paɪɪtɪ) *n, pl* **pieties. 1** dutiful devotion to God and observance of religious principles. **2** the quality of being pious. **3** a pious action, saying, etc. **4** *Now rare.* devotion and obedience to parents or superiors. ORIG C13 *piete,* from OF, from L *pietās* piety, dutifulness, from *pius* pious

piezoelectric effect (paɪˌiːzəʊɪ'lɛktrɪk) *or* **piezoelectricity** (paɪˌiːzəʊɪlɛk'trɪsɪtɪ) *n Physics.* **a** the production of electricity or electric polarity by applying a mechanical stress to certain crystals. **b** the converse effect in which stress is produced in a crystal as a result of an applied potential difference. ORIG C19: from Gk *piezein* to press
▸ **piˌezoe'lectrically** *adv*

piffle (ˈpɪfᵊl) *Inf.* ◆ *n* **1** nonsense. ◆ *vb* **piffles, piffling, piffled. 2** (*intr*) to talk or behave feebly. ORIG C19: from ?

piffling (ˈpɪflɪŋ) *adj Inf.* worthless; trivial.

pig (pɪg) *n* **1** any artiodactyl mammal of an African and Eurasian family, esp. the domestic pig, typically having a long head with a movable snout and a thick bristle-covered skin. Related adj: **porcine. 2** *Inf.* a dirty, greedy, or bad-mannered person. **3** the meat of swine; pork. **4** *Derog.* a slang word for **policeman. 5a** a mass of metal cast into a simple shape. **5b** the mould used. **6** *Brit. inf.* something that is difficult or unpleasant. **7 a pig in a poke.** something bought or received without prior sight or knowledge. **8 make a pig of oneself.** *Inf.* to overindulge oneself. ◆ *vb* **pigs, pigging, pigged. 9** (*intr*) (of a sow) to give birth. **10** (*intr*) Also: **pig it.** *Inf.* to live in squalor. **11** (*tr*) *Inf.* to devour (food) greedily. ORIG C13 *pigge,* from ?

pigeon[1] (ˈpɪdʒɪn) *n* **1** any of numerous related birds having a heavy body, small head, short legs, and long pointed wings. **2** *Sl.* a victim or dupe. ORIG C14: from OF *pijon* young dove, from LL *pīpiō* young bird, from *pīpīre* to chirp

pigeon[2] (ˈpɪdʒɪn) *n Brit. inf.* concern or responsibility (often in **it's his, her,** etc., **pigeon**). ORIG C19: altered from PIDGIN

pigeon breast *n* a deformity of the chest characterized by an abnormal protrusion of the breastbone, caused by rickets.

pigeonhole (ˈpɪdʒɪnˌhəʊl) *n* **1** a small compartment for papers, letters, etc., as in a bureau. **2** a hole or recess in a dovecote for pigeons to nest in. ◆ *vb* **pigeonholes, pigeonholing, pigeonholed.** (*tr*) **3** to put aside or defer. **4** to classify or categorize.

pigeon-toed *adj* having the toes turned inwards.

pigface (ˈpɪgˌfeɪs) *n Austral.* a creeping succulent plant having bright-coloured flowers and red fruits and often grown for ornament.

piggery (ˈpɪgərɪ) *n, pl* **piggeries. 1** a place where pigs are kept. **2** great greediness.

piggish (ˈpɪgɪʃ) *adj* **1** like a pig, esp. in appetite or manners. **2** *Inf., chiefly Brit.* obstinate or mean.
▸ **ˈpiggishly** *adv* ▸ **ˈpiggishness** *n*

Piggott ★ (ˈpɪgət) *n* **Lester (Keith).** born 1935, British flat-racing jockey: he won the Derby nine times.

piggy (ˈpɪgɪ) *n, pl* **piggies. 1** a child's word for a **pig. 2** a child's word for a **toe.** ◆ *adj* **piggier, piggiest. 3** another word for **piggish.**

piggyback (ˈpɪgɪˌbæk) *or* **pickaback** *n* **1** a ride on the back and shoulders of another person. **2** a system whereby a vehicle, aircraft, etc., is transported for part of its journey on another vehicle. ◆ *adv* **3** on the back and shoulders of another person. **4** on or as an addition. ◆ *adj* **5** of or for a piggyback: *a piggyback ride; piggyback lorry trains.* **6** of or relating to a type of heart transplant in which the transplanted heart functions in conjunction with the patient's own heart.

piggy bank *n* a child's coin bank shaped like a pig with a slot for coins.

pig-headed *adj* stupidly stubborn.
▸ **ˌpig-ˈheadedly** *adv* ▸ **ˌpig-ˈheadedness** *n*

pig iron *n* crude iron produced in a blast furnace and poured into moulds.

Pig Island ★ *n NZ inf.* New Zealand.
▸ **Pig Islander** *n*

piglet (ˈpɪglɪt) *n* a young pig.

pigmeat (ˈpɪgˌmiːt) *n* a less common name for pork, ham, or bacon.

pigment (ˈpɪgmənt) *n* **1** a substance occurring in plant or animal tissue and producing a characteristic colour. **2** any substance used to impart colour. **3** a powder that is mixed with a liquid to give a paint, ink, etc. ORIG C14: from L *pigmentum,* from *pingere* to paint
▸ **ˈpigmentary** *adj*

pigmentation (ˌpɪgmənˈteɪʃən) *n* **1** coloration in plants, animals, or man caused by the presence of pigments. **2** the deposition of pigment in animals, plants, or man.

Pigmy (ˈpɪgmɪ) *n, pl* **Pigmies.** a variant spelling of **Pygmy.**

pignut (ˈpɪgˌnʌt) *n* **1** Also called: **hognut. 1a** the bitter nut of any of several North American hickory trees. **1b** any of the trees bearing such a nut. **2** another name for **earthnut.**

pig-root *vb* (*intr*) *Austral. & NZ sl.* (of a horse) to buck slightly.

pigs (pɪgz) *interj Austral. sl.* an expression of derision or disagreement. Also: **pig's arse, pig's bum.**

Pigs ★ (pɪgz) *n* **Bay of.** See **Bay of Pigs.**

pigskin (ˈpɪgˌskɪn) *n* **1** the skin of the domestic pig. **2** leather made of this skin. **3** *US & Canad. inf.* a football. ◆ *adj* **4** made of pigskin.

pigsticking (ˈpɪgˌstɪkɪŋ) *n* the sport of hunting wild boar.
▸ **ˈpigˌsticker** *n*

pigsty (ˈpɪgˌstaɪ) *or US & Canad.* **pigpen** *n, pl* **pigsties** *or US & Canad.* **pigpens. 1** a pen for pigs. **2** *Brit.* an untidy place.

pigswill (ˈpɪgˌswɪl) *n* waste food or other edible matter fed to pigs. Also called: **pig's wash.**

pigtail (ˈpɪgˌteɪl) *n* **1** a plait of hair or one of two plaits on either side of the face. **2** a twisted roll of tobacco.

pika (ˈpaɪkə) *n* a burrowing mammal of mountainous regions of North America and Asia, having short rounded ears, a rounded body, and rudimentary tail. ORIG C19: from E Siberian *piika*

pikau (ˈpiːkaʊ) *n NZ.* a pack, knapsack, or rucksack. ORIG Maori

pike[1] (paɪk) *n, pl* **pike** *or* **pikes. 1** any of several large predatory freshwater teleost fishes with a broad flat snout, strong teeth, and elongated body covered with small scales. **2** any of various similar fishes. ORIG C14: short for *pikefish,* from OE *pīc* point, with reference to the shape of its jaw

pike[2] (paɪk) *n* **1** a medieval weapon consisting of a metal spearhead joined to a long pole. **2** a point or spike. ◆ *vb* **pikes, piking, piked. 3** (*tr*) to pierce using a pike. ORIG OE *pīc* point, from ?
▸ **ˈpikeman** *n*

pike[3] (paɪk) *n* short for **turnpike** (sense 1).

pike[4] (paɪk) *n Northern English dialect.* a pointed or conical hill. ORIG OE *pīc*

pike[5] (paɪk) *or* **piked** (paɪkt) *adj* (of the body position of a diver) bent at the hips but with the legs straight.

pike[6] (paɪk) *vb* **pikes, piking, piked.** (*intr;* foll. by *out*) *Austral. sl.* to shirk. ORIG from PIKER

pikeperch (ˈpaɪkˌpɜːtʃ) *n, pl* **pikeperch** *or* **pikeperches.** any of various pikelike freshwater teleost fishes of the perch family of Europe.

piker (ˈpaɪkə) *n US, Austral., & NZ sl.* **1** a person who will not accept a challenge; shirker. **2** a mean person. ORIG C19: from *Pike* county, Missouri, US

Pikes Peak ★ *n* a mountain in central Colorado, in the Rockies. Height: 4300 m (14 109 ft).

pikestaff (ˈpaɪkˌstɑːf) *n* the wooden handle of a pike.

pilaster (pɪˈlæstə) *n* a shallow rectangular column attached to the face of a wall. ORIG C16: from F *pilastre,* from L *pīla* pillar
▸ **piˈlastered** *adj*

Pilate ★ (ˈpaɪlət) *n* **Pontius** (ˈpɒnʃəs, ˈpɒntɪəs). Roman procurator of Judaea (?26–?36 A.D.), who ordered the crucifixion of Jesus, allegedly reluctantly against his better judgment.

Pilates (pɪˈlɑːtiːz) *n* a system of gentle exercise performed lying down that stretches and lengthens the muscles, designed to improve posture, flexibility, etc. ORIG C20: named after Joseph *Pilates* (1880–1967), its German inventor

Pilatus ★ (*German* piˈlaːtʊs) *n* a mountain in central Switzerland, in Unterwalden canton: derives its name from the legend that the body of Pontius Pilate lay in a former lake on the mountain. Height: 2122 m (6962 ft).

pilau (pɪˈlaʊ), **pilaf, pilaff** (ˈpɪlæf), *or* **pilaw** (pɪˈlɔː) *n* a dish originating from the East, consisting of rice flavoured with spices and cooked in stock, to which meat, poultry, or fish may be added. ORIG C17: from Turkish *pilāw,* from Persian

pilchard (ˈpɪltʃəd) *n* a European food fish of the herring family, with a rounded body covered with large scales. ORIG C16 *pylcher,* from ?

Pilcomayo ★ (*Spanish* pilko'majo) *n* a river in S central South America, rising in W central Bolivia and flowing southeast, forming the border between Argentina and Paraguay, to the Paraguay River at Asunción. Length: about 1600 km (1000 miles).

pile[1] (paɪl) *n* **1** a collection of objects laid on top of one another; heap; mound. **2** *Inf.* a large amount of money (esp. in **make a pile**). **3** (*often pl*) *Inf.* a large amount: *a pile of work.* **4** a less common word for **pyre. 5** a large building or group of buildings. **6** *Physics.* a structure of uranium and a moderator used for producing atomic energy; nuclear reactor. ◆ *vb* **piles, piling, piled. 7** (often foll. by *up*) to collect or be collected into or as if into a pile: *snow piled up in the drive.* **8** (*intr;* foll. by *in, into, off, out,* etc.) to move in a group, esp. in a hurried or disorganized manner: *to pile off the bus.* **9 pile it on.** *Inf.* to exaggerate. ◆ See also **pile up.** ORIG C15: via OF from L *pīla* stone pier

pile[2] (paɪl) *n* **1** a long column of timber, concrete, or steel, driven into the ground as a foundation for a structure. ◆ *vb* **piles, piling, piled.** (*tr*) **2** to drive (piles) into the ground. **3** to support (a structure) with piles. ORIG OE *pīl,* from L *pīlum*

pile[3] (paɪl) *n* **1** the yarns in a fabric that stand up or out from the weave, as in carpeting, velvet, etc. **2** soft fine hair, fur, wool, etc. ORIG C15: from Anglo-Norman *pyle,* from L *pilus* hair

pileate ('paɪlɪɪt, -ˌeɪt, 'pɪl-) *or* **pileated** ('paɪlɪˌeɪtɪd, 'pɪl-) *adj* **1** (of birds) having a crest. **2** *Bot.* having a pileus. ORIG C18: from L *pīleātus* wearing a felt cap, from PILEUS

pile-driver *n* a machine that drives piles into the ground.

pileous ('paɪlɪəs, 'pɪl-) *adj Biol.* **1** hairy. **2** of or relating to hair. ORIG C19: ult. from L *pilus* a hair

piles (paɪlz) *pl n* a nontechnical name for **haemorrhoids.** ORIG C15: from L *pilae* balls (referring to the external piles)

pileum ('paɪlɪəm, 'pɪl-) *n, pl* **pilea** (-lɪə). the top of a bird's head from the base of the bill to the occiput. ORIG C19: NL, from L PILEUS

pile up *vb* (*adv*) **1** to gather or be gathered in a pile. **2** *Inf.* to crash or cause to crash. ◆ *n* **pile-up. 3** *Inf.* a multiple collision of vehicles.

pileus ('paɪlɪəs) *n, pl* **pilei** (-lɪˌaɪ). the upper cap-shaped part of a mushroom. ORIG C18: (botanical use): NL, from L: felt cap

pilewort ('paɪlˌwɜːt) *n* any of several plants, such as lesser celandine, thought to be effective in treating piles.

pilfer ('pɪlfə) *vb* to steal (minor items), esp. in small quantities. ORIG C14 *pylfre* (n) from OF *pelfre* booty
▸ **'pilferage** *n* ▸ **'pilferer** *n*

pilgrim ('pɪlgrɪm) *n* **1** a person who undertakes a journey to a sacred place. **2** any wayfarer. ORIG C12: from Provençal *pelegrin,* from L *peregrīnus* foreign, from *per* through + *ager* land

pilgrimage ('pɪlgrɪmɪdʒ) *n* **1** a journey to a shrine or other sacred place. **2** a journey or long search made for exalted or sentimental reasons. ◆ *vb* **pilgrimages, pilgrimaging, pilgrimaged. 3** (*intr*) to make a pilgrimage.

Pilgrim Fathers *or* **Pilgrims** *pl n* **the.** the English Puritans who sailed on the Mayflower to New England, where they founded Plymouth Colony in SE Massachusetts (1620).

piliferous (paɪ'lɪfərəs) *adj* (esp. of plants) bearing or ending in a hair or hairs. ORIG C19: from L *pilus* hair + -FEROUS
▸ **'piliˌform** *adj*

piling ('paɪlɪŋ) *n* **1** the act of driving piles. **2** a number of piles. **3** a structure formed of piles.

Pílion ★ ('piljɔn) *n* transliteration of the Modern Greek name for **Pelion.**

pill[1] (pɪl) *n* **1** a small spherical or ovoid mass of a medicinal substance, intended to be swallowed whole. **2 the pill.** (*sometimes cap.*) *Inf.* an oral contraceptive. **3** something unpleasant that must be endured (esp. in **bitter pill to swallow**). **4** *Sl.* a ball or disc. **5** *Sl.* an unpleasant or boring person. ◆ *vb* **6** (*tr*) to give pills to. ORIG C15: from MFlemish *pille,* from L *pilula* a little ball, from *pila* ball

pill[2] (pɪl) *vb* **1** *Arch. or dialect.* to peel or skin (something). **2** *Arch.* to pillage or plunder (a place, etc.). ORIG OE *pilian,* from L *pilāre* to strip

pillage ('pɪlɪdʒ) *vb* **pillages, pillaging, pillaged. 1** to rob (a town, village, etc.) of (booty or spoils). ◆ *n* **2** the act of pillaging. **3** something obtained by pillaging; booty. ORIG C14: via OF from *piller* to despoil, prob. from *peille* rag, from L *pīleus* felt cap
▸ **'pillager** *n*

pillar ('pɪlə) *n* **1** an upright structure of stone, brick, metal, etc. that supports a superstructure. **2** something resembling this in shape or function: *a pillar of smoke.* **3** a prominent supporter: *a pillar of the Church.* **4 from pillar to post.** from one place to another. ORIG C13: from OF *pilier,* from L *pīla*

pillar box *n* (in Britain) a red pillar-shaped public letter box situated on a pavement.

Pillars of Hercules ★ *pl n* the two promontories at the E end of the Strait of Gibraltar: the Rock of Gibraltar on the European side and the Jebel Musa on the African side; according to legend, formed by Hercules.

pillbox ('pɪlˌbɒks) *n* **1** a box for pills. **2** a small enclosed fortified emplacement, made of reinforced concrete. **3** a small round hat.

pillion ('pɪljən) *n* **1** a seat or place behind the rider of a motorcycle, scooter, horse, etc. ◆ *adv* **2** on a pillion: *to ride pillion.* ORIG C16: from Gaelic; cf. Scot. *pillean,* Irish *pillīn* couch

pilliwinks ('pɪlɪˌwɪŋks) *pl n* a medieval instrument of torture for the fingers. ORIG C14: from ?

pillock ('pɪlək) *n Brit. sl.* a stupid or annoying person. ORIG C14: from Scand. dialect *pillicock* penis

pillory ('pɪlərɪ) *n, pl* **pillories. 1** a wooden framework into which offenders were formerly locked by the neck and wrists and exposed to public abuse and ridicule. **2** exposure to public scorn or abuse. ◆ *vb* **pillories, pillorying, pilloried.** (*tr*) **3** to expose to public scorn or ridicule. **4** to punish by putting in a pillory. ORIG C13: from Anglo-L *pillorium,* from OF *pilori,* from ?

pillow ('pɪləʊ) *n* **1** a cloth case stuffed with feathers, foam rubber, etc., used to support the head, esp. during sleep. **2** Also called: **cushion.** a padded cushion or board on which pillow lace is made. **3** anything like a pillow in shape or function. ◆ *vb* (*tr*) **4** to rest (one's head) on or as if on a pillow. **5** to serve as a pillow for. ORIG OE *pylwe,* from L *pulvīnus* cushion

pillowcase ('pɪləʊˌkeɪs) *or* **pillowslip** ('pɪləʊˌslɪp) *n* a removable washable cover of cotton, linen, nylon, etc., for a pillow.

pillow fight *n* a mock fight in which participants thump each other with pillows.

pillow lace *n* lace made by winding thread around bobbins on a padded cushion or board. Cf. **point lace.**

pillow talk *n* confidential talk between sexual partners in bed.

Pílos ★ ('pilɔs) *n* transliteration of the Modern Greek name for **Pylos.**

pilose ('paɪləʊz) *adj Biol.* covered with fine soft hairs: *pilose leaves.* ORIG C18: from L *pilōsus,* from *pilus* hair
▸ **pilosity** (paɪ'lɒsɪtɪ) *n*

pilot ('paɪlət) *n* **1** a person who is qualified to operate an aircraft or spacecraft in flight. **2a** a person who is qualified to steer or guide a ship into or out of a port, river mouth, etc. **2b** (*as modifier*): *a pilot ship.* **3** a person who steers a ship. **4** a person who acts as a leader or guide. **5** *Machinery.* a guide used to assist in joining two mating parts together. **6** an experimental programme on radio or television. **7** (*modifier*) serving as a test or trial: *a pilot project.* **8** (*modifier*) serving as a guide: *a pilot beacon.* ◆ *vb* (*tr*) **9** to act as pilot of. **10** to control the course of. **11** to guide or lead (a project, people, etc.). ORIG C16: from F *pilote,* from Med. L *pilotus,* ult. from Gk *pēdon* oar

pilotage ('paɪlətɪdʒ) *n* **1** the act of piloting an aircraft or ship. **2** a pilot's fee.

pilot balloon *n* a meteorological balloon used to observe air currents.

pilot fish *n* a small fish of tropical and subtropical seas, marked with dark vertical bands: often accompanies sharks.

pilot house *n Naut.* an enclosed structure on the bridge of a vessel from which it can be navigated; a wheelhouse.

pilot lamp *n* a small light in an electric circuit or device that lights when the current is on.

pilot light *n* **1** a small auxiliary flame that ignites the main burner of a gas appliance. **2** a small electric light used as an indicator.

pilot officer *n* the most junior commissioned rank in the British Royal Air Force and in certain other air forces.

pilot study *n* a small-scale experiment undertaken to decide whether and how to launch a full-scale project.

Pils (pɪlz, pɪls) *n* a type of lager-like beer. ORIG C20: abbrev. of PILSNER

Pilsen ★ ('pɪlzən) *n* the German name for **Plzeň**.

Pilsner ('pɪlznə) *or* **Pilsener** *n* a type of pale beer with a strong flavour of hops. ORIG after PILSEN, where it was orig. brewed

Pilsudski ★ (*Polish* piw'sutski) *n* **Józef** ('juzɛf). 1867–1935, Polish nationalist leader and statesman; president (1918–21) and premier (1926–28; 1930).

pilule ('pɪlju:l) *n* a small pill. ORIG C16: via F from L *pilula* little ball, from *pila* ball
▸ **'pilular** *adj*

pimento (pɪ'mɛntəʊ) *n, pl* **pimentos.** another name for **allspice** or **pimiento.** ORIG C17: from Sp. *pimiento* pepper plant, from Med. L *pigmenta* spiced drink, from L *pigmentum* PIGMENT

pi meson *n* another name for **pion.**

pimiento (pɪ'mjɛntəʊ, -'mɛn-) *n, pl* **pimientos.** a Spanish pepper with a red fruit used as a vegetable. Also called: **pimento.** ORIG var. of PIMENTO

pimp[1] (pɪmp) *n* **1** a man who solicits for a prostitute or brothel. **2** a man who procures sexual gratification for another; procurer; pander. ◆ *vb* **3** (*intr*) to act as a pimp. ORIG C17: from ?

pimp[2] (pɪmp) *Sl., chiefly Austral. & NZ.* ◆ *n* **1** a spy or informer. ◆ *vb* **2** (*intr;* often foll. by *on*) to inform (on). ORIG from ?

pimpernel ('pɪmpə,nɛl, -nᵊl) *n* any of several plants, such as the scarlet pimpernel, typically having small star-shaped flowers. ORIG C15: from OF *pimpernelle,* ult. from L *piper* PEPPER

pimple ('pɪmpᵊl) *n* a small round usually inflamed swelling of the skin. ORIG C14: rel. to OE *pipilian* to break out in spots
▸ **'pimpled** *adj* ▸ **'pimply** *adj* ▸ **'pimpliness** *n*

pin (pɪn) *n* **1** a short stiff straight piece of wire pointed at one end and either rounded or having a flattened head at the other: used mainly for fastening pieces of cloth, paper, etc. **2** short for **cotter pin, hairpin, panel pin, rolling pin,** or **safety pin. 3** an ornamental brooch, esp. a narrow one. **4** a badge worn fastened to the clothing by a pin. **5** something of little or no importance (esp. in **not care** *or* **give a pin (for)**). **6** a peg or dowel. **7** anything resembling a pin in shape, function, etc. **8** (in various bowling games) a usually club-shaped wooden object set up in groups as a target. **9** Also called: **safety pin.** a clip on a hand grenade that prevents its detonation until removed or released. **10** *Naut.* **10a** See **belaying pin. 10b** the sliding closure for a shackle. **11** *Music.* a metal tuning peg on a piano. **12** *Surgery.* a metal rod, esp. of stainless steel, for holding together adjacent ends of fractured bones during healing. **13** *Chess.* a position in which a piece is pinned against a more valuable piece or the king. **14** *Golf.* the flagpole marking the hole on a green. **15** (*usually pl*) *Inf.* a leg. ◆ *vb* **pins, pinning, pinned.** (*tr*) **16** to attach, hold, or fasten with or as if with a pin or pins. **17** to transfix with a pin, spear, etc. **18** (foll. by *on*) *Inf.* to place (the blame for something): *he pinned the charge on his accomplice.* **19** *Chess.* to cause (an enemy piece) to be effectively immobilized since moving it would reveal a check or expose a more valuable piece to capture. ◆ See also **pin down.** ORIG OE *pinn*

PIN (pɪn) *n acronym for* personal identification number: a number used by a holder of a cash card or credit card used in EFTPOS.

pinaceous (paɪ'neɪʃəs) *adj* of, relating to, or belonging to a family of conifers with needle-like leaves: includes pine, spruce, fir, larch, and cedar. ORIG C19: via NL from L *pīnus* a pine

pinafore ('pɪnə,fɔ:) *n* **1** *Chiefly Brit.* an apron, esp. one with a bib. **2** Also called: **pinafore dress.** a dress with a sleeveless bodice or bib top, worn over a jumper or blouse. ORIG C18: from PIN + AFORE

Pinar del Río ★ (*Spanish* pi'nar ðel 'rrio) *n* a city in W Cuba: tobacco industry. Pop.: 128 570 (1994 est.).

pinaster (paɪ'næstə) *n* a Mediterranean pine tree with paired needles and prickly cones. Also called: **maritime** (*or* **cluster**) **pinaster.** ORIG C16: from L: wild pine, from *pīnus* pine

pinball ('pɪn,bɔ:l) *n* **a** a game in which the player shoots a small ball through several hazards on a table, electrically operated machine, etc. **b** (*as modifier*): *a pinball machine.*

pince-nez ('pæns,neɪ, 'pɪns-; *French* pɛ̃sne) *n, pl* **pince-nez.** eyeglasses that are held in place only by means of a clip over the bridge of the nose. ORIG C19: F, lit.: pinch-nose

pincers ('pɪnsəz) *pl n* **1** Also called: **pair of pincers.** a gripping tool consisting of two hinged arms with handles at one end and, at the other, curved bevelled jaws that close on the workpiece. **2** the pair or pairs of jointed grasping appendages in lobsters and certain other arthropods. ORIG C14: from OF *pinceour,* from OF *pincier* to pinch

pinch (pɪntʃ) *vb* **1** to press (something, esp. flesh) tightly between two surfaces, esp. between a finger and thumb. **2** to confine, squeeze, or painfully press (toes, fingers, etc.) because of lack of space: *these shoes pinch.* **3** (*tr*) to cause stinging pain to: *the cold pinched his face.* **4** (*tr*) to make thin or drawn-looking, as from grief, lack of food, etc. **5** (usually foll. by *on*) to provide (oneself or another person) with meagre allowances, amounts, etc. **6 pinch pennies.** to live frugally because of meanness or to economize. **7** (usually foll. by *off, out,* or *back*) to remove the tips of (buds, shoots, etc.) to correct or encourage growth. **8** (*tr*) *Inf.* to steal or take without asking. **9** (*tr*) *Inf.* to arrest. ◆ *n* **10** a squeeze or sustained nip. **11** the quantity of a substance, such as salt, that can be taken between a thumb and finger. **12** a very small quantity. **13** (usually preceded by *the*) sharp, painful, or extreme stress, need, etc.: *feeling the pinch of poverty.* **14** *Sl.* a robbery. **15** *Sl.* a police raid or arrest. **16 at a pinch.** if absolutely necessary. ORIG C16: prob. from OF *pinchier* (unattested)

pinchbeck ('pɪntʃ,bɛk) *n* **1** an alloy of copper and zinc, used as imitation gold. **2** a spurious or cheap imitation. ◆ *adj* **3** made of pinchbeck. **4** sham or cheap. ORIG C18 (the alloy), C19 (something spurious): after C. *Pinchbeck* (?1670–1732), E watchmaker who invented it

pinchpenny ('pɪntʃ,pɛnɪ) *adj* **1** niggardly; miserly. ◆ *n, pl* **pinchpennies. 2** a miserly person.

Pinckney ★ ('pɪŋknɪ) *n* **Charles Cotesworth.** 1746–1825, US statesman, who was a member of the convention that framed the US Constitution (1787).

Pincus ★ ('pɪŋkəs) *n* **Gregory Goodwin.** 1903–67, US physiologist, whose work on steroid hormones led to the development of the first contraceptive pill.

pincushion ('pɪn,kʊʃən) *n* a small well-padded cushion in which pins are stuck ready for use.

Pindar ★ ('pɪndə) *n* ?518–?438 B.C., Greek lyric poet, noted for his *Epinikia,* odes commemorating victories in the Greek games.
▸ **Pindaric** (pɪn'dærɪk) *adj*

pin down *vb* (*tr, adv*) **1** to force (someone) to make a decision or carry out a promise. **2** to define clearly: *he had a vague suspicion that he couldn't quite pin down.* **3** to confine to a place.

Pindus ★ ('pɪndəs) *n* a mountain range in central Greece between Epirus and Thessaly. Highest peak: Mount Smólikas, 2633 m (8639 ft). Modern Greek name: **Píndhos** ('pinðɔs).

pine[1] (paɪn) *n* **1** any of a genus of evergreen resinous coniferous trees of the N hemisphere, with long needle-shaped leaves (**pine needles**) and brown cones. **2** the wood of any of these trees. ORIG OE *pīn,* from L *pīnus* pine

pine² (paɪn) *vb* **pines, pining, pined. 1** (*intr;* often foll. by *for* or an infinitive) to feel great longing or desire; yearn. **2** (*intr;* often foll. by *away*) to become ill or thin through worry, longing, etc. ORIG OE *pīnian* to torture, from *pīn* pain, from Med. L *pēna,* from L *poena* PAIN

pineal eye ('pɪnɪəl) *n* an outgrowth of the pineal gland that forms an eyelike structure on the top of the head in certain cold-blooded vertebrates. ORIG C19: from F, from L *pīnea* pine cone

pineal gland *or* **body** *n* a pea-sized organ situated at the base of the brain that secretes a hormone, melatonin, into the bloodstream. Technical names: **epiphysis, epiphysis cerebri.**

pineapple ('paɪn,æpᵊl) *n* **1** a tropical American plant cultivated for its large fleshy edible fruit. **2** the fruit of this plant, consisting of an inflorescence clustered around a fleshy axis and surmounted by a tuft of leaves. **3** *Mil. sl.* a hand grenade. ORIG C14 *pinappel* pine cone; C17: applied to the fruit because of its appearance

pine cone *n* the seed-producing structure of a pine tree. See **cone** (sense 3a).

pine marten *n* a marten of N European and Asian coniferous woods, having dark brown fur with a creamy-yellow patch on the throat.

pinene ('paɪni:n) *n* either of two isomeric terpenes, found in many essential oils and constituting the main part of oil of turpentine. ORIG C20: from PINE¹ + -ENE

pine nut *or* **kernel** *n* the edible seed of certain pine trees.

Pinero ★ (pɪ'nɪərəʊ) *n* Sir **Arthur Wing.** 1855–1934, British dramatist. His works include the farce *Dandy Dick* (1887) and the problem play *The Second Mrs Tanqueray* (1893).

Pines ★ (paɪnz) *n* **Isle of.** the former name of the (Isle of) **Youth.**

pine tar *n* a brown or black semisolid, produced by the destructive distillation of pine wood, used in roofing compositions, paints, medicines, etc.

pinfeather ('pɪn,fɛðə) *n Ornithol.* a feather emerging from the skin and still enclosed in its horny sheath.

pinfold ('pɪn,fəʊld) *n* **1** a pound for stray cattle. ◆ *vb* **2** (*tr*) to gather or confine in or as if in a pinfold. ORIG OE *pundfald*

ping (pɪŋ) *n* **1** a short high-pitched resonant sound, as of a bullet striking metal or a sonar echo. ◆ *vb* **2** (*intr*) to make such a noise. ORIG C19: imit.

pinger ('pɪŋə) *n* a device that makes a pinging sound, esp. one that can be preset to ring at a particular time.

Ping-Pong ('pɪŋ,pɒŋ) *n Trademark.* another name for **table tennis.** Also: **ping pong.**

pinhead ('pɪn,hɛd) *n* **1** the head of a pin. **2** something very small. **3** *Inf.* a stupid person.
▸ **'pin,headed** *adj* ▸ **'pin,headedness** *n*

pinhole ('pɪn,həʊl) *n* a small hole made with or as if with a pin.

pinion¹ ('pɪnjən) *n* **1** *Chiefly poetic.* a bird's wing. **2** the part of a bird's wing including the flight feathers. ◆ *vb* (*tr*) **3** to hold or bind (the arms) of (a person) so as to restrain or immobilize him. **4** to confine or shackle. **5** to make (a bird) incapable of flight by removing the flight feathers. ORIG C15: from OF *pignon* wing, from L *pinna* wing

pinion² ('pɪnjən) *n* a cogwheel that engages with a larger wheel or rack. ORIG C17: from F *pignon* cogwheel, from OF *peigne* comb, from L *pecten*

Piniós ★ (pi'njɔs) *n* transliteration of the Modern Greek name for the **Salambria.**

pink¹ (pɪŋk) *n* **1** a pale reddish colour. **2** pink cloth or clothing: *dressed in pink.* **3** any of various Old World plants, such as the garden pink, cultivated for their fragrant flowers. See also **carnation** (sense 1). **4** the flower of any of these plants. **5** the highest or best degree, condition, etc. (esp. in **in the pink**). **6a** a huntsman's scarlet coat. **6b** a huntsman who wears a scarlet coat. ◆ *adj* **7** of the colour pink. **8** *Brit. inf.* left-wing. **9** *Inf.* of or relating to homosexuals or homosexuality: *the pink vote.* **10** (of a huntsman's coat) scarlet or red. ◆ *vb* **11** (*intr*) another word for **knock** (sense 7). ORIG C16 (the flower), C18 (the colour): ? short for PINKEYE
▸ **'pinkish** *or* **'pinky** *adj* ▸ **'pinkness** *n*

pink² (pɪŋk) *vb* (*tr*) **1** to prick lightly with a sword, etc. **2** to decorate (leather, etc.) with a perforated or punched pattern. **3** to cut with pinking shears. ORIG C14: ? of Low G origin

pink³ (pɪŋk) *n* a sailing vessel with a narrow overhanging transom. ORIG C15: from MDu. *pinke,* from ?

Pinkerton ★ ('pɪŋkətən) *n* **Allan.** 1819–84, US private detective, born in Scotland. He founded the first detective agency in the US (1850) and organized an intelligence system for the Federal States of America (1861).

pinkeye ('pɪŋk,aɪ) *n* **1** Also called: **acute conjunctivitis.** an acute contagious inflammation of the conjunctiva of the eye, characterized by redness, discharge, etc. **2** Also called: **infectious keratitis.** a similar condition affecting the cornea of horses and cattle. ORIG C16: partial translation of obs. Du. *pinck oogen* small eyes

pinkie *or* **pinky** ('pɪŋkɪ) *n, pl* **pinkies.** *Scot., US, & Canad.* the little finger. ORIG C19: from Du. *pinkje*

pinking shears *pl n* scissors with a serrated edge on one or both blades, producing a wavy edge to material cut, thus preventing fraying.

pink salmon *n* **1** any salmon having pale pink flesh. **2** the flesh of such a fish.

pin money *n* **1** an allowance by a husband to his wife for personal expenditure. **2** money saved or earned for incidental expenses.

pinna ('pɪnə) *n, pl* **pinnae** (-ni:) *or* **pinnas. 1** any leaflet of a pinnate compound leaf. **2** *Zool.* a feather, wing, fin, etc. **3** another name for **auricle** (sense 2). ORIG C18: via NL from L: wing

pinnace ('pɪnɪs, -əs) *n* any of various kinds of ship's tender. ORIG C16: from F *pinace,* ?from OSp. *pinaza,* lit.: something made of pine, ult. from L *pīnus* pine

pinnacle ('pɪnəkᵊl) *n* **1** the highest point, esp. of fame, success, etc. **2** a towering peak, as of a mountain. **3** a slender upright structure in the form of a spire on the top of a buttress, gable, or tower. ◆ *vb* **pinnacles, pinnacling, pinnacled.** (*tr*) **4** to set as on a pinnacle. **5** to furnish with a pinnacle or pinnacles. **6** to crown with a pinnacle. ORIG C14: via OF from LL *pinnāculum* a peak, from L *pinna* wing

pinnate ('pɪneɪt, 'pɪnɪt) *adj* **1** like a feather in appearance. **2** (of compound leaves) having the leaflets growing opposite each other in pairs on either side of the stem. ORIG C18: from L *pinnātus,* from *pinna* feather
▸ **'pinnately** *adv* ▸ **pin'nation** *n*

pinniped ('pɪnɪ,pɛd) *adj* **1** of, relating to, or belonging to an order of aquatic placental mammals having a streamlined body and limbs specialized as flippers: includes seals, sea lions, and the walrus. ◆ *n* **2** any pinniped animal. ORIG C19: from NL *pinnipēs,* from L *pinna* fin + *pēs* foot

pinnule ('pɪnju:l) *n* **1** any of the lobes of a leaflet of a pinnate compound leaf, which is itself pinnately divided. **2** *Zool.* any feather-like part, such as any of the arms of a sea lily. ORIG C16: from L *pinnula,* dim. of *pinna* feather
▸ **'pinnular** *adj*

pinny ('pɪnɪ) *n, pl* **pinnies.** a child's or informal name for **pinafore** (sense 1).

Pinochet ★ ('pi:nə,ʃeɪ) *n* **Augusto** (**Ugarte**) (au'gusto). born 1915, Chilean general and statesman; president of Chile (1974–90), following his overthrow of Allende (1973).

pinochle *or* **pinocle** ('pi:nʌkᵊl) *n* **1** a card game for two to four players similar to bezique. **2** the combination of queen of spades and jack of diamonds in this game. ORIG C19: from ?

pinotage ('pɪnəta:ʒ) *n* **1** a red grape variety of South Africa, a cross between the Pinot Noir and the Hermitage. **2** any of the red wines made from this grape.

★ people and places

Pinot Noir (piːˈnəʊ nwɑː) *n* **1** a variety of black grape, grown esp. for wine-making. **2** any of the red wines made from this grape. ORIG F

pinpoint (ˈpɪnˌpɔɪnt) *vb* (*tr*) **1** to locate or identify exactly: *to pinpoint a problem; to pinpoint a place on a map.* ♦ *n* **2** an insignificant or trifling thing. **3** the point of a pin. **4** (*modifier*) exact: *a pinpoint aim.*

pinprick (ˈpɪnˌprɪk) *n* **1** a slight puncture made by or as if by a pin. **2** a small irritation. ♦ *vb* **3** (*tr*) to puncture with or as if with a pin.

pins and needles *n* (*functioning as sing*) *Inf.* **1** a tingling sensation in the fingers, toes, legs, etc., caused by the return of normal blood circulation after its temporary impairment. **2 on pins and needles.** in a state of anxious suspense.

Pinsent ★ (ˈpɪnˌsɛnt) *n* **Matthew** (**Clive**). born 1970, British oarsman: won three gold medals in rowing events at three consecutive Olympic Games (1992, 1996, and 2000).

Pinsk ★ (*Russian* pinsk) *n* a city in SW Belarus: capital of a principality (13th–14th centuries). Pop.: 130 000 (1996 est.).

pinstripe (ˈpɪnˌstraɪp) *n* (in textiles) a very narrow stripe in fabric or the fabric itself.

pint (paɪnt) *n* **1** a unit of liquid measure of capacity equal to one eighth of a gallon. 1 Brit. pint is equal to 0.568 litre, 1 US pint to 0.473 litre. **2** a unit of dry measure of capacity equal to one half of a quart. 1 US dry pint is equal to one sixty-fourth of a US bushel or 0.5506 litre. **3** a measure having such a capacity. **4** *Brit. inf.* **4a** a pint of beer. **4b** a drink of beer: *he's gone out for a pint.* ORIG C14: from OF *pinte,* from ?; ?from Med. L *pincta* marks used in measuring liquids, ult. from L *pingere* to paint

pinta (ˈpaɪntə) *n Inf.* a pint of milk. ORIG C20: phonetic rendering of *pint of*

pintail (ˈpɪnˌteɪl) *n, pl* **pintails** *or* **pintail.** a greyish-brown duck with a pointed tail.

Pinter ★ (ˈpɪntə) *n* **Harold.** born 1930, British dramatist. His plays, such as *The Caretaker* (1960), *The Homecoming* (1965), and *Ashes to Ashes* (1996), are noted for their equivocal and halting dialogue.

pintle (ˈpɪntᵊl) *n* **1** a pin or bolt forming the pivot of a hinge. **2** the link bolt, hook, or pin on a vehicle's towing bracket. **3** the needle or plunger of the injection valve of an oil engine. ORIG OE *pintel* penis

pinto (ˈpɪntəʊ) *US & Canad.* ♦ *adj* **1** marked with patches of white; piebald. ♦ *n, pl* **pintos. 2** a pinto horse. ORIG C19: from American Sp. (orig.: painted, spotted), ult. from L *pingere* to paint

pint-size *or* **pint-sized** *adj Inf.* very small.

pin tuck *n* a narrow, ornamental fold, esp. used on shirt fronts and dress bodices.

Pinturicchio (*Italian* pintuˈrikkjo) *or* **Pintoricchio** ★ (*Italian* pintoˈrikkjo) *n* real name *Bernardino di Betto.* ?1454–1513, Italian painter of the Umbrian school.

pin-up *n* **1** *Inf.* **1a** a picture of a sexually attractive person, esp. when partially or totally undressed. **1b** (*as modifier*): *a pin-up magazine.* **2** *Sl.* a person who has appeared in such a picture. **3** a photograph of a famous personality.

pinus radiata (ˈpaɪnəs ˌreɪdɪˈɑːtə) *n* a pine tree grown in New Zealand and Australia to produce building timber.

pinwheel (ˈpɪnˌwiːl) *n* another name for a **Catherine wheel** (sense 1).

pinworm (ˈpɪnˌwɜːm) *n* a parasitic nematode worm, infecting the colon, rectum, and anus of humans. Also called: **threadworm.**

piny (ˈpaɪnɪ) *adj* **pinier, piniest.** of, resembling, or covered with pine trees.

Pinyin (ˈpɪnˈjɪn) *n* a system of spelling used to transliterate Chinese characters into the Roman alphabet.

Pinzón ★ (*Spanish* pinˈθɔn) *n* **1 Martín Alonzo** (marˈtin aˈlɔnθo). ?1440–93, Spanish navigator, who commanded the *Pinta* on Columbus' first expedition (1492–93). **2** his brother, **Vicente Yáñez** (biˈθente ˈjaɲεθ). ?1460–?1524, Spanish navigator, who commanded the *Niña* on Columbus' first expedition (1492–93).

★ people and places

pion (ˈpaɪɒn) *or* **pi meson** *n Physics.* a meson having a positive or negative charge and a rest mass 273 times that of the electron, or no charge and a rest mass 264 times that of the electron. ORIG C20: from Gk letter PI + -ON

pioneer (ˌpaɪəˈnɪə) *n* **1a** a colonist, explorer, or settler of a new land, region, etc. **1b** (*as modifier*): *a pioneer wagon.* **2** an innovator or developer of something new. **3** *Mil.* a member of an infantry group that digs entrenchments, makes roads, etc. ♦ *vb* **4** to be a pioneer (in or of). **5** (*tr*) to initiate, prepare, or open up: *to pioneer a medical programme.* ORIG C16: from OF *paonier* infantryman, from *paon* PAWN[2]

pious (ˈpaɪəs) *adj* **1** having or expressing reverence for a god or gods; religious; devout. **2** marked by reverence. **3** marked by false reverence; sanctimonious. **4** sacred; not secular. ORIG C17: from L *pius*
▸ **ˈpiously** *adv* ▸ **ˈpiousness** *n*

pip[1] (pɪp) *n* **1** the seed of a fleshy fruit, such as an apple or pear. **2** any of the segments marking the surface of a pineapple. ORIG C18: short for PIPPIN

pip[2] (pɪp) *n* **1** a short high-pitched sound, a sequence of which can act as a time signal, esp. on radio. **2** a radar blip. **3a** a device, such as a spade, diamond, heart, or club on a playing card. **3b** any of the spots on dice or dominoes. **4** *Inf.* the emblem worn on the shoulder by junior officers in the British Army, indicating their rank. ♦ *vb* **pips, pipping, pipped. 5** (of a young bird) **5a** (*intr*) to chirp; peep. **5b** to pierce (the shell of its egg) while hatching. **6** (*intr*) to make a short high-pitched sound. ORIG C16 (in the sense: spot); C17 (vb); C20 (in the sense: short high-pitched sound): ? imit.

pip[3] (pɪp) *n* **1** a contagious disease of poultry characterized by the secretion of thick mucus in the mouth and throat. **2** *Facetious sl.* a minor human ailment. **3** *Brit. sl.* a bad temper or depression (esp. in **give** (**someone**) **the pip**). ♦ *vb* **pips, pipping, pipped. 4** *Brit. sl.* to cause to be annoyed or depressed. ORIG C15: from MDu. *pippe,* ult. from L *pituita* phlegm

pip[4] (pɪp) *vb* **pips, pipping, pipped.** (*tr*) *Brit. sl.* **1** to wound, esp. with a gun. **2** to defeat (a person), esp. when his or her success seems certain (often in **pip at the post**). **3** to blackball or ostracize. ORIG C19 (orig. in the sense: to blackball): prob. from PIP[2]

pipal (ˈpiːpᵊl) *n* a variant of **peepul.**

pipe[1] (paɪp) *n* **1** a long tube of metal, plastic, etc., used to convey water, oil, gas, etc. **2** a long tube or case. **3** an object made in various shapes and sizes, consisting of a small bowl with an attached tubular stem, in which tobacco or other substances are smoked. **4** Also called: **pipeful.** the amount of tobacco that fills the bowl of a pipe. **5 put that in your pipe and smoke it.** *Inf.* accept that fact if you can. **6** *Zool., bot.* any of various hollow organs, such as the respiratory passage of certain animals. **7a** any musical instrument whose sound production results from the vibration of an air column in a simple tube. **7b** any of the tubular devices on an organ. **8 the pipes.** See **bagpipes. 9** a shrill voice or sound, as of a bird. **10a** a boatswain's pipe. **10b** the sound it makes. **11** (*pl*) *Inf.* the respiratory tract or vocal cords. **12** *Metallurgy.* a conical hole in the head of an ingot. **13** a cylindrical vein of rich ore. **14** Also called: **volcanic pipe.** a vertical cylindrical passage in a volcano through which molten lava is forced during eruption. ♦ *vb* **pipes, piping, piped. 15** to play (music) on a pipe. **16** (*tr*) to summon or lead by a pipe: *to pipe the dancers.* **17** to utter (something) shrilly. **18a** to signal orders to (the crew) by a boatswain's pipe. **18b** (*tr*) to signal the arrival or departure of: *to pipe the admiral aboard.* **19** (*tr*) to convey (water, gas, etc.) by a pipe or pipes. **20** (*tr*) to provide with pipes. **21** (*tr*) to trim (an article, esp. of clothing) with piping. **22** to force cream or icing, etc., through a shaped nozzle to decorate food. ♦ See also **pipe down, pipe up.** ORIG OE *pīpe* (n), *pīpian* (vb), ult. from L *pīpāre* to chirp

pipe[2] (paɪp) *n* **1** a large cask for wine, oil, etc. **2** a measure of capacity for wine equal to four barrels or 105 Brit. gallons. **3** a cask holding this quantity with its contents. ORIG C14: via OF (in the sense: tube), ult. from L *pīpāre* to chirp

pipe bomb *n* a small explosive device hidden in a pipe or drain, detonated by means of a timer.

pipeclay ('paɪpˌkleɪ) *n* **1** a fine white pure clay, used in the manufacture of tobacco pipes and pottery and for whitening leather and similar materials. ◆ *vb* **2** (*tr*) to whiten with pipeclay.

pipe cleaner *n* a short length of thin wires twisted so as to hold tiny tufts of yarn: used to clean the stem of a tobacco pipe.

piped music *n* light popular music prerecorded and played through amplifiers in a shop, restaurant, factory, etc., as background music.

pipe down *vb* (*intr, adv*) *Inf.* to stop talking, making noise, etc.

pipe dream *n* a fanciful or impossible plan or hope. ORIG alluding to dreams produced by smoking an opium pipe

pipefish ('paɪpˌfɪʃ) *n, pl* **pipefish** *or* **pipefishes.** any of various teleost fishes having a long tubelike snout and an elongated body covered with bony plates. Also called: **needlefish.**

pipefitting ('paɪpˌfɪtɪŋ) *n* **a** the act or process of bending and joining pipes. **b** the branch of plumbing involving this.
▸ **'pipeˌfitter** *n*

pipeline ('paɪpˌlaɪn) *n* **1** a long pipe used to transport oil, natural gas, etc. **2** a medium of communication, esp. a private one. **3 in the pipeline.** in the process of being completed, delivered, or produced. ◆ *vb* **pipelines, pipelining, pipelined.** (*tr*) **4** to convey by pipeline. **5** to supply with a pipeline.

pipe major *n* the noncommissioned officer responsible for the training of a pipe band.

pipe organ *n* another name for **organ** (the musical instrument).

piper ('paɪpə) *n* **1** a person who plays a pipe or bagpipes. **2 pay the piper and call the tune.** to bear the cost of an undertaking and control it.

Piper ★ ('paɪpə) *n* **John.** 1903–92, British artist. An official war artist in World War II, he is known also for his stained glass in Coventry Cathedral.

piperidine (pɪ'pɛrɪˌdiːn) *n* a liquid compound with a peppery ammoniacal odour: used in making rubbers and curing epoxy resins.

piperine ('pɪpəˌraɪn) *n* an alkaloid that is the active ingredient of pepper, used as a flavouring and as an insecticide. ORIG C19: from L *piper* PEPPER

piperonal ('pɪpərəʊˌnæl) *n* a white fragrant aldehyde used in flavourings, perfumery, and suntan lotions.

pipette (pɪ'pɛt) *n* a calibrated glass tube drawn to a fine bore at one end, filled by sucking liquid into the bulb, and used to transfer or measure known volumes of liquid. ORIG C19: via F: little pipe

pipe up *vb* (*intr, adv*) **1** to commence singing or playing a musical instrument: *the band piped up.* **2** to speak up, esp. in a shrill voice.

pipi ('pɪpiː) *n, pl* **pipi** *or* **pipis. 1** an edible shellfish of New Zealand. **2** an Australian mollusc of sandy beaches, widely used as bait. ORIG from Maori

piping ('paɪpɪŋ) *n* **1** pipes collectively, as in the plumbing of a house. **2** a cord of icing, whipped cream, etc., often used to decorate desserts and cakes. **3** a thin strip of covered cord or material, used to edge hems, etc. **4** the sound of a pipe or bagpipes. **5** the art or technique of playing a pipe or bagpipes. **6** a shrill voice or sound, esp. a whistling sound. ◆ *adj* **7** making a shrill sound. **8 piping hot.** extremely hot.

pipistrelle (ˌpɪpɪ'strɛl) *n* any of a genus of numerous small brownish insectivorous bats, occurring in most parts of the world. ORIG C18: via F from It. *pipistrello,* from L *vespertīliō* a bat, from *vesper* evening, because of its nocturnal habits

pipit ('pɪpɪt) *n* any of various songbirds, esp. the **meadow pipit,** having brownish speckled plumage and a long tail. ORIG C18: prob. imit.

pipkin ('pɪpkɪn) *n* a small earthenware vessel. ORIG C16: ? dim. of PIPE[2]; see -KIN

pippin ('pɪpɪn) *n* any of several varieties of eating apple. ORIG C13: from OF *pepin,* from ?

pipsissewa (pɪp'sɪsəwə) *n* any of several ericaceous plants of an Asian and American genus, having jagged evergreen leaves and white or pinkish flowers. Also called: **wintergreen.** ORIG C19: from Algonquian *pipisisikweu,* lit.: it breaks it into pieces, so called because believed to be efficacious in treating bladder stones

pipsqueak ('pɪpˌskwiːk) *n Inf.* a person or thing that is insignificant or contemptible.

piquant ('piːkənt, -kɑːnt) *adj* **1** having an agreeably pungent or tart taste. **2** lively or stimulating to the mind. ORIG C16: from F (lit.: prickling), from *piquer* to prick, goad
▸ **'piquancy** *n* ▸ **'piquantly** *adv*

pique (piːk) *n* **1** a feeling of resentment or irritation, as from having one's pride wounded. ◆ *vb* **piques, piquing, piqued.** (*tr*) **2** to cause to feel resentment or irritation. **3** to excite or arouse. **4** (foll. by *on* or *upon*) to pride or congratulate (oneself). ORIG C16: from F, from *piquer* to prick

piqué ('piːkeɪ) *n* a close-textured fabric of cotton, silk, or spun rayon woven with lengthwise ribs. ORIG C19: from F *piqué* pricked, from *piquer* to prick

piquet (pɪ'kɛt, -'keɪ) *n* a card game for two people played with a reduced pack. ORIG C17: from F, from ?

piracy ('paɪrəsɪ) *n, pl* **piracies. 1** *Brit.* robbery on the seas. **2** a felony, such as robbery or hijacking, committed aboard a ship or aircraft. **3** the unauthorized use or appropriation of patented or copyrighted material, ideas, etc. ORIG C16: from Anglo-L *pirātia,* from LGk *peirāteia;* see PIRATE

Piraeus *or* **Peiraeus** ★ (paɪ'riːəs, pɪ'reɪ-) *n* a port in SE Greece, adjoining Athens: the country's chief port; founded in the 5th century B.C. as the port of Athens. Pop.: 169 622 (1991). Modern Greek name: **Piraiévs** (ˌpirɛ'ɛfs).

Pirandello ★ (*Italian* piran'dɛllo) *n* **Luigi** (lu'iːdʒi). 1867–1936, Italian dramatist and writer. His plays include *Six Characters in Search of an Author* (1921) and *Henry IV* (1922): Nobel prize for literature 1934.

Piranesi ★ (*Italian* pira'neːsi) *n* **Giambattista** (dʒambat'tista). 1720–78, Italian etcher and architect: etchings include *Imaginary Prisons* and *Views of Rome.*

piranha *or* **piraña** (pɪ'rɑːnjə) *n* any of various small freshwater voracious fishes of tropical America, having strong jaws and sharp teeth. ORIG C19: via Port. from Tupi: fish with teeth, from *pirá* fish + *sainha* tooth

pirate ('paɪrɪt) *n* **1** a person who commits piracy. **2a** a vessel used by pirates. **2b** (*as modifier*): *a pirate ship.* **3** a person who illicitly uses or appropriates someone else's literary, artistic, or other work. **4a** a person or group of people who broadcast illegally. **4b** (*as modifier*): *a pirate radio station.* ◆ *vb* **pirates, pirating, pirated. 5** (*tr*) to use, appropriate, or reproduce (artistic work, ideas, etc.) illicitly. ORIG C15: from L *pīrāta,* from Gk *peirātēs* one who attacks, from *peira* an attack
▸ **pi'ratical** *or* **piratic** (paɪ'rætɪk) *adj* ▸ **pi'ratically** *adv*

Pirithoüs ★ (paɪ'rɪθəʊəs) *n Greek myth.* a prince of the Lapiths, who accomplished many great deeds with his friend Theseus.

pirogue (pɪ'rəʊg) *or* **piragua** (pɪ'rɑːgwə, -'ræg-) *n* any of various kinds of dugout canoes. ORIG C17: via F from Sp., of Amerind origin

pirouette (ˌpɪrʊ'ɛt) *n* **1** a body spin, esp. in dancing, on the toes or the ball of the foot. ◆ *vb* **pirouettes, pirouetting, pirouetted. 2** (*intr*) to perform a pirouette. ORIG C18: from F, from OF *pirouet* spinning top

Pisa ★ ('piːzə; *Italian* 'piːsa) *n* a city in Tuscany, NW Italy, near the mouth of the River Arno: flourishing maritime republic (11th–12th centuries), contains a university (1343), a cathedral (1063), and the Leaning Tower (begun in 1174 and about 5 m (17 ft) from perpendicular); tourism. Pop.: 102 150 (1990).

Pisanello ★ (*Italian* pisa'nɛllo) *n* **Antonio** (an'tɔːnjo). ?1395–?1455, Italian painter and medallist in the International Gothic style: best known for his portrait medals and drawings of animals.

Pisano ★ (*Italian* pi'saːno) *n* **1 Giovanni** (dʒo'vanni).

?1250–?1320, Italian sculptor, noted for his pulpit in St Andrea, Pistoia. **2** his father, **Nicola** (ni'kɔ:la). ?1220–?84, Italian sculptor, who pioneered the classical style: noted esp. for his pulpit in the baptistry of Pisa Cathedral.

piscatorial (ˌpɪskə'tɔ:rɪəl) *or* **piscatory** ('pɪskətərɪ, -trɪ) *adj* **1** of or relating to fish, fishing, or fishermen. **2** devoted to fishing. ORIG C19: from L *piscātōrius,* from *piscātor* fisherman
▸ **ˌpisca'torially** *adv*

Pisces ('paɪsi:z, 'pɪ-) *n, Latin genitive* **Piscium** ('paɪsɪəm). **1** *Astron.* a faint extensive zodiacal constellation lying between Aquarius and Aries on the ecliptic. **2** *Astrol.* Also called: the **Fishes.** the twelfth sign of the zodiac. The sun is in this sign between about Feb. 19 and March 20. **3a** a taxonomic group that comprises all fishes. See **fish** (sense 1). **3b** a taxonomic group that comprises the bony fishes only. See **teleost.** ORIG C14: L: the fish (pl)

pisci- *combining form.* fish: *pisciculture.* ORIG from L *piscis*

pisciculture ('pɪsɪˌkʌltʃə) *n* the rearing and breeding of fish under controlled conditions.
▸ **ˌpisci'cultural** *adj* ▸ **ˌpisci'culturist** *n, adj*

piscina (pɪ'si:nə) *n, pl* **piscinae** (-ni:) *or* **piscinas.** *RC Church.* a stone basin, with a drain, in a church or sacristy where water used at Mass is poured away. ORIG C16: from L: fish pond, from *piscis* a fish

piscine ('pɪsaɪn) *adj* of, relating to, or resembling a fish.

piscivorous (pɪ'sɪvərəs) *adj* feeding on fish.

Pisgah ★ ('pɪzgə) *n* **Mount.** *Old Testament.* the mountain slopes to the northeast of the Dead Sea, from one of which, Mount Nebo, Moses viewed Canaan.

pish (pʃ, pɪʃ) *interj* **1** an exclamation of impatience or contempt. ◆ *vb* **2** to make this exclamation at (someone or something).

Pishpek ★ (pɪʃ'pɛk) *n* a variant transliteration of the Kyrgyz name for **Bishkek.**

pisiform ('pɪsɪˌfɔ:m) *adj* **1** *Zool., bot.* resembling a pea. ◆ *n* **2** a small pealike bone on the ulnar side of the carpus. ORIG C18: via NL from L *pīsum* pea + *forma* shape

Pisistratus ★ (paɪ'sɪstrətəs) *n* ?600–527 B.C., tyrant of Athens: he established himself in firm control of the city following his defeat of his aristocratic rivals at Pallene (546).

pismire ('pɪsˌmaɪə) *n* an archaic or dialect word for an **ant.** ORIG C14 (lit.: urinating ant, from the odour of formic acid): from PISS + obs. *mire* ant, from ON

piss (pɪs) *Sl.* ◆ *vb* **1** (*intr*) *Taboo.* to urinate. **2** (*tr*) *Taboo.* to discharge as or in one's urine: *to piss blood.* ◆ *n* **3** *Taboo.* an act of urinating. **4** *Taboo.* urine. **5 take the piss.** to tease or make fun of someone or something. ORIG C13: from OF *pisser,* prob. imit.

Pissarro ★ (pɪ'sɑ:rəʊ; *French* pisaro) *n* **Camille** (kamij). 1830–1903, French impressionist painter, esp. of landscapes.

piss artist *n Sl.* **1** a boastful or incompetent person. **2** a person who drinks heavily and gets drunk frequently.

pissed (pɪst) *adj Sl.* **1** *Brit. taboo.* drunk. **2** *US.* annoyed, irritated, or disappointed.

piss off *vb* (*adv*) *Taboo sl.* **1** (*tr; often passive*) to annoy, irritate, or disappoint. **2** (*intr*) *Chiefly Brit.* to go away; depart: often used to dismiss a person.

piss-poor *adj Sl.* of a very low standard; bad.

piss-up *n Sl.* a party involving a considerable amount of drinking.

pistachio (pɪ'stɑ:ʃɪˌəʊ) *n, pl* **pistachios. 1** a tree of the Mediterranean region and W Asia, with small hard-shelled nuts. **2** Also called: **pistachio nut.** the nut of this tree, having an edible green kernel. **3** the sweet flavour of the pistachio nut, used in ice creams, etc. ◆ *adj* **4** of a yellowish-green colour. ORIG C16: via It. & L from Gk *pistakion* pistachio nut, from *pistakē* pistachio tree, from Persian *pistah*

piste (pi:st) *n* a slope or course for skiing. ORIG C18: via OF from OIt. *pista,* from *pistare* to tread down

pistil ('pɪstɪl) *n* the female reproductive part of a flower, consisting of one or more separate or fused carpels. ORIG C18: from L *pistillum* pestle

pistillate ('pɪstɪlɪt, -ˌleɪt) *adj* (of plants) **1** having pistils but no anthers. **2** having or producing pistils.

Pistoia ★ (*Italian* pis'to:ja) *n* a city in N Italy, in N Tuscany: scene of the defeat and death of Catiline in 62 B.C. Pop.: 89 972 (1990).

pistol ('pɪstᵊl) *n* **1** a short-barrelled handgun. **2 hold a pistol to a person's head.** to threaten a person in order to force him or her to do what one wants. ◆ *vb* **pistols, pistolling, pistolled** *or US* **pistols, pistoling, pistoled. 3** (*tr*) to shoot with a pistol. ORIG C16: from F *pistole,* from G, from Czech *pišt'ala* pistol, pipe

pistole (pɪs'təʊl) *n* any of various gold coins of varying value, formerly used in Europe. ORIG C16: from OF, shortened from *pistolet,* lit.: little PISTOL

pistol grip *n* **a** a handle shaped like the butt of a pistol. **b** (*as modifier*): *a pistol-grip camera.*

pistol-whip *vb* **pistol-whips, pistol-whipping, pistol-whipped.** (*tr*) *US.* to beat or strike with a pistol barrel.

piston ('pɪstən) *n* a disc or cylindrical part that slides to and fro in a hollow cylinder. In an internal-combustion engine it is attached by a pivoted connecting rod to a crankshaft or flywheel, thus converting reciprocating motion into rotation. ORIG C18: via F from OIt. *pistone,* from *pistare* to grind, from L *pinsere* to beat

piston ring *n* a split ring that fits into a groove on the rim of a piston to provide a spring-loaded seal against the cylinder wall.

piston rod *n* **1** the rod that connects the piston of a reciprocating steam engine to the crosshead. **2** a less common name for a **connecting rod.**

pit¹ (pɪt) *n* **1** a large, usually deep opening in the ground. **2a** a mine or excavation, esp. for coal. **2b** the shaft in a mine. **2c** (*as modifier*): *pit pony; pit prop.* **3** a concealed danger or difficulty. **4 the pit.** hell. **5** Also called: **orchestra pit.** the area that is occupied by the orchestra in a theatre, located in front of the stage. **6** an enclosure for fighting animals or birds. **7** *Anat.* **7a** a small natural depression on the surface of a body, organ, or part. **7b** the floor of any natural bodily cavity: *the pit of the stomach.* **8** *Pathol.* a small indented scar at the site of a former pustule; pockmark. **9** a working area at the side of a motor-racing track for servicing or refuelling vehicles. **10** a section on the floor of a commodity exchange devoted to a special line of trading. **11** the ground floor of the auditorium of a theatre. **12** another word for **pitfall** (sense 2). ◆ *vb* **pits, pitting, pitted. 13** (*tr; often foll. by against*) to match in opposition, esp. as antagonists. **14** to mark or become marked with pits. **15** (*tr*) to place or bury in a pit. ORIG OE *pytt,* from L *puteus*

pit² (pɪt) *Chiefly US & Canad.* ◆ *n* **1** the stone of a cherry, etc. ◆ *vb* **pits, pitting, pitted.** (*tr*) **2** to extract the stone from (a fruit). ORIG C19: from Du.: kernel

pitapat ('pɪtəˌpæt) *adv* **1** with quick light taps. ◆ *vb* **pitapats, pitapatting, pitapatted. 2** (*intr*) to make quick light taps. ◆ *n* **3** such taps. ORIG C16: imit.

pit bull terrier *n* a dog resembling the Staffordshire bull terrier but somewhat larger: originally developed for dogfighting.

Pitcairn Island ★ (pɪt'kɛən, 'pɪtkɛən) *n* an island in the S Pacific: forms with other islands a UK overseas territory; uninhabited until the landing in 1790 of the mutineers of H.M.S. *Bounty* and their Tahitian companions. Pop.: 54 (1995). Area: 4.6 sq. km (1.75 sq. miles).

pitch¹ (pɪtʃ) *vb* **1** to hurl or throw (something); cast; fling. **2** (*usually tr*) to set up (a camp, tent, etc.). **3** (*tr*) to aim or fix (something) at a particular level, position, style, etc.: *if you advertise privately you may pitch the price too low.* **4** (*tr*) to aim to sell (a product) to a specified market or on a specified basis. **5** (*intr*) to slope downwards. **6** (*intr*) to fall forwards or downwards. **7** (*intr*) (of a vessel) to dip and raise its bow and stern alternately. **8** *Cricket.* to bowl (a ball) so that it bounces on a certain part of the wicket, or (of a ball) to bounce on a certain part of the wicket. **9** (*intr*) (of a missile, aircraft, etc.) to deviate from a stable flight attitude by movement of the longitudinal axis about the lateral axis. **10** (*tr*) (in golf, etc.) to hit (a ball) steeply into the air. **11** (*tr*) *Music.* **11a** to sing or play accurately (a note, interval, etc.). **11b** (*usually passive*) (of a wind instrument) to specify or indicate its basic key or harmonic series by its size, manufacture, etc. **12** *Baseball, softball.* **12a** (*tr*) to throw (a ball) to a batter. **12b** (*intr*) to act as a pitcher in a game. ◆ *n* **13** the degree of elevation or depression. **14a** the angle of descent of a downward slope. **14b** such a slope. **15** the extreme height or depth. **16** *Mountaineering.* a section of a route between two belay points. **17** the degree of slope of a roof. **18** the distance between corresponding points on adjacent members of a body of regular form, esp. the distance between teeth on a gearwheel or between threads on a screw thread. **19** the pitching motion of a ship, missile, etc. **20** *Music.* **20a** the height or depth of a note as determined by its frequency relative to that of other notes: *high pitch; low pitch.* **20b** an absolute frequency assigned to a specific note, fixing the relative frequencies of all other notes. **21** *Cricket.* the rectangular area between the stumps, 22 yards long and 10 feet wide; the wicket. **22** the act or manner of pitching a ball, as in cricket, etc. **23** *Chiefly Brit.* a vendor's station, esp. on a pavement. **24** *Sl.* a persuasive sales talk, esp. one routinely repeated. **25** *Chiefly Brit.* (in many sports) the field of play. **26** *Golf.* Also called: **pitch shot.** an approach shot in which the ball is struck in a high arc. **27** **queer someone's pitch.** *Brit. inf.* to upset someone's plans. ◆ See also **pitch in, pitch into.** ORIG C13 *picchen*

pitch[2] (pɪtʃ) *n* **1** any of various heavy dark viscid substances obtained as a residue from the distillation of tars. **2** any of various similar substances, such as asphalt, occurring as natural deposits. **3** crude turpentine obtained as sap from pine trees. ◆ *vb* **4** (*tr*) to apply pitch to (something). ORIG OE *pic,* from L *pix*

pitch-black *adj* **1** extremely dark; unlit: *the room was pitch-black.* **2** of a deep black colour.

pitchblende (ˈpɪtʃˌblɛnd) *n* a blackish mineral that occurs in veins, frequently associated with silver: the principal source of uranium and radium. ORIG C18: partial translation of G *Pechblende,* from *Pech* PITCH[2] (from its black colour) + BLENDE

pitch-dark *adj* extremely or completely dark.

pitched battle *n* **1** a battle ensuing from the deliberate choice of time and place. **2** any fierce encounter, esp. one with large numbers.

pitcher[1] (ˈpɪtʃə) *n* a large jug, usually rounded with a narrow neck and often of earthenware, used mainly for holding water. ORIG C13: from OF *pichier,* from Med. L *picārium,* var. of *bicārium* BEAKER

pitcher[2] (ˈpɪtʃə) *n Baseball.* the player on the fielding team who throws the ball to the batter.

pitcher plant *n* any of various insectivorous plants, having leaves modified to form pitcher-like organs that attract and trap insects, which are then digested.

pitchfork (ˈpɪtʃˌfɔːk) *n* **1** a long-handled fork with two or three long curved tines for tossing hay. ◆ *vb* (*tr*) **2** to use a pitchfork on (something). **3** to thrust (someone) unwillingly into a position.

pitch in *vb* (*intr, adv*) **1** to cooperate or contribute. **2** to begin energetically.

pitch into *vb* (*intr, prep*) *Inf.* **1** to assail physically or verbally. **2** to get on with doing (something).

pitch pine *n* **1** any of various coniferous trees of North America: valued as a source of turpentine and pitch. **2** the wood of any of these trees.

pitch pipe *n* a small pipe that sounds a note or notes of standard frequency. It is used for establishing the correct starting note for unaccompanied singing.

pitchy (ˈpɪtʃɪ) *adj* **pitchier, pitchiest. 1** full of or covered with pitch. **2** resembling pitch.
▸ **ˈpitchiness** *n*

piteous (ˈpɪtɪəs) *adj* exciting or deserving pity.
▸ **ˈpiteously** *adv* ▸ **ˈpiteousness** *n*

pitfall (ˈpɪtˌfɔːl) *n* **1** an unsuspected difficulty or danger. **2** a trap in the form of a concealed pit, designed to catch men or wild animals. ORIG OE *pytt* PIT[1] + *fealle* trap

pith (pɪθ) *n* **1** the soft fibrous tissue lining the inside of the rind in fruits such as the orange. **2** the essential or important part, point, etc. **3** weight; substance. **4** *Bot.* the central core of unspecialized cells surrounded by conducting tissue in stems. **5** the soft central part of a bone, feather, etc. ◆ *vb* (*tr*) **6** to kill (animals) by severing the spinal cord. **7** to remove the pith from (a plant). ORIG OE *pitha*

pithead (ˈpɪtˌhɛd) *n* the top of a mine shaft and the buildings, hoisting gear, etc., around it.

pithecanthropus (ˌpɪθɪkænˈθrəʊpəs) *n, pl* **pithecanthropi** (-ˌpaɪ). any primitive apelike man of the former genus *Pithecanthropus,* now included in the genus *Homo.* See **Java man.** ORIG C19: NL, from Gk *pithēkos* ape + *anthrōpos* man

pith helmet *n* a lightweight hat made of the pith of the sola, an E Indian swamp plant, that protects the wearer from the sun. Also called: **topee, topi.**

pithos (ˈpɪθɒs, ˈpaɪ-) *n, pl* **pithoi** (-θɔɪ). a large ceramic container for oil or grain. ORIG from Gk

pithy (ˈpɪθɪ) *adj* **pithier, pithiest. 1** terse and full of meaning or substance. **2** of, resembling, or full of pith.
▸ **ˈpithily** *adv* ▸ **ˈpithiness** *n*

pitiable (ˈpɪtɪəbᵊl) *adj* exciting or deserving pity or contempt.
▸ **ˈpitiableness** *n* ▸ **ˈpitiably** *adv*

pitiful (ˈpɪtɪfʊl) *adj* **1** arousing or deserving pity. **2** arousing or deserving contempt. **3** *Arch.* full of pity or compassion.
▸ **ˈpitifully** *adv* ▸ **ˈpitifulness** *n*

pitiless (ˈpɪtɪlɪs) *adj* having or showing little or no pity or mercy.
▸ **ˈpitilessly** *adv* ▸ **ˈpitilessness** *n*

pitman (ˈpɪtmən) *n, pl* **pitmen.** *Chiefly Scot. & N English.* a person who works in a pit, esp. a coal miner.

Pitman ★ (ˈpɪtmən) *n* Sir **Isaac.** 1813–97, British inventor of a system of phonetic shorthand (1837).

piton (ˈpiːtɒn) *n Mountaineering.* a metal spike that may be driven into a crevice and used to secure a rope, etc. ORIG C20: from F: ringbolt

pits (pɪts) *pl n* **the.** *Sl.* the worst possible person, place, or thing. ORIG C20: from ? *armpits*

pit stop *n* **1** *Motor racing.* a brief stop made at a pit by a racing car for repairs, refuelling, etc. **2** *Inf.* any stop made during a car journey for refreshment, rest, or refuelling.

Pitt ★ (pɪt) *n* **1 William,** known as *Pitt the Elder,* 1st Earl of Chatham. 1708–78, British statesman. He was first minister (1756–57; 1757–61; 1766–68) and achieved British victory in the Seven Years' War (1756–63). **2** his son **William,** known as *Pitt the Younger.* 1759–1806, British statesman. As prime minister (1783–1801; 1804–06), he carried through important fiscal and tariff reforms. From 1793, his attention was focused on the wars with revolutionary and Napoleonic France.

pitta bread *or* **pitta** (ˈpɪtə) *n* a flat rounded slightly leavened bread, originally from the Middle East. ORIG from Mod. Gk: a cake

pittance (ˈpɪtᵊns) *n* a small amount or portion, esp. a meagre allowance of money. ORIG C16: from OF *pietance* ration, ult. from L *pietās* duty

pitter-patter (ˈpɪtəˌpætə) *n* **1** the sound of light rapid taps or pats, as of raindrops. ◆ *vb* **2** (*intr*) to make such a sound. ◆ *adv* **3** with such a sound.

Pittsburgh ★ (ˈpɪtsbɜːg) *n* a port in SW Pennsylvania, at the confluence of the Allegheny and Monongahela Rivers, which form the Ohio River: settled around Fort Pitt in 1758; developed rapidly with the discovery of iron deposits and one of the world's richest coalfields; the largest river port in the US and an important industrial centre, formerly with large steel mills. Pop.: 350 363 (1996 est.).

pituitary (pɪˈtjuːɪtərɪ) *n, pl* **pituitaries. 1** See **pituitary gland.** ◆ *adj* **2** of or relating to the pituitary gland. ORIG C17: from LL *pītuītārius* slimy, from *pītuīta* phlegm

pituitary gland *or* **body** *n* the master endocrine gland, attached by a stalk to the base of the brain. Its two lobes secrete hormones affecting skeletal growth, development of the sex glands, and the functioning of the other endocrine glands.

pit viper *n* any venomous snake of a New World family,

having a heat-sensitive organ in a pit on each side of the head: includes the rattlesnakes.

pity ('pɪtɪ) *n, pl* **pities. 1** sympathy or sorrow felt for the sufferings of another. **2 have** (*or* **take**) **pity on.** to have sympathy or show mercy for. **3** something that causes regret. **4** an unfortunate chance: *what a pity you can't come.* ◆ *vb* **pities, pitying, pitied.** (*tr*) **5** to feel pity for. ORIG C13: from OF *pité,* from L *pietās* duty
▸ **'pitying** *adj* ▸ **'pityingly** *adv*

pityriasis (ˌpɪtəˈraɪəsɪs) *n* any of a group of skin diseases characterized by the shedding of dry flakes of skin. ORIG C17: via NL from Gk *pituriasis* scurfiness, from *pituron* bran

più (pju:) *adv* (*in combination*) *Music.* more (quickly, etc.): *più allegro.* ORIG It., from L *plus* more

piupiu ('pi:u:ˌpi:u:) *n* a skirt made from leaves of the New Zealand flax, worn by Maoris on ceremonial occasions. ORIG from Maori

Piura ★ (*Spanish* 'pjura) *n* a city in NW Peru: the oldest colonial city in Peru, founded by Pizarro in 1532; commercial centre of an agricultural district. Pop.: 277 964 (1993).

Pius II ★ ('paɪəs) *n* pen name *Aeneas Silvius,* original name *Enea Silvio de' Piccolomini.* 1405–64, Italian ecclesiastic, humanist, poet, and historian; pope (1458–64).

Pius IV ★ *n* original name *Giovanni Angelo de' Medici.* 1499–1565, pope (1559–65). He reconvened the Council of Trent (1562), confirming its final decrees.

Pius V ★ *n* **Saint.** original name *Michele Ghislieri.* 1504–72, pope (1566–72). He attempted to enforce the reforms decreed by the Council of Trent, excommunicated Elizabeth I of England (1570), and organized the alliance that defeated the Turks at Lepanto (1571). Feast day: Apr. 30.

Pius VII ★ *n* original name *Luigi Barnaba Chiaramonti.* 1740–1823, Italian ecclesiastic; pope (1800–23). He concluded a concordat with Napoleon (1801) but resisted his annexation of the Papal States (1809).

Pius IX ★ *n* original name *Giovanni Maria Mastai-Ferretti.* 1792–1878, Italian ecclesiastic; pope (1846–78). He decreed the dogma of the Immaculate Conception (1854) and convened the Vatican Council, which laid down the doctrine of papal infallibility (1870).

Pius X ★ *n* **Saint.** original name *Giuseppe Sarto.* 1835–1914, Italian ecclesiastic; pope (1903–14). He condemned Modernism (1907) and initiated a new codification of canon law. Feast day: Aug. 21.

Pius XI ★ *n* original name *Achille Ratti.* 1857–1939, Italian ecclesiastic; pope (1922–39). He signed the Lateran Treaty (1929), by which the Vatican City was recognized as an independent state.

Pius XII ★ *n* original name *Eugenio Pacelli.* 1876–1958, Italian ecclesiastic; pope (1939–58): his attitude towards Nazi German anti-Semitism has been a matter of controversy.

pivot ('pɪvət) *n* **1** a short shaft or pin supporting something that turns; fulcrum. **2** the end of a shaft or arbor that terminates in a bearing. **3** a person or thing upon which progress, success, etc., depends. **4** the person or position from which a military formation takes its reference when altering position, etc. ◆ *vb* **5** (*tr*) to mount on or provide with a pivot or pivots. **6** (*intr*) to turn on or as if on a pivot. ORIG C17: from OF

pivotal ('pɪvət°l) *adj* **1** of, involving, or acting as a pivot. **2** of crucial importance.

pix[1] (pɪks) *n* a plural of **pic.**

pix[2] (pɪks) *n* a less common spelling of **pyx.**

pixel ('pɪksel) *n* any of a number of very small picture elements that make up a picture, as on a visual display unit. ORIG C20: from *pix* pictures + *el*(*ement*)

pixie *or* **pixy** ('pɪksɪ) *n, pl* **pixies.** (in folklore) a fairy or elf. ORIG C17: from ?

pixilated *or* **pixillated** ('pɪksɪˌleɪtɪd) *adj Chiefly US.* **1** eccentric or whimsical. **2** *Sl.* drunk. ORIG C20: from PIXIE + *-lated,* as in *stimulated, titillated,* etc.

Pizarro ★ (pɪ'zɑ:rəʊ; *Spanish* pi'θarrɔ) *n* **Francisco** (fran'θisko). ?1475–1541, Spanish conqueror of Peru. He landed in Peru (1532), murdered the Inca King Atahualpa (1533), and founded Lima as the new capital of Peru (1535). He was murdered by his own followers.

pizza ('pi:tsə) *n* a dish of Italian origin consisting of a baked disc of dough covered with cheese and tomatoes, plus ham, mushrooms, etc. ORIG C20: from It., ?from Vulgar L *picea* (unattested), ? rel. to Mod. Gk *pitta* cake

pizzazz *or* **pizazz** (pə'zæz) *n Inf.* an attractive combination of energy and style; sparkle. Also: **bezazz.** ORIG C20: ?

pizzeria (ˌpi:tsə'ri:ə) *n* a place where pizzas are made, sold, or eaten.

pizzicato (ˌpɪtsɪ'kɑ:təʊ) *Music.* ◆ *adj, adv* **1** (in music for the violin family) to be plucked with the finger. ◆ *n* **2** this style or technique of playing. ORIG C19: from It.: pinched, from *pizzicare* to twist

pizzle ('pɪz°l) *n Arch. or dialect.* the penis of an animal, esp. a bull. ORIG C16: of Gmc origin

pk *pl* **pks** *abbrev. for:* **1** pack. **2** park. **3** peak.

pkg. *pl* **pkgs.** *abbrev. for* package.

pl *abbrev. for:* **1** place. **2** plate. **3** plural.

Pl. (in street names) *abbrev. for* Place.

PLA *abbrev. for* Port of London Authority.

plaas (plɑ:s) *n S. African.* a farm. ORIG from Afrik., from Du.

placable ('plækəb°l) *adj* easily placated or appeased. ORIG C15: via OF from L *plācābilis,* from *plācāre* to appease
▸ **ˌplaca'bility** *n*

placard ('plækɑ:d) *n* **1** a notice for public display; poster. **2** a small plaque or card. ◆ *vb* (*tr*) **3** to post placards on or in. **4** to advertise by placards. **5** to display as a placard. ORIG C15: from OF *plaquart,* from *plaquier* to plate, lay flat; see PLAQUE

placate (plə'keɪt) *vb* **placates, placating, placated.** (*tr*) to pacify or appease. ORIG C17: from L *plācāre*
▸ **pla'cation** *n* ▸ **pla'catory** *adj*

place (pleɪs) *n* **1** a particular point or part of space or of a surface, esp. that occupied by a person or thing. **2** a geographical point, such as a town, city, etc. **3** a position or rank in a sequence or order. **4** an open square lined with houses in a city or town. **5** space or room. **6** a house or living quarters. **7** a country house with grounds. **8** any building or area set aside for a specific purpose. **9** a passage in a book, play, film, etc.: *to lose one's place.* **10** proper, right, or customary surroundings (esp. in **out of place, in place**). **11** right, prerogative, or duty: *it is your place to give a speech.* **12** appointment, position, or job: *a place at college.* **13** position, condition, or state: *if I were in your place.* **14a** a space or seat, as at a dining table. **14b** (*as modifier*): *place mat.* **15** *Maths.* the relative position of a digit in a number. **16** any of the best times in a race. **17** *Horse racing.* **17a** *Brit., Austral., & NZ.* the first, second, or third position at the finish. **17b** *US & Canad.* the first or usually the second position at the finish. **17c** (*as modifier*): *a place bet.* **18 all over the place.** in disorder or disarray. **19 give place (to).** to make room (for) or be superseded (by). **20 go places.** *Inf.* **20a** to travel. **20b** to become successful. **21 in place of. 21a** instead of; in lieu of: *go in place of my sister.* **21b** in exchange for: *he gave her it in place of her ring.* **22 know one's place.** to be aware of one's inferior position. **23 put someone in his** (*or* **her**) **place.** to humble someone who is arrogant, conceited, forward, etc. **24 take one's place.** to take up one's usual or specified position. **25 take place.** to happen or occur. **26 take the place of.** to be a substitute for. ◆ *vb* **places, placing, placed.** (*mainly tr*) **27** to put or set in a particular or appropriate place. **28** to find or indicate the place of. **29** to identify or classify by linking with an appropriate context: *to place a face.* **30** to regard or view as being: *to place prosperity above sincerity.* **31** to make (an order, bet, etc.). **32** to find a home or job for (someone). **33** to appoint to an office or position. **34** (often foll. by *with*) to put under the care (of). **35** to direct or aim carefully. **36** (*passive*) *Brit.* to cause (a racehorse, greyhound, athlete, etc.) to arrive in first, second, third, or sometimes fourth place. **37** (*intr*) *US & Canad.* (of a racehorse, greyhound, etc.) to finish among the first three in a contest, esp. in second position. **38** to invest (funds). **39** (*tr*) to insert (an advertisement) in a newspaper, journal, etc. ORIG C13: via OF from L *platēa* courtyard, from Gk *plateia,* from *platus* broad

placebo (plə'siːbəʊ) *n, pl* **placebos** *or* **placeboes. 1** *Med.* an inactive substance administered to a patient usually to compare its effects with those of a real drug but sometimes for the psychological benefit to the patient through his believing he is receiving treatment. **2** something said or done to please or humour another. **3** *RC Church.* a traditional name for the vespers of the office for the dead. ORIG C13 (in the ecclesiastical sense): from L *Placebo Domino* I shall please the Lord; C19 (in the medical sense)

placebo effect *n Med.* a positive therapeutic effect claimed by a patient after receiving a placebo believed by him to be an active drug.

place card *n* a card placed on a dinner table before a seat, indicating who is to sit there.

place kick *Football, etc.* ◆ *n* **1** a kick in which the ball is placed in position before it is kicked. ◆ *vb* **place-kick. 2** to kick (a ball) in this way.

placement ('pleɪsmənt) *n* **1** the act of placing or the state of being placed. **2** arrangement or position. **3** the process of finding employment.

placenta (plə'sɛntə) *n, pl* **placentas** *or* **placentae** (-tiː). **1** the vascular organ formed in the uterus of most mammals during pregnancy, consisting of both maternal and embryonic tissues and providing oxygen and nutrients for the fetus. **2** *Bot.* the part of the ovary of flowering plants to which the ovules are attached. ORIG C17: via L from Gk *plakoeis* flat cake, from *plax* flat
▸ **pla'cental** *adj*

placer ('plæsə) *n* **a** surface sediment containing particles of gold or some other valuable mineral. **b** (*in combination*): *placer-mining.* ORIG C19: from American Sp.: deposit, from Sp. *plaza* PLACE

place setting *n* the cutlery, crockery, and glassware laid for one person at a dining table.

placet ('pleɪsɛt) *n* a vote or expression of assent by saying *placet.* ORIG C16: from L, lit.: it pleases

placid ('plæsɪd) *adj* having a calm appearance or nature. ORIG C17: from L *placidus* peaceful
▸ **placidity** (plə'sɪdɪtɪ) *or* **'placidness** *n* ▸ **'placidly** *adv*

placing ('pleɪsɪŋ) *n Stock Exchange.* a method of issuing securities to the public using an intermediary, such as a stockbroking firm.

placket ('plækɪt) *n Dressmaking.* **1** a piece of cloth sewn in under a closure with buttons, zips, etc. **2** the closure itself. ORIG C16: ?from MDu. *plackaet* breastplate, from Med. L *placca* metal plate

placoid ('plækɔɪd) *adj* **1** platelike or flattened. **2** (of the scales of sharks) toothlike; composed of dentine with an enamel tip and basal pulp cavity. ORIG C19: from Gk *plac-, plax* flat

plafond (plə'fɒn; *French* plafɔ̃) *n* a ceiling, esp. one having ornamentation. ORIG C17: from F, from *plat* flat + *fond* bottom, from L *fundus*

plagal ('pleɪgᵊl) *adj* **1** (of a cadence) progressing from the subdominant to the tonic chord, as in the *Amen* of a hymn. **2** (of a mode) commencing upon the dominant of an authentic mode, but sharing the same final as the authentic mode. ◆ Cf. **authentic** (sense 5). ORIG C16: from Med. L *plagālis,* from *plaga,* ?from Gk *plagos* side

plage (plɑːʒ) *n Astron.* a bright patch in the sun's chromosphere. ORIG F, lit.: beach

plagiarism ('pleɪdʒəˌrɪzəm) *n* **1** the act of plagiarizing. **2** something plagiarized. ORIG C17: from L *plagiārus* plunderer, from *plagium* kidnapping
▸ **'plagiarist** *n* ▸ **ˌplagia'ristic** *adj*

plagiarize *or* **plagiarise** ('pleɪdʒəˌraɪz) *vb* **plagiarizes, plagiarizing, plagiarized** *or* **plagiarises, plagiarising, plagiarised.** to appropriate (ideas, passages, etc.) from (another work or author).
▸ **'plagiaˌrizer** *or* **'plagiaˌriser** *n*

plagioclase ('pleɪdʒɪəʊˌkleɪz) *n* a series of feldspar minerals consisting of a mixture of sodium and calcium aluminium silicates in triclinic crystalline form. ORIG C19: from Gk, from *plagos* side + -CLASE
▸ **plagioclastic** (ˌpleɪdʒɪəʊ'klæstɪk) *adj*

plague (pleɪg) *n* **1** any widespread and usually highly contagious disease with a high fatality rate. **2** an infectious disease of rodents, esp. rats, transmitted to man by the bite of the rat flea. **3** See **bubonic plague. 4** something that afflicts or harasses. **5** *Inf.* an annoyance or nuisance. **6** a pestilence, affliction, or calamity on a large scale, esp. when regarded as sent by God. ◆ *vb* **plagues, plaguing, plagued.** (*tr*) **7** to afflict or harass. **8** to bring down a plague upon. **9** *Inf.* to annoy. ORIG C14: from LL *plāga* pestilence, from L: a blow

plaguy *or* **plaguey** ('pleɪgɪ) *Arch., inf.* ◆ *adj* **1** disagreeable or vexing. ◆ *adv* **2** disagreeably or annoyingly.
▸ **'plaguily** *adv*

plaice (pleɪs) *n, pl* **plaice** *or* **plaices. 1** a European flatfish having an oval brown body marked with red or orange spots and valued as a food fish. **2** *US & Canad.* any of various other related fishes. ORIG C13: from OF *plaïz,* from LL *platessa* flatfish, from Gk *platus* flat

plaid (plæd, pleɪd) *n* **1** a long piece of cloth of a tartan pattern, worn over the shoulder as part of Highland costume. **2a** a crisscross weave or cloth. **2b** (*as modifier*): *a plaid scarf.* ORIG C16: from Scot. Gaelic *plaide,* from ?

Plaid Cymru (ˌplaɪd 'kʌmrɪ) *n* the Welsh nationalist party. Official name: **Plaid Cymru, the Party of Wales.** ORIG Welsh

plain[1] (pleɪn) *adj* **1** flat or smooth; level. **2** not complicated; clear: *the plain truth.* **3** not difficult; simple or easy: *a plain task.* **4** honest or straightforward. **5** lowly, esp. in social rank or education. **6** without adornment or show: *a plain coat.* **7** (of fabric) without pattern or of simple untwilled weave. **8** not attractive. **9** not mixed; simple: *plain vodka.* **10** (of knitting) done in plain stitch. ◆ *n* **11** a level or almost level tract of country. **12** a simple stitch in knitting made by passing the wool round the front of the needle. ◆ *adv* **13** (intensifier): *just plain tired.* ORIG C13: from OF: simple, from L *plānus* level, clear
▸ **'plainly** *adv* ▸ **'plainness** *n*

plain[2] (pleɪn) *vb* a dialect or poetic word for **complain.** ORIG C14 *pleignen,* from OF *plaindre* to lament, from L *plangere* to beat

plainchant ('pleɪnˌtʃɑːnt) *n* another name for **plainsong.** ORIG C18: from F, for Med. L *cantus plānus*

plain chocolate *n* chocolate with a slightly bitter flavour and dark colour.

plain clothes *pl n* **a** ordinary clothes, as distinguished from uniform, as worn by a police detective on duty. **b** (*as modifier*): *a plain-clothes policeman.*

plain flour *n* flour to which no raising agent has been added.

plain sailing *n* **1** *Inf.* smooth or easy progress. **2** *Naut.* sailing in a body of water that is unobstructed; clear sailing.

plainsman ('pleɪnzmən) *n, pl* **plainsmen.** a person who lives in a plains region, esp. in the Great Plains of North America.

Plains of Abraham ★ *n* (*functioning as sing*) a field in E Canada between Quebec City and the St Lawrence River: site of an important British victory (1759) in the Seven Years' War, which cost the French their possession of Canada.

plainsong ('pleɪnˌsɒŋ) *n* the style of unison unaccompanied vocal music used in the medieval Church, esp. in Gregorian chant. ORIG C16: translation of Med. L *cantus plānus*

plain-spoken *adj* candid; frank; blunt.

plaint (pleɪnt) *n* **1** *Arch.* a complaint or lamentation. **2** *Law.* a statement in writing of grounds of complaint made to a court of law. ORIG C13: from OF *plainte,* from L *planctus* lamentation, from *plangere* to beat

plaintiff ('pleɪntɪf) *n* a person who brings a civil action in a court of law. ORIG C14: from legal F *plaintif,* from OF *plaintif* (adj) complaining, from *plainte* PLAINT

plaintive ('pleɪntɪv) *adj* expressing melancholy; mournful. ORIG C14: from OF *plaintif* grieving, from PLAINT
▸ **'plaintively** *adv* ▸ **'plaintiveness** *n*

plait (plæt) *n* **1** a length of hair, etc., that has been plaited. **2** a rare spelling of **pleat.** ◆ *vb* **3** (*tr*) to intertwine (strands or strips) in a pattern. ORIG C15 *pleyt,* from OF *pleit,* from L *plicāre* to fold

plan (plæn) *n* **1** a detailed scheme, method, etc., for attaining an objective. **2** (*sometimes pl*) a proposed, usually tentative idea for doing something. **3** a drawing to scale of a horizontal section through a building taken at a given level. **4** an outline, sketch, etc. ◆ *vb* **plans, planning, planned. 5** to form a plan (for) or make plans (for). **6** (*tr*) to make a plan of (a building). **7** (*tr; takes a clause as object or an infinitive*) to have in mind as a purpose; intend. ORIG C18: via F from L *plānus* flat

planar ('pleɪnə) *adj* **1** of or relating to a plane. **2** lying in one plane; flat. ORIG C19: from LL *plānāris* on level ground, from L *plānus* flat

planarian (plə'nɛərɪən) *n* any of various free-living mostly aquatic flatworms, having a three-branched intestine. ORIG C19: from NL *Plānāria* type genus, from LL *plānārius* flat; see PLANE[1]

planar process *n* a method of producing diffused junctions in semiconductor devices. A pattern of holes is etched into an oxide layer formed on a silicon substrate, into which impurities are diffused through the holes.

planchet ('plɑːntʃɪt) *n* a piece of metal ready to be stamped as a coin, medal, etc.; flan. ORIG C17: from F: little board, from *planche* PLANK

planchette (plɑːn'ʃɛt) *n* a heart-shaped board on wheels, on which messages are written under supposed spirit guidance. ORIG C19: from F: little board, from *planche* PLANK

Planck ★ (plæŋk; *German* plaŋk) *n* **Max (Karl Ernst Ludwig)** (maks). 1858–1947, German physicist who first formulated the quantum theory (1900): Nobel prize for physics 1918.

Planck constant *or* **Planck's constant** *n* a fundamental constant equal to the energy of any quantum of radiation divided by its frequency.

plane[1] (pleɪn) *n* **1** *Maths.* a flat surface in which a straight line joining any two of its points lies entirely on that surface. **2** a level surface. **3** a level of existence, attainment, etc. **4a** short for **aeroplane. 4b** a wing or supporting surface of an aircraft. ◆ *adj* **5** level or flat. **6** *Maths.* lying entirely in one plane. ◆ *vb* **planes, planing, planed.** (*intr*) **7** to glide. **8** (of a boat) to rise partly and skim over the water when moving at a certain speed. ORIG C17: from L *plānum* level surface

plane[2] (pleɪn) *n* **1** a tool with a steel blade set obliquely in a wooden or iron body, for smoothing timber surfaces, cutting grooves, etc. **2** a flat tool, usually metal, for smoothing the surface of clay or plaster in a mould. ◆ *vb* **planes, planing, planed.** (*tr*) **3** to smooth or cut (timber, etc.) using a plane. **4** (often foll. by *off*) to remove using a plane. ORIG C14: via OF from LL *plāna* plane, from *plānāre* to level

plane[3] (pleɪn) *n* See **plane tree.**

plane geometry *n* the study of the properties of plane curves, figures, etc.

plane polarization *n* a type of polarization in which waves of light or other radiation are restricted to vibration in a single plane.

planet ('plænɪt) *n* **1** Also called: **major planet**. any of the nine celestial bodies, Mercury, Venus, Earth, Mars, Jupiter, Saturn, Uranus, Neptune, or Pluto, that revolve around the sun in elliptical orbits. **2** any celestial body revolving around a star. **3** *Astrol.* any of the planets of the solar system, excluding the earth but including the sun and moon, each thought to rule one or sometimes two signs of the zodiac. ORIG C12: via OF from LL *planēta,* from Gk *planētēs* wanderer, from *planaein* to wander

plane table *n* a surveying instrument consisting of a drawing board mounted on adjustable legs.

planetarium (ˌplænɪ'tɛərɪəm) *n, pl* **planetariums** *or* **planetaria** (-ɪə). **1** an instrument for simulating the apparent motions of the sun, moon, and planets by projecting images of these bodies onto a domed ceiling. **2** a building in which such an instrument is housed. **3** a model of the solar system.

planetary ('plænɪtərɪ, -trɪ) *adj* **1** of a planet. **2** mundane; terrestrial. **3** wandering or erratic. **4** *Astrol.* under the influence of one of the planets. **5** (of a gear) having an axis that rotates around that of another gear.

planetesimal hypothesis (ˌplænɪ'tɛsɪməl) *n* the discredited theory that the close passage of a star to the sun caused many small bodies (**planetesimals**) to be drawn from the sun, eventually coalescing to form the planets. ORIG C20: *planetesimal,* from PLANET + INFINITESIMAL

planetoid ('plænɪˌtɔɪd) *n* another name for **asteroid** (sense 1).

▸ ˌ**plane'toidal** *adj*

plane tree *or* **plane** *n* a tree with ball-shaped heads of fruit and leaves with pointed lobes. ORIG C14 *plane,* from OF, from L *platanus,* from Gk, from *platos* wide, referring to the leaves AC

planet Zog (zɒg) *n Brit. inf.* a place or situation that is far removed from reality or what is happening: *those of you who've been on planet Zog for the last ten years.*

plangent ('plændʒənt) *adj* **1** having a loud deep sound. **2** resonant and mournful. ORIG C19: from L *plangere* to beat (esp. the breast, in grief)

planimeter (plæ'nɪmɪtə) *n* a mechanical instrument for measuring the area of an irregular plane figure by moving a point attached to an arm.

▸ **pla'nimetry** *n*

planish ('plænɪʃ) *vb* (*tr*) to give a final finish to (metal, etc.) by hammering or rolling. ORIG C16: from OF *planir* to smooth out, from L *plānus* flat

planisphere ('plænɪˌsfɪə) *n* a projection or representation of all or part of a sphere on a plane surface. ORIG C14: from Med. L *plānisphaerium,* from L *plānus* flat + Gk *sphaira* globe

plank (plæŋk) *n* **1** a stout length of sawn timber. **2** something that supports or sustains. **3** one of the policies in a political party's programme. **4 walk the plank.** to be forced by pirates, etc., to walk to one's death off the end of a plank jutting out from the side of a ship. ◆ *vb* **5** (*tr*) to cover or provide with planks. ORIG C13: from OF *planke,* from LL *planca* board, from *plancus* flat-footed

planking ('plæŋkɪŋ) *n* a number of planks.

plankton ('plæŋktən) *n* the organisms inhabiting the surface layer of a sea or lake, consisting of small drifting plants and animals. ORIG C19: via G from Gk *planktos* wandering, from *plazesthai* to roam

planned economy *n* another name for **command economy.**

planned obsolescence *n* the policy of deliberately limiting the life of a product in order to encourage the purchaser to replace it. Also called: **built-in obsolescence.**

planner ('plænə) *n* **1** a person who makes plans, esp. for the development of a town, building, etc. **2** a chart for recording future appointments, tasks, goals, etc.

planning permission *n* (in Britain) formal permission granted by a local authority for the development or changed use of land or buildings.

plano- *or sometimes before a vowel* **plan-** *combining form.* indicating flatness or planeness: *plano-concave.* ORIG from L *plānus* flat

plano-concave (ˌpleɪnəʊ'kɒnkeɪv) *adj* (of a lens) having one side concave and the other plane.

plano-convex (ˌpleɪnəʊ'kɒnvɛks) *adj* (of a lens) having one side convex and the other plane.

plant[1] (plɑːnt) *n* **1** any living organism that typically synthesizes its food from inorganic substances, lacks specialized sense organs, and has no powers of locomotion. **2** such an organism that is smaller than a shrub or tree; a herb. **3** a cutting, seedling, or similar structure, esp. when ready for transplantation. **4** *Inf.* a thing positioned secretly for discovery by another, esp. in order to incriminate an innocent person. **5** *Inf.* a person, placed in an audience, whose rehearsed responses, etc., seem spontaneous to the rest of the audience. **6** *Inf.* a person placed secretly in a group or organization to obtain information, etc. ◆ *vb* (*tr*) **7** (often foll. by *out*) to set (seeds, crops, etc.) into (ground) to grow. **8** to place firmly in position. **9** to establish; found. **10** (foll. by *with*) to stock or furnish. **11** to implant in the mind. **12** *Sl.* to deliver (a blow). **13** *Inf.* to position or hide, esp. in order to deceive

or observe. **14** *Inf.* to hide or secrete, esp. for some illegal purpose or in order to incriminate someone. ORIG OE, from *planta* a shoot
▸ **'plantable** *adj*

plant[2] (plɑːnt) *n* **1** the land, buildings, and equipment used in carrying on an industry or business. **2** a factory or workshop. **3** mobile mechanical equipment for construction, road-making, etc. ORIG C20: special use of PLANT[1]

Plantagenet ★ (plænˈtædʒɪnɪt) *n* a line of English kings, ruling from the ascent of Henry II (1154) to the death of Richard III (1485). ORIG C12: from OF, lit.: sprig of broom, with reference to the crest of the Angevin kings, from L *planta* sprig + *genista* broom

plantain[1] (ˈplæntɪn) *n* any of various N temperate plants, esp. the great plantain, which has a rosette of broad leaves and a slender spike of small greenish flowers. See also **ribwort.** ORIG C14 *plauntein,* from OF, from L *plantāgō,* from *planta* sole of the foot

plantain[2] (ˈplæntɪn) *n* a large tropical plant with a green-skinned banana-like fruit which is eaten as a staple food in many tropical regions. ORIG C16: Sp. *platano* plantain, PLANE TREE

plantain lily *n* any of several Asian plants of the genus *Hosta,* having broad ribbed leaves.

plantar (ˈplæntə) *adj* of or on the sole of the foot. ORIG C18: from L *plantāris,* from *planta* sole of the foot

plantation (plænˈteɪʃən) *n* **1** an estate, esp. in tropical countries, where cash crops such as rubber, oil palm, etc., are grown on a large scale. **2** a group of cultivated trees or plants. **3** (formerly) a colony or group of settlers.

planter (ˈplɑːntə) *n* **1** the owner or manager of a plantation. **2** a machine designed for rapid and efficient planting of seeds. **3** a colonizer or settler. **4** a decorative pot for house plants.

plantigrade (ˈplæntɪˌgreɪd) *adj* **1** walking with the entire sole of the foot touching the ground, as man and bears. ◆ *n* **2** a plantigrade animal. ORIG C19: via F from NL *plantigradus,* from L *planta* sole of the foot + *gradus* a step

plant louse *n* another name for an **aphid.**

plaque (plæk, plɑːk) *n* **1** an ornamental or commemorative inscribed tablet. **2** a small flat brooch or badge. **3** *Pathol.* any small abnormal patch on or within the body. **4** short for **dental plaque.** ORIG C19: from F, from *plaquier* to plate, from MDu. *placken* to beat into a thin plate

plash (plæʃ) *vb, n* a less common word for **splash.** ORIG OE *plæsc,* prob. imit.
▸ **'plashy** *adj*

-plasia *or* **-plasy** *n combining form.* indicating growth, development, or change. ORIG from NL, from Gk *plasis* a moulding, from *plassein* to mould

plasm (ˈplæzəm) *n* **1** protoplasm of a specified type: *germ plasm.* **2** a variant of **plasma.**

-plasm *n combining form.* (in biology) indicating the material forming cells: *protoplasm; cytoplasm.* ORIG from Gk *plasma* something moulded; see PLASMA
▸ **-plasmic** *adj combining form.*

plasma (ˈplæzmə) *or* **plasm** *n* **1** the clear yellowish fluid portion of blood or lymph in which the corpuscles and cells are suspended. **2** Also called: **blood plasma.** a sterilized preparation of such fluid, taken from the blood, for use in transfusions. **3** a former name for **protoplasm** or **cytoplasm.** **4** *Physics.* a hot ionized gas containing positive ions and electrons. **5** a green variety of chalcedony. ORIG C18: from LL: something moulded, from Gk, from *plassein* to mould
▸ **plasmatic** (plæzˈmætɪk) *or* **'plasmic** *adj*

plasma torch *n* an electrical device for converting a gas into a plasma, used for melting metal, etc.

plasmid (ˈplæzmɪd) *n* a small circle of bacterial DNA that is independent of the main bacterial chromosome. Plasmids often contain genes for drug resistances and can be transmitted between bacteria of the same and different species: used in genetic engineering. ORIG C20: from PLASM + -ID[1]

plasmodium (plæzˈməʊdɪəm) *n, pl* **plasmodia** (-dɪə). **1** an amoeboid mass of protoplasm, containing many nuclei: a stage in the life cycle of certain organisms. **2** a parasitic protozoan which causes malaria. ORIG C19: NL; see PLASMA, -ODE[1]
▸ **plas'modial** *adj*

plasmolysis (plæzˈmɒlɪsɪs) *n* the shrinkage of protoplasm away from cell walls that occurs as a result of excessive water loss, esp. in plant cells.

Plassey ★ (ˈplæsɪ) *n* a village in NE India, in W Bengal: scene of Clive's victory (1757) over Siraj-ud-daula, which established British supremacy over India.

-plast *n combining form.* indicating a living cell or particle of living matter: *protoplast.* ORIG from Gk *plastos* formed, from *plassein* to form

plaster (ˈplɑːstə) *n* **1** a mixture of lime, sand, and water that is applied to a wall or ceiling as a soft paste that hardens when dry. **2** *Brit., Austral., & NZ.* an adhesive strip of material for dressing a cut, wound, etc. **3** short for **mustard plaster** or **plaster of Paris.** ◆ *vb* **4** to coat (a wall, ceiling, etc.) with plaster. **5** (*tr*) to apply like plaster: *she plastered make-up on her face.* **6** (*tr*) to cause to lie flat or to adhere. **7** (*tr*) to apply a plaster cast to. **8** (*tr*) *Sl.* to strike or defeat with great force. ORIG OE, from Med. L *plastrum* medicinal salve, building plaster, via L from Gk *emplastron* curative dressing
▸ **'plasterer** *n*

plasterboard (ˈplɑːstəˌbɔːd) *n* a thin rigid board, in the form of a layer of plaster compressed between two layers of fibreboard, used to form or cover walls, etc.

plastered (ˈplɑːstəd) *adj Sl.* intoxicated; drunk.

plaster of Paris *n* **1** a white powder that sets to a hard solid when mixed with water, used for making sculptures and casts, as an additive for lime plasters, and for making casts for setting broken limbs. **2** the hard plaster produced when this powder is mixed with water. ORIG C15: from Med. L *plastrum parisiense,* orig. made from the gypsum of *Paris*

plastic (ˈplæstɪk) *n* **1** any one of a large number of synthetic materials that have a polymeric structure and can be moulded when soft and then set. Plastics are used in the manufacture of many articles and in coatings, artificial fibres, etc. ◆ *adj* **2** made of plastic. **3** easily influenced; impressionable. **4** capable of being moulded or formed. **5a** of moulding or modelling: *the plastic arts.* **5b** produced or apparently produced by moulding: *the plastic draperies of Giotto's figures.* **6** having the power to form or influence: *the plastic forces of the imagination.* **7** *Biol.* able to change, develop, or grow: *plastic tissues.* **8** *Sl.* superficially attractive yet unoriginal or artificial: *plastic food.* ORIG C17: from L *plasticus* relating to moulding, from Gk *plastikos,* from *plassein* to form
▸ **'plastically** *adv* ▸ **plasticity** (plæˈstɪsɪtɪ) *n*

-plastic *adj combining form.* growing or forming. ORIG from Gk *plastikos;* see PLASTIC

plastic bomb *n* a bomb consisting of plastic explosive fitted around a detonator.

plastic bullet *n* a bullet consisting of a cylinder of plastic about four inches long, generally causing less severe injuries than an ordinary bullet, and used esp. for riot control. Also called: **baton round.**

plastic explosive *n* an adhesive jelly-like explosive substance.

Plasticine (ˈplæstɪˌsiːn) *n Trademark.* a soft coloured material used, esp. by children, for modelling.

plasticize *or* **plasticise** (ˈplæstɪˌsaɪz) *vb* **plasticizes, plasticizing, plasticized** *or* **plasticises, plasticising, plasticised.** to make or become plastic, as by the addition of a plasticizer.
▸ **ˌplasticiˈzation** *or* **ˌplasticiˈsation** *n*

plasticizer *or* **plasticiser** (ˈplæstɪˌsaɪzə) *n* any of a number of substances added to materials. Their uses include softening and improving the flexibility of plastics and preventing dried paint coatings from becoming too brittle.

plastic money *n* credit cards as opposed to cash.

plastic surgery *n* the branch of surgery concerned

with therapeutic or cosmetic repair or re-formation of missing, injured, or malformed tissues or parts.
▸ **plastic surgeon** *n*

plastid (ˈplæstɪd) *n* any of various small particles in the cells of plants and some animals which contain starch, oil, protein, etc. ORIG C19: via G from Gk *plastēs* sculptor, from *plassein* to form

plastron (ˈplæstrən) *n* the bony plate forming the ventral part of the shell of a tortoise or turtle. ORIG C16: via F from It. *piastrone*, from *piastra* breastplate, from L *emplastrum* PLASTER
▸ ˈ**plastral** *adj*

-plasty *n combining form.* indicating plastic surgery: *rhinoplasty.* ORIG from Gk *-plastia;* see -PLAST

plat[1] (plæt) *n* a small area of ground; plot. ORIG C16 (also in ME place names): orig. a var. of PLOT[2]

plat[2] (plæt) *vb* **plats, platting, platted,** *n* a dialect variant spelling of **plait.** ORIG C16

Plata ★ (*Spanish* ˈplata) *n* **Río de la** (ˈrio de la). an estuary on the SE coast of South America, between Argentina and Uruguay, formed by the Uruguay and Paraná Rivers. Length: 275 km (171 miles). Width: (at its mouth) 225 km (140 miles). Also called: **La Plata.** English name: (River) **Plate.**

Plataea ★ (pləˈtiːə) *n* an ancient city in S Boeotia, traditionally an ally of Athens: scene of the defeat of a great Persian army by the Greeks in 479 B.C.

platan (ˈplætᵊn) *n* another name for **plane tree.** ORIG C14: see PLANE TREE

plat du jour (ˈplɑː də ˈʒʊə; *French* pla dy zur) *n, pl* **plats du jour** (ˈplɑːz də ˈʒʊə; *French* pla dy zur). the specially prepared or recommended dish of the day on a restaurant's menu. ORIG F, lit.: dish of the day

plate (pleɪt) *n* **1a** a shallow usually circular dish made of porcelain, earthenware, glass, etc., on which food is served. **1b** (*as modifier*): *a plate rack.* **2a** Also called: **plateful.** the contents of a plate. **2b** *Austral. & NZ.* a plate of cakes, sandwiches, etc., brought by a guest to a party: *everyone was asked to bring a plate.* **3** an entire course of a meal: *a cold plate.* **4** any shallow receptacle, esp. for receiving a collection in church. **5** flat metal of uniform thickness obtained by rolling, usually having a thickness greater than about three millimetres. **6** a thin coating of metal usually on another metal, as produced by electrodeposition. **7** metal or metalware that has been coated in this way: *Sheffield plate.* **8** dishes, cutlery, etc., made of gold or silver. **9** a sheet of metal, plastic, rubber, etc., having a printing surface produced by a process such as stereotyping. **10** a print taken from such a sheet or from a woodcut. **11** a thin flat sheet of a substance, such as metal or glass. **12** a small piece of metal, plastic, etc., designed to bear an inscription and to be fixed to another surface. **13** armour made of overlapping or articulated pieces of thin metal. **14** *Photog.* a sheet of glass, or sometimes metal, coated with photographic emulsion on which an image can be formed by exposure to light. **15** a device for straightening teeth. **16** an informal word for **denture** (sense 1). **17** *Anat.* any flat platelike structure. **18a** a cup awarded to the winner of a sporting contest, esp. a horse race. **18b** a race or contest for such a prize. **19** any of the rigid layers of the earth's lithosphere. **20** *Electronics, chiefly US.* the anode in an electronic valve. **21** a horizontal timber joist that supports rafters. **22** a light horseshoe for flat racing. **23** *RC Church.* Also called: **Communion plate.** a flat plate held under the chin of a communicant in order to catch any fragments of the consecrated Host. **24 on a plate.** acquired without trouble: *he was handed the job on a plate.* **25 on one's plate.** waiting to be done or dealt with. ◆ *vb* **plates, plating, plated.** (*tr*) **26** to coat (a surface, usually metal) with a thin layer of other metal by electrolysis, etc. **27** to cover with metal plates, as for protection. **28** *Printing.* to make a stereotype or electrotype from (type or another plate). **29** to form (metal) into plate, esp. by rolling. ORIG C13: from OF: thin metal sheet, something flat, from Vulgar L *plattus* (unattested)

Plate ★ (pleɪt) *n* **River.** the English name for the (Río de la) **Plata.**

plateau (ˈplætəʊ) *n, pl* **plateaus** *or* **plateaux** (-əʊz). **1** a wide mainly level area of elevated land. **2** a relatively long period of stability; levelling off: *the rising prices reached a plateau.* ◆ *vb* (*intr*) **3** to remain at a stable level for a relatively long period. ORIG C18: from F, from OF *platel* something flat, from *plat* flat

Plateau ★ (ˈplætəʊ) *n* a state of central Nigeria, formed in 1976 from part of Benue-Plateau State: tin mining. Capital: Jos. Pop.: 3 671 498 (1995 est.). Area: 58 030 sq. km (22 405 sq. miles).

plated (ˈpleɪtɪd) *adj* **a** coated with a layer of metal. **b** (*in combination*): *gold-plated.*

plate glass *n* glass formed into a sheet by rolling, used for windows, etc.

platelayer (ˈpleɪtˌleɪə) *n Brit.* a workman who lays and maintains railway track. US equivalent: **trackman.**

platelet (ˈpleɪtlɪt) *n* a minute particle occurring in the blood of vertebrates and involved in the clotting of the blood. ORIG C19: a small PLATE

platen (ˈplætᵊn) *n* **1** a flat plate in a printing press that presses the paper against the type. **2** the roller on a typewriter, against which the keys strike. ORIG C15: from OF *platine*, from *plat* flat

plater (ˈpleɪtə) *n* **1** a person or thing that plates. **2** *Horse racing.* a mediocre horse entered chiefly for minor races.

plate tectonics *n* (*functioning as sing*) *Geol.* the study of the earth's crust with reference to the theory that the lithosphere is divided into rigid blocks (plates) that float on semimolten rock and are thus able to interact with each other at their boundaries.

platform (ˈplætfɔːm) *n* **1** a raised floor or other horizontal surface. **2** a raised area at a railway station, from which passengers have access to the trains. **3** See **drilling platform. 4** the declared principles, aims, etc., of a political party, etc. **5a** the thick raised sole of some shoes. **5b** (*as modifier*): *platform shoes.* **6** a vehicle or level place on which weapons are mounted and fired. **7** a specific type of computer hardware or computer operating system. ORIG C16: from F *plateforme*, from *plat* flat + *forme* layout

platform ticket *n* a ticket for admission to railway platforms but not for travel.

Plath ★ (plæθ) *n* **Sylvia.** 1932–63, US poet living in England. She wrote two volumes of verse, *The Colossus* (1960) and *Ariel* (1965), and a novel, *The Bell Jar* (1963).

plating (ˈpleɪtɪŋ) *n* **1** a coating or layer of material, esp. metal. **2** a layer or covering of metal plates.

platiniridium (ˌplætɪnɪˈrɪdɪəm) *n* any alloy of platinum and iridium.

platinize *or* **platinise** (ˈplætɪˌnaɪz) *vb* **platinizes, platinizing, platinized** *or* **platinises, platinising, platinised.** (*tr*) to coat with platinum.
▸ ˌ**platiniˈzation** *or* ˌ**platiniˈsation** *n*

platinum (ˈplætɪnəm) *n* a ductile malleable silvery-white metallic element, very resistant to heat and chemicals: used in jewellery, laboratory apparatus, electrical contacts, dentistry, electroplating, and as a catalyst. Symbol: Pt; atomic no.: 78; atomic wt.: 195.08. ORIG C19: NL, from Sp. *platina* silvery element, from *plata* silver, from Provençal: silver plate + the suffix *-um*

platinum black *n Chem.* a black powder consisting of very finely divided platinum metal.

platinum-blond *or* (*fem*) **platinum-blonde** *adj* **1** (of hair) of a pale silver-blond colour. **2a** having hair of this colour. **2b** (*as n*): *she was a platinum blonde.*

platinum disc *n* **1** (in Britain) an LP record certified to have sold 300 000 copies or a single certified to have sold 600 000 copies. **2** (in the US) an LP record or single certified to have sold one million copies.

platinum metal *n* any of the group of precious metallic elements consisting of ruthenium, rhodium, palladium, osmium, iridium, and platinum.

platitude (ˈplætɪˌtjuːd) *n* **1** a trite, dull, or obvious remark. **2** staleness or insipidity of thought or language; triteness. ORIG C19: from F, lit.: flatness, from *plat* flat
▸ ˌ**platiˈtudinous** *adj*

platitudinize *or* **platitudinise** (ˌplætɪˈtjuːdɪˌnaɪz) *vb* **platitudinizes, platitudinizing, platitudinized** *or* **platitudinises,**

platitudinising, platitudinised. (*intr*) to speak or write in platitudes.

Plato ★ ('pleɪtəʊ) *n* ?427–?347 B.C., Greek philosopher: with his teacher Socrates and his pupil Aristotle, he is regarded as the initiator of western philosophy. His distinction between objects of sense perception and the universal Ideas or Forms of which they are an expression is formulated in such dialogues as *Phaedo, Symposium,* and *The Republic.*

Platonic (plə'tɒnɪk) *adj* **1** of or relating to Plato or his teachings. **2** (*often not cap.*) free from physical desire: *Platonic love.*
▸ **Pla'tonically** *adv*

Platonic solid *n* any of the five possible regular polyhedrons: cube, tetrahedron, octahedron, icosahedron, and dodecahedron.

Platonism ('pleɪtəˌnɪzəm) *n* the teachings of Plato and his followers; esp. the philosophical theory that the meanings of general words are real entities (Forms) and that particular objects have properties in common by virtue of their relationship with these Forms.
▸ **'Platonist** *n*

platoon (plə'tu:n) *n* **1** *Mil.* a subunit of a company, usually comprising three sections of ten to twelve men. **2** a group of people sharing a common activity, etc. ORIG C17: from F *peloton* little ball, group of men, from *pelote* ball; see PELLET

Plattdeutsch (*German* 'platdɔytʃ) *n* another name for **Low German.** ORIG lit.: flat German

Platte ★ (plæt) *n* a river system of the central US, formed by the confluence of the **North Platte** and **South Platte** at North Platte, Nebraska: flows generally east to the Missouri River. Length: 499 km (310 miles).

platteland ('platəˌlant) *n* **the.** (in South Africa) the country districts or rural areas. ORIG C20: from Afrik., from Du. *plat* flat + *land* country

platter ('plætə) *n* **1** a large shallow usually oval dish or plate. **2** a course of a meal, usually consisting of several different foods served on the same plate: *a seafood platter.* ORIG C14: from Anglo-Norman *plater,* from *plat* dish, from OF *plat* flat; see PLATE

platy- *combining form.* indicating something flat, as **platyhelminth,** the flatworm. ORIG from Gk *platus* flat

platypus ('plætɪpəs) *n, pl* **platypuses.** See **duck-billed platypus.** ORIG C18: NL, from PLATY- + *-pus,* from Gk *pous* foot

platyrrhine ('plætɪˌraɪn) *or* **platyrrhinian** (ˌplætɪ'rɪnɪən) *adj* **1** (esp. of New World monkeys) having widely separated nostrils opening to the side of the face. **2** (of a human) having an unusually short wide nose. ORIG C19: from NL *platyrrhinus,* from PLATY- + *-rrhinus,* from Gk *rhis* nose

plaudit ('plɔ:dɪt) *n* (*usually pl*) **1** an expression of enthusiastic approval. **2** a round of applause. ORIG C17: from earlier *plauditē,* from L: applaud!, from *plaudere* to APPLAUD

Plauen ★ (*German* 'plauən) *n* a city in E central Germany, in Saxony: textile centre. Pop.: 70 860 (1991).

plausible ('plɔ:zɪbᵊl) *adj* **1** apparently reasonable, valid, truthful, etc.: *a plausible excuse.* **2** apparently trustworthy or believable: *a plausible speaker.* ORIG C16: from L *plausibilis* worthy of applause, from *plaudere* to APPLAUD
▸ ˌ**plausi'bility** *or* **'plausibleness** *n* ▸ **'plausibly** *adv*

Plautus ★ ('plɔ:təs) *n* **Titus Maccius** ('taɪtəs 'mæksɪəs). ?254–?184 B.C., Roman comic dramatist. His 21 extant works, adapted from Greek plays, esp. those by Menander, include *Menaechmi* (the basis of Shakespeare's *The Comedy of Errors*), *Miles Gloriosus, Rudens,* and *Captivi.*

play (pleɪ) *vb* **1** to occupy oneself in (a sport or diversion). **2** (*tr*) to contend against (an opponent) in a sport or game: *Ed played Tony at chess and lost.* **3** to fulfil or cause to fulfil (a particular role) in a team game: *he plays in the defence.* **4** (*intr;* often foll. by *about* or *around*) to behave carelessly, esp. in a way that is unconsciously cruel or hurtful: *to play about with a young girl's affections.* **5** (when *intr,* often foll. by *at*) to perform or act the part (of) in or as in a dramatic production. **6** to perform (a dramatic production). **7a** to have the ability to perform on (a musical instrument): *David plays the harp.* **7b** to perform as specified: *he plays out of tune.* **8** (*tr*) **8a** to reproduce (a piece of music, note, etc.) on an instrument. **8b** to perform works by: *to play Brahms.* **9** to discharge or cause to discharge: *he played the water from the hose onto the garden.* **10** to cause (a radio, etc.) to emit sound. **11** to move freely, quickly, or irregularly: *lights played on the scenery.* **12** (*tr*) *Stock Exchange.* to speculate or operate aggressively for gain in (a market). **13** (*tr*) *Angling.* to attempt to tire (a hooked fish) by alternately letting out and reeling in line. **14** to put (a card, counter, piece, etc.) into play. **15** to gamble. **16 play fair** (*or* **false**). (often foll. by *with*) to prove oneself fair (*or* unfair) in one's dealings. **17 play for time.** to delay the outcome of some activity so as to gain time to one's own advantage. **18 play into the hands of.** to act directly to the advantage of (an opponent). ◆ *n* **19** a dramatic composition written for performance by actors on a stage, etc.; drama. **20** the performance of a dramatic composition. **21a** games, exercise, or other activity undertaken for pleasure, esp. by children. **21b** (*in combination): playroom.* **22** conduct: *fair play.* **23** the playing of a game or the period during which a game is in progress: *rain stopped play.* **24** *US.* a manoeuvre in a game: *a brilliant play.* **25** the situation of a ball, etc., that is within the defined area and being played according to the rules (in **in play, out of play**). **26** gambling. **27** activity or operation: *the play of the imagination.* **28** freedom of movement: *too much play in the rope.* **29** light, free, or rapidly shifting motion: *the play of light on the water.* **30** fun, jest, or joking: *I only did it in play.* **31 call into play.** to bring into operation. **32 make a play for.** *Inf.* to make an obvious attempt to gain. ◆ See also **play along, playback,** etc. ORIG OE *plega* (n), *plegan* (vb)
▸ **'playable** *adj*

play-act *vb* **1** (*intr*) to pretend or make believe. **2** (*intr*) to behave in an overdramatic or affected manner. **3** to act in or as in (a play).
▸ **'play-ˌacting** *n* ▸ **'play-ˌactor** *n*

play along *vb* (*adv*) **1** (*intr;* usually foll. by *with*) to cooperate (with), esp. as a temporary measure. **2** (*tr*) to manipulate as if in a game, esp. for one's own advantage: *he played the widow along until she gave him her money.*

playback ('pleɪˌbæk) *n* **1** the act or process of reproducing a recording, esp. on magnetic tape. **2** the part of a tape recorder serving to reproduce or used for reproducing recorded material. ◆ *vb* **play back.** (*adv*) **3** to reproduce (recorded material) on (a magnetic tape) by means of a tape recorder.

playbill ('pleɪˌbɪl) *n* **1** a poster or bill advertising a play. **2** the programme of a play.

playboy ('pleɪˌbɔɪ) *n* a man, esp. one of private means, who devotes himself to the pleasures of nightclubs, female company, etc.

play down *vb* (*tr, adv*) to make little or light of; minimize the importance of.

player ('pleɪə) *n* **1** a person who participates in or is skilled at some game or sport. **2** a person who plays a game or sport professionally. **3** a person who plays a musical instrument. **4** an actor. **5** *Inf.* a participant, esp. a powerful one, in a particular field of activity: *a leading city player.*

Player ★ ('pleɪə) *n* **Gary** ('gærɪ). born 1935, South African professional golfer: won the British Open Championship (1959; 1968; 1974) and the US Open Championship (1965).

player piano *n* a mechanical piano; Pianola.

playful ('pleɪful) *adj* **1** full of high spirits and fun: *a playful kitten.* **2** good-natured and humorous: *a playful remark.*
▸ **'playfully** *adv*

playgoer ('pleɪˌgəʊə) *n* a person who goes to theatre performances, esp. frequently.

playground ('pleɪˌgraʊnd) *n* **1** an outdoor area for children's play, esp. one having swings, slides, etc., or adjoining a school. **2** a place popular as a sports or holiday resort.

playgroup ('pleɪˌgru:p) *n* a regular meeting of small children for supervised creative play.

playhouse (ˈpleɪˌhaʊs) *n* **1** a theatre. **2** *US.* a small house for children to play in.

playing card *n* one of a pack of 52 rectangular pieces of stiff card, used for playing a wide variety of games, each card having one or more symbols of the same kind on the face, but an identical design on the reverse.

playing field *n Chiefly Brit.* a field or open space used for sport.

playlet (ˈpleɪlɪt) *n* a short play.

playlist (ˈpleɪˌlɪst) *n* **1** a list of records chosen for playing, as on a radio station. **2** a list of tracks to be played in a particular order on a CD player. ◆ *vb* **3** (*tr*) to put (a song or record) on a playlist.

playmaker (ˈpleɪˌmeɪkə) *n Sport.* a player whose role is to create scoring opportunities for his or her team-mates.

playmate (ˈpleɪˌmeɪt) *or* **playfellow** *n* a friend or partner in play or recreation.

play off *vb* (*adv*) **1** (*tr;* usually foll. by *against*) to manipulate as if in playing a game: *to play one person off against another.* **2** (*intr*) to take part in a play-off. ◆ *n* **play-off.** **3** *Sport.* an extra contest to decide the winner when competitors are tied. **4** *Chiefly US & Canad.* a contest or series of games to determine a championship.

play on *vb* (*intr*) **1** (*adv*) to continue to play. **2** (*prep*) Also: **play upon.** to exploit or impose upon (the feelings or weakness of another).

play on words *n* another term for **pun**[1].

playpen (ˈpleɪˌpen) *n* a small enclosure, usually portable, in which a young child can be left to play in safety.

playschool (ˈpleɪˌskuːl) *n* an informal nursery group for preschool children.

plaything (ˈpleɪˌθɪŋ) *n* **1** a toy. **2** a person regarded or treated as a toy.

playtime (ˈpleɪˌtaɪm) *n* a time for play or recreation, esp. the school break.

play up *vb* (*adv*) **1** (*tr*) to highlight: *to play up one's best features.* **2** *Brit. inf.* to behave irritatingly (towards). **3** (*intr*) *Brit. inf.* (of a machine, etc.) to function erratically: *the car is playing up again.* **4** to hurt; give (one) trouble: *my back's playing up again.* **5** **play up to. 5a** to support (another actor) in a performance. **5b** to try to gain favour with by flattery.

playwright (ˈpleɪˌraɪt) *n* a person who writes plays.

plaza (ˈplɑːzə) *n* **1** an open space or square, esp. in Spain. **2** *Chiefly US & Canad.* a modern complex of shops, buildings, and parking areas. ORIG C17: from Sp., from L *platēa* courtyard; see PLACE

plc *or* **PLC** *abbrev. for* public limited company.

plea (pliː) *n* **1** an earnest entreaty or request. **2a** *Law.* something alleged by or on behalf of a party to legal proceedings in support of his claim or defence. **2b** *Criminal law.* the answer made by an accused to the charge: *a plea of guilty.* **2c** (in Scotland and formerly in England) a suit or action at law. **3** an excuse, justification, or pretext: *he gave the plea of a previous engagement.* ORIG C13: from Anglo-Norman *plai,* from OF *plaid* lawsuit, from Med. L *placitum* court order (lit.: what is pleasing), from L *placēre* to please

plea bargaining *n* an agreement between the prosecution and defence, sometimes including the judge, in which the accused agrees to plead guilty to a lesser charge in return for more serious charges being dropped.

plead (pliːd) *vb* **pleads, pleading; pleaded, plead** (plɛd), *or esp. Scot. & US.* **pled.** **1** (when *intr,* often foll. by *with*) to appeal earnestly or humbly (to). **2** (*tr; may take a clause as object*) to give as an excuse: *to plead ignorance.* **3** *Law.* to declare oneself to be (guilty or not guilty) in answer to the charge. **4** *Law.* to advocate (a case) in a court of law. **5** (*intr*) *Law.* **5a** to file pleadings. **5b** to address a court as an advocate. ORIG C13: from OF *plaidier,* from Med. L *placitāre* to have a lawsuit, from L *placēre* to please
▸ **ˈpleadable** *adj* ▸ **ˈpleader** *n*

pleadings (ˈpliːdɪŋz) *pl n Law.* the formal written statements presented alternately by the plaintiff and defendant in a lawsuit.

pleasance (ˈplɛzəns) *n* **1** a secluded part of a garden laid out with trees, walks, etc. **2** *Arch.* enjoyment or pleasure. ORIG C14 *plesaunce,* from OF *plaisance,* ult. from *plaisir* to PLEASE

pleasant (ˈplɛzᵊnt) *adj* **1** giving or affording pleasure; enjoyable. **2** having pleasing or agreeable manners, appearance, habits, etc. **3** *Obs.* merry and lively. ORIG C14: from OF *plaisant,* from *plaisir* to PLEASE
▸ **ˈpleasantly** *adv*

Pleasant Island ★ *n* the former name of **Nauru.**

pleasantry (ˈplɛzᵊntrɪ) *n, pl* **pleasantries.** **1** (*often pl*) an agreeable or amusing remark, etc., often one made in order to be polite: *they exchanged pleasantries.* **2** an agreeably humorous manner or style. ORIG C17: from F *plaisanterie,* from *plaisant* PLEASANT

please (pliːz) *vb* **pleases, pleasing, pleased.** **1** to give satisfaction, pleasure, or contentment to (a person). **2** to be the will of or have the will (to): *if it pleases you; the court pleases.* **3** **if you please.** if you will or wish, sometimes used in ironic exclamation. **4** **pleased with.** happy because of. **5** **please oneself.** to do as one likes. ◆ *adv* **6** (*sentence modifier*) used in making polite requests, pleading, etc. **7** **yes please.** a polite formula for accepting an offer, invitation, etc. ORIG C14 *plese,* from OF *plaisir,* from L *placēre*
▸ **pleased** *adj* ▸ **pleasedly** (ˈpliːzɪdlɪ) *adv*

Pleasence ★ (ˈplɛzəns) *n* **Donald.** 1919–95, British actor. His films include *Dr Crippen* (1962) and *Cul de Sac* (1966).

pleasing (ˈpliːzɪŋ) *adj* giving pleasure; likable or gratifying.
▸ **ˈpleasingly** *adv*

pleasurable (ˈplɛʒərəbᵊl) *adj* enjoyable, agreeable, or gratifying.
▸ **ˈpleasurably** *adv*

pleasure (ˈplɛʒə) *n* **1** an agreeable or enjoyable sensation or emotion: *the pleasure of hearing good music.* **2** something that gives enjoyment: *his garden was his only pleasure.* **3a** amusement, recreation, or enjoyment. **3b** (*as modifier*): *a pleasure ground.* **4** *Euphemistic.* sexual gratification: *he took his pleasure of her.* **5** a person's preference. ◆ *vb* **pleasures, pleasuring, pleasured.** **6** (when *intr,* often foll. by *in*) to give pleasure to or take pleasure (in). ORIG C14 *plesir,* from OF

pleat (pliːt) *n* **1** any of various types of fold formed by doubling back fabric, etc., and pressing, stitching, or steaming into place. ◆ *vb* **2** (*tr*) to arrange (material, part of a garment, etc.) in pleats. ORIG C16: var. of PLAIT

pleb (plɛb) *n* **1** short for **plebeian.** **2** *Brit. inf., often derog.* a common vulgar person.

plebeian (pləˈbiːən) *adj* **1** of or characteristic of the common people, esp. those of ancient Rome. **2** lacking refinement; philistine or vulgar: *plebeian tastes.* ◆ *n* **3** one of the common people, esp. one of the Roman plebs. **4** a person who is coarse, vulgar, etc. ORIG C16: from L *plēbēius* of the people, from *plēbs* the common people of ancient Rome
▸ **pleˈbeianˌism** *n*

plebiscite (ˈplɛbɪˌsaɪt, -sɪt) *n* **1** a direct vote by the electorate of a state, region, etc., on some question, usually of national importance. **2** any expression of public opinion on some matter. ◆ See also **referendum.** ORIG C16: from OF *plēbiscite,* from L *plēbiscītum* decree of the people, from *plēbs* the populace + *scīscere* to decree, from *scīre* to know
▸ **plebiscitary** (pləˈbɪsɪtərɪ, -trɪ) *adj*

plectrum (ˈplɛktrəm) *n, pl* **-trums** *or* **-tra** (-trə). any implement for plucking a string, such as a small piece of plastic, wood, etc., used to strum a guitar. ORIG C17: from L, from Gk *plektron,* from *plessein* to strike

pled (plɛd) *vb US or* (*esp. in legal usage*) *Scot.* a past tense and past participle of **plead.**

pledge (plɛdʒ) *n* **1** a formal or solemn promise or agreement. **2a** collateral for the payment of a debt or the performance of an obligation. **2b** the condition of being collateral (esp. in **in pledge**). **3** a token: *the gift is a pledge of their sincerity.* **4** an assurance of support or goodwill, conveyed by drinking a toast: *we drank a pledge to their success.* **5** a person who binds himself or herself, as by becoming bail or surety for another. **6** **take** *or* **sign the pledge.** to make a vow to abstain from alcoholic drink. ◆ *vb* **pledges,**

pledging, pledged. 7 to promise formally or solemnly. **8** (*tr*) to bind by or as if by a pledge: *they were pledged to secrecy.* **9** to give or offer (one's word, freedom, property, etc.) as a guarantee, as for the repayment of a loan. **10** to drink a toast to (a person, cause, etc.). ORIG C14: from OF *plege,* from LL *plebium* security, from *plebīre* to pledge, of Gmc origin
▸ **'pledgable** *adj* ▸ **'pledger** *or* **'pledgor** *n*

pledgee (plɛdʒ'iː) *n* **1** a person to whom a pledge is given. **2** a person to whom property is delivered as a pledge.

pledget ('plɛdʒɪt) *n* a small flattened pad of wool, cotton, etc., esp. for use as a pressure bandage to be applied to wounds. ORIG C16: from ?

-plegia *n combining form.* indicating a specified type of paralysis: *paraplegia.* ORIG from Gk, from *plēgē* stroke, from *plēssein* to strike
▸ **-plegic** *adj and n combining form.*

pleiad ('plaɪəd) *n* a brilliant or talented group, esp. one with seven members. ORIG C16: orig. F *Pléiade,* name given by Ronsard to himself and six other poets, ult. after the PLEIADES

Pleiades ★ ('plaɪəˌdiːz) *pl n Greek myth.* the seven daughters of Atlas, placed as stars in the sky either to save them from the pursuit of Orion or, in another account, after they had killed themselves for grief over the death of their half-sisters the Hyades.

Pleiocene ('plaɪəʊˌsiːn) *adj, n* a variant spelling of **Pliocene.**

Pleistocene ('plaɪstəˌsiːn) *adj* **1** of, denoting, or formed in the first epoch of the Quaternary period. It was characterized by extensive glaciations of the N hemisphere and the evolutionary development of man. ◆ *n* **2 the.** the Pleistocene epoch or rock series. ORIG C19: from Gk *pleistos* most + *kainos* recent

plenary ('pliːnərɪ, 'plɛn-) *adj* **1** full, unqualified, or complete: *plenary powers; plenary indulgence.* **2** (of assemblies, councils, etc.) attended by all the members. ORIG C15: from LL *plēnārius,* from L *plēnus* full
▸ **'plenarily** *adv*

plenipotentiary (ˌplɛnɪpə'tɛnʃərɪ) *adj* **1** (esp. of a diplomatic envoy) invested with or possessing full authority. **2** conferring full authority. **3** (of power or authority) full; absolute. ◆ *n, pl* **plenipotentiaries. 4** a person invested with full authority to transact business, esp. a diplomat authorized to represent a country. See also **envoy**[1] (sense 1). ORIG C17: from Med. L *plēnipotentiārius,* from L *plēnus* full + *potentia* POWER

plenitude ('plɛnɪˌtjuːd) *n* **1** abundance. **2** the condition of being full or complete. ORIG C15: via OF from L *plēnitūdō,* from *plēnus* full

plenteous ('plɛntɪəs) *adj* **1** ample; abundant: *a plenteous supply of food.* **2** producing or yielding abundantly: *a plenteous grape harvest.* ORIG C13 *plenteus,* from OF, from *plentif,* from *plenté* PLENTY
▸ **'plenteously** *adv* ▸ **'plenteousness** *n*

plentiful ('plɛntɪfʊl) *adj* **1** ample; abundant. **2** having or yielding an abundance: *a plentiful year.*
▸ **'plentifully** *adv* ▸ **'plentifulness** *n*

plenty ('plɛntɪ) *n, pl* **plenties. 1** (often foll. by *of*) a great number, amount, or quantity; lots: *plenty of time; there are plenty of cars on display here.* **2** ample supplies or resources: *the age of plenty.* **3 in plenty.** existing in abundance: *food in plenty.* ◆ *determiner* **4a** very many; ample: *plenty of people believe in ghosts.* **4b** (*as pron*): *that's plenty, thanks.* ◆ *adv* **5** *Inf.* fully or abundantly: *the coat was plenty big enough.* ORIG C13: from OF *plenté,* from LL *plēnitās* fullness, from L *plēnus* full

Plenty ★ ('plɛntɪ) *n* **Bay of.** a large bay of the Pacific on the NE coast of the North Island, New Zealand.

plenum ('pliːnəm) *n, pl* **plenums** *or* **plena** (-nə). **1** an enclosure containing gas at a higher pressure than the surrounding environment. **2** a fully attended meeting. **3** (esp. in the philosophy of the Stoics) space regarded as filled with matter. ORIG C17: from L: space filled with matter, from *plēnus* full

pleochroism (plɪ'ɒkrəʊˌɪzəm) *n* a property of certain crystals of absorbing light waves selectively and therefore of showing different colours when looked at from different directions. ORIG C19: from Gk *pleiōn* more, from *polus* many + *-chroism* from *khrōs* skin colour
▸ **pleochroic** (ˌpliːə'krəʊɪk) *adj*

pleomorphism (ˌpliːə'mɔːfɪzəm) *or* **pleomorphy** ('pliːəˌmɔːfɪ) *n* **1** the occurrence of more than one different form in the life cycle of a plant or animal. **2** another word for **polymorphism** (sense 2).
▸ **ˌpleo'morphic** *adj*

pleonasm ('pliːəˌnæzəm) *n Rhetoric.* **1** the use of more words than necessary or an instance of this, such as *a tiny little child.* **2** a word or phrase that is superfluous. ORIG C16: from L *pleonasmus,* from Gk *pleonasmos* excess, from *pleonazein* to be redundant
▸ **ˌpleo'nastic** *adj*

plesiosaur ('pliːsɪəˌsɔː) *n* any of various marine reptiles of Jurassic and Cretaceous times, having a long neck, short tail, and paddle-like limbs. ORIG C19: from NL *plēsiosaurus,* from Gk *plēsios* near + *sauros* a lizard

plethora ('plɛθərə) *n* **1** superfluity or excess; overabundance. **2** *Pathol., obs.* a condition caused by dilation of superficial blood vessels, characterized esp. by a reddish face. ORIG C16: via Med. L from Gk *plēthōrē* fullness, from *plēthein* to grow full
▸ **plethoric** (plɛ'θɒrɪk) *adj*

pleura ('plʊərə) *n, pl* **pleurae** ('plʊəriː). the thin transparent membrane enveloping the lungs and lining the walls of the thoracic cavity. ORIG C17: via Med. L from Gk: side, rib
▸ **'pleural** *adj*

pleurisy ('plʊərɪsɪ) *n* inflammation of the pleura, characterized by pain that is aggravated by deep breathing or coughing. ORIG C14: from OF *pleurisie,* from LL, from Gk *pleuritis,* from *pleura* side
▸ **pleuritic** (plʊ'rɪtɪk) *adj, n*

pleuro- *or before a vowel* **pleur-** *combining form.* **1** of or relating to the side. **2** indicating the pleura. ORIG from Gk *pleura* side

pleuropneumonia (ˌplʊərəʊnjuː'məʊnɪə) *n* the combined disorder of pleurisy and pneumonia.

Pleven (*Bulgarian* 'plɛvɛn) *or* **Plevna** ★ (*Bulgarian* 'plɛvna) *n* a town in N Bulgaria: taken by Russia from the Turks in 1877 after a siege of 143 days. Pop.: 125 029 (1996 est.).

Plexiglas ('plɛksɪˌglɑːs) *n US trademark.* a transparent plastic, polymethylmethacrylate, used for combs, plastic sheeting, etc.

plexor ('plɛksə) *or* **plessor** *n Med.* a small hammer with a rubber head for use in percussion of the chest and testing reflexes. ORIG C19: from Gk *plēxis* a stroke, from *plēssein* to strike

plexus ('plɛksəs) *n, pl* **plexuses** *or* **plexus. 1** any complex network of nerves, blood vessels, or lymphatic vessels. **2** an intricate network or arrangement. ORIG C17: NL, from L *plectere* to braid

pliable ('plaɪəb[ə]l) *adj* easily moulded, bent, influenced, or altered.
▸ **ˌplia'bility** *or* **'pliableness** *n* ▸ **'pliably** *adv*

pliant ('plaɪənt) *adj* **1** easily bent; supple: *a pliant young tree.* **2** adaptable; yielding readily to influence; compliant. ORIG C14: from OF, from *plier* to fold; see PLY[2]
▸ **'pliancy** *n* ▸ **'pliantly** *adv*

plicate ('plaɪkeɪt) *or* **plicated** *adj* having or arranged in parallel folds or ridges; pleated: *a plicate leaf; plicate rock strata.* ORIG C18: from L *plicātus* folded, from *plicāre* to fold
▸ **pli'cation** *n*

plié ('pliːeɪ) *n* a classic ballet practice posture with back erect and knees bent. ORIG F: bent

plier ('plaɪə) *n* a person who plies a trade.

pliers ('plaɪəz) *pl n* a gripping tool consisting of two hinged arms usually with serrated jaws. ORIG C16: from PLY[1]

plight[1] (plaɪt) *n* a condition of extreme hardship, danger, etc. ORIG C14 *plit,* from OF *pleit* fold; prob. infl. by OE *pliht* PLIGHT[2]

plight[2] (plaɪt) *vb* (*tr*) **1** to promise formally or pledge (al-

★ people and places

legiance, support, etc.). **2 plight one's troth.** to make a promise, esp. of marriage. ♦ *n* **3** *Arch. or dialect.* a solemn promise, esp. of engagement; pledge. ORIG OE *pliht* peril
▸ **'plighter** *n*

plimsoll *or* **plimsole** ('plɪmsəl) *n Brit.* a light rubber-soled canvas shoe worn for various sports. Also called: **gym shoe, sandshoe.** ORIG C20: from the resemblance of the sole to a Plimsoll line

Plimsoll line ('plɪmsəl) *n* another name for **load line.** ORIG C19: after Samuel *Plimsoll* (1824–98), Brit. politician who advocated its adoption

plinth (plɪnθ) *n* **1** the rectangular slab or block that forms the lowest part of the base of a column, statue, pedestal, or pier. **2** Also called: **plinth course.** the lowest part of the wall of a building, esp. one that is formed of a course of stone or brick. **3** a flat block on either side of a doorframe, where the architrave meets the skirting. ORIG C17: from L *plinthus,* from Gk *plinthos* brick

Pliny ★ ('plɪnɪ) *n* **1** known as *Pliny the Elder.* Latin name *Gaius Plinius Secundus.* 23–79 A.D., Roman writer, the author of the encyclopedic *Natural History* (77). **2** his nephew, known as *Pliny the Younger.* Latin name *Gaius Plinius Caecilius Secundus.* ?62–?113 A.D., Roman writer and administrator, noted for his letters.

Pliocene *or* **Pleiocene** ('plaɪəʊˌsiːn) *adj* **1** of, denoting, or formed in the last epoch of the Tertiary period, during which many modern mammals appeared. ♦ *n* **2 the.** the Pliocene epoch or rock series. ORIG C19: from Gk *pleiōn* more, from *polus* many + *-cene* from *kainos* recent

plissé ('pliːseɪ, 'plɪs-) *n* **1** fabric with a wrinkled finish, achieved by treatment involving caustic soda: *cotton plissé.* **2** such a finish on a fabric. ORIG F: pleated

PLO *abbrev. for* Palestine Liberation Organization.

Płock ★ (plɒk; *Polish* pwɔtsk) *n* a town in central Poland, on the River Vistula: several Polish kings are buried in the cathedral: oil refining, petrochemical works. Pop.: 126 900 (1996 est.).

plod (plɒd) *vb* **plods, plodding, plodded. 1** to make (one's way) or walk along (a path, etc.) with heavy usually slow steps. **2** (*intr*) to work slowly and perseveringly. ♦ *n* **3** the act of plodding. **4** *Brit.* a slang word for **policeman.** ORIG C16: imit.
▸ **'plodder** *n* ▸ **'plodding** *adj* ▸ **'ploddingly** *adv*

Ploeşti ★ (*Romanian* plo'jeʃtj) *n* a city in SE central Romania: centre of the Romanian petroleum industry. Pop.: 254 136 (1994 est.).

-ploid *adj and n combining form.* indicating a specific multiple of a single set of chromosomes: *diploid.* ORIG from Gk *-pl(oos)* -fold + -OID
▸ **-ploidy** *n combining form.*

plonk[1] (plɒŋk) *vb* **1** (often foll. by *down*) to drop or be dropped heavily: *he plonked the money on the table.* ♦ *n* **2** the act or sound of plonking. ORIG var. of PLUNK

plonk[2] (plɒŋk) *n Inf.* alcoholic drink, usually wine, esp. of inferior quality. ORIG C20: ?from F *blanc* white, as in *vin blanc* white wine

plonker ('plɒŋkə) *n Sl.* a stupid person. ORIG C20: from PLONK[1]

plop (plɒp) *n* **1** the characteristic sound made by an object dropping into water without a splash. ♦ *vb* **plops, plopping, plopped. 2** to fall or cause to fall with the sound of a plop: *the stone plopped into the water.* ♦ *interj* **3** an exclamation imitative of this sound: *to go plop.* ORIG C19: imit.

plosion ('pləʊʒən) *n Phonetics.* the sound of an abrupt break or closure, esp. the audible release of a stop. Also called: **explosion.**

plosive ('pləʊsɪv) *Phonetics.* ♦ *adj* **1** accompanied by plosion. ♦ *n* **2** a plosive consonant; stop. ORIG C20: from F, from *explosif* EXPLOSIVE

plot[1] (plɒt) *n* **1** a secret plan to achieve some purpose, esp. one that is illegal or underhand. **2** the story or plan of a play, novel, etc. **3** *Mil.* a graphic representation of an individual or tactical setting that pinpoints an artillery target. **4** *Chiefly US.* a diagram or plan. **5 lose the plot.** *Inf.* to lose one's ability or judgment in a given situation. ♦ *vb* **plots, plotting, plotted. 6** to plan secretly (something illegal, revolutionary, etc.); conspire. **7** (*tr*) to mark (a course, as of a ship or aircraft) on a map. **8** (*tr*) to make a plan or map of. **9a** to locate and mark (points) on a graph by means of coordinates. **9b** to draw (a curve) through these points. **10** (*tr*) to construct the plot of (a literary work, etc.). ORIG C16: from PLOT[2], infl. by obs. *complot* conspiracy, from OF, from ?
▸ **'plotter** *n*

plot[2] (plɒt) *n* a small piece of land: *a vegetable plot.* ORIG OE

Plotinus ★ (plɒ'taɪnəs) *n* ?205–?270 A.D., Roman Neo-Platonist philosopher, born in Egypt.

plough *or esp. US* **plow** (plaʊ) *n* **1** an agricultural implement with sharp blades for cutting or turning over the earth. **2** any of various similar implements, such as a device for clearing snow. **3** ploughed land. **4 put one's hand to the plough.** to begin or undertake a task. ♦ *vb* **5** to till (the soil, etc.) with a plough. **6** to make (furrows or grooves) in (something) with or as if with a plough. **7** (when *intr,* usually foll. by *through*) to move (through something) in the manner of a plough. **8** (*intr;* foll. by *through*) to work at slowly or perseveringly. **9** (*intr;* foll. by *into* or *through*) (of a vehicle) to run uncontrollably into something in its path. **10** (*intr*) *Brit. sl.* to fail an examination. ORIG OE *plōg* plough land
▸ **'plougher** *or esp. US* **'plower** *n*

Plough (plaʊ) *n* **the.** the group of the seven brightest stars in the constellation Ursa Major. Also called: **Charles's Wain.** Usual US name: the **Big Dipper.**

plough back *vb* (*tr, adv*) to reinvest (the profits of a business) in the same business.

ploughman *or esp. US* **plowman** ('plaʊmən) *n, pl* **ploughmen** *or esp. US* **plowmen.** a man who ploughs, esp. using horses.

ploughman's lunch *n* a snack lunch, served esp. in a pub, consisting of bread and cheese with pickle.

ploughshare *or esp. US* **plowshare** ('plaʊˌʃɛə) *n* the horizontal pointed cutting blade of a mouldboard plough.

Plovdiv ★ (*Bulgarian* 'plɔvdif) *n* a city in S Bulgaria on the Maritsa River: the second largest town in Bulgaria; conquered by Philip II of Macedonia in 341 B.C.; capital of Roman Thracia; commercial centre of a rich agricultural region. Pop.: 344 326 (1996 est.). Greek name: **Philippopolis.**

plover ('plʌvə) *n* **1** any of a family of shore birds, typically having a round head, straight bill, and large pointed wings. **2 green plover.** another name for **lapwing.** ORIG C14: from OF *plovier* rainbird, from L *pluvia* rain

plow (plaʊ) *n, vb* the usual US spelling of **plough.**

ploy (plɔɪ) *n* **1** a manoeuvre or tactic in a game, conversation, etc. **2** any business, job, hobby, etc., with which one is occupied: *angling is his latest ploy.* **3** *Chiefly Brit.* a frolic, escapade, or practical joke. ORIG C18: orig. Scot. & N English, obs. n sense of EMPLOY meaning an occupation

PLP (in Britain) *abbrev. for* Parliamentary Labour Party.

PLR *abbrev. for* Public Lending Right.

pluck (plʌk) *vb* **1** (*tr*) to pull off (feathers, fruit, etc.) from (a fowl, tree, etc.). **2** (when *intr,* foll. by *at*) to pull or tug. **3** (*tr;* foll. by *off, away,* etc.) *Arch.* to pull (something) forcibly or violently (from something or someone). **4** (*tr*) to sound (the strings) of (a musical instrument) with the fingers, a plectrum, etc. **5** (*tr*) *Sl.* to fleece or swindle. ♦ *n* **6** courage, usually in the face of difficulties or hardship. **7** a sudden pull or tug. **8** the heart, liver, and lungs, esp. of an animal used for food. ORIG OE *pluccian, plyccan*
▸ **'plucker** *n*

pluck up *vb* (*tr, adv*) **1** to pull out; uproot. **2** to muster (courage, one's spirits, etc.).

plucky ('plʌkɪ) *adj* **pluckier, pluckiest.** having or showing courage in the face of difficulties, danger, etc.
▸ **'pluckily** *adv* ▸ **'pluckiness** *n*

plug (plʌg) *n* **1** a piece of wood, cork, or other material, used to stop up holes or waste pipes or as a wedge for taking a screw or nail. **2** a device having one or more pins to which an electric cable is attached: used to make an elec-

trical connection when inserted into a socket. **3** Also called: **volcanic plug.** a mass of solidified magma filling the neck of an extinct volcano. **4** See **sparking plug. 5a** a cake of pressed or twisted tobacco, esp. for chewing. **5b** a small piece of such a cake. **6** *Inf.* a favourable mention of a product, show, etc., as on television. ◆ *vb* **plugs, plugging, plugged. 7** (*tr*) to stop up or secure (a hole, gap, etc.) with or as if with a plug. **8** (*tr*) to insert or use (something) as a plug: *to plug a finger into one's ear.* **9** (*tr*) *Inf.* to make favourable and often-repeated mentions of (a song, product, show, etc.), as on television. **10** (*tr*) *Sl.* to shoot: *he plugged six rabbits.* **11** (*tr*) *Sl.* to punch. **12** (*intr;* foll. by *along, away,* etc.) *Inf.* to work steadily or persistently. ORIG C17: from MDu. *plugge*
▸ **'plugger** *n*

plug-and-play *adj Computing.* capable of detecting the addition of a new input or output device and automatically activating the appropriate control software.

plugged in *adj Sl.* up to date; abreast of the times.

plughole ('plʌɡˌhəʊl) *n* a hole in a sink, etc., through which waste water drains and which can be closed with a plug.

plug in *vb* (*tr, adv*) **1** to connect (an electrical appliance, etc.) with a power source by means of an electrical plug. ◆ *n* **plug-in. 2a** a device that can be connected by means of a plug. **2b** (*as modifier*): *a plug-in heater.* **3** *Computing.* **3a** a module or piece of software that can be added to a system to provide extra functions or features. **3b** (*as modifier*): *plug-in memory cards.*

plug-ugly *adj* **1** *Inf.* extremely ugly. ◆ *n, pl* **plug-uglies. 2** *US sl.* a city tough; ruffian. ORIG C19: from ?

plum (plʌm) *n* **1** a small rosaceous tree with an edible oval fruit that is purple, yellow, or green and contains an oval stone. **2** the fruit of this tree. **3** a raisin, as used in a cake or pudding. **4a** a dark reddish-purple colour. **4b** (*as adj*): *a plum carpet.* **5** *Inf.* **5a** something of a superior or desirable kind, such as a financial bonus. **5b** (*as modifier*): *a plum job.* ORIG OE *plūme*

plumage ('pluːmɪdʒ) *n* the layer of feathers covering the body of a bird. ORIG C15: from OF, from *plume* feather, from L *plūma* down

plumate ('pluːmeɪt, -mɪt) *or* **plumose** *adj Zool., bot.* **1** of or possessing feathers or plumes. **2** covered with small hairs: *a plumate seed.* ORIG C19: from L *plumātus* covered with feathers; see PLUME

plumb (plʌm) *n* **1** a weight, usually of lead, suspended at the end of a line and used to determine water depth or verticality. **2** the perpendicular position of a freely suspended plumb line (esp. in **out of plumb, off plumb**). ◆ *adv also* **plum. 3** in a vertical or perpendicular line or direction. **4** *Inf., chiefly US.* (intensifier): *plumb stupid.* **5** *Inf.* exactly; precisely. ◆ *vb* **6** (*tr;* often foll. by *up*) to test the alignment of or adjust to the vertical with a plumb line. **7** (*tr*) to experience (the worst extremes of): *to plumb the depths of despair.* **8** (*tr*) to understand or master (something obscure): *to plumb a mystery.* **9** to connect or join (a device such as a tap) to a water pipe or drainage system. ORIG C13: from OF *plomb* (unattested) lead line, from *plon* lead, from L *plumbum*
▸ **'plumbable** *adj*

plumbago (plʌm'beɪɡəʊ) *n, pl* **plumbagos. 1** a plant of warm regions, having clusters of blue, white, or red flowers. **2** another name for **graphite.** ORIG C17: from L: lead ore, translation of Gk *polubdaina,* from *polubdos* lead

plumber ('plʌmə) *n* a person who installs and repairs pipes, fixtures, etc., for water, drainage, and gas. ORIG C14: from OF *plommier* worker in lead, from LL *plumbārius,* from L *plumbum* lead

plumbing ('plʌmɪŋ) *n* **1** the trade or work of a plumber. **2** the pipes, fixtures, etc., used in a water, drainage, or gas installation. **3** the act or procedure of using a plumb.

plumbism ('plʌmˌbɪzəm) *n* chronic lead poisoning. ORIG C19: from L *plumbum* lead

plumb line *n* a string with a metal weight, or **plumb bob,** at one end that, when suspended, points directly towards the earth's centre of gravity and so is used to determine verticality, depth, etc.

plumb rule *n* a plumb line attached to a narrow board, used by builders, surveyors, etc.

plume (pluːm) *n* **1** a feather, esp. one that is large or ornamental. **2** a feather or cluster of feathers worn esp. formerly as a badge or ornament in a headband, hat, etc. **3** *Biol.* any feathery part. **4** something that resembles a plume: *a plume of smoke.* **5** a token or decoration of honour; prize. ◆ *vb* **plumes, pluming, plumed.** (*tr*) **6** to adorn with feathers or plumes. **7** (of a bird) to clean or preen (itself or its feathers). **8** (foll. by *on* or *upon*) to pride or congratulate (oneself). ORIG C14: from OF, from L *plūma* downy feather

plummet ('plʌmɪt) *vb* **plummets, plummeting, plummeted. 1** (*intr*) to drop down; plunge. ◆ *n* **2** the weight on a plumb line; plumb bob. **3** a lead plumb used by anglers. ORIG C14: from OF *plommet* ball of lead, from *plomb* lead, from L *plumbum*

plummy ('plʌmɪ) *adj* **plummier, plummiest. 1** of, full of, or resembling plums. **2** *Brit. inf.* (of speech) deep, refined, and somewhat drawling. **3** *Brit. inf.* choice; desirable.

plumose ('pluːməʊs, -məʊz) *adj* another word for **plumate.** ORIG C17: from L *plūmōsus* feathery

plump[1] (plʌmp) *adj* **1** well filled out or rounded; chubby: *a plump turkey.* **2** bulging; full: *a plump wallet.* ◆ *vb* **3** (often foll. by *up* or *out*) to make or become plump: *to plump up a pillow.* ORIG C15 (meaning: dull, rude), C16 (in current senses): ?from MDu. *plomp* blunt
▸ **'plumply** *adv* ▸ **'plumpness** *n*

plump[2] (plʌmp) *vb* **1** (often foll. by *down, into,* etc.) to drop or fall suddenly and heavily. **2** (*intr;* foll. by *for*) to give support (to) or make a choice (of) one out of a group or number. ◆ *n* **3** a heavy abrupt fall or the sound of this. ◆ *adv* **4** suddenly or heavily. **5** straight down; directly: *the helicopter landed plump in the middle of the field.* ◆ *adj, adv* **6** in a blunt, direct, or decisive manner. ORIG C14: prob. imit.

plum pudding *n Brit.* a boiled or steamed pudding made with flour, suet, sugar, and dried fruit.

plumule ('pluːmjuːl) *n* **1** the embryonic shoot of seed-bearing plants. **2** a down feather of young birds. ORIG C18: from LL *plūmula* a little feather

plumy ('pluːmɪ) *adj* **plumier, plumiest. 1** plumelike; feathery. **2** consisting of, covered with, or adorned with feathers.

plunder ('plʌndə) *vb* **1** to steal (valuables, goods, sacred items, etc.) from (a town, church, etc.) by force, esp. in time of war; loot. **2** (*tr*) to rob or steal (choice or desirable things) from (a place): *to plunder an orchard.* ◆ *n* **3** anything taken by plundering; booty. **4** the act of plundering; pillage. ORIG C17: prob. from Du. *plunderen* (orig.: to plunder household goods)
▸ **'plunderer** *n*

plunge (plʌndʒ) *vb* **plunges, plunging, plunged. 1** (usually foll. by *into*) to thrust or throw (something, oneself, etc.): *they plunged into the sea.* **2** to throw or be thrown into a certain condition: *the room was plunged into darkness.* **3** (usually foll. by *into*) to involve or become involved deeply (in). **4** (*intr*) to move or dash violently or with great speed or impetuosity. **5** (*intr*) to descend very suddenly or steeply: *the ship plunged in heavy seas; a plunging neckline.* **6** (*intr*) *Inf.* to speculate or gamble recklessly, for high stakes, etc. ◆ *n* **7** a leap or dive. **8** *Inf.* a swim; dip. **9** a pitching or tossing motion. **10 take the plunge.** *Inf.* to resolve to do something dangerous or irrevocable. ORIG C14: from OF *plongier,* from Vulgar L *plumbicāre* (unattested) to sound with a plummet, from L *plumbum* lead

plunger ('plʌndʒə) *n* **1** a rubber suction cup used to clear blocked drains, etc. **2** a device or part of a machine that has a plunging or thrusting motion; piston. **3** *Inf.* a reckless gambler.

plunk (plʌŋk) *vb* **1** to pluck (the strings) of (a banjo, etc.) or (of such an instrument) to give forth a sound when plucked. **2** (often foll. by *down*) to drop or be dropped, esp. heavily or suddenly. ◆ *n* **3** the act or sound of plunking. ORIG C20: imit.

Plunket *or* **Plunkett** ★ ('plʌŋkɪt) *n* **Saint Oliver.** 1629–81, Irish Roman Catholic churchman and martyr;

★ people and places

wrongly executed as a supposed conspirator in the Popish Plot (1678). Feast day: July 11.

pluperfect (plu:ˈpɜ:fɪkt) *adj, n Grammar.* another term for **past perfect.** ORIG C16: from L *plūs quam perfectum* more than perfect

plural (ˈplʊərəl) *adj* **1** containing, involving, or composed of more than one. **2** denoting a word indicating that more than one referent is being referred to or described. ◆ *n* **3** *Grammar.* **3a** the plural number. **3b** a plural form. ORIG C14: from OF *plurel,* from LL *plūrālis* concerning many, from L *plūs* more
▸ ˈ**plurally** *adv*

pluralism (ˈplʊərəˌlɪzəm) *n* **1** the holding by a single person of more than one ecclesiastical benefice or office; plurality. **2** *Sociol.* a theory of society as several autonomous but interdependent groups. **3** the existence in a society of groups having distinctive ethnic origin, cultural forms, religions, etc. **4** *Philosophy.* **4a** the metaphysical doctrine that reality consists of more than two basic types of substance. Cf. **monism** (sense 1), **dualism** (sense 2). **4b** the metaphysical doctrine that reality consists of independent entities rather than one unchanging whole.
▸ ˈ**pluralist** *n, adj* ▸ ˌ**pluralˈistic** *adj*

plurality (plʊəˈrælɪtɪ) *n, pl* **pluralities. 1** the state of being plural. **2** *Maths.* a number greater than one. **3** the US term for **relative majority. 4** a large number. **5** the greater number; majority. **6** another word for **pluralism** (sense 1).

pluralize *or* **pluralise** (ˈplʊərəˌlaɪz) *vb* **pluralizes, pluralizing, pluralized** *or* **pluralises, pluralising, pluralised. 1** (*intr*) to hold more than one ecclesiastical benefice or office at the same time. **2** to make or become plural.

pluri- *combining form.* denoting several. ORIG from L *plur-, plus* more, *plures* several

plus (plʌs) *prep* **1** increased by the addition of: *four plus two.* **2** with or with the addition of: *a good job, plus a new car.* ◆ *adj* **3** (*prenominal*) indicating or involving addition: *a plus sign.* **4** another word for **positive** (senses 7, 8). **5** on the positive part of a scale or coordinate axis: *a value of +x.* **6** indicating the positive side of an electrical circuit. **7** involving advantage: *a plus factor.* **8** (*postpositive*) *Inf.* having a value above that which is stated: *she had charm plus.* **9** (*postpositive*) slightly above a specified standard: *he received a B+ grade for his essay.* ◆ *n* **10** short for **plus sign. 11** a positive quantity. **12** *Inf.* something positive or to the good. **13** a gain, surplus, or advantage. ◆ Mathematical symbol: + ORIG C17: from L: more

> **USAGE NOTE** *Plus, together with,* and *along with* do not create compound subjects in the way that *and* does: the number of the verb depends on that of the subject to which *plus, together with,* or *along with* is added: *this task, plus all the others, was* (not *were*) *undertaken by the government; the doctor, together with the nurses, was* (not *were*) *waiting for the patient.*

plus fours *pl n* men's baggy knickerbockers reaching below the knee, now only worn for golf, etc. ORIG C20: because made with four inches of material to hang over at the knee

plush (plʌʃ) *n* **1** a fabric with a cut pile that is longer and softer than velvet. ◆ *adj* **2** Also: **plushy.** *Inf.* lavishly appointed; rich; costly. ORIG C16: from F *pluche,* from OF *peluchier* to pluck, ult. from L *pilus* a hair
▸ ˈ**plushly** *adv*

plus sign *n* the symbol +, indicating addition or positive quantity.

Plutarch ★ (ˈplu:tɑ:k) *n* ?46–?120 A.D., Greek biographer and philosopher, noted for his *Parallel Lives* of distinguished Greeks and Romans.

Pluto[1] ★ (ˈplu:təʊ) *n Classical myth.* the god of the underworld; Hades.
▸ **Pluˈtonian** *adj*

Pluto[2] (ˈplu:təʊ) *n* the smallest planet and the farthest known from the sun. ORIG L, from Gk *Ploutōn,* lit.: the rich one

plutocracy (plu:ˈtɒkrəsɪ) *n, pl* **plutocracies. 1** the rule of society by the wealthy. **2** a state or government characterized by the rule of the wealthy. **3** a class that exercises power by virtue of its wealth. ORIG C17: from Gk *ploutokratia,* from *ploutos* wealth + *-kratia* rule
▸ **plutocratic** (ˌplu:təˈkrætɪk) *adj* ▸ ˌ**plutoˈcratically** *adv*

plutocrat (ˈplu:təˌkræt) *n* a member of a plutocracy.

pluton (ˈplu:tɒn) *n* any mass of igneous rock that has solidified below the surface of the earth. ORIG C20: back formation from PLUTONIC

plutonic (plu:ˈtɒnɪk) *adj* (of igneous rocks) derived from magma that has cooled and solidified below the surface of the earth. ORIG C20: after PLUTO[1]

plutonium (plu:ˈtəʊnɪəm) *n* a highly toxic metallic transuranic element. It occurs in trace amounts in uranium ores and is produced in a nuclear reactor by neutron bombardment of uranium-238. The most stable isotope, **plutonium-239,** readily undergoes fission and is used as a reactor fuel. Symbol: Pu; atomic no.: 94; half-life of ^{239}Pu: 24 360 years. ORIG C20: after PLUTO[2] because Pluto lies beyond Neptune and plutonium was discovered soon after NEPTUNIUM

Plutus ★ (ˈplu:tʊs) *n* the Greek god of wealth. ORIG from Gk *ploutos* wealth

pluvial (ˈplu:vɪəl) *adj* **1** of, characterized by, or due to the action of rain; rainy. ◆ *n* **2** *Geol.* a period of persistent rainfall. ORIG C17: from L *pluviālis* rainy, from *pluvia* rain

pluviometer (ˌplu:vɪˈɒmɪtə) *n* another name for **rain gauge.**
▸ **pluviometric** (ˌplu:vɪəˈmɛtrɪk) *adj* ▸ ˌ**pluvioˈmetrically** *adv*

ply[1] (plaɪ) *vb* **plies, plying, plied.** (*mainly tr*) **1** to carry on, pursue, or work at (a job, trade, etc.). **2** to manipulate or wield (a tool, etc.). **3** to sell (goods, wares, etc.), esp. at a regular place. **4** (usually foll. by *with*) to provide (with) or subject (to) repeatedly or persistently: *he plied us with drink; he plied the speaker with questions.* **5** (*intr*) to work steadily or diligently. **6** (*also intr*) (esp. of a ship, etc.) to travel regularly along (a route) or in (an area): *to ply the trade routes.* ORIG C14 *plye,* short for *aplye* to APPLY

ply[2] (plaɪ) *n, pl* **plies. 1a** a layer, fold, or thickness, as of yarn. **1b** (*in combination*): *four-ply.* **2** a thin sheet of wood glued to other similar sheets to form plywood. **3** one of the strands twisted together to make rope, yarn, etc. ORIG C15: from OF *pli* fold, from *plier* to fold, from L *plicāre*

Plymouth ★ (ˈplɪməθ) *n* **1** a port in SW England, in SW Devon on **Plymouth Sound** (an inlet of the English Channel): Britain's chief port in Elizabethan times; the last port visited by the Pilgrim Fathers in the *Mayflower* before sailing to America; naval base; seat of the University of Plymouth (1992). Pop.: 245 295 (1991). **2** a unitary authority in SW England. Pop.: 255 800 (1996 est.). Area: 76 sq. km (30 sq. miles). **3** a city in SE Massachusetts, on **Plymouth Bay**: the first permanent European settlement in New England; founded by the Pilgrim Fathers. Pop.: 45 608 (1990).

Plymouth Brethren *pl n* a religious sect founded about 1827, strongly Puritanical in outlook and having no organized ministry.

plywood (ˈplaɪˌwʊd) *n* a structural board consisting of thin layers of wood glued together under pressure, with the grain of one layer at right angles to the grain of the adjoining layer.

Plzeň ★ (*Czech* ˈplzɛnj) *n* an industrial city in the W Czech Republic. Pop.: 171 908 (1995 est.). German name: **Pilsen.**

pm *abbrev. for* premium.

Pm *the chemical symbol for* promethium.

PM *abbrev. for:* **1** Past Master (of a fraternity). **2** Paymaster. **3** Postmaster. **4** Prime Minister. **5** *Mil.* Provost Marshal.

p.m., P.M., pm, *or* **PM** *abbrev. for:* **1** (indicating the time from midday to midnight) post meridiem. ORIG L: after noon **2** postmortem (examination).

PMG *abbrev. for:* **1** Paymaster General. **2** Postmaster General.

PMS *abbrev. for* premenstrual syndrome.

PMT *abbrev. for* premenstrual tension.

PNdB *abbrev. for* perceived noise decibel.

pneumatic (njuˈmætɪk) *adj* **1** of or concerned with air, gases, or wind. **2** (of a machine or device) operated by compressed air or by a vacuum. **3** containing compressed air: *a pneumatic tyre.* **4** (of the bones of birds) containing air spaces which reduce their weight as an adaptation to flying. ◆ *n* **5** a pneumatic tyre. ORIG C17: from LL *pneumaticus* of air or wind, from Gk, from *pneuma* breath, wind
▸ **pneuˈmatically** *adv*

pneumatics (njuˈmætɪks) *n* (*functioning as sing*) the branch of physics concerned with the mechanical properties of gases, esp. air.

pneumatology (ˌnjuːməˈtɒlədʒɪ) *n* **1** the branch of theology concerned with the Holy Ghost and other spiritual beings. **2** an obsolete name for **psychology** (the science).

pneumatophore (njuːˈmætəʊˌfɔː) *n* **1** a specialized root of certain swamp plants, such as the mangrove, that branches upwards and undergoes gaseous exchange with the atmosphere. **2** a polyp such as the Portuguese man-of-war, that is specialized as a float.

pneumococcus (ˌnjuːməʊˈkɒkəs) *n, pl* **pneumococci** (-ˈkɒkaɪ, -ˈkɒksaɪ, -ˈkɒkiː). a bacterium that causes pneumonia.

pneumoconiosis (ˌnjuːməʊˌkəʊnɪˈəʊsɪs) *or* **pneumonoconiosis** (ˌnjuːmənəʊˌkəʊnɪˈəʊsɪs) *n* any disease of the lungs or bronchi caused by the inhalation of metallic or mineral particles. ORIG C19: shortened from *pneumonoconiosis,* from Gk *pneumōn* lung + *-coniosis,* from *konis* dust

pneumoencephalogram (ˌnjuːməʊɛnˈsɛfələˌgræm) *n* See **encephalogram.**

pneumogastric (ˌnjuːməʊˈgæstrɪk) *adj Anat.* **1** of or relating to the lungs and stomach. **2** a former term for **vagus.**

pneumonectomy (ˌnjuːməʊˈnɛktəmɪ) *or* **pneumectomy** *n, pl* **pneumonectomies** *or* **pneumectomies.** the surgical removal of a lung or part of a lung. ORIG C20: from Gk *pneumōn* lung + -ECTOMY

pneumonia (njuːˈməʊnɪə) *n* inflammation of one or both lungs, in which the air sacs (alveoli) become filled with liquid. ORIG C17: NL from Gk from *pneumōn* lung
▸ **pneumonic** (njuːˈmɒnɪk) *adj*

pneumothorax (ˌnjuːməʊˈθɔːræks) *n* the abnormal presence of air between the lung and the wall of the chest (pleural cavity), resulting in collapse of the lung.

PNI *abbrev. for* psychoneuroimmunology.

p-n junction *n Electronics.* a boundary between a p-type and n-type semiconductor that functions as a rectifier and is used in diodes and junction transistors.

Pnom Penh ★ (ˈnɒm ˈpɛn) *n* a variant spelling of **Phnom Penh.**

po (pəʊ) *n, pl* **pos.** *Brit.* an informal word for **chamber pot.** ORIG C19: from POT[1]

Po[1] *the chemical symbol for* polonium.

Po[2] ★ (pəʊ) *n* a river in N Italy, rising in the Cottian Alps and flowing northeast to Turin, then east to the Adriatic: the longest river in Italy. Length: 652 km (405 miles). Latin name: **Padus.**

PO *abbrev. for:* **1** Personnel Officer. **2** petty officer. **3** Pilot Officer. **4** Also: **p.o.** postal order. **5** Post Office.

poach[1] (pəʊtʃ) *vb* **1** to catch (game, fish, etc.) illegally by trespassing on private property. **2** to encroach on or usurp (another person's rights, duties, etc.) or steal (an idea, employee, etc.). **3** *Tennis, badminton, etc.* to take or play (shots that should belong to one's partner). **4** to break up (land) into wet muddy patches, as by riding over it. ORIG C17: from OF *pocher,* of Gmc origin
▸ **ˈpoacher** *n*

poach[2] (pəʊtʃ) *vb* to simmer (eggs, fish, etc.) very gently in water, milk, stock, etc. ORIG C15: from OF *pochier* to enclose in a bag (as the yolks are enclosed by the whites)
▸ **ˈpoacher** *n*

Pocahontas ★ (ˌpɒkəˈhɒntəs) *n* original name *Matoaka;* married name *Rebecca Rolfe.* ?1595–1617, American Indian, who allegedly saved the colonist Captain John Smith from being killed.

pochard (ˈpəʊtʃəd) *n, pl* **pochards** *or* **pochard.** any of various diving ducks, esp. a European variety, the male of which has a grey-and-black body and a reddish head. ORIG C16: from ?

pock (pɒk) *n* **1** any pustule resulting from an eruptive disease, esp. from smallpox. **2** another word for **pockmark** (sense 1). ORIG OE *pocc*
▸ **ˈpocky** *adj*

pocket (ˈpɒkɪt) *n* **1** a small bag or pouch in a garment for carrying small articles, money, etc. **2** any bag or pouch or anything resembling this. **3** *S. African.* a bag or sack of vegetables or fruit. **4** a cavity in the earth, etc., such as one containing ore. **5** a small enclosed or isolated area: *a pocket of resistance.* **6** any of the six holes with pouches or nets let into the corners and sides of a billiard table. **7 in one's pocket.** under one's control. **8 in** *or* **out of pocket.** having made a profit or loss. **9 line one's pockets.** to make money, esp. by dishonesty when in a position of trust. **10** (*modifier*) small: *a pocket edition.* ◆ *vb* **pockets, pocketing, pocketed.** (*tr*) **11** to put into one's pocket. **12** to take surreptitiously or unlawfully; steal. **13** (*usually passive*) to confine in or as if in a pocket. **14** to conceal or keep back: *he pocketed his pride and asked for help.* **15** *Billiards, etc.* to drive (a ball) into a pocket. ORIG C15: from Anglo-Norman *poket* a little bag, from *poque* bag, from MDu. *poke* bag
▸ **ˈpocketless** *adj*

pocket battleship *n* a small heavily armed battle cruiser specially built to conform with treaty limitations on tonnage and armament.

pocket billiards *n* (*functioning as sing*) any game played on a table in which the object is to pocket the balls, esp. snooker or pool.

pocketbook (ˈpɒkɪtˌbʊk) *n* **1** *Chiefly US.* a small bag or case for money, papers, etc. **2** a pocket-sized notebook.

pocket borough *n* (before the Reform Act of 1832) an English borough constituency controlled by one person or family who owned the land.

pocketful (ˈpɒkɪtful) *n, pl* **pocketfuls.** as much as a pocket will hold.

pocketknife (ˈpɒkɪtˌnaɪf) *n, pl* **pocketknives.** a small knife with one or more blades that fold into the handle; penknife.

pocket money *n* **1** *Brit.* a small weekly sum of money given to children by parents as an allowance. **2** money for day-to-day spending, incidental expenses, etc.

pockmark (ˈpɒkˌmɑːk) *n* **1** Also called: **pock.** a pitted scar left on the skin after the healing of a smallpox or similar pustule. **2** any pitting of a surface that resembles such scars. ◆ *vb* **3** (*tr*) to scar or pit with pockmarks.

poco (ˈpəʊkəʊ; *Italian* ˈpɔːko) *or* **un poco** *adj, adv* (*in combination*) *Music.* a little; to a small degree. ORIG from It.: little, from L *paucus* few

poco a poco *adv* (*in combination*) *Music.* little by little: *poco a poco rall.* ORIG It.

pod (pɒd) *n* **1a** the fruit of any leguminous plant, consisting of a long two-valved case that contains seeds. **1b** the seedcase as distinct from the seeds. **2** any similar fruit. **3** a streamlined structure attached to an aircraft and used to house a jet engine, fuel tank, armament, etc. ◆ *vb* **pods, podding, podded. 4** (*tr*) to remove the pod from. ORIG C17: ? back formation from earlier *podware* bagged vegetables

-pod *or* **-pode** *n combining form.* indicating a certain type or number of feet: *arthropod; tripod.* ORIG from Gk *-podos* footed, from *pous* foot

podagra (pəˈdægrə) *n* gout of the foot or big toe. ORIG C15: via L from Gk, from *pous* foot + *agra* a trap

poddy (ˈpɒdɪ) *n, pl* **poddies.** *Austral.* a handfed calf or lamb. ORIG ?from *poddy* (adj) fat

Podgorica *or* **Podgoritsa** ★ (*Russian* ˈpɔdgɔˌriːtsa) *n* a city in Yugoslavia, the capital of Montenegro. Pop.: 117 875 (1991). Former name (1946–91): **Titograd.**

podgy (ˈpɒdʒɪ) *adj* **podgier, podgiest. 1** short and fat; chubby. **2** (of the face, arms, etc.) unpleasantly chubby and pasty-looking. ORIG C19: from *podge* a short plump person
▸ **ˈpodgily** *adv* ▸ **ˈpodginess** *n*

podium ('pəʊdɪəm) *n, pl* **podiums** *or* **podia** (-dɪə). **1** a small raised platform used by lecturers, conductors, etc. **2** a plinth that supports a colonnade or wall. **3** a low wall surrounding the arena of an ancient amphitheatre. **4** *Zool.* any footlike organ, such as the tube foot of a starfish. ORIG C18: from L: platform, from Gk *podion* little foot, from *pous* foot

-podium *n combining form.* a part resembling a foot: *pseudopodium.* ORIG from NL: footlike; see PODIUM

Podolsk ★ (*Russian* pa'dɔljsk) *n* an industrial city in W Russia, near Moscow. Pop.: 202 000 (1995 est.).

podophyllin (ˌpɒdəʊ'fɪlɪn) *n* a bitter yellow resin obtained from the dried underground stems of the May apple and mandrake: used as a cathartic. ORIG C19: from NL *Podophyllum,* genus of herbs, from *podo-,* from Gk *pous* foot + *phullon* leaf

-podous *adj combining form.* having feet of a certain kind or number: *cephalopodous.*

podzol ('pɒdzɒl) *or* **podsol** ('pɒdsɒl) *n* a type of soil characteristic of coniferous forest regions having a greyish-white colour in its upper layers from which certain minerals have leached. ORIG C20: from Russian: ash ground

Poe ★ (pəʊ) *n* **Edgar Allan.** 1809–49, US short-story writer, poet, and critic. Most of his short stories, such as *The Fall of the House of Usher* (1839) and the *Tales of the Grotesque and Arabesque* (1840), are about death and madness.

poem ('pəʊɪm) *n* **1** a composition in verse, usually characterized by words chosen for their sound and suggestive power as well as for their sense, and using such techniques as metre, rhyme, and alliteration. **2** a literary composition that is not in verse but exhibits the intensity of imagination and language common to it: *a prose poem.* **3** anything resembling a poem in beauty, effect, etc. ORIG C16: from L *poēma,* from Gk, var. of *poiēma* something created, from *poiein* to make

poep (pʊp) *n S. African taboo sl.* **1** an emission of intestinal gas from the anus. **2** a mean or despicable person. ORIG Afrik.

poesy ('pəʊɪzɪ) *n, pl* **poesies. 1** an archaic word for **poetry. 2** *Poetic.* the art of writing poetry. ORIG C14: via OF from L *poēsis,* from Gk, from *poiēsis* poetic art, from *poiein* to make

poet ('pəʊɪt) *or* (*sometimes when fem*) **poetess** *n* **1** a person who writes poetry. **2** a person with great imagination and creativity. ORIG C13: from L *poēta,* from Gk *poiētēs* maker, poet

poetaster (ˌpəʊɪ'tæstə, -'teɪ-) *n* a writer of inferior verse. ORIG C16: from Med. L; see POET, -ASTER

poetic (pəʊ'ɛtɪk) *or* **poetical** *adj* **1** of poetry. **2** characteristic of poetry, as in being elevated, sublime, etc. **3** characteristic of a poet. **4** recounted in verse.
▸ **po'etically** *adv*

poeticize, poeticise (pəʊ'ɛtɪˌsaɪz) *or* **poetize, poetise** ('pəʊɪˌtaɪz) *vb* **poeticizes, poeticizing, poeticized; poeticises, poeticising, poeticised** *or* **poetizes, poetizing, poetized; poetises, poetising, poetised. 1** (*tr*) to put into poetry or make poetic. **2** (*intr*) to speak or write poetically.

poetic justice *n* fitting retribution.

poetic licence *n* justifiable departure from conventional rules of form, fact, etc., as in poetry.

poetics (pəʊ'ɛtɪks) *n* (*usually functioning as sing*) **1** the principles and forms of poetry or the study of these. **2** a treatise on poetry.

poet laureate *n, pl* **poets laureate.** *Brit.* the poet appointed as court poet of Britain and given a post in the Royal Household.

poetry ('pəʊɪtrɪ) *n* **1** literature in metrical form; verse. **2** the art or craft of writing verse. **3** poetic qualities, spirit, or feeling in anything. **4** anything resembling poetry in rhythm, beauty, etc. ORIG C14: from Med. L *poētria,* from L *poēta* POET

po-faced *adj* **1** wearing a disapproving stern expression. **2** narrow-minded; strait-laced. ORIG C20: from PO + POKER-FACED

pogey *or* **pogy** ('pəʊgɪ) *n, pl* **pogeys** *or* **pogies.** *Canad. sl.* **1** financial or other relief given to the unemployed by the government. **2** unemployment insurance. **3a** the office distributing relief to the unemployed. **3b** (*as modifier*): *pogey clothes.*

pogo stick ('pəʊgəʊ) *n* a stout pole with a handle at the top, steps for the feet and a spring at the bottom, so that the user can spring up, down, and along on it. ORIG C20: from ?

pogrom ('pɒgrəm) *n* an organized persecution or extermination of an ethnic group, esp. of Jews. ORIG C20: via Yiddish from Russian: destruction, from *po-* like + *grom* thunder

Pohai ★ (ˌpəʊ'haɪ) *n* a variant transliteration of the Chinese name for **Bohai.**

pohutukawa (pəˌhuːtuː'kɑːwə) *n* a New Zealand tree which grows on the coast and produces red flowers in the summer. Also called: **Christmas tree.**

poi (pɔɪ) *n NZ.* a ball of woven New Zealand flax swung rhythmically by Maori women while performing poi dances.

poi dance *n NZ.* a women's formation dance that involves singing and manipulating a poi.

-poiesis *n combining form.* indicating the act of making or producing something specified. ORIG from Gk, from *poiēsis* a making; see POESY
▸ **-poietic** *adj combining form.*

poignant ('pɔɪnjənt, -nənt) *adj* **1** sharply distressing or painful to the feelings. **2** to the point; cutting or piercing: *poignant wit.* **3** keen or pertinent in mental appeal: *a poignant subject.* **4** pungent in smell. ORIG C14: from OF, from L *pungens* pricking, from *pungere* to sting
▸ **'poignancy** *or* **'poignance** *n* ▸ **'poignantly** *adv*

poikilothermic (ˌpɔɪkɪləʊ'θɜːmɪk) *or* **poikilothermal** (ˌpɔɪkɪləʊ'θɜːməl) *adj* (of all animals except birds and mammals) having a body temperature that varies with the temperature of the surroundings. ORIG C19: from Gk *poikilos* various + THERMAL
▸ **ˌpoikilo'thermy** *n*

Poincaré ★ (*French* pwɛ̃kare) *n* **1 Jules Henri** (ʒyl ɑ̃ri). 1854–1912, French mathematician, physicist, and philosopher. He made important contributions to the theory of functions and to astronomy and electromagnetic theory. **2** his cousin, **Raymond** (rɛmɔ̃). 1860–1934, French statesman; premier of France (1912–13; 1922–24; 1926–29); president (1913–20).

poinciana (ˌpɔɪnsɪ'ɑːnə) *n* a tree of a tropical genus having large orange or red flowers. ORIG C17: NL, after M. de *Poinci,* 17th-cent. governor of the French Antilles

poind (pɪnd) *vb* (*tr*) *Scots Law.* **1** to take (property of a debtor, etc.) in execution of distress; distrain. **2** to impound (stray cattle, etc.). ORIG C15: from Scot., var. of OE *pyndan* to impound

poinsettia (pɔɪn'sɛtɪə) *n* a shrub of Mexico and Central America, widely cultivated for its showy scarlet bracts, which resemble petals. ORIG C19: NL, after J. P. *Poinsett* (1799–1851), US Minister to Mexico

point (pɔɪnt) *n* **1** a dot or tiny mark. **2** a location, spot, or position. **3** any dot used in writing or printing, such as a decimal point or a full stop. **4** the sharp tapered end of a pin, knife, etc. **5** *Maths.* **5a** a geometric element having no dimensions whose position is located by means of its coordinates. **5b** a location: *point of inflection.* **6** a small promontory. **7** a specific condition or degree. **8** a moment: *at that point he left the room.* **9** a reason, aim, etc.: *the point of this exercise is to train new teachers.* **10** an essential element in an argument: *I take your point.* **11** a suggestion or tip. **12** a detail or item. **13** a characteristic, physical attribute, etc.: *he has his good points.* **14** a distinctive characteristic or quality of an animal, esp. one used as a standard in judging livestock. **15** (*often pl*) any of the extremities, such as the tail, ears, or feet, of a domestic animal. **16** (*often pl*) *Ballet.* the tip of the toes. **17** a single unit for measuring or counting, as in the scoring of a game. **18** *Printing.* a unit of measurement equal to one twelfth of a pica. There are approximately 72 points to the inch. **19** *Finance.* a unit of value used to quote security and commodity prices and their fluctuations. **20** *Navigation.* **20a** one of the 32 marks on the compass indicating direction. **20b** the angle of 11°15′ between two adjacent marks. **21** *Cricket.* a fielding position at right angles to the batsman on the off side and relatively near the pitch. **22** either of the two electrical contacts that make or break the current flow in the distributor of an internal-combustion engine. **23** *Brit., Austral., & NZ.* (*often pl*) a junction of railway tracks in which a pair of rails can be moved so that a train can be directed onto either of two lines. US and Canad. equivalent: **switch. 24** (*often pl*) a piece of ribbon, cord, etc., with metal tags at the end: used during the 16th and 17th centuries to fasten clothing. **25** *Brit.* short for **power point. 26** the position of the body of a pointer or setter when it discovers game. **27** *Boxing.* a mark awarded for a scoring blow, knockdown, etc. **28** any diacritic used in a writing system, esp. in a phonetic transcription, to indicate modifications of vowels or consonants. **29** *Jewellery.* a unit of weight equal to 0.01 carat. **30** the act of pointing. **31 beside the point.** irrelevant. **32 case in point.** a specific or relevant instance. **33 make a point of. 33a** to make (something) one's regular habit. **33b** to do (something) because one thinks it important. **34 not to put too fine a point on it.** to speak plainly and bluntly. **35 on** (*or* **at**) **the point of.** at the moment immediately before: *on the point of leaving the room.* **36 score points off.** to gain an advantage at someone else's expense. **37 to the point.** relevant. **38 up to a point.** not completely. ♦ *vb* **39** (usually foll. by *at* or *to*) to indicate the location or direction of by or as by extending (a finger or other pointed object) towards it: *he pointed to the front door; don't point that gun at me.* **40** (*intr;* usually foll. by *at* or *to*) to indicate or identify a specific person or thing among several: *all evidence pointed to Donald as the murderer.* **41** (*tr*) to direct or face in a specific direction: *point me in the right direction.* **42** (*tr*) to sharpen or taper. **43** (*intr*) (of gun dogs) to indicate the place where game is lying by standing rigidly with the muzzle turned in its direction. **44** (*tr*) to finish or repair the joints of (brickwork, masonry, etc.) with mortar or cement. **45** (*tr*) *Music.* to mark (a psalm text) with vertical lines to indicate the points at which the music changes during chanting. **46** (*tr*) *Phonetics.* to provide (a letter or letters) with diacritics. **47** (*tr*) to provide (a Hebrew or similar text) with vowel points. ♦ See also **point off, point out, point up.** ORIG C13: from OF: spot, from L *punctum* a point, from *pungere* to pierce

point after *n American football.* a score given for a successful kick between the goalposts and above the crossbar, following a touchdown.

point-blank *adj* **1a** aimed or fired at a target so close that it is unnecessary to make allowance for the drop in the course of the projectile. **1b** permitting such aim or fire without loss of accuracy: *at point-blank range.* **2** aimed or fired at nearly zero range. **3** plain or blunt: *a point-blank question.* ♦ *adv* **4** directly or straight. **5** plainly or bluntly. ORIG C16: from POINT + BLANK (in the sense: centre spot of an archery target)

Point de Galle ★ (pɔɪnt də ˈgɑːlə) *n* a former name of **Galle.**

point duty *n* **1** the stationing of a policeman or traffic warden at a road junction to control and direct traffic. **2** the position at the head of a military control, regarded as being the most dangerous.

pointe (pɔɪnt) *n Ballet.* the tip of the toe (esp. in **on pointes**). ORIG from F: point

Pointe-à-Pitre ★ (*French* pwɛ̃tapitrə) *n* the chief port of Guadeloupe, on SW Grande Terre Island in the Caribbean. Pop.: 26 029 (1990).

pointed (ˈpɔɪntɪd) *adj* **1** having a point. **2** cutting or incisive: *a pointed wit.* **3** obviously directed at a particular person or aspect: *pointed criticism.* **4** emphasized or made conspicuous: *pointed ignorance.* **5** (of an arch or style of architecture) Gothic. **6** *Music.* (of a psalm text) marked to show changes in chanting. **7** (of Hebrew text) with vowel points marked.
▸ ˈ**pointedly** *adv*

Pointe-Noire ★ (*French* pwɛ̃twar) *n* a port in S Congo-Brazzaville, on the Atlantic: the country's chief port and former capital (1950–58). Pop.: 576 206 (1995 est.).

pointer (ˈpɔɪntə) *n* **1** a person or thing that points. **2** an indicator on a measuring instrument. **3** a long rod or cane used by a lecturer to point to parts of a map, blackboard, etc. **4** one of a breed of large smooth-coated gun dogs, usually white with black, liver, or lemon markings. **5** a helpful piece of information.

pointillism (ˈpwæntɪˌlɪzəm) *n* the technique of painting elaborated from impressionism, in which dots of unmixed colour are juxtaposed on a white ground so that from a distance they fuse in the viewer's eye into appropriate intermediate tones. ORIG C19: from F, from *pointiller* to mark with tiny dots, from *pointille* little point, from It., from *punto* POINT
▸ ˈ**pointillist** *n, adj*

pointing (ˈpɔɪntɪŋ) *n* the act or process of repairing or finishing joints in brickwork, masonry, etc., with mortar.

point lace *n* lace made by a needle with buttonhole stitch on a paper pattern. Also called: **needlepoint.** Cf. **pillow lace.**

pointless (ˈpɔɪntlɪs) *adj* **1** without a point. **2** without meaning, relevance, or force. **3** *Sport.* without a point scored.
▸ ˈ**pointlessly** *adv*

point off *vb* (*tr, adv*) to mark off from the right-hand side (a number of decimal places) in a whole number to create a mixed decimal: *point off three decimal places in 12345 and you get 12.345.*

point of honour *n, pl* **points of honour.** a circumstance, event, etc., that involves the defence of one's principles, social honour, etc.

point of no return *n* **1** a point at which an irreversible commitment must be made to an action, progression, etc. **2** a point in a journey at which, if one continues, supplies will be insufficient for a return to the starting place.

point of order *n, pl* **points of order.** a question raised in a meeting as to whether the rules governing procedures are being breached.

point of sale *n* (in retail distribution) **a** the place at which a sale is made. Abbrev.: **POS. b** (*as modifier*): *a point-of-sale display.*

point of view *n, pl* **points of view. 1** a position from which someone or something is observed. **2** a mental viewpoint or attitude.

point out *vb* (*tr, adv*) to indicate or specify.

pointsman (ˈpɔɪntsˌmæn, -mən) *n, pl* **pointsmen. 1** a person who operates railway points. **2** a policeman or traffic warden on point duty.

point source *n Optics.* a source of light or other radiation that can be considered to have negligible dimensions.

points system *n Brit.* a system used to assess applicants' eligibility for local authority housing, based on (points awarded for) such factors as the length of time the applicant has lived in the area, how many children are in the family, etc.

point-to-point *n Brit.* a steeplechase organized by a recognized hunt or other body, usually restricted to amateurs riding horses that have been regularly used in hunting.

point up *vb* (*tr, adv*) to emphasize, esp. by identifying: *he pointed up the difficulties.*

poise[1] (pɔɪz) *n* **1** composure or dignity of manner. **2** physical balance. **3** equilibrium; stability. **4** the position of hovering. ♦ *vb* **poises, poising, poised. 5** to be or cause to be balanced or suspended. **6** (*tr*) to hold, as in readiness: *to poise a lance.* ORIG C16: from OF *pois* weight, from L *pēnsum,* from *pendere* to weigh

poise[2] (pwɑːz, pɔɪz) *n* the cgs unit of viscosity; the viscosity of a fluid in which a tangential force of 1 dyne per square centimetre maintains a difference in velocity of 1 centimetre per second between two parallel planes 1 centimetre apart. Symbol: P ORIG C20: after Jean Louis Marie *Poiseuille* (1799–1869), F physician

poised (pɔɪzd) *adj* **1** self-possessed; dignified. **2** balanced and prepared for action.

poison (ˈpɔɪzᵊn) *n* **1** any substance that can impair function or otherwise injure the body. **2** something that de-

stroys, corrupts, etc. **3** a substance that retards a chemical reaction or the activity of a catalyst. **4** a substance that absorbs neutrons in a nuclear reactor and thus slows down the reaction. ◆ *vb* (*tr*) **5** to give poison to (a person or animal), esp. with intent to kill. **6** to add poison to. **7** to taint or infect with or as if with poison. **8** (foll. by *against*) to turn (a person's mind) against: *he poisoned her mind against me.* **9** to retard or stop (a chemical or nuclear reaction) by the action of a poison. ORIG C13: from OF *puison* potion, from L *pōtiō* a drink, esp. a poisonous one, from *pōtāre* to drink
▸ **'poisoner** *n*

poison ivy *n* any of several North American shrubs or climbing plants that cause an itching rash on contact.

poisonous ('pɔɪzənəs) *adj* **1** having the effects or qualities of a poison. **2** capable of killing or inflicting injury. **3** corruptive or malicious.
▸ **'poisonously** *adv* ▸ **'poisonousness** *n*

poison-pen letter *n* a letter written in malice, usually anonymously, and intended to abuse, frighten, or insult the recipient.

poison pill *n Finance.* a tactic used by a company fearing an unwelcome takeover bid, in which the value of the company is automatically reduced, as by the sale of an issue of shares having an option unfavourable to the bidders, if the bid is successful.

poison sumach *n* a swamp shrub of the southeastern US that causes an itching rash on contact with the skin.

Poisson distribution ('pwɑːsᵊn) *n Statistics.* a distribution that represents the number of events occurring randomly in a fixed time at an average rate λ. ORIG C19: after S. D. *Poisson* (1781–1840), F mathematician

Poitiers ★ (*French* pwatje) *n* a city in S central France: capital of the former province of Poitou until 1790; scene of the battle (1356) in which the English under the Black Prince defeated the French; university (1432). Pop.: 78 894 (1990).

Poitou ★ (*French* pwatu) *n* a former province of W central France, on the Atlantic. Chief town: Poitiers.

Poitou-Charentes ★ (*French* pwatuʃarɑ̃t) *n* a region of W central France, on the Bay of Biscay: mainly low-lying.

poke[1] (pəuk) *vb* **pokes, poking, poked. 1** (*tr*) to jab or prod, as with the elbow, a stick, etc. **2** (*tr*) to make (a hole) by or as by poking. **3** (when *intr*, often foll. by *at*) to thrust (at). **4** (*tr*) *Inf.* to hit with the fist; punch. **5** (usually foll. by *in, through,* etc.) to protrude or cause to protrude: *don't poke your arm out of the window.* **6** (*tr*) to stir (a fire, etc.) by poking. **7** (*intr*) to meddle or intrude. **8** (*intr;* often foll. by *about* or *around*) to search or pry. **9 poke one's nose into.** to interfere with or meddle in. ◆ *n* **10** a jab or prod. **11** *Inf.* a blow with one's fist; punch. ORIG C14: from Low G & MDu. *poken* to prod

poke[2] (pəuk) *n* **1** *Dialect.* a pocket or bag. **2 a pig in a poke.** See **pig.** ORIG C13: from OF *poque,* of Gmc origin

poke[3] (pəuk) *n* **1** Also called: **poke bonnet.** a bonnet with a brim that projects at the front, popular in the 18th and 19th centuries. **2** the brim itself. ORIG C18: from POKE[1] (in the sense: to project)

poker[1] ('pəukə) *n* a metal rod, usually with a handle, for stirring a fire.

poker[2] ('pəukə) *n* a card game of bluff and skill in which bets are made on the hands dealt, the highest-ranking hand winning the pool. ORIG C19: prob. from F *poque* similar card game

poker face *n Inf.* a face without expression, as that of a poker player attempting to conceal the value of his cards.
▸ **'poker-ˌfaced** *adj*

poker machine *n Austral. & NZ.* a fruit machine.

pokerwork ('pəukəˌwɜːk) *n* the art of producing pictures or designs on wood by charring it with a heated tool.

pokeweed ('pəukˌwiːd), **pokeberry,** *or* **pokeroot** *n* a tall North American plant that has a poisonous purple root used medicinally. ORIG C18 *poke,* from Algonquian *puccoon* plant used in dyeing, from *pak* blood

pokie ('pəukɪ) *n Austral. inf.* short for **poker machine.**

poky *or* **pokey** ('pəukɪ) *adj* **pokier, pokiest. 1** (esp. of rooms) small and cramped. **2** *Inf., chiefly US.* without speed or energy; slow. ORIG C19: from POKE[1] (in sl. sense: to confine)
▸ **'pokily** *adv* ▸ **'pokiness** *n*

pol. *abbrev. for:* **1** political. **2** politics.

Pol. *abbrev. for:* **1** Poland. **2** Polish.

Pola ★ ('pɔːla) *n* the Italian name for **Pula.**

Poland ★ ('pəulənd) *n* a republic in central Europe, on the Baltic: first united in the 10th century; dissolved after the third partition effected by Austria, Russia, and Prussia in 1795; re-established independence in 1918; invaded by Germany in 1939; ruled by a Communist government from 1947 to 1989, when a multiparty system was introduced. It consists chiefly of a low undulating plain in the north, rising to a low plateau in the south, with the Sudeten and Carpathian Mountains along the S border. Official language: Polish. Religion: Roman Catholic majority. Currency: zloty. Capital: Warsaw. Pop.: 38 694 000 (1999 est.). Area: 311 730 sq. km (120 359 sq. miles). Polish name: **Polska.**

Polanski ★ (pə'lænskɪ) *n* **Roman.** born 1933, Polish film director with a taste for the macabre, as in *Repulsion* (1965) and *Rosemary's Baby* (1968): later films include *Tess* (1980) and *Death and the Maiden* (1995).

polar ('pəulə) *adj* **1** at, near, or relating to either of the earth's poles or the area inside the Arctic or Antarctic Circles: *polar regions.* **2** having or relating to a pole or poles. **3** pivotal or guiding in the manner of the Pole Star. **4** directly opposite, as in tendency or character. **5** *Chem.* (of a molecule) having an uneven distribution of electrons and thus a permanent dipole moment: *water has polar molecules.*

polar bear *n* a white carnivorous bear of coastal regions of the North Pole.

polar circle *n* a term for either the **Arctic Circle** or **Antarctic Circle.**

polar coordinates *pl n* a pair of coordinates for locating a point in a plane by means of the length of a radius vector, *r,* which pivots about the origin to establish the angle, θ, that the position of the point makes with a fixed line. Usually written (*r,* θ).

polar distance *n* the angular distance of a star, planet, etc., from the celestial pole; the complement of the declination.

polar front *n Meteorol.* a front dividing cold polar air from warmer temperate or tropical air.

Polari (pə'lɑːrɪ) *n* an English slang derived from the Lingua Franca of Mediterranean ports; brought to England by sailors from the 16th century onwards. ORIG C19: from It. *parlare* to speak

polarimeter (ˌpəulə'rɪmɪtə) *n* an instrument for measuring the polarization of light.
▸ **polarimetric** (ˌpəulərɪ'mɛtrɪk) *adj*

Polaris (pə'lɑːrɪs) *n* **1** Also called: the **Pole Star,** the **North Star.** the brightest star in the constellation Ursa Minor, situated slightly less than 1° from the north celestial pole. **2** a type of US two-stage intermediate-range ballistic missile, usually fired by a submerged submarine. ORIG from Med. L *stella polāris* polar star

polariscope (pəu'lærɪˌskəup) *n* an instrument for detecting polarized light or for observing objects under polarized light, esp. for detecting strain in transparent materials.

polarity (pəu'lærɪtɪ) *n, pl* **polarities. 1** the condition of having poles. **2** the condition of a body or system in which it has opposing physical properties, esp. magnetic poles or electric charge. **3** the particular state of a part that has polarity: *an electrode with positive polarity.* **4** the state of having or expressing two directly opposite tendencies, opinions, etc.

polarization *or* **polarisation** (ˌpəulərai'zeɪʃən) *n* **1** the condition of having or giving polarity. **2** *Physics.* the phenomenon in which waves of light or other radiation are restricted to certain directions of vibration.

polarize *or* **polarise** ('pəuləˌraɪz) *vb* **polarizes, polarizing, polarized** *or* **polarises, polarising, polarised. 1** to acquire or

cause to acquire polarity or polarization. **2** (*tr*) to cause (people) to adopt extreme opposing positions: *to polarize opinion.*
▸ **ˈpolarˌizer** *or* **ˈpolarˌiser** *n*

polar lights *pl n* the aurora borealis in the N hemisphere or the aurora australis in the S hemisphere.

polarography (ˌpəʊləˈrɒgrəfɪ) *n* a technique for analysing and studying ions in solution by using an electrolytic cell with a very small cathode and obtaining a graph (**polarogram**) of the current against the potential to determine the concentration and nature of the ions.

Polaroid (ˈpəʊləˌrɔɪd) *n Trademark.* **1** a type of plastic sheet that can polarize a transmitted beam of normal light because it is composed of long parallel molecules. It only transmits plane-polarized light if these molecules are parallel to the plane of polarization. **2 Polaroid Land Camera.** any of several types of camera yielding a finished print by means of a special developing and processing technique that occurs inside the camera and takes only a few seconds. **3** (*pl*) sunglasses with lenses made from Polaroid plastic.

polder (ˈpəʊldə, ˈpɒl-) *n* a stretch of land reclaimed from the sea or a lake, esp. in the Netherlands. ORIG C17: from MDu. *polre*

pole[1] (pəʊl) *n* **1** a long slender usually round piece of wood, metal, or other material. **2** the piece of timber on each side of which a pair of carriage horses are hitched. **3** another name for **rod** (sense 7). **4 up the pole.** *Brit., Austral., & NZ inf.* **4a** slightly mad. **4b** mistaken; on the wrong track. ◆ *vb* **poles, poling, poled. 5** (*tr*) to strike or push with a pole. **6** (*tr*) **6a** to set out (an area of land or garden) with poles. **6b** to support (a crop, such as hops) on poles. **7** to punt (a boat). ORIG OE *pāl,* from L *pālus* a stake

pole[2] (pəʊl) *n* **1** either of the two antipodal points where the earth's axis of rotation meets the earth's surface. See also **North Pole, South Pole. 2** *Physics.* **2a** either of the two regions at the extremities of a magnet to which the lines of force converge. **2b** either of two points at which there are opposite electric charges, as at the terminals of a battery. **3** *Biol.* either end of the axis of a cell, spore, ovum, or similar body. **4** either of two mutually exclusive or opposite actions, opinions, etc. **5 poles apart** (*or* **asunder**). having widely divergent opinions, tastes, etc. ORIG C14: from L *polus* end of an axis, from Gk *polos* pivot

Pole[1] (pəʊl) *n* a native, inhabitant, or citizen of Poland or a speaker of Polish.

Pole[2] ★ (pəʊl) *n* **Reginald.** 1500–58, English cardinal; last Roman Catholic archbishop of Canterbury (1556–58).

poleaxe *or US* **poleax** (ˈpəʊlˌæks) *n* **1** another term for a battle-axe or a butcher's axe. ◆ *vb* **poleaxes, poleaxing, poleaxed. 2** (*tr*) to hit or fell with or as if with a poleaxe. ORIG C14 *pollax* battle-axe, from POLL + AXE

polecat (ˈpəʊlˌkæt) *n, pl* **polecats** *or* **polecat. 1** a dark brown musteline mammal of Europe, Asia, and N Africa, that is closely related to but larger than the weasel and gives off an unpleasant smell. **2** *US.* a nontechnical name for **skunk** (sense 1). ORIG C14 *polcat,* ?from OF *pol* cock, from L *pullus,* + CAT; from its preying on poultry

polemic (pəˈlɛmɪk) *adj also* **polemical. 1** of or involving dispute or controversy. ◆ *n* **2** an argument or controversy, esp. over a doctrine, belief, etc. **3** a person engaged in such controversy. ORIG C17: from Med. L *polemicus,* from Gk *polemikos* relating to war, from *polemos* war
▸ **poˈlemically** *adv* ▸ **polemicist** (pəˈlɛmɪsɪst) *n*

polemics (pəˈlɛmɪks) *n* (*functioning as sing*) the art or practice of dispute or argument, as in attacking or defending a doctrine or belief.

pole position *n* **1** (in motor racing) the starting position on the inside of the front row, generally considered the best one. **2** an advantageous starting position.

pole star *n* a guiding principle, rule, etc.

Pole Star *n* **the.** the star closest to the N celestial pole at any particular time. At present this is Polaris, but it will eventually be replaced owing to precession of the earth's axis.

pole vault *n* **1 the.** a field event in which competitors attempt to clear a high bar with the aid of an extremely flexible long pole. ◆ *vb* **pole-vault. 2** (*intr*) to perform a pole vault or compete in the pole vault.
▸ **ˈpole-ˌvaulter** *n*

poley (ˈpəʊlɪ) *adj Austral.* (of cattle) hornless or polled.

police (pəˈliːs) *n* **1** (often preceded by *the*) the organized civil force of a state, concerned with maintenance of law and order. **2** (*functioning as pl*) the members of such a force collectively. **3** any organized body with a similar function: *security police.* ◆ *vb* **polices, policing, policed.** (*tr*) **4** to regulate, control, or keep in order by means of a police or similar force. **5** to observe or record the activity or enforcement of: *a committee was set up to police the new agreement on picketing.* ORIG C16: via F from L *polītīa* administration; see POLITY

police dog *n* a dog, often an Alsatian, trained to help the police, as in tracking.

policeman (pəˈliːsmən) *or* (*fem*) **policewoman** *n, pl* **policemen** *or* **policewomen.** a member of a police force, esp. one holding the rank of constable.

police officer *n* a member of a police force, esp. a constable; policeman.

police procedural *n* a novel, film, or television drama that deals realistically with police work.

police state *n* a state or country in which a repressive government maintains control through the police.

police station *n* the office or headquarters of the police force of a district.

policing (pəˈliːsɪŋ) *n* the policies, techniques, and practice of a police force in keeping order, preventing crime, etc.

policy[1] (ˈpɒlɪsɪ) *n, pl* **policies. 1** a plan of action adopted or pursued by an individual, government, party, business, etc. **2** wisdom, shrewdness, or sagacity. **3** (*often pl*) *Scot.* the improved grounds surrounding a country house. ORIG C14: from OF *policie,* from L *polītīa* administration, POLITY

policy[2] (ˈpɒlɪsɪ) *n, pl* **policies.** a document containing a contract of insurance. ORIG C16: from OF *police* certificate, from OIt. from L *apodixis* proof, from Gk *apodeixis*
▸ **ˈpolicyˌholder** *n*

Polignac ★ (*French* pɔliɲak) *n* **Prince de,** title of *Auguste Jules Armand Marie de Polignac.* 1780–1847, French statesman; prime minister (1829–30) to Charles X.

polio (ˈpəʊlɪəʊ) *n* short for **poliomyelitis.**

poliomyelitis (ˌpəʊlɪəʊˌmaɪəˈlaɪtɪs) *n* an acute infectious viral disease, esp. affecting children. In its paralytic form the brain and spinal cord are involved, causing paralysis and wasting of muscle. Also called: **infantile paralysis.** ORIG C19: NL, from Gk *polios* grey + *muelos* marrow

polish (ˈpɒlɪʃ) *vb* **1** to make or become smooth and shiny by rubbing, esp. with wax or an abrasive. **2** (*tr*) to make perfect or complete. **3** to make or become elegant or refined. ◆ *n* **4** a finish or gloss. **5** the act of polishing. **6** a substance used to produce a shiny, often protective surface. **7** elegance or refinement, esp. in style, manner, etc. ORIG C13 *polis,* from OF *polir,* from L *polīre* to polish
▸ **ˈpolisher** *n*

Polish (ˈpəʊlɪʃ) *adj* **1** of, relating to, or characteristic of Poland, its people, or their language. ◆ *n* **2** the official language of Poland.

Polish Corridor ★ *n* the strip of land through E Pomerania providing Poland with access to the sea (1919–39), given to her in 1919 in the Treaty of Versailles, and separating East Prussia from the rest of Germany. It is now part of Poland.

polished (ˈpɒlɪʃt) *adj* **1** accomplished: *a polished actor.* **2** impeccably or professionally done: *a polished performance.* **3** (of rice) milled to remove the outer husk.

polish off *vb* (*tr, adv*) *Inf.* **1** to finish or process completely. **2** to dispose of or kill.

polish up *vb* (*adv*) **1** to make or become smooth and shiny by polishing. **2** (when *intr,* foll. by *on*) to study or practise until adept (at): *he's polishing up on his German.*

Politburo (ˈpɒlɪtˌbjʊərəʊ) *n* **1** the executive and policy-making committee of a Communist Party. **2** the supreme policy-making authority in most Communist countries. ORIG C20: from Russian: contraction of *Politicheskoe Buro* political bureau

polite (pəˈlaɪt) *adj* **1** showing a great regard for others, as in manners, etc.; courteous. **2** cultivated or refined: *polite society*. **3** elegant or polished: *polite letters*. ORIG C15: from L *polītus* polished
▸ **poˈlitely** *adv* ▸ **poˈliteness** *n*

politesse (ˌpɒlɪˈtɛs) *n* formal or genteel politeness. ORIG C18: via F from It. *politezza,* ult. from L *polīre* to polish

Politian ★ (pəʊˈlɪʃən, pɒ-) *n* Italian name *Angelo Polliziano;* original name *Angelo Ambrogini*. 1454–94, Florentine humanist and poet.

politic (ˈpɒlɪtɪk) *adj* **1** artful or shrewd; ingenious. **2** crafty or unscrupulous; cunning. **3** wise or prudent, esp. in statesmanship: *a politic choice*. **4** an archaic word for **political**. ◆ See also **body politic**. ORIG C15: from OF *politique,* from L *polīticus* concerning civil administration, from Gk, from *politēs* citizen, from *polis* city
▸ **ˈpoliticly** *adv*

political (pəˈlɪtɪkᵊl) *adj* **1** of or relating to the state, government, public administration, etc. **2a** of or relating to government policy-making as distinguished from administration or law. **2b** of or relating to the civil aspects of government as distinguished from the military. **3** of, dealing with, or relating to politics: *a political person*. **4** of or relating to the parties and the partisan aspects of politics. **5** organized with respect to government: *a political unit*.
▸ **poˈlitically** *adv*

political economy *n* the former name for **economics** (sense 1).

politically correct *adj* demonstrating progressive ideals, esp. by avoiding vocabulary that is considered offensive, discriminatory, or judgmental, esp. concerning race, gender, and sexuality. Abbrev.: **PC**.
▸ **political correctness** *n*

political prisoner *n* a person imprisoned for holding or expressing particular political beliefs.

political science *n* the study of the state, government, and politics: one of the social sciences.
▸ **political scientist** *n*

politician (ˌpɒlɪˈtɪʃən) *n* **1** a person actively engaged in politics, esp. a full-time professional member of a deliberative assembly. **2** a person who is experienced or skilled in government or administration; statesman. **3** *Disparaging, chiefly US*. a person who engages in politics out of a wish for personal gain.

politicize *or* **politicise** (pəˈlɪtɪˌsaɪz) *vb* **politicizes, politicizing, politicized** *or* **politicises, politicising, politicised. 1** (*tr*) to render political in tone, interest, or awareness. **2** (*intr*) to participate in political discussion or activity.
▸ **poˌliticiˈzation** *or* **poˌliticiˈsation** *n*

politicking (ˈpɒlɪtɪkɪŋ) *n* political activity, esp. seeking votes.

politico (pəˈlɪtɪˌkəʊ) *n, pl* **politicos**. *Chiefly US*. an informal word for a **politician** (senses 1, 3). ORIG C17: from It. or Sp.

politics (ˈpɒlɪtɪks) *n* **1** (*functioning as sing*) the art and science of directing and administrating states and other political units; government. **2** (*functioning as sing*) the complex or aggregate of relationships of people in society, esp. those relationships involving authority or power. **3** (*functioning as pl*) political activities or affairs: *party politics*. **4** (*functioning as sing*) the business or profession of politics. **5** (*functioning as sing or pl*) any activity concerned with the acquisition of power, etc.: *company politics are frequently vicious*. **6** manoeuvres or factors leading up to or influencing (something): *the politics of the decision*. **7** (*functioning as pl*) opinions, sympathies, etc., with respect to politics: *his conservative politics*.

polity (ˈpɒlɪtɪ) *n, pl* **polities. 1** a form of government or organization of a society, etc.; constitution. **2** a politically organized society, etc. **3** the management of public affairs. **4** political organization. ORIG C16: from L *polītīa,* from Gk *politeia* citizenship, civil administration, from *politēs* citizen, from *polis* city

Polk ★ (pəʊk) *n* **James Knox**. 1795–1849, US statesman; 11th president of the US (1845–49). During his administration, Texas and territory now included in New Mexico, Colorado, Utah, Nevada, Arizona, Oregon, and California were added to the Union.

polka (ˈpɒlkə) *n* **1** a 19th-century Bohemian dance with three steps and a hop, in fast duple time. **2** a piece of music composed for or in the rhythm of this dance. ◆ *vb* **polkas, polkaing, polkaed. 3** (*intr*) to dance a polka. ORIG C19: via F from Czech *pulka* half-step

polka dot *n* one of a pattern of small circular regularly spaced spots on a fabric.

poll (pəʊl) *n* **1** the casting, recording, or counting of votes in an election; a voting. **2** the result of such a voting: *a heavy poll*. **3** Also called: **opinion poll. 3a** a canvassing of a representative sample of people on some question in order to determine the general opinion. **3b** the results of such a canvassing. **4** any counting or enumeration, esp. for taxation or voting purposes. **5** the back part of the head of an animal. ◆ *vb* (*mainly tr*) **6** to receive (a vote or quantity of votes): *he polled 10 000 votes*. **7** to receive, take, or record the votes of: *he polled the whole town*. **8** to canvass (a person, group, area, etc.) as part of a survey of opinion. **9** (*sometimes intr*) to cast (a vote) in an election. **10** to clip or shear. **11** to remove or cut short the horns of (cattle). ORIG C13 (in the sense: a human head) & C17 (in the sense: votes): from MLow G *polle* hair of the head, head, top of a tree

pollack *or* **pollock** (ˈpɒlək) *n, pl* **pollacks, pollack** *or* **pollocks, pollock**. a gadoid food fish that has a projecting lower jaw and occurs in northern seas. ORIG C17: from earlier Scot. *podlok,* from ?

Pollack ★ (ˈpɒlək) *n* **Sydney**. born 1934, US film director. His films include *Tootsie* (1982), *Out of Africa* (1986), and *The Firm* (1993).

Pollaiuolo ★ (*Italian* pollajˈwɔːlo) *n* **1 Antonio** (anˈtɔːnjo), ?1432–98, Florentine painter, sculptor, goldsmith, and engraver: his paintings include the *Martyrdom of St Sebastian*. **2** his brother **Piero** (ˈpjɛːro). ?1443–96, Florentine painter and sculptor.

pollan (ˈpɒlən) *n* any of several varieties of whitefish that occur in lakes in Northern Ireland. ORIG C18: prob. from Irish *poll* lake

pollard (ˈpɒləd) *n* **1** an animal, such as a sheep or deer, that has either shed its horns or antlers or has had them removed. **2** a tree that has had its branches cut back to encourage a more bushy growth. ◆ *vb* **3** (*tr*) to convert into a pollard; poll. ORIG C16: hornless animal; see POLL

pollen (ˈpɒlən) *n* a substance produced by the anthers of seed-bearing plants, consisting of numerous fine grains containing the male gametes. ORIG C16: from L: powder
▸ **pollinic** (pəˈlɪnɪk) *adj*

Pollen ★ (ˈpɒlən) *n* **Daniel**. 1813–96, New Zealand statesman, born in Ireland: prime minister of New Zealand (1876).

pollen analysis *n* another name for **palynology**.

pollen count *n* a measure of the pollen present in the air over a 24-hour period, often published to enable sufferers from hay fever to predict the severity of their attacks.

pollex (ˈpɒlɛks) *n, pl* **pollices** (-lɪˌsiːz). the first digit of the forelimb of amphibians, reptiles, birds, and mammals, such as the thumb of man. ORIG C19: from L: thumb, big toe
▸ **pollical** (ˈpɒlɪkᵊl) *adj*

pollinate (ˈpɒlɪˌneɪt) *vb* **pollinates, pollinating, pollinated**. (*tr*) to transfer pollen from the anthers to the stigma of (a flower).
▸ **ˌpolliˈnation** *n* ▸ **ˈpolliˌnator** *n*

polling booth *n* a semienclosed space in which a voter stands to mark a ballot paper during an election.

polling station *n* a building, such as a school, designated as the place to which voters go during an election in order to cast their votes.

polliwog *or* **pollywog** (ˈpɒlɪˌwɒg) *n Dialect, US, & Canad*. a tadpole. ORIG C15 *polwygle*

Pollock ★ (ˈpɒlək) *n* **1** Sir **Frederick**. 1845–1937, British legal scholar: with Maitland, he wrote *History of English Law before the Time of Edward I* (1895). **2 Jackson**. 1912–56,

US abstract expressionist painter; chief exponent of action painting in the US.

pollster ('pəʊlstə) *n* a person who conducts opinion polls.

poll tax *n* **1** a tax levied per head of adult population. **2** an informal name for **community charge.**

pollutant (pə'lu:tᵊnt) *n* a substance that pollutes, esp. a chemical produced as a waste product of an industrial process.

pollute (pə'lu:t) *vb* **pollutes, polluting, polluted.** (*tr*) **1** to contaminate, as with poisonous or harmful substances. **2** to make morally corrupt. **3** to desecrate. ORIG C14 *polute,* from L *polluere* to defile
▸ **pol'luter** *n* ▸ **pol'lution** *n*

Pollux ★ ('pɒləks) *n Classical myth.* See **Castor and Pollux.**

Pollyanna (ˌpɒlɪ'ænə) *n* a person who is optimistic. ORIG C20: after the chief character in *Pollyanna* (1913), a novel by Eleanor Porter (1868–1920), US writer

polo ('pəʊləʊ) *n* **1** a game similar to hockey played on horseback using long-handled mallets (**polo sticks**) and a wooden ball. **2** short for **water polo. 3** Also called: **polo neck. 3a** a collar on a garment, worn rolled over to fit closely round the neck. **3b** a garment, esp. a sweater, with such a collar. ORIG C19: from Balti (dialect of Kashmir): ball, from Tibetan *pulu*

Polo ★ ('pəʊləʊ) *n* **Marco** ('mɑ:kəʊ). 1254–1324, Venetian merchant, famous for his account of his travels in Asia. After travelling overland to China (1271–75), he spent 17 years serving Kublai Khan before returning to Venice by sea (1292–95).

polonaise (ˌpɒlə'neɪz) *n* **1** a ceremonial marchlike dance in three-four time from Poland. **2** a piece of music composed for or in the rhythm of this dance. **3** a woman's costume with a tight bodice and an overskirt drawn back to show a decorative underskirt. ORIG C18: from F *danse polonaise* Polish dance

polonium (pə'ləʊnɪəm) *n* a very rare radioactive element that occurs in trace amounts in uranium ores. Symbol: Po; atomic no.: 84; half-life of most stable isotope, ^{209}Po: 103 years. ORIG C19: NL, from Med. L *Polōnia* Poland; in honour of the nationality of its discoverer, Marie Curie

polony (pə'ləʊnɪ) *n, pl* **polonies.** *Brit.* another name for **bologna sausage.**

polo shirt *n* a knitted cotton short-sleeved shirt with a collar and three-button opening at the neck.

Pol Pot ★ ('pɒl 'pɒt) *n* original name *Kompong Thom.* 1925–98, Cambodian Communist leader; prime minister of Kampuchea (1976; 1977–79); his policies led to the deaths of thousands in labour camps: overthrown by Vietnamese forces.

Polska ★ ('pɔlska) *n* the Polish name for **Poland.**

Poltava ★ (*Russian* pal'tavə) *n* a city in E Ukraine: scene of the victory (1709) of the Russians under Peter the Great over the Swedes under Charles XII. Pop.: 321 000 (1996 est.).

poltergeist ('pɒltəˌgaɪst) *n* a spirit believed to manifest its presence by noises and acts of mischief, such as throwing furniture about. ORIG C19: from G, from *poltern* to be noisy + *Geist* GHOST

poltroon (pɒl'tru:n) *n* an abject or contemptible coward. ORIG C16: from OF *poultron,* from OIt. *poltrone* lazy good-for-nothing, apparently from *poltrīre* to lie indolently in bed

poly ('pɒlɪ) *n, pl* **polys.** *Inf.* short for **polytechnic.**

poly- *combining form.* **1** more than one; many or much: *polyhedron.* **2** having an excessive or abnormal number or amount: *polyphagia.* ORIG from Gk *polus* much, many

polyamide (ˌpɒlɪ'æmaɪd, -mɪd) *n* any of a class of synthetic polymeric materials, including nylon.

polyandry ('pɒlɪˌændrɪ) *n* **1** the practice or condition of being married to more than one husband at the same time. **2** the practice in animals of a female mating with more than one male during one breeding season. **3** the condition in flowers of having a large indefinite number of stamens. ORIG C18: from Gk *poluandria,* from POLY- + *-andria* from *anēr* man
▸ **ˌpoly'androus** *adj*

polyanthus (ˌpɒlɪ'ænθəs) *n, pl* **polyanthuses.** any of several hybrid garden primroses with brightly coloured flowers. ORIG C18: NL, from Gk: having many flowers

polyatomic (ˌpɒlɪə'tɒmɪk) *adj* (of a molecule) containing more than two atoms.

poly bag ('pɒlɪ) *n Brit. inf.* a polythene bag, esp. one used to store or protect food or household articles.

polybasic (ˌpɒlɪ'beɪsɪk) *adj* (of an acid) having two or more replaceable hydrogen atoms per molecule.

Polybius ★ (pəʊ'lɪbɪəs) *n* ?205–?123 B.C., Greek historian, who wrote in 40 books a history of Rome from 264 B.C. to 146 B.C.

polycarboxylate (ˌpɒlɪkɑ:'bɒksɪˌleɪt) *n* a salt or ester of a polycarboxylic acid. Polycarboxylate esters are used in certain detergents.

polycarboxylic acid (ˌpɒlɪˌkɑ:bɒk'sɪlɪk) *n* a type of carboxylic acid containing two or more carboxyl groups.

Polycarp ★ ('pɒlɪˌkɑ:p) *n* **Saint.** ?69–?155 A.D., Christian martyr and bishop of Smyrna, noted for his letter to the church at Philippi. Feast day: Feb. 23.

polycarpic (ˌpɒlɪ'kɑ:pɪk) *or* **polycarpous** *adj* (of a plant) able to produce flowers and fruit several times in succession.
▸ **'polyˌcarpy** *n*

polycentrism (ˌpɒlɪ'sɛntrɪzəm) *n* (formerly) the fact or advocacy of the existence of more than one predominant ideological or political centre in a political system, alliance, etc., in the Communist world.

polychaete ('pɒlɪˌki:t) *n* **1** a marine annelid worm having a distinct head and paired fleshy appendages (parapodia) that bear bristles and are used in swimming. ◆ *adj also* **polychaetous. 2** of or denoting such a creature. ORIG C19: from NL, from Gk *polukhaitēs* having much hair

polychromatic (ˌpɒlɪkrəʊ'mætɪk), **polychromic** (ˌpɒlɪ'krəʊmɪk), *or* **polychromous** *adj* **1** having various or changing colours. **2** (of light or other radiation) containing radiation with more than one wavelength.
▸ **polychromatism** (ˌpɒlɪ'krəʊməˌtɪzəm) *n*

polyclinic (ˌpɒlɪ'klɪnɪk) *n* a hospital or clinic able to treat a wide variety of diseases.

Polyclitus, Polycleitus (ˌpɒlɪ'klaɪtəs), *or* **Polycletus** ★ (ˌpɒlɪ'kli:təs) *n* 5th-century B.C. Greek sculptor, noted particularly for his idealized bronze sculptures of the male nude, such as the *Doryphoros.*

polycotton ('pɒlɪkɒtᵊn) *n* a fabric made from a mixture of polyester and cotton.

polycotyledon (ˌpɒlɪˌkɒtɪ'li:dᵊn) *n* any of various plants, esp. gymnosperms, that have or appear to have more than two cotyledons.
▸ **ˌpolyˌcoty'ledonous** *adj*

Polycrates ★ (pə'lɪkrəˌti:z) *n* died ?522 B.C., Greek tyrant of Samos, who was crucified by a Persian satrap.

polycyclic (ˌpɒlɪ'saɪklɪk) *adj* **1** (of a molecule or compound) having molecules that contain two or more closed rings of atoms. **2** *Biol.* having two or more rings or whorls: *polycyclic shells.* ◆ *n* **3** a polycyclic compound.

polycystic (ˌpɒlɪ'sɪstɪk) *adj Med.* containing many cysts: *a polycystic ovary.*

polydactyl (ˌpɒlɪ'dæktɪl) *adj also* **polydactylous. 1** (of man and other vertebrates) having more than the normal number of digits. ◆ *n* **2** a human or other vertebrate having more than the normal number of digits.

Polydeuces ★ (ˌpɒlɪ'dju:si:z) *n* the Greek name of **Pollux.** See **Castor and Pollux.**

polyester (ˌpɒlɪ'ɛstə) *n* any of a large class of synthetic materials that are polymers containing recurring -COO-groups: used as plastics, textile fibres, and adhesives.

polyethene (ˌpɒlɪ'ɛθi:n) *n* the systematic name for **polythene.**

polyethylene (ˌpɒlɪ'ɛθɪˌli:n) *n* another name for **polythene.**

polygamy (pə'lɪgəmɪ) *n* **1** the practice of having more than one wife or husband at the same time. **2** the condition of having male, female, and hermaphrodite flowers on the same plant or on separate plants of the same spe-

cies. **3** the practice in male animals of having more than one mate during one breeding season. ORIG C16: via F from Gk *polugamia*
▸ **po'lygamist** *n* ▸ **po'lygamous** *adj* ▸ **po'lygamously** *adv*

polygene ('pɒlɪˌdʒiːn) *n* any of a group of genes that each produce a small quantitative effect on a particular characteristic, such as height.

polygenesis (ˌpɒlɪ'dʒɛnɪsɪs) *n* **1** *Biol.* evolution of organisms from different ancestral groups. **2** the hypothetical descent of different races from different ultimate ancestors.
▸ **polygenetic** (ˌpɒlɪdʒɪ'nɛtɪk) *adj*

polyglot ('pɒlɪˌglɒt) *adj* **1** having a command of many languages. **2** written in or containing many languages. ◆ *n* **3** a person with a command of many languages. **4** a book, esp. a Bible, containing several versions of the same text written in various languages. **5** a mixture of languages. ORIG C17: from Gk *poluglōttos,* lit.: many-tongued

Polygnotus ★ (ˌpɒlɪg'nəʊtəs) *n* 5th century B.C., Greek painter: associated with Cimon in rebuilding Athens.

polygon ('pɒlɪˌgɒn) *n* a closed plane figure bounded by three or more straight sides that meet in pairs in the same number of vertices and do not intersect other than at these vertices. Specific polygons are named according to the number of sides, such as triangle, pentagon, etc. ORIG C16: via L from Gk *polugōnon* figure with many angles
▸ **polygonal** (pə'lɪgənᵊl) *adj* ▸ **po'lygonally** *adv*

polygonum (pə'lɪgənəm) *n* a plant having stems with knotlike joints and spikes of small white, green, or pink flowers. ORIG C18: NL, from Gk *polugonon* knotgrass, from *polu-* POLY- + *-gonon,* from *gonu* knee

polygraph ('pɒlɪˌgrɑːf) *n* **1** an instrument for the simultaneous recording of several involuntary physiological activities, including pulse rate and perspiration, used esp. as a lie detector. **2** a device for producing copies of written matter. ORIG C18: from Gk *polugraphos* writing copiously

polygyny (pə'lɪdʒɪnɪ) *n* **1** the practice or condition of being married to more than one wife at the same time. **2** the practice in animals of a male mating with more than one female during one breeding season. **3** the condition in flowers of having many styles. ORIG C18: from POLY- + *-gyny,* from Gk *gunē* a woman
▸ **po'lygynous** *adj*

polyhedron (ˌpɒlɪ'hiːdrən) *n, pl* **polyhedrons** *or* **polyhedra** (-drə). a solid figure consisting of four or more plane faces (all polygons), pairs of which meet along an edge, three or more edges meeting at a vertex. Specific polyhedrons are named according to the number of faces, such as tetrahedron, icosahedron, etc. ORIG C16: from Gk *poluedron,* from POLY- + *hedron* side
▸ **ˌpoly'hedral** *adj*

Polyhymnia ★ (ˌpɒlɪ'hɪmnɪə) *n Greek myth.* the Muse of singing, mime, and sacred dance. ORIG L, from Gk *Polumnia* full of songs

polymath ('pɒlɪˌmæθ) *n* a person of great and varied learning. ORIG C17: from Gk *polumathēs* having much knowledge
▸ **polymathy** (pə'lɪməθɪ) *n*

polymer ('pɒlɪmə) *n* a naturally occurring or synthetic compound, such as starch or Perspex, that has large molecules made up of many relatively simple repeated units.
▸ **polymerism** (pə'lɪməˌrɪzəm, 'pɒlɪmə-) *n*

polymerase ('pɒlɪməˌreɪs, -ˌreɪz) *n* any enzyme that catalyses the synthesis of a polymer, esp. the synthesis of DNA or RNA.

polymeric (ˌpɒlɪ'mɛrɪk) *adj* of, concerned with, or being a polymer: *a polymeric compound.* ORIG C19: from Gk *polumerēs* having many parts

polymerization *or* **polymerisation** (pəˌlɪməraɪ'zeɪʃən, ˌpɒlɪməraɪ-) *n* the act or process of forming a polymer or copolymer.

polymerize *or* **polymerise** ('pɒlɪməˌraɪz, pə'lɪmə-) *vb* **polymerizes, polymerizing, polymerized** *or* **polymerises, polymerising, polymerised.** to react or cause to react to form a polymer.

polymerous (pə'lɪmərəs) *adj Biol.* having or being composed of many parts.

polymorph ('pɒlɪˌmɔːf) *n* a species of animal or plant, or a crystalline form of a chemical compound, that exhibits polymorphism. ORIG C19: from Gk *polumorphos* having many forms

polymorphic function *n Computing.* a function in a computer program that can deal with a number of different types of data.

polymorphism (ˌpɒlɪ'mɔːfɪzəm) *n* **1** the occurrence of more than one form of individual in a single species within an interbreeding population. **2** the existence or formation of different types of crystal of the same chemical compound.

polymorphous (ˌpɒlɪ'mɔːfəs) *or* **polymorphic** *adj* **1** having, taking, or passing through many different forms or stages. **2** exhibiting or undergoing polymorphism.

Polynesia ★ (ˌpɒlɪ'niːʒə, -ʒɪə) *n* one of the three divisions of islands in the Pacific, the others being Melanesia and Micronesia: includes Samoa, Society, Marquesas, Mangareva, Tuamotu, Cook, and Tubuai Islands, and Tonga. ORIG C18: via F from POLY- + Gk *nēsos* island

Polynesian (ˌpɒlɪ'niːʒən, -ʒɪən) *adj* **1** of or relating to Polynesia, its people, or any of their languages. ◆ *n* **2** a member of the people that inhabit Polynesia, generally of Caucasoid features with light skin and wavy hair. **3** a branch of the Malayo-Polynesian family of languages, including Maori and Hawaiian.

polyneuritis (ˌpɒlɪnjʊ'raɪtɪs) *n* inflammation of many nerves at the same time.

Polynices ★ (ˌpɒlɪ'naɪsiːz) *n Greek myth.* a son of Oedipus and Jocasta, for whom the Seven Against Thebes sought to regain Thebes. He and his brother Eteocles killed each other in single combat before its walls.

polynomial (ˌpɒlɪ'nəʊmɪəl) *adj* **1** of, consisting of, or referring to two or more names or terms. ◆ *n* **2a** a mathematical expression consisting of a sum of terms each of which is the product of a constant and one or more variables raised to a positive or zero integral power. **2b** Also called: **multinomial.** any mathematical expression consisting of the sum of a number of terms. **3** *Biol.* a taxonomic name consisting of more than two terms, such as *Parus major minor* in which *minor* designates the subspecies.

polynucleotide (ˌpɒlɪ'njuːklɪəˌtaɪd) *n Biochem.* a molecular chain of nucleotides chemically bonded by a series of ester linkages between the phosphoryl group of one nucleotide and the hydroxyl group of the sugar in the adjacent nucleotide.

polynya ('pɒlənˌjɑː) *n* a stretch of open water surrounded by ice, esp. near the mouths of large rivers, in arctic seas. ORIG C19: from Russian, from *poly* open

polyp ('pɒlɪp) *n* **1** *Zool.* one of the two forms of individual that occur in coelenterates. It usually has a hollow cylindrical body with a ring of tentacles around the mouth. **2** Also called: **polypus.** *Pathol.* a small growth arising from the surface of a mucous membrane. ORIG C16 *polip,* from F *polype* nasal polyp, from L *pōlypus,* from Gk *polupous* having many feet
▸ **'polypous** *or* **'polypoid** *adj*

polypeptide (ˌpɒlɪ'pɛptaɪd) *n* any of a group of natural or synthetic polymers made up of amino acids chemically linked together; includes the proteins.

polypetalous (ˌpɒlɪ'pɛtələs) *adj* (of flowers) having many distinct or separate petals.

polyphagia (ˌpɒlɪ'feɪdʒə) *n* **1** an abnormal desire to consume excessive amounts of food. **2** the habit of certain animals, esp. certain insects, of feeding on many different types of food. ORIG C17: NL, from Gk, from *poluphagos* eating much
▸ **polyphagous** (pə'lɪfəgəs) *adj*

polyphase ('pɒlɪˌfeɪz) *adj* **1** (of an electrical system, circuit, or device) having or using alternating voltages of the same frequency, the phases of which are cyclically displaced by fractions of a period. **2** having more than one phase.

Polyphemus ★ (ˌpɒlɪ'fiːməs) *n Greek myth.* a cyclops

who imprisoned Odysseus and his companions in his cave. To effect his escape, Odysseus blinded him.

polyphone (ˈpɒlɪˌfəʊn) *n* a letter or character having more than one phonetic value, such as *c* in English.

polyphonic (ˌpɒlɪˈfɒnɪk) *adj* **1** *Music.* composed of relatively independent parts; contrapuntal. **2** many-voiced. **3** *Phonetics.* denoting a polyphone.
▸ **ˌpolyˈphonically** *adv*

polyphony (pəˈlɪfənɪ) *n, pl* **polyphonies. 1** polyphonic style of composition or a piece of music utilizing it. **2** the use of polyphones in a writing system. ORIG C19: from Gk *poluphōnia* diversity of tones
▸ **poˈlyphonous** *adj* ▸ **poˈlyphonously** *adv*

polyploid (ˈpɒlɪˌplɔɪd) *adj* (of cells, organisms, etc.) having more than twice the basic (haploid) number of chromosomes.
▸ **ˌpolyˈploidal** *adj* ▸ **ˈpolyˌploidy** *n*

polypod (ˈpɒlɪˌpɒd) *adj* **1** (esp. of insect larvae) having many legs or similar appendages. ◆ *n* **2** an animal of this type.

polypody (ˈpɒlɪˌpəʊdɪ) *n, pl* **polypodies.** any of various ferns having deeply divided leaves and round naked sporangia. ORIG C15: from L *polypodium,* from Gk, from POLY- + *pous* foot

polypropylene (ˌpɒlɪˈprəʊpɪˌliːn) *n* any of various tough flexible synthetic thermoplastic materials made by polymerizing propylene. Systematic name: **polypropene** (ˌpɒlɪˈprəʊpiːn).

polypus (ˈpɒlɪpəs) *n, pl* **polypi** (-paɪ). *Pathol.* another word for **polyp** (sense 2). ORIG C16: via L from Gk: POLYP

polysaccharide (ˌpɒlɪˈsækəˌraɪd, -rɪd) *or* **polysaccharose** (ˌpɒlɪˈsækəˌrəʊz, -ˌrəʊs) *n* any one of a class of carbohydrates whose molecules contain linked monosaccharide units: includes starch, inulin, and cellulose.

polysemy (ˌpɒlɪˈsiːmɪ, pəˈlɪsəmɪ) *n* the existence of several meanings in a single word. ORIG C20: from NL *polysēmia,* from Gk *polusēmos* having many meanings
▸ **ˌpolyˈsemous** *adj*

polysomic (ˌpɒlɪˈsəʊmɪk) *adj* of, relating to, or designating a basically diploid chromosome complement, in which some but not all the chromosomes are represented more than twice.

polystyrene (ˌpɒlɪˈstaɪriːn) *n* a synthetic thermoplastic material obtained by polymerizing styrene; used as a white rigid foam (**expanded polystyrene**) for insulating and packing and as a glasslike material in light fittings.

polysyllable (ˈpɒlɪˌsɪləbᵊl) *n* a word consisting of more than two syllables.
▸ **polysyllabic** (ˌpɒlɪsɪˈlæbɪk) *adj* ▸ **ˌpolysylˈlabically** *adv*

polysyndeton (ˌpɒlɪˈsɪndɪtən) *n Rhetoric.* the use of several conjunctions in close succession, esp. where some might be omitted, as in *he ran and jumped and laughed for joy.* ORIG C16: POLY- + *-syndeton,* from Gk *sundetos* bound together

polytechnic (ˌpɒlɪˈtɛknɪk) *n* **1** *Brit.* (formerly) a college offering advanced courses in many fields at and below degree standard. ◆ *adj* **2** of or relating to technical instruction and training. ORIG C19: via F from Gk *polutekhnos* skilled in many arts

polytetrafluoroethylene (ˌpɒlɪˌtɛtrəˌfluərəʊˈɛθɪˌliːn) *n* a white thermoplastic material with a waxy texture, made by polymerizing tetrafluoroethylene. It is used for making gaskets, hoses, insulators, bearings, and for coating metal surfaces. Abbrev.: **PTFE.** Also called (trademark): **Teflon.**

polytheism (ˈpɒlɪθiːˌɪzəm, ˌpɒlɪˈθiːɪzəm) *n* the worship of or belief in more than one god.
▸ **ˌpolytheˈistic** *adj* ▸ **ˌpolytheˈistically** *adv*

polythene (ˈpɒlɪˌθiːn) *n* any one of various light thermoplastic materials made from ethylene with properties depending on the molecular weight of the polymer. Systematic name: **polyethene.** Also called: **polyethylene.**

polytonality (ˌpɒlɪtəʊˈnælɪtɪ) *or* **polytonalism** (ˌpɒlɪˈtəʊnəˌlɪzəm) *n Music.* the simultaneous use of more than two different keys or tonalities.
▸ **ˌpolyˈtonal** *adj* ▸ **ˌpolyˈtonally** *adv*

polyunsaturated (ˌpɒlɪʌnˈsætʃəˌreɪtɪd) *adj* of or relating to a class of animal and vegetable fats, the molecules of which consist of long carbon chains with many double bonds. Polyunsaturated compounds are less likely to be converted into cholesterol in the body. See also **monounsaturated.**

polyurethane (ˌpɒlɪˈjʊərəˌθeɪn) *n* a class of synthetic materials commonly used as a foam for insulation and packing.

polyvalent (ˌpɒlɪˈveɪlənt, pəˈlɪvələnt) *adj* **1** *Chem.* having more than one valency. **2** (of a vaccine) effective against several strains of the same disease-producing microorganism, antigen, or toxin.
▸ **ˌpolyˈvalency** *n*

polyvinyl (ˌpɒlɪˈvaɪnɪl, -ˈvaɪnᵊl) *n* (*modifier*) designating a plastic or resin formed by polymerization of a vinyl derivative.

polyvinyl acetate *n* a colourless odourless tasteless resin used in emulsion paints, adhesives, sealers, a substitute for chicle in chewing gum, and for sealing porous surfaces.

polyvinyl chloride *n* the full name of **PVC.**

polyvinyl resin *n* any of a class of thermoplastic resins made by polymerizing a vinyl compound. The commonest type is PVC.

Polyxena ★ (pɒˈlɪksɪnə) *n Greek myth.* a daughter of King Priam of Troy, who was sacrificed on the command of Achilles' ghost.

polyzoan (ˌpɒlɪˈzəʊən) *n, adj* another word for **bryozoan.** ORIG C19: from NL, *Polyzoa* class name, from POLY- + *-zoan,* from Gk *zoion* an animal

pom (pɒm) *n Austral. & NZ sl.* short for **pommy.**

POM *abbrev. for* prescription only medicine (*or* medication). Cf. **OTC.**

pomace (ˈpʌmɪs) *n* **1** the pulpy residue of apples or similar fruit after crushing and pressing, as in cider-making. **2** any pulpy substance left after crushing, mashing, etc. ORIG C16: from Med. L *pōmācium* cider, from L *pōmum* apple

pomaceous (pɒˈmeɪʃəs) *adj* of, relating to, or bearing pomes, such as the apple and quince trees. ORIG C18: from NL *pōmāceus,* from L *pōmum* apple

pomade (pəˈmɑːd) *n* **1** a perfumed oil or ointment put on the hair, as to make it smooth and shiny. ◆ *vb* **pomades, pomading, pomaded. 2** (*tr*) to put pomade on. ◆ Also: **pomatum.** ORIG C16: from F *pommade,* from It. *pomato* (orig. made partly from apples), from L *pōmum* apple

pomander (pəʊˈmændə) *n* **1** a mixture of aromatic substances in a sachet or an orange, formerly carried as scent or as a protection against disease. **2** a container for such a mixture. ORIG C15: from OF *pome d'ambre,* from Med. L *pōmum ambrae* apple of amber

Pombal ★ (*Portuguese* pomˈbal) *n* **Marquês de** (mərkeʃ ˈdəː). title of *Sebastião José de Carvalho e Mello.* 1699–1782, Portuguese statesman, who dominated Portuguese government from 1750 to 1777 and instituted many administrative and economic reforms.

pome (pəʊm) *n* the fleshy fruit of the apple and related plants, consisting of an enlarged receptacle enclosing the ovary and seeds. ORIG C15: from OF, from LL *pōma,* pl. of L *pōmum* apple

pomegranate (ˈpɒmɪˌgrænɪt, ˈpɒmˌgrænɪt) *n* **1** an Asian shrub or small tree cultivated in semitropical regions for its edible fruit. **2** the many-chambered globular fruit of this tree, which has tough reddish rind, juicy red pulp, and many seeds. ORIG C14: from OF *pome grenate,* from L *pōmum* apple + *grenate,* from *grānātus* full of seeds

pomelo (ˈpɒmɪˌləʊ) *n, pl* **pomelos. 1** Also called: **shaddock.** the edible yellow fruit, resembling a grapefruit, of a tropical tree widely grown in oriental regions. **2** *US.* another name for **grapefruit.** ORIG C19: from Du. *pompelmoes*

Pomerania ★ (ˌpɒməˈreɪnɪə) *n* a region of N central Europe, extending along the S coast of the Baltic Sea from Stralsund to the Vistula River: now chiefly in Poland, with a small area in NE Germany. German name: **Pommern.** Polish name: **Pomorze.**

Pomeranian (ˌpɒməˈreɪnɪən) *adj* **1** of or relating to Pomerania. ◆ *n* **2** a breed of toy dog of the spitz type with a long thick straight coat.

pomfret (ˈpʌmfrɪt, ˈpɒm-) *or* **pomfret-cake** *n* a small black rounded confection of liquorice. Also called: **Pontefract cake.** ORIG C19: from *Pomfret,* earlier form of PONTEFRACT, where orig. made

pomiculture (ˈpɒmɪˌkʌltʃə) *n* the cultivation of fruit. ORIG C19: from L *pōmum* fruit + CULTURE

pommel (ˈpʌməl, ˈpɒm-) *n* **1** the raised part on the front of a saddle. **2** a knob at the top of a sword or similar weapon. ◆ *vb* **pommels, pommelling, pommelled** *or US* **pommels, pommeling, pommeled. 3** a less common word for **pummel.** ORIG C14: from OF *pomel* knob, from Vulgar L *pōmellum* (unattested) little apple, from L *pōmum* apple

Pommern ★ (ˈpɔmərn) *n* the German name for **Pomerania.**

pommy (ˈpɒmɪ) *n, pl* **pommies.** (*sometimes cap.*) *Sl.* a mildly offensive word used by Australians and New Zealanders for a British person. Sometimes shortened to **pom.** ORIG C20: from ?, ? a blend of IMMIGRANT & POMEGRANATE (alluding to the red cheeks of British immigrants)

pomology (pɒˈmɒlədʒɪ) *n* the branch of horticulture concerned with the study and cultivation of fruit. ORIG C19: from NL *pōmologia,* from L *pōmum* fruit
▸ **pomological** (ˌpɒməˈlɒdʒɪkᵊl) *adj*

Pomona[1] ★ (pəˈməʊnə) *n* another name for **Mainland** (in the Orkneys).

Pomona[2] ★ (pəˈməʊnə) *n* the Roman goddess of fruit trees.

Pomorze ★ (pɔˈmɔʒɛ) *n* the Polish name for **Pomerania.**

pomp (pɒmp) *n* **1** stately or magnificent display; ceremonial splendour. **2** vain display, esp. of dignity or importance. **3** *Obs.* a procession or pageant. ORIG C14: from OF *pompe,* from L *pompa* procession, from Gk *pompē*

pompadour (ˈpɒmpəˌdʊə) *n* an early 18th-century hairstyle for women, having the front hair arranged over a pad to give it greater height and bulk. ORIG C18: after the Marquise de POMPADOUR, who originated it

Pompadour ★ (*French* pɔ̃padur) *n* **Marquise de,** title of *Jeanne Antoinette Poisson.* 1721–64, mistress of Louis XV of France (1745–64), whom she greatly influenced.

pompano (ˈpɒmpəˌnəʊ) *n, pl* **pompano** *or* **pompanos. 1** any of several food fishes of American coastal regions of the Atlantic. **2** a spiny-finned food fish of North American coastal regions of the Pacific. ORIG C19: from Sp. *pámpano,* from ?

Pompeii ★ (pɒmˈpeɪiː) *n* an ancient city in Italy, southeast of Naples: buried by an eruption of Vesuvius (79 A.D.); excavation of the site, which is extremely well preserved, began in 1748.
▸ **Pompeiian** (pɒmˈpeɪən, -ˈpiː-) *adj, n*

Pompey[1] ★ (ˈpɒmpɪ) *n* an informal name for **Portsmouth.**

Pompey[2] ★ (ˈpɒmpɪ) *n* called *Pompey the Great;* Latin name *Gnaeus Pompeius Magnus.* 106–48 B.C., Roman general and statesman; a member with Caesar and Crassus of the first triumvirate (60). He later quarrelled with Caesar, who defeated him at Pharsalus (48). He fled to Egypt and was murdered.

Pompidou ★ (*French* pɔ̃pidu) *n* **Georges** (ʒɔrʒ). 1911–74, French statesman; president of France (1969–74).

pompom (ˈpɒmpɒm) *or* **pompon** *n* **1** a ball of tufted silk, wool, feathers, etc., worn on a hat for decoration. **2a** the small globelike flower head of certain varieties of dahlia and chrysanthemum. **2b** (*as modifier*): *pompom dahlia.* ORIG C18: from F, from OF *pompe* knot of ribbons, from ?

pom-pom (ˈpɒmpɒm) *n* an automatic rapid-firing small-calibre cannon, esp. a type of anti-aircraft cannon used in World War II. Also called: **pompom.** ORIG C19: imit.

pomposo (pɒmˈpəʊsəʊ) *adv Music.* in a pompous manner. ORIG It.

pompous (ˈpɒmpəs) *adj* **1** exaggeratedly or ostentatiously dignified or self-important. **2** ostentatiously lofty in style: *a pompous speech.* **3** *Rare.* characterized by ceremonial pomp or splendour.
▸ **pomposity** (pɒmˈpɒsɪtɪ) *or* **ˈpompousness** *n* ▸ **ˈpompously** *adv*

ˈpon (pɒn) *Poetic or arch. contraction of* upon.

ponce (pɒns) *Derog. sl., chiefly Brit.* ◆ *n* **1** a man given to ostentatious or effeminate display. **2** another word for **pimp[1].** ◆ *vb* **ponces, poncing, ponced. 3** (*intr;* often foll. by *around* or *about*) to act like a ponce. ORIG C19: from Polari, from Sp. *pu(n)to* male prostitute or F *pront* prostitute
▸ **ˈponcy** *or* **ˈponcey** *adj*

Ponce ★ (*Spanish* ˈpɔnθe) *n* a port in S Puerto Rico, on the Caribbean: the second largest town on the island; settled in the 16th century. Pop.: 189 988 (1996 est.).

Ponce de León ★ (ˈpɒns də ˈliːən; *Spanish* ˈpɔnθe ðe leˈɔn) *n* **Juan** (xwan). ?1460–1521, Spanish explorer. He settled (1509) and governed (1510–12) Puerto Rico and discovered (1513) Florida.

poncho (ˈpɒntʃəʊ) *n, pl* **ponchos.** a cloak of a kind originally worn in South America, made of a rectangular or circular piece of cloth with a hole in the middle for the head. ORIG C18: from American Sp., of Amerind origin, from *pantho* woollen material

pond (pɒnd) *n* a pool of still water, often artificially created. ORIG C13 *ponde* enclosure

ponder (ˈpɒndə) *vb* (when *intr,* sometimes foll. by *on* or *over*) to give thorough or deep consideration (to); meditate (upon). ORIG C14: from OF *ponderer,* from L *ponderāre* to weigh, consider, from *pondus* weight
▸ **ˈponderable** *adj*

ponderous (ˈpɒndərəs) *adj* **1** heavy; huge. **2** (esp. of movement) lacking ease or lightness; lumbering or graceless. **3** dull or laborious: *a ponderous oration.* ORIG C14: from L *ponderōsus* of great weight, from *pondus* weight
▸ **ˈponderously** *adv* ▸ **ˈponderousness** *or* **ponderosity** (ˌpɒndəˈrɒsɪtɪ) *n*

Pondicherry ★ (ˌpɒndɪˈtʃerɪ) *n* **1** a Union Territory of SE India: transferred from French to Indian administration in 1954 and made a Union Territory in 1962. Capital: Pondicherry. Pop.: 894 000 (1994 est.). Area: 479 sq. km (185 sq. miles). **2** a port in SE India, capital of the Union Territory of Pondicherry, on the Coromandel Coast. Pop.: 203 065 (1991).

pond lily *n* another name for **water lily.**

pondok (ˈpɒndɒk) *or* **pondokkie** *n* (in southern Africa) a crudely made house built of tin sheet, reeds, etc. ORIG C20: from Malay *pondók* leaf house

Pondoland ★ (ˈpɒndəʊˌlænd) *n* an area of SE South Africa, inhabited chiefly by the Pondo people.

pond scum *n* a greenish layer floating on the surface of stagnant waters, consisting of algae.

pondweed (ˈpɒndˌwiːd) *n* **1** any of various water plants of the genus *Potamogeton,* which grow in ponds and slow streams. **2** Also called: **waterweed.** *Brit.* any of various water plants, such as mare's-tail, that have thin or much-divided leaves.

pone[1] (pəʊn, ˈpəʊnɪ) *n Cards.* the player to the right of the dealer, or the nondealer in two-handed games. ORIG C19: from L: put!, that is, play, from *ponere* to put

pone[2] (pəʊn) *n Southern US.* bread made of maize. Also called: **pone bread, corn pone.** ORIG C17: of Amerind origin

pong (pɒŋ) *Brit. inf.* ◆ *n* **1** a disagreeable or offensive smell; stink. ◆ *vb* **2** (*intr*) to stink. ORIG C20: ?from Romany *pan* to stink
▸ **ˈpongy** *adj*

ponga (ˈpɒŋə) *n* a tall New Zealand tree fern with large leathery leaves.

pongee (pɒnˈdʒiː, ˈpɒndʒiː) *n* **1** a thin plain-weave silk fabric from China or India, left in its natural colour. **2** a cotton or rayon fabric similar to this. ORIG C18: from Mandarin Chinese (Peking) *pen-chī* woven at home, from *pen* own + *chi* loom

pongid (ˈpɒŋgɪd, ˈpɒndʒɪd) *n* **1** any primate of the family Pongidae, which includes the gibbons and the great apes. ◆ *adj* **2** of this family. ORIG from NL *Pongo* type genus, from Congolese *mpongo* ape

pongo (ˈpɒŋgəʊ) *n, pl* **pongos.** an anthropoid ape, esp. an orang-utan or (formerly) a gorilla. ORIG C17: from Congolese *mpongo*

poniard (ˈpɒnjəd) *n* **1** a small dagger with a slender blade. ◆ *vb* **2** (*tr*) to stab with a poniard. ORIG C16: from OF *poignard,* from *poing* fist, from L *pugnus*

pons Varolii (pɒnz vəˈrəʊlɪˌaɪ) *n, pl* **pontes Varolii** (ˈpɒntiːz). a broad white band of connecting nerve fibres that bridges the hemispheres of the cerebellum in mammals. Sometimes shortened to **pons.** ORIG C16: NL, lit.: bridge of Varoli, after Costanzo *Varoli* (?1543–75), It. anatomist

Ponta Delgada ★ (*Portuguese* ˈpontə ðɛlˈgaðə) *n* a port in the E Azores, on S São Miguel Island: chief commercial centre of the archipelago. Pop.: 21 091 (1991 est.).

Pontchartrain ★ (ˈpɒntʃəˌtreɪn) *n* **Lake.** a shallow lagoon in SE Louisiana, linked with the Gulf of Mexico by a narrow channel, the **Rigolets:** resort and fishing centre. Area: 1620 sq. km (625 sq. miles).

Pontefract ★ (ˈpɒntɪˌfrækt) *n* an industrial town in N England, in Wakefield, in West Yorkshire: castle (1069), in which Richard II was imprisoned and murdered (1400). Pop.: 28 358 (1991).

Pontevedra ★ (*Spanish* pɔnteˈβeðra) *n* a port in NW Spain: takes its name from a 12-arched Roman bridge, the Pons Vetus. Pop.: 74 850 (1991).

Pontiac ★ (ˈpɒntɪˌæk) *n* died 1769, chief of the Ottawa Indians, who led a rebellion against the British (1763–66).

Pontianak ★ (ˌpɒntɪˈɑːnæk) *n* a port in Indonesia, on W coast of Borneo almost exactly on the equator. Pop.: 449 100 (1995 est.).

Pontic (ˈpɒntɪk) *adj* denoting or relating to the Black Sea. ORIG C15: from L *Ponticus,* from Gk, from *Pontos* PONTUS

pontifex (ˈpɒntɪˌfɛks) *n, pl* **pontifices** (pɒnˈtɪfɪˌsiːz). (in ancient Rome) any of the senior members of the Pontifical College, presided over by the **Pontifex Maximus.** ORIG C16: from L, ?from Etruscan but infl. by folk etymology as if meaning lit.: bridge-maker

pontiff (ˈpɒntɪf) *n* a former title of the pagan high priest at Rome, later used of popes and occasionally of other bishops, and now confined to the pope. ORIG C17: from F *pontife,* from L PONTIFEX

pontifical (pɒnˈtɪfɪkᵊl) *adj* **1** of, relating to, or characteristic of a pontiff. **2** having an excessively authoritative manner; pompous. ◆ *n* **3** *RC Church, Church of England.* a book containing the prayers and ritual instructions for ceremonies restricted to a bishop.
▸ **ponˈtifically** *adv*

pontificals (pɒnˈtɪfɪkᵊlz) *pl n Chiefly RC Church.* the insignia and special vestments worn by a bishop, esp. when celebrating High Mass.

pontificate *vb* (pɒnˈtɪfɪˌkeɪt), **pontificates, pontificating, pontificated.** (*intr*) **1** to speak or behave in a pompous or dogmatic manner. **2** to serve or officiate at a Pontifical Mass. ◆ *n* (pɒnˈtɪfɪkɪt). **3** the office or term of office of a pope.

Pontine Marshes ★ (ˈpɒntaɪn) *pl n* an area of W Italy, southeast of Rome: formerly malarial swamps, drained in 1932–34 after numerous attempts since 160 B.C. had failed. Italian name: **Agro Pontino** (ˈɑːgro ponˈtiːno)

Pontius Pilate ★ (ˈpɒnʃəs, ˈpɒntɪəs ˈpaɪlət) *n* See **Pilate.**

pontoon[1] (pɒnˈtuːn) *n* **a** a watertight float or vessel used where buoyancy is required in water, as in supporting a bridge, in salvage work, or where a temporary or mobile structure is required in military operations. **b** (*as modifier*): *a pontoon bridge.* ORIG C17: from F *ponton,* from L *pontō* punt, from *pōns* bridge

pontoon[2] (pɒnˈtuːn) *n* a gambling game in which players try to obtain card combinations worth 21 points. Also called: **twenty-one** (esp. US), **vingt-et-un.** ORIG C20: prob. an alteration of F *vingt-et-un,* lit.: twenty-one

Pontoppidan ★ (*Danish* pɔnˈtɔbidan) *n* **Henrik** (ˈhɛnrək). 1857–1943, Danish novelist and short-story writer, author of the novel sequences *The Promised Land* (1891–95), *Lykke-Per* (1898–1904), and *The Empire of Death* (1912–16). Nobel prize for literature 1917.

Pontormo ★ (*Italian* ponˈtormo) *n* **Jacopo da** (ˈjaːkopo da). original name *Jacopo Carrucci.* 1494–1556, Italian mannerist painter.

Pontus ★ (ˈpɒntəs) *n* an ancient region of NE Asia Minor, on the Black Sea: became a kingdom in the 4th century B.C.; at its height under Mithridates VI (about 115–63 B.C.), when it controlled all Asia Minor; defeated by the Romans in the mid-1st century B.C.

Pontus Euxinus ★ (juːkˈsaɪnəs) *n* the Latin name of the **Black Sea.**

Pontypool ★ (ˌpɒntɪˈpuːl) *n* an industrial town in E Wales, in Torfaen: famous for lacquered ironware in the 18th century. Pop.: 35 564 (1991).

Pontypridd ★ (ˌpɒntɪˈpriːð) *n* an industrial town in S Wales, in Rhondda, Cynon, Taff. Pop.: 28 487 (1991).

pony (ˈpəʊnɪ) *n, pl* **ponies. 1** any of various breeds of small horse, usually under 14.2 hands. **2** a small drinking glass, esp. for liqueurs. **3** anything small of its kind. **4** *Brit. sl.* a sum of £25, esp. in bookmaking. **5** Also called: **trot.** *US sl.* a translation used by students, often illicitly; crib. ORIG C17: from Scot. *powney,* ?from obs. F *poulenet* a little colt, from L *pullus* young animal, foal

ponytail (ˈpəʊnɪˌteɪl) *n* a hairstyle in which the hair is gathered together tightly by a band into a bunch at the back of the head.

pony trekking *n* the act of riding ponies cross-country, esp. as a pastime.

pooch (puːtʃ) *n Chiefly US & Canad.* a slang word for **dog.** ORIG from ?

poodle (ˈpuːdᵊl) *n* **1** a breed of dog with curly hair, which is generally clipped from ribs to tail. **2** a servile person; lackey. ORIG C19: from G *Pudel,* short for *Pudelhund,* from *pudeln* to splash + *Hund* dog; formerly trained as water dogs

poof (pʊf, puːf), **poove** (puːv), *or* **poofter** (ˈpuːftə) *n Brit. & Austral. derog. sl.* a male homosexual. ORIG C20: from F *pouffe* puff
▸ **ˈpoofy** *adj*

pooh (puː) *interj* an exclamation of disdain, contempt, or disgust.

Pooh-Bah (ˈpuːˈbɑː) *n* a pompous self-important official holding several offices at once and fulfilling none of them. ORIG C19: after the character, the Lord-High-Everything-Else, in *The Mikado* (1885), by Gilbert & Sullivan

pooh-pooh (ˈpuːˈpuː) *vb* (*tr*) to express disdain or scorn for; dismiss or belittle.

pool[1] (puːl) *n* **1** a small body of still water, usually fresh; small pond. **2** a small isolated collection of spilt liquid; puddle: *a pool of blood.* **3** a deep part of a stream or river where the water runs very slowly. **4** an underground accumulation of oil or gas. **5** See **swimming pool.** ORIG OE *pōl*

pool[2] (puːl) *n* **1** any communal combination of resources, funds, etc.: *a typing pool.* **2** the combined stakes of the betters in many gambling games; kitty. **3** *Commerce.* a group of producers who agree to establish and maintain output levels and high prices, each member of the group being allocated a maximum quota. **4** *Finance, chiefly US.* a joint fund organized by security-holders for speculative or manipulative purposes on financial markets. **5** any of various billiard games in which the object is to pot all the balls with the cue ball, esp. that played with 15 coloured and numbered balls. ◆ *vb* (*tr*) **6** to combine (investments, money, interests, etc.) into a common fund, as for a joint enterprise. **7** *Commerce.* to organize a pool of (enterprises). ORIG C17: from F *poule,* lit.: hen used to signify stakes in a card game, from Med. L *pulla* hen, from L *pullus* young animal

Poole ★ (puːl) *n* **1** a port and resort in S England, in Dorset on **Poole Harbour;** seat of Bournemouth University (1992). Pop.: 138 479 (1991). **2** a unitary authority in S England, in Dorset. Pop.: 139 200 (1996 est.). Area: 37 sq. km (14 sq. miles).

Pool Malebo ★ (ˈpuːl məˈliːbəʊ) *n* the Congolese name for **Stanley Pool.**

pools (puːlz) *pl n* **the** *Brit.* an organized nationwide principally postal gambling pool betting on the result of football matches. Also called: **football pools.**

Poona *or* **Pune** ★ (ˈpuːnə) *n* a city in W India, in W Maharashtra: under British rule served as the seasonal capital of the Bombay Presidency. Pop.: 1 566 651 (1991).

poop[1] (puːp) *Naut.* ◆ *n* **1** a raised structure at the stern of a vessel, esp. a sailing ship. **2** Also called: **poop deck.** a raised deck at the stern of a ship. ◆ *vb* **3** (*tr*) (of a wave or sea) to break over the stern of (a vessel). **4** (*intr*) (of a vessel) to ship a wave or sea over the stern, esp. repeatedly. ORIG C15: from OF *pupe,* from L *puppis*

poop[2] (puːp) *vb US & Canad. sl.* **1** (*tr; usually passive*) to cause to become exhausted; tire: *he was pooped after the race.* **2** (*intr;* usually foll. by *out*) to give up or fail: *he pooped out of the race.* ORIG C14 *poupen* to blow, ? imit.

poop[3] (puːp) *Inf.* ◆ *vb* (*intr*) **1** to defecate. ◆ *n* **2** faeces; excrement. ORIG perhaps related to POOP[2]

pooper-scooper *n* a device used to remove dogs' excrement from public areas. ORIG C20: POOP[3] + -ER[1] + SCOOP

Poopó ★ (*Spanish* pooˈpo) *n* **Lake.** a lake in SW Bolivia, at an altitude of 3688 m (12 100 ft): fed by the Desaguadero River. Area: 2540 sq. km (980 sq. miles).

poor (pʊə, pɔː) *adj* **1** lacking financial or other means of subsistence; needy. **2** characterized by or indicating poverty: *the country had a poor economy.* **3** scanty or inadequate: *a poor salary.* **4** (when *postpositive,* usually foll. by *in*) badly supplied (with resources, etc.): *a region poor in wild flowers.* **5** inferior. **6** contemptible or despicable. **7** disappointing or disagreeable: *a poor play.* **8** (*prenominal*) deserving of pity; unlucky: *poor John is ill again.* ORIG C13: from OF *povre,* from L *pauper*
▸ ˈ**poorness** *n*

poor box *n* a box, esp. one in a church, used for the collection of alms or money for the poor.

poorhouse (ˈpʊəˌhaʊs, ˈpɔː-) *n* another name for **workhouse** (sense 1).

poor law *n English history.* a law providing for the relief or support of the poor from parish funds.

poorly (ˈpʊəlɪ, ˈpɔː-) *adv* **1** badly. ◆ *adj* **2** (*usually postpositive*) *Inf.* in poor health; rather ill.

poort (pʊət) *n* (in South Africa) a steep narrow mountain pass, usually following a river or stream. ORIG C19: from Afrik., from Du.: gateway

poor White *n Often offens.* **a** a poverty-stricken and underprivileged White person, esp. in the southern US and South Africa. **b** (*as modifier*): *poor White trash.*

pop[1] (pɒp) *vb* **pops, popping, popped. 1** to make or cause to make a light sharp explosive sound. **2** to burst open with such a sound. **3** (*intr;* often foll. by *in, out,* etc.) *Inf.* to come (to) or go (from) rapidly or suddenly. **4** (*intr*) (esp. of the eyes) to protrude: *her eyes popped with amazement.* **5** to shoot at (a target) with a firearm. **6** (*tr*) to place with a sudden movement: *she popped some tablets into her mouth.* **7** (*tr*) *Inf.* to pawn: *he popped his watch yesterday.* **8** (*tr*) *Sl.* to take (a drug) in pill form or as an injection. **9 pop the question.** *Inf.* to propose marriage. ◆ *n* **10** a light sharp explosive sound; crack. **11** *Inf.* a flavoured nonalcoholic carbonated beverage. ◆ *adv* **12** with a popping sound. ◆ See also **pop off.** ORIG C14: imit.

pop[2] (pɒp) *n* **1a** music of general appeal, esp. among young people, that originated as a distinctive genre in the 1950s. It is generally characterized by a heavy rhythmic element and the use of electrical amplification. **1b** (*as modifier*): *a pop group.* **2** *Inf.* a piece of popular or light classical music. ◆ *adj* **3** *Inf.* short for **popular.**

pop[3] (pɒp) *n* **1** an informal word for **father. 2** *Inf.* a name used in addressing an old man.

POP *abbrev. for* Post Office Preferred (size of envelopes, etc.).

pop. *abbrev. for:* **1** popular(ly). **2** population.

pop art *n* a movement in modern art that imitates the methods, styles, and themes of popular culture and mass media, such as comic strips, advertising, and science fiction.

popcorn (ˈpɒpˌkɔːn) *n* **1** a variety of maize having hard pointed kernels that puff up and burst when heated. **2** the puffed edible kernels of this plant.

pope (pəʊp) *n* **1** (*often cap.*) the bishop of Rome as head of the Roman Catholic Church. **2** *Eastern Orthodox Churches.* a title sometimes given to a parish priest or to the Greek Orthodox patriarch of Alexandria. ORIG OE *papa,* from Church L: bishop, esp. of Rome, from LGk *papas* father-in-God, from Gk *pappas* father
▸ ˈ**popedom** *n*

Pope ★ (pəʊp) *n* **Alexander.** 1688–1744, British poet, regarded as the most brilliant satirist of the Augustan period. His works include *The Rape of the Lock* (1712–14), *The Dunciad* (1728; 1742), *An Essay on Man* (1733–34), and *Imitations of Horace* (1733–38).

popery (ˈpəʊpərɪ) *n* a derogatory name for **Roman Catholicism.**

popeyed (ˈpɒpˌaɪd) *adj* **1** having bulging prominent eyes. **2** staring in astonishment.

popgun (ˈpɒpˌgʌn) *n* a toy gun that fires a pellet or cork by means of compressed air.

popinjay (ˈpɒpɪnˌdʒeɪ) *n* **1** a conceited, foppish, or excessively talkative person. **2** an archaic word for **parrot. 3** the figure of a parrot used as a target. ORIG C13 *papeniai,* from OF *papegay* a parrot, from Sp., from Ar. *babaghā*

popish (ˈpəʊpɪʃ) *adj Derog.* belonging to or characteristic of Roman Catholicism.

poplar (ˈpɒplə) *n* **1** a tree of N temperate regions, having triangular leaves, flowers borne in catkins, and light soft wood. **2** *US.* the tulip tree. ORIG C14: from OF *poplier,* from L *pōpulus*

poplin (ˈpɒplɪn) *n* a strong fabric, usually of cotton, in plain weave with fine ribbing. ORIG C18: from F *papeline,* ?from *Poperinge,* a centre of textile manufacture in Flanders

popliteal (pɒpˈlɪtɪəl, ˌpɒplɪˈtiːəl) *adj* of, relating to, or near the part of the leg behind the knee. ORIG C18: from NL *popliteus* the muscle behind the knee joint, from L *poples* the ham of the knee

Popocatépetl ★ (ˌpɒpəˈkætəpɛtᵊl, -ˌkætəˈpɛtᵊl; *Spanish* popokaˈtepetl) *n* a volcano in SE central Mexico, southeast of Mexico City. Height: 5452 m (17 887 ft).

pop off *vb* (*intr, adv*) *Inf.* **1** to depart suddenly or unexpectedly. **2** to die, esp. suddenly.

Popov ★ (*Russian* paˈpɔf) *n* **Alexander Stepanovich** (alɪkˈsandᵊr stɪˈpanəvitʃ). 1859–1906, Russian physicist, the first to use an aerial in experiments with radio waves.

poppadom *or* **poppadum** (ˈpɒpədəm) *n* a thin round crisp Indian bread, fried or roasted and served with curry, etc. ORIG from Hindi

popper (ˈpɒpə) *n* **1** a person or thing that pops. **2** *Brit.* an informal name for **press stud. 3** *Chiefly US & Canad.* a container for cooking popcorn in. **4** *Sl.* an amyl nitrite capsule, crushed and inhaled by drug users.

Popper ★ (ˈpɒpə) *n* Sir **Karl.** 1902–94, British philosopher, born in Vienna. His works include *The Logic of Scientific Discovery* (1934), *The Open Society and its Enemies* (1945), and *Objective Knowledge* (1972).
▸ **Popperian** (pɒˈpɪərɪən) *n, adj*

poppet (ˈpɒpɪt) *n* **1** a term of affection for a small child or sweetheart. **2** Also called: **poppet valve.** a mushroom-shaped valve that is lifted from its seating by applying an axial force to its stem. **3** *Naut.* a temporary supporting brace for a vessel hauled on land. ORIG C14: early var. of PUPPET

popping crease *n Cricket.* a line four feet in front of and parallel with the bowling crease, at or behind which the batsman stands. ORIG C18: from POP[1] (in the obs. sense: to hit) + CREASE

popple (ˈpɒpᵊl) *vb* **popples, poppling, poppled.** (*intr*) **1** (of boiling water or a choppy sea) to heave or toss; bubble. **2** (often foll. by *along*) (of a stream or river) to move with an irregular tumbling motion. ORIG C14: imit.

poppy (ˈpɒpɪ) *n, pl* **poppies. 1** any of numerous papaveraceous plants having red, orange, or white flowers and a milky sap. **2** any of several similar or related plants, such as the California poppy and Welsh poppy. **3**

any of the drugs, such as opium, that are obtained from these plants. **4a** a strong red to reddish-orange colour. **4b** (*as adj*): *a poppy dress.* **5** an artificial red poppy flower worn to mark Remembrance Sunday. ORIG OE *popæg,* ult. from L *papāver*

poppycock ('pɒpɪˌkɒk) *n Inf.* nonsense. ORIG C19: from Du. dialect *pappekak,* lit.: soft excrement

Poppy Day *n* an informal name for **Remembrance Sunday.**

poppyhead ('pɒpɪˌhɛd) *n* **1** the hard dry seed-containing capsule of a poppy. **2** a carved ornament, esp. one used on the top of the end of a pew or bench in Gothic church architecture.

poppy seed *n* the small grey seeds of the opium poppy, used esp. on loaves.

pop socks *pl n* knee-length nylon stockings.

popsy ('pɒpsɪ) *n, pl* **popsies.** *Old-fashioned Brit. sl.* an attractive young woman. ORIG C19: dim. from *pop,* shortened from POPPET; orig. a nursery term

populace ('pɒpjʊləs) *n* (*sometimes functioning as pl*) **1** local inhabitants. **2** the common people; masses. ORIG C16: via F from It. *popolaccio* the common herd, from *popolo* people, from L *populus*

popular ('pɒpjʊlə) *adj* **1** widely favoured or admired. **2** favoured by an individual or limited group: *I'm not very popular with her.* **3** prevailing among the general public; common: *popular discontent.* **4** appealing to or comprehensible to the layman: *a popular lecture on physics.* ◆ *n* **5** (*usually pl*) a cheap newspaper with a mass circulation. ORIG C15: from L *populāris* of the people, democratic
▸ **popularity** (ˌpɒpjʊ'lærɪtɪ) *n* ▸ **'popularly** *adv*

popular front *n* (*often cap.*) any of the left-wing groups or parties that were organized from 1935 onwards to oppose the spread of fascism.

popularize *or* **popularise** ('pɒpjʊləˌraɪz) *vb* **popularizes, popularizing, popularized** *or* **popularises, popularising, popularised.** (*tr*) **1** to make popular. **2** to make or cause to become easily understandable or acceptable.
▸ **ˌpopulari'zation** *or* **ˌpopulari'sation** *n* ▸ **'popularˌizer** *or* **'popularˌiser** *n*

populate ('pɒpjʊˌleɪt) *vb* **populates, populating, populated.** (*tr*) **1** (*often passive*) to live in; inhabit. **2** to provide a population for; colonize or people. ORIG C16: from Med. L *populāre,* from L *populus* people

population (ˌpɒpjʊ'leɪʃən) *n* **1** (*sometimes functioning as pl*) all the persons inhabiting a specified place. **2** the number of such inhabitants. **3** (*sometimes functioning as pl*) all the people of a particular class in a specific area: *the Chinese population of San Francisco.* **4** the act or process of providing a place with inhabitants; colonization. **5** *Ecology.* a group of individuals of the same species inhabiting a given area. **6** *Astron.* either of two main groups of stars classified according to age and location. **7** *Statistics.* the entire aggregate of individuals or items from which samples are drawn.

population explosion *n* a rapid increase in the size of a population caused by such factors as a sudden decline in infant mortality or an increase in life expectancy.

population pyramid *n* a pyramid-shaped diagram illustrating the age distribution of a population: the youngest are represented by a rectangle at the base, the oldest by one at the apex.

populism ('pɒpjʊˌlɪzəm) *or* **popularism** *n* the practice, esp. by a politician of making a calculated appeal to the interests, tastes, or prejudices of ordinary people.

populist ('pɒpjʊˌlɪst) *adj* **1** appealing to the interests or prejudices of ordinary people. ◆ *n* **2** a person, esp. a politician, who appeals to the interests or prejudices of ordinary people.

Populist ('pɒpjʊlɪst) *n* **1** *US history.* a member of the People's Party, formed largely by agrarian interests to contest the 1892 presidential election. ◆ *adj* **2** of or relating to the People's Party or any individual or movement with similar aims. Also: **Populistic.**
▸ **'Popuˌlism** *n*

populous ('pɒpjʊləs) *adj* containing many inhabitants. ORIG C15: from LL *populōsus*
▸ **'populously** *adv* ▸ **'populousness** *n*

porangi ('pɔːræŋɪ) *adj NZ inf.* crazy; mad. ORIG from Maori

porbeagle ('pɔːˌbiːgᵊl) *n* any of several voracious sharks of northern seas. Also called: **mackerel shark.** ORIG C18: from Cornish *porgh-bugel,* from ?

porcelain ('pɔːslɪn) *n* **1** a more or less translucent ceramic material, the principal ingredients being kaolin and petuntse (hard paste) or other clays, bone ash, etc. **2** an object made of this or such objects collectively. **3** (*modifier*) of, relating to, or made from this material: *a porcelain cup.* ORIG C16: from F *porcelaine,* from It. *porcellana* cowrie shell, lit.: relating to a sow, from *porcella* little sow, from *porca* sow, from L; see PORK
▸ **porcellaneous** (ˌpɔːsə'leɪnɪəs) *adj*

porch (pɔːtʃ) *n* **1** a low structure projecting from the doorway of a house and forming a covered entrance. **2** *US & Canad.* a veranda. ORIG C13: from F *porche,* from L *porticus* portico

porcine ('pɔːsaɪn) *adj* of or characteristic of pigs. ORIG C17: from L *porcīnus,* from *porcus* a pig

porcupine ('pɔːkjʊˌpaɪn) *n* any of various large rodents that have a body covering of protective spines or quills. ORIG C14 *porc despyne* pig with spines, from OF *porc espin;* see PORK, SPINE
▸ **'porcuˌpinish** *adj* ▸ **'porcuˌpiny** *adj*

porcupine fish *n* any of various fishes of temperate and tropical seas having a body that is covered with sharp spines and can be inflated into a globe. Also called: **globefish.**

porcupine grass *n Austral.* another name for **spinifex.**

porcupine provisions *pl n Finance.* provisions, such as poison pills or staggered directorships, made in the bylaws of a company to deter takeover bids. Also called: **shark repellents.**

pore[1] (pɔː) *vb* **pores, poring, pored.** (*intr*) **1** (foll. by *over*) to make a close intent examination or study (of): *he pored over the documents for several hours.* **2** (foll. by *over, on,* or *upon*) to think deeply (about). **3** (foll. by *over, on,* or *upon*) *Rare.* to gaze fixedly (upon). ORIG C13 *pouren*

> **USAGE NOTE** See at **pour.**

pore[2] (pɔː) *n* **1** any small opening in the skin or outer surface of an animal. **2** *Bot.* any small aperture, esp. that of a stoma, through which water vapour and gases pass. **3** any other small hole, such as a space in a rock, etc. ORIG C14: from LL *porus,* from Gk *poros* passage, pore

porgy ('pɔːgɪ) *n, pl* **porgy** *or* **porgies.** any of various perchlike fishes, many of which occur in American Atlantic waters. ORIG C18: from Sp. *pargo,* from L *phager,* from Gk *phagros* sea bream

Pori ★ (*Finnish* 'pɔri) *n* a port in SW Finland, on the Gulf of Bothnia. Pop.: 76 561 (1994). Swedish name: **Björneborg.**

poriferan (pɔː'rɪfərən) *n* any invertebrate of the phylum *Porifera,* which comprises the sponges. ORIG C19: from NL *porifer* bearing pores

Porirua ★ (ˌpɔːrɪ'ruːə) *n* a city in New Zealand, on the North Island, north of Wellington. Pop.: 46 601 (1991).

pork (pɔːk) *n* the flesh of pigs used as food. ORIG C13: from OF *porc,* from L *porcus* pig

porker ('pɔːkə) *n* a pig, esp. a young one, fattened to provide meat.

pork pie *n* **1** a pie filled with minced seasoned pork. **2** See **porky**[2].

porkpie hat ('pɔːkˌpaɪ) *n* a hat with a round flat crown and a brim that can be turned up or down.

porky[1] ('pɔːkɪ) *adj* **porkier, porkiest. 1** characteristic of pork. **2** *Inf.* fat; obese.

porky[2] ('pɔːkɪ) *n, pl* **porkies.** *Brit. sl.* a lie. Also called: **pork pie.** ORIG from rhyming slang *pork pie* lie

porn (pɔːn) *or* **porno** ('pɔːnəʊ) *n, adj Inf.* short for **pornography** or **pornographic.**

pornography (pɔː'nɒgrəfɪ) *n* **1** writings, pictures, films, etc., designed to stimulate sexual excitement. **2** the production of such material. ◆ Sometimes (informal)

★ people and places

shortened to **porn** or **porno.** ORIG C19: from Gk *pornographos* writing of harlots
▸ **por'nographer** *n* ▸ **pornographic** (ˌpɔːnəˈgræfɪk) *adj* ▸ **ˌporno'graphically** *adv*

poromeric (ˌpɔːrəˈmɛrɪk) *adj* **1** (of a plastic) permeable to water vapour. ◆ *n* **2** a substance having this characteristic, esp. one used in place of leather in making shoe uppers. ORIG C20: from PORO(SITY) + (POLY)MER + -IC

porous (ˈpɔːrəs) *adj* **1** permeable to water, air, or other fluids. **2** having pores. **3** easy to cross or penetrate: *the porous border into Thailand; the most porous defence in the league.* ORIG C14: from Med. L *porōsus,* from LL *porus* PORE[2]
▸ **'porously** *adv* ▸ **porosity** (pɔːˈrɒsɪtɪ) *or* **'porousness** *n*

porphyria (pɔːˈfɪrɪə) *n* a hereditary disease of body metabolism, producing abdominal pain, mental confusion, etc. ORIG C19: from NL, from *porphyrin* a purple substance excreted by patients suffering from this condition, from Gk *porphura* purple

porphyry (ˈpɔːfɪrɪ) *n, pl* **porphyries. 1** a reddish-purple rock consisting of large crystals of feldspar in a finer groundmass of feldspar, hornblende, etc. **2** any igneous rock with large crystals embedded in a finer groundmass of minerals. ORIG C14 *porfurie,* from LL, from Gk *porphuritēs (lithos)* purple (stone), from *porphuros* purple
▸ **ˌporphy'ritic** *adj*

Porphyry ★ (ˈpɔːfɪrɪ) *n* original name *Malchus.* 232–305 A.D., Greek Neo-Platonist philosopher, born in Syria; disciple and biographer of Plotinus.

porpoise (ˈpɔːpəs) *n, pl* **porpoises** *or* **porpoise.** any of various small cetacean mammals having a blunt snout and many teeth. ORIG C14: from F *pourpois,* from Med. L *porcopiscus,* from L *porcus* pig + *piscis* fish

porridge (ˈpɒrɪdʒ) *n* **1** a dish made from oatmeal or another cereal, cooked in water or milk to a thick consistency. **2** *Sl.* a term of imprisonment. ORIG C16: var. (infl. by ME *porray* pottage) of POTTAGE

porringer (ˈpɒrɪndʒə) *n* a small dish, often with a handle, for soup, porridge, etc. ORIG C16: changed from ME *potinger, poteger,* from OF, from *potage* soup; see POTTAGE

Porsena (ˈpɔːsɪnə) *or* **Porsenna** ★ (pɔːˈsɛnə) *n* **Lars** (lɑːz). 6th century B.C., a legendary Etruscan king, alleged to have besieged Rome in a vain attempt to reinstate Tarquinius Superbus on the throne.

port[1] (pɔːt) *n* **1** a town or place alongside navigable water with facilities for the loading and unloading of ships. **2** See **port of entry.** ORIG OE, from L *portus*

port[2] (pɔːt) *n* **1** Also called (formerly): **larboard.** the left side of an aircraft or vessel when facing the nose or bow. Cf. **starboard** (sense 1). ◆ *vb* **2** to turn or be turned towards the port. ORIG C17: from ?

port[3] (pɔːt) *n* a sweet fortified dessert wine. ORIG C17: after *Oporto,* Portugal, from where it came orig.

port[4] (pɔːt) *n* **1** *Naut.* **1a** an opening in the side of a ship, fitted with a watertight door, for access to the holds. **1b** See **porthole** (sense 1). **2** a small opening in a wall, armoured vehicle, etc., for firing through. **3** an aperture by which fluid enters or leaves the cylinder head of an engine, compressor, etc. **4** *Electronics.* a logic circuit for the input and ouput of data. **5** *Chiefly Scot.* a gate in a town or fortress. ORIG OE, from L *porta* gate

port[5] (pɔːt) *vb (tr) Mil.* to carry (a rifle, etc.) in a position diagonally across the body with the muzzle near the left shoulder. ORIG C14: from OF, from *porter* to carry, from L *portāre*

port[6] (pɔːt) *n Austral.* (esp. in Queensland) a suitcase or school case. ORIG C20: shortened from PORTMANTEAU

Port. *abbrev. for:* **1** Portugal. **2** Portuguese.

portable (ˈpɔːtəbᵊl) *adj* **1** able to be carried or moved easily, esp. by hand. **2** (of computer software, files, etc.) able to be transferred from one type of computer system to another. ◆ *n* **3** an article designed to be readily carried by hand, such as a television, typewriter, etc. ORIG C14: from LL *portābilis,* from L *portāre* to carry
▸ **ˌporta'bility** *n* ▸ **'portably** *adv*

Port Adelaide ★ *n* the chief port of South Australia, near Adelaide on St Vincent Gulf. Pop.: 39 000 (latest est.).

Portadown ★ (ˌpɔːtəˈdaʊn) *n* a town in S Northern Ireland, in the district of Armagh. Pop.: 21 299 (1991).

portage (ˈpɔːtɪdʒ) *n* **1** the act of carrying; transport. **2** the cost of carrying or transporting. **3** the transporting of boats, supplies, etc., overland between navigable waterways. **4** the route used for such transport. ◆ *vb* **portages, portaging, portaged. 5** to transport (boats, supplies, etc.) thus. ORIG C15: from F, from OF *porter* to carry

Portakabin (ˈpɔːtəˌkæbɪn) *n Trademark.* a portable building quickly set up for use as a temporary office, etc.

portal (ˈpɔːtᵊl) *n* **1** an entrance, gateway, or doorway, esp. one that is large and impressive. **2** an Internet site providing links to other sites. ◆ *adj* **3** *Anat.* of or relating to a portal vein: *hepatic portal system.* ORIG C14: via OF from Med. L *portāle,* from L *porta* gate

portal vein *n* any vein connecting two capillary networks, esp. in the liver.

portamento (ˌpɔːtəˈmɛntəʊ) *n, pl* **portamenti** (-tɪ). *Music.* a smooth slide from one note to another in which intervening notes are not separately discernible. ORIG C18: from It.: a carrying, from L *portāre* to carry

Port Arthur ★ *n* **1** a former penal settlement (1833–70) in Australia, on the S coast of the Tasman Peninsula, Tasmania. **2** the former name of **Lüshun.**

portative (ˈpɔːtətɪv) *adj* **1** a less common word for **portable. 2** concerned with the act of carrying. ORIG C14: from F, from L *portāre* to carry

Port-au-Prince ★ (ˈpɔːtəʊˈprɪns; *French* pɔrtoprɛ̃s) *n* the capital and chief port of Haiti, in the south on the Gulf of Gonaïves: founded in 1749 by the French; university (1944). Pop.: 846 247 (1995 est.).

Port Blair ★ (blɛə) *n* the capital of the Indian Union Territory of the Andaman and Nicobar Islands, a port on the SE coast of South Andaman Island: a former penal colony. Pop.: 74 955 (1991).

portcullis (pɔːtˈkʌlɪs) *n* an iron or wooden grating suspended vertically in grooves in the gateway of a castle or town and able to be lowered so as to bar the entrance. ORIG C14 *port colice,* from OF *porte coleïce* sliding gate, from *porte* door + *coleïce,* from *couler* to slide, from LL *cōlāre* to filter

Porte (pɔːt) *n* short for Sublime Porte; the court or government of the Ottoman Empire. ORIG C17: shortened from F *Sublime Porte* High Gate, rendering the Turkish title *Babi Ali,* the imperial gate, regarded as the seat of government

porte-cochere (ˌpɔːtkɒˈʃɛə) *n* **1** a large covered entrance for vehicles leading into a courtyard. **2** a large roof projecting over a drive to shelter travellers entering or leaving vehicles. ORIG C17: from F: carriage entrance

Port Elizabeth ★ *n* a port in S South Africa, on Algoa Bay: motor-vehicle manufacture and fruit canning; resort. Pop.: 303 353 (1991).

portend (pɔːˈtɛnd) *vb (tr)* to give warning of; foreshadow. ORIG C15: from L *portendere* to indicate

portent (ˈpɔːtɛnt) *n* **1** a sign of a future event; omen. **2** momentous or ominous significance: *a cry of dire portent.* **3** a marvel. ORIG C16: from L *portentum* sign, from *portendere* to portend

portentous (pɔːˈtɛntəs) *adj* **1** of momentous or ominous significance. **2** miraculous, amazing, or awe-inspiring. **3** self-important or pompous.

porter[1] (ˈpɔːtə) *n* **1** a person employed to carry luggage, parcels, supplies, etc., at a railway station or hotel. **2** (in hospitals) a person employed to move patients from place to place. **3** *US & Canad.* a railway employee who waits on passengers, esp. in a sleeper. ORIG C14: from OF *portour,* from LL *portātōr,* from L *portāre* to carry
▸ **'porterage** *n*

porter[2] (ˈpɔːtə) *n* **1** *Chiefly Brit.* a person in charge of a gate or door; doorman or gatekeeper. **2** a person employed as a caretaker and doorkeeper who also answers inquiries. **3** a person in charge of the maintenance of a building, esp. a block of flats. ORIG C13: from OF *portier,* from LL *portārius,* from L *porta* door

porter[3] ('pɔːtə) *n Brit.* a dark sweet ale brewed from black malt. ORIG C18: from *porter's ale,* apparently because it was a favourite beverage of porters

Porter ★ ('pɔːtə) *n* **1 Cole.** 1893–1964, US composer and lyricist of musical comedies. His most popular songs include *Night and Day* and *Let's Do It.* **2 George,** 1st Baron. born 1920, British chemist, who shared a Nobel prize for chemistry in 1967 for his work on flash photolysis. **3 Katherine Anne.** 1894–1980, US short-story writer and novelist. Her collections of stories include *Flowering Judas* (1930) and *Pale Horse, Pale Rider* (1939). **4 Peter.** born 1929, Australian poet, living in Britain. **5 Rodney Robert.** 1917–85, British biochemist: shared the Nobel prize for physiology or medicine (1972) for determining the structure of an antibody.

porterhouse ('pɔːtəˌhaʊs) *n* **1** Also called: **porterhouse steak.** a thick choice steak of beef cut from the middle ribs or sirloin. **2** (formerly) a place in which porter, beer, etc., and sometimes chops and steaks, were served. ORIG C19 (sense 1): said to be after a porterhouse in New York

portfire ('pɔːtˌfaɪə) *n* a slow-burning fuse used for firing rockets and fireworks and, in mining, for igniting explosives. ORIG C17: from F *porte-feu,* from *porter* to carry + *feu* fire

portfolio (pɔːt'fəʊlɪəʊ) *n, pl* **portfolios. 1** a flat case, esp. of leather, used for carrying maps, drawings, etc. **2** the contents of such a case, such as drawings or photographs, that demonstrate recent work. **3** such a case used for carrying ministerial or state papers. **4** the responsibilities or role of the head of a government department: *the portfolio for foreign affairs.* **5 Minister without portfolio.** a cabinet minister who is not responsible for any government department. **6** the complete investments held by an individual investor or a financial organization. ORIG C18: from It. *portafoglio,* from *portāre* to carry + *foglio* leaf, from L *folium*

portfolio management *n* the service provided by an investment adviser who manages a financial portfolio on behalf of the investor.

Port-Gentil ★ (*French* pɔrʒɑ̃ti) *n* the chief port of Gabon, in the west near the mouth of the Ogooué River: oil refinery. Pop.: 80 841 (1993).

Port Harcourt ★ ('hɑːkət, -kɔːt) *n* a port in S Nigeria, capital of Rivers state on the Niger delta: the nation's second largest port; industrial centre. Pop.: 410 000 (1996 est.).

porthole ('pɔːtˌhəʊl) *n* **1** a small aperture in the side of a vessel to admit light and air, fitted with a watertight cover. Sometimes shortened to **port. 2** an opening in a wall or parapet through which a gun can be fired.

portico ('pɔːtɪkəʊ) *n, pl* **porticoes** *or* **porticos. 1** a covered entrance to a building; porch. **2** a covered walkway in the form of a roof supported by columns or pillars, esp. one built on to the exterior of a building. ORIG C17: via It. from L *porticus*

portière (ˌpɔːtɪ'ɛə; *French* pɔrtjɛr) *n* a curtain hung in a doorway. ORIG C19: via F from Med. L *portāria,* from L *porta* door
▸ ˌ**porti'èred** *adj*

Porţile de Fier ★ (pɔr'tsiːlɛ dɛ 'fjɛr) *n* the Romanian name for the **Iron Gate.**

portion ('pɔːʃən) *n* **1** a part of a whole. **2** a part allotted or belonging to a person or group. **3** an amount of food served to one person; helping. **4** *Law.* **4a** a share of property, esp. one coming to a child from the estate of his parents. **4b** a dowry. **5** a person's lot or destiny. ◆ *vb (tr)* **6** to divide up; share out. **7** to give a share to (a person). ORIG C13: via OF from L *portiō*
▸ '**portionless** *adj*

Port Jackson ★ *n* an inlet of the Pacific on the coast of SE Australia, forming a fine natural harbour: site of the city of Sydney, spanned by Sydney Harbour Bridge.

Portland[1] ★ ('pɔːtlənd) *n* **1 Isle of.** a rugged limestone peninsula in SW England, in Dorset, connected to the mainland by a narrow isthmus and by Chesil Bank: the lighthouse of **Portland Bill** lies at the S tip; famous for the quarrying of **Portland stone,** a fine building material. Pop.: 13 000 (latest est.). **2** an inland port in NW Oregon, on the Willamette River: the largest city in the state; shipbuilding and chemical industries. Pop.: 480 824 (1996 est.). **3** a port in SW Maine, on Casco Bay: the largest city in the state; settled by Englishmen in 1632, destroyed successively by French, Indian, and British attacks, and rebuilt; capital of Maine (1820–32). Pop.: 62 466 (1992 est.).

Portland[2] ★ ('pɔːtlənd) *n* **3rd Duke of.** title of *William Henry Cavendish Bentinck.* 1738–1809, British statesman; prime minister (1783; 1807–09); father of Lord William Cavendish Bentinck.

Portland cement *n* a cement that hardens under water and is made by heating clay and crushed chalk or limestone. ORIG C19: after the Isle of PORTLAND, because its colour resembles that of the stone quarried there

Portlaoise ★ (ˌpɔːt'liːʃə) *n* a town in central Republic of Ireland, county town of Laois: site of a top-security prison. Pop.: 9500 (1990 est.).

Port Louis ★ ('luːɪs, 'luːɪ) *n* the capital and chief port of Mauritius, on the NW coast on the Indian Ocean. Pop.: 145 584 (1995 est.).

portly ('pɔːtlɪ) *adj* **portlier, portliest. 1** stout or corpulent. **2** *Arch.* stately; impressive. ORIG C16: from PORT[5] (in the sense: deportment)
▸ '**portliness** *n*

Port Lyautey ★ (ljəʊ'teɪ) *n* the former name (1932–56) of **Mina Hassan Tani.**

portmanteau (pɔːt'mæntəʊ) *n, pl* **portmanteaus** *or* **portmanteaux** (-təʊz). **1** (formerly) a large travelling case made of stiff leather, esp. one hinged at the back so as to open out into two compartments. **2** (*modifier*) embodying several uses or qualities: *the heroine is a portmanteau figure of all the virtues.* ORIG C16: from F: cloak carrier

portmanteau word *n* another name for **blend** (sense 7). ORIG C19: from the idea that two meanings are packed into one word

Port Moresby ★ ('mɔːzbɪ) *n* the capital and chief port of Papua New Guinea, on the SE coast on the Gulf of Papua: important Allied base in World War II. Pop.: 193 242 (1990).

Port Nicholson ★ *n* **1** the first British settlement in New Zealand, established on Wellington Harbour in 1840: grew into Wellington. **2** the former name for Wellington Harbour.

Pôrto ★ ('portu) *n* the Portuguese name for **Oporto.**

Pôrto Alegre ★ (*Portuguese* 'portu a'lɛgri) *n* a port in S Brazil, capital of the Rio Grande do Sul state: the country's chief inland port; the chief commercial centre of S Brazil, with two universities (1936 and 1948). Pop (city): 1 237 223 (1991); (urban area): 3 349 000 (1995).

Portobello ★ (ˌpɔːtəʊ'bɛləʊ) *n* a small port in Panama, on the Caribbean northeast of Colón: the most important port in South America in colonial times; declined with the opening of the Panama Canal. Pop.: 3026 (1990 est.).

port of call *n* **1** a port where a ship stops. **2** any place visited on a traveller's itinerary.

port of entry *n Law.* an airport, harbour, etc., where customs officials are stationed to supervise the entry into and exit from a country of persons and merchandise.

Port of Spain ★ *n* the capital and chief port of Trinidad and Tobago, on the W coast of Trinidad. Pop.: 52 000 (1995 est.).

Porto Novo ★ ('pɔːtəʊ 'nəʊvəʊ) *n* the capital of Benin, in the southwest on a coastal lagoon: formerly a centre of Portuguese settlement and the slave trade. Pop.: 200 000 (1994 est.).

Porto Rico ★ ('pɔːtə 'riːkəʊ) *n* the former name (until 1932) of **Puerto Rico.**
▸ **Porto Rican** *adj, n*

Pôrto Velho ★ (*Portuguese* 'portu 'vɛʎu) *n* a city in W Brazil, capital of the federal territory of Rondônia on the Madeira River. Pop.: 226 198 (1991).

Port Phillip Bay *or* **Port Phillip** ★ *n* a bay in SE Australia, which forms the harbour of Melbourne.

portrait ('pɔːtrɪt, -treɪt) *n* **1** a painting or other likeness of

an individual, esp. of the face. **2** a verbal description, esp. of a person's character. ◆ *adj* **3** *Printing.* (of an illustration in a book, magazine, etc.) of greater height than width. Cf. **landscape** (sense 5a). ORIG C16: from F, from *portraire* to PORTRAY
▸ **'portraitist** *n*

portraiture ('pɔːtrɪtʃə) *n* **1** the practice or art of making portraits. **2a** a portrait. **2b** portraits collectively. **3** a verbal description.

portray (pɔː'treɪ) *vb* (*tr*) **1** to make a portrait of. **2** to depict in words. **3** to play the part of (a character) in a play or film. ORIG C14: from OF *portraire* to depict, from L *prōtrahere* to drag forth
▸ **por'trayal** *n* ▸ **por'trayer** *n*

Port Royal ★ *n* **1** a fortified town in SE Jamaica, at the entrance to Kingston harbour: capital of Jamaica in colonial times. **2** the former name (until 1710) of **Annapolis Royal.**

Port Said ★ ('sɑːiːd, saɪd) *n* a port in NE Egypt, at the N end of the Suez Canal: founded in 1859 when the Suez Canal was begun; became the largest coaling station in the world and later an oil-bunkering port; damaged in the Arab–Israeli wars of 1967 and 1973. Pop.: 460 000 (1994 est.).

Port-Salut ('pɔː sə'luː; *French* pɔrsaly) *n* a mild semihard whole-milk cheese of a round flat shape. Also called: **Port du Salut.** ORIG C19: named after the Trappist monastery at *Port du Salut* in NW France where it was first made

Portsmouth ★ ('pɔːtsməθ) *n* **1** a port in S England, in Hampshire on the English Channel: Britain's chief naval base; seat of the University of Portsmouth (1992). Pop.: 174 690 (1991). Informal name: **Pompey. 2** a unitary authority in S England, in Hampshire. Pop.: 190 400 (1996 est.). Area: 37 sq. km (14 sq. miles). **3** a port in SE Virginia, on the Elizabeth River: naval base; shipyards. Pop.: 101 308 (1996 est.).

Port Sudan ★ *n* the chief port of the Sudan, in the NE on the Red Sea. Pop.: 305 385 (1993).

Port Talbot ★ ('tɔːlbət, 'tæl-) *n* a port in SE Wales, on Swansea Bay: established as a coal port in the mid-19th century. Pop.: 37 647 (1991).

Portugal ★ ('pɔːtjʊgᵊl) *n* a republic in SW Europe, on the Atlantic: became an independent monarchy in 1139 and expelled the Moors in 1249 after more than four centuries of Muslim rule; became a republic in 1910; under the dictatorship of Salazar from 1932 until 1968, when he was succeeded by Dr Caetano, who was overthrown by a junta in 1974: constitutional government was restored in 1976; a member of the European Union. Official language: Portuguese. Religion: Roman Catholic. Currency: escudo and euro. Capital: Lisbon. Pop.: 9 988 000 (1999 est.). Area: 91 231 sq. km (35 456 sq. miles).

Portuguese (ˌpɔːtjʊ'giːz) *n* **1** the official language of Portugal and Brazil; it belongs to the Romance group of the Indo-European family. **2** (*pl* **Portuguese**) a native, citizen, or inhabitant of Portugal. ◆ *adj* **3** of Portugal, its inhabitants, or their language.

Portuguese East Africa ★ *n* a former name (until 1975) of **Mozambique.**

Portuguese Guinea ★ *n* the former name (until 1974) of **Guinea-Bissau.**
▸ **Portuguese Guinean** *adj, n*

Portuguese India ★ *n* a former Portuguese overseas province on the W coast of India, consisting of Goa, Daman, and Diu: established between 1505 and 1510; annexed by India in 1961.

Portuguese man-of-war *n* any of several large hydrozoans having an aerial float and long stinging tentacles. Sometimes shortened to **man-of-war.**

Portuguese Timor ★ *n* a former name for **East Timor.**

Portuguese West Africa ★ *n* a former name (until 1975) of **Angola.**

portulaca (ˌpɔːtjʊ'lækə, -'leɪkə) *n* any of a genus of plants of tropical and subtropical America, having yellow, pink, or purple showy flowers. ORIG C16: from L: PURSLANE

POS *abbrev. for* point of sale.

pose[1] (pəʊz) *vb* **poses, posing, posed. 1** to assume or cause to assume a physical attitude, as for a photograph or painting. **2** (*intr;* often foll. by *as*) to present oneself (as something one is not). **3** (*intr*) to affect an attitude in order to impress others. **4** (*tr*) to put forward or ask: *to pose a question.* **5** (*intr*) *Sl.* to adopt a particular style of appearance and stand or strut around, esp. in bars, discotheques, etc., in order to attract attention. ◆ *n* **6** a physical attitude, esp. one deliberately adopted for an artist or photographer. **7** a mode of behaviour that is adopted for effect. ORIG C14: from OF *poser* to set in place, from LL *pausāre* to cease, put down (infl. by L *pōnere* to place)

pose[2] (pəʊz) *vb* **poses, posing, posed.** (*tr*) *Rare.* to puzzle or baffle. ORIG C16: from obs. *appose,* from L *appōnere* to put to

Poseidon (pɒ'saɪdᵊn) ★ *n Greek myth.* the god of the sea and of earthquakes; brother of Zeus, Hades, and Hera. He is generally depicted in art wielding a trident. Roman counterpart: **Neptune.**

Posen ★ ('poːzən) *n* the German name for **Poznań.**

poser[1] ('pəʊzə) *n* **1** a person who poses. **2** *Inf.* a person who likes to be seen in trendsetting clothes in fashionable bars, discos, etc.

poser[2] ('pəʊzə) *n* a baffling or insoluble question.

poseur (pəʊ'zɜː) *n* a person who strikes an attitude or assumes a pose in order to impress others. ORIG C19: from F, from *poser* to POSE[1]

posh (pɒʃ) *adj Inf., chiefly Brit.* **1** smart, elegant, or fashionable. **2** upper-class or genteel. ORIG C19: often said to be an acronym of *port out, starboard home,* the most desirable location for a cabin in British ships sailing to & from the East, being the shaded side; but more likely from obs. sl. *posh* (n) a dandy

posit ('pɒzɪt) *vb* (*tr*) **1** to assume or put forward as fact or the factual basis for an argument; postulate. **2** to put in position. ORIG C17: from L *pōnere* to place

position (pə'zɪʃən) *n* **1** place, situation, or location: *he took up a position to the rear.* **2** the appropriate or customary location: *the telescope is in position for use.* **3** the manner in which a person or thing is placed; arrangement. **4** *Mil.* an area or point occupied for tactical reasons. **5** point of view; stand: *what's your position on this issue?* **6** social status, esp. high social standing. **7** a post of employment; job. **8** the act of positing a fact or viewpoint. **9** something posited, such as an idea. **10** *Sport.* the part of a field or playing area where a player is placed or where he generally operates. **11** *Music.* the vertical spacing or layout of the written notes in a chord. **12** (in classical prosody) the situation in which a short vowel may be regarded as long, that is, when it occurs before two or more consonants. **13** *Finance.* the market commitment of a dealer in securities, currencies, or commodities: *a short position.* **14 in a position.** (foll. by an infinitive) able (to). ◆ *vb* (*tr*) **15** to put in the proper or appropriate place; locate. **16** *Sport.* to place (oneself or another player) in a particular part of the field or playing area. ORIG C15: from LL *positiō* a positioning, affirmation, from *pōnere* to place
▸ **po'sitional** *adj*

positional notation *n* the method of denoting numbers by the use of a finite number of digits, each digit having its value multiplied by its place value, as in 936 = (9 × 100) + (3 × 10) + 6.

position audit *n Commerce.* a systematic assessment of the current strengths and weaknesses of an organization as a prerequisite for future strategic planning.

positive ('pɒzɪtɪv) *adj* **1** expressing certainty or affirmation: *a positive answer.* **2** possessing actual or specific qualities; real: *a positive benefit.* **3** tending to emphasize what is good or laudable; constructive: *he takes a very positive attitude when correcting pupils' mistakes.* **4** tending towards progress or improvement. **5** *Philosophy.* constructive rather than sceptical. **6** (*prenominal*) *Inf.* (intensifier): *a positive delight.* **7** *Maths.* having a value greater than zero: *a positive number.* **8** *Maths.* **8a** measured in a direction opposite to that regarded as negative. **8b** having

the same magnitude as but opposite sense to an equivalent negative quantity. **9** *Grammar.* denoting the usual form of an adjective as opposed to its comparative or superlative form. **10** *Physics.* **10a** (of an electric charge) having an opposite polarity to the charge of an electron and the same polarity as the charge of a proton. **10b** (of a body, system, ion, etc.) having a positive electric charge. **11** short for **electropositive.** **12** *Med.* (of the results of an examination or test) indicating the presence of a suspected disorder or organism. **13** *Economics.* of or denoting an analysis that is free of ethical, political, or value judgments. ◆ *n* **14** something that is positive. **15** *Maths.* a quantity greater than zero. **16** *Photog.* a print or slide showing a photographic image whose colours or tones correspond to those of the original subject. **17** *Grammar.* the positive degree of an adjective or adverb. **18** a positive object, such as a terminal or plate in a voltaic cell. ORIG C13: from LL *positīvus,* from *pōnere* to place
▸ **'positiveness** *or* **,posi'tivity** *n*

positive discrimination *n* the provision of special opportunities for a disadvantaged group.

positive feedback *n* See **feedback** (sense 2).

positively ('pɒzɪtɪvlɪ) *adv* **1** in a positive manner. **2** (intensifier): *he disliked her; in fact, he positively hated her.*

positive vetting *n* the checking of a person's background, to assess his suitability for a position that may involve national security.

positivism ('pɒzɪtɪ,vɪzəm) *n* **1** a form of empiricism, esp. as established by Auguste Comte, that rejects metaphysics and theology and holds that experimental investigation and observation are the only sources of substantial knowledge. See also **logical positivism.** **2** the quality of being definite, certain, etc.
▸ **'positivist** *n, adj*

positron ('pɒzɪ,trɒn) *n Physics.* the antiparticle of the electron, having the same mass but an equal and opposite charge. ORIG C20: from *posi(tive + elec)tron*

positron emission tomography *n* a technique for assessing brain activity and function by recording the emission of positrons when radioactively labelled glucose, introduced into the brain, is metabolized.

positronium (,pɒzɪ'trəʊnɪəm) *n Physics.* a short-lived entity consisting of a positron and an electron bound together.

posology (pə'sɒlədʒɪ) *n* the branch of medicine concerned with the determination of appropriate doses of drugs or agents. ORIG C19: from F *posologie,* from Gk *posos* how much

poss. *abbrev. for:* **1** possession. **2** possessive. **3** possible. **4** possibly.

posse ('pɒsɪ) *n* **1** *US.* short for **posse comitatus,** the able-bodied men of a district forming a group upon whom the sheriff may call for assistance in maintaining law and order. **2** *Sl.* a Jamaican street gang in the US. **3** *Inf.* a group of friends or associates. **4** (in W Canada) a troop of trained horses and riders who perform at stampedes. **5** *Law.* possibility (esp. in **in posse**). ORIG C16: from Med. L (n): power, from L (vb): to be able

posse comitatus (,kɒmɪ'tɑːtəs) *n* the formal legal term for **posse** (sense 1). ORIG Med. L: strength (manpower) of the county

possess (pə'zɛs) *vb (tr)* **1** to have as one's property; own. **2** to have as a quality, characteristic, etc.: *to possess good eyesight.* **3** to have knowledge of: *to possess a little French.* **4** to gain control over or dominate: *whatever possessed you to act so foolishly?* **5** (foll. by *of*) to cause to be the owner or possessor: *I am possessed of the necessary information.* **6** to have sexual intercourse with. **7** *Now rare.* to maintain (oneself or one's feelings) in a certain state or condition: *possess yourself in patience until I tell you the news.* ORIG C15: from OF *possesser,* from L *possidēre*
▸ **pos'sessor** *n* ▸ **pos'sessory** *adj*

possessed (pə'zɛst) *adj* **1** (foll. by *of*) owning or having. **2** (*usually postpositive*) under the influence of a powerful force, such as a spirit or strong emotion. **3** a less common term for **self-possessed.**

possession (pə'zɛʃən) *n* **1** the act of possessing or state of being possessed: *in possession of the crown.* **2** anything that is owned or possessed. **3** (*pl*) wealth or property. **4** the state of being controlled by or as if by evil spirits. **5** the occupancy of land, property, etc., whether or not accompanied by ownership: *to take possession of a house.* **6** a territory subject to a foreign state: *colonial possessions.* **7** *Sport.* control of the ball, puck, etc., as exercised by a player or team: *he got possession in his own half.*

possessive (pə'zɛsɪv) *adj* **1** of or relating to possession. **2** having or showing an excessive desire to possess or dominate: *a possessive husband.* **3** *Grammar.* **3a** another word for **genitive.** **3b** denoting an inflected form of a noun or pronoun used to convey the idea of possession, association, etc., as *my* or *Harry's.* ◆ *n* **4** *Grammar.* **4a** the possessive case. **4b** a word or speech element in the possessive case.
▸ **pos'sessively** *adv* ▸ **pos'sessiveness** *n*

posset ('pɒsɪt) *n* a drink of hot milk curdled with ale, beer, etc., flavoured with spices, formerly used as a remedy for colds. ORIG C15 *poshoote,* from ?

possibility (,pɒsɪ'bɪlɪtɪ) *n, pl* **possibilities.** **1** the state or condition of being possible. **2** anything that is possible. **3** a competitor, candidate, etc., who has a moderately good chance of winning, being chosen, etc. **4** (*often pl*) a future prospect or potential: *my new house has great possibilities.*

possible ('pɒsɪbᵊl) *adj* **1** capable of existing, taking place, or proving true without contravention of any natural law. **2** capable of being achieved: *it is not possible to finish in three weeks.* **3** having potential: *the idea is a possible money-spinner.* **4** feasible but less than probable: *it is possible that man will live on Mars.* **5** *Logic.* (of a statement, formula, etc.) capable of being true under some interpretation or in some circumstances. ◆ *n* **6** another word for **possibility** (sense 3). ORIG C14: from L *possibilis* that may be, from *posse* to be able

> **USAGE NOTE** Although it is very common to talk about something being *very possible* or *more possible,* these uses are thought by some to be incorrect, since *possible* describes an absolute state, and therefore something can only be *possible* or *not possible: it is very likely* (not *very possible*) *that he will resign; it has now become easier* (not *more possible*) *to obtain an entry visa.*

possibly ('pɒsɪblɪ) *sentence substitute, adv* **1a** perhaps or maybe. **1b** (*as sentence modifier*): *possibly he'll come.* ◆ *adv* **2** by any chance; at all: *he can't possibly come.*

possum ('pɒsəm) *n* **1** an informal name for **opossum.** **2** an Australian and New Zealand name for **phalanger.** **3 play possum.** to pretend to be dead, ignorant, asleep, etc., in order to deceive an opponent. **4 stir the possum** *Austral. sl.* to cause trouble.

post[1] (pəʊst) *n* **1** a length of wood, metal, etc., fixed upright to serve as a support, marker, point of attachment, etc. **2** *Horse racing.* **2a** either of two upright poles marking the beginning (**starting post**) and end (**winning post**) of a racecourse. **2b** the finish of a horse race. ◆ *vb (tr)* **3** (sometimes foll. by *up*) to fasten or put up (a notice) in a public place. **4** to announce by or as if by means of a poster: *to post banns.* **5** to publish (a name) on a list. **6** to denounce publicly; brand. ORIG OE, from L *postis*

post[2] (pəʊst) *n* **1** a position to which a person is appointed or elected; appointment; job. **2** a position to which a person, such as a sentry, is assigned for duty. **3** a permanent military establishment. **4** *Brit.* either of two military bugle calls (**first post** and **last post**) giving notice of the time to retire for the night. **5** See **trading post.** ◆ *vb* **6** *(tr)* to assign to or station at a particular place or position. **7** *Chiefly Brit.* to transfer to a different unit or ship on taking up a new appointment, etc. ORIG C16: from F *poste,* from It. *posto,* ult. from L *pōnere* to place

post[3] (pəʊst) *n* **1** *Chiefly Brit.* letters, packages, etc., that are transported and delivered by the Post Office; mail. **2** *Chiefly Brit.* a single collection or delivery of mail. **3** *Brit.* an official system of mail delivery. **4** (formerly) any of a series of stations furnishing relays of men and horses to deliver mail over a fixed route. **5** a rider who carried mail between such stations. **6** *Brit.* a postbox or post office: *take this to the post.* **7** any of various book sizes, esp. 5¼ by

8¼ inches (**post octavo**). **8 by return of post.** *Brit.* by the next mail in the opposite direction. ◆ *vb* **9** (*tr*) *Chiefly Brit.* to send by post. US and Canad. word: **mail.** **10** (*tr*) *Book-keeping.* **10a** to enter (an item) in a ledger. **10b** (often foll. by *up*) to compile or enter all paper items in (a ledger). **11** (*tr*) to inform of the latest news. **12** (*intr*) (formerly) to travel with relays of post horses. **13** *Arch.* to travel or dispatch with speed; hasten. ◆ *adv* **14** with speed; rapidly. **15** (formerly) by means of post horses. ORIG C16: via F from It. *poste,* from L *posita* something placed, from *pōnere* to put

post- *prefix* **1** after in time or sequence; following; subsequent: *postgraduate.* **2** behind; posterior to: *postorbital.* ORIG from L, from *post* after, behind

postage ('pəʊstɪdʒ) *n* **a** the charge for delivering a piece of mail. **b** (*as modifier*): *postage charges.*

postage meter *n Chiefly US & Canad.* a postal franking machine. Also called: **postal meter.**

postage stamp *n* **1** a printed paper label with a gummed back for attaching to mail as an official indication that the required postage has been paid. **2** a mark printed on an envelope, etc., serving the same function.

postal ('pəʊstᵊl) *adj* of or relating to a Post Office or to the mail-delivery service.
▸ **'postally** *adv*

postal note *n Austral.* the usual name for **postal order.**

postal order *n* a written order for the payment of a sum of money, to a named payee, obtainable and payable at a post office.

postbag ('pəʊstˌbæg) *n* **1** *Chiefly Brit.* another name for **mailbag. 2** the mail received by a magazine, radio programme, public figure, etc.

postbox ('pəʊstˌbɒks) *n* another name for **letter box** (sense 2).

postcard ('pəʊstˌkɑːd) *n* a card, often bearing a photograph, picture, etc., on one side (**picture postcard**), for sending a message by post without an envelope. Also called (US): **postal card.**

post chaise *n* a closed four-wheeled horse-drawn coach used as a rapid means for transporting mail and passengers in the 18th and 19th centuries. ORIG C18: from POST[3] + CHAISE

postclassical (pəʊst'klæsɪkᵊl) *adj* (esp. of Greek or Roman literature) later than the classical period.

postcode ('pəʊstˌkəʊd) *n* a code of letters and digits used as part of a postal address to aid the sorting of mail. Also called: **postal code.** US name: **zip code.**

postconsonantal (pəʊstˌkɒnsə'næntᵊl) *adj* (of a speech sound) immediately following a consonant.

postdate (pəʊst'deɪt) *vb* **postdates, postdating, postdated.** (*tr*) **1** to write a future date on (a document, etc.), as on a cheque to prevent it being paid until then. **2** to assign a date to (an event, period, etc.) that is later than its previously assigned date of occurrence. **3** to be or occur at a later date than.

postdoctoral (pəʊst'dɒktərəl) *adj* of, relating to, or designating studies, research, or professional work above the level of a doctorate.

poster ('pəʊstə) *n* **1** a large printed picture, used for decoration. **2** a placard or bill posted in a public place as an advertisement. **3** a person who posts bills.

poster boy *or* (*fem*) **poster girl** *n* **1** a person who appears on a poster. **2** a person who typifies or represents a particular characteristic, cause, opinion, etc.: *a poster girl for late motherhood.* ◆ Also called: **poster child.**

poste restante ('pəʊst rɪ'stænt) *n* **1** an address on mail indicating that it should be kept at a specified post office until collected by the addressee. **2** the mail-delivery service or post-office department that handles mail having this address. ◆ US and Canad. equivalent: **general delivery.** ORIG F, lit.: mail remaining

posterior (pɒ'stɪərɪə) *adj* **1** situated at the back of or behind something. **2** coming after or following another in a series. **3** coming after in time. ◆ *n* **4** the buttocks; rump. ORIG C16: from L: latter, from *posterus* coming next, from *post* after
▸ **pos'teriorly** *adv*

posterity (pɒ'stɛrɪtɪ) *n* **1** future or succeeding generations. **2** all of one's descendants. ORIG C14: from F *postérité,* from L *posteritās,* from *posterus* coming after, from *post* after

postern ('pɒstən) *n* a back door or gate, esp. one that is for private use. ORIG C13: from OF *posterne,* from LL *posterula (jānua)* a back (entrance), from *posterus* coming behind

poster paint *or* **colour** *n* a gum-based opaque watercolour paint used for writing posters, etc.

postfeminist (pəʊst'fɛmɪnɪst) *adj* **1** resulting from or including the beliefs and ideas of feminism. **2** differing from or showing moderation of these beliefs and ideas. ◆ *n* **3** a person who believes in or advocates any of the ideas that have developed from the feminist movement.

post-Fordism (pəʊst'fɔːdˌɪzəm) *n* the idea that modern industrial production has moved away from mass production in huge factories, as pioneered by Henry Ford, towards specialized markets based on small flexible manufacturing units.
▸ **post-'Fordist** *adj*

post-free *adv, adj* **1** *Brit.* with the postage prepaid; postpaid. **2** free of postal charge.

postglacial (pəʊst'gleɪsɪəl, -ʃəl) *adj* formed or occurring after a glacial period.

postgraduate (pəʊst'grædjʊɪt) *n* **1** a student who has obtained a degree from a university, etc., and is pursuing studies for a more advanced qualification. **2** (*modifier*) of or relating to such a student or his or her studies. ◆ Also (US and Canad.): **graduate.**

posthaste ('pəʊst'heɪst) *adv* **1** with great haste. ◆ *n* **2** *Arch.* great haste.

post horn *n* a simple valveless natural horn consisting of a long tube of brass or copper.

post horse *n* (formerly) a horse kept at an inn or post house for use by postriders or for hire to travellers.

post house *n* (formerly) a house or inn where horses were kept for postriders or for hire to travellers.

posthumous ('pɒstjʊməs) *adj* **1** happening or continuing after one's death. **2** (of a book, etc.) published after the author's death. **3** (of a child) born after the father's death. ORIG C17: from L *postumus* the last, but modified as though from L *post* after + *humus* earth, that is, after the burial
▸ **'posthumously** *adv*

posthypnotic suggestion (ˌpəʊsthɪp'nɒtɪk) *n* a suggestion made to the subject while he is in a hypnotic trance, to be acted upon at some time after emerging from the trance.

postiche (pɒ'stiːʃ) *adj* **1** (of architectural ornament) inappropriately applied; sham. **2** false or artificial; spurious. ◆ *n* **3** another term for **hairpiece** (sense 2). **4** anything that is false; sham or pretence. ORIG C19: from F, from It. *apposticcio* (n), from LL *appositīcius* (adj); see APPOSITE

postilion *or* **postillion** (pɒ'stɪljən) *n* a person who rides the near horse of the leaders in order to guide a team of horses drawing a coach. ORIG C16: from F *postillon,* from It. *postiglione,* from *posta* POST[3]

postimpressionism (ˌpəʊstɪm'prɛʃəˌnɪzəm) *n* a movement in painting in France at the end of the 19th century which rejected the naturalism and momentary effects of impressionism but adapted its use of pure colour to paint subjects with greater subjective emotion.
▸ **ˌpostim'pressionist** *n, adj*

post-industrial (ˌpəʊstɪn'dʌstrɪəl) *adj* denoting work or a society that is no longer based on heavy industry.

posting ('pəʊstɪŋ) *n* **1** an appointment to a position or post, usually in another town or country. **2** *Computing.* an electronic message sent to a bulletin board, website, etc., and intended for access by every user.

postliminy (pəʊst'lɪmɪnɪ) *or* **postliminium** (ˌpəʊstlɪ'mɪnɪəm) *n, pl* **postliminies** *or* **postliminia** (-ɪə). *International law.* the right by which persons and property seized in war are restored to their former status on recovery. ORIG C17: from L *post* behind + *limen, liminis* threshold

postlude ('pəʊstluːd) *n Music.* a final or concluding piece or movement. ORIG C19: from POST- + *-lude,* from L *lūdus* game; cf. PRELUDE

postman ('pəʊstmən) *or (fem)* **postwoman** *n, pl* **postmen** *or* **postwomen.** a person who carries and delivers mail as a profession.

postman's knock *n* a children's party game in which a kiss is exchanged for a pretend letter.

postmark ('pəʊstˌmɑːk) *n* **1** any mark stamped on mail by postal officials, usually showing the date and place of posting. ◆ *vb* **2** (*tr*) to put such a mark on (mail).

postmaster ('pəʊstˌmɑːstə) *n* **1** Also (*fem*) **postmistress.** an official in charge of a local post office. **2** the person responsible for managing the electronic mail at a site.

postmaster general *n, pl* **postmasters general.** the executive head of the postal service in certain countries.

postmeridian (ˌpəʊstmə'rɪdɪən) *adj* after noon; in the afternoon or evening. ORIG C17: from L *postmerīdiānus* in the afternoon

post meridiem ('pəʊst mə'rɪdɪəm) the full form of **p.m.** ORIG C17: L: after noon

post mill *n* a windmill built around a central post on which the whole mill can be turned so that the sails catch the wind.

postmillennialism (ˌpəʊstmɪ'lɛnɪəˌlɪzəm) *n Christian theol.* the doctrine or belief that the Second Coming of Christ will be preceded by the millennium.
▸ **ˌpostmil'lennialist** *n*

postmodernism (pəʊst'mɒdəˌnɪzəm) *n* (in the arts, architecture, etc.) a style and school of thought that rejects the dogma and practices of any form of modernism; in architecture it contrasts with international modernism and features elements from several periods, esp. the Classical, often with ironic use of decoration.
▸ **post'modernist** *n, adj*

postmortem (pəʊst'mɔːtəm) *adj* **1** (*prenominal*) occurring after death. ◆ *n* **2** analysis or study of a recent event: *a postmortem on a game of chess.* **3** See **postmortem examination.** ORIG C18: from L, lit.: after death

postmortem examination *n* dissection and examination of a dead body to determine the cause of death. Also called: **autopsy, necropsy.**

postnatal (pəʊst'neɪtᵊl) *adj* of or relating to the period after childbirth.

post-obit (pəʊst'əʊbɪt, -'ɒbɪt) *Chiefly law.* ◆ *n* **1** a bond given by a borrower, payable after the death of a specified person, esp. one given to a moneylender by an expectant heir promising to repay when his interest falls into possession. ◆ *adj* **2** taking effect after death. ORIG C18: from L *post obitum* after death

post office *n* a building or room where postage stamps are sold and other postal business is conducted.

Post Office *n* a government department or authority in many countries responsible for postal services and often telecommunications.

post office box *n* a private numbered place in a post office, in which letters received are kept until called for.

postoperative (pəʊst'ɒpərətɪv) *adj* of or occurring in the period following a surgical operation.

post-paid *adv, adj* with the postage prepaid.

postpone (pəʊst'pəʊn, pə'spəʊn) *vb* **postpones, postponing, postponed.** (*tr*) **1** to put off or delay until a future time. **2** to put behind in order of importance; defer. ORIG C16: from L *postpōnere* to put after
▸ **post'ponement** *n*

postpositive (pəʊst'pɒzɪtɪv) *adj* **1** (of an adjective or other modifier) placed after the word modified, either immediately after, as in *two men abreast,* or as part of a complement, as in *those men are bad.* ◆ *n* **2** a postpositive modifier.

postprandial (pəʊst'prændɪəl) *adj usually humorous.* after a meal.

postrider ('pəʊstˌraɪdə) *n* (formerly) a person who delivered post on horseback.

postscript ('pəʊsˌskrɪpt, 'pəʊst-) *n* **1** a message added at the end of a letter, after the signature. **2** any supplement, as to a document or book. ORIG C16: from LL *postscribere* to write after

poststructuralism (pəʊst'strʌktʃərəˌlɪzəm) *n* an approach to literature that, proceeding from the tenets of structuralism, maintains that, as words have no absolute meaning, any text is open to an unlimited range of interpretations.
▸ **post'structuralist** *n, adj*

post-traumatic stress disorder *n* a psychological condition, characterized by anxiety, withdrawal, and a proneness to physical illness, that may follow a traumatic experience.

postulant ('pɒstjʊlənt) *n* a person who makes a request or application, esp. a candidate for admission to a religious order. ORIG C18: from L *postulāns* asking, from *postulāre* to ask

postulate *vb* ('pɒstjʊˌleɪt), **postulates, postulating, postulated.** (*tr; may take a clause as object*) **1** to assume to be true or existent; take for granted. **2** to ask, demand, or claim. **3** to nominate (a person) to a post or office subject to approval by a higher authority. ◆ *n* ('pɒstjʊlɪt). **4** something taken as self-evident or assumed as the basis of an argument. **5** a prerequisite. **6** a fundamental principle. **7** *Logic, maths.* an unproved statement that should be taken for granted: used as an initial premise in a process of reasoning. ORIG C16: from L *postulāre* to ask for
▸ **ˌpostu'lation** *n*

postulator ('pɒstjʊˌleɪtə) *n RC Church.* a person who presents a plea for the beatification or canonization of some deceased person.

posture ('pɒstʃə) *n* **1** a position or attitude of the limbs or body. **2** a characteristic manner of bearing the body: *good posture.* **3** the disposition of the parts of a visible object. **4** a mental attitude. **5** a state or condition. **6** a false or affected attitude; pose. ◆ *vb* **postures, posturing, postured. 7** to assume or cause to assume a bodily attitude. **8** (*intr*) to assume an affected posture; pose. ORIG C17: via F from It. *postura,* from L *positūra,* from *pōnere* to place
▸ **'postural** *adj* ▸ **'posturer** *n*

postviral syndrome (ˌpəʊst'vaɪrəl) *n* another name for **chronic fatigue syndrome.** Abbrev.: **PVS.**

postwar (pəʊst'wɔː) *adj* happening or existing after a war.

posy ('pəʊzɪ) *n, pl* **posies. 1** a small bunch of flowers. **2** *Arch.* a brief motto or inscription, esp. one on a trinket or a ring. ORIG C16: var. of POESY

pot[1] (pɒt) *n* **1** a container, usually round and deep and often having a handle and lid, used for cooking and other domestic purposes. **2** the amount that a pot will hold; potful. **3** a large mug or tankard. **4** *Austral.* any of various measures used for serving beer. **5** the money or stakes in the pool in gambling games. **6** a wicker trap for catching fish, esp. crustaceans: *a lobster pot.* **7** *Billiards, etc.* a shot by which a ball is pocketed. **8** a chamber pot, esp. a small one designed for a baby or toddler. **9** (*often pl*) *Inf.* a large amount (esp. of money). **10** *Inf.* a prize or trophy. **11** *Chiefly Brit.* short for **chimneypot. 12** short for **flowerpot, teapot. 13** See **potbelly. 14 go to pot.** to go to ruin. ◆ *vb* **pots, potting, potted.** (*mainly tr*) **15** to put or preserve (meat, etc.) in a pot. **16** to plant (a cutting, seedling, etc.) in soil in a flowerpot. **17** to cause (a baby or toddler) to use or sit on a pot. **18** to shoot (game) for food rather than for sport. **19** (*also intr*) to shoot casually or without careful aim. **20** (*also intr*) to shape clay as a potter. **21** *Billiards, etc.* to pocket (a ball). **22** *Inf.* to capture or win. ORIG LOE *pott,* from Med. L *pottus* (unattested), ?from L *pōtus* a drink

pot[2] (pɒt) *n Sl.* cannabis used as a drug in any form. ORIG C20: ? shortened from Mexican Indian *potiguaya*

potable ('pəʊtəbᵊl) *adj* drinkable. ORIG C16: from LL *pōtābilis* drinkable, from L *pōtāre* to drink
▸ **ˌpota'bility** *n*

potae ('pɔtaɪ) *n NZ.* a hat. ORIG Maori

potage *French.* (pɔtaʒ; *English* pəʊ'tɑːʒ) *n* any thick soup. ORIG C16: from OF; see POTTAGE

potamic (pə'tæmɪk) *adj* of or relating to rivers. ORIG C19: from Gk *potamos* river

potash ('pɒtˌæʃ) *n* **1** another name for **potassium carbonate**

or **potassium hydroxide. 2** potassium chemically combined in certain compounds: *chloride of potash.* ORIG C17 *pot ashes,* translation of obs. Du. *potaschen;* because orig. obtained by evaporating the lye of wood ashes in pots

potassium (pəˈtæsɪəm) *n* a light silvery element of the alkali metal group that is highly reactive and rapidly oxidizes in air. Symbol: K; atomic no.: 19; atomic wt.: 39.098. ORIG C19: NL *potassa* potash
▸ **poˈtassic** *adj*

potassium-argon dating *n* a technique for determining the age of minerals based on the occurrence in natural potassium of a small fixed amount of radioisotope ^{40}K that decays to the stable argon isotope ^{40}Ar with a half-life of 1.28×10^9 years. Measurement of the ratio of these isotopes thus gives the age of the mineral.

potassium bromide *n* a white crystalline soluble substance with a bitter saline taste used in making photographic papers and plates and in medicine as a sedative. Formula: KBr.

potassium carbonate *n* a white odourless substance used in making glass and soft soap and as an alkaline cleansing agent. Formula: K_2CO_3.

potassium chlorate *n* a white crystalline soluble substance used in explosives and as a disinfectant and bleaching agent. Formula: $KClO_3$.

potassium cyanide *n* a white poisonous granular soluble solid substance used in photography. Formula: KCN.

potassium hydrogen tartrate *n* a white soluble crystalline salt used in baking powders, soldering fluxes, and laxatives. Formula: $KHC_4H_4O_6$. Also called: **cream of tartar.**

potassium hydroxide *n* a white deliquescent alkaline solid used in the manufacture of soap, liquid shampoos, and detergents. Formula: KOH.

potassium nitrate *n* a colourless or white crystalline compound used in gunpowders, pyrotechnics, fertilizers, and as a preservative for foods (**E 252**). Formula: KNO_3. Also called: **saltpetre, nitre.**

potassium permanganate *n* a dark purple poisonous odourless soluble crystalline solid, used as a bleach, disinfectant, and antiseptic. Formula: $KMnO_4$. Systematic name: **potassium manganate(VII).**

potation (pəʊˈteɪʃən) *n* **1** the act of drinking. **2** a drink or draught, esp. of alcoholic drink. ORIG C15: from L *pōtātiō,* from *pōtāre* to drink

potato (pəˈteɪtəʊ) *n, pl* **potatoes. 1a** a plant of South America widely cultivated for its edible tubers. **1b** the starchy oval tuber of this plant, which has a brown or red skin and is cooked and eaten as a vegetable. **2** any of various similar plants, esp. the sweet potato. ORIG C16: from Sp. *patata* white potato, from Taino *batata* sweet potato

potato beetle *n* another name for the **Colorado beetle.**

potato chip *n* (*usually pl*) **1** another name for **chip** (sense 4). **2** the US, Canad., Austral., and NZ term for **crisp** (sense 10).

potato crisp *n* (*usually pl*) another name for **crisp** (sense 10).

potbelly (ˈpɒtˌbɛlɪ) *n, pl* **potbellies. 1** a protruding or distended belly. **2** a person having such a belly.
▸ **ˈpotˌbellied** *adj*

potboiler (ˈpɒtˌbɔɪlə) *n Inf.* an artistic work of little merit produced quickly to make money.

pot-bound *adj* (of a pot plant) having grown to fill all the available root space and therefore lacking room for continued growth.

potboy (ˈpɒtˌbɔɪ) *or* **potman** (ˈpɒtmən) *n, pl* **potboys** *or* **potmen.** *Chiefly Brit.* (esp. formerly) a man employed at a public house to serve beer, etc.

potch (pɒtʃ) *n Chiefly Austral., sl.* inferior quality opal. ORIG C20: from ?

poteen (ˈpɒtiːn) *or* **poitín** (pɒˈtʃiːn) *n* (in Ireland) illicit spirit, often distilled from potatoes. ORIG C19: from Irish *poitín* little pot, from *pota* pot

Potemkin *or* **Potyomkin** ★ (pɒˈtɛmkɪn; *Russian* paˈtjɔmkin) *n* **Grigori Aleksandrovich** (griˈgɔrij alɪkˈsandrəvitʃ). 1739–91, Russian soldier and statesman; lover of Catherine II, whose favourite he remained until his death.

potent¹ (ˈpəʊtᵊnt) *adj* **1** possessing great strength; powerful. **2** (of arguments, etc.) persuasive or forceful. **3** influential or authoritative. **4** tending to produce violent physical or chemical effects: *a potent poison.* **5** (of a male) capable of having sexual intercourse. ORIG C15: from L *potēns* able, from *posse* to be able
▸ **ˈpotency** *or* **ˈpotence** *n* ▸ **ˈpotently** *adv*

potent² (ˈpəʊtᵊnt) *adj Heraldry.* (of a cross) having flat bars across the ends of the arms. ORIG C17: from obs. *potent* a crutch, from L *potentia* power

potentate (ˈpəʊtᵊnˌteɪt) *n* a ruler or monarch. ORIG C14: from LL *potentātus,* from L: rule, from *potens* powerful, from *posse* to be able

potential (pəˈtɛnʃəl) *adj* **1a** possible but not yet actual. **1b** (*prenominal*) capable of being or becoming; latent. **2** *Grammar.* (of a verb) expressing possibility, as English *may* and *might.* ◆ *n* **3** latent but unrealized ability: *Jones has great potential as a sales manager.* **4** *Grammar.* a potential verb or verb form. **5** short for **electric potential.** ORIG C14: from OF *potencial,* from LL *potentiālis,* from L *potentia* power
▸ **poˈtentially** *adv*

potential difference *n* the difference in electric potential between two points in an electric field; the work that has to be done in transferring unit positive charge from one point to the other, measured in volts. Abbrev.: **pd.**

potential energy *n* the energy of a body or system as a result of its position in an electric, magnetic, or gravitational field. Abbrev.: **PE.**

potentiality (pəˌtɛnʃɪˈælɪtɪ) *n, pl* **potentialities. 1** latent or inherent capacity for growth, fulfilment, etc. **2** a person or thing that possesses this.

potentiate (pəˈtɛnʃɪˌeɪt) *vb* **potentiates, potentiating, potentiated.** (*tr*) **1** to cause to be potent. **2** *Med.* to increase (the individual action or effectiveness) of two drugs by administering them in combination.

potentilla (ˌpəʊtᵊnˈtɪlə) *n* any rosaceous plant or shrub of the N temperate genus *Potentilla,* having five-petalled flowers. ORIG C16: NL, from Med. L: garden valerian, from L *potēns* powerful

potentiometer (pəˌtɛnʃɪˈɒmɪtə) *n* **1** an instrument for determining a potential difference of electromotive force. **2** a device used in electronic circuits, esp. as a volume control. Sometimes shortened to **pot.**
▸ **poˌtentiˈometry** *n*

potful (ˈpɒtfʊl) *n* the amount held by a pot.

pother (ˈpɒðə) *n* **1** a commotion, fuss, or disturbance. **2** a choking cloud of smoke, dust, etc. ◆ *vb* **3** to make or be troubled or upset. ORIG C16: from ?

potherb (ˈpɒtˌhɜːb) *n* any plant having leaves, flowers, stems, etc., that are used in cooking.

pothole (ˈpɒtˌhəʊl) *n* **1** *Geog.* **1a** a deep hole in limestone areas resulting from action by running water. **1b** a circular hole in the bed of a river produced by abrasion. **2** a deep hole produced in a road surface by wear or weathering.

potholing (ˈpɒtˌhəʊlɪŋ) *n Brit.* a sport in which participants explore underground caves.
▸ **ˈpotˌholer** *n*

pothook (ˈpɒtˌhʊk) *n* **1** a curved or S-shaped hook used for suspending a pot over a fire. **2** a long hook used for lifting hot pots, lids, etc. **3** an S-shaped mark, often made by children when learning to write.

pothouse (ˈpɒtˌhaʊs) *n Brit.* (formerly) a small tavern or pub.

pothunter (ˈpɒtˌhʌntə) *n* **1** a person who hunts for profit without regard to the rules of sport. **2** *Inf.* a person who enters competitions for the sole purpose of winning prizes.

potion (ˈpəʊʃən) *n* a drink, esp. of medicine, poison, or some supposedly magic beverage. ORIG C13: via OF from L *pōtiō* a drink, esp. a poisonous one, from *pōtāre* to drink

Potiphar ★ ('pɒtɪfə) *n Old Testament.* one of Pharaoh's officers, who bought Joseph as a slave (Genesis 37:36).

potlatch ('pɒtˌlætʃ) *n Anthropol.* a competitive ceremonial activity among certain North American Indians, involving a lavish distribution of gifts to emphasize the wealth and status of the chief or clan. ORIG C19: of Amerind origin, from *patshatl* a present

pot luck *n Inf.* **1** whatever food happens to be available without special preparation. **2** whatever is available (esp. in **take pot luck**).

pot marigold *n* a Central European and Mediterranean plant grown for its rayed orange-and-yellow showy flowers.

Potomac ★ (pə'təʊmək) *n* a river in the E central US, rising in the Appalachian Mountains of West Virginia: flows northeast, then generally southeast to Chesapeake Bay. Length (from the confluence of headstreams): 462 km (287 miles).

potometer (pə'tɒmɪtə) *n* an apparatus that measures the rate of water uptake by a plant or plant part. ORIG from L *pōtāre* to drink + -METER

potoroo (ˌpɒtə'ruː) *n* another name for **kangaroo rat.** ORIG from Abor.

Potosí ★ (*Spanish* poto'si) *n* a city in S Bolivia, at an altitude of 4066 m (13 340 ft): one of the highest cities in the world; developed with the discovery of local silver in 1545; tin mining; university (1571). Pop.: 123 327 (1993 est.).

potpourri (ˌpəʊ'pʊərɪ) *n, pl* **potpourris. 1** a collection of mixed flower petals dried and preserved in a pot to scent the air. **2** a collection of unrelated items; miscellany. **3** a medley of popular tunes. ORIG C18: from F, lit.: rotten pot, translation of Sp. *olla podrida* miscellany

pot roast *n* meat cooked slowly in a covered pot with very little water.

Potsdam ★ ('pɒtsdæm; *German* 'pɔtsdam) *n* a city in Germany, the capital of Brandenburg on the Havel River: residence of Prussian kings and German emperors and scene of the **Potsdam Conference** of 1945. Pop.: 136 619 (1996 est.).

potsherd ('pɒtˌʃɜːd) *or* **potshard** ('pɒtˌʃɑːd) *n* a broken fragment of pottery. ORIG C14: from POT[1] + *schoord* piece of broken crockery; see SHARD

pot shot *n* **1** a chance shot taken casually, hastily, or without careful aim. **2** a shot fired to kill game in disregard of the rules of sport. **3** a shot fired at quarry within easy range.

pot still *n* a type of still in which heat is applied directly to the pot in which the wash is contained: used in distilling whisky.

pottage ('pɒtɪdʒ) *n* a thick soup. ORIG C13: from OF *potage* contents of a pot, from *pot* POT[1]

potted ('pɒtɪd) *adj* **1** placed or grown in a pot. **2** cooked or preserved in a pot: *potted shrimps.* **3** *Inf.* abridged: *a potted version of a novel.*

potter[1] ('pɒtə) *n* a person who makes pottery.

potter[2] ('pɒtə) *or esp. US & Canad.* **putter** *vb* **1** (*intr;* often foll. by *about* or *around*) to busy oneself in a desultory though agreeable manner. **2** (*intr;* often foll. by *along* or *about*) to move with little energy or direction: *to potter about town.* **3** (*tr;* usually foll. by *away*) to waste (time): *to potter the day away.* ORIG C16 (in the sense: to poke repeatedly): from OE *potian* to thrust
▸ **'potterer** *or esp. US* **'putterer** *n*

Potter ★ ('pɒtə) *n* **1** (**Helen**) **Beatrix.** 1866–1943, British author and illustrator of children's animal stories, such as *The Tale of Peter Rabbit* (1902). **2 Dennis** (**Christopher George**). 1935–94, British playwright. His TV successes include *Pennies from Heaven* (1978) and *The Singing Detective* (1986). **3 Paulus.** 1625–54, Dutch painter, esp. of animals.

Potteries ★ ('pɒtərɪz) *pl n* **the.** (*sometimes functioning as sing*) a region of W central England, in Staffordshire, in which the china industries are concentrated.

potter's field *n* **1** *New Testament.* the land bought by the Sanhedrin with the money paid for the betrayal of Jesus, to be used as a burial place for strangers (Acts 1:19; Matthew 27:7). **2** *US.* a cemetery where the poor or unidentified are buried at the public's expense.

potter's wheel *n* a device with a horizontal rotating disc, on which clay is shaped by hand.

pottery ('pɒtərɪ) *n, pl* **potteries. 1** articles made from earthenware and baked in a kiln. **2** a place where such articles are made. **3** the craft or business of making such articles. ORIG C15: from OF *poterie,* from *potier* potter, from *pot* POT[1]

potting shed *n* a building in which plants are set in flowerpots and in which empty pots, potting compost, etc., are stored.

pottle ('pɒtᵊl) *n Arch.* a liquid measure equal to half a gallon. ORIG C14 *potel,* from OF: a small POT[1]

potto ('pɒtəʊ) *n, pl* **pottos.** a short-tailed prosimian primate having vertebral spines protruding through the skin in the neck region. Also called: **kinkajou.** ORIG C18: of W African origin

Pott's disease (pɒts) *n* a disease of the spine, characterized by weakening and gradual disintegration of the vertebrae. ORIG C18: after Percivall *Pott* (1714–88), Brit. surgeon

Pott's fracture *n* a fracture of the lower part of the fibula, usually with the dislocation of the ankle. ORIG C18: see POTT'S DISEASE

potty[1] ('pɒtɪ) *adj* **pottier, pottiest.** *Brit. inf.* **1** foolish or slightly crazy. **2** trivial or insignificant. **3** (foll. by *about*) very keen (on). ORIG C19: ?from POT[1]
▸ **'pottiness** *n*

potty[2] ('pɒtɪ) *n, pl* **potties.** a child's word for **chamber pot.**

Potyomkin ★ (*Russian* pa'tjɔmkin) *n* a variant spelling of **Potemkin.**

pouch (paʊtʃ) *n* **1** a small flexible baglike container: *a tobacco pouch.* **2** a saclike structure in any of various animals, such as the cheek fold in rodents. **3** *Anat.* any sac, pocket, or pouchlike cavity. **4** a Scot. word for **pocket.** ◆ *vb* **5** (*tr*) to place in or as if in a pouch. **6** to arrange or become arranged in a pouchlike form. **7** (*tr*) (of certain birds and fishes) to swallow. ORIG C14: from OF *pouche,* from OF *poche* bag
▸ **'pouchy** *adj*

pouf *or* **pouffe** (puːf) *n* **1** a large solid cushion used as a seat. **2a** a woman's hairstyle, fashionable esp. in the 18th century, in which the hair is piled up in rolled puffs. **2b** a pad set in the hair to make such puffs. **3** (*also* pʊf). *Brit. derog. sl.* less common spellings of **poof.** ORIG C19: from F

poulard *or* **poularde** ('puːlɑːd) *n* a hen that has been spayed for fattening. Cf. **capon.** ORIG C18: from OF *pollarde,* from *polle* hen

Poulenc ★ (*French* pulɛ̃k) *n* **Francis** (frɑ̃sis). 1899–1963, French composer; a member of Les Six. His works include the operas *Les Mamelles de Tirésias* (1947) and *Dialogues des Carmélites* (1957), and the ballet *Les Biches* (1924).

poult (pəʊlt) *n* the young of a gallinaceous bird, esp. of domestic fowl. ORIG C15: var. of *poulet* PULLET

poulterer ('pəʊltərə) *n Brit.* another word for a **poultryman.** ORIG C17: from obs. *poulter,* from OF *pouletier,* from *poulet* PULLET

poultice ('pəʊltɪs) *n Med.* a local moist and often heated application for the skin used to improve the circulation, treat inflamed areas, etc. ORIG C16: from earlier *pultes,* from L *puls* a thick porridge

poultry ('pəʊltrɪ) *n* domestic fowls collectively. ORIG C14: from OF *pouletrie,* from *pouletier* poultry dealer

poultryman ('pəʊltrɪmən) *or* **poulterer** *n, pl* **poultrymen** *or* **poulterers. 1** Also called: **chicken farmer.** a person who rears domestic fowls for their eggs or meat. **2** a dealer in poultry.

pounce[1] (paʊns) *vb* **pounces, pouncing, pounced. 1** (*intr;* often foll. by *on* or *upon*) to spring or swoop, as in capturing prey. ◆ *n* **2** the act of pouncing; a spring or swoop. **3** the claw of a bird of prey. ORIG C17: apparently from ME *punson* pointed tool
▸ **'pouncer** *n*

pounce[2] (pauns) *n* **1** a very fine resinous powder, esp. of cuttlefish bone, formerly used to dry ink. **2** a fine powder, esp. of charcoal, that is tapped through perforations in paper in order to transfer the design to another surface. ♦ *vb* **pounces, pouncing, pounced.** (*tr*) **3** to dust (paper) with pounce. **4** to transfer (a design) by means of pounce. ORIG C18: from OF *ponce*, from L *pūmex* pumice

pouncet box ('paunsɪt) *n* a box with a perforated top used for perfume. ORIG C16 *pouncet*, ? alteration of *pounced* perforated

pound[1] (paund) *vb* **1** (when *intr*, often foll. by *on* or *at*) to strike heavily and often. **2** (*tr*) to beat to a pulp; pulverize. **3** (*tr*; foll. by *out*) to produce, as by typing heavily. **4** to walk or move with heavy steps or thuds. **5** (*intr*) to throb heavily. ♦ *n* **6** the act of pounding. ORIG OE *pūnian*
▸ **'pounder** *n*

pound[2] (paund) *n* **1** an avoirdupois unit of weight that is divided into 16 ounces and is equal to 0.453 592 kilograms. Abbrev.: **lb. 2** a troy unit of weight divided into 12 ounces equal to 0.373 242 kilograms. **3a** the standard monetary unit of the United Kingdom, divided into 100 pence. Official name: **pound sterling. 3b** (*as modifier*): *a pound coin*. **4** the standard monetary unit of various other countries, including Cyprus, Egypt, Israel, and Syria. **5** Also called: **pound Scots.** a former Scottish monetary unit originally worth an English pound but later declining in value to 1 shilling 8 pence. ORIG OE *pund*, from L *pondō*

pound[3] (paund) *n* **1** an enclosure for keeping officially removed vehicles or distrained goods or animals, esp. stray dogs. **2** a place where people are confined. **3** a trap for animals. ♦ *vb* **4** (*tr*) to confine in or as if in a pound; impound, imprison, or restrain. ORIG C14: from LOE *pund-*, as in *pundfeald* PINFOLD

Pound ★ (paund) *n* **Ezra** (**Loomis**). 1885–1972, US poet, translator, and critic, living in Europe. Indicted for treason by the US government (1945) for pro-Fascist broadcasts during World War II, he was committed to a mental hospital until 1958. His life work, the *Cantos* (1925–70), is an unfinished sequence of poems, which incorporates mythological and historical materials in several languages as well as political, economic, and autobiographical elements.

poundage ('paundɪdʒ) *n* **1** a charge of so much per pound of weight. **2** a charge of so much per pound sterling. **3** a weight expressed in pounds.

poundal ('paundᵊl) *n* the fps unit of force; the force that imparts an acceleration of 1 foot per second per second to a mass of 1 pound. Abbrev.: **pdl.** ORIG C19: from POUND[2] + QUINTAL

pound cost averaging *n Stock Exchange.* a method of accumulating capital by investing a fixed sum in a particular security at regular intervals, in order to achieve an average purchase price below the arithmetic average of the market prices on the purchase dates.

-pounder ('paundə) *n* (*in combination*) **1** something weighing a specified number of pounds: *a 200-pounder*. **2** something worth a specified number of pounds: *a ten-pounder*. **3** a gun that discharges a shell weighing a specified number of pounds: *a two-pounder*.

pound sterling *n* See **pound**[2] (sense 3).

pour (pɔː) *vb* **1** to flow or cause to flow in a stream. **2** (*tr*) to emit in a profuse way. **3** (*intr*; often foll. by *down*) Also: **pour with rain.** to rain heavily. **4** (*intr*) to move together in large numbers; swarm. **5** (*intr*) to serve tea, coffee, etc.: *shall I pour?* **6 it never rains but it pours.** events, esp. unfortunate ones, come in rapid succession. **7 pour oil on troubled waters.** to calm a quarrel, etc. ♦ *n* **8** a pouring, downpour, etc. ORIG C13: from ?
▸ **'pourer** *n*

> **USAGE NOTE** The verbs *pour* and *pore* are sometimes confused: *she poured cream over her strudel; she pored* (not *poured*) *over the manuscript.*

pourboire *French.* (purbwar) *n* a tip; gratuity. ORIG lit.: for drinking

poussin *French.* (pusɛ̃) *n* a young chicken reared for eating.

Poussin ★ (*French* pusɛ̃) *n* **Nicolas** (nikɔla). 1594–1665, French painter, regarded as a leader of French classical painting. He is best known for the austere historical and biblical paintings and landscapes of his later years.

pout[1] (paut) *vb* **1** to thrust out (the lips), as when sullen or (of the lips) to be thrust out. **2** (*intr*) to swell out; protrude. **3** (*tr*) to utter with a pout. ♦ *n* **4** Also: **the pouts.** a fit of sullenness. **5** the act or state of pouting. ORIG C14: from ?
▸ **'poutingly** *adv*

pout[2] (paut) *n, pl* **pout** *or* **pouts. 1** short for **eelpout. 2** Also called: **horned pout.** a N American catfish with barbels round the mouth. **3** any of various gadoid food fishes. ORIG OE *-pūte*, as in *ǣlepūte* eelpout

pouter ('pautə) *n* **1** a person or thing that pouts. **2** a breed of domestic pigeon with a large crop capable of being greatly puffed out.

poutine (ˌpuː'tiːn) *n Canad.* a dish of cheese curds, French fried potatoes, and sauce. ORIG from F

poverty ('pɒvətɪ) *n* **1** the condition of being without adequate food, money, etc. **2** scarcity: *a poverty of wit*. **3** a lack of elements conducive to fertility in soil. ORIG C12: from OF *poverté*, from L *paupertās* restricted means, from *pauper* poor

poverty-stricken *adj* suffering from extreme poverty.

poverty trap *n* the situation of being unable to raise one's living standard because one is dependent on state benefits which are reduced or withdrawn if one gains any extra income.

pow (pau) *interj* an exclamation imitative of a collision, explosion, etc.

POW *abbrev. for* prisoner of war.

powan ('pauən) *n* a freshwater whitefish occurring in some Scottish lakes. ORIG C17: Scot. var. of POLLAN

powder ('paudə) *n* **1** a substance in the form of tiny loose particles. **2** any of various preparations in this form, such as gunpowder, face powder, or soap powder. ♦ *vb* **3** to turn into powder; pulverize. **4** (*tr*) to cover or sprinkle with or as if with powder. ORIG C13: from OF *poldre*, from L *pulvis* dust
▸ **'powderer** *n* ▸ **'powdery** *adj*

powder blue *n* a dusty pale blue colour.

powder burn *n* a superficial burn of the skin caused by a momentary intense explosion.

powder flask *n* a small flask or case formerly used to carry gunpowder.

powder horn *n* a powder flask consisting of the hollow horn of an animal.

powder keg *n* **1** a small barrel to hold gunpowder. **2** a potential source of violence, disaster, etc.

powder metallurgy *n* the science and technology of producing solid metal components from metal powder by compaction and sintering.

powder monkey *n* (formerly) a boy who carried powder from the magazine to the guns on warships.

powder puff *n* a soft pad of fluffy material used for applying cosmetic powder to the skin.

powder room *n* a ladies' cloakroom.

powdery mildew *n* a plant disease characterized by a white powdery growth on stems and leaves, caused by parasitic fungi.

Powell ★ ('pauəl) *n* **1** ('pəuəl). **Anthony** (**Dymoke**). 1905–2000, British novelist, best known for his sequence of novels *A Dance to the Music of Time* (1951–75). **2 Cecil Frank.** 1903–69, British physicist, who was awarded the Nobel prize for physics (1950) for his discovery of the pi-meson. **3 Earl,** known as *Bud Powell*. 1924–1966, US modern-jazz pianist. **4** (**John**) **Enoch.** 1912–98, British politician. An opponent of Commonwealth immigration, he resigned from the Conservative Party, returning to Parliament as a United Ulster Unionist Council member (1974–87). **5 Michael.** 1905–90, British film writer, producer, and director, best known for his collaboration

(1942–57) with Emeric Pressburger. Films include *The Life and Death of Colonel Blimp* (1943), *A Matter of Life and Death* (1946), and *Peeping Tom* (1960).

power ('pauə) *n* **1** ability to do something. **2** (*often pl*) a specific ability, capacity, or faculty. **3** political, financial, social, etc., force or influence. **4** control or dominion or a position of control, dominion, or authority. **5** a state or other political entity with political, industrial, or military strength. **6** a person or group that exercises control, influence, or authority: *he's a power in the state.* **7** a prerogative, privilege, or liberty. **8** legal authority to act for another. **9a** a military force. **9b** military potential. **10** *Maths.* **10a** the value of a number or quantity raised to some exponent. **10b** another name for **exponent** (sense 4). **11** *Physics, engineering.* a measure of the rate of doing work expressed as the work done per unit time. It is measured in watts, horsepower, etc. **12a** the rate at which electrical energy is fed into or taken from a device or system. It is measured in watts. **12b** (*as modifier*): *a power amplifier.* **13** the ability to perform work. **14a** mechanical energy as opposed to manual labour. **14b** (*as modifier*): *a power tool.* **15** a particular form of energy: *nuclear power.* **16a** a measure of the ability of a lens or optical system to magnify an object. **16b** another word for **magnification. 17** *Inf.* a large amount: *a power of good.* **18 in one's power.** (*often foll. by an infinitive*) able or allowed (to). **19 in (someone's) power.** under the control of (someone). **20 the powers that be.** established authority. ◆ *vb* **21** (*tr*) to give or provide power to. **22** (*tr*) to fit (a machine) with a motor or engine. **23** *Inf.* to move or cause to move by the exercise of physical power. ORIG C13: from Anglo-Norman *poer,* from Vulgar L *potēre* (unattested), from L *posse* to be able

power amplifier *n Electronics.* an amplifier that is usually the final amplification stage in a device and is designed to give the required power output.

power-assisted *adj* (of a mechanism) helped by mechanical or hydraulic power: *power-assisted steering; power-assisted brakes.*

powerboat ('pauə,bəut) *n* a boat, esp. a fast one, propelled by an inboard or outboard motor.

powerboating ('pauə,bəutɪŋ) *n* the sport of driving powerboats in racing competitions.

power broker *n* a person with power and influence, esp. one who operates behind the scenes.

power cut *n* a temporary interruption or reduction in the supply of electrical power.

power dive *n* **1** a steep dive by an aircraft with its engines at high power. ◆ *vb* **power-dive, power-dives, power-diving, power-dived. 2** to cause (an aircraft) to perform a power dive or (of an aircraft) to perform a power dive.

power dressing *n* a style of dressing in severely tailored suits, adopted by some women executives to project an image of efficiency.

powerful ('pauəful) *adj* **1** having great power. **2** extremely effective or efficient: *a powerful drug.* ◆ *adv* **3** *Dialect.* very: *he ran powerful fast.*
▸ **'powerfully** *adv* ▸ **'powerfulness** *n*

powerhouse ('pauə,haus) *n* **1** an electrical generating station or plant. **2** *Inf.* a forceful or powerful person or thing.

powerless ('pauəlɪs) *adj* without power or authority.
▸ **'powerlessly** *adv* ▸ **'powerlessness** *n*

power lunch *n* a high-powered business meeting conducted over lunch.

power of attorney *n* **1** legal authority to act for another person in certain specified matters. **2** the document conferring such authority.

power pack *n* a device for converting the current from a supply into direct or alternating current at the voltage required by a particular electrical or electronic device.

power plant *n* **1** the complex, including machinery, associated equipment, and the structure housing it, that is used in the generation of power, esp. electrical power. **2** the equipment supplying power to a particular machine.

power point *n* an electrical socket mounted on or recessed into a wall.

power-sharing *n* a political arrangement in which opposing groups in a society participate in government.

power station *n* an electrical generating station.

power steering *n* a form of steering used on vehicles, where the torque applied to the steering wheel is augmented by engine power. Also called: **power-assisted steering.**

power structure *n* the structure or distribution of power and authority in a community.

power walking *n* walking at a brisk pace while pumping the arms as part of an aerobic exercise.

Powhatan ★ (,pauhə'tæn, pau'hætən) *n* American Indian name *Wahunsonacock.* died 1618, American Indian chief of a confederacy of tribes; father of Pocahontas.

powwow ('pau,wau) *n* **1** a talk, conference, or meeting. **2** a magical ceremony of certain North American Indians. **3** (among certain North American Indians) a medicine man. **4** a meeting of North American Indians. ◆ *vb* **5** (*intr*) to hold a powwow. ORIG C17: of Amerind origin

Powys[1] ★ ('pauɪs) *n* a county in E Wales, formed in 1974 from most of Breconshire, Montgomeryshire, and Radnorshire. Administrative centre: Llandrindod Wells. Pop.: 122 000 (1995 est.). Area: 5077 sq. km (1960 sq. miles).

Powys[2] ★ ('pəuɪs) *n* **1 John Cowper** ('ku:pə). 1872–1963, British novelist, essayist, and poet, who spent much of his life in the US. His novels include *Wolf Solent* (1929) and *A Glastonbury Romance* (1932). **2** his brother, **T(heodore) F(rancis).** 1875–1953, British writer, noted for such religious fables as *Mr Weston's Good Wine* (1927).

pox (pɒks) *n* **1** any disease characterized by the formation of pustules on the skin that often leave pockmarks when healed. **2** (usually preceded by *the*) an informal name for **syphilis. 3 a pox on (someone *or* something).** (*interj*) *Arch.* an expression of intense disgust or aversion. ORIG C15: changed from *pocks,* pl. of POCK

Poyang *or* **P'o-yang** ★ ('pɔ:'jæŋ) *n* a lake in E China, in N Jiangxi province, connected by canal with the Yangtze River: the second largest lake in China. Area (at its greatest): 2780 sq. km (1073 sq. miles).

Poznań ★ (*Polish* 'pɔznajn) *n* a city in W Poland, on the Warta River: the centre of Polish resistance to German rule (1815–1918, 1939–45). Pop.: 581 800 (1996 est.). German name: **Posen.**

Pozsony ★ ('poʒonj) *n* the Hungarian name for **Bratislava.**

pozzuolana (,pɒtswə'lɑ:nə) *or* **pozzolana** (,pɒtsə'lɑ:nə) *n* **1** a type of porous volcanic ash used in making hydraulic cements. **2** any of various artificial substitutes for this ash used in cements. ORIG C18: from It.: of POZZUOLI

Pozzuoli ★ (*Italian* pot'tswɔ:li) *n* a port in SW Italy, in Campania on the **Gulf of Pozzuoli** (an inlet of the Bay of Naples): in a region of great volcanic activity; founded in the 6th century B.C. by the Greeks. Pop.: 65 025 (1987 est.).

pp *abbrev. for:* **1** past participle. **2** (in formal correspondence) per pro. ORIG L: *per procurationem*: by delegation to ◆ **3** *Music. symbol for* pianissimo.

> **USAGE NOTE** In formal correspondence, when Brenda Smith is signing on behalf of Peter Jones, she should write *Peter Jones pp* (or *per pro*) *Brenda Smith,* not the other way about.

pp *or* **PP** *abbrev. for:* **1** parcel post. **2** post-paid. **3** (in prescriptions) post prandium. ORIG L: after a meal **4** prepaid.

PP *abbrev. for:* **1** Parish Priest. **2** past President.

pp. *abbrev. for* pages.

ppd *abbrev. for:* **1** post-paid. **2** prepaid.

PPE *abbrev. for* philosophy, politics, and economics: a university course.

ppm *Chem. abbrev. for* parts per million.

PPP *abbrev. for* purchasing power parity: a rate of exchange between two currencies that gives them equal purchasing powers in their own economies.

ppr *or* **p.pr.** *abbrev. for* present participle.

PPS *abbrev. for:* **1** parliamentary private secretary. **2** Also: **pps** post postscriptum. ORIG L: after postscript; additional postscript

PQ *abbrev. for:* **1** (in Canada) Parti Québecois. **2** Province of Quebec.

pr *abbrev. for:* **1** (*pl* **prs**) pair. **2** paper. **3** power.

Pr *the chemical symbol for* praseodymium.

PR *abbrev. for:* **1** proportional representation. **2** public relations. **3** Puerto Rico.

pr. *abbrev. for:* **1** price. **2** pronoun.

practicable ('præktɪkəbᵊl) *adj* **1** capable of being done; feasible. **2** usable. ORIG C17: from F *praticable,* from *pratiquer* to practise; see PRACTICAL
▸ **ˌpracticaˈbility** *or* **ˈpracticableness** *n* ▸ **ˈpracticably** *adv*

> **USAGE NOTE** See at **practical.**

practical ('præktɪkᵊl) *adj* **1** of or concerned with experience or actual use; not theoretical. **2** of or concerned with ordinary affairs, work, etc. **3** adapted or adaptable for use. **4** of, involving, or trained by practice. **5** being such for all general purposes; virtual. ◆ *n* **6** an examination or lesson in a practical subject. ORIG C17: from earlier *practic,* from F *pratique,* via LL from Gk *praktikos,* from *prassein* to experience
▸ **ˌpractiˈcality** *or* **ˈpracticalness** *n*

> **USAGE NOTE** A distinction is usually made between *practical* and *practicable. Practical* refers to a person, idea, project, etc., as being more concerned with or relevant to practice than theory: *he is a very practical person; the idea had no practical application. Practicable* refers to a project or idea as being capable of being done or put into effect: *the plan was expensive, yet practicable.*

practical joke *n* a prank or trick usually intended to make the victim appear foolish.
▸ **practical joker** *n*

practically ('præktɪkəlɪ, -klɪ) *adv* **1** virtually; almost: *it rained practically every day.* **2** in actuality rather than in theory: *what can we do practically to help?*

practice ('præktɪs) *n* **1** a usual or customary action: *it was his practice to rise at six.* **2** repetition of an activity in order to achieve mastery and fluency: *they had one last practice the day before the show.* **3** the condition of having mastery of a skill or activity through repetition (esp. in **in practice, out of practice**). **4** the exercise of a profession: *he set up practice as a lawyer.* **5** the act of doing something: *he put his plans into practice.* **6** the established method of conducting proceedings in a court of law. ◆ *vb* **practices, practicing, practiced. 7** the US spelling of **practise.** ORIG C16: from Med. L *practicāre* to practise, from Gk *praktikē* practical work, from *prattein* to do

practise *or US* **practice** ('præktɪs) *vb* **practises, practising, practised** *or US* **practices, practicing, practiced. 1** to do or cause to do repeatedly in order to gain skill. **2** (*tr*) to do (something) habitually or frequently: *they practise ritual murder.* **3** to observe or pursue (something): *to practise Christianity.* **4** to work at (a profession, etc.): *he practises medicine.* ORIG C15: see PRACTICE

practised *or US* **practiced** ('præktɪst) *adj* **1** expert; skilled; proficient. **2** acquired or perfected by practice.

practitioner (præk'tɪʃənə) *n* **1** a person who practises a profession or art. **2** *Christian Science.* a person authorized to practise spiritual healing. ORIG C16: from *practician,* from OF, from *pratiquer* to PRACTISE

Prader-Willi syndrome (ˌprɑːdə'vɪlɪ) *n* a congenital condition characterized by obsessive eating, obesity, mental retardation, and small genitalia. ORIG C20: after Andrea *Prader* (b. 1919) and H. *Willi* (b. 1900), Swiss paediatricians

Prado ★ ('prɑːdəʊ) *n* an art gallery in Madrid housing an important collection of Spanish paintings.

prae- *prefix* an archaic variant of **pre-.**

praedial *or* **predial** ('priːdɪəl) *adj* **1** of or relating to land, farming, etc. **2** attached to or occupying land. ORIG C16: from Med. L *praediālis,* from L *praedium* farm, estate

praesidium (prɪ'sɪdɪəm) *n* a variant of **presidium.**

praetor *or esp. US* **pretor** ('priːtə, -tɔː) *n* (in ancient Rome) any of several senior magistrates ranking just below the consuls. ORIG C15: from L: one who leads the way, prob. from *praeīre,* from *prae-* before + *īre* to go
▸ **praeˈtorian** *or* **preˈtorian** *adj, n* ▸ **ˈpraetorship** *or* **ˈpretorship** *n*

Praetorius ★ (*German* prɛ'toːrius) *n* **Michael** ('mɪçaeːl). 1571–1621, German composer and musicologist, noted esp. for his description of contemporary musical practices and instruments, *Syntagma musicum* (1615–19).

pragmatic (præg'mætɪk) *adj* **1** advocating behaviour dictated more by practical consequences than by theory. **2** *Philosophy.* of pragmatism. **3** involving everyday or practical business. **4** of or concerned with the affairs of a state or community. **5** *Rare.* meddlesome; officious. Also (for senses 3, 5): **pragmatical.** ORIG C17: from LL *prāgmaticus,* from Gk *prāgmatikos* from *pragma* act, from *prattein* to do
▸ **pragˌmatiˈcality** *n* ▸ **pragˈmatically** *adv*

pragmatic sanction *n* an edict, decree, or ordinance issued with the force of fundamental law by a sovereign.

pragmatism ('prægməˌtɪzəm) *n* **1** action or policy dictated by consideration of the practical consequences rather than by theory. **2** *Philosophy.* the doctrine that the content of a concept consists only in its practical applicability.
▸ **ˈpragmatist** *n, adj*

Prague ★ (prɑːg) *n* the capital and largest city of the Czech Republic, on the Vltava River: a rich commercial centre during the Middle Ages; site of Charles University (1348) and a technical university (1707); scene of defenestrations (1419 and 1618) that contributed to the outbreak of the Hussite Wars and the Thirty Years' War respectively. Pop.: 1 209 855 (1996 est.). Czech name: **Praha.**

Praha ★ ('praha) *n* the Czech name for **Prague.**

prairie ('prɛərɪ) *n* (*often pl*) a treeless grassy plain of the central US and S Canada. ORIG C18: from F, from OF *praierie,* from L *prātum* meadow

prairie chicken, fowl, grouse, *or* **hen** *n* either of two mottled brown-and-white grouse of North America.

prairie dog *n* any of several rodents that live in large complex burrows in the prairies of North America. Also called: **prairie marmot.**

prairie-dogging *n* (of workers in an open-plan office) the practice of looking over the top of one's partition in order to discover the source of or reason for a commotion. ORIG C20: after the actions of a PRAIRIE DOG, which stands on its hind legs to get a better view of something

prairie oyster *n* a drink consisting of raw unbeaten egg, vinegar or Worcester sauce, salt, and pepper: a supposed cure for a hangover.

Prairie Provinces ★ *pl n* the Canadian provinces of Manitoba, Saskatchewan, and Alberta, which lie in the N Great Plains region of North America: the chief wheat and petroleum producing area of Canada.

prairie schooner *n Chiefly US.* a horse-drawn covered wagon used in the 19th century to cross the prairies of North America.

prairie wolf *n* another name for **coyote.**

praise (preɪz) *n* **1** the act of expressing commendation, admiration, etc. **2** the rendering of homage and gratitude to a deity. **3 sing someone's praises.** to commend someone highly. ◆ *vb* **praises, praising, praised.** (*tr*) **4** to express commendation, admiration, etc., for. **5** to proclaim the glorious attributes of (a deity) with homage and thanksgiving. ORIG C13: from OF *preisier,* from LL *pretiāre* to esteem highly, from L *pretium* prize

praiseworthy ('preɪzˌwɜːðɪ) *adj* deserving of praise; commendable.
▸ **ˈpraiseˌworthily** *adv* ▸ **ˈpraiseˌworthiness** *n*

Prakrit ('prɑːkrɪt) *n* any of the vernacular Indic languages as distinguished from Sanskrit: spoken from

about 300 B.C. to the Middle Ages. ORIG C18: from Sansk. *prākrta* original
▸ **Pra'kritic** *adj*

praline ('prɑːliːn) *n* **1** a confection of nuts with caramelized sugar. **2** Also called: **sugared almond.** a sweet consisting of an almond encased in sugar. ORIG C18: from F, after César de Choiseul, comte de Plessis-*Praslin* (1598–1675), F field marshal whose chef first concocted it

pralltriller ('prɑːlˌtrɪlə) *n* an ornament used in 18th-century music consisting of an inverted mordent with an added initial upper note. ORIG G: bouncing trill

pram[1] (præm) *n Brit.* a cotlike four-wheeled carriage for a baby. US term: **baby carriage.** ORIG C19: shortened & altered from PERAMBULATOR

pram[2] (prɑːm) *n Naut.* a light tender with a flat bottom and a bow formed from the ends of the side and bottom planks meeting in a small raised transom. ORIG C16: from MDu. *prame*

prance (prɑːns) *vb* **prances, prancing, pranced. 1** (*intr*) to swagger or strut. **2** (*intr*) to caper, gambol, or dance about. **3** (*intr*) (of a horse) to move with high lively springing steps. **4** (*tr*) to cause to prance. ◆ *n* **5** the act or an instance of prancing. ORIG C14 *prauncen,* from ?
▸ **'prancer** *n* ▸ **'prancing** *adj*

prandial ('prændɪəl) *adj Facetious.* of or relating to a meal. ORIG C19: from L *prandium* meal, luncheon

prang (præŋ) *Chiefly Brit. sl.* ◆ *n* **1** an accident or crash in an aircraft, car, etc. **2** an aircraft bombing raid. ◆ *vb* **3** to crash or damage (an aircraft, car, etc.). **4** to damage (a town, etc.) by bombing. ORIG C20: ? imit.

prank[1] (præŋk) *n* a mischievous trick or joke. ORIG C16: from ?
▸ **'prankish** *adj* ▸ **'prankster** *n*

prank[2] (præŋk) *vb* **1** (*tr*) to dress or decorate showily or gaudily. **2** (*intr*) to make an ostentatious display. ORIG C16: from MDu. *pronken*

prase (preɪz) *n* a light green translucent variety of chalcedony. ORIG C14: from F, from L *prasius* a leek-green stone, from Gk *prasios,* from *prason* a leek

praseodymium (ˌpreɪzɪəʊ'dɪmɪəm) *n* a malleable ductile silvery-white element of the lanthanide series of metals. Symbol: Pr; atomic no.: 59; atomic wt.: 140.91. ORIG C20: NL, from Gk *prasios* of a leek-green colour + DIDYMIUM

Pratchett ★ ('prætʃɪt) *n* **Terry.** born 1948, British novelist. His best-known work is a series of fantasy novels, *Discworld,* which began with *The Colour of Magic* (1983); *Hogfather* (1996) was the 20th novel in this series.

prate (preɪt) *vb* **prates, prating, prated. 1** (*intr*) to talk idly and at length; chatter. **2** (*tr*) to utter in an idle or empty way. ◆ *n* **3** idle or trivial talk; chatter. ORIG C15: of Gmc origin
▸ **'prater** *n* ▸ **'prating** *adj*

pratfall ('prætˌfɔːl) *n US & Canad. sl.* a fall upon one's buttocks. ORIG C20: from C16 *prat* buttocks (from ?) + FALL

pratincole ('prætɪŋˌkəʊl, 'preɪ-) *n* any of various swallow-like shore birds of the Old World, having long pointed wings, short legs, and a short bill. ORIG C18: from NL *pratincola* field-dwelling, from L *prātum* meadow + *incola* inhabitant

Prato ★ (*Italian* 'praːto) *n* a walled city in central Italy, in Tuscany: woollen industry. Pop.: 167 991 (1996 est.). Official name: **Prato in Toscana** (in tos'kaːna).

prattle ('prætᵊl) *vb* **prattles, prattling, prattled. 1** (*intr*) to talk in a foolish or childish way; babble. **2** (*tr*) to utter in a foolish or childish way. ◆ *n* **3** foolish or childish talk. ORIG C16: from MLow G *pratelen* to chatter
▸ **'prattler** *n* ▸ **'prattling** *adj*

prau (praʊ) *n* a variant of **proa.**

prawn (prɔːn) *n* **1** any of various small edible marine decapod crustaceans having a slender flattened body with a long tail and two pairs of pincers. **2 come the raw prawn with.** *Austral. inf.* to attempt to deceive. ORIG C15: from ?

praxis ('præksɪs) *n, pl* **praxes** ('præksiːz) *or* **praxises. 1** the practice of a field of study, as opposed to the theory. **2** a practical exercise. **3** accepted practice or custom. ORIG C16: via Med. L from Gk: deed, action, from *prassein* to do

Praxiteles ★ (præk'sɪtɪˌliːz) *n* 4th-century B.C. Greek sculptor: his works include statues of Hermes at Olympia, which survives, and of Aphrodite at Cnidus.

pray (preɪ) *vb* **1** (when *intr,* often foll. by *for;* when *tr, usually takes a clause as object*) to utter prayers (to God or other object of worship). **2** (when *tr, usually takes a clause as object or an infinitive*) to beg or implore: *she prayed to be allowed to go.* ◆ *sentence substitute.* **3** *Arch.* I beg you; please: *pray, leave us alone.* ORIG C13: from OF *preier,* from L *precārī* to implore, from *prex* an entreaty

prayer[1] (prɛə) *n* **1** a personal communication or petition addressed to a deity, esp. in the form of supplication, adoration, praise, contrition, or thanksgiving. **2** a similar personal communication that does not involve adoration, addressed to beings closely associated with a deity, such as saints. **3** the practice of praying: *prayer is our solution to human problems.* **4** (*often pl*) a form of devotion spent mainly or wholly praying: *morning prayers.* **5** (*cap. when part of a recognized name*) a form of words used in praying: *the Lord's Prayer.* **6** an object or benefit prayed for. **7** an earnest request or entreaty. ORIG C13 *preiere,* from OF, from Med. L, from L *precārius* obtained by begging, from *prex* prayer
▸ **'prayerful** *adj*

prayer[2] ('preɪə) *n* a person who prays.

prayer book (prɛə) *n* a book containing the prayers used at church services or recommended for private devotions.

prayer rug (prɛə) *n* the small carpet on which a Muslim kneels and prostrates himself or herself while saying prayers. Also called: **prayer mat.**

prayer wheel (prɛə) *n Buddhism.* (esp. in Tibet) a wheel or cylinder inscribed with or containing prayers, each revolution of which is counted as an uttered prayer, so that such prayers can be repeated by turning it.

praying mantis *or* **mantid** *n* another name for **mantis.**

PRB *abbrev. for* Pre-Raphaelite Brotherhood.

pre- *prefix* before in time, position, etc.: *predate; preeminent.* ORIG from L *prae* before

preach (priːtʃ) *vb* **1** to make known (religious truth) or give religious or moral instruction or exhortation in (sermons). **2** to advocate (a virtue, action, etc.), esp. in a moralizing way. ORIG C13: from OF *prechier,* from Church L *praedicāre,* from L: to proclaim in public; see PREDICATE

preacher ('priːtʃə) *n* a person who preaches, esp. a Protestant clergyman.

preachify ('priːtʃɪˌfaɪ) *vb* **preachifies, preachifying, preachified.** (*intr*) *Inf.* to preach or moralize in a tedious manner.
▸ **ˌpreachifi'cation** *n*

preachment ('priːtʃmənt) *n* **1** the act of preaching. **2** a tedious or pompous sermon.

preachy ('priːtʃɪ) *adj* **preachier, preachiest.** *Inf.* inclined to or marked by preaching.

preacquisition profit (ˌpriːækwɪ'zɪʃən) *n* the retained profit of a company earned before a takeover and therefore not eligible for distribution as a dividend to the shareholders of the acquiring company.

preamble (priː'æmbᵊl) *n* **1** a preliminary or introductory statement, esp. attached to a statute setting forth its purpose. **2** a preliminary event, fact, etc. ORIG C14: from OF *préambule,* from LL *praeambulum,* from L *prae-* before + *ambulāre* to walk

preamplifier (priː'æmplɪˌfaɪə) *n* an electronic amplifier used to improve the signal-to-noise ratio of an electronic device. It boosts a low-level signal to an intermediate level before it is transmitted to the main amplifier.

prebend ('prɛbənd) *n* **1** the stipend assigned by a cathedral or collegiate church to a canon or member of the chapter. **2** the land, tithe, or other source of such a stipend. **3** a less common word for **prebendary. 4** *Church of England.* the office of a prebendary. ORIG C15: from OF

prébende, from Med. L *praebenda* stipend, from L *praebēre* to offer, from *prae* forth + *habēre* to have
▸ **prebendal** (prɪ'bɛndᵊl) *adj*

prebendary ('prɛbəndərɪ, -drɪ) *n, pl* **prebendaries. 1** a canon or member of the chapter of a cathedral or collegiate church who holds a prebend. **2** *Church of England.* an honorary canon with the title of prebendary.

Precambrian *or* **Pre-Cambrian** (priː'kæmbrɪən) *adj* **1** of, denoting, or formed in the earliest geological era, which lasted for about 4 000 000 000 years before the Cambrian period. ◆ *n* **2 the.** the Precambrian era.

precancel (priː'kænsᵊl) *vb* **precancels, precancelling, precancelled** *or US* **precancels, precanceling, precanceled.** (*tr*) to cancel (postage stamps) before placing them on mail.

precancerous *adj* (esp. of cells) displaying characteristics that may develop into cancer.

precarious (prɪ'kɛərɪəs) *adj* **1** liable to failure or catastrophe; insecure; perilous. **2** *Arch.* dependent on another's will. ORIG C17: from L *precārius* obtained by begging, from *prex* PRAYER[1]
▸ **pre'cariously** *adv* ▸ **pre'cariousness** *n*

precast ('priːˌkɑːst) *adj* (esp. of concrete when employed as a structural element in building) cast in a particular form before being used.

precaution (prɪ'kɔːʃən) *n* **1** an action taken to avoid a dangerous or undesirable event. **2** caution practised beforehand; circumspection. ORIG C17: from F, from LL *praecautiō,* from L, from *prae* before + *cavēre* to beware
▸ **pre'cautionary** *adj*

precede (prɪ'siːd) *vb* **precedes, preceding, preceded. 1** to go or be before (someone or something) in time, place, rank, etc. **2** (*tr*) to preface or introduce. ORIG C14: via OF from L *praecēdere* to go before

precedence ('prɛsɪdəns) *or* **precedency** *n* **1** the act of preceding or the condition of being precedent. **2** the ceremonial order or priority to be observed on formal occasions: *the officers are seated according to precedence.* **3** a right to preferential treatment: *I take precedence over you.*

precedent *n* ('prɛsɪdənt). **1** *Law.* a judicial decision that serves as an authority for deciding a later case. **2** an example or instance used to justify later similar occurrences. ◆ *adj* (prɪ'siːdᵊnt, 'prɛsɪdənt). **3** preceding.

precedented ('prɛsɪˌdɛntɪd) *adj* (of a decision, etc.) supported by having a precedent.

precedential (ˌprɛsɪ'dɛnʃəl) *adj* **1** of or serving as a precedent. **2** having precedence.

preceding (prɪ'siːdɪŋ) *adj* (*prenominal*) going or coming before; former.

precentor (prɪ'sɛntə) *n* **1** a cleric who directs the choral services in a cathedral. **2** a person who leads a congregation or choir in the sung parts of church services. ORIG C17: from LL *praecentor,* from *prae* before + *canere* to sing
▸ **precentorial** (ˌpriːsɛn'tɔːrɪəl) *adj* ▸ **pre'centorˌship** *n*

precept ('priːsɛpt) *n* **1** a rule or principle for action. **2** a guide or rule for morals; maxim. **3** a direction, esp. for a technical operation. **4** *Law.* **4a** a writ or warrant. **4b** (in England) an order to collect money under a rate. ORIG C14: from L *praeceptum* injunction, from *praecipere* to admonish, from *prae* before + *capere* to take
▸ **pre'ceptive** *adj*

preceptor (prɪ'sɛptə) *n Rare.* a tutor or instructor.
▸ **preceptorial** (ˌpriːsɛp'tɔːrɪəl) *or* **pre'ceptoral** *adj* ▸ **pre'ceptress** *fem n*

precession (prɪ'sɛʃən) *n* **1** the act of preceding. **2** See **precession of the equinoxes. 3** the motion of a spinning body, such as a top, gyroscope, or planet, in which it wobbles so that the axis of rotation sweeps out a cone. ORIG C16: from LL *praecessiō,* from L *praecādere* to precede
▸ **pre'cessional** *adj* ▸ **pre'cessionally** *adv*

precession of the equinoxes *n* the slightly earlier occurrence of the equinoxes each year due to the slow continuous westward shift of the equinoctial points along the ecliptic.

precinct ('priːsɪŋkt) *n* **1a** an enclosed area or building marked by a fixed boundary such as a wall. **1b** such a boundary. **2** an area in a town, often closed to traffic, that is designed or reserved for a particular activity: *a shopping precinct.* **3** *US.* **3a** a district of a city for administrative or police purposes. **3b** a polling district. ORIG C15: from Med. L *praecinctum* (something) surrounded, from L *praecingere* to gird around

precincts ('priːsɪŋkts) *pl n* the surrounding region or area.

preciosity (ˌprɛʃɪ'ɒsɪtɪ) *n, pl* **preciosities.** fastidiousness or affectation.

precious ('prɛʃəs) *adj* **1** beloved; dear; cherished. **2** very costly or valuable. **3** very fastidious or affected, as in speech, manners, etc. **4** *Inf.* worthless: *you and your precious ideas!* ◆ *adv* **5** *Inf.* (intensifier): *there's precious little left.* ORIG C13: from OF *precios,* from L *pretiōsus* valuable, from *pretium* price
▸ **'preciously** *adv* ▸ **'preciousness** *n*

precious metal *n* gold, silver, or platinum.

precious stone *n* any of certain rare minerals, such as diamond, ruby, or opal, that are highly valued as gemstones.

precipice ('prɛsɪpɪs) *n* **1** the steep sheer face of a cliff or crag. **2** the cliff or crag itself. ORIG C16: from L *praecipitium* steep place, from *praeceps* headlong
▸ **'precipiced** *adj*

precipitant (prɪ'sɪpɪtənt) *adj* **1** hasty or impulsive; rash. **2** rushing or falling rapidly or without heed. **3** abrupt or sudden. ◆ *n* **4** *Chem.* a substance that causes a precipitate to form.
▸ **pre'cipitance** *or* **pre'cipitancy** *n*

precipitate *vb* (prɪ'sɪpɪˌteɪt), **precipitates, precipitating, precipitated. 1** (*tr*) to cause to happen too soon; bring on. **2** to throw or fall from or as from a height. **3** to cause (moisture) to condense and fall as snow, rain, etc., or (of moisture, rain, etc.) to condense and fall thus. **4** *Chem.* to undergo or cause to undergo a process in which a dissolved substance separates from solution as a fine suspension of solid particles. ◆ *adj* (prɪ'sɪpɪtɪt). **5** rushing ahead. **6** done rashly or with undue haste. **7** sudden and brief. ◆ *n* (prɪ'sɪpɪtɪt). **8** *Chem.* a precipitated solid. ORIG C16: from L *praecipitāre* to throw down headlong, from *praeceps* steep, from *prae* before + *caput* head
▸ **pre'cipitable** *adj* ▸ **preˌcipita'bility** *n* ▸ **pre'cipitately** *adv* ▸ **pre'cipiˌtator** *n*

precipitation (prɪˌsɪpɪ'teɪʃən) *n* **1** *Meteorol.* **1a** rain, snow, sleet, dew, etc., formed by condensation of water vapour in the atmosphere. **1b** the deposition of these on the earth's surface. **2** the formation of a chemical precipitate. **3** the act of precipitating or the state of being precipitated. **4** rash or undue haste.

precipitous (prɪ'sɪpɪtəs) *adj* **1** resembling a precipice. **2** very steep. **3** hasty or precipitate.
▸ **pre'cipitously** *adv* ▸ **pre'cipitousness** *n*

> **USAGE NOTE** Some people think the use of *precipitous* to mean 'hasty' is incorrect, and that *precipitate* should be used instead.

precis *or* **précis** ('preɪsiː) *n, pl* **precis** *or* **précis** ('preɪsiːz). **1** a summary of a text; abstract. ◆ *vb* **2** (*tr*) to make a precis of. ORIG C18: from F: PRECISE

precise (prɪ'saɪs) *adj* **1** strictly correct in amount or value: *a precise sum.* **2** particular: *this precise location.* **3** using or operating with total accuracy: *precise instruments.* **4** strict in observance of rules, standards, etc.: *a precise mind.* ORIG C16: from F *précis,* from L *praecīdere* to curtail, from *prae* before + *caedere* to cut
▸ **pre'cisely** *adv* ▸ **pre'ciseness** *n*

precision (prɪ'sɪʒən) *n* **1** the quality of being precise; accuracy. **2** (*modifier*) characterized by a high degree of exactness: *precision grinding.* ORIG C17: from L *praecīsiō* a cutting off; see PRECISE
▸ **pre'cisionism** *n* ▸ **pre'cisionist** *n*

preclassical (prɪ'klæsɪkᵊl) *adj* (of music, literature, etc.) before a period regarded as classical.

preclude (prɪ'kluːd) *vb* **precludes, precluding, precluded.** (*tr*) **1** to exclude or debar. **2** to make impossible, esp. beforehand. ORIG C17: from L *praeclūdere* to shut up, from *prae* before + *claudere* to close
▸ **preclusion** (prɪ'kluːʒən) *n* ▸ **preclusive** (prɪ'kluːsɪv) *adj*

precocial (prɪˈkəʊʃəl) *adj* **1** denoting birds whose young, after hatching, are covered with down and capable of leaving the nest within a few days. ◆ *n* **2** a precocial bird. ◆ Cf. **altricial.**

precocious (prɪˈkəʊʃəs) *adj* **1** ahead in development, such as the mental development of a child. **2** *Bot.* flowering or ripening early. ORIG C17: from L *praecox,* from *prae* early + *coquere* to ripen
▸ **preˈcociously** *adv* ▸ **preˈcociousness** *or* **precocity** (prɪˈkɒsɪtɪ) *n*

precognition (ˌpriːkɒgˈnɪʃən) *n Psychol.* the alleged ability to foresee future events. ORIG C17: from LL *praecognitiō* foreknowledge, from *praecognoscere* to foresee
▸ **precognitive** (priːˈkɒgnɪtɪv) *adj*

preconceive (ˌpriːkənˈsiːv) *vb* **preconceives, preconceiving, preconceived.** (*tr*) to form an idea of beforehand.
▸ **preconception** (ˌpriːkənˈsɛpʃən) *n*

precondition (ˌpriːkənˈdɪʃən) *n* **1** a necessary or required condition; prerequisite. ◆ *vb* **2** (*tr*) *Psychol.* to present successively two stimuli to (an organism) without reinforcement so that they become associated; if a response is then conditioned to the second stimulus on its own, the same response will be evoked by the first stimulus.

preconize *or* **preconise** (ˈpriːkəˌnaɪz) *vb* **preconizes, preconizing, preconized** *or* **preconises, preconising, preconised.** (*tr*) **1** to announce or commend publicly. **2** to summon publicly. **3** (of the pope) to approve the appointment of (a nominee) to one of the higher dignities in the Roman Catholic Church. ORIG C15: from Med. L *praecōnīzāre* to make an announcement, from L *praecō* herald
▸ **ˌpreconiˈzation** *or* **ˌpreconiˈsation** *n*

precursor (prɪˈkɜːsə) *n* **1** a person or thing that precedes and announces someone or something to come. **2** a predecessor. **3** a chemical substance that gives rise to another more important substance. ORIG C16: from L *praecursor* one who runs in front, from *praecurrere,* from *prae* in front + *currere* to run

precursory (prɪˈkɜːsərɪ) *or* **precursive** *adj* **1** serving as a precursor. **2** preliminary.

pred. *abbrev. for* predicate.

predacious *or* **predaceous** (prɪˈdeɪʃəs) *adj* (of animals) habitually hunting and killing other animals for food. ORIG C18: from L *praeda* plunder
▸ **preˈdaciousness, preˈdaceousness,** *or* **predacity** (prɪˈdæsɪtɪ) *n*

predate (priːˈdeɪt) *vb* **predates, predating, predated.** (*tr*) **1** to affix a date to (a document, paper, etc.) that is earlier than the actual date. **2** to assign a date to (an event, period, etc.) that is earlier than the actual or previously assigned date of occurrence. **3** to be or occur at an earlier date than; precede in time.

predation (prɪˈdeɪʃən) *n* a relationship between two species of animal in a community, in which one hunts, kills, and eats the other.

predator (ˈprɛdətə) *n* **1** any carnivorous animal. **2** a predatory person or thing.

predatory (ˈprɛdətərɪ) *adj* **1** *Zool.* another word for **predacious. 2** of or characterized by plundering, robbing, etc. ORIG C16: from L *praedātōrius* rapacious, from *praedārī* to pillage, from *praeda* booty
▸ **ˈpredatorily** *adv* ▸ **ˈpredatoriness** *n*

predecease (ˌpriːdɪˈsiːs) *vb* **predeceases, predeceasing, predeceased.** to die before (some other person).

predecessor (ˈpriːdɪˌsɛsə) *n* **1** a person who precedes another, as in an office. **2** something that precedes something else. **3** an ancestor. ORIG C14: via OF from LL *praedēcessor,* from *prae* before + *dēcēdere* to go away

predella (prɪˈdɛlə) *n, pl* **predelle** (-liː). **1** a painting or a series of small paintings in a long strip forming the lower edge of an altarpiece or the face of an altar step. **2** a platform in a church upon which the altar stands. ORIG C19: from It.: step, prob. from OHG *bret* board

predestinarian (ˌpriːdɛstɪˈnɛərɪən) *n* **1** a person who believes in divine predestination. ◆ *adj* **2** of or relating to predestination or those who believe in it.

predestinate *vb* (priːˈdɛstɪˌneɪt), **predestinates, predestinating, predestinated. 1** another word for **predestine.** ◆ *adj* (priːˈdɛstɪnɪt, -ˌneɪt). **2** predestined.

predestination (priːˌdɛstɪˈneɪʃən) *n* **1** *Christian theol.* **1a** the act of God foreordaining every event from eternity. **1b** the doctrine or belief, esp. associated with Calvin, that the final salvation of some of mankind is foreordained from eternity by God. **2** the act of predestining or the state of being predestined.

predestine (priːˈdɛstɪn) *or* **predestinate** *vb* **predestines, predestining, predestined** *or* **predestinates, predestinating, predestinated.** (*tr*) **1** to determine beforehand. **2** *Christian theol.* (of God) to decree from eternity (any event, esp. the final salvation of individuals). ORIG C14: from L *praedestināre* to resolve beforehand

predetermine (ˌpriːdɪˈtɜːmɪn) *vb* **predetermines, predetermining, predetermined.** (*tr*) **1** to determine beforehand. **2** to influence or bias.
▸ **ˌpredeˈterminable** *adj* ▸ **ˌpredeˈterminate** *adj* ▸ **ˌpredeˌtermiˈnation** *n*

predicable (ˈprɛdɪkəbᵊl) *adj* **1** capable of being predicated or asserted. ◆ *n* **2** a quality that can be predicated. **3** *Logic, obs.* any of the five Aristotelian classes of predicates, namely genus, species, difference, property, and relation. ORIG C16: from L *praedicābilis,* from *praedicāre* to assert publicly; see PREDICATE
▸ **ˌpredicaˈbility** *n*

predicament *n* **1** (prɪˈdɪkəmənt) a perplexing, embarrassing, or difficult situation. **2** (ˈprɛdɪkəmənt). *Logic.* a logical category. ORIG C14: from LL *praedicāmentum* what is predicated, from *praedicāre* to announce; see PREDICATE

predicant (ˈprɛdɪkənt) *adj* **1** of or relating to preaching. ◆ *n* **2** a member of a religious order founded for preaching, esp. a Dominican. ORIG C17: from L *praedicāns* preaching, from *praedicāre* to say publicly; see PREDICATE

predicate *vb* (ˈprɛdɪˌkeɪt), **predicates, predicating, predicated.** (*mainly tr*) **1** (*also intr; when tr, may take a clause as object*) to declare or affirm. **2** to imply or connote. **3** (foll. by *on* or *upon*) *Chiefly US.* to base (a proposition, argument, etc.). **4** *Logic.* to assert (a property or condition) of the subject of a proposition. ◆ *n* (ˈprɛdɪkɪt). **5** *Grammar.* the part of a sentence in which something is asserted or denied of the subject of a sentence. **6** *Logic.* a term, property, or condition that is affirmed or denied concerning the subject of a proposition. ◆ *adj* (ˈprɛdɪkɪt). **7** of or relating to something that has been predicated. ORIG C16: from L *praedicāre* to assert publicly, from *prae* in front + *dīcere* to say
▸ **ˌprediˈcation** *n*

predicate calculus *n* the system of symbolic logic concerned not only with relations between propositions as wholes but also with the representation by symbols of individuals and predicates in propositions. See also **propositional calculus.**

predicative (prɪˈdɪkətɪv) *adj Grammar.* relating to or occurring within the predicate of a sentence: *a predicative adjective.* Cf. **attributive.**
▸ **preˈdicatively** *adv*

predict (prɪˈdɪkt) *vb* (*tr; may take a clause as object*) to state or make a declaration about in advance; foretell. ORIG C17: from L *praedīcere* to mention beforehand
▸ **preˈdictable** *adj* ▸ **preˌdictaˈbility** *n* ▸ **preˈdictably** *adv* ▸ **preˈdictive** *adj* ▸ **preˈdictor** *n*

prediction (prɪˈdɪkʃən) *n* **1** the act of predicting. **2** something predicted; a forecast.

predigest (ˌpriːdaɪˈdʒɛst, -dɪ-) *vb* (*tr*) to treat (food) artificially to aid subsequent digestion in the body.
▸ **ˌprediˈgestion** *n*

predikant (ˌprɛdɪˈkænt) *n* a minister in the Dutch Reformed Church, esp. in South Africa. ORIG from Du., from OF *predicant,* from LL, from *praedicāre* to PREACH

predilection (ˌpriːdɪˈlɛkʃən) *n* a predisposition, preference, or bias. ORIG C18: from F *prédilection,* from Med. L *praedīligere* to prefer, from L *prae* before + *dīligere* to love

predispose (ˌpriːdɪˈspəʊz) *vb* **predisposes, predisposing, predisposed.** (*tr*) (often foll. by *to* or *towards*) to incline or make (someone) susceptible to something beforehand.
▸ **ˌpredisˈposal** *n* ▸ **ˌpredispoˈsition** *n*

prednisolone (prɛdˈnɪsəˌləʊn) *n* a steroid drug derived from prednisone and having the same uses as cortisone. ORIG C20: altered from PREDNISONE

prednisone (ˈprɛdnɪˌsəʊn) *n* a steroid drug derived from cortisone and having the same uses. ORIG C20: perhaps from PRE(GNANT) + -D(IE)N(E) + (CORT)ISONE

predominant (prɪˈdɒmɪnənt) *adj* **1** superior in power, influence, etc., over others. **2** prevailing.
▸ **preˈdominance** *n* ▸ **preˈdominantly** *adv*

predominate *vb* (prɪˈdɒmɪˌneɪt), **predominates, predominating, predominated.** (*intr*) **1** (often foll. by *over*) to have power, influence, or control. **2** to prevail or preponderate. ◆ *adj* (prɪˈdɒmɪnɪt). **3** another word for **predominant.** ORIG C16: from Med. L *praedominārī*, from L *prae* before + *dominārī* to bear rule
▸ **preˈdominately** *adv* ▸ **preˌdomiˈnation** *n*

pre-eclampsia (ˌpriːɪˈklæmpsɪə) *n* a serious condition that can occur late in pregnancy. If not treated it can lead to eclampsia.

pre-embryo (priːˈɛmbrɪˌəʊ) *n, pl* **pre-embryos.** the structure formed after fertilization of an ovum but before differentiation of embryonic tissue.

pre-eminent (prɪˈɛmɪnənt) *adj* extremely eminent or distinguished; outstanding.
▸ **pre-ˈeminence** *n* ▸ **pre-ˈeminently** *adv*

pre-empt (prɪˈɛmpt) *vb* **1** (*tr*) to acquire in advance of or to the exclusion of others; appropriate. **2** (*tr*) *Chiefly US.* to occupy (public land) in order to acquire a prior right to purchase. **3** (*intr*) *Bridge.* to make a high opening bid, often on a weak hand, to shut out opposition bidding.
▸ **pre-ˈemptor** *n*

pre-emption (prɪˈɛmpʃən) *n* **1** *Law.* the purchase of or right to purchase property in preference to others. **2** *International law.* the right of a government to intercept and seize property of the subjects of another state while in transit, esp. in time of war. ORIG C16: from Med. L *praeemptiō*, from *praeemere* to buy beforehand

pre-emptive (prɪˈɛmptɪv) *adj* **1** of, involving, or capable of pre-emption. **2** *Bridge.* (of a high bid) made to shut out opposition bidding. **3** *Mil.* designed to reduce or destroy an enemy's attacking strength before it can use it: *a pre-emptive strike.*

preen (priːn) *vb* **1** (of birds) to maintain (feathers) in a healthy condition by arrangement, cleaning, and other contact with the bill. **2** to dress or array (oneself) carefully; primp. **3** (usually foll. by *on*) to pride or congratulate (oneself). ORIG C14 *preinen*, prob. from *prunen*, infl. by *prenen* to prick; suggestive of the pricking movement of the bird's beak
▸ **ˈpreener** *n*

pre-exist (ˌpriːɪgˈzɪst) *vb* (*intr*) to exist at an earlier time.
▸ **ˌpre-exˈistent** *adj* ▸ **ˌpre-exˈistence** *n*

pref. *abbrev. for:* **1** preface. **2** prefatory. **3** preference. **4** preferred. **5** prefix.

prefab (ˈpriːˌfæb) *n* a building that is prefabricated, esp. a small house.

prefabricate (priːˈfæbrɪˌkeɪt) *vb* **prefabricates, prefabricating, prefabricated.** (*tr*) to manufacture sections of (a building) so that they can be easily transported to and rapidly assembled on a building site.
▸ **preˌfabriˈcation** *n*

preface (ˈprɛfɪs) *n* **1** a statement written as an introduction to a literary or other work, typically explaining its scope, intention, method, etc.; foreword. **2** anything introductory. ◆ *vb* **prefaces, prefacing, prefaced.** (*tr*) **3** to furnish with a preface. **4** to serve as a preface to. ORIG C14: from Med. L *praefātia*, from L *praefātiō* a saying beforehand, from *praefārī* to utter in advance
▸ **ˈprefacer** *n*

prefatory (ˈprɛfətərɪ, -trɪ) *or* **prefatorial** (ˌprɛfəˈtɔːrɪəl) *adj* of or serving as a preface; introductory. ORIG C17: from L *praefārī* to say in advance

prefect (ˈpriːfɛkt) *n* **1** (in France, Italy, etc.) the chief administrative officer in a department. **2** (in France, etc.) the head of a police force. **3** *Brit., Austral., & NZ.* a schoolchild appointed to a position of limited power over his or her fellows. **4** (in ancient Rome) any of several magistrates or military commanders. **5** *RC Church.* one of two senior masters in a Jesuit school or college. ORIG C14: from L *praefectus* one put in charge, from *praeficere* to place in authority over, from *prae* before + *facere* to do
▸ **prefectorial** (ˌpriːfɛkˈtɔːrɪəl) *adj*

prefecture (ˈpriːfɛkˌtjʊə) *n* **1** the office, position, or area of authority of a prefect. **2** the official residence of a prefect in France, etc.

prefer (prɪˈfɜː) *vb* **prefers, preferring, preferred. 1** (when *tr, may take a clause as object or an infinitive*) to like better or value more highly: *I prefer to stand.* **2** *Law.* (esp. of the police) to put (charges) before a court, magistrate, etc., for consideration and judgment. **3** (*tr; often passive*) to advance in rank over another or others; promote. ORIG C14: from L *praeferre* to carry in front, prefer

> **USAGE NOTE** Normally, *to* is used after *prefer* and *preferable*, not *than*: *I prefer Brahms to Tchaikovsky; a small income is preferable to no income at all; I prefer snowboarding to skiing.* However, *than* or *rather than* should be used to link infinitives: *people who prefer to do rather than to talk.*

preferable (ˈprɛfərəbᵊl) *adj* preferred or more desirable.
▸ **ˈpreferably** *adv*

> **USAGE NOTE** Since *preferable* already means 'more desirable' it is better when writing not to say something is *more preferable* or *most preferable.* The generally preferred pronunciation of this word in British English is with the stress on the first syllable, though it is occasionally heard with the second syllable stressed, in line with the verb. See also at **prefer.**

preference (ˈprɛfərəns, ˈprɛfrəns) *n* **1** the act of preferring. **2** something or someone preferred. **3** *International trade.* the granting of favour or precedence to particular foreign countries, as by levying differential tariffs.

preference shares *pl n Brit. & Austral.* fixed-interest shares issued by a company and giving their holders a prior right over ordinary shareholders to payment of dividend and to repayment of capital if the company is liquidated. US and Canad. name: **preferred stock.** Cf. **ordinary shares, preferred ordinary shares.**

preferential (ˌprɛfəˈrɛnʃəl) *adj* **1** showing or resulting from preference. **2** giving, receiving, or originating from preference in international trade.
▸ **ˌpreferˈentially** *adv*

preferment (prɪˈfɜːmənt) *n* **1** the act of promoting to a higher position, office, etc. **2** the state of being preferred for promotion or social advancement. **3** the act of preferring.

preferred ordinary shares *pl n Brit.* shares issued by a company that rank between preference shares and ordinary shares in the payment of dividends. Cf. **preference shares, ordinary shares.**

prefigure (priːˈfɪgə) *vb* **prefigures, prefiguring, prefigured.** (*tr*) **1** to represent or suggest in advance. **2** to imagine beforehand.
▸ **ˌprefiguˈration** *n* ▸ **preˈfigurement** *n*

prefix *n* (ˈpriːfɪks). **1** *Grammar.* an affix that precedes the stem to which it is attached, as for example *un-* in *unhappy.* Cf. **suffix** (sense 1). **2** something coming or placed before. ◆ *vb* (priːˈfɪks, ˈpriːfɪks). (*tr*) **3** to put or place before. **4** *Grammar.* to add (a morpheme) as a prefix to the beginning of a word.
▸ **prefixion** (priːˈfɪkʃən) *n*

prefrontal (priːˈfrʌntᵊl) *adj* in or relating to the foremost part of the frontal lobe of the brain.

preglacial (priːˈgleɪsɪəl, -ʃəl) *adj* formed or occurring before a glacial period, esp. before the Pleistocene epoch.

pregnable (ˈprɛgnəbᵊl) *adj* capable of being assailed or captured. ORIG C15 *prenable*, from OF *prendre* to take, from L *prehendere* to catch

pregnant (ˈprɛgnənt) *adj* **1** carrying a fetus or fetuses within the womb. **2** full of meaning or significance. **3** in-

ventive or imaginative. **4** prolific or fruitful. ORIG C16: from L *praegnāns* with child, from *prae* before + *(g)nascī* to be born
▸ **'pregnancy** *n* ▸ **'pregnantly** *adv*

prehensile (prɪ'hɛnsaɪl) *adj* adapted for grasping, esp. by wrapping around a support: *a prehensile tail.* ORIG C18: from F *préhensile,* from L *prehendere* to grasp
▸ **prehensility** (ˌpriːhɛn'sɪlɪtɪ) *n*

prehension (prɪ'hɛnʃən) *n* **1** the act of grasping. **2** apprehension by the mind.

prehistoric (ˌpriːhɪ'stɒrɪk) *or* **prehistorical** *adj* of or relating to man's development before the appearance of the written word.
▸ **ˌprehis'torically** *adv* ▸ **pre'history** *n*

pre-ignition (ˌpriːɪg'nɪʃən) *n* ignition of all or part of the explosive charge in an internal-combustion engine before the exact instant necessary for correct operation.

prejudge (priː'dʒʌdʒ) *vb* **prejudges, prejudging, prejudged.** (*tr*) to judge beforehand, esp. without sufficient evidence.

prejudice ('prɛdʒʊdɪs) *n* **1** an opinion formed beforehand, esp. an unfavourable one based on inadequate facts. **2** the act or condition of holding such opinions. **3** intolerance of or dislike for people of a specific race, religion, etc. **4** disadvantage or injury resulting from prejudice. **5 in** (*or* **to**) **the prejudice of.** to the detriment of. **6 without prejudice.** *Law.* without dismissing or detracting from an existing right or claim. ◆ *vb* **prejudices, prejudicing, prejudiced.** (*tr*) **7** to cause to be prejudiced. **8** to disadvantage or injure by prejudice. ORIG C13: from OF *préjudice,* from L *praejūdicium,* from *prae* before + *jūdicium* sentence, from *jūdex* a judge

prejudicial (ˌprɛdʒʊ'dɪʃəl) *adj* causing prejudice; damaging.
▸ **ˌpreju'dicially** *adv*

prelacy ('prɛləsɪ) *n, pl* **prelacies. 1** Also called: **prelature. 1a** the office or status of a prelate. **1b** prelates collectively. **2** *Often derog.* government of the Church by prelates.

prelapsarian (ˌpriːlæp'sɛərɪən) *adj* of or relating to the human state before the Fall: *prelapsarian innocence.*

prelate ('prɛlɪt) *n* a Church dignitary of high rank, such as a cardinal, bishop, or abbot. ORIG C13: from OF *prélat,* from Church L *praelātus,* from L *praeferre* to hold in special esteem
▸ **prelatic** (prɪ'lætɪk) *or* **pre'latical** *adj*

preliminaries (prɪ'lɪmɪnərɪz) *pl n* the full word for **prelims.**

preliminary (prɪ'lɪmɪnərɪ) *adj* **1** (*usually prenominal*) occurring before or in preparation; introductory. ◆ *n, pl* **preliminaries. 2** a preliminary event or occurrence. **3** an eliminating contest held before the main competition. ORIG C17: from NL *praelīminăris,* from L *prae* before + *līmen* threshold
▸ **pre'liminarily** *adv*

prelims ('priːlɪmz, prɪ'lɪmz) *pl n* **1** Also called: **front matter.** the pages of a book, such as the title page and contents, before the main text. **2** the first public examinations taken for the bachelor's degree in some universities. **3** (in Scotland) the school examinations taken before public examinations. ORIG C19: a contraction of PRELIMINARIES

preloved ('priːˌlʌvd) *adj Austral. inf.* previously owned or used; second-hand.

prelude ('prɛljuːd) *n* **1a** a piece of music that precedes a fugue, or forms the first movement of a suite, or an introduction to an act in an opera, etc. **1b** (esp. for piano) a self-contained piece of music. **2** an introduction or preceding event, occurrence, etc. ◆ *vb* **preludes, preluding, preluded. 3** to serve as a prelude to (something). **4** (*tr*) to introduce by a prelude. ORIG C16: from Med. L *praelūdium,* from *prae* before + L *lūdere* to play
▸ **preludial** (prɪ'ljuːdɪəl) *adj*

premarital (priː'mærɪtᵊl) *adj* (esp. of sexual relations) occurring before marriage.

premature (ˌprɛmə'tjʊə, 'prɛməˌtjʊə) *adj* **1** occurring or existing before the normal or expected time. **2** impulsive or hasty: *a premature judgment.* **3** (of an infant) born before the end of the full period of gestation. ORIG C16: from L *praemātūrus* very early, from *prae* in advance + *mātūrus* ripe
▸ **ˌprema'turely** *adv*

premedical (priː'mɛdɪkᵊl) *adj* **1** of or relating to a course of study prerequisite for entering medical school. **2** of or relating to a person engaged in such a course of study.

premedication (ˌpriːmɛdɪ'keɪʃən) *n Surgery.* any drugs administered to sedate and otherwise prepare a patient for general anaesthesia.

premeditate (prɪ'mɛdɪˌteɪt) *vb* **premeditates, premeditating, premeditated.** to plan or consider (something, such as a violent crime) beforehand.
▸ **pre'mediˌtator** *n*

premeditation (prɪˌmɛdɪ'teɪʃən) *n* **1** *Law.* prior resolve to do some act or to commit a crime. **2** the act of premeditating.

premenstrual syndrome *or* **tension** *n* symptoms, esp. nervous tension, that may be experienced because of hormonal changes in the days before a menstrual period starts. Abbrevs.: **PMS, PMT.**

premier ('prɛmjə) *n* **1** another name for **prime minister. 2** any of the heads of government of the Canadian provinces and the Australian states. **3** *Austral.* a team that wins a premiership. ◆ *adj* (*prenominal*) **4** first in importance, rank, etc. **5** first in occurrence; earliest. ORIG C15: from OF: first, from L *prīmārius* principal, from *prīmus* first

premiere ('prɛmɪˌɛə, 'prɛmɪə) *n* **1** the first public performance of a film, play, opera, etc. **2** the leading lady in a theatre company. ◆ *vb* **premieres, premiering, premiered. 3** (*tr*) to give a premiere of: *the show will be premiered on Broadway.* ORIG C19: from F, fem of *premier* first

premiership ('prɛmjəʃɪp) *n* **1** the office of premier. **2a** a championship competition held among a number of sporting clubs. **2b** a victory in such a championship.

premillennialism (ˌpriːmɪ'lɛnɪəˌlɪzəm) *n* the doctrine or belief that the millennium will be preceded by the Second Coming of Christ.
▸ **ˌpremil'lennialist** *n* ▸ **ˌpremille'narian** *n, adj*

Preminger ★ ('prɛmɪndʒə) *n* **Otto (Ludwig).** 1906–86, US film director, born in Austria. His films include *Carmen Jones* (1954) and *Anatomy of a Murder* (1959).

premise *n* ('prɛmɪs), also **premiss. 1** *Logic.* a statement that is assumed to be true for the purpose of an argument from which a conclusion is drawn. ◆ *vb* (prɪ'maɪz, 'prɛmɪs), **premises, premising, premised. 2** (when *tr, may take a clause as object*) to state or assume (a proposition) as a premise in an argument, etc. ORIG C14: from OF *prémisse,* from Med. L *praemissa* sent on before, from L *praemittere* to dispatch in advance

premises ('prɛmɪsɪz) *pl n* **1** a piece of land together with its buildings, esp. considered as a place of business. **2** *Law.* (in a deed, etc.) the matters referred to previously; the aforesaid.

premium ('priːmɪəm) *n* **1** an amount paid in addition to a standard rate, price, wage, etc.; bonus. **2** the amount paid or payable, usually in regular instalments, for an insurance policy. **3** the amount above nominal or par value at which something sells. **4** an offer of something free or at a reduced price as an inducement to buy a commodity or service. **5** a prize given to the winner of a competition. **6** *US.* an amount sometimes charged for a loan of money in addition to the interest. **7** great value or regard: *to put a premium on someone's services.* **8 at a premium. 8a** in great demand, usually because of scarcity. **8b** above par. ORIG C17: from L *praemium* prize

Premium Savings Bonds *pl n* (in Britain) bonds issued by the Treasury since 1956 for purchase by the public. No interest is paid but there is a monthly draw for cash prizes of various sums. Also called: **premium bonds.**

premolar (priː'məʊlə) *adj* **1** situated before a molar tooth. ◆ *n* **2** any one of eight bicuspid teeth in the human adult, two on each side of both jaws between the first molar and the canine.

premonition (ˌprɛmə'nɪʃən) *n* **1** an intuition of a future, usually unwelcome, occurrence; foreboding. **2** an early

warning of a future event. ORIG C16: from LL *praemonitiō*, from L *praemonēre* to admonish beforehand, from *prae* before + *monēre* to warn
▸ **premonitory** (prɪˈmɒnɪtərɪ, -trɪ) *adj*

Premonstratensian (ˌpriːmɒnstrəˈtɛnsɪən) *adj* **1** of or denoting an order of regular canons founded in 1119 at Prémontré, in France. ◆ *n* **2** a member of this order.

prenatal (priːˈneɪtᵊl) *adj* **1** occurring or present before birth; during pregnancy. ◆ *n* **2** *Inf.* a prenatal examination. ◆ Also: **antenatal.**

prenominal (priːˈnɒmɪnᵊl) *adj* placed before a noun, esp. (of an adjective or sense of an adjective) used only before a noun.

prentice (ˈprɛntɪs) *n* an archaic word for **apprentice.**

prenuptial agreement *n* a contract made between a man and woman before they marry, agreeing on the distribution of their assets in the event of divorce.

preoccupation (priːˌɒkjʊˈpeɪʃən) *n* **1** the state of being preoccupied, esp. mentally. **2** something that preoccupies the mind.

preoccupied (priːˈɒkjʊˌpaɪd) *adj* **1** engrossed or absorbed in something, esp. one's own thoughts. **2** already occupied or used.

preoccupy (priːˈɒkjʊˌpaɪ) *vb* **preoccupies, preoccupying, preoccupied.** (*tr*) **1** to engross the thoughts or mind of. **2** to occupy before or in advance of another. ORIG C16: from L *praeoccupāre* to capture in advance

preordain (ˌpriːɔːˈdeɪn) *vb* (*tr*) to ordain, decree, or appoint beforehand.

prep (prɛp) *n Inf.* **1** short for **preparation** (sense 5) or (chiefly US) **preparatory school.** ◆ *vb* **preps, prepping, prepped. 2** (*tr*) to prepare (a patient) for a medical operation or procedure.

prep. *abbrev. for:* **1** preparation. **2** preparatory. **3** preposition.

preparation (ˌprɛpəˈreɪʃən) *n* **1** the act or process of preparing. **2** the state of being prepared; readiness. **3** (*often pl*) a measure done in order to prepare for something; provision: *to make preparations for something.* **4** something that is prepared, esp. a medicine. **5** (esp. in a boarding school) **5a** homework. **5b** the period reserved for this. Usually shortened to **prep. 6** *Music.* **6a** the anticipation of a dissonance so that the note producing it in one chord is first heard in the preceding chord as a consonance. **6b** a note so employed.

preparative (prɪˈpærətɪv) *adj* **1** preparatory. ◆ *n* **2** something that prepares.
▸ **preˈparatively** *adv*

preparatory (prɪˈpærətərɪ, -trɪ) *adj* **1** serving to prepare. **2** introductory. **3** occupied in preparation. **4 preparatory to.** before: *a drink preparatory to eating.*
▸ **preˈparatorily** *adv*

preparatory school *n* **1** (in Britain) a private school, usually single-sex and for children between the ages of 6 and 13, generally preparing pupils for public school. **2** (in the US) a private secondary school preparing pupils for college. ◆ Often shortened to **prep school.**

prepare (prɪˈpɛə) *vb* **prepares, preparing, prepared. 1** to make ready or suitable in advance for some use, event, etc.: *to prepare a meal; to prepare to go.* **2** to put together using parts or ingredients; construct. **3** (*tr*) to equip or outfit, as for an expedition. **4** (*tr*) *Music.* to soften the impact of (a dissonant note) by the use of preparation. **5 be prepared.** (*foll. by an infinitive*) to be willing and able: *I'm not prepared to reveal these figures.* ORIG C15: from L *praeparāre*, from *prae* before + *parāre* to make ready
▸ **preˈparer** *n*

preparedness (prɪˈpɛərɪdnɪs) *n* the state of being prepared, esp. militarily ready for war.

prepay (priːˈpeɪ) *vb* **prepays, prepaying, prepaid.** (*tr*) to pay for in advance.
▸ **preˈpayable** *adj*

prepense (prɪˈpɛns) *adj* (*postpositive*) (usually in legal contexts) premeditated (esp. in **malice prepense**). ORIG C18: from Anglo-Norman *purpensé*, from OF *purpenser* to consider in advance, from L *pēnsāre* to consider

preponderant (prɪˈpɒndərənt) *adj* greater in weight, force, influence, etc.
▸ **preˈponderance** *n* ▸ **preˈponderantly** *adv*

preponderate (prɪˈpɒndəˌreɪt) *vb* **preponderates, preponderating, preponderated.** (*intr*) **1** (often foll. by *over*) to be more powerful, important, numerous, etc. (than). **2** to be of greater weight than something else. ORIG C17: from LL *praeponderāre* to be of greater weight, from *pondus* weight
▸ **preˌponderˈation** *n*

preposition (ˌprɛpəˈzɪʃən) *n* a word or group of words used before a noun or pronoun to relate it grammatically or semantically to some other constituent of a sentence. ORIG C14: from L *praepositiō* a putting before, from *pōnere* to place
▸ **ˌprepoˈsitional** *adj* ▸ **ˌprepoˈsitionally** *adv*

> **USAGE NOTE** The practice of ending a sentence with a preposition (*Venice is a place I should like to go to*) was formerly regarded as incorrect, but is now acceptable and is the preferred form in many contexts.

prepossess (ˌpriːpəˈzɛs) *vb* (*tr*) **1** to preoccupy or engross mentally. **2** to influence in advance, esp. to make a favourable impression on beforehand.
▸ **ˌpreposˈsession** *n*

prepossessing (ˌpriːpəˈzɛsɪŋ) *adj* creating a favourable impression; attractive.

preposterous (prɪˈpɒstərəs) *adj* contrary to nature, reason, or sense; absurd; ridiculous. ORIG C16: from L *praeposterus* reversed, from *prae* in front + *posterus* following
▸ **preˈposterously** *adv* ▸ **preˈposterousness** *n*

prepotency (prɪˈpəʊtᵊnsɪ) *n* **1** the quality of possessing greater power or influence. **2** *Genetics.* the ability of one parent to transmit more characteristics to its offspring than the other parent. **3** *Bot.* the ability of pollen from one source to bring about fertilization more readily than that from other sources.
▸ **preˈpotent** *adj*

preppy (ˈprɛpɪ) *Inf.* ◆ *adj* **1** of or denoting a style of neat, understated, and often expensive clothes; young but classic. ◆ *n, pl* **preppies. 2** a person exhibiting such style. ORIG C20: orig. US, from *preppy* a person who attends a PREPARATORY SCHOOL

prep school *n Inf.* See **preparatory school.**

prepuce (ˈpriːpjuːs) *n* **1** the retractable fold of skin covering the tip of the penis. Nontechnical name: **foreskin. 2** a similar fold of skin covering the tip of the clitoris. ORIG C14: from L *praepūtium*

prequel (ˈpriːkwəl) *n* a novel or film dealing with events that happened before events in an earlier novel or film, usually made to exploit the success of the earlier work. ORIG C20: from PRE- + (*se*)*quel*

Pre-Raphaelite (ˌpriːˈræfəlaɪt) *n* **1** a member of the **Pre-Raphaelite Brotherhood,** an association of painters and writers founded in 1848 to revive the fidelity to nature and the vivid realistic colour considered typical of Italian painting before Raphael. ◆ *adj* **2** of, in the manner of, or relating to Pre-Raphaelite painting and painters.
▸ **ˌPre-ˈRaphaelitˌism** *n*

prerequisite (priːˈrɛkwɪzɪt) *adj* **1** required as a prior condition. ◆ *n* **2** something required as a prior condition.

prerogative (prɪˈrɒgətɪv) *n* **1** an exclusive privilege or right exercised by a person or group of people holding a particular office or hereditary rank. **2** any privilege or right. **3** a power, privilege, or immunity restricted to a sovereign or sovereign government. ◆ *adj* **4** having or able to exercise a prerogative. ORIG C14: from L *praerogātīva* privilege, earlier: group with the right to vote first, from *prae* before + *rogāre* to ask

pres. *abbrev. for:* **1** present (time). **2** presidential.

Pres. *abbrev. for* President.

presage *n* (ˈprɛsɪdʒ). **1** an intimation or warning of something about to happen; portent; omen. **2** a sense of what is about to happen; foreboding. ◆ *vb* (ˈprɛsɪdʒ,

prɪ'seɪdʒ). **presages, presaging, presaged.** (*tr*) **3** to have a presentiment of. **4** to give a forewarning of; portend. ORIG C14: from L *praesāgium,* from *praesāgīre* to perceive beforehand
▸ **pre'sageful** *adj* ▸ **pre'sager** *n*

presale ('priː,seɪl) *n* the practice of arranging the sale of a product before it is available.
▸ **pre'sell** *vb* (*tr*)

presbyopia (,prɛzbɪ'əʊpɪə) *n* a progressively diminishing ability of the eye to focus, noticeable from middle to old age, caused by loss of elasticity of the crystalline lens. ORIG C18: NL, from Gk *presbus* old man + *ōps* eye
▸ **presbyopic** (,prɛzbɪ'ɒpɪk) *adj*

presbyter ('prɛzbɪtə) *n* **1a** an elder of a congregation in the early Christian Church. **1b** (in some Churches having episcopal politics) an official who is subordinate to a bishop and has administrative and sacerdotal functions. **2** (in some hierarchical Churches) another name for **priest**. **3** (in the Presbyterian Church) an elder. ORIG C16: from LL, from Gk *presbuteros* an older man, from *presbus* old man
▸ **,presby'terial** *adj*

presbyterian (,prɛzbɪ'tɪərɪən) *adj* **1** of or designating Church government by presbyters or lay elders. ◆ *n* **2** an upholder of this type of Church government.
▸ **,presby'terianism** *n*

Presbyterian (,prɛzbɪ'tɪərɪən) *adj* **1** of or relating to any of various Protestant Churches governed by presbyters or lay elders and adhering to various modified forms of Calvinism. ◆ *n* **2** a member of a Presbyterian Church.
▸ **,Presby'terianism** *n*

presbytery ('prɛzbɪtərɪ) *n, pl* **presbyteries. 1** *Presbyterian Church.* **1a** a local Church court. **1b** the congregations within the jurisdiction of any such court. **2** the part of a church east of the choir, in which the main altar is situated; a sanctuary. **3** presbyters or elders collectively. **4** *RC Church.* the residence of a parish priest. ORIG C15: from OF *presbiterie,* from Church L, from Gk *presbyterion;* see PRESBYTER

prescience ('prɛsɪəns) *n* knowledge of events before they take place; foreknowledge. ORIG C14: from L *praescīre* to foreknow
▸ **'prescient** *adj*

Prescott ★ ('prɛskət) *n* **1 John Leslie.** born 1938, British politician: deputy prime minister from 1997. **2 William Hickling** ('hɪklɪŋ). 1796–1859, US historian.

prescribe (prɪ'skraɪb) *vb* **prescribes, prescribing, prescribed. 1** (*tr*) to lay down as a rule or directive. **2** *Med.* to recommend or order the use of (a drug or other remedy). ORIG C16: from L *praescrībere* to write previously
▸ **pre'scriber** *n*

prescript ('priːskrɪpt) *n* something laid down or prescribed. ORIG C16: from L *praescriptum* something written down beforehand, from *praescrībere* to PRESCRIBE

prescription (prɪ'skrɪpʃən) *n* **1a** written instructions from a physician to a pharmacist stating the form, dosage, strength, etc., of a drug to be issued to a specific patient. **1b** the drug or remedy prescribed. **2a** written instructions for an optician specifying the lenses needed to correct defects of vision. **2b** (*as modifier*): *prescription glasses.* **3** the act of prescribing. **4** something that is prescribed. **5** a long-established custom or a claim based on one. **6** *Law.* **6a** the uninterrupted possession of property over a stated time, after which a right or title is acquired (**positive prescription**). **6b** the barring of adverse claims to property, etc., after a specified time has elapsed, allowing the possessor to acquire title (**negative prescription**). ORIG C14: from legal L *praescriptiō* an order; see PRESCRIBE

prescriptive (prɪ'skrɪptɪv) *adj* **1** making or giving directions, rules, or injunctions. **2** sanctioned by long-standing custom. **3** based upon legal prescription: *a prescriptive title.*
▸ **pre'scriptively** *adv* ▸ **pre'scriptiveness** *n*

presence ('prɛzəns) *n* **1** the state or fact of being present. **2** immediate proximity. **3** personal appearance or bearing, esp. of a dignified nature. **4** an imposing or dignified personality. **5** an invisible spirit felt to be nearby. **6** *Electronics.* a recording control that boosts mid-range frequencies. **7** *Obs.* assembly or company. ORIG C14: via OF from L *praesentia* a being before, from *praeesse* to be before

presence chamber *n* the room in which a great person, such as a monarch, receives guests, assemblies, etc.

presence of mind *n* the ability to remain calm and act constructively during times of crisis.

presenile dementia (priː'siːnaɪl) *n* a form of dementia, of unknown cause, starting before a person is old.

present[1] ('prɛz^ənt) *adj* **1** (*prenominal*) in existence at the time at which something is spoken or written. **2** (*postpositive*) being in a specified place, thing, etc.: *the murderer is present in this room.* **3** (*prenominal*) now being dealt with or under discussion: *the present author.* **4** *Grammar.* denoting a tense of verbs used when the action or event described is occurring at the time of utterance or when the speaker does not wish to make any explicit temporal reference. **5** *Arch.* instant: *present help is at hand.* ◆ *n* **6** *Grammar.* **6a** the present tense. **6b** a verb in this tense. **7 at present.** now. **8 for the present.** for the time being; temporarily. **9 the present.** the time being; now. ◆ See also **presents.** ORIG C13: from L *praesens,* from *praeesse* to be in front of

present[2] *vb* (prɪ'zɛnt). (*mainly tr*) **1** to introduce (a person) to another, esp. to someone of higher rank. **2** to introduce to the public: *to present a play.* **3** to introduce and compere (a radio or television show). **4** to show; exhibit: *he presented a brave face to the world.* **5** to bring or suggest to the mind: *to present a problem.* **6** to put forward; submit: *she presented a proposal for a new book.* **7** to award: *to present a prize; to present a university with a foundation scholarship.* **8** to offer formally: *to present one's compliments.* **9** to hand over for action or settlement: *to present a bill.* **10** to depict in a particular manner: *the actor presented Hamlet as a very young man.* **11** to salute someone with (one's weapon) (usually in **present arms**). **12** to aim (a weapon). **13** to nominate (a clergyman) to a bishop for institution to a benefice in his diocese. **14** to lay (a charge, etc.) before a court, magistrate, etc., for consideration or trial. **15** to bring a formal charge or accusation against (a person); indict. **16** (*intr*) *Med.* to seek treatment for a particular problem: *she presented with postnatal depression.* **17** (*intr*) *Inf.* to produce a specified impression: *she presents well in public.* **18 present oneself.** to appear, esp. at a specific time and place. ◆ *n* ('prɛz^ənt). **19** a gift. ORIG C13: from OF *presenter,* from L *praesentāre* to exhibit, from *praesens* PRESENT[1]

presentable (prɪ'zɛntəb^əl) *adj* **1** fit to be presented or introduced to other people. **2** fit to be displayed or offered.
▸ **pre'sentableness** *or* **pre,senta'bility** *n* ▸ **pre'sentably** *adv*

presentation (,prɛzən'teɪʃən) *n* **1** the act of presenting or state of being presented. **2** the manner of presenting; delivery or overall impression. **3** a verbal report, often with illustrative material: *a presentation on the company results.* **4a** an offering, as of a gift. **4b** (*as modifier*): *a presentation copy of a book.* **5** a performance or representation, as of a play. **6** the formal introduction of a person, as at court; debut. **7** the act or right of nominating a member of the clergy to a benefice.
▸ **,presen'tational** *adj*

presentationism (,prɛzən'teɪʃə,nɪzəm) *n Philosophy.* the theory that objects are identical with our perceptions of them. Cf. **representationalism.**
▸ **,presen'tationist** *n, adj*

presentative (prɪ'zɛntətɪv) *adj* **1** *Philosophy.* able to be known or perceived immediately. **2** conferring the right of ecclesiastical presentation.

present-day *n* (*modifier*) of the modern day; current: *I don't like present-day fashions.*

presenteeism (,prɛzən'tiːɪzəm) *n* the practice of persistently working longer hours and taking fewer holidays than the terms of one's employment demand. ORIG C20: a play on ABSENTEEISM

presenter (prɪ'zɛntə) *n* **1** a person who presents something or someone. **2** *Radio, television.* a person who introduces a show, links items, etc.

presentient (prɪ'sɛnʃənt) *adj* characterized by or experiencing a presentiment. ORIG C19: from L *praesentiens,* from *praesentire,* from *prae-* PRE- + *sentire* to feel

presentiment (prɪˈzɛntɪmənt) *n* a sense of something about to happen; premonition. ORIG C18: from obs. F, from *pressentir* to sense beforehand

presently (ˈprɛzəntlɪ) *adv* **1** in a short while; soon. **2** at the moment. **3** an archaic word for **immediately**.

presentment (prɪˈzɛntmənt) *n* **1** the act of presenting or state of being presented; presentation. **2** something presented, such as a picture, play, etc. **3** *Law.* a statement on oath by a jury of something within their own knowledge or observation. **4** *Commerce.* the presenting of a bill of exchange, promissory note, etc.

present participle (ˈprɛzᵊnt) *n* a participial form of verbs used adjectivally when the action it describes is contemporaneous with that of the main verb of a sentence and also used in the formation of certain compound tenses. In English this form ends in *-ing.*

present perfect (ˈprɛzᵊnt) *adj, n Grammar.* another term for **perfect** (senses 8, 10).

presents (ˈprɛzənts) *pl n Law.* used in a deed or document to refer to itself: *know all men by these presents.*

preservative (prɪˈzɜːvətɪv) *n* **1** something that preserves, esp. a chemical added to foods. ◆ *adj* **2** tending or intended to preserve.

preserve (prɪˈzɜːv) *vb* **preserves, preserving, preserved.** (*mainly tr*) **1** to keep safe from danger or harm; protect. **2** to protect from decay or dissolution; maintain: *to preserve old buildings.* **3** to maintain possession of; keep up: *to preserve a façade of indifference.* **4** to prevent from decomposition or chemical change. **5** to prepare (food), as by salting, so that it will resist decomposition. **6** to make preserves of (fruit, etc.). **7** to rear and protect (game) in restricted places for hunting or fishing. **8** (*intr*) to maintain protection for game in preserves. ◆ *n* **9** something that preserves or is preserved. **10** a special domain: *archaeology is the preserve of specialists.* **11** (*usually pl*) fruit, etc., prepared by cooking with sugar. **12** areas where game is reared for private hunting or fishing. ORIG C14: via OF, from LL *praeservāre,* lit.: to keep safe in advance, from L *prae* before + *servāre* to keep safe
▸ **preˈservable** *adj* ▸ **preservation** (ˌprɛzəˈveɪʃən) *n* ▸ **preˈserver** *n*

preset *vb* (priːˈsɛt), **presets, presetting, preset.** (*tr*) **1** to set (a timing device) so that something begins to operate at the time specified. ◆ *n* (ˈpriːsɛt). **2** *Electronics.* a control, such as a variable resistor, that is not as accessible as the main controls and is used to set initial conditions.

preshrunk (priːˈʃrʌŋk) *adj* (of fabrics) having undergone shrinking during manufacture so that further shrinkage will not occur.

preside (prɪˈzaɪd) *vb* **presides, presiding, presided.** (*intr*) **1** to sit in or hold a position of authority, as over a meeting. **2** to exercise authority; control. ORIG C17: via F from L *praesidēre* to superintend, from *prae* before + *sedēre* to sit

presidency (ˈprɛzɪdənsɪ) *n, pl* **presidencies. 1** the office, dignity, or term of a president. **2** (*often cap.*) the office of president of a republic, esp. of the President of the US.

president (ˈprɛzɪdənt) *n* **1** (*often cap.*) the head of state of a republic, esp. of the US. **2** (in the US) the chief executive officer of a company, corporation, etc. **3** a person who presides over an assembly, meeting, etc. **4** the chief executive officer of certain establishments of higher education. ORIG C14: via OF from LL *praesidens* ruler; see PRESIDE
▸ **presidential** (ˌprɛzɪˈdɛnʃəl) *adj* ▸ **ˌpresiˈdentially** *adv* ▸ **ˈpresidentship** *n*

presidium *or* **praesidium** (prɪˈsɪdɪəm) *n* **1** (*often cap.*) (in Communist countries) a permanent committee of a larger body, such as a legislature, that acts for it when it is in recess. **2** a collective presidency. ORIG C20: from Russian *prezidium,* from L *praesidium,* from *praesidēre* to superintend; see PRESIDE

Presley ★ (ˈprɛzlɪ) *n* **Elvis** (**Aaron** *or* **Aron**). 1935–77, US rock and roll singer. His recordings include "That's All Right (Mama)" (1954), "Heartbreak Hotel" (1956), "Hound Dog" (1956), numbers from the films *Loving You* and *Jailhouse Rock* (both 1957), and *Elvis is Back* (1960).

press[1] (prɛs) *vb* **1** to apply or exert weight, force, or steady pressure (on): *he pressed the button on the camera.* **2** (*tr*) to squeeze or compress so as to alter in shape. **3** to apply heat or pressure to (clothing) so as to smooth out creases. **4** to make (objects) from soft material by pressing with a mould, etc., esp. to make gramophone records from plastic. **5** (*tr*) to clasp; embrace. **6** (*tr*) to extract or force out (juice) by pressure (from). **7** (*tr*) to force or compel. **8** to importune (a person) insistently: *they pressed for an answer.* **9** to harass or cause harassment. **10** (*tr*) to plead or put forward strongly: *to press a claim.* **11** (*intr*) to be urgent. **12** (*tr; usually passive*) to have little of: *we're hard pressed for time.* **13** (when *intr,* often foll. by *on* or *forward*) to hasten or advance or cause to hasten or advance in a forceful manner. **14** (*intr*) to crowd; push. **15** (*tr*) *Arch.* to trouble or oppress. ◆ *n* **16** any machine that exerts pressure to form, shape, or cut materials or to extract liquids, compress solids, or hold components together while an adhesive joint is formed. **17** See **printing press. 18** the art or process of printing. **19 to (the) press.** to be printed: *when is this book going to press?* **20 the press. 20a** news media collectively, esp. newspapers. **20b** (*as modifier*): *press relations.* **21** the opinions and reviews in the newspapers, etc.: *the play received a poor press.* **22** the act of pressing or state of being pressed. **23** the act of crowding or pushing together. **24** a closely packed throng; crowd. **25** a cupboard, esp. a large one used for storing clothes or linen. **26** a wood or metal clamp to prevent tennis rackets, etc., from warping when not in use. ORIG C14 *pressen,* from OF *presser,* from L, from *premere* to press

press[2] (prɛs) *vb* (*tr*) **1** to recruit (men) by forcible measures for military service. **2** to use for a purpose other than intended (esp. in **press into service**). ◆ *n* **3** recruitment into military service by forcible measures, as by a press gang. ORIG C16: back formation from *prest* to recruit soldiers; also infl. by PRESS[1]

press agent *n* a person employed to obtain favourable publicity, such as notices in newspapers, for an organization, actor, etc.

press box *n* an area reserved for reporters, as in a sports stadium.

Pressburg ★ (ˈprɛsbʊrk) *n* the German name for **Bratislava.**

Pressburger ★ (ˈprɛsˌbɜːgə) *n* **Emeric** (ˈɛmərɪk). 1902–88, Hungarian film writer and producer, living in Britain: best known for his collaboration (1942–57) with Michael Powell. Films include *The Life and Death of Colonel Blimp* (1943), *I Know Where I'm Going* (1944), and *A Matter of Life and Death* (1945).

press conference *n* an interview for press reporters given by a politician, film star, etc.

press fit *n Engineering.* a type of fit for mating parts, usually tighter than a sliding fit, used when the parts do not have to move relative to each other.

press gallery *n* an area for newspaper reporters, esp. in a legislative assembly.

press gang *n* **1** (formerly) a detachment of men used to press civilians for service in the navy or army. ◆ *vb* **press-gang.** (*tr*) **2** to force (a person) to join the navy or army by a press gang. **3** to induce (a person) to perform a duty by forceful persuasion.

pressing (ˈprɛsɪŋ) *adj* **1** demanding immediate attention. **2** persistent or importunate. ◆ *n* **3** a large specified number of gramophone records produced at one time from a master record. **4** *Football.* the tactic of trying to stay very close to the opposition when they are in possession of the ball.
▸ **ˈpressingly** *adv*

pressman (ˈprɛsmən, -ˌmæn) *n, pl* **pressmen. 1** a journalist. **2** a person who operates a printing press.

press of sail *n Naut.* the most sail a vessel can carry under given conditions. Also called: **press of canvas.**

press release *n* an official announcement or account of a news item circulated to the press.

pressroom (ˈprɛsˌruːm, -ˌrʊm) *n* the room in a printing establishment that houses the printing presses.

press stud *n* a fastening device consisting of one part with a projecting knob that snaps into a hole on another like part, used esp. on clothing. Canad. equivalent: **dome fastener**.

press-up *n* an exercise in which the body is alternately raised from and lowered to the floor by the arms only, the trunk being kept straight. Also called (US and Canad.): **push-up**.

pressure (ˈprɛʃə) *n* **1** the state of pressing or being pressed. **2** the exertion of force by one body on the surface of another. **3** a moral force that compels: *to bring pressure to bear.* **4** urgent claims or demands: *to work under pressure.* **5** a burdensome condition that is hard to bear: *the pressure of grief.* **6** the force applied to a unit area of a surface, usually measured in pascals, millibars, torrs, or atmospheres. **7** short for **atmospheric pressure** or **blood pressure**. ◆ *vb* **pressures, pressuring, pressured.** (*tr*) **8** to constrain or compel, as by moral force. **9** another word for **pressurize**. ORIG C14: from LL *pressūra* a pressing, from L *premere* to press

pressure cooker *n* a strong hermetically sealed pot in which food may be cooked quickly under pressure at a temperature above the normal boiling point of water.
▸ **ˈpressure-ˌcook** *vb*

pressure group *n* a group of people who seek to exert pressure on legislators, public opinion, etc., in order to promote their own ideas or welfare.

pressure point *n* any of several points on the body above an artery that, when firmly pressed, will control bleeding from the artery at a point farther away from the heart.

pressure suit *n* an inflatable suit worn by a person flying at high altitudes or in space, to provide protection from low pressure.

pressurize *or* **pressurise** (ˈprɛʃəˌraɪz) *vb* **pressurizes, pressurizing, pressurized** *or* **pressurises, pressurising, pressurised.** (*tr*) **1** to increase the pressure in (an enclosure, such as an aircraft cabin) in order to maintain approximately atmospheric pressure when the external pressure is low. **2** to increase pressure on (a fluid). **3** to make insistent demands of (someone); coerce.
▸ **ˌpressuriˈzation** *or* **ˌpressuriˈsation** *n*

pressurized-water reactor *n* a type of nuclear reactor that uses water under pressure as both coolant and moderator.

presswork (ˈprɛsˌwɜːk) *n* the operation of, or matter printed by, a printing press.

Prestel (ˈprɛstɛl) *n Trademark.* (in Britain) the viewdata service operated by British Telecom.

Prester John ★ (ˈprɛstə) *n* a legendary Christian priest and king, believed in the Middle Ages to have ruled in the Far East, but identified in the 14th century with the king of Ethiopia. ORIG C14 *Prestre Johan*, from Med. L *presbyter Iohannes* Priest John

prestidigitation (ˌprɛstɪˌdɪdʒɪˈteɪʃən) *n* another name for **sleight of hand**. ORIG C19: from F: quick-fingeredness, from L *praestigiae* tricks, prob. infl. by F *preste* nimble, & L *digitus* finger
▸ **ˌprestiˈdigiˌtator** *n*

prestige (prɛˈstiːʒ) *n* **1** high status or reputation achieved through success, influence, wealth, etc.; renown. **2a** the power to impress; glamour. **2b** (*modifier*): *a prestige car.* ORIG C17: via F from L *praestigiae* tricks
▸ **prestigious** (prɛˈstɪdʒəs) *adj*

prestissimo (prɛˈstɪsɪˌməʊ) *Music.* ◆ *adj, adv* **1** to be played as fast as possible. ◆ *n, pl* **prestissimos. 2** a piece to be played in this way. ORIG C18: from It.: very quickly, from *presto* fast

presto (ˈprɛstəʊ) *adj, adv* **1** *Music.* to be played very fast. ◆ *adv* **2** immediately (esp. in **hey presto**). ◆ *n, pl* **prestos. 3** *Music.* a passage directed to be played very quickly. ORIG C16: from It.: fast, from LL *praestus* (adj) ready to hand, L *praestō* (adv) present

Preston ★ (ˈprɛstən) *n* a town in NW England, administrative centre of Lancashire, on the River Ribble: developed as a weaving centre (17th–18th centuries); seat of the University of Central Lancashire (1992). Pop.: 177 660 (1991).

Prestonpans ★ (ˌprɛstənˈpænz) *n* a small town and resort in SE Scotland, in East Lothian on the Firth of Forth: scene of the battle (1745) in which the Jacobite army of Prince Charles Edward defeated government forces under Sir John Cope. Pop.: 7014 (1991).

prestressed concrete (ˌpriːˈstrɛst) *n* concrete that contains steel wires that are stretched to counteract the stresses that will occur under load.

Prestwich ★ (ˈprɛstwɪtʃ) *n* a town in Bury, in NW England, in Greater Manchester. Pop.: 31 801 (1991).

Prestwick ★ (ˈprɛstwɪk) *n* a town in SW Scotland, in South Ayrshire on the Firth of Clyde; international airport, golf course: tourism. Pop.: 13 705 (1991).

presumably (prɪˈzjuːməblɪ) *adv* (*sentence modifier*) one supposes that: *presumably he won't see you, if you're leaving tomorrow.*

presume (prɪˈzjuːm) *vb* **presumes, presuming, presumed. 1** (when *tr, often takes a clause as object*) to take (something) for granted; assume. **2** (when *tr, often foll. by an infinitive*) to dare (to do something): *do you presume to copy my work?* **3** (*intr;* foll. by *on* or *upon*) to rely or depend: *don't presume on his agreement.* **4** (*intr;* foll. by *on* or *upon*) to take advantage (of): *don't presume upon his good nature too far.* **5** (*tr*) *Law.* to take as proved until contrary evidence is produced. ORIG C14: via OF from L *praesūmere* to take in advance, from *prae* before + *sūmere* to ASSUME
▸ **presumedly** (prɪˈzjuːmɪdlɪ) *adv* ▸ **preˈsuming** *adj*

presumption (prɪˈzʌmpʃən) *n* **1** the act of presuming. **2** bold or insolent behaviour. **3** a belief or assumption based on reasonable evidence. **4** a basis on which to presume. **5** *Law.* an inference of the truth of a fact from other facts proved. ORIG C13: via OF from L *praesumptiō* anticipation, from *praesūmere* to take beforehand; see PRESUME

presumptive (prɪˈzʌmptɪv) *adj* **1** based on presumption or probability. **2** affording reasonable ground for belief.
▸ **preˈsumptively** *adv*

presumptuous (prɪˈzʌmptjʊəs) *adj* characterized by presumption or tending to presume; bold; forward.
▸ **preˈsumptuously** *adv* ▸ **preˈsumptuousness** *n*

presuppose (ˌpriːsəˈpəʊz) *vb* **presupposes, presupposing, presupposed.** (*tr*) **1** to take for granted. **2** to require as a necessary prior condition.
▸ **presupposition** (ˌpriːsʌpəˈzɪʃən) *n*

preteen (priːˈtiːn) *n* a boy or girl approaching his or her teens.

pretence *or US* **pretense** (prɪˈtɛns) *n* **1** the act of pretending. **2** a false display; affectation. **3** a claim, esp. a false one, to a right, title, or distinction. **4** make-believe. **5** a pretext.

pretend (prɪˈtɛnd) *vb* **1** (when *tr, usually takes a clause as object or an infinitive*) to claim or allege (something untrue). **2** (*tr; may take a clause as object or an infinitive*) to make believe, as in a play: *you pretend to be Ophelia.* **3** (*intr;* foll. by *to*) to present a claim, esp. a dubious one: *to pretend to the throne.* **4** (*intr;* foll. by *to*) *Obs.* to aspire as a candidate or suitor (for). ◆ *adj* **5** make-believe; imaginary. ORIG C14: from L *praetendere* to stretch forth, feign

pretender (prɪˈtɛndə) *n* **1** a person who pretends or makes false allegations. **2** a person who mounts a claim, as to a throne or title.

pretension (prɪˈtɛnʃən) *n* **1** (*often pl*) a false claim, esp. to merit, worth, or importance. **2** a specious or unfounded allegation; pretext. **3** the quality of being pretentious.

pretentious (prɪˈtɛnʃəs) *adj* **1** making claim to distinction or importance, esp. undeservedly. **2** ostentatious.
▸ **preˈtentiously** *adv* ▸ **preˈtentiousness** *n*

preterite *or esp. US* **preterit** (ˈprɛtərɪt) *Grammar.* ◆ *n* **1** a tense of verbs used to relate past action, formed in English by inflection of the verb, as *jumped, swam.* **2** a verb in this tense. ◆ *adj* **3** denoting this tense. ORIG C14: from LL *praeteritum* (*tempus*) past (time), from L *praeterīre* to go by, from *preter-* beyond + *īre* to go

preterm (priːˈtɜːm) *adj* **1** (of a baby) born prematurely. ◆ *adv* **2** prematurely.

pretermit (ˌpriːtəˈmɪt) *vb* **pretermits, pretermitting, pretermitted.** (*tr*) *Rare.* **1** to disregard. **2** to fail to do; neglect;

omit. ORIG C16: from L *praetermittere* to let pass, from *preter-* beyond + *mittere* to send

preternatural (ˌpriːtəˈnætʃrəl) *adj* **1** beyond what is ordinarily found in nature; abnormal. **2** another word for **supernatural.** ORIG C16: from Med. L *praeternātūrālis,* from L *praeter natūram* beyond the scope of nature
▸ **ˌpreterˈnaturally** *adv*

pretext (ˈpriːtɛkst) *n* **1** a fictitious reason given in order to conceal the real one. **2** a pretence. ORIG C16: from L *praetextum* disguise, from *praetexere* to weave in front, disguise

pretor (ˈpriːtə, -tɔː) *n* a variant (esp. US) spelling of **praetor.**

Pretoria ★ (prɪˈtɔːrɪə) *n* a city in N South Africa, the administrative capital of South Africa: two universities (1873, 1930); large steelworks. Pop.: 525 583 (1991).

Pretorius ★ (prɪˈtɔːrɪəs) *n* **1** **Andries Wilhelmus Jacobus** (ˈɑndriːs wɪlˈhɛlmys jaːˈkoːbys). 1799–1853, a Boer leader in the Great Trek (1838) to escape British sovereignty; he also led an expedition to the Transvaal (1848). The town Pretoria was named after him. **2** his son, **Marthinus Wessels** (marˈtiːnys ˈwɛsəls). 1819–1901, first president of the South African Republic (1857–71) and of the Orange Free State (1859–63).

prettify (ˈprɪtɪˌfaɪ) *vb* **prettifies, prettifying, prettified.** (*tr*) to make pretty, esp. in a trivial fashion; embellish.
▸ **ˌprettifiˈcation** *n* ▸ **ˈprettiˌfier** *n*

pretty (ˈprɪtɪ) *adj* **prettier, prettiest. 1** pleasing or appealing in a delicate or graceful way. **2** dainty, neat, or charming. **3** *Inf., often ironical.* excellent, grand, or fine: *here's a pretty mess!* **4** commendable; good of its kind: *he replied with a pretty wit.* **5** *Inf.* effeminate; foppish. **6** *Arch. or Scot.* vigorous or brave. **7 sitting pretty.** *Inf.* well placed or established financially, socially, etc. ◆ *n, pl* **pretties. 8** a pretty person or thing. ◆ *adv Inf.* **9** fairly; somewhat. **10** very. ◆ *vb* **pretties, prettying, prettied. 11** (*tr;* often foll. by *up*) to make pretty; adorn. ORIG OE *prættig* clever
▸ **ˈprettily** *adv* ▸ **ˈprettiness** *n*

pretty-pretty *adj Inf.* excessively or ostentatiously pretty.

pretzel (ˈprɛtsəl) *n* a brittle savoury biscuit, in the form of a knot or stick, eaten esp. in Germany and the US. ORIG C19: from G, from OHG *brezitella*

Preussen ★ (ˈprɔysən) *n* the German name for **Prussia.**

prevail (prɪˈveɪl) *vb* (*intr*) **1** (often foll. by *over* or *against*) to prove superior; gain mastery: *skill will prevail.* **2** to be the most important feature; be prevalent. **3** to exist widely; be in force. **4** (often foll. by *on* or *upon*) to succeed in persuading or inducing. ORIG C14: from L *praevalēre* to be superior in strength
▸ **preˈvailer** *n*

prevailing (prɪˈveɪlɪŋ) *adj* **1** generally accepted; widespread: *the prevailing opinion.* **2** most frequent; predominant: *the prevailing wind is from the north.*
▸ **preˈvailingly** *adv*

prevalent (ˈprɛvələnt) *adj* **1** widespread or current. **2** superior in force or power; predominant.
▸ **ˈprevalence** *n* ▸ **ˈprevalently** *adv*

prevaricate (prɪˈværɪˌkeɪt) *vb* **prevaricates, prevaricating, prevaricated.** (*intr*) to speak or act falsely or evasively with intent to deceive. ORIG C16: from L *praevāricārī* to walk crookedly, from *prae* beyond + *vāricare* to straddle the legs
▸ **preˌvariˈcation** *n* ▸ **preˈvariˌcator** *n*

prevent (prɪˈvɛnt) *vb* **1** (*tr*) to keep from happening, esp. by taking precautionary action. **2** (*tr;* often foll. by *from*) to keep (someone from doing something). **3** (*intr*) to interpose or act as a hindrance. **4** (*tr*) *Arch.* to anticipate or precede. ORIG C15: from L *praevenīre,* from *prae* before + *venīre* to come
▸ **preˈventable** *or* **preˈventible** *adj* ▸ **preˈventably** *or* **preˈventibly** *adv*

prevention (prɪˈvɛnʃən) *n* **1** the act of preventing. **2** a hindrance or impediment.

preventive (prɪˈvɛntɪv) *adj* **1** tending or intended to prevent or hinder. **2** *Med.* tending to prevent disease; prophylactic. **3** (in Britain) of, relating to, or belonging to the customs and excise service or the coastguard. ◆ *n* **4** something that serves to prevent or hinder. **5** *Med.* any drug or agent that tends to prevent disease. Also (for senses 1, 2, 4, 5): **preventative.**
▸ **preˈventively** *or* **preˈventatively** *adv*

> **USAGE NOTE** *Preventive* is generally used in preference to *preventative* in medical contexts and otherwise, and is about twice as common in the Bank of English. Overall, *preventative* is much less frequent in American than in British sources.

Prévert ★ (*French* prevɛr) *n* **Jacques** (ʒak). 1900–77, Parisian poet, satirist, and writer of film scripts, noted esp. for his song poems. He was a member of the surrealist group from 1925 to 1929.

preview (ˈpriːvjuː) *n* **1** an advance view or sight. **2** an advance showing before public presentation of a film, art exhibition, etc., usually before an invited audience. ◆ *vb* **3** (*tr*) to view in advance.

Previn ★ (ˈprɛvɪn) *n* **André** (ˈɒndreɪ). born 1929, US orchestral conductor, born in Germany; living in Britain.

previous (ˈpriːvɪəs) *adj* **1** (*prenominal*) existing or coming before something else. **2** (*postpositive*) *Inf.* taking place or done too soon; premature. **3 previous to.** before. ORIG C17: from L *praevius* leading the way, from *prae* before + *via* way
▸ **ˈpreviously** *adv* ▸ **ˈpreviousness** *n*

previous question *n* **1** (in the House of Commons) a motion to drop the present topic under debate, put in order to prevent a vote. **2** (in the House of Lords and US legislative bodies) a motion to vote on a bill without delay.

previse (prɪˈvaɪz) *vb* **previses, prevising, prevised.** (*tr*) *Rare.* **1** to predict or foresee. **2** to notify in advance. ORIG C16: from L *praevidēre* to foresee
▸ **prevision** (prɪˈvɪʒən) *n*

Prévost d'Exiles ★ (*French* prevo dɛgzil) *n* **Antoine François** (ɑ̃twan frɑ̃swa), known as *Abbé Prévost.* 1697–1763, French novelist, noted for his romance *Manon Lescaut* (1731), which served as the basis for operas by Puccini and Massenet.

prey (preɪ) *n* **1** an animal hunted or captured by another for food. **2** a person or thing that becomes the victim of a hostile person, influence, etc. **3 bird** *or* **beast of prey.** a bird or animal that preys on others for food. **4** an archaic word for **booty.** ◆ *vb* (*intr;* often foll. by *on* or *upon*) **5** to hunt food by killing other animals. **6** to make a victim (of others), as by profiting at their expense. **7** to exert a depressing or obsessive effect (on the mind, spirits, etc.). ORIG C13: from OF *preie,* from L *praeda* booty
▸ **ˈpreyer** *n*

Priam ★ (ˈpraɪəm) *n Greek myth.* the last king of Troy, killed at its fall. He was father by Hecuba of Hector, Paris, and Cassandra.

priapic (praɪˈæpɪk, -ˈeɪ-) *or* **priapean** (ˌpraɪəˈpiːən) *adj* **1** (*sometimes cap.*) of or relating to Priapus. **2** a less common word for **phallic.**

priapism (ˈpraɪəˌpɪzəm) *n Pathol.* prolonged painful erection of the penis, caused by neurological disorders, etc. ORIG C17: from LL *priāpismus,* ult. from Gk PRIAPUS

Priapus ★ (praɪˈeɪpəs) *n* **1** (in classical antiquity) the god of the male procreative power and of gardens and vineyards. **2** (*often not cap.*) a representation of the penis.

Pribilof Islands ★ (ˈprɪbɪləf) *pl n* a group of islands in the Bering Sea, off SW Alaska, belonging to the US: the breeding ground of the northern fur seal. Area: about 168 sq. km (65 sq. miles). Also called: **Fur Seal Islands.**

price (praɪs) *n* **1** the sum in money or goods for which anything is or may be bought or sold. **2** the cost at which anything is obtained. **3** the cost of bribing a person. **4** a sum of money offered as a reward for a capture or killing. **5** value or worth, esp. high worth. **6** *Gambling.* another word for **odds. 7 at any price.** whatever the price or cost. **8 at a price.** at a high price. **9 what price (something)?** what are the chances of (something) happening now? ◆ *vb* **prices, pricing, priced.** (*tr*) **10** to fix the price of. **11** to discover the price of. **12 price out of the market.** to charge so

highly for as to prevent the sale, hire, etc., of. ORIG C13 *pris,* from OF, from L *pretium*
▸ **'pricer** *n*

price control *n* the establishment and maintenance of maximum price levels for basic goods and services by a government.

price-dividend ratio *n* the ratio of the price of a share on a stock exchange to the dividends per share paid in the previous year, used as a measure of a company's potential as an investment. Abbrevs.: **P-D ratio, PDR.**

price-earnings ratio *n* the ratio of the price of a share on the stock exchange to the earnings per share, used as a measure of a company's future profitability. Abbrev.: **P-E ratio.**

price-fixing *n* **1** the setting of prices by agreement among producers and distributors. **2** another name for **price control** or **resale price maintenance.**

price leadership *n Marketing.* the setting of the price of a product or service by a dominant firm at a level that competitors can match, in order to avoid a price war.

priceless ('praɪslɪs) *adj* **1** of inestimable worth; invaluable. **2** *Inf.* extremely amusing or ridiculous.
▸ **'pricelessly** *adv* ▸ **'pricelessness** *n*

price ring *n* a group of traders formed to maintain the prices of their goods.

price-sensitive *adj* likely to affect the price of property, esp. shares and securities: *price-sensitive information.*

pricey *or* **pricy** ('praɪsɪ) *adj* **pricier, priciest.** an informal word for **expensive.**

prick (prɪk) *vb* (*mainly tr*) **1a** to make (a small hole) in (something) by piercing lightly with a sharp point. **1b** to wound in this manner. **2** (*intr*) to cause or have a piercing or stinging sensation. **3** to cause to feel a sharp emotional pain: *knowledge of such poverty pricked his conscience.* **4** to puncture. **5** to outline by dots or punctures. **6** (*also intr;* usually foll. by *up*) to rise or raise erect: *the dog pricked his ears up.* **7** (usually foll. by *out* or *off*) to transplant (seedlings) into a larger container. **8** *Arch.* to urge on, esp. to spur a horse on. **9 prick up one's ears.** to start to listen attentively; become interested. ◆ *n* **10** the act of pricking or the sensation of being pricked. **11** a mark made by a sharp point; puncture. **12** a sharp emotional pain: *a prick of conscience.* **13** a taboo slang word for **penis. 14** *Sl., derog.* an obnoxious or despicable person. **15** an instrument or weapon with a sharp point. **16** the track of an animal, esp. a hare. **17 kick against the pricks.** to hurt oneself by struggling against something in vain. ORIG OE *prica* point, puncture
▸ **'pricker** *n*

pricket ('prɪkɪt) *n* **1** a male deer in the second year of life having unbranched antlers. **2** a sharp metal spike on which to stick a candle. ORIG C14 *priket,* from *prik* PRICK

prickle ('prɪkᵊl) *n* **1** *Bot.* a pointed process arising from the outer layer of a stem, leaf, etc., and containing no woody tissue. Cf. **thorn. 2** a pricking or stinging sensation. ◆ *vb* **prickles, prickling, prickled. 3** to feel or cause to feel a stinging sensation. **4** (*tr*) to prick, as with a thorn. ORIG OE *pricel*

prickly ('prɪklɪ) *adj* **pricklier, prickliest. 1** having or covered with prickles. **2** stinging. **3** irritable. **4** full of difficulties: *a prickly problem.*
▸ **'prickliness** *n*

prickly heat *n* a nontechnical name for **miliaria.**

prickly pear *n* **1** any of various tropical cactuses having flattened or cylindrical spiny joints and oval fruit that is edible in some species. **2** the fruit of any of these plants.

pride (praɪd) *n* **1** a feeling of honour and self-respect; a sense of personal worth. **2** excessive self-esteem; conceit. **3** a source of pride. **4** satisfaction or pleasure in one's own or another's success, achievements, etc. (esp. in **take (a) pride in**). **5** the better or superior part of something. **6** the most flourishing time. **7** a group (of lions). **8** courage; spirit. **9** *Arch.* pomp or splendour. **10 pride of place.** the most important position. ◆ *vb* **prides, priding, prided. 11** (*tr;* foll. by *on* or *upon*) to take pride in (oneself) for. ORIG OE *prȳda*
▸ **'prideful** *adj* ▸ **'pridefully** *adv*

Pride ★ (praɪd) *n* **Thomas.** died 1658, soldier on the Parliamentary side during the Civil War. He expelled members of the Long Parliament hostile to the army (**Pride's Purge,** 1648) and signed Charles I's death warrant.

prie-dieu (priː'djɜː) *n* a piece of furniture consisting of a low surface for kneeling upon and a narrow front surmounted by a rest, for use when praying. ORIG C18: from F, from *prier* to pray + *Dieu* God

prier *or* **pryer** ('praɪə) *n* a person who pries.

priest (priːst) *n* **1** a person ordained to act as a mediator between God and man in administering the sacraments, preaching, etc. **2** (in episcopal Churches) a minister in the second grade of the hierarchy of holy orders, ranking below a bishop but above a deacon. **3** a minister of any religion. **4** an official who offers sacrifice on behalf of the people and performs other religious ceremonies. ◆ *vb* **5** (*tr*) to make a priest; ordain. ORIG OE *prēost,* apparently from PRESBYTER
▸ **'priestess** *fem n* ▸ **'priest,hood** *n* ▸ **'priest,like** *adj*
▸ **'priestly** *adj*

priestcraft ('priːst,krɑːft) *n* **1** the art and skills involved in the work of a priest. **2** *Derog.* the influence of priests upon politics.

priest-hole *or* **priest's hole** *n* a secret chamber in certain houses in England, built as a hiding place for Roman Catholic priests when they were proscribed in the 16th and 17th centuries.

Priestley ★ ('priːstlɪ) *n* **1 J(ohn) B(oynton).** 1894–1984, British author. His works include the novels *The Good Companions* (1929) and *Angel Pavement* (1930) and the comedy *Laburnum Grove* (1933). **2 Joseph.** 1733–1804, British chemist, political theorist, and clergyman, in the US from 1794. He discovered oxygen (1774) independently of Scheele and isolated and described many other gases.

prig[1] (prɪg) *n* a person who is smugly self-righteous and narrow-minded. ORIG C18: from ?
▸ **'priggery** *or* **'priggishness** *n* ▸ **'priggish** *adj* ▸ **'priggishly** *adv*

prig[2] (prɪg) *Brit. arch. sl.* ◆ *vb* **prigs, prigging, prigged. 1** another word for **steal.** ◆ *n* **2** another word for **thief.** ORIG C16: from ?

Prigogine ★ (*French* prigɔʒin) *n* **Ilya** (ilja), Viscount. born 1917, Belgian chemist, born in Russia: Nobel prize for chemistry 1977 for his work on nonequilibrium thermodynamics.

prim (prɪm) *adj* **primmer, primmest. 1** affectedly proper, precise, or formal. ◆ *vb* **prims, primming, primmed. 2** (*tr*) to make prim. **3** to purse (the mouth) primly or (of the mouth) to be so pursed. ORIG C18: from ?
▸ **'primly** *adv* ▸ **'primness** *n*

prima ballerina ('priːmə) *n* a leading female ballet dancer. ORIG from It., lit.: first ballerina

primacy ('praɪməsɪ) *n, pl* **primacies. 1** the state of being first in rank, grade, etc. **2** *Christianity.* the office, rank, or jurisdiction of a primate, senior bishop, or pope.

prima donna ('priːmə 'dɒnə) *n, pl* **prima donnas. 1** a leading female operatic star. **2** *Inf.* a temperamental person. ORIG C19: from It.: first lady

prima facie ('praɪmə 'feɪʃɪ) *adv* at first sight; as it seems at first. ORIG C15: from L, from *prīmus* first + *faciēs* FACE

prima-facie evidence *n Law.* evidence that is sufficient to establish a fact or to raise a presumption of the truth unless controverted.

primal ('praɪməl) *adj* **1** first or original. **2** chief or most important. ORIG C17: from Med. L *prīmālis,* from L *prīmus* first

primaquine ('praɪmə,kwiːn) *n* a synthetic drug used in the treatment of malaria. ORIG C20: from *prima-,* from L *prīmus* first + QUIN(OLIN)E

primarily ('praɪmərɪlɪ, praɪ'mærɪlɪ, -'mɛərɪlɪ) *adv* **1** principally; chiefly; mainly. **2** at first; originally.

primary ('praɪmərɪ) *adj* **1** first in importance, degree, rank, etc. **2** first in position or time, as in a series. **3** fundamental; basic. **4** being the first stage; elementary. **5** (*prenominal*) of or relating to the education of children up to the age of 11. **6** (of the flight feathers of a bird's wing) growing from the manus. **7a** being the part of an electric circuit, such as a transformer, in which a changing current induces a current in a neighbouring circuit: *a primary coil.* **7b** (of a current) flowing in such a circuit. **8a** (of a product) consisting of a natural raw material; unmanufactured. **8b** (of production or industry) involving the extraction or winning of such products. **9** (of Latin, Greek, or Sanskrit tenses) referring to present or future time. **10** *Geol., obs.* relating to the Palaeozoic or earlier eras. ◆ *n, pl* **primaries. 11** a person or thing that is first in rank, occurrence, etc. **12** (in the US) a preliminary election in which the voters of a state or region choose a party's convention delegates, nominees for office, etc. Full name: **primary election. 13** short for **primary colour** or **primary school. 14** any of the flight feathers growing from the manus of a bird's wing. **15** a primary coil, winding, inductance, or current in an electric circuit. **16** *Astron.* a celestial body around which one or more specified secondary bodies orbit: *the sun is the primary of the earth.* ORIG C15: from L *prīmārius* principal, from *prīmus* first

primary accent *or* **stress** *n Linguistics.* the strongest accent in a word or breath group, as that on the first syllable of *agriculture.*

primary cell *n* an electric cell that generates an electromotive force by the direct and usually irreversible conversion of chemical energy into electrical energy. Also called: **voltaic cell.**

primary colour *n* **1** any of three colours (usually red, green, and blue) that can be mixed to match any other colour, including white light but excluding black. **2** any one of the colours cyan, magenta, or yellow. An equal mixture of the three produces a black pigment. **3** any one of the colours red, yellow, green, or blue. All other colours look like a mixture of two or more of these colours.

primary school *n* **1** (in England and Wales) a school for children below the age of 11. It is usually divided into an infant and a junior section. **2** (in Scotland) a school for children below the age of 12. **3** (in the US and Canad.) a school equivalent to the first three or four grades of elementary school.

primate¹ ('praɪmeɪt) *n* **1** any placental mammal of the order *Primates,* typically having flexible hands, good eyesight, and, in the higher apes, a highly developed brain: includes lemurs, apes, and man. ◆ *adj* **2** of, relating to, or belonging to the order *Primates.* ORIG C18: from NL *primates,* pl. of *prīmās* principal, from *prīmus* first
▸ **primatial** (praɪ'meɪʃəl) *adj*

primate² ('praɪmeɪt) *n* **1** another name for an **archbishop. 2 Primate of all England.** the Archbishop of Canterbury. **3 Primate of England.** the Archbishop of York. ORIG C13: from OF, from L *prīmās* principal, from *prīmus* first

prime (praɪm) *adj* **1** (*prenominal*) first in quality or value; first-rate. **2** (*prenominal*) fundamental; original. **3** (*prenominal*) first in importance; chief. **4** *Maths.* **4a** having no factors except itself or one: $x^2 + x + 3$ *is a prime polynomial.* **4b** (foll. by *to*) having no common factors (with): *20 is prime to 21.* **5** *Finance.* having the best credit rating: *prime investments.* ◆ *n* **6** the time when a thing is at its best. **7** a period of power, vigour, etc. (esp. in **the prime of life**). **8** *Maths.* short for **prime number. 9** *Chiefly RC Church.* the second of the seven canonical hours of the divine office, originally fixed for the first hour of the day, at sunrise. **10** the first of eight basic positions from which a parry or attack can be made in fencing. ◆ *vb* **primes, priming, primed. 11** to prepare (something). **12** (*tr*) to apply a primer, such as paint or size, to (a surface). **13** (*tr*) to fill (a pump) with its working fluid before starting, in order to expel air from it before starting. **14 prime the pump. 14a** See **pump priming. 14b** to make an initial input in order to set a process going. **15** (*tr*) to increase the quantity of fuel in the float chamber of (a carburettor) in order to facilitate the starting of an engine. **16** (*tr*) to insert a primer into (a gun, mine, etc.) preparatory to detonation or firing. **17** (*tr*) to provide with facts beforehand; brief. ORIG (adj) C14: from L *prīmus* first; (n) C13: from L *prīma* (*hora*) the first (hour); (vb) C16: from ?
▸ **'primeness** *n*

prime cost *n* the portion of the cost of a commodity that varies directly with the amount of it produced, principally comprising materials and labour. Also called: **variable cost.**

prime meridian *n* the 0° meridian from which the other meridians are calculated, usually taken to pass through Greenwich.

prime minister *n* **1** the head of a parliamentary government. **2** the chief minister of a sovereign or a state.

prime mover *n* **1** the original force behind an idea, enterprise, etc. **2a** the source of power, such as fuel, wind, electricity, etc., for a machine. **2b** the means of extracting power from such a source, such as a steam engine.

prime number *n* an integer that cannot be factorized into other integers but is only divisible by itself or 1, such as 2, 3, 5, 7, and 11.

primer¹ ('praɪmə) *n* an introductory text, such as a school textbook. ORIG C14: via Anglo-Norman, from Med. L *primārius* (*liber*) a first (book), from L *prīmārius* PRIMARY

primer² ('praɪmə) *n* **1** a person or thing that primes. **2** a device, such as a tube containing explosive, for detonating the main charge in a gun, mine, etc. **3** a substance, such as paint, applied to a surface as a base, sealer, etc. ORIG C15: see PRIME (vb)

prime rate *n* the lowest commercial interest rate charged by a bank at a particular time.

prime time *n* the peak viewing time on television, for which advertising rates are the highest.

primeval *or* **primaeval** (praɪ'miːvᵊl) *adj* of or belonging to the first ages of the world. ORIG C17: from L *prīmaevus* youthful, from *prīmus* first + *aevum* age
▸ **pri'mevally** *or* **pri'maevally** *adv*

priming ('praɪmɪŋ) *n* **1** something used to prime. **2** a substance used to ignite an explosive charge.

primitive ('prɪmɪtɪv) *adj* **1** of or belonging to the beginning; original. **2** characteristic of an early state, esp. in being crude or uncivilized: *a primitive dwelling.* **3** *Anthropol.* denoting a preliterate and nonindustrial social system. **4** *Biol.* of, relating to, or resembling an early stage in development: *primitive amphibians.* **5** showing the characteristics of primitive painters; untrained, childlike, or naive. **6** *Geol.* of or denoting rocks formed in or before the Palaeozoic era. **7** denoting a word from which another word is derived, as for example *hope,* from which *hopeless* is derived. **8** *Protestant theol.* of or associated with a group that breaks away from a sect, denomination, or Church in order to return to what is regarded as the original simplicity of the Gospels. ◆ *n* **9** a primitive person or thing. **10a** an artist whose work does not conform to traditional standards of Western painting, such as a painter from an African civilization. **10b** a painter of the pre-Renaissance era in European painting. **10c** a painter of any era whose work appears childlike or untrained. ◆ Also called (for a, c): **naive. 11** a work by such an artist. **12** a word from which another word is derived. **13** *Maths.* a curve or other form from which another is derived. ORIG C14: from L *prīmitīvus* earliest of its kind from *prīmus* first
▸ **'primitively** *adv* ▸ **'primitiveness** *n*

primitivism ('prɪmɪtɪˌvɪzəm) *n* **1** the condition of being primitive. **2** the belief that the value of primitive cultures is superior to that of the modern world.
▸ **'primitivist** *n, adj*

primo ('priːməʊ) *n, pl* **primos** *or* **primi** (-miː). *Music.* **1** the upper or right-hand part of a piano duet. **2 tempo primo.** at the same speed as at the beginning of the piece. ORIG It.: first, from L *prīmus*

Primo de Rivera ★ (*Spanish* 'primo de ri'βera) *n* **1 José Antonio** (xo'se an'tonjo). 1903–36, Spanish politician; founded Falangism in 1933. **2** his father, **Miguel** (mi'ɣɛl). 1870–1930, Spanish general; dictator of Spain (1923–30).

primogenitor (ˌpraɪməʊ'dʒɛnɪtə) *n* **1** a forefather; ancestor. **2** an earliest parent or ancestor, as of a race. ORIG C17: alteration of PROGENITOR after PRIMOGENITURE

primogeniture (ˌpraɪməʊ'dʒɛnɪtʃə) *n* **1** the state of being a first-born. **2** *Law.* the right of an eldest son to succeed to the estate of his ancestor to the exclusion of all

others. ORIG C17: from Med. L *prīmōgenitūra* birth of a first child, from L *prīmō* at first + LL *genitūra* a birth
▸ **primogenitary** (ˌpraɪməʊˈdʒɛnɪtərɪ, -trɪ) *adj*

primordial (praɪˈmɔːdɪəl) *adj* **1** existing at or from the beginning; primeval. **2** constituting an origin; fundamental. **3** *Biol.* relating to an early stage of development. ORIG C14: from LL *prīmōrdiālis* original, from L *prīmus* first + *ōrdīrī* to begin
▸ **priˌmordiˈality** *n* ▸ **priˈmordially** *adv*

primp (prɪmp) *vb* to dress (oneself), esp. in fine clothes; prink. ORIG C19: prob. from PRIM

primrose (ˈprɪmˌrəʊz) *n* **1** any of various temperate plants of the genus *Primula,* esp. a European variety which has pale yellow flowers. **2** short for **evening primrose.** **3** Also called: **primrose yellow.** a light yellow, sometimes with a greenish tinge. ◆ *adj* **4** of or abounding in primroses. **5** of the colour primrose. ORIG C15: from OF *primerose,* from Med. L *prīma rosa* first rose

primrose path *n* (often preceded by *the*) a pleasurable way of life.

primula (ˈprɪmjʊlə) *n* any plant of the N temperate genus *Primula,* having white, yellow, pink, or purple funnel-shaped flowers with five spreading petals: includes the primrose, oxlip, cowslip, and polyanthus. ORIG C18: NL, from Med. L *prīmula (vēris)* little first one (of the spring)

primum mobile *Latin.* (ˈpraɪmʊm ˈməʊbɪlɪ) *n* **1** a prime mover. **2** *Astron.* the outermost empty sphere in the Ptolemaic system that was thought to revolve around the earth from east to west in 24 hours carrying with it the inner spheres of the planets, sun, moon, and fixed stars. ORIG C15: from Med. L: first moving (thing)

Primus (ˈpraɪməs) *n Trademark.* a portable paraffin cooking stove, used esp. by campers. Also called: **Primus stove.**

prince (prɪns) *n* **1** (in Britain) a son of the sovereign or of one of the sovereign's sons. **2** a nonreigning male member of a sovereign family. **3** the monarch of a small territory that was at some time subordinate to an emperor or king. **4** any monarch. **5** a nobleman in various countries, such as Italy and Germany. **6** an outstanding member of a specified group: *a merchant prince.* ORIG C13: via OF from L *princeps* first man, ruler
▸ **ˈprincedom** *n* ▸ **ˈprinceˌlike** *adj*

Prince ★ (prɪns) *n* full name *Prince Rogers Nelson.* born 1958, US rock musician. His albums include *Dirty Mind* (1981), *Purple Rain* (1984), and *Emancipation* (1996). He changed his stage name to a symbol and is often referred to as 'The Artist (formerly known as Prince)'.

prince consort *n* the husband of a female sovereign, who is himself a prince.

Prince Edward Island ★ *n* an island in the Gulf of St Lawrence that constitutes the smallest Canadian province. Capital: Charlottetown. Pop.: 137 796 (1999 est.). Area: 5656 sq. km (2184 sq. miles). Abbrev.: **PE.**
▸ **Prince Edward Islander** *n*

princeling (ˈprɪnslɪŋ) *n* **1** a young prince. **2** Also called: **princelet.** the ruler of an insignificant territory.

princely (ˈprɪnslɪ) *adj* **princelier, princeliest. 1** generous or lavish. **2** of or characteristic of a prince. ◆ *adv* **3** in a princely manner.
▸ **ˈprinceliness** *n*

Prince of Darkness *n* another name for **Satan.**

Prince of Peace *n Bible.* the future Messiah (Isaiah 9:6): held by Christians to be Christ.

Prince of Wales[1] *n* the eldest son and heir apparent of the British sovereign.

Prince of Wales[2] ★ *n* **Cape.** a cape in W Alaska, on the Bering Strait opposite the coast of extreme NE Russia: the westernmost point of North America.

Prince of Wales Island ★ *n* **1** an island in N Canada, in the Northwest Territories. Area: about 36 000 sq. km (14 000 sq. miles). **2** an island in SE Alaska, the largest island in the Alexander Archipelago. Area: about 4000 sq. km (1500 sq. miles). **3** an island in NE Australia, in N Queensland in the Torres Strait. **4** the former name (until about 1867) of the island of **Penang.**

prince regent *n* a prince who acts as regent during the minority, disability, or absence of the legal sovereign.

Prince Regent ★ *n* George IV as regent of Great Britain and Ireland during the insanity of his father (1811–20).

Prince Rupert ★ *n* a port in W Canada, on the coast of British Columbia: one of the W termini of the Canadian National transcontinental railway. Pop.: 16 620 (1991).

prince's-feather *n* **1** a garden plant with spikes of bristly brownish-red flowers. **2** a tall tropical plant with hanging spikes of pink flowers.

princess (prɪnˈsɛs) *n* **1** (in Britain) a daughter of the sovereign or of one of the sovereign's sons. **2** a nonreigning female member of a sovereign family. **3** the wife and consort of a prince. **4** *Arch.* a female sovereign. **5** Also: **princess dress.** a style of dress having a fitted bodice and A-line skirt without a seam at the waistline.

princess royal *n* **1** the eldest daughter of a British or (formerly) a Prussian sovereign. **2** (*caps.*) the title of Princess Anne.

Princeton ★ (ˈprɪnstən) *n* a town in central New Jersey: settled by Quakers in 1696; an important educational centre, seat of Princeton University (founded at Elizabeth in 1747 and moved here in 1756); scene of the battle (1777) during the War of American Independence in which Washington's troops defeated the British on the university campus. Pop.: 12 016 (1990).

principal (ˈprɪnsɪpᵊl) *adj* (*prenominal*) **1** first in importance, rank, value, etc. **2** denoting capital or property as opposed to interest, etc. ◆ *n* **3** a person who is first in importance or directs some event, organization, etc. **4** *Law.* **4a** a person who engages another to act as his or her agent. **4b** an active participant in a crime. **4c** the person primarily liable to fulfil an obligation. **5** the head of a school or other educational institution. **6** (in Britain) a civil servant of an executive grade who is in charge of a section. **7** the leading performer in a play. **8** *Finance.* **8a** capital or property, as contrasted with income. **8b** the original amount of a debt on which interest is calculated. **9** a main roof truss or rafter. **10** *Music.* either of two types of open diapason organ stops. ORIG C13: via OF from L *principālis* chief, from *princeps* chief man
▸ **ˈprincipally** *adv* ▸ **ˈprincipalship** *n*

> **USAGE NOTE** See at **principle.**

principal boy *n* the leading male role in a pantomime, traditionally played by a woman.

principality (ˌprɪnsɪˈpælɪtɪ) *n, pl* **principalities. 1** a territory ruled by a prince or from which a prince draws his title. **2** the authority of a prince.

principal nursing officer *n* a grade of nurse concerned with administration in the British National Health Service.

principal parts *pl n Grammar.* the main inflected forms of a verb, from which all other inflections may be deduced.

principate (ˈprɪnsɪˌpeɪt) *n* **1** a state ruled by a prince. **2** a form of rule in the early Roman Empire in which some republican forms survived.

Príncipe ★ (ˈprɪnsɪpiː; *Portuguese* ˈprĩsipə) *n* an island in the Gulf of Guinea, off the W coast of Africa: part of São Tomé e Principe. Area: 150 sq. km (58 sq. miles).

principle (ˈprɪnsɪpᵊl) *n* **1** a standard or rule of personal conduct: *he would stoop to anything – he has no principles.* **2** a set of such moral rules: *he was a man of principle.* **3** a fundamental or general truth. **4** the essence of something. **5** a source; origin. **6** a law concerning a natural phenomenon or the behaviour of a system: *the principle of the conservation of mass.* **7** *Chem.* a constituent of a substance that gives the substance its characteristics. **8 in principle.** in theory. **9 on principle.** because of or in demonstration of a principle. ORIG C14: from L *principium* beginning, basic tenet

> **USAGE NOTE** *Principle* and *principal* are often confused: *the principal* (not *principle*) *reason for his departure; the plan was approved in principle* (not *principal*).

principled ('prɪnsɪpᵊld) *adj* **a** having high moral principles. **b** (*in combination*): *high-principled.*

prink (prɪŋk) *vb* **1** to dress (oneself, etc.) finely; deck out. **2** (*intr*) to preen oneself. ORIG C16: prob. changed from PRANK² (to adorn)

print (prɪnt) *vb* **1** to reproduce (text, pictures, etc.), esp. in large numbers, by applying ink to paper or other material. **2** to produce or reproduce (a manuscript, data, etc.) in print, as for publication. **3** to write (letters, etc.) in the style of printed matter. **4** to mark or indent (a surface) by pressing (something) onto it. **5** to produce a photographic print from (a negative). **6** (*tr*) to fix in the mind or memory. **7** (*tr*) to make (a mark) by applying pressure. ◆ *n* **8** printed matter such as newsprint. **9** a printed publication such as a book. **10 in print. 10a** in printed or published form. **10b** (of a book, etc.) offered for sale by the publisher. **11 out of print.** no longer available from a publisher. **12** a design or picture printed from an engraved plate, wood block, or other medium. **13** printed text, esp. with regard to the typeface: *small print.* **14** a positive photographic image produced from a negative image on film. **15a** a fabric with a printed design. **15b** (*as modifier*): *a print dress.* **16a** a mark made by pressing something onto a surface. **16b** a stamp, die, etc., that makes such an impression. **17** See **fingerprint.** ◆ See also **print out.** ORIG C13 *priente,* from OF: something printed, from *preindre* to make an impression, from L *premere* to press
▸ **'printable** *adj*

printed circuit *n* an electronic circuit in which certain components and the connections between them are formed by etching a metallic coating or by electrodeposition on one or both sides of a thin insulating board.

printer ('prɪntə) *n* **1** a person or business engaged in printing. **2** a machine or device that prints. **3** *Computing.* an output device for printing results on paper.

printer's devil *n* an apprentice or errand boy in a printing establishment.

printing ('prɪntɪŋ) *n* **1** the business or art of producing printed matter. **2** printed text. **3** Also called: **impression.** all the copies of a book, etc., printed at one time. **4** a form of writing in which letters resemble printed letters.

printing press *n* any of various machines used for printing.

printmaker ('prɪnt,meɪkə) *n* a person who makes print or prints, esp. a craftsman or artist.

print out *vb* (*tr, adv*) **1** (of a computer output device) to produce (printed information). ◆ *n* **print-out, printout. 2** such printed information.

print shop *n* a place in which printing is carried out.

prion ('pri:ɒn) *n* a protein in the brain, an abnormal transmissible form of which is thought to be the agent responsible for certain spongiform encephalopathies, such as BSE, scrapie, Creutzfeldt-Jakob disease, and kuru. ORIG C20: from *pr(oteinaceous) i(nfectious particle)* + -ON

prior¹ ('praɪə) *adj* **1** (*prenominal*) previous. **2 prior to.** before; until. ORIG C18: from L: previous

prior² ('praɪə) *n* **1** the superior of a community in certain religious orders. **2** the deputy head of a monastery or abbey, immediately below the abbot. ORIG C11: from LL: head, from L (adj): previous, from OL *pri* before
▸ **'priorate** *n* ▸ **'prioress** *fem n*

Prior ★ ('praɪə) *n* **Matthew.** 1664–1721, English poet and diplomat, noted for his occasional verse.

priority (praɪ'ɒrɪtɪ) *n, pl* **priorities. 1** the condition of being prior; antecedence; precedence. **2** the right of precedence over others. **3** something given specified attention: *my first priority.*

priory ('praɪərɪ) *n, pl* **priories.** a religious house governed by a prior, sometimes being subordinate to an abbey. ORIG C13: from Med. L *priōria*

Pripet ★ ('pri:pɪt) *n* a river in E Europe, rising in NW Ukraine and flowing northeast into Belarus across the **Pripet Marshes** (the largest swamp in Europe), then east into the Dnieper River. Length: about 800 km (500 miles). Russian name: **Pripyat** ('prɪpjətj).

Priscian ★ ('prɪʃɪən) *n* Latin name *Priscianus Caesariensis.* 6th century A.D., Latin grammarian.

prise *or* **prize** (praɪz) *vb* **prises, prising, prised** *or* **prizes, prizing, prized.** (*tr*) **1** to force open by levering. **2** to extract or obtain with difficulty: *they had to prise the news out of him.* ORIG C17: from OF *prise* a taking, from *prendre* to take, from L *prehendere;* see PRIZE¹

prism ('prɪzəm) *n* **1** a transparent polygonal solid, often having triangular ends and rectangular sides, for dispersing light into a spectrum or for reflecting light: used in binoculars, periscopes, etc. **2** *Maths.* a polyhedron having parallel bases and sides that are parallelograms. ORIG C16: from Med. L *prisma,* from Gk: something shaped by sawing, from *prizein* to saw

prismatic (prɪz'mætɪk) *adj* **1** of or produced by a prism. **2** exhibiting bright spectral colours: *prismatic light.* **3** *Crystallog.* another word for **orthorhombic.**
▸ **pris'matically** *adv*

prison ('prɪzᵊn) *n* **1** a public building used to house convicted criminals and accused persons awaiting trial. **2** any place of confinement. ORIG C12: from OF *prisun,* from L *prēnsiō* a capturing, from *prehendere* to lay hold of

prisoner ('prɪzənə) *n* **1** a person kept in custody as a punishment for a crime, while awaiting trial, or for some other reason. **2** a person confined by any of various restraints: *we are all prisoners of time.* **3 take (someone) prisoner.** to capture and hold (someone) as a prisoner.

prisoner of war *n* a person, esp. a serviceman, captured by an enemy in time of war. Abbrev.: **POW.**

prisoner's base *n* a children's game involving two teams, members of which chase and capture each other.

prissy ('prɪsɪ) *adj* **prissier, prissiest.** fussy and prim, esp. in a prudish way. ORIG C20: prob. from PRIM + SISSY
▸ **'prissily** *adv* ▸ **'prissiness** *n*

Priština ★ (*Serbo-Croat* 'pri:ʃtina) *n* a city in S Yugoslavia, in Serbia, capital of the Kosovo-Metohija autonomous region: under Turkish control until 1912; nearby is the 14th-century Gračanica monastery. Pop.: 155 499 (1991).

pristine ('prɪstaɪn, -ti:n) *adj* **1** of or involving the earliest period, state, etc.; original. **2** pure; uncorrupted. **3** fresh, clean, and unspoiled: *his pristine new car.* ORIG C15: from L *pristinus* primitive

> **USAGE NOTE** The use of *pristine* to mean 'fresh, clean, and unspoiled' was formerly considered by some people to be incorrect, but is now generally acceptable.

Pritchett ★ ('prɪtʃɪt) *n* Sir **V(ictor) S(awdon).** 1900–97, British short-story writer, novelist, essayist, and autobiographer.

prithee ('prɪðɪ) *interj Arch.* pray thee; please. ORIG C16: shortened from *I pray thee*

privacy ('praɪvəsɪ, 'prɪvəsɪ) *n* **1** the condition of being private. **2** secrecy.

private ('praɪvɪt) *adj* **1** not widely or publicly known: *they had private reasons for the decision.* **2** confidential; secret: *a private conversation.* **3** not for general or public use: *a private bathroom.* **4** of or provided by a private individual or organization rather than by the state. **5** (*prenominal*) individual; special: *my own private recipe.* **6** (*prenominal*) having no public office, rank, etc.: *a private man.* **7** (*prenominal*) denoting a soldier of the lowest military rank. **8** (of a place) retired; not overlooked. ◆ *n* **9** a soldier of the lowest rank in many armies and marine corps. **10 in private.** in secret. ORIG C14: from L *prīvātus* belonging to one individual, withdrawn from public life, from *prīvāre* to deprive
▸ **'privately** *adv*

private bill *n* a bill presented to Parliament or Congress on behalf of a private individual, corporation, etc.

private company *n* a limited company that does not issue shares for public subscription and whose owners do not enjoy an unrestricted right to transfer their shareholdings. Cf. **public company.**

private detective *n* an individual privately employed

to investigate a crime or make other inquiries. Also called: **private investigator.**

private enterprise *n* economic activity undertaken by private individuals or organizations under private ownership.

privateer (ˌpraɪvəˈtɪə) *n* **1** an armed privately owned vessel commissioned for war service by a government. **2** Also called: **privateersman.** a member of the crew of a privateer. **3** a competitor, esp. in motor racing, who is privately financed rather than sponsored by a manufacturer. ◆ *vb* **4** (*intr*) to serve as a privateer.

private eye *n Inf.* a private detective.

Private Finance Initiative *n* (in Britain) a government scheme to encourage private investment in public projects. Abbrev.: **PFI.**

private health insurance *n* insurance against the need for medical treatment as a private patient.

private hotel *n* **1** a hotel in which the proprietor has the right to refuse to accept a person as a guest. **2** *Austral. & NZ.* a hotel not having a licence to sell alcoholic liquor.

private income *n* an income from sources other than employment, such as investment. Also called: **private means.**

private life *n* the social life or personal relationships of an individual, esp. of a celebrity.

private member *n* a member of a legislative assembly not having an appointment in the government.

private member's bill *n* a parliamentary bill sponsored by a Member of Parliament who is not a government minister.

private parts *or* **privates** *pl n* euphemistic terms for **genitals.**

private patient *n Brit.* a patient receiving medical treatment not paid for by the National Health Service.

private pay bed *n* (in Britain) a hospital bed reserved for private patients who are charged by the health service for use of hospital facilities.

private practice *n Brit.* medical practice that is not part of the National Health Service.

private school *n* a school under the financial and managerial control of a private body, accepting mostly fee-paying pupils.

private secretary *n* **1** a secretary entrusted with the personal and confidential matters of a business executive. **2** a civil servant who acts as aide to a minister or senior government official.

private sector *n* the part of a country's economy that consists of privately owned enterprises.

privation (praɪˈveɪʃən) *n* **1** loss or lack of the necessities of life, such as food and shelter. **2** hardship resulting from this. **3** the state of being deprived. ORIG C14: from L *prīvātiō* deprivation

privative (ˈprɪvətɪv) *adj* **1** causing privation. **2** expressing lack or negation, as for example the English suffix *-less* and prefix *un-*. ORIG C16: from L *prīvātīvus* indicating loss
▸ **ˈprivatively** *adv*

privatize *or* **privatise** (ˈpraɪvɪˌtaɪz) *vb* **privatizes, privatizing, privatized** *or* **privatises, privatising, privatised.** (*tr*) to take into, or return to, private ownership, a company or concern that has previously been owned by the state.
▸ **ˌprivatiˈzation** *or* **ˌprivatiˈsation** *n*

privet (ˈprɪvɪt) *n* **a** any of a genus of shrubs, esp. one having oval dark green leaves, white flowers, and purplish-black berries. **b** (*as modifier*): *a privet hedge.* ORIG C16: from ?

privilege (ˈprɪvɪlɪdʒ) *n* **1** a benefit, immunity, etc., granted under certain conditions. **2** the advantages and immunities enjoyed by a small usually powerful group or class, esp. to the disadvantage of others: *one of the obstacles to social harmony is privilege.* **3** *US Stock Exchange.* a speculative contract permitting its purchaser to make optional purchases or sales of securities at a specified time over a limited period. ◆ *vb* **privileges, privileging, privileged.** (*tr*) **4** to bestow a privilege or privileges upon. **5** (foll. by *from*) to free or exempt. ORIG C12: from OF *privilège,* from L *prīvilēgium* law relevant to rights of an individual, from *prīvus* an individual + *lēx* law

privileged (ˈprɪvɪlɪdʒd) *adj* **1** enjoying or granted as a privilege or privileges. **2** *Law.* **2a** not actionable as a libel or slander. **2b** (of a communication, document, etc.) that a witness cannot be compelled to divulge.

privity (ˈprɪvɪtɪ) *n, pl* **privities. 1** a legally recognized relationship existing between two parties, such as that between the parties to a contract: *privity of contract.* **2** secret knowledge that is shared. ORIG C13: from OF *priveté*

privy (ˈprɪvɪ) *adj* **privier, priviest. 1** (*postpositive;* foll. by *to*) participating in the knowledge of something secret. **2** *Arch.* secret, hidden, etc. ◆ *n, pl* **privies. 3** a lavatory, esp. an outside one. **4** *Law.* a person in privity with another. See **privity.** ORIG C13: from OF *privé* something private, from L *prīvātus* PRIVATE
▸ **ˈprivily** *adv*

privy council *n* **1** the council of state of a monarch, esp. formerly. **2** *Arch.* a secret council.

Privy Council *n* **1** the private council of the British sovereign, consisting of all current and former ministers of the Crown and other distinguished subjects, all of whom are appointed for life. **2** (in Canada) a ceremonial body of advisers of the governor general, the chief of them being the Federal cabinet ministers.
▸ **Privy Counsellor** *n*

privy purse *n* (*often cap.*) **1** an allowance voted by Parliament for the private expenses of the monarch. **2** an official of the royal household responsible for dealing with the monarch's private expenses. Full name: **Keeper of the Privy Purse.**

privy seal *n* (*often cap.*) (in Britain) a seal affixed to certain documents issued by royal authority: of less importance than the great seal.

Prix Goncourt (*French* pri) *n* an annual prize for a work of French fiction. ORIG C20: after the Académie GONCOURT

prize[1] (praɪz) *n* **1a** a reward or honour for having won a contest, competition, etc. **1b** (*as modifier*): *prize jockey; prize essay.* **2** something given to the winner of any game of chance, lottery, etc. **3** something striven for. **4** any valuable property captured in time of war, esp. a vessel. ORIG C14: from OF *prise* a capture, from L *prehendere* to seize; infl. by ME *prise* reward

prize[2] (praɪz) *vb* **prizes, prizing, prized.** (*tr*) to esteem greatly; value highly. ORIG C15 *prise,* from OF *preisier* to PRAISE

prize court *n Law.* a court having jurisdiction to determine how property captured at sea in wartime is to be distributed.

prizefight (ˈpraɪzˌfaɪt) *n* a boxing match for a prize or purse.
▸ **ˈprizeˌfighter** *n* ▸ **ˈprizeˌfighting** *n*

prize ring *n* **1** the enclosed area or ring used by prizefighters. **2 the prize ring.** the sport of prizefighting.

pro[1] (prəʊ) *adv* **1** in favour of a motion, issue, course of action, etc. ◆ *prep* **2** in favour of. ◆ *n, pl* **pros. 3** (*usually pl*) an argument or vote in favour of a proposal or motion. See also **pros and cons.** ORIG from L *prō* (prep) in favour of

pro[2] (prəʊ) *n, pl* **pros,** *adj Inf.* **1** short for **professional. 2** a prostitute. ORIG C19

PRO *abbrev. for:* **1** Public Records Office. **2** public relations officer.

pro-[1] *prefix* **1** in favour of; supporting: *pro-Chinese.* **2** acting as a substitute for: *proconsul; pronoun.* ORIG from L *prō* (adv & prep). In compound words borrowed from L, *prō-* indicates: forward, out (*project*); away from (*prodigal*); onward (*proceed*); in front of (*provide, protect*); on behalf of (*procure*); substitute for (*pronominal*); and sometimes intensive force (*promiscuous*)

pro-[2] *prefix* before in time or position; anterior; forward: *prognathous.* ORIG from Gk *pro* (prep) before (in time, position, etc.)

proa (ˈprəʊə) *or* **prau** *n* any of several kinds of canoe-like boats used in the South Pacific, esp. one equipped with an outrigger and sails. ORIG C16: from Malay *parāhū* a boat

proactive (prəʊ'æktɪv) *adj* **1** tending to initiate change rather than reacting to events. **2** *Psychol.* of or denoting a mental process that affects a subsequent process. ORIG C20: from PRO-[2] + (RE)ACTIVE

pro-am ('prəʊ'æm) *adj* **1** (of a golf tournament, etc.) involving both professional and amateur players. ◆ *n* **2** a sporting tournament involving both professional and amateur players.

probability (ˌprɒbə'bɪlɪtɪ) *n, pl* **probabilities. 1** the condition of being probable. **2** an event or other thing that is probable. **3** *Statistics.* a measure of the degree of confidence one may have in the occurrence of an event, measured on a scale from zero (impossibility) to one (certainty).

probable ('prɒbəb°l) *adj* **1** likely to be or to happen but not necessarily so. **2** most likely: *the probable cause of the accident.* ◆ *n* **3** a person who is probably to be chosen for a team, event, etc. ORIG C14: via OF from L *probābilis* that may be proved, from *probāre* to prove

probably ('prɒbəblɪ) *adv* **1** (*sentence modifier*) in all likelihood or probability: *I'll probably see you tomorrow.* ◆ *sentence substitute.* **2** I believe such a thing may be the case.

proband ('prəʊbænd) *n* another name (esp. US) for **propositus.** ORIG C20: from L *probandus, probāre* to test

probang ('prəʊbæŋ) *n Surgery.* a long flexible rod, often with a small sponge at one end, for inserting into the oesophagus, as to apply medication. ORIG C17: var., apparently by association with PROBE, of *provang,* coined by W. Rumsey (1584–1660), Welsh judge, its inventor; from ?

probate ('prəʊbɪt, -beɪt) *n* **1** the process of officially proving the validity of a will. **2** the official certificate stating a will to be genuine and conferring on the executors power to administer the estate. **3** (*modifier*) relating to probate: *a probate court.* ◆ *vb* **probates, probating, probated. 4** (*tr*) *Chiefly US.* to establish officially the validity of (a will). ORIG C15: from L *probāre* to inspect

probation (prə'beɪʃən) *n* **1** a system of dealing with offenders by placing them under the supervision of a probation officer. **2 on probation. 2a** under the supervision of a probation officer. **2b** undergoing a test period. **3** a trial period, as for a teacher.
▸ **pro'bational** *or* **pro'bationary** *adj*

probationer (prə'beɪʃənə) *n* a person on probation.

probation officer *n* an officer of a court who supervises offenders placed on probation and assists and befriends them.

probe (prəʊb) *vb* **probes, probing, probed. 1** (*tr*) to search into closely. **2** to examine (something) with or as if with a probe. ◆ *n* **3** something that probes or tests. **4** *Surgery.* a slender instrument for exploring a wound, sinus, etc. **5** a thorough inquiry, such as one by a newspaper into corrupt practices. **6** *Electronics.* a lead connecting to or containing a monitoring circuit used for testing. **7** anything which provides or acts as a coupling, esp. a flexible tube extended from an aircraft to link it with another so that it can refuel. **8** See **space probe.** ORIG C16: from Med. L *proba* investigation, from L *probāre* to test
▸ **'probeable** *adj* ▸ **'prober** *n*

probiotic (ˌprəʊbaɪ'ɒtɪk) *n* **1** a harmless bacterium that helps to protect the body from harmful bacteria. ◆ *adj* **2** of or relating to probiotics: *probiotic yoghurt.* ORIG C20: from PRO-[1] + (ANTI)BIOTIC

probity ('prəʊbɪtɪ) *n* confirmed integrity. ORIG C16: from L *probitās* honesty, from *probus* virtuous

problem ('prɒbləm) *n* **1a** any thing, matter, person, etc., that is difficult to deal with. **1b** (*as modifier*): *a problem child.* **2** a puzzle, question, etc., set for solution. **3** *Maths.* a statement requiring a solution usually by means of several operations or constructions. **4** (*modifier*) designating a literary work that deals with difficult moral questions: *a problem play.* ORIG C14: from LL *problēma,* from Gk: something put forward

problematic (ˌprɒblə'mætɪk) *or* **problematical** *adj* **1** having the nature of a problem; uncertain; questionable. **2** *Logic, obs.* (of a proposition) asserting that a property may or may not hold.
▸ **ˌproblem'atically** *adv*

pro bono publico *Latin.* ('prəʊ 'bəʊnəʊ 'pʊblɪkəʊ) for the public good.

proboscidean *or* **proboscidian** (ˌprəʊbɒ'sɪdɪən) *adj* **1** of or belonging to an order of massive herbivorous placental mammals having tusks and a long trunk: contains the elephants. ◆ *n* **2** any proboscidean animal.

proboscis (prəʊ'bɒsɪs) *n, pl* **proboscises** *or* **proboscides** (-sɪˌdiːz). **1** a long flexible prehensile trunk or snout, as of an elephant. **2** the elongated mouthpart of certain insects. **3** any similar organ. **4** *Inf., facetious.* a person's nose. ORIG C17: via L from Gk *proboskis* trunk of an elephant, from *boskein* to feed

procaine ('prəʊkeɪn, prəʊ'keɪn) *n* a colourless or white crystalline water-soluble substance used, as **procaine hydrochloride**, as a local anaesthetic. ORIG C20: from PRO-[1] + (CO)CAINE

procathedral (ˌprəʊkə'θiːdrəl) *n* a church serving as a cathedral.

procedure (prə'siːdʒə) *n* **1** a way of acting or progressing, esp. an established method. **2** the established form of conducting the business of a legislature, the enforcement of a legal right, etc. **3** *Computing.* another name for **subroutine.**
▸ **pro'cedural** *adj* ▸ **pro'cedurally** *adv*

proceed (prə'siːd) *vb* (*intr*) **1** (often foll. by *to*) to advance or carry on, esp. after stopping. **2** (often foll. by *with*) to continue: *he proceeded with his reading.* **3** (often foll. by *against*) to institute or carry on a legal action. **4** to originate; arise: *evil proceeds from the heart.* ORIG C14: from L *prōcēdere* to advance
▸ **pro'ceeder** *n*

proceeding (prə'siːdɪŋ) *n* **1** an act or course of action. **2a** a legal action. **2b** any step taken in a legal action. **3** (*pl*) the minutes of the meetings of a society, etc. **4** (*pl*) legal action; litigation. **5** (*pl*) the events of an occasion.

proceeds ('prəʊsiːdz) *pl n* **1** the profit or return derived from a commercial transaction, investment, etc. **2** the result, esp. the total sum, accruing from some undertaking.

process[1] ('prəʊses) *n* **1** a series of actions which produce a change or development: *the process of digestion.* **2** a method of doing or producing something. **3** progress or course of time. **4 in the process of.** during or in the course of. **5a** a summons commanding a person to appear in court. **5b** the whole proceedings in an action at law. **6** a natural outgrowth or projection of a part or organism. **7** (*modifier*) relating to the general preparation of a printing forme or plate by the use, at some stage, of photography. ◆ *vb* (*tr*) **8** to subject to a routine procedure; handle. **9** to treat or prepare by a special method, esp. to treat (food) in order to preserve it: *to process cheese.* **10a** to institute legal proceedings against. **10b** to serve a process on. **11** *Photog.* **11a** to develop, rinse, fix, wash, and dry (exposed film, etc.). **11b** to produce final prints or slides from (undeveloped film). **12** *Computing.* to perform operations on (data) according to programmed instructions in order to obtain the required information. ORIG C14: from OF *procès,* from L *prōcessus* an advancing, from *prōcēdere* to proceed

process[2] (prə'ses) *vb* (*intr*) to proceed in a procession. ORIG C19: back formation from PROCESSION

process industry *n* a manufacturing industry, such as oil refining, which converts bulk raw materials into a workable form.

procession (prə'seʃən) *n* **1** the act of proceeding in a regular formation. **2** a group of people or things moving forwards in an orderly, regular, or ceremonial manner. **3** *Christianity.* the emanation of the Holy Spirit. ◆ *vb* **4** (*intr*) *Rare.* to go in procession. ORIG C12: via OF from L *prōcessiō* a marching forwards

processional (prə'seʃənəl) *adj* **1** of or suitable for a procession. ◆ *n* **2** *Christianity.* **2a** a book containing the prayers, hymns, etc., prescribed for processions. **2b** a hymn, etc., used in a procession.

processor ('prəʊsesə) *n* **1** *Computing.* another name for **central processing unit. 2** a person or thing that carries out a process.

process-server *n* a sheriff's officer who serves legal documents such as writs for appearance in court.

procès-verbal *French.* (prɔsɛverbal) *n, pl* **-baux** (-bo). a written record of an official proceeding; minutes. ORIG C17: from F: see PROCESS, VERBAL

pro-choice *adj* (of an organization, pressure group, etc.) supporting the right of a woman to have an abortion. Cf. **pro-life.**

prochronism ('prəukrə,nɪzəm) *n* an error in dating that places an event earlier than it actually occurred. ORIG C17: from PRO-[2] + Gk *khronos* time + -ISM, by analogy with ANACHRONISM

proclaim (prə'kleɪm) *vb* (*tr*) **1** (*may take a clause as object*) to announce publicly. **2** (*may take a clause as object*) to indicate plainly. **3** to praise or extol. ORIG C14: from L *prōclāmāre* to shout aloud
▸ **proclamation** (,prɒklə'meɪʃən) *n* ▸ **pro'claimer** *n* ▸ **proclamatory** (prə'klæmətərɪ, -trɪ) *adj*

proclitic (prəu'klɪtɪk) *adj* **1a** denoting a monosyllabic word or form having no stress and pronounced as a prefix of the following word, as in English *'t* for *it* in *'twas.* **1b** (in classical Greek) denoting a word that throws its accent onto the following word. ◆ *n* **2** a proclitic word or form. ORIG C19: from NL *proclīticus,* from Gk *proklinein* to lean forwards; on the model of ENCLITIC

proclivity (prə'klɪvɪtɪ) *n, pl* **proclivities.** a tendency or inclination. ORIG C16: from L *prōclīvitās,* from *prōclīvis* steep, from *clīvus* a slope

Proclus ★ ('prəukləs, 'prɒk-) *n* ?410–485 A.D., Greek Neo-Platonist philosopher.

Procne ★ ('prɒknɪ) *n Greek myth.* a princess of Athens, who punished her husband for raping her sister Philomela by feeding him the flesh of their son. She was changed at her death into a swallow. See **Philomela.**

proconsul (prəu'kɒns°l) *n* **1** a governor of a colony or other dependency. **2** (in ancient Rome) the governor of a senatorial province.
▸ **proconsular** (prəu'kɒnsjulə) *adj*

Procopius ★ (prəu'kəupɪəs) *n* ?490–?562 A.D., Byzantine historian, noted for his account of the wars of Justinian I against the Persians, Vandals, and Ostrogoths.

procrastinate (prəu'kræstɪ,neɪt, prə-) *vb* **procrastinates, procrastinating, procrastinated.** (*usually intr*) to put off (an action) until later; delay. ORIG C16: from L *prōcrāstināre* to postpone until tomorrow, from PRO-[1] + *crās* tomorrow
▸ **pro,crasti'nation** *n* ▸ **pro'crasti,nator** *n*

procreate ('prəukrɪ,eɪt) *vb* **procreates, procreating, procreated. 1** to beget or engender (offspring). **2** (*tr*) to bring into being. ORIG C16: from L *prōcreāre,* from PRO-[1] + *creāre* to create
▸ **'procreant** *or* **'procre,ative** *adj* ▸ **,procre'ation** *n* ▸ **'procre,ator** *n*

Procrustean (prəu'krʌstɪən) *adj* tending or designed to produce conformity by violent or ruthless methods.

Procrustes ★ (prəu'krʌstiːz) *n Greek myth.* a robber, who put travellers in his bed, stretching or lopping off their limbs so that they fitted it. ORIG C16: from Gk *Prokroustēs* the stretcher, from *prokrouein* to extend by hammering out

proctology (prɒk'tɒlədʒɪ) *n* the branch of medical science concerned with the rectum. ORIG from Gk *prōktos* rectum + -OLOGY

proctor ('prɒktə) *n* **1** a member of the staff of certain universities having duties including the enforcement of discipline. **2** (formerly) an agent, esp. one engaged to conduct another's case in a court. **3** *Church of England.* one of the elected representatives of the clergy in Convocation. ORIG C14: syncopated var. of PROCURATOR
▸ **proctorial** (prɒk'tɔːrɪəl) *adj*

procumbent (prəu'kʌmbənt) *adj* **1** (of stems) trailing loosely along the ground. **2** leaning forwards or lying on the face. ORIG C17: from L *prōcumbere* to fall forwards

procurator ('prɒkju,reɪtə) *n* **1** (in ancient Rome) a civil official of the emperor's administration, often employed as the governor of a minor province. **2** *Rare.* a person engaged by another to manage his affairs. ORIG C13: from L: a manager, from *prōcūrāre* to attend to
▸ **procuracy** ('prɒkjurəsɪ) *or* **'procu,ratorship** *n* ▸ **procuratorial** (,prɒkjurə'tɔːrɪəl) *adj*

procurator fiscal *n* (in Scotland) a legal officer who performs the functions of public prosecutor and coroner.

procure (prə'kjuə) *vb* **procures, procuring, procured. 1** (*tr*) to obtain or acquire; secure. **2** to obtain (women or girls) to act as prostitutes. ORIG C13: from L *prōcūrāre* to look after
▸ **pro'curable** *adj* ▸ **pro'curement, pro'cural,** *or* **procuration** (,prɒkju'reɪʃən) *n*

procurer (prə'kjuərə) *n* a person who procures, esp. one who procures women as prostitutes.

prod (prɒd) *vb* **prods, prodding, prodded. 1** to poke or jab with or as if with a pointed object. **2** (*tr*) to rouse to action. ◆ *n* **3** the act or an instance of prodding. **4** a sharp object. **5** a stimulus or reminder. ORIG C16: from ?
▸ **'prodder** *n*

prod. *abbrev. for:* **1** produce. **2** produced. **3** product.

Prodi ★ ('prəudɪ) *n* **Romano.** born 1939, Italian statesman and economist: prime minister of Italy (1996–98); president of the European Commission from 1999.

prodigal ('prɒdɪg°l) *adj* **1** recklessly wasteful or extravagant, as in disposing of goods or money. **2** lavish: *prodigal of compliments.* ◆ *n* **3** a person who spends lavishly or squanders money. ORIG C16: from Med. L *prōdigālis* wasteful, from L, from *prōdigere* to squander, from *agere* to drive
▸ **,prodi'gality** *n* ▸ **'prodigally** *adv*

prodigious (prə'dɪdʒəs) *adj* **1** vast in size, extent, power, etc. **2** wonderful or amazing. ORIG C16: from L *prōdigiōsus* marvellous, from *prōdigium;* see PRODIGY
▸ **pro'digiously** *adv* ▸ **pro'digiousness** *n*

prodigy ('prɒdɪdʒɪ) *n, pl* **prodigies. 1** a person, esp. a child, of unusual or marvellous talents. **2** anything that is a cause of wonder. **3** something monstrous or abnormal. ORIG C16: from L *prōdigium* an unnatural happening

prodrug ('prəu,drʌg) *n* a compound that is itself biologically inactive but is metabolized in the body to produce an active therapeutic drug.

produce *vb* (prə'djuːs), **produces, producing, produced. 1** to bring (something) into existence; yield. **2** (*tr*) to make: *she produced a delicious dinner.* **3** (*tr*) to give birth to. **4** (*tr*) to present to view: *to produce evidence.* **5** (*tr*) to bring before the public: *he produced a film last year.* **6** (*tr*) to act as producer of. **7** (*tr*) *Geom.* to extend (a line). ◆ *n* ('prɒdjuːs). **8** anything produced; a product. **9** agricultural products collectively: *farm produce.* ORIG C15: from L *prōdūcere* to bring forward
▸ **pro'ducible** *adj* ▸ **pro,duci'bility** *n*

producer (prə'djuːsə) *n* **1** a person or thing that produces. **2** *Brit.* a person responsible for the artistic direction of a play. **3** *US & Canad.* a person who organizes the stage production of a play, including the finance, management, etc. **4** the person who takes overall administrative responsibility for a film or television programme. Cf. **director** (sense 4). **5** the person who supervises the arrangement, recording, and mixing of a record. **6** *Econ.* a person or business enterprise that generates goods or services for sale. Cf. **consumer** (sense 1). **7** *Chem.* an apparatus or plant for making producer gas.

producer gas *n* a mixture of carbon monoxide and nitrogen produced by passing air over hot coke, used mainly as a fuel.

product ('prɒdʌkt) *n* **1** something produced by effort, or some mechanical or industrial process. **2** the result of some natural process. **3** a result or consequence. **4** *Maths.* the result of the multiplication of two or more numbers, quantities, etc. ORIG C15: from L *prōductum* (something) produced, from *prōdūcere* to bring forth

product differentiation *n Commerce.* the real or illusory distinction between competing products in a market.

production (prə'dʌkʃən) *n* **1** the act of producing. **2** anything that is produced; a product. **3** the amount produced or the rate at which it is produced. **4** *Econ.* the creation or manufacture of goods and services with exchange value. **5** any work created as a result of literary or

★ people and places

artistic effort. **6** the presentation of a play, opera, etc. **7** *Brit.* the artistic direction of a play. **8** (*modifier*) manufactured by mass production: *a production model of a car.*
▸ **pro'ductional** *adj*

production line *n* a factory system in which parts or components of the end product are transported by a conveyor through a number of different sites at each of which a manual or machine operation is performed on them.

productive (prə'dʌktɪv) *adj* **1** producing or having the power to produce; fertile. **2** yielding favourable results. **3** *Econ.* **3a** producing goods and services that have exchange value: *productive assets.* **3b** relating to such production: *the productive processes of an industry.* **4** (*postpositive;* foll. by *of*) resulting in: *productive of good results.*
▸ **pro'ductively** *adv* ▸ **pro'ductiveness** *n*

productivity (ˌprɒdʌk'tɪvɪtɪ) *n* **1** the output of an industrial concern in relation to the materials, labour, etc., it employs. **2** the state of being productive.

product liability *n* the liability to the public of a manufacturer or trader for selling a faulty product.

product life cycle *n Marketing.* the four stages (introduction, growth, maturity, and decline) into one of which the sales of a product fall during its market life.

product line *n Marketing.* a group of related products marketed by the same company.

product placement *n* the practice of a company paying for its product to be placed in a prominent position in a film or television programme as a form of advertising.

proem ('prəuɛm) *n* an introduction or preface, such as to a work of literature. ORIG C14: from L *prooemium* introduction, from Gk *prooimion,* from PRO-[2] + *hoimē* song
▸ **proemial** (prəu'i:mɪəl) *adj*

proenzyme (prəu'ɛnzaɪm) *n* the inactive form of an enzyme; zymogen.

Prof. *abbrev. for* Professor.

profane (prə'feɪn) *adj* **1** having or indicating contempt, irreverence, or disrespect for a divinity or something sacred. **2** not designed for religious purposes; secular. **3** not initiated into the inner mysteries or sacred rites. **4** coarse or blasphemous: *profane language.* ◆ *vb* **profanes, profaning, profaned.** (*tr*) **5** to treat (something sacred) with irreverence. **6** to put to an unworthy use. ORIG C15: from L *profānus* outside the temple
▸ **profanation** (ˌprɒfə'neɪʃən) *n* ▸ **pro'fanely** *adv* ▸ **pro'faneness** *n* ▸ **pro'faner** *n*

profanity (prə'fænɪtɪ) *n, pl* **profanities. 1** the state or quality of being profane. **2** vulgar or irreverent action, speech, etc.

profess (prə'fɛs) *vb* **1** (*tr*) to affirm or acknowledge: *to profess ignorance; to profess a belief in God.* **2** (*tr*) to claim (something), often insincerely or falsely: *to profess to be a skilled driver.* **3** to receive or be received into a religious order, as by taking vows. ORIG C14: from L *prōfitērī* to confess openly

professed (prə'fɛst) *adj* (*prenominal*) **1** avowed or acknowledged. **2** alleged or pretended. **3** professing to be qualified as: *a professed philosopher.* **4** having taken vows of a religious order.
▸ **professedly** (prə'fɛsɪdlɪ) *adv*

profession (prə'fɛʃən) *n* **1** an occupation requiring special training in the liberal arts or sciences, esp. one of the three learned professions, law, theology, or medicine. **2** the body of people in such an occupation. **3** an avowal; declaration. **4** Also called: **profession of faith.** a declaration of faith in a religion, esp. as made on entering the Church or an order belonging to it. ORIG C13: from Med. L *professiō* the taking of vows upon entering a religious order, from L: public acknowledgment; see PROFESS

professional (prə'fɛʃənᵊl) *adj* **1** of, suitable for, or engaged in as a profession. **2** engaging in an activity as a means of livelihood. **3a** extremely competent in a job, etc. **3b** (of a piece of work or anything performed) produced with competence or skill. **4** undertaken or performed by people who are paid. ◆ *n* **5** a person who belongs to one of the professions. **6** a person who engages for his or her livelihood in some activity also pursued by amateurs. **7** a person who engages in an activity with great competence. **8** an expert player of a game who gives instruction, esp. to members of a club by whom he or she is hired.
▸ **pro'fessionaˌlism** *n* ▸ **pro'fessionally** *adv*

professional foul *n Football.* a deliberate foul committed as a last-ditch tactic to prevent an opponent from scoring.

professor (prə'fɛsə) *n* **1** the principal teacher in a field of learning at a university or college; a holder of a university chair. **2** *Chiefly US & Canad.* any teacher in a university or college. **3** a person who professes his or her opinions, beliefs, etc. ORIG C14: from Med. L: one who has made his profession in a religious order, from L: a public teacher; see PROFESS
▸ **professorial** (ˌprɒfɪ'sɔ:rɪəl) *adj* ▸ **ˌprofes'sorially** *adv* ▸ **ˌprofes'soriate** *or* **pro'fessorship** *n*

proffer ('prɒfə) *vb* **1** (*tr*) to offer for acceptance. ◆ *n* **2** the act of proffering. ORIG C13: from OF *proffrir,* from PRO-[1] + *offrir* to offer

proficient (prə'fɪʃənt) *adj* **1** having great facility (in an art, occupation, etc.); skilled. ◆ *n* **2** an expert. ORIG C16: from L *prōficere* to make progress
▸ **pro'ficiency** *n* ▸ **pro'ficiently** *adv*

profile ('prəufaɪl) *n* **1** a side view or outline of an object, esp. of a human head. **2** a short biographical sketch. **3** a graph, table, etc., representing the extent to which a person, field, or object exhibits various tested characteristics: *a population profile.* **4** a vertical section of soil or rock showing the different layers. **5** the outline of the shape of a river valley either from source to mouth (**long profile**) or at right angles to the flow of the river (**cross profile**). ◆ *vb* **profiles, profiling, profiled. 6** (*tr*) to draw, write, or make a profile of. ORIG C17: from It. *profilo,* from *profilare* to sketch lightly, from L *fīlum* thread
▸ **'profiler** *or* **profilist** ('prəufɪlɪst) *n*

profile component *n Brit. education.* attainment targets in different subjects brought together for the general assessment of a pupil.

profit ('prɒfɪt) *n* **1** (*often pl*) excess of revenues over outlays and expenses in a business enterprise. **2** the monetary gain derived from a transaction. **3** income derived from property or an investment, as contrasted with capital gains. **4a** *Econ.* the income accruing to a successful entrepreneur and held to be the motivating factor of a capitalist economy. **4b** (*as modifier*): *the profit motive.* **5** a gain, benefit, or advantage. ◆ *vb* **6** to gain or cause to gain profit. ORIG C14: from L *prōfectus* advance, from *prōficere* to make progress
▸ **'profitless** *adj*

profitable ('prɒfɪtəbᵊl) *adj* affording gain or profit.
▸ **ˌprofita'bility** *n* ▸ **'profitably** *adv*

profit and loss *n Book-keeping.* an account compiled at the end of a financial year showing that year's revenue and expense items and indicating gross and net profit or loss.

profit centre *n* a section of a commercial organization which is allocated financial targets in its own right.

profiteer (ˌprɒfɪ'tɪə) *n* **1** a person who makes excessive profits, esp. by charging exorbitant prices for goods in short supply. ◆ *vb* **2** (*intr*) to make excessive profits.

profiterole ('prɒfɪtəˌrəul, prə'fɪtəˌrəul) *n* a small case of choux pastry with a sweet or savoury filling. ORIG C16: from F, lit.: a small profit

profit-sharing *n* a system in which a portion of the net profit of a business is distributed to its employees, usually in proportion to their wages or their length of service.

profit taking *n* selling commodities, securities, etc., at a profit after a rise in market values or before an expected fall in values.

profligate ('prɒflɪgɪt) *adj* **1** shamelessly immoral or debauched. **2** wildly extravagant or wasteful. ◆ *n* **3** a profligate person. ORIG C16: from L *prōflīgātus* corrupt, from *prōflīgāre* to overthrow, from PRO-[1] + *flīgere* to beat
▸ **profligacy** ('prɒflɪgəsɪ) *n* ▸ **'profligately** *adv*

pro forma ('prəʊ 'fɔːmə) *adj* **1** prescribing a set form or procedure. ♦ *adv* **2** performed in a set manner. ORIG L: for form's sake

profound (prə'faʊnd) *adj* **1** penetrating deeply into subjects or ideas: *a profound mind.* **2** showing or requiring great knowledge or understanding: *a profound treatise.* **3** situated at or extending to a great depth. **4** stemming from the depths of one's nature: *profound regret.* **5** intense or absolute: *profound silence.* **6** thoroughgoing; extensive: *profound changes.* ♦ *n* **7** *Arch. or literary.* a great depth; abyss. ORIG C14: from OF *profund,* from L *profundus* deep, from *fundus* bottom
▸ **pro'foundly** *adv* ▸ **profundity** (prə'fʌndɪtɪ) *n*

Profumo ★ (prə'fjuːməʊ) *n* **John (Dennis).** born 1915, British Conservative politician; secretary of state for war (1960–63). He resigned after a scandal that threatened Macmillan's government.

profuse (prə'fjuːs) *adj* **1** plentiful or abundant: *profuse compliments.* **2** (often foll. by *in*) free or generous in the giving (of): *profuse in thanks.* ORIG C15: from L *profundere* to pour lavishly
▸ **pro'fusely** *adv* ▸ **pro'fuseness** *or* **pro'fusion** *n*

progenitive (prəʊ'dʒɛnɪtɪv) *adj* capable of bearing offspring.
▸ **pro'genitiveness** *n*

progenitor (prəʊ'dʒɛnɪtə) *n* **1** a direct ancestor. **2** an originator or founder. ORIG C14: from L: ancestor, from *gignere* to beget

progeny ('prɒdʒɪnɪ) *n, pl* **progenies. 1** the immediate descendant or descendants of a person, animal, etc. **2** a result or outcome. ORIG C13: from L *prōgeniēs* lineage; see PROGENITOR

progesterone (prəʊ'dʒɛstəˌrəʊn) *n* a steroid hormone, secreted mainly by the corpus luteum in the ovary, that prepares and maintains the uterus for pregnancy. ORIG C20: from PRO-[1] + GE(STATION) + STER(OL) + -ONE

progestogen (prəʊ'dʒɛstədʒən) *or* **progestin** (prə'dʒɛstɪn) *n* any of a group of steroid hormones with progesterone-like activity, used in oral contraceptives and in treating gynaecological disorders.

prognathous (prɒg'neɪθəs) *or* **prognathic** (prɒg'næθɪk) *adj* having a projecting lower jaw. ORIG C19: from PRO-[2] + Gk *gnathos* jaw

prognosis (prɒg'nəʊsɪs) *n, pl* **prognoses** (-'nəʊsiːz). **1** *Med.* a prediction of the course or outcome of a disease. **2** any prediction. ORIG C17: via L from Gk: knowledge beforehand

prognostic (prɒg'nɒstɪk) *adj* **1** of or serving as a prognosis. **2** predicting. ♦ *n* **3** *Med.* any symptom or sign used in making a prognosis. **4** a sign of some future occurrence. ORIG C15: from OF *pronostique,* from L *prognōsticum,* from Gk, from *progignōskein* to know in advance

prognosticate (prɒg'nɒstɪˌkeɪt) *vb* **prognosticates, prognosticating, prognosticated. 1** to foretell (future events); prophesy. **2** (*tr*) to foreshadow or portend. ORIG C16: from Med. L *prognōsticāre* to predict
▸ **progˌnosti'cation** *n* ▸ **prog'nosticative** *adj* ▸ **prog'nostiˌcator** *n*

program *or* (*sometimes*) **programme** ('prəʊgræm) *n* **1** a sequence of coded instructions fed into a computer, enabling it to perform specified logical and arithmetical operations on data. ♦ *vb* **programs** *or* **programmes, programming, programmed. 2** (*tr*) to feed a program into (a computer). **3** (*tr*) to arrange (data) in a suitable form so that it can be processed by a computer. **4** (*intr*) to write a program.
▸ **'programmer** *n*

USAGE NOTE The spelling *program* is the generally used US spelling of *programme* in all its senses, and is also the generally preferred spelling when referring to *computer programs.*

programmable *or* **programable** (prəʊ'græməbəl) *adj* capable of being programmed for automatic operation or computer processing.

programme *or US* **program** ('prəʊgræm) *n* **1** a written or printed list of the events, performers, etc., in a public performance. **2** a performance presented at a scheduled time, esp. on radio or television. **3** a specially arranged selection of things to be done: *what's the programme for this afternoon?* **4** a plan, schedule, or procedure. **5** a syllabus or curriculum. ♦ *vb* **programmes, programming, programmed** *or US* **programs, programing, programed. 6** to design or schedule (something) as a programme. ♦ *n, vb* **7** *Computing.* a variant spelling of **program.** ORIG C17: from LL *programma,* from Gk: written public notice, from PRO-[2] + *graphein* to write
▸ **ˌprogram'matic** *adj*

programmed learning *n* a teaching method in which the material to be learned is broken down into easily understandable parts on which the pupil is able to test himself.

programme music *n* music that is intended to depict or evoke a scene or idea.

programme of study *n Brit. education.* the prescribed syllabus that pupils must be taught at each key stage in the National Curriculum.

programming language *n* a simple language system designed to facilitate the writing of computer programs.

program statement *n* a single instruction in a computer program.

program trading *n* trading on international stock exchanges using a computer program to exploit differences between stock index futures and actual share prices on world equity markets.

progress *n* ('prəʊgrɛs). **1** movement forwards, esp. towards a place or objective. **2** satisfactory development or advance. **3** advance towards completion or perfection. **4** (*modifier*) of or relating to progress: *a progress report.* **5** (formerly) a stately royal journey. **6 in progress.** taking place. ♦ *vb* (prə'grɛs). **7** (*intr*) to move forwards or onwards. **8** (*intr*) to move towards completion or perfection. **9** (*tr*) to be responsible for the satisfactory progress of (a project, etc.) to completion. ORIG C15: from L *prōgressus,* from *prōgredī* to advance, from *gradī* to step

progression (prə'grɛʃən) *n* **1** the act of progressing; advancement. **2** the act or an instance of moving from one thing in a sequence to the next. **3** *Maths.* a sequence of numbers in which each term differs from the succeeding term by a constant relation. See also **arithmetic progression, geometric progression, harmonic progression. 4** *Music.* movement from one note or chord to the next.
▸ **pro'gressional** *adj*

progressive (prə'grɛsɪv) *adj* **1** of or relating to progress. **2** progressing by steps or degrees. **3** (*often cap.*) favouring or promoting political or social reform: *a progressive policy.* **4** denoting an educational system that allows flexibility in learning procedures, based on activities determined by the needs and capacities of the individual child. **5** (esp. of a disease) advancing in severity, complexity, or extent. **6** (of a dance, card game, etc.) involving a regular change of partners. **7** denoting an aspect of verbs in some languages, including English, used to express continuous activity: *a progressive aspect of the verb "to walk" is "is walking".* ♦ *n* **8** a person who advocates progress, as in education, politics, etc. **9a** the progressive aspect of a verb. **9b** a verb in this aspect.
▸ **pro'gressively** *adv* ▸ **pro'gressiveness** *n* ▸ **pro'gressivism** *n* ▸ **pro'gressivist** *n*

progress payment *n* an instalment of a larger payment made to a contractor for work carried out up to a specified stage of the job.

prohibit (prə'hɪbɪt) *vb* (*tr*) **1** to forbid by law or other authority. **2** to hinder or prevent. ORIG C15: from L *prohibēre* to prevent, from PRO-[1] + *habēre* to hold
▸ **pro'hibiter** *or* **pro'hibitor** *n*

prohibition (ˌprəʊɪ'bɪʃən) *n* **1** the act of prohibiting or state of being prohibited. **2** an order or decree that prohibits. **3** (*sometimes cap.*) (esp. in the US) a policy of legally forbidding the manufacture, sale, or consumption of alcoholic beverages. **4** *Law.* an order of a superior court forbidding an inferior court to determine a matter outside its jurisdiction.
▸ **ˌprohi'bitionary** *adj* ▸ **ˌprohi'bitionist** *n*

★ people and places

Prohibition (ˌprəʊɪˈbɪʃən) *n* the period (1920–33) when the manufacture, sale, and transportation of intoxicating liquors was banned in the US.
▸ **ˌProhiˈbitionist** *n*

prohibitive (prəˈhɪbɪtɪv) *or (less commonly)* **prohibitory** (prəˈhɪbɪtərɪ, -trɪ) *adj* **1** prohibiting or tending to prohibit. **2** (esp. of prices) tending or designed to discourage sale or purchase.
▸ **proˈhibitively** *adv* ▸ **proˈhibitiveness** *n*

project *n* (ˈprɒdʒɛkt). **1** a proposal, scheme, or design. **2a** a task requiring considerable or concerted effort, such as one by students. **2b** the subject of such a task. ◆ *vb* (prəˈdʒɛkt). **3** (*tr*) to propose or plan. **4** (*tr*) to throw forwards. **5** to jut or cause to jut out. **6** (*tr*) to make a prediction based on known data and observations. **7** (*tr*) to transport in the imagination: *to project oneself into the future.* **8** (*tr*) to cause (an image) to appear on a surface. **9** to cause (one's voice) to be heard clearly at a distance. **10** *Psychol.* **10a** (*intr*) (esp. of a child) to believe that others share one's subjective mental life. **10b** to impute to others (one's hidden desires). **11** (*tr*) *Geom.* to draw a projection of. **12** (*intr*) to communicate effectively, esp. to a large gathering. ORIG C14: from L *prōicere* to throw down

projectile (prəˈdʒɛktaɪl) *n* **1** an object thrown forwards. **2** any self-propelling missile, esp. a rocket. **3** any object that can be fired from a gun, such as a shell. ◆ *adj* **4** designed to be hurled forwards. **5** projecting forwards. **6** *Zool.* another word for **protrusile.** ORIG C17: from NL *prōjectilis* jutting forwards

projection (prəˈdʒɛkʃən) *n* **1** the act of projecting or the state of being projected. **2** a part that juts out. **3** See **map projection. 4** the representation of a line, figure, or solid on a given plane as it would be seen from a particular direction or in accordance with an accepted set of rules. **5** a scheme or plan. **6** a prediction based on known evidence and observations. **7a** the process of showing film on a screen. **7b** the images shown. **8** *Psychol.* **8a** the belief that others share one's subjective mental life. **8b** the process of projecting one's own hidden desires and impulses.
▸ **proˈjectional** *adj* ▸ **proˈjective** *adj*

projectionist (prəˈdʒɛkʃənɪst) *n* a person responsible for the operation of film projection machines.

projective geometry *n* the branch of geometry concerned with the properties of solids that are invariant under projection and section.

projector (prəˈdʒɛktə) *n* **1** an optical instrument that projects an enlarged image of individual slides. Full name: **slide projector. 2** an optical instrument in which a film is wound past a lens so that the frames can be viewed as a continuously moving sequence. Full name: **film** *or* **cine projector. 3** a device for projecting a light beam. **4** a person who devises projects.

prokaryote *or* **procaryote** (prəʊˈkærɪɒt) *n* any organism of the kingdom *Prokaryotae* having cells in which the genetic material is in a single filament of DNA, not enclosed in a nucleus. Cf. **eukaryote.** ORIG from PRO-[2] + KARYO- + *-ote* as in *zygote*
▸ **prokaryotic** *or* **procaryotic** (prəʊˌkærɪˈɒtɪk) *adj*

Prokofiev ★ (prəˈkɒfɪˌɛf; *Russian* praˈkɔfjɪf) *n* **Sergei Sergeyevich** (sɪrˈgjej sɪrˈgjejɪvitʃ). 1891–1953, Soviet composer. His compositions include the orchestral fairy tale *Peter and the Wolf* (1936), the opera *The Love for Three Oranges* (1921), and seven symphonies.

Prokopyevsk ★ (*Russian* praˈkɔpjɪfsk) *n* a city in S Russia: the chief coal-mining centre of the Kuznetsk Basin. Pop.: 253 000 (1995 est.).

prolactin (prəʊˈlæktɪn) *n* a gonadotrophic hormone secreted by the anterior lobe of the pituitary gland. In mammals it stimulates the secretion of progesterone by the corpus luteum and initiates and maintains lactation.

prolapse (ˈprəʊlæps, prəʊˈlæps) *Pathol.* ◆ *n* **1** Also: **prolapsus** (prəʊˈlæpsəs). the sinking or falling down of an organ or part, esp. the womb. ◆ *vb* **prolapses, prolapsing, prolapsed.** (*intr*) **2** (of an organ, etc.) to sink from its normal position. ORIG C17: from L *prōlābi* to slide along

prolate (ˈprəʊleɪt) *adj* having a polar diameter of greater length than the equatorial diameter. Cf. **oblate**[1]. ORIG C17: from L *prōferre* to enlarge
▸ **ˈprolately** *adv*

prole (prəʊl) *n, adj Derog. sl., chiefly Brit.* short for **proletarian.**

prolegomenon (ˌprəʊlɛˈgɒmɪnən) *n, pl* **prolegomenona** (-nə). (*often pl*) a preliminary discussion, esp. a formal critical introduction to a lengthy text. ORIG C17: from Gk, from *prolegein,* from PRO-[2] + *legein* to say
▸ **ˌproleˈgomenal** *adj*

prolepsis (prəʊˈlɛpsɪs) *n, pl* **prolepses** (-siːz). **1** a rhetorical device by which objections are anticipated and answered in advance. **2** use of a word after a verb in anticipation of its becoming applicable through the action of the verb, as *flat* in *hammer it flat.* ORIG C16: via LL from Gk: anticipation, from *prolambanein* to anticipate, from PRO-[2] + *lambanein* to take
▸ **proˈleptic** *adj*

proletarian (ˌprəʊlɪˈtɛərɪən) *adj* **1** of or belonging to the proletariat. ◆ *n* **2** a member of the proletariat. ORIG C17: from L *prōlētārius* one whose only contribution to the state was his offspring, from *prōlēs* offspring
▸ **ˌproleˈtarianism** *n*

proletariat (ˌprəʊlɪˈtɛərɪət) *n* **1** all wage-earners collectively. **2** the lower or working class. **3** (in Marxist theory) the class of wage-earners, esp. industrial workers, in a capitalist society, whose only possession of significant material value is their labour. **4** (in ancient Rome) the lowest class of citizens, who had no property. ORIG C19: via F from L *prōlētārius* PROLETARIAN

pro-life *adj* (of an organization, pressure group, etc.) supporting the right to life of the unborn; against abortion, experiments on embryos, etc.
▸ **ˌpro-ˈlifer** *n*

proliferate (prəˈlɪfəˌreɪt) *vb* **proliferates, proliferating, proliferated. 1** to grow or reproduce (new parts, cells, etc.) rapidly. **2** to grow or increase rapidly. ORIG C19: from Med. L *prōlifer* having offspring, from L *prōlēs* offspring + *ferre* to bear
▸ **proˌliferˈation** *n* ▸ **proˈliferative** *adj*

prolific (prəˈlɪfɪk) *adj* **1** producing fruit, offspring, etc., in abundance. **2** producing constant or successful results. **3** (often foll. by *in* or *of*) rich or fruitful. ORIG C17: from Med. L *prōlificus,* from L *prōlēs* offspring
▸ **proˈlifically** *adv* ▸ **proˈlificness** *or* **proˈlificacy** *n*

prolix (ˈprəʊlɪks, prəʊˈlɪks) *adj* **1** (of a speech, book, etc.) so long as to be boring. **2** long-winded. ORIG C15: from L *prōlixus* stretched out widely, from *līquī* to flow
▸ **proˈlixity** *n* ▸ **proˈlixly** *adv*

prolocutor (prəʊˈlɒkjʊtə) *n* a chairman, esp. of the lower house of clergy in a convocation of the Anglican Church. ORIG C15: from L: advocate, from *loqui* to speak
▸ **proˈlocutorship** *n*

PROLOG *or* **Prolog** (ˈprəʊlɒg) *n* a computer programming language based on mathematical logic. ORIG C20: from *pro(gramming in) log(ic)*

prologue *or US (often)* **prolog** (ˈprəʊlɒg) *n* **1** the prefatory lines introducing a play or speech. **2** a preliminary act or event. **3** (in early opera) **3a** an introductory scene in which a narrator summarizes the main action of the work. **3b** a brief independent play preceding the opera, esp. one in honour of a patron. ◆ *vb* **prologues, prologuing, prologued** *or US* **prologs, prologing, prologed. 4** (*tr*) to introduce with a prologue. ORIG C13: from L *prologus,* from Gk, from PRO-[2] + *logos* discourse

prolong (prəˈlɒŋ) *vb* (*tr*) to lengthen; extend. ORIG C15: from LL *prōlongāre* to extend, from L PRO-[1] + *longus* long
▸ **prolongation** (ˌprəʊlɒŋˈgeɪʃən) *n*

prolusion (prəˈluːʒən) *n* **1** a preliminary written exercise. **2** an introductory essay. ORIG C17: from L *prōlūsiō,* from *prōlūdere* to practise beforehand, from PRO-[1] + *lūdere* to play
▸ **prolusory** (prəˈluːzərɪ) *adj*

prom (prɒm) *n* **1** *Brit.* short for **promenade** (sense 1) or **promenade concert. 2** *US & Canad. inf.* a formal dance held at a high school or college.

PROM (prɒm) *n Computing. acronym for* programmable read only memory.

promenade (ˌprɒməˈnɑːd) *n* **1** *Chiefly Brit.* a public walk, esp. at a seaside resort. **2** a leisurely walk, esp. one in a public place for pleasure or display. **3** a marchlike step in dancing. **4** a marching sequence in a square or country dance. ◆ *vb* **promenades, promenading, promenaded. 5** to take a promenade in or through (a place). **6** (*intr*) *Dancing.* to perform a promenade. **7** (*tr*) to display or exhibit (someone or oneself) on or as if on a promenade. ORIG C16: from F, from *promener* to lead out for a walk, from LL *prōmināre* to drive (cattle) along, from *mināre* to drive, prob. from *minārī* to threaten
▸ **ˌpromeˈnader** *n*

promenade concert *n* a concert at which some of the audience stand rather than sit.

promenade deck *n* an upper covered deck of a passenger ship for the use of the passengers.

promethazine (prəʊˈmɛθəˌziːn) *n* an antihistamine drug used to treat allergies and to prevent vomiting. ORIG C20: from PRO(PYL) + (*di*)*meth*(*ylamine*) + (*phenothi*)*azine*

Promethean (prəˈmiːθɪən) *adj* **1** of or relating to Prometheus. **2** creative, original, or life-enhancing.

Prometheus ★ (prəˈmiːθɪəs) *n Greek myth.* a Titan, who stole fire from Olympus to give to mankind and in punishment was chained to a rock, where an eagle tore at his liver until Hercules freed him.

promethium (prəˈmiːθɪəm) *n* a radioactive element of the lanthanide series artificially produced by the fission of uranium. Symbol: Pm; atomic no.: 61; half-life of most stable isotope, ^{145}Pm: 17.7 years. ORIG C20: NL from PROMETHEUS

prominence (ˈprɒmɪnəns) *n* **1** the state of being prominent. **2** something that is prominent, such as a protuberance. **3** relative importance. **4** *Astron.* an eruption of incandescent gas from the sun's surface, visible during a total eclipse.

prominent (ˈprɒmɪnənt) *adj* **1** jutting or projecting outwards. **2** standing out from its surroundings; noticeable. **3** widely known; eminent. ORIG C16: from L *prōminēre* to jut out, from PRO-[1] + *ēminēre* to project
▸ **ˈprominently** *adv*

promiscuous (prəˈmɪskjʊəs) *adj* **1** indulging in casual and indiscriminate sexual relationships. **2** consisting of a number of dissimilar parts or elements mingled indiscriminately. **3** indiscriminate in selection. **4** casual or heedless. ORIG C17: from L *prōmiscuus* indiscriminate, from PRO-[1] + *miscēre* to mix
▸ **proˈmiscuously** *adv* ▸ **promiscuity** (ˌprɒmɪˈskjuːɪtɪ) *or* **proˈmiscuousness** *n*

promise (ˈprɒmɪs) *vb* **promises, promising, promised. 1** (often foll. by *to;* when *tr, may take a clause as object or an infinitive*) to give an assurance of (something to someone): *I promise that I will come.* **2** (*tr*) to undertake to give (something to someone): *he promised me a car for my birthday.* **3** (when *tr, takes an infinitive*) to cause people to expect that one is likely (to be or do something): *she promises to be a fine soprano.* **4** (*tr; usually passive*) *Obs.* to betroth: *I'm promised to Bill.* **5** (*tr*) to assure (someone) of the authenticity or inevitability of something: *there'll be trouble, I promise you.* ◆ *n* **6** an assurance given by one person to another agreeing or guaranteeing to do or not to do something. **7** indication of forthcoming excellence: *a writer showing considerable promise.* **8** the thing of which an assurance is given. ORIG C14: from L *prōmissum* a promise, from *prōmittere* to send forth
▸ **ˌpromiˈsee** *n* ▸ **ˈpromiser** *or* (*Law*) **ˈpromisor** *n*

Promised Land ★ *n* **1** *Old Testament.* the land of Canaan, promised by God to Abraham and his descendants as their heritage (Genesis 12:7). **2** *Christianity.* heaven. **3** any longed-for place where one expects to find greater happiness.

promising (ˈprɒmɪsɪŋ) *adj* showing promise of future success.
▸ **ˈpromisingly** *adv*

promissory (ˈprɒmɪsərɪ) *adj* **1** containing, relating to, or having the nature of a promise. **2** *Insurance.* stipulating how the provisions of an insurance contract will be fulfilled.

promissory note *n Commerce, chiefly US.* a document containing a signed promise to pay a stated sum of money to a specified person at a designated date or on demand. Also called: **note, note of hand.**

promo (ˈprəʊməʊ) *n, pl* **promos.** *Inf.* something used to promote a product, esp. a videotape film used to promote a pop record. ORIG C20: shortened from *promotion*

promontory (ˈprɒməntərɪ, -trɪ) *n, pl* **promontories. 1** a high point of land, esp. of rocky coast, that juts out into the sea. **2** *Anat.* any of various projecting structures. ORIG C16: from L *prōmunturium* headland

promote (prəˈməʊt) *vb* **promotes, promoting, promoted.** (*tr*) **1** to encourage the progress or existence of. **2** to raise to a higher rank, status, etc. **3** to advance (a pupil or student) to a higher course, class, etc. **4** to work for: *to promote reform.* **5** to encourage the sale of (a product) by advertising or securing financial support. ORIG C14: from L *prōmovēre* to push onwards
▸ **proˈmotion** *n* ▸ **proˈmotional** *adj*

promoter (prəˈməʊtə) *n* **1** a person or thing that promotes. **2** a person who helps to organize, develop, or finance an undertaking. **3** a person who organizes and finances a sporting event, esp. a boxing match.

prompt (prɒmpt) *adj* **1** performed or executed without delay. **2** quick or ready to act or respond. ◆ *adv* **3** *Inf.* punctually. ◆ *vb* **4** (*tr*) to urge (someone to do something). **5** to remind (an actor, singer, etc.) of lines forgotten during a performance. **6** (*tr*) to refresh the memory of. **7** (*tr*) to give rise to by suggestion: *his affairs will prompt discussion.* ◆ *n* **8** *Commerce.* **8a** the time limit allowed for payment of the debt incurred by purchasing on credit. **8b** Also called: **prompt note.** a memorandum sent to a purchaser to remind him of the time limit and the sum due. **9** anything that serves to remind. ORIG C15: from L *promptus* evident, from *prōmere* to produce, from *emere* to buy
▸ **ˈpromptly** *adv* ▸ **ˈpromptness** *n*

prompter (ˈprɒmptə) *n* **1** a person offstage who reminds the actors of forgotten lines or cues. **2** a person, thing, etc., that prompts.

promptitude (ˈprɒmptɪˌtjuːd) *n* the quality of being prompt; punctuality.

prompt side *n Theatre.* the side of the stage where the prompter is, usually to the actor's left in Britain and to his right in the United States.

promulgate (ˈprɒməlˌgeɪt) *vb* **promulgates, promulgating, promulgated.** (*tr*) **1** to put into effect (a law, decree, etc.), esp. by formal proclamation. **2** to announce officially. **3** to make widespread. ORIG C16: from L *prōmulgāre* to bring to public knowledge
▸ **ˌpromulˈgation** *n* ▸ **ˈpromulˌgator** *n*

pron. *abbrev. for:* **1** pronominal. **2** pronoun. **3** pronounced. **4** pronunciation.

pronate (prəʊˈneɪt) *vb* **pronates, pronating, pronated.** (*tr*) to turn (the forearm or hand) so that the palmar surface is directed downwards. ORIG C19: from LL *prōnāre* to bow
▸ **proˈnation** *n* ▸ **proˈnator** *n*

prone (prəʊn) *adj* **1** lying flat or face downwards; prostrate. **2** sloping or tending downwards. **3** having an inclination to do something. ORIG C14: from L *prōnus* bent forward, from PRO-[1]
▸ **ˈpronely** *adv* ▸ **ˈproneness** *n*

-prone *adj combining form.* liable or disposed to suffer: *accident-prone.*

prong (prɒŋ) *n* **1** a sharply pointed end of an instrument, such as on a fork. **2** any pointed projecting part. ◆ *vb* **3** (*tr*) to prick or spear with or as if with a prong. ORIG C15
▸ **pronged** *adj*

pronghorn (ˈprɒŋˌhɔːn) *n* a ruminant mammal inhabiting rocky deserts of North America and having small branched horns. Also called: **American antelope.**

pronominal (prəʊˈnɒmɪnᵊl) *adj* relating to or playing the part of a pronoun. ORIG C17: from LL *prōnōminālis,* from *prōnōmen* a PRONOUN
▸ **proˈnominally** *adv*

pronoun (ˈprəʊˌnaʊn) *n* one of a class of words that serves to replace a noun or noun phrase that has already

★ people and places

been or is about to be mentioned in the sentence or context. Abbrev.: **pron.** ORIG C16: from L *prōnōmen*, from PRO-[1] + *nōmen* noun

pronounce (prəˈnauns) *vb* **pronounces, pronouncing, pronounced. 1** to utter or articulate (a sound or sounds). **2** (*tr*) to utter (words) in the correct way. **3** (*tr; may take a clause as object*) to proclaim officially: *I now pronounce you man and wife.* **4** (when *tr, may take a clause as object*) to declare as one's judgment: *to pronounce the death sentence upon someone.* ORIG C14: from L *prōnuntiāre* to announce
▸ **proˈnounceable** *adj* ▸ **proˈnouncer** *n*

pronounced (prəˈnaunst) *adj* **1** strongly marked or indicated. **2** (of a sound) articulated with vibration of the vocal cords; voiced.
▸ **pronouncedly** (prəˈnaunsɪdlɪ) *adv*

pronouncement (prəˈnaunsmənt) *n* **1** an official or authoritative announcement. **2** the act of declaring or uttering formally.

pronto (ˈprɒntəu) *adv Inf.* at once. ORIG C20: from Sp.: quick, from L *promptus* PROMPT

pronunciation (prəˌnʌnsɪˈeɪʃən) *n* **1** the act, instance, or manner of pronouncing sounds. **2** the supposedly correct manner of pronouncing sounds in a given language. **3** a phonetic transcription of a word.

> **USAGE NOTE** The segment *-un-* in this word should be pronounced as in *unkind*, not as in the verb *pronounce*. Occasionally *pronunciation* is misspelt and an *o* added after the *u*.

proof (pru:f) *n* **1** any evidence that establishes or helps to establish the truth, validity, quality, etc., of something. **2** *Law.* the whole body of evidence upon which the verdict of a court is based. **3** *Maths, logic.* a sequence of steps or statements that establishes the truth of a proposition. **4** the act of testing the truth of something (esp. in **put to the proof**). **5** *Scots Law.* trial before a judge without a jury. **6** *Printing.* a trial impression made from composed type for the correction of errors. **7** (in engraving, etc.) a print made by an artist for his or her own satisfaction before the plate is handed over to a professional printer. **8** *Photog.* a trial print from a negative. **9a** the alcoholic strength of proof spirit. **9b** the strength of a liquor as measured on a scale in which the strength of proof spirit is 100 degrees. ◆ *adj* **10** (*usually postpositive; foll. by against*) impervious (to): *the roof is proof against rain.* **11** having the alcoholic strength of proof spirit. **12** of proved impenetrability: *proof armour.* ◆ *vb* **13** (*tr*) to take a proof from (type matter, a plate, etc.). **14** to proofread (text) or inspect (a print, etc.), as for approval. **15** to render (something) proof, esp. to waterproof. ORIG C13: from OF *preuve* a test, from LL *proba*, from L *probāre* to test

-proof *adj, vb combining form.* (to make) impervious to; secure against (damage by): *waterproof.* ORIG from PROOF (adj)

proofread (ˈpru:fˌri:d) *vb* **proofreads, proofreading, proofread** (-ˌrɛd). to read (copy or printer's proofs) and mark errors to be corrected.
▸ **ˈproofˌreader** *n*

proof spirit *n* (in Britain) a mixture of alcohol and water or an alcoholic beverage that contains 49.28 per cent of alcohol by weight, 57.1 per cent by volume at 51°F: used until 1980 as a standard of alcoholic liquids.

prop[1] (prɒp) *vb* **props, propping, propped.** (*tr;* often foll. by *up*) **1** to support with a rigid object, such as a stick. **2** (usually also foll. by *against*) to place or lean. **3** to sustain or support. ◆ *n* **4** something that gives rigid support, such as a stick. **5** short for **clothes prop. 6** a person or thing giving support, as of a moral nature. **7** *Rugby.* either of the forwards at either end of the front row of a scrum. ORIG C15: rel. to M Du. *proppe* vine prop

prop[2] (prɒp) *n* short for **property** (sense 8).

prop[3] (prɒp) *n* an informal word for **propeller.**

prop. *abbrev. for:* **1** proper(ly). **2** property. **3** proposition. **4** proprietor.

propaedeutic (ˌprəupɪˈdju:tɪk) *n* **1** (*often pl*) preparatory instruction basic to further study of an art or science. ◆ *adj also* **propaedeutical. 2** of, relating to, or providing such instruction. ORIG C19: from Gk *propaideuein* to teach in advance, from PRO-[2] + *paideuein* to rear

propaganda (ˌprɒpəˈgændə) *n* **1** the organized dissemination of information, allegations, etc., to assist or damage the cause of a government, movement, etc. **2** such information, allegations, etc. ORIG C18: from It., use of *propāgandā* in the NL title *Sacra Congregatio de Propaganda Fide* Sacred Congregation for Propagating the Faith
▸ **ˌpropaˈgandism** *n* ▸ **ˌpropaˈgandist** *n, adj*

Propaganda (ˌprɒpəˈgændə) *n RC Church.* a congregation responsible for directing the work of the foreign missions.

propagandize *or* **propagandise** (ˌprɒpəˈgænˌdaɪz) *vb* **propagandizes, propagandizing, propagandized** *or* **propagandises, propagandising, propagandised. 1** (*tr*) to spread by, or subject to, propaganda. **2** (*intr*) to spread or organize propaganda.

propagate (ˈprɒpəˌgeɪt) *vb* **propagates, propagating, propagated. 1** *Biol.* to reproduce or cause to reproduce; breed. **2** (*tr*) *Horticulture.* to produce (plants) by layering, grafting, cuttings, etc. **3** (*tr*) to promulgate. **4** *Physics.* to transmit, esp. in the form of a wave: *to propagate sound.* **5** (*tr*) to transmit (characteristics) from one generation to the next. ORIG C16: from L *propāgāre* to increase (plants) by cuttings, from *propāgēs* a cutting, from *pangere* to fasten
▸ **ˌpropaˈgation** *n* ▸ **ˌpropaˈgational** *adj* ▸ **ˈpropagative** *adj*
▸ **ˈpropaˌgator** *n*

propane (ˈprəupeɪn) *n* a flammable gaseous alkane found in petroleum and used as a fuel. Formula: $CH_3CH_2CH_3$. ORIG C19: from PROPIONIC (ACID) + -ANE

propanoic acid (ˌprəupəˈnəuɪk) *n* a colourless liquid carboxylic acid used in inhibiting the growth of moulds in bread. Formula: CH_3CH_2COOH. Former name: **propionic acid.** ORIG C20: from PROPANE + -OIC

pro patria *Latin.* (ˈprəu ˈpætrɪˌɑ:) for one's country.

propel (prəˈpɛl) *vb* **propels, propelling, propelled.** (*tr*) to impel, drive, or cause to move forwards. ORIG C15: from L *prōpellere*
▸ **proˈpellant** *or* **proˈpellent** *n*

propeller (prəˈpɛlə) *n* **1** a device having blades radiating from a central hub that is rotated to produce thrust to propel a ship, aircraft, etc. **2** a person or thing that propels.

propelling pencil *n* a pencil consisting of a metal or plastic case containing a replaceable lead. As the point is worn away the lead can be extended, usually by turning part of the case.

propene (ˈprəupi:n) *n* a colourless gaseous alkene obtained by cracking petroleum. Formula: $CH_3CH{:}CH_2$. Also called: **propylene.**

propensity (prəˈpɛnsɪtɪ) *n, pl* **propensities. 1** a natural tendency. **2** *Obs.* partiality. ORIG C16: from L *prōpensus* inclined to, from *prōpendēre* to hang forwards

proper (ˈprɒpə) *adj* **1** (*usually prenominal*) appropriate or usual: *in its proper place.* **2** suited to a particular purpose: *use the proper knife to cut the bread.* **3** correct in behaviour. **4** vigorously or excessively moral. **5** up to a required or regular standard. **6** (*immediately postpositive*) (of an object, quality, etc.) referred to so as to exclude anything not directly connected with it: *his claim is connected with the deed proper.* **7** (*postpositive;* foll. by *to*) belonging to or characteristic of a person or thing. **8** (*prenominal*) *Brit. inf.* (intensifier): *I felt a proper fool.* **9** (*usually postpositive*) (of heraldic colours) considered correct for the natural colour of the object depicted: *three martlets proper.* **10** *Arch.* pleasant or good. **11 good and proper.** *Inf.* thoroughly. ◆ *n* **12** the parts of the Mass that vary according to the particular day or feast on which the Mass is celebrated. ORIG C13: via OF from L *prōprius* special
▸ **ˈproperly** *adv* ▸ **ˈproperness** *n*

proper fraction *n* a fraction in which the numerator has a lower absolute value than the denominator, as ½ or $x/(3 + x^2)$.

proper motion *n* the very small continuous change in the direction of motion of a star relative to the sun.

proper noun *or* **name** *n* the name of a person, place, or object, as for example *Iceland, Patrick,* or *Uranus.* Cf. **common noun.**

propertied ('prɒpətɪd) *adj* owning land or property.

Propertius ★ (prə'pɜːʃɪəs, -ʃəs) *n* **Sextus** ('sɛkstəs). ?50–?15 B.C., Roman elegiac poet.

property ('prɒpətɪ) *n, pl* **properties. 1** something of value, either tangible, such as land, or intangible, such as copyrights. **2** *Law.* the right to possess, use, and dispose of anything. **3** possessions collectively. **4a** land or real estate. **4b** (*as modifier*): *property rights.* **5** *Chiefly Austral.* a ranch or station. **6** a quality or characteristic attribute, such as the density or strength of a material. **7** *Logic, obs.* Also called: **proprium** ('prəʊpɪəm). an attribute that is not essential to a species but is common and peculiar to it. **8** any movable object used on the set of a stage play or film. Usually shortened to **prop.** ORIG C13: from OF *propriété,* from L *proprietās* something personal, from *proprius* one's own

property bond *n* a bond issued by a life-assurance company, the premiums for which are invested in a property-owning fund.

property centre *n* a service for buying and selling property, including conveyancing, provided by a group of local solicitors. In full: **solicitors' property centre.**

property man *n* a member of the stage crew in charge of the stage properties. Usually shortened to **propman.**

prophecy ('prɒfɪsɪ) *n, pl* **prophecies. 1a** a message of divine truth revealing God's will. **1b** the act of uttering such a message. **2** a prediction or guess. **3** the charismatic endowment of a prophet. ORIG C13: ult. from Gk *prophētēs* PROPHET

prophesy ('prɒfɪˌsaɪ) *vb* **prophesies, prophesying, prophesied. 1** to foretell (something) by or as if by divine inspiration. **2** (*intr*) *Arch.* to give instructions in religious subjects. ORIG C14 *prophecien,* from PROPHECY
▸ **'propheˌsiable** *adj* ▸ **'propheˌsier** *n*

prophet ('prɒfɪt) *n* **1** a person who supposedly speaks by divine inspiration, esp. one through whom a divinity expresses his will. **2** a person who predicts the future: *a prophet of doom.* **3** a spokesman for a movement, doctrine, etc. ORIG C13: from OF *prophète,* from L, from Gk *prophētēs* one who declares the divine will, from PRO-[2] + *phanai* to speak
▸ **'prophetess** *fem n*

Prophet ('prɒfɪt) *n* **the. 1** the principal designation of Mohammed as the founder of Islam. **2** a name for Joseph Smith as the founder of the Mormon Church.

prophetic (prə'fɛtɪk) *adj* **1** of or relating to a prophet or prophecy. **2** of the nature of a prophecy; predictive.
▸ **pro'phetically** *adv*

prophylactic (ˌprɒfɪ'læktɪk) *adj* **1** protecting from or preventing disease. **2** protective or preventive. ◆ *n* **3** a prophylactic drug or device. **4** *Chiefly US.* another name for **condom.** ORIG C16: via F from Gk *prophulaktikos,* from *prophulassein* to guard by taking advance measures, from PRO-[2] + *phulax* a guard

prophylaxis (ˌprɒfɪ'læksɪs) *n* the prevention of disease or control of its possible spread.

propinquity (prə'pɪŋkwɪtɪ) *n* **1** nearness in place or time. **2** nearness in relationship. ORIG C14: from L *propinquitās,* from *propinquus* near, from *prope* nearby

propionic acid (ˌprəʊpɪ'ɒnɪk) *n* the former name for **propanoic acid.** ORIG C19: from Gk *pro-* first + *pionic,* from *piōn* fat, because it is first in order of the fatty acids

propitiate (prə'pɪʃɪˌeɪt) *vb* **propitiates, propitiating, propitiated.** (*tr*) to appease or make well disposed; conciliate. ORIG C17: from L *propitiāre,* from *propitius* gracious
▸ **pro'pitiable** *adj* ▸ **proˌpiti'ation** *n* ▸ **pro'pitiative** *adj* ▸ **pro'pitiˌator** *n* ▸ **pro'pitiatory** *adj*

propitious (prə'pɪʃəs) *adj* **1** favourable; auguring well. **2** gracious or favourably inclined. ORIG C15: from L *propitius* well disposed, from *prope* close to
▸ **pro'pitiously** *adv* ▸ **pro'pitiousness** *n*

propjet ('prɒpˌdʒɛt) *n* another name for **turboprop.**

propolis ('prɒpəlɪs) *n* a greenish-brown resinous aromatic substance collected by bees from the buds of trees for use in the construction of hives. Also called: **bee glue, hive dross.** ORIG C17: via L from Gk: suburb, bee glue, from *pro-* before + *polis* city

proponent (prə'pəʊnənt) *n* a person who argues in favour of something or puts forward a proposal, etc. ORIG C16: from L *prōpōnere* to PROPOSE

Propontis ★ (prə'pɒntɪs) *n* the ancient name for (the Sea of) **Marmara.**

proportion (prə'pɔːʃən) *n* **1** relative magnitude or extent; ratio. **2** correct or desirable relationship between parts; symmetry. **3** a part considered with respect to the whole. **4** (*pl*) dimensions or size: *a building of vast proportions.* **5** a share or quota. **6** a relationship that maintains a constant ratio between two variable quantities: *prices increase in proportion to manufacturing costs.* **7** *Maths.* a relationship between four numbers or quantities in which the ratio of the first pair equals the ratio of the second pair. ◆ *vb* (*tr*) **8** to adjust in relative amount, size, etc. **9** to cause to be harmonious in relationship of parts. ORIG C14: from L *prōportiō,* from *prō portione,* lit.: for (its, one's) PORTION
▸ **pro'portionable** *adj* ▸ **pro'portionably** *adv* ▸ **pro'portionment** *n*

proportional (prə'pɔːʃənᵊl) *adj* **1** of, involving, or being in proportion. ◆ *n* **2** *Maths.* an unknown term in a proportion: *in a/b = c/x, x is the fourth proportional.*
▸ **proˌportion'ality** *n* ▸ **pro'portionally** *adv*

proportional representation *n* representation of parties in an elective body in proportion to the votes they win. Abbrev.: **PR.** Cf. **first-past-the-post.** See also **Additional Member System, Alternative Vote, party list, Single Transferable Vote.**

proportionate *adj* (prə'pɔːʃənɪt). **1** being in proper proportion. ◆ *vb* (prə'pɔːʃəˌneɪt), **proportionates, proportionating, proportionated. 2** (*tr*) to make proportionate.
▸ **pro'portionately** *adv*

proposal (prə'pəʊzᵊl) *n* **1** the act of proposing. **2** something proposed, as a plan. **3** an offer, esp. of marriage.

propose (prə'pəʊz) *vb* **proposes, proposing, proposed. 1** (when *tr, may take a clause as object*) to put forward (a plan, etc.) for consideration. **2** (*tr*) to nominate, as for a position. **3** (*tr*) to intend (to do something): *I propose to leave town now.* **4** (*tr*) to announce the drinking of (a toast). **5** (*intr;* often foll. by *to*) to make an offer of marriage. ORIG C14: from OF *proposer,* from L *prōpōnere* to display, from PRO-[1] + *pōnere* to place
▸ **pro'posable** *adj* ▸ **pro'poser** *n*

proposition (ˌprɒpə'zɪʃən) *n* **1** a proposal for consideration. **2** *Philosophy.* the content of a sentence that affirms or denies something and is capable of being true or false. **3** *Maths.* a statement or theorem, usually containing its proof. **4** *Inf.* a person or matter to be dealt with: *he's a difficult proposition.* **5** *Inf.* an invitation to engage in sexual intercourse. ◆ *vb* **6** (*tr*) to propose a plan, deal, etc., to, esp. to engage in sexual intercourse. ORIG C14 *proposicioun,* from L *prōpositiō* a setting forth; see PROPOSE
▸ **ˌpropo'sitional** *adj*

propositional calculus *n* the system of symbolic logic concerned only with the relations between propositions as wholes, taking no account of their internal structure. Cf. **predicate calculus.**

propositus (prə'pɒzɪtəs) *or* (*fem*) **proposita** (prə'pɒzɪtə) *n, pl* **propositi** (-ˌtaɪ) *or* (*fem*) **propositae** (-tiː). *Med.* the first patient to be investigated in a family study, to whom all relationships are referred. Also called (esp. US): **proband.**

propound (prə'paʊnd) *vb* (*tr*) **1** to put forward for consideration. **2** *English law.* to produce (a will or similar instrument) to the proper court or authority for its validity to be established. ORIG C16 *propone,* from L *prōpōnere* to set forth, from PRO-[1] + *pōnere* to place
▸ **pro'pounder** *n*

propranolol (prəʊ'prænəˌlɒl) *n* a drug used in the treatment of heart disease.

proprietary (prə'praɪɪtərɪ, -trɪ) *adj* **1** of or belonging to property or proprietors. **2** privately owned and controlled. **3** *Med.* denoting a drug manufactured and distributed under a trade name. ◆ *n, pl* **proprietaries. 4** *Med.* a proprietary drug. **5** a proprietor or proprietors collec-

tively. **6a** right to property. **6b** property owned. **7** (in Colonial America) an owner of a **proprietary colony,** a colony which was granted by the Crown to a particular person or group. ORIG C15: from LL *proprietārius* an owner, from *proprius* one's own
▸ **pro'prietarily** *adv*

proprietary name *n* a name which is restricted in use by virtue of being a trade name.

proprietor (prə'praɪətə) *n* **1** an owner of a business. **2** a person enjoying exclusive right of ownership to some property.
▸ **proprietorial** (prə,praɪə'tɔːrɪəl) *adj* ▸ **pro'prietress** *or* **pro'prietrix** *fem n*

propriety (prə'praɪətɪ) *n, pl* **proprieties. 1** the quality or state of being appropriate or fitting. **2** conformity to the prevailing standard of behaviour, speech, etc. **3 the proprieties.** the standards of behaviour considered correct by polite society. ORIG C15: from OF *propriété,* from L *proprietās* a peculiarity, from *proprius* one's own

proprioceptor (,prəuprɪə'sɛptə) *n Physiol.* any receptor, as in the gut, blood vessels, muscles, etc., that supplies information about the state of the body. ORIG C20: from *proprio-,* from L *proprius* one's own + RECEPTOR
▸ **,proprio'ceptive** *adj*

proptosis (prɒp'təusɪs) *n, pl* **proptoses** (-siːz). *Pathol.* the forward displacement of an organ or part, such as the eyeball. ORIG C17: via LL from Gk, from *propiptein* to fall forwards

propulsion (prə'pʌlʃən) *n* **1** the act of propelling or the state of being propelled. **2** a propelling force. ORIG C15: from L *prōpellere* to propel
▸ **propulsive** (prə'pʌlsɪv) *or* **pro'pulsory** *adj*

propyl ('prəupɪl) *n* (*modifier*) of or containing the monovalent group of atoms C_3H_7-. ORIG C19: from PROP(IONIC ACID) + -YL

propylaeum (,prɒpɪ'liːəm) *or* **propylon** ('prɒpɪ,lɒn) *n, pl* **propylaea** (-'liːə) *or* **propylons, propyla** (-lə). a portico, esp. one that forms the entrance to a temple. ORIG C18: via L from Gk *propulaion* before the gate, from PRO-[2] + *pulē* gate

propylene ('prəupɪ,liːn) *n* another name for **propene.** ORIG C19

propylene glycol *n* a colourless viscous compound used as an antifreeze and brake fluid. Formula: $CH_3CH(OH)CH_2OH$. Systematic name: **1,2-dihydroxypropane.**

pro rata ('prəu 'rɑːtə) in proportion. ORIG Med. L

prorate (prəu'reɪt, 'prəureɪt) *vb* **prorates, prorating, prorated.** *Chiefly US & Canad.* to divide, assess, or distribute proportionately. ORIG C19: from PRO RATA
▸ **pro'ratable** *adj* ▸ **pro'ration** *n*

prorogue (prə'rəug) *vb* **prorogues, proroguing, prorogued.** to discontinue the meetings of (a legislative body) without dissolving it. ORIG C15: from L *prorogāre,* lit.: to ask publicly
▸ **prorogation** (,prəurə'geɪʃən) *n*

prosaic (prəu'zeɪɪk) *adj* **1** lacking imagination. **2** having the characteristics of prose. ORIG C16: from LL *prōsaicus,* from L *prōsa* PROSE
▸ **pro'saically** *adv*

pros and cons *pl n* the various arguments in favour of and against a motion, course of action, etc. ORIG C16: from L *prō* for + *con,* from *contrā* against

proscenium (prə'siːnɪəm) *n, pl* **proscenia** (-nɪə) *or* **prosceniums. 1** the arch or opening separating the stage from the auditorium together with the area immediately in front of the arch. **2** (in ancient theatres) the stage itself. ORIG C17: via L from Gk *proskēnion,* from *pro-* before + *skēnē* scene

prosciutto (prəu'ʃuːtəu; *Italian* pro'ʃutto) *n* cured ham from Italy: usually served as an hors d'oeuvre. ORIG It., lit.: dried beforehand

proscribe (prəu'skraɪb) *vb* **proscribes, proscribing, proscribed.** (*tr*) **1** to condemn or prohibit. **2** to outlaw; banish; exile. ORIG C16: from L *prōscrībere* to put up a public notice, from *prō-* in public + *scrībere* to write
▸ **pro'scriber** *n* ▸ **proscription** (prəu'skrɪpʃən) *n*

prose (prəuz) *n* **1** spoken or written language distinguished from poetry by its lack of a marked metrical structure. **2** a passage set for translation into a foreign language. **3** commonplace or dull discourse, expression, etc. **4** (*modifier*) written in prose. **5** (*modifier*) matter-of-fact. ◆ *vb* **proses, prosing, prosed. 6** to write (something) in prose. **7** (*intr*) to speak or write in a tedious style. ORIG C14: via OF from L *prōsa ōrātiō* straightforward speech, from *prorsus* prosaic, from *prōvertere* to turn forwards
▸ **'prose,like** *adj*

prosecute ('prɒsɪ,kjuːt) *vb* **prosecutes, prosecuting, prosecuted. 1** (*tr*) to bring a criminal action against (a person). **2** (*intr*) **2a** to seek redress by legal proceedings. **2b** to institute or conduct a prosecution. **3** (*tr*) to practise (a profession or trade). **4** (*tr*) to continue to do (a task, etc.). ORIG C15: from L *prōsequī* to follow
▸ **'prose,cutable** *adj* ▸ **'prose,cutor** *n*

prosecution (,prɒsɪ'kjuːʃən) *n* **1** the act of prosecuting or the state of being prosecuted. **2a** the institution and conduct of legal proceedings against a person. **2b** the proceedings brought in the name of the Crown to put an accused on trial. **3** the lawyers acting for the Crown to put the case against a person. **4** the following up or carrying on of something begun.

proselyte ('prɒsɪ,laɪt) *n* **1** a person newly converted to a religious faith, esp. a Gentile converted to Judaism. ◆ *vb* **proselytes, proselyting, proselyted. 2** a less common word for **proselytize.** ORIG C14: from Church L *prosēlytus,* from Gk *prosēlutos* recent arrival, convert, from *proserchesthai* to draw near
▸ **proselytism** ('prɒsɪlɪ,tɪzəm) *n* ▸ **proselytic** (,prɒsɪ'lɪtɪk) *adj*

proselytize *or* **proselytise** ('prɒsɪlɪ,taɪz) *vb* **proselytizes, proselytizing, proselytized** *or* **proselytises, proselytising, proselytised.** to convert (someone) from one religious faith to another.
▸ **'proselyt,izer** *or* **'proselyt,iser** *n*

prosencephalon (,prɒsɛn'sɛfəlɒn) *n, pl* **prosencephala** (-lə). the part of the brain that develops from the anterior portion of the neural tube. Nontechnical name: **forebrain.** ORIG C19: from NL, from Gk *prosō* forward + *enkephalos* brain

prosenchyma (prɒs'ɛŋkɪmə) *n* a plant tissue consisting of long narrow cells with pointed ends: occurs in conducting tissue. ORIG C19: from NL, from Gk *pros-* towards + *enkhuma* infusion

Proserpina ★ (prəu'sɜːpɪnə) *n* the Roman goddess of the underworld. Greek counterpart: **Persephone.**

prosimian (prəu'sɪmɪən) *n* **1** any of a primitive suborder of primates, including lemurs, lorises, and tarsiers. ◆ *adj* **2** of or belonging to this suborder. ORIG C19: via NL from L *sīmia* ape

prosit *German.* ('proːzɪt) *sentence substitute.* good health! cheers! ORIG G, from L, lit.: may it prove beneficial

prosody ('prɒsədɪ) *n* **1** the study of poetic metre and of the art of versification. **2** a system of versification. **3** the patterns of stress and intonation in a language. ORIG C15: from L *prosōdia* accent of a syllable, from Gk *prosōidia* song set to music, from *pros* towards + *ōidē,* from *aoidē* song; see ODE
▸ **prosodic** (prə'sɒdɪk) *adj* ▸ **'prosodist** *n*

prosopopoeia *or* **prosopopeia** (,prɒsəpə'piːə) *n* **1** *Rhetoric.* another word for **personification. 2** a figure of speech that represents an imaginary, absent, or dead person speaking or acting. ORIG C16: via L from Gk *prosōpopoiia* dramatization, from *prosōpon* face + *poiein* to make

prospect *n* ('prɒspɛkt). **1** (*sometimes pl*) a probability of future success. **2** a view or scene. **3** a mental outlook. **4** expectation, or what one expects. **5** a prospective buyer, project, etc. **6** a survey or observation. **7** *Mining.* **7a** a known or likely deposit of ore. **7b** the location of a deposit of ore. **7c** the yield of mineral obtained from a sample of ore. ◆ *vb* (prə'spɛkt). **8** (when *intr,* often foll. by *for*) to explore (a region) for gold or other valuable minerals. **9** (*tr*) to work (a mine) to discover its profitability. **10** (*intr;* often foll. by *for*) to search (for). ORIG C15: from L *prōspectus* distant view, from *prōspicere* to look into the distance

★ people and places

prospective (prəˈspɛktɪv) *adj* **1** looking towards the future. **2** (*prenominal*) expected or likely.
▸ **proˈspectively** *adv*

prospector (prəˈspɛktə) *n* a person who searches for gold, petroleum, etc.

prospectus (prəˈspɛktəs) *n, pl* **prospectuses. 1** a formal statement giving details of a forthcoming event, such as the issue of shares. **2** a brochure giving details of courses, as at a school.

prosper (ˈprɒspə) *vb* (*usually intr*) to thrive, succeed, etc., or cause to thrive, etc., in a healthy way. ORIG C15: from L *prosperāre* to succeed, from *prosperus* fortunate, from PRO-[1] + *spēs* hope

prosperity (prɒˈspɛrɪtɪ) *n* the condition of prospering; success or wealth.

prosperous (ˈprɒspərəs) *adj* **1** flourishing; prospering. **2** wealthy.
▸ **ˈprosperously** *adv*

Prost ★ (*French* prɔst) *n* **Alain** (alɛ̃). born 1955, French motor-racing driver: world champion 1985, 1986, 1989, and 1993.

prostaglandin (ˌprɒstəˈglændɪn) *n* any of a group of hormone-like compounds found in all mammalian tissues, which stimulate the muscles of the uterus and affect the blood vessels; used to induce abortion or birth. ORIG C20: from *prosta(te) gland* + -IN; orig. believed to be secreted by the prostate gland

prostate (ˈprɒsteɪt) *n* **1** Also called: **prostate gland.** a gland in male mammals that surrounds the neck of the bladder and secretes a liquid constituent of the semen. ◆ *adj* **2** Also: **prostatic** (prɒˈstætɪk). of the prostate gland. ◆ See also **PSA.** ORIG C17: via Med. L from Gk *prostatēs* something standing in front (of the bladder), from *pro-* in front + *histanai* to cause to stand

prosthesis (ˈprɒsθɪsɪs) *n, pl* **prostheses** (-ˌsiːz). **1** *Surgery.* **1a** the replacement of a missing bodily part with an artificial substitute. **1b** an artificial part such as a limb, eye, or tooth. **2** *Linguistics.* another word for **prothesis.** ORIG C16: via LL from Gk: an addition, from *prostithenai* to add, from *pros-* towards + *tithenai* to place
▸ **prosthetic** (prɒsˈθɛtɪk) *adj* ▸ **prosˈthetically** *adv*

prosthetics (prɒsˈθɛtɪks) *n* (*functioning as sing*) the branch of surgery concerned with prosthesis.

prostitute (ˈprɒstɪˌtjuːt) *n* **1** a woman who engages in sexual intercourse for money. **2** a man who engages in such activity, esp. in homosexual practices. **3** a person who offers his or her talent for unworthy purposes. ◆ *vb* **prostitutes, prostituting, prostituted.** (*tr*) **4** to offer (oneself or another) in sexual intercourse for money. **5** to offer for unworthy purposes. ORIG C16: from L *prōstituere* to expose to prostitution, from *prō-* in public + *statuere* to cause to stand
▸ **ˌprostiˈtution** *n* ▸ **ˈprostiˌtutor** *n*

prostrate *adj* (ˈprɒstreɪt). **1** lying face downwards, as in submission. **2** exhausted physically or emotionally. **3** helpless or defenceless. **4** (of a plant) growing closely along the ground. ◆ *vb* (prɒˈstreɪt), **prostrates, prostrating, prostrated.** (*tr*) **5** to cast (oneself) down, as in submission. **6** to lay or throw down flat. **7** to make helpless. **8** to make exhausted. ORIG C14: from L *prōsternere* to throw to the ground, from *prō-* before + *sternere* to lay low
▸ **prosˈtration** *n*

> **USAGE NOTE** This word is sometimes wrongly used where *prostate* is meant: *prostate* (not *prostrate*) *cancer.*

prostyle (ˈprəustaɪl) *adj* **1** (of a building) having a row of columns in front, esp. as in the portico of a Greek temple. ◆ *n* **2** a prostyle building, portico, etc. ORIG C17: from L *prostȳlos*, from Gk: with pillars in front, from PRO-[2] + *stulos* pillar

prosy (ˈprəuzɪ) *adj* **prosier, prosiest. 1** of the nature of or similar to prose. **2** dull, tedious, or long-winded.
▸ **ˈprosily** *adv* ▸ **ˈprosiness** *n*

Prot. *abbrev. for:* **1** Protectorate. **2** Protestant.

protactinium (ˌprəutækˈtɪnɪəm) *n* a toxic radioactive element that occurs in uranium ores and is produced by neutron irradiation of thorium. Symbol: Pa; atomic no.: 91; half-life of most stable isotope, ^{231}Pa: 32 500 years.

protagonist (prəuˈtægənɪst) *n* **1** the principal character in a play, story, etc. **2** a supporter, esp. when important or respected, of a cause, party, etc. ORIG C17: from Gk *prōtagōnistēs*, from *prōtos* first + *agōnistēs* actor
▸ **proˈtagonism** *n*

Protagoras ★ (prəuˈtægəˌræs) *n* ?485–?411 B.C., Greek philosopher and sophist, famous for his dictum "Man is the measure of all things."

protasis (ˈprɒtəsɪs) *n, pl* **protases** (-siːz). **1** *Logic, grammar.* the antecedent of a conditional statement, such as *it rains* in *if it rains the game will be cancelled.* **2** (in classical drama) the introductory part of a play. ORIG C17: via L from Gk: a proposal, from *pro-* before + *teinein* to extend

protea (ˈprəutɪə) *n* a shrub of tropical and southern Africa, having flowers with coloured bracts arranged in showy heads. ORIG C20: from NL, from PROTEUS

protean (prəuˈtiːən, ˈprəutɪən) *adj* readily taking on various shapes or forms; variable. ORIG C16: from PROTEUS

protease (ˈprəutɪˌeɪs) *n* any enzyme involved in proteolysis. ORIG C20: from PROTEIN + -ASE

protease inhibitor *n* any one of a class of antiviral drugs that impair the growth and replication of HIV by inhibiting the action of protease produced by the virus: used in the treatment of AIDS.

protect (prəˈtɛkt) *vb* (*tr*) **1** to defend from trouble, harm, etc. **2** *Econ.* to assist (domestic industries) by the imposition of protective tariffs on imports. **3** *Commerce.* to provide funds in advance to guarantee payment of (a note, etc.). ORIG C16: from L *prōtegere* to cover before

protectant (prəˈtɛktənt) *n* a chemical substance that affords protection, as against frost, rust, insects, etc.

protection (prəˈtɛkʃən) *n* **1** the act of protecting or the condition of being protected. **2** something that protects. **3a** the imposition of duties on imports, for the protection of domestic industries against overseas competition, etc. **3b** Also called: **protectionism.** the system or theory of such restrictions. **4** *Inf.* **4a** Also called: **protection money.** money demanded by gangsters for freedom from molestation. **4b** freedom from molestation purchased in this way.
▸ **proˈtectionˌism** *n* ▸ **proˈtectionist** *n, adj*

protective (prəˈtɛktɪv) *adj* **1** giving or capable of giving protection. **2** *Econ.* of or intended for protection of domestic industries. ◆ *n* **3** something that protects. **4** a condom.
▸ **proˈtectively** *adv* ▸ **proˈtectiveness** *n*

protective coloration *n* the coloration of an animal that enables it to blend with its surroundings and therefore escape the attention of predators.

protector (prəˈtɛktə) *n* **1** a person or thing that protects. **2** *History.* a person who exercised royal authority during the minority, absence, or incapacity of the monarch.
▸ **proˈtectress** *fem n*

Protector (prəˈtɛktə) *n* short for **Lord Protector,** the title borne by Oliver Cromwell (1653–58) and by Richard Cromwell (1658–59) as heads of state during the period known as the Protectorate.

protectorate (prəˈtɛktərɪt) *n* **1a** a territory largely controlled by but not annexed to a stronger state. **1b** the relation of a protecting state to its protected territory. **2** the office or period of office of a protector.

protégé *or* (*fem*) **protégée** (ˈprəutɪˌʒeɪ) *n* a person who is protected and aided by the patronage of another. ORIG C18: from F *protéger* to PROTECT

protein (ˈprəutiːn) *n* any of a large group of nitrogenous compounds of high molecular weight that are essential constituents of all living organisms. ORIG C19: via G from Gk *prōteios* primary, from *protos* first + -IN
▸ **ˌproteinˈaceous, proˈteinic,** *or* **proˈteinous** *adj*

pro tempore *Latin.* (ˈprəu ˈtɛmpərɪ) *adv, adj* for the time being. Often shortened to **pro tem** (ˈprəu ˈtɛm).

proteolysis (ˌprəutɪˈɒlɪsɪs) *n* the hydrolysis of proteins

into simpler compounds by the action of enzymes. ORIG C19: from NL, from *proteo-* (from PROTEIN) + -LYSIS
▸ **proteolytic** (ˌprəʊtɪəˈlɪtɪk) *adj*

protest *n* (ˈprəʊtɛst). **1a** public, often organized, manifestation of dissent. **1b** (*as modifier*): *a protest march*. **2** a formal or solemn objection. **3** a formal notarial statement drawn up on behalf of a creditor and declaring that the debtor has dishonoured a bill of exchange, etc. **4** the act of protesting. ◆ *vb* (prəˈtɛst). **5** (when *intr*, foll. by *against, at, about*, etc.; when *tr, may take a clause as object*) to make a strong objection (to something, esp. a supposed injustice or offence). **6** (when *tr, may take a clause as object*) to disagree; object: *"I'm O.K." she protested*. **7** (when *tr, may take a clause as object*) to assert in a formal or solemn manner. **8** (*tr*) *Chiefly US*. to object forcefully to: *a women's rights group at the University of Kansas is protesting violence against women*. **9** (*tr*) to declare formally that (a bill of exchange or promissory note) has been dishonoured. ORIG C14: from L *prōtestārī* to make a formal declaration, from *prō-* before + *testārī* to assert
▸ **proˈtestant** *adj, n* ▸ **proˈtester** *or* **proˈtestor** *n* ▸ **proˈtestingly** *adv*

Protestant (ˈprɒtɪstənt) *n* **a** an adherent of Protestantism. **b** (*as modifier*): *the Protestant Church*.

Protestantism (ˈprɒtɪstənˌtɪzəm) *n* the religion of any of the Churches of Western Christendom that are separated from the Roman Catholic Church and adhere substantially to principles established during the Reformation.

protestation (ˌprəʊtɛsˈteɪʃən) *n* **1** the act of protesting. **2** a strong declaration.

Proteus ★ (ˈprəʊtɪəs) *n Greek myth*. a prophetic sea god capable of changing his shape at will.

prothalamion (ˌprəʊθəˈleɪmɪən) *or* **prothalamium** *n, pl* **prothalamia** (-mɪə). a song or poem in celebration of a marriage. ORIG C16: from Gk *pro-* before + *thalamos* marriage

prothallus (prəʊˈθæləs) *or* **prothallium** (prəʊˈθælɪəm) *n, pl* **prothalli** (-laɪ) *or* **prothallia** (-lɪə). *Bot*. the small flat green disc of tissue that bears the reproductive organs of ferns, horsetails, and club mosses. ORIG C19: from NL, from *pro-* before + Gk *thallus* a young shoot

prothesis (ˈprɒθɪsɪs) *n, pl* **protheses** (-siːz). **1** a development of a language by which a syllable is prefixed to a word to facilitate pronunciation: *Latin "scala" gives Spanish "escala" by prothesis*. **2** *Eastern Orthodox Church*. the solemn preparation of the Eucharistic elements before consecration. ORIG C16: via LL from Gk: a setting out in public, from *pro-* forth + *thesis* a placing
▸ **prothetic** (prəˈθɛtɪk) *adj* ▸ **proˈthetically** *adv*

prothrombin (prəʊˈθrɒmbɪn) *n Biochemistry*. a zymogen found in blood that gives rise to thrombin on activation.

protist (ˈprəʊtɪst) *n* (in some classification systems) any organism belonging to a large group, including bacteria, protozoans, and fungi, regarded as distinct from plants and animals. The group is usually now restricted to protozoans, unicellular algae, and simple fungi. Cf. **protoctist**. ORIG C19: from NL *Protista* most primitive organisms, from Gk *prōtistos* the very first, from *prōtos* first

protium (ˈprəʊtɪəm) *n* the most common isotope of hydrogen, having a mass number of 1. ORIG C20: NL, from PROTO- + -IUM

proto- *or sometimes before a vowel* **prot-** *combining form*. **1** first: *protomartyr*. **2** primitive or original: *prototype*. **3** first in a series of chemical compounds: *protoxide*. ORIG from Gk *prōtos* first, from *pro* before

protocol (ˈprəʊtəˌkɒl) *n* **1** the formal etiquette and procedure for state and diplomatic ceremonies. **2** a record of an agreement, esp. in international negotiations, etc. **3a** an amendment to a treaty or convention. **3b** an annexe appended to a treaty to deal with subsidiary matters. **4** *Chiefly US*. a record of data or observations on a particular experiment or proceeding. **5** *Computing*. the set form in which data must be presented for handling by a particular computer configuration, esp. in the transmission of information between different computer systems. ORIG C16: from Med. L *prōtocollum*, from LGk *prōtokollon* sheet glued to the front of a manuscript, from PROTO- + *kolla* glue

protoctist (prəʊˈtɒktɪst) *n* (in modern biological classifications) any unicellular or simple multicellular organism belonging to the kingdom that includes protozoans, algae, and slime moulds. ORIG C19: from NL *protoctista*, ?from Gk *prototokos* first born

protohuman (ˌprəʊtəʊˈhjuːmən) *n* **1** any of various prehistoric primates that resembled modern man. ◆ *adj* **2** of these primates.

Proto-Indo-European *n* the prehistoric unrecorded language that was the ancestor of all Indo-European languages.

protomartyr (ˌprəʊtəʊˈmɑːtə) *n* **1** St Stephen as the first Christian martyr. **2** the first martyr to lay down his or her life in any cause.

proton (ˈprəʊtɒn) *n* a stable, positively charged elementary particle, found in atomic nuclei in numbers equal to the atomic number of the element. ORIG C20: from Gk *prōtos* first

protoplasm (ˈprəʊtəˌplæzəm) *n Biol*. the living contents of a cell: a complex translucent colourless colloidal substance. ORIG C19: from NL, from PROTO- + Gk *plasma* form
▸ ˌ**protoˈplasmic**, ˌ**protoˈplasmal**, *or* ˌ**protoplasˈmatic** *adj*

prototype (ˈprəʊtəˌtaɪp) *n* **1** one of the first units manufactured of a product, which is tested so that the design can be changed if necessary before the product is manufactured commercially. **2** a person or thing that serves as an example of a type. **3** *Biol*. the ancestral or primitive form of a species.
▸ ˌ**protoˈtypal, prototypic** (ˌprəʊtəˈtɪpɪk), *or* ˌ**protoˈtypical** *adj*

protozoan (ˌprəʊtəˈzəʊən) *n, pl* **protozoa** (-ˈzəʊə). **1** Also **protozoon**. any of various minute unicellular organisms formerly regarded as invertebrates of the phylum *Protozoa*, but now usually classified in certain phyla of protoctists. Protozoans include amoebas and foraminifers. ◆ *adj also* **protozoic**. **2** of or belonging to protozoans. ORIG C19: via NL from Gk PROTO- + *zoion* animal

protract (prəˈtrækt) *vb* (*tr*) **1** to lengthen or extend (a speech, etc.). **2** (of a muscle) to draw, thrust, or extend (a part, etc.) forwards. **3** to plot using a protractor and scale. ORIG C16: from L *prōtrahere* to prolong, from PRO-[1] + *trahere* to drag
▸ **proˈtracted** *adj* ▸ **protractedly** *adv* ▸ **proˈtraction** *n*

protractile (prəˈtræktaɪl) *adj* able to be extended: *protractile muscle*.

protractor (prəˈtræktə) *n* **1** an instrument for measuring or drawing angles, usually a flat semicircular transparent plastic sheet graduated in degrees. **2** *Anat*. a former term for **extensor**.

protrude (prəˈtruːd) *vb* **protrudes, protruding, protruded**. **1** to thrust forwards or outwards. **2** to project or cause to project. ORIG C17: from L, from PRO-[2] + *trudere* to thrust
▸ **proˈtrusion** *n* ▸ **proˈtrusive** *adj*

protrusile (prəˈtruːsaɪl) *adj Zool*. capable of being thrust forwards: *protrusile jaws*.

protuberant (prəˈtjuːbərənt) *adj* swelling out; bulging. ORIG C17: from LL *prōtūberāre* to swell, from PRO-[1] + *tūber* swelling
▸ **proˈtuberance** *or* **proˈtuberancy** *n* ▸ **proˈtuberantly** *adv*

proud (praʊd) *adj* **1** (foll. by *of*, an infinitive, or a clause) pleased or satisfied, as with oneself, one's possessions, achievements, etc. **2** feeling honoured or gratified by some distinction. **3** having an inordinately high opinion of oneself; haughty. **4** characterized by or proceeding from a sense of pride: *a proud moment*. **5** having a proper sense of self-respect. **6** stately or distinguished. **7** bold or fearless. **8** (of a surface, edge, etc.) projecting or protruding. **9** (of animals) restive or excited, often sexually. ◆ *adv* **10 do (someone) proud**. **10a** to entertain (someone) on a grand scale: *they did us proud at the hotel*. **10b** to honour (someone): *his honesty did him proud*. ORIG LOE *prūd*, from OF *prud, prod* brave, from LL *prōde* useful, from L *prōdesse* to be of value
▸ ˈ**proudly** *adv* ▸ ˈ**proudness** *n*

proud flesh *n* a mass of tissue formed around a healing wound.

Proudhon ★ (*French* prudɔ̃) *n* **Pierre Joseph** (pjɛr ʒozɛf). 1809–65, French socialist, whose pamphlet *What is Property?* (1840) declared that property is theft.

Proust ★ (*French* prust) *n* **1 Joseph Louis** (ʒozɛf lwi). 1754–1826, French chemist, who formulated the law of constant proportions. **2 Marcel** (marsɛl). 1871–1922, French novelist whose long novel *À la recherche du temps perdu* (1913–27) deals with themes such as art, time, memory, and society.

Prov. *abbrev. for:* **1** Provençal. **2** *Bible.* Proverbs. **3** Province. **4** Provost.

prove (pruːv) *vb* **proves, proving, proved; proved** *or* **proven.** (*mainly tr*) **1** (*may take a clause as object or an infinitive*) to demonstrate the truth or validity of, esp. by using an established sequence of procedures. **2** to establish the quality of, esp. by experiment. **3** *Law.* to establish the genuineness of (a will). **4** to show (oneself) able or courageous. **5** (*copula*) to be found (to be): *this has proved useless.* **6** (*intr*) (of dough) to rise in a warm place before baking. ORIG C12: from OF *prover,* from L *probāre* to test, from *probus* honest
▸ **'provable** *adj* ▸ **'provably** *adv* ▸ **,prova'bility** *n*

proven ('pruːvᵊn, 'prəʊ-) *vb* **1** a past participle of **prove. 2** See **not proven.** ◆ *adj* **3** tried; tested: *a proven method.*

provenance ('prɒvɪnəns) *n* a place of origin, as of a work of art. ORIG C19: from F, from *provenir,* from L *prōvenīre* to originate, from *venīre* to come

Provençal (,prɒvɒn'sɑːl; *French* prɔvɑ̃sal) *adj* **1** denoting or characteristic of Provence, its inhabitants, their dialect of French, or their Romance language. ◆ *n* **2** a language of Provence, closely related to French and Italian, belonging to the Romance group of the Indo-European family. **3** a native or inhabitant of Provence.

Provence ★ (*French* prɔvɑ̃s) *n* a former province of SE France, on the Mediterranean, and the River Rhône: forms part of the administrative region of Provence-Alpes-Côte d'Azur.

provender ('prɒvɪndə) *n* **1** fodder for livestock. **2** food in general. ORIG C14: from OF *provendre,* from LL *praebenda* grant, from L *praebēre* to proffer

proverb ('prɒvɜːb) *n* **1** a short memorable saying embodying some commonplace fact. **2** a person or thing exemplary of a characteristic: *Antarctica is a proverb for extreme cold.* **3** *Bible.* a wise saying providing guidance. ORIG C14: via OF from L *prōverbium,* from *verbum* word

proverbial (prə'vɜːbɪəl) *adj* **1** (*prenominal*) commonly or traditionally referred to as an example of some peculiarity, characteristic, etc. **2** of, embodied in, or resembling a proverb.
▸ **pro'verbially** *adv*

provide (prə'vaɪd) *vb* **provides, providing, provided.** (*mainly tr*) **1** to furnish or supply. **2** to afford; yield: *this meeting provides an opportunity to talk.* **3** (*intr;* often foll. by *for* or *against*) to take careful precautions: *he provided against financial ruin by wise investment.* **4** (*intr;* foll. by *for*) to supply means of support (to): *he provides for his family.* **5** (of a person, law, etc.) to state as a condition; stipulate. **6** to confer and induct into ecclesiastical offices. ORIG C15: from L *prōvidēre* to provide for, from *prō-* beforehand + *vidēre* to see
▸ **pro'vider** *n*

providence ('prɒvɪdəns) *n* **1a** *Christianity.* God's foreseeing protection and care of his creatures. **1b** such protection and care as manifest by some other force. **2** a supposed manifestation of such care and guidance. **3** the foresight or care exercised by a person in the management of his affairs.

Providence[1] ('prɒvɪdəns) *n Christianity.* God, esp. as showing foreseeing care of his creatures.

Providence[2] ★ ('prɒvɪdəns) *n* a port in NE Rhode Island, capital of the state, at the head of Narragansett Bay: founded by Roger Williams in 1636. Pop.: 152 558 (1996 est.).

provident ('prɒvɪdənt) *adj* **1** providing for future needs. **2** exercising foresight in the management of one's affairs. **3** characterized by foresight. ORIG C15: from L *prōvidens* foreseeing, from *prōvidēre* to PROVIDE
▸ **'providently** *adv*

providential (,prɒvɪ'dɛnʃəl) *adj* characteristic of or presumed to proceed from or as if from divine providence.
▸ **,provi'dentially** *adv*

provident society *n* a mutual insurance society catering esp. for those on a low income, providing sickness, death, and pension benefits.

providing (prə'vaɪdɪŋ) *or* **provided** *conj* (*subordinating;* sometimes foll. by *that*) on the condition or understanding (that): *I'll play, providing you pay me.*

province ('prɒvɪns) *n* **1** a territory governed as a unit of a country or empire. **2** (*pl;* usually preceded by *the*) those parts of a country lying outside the capital and other large cities and regarded as outside the mainstream of sophisticated culture. **3** an area of learning, activity, etc. **4** the extent of a person's activities or office. **5** an ecclesiastical territory, having an archbishop or metropolitan at its head. **6** an administrative and territorial subdivision of a religious order. **7** *History.* a region of the Roman Empire outside Italy ruled by a governor from Rome. ORIG C14: from OF, from L *prōvincia* conquered territory

Provincetown ★ ('prɒvɪns,taʊn) *n* a village in SE Massachusetts, at the tip of Cape Cod: scene of the first landing place of the Pilgrims (1620) and of the signing of the Mayflower Compact (1620). Pop.: 3374 (1990).

provincewide ('prɒvɪns,waɪd) *Canad.* ◆ *adj* **1** covering or available to the whole of a province: *a provincewide referendum.* ◆ *adv* **2** throughout a province: *an advertising campaign to go provincewide.*

provincial (prə'vɪnʃəl) *adj* **1** of or connected with a province. **2** characteristic of or connected with the provinces. **3** having attitudes and opinions supposedly common to people living in the provinces; unsophisticated; limited. **4** *NZ.* denoting a football team representing a province, one of the historical administrative areas of New Zealand. ◆ *n* **5** a person lacking the sophistications of city life; rustic or narrow-minded individual. **6** a person coming from or resident in a province or the provinces. **7** the head of an ecclesiastical province. **8** the head of a territorial subdivision of a religious order.
▸ **provinciality** (prə,vɪnʃɪ'ælɪtɪ) *n* ▸ **pro'vincially** *adv*

provincialism (prə'vɪnʃə,lɪzəm) *n* **1** narrowness of mind; lack of sophistication. **2** a word or attitude characteristic of a provincial. **3** attention to the affairs of one's local area rather than the whole nation. **4** the state or quality of being provincial.

provirus ('prəʊ,vaɪrəs) *n* the inactive form of a virus in a host cell.

provision (prə'vɪʒən) *n* **1** the act of supplying food, etc. **2** something that is supplied. **3** preparations (esp. in **make provision for**). **4** (*pl*) food and other necessities, as for an expedition. **5** a condition or stipulation incorporated in a document; proviso. **6** the conferring of and induction into ecclesiastical offices. ◆ *vb* **7** (*tr*) to supply with provisions. ORIG C14: from L *prōvīsiō* a providing; see PROVIDE
▸ **pro'visioner** *n*

provisional (prə'vɪʒənᵊl) *adj* subject to later alteration; temporary or conditional: *a provisional decision.*
▸ **pro'visionally** *adv*

Provisional (prə'vɪʒənᵊl) *adj* **1** designating one of the two factions of the IRA and Sinn Féin that have existed since a split in late 1969. The Provisional movement advocates terrorism to achieve Irish unity. ◆ *n* **2** Also called: **Provo.** a member of the Provisional IRA or Sinn Féin.

proviso (prə'vaɪzəʊ) *n, pl* **provisos** *or* **provisoes. 1** a clause in a document or contract that embodies a condition or stipulation. **2** a condition or stipulation. ORIG C15: from Med. L *prōvīsō quod* it being provided that, from L *prōvīsus* provided

provisory (prə'vaɪzərɪ) *adj* **1** containing a proviso; conditional. **2** provisional. **3** making provision.
▸ **pro'visorily** *adv*

Provo ('prəʊvəʊ) *n, pl* **Provos.** another name for a **Provisional** (sense 2).

provocation (ˌprɒvəˈkeɪʃən) *n* **1** the act of provoking or inciting. **2** something that causes indignation, anger, etc.

provocative (prəˈvɒkətɪv) *adj* serving or intended to provoke or incite, esp. to anger or sexual desire: *a provocative look; a provocative remark.*
▸ **proˈvocatively** *adv*

provoke (prəˈvəuk) *vb* **provokes, provoking, provoked.** (*tr*) **1** to anger or infuriate. **2** to incite or stimulate. **3** to promote (anger, etc.) in a person. **4** to cause; bring about: *the accident provoked an inquiry.* ORIG C15: from L *prōvocāre* to call forth
▸ **proˈvoking** *adj* ▸ **proˈvokingly** *adv*

provost (ˈprɒvəst) *n* **1** the head of certain university colleges or schools. **2** (in Scotland) the chairman and civic head of certain district councils or (formerly) of a burgh council. Cf. **convener** (sense 2). **3** *Church of England.* the senior dignitary of one of the more recent cathedral foundations. **4** *RC Church.* **4a** the head of a cathedral chapter. **4b** (formerly) the member of a monastic community second in authority under the abbot. **5** (in medieval times) an overseer, steward, or bailiff. ORIG OE *profost,* from Med. L *prōpositus* placed at the head (of), from L *praepōnere* to place first

provost marshal (prəˈvəu) *n* the officer in charge of military police in a camp or city.

prow (prau) *n* the bow of a vessel. ORIG C16: from OF *proue,* from L *prora,* from Gk *prōra*

prowess (ˈprauɪs) *n* **1** outstanding or superior skill or ability. **2** bravery or fearlessness, esp. in battle. ORIG C13: from OF *proesce,* from *prou* good

prowl (praul) *vb* **1** (when *intr,* often foll. by *around* or *about*) to move stealthily around (a place) as if in search of prey or plunder. ◆ *n* **2** the act of prowling. **3 on the prowl. 3a** moving around stealthily. **3b** pursuing members of the opposite sex. ORIG C14 *prollen,* from ?
▸ **ˈprowler** *n*

prox. *abbrev. for* proximo (next month).

proximal (ˈprɒksɪməl) *adj Anat.* situated close to the centre, median line, or point of attachment or origin.
▸ **ˈproximally** *adv*

proximate (ˈprɒksɪmɪt) *adj* **1** next or nearest in space or time. **2** very near; close. **3** immediately preceding or following in a series. **4** a less common word for **approximate.** ORIG C16: from LL *proximāre* to draw near, from L *proximus* next, from *prope* near
▸ **ˈproximately** *adv*

proximity (prɒkˈsɪmɪtɪ) *n* **1** nearness in space or time. **2** nearness or closeness in a series. ORIG C15: from L *proximitās* closeness; see PROXIMATE

proximo (ˈprɒksɪməu) *adv Now rare except when abbreviated in formal correspondence.* in or during the next or coming month: *a letter of the seventh proximo.* Abbrev.: **prox.** Cf. **instant, ultimo.** ORIG C19: from L: in or on the next

proxy (ˈprɒksɪ) *n, pl* **proxies. 1** a person authorized to act on behalf of someone else; agent: *vote by proxy.* **2** authority, esp. in the form of a document, given to a person to act on behalf of someone else. ORIG C15 *prokesye,* from *procuracy,* from L *prōcūrātiō* procuration; see PROCURE

Prozac (ˈprəuzæk) *n Trademark.* a drug that prolongs the action of serotonin in the brain; used as an antidepressant.

PRP *abbrev. for:* **1** performance-related pay. **2** profit-related pay.

PRT *abbrev. for* petroleum revenue tax.

prude (pruːd) *n* a person who affects or shows an excessively modest, prim, or proper attitude, esp. regarding sex. ORIG C18: from F, from *prudefemme,* from OF *prode femme* respectable woman; see PROUD
▸ **ˈprudery** *n* ▸ **ˈprudish** *adj* ▸ **ˈprudishly** *adv*

prudence (ˈpruːdəns) *n* **1** caution in practical affairs; discretion. **2** care taken in the management of one's resources. **3** consideration for one's own interests. **4** the quality of being prudent.

prudent (ˈpruːdᵊnt) *adj* **1** discreet or cautious in managing one's activities; circumspect. **2** practical and careful in providing for the future. **3** exercising good judgment. ORIG C14: from L *prūdēns* far-sighted, from *prōvidens* acting with foresight; see PROVIDENT
▸ **ˈprudently** *adv*

prudential (pruːˈdɛnʃəl) *adj* **1** characterized by or resulting from prudence. **2** exercising sound judgment.
▸ **pruˈdentially** *adv*

Prudentius ★ (pruːˈdɛnʃəs) *n* **Aurelius Clemens** (ɔːˈriːlɪəs ˈklɛmɛnz). 348–410 A.D., Latin Christian poet, born in Spain. His works include the allegory *Psychomachia.*

Prud'hon ★ (*French* prydɔ̃) *n* **Pierre Paul** (pjɛr pɔl). 1758–1823, French painter, noted for the romantic and mysterious aura of his portraits.

pruinose (ˈpruːɪˌnəus, -ˌnəuz) *adj Bot.* coated with a powdery or waxy bloom. ORIG C19: from L *pruīnōsus* frost-covered, from *pruīna* hoarfrost

prune¹ (pruːn) *n* **1** a purplish-black partially dried fruit of any of several varieties of plum tree. **2** *Sl., chiefly Brit.* a dull or foolish person. **3 prunes and prisms.** denoting an affected and mincing way of speaking. ORIG C14: from OF *prune,* from L *prūnum* plum, from Gk *prounon*

prune² (pruːn) *vb* **prunes, pruning, pruned. 1** to remove (dead or superfluous twigs, branches, etc.) from (a tree, shrub, etc.), esp. by cutting off. **2** to remove (anything undesirable or superfluous) from (a book, etc.). ORIG C15: from OF *proignier* to clip, prob. from *provigner* to prune vines, ult. from L *propāgo* a cutting
▸ **ˈprunable** *adj* ▸ **ˈpruner** *n*

prunella (pruːˈnɛlə) *n* a strong fabric, esp. a twill-weave worsted, formerly used for academic gowns and the uppers of some shoes. ORIG C17: ?from *prunelle,* a green French liqueur, with reference to the colour of the cloth

pruning hook *n* a tool with a curved steel blade terminating in a hook, used for pruning.

prurient (ˈpruərɪənt) *adj* **1** unusually or morbidly interested in sexual thoughts or practices. **2** exciting lustfulness. ORIG C17: from L *prūrīre* to lust after, itch
▸ **ˈprurience** *n* ▸ **ˈpruriently** *adv*

prurigo (pruəˈraɪgəu) *n* a chronic inflammatory disease of the skin characterized by intense itching. ORIG C19: from L: an itch
▸ **pruriginous** (pruəˈrɪdʒɪnəs) *adj*

pruritus (pruəˈraɪtəs) *n Pathol.* any intense sensation of itching. ORIG C17: from L: an itching; see PRURIENT
▸ **pruritic** (pruəˈrɪtɪk) *adj*

Prus. *abbrev. for* Prussia(n).

Prussia ★ (ˈprʌʃə) *n* a former German state in N and central Germany, extending from France and the Low Countries to the Baltic Sea and Poland: developed as the chief military power of the Continent, leading the North German Confederation from 1867–71, when the German Empire was established; dissolved in 1947 and divided between East and West Germany, Poland, and the former Soviet Union. Area: (in 1939) 294 081 sq. km (113 545 sq. miles). German name: **Preussen.**

Prussian (ˈprʌʃən) *adj* **1** of Prussia, or its people, esp. of the Junkers and their military tradition. ◆ *n* **2** a native or inhabitant of Prussia. **3 Old Prussian.** the extinct Baltic language of the non-German inhabitants of Prussia.

Prussian blue *n* **1** any of a number of blue pigments containing ferrocyanide or ferricyanide ions. **2a** the blue or deep greenish-blue colour of this. **2b** (*as adj*): *a Prussian-blue carpet.*

prussic acid (ˈprʌsɪk) *n* the extremely poisonous aqueous solution of hydrogen cyanide. ORIG C18: from F *acide prussique* Prussian acid, because obtained from Prussian blue

Prut ★ (*Russian* prut) *n* a river in E Europe, rising in SW Ukraine and flowing generally southeast, forming part of the border between Romania and Moldova, to join the River Danube. Length: 853 km (530 miles).

pry¹ (praɪ) *vb* **pries, prying, pried. 1** (*intr;* often foll. by *into*) to make an impertinent or uninvited inquiry (about a private matter, topic, etc.). ◆ *n, pl* **pries. 2** the act of prying. **3** a person who pries. ORIG C14: from ?

pry² (praɪ) *vb* **pries, prying, pried.** the US and Canad. word for **prise.** ORIG C14: from ?

pryer ('praɪə) *n* a variant spelling of **prier**.

Prynne ★ (prɪn) *n* **William.** 1600–69, English Puritan leader and pamphleteer, whose ears were cut off in punishment for his attacks on Laud.

Przemyśl ★ (*Polish* 'pʃɛmiʃl) *n* a city in SE Poland, near the border with Ukraine on the San River: a fortress in the early Middle Ages; belonged to Austria (1722–1918). Pop.: 67 000 (1989 est.).

Przewalski's horse (ˌpɜːʒə'vælskɪz) *n* a wild horse of W Mongolia, having an erect mane and no forelock: extinct in the wild, a few survive in captivity. ORIG C19: after the Russian explorer Nikolai *Przewalski* (1839–88), who discovered it

PS *abbrev. for:* **1** Passenger Steamer. **2** Police Sergeant. **3** Also: **ps.** postscript. **4** private secretary. **5** prompt side.

Ps. *or* **Psa.** *Bible. abbrev. for* Psalm(s).

PSA *abbrev. for* prostatic specific antigen: an enzyme secreted by the prostate gland, increased levels of which are found in the blood of patients with cancer of the prostate.

psalm (sɑːm) *n* **1** (*often cap.*) any of the sacred songs that constitute a book (Psalms) of the Old Testament. **2** a musical setting of one of these. **3** any sacred song. ORIG OE, from LL *psalmus,* from Gk *psalmos* song accompanied on the harp, from *psallein* to play (the harp)
▸ **psalmic** ('sɑːmɪk, 'sæl-) *adj*

psalmist ('sɑːmɪst) *n* the composer of a psalm or psalms, esp. (when *cap.* and preceded by *the*) David, traditionally regarded as the author of The Book of Psalms.

psalmody ('sɑːmədɪ, 'sæl-) *n, pl* **psalmodies. 1** the act of singing psalms or hymns. **2** the art of setting psalms to music. ORIG C14: via LL from Gk *psalmōdia* singing accompanied by a harp, from *psalmos* (see PSALM) + *ōidē* ODE
▸ **'psalmodist** *n* ▸ **psalmodic** (sæl'mɒdɪk) *adj*

Psalter ('sɔːltə) *n* **1** another name for the Book of Psalms, esp. in the version in the Book of Common Prayer. **2** a translation, musical, or metrical version of the Psalms. **3** a book containing a version of Psalms. ORIG OE *psaltere,* from LL *psaltērium,* from Gk *psaltērion* stringed instrument, from *psallein* to play a stringed instrument

psalterium (sɔːl'tɪərɪəm) *n, pl* **psalteria** (-'tɪərɪə). the third compartment of the stomach of ruminants. Also called: **omasum.** ORIG C19: from L *psaltērium* PSALTER; from the similarity of its folds to the pages of a book

psaltery ('sɔːltərɪ) *n, pl* **psalteries.** *Music.* an ancient stringed instrument similar to the lyre, but having a trapezoidal sounding board over which the strings are stretched.

p's and q's *pl n* behaviour; manners (esp. in **mind one's p's and q's**). ORIG altered from *p(lea)se and (than)k yous*

PSBR (in Britain) *abbrev. for* public sector borrowing requirement; the money required by the public sector of the economy for expenditure on items that are not financed from income.

psephology (sɛ'fɒlədʒɪ) *n* the statistical and sociological study of elections. ORIG C20: from Gk *psephos* pebble, vote + -LOGY, from the ancient Greeks' custom of voting with pebbles
▸ **psephological** (ˌsɛfə'lɒdʒɪkᵊl) *adj* ▸ **ˌpsepho'logically** *adv* ▸ **pse'phologist** *n*

pseud (sjuːd) *n* **1** *Inf.* a false or pretentious person. ◆ *adj* **2** another word for **pseudo**.

Pseudepigrapha (ˌsjuːdɪ'pɪgrəfə) *pl n* various Jewish writings from the first century B.C. to the first century A.D. that claim to have been divinely revealed but which have been excluded from the Greek canon of the Old Testament. ORIG C17: from Gk *pseudepigraphos* falsely entitled, from PSEUDO- + *epigraphein* to inscribe
▸ **Pseudepigraphic** (ˌsjuːdɛpɪ'græfɪk) *or* **ˌPseudepi'graphical** *adj*

pseudo ('sjuːdəʊ) *adj Inf.* not genuine.

pseudo- *or sometimes before a vowel* **pseud-** *combining form.* **1** false, pretending, or unauthentic: *pseudo-intellectual.* **2** having a close resemblance to: *pseudopodium.* ORIG from Gk *pseudēs* false, from *pseudein* to lie

pseudocarp ('sjuːdəʊˌkɑːp) *n* a fruit, such as the apple, that includes parts other than the ripened ovary.
▸ **ˌpseudo'carpous** *adj*

pseudoephedrine (ˌsjuːdəʊ'ɛfɪˌdriːn, -drɪn) *n* a drug similar in action to ephedrine, used extensively as a decongestant.

pseudomorph ('sjuːdəʊˌmɔːf) *n* a mineral that has an uncharacteristic crystalline form as a result of assuming the shape of another mineral that it has replaced.
▸ **ˌpseudo'morphic** *or* **ˌpseudo'morphous** *adj* ▸ **ˌpseudo'morphism** *n*

pseudonym ('sjuːdəˌnɪm) *n* a fictitious name adopted esp. by an author. ORIG C19: via F from Gk *pseudōnumon*
▸ **ˌpseudo'nymity** *n* ▸ **pseudonymous** (sjuː'dɒnɪməs) *adj*

pseudopodium (ˌsjuːdəʊ'pəʊdɪəm) *n, pl* **pseudopodia** (-dɪə). a temporary projection from the cell of a protozoan, etc., used for feeding and locomotion.

pseudovector (ˌsjuːdəʊ'vɛktə) *n Maths.* a variable quantity, such as angular momentum, that has magnitude and orientation with respect to an axis.

psf *abbrev. for* pounds per square foot.

pshaw (pʃɔː) *interj Becoming rare.* an exclamation of disgust, impatience, disbelief, etc.

psi[1] (psaɪ) *n* **1** the 23rd letter of the Greek alphabet (Ψ, ψ), a composite consonant, transliterated as *ps.* **2** paranormal or psychic phenomena collectively.

psi[2] *abbrev. for* pounds per square inch.

psilocybin (ˌsɪlə'saɪbɪn, ˌsaɪlə-) *n* a crystalline phosphate ester that is the active principle of the hallucinogenic fungus *Psilocybe mexicana.* Formula: $C_{12}H_{17}N_2O_4P$. ORIG C20: from NL *Psilocybe* (from Gk *psilos* bare + *kubē* head) + -IN

psi particle *n* See **J/psi particle.**

psittacine ('sɪtəˌsaɪn, -sɪn) *adj* of, relating to, or resembling a parrot. ORIG C19: from LL *psittacīnus,* from L *psittacus* a parrot

psittacosis (ˌsɪtə'kəʊsɪs) *n* a disease of parrots that can be transmitted to man, in whom it produces pneumonia. Also called: **parrot fever.** ORIG C19: from NL, from L *psittacus* a parrot, from Gk *psittakos;* see -OSIS

Pskov ★ (*Russian* pskɔf) *n* **1** a city in NW Russia, on the Velikaya River: one of the oldest Russian cities, at its height in the 13th and 14th centuries. Pop.: 207 000 (1995 est.). **2 Lake.** the S part of Lake Peipus in NW Russia, linked to the main part by a channel 24 km (15 miles) long. Area: about 1000 sq. km (400 sq. miles).

psoas ('səʊəs) *n* either of two muscles of the loins that aid in flexing and rotating the thigh. ORIG C17: from NL, from Gk *psoai* (pl)

psoriasis (sə'raɪəsɪs) *n* a skin disease characterized by the formation of reddish spots and patches covered with silvery scales. ORIG C17: via NL from Gk: itching disease, from *psōra* itch
▸ **psoriatic** (ˌsɔːrɪ'ætɪk) *adj*

psst (pst) *interj* an exclamation made to attract someone's attention, esp. one made surreptitiously.

PST (in the US and Canada) *abbrev. for* Pacific Standard Time.

PSV (in Britain) *abbrev. for* public service vehicle (now called passenger carrying vehicle).

psych *or* **psyche** (saɪk) *vb* **psychs** *or* **psyches, psyching, psyched.** (*tr*) *Inf.* to psychoanalyse. See also **psych out, psych up.** ORIG C20: shortened from PSYCHOANALYSE

psyche ('saɪkɪ) *n* the human mind or soul. ORIG C17: from L, from Gk *psukhē* breath, soul

Psyche ★ ('saɪkɪ) *n Greek myth.* a beautiful girl loved by Eros (Cupid), who became the personification of the soul.

psychedelic (ˌsaɪkɪ'dɛlɪk) *adj* **1** relating to or denoting new or altered perceptions or sensory experiences, as through the use of hallucinogenic drugs. **2** denoting any of the drugs, esp. LSD, that produce these effects. **3** *Inf.* (of painting, etc.) having the vivid colours and complex patterns popularly associated with the visual effects of psychedelic states. ORIG C20: from PSYCHE + Gk *delos* visible
▸ **ˌpsyche'delically** *adv*

psychiatry (saɪ'kaɪətrɪ) *n* the branch of medicine concerned with the diagnosis and treatment of mental disorders.
▸ **psychiatric** (ˌsaɪkɪ'ætrɪk) *or* **ˌpsychi'atrical** *adj* ▸ **ˌpsychi'atrically** *adv* ▸ **psy'chiatrist** *n*

psychic ('saɪkɪk) *adj* **1a** outside the possibilities defined by natural laws, as mental telepathy. **1b** (of a person) sensitive to forces not recognized by natural laws. **2** mental as opposed to physical. ◆ *n* **3** a person who is sensitive to parapsychological forces or influences.
▸ **'psychical** *adj* ▸ **'psychically** *adv*

psycho ('saɪkəʊ) *n, pl* **psychos,** *adj* an informal word for **psychopath** or **psychopathic.**

psycho- *or sometimes before a vowel* **psych-** *combining form.* indicating the mind or psychological or mental processes: *psychology.* ORIG from Gk *psukhē* spirit, breath

psychoactive (ˌsaɪkəʊ'æktɪv) *adj* (of drugs such as LSD and barbiturates) capable of affecting mental activity. Also: **psychotropic.**

psychoanalyse *or esp. US* **psychoanalyze** (ˌsaɪkəʊ'ænəˌlaɪz) *vb* **psychoanalyses, psychoanalysing, psychoanalysed** *or US* **psychoanalyzes, psychoanalyzing, psychoanalyzed.** (*tr*) to examine or treat (a person) by psychoanalysis.

psychoanalysis (ˌsaɪkəʊə'nælɪsɪs) *n* a method of studying the mind and treating mental and emotional disorders based on revealing and investigating the role of the unconscious mind.
▸ **psychoanalyst** (ˌsaɪkəʊ'ænəlɪst) *n* ▸ **psychoanalytic** (ˌsaɪkəʊˌænə'lɪtɪk) *or* **ˌpsychoˌana'lytical** *adj* ▸ **ˌpsychoˌana'lytically** *adv*

psychobiology (ˌsaɪkəʊbaɪ'ɒlədʒɪ) *n Psychol.* the attempt to understand the psychology of organisms in terms of their biological functions and structures.
▸ **psychobiological** (ˌsaɪkəʊˌbaɪə'lɒdʒɪkᵊl) *adj* ▸ **ˌpsychobi'ologist** *n*

psychochemical (ˌsaɪkəʊ'kɛmɪkᵊl) *n* **1** any of various chemicals whose primary effect is the alteration of the normal state of consciousness. ◆ *adj* **2** of such compounds.

psychodrama ('saɪkəʊˌdrɑːmə) *n* **1** *Psychiatry.* a form of group therapy in which individuals act out situations from their past. **2** a film, television drama, etc., in which the psychological development of the characters is emphasized.

psychodynamics (ˌsaɪkəʊdaɪ'næmɪks) *n* (*functioning as sing*) *Psychol.* the study of interacting motives and emotions.
▸ **ˌpsychody'namic** *adj*

psychogenic (ˌsaɪkəʊ'dʒɛnɪk) *adj Psychol.* (esp. of disorders or symptoms) of mental, rather than organic, origin.
▸ **ˌpsycho'genically** *adv*

psychokinesis (ˌsaɪkəʊkɪ'niːsɪs, -kaɪ-) *n* (in parapsychology) alteration of the state of an object supposedly by mental influence alone. ORIG C20: from PSYCHO- + Gk *kinēsis* motion

psycholinguistics (ˌsaɪkəʊlɪŋ'gwɪstɪks) *n* (*functioning as sing*) the psychology of language, including language acquisition by children, language disorders, etc.
▸ **ˌpsycho'linguist** *n*

psychological (ˌsaɪkə'lɒdʒɪkᵊl) *adj* **1** of or relating to psychology. **2** of or relating to the mind or mental activity. **3** having no real or objective basis; arising in the mind: *his backaches are all psychological.* **4** affecting the mind.
▸ **ˌpsycho'logically** *adv*

psychological moment *n* the most appropriate time for producing a desired effect.

psychological warfare *n* the application of psychology, esp. to attempts to influence morale in time of war.

psychologize *or US* **psychologise** (saɪ'kɒləˌdʒaɪz) *vb* **psychologizes, psychologizing, psychologized** *or US* **psychologises, psychologising, psychologised.** (*intr*) **1** to make interpretations of mental processes. **2** to carry out investigation in psychology.

psychology (saɪ'kɒlədʒɪ) *n, pl* **psychologies. 1** the scientific study of all forms of human and animal behaviour. **2** *Inf.* the mental make-up of an individual that causes that person to think or act in the way he or she does.
▸ **psy'chologist** *n*

psychometrics (ˌsaɪkəʊ'mɛtrɪks) *n* (*functioning as sing*) **1** the branch of psychology concerned with the design and use of psychological tests. **2** the application of statistical techniques to psychological testing.

psychometry (saɪ'kɒmɪtrɪ) *n Psychol.* **1** measurement and testing of mental states and processes. **2** (in parapsychology) the supposed ability to deduce facts about events by touching objects related to them.
▸ **psychometric** (ˌsaɪkəʊ'mɛtrɪk) *or* **ˌpsycho'metrical** *adj* ▸ **ˌpsycho'metrically** *adv*

psychomotor (ˌsaɪkəʊ'məʊtə) *adj* of, relating to, or characterizing movements of the body associated with mental activity.

psychoneuroimmunology (ˌsaɪkəʊˌnjʊərəʊˌɪmjʊ'nɒlədʒɪ) *n* the study of the psychological factors that affect the immune system. Abbrev.: **PNI.**

psychoneurosis (ˌsaɪkəʊnjʊ'rəʊsɪs) *n, pl* **psychoneuroses** (-'rəʊsiːz). another word for **neurosis.**

psychopath ('saɪkəʊˌpæθ) *n* a person with a personality disorder characterized by a tendency to commit antisocial and sometimes violent acts without feeling guilt.
▸ **ˌpsycho'pathic** *adj* ▸ **ˌpsycho'pathically** *adv*

psychopathology (ˌsaɪkəʊpə'θɒlədʒɪ) *n* the scientific study of mental disorders.
▸ **psychopathological** (ˌsaɪkəʊˌpæθə'lɒdʒɪkᵊl) *adj*

psychopathy (saɪ'kɒpəθɪ) *n* any mental disorder or disease.

psychopharmacology (ˌsaɪkəʊˌfɑːmə'kɒlədʒɪ) *n* the study of drugs that affect the mind.

psychophysics (ˌsaɪkəʊ'fɪzɪks) *n* (*functioning as sing*) the branch of psychology concerned with the relationship between physical stimuli and their effects in the mind.
▸ **ˌpsycho'physical** *adj*

psychophysiology (ˌsaɪkəʊˌfɪzɪ'ɒlədʒɪ) *n* the branch of psychology concerned with the physiological basis of mental processes.
▸ **psychophysiological** (ˌsaɪkəʊˌfɪzɪə'lɒdʒɪkᵊl) *adj*

psychosexual (ˌsaɪkəʊ'sɛksjʊəl) *adj* of or relating to the mental aspects of sex, such as sexual fantasies.
▸ **ˌpsycho'sexually** *adv*

psychosis (saɪ'kəʊsɪs) *n, pl* **psychoses** (-'kəʊsiːz). any form of severe mental disorder in which the individual's contact with reality becomes highly distorted. ORIG C19: NL, from PSYCHO- + -OSIS

psychosocial (ˌsaɪkəʊ'səʊʃəl) *adj* of or relating to processes or factors that are both social and psychological in origin.

psychosomatic (ˌsaɪkəʊsə'mætɪk) *adj* of disorders, such as stomach ulcers, thought to be caused or aggravated by psychological factors such as stress.

psychosurgery (ˌsaɪkəʊ'sɜːdʒərɪ) *n* any surgical procedure on the brain, such as a frontal lobotomy, to relieve serious mental disorders.
▸ **psychosurgical** (ˌsaɪkəʊ'sɜːdʒɪkᵊl) *adj*

psychotherapy (ˌsaɪkəʊ'θɛrəpɪ) *n* the treatment of nervous disorders by psychological methods.
▸ **ˌpsychoˌthera'peutic** *adj* ▸ **ˌpsychoˌthera'peutically** *adv* ▸ **ˌpsycho'therapist** *n*

psychotic (saɪ'kɒtɪk) *Psychiatry.* ◆ *adj* **1** of or characterized by psychosis. ◆ *n* **2** a person suffering from psychosis.
▸ **psy'chotically** *adv*

psychotomimetic (saɪˌkɒtəʊmɪ'mɛtɪk) *adj* (of drugs such as LSD and mescaline) capable of inducing psychotic symptoms.

psych out *vb* (*mainly tr, adv*) *Inf.* **1** to guess correctly the intentions of (another). **2** to analyse (a problem, etc.) psychologically. **3** to intimidate or frighten.

psychrometer (saɪ'krɒmɪtə) *n* a type of hygrometer consisting of two thermometers, one of which has a dry bulb and the other a bulb that is kept moist and ventilated.

psych up *vb* (*tr, adv*) *Inf.* to get (oneself or another) into a state of psychological readiness for an action, performance, etc.

pt *abbrev. for:* **1** part. **2** patient. **3** payment. **4** point. **5** port. **6** pro tempore.

Pt *abbrev. for* (in place names): **1** Point. **2** Port. ◆ **3.** *the chemical symbol for* platinum.

PT *abbrev. for:* **1** physical therapy. **2** physical training. **3** postal telegraph.

pt. *abbrev. for:* **1** pint. **2** preterite.

PTA *abbrev. for:* **1** Parent Teacher Association. **2** (in Britain) Passenger Transport Authority.

Ptah ★ (ptɑː, tɑː) *n* (in ancient Egypt) a major god worshipped as the creative power, esp. at Memphis.

ptarmigan (ˈtɑːmɪgən) *n, pl* **ptarmigans** *or* **ptarmigan.** any of several arctic and subarctic grouse, esp. one which has a white winter plumage. ORIG C16: changed (? infl. by Gk *pteron* wing) from Scot. Gaelic *tarmachan,* from ?

Pte *Mil. abbrev. for* private.

pteridology (ˌtɛrɪˈdɒlədʒɪ) *n* the branch of botany concerned with the study of ferns. ORIG C19: from *pterido-,* from Gk *pteris* fern + -LOGY
▸ **pteridological** (ˌtɛrɪdəʊˈlɒdʒɪkəl) *adj*

pteridophyte (ˈtɛrɪdəʊˌfaɪt) *n* (in traditional classification) a plant, such as a fern, horsetail, or club moss, reproducing by spores and having vascular tissue, roots, stems, and leaves. In modern classifications these plants are placed in separate phyla. ORIG C19: from *pterido-,* from Gk *pteris* fern + -PHYTE

ptero- *combining form.* a wing, or a part resembling a wing: *pterodactyl.* ORIG from Gk *pteron*

pterodactyl (ˌtɛrəˈdæktɪl) *n* an extinct flying reptile having membranous wings supported on an elongated fourth digit.

pteropod (ˈtɛrəˌpɒd) *n* a small marine gastropod mollusc in which the foot is expanded into two winglike lobes for swimming. Also called: **sea butterfly.**

pterosaur (ˈtɛrəˌsɔː) *n* any of an order of extinct flying reptiles of Jurassic and Cretaceous times: included the pterodactyls.

-pterous *or* **-pteran** *adj combining form.* indicating a specified number or type of wings: *dipterous.* ORIG from Gk *-pteros,* from *pteron* wing

pterygoid process (ˈtɛrɪˌgɔɪd) *n Anat.* either of two long bony plates extending downwards from each side of the sphenoid bone within the skull. ORIG C18 *pterygoid,* from Gk *pterugoeidēs,* from *pterux* wing; see -OID

PTN *abbrev. for* public telephone network: the telephone network provided in Britain by British Telecom.

PTO *or* **pto** *abbrev. for* please turn over.

Ptolemaic (ˌtɒlɪˈmeɪɪk) *adj* **1** of or relating to the ancient astronomer Ptolemy or to his conception of the universe. **2** of or relating to the Macedonian dynasty that ruled Egypt from the death of Alexander the Great (323 B.C.) to the death of Cleopatra (30 B.C.).

Ptolemaic system *n* the theory of planetary motion developed by Ptolemy from the hypotheses of earlier philosophers, stating that the earth lay at the centre of the universe with the sun, the moon, and the known planets revolving around it in complicated orbits. Beyond the largest of these orbits lay a sphere of fixed stars.

Ptolemy ★ (ˈtɒlɪmɪ) *n* Latin name *Claudius Ptolemaeus.* 2nd-century A.D. Greek astronomer, mathematician, and geographer. His *Geography* was the standard geographical textbook until the discoveries of the 15th century. His system of astronomy (see **Ptolemaic system**) remained undisputed until Copernicus.

Ptolemy I ★ *n* called *Ptolemy Soter.* ?367–283 B.C., king of Egypt (323–285 B.C.), a general of Alexander the Great, who obtained Egypt on Alexander's death and founded the Ptolemaic dynasty.

Ptolemy II ★ *n* called *Philadelphus.* 309–246 B.C., the son of Ptolemy I; king of Egypt (285–246). Under his rule the power, prosperity, and culture of Egypt was at its height.

ptomaine *or* **ptomain** (ˈtəʊmeɪn) *n* any of a group of amines formed by decaying organic matter. ORIG C19: from It. *ptomaina,* from Gk *ptoma* corpse, from *piptein* to fall

ptomaine poisoning *n* a popular term for **food poisoning.** Ptomaines were once erroneously thought to be a cause of food poisoning.

ptosis (ˈtəʊsɪs) *n, pl* **ptoses** (ˈtəʊsiːz). prolapse or drooping of a part, esp. the eyelid. ORIG C18: from Gk: a falling
▸ **ptotic** (ˈtɒtɪk) *adj*

PTSD *abbrev. for* post-traumatic stress disorder.

pty *Austral., NZ, & S. African. abbrev. for* proprietary.

ptyalin (ˈtaɪəlɪn) *n Biochemistry.* an amylase secreted in the saliva of man and other animals. ORIG C19: from Gk *ptualon* saliva, from *ptuein* to spit

p-type *adj* **1** (of a semiconductor) having a density of mobile holes in excess of that of conduction electrons. **2** associated with or resulting from the movement of holes in a semiconductor: *p-type conductivity.*

Pu *the chemical symbol for* plutonium.

pub (pʌb) *n* **1** *Chiefly Brit.* a building with a bar and one or more public rooms licensed for the sale and consumption of alcoholic drink, often also providing light meals. Formal name: **public house.** **2** *Austral. & NZ.* a hotel. ◆ *vb* **pubs, pubbing, pubbed.** **3** (*intr*) *Inf.* to visit a pub or pubs (esp. in **go pubbing**).

pub. *abbrev. for:* **1** public. **2** publication. **3** published. **4** publisher. **5** publishing.

pub-crawl *Inf., chiefly Brit.* ◆ *n* **1** a drinking tour of a number of pubs or bars. ◆ *vb* **2** (*intr*) to make such a tour.

puberty (ˈpjuːbətɪ) *n* the period at the beginning of adolescence when the sex glands become functional. Also called: **pubescence.** ORIG C14: from L *pūbertās* maturity, from *pūber* adult
▸ **ˈpubertal** *adj*

pubes (ˈpjuːbiːz) *n, pl* **pubes.** **1** the region above the external genital organs, covered with hair from the time of puberty. **2** pubic hair. **3** the pubic bones. **4** the plural of **pubis.** ORIG from L

pubescent (pjuːˈbɛsənt) *adj* **1** arriving or arrived at puberty. **2** (of certain plants and animals or their parts) covered with a layer of fine short hairs or down. ORIG C17: from L *pūbēscere* to reach manhood, from *pūber* adult
▸ **puˈbescence** *n*

pubic (ˈpjuːbɪk) *adj* of or relating to the pubes or pubis: *pubic hair.*

pubis (ˈpjuːbɪs) *n, pl* **pubes.** one of the three sections of the hipbone that forms part of the pelvis. ORIG C16: shortened from NL *os pūbis* bone of the PUBES

public (ˈpʌblɪk) *adj* **1** of or concerning the people as a whole. **2** open to all: *public gardens.* **3** performed or made openly: *public proclamation.* **4** (*prenominal*) well-known: *a public figure.* **5** (*usually prenominal*) maintained at the expense of, serving, or for the use of a community: *a public library.* **6** open, acknowledged, or notorious: *a public scandal.* **7 go public.** (of a private company) to issue shares for subscription by the public. ◆ *n* **8** the community or people in general. **9** a section of the community grouped because of a common interest, activity, etc.: *the racing public.* ORIG C15: from L *pūblicus,* changed from *pōplicus* of the people, from *populus* people
▸ **ˈpublicly** *adv*

public-address system *n* a system of microphones, amplifiers, and loudspeakers for increasing the sound level, used in auditoriums, public gatherings, etc. Sometimes shortened to **PA system.**

publican (ˈpʌblɪkən) *n* **1** (in Britain) a person who keeps a public house. **2** (in ancient Rome) a public contractor, esp. one who farmed the taxes of a province. ORIG C12: from OF *publicain,* from L *pūblicānus* tax gatherer, from *pūblicum* state revenues

publication (ˌpʌblɪˈkeɪʃən) *n* **1** the act or process of publishing a printed work. **2** any printed work offered for sale or distribution. **3** the act or an instance of making information public. ORIG C14: via OF from L *pūblicātiō* confiscation of property, from *pūblicāre* to seize for public use

public bar *n Brit.* a bar in a public house usually serving drinks at a cheaper price than in the lounge bar.

public company *n* a limited company whose shares may be purchased by the public and traded freely on the open market and whose share capital is not less than a statutory minimum; public limited company. Cf. **private company.**

public convenience *n* a public lavatory.

public corporation *n* (in Britain) an organization established to run a nationalized industry or state-owned enterprise. The chairman and board members are appointed by a government minister, and the government has overall control.

public domain *n* **1** the status of a published work upon which the copyright has expired or which has not been subject to copyright. **2 in the public domain.** generally known or accessible.

public enemy *n* a notorious person, such as a criminal, who is regarded as a menace to the public.

public house *n* **1** *Brit.* the formal name for a **pub. 2** *US & Canad.* an inn, tavern, or small hotel.

publicist ('pʌblɪsɪst) *n* **1** a person who publicizes something, esp. a press or publicity agent. **2** a journalist. **3** *Rare.* a person learned in public or international law.

publicity (pʌ'blɪsɪtɪ) *n* **1a** the technique or process of attracting public attention to people, products, etc., as by the use of the mass media. **1b** (*as modifier*): *a publicity agent.* **2** public interest aroused by such a technique or process. **3** information used to draw public attention to people, products, etc. **4** the state of being public. ORIG C18: via F from Med. L *pūblicitās;* see PUBLIC

publicize *or* **publicise** ('pʌblɪˌsaɪz) *vb* **publicizes, publicizing, publicized** *or* **publicises, publicising, publicised.** (*tr*) to bring to public notice; advertise.

Public Lending Right *n* the right of authors to receive payment when their books are borrowed from public libraries.

public-liability insurance *n* (in Britain) a form of insurance, compulsory for any business in contact with the public, which pays compensation to a member of the public suffering injury or damage as a result of the policyholder or his employees failing to take reasonable care.

public limited company *n* another name for **public company.** Abbrev.: **plc** *or* **PLC.**

public nuisance *n* **1** *Law.* an illegal act causing harm to members of a community rather than to any individual. **2** *Inf.* a person generally considered objectionable.

public opinion *n* the attitude of the public, esp. as a factor in determining action, policy, etc.

public prosecutor *n Law.* an official in charge of prosecuting important cases.

Public Record Office *n* an institution in which official records are stored and kept available for inspection by the public.

public relations *n* (*functioning as sing or pl*) **1a** the practice of creating, promoting, or maintaining goodwill and a favourable image among the public towards an institution, public body, etc. **1b** the professional staff employed for this purpose. Abbrev.: **PR. 1c** the techniques employed. **1d** (*as modifier*): *the public-relations industry.* **2** the relationship between an organization and the public.

public school *n* **1** (in England and Wales) a private independent fee-paying secondary school. **2** in certain Canadian provinces, a public elementary school as distinguished from a separate school. **3** (in the US) any school that is part of a free local educational system.

public sector *n* the part of an economy which consists of state-owned institutions, including nationalized industries and services provided by local authorities.

public servant *n* **1** an elected or appointed holder of a public office. **2** the Austral. and NZ equivalent of **civil servant.**

public service *n* the Austral. and NZ equivalent of the **civil service.**

public-spirited *adj* having or showing active interest in the good of the community.

public utility *n* an enterprise concerned with the provision to the public of essentials, such as electricity or water. Also called (in the US): **public-service corporation.**

public works *pl n* engineering projects and other constructions, financed and undertaken by a government for the community.

publish ('pʌblɪʃ) *vb* **1** to produce and issue (a book, journal, music, electronic material, etc.) for distribution. **2** (*intr*) to have one's work issued for publication. **3** (*tr*) to announce formally or in public. **4** (*tr*) to communicate (defamatory matter) to someone other than the person defamed: *to publish a libel.* ORIG C14: from OF *puplier,* from L *pūblicāre* to make PUBLIC
▸ **'publishable** *adj*

publisher ('pʌblɪʃə) *n* **1** a company or person engaged in publishing periodicals, books, music, etc. **2** *US & Canad.* the proprietor of a newspaper.

Puccini ★ (pu'tʃi:nɪ) *n* **Giacomo** ('dʒa:komo). 1858–1924, Italian operatic composer, noted for the dramatic realism of his operas, which include *Manon Lescaut* (1893), *La Bohème* (1896), *Tosca* (1900), and *Madame Butterfly* (1904).

puce (pju:s) *n, adj* (of) a colour varying from deep red to dark purplish brown. ORIG C18: shortened from F *couleur puce* flea colour, from L *pūlex* flea

puck[1] (pʌk) *n* **1** a small disc of hard rubber used in ice hockey. **2** a stroke at the ball in hurling. **3** *Irish sl.* a sharp blow. ◆ *vb* (*tr*) **4** to strike (the ball) in hurling. **5** *Irish sl.* to strike hard; punch. ORIG C19: from ?

puck[2] (pʌk) *n* a mischievous or evil spirit. ORIG OE *pūca,* from ?
▸ **'puckish** *adj*

pucka ('pʌkə) *adj* a less common spelling of **pukka.**

pucker ('pʌkə) *vb* **1** to gather (a soft surface such as the skin) into wrinkles, or (of such a surface) to be so gathered. ◆ *n* **2** a wrinkle, crease, or irregular fold. ORIG C16: ? rel. to POKE[2], from the baglike wrinkles

pudding ('pʊdɪŋ) *n* **1** a sweetened usually cooked dessert made in many forms and of various ingredients. **2** a savoury dish, usually consisting partially of pastry or batter: *steak-and-kidney pudding.* **3** the dessert course in a meal. **4** a sausage-like mass of meat, oatmeal, etc., stuffed into a prepared skin or bag and boiled. ORIG C13 *poding*
▸ **'puddingy** *adj*

pudding stone *n* a conglomerate rock in which there is a difference in colour and composition between the pebbles and the matrix.

puddle ('pʌdᵊl) *n* **1** a small pool of water, esp. of rain. **2** a small pool of any liquid. **3** a worked mixture of wet clay and sand that is impervious to water and is used to line a pond or canal. ◆ *vb* **puddles, puddling, puddled.** (*tr*) **4** to make (clay, etc.) into puddle. **5** to subject (iron) to puddling. ORIG C14 *podel,* dim. of OE *pudd* ditch, from ?
▸ **'puddler** *n* ▸ **'puddly** *adj*

puddling ('pʌdlɪŋ) *n* a process for converting pig iron into wrought iron by heating it with ferric oxide in a furnace and stirring it to oxidize the carbon.

pudency ('pju:dᵊnsɪ) *n* modesty or prudishness. ORIG C17: from LL *pudentia,* from L *pudēre* to feel shame

pudendum (pju:'dɛndəm) *n, pl* **pudenda** (-də). (*often pl*) the human external genital organs collectively, esp. of a female. ORIG C17: from LL, from L *pudenda* the shameful (parts), from *pudēre* to be ashamed
▸ **pu'dendal** *or* **pudic** ('pju:dɪk) *adj*

pudgy ('pʌdʒɪ) *adj* **pudgier, pudgiest.** a variant spelling (esp. US) of **podgy.** ORIG C19: from ?
▸ **'pudgily** *adv* ▸ **'pudginess** *n*

Pudsey ★ ('pʌdzɪ) *n* a town in N England, in Leeds unitary authority, in West Yorkshire. Pop.: 31 636 (1991).

Puebla ★ (*Spanish* 'pweβla) *n* **1** an inland state of S central Mexico, situated on the Anáhuac Plateau. Capital: Puebla. Pop.: 4 792 156 (1997 est.). Area: 33 919 sq. km (13 096 sq. miles). **2** a city in S Mexico, capital of Puebla state: founded in 1532; university (1537). Pop.:

1 007 170 (1990). Full name: **Puebla de Zaragoza** (de θara'ɣoθa).

pueblo ('pwɛbləu; *Spanish* 'pweβlo) *n, pl* **pueblos** (-ləuz; *Spanish* -los). **1** a communal village, built by certain Indians of the southwestern US and parts of Latin America, consisting of one or more flat-roofed houses. **2** (in Spanish America) a village or town. ORIG C19: from Sp.: people, from L *populus*

Pueblo[1] ('pwɛbləu) *n, pl* **Pueblo** *or* **Pueblos.** a member of any of the North American Indian peoples who live in pueblos.

Pueblo[2] ★ ('pwɛbləu) *n* a city in the US, in Colorado: a centre of the steel industry. Pop.: 99 406 (1996 est.).

puerile ('pjuəraɪl) *adj* **1** exhibiting silliness; immature; trivial. **2** of or characteristic of a child. ORIG C17: from L *puerīlis* childish, from *puer* a boy
▸ **'puerilely** *adv* ▸ **puerility** (pjuə'rɪlɪtɪ) *n*

puerperal (pju:'ɜ:pərəl) *adj* of or occurring during the period following childbirth. ORIG C18: from NL *puerperālis,* from L *puerperium* childbirth, ult. from *puer* boy + *parere* to bear

puerperal fever *n* a serious, formerly widespread, form of blood poisoning caused by infection contracted during childbirth.

puerperal psychosis *n* a mental disorder sometimes occurring in women after childbirth, characterized by deep depression.

Puerto Rico ★ ('pwɜ:təu 'ri:kəu, 'pwɛə-) *n* an autonomous commonwealth (in association with the US) occupying the smallest and easternmost of the Greater Antilles in the Caribbean: one of the most densely populated areas in the world; ceded by Spain to the US in 1899. Currency: US dollar. Capital: San Juan. Pop.: 3 888 000 (1999 est.). Area: 9104 sq. km (3515 sq. miles). Former name (until 1932): **Porto Rico.** Abbrev.: **PR.**
▸ **Puerto Rican** *adj, n*

puff (pʌf) *n* **1** a short quick gust or emission, as of wind, smoke, etc. **2** the amount of wind, smoke, etc., released in a puff. **3** the sound made by a puff. **4** an instance of inhaling and expelling the breath as in smoking. **5** a light aerated pastry usually filled with cream, jam, etc. **6** a powder puff. **7** exaggerated praise, as of a book, product, etc., esp. through an advertisement. **8** a piece of clothing fabric gathered up so as to bulge in the centre while being held together at the edges. **9** a cylindrical roll of hair pinned in place in a coiffure. **10** *US.* a quilted bed cover. **11** one's breath (esp. in **out of puff**). **12** *Derog. sl.* a male homosexual. ◆ *vb* **13** to blow or breathe or cause to blow or breathe in short quick draughts. **14** (*tr; often foll. by out; usually passive*) to cause to be out of breath. **15** to take draws at (a cigarette, etc.). **16** (*intr*) to move with or by the emission of puffs: *the steam train puffed up the incline.* **17** (often foll. by *up, out,* etc.) to swell, as with air, pride, etc. **18** (*tr*) to praise with exaggerated empty words, often in advertising. **19** (*tr*) to apply (powder, dust, etc.) to (something). ORIG OE *pyffan*
▸ **'puffy** *adj*

puff adder *n* **1** a large venomous African viper that inflates its body when alarmed. **2** another name for **hognose snake.**

puffball ('pʌf,bɔ:l) *n* **1** any of various fungi having a round fruiting body that discharges a cloud of brown spores when mature. **2** short for **puffball skirt.**

puffball skirt *n* a skirt or a dress with a skirt that puffs out wide and is nipped into a narrow hem.

puffer ('pʌfə) *n* **1** a person or thing that puffs. **2** Also called: **blowfish, globefish.** a marine fish with an elongated spiny body that can be inflated to form a globe.

puffin ('pʌfɪn) *n* any of various northern diving birds, having a black-and-white plumage and a brightly coloured vertically flattened bill. ORIG C14: ? of Cornish origin

puff pastry *or US* **puff paste** *n* a dough used for making a rich flaky pastry.

puff-puff *n Brit.* a children's name for a steam locomotive or railway train.

pug[1] (pʌg) *n* a small compact breed of dog with a smooth coat, lightly curled tail, and a short wrinkled nose. ORIG C16: from ?
▸ **'puggish** *adj*

pug[2] (pʌg) *vb* **pugs, pugging, pugged.** (*tr*) **1** to mix (clay) with water to form a malleable mass or paste, often in a **pug mill. 2** to fill or stop with clay or a similar substance. ORIG C19: from ?

pug[3] (pʌg) *n* a slang name for **boxer** (sense 1). ORIG C20: shortened from PUGILIST

Puget Sound ★ ('pju:dʒɪt) *n* an inlet of the Pacific in NW Washington. Length: about 130 km (80 miles).

pugging ('pʌgɪŋ) *n* material such as clay, sawdust, etc., inserted between wooden flooring and ceiling to deaden sound. Also called: **pug.**

puggree, pugree ('pʌgrɪ) *or* **puggaree, pugaree** ('pʌgərɪ) *n* **1** the usual Indian word for **turban. 2** a scarf, usually pleated, around the crown of some hats, esp. sun helmets. ORIG C17: from Hindi *pagrī,* from Sansk. *parikara*

pugilism ('pju:dʒɪ,lɪzəm) *n* the art, practice, or profession of fighting with the fists; boxing. ORIG C18: from L *pugil* a boxer
▸ **'pugilist** *n* ▸ **,pugi'listic** *adj* ▸ **,pugi'listically** *adv*

Pugin ★ ('pju:dʒɪn) *n* **Augustus** (**Welby Northmore**). 1812–52, British architect; a leader of the Gothic Revival. He collaborated with Sir Charles Barry on the Palace of Westminster (begun 1836).

Puglia ★ ('puʎʎa) *n* the Italian name for **Apulia.**

pugnacious (pʌg'neɪʃəs) *adj* readily disposed to fight; belligerent. ORIG C17: from L *pugnāx*
▸ **pug'naciously** *adv* ▸ **pugnacity** (pʌg'næsɪtɪ) *n*

pug nose *n* a short stubby upturned nose. ORIG C18: from PUG[1]
▸ **'pug-,nosed** *adj*

puisne ('pju:nɪ) *adj* (esp. of a subordinate judge) of lower rank. ORIG C16: from Anglo-F, from OF *puisné* born later, from L *posteā* afterwards + *nascī* to be born

puissance ('pju:ɪsᵊns, 'pwi:sɑ:ns) *n* **1** a competition in showjumping that tests a horse's ability to jump large obstacles. **2** *Arch. or poetic.* power. ORIG C15: from OF; see PUISSANT

puissant ('pju:ɪsᵊnt) *adj Arch. or poetic.* powerful. ORIG C15: from OF, ult. from L *potēns* mighty, from *posse* to have power
▸ **'puissantly** *adv*

puke (pju:k) *Sl.* ◆ *vb* **pukes, puking, puked. 1** to vomit. ◆ *n* **2** the act of vomiting. **3** the matter vomited. ORIG C16: prob. imit.

pukeko ('pukəkəu) *n, pl* **pukekos.** a New Zealand wading bird with bright plumage. ORIG from Maori

pukka *or* **pucka** ('pʌkə) *adj Anglo-Indian.* properly or perfectly done, constructed, etc.; good; genuine. ORIG C17: from Hindi *pakkā* firm, from Sansk. *pakva*

puku ('puku:) *n NZ inf.* the stomach; belly. ORIG Maori

Pula ★ (*Serbo-Croat* 'pu:la) *n* a port in NW Croatia, at the S tip of the Istrian Peninsula: made a Roman military base in 178 B.C.; became the main Austro-Hungarian naval station and passed to Italy in 1919, then to Yugoslavia (1947–91). Pop.: 62 300 (1991). Latin name: **Pietas Julia** (paɪ'eɪtæs 'ju:lɪə). Italian name: **Pola.**

Pulau Pinang ★ ('pulau pɪ'næŋ) *n* another name for **Penang.**

pulchritude ('pʌlkrɪ,tju:d) *n Formal or literary.* physical beauty. ORIG C15: from L *pulchritūdō,* from *pulcher* beautiful
▸ **,pulchri'tudinous** *adj*

pule (pju:l) *vb* **pules, puling, puled.** (*intr*) to cry plaintively; whimper. ORIG C16: ? imit.
▸ **'puler** *n*

Pulitzer ★ ('pulɪtsə) *n* **Joseph.** 1847–1911, US newspaper publisher, born in Hungary. He established the Pulitzer prizes.

Pulitzer prize *n* one of a group of prizes established by Joseph Pulitzer and awarded yearly since 1917 for excellence in American journalism, literature, and music.

pull (pul) *vb* (*mainly tr*) **1** (*also intr*) to exert force on (an ob-

ject) so as to draw it towards the source of the force. **2** to remove; extract: *to pull a tooth.* **3** to strip of feathers, hair, etc.; pluck. **4** to draw the entrails from (a fowl). **5** to rend or tear. **6** to strain (a muscle or tendon). **7** (usually foll. by *off*) *Inf.* to bring about: *to pull off a million-pound deal.* **8** (often foll. by *on*) *Inf.* to draw out (a weapon) for use: *he pulled a knife on his attacker.* **9** *Inf.* to attract: *the pop group pulled a crowd.* **10** (*also intr*) *Sl.* to attract (a sexual partner). **11** (*intr;* usually foll. by *on* or *at*) to drink or inhale deeply: *to pull at one's pipe.* **12** to make (a grimace): *to pull a face.* **13** (*also intr;* foll. by *away, out, over,* etc.) to move (a vehicle) or (of a vehicle) to be moved in a specified manner. **14** (*intr*) to possess or exercise the power to move: *this car doesn't pull well on hills.* **15** to withdraw or remove: *the board decided to pull their support.* **16** *Printing.* to take (a proof) from type. **17** *Golf, baseball, etc.* to hit (a ball) so that it veers away from the direction in which the player intended to hit it. **18** *Cricket.* to hit (a ball pitched straight or on the off side) to the leg side. **19** *Hurling.* to strike (a fast-moving ball) in the same direction as it is already moving. **20** (*also intr*) to row (a boat) or take a stroke of (an oar) in rowing. **21** (of a rider) to restrain (a horse), esp. to prevent it from winning a race. **22 pull a fast one.** *Sl.* to play a sly trick. **23 pull apart** *or* **to pieces.** to criticize harshly. **24 pull (one's) punches. 24a** *Inf.* to restrain the force of one's criticisms or actions. **24b** *Boxing.* to restrain the force of one's blows. ◆ *n* **25** an act or an instance of pulling or being pulled. **26** the force or effort used in pulling: *the pull of the moon affects the tides.* **27** the act or an instance of taking in drink or smoke. **28** *Printing.* a proof taken from type: *the first pull was smudged.* **29** something used for pulling, such as a handle. **30** *Inf.* special advantage or influence: *his uncle is chairman of the company, so he has quite a lot of pull.* **31** *Inf.* the power to attract attention or support. **32** a period of rowing. **33** a single stroke of an oar in rowing. **34** the act of pulling the ball in golf, cricket, etc. **35** the act of reining in a horse. ◆ See also **pull down, pull in,** etc. ORIG OE *pullian*
▸ **'puller** *n*

pull down *vb* (*tr, adv*) to destroy or demolish: *the old houses were pulled down.*

pullet ('pʊlɪt) *n* a young hen of the domestic fowl, less than one year old. ORIG C14: from OF *poulet* chicken, from L *pullus* a young animal or bird

pulley ('pʊlɪ) *n* **1** a wheel with a grooved rim in which a rope can run in order to change the direction of a force applied to the rope, etc. **2** a number of such wheels pivoted in parallel in a block, used to raise heavy loads. **3** a wheel with a flat, convex, or grooved rim mounted on a shaft and driven by or driving a belt passing around it. ORIG C14 *poley,* from OF *polie,* from Vulgar L *polidium* (unattested), apparently from LGk *polidion* (unattested) a little pole, from Gk *polos* axis

pull in *vb* (*adv*) **1** (*intr;* often foll. by *to*) to reach a destination: *the train pulled in at the station.* **2** (*intr*) Also: **pull over.** (of a motor vehicle) **2a** to draw in to the side of the road. **2b** to stop (at a café, lay-by, etc.). **3** (*tr*) to attract: *his appearance will pull in the crowds.* **4** (*tr*) *Sl.* to arrest. **5** (*tr*) to earn or gain (money). ◆ *n* **pull-in. 6** *Brit.* a roadside café, esp. for lorry drivers.

Pullman ('pʊlmən) *n, pl* **Pullmans.** a luxurious railway coach. Also called: **Pullman car.** ORIG C19: after G. M. *Pullman* (1831–97), its US inventor

pull off *vb* (*tr*) **1** to remove (clothing) forcefully. **2** (*adv*) to succeed in performing (a difficult feat).

pull out *vb* (*adv*) **1** (*tr*) to extract. **2** (*intr*) to depart: *the train pulled out of the station.* **3** *Mil.* to withdraw or be withdrawn: *the troops were pulled out of the ruined city.* **4** (*intr*) (of a motor vehicle) **4a** to draw away from the side of the road. **4b** to draw out from behind another vehicle to overtake. **5** (*intr*) to abandon a position or situation. **6** (foll. by *of*) to level out (from a dive). ◆ *n* **pull-out. 7** an extra leaf of a book that folds out. **8** a removable section of a magazine, etc.

pullover ('pʊl,əʊvə) *n* a garment, esp. a sweater, that is pulled on over the head.

pull through *vb* to survive or recover or cause to survive or recover, esp. after a serious illness or crisis. Also: **pull round.**

pull together *vb* **1** (*intr, adv*) to cooperate, or work harmoniously. **2 pull oneself together.** *Inf.* to regain one's self-control or composure.

pullulate ('pʌlju,leɪt) *vb* **pullulates, pullulating, pullulated.** (*intr*) **1** (of animals, etc.) to breed abundantly. **2** (of plants) to sprout, bud, or germinate. ORIG C17: from L *pullulāre* to sprout, from *pullulus* a baby animal, from *pullus* young animal
▸ **,pullu'lation** *n*

pull up *vb* (*adv*) **1** (*tr*) to remove by the roots. **2** (often foll. by *with* or *on*) to move level (with) or ahead (of), esp. in a race. **3** to stop: *the car pulled up suddenly.* **4** (*tr*) to rebuke. ◆ *n* **pull-up. 5** an exercise in which a person hangs by the arms from a bar and pulls to lift his or her body. **6** *Brit.* a roadside café; pull-in.

pulmonary ('pʌlmənərɪ, 'pʊl-) *adj* **1** of or affecting the lungs. **2** having lungs or lunglike organs. ORIG C18: from L *pulmōnārius,* from *pulmō* a lung

pulmonary artery *n* either of the two arteries that convey oxygen-depleted blood from the heart to the lungs.

pulmonary vein *n* any one of the four veins that convey oxygen-rich blood from the lungs to the heart.

pulp (pʌlp) *n* **1** soft or fleshy plant tissue, such as the succulent part of a fleshy fruit. **2** a moist mixture of cellulose fibres, as obtained from wood, from which paper is made. **3a** a magazine or book containing trite or sensational material, and usually printed on cheap rough paper. **3b** (*as modifier*): *a pulp novel.* **4** *Dentistry.* the soft innermost part of a tooth, containing nerves and blood vessels. **5** any soft soggy mass. **6** *Mining.* pulverized ore. ◆ *vb* **7** to reduce (a material) to pulp or (of a material) to be reduced to pulp. **8** (*tr*) to remove the pulp from (fruit, etc.). ORIG C16: from L *pulpa*
▸ **'pulpy** *adj*

pulpit ('pʊlpɪt) *n* **1** a raised platform, usually surrounded by a barrier, set up in churches as the appointed place for preaching, etc. **2** a medium for expressing an opinion, such as a newspaper column. **3** (usually preceded by *the*) **3a** the preaching of the Christian message. **3b** the clergy or their influence. ORIG C14: from L *pulpitum* a platform

pulpwood ('pʌlp,wʊd) *n* pine, spruce, or any other soft wood used to make paper.

pulque ('pʊlkɪ) *n* a light alcoholic drink from Mexico made from the juice of various agave plants. ORIG C17: from Mexican Sp., apparently from Nahuatl, from *puliuhqui* decomposed, since it will only keep for a day

pulsar ('pʌl,sɑː) *n* any of a number of very small stars first discovered in 1967, which rotate fast, emitting regular pulses of polarized radiation. ORIG C20: from PULS(ATING ST)AR, on the model of QUASAR

pulsate (pʌl'seɪt) *vb* **pulsates, pulsating, pulsated.** (*intr*) **1** to expand and contract with a rhythmic beat; throb. **2** *Physics.* to vary in intensity, magnitude, etc. **3** to quiver or vibrate. ORIG C18: from L *pulsāre* to push
▸ **pulsative** ('pʌlsətɪv) *adj* ▸ **pul'sation** *n* ▸ **pul'sator** *n*
▸ **pulsatory** ('pʌlsətərɪ, -trɪ) *adj*

pulsatilla (,pʌlsə'tɪlə) *n* any of a genus of plants related to the anemone, with feathery or hairy foliage. ORIG C16: from Med. L, from *pulsāta* beaten (by the wind)

pulsating star *n* a type of variable star, the variation in brightness resulting from expansion and subsequent contraction of the star.

pulse[1] (pʌls) *n* **1** *Physiol.* **1a** the rhythmic contraction and expansion of an artery at each beat of the heart. **1b** a single such pulsation. **2** *Physics, electronics.* **2a** a transient sharp change in some quantity normally constant in a system. **2b** one of a series of such transient disturbances, usually recurring at regular intervals. **3a** a recurrent rhythmic series of beats, vibrations, etc. **3b** any single beat, wave, etc., in such a series. **4** an inaudible electronic "ping" to operate a slide projector. **5** bustle, vitality, or excitement: *the pulse of a city.* **6 keep one's finger on the pulse.** to be well informed about current events, opinions, etc. ◆ *vb* **pulses, pulsing, pulsed. 7** (*intr*) to beat, throb, or vibrate. **8** (*tr*) to provide an electronic pulse to operate (a slide projector). ORIG C14 *pous,* from L *pulsus* a beating, from *pellere* to beat
▸ **'pulseless** *adj*

pulse² (pʌls) *n* **1** the edible seeds of any of several leguminous plants, such as peas, beans, and lentils. **2** the plant producing any of these. ORIG C13 *pols,* from OF, from L *puls* pottage of pulse

pulsejet ('pʌlsˌdʒɛt) *n* a type of ramjet engine in which air is admitted through movable vanes that are closed by the pressure resulting from each intermittent explosion of the fuel in the combustion chamber, thus causing a pulsating thrust. Also called: **pulsejet engine, pulsojet.**

pulse modulation *n Electronics.* a type of modulation in which a train of pulses is used as the carrier wave, one or more of its parameters, such as amplitude, being modulated or modified in order to carry information.

pulsimeter (pʌl'sɪmɪtə) *n Med.* an instrument for measuring the rate of the pulse.

pulverize *or* **pulverise** ('pʌlvəˌraɪz) *vb* **pulverizes, pulverizing, pulverized** *or* **pulverises, pulverising, pulverised. 1** to reduce (a substance) to fine particles, as by grinding, or (of a substance) to be so reduced. **2** *(tr)* to destroy completely. ORIG C16: from LL *pulverizare,* from L *pulvis* dust ▸ **'pulverˌizable** *or* **'pulverˌisable** *adj* ▸ **ˌpulveri'zation** *or* **ˌpulveri'sation** *n* ▸ **'pulverˌizer** *or* **'pulverˌiser** *n*

pulverulent (pʌl'vɛrʊlənt) *adj* consisting of, covered with, or crumbling to dust or fine particles. ORIG C17: from L *pulverulentus,* from *pulvis* dust

puma ('pjuːmə) *n* a large American feline mammal that resembles a lion, having a plain greyish-brown coat and long tail. Also called: **cougar, mountain lion.** ORIG C18: via Sp. from Quechua

pumice ('pʌmɪs) *n* **1** Also called: **pumice stone.** a light porous volcanic rock used for scouring and, in powdered form, as an abrasive and for polishing. ◆ *vb* **pumices, pumicing, pumiced. 2** *(tr)* to rub or polish with pumice. ORIG C15 *pomys,* from OF *pomis,* from L *pūmex* ▸ **pumiceous** (pjuː'mɪʃəs) *adj*

pummel ('pʌməl) *vb* **pummels, pummelling, pummelled** *or US* **pummels, pummeling, pummeled.** *(tr)* to strike repeatedly with or as if with the fists. Also (less commonly): **pommel.** ORIG C16: see POMMEL

pump¹ (pʌmp) *n* **1** any device for compressing, driving, raising, or reducing the pressure of a fluid, esp. by means of a piston or set of rotating impellers. **2** *Biol.* a mechanism for the active transport of ions, such as protons, calcium ions, and sodium ions, across cell membranes: *a sodium pump.* ◆ *vb* **3** (when *tr,* usually foll. by *from, out,* etc.) to raise or drive (air, liquid, etc., esp. into or from something) with a pump. **4** *(tr;* usually foll. by *in* or *into)* to supply in large amounts: *to pump capital into a project.* **5** *(tr)* to deliver (bullets, etc.) repeatedly. **6** to operate (something, esp. a handle) in the manner of a pump or (of something) to work in this way: *to pump the pedals of a bicycle.* **7** *(tr)* to obtain (information) from (a person) by persistent questioning. **8** *(intr;* usually foll. by *from* or *out of)* (of liquids) to flow freely in large spurts: *oil pumped from the fissure.* **9 pump iron.** *Sl.* to exercise with weights; do body-building exercises. ORIG C15: from MDu. *pumpe* pipe, prob. from Sp. *bomba,* imit.

pump² (pʌmp) *n* **1** a low-cut low-heeled shoe without fastenings, worn esp. for dancing. **2** a type of shoe with a rubber sole, used in games such as tennis; plimsoll. ORIG C16: from ?

pumpernickel ('pʌmpəˌnɪkᵊl) *n* a slightly sour black bread, originating in Germany, made of coarse rye flour. ORIG C18: from G, from ?

pumpkin ('pʌmpkɪn) *n* **1** any of several creeping plants of the genus *Cucurbita.* **2** the large round fruit of any of these plants, which has a thick orange rind, pulpy flesh, and numerous seeds. ORIG C17: from earlier *pumpion,* from OF, from L *pepo,* from Gk, from *peptein* to ripen

pump priming *n* **1** the process of introducing fluid into a pump to improve starting and to expel air from it. **2** government expenditure designed to stimulate economic activity in stagnant or depressed areas. **3** another term for **deficit financing.**

pun¹ (pʌn) *n* **1** the use of words to exploit ambiguities and innuendoes for humorous effect; a play on words. An example is: *"Ben Battle was a soldier bold, And used to war's alarms: But a cannonball took off his legs, So he laid down his arms."* (Thomas Hood). ◆ *vb* **puns, punning, punned. 2** *(intr)* to make puns. ORIG C17: ?from It. *puntiglio* wordplay; see PUNCTILIO

pun² (pʌn) *vb* **puns, punning, punned.** *(tr) Brit.* to pack (earth, rubble, etc.) by pounding. ORIG C16: var. of POUND¹

puna *Spanish.* ('puna) *n* **1** a high cold dry plateau. **2** another name for **mountain sickness.** ORIG C17: from American Sp., of Amerind origin

Punakha *or* **Punaka** ★ ('puːnəkə) *n* a town in W central Bhutan: a former capital of the country.

punch¹ (pʌntʃ) *vb* **1** to strike at, esp. with a clenched fist. **2** *(tr) Western US.* to herd or drive (cattle), esp. for a living. **3** *(tr)* to poke with a stick, etc. ◆ *n* **4** a blow with the fist. **5** *Inf.* point or vigour: *his arguments lacked punch.* ORIG C15: ? var. of *pounce,* from OF *poinçonner* to stamp ▸ **'puncher** *n*

punch² (pʌntʃ) *n* **1** a tool or machine for piercing holes in a material. **2** a tool or machine used for stamping a design on something or shaping it by impact. **3** the solid die of a punching machine. **4** *Computing.* a device for making holes in a card or paper tape. ◆ *vb* **5** *(tr)* to pierce, cut, stamp, shape, or drive with a punch. ORIG C14: shortened from *puncheon,* from OF *ponçon;* see PUNCHEON²

punch³ (pʌntʃ) *n* any mixed drink containing fruit juice and, usually, alcoholic liquor, generally hot and spiced. ORIG C17: ?from Hindi *pāñch,* from Sansk. *pañca* five; it orig. had five ingredients

Punch (pʌntʃ) *n* the main character in the traditional children's puppet show **Punch and Judy.**

punchbag ('pʌntʃˌbæg) *n* a suspended stuffed bag that is punched for exercise, esp. boxing training. Also called (US and Canad.): **punching bag.**

punchball ('pʌntʃˌbɔːl) *n* **1** a stuffed or inflated ball, supported by a flexible rod, that is punched for exercise, esp. boxing training. **2** *US.* a game resembling baseball.

punchbowl ('pʌntʃˌbəʊl) *n* **1** a large bowl for serving punch, often having small drinking glasses hooked around the rim. **2** *Brit.* a bowl-shaped depression in the land.

punch-drunk *adj* **1** demonstrating or characteristic of the behaviour of a person who has suffered repeated blows to the head, esp. a professional boxer. **2** dazed; stupefied.

punched card *or esp. US* **punch card** *n* a card on which data can be coded in the form of punched holes, formerly used in computing.

punched tape *or US (sometimes)* **perforated tape** *n* other terms for **paper tape.**

puncheon¹ ('pʌntʃən) *n* a large cask of variable capacity, usually between 70 and 120 gallons. ORIG C15 *poncion,* from OF *ponchon,* from ?

puncheon² ('pʌntʃən) *n* **1** a short wooden post used as a vertical strut. **2** a less common name for **punch²** (sense 1). ORIG C14 *ponson,* from OF *ponçon,* from L *punctiō* a puncture, from *pungere* to prick

Punchinello (ˌpʌntʃɪ'nɛləʊ) *n, pl* **Punchinellos** *or* **Punchinelloes. 1** a clown from Italian puppet shows, the prototype of Punch. **2** *(sometimes not cap.)* any grotesque or absurd character. ORIG C17: from earlier *Polichinello,* from It. *Polecenella,* from *pulcino* chicken, ult. from L *pullus* young animal

punch line *n* the culminating part of a joke, funny story, etc., that gives it its point.

punch-up *n Brit. inf.* a fight or brawl.

punchy ('pʌntʃɪ) *adj* **punchier, punchiest. 1** an informal word for **punch-drunk. 2** *Inf.* incisive or forceful. ▸ **'punchily** *adv* ▸ **'punchiness** *n*

punctate ('pʌŋkteɪt) *adj* having or marked with minute spots or depressions. ORIG C18: from NL *punctātus,* from L *punctum* a point ▸ **punc'tation** *n*

punctilio (pʌŋk'tɪlɪˌəʊ) *n, pl* **punctilios. 1** strict attention to minute points of etiquette. **2** a petty formality or fine point of etiquette. ORIG C16: from It. *puntiglio* small point, from L *punctum* point

punctilious (pʌŋk'tɪlɪəs) *adj* **1** paying scrupulous attention to correctness in etiquette. **2** attentive to detail.
▸ **punc'tiliously** *adv* ▸ **punc'tiliousness** *n*

punctual ('pʌŋktjʊəl) *adj* **1** arriving or taking place at an arranged time. **2** (of a person) having the characteristic of always keeping to arranged times. **3** *Obs.* precise; exact. **4** *Maths.* consisting of or confined to a point. ORIG C14: from Med. L *punctuālis* concerning detail, from L *punctum* point
▸ ˌ**punctu'ality** *n* ▸ '**punctually** *adv*

punctuate ('pʌŋktjʊˌeɪt) *vb* **punctuates, punctuating, punctuated.** (*mainly tr*) **1** (*also intr*) to insert punctuation marks into (a written text). **2** to interrupt or insert at frequent intervals: *a meeting punctuated by heckling.* **3** to give emphasis to. ORIG C17: from Med. L *punctuāre* to prick, from L, from *pungere* to puncture

punctuation (ˌpʌŋktjʊ'eɪʃən) *n* **1** the use of symbols not belonging to the alphabet of a writing system to indicate aspects of the intonation and meaning not otherwise conveyed in the written language. **2** the symbols used for this purpose.

punctuation mark *n* any of the signs used in punctuation, such as a comma.

puncture ('pʌŋktʃə) *n* **1** a small hole made by a sharp object. **2** a perforation and loss of pressure in a pneumatic tyre. **3** the act of puncturing or perforating. ◆ *vb* **punctures, puncturing, punctured.** **4** (*tr*) to pierce a hole in (something) with a sharp object. **5** to cause (something pressurized, esp. a tyre) to lose pressure by piercing, or (of a tyre, etc.) to collapse in this way. **6** (*tr*) to depreciate (a person's self-esteem, pomposity, etc.). ORIG C14: from L *punctūra,* from *pungere* to prick

pundit ('pʌndɪt) *n* **1** an expert. **2** (formerly) a learned person. **3** Also: **pandit.** a Brahman learned in Sanskrit, Hindu religion, philosophy or law. ORIG C17: from Hindi *pandit,* from Sansk. *pandita* learned man

Pune ★ ('puːnə) *n* another name for **Poona.**

punga ('pʌŋə) *n* a variant spelling of **ponga.**

pungent ('pʌndʒənt) *adj* **1** having an acrid smell or sharp bitter flavour. **2** (of wit, satire, etc.) biting; caustic. **3** *Biol.* ending in a sharp point. ORIG C16: from L *pungens* piercing, from *pungere* to prick
▸ '**pungency** *n* ▸ '**pungently** *adv*

Punic ('pjuːnɪk) *adj* **1** of or relating to ancient Carthage or the Carthaginians. **2** treacherous; faithless. ◆ *n* **3** the language of the Carthaginians; a late form of Phoenician. ORIG C15: from L *Pūnicus,* var. of *Poenicus* Carthaginian, from Gk *Phoinix*

punish ('pʌnɪʃ) *vb* **1** to force (someone) to undergo a penalty for some crime or misdemeanour. **2** (*tr*) to inflict punishment for (some crime, etc.). **3** (*tr*) to treat harshly, esp. as by overexertion: *to punish a horse.* **4** (*tr*) *Inf.* to consume in large quantities: *to punish the bottle.* ORIG C14 *punisse,* from OF *punir,* from L *pūnīre* to punish, from *poena* penalty
▸ '**punishable** *adj* ▸ '**punisher** *n* ▸ '**punishing** *adj*

punishment ('pʌnɪʃmənt) *n* **1** a penalty for a crime or offence. **2** the act of punishing or state of being punished. **3** *Inf.* rough treatment.

punitive ('pjuːnɪtɪv) *adj* relating to, involving, or with the intention of inflicting punishment: *a punitive expedition.* ORIG C17: from Med. L *pūnītīvus* concerning punishment, from L *pūnīre* to punish
▸ '**punitively** *adv*

Punjab ★ (pʌn'dʒɑːb, 'pʌndʒɑːb) *n* **1** (formerly) a province in NW British India: divided between India and Pakistan in 1947. **2** a state of NW India: reorganized in 1966 as a Punjabi-speaking state, a large part forming the new state of Haryana; mainly agricultural. Capital: Chandigarh. Pop.: 21 695 000 (1994 est.). Area: 50 255 sq. km (19 403 sq. miles). **3** a province of W Pakistan: created in 1947. Capital: Lahore. Pop.: 54 000 000 (latest est.). Area: 205 344 sq. km (127 595 sq. miles).

Punjabi (pʌn'dʒɑːbɪ) *n* **1** (*pl* **Punjabis**) a member of the chief people of the Punjab. **2** the language of the Punjab, belonging to the Indic branch of the Indo-European family. ◆ *adj* **3** of the Punjab, its people, or their language.

Punjab States ★ *pl n* (formerly) a group of states in NW India, amalgamated in 1956 with Punjab state.

punk[1] (pʌŋk) *n* **1** a youth movement of the late 1970s, characterized by anti-Establishment slogans and outrageous clothes and hairstyles. **2** an inferior, rotten, or worthless person or thing. **3** worthless articles collectively. **4** short for **punk rock.** **5** *Obs.* a young male homosexual; catamite. **6** *Obs.* a prostitute. ◆ *adj* **7** rotten or worthless. ORIG C16: from ?

punk[2] (pʌŋk) *n* dried decayed wood or other substance that smoulders when ignited: used as tinder. ORIG C18: from ?

punka *or* **punkah** ('pʌŋkə) *n* **1** a fan made of a palm leaf or leaves. **2** a large fan made of palm leaves, etc., worked mechanically to cool a room. ORIG C17: from Hindi *pankhā,* from Sansk. *paksaka* fan, from *paksa* wing

punk rock *n* a fast abrasive style of rock music of the late 1970s, characterized by aggressive lyrics and performance, usually expressing rage and frustration.
▸ **punk rocker** *n*

punnet ('pʌnɪt) *n Chiefly Brit.* a small basket for fruit. ORIG C19: ? dim. of dialect *pun* POUND[2]

punster ('pʌnstə) *n* a person who is fond of making puns, esp. one who makes a tedious habit of this.

punt[1] (pʌnt) *n* **1** an open flat-bottomed boat with square ends, propelled by a pole. ◆ *vb* **2** to propel (a boat, esp. a punt) by pushing with a pole on the bottom of a river, etc. ORIG OE *punt* shallow boat, from L *pontō* punt

punt[2] (pʌnt) *n* **1** a kick in certain sports, such as rugby, in which the ball is released and kicked before it hits the ground. **2** any long high kick. ◆ *vb* **3** to kick (a ball, etc.) using a punt. ORIG C19: ? var. of dialect *bunt* to push

punt[3] (pʌnt) *Chiefly Brit.* ◆ *vb* **1** (*intr*) to gamble; bet. ◆ *n* **2** a gamble or bet, esp. against the bank, as in roulette, or on horses. **3** Also called: **punter.** a person who bets. **4 take a punt at.** *Austral. & NZ inf.* to make an attempt at. ORIG C18: from F *ponter* to punt, from *ponte* bet laid against the banker, from Sp. *punto* point, from L *punctum*

punt[4] (pʊnt) *n* the Irish pound. ORIG Irish Gaelic: pound

Punta Arenas ★ (*Spanish* 'punta a'renas) *n* a port in S Chile, on the Strait of Magellan: the southernmost city in the world. Pop.: 117 206 (1995 est.). Former name: **Magallanes.**

punter[1] ('pʌntə) *n* a person who punts a boat.

punter[2] ('pʌntə) *n* a person who kicks a ball.

punter[3] ('pʌntə) *n* **1** a person who gambles or bets. **2** *Sl.* any client or customer, esp. a prostitute's client. **3** *Sl.* a victim of a con man.

puny ('pjuːnɪ) *adj* **punier, puniest.** **1** small and weakly. **2** paltry; insignificant. ORIG C16: from OF *puisne* PUISNE
▸ '**puniness** *n*

pup (pʌp) *n* **1a** a young dog; puppy. **1b** the young of various other animals, such as the seal. **2 in pup.** (of a bitch) pregnant. **3** *Inf., chiefly Brit.* a conceited young man (esp. in **young pup**). **4 sell (someone) a pup.** to swindle (someone) by selling him or her something worthless. ◆ *vb* **pups, pupping, pupped.** **5** (of dogs, seals, etc.) to give birth to (young). ORIG C18: back formation from PUPPY

pupa ('pjuːpə) *n, pl* **pupae** (-piː) *or* **pupas.** an insect at the immobile nonfeeding stage of development between larva and adult, when many internal changes occur. ORIG C19: via NL, from L: a doll
▸ '**pupal** *adj*

pupate (pjuː'peɪt) *vb* **pupates, pupating, pupated.** (*intr*) (of an insect larva) to develop into a pupa.
▸ **pu'pation** *n*

pupil[1] ('pjuːpᵊl) *n* **1** a student who is taught by a teacher. **2** *Civil & Scots Law.* a boy under 14 or a girl under 12 who is in the care of a guardian. ORIG C14: from L *pupillus* an orphan, from *pūpus* a child
▸ '**pupillage** *or US* '**pupilage** *n* ▸ '**pupillary** *or* '**pupilary** *adj*

pupil[2] ('pjuːpᵊl) *n* the dark circular aperture at the centre of the iris of the eye, through which light enters. ORIG C16: from L *pūpilla,* dim. of *pūpa* doll; from the tiny reflections in the eye
▸ '**pupillary** *or* '**pupilary** *adj*

pupiparous (pjuː'pɪpərəs) *adj* (of certain dipterous flies)

★ people and places

producing young that have already reached the pupa stage at the time of hatching. ORIG C19: from NL *pupiparus,* from PUPA + *parere* to bring forth

puppet ('pʌpɪt) *n* **1a** a small doll or figure moved by strings attached to its limbs or by the hand inserted in its cloth body. **1b** (*as modifier*): *a puppet theatre.* **2a** a person, state, etc., that appears independent but is controlled by another. **2b** (*as modifier*): *a puppet government.* ORIG C16 *popet,* ?from OF *poupette* little doll, ult. from L *pūpa* doll

puppeteer (ˌpʌpɪ'tɪə) *n* a person who manipulates puppets.

puppetry ('pʌpɪtrɪ) *n* **1** the art of making and manipulating puppets and presenting puppet shows. **2** unconvincing or specious presentation.

puppy ('pʌpɪ) *n, pl* **puppies. 1** a young dog; pup. **2** *Inf., contemptuous.* a brash or conceited young man; pup. ORIG C15 *popi,* from OF *popée* doll
▸ **'puppyhood** *n* ▸ **'puppyish** *adj*

puppy fat *n* fatty tissue that develops in childhood or adolescence and usually disappears with maturity.

puppy love *n* another term for **calf love.**

Purana (pʊ'rɑːnə) *n* any of a class of Sanskrit writings not included in the Vedas, characteristically recounting the birth and deeds of Hindu gods and the creation of the universe. ORIG C17: from Sansk.: ancient, from *purā* formerly

Purbeck marble *or* **stone** ('pɜːbɛk) *n* a fossil-rich limestone that takes a high polish. ORIG C15: after *Purbeck,* Dorset, where quarried

purblind ('pɜːˌblaɪnd) *adj* **1** partly or nearly blind. **2** lacking in insight or understanding; obtuse. ORIG C13: see PURE, BLIND

Purcell ★ ('pɜːs^əl) *n* **1 Edward Mills.** 1912–97, US physicist, noted for his work on the magnetic moments of atomic nuclei: shared the Nobel prize for physics 1952. **2 Henry.** ?1659–95, English composer. His works include the opera *Dido and Aeneas* (1689), music for the theatrical pieces *King Arthur* (1691) and *The Fairy Queen* (1692) and several choral odes.

purchase ('pɜːtʃɪs) *vb* **purchases, purchasing, purchased.** (*tr*) **1** to obtain (goods, etc.) by payment. **2** to obtain by effort, sacrifice, etc.: *to purchase one's freedom.* **3** to draw or lift (a load) with mechanical apparatus. ◆ *n* **4** something that is purchased. **5** the act of buying. **6** acquisition of an estate by any lawful means other than inheritance. **7** the mechanical advantage achieved by a lever. **8** a firm foothold, grasp, etc., as for climbing something. ORIG C13: from OF *porchacier* to strive to obtain; see CHASE[1]
▸ **'purchasable** *adj* ▸ **'purchaser** *n*

purchase tax *n* (in Britain, formerly) a tax levied on nonessential consumer goods and added to selling prices by retailers.

purdah ('pɜːdə) *n* **1** the custom in some Muslim and Hindu communities of keeping women in seclusion, with clothing that conceals them completely when they go out. **2** a screen in a Hindu house used to keep the women out of view. ORIG C19: from Hindi *parda* veil, from Persian *pardah*

pure (pjʊə) *adj* **1** not mixed with any extraneous or dissimilar materials, elements, etc. **2** free from tainting or polluting matter: *pure water.* **3** free from moral taint or defilement: *pure love.* **4** (*prenominal*) (intensifier): *a pure coincidence.* **5** (of a subject, etc.) studied in its theoretical aspects rather than for its practical applications: *pure mathematics.* **6** (of a vowel) pronounced with more or less unvarying quality without any glide. **7** (of a consonant) not accompanied by another consonant. **8** of unmixed descent. **9** *Genetics, biol.* breeding true; homozygous. ORIG C13: from OF *pur,* from L *pūrus* unstained
▸ **'purely** *adv* ▸ **'pureness** *n*

purebred *adj* ('pjʊə'brɛd). **1** denoting a pure strain obtained through many generations of controlled breeding. ◆ *n* ('pjʊəˌbrɛd). **2** a purebred animal.

purée ('pjʊəreɪ) *n* **1** a smooth thick pulp of sieved fruit, vegetables, meat, or fish. ◆ *vb* **purées, puréeing, puréed. 2** (*tr*) to make (cooked foods) into a purée. ORIG C19: from F *purer* to PURIFY

purfle ('pɜːf^əl) *n also* **purfling. 1** a ruffled or curved ornamental band, as on clothing, furniture, etc. ◆ *vb* **purfles, purfling, purfled. 2** (*tr*) to decorate with such a band. ORIG C14: from OF *purfiler* to decorate with a border, from *fil* thread, from L *fīlum*

purgation (pɜː'geɪʃən) *n* the act of purging or state of being purged; purification.

purgative ('pɜːgətɪv) *Med.* ◆ *n* **1** a drug or agent for purging the bowels. ◆ *adj* **2** causing evacuation of the bowels.
▸ **'purgatively** *adv*

purgatory ('pɜːgətərɪ, -trɪ) *n* **1** *Chiefly RC Church.* a state or place in which the souls of those who have died in a state of grace are believed to undergo a limited amount of suffering to expiate their venial sins. **2** a place or condition of suffering or torment, esp. one that is temporary. ORIG C13: from OF *purgatoire,* from Med. L *pūrgātōrium,* lit.: place of cleansing, from L *pūrgāre* to purge
▸ **ˌpurga'torial** *adj*

purge (pɜːdʒ) *vb* **purges, purging, purged. 1** (*tr*) to rid (something) of (impure elements). **2** (*tr*) to rid (a state, political party, etc.) of (dissident people). **3** (*tr*) **3a** to empty (the bowels) by evacuation of faeces. **3b** to cause (a person) to evacuate his or her bowels. **4a** to clear (a person) of a charge. **4b** to free (oneself) of guilt, as by atonement. **5** (*intr*) to be purified. ◆ *n* **6** the act or process of purging. **7** the elimination of opponents or dissidents from a state, political party, etc. **8** a purgative drug or agent. ORIG C14: from OF *purger,* from L *pūrgāre* to purify

Puri ★ ('pʊəriː, pʊə'riː) *n* a port in E India, in Orissa on the Bay of Bengal: 12th-century temple of Jagannath. Pop.: 125 199 (1991).

purificator ('pjʊərɪfɪˌkeɪtə) *n Christianity.* a small white linen cloth used to wipe the chalice and paten at the Eucharist.

purify ('pjʊərɪˌfaɪ) *vb* **purifies, purifying, purified. 1** to free (something) of contaminating or debasing matter. **2** (*tr*) to free (a person, etc.) from sin or guilt. **3** (*tr*) to make clean, as in a ritual. ORIG C14: from OF *purifier,* from LL *pūrificāre* to cleanse, from *pūrus* pure + *facere* to make
▸ **ˌpurifi'cation** *n* ▸ **purificatory** ('pjʊərɪfɪˌkeɪtərɪ, -trɪ) *adj*
▸ **'puriˌfier** *n*

Purim ('pʊərɪm; *Hebrew* puː'riːm) *n* a Jewish holiday in February or March to commemorate the deliverance of the Jews from the massacre planned by Haman (Esther 9). ORIG Heb. *pūrīm,* pl. of *pūr* lot; from the casting of lots by Haman

purine ('pjʊəriːn) *or* **purin** ('pjʊərɪn) *n* **1** a colourless crystalline solid that can be prepared from uric acid. Formula: $C_5H_5N_4$. **2** Also called: **purine base.** any of a number of nitrogenous bases that are derivatives of purine. ORIG C19: from G *Purin*

puriri (puː'riːriː) *n* a New Zealand tree with hard timber and red berries. ORIG from Maori

purism ('pjʊəˌrɪzəm) *n* insistence on traditional canons of correctness of form or purity of style or content.
▸ **'purist** *adj, n* ▸ **pu'ristic** *adj*

puritan ('pjʊərɪt^ən) *n* **1** a person who adheres to strict moral or religious principles, esp. one opposed to luxury and sensual enjoyment. ◆ *adj* **2** characteristic of a puritan. ORIG C16: from LL *pūritās* purity
▸ **'puritanˌism** *n*

Puritan ('pjʊərɪt^ən) (in the late 16th and 17th centuries) ◆ *n* **1** any of the extreme English Protestants who wished to purify the Church of England of most of its ceremony and other aspects that they deemed to be Catholic. ◆ *adj* **2** of or relating to the Puritans.
▸ **'Puritanˌism** *n*

puritanical (ˌpjʊərɪ'tænɪk^əl) *adj* **1** *Usually disparaging.* strict in moral or religious outlook, esp. in shunning sensual pleasures. **2** (*sometimes cap.*) of or relating to a puritan or the Puritans.
▸ **ˌpuri'tanically** *adv*

purity ('pjʊərɪtɪ) *n* the state or quality of being pure.

purl[1] (pɜːl) *n* **1** a knitting stitch made by doing a plain stitch backwards. **2** a decorative border, as of lace. **3** gold or silver wire thread. ◆ *vb* **4** to knit in purl stitch. **5** to edge (something) with a purl. ◆ Also (for senses 2, 3, 5): **pearl.** ORIG C16: from dialect *pirl* to twist into a cord

purl[2] (pɜːl) *vb* **1** (*intr*) (of a stream, etc.) to flow with a gentle swirling or rippling movement and a murmuring sound. ◆ *n* **2** a swirling movement of water; eddy. **3** a murmuring sound, as of a shallow stream. ORIG C16: rel. to Norwegian *purla* to bubble

purler[1] ('pɜːlə) *n Inf.* a headlong or spectacular fall (esp. in **come a purler**).

purler[2] ('pɜːlə) *n Austral. sl.* something outstanding in its class. ORIG from ?

purlieu ('pɜːljuː) *n* **1** *English history.* land on the edge of a forest once included within the bounds of the royal forest but later separated although still subject to some of the forest laws. **2** (*usually pl*) a neighbouring area; outskirts. **3** (*often pl*) a place one frequents; haunt. ORIG C15 *purlewe,* from Anglo-F *puralé* a going through (infl. also by OF *lieu* place), from OF *puraler,* from *pur* through + *aler* to go

purlin *or* **purline** ('pɜːlɪn) *n* a horizontal beam that supports the common rafters of a roof and is carried by the principal rafters or trusses. ORIG C15: from ?

purloin (pɜː'lɔɪn) *vb* to steal. ORIG C15: from OF *porloigner* to put at a distance, from *por-* for + *loin* distant, from L *longus* long
▸ **pur'loiner** *n*

purple ('pɜːpᵊl) *n* **1** a colour between red and blue. **2** a dye or pigment producing such a colour. **3** cloth of this colour, often used to symbolize royalty or nobility. **4** (usually preceded by *the*) high rank; nobility. **5a** the official robe of a cardinal. **5b** the rank of a cardinal as signified by this. ◆ *adj* **6** of the colour purple. **7** (of writing) excessively elaborate or full of imagery: *purple prose.* ORIG OE, from L *purpura* purple dye, from Gk *porphura* the purple fish (murex)
▸ **'purpleness** *n* ▸ **'purplish** *or* **'purply** *adj*

purple heart *n* **1** any of several tropical American trees. **2** *Inf., chiefly Brit.* a heart-shaped purple tablet consisting mainly of amphetamine.

Purple Heart *n* a decoration awarded to members of the US Armed Forces for a wound received in action.

purple patch *n* **1** Also called: **purple passage.** a section in a piece of writing characterized by fanciful or ornate language. **2** *Sl.* a period of good fortune.

purport *vb* (pɜː'pɔːt). (*tr*) **1** to claim to be (true, official, etc.) by manner or appearance, esp. falsely. **2** (esp. of speech or writing) to signify or imply. ◆ *n* ('pɜːpɔːt). **3** meaning; significance. **4** object; intention. ORIG C15: from Anglo-F: contents, from OF *porporter* to convey, from L *portāre*

purpose ('pɜːpəs) *n* **1** the reason for which anything is done, created, or exists. **2** a fixed design or idea that is the object of an action or other effort. **3** determination: *a man of purpose.* **4** practical advantage or use: *to work to good purpose.* **5** that which is relevant (esp. in **to** *or* **from the purpose**). **6** *Arch.* purport. **7 on purpose.** intentionally. ◆ *vb* **purposes, purposing, purposed. 8** (*tr*) to intend or determine to do (something). ORIG C13: from OF *porpos,* from *porposer* to plan, from L *prōpōnere* to PROPOSE
▸ **'purposeless** *adj*

purpose-built *adj* made to serve a specific purpose.

purposeful ('pɜːpəsfʊl) *adj* **1** having a definite purpose in view. **2** determined.
▸ **'purposefully** *adv* ▸ **'purposefulness** *n*

USAGE NOTE Someone who is *purposeful* has an aim in mind and is determined to achieve it. Probably because the adjective conveys the idea of having such an aim, the adverb *purposefully* is sometimes wrongly used where *purposely* is meant: *he had purposely* (not *purposefully*) *left the door unlocked.* The use of *purposefully* in the following example is correct: *she rose purposefully from her chair to confront them…*

purposely ('pɜːpəslɪ) *adv* on purpose.

USAGE NOTE See at **purposeful.**

purposive ('pɜːpəsɪv) *adj* **1** having or indicating conscious intention. **2** serving a purpose; useful.
▸ **'purposively** *adv* ▸ **'purposiveness** *n*

purpura ('pɜːpjʊrə) *n Pathol.* any of several blood diseases causing purplish spots on the skin due to subcutaneous bleeding. ORIG C18: via L from Gk *porphura* a shellfish yielding purple dye

purr (pɜː) *vb* **1** (*intr*) (esp. of cats) to make a low vibrant sound, usually considered as expressing pleasure, etc. **2** (*tr*) to express (pleasure, etc.) by this sound or by a sound suggestive of purring. ◆ *n* **3** a purring sound. ORIG C17: imit.

purse (pɜːs) *n* **1** a small bag or pouch for carrying money, esp. coins. **2** *US & Canad.* a woman's handbag. **3** anything resembling a small bag or pouch in form or function. **4** wealth; funds; resources. **5** a sum of money that is offered, esp. as a prize. ◆ *vb* **purses, pursing, pursed. 6** (*tr*) to contract (the mouth, lips, etc.) into a small rounded shape. ORIG OE *purs,* prob. from LL *bursa* bag, ult. from Gk: leather

purser ('pɜːsə) *n* an officer aboard a ship or aircraft who keeps the accounts and attends to the welfare of the passengers.

purse seine *n* a large net that encloses fish and is then closed at the bottom by means of a line resembling the string formerly used to draw shut the neck of a money pouch.

purse strings *pl n* control of expenditure (esp. in **hold** *or* **control the purse strings**).

purslane ('pɜːslɪn) *n* a plant with fleshy leaves used (esp. formerly) in salads and as a potherb. ORIG C14 *purcelane,* from OF *porcelaine,* from LL, from L *porcillāca,* var. of *portulāca*

pursuance (pə'sjuːəns) *n* the carrying out or pursuing of an action, plan, etc.

pursuant (pə'sjuːənt) *adj* **1** (*usually postpositive;* often foll. by *to*) *Chiefly law.* in agreement or conformity. **2** *Arch.* pursuing. ORIG C17: rel. to ME *poursuivant* following after, from OF; see PURSUE
▸ **pur'suantly** *adv*

pursue (pə'sjuː) *vb* **pursues, pursuing, pursued.** (*mainly tr*) **1** (*also intr*) to follow (a fugitive, etc.) in order to capture or overtake. **2** to follow closely or accompany: *ill health pursued her.* **3** to seek or strive to attain (some desire, etc.). **4** to follow the precepts of (a plan, policy, etc.). **5** to apply oneself to (studies, interests, etc.). **6** to follow persistently or seek to become acquainted with. **7** to continue to discuss or argue (a point, subject, etc.). ORIG C13: from Anglo-Norman *pursiwer,* from OF *poursivre,* from L *prōsequī* to follow after
▸ **pur'suer** *n*

pursuit (pə'sjuːt) *n* **1a** the act of pursuing. **1b** (*as modifier*): *a pursuit plane.* **2** an occupation or pastime. **3** (in cycling) a race in which the riders set off at intervals along the track and attempt to overtake each other. ORIG C14: from OF *poursieute,* from *poursivre* to PURSUE

pursuivant ('pɜːsɪvənt) *n* **1** the lowest rank of heraldic officer. **2** *History.* a state or royal messenger. **3** *History.* a follower or attendant. ORIG C14: from OF, from *poursivre* to PURSUE

purulent ('pjʊərʊlənt) *adj* of, relating to, or containing pus. ORIG C16: from L *pūrulentus,* from *pūs*
▸ **'purulence** *n* ▸ **'purulently** *adv*

Purús ★ (*Spanish, Portuguese* pu'rus) *n* a river in NW central South America, rising in SE Peru and flowing northeast to the Amazon. Length: about 3200 km (2000 miles).

purvey (pə'veɪ) *vb* (*tr*) **1** to sell or provide (commodities, esp. foodstuffs) on a large scale. **2** to publish (lies, scandal, etc.). ORIG C13: from OF *porveeir,* from L *prōvidēre* to PROVIDE
▸ **pur'veyor** *n*

purveyance (pə'veɪəns) *n* **1** *History.* the collection or requisition of provisions for a sovereign. **2** *Rare.* the act of purveying.

purview ('pɜːvjuː) *n* **1** scope of operation. **2** breadth or range of outlook. **3** *Law.* the body of a statute, containing the enacting clauses. ORIG C15: from Anglo-Norman *purveu,* from *porveeir* to furnish; see PURVEY

pus (pʌs) *n* the yellow or greenish fluid product of inflammation. ORIG C16: from L *pūs*

Pusan ★ ('puː'sæn) *n* a port in SE South Korea, on the Korea Strait: the second largest city and chief port of the country; industrial centre; two universities. Pop.: 3 813 814 (1995).

Pusey ★ ('pjuːzɪ) *n* **Edward Bouverie** ('buːvərɪ). 1800–82, British ecclesiastic; a leader with Keble and Newman of the Oxford Movement.

push (pʊʃ) *vb* **1** (when *tr,* often foll. by *off, away,* etc.) to apply steady force to in order to move. **2** to thrust (one's way) through something, such as a crowd. **3** (*tr*) to encourage or urge (a person) to some action, decision, etc. **4** (when *intr,* often foll. by *for*) to be an advocate or promoter (of): *to push for acceptance of one's theories.* **5** (*tr*) to use one's influence to help (a person): *to push one's own candidate.* **6** to bear upon (oneself or another person) in order to achieve better results, etc. **7** *Cricket, etc.* to hit (a ball) with a stiff pushing stroke. **8** (*tr*) *Inf.* to sell (narcotic drugs) illegally. **9** (*intr;* foll. by *out, into,* etc.) to extend: *the cliffs pushed out to the sea.* **10 push one's luck** *or* **push it. 10a** to take undue risks, esp. through overconfidence. **10b** (*intr*) to act overconfidently. ◆ *n* **11** the act of pushing; thrust. **12** a part or device that is pressed to operate some mechanism. **13** *Inf.* drive, energy, etc. **14** *Inf.* a special effort or attempt to advance, as of an army: *to make a push.* **15** *Austral. sl.* a group, gang, or clique. **16** *Cricket, etc.* a stiff pushing stroke. **17 at a push.** *Inf.* with difficulty; only just. **18 the push.** *Inf., chiefly Brit.* dismissal, esp. from employment. ◆ See also **push off, push in,** etc. ORIG C13: from OF *pousser,* from L *pulsāre,* from *pellere* to drive

push-bike *n Brit.* an informal name for **bicycle.**

push button *n* **1** an electrical switch operated by pressing a button, which closes or opens a circuit. ◆ *modifier.* **push-button. 2a** operated by a push button: *a push-button radio.* **2b** initiated as simply as by pressing a button: *push-button warfare.*

pushcart ('pʊʃˌkɑːt) *n* another name (esp. US and Canad.) for **barrow**[1] (sense 3).

pushchair ('pʊʃˌtʃɛə) *n* a usually collapsible chair-shaped carriage for a small child. Also called: **baby buggy, buggy.** US and Canad. word: **stroller.** Austral. words: **pusher, stroller.**

pushed (pʊʃt) *adj* (often foll. by *for*) *Inf.* short (of) or in need (of time, money, etc.).

pusher ('pʊʃə) *n* **1** *Inf.* a person who sells illegal drugs, esp. narcotics such as heroin. **2** *Inf.* an aggressively ambitious person. **3** a person or thing that pushes. **4** *Austral.* the usual name for **pushchair.**

push in *vb* (*intr, adv*) to force one's way into a group of people, queue, etc.

pushing ('pʊʃɪŋ) *adj* **1** enterprising or aggressively ambitious. **2** impertinently self-assertive. ◆ *adv* **3** almost or nearly (a certain age, speed, etc.): *pushing fifty.*
▸ **'pushingly** *adv*

Pushkin[1] ★ ('pʊʃkɪn) *n* a town in NW Russia: site of the imperial summer residence and Catherine the Great's palace. Pop.: 97 000 (1989). Former name: **Tsarskoye Selo** (1708–1937).

Pushkin[2] ★ ('pʊʃkɪn) *n* **Aleksander Sergeyevich** (alɪk'sandr sɪr'gjejɪvitʃ). 1799–1837, Russian poet, novelist, and dramatist. His works include the verse novel *Eugene Onegin* (1833), the tragedy *Boris Godunov* (1825), and the novel *The Captain's Daughter* (1836).

push money *n* a cash inducement provided by a manufacturer or distributor for a retailer or his staff, to reward successful selling.

push off *vb* (*adv*) **1** Also: **push out.** to move into open water, as by being cast off from a mooring. **2** (*intr*) *Inf.* to go away; leave.

pushover ('pʊʃˌəʊvə) *n Inf.* **1** something that is easily achieved. **2** a person, team, etc., that is easily taken advantage of or defeated.

push-pull *n* (*modifier*) using two similar electronic devices made to operate out of phase with each other to produce a signal that replicates the input waveform: *a push-pull amplifier.*

push-start *vb* (*tr*) **1** to start (a motor vehicle) by pushing it while it is in gear, thus turning the engine. ◆ *n* **2** this process.

push through *vb* (*tr*) to compel to accept: *the bill was pushed through Parliament.*

Pushto ('pʌʃtəʊ) *or* **Pushtu** ('pʌʃtuː) *n, adj* variant spellings of **Pashto.**

push-up *n* the US and Canad. term for **press-up.**

pushy ('pʊʃɪ) *adj* **pushier, pushiest.** *Inf.* **1** offensively assertive. **2** aggressively or ruthlessly ambitious.
▸ **'pushily** *adv* ▸ **'pushiness** *n*

pusillanimous (ˌpjuːsɪ'lænɪməs) *adj* characterized by a lack of courage or determination. ORIG C16: from LL *pusillanimis* from L *pusillus* weak + *animus* courage
▸ **pusillanimity** (ˌpjuːsɪlə'nɪmɪtɪ) *n* ▸ **ˌpusil'lanimously** *adv*

puss (pʊs) *n* **1** an informal name for a **cat. 2** *Sl.* a girl or woman. **3** an informal name for a **hare.** ORIG C16: rel. to MLow G *pūs*

pussy[1] ('pʊsɪ) *n, pl* **pussies. 1** Also called: **puss, pussycat.** an informal name for a **cat. 2** a furry catkin. **3** *Taboo sl.* the female pudenda. **4** *Sl., chiefly US.* an ineffectual or timid man. ORIG C18: from PUSS

pussy[2] ('pʌsɪ) *adj* **pussier, pussiest.** containing or full of pus.

pussycat ('pʊsɪˌkæt) *n* **1** an informal or child's name for **cat**[1]. **2** *Brit. inf.* an endearing or gentle person.

pussyfoot ('pʊsɪˌfʊt) *vb* (*intr*) *Inf.* **1** to move about stealthily or warily like a cat. **2** to avoid committing oneself.

pussy willow ('pʊsɪ) *n* a willow tree with silvery silky catkins.

pustulant ('pʌstjʊlənt) *adj* **1** causing the formation of pustules. ◆ *n* **2** an agent causing such formation.

pustulate *vb* ('pʌstjʊˌleɪt), **pustulates, pustulating, pustulated. 1** to form or cause to form into pustules. ◆ *adj* ('pʌstjʊlɪt). **2** covered with pustules.
▸ **ˌpustu'lation** *n*

pustule ('pʌstjuːl) *n* **1** a small inflamed elevated area of skin containing pus. **2** any spot resembling a pimple. ORIG C14: from L *pustula* a blister, var. of *pūsula*
▸ **pustular** ('pʌstjʊlə) *adj*

put (pʊt) *vb* **puts, putting, put.** (*mainly tr*) **1** to cause to be (in a position or place): *to put a book on the table.* **2** to cause to be (in a state, relation, etc.): *to put one's things in order.* **3** (foll. by *to*) to cause (a person) to experience or suffer: *to put to death.* **4** to set or commit (to an action, task, or duty), esp. by force: *he put him to work.* **5** to render or translate: *to put into English.* **6** to set (words) in a musical form (esp. in **put to music**). **7** (foll. by *at*) to estimate: *he put the distance at fifty miles.* **8** (foll. by *to*) to utilize: *he put his knowledge to use.* **9** (foll. by *to*) to couple (a female animal) with a male for breeding: *the farmer put his heifer to the bull.* **10** to express: *to put it bluntly.* **11** to make (an end or limit): *he put an end to the proceedings.* **12** to present for consideration; propose: *he put the question to the committee.* **13** to invest (money) in or expend (time, energy, etc.) on: *he put five thousand pounds into the project.* **14** to impart: *to put zest into a party.* **15** to throw or cast. **16 not know where to put oneself.** to feel embarrassed. **17 stay put.** to remain in one place; keep one's position. ◆ *n* **18** a throw, esp. in putting the shot. **19** Also called: **put option.** *Stock Exchange.* an option to sell a stated number of securities at a specified price during a limited period. ◆ See also **put about, put across,** etc. ORIG C12 *puten* to push

put about *vb* (*adv*) **1** *Naut.* to change course. **2** (*tr*) to make widely known: *he put about the news of the air disaster.* **3** (*tr; usually passive*) to disconcert or disturb.

put across *vb* (*tr*) **1** (*adv*) to communicate in a comprehensible way: *he couldn't put things across very well.* **2 put one across.** *Inf.* to get (someone) to believe a claim, excuse, etc., by deception: *they put one across their teacher.*

put aside *vb* (*tr, adv*) **1** to move (an object, etc.) to one side, esp. in rejection. **2** to save: *to put money aside for a rainy day.* **3** to disregard: *let us put aside our differences.*

putative ('pjuːtətɪv) *adj* (*prenominal*) **1** commonly re-

garded as being: *the putative father.* **2** considered to exist or have existed; inferred. ORIG C15: from LL *putātīvus* supposed, from L *putāre* to consider
▸ **'putatively** *adv*

put away *vb* (*tr, adv*) **1** to return (something) to the proper place. **2** to save: *to put away money for the future.* **3** to lock up in a prison, mental institution, etc.: *they put him away for twenty years.* **4** to eat or drink, esp. in large amounts.

put back *vb* (*tr, adv*) **1** to return to its former place. **2** to move to a later time: *the wedding was put back a fortnight.* **3** to impede the progress of: *the strike put back production.*

put by *vb* (*tr, adv*) to set aside for the future; save.

put down *vb* (*tr, adv*) **1** to make a written record of. **2** to repress: *to put down a rebellion.* **3** to consider: *they put him down for an ignoramus.* **4** to attribute: *I put the mistake down to inexperience.* **5** to put (an animal) to death, because of old age or illness. **6** to table on the agenda: *the MPs put down a motion on the increase in crime.* **7** *Sl.* to reject or humiliate. ◆ *n* **put-down.** **8** a cruelly crushing remark.

put forth *vb* (*tr, adv*) *Formal.* **1** to propose. **2** (of a plant) to produce or bear (leaves, etc.).

put forward *vb* (*tr, adv*) **1** to propose; suggest. **2** to offer the name of; nominate.

Putin ★ ('pu:tɪn) *n* **Vladimir** (**Vladimirovich**). born 1952, Russian statesman: prime minister (1999); acting president (1999–2000) following Boris Yeltsin's resignation; president from 2000.

put in *vb* (*adv*) **1** (*intr*) *Naut.* to bring a vessel into port. **2** (often foll. by *for*) to apply (for a job, etc.). **3** (*tr*) to submit: *he put in his claims form.* **4** to intervene with (a remark) during a conversation. **5** (*tr*) to devote (time, effort, etc.): *he put in three hours overtime last night.* **6** (*tr*) to establish or appoint: *he put in a manager.* **7** (*tr*) *Cricket.* to cause to bat: *England won the toss and put the visitors in to bat.*

Putnam ★ ('pʌtnəm) *n* **1 Israel.** 1718–90, American general in the War of Independence. **2** his cousin **Rufus.** 1738–1824, American soldier in the War of Independence; surveyor general of the US (1796–1803).

put off *vb* (*tr*) **1** (*adv*) to postpone: *they have put off the dance until tomorrow.* **2** (*adv*) to evade (a person) by postponement or delay: *they tried to put him off, but he came anyway.* **3** (*adv*) to cause aversion: *he was put off by her appearance.* **4** (*prep*) to cause to lose interest in: *the accident put him off driving.*

put on *vb* (*tr, mainly adv*) **1** to clothe oneself in. **2** (*usually passive*) to adopt (an attitude or feeling) insincerely: *his misery was just put on.* **3** to present (a play, show, etc.). **4** to add: *she put on weight.* **5** to cause (an electrical device) to function. **6** (*also prep*) to wager (money) on a horse race, game, etc. **7** (*also prep*) to impose: *to put a tax on cars.* **8** *Cricket.* to cause (a bowler) to bowl.

put out *vb* (*tr, adv*) **1** (*often passive*) **1a** to annoy; anger. **1b** to disturb; confuse. **2** to extinguish (a fire, light, etc.). **3** to poke forward: *to put out one's tongue.* **4** to be a source of inconvenience to: *I hope I'm not putting you out.* **5** to publish; broadcast: *the authorities put out a leaflet.* **6** to render unconscious. **7** to dislocate: *he put out his shoulder in the accident.* **8** to give out (work to be done) at different premises. **9** to lend (money) at interest. **10** *Cricket, etc.* to dismiss (a player or team).

put over *vb* (*tr, adv*) **1** *Inf.* to communicate (facts, information, etc.). **2** *Chiefly US.* to postpone. **3 put** (**a fast**) **one over on.** *Inf.* to get (someone) to believe a claim, excuse, etc., by deception: *he put one over on his boss.*

put-put ('pʌt,pʌt) *Inf.* ◆ *n* **1** a light chugging or popping sound, as made by a petrol engine. ◆ *vb* **put-puts, put-putting, put-putted.** **2** (*intr*) to make such a sound.

putrefy ('pju:trɪ,faɪ) *vb* **putrefies, putrefying, putrefied.** (of organic matter) to decompose or rot with an offensive smell. ORIG C15: from OF *putrefier* + L *putrefacere,* from *puter* rotten + *facere* to make
▸ **putrefaction** (,pju:trɪ'fækʃən) *n* ▸ **,putre'factive** *or* **putrefacient** (,pju:trɪ'feɪʃənt) *adj*

putrescent (pju:'trɛsᵊnt) *adj* **1** becoming putrid; rotting. **2** characterized by or undergoing putrefaction. ORIG C18: from L *putrescere* to become rotten
▸ **pu'trescence** *n*

putrid ('pju:trɪd) *adj* **1** (of organic matter) in a state of decomposition: *putrid meat.* **2** morally corrupt. **3** sickening; foul: *a putrid smell.* **4** *Inf.* deficient in quality or value: *a putrid film.* ORIG C16: from L *putridus,* from *putrēre* to be rotten
▸ **pu'tridity** *or* **'putridness** *n* ▸ **'putridly** *adv*

putsch (putʃ) *n* a violent and sudden uprising; political revolt. ORIG C20: from G, from Swiss G: a push, imit.

putt (pʌt) *Golf.* ◆ *n* **1** a stroke on the green with a putter to roll the ball into or near the hole. ◆ *vb* **2** to strike (the ball) in this way. ORIG C16: of Scot. origin

puttee *or* **putty** ('pʌtɪ) *n, pl* **puttees** *or* **putties.** (*usually pl*) a strip of cloth worn wound around the leg from the ankle to the knee, esp. as part of a military uniform in World War I. ORIG C19: from Hindi *paṭṭī,* from Sansk. *paṭṭikā,* from *paṭṭa* cloth

putter[1] ('pʌtə) *n Golf.* **1** a club for putting, usually having a solid metal head. **2** a golfer who putts: *he is a good putter.*

putter[2] ('pʌtə) *vb* the usual US and Canad. word for **potter**[2].
▸ **'putterer** *n*

putter[3] ('putə) *n* **1** a person who puts: *the putter of a question.* **2** a person who puts the shot.

put through *vb* (*tr, mainly adv*) **1** to carry out to a conclusion: *he put through his plan.* **2** (*also prep*) to organize the processing of: *she put through his application to join the organization.* **3** to connect by telephone. **4** to make (a telephone call).

putting green ('pʌtɪŋ) *n* **1** (on a golf course) the area of closely mown grass at the end of a fairway where the hole is. **2** an area of smooth grass with several holes for putting games.

Puttnam ★ ('pʌtnəm) *n* **David,** Baron. born 1941, British film producer. Films include *Chariots of Fire* (1981), *The Killing Fields* (1984), and *Memphis Belle* (1990).

putto ('putəʊ) *n, pl* **putti** (-ti:). a representation of a small boy, a cherub or cupid, esp. in baroque painting or sculpture. ORIG from It., from L *putus* boy

putty ('pʌtɪ) *n, pl* **putties.** **1** a stiff paste made of whiting and linseed oil that is used to fix glass into frames and to fill cracks in woodwork, etc. **2** any substance with a similar function or appearance. **3** a mixture of lime and later with sand or plaster of Paris used on plaster as a finishing coat. **4** (*as modifier*): *a putty knife.* **5** a person who is easily influenced: *he's putty in her hands.* **6a** a colour varying from greyish yellow to greyish brown. **6b** (*as adj*): *putty wool.* ◆ *vb* **putties, puttying, puttied.** **7** (*tr*) to fix, fill, or coat with putty. ORIG C17: from F *potée* a potful

Putumayo ★ (*Spanish* putu'majo) *n* a river in NW South America, rising in S Colombia and flowing southeast as most of the border between Colombia and Peru, entering the Amazon in Brazil: scene of the Putumayo rubber scandal (1910–11) during the rubber boom, in which many Indians were enslaved and killed by rubber exploiters. Length: 1578 km (980 miles). Brazilian name: **Içá.**

put up *vb* (*adv, mainly tr*) **1** to build; erect: *to put up a statue.* **2** to accommodate or be accommodated at: *can you put me up for tonight?* **3** to increase (prices). **4** to submit (a plan, case, etc.). **5** to offer: *to put a house up for sale.* **6** to give: *to put up a good fight.* **7** to provide (money) for: *they put up five thousand for the new project.* **8** to preserve or can (jam, etc.). **9** to pile up (long hair) on the head in any of several styles. **10** (*also intr*) to nominate or be nominated as a candidate: *he put up for president.* **11** *Arch.* to return (a weapon) to its holder: *put up your sword!* **12 put up to.** **12a** to inform or instruct (a person) about (tasks, duties, etc.). **12b** to incite to. **13 put up with.** *Inf.* to endure; tolerate. ◆ *adj* **put-up.** **14** dishonestly or craftily prearranged (esp. in **put-up job**).

put upon *vb* (*intr, prep; usually passive*) **1** to presume on (a person's generosity, good nature, etc.): *he's always being put upon.* **2** to impose hardship on: *he was sorely put upon.*

putz (pʌts) *n US sl.* a despicable or stupid person. ORIG from Yiddish *puts* ornament

Puvis de Chavannes ★ (*French* pyvis də ʃavan) *n* **Pierre Cécile** (pjɛr sesil). 1824–98, French mural painter.

Puy de Dôme ★ (pwi də dom) *n* **1** a department of central France in Auvergne region. Capital: Clermont-Ferrand. Pop.: 598 210 (1990). Area: 8016 sq. km (3094 sq. miles). **2** a mountain in central France, in the Auvergne Mountains: a volcanic plug. Height: 1485 m (4872 ft).

Puy de Sancy ★ (*French* pwi də sɑ̃si) *n* a mountain in S central France: highest peak of the Monts Dore. Height: 1886 m (6188 ft).

Pu-yi ★ (ˈpuːˈjiː) *n* **Henry.** 1906–67, last emperor of China as Xuan-Tong (1908–12); emperor of the Japanese puppet state of Manchukuo as Kang-de (1934–45).

puzzle (ˈpʌzᵊl) *vb* **puzzles, puzzling, puzzled. 1** to perplex or be perplexed. **2** (*intr;* foll. by *over*) to ponder about the cause of: *he puzzled over her absence.* **3** (*tr;* usually foll. by *out*) to solve by mental effort: *he puzzled out the meaning.* ◆ *n* **4** a person or thing that puzzles. **5** a problem that cannot be easily solved. **6** the state of being puzzled. **7** a toy, game, or question presenting a problem that requires skill or ingenuity for its solution. ORIG C16: from ? ▸ **ˈpuzzlement** *n* ▸ **ˈpuzzler** *n* ▸ **ˈpuzzling** *adj* ▸ **ˈpuzzlingly** *adv*

PVC *abbrev. for* polyvinyl chloride; a synthetic thermoplastic material made by polymerizing vinyl chloride. The flexible forms are used in insulation, shoes, etc. Rigid PVC is used for moulded articles.

PVS *abbrev. for:* **1** persistent vegetative state. **2** postviral syndrome.

Pvt. *Mil. abbrev. for* private.

PW *abbrev. for* policewoman.

PWA *abbrev. for* person with AIDS.

PWR *abbrev. for* pressurized-water reactor.

pyaemia *or* **pyemia** (paɪˈiːmɪə) *n* blood poisoning characterized by pus-forming microorganisms in the blood. ORIG C19: from NL, from Gk *puon* pus + *haima* blood ▸ **pyˈaemic** *or* **pyˈemic** *adj*

Pydna ★ (ˈpɪdnə) *n* a town in ancient Macedonia: site of a major Roman victory over the Macedonians, resulting in the downfall of their kingdom (168 B.C.).

pye-dog, pie-dog, *or* **pi-dog** (ˈpaɪˌdɒg) *n* an ownerless half-wild Asian dog. ORIG C19: Anglo-Indian, from Hindi *pāhī* outsider

pyelitis (ˌpaɪəˈlaɪtɪs) *n* inflammation of the pelvis of the kidney. ORIG C19: NL, from Gk *puelos* trough ▸ **pyelitic** (ˌpaɪəˈlɪtɪk) *adj*

Pygmalion ★ (pɪgˈmeɪlɪən) *n Greek myth.* a king of Cyprus, who fell in love with the statue of a woman he had sculpted and which his prayers brought to life as Galatea.

pygmy *or* **pigmy** (ˈpɪgmɪ) *n, pl* **pygmies** *or* **pigmies. 1** an abnormally undersized person. **2** something that is a very small example of its type. **3** a person of little importance or significance. **4** (*modifier*) very small. ORIG C14 *pigmeis* the Pygmies, from L *Pygmaeus* a Pygmy, from Gk *pugmaios* undersized, from *pugmē* fist ▸ **pygmaean** *or* **pygmean** (pɪgˈmiːən) *adj*

Pygmy *or* **Pigmy** (ˈpɪgmɪ) *n, pl* **Pygmies** *or* **Pigmies.** a member of one of the dwarf peoples of Equatorial Africa, noted for their hunting and forest culture.

pyinkado (pjɪŋˈkɑːdəʊ) *n, pl* **pyinkados. 1** a leguminous tree, native to India and Myanmar. **2** the heavy durable timber of this tree, used for construction. ORIG C19: from Burmese

pyjamas *or US* **pajamas** (pəˈdʒɑːməz) *pl n* **1** loose-fitting nightclothes comprising a jacket or top and trousers. **2** full loose-fitting ankle-length trousers worn by either sex in various Eastern countries. ORIG C19: from Hindi, from Persian *pai* leg + *jāma* garment

pyknic (ˈpɪknɪk) *adj* characterized by a broad squat fleshy physique with a large chest and abdomen. ORIG C20: from Gk *puknos* thick

pylon (ˈpaɪlən) *n* **1** a large vertical steel tower-like structure supporting high-tension electrical cables. **2** a post or tower for guiding pilots or marking a turning point in a race. **3** a streamlined aircraft structure for attaching an engine pod, etc., to the main body of the aircraft. **4** a monumental gateway, such as one at the entrance to an ancient Egyptian temple. ORIG C19: from Gk *pulōn* a gateway

pylorus (paɪˈlɔːrəs) *n, pl* **pylori** (-raɪ). the small circular opening at the base of the stomach through which partially digested food passes to the duodenum. ORIG C17: via LL from Gk *pulōrus* gatekeeper, from *pulē* gate + *ouros* guardian

Pylos ★ (ˈpaɪlɒs) *n* a port in SW Greece, in the SW Peloponnese; scene of a defeat of the Spartans by the Athenians (425 B.C.) during the Peloponnesian War and of the Battle of Navarino (see **Navarino**). Italian name: **Navarino.** Modern Greek name: **Pílos.**

Pym ★ (pɪm) *n* **John.** ?1584–1643, leading English parliamentarian during the events leading to the Civil War: prominent in the impeachment of Buckingham (1626) and of Strafford and Laud (1640).

Pynchon ★ (ˈpɪntʃən) *n* **Thomas.** born 1937, US novelist, author of *V* (1963), *The Crying of Lot 49* (1967), *Gravity's Rainbow* (1973), and *Mason and Dixon* (1997).

pyo- *or before a vowel* **py-** *combining form.* denoting pus: *pyosis.* ORIG from Gk *puon*

Pyongyang *or* **P'yŏng-yang** ★ (ˈpjɒŋˈjæŋ) *n* the capital of North Korea, in the southwest on the Taedong River: industrial centre; university (1946). Pop.: 2 355 000 (1987 est.).

pyorrhoea *or esp. US* **pyorrhea** (ˌpaɪəˈrɪə) *n* inflammation of the gums characterized by the discharge of pus and loosening of the teeth; periodontal disease. ▸ **ˌpyorˈrhoeal, ˌpyorˈrhoeic** *or esp. US* **ˌpyorˈrheal, ˌpyorˈrheic** *adj*

pyracantha (ˌpaɪrəˈkænθə) *n* any of a genus of shrubs with yellow, orange, or scarlet berries, widely cultivated for ornament. ORIG C17: from Gk *purakantha,* from PYRO- + *akantha* thorn

pyramid (ˈpɪrəmɪd) *n* **1** a huge masonry construction that has a square base and, as in the case of the ancient Egyptian royal tombs, four sloping triangular sides. **2** an object or structure resembling such a construction. **3** *Maths.* a solid having a polygonal base and triangular sides that meet in a common vertex. **4** *Crystallography.* a crystal form in which three planes intersect all three axes of the crystal. **5** *Finance.* a group of enterprises containing a series of holding companies structured so that the top holding company controls the entire group with a relatively small proportion of the total capital invested. **6** (*pl*) a game similar to billiards. ◆ *vb* **pyramids, pyramiding, pyramided. 7** to build up or be arranged in the form of a pyramid. **8** *Finance.* to form (companies) into a pyramid. ORIG C16 (earlier *pyramis*): from L *pyramis,* from Gk *puramis,* prob. from Egyptian ▸ **pyramidal** (pɪˈræmɪdᵊl), **ˌpyraˈmidical,** *or* **ˌpyraˈmidic** *adj* ▸ **pyˈramidally** *or* **ˌpyraˈmidically** *adv*

pyramid selling *n* a practice adopted by some manufacturers of advertising for distributors and selling them batches of goods. The first distributors then advertise for more distributors who are sold subdivisions of the original batches at an increased price. This process continues until the final distributors are left with a stock that is unsaleable except at a loss.

Pyramus and Thisbe ★ (ˈpɪrəməs; ˈθɪzbɪ) *n* (in Greek legend) two lovers of Babylon: Pyramus, wrongly supposing Thisbe to be dead, killed himself and she, encountering him in his death throes, did the same.

pyre (ˈpaɪə) *n* a pile of wood or other combustible material, esp. one for cremating a corpse. ORIG C17: from L *pyra,* from Gk *pura* hearth, from *pur* fire

Pyrenees ★ (ˌpɪrəˈniːz) *pl n* a mountain range between France and Spain, extending from the Bay of Biscay to the Mediterranean. Highest peak: Pico de Aneto, 3404 m (11 168 ft). ▸ **ˌPyreˈnean** *adj*

Pyrénées *or* **Pyrénées-Atlantiques** ★ (*French* pirenezatlɑ̃tik) *n* a department of SW France in Aquitaine region. Capital: Pau. Pop.: 590 992 (1994 est.).

Area: 7712 sq. km (3008 sq. miles). Former name: **Basses-Pyrénées.**

Pyrénées-Orientales ★ (*French* pirenezɔrjɑ̃tal) *n* a department of S France, in Languedoc-Roussillon region. Capital: Perpignan. Pop.: 375 018 (1994 est.). Area: 4144 sq. km (1616 sq. miles).

pyrethrin (paɪˈriːθrɪn) *n* either of two oily compounds found in pyrethrum and used as insecticides. ORIG C19: from PYRETHRUM + -IN

pyrethrum (paɪˈriːθrəm) *n* **1** any of several cultivated Eurasian chrysanthemums with white, pink, red, or purple flowers. **2** any insecticide prepared from the dried flowers of any of these plants. ORIG C16: via L from Gk *purethron* feverfew, prob. from *puretos* fever; see PYRETIC

pyretic (paɪˈrɛtɪk) *adj Pathology.* of, relating to, or characterized by fever. ORIG C18: from NL *pyreticus,* from Gk *puretos* fever, from *pur* fire

Pyrex (ˈpaɪrɛks) *n Trademark.* **a** any of a variety of glasses that have low coefficients of expansion, making them suitable for heat-resistant glassware used in cookery and chemical apparatus. **b** (*as modifier*): *a Pyrex dish.*

pyrexia (paɪˈrɛksɪə) *n* a technical name for **fever.** ORIG C18: from NL, from Gk *purexis,* from *puressein* to be feverish, from *pur* fire
▸ **pyˈrexial** *or* **pyˈrexic** *adj*

pyridine (ˈpɪrɪˌdiːn) *n* a colourless hygroscopic liquid heterocyclic compound with a characteristic odour: used as a solvent and in preparing other organic chemicals. Formula: C_5H_5N. ORIG C19: from PYRO- + -ID[2] + -INE[2]

pyridoxine (ˌpɪrɪˈdɒksiːn) *n Biochemistry.* a derivative of pyridine that is a precursor of the compounds pyridoxal and pyridoxamine. Also called: **vitamin B_6.**

pyrimidine (paɪˈrɪmɪˌdiːn) *n* **1** a liquid or crystalline organic compound with a penetrating odour. Formula: $C_4H_4N_2$. **2** Also called: **pyrimidine base.** any of a number of similar compounds having a basic structure that is derived from pyrimidine, and which are constituents of nucleic acids. ORIG C20: var. of PYRIDINE

pyrite (ˈpaɪraɪt) *n* a yellow mineral consisting of iron sulphide in cubic crystalline form. It occurs in igneous and metamorphic rocks and in veins, associated with various metals, and is used mainly in the manufacture of sulphuric acid and paper. Formula: FeS_2. Also called: **iron pyrites, pyrites.** ORIG C16: from L *pyrites* flint, from Gk *puritēs (lithos)* fire(stone), from *pur* fire
▸ **pyritic** (paɪˈrɪtɪk) *or* **pyˈritous** *adj*

pyrites (paɪˈraɪtiːz; *in combination* ˈpaɪraɪts) *n, pl* **pyrites. 1** another name for **pyrite. 2** any of a number of other disulphides of metals, esp. of copper and tin.

pyro- *or before a vowel* **pyr-** *combining form.* **1** denoting fire or heat: *pyromania; pyrometer.* **2** *Chem.* denoting a new substance obtained by heating another: *pyroboric acid is obtained by heating boric acid.* **3** *Mineralogy.* **3a** having a property that changes upon the application of heat. **3b** having a flame-coloured appearance: *pyroxylin.* ORIG from Gk *pur* fire

pyroelectricity (ˌpaɪrəʊɪlɛkˈtrɪsɪtɪ) *n* the development of opposite charges at the ends of the axis of certain crystals as a result of a change in temperature.

pyrogallol (ˌpaɪrəʊˈgælɒl) *n* a crystalline soluble phenol with weakly acidic properties: used as a photographic developer and for absorbing oxygen in gas analysis. Formula: $C_6H_3(OH)_3$. ORIG C20: from PYRO- + GALL(IC ACID) + -OL[1]

pyrogenic (ˌpaɪrəʊˈdʒɛnɪk) *or* **pyrogenous** (paɪˈrɒdʒɪnəs) *adj* **1** produced by or producing heat. **2** *Pathology.* causing or resulting from fever. **3** *Geol.* less common words for **igneous.**

pyrography (paɪˈrɒgrəfɪ) *n* another name for **pokerwork.**

pyroligneous (ˌpaɪrəʊˈlɪgnɪəs) *or* **pyrolignic** *adj* (of a substance) produced by the action of heat on wood, esp. by destructive distillation.

pyrolysis (paɪˈrɒlɪsɪs) *n* **1** the application of heat to chemical compounds in order to cause decomposition. **2** such chemical decomposition.
▸ **pyrolytic** (ˌpaɪrəʊˈlɪtɪk) *adj*

pyromania (ˌpaɪrəʊˈmeɪnɪə) *n Psychiatry.* the uncontrollable impulse and practice of setting things on fire.
▸ **ˌpyroˈmaniˌac** *n*

pyrometer (paɪˈrɒmɪtə) *n* an instrument for measuring high temperatures, esp. by measuring the brightness or total quantity of the radiation produced.
▸ **pyrometric** (ˌpaɪrəʊˈmɛtrɪk) *or* **ˌpyroˈmetrical** *adj*
▸ **ˌpyroˈmetrically** *adv* ▸ **pyˈrometry** *n*

pyrope (ˈpaɪrəʊp) *n* a deep yellowish-red garnet that consists of magnesium aluminium silicate and is used as a gemstone. ORIG C14 (used loosely of a red gem; modern sense C19): from OF *pirope,* from L *pyrōpus* bronze, from Gk *purōpus* fiery-eyed

pyrophoric (ˌpaɪrəʊˈfɒrɪk) *adj* **1** (of a chemical) igniting spontaneously on contact with air. **2** (of an alloy) producing sparks when struck or scraped: *lighter flints are made of pyrophoric alloy.* ORIG C19: from NL *pyrophorus,* from Gk *purophoros* fire-bearing, from *pur* fire + *pherein* to bear

pyrosis (paɪˈrəʊsɪs) *n Pathology.* a technical name for **heartburn.** ORIG C18: from NL, from Gk: a burning, from *puroun* to burn, from *pur* fire

pyrostat (ˈpaɪrəʊˌstæt) *n* **1** a device that activates an alarm or extinguisher in the event of a fire. **2** a thermostat for use at high temperatures.
▸ **ˌpyroˈstatic** *adj*

pyrotechnics (ˌpaɪrəʊˈtɛknɪks) *n* **1** (*functioning as sing*) the art of making fireworks. **2** (*functioning as sing or pl*) a firework display. **3** (*functioning as sing or pl*) brilliance of display, as in the performance of music.
▸ **ˌpyroˈtechnic** *or* **ˌpyroˈtechnical** *adj*

pyroxene (paɪˈrɒksiːn) *n* any of a large group of minerals consisting of the silicates of magnesium, iron, and calcium. They occur in basic igneous rocks. ORIG C19: PYRO- + *-xene* from Gk *xenos* foreign, because mistakenly thought to have originated elsewhere when found in igneous rocks

pyroxylin (paɪˈrɒksɪlɪn) *n* a yellow substance obtained by nitrating cellulose with a mixture of nitric and sulphuric acids; guncotton: used to make collodion, plastics, lacquers, and adhesives.

pyrrhic (ˈpɪrɪk) *Prosody.* ◆ *n* **1** a metrical foot of two short or unstressed syllables. ◆ *adj* **2** of or composed in pyrrhics. ORIG C16: via L, from Gk *purrhikhē,* said to be after its inventor *Purrhikhos*

Pyrrhic victory *n* a victory in which the victor's losses are as great as those of the defeated. Also called: **Cadmean victory.** ORIG after PYRRHUS, who defeated the Romans at Asculum in 279 B.C. but suffered heavy losses

Pyrrho ★ (ˈpɪrəʊ) *n* ?365–?275 B.C., Greek philosopher; founder of scepticism. He maintained that true wisdom and happiness lie in suspension of judgment, since certain knowledge is impossible to attain.
▸ **ˈPyrrhonism** *n* ▸ **ˈPyrrhonist** *n, adj*

Pyrrhus ★ (ˈpɪrəs) *n* **1** 319–272 B.C., king of Epirus (306–272). He invaded Italy but was ultimately defeated by the Romans (275 B.C.). **2** another name for **Neoptolemus.**
▸ **ˈPyrrhic** *adj*

pyruvic acid (paɪˈruːvɪk) *n* a liquid formed during the metabolism of proteins and carbohydrates, helping to release energy to the body. ORIG C19: from PYRO- + L *ūva* grape

Pythagoras ★ (paɪˈθægərəs) *n* ?580–?500 B.C., Greek philosopher and mathematician. He founded a religious brotherhood, which followed a life of strict asceticism and greatly influenced the development of mathematics and its application to music and astronomy.

Pythagoras' theorem *n* the theorem that in a right-angled triangle the square of the length of the hypotenuse equals the sum of the squares of the other two sides.

Pythagorean (paɪˌθægəˈriːən) *adj* **1** of or relating to Pythagoras. ◆ *n* **2** a follower of Pythagoras.

Pytheas ★ (ˈpɪθɪəs) *n* 4th century B.C., Greek navigator. He was the first Greek to visit and describe the coasts of Spain, France, and the British Isles and may have reached Iceland.

Pythia ★ ('pɪθɪə) *n Greek myth.* the priestess of Apollo at Delphi, who transmitted the oracles.

Pythian ('pɪθɪən) *adj also* **Pythic. 1** of or relating to Delphi or its oracle. ◆ *n* **2** the priestess of Apollo at the oracle of Delphi. ORIG C16: via L *Pȳthius* from Gk *Puthios* of Delphi

python ('paɪθən) *n* any of a family of large non-venomous snakes of Africa, S Asia, and Australia. They can reach a length of more than 20 feet and kill their prey by constriction. ORIG C16: NL, after PYTHON
▸ **pythonic** (paɪ'θɒnɪk) *adj*

Python ★ ('paɪθən) *n Greek myth.* a dragon, killed by Apollo at Delphi.

pythoness ('paɪθənɛs) *n* a woman, such as Apollo's priestess at Delphi, believed to be possessed by an oracular spirit. ORIG C14 *phitonesse,* ult. from Gk *Puthōn* PYTHON

pyuria (paɪ'jʊərɪə) *n Pathol.* any condition characterized by the presence of pus in the urine. ORIG C19: from NL, from Gk *puon* pus + *ouron* urine

pyx (pɪks) *n* **1** Also called: **pyx chest.** the chest in which coins from the British mint are placed to be tested for weight, etc. **2** *Christianity.* any receptacle in which the Eucharistic Host is kept. ORIG C14: from L *pyxis* small box, from Gk, from *puxos* box tree

pyxidium (pɪk'sɪdɪəm) *or* **pyxis** ('pɪksɪs) *n, pl* **pyxidia** (-ɪə) *or* **pyxides** ('pɪksɪˌdiːz). the dry fruit of such plants as the plantain: a capsule whose upper part falls off when mature so that the seeds are released. ORIG C19: via NL from Gk *puxidion* a little box, from *puxis* box

pyxis ('pɪksɪs) *n, pl* **pyxides** ('pɪksɪˌdiːz). **1** a small box used by the ancient Greeks and Romans to hold medicines, etc. **2** another name for **pyxidium.** ORIG C14: via L from Gk: box

Qq

q *or* **Q** (kjuː) *n, pl* **q's, Q's,** *or* **Qs. 1** the 17th letter of the English alphabet. **2** a speech sound represented by this letter.

q *symbol for* quintal.

Q *symbol for:* **1** *Physics.* heat. **2** *Chess.* queen. **3** question. **4** Q factor.

q. *abbrev. for:* **1** quart. **2** quarter. **3** quarterly. **4** query. **5** question. **6** quire.

Q. *abbrev. for:* **1** quartermaster. **2** (*pl* **Qq., qq.**) Also: **q.** quarto. **3** Quebec. **4** Queen. **5** question.

Qabis ★ (ˈkɑːbɪs) *n* the Arabic name for **Gabès.**

Qaboos bin Said ★ (kəˈbuːs bɪn ˈsaɪd) *n* born 1940, sultan of Oman from 1970.

Qaddafi ★ (gəˈdɑːfɪ) *n* **Moamar al** (ˈməʊəˌmɑː ˌæl). See (Moamar al) **Gaddafi.**

qadi (ˈkɑːdɪ, ˈkeɪdɪ) *n, pl* **qadis.** a variant spelling of **cadi.**

Qairwan ★ (kaɪəˈwɑːn) *n* a variant of **Kairouan.**

QANTAS (ˈkwɒntəs) *n* the national airline of Australia. ORIG C20: from *Q(ueensland) a(nd) N(orthern) T(erritory) A(erial) S(ervices Ltd.)*

Qaraghandy ★ (*Kazakh* karaɣanˈdɪ) *n* a variant transliteration of the Kazakh name for **Karaganda.**

QARANC *abbrev. for* Queen Alexandra's Royal Army Nursing Corps.

Qatar *or* **Katar** ★ (kæˈtɑː) *n* a state in E Arabia, occupying a peninsula in the Persian Gulf: under Persian rule until the 19th century; became a British protectorate in 1916; declared independence in 1971; exports petroleum and natural gas. Official language: Arabic. Official religion: (Sunni) Muslim. Currency: riyal. Capital: Doha. Pop.: 589 000 (1999 est.). Area: about 11 000 sq. km (4250 sq. miles).
▸ **Qaˈtari** *or* **Kaˈtari** *adj, n*

Qattara Depression ★ (kəˈtɑːrə) *n* an arid basin in the Sahara, in NW Egypt, impassable to vehicles. Area: about 18 000 sq. km (7000 sq. miles). Lowest point: 133 m (435 ft) below sea level.

qawwali (kəˈvɑːlɪ) *n* an Islamic religious song, esp. in Asia.

QB *abbrev. for* Queen's Bench.

QC *abbrev. for* Queen's Counsel.

QED *abbrev. for:* **1** quantum electrodynamics. **2** quod erat demonstrandum. ORIG L: which was to be shown or proved

Qeshm (ˈkɛʃəm) *or* **Qishm** ★ *n* **1** the largest island in the Persian Gulf: part of Iran. Area: 1336 sq. km (516 sq. miles). **2** the chief town of this island.

Q factor *n* **1** a measure of the relationship between stored energy and rate of energy dissipation in certain electrical components, devices, etc. **2** Also called: **Q value.** the heat released in a nuclear reaction. ◆ Symbol: Q ORIG C20: short for *quality factor*

Q fever *n* an acute disease characterized by fever and pneumonia, transmitted to man by a rickettsia. ORIG C20: from *q(uery) fever* (the cause being orig. unknown)

qi (tʃiː) *n* a variant spelling of **chi**[2].

Qingdao (ˈtʃɪŋˈdaʊ), **Tsingtao,** *or* **Chingtao** ★ *n* a port in E China, in E Shandong province on Jiazhou Bay, developed as a naval base and fort in 1891. Shandong university (1926). Pop.: 2 060 000 (1991 est.).

Qinghai, Tsinghai, *or* **Chinghai** ★ (ˈtʃɪŋˈhaɪ) *n* **1** a province of NW China: consists largely of mountains and high plateaus. Capital: Xining. Pop.: 4 960 000 (1997 est.). Area: 721 000 sq. km (278 400 sq. miles). **2** the Pinyin transliteration of the Chinese name for **Koko Nor.**

Qiqihar, Chichihaerh, Ch'i-ch'i-haerh, *or* **Tsitsihar** ★ (ˈtʃiːˌtʃiːˈhɑː) *n* a city in NE China, in Heilongjiang province on the Nonni River. Pop.: 1 380 000 (1991 est.).

Qishm ★ (ˈkɪʃəm) *n* a variant of **Qeshm.**

Qld *or* **QLD** *abbrev. for* Queensland.

QM *abbrev. for* Quartermaster.

QMG *abbrev. for* Quartermaster General.

QMV *abbrev. for* Qualified Majority Voting.

Qom (kɒm), **Qum,** *or* **Kum** ★ *n* a city in NW central Iran: a place of pilgrimage for Shiite Muslims. Pop.: 780 453 (1994 est.).

qr. *pl* **qrs.** *abbrev. for:* **1** quarter. **2** quarterly. **3** quire.

Q-ship *n* a merchant ship with concealed guns, used to decoy enemy ships. ORIG C20: from Q short for QUERY

QSM (in New Zealand) *abbrev. for* Queen's Service Medal.

QSO *abbrev. for:* **1** quasi-stellar object. **2** (in New Zealand) Queen's Service Order.

qt *pl* **qt** *or* **qts** *abbrev. for* quart.

q.t. *Inf.* **1** *abbrev. for* quiet. **2 on the q.t.** secretly.

qua (kweɪ, kwɑː) *prep* in the capacity of; by virtue of being. ORIG C17: from L, ablative sing (fem) of *qui* who

quack[1] (kwæk) *vb* (*intr*) **1** (of a duck) to utter a harsh guttural sound. **2** to make a noise like a duck. ◆ *n* **3** the sound made by a duck. ORIG C17: imit.

quack[2] (kwæk) *n* **1a** an unqualified person who claims medical knowledge or other skills. **1b** (*as modifier*): *a quack doctor.* **2** *Brit., Austral., & NZ inf.* a doctor; physician or surgeon. ◆ *vb* **3** (*intr*) to act in the manner of a quack. ORIG C17: short for QUACKSALVER
▸ **ˈquackish** *adj*

quackery (ˈkwækərɪ) *n, pl* **quackeries.** the activities or methods of a quack.

quack grass *n* another name for **couch grass.**

quacksalver (ˈkwækˌsælvə) *n* an archaic word for **quack**[2]. ORIG C16: from Du., from *quack,* apparently: to hawk + *salf* SALVE

quad[1] (kwɒd) *n* short for **quadrangle.**

quad[2] (kwɒd) *n Printing.* a block of type metal used for spacing. ORIG C19: shortened from QUADRAT

quad[3] (kwɒd) *n* short for **quadruplet.**

quad[4] (kwɒd) *n, adj Inf.* short for **quadraphonics** *or* **quadraphonic.**

quad bike *or* **quad** *n* a vehicle like a motorcycle, with four large wheels, designed for agricultural, sporting, and other off-road uses.

Quadragesima (ˌkwɒdrəˈdʒɛsɪmə) *n* the first Sunday in Lent. Also called: **Quadragesima Sunday.** ORIG C16: from Med. L *quadrāgēsima dies* the fortieth day

Quadragesimal (ˌkwɒdrəˈdʒɛsɪməl) *adj* of, relating to, or characteristic of Lent.

quadrangle (ˈkwɒdˌræŋgᵊl) *n* **1** *Geom.* a plane figure consisting of four points connected by four lines. **2** a rectangular courtyard, esp. one having buildings on all four sides. **3** the building surrounding such a courtyard. ORIG C15: from LL *quadrangulum* figure having four corners
▸ **quadrangular** (kwɒˈdræŋgjʊlə) *adj*

quadrant (ˈkwɒdrənt) *n* **1** *Geom.* **1a** a quarter of the circumference of a circle. **1b** the area enclosed by two perpendicular radii of a circle. **1c** any of the four sections into which a plane is divided by two coordinate axes. **2** a piece of a mechanism in the form of a quarter circle. **3** an instrument formerly used in astronomy and navigation for measuring the altitudes of stars. ORIG C14: from L *quadrāns* a quarter
▸ **quadrantal** (kwɒˈdræntᵊl) *adj*

quadraphonics *or* **quadrophonics** (ˌkwɒdrəˈfɒnɪks)

★ people and places

n (functioning as sing) a system of sound recording and reproduction that uses four independent loudspeakers to give directional sources of sound.
▸ **ˌquadraˈphonic** *or* **ˌquadroˈphonic** *adj*

quadrat (ˈkwɒdrət) *n* **1** *Ecology.* an area of vegetation selected at random for study. **2** *Printing.* an archaic name for **quad**[2]. ORIG C14 (meaning "a square"): var. of QUADRATE

quadrate *n* (ˈkwɒdrɪt, -ˌdreɪt). **1** a cube, square, or a square or cubelike object. **2** one of a pair of bones of the upper jaw of fishes, amphibians, reptiles, and birds. ◆ *adj* (ˈkwɒdrɪt, -ˌdreɪt). **3** of or relating to this bone. **4** square or rectangular. ◆ *vb* (kwɒˈdreɪt), **quadrates, quadrating, quadrated. 5** *(tr)* to make square or rectangular. **6** (often foll. by *with*) to conform or cause to conform. ORIG C14: from L *quadrāre* to make square

quadratic (kwɒˈdrætɪk) *Maths.* ◆ *n* **1** Also called: **quadratic equation.** an equation containing one or more terms in which the variable is raised to the power of two, but to no higher power. ◆ *adj* **2** of or relating to the second power.

quadrature (ˈkwɒdrətʃə) *n* **1** *Maths.* the process of determining a square having an area equal to that of a given figure or surface. **2** the process of making square or dividing into squares. **3** *Astron.* a configuration in which two celestial bodies form an angle of 90° with a third body. **4** *Electronics.* the relationship between two waves that are 90° out of phase.

quadrella (kwɒˈdrɛlə) *n Austral.* a form of betting in which the punter must select the winner of four specified races.

quadrennial (kwɒˈdrɛnɪəl) *adj* **1** occurring every four years. **2** lasting four years. ◆ *n* **3** a period of four years.
▸ **quadˈrennially** *adv*

quadrennium (kwɒˈdrɛnɪəm) *n, pl* **quadrenniums** *or* **quadrennia** (-nɪə). a period of four years. ORIG C17: from L *quadriennium,* from QUADRI- + *annus* year

quadri- *or before a vowel* **quadr-** *combining form.* four: *quadrilateral.* ORIG from L; cf. *quattuor* four

quadric (ˈkwɒdrɪk) *Maths.* ◆ *adj* **1** having or characterized by an equation of the second degree. **2** of the second degree. ◆ *n* **3** a quadric curve, surface, or function.

quadriceps (ˈkwɒdrɪˌsɛps) *n, pl* **quadricepses** (-ˌsɛpsɪz) *or* **quadriceps.** *Anat.* a large four-part muscle of the front of the thigh, which extends the leg. ORIG C19: NL, from QUADRI- + *-ceps* as in BICEPS

quadrifid (ˈkwɒdrɪfɪd) *adj Bot.* divided into four lobes or other parts: *quadrifid leaves.*

quadrilateral (ˌkwɒdrɪˈlætərəl) *adj* **1** having or formed by four sides. ◆ *n* **2** Also called: **tetragon.** a polygon having four sides.

quadrille[1] (kwɒˈdrɪl) *n* **1** a square dance for four couples. **2** a piece of music for such a dance. ORIG C18: via F from Sp. *cuadrilla,* dim. of *cuadro* square, from L *quadra*

quadrille[2] (kwɒˈdrɪl, kwə-) *n* an old card game for four players. ORIG C18: from F, from Sp. *cuartillo,* from *cuarto* fourth, from L *quartus,* infl. by QUADRILLE[1]

quadrillion (kwɒˈdrɪljən) *n, pl* **quadrillions** *or* **quadrillion. 1** (in Britain, France, and Germany) the number represented as one followed by 24 zeros (10^{24}). US and Canad. word: **septillion. 2** (in the US and Canada) the number represented as one followed by 15 zeros (10^{15}). ◆ *determiner* **3** amounting to this number: *a quadrillion atoms.* ORIG C17: from F *quadrillon,* from QUADRI- + *-illion,* on the model of *million*
▸ **quadˈrillionth** *adj*

quadrinomial (ˌkwɒdrɪˈnəʊmɪəl) *n* an algebraic expression containing four terms.

quadriplegia (ˌkwɒdrɪˈpliːdʒɪə) *n* paralysis of all four limbs. Also called: **tetraplegia.** ORIG C20: from QUADRI- + Gk *plēssein* to strike
▸ **quadriplegic** (ˌkwɒdrɪˈpliːdʒɪk) *adj*

quadrivalent (ˌkwɒdrɪˈveɪlənt) *adj Chem.* another word for **tetravalent.**
▸ **ˌquadriˈvalency** *or* **ˌquadriˈvalence** *n*

quadrivium (kwɒˈdrɪvɪəm) *n, pl* **quadrivia** (-ɪə). (in medieval learning) a course consisting of arithmetic, geometry, astronomy, and music. ORIG from Med. L, from L: crossroads, from QUADRI- + *via* way

quadroon (kwɒˈdruːn) *n* a person who is one-quarter Black. ORIG C18: from Sp. *cuarterón,* from *cuarto* quarter, from L *quartus*

quadrumanous (kwɒˈdruːmənəs) *adj* (of monkeys and apes) having all four feet specialized for use as hands. ORIG C18: from NL *quadrumanus,* from QUADRI- + L *manus* hand

quadruped (ˈkwɒdrʊˌpɛd) *n* **1** an animal, esp. a mammal, that has all four limbs specialized for walking. ◆ *adj* **2** having four feet. ORIG C17: from L *quadrupēs,* from *quadru-* (see QUADRI-) + *pēs* foot
▸ **quadrupedal** (kwɒˈdruːpɪdᵊl) *adj*

quadruple (ˈkwɒdrʊpᵊl, kwɒˈdruːpᵊl) *vb* **quadruples, quadrupling, quadrupled. 1** to multiply by four or increase fourfold. ◆ *adj* **2** four times as much or as many; fourfold. **3** consisting of four parts. **4** *Music.* having four beats in each bar. ◆ *n* **5** a quantity or number four times as great as another. ORIG C16: via OF from L *quadruplus,* from *quadru-* (see QUADRI-) + *-plus* -fold
▸ **ˈquadruply** *adv*

quadruplet (ˈkwɒdrʊplɪt, kwɒˈdruːplɪt) *n* **1** one of four offspring born at one birth. **2** a group of four similar things. **3** *Music.* a group of four notes to be played in a time value of three.

quadruplicate *adj* (kwɒˈdruːplɪkɪt). **1** fourfold or quadruple. ◆ *vb* (kwɒˈdruːplɪˌkeɪt), **quadruplicates, quadruplicating, quadruplicated. 2** to multiply or be multiplied by four. ◆ *n* (kwɒˈdruːplɪkɪt). **3** a group or set of four things. ORIG C17: from L *quadruplicāre* to increase fourfold

quaestor (ˈkwiːstə) *or US (sometimes)* **questor** (ˈkwɛstə) *n* any of several magistrates of ancient Rome, usually a financial administrator. ORIG C14: from L, from *quaerere* to inquire
▸ **quaestorial** (kwɛˈstɔːrɪəl) *adj*

quaff (kwɒf) *vb* to drink heartily or in one draught. ORIG C16: ? imit.; cf. MLow G *quassen* to eat or drink excessively
▸ **ˈquaffer** *n*

quag (kwæg) *n* a quagmire. ORIG C16: ? rel. to QUAKE

quagga (ˈkwægə) *n, pl* **quaggas** *or* **quagga.** a recently extinct member of the horse family of southern Africa: it had zebra-like stripes on the head and shoulders. ORIG C18: from obs. Afrik., from Khoikhoi *quăgga*

quaggy (ˈkwægɪ) *adj* **quaggier, quaggiest. 1** resembling a quagmire; boggy. **2** soft or flabby.

quagmire (ˈkwægˌmaɪə) *n* **1** a soft wet area of land that gives way under the feet; bog. **2** an awkward, complex, or embarrassing situation. ORIG C16: from QUAG + MIRE

quahog (ˈkwɑːˌhɒg) *n* an edible clam native to the Atlantic coast of North America, having a large heavy rounded shell. ORIG C18: from Amerind, short for *poquauhock,* from *pohkeni* dark + *hogki* shell

quaich *or* **quaigh** (kweɪx) *n Scot.* a small shallow drinking cup, usually with two handles. ORIG from Gaelic *cuach* cup

Quai d'Orsay ★ *(French* ke dɔrsɛ) *n* the quay along the S bank of the Seine, Paris, where the French foreign office is situated.

quail[1] (kweɪl) *n, pl* **quails** *or* **quail.** any of various small Old World game birds having rounded bodies and small tails. ORIG C14: from OF *quaille,* from Med. L *quaccula,* prob. imit.

quail[2] (kweɪl) *vb (intr)* to shrink back with fear; cower. ORIG C15: ?from OF *quailler,* from L *coāgulāre* to curdle

quaint (kweɪnt) *adj* **1** attractively unusual, esp. in an old-fashioned style. **2** odd or inappropriate. ORIG C13 (in the sense: clever): from OF *cointe,* from L *cognitus* known, from *cognoscere* to ascertain
▸ **ˈquaintly** *adv* ▸ **ˈquaintness** *n*

quair (kwɛə) *n Scot.* a book. ORIG var. of QUIRE[1]

quake (kweɪk) *vb* **quakes, quaking, quaked.** *(intr)* **1** to shake or tremble with or as with fear. **2** to convulse or quiver, as from instability. ◆ *n* **3** a quaking. **4** *Inf.* an earthquake. ORIG OE *cwacian*

Quaker (ˈkweɪkə) *n* **1** a member of the Religious Society of Friends, a Christian sect founded by George Fox about 1650. Quakers reject sacraments, ritual, and formal min-

istry, and have promoted many causes for social reform. ◆ *adj* **2** of the Religious Society of Friends or its beliefs or practices. ORIG C17: orig. a derog. nickname
▸ **'Quakeress** *fem n* ▸ **'Quakerish** *adj* ▸ **'Quakerism** *n*

quaking ('kweɪkɪŋ) *adj* unstable or unsafe to walk on, as a bog or quicksand.

quaking grass *n* any of various grasses having delicate branches that shake in the wind.

quaky ('kweɪkɪ) *adj* **quakier, quakiest.** inclined to quake; shaky.
▸ **'quakiness** *n*

qualification (ˌkwɒlɪfɪ'keɪʃən) *n* **1** an official record of achievement awarded on the successful completion of a course of training or passing of an examination. **2** an ability, quality, or attribute, esp. one that fits a person to perform a particular job or task. **3** a condition that modifies or limits; restriction. **4** a qualifying or being qualified.

qualified ('kwɒlɪˌfaɪd) *adj* **1** having the abilities, qualities, attributes, etc., necessary to perform a particular job or task. **2** limited, modified, or restricted; not absolute.

Qualified Majority Voting *n* a voting system, used by the EU Council of Ministers, by which resolutions concerning certain areas of policy may be passed without unanimity. Abbrev.: **QMV.**

qualify ('kwɒlɪˌfaɪ) *vb* **qualifies, qualifying, qualified. 1** to provide or be provided with the abilities or attributes necessary for a task, office, duty, etc.: *his degree qualifies him for the job.* **2** (*tr*) to make less strong, harsh, or violent; moderate or restrict. **3** (*tr*) to modify or change the strength or flavour of. **4** (*tr*) *Grammar.* another word for **modify. 5** (*tr*) to attribute a quality to; characterize. **6** (*intr*) to progress to the final stages of a competition, as by winning preliminary contests. ORIG C16: from OF *qualifier,* from Med. L *quālificāre* to characterize, from L *quālis* of what kind + *facere* to make
▸ **'qualiˌfiable** *adj* ▸ **'qualiˌfier** *n*

qualitative ('kwɒlɪtətɪv) *adj* involving or relating to distinctions based on quality or qualities.
▸ **'qualitatively** *adv*

qualitative analysis *n* See **analysis** (sense 4).

quality ('kwɒlɪtɪ) *n, pl* **qualities. 1** a distinguishing characteristic or attribute. **2** the basic character or nature of something. **3** a feature of personality. **4** degree or standard of excellence, esp. a high standard. **5** (formerly) high social status or the distinction associated with it. **6** musical tone colour; timbre. **7** *Logic.* the characteristic of a proposition that makes it affirmative or negative. **8** *Phonetics.* the distinctive character of a vowel, determined by the configuration of the mouth, tongue, etc. **9** (*modifier*) having or showing excellence or superiority: *a quality product.* ORIG C13: from OF *qualité,* from L *quālitās* state, from *quālis* of what sort

quality control *n* control of the quality of a manufactured product, usually by statistical sampling techniques.

quality time *n* a short period during the day in which a person gives the whole of his or her attention to some matter other than work, esp. family relationships.

qualm (kwɑːm) *n* **1** a sudden feeling of sickness or nausea. **2** a pang of doubt, esp. concerning moral conduct; scruple. **3** a sudden sensation of misgiving. ORIG OE *cwealm* death or plague
▸ **'qualmish** *adj*

quandary ('kwɒndrɪ) *n, pl* **quandaries.** a difficult situation; predicament. ORIG C16: from ?; ? rel. to L *quandō* when

quandong, quandang ('kwɒnˌdɒŋ), *or* **quantong** ('kwɒnˌtɒŋ) *n* **1** Also called: **native peach. 1a** a small Australian tree. **1b** the edible fruit or nut of this tree. **2** *Austral. sl.* a sponger or parasite. **3 silver quandong. 3a** an Australian tree. **3b** its timber. ORIG from Abor.

quango ('kwæŋgəʊ) *n, pl* **quangos.** a semipublic government-financed administrative body whose members are appointed by the government. ORIG C20: *qu(asi-) a(utonomous) n(on) g(overnmental) o(rganization)*

quangocracy (kwæŋ'gɒkrəsɪ) *n, pl* **quangocracies. 1** the control or influence ascribed to quangos. **2** quangos collectively.

quant[1] (kwɒnt) *n* **1** a long pole for propelling a boat, esp. a punt. ◆ *vb* **2** to propel (a boat) with a quant. ORIG C15: prob. from L *contus* pole, from Gk *kontos*

quant[2] (kwɒnt) *n Inf.* a highly paid analyst with a degree in a quantitative science, employed by a financial house to predict price movements of securities, commodities, etc. ORIG C20: from QUANTITATIVE

Quant ★ (kwɒnt) *n* **Mary.** born 1934, British fashion designer.

quanta ('kwɒntə) *n* the plural of **quantum.**

quantic ('kwɒntɪk) *n* a homogeneous function of two or more variables in a rational and integral form. ORIG C19: from L *quantus* how great

quantifier ('kwɒntɪˌfaɪə) *n* **1** *Logic.* a symbol indicating the quantity of a term: *the existential quantifier corresponds to the words "there is something, such that".* **2** *Grammar.* a word or phrase, such as *some, all,* or *no,* expressing quantity.

quantify ('kwɒntɪˌfaɪ) *vb* **quantifies, quantifying, quantified.** (*tr*) **1** to discover or express the quantity of. **2** *Logic.* to specify the quantity of (a term) by using a quantifier, such as *all, some,* or *no.* ORIG C19: from Med. L *quantificāre,* from L *quantus* how much + *facere* to make
▸ **'quantifiable** *adj* ▸ **ˌquantifi'cation** *n*

quantitative ('kwɒntɪtətɪv) *or* **quantitive** *adj* **1** involving or relating to considerations of amount or size. **2** capable of being measured. **3** *Prosody.* of a metrical system that is based on the length of syllables.
▸ **'quantitatively** *or* **'quantitively** *adv*

quantitative analysis *n* See **analysis** (sense 4).

quantity ('kwɒntɪtɪ) *n, pl* **quantities. 1a** a specified or definite amount, number, etc. **1b** (*as modifier*): *a quantity estimate.* **2** the aspect of anything that can be measured, weighed, counted, etc. **3 unknown quantity.** a person or thing whose action, effort, etc., is unknown or unpredictable. **4** a large amount. **5** *Maths.* an entity having a magnitude that may be denoted by a numerical expression. **6** *Physics.* a specified magnitude or amount. **7** *Logic.* the characteristic of a proposition that makes it universal or particular. **8** *Prosody.* the relative duration of a syllable or the vowel in it. ORIG C14: from OF *quantité,* from L *quantitās* amount, from *quantus* how much

> **USAGE NOTE** The use of a plural noun after *quantity of* as in *a large quantity of bananas* was formerly considered incorrect, but is now acceptable.

quantity surveyor *n* a person who estimates the cost of the materials and labour necessary for a construction job.

quantize *or* **quantise** ('kwɒntaɪz) *vb* **quantizes, quantizing, quantized** *or* **quantises, quantising, quantised.** (*tr*) **1** *Physics.* to restrict (a physical quantity) to one of a set of fixed values. **2** *Maths.* to limit to values that are multiples of a basic unit.
▸ **ˌquanti'zation** *or* **ˌquanti'sation** *n*

quantum ('kwɒntəm) *n, pl* **quanta. 1** *Physics.* **1a** the smallest quantity of some physical property that a system can possess according to the quantum theory. **1b** a particle with such a unit of energy. **2** amount or quantity, esp. a specific amount. ◆ *adj* **3** of or designating a major breakthrough or sudden advance: *a quantum leap forward.* ORIG C17: from L *quantus* (adj) how much

quantum electrodynamics *n Physics.* the study of electromagnetic radiation and its interaction with charged particles in terms of quantum theory. Abbrev.: **QED.**

quantum mechanics *n* (*functioning as sing*) the branch of mechanics, based on the quantum theory, used for interpreting the behaviour of elementary particles and atoms, which do not obey Newtonian mechanics.

quantum meruit *Latin.* ('mɛruːɪt) as much as he has earned.

quantum number *n Physics.* one of a set of integers or half-integers characterizing the energy states of a particle or system of particles.

quantum theory *n* a theory concerning the behaviour of physical systems based on the idea that they can only possess certain properties, such as energy and angular momentum, in discrete amounts (quanta).

quaquaversal (ˌkwɑːkwəˈvɜːsəl) *adj Geol.* directed outwards in all directions from a common centre. ORIG C18: from L *quāquā* in every direction + *versus* towards

quarantine (ˈkwɒrənˌtiːn) *n* **1** a period of isolation or detention, esp. of persons or animals arriving from abroad, to prevent the spread of disease. **2** the place where such detention is enforced. **3** any period or state of enforced isolation. ◆ *vb* **quarantines, quarantining, quarantined.** **4** (*tr*) to isolate in or as if in quarantine. ORIG C17: from It. *quarantina* period of forty days, from *quaranta* forty, from L *quadrāgintā*

quarantine flag *n Naut.* the yellow signal flag for the letter Q, flown alone from a vessel to indicate that there is no disease aboard or, with a second signal flag, to indicate that there is disease aboard. Also called: **yellow jack.**

quark[1] (kwɑːk) *n Physics.* any of a set of six elementary particles that, together with their antiparticles, are thought to be fundamental units of all baryons and mesons but unable to exist in isolation. ORIG C20: coined by James JOYCE in the novel *Finnegans Wake*, and given special application in physics

quark[2] (kwɑːk) *n* a type of low-fat soft cheese. ORIG from G

Quarles ★ (kwɔːlz, kwɑːlz) *n* **Francis.** 1592–1644, English poet.

quarrel[1] (ˈkwɒrəl) *n* **1** an angry disagreement; argument. **2** a cause of dispute; grievance. ◆ *vb* **quarrels, quarrelling, quarrelled** *or US* **quarrels, quarreling, quarreled.** (*intr; often foll. by with*) **3** to engage in a disagreement or dispute; argue. **4** to find fault; complain. ORIG C14: from OF *querele*, from L *querēlla* complaint, from *querī* to complain ▸ ˈ**quarreller** *or US* ˈ**quarreler** *n*

quarrel[2] (ˈkwɒrəl) *n* **1** an arrow having a four-edged head, fired from a crossbow. **2** a small square or diamond-shaped pane of glass. ORIG C13: from OF *quarrel* pane, from Med. L *quadrellus*, dim. of L *quadrus* square

quarrelsome (ˈkwɒrəlsəm) *adj* inclined to quarrel or disagree; belligerent.

quarrian *or* **quarrion** (ˈkwɒrɪən) *n* a cockatiel of inland Australia that feeds on seeds and grasses. ORIG C20: prob. from Abor.

quarry[1] (ˈkwɒrɪ) *n, pl* **quarries.** **1** an open surface excavation for the extraction of building stone, slate, marble, etc. **2** a copious source, esp. of information. ◆ *vb* **quarries, quarrying, quarried.** **3** to extract (stone, slate, etc.) from or as if from a quarry. **4** (*tr*) to excavate a quarry in. **5** to obtain (something) diligently and laboriously. ORIG C15: from OF *quarriere*, from *quarre* (unattested) square-shaped stone, from L *quadrāre* to make square

quarry[2] (ˈkwɒrɪ) *n, pl* **quarries.** **1** an animal, etc., that is hunted, esp. by other animals; prey. **2** anything pursued. ORIG C14 *quirre* entrails offered to the hounds, from OF *cuirée* what is placed on the hide, from *cuir* hide, from L *corium* leather; prob. also infl. by OF *coree* entrails, from L *cor* heart

quarryman (ˈkwɒrɪmən) *n, pl* **quarrymen.** a man who works in or manages a quarry.

quarry tile *n* an unglazed floor tile.

quart (kwɔːt) *n* **1** a unit of liquid measure equal to a quarter of a gallon or two pints. 1 US quart (0.946 litre) is equal to 0.8326 UK quart. 1 UK quart (1.136 litres) is equal to 1.2009 US quarts. **2** a unit of dry measure equal to 2 pints or one eighth of a peck. ORIG C14: from OF *quarte*, from L *quartus* fourth

quartan (ˈkwɔːtᵊn) *adj* (of a fever) occurring every third day. ORIG C13: from L *febris quartāna* fever occurring every fourth day, reckoned inclusively

quarte (kɑːt) *n* the fourth of eight basic positions from which a parry or attack can be made in fencing. ORIG C18: F from OF *quarte*, from L *quartus* fourth

quarter (ˈkwɔːtə) *n* **1** one of four equal parts of an object, quantity, etc. **2** the fraction equal to one divided by four (¼). **3** *US, Canad., etc.* a 25-cent piece. **4** a unit of weight equal to a quarter of a hundredweight. 1 US quarter is equal to 25 pounds; 1 Brit. quarter is equal to 28 pounds. **5** short for **quarter-hour.** **6** a fourth part of a year; three months. **7** *Astron.* **7a** one fourth of the moon's period of revolution around the earth. **7b** either of two phases of the moon when half of the lighted surface is visible. **8** *Inf.* a unit of weight equal to a quarter of a pound or 4 ounces. **9** *Brit.* a unit of capacity for grain, etc., usually equal to 8 UK bushels. **10** *Sport.* one of the four periods into which certain games are divided. **11** *Naut.* the part of a vessel's side towards the stern. **12** a region or district of a town or city: *the Spanish quarter.* **13** a region, direction, or point of the compass. **14** (*sometimes pl*) an unspecified person or group of people: *to get word from the highest quarter.* **15** mercy or pity, as shown to a defeated opponent (esp. in **ask for** *or* **give quarter**). **16** any of the four limbs, including the adjacent parts, of a quadruped or bird. **17** *Heraldry.* one of four quadrants into which a shield may be divided. ◆ *vb* **18** (*tr*) to divide into four equal parts. **19** (*tr*) to divide into any number of parts. **20** (*tr*) (esp. formerly) to dismember (a human body). **21** to billet or be billeted in lodgings, esp. (of military personnel) in civilian lodgings. **22** (*intr*) (of hounds) to range over an area of ground in search of game or the scent of quarry. **23** (*intr*) *Naut.* (of the wind) to blow onto a vessel's quarter. **24** (*tr*) *Heraldry.* **24a** to divide (a shield) into four separate bearings. **24b** to place (one set of arms) in diagonally opposite quarters to another. ◆ *adj* **25** being or consisting of one of four equal parts. ◆ See also **quarters.** ORIG C13: from OF *quartier*, from L *quartārius* a fourth part, from *quartus* fourth

quarterback (ˈkwɔːtəˌbæk) *n* a player in American football who directs attacking play.

quarter-bound *adj* (of a book) having a binding consisting of two types of material, the better type being used on the spine.

quarter day *n* any of four days in the year when certain payments become due. In England, Wales, and Northern Ireland these are Lady Day, Midsummer's Day, Michaelmas, and Christmas. In Scotland they are Candlemas, Whit Sunday, Lammas, and Martinmas.

quarterdeck (ˈkwɔːtəˌdɛk) *n Naut.* the after part of the upper deck of a ship, traditionally the deck for official or ceremonial use.

quartered (ˈkwɔːtəd) *adj* **1** *Heraldry.* (of a shield) divided into four sections, each having contrasting arms or having two sets of arms, each repeated in diagonally opposite corners. **2** (of a log) sawn into four equal parts along two diameters at right angles to each other.

quarterfinal (ˌkwɔːtəˈfaɪnᵊl) *n* the round before the semifinal in a competition.

quarter-hour *n* **1** a period of 15 minutes. **2** either of the points on a timepiece that mark 15 minutes before or after the hour.

quartering (ˈkwɔːtərɪŋ) *n* **1** *Mil.* the allocation of accommodation to service personnel. **2** *Heraldry.* **2a** the marshalling of several coats of arms on one shield, usually representing intermarriages. **2b** any coat of arms marshalled in this way.

quarterlight (ˈkwɔːtəˌlaɪt) *n Brit.* a small pivoted window in the door of a car for ventilation.

quarterly (ˈkwɔːtəlɪ) *adj* **1** occurring, done, paid, etc., at intervals of three months. **2** of, relating to, or consisting of a quarter. ◆ *n, pl* **quarterlies.** **3** a periodical issued every three months. ◆ *adv* **4** once every three months.

quartermaster (ˈkwɔːtəˌmɑːstə) *n* **1** an officer responsible for accommodation, food, and equipment in a military unit. **2** a rating in the navy, usually a petty officer, with particular responsibility for navigational duties.

quarter-miler *n* an athlete who specializes in running the quarter mile or in running 400-metre races.

quartern (ˈkwɔːtən) *n* **1** a fourth part of certain weights or measures. **2** Also called: **quartern loaf.** *Brit.* **2a** a type of loaf 4 inches square. **2b** any loaf weighing 1600 g. ORIG C13: from OF *quarteron*, from *quart* a quarter

quarter note *n* the usual US and Canad. name for **crotchet** (sense 1).

quarter plate *n* a photographic plate measuring 3¼ × 4¼ inches (8.3 × 10.8 cm).

quarters (ˈkwɔːtəz) *pl n* **1** accommodation, esp. as provided for military personnel. **2** the stations assigned to crew members of a warship: *general quarters.*

quarter sessions *n* (*functioning as sing or pl*) (formerly) any of various courts held four times a year before justices of the peace or a recorder.

quarterstaff ('kwɔːtəˌstɑːf) *n, pl* **quarterstaves** (-ˌsteɪvz). a stout iron-tipped wooden staff about 6ft long, formerly used as a weapon. ORIG C16: from ?

quarter tone *n Music.* a quarter of a whole tone.

quartet *or* **quartette** (kwɔː'tɛt) *n* **1** a group of four singers or instrumentalists or a piece of music composed for such a group. **2** any group of four. ORIG C18: from It. *quartetto,* dim. of *quarto* fourth

quartic ('kwɔːtɪk) *adj, n* another word for **biquadratic.** ORIG C19: from L *quartus* fourth

quartile ('kwɔːtaɪl) *n* **1** *Statistics.* one of three values of a variable dividing its distribution into four groups with equal frequencies. ◆ *adj* **2** *Statistics.* of a quartile. **3** *Astrol.* denoting an aspect of two heavenly bodies when their longitudes differ by 90°. ORIG C16: from Med. L *quartīlis,* from L *quartus* fourth

quarto ('kwɔːtəʊ) *n, pl* **quartos.** a book size resulting from folding a sheet of paper into four leaves or eight pages. ORIG C16: from NL *in quartō* in quarter

quartz (kwɔːts) *n* a hard glossy mineral consisting of silicon dioxide in crystalline form. It occurs as colourless rock crystal and as several impure coloured varieties including agate, chalcedony, flint, and amethyst. Formula: SiO_2. ORIG C18: from G *Quarz,* of Slavic origin

quartz clock *or* **watch** *n* a clock or watch that is operated by a vibrating quartz crystal.

quartz crystal *n* a thin plate or rod cut from a piece of piezoelectric quartz and ground so that it vibrates at a particular frequency.

quartz glass *n* a colourless glass composed of almost pure silica, resistant to very high temperatures.

quartz-iodine lamp *or* **quartz lamp** *n* a type of tungsten-halogen lamp containing small amounts of iodine and having a quartz envelope, operating at high temperature and producing an intense light for use in car headlamps, etc.

quartzite ('kwɔːtsaɪt) *n* **1** a sandstone composed of quartz. **2** a very hard rock consisting of intergrown quartz crystals.

quasar ('kweɪzɑː, -sɑː) *n* any of a class of quasi-stellar objects that emit an immense amount of energy in the form of light, infrared radiation, etc., from a compact source. They are extremely distant and hence the youngest objects observed in the universe, and their energy generation is thought to involve a black hole located in a galaxy. ORIG C20: *quasi(i-stell)ar (object)*

quash (kwɒʃ) *vb* (*tr*) **1** to subdue forcefully and completely. **2** to annul or make void (a law, etc.). **3** to reject (an indictment, etc.) as invalid. ORIG C14: from OF *quasser,* from L *quassāre* to shake

quasi- *combining form.* **1** almost but not really; seemingly: *a quasi-religious cult.* **2** resembling but not actually being; so-called: *a quasi-scholar.* ORIG from L, lit.: as if

Quasimodo ★ (*Italian* kwa'ziːmodo) *n* **Salvatore** (salva'toːre). 1901–68, Italian poet: Nobel prize for literature 1959.

quasi-stellar object ('kwɑːzɪ, 'kweɪsaɪ) *n* a member of any of several classes of astronomical bodies, including **quasars** and **quasi-stellar galaxies,** both of which have exceptionally large red shifts. Abbrev.: **QSO.**

quassia ('kwɒʃə) *n* **1** any of a genus of tropical American trees having bitter bark and wood. **2** the wood of this tree or a bitter compound extracted from it, formerly used as a tonic and vermifuge, now used in insecticides. ORIG C18: from NL, after Graman *Quassi,* a slave who discovered (1730) the medicinal value of the root

quatercentenary (ˌkwætəsɛn'tiːnərɪ) *n, pl* **quatercentenaries.** a 400th anniversary. ORIG C19: from L *quater* four times + CENTENARY
▸ ˌ**quatercen'tennial** (ˌkwætəsɛn'tɛnɪəl) *adj, n*

quaternary (kwə'tɜːnərɪ) *adj* **1** consisting of fours or by fours. **2** fourth in a series. **3** *Chem.* containing or being an atom bound to four other atoms or groups. ◆ *n, pl* **quaternaries. 4** the number four or a set of four. ORIG C15: from L *quaternārius* each containing four, from *quaternī* by fours, from *quattuor* four

Quaternary (kwə'tɜːnərɪ) *adj* **1** of or denoting the most recent period of geological time, which succeeded the Tertiary period one million years ago. ◆ *n* **2 the.** the Quaternary period or rock system.

quaternion (kwə'tɜːnɪən) *n* **1** *Maths.* a generalized complex number consisting of four components, $x = x_0 + x_1i + x_2j + x_3k$, where x, $x_0 \ldots x_3$ are real numbers and $i^2 = j^2 = k^2 = -1$, $ij = -ji = k$, etc. **2** a set of four. ORIG C14: from LL, from L *quaternī* four at a time

Quathlamba ★ (kwɑːt'lɑːmbɑː) *n* the Sotho name for the **Drakensberg.**

quatrain ('kwɒtreɪn) *n* a stanza or poem of four lines. ORIG C16: from F, from *quatre* four, from L *quattuor*

Quatre Bras ★ (*French* katrə bra) *n* a village in Belgium near Brussels; site of a battle in June 1815 where Wellington defeated the French under Marshal Ney, immediately preceding the battle of Waterloo.

quatrefoil ('kætrəˌfɔɪl) *n* **1** a leaf composed of four leaflets. **2** *Archit.* a carved ornament having four foils arranged about a common centre. ORIG C15: from OF, from *quatre* four + *-foil* leaflet

quattrocento (ˌkwætrəʊ'tʃɛntəʊ) *n* the 15th century, esp. in reference to Renaissance Italian art and literature. ORIG It., lit.: four hundred (short for fourteen hundred)

quaver ('kweɪvə) *vb* **1** to say or sing (something) with a trembling voice. **2** (*intr*) (esp. of the voice) to quiver or tremble. **3** (*intr*) *Rare.* to sing or play trills. ◆ *n* **4** *Music.* a note having the time value of an eighth of a semibreve. Usual US and Canad. name: **eighth note. 5** a tremulous sound or note. ORIG C15 (in the sense: to vibrate): from *quaven* to tremble, of Gmc origin
▸ '**quavering** *adj* ▸ '**quaveringly** *adv*

quay (kiː) *n* a wharf, typically one built parallel to the shoreline. ORIG C14 *keye,* from OF *kai,* of Celtic origin

quayage ('kiːɪdʒ) *n* **1** a system of quays. **2** a charge for the use of a quay.

Quayle ★ (kweɪl) *n* Sir (**John**) **Anthony.** 1913–89, British actor and producer: director (1948–56) of the Shakespeare Memorial Theatre.

quayside ('kiːˌsaɪd) *n* the edge of a quay along the water.

Que. *abbrev. for* Quebec.

quean (kwiːn) *n* **1** *Arch.* **1a** a boisterous impudent woman. **1b** a prostitute. **2** *Scot.* an unmarried girl. ORIG OE *cwene*

queasy ('kwiːzɪ) *adj* **queasier, queasiest. 1** having the feeling that one is about to vomit; nauseous. **2** feeling or causing uneasiness. ORIG C15: from ?
▸ '**queasily** *adv* ▸ '**queasiness** *n*

Quebec ★ (kwɪ'bɛk, kə-, kɛ-) *n* **1** a province of E Canada: the largest Canadian province; a French colony from 1608 to 1763, when it passed to Britain; a large proportion of the population is French-speaking and there is a strong secessionist movement; lying mostly on the Canadian Shield, it has vast areas of forest and extensive tundra and is populated mostly in the plain around the St Lawrence River. Capital: Quebec. Pop.: 7 363 262 (1999 est.). Area: 1 540 680 sq. km (594 860 sq. miles). Abbrev.: **PQ. 2** a port in E Canada, capital of the province of Quebec, situated on the St Lawrence River: founded in 1608 by Champlain; scene of the battle of the Plains of Abraham (1759), by which the British won Canada from the French. Pop.: 167 517 (1991).
▸ **Que'becker** *or* **Que'becer** *n*

Québecois (*French* kebɛkwa) *n, pl* **Québecois** (-kwa). a native or inhabitant of the province of Quebec, esp. a French-speaking one.
▸ **Québecoise** (*French* kebɛkwaz) *fem n*

quebracho (keɪ'brɑːtʃəʊ) *n, pl* **quebrachos** (-tʃəʊz). **1** either of two South American trees having a tannin-rich hard wood used in tanning and dyeing. **2** a South American tree, whose bark yields alkaloids used in medicine and tanning. **3** the wood or bark of any of these trees. ORIG C19: from American Sp., from *quiebracha,* from *quebrar* to break (from L *crepāre* to rattle) + *hacha* axe (from F)

Quechua ('kɛtʃwə) *n* **1** (*pl* **Quechuas** *or* **Quechua**) a member

of any of a group of South American Indian peoples of the Andes, including the Incas. **2** the language or family of languages spoken by these peoples.
▸ **'Quechuan** *adj, n*

queen (kwi:n) *n* **1** a female sovereign who is the official ruler or head of state. **2** the wife of a king. **3** a woman or a thing personified as a woman considered the best or most important of her kind: *the queen of ocean liners*. **4** *Sl.* an effeminate male homosexual. **5** the only fertile female in a colony of bees, ants, etc. **6** an adult female cat. **7** a playing card bearing the picture of a queen. **8** the most powerful chess piece, able to move in a straight line in any direction or diagonally. ◆ *vb* **9** *Chess.* to promote (a pawn) to a queen when it reaches the eighth rank. **10** (*tr*) to crown as queen. **11** (*intr*) to reign as queen. **12 queen it.** (often foll. by *over*) *Inf.* to behave in an overbearing manner. ORIG OE *cwēn*

Queen-Anne *n* **1** a style of furniture popular in England about 1700–20 and in America about 1720–70, characterized by walnut veneer and cabriole legs. ◆ *adj* **2** in or of this style. **3** of a style of architecture popular in early 18th-century England, characterized by red-brick construction with classical ornamentation.

Queen Anne's lace *n* another name for the **wild carrot**.

queen bee *n* **1** the fertile female bee in a hive. **2** *Inf.* a woman in a position of dominance over her associates.

Queenborough in Sheppey ★ ('kwi:nbərə; 'ʃɛpɪ) *n* a town in SE England, in Kent: formed in 1968 by the amalgamation of Queenborough, Sheerness, and Sheppey. Pop.: 30 790 (1991).

Queen Charlotte Islands ★ *pl n* a group of about 150 islands off the W coast of Canada: part of British Columbia. Pop.: 5316 (1991). Area: 9596 sq. km (3705 sq. miles).

queen consort *n* the wife of a reigning king.

queen dowager *n* the widow of a king.

Queen Elizabeth Islands ★ *pl n* a group of islands off the N coast of Canada: the northernmost islands of the Canadian Arctic archipelago, lying N of latitude 74°N; part of the Northwest Territories. Area: about 390 000 sq. km (150 000 sq. miles).

queenly ('kwi:nlɪ) *adj* **queenlier, queenliest. 1** resembling or appropriate to a queen. ◆ *adv* **2** in a manner appropriate to a queen.

Queen Mab ★ (mæb) *n* (in British folklore) a bewitching fairy who rules over men's dreams.

Queen Maud Land ★ (mɔ:d) *n* the large section of Antarctica between Coats Land and Enderby Land: claimed by Norway in 1939.

Queen Maud Range ★ *n* a mountain range in Antarctica, in S Ross Dependency, extending for about 800 km (500 miles).

queen mother *n* the widow of a former king who is also the mother of the reigning sovereign.

queen olive *n* a variety of olive having large fleshy fruit suitable for pickling.

queen post *n* one of a pair of vertical posts that connect the tie beam of a truss to the principal rafters. Cf. **king post**.

Queens ★ (kwi:nz) *n* a borough of E New York City, on Long Island. Pop.: 1 951 598 (1990).

Queen's Award *n* either of two awards instituted by royal warrant (1976) for increased export earnings by a British firm (**Queen's Award for Export Achievement**) or for an advance in technology (**Queen's Award for Technological Achievement**).

Queen's Bench *n* (in England when the sovereign is female) one of the divisions of the High Court of Justice.

Queensberry rules ('kwi:nzbərɪ) *pl n* **1** the code of rules followed in modern boxing. **2** *Inf.* gentlemanly conduct, esp. in a dispute. ORIG C19: after the ninth Marquess of *Queensberry*, who originated the rules in 1869

Queen's Counsel *n* (when the sovereign is female) **1** a barrister (in England and Wales) or an advocate (in Scotland) appointed Counsel to the Crown by the sovereign on the recommendation of the Lord Chancellor (in England and Wales) or the Lord President (in Scotland). **2** (in Australia) a similar appointment, usually made on the recommendation of the Chief Justice of each state, through the state governor. **3** (in Canada) an honorary title which may be bestowed by the government on lawyers with long experience.

Queen's County ★ *n* the former name of **Laois**.

Queen's English *n* (when the British sovereign is female) standard Southern British English.

queen's evidence *n English & Canad. law.* (when the sovereign is female) evidence given for the Crown against former associates in crime by an accomplice (esp. in **turn queen's evidence**). US equivalent: **state's evidence**.

Queen's Guide *n* (in Britain and the Commonwealth when the sovereign is female) a Guide who has passed the highest tests of proficiency.

queen's highway *n* **1** (in Britain when the sovereign is female) any public road or right of way. **2** (in Canada) a main road maintained by the provincial government.

queen-size *or* **queen-sized** *adj* (of a bed, etc.) larger or longer than normal size but smaller or shorter than king-size.

Queensland ★ ('kwi:nz,lænd, -lənd) *n* a state of NE Australia: fringed on the Pacific side by the Great Barrier Reef; the Great Dividing Range lies in the east, separating the coastal lowlands from the dry Great Artesian Basin in the south. Capital: Brisbane. Pop.: 3 368 850 (1996). Area: 1 727 500 sq. km (667 000 sq. miles).
▸ **'Queens,lander** *n*

Queensland nut *n* another name for **macadamia**.

Queen's Scout *n* (in Britain and the Commonwealth when the sovereign is female) a Scout who has passed the highest tests of proficiency. US equivalent: **Eagle Scout**.

queer (kwɪə) *adj* **1** differing from the normal or usual; odd or strange. **2** dubious; shady. **3** faint, giddy, or queasy. **4** *Inf., derog.* homosexual. **5** *Inf.* eccentric or slightly mad. **6** *Sl.* worthless or counterfeit. ◆ *n* **7** *Inf., derog.* a homosexual. ◆ *vb* (*tr*) *Inf.* **8** to spoil or thwart (esp. in **queer someone's pitch**). **9** to put in a difficult position. ORIG C16: ? from G *quer* oblique, ult. from OHG *twërh*
▸ **'queerly** *adv* ▸ **'queerness** *n*

> **USAGE NOTE** Although the term *queer* meaning 'gay' is still considered derogatory when used by non-gays, it is now being used by gay people themselves as a positive term in certain contexts, such as *queer politics, queer cinema*. Nevertheless, many gay people would not wish to have the term applied to them, nor would they use it of themselves.

queer fish *n Brit. inf.* an odd person.

queer street *n* (*sometimes cap.*) *Inf.* a difficult situation, such as debt or bankruptcy (in **in queer street**).

quell (kwɛl) *vb* (*tr*) **1** to suppress (rebellion, etc.); subdue. **2** to overcome or allay. ORIG OE *cwellan* to kill
▸ **'queller** *n*

Quelpart ★ ('kwɛl,pɑ:t) *n* another name for **Cheju**.

Quemoy ★ (kɛ'mɔɪ) *n* an island in Formosa Strait, off the SE coast of China: administratively part of Taiwan. Pop.: 53 237 (1996 est.). Area: 130 sq. km (50 sq. miles).

quench (kwɛntʃ) *vb* (*tr*) **1** to satisfy (one's thirst, desires, etc.); slake. **2** to put out (a fire, etc.); extinguish. **3** to put down; suppress; subdue. **4** to cool (hot metal) by plunging it into cold water. ORIG OE *ācwencan* to extinguish
▸ **'quenchable** *adj* ▸ **'quencher** *n*

Queneau ★ (*French* kəno) *n* **Raymond** (rɛmɔ̃). 1903–76, French writer, whose novels include *Zazie dans le métro* (1959).

quenelle (kə'nɛl) *n* a ball of sieved meat or fish. ORIG C19: from F, from G *Knödel* dumpling, from OHG *knodo* knot

Querétaro ★ (*Spanish* ke'retaro) *n* **1** an inland state of central Mexico: economy based on agriculture and mining. Capital: Querétaro. Pop.: 1 297 575 (1997 est.). Area: 11 769 sq. km (4544 sq. miles). **2** a city in central Mexico, capital of Querétaro state: scene of the signing (1848) of the treaty ending the US-Mexican War and of the execution of Emperor Maximilian (1867). Pop.: 385 503 (1990).

querist ('kwɪərɪst) *n* a person who makes inquiries or queries; questioner.

quern (kwɜːn) *n* a stone hand mill for grinding corn. ORIG OE *cweorn*

quernstone ('kwɜːnˌstəʊn) *n* **1** another name for **millstone** (sense 1). **2** one of the two stones used in a quern.

querulous ('kwɛrʊləs, 'kwɛrjʊ-) *adj* **1** inclined to make whining or peevish complaints. **2** characterized by or proceeding from a complaining fretful attitude or disposition. ORIG C15: from L *querulus,* from *querī* to complain
▸ '**querulously** *adv* ▸ '**querulousness** *n*

query ('kwɪərɪ) *n, pl* **queries. 1** a question, esp. one expressing doubt. **2** a question mark. ◆ *vb* **queries, querying, queried.** (*tr*) **3** to express uncertainty, doubt, or an objection concerning (something). **4** to express as a query. **5** *US.* to put a question to (a person); ask. ORIG C17: from earlier *quere,* from L *quaerē* ask!, from *quaerere* to seek

query language *n Computing.* the instructions and procedures used to retrieve information from a database.

Quesnay ★ (*French* kɛnɛ) *n* **François** (frɑ̃swa). 1694–1774, French political economist, encyclopedist, and physician, noted for his *Tableau économique* (1758).

quest (kwɛst) *n* **1** a looking for or seeking; search. **2** (in medieval romance) an expedition by a knight or knights to accomplish a task, such as finding the Holy Grail. **3** the object of a search; a goal or target. ◆ *vb* (*mainly intr*) **4** (foll. by *for* or *after*) to go in search (of). **5** (of dogs, etc.) to search for game. **6** (*also tr*) *Arch.* to seek. ORIG C14: from OF *queste,* from L *quaesita* sought, from *quaerere* to seek
▸ '**quester** *n* ▸ '**questing** *adj* ▸ '**questingly** *adv*

question ('kwɛstʃən) *n* **1** a form of words addressed to a person in order to elicit information or evoke a response; interrogative sentence. **2** a point at issue: *it's only a question of time until she dies.* **3** a difficulty or uncertainty. **4a** an act of asking. **4b** an investigation into some problem. **5** a motion presented for debate. **6 put the question.** to require members of a deliberative assembly to vote on a motion presented. **7** *Law.* a matter submitted to a court or other tribunal. **8 beyond (all) question.** beyond (any) dispute or doubt. **9 call in** *or* **into question. 9a** to make (something) the subject of disagreement. **9b** to cast doubt upon the truth, etc., of (something). **10 in question.** under discussion: *this is the man in question.* **11 out of the question.** beyond consideration; unthinkable or impossible. **12 put to the question.** (formerly) to interrogate by torture. ◆ *vb* (*mainly tr*) **13** to put a question or questions to (a person); interrogate. **14** to make (something) the subject of dispute. **15** to express uncertainty about the truth of (something); doubt. ORIG C13: via OF from L *quaestiō,* from *quaerere* to seek
▸ '**questioner** *n*

questionable ('kwɛstʃənəbᵊl) *adj* **1** (esp. of a person's morality or honesty) admitting of some doubt; dubious. **2** of disputable value or authority.
▸ '**questionableness** *n* ▸ '**questionably** *adv*

questioning ('kwɛstʃənɪŋ) *adj* **1** proceeding from or characterized by a feeling of doubt or uncertainty. **2** intellectually inquisitive: *a questioning mind.*
▸ '**questioningly** *adv*

questionless ('kwɛstʃənlɪs) *adj* **1** blindly adhering; unquestioning. **2** a less common word for **unquestionable.**
▸ '**questionlessly** *adv*

question mark *n* **1** the punctuation mark **?**, used at the end of questions and in other contexts where doubt or ignorance is implied. **2** this mark used for any other purpose, as to draw attention to a possible mistake.

question master *n Brit.* the chairman of a quiz or panel game.

questionnaire (ˌkwɛstʃə'nɛə, ˌkɛs-) *n* a set of questions on a form, submitted to a number of people in order to collect statistical information.

> **USAGE NOTE** The most generally heard pronunciation of the first syllable of this word is the naturalized one, *kwes.* The French-sounding pronunciation *kes* is much less common, and may sound affected to certain people.

question time *n* (in parliamentary bodies of the British type) the time set aside each day for questions to government ministers.

Quetta ★ ('kwɛtə) *n* a city in W central Pakistan, at an altitude of 1650 m (5500 ft): a summer resort, military station, and trading centre. Pop.: 300 000 (latest est.).

quetzal ('kɛtsəl) *n, pl* **quetzals** *or* **quetzales** (-'sɑːlɛs). **1** a crested bird of Central and N South America, which has a brilliant green, red, and white plumage and, in the male, long tail feathers. **2** the standard monetary unit of Guatemala. ORIG via American Sp. from Nahuatl *quetzalli* brightly coloured tail feather

Quetzalcoatl ★ (ˌkɛtsəlkəʊ'ætᵊl) *n* a god of the Aztecs and Toltecs, represented as a feathered serpent.

queue (kjuː) *Chiefly Brit.* ◆ *n* **1** a line of people, vehicles, etc., waiting for something. **2** *Computing.* a list in which entries are deleted from one end and inserted at the other. **3** a pigtail. ◆ *vb* **queues, queuing** *or* **queueing, queued. 4** (*intr,* often foll. by *up*) to form or remain in a line while waiting. **5** *Computing.* to arrange (a number of programs) in a predetermined order for accessing by a computer. ◆ Usual US word (senses 1, 4): **line.** ORIG C16 (in the sense: tail); C18 (in the sense: pigtail): via F from L *cauda* tail

queue-jump *vb* (*intr*) **1** to take a place in a queue ahead of those already queuing; push in. **2** to obtain some advantage out of turn or unfairly.
▸ '**queue-**ˌ**jumper** *n*

Quezon City ★ ('keɪzɒn) *n* a city in the Philippines, on central Luzon adjoining Manila: capital of the Philippines from 1948 to 1976; seat of the University of the Philippines (1908). Pop.: 1 676 644 (1994 est.).

Quezon y Molina ★ ('keɪzɒn iː mɒ'liːnə; *Spanish* ke'θɔn i mo'lina) *n* **Manuel Luis** (ma'nwɛl lwis). 1878–1944, Philippine statesman: first president of the Philippines (from 1935) and head of the government in exile after the Japanese conquest in World War II.

quibble ('kwɪbᵊl) *vb* **quibbles, quibbling, quibbled.** (*intr*) **1** to make trivial objections. **2** *Arch.* to play on words; pun. ◆ *n* **3** a trivial objection or equivocation, esp. one used to avoid an issue. **4** *Arch.* a pun. ORIG C17: prob. from obs. *quib,* ?from L *quibus* (from *quī* who, which), as used in legal documents, with reference to their obscure phraseology
▸ '**quibbler** *n* ▸ '**quibbling** *adj*

Quiberon ★ (*French* kibrɔ̃) *n* a peninsula of NW France, on the S coast of Brittany: a naval battle was fought off its coast in 1759 during the Seven Years' War, in which the British defeated the French.

quiche (kiːʃ) *n* an open savoury tart with an egg custard filling to which bacon, onion, cheese, etc., are added. ORIG F, from G *Kuchen* cake

quick (kwɪk) *adj* **1** performed or occurring during a comparatively short time: *a quick move.* **2** lasting a short time; brief. **3** accomplishing something in a time that is shorter than normal: *a quick worker.* **4** characterized by rapidity of movement; fast. **5** immediate or prompt. **6** (*postpositive*) eager or ready to perform (an action): *quick to criticize.* **7** responsive to stimulation; alert; lively. **8** eager or enthusiastic for learning. **9** easily excited or aroused. **10** nimble in one's movements or actions; deft: *quick fingers.* **11** *Arch.* **11a** alive; living. **11b** (*as n*) living people (esp. in **the quick and the dead**). **12 quick with child.** *Arch.* pregnant. ◆ *n* **13** any area of sensitive flesh, esp. that under a toenail or fingernail. **14** the most important part (of a thing). **15 cut (someone) to the quick.** to hurt (someone's) feelings deeply. ◆ *adv Inf.* **16** in a rapid manner; swiftly. **17** soon: *I hope he comes quick.* ◆ *sen-*

tence substitute. **18** a command to perform an action immediately. ORIG OE *cwicu* living
▸ **'quickly** *adv* ▸ **'quickness** *n*

quick-change artist *n* an actor or entertainer who undertakes several rapid changes of costume during his performance.

quicken ('kwɪkən) *vb* **1** to make or become faster; accelerate. **2** to impart to or receive vigour, enthusiasm, etc.: *science quickens man's imagination.* **3** to make or become alive; revive. **4a** (of an unborn fetus) to begin to show signs of life. **4b** (of a pregnant woman) to reach the stage of pregnancy at which movements of the fetus can be felt.

quick-freeze *vb* **quick-freezes, quick-freezing, quick-froze, quick-frozen.** (*tr*) to preserve (food) by subjecting it to rapid refrigeration at temperatures of 0°C or lower.

quickie ('kwɪkɪ) *n Inf.* **1** Also called (esp. Brit.): **quick one.** a speedily consumed alcoholic drink. **2a** anything made or done rapidly. **2b** (*as modifier*): *a quickie divorce.*

quicklime ('kwɪk,laɪm) *n* another name for **calcium oxide.**

quick march *n* **1** a march at quick time or the order to proceed at such a pace. ◆ *interj* **2** a command to commence such a march.

quicksand ('kwɪk,sænd) *n* a deep mass of loose wet sand that sucks anything on top of it inextricably into it.

quickset ('kwɪk,set) *Chiefly Brit.* ◆ *n* **1a** a plant or cutting, esp. of hawthorn, set so as to form a hedge. **1b** such plants or cuttings collectively. **2** a hedge composed of such plants. ◆ *adj* **3** composed of such plants.

quicksilver ('kwɪk,sɪlvə) *n* **1** another name for **mercury** (sense 1). ◆ *adj* **2** rapid or unpredictable in movement or change.

quickstep ('kwɪk,stɛp) *n* **1** a modern ballroom dance in rapid quadruple time. **2** a piece of music composed for or in the rhythm of this dance. ◆ *vb* **quicksteps, quickstepping, quickstepped.** **3** (*intr*) to perform this dance.

quick-tempered *adj* readily roused to anger; irascible.

quickthorn ('kwɪk,θɔ:n) *n* hawthorn, esp. when planted as a hedge. ORIG C17: prob. from *quick* in the sense "fast-growing": cf. QUICKSET

quick time *n Mil.* the normal marching rate of 120 paces to the minute.

quick-witted *adj* having a keenly alert mind, esp. as used to avert danger, make effective reply, etc.
▸ **,quick-'wittedly** *adv* ▸ **,quick-'wittedness** *n*

quid[1] (kwɪd) *n* a piece of tobacco, suitable for chewing. ORIG OE *cwidu* chewing resin

quid[2] (kwɪd) *n, pl* **quid.** *Brit. sl.* **1** a pound (sterling). **2** (**be**) **quids in.** (to be) in a very favourable or advantageous position. ORIG C17: from ?

quiddity ('kwɪdɪtɪ) *n, pl* **quiddities. 1** the essential nature of something. **2** a petty or trifling distinction; quibble. ORIG C16: from Med. L *quidditās,* from L *quid* what

quidnunc ('kwɪd,nʌŋk) *n* a person eager to learn news and scandal; gossipmonger. ORIG C18: from L, lit.: what now

quid pro quo ('kwɪd prəʊ 'kwəʊ) *n, pl* **quid pro quos. 1** a reciprocal exchange. **2** something given in compensation, esp. an advantage or object given in exchange for another. ORIG C16: from L: something for something

quiescent (kwɪ'ɛsᵊnt) *adj* quiet, inactive, or dormant. ORIG C17: from L *quiescere* to rest
▸ **qui'escence** *or* **qui'escency** *n* ▸ **qui'escently** *adv*

quiet ('kwaɪət) *adj* **1** characterized by an absence of noise. **2** calm or tranquil: *the sea is quiet tonight.* **3** free from activities, distractions, etc.; untroubled: *a quiet life.* **4** short of work, orders, etc.; not busy: *business is quiet today.* **5** private; not public; secret: *a quiet word with someone.* **6** free from anger, impatience, or other extreme emotion. **7** free from pretentiousness; modest or reserved: *quiet humour.* **8** *Astron.* (of the sun) exhibiting a very low number of sunspots, solar flares, etc.; inactive. ◆ *n* **9** the state of being silent, peaceful, or untroubled. **10 on the quiet.** without other people knowing. ◆ *vb* **11** a less common word for **quieten.** ORIG C14: from L *quiētus,* p.p. of *quiēscere* to rest, from *quiēs* repose
▸ **'quietness** *n*

quieten ('kwaɪətᵊn) *vb Chiefly Brit.* **1** (often foll. by *down*) to make or become calm, silent, etc. **2** (*tr*) to allay (fear, doubts, etc.).

quietism ('kwaɪə,tɪzəm) *n* **1** a form of religious mysticism originating in Spain in the late 17th century, requiring complete passivity to God's will. **2** passivity and calmness of mind towards external events.
▸ **'quietist** *n, adj*

quietly ('kwaɪətlɪ) *adv* **1** in a quiet manner. **2 just quietly.** *Austral.* confidentially.

quietude ('kwaɪə,tju:d) *n* the state or condition of being quiet, peaceful, calm, or tranquil.

quietus (kwaɪ'i:təs, -'eɪtəs) *n, pl* **quietuses. 1** anything that serves to quash, eliminate, or kill. **2** a release from life; death. **3** the discharge or settlement of debts, duties, etc. ORIG C16: from L *quiētus est,* lit.: he is at rest

quiff (kwɪf) *n Brit.* a tuft of hair brushed up above the forehead. ORIG C19: from ?

quill (kwɪl) *n* **1a** any of the large stiff feathers of the wing or tail of a bird. **1b** the long hollow part of a feather; calamus. **2** Also called: **quill pen.** a feather made into a pen for writing. **3** any of the stiff hollow spines of a porcupine or hedgehog. **4** a device, formerly made from a crow quill, for plucking a harpsichord string. **5** a small roll of bark, esp. one of dried cinnamon. **6** a bobbin or spindle. **7** a fluted fold, as in a ruff. ◆ *vb* (*tr*) **8** to wind (thread, etc.) onto a spool or bobbin. **9** to make or press fluted folds in (a ruff, etc.). ORIG C15 (in the sense: hollow reed or pipe): from ?; cf. MLow G *quiele* quill

Quilmes ★ (*Spanish* 'kilmes) *n* a city in E Argentina: a resort and suburb of Buenos Aires. Pop.: 509 445 (1991).

quilt (kwɪlt) *n* **1** a cover for a bed, consisting of a soft filling sewn between two layers of material, usually with crisscross seams. **2** short for **continental quilt. 3** a bedspread. **4** anything resembling a quilt. ◆ *vb* (*tr*) **5** to stitch together (two pieces of fabric) with (a thick padding or lining) between them. **6** to create (a garment, etc.) in this way. **7** to pad with material. ORIG C13: from OF *coilte* mattress, from L *culcita* stuffed item of bedding
▸ **'quilted** *adj* ▸ **'quilter** *n*

quilting ('kwɪltɪŋ) *n* **1** material for quilts. **2** the act of making a quilt. **3** quilted work.

Quimper ★ (*French* kɛ̃pɛr) *n* a city in NW France: capital of Finistère department. Pop.: 62 540 (1990).

quin (kwɪn) *n Brit.* short for **quintuplet** (sense 1). US and Canad. word: **quint.**

quinary ('kwaɪnərɪ) *adj* **1** of or by fives. **2** fifth in a series. **3** (of a number system) having a base of five. ORIG C17: from L *quīnārius* containing five, from *quīnī* five each

quince (kwɪns) *n* **1** a small widely cultivated Asian tree with edible pear-shaped fruits. **2** the fruit of this tree, much used in preserves. ORIG C14 *qwince* pl. of *quyn,* from OF *coin,* from L *cotōneum,* from Gk *kudōnion* quince

quincentenary (,kwɪnsɛn'ti:nərɪ) *n, pl* **quincentenaries.** a 500th anniversary. ORIG C19: irregularly from L *quinque* five + CENTENARY
▸ **quincentennial** (,kwɪnsɛn'tɛnɪəl) *adj, n*

quincunx ('kwɪnkʌŋks) *n* a group of five objects arranged in the shape of a rectangle with one at each of the four corners and the fifth in the centre. ORIG C17: from L: five twelfths, from *quinque* five + *uncia* twelfth; in ancient Rome, this was a coin worth five twelfths of an AS[2] and marked with five spots
▸ **quincuncial** (kwɪn'kʌnʃəl) *adj*

Quine ★ (kwaɪn) *n* **Willard van Orman.** 1908–2000, US philosopher. His works include *Word and Object* (1960), *Philosophy of Logic* (1970), *The Roots of Reference* (1973), and *The Logic of Sequences* (1990).

quinella (kwɪ'nɛlə) *n Austral.* a form of betting in which the punter must select the first and second place winners, in any order. ORIG from American Sp. *quiniela*

Qui Nhong ★ ('kwi: 'njɒŋ) *n* a port in SE Vietnam, on the South China Sea. Pop.: 163 385 (1992 est.).

quinidine ('kwɪnɪ,di:n) *n* a crystalline alkaloid drug used to treat heart arrhythmias.

quinine (kwɪ'ni:n; *US* 'kwaɪnaɪn) *n* a bitter crystalline alkaloid extracted from cinchona bark, the salts of which are used as a tonic, analgesic, etc., and in malaria therapy. ORIG C19: from Sp. *quina* cinchona bark, from Quechua *kina* bark

Quinn ★ (kwɪn) *n* **Anthony**. born 1915, US film actor, born in Mexico: his films include *La Strada* (1954) and *Zorba the Greek* (1964).

quinol ('kwɪnɒl) *n* another name for **hydroquinone**.

quinoline ('kwɪnəˌliːn, -lɪn) *n* an oily colourless insoluble compound synthesized by heating aniline, nitrobenzene, glycerol, and sulphuric acid: used as a food preservative and in the manufacture of dyes and antiseptics. Formula: C_9H_7N.

quinquagenarian (ˌkwɪŋkwədʒɪ'nɛərɪən) *n* **1** a person between 50 and 59 years old. ◆ *adj* **2** being between 50 and 59 years old. **3** of a quinquagenarian. ORIG C16: from L *quinquāgēnārius* containing fifty, from *quinquāgēnī* fifty each

Quinquagesima (ˌkwɪŋkwə'dʒɛsɪmə) *n* the Sunday preceding Lent. Also called: **Quinquagesima Sunday**. ORIG C14: via Med. L from L *quinquāgēsima diēs* fiftieth day

quinquecentenary (ˌkwɪŋkwɪsɛn'tiːnərɪ) *n, pl* **quinquecentenaries**. another name for **quincentenary**.

quinquennial (kwɪn'kwɛnɪəl) *adj* **1** occurring once every five years or over a period of five years. ◆ *n* **2** a fifth anniversary.
▸ **quin'quennially** *adv*

quinquennium (kwɪn'kwɛnɪəm) *n, pl* **quinquennia** (-nɪə). a period or cycle of five years. ORIG C17: from L *quinque* five + *annus* year

quinquereme (ˌkwɪŋkwɪ'riːm) *n* an ancient Roman galley with five banks of oars. ORIG C16: from L *quinquerēmis*, from *quinque-* five + *rēmus* oar

quinquevalent (ˌkwɪŋkwɪ'veɪlənt) *adj Chem.* another word for **pentavalent**.
▸ **ˌquinque'valency** *or* **ˌquinque'valence** *n*

quinsy ('kwɪnzɪ) *n* inflammation of the tonsils and surrounding tissues with the formation of abscesses. ORIG C14: via OF & Med. L from Gk *kunankhē*, from *kuōn* dog + *ankhein* to strangle

quint[1] *n* **1** (kwɪnt). an organ stop sounding a note a fifth higher. **2** (kɪnt). *Piquet.* a sequence of five cards in the same suit. ORIG C17: from F *quinte*, from L *quintus* fifth

quint[2] (kwɪnt) *n* the US and Canad. word for **quin**.

quintain ('kwɪntɪn) *n* (esp. in medieval Europe) a post or target set up for tilting exercises for mounted knights or foot soldiers. ORIG C14: from OF *quintaine*, from L: street in a Roman camp between the fifth & sixth maniples (the maniple was a unit of 120–200 soldiers in ancient Rome), from *quintus* fifth

quintal ('kwɪntᵊl) *n* **1** a unit of weight equal to (esp. in Britain) 112 pounds or (esp. in US) 100 pounds. **2** a unit of weight equal to 100 kilograms. ORIG C15: via OF from Ar. *qintār*, possibly from L *centēnārius* consisting of a hundred

quintan ('kwɪntən) *adj* (of a fever) occurring every fourth day. ORIG C17: from L *febris quintāna* fever occurring every fifth day, reckoned inclusively

Quintana Roo ★ (*Spanish* kin'tana 'rɔo) *n* a state of SE Mexico, on the E Yucatán Peninsula: hot, humid, forested, and inhabited chiefly by Maya Indians. Capital: Chetumal. Pop.: 772 803 (1997 est.). Area: 50 350 sq. km (19 463 sq. miles).

quinte (kænt) *n* the fifth of eight basic positions from which a parry or attack can be made in fencing. ORIG C18: F from L *quintus* fifth

quintessence (kwɪn'tɛsəns) *n* **1** the most typical representation of a quality, state, etc. **2** an extract of a substance containing its principle in its most concentrated form. **3** (in ancient philosophy) ether, the fifth essence or element, which was thought to be the constituent matter of the heavenly bodies and latent in all things. ORIG C15: via F from Med. L *quinta essentia* the fifth essence, translation of Gk
▸ **quintessential** (ˌkwɪntɪ'sɛnʃəl) *adj* ▸ **ˌquintes'sentially** *adv*

quintet *or* **quintette** (kwɪn'tɛt) *n* **1** a group of five singers or instrumentalists or a piece of music composed for such a group. **2** any group of five. ORIG C19: from It. *quintetto*, from *quinto* fifth

quintillion (kwɪn'tɪljən) *n, pl* **quintillions** *or* **quintillion**. **1** (in Britain, France, and Germany) the number represented as one followed by 30 zeros (10^{30}). US and Canad. word: **nonillion**. **2** (in the US and Canada) the number represented as one followed by 18 zeros (10^{18}). Brit. word: **trillion**. ORIG C17: from L *quintus* fifth + *-illion*, as in MILLION
▸ **quin'tillionth** *adj*

quintuple ('kwɪntjʊpᵊl, kwɪn'tjuːpᵊl) *vb* **quintuples, quintupling, quintupled**. **1** to multiply by five. ◆ *adj* **2** five times as much or as many; fivefold. **3** consisting of five parts. ◆ *n* **4** a quantity or number five times as great as another. ORIG C16: from F, from L *quintus*, on the model of QUADRUPLE

quintuplet ('kwɪntjʊplɪt, kwɪn'tjuːplɪt) *n* **1** one of five offspring born at one birth. **2** a group of five similar things. **3** *Music.* a group of five notes to be played in a time value of three or four.

quintuplicate *adj* (kwɪn'tjuːplɪkɪt). **1** fivefold or quintuple. ◆ *vb* (kwɪn'tjuːplɪˌkeɪt), **quintuplicates, quintuplicating, quintuplicated**. **2** to multiply or be multiplied by five. ◆ *n* (kwɪn'tjuːplɪkɪt). **3** a group or set of five things.

quip (kwɪp) *n* **1** a sarcastic remark. **2** a witty saying. **3** *Arch.* another word for **quibble**. ◆ *vb* **quips, quipping, quipped**. **4** (*intr*) to make a quip. ORIG C16: from earlier *quippy*, prob. from L *quippe* indeed, to be sure
▸ **'quipster** *n*

quire[1] ('kwaɪə) *n* **1** a set of 24 or 25 sheets of paper. **2** four sheets of paper folded to form 16 pages. **3** a set of all the sheets in a book. ORIG C15 *quayer*, from OF *quaier*, from L *quaternī* four at a time, from *quater* four times

quire[2] ('kwaɪə) *n* an obsolete spelling of **choir**.

Quirinal ★ ('kwɪrɪnᵊl) *n* one of the seven hills on which ancient Rome was built.

Quirinus ★ (kwɪ'raɪnəs) *n Roman myth.* a god of war, who came to be identified with the deified Romulus.

quirk (kwɜːk) *n* **1** a peculiarity of character; mannerism or foible. **2** an unexpected twist or turn: *a quirk of fate*. **3** a continuous groove in an architectural moulding. **4** a flourish, as in handwriting. ORIG C16: from ?
▸ **'quirky** *adj* ▸ **'quirkiness** *n*

quirt (kwɜːt) *US & S. African.* ◆ *n* **1** a whip with a leather thong at one end. ◆ *vb* (*tr*) **2** to strike with a quirt. ORIG C19: from Sp. *cuerda* CORD

quisling ('kwɪzlɪŋ) *n* a traitor who aids an occupying enemy force; collaborator. ORIG C20: after Major Vidkun *Quisling* (1887–1945), Norwegian collaborator with the Nazis

quit (kwɪt) *vb* **quits, quitting, quitted** *or* **quit**. **1** (*tr*) to depart from; leave. **2** to resign; give up (a job). **3** (*intr*) (of a tenant) to give up occupancy of premises and leave them. **4** to desist or cease from (something or doing something). **5** (*tr*) to pay off (a debt). **6** (*tr*) *Arch.* to conduct or acquit (oneself); comport (oneself). ◆ *adj* **7** (*usually predicative; foll. by of*) free (from); released (from). ORIG C13: from OF *quitter*, from L *quiētus* QUIET

quitch grass (kwɪtʃ) *n* another name for **couch grass**. Sometimes shortened to **quitch**. ORIG OE *cwice*; ? rel. to *cwicu* living, QUICK (with the implication that the grass cannot be killed)

quitclaim ('kwɪtˌkleɪm) *Law.* ◆ *n* **1** a renunciation of a claim or right. ◆ *vb* **2** (*tr*) to renounce (a claim). ORIG C14: from Anglo-F *quiteclame*, from *quite* QUIT + *clamer* to declare (from L *clamāre* to shout)

quite (kwaɪt) *adv* **1** completely or absolutely: *you're quite right*. **2** (*not used with a negative*) somewhat: *she's quite pretty*. **3** in actuality; truly. **4 quite a** *or* **an**. (*not used with a negative*) of an exceptional, considerable, or noticeable kind: *quite a girl*. **5 quite something**. a remarkable or noteworthy thing or person. ◆ *sentence substitute*. **6** Also: **quite so**. an expression used to indicate agreement. ORIG C14: adverbial use of *quite* (adj) QUIT

USAGE NOTE See at **very**.

Quito ★ ('ki:təʊ; *Spanish* 'kito) *n* the capital of Ecuador, in the north at an altitude of 2850 m (9350 ft), just south of the equator: the oldest capital in South America, existing many centuries before the Incan conquest in 1487; a cultural centre since the beginning of Spanish rule (1534); two universities. Pop.: 1 487 513 (1997 est.).

quitrent ('kwɪt,rɛnt) *n* (formerly) a rent payable by a freeholder or copyholder to his lord in lieu of services.

quits (kwɪts) *adj* (*postpositive*) *Inf.* **1** on an equal footing; even. **2 call it quits.** to agree to end a dispute, contest, etc., agreeing that honours are even.

quittance ('kwɪtᵊns) *n* **1** release from debt or other obligation. **2** a receipt or other document certifying this. ORIG C13: from OF, from *quitter* to release from obligation; see QUIT

quitter ('kwɪtə) *n* a person who gives up easily.

quiver¹ ('kwɪvə) *vb* **1** (*intr*) to shake with a tremulous movement; tremble. ◆ *n* **2** the state, process, or noise of shaking or trembling. ORIG C15: from obs. *cwiver* quick, nimble
▸ **'quivering** *adj* ▸ **'quivery** *adj*

quiver² ('kwɪvə) *n* a case for arrows. ORIG C13: from OF *cuivre*

qui vive (,ki: 'vi:v) *n* **on the qui vive.** on the alert; attentive. ORIG C18: from F, lit.: long live who?, sentry's challenge (equivalent to "Whose side are you on?")

Quixote ('kwɪksət; *Spanish* ki'xote) *n* See **Don Quixote.**

quixotic (kwɪk'sɒtɪk) *adj* preoccupied with an unrealistically optimistic or chivalrous approach to life; impractically idealistic. ORIG C18: after DON QUIXOTE
▸ **quix'otically** *adv*

quiz (kwɪz) *n, pl* **quizzes. 1a** an entertainment in which the knowledge of the players is tested by a series of questions. **1b** (*as modifier*): *a quiz programme.* **2** any set of quick questions designed to test knowledge. **3** an investigation by close questioning. **4** *Obs.* a practical joke. **5** *Obs.* a puzzling individual. **6** *Obs.* a person who habitually looks quizzically at others. ◆ *vb* **quizzes, quizzing, quizzed.** (*tr*) **7** to investigate by close questioning; interrogate. **8** *US & Canad. inf.* to test the knowledge of (a student or class). **9** (*tr*) *Obs.* to look quizzically at, esp. through a small monocle. ORIG C18: from ?
▸ **'quizzer** *n*

quizzical ('kwɪzɪkᵊl) *adj* questioning and mocking or supercilious.
▸ **'quizzically** *adv*

Qum ★ (kʊm) *n* a variant of **Qom.**

Qumran ★ ('kʊmrɑ:n) *n* See **Khirbet Qumran.**

Qungur ★ ('kʊŋgʊə) *n* a variant transliteration of the Chinese name for **Kongur Shan.**

quod (kwɒd) *n* *Chiefly Brit.* a slang word for **jail.** ORIG C18: from ?

quod erat demonstrandum *Latin.* ('kwɒd 'ɛræt ,dɛmən'strændʊm) (at the conclusion of a proof, esp. of a theorem in Euclidean geometry) which was to be proved. Abbrev.: **QED.**

quodlibet ('kwɒdlɪ,bɛt) *n* **1** a light piece of music. **2** a subtle argument, esp. one prepared as an exercise on a theological topic. ORIG C14: from L, from *quod* what + *libet* pleases, that is, whatever you like

quoin (kwɔɪn, kɔɪn) *n* **1** an external corner of a wall. **2** a stone forming the external corner of a wall. **3** another name for **keystone** (sense 1). **4** *Printing.* a wedge or an expanding device used to lock type up in a chase. **5** a wedge used for any of various other purposes. ORIG C16: var. of *coin* (in former sense of corner)

quoit (kɔɪt) *n* a ring of iron, plastic, etc., used in the game of quoits. ORIG C15: from ?

quoits (kɔɪts) *pl n* (*usually functioning as sing*) a game in which quoits are tossed at a stake in the ground in attempts to encircle it.

quokka ('kwɒkə) *n* a small wallaby of Western Australia, now rare. ORIG of Abor. origin

quondam ('kwɒndæm) *adj* (*prenominal*) of an earlier time; former. ORIG C16: from L

quorate ('kwɔ:,reɪt) *adj Brit.* consisting of or being a quorum: *the meeting was quorate.*

Quorn (kwɔ:n) *n Trademark.* a vegetable protein developed from a type of fungus and used as a meat substitute.

quorum ('kwɔ:rəm) *n* a minimum number of members in an assembly, etc., required to be present before any business can be transacted. ORIG C15: from L, lit.: of whom, occurring in L commissions in the formula *quorum vos...duos* (etc.) *volumus* of whom we wish that you be...two (etc.)

quota ('kwəʊtə) *n* **1** the proportional share or part that is due from, due to, or allocated to a person or group. **2** a prescribed number or quantity, as of items to be imported or students admitted to a college, etc. ORIG C17: from L *quota pars* how big a share?, from *quotus* of what number

quotable ('kwəʊtəbᵊl) *adj* apt or suitable for quotation.
▸ **,quota'bility** *n*

quotation (kwəʊ'teɪʃən) *n* **1** a phrase or passage from a book, speech, etc., remembered and repeated, usually with an acknowledgment of its source. **2** the act or habit of quoting. **3a** a cost estimate for goods or services given to a prospective client. **3b** the current market price of a commodity, security, etc. **4** *Printing.* a quad used to fill up spaces.

quotation mark *n* either of the punctuation marks used to begin or end a quotation, respectively " and " or ' and '. Also called: **inverted comma.**

quote (kwəʊt) *vb* **quotes, quoting, quoted. 1** to recite a quotation. **2** (*tr*) to put quotation marks round (a phrase, etc.). **3a** to give (a cost estimate for specified goods or services) to a prospective client. **3b** to state (the current market price) of (a security or commodity). ◆ *n* **4** an informal word for **quotation. 5** (*often pl*) an informal word for **quotation mark.** ◆ *interj* **6** an expression used to indicate that the words that follow it form a quotation. ORIG C14: from Med. L *quotāre* to assign reference numbers to passages, from L *quot* how many

quoted company *n* a company whose shares are quoted on a stock exchange.

quote-driven *adj* denoting an electronic market system, esp. for stock exchanges, in which prices are determined by quotations made by market makers or dealers. Cf. **order-driven.**

quote-unquote *interj* an expression used before or part before and part after a quotation to identify it as such, and sometimes to dissociate the writer or speaker from it.

quoth (kwəʊθ) *vb Arch.* (used with all pronouns except *thou* and *you,* and with nouns) said. ORIG OE *cwæth,* third person sing of *cwethan* to say

quotha ('kwəʊθə) *interj Arch.* an expression of mild sarcasm, used in picking up a word or phrase used by someone else. ORIG C16: from *quoth a* quoth he

quotidian (kwəʊ'tɪdɪən) *adj* **1** (esp. of fever) recurring daily. **2** commonplace. ◆ *n* **3** a fever characterized by attacks that recur daily. ORIG C14: from L *quotīdiānus,* var. of *cottīdiānus* daily

quotient ('kwəʊʃənt) *n* **1a** the result of the division of one number or quantity by another. **1b** the integral part of the result of division. **2** a ratio of two numbers or quantities to be divided. ORIG C15: from L *quotiens* how often

quo vadis ('kwəʊ 'vɑ:dɪs) whither goest thou? ORIG L from the Vulgate version of John 16:5

quo warranto ('kwəʊ wɒ'ræntəʊ) *n Law.* a proceeding initiated to determine or (formerly) a writ demanding by what authority a person claims an office, franchise, or privilege. ORIG from Med. L: by what warrant

Qur'an (kʊ'rɑ:n, -'ræn) *n* a variant spelling of **Koran.**

q.v. (denoting a cross-reference) *abbrev. for* quod vide. ORIG NL: which (word, item, etc.) see

qwerty *or* **QWERTY keyboard** ('kwɜ:tɪ) *n* the standard English language typewriter keyboard layout with the characters q, w, e, r, t, and y at the top left of the keyboard.

Rr

r *or* **R** (ɑː) *n, pl* **r's, R's,** *or* **Rs. 1** the 18th letter of the English alphabet. **2** a speech sound represented by this letter. **3** See **three Rs.**

R *symbol for:* **1** *Chem.* gas constant. **2** *Chem.* radical. **3** *Currency.* **3a** rand. **3b** rupee. **4** Réaumur (scale). **5** *Physics, electronics.* resistance. **6** roentgen *or* röntgen. **7** *Chess.* rook. **8** Royal. **9** (in the US and Australia) **9a** restricted exhibition (used to describe a category of film certified as unsuitable for viewing by anyone under the age of 18). **9b** (*as modifier*): *an R film.*

r. *abbrev. for:* **1** rare. **2** recto. **3** Also: **r** rod (unit of length). **4** ruled. **5** *Cricket.* run(s).

R. *abbrev. for:* **1** rabbi. **2** rector. **3** Regiment. **4** Regina. ORIG L: Queen **5** Republican. **6** Rex. ORIG L: King **7** River. **8** Royal.

R. *or* **r.** *abbrev. for:* **1** radius. **2** railway. **3** registered (trademark). **4** right. **5** river. **6** road. **7** rouble.

Ra[1] *the chemical symbol for* radium.

Ra[2] (rɑː) *or* **Re** ★ *n* the ancient Egyptian sun god, depicted as a man with a hawk's head surmounted by a solar disc and serpent.

RA *abbrev. for:* **1** rear admiral. **2** *Astron.* right ascension. **3** (in Britain) Royal Academician *or* Academy. **4** (in Britain) Royal Artillery.

RAAF *abbrev. for* Royal Australian Air Force.

Rabat ★ (rəˈbɑːt) *n* the capital of Morocco, on the Atlantic coast, served by the port of Salé: became a fortified military centre in the 12th century and a Corsair republic in the 17th century. Pop. (with Salé): 1 386 000 (1994 est.).

Rabaul ★ (rɑːˈbaul) *n* a port in Papua New Guinea, on NE New Britain Island, in the Bismarck Archipelago: capital of the Territory of New Guinea until 1941; almost surrounded by volcanoes. Pop.: 17 022 (1990).

Rabbath Ammon ★ (ˈræbəθ ˈæmən) *n Old Testament.* the ancient royal city of the Ammonites, on the site of modern Amman.

rabbet (ˈræbɪt) *or* **rebate** *n* **1** a recess, groove, or step, usually of rectangular section, cut into a piece of timber to receive a mating piece. ◆ *vb* **rabbets, rabbeting, rabbeted** *or* **rebates, rebating, rebated.** (*tr*) **2** to cut a rabbet in (timber). **3** to join (pieces of timber) using a rabbet. ORIG C15: from OF *rabattre* to beat down

rabbi (ˈræbaɪ) *n, pl* **rabbis. 1** the spiritual leader of a Jewish congregation; the chief religious minister of a synagogue. **2** a scholar learned in Jewish Law, esp. one authorized to teach it. ORIG Heb., from *rabh* master + -*ī* my

rabbinate (ˈræbɪnɪt) *n* **1** the position, function, or tenure of office of a rabbi. **2** rabbis collectively.

rabbinic (rəˈbɪnɪk) *or* **rabbinical** (rəˈbɪnɪkᵊl) *adj* of or relating to the rabbis, their teachings, writings, views, language, etc.
▸ **rabˈbinically** *adv*

Rabbinic (rəˈbɪnɪk) *n* the form of the Hebrew language used by the rabbis of the Middle Ages.

rabbit (ˈræbɪt) *n, pl* **rabbits** *or* **rabbit. 1** any of various common gregarious burrowing mammals of Europe and North Africa. They are closely related and similar to hares but are smaller and have shorter ears. **2** the fur of such an animal. **3** *Brit. inf.* a poor performer at a game or sport. ◆ *vb* **4** (*intr*) to hunt or shoot rabbits. **5** (*intr*) (often foll. by *on* or *away*) *Brit. inf.* to talk inconsequentially; chatter. ORIG C14: ?from Walloon *robett,* dim. of Flemish *robbe* rabbit, from ?

rabbit fever *n Pathol.* another name for **tularaemia.**

rabbit punch *n* a short sharp blow to the back of the neck that can cause loss of consciousness or even death. Austral. name: **rabbit killer.**

rabble (ˈræbᵊl) *n* **1** a disorderly crowd; mob. **2 the rabble.** *Contemptuous.* the common people. ORIG C14 (in the sense: a pack of animals): from ?

rabble-rouser *n* a person who manipulates the passions of the mob; demagogue.
▸ **ˈrabble-ˌrousing** *adj, n*

Rabelais ★ (ˈræbəˌleɪ; *French* rablɛ) *n* **François** (frɑ̃swa). ?1494–1553, French writer, noted for his *Gargantua and Pantagruel* (1534).

Rabelaisian (ˌræbəˈleɪzɪən, -ʒən) *adj* **1** of, relating to, or resembling the work of Rabelais, esp. by broad, often bawdy, humour and sharp satire. ◆ *n* **2** a student or admirer of Rabelais.
▸ **ˌRabeˈlaisianism** *n*

Rabi ★ (ˈrɑːbɪ) *n* **Isidor Isaac.** 1898–1988, US physicist, born in Austria, who devised the atomic and molecular beam resonance method of observing atomic spectra. Nobel prize for physics 1944.

rabid (ˈræbɪd, ˈreɪ-) *adj* **1** relating to or having rabies. **2** zealous; fanatical; violent; raging. ORIG C17: from L *rabidus* frenzied, from *rabere* to be mad
▸ **rabidity** (rəˈbɪdɪtɪ) *or* **ˈrabidness** *n* ▸ **ˈrabidly** *adv*

rabies (ˈreɪbiːz) *n Pathol.* an acute infectious viral disease of the nervous system transmitted by the saliva of infected animals, esp. dogs. ORIG C17: from L: madness, from *rabere* to rave
▸ **rabic** (ˈræbɪk) *or* **rabietic** (ˌreɪbɪˈɛtɪk) *adj*

Rabin ★ (ræˈbiːn) *n* **Yitzhak** (ˈjɪtzæk). 1922–95, Israeli statesman; prime minister (1974–77; 1992–95); shared Nobel peace prize 1994.

RAC *abbrev. for:* **1** Royal Armoured Corps. **2** Royal Automobile Club.

raccoon *or* **racoon** (rəˈkuːn) *n, pl* **raccoons, raccoon** *or* **racoons, racoon. 1** an omnivorous mammal, esp. the **North American raccoon,** inhabiting forests of North and Central America. Raccoons have a pointed muzzle, long tail, and greyish-black fur with black bands around the tail and across the face. **2** the fur of the raccoon. ORIG C17: from Algonquian *ärähkun,* from *ärähkuněm* he scratches with his hands

race[1] (reɪs) *n* **1** a contest of speed, as in running, etc. **2** any competition or rivalry. **3** rapid or constant onward movement: *the race of time.* **4** a rapid current of water, esp. one through a narrow channel that has a tidal range greater at one end than the other. **5** a channel of a stream, esp. one for conducting water to or from a water wheel for energy: *a mill race.* **6a** a channel or groove that contains ball bearings or roller bearings. **6b** the inner or outer cylindrical ring in a ball bearing or roller bearing. **7** *Austral. & NZ.* a narrow passage or enclosure in a sheep yard through which sheep pass individually, as to a sheep dip. **8** *Austral.* a wire tunnel through which footballers pass from the changing room onto a football field. **9** *Arch.* the span or course of life. ◆ *vb* **races, racing, raced. 10** to engage in a contest of speed with (another). **11** to cause (animals, etc.) to engage in a race: *to race pigeons.* **12** to move or go as fast as possible. **13** to run (an engine, propeller, etc.) or (of an engine, propeller, etc.) to run at high speed, esp. after reduction of the load. ◆ See also **races.** ORIG C13: from ON *rās* running

race[2] (reɪs) *n* **1** a group of people of common ancestry, distinguished from others by physical characteristics, such as hair type, colour of skin, stature, etc. **2 the human race.** human beings collectively. **3** a group of animals or plants having common characteristics that distinguish them from other members of the same species, usually forming a geographically isolated group; subspecies. **4** a group of people sharing the same interests, characteristics, etc.: *race of authors.* ORIG C16: from F, from It. *razza,* from ?

Race ★ (reɪs) *n* **Cape.** a cape at the SE extremity of Newfoundland, Canada.

★ people and places

racecard ('reɪsˌkɑːd) *n* a card at a race meeting with the races and runners, etc., printed on it.

racecourse ('reɪsˌkɔːs) *n* a long broad track, over which horses are raced. Also called (esp. US and Canad.): **racetrack.**

racehorse ('reɪsˌhɔːs) *n* a horse specially bred for racing.

raceme (rə'siːm) *n* an inflorescence in which the flowers are borne along the main stem. ORIG C18: from L *racēmus* bunch of grapes
▸ **racemose** ('ræsɪˌməʊs, -məʊz) *adj*

race meeting *n* a prearranged fixture for racing horses (or greyhounds) over a set course.

racemic (rə'siːmɪk, -'sɛm-) *adj Chem.* of, or being a mixture of dextrorotatory and laevorotatory isomers in such proportions that the mixture has no optical activity. ORIG C19: from RACEME + -IC
▸ **racemism** ('ræsɪˌmɪzəm) *n*

racer ('reɪsə) *n* **1** a person, animal, or machine that races. **2** a turntable used to traverse a heavy gun. **3** any of several slender nonvenomous North American snakes, such as the **striped racer.**

race relations *n* **1** (*functioning as pl*) the relations between members of two or more human races, esp. within a single community. **2** (*functioning as sing*) the branch of sociology concerned with such relations.

race riot *n* a riot among members of different races in the same community.

races ('reɪsɪz) *pl n* **the races.** a series of contests of speed between horses (or greyhounds) over a set course.

racetrack ('reɪsˌtræk) *n* **1** a circuit or course, esp. an oval one, used for motor racing, etc. **2** the usual US and Canad. word for **racecourse.**

raceway ('reɪsˌweɪ) *n* **1** another word for **race**[1] (senses 5, 6). **2** *Chiefly US.* a racetrack.

Rachel ★ ('reɪtʃəl) *n Old Testament.* the second wife of Jacob; mother of Joseph and Benjamin (Genesis 29–35).

rachis *or* **rhachis** ('reɪkɪs) *n, pl* **rachises, rhachises** *or* **rachides, rhachides** ('rækɪˌdiːz, 'reɪ-). **1** *Bot.* the main axis or stem of an inflorescence or compound leaf. **2** *Ornithol.* the shaft of a feather, esp. the part that carries the barbs. **3** another name for **spinal column.** ORIG C17: via NL from Gk *rhakhis* ridge
▸ **rachial, rhachial** ('reɪkɪəl) *or* **rachidial, rhachidial** (rə'kɪdɪəl) *adj*

rachitis (rə'kaɪtɪs) *n Pathol.* another name for **rickets.**
▸ **rachitic** (rə'kɪtɪk) *adj*

Rachmaninoff *or* **Rachmaninov** ★ (ræk'mænɪˌnɒf; *Russian* rax'maninəf) *n* **Sergei Vassilievich** (sɪr'gjej va'siljɪvitʃ). 1873–1943, Russian pianist and composer, in the US from 1917. Works include three symphonies, four piano concertos, operas, and piano music.

Rachmanism ('rækməˌnɪzəm) *n* extortion or exploitation by a landlord of tenants of slum property. ORIG C20: after *Perec Rachman* (1920–62), Brit. property-owner

racial ('reɪʃəl) *adj* **1** denoting or relating to the division of the human species into races on grounds of physical characteristics. **2** characteristic of any such group.
▸ **'racially** *adv*

Racine ★ (*French* rasin) *n* **Jean Baptiste** (ʒɑ̃ batist). 1639–99, French poet and dramatist. His plays include *Andromaque* (1667) and *Phèdre* (1677).

racism ('reɪsɪzəm) *or* **racialism** ('reɪʃəˌlɪzəm) *n* **1** the belief that races have distinctive cultural characteristics determined by hereditary factors and that this endows some races with an intrinsic superiority. **2** abusive or aggressive behaviour towards members of another race on the basis of such a belief.
▸ **'racist** *or* **'racialist** *n, adj*

rack[1] (ræk) *n* **1** a framework for holding, carrying, or displaying a specific load or object. **2** a toothed bar designed to engage a pinion to form a mechanism that will adjust the position of something. **3** (preceded by *the*) an instrument of torture that stretched the body of the victim. **4** a cause or state of mental or bodily stress, suffering, etc. (esp. in **on the rack**). **5** *US & Canad.* (in pool, snooker, etc.) **5a** the triangular frame used to arrange the balls for the opening shot. **5b** the balls so grouped. Brit. equivalent: **frame.** ◆ *vb* (*tr*) **6** to torture on the rack. **7** to cause great suffering to: *guilt racked his conscience.* **8** to strain or shake (something) violently: *the storm racked the town.* **9** to place or arrange in or on a rack. **10** to move (parts of machinery or a mechanism) using a toothed rack. **11** to raise (rents) exorbitantly. **12 rack one's brains.** to strain in mental effort. ORIG C14 *rekke,* prob. from MDu. *rec* framework
▸ **'racker** *n*

> **USAGE NOTE** See at **wrack**[1].

rack[2] (ræk) *n* destruction; wreck (obs. except in **go to rack and ruin**). ORIG C16: var. of WRACK[1]

rack[3] (ræk) *n* another word for **single-foot.** ORIG C16: ? based on ROCK[2]

rack[4] (ræk) *n* **1** a group of broken clouds moving in the wind. ◆ *vb* **2** (*intr*) (of clouds) to be blown along by the wind. ORIG OE *wrǣc* what is driven

rack[5] (ræk) *vb* (*tr*) to clear (wine, beer, etc.) as by siphoning it off from the dregs. ORIG C15: from OProvençal *arraca,* from *raca* dregs of grapes after pressing

rack-and-pinion *n* **1** a device for converting rotary into linear motion and vice versa, in which a gearwheel (the pinion) engages with a flat toothed bar (the rack). ◆ *adj* **2** (of a type of steering gear in motor vehicles) having a track rod with a rack along part of its length that engages with a pinion attached to the steering column.

racket[1] ('rækɪt) *n* **1** a noisy disturbance or loud commotion; clamour; din. **2** an illegal enterprise carried on for profit, such as extortion, fraud, etc. **3** *Sl.* a business or occupation: *what's your racket?* **4** *Music.* a medieval woodwind instrument of deep bass pitch. ◆ *vb* **5** (*intr;* often foll. by *about*) *Now rare.* to go about gaily or noisily, in search of pleasure, etc. ORIG C16: prob. imit.
▸ **'rackety** *adj*

racket[2] *or* **racquet** ('rækɪt) *n* **1** a bat consisting of an open network of strings stretched in an oval frame with a handle, used to strike a tennis ball, etc. **2** a snowshoe shaped like a tennis racket. ◆ *vb* **3** (*tr*) to strike (a ball, etc.) with a racket. ◆ See also **rackets.** ORIG C16: from F *raquette,* from Ar. *rāhat* palm of the hand

racketeer (ˌrækɪ'tɪə) *n* **1** a person engaged in illegal enterprises for profit. ◆ *vb* **2** (*intr*) to operate an illegal enterprise.
▸ **ˌracket'eering** *n*

racket press *n* a device consisting of a frame closed by a spring mechanism, for keeping taut the strings of a tennis racket, squash racket, etc.

rackets ('rækɪts) *n* (*functioning as sing*) **a** a game similar to squash played in a four-walled court by two or four players using rackets and a small hard ball. **b** (*as modifier*): *a rackets court.*

Rackham ★ ('rækəm) *n* **Arthur.** 1867–1939, British book illustrator, esp. of fairy tales.

rack railway *n* a steep mountain railway having a middle rail fitted with a rack that engages a pinion on the locomotive to provide traction. Also called: **cog railway.**

rack-rent *n* **1** a high rent that annually equals the value of the property upon which it is charged. **2** any extortionate rent. ◆ *vb* **3** to charge an extortionate rent for.
▸ **'rack-ˌrenter** *n*

rack saw *n Building trades.* a wide-toothed saw.

racon ('reɪkɒn) *n* another name for **radar beacon.** ORIG C20: from RA(DAR) + (BEA)CON

raconteur (ˌrækɒn'tɜː) *n* a person skilled in telling stories. ORIG C19: F, from *raconter* to tell

racoon (rə'kuːn) *n, pl* **racoons** *or* **racoon.** a variant spelling of **raccoon.**

racquet ('rækɪt) *n* a variant spelling of **racket**[2].

racy ('reɪsɪ) *adj* **racier, raciest. 1** (of a person's manner, literary style, etc.) having a distinctively lively and spirited quality. **2** having a characteristic or distinctive flavour: *a racy wine.* **3** suggestive; slightly indecent; risqué.
▸ **'racily** *adv* ▸ **'raciness** *n*

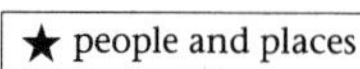

rad[1] (ræd) *n* a former unit of absorbed ionizing radiation dose equivalent to an energy absorption per unit mass of 0.01 joule per kilogram of irradiated material. ORIG C20: from RADIATION

rad[2] *symbol for* radian.

rad. *abbrev. for:* **1** radical. **2** radius.

RADA ('rɑːdə) *n* (in Britain) *acronym for* Royal Academy of Dramatic Art.

radar ('reɪdɑː) *n* **1** a method for detecting the position and velocity of a distant object. A narrow beam of extremely high-frequency radio pulses is transmitted and reflected by the object back to the transmitter. The direction of the reflected beam and the time between transmission and reception of a pulse determine the position of the object. **2** the equipment used in such detection. ORIG C20: *ra(dio) d(etecting) a(nd) r(anging)*

radar astronomy *n* the use of radar to map the surfaces of the planets, their satellites, and other bodies.

radar beacon *n* a device for transmitting a coded radar signal in response to a signal from an aircraft or ship. The coded signal is then used by the navigator to determine his position. Also called: **racon.**

radarscope ('reɪdɑːˌskəʊp) *n* a cathode-ray oscilloscope on which radar signals can be viewed.

radar trap *n* a device using radar to detect motorists who exceed the speed limit.

Radcliffe ★ ('rædklɪf) *n* **Ann.** 1764–1823, British novelist, noted for her Gothic romance *The Mysteries of Udolpho* (1794).

raddle ('rædᵊl) *vb* **raddles, raddling, raddled. 1** (*tr*) *Chiefly Brit.* to paint (the face) with rouge. ◆ *n, vb* **2** another word for **ruddle.** ORIG C16: var. of RUDDLE

raddled ('rædᵊld) *adj* (esp. of a person) unkempt or rundown in appearance.

Radetzky ★ (*German* ra'dɛtski) *n* Count **Joseph** ('joːzɛf). 1766–1858, Austrian field marshal: served in the war against Sardinia (1848–49): governor of Lombardy-Venetia in N Italy (1849-57).

radial ('reɪdɪəl) *adj* **1** (of lines, etc.) emanating from a common central point; arranged like the radii of a circle. **2** of, like, or relating to a radius or ray. **3** short for **radial-ply. 4** *Anat.* of or relating to the radius or forearm. **5** *Astron.* (of velocity) in a direction along the line of sight of a celestial object and measured by means of the red shift (or blue shift) of the spectral lines of the object. ◆ *n* **6** a radial part or section. ORIG C16: from Med. L *radiālis,* from RADIUS
▸ **'radially** *adv*

radial engine *n* an internal-combustion engine having a number of cylinders arranged about a central crankcase.

radial-ply *adj* (of a motor tyre) having the fabric cords in the outer casing running radially to enable the sidewalls to be flexible.

radial symmetry *n* a type of structure of an organism in which a vertical cut through the axis in any of two or more planes produces two halves that are mirror images of each other. Cf. **bilateral symmetry.**

radian ('reɪdɪən) *n* an SI unit of plane angle; the angle between two radii of a circle that cut off on the circumference an arc equal in length to the radius. 1 radian is equivalent to 57.296 degrees. Symbol: rad. ORIG C19: from RADIUS

radiance ('reɪdɪəns) *or* **radiancy** *n, pl* **radiances** *or* **radiancies. 1** the quality or state of being radiant. **2** a measure of the amount of electromagnetic radiation leaving or arriving at a point on a surface.

radiant ('reɪdɪənt) *adj* **1** sending out rays of light; bright; shining. **2** characterized by health, happiness, etc.: *a radiant smile.* **3** emitted or propagated by or as radiation; radiated: *radiant heat.* **4** sending out heat by radiation: *a radiant heater.* **5** *Physics.* (of a physical quantity in photometry) evaluated by absolute energy measurements: *radiant flux.* ◆ *n* **6** a point or object that emits radiation, esp. the part of a heater that gives out heat. **7** *Astron.* the point in the sky from which a meteor shower appears to emanate. ORIG C15: from L *radiāre* to shine, from *radius* ray of light
▸ **'radiancy** *n* ▸ **'radiantly** *adv*

radiant energy *n* energy that is emitted or propagated in the form of particles or electromagnetic radiation.

radiant heat *n* heat transferred in the form of electromagnetic radiation rather than by conduction or convection; infrared radiation.

radiata pine (ˌreɪdɪ'ɑːtə) *n* a pine tree grown in Australia and New Zealand to produce building timber. Often shortened to **radiata.** ORIG from NL

radiate *vb* ('reɪdɪˌeɪt), **radiates, radiating, radiated. 1** Also: **eradiate.** to emit (heat, light, or other forms of radiation) or (of heat, light, etc.) to be emitted as radiation. **2** (*intr*) (of lines, beams, etc.) to spread out from a centre or be arranged in a radial pattern. **3** (*tr*) (of a person) to show (happiness, etc.) to a great degree. ◆ *adj* ('reɪdɪɪt, -ˌeɪt). **4** having rays; radiating. **5** (of a capitulum) consisting of ray flowers. **6** (of animals) showing radial symmetry. ORIG C17: from L *radiāre* to emit rays
▸ **'radiative** *adj*

radiation (ˌreɪdɪ'eɪʃən) *n* **1** *Physics.* **1a** the emission or transfer of radiant energy as particles, electromagnetic waves, sound, etc. **1b** the particles, etc., emitted, esp. the particles and gamma rays emitted in nuclear decay. **2** Also called: **radiation therapy.** *Med.* treatment using a radioactive substance. **3** the act, state, or process of radiating or being radiated.
▸ **ˌradi'ational** *adj*

radiation sickness *n Pathol.* illness caused by overexposure of the body to ionizing radiations from radioactive material or X-rays.

radiator ('reɪdɪˌeɪtə) *n* **1** a device for heating a room, building, etc., consisting of a series of pipes through which hot water or steam passes. **2** a device for cooling an internal-combustion engine, consisting of thin-walled tubes through which water passes. **3** *Electronics.* the part of an aerial or transmission line that radiates electromagnetic waves.

radical ('rædɪkᵊl) *adj* **1** of, relating to, or characteristic of the basic or inherent constitution of a person or thing; fundamental: *a radical fault.* **2** concerned with or tending to concentrate on fundamental aspects of a matter; searching or thoroughgoing: *radical thought.* **3** favouring or tending to produce extreme or fundamental changes in political, economic, or social conditions, institutions, etc.: *a radical party.* **4** *Med.* (of treatment) aimed at removing the source of a disease: *radical surgery.* **5** *Sl., chiefly US.* very good; excellent. **6** of or arising from the root or the base of the stem of a plant: *radical leaves.* **7** *Maths.* of, relating to, or containing roots of numbers or quantities. **8** *Linguistics.* of or relating to the root of a word. ◆ *n* **9** a person who favours extreme or fundamental change in existing institutions or in political, social, or economic conditions. **10** *Maths.* a root of a number or quantity, such as $\sqrt[3]{5}$. **11** *Chem.* **11a** short for **free radical. 11b** another name for **group** (sense 9). **12** *Linguistics.* another word for **root**[1] (sense 8). ORIG C14: from LL *rādīcālis* having roots, from L *rādix* a root
▸ **'radicalness** *n*

radicalism ('rædɪkəˌlɪzəm) *n* **1** the principles, desires, or practices of political radicals. **2** a radical movement, esp. in politics.
▸ **ˌradical'istic** *adj* ▸ **ˌradical'istically** *adv*

radically ('rædɪkəlɪ) *adv* thoroughly; completely; fundamentally: *to alter radically.*

radical sign *n* the symbol √ placed before a number or quantity to indicate the extraction of a root, esp. a square root. The value of a higher root is indicated by a raised digit in front of the symbol, as in $\sqrt[3]{}$.

radicand ('rædɪˌkænd, ˌrædɪ'kænd) *n* a number or quantity from which a root is to be extracted, usually preceded by a radical sign: 3 *is the radicand of* $\sqrt{3}$. ORIG C20: from L *rādīcandum,* lit.: that which is to be rooted, from *rādīcāre,* from *rādīx* root

radicchio (ræ'diːkɪəʊ) *n, pl* **radicchios.** an Italian variety of chicory, having purple leaves streaked with white that are eaten raw in salads.

radices ('reɪdɪˌsiːz) *n* a plural of **radix**.

radicle ('rædɪkᵊl) *n* **1** *Bot.* **1a** the part of the embryo of seed-bearing plants that develops into the main root. **1b** a very small root or rootlike part. **2** *Anat.* any bodily structure resembling a rootlet, esp. one of the smallest branches of a vein or nerve. **3** *Chem.* a variant spelling of **radical** (sense 11). ORIG C18: from L *rādīcula*, from *rādīx* root

Radiguet ★ (*French* radigɛ) *n* **Raymond** (rɛmɔ̃). 1903–23, French novelist; the author of *The Devil in the Flesh* (1923).

radii ('reɪdɪˌaɪ) *n* a plural of **radius**.

radio ('reɪdɪəʊ) *n, pl* **radios. 1** the use of electromagnetic waves, lying in the radio-frequency range, for broadcasting, two-way communications, etc. **2** an electronic device designed to receive, demodulate, and amplify radio signals from sound broadcasting stations, etc. **3** the broadcasting, content, etc., of radio programmes: *he thinks radio is poor these days.* **4** the occupation or profession concerned with any aspect of the broadcasting of radio programmes. **5** short for **radiotelegraph, radiotelegraphy,** or **radiotelephone. 6** (*modifier*) **6a** of, relating to, or sent by radio signals: *a radio station.* **6b** of, concerned with, using, or operated by radio frequencies: *radio spectrum.* **6c** relating to or produced for radio: *radio drama.* ◆ *vb* **radios, radioing, radioed. 7** to transmit (a message, etc.) to (a person, etc.) by means of radio waves. ◆ Also called (esp. Brit.): **wireless.** ORIG C20: short for *radiotelegraphy*

radio- *combining form.* **1** denoting radio, broadcasting, or radio frequency: *radiogram.* **2** indicating radioactivity or radiation: *radiocarbon; radiochemistry.* ORIG from F, from L *radius* ray

radioactive (ˌreɪdɪəʊ'æktɪv) *adj* exhibiting, using, or concerned with radioactivity.
▸ **ˌradio'actively** *adv*

radioactive dating *n* another term for **radiometric dating.**

radioactive decay *n* disintegration of a nucleus that occurs spontaneously or as a result of electron capture. Also called: **disintegration.**

radioactive series *n Physics.* a series of nuclides each of which undergoes radioactive decay into the next member of the series, ending with a stable element, usually lead.

radioactive tracer *n Med.* See **tracer** (sense 3).

radioactive waste *n* any waste material containing radionuclides. Also called: **nuclear waste.**

radioactivity (ˌreɪdɪəʊæk'tɪvɪtɪ) *n* the spontaneous emission of radiation from atomic nuclei. The radiation can consist of alpha, beta, or gamma radiation.

radio astronomy *n* a branch of astronomy in which a radio telescope is used to detect and analyse radio signals received on earth from radio sources in space.

radio beacon *n* a fixed radio transmitting station that broadcasts a characteristic signal by means of which a vessel or aircraft can determine its bearing or position.

radiobiology (ˌreɪdɪəʊbaɪ'ɒlədʒɪ) *n* the branch of biology concerned with the effects of radiation on living organisms and the study of biological processes using radioactive substances as tracers.
▸ **radiobiological** (ˌreɪdɪəʊˌbaɪə'lɒdʒɪkᵊl) *adj* ▸ **ˌradioˌbio'logically** *adv* ▸ **ˌradiobi'ologist** *n*

radiocarbon (ˌreɪdɪəʊ'kɑːbᵊn) *n* a radioactive isotope of carbon, esp. carbon-14. See **carbon** (sense 1).

radiocarbon dating *n* See **carbon dating.**

radiochemistry (ˌreɪdɪəʊ'kɛmɪstrɪ) *n* the chemistry of radioactive elements and their compounds.
▸ **ˌradio'chemical** *adj* ▸ **ˌradio'chemist** *n*

radio compass *n* any navigational device that gives a bearing by determining the direction of incoming radio waves transmitted from a particular radio station or beacon. See also **goniometer** (sense 2).

radio control *n* remote control by means of radio signals from a transmitter.
▸ **'radio-con'trolled** *adj*

radioelement (ˌreɪdɪəʊ'ɛlɪmənt) *n* an element that is naturally radioactive.

radio frequency *n* **1a** any frequency that lies in the range 10 kilohertz to 300 000 megahertz and can be used for broadcasting. Abbrevs.: **rf, RF. 1b** (*as modifier*): *a radio-frequency amplifier.* **2** the frequency transmitted by a particular radio station.

radio galaxy *n* a galaxy that is a strong emitter of radio waves.

radiogram ('reɪdɪəʊˌgræm) *n* **1** *Brit.* a unit comprising a radio and record player. **2** a message transmitted by radiotelegraphy. **3** another name for **radiograph.**

radiograph ('reɪdɪəʊˌgrɑːf) *n* an image produced on a specially sensitized photographic film or plate by radiation, usually by X-rays or gamma rays.

radiography (ˌreɪdɪ'ɒgrəfɪ) *n* the production of radiographs of opaque objects for use in medicine, surgery, industry, etc.
▸ **ˌradi'ographer** *n* ▸ **radiographic** (ˌreɪdɪəʊ'græfɪk) *adj* ▸ **ˌradio'graphically** *adv*

radioimmunoassay ('reɪdɪəʊˌɪmjʊnəʊ'æseɪ) *n* a sensitive immunological assay, making use of radioactive labelling, of such things as hormone levels in the blood.

radioisotope (ˌreɪdɪəʊ'aɪsətəʊp) *n* a radioactive isotope.
▸ **radioisotopic** (ˌreɪdɪəʊˌaɪsə'tɒpɪk) *adj*

radiolarian (ˌreɪdɪəʊ'lɛərɪən) *n* any of various marine protozoans typically having a siliceous shell and stiff radiating cytoplasmic projections. ORIG C19: from NL *Radiolaria,* from LL *radiolus* little sunbeam, from L *radius* ray

radiology (ˌreɪdɪ'ɒlədʒɪ) *n* the use of X-rays and radioactive substances in the diagnosis and treatment of disease.
▸ **ˌradi'ologist** *n*

radiometer (ˌreɪdɪ'ɒmɪtə) *n* any instrument for the detection or measurement of radiant energy.
▸ **radiometric** (ˌreɪdɪəʊ'mɛtrɪk) *adj* ▸ **ˌradi'ometry** *n*

radiometric dating *n* any method of dating material based on the decay of its constituent radioactive atoms, such as potassium-argon dating or rubidium-strontium dating. Also called: **radioactive dating.**

radiopager ('reɪdɪəʊˌpeɪdʒə) *n* a small radio receiver fitted with a buzzer to alert a person to telephone their home, office, etc., to receive a message.
▸ **'radioˌpaging** *n*

radiopaque (ˌreɪdɪəʊ'peɪk) *or* **radio-opaque** *adj* not permitting X-rays or other radiation to pass through.
▸ **radiopacity** (ˌreɪdɪəʊ'pæsɪtɪ) *or* **ˌradio-o'pacity** *n*

radio receiver *n* an apparatus that receives incoming modulated radio waves and converts them into sound.

radioscopy (ˌreɪdɪ'ɒskəpɪ) *n* another word for **fluoroscopy.**
▸ **radioscopic** (ˌreɪdɪəʊ'skɒpɪk) *adj* ▸ **ˌradio'scopically** *adv*

radiosonde ('reɪdɪəʊˌsɒnd) *n* an airborne instrument to send meteorological information back to earth by radio. ORIG C20: RADIO- + F *sonde* sounding line

radio source *n* a celestial object, such as a supernova remnant or quasar, that is a source of radio waves.

radio spectrum *n* the range of electromagnetic frequencies used in radio transmission, between 10 kilohertz and 300 000 megahertz.

radio star *n* a former name for **radio source.**

radiotelegraphy (ˌreɪdɪəʊtɪ'lɛgrəfɪ) *n* a type of telegraphy in which messages (formerly in Morse code) are transmitted by radio waves.
▸ **ˌradio'teleˌgraph** *vb, n* ▸ **radiotelegraphic** (ˌreɪdɪəʊˌtɛlɪ'græfɪk) *adj*

radiotelephone (ˌreɪdɪəʊ'tɛlɪˌfəʊn) *n* **1** a device for communications by means of radio waves rather than by transmitting along wires or cables. ◆ *vb* **radiotelephones, radiotelephoning, radiotelephoned. 2** to telephone (a person) by radiotelephone.
▸ **radiotelephonic** (ˌreɪdɪəʊˌtɛlɪ'fɒnɪk) *adj* ▸ **radiotelephony** (ˌreɪdɪəʊtɪ'lɛfənɪ) *n*

radio telescope *n* an instrument consisting of an antenna or system of antennas connected to one or more radio receivers, used in radio astonomy to detect and analyse radio waves from space.

radioteletype (ˌreɪdɪəʊ'tɛlɪˌtaɪp) *n* **1** a teleprinter that transmits or receives information by means of radio waves. **2** a network of such devices widely used for communicating news, messages, etc. Abbrevs.: **RTT, RTTY.**

radiotherapy (ˌreɪdɪəʊ'θɛrəpɪ) *n* the treatment of disease by means of alpha or beta particles emitted from an implanted or ingested radioisotope, or by means of a beam of high-energy radiation. Cf. **chemotherapy.**
▸ **radiotherapeutic** (ˌreɪdɪəʊˌθɛrə'pjuːtɪk) *adj* ▸ **ˌradio'therapist** *n*

radio wave *n* an electromagnetic wave of radio frequency.

radish ('rædɪʃ) *n* **1** any of a genus of plants of Europe and Asia, with petals arranged like a cross, cultivated for their edible roots. **2** the root of this plant, which has a pungent taste and is eaten raw in salads. ORIG OE *rǣdīc,* from L *rādīx* root

radium ('reɪdɪəm) *n* **a** a highly radioactive luminescent white element of the alkaline earth group of metals. It occurs in pitchblende and other uranium ores. Symbol: Ra; atomic no.: 88; half-life of most stable isotope, ^{226}Ra: 1620 years. **b** (*as modifier*): *radium needle.* ORIG C20: from L *radius* ray

radium therapy *n* treatment of disease, esp. cancer, by exposing affected tissues to radiation from radium.

radius ('reɪdɪəs) *n, pl* **radii** *or* **radiuses. 1** a straight line joining the centre of a circle or sphere to any point on the circumference or surface. **2** the length of this line, usually denoted by the symbol *r.* **3** *Anat.* the outer, slightly shorter of the two bones of the human forearm, extending from the elbow to the wrist. **4** a corresponding bone in other vertebrates. **5** any of the veins of an insect's wing. **6** a group of ray flowers, occurring in such plants as the daisy. **7a** any radial or radiating part, such as a spoke. **7b** (*as modifier*): *a radius arm.* **8** a circular area of a size indicated by the length of its radius: *the police stopped every lorry within a radius of four miles.* **9** the operational limit of a ship, aircraft, etc. ORIG C16: from L: rod, ray, spoke

radix ('reɪdɪks) *n, pl* **radices** *or* **radixes. 1** *Maths.* any number that is the base of a number system or of a system of logarithms: *10 is the radix of the decimal system.* **2** *Biol.* the root or point of origin of a part or organ. **3** *Linguistics.* a less common word for **root**[1] (sense 8). ORIG C16: from L *rādīx* root

radix point *n* a point, such as the decimal point in the decimal system, separating the integral part of a number from the fractional part.

Radnorshire ('rædnəˌʃɪə, -ʃə) *or* **Radnor** ★ *n* (until 1974) a county of E Wales, now part of Powys.

Radom ★ (*Polish* 'radɔm) *n* a city in E Poland: under Austria from 1795 to 1815 and Russia from 1815 to 1918. Pop.: 232 300 (1995 est.).

radome ('reɪdəʊm) *n* a protective housing for a radar antenna made from a material that is transparent to radio waves. ORIG C20: RA(DAR) + DOME

radon ('reɪdɒn) *n* a colourless radioactive element of the rare gas group, the most stable isotope of which, radon-222, is a decay product of radium. Symbol: Rn; atomic no.: 86; half-life of ^{222}Rn: 3.82 days. ORIG C20: from RADIUM + -ON

radula ('rædjʊlə) *n, pl* **radulae** (-ˌliː). a horny tooth-bearing strip on the tongue of molluscs that is used for rasping food. ORIG C19: from LL: a scraping iron, from L *rādere* to scrape
▸ **'radular** *adj*

Raeburn ★ ('reɪˌbɜːn) *n* Sir **Henry.** 1756–1823, Scottish portrait painter.

RAF (*Not standard* ræf) *abbrev. for* Royal Air Force.

Rafferty ('ræfətɪ) *or* **Rafferty's rules** *pl n Austral. & NZ sl.* no rules at all. ORIG C20: from ?

raffia *or* **raphia** ('ræfɪə) *n* **1** a palm tree, native to Madagascar, that has large plumelike leaves, the stalks of which yield a useful fibre. **2** the fibre obtained from this plant, used for weaving, etc. **3** any of several related palms or the fibre obtained from them. ORIG C19: from Malagasy

raffish ('ræfɪʃ) *adj* **1** careless or unconventional in dress, manners, etc.; rakish. **2** tawdry; flashy; vulgar. ORIG C19: from *raff* rubbish, rabble
▸ **'raffishly** *adv* ▸ **'raffishness** *n*

raffle ('ræfᵊl) *n* **1a** a lottery in which the prizes are goods rather than money. **1b** (*as modifier*): *a raffle ticket.* ◆ *vb* **raffles, raffling, raffled. 2** (*tr;* often foll. by *off*) to dispose of (goods) in a raffle. ORIG C14 (a dice game): from OF, from ?
▸ **'raffler** *n*

Raffles ★ ('ræfᵊlz) *n* Sir **Thomas Stamford.** 1781–1826, British colonial administrator: founded Singapore (1819) as a station for the British East India Company.

rafflesia (ræ'fliːzɪə) *n* any of various tropical Asian parasitic leafless plants, the flowers of which grow up to 45 cm (18 inches) across, smell of putrid meat, and are pollinated by carrion flies. ORIG C19: NL, after Sir Stamford RAFFLES, who discovered it

Rafsanjani ★ (ˌræfsæn'dʒɑːnɪ) *n* **Ali Akbar Hashemi.** born 1934, Iranian politician: president of Iran (1989–97).

raft[1] (rɑːft) *n* **1** a buoyant platform of logs, planks, etc., used as a vessel or moored platform. **2** a thick slab of reinforced concrete laid over soft ground to provide a foundation for a building. ◆ *vb* **3** to convey on or travel by raft, or make a raft from. ORIG C15: from ON *raptr* RAFTER

raft[2] (rɑːft) *n Inf.* a large collection or amount: *a raft of old notebooks discovered in a cupboard.*

rafter ('rɑːftə) *n* any one of a set of parallel sloping beams that form the framework of a roof. ORIG OE *ræfter*

RAFVR *abbrev. for* Royal Air Force Volunteer Reserve.

rag[1] (ræg) *n* **1a** a small piece of cloth, such as one torn from a discarded garment, or such pieces of cloth collectively. **1b** (*as modifier*): *a rag doll.* **2** a fragmentary piece of any material; scrap; shred. **3** *Inf.* a newspaper, esp. one considered as worthless, sensational, etc. **4** *Inf.* an item of clothing. **5** *Inf.* a handkerchief. **6** *Brit. sl., esp. naval.* a flag or ensign. **7 from rags to riches.** *Inf.* **7a** from poverty to great wealth. **7b** (*as modifier*): *a rags-to-riches tale.* ORIG C14: prob. back formation from RAGGED from OE *raggig*

rag[2] (ræg) *vb* **rags, ragging, ragged.** (*tr*) **1** to draw attention facetiously and persistently to the shortcomings of (a person). **2** *Brit.* to play rough practical jokes on. ◆ *n* **3** *Brit.* a boisterous practical joke. **4** (in British universities, etc.) **4a** a period in which various events are organized to raise money for charity. **4b** (*as modifier*): *rag day.* ORIG C18: from ?

rag[3] (ræg) *Jazz.* ◆ *n* **1** a piece of ragtime music. ◆ *vb* **rags, ragging, ragged. 2** (*tr*) to compose or perform in ragtime. ORIG C20: from RAGTIME

raga ('rɑːgə) *n* (in Indian music) **1** any of several conventional patterns of melody and rhythm that form the basis for freely interpreted compositions. **2** a composition based on one of these patterns. ORIG C18: from Sansk. *rāga* tone, colour

ragamuffin ('rægəˌmʌfɪn) *n* **1** a ragged unkempt person, esp. a child. **2** another name for **ragga.** ORIG C14 *Ragamoffyn,* a demon in the poem *Piers Plowman* (1393); prob. based on RAG[1]

rag-and-bone man *n Brit.* a man who buys and sells discarded clothing, etc. US equivalent: **junkman.**

ragbag ('rægˌbæg) *n* **1** a bag for storing odd rags. **2** a confused assortment; jumble.

ragbolt ('rægˌbəʊlt) *n* a bolt that has angled projections on it to prevent it working loose.

rage (reɪdʒ) *n* **1** intense anger; fury. **2** violent movement or action, esp. of the sea, wind, etc. **3** great intensity of hunger or other feelings. **4** aggressive behaviour associated with a specified environment or activity: *road rage; school rage.* **5** a fashion or craze (esp. in **all the rage**). **6** *Austral. & NZ inf.* a dance or party. ◆ *vb* **rages, raging, raged.** (*intr*) **7** to feel or exhibit intense anger. **8** (esp. of storms, fires, etc.) to move or surge with great violence. **9** (esp. of a disease) to spread rapidly and uncontrollably. **10** *Aus-*

tral. & NZ inf. to have a good time. ORIG C13: via OF from L *rabiēs* madness

ragga ('rægə) *n* a dance-oriented style of reggae. Also called: **ragamuffin**. ORIG C20: shortened from RAGAMUFFIN

ragged ('rægɪd) *adj* **1** (of clothes) worn to rags; tattered. **2** (of a person) dressed in tattered clothes. **3** having a neglected or unkempt appearance: *ragged weeds*. **4** having a rough or uneven surface or edge; jagged. **5** uneven or irregular: *a ragged beat; a ragged shout*. ORIG C13: prob. from *ragge* RAG[1]
▸ **'raggedly** *adv* ▸ **'raggedness** *n*

ragged robin *n* a plant related to the carnation family and native to Europe and Asia, that has pink or white flowers with ragged petals. See also **catchfly**.

raggedy ('rægɪdɪ) *adj Inf., chiefly US & Canad.* somewhat ragged; tattered: *a raggedy doll*.

ragi, raggee, *or* **raggy** ('rægɪ) *n* a cereal grass, cultivated in Africa and Asia for its edible grain. ORIG C18: from Hindi

raglan ('ræglən) *n* **1** a coat, jumper, etc., with sleeves that continue to the collar instead of having armhole seams. ◆ *adj* **2** cut in this design: *a raglan sleeve*. ORIG C19: after Lord RAGLAN

Raglan ★ ('ræglən) *n* **Fitzroy James Henry Somerset,** 1st Baron Raglan. 1788–1855, British field marshal: commanded British troops (1854–55) in the Crimean War.

ragout (ræ'gu:) *n* **1** a richly seasoned stew of meat and vegetables. ◆ *vb* **ragouts** (-'gu:z), **ragouting** (-'gu:ɪŋ), **ragouted** (-'gu:d). **2** (*tr*) to make into a ragout. ORIG C17: from F, from *ragoûter* to stimulate the appetite again, from *ra-* RE- + *goûter* from L *gustāre* to taste

rag-rolling *n* a decorating technique in which paint is applied with a roughly folded cloth in order to create a marbled effect.

ragtag ('ræg,tæg) *n Derog.* the common people; rabble (esp. in **ragtag and bobtail**). ORIG C19: from RAG[1] + TAG[1]

ragtime ('ræg,taɪm) *n* a style of jazz piano music, developed by Scott Joplin around 1900, having a two-four rhythm base and a syncopated melody. ORIG C20: prob. from RAGGED + TIME

rag trade *n Inf.* the clothing business.

Ragusa ★ (*Italian* ra'gu:za) *n* **1** an industrial town in SE Sicily. Pop.: 68 850 (1990). **2** the Italian name (until 1918) for **Dubrovnik**.

ragweed ('ræg,wi:d) *n* a North American plant of the composite family such as the **common ragweed**. Its green tassel-like flowers produce large amounts of pollen, which causes hay fever. Also called: **ambrosia**.

ragworm ('ræg,wɜ:m) *n* any polychaete worm living chiefly in burrows in sand and having a flattened body with a row of fleshy lateral appendages along each side. US name: **clamworm**.

ragwort ('ræg,wɜ:t) *n* any of several European plants of the composite family that have yellow daisy-like flowers. See also **groundsel**.

rah (rɑ:) *interj Inf., chiefly US.* short for **hurrah**.

rai (raɪ) *n* a type of Algerian popular music based on traditional Algerian music influenced by modern Western pop. ORIG C20: Ar., lit.: opinion

raid (reɪd) *n* **1** a sudden surprise attack. **2** a surprise visit by police searching for criminals or illicit goods: *a fraud-squad raid*. ◆ *vb* **3** to make a raid against (a person, thing, etc.). **4** to sneak into (a place) in order to take something, steal, etc.: *raiding the larder*. ◆ See also **bear raid, dawn raid, ram raid**. ORIG C15: Scot. dialect, from OE *rād* military expedition
▸ **'raider** *n*

rail[1] (reɪl) *n* **1** a horizontal bar of wood, etc., supported by vertical posts, functioning as a fence, barrier, etc. **2** a horizontal bar fixed to a wall on which to hang things: *a picture rail*. **3** a horizontal framing member in a door. Cf. **stile**[2]. **4** short for **railing. 5** one of a pair of parallel bars laid on a track, roadway, etc., that serve as a guide and running surface for the wheels of a train, tramcar, etc. **6a** short for **railway. 6b** (*as modifier*): *rail transport*. **7** *Naut.* a trim for finishing the top of a bulwark. **8 off the rails. 8a** into or in a state of disorder. **8b** eccentric or mad. ◆ *vb* (*tr*) **9** to provide with a rail or railings. **10** (usually foll. by *in* or *off*) to fence (an area) with rails. ORIG C13: from OF *raille* rod, from L *rēgula* ruler

rail[2] (reɪl) *vb* (*intr;* foll. by *at* or *against*) to complain bitterly or vehemently. ORIG C15: from OF *railler* to mock, from OProvençal *ralhar* to chatter, from LL *ragere* to yell
▸ **'railer** *n*

rail[3] (reɪl) *n* any of various small cranelike wading marsh birds with short wings and neck, long legs, and dark plumage. ORIG C15: from OF *raale,* ?from L *rādere* to scrape

railcar ('reɪl,kɑ:) *n* a passenger-carrying railway vehicle consisting of a single coach with its own power unit.

railcard ('reɪl,kɑ:d) *n Brit.* a card issued to students or senior citizens to entitle them to cheap rail fares.

railhead ('reɪl,hɛd) *n* **1** a terminal of a railway. **2** the farthest point reached by completed track on an unfinished railway.

railing ('reɪlɪŋ) *n* **1** (*often pl*) a fence, balustrade, or barrier that consists of rails supported by posts. **2** rails collectively or material for making rails.

raillery ('reɪlərɪ) *n, pl* **railleries. 1** light-hearted satire or ridicule; banter. **2** a bantering remark. ORIG C17: from F, from *railler* to tease; see RAIL[2]

railroad ('reɪl,rəʊd) *n* **1** the usual US word for **railway**. ◆ *vb* **2** (*tr*) *Inf.* to force (a person) into (an action) with haste or by unfair means.

railway ('reɪl,weɪ) *or US* **railroad** *n* **1** a permanent track composed of a line of parallel metal rails fixed to sleepers, for transport of passengers and goods in trains. **2** any track for the wheels of a vehicle to run on: *a cable railway*. **3** the entire equipment, rolling stock, buildings, property, and system of tracks used in such a transport system. **4** the organization responsible for operating a railway network. **5** (*modifier*) of, relating to, or used on a railway: *a railway engine*.

raiment ('reɪmənt) *n Arch. or poetic.* attire; clothing. ORIG C15: from *arrayment,* from OF *areement;* see ARRAY

rain (reɪn) *n* **1a** precipitation from clouds in the form of drops of water, formed by the condensation of water vapour in the atmosphere. **1b** a fall of rain; shower. **1c** (*in combination*): *a raindrop*. **2** a large quantity of anything falling rapidly or in quick succession: *a rain of abuse*. **3 (come) rain or (come) shine.** regardless of the weather or circumstances. **4 right as rain.** *Brit. inf.* perfectly all right. ◆ *vb* **5** (*intr;* with *it* as subject) to be the case that rain is falling. **6** (often with *it* as subject) to fall or cause to fall like rain. **7** (*tr*) to bestow in large measure: *to rain abuse on someone*. **8 rained off.** cancelled or postponed on account of rain. US and Canad. term: **rained out**. ◆ See also **rains**. ORIG OE *regn*
▸ **'rainless** *adj*

rainbird ('reɪn,bɜ:d) *n* any of various birds whose cry is supposed to portend rain, such as the green woodpecker in Britain and Burchell's coucal in South Africa.

rainbow ('reɪn,bəʊ) *n* **1a** a bow-shaped display in the sky of the colours of the spectrum, caused by the refraction and reflection of the sun's rays through rain. **1b** (*as modifier*): *a rainbow pattern*. **2** an illusory hope: *to chase rainbows*. **3** (*modifier*) of or relating to a political grouping together by several minorities, esp. of different races: *the rainbow coalition*.

Rainbow Bridge ★ *n* a natural stone bridge over a creek in SE Utah. Height: 94 m (309 ft). Span: 85 m (278 ft).

rainbow nation *n S. African.* an epithet, alluding to its multiracial population, of **South Africa**. ORIG C20: coined by Nelson MANDELA following the end of apartheid

rainbow trout *n* a freshwater trout of North American origin, marked with many black spots and two longitudinal red stripes.

rain check *n US & Canad.* **1** a ticket stub for a baseball game that allows readmission on a future date if the event is cancelled because of rain. **2** the deferral of acceptance of an offer. **3 take a rain check.** *Inf.* to accept or request the postponement of an offer.

raincoat (ˈreɪnˌkəʊt) *n* a coat made of a waterproof material.

rainfall (ˈreɪnˌfɔːl) *n* **1** precipitation in the form of raindrops. **2** *Meteorol.* the amount of precipitation in a specified place and time.

rainforest (ˈreɪnˌfɒrɪst) *n* dense forest found in tropical areas of heavy rainfall.

rain gauge *n* an instrument for measuring rainfall or snowfall, consisting of a cylinder covered by a funnel-like lid.

Rainier ★ (ˈreɪnɪə; reɪˈnɪə, rə-) *n* **Mount.** a mountain in W Washington State: the highest mountain in the state and in the Cascade Range. Height: 4392 m (14 410 ft).

Rainier III ★ (ˈreɪnɪˌeɪ; *French* rɛnje) *n* full name *Rainier Louis Henri Maxence Bertrand de Grimaldi.* born 1923, ruling prince of Monaco from 1949.

rainproof (ˈreɪnˌpruːf) *adj* **1** Also: **ˈrainˌtight.** (of garments, materials, etc.) impermeable to rainwater. ◆ *vb* **2** (*tr*) to make rainproof.

rains (reɪnz) *pl n* **the rains.** the season of heavy rainfall, esp. in the tropics.

rain shadow *n* the relatively dry area on the leeward side of high ground in the path of rain-bearing winds.

rainstorm (ˈreɪnˌstɔːm) *n* a storm with heavy rain.

rainwater (ˈreɪnˌwɔːtə) *n* pure water from rain (as distinguished from spring water, tap water, etc., which may contain minerals and impurities).

rainy (ˈreɪnɪ) *adj* **rainier, rainiest. 1** characterized by a large rainfall: *a rainy climate.* **2** wet or showery; bearing rain.
▸ **ˈrainily** *adv* ▸ **ˈraininess** *n*

rainy day *n* a future time of need, esp. financial.

Rais *or* **Retz** ★ (*French* rɛ) *n* **Gilles de** (ʒil də). 1404–40, French nobleman who fought with Joan of Arc: marshal of France (1429–40). He was executed for the torture and murder of more than 140 children.

raise (reɪz) *vb* **raises, raising, raised.** (*mainly tr*) **1** to move or elevate to a higher position or level; lift. **2** to set or place in an upright position. **3** to construct, build, or erect: *to raise a barn.* **4** to increase in amount, size, value, etc.: *to raise prices.* **5** to increase in degree, strength, intensity, etc.: *to raise one's voice.* **6** to advance in rank or status; promote. **7** to arouse or awaken from sleep or death. **8** to stir up or incite; activate: *to raise a mutiny.* **9 raise Cain** (*or* **the devil, hell, the roof,** etc.). **9a** to create a disturbance, esp. by making a great noise. **9b** to protest vehemently. **10** to give rise to; cause or provoke: *to raise a smile.* **11** to put forward for consideration: *to raise a question.* **12** to cause to assemble or gather together: *to raise an army.* **13** to grow or cause to grow: *to raise a crop.* **14** to bring up; rear: *to raise a family.* **15** to cause to be heard or known; utter or express: *to raise a shout.* **16** to bring to an end; remove: *to raise a siege.* **17** to cause (bread, etc.) to rise, as by the addition of yeast. **18** *Poker.* to bet more than (the previous player). **19** *Bridge.* to bid (one's partner's suit) at a higher level. **20** *Naut.* to cause (something) to seem to rise above the horizon by approaching: *we raised land after 20 days.* **21** to establish radio communications with: *we raised Moscow last night.* **22** to obtain (money, funds, etc.). **23** to bring (a surface, a design, etc.) into relief; cause to project. **24** to cause (a blister, etc.) to form on the skin. **25** *Maths.* to multiply (a number) by itself a specified number of times: *8 is 2 raised to the power 3.* **26 raise one's glass** (**to**). to drink a toast (to). **27 raise one's hat.** *Old-fashioned.* to take one's hat briefly off one's head as a greeting or mark of respect. ◆ *n* **28** the act or an instance of raising. **29** *Chiefly US & Canad.* an increase, esp. in salary, wages, etc.; rise. ORIG C12: from ON *reisa*
▸ **ˈraisable** *or* **ˈraiseable** *adj*

raised beach *n* a wave-cut platform raised above the shoreline by a relative fall in the water level.

raisin (ˈreɪzᵊn) *n* a dried grape. ORIG C13: from OF: grape, ult. from L *racēmus* cluster of grapes
▸ **ˈraisiny** *adj*

raison d'être *French.* (rɛzɔ̃ dɛtrə) *n, pl* ***raisons d'être*** (rɛzɔ̃ dɛtrə). reason or justification for existence.

raita (ˈraɪtə) *n* an Indian dish of finely chopped cucumber, peppers, mint, etc., in yogurt, served with curries. ORIG C20: from Hindi

raj (rɑːdʒ) *n* **1** (in India) government; rule. **2** (cap. and preceded by *the*) the British government in India before 1947. ORIG C19: from Hindi, from Sansk., from *rājati* he rules

rajah *or* **raja** (ˈrɑːdʒə) *n* **1** (in India, formerly) a ruler: sometimes used as a title preceding a name. **2** a Malayan or Javanese prince or chieftain. ORIG C16: from Hindi, from Sansk. *rājan* king

Rajasthan ★ (ˌrɑːdʒəˈstɑːn) *n* a state of NW India, bordering on Pakistan: formed in 1958; contains the Thar Desert in the west. Capital: Jaipur. Pop.: 48 040 000 (1994 est.). Area: 342 239 sq. km (132 111 sq. miles).

Rajkot ★ (ˈrɑːdʒkəʊt) *n* a city in W India, in S Gujarat. Pop.: 559 407 (1991).

Rajput *or* **Rajpoot** (ˈrɑːdʒpʊt) *n Hinduism.* one of a Hindu military caste claiming descent from the Kshatriya, the original warrior caste. ORIG C16: from Hindi, from Sansk. *rājan* king

Rajputana ★ (ˌrɑːdʒpʊˈtɑːnə) *n* a former group of princely states in NW India: now mostly part of Rajasthan.

Rakata ★ (rəˈkɑːtə) *n* another name for **Krakatoa.**

rake[1] (reɪk) *n* **1** a hand implement consisting of a row of teeth set in a headpiece attached to a long shaft and used for gathering hay, straw, etc., or for smoothing loose earth. **2** any of several mechanical farm implements equipped with rows of teeth or rotating wheels mounted with tines and used to gather hay, straw, etc. **3** any of various implements similar in shape or function. **4** the act of raking. ◆ *vb* **rakes, raking, raked. 5** to scrape, gather, or remove (leaves, refuse, etc.) with a rake. **6** to level or prepare (a surface) with a rake. **7** (*tr; sometimes foll. by out*) to clear (ashes, etc.) from (a fire). **8** (*tr; foll. by up or together*) to gather (items or people) with difficulty, as from a scattered area or limited supply. **9** (*tr; often foll. by through, over,* etc.) to search or examine carefully. **10** (when *intr*, foll. by *against, along,* etc.) to scrape or graze: *the ship raked the side of the quay.* **11** (*tr*) to direct (gunfire) along the length of (a target): *machine-guns raked the column.* **12** (*tr*) to sweep (one's eyes) along the length of (something); scan. ◆ See also **rake in, rake-off,** etc. ORIG OE *raca*
▸ **ˈraker** *n*

rake[2] (reɪk) *n* a dissolute man, esp. one in fashionable society; roué. ORIG C17: short for *rakehell* a dissolute man

rake[3] (reɪk) *vb* **rakes, raking, raked.** (*mainly intr*) **1** to incline from the vertical by a perceptible degree, esp. (of a ship's mast) towards the stern. **2** (*tr*) to construct with a backward slope. ◆ *n* **3** the degree to which an object, such as a ship's mast, inclines from the perpendicular, esp. towards the stern. **4** *Theatre.* the slope of a stage from the back towards the footlights. **5** the angle between the working face of a cutting tool and a plane perpendicular to the surface of the workpiece. ORIG C17: from ?; ? rel. to G *ragen* to project, Swedish *raka*

rake in *vb* (*tr, adv*) *Inf.* to acquire (money) in large amounts.

rake-off *Sl.* ◆ *n* **1** a share of profits, esp. one that is illegal or given as a bribe. ◆ *vb* **rake off. 2** (*tr, adv*) to take or receive (such a share of profits).

rake up *vb* (*tr, adv*) to revive, discover, or bring to light (something forgotten): *to rake up an old quarrel.*

raki *or* **rakee** (rɑːˈkiː, ˈrækɪ) *n* a strong spirit distilled in Turkey from grain, usually flavoured with aniseed or other aromatics. ORIG C17: from Turkish *rāqī*

rakish[1] (ˈreɪkɪʃ) *adj* dissolute; profligate. ORIG C18: from RAKE[2]
▸ **ˈrakishly** *adv* ▸ **ˈrakishness** *n*

rakish[2] (ˈreɪkɪʃ) *adj* **1** dashing; jaunty: *a hat set at a rakish angle.* **2** *Naut.* (of a ship or boat) having lines suggestive of speed. ORIG C19: prob. from RAKE[3]

rale *or* **râle** (rɑːl) *n Med.* an abnormal crackling sound heard on auscultation of the chest, usually caused by the accumulation of fluid in the lungs. ORIG C19: from F, from *râler* to breathe with a rattling sound

Raleigh[1] ★ ('rɔːlɪ, 'rɑː-) *n* a city in E central North Carolina, capital of the state. Pop.: 236 707 (1994 est.).

Raleigh[2] *or* **Ralegh** ★ ('rɔːlɪ, 'rɑː-) *n* Sir **Walter.** ?1552–1618, English explorer and writer; favourite of Elizabeth I: introduced tobacco and potatoes into England. He was imprisoned (1603–16) for conspiracy under James I and subsequently beheaded.

rallentando (ˌrælɛn'tændəʊ) *adj, adv Music.* becoming slower. Also: **ritardando.** ORIG C19: It., from *rallentare* to slow down

rally[1] ('rælɪ) *vb* **rallies, rallying, rallied. 1** to bring (a group, unit, etc.) into order, as after dispersal, or (of such a group) to reform and come to order. **2** (when *intr*, foll. by *to*) to organize (supporters, etc.) for a common cause or (of such people) to come together for a purpose. **3** to summon up (one's strength, spirits, etc.) or (of a person's health, strength, or spirits) to revive or recover. **4** (*intr*) *Stock Exchange.* to increase sharply after a decline. **5** (*intr*) *Tennis, squash, etc.* to engage in a rally. ◆ *n, pl* **rallies. 6** a large gathering of people for a common purpose. **7** a marked recovery of strength or spirits, as during illness. **8** a return to order after dispersal or rout, as of troops, etc. **9** *Stock Exchange.* a sharp increase in price or trading activity after a decline. **10** *Tennis, squash, etc.* an exchange of several shots before one player wins the point. **11** a type of motoring competition over public roads. ORIG C16: from OF *rallier*, from RE- + *alier* to unite
▸ **'rallier** *n*

rally[2] ('rælɪ) *vb* **rallies, rallying, rallied.** to mock or ridicule (someone) in a good-natured way; chaff; tease. ORIG C17: from OF *railler* to tease; see RAIL[2]

rallycross ('rælɪˌkrɒs) *n* a form of motor sport in which cars race over a one-mile circuit of rough grass with some hard-surfaced sections.

rally round *vb* (*intr*) to come to the aid of (someone); offer moral or practical support.

ram (ræm) *n* **1** an uncastrated adult male sheep. **2** a piston or moving plate, esp. one driven hydraulically or pneumatically. **3** the falling weight of a pile driver. **4** short for **battering ram. 5** a pointed projection in the stem of an ancient warship for puncturing the hull of enemy ships. **6** a warship equipped with a ram. ◆ *vb* **rams, ramming, rammed. 7** (*tr*; usually foll. by *into*) to force or drive, as by heavy blows: *to ram a post into the ground.* **8** (of a moving object) to crash with force (against another object) or (of two moving objects) to collide in this way. **9** (*tr*; often foll. by *in* or *down*) to stuff or cram (something into a hole, etc.). **10** (*tr*; foll. by *onto, against,* etc.) to thrust violently: *he rammed the books onto the desk.* **11** (*tr*) to present (an idea, argument, etc.) forcefully or aggressively (esp. in **ram (something) down someone's throat**). **12** (*tr*) to drive (a charge) into a firearm. ORIG OE *ramm*
▸ **'rammer** *n*

Ram (ræm) *n* **the.** the constellation Aries, the first sign of the zodiac.

RAM[1] (ræm) *n Computing. acronym for* random access memory: semiconductor memory in which all storage locations can be rapidly accessed in the same amount of time. It forms the main memory of a computer, used by applications to perform tasks while the device is operating.

RAM[2] *abbrev. for* Royal Academy of Music.

Ramadan *or* **Rhamadhan** (ˌræmə'dɑːn) *n* **1** the ninth month of the Muslim year, lasting 30 days, during which strict fasting is observed from sunrise to sunset. **2** the fast itself. ORIG C16: from Ar., lit.: the hot month, from *ramad* dryness

Ramakrishna ★ (ˌrɑːmə'krɪʃnə) *n* **Sri** (sriː). 1834–86, Hindu yogi and religious reformer.

Raman effect ('rɑːmən) *n* the change in wavelength of light that is scattered by electrons within a material: used in **Raman spectroscopy** for studying molecules. ORIG C20: after Sir Chandasekhara *Raman* (1888–1970), Indian physicist

Ramat Gan ★ (rɑː'mɑːt 'gɑːn) *n* a city in Israel, E of Tel Aviv. Pop.: 121 700 (1996 est.).

Rambert ★ ('rɒmbɛə) *n* Dame **Marie.** 1888–1982, British ballet dancer and teacher, born in Poland: founded the **Ballet Rambert** (1926).

ramble ('ræmb°l) *vb* **rambles, rambling, rambled.** (*intr*) **1** to stroll about freely, as for relaxation, with no particular direction. **2** (of paths, streams, etc.) to follow a winding course; meander. **3** to grow or develop in a random fashion. **4** (of speech, writing, etc.) to lack organization. ◆ *n* **5** a leisurely stroll, esp. in the countryside. ORIG C17: prob. rel. to MDu. *rammelen* to ROAM (of animals)

rambler ('ræmblə) *n* **1** a weak-stemmed plant that straggles over other vegetation. **2** a person who rambles, esp. one who takes country walks. **3** a person who lacks organization in his or her speech or writing.

rambling ('ræmblɪŋ) *adj* **1** straggling or sprawling haphazardly: *a rambling old house.* **2** (of speech or writing) diffuse and disconnected. **3** (of a plant, esp. a rose) climbing and straggling. **4** nomadic; wandering.

Ramboesque (ˌræmbəʊ'ɛsk) *adj* looking or behaving like or characteristic of Rambo, a mindlessly brutal fictional film character.
▸ **'Rambo,ism** *n*

Rambouillet ★ (*French* rɑ̃bujɛ) *n* a town in N France, in the Yvelines department: site of the summer residence of French presidents. Pop.: 25 300 (1990).

rambunctious (ræm'bʌŋkʃəs) *adj Inf.* boisterous; unruly. ORIG C19: prob. from Icelandic *ram* (intensifying prefix) + *-bunctious*, from BUMPTIOUS
▸ **ram'bunctiousness** *n*

rambutan (ræm'buːtᵊn) *n* **1** a tree related to the soapberry, native to SE Asia, that has bright red edible fruit covered with hairs. **2** the fruit of this tree. ORIG C18: from Malay, from *rambut* hair

RAMC *abbrev. for* Royal Army Medical Corps.

Rameau ★ (*French* ramo) *n* **Jean Philippe** (ʒɑ̃ filip). 1683–1764, French composer. His works include the opera *Castor et Pollux* (1737) and his *Traité de l'harmonie* (1722) was important in the development of harmony.

ramekin *or* **ramequin** ('ræmɪkɪn) *n* **1** a savoury dish made from a cheese mixture baked in a fireproof container. **2** the container itself. ORIG C18: F *ramequin*, of Gmc origin

Rameses ★ ('ræmɪˌsiːz) *n* a variant of **Ramses.**

ramification (ˌræmɪfɪ'keɪʃən) *n* **1** the act or process of ramifying or branching out. **2** an offshoot or subdivision. **3** a structure of branching parts.

ramify ('ræmɪˌfaɪ) *vb* **ramifies, ramifying, ramified. 1** to divide into branches or branchlike parts. **2** (*intr*) to develop complicating consequences. ORIG C16: from F *ramifier*, from L *rāmus* branch + *facere* to make

Ramillies ★ ('ræmɪliːz; *French* ramiji) *n* a village in central Belgium where the Duke of Marlborough defeated the French in 1706.

ramjet *or* **ramjet engine** ('ræmˌdʒɛt) *n* **a** a type of jet engine in which fuel is burned in a duct using air compressed by the forward speed of the aircraft. **b** an aircraft powered by such an engine.

ramose ('reɪməʊs, ræ'məʊs) *or* **ramous** ('reɪməs) *adj* having branches. ORIG C17: from L *rāmōsus*, from *rāmus* branch
▸ **'ramosely** *or* **'ramously** *adv* ▸ **ramosity** (ræ'mɒsɪtɪ) *n*

ramp (ræmp) *n* **1** a sloping floor, path, etc., that joins two surfaces at different levels. **2** a place where the level of a road surface changes because of roadworks. **3** a movable stairway by which passengers enter and leave an aircraft. **4** the act of ramping. **5** *Brit. sl.* a swindle, esp. one involving exorbitant prices. ◆ *vb* **6** (*intr*) (often foll. by *about* or *around*) (esp. of animals) to rush around in a wild excited manner. **7** (*intr*) to act in a violent or threatening manner (esp. in **ramp and rage**). **8** (*tr*) *Finance.* to buy (a security) in the market with the object of raising its price and enhancing the image of the company behind it for financial gain. ORIG C18 (n): from C13 *rampe*, from OF *ramper* to crawl or rear, prob. of Gmc origin

rampage *vb* (ræm'peɪdʒ), **rampages, rampaging, rampaged. 1** (*intr*) to rush about in a violent or agitated fashion. ◆ *n* ('ræmpeɪdʒ, ræm'peɪdʒ). **2** angry or destructive behav-

iour. **3 on the rampage.** behaving violently or destructively. ORIG C18: from Scot., from ?; ? based on RAMP
▸ **ram'pageous** *adj* ▸ **ram'pageously** *adv* ▸ **'rampager** *n*

rampant ('ræmpənt) *adj* **1** unrestrained or violent in behaviour, etc. **2** growing or developing unchecked. **3** (*postpositive*) *Heraldry.* (of a beast) standing on the hind legs, the right foreleg raised above the left. **4** (of an arch) having one abutment higher than the other. ORIG C14: from OF *ramper* to crawl, rear; see RAMP
▸ **'rampancy** *n* ▸ **'rampantly** *adv*

rampart ('ræmpɑːt) *n* **1** the surrounding embankment of a fort, often including any walls, parapets, etc., that are built on the bank. **2** any defence or bulwark. ◆ *vb* **3** (*tr*) to provide with a rampart; fortify. ORIG C16: from OF, from RE- + *emparer* to take possession of, from OProvençal *antparar,* from L *ante* before + *parāre* to prepare

rampike ('ræmˌpaɪk) *n Canad.* a tall tree that has been burned or is bare of branches.

rampion ('ræmpɪən) *n* a plant, native to Europe and Asia, that has clusters of bell-shaped bluish flowers and an edible white tuberous root used in salads. ORIG C16: prob. from OF *raiponce,* from OIt. *raponzo,* from *rapa* turnip, from L *rāpum*

Rampur ★ ('ræmpʊə) *n* a city in N India, in N Uttar Pradesh. Pop.: 243 742 (1991).

ram raid *n Inf.* a raid in which a stolen car is driven through a shop window in order to steal goods from the shop.
▸ **ram raiding** *n* ▸ **ram raider** *n*

ramrod ('ræmˌrɒd) *n* **1** a rod for cleaning the barrel of a rifle, etc. **2** a rod for ramming in the charge of a muzzle-loading firearm.

Ramsay ★ ('ræmzɪ) *n* **1 Allan.** ?1686–1758, Scottish writer and bookseller, noted esp. for his comedy *The Gentle Shepherd* (1725). He introduced the circulating library to Scotland. **2** his son, **Allan.** 1713–84, Scottish portrait painter. **3 James Andrew Broun.** See (1st Marquis and 10th Earl of) **Dalhousie. 4** Sir **William.** 1852–1916, Scottish chemist. He discovered several rare gases: Nobel prize for chemistry 1904.

Ramses ('ræmsiːz) *or* **Rameses** ★ *n* any of 12 kings of ancient Egypt, who ruled from ?1315 to ?1090 B.C.

Ramses II *or* **Rameses II** ★ *n* died ?1225 B.C., king of ancient Egypt (?1292–?25). His reign was marked by the construction of such monuments as the temple at Abu Simbel.

Ramses III *or* **Rameses III** ★ *n* died ?1167 B.C., king of ancient Egypt (?1198–?67).

Ramsey ★ ('ræmzɪ) *n* Sir **Alf**(**red Ernest**). 1922–99, English footballer and football manager, who played for England 32 times and managed England when they won the World Cup (1966).

Ramsgate ★ ('ræmzˌgeɪt) *n* a port and resort in SE England, in E Kent on the North Sea coast. Pop.: 37 895 (1991).

ramshackle ('ræmˌʃækᵊl) *adj* (esp. of buildings) rickety, shaky, or derelict. ORIG C17 *ramshackled,* from obs. *ransackle* to RANSACK

ramsons ('ræmzənz, -sənz) *pl n* (*usually functioning as sing*) **1** a broad-leaved garlic native to Europe and Asia. **2** the bulbous root of this plant, eaten as a relish. ORIG OE *hramesa*

ran (ræn) *vb* the past tense of **run.**

RAN *abbrev. for* Royal Australian Navy.

Rancagua ★ (*Spanish* raŋ'kagwa) *n* a city in central Chile. Pop.: 193 755 (1995 est.).

ranch (rɑːntʃ) *n* **1** a large tract of land, esp. one in North America, together with the necessary personnel, buildings, and equipment, for rearing livestock, esp. cattle. **2a** any large farm for the rearing of a particular kind of livestock or crop: *a mink ranch.* **2b** the buildings, land, etc., connected with it. ◆ *vb* **3** (*intr*) to run a ranch. **4** (*tr*) to raise (animals) on or as if on a ranch. ORIG C19: from Mexican Sp. *rancho* small farm
▸ **'rancher** *n*

rancherie ('rɑːntʃərɪ) *n* (in British Columbia, Canada) a settlement of North American Indians, esp. on a reserve. ORIG from Sp. *rancheria*

Ranchi ★ ('ræntʃɪ) *n* an industrial city in E India, in S Bihar between the coal and iron belts of the Chota Nagpur Plateau. Pop.: 599 306 (1991).

rancid ('rænsɪd) *adj* **1** (of food) having an unpleasant stale taste or smell as the result of decomposition. **2** (of a taste or smell) rank or sour; stale. ORIG C17: from L *rancidus,* from *rancēre* to stink
▸ **rancidity** (ræn'sɪdɪtɪ) *or* **'rancidness** *n*

rancour *or US* **rancor** ('ræŋkə) *n* malicious resentfulness or hostility; spite. ORIG C14: from OF, from LL *rancor* rankness
▸ **'rancorous** *adj* ▸ **'rancorously** *adv*

rand[1] (rænd, rɒnt) *n* the standard monetary unit of South Africa, divided into 100 cents. ORIG C20: from Afrik., from WITWATERSRAND, referring to the gold-mining there; rel. to RAND[2]

rand[2] (rænd) *n* **1** *Shoemaking.* a leather strip put in the heel of a shoe before the lifts are put on. **2** *Dialect.* **2a** a strip or margin; border. **2b** a strip of cloth; selvage. ORIG OE; rel. to OHG *rant* border, rim of a shield, ON *rönd* shield, rim

Rand ★ (rænd) *n* **the.** short for **Witwatersrand.**

R & B *abbrev. for* rhythm and blues.

R & D *abbrev. for* research and development.

Randers ★ (*Danish* 'randərs) *n* a port and industrial centre in Denmark, in E Jutland on **Randers Fjord** (an inlet of the Kattegat). Pop.: 61 435 (1995).

Randolph ★ ('rændɒlf, -dəlf) *n* **1 Edmund Jennings,** 1753–1813, US politician. He helped to frame the US constitution (1787), attorney general (1789–94), and secretary of state (1794–95). **2 John,** called *Randolph of Roanoke.* 1773–1833, US politician: opposed the Missouri Compromise (1820) that outlawed slavery. **3** Sir **Thomas,** 1st Earl of Moray. died 1332, Scottish soldier: regent after the death of Robert the Bruce (1329).

random ('rændəm) *adj* **1** lacking any definite plan or prearranged order; haphazard: *a random selection.* **2** *Statistics.* **2a** having a value which cannot be determined but only described in terms of probability: *a random variable.* **2b** chosen without regard to any characteristics of the individual members of the population so that each has an equal chance of being selected: *random sampling.* ◆ *n* **3 at random.** not following any prearranged order. ORIG C14: from OF *randon,* from *randir* to gallop, of Gmc origin
▸ **'randomly** *adv* ▸ **'randomness** *n*

random access *n* another name for **direct access.**

randomize *or* **randomise** ('rændəˌmaɪz) *vb* **randomizes, randomizing, randomized** *or* **randomises, randomising, randomised.** (*tr*) to set up (a selection process, sample, etc.) in a deliberately random way in order to enhance the statistical validity of any results obtained.
▸ **ˌrandomi'zation** *or* **ˌrandomi'sation** *n* ▸ **'randomˌizer** *or* **'randomˌiser** *n*

random walk theory *n Stock Exchange.* the theory that the future movement of share prices does not reflect past movements and therefore will not follow a discernible pattern.

R and R *US mil. abbrev. for* rest and recreation.

randy ('rændɪ) *adj* **randier, randiest. 1** *Inf., chiefly Brit.* sexually eager or lustful. **2** *Chiefly Scot.* lacking any sense of propriety; reckless. ◆ *n, pl* **randies. 3** *Chiefly Scot.* a rude or reckless person. ORIG C17: prob. from obs. *rand* to RANT
▸ **'randily** *adv* ▸ **'randiness** *n*

ranee ('rɑːnɪ) *n* a variant spelling of **rani.**

rang (ræŋ) *vb* the past tense of **ring**[2].

USAGE NOTE See at **ring**[2].

rangatira (ˌrʌŋgə'tɪərə) *n NZ.* a Maori chief of either sex. ORIG from Maori

range (reɪndʒ) *n* **1** the limits within which a person or thing can function effectively: *the violin has a range of five octaves.* **2** the limits within which any fluctuation takes place: *a range of values.* **3** the total products of a manufacturer, designer, or stockist: *the new spring range.* **4a** the maximum effective distance of a projectile fired from a weapon. **4b** the distance between a target and a weapon. **5** an area set aside for shooting practice or rocket testing. **6** the total distance which a ship, aircraft, or land vehicle is capable of covering without taking on fresh fuel: *the range of this car is about 160 miles.* **7** *Maths.* (of a function or variable) the set of values that a function or variable can take. **8** *US & Canad.* **8a** an extensive tract of open land on which livestock can graze. **8b** (*as modifier*): *range cattle.* **9** the geographical region in which a species of plant or animal normally grows or lives. **10** a rank, row, or series of items. **11** a series or chain of mountains. **12** a large stove with burners and one or more ovens, usually heated by solid fuel. **13** the act or process of ranging. ◆ *vb* **ranges, ranging, ranged. 14** to establish or be situated in a line, row, or series. **15** (*tr; often reflexive,* foll. by *with*) to put into a specific category; classify: *she ranges herself with the angels.* **16** (foll. by *on*) to aim or point (a telescope, gun, etc.) or (of a gun, telescope, etc.) to be pointed or aimed. **17** to establish the distance of (a target) from (a weapon). **18** (*intr*) (of a gun or missile) to have a specified range. **19** (when *intr,* foll. by *over*) to wander about (in) an area; roam (over). **20** (*intr;* foll. by *over*) (of an animal or plant) to live or grow in its normal habitat. **21** (*tr*) to put (cattle) to graze on a range. **22** (*intr*) to fluctuate within specific limits. **23** (*intr*) to extend or run in a specific direction. **24** (*intr*) *Naut.* (of a vessel) to swing back and forth while at anchor. **25** (*tr*) to make (lines of printers' type) level or even at the margin. ORIG C13: from OF: row, from *ranger* to position, from *renc* line

rangefinder ('reɪndʒˌfaɪndə) *n* an instrument for determining the distance of an object from the observer, esp. in order to sight a gun or focus a camera.

ranger ('reɪndʒə) *n* **1** (*sometimes cap.*) an official in charge of a forest, park, nature reserve, etc. **2** *Orig. US.* a person employed to patrol a State or national park. Brit. equivalent: **warden. 3** *US.* one of a body of armed troops employed to police a State or district: *a Texas ranger.* **4** (in the US) a commando specially trained in making raids. **5** a person who wanders about; a rover.

Ranger *or* **Ranger Guide** ('reɪndʒə) *n Brit.* a member of the senior branch of the Guides.

rangiora (ˌræŋgɪ'ɔːrə) *n* a broad-leaved shrub of New Zealand. ORIG from Maori

Rangoon ★ (ræŋ'guːn) *n* the former name (until 1989) of **Yangon.**

rangy ('reɪndʒɪ) *adj* **rangier, rangiest. 1** having long slender limbs. **2** adapted to wandering or roaming. **3** allowing considerable freedom of movement; spacious.
▸ **'rangily** *adv* ▸ **'ranginess** *n*

rani *or* **ranee** ('rɑːnɪ) *n* an Indian queen or princess; the wife of a rajah. ORIG C17: from Hindi: queen, from Sansk. *rājñī*

Ranjit Singh ★ ('rʌndʒɪt 'sɪŋ) *n* called *the Lion of the Punjab.* 1780–1839; founder of the Sikh kingdom in the Punjab.

rank[1] (ræŋk) *n* **1** a position, esp. an official one, within a social organization: *the rank of captain.* **2** high social or other standing; status. **3** a line or row of people or things. **4** the position of an item in any ordering or sequence. **5** *Brit.* a place where taxis wait to be hired. **6** a line of soldiers drawn up abreast of each other. **7** any of the eight horizontal rows of squares on a chessboard. **8 close ranks.** to maintain discipline or solidarity. **9 pull rank.** to get one's own way by virtue of one's superior position or rank. **10 rank and file. 10a** the ordinary soldiers, excluding the officers. **10b** the great mass or majority of any group, as opposed to the leadership. **10c** (*modifier*): *rank-and-file support.* ◆ *vb* **11** (*tr*) to arrange (people or things) in rows or lines; range. **12** to accord or be accorded a specific position in an organization or group. **13** (*tr*) to array a set of objects as a sequence: *to rank students by their test scores.* **14** (*intr*) to be important; rate: *money ranks low in her order of priorities.* **15** *Chiefly US.* to take precedence or surpass in rank. ORIG C16: from OF *ranc* row, rank, of Gmc origin

rank[2] (ræŋk) *adj* **1** showing vigorous and profuse growth: *rank weeds.* **2** highly offensive or disagreeable, esp. in smell or taste. **3** (*prenominal*) complete or absolute; utter: *a rank outsider.* **4** coarse or vulgar; gross: *his language was rank.* ORIG OE *ranc* straight, noble
▸ **'rankly** *adv* ▸ **'rankness** *n*

Rank ★ *n* **1** (ræŋk). **J**(**oseph**) **Arthur,** 1st Baron. 1888–1972, British industrialist and film executive. **2** (*German* raŋk). **Otto** ('ɔto). 1884–1939, Austrian psychoanalyst.

ranker ('ræŋkə) *n* **1** a soldier in the ranks. **2** a commissioned officer who entered service as a noncommissioned recruit.

ranking ('ræŋkɪŋ) *adj* **1** *Chiefly US & Canad.* prominent; high ranking. **2** *Caribbean sl.* possessed of style; exciting. ◆ *n* **3** a position on a scale; rating: *a ranking in a tennis tournament.*

rankle ('ræŋk^{ə}l) *vb* **rankles, rankling, rankled.** (*intr*) to cause severe and continuous irritation, anger, or bitterness; fester. ORIG C14 *ranclen,* from OF *draoncle* ulcer, from L *dracunculus* dim. of *dracō* serpent

ransack ('rænsæk) *vb* (*tr*) **1** to search through every part of (a house, box, etc.); examine thoroughly. **2** to plunder; pillage. ORIG C13: from ON *rann* house + *saka* to search
▸ **'ransacker** *n*

ransom ('rænsəm) *n* **1** the release of captured prisoners, property, etc., on payment of a stipulated price. **2** the price demanded or stipulated for such a release. **3 hold to ransom. 3a** to keep (prisoners, etc.) in confinement until payment for their release is received. **3b** to attempt to force (a person) to comply with one's demands. **4 a king's ransom.** a very large amount of money or valuables. ◆ *vb* (*tr*) **5** to pay a stipulated price and so obtain the release of (prisoners, property, etc.). **6** to set free (prisoners, property, etc.) upon receiving the payment demanded. **7** to redeem; rescue: *Christ ransomed men from sin.* ORIG C14: from OF *ransoun,* from L *redemptiō* a buying back
▸ **'ransomer** *n*

Ransom ★ ('rænsəm) *n* **John Crowe.** 1888–1974, US poet and critic.

Ransome ★ ('rænsəm) *n* **Arthur.** 1884–1967, British writer, best known for his childrens' books, including *Swallows and Amazons* (1930).

rant (rænt) *vb* **1** to utter (something) in loud, violent, or bombastic tones. ◆ *n* **2** loud, declamatory, or extravagant speech; bombast. ORIG C16: from Du. *ranten* to rave
▸ **'ranter** *n* ▸ **'ranting** *adj, n* ▸ **'rantingly** *adv*

ranunculaceous (rəˌnʌŋkjʊ'leɪʃəs) *adj* of, relating to, or belonging to a N temperate family of flowering plants typically having flowers with five petals and numerous anthers and styles. The family includes the buttercup, clematis, and columbine.

ranunculus (rə'nʌŋkjʊləs) *n, pl* **ranunculuses** *or* **ranunculi** (-ˌlaɪ). any of a genus of ranunculaceous plants having finely divided leaves and typically yellow five-petalled flowers. The genus includes buttercup, crowfoot, and spearwort. ORIG C16: from L: tadpole, from *rāna* frog

RAOC *abbrev. for* Royal Army Ordnance Corps.

rap[1] (ræp) *vb* **raps, rapping, rapped. 1** to strike (a fist, stick, etc.) against (something) with a sharp quick blow; knock. **2** (*intr*) to make a sharp loud sound, esp. by knocking. **3** (*tr*) to rebuke or criticize sharply. **4** (*tr;* foll. by *out*) to put (forth) in sharp rapid speech; utter in an abrupt fashion: *to rap out orders.* **5** (*intr*) *Sl.* to talk, esp. volubly. **6** (*intr*) to perform a rhythmic monologue with musical backing. **7 rap over the knuckles.** to reprimand. ◆ *n* **8** a sharp quick blow or the sound produced by such a blow. **9** a sharp rebuke or criticism. **10** *Sl.* voluble talk; chatter. **11a** a fast, rhythmic monologue over a musical backing. **11b** (*as modifier*): *rap music.* **12 beat the rap.** *US & Canad. sl.* to escape punishment or be acquitted of a crime. **13 take the rap.** *Sl.* to suffer the punishment for a crime, whether guilty or not. ORIG C14: prob. from ON; cf. Swedish *rappa* to beat

rap[2] (ræp) *n* (*used with a negative*) the least amount (esp. in **not care a rap**). ORIG C18: prob. from *ropaire* counterfeit coin formerly current in Ireland

rap[3] (ræp) *vb* **raps, rapping, rapped.** *n Austral. inf.* a variant spelling of **wrap** (senses 8, 14).

rapacious (rə'peɪʃəs) *adj* **1** practising pillage or rapine. **2**

greedy or grasping. **3** (of animals, esp. birds) subsisting by catching living prey. ORIG C17: from L *rapāx,* from *rapere* to seize
▸ **ra'paciously** *adv* ▸ **rapacity** (rə'pæsɪtɪ) *or* **ra'paciousness** *n*

Rapacki ★ (*Polish* ra'patski) *n* **Adam** ('adam). 1909–70, Polish politician: foreign minister (1956–68); his proposal to denuclearize eastern Europe (the **Rapacki Plan**) was rejected by the West because of Soviet predominance in conventional weapons.

Rapallo ★ (*Italian* ra'pallo) *n* a port and resort in NW Italy, in Liguria on the **Gulf of Rapallo** (an inlet of the Ligurian Sea): scene of the signing of two treaties after World War I. Pop.: 30 000 (1990 est.).

Rapa Nui ★ ('rɑːpɑː 'nuːɪ) *n* another name for **Easter Island.**

rape[1] (reɪp) *n* **1** the offence of forcing a person, esp. a woman, to submit to sexual intercourse against that person's will. **2** the act of despoiling a country in warfare. **3** any violation or abuse: *the rape of justice.* **4** *Arch.* abduction: *the rape of the Sabine women.* ◆ *vb* **rapes, raping, raped.** (*mainly tr*) **5** to commit rape upon (a person). **6** *Arch.* to carry off by force; abduct. ORIG C14: from L *rapere* to seize
▸ **'rapist** *n*

rape[2] (reɪp) *n* a Eurasian plant that is cultivated for its seeds, **rapeseed,** which yield a useful oil, **rape oil,** and as a fodder plant. Also called: **colza, cole.** ORIG C14: from L *rāpum* turnip

rape[3] (reɪp) *n* (*often pl*) the skins and stalks of grapes left after wine-making: used in making vinegar. ORIG C17: from F *râpe,* of Gmc origin

Raphael ★ ('ræfeɪəl) *n* **1** *Bible.* one of the archangels; the angel of healing and the guardian of Tobias (Tobit 3:17; 5-12). Feast day: Sept. 29. **2** original name *Raffaello Santi* or *Sanzio.* 1483–1520, Italian painter and architect; his paintings include the *Sistine Madonna* (?1513).
▸ **,Raphael'esque** *adj*

raphia ('ræfɪə) *n* a variant spelling of **raffia.**

raphide ('reɪfaɪd) *or* **raphis** ('reɪfɪs) *n, pl* **raphides** ('ræfɪ,diːz). needle-shaped crystals, usually of calcium oxalate, that occur in many plant cells. ORIG C18: from F, from Gk *rhaphis* needle

rapid ('ræpɪd) *adj* **1** (of an action) performed or occurring during a short interval of time; quick. **2** acting or moving quickly; fast: *a rapid worker.* ◆ See also **rapids.** ORIG C17: from L *rapidus* tearing away, from *rapere* to seize
▸ **'rapidly** *adv* ▸ **rapidity** (rə'pɪdɪtɪ) *or* **'rapidness** *n*

rapid eye movement *n* movement of the eyeballs during paradoxical sleep, while the sleeper is dreaming. Abbrev.: **REM.**

rapid fire *n* **1** a fast rate of gunfire. ◆ *adj* **rapid-fire. 2** firing shots rapidly. **3** done, delivered, or occurring in rapid succession.

rapids ('ræpɪdz) *pl n* part of a river where the water is very fast and turbulent.

rapier ('reɪpɪə) *n* **1** a long narrow two-edged sword with a guarded hilt, used as a thrusting weapon, popular in the 16th and 17th centuries. **2** a smaller single-edged 18th-century sword, used principally in France. ORIG C16: from OF *espee rapiere,* lit.: rasping sword

rapine ('ræpaɪn) *n* the seizure of property by force; pillage. ORIG C15: from L *rapīna* plundering, from *rapere* to snatch

rappee (ræ'piː) *n* a moist English snuff. ORIG C18: from F *tabac râpé,* lit.: scraped tobacco

rappel (ræ'pɛl) *vb* **rappels, rappelling, rappelled,** *n* **1** another word for **abseil.** ◆ *n* **2** (formerly) a drumbeat to call soldiers to arms. ORIG C19: from F, from *rappeler* to call back, from L *appellāre* to summon

rapport (ræ'pɔː) *n* (often foll. by *with*) a sympathetic relationship or understanding. See also **en rapport.** ORIG C15: from F, from *rapporter* to bring back, from RE- + *aporter,* from L *apportāre,* from *ad* to + *portāre* to carry

rapprochement *French.* (raprɔʃmɑ̃) *n* a resumption of friendly relations, esp. between two countries. ORIG C19: lit.: bringing closer

rapscallion (ræp'skæljən) *n* a disreputable person; rascal or rogue. ORIG C17: from earlier *rascallion;* see RASCAL

rapt[1] (ræpt) *adj* **1** totally absorbed; engrossed; spellbound, esp. through or as if through emotion: *rapt with wonder.* **2** characterized by or proceeding from rapture: *a rapt smile.* ORIG C14: from L *raptus* carried away, from *rapere* to seize
▸ **'raptly** *adv*

rapt[2] (ræpt) *adj Austral. inf.* Also: **wrapped.** very pleased; delighted.

raptor ('ræptə) *n* another name for **bird of prey.** ORIG C17: from L: plunderer, from *rapere* to take by force

raptorial (ræp'tɔːrɪəl) *adj Zool.* **1** (of the feet of birds) adapted for seizing prey. **2** of or relating to birds of prey. ORIG C19: from L *raptor* robber, from *rapere* to snatch

rapture ('ræptʃə) *n* **1** the state of mind resulting from feelings of high emotion; joyous ecstasy. **2** (*often pl*) an expression of ecstatic joy. **3** the act of transporting a person from one sphere of existence to another. ◆ *vb* **raptures, rapturing, raptured. 4** (*tr*) *Arch. or literary.* to enrapture. ORIG C17: from Med. L *raptūra,* from L *raptus* RAPT[1]
▸ **'rapturous** *adj*

RAR *abbrev. for* Royal Australian Regiment.

rara avis ('rɛərə 'eɪvɪs) *n, pl* **rarae aves** ('rɛəriː 'eɪviːz). an unusual, uncommon, or exceptional person or thing. ORIG L: rare bird

rare[1] (rɛə) *adj* **1** not widely known; not frequently used or experienced; uncommon or unusual: *a rare word.* **2** not widely distributed; not generally occurring: *a rare herb.* **3** (of a gas, esp. the atmosphere at high altitudes) having a low density; thin; rarefied. **4** uncommonly great; extreme: *kind to a rare degree.* **5** exhibiting uncommon excellence: *rare skill.* ORIG C14: from L *rārus* sparse
▸ **'rareness** *n*

rare[2] (rɛə) *adj* (of meat, esp. beef) very lightly cooked. ORIG OE *hrēr;* rel. to *hreaw* RAW

rarebit ('rɛəbɪt) *n* another term for **Welsh rabbit.** ORIG C18: by folk etymology from (WELSH) RABBIT; see RARE[2], BIT[1]

rare earth *n* **1** any oxide of a lanthanide. **2** Also called: **rare-earth element.** any element of the lanthanide series.

raree show ('rɛəriː) *n* **1** a street show or carnival. **2** another name for **peepshow.** ORIG C17: *raree* from RARE[1]

rarefaction (,rɛərɪ'fækʃən) *or* **rarefication** (,rɛərɪfɪ'keɪʃən) *n* the act or process of making less dense or the state of being less dense.
▸ **,rare'factive** *adj*

rarefied ('rɛərɪ,faɪd) *adj* **1** exalted in nature or character; lofty: *a rarefied spiritual existence.* **2** current within only a small group. **3** thin: *air rarefied at altitude.*

rarefy ('rɛərɪ,faɪ) *vb* **rarefies, rarefying, rarefied.** to make or become rarer or less dense; thin out. ORIG C14: from OF *raréfier,* from L *rārēfacere,* from *rārus* RARE[1] + *facere* to make
▸ **'rare,fiable** *adj* ▸ **'rare,fier** *n*

rare gas *n* another name for **inert gas.**

rarely ('rɛəlɪ) *adv* **1** hardly ever; seldom. **2** to an unusual degree; exceptionally. **3** *Dialect.* uncommonly well; excellently: *he did rarely at market yesterday.*

> **USAGE NOTE** Since *rarely* means *hardly ever,* in writing you should not use *rarely ever,* even though it is quite often used in speaking for extra emphasis.

raring ('rɛərɪŋ) *adj* ready; willing; enthusiastic (esp. in **raring to go**). ORIG C20: from *rare,* var. of REAR[2]

rarity ('rɛərɪtɪ) *n, pl* **rarities. 1** a rare person or thing, esp. something valued because it is uncommon. **2** the state of being rare.

Rarotonga ★ (,rɛərə'tɒŋgə) *n* an island in the S Pacific, in the SW Cook Islands: the chief island of the group. Chief settlement: Avarua. Pop.: 9281 (1986). Area: 67 sq. km (26 sq. miles).

rasbora (ræz'bɔːrə) *n* any of the small cyprinid fishes of tropical Asia and East Africa. Many species are brightly coloured and are popular aquarium fishes. ORIG from NL, from an East Indian language

rascal ('rɑːskᵊl) *n* **1** a disreputable person; villain. **2** a mischievous or impish rogue. **3** an affectionate or mildly reproving term, esp. for a child: *you little rascal.* **4** *Obs.* a person of lowly birth. ◆ *adj* **5** (*prenominal*) *Obs.* **5a** belonging to the rabble. **5b** dishonest; knavish. ORIG C14: from OF *rascaille* rabble, ?from OF *rasque* mud

rascality (rɑː'skælɪtɪ) *n, pl* **rascalities.** mischievous or disreputable character or action.

rascally ('rɑːskəlɪ) *adj* **1** dishonest or mean; base. ◆ *adv* **2** in a dishonest or mean fashion.

rase (reɪz) *vb* **rases, rasing, rased.** a variant spelling of **raze.**

rash[1] (ræʃ) *adj* **1** acting without due thought; impetuous. **2** resulting from excessive haste or impetuosity: *a rash word.* ORIG C14: from OHG *rasc* hurried, clever
▸ **'rashly** *adv* ▸ **'rashness** *n*

rash[2] (ræʃ) *n* **1** *Pathol.* any skin eruption. **2** a series of unpleasant and unexpected occurrences: *a rash of forest fires.* ORIG C18: from OF *rasche,* from *raschier* to scratch, from L *rādere* to scrape

rasher ('ræʃə) *n* a thin slice of bacon or ham. ORIG C16: from ?

Rashid[1] ★ (ræ'ʃiːd) *n* the Egyptian name for **Rosetta.**

Rashid[2] ★ (ræ'ʃiːd) *n* **Harun al-.** See **Harun al-Rashid.**

Rasht (ræʃt) *or* **Resht** ★ *n* a city in NW Iran, near the Caspian Sea: agricultural and commercial centre in a rice-growing area. Pop.: 374 475 (1994 est.).

Rask ★ (*Danish* rasg) *n* **Rasmus Christian** ('rasmus 'kresdjan). 1787–1832, Danish philologist. He pioneered comparative philology with his work on Old Norse (1818).

Rasmussen ★ (*Danish* 'rasmusən) *n* **Knud Johan Victor** (knuð jo'han 'viktɔr). 1879–1933, Danish arctic explorer and ethnologist. He led several expeditions through the Arctic in support of his theory that the North American Indians were originally migrants from Asia.

rasp (rɑːsp) *n* **1** a harsh grating noise. **2** a coarse file with rows of raised teeth. ◆ *vb* **3** (*tr*) to scrape or rub (something) roughly, esp. with a rasp; abrade. **4** to utter with or make a harsh grating noise. **5** to irritate (one's nerves); grate (upon). ORIG C16: from OF *raspe,* of Gmc origin; cf. OHG *raspōn* to scrape
▸ **'rasper** *n* ▸ **'rasping** *adj* ▸ **'raspish** *adj*

raspberry ('rɑːzbərɪ, -brɪ) *n, pl* **raspberries. 1** a prickly rosaceous shrub of North America and Europe that has pinkish-white flowers and typically red berry-like fruits (drupelets). See also **bramble. 2a** the fruit of any such plant. **2b** (*as modifier*): *raspberry jelly.* **3a** a dark purplish-red colour. **3b** (*as adj*): *a raspberry dress.* **4** a spluttering noise made with the tongue and lips to express contempt (esp. in **blow a raspberry**). ORIG C17: from earlier *raspis* raspberry, from ? + BERRY

Rasputin ★ (ræ'spjuːtɪn; *Russian* ras'putin) *n* **Grigori Efimovich** (gri'gɔrij jɪ'fiməvitʃ). ?1871–1916, Siberian monk, notorious for his debauchery and his influence over Tsarina Alexandra: assassinated by a group of Russian noblemen.

Ras Tafari ★ (ræs tə'fɑːrɪ) *n* See **Haile Selassie.**

Rastafarian (ˌræstə'fɛərɪən) *n* **1** a member of an originally Jamaican religion that regards Ras Tafari, the former emperor of Ethiopia, Haile Selassie, as God. ◆ *adj* **2** of, characteristic of, or relating to the Rastafarians. ◆ Often shortened to **Rasta.**

raster ('ræstə) *n* a pattern of horizontal scanning lines, esp. those traced by an electron beam on a television screen or those in a digitized bitmap image. ORIG C20: via G from L: rake, from *rādere* to scrape

rat (ræt) *n* **1** any of numerous long-tailed Old World rodents, that are similar to but larger than mice and are now distributed all over the world. **2** *Inf.* a person who deserts his or her friends or associates, esp. in time of trouble. **3** *Inf.* a worker who works during a strike; blackleg; scab. **4** *Inf.* a despicable person. **5 have** *or* **be rats.** *Austral. sl.* to be mad or eccentric. **6 smell a rat.** to detect something suspicious. ◆ *vb* **rats, ratting, ratted. 7** (*intr;* usually foll. by *on*) **7a** to divulge secret information (about); betray the trust (of). **7b** to default (on); abandon. **8** to hunt and kill rats. ORIG OE *rætt*

rata ('rɑːtə) *n* a New Zealand tree with red flowers. ORIG from Maori

ratable *or* **rateable** ('reɪtəbᵊl) *adj* **1** able to be rated or evaluated. **2** *Brit.* (of property) liable to payment of rates.
▸ **ˌrata'bility** *or* **ˌratea'bility** *n* ▸ **'ratably** *or* **'rateably** *adv*

ratable value *n Brit.* (formerly) a fixed value assigned to a property by a local authority, on the basis of which variable annual rates are charged.

ratafia (ˌrætə'fɪə) *or* **ratafee** (ˌrætə'fiː) *n* **1** any liqueur made from fruit or from brandy with added fruit. **2** a flavouring essence made from almonds. **3** *Chiefly Brit.* Also called: **ratafia biscuit.** a small macaroon flavoured with almonds. ORIG C17: from West Indian Creole F

ratan (ræ'tæn) *n* a variant spelling of **rattan.**

rat-arsed *adj Brit. sl.* drunk.

rat-a-tat-tat ('rætəˌtæt'tæt) *or* **rat-a-tat** ('rætə'tæt) *n* the sound of knocking on a door.

ratatouille (ˌrætə'twiː) *n* a vegetable casserole made of tomatoes, aubergines, peppers, etc., fried in oil and stewed slowly. ORIG C19: from F, from *touiller* to stir, from L, from *tudes* hammer

ratbag ('rætˌbæg) *n Sl.* an eccentric, stupid, or unreliable person.

rat-catcher *n* a person whose job is to destroy or drive away vermin, esp. rats.

ratchet ('rætʃɪt) *n* **1** a device in which a toothed rack or wheel is engaged by a pawl to permit motion in one direction only. **2** the toothed rack or wheel forming part of such a device. ORIG C17: from F *rochet,* from OF *rocquet* blunt head of a lance, of Gmc origin

ratchet effect *n Econ.* an effect that occurs when a price or wage increases as a result of temporary pressure but fails to fall back when the pressure is removed.

rate[1] (reɪt) *n* **1** a quantity or amount considered in relation to or measured against another quantity or amount: *a rate of 70 miles an hour.* **2a** a price or charge with reference to a standard or scale: *rate of interest.* **2b** (*as modifier*): *a rate card.* **3** a charge made per unit for a commodity, service, etc. **4** See **rates. 5** the relative speed of progress or change of something variable; pace: *the rate of production has doubled.* **6a** relative quality; class or grade. **6b** (*in combination*): *first-rate ideas.* **7 at any rate.** in any case; at all events; anyway. ◆ *vb* **rates, rating, rated.** (*mainly tr*) **8** (*also intr*) to assign or receive a position on a scale of relative values; rank: *he is rated fifth in the world.* **9** to estimate the value of; evaluate: *we rate your services highly.* **10** to be worthy of; deserve: *this hotel does not rate four stars.* **11** to consider; regard: *I rate him among my friends.* **12** *Brit.* to assess the value of (property) for the purpose of local taxation. ORIG C15: from OF, from Med. L *rata,* from L *prō ratā parte* according to a fixed proportion, from *ratus* fixed, from *rērī* to think, decide

rate[2] (reɪt) *vb* **rates, rating, rated.** (*tr*) to scold or criticize severely; rebuke harshly. ORIG C14: ? rel. to Swedish *rata* to chide

rateable ('reɪtəbᵊl) *adj* a variant spelling of **ratable.**

rate-cap ('reɪtˌkæp) *vb* **rate-caps, rate-capping, rate-capped.** (*tr*) (formerly in Britain) to impose on (a local authority) an upper limit on the rate it may levy.
▸ **'rate-ˌcapping** *n*

ratel ('reɪtᵊl) *n* **1** a carnivorous mammal related to the badger family, inhabiting wooded regions of Africa and S Asia. It has a massive body, strong claws, and a thick coat that is paler on the back. It feeds on honey and small animals. **2** *S. African.* a six-wheeled armoured vehicle. ORIG C18: from Afrik.

rate of exchange *n* See **exchange rate.**

rate of return *n Finance.* the ratio of the annual income from an investment to the original investment, often expressed as a percentage.

ratepayer ('reɪtˌpeɪə) *n* **1** (in Canada) a person subject to local rates, esp. a householder. **2** (in Britain) a person subject to local nondomestic rates.

rates (reɪts) *pl n* (in Canada and Britain) a tax levied on property (in Britain on business and other nondomestic property only) by a local authority.

Rathenau ★ (*German* 'ra:tənau) *n* **Walther** ('valtər). 1867–1922, German industrialist, who organized the war industries during World War I; minister of reconstruction (1921) and of foreign affairs (1922): largely responsible for the treaty of Rapallo with Russia: assassinated.

rather ('rɑːðə) *adv* (*in senses 1-4, not used with a negative*) **1** relatively or fairly; somewhat: *it's rather dull.* **2** to a significant or noticeable extent; quite: *she's rather pretty.* **3** to a limited extent or degree: *I rather thought that was the case.* **4** with better or more just cause: *this text is rather to be deleted than rewritten.* **5** more readily or willingly; sooner: *I would rather not see you tomorrow.* ◆ *sentence connector.* **6** on the contrary: *it's not cold. Rather, it's very hot.* ◆ *sentence substitute.* ('rɑː'ðɜː). **7** an expression of strong affirmation: *Is it worth seeing? Rather!* ORIG OE *hrathor* comp. of *hræth* READY, quick

> **USAGE NOTE** Both *would* and *had* are used with *rather* in sentences such as *I would rather* (or *had rather*) *go to the film than to the play. Had rather* is less common and now widely regarded as slightly old-fashioned.

ratify ('rætɪˌfaɪ) *vb* **ratifies, ratifying, ratified.** (*tr*) to give formal approval or consent to. ORIG C14: via OF from L *ratus* fixed (see RATE[1]) + *facere* to make
▸ **'ratiˌfiable** *adj* ▸ **ˌratifi'cation** *n* ▸ **'ratiˌfier** *n*

rating[1] ('reɪtɪŋ) *n* **1** a classification according to order or grade; ranking. **2** an ordinary seaman. **3** *Sailing.* a handicap assigned to a racing boat based on its dimensions, draught, etc. **4** the estimated financial or credit standing of a business enterprise or individual. **5** *Radio, television, etc.* a figure based on statistical sampling indicating what proportion of the total audience tune in to a specific programme.

rating[2] ('reɪtɪŋ) *n* a sharp scolding or rebuke.

ratio ('reɪʃɪəʊ) *n, pl* **ratios. 1** a measure of the relative size of two classes expressible as a proportion: *the ratio of boys to girls is 2 to 1.* **2** *Maths.* a quotient of two numbers or quantities. See also **proportion** (sense 6). ORIG C17: from L: a reckoning, from *rērī* to think

ratiocinate (ˌrætɪ'ɒsɪˌneɪt) *vb* **ratiocinates, ratiocinating, ratiocinated.** (*intr*) to think or argue logically and methodically; reason. ORIG C17: from L *ratiōcinārī* to calculate, from *ratiō* REASON
▸ **ˌratiˌoci'nation** *n* ▸ **ˌrati'ociˌnative** *adj* ▸ **ˌrati'ociˌnator** *n*

ration ('ræʃən) *n* **1a** a fixed allowance of food, provisions, etc., esp. a statutory one for civilians in time of scarcity or soldiers in time of war. **1b** (*as modifier*): *a ration book.* **2** a sufficient or adequate amount: *you've had your ration of television for today.* ◆ *vb* (*tr*) **3** (often foll. by *out*) to distribute (provisions), esp. to an army. **4** to restrict the distribution or consumption of (a commodity) by (people): *the government has rationed sugar.* ◆ See also **rations.** ORIG C18: via F from L *ratiō* REASON

rational ('ræʃən[ə]l) *adj* **1** using reason or logic in thinking out a problem. **2** in accordance with the principles of logic or reason; reasonable. **3** of sound mind; sane: *the patient seemed rational.* **4** endowed with the capacity to reason: *rational beings.* **5** *Maths.* **5a** expressible as a ratio of two integers. **5b** (of an expression, equation, etc.) containing no variable either in irreducible radical form or raised to a fractional power. ◆ *n* **6** a rational number. ORIG C14: from L *ratiōnālis,* from *ratiō* REASON
▸ **ˌratio'nality** *n* ▸ **'rationally** *adv* ▸ **'rationalness** *n*

rationale (ˌræʃə'nɑːl) *n* a reasoned exposition, esp. one defining the fundamental reasons for an action, etc. ORIG C17: from NL, from L *ratiōnālis*

rationalism ('ræʃənəˌlɪzəm) *n* **1** reliance on reason rather than intuition to justify one's beliefs or actions. **2** *Philosophy.* the doctrine that knowledge is acquired by reason without regard to experience. **3** the belief that knowledge and truth are ascertained by rational thought and not by divine or supernatural revelation.
▸ **'rationalist** *n* ▸ **ˌrational'istic** *adj* ▸ **ˌrational'istically** *adv*

rationalize *or* **rationalise** ('ræʃənəˌlaɪz) *vb* **rationalizes, rationalizing, rationalized** *or* **rationalises, rationalising, rationalised. 1** to justify (one's actions) with plausible reasons, esp. after the event. **2** to apply logic or reason to (something). **3** (*tr*) to eliminate unnecessary equipment, etc., from (a group of businesses, factory, etc.), in order to make it more efficient. **4** (*tr*) *Maths.* to eliminate radicals without changing the value of (an expression) or the roots of (an equation).
▸ **ˌrationali'zation** *or* **ˌrationali'sation** *n* ▸ **'rationalˌizer** *or* **'rationalˌiser** *n*

rational number *n* any real number of the form *a/b*, where *a* and *b* are integers and *b* is not zero, as 7 or 7/3.

rations ('ræʃənz) *pl n* (*sometimes sing*) a fixed daily allowance of food, esp. to military personnel or when supplies are limited.

Ratisbon ★ ('rætɪzˌbɒn) *n* the former English name for **Regensburg.**

ratite ('rætaɪt) *adj* **1** (of flightless birds) having a breastbone that lacks a keel for the attachment of flight muscles. **2** of or denoting the flightless birds, that have a flat breastbone, feathers lacking vanes, and reduced wings. ◆ *n* **3** a bird, such as an ostrich that belongs to this group; a flightless bird. ORIG C19: from L *ratis* raft

rat kangaroo *n* any of several ratlike kangaroos that occur in Australia and Tasmania.

ratline *or* **ratlin** ('rætlɪn) *n* *Naut.* any of a series of light lines tied across the shrouds of a sailing vessel for climbing aloft. ORIG C15: from ?

ratoon *or* **rattoon** (ræ'tuːn) *n* **1** a new shoot that grows from near the root of crop plants, esp. the sugar cane, after the old growth has been cut back. ◆ *vb* **2** to propagate by such a growth. ORIG C18: from Sp. *retoño,* from RE- + *otoñar* to sprout in autumn, from *otoño* AUTUMN

ratpack ('rætˌpæk) *n* *Derog. sl.* those members of the press who pursue celebrities and give wide, often intrusive, coverage of their private lives: *the royal ratpack.*

rat race *n* a continual routine of hectic competitive activity: *working in the City is a real rat race.*

rat-running *n* the practice of driving through residential side streets to avoid congested main roads.
▸ **'rat-ˌrun** *n* ▸ **'rat-ˌrunner** *n*

ratsbane ('rætsˌbeɪn) *n* rat poison, esp. arsenic oxide.

rat-tail *n* **1a** a horse's tail that has no hairs. **1b** a horse having such a tail. **2** a style of spoon in which the line of the handle is prolonged in a tapering moulding along the back of the bowl.

rattan *or* **ratan** (ræ'tæn) *n* **1** a climbing palm having tough stems used for wickerwork and canes. **2** the stems of such a plant collectively. **3** a stick made from one of these stems. ORIG C17: from Malay *rōtan*

ratter ('rætə) *n* **1** a dog or cat that catches and kills rats. **2** another word for **rat** (sense 3).

Rattigan ★ ('rætɪgən) *n* Sir **Terence Mervyn.** 1911–77, British playwright. His plays include *The Winslow Boy* (1946) and *Ross* (1960).

rattle ('ræt[ə]l) *vb* **rattles, rattling, rattled. 1** to make a rapid succession of short sharp sounds, as of loose pellets colliding when shaken in a container. **2** to shake with such a sound. **3** to send, move, drive, etc., with such a sound: *the car rattled along the country road.* **4** (*intr;* foll. by *on*) to chatter idly: *he rattled on about his work.* **5** (*tr;* foll. by *off, out,* etc.) to recite perfunctorily or rapidly. **6** (*tr*) *Inf.* to disconcert; make frightened or anxious. ◆ *n* **7** a rapid succession of short sharp sounds. **8** a baby's toy filled with small pellets that rattle when shaken. **9** a series of loosely connected horny segments on the tail of a rattlesnake, vibrated to produce a rattling sound. **10** any of various European scrophulariaceous plants having a capsule in which the seeds rattle, such as the **red rattle** and the **yellow rattle. 11** idle chatter. **12** *Med.* another name for **rale.** ORIG C14: from MDu. *ratelen,* imit.
▸ **'rattly** *adj*

Rattle ★ ('ræt[ə]l) *n* Sir **Simon.** born 1955, British conductor.

rattler ('rætlə) *n* **1** a person or thing that rattles. **2** *Inf.* a rattlesnake.

rattlesnake ('rætᵊlˌsneɪk) *n* any of the venomous New World snakes such as the **black** or **timber rattlesnake** belonging to the family of pit vipers. They have a series of loose horny segments on the tail that are vibrated to produce a buzzing or whirring sound.

rattletrap ('rætᵊlˌtræp) *n Inf.* a broken-down old vehicle, esp. an old car.

rattling ('rætlɪŋ) *adv Inf.* (intensifier qualifying something good, fine, etc.): *a rattling good lunch.*

ratty ('rætɪ) *adj* **rattier, rattiest. 1** *Brit. & NZ inf.* irritable; annoyed. **2** *Inf.* (of the hair) straggly, unkempt, or greasy. **3** *US & Canad. sl.* shabby; dilapidated. **4** *Austral. sl.* mad, eccentric, or odd. **5** of, like, or full of rats.
▸ **'rattily** *adv* ▸ **'rattiness** *n*

Ratushinskaya ★ (ˌrætu'ʃɪnskaɪjə) *n* **Irina** (ɪ'riːnə). born 1954, Russian poet and writer, living in Britain: imprisoned (1983–86) in a Soviet labour camp on charges of subversion. Her publications include *No, I'm Not Afraid* (1986), *Grey is the Colour of Hope* (1988), and *The Odessans* (1992).

raucous ('rɔːkəs) *adj* (of voices, cries, etc.) harshly or hoarsely loud. ORIG C18: from L *raucus* hoarse
▸ **'raucously** *adv* ▸ **'raucousness** *n*

raunchy ('rɔːntʃɪ) *adj* **raunchier, raunchiest.** *Sl.* **1** openly sexual; lusty; earthy. **2** *Chiefly US.* slovenly; dirty. ORIG C20: from ?
▸ **'raunchily** *adv* ▸ **'raunchiness** *n*

raupo ('raʊpəʊ) *n, pl* **raupos.** a marsh reed common in New Zealand. ORIG from Maori

Rauschenberg ★ ('raʊʃənbɜːg) *n* **Robert.** born 1925, US exponent of pop art.

rauwolfia (rɔː'wʊlfɪə, raʊ-) *n* **1** a tropical flowering tree or shrub of SE Asia with latex in its stem. **2** the powdered root of this plant: a source of various drugs, esp. reserpine. ORIG C19: NL, after Leonhard *Rauwolf* (died 1596), G botanist

ravage ('rævɪdʒ) *vb* **ravages, ravaging, ravaged. 1** to cause extensive damage to. ◆ *n* **2** (*often pl*) destructive action: *the ravages of time.* ORIG C17: from F, from OF *ravir* to snatch away, RAVISH
▸ **'ravager** *n*

rave (reɪv) *vb* **raves, raving, raved. 1** to utter (something) in a wild or incoherent manner, as when delirious. **2** (*intr*) to speak in an angry uncontrolled manner. **3** (*intr*) (of the sea, wind, etc.) to rage or roar. **4** (*intr; foll. by over or about*) *Inf.* to write or speak (about) with great enthusiasm. **5** (*intr*) *Brit. sl.* to enjoy oneself wildly or uninhibitedly. ◆ *n* **6** *Inf.* **6a** enthusiastic or extravagant praise. **6b** (*as modifier*): *a rave review.* **7** *Brit. sl.* **7a** Also called: **rave-up.** a party. **7b** a professionally organized party for young people, with electronic dance music, sometimes held in a field or disused building. **8** a name given to various types of dance music, such as techno, that feature fast electronic rhythm. ORIG C14 *raven,* apparently from OF *resver* to wander

ravel ('rævᵊl) *vb* **ravels, ravelling, ravelled** *or US* **ravels, raveling, raveled. 1** to tangle (threads, fibres, etc.) or (of threads, etc.) to become entangled. **2** (often foll. by *out*) to tease or draw out (the fibres of a fabric) or (of a fabric) to fray out in loose ends; unravel. **3** (*tr;* usually foll. by *out*) to disentangle or resolve: *to ravel out a complicated story.* ◆ *n* **4** a tangle or complication. ORIG C16: from MDu. *ravelen*
▸ **'raveller** *n* ▸ **'ravelly** *adj*

Ravel ★ (*French* ravɛl) *n* **Maurice (Joseph)** (mɔris). 1875–1937, French composer, whose works include *Le Tombeau de Couperin* (1917) for piano, *Boléro* (1928) for orchestra, and the ballet *Daphnis et Chloé* (1912).

raven[1] ('reɪvᵊn) *n* **1** a large passerine bird of the crow family, having a large straight bill, long wedge-shaped tail, and black plumage. **2a** a shiny black colour. **2b** (*as adj*): *raven hair.* ORIG OE *hræfn*

raven[2] ('rævᵊn) *vb* **1** to seize or seek (plunder, prey, etc.). **2** to eat (something) voraciously or greedily. ORIG C15: from OF *raviner* to attack impetuously; see RAVENOUS

ravening ('rævənɪŋ) *adj* (of animals) voracious; predatory.
▸ **'raveningly** *adv*

Ravenna ★ (rə'vɛnə; *Italian* ra'venna) *n* a city and port in NE Italy, in Emilia-Romagna: capital of the Western Roman Empire from 402 to 476, of the Goths from 493 to 526, and of the Byzantine province from 584 to 751; famous for its ancient mosaics. Pop.: 137 216 (1996 est.).

ravenous ('rævənəs) *adj* **1** famished; starving. **2** rapacious; voracious. ORIG C16: from OF *ravineux,* from L *rapīna* plunder, from *rapere* to seize
▸ **'ravenously** *adv* ▸ **'ravenousness** *n*

raver ('reɪvə) *n* **1** *Brit. sl.* a person who leads a wild or uninhibited social life. **2** *Sl.* a person who enjoys rave music, esp. one who frequents raves.

ravine (rə'viːn) *n* a deep narrow steep-sided valley. ORIG C15: from OF: torrent, from L *rapīna* robbery, infl. by L *rapidus* RAPID, both from *rapere* to snatch

raving ('reɪvɪŋ) *adj* **1a** delirious; frenzied. **1b** (*as adv*): *raving mad.* **2** *Inf.* (intensifier): *a raving beauty.* ◆ *n* **3** (*usually pl*) frenzied or wildly extravagant talk or utterances.
▸ **'ravingly** *adv*

ravioli (ˌrævɪ'əʊlɪ) *n* small squares of pasta containing a savoury mixture of meat, cheese, etc. ORIG C19: It. dialect, lit.: little turnips, from It. *rava* turnip, from L *rāpa*

ravish ('rævɪʃ) *vb* (*tr*) **1** (*often passive*) to enrapture. **2** to rape. **3** *Arch.* to carry off by force. ORIG C13: from OF *ravir,* from L *rapere* to seize
▸ **'ravisher** *n* ▸ **'ravishment** *n*

ravishing ('rævɪʃɪŋ) *adj* delightful; lovely; entrancing.
▸ **'ravishingly** *adv*

raw (rɔː) *adj* **1** (of food) not cooked. **2** (*prenominal*) in an unfinished, natural, or unrefined state; not treated by manufacturing or other processes: *raw materials.* **3** (of the skin, a wound, etc.) having the surface exposed or abraded, esp. painfully. **4** (of an edge of material) unhemmed; liable to fray. **5** ignorant, inexperienced, or immature: *a raw recruit.* **6** (*prenominal*) not selected or modified: *raw statistics.* **7** frank or realistic: *a raw picture of a marriage.* **8** (of spirits) undiluted. **9** *Chiefly US.* coarse, vulgar, or obscene. **10** (of the weather) harshly cold and damp. **11** *Inf.* unfair; unjust (esp. in **a raw deal**). ◆ *n* **12 in the raw. 12a** *Inf.* without clothes; naked. **12b** in a natural or unmodified state. **13 the raw.** *Brit. inf.* a sensitive point: *his criticism touched me on the raw.* ORIG OE *hreaw*
▸ **'rawish** *adj* ▸ **'rawly** *adv* ▸ **'rawness** *n*

Rawalpindi ★ (rɔːl'pɪndɪ) *n* an ancient city in N Pakistan: interim capital of Pakistan (1959–67) during the building of Islamabad. Pop.: 1 290 000 (1995 est.).

rawboned ('rɔː'bəʊnd) *adj* having a lean bony physique.

rawhide ('rɔːˌhaɪd) *n* **1** untanned hide. **2** a whip or rope made of strips cut from such a hide.

rawhide hammer *n* a hammer, used to avoid damaging a surface, having a head consisting of a metal tube from each end of which a tight roll of hide protrudes.

rawinsonde ('reɪwɪnˌsɒnd) *n* a hydrogen balloon carrying meteorological instruments and a radar target, enabling the velocity of winds in the atmosphere to be measured. ORIG C20: blend of *radar* + *wind* + *radiosonde*

Rawlplug ('rɔːlplʌg) *n Trademark.* a short fibre or plastic tube used to provide a fixing in a wall for a screw.

raw material *n* **1** material on which a particular manufacturing process is carried out. **2** a person or thing regarded as suitable for some particular purpose: *raw material for the army.*

raw silk *n* **1** untreated silk fibres reeled from the cocoon. **2** fabric woven from such fibres.

Rawsthorne ★ ('rɔːsˌθɔːn) *n* **Alan.** 1905–71, British composer, whose works include three symphonies, several concertos, and a set of *Symphonic Studies* (1939).

ray[1] (reɪ) *n* **1** a narrow beam of light; gleam. **2** a slight indication: *a ray of solace.* **3** *Maths.* a straight line extending from a point. **4** a thin beam of electromagnetic radiation or particles. **5** any of the bony or cartilaginous spines of the fin of a fish that form the support for the soft part of the fin. **6** any of the arms or branches of a starfish. **7** *Bot.* any strand of tissue that runs radially through the vascular tissue of some higher plants. ◆ *vb* **8** (of an object) to emit (light) in rays or (of light) to issue in the form of rays. **9** (*intr*) (of lines, etc.) to extend in rays or on radiating paths. **10** (*tr*) to adorn (an ornament, etc.) with rays or radiating lines. ORIG C14: from OF *rai,* from L *radius* spoke

ray[2] (reɪ) *n* any of various marine selachian fishes typically having a flattened body, greatly enlarged winglike pectoral fins, gills on the undersurface of the fins, and a long whiplike tail. ORIG C14: from OF *raie,* from L *raia*

ray[3] (reɪ) *n Music.* (in tonic sol-fa) the second degree of any major scale; supertonic. ORIG C18: later variant of *re;* see GAMUT

Ray[1] ★ (reɪ) *n* **Cape.** a promontory in SW Newfoundland, Canada.

Ray[2] ★ (reɪ) *n* **1 John.** 1627–1705, English naturalist, noted for his botanical classification. **2 Man,** real name *Emmanuel Rudnitsky.* 1890–1976, US surrealist photographer. **3 Satyajit** ('sætjədʒɪt). 1921–92, Indian film director. His films include *Pather Panchali* (1955), *The World of Apu* (1959), and *The Stranger* (1992).

Raybans ('reɪˌbænz) *pl n Trademark.* a brand of sunglasses.

ray flower *or* **floret** *n* any of the small strap-shaped flowers in the flower head of certain composite plants, such as the daisy.

ray gun *n* (in science fiction) a gun that emits rays to paralyse, stun, or destroy.

Rayleigh ★ ('reɪlɪ) *n* **Lord,** title of *John William Strutt.* 1842–1919, British physicist: Nobel prize for physics (1904) for his work on sound and the scattering of radiation.

rayless ('reɪlɪs) *adj* **1** dark; gloomy. **2** lacking rays: *a rayless flower.*

raylet ('reɪlɪt) *n* a small ray.

rayon ('reɪɒn) *n* **1** any of a number of textile fibres made from wood pulp or other forms of cellulose. **2** any fabric made from such a fibre. **3** (*as modifier*): *a rayon shirt.* ORIG C20: from F, from OF *rai* RAY[1]

raze *or* **rase** (reɪz) *vb* **razes, razing, razed** *or* **rases, rasing, rased.** (*tr*) **1** to demolish (buildings, etc.) completely (esp. in **raze to the ground**). **2** to delete; erase. **3** *Arch.* to graze. ORIG C16: from OF *raser,* from L *rādere* to scrape
▸ **'razer** *or* **'raser** *n*

razoo (rɑː'zuː) *n, pl* **razoos.** *Austral. & NZ inf.* an imaginary coin: *not a brass razoo; they took every last razoo.* ORIG C20: from ?

razor ('reɪzə) *n* **1** a sharp implement used esp. for shaving the face. **2 on a razor's edge** *or* **razor-edge.** in an acute dilemma. ◆ *vb* **3** (*tr*) to cut or shave with a razor. ORIG C13: from OF *raseor,* from *raser* to shave; see RAZE

razorback ('reɪzəˌbæk) *n* **1** Also called: **finback.** another name for the **common rorqual** (see **rorqual**). **2** a wild pig of the US, having a narrow body, long legs, and a ridged back.

razorbill ('reɪzəˌbɪl) *or* **razor-billed auk** *n* a common auk of the North Atlantic, having a thick laterally compressed bill with white markings.

razor blade *n* a small rectangular piece of metal sharpened on one or both long edges for use in a razor for shaving.

razor-shell *n* any of various sand-burrowing bivalve molluscs which have a long tubular shell. US name: **razor clam.**

razor wire *n* strong wire with pieces of sharp metal set across it at close intervals.

razz (ræz) *US & Canad. sl.* ◆ *vb* **1** (*tr*) to make fun of; deride. ◆ *n* **2** short for **raspberry** (sense 4).

razzle ('ræzᵊl) *n Inf.* **on the razzle.** out enjoying oneself or celebrating, esp. while drinking freely. ORIG C20: from RAZZLE-DAZZLE

razzle-dazzle ('ræzᵊl'dæzᵊl) *or* **razzmatazz** ('ræzmə'tæz) *n Sl.* **1** noisy or showy fuss or activity. **2** a spree or frolic. ORIG C19: rhyming compound from DAZZLE

Rb *the chemical symbol for* rubidium.

RBT *abbrev. for* random breath testing.

RC *abbrev. for:* **1** Red Cross. **2** Roman Catholic.

RCA *abbrev. for:* **1** (formerly) Radio Corporation of America. **2** Royal College of Art.

RCAF *abbrev. for* Royal Canadian Air Force.

RC CH *abbrev. for* Roman Catholic Church.

RCM *abbrev. for* Royal College of Music.

RCMP *abbrev. for* Royal Canadian Mounted Police.

RCN *abbrev. for:* **1** Royal Canadian Navy. **2** Royal College of Nursing.

RCP *abbrev. for* Royal College of Physicians.

RCS *abbrev. for:* **1** Royal College of Science. **2** Royal College of Surgeons. **3** Royal Corps of Signals.

rd *abbrev. for:* **1** road. **2** rod (unit of length). **3** round. **4** *Physics.* rutherford.

Rd *abbrev. for* Road.

RDA *abbrev. for:* **1** recommended daily (*or* dietary) amount (*or* allowance). **2** (in England) Regional Development Agency.

RDC (in Britain, formerly) *abbrev. for* Rural District Council.

re[1] (reɪ, riː) *n Music.* the syllable used in the fixed system of solmization for the note D. ORIG C14: see GAMUT

re[2] (riː) *prep* with reference to. ORIG C18: from L *rē,* ablative case of *rēs* thing

> **USAGE NOTE** In contexts such as *re your letter, your remarks have been noted* or *he spoke to me re your complaint, re* is common in business or official correspondence. In spoken and in general written English *with reference to* is preferable in the former case and *about* or *concerning* in the latter. Even in business correspondence, the use of *re* is often restricted to the letter heading.

Re[1] ★ (reɪ) *n* another name for **Ra**[2].

Re[2] *the chemical symbol for* rhenium.

RE *abbrev. for:* **1** Religious Education. **2** Royal Engineers.

re- *prefix* **1** indicating return to a previous condition, withdrawal, etc.: *rebuild; renew.* **2** indicating repetition of an action: *remarry.* ORIG L

> **USAGE NOTE** Verbs beginning with *re-* indicate repetition or restoration. It is unnecessary to add an adverb such as *back* or *again*: *this must not occur again* (not *recur again*); *we recounted the votes* (not *recounted the votes again,* which implies that the votes were counted three times, not twice).

reach (riːtʃ) *vb* **1** (*tr*) to arrive at or get to (a place, person, etc.) in the course of movement or action: *to reach the office.* **2** to extend as far as (a point or place): *to reach the ceiling; can you reach?* **3** (*tr*) to come to (a certain condition or situation): *to reach the point of starvation.* **4** (*intr*) to extend in influence or operation: *the Roman conquest reached throughout England.* **5** (*tr*) *Inf.* to pass or give (something to a person) with the outstretched hand. **6** (*intr;* foll. by *out, for,* or *after*) to make a movement (towards), as if to grasp or touch. **7** (*tr*) to make contact or communication with (someone): *we tried to reach him all day.* **8** (*tr*) to strike, esp. in fencing or boxing. **9** (*tr*) to amount to (a certain sum): *to reach five million.* **10** (*intr*) *Naut.* to sail on a tack with the wind on or near abeam. ◆ *n* **11** the act of reaching. **12** the extent or distance of reaching: *within reach.* **13** the range of influence, power, etc. **14** an open stretch of water, esp. on a river. **15** *Naut.* the direction or distance sailed by a vessel on one tack. **16** *Advertising.* the proportion of a market that an advertiser hopes to reach at least once in a campaign. ORIG OE *rǣcan*
▸ **'reachable** *adj* ▸ **'reacher** *n*

reach-me-down *n* **1a** (*often pl*) a cheaply ready-made or second-hand garment. **1b** (*as modifier*): *reach-me-down finery.* **2** (*modifier*) not original; derivative: *reach-me-down ideas.*

react (rɪ'ækt) *vb* **1** (*intr;* foll. by *to, upon,* etc.) (of a person or thing) to act in response to another person, a stimulus, etc. **2** (*intr;* foll. by *against*) to act in an opposing or contrary manner. **3** (*intr*) *Physics.* to exert an equal force in the opposite direction to an acting force. **4** *Chem.* to undergo or cause to undergo a chemical reaction. ORIG C17: from LL *reagere,* from RE- + L *agere* to do

re-act (riː'ækt) *vb* (*tr*) to act or perform again.

reactance (rɪ'æktəns) *n* the opposition to the flow of alternating current by the capacitance or inductance of an electrical circuit.

reactant (rɪ'æktənt) *n* a substance that participates in a chemical reaction.

reaction (rɪ'ækʃən) *n* **1** a response to some foregoing action or stimulus. **2** the reciprocal action of two things acting together. **3** opposition to change, esp. political change, or a desire to return to a former system. **4** a response indicating a person's feelings or emotional attitude. **5** *Med.* **5a** any effect produced by the action of a drug. **5b** any effect produced by a substance (allergen) to which a person is allergic. **6** *Chem.* a process that involves changes in the structure and energy content of atoms, molecules, or ions. **7** the equal and opposite force that acts on a body whenever it exerts a force on another body.
▸ **re'actional** *adj*

> **USAGE NOTE** *Reaction* is used to refer both to an instant response (*her reaction was one of amazement*) and to a considered response in the form of a statement (*the Minister gave his reaction to the court's decision*). Some people think this second use is incorrect.

reactionary (rɪ'ækʃənərɪ, -ʃənrɪ) *or* **reactionist** *adj* **1** of, relating to, or characterized by reaction, esp. against radical political or social change. ◆ *n, pl* **reactionaries** *or* **reactionists. 2** a person opposed to radical change.
▸ **re'actionism** *n*

reaction engine *or* **motor** *n* an engine, such as a jet engine, that ejects gas at high velocity and develops its thrust from the ensuing reaction.

reaction turbine *n* a turbine in which the working fluid is accelerated by expansion in both the static nozzles and the rotor blades.

reactivate (rɪ'æktɪˌveɪt) *vb* **reactivates, reactivating, reactivated.** (*tr*) to make (something) active again.
▸ **reˌacti'vation** *n*

reactive (rɪ'æktɪv) *adj* **1** readily partaking in chemical reactions: *sodium is a reactive metal.* **2** of, concerned with, or having a reactance. **3** responsive to stimulus. **4** (of mental illnesses) precipitated by an external cause.
▸ **reactivity** (ˌriːæk'tɪvɪtɪ) *or* **re'activeness** *n*

reactor (rɪ'æktə) *n* **1** short for **nuclear reactor. 2** a vessel in which a chemical reaction takes occurs. **3** a coil of low resistance and high inductance that introduces reactance into a circuit. **4** *Med.* a person sensitive to a particular drug or agent. **5** *Chem.* a substance that takes part in a reaction.

read¹ (riːd) *vb* **reads, reading, read** (rɛd). **1** to comprehend the meaning of (something written or printed) by looking at and interpreting the written or printed characters. **2** (when *tr,* often foll. by *out*) to look at, interpret, and speak aloud (something written or printed). **3** (*tr*) to interpret the significance or meaning of through scrutiny and recognition: *to read a map.* **4** (*tr*) to interpret or understand the meaning of (signs, characters, etc.) other than by visual means: *to read Braille.* **5** (*tr*) to have sufficient knowledge of (a language) to understand the written or printed word. **6** (*tr*) to discover or make out the true nature or mood of: *to read someone's mind.* **7** to interpret or understand (something read) in a specified way: *I read this speech as satire.* **8** (*tr*) to adopt as a reading in a particular passage: *for "boon" read "bone".* **9** (*intr*) to have or contain a certain form or wording: *the sentence reads as follows.* **10** to undertake a course of study in (a subject): *to read history.* **11** to gain knowledge by reading: *he read about the war.* **12** (*tr*) to register, indicate, or show: *the meter reads 100.* **13** (*tr*) to put into a specified condition by reading: *to read a child to sleep.* **14** (*tr*) to hear and understand, esp. when using a two-way radio: *we are reading you loud and clear.* **15** *Computing.* to obtain (data) from a storage device, such as magnetic tape. **16 read a lesson** (*or* **lecture**). *Inf.* to censure or reprimand. ◆ *n* **17** matter suitable for reading: *this book is a very good read.* **18** the act or a spell of reading. ◆ See also **read into, read out,** etc. ORIG OE *rǣdan* to advise, explain

read² (rɛd) *vb* **1** the past tense and past participle of **read¹**. ◆ *adj* **2** having knowledge gained from books (esp. in **widely read** and **well-read**). **3 take (something) as read.** to take (something) for granted as a fact; understand or presume.

readable ('riːdəbᵊl) *adj* **1** (of handwriting, etc.) able to be read or deciphered; legible. **2** (of style of writing) interesting, easy, or pleasant to read.
▸ **ˌreada'bility** *or* **'readableness** *n* ▸ **'readably** *adv*

Reade ★ (riːd) *n* **Charles.** 1814–84, British novelist: author of *The Cloister and the Hearth* (1861).

reader ('riːdə) *n* **1** a person who reads. **2** *Chiefly Brit.* a member of staff below a professor but above a senior lecturer at a university. **3a** a book that is part of a planned series for those learning to read. **3b** a standard textbook, esp. for foreign-language learning. **4** a person who reads aloud in public. **5** a person who reads and assesses the merit of manuscripts submitted to a publisher. **6** a proofreader. **7** short for **lay reader.**

readership ('riːdəʃɪp) *n* all the readers collectively of a publication or author: *a readership of five million.*

reading ('riːdɪŋ) *n* **1a** the act of a person who reads. **1b** (*as modifier*): *a reading room.* **2a** ability to read. **2b** (*as modifier*): *a child of reading age.* **3** any matter that can be read; written or printed text. **4** a public recital or rendering of a literary work. **5** the form of a particular word or passage in a given text, esp. where more than one version exists. **6** an interpretation, as of a piece of music, a situation, or something said or written. **7** knowledge gained from books: *a person of little reading.* **8** a measurement indicated by a gauge, dial, scientific instrument, etc. **9** *Parliamentary procedure.* **9a** the formal recital of the body or title of a bill in a legislative assembly in order to begin one of the stages of its passage. **9b** one of the three stages in the passage of a bill through a legislative assembly. See **first reading, second reading, third reading. 10** the formal recital of something written, esp. a will.

Reading ★ ('rɛdɪŋ) *n* **1** a town in S England, in Berkshire, on the River Thames: seat of The University of Reading (1892). Pop.: 134 600 (1991). **2** a unitary authority in S England, in Berkshire. Pop.: 142 900 (1996 est.). Area: 37 sq. km (14 sq. miles).

read into (riːd) *vb* (*tr, prep*) to discern in or infer from a statement (meanings not intended by the speaker or writer).

read out (riːd) *vb* (*adv*) **1** (*tr*) to read (something) aloud. **2** to retrieve (information) from a computer memory or storage device. **3** (*tr*) *US & Canad.* to expel (someone) from a political party or other society. ◆ *n* **read-out. 4a** the act of retrieving information from a computer memory or storage device. **4b** the information retrieved.

read up (riːd) *vb* (*adv;* when *intr,* often foll. by *on*) to acquire information about (a subject) by reading intensively.

read-write head ('riːd'raɪt) *n Computing.* an electromagnet that can both read and write information on a magnetic tape or disk.

ready ('rɛdɪ) *adj* **readier, readiest. 1** in a state of completion or preparedness, as for use or action. **2** willing or eager: *ready helpers.* **3** prompt or rapid: *a ready response.* **4** (*prenominal*) quick in perceiving; intelligent: *a ready mind.* **5** (*postpositive*) (foll. by *to*) on the point (of) or liable (to): *ready to collapse.* **6** (*postpositive*) conveniently near (esp. in **ready to hand**). **7 make** *or* **get ready.** to prepare (oneself or something) for use or action. ◆ *n* **8** *Inf.* (*often preceded by* the) short for **ready money. 9 at** *or* **to the ready. 9a** (of a rifle) in the position adopted prior to aiming and firing. **9b** poised for use or action: *with pen at the ready.* ◆ *vb* **readies, readying, readied. 10** (*tr*) to put in a state of readiness; prepare. ORIG OE (*ge*)*rǣde*
▸ **'readily** *adv* ▸ **'readiness** *n*

ready-made *adj* **1** made for purchase and immediate

use by any customer. **2** extremely convenient or ideally suited: *a ready-made solution.* **3** unoriginal or conventional: *ready-made phrases.* ◆ *n* **4** a ready-made article, esp. a garment.

ready-mix *n* **1** (*modifier*) consisting of ingredients blended in advance, esp. of food that is ready to cook or eat after addition of milk or water: *a ready-mix cake.* **2** concrete that is mixed before or during delivery to a building site.

ready money *or* **cash** *n* funds for immediate use; cash. Also: **the ready, the readies.**

ready reckoner *n* a table of numbers for facilitating simple calculations, esp. for working out interest, etc.

ready-to-wear *adj* (**ready to wear** *when postpositive*). **1** (of clothes) not tailored for the wearer; of a standard size. ◆ *n* **2** an article or suit of such clothes.

reafforest (ˌriːəˈfɒrɪst) *or* **reforest** *vb* (*tr*) to replant (an area that was formerly forested).
▸ **ˌreafˌforestˈation** *or* **ˌreforestˈation** *n*

Reagan ★ (ˈreɪgən) *n* **Ronald.** born 1911, US film actor and Republican statesman: Governor of California (1966–74): 40th president of the US (1981–89).

reagent (riːˈeɪdʒənt) *n* a substance for use in a chemical reaction, esp. for use in chemical synthesis and analysis.

real[1] (rɪəl) *adj* **1** existing or occurring in the physical world; not imaginary, fictitious, or theoretical; actual. **2** (*prenominal*) true; actual; not false: *the real reason.* **3** (*prenominal*) deserving the name; rightly so called: *a real friend.* **4** not artificial or simulated; genuine: *real fur.* **5** (of food, etc.) traditionally made and having a distinct flavour: *real ale; real cheese.* **6** *Philosophy.* existent or relating to actual existence (as opposed to nonexistent, potential, contingent, or apparent). **7** (*prenominal*) *Econ.* (of prices, incomes, etc.) considered in terms of purchasing power rather than nominal currency value. **8** (*prenominal*) denoting or relating to immovable property such as land and tenements: *real estate.* **9** *Maths.* involving or containing real numbers alone; having no imaginary part. **10** *Inf.* (intensifier): *a real genius.* **11 the real thing.** the genuine article, not a substitute. ◆ *n* **12 for real.** *Sl.* not as a test or trial; in earnest. **13 the real.** that which exists in fact; reality. ORIG C15: from OF *réel,* from LL *reālis,* from L *rēs* thing
▸ **ˈrealness** *n*

real[2] (reɪˈɑːl) *n, pl* **reals** *or* **reales** (*Spanish* reˈales). a former small Spanish or Spanish-American silver coin. ORIG C17: from Sp., lit.: royal, from L *rēgālis;* see REGAL

real ale *n* any beer which is allowed to ferment in the barrel and which is pumped up from the keg without using carbon dioxide.

real estate *n* another term, chiefly US and Canad., for **real property.**

realgar (rɪˈælgə) *n* a rare orange-red soft mineral consisting of arsenic sulphide in monoclinic crystalline form. ORIG C14: via Med. L from Ar. *rahj al-ghar* powder of the mine

realism (ˈrɪəˌlɪzəm) *n* **1** awareness or acceptance of the physical universe, events, etc., as they are, as opposed to the abstract or ideal. **2** a style of painting and sculpture that seeks to represent the familiar or typical in real life. **3** any similar style in other arts, esp. literature. **4** *Philosophy.* the thesis that general terms refer to entities that have a real existence separate from the individuals which fall under them. **5** *Philosophy.* the theory that physical objects continue to exist whether they are perceived or not.
▸ **ˈrealist** *n*

realistic (ˌrɪəˈlɪstɪk) *adj* **1** showing awareness and acceptance of reality. **2** practical or pragmatic rather than ideal or moral. **3** (of a book, etc.) depicting what is real and actual. **4** of or relating to philosophical realism.
▸ **ˌrealˈistically** *adv*

reality (rɪˈælɪtɪ) *n, pl* **realities. 1** the state of things as they are or appear to be, rather than as one might wish them to be. **2** something that is real. **3** the state of being real. **4** *Philosophy.* **4a** that which exists, independent of human awareness. **4b** the totality of facts. **5 in reality.** actually; in fact.

reality principle *n Psychoanal.* control of behaviour by the ego to meet the conditions imposed by the external world.

reality TV *n* television programmes focusing on members of the public living in conditions created especially by the programme makers.

realize *or* **realise** (ˈrɪəˌlaɪz) *vb* **realizes, realizing, realized** *or* **realises, realising, realised. 1** (when *tr, may take a clause as object*) to become conscious or aware of (something). **2** (*tr, often passive*) to bring (a plan, ambition, etc.) to fruition. **3** (*tr*) to give (a drama or film) the appearance of reality. **4** (*tr*) (of goods, property, etc.) to sell for or make (a certain sum): *this table realized £800.* **5** (*tr*) to convert (property or goods) into cash. **6** (*tr*) (of a musicologist or performer) to reconstruct (a composition) from an incomplete set of parts.
▸ **ˈrealˌizable** *or* **ˈrealˌisable** *adj* ▸ **ˈrealˌizably** *or* **ˈrealˌisably** *adv* ▸ **ˌrealiˈzation** *or* **ˌrealiˈsation** *n* ▸ **ˈrealˌizer** *or* **ˈrealˌiser** *n*

real life *n* actual human life, as lived by real people, esp. contrasted with the lives of fictional characters: *miracles don't happen in real life.*

really (ˈrɪəlɪ) *adv* **1** in reality; in actuality; assuredly: *it's really quite harmless.* **2** truly; genuinely: *really beautiful.* ◆ *interj* **3** an exclamation of dismay, disapproval, doubt, surprise, etc. **4 not really?** an exclamation of surprise or polite doubt.

USAGE NOTE See at **very.**

realm (rɛlm) *n* **1** a royal domain; kingdom: *peer of the realm.* **2** a field of interest, study, etc.: *the realm of the occult.* ORIG C13: from OF *reialme,* from L *regimen* rule, infl. by OF *reial,* from L *rēgālis* REGAL

real number *n* any rational or irrational number. See **number.**

real presence *n* the doctrine that the body of Christ is actually present in the Eucharist.

real property *n Property law.* immovable property, esp. freehold land. Cf. **personal property.**

real tennis *n* an ancient form of tennis played in a four-walled indoor court.

real-time *adj* denoting or relating to a data-processing system in which a computer is on-line to a source of data and processes the data as it is generated.

realtor (ˈrɪəltə, -ˌtɔː) *n* a US word for an **estate agent,** esp. an accredited one. ORIG C20: from REALTY + -OR[1]

realty (ˈrɪəltɪ) *n* another term for **real property.**

ream[1] (riːm) *n* **1** a number of sheets of paper, formerly 480 sheets (**short ream**), now 500 sheets (**long ream**) or 516 sheets (**printer's ream** or **perfect ream**). One ream is equal to 20 quires. **2** (*often pl*) *Inf.* a large quantity, esp. of written matter: *he wrote reams.* ORIG C14: from OF, from Sp., from Ar. *rizmah* bale

ream[2] (riːm) *vb* (*tr*) **1** to enlarge (a hole) by use of a reamer. **2** *US.* to extract (juice) from (a citrus fruit) using a reamer. ORIG C19: ?from C14 *remen* to open up, from OE *rȳman* to widen

reamer (ˈriːmə) *n* **1** a steel tool with a cylindrical or tapered shank around which longitudinal teeth are ground, used for smoothing the bores of holes accurately to size. **2** *US.* a utensil with a conical projection used for extracting juice from citrus fruits.

reap (riːp) *vb* **1** to cut or harvest (a crop) from (a field). **2** (*tr*) to gain or get (something) as a reward for or result of some action or enterprise. ORIG OE *riopan*
▸ **ˈreapable** *adj*

reaper (ˈriːpə) *n* **1** a person who reaps or a machine for reaping. **2 the grim reaper.** death.

rear[1] (rɪə) *n* **1** the back or hind part. **2** the area or position that lies at the back: *a garden at the rear of the house.* **3** the section of a military force farthest from the front. **4** an informal word for **buttocks** (see **buttock**). **5 bring up the rear.** to be at the back in a procession, race, etc. **6 in the rear.** at the back. **7** (*modifier*) of or in the rear: *the rear side.* ORIG C17: prob. from REARWARD or REARGUARD

★ people and places

rear[2] (rɪə) *vb* **1** (*tr*) to care for and educate (children) until maturity; raise. **2** (*tr*) to breed (animals) or grow (plants). **3** (*tr*) to place or lift (a ladder, etc.) upright. **4** (*tr*) to erect (a monument, building, etc.). **5** (*intr; often foll. by up*) (esp. of horses) to lift the front legs in the air and stand nearly upright. **6** (*intr; often foll. by up or over*) (esp. of tall buildings) to rise high; tower. **7** (*intr*) to start with anger, resentment, etc. ORIG OE *ræran*
▸ **'rearer** *n*

rear admiral *n* an officer holding flag rank in any of certain navies, junior to a vice admiral.

Reardon ★ ('rɪədən) *n* **Ray.** born 1932, Welsh snooker player: world champion 1970, 1973–76, 1978.

rearguard ('rɪə,gɑːd) *n* **1** a detachment detailed to protect the rear of a military formation, esp. in retreat. **2** an entrenched or conservative element, as in a political party. **3** (*modifier*) of, relating to, or characteristic of a rearguard: *a rearguard action.* ORIG C15: from OF *rereguarde,* from *rer,* from L *retro* back + *guarde* GUARD

rear light *or* **lamp** *n* a red light, usually one of a pair, attached to the rear of a motor vehicle. Also called: **tail-light, tail lamp.**

rearm (riː'ɑːm) *vb* **1** to arm again. **2** (*tr*) to equip (an army, etc.) with better weapons.
▸ **re'armament** *n*

rearmost ('rɪə,məʊst) *adj* nearest the rear; coming last.

rear-view mirror *n* a mirror on a motor vehicle enabling the driver to see traffic behind him.

rearward ('rɪəwəd) *adj, adv* **1** Also (for adv only): **rearwards.** towards or in the rear. ◆ *n* **2** a position in the rear, esp. the rear division of a military formation. ORIG C14 (*as n:* the part of an army behind the main body of troops): from Anglo-F *rerewarde,* var. of *reregarde;* see REARGUARD

Rea Silvia ★ ('rɪə 'sɪlvɪə) *n* a variant spelling of **Rhea Silvia.**

reason ('riːzᵊn) *n* **1** the faculty of rational argument, deduction, judgment, etc. **2** sound mind; sanity. **3** a cause or motive, as for a belief, action, etc. **4** an argument in favour or a justification for something. **5** *Philosophy.* the intellect regarded as a source of knowledge, as contrasted with experience. **6** *Logic.* a premise of an argument in favour of the given conclusion. **7 by reason of.** because of. **8 in** *or* **within reason.** within moderate or justifiable bounds. **9 it stands to reason.** it is logical or obvious. **10 listen to reason.** to be persuaded peaceably. **11 reasons of State.** political justifications for an immoral act. ◆ *vb* **12** (when *tr, takes a clause as object*) to think logically or draw (logical conclusions) from facts or premises. **13** (*intr; usually foll. by with*) to seek to persuade by reasoning. **14** (*tr; often foll. by out*) to work out or resolve (a problem) by reasoning. ORIG C13: from OF *reisun,* from L *ratiō* reckoning, from *rērī* to think
▸ **'reasoner** *n*

> **USAGE NOTE** The expression *the reason is because...* should be avoided. Instead one should say either *this is because...* or *the reason is that...*

reasonable ('riːzənəbᵊl) *adj* **1** showing reason or sound judgment. **2** having the ability to reason. **3** having modest or moderate expectations. **4** moderate in price. **5** fair; average: *reasonable weather.*
▸ **'reasonably** *adv* ▸ **'reasonableness** *n*

reasoned ('riːzᵊnd) *adj* well thought-out or well presented: *a reasoned explanation.*

reasoning ('riːzənɪŋ) *n* **1** the act or process of drawing conclusions from facts, evidence, etc. **2** the arguments, proofs, etc., so adduced.

reassure (,riːə'ʃʊə) *vb* **reassures, reassuring, reassured.** (*tr*) **1** to relieve (someone) of anxieties; restore confidence to. **2** to insure again.
▸ **,reas'surance** *n* ▸ **,reas'surer** *n* ▸ **,reas'suringly** *adv*

Réaumur ('reɪə,mjʊə) *adj* indicating measurement on the Réaumur scale.

Réaumur scale *n* a scale of temperature in which the freezing point of water is taken as 0° and the boiling point as 80°. ORIG C18: after René de *Réaumur* (1683–1757), F physicist, who introduced it

reave (riːv) *vb* **reaves, reaving, reaved** *or* **reft.** *Arch.* **1** to carry off (property, prisoners, etc.) by force. **2** (*tr; foll. by of*) to deprive; strip. See **reive.** ORIG OE *reāfian*

rebadge (,riː'bædʒ) *vb* (*tr*) to relaunch (a product) under a new name, brand, or logo.

rebarbative (rɪ'bɑːbətɪv) *adj* fearsome; forbidding. ORIG C19: from F *rébarbatif,* from OF *rebarber* to repel (an enemy)

rebate[1] *n* ('riːbeɪt). **1** a refund of a fraction of the amount payable; discount. ◆ *vb* (rɪ'beɪt), **rebates, rebating, rebated.** (*tr*) **2** to deduct (a part) of a payment from (the total). **3** *Arch.* to reduce. ORIG C15: from OF *rabattre* to beat down, hence reduce, from RE- + *abatre* to put down
▸ **re'batable** *or* **re'bateable** *adj* ▸ **'rebater** *n*

rebate[2] ('riːbeɪt, 'ræbɪt) *n, vb* **rebates, rebating, rebated.** another word for **rabbet.**

rebec *or* **rebeck** ('riːbɛk) *n* a medieval stringed instrument resembling the violin but having a lute-shaped body. ORIG C16: from OF *rebebe,* from Ar. *rebāb;* ? infl. by OF *bec* beak

Rebecca ★ (rɪ'bɛkə) *n Old Testament.* the sister of Laban, who became the wife of Isaac and the mother of Esau and Jacob (Genesis 24–27). Douay spelling: **Rebekah.**

rebel *vb* (rɪ'bɛl), **rebels, rebelling, rebelled.** (*intr; often foll. by against*) **1** to resist or rise up against a government or authority, esp. by force of arms. **2** to dissent from an accepted moral code or convention of behaviour, etc. **3** to show repugnance (towards). ◆ *n* ('rɛbᵊl). **4a** a person who rebels. **4b** (*as modifier*): *a rebel soldier.* **5** a person who dissents from some accepted moral code or convention of behaviour, etc. ORIG C13: from OF *rebelle,* from L *rebellis* insurgent, from RE- + *bellum* war

rebellion (rɪ'bɛljən) *n* **1** organized opposition to a government or other authority. **2** dissent from an accepted moral code or convention of behaviour, etc. ORIG C14: via OF from L *rebelliō* revolt (of those conquered); see REBEL

rebellious (rɪ'bɛljəs) *adj* **1** showing a tendency towards rebellion. **2** (of a problem, etc.) difficult to overcome; refractory.
▸ **re'belliously** *adv* ▸ **re'belliousness** *n*

rebirth (riː'bɜːθ) *n* **1** a revival or renaissance: *the rebirth of learning.* **2** a second or new birth.

reboot (riː'buːt) *vb* to shut down and then restart (a computer system) or (of a computer system) to shut down and restart.

rebore *n* ('riː,bɔː). **1** the process of boring out the cylinders of a worn reciprocating engine and fitting oversize pistons. ◆ *vb* (riː'bɔː), **rebores, reboring, rebored. 2** (*tr*) to carry out this process.

rebound *vb* (rɪ'baʊnd). (*intr*) **1** to spring back, as from a sudden impact. **2** to misfire, esp. so as to hurt the perpetrator. ◆ *n* ('riːbaʊnd). **3** the act or an instance of rebounding. **4 on the rebound. 4a** in the act of springing back. **4b** *Inf.* in a state of recovering from rejection, etc.: *he married her on the rebound from an unhappy love affair.* ORIG C14: from OF *rebondir,* from RE- + *bondir* to BOUND[2]

rebounder (rɪ'baʊndə) *n* a type of small trampoline used for aerobic exercising.

rebozo (rɪ'bəʊzəʊ) *n, pl* **rebozos.** a long wool or linen scarf covering the shoulders and head, worn by Latin American women. ORIG C19: from Sp., from *rebozar* to muffle

rebrand (,riː'brænd) *vb* (*tr*) to change or update the image of (an organization or product).

rebuff (rɪ'bʌf) *vb* (*tr*) **1** to snub, reject, or refuse (help, sympathy, etc.). **2** to beat back (an attack); repel. ◆ *n* **3** a blunt refusal or rejection; snub. ORIG C16: from OF *rebuffer,* from It., from *ribuffo* a reprimand, from *ri-* RE- + *buffo* puff, gust, apparently imit.

rebuke (rɪ'bjuːk) *vb* **rebukes, rebuking, rebuked. 1** (*tr*) to scold or reprimand (someone). ◆ *n* **2** a reprimand or scolding. ORIG C14: from OF *rebuker,* from RE- + *buchier* to hack down, from *busche* log, of Gmc origin
▸ **re'bukable** *adj* ▸ **re'buker** *n* ▸ **re'bukingly** *adv*

rebus ('riːbəs) *n, pl* **rebuses. 1** a puzzle consisting of pictures, symbols, etc., representing syllables and words; the word *hear* might be represented by H and a picture of an ear. **2** a heraldic device that is a pictorial representation of the name of the bearer. ORIG C17: from F *rébus,* from L *rēbus* by things, from RES

rebut (rɪ'bʌt) *vb* **rebuts, rebutting, rebutted.** (*tr*) to refute or disprove, esp. by offering a contrary contention. ORIG C13: from OF *reboter,* from RE- + *boter* to thrust, BUTT[3]
▸ **re'buttable** *adj* ▸ **re'buttal** *n*

rebutter (rɪ'bʌtə) *n* **1** *Law.* a defendant's pleading in reply to a plaintiff's surrejoinder. **2** a person who rebuts.

rec. *abbrev. for:* **1** receipt. **2** recipe. **3** record.

recalcitrant (rɪ'kælsɪtrənt) *adj* **1** not susceptible to control; refractory. ◆ *n* **2** a recalcitrant person. ORIG C19: via F from L, from RE- + *calcitrāre* to kick, from *calx* heel
▸ **re'calcitrance** *n*

recalescence (ˌriːkə'lɛsəns) *n* a sudden spontaneous increase in the temperature of cooling iron. ORIG C19: from L *recalēscere* to grow warm again, from RE- + *calēscere,* from *calēre* to be hot
▸ **ˌrecal'esce** *vb* (*intr*) ▸ **ˌreca'lescent** *adj*

recall (rɪ'kɔːl) *vb* (*tr*) **1** (*may take a clause as object*) to bring back to mind; recollect. **2** to order to return. **3** to revoke or take back. **4** to cause (one's thoughts, attention, etc.) to return from a reverie or digression. ◆ *n* **5** the act of recalling or state of being recalled. **6** revocation or cancellation. **7** the ability to remember things. **8** *Mil.* (formerly) a signal to call back troops, etc. **9** *US.* the process by which elected officials may be deprived of office by popular vote.
▸ **re'callable** *adj*

recant (rɪ'kænt) *vb* to repudiate or withdraw (a former belief or statement), esp. formally in public. ORIG C16: from L *recantāre,* from RE- + *cantāre* to sing
▸ **recantation** (ˌriːkæn'teɪʃən) *n* ▸ **re'canter** *n*

recap *vb* ('riːˌkæp, riː'kæp), **recaps, recapping, recapped,** *n* ('riːˌkæp). *Inf.* short for **recapitulate** *or* **recapitulation.**
▸ **re'cappable** *adj*

recapitulate (ˌriːkə'pɪtjʊˌleɪt) *vb* **recapitulates, recapitulating, recapitulated. 1** to restate the main points of (an argument, speech, etc.). **2** (*tr*) (of an animal) to repeat (stages of its evolutionary development) during the embryonic stages of its life. ORIG C16: from LL *recapitulāre,* lit.: to put back under headings; see CAPITULATE
▸ **ˌreca'pitulative** *or* **ˌreca'pitulatory** *adj*

recapitulation (ˌriːkəˌpɪtjʊ'leɪʃən) *n* **1** the act of recapitulating, esp. summing up, as at the end of a speech. **2** Also called: **palingenesis.** *Biol.* the apparent repetition in the embryonic development of an animal of the changes that occurred during its evolutionary history. **3** *Music.* the repeating of earlier themes, esp. in the final section of a movement in sonata form.

recapture (riː'kæptʃə) *vb* **recaptures, recapturing, recaptured.** (*tr*) **1** to capture or take again. **2** to recover, renew, or repeat (a lost or former ability, sensation, etc.). ◆ *n* **3** the act of recapturing or fact of being recaptured.

recce ('rɛkɪ) *n, vb* **recces, recceing, recced** *or* **recceed.** a slang word for **reconnaissance** or **reconnoitre.**

recd *or* **rec'd** *abbrev. for* received.

recede (rɪ'siːd) *vb* **recedes, receding, receded.** (*intr*) **1** to withdraw from a point or limit; go back: *the tide receded.* **2** to become more distant: *hopes of rescue receded.* **3** to slope backwards: *apes have receding foreheads.* **4a** (of a man's hair) to cease to grow at the temples and above the forehead. **4b** (of a man) to start to go bald in this way. **5** to decline in value. **6** (usually foll. by *from*) to draw back or retreat, as from a promise. ORIG C15: from L *recēdere* to go back, from RE- + *cēdere* to yield

re-cede (riː'siːd) *vb* **re-cedes, re-ceding, re-ceded.** (*tr*) to restore to a former owner.

receipt (rɪ'siːt) *n* **1** a written acknowledgment by a receiver of money, goods, etc., that payment or delivery has been made. **2** the act of receiving or fact of being received. **3** (*usually pl*) an amount or article received. **4** *Obs.* another word for **recipe.** ◆ *vb* **5** (*tr*) to acknowledge payment of (a bill), as by marking it. ORIG C14: from OF *receite,* from Med. L *recepta,* from L *recipere* to RECEIVE

receivable (rɪ'siːvəbəl) *adj* **1** suitable for or capable of being received, esp. as payment or legal tender. **2** (of a bill, etc.) awaiting payment: *accounts receivable.* ◆ *n* **3** (*usually pl*) the part of the assets of a business represented by accounts due for payment.

receive (rɪ'siːv) *vb* **receives, receiving, received.** (*mainly tr*) **1** to take (something offered) into one's hand or possession. **2** to have (an honour, blessing, etc.) bestowed. **3** to accept delivery or transmission of (a letter, etc.). **4** to be informed of (news). **5** to hear and consent to or acknowledge (a confession, etc.). **6** (of a container) to take or hold (a substance or certain amount). **7** to support or sustain (the weight of something); bear. **8** to apprehend or perceive (ideas, etc.). **9** to experience, undergo, or meet with: *to receive a crack on the skull.* **10** (*also intr*) to be at home to (visitors). **11** to greet or welcome (guests), esp. in formal style. **12** to admit (a person) to a place, society, condition, etc.: *he was received into the priesthood.* **13** to accept or acknowledge (a precept or principle) as true or valid. **14** to convert (incoming radio signals) into sounds, pictures, etc., by means of a receiver. **15** (*also intr*) *Tennis, etc.* to play at the other end from the server. **16** (*also intr*) to partake of (the Christian Eucharist). **17** (*intr*) *Chiefly Brit.* to buy and sell stolen goods. ORIG C13: from OF *receivre,* from L *recipere,* from RE- + *capere* to take

received (rɪ'siːvd) *adj* generally accepted or believed: *received wisdom.*

Received Pronunciation *n* the accent of standard Southern British English. Abbrev.: **RP.**

receiver (rɪ'siːvə) *n* **1** a person who receives something; recipient. **2** a person appointed by a court to manage property pending the outcome of litigation, during the infancy of the owner, or after the owner has been declared bankrupt or insane. **3** *Chiefly Brit.* a person who receives stolen goods knowing that they have been stolen. **4** the equipment in a telephone, radio, or television that receives incoming electrical signals or modulated radio waves and converts them into the original audio or video signals. **5** the detachable part of a telephone that is held to the ear. **6** *Chem.* a vessel in which the distillate is collected during distillation. **7** *US sport.* a player whose function is to receive the ball.

receivership (rɪ'siːvəʃɪp) *n Law.* **1** the office or function of a receiver. **2** the condition of being administered by a receiver.

receiving order *n Brit.* a court order appointing a receiver to manage the property of a debtor or bankrupt.

recension (rɪ'sɛnʃən) *n* **1** a critical revision of a literary work. **2** a text revised in this way. ORIG C17: from L *recēnsiō,* from *recēnsēre,* from RE- + *cēnsēre* to assess

recent ('riːsənt) *adj* having appeared, happened, or been made not long ago; modern, fresh, or new. ORIG C16: from L *recens* fresh; rel. to Gk *kainos* new
▸ **'recently** *adv* ▸ **'recentness** *or* **'recency** *n*

Recent ('riːsənt) *adj, n Geol.* another word for **Holocene.**

receptacle (rɪ'sɛptəkəl) *n* **1** an object that holds something; container. **2** *Bot.* **2a** the enlarged or modified tip of the flower stalk that bears the parts of the flower. **2b** the part of lower plants that bears the reproductive organs or spores. ORIG C15: from L *receptāculum* store-place, from *receptāre,* from *recipere* to RECEIVE

reception (rɪ'sɛpʃən) *n* **1** the act of receiving or state of being received. **2** the manner in which something, such as a guest or a new idea, is received: *a cold reception.* **3** a formal party for guests, such as after a wedding. **4** an area in an office, hotel, etc., where visitors or guests are received and appointments or reservations dealt with. **5** short for **reception room. 6** the quality or fidelity of a received radio or television broadcast: *the reception was poor.* ORIG C14: from L *receptiō,* from *recipere* to RECEIVE

reception centre *n* a place to which distressed people, such as vagrants, addicts, victims of a disaster, refugees, etc., go pending more permanent arrangements.

reception class *n* in the UK, the class in primary schools for the youngest children attending school for the first time.

receptionist (rɪ'sɛpʃənɪst) *n* a person employed in an office, surgery, etc., to receive clients or guests, arrange appointments, etc.

reception room *n* **1** a room in a private house suitable for entertaining guests. **2** a room in a hotel suitable for receptions, etc.

receptive (rɪ'sɛptɪv) *adj* **1** able to apprehend quickly. **2** tending to receive new ideas or suggestions favourably. **3** able to hold or receive.
▸ **re'ceptively** *adv* ▸ **receptivity** (ˌriːsɛp'tɪvɪtɪ) *or* **re'ceptiveness** *n*

receptor (rɪ'sɛptə) *n* **1** *Physiol.* a sensory nerve ending that changes specific stimuli into nerve impulses. **2** any of various devices that receive information, signals, etc.

recess *n* (rɪ'sɛs, 'riːsɛs). **1** a space, such as a niche or alcove, set back or indented. **2** (*often pl*) a secluded or secret place: *recesses of the mind.* **3** a cessation of business, such as the closure of Parliament during a vacation. **4** *Anat.* a small cavity or depression in a bodily organ. **5** *US & Canad.* a break between classes at a school. ◆ *vb* (rɪ'sɛs). **6** (*tr*) to place or set (something) in a recess. **7** (*tr*) to build a recess in (a wall, etc.). ORIG C16: from L *recessus* a retreat, from *recēdere* to RECEDE

recession[1] (rɪ'sɛʃən) *n* **1** a temporary depression in economic activity or prosperity. **2** the withdrawal of the clergy and choir in procession after a church service. **3** the act of receding. **4** a part of a building, wall, etc., that recedes. ORIG C17: from L *recessio;* see RECESS

recession[2] (riː'sɛʃən) *n* the act of restoring possession to a former owner. ORIG C19: from RE- + CESSION

recessional (rɪ'sɛʃənᵊl) *adj* **1** of or relating to recession. ◆ *n* **2** a hymn sung as the clergy and choir withdraw after a church service.

recessive (rɪ'sɛsɪv) *adj* **1** tending to recede or go back. **2** *Genetics.* **2a** (of a gene) capable of producing its characteristic phenotype in the organism only when its allele is identical. **2b** (of a character) controlled by such a gene. Cf. **dominant** (sense 4). **3** *Linguistics.* (of stress) tending to be placed on or near the initial syllable of a polysyllabic word. ◆ *n* **4** *Genetics.* a recessive gene or character.
▸ **re'cessively** *adv* ▸ **re'cessiveness** *n*

recharge (ˌriː'tʃɑːdʒ) *vb* **recharges, recharging, recharged.** (*tr*) **1** to cause (an accumulator, capacitor, etc.) to take up and store electricity again. **2** to revive or renew (one's energies) (esp. in **recharge one's batteries**).
▸ **re'chargeable** *adj*

recherché (rə'ʃɛəʃeɪ) *adj* **1** known only to connoisseurs; choice or rare. **2** studiedly refined or elegant. ORIG C18: from F: p.p. of *rechercher* to make a thorough search for

recidivism (rɪ'sɪdɪˌvɪzəm) *n* habitual relapse into crime. ORIG C19: from L *recidīvus* falling back, from RE- + *cadere* to fall
▸ **re'cidivist** *n, adj* ▸ **reˌcidi'vistic** *or* **re'cidivous** *adj*

Recife ★ (rɛ'siːfə) *n* a port at the easternmost point of Brazil on the Atlantic: capital of Pernambuco state; built partly on an island, with many waterways and bridges. Pop. (urban area): 3 168 000 (1995). Former name: **Pernambuco.**

recipe ('rɛsɪpɪ) *n* **1** a list of ingredients and directions for making something, esp. when preparing food. **2** *Med.* (formerly) a medical prescription. **3** a method for achieving some desired objective: *a recipe for success.* ORIG C14: from L, lit.: take (it)! from *recipere* to take

recipient (rɪ'sɪpɪənt) *n* **1** a person who or thing that receives. ◆ *adj* **2** receptive. ORIG C16: via F from L, from *recipere* to RECEIVE
▸ **re'cipience** *or* **re'cipiency** *n*

reciprocal (rɪ'sɪprəkᵊl) *adj* **1** of, relating to, or designating something given by each of two people, countries, etc., to the other; mutual: *reciprocal trade.* **2** given or done in return: *a reciprocal favour.* **3** (of a pronoun) indicating that action is given and received by each subject; for example, *each other* in *they started to shout at each other.* **4** *Maths.* of or relating to a number or quantity divided into one. ◆ *n* **5** something that is reciprocal. **6** Also called: **inverse.** *Maths.* a number or quantity that when multiplied by a given number or quantity gives a product of one: *the reciprocal of 2 is 0.5.* ORIG C16: from L *reciprocus* alternating
▸ **reˌcipro'cality** *n* ▸ **re'ciprocally** *adv*

reciprocate (rɪ'sɪprəˌkeɪt) *vb* **reciprocates, reciprocating, reciprocated.** **1** to give or feel in return. **2** to move or cause to move backwards and forwards. **3** (*intr*) to be correspondent or equivalent. ORIG C17: from L *reciprocāre,* from *reciprocus* RECIPROCAL
▸ **reˌcipro'cation** *n* ▸ **re'ciprocative** *or* **re'ciproˌcatory** *adj* ▸ **re'ciproˌcator** *n*

reciprocating engine *n* an engine in which one or more pistons move backwards and forwards inside a cylinder or cylinders.

reciprocity (ˌrɛsɪ'prɒsɪtɪ) *n* **1** reciprocal action or relation. **2** a mutual exchange of commercial or other privileges. ORIG C18: via F from L *reciprocus* RECIPROCAL

recision (rɪ'sɪʒən) *n* the act of cancelling or rescinding; annulment: *the recision of a treaty.* ORIG C17: from L *recīsiō,* from *recīdere* to cut back

recital (rɪ'saɪtᵊl) *n* **1** a musical performance by a soloist or soloists. **2** the act of reciting or repeating something learned or prepared. **3** an account, narration, or description. **4** (*often pl*) *Law.* the preliminary statement in a deed showing the reason for its existence and explaining the operative part.
▸ **re'citalist** *n*

recitation (ˌrɛsɪ'teɪʃən) *n* **1a** the act of reciting from memory. **1b** a formal reading of verse before an audience. **2** something recited.

recitative[1] (ˌrɛsɪtə'tiːv) *n* a passage in a musical composition, esp. the narrative parts in an oratorio, reflecting the natural rhythms of speech. ORIG C17: from It. *recitativo;* see RECITE

recitative[2] (rɪ'saɪtətɪv) *adj* of or relating to recital.

recite (rɪ'saɪt) *vb* **recites, reciting, recited.** **1** to repeat (a poem, etc.) aloud from memory before an audience. **2** (*tr*) to give a detailed account of. **3** (*tr*) to enumerate (examples, etc.). ORIG C15: from L *recitāre* to cite again, from RE- + *citāre* to summon
▸ **re'citable** *adj* ▸ **re'citer** *n*

reck (rɛk) *vb Arch.* (*used mainly with a negative*) **1** to mind or care about (something): *to reck nought.* **2** (*usually impersonal*) to concern or interest (someone). ORIG OE *reccan*

reckless ('rɛklɪs) *adj* having or showing no regard for danger or consequences; heedless; rash: *a reckless driver.* ORIG OE *recceleās;* see RECK, -LESS
▸ **'recklessly** *adv* ▸ **'recklessness** *n*

Recklinghausen ★ (*German* rɛklɪŋ'hauzən) *n* an industrial city in NW Germany, in North Rhine-Westphalia on the N edge of the Ruhr. Pop.: 127 216 (1996 est.).

reckon ('rɛkən) *vb* **1** to calculate or ascertain by calculating; compute. **2** (*tr*) to include; count as part of a set or class. **3** (*usually passive*) to consider or regard: *he is reckoned clever.* **4** (when *tr, takes a clause as object*) to think or suppose; be of the opinion: *I reckon you don't know.* **5** (*intr;* foll. by *with*) to settle accounts (with). **6** (*intr;* foll. by *with* or *without*) to take into account or fail to take into account: *they reckoned without John.* **7** (*intr;* foll. by *on* or *upon*) to rely or depend: *I reckon on your support.* **8** (*tr*) *Inf.* to have a high opinion of. **9 to be reckoned with.** of considerable importance or influence. ORIG OE (*ge*)*recenian* recount

reckoner ('rɛkənə) *n* any of various devices or tables used to facilitate reckoning, esp. a ready reckoner.

reckoning ('rɛkənɪŋ) *n* **1** the act of counting or calculating. **2** settlement of an account or bill. **3** a bill or account. **4** retribution for one's actions (esp. in **day of reckoning**). **5** *Navigation.* short for **dead reckoning.**

reclaim (rɪ'kleɪm) *vb* (*tr*) **1** to claim back: *reclaim baggage.* **2** to convert (desert, marsh, etc.) into land suitable for growing crops. **3** to recover (useful substances) from waste products. **4** to convert (someone) from sin, folly, vice, etc. ◆ *n* **5** the act of reclaiming or state of being reclaimed. ORIG C13: from OF *réclamer,* from L *reclāmāre* to cry out, from RE- + *clāmāre* to shout
▸ **re'claimable** *adj* ▸ **re'claimant** *or* **re'claimer** *n*

reclamation (ˌrɛklə'meɪʃən) *n* **1** the conversion of desert, marsh, etc., into land suitable for cultivation. **2** the recovery of useful substances from waste products. **3** the act of reclaiming or state of being reclaimed.

réclame *French.* (reklam) *n* **1** public acclaim or attention; publicity. **2** the capacity for attracting publicity.

reclinate ('rɛklɪˌneɪt) *adj Bot.* naturally curved or bent backwards so that the upper part rests on the ground. ORIG C18: from L *reclīnātus* bent back

recline (rɪ'klaɪn) *vb* **reclines, reclining, reclined.** to rest in a leaning position. ORIG C15: from OF *recliner,* from L *reclīnāre,* from RE- + *clīnāre* to LEAN[1]
▸ **re'clinable** *adj* ▸ **reclination** (ˌrɛklɪ'neɪʃən) *n*

recliner (rɪ'klaɪnə) *n* a person or thing that reclines, esp. a type of armchair having a back that can be adjusted to slope at various angles.

recluse (rɪ'klu:s) *n* **1** a person who lives in seclusion, esp. to devote himself or herself to prayer and religious meditation; a hermit. ◆ *adj* **2** solitary; retiring. ORIG C13: from OF *reclus,* from LL *reclūdere* to shut away, from L RE- + *claudere* to close
▸ **reclusion** (rɪ'klu:ʒən) *n* ▸ **re'clusive** *adj*

recognition (ˌrɛkəg'nɪʃən) *n* **1** the act of recognizing or fact of being recognized. **2** acceptance or acknowledgment of a claim, duty, etc. **3** a token of thanks. **4** formal acknowledgment of a government or of the independence of a country. ORIG C15: from L *recognitiō,* from *recognoscere,* from RE- + *cognoscere* to know
▸ **recognitive** (rɪ'kɒgnɪtɪv) *or* **re'cognitory** *adj*

recognizance *or* **recognisance** (rɪ'kɒgnɪzəns) *n Law.* **a** a bond entered into before a court or magistrate by which a person binds himself to do a specified act, as to appear in court on a stated day, keep the peace, or pay a debt. **b** a monetary sum pledged to the performance of such an act. ORIG C14: from OF *reconoissance,* from *reconoistre* to RECOGNIZE
▸ **re'cognizant** *or* **re'cognisant** *adj*

recognize *or* **recognise** ('rɛkəgˌnaɪz) *vb* **recognizes, recognizing, recognized** *or* **recognises, recognising, recognised.** (*tr*) **1** to perceive (a person or thing) to be the same as or belong to the same class as something previously seen or known; know again. **2** to accept or be aware of (a fact, problem, etc.): *to recognize necessity.* **3** to give formal acknowledgment of the status or legality of (a government, a representative, etc.). **4** *Chiefly US & Canad.* to grant (a person) the right to speak in a deliberative body. **5** to give a token of thanks for (a service rendered, etc.). **6** to make formal acknowledgment of (a claim, etc.). **7** to show approval or appreciation of (something good). **8** to acknowledge or greet (a person). ORIG C15: from L *recognoscere,* from RE- + *cognoscere* to know
▸ **'recogˌnizable** *or* **'recogˌnisable** *adj* ▸ **ˌrecogˌniza'bility** *or* **ˌrecogˌnisa'bility** *n* ▸ **'recogˌnizably** *or* **'recogˌnisably** *adv* ▸ **'recogˌnizer** *or* **'recogˌniser** *n*

recoil *vb* (rɪ'kɔɪl). (*intr*) **1** to jerk back, as from an impact or violent thrust. **2** (often foll. by *from*) to draw back in fear, horror, or disgust. **3** (foll. by *on* or *upon*) to go wrong, esp. so as to hurt the perpetrator. **4** (of an atom, etc.) to change momentum as a result of the emission of a particle. ◆ *n* (rɪ'kɔɪl, 'ri:kɔɪl). **5a** the backward movement of a gun when fired. **5b** the distance moved. **6** the motion acquired by an atom, etc., as a result of its emission of a particle. **7** the act of recoiling. ORIG C13: from OF *reculer,* from RE- + *cul* rump, from L *cūlus*
▸ **re'coiler** *n*

recollect (ˌrɛkə'lɛkt) *vb* (when *tr, often takes a clause as object*) to recall from memory; remember. ORIG C16: from L *recolligere,* from RE- + *colligere* to COLLECT
▸ **ˌrecol'lection** *n* ▸ **ˌrecol'lective** *adj* ▸ **ˌrecol'lectively** *adv*

recombinant (ri:'kɒmbɪnənt) *Genetics.* ◆ *adj* **1** produced by the combining of genetic material from more than one origin. ◆ *n* **2** a chromosome, cell, organism, etc., the genetic makeup of which results from recombination.

recombinant DNA *n* DNA molecules that are extracted from different sources and chemically joined together.

recombination (ˌri:kɒmbɪ'neɪʃən) *n Genetics.* any of several processes by which genetic material of different origins becomes combined.

recommend (ˌrɛkə'mɛnd) *vb* (*tr*) **1** (*may take a clause as object or an infinitive*) to advise as the best course or choice; counsel. **2** to praise or commend: *to recommend a new book.* **3** to make attractive or advisable: *the trip has little to recommend it.* **4** *Arch.* to entrust (a person or thing) to someone else's care; commend. ORIG C14: via Med. L from L RE- + *commendāre* to COMMEND
▸ **ˌrecom'mendable** *adj* ▸ **ˌrecom'mendatory** *adj* ▸ **ˌrecom'mender** *n*

recommendation (ˌrɛkəmɛn'deɪʃən) *n* **1** the act of recommending. **2** something that recommends, esp. a letter. **3** something that is recommended, such as a course of action.

recommit (ˌri:kə'mɪt) *vb* **recommits, recommitting, recommitted.** (*tr*) **1** to send (a bill) back to a committee for further consideration. **2** to commit again.
▸ **ˌrecom'mitment** *or* **ˌrecom'mittal** *n*

recompense ('rɛkəmˌpɛns) *vb* **recompenses, recompensing, recompensed.** (*tr*) **1** to pay or reward for service, work, etc. **2** to compensate for loss, injury, etc. ◆ *n* **3** compensation for loss, injury, etc. **4** reward, remuneration, or repayment. ORIG C15: from OF *recompenser,* from L RE- + *compensāre* to balance in weighing
▸ **'recomˌpensable** *adj* ▸ **'recomˌpenser** *n*

reconcile ('rɛkənˌsaɪl) *vb* **reconciles, reconciling, reconciled.** (*tr*) **1** (*often passive;* usually foll. by *to*) to make (oneself or another) no longer opposed; cause to acquiesce in something unpleasant: *she reconciled herself to poverty.* **2** to become friendly with (someone) after estrangement or to re-establish friendly relations between (two or more people). **3** to settle (a quarrel). **4** to make (two apparently conflicting things) compatible or consistent with each other. **5** to reconsecrate (a desecrated church, etc.). ORIG C14: from L *reconciliāre,* from RE- + *conciliāre* to make friendly, CONCILIATE
▸ **'reconˌcilement** *n* ▸ **'reconˌciler** *n* ▸ **reconciliation** (ˌrɛkənˌsɪlɪ'eɪʃən) *n* ▸ **reconciliatory** (ˌrɛkən'sɪlɪətərɪ, -trɪ) *adj*

recondite (rɪ'kɒndaɪt, 'rɛkənˌdaɪt) *adj* **1** requiring special knowledge; abstruse. **2** dealing with abstruse or profound subjects. ORIG C17: from L *reconditus* hidden away, from RE- + *condere* to conceal
▸ **re'conditely** *adv* ▸ **re'conditeness** *n*

recondition (ˌri:kən'dɪʃən) *vb* (*tr*) to restore to good condition or working order: *to recondition an engine.*
▸ **ˌrecon'ditioned** *adj*

reconnaissance (rɪ'kɒnɪsəns) *n* **1** the act of reconnoitring. **2** the process of obtaining information about the position, etc., of an enemy. **3** a preliminary inspection of an area of land. ORIG C18: from F, from OF *reconoistre* to explore, RECOGNIZE

reconnoitre *or US* **reconnoiter** (ˌrɛkə'nɔɪtə) *vb* **reconnoitres, reconnoitring, reconnoitred** *or US* **reconnoiters, reconnoitering, reconnoitered. 1** to survey or inspect (an enemy's position, region of land, etc.). ◆ *n* **2** the act or process of reconnoitring; a reconnaissance. ORIG C18: from obs. F *reconnoître* to inspect, explore; see RECOGNIZE
▸ **ˌrecon'noitrer** *or US* **ˌrecon'noiterer** *n*

reconsider (ˌri:kən'sɪdə) *vb* to consider (something) again, with a view to changing one's policy or course of action.
▸ **ˌreconˌsider'ation** *n*

reconstitute (ri:'kɒnstɪˌtju:t) *vb* **reconstitutes, reconstituting, reconstituted.** (*tr*) **1** to restore (food, etc.) to its former or natural state, as by the addition of water to a concentrate. **2** to reconstruct; form again.
▸ **reconstituent** (ˌri:kən'stɪtjʊənt) *adj, n* ▸ **ˌreconsti'tution** *n*

reconstruct (ˌri:kən'strʌkt) *vb* (*tr*) **1** to construct or form again; rebuild. **2** to form a picture of (a crime, past event, etc.) by piecing together evidence.
▸ **ˌrecon'structible** *adj* ▸ **ˌrecon'struction** *n* ▸ **ˌrecon'structive** *or* **ˌrecon'structional** *adj* ▸ **ˌrecon'structor** *n*

reconvert (ˌri:kən'vɜ:t) *vb* (*tr*) **1** to change (something) back to a previous state or form. **2** to bring (someone) back to his or her former religion.
▸ **reconversion** (ˌri:kən'vɜ:ʃən) *n*

record *n* ('rɛkɔ:d). **1** an account in permanent form, esp. in writing, preserving knowledge or information. **2** a

written account of some transaction that serves as legal evidence of the transaction. **3** a written official report of the proceedings of a court of justice or legislative body. **4** anything serving as evidence or as a memorial: *the First World War is a record of human folly.* **5** (*often pl*) information or data on a specific subject collected methodically over a long period: *weather records.* **6a** the best or most outstanding amount, rate, height, etc., ever attained, as in some field of sport: *a world record.* **6b** (*as modifier*): *a record time.* **7** the sum of one's recognized achievements, career, or performance. **8** a list of crimes of which an accused person has previously been convicted. **9 have a record.** to be a known criminal. **10** Also called: **gramophone record, disc.** a thin disc of a plastic material upon which sound has been recorded. Each side has a spiral groove, which undulates in accordance with the frequency and amplitude of the sound. **11** the markings made by a recording instrument such as a seismograph. **12** *Computing.* a group of data or piece of information preserved as a unit in machine-readable form. **13 for the record.** for the sake of strict factual accuracy. **14 go on record.** to state one's views publicly. **15 off the record.** confidential or confidentially. **16 on record. 16a** stated in a public document. **16b** publicly known. **17 set** *or* **put the record straight.** to correct an error. ◆ *vb* (rɪ'kɔːd). (*mainly tr*) **18** to set down in some permanent form so as to preserve the true facts of: *to record the minutes of a meeting.* **19** to contain or serve to relate (facts, information, etc.). **20** to indicate, show, or register: *his face recorded his disappointment.* **21** to remain as or afford evidence of: *these ruins record the life of the Romans in Britain.* **22** (*also intr*) to make a recording of (music, speech, etc.) for reproduction, esp. on a record player or tape recorder, or for later broadcasting. **23** (*also intr*) (of an instrument) to register or indicate (information) on a scale: *the barometer recorded a low pressure.* ORIG C13: from OF *recorder,* from L *recordārī* to remember, from RE- + *cor* heart
▸ **re'cordable** *adj*

recorded delivery *n* a Post Office service by which an official record of posting and delivery is obtained for a letter or package.

recorder (rɪ'kɔːdə) *n* **1** a person who records, such as an official or historian. **2** something that records, esp. an apparatus that provides a permanent record of experiments, etc. **3** short for **tape recorder. 4** *Music.* a wind instrument of the flute family, blown through a fipple in the mouth end, having a reedlike quality of tone. **5** (in England) a barrister or solicitor of at least ten years' standing appointed to sit as a part-time judge in the crown court.
▸ **re'cordership** *n*

recording (rɪ'kɔːdɪŋ) *n* **1a** the act or process of making a record, esp. of sound on a gramophone record or magnetic tape. **1b** (*as modifier*): *recording studio.* **2** the record or tape so produced. **3** something that has been recorded, esp. a radio or television programme.

Recording Angel *n* an angel who supposedly keeps a record of every person's good and bad acts.

record of achievement *n Brit.* a statement of the personal and educational development of each pupil.

record player *n* a device for reproducing the sounds stored on a record. A stylus vibrates in accordance with the undulations of the walls of the groove in the record as it rotates.

recount (rɪ'kaʊnt) *vb* (*tr*) to tell the story or details of; narrate. ORIG C15: from OF *reconter,* from RE- + *conter* to tell; see COUNT[1]
▸ **re'countal** *n*

re-count *vb* (riː'kaʊnt). **1** to count (votes, etc.) again. ◆ *n* ('riːˌkaʊnt). **2** a second or further count, esp. of votes in an election.

recoup (rɪ'kuːp) *vb* **1** to regain or make good (a financial or other loss). **2** (*tr*) to reimburse or compensate (someone), as for a loss. **3** *Law.* to keep back (something due), having rightful claim to do so. ◆ *n* **4** *Rare.* the act of recouping; recoupment. ORIG C15: from OF *recouper* to cut back, from RE- + *couper,* from *coper* to behead
▸ **re'coupable** *adj* ▸ **re'coupment** *n*

recourse (rɪ'kɔːs) *n* **1** the act of resorting to a person, course of action, etc., in difficulty (esp. in **have recourse to**). **2** a person, organization, or course of action that is turned to for help, etc. **3** the right to demand payment, esp. from the drawer or endorser of a bill of exchange or other negotiable instrument when the person accepting it fails to pay. **4 without recourse.** a qualified endorsement on such a negotiable instrument, by which the endorser protects himself from liability to subsequent holders. ORIG C14: from OF *recours,* from LL *recursus* a running back, from RE- + L *currere* to run

recover (rɪ'kʌvə) *vb* **1** (*tr*) to find again or obtain the return of (something lost). **2** to regain (loss of money, time, etc.). **3** (of a person) to regain (health, spirits, composure, etc.). **4** to regain (a former and better condition): *industry recovered after the war.* **5** *Law.* **5a** (*tr*) to gain (something) by the judgment of a court of law: *to recover damages.* **5b** (*intr*) to succeed in a lawsuit. **6** (*tr*) to obtain (useful substances) from waste. **7** (*intr*) (in fencing, rowing, etc.) to make a recovery. ORIG C14: from OF *recoverer,* from L *recuperāre* RECUPERATE
▸ **re'coverable** *adj* ▸ **reˌcovera'bility** *n* ▸ **re'coverer** *n*

re-cover (riː'kʌvə) *vb* (*tr*) **1** to cover again. **2** to provide (furniture, etc.) with a new cover.

recovery (rɪ'kʌvərɪ) *n, pl* **recoveries. 1** the act or process of recovering, esp. from sickness, a shock, or a setback. **2** restoration to a former or better condition. **3** the regaining of something lost. **4** the extraction of useful substances from waste. **5** the retrieval of a space capsule after a spaceflight. **6** *Law.* the obtaining of a right, etc., by the judgment of a court. **7** *Fencing.* a return to the position of guard after making an attack. **8** *Swimming, rowing, etc.* the action of bringing the arm, an oar, etc., forward for another stroke. **9** *Golf.* a stroke played from the rough or a bunker to the fairway or green.

recovery stock *n Stock Exchange.* a security that has fallen in price but is believed to have the ability to recover.

recreant ('rɛkrɪənt) *Arch.* ◆ *adj* **1** cowardly; faint-hearted. **2** disloyal. ◆ *n* **3** a disloyal or cowardly person. ORIG C14: from OF, from *recroire* to surrender, from RE- + L *crēdere* to believe
▸ **'recreance** *or* **'recreancy** *n* ▸ **'recreantly** *adv*

recreate ('rɛkrɪˌeɪt) *vb* **recreates, recreating, recreated.** *Rare.* to amuse (oneself or someone else). ORIG C15: from L *recreāre* to invigorate, renew, from RE- + *creāre* to CREATE
▸ **'recreative** *adj* ▸ **'recreatively** *adv* ▸ **'recreˌator** *n*

re-create (ˌriːkrɪ'eɪt) *vb* **re-creates, re-creating, re-created.** to create anew; reproduce.
▸ **ˌre-cre'ation** *n* ▸ **ˌre-cre'ator** *n*

recreation (ˌrɛkrɪ'eɪʃən) *n* **1** refreshment of health or spirits by relaxation and enjoyment. **2** an activity that promotes this. **3a** an interval of free time between school lessons. **3b** (*as modifier*): *recreation period.*

recreational (ˌrɛkrɪ'eɪʃənᵊl) *adj* **1** of, relating to, or used for recreation: *recreational facilities.* **2** (of a drug) taken for pleasure rather than for medical reasons or because of an addiction.

recreational vehicle *n Chiefly US.* a large vanlike vehicle equipped to be lived in. Abbrev.: **RV.**

recriminate (rɪ'krɪmɪˌneɪt) *vb* **recriminates, recriminating, recriminated.** (*intr*) to return an accusation against someone or engage in mutual accusations. ORIG C17: via Med. L, from L *crīmināri* to accuse, from *crīmen* accusation
▸ **reˌcrimi'nation** *n* ▸ **re'criminative** *or* **re'criminatory** *adj*
▸ **re'crimiˌnator** *n*

recrudesce (ˌriːkruː'dɛs) *vb* **recrudesces, recrudescing, recrudesced.** (*intr*) (of a disease, trouble, etc.) to break out or appear again after a period of dormancy. ORIG C19: from L *recrūdēscere,* from RE- + *crūdēscere* to grow worse, from *crūdus* bloody, raw
▸ **ˌrecru'descence** *n*

recruit (rɪ'kruːt) *vb* **1a** to enlist (men) for military service. **1b** to raise or strengthen (an army, etc.) by enlistment. **2** (*tr*) to enrol or obtain (members, support, etc.). **3** to furnish or be furnished with a fresh supply; renew. **4** *Arch.* to recover (health, spirits, etc.). ◆ *n* **5** a newly joined member of a military service. **6** any new member or sup-

porter. ORIG C17: from F *recrute* lit.: new growth, from *recroître,* from L, from RE- + *crēscere* to grow
▸ **re'cruitable** *adj* ▸ **re'cruiter** *n* ▸ **re'cruitment** *n*

recta ('rɛktə) *n* a plural of **rectum.**

rectal ('rɛktəl) *adj* of or relating to the rectum.
▸ **'rectally** *adv*

rectangle ('rɛk,tæŋgəl) *n* a parallelogram having four right angles. ORIG C16: from Med. L *rectangulum,* from L *rectus* straight + *angulus* angle

rectangular (rɛk'tæŋgjʊlə) *adj* **1** shaped like a rectangle. **2** having or relating to right angles. **3** mutually perpendicular: *rectangular coordinates.* **4** having a base or section shaped like a rectangle.
▸ **rec,tangu'larity** *n* ▸ **rec'tangularly** *adv*

rectangular coordinates *pl n* the Cartesian coordinates in a system of mutually perpendicular axes.

rectangular hyperbola *n* a hyperbola with perpendicular asymptotes.

recti ('rɛktaɪ) *n* the plural of **rectus.**

recti- *or before a vowel* **rect-** *combining form.* straight or right: *rectangle.* ORIG from L *rectus*

rectifier ('rɛktɪ,faɪə) *n* **1** an electronic device that converts an alternating current to a direct current. **2** *Chem.* an apparatus for condensing a hot vapour to a liquid in distillation; condenser. **3** a thing or person that rectifies.

rectify ('rɛktɪ,faɪ) *vb* **rectifies, rectifying, rectified.** (*tr*) **1** to put right; correct; remedy. **2** to separate (a substance) from a mixture or refine (a substance) by fractional distillation. **3** to convert (alternating current) into direct current. **4** *Maths.* to determine the length of (a curve). ORIG C14: via OF from Med. L *rectificāre,* from L *rectus* straight + *facere* to make
▸ **'recti,fiable** *adj* ▸ **,rectifi'cation** *n*

rectilinear (,rɛktɪ'lɪnɪə) *or* **rectilineal** *adj* **1** in, moving in, or characterized by a straight line. **2** consisting of, bounded by, or formed by a straight line.
▸ **,recti'linearly** *or* **,recti'lineally** *adv*

rectitude ('rɛktɪ,tju:d) *n* **1** moral or religious correctness. **2** correctness of judgment. ORIG C15: from LL *rectitūdō,* from L *rectus* right, from *regere* to rule

recto ('rɛktəʊ) *n, pl* **rectos. 1** the front of a sheet of printed paper. **2** the right-hand pages of a book. Cf. **verso** (sense 1b). ORIG C19: from L *rectō foliō* on the right-hand page

rectocele ('rɛktəʊ,si:l) *n Pathol.* a protrusion or herniation of the rectum into the vagina.

rector ('rɛktə) *n* **1** *Church of England.* a clergyman in charge of a parish in which, as its incumbent, he would formerly have been entitled to the whole of the tithes. **2** *RC Church.* a cleric in charge of a college, religious house, or congregation. **3** *Protestant Episcopal Church.* a clergyman in charge of a parish. **4** *Chiefly Brit.* the head of certain schools, colleges, or universities. **5** (in Scotland) a high-ranking official in a university. **6** (in South Africa) a principal of an Afrikaans university. ORIG C14: from L: director, ruler, from *regere* to rule
▸ **'rectorate** *n* ▸ **rectorial** (rɛk'tɔ:rɪəl) *adj* ▸ **'rectorship** *n*

rectory ('rɛktərɪ) *n, pl* **rectories. 1** the official house of a rector. **2** *Church of England.* the office and benefice of a rector.

rectrix ('rɛktrɪks) *n, pl* **rectrices** ('rɛktrɪ,si:z, rɛk'traɪsi:z). any of the large stiff feathers of a bird's tail, used in controlling the direction of flight. ORIG C17: from LL, fem of L *rector* RECTOR
▸ **rectricial** (rɛk'trɪʃəl) *adj*

rectum ('rɛktəm) *n, pl* **rectums** *or* **recta.** the lower part of the alimentary canal, between the sigmoid flexure of the colon and the anus. ORIG C16: from NL *rectum intestinum* the straight intestine

rectus ('rɛktəs) *n, pl* **recti.** *Anat.* a straight muscle. ORIG C18: from NL *rectus musculus*

recumbent (rɪ'kʌmbənt) *adj* **1** lying down; reclining. **2** (of an organ) leaning or resting against another organ. ORIG C17: from L *recumbere* to lie back, from RE- + *cumbere* to lie
▸ **re'cumbence** *or* **re'cumbency** *n* ▸ **re'cumbently** *adv*

recuperate (rɪ'ku:pə,reɪt, -'kju:-) *vb* **recuperates, recuperating, recuperated. 1** (*intr*) to recover from illness or exhaustion. **2** to recover (financial losses, etc.). ORIG C16: from L *recuperāre* to recover, from RE- + *capere* to gain
▸ **re,cuper'ation** *n* ▸ **re'cuperative** *adj*

recur (rɪ'kɜ:) *vb* **recurs, recurring, recurred.** (*intr*) **1** to happen again. **2** (of a thought, etc.) to come back to the mind. **3** (of a problem, etc.) to come up again. **4** *Maths.* (of a digit or group of digits) to be repeated an infinite number of times at the end of a decimal fraction. ORIG C15: from L *recurrere,* from RE- + *currere* to run
▸ **re'curring** *adj*

recurrent (rɪ'kʌrənt) *adj* **1** tending to happen again or repeatedly. **2** *Anat.* (of certain nerves, etc.) turning back, so as to run in the opposite direction.
▸ **re'currence** *n* ▸ **re'currently** *adv*

recurrent fever *n* another name for **relapsing fever.**

recurring decimal *n* a rational number that contains a pattern of digits repeated indefinitely after the decimal point.

recursion (rɪ'kɜ:ʃən) *n* **1** the act or process of returning or running back. **2** *Maths, logic.* the application of a function to its own values to generate an infinite sequence of values. ORIG C17: from L *recursio,* from *recurrere* RECUR
▸ **re'cursive** *adj*

recurve (rɪ'kɜ:v) *vb* **recurves, recurving, recurved.** to curve or bend (something) back or down or (of something) to be so curved or bent. ORIG C16: from L *recurvāre,* from RE- + *curvāre* to CURVE

recusant ('rɛkjʊzənt) *n* **1** (in 16th to 18th century England) a Roman Catholic who did not attend the services of the Church of England. **2** any person who refuses to submit to authority. ◆ *adj* **3** (formerly, of Catholics) refusing to attend services of the Church of England. **4** refusing to submit to authority. ORIG C16: from L *recūsāns* refusing, from *recūsāre,* from RE- + *causārī* to dispute, from *causa* a CAUSE
▸ **'recusance** *or* **'recusancy** *n*

recycle (ri:'saɪkəl) *vb* **recycles, recycling, recycled.** (*tr*) **1** to pass (a substance) through a system again for further treatment or use. **2** to reclaim (packaging or products with a limited useful life) for further use: *to recycle water.* ◆ *n* **3** the repetition of a fixed sequence of events.
▸ **re'cyclable** *or* **re'cycleable** *adj*

red[1] (rɛd) *n* **1** any of a group of colours, such as that of a ripe tomato or fresh blood. **2** a pigment or dye of or producing these colours. **3** red cloth or clothing: *dressed in red.* **4** a red ball in snooker, etc. **5** (in roulette) one of two colours on which players may place even bets. **6** *Inf.* red wine: *a bottle of red.* **7 in the red.** *Inf.* in debt. **8 see red.** *Inf.* to become very angry. ◆ *adj* **redder, reddest. 9** of the colour red. **10** reddish in colour or having parts or marks that are reddish: *red deer.* **11** having the face temporarily suffused with blood, being a sign of anger, shame, etc. **12** (of the complexion) rosy; florid. **13** (of the eyes) bloodshot. **14** (of the hands) stained with blood. **15** bloody or violent: *red revolution.* **16** denoting the highest degree of urgency in an emergency; used by the police and the army and informally (esp. in the phrase **red alert**). **17** (of wine) made from black grapes and coloured by their skins. ◆ *vb* **reds, redding, redded. 18** another word for **redden.** ORIG OE *rēad*
▸ **'reddish** *adj* ▸ **'redness** *n*

red[2] (rɛd) *vb* **reds, redding, red** *or* **redded.** (*tr*) a variant spelling of **redd.**

Red (rɛd) *Inf.* ◆ *adj* **1** Communist, Socialist, or Soviet. **2** radical, leftist, or revolutionary. ◆ *n* **3** a member or supporter of a Communist or Socialist Party or a national of the Soviet Union. **4** a radical, leftist, or revolutionary. ORIG C19: from the colour chosen to symbolize revolutionary socialism

redact (rɪ'dækt) *vb* (*tr*) **1** to compose or draft (an edict, proclamation, etc.). **2** to put (a literary work, etc.) into appropriate form for publication; edit. ORIG C15: from L *redigere* to bring back, from *red-* RE- + *agere* to drive
▸ **re'daction** *n* ▸ **re'dactional** *adj* ▸ **re'dactor** *n*

red admiral *n* a butterfly of temperate Europe and Asia, having black wings with red and white markings. See also **white admiral.**

red algae *pl n* the numerous algae which contain a red

pigment in addition to chlorophyll. The group includes carrageen and dulse.

Red Army Faction *n* another name for **Baader-Meinhof Gang.**

redback ('rɛd,bæk) *n Austral.* a small, venomous spider, the female of which has a red stripe on its back. Also called: **redback spider.**

red bark *n* a kind of cinchona containing a high proportion of alkaloids.

red biddy *n Inf.* cheap red wine fortified with methylated spirits.

red blood cell *n* another name for **erythrocyte.**

red-blooded *adj Inf.* vigorous; virile.
▸ **,red-'bloodedness** *n*

red book *n Brit.* (sometimes caps.) a government publication bound in red, esp. the Treasury's annual forecast of revenue, expenditure, growth, and inflation.

redbreast ('rɛd,brɛst) *n* any of various birds having a red breast, esp. the Old World robin.

redbrick ('rɛd,brɪk) *n (modifier)* denoting, relating to, or characteristic of a provincial British university of relatively recent foundation.

Redbridge ★ ('rɛd,brɪdʒ) *n* a borough of NE Greater London: includes part of Epping Forest. Pop.: 225 100 (1994 est.). Area: 56 sq. km (22 sq. miles).

redcap ('rɛd,kæp) *n* **1** *Brit. inf.* a military policeman. **2** *US & Canad.* a porter at an airport or station.

Redcar and Cleveland ★ ('rɜdkɑː) *n* a unitary authority in NE England, in North Yorkshire. Pop.: 144 000 (1996 est.). Area: 240 sq. km (93 sq. miles).

red card *Soccer, etc.* ◆ *n* **1** a card of a red colour displayed by a referee to indicate that a player has been sent off. ◆ *vb* **red-card. 2** *(tr)* to send off (a player).

red carpet *n* **1** a strip of red carpeting laid for important dignitaries to walk on. **2a** deferential treatment accorded to a person of importance. **2b** *(as modifier): a red-carpet reception.*

red cedar *n* **1** any of several North American coniferous trees, esp. a juniper that has fragrant reddish wood. **2** the wood of any of these trees. **3** any of several Australian timber trees.

red cent *n (used with a negative) Inf., chiefly US.* a cent considered as a trivial amount of money (esp. in **not have a red cent,** etc.).

Red China ★ *n* an unofficial name for (the People's Republic of) **China.**

redcoat ('rɛd,kəʊt) *n* **1** (formerly) a British soldier. **2** *Canad. inf.* another name for **Mountie.**

red coral *n* any of several corals, the skeletons of which are pinkish red in colour and used to make ornaments, etc.

red corpuscle *n* another name for **erythrocyte.**

Red Crescent *n* the emblem of the Red Cross Society in a Muslim country.

Red Cross *n* **1** an international humanitarian organization (**Red Cross Society**) formally established by the Geneva Convention of 1864. **2** the emblem of this organization, consisting of a red cross on a white background.

redcurrant (,rɛd'kʌrənt) *n* **1** a N temperate shrub having greenish flowers and small edible rounded red berries. **2a** the fruit of this shrub. **2b** *(as modifier): redcurrant jelly.*

redd *or* **red** (rɛd) *Scot. & N English dialect.* ◆ *vb* **redds, redding, redd** *or* **redded. 1** *(tr;* often foll. by *up)* to bring order to; tidy (up). ◆ *n* **2** the act or an instance of redding. ORIG C15: *redden* to clear, ? a variant of RID
▸ **'redder** *n*

red deer *n* a large deer formerly widely distributed in the woodlands of Europe and Asia. The coat is reddish brown in summer and the short tail is surrounded by a patch of light-coloured hair.

Red Deer ★ *n* **1** a town in S Alberta on the Red Deer River: trade centre for mixed farming, dairying region, and natural gas processing. Pop: 58 134 (1991). **2** a river in W Canada, in SW Alberta, flowing southeast into the South Saskatchewan River. Length: about 620 km (385 miles). **3** a river in W Canada, flowing east through **Red Deer Lake** into Lake Winnipegosis. Length: about 225 km (140 miles).

redden ('rɛdᵊn) *vb* **1** to make or become red. **2** *(intr)* to flush with embarrassment, anger, etc.

Redding ★ ('rɛdɪŋ) *n* **Otis.** 1941–67, US singer and songwriter. His recordings include "Respect" (1965).

Redditch ★ ('rɛdɪtʃ) *n* a town in W central England, in Hereford and Worcester: designated a new town in the mid-1960s; metal-working industries. Pop.: 73 372 (1991).

reddle ('rɛdᵊl) *n, vb* **reddles, reddling, reddled.** a variant spelling of **ruddle.**

red duster *n Brit.* an informal name for the **Red Ensign.**

red dwarf *n* one of a class of stars of relatively small mass and low luminosity.

rede (riːd) *Arch.* ◆ *n* **1** advice or counsel. **2** an explanation. ◆ *vb* **redes, reding, reded.** *(tr)* **3** to advise; counsel. **4** to explain. ORIG OE *rǣdan* to rule

red earth *n* a clayey zonal soil of tropical savanna lands, formed by extensive chemical weathering and coloured by iron compounds.

redeem (rɪ'diːm) *vb (tr)* **1** to recover possession or ownership of by payment of a price or service; regain. **2** to convert (bonds, shares, etc.) into cash. **3** to pay off (a loan, etc.). **4** to recover (something pledged, mortgaged, or pawned). **5** to convert (paper money) into bullion or specie. **6** to fulfil (a promise, pledge, etc.). **7** to exchange (coupons, etc.) for goods. **8** to reinstate in someone's estimation or good opinion: *he redeemed himself by his altruistic action.* **9** to make amends for. **10** to recover from captivity, esp. by a money payment. **11** *Christianity.* (of Christ as Saviour) to free (humanity) from sin by death on the Cross. ORIG C15: from OF *redimer,* from L *redimere,* from *red-* RE- + *emere* to buy
▸ **re'deemable** *or* **re'demptible** *adj* ▸ **re'deemer** *n*

Redeemer (rɪ'diːmə) *n* **the.** Jesus Christ as having brought redemption to mankind.

redeeming (rɪ'diːmɪŋ) *adj* serving to compensate for faults or deficiencies.

redemption (rɪ'dɛmpʃən) *n* **1** the act or process of redeeming. **2** the state of being redeemed. **3** *Christianity.* **3a** deliverance from sin through the incarnation, sufferings, and death of Christ. **3b** atonement for guilt. ORIG C14: via OF from L *redemptiō* a buying back; see REDEEM
▸ **re'demptional, re'demptive,** *or* **re'demptory** *adj* ▸ **re'demptively** *adv*

redemption yield *n Stock Exchange.* the yield produced by a redeemable gilt-edged security taking into account the annual interest it pays and an annualized amount to account for any profit or loss when it is redeemed.

Red Ensign *n* the ensign of the British Merchant Navy, having the Union Jack on a red background at the upper corner of the vertical edge alongside the hoist. It was also the national flag of Canada until 1965.

redeploy (,riːdɪ'plɔɪ) *vb* **1** to assign new positions or tasks to (labour, troops, etc.). **2** *S. African.* to assign (an employee) to a new position after some embarrassment or display of incompetence.
▸ **,rede'ployment** *n*

redevelopment area (,riːdɪ'vɛləpmənt) *n* an urban area in which all or most of the buildings are demolished and rebuilt.

redeye ('rɛd,aɪ) *n* **1** *US sl.* inferior whisky. **2** *Sl., chiefly US.* a flight that departs late at night and arrives early next morning. **3** another name for **rudd. 4** *Canad. sl.* a drink incorporating beer and tomato juice.

red-faced *adj* **1** flushed with embarrassment or anger. **2** having a florid complexion.
▸ **red-facedly** (,rɛd'feɪsɪdlɪ, -'feɪstlɪ) *adv*

redfin ('rɛd,fɪn) *n* any of various small cyprinid fishes with reddish fins.

redfish ('rɛd,fɪʃ) *n, pl* **redfish** *or* **redfishes. 1** a male salmon that has recently spawned. Cf. **blackfish** (sense 2). **2** *Canad.* another name for **kokanee.**

★ people and places

red flag *n* **1** a symbol of socialism, communism, or revolution. **2** a warning of danger or a signal to stop.

Redford ★ ('rɛdfəd) *n* **Robert.** born 1937, US film actor and director. His films as an actor include *Butch Cassidy and the Sundance Kid* (1969), *The Sting* (1973), and *Up Close and Personal* (1996) and as director *Ordinary People* (1980) and *The Horse Whisperer* (1998).

red fox *n* the common fox of Europe and N America, which has a reddish-brown coat.

red giant *n* a giant star that emits red light.

Redgrave ★ ('rɛd,greɪv) *n* **1 Lynn.** born 1944, British stage and film actress. Her films include *Georgy Girl* (1966) and *Getting It Right* (1989). **2** her father, Sir **Michael.** 1908–85, British actor. Among his films are *The Dam Busters* (1955) and *The Go-Between* (1971). **3** Sir **Steve.** born 1962, British oarsman: won five gold medals in rowing events at five consecutive Olympic Games (1984, 1988, 1992, 1996, and 2000). **4 Vanessa.** born 1937, British actress, elder daughter of Sir Michael Redgrave; her films include *Isadora* (1968), *Howard's End* (1992), and *Déjà Vu* (1998): noted also for her left-wing politics.

red grouse *n* a reddish-brown grouse of upland moors of Great Britain.

Red Guard *n* a member of a Communist Chinese youth movement that attempted to effect the Cultural Revolution (1966–69).

red-handed *adj* (*postpositive*) in the act of committing a crime or doing something wrong or shameful (esp. in **catch red-handed**). ORIG C19 (earlier, C15 *red hand*)
▸ **,red-'handedly** *adv* ▸ **,red-'handedness** *n*

red hat *n* the broad-brimmed crimson hat given to cardinals as the symbol of their rank.

redhead ('rɛd,hɛd) *n* a person with red hair.
▸ **'red,headed** *adj*

red heat *n* **1** the temperature at which a substance is red-hot. **2** the state or condition of being red-hot.

red herring *n* **1** anything that diverts attention from a topic or line of inquiry. **2** a herring cured by salting and smoking.

red-hot *adj* **1** (esp. of metal) heated to the temperature at which it glows red. **2** extremely hot. **3** keen, excited, or eager. **4** furious; violent: *red-hot anger.* **5** very recent or topical: *red-hot information.* **6** *Austral. sl.* extreme, unreasonable, or unfair.

red-hot poker *n* a liliaceous plant: widely cultivated for its showy spikes of red or yellow flowers.

Red Indian *n, adj* another name, now considered offensive, for **American Indian.** ORIG see REDSKIN

redingote ('rɛdɪŋ,gəʊt) *n* **1** a man's full-skirted outer coat of the 18th and 19th centuries. **2** a woman's coat of the 18th century, with an open-fronted skirt, revealing a decorative underskirt. **3** a woman's coat with a close-fitting top and a full skirt. ORIG C19: from F, from E *riding coat*

redintegrate (rɛ'dɪntɪ,greɪt) *vb* **redintegrates, redintegrating, redintegrated.** (*tr*) to make whole or complete again; restore to a perfect state; renew. ORIG C15: from L *redintegrāre* to renew, from *red-* RE- + *integer* complete
▸ **re,dinte'gration** *n* ▸ **red'integrative** *adj*

redistribution (,riːdɪstrɪ'bjuːʃən) *n* **1** the act or an instance of distributing again. **2** a revision of the number of seats in the Canadian House of Commons allocated to each province, made every ten years on the basis of a new census.

redivivus (,rɛdɪ'vaɪvəs) *adj Rare.* returned to life; revived. ORIG C17: from LL, from L *red-* RE- + *vīvus* alive

red lead (lɛd) *n* a bright-red poisonous insoluble oxide of lead.

red-letter day *n* a memorably important or happy occasion. ORIG C18: from the red letters used in ecclesiastical calendars to indicate saints' days and feasts

red light *n* **1** a signal to stop, esp. a red traffic signal. **2** a danger signal. **3a** a red lamp indicating that a house is a brothel. **3b** (*as modifier*): *a red-light district.*

redline ('rɛd,laɪn) *vb* **redlines, redlining, redlined.** (*tr*) (esp. of a bank or group of banks) to refuse to consider giving a loan to (a person or country) because of the presumed risks involved.

red meat *n* any meat that is dark in colour, esp. beef and lamb. Cf. **white meat.**

Redmond ★ ('rɛdmənd) *n* **John Edward.** 1856–1918, Irish politician.

red mullet *n* a food fish of European waters with a pair of long barbels beneath the chin and a reddish coloration. US name: **goatfish.**

redneck ('rɛd,nɛk) *n Disparaging.* **1** (in the southwestern US) a poor uneducated White farm worker. **2** a person or institution that is extremely reactionary. ◆ *adj* **3** reactionary and bigoted: *redneck laws.*

redo (riː'duː) *vb* **redoes, redoing, redid, redone.** (*tr*) **1** to do over again. **2** *Inf.* to redecorate, esp. thoroughly: *we redid the house last summer.*

red ochre *n* any of various natural red earths containing ferric oxide: used as pigments.

redolent ('rɛdəʊlənt) *adj* **1** having a pleasant smell; fragrant. **2** (*postpositive;* foll. by *of* or *with*) having the odour or smell (of): *a room redolent of flowers.* **3** (*postpositive;* foll. by *of* or *with*) reminiscent or suggestive (of): *a picture redolent of the 18th century.* ORIG C14: from L *redolens* smelling (of), from *redolēre* to give off an odour, from *red-* RE- + *olēre* to smell
▸ **'redolence** *or* **'redolency** *n* ▸ **'redolently** *adv*

Redon ★ (*French* rədɔ̃) *n* **Odilon** (ɔdilɔ̃). 1840–1916, French painter.

redouble (rɪ'dʌbᵊl) *vb* **redoubles, redoubling, redoubled. 1** to make or become much greater in intensity, number, etc.: *to redouble one's efforts.* **2** to send back (sounds) or (of sounds) to be sent back. **3** *Bridge.* to double (an opponent's double). ◆ *n* **4** the act of redoubling.

redoubt (rɪ'daʊt) *n* **1** an outwork or fieldwork defending a hilltop, pass, etc. **2** a temporary defence work built inside a fortification as a last defensive position. ORIG C17: via F from obs. It. *ridotta,* from Med. L *reductus* shelter, from L *redūcere,* from RE- + *dūcere* to lead

redoubtable (rɪ'daʊtəbᵊl) *adj* **1** to be feared; formidable. **2** worthy of respect. ORIG C14: from OF, from *redouter* to dread, from RE- + *douter* to be afraid, DOUBT
▸ **re'doubtableness** *n* ▸ **re'doubtably** *adv*

redound (rɪ'daʊnd) *vb* **1** (*intr;* foll. by *to*) to have an advantageous or disadvantageous effect (on): *brave deeds redound to your credit.* **2** (*intr;* foll. by *on* or *upon*) to recoil or rebound. **3** (*tr*) *Arch.* to reflect; bring: *his actions redound dishonour upon him.* ORIG C14: from OF *redonder,* from L *redundāre* to stream over, from *red-* RE- + *undāre* to rise in waves

redox ('riːdɒks) *n* (*modifier*) another term for **oxidation-reduction.** ORIG C20: from RED(UCTION) + OX(IDATION)

red pepper *n* **1** any of several varieties of the pepper plant cultivated for their hot pungent red podlike fruits. **2** the fruit of any of these plants. **3** the ripe red fruit of the sweet pepper. **4** another name for **cayenne pepper.**

Red Planet *n* **the.** an informal name for **Mars**[2].

redpoll ('rɛd,pɒl) *n* either of two widely distributed types of finches, having a greyish-brown plumage with a red crown and pink breast.

red rag *n* a provocation; something that infuriates. ORIG so called because red objects supposedly infuriate bulls

redress (rɪ'drɛs) *vb* (*tr*) **1** to put right (a wrong), esp. by compensation; make reparation for. **2** to correct or adjust (esp. in **redress the balance**). **3** to make compensation to (a person) for a wrong. ◆ *n* **4** the act or an instance of setting right a wrong; remedy or cure. **5** compensation, amends, or reparation for a wrong, injury, etc. ORIG C14: from OF *redrecier* to set up again, from RE- + *drecier* to straighten; see DRESS
▸ **re'dressable** *or* **re'dressible** *adj* ▸ **re'dresser** *or* **re'dressor** *n*

re-dress (riː'drɛs) *vb* (*tr*) to dress (something) again.

red ribbon *n Canad.* an award presented for coming first in a competition.

Red River ★ *n* **1** Also called: **Red River of the South.** a river in the S central US, flowing east from N Texas through Arkansas into the Mississippi in Louisiana. Length: 1639 km (1018 miles). **2** a river in the northern US, flowing north as the border between North Dakota and Minnesota and into Lake Winnipeg, Canada. Length: 515 km (320 miles). **3** a river in SE Asia, rising in SW China in Yünnan province and flowing southeast across N Vietnam to the Gulf of Tongkin: the chief river of N Vietnam, with an extensive delta. Length: 500 km (310 miles). Vietnamese name: **Song Koi.**

Red River cart *n Canad. history.* a strongly-built, two-wheeled, ox- or horse-drawn cart used in W Canada.

red rose *n English history.* the emblem of the House of Lancaster.

red salmon *n* any salmon having reddish flesh, esp. the sockeye salmon.

Red Sea ★ *n* a long narrow sea between Arabia and NE Africa, linked with the Mediterranean in the north by the Suez Canal and with the Indian Ocean in the south: occasionally reddish in appearance through algae. Area: 438 000 sq. km (169 000 sq. miles).

redshank (ˈrɛdˌʃæŋk) *n* any of various large common European sandpipers, esp. the **spotted redshank,** having red legs.

red shift *n* a shift in the lines of the spectrum of an astronomical object towards a longer wavelength (the red end of an optical spectrum), relative to the wavelength of these lines in the terrestrial spectrum, usually as a result of the Doppler effect caused by the recession of the object.

redskin (ˈrɛdˌskɪn) *n* an informal name, now considered offensive, for an **American Indian.** ORIG so called because one now extinct tribe painted themselves with red ochre

red snapper *n* any of various marine percoid food fishes of the snapper family, having a reddish coloration, common in American coastal regions of the Atlantic.

red spider *n* short for **red spider mite** (see **spider mite**).

Red Spot *n* See **Great Red Spot.**

red squirrel *n* a reddish-brown squirrel, inhabiting woodlands of Europe and parts of Asia.

redstart (ˈrɛdˌstɑːt) *n* **1** a European songbird of the thrush family: the male has a black throat, orange-brown tail and breast, and grey back. **2** a North American warbler. ORIG OE *rēad* red + *steort* tail

red tape *n* obstructive official routine or procedure; time-consuming bureaucracy. ORIG C18: from the red tape used to bind official government documents

reduce (rɪˈdjuːs) *vb* **reduces, reducing, reduced.** (*mainly tr*) **1** (*also intr*) to make or become smaller in size, number, etc. **2** to bring into a certain state, condition, etc.: *to reduce a forest to ashes; he was reduced to tears.* **3** (*also intr*) to make or become slimmer; lose or cause to lose excess weight. **4** to impoverish (esp. in **in reduced circumstances**). **5** to bring into a state of submission to one's authority; subjugate: *the whole country was reduced after three months.* **6** to bring down the price of (a commodity). **7** to lower the rank or status of; demote: *reduced to the ranks.* **8** to set out systematically as an aid to understanding; simplify: *his theories have been reduced in a treatise.* **9** *Maths.* to modify or simplify the form of (an expression or equation), esp. by substitution of one term by another. **10** *Cookery.* to make (a sauce, stock, etc.) more concentrated by boiling away some of the water in it. **11** to thin out (paint) by adding oil, turpentine, etc. **12** (*also intr*) *Chem.* **12a** to undergo or cause to undergo a chemical reaction with hydrogen. **12b** to lose or cause to lose oxygen atoms. **12c** to undergo or cause to undergo an increase in the number of electrons. **13** *Photog.* to lessen the density of (a negative or print). **14** *Surgery.* to manipulate or reposition (a broken or displaced bone, organ, or part) back to its normal site. ORIG C14: from L *redūcere* to bring back, from RE- + *dūcere* to lead
▸ **reˈducible** *adj* ▸ **reˌduciˈbility** *n* ▸ **reˈducibly** *adv*

reducer (rɪˈdjuːsə) *n* **1** *Photog.* a chemical solution used to lessen the density of a negative or print by oxidizing some of the blackened silver to soluble silver compounds. **2** a pipe fitting connecting two pipes of different diameters. **3** a person or thing that reduces.

reducing agent *n Chem.* a substance that reduces another substance in a chemical reaction, being itself oxidized in the process.

reducing glass *n* a lens or curved mirror that produces an image smaller than the object observed.

reductase (rɪˈdʌkteɪz) *n* any enzyme that catalyses a biochemical reduction reaction. ORIG C20: from REDUCTION + -ASE

reductio ad absurdum (rɪˈdʌktɪəʊ æd æbˈsɜːdəm) *n* **1** a method of disproving a proposition by showing that its inevitable consequences would be absurd. **2** a method of indirectly proving a proposition by assuming its negation to be true and showing that this leads to an absurdity. **3** application of a principle or proposed principle to an instance in which it is absurd. ORIG L, lit.: reduction to the absurd

reduction (rɪˈdʌkʃən) *n* **1** the act or process or an instance of reducing. **2** the state or condition of being reduced. **3** the amount by which something is reduced. **4** a form of an original resulting from a reducing process, such as a copy on a smaller scale. **5** *Maths.* **5a** the process of converting a fraction into its decimal form. **5b** the process of dividing out the common factors in the numerator and denominator of a fraction.
▸ **reˈductive** *adj*

reduction formula *n Maths.* a formula expressing the values of a trigonometric function of any angle greater than 90° in terms of a function of an acute angle.

reductionism (rɪˈdʌkʃəˌnɪzəm) *n* **1** the analysis of complex things, data, etc., into less complex constituents. **2** *Often disparaging.* any theory or method that holds that a complex idea, system, etc., can be completely understood in terms of its simpler parts or components.
▸ **reˈductionist** *n, adj* ▸ **reˌductionˈistic** *adj*

redundancy (rɪˈdʌndənsɪ) *n, pl* **redundancies. 1a** the state or condition of being redundant or superfluous, esp. superfluous in one's job. **1b** (*as modifier*): *a redundancy payment.* **2** excessive proliferation or profusion, esp. of superfluity.

redundant (rɪˈdʌndənt) *adj* **1** surplus to requirements; unnecessary or superfluous. **2** verbose or tautological. **3** deprived of one's job because it is no longer necessary. ORIG C17: from L *redundans* overflowing, from *redundāre* to stream over; see REDOUND
▸ **reˈdundantly** *adv*

red underwing *n* a large noctuid moth having hind wings coloured red and black.

reduplicate *vb* (rɪˈdjuːplɪˌkeɪt), **reduplicates, reduplicating, reduplicated. 1** to make or become double; repeat. **2** to repeat (a sound or syllable) in a word or (of a sound or syllable) to be repeated. ◆ *adj* (rɪˈdjuːplɪkɪt). **3** doubled or repeated. **4** (of petals or sepals) having the margins curving outwards.
▸ **reˌdupliˈcation** *n* ▸ **reˈduplicative** *adj*

red-water *n* a disease of cattle which destroys the red blood cells, characterized by the passage of red or blackish urine.

redwing (ˈrɛdˌwɪŋ) *n* a small European thrush having a speckled breast, reddish flanks, and brown back.

redwood (ˈrɛdˌwʊd) *n* a giant coniferous tree of coastal regions of California, having reddish fibrous bark and durable timber.

reebok (ˈriːbʌk, -bɒk) *n, pl* **reeboks** *or* **reebok.** a variant spelling of **rhebuck** *or* **rhebok.**

re-echo (riːˈɛkəʊ) *vb* **re-echoes, re-echoing, re-echoed. 1** to echo (a sound that is already an echo); resound. **2** (*tr*) to repeat like an echo.

reed (riːd) *n* **1** any of various widely distributed tall grasses that grow in swamps and shallow water and have jointed hollow stalks. **2** the stalk, or stalks collectively, of any of these plants, esp. as used for thatching. **3** *Music.* **3a** a thin piece of cane or metal inserted into the tubes of certain wind instruments, which sets in vibration the air column inside the tube. **3b** a wind instrument or organ pipe that sounds by means of a reed. **4** one of the several

★ people and places

vertical parallel wires on a loom that may be moved upwards to separate the warp threads. **5** a small semicircular architectural moulding. **6** an archaic word for **arrow**. **7** **broken reed**. a weak, unreliable, or ineffectual person. ◆ *vb* (*tr*) **8** to fashion into or supply with reeds or reeding. **9** to thatch using reeds. ORIG OE *hreod*

Reed ★ (riːd) *n* **1** Sir **Carol**. 1906–76, British film director. His films include *The Third Man* (1949) and *Oliver!* (1968). **2** **Lou**. born 1942, US rock singer, songwriter, and guitarist: member of the Velvet Underground (1965–70). His albums include *Transformer* (1972) and *Magic and Loss* (1992). **3** **Walter**. 1851–1902, US physician, who proved that yellow fever is transmitted by mosquitoes (1900).

reedbuck (ˈriːdˌbʌk) *n, pl* **reedbucks** *or* **reedbuck**. an antelope of Africa south of the Sahara, having a buff-coloured coat and inward-curving horns.

reed bunting *n* a common European bunting that has a brown streaked plumage with, in the male, a black head.

reed grass *n* a tall perennial grass of rivers and ponds of Europe, Asia, and Canada.

reeding (ˈriːdɪŋ) *n* **1** a set of small semicircular architectural mouldings. **2** the milling on the edges of a coin.

reedling (ˈriːdlɪŋ) *n* a titlike Eurasian songbird, common in reed beds, which belongs to the family of Old World flycatchers and has a tawny back and tail and, in the male, a grey-and-black head. Also called: **bearded tit**.

reed mace *n* a tall reedlike marsh plant, with straplike leaves and flowers in long brown spikes. Also called: (popularly) **bulrush, cat's-tail**.

reed organ *n* **1** a wind instrument, such as the harmonium, accordion, or harmonica, in which the sound is produced by reeds, each reed producing one note only. **2** a type of pipe organ in which all the pipes are fitted with reeds.

reed pipe *n* an organ pipe sounded by a vibrating reed.

reed stop *n* an organ stop controlling a rank of reed pipes.

reed warbler *n* any of various common Old World warblers that inhabit marshy regions and have a brown plumage.

reedy (ˈriːdɪ) *adj* **reedier, reediest**. **1** (of a place) abounding in reeds. **2** of or like a reed. **3** having a tone like a reed instrument; shrill or piping.
▸ ˈ**reedily** *adv* ▸ ˈ**reediness** *n*

reef[1] (riːf) *n* **1** a ridge of rock, sand, coral, etc., the top of which lies close to the surface of the sea. **2** a vein of ore, esp. one of gold-bearing quartz. **3** (*cap.*) **the. 3a** the Great Barrier Reef in Australia. **3b** the Witwatersrand in South Africa, a gold-bearing ridge. ORIG C16: from MDu. *ref*, from ON *rif* RIB[1], REEF[2]

reef[2] (riːf) *Naut.* ◆ *n* **1** the part gathered in when sail area is reduced, as in a high wind. ◆ *vb* **2** to reduce the area of (sail) by taking in a reef. **3** (*tr*) to shorten or bring inboard (a spar). ORIG C14: from MDu. *rif; rel. to ON *rif* reef, RIB[1]

Reef ★ (riːf) *n* **the. 1** another name for **Great Barrier Reef**. **2** another name for **Witwatersrand**.

reefer (ˈriːfə) *n* **1** *Naut.* a person who reefs, such as a midshipman. **2** another name for **reefing jacket**. **3** *Sl.* a hand-rolled cigarette containing cannabis. ORIG C19: from REEF[2]; applied to the cigarette from its resemblance to the rolled reef of a sail

reefing jacket *n* a man's short double-breasted jacket of sturdy wool.

reef knot *n* a knot consisting of two overhand knots turned opposite ways. Also called: **square knot**.

reef point *n Naut.* one of several short lengths of line stitched through a sail for tying a reef.

reek (riːk) *vb* **1** (*intr*) to give off or emit a strong unpleasant odour; smell or stink. **2** (*intr;* often foll. by *of*) to be permeated (by): *the letter reeks of subservience*. **3** (*tr*) to treat with smoke; fumigate. **4** (*tr*) *Chiefly dialect.* to give off or emit (smoke, fumes, etc.). ◆ *n* **5** a strong offensive smell; stink. **6** *Chiefly dialect.* smoke or steam; vapour. ORIG OE *rēocan*
▸ ˈ**reeky** *adj*

reel[1] (riːl, rɪəl) *n* **1** any of various cylindrical objects or frames that turn on an axis and onto which film, tape, wire, etc., may be wound. US equivalent: **spool**. **2** *Angling.* a device for winding, casting, etc., consisting of a revolving spool with a handle, attached to a fishing rod. ◆ *vb* (*tr*) **3** to wind (cotton, thread, etc.) onto a reel. **4** (foll. by *in, out,* etc.) to wind or draw with a reel: *to reel in a fish*. ORIG OE *hrēol*
▸ ˈ**reelable** *adj* ▸ ˈ**reeler** *n*

reel[2] (riːl, rɪəl) *vb* (*mainly intr*) **1** to sway, esp. under the shock of a blow or through dizziness or drunkenness. **2** to whirl about or have the feeling of whirling about: *his brain reeled*. ◆ *n* **3** a staggering or swaying motion or sensation. ORIG C14 *relen*, prob. from REEL[1]

reel[3] (riːl, rɪəl) *n* **1** any of various lively Scottish dances for a fixed number of couples who combine in square and circular formations. **2** a piece of music composed for or in the rhythm of this dance. ORIG C18: from REEL[2]

reel-fed *adj Printing.* involving or printing on a web of paper: *a reel-fed press*.

reelman (ˈriːlmən, ˈrɪəl-) *n, pl* **reelmen**. *Austral. & NZ.* (formerly) the member of a beach life-saving team who controlled the reel on which the line was wound.

reel off *vb* (*tr, adv*) to recite or write fluently and without apparent effort.

reel-to-reel *adj* **1** (of magnetic tape) wound from one reel to another in use. **2** (of a tape recorder) using magnetic tape wound from one reel to another, as opposed to cassettes.

re-entrant (riːˈɛntrənt) *adj* **1** (of an angle) pointing inwards. ◆ *n* **2** an angle or part that points inwards.

re-entry (riːˈɛntrɪ) *n, pl* **re-entries**. **1** the act of retaking possession of land, etc. **2** the return of a spacecraft into the earth's atmosphere.

re-entry vehicle *n* the portion of a ballistic missile that carries a nuclear warhead and re-enters the earth's atmosphere.

reeve[1] (riːv) *n* **1** *English history.* the local representative of the king in a shire until the early 11th century. **2** (in medieval England) a manorial steward who supervised the daily affairs of the manor. **3** *Canad. government.* (in some provinces) a president of a local council, esp. in a rural area. **4** (formerly) a minor local official in England and the US. ORIG OE *gerēva*

reeve[2] (riːv) *vb* **reeves, reeving, reeved** *or* **rove**. (*tr*) *Naut.* **1** to pass (a rope or cable) through an eye or other narrow opening. **2** to fasten by passing through or around something. ORIG C17: ?from Du. *rēven* REEF[2]

reeve[3] (riːv) *n* the female of the ruff (the bird). ORIG C17: from ?

re-export *vb* (ˌriːɪkˈspɔːt, ˌriːˈɛkspɔːt). **1** to export (imported goods, esp. after processing). ◆ *n* (riːˈɛkspɔːt). **2** the act of re-exporting. **3** a re-exported commodity.
▸ ˌ**re-exporˈtation** *n* ▸ ˌ**re-exˈporter** *n*

ref (rɛf) *n Inf.* short for **referee**.

ref. *abbrev. for:* **1** referee. **2** reference. **3** reformed.

refection (rɪˈfɛkʃən) *n* refreshment with food and drink. ORIG C14: from L *refectiō* a restoring, from *reficere*, from RE- + *facere* to make

refectory (rɪˈfɛktərɪ, -trɪ) *n, pl* **refectories**. a dining hall in a religious or academic institution. ORIG C15: from LL *refectōrium*, from L *refectus* refreshed

refectory table *n* a long narrow dining table.

refer (rɪˈfɜː) *vb* **refers, referring, referred**. (often foll. by *to*). **1** (*intr*) to make mention (of). **2** (*tr*) to direct the attention of (someone) for information, facts, etc.: *the reader is referred to Chomsky, 1965*. **3** (*intr*) to seek information (from): *he referred to his notes*. **4** (*intr*) to be relevant (to); pertain or relate (to). **5** (*tr*) to assign or attribute: *Cromwell referred his victories to God*. **6** (*tr*) to hand over for consideration, reconsideration, or decision: *to refer a complaint to another department*. **7** (*tr*) to hand back to the originator as unacceptable or unusable. **8** (*tr*) *Brit.* to fail (a student) in an examination. **9** **refer to drawer**. a request by a bank that the payee consult the drawer concerning a cheque payable by that bank. **10** (*tr*) to direct (a patient, client, etc.) to another doctor, agency, etc. ORIG C14: from L *referre*, from RE- + *ferre* to BEAR[1]

★ people and places

▸ **referable** (ˈrɛfərəbᵊl) *or* **referrable** (rɪˈfɜːrəbᵊl) *adj* ▸ **reˈferral** *n* ▸ **reˈferrer** *n*

> **USAGE NOTE** The not uncommon addition of *back* to *refer* is often unnecessary, since this meaning is already contained in the *re-* of *refer*: *this refers to* (not *back to*) *what has already been said*. However, when *refer* is used in the sense of returning a document or question for further consideration to the person from whom it came, it may be appropriate to say *he referred the matter back*.

referee (ˌrɛfəˈriː) *n* **1** a person to whom reference is made, esp. for an opinion, information, or a decision. **2** the umpire or judge in any of various sports, esp. football and boxing. **3** a person who is willing to testify to the character or capabilities of someone. **4** *Law*. a person appointed by a court to report on a matter. ◆ *vb* **referees, refereeing, refereed. 5** to act as a referee (in); preside (over).

reference (ˈrɛfərəns, ˈrɛfrəns) *n* **1** the act or an instance of referring. **2** something referred, esp. proceedings submitted to a referee in law. **3** a direction of the attention to a passage elsewhere or to another book, etc. **4** a book or passage referred to. **5** a mention or allusion: *this book contains several references to the Civil War*. **6** the relation between a word or phrase and the object or idea to which it refers. **7a** a source of information or facts. **7b** (*as modifier*): *a reference book; a reference library*. **8** a written testimonial regarding one's character or capabilities. **9** a person referred to for such a testimonial. **10a** (foll. by *to*) relation or delimitation, esp. to or by membership of a specific group: *without reference to sex or age*. **10b** (*as modifier*): *a reference group*. **11 terms of reference.** the specific limits of responsibility that determine the activities of an investigating body, etc. ◆ *vb* **references, referencing, referenced.** (*tr*) **12** to furnish or compile a list of references for (a publication, etc.). **13** to make a reference to; refer to. ◆ *prep* **14** *Business jargon*. with reference to: *reference your letter of the 9th inst*. Abbrev.: **re.**
▸ **referential** (ˌrɛfəˈrɛnʃəl) *adj*

referendum (ˌrɛfəˈrɛndəm) *n, pl* **referendums** *or* **referenda** (-də). **1** submission of an issue of public importance to the direct vote of the electorate. **2** a vote on such a measure. ◆ See also **plebiscite.** ORIG C19: from L: something to be carried back, from *referre* to REFER

referent (ˈrɛfərənt) *n* the object or idea to which a word or phrase refers. ORIG C19: from L *referens* from *referre* to REFER

referred pain *n Psychol.* pain felt at some place other than its actual place of origin.

refill *vb* (riːˈfɪl). **1** to fill (something) again. ◆ *n* (ˈriːfɪl). **2** a replacement for a consumable substance in a permanent container. **3** a second or subsequent filling.
▸ **reˈfillable** *adj*

refine (rɪˈfaɪn) *vb* **refines, refining, refined. 1** to make or become free from impurities or foreign matter; purify. **2** (*tr*) to separate (a mixture) into pure constituents, as in an oil refinery. **3** to make or become elegant or polished. **4** (*intr*; often foll. by *on* or *upon*) to enlarge or improve (upon) by making subtle or fine distinctions. **5** (*tr*) to make (language) more subtle or polished. ORIG C16: from RE- + FINE[1]
▸ **reˈfinable** *adj* ▸ **reˈfiner** *n*

refined (rɪˈfaɪnd) *adj* **1** not coarse or vulgar; genteel, elegant, or polite. **2** subtle; discriminating. **3** freed from impurities; purified.

refinement (rɪˈfaɪnmənt) *n* **1** the act of refining or the state of being refined. **2** a fine or delicate point or distinction; a subtlety. **3** fineness or precision of thought, expression, manners, etc. **4** an improvement to a piece of equipment, etc.

refinery (rɪˈfaɪnərɪ) *n, pl* **refineries.** a factory for the purification of some crude material, such as sugar, oil, etc.

refit *vb* (riːˈfɪt), **refits, refitting, refitted. 1** to make or be made ready for use again by repairing, re-equipping, or resupplying. ◆ *n* (ˈriːˌfɪt). **2** a repair or re-equipping, as of a ship, for further use.
▸ **reˈfitment** *n*

refl. *abbrev. for:* **1** reflection. **2** reflective. **3** reflex(ive).

reflate (riːˈfleɪt) *vb* **reflates, reflating, reflated.** to inflate or be inflated again. ORIG C20: back formation from REFLATION

reflation (riːˈfleɪʃən) *n* **1** an increase in economic activity. **2** an increase in the supply of money and credit designed to cause such economic activity. ◆ Cf. **inflation** (sense 2). ORIG C20: from RE- + *-flation*, as in INFLATION

reflect (rɪˈflɛkt) *vb* **1** to undergo or cause to undergo a process in which light, other electromagnetic radiation, sound, particles, etc., are thrown back after impinging on a surface. **2** (of a mirror, etc.) to form an image of (something) by reflection. **3** (*tr*) to show or express: *his tactics reflect his desire for power*. **4** (*tr*) to bring as a consequence: *their success reflected great credit on them*. **5** (*intr*; foll. by *on* or *upon*) to cause to be regarded in a specified way: *her behaviour reflects well on her*. **6** (*intr*; often foll. by *on* or *upon*) to cast dishonour or honour, credit or discredit, etc. (on). **7** (*intr*; usually foll. by *on*) to think, meditate, or ponder. ORIG C15: from L *reflectere*, from RE- + *flectere* to bend
▸ **reˈflectingly** *adv*

reflectance (rɪˈflɛktəns) *or* **reflection factor** *n* a measure of the ability of a surface to reflect light or other electromagnetic radiation, equal to the ratio of the reflected flux to the incident flux.

reflecting telescope *n* a type of telescope in which the initial image is formed by a concave mirror. Also called: **reflector.** Cf. **refracting telescope.**

reflection *or* **reflexion** (rɪˈflɛkʃən) *n* **1** the act of reflecting or the state of being reflected. **2** something reflected or the image so produced, as by a mirror. **3** careful or long consideration or thought. **4** attribution of discredit or blame. **5** *Maths*. a transformation in which the direction of one axis is reversed or changes the polarity of one of the variables. **6** *Anat*. the bending back of a structure or part upon itself.
▸ **reˈflectional** *or* **reˈflexional** *adj*

reflection density *n Physics*. a measure of the extent to which a surface reflects light or other electromagnetic radiation. Symbol: *D*

reflective (rɪˈflɛktɪv) *adj* **1** characterized by quiet thought or contemplation. **2** capable of reflecting: *a reflective surface*. **3** produced by reflection.
▸ **reˈflectively** *adv*

reflectivity (ˌriːflɛkˈtɪvɪtɪ) *n* **1** *Physics*. a measure of the ability of a surface to reflect radiation, equal to the reflectance of a layer of material sufficiently thick for the reflectance not to depend on the thickness. **2** Also: **reflectiveness.** the quality or capability of being reflective.

reflector (rɪˈflɛktə) *n* **1** a person or thing that reflects. **2** a surface or object that reflects light, sound, heat, etc. **3** another name for **reflecting telescope.**

reflet (rəˈfleɪ) *n* an iridescent glow or lustre, as on ceramic ware. ORIG C19: from F: a reflection, from It. *riflesso*, from L *reflexus*, from *reflectere* to reflect

reflex *n* (ˈriːflɛks). **1a** an immediate involuntary response, such as coughing, evoked by a given stimulus. **1b** (*as modifier*): *a reflex action*. See also **reflex arc. 2a** a mechanical response to a particular situation, involving no conscious decision. **2b** (*as modifier*): *a reflex response*. **3** a reflection; an image produced by or as if by reflection. ◆ *adj* (ˈriːflɛks). **4** *Maths*. (of an angle) between 180° and 360°. **5** (*prenominal*) turned, reflected, or bent backwards. ◆ *vb* (rɪˈflɛks). **6** (*tr*) to bend, turn, or reflect backwards. ORIG C16: from L *reflexus* bent back, from *reflectere* to reflect
▸ **reˈflexible** *adj* ▸ **reˌflexiˈbility** *n*

reflex arc *n Physiol.* the neural pathway over which impulses travel to produce a reflex action.

reflex camera *n* a camera in which the image is composed and focused on a ground-glass viewfinder screen.

reflexion (rɪˈflɛkʃən) *n Brit.* a less common spelling of **reflection.**
▸ **reˈflexional** *adj*

reflexive (rɪˈflɛksɪv) *adj* **1** denoting a class of pronouns that refer back to the subject of a sentence or clause. Thus, in *that man thinks a great deal of himself,* the pronoun *himself* is reflexive. **2** denoting a verb used transitively with the reflexive pronoun as its direct object, as in *to dress oneself.* **3** *Physiol.* of or relating to a reflex. ◆ *n* **4** a reflexive pronoun or verb.
▸ **reˈflexively** *adv* ▸ **reˈflexiveness** *or* **reflexivity** (ˌriːflɛkˈsɪvɪtɪ) *n*

reflexology (ˌriːflɛkˈsɒlədʒɪ) *n* a form of therapy in alternative medicine in which the soles of the feet are massaged: designed to stimulate the blood supply and nerves and thus relieve tension.
▸ **ˌreflexˈologist** *n*

reflux (ˈriːflʌks) *vb* **1** *Chem.* to boil or be boiled in a vessel attached to a condenser, so that the vapour condenses and flows back into the vessel. ◆ *n* **2** *Chem.* **2a** an act of refluxing. **2b** (*as modifier*): *a reflux condenser.* **3** the act or an instance of flowing back; ebb. ORIG C15: from Med. L *refluxus,* from L *refluere* to flow back

reflux oesophagitis (iːˌsɒfəˈdʒaɪtɪs) *n* inflammation of the gullet caused by regurgitation of stomach acids, producing heartburn: may be associated with a hiatus hernia.

reform (rɪˈfɔːm) *vb* **1** (*tr*) to improve (an existing institution, law, etc.) by alteration or correction of abuses. **2** to give up or cause to give up a reprehensible habit or immoral way of life. ◆ *n* **3** an improvement or change for the better, esp. as a result of correction of legal or political abuses or malpractices. **4** a principle, campaign, or measure aimed at achieving such change. **5** improvement of morals or behaviour. ORIG C14: via OF from L *reformāre* to form again
▸ **reˈformable** *adj* ▸ **reˈformative** *adj* ▸ **reˈformer** *n*

re-form (riːˈfɔːm) *vb* to form anew.
▸ **ˌre-forˈmation** *n*

reformation (ˌrɛfəˈmeɪʃən) *n* **1** the act or an instance of reforming or the state of being reformed. **2** (*usually cap.*) a religious and political movement of 16th-century Europe that began as an attempt to reform the Roman Catholic Church and resulted in the establishment of the Protestant Churches.
▸ **ˌreforˈmational** *adj*

reformatory (rɪˈfɔːmətərɪ, -trɪ) *n, pl* **reformatories. 1** Also called: **reform school.** (formerly) a place of instruction where young offenders were sent for corrective training. ◆ *adj* **2** having the purpose or function of reforming.

Reformed (rɪˈfɔːmd) *adj* **1** of or designating a Protestant Church, esp. the Calvinist. **2** of or designating Reform Judaism.

reformism (rɪˈfɔːmɪzəm) *n* a doctrine advocating reform, esp. political or religious reform rather than abolition.
▸ **reˈformist** *n, adj*

Reform Judaism *n* a movement in Judaism that does not require strict observance of the law, but adapts to the contemporary world.

refract (rɪˈfrækt) *vb* **1** to cause to undergo refraction. **2** (*tr*) to measure the amount of refraction of (the eye, a lens, etc.). ORIG C17: from L *refractus* broken up, from *refringere,* from RE- + *frangere* to break
▸ **reˈfractable** *adj* ▸ **reˈfractive** *adj*

refracting telescope *n* a type of telescope in which the image is formed by a set of lenses. Also called: **refractor.** Cf. **reflecting telescope.**

refraction (rɪˈfrækʃən) *n* **1** *Physics.* the change in direction of a propagating wave, such as light or sound, in passing from one medium to another in which it has a different velocity. **2** the amount by which a wave is refracted. **3** the ability of the eye to refract light.
▸ **reˈfractional** *adj*

refractive index *n Physics.* a measure of the extent to which a medium refracts light; the ratio of the speed of light in free space to that in the medium.

refractometer (ˌriːfrækˈtɒmɪtə) *n* any instrument for measuring the refractive index.
▸ **refractometric** (rɪˌfræktəˈmɛtrɪk) *adj* ▸ **ˌrefracˈtometry** *n*

refractor (rɪˈfræktə) *n* **1** an object or material that refracts. **2** another name for **refracting telescope.**

refractory (rɪˈfræktərɪ) *adj* **1** unmanageable or obstinate. **2** *Med.* not responding to treatment. **3** *Physiol.* (of a nerve or muscle) incapable of responding to stimulation. **4** (of a material) able to withstand high temperatures without fusion or decomposition. ◆ *n, pl* **refractories. 5** a material, such as fire clay, that is able to withstand high temperatures.
▸ **reˈfractorily** *adv* ▸ **reˈfractoriness** *n*

refrain[1] (rɪˈfreɪn) *vb* (*intr;* usually foll. by *from*) to abstain (from action); forbear. ORIG C14: from L *refrēnāre* to check with a bridle, from RE- + *frēnum* a bridle
▸ **reˈfrainer** *n* ▸ **reˈfrainment** *n*

refrain[2] (rɪˈfreɪn) *n* **1** a regularly recurring melody, such as the chorus of a song. **2** a much repeated saying or idea. ORIG C14: via OF, ult. from L *refringere* to break into pieces

refrangible (rɪˈfrændʒɪbᵊl) *adj* capable of being refracted. ORIG C17: from L *refringere* to break up, from RE- + *frangere* to break
▸ **reˌfrangiˈbility** *or* **reˈfrangibleness** *n*

refresh (rɪˈfrɛʃ) *vb* **1** (*usually tr or reflexive*) to make or become fresh or vigorous, as through rest, drink, or food; revive or reinvigorate. **2** (*tr*) to enliven (something worn or faded), as by adding new decorations. **3** to pour cold water over previously blanched and drained food. **4** (*tr*) to stimulate (the memory, etc.). **5** (*tr*) to replenish, as with new equipment or stores. ORIG C14: from OF *refreschir;* see RE-, FRESH
▸ **reˈfresher** *n* ▸ **reˈfreshing** *adj*

refresher course *n* a short educational course for people to review their subject and developments in it.

refreshment (rɪˈfrɛʃmənt) *n* **1** the act of refreshing or the state of being refreshed. **2** (*pl*) snacks and drinks served as a light meal.

refrigerant (rɪˈfrɪdʒərənt) *n* **1** a fluid capable of changes of phase at low temperatures: used as the working fluid of a refrigerator. **2** a cooling substance, such as ice or solid carbon dioxide. **3** *Med.* an agent that provides a sensation of coolness or reduces fever. ◆ *adj* **4** causing cooling or freezing.

refrigerate (rɪˈfrɪdʒəˌreɪt) *vb* **refrigerates, refrigerating, refrigerated.** to make or become frozen or cold, esp. for preservative purposes; chill or freeze. ORIG C16: from L *refrīgerāre* to make cold, from RE- + *frīgus* cold
▸ **reˌfrigerˈation** *n* ▸ **reˈfrigerative** *adj* ▸ **reˈfrigeratory** *adj, n*

refrigerator (rɪˈfrɪdʒəˌreɪtə) *n* a chamber in which food, drink, etc., are kept cool. Informal name: **fridge.**

refringent (rɪˈfrɪndʒənt) *adj Physics.* of, concerned with, or causing refraction; refractive. ORIG C18: from L *refringere;* see REFRACT
▸ **reˈfringency** *or* **reˈfringence** *n*

reft (rɛft) *vb* a past tense and past participle of **reave.**

refuel (riːˈfjuːəl) *vb* **refuels, refuelling, refuelled** *or US* **refuels, refueling, refueled.** to supply or be supplied with fresh fuel.

refuge (ˈrɛfjuːdʒ) *n* **1** shelter or protection, as from the weather or danger. **2** any place, person, action, or thing that offers protection, help, or relief. ORIG C14: via OF from L *refugium,* from *refugere,* from RE- + *fugere* to escape

refugee (ˌrɛfjʊˈdʒiː) *n* **a** a person who has fled from some danger or problem, esp. political persecution. **b** (*as modifier*): *a refugee camp.*
▸ **ˌrefuˈgeeism** *n*

refugee capital *n Finance.* money from abroad invested, esp. for a short term, in the country offering the highest interest rate.

refugium (rɪˈfjuːdʒɪəm) *n, pl* **refugia** (-dʒɪə). a geographical region that has remained unaltered by a climatic change affecting surrounding regions and that therefore forms a haven for relict fauna and flora. ORIG C20: L: REFUGE

refulgent (rɪˈfʌldʒənt) *adj Literary.* shining, brilliant, or radiant. ORIG C16: from L *refulgēre,* from RE- + *fulgēre* to shine
▸ **reˈfulgence** *or* **reˈfulgency** *n* ▸ **reˈfulgently** *adv*

refund *vb* (rɪˈfʌnd). (*tr*) **1** to give back (money, etc.), as

when an article purchased is unsatisfactory. **2** to reimburse (a person). ◆ *n* ('riː,fʌnd). **3** return of money to a purchaser or the amount so returned. ORIG C14: from L *refundere,* from RE- + *fundere* to pour
▸ **re'fundable** *adj* ▸ **re'funder** *n*

re-fund (riː'fʌnd) *vb* (*tr*) *Finance.* to discharge (an old or matured debt) by new borrowing, as by a new bond issue. ORIG C20: from RE- + FUND

refurbish (riː'fɜːbɪʃ) *vb* (*tr*) to renovate, re-equip, or restore.
▸ **re'furbishment** *n*

refusal (rɪ'fjuːzᵊl) *n* **1** the act or an instance of refusing. **2** the opportunity to reject or accept; option.

refuse[1] (rɪ'fjuːz) *vb* **refuses, refusing, refused. 1** (*tr*) to decline to accept (something offered): *to refuse promotion.* **2** to decline to give or grant (something) to (a person, etc.). **3** (when *tr, takes an infinitive*) to express determination not (to do something); decline: *he refuses to talk about it.* **4** (of a horse) to be unwilling to take (a jump). ORIG C14: from OF *refuser,* from L *refundere* to pour back
▸ **re'fusable** *adj* ▸ **re'fuser** *n*

refuse[2] ('rɛfjuːs) *n* **a** anything thrown away; waste; rubbish. **b** (*as modifier*): *a refuse collection.* ORIG C15: from OF *refuser* to REFUSE[1]

refusenik *or* **refusnik** (rɪ'fjuːznɪk) *n* **1** (formerly) a Jew in the Soviet Union who had been refused permission to emigrate. **2** a person who refuses to cooperate with a system or comply with a law because of a moral conviction. ORIG C20: from REFUSE[1] + -NIK

refute (rɪ'fjuːt) *vb* **refutes, refuting, refuted.** (*tr*) to prove (a statement, theory, charge, etc.) of (a person) to be false or incorrect; disprove. ORIG C16: from L *refūtāre* to rebut
▸ **refutable** ('rɛfjʊtəbᵊl, rɪ'fjuː-) *adj* ▸ **'refutably** *adv* ▸ **,refu'tation** *n* ▸ **re'futer** *n*

> **USAGE NOTE** The use of *refute* to mean *deny* as in *I'm not refuting the fact that...* is thought by some people to be incorrect. In careful writing it may be advisable to use *refute* only where there is an element of disproving something through argument and evidence, as in *we haven't got evidence to refute their hypothesis.*

reg. *abbrev. for:* **1** regiment. **2** register(ed). **3** registrar. **4** regular(ly). **5** regulation.

regain (rɪ'geɪn) *vb* (*tr*) **1** to take or get back; recover. **2** to reach again.
▸ **re'gainer** *n*

regal ('riːgᵊl) *adj* of, relating to, or befitting a king or queen; royal. ORIG C14: from L *rēgālis,* from *rēx* king
▸ **re'gality** *n* ▸ **'regally** *adv*

regale (rɪ'geɪl) *vb* **regales, regaling, regaled.** (*tr;* usually foll. by *with*) **1** to give delight or amusement to: *he regaled them with stories.* **2** to provide with choice or abundant food or drink. ◆ *n* **3** *Arch.* **3a** a feast. **3b** a delicacy of food or drink. ORIG C17: from F *régaler,* from *gale* pleasure
▸ **re'galement** *n*

regalia (rɪ'geɪlɪə) *n* (*pl, sometimes functioning as sing*) **1** the ceremonial emblems or robes of royalty, high office, an order, etc. **2** any splendid or special clothes; finery. ORIG C16: from Med. L: royal privileges, from L *rēgālis* REGAL

regard (rɪ'gɑːd) *vb* **1** to look closely or attentively at (something or someone); observe steadily. **2** (*tr*) to hold (a person or thing) in respect, admiration, or affection: *we regard your work very highly.* **3** (*tr*) to look upon or consider in a specified way: *she regarded her brother as her responsibility.* **4** (*tr*) to relate to; concern; have a bearing on. **5** to take notice of or pay attention to (something); heed: *he has never regarded the conventions.* **6 as regards.** (*prep*) in respect of; concerning. ◆ *n* **7** a gaze; look. **8** attention; heed: *he spends without regard to his bank balance.* **9** esteem, affection, or respect. **10** reference, relation, or connection (esp. in **with regard to** *or* **in regard to**). **11** (*pl*) good wishes or greetings (esp. in **with kind regards,** used at the close of a letter). **12 in this regard.** on this point. ORIG C14: from OF *regarder* to look at, care about, from RE- + *garder* to GUARD

> **USAGE NOTE** In writing, care should be taken to avoid putting *with regards to* instead of *with regard to.* This mistake is common, particularly in speaking, perhaps under the influence of the phrase *as regards.*

regardant (rɪ'gɑːdᵊnt) *adj* (*usually postpositive*) *Heraldry.* (of a beast) shown looking backwards over its shoulder. ORIG C15: from OF; see REGARD

regardful (rɪ'gɑːdfʊl) *adj* **1** (often foll. by *of*) showing regard (for); heedful (of). **2** showing regard, respect, or consideration.
▸ **re'gardfully** *adv*

regarding (rɪ'gɑːdɪŋ) *prep* in respect of; on the subject of.

regardless (rɪ'gɑːdlɪs) *adj* **1** (usually foll. by *of*) taking no regard or heed; heedless. ◆ *adv* **2** in spite of everything; disregarding drawbacks.
▸ **re'gardlessly** *adv* ▸ **re'gardlessness** *n*

regatta (rɪ'gætə) *n* an organized series of races of yachts, rowing boats, etc. ORIG C17: from obs. It. *rigatta* contest, from ?

regd *abbrev. for* registered.

regelation (,riːdʒɪ'leɪʃən) *n* the rejoining together of two pieces of ice as a result of melting under pressure at the interface between them and subsequent refreezing.
▸ **'rege,late** *vb*

regency ('riːdʒənsɪ) *n, pl* **regencies. 1** government by a regent. **2** the office of a regent. **3** a territory under the jurisdiction of a regent. ORIG C15: from Med. L *regentia,* from L *regere* to rule

Regency ('riːdʒənsɪ) *n* (preceded by *the*) **1** (in Britain) the period (1811–20) of the regency of the Prince of Wales (later George IV). **2** (in France) the period (1715-23) of the regency of Philip, Duke of Orleans. ◆ *adj* **3** characteristic of or relating to the Regency periods or to the styles of architecture, art, etc., produced in them.

regenerate *vb* (rɪ'dʒɛnə,reɪt), **regenerates, regenerating, regenerated. 1** to undergo or cause to undergo moral, spiritual, or physical renewal or invigoration. **2** to form or be formed again; come or bring into existence once again. **3** to replace (lost or damaged tissues or organs) by new growth, or to cause (such tissues) to be replaced. **4** (*tr*) *Electronics.* to use positive feedback to improve the demodulation and amplification of a signal. ◆ *adj* (rɪ'dʒɛnərɪt). **5** morally, spiritually, or physically renewed or reborn.
▸ **re'generacy** *n* ▸ **re,gener'ation** *n* ▸ **re'generative** *adj* ▸ **re'generatively** *adv* ▸ **re'gener,ator** *n*

Regensburg ★ (*German* 'reːgənsbʊrk) *n* a city in SE Germany, in Bavaria on the River Danube: a free Imperial city from 1245 and the leading commercial city of S Germany in the 12th and 13th centuries; the Imperial Diet was held in the town hall from 1663 to 1806. Pop.: 125 836 (1996 est.). Former English name: **Ratisbon.**

regent ('riːdʒənt) *n* **1** the ruler or administrator of a country during the minority, absence, or incapacity of its monarch. **2** *US & Canad.* a member of the governing board of certain schools and colleges. ◆ *adj* **3** (*usually postpositive*) acting or functioning as a regent: *a queen regent.* ORIG C14: from L *regēns,* from *regere* to rule
▸ **'regental** *adj* ▸ **'regentship** *n*

regent-bird *n Austral.* a bowerbird, the male of which has showy yellow and velvety-black plumage. ORIG after the PRINCE REGENT

Regents Park ★ *n* a park in central London, laid out as Marylebone Park by John Nash; now known for the London Zoo, its open-air theatre, and Nash's curved terraces.

Reger ★ (*German* 'reːgər) *n* **Max** (maks). 1873–1916, German composer, esp. of organ works.

reggae ('rɛgeɪ) *n* a type of West Indian popular music having four beats to the bar, the upbeat being strongly accented. ORIG C20: of West Indian origin

Reggio di Calabria ★ (*Italian* 'reddʒo di ka'laːbrja) *n* a port in S Italy, in Calabria on the Strait of Messina:

founded about 720 B.C. by Greek colonists. Pop.: 179 623 (1996 est.).

Reggio nell'Emilia ★ (*Italian* 'reddʒo nelle'miːlja) *n* a city in N central Italy, in Emilia-Romagna: founded in the 2nd century B.C. by Marcus Aemilius Lepidus; ruled by the Este family in the 15th–18th centuries. Pop.: 135 406 (1996 est.).

regicide ('rɛdʒɪˌsaɪd) *n* **1** the killing of a king. **2** a person who kills a king. ORIG C16: from L *rēx* king + -CIDE
▸ ˌ**regi'cidal** *adj*

regime *or* **régime** (reɪ'ʒiːm) *n* **1** a system of government or a particular administration: *a fascist regime.* **2** a social system or order. **3** another word for **regimen** (sense 1). ORIG C18: from F, from L *regimen* guidance, from *regere* to rule

regimen ('rɛdʒɪˌmɛn) *n* **1** Also called: **regime.** a systematic course of therapy, often including a recommended diet. **2** administration or rule. ORIG C14: from L: guidance

regiment *n* ('rɛdʒɪmənt). **1** a military formation varying in size from a battalion to a number of battalions. **2** a large number in regular or organized groups. ◆ *vb* ('rɛdʒɪˌmɛnt). (*tr*) **3** to force discipline or order on, esp. in a domineering manner. **4** to organize into a regiment. **5** to form into organized groups. ORIG C14: via OF from LL *regimentum* government, from L *regere* to rule
▸ ˌ**regi'mental** *adj* ▸ ˌ**regi'mentally** *adv* ▸ ˌ**regimen'tation** *n*

regimentals (ˌrɛdʒɪ'mɛntᵊlz) *pl n* **1** the uniform and insignia of a regiment. **2** military dress.

Regin ★ ('reɪgɪn) *n Norse myth.* a dwarf smith, tutor of Sigurd, whom he encouraged to kill Fafnir for the gold he guarded.

Regina[1] (rɪ'dʒaɪnə) *n* queen: now used chiefly in documents, inscriptions, etc. Cf. **Rex.** ORIG L

Regina[2] ★ (rɪ'dʒaɪnə) *n* a city in W Canada, capital and largest city of Saskatchewan: founded in 1882 as Pile O'Bones. Pop.: 179 178 (1991).

Regiomontanus ★ (ˌriːdʒɪəʊmɒn'teɪnəs, -'tɑː-, -'tæn-) *n* original name *Johann Müller.* 1436–76, German mathematician and astronomer.

region ('riːdʒən) *n* **1** any large, indefinite, and continuous part of a surface or space. **2** an area considered as a unit for geographical, functional, social, or cultural reasons. **3** an administrative division of a country, or a Canadian province. **4** a realm or sphere of activity or interest. **5** range, area, or scope: *in what region is the price likely to be?* **6** a division or part of the body: *the lumbar region.* ORIG C14: from L *regiō,* from *regere* to govern

regional ('riːdʒənᵊl) *adj* of, characteristic of, or limited to a region.
▸ '**regionally** *adv*

regionalism ('riːdʒənəˌlɪzəm) *n* **1** division of a country into administrative regions having partial autonomy. **2** loyalty to one's home region; regional patriotism.
▸ '**regionalist** *n, adj*

régisseur *French.* (reʒisœr) *n* an official in a dance company with varying duties, usually including directing productions. ORIG F, from *régir* to manage

register ('rɛdʒɪstə) *n* **1** an official or formal list recording names, events, or transactions. **2** the book in which such a list is written. **3** an entry in such a list. **4** a recording device that accumulates data, totals sums of money, etc.: *a cash register.* **5** a movable plate that controls the flow of air into a furnace, chimney, room, etc. **6** *Music.* **6a** the timbre characteristic of a certain manner of voice production. **6b** any of the stops on an organ as classified in respect of its tonal quality: *the flute register.* **7** *Printing.* the exact correspondence of lines of type, etc., on the two sides of a printed sheet of paper. **8** a form of a language associated with a particular social situation or subject matter. **9** the act or an instance of registering. ◆ *vb* **10** (*tr*) to enter or cause someone to enter (an event, person's name, ownership, etc.) on a register. **11** to show or be shown on a scale or other measuring instrument: *the current didn't register on the meter.* **12** to show or be shown in a person's face, bearing, etc.: *his face registered surprise.* **13** (*intr*) *Inf.* to have an effect; make an impression: *the news of her uncle's death just did not register.* **14** to send (a letter, package, etc.) by registered post. **15** (*tr*) *Printing.* to adjust (a printing press, forme, etc.) to ensure that the printed matter is in register. ORIG C14: from Med. L *registrum,* from L *regerere* to transcribe, from RE- + *gerere* to bear
▸ '**registrable** *adj*

Registered General Nurse *n* (in Britain) a nurse who has completed a three-year training course and has been registered with the United Kingdom Central Council for Nursing, Midwifery, and Health Visiting. Abbrev.: **RGN.**

registered post *n* **1** a Post Office service by which compensation is paid for loss or damage to mail for which a registration fee has been paid. **2** mail sent by this service.

Registered Trademark *n* See **trademark** (sense 1).

register office *n Brit.* a government office where civil marriages are performed and births, marriages, and deaths are recorded. Often called: **registry office.**

register ton *n* the full name for **ton**[1] (sense 6).

registrar (ˌrɛdʒɪ'strɑː, 'rɛdʒɪˌstrɑː) *n* **1** a person who keeps official records. **2** an administrative official responsible for student records, enrolment procedure, etc., in a school, college, or university. **3** *Brit. & NZ.* a hospital doctor senior to a houseman but junior to a consultant. **4** *Austral.* the chief medical administrator of a large hospital. **5** *Chiefly US.* a person employed by a company to maintain a register of its security issues.
▸ '**regisˌtrarship** *n*

registration (ˌrɛdʒɪ'streɪʃən) *n* **1a** the act of registering or state of being registered. **1b** (*as modifier*): *a registration number.* **2** an entry in a register. **3** a group of people, such as students, who register at a particular time. **4** *Austral.* **4a** a tax payable by the owner of a motor vehicle. **4b** the period paid for.

registration document *n Brit.* a document giving identification details of a motor vehicle, including its manufacturer, date of registration, and owner's name.

registration number *n* a sequence of letters and numbers assigned to a motor vehicle when it is registered, usually indicating the year and place of registration, displayed on numberplates at the front and rear of the vehicle.

registration plate *n Austral. & NZ.* the numberplate of a vehicle.

registry ('rɛdʒɪstrɪ) *n, pl* **registries. 1** a place where registers are kept. **2** the registration of a ship's country of origin: *a ship of Liberian registry.* **3** another word for **registration.**

registry office *n Brit.* another term for **register office.**

Regius professor ('riːdʒɪəs) *n Brit.* a person appointed by the Crown to a university chair founded by a royal patron. ORIG C17: *regius,* from L: royal, from *rex* king

reglet ('rɛglɪt) *n* **1** a flat narrow architectural moulding. **2** *Printing.* a strip of oiled wood used for spacing between lines. ORIG C16: from OF, lit.: a little rule, from *régle* rule, from L *rēgula*

regmaker ('rɛxˌmɑːkə) *n S. African.* a drink to relieve the symptoms of a hangover. ORIG from Afrik., right maker

regnal ('rɛgnəl) *adj* **1** of a sovereign or reign. **2** designating a year of a sovereign's reign calculated from the date of accession. ORIG C17: from Med. L *rēgnālis,* from L *rēgnum* sovereignty; see REIGN

regnant ('rɛgnənt) *adj* **1** (*postpositive*) reigning. **2** prevalent; current. ORIG C17: from L *regnāre* to REIGN
▸ '**regnancy** *n*

regorge (rɪ'gɔːdʒ) *vb* **regorges, regorging, regorged. 1** (*tr*) to vomit up; disgorge. **2** (*intr*) (esp. of water) to flow or run back. ORIG C17: from F *regorger;* see GORGE

regress *vb* (rɪ'grɛs). **1** (*intr*) to return or revert, as to a former place, condition, or mode of behaviour. **2** (*tr*) *Statistics.* to measure the extent to which (a dependent variable) is associated with one or more independent variables. ◆ *n* ('riːgrɛs). **3** movement in a backward direction; retrogression. ORIG C14: from L *regressus,* from *regredī* to go back, from RE- + *gradī* to go
▸ **re'gressive** *adj* ▸ **re'gressor** *n*

regression (rɪ'grɛʃən) *n* **1** *Psychol.* the adoption by an adult of behaviour more appropriate to a child. **2** *Statistics.* **2a** the measure of the association between one variable (the dependent variable) and other variables (the independent variables). **2b** (*as modifier*): *regression curve.* **3** *Geol.* the retreat of the sea from the land. **4** the act of regressing.

regret (rɪˈgrɛt) *vb* **regrets, regretting, regretted.** (*tr*) **1** (*may take a clause as object or an infinitive*) to feel sorry, repentant, or upset about. **2** to bemoan or grieve the death or loss of. ◆ *n* **3** a sense of repentance, guilt, or sorrow. **4** a sense of loss or grief. **5** (*pl*) a polite expression of sadness, esp. in a formal refusal of an invitation. ORIG C14: from OF *regreter,* from ON
▸ **reˈgretful** *adj* ▸ **reˈgretfully** *adv* ▸ **reˈgretfulness** *n* ▸ **reˈgrettable** *adj* ▸ **reˈgrettably** *adv*

> **USAGE NOTE** *Regretful* and *regretfully* are sometimes wrongly used where *regrettable* and *regrettably* are meant. A simple way of making the distinction is that when you regret something you have done, you are *regretful: he gave a regretful smile; he smiled regretfully.* In contrast, when you are sorry about an occurrence you did not yourself cause, you view the occurrence as *regrettable: this is a regrettable* (not *regretful*) *mistake; regrettably* (not *regretfully,* i.e. because of circumstances beyond my control) *I shall be unable to attend.*

regroup (riːˈgruːp) *vb* **1** to reorganize (military forces), esp. after an attack or a defeat. **2** (*tr*) to rearrange into a new grouping.

Regt *abbrev. for:* **1** Regent. **2** Regiment.

regulable (ˈrɛgjʊləbᵊl) *adj* able to be regulated.

regular (ˈrɛgjʊlə) *adj* **1** normal, customary, or usual. **2** according to a uniform principle, arrangement, or order. **3** occurring at fixed or prearranged intervals: *a regular call on a customer.* **4** following a set rule or normal practice; methodical or orderly. **5** symmetrical in appearance or form; even: *regular features.* **6** (*prenominal*) organized, elected, conducted, etc., in a proper or officially prescribed manner. **7** (*prenominal*) officially qualified or recognized: *he's not a regular doctor.* **8** (*prenominal*) (intensifier): *a regular fool.* **9** *US & Canad. inf.* likable, dependable, or nice: *a regular guy.* **10** denoting or relating to the personnel or units of the permanent military services: *a regular soldier.* **11** (of flowers) having any of their parts, esp. petals, alike in size, etc.; symmetrical. **12** *Grammar.* following the usual pattern of formation in a language. **13** *Maths.* **13a** (of a polygon) equilateral and equiangular. **13b** (of a polyhedron) having identical regular polygons as faces. **13c** (of a prism) having regular polygons as bases. **13d** (of a pyramid) having a regular polygon as a base and the altitude passing through the centre of the base. **14** *Bot.* (of a flower) having radial symmetry. **15** (*postpositive*) subject to the rule of an established religious order or community: *canons regular.* ◆ *n* **16** a professional long-term serviceman in a military unit. **17** *Inf.* a person who does something regularly, such as attending a theatre. **18** a member of a religious order or congregation, as contrasted with a secular. ORIG C14: from OF *reguler,* from L *rēgulāris* of a bar of wood or metal, from *rēgula* ruler, model
▸ **ˌreguˈlarity** *n* ▸ **ˈregularˌize** *or* **ˈregularˌise** *vb* ▸ **ˈregularly** *adv*

regulate (ˈrɛgjʊˌleɪt) *vb* **regulates, regulating, regulated.** (*tr*) **1** to adjust (the amount of heat, sound, etc.) as required; control. **2** to adjust (an instrument or appliance) so that it operates correctly. **3** to bring into conformity with a rule, principle, or usage. ORIG C17: from LL *rēgulāre* to control, from L *rēgula* ruler
▸ **ˈregulative** *or* **ˈregulatory** *adj* ▸ **ˈregulatively** *adv*

regulation (ˌrɛgjʊˈleɪʃən) *n* **1** the act or process of regulating. **2** a rule, principle, or condition that governs procedure or behaviour. **3** (*modifier*) as required by official rules: *regulation uniform.* **4** (*modifier*) normal; usual; conforming to accepted standards: *a regulation haircut.*

regulator (ˈrɛgjʊˌleɪtə) *n* **1** a person or thing that regulates. **2** the mechanism by which the speed of a timepiece is regulated. **3** any of various mechanisms or devices, such as a governor valve, for controlling fluid flow, pressure, temperature, etc.

regulo (ˈrɛgjʊləʊ) *n* any of a number of temperatures to which a gas oven may be set: *cook at regulo 4.* ORIG C20: from *Regulo,* trademark for a type of thermostatic control on gas ovens

regulus (ˈrɛgjʊləs) *n, pl* **reguluses** *or* **reguli** (-ˌlaɪ). impure metal forming beneath the slag during the smelting of ores. ORIG C16: from L: a petty king, from *rēx* king; formerly used for *antimony,* because it combines readily with gold, the king of metals
▸ **ˈreguline** *adj*

Regulus ★ (ˈrɛgjʊləs) *n* **Marcus Atilius** (ˈmɑːkəs əˈtɪlɪəs). died ?250 B.C., Roman general; consul (267; 256). Captured by the Carthaginians in the First Punic War, he was sent to Rome with the enemy's peace terms, which he advised the Senate to reject, and was tortured to death on his return to Carthage.

regurgitate (rɪˈgɜːdʒɪˌteɪt) *vb* **regurgitates, regurgitating, regurgitated. 1** to vomit forth (partially digested food). **2** (of some birds and animals) to bring back to the mouth (undigested or partly digested food to feed the young). **3** (*intr*) to be cast up or out, esp. from the mouth. **4** (*intr*) *Med.* (of blood) to flow in a direction opposite to the normal one, esp. through a defective heart valve. ORIG C17: from Med. L *regurgitāre,* from RE- + *gurgitāre* to flood, from L *gurges* whirlpool
▸ **reˈgurgitant** *n, adj* ▸ **reˌgurgiˈtation** *n*

rehabilitate (ˌriːəˈbɪlɪˌteɪt) *vb* **rehabilitates, rehabilitating, rehabilitated.** (*tr*) **1** to help (a physically or mentally disabled person or an ex-prisoner) to readapt to society or a new job, as by vocational guidance, retraining, or therapy. **2** to restore to a former position or rank. **3** to restore the good reputation of. ORIG C16: from Med. L *rehabilitāre* to restore, from RE- + L *habilitās* skill
▸ **ˌrehaˌbiliˈtation** *n* ▸ **ˌrehaˈbilitative** *adj*

Rehabilitation Department *n NZ.* a government department set up after World War II to assist ex-servicemen. Often shortened to **rehab.**

rehash *vb* (riːˈhæʃ). **1** (*tr*) to rework, reuse, or make over (old or already used material). ◆ *n* (ˈriːˌhæʃ). **2** something consisting of old, reworked, or reused material. ORIG C19: from RE- + HASH[1] (to chop into pieces)

rehearsal (rɪˈhɜːsᵊl) *n* **1** a session of practising a play, concert, etc., in preparation for public performance. **2 in rehearsal.** being prepared for public performance.

rehearse (rɪˈhɜːs) *vb* **rehearses, rehearsing, rehearsed. 1** to practise (a play, concert, etc.), in preparation for public performance. **2** (*tr*) to run through; recount; recite: *he rehearsed the grievances of the committee.* **3** (*tr*) to train or drill (a person) for public performance. ORIG C16: from Anglo-Norman *rehearser,* from OF *rehercier* to harrow a second time, from RE- + *herce* harrow
▸ **reˈhearser** *n*

reheat *vb* (riːˈhiːt). **1** to heat or be heated again: *to reheat yesterday's soup.* **2** (*tr*) to add fuel to (the exhaust gases of an aircraft jet engine) to produce additional heat and thrust. ◆ *n* (ˈriːˌhiːt), *also* **reheating. 3** a process in which additional fuel is ignited in the exhaust gases of a jet engine to produce additional thrust.
▸ **reˈheater** *n*

rehoboam (ˌriːəˈbəʊəm) *n* a wine bottle holding the equivalent of six normal bottles. ORIG after *Rehoboam,* a son of King Solomon, from Heb., lit.: the nation is enlarged

Reich (raɪk) *n* **1** the Holy Roman Empire (962–1806) (**First Reich**). **2** the Hohenzollern empire in Germany from 1871 to 1918 (**Second Reich**). **3** the Nazi dictatorship (1933–45) in Germany (**Third Reich**). ORIG G: kingdom

Reichenberg ★ (ˈraiçənbɛrk) *n* the German name for **Liberec.**

Reichsmark (ˈraɪksˌmɑːk) *n, pl* **Reichsmarks** *or* **Reichsmark.** the standard monetary unit of Germany between 1924 and 1948.

Reichstag (ˈraɪksˌtɑːg) *n* **1** the legislative assembly of Germany (1867–1933). **2** the building in Berlin in which this assembly met.

Reid ★ (riːd) *n* **1** Sir **George Houston.** 1845–1918, Australian statesman, born in Scotland: premier of New South Wales (1894–99); prime minister of Australia (1904–05).

2 John. born 1947, British Labour politician: secretary of state for Northern Ireland from 2001. **3 Thomas.** 1710–96, Scottish philosopher: his books include *Enquiry into the Human Mind on the Principles of Common Sense* (1764).

reify (ˈriːɪˌfaɪ) *vb* **reifies, reifying, reified.** (*tr*) to consider or make (an abstract idea or concept) real or concrete. ORIG C19: from L *rēs* thing
▸ **ˌreifiˈcation** *n* ▸ **ˌreifiˈcatory** *adj* ▸ **ˈreiˌfier** *n*

Reigate ★ (ˈraɪɡɪt, -ɡeɪt) *n* a town in S England, in Surrey at the foot of the North Downs. Pop.: 47 602 (1991).

reign (reɪn) *n* **1** the period during which a monarch is the official ruler of a country. **2** a period during which a person or thing is dominant or powerful: *the reign of violence.* ◆ *vb* (*intr*) **3** to exercise the power and authority of a sovereign. **4** to be accorded the rank and title of a sovereign without having ruling authority. **5** to predominate; prevail: *darkness reigns.* **6** (*usually present participle*) to be the most recent winner of a contest, etc.: *the reigning champion.* ORIG C13: from OF *reigne,* from L *rēgnum* kingdom, from *rēx* king

> **USAGE NOTE** *Reign* is sometimes wrongly written for *rein* in certain phrases: *he gave full rein* (not *reign*) *to his feelings; it will be necessary to rein in* (not *reign in*) *public spending.*

reiki (ˈreɪkɪ) *n* a form of therapy in which the practitioner is believed to channel energy into the patient in order to encourage healing or restore well-being. ORIG Japanese, from *rei* universal + *ki* life force

reimburse (ˌriːɪmˈbɜːs) *vb* **reimburses, reimbursing, reimbursed.** (*tr*) to repay or compensate (someone) for (money already spent, losses, damages, etc.). ORIG C17: from RE- + *imburse,* from Med. L *imbursāre* to put in a moneybag, from *bursa* PURSE
▸ **ˌreimˈbursable** *adj* ▸ **ˌreimˈbursement** *n* ▸ **ˌreimˈburser** *n*

reimport *vb* (ˌriːɪmˈpɔːt, riːˈɪmpɔːt). **1** (*tr*) to import (goods manufactured from exported raw materials). ◆ *n* (riːˈɪmpɔːt). **2** the act of reimporting. **3** a reimported commodity.
▸ **ˌreimporˈtation** *n*

Reims *or* **Rheims** ★ (riːmz; *French* rɛ̃s) *n* a city in NE France: scene of the coronation of most French monarchs. Pop.: 185 164 (1990).

rein (reɪn) *n* **1** (*often pl*) one of a pair of long straps, usually connected together and made of leather, used to control a horse. **2** a similar device used to control a very young child. **3** any form or means of control: *to take up the reins of government.* **4** the direction in which a rider turns (in **on a left rein**). **5** something that restrains, controls, or guides. **6 give (a) free rein.** to allow considerable freedom; remove restraints. **7 keep a tight rein on.** to control carefully; limit: *we have to keep a tight rein on expenditure.* ◆ *vb* **8** (*tr*) to check, restrain, hold back, or halt with or as if with reins. **9** to control or guide (a horse) with a rein or reins: *they reined left.* ◆ See also **rein in.** ORIG C13: from OF *resne,* from L *retinēre* to hold back, from RE- + *tenēre* to hold

> **USAGE NOTE** See at **reign.**

reincarnate *vb* (ˌriːɪnˈkɑːˌneɪt), **reincarnates, reincarnating, reincarnated.** (*tr; often passive*) **1** to cause to undergo reincarnation; be born again. ◆ *adj* (ˌriːɪnˈkɑːnɪt). **2** born again in a new body.

reincarnation (ˌriːɪnkɑːˈneɪʃən) *n* **1** the belief that on the death of the body the soul transmigrates to or is born again in another body. **2** the incarnation or embodiment of a soul in a new body after it has left the old one at physical death. **3** embodiment again in a new form, as of a principle or idea.
▸ **ˌreincarˈnationist** *n, adj*

reindeer (ˈreɪnˌdɪə) *n, pl* **reindeer** *or* **reindeers.** a large deer, having large branched antlers in the male and female and inhabiting the arctic regions. It also occurs in North America, where it is known as a caribou. ORIG C14: from ON *hreindýri,* from *hreinn* reindeer + *dyr* animal

Reindeer Lake ★ *n* a lake in W Canada, in Saskatchewan and Manitoba: drains into the Churchill River via the **Reindeer River.** Area: 6390 sq. km (2467 sq. miles).

reindeer moss *n* any of various lichens which occur in arctic and subarctic regions, providing food for reindeer.

reinforce (ˌriːɪnˈfɔːs) *vb* **reinforces, reinforcing, reinforced.** (*tr*) **1** to give added strength or support to. **2** to give added emphasis to; stress or increase: *his rudeness reinforced my determination.* **3** to give added support to (a military force) by providing more men, supplies, etc. ORIG C17: from F *renforcer*
▸ **ˌreinˈforcement** *n*

reinforced concrete *n* concrete with steel bars, mesh, etc., embedded in it to enable it to withstand tensile and shear stresses.

reinforced plastic *n* plastic with fibrous matter, such as carbon fibre, embedded in it to strengthen it.

Reinhardt ★ (ˈraɪnˌhɑːt) *n* **1 Django** (ˈdʒæŋɡəʊ), real name *Jean Baptiste Reinhardt.* 1910–53, Belgian jazz guitarist, whose work was greatly influenced by Gypsy music. With Stéphane Grappelli, he led the quintet of the Hot Club of France between 1934 and 1939. **2 Max,** original name *Max Goldmann.* 1873–1943, Austrian theatre producer and director, in the US after 1933.

rein in *vb* (*adv*) to stop (a horse) by pulling on the reins.

reins (reɪnz) *pl n Arch.* the kidneys or loins. ORIG C14: from OF, from L *rēnēs* the kidneys

reinstate (ˌriːɪnˈsteɪt) *vb* **reinstates, reinstating, reinstated.** (*tr*) to restore to a former rank or condition.
▸ **ˌreinˈstatement** *n* ▸ **ˌreinˈstator** *n*

reinsurer (ˌriːɪnˈʃʊərə) *n* an insurance company which will accept business from other insurance companies, thus enabling the risks to be spread.
▸ **ˌreinˈsurance** *n*

reinvent (ˌriːɪnˈvɛnt) *vb* (*tr*) **1** to replace (a product, etc.) with an entirely new version. **2** to duplicate (something that already exists) in what is therefore a wasted effort (esp. in **reinvent the wheel**).

reissue (ˌriːˈɪʃjuː) *n* **1** a book, record, etc., that is published or released again after being unavailable for a time. ◆ *vb* **2** (*tr*) to publish or release (a book, record, etc.) again after a period of unavailability.

reiterate (riːˈɪtəˌreɪt) *vb* **reiterates, reiterating, reiterated.** (*tr; may take a clause as object*) to say or do again or repeatedly. ORIG C16: from L *reiterāre,* from RE- + *iterāre* to do again, from *iterum* again
▸ **reˌiterˈation** *n* ▸ **reˈiterative** *adj* ▸ **reˈiteratively** *adv*

Reith ★ (riːθ) *n* **John** (**Charles Walsham**), 1st Baron. 1889–1971, British public servant: first general manager (1922–27) and first director general (1927–38) of the BBC.
▸ **ˈReithian** *or* **ˈReithean** *adj*

reive (riːv) *vb* **reives, reiving, reived.** (*intr*) *Scot. & N English dialect.* to go on a plundering raid. ORIG var. of REAVE
▸ **ˈreiver** *n*

reject *vb* (rɪˈdʒɛkt). (*tr*) **1** to refuse to accept, use, believe, etc. **2** to throw out as useless or worthless; discard. **3** to rebuff (a person). **4** (of an organism) to fail to accept (a foreign tissue graft or organ transplant). ◆ *n* (ˈriːdʒɛkt). **5** something rejected as imperfect, unsatisfactory, or useless. ORIG C15: from L *rēicere* to throw back, from RE- + *jacere* to hurl
▸ **reˈjecter** *or* **reˈjector** *n* ▸ **reˈjection** *n* ▸ **reˈjective** *adj*

rejig (riːˈdʒɪɡ) *vb* **rejigs, rejigging, rejigged.** (*tr*) **1** to re-equip (a factory or plant). **2** *Inf.* to rearrange, manipulate, etc., sometimes in an unscrupulous way. ◆ *n* **3** the act or process of rejigging.
▸ **reˈjigger** *n*

rejoice (rɪˈdʒɔɪs) *vb* **rejoices, rejoicing, rejoiced.** (when *tr, takes a clause as object or an infinitive;* when *intr,* often foll. by *in*) to feel or express great joy or happiness. ORIG C14: from OF *resjoir,* from RE- + *joir* to be glad, from L *gaudēre* to rejoice
▸ **reˈjoicer** *n*

rejoin[1] (riːˈdʒɔɪn) *vb* **1** to come again into company with (someone or something). **2** (*tr*) to put or join together again; reunite.

★ people and places

rejoin[2] (rɪˈdʒɔɪn) *vb (tr)* **1** to answer or reply. **2** *Law.* to answer (a plaintiff's reply). ORIG C15: from OF *rejoign-*, stem of *rejoindre;* see RE-, JOIN

rejoinder (rɪˈdʒɔɪndə) *n* **1** a reply or response to a question or remark. **2** *Law.* (in pleading) the answer made by a defendant to the plaintiff's reply. ORIG C15: from OF *rejoindre* to REJOIN[2]

rejuvenate (rɪˈdʒuːvɪˌneɪt) *vb* **rejuvenates, rejuvenating, rejuvenated.** *(tr)* **1** to give new youth, restored vitality, or youthful appearance to. **2** *(usually passive) Geog.* to cause (a river) to begin eroding more vigorously to a new lower base level. ORIG C19: from RE- + L *juvenis* young
▸ **reˌjuveˈnation** *n* ▸ **reˈjuveˌnator** *n*

rejuvenesce (rɪˌdʒuːvəˈnɛs) *vb* **rejuvenesces, rejuvenescing, rejuvenesced.** **1** to make or become youthful or restored to vitality. **2** *Biol.* to convert (cells) or (of cells) to be converted into a more active form.
▸ **reˌjuveˈnescence** *n* ▸ **reˌjuveˈnescent** *adj*

rel. *abbrev. for:* **1** relating. **2** relative(ly). **3** released. **4** religion. **5** religious.

relapse (rɪˈlæps) *vb* **relapses, relapsing, relapsed.** *(intr)* **1** to lapse back into a former state or condition, esp. one involving bad habits. **2** to become ill again after apparent recovery. ◆ *n* **3** the act or an instance of relapsing. **4** the return of ill health after an apparent or partial recovery. ORIG C16: from L *relabī*, from RE- + *labī* to slip, slide
▸ **reˈlapser** *n*

relapsing fever *n* any of various infectious diseases characterized by recurring fever, caused by the bite of body lice or ticks. Also called: **recurrent fever.**

relata (rɪˈleɪtə) *n* the plural of **relatum.**

relate (rɪˈleɪt) *vb* **relates, relating, related.** **1** *(tr)* to tell or narrate (a story, etc.). **2** (often foll. by *to*) to establish association (between two or more things) or (of something) to have relation or reference (to something else). **3** *(intr;* often foll. by *to)* to form a sympathetic or significant relationship (with other people, things, etc.). ORIG C16: from L *relātus* brought back, from *referre*, from RE- + *ferre* to bear
▸ **reˈlatable** *adj* ▸ **reˈlater** *n*

related (rɪˈleɪtɪd) *adj* **1** connected; associated. **2** connected by kinship or marriage. **3** (in diatonic music) denoting or relating to a key that has notes in common with another key or keys.
▸ **reˈlatedness** *n*

relation (rɪˈleɪʃən) *n* **1** the state or condition of being related or the manner in which things are related. **2** connection by blood or marriage; kinship. **3** a person who is connected by blood or marriage; relative. **4** reference or regard (esp. in **in** *or* **with relation to**). **5** the position, association, connection, or status of one person or thing with regard to another. **6** the act of relating or narrating. **7** an account or narrative. **8** *Law.* the statement of grounds of complaint made by a relator. **9** *Logic, maths.* **9a** an association between ordered pairs of objects, numbers, etc., such as ... is greater than .... **9b** the set of ordered pairs whose members have such an association. ◆ See also **relations.** ORIG C14: from L *relātiō* a narration, a relation (between philosophical concepts)

relational (rɪˈleɪʃənᵊl) *adj* **1** *Grammar.* indicating or expressing syntactic relation, as for example the case endings in Latin. **2** having relation or being related. **3** *Computing.* based on data that is interconnected, often in tabular form.

relations (rɪˈleɪʃənz) *pl n* **1** social, political, or personal connections or dealings between or among individuals, groups, nations, etc. **2** family or relatives. **3** *Euphemistic.* sexual intercourse.

relationship (rɪˈleɪʃənʃɪp) *n* **1** the state of being connected or related. **2** association by blood or marriage; kinship. **3** the mutual dealings, connections, or feelings that exist between two countries, people, etc. **4** an emotional or sexual affair or liaison.

relative (ˈrɛlətɪv) *adj* **1** having meaning or significance only in relation to something else; not absolute. **2** *(prenominal)* (of a scientific quantity) being measured or stated relative to some other substance or measurement: *relative density.* **3** *(prenominal)* comparative or respective: *the relative qualities of speed and accuracy.* **4** *(postpositive;* foll. by *to)* in proportion (to); corresponding (to): *earnings relative to production.* **5** having reference (to); pertinent (to). **6** *Grammar.* denoting or belonging to a class of words that function as subordinating conjunctions in introducing relative clauses such as *who, which,* and *that.* Cf. **demonstrative. 7** *Grammar.* denoting or relating to a clause (**relative clause**) that modifies a noun or pronoun occurring earlier in the sentence. **8** (of a musical key or scale) having the same key signature as another key or scale. ◆ *n* **9** a person who is related by blood or marriage; relation. **10** a relative pronoun, clause, or grammatical construction. ORIG C16: from LL *relātīvus* referring
▸ **ˈrelatively** *adv* ▸ **ˈrelativeness** *n*

relative aperture *n Photog.* the ratio of the equivalent focal length of a lens to the effective aperture of the lens.

relative atomic mass *n* the ratio of the average mass per atom of the naturally occurring form of an element to one-twelfth of the mass of an atom of carbon-12. Symbol: A_r Abbrev.: **r.a.m.** Former name: **atomic weight.**

relative density *n* the ratio of the density of a substance to the density of a standard substance under specified conditions. For liquids and solids the standard is usually water at 4°C. For gases the standard is air or hydrogen at the same temperature and pressure as the substance. See also **specific gravity, vapour density.**

relative frequency *n Statistics.* the ratio of the actual number of favourable events to the total possible number of events.

relative humidity *n* the mass of water vapour present in the air expressed as a percentage of the mass present in an equal volume of saturated air at the same temperature.

relative majority *n Brit.* the excess of votes or seats won by the winner of an election over the runner-up when no candidate or party has more than 50 per cent. Cf. **absolute majority.**

relative molecular mass *n* the sum of all the relative atomic masses of the atoms in a molecule; the ratio of the average mass per molecule of a specified isotopic composition of a substance to one-twelfth the mass of an atom of carbon-12. Symbol: M_r Abbrev.: **r.m.m.** Former name: **molecular weight.**

relative permeability *n* the ratio of the permeability of a medium to that of free space.

relative permittivity *n* the ratio of the permittivity of a substance to that of free space.

relativism (ˈrɛlətɪˌvɪzəm) *n* any theory holding that truth or moral or aesthetic value, etc., is not universal or absolute but may differ between individuals or cultures.
▸ **ˈrelativist** *n, adj* ▸ **ˌrelativˈistic** *adj*

relativity (ˌrɛləˈtɪvɪtɪ) *n* **1** either of two theories developed by Albert Einstein, the **special theory of relativity,** which requires that the laws of physics shall be the same as seen by any two different observers in uniform relative motion, and the **general theory of relativity,** which considers observers with relative acceleration and leads to a theory of gravitation. **2** the state or quality of being relative.

relator (rɪˈleɪtə) *n* **1** a person who relates a story; narrator. **2** *English law.* a person who gives information upon which the attorney general brings an action.

relatum (rɪˈleɪtəm) *n, pl* **relata** (-tə). *Logic.* one of the objects between which a relation is said to hold.

relax (rɪˈlæks) *vb* **1** to make (muscles, a grip, etc.) less tense or rigid or (of muscles, a grip, etc.) to become looser or less rigid. **2** *(intr)* to take rest, as from work or effort. **3** to lessen the force of (effort, concentration) or (of effort) to become diminished. **4** to make (rules or discipline) less rigid or strict or (of rules, etc.) to diminish in severity. **5** *(intr)* (of a person) to become less formal; unbend. ORIG C15: from L *relaxāre* to loosen, from RE- + *laxāre*, from *laxus* loose
▸ **reˈlaxed** *adj* ▸ **relaxedly** (rɪˈlæksɪdlɪ) *adv* ▸ **reˈlaxer** *n*

relaxant (rɪˈlæksᵊnt) *n* **1** *Med.* a drug or agent that relaxes, esp. one that relaxes tense muscles. ◆ *adj* **2** of or tending to produce relaxation.

relaxation (ˌriːlækˈseɪʃən) *n* **1** rest or refreshment, as after work or effort; recreation. **2** a form of rest or recreation: *his relaxation is cricket.* **3** a partial lessening of a punishment, duty, etc. **4** the act of relaxing or state of being relaxed. **5** *Physics.* the return of a system to equilibrium after a displacement from this state.

relaxin (rɪˈlæksɪn) *n* **1** a mammalian polypeptide hormone secreted during pregnancy, which relaxes the pelvic ligaments. **2** a preparation of this hormone, used to facilitate childbirth. ORIG C20: from RELAX + -IN

relay *n* (ˈriːleɪ). **1** a person or team of people relieving others, as on a shift. **2** a fresh team of horses, etc., posted along a route to relieve others. **3** the act of relaying or process of being relayed. **4** short for **relay race. 5** an automatic device that controls a valve, switch, etc., by means of an electric motor, solenoid, or pneumatic mechanism. **6** *Electronics.* an electrical device in which a small change in current or voltage controls the switching on or off of circuits. **7** *Radio.* **7a** a combination of a receiver and transmitter designed to receive radio signals and retransmit them. **7b** *(as modifier): a relay station.* ◆ *vb* (rɪˈleɪ). *(tr)* **8** to carry or spread (news or information) by relays. **9** to supply or replace with relays. **10** to retransmit (a signal) by means of a relay. **11** *Brit.* to broadcast (a performance) by sending out signals through a transmitting station. ORIG C15 *relaien,* from OF *relaier* to leave behind, from RE- + *laier* to leave, ult. from L *laxāre* to loosen

relay race *n* a race between two or more teams of contestants in which each contestant covers a specified portion of the distance.

release (rɪˈliːs) *vb* **releases, releasing, released.** *(tr)* **1** to free (a person or animal) from captivity or imprisonment. **2** to free (someone) from obligation or duty. **3** to free (something) from (one's grip); let fall. **4** to issue (a record, film, or book) for sale or circulation. **5** to make (news or information) known or allow (news, etc.) to be made known. **6** *Law.* to relinquish (a right, claim, or title) in favour of someone else. ◆ *n* **7** the act of freeing or state of being freed. **8** the act of issuing for sale or publication. **9** something issued for sale or public showing, esp. a film or a record: *a new release from Bob Dylan.* **10** a news item, etc., made available for publication, broadcasting, etc. **11** *Law.* the surrender of a claim, right, title, etc., in favour of someone else. **12** a control mechanism for starting or stopping an engine. **13** the control mechanism for the shutter in a camera. ORIG C13: from OF *relesser,* from L *relaxāre* to slacken
▸ **reˈleaser** *n*

relegate (ˈrɛlɪˌɡeɪt) *vb* **relegates, relegating, relegated.** *(tr)* **1** to move to a position of less authority, importance, etc.; demote. **2** *(usually passive) Chiefly Brit.* to demote (a football team, etc.) to a lower division. **3** to assign or refer (a matter) to another. **4** (foll. by *to*) to banish or exile. **5** to assign (something) to a particular group or category. ORIG C16: from L *relēgāre,* from RE- + *lēgāre* to send
▸ **ˈreleˌgatable** *adj* ▸ **ˌreleˈgation** *n*

relent (rɪˈlɛnt) *vb (intr)* **1** to change one's mind about some decision, esp. a harsh one; become more mild or amenable. **2** (of the pace or intensity of something) to slacken. **3** (of the weather) to become more mild. ORIG C14: from RE- + L *lentāre* to bend, from *lentus* flexible

relentless (rɪˈlɛntlɪs) *adj* **1** (of an enemy, etc.) implacable; inflexible; inexorable. **2** (of pace or intensity) sustained; unremitting.
▸ **reˈlentlessly** *adv* ▸ **reˈlentlessness** *n*

Relenza (rɪˈlɛnzə) *n Trademark.* a preparation of an antiviral drug, zanamivir, used in the treatment of influenza to reduce the duration and severity of the illness.

relevant (ˈrɛlɪvənt) *adj* having direct bearing on the matter in hand; pertinent. ORIG C16: from Med. L *relevans,* from L *relevāre,* from RE- + *levāre* to raise, RELIEVE
▸ **ˈrelevance** *or* **ˈrelevancy** *n* ▸ **ˈrelevantly** *adv*

reliable (rɪˈlaɪəbᵊl) *adj* able to be trusted; dependable.
▸ **reˌliaˈbility** *or* **reˈliableness** *n* ▸ **reˈliably** *adv*

reliance (rɪˈlaɪəns) *n* **1** dependence, confidence, or trust. **2** something or someone upon which one relies.
▸ **reˈliant** *adj* ▸ **reˈliantly** *adv*

relic (ˈrɛlɪk) *n* **1** something that has survived from the past, such as an object or custom. **2** something treasured for its past associations; keepsake. **3** *(usually pl)* a remaining part or fragment. **4** *RC Church, Eastern Church.* part of the body of a saint or his belongings, venerated as holy. **5** *Inf.* an old or old-fashioned person or thing. **6** *(pl) Arch.* the remains of a dead person; corpse. ORIG C13: from OF *relique,* from L *reliquiae* remains, from *relinquere* to leave behind

relict (ˈrɛlɪkt) *n* **1** *Ecology.* **1a** a group of animals or plants that exists as a remnant of a formerly widely distributed group. **1b** *(as modifier): a relict fauna.* **2** *Geol.* a mountain, lake, glacier, etc., that is a remnant of a pre-existing formation after a destructive process has occurred. **3** an archaic word for **widow. 4** an archaic word for **relic.** ORIG C16: from L *relictus* left behind, from *relinquere* to RELINQUISH

relief (rɪˈliːf) *n* **1** a feeling of cheerfulness or optimism that follows the removal of anxiety, pain, or distress. **2** deliverance from or alleviation of anxiety, pain, etc. **3a** help or assistance, as to the poor or needy. **3b** *(as modifier): relief work.* **4** a diversion from monotony. **5** a person who replaces another at some task or duty. **6** a bus, plane, etc., that carries additional passengers when a scheduled service is full. **7** a road (**relief road**) carrying traffic round an urban area; bypass. **8a** the act of freeing a beleaguered town, fortress, etc.: *the relief of Mafeking.* **8b** *(as modifier): a relief column.* **9** Also called: **relievo, rilievo.** *Sculpture, archit.* **9a** the projection of forms or figures from a flat ground, so that they are partly or wholly free of it. **9b** a piece of work of this kind. **10** a printing process that employs raised surfaces from which ink is transferred to the paper. **11** any vivid effect resulting from contrast: *comic relief.* **12** variation in altitude in an area; difference between highest and lowest level. **13** *Law.* redress of a grievance or hardship: *to seek relief through the courts.* **14 on relief.** *US & Canad.* (of people) in receipt of government aid because of personal need. ORIG C14: from OF, from *relever;* see RELIEVE

relief map *n* a map that shows the configuration and height of the land surface, usually by means of contours.

relieve (rɪˈliːv) *vb* **relieves, relieving, relieved.** *(tr)* **1** to bring alleviation of (pain, distress, etc.) to (someone). **2** to bring aid or assistance to (someone in need, etc.). **3** to take over the duties or watch of (someone). **4** to bring aid or a relieving force to (a besieged town, etc.). **5** to free (someone) from an obligation. **6** to make (something) less unpleasant, arduous, or monotonous. **7** to bring into relief or prominence, as by contrast. **8** (foll. by *of*) *Inf.* to take from: *the thief relieved him of his watch.* **9 relieve oneself.** to urinate or defecate. ORIG C14: from OF *relever,* from L *relevāre* to lift up, relieve, from RE- + *levāre* to lighten
▸ **reˈlievable** *adj* ▸ **reˈliever** *n*

relieved (rɪˈliːvd) *adj (postpositive;* often foll. by *at, about,* etc.) experiencing relief, esp. from worry or anxiety.

religieuse *French.* (rəliʒjøz) *n* a nun. ORIG C18: fem of RELIGIEUX

religieux *French.* (rəliʒjø) *n, pl* ***religieux*** (-ʒjø). a member of a monastic order or clerical body. ORIG C17: from L *religiōsus* religious

religion (rɪˈlɪdʒən) *n* **1** belief in, worship of, or obedience to a supernatural power or powers considered to be divine or to have control of human destiny. **2** any formal or institutionalized expression of such belief: *the Christian religion.* **3** the attitude and feeling of one who believes in a transcendent controlling power or powers. **4** *Chiefly RC Church.* the way of life entered upon by monks and nuns: *to enter religion.* **5** something of overwhelming importance to a person: *football is his religion.* ORIG C12: via OF from L *religiō* fear of the supernatural, piety, prob. from *religāre,* from RE- + *ligāre* to bind

religionism (rɪˈlɪdʒəˌnɪzəm) *n* extreme religious fervour.
▸ **reˈligionist** *n, adj*

religiose (rɪˈlɪdʒɪˌəʊs) *adj* affectedly or extremely pious; sanctimoniously religious.
▸ **reˈligiˌosely** *adv* ▸ **religiosity** (rɪˌlɪdʒɪˈɒsɪtɪ) *n*

religious (rɪˈlɪdʒəs) *adj* **1** of, relating to, or concerned with religion. **2a** pious; devout; godly. **2b** *(as collective n;*

preceded by *the*): *the religious*. **3** appropriate to or in accordance with the principles of a religion. **4** scrupulous, exact, or conscientious. **5** *Christianity*. of or relating to a way of life dedicated to religion and defined by a monastic rule. ◆ *n* **6** *Christianity*. a monk or nun.
▸ **re'ligiously** *adv* ▸ **re'ligiousness** *n*

Religious Society of Friends *n* the official name for the **Quakers**.

relinquish (rɪ'lɪŋkwɪʃ) *vb* (*tr*) **1** to give up (a task, struggle, etc.); abandon. **2** to surrender or renounce (a claim, right, etc.). **3** to release; let go. ORIG C15: from F *relinquir*, from L *relinquere*, from RE- + *linquere* to leave
▸ **re'linquisher** *n* ▸ **re'linquishment** *n*

reliquary ('rɛlɪkwərɪ) *n, pl* **reliquaries**. a receptacle or repository for relics, esp. relics of saints. ORIG C17: from OF *reliquaire*, from *relique* RELIC

relique (rə'li:k, 'rɛlɪk) *n* an archaic spelling of **relic**.

reliquiae (rɪ'lɪkwɪˌi:) *pl n* fossil remains of animals or plants. ORIG C19: from L: remains

relish ('rɛlɪʃ) *vb* (*tr*) **1** to savour or enjoy (an experience) to the full. **2** to anticipate eagerly; look forward to. **3** to enjoy the taste or flavour of (food, etc.); savour. ◆ *n* **4** liking or enjoyment, as of something eaten or experienced (esp. in **with relish**). **5** pleasurable anticipation: *he didn't have much relish for the idea*. **6** an appetizing or spicy food added to a main dish to enhance its flavour. **7** an appetizing taste or flavour. **8** a zestful trace or touch: *there was a certain relish in all his writing*. ORIG C16: from earlier *reles* aftertaste, from OF, from *relaisser* to leave behind; see RELEASE
▸ **'relishable** *adj*

relive (ri:'lɪv) *vb* **relives, reliving, relived.** (*tr*) to experience (a sensation, event, etc.) again, esp. in the imagination.
▸ **re'livable** *adj*

relocate (ˌri:ləʊ'keɪt) *vb* **relocates, relocating, relocated.** to move or be moved to a new place, esp. (of an employee, a business, etc.) to a new area or place of employment.
▸ **ˌrelo'cation** *n*

reluctance (rɪ'lʌktəns) *or* **reluctancy** *n* **1** lack of eagerness or willingness; disinclination. **2** *Physics*. a measure of the resistance of a closed magnetic circuit to a magnetic flux. ORIG C16: from L *reluctārī* to resist, from RE- + *luctārī* to struggle

reluctant (rɪ'lʌktənt) *adj* not eager; unwilling; disinclined. ORIG C17: from L *reluctārī* to resist
▸ **re'luctantly** *adv*

reluctivity (ˌrɛlʌk'tɪvɪtɪ) *n, pl* **reluctivities.** *Physics*. a specific or relative reluctance of a magnetic material. ORIG C19: from obs. *reluct* to struggle + *-ivity*

rely (rɪ'laɪ) *vb* **relies, relying, relied.** (*intr*; foll. by *on* or *upon*) **1** to be dependent (on): *he relies on his charm*. **2** to have trust or confidence (in): *you can rely on us*. ORIG C14: from OF *relier* to fasten together, from L *religāre*, from RE- + *ligāre* to tie

REM *abbrev. for* rapid eye movement.

remain (rɪ'meɪn) *vb* (*mainly intr*) **1** to stay behind or in the same place: *to remain at home*. **2** (*copula*) to continue to be: *to remain cheerful*. **3** to be left, as after use, the passage of time, etc. **4** to be left to be done, said, etc.: *it remains to be pointed out*. ORIG C14: from OF *remanoir*, from L *remanēre*, from RE- + *manēre* to stay

remainder (rɪ'meɪndə) *n* **1** a part or portion that is left, as after use, subtraction, expenditure, the passage of time, etc.: *the remainder of the milk*. **2** *Maths*. **2a** the amount left over when one quantity cannot be exactly divided by another: *for 10 ÷ 3, the remainder is 1*. **2b** another name for **difference** (sense 7). **3** *Property law*. a future interest in property; an interest in a particular estate that will pass to one at some future date, as on the death of the current possessor. **4** a number of copies of a book left unsold when demand ceases, which are sold at a reduced price. ◆ *vb* **5** (*tr*) to sell (copies of a book) as a remainder.

remains (rɪ'meɪnz) *pl n* **1** any pieces, fragments, etc., that are left unused or still extant, as after use, consumption, the passage of time: *archaeological remains*. **2** the body of a dead person; corpse. **3** Also called: **literary remains**. the unpublished writings of an author at the time of his or her death.

remake *n* ('ri:ˌmeɪk). **1** something that is made again, esp. a new version of an old film. **2** the act of making again. ◆ *vb* (ri:'meɪk), **remakes, remaking, remade. 3** (*tr*) to make again or anew.

remand (rɪ'mɑ:nd) *vb* (*tr*) **1** *Law*. (of a court or magistrate) to send (a prisoner or accused person) back into custody. **2** to send back. ◆ *n* **3** the sending of a prisoner or accused person back into custody to await trial. **4** the act of remanding or state of being remanded. **5 on remand.** in custody or on bail awaiting trial. ORIG C15: from Med. L *remandāre* to send back word, from L RE- + *mandāre* to command

remand centre *n* (in Britain) an institution to which accused persons are sent for detention while awaiting appearance before a court.

remanence ('rɛmənəns) *n Physics*. the ability of a material to retain magnetization after the removal of the magnetizing field. ORIG C17: from L *remanēre* to stay behind

remark (rɪ'mɑ:k) *vb* **1** (when *intr*, often foll. by *on* or *upon*; when *tr, may take a clause as object*) to pass a casual comment (about); reflect in informal speech or writing. **2** (*tr; may take a clause as object*) to perceive; observe; notice. ◆ *n* **3** a brief casually expressed thought or opinion. **4** notice, comment, or observation: *the event passed without remark*. **5** a variant of **remarque**. ORIG C17: from OF *remarquer* to observe, from RE- + *marquer* to note, MARK[1]
▸ **re'marker** *n*

remarkable (rɪ'mɑ:kəbᵊl) *adj* **1** worthy of note or attention: *a remarkable achievement*. **2** unusual, striking, or extraordinary: *a remarkable sight*.
▸ **re'markableness** *n* ▸ **re'markably** *adv*

remarque (rɪ'mɑ:k) *n* a mark in the margin of an engraved plate to indicate the stage of production. ORIG C19: from F; see REMARK

Remarque ★ (rɪ'mɑ:k) *n* **Erich Maria** ('e:rɪç ma'ri:a). 1898–1970, US novelist, born in Germany, noted for his novel *All Quiet on the Western Front* (1929).

remaster (ri:'mɑ:stə) *vb* (*tr*) to make a new master audio recording, now usually digital, from (an earlier original recording), in order to produce compact discs or stereo records with improved sound reproduction.

Rembrandt ★ ('rɛmbrænt) *n* full name *Rembrandt Harmensz* (or *Harmenszoon*) *van Rijn* (or *van Ryn*). 1606–69, Dutch painter, noted for his portraits, esp. *The Nightwatch* (1642).
▸ **ˌRembrandt'esque** *adj*

REME ('ri:mɪ) *n acronym for* Royal Electrical and Mechanical Engineers.

remedial (rɪ'mi:dɪəl) *adj* **1** affording a remedy; curative. **2** denoting or relating to special teaching for backward and slow learners: *remedial education*.
▸ **re'medially** *adv*

remediation (rɪˌmi:dɪ'eɪʃən) *n* the action of remedying something, esp. the reversal or stopping of damage to the environment.

remedy ('rɛmɪdɪ) *n, pl* **remedies. 1** (usually foll. by *for* or *against*) any drug or agent that cures a disease or controls its symptoms. **2** (usually foll. by *for* or *against*) anything that serves to cure defects, improve conditions, etc.: *a remedy for industrial disputes*. **3** the legally permitted variation from the standard weight or quality of coins. ◆ *vb* (*tr*) **4** to relieve or cure (a disease, etc.) by a remedy. **5** to put to rights (a fault, error, etc.); correct. ORIG C13: from Anglo-Norman *remedie*, from L *remedium* a cure, from *remedērī*, from RE- + *medērī* to heal
▸ **remediable** (rɪ'mi:dɪəbᵊl) *adj* ▸ **re'mediably** *adv* ▸ **'remediless** *adj*

remember (rɪ'mɛmbə) *vb* **1** to become aware of (something forgotten) again; bring back to one's consciousness. **2** to retain (an idea, intention, etc.) in one's conscious mind: *remember to do one's shopping*. **3** (*tr*) to give money, etc., to (someone), as in a will or in tipping. **4** (*tr*; foll. by *to*) to mention (a person's name) to another person, as by way of greeting: *remember me to your mother*. **5** (*tr*) to mention (a person) favourably, as in prayer. **6** (*tr*) to commemorate (a person, event, etc.): *to remember the dead of the wars*. **7 remember oneself.** to recover one's good

manners after a lapse. ORIG C14: from OF *remembrer*, from LL *rememorārī* to recall to mind, from L RE- + *memor* mindful
▸ **re'memberer** *n*

remembrance (rɪ'mɛmbrəns) *n* **1** the act of remembering or state of being remembered. **2** something that is remembered; reminiscence. **3** a memento or keepsake. **4** the extent in time of one's power of recollection. **5** the act of honouring some past event, person, etc.

Remembrance Day *n* **1** (in Britain) another name for **Remembrance Sunday**. **2** (in Canada) a statutory holiday observed on November 11 in memory of the dead of both World Wars.

remembrancer (rɪ'mɛmbrənsə) *n* **1** *Arch.* a reminder, memento, or keepsake. **2** (*usually cap.*) (in Britain) any of several officials of the Exchequer, esp. one (**Queen's** *or* **King's Remembrancer**) whose duties include collecting debts due to the Crown. **3** (*usually cap.*) an official (**City Remembrancer**) appointed by the Corporation of the City of London to represent its interests to Parliament.

Remembrance Sunday *n* (in Britain) the Sunday closest to November 11, on which the dead of both World Wars are commemorated. Also called: **Remembrance Day**.

remex ('ri:mɛks) *n, pl* **remiges** ('rɛmɪˌdʒi:z). any of the large flight feathers of a bird's wing. ORIG C18: from L: rower, from *rēmus* oar
▸ **remigial** (rɪ'mɪdʒɪəl) *adj*

remind (rɪ'maɪnd) *vb* (*tr; usually foll. by of; may take a clause as object or an infinitive*) to cause (a person) to remember (something or to do something); put (a person) in mind (of something): *remind me to phone home; flowers remind me of holidays.*
▸ **re'minder** *n*

remindful (rɪ'maɪndfʊl) *adj* **1** serving to remind. **2** (*postpositive*) mindful.

reminisce (ˌrɛmɪ'nɪs) *vb* **reminisces, reminiscing, reminisced.** (*intr*) to talk or write about old times, past experiences, etc.

reminiscence (ˌrɛmɪ'nɪsəns) *n* **1** the act of recalling or narrating past experiences. **2** (*often pl*) some past experience, event, etc., that is recalled. **3** an event, phenomenon, or experience that reminds one of something else. **4** *Philosophy.* the doctrine that the mind has seen the universal forms of all things in a previous disembodied existence.

reminiscent (ˌrɛmɪ'nɪsᵊnt) *adj* **1** (*postpositive;* foll. by *of*) stimulating memories (of) or comparisons (with). **2** characterized by reminiscence. **3** (of a person) given to reminiscing. ORIG C18: from L *reminiscī* to call to mind, from RE- + *mēns* mind
▸ ˌ**remi'niscently** *adv*

remise (rɪ'maɪz) *vb* **remises, remising, remised. 1** (*tr*) *Law.* to give up or relinquish (a right, claim, etc.). **2** (*intr*) *Fencing.* to make a remise. ◆ *n* **3** *Fencing.* a second thrust made on the same lunge after the first has missed. **4** *Obs.* a coach house. ORIG C17: from F *remettre* to put back, from L *remittere,* from RE- + *mittere* to send

remiss (rɪ'mɪs) *adj* (*postpositive*) **1** lacking in care or attention to duty; negligent. **2** lacking in energy. ORIG C15: from L *remissus,* from *remittere,* from RE- + *mittere* to send
▸ **re'missly** *adv* ▸ **re'missness** *n*

remissible (rɪ'mɪsɪbᵊl) *adj* able to be remitted. ORIG C16: from L *remissibilis;* see REMIT
▸ **reˌmissi'bility** *n*

remission (rɪ'mɪʃən) *or* (*less commonly*) **remittal** (rɪ'mɪtᵊl) *n* **1** the act of remitting or state of being remitted. **2** a reduction of the term of a sentence of imprisonment, as for good conduct. **3** forgiveness for sin. **4** discharge or release from penalty, obligation, etc. **5** lessening of intensity; abatement, as in the symptoms of a disease. **6** *Rare.* the act of sending a remittance.
▸ **re'missive** *adj* ▸ **re'missively** *adv*

remit *vb* (rɪ'mɪt), **remits, remitting, remitted.** (*mainly tr*) **1** (*also intr*) to send (payment, etc.), as for goods or service, esp. by post. **2** *Law.* (esp. of an appeal court) to send back (a case) to an inferior court for further consideration. **3** to cancel or refrain from exacting (a penalty or punishment). **4** (*also intr*) to relax (pace, intensity, etc.) or (of pace) to slacken or abate. **5** to postpone; defer. **6** *Arch.* to pardon or forgive (crime, sins, etc.). ◆ *n* ('ri:mɪt, rɪ'mɪt). **7** area of authority (of a committee, etc.). **8** *Law.* the transfer of a case from one court or jurisdiction to another. **9** the act of remitting. ORIG C14: from L *remittere,* from RE- + *mittere* to send
▸ **re'mittable** *adj* ▸ **re'mitter** *n*

remittance (rɪ'mɪtəns) *n* **1** payment for goods or services received or as an allowance, esp. when sent by post. **2** the act of remitting.

remittance man *n* a man living abroad on money sent from home, esp. in the days of the British Empire.

remittent (rɪ'mɪtᵊnt) *adj* (of the symptoms of a disease) characterized by periods of diminished severity.
▸ **re'mittence** *n* ▸ **re'mittently** *adv*

remix *vb* (ri:'mɪks). **1** to change the balance and separation of (a recording). ◆ *n* ('ri:ˌmɪks). **2** a remixed version of a recording.

remnant ('rɛmnənt) *n* **1** (*often pl*) a part left over after use, processing, etc. **2** a surviving trace or vestige: *a remnant of imperialism.* **3** a piece of material from the end of a roll. ◆ *adj* **4** remaining; left over. ORIG C14: from OF *remenant* remaining, from *remanoir* to REMAIN

remonetize *or* **remonetise** (ri:'mʌnɪˌtaɪz) *vb* **remonetizes, remonetizing, remonetized** *or* **remonetises, remonetising, remonetised.** (*tr*) to reinstate as legal tender: *to remonetize silver.*
▸ **reˌmoneti'zation** *or* **reˌmoneti'sation** *n*

remonstrance (rɪ'mɒnstrəns) *n* **1** the act of remonstrating. **2** a protest or reproof, esp. a petition protesting against something.

remonstrant (rɪ'mɒnstrənt) *n* **1** a person who remonstrates, esp. one who signs a remonstrance. ◆ *adj* **2** *Rare.* remonstrating.

remonstrate ('rɛmənˌstreɪt) *vb* **remonstrates, remonstrating, remonstrated.** (*intr*) (usually foll. by *with, against,* etc.) to argue in protest or objection: *to remonstrate with the government.* ORIG C16: from Med. L *remonstrāre* to point out (errors, etc.), from L RE- + *monstrāre* to show
▸ ˌ**remon'stration** *n* ▸ **remonstrative** (rɪ'mɒnstrətɪv) *adj*
▸ '**remonˌstrator** *n*

remontant (rɪ'mɒntənt) *adj* **1** (esp. of roses) flowering more than once in a single season. ◆ *n* **2** a rose having such a growth. ORIG C19: from F: coming up again, from *remonter*

remora ('rɛmərə) *n* a marine spiny-finned fish which has a flattened elongated body and attaches itself to larger fish, rocks, etc., by a sucking disc on the top of the head. ORIG C16: from L, from RE- + *mora* delay; from its alleged habit of delaying ships

remorse (rɪ'mɔ:s) *n* **1** a sense of deep regret and guilt for some misdeed. **2** compunction; pity; compassion. ORIG C14: from Med. L *remorsus* a gnawing, from L *remordēre,* from RE- + *mordēre* to bite
▸ **re'morseful** *adj* ▸ **re'morsefully** *adv* ▸ **re'morsefulness** *n*
▸ **re'morseless** *adj*

remote (rɪ'məʊt) *adj* **1** located far away; distant. **2** far from society or civilization; out-of-the-way. **3** distant in time. **4** distantly related or connected: *a remote cousin.* **5** slight or faint (esp. in **not the remotest idea**). **6** (of a person's manner) aloof or abstracted. **7** operated from a distance; remote-controlled: *a remote monitor.* ORIG C15: from L *remōtus* far removed, from *removēre,* from RE- + *movēre* to move
▸ **re'motely** *adv* ▸ **re'moteness** *n*

remote access *n Computing.* access to a computer from a physically separate terminal.

remote control *n* control of a system or activity from a distance, usually by radio, ultrasonic, or electrical signals.
▸ **reˌmote-con'trolled** *adj*

remote sensor *n* any instrument, such as a radar device or camera, that scans the earth or another planet from space in order to collect data about some aspect of it.
▸ **remote sensing** *adj, n*

rémoulade (ˌrɛməˈleɪd) *n* a mayonnaise sauce flavoured with herbs, mustard, and capers, served with salads, cold meat, etc. ORIG C19: from F, from dialect *ramolas* horseradish, from L *armoracea*

remould *vb* (ˌriːˈməʊld). (*tr*) **1** to mould again. **2** to bond a new tread onto the casing of (a worn pneumatic tyre). ◆ *n* (ˈriːˌməʊld). **3** a tyre made by this process.

remount *vb* (riːˈmaʊnt). **1** to get on (a horse, bicycle, etc.) again. **2** (*tr*) to mount (a picture, jewel, exhibit, etc.) again. ◆ *n* (ˈriːˌmaʊnt). **3** a fresh horse.

removal (rɪˈmuːvᵊl) *n* **1** the act of removing or state of being removed. **2a** a change of residence. **2b** (*as modifier*): *a removal company.* **3** dismissal from office.

removalist (rɪˈmuːvəlɪst) *n Austral.* a person or company that transports household effects to a new home.

remove (rɪˈmuːv) *vb* **removes, removing, removed.** (*mainly tr*) **1** to take away and place elsewhere. **2** to dismiss (someone) from office. **3** to do away with; abolish; get rid of. **4** *Euphemistic.* to assassinate; kill. **5** (*intr*) *Formal.* to change the location of one's home or place of business. ◆ *n* **6** the act of removing, esp. (formal) a removal of one's residence or place of work. **7** the degree of difference: *only one remove from madness.* **8** *Brit.* (in certain schools) a class or form. ORIG C14: from OF *removoir,* from L *removēre;* see MOVE
▸ **reˈmovable** *adj* ▸ **reˌmovaˈbility** *n* ▸ **reˈmover** *n*

removed (rɪˈmuːvd) *adj* **1** separated by distance or abstract distinction. **2** (*postpositive*) separated by a degree of descent or kinship: *the child of a person's first cousin is his first cousin once removed.*

Remscheid ★ (*German* ˈrɛmʃait) *n* an industrial city in W Germany, in North Rhine-Westphalia. Pop.: 122 260 (1996 est.).

remunerate (rɪˈmjuːnəˌreɪt) *vb* **remunerates, remunerating, remunerated.** (*tr*) to reward or pay for work, service, etc. ORIG C16: from L *remūnerārī* to reward, from RE- + *mūnerāre* to give, from *mūnus* a gift
▸ **reˌmunerˈation** *n* ▸ **reˈmunerable** *adj* ▸ **reˈmunerative** *adj* ▸ **reˈmuneratively** *adv* ▸ **reˈmunerˌator** *n*

Remus ★ (ˈriːməs) *n Roman myth.* the brother of Romulus.

renaissance (rəˈneɪsəns, ˈrɛnəˌsɑːns) *or* **renascence** *n* a revival or rebirth, esp. of culture and learning. ORIG C19: from F, from L RE- + *nascī* to be born

Renaissance (rəˈneɪsəns, ˈrɛnəˌsɑːns) *n* **1** the. the great revival of art, literature, and learning in Europe in the 14th, 15th, and 16th centuries. **2** the spirit, culture, art, science, and thought of this period. ◆ *adj* **3** of, characteristic of, or relating to the Renaissance, its culture, etc.

renal (ˈriːnᵊl) *adj* of, relating to, resembling, or situated near the kidney. ORIG C17: from F, from LL *rēnālis,* from L *rēnēs* kidneys, from ?

renal pelvis *n* a small funnel-shaped cavity of the kidney into which urine is discharged before passing into the ureter.

Renan ★ (*French* rənɑ̃) *n* **(Joseph) Ernest** (ɛrnɛst). 1823–92, French philosopher, theologian, and historian; best known for his *Life of Jesus* (1863).

renascent (rɪˈnæsᵊnt, -ˈneɪ-) *adj* becoming active or vigorous again; reviving: *renascent nationalism.* ORIG C18: from L *renascī* to be born again

rencounter (rɛnˈkaʊntə) *Arch.* ◆ *n also* **rencontre** (rɛnˈkɒntə). **1** an unexpected meeting. **2** a hostile clash, as of two armies, adversaries, etc.; skirmish. ◆ *vb* **3** to meet (someone) unexpectedly. ORIG C16: from F *rencontre,* from *rencontrer;* as ENCOUNTER

rend (rɛnd) *vb* **rends, rending, rent. 1** to tear with violent force or to be torn in this way; rip. **2** (*tr*) to tear or pull (one's clothes, etc.), esp. as a manifestation of rage or grief. **3** (*tr*) (of a noise or cry) to disturb (the silence) with a shrill or piercing tone. ORIG OE *rendan*
▸ **ˈrendible** *adj*

Rendell ★ (ˈrɛndᵊl, rɛnˈdɛl) *n* **Ruth (Barbara),** Baroness. born 1930, British author of detective novels, such as *Wolf to the Slaughter* (1967), and psychological thrillers, such as *The Lake of Darkness* (1980) and (under the name Barbara Vine) *A Fatal Inversion* (1987) and *No Night is Too Long* (1994).

render (ˈrɛndə) *vb* (*tr*) **1** to present or submit (accounts, etc.) for payment, etc. **2** to give or provide (aid, charity, a service, etc.). **3** to show (obedience), as expected. **4** to give or exchange, as by way of return or requital: *to render blow for blow.* **5** to cause to become: *grief had rendered him simple-minded.* **6** to deliver (a verdict or opinion) formally. **7** to portray or depict (something), as in painting, music, or acting. **8** to translate (something). **9** (sometimes foll. by *up*) to yield or give: *the tomb rendered up its secret.* **10** (often foll. by *back*) to return (something); give back. **11** to cover the surface of (brickwork, etc.) with a coat of plaster. **12** (often foll. by *down*) to extract (fat) from (meat) by melting. ◆ *n* **13** a first thin coat of plaster applied to a surface. **14** one who or that which rends. ORIG C14: from OF *rendre,* from L *reddere* to give back (infl. by L *prendere* to grasp), from RE- + *dare* to give
▸ **ˈrenderable** *adj* ▸ **ˈrenderer** *n* ▸ **ˈrendering** *n*

rendezvous (ˈrɒndɪˌvuː) *n, pl* **rendezvous** (-ˌvuːz). **1** a meeting or appointment to meet at a specified time and place. **2** a place where people meet. ◆ *vb* (*intr*) **3** to meet at a specified time or place. ORIG C16: from F, from *rendez-vous!* present yourselves! from *se rendre* to present oneself; see RENDER

rendition (rɛnˈdɪʃən) *n* **1** a performance of a musical composition, dramatic role, etc. **2** a translation. **3** the act of rendering. ORIG C17: from obs. F, from LL *redditiō;* see RENDER

renegade (ˈrɛnɪˌgeɪd) *n* **1a** a person who deserts his or her cause or faith for another; traitor. **1b** (*as modifier*): *a renegade priest.* **2** any outlaw or rebel. ORIG C16: from Sp. *renegado,* ult. from L RE- + *negāre* to deny

renege *or* **renegue** (rɪˈniːg, -ˈneɪg) *vb* **reneges, reneging, reneged** *or* **renegues, reneguing, renegued. 1** (*intr;* often foll. by *on*) to go back (on one's promise, etc.). ◆ *vb, n* **2** *Cards.* other words for **revoke.** ORIG C16 (in the sense: to deny, renounce): from Med. L *renegāre* to renounce
▸ **reˈneger** *or* **reˈneguer** *n*

renew (rɪˈnjuː) *vb* (*mainly tr*) **1** to take up again. **2** (*also intr*) to begin (an activity) again; recommence. **3** to restate or reaffirm (a promise, etc.). **4** (*also intr*) to make (a lease, etc.) valid for a further period. **5** to regain or recover (vigour, strength, activity, etc.). **6** to restore to a new or fresh condition. **7** to replace (an old or worn-out part or piece). **8** to replenish (a supply, etc.).
▸ **reˈnewable** *adj* ▸ **reˈnewal** *n* ▸ **reˈnewer** *n*

renewable energy *n* another name for **alternative energy.**

renewables *pl n* sources of alternative energy, such as wind and wave power.

Renfrew ★ (ˈrɛnfruː) *n* an industrial town in W central Scotland, in Renfrewshire. Pop.: 20 764 (1991).

Renfrewshire ★ (ˈrɛnfruːʃɪə, -ʃə) *n* **1** a council area of W central Scotland, on the River Clyde W of Glasgow: corresponds to part of the historic county of Renfrewshire. Administrative centre: Paisley. Pop.: 178 550 (1996 est.). Area: 261 sq. km (101 sq. miles). **2** a historic county of W central Scotland, on the Firth of Clyde: now covered by the council areas of Renfrewshire, East Renfrewshire, and Inverclyde.

Reni ★ (*Italian* ˈrɛːni) *n* **Guido** (ˈgwiːdo). 1575–1642, Italian baroque painter.

reni- *combining form.* kidney or kidneys: *reniform.* ORIG from L *rēnēs*

reniform (ˈrɛnɪˌfɔːm) *adj* having the shape or profile of a kidney: *a reniform leaf.*

renin (ˈriːnɪn) *n* a proteolytic enzyme secreted by the kidneys, which plays an important part in the maintenance of blood pressure. ORIG C20: from RENI- + -IN

Rennes ★ (*French* rɛn) *n* a city in NW France: the ancient capital of Brittany. Pop.: 203 533 (1990).

rennet (ˈrɛnɪt) *n* **1** the membrane lining the fourth stomach of a young calf. **2** a substance prepared esp. from the stomachs of calves and used for curdling milk in making cheese. ORIG C15: rel. to OE *gerinnan* to curdle, RUN

rennin (ˈrɛnɪn) *n* an enzyme that occurs in gastric juice and is an active constituent of rennet. It coagulates milk. ORIG C20: from RENNET + -IN

Reno ★ ('riːnəʊ) *n* a city in W Nevada, at the foot of the Sierra Nevada: noted as a divorce, wedding, and gambling centre by reason of its liberal laws. Pop.: 150 620 (1995 est.).

Renoir ★ ('rɛnwɑː; *French* rənwar) *n* **1 Jean** (ʒɑ̃). 1894–1979, French film director: his films include *La grande illusion* (1937) and *Diary of a Chambermaid* (1945). **2** his father, **Pierre Auguste** (pjɛr ogyst). 1841–1919, French impressionist painter, noted for such works as *Les Parapluies* and his later nudes.

renounce (rɪ'naʊns) *vb* **renounces, renouncing, renounced. 1** (*tr*) to give up formally (a claim or right): *to renounce a title.* **2** (*tr*) to repudiate: *to renounce Christianity.* **3** (*tr*) to give up (some habit, etc.) voluntarily: *to renounce one's old ways.* **4** (*intr*) *Cards.* to fail to follow suit because one has no more cards of the suit led. ◆ *n* **5** *Cards.* a failure to follow suit. ORIG C14: from OF *renoncer,* from L *renuntiāre,* from RE- + *nuntiāre* to announce, from *nuntius* messenger
▸ **re'nouncement** *n* ▸ **re'nouncer** *n*

renovate ('rɛnə,veɪt) *vb* **renovates, renovating, renovated.** (*tr*) **1** to restore (something) to good condition. **2** to revive or refresh (one's spirits, health, etc.). ORIG C16: from L *renovāre,* from RE- + *novāre* to make new
▸ **,reno'vation** *n* ▸ **'reno,vative** *adj* ▸ **'reno,vator** *n*

renown (rɪ'naʊn) *n* widespread reputation, esp. of a good kind; fame. ORIG C14: from Anglo-Norman *renoun,* from OF *renom,* from *renomer* to celebrate, from RE- + *nomer* to name, from L *nōmināre*
▸ **re'nowned** *adj*

rent¹ (rɛnt) *n* **1** a payment made periodically by a tenant to a landlord or owner for the occupation or use of land, buildings, etc. **2** *Econ.* the return derived from the cultivation of land in excess of production costs. **3 for rent.** *Chiefly US & Canad.* available for use and occupation subject to the payment of rent. ◆ *vb* **4** (*tr*) to grant (a person) the right to use one's property in return for periodic payments. **5** (*tr*) to occupy or use (property) in return for periodic payments. **6** (*intr; often foll. by at*) to be let or rented (for a specified rental). ORIG C12: from OF *rente* revenue, from Vulgar L *rendere* (unattested) to yield; see RENDER
▸ **'rentable** *adj* ▸ **'renter** *n*

rent² (rɛnt) *n* **1** a slit or opening made by tearing or rending. **2** a breach or division. ◆ *vb* **3** the past tense and past participle of **rend.**

rent-a- *prefix* **1** denoting a rental service. **2** *Derog. or facetious.* denoting a person or group that performs a function as if hired from a rental service: *rent-a-mob.*

rental ('rɛntᵊl) *n* **1a** the amount paid by a tenant as rent. **1b** an income derived from rents received. **2** property available for renting. ◆ *adj* **3** of or relating to rent.

rent boy *n* a young male prostitute.

rent control *n* regulation by law of the rent a landlord can charge for domestic accommodation and of his right to evict tenants.

rent-free *adj, adv* without payment of rent.

rentier *French.* (rɑ̃tje) *n* a person whose income consists primarily of fixed unearned amounts, such as rent or interest. ORIG from *rente;* see RENT¹

rent-roll *n* **1** a register of lands and buildings owned by a person, company, etc., showing the rent due from each tenant. **2** the total income arising from rented property.

renunciation (rɪ,nʌnsɪ'eɪʃən) *n* **1** the act or an instance of renouncing. **2** a formal declaration renouncing something. **3** *Stock Exchange.* the surrender to another of the rights to buy new shares in a rights issue. ORIG C14: from L *renunciātiō* a declaration, from *renuntiāre* to report
▸ **re'nunciative** *or* **re'nunciatory** *adj*

rep¹ *or* **repp** (rɛp) *n* a silk, wool, rayon, or cotton fabric with a transversely corded surface. ORIG C19: from F *reps,* ?from E *ribs*
▸ **repped** *adj*

rep² (rɛp) *n Theatre.* short for **repertory company.**

rep³ (rɛp) *n* **1** short for **representative** (sense 2). **2** *NZ inf.* a rugby player selected to represent his district.

rep⁴ (rɛp) *n US inf.* short for **reputation.**

rep. *abbrev. for:* **1** report. **2** reporter. **3** reprint.

Rep. *abbrev. for:* **1** *US.* Representative. **2** Republic. **3** *US.* Republican.

repair¹ (rɪ'pɛə) *vb* (*tr*) **1** to restore (something damaged or broken) to good condition or working order. **2** to heal (a breach or division) in (something): *to repair a broken marriage.* **3** to make amends for (a mistake, injury, etc.). ◆ *n* **4** the act, task, or process of repairing. **5** a part that has been repaired. **6** state or condition: *in good repair.* ORIG C14: from OF *reparer,* from L *reparāre,* from RE- + *parāre* to make ready
▸ **re'pairable** *adj* ▸ **re'pairer** *n*

repair² (rɪ'pɛə) *vb* (*intr*) **1** (usually foll. by *to*) to go (to a place). **2** (usually foll. by *to*) to have recourse (to) for help, etc.: *to repair to one's lawyer.* ◆ *n* **3** a haunt or resort. ORIG C14: from OF *repairier,* from LL *repatriāre* to return to one's native land, from L RE- + *patria* fatherland

repairman (rɪ'pɛə,mæn) *n, pl* **repairmen.** a man whose job it is to repair machines, etc.

repand (rɪ'pænd) *adj Bot.* having a wavy margin: *a repand leaf.* ORIG C18: from L *repandus* bent backwards, from RE- + *pandus* curved
▸ **re'pandly** *adv*

reparable ('rɛpərəbᵊl, 'rɛprə-) *adj* able to be repaired, recovered, or remedied. ORIG C16: from L *reparābilis,* from *reparāre* to REPAIR¹
▸ **'reparably** *adv*

reparation (,rɛpə'reɪʃən) *n* **1** the act or process of making amends. **2** (*usually pl*) compensation exacted as an indemnity from a defeated nation by the victors. **3** the act or process of repairing or state of having been repaired. ORIG C14 *reparacioun,* ult. from L *reparāre* to REPAIR¹
▸ **reparative** (rɪ'pærətɪv) *or* **re'paratory** *adj*

repartee (,rɛpɑː'tiː) *n* **1** a sharp, witty, or aphoristic remark made as a reply. **2** skill in making sharp witty replies. ORIG C17: from F *repartie,* from *repartir* to retort, from RE- + *partir* to go away

repast (rɪ'pɑːst) *n* a meal or the food provided at a meal: *a light repast.* ORIG C14: from OF, from *repaistre* to feed, from LL *repāscere,* from L RE- + *pāscere* to feed, pasture (of animals)

repatriate *vb* (riː'pætrɪ,eɪt), **repatriates, repatriating, repatriated.** (*tr*) **1** to send back (a refugee, prisoner of war, etc.) to the country of his birth or citizenship. **2** to send back (a sum of money previously invested abroad) to its country of origin. ◆ *n* (riː'pætrɪɪt). **3** a person who has been repatriated. ORIG C17: from LL *repatriāre,* from L RE- + *patria* fatherland
▸ **re,patri'ation** *n*

repay (rɪ'peɪ) *vb* **repays, repaying, repaid. 1** to pay back (money, etc.) to (a person); refund or reimburse. **2** to make a return for (something): *to repay kindness.*
▸ **re'payable** *adj* ▸ **re'payment** *n*

repeal (rɪ'piːl) *vb* (*tr*) **1** to annul or rescind officially; revoke: *these laws were repealed.* ◆ *n* **2** an instance or the process of repealing; annulment. ORIG C14: from OF *repeler,* from RE- + *apeler* to call, APPEAL
▸ **re'pealable** *adj* ▸ **re'pealer** *n*

repeat (rɪ'piːt) *vb* **1** (when *tr, may take a clause as object*) to do or experience (something) again once or several times, esp. to say or write (something) again. **2** (*intr*) to occur more than once: *the last figure repeats.* **3** (*tr; may take a clause as object*) to reproduce (the words, sounds, etc.) uttered by someone else; echo. **4** (*tr*) to utter (a poem, etc.) from memory; recite. **5** (*intr*) (of food) to be tasted again after ingestion as the result of belching. **6** (*tr; may take a clause as object*) to tell to another person (the secrets imparted to one by someone else). **7** (*intr*) (of a clock) to strike the hour or quarter-hour just past. **8** (*intr*) *US.* to vote (illegally) more than once in a single election. **9 repeat oneself.** to say or do the same thing more than once, esp. so as to be tedious. ◆ *n* **10a** the act or an instance of repeating. **10b** (*as modifier*): *a repeat performance.* **11** a word, action, etc., that is repeated. **12** an order made out for goods, etc., that duplicates a previous order. **13** *Radio, television.* a broadcast of a programme which has been broadcast before. **14** *Music.* a passage that is an

exact restatement of the passage preceding it. ORIG C14: from OF *repeter,* from L *repetere,* from RE- + *petere* to seek
▸ **re'peatable** *adj*

> **USAGE NOTE** Since *again* is part of the meaning of *repeat,* it is better in writing not to say that something is *repeated again.*

repeated (rɪ'pi:tɪd) *adj* done, made, or said again and again; continual.
▸ **re'peatedly** *adv*

repeater (rɪ'pi:tə) *n* **1** a person or thing that repeats. **2** Also called: **repeating firearm.** a firearm capable of discharging several shots without reloading. **3** a timepiece that strikes the hour or quarter-hour just past, when a spring is pressed. **4** a device that amplifies incoming electrical signals and retransmits them.

repeating decimal *n* another name for **recurring decimal.**

repechage (ˌrɛpɪ'ʃɑ:ʒ) *n* a heat of a competition, esp. in rowing or fencing, in which eliminated contestants have another chance to qualify for the next round or the final. ORIG C19: from F *repêchage,* lit.: fishing out again, from RE- + *pêcher* to fish + -AGE

repel (rɪ'pɛl) *vb* **repels, repelling, repelled.** (*mainly tr*) **1** to force or drive back (something or somebody). **2** (*also intr*) to produce a feeling of aversion or distaste in (someone or something); be disgusting (to). **3** to be effective in keeping away, controlling, or resisting: *a spray that repels flies.* **4** to have no affinity for; fail to mix with or absorb: *water and oil repel each other.* **5** to disdain to accept (something); turn away from or spurn: *she repelled his advances.* ORIG C15: from L *repellere,* from RE- + *pellere* to push
▸ **re'peller** *n* ▸ **re'pellingly** *adv*

> **USAGE NOTE** See at **repulse.**

repellent (rɪ'pɛlənt) *adj* **1** distasteful or repulsive. **2** driving or forcing away or back; repelling. ◆ *n also* **repellant. 3** something, esp. a chemical substance, that repels: *insect repellent.* **4** a substance with which fabrics are treated to increase their resistance to water.
▸ **re'pellence** *or* **re'pellency** *n* ▸ **re'pellently** *adv*

repent[1] (rɪ'pɛnt) *vb* to feel remorse (for); be contrite (about); show penitence (for). ORIG C13: from OF *repentir,* from RE- + *pentir,* from L *paenitēre* to repent
▸ **re'penter** *n*

repent[2] ('ri:pᵊnt) *adj Bot.* lying or creeping along the ground: *repent stems.* ORIG C17: from L *rēpere* to creep

repentance (rɪ'pɛntəns) *n* **1** remorse or contrition for one's past actions. **2** an act or the process of being repentant; penitence.
▸ **re'pentant** *adj*

repercussion (ˌri:pə'kʌʃən) *n* **1** (*often pl*) a result or consequence of an action or event: *the repercussions of the war are still felt.* **2** a recoil after impact; a rebound. **3** a reflection, esp. of sound; echo or reverberation. ORIG C16: from L *repercussiō,* from *repercutere* to strike back
▸ ˌ**reper'cussive** *adj*

repertoire ('rɛpəˌtwɑ:) *n* **1** all the works collectively that a company, actor, etc., is competent to perform. **2** the entire stock of things available in a field or of a kind. **3 in repertoire.** denoting the performance of two or more plays, etc., by the same company in the same venue on different evenings over a period of time: *"Tosca" returns to Leeds next month in repertoire with "Wozzeck".* ORIG C19: from F, from LL *repertōrium* inventory; see REPERTORY

repertory ('rɛpətərɪ, -trɪ) *n, pl* **repertories. 1** the entire stock of things available in a field or of a kind; repertoire. **2** a place where a stock of things is kept; repository. **3** short for **repertory company.** ORIG C16: from LL *repertōrium* storehouse, from L *reperīre* to obtain, from RE- + *parere* to bring forth
▸ **repertorial** (ˌrɛpə'tɔ:rɪəl) *adj*

repertory company *n* a theatrical company that performs plays from a repertoire. US name: **stock company.**

repetend ('rɛpɪˌtɛnd) *n* **1** *Maths.* the digit in a recurring decimal that repeats itself. **2** anything repeated. ORIG C18: from L *repetendum* what is to be repeated, from *repetere* to REPEAT

répétiteur *French.* (repetitœr) *n* a member of an opera company who coaches the singers.

repetition (ˌrɛpɪ'tɪʃən) *n* **1** the act or an instance of repeating; reiteration. **2** a thing, word, action, etc., that is repeated. **3** a replica or copy.
▸ **repetitive** (rɪ'pɛtɪtɪv) *adj*

repetitious (ˌrɛpɪ'tɪʃəs) *adj* characterized by unnecessary repetition.
▸ ˌ**repe'titiously** *adv* ▸ ˌ**repe'titiousness** *n*

repetitive strain *or* **stress injury** *n* a condition, characterized by arm or wrist pains, that can affect musicians, computer operators, etc., who habitually perform awkward hand movements. Abbrev.: **RSI.**

repine (rɪ'paɪn) *vb* **repines, repining, repined.** (*intr*) to be fretful or low-spirited through discontent. ORIG C16: from RE- + PINE[2]

replace (rɪ'pleɪs) *vb* **replaces, replacing, replaced.** (*tr*) **1** to take the place of; supersede. **2** to substitute a person or thing for (another); put in place of: *to replace an old pair of shoes.* **3** to restore to its rightful place.
▸ **re'placeable** *adj* ▸ **re'placer** *n*

replacement (rɪ'pleɪsmənt) *n* **1** the act or process of replacing. **2** a person or thing that replaces another.

replay *n* ('ri:ˌpleɪ). **1** Also called: **action replay.** a showing again of a sequence of action in slow motion immediately after it happens. **2** a second match between a pair or group of contestants. ◆ *vb* (ri:'pleɪ). **3** to play again (a record, sporting contest, etc.).

replenish (rɪ'plɛnɪʃ) *vb* (*tr*) **1** to make full or complete again by supplying what has been used up. **2** to put fresh fuel on (a fire). ORIG C14: from OF *replenir,* from RE- + *plenir,* from L *plēnus* full
▸ **re'plenisher** *n* ▸ **re'plenishment** *n*

replete (rɪ'pli:t) *adj* (*usually postpositive*) **1** (often foll. by *with*) copiously supplied (with); abounding (in). **2** having one's appetite completely or excessively satisfied; gorged; satiated. ORIG C14: from L *replētus,* from *replēre,* from RE- + *plēre* to fill
▸ **re'pletely** *adv* ▸ **re'pleteness** *n* ▸ **re'pletion** *n*

replevin (rɪ'plɛvɪn) *Law.* ◆ *n* **1** the recovery of goods unlawfully taken, made subject to establishing the validity of the recovery in a legal action and returning the goods if the decision is adverse. **2** (formerly) a writ of replevin. ◆ *vb* **3** another word for **replevy.** ORIG C15: from Anglo-F, from OF *replevir* to give security for, from RE- + *plevir* to PLEDGE

replevy (rɪ'plɛvɪ) *Law.* ◆ *vb* **replevies, replevying, replevied.** (*tr*) **1** to recover possession of (goods) by replevin. ◆ *n, pl* **replevies. 2** another word for **replevin.** ORIG C15: from OF *replevir;* see REPLEVIN
▸ **re'pleviable** *or* **re'plevisable** *adj*

replica ('rɛplɪkə) *n* an exact copy or reproduction, esp. on a smaller scale. ORIG C19: from It., lit.: a reply, from *replicare,* from L: to bend back, repeat

replicate *vb* ('rɛplɪˌkeɪt), **replicates, replicating, replicated.** (*mainly tr*) **1** (*also intr*) to make or be a copy (of); reproduce. **2** to fold (something) over on itself; bend back. ◆ *adj* ('rɛplɪkɪt). **3** folded back on itself: *a replicate leaf.* ORIG C19: from L *replicātus* bent back; see REPLICA
▸ ˌ**repli'cation** *n* ▸ **'replicative** *adj*

reply (rɪ'plaɪ) *vb* **replies, replying, replied.** (*mainly intr*) **1** to make answer (to) in words or writing or by an action; respond. **2** (*tr; takes a clause as object*) to say (something) in answer: *he replied that he didn't want to come.* **3** *Law.* to answer a defendant's plea. **4** to return (a sound); echo. ◆ *n, pl* **replies. 5** an answer; response. **6** the answer made by a plaintiff or petitioner to a defendant's case. ORIG C14: from OF *replier* to fold again, reply, from L *replicāre,* from RE- + *plicāre* to fold
▸ **re'plier** *n*

repo ('ri:pəʊ) *n Inf.* short for: **1** repurchase agreement. **2a** repossession of property. **2b** (*as modifier*): *a repo car.*

repoint (ˌriːˈpɔɪnt) *vb* (*tr*) to repair the joints of (brickwork, masonry, etc.) with mortar or cement.

report (rɪˈpɔːt) *n* **1** an account prepared after investigation and published or broadcast. **2** a statement made widely known; rumour: *according to report, he is not dead.* **3** an account of the deliberations of a committee, body, etc.: *a report of parliamentary proceedings.* **4** *Brit.* a statement on the progress of each schoolchild. **5** a written account of a case decided at law. **6** comment on a person's character or actions; reputation: *he is of good report here.* **7** a sharp loud noise, esp. one made by a gun. ◆ *vb* (when *tr, may take a clause as object;* when *intr,* often foll. by *on*) **8** to give an account (of); describe. **9** to give an account of the results of an investigation (into): *to report on housing conditions.* **10** (of a committee, legislative body, etc.) to make a formal report on (a bill). **11** (*tr*) to complain about (a person), esp. to a superior. **12** to present (oneself) or be present at an appointed place or for a specific purpose: *report to the manager's office.* **13** (*intr*) to say or show that one is (in a certain state): *to report fit.* **14** (*intr;* foll. by *to*) to be responsible (to) and under the authority (of). **15** (*intr*) to act as a reporter. **16** *Law.* to take down in writing details of (the proceedings of a court of law, etc.) as a record or for publication. ORIG C14: from OF, from *reporter,* from L *reportāre,* from RE- + *portāre* to carry
▸ **reˈportable** *adj* ▸ **reˈportedly** *adv*

reportage (rɪˈpɔːtɪdʒ, ˌrɛpɔːˈtɑːʒ) *n* **1** the act or process of reporting news or other events of general interest. **2** a journalist's style of reporting.

reported speech *n* another term for **indirect speech**.

reporter (rɪˈpɔːtə) *n* **1** a person who reports, esp. one employed to gather news for a newspaper or broadcasting organization. **2** a person authorized to report the proceedings of a legislature.

report stage *n* the stage preceding the third reading in the passage of a bill through Parliament.

repose[1] (rɪˈpəʊz) *n* **1** a state of quiet restfulness; peace or tranquillity. **2** dignified calmness of manner; composure. ◆ *vb* **reposes, reposing, reposed. 3** to lie or lay down at rest. **4** (*intr*) to lie when dead, as in the grave. **5** (*intr;* foll. by *on, in,* etc.) *Formal.* to be based (on): *your plan reposes on a fallacy.* ORIG C15: from OF *reposer,* from LL *repausāre,* from RE- + *pausāre* to stop
▸ **reˈposal** *n* ▸ **reˈposer** *n* ▸ **reˈposeful** *adj* ▸ **reˈposefully** *adv*

repose[2] (rɪˈpəʊz) *vb* **reposes, reposing, reposed.** (*tr*) **1** to put (trust) in a person or thing. **2** to place or put (an object) somewhere. ORIG C15: from L *repōnere* to store up, from RE- + *pōnere* to put
▸ **reˈposal** *n*

reposition (ˌriːpəˈzɪʃən) *n* **1** the act or process of depositing or storing. ◆ *vb* (*tr*) **2** to place in a new position. **3** to target (a product or brand) at a new market by changing its image.

repository (rɪˈpɒzɪtərɪ, -trɪ) *n, pl* **repositories. 1** a place or container in which things can be stored for safety. **2** a place where things are kept for exhibition; museum. **3** a place of burial; sepulchre. **4** a person to whom a secret is entrusted; confidant. ORIG C15: from L *repositōrium,* from *repōnere* to place

repossess (ˌriːpəˈzɛs) *vb* (*tr*) to take back possession of (property), esp. for nonpayment of money due under a hire-purchase agreement.
▸ **repossession** (ˌriːpəˈzɛʃən) *n* ▸ ˌ**reposˈsessor** *n*

repoussé (rəˈpuːseɪ) *adj* **1** raised in relief, as a design on a thin piece of metal hammered through from the underside. ◆ *n* **2** a design or surface made in this way. ORIG C19: from F, from *repousser,* from RE- + *pousser* to PUSH

repp (rɛp) *n* a variant spelling of **rep**[1].

reprehend (ˌrɛprɪˈhɛnd) *vb* (*tr*) to find fault with; criticize. ORIG C14: from L *reprehendere* to hold fast, rebuke, from RE- + *prendere* to grasp
▸ ˌ**repreˈhender** *n* ▸ ˌ**repreˈhension** *n*

reprehensible (ˌrɛprɪˈhɛnsɪbᵊl) *adj* open to criticism or rebuke; blameworthy. ORIG C14: from LL *reprehensibilis,* from L *reprehendere;* see REPREHEND
▸ ˌ**repreˌhensiˈbility** *n* ▸ ˌ**repreˈhensibly** *adv*

represent (ˌrɛprɪˈzɛnt) *vb* (*tr*) **1** to stand as an equivalent of; correspond to. **2** to act as a substitute or proxy (for). **3** to act as or be the authorized delegate or agent for (a person, country, etc.): *an MP represents his constituency.* **4** to serve or use as a means of expressing: *letters represent the sounds of speech.* **5** to exhibit the characteristics of; exemplify; typify: *romanticism in music is represented by Beethoven.* **6** to present an image of through the medium of a picture or sculpture; portray. **7** to bring clearly before the mind. **8** to set forth in words; state or explain. **9** to describe as having a specified character or quality: *he represented her as a saint.* **10** to act out the part of on stage; portray. ORIG C14: from L *repraesentāre* to exhibit, from RE- + *praesentāre* to PRESENT[2]
▸ ˌ**repreˈsentable** *adj* ▸ ˌ**repreˌsentaˈbility** *n*

re-present (ˌriːprɪˈzɛnt) *vb* (*tr*) to present again.
▸ **re-presentation** (ˌriːˌprɛzənˈteɪʃən) *n*

representation (ˌrɛprɪzɛnˈteɪʃən) *n* **1** the act or an instance of representing or the state of being represented. **2** anything that represents, such as a verbal or pictorial portrait. **3** anything that is represented, such as an image brought clearly to mind. **4** the principle by which delegates act for a constituency. **5** a body of representatives. **6** an instance of acting for another in a particular capacity, such as executor. **7** a dramatic production or performance. **8** (*often pl*) a statement of facts, true or alleged, esp. one set forth by way of remonstrance or expostulation.

representational (ˌrɛprɪzɛnˈteɪʃənᵊl) *adj* **1** *Art.* depicting objects, scenes, etc., directly as seen; naturalistic. **2** of or relating to representation.

representationalism (ˌrɛprɪzɛnˈteɪʃənəˌlɪzəm) *or* **representationism** *n* **1** *Philosophy.* the doctrine that in perceptions of objects what is before the mind is not the object but a representation of it. Cf. **presentationism. 2** *Art.* the practice of depicting objects, scenes, etc., directly as seen.
▸ ˌ**represenˌtationalˈistic** *adj* ▸ ˌ**represenˈtationist** *n, adj*

representative (ˌrɛprɪˈzɛntətɪv) *n* **1** a person or thing that represents another. **2** a person who represents and tries to sell the products or services of a firm. **3** a typical example. **4** a person representing a constituency in a deliberative, legislative, or executive body, esp. (*cap.*) a member of the **House of Representatives** (the lower house of Congress). ◆ *adj* **5** serving to represent; symbolic. **6a** exemplifying a class or kind; typical. **6b** containing or including examples of all the interests, types, etc., in a group. **7** acting as deputy or proxy for another. **8** representing a constituency or the whole people in the process of government: *a representative council.* **9** of or relating to the political representation of the people: *representative government.* **10** of or relating to a mental picture or representation.
▸ ˌ**repreˈsentatively** *adv* ▸ ˌ**repreˈsentativeness** *n*

repress (rɪˈprɛs) *vb* (*tr*) **1** to keep (feelings, etc.) under control; suppress or restrain. **2** to put into a state of subjugation: *to repress a people.* **3** *Psychol.* to banish (unpleasant thoughts) from one's conscious mind. ORIG C14: from L *reprimere* to press back, from RE- + *premere* to PRESS[1]
▸ **reˈpressed** *adj* ▸ **reˈpresser** *or* **reˈpressor** *n* ▸ **reˈpressible** *adj* ▸ **reˈpression** *n* ▸ **reˈpressive** *adj*

reprieve (rɪˈpriːv) *vb* **reprieves, reprieving, reprieved.** (*tr*) **1** to postpone or remit the punishment of (a person, esp. one condemned to death). **2** to give temporary relief to (a person or thing), esp. from otherwise irrevocable harm. ◆ *n* **3** a postponement or remission of punishment. **4** a warrant granting a postponement. **5** a temporary relief from pain or harm; respite. ORIG C16: from OF *repris* (something) taken back, from *reprendre,* from L *reprehendere;* ? also infl. by obs. E *repreve* to reprove
▸ **reˈprievable** *adj* ▸ **reˈpriever** *n*

reprimand (ˈrɛprɪˌmɑːnd) *n* **1** a reproof or formal admonition; rebuke. ◆ *vb* **2** (*tr*) to admonish or rebuke, esp. formally. ORIG C17: from F *réprimande,* from L *reprimenda* (things) to be repressed; see REPRESS
▸ ˌ**repriˈmanding** *adj*

reprint *n* (ˈriːˌprɪnt). **1** a reproduction in print of any matter already published. **2** a reissue of a printed work using the same type, plates, etc., as the original. ◆ *vb* (riːˈprɪnt). **3** (*tr*) to print again.
▸ **reˈprinter** *n*

reprisal (rɪ'praɪzᵊl) *n* **1** the act or an instance of retaliation in any form. **2** (*often pl*) retaliatory action against an enemy in wartime. **3** (formerly) the forcible seizure of the property or subjects of one nation by another. ORIG C15: from OF *reprisaille,* from OIt., from *riprendere* to recapture, from L *reprehendere;* see REPREHEND

reprise (rɪ'pri:z) *Music.* ◆ *n* **1** the repeating of an earlier theme. ◆ *vb* **reprises, reprising, reprised. 2** to repeat (an earlier theme). ORIG C14: from OF, from *reprendre* to take back, from L *reprehendere;* see REPREHEND

repro ('ri:prəʊ) *n, pl* **repros. 1** short for **reproduction** (sense 2): *repro furniture.* **2** short for **reproduction proof.**

reproach (rɪ'prəʊtʃ) *vb* (*tr*) **1** to impute blame to (a person) for an action or fault; rebuke. ◆ *n* **2** the act of reproaching. **3** rebuke or censure; reproof. **4** disgrace or shame: *to bring reproach upon one's family.* **5 above** *or* **beyond reproach.** perfect; beyond criticism. ORIG C15: from OF *reprochier,* from L RE- + *prope* near
▸ **re'proachable** *adj* ▸ **re'proacher** *n* ▸ **re'proachingly** *adv*

reproachful (rɪ'prəʊtʃfʊl) *adj* full of or expressing reproach.
▸ **re'proachfully** *adv* ▸ **re'proachfulness** *n*

reprobate ('rɛprəʊˌbeɪt) *adj* **1** morally unprincipled; depraved. **2** *Christianity.* condemned to eternal punishment in hell. ◆ *n* **3** an unprincipled, depraved, or damned person. **4** a disreputable or roguish person. ◆ *vb* **reprobates, reprobating, reprobated.** (*tr*) **5** to disapprove of; condemn. **6** (of God) to condemn to eternal punishment in hell. ORIG C16: from LL *reprobātus* held in disfavour, from L RE- + *probāre* to test, APPROVE
▸ **reprobacy** ('rɛprəbəsɪ) *n* ▸ **'reproˌbater** *n* ▸ **ˌrepro'bation** *n*

reprocess (ri:'prəʊsɛs) *vb* (*tr*) to treat again (something already made and used) in order to make it reusable in some form.
▸ **re'processing** *n, adj*

reproduce (ˌri:prə'dju:s) *vb* **reproduces, reproducing, reproduced.** (*mainly tr*) **1** to make a copy, representation, or imitation of; duplicate. **2** (*also intr*) *Biol.* to undergo or cause to undergo a process of reproduction. **3** to produce again; bring back into existence again; re-create. **4** (*intr*) to come out (well, badly, etc.) when copied.
▸ **ˌrepro'ducer** *n* ▸ **ˌrepro'ducible** *adj* ▸ **ˌrepro'ducibly** *adv* ▸ **ˌreproˌduci'bility** *n*

reproduction (ˌri:prə'dʌkʃən) *n* **1** *Biol.* any of various processes, either sexual or asexual, by which an animal or plant produces one or more individuals similar to itself. **2a** an imitation or facsimile of a work of art. **2b** (*as modifier*): *a reproduction portrait.* **3** the quality of sound from an audio system. **4** the act or process of reproducing.

reproduction proof *n Printing.* a proof of very good quality used for photographic reproduction to make a printing plate.

reproductive (ˌri:prə'dʌktɪv) *adj* of, relating to, characteristic of, or taking part in reproduction.
▸ **ˌrepro'ductively** *adv* ▸ **ˌrepro'ductiveness** *n*

reprography (rɪ'prɒgrəfɪ) *n* the art or process of copying, reprinting, or reproducing printed material.
▸ **reprographic** (ˌrɛprə'græfɪk) *adj* ▸ **ˌrepro'graphically** *adv*

reproof (rɪ'pru:f) *n* an act or expression of rebuke or censure. Also: **reproval** (rɪ'pru:vᵊl). ORIG C14 *reproffe,* from OF *reprove,* from LL *reprobāre* to disapprove of; see REPROBATE

re-proof (ri:'pru:f) *vb* (*tr*) **1** to treat (a coat, jacket, etc.) so as to renew its texture, waterproof qualities, etc. **2** to provide a new proof of (a book, galley, etc.).

reprove (rɪ'pru:v) *vb* **reproves, reproving, reproved.** (*tr*) to rebuke or scold. ORIG C14: from OF *reprover,* from LL *reprobāre,* from L RE- + *probāre* to examine
▸ **re'provable** *adj* ▸ **re'prover** *n* ▸ **re'provingly** *adv*

reptant ('rɛptənt) *adj Biol.* creeping, crawling, or lying along the ground. ORIG C17: from L *reptāre* to creep

reptile ('rɛptaɪl) *n* **1** any of the cold-blooded vertebrates characterized by lungs, an outer covering of horny scales or plates, and young produced in eggs, such as the tortoises, turtles, snakes, lizards, and crocodiles. **2** a grovelling insignificant person: *you miserable little reptile!* ◆ *adj* **3** creeping, crawling, or squirming. ORIG C14: from LL *reptilis* creeping, from L *rēpere* to crawl
▸ **reptilian** (rɛp'tɪlɪən) *n, adj*

Repton ★ ('rɛptᵊn) *n* **Humphry.** 1752–1818, British landscape gardener.

republic (rɪ'pʌblɪk) *n* **1** a form of government in which the people or their elected representatives possess the supreme power. **2** a political or national unit possessing such a form of government. **3** a constitutional form in which the head of state is an elected or nominated president. ORIG C17: from F *république,* from L *rēspublica,* lit.: the public thing, from *rēs* thing + *publica* PUBLIC

republican (rɪ'pʌblɪkən) *adj* **1** of, resembling, or relating to a republic. **2** supporting or advocating a republic. ◆ *n* **3** a supporter or advocate of a republic.

Republican (rɪ'pʌblɪkən) *adj* **1** of, belonging to, or relating to a Republican Party. **2** of, belonging to, or relating to the Irish Republican Army. ◆ *n* **3** a member or supporter of a Republican Party. **4** a member or supporter of the Irish Republican Army.

republicanism (rɪ'pʌblɪkəˌnɪzəm) *n* **1** the principles or theory of republican government. **2** support for a republic. **3** (*often cap.*) support for a Republican Party.

Republican Party *n* **1** one of the two major political parties in the US: established around 1854. **2** any of a number of political parties in other countries, usually so named to indicate their opposition to monarchy.

Republic of Ireland ★ *n* See **Ireland**[1] (sense 2).

repudiate (rɪ'pju:dɪˌeɪt) *vb* **repudiates, repudiating, repudiated.** (*tr*) **1** to reject the authority or validity of; refuse to accept or ratify. **2** to refuse to acknowledge or pay (a debt). **3** to cast off or disown (a son, lover, etc.). ORIG C16: from L *repudiāre* to put away, from *repudium* separation, divorce, from RE- + *pudēre* to be ashamed
▸ **re'pudiable** *adj* ▸ **reˌpudi'ation** *n* ▸ **re'pudiative** *adj* ▸ **re'pudiˌator** *n*

repugnant (rɪ'pʌgnənt) *adj* **1** repellent to the senses; causing aversion. **2** distasteful; offensive; disgusting. **3** contradictory; inconsistent or incompatible. ORIG C14: from L *repugnāns* resisting, from *repugnāre,* from RE- + *pugnāre* to fight
▸ **re'pugnance** *n* ▸ **re'pugnantly** *adv*

repulse (rɪ'pʌls) *vb* **repulses, repulsing, repulsed.** (*tr*) **1** to drive back or ward off (an attacking force); repel; rebuff. **2** to reject with coldness or discourtesy: *she repulsed his advances.* ◆ *n* **3** the act or an instance of driving back or warding off; rebuff. **4** a cold discourteous rejection or refusal. ORIG C16: from L *repellere* to drive back
▸ **re'pulser** *n*

> **USAGE NOTE** Some people think that the use of *repulse* in sentences such as *he was repulsed by what he saw* is incorrect and that the correct word is *repel.*

repulsion (rɪ'pʌlʃən) *n* **1** a feeling of disgust or aversion. **2** *Physics.* a force separating two objects, such as the force between two like electric charges.

repulsive (rɪ'pʌlsɪv) *adj* **1** causing or occasioning repugnance; loathsome; disgusting or distasteful. **2** tending to repel, esp. by coldness and discourtesy. **3** *Physics.* concerned with, producing, or being a repulsion.
▸ **re'pulsively** *adv* ▸ **re'pulsiveness** *n*

repurchase (ri:'pɜ:tʃɪs) *vb* **1** (*tr*) to buy back or buy again (goods, securities, assets, etc.). ◆ *n* **2** an act or instance of repurchasing.

reputable ('rɛpjʊtəbᵊl) *adj* **1** having a good reputation; honoured, trustworthy, or respectable. **2** (of words) acceptable as good usage; standard.
▸ **'reputably** *adv*

reputation (ˌrɛpjʊ'teɪʃən) *n* **1** the estimation in which a person or thing is generally held; opinion. **2** a high opinion generally held about a person or thing; esteem. **3** notoriety or fame, esp. for some specified characteristic. ORIG C14: from L *reputātiō,* from *reputāre* to calculate; see REPUTE

repute (rɪ'pju:t) *vb* **reputes, reputing, reputed. 1** (*tr; usually* *passive*) to consider (a person or thing) to be as specified: *he is reputed to be rich.* ◆ *n* **2** public estimation; reputation: *a writer of little repute.* ORIG C15: from OF *reputer,* from L *reputāre,* from RE- + *putāre* to think

reputed (rɪ'pju:tɪd) *adj* (*prenominal*) generally reckoned or considered; supposed: *the reputed writer of two epic poems.*
▸ **re'putedly** *adv*

request (rɪ'kwɛst) *vb* (*tr*) **1** to express a desire for, esp. politely; ask for or demand: *to request a bottle of wine.* ◆ *n* **2** the act or an instance of requesting, esp. in the form of a written statement, etc.; petition or solicitation. **3 by request.** in accordance with someone's desire. **4 in request.** in demand; popular: *he is in request all over the world.* **5 on request.** on the occasion of a demand or request: *application forms are available on request.* ORIG C14: from OF *requeste,* from Vulgar L *requaerere;* see REQUIRE, QUEST
▸ **re'quester** *n*

request stop *n* a point on a route at which a bus, etc., will stop only if signalled to do so. US equivalent: **flag stop.**

Requiem ('rɛkwɪəm) *n* **1** *RC Church.* a Mass celebrated for the dead. **2** a musical setting of this Mass. **3** any piece of music composed or performed as a memorial to a dead person. ORIG C14: from L *requiēs* rest, from the introit, *Requiem aeternam dona eis* Rest eternal grant unto them

requiem shark *n* any of a family of sharks occurring mostly in tropical seas and characterized by a nictitating membrane.

requiescat (ˌrɛkwɪ'ɛskæt) *n* a prayer for the repose of the souls of the dead. ORIG L, from *requiescat in pace* may he rest in peace

require (rɪ'kwaɪə) *vb* **requires, requiring, required.** (*mainly tr; may take a clause as object or an infinitive*) **1** to have need of; depend upon; want. **2** to impose as a necessity; make necessary: *this work requires precision.* **3** (*also intr*) to make formal request (for); insist upon. **4** to call upon or oblige (a person) authoritatively; order or command: *to require someone to account for his actions.* ORIG C14: from OF *requerre,* via Vulgar L from L *requīrere* to seek to know; also infl. by *quaerere* to seek
▸ **re'quirer** *n*

> **USAGE NOTE** The use of *require to* as in *I require to see the manager* or *you require to complete a special form* is thought by many people to be incorrect: *I need to see the manager; you are required to complete a special form.*

requirement (rɪ'kwaɪəmənt) *n* **1** something demanded or imposed as an obligation. **2** a thing desired or needed. **3** the act or an instance of requiring.

requisite ('rɛkwɪzɪt) *adj* **1** absolutely essential; indispensable. ◆ *n* **2** something indispensable; necessity. ORIG C15: from L *requisītus* sought after, from *requīrere* to seek for
▸ **'requisitely** *adv*

requisition (ˌrɛkwɪ'zɪʃən) *n* **1** a request or demand, esp. an authoritative or formal one. **2** an official form on which such a demand is made. **3** the act of taking something over, esp. temporarily for military or public use. ◆ *vb* (*tr*) **4** to demand and take for use, esp. by military or public authority. **5** (*may take an infinitive*) to require (someone) formally to do (something): *to requisition a soldier to drive an officer's car.*
▸ ˌ**requi'sitionary** *adj* ▸ ˌ**requi'sitionist** *n*

requite (rɪ'kwaɪt) *vb* **requites, requiting, requited.** (*tr*) to make return to (a person for a kindness or injury); repay with a similar action. ORIG C16: RE- + obs. *quite* to discharge, repay; see QUIT
▸ **re'quitable** *adj* ▸ **re'quital** *n* ▸ **re'quitement** *n* ▸ **re'quiter** *n*

reredos ('rɪədɒs) *n* **1** a screen or wall decoration at the back of an altar. **2** another word for **fireback.** ORIG C14: from OF *areredos,* from *arere* behind + *dos* back, from L *dorsum*

rerun *vb* (ri:'rʌn), **reruns, rerunning, reran, rerun.** (*tr*) **1** to broadcast or put on (a film, etc.) again. **2** to run (a race, etc.) again. ◆ *n* ('ri:ˌrʌn). **3** a film, etc., that is broadcast again; repeat. **4** a race that is run again. **5** *Computing.* the repeat of a part of a computer program.

res (reɪs) *n, pl* **res.** *Latin.* a thing, matter, or object.

res. *abbrev. for:* **1** research. **2** reserve. **3** residence. **4** resides. **5** resigned. **6** resolution.

resale price maintenance ('ri:seɪl) *n* the practice by which a manufacturer establishes a fixed or minimum price for the resale of a brand product by retailers or other distributors. US equivalent: **fair trade.** Abbrev.: **rpm.**

reschedule (ri:'ʃɛdju:l; *also, esp. US* -'skɛdʒuəl) *vb* (*tr*) **1** to change the time, date, or schedule of. **2** to arrange a revised schedule for repayment of (a debt).

rescind (rɪ'sɪnd) *vb* (*tr*) to annul or repeal. ORIG C17: from L *rēscindere* to cut off, from *re-* (intensive) + *scindere* to cut
▸ **re'scindable** *adj* ▸ **re'scinder** *n* ▸ **re'scindment** *n*

rescission (rɪ'sɪʒən) *n* **1** the act of rescinding. **2** *Law.* the right to have a contract set aside if it has been entered into mistakenly, as a result of misrepresentation, undue influence, etc.

rescript ('ri:ˌskrɪpt) *n* **1** (in ancient Rome) a reply by the emperor to a question on a point of law. **2** any official announcement or edict; a decree. **3** something rewritten. ORIG C16: from L *rēscriptum* reply, from *rēscribere* to write back

rescue ('rɛskju:) *vb* **rescues, rescuing, rescued.** (*tr*) **1** to bring (someone or something) out of danger, etc.; deliver or save. **2** to free (a person) from legal custody by force. **3** *Law.* to seize (goods) by force. ◆ *n* **4a** the act or an instance of rescuing. **4b** (*as modifier*): *a rescue party.* **5** the forcible removal of a person from legal custody. **6** *Law.* the forcible seizure of goods or property. ORIG C14: *rescowen,* from OF *rescourre,* from RE- + *escourre* to pull away, from L *excutere* to shake off, from *quatere* to shake
▸ **'rescuer** *n*

research (rɪ'sɜ:tʃ) *n* **1** systematic investigation to establish facts or collect information on a subject. ◆ *vb* **2** to carry out investigations into (a subject, etc.). ORIG C16: from OF *recercher* to seek, search again, from RE- + *cercher* to SEARCH
▸ **re'searchable** *adj* ▸ **re'searcher** *n*

research and development *n* a commercial company's application of scientific research to develop new products. Abbrev.: **R & D.**

reseat (ri:'si:t) *vb* (*tr*) **1** to show (a person) to a new seat. **2** to put a new seat on (a chair, etc.). **3** to provide new seats for (a theatre, etc.). **4** to re-form the seating of (a valve).

resect (rɪ'sɛkt) *vb* (*tr*) *Surgery.* to cut out part of (a bone, organ, or other structure or part). ORIG C17: from L *resecāre,* from RE- + *secāre* to cut

resection (rɪ'sɛkʃən) *n* **1** *Surgery.* excision of part of a bone, organ, or other part. **2** *Surveying.* a method of fixing the position of a point by making angular observations to three fixed points.
▸ **re'sectional** *adj*

resemblance (rɪ'zɛmbləns) *n* **1** the state or quality of resembling; likeness or similarity. **2** the degree or extent to which a likeness exists. **3** semblance; likeness.
▸ **re'semblant** *adj*

resemble (rɪ'zɛmbᵊl) *vb* **resembles, resembling, resembled.** (*tr*) to possess some similarity to; be like. ORIG C14: from OF *resembler,* from RE- + *sembler* to look like, from L *similis* like
▸ **re'sembler** *n*

resent (rɪ'zɛnt) *vb* (*tr*) to feel bitter, indignant, or aggrieved at. ORIG C17: from F *ressentir,* from RE- + *sentir* to feel, from L *sentīre* to perceive; see SENSE
▸ **re'sentful** *adj* ▸ **re'sentment** *n*

reserpine ('rɛsəpɪn) *n* an insoluble alkaloid, extracted from the roots of a rauwolfia, used medicinally to lower blood pressure and as a sedative and tranquillizer. ORIG C20: from G *Reserpin,* prob. from the NL name of the plant

reservation (ˌrɛzə'veɪʃən) *n* **1** the act or an instance of reserving. **2** something reserved, esp. accommodation or a seat. **3** (*often pl*) a stated or unstated qualification of opinion that prevents one's wholehearted acceptance of a proposal, etc. **4** an area of land set aside, esp. (in the US) for American Indian peoples. **5** *Brit.* the strip of land between the two carriageways of a dual carriageway. **6** the act or process of keeping back, esp. for oneself; withholding. **7** *Law.* a right or interest retained by the grantor in property dealings.

reserve (rɪ'zɜːv) *vb* **reserves, reserving, reserved.** (*tr*) **1** to keep back or set aside, esp. for future use or contingency; withhold. **2** to keep for oneself; retain: *I reserve the right to question these men later.* **3** to obtain or secure by advance arrangement: *I have reserved two tickets for tonight's show.* **4** to delay delivery of (a judgment). ◆ *n* **5a** something kept back or set aside, esp. for future use or contingency. **5b** (*as modifier*): *a reserve stock.* **6** the state or condition of being reserved: *I have plenty in reserve.* **7** a tract of land set aside for a special purpose: *a nature reserve.* **8** *Austral. & NZ.* a public park. **9** the usual Canadian name for **reservation** (sense 4). **10** *Sport.* a substitute. **11** (*often pl*) **11a** a part of an army not committed to immediate action in a military engagement. **11b** that part of a nation's armed services not in active service. **12** coolness or formality of manner; restraint, silence, or reticence. **13** (*often pl*) *Finance.* liquid assets or a portion of capital not invested or a portion of profits not distributed by a bank or business enterprise and held to meet future liabilities or contingencies. **14 without reserve.** without reservations; fully. ORIG C14: from OF *reserver,* from L *reservāre,* from RE- + *servāre* to keep
▸ **re'servable** *adj* ▸ **re'server** *n*

re-serve (riː'sɜːv) *vb* **re-serves, re-serving, re-served.** (*tr*) to serve again.

reserve bank *n* one of the twelve banks forming part of the US Federal Reserve System.

reserve currency *n* foreign currency that is acceptable as a medium of international payments and is held in reserve by many countries.

reserved (rɪ'zɜːvd) *adj* **1** set aside for use by a particular person. **2** cool or formal in manner; restrained or reticent. **3** destined; fated: *a man reserved for greatness.*
▸ **reservedly** (rɪ'zɜːvɪdlɪ) *adv* ▸ **re'servedness** *n*

reserved list *n Brit.* a list of retired naval, army, or air-force officers available for recall to active service in an emergency.

reserved occupation *n Brit.* an occupation from which one will not be called up for military service in time of war.

reserve-grade *adj Austral.* denoting a sporting team of the second rank in a club.

reserve price *n Brit.* the minimum price acceptable to the owner of property being auctioned or sold. Also called (esp. Scot. and US): **upset price.**

reserve tranche *n* the quota of 25 per cent to which a member of the IMF has unconditional access. Prior to 1978 it was paid in gold and known as the **gold tranche.**

reservist (rɪ'zɜːvɪst) *n* one who serves in the reserve formations of a nation's armed forces.

reservoir ('rɛzəˌvwɑː) *n* **1** a natural or artificial lake or large tank used for collecting and storing water for community use. **2** *Biol.* a cavity in an organism containing fluid. **3** a place where a great stock of anything is accumulated. **4** a large supply of something: *a reservoir of talent.* ORIG C17: from F *réservoir,* from *réserver* to RESERVE

reservoir rock *n* porous and permeable rock containing producible oil or gas in its pore spaces.

reset[1] *vb* (riː'sɛt), **resets, resetting, reset.** (*tr*) **1** to set again (a broken bone, matter in type, a gemstone, etc.). **2** to restore (a gauge, etc.) to zero. ◆ *n* ('riːˌsɛt). **3** the act or an instance of setting again. **4** a thing that is set again.
▸ **re'setter** *n*

reset[2] *Scot.* ◆ *vb* (riː'sɛt), **resets, resetting, reset. 1** to receive or handle goods knowing they have been stolen. ◆ *n* ('riːsɛt). **2** the receiving of stolen goods. ORIG C14: from OF *receter,* from L *receptāre,* from *recipere* to receive
▸ **re'setter** *n*

res gestae ('dʒɛstiː) *pl n* **1** things done or accomplished; achievements. **2** *Law.* incidental facts and circumstances that are admissible in evidence because they explain the matter at issue. ORIG L

Resht ★ (rɛʃt) *n* a variant of **Rasht.**

reside (rɪ'zaɪd) *vb* **resides, residing, resided.** (*intr*) *Formal.* **1** to live permanently (in a place); have one's home (in): *he resides in London.* **2** (of things, qualities, etc.) to be inherently present (in); be vested (in): *political power resides in military strength.* ORIG C15: from L *residēre* to sit back, from RE- + *sedēre* to sit
▸ **re'sider** *n*

residence ('rɛzɪdəns) *n* **1** the place in which one resides; abode or home. **2** a large imposing house; mansion. **3** the fact of residing in a place or a period of residing. **4 in residence. 4a** actually resident: *the Queen is in residence.* **4b** designating a creative artist resident and active for a set period at a college, gallery, etc.: *writer in residence.*

residency ('rɛzɪdənsɪ) *n, pl* **residencies. 1** a variant of **residence. 2** a regular series of concerts by a band or singer at one venue. **3** *US & Canad.* the period, following internship, during which a physician undergoes specialized training. **4** (in India, formerly) the official house of the governor general at the court of a native prince.

resident ('rɛzɪdənt) *n* **1** a person who resides in a place. **2** (esp. formerly) a representative of the British government in a British protectorate. **3** (in India, formerly) a representative of the British governor general at the court of a native prince. **4** a bird or animal that does not migrate. **5** *Brit. & NZ.* a junior doctor who lives in the hospital where he or she works. **6** *US & Canad.* a physician who lives in the hospital while undergoing specialist training after completing his or her internship. ◆ *adj* **7** living in a place; residing. **8** living or staying at a place in order to discharge a duty, etc. **9** (of qualities, etc.) existing or inherent (in). **10** (of birds and animals) not in the habit of migrating.
▸ **'residentship** *n*

residential (ˌrɛzɪ'dɛnʃəl) *adj* **1** suitable for or allocated for residence: *a residential area.* **2** relating to residence.
▸ **ˌresi'dentially** *adv*

residential school *n* (in Canada) a boarding school maintained by the Canadian government for Indian and Inuit children from sparsely populated settlements.

residentiary (ˌrɛzɪ'dɛnʃərɪ) *adj* **1** residing in a place, esp. officially. **2** obliged to reside in an official residence: *a residentiary benefice.* ◆ *n, pl* **residentiaries. 3** a member of the clergy obliged to reside in the place of his or her official appointment.

residual (rɪ'zɪdjʊəl) *adj* **1** of, relating to, or designating a residue or remainder; remaining; leftover. **2** *US.* of or relating to the payment of residuals. ◆ *n* **3** something left over as a residue; remainder. **4** *Statistics.* **4a** the difference between the mean of a set of observations and one particular observation. **4b** the difference between the numerical value of one particular observation and the theoretical result. **5** (*often pl*) payment made to an actor, musician, etc., for subsequent use of film in which the person appears.
▸ **re'sidually** *adv*

residual unemployment *n* the unemployment that remains in periods of full employment, as a result of those mentally, physically, or emotionally unfit to work.

residuary (rɪ'zɪdjʊərɪ) *adj* **1** of, relating to, or constituting a residue; residual. **2** *Law.* entitled to the residue of an estate after payment of debts and distribution of specific gifts.

residue ('rɛzɪˌdjuː) *n* **1** matter remaining after something has been removed. **2** *Law.* what is left of an estate after the discharge of debts and distribution of specific gifts. ORIG C14: from OF *residu,* from L *residuus* remaining over, from *residēre* to stay behind

residuum (rɪ'zɪdjʊəm) *n, pl* **residua** (-jʊə). a more formal word for **residue.**

resign (rɪ'zaɪn) *vb* **1** (when *intr,* often foll. by *from*) to give up tenure of (a job, office, etc.). **2** (*tr*) to reconcile (oneself) to; yield: *to resign oneself to death.* **3** (*tr*) to give up (a right, claim, etc.); relinquish. ORIG C14: from OF

resigner, from L *resignāre* to unseal, destroy, from RE- + *signāre* to seal
▸ **re'signer** *n*

re-sign (riː'saɪn) *vb* to sign again.

resignation (ˌrɛzɪg'neɪʃən) *n* **1** the act of resigning. **2** a formal document stating one's intention to resign. **3** a submissive unresisting attitude; passive acquiescence.

resigned (rɪ'zaɪnd) *adj* characteristic of or proceeding from an attitude of resignation; acquiescent or submissive.
▸ **resignedly** (rɪ'zaɪnɪdlɪ) *adv* ▸ **re'signedness** *n*

resile (rɪ'zaɪl) *vb* **resiles, resiling, resiled.** (*intr*) to spring or shrink back; recoil or resume original shape. ORIG C16: from OF *resilir,* from L *resilīre* to jump back, from RE- + *salīre* to jump
▸ **re'silement** *n*

resilient (rɪ'zɪlɪənt) *adj* **1** (of an object) capable of regaining its original shape or position after bending, stretching, or other deformation; elastic. **2** (of a person) recovering easily and quickly from illness, hardship, etc.
▸ **re'silience** *or* **re'siliency** *n* ▸ **re'siliently** *adv*

resin ('rɛzɪn) *n* **1** any of a group of solid or semisolid amorphous compounds that are obtained directly from certain plants as exudations. **2** any of a large number of synthetic, usually organic, materials that have a polymeric structure, esp. such a substance in a raw state before it is moulded or treated with plasticizer, etc. ◆ *vb* **3** (*tr*) to treat or coat with resin. ORIG C14: from OF *resine,* from L *rēsīna,* from Gk *rhētinē* resin from a pine
▸ **'resinous** *adj* ▸ **'resinously** *adv* ▸ **'resinousness** *n*

resinate ('rɛzɪˌneɪt) *vb* **resinates, resinating, resinated.** (*tr*) to impregnate with resin.

resipiscence (ˌrɛsɪ'pɪsəns) *n Literary.* acknowledgment that one has been mistaken. ORIG C16: from LL *resipiscentia,* from *resipiscere* to recover one's senses, from L *sapere* to know
▸ **ˌresi'piscent** *adj*

resist (rɪ'zɪst) *vb* **1** to stand firm (against); not yield (to); fight (against). **2** (*tr*) to withstand the deleterious action of; be proof against: *to resist corrosion.* **3** (*tr*) to oppose; refuse to accept or comply with: *to resist arrest.* **4** (*tr*) to refrain from, esp. in spite of temptation (esp. in **cannot resist** (**something**)). ◆ *n* **5** a substance used to protect something, esp. a coating that prevents corrosion. ORIG C14: from L *resistere,* from RE- + *sistere* to stand firm
▸ **re'sister** *n* ▸ **re'sistible** *adj* ▸ **reˌsisti'bility** *n* ▸ **re'sistibly** *adv* ▸ **re'sistless** *adj*

resistance (rɪ'zɪstəns) *n* **1** the act or an instance of resisting. **2** the capacity to withstand something, esp. the body's natural capacity to withstand disease. **3a** the opposition to a flow of electric current through a circuit component, medium, or substance. It is measured in ohms. Symbol: R **3b** (*as modifier*): *a resistance thermometer.* **4** any force that tends to retard or oppose motion: *air resistance; wind resistance.* **5 line of least resistance.** the easiest, but not necessarily the best or most honourable, course of action. **6** See **passive resistance.**
▸ **re'sistant** *adj, n*

Resistance (rɪ'zɪstəns) *n* **the.** an illegal organization fighting for national liberty in a country under enemy occupation.

resistance thermometer *n* an accurate type of thermometer in which temperature is calculated from the resistance of a coil of wire or of a semiconductor placed at the point at which the temperature is to be measured.

Resistencia ★ (*Spanish* rɛsis'tenθja) *n* a city in NE Argentina, on the Paraná River. Pop.: 292 350 (1991).

resistivity (ˌriːzɪs'tɪvɪtɪ) *n* **1** the electrical property of a material that determines the resistance of a piece of given dimensions. It is measured in ohms. Former name: **specific resistance.** **2** the power or capacity to resist; resistance.

resistor (rɪ'zɪstə) *n* an electrical component designed to introduce a known value of resistance into a circuit.

resit *vb* (riː'sɪt), **resits, resitting, resat.** (*tr*) **1** to sit (an examination) again. ◆ *n* ('riːsɪt). **2** an examination which one must sit again.

★ people and places

res judicata (ˌdʒuːdɪ'kɑːtə) *or* **res adjudicata** *n Law.* a matter already adjudicated upon that cannot be raised again. ORIG L

Resnais ★ (*French* rɛnɛ) *n* **Alain** (alɛ̃). born 1922, French film director, whose films include *Hiroshima mon amour* (1959) and *Un Connait la chanson* (1998).

resoluble (rɪ'zɒljub^əl, 'rɛzəl-) *adj* another word for **resolvable.**

re-soluble (riː'sɒljub^əl) *adj* capable of being dissolved again.
▸ **re-'solubleness** *or* **re-ˌsolu'bility** *n* ▸ **re-'solubly** *adv*

resolute ('rɛzəˌluːt) *adj* **1** firm in purpose or belief; steadfast. **2** characterized by resolution; determined: *a resolute answer.* ORIG C16: from L *resolutus,* from *resolvere* to RESOLVE
▸ **'resoˌlutely** *adv* ▸ **'resoˌluteness** *n*

resolution (ˌrɛzə'luːʃən) *n* **1** the act or an instance of resolving. **2** firmness or determination. **3** something resolved or determined; decision. **4** a formal expression of opinion by a meeting. **5** a judicial decision on some matter; verdict; judgment. **6** the act of separating something into its constituent parts or elements. **7** *Med.* subsidence of the symptoms of a disease, esp. the disappearance of inflammation without pus. **8** *Music.* the process in harmony whereby a dissonant note or chord is followed by a consonant one. **9** the ability of a television or film image to reproduce fine detail. **10** *Physics.* another word for **resolving power.**
▸ **ˌreso'lutioner** *or* **ˌreso'lutionist** *n*

resolvable (rɪ'zɒlvəb^əl) *or* **resoluble** *adj* able to be resolved or analysed.
▸ **reˌsolva'bility, reˌsolu'bility** *or* **re'solvableness, re'solubleness** *n*

resolve (rɪ'zɒlv) *vb* **resolves, resolving, resolved.** (*mainly tr*) **1** (*takes a clause as object or an infinitive*) to decide or determine firmly. **2** to express (an opinion) formally, esp. by a vote. **3** (*also intr;* usually foll. by *into*) to separate or cause to separate (into) (constituent parts). **4** (*usually reflexive*) to change; alter: *the ghost resolved itself into a tree.* **5** to make up the mind of; cause to decide: *the tempest resolved him to stay at home.* **6** to find the answer or solution to. **7** to explain away or dispel: *to resolve a doubt.* **8** to bring to an end; conclude: *to resolve an argument.* **9** *Med.* to cause (an inflammation) to subside, esp. without the formation of pus. **10** *Music.* (*also intr*) to follow (a dissonant note or chord) by one producing a consonance. **11** *Physics.* to distinguish between (separate parts) of (an image) as in a microscope, telescope, or other optical instrument. ◆ *n* **12** something determined or decided; resolution: *he had made a resolve to work all day.* **13** firmness of purpose; determination: *nothing can break his resolve.* ORIG C14: from L *resolvere* to unfasten, reveal, from RE- + *solvere* to loosen
▸ **re'solvable** *adj* ▸ **reˌsolva'bility** *n* ▸ **re'solver** *n*

resolved (rɪ'zɒlvd) *adj* fixed in purpose or intention; determined.
▸ **resolvedly** (rɪ'zɒlvɪdlɪ) *adv* ▸ **re'solvedness** *n*

resolvent (rɪ'zɒlvənt) *adj* **1** serving to dissolve or separate something into its elements; resolving. ◆ *n* **2** a drug or agent able to reduce swelling or inflammation.

resolving power *n* **1** Also called: **resolution.** *Physics.* the ability of a microscope or telescope to produce separate images of closely placed objects. **2** *Photog.* the ability of an emulsion to show up fine detail in an image.

resonance ('rɛzənəns) *n* **1** the condition or quality of being resonant. **2** sound produced by a body vibrating in sympathy with a neighbouring source of sound. **3** the condition of a body or system when it is subjected to a periodic disturbance of the same frequency as the natural frequency of the body or system. **4** amplification of speech sounds by sympathetic vibration in the bone structure of the head and chest, resounding in the cavities of the nose, mouth, and pharynx. **5** *Electronics.* the condition of an electrical circuit when the frequency is such that the capacitive and inductive reactances are equal in magnitude. **6** *Med.* the sound heard when tapping a hollow bodily structure, esp. the chest or abdomen. **7** *Chem.* the phenomenon in which the electronic structure of a molecule can be represented by two or more hypothetical structures involving single, double, and triple chemical bonds. **8** *Physics.* the condition of a system in which there is a sharp maximum probability for the absorption of electromagnetic radiation or capture of particles. ORIG C16: from L *resonāre* to RESOUND

resonant ('rɛzənənt) *adj* **1** resounding or re-echoing. **2** producing resonance: *resonant walls.* **3** full of, or intensified by, resonance: *a resonant voice.*
▸ **'resonantly** *adv*

resonate ('rɛzəˌneɪt) *vb* **resonates, resonating, resonated. 1** to resound or cause to resound; reverberate. **2** *Chem., electronics.* to exhibit or cause to exhibit resonance. ORIG C19: from L *resonāre*
▸ **ˌreso'nation** *n*

resonator ('rɛzəˌneɪtə) *n* any body or system that displays resonance, esp. a tuned electrical circuit or a conducting cavity in which microwaves are generated by a resonant current.

resorb (rɪ'sɔːb) *vb* (*tr*) to absorb again. ORIG C17: from L *resorbēre,* from RE- + *sorbēre* to suck in
▸ **re'sorbent** *adj* ▸ **re'sorptive** *adj*

resorcinol (rɪ'zɔːsɪˌnɒl) *n* a colourless crystalline phenol, used in making dyes, drugs, resins, and adhesives. Formula: $C_6H_4(OH)_2$. ORIG C19: NL, from RESIN + *orcinol,* a crystalline solid
▸ **re'sorcinal** *adj*

resorption (rɪ'sɔːpʃən) *n* **1** the process of resorbing or the state of being resorbed. **2** *Geol.* the remelting of a mineral by magma, resulting in a new crystal form being produced.

resort (rɪ'zɔːt) *vb* (*intr*) **1** (usually foll. by *to*) to have recourse (to) for help, use, etc.: *to resort to violence.* **2** to go, esp. often or habitually: *to resort to the beach.* ◆ *n* **3** a place to which many people go for recreation, etc.: *a holiday resort.* **4** the use of something as a means, help, or recourse. **5 last resort.** the last possible course of action open to one. ORIG C14: from OF *resortir,* from RE- + *sortir* to emerge
▸ **re'sorter** *n*

re-sort (riː'sɔːt) *vb* (*tr*) to sort again.

resound (rɪ'zaʊnd) *vb* (*intr*) **1** to ring or echo with sound; reverberate. **2** to make a prolonged echoing noise: *the trumpet resounded.* **3** (of sounds) to echo or ring. **4** to be widely famous: *his fame resounded throughout India.* ORIG C14: from OF *resoner,* from L *resonāre* to sound again

re-sound (riː'saʊnd) *vb* to sound or cause to sound again.

resounding (rɪ'zaʊndɪŋ) *adj* **1** clear and emphatic: *a resounding vote of confidence.* **2** resonant; reverberating: *a resounding slap.*
▸ **re'soundingly** *adv*

resource (rɪ'zɔːs, -'sɔːs) *n* **1** capability, ingenuity, and initiative; quick-wittedness: *a man of resource.* **2** (*often pl*) a source of economic wealth, esp. of a country or business enterprise. **3** a supply or source of aid or support; something resorted to in time of need. **4** a means of doing something; expedient. ORIG C17: from OF *ressourse* relief, from *resourdre,* from L *resurgere,* from RE- + *surgere* to rise
▸ **re'sourceless** *adj*

resourceful (rɪ'zɔːsfʊl, -'sɔːs-) *adj* ingenious, capable, and full of initiative.
▸ **re'sourcefully** *adv* ▸ **re'sourcefulness** *n*

respect (rɪ'spɛkt) *n* **1** an attitude of deference, admiration, or esteem; regard. **2** the state of being honoured or esteemed. **3** a detail, point, or characteristic: *they differ in some respects.* **4** reference or relation (esp. in **in respect of, with respect to**). **5** polite or kind regard; consideration: *respect for people's feelings.* **6** (*often pl*) an expression of esteem or regard (esp. in **pay one's respects**). ◆ *vb* (*tr*) **7** to have an attitude of esteem towards: *to respect one's elders.* **8** to pay proper attention to; not violate: *to respect Swiss neutrality.* **9** *Arch.* to concern or refer to. ORIG C14: from L *rēspicere* to look back, pay attention to, from RE- + *specere* to look
▸ **re'specter** *n*

respectable (rɪ'spɛktəb[ə]l) *adj* **1** having or deserving the respect of other people; estimable; worthy. **2** having good social standing or reputation. **3** having socially or conventionally acceptable morals, etc.: *a respectable woman.* **4** relatively or fairly good; considerable: *a respectable salary.* **5** fit to be seen by other people; presentable.
▸ **reˌspecta'bility** *n* ▸ **re'spectably** *adv*

respectful (rɪ'spɛktfʊl) *adj* full of, showing, or giving respect.
▸ **re'spectfully** *adv* ▸ **re'spectfulness** *n*

respecting (rɪ'spɛktɪŋ) *prep* concerning; regarding.

respective (rɪ'spɛktɪv) *adj* belonging or relating separately to each of several people or things; several: *we took our respective ways home.*
▸ **re'spectiveness** *n*

respectively (rɪ'spɛktɪvlɪ) *adv* (in listing a number of items or attributes that refer to another list) separately in the order given: *he gave Janet and John a cake and a chocolate respectively.*

Respighi ★ (*Italian* res'piːgi) *n* **Ottorino** (otto'riːno). 1879–1936, Italian composer, noted esp. for his operas and ballet music.

respirable ('rɛspɪrəb[ə]l) *adj* **1** able to be breathed. **2** suitable or fit for breathing.
▸ **ˌrespira'bility** *n*

respiration (ˌrɛspɪ'reɪʃən) *n* **1** the process in living organisms of taking in oxygen from the surroundings and giving out carbon dioxide. **2** the chemical breakdown of complex organic substances that takes place in the cells and tissues of animals and plants, during which energy is released and carbon dioxide produced.
▸ **respiratory** ('rɛspɪrətərɪ, -trɪ) *or* **ˌrespi'rational** *adj*

respirator ('rɛspɪˌreɪtə) *n* **1** an apparatus for providing long-term artificial respiration. **2** a device worn over the mouth and nose to prevent inhalation of noxious fumes or to warm cold air before it is breathed.

respiratory failure *n* a condition in which the respiratory system is unable to provide an adequate supply of oxygen or to remove carbon dioxide efficiently.

respiratory quotient *n Biol.* the ratio of the volume of carbon dioxide expired to the volume of oxygen consumed by an organism, tissue, or cell in a given time.

respiratory system *n* the specialized organs, collectively, concerned with external respiration: in humans and other mammals it includes the trachea, bronchi, bronchioles, lungs, and diaphragm.

respire (rɪ'spaɪə) *vb* **respires, respiring, respired. 1** to inhale and exhale (air); breathe. **2** (*intr*) to undergo the process of respiration. ORIG C14: from L *rēspīrāre* to exhale, from RE- + *spīrāre* to breathe

respite ('rɛspɪt, -paɪt) *n* **1** a pause from exertion; interval of rest. **2** a temporary delay. **3** a temporary stay of execution; reprieve. ◆ *vb* **respites, respiting, respited. 4** (*tr*) to grant a respite to; reprieve. ORIG C13: from OF *respit,* from L *respectus* a looking back; see RESPECT

resplendent (rɪ'splɛndənt) *adj* having a brilliant or splendid appearance. ORIG C15: from L *rēsplendēre,* from RE- + *splendēre* to shine
▸ **re'splendence** *or* **re'splendency** *n* ▸ **re'splendently** *adv*

respond (rɪ'spɒnd) *vb* **1** to state or utter (something) in reply. **2** (*intr*) to act in reply; react: *to respond by issuing an invitation.* **3** (*intr;* foll. by *to*) to react favourably: *this patient will respond to treatment.* **4** an archaic word for **correspond.** ◆ *n* **5** *Archit.* a pilaster or an engaged column that supports an arch or a lintel. **6** *Christianity.* a choral anthem chanted in response to a lesson read. ORIG C14: from OF *respondre,* from L *rēspondēre* to return like for like, from RE- + *spondēre* to pledge
▸ **re'spondence** *or* **re'spondency** *n* ▸ **re'sponder** *n*

respondent (rɪ'spɒndənt) *n* **1** *Law.* a person against whom a petition is brought. ◆ *adj* **2** a less common word for **responsive.**

response (rɪ'spɒns) *n* **1** the act of responding; reply or reaction. **2** *Bridge.* a bid replying to a partner's bid or double. **3** (*usually pl*) *Christianity.* a short sentence or phrase recited or sung in reply to the officiant at a church service. **4** *Electronics.* the ratio of the output to the input level of an electrical device. **5** a glandular, muscular, or electrical reaction that arises from stimulation of the

nervous system. ORIG C14: from L *rēsponsum* answer, from *rēspondēre* to RESPOND
▸ **re'sponseless** *adj*

responser *or* **responsor** (rɪ'spɒnsə) *n* a radio or radar receiver used to receive and display signals from a transponder.

responsibility (rɪˌspɒnsɪ'bɪlɪtɪ) *n, pl* **responsibilities. 1** the state or position of being responsible. **2** a person or thing for which one is responsible.

responsible (rɪ'spɒnsɪbᵊl) *adj* **1** (*postpositive;* usually foll. by *for*) having control or authority (over). **2** (*postpositive;* foll. by *to*) being accountable for one's actions and decisions (to): *responsible to one's commanding officer.* **3** (of a position, duty, etc.) involving decision and accountability. **4** (often foll. by *for*) being the agent or cause (of some action): *responsible for a mistake.* **5** able to take rational decisions without supervision; accountable for one's own actions. **6** able to meet financial obligations; of sound credit. ORIG C16: from L *rēsponsus,* from *rēspondēre* to RESPOND
▸ **re'sponsibleness** *n* ▸ **re'sponsibly** *adv*

responsive (rɪ'spɒnsɪv) *adj* **1** reacting or replying quickly or favourably, as to a suggestion, initiative, etc. **2** (of an organism) reacting to a stimulus.
▸ **re'sponsively** *adv* ▸ **re'sponsiveness** *n*

responsory (rɪ'spɒnsərɪ) *n, pl* **responsories.** an anthem or chant recited or sung after a lesson in a church service. ORIG C15: from LL *rēsponsōrium,* from L *rēspondēre* to answer

rest¹ (rɛst) *n* **1a** relaxation from exertion or labour. **1b** (*as modifier*): *a rest period.* **2** repose; sleep. **3** any relief or refreshment, as from worry. **4** calm; tranquillity. **5** death regarded as repose: *eternal rest.* **6** cessation from motion. **7 at rest. 7a** not moving. **7b** calm. **7c** dead. **7d** asleep. **8** a pause or interval. **9** a mark in a musical score indicating a pause of specific duration. **10** *Prosody.* a pause at the end of a line; caesura. **11** a shelter or lodging: *a seaman's rest.* **12** a thing or place on which to put something for support or to steady it. **13** *Billiards, snooker.* any of various special poles sometimes used as supports for the cue. **14 come to rest.** to slow down and stop. **15 lay to rest.** to bury (a dead person). **16 set (someone's mind) at rest.** to reassure (someone) or settle (someone's mind). ◆ *vb* **17** to take or give rest, as by sleeping, lying down, etc. **18** to place or position (oneself, etc.) for rest or relaxation. **19** (*tr*) to place or position for support or steadying: *to rest one's elbows on the table.* **20** (*intr*) to be at ease; be calm. **21** to cease or cause to cease from motion or exertion. **22** (*intr*) to remain without further attention or action: *let the matter rest.* **23** to direct (one's eyes) or (of one's eyes) to be directed: *her eyes rested on the child.* **24** to depend or cause to depend; base; rely: *the whole argument rests on one crucial fact.* **25** (*intr;* foll. by *with, on, upon,* etc.) to be a responsibility (of): *it rests with us to apportion blame.* **26** *Law.* to finish the introduction of evidence in (a case). **27** to put pastry in a cool place to allow the gluten to contract. **28 rest on one's oars.** to stop doing anything for a time. ORIG OE *ræst, reste,* of Gmc origin
▸ **'rester** *n*

rest² (rɛst) *n* (usually preceded by *the*) **1** something left or remaining; remainder. **2** the others: *the rest of the world.* ◆ *vb* **3** (*copula*) to continue to be (as specified); remain: *rest assured.* ORIG C15: from OF *rester* to remain, from L *rēstāre,* from RE- + *stāre* to stand

rest area *n Austral. & NZ.* a motorists' stopping place, usually off a highway, equipped with tables, seats, etc.

restaurant ('rɛstəˌrɒŋ, 'rɛstrɒŋ) *n* a commercial establishment where meals are prepared and served to customers. ORIG C19: from F, from *restaurer* to RESTORE

restaurant car *n Brit.* a railway coach in which meals are served. Also called: **dining car.**

restaurateur (ˌrɛstərə'tɜː) *n* a person who owns or runs a restaurant. ORIG C18: via F from LL *restaurātor,* from L *restaurāre* to RESTORE

> **USAGE NOTE** Although the spelling *restauranteur* occurs frequently, it is a misspelling and should be avoided.

rest-cure *n* **1** a rest taken as part of a course of medical treatment, so as to relieve stress, anxiety, etc. **2** an easy time or assignment: usually used with a negative: *it's no rest-cure, I assure you.*

restful ('rɛstfʊl) *adj* **1** giving or conducive to rest. **2** being at rest; tranquil; calm.
▸ **'restfully** *adv* ▸ **'restfulness** *n*

restharrow ('rɛstˌhærəʊ) *n* any of a genus of Eurasian papilionaceous plants with tough woody stems and roots. ORIG C16: from *rest,* var. of ARREST (to hinder, stop) + HARROW

resting ('rɛstɪŋ) *adj* **1** not moving or working; at rest. **2** *Euphemistic.* (of an actor) out of work. **3** (esp. of plant spores) undergoing a period of dormancy before germination.

restitution (ˌrɛstɪ'tjuːʃən) *n* **1** the act of giving back something that has been lost or stolen. **2** *Law.* compensating for loss or injury by reverting as far as possible to the original position. **3** the return of an object or system to its original state, esp. after elastic deformation. ORIG C13: from L *rēstitūtiō,* from *rēstituere* to rebuild, from RE- + *statuere* to set up
▸ **'restiˌtutive** *or* **ˌresti'tutory** *adj*

restive ('rɛstɪv) *adj* **1** restless, nervous, or uneasy. **2** impatient of control or authority. ORIG C16: from OF *restif* balky, from *rester* to remain
▸ **'restively** *adv* ▸ **'restiveness** *n*

restless ('rɛstlɪs) *adj* **1** unable to stay still or quiet. **2** ceaselessly active or moving: *the restless wind.* **3** worried; anxious; uneasy. **4** not restful; without repose: *a restless night.*
▸ **'restlessly** *adv* ▸ **'restlessness** *n*

rest mass *n* the mass of an object that is at rest relative to an observer. It is the mass used in Newtonian mechanics.

restoration (ˌrɛstə'reɪʃən) *n* **1** the act of restoring to a former or original condition, place, etc. **2** the giving back of something lost, stolen, etc. **3** something restored, replaced, or reconstructed. **4** a model or representation of an extinct animal, etc. **5** (*usually cap.*) *Brit. history.* the re-establishment of the monarchy in 1660 or the reign of Charles II (1660–85).

restorative (rɪ'stɒrətɪv) *adj* **1** tending to revive or renew health, spirits, etc. ◆ *n* **2** anything that restores or revives, esp. a drug.

restore (rɪ'stɔː) *vb* **restores, restoring, restored.** (*tr*) **1** to return (something) to its original or former condition. **2** to bring back to health, good spirits, etc. **3** to return (something lost, stolen, etc.) to its owner. **4** to reintroduce or re-enforce: *to restore discipline.* **5** to reconstruct (an extinct animal, etc.). ORIG C13: from OF, from L *rēstaurāre* to rebuild, from RE- + *-staurāre,* as in *instaurāre* to renew
▸ **re'storable** *adj* ▸ **re'storer** *n*

restrain (rɪ'streɪn) *vb* (*tr*) **1** to hold (someone) back from some action, esp. by force. **2** to deprive (someone) of liberty, as by imprisonment. **3** to limit or restrict. ORIG C14 *restreyne,* from OF *restreindre,* from L *rēstringere,* from RE- + *stringere* to draw, bind
▸ **re'strainable** *adj* ▸ **restrainedly** (rɪ'streɪnɪdlɪ) *adv* ▸ **re'strainer** *n*

restraint (rɪ'streɪnt) *n* **1** the ability to control or moderate one's impulses, passions, etc. **2** the act of restraining or the state of being restrained. **3** something that restrains; restriction. ORIG C15: from OF *restreinte,* from *restreindre* to RESTRAIN

restraint of trade *n* action interfering with the freedom to compete in business.

restrict (rɪ'strɪkt) *vb* (often foll. by *to*) to confine or keep within certain, often specified, limits or selected bounds. ORIG C16: from L *rēstrictus* bound up, from *rēstringere;* see RESTRAIN

restricted (rɪ'strɪktɪd) *adj* **1** limited or confined. **2** not accessible to the general public or (*esp. US*) out of bounds to military personnel. **3** *Brit.* denoting a zone in which a speed limit or waiting restrictions for vehicles apply.
▸ **re'strictedly** *adv* ▸ **re'strictedness** *n*

restriction (rɪ'strɪkʃən) *n* **1** something that restricts; a re-

strictive measure, law, etc. **2** the act of restricting or the state of being restricted.
▸ **re'strictionist** *n, adj*

restrictive (rɪ'strɪktɪv) *adj* **1** restricting or tending to restrict. **2** *Grammar.* denoting a relative clause or phrase that restricts the number of possible referents of its antecedent. The relative clause in *Americans who live in New York* is restrictive; the relative clause in *Americans, who are generally extrovert,* is nonrestrictive.
▸ **re'strictively** *adv* ▸ **re'strictiveness** *n*

restrictive practice *n Brit.* **1** a trading agreement against the public interest. **2** a practice of a union or other group tending to limit the freedom of other workers or employers.

rest room *n* a room in a public building with toilets, washbasins, and, sometimes, couches.

restructure (riː'strʌktʃə) *vb* (*tr*) to organize (a system, business, society, etc.) in a different way: *radical attempts to restructure the economy.*
▸ **re'structuring** *n*

result (rɪ'zʌlt) *n* **1** something that ensues from an action, policy, etc.; outcome; consequence. **2** a number, quantity, or value obtained by solving a mathematical problem. **3** *US.* a decision of a legislative body. **4** (*often pl*) the final score or outcome of a sporting contest. **5** a favourable result, esp. a victory or success. ◆ *vb* (*intr*) **6** (often foll. by *from*) to be the outcome or consequence (of). **7** (foll. by *in*) to issue or terminate (in a specified way, etc.); end: *to result in tragedy.* ORIG C15: from L *resultāre* to rebound, spring from, from RE- + *saltāre* to leap

resultant (rɪ'zʌltənt) *adj* **1** that results; resulting. ◆ *n* **2** *Maths, physics.* a single vector that is the vector sum of two or more other vectors.

resume (rɪ'zjuːm) *vb* **resumes, resuming, resumed. 1** to begin again or go on with (something interrupted). **2** (*tr*) to occupy again, take back, or recover: *to resume one's seat; resume the presidency.* **3** *Arch.* to summarize; make a résumé of. ORIG C15: from L *resūmere,* from RE- + *sūmere* to take up
▸ **re'sumable** *adj* ▸ **re'sumer** *n*

résumé ('rɛzjʊˌmeɪ) *n* **1** a short descriptive summary, as of events, etc. **2** *US & Canad.* another name for **curriculum vitae.** ORIG C19: from F, from *résumer* to RESUME

resumption (rɪ'zʌmpʃən) *n* the act of resuming or beginning again. ORIG C15: via OF from LL *resumptiō,* from L *resūmere* to RESUME
▸ **re'sumptive** *adj* ▸ **re'sumptively** *adv*

resupinate (rɪ'sjuːpɪnɪt) *adj Bot.* (of plant parts) reversed or inverted in position, so as to appear to be upside down. ORIG C18: from L *resupīnātus* bent back, from *resupīnāre,* from RE- + *supīnāre* to place on the back
▸ **reˌsupi'nation** *n*

resurge (rɪ'sɜːdʒ) *vb* **resurges, resurging, resurged.** (*intr*) *Rare.* to rise again as if from the dead. ORIG C16: from L *resurgere* to rise again, reappear, from RE- + *surgere* to lift, arise

resurgent (rɪ'sɜːdʒənt) *adj* rising again, as to new life, vigour, etc.: *resurgent nationalism.*
▸ **re'surgence** *n*

resurrect (ˌrɛzə'rɛkt) *vb* **1** to rise or raise from the dead; bring or be brought back to life. **2** (*tr*) to bring back into use or activity; revive. **3** (*tr*) *Facetious.* (formerly) to exhume and steal (a body) from its grave.

resurrection (ˌrɛzə'rɛkʃən) *n* **1** a supposed act or instance of a dead person coming back to life. **2** belief in the possibility of this as part of a religious or mystical system. **3** the condition of those who have risen from the dead: *we shall all live in the resurrection.* **4** (*usually cap.*) *Christian theol.* the rising again of Christ from the tomb three days after his death. **5** (*usually cap.*) the rising again from the dead of all men at the Last Judgment. ORIG C13: via OF from LL *resurrectiō,* from L *resurgere* to rise again
▸ **ˌresur'rectional** *or* **ˌresur'rectionary** *adj*

resurrectionism (ˌrɛzə'rɛkʃəˌnɪzəm) *n* belief that men will rise again from the dead, esp. according to Christian doctrine.

resurrectionist (ˌrɛzə'rɛkʃənɪst) *n* **1** *Facetious.* (formerly) a body snatcher. **2** a person who believes in the Resurrection.

resurrection plant *n* any of several unrelated desert plants that form a tight ball when dry and unfold and bloom when moistened.

resuscitate (rɪ'sʌsɪˌteɪt) *vb* **resuscitates, resuscitating, resuscitated.** (*tr*) to restore to consciousness; revive. ORIG C16: from L *resuscitāre,* from RE- + *suscitāre* to raise, from *sub-* up from below + *citāre* to rouse, from *citus* quick
▸ **reˌsusci'tation** *n* ▸ **re'suscitative** *adj* ▸ **re'susciˌtator** *n*

ret (rɛt) *vb* **rets, retting, retted.** (*tr*) to moisten or soak (flax, hemp, etc.) in order to separate the fibres from the woody tissue by beating. ORIG C15: of Gmc origin

ret. *abbrev. for:* **1** retain. **2** retired. **3** return(ed).

retable (rɪ'teɪb^{ə}l) *n* an ornamental screenlike structure above and behind an altar. ORIG C19: from F, from Sp. *retablo,* from L *retrō* behind + *tabula* board

retail ('riːteɪl) *n* **1** the sale of goods individually or in small quantities to consumers. Cf. **wholesale.** ◆ *adj* **2** of, relating to, or engaged in such selling: *retail prices.* ◆ *adv* **3** in small amounts or at a retail price. ◆ *vb* **4** to sell or be sold in small quantities to consumers. **5** (rɪ'teɪl). (*tr*) to relate (gossip, scandal, etc.) in detail. ORIG C14: from OF *retaillier,* from RE- + *taillier* to cut; see TAILOR
▸ **'retailer** *n*

retail price index *n* a measure of the changes in the average level of retail prices of selected goods, usually on a monthly basis. Abbrev.: **RPI.**

retail therapy *n Jocular.* the action of shopping for clothes, etc., esp. to cheer oneself up.

retain (rɪ'teɪn) *vb* (*tr*) **1** to keep in one's possession. **2** to be able to hold or contain: *soil that retains water.* **3** (of a person) to be able to remember (information, etc.) without difficulty. **4** to hold in position. **5** to keep for one's future use, as by paying a retainer or nominal charge. **6** *Law.* to engage the services of (a barrister) by payment of a preliminary fee. ORIG C14: from OF *retenir,* from L *retinēre* to hold back, from RE- + *tenēre* to hold
▸ **re'tainable** *adj* ▸ **re'tainment** *n*

retained object *n Grammar.* a direct or indirect object of a passive verb. The phrase *the drawings* in *she was given the drawings* is a retained object.

retainer (rɪ'teɪnə) *n* **1** *History.* a supporter or dependant of a person of rank. **2** a servant, esp. one who has been with a family for a long time. **3** a clip, frame, or similar device that prevents a part of a machine, etc., from moving. **4** a fee paid in advance to secure first option on the services of a barrister, jockey, etc. **5** a reduced rent paid for a flat, etc., to reserve it for future use.

retaining wall *n* a wall constructed to hold back earth, loose rock, etc. Also called: **revetment.**

retake *vb* (riː'teɪk), **retakes, retaking, retook, retaken.** (*tr*) **1** to take back or capture again: *to retake a fortress.* **2** *Films.* to shoot (a scene) again. **3** to tape (a recording) again. ◆ *n* ('riːˌteɪk). **4** *Films.* a rephotographed scene. **5** a retaped recording.
▸ **re'taker** *n*

retaliate (rɪ'tælɪˌeɪt) *vb* **retaliates, retaliating, retaliated.** (*intr*) **1** to take retributory action, esp. by returning some injury or wrong in kind. **2** to cast (accusations) back upon a person. ORIG C17: from LL *retāliāre,* from L RE- + *tālis* of such kind
▸ **reˌtali'ation** *n* ▸ **re'taliative** *or* **re'taliatory** *adj*

retard (rɪ'tɑːd) *vb* (*tr*) to delay or slow down (the progress or speed) of (something). ORIG C15: from OF *retarder,* from L *retardāre,* from RE- + *tardāre* to make slow, from *tardus* sluggish

retardant (rɪ'tɑːd^{ə}nt) *n* **1** a substance that reduces the rate of a chemical reaction. ◆ *adj* **2** having a slowing effect.

retardation (ˌriːtɑː'deɪʃən) *or* **retardment** (rɪ'tɑːdmənt) *n* **1** the act of retarding or the state of being retarded. **2** something that retards.
▸ **re'tardative** *or* **re'tardatory** *adj*

retarded (rɪ'tɑːdɪd) *adj* underdeveloped, usually mentally and esp. having an IQ of 70 to 85.

retarder (rɪ'tɑːdə) *n* **1** a person or thing that retards. **2** a substance added to slow down the rate of a chemical change, such as one added to cement to delay its setting.

retch (rɛtʃ, riːtʃ) *vb* **1** (*intr*) to undergo an involuntary spasm of ineffectual vomiting. ♦ *n* **2** an involuntary spasm of ineffectual vomiting. ORIG OE *hrǣcan;* rel. to ON *hrǣkja* to spit

retd *abbrev. for:* **1** retired. **2** retained. **3** returned.

rete (ˈriːtɪ) *n, pl* **retia** (ˈriːʃɪə, -tɪə). *Anat.* any network of nerves or blood vessels; plexus. ORIG C14 (referring to a metal network used with an astrolabe): from L *rēte* net
▸ **retial** (ˈriːʃɪəl) *adj*

retention (rɪˈtɛnʃən) *n* **1** the act of retaining or state of being retained. **2** the capacity to hold or retain liquid, etc. **3** the capacity to remember. **4** *Pathol.* the abnormal holding within the body of urine, faeces, etc. **5** *Commerce.* a sum of money owed to a contractor but not paid for an agreed period as a safeguard against the appearance of any faults. **6** (*pl*) *Account.* profits earned by a company but not distributed as dividends; retained earnings. ORIG C14: from L *retentiō,* from *retinēre* to RETAIN

retentive (rɪˈtɛntɪv) *adj* having the capacity to retain or remember.
▸ **reˈtentively** *adv* ▸ **reˈtentiveness** *n*

Réti ★ (ˈreɪtɪ) *n* **Richard.** 1889–1929, Hungarian chess player.

retiarius (ˌriːtɪˈɛərɪəs, ˌriːʃɪ-) *n, pl* **retiarii** (-ˈɛərɪˌaɪ). (in ancient Rome) a gladiator armed with a net and trident. ORIG L, from *rēte* net

reticent (ˈrɛtɪsənt) *adj* not communicative; not saying all that one knows; taciturn; reserved. ORIG C19: from L *reticēre* to keep silent, from RE- + *tacēre* to be silent
▸ **ˈreticence** *n* ▸ **ˈreticently** *adv*

> **USAGE NOTE** This word is quite commonly used nowadays as a synonym of *reluctant* and followed by *to* and a verb. In careful writing it is advisable to avoid this use, since many people would regard it as mistaken.

reticle (ˈrɛtɪkᵊl) *or* (*less commonly*) **reticule** *n* a network of fine lines, wires, etc., placed in the focal plane of an optical instrument. ORIG C17: from L *rēticulum* a little net, from *rēte* net

reticulate *adj* (rɪˈtɪkjʊlɪt) *also* **reticular. 1** in the form of a network or having a network of parts: *a reticulate leaf.* ♦ *vb* (rɪˈtɪkjʊˌleɪt), **reticulates, reticulating, reticulated. 2** to form or be formed into a net. ORIG C17: from LL *rēticulātus* made like a net
▸ **reˈticulately** *adv* ▸ **reˌticuˈlation** *n*

reticule (ˈrɛtɪˌkjuːl) *n* **1** (formerly) a woman's small bag or purse, usually with a drawstring and made of net, beading, brocade, etc. **2** a less common variant of **reticle.** ORIG C18: from F *réticule,* from L *rēticulum* RETICLE

reticulum (rɪˈtɪkjʊləm) *n, pl* **reticula** (-lə). **1** any fine network, esp. one in the body composed of cells, fibres, etc. **2** the second compartment of the stomach of ruminants. ORIG C17: from L: little net, from *rēte* net

retiform (ˈriːtɪˌfɔːm, ˈrɛt-) *adj Rare.* netlike; reticulate. ORIG C17: from L *rēte* net + *forma* shape

retina (ˈrɛtɪnə) *n, pl* **retinas** *or* **retinae** (-ˌniː). the light-sensitive membrane forming the inner lining of the posterior wall of the eyeball. ORIG C14: from Med. L, ?from L *rēte* net
▸ **ˈretinal** *adj*

retinene (ˈrɛtɪˌniːn) *n* a yellow pigment, the aldehyde of vitamin A, that is involved in the formation of rhodopsin. ORIG C20: from RETINA + -ENE

retinitis (ˌrɛtɪˈnaɪtɪs) *n* inflammation of the retina. ORIG C20: from NL, from RETINA + -ITIS

retinoscopy (ˌrɛtɪˈnɒskəpɪ) *n Ophthalmol.* a procedure for detecting errors of refraction in the eye by means of an instrument (**retinoscope**) that reflects a beam of light from a mirror into the eye.
▸ **retinoscopic** (ˌrɛtɪnəˈskɒpɪk) *adj* ▸ **ˌretinoˈscopically** *adv* ▸ **ˌretiˈnoscopist** *n*

retinue (ˈrɛtɪˌnjuː) *n* a body of aides and retainers attending an important person. ORIG C14: from OF *retenue,* from *retenir* to RETAIN

retiral (rɪˈtaɪərᵊl) *n esp. Scot.* the act of retiring; retirement.

retire (rɪˈtaɪə) *vb* **retires, retiring, retired.** (*mainly intr*) **1** (*also tr*) to give up or to cause (a person) to give up his or her work, esp. on reaching pensionable age. **2** to go away, as into seclusion, for recuperation, etc. **3** to go to bed. **4** to recede or disappear: *the sun retired behind the clouds.* **5** to withdraw from a sporting contest, esp. because of injury. **6** (*also tr*) to pull back (troops, etc.) from battle or (of troops, etc.) to fall back. **7** (*tr*) to remove (money, bonds, shares, etc.) from circulation. ORIG C16: from F *retirer,* from OF RE- + *tirer* to pull, draw
▸ **reˈtired** *adj* ▸ **reˈtirement** *n* ▸ **reˈtirer** *n*

retirement pension *n Brit.* a weekly payment made by the government to a retired man over 65 or a woman over 60.

retirement relief *n* (in Britain) relief from capital-gains tax given to persons over 60 when disposing of business assets.

retiring (rɪˈtaɪərɪŋ) *adj* shunning contact with others; shy; reserved.
▸ **reˈtiringly** *adv*

retool (riːˈtuːl) *vb* **1** to replace, re-equip, or rearrange the tools in (a factory, etc.). **2** (*tr*) *Chiefly US & Canad.* to revise or reorganize.

retort[1] (rɪˈtɔːt) *vb* **1** (when *tr, takes a clause as object*) to utter (something) quickly, wittily, or angrily, in response. **2** to use (an argument) against its originator. ♦ *n* **3** a sharp, angry, or witty reply. **4** an argument used against its originator. ORIG C16: from L *retorquēre,* from RE- + *torquēre* to twist, wrench
▸ **reˈtorter** *n*

retort[2] (rɪˈtɔːt) *n* **1** a glass vessel with a long tapering neck that is bent down, used for distillation. **2** a vessel used for heating ores in the production of metals or heating coal to produce gas. ♦ *vb* **3** (*tr*) to heat in a retort. ORIG C17: from F *retorte,* from Med. L *retorta,* from L *retorquēre* to twist back; see RETORT[1]

retouch (riːˈtʌtʃ) *vb* (*tr*) **1** to restore, correct, or improve (a painting, make-up, etc.) with new touches. **2** *Photog.* to alter (a negative or print) by painting over blemishes or adding details. ♦ *n* **3** the art or practice of retouching. **4** a detail that is the result of retouching. **5** a photograph, painting, etc., that has been retouched.
▸ **reˈtoucher** *n*

retrace (rɪˈtreɪs) *vb* **retraces, retracing, retraced.** (*tr*) **1** to go back over (one's steps, a route, etc.) again. **2** to go over (a past event) in the mind; recall. **3** to go over (a story, account, etc.) from the beginning.

re-trace (riːˈtreɪs) *vb* **re-traces, re-tracing, re-traced.** (*tr*) to trace (a map, etc.) again.

retract (rɪˈtrækt) *vb* **1** (*tr*) to draw in (a part or appendage): *a snail can retract its horns; to retract the landing gear of an aircraft.* **2** to withdraw (a statement, opinion, charge, etc.) as invalid or unjustified. **3** to go back on (a promise or agreement). ORIG C16: from L *retractāre* to withdraw, from *tractāre,* from *trahere* to drag
▸ **reˈtractable** *or* **reˈtractible** *adj* ▸ **reˈtraction** *n* ▸ **reˈtractive** *adj*

retractile (rɪˈtræktaɪl) *adj* capable of being drawn in: *the retractile claws of a cat.*
▸ **retractility** (ˌriːtrækˈtɪlɪtɪ) *n*

retractor (rɪˈtræktə) *n* **1** *Anat.* any of various muscles that retract an organ or part. **2** *Surgery.* an instrument for holding back an organ or part. **3** a person or thing that retracts.

retral (ˈriːtrəl, ˈrɛtrəl) *adj Rare.* at, near, or towards the back. ORIG C19: from L *retrō* backwards
▸ **ˈretrally** *adv*

retread *vb* (riːˈtrɛd), **retreads, retreading, retreaded. 1** (*tr*) another word for **remould** (sense 2). ♦ *n* (ˈriːˌtrɛd). **2** another word for **remould** (sense 3). **3** *NZ sl.* a pensioner who has resumed employment, esp. in the same profession as formerly. **4** a film, piece of music, etc., that is a superficially altered version of an earlier original.

★ people and places

re-tread (riː'trɛd) *vb* **re-treads, re-treading, re-trod, re-trodden** *or* **re-trod.** (*tr*) to tread (one's steps, etc.) again.

retreat (rɪ'triːt) *vb* (*mainly intr*) **1** *Mil.* to withdraw or retire in the face of or from action with an enemy. **2** to retire or withdraw, as to seclusion or shelter. **3** (of a person's features) to slope back; recede. **4** (*tr*) *Chess.* to move (a piece) back. ◆ *n* **5** the act of retreating or withdrawing. **6** *Mil.* **6a** a withdrawal or retirement in the face of the enemy. **6b** a bugle call signifying withdrawal or retirement. **7** retirement or seclusion. **8** a place to which one may retire for religious contemplation. **9** a period of seclusion, esp. for religious contemplation. **10** an institution for the care and treatment of the mentally ill, infirm, elderly, etc. ORIG C14: from OF *retret,* from *retraire* to withdraw, from L *retrahere* to pull back

retrench (rɪ'trɛntʃ) *vb* **1** to reduce (costs); economize. **2** (*tr*) to shorten, delete, or abridge. ORIG C17: from OF *retrenchier,* from RE- + *trenchier* to cut, from L *truncāre* to lop
► **re'trenchment** *n*

retribution (ˌrɛtrɪ'bjuːʃən) *n* **1** the act of punishing or taking vengeance for wrongdoing, sin, or injury. **2** punishment or vengeance. ORIG C14: via OF from Church L *retribūtiō,* from L *retribuere,* from RE- + *tribuere* to pay
► **retributive** (rɪ'trɪbjʊtɪv) *adj* ► **re'tributively** *adv*

retrieval (rɪ'triːvᵊl) *n* **1** the act or process of retrieving. **2** the possibility of recovery, restoration, or rectification. **3** a computer operation that recalls data from a file.

retrieve (rɪ'triːv) *vb* **retrieves, retrieving, retrieved.** (*mainly tr*) **1** to get or fetch back again; recover. **2** to bring back to a more satisfactory state; revive. **3** to rescue or save. **4** to recover or make newly available (stored information) from a computer system. **5** (*also intr*) (of dogs) to find and fetch (shot game, etc.). **6** *Tennis, etc.* to return successfully (a shot difficult to reach). **7** to recall; remember. ◆ *n* **8** the act of retrieving. **9** the chance of being retrieved. ORIG C15: from OF *retrover,* from RE- + *trouver* to find, ?from Vulgar L *tropāre* (unattested) to compose
► **re'trievable** *adj*

retriever (rɪ'triːvə) *n* **1** one of a breed of large dogs that can be trained to retrieve game. **2** any dog used to retrieve shot game. **3** a person or thing that retrieves.

retro ('rɛtrəʊ) *n, pl* **retros. 1** short for **retrorocket.** ◆ *adj* **2** denoting something associated with or revived from the past: *retro fashion.*

retro- *prefix* **1** back or backwards: *retroactive.* **2** located behind: *retrochoir.* ORIG from L *retrō* behind, backwards

retroact ('rɛtrəʊˌækt) *vb* (*intr*) **1** to act in opposition. **2** to influence or have reference to past events.
► ˌ**retro'action** *n*

retroactive (ˌrɛtrəʊ'æktɪv) *adj* **1** applying or referring to the past: *retroactive legislation.* **2** effective from a date or for a period in the past.
► ˌ**retro'actively** *adv* ► ˌ**retroac'tivity** *n*

retrocede (ˌrɛtrəʊ'siːd) *vb* **retrocedes, retroceding, retroceded. 1** (*tr*) to give back; return. **2** (*intr*) to go back; recede.
► **retrocession** (ˌrɛtrəʊ'sɛʃən) *or* ˌ**retro'cedence** *n* ► ˌ**retro'cessive** *or* ˌ**retro'cedent** *adj*

retrochoir ('rɛtrəʊˌkwaɪə) *n* the space in a large church or cathedral behind the high altar.

retrofire ('rɛtrəʊˌfaɪə) *n* **1** the act of firing a retrorocket. **2** the moment at which it is fired.

retrofit ('rɛtrəʊˌfɪt) *vb* **retrofits, retrofitting, retrofitted.** (*tr*) to equip (a vehicle, piece of equipment, etc.) with new parts, safety devices, etc., after manufacture.

retroflex ('rɛtrəʊˌflɛks) *or* **retroflexed** *adj* **1** bent or curved backwards. **2** *Phonetics.* of or involving retroflexion. ORIG C18: from L *retrōflexus,* from *retrōflectere,* from RETRO- + *flectere* to bend

retroflexion *or* **retroflection** (ˌrɛtrəʊ'flɛkʃən) *n* **1** the act or condition of bending or being bent backwards. **2** the act of turning the tip of the tongue upwards and backwards in the articulation of a vowel or a consonant.

retrograde ('rɛtrəʊˌgreɪd) *adj* **1** moving or bending backwards. **2** (esp. of order) reverse or inverse. **3** tending towards an earlier worse condition; declining or deteriorating. **4** *Astron.* **4a** occurring or orbiting in a direction opposite to that of the earth's motion around the sun. Cf. **direct** (sense 18). **4b** occurring or orbiting in a direction around a planet opposite to the planet's rotational direction. **4c** appearing to move in a clockwise direction due to the rotational period exceeding the period of revolution around the sun: *Venus has retrograde rotation.* ◆ *vb* **retrogrades, retrograding, retrograded.** (*intr*) **5** to move in a retrograde direction; retrogress. ORIG C14: from L *retrōgradī,* from *gradi* to walk, go
► ˌ**retrogra'dation** *n* ► '**retroˌgradely** *adv*

retrogress (ˌrɛtrəʊ'grɛs) *vb* (*intr*) **1** to go back to an earlier, esp. worse, condition; degenerate or deteriorate. **2** to move backwards; recede. ORIG C19: from L *retrōgressus* having moved backwards; see RETROGRADE
► ˌ**retro'gression** *n* ► ˌ**retro'gressive** *adj* ► ˌ**retro'gressively** *adv*

retrorocket ('rɛtrəʊˌrɒkɪt) *n* a small auxiliary rocket engine on a larger rocket, missile, or spacecraft, that produces thrust in the opposite direction to the direction of flight in order to decelerate. Often shortened to **retro.**

retrorse (rɪ'trɔːs) *adj* (esp. of plant parts) pointing backwards. ORIG C19: from L *retrōrsus,* from *retrōversus* turned back, from RETRO- + *vertere* to turn
► **re'trorsely** *adv*

retrospect ('rɛtrəʊˌspɛkt) *n* the act of surveying things past (often in **in retrospect**). ORIG C17: from L *retrōspicere* to look back, from RETRO- + *specere* to look
► ˌ**retro'spection** *n*

retrospective (ˌrɛtrəʊ'spɛktɪv) *adj* **1** looking or directed backwards, esp. in time; characterized by retrospection. **2** applying to the past; retroactive. ◆ *n* **3** an exhibition of an artist's life's work.
► ˌ**retro'spectively** *adv*

retroussé (rə'truːseɪ) *adj* (of a nose) turned up. ORIG C19: from F *retrousser* to tuck up

retroversion (ˌrɛtrəʊ'vɜːʃən) *n* **1** the act of turning or condition of being turned backwards. **2** the condition of a part or organ, esp. the uterus, that is turned backwards.
► '**retroˌverted** *adj*

Retrovir ('rɛtrəʊˌvɪə) *n Trademark.* a brand name for **zidovudine.**

retrovirus ('rɛtrəʊˌvaɪrəs) *n* any of several viruses that are able to reverse the normal flow of genetic information from DNA to RNA by transcribing RNA into DNA: many retroviruses are known to cause cancer in animals.
► '**retroˌviral** *adj*

retsina (rɛt'siːnə) *n* a Greek wine flavoured with resin. ORIG Mod. Gk, from It. *resina* RESIN

retune (riː'tjuːn) *vb* **retunes, retuning, retuned.** (*tr*) **1** to tune (a musical instrument) differently or again. **2** to tune (a radio, television, etc.) to another frequency.

return (rɪ'tɜːn) *vb* **1** (*intr*) to come back to a former place or state. **2** (*tr*) to give, take, or carry back; replace or restore. **3** (*tr*) to repay or recompense, esp. with something of equivalent value: *return the compliment.* **4** (*tr*) to earn or yield (profit or interest) as an income from an investment or venture. **5** (*intr*) to come back or revert in thought or speech: *I'll return to that later.* **6** (*intr*) to recur or reappear: *the symptoms have returned.* **7** to answer or reply. **8** (*tr*) to vote into office; elect. **9** (*tr*) *Law.* (of a jury) to deliver or render (a verdict). **10** (*tr*) to submit (a report, etc.) about (someone or something) to someone in authority. **11** (*tr*) *Cards.* to lead back (the suit led by one's partner). **12** (*tr*) *Ball games.* to hit, throw, or play (a ball) back. **13 return thanks.** (of Christians) to say grace before a meal. ◆ *n* **14** the act or an instance of coming back. **15** something that is given or sent back, esp. unsatisfactory merchandise or a theatre ticket for resale. **16** the act or an instance of putting, sending, or carrying back; replacement or restoration. **17** (*often pl*) the yield or profit from an investment or venture. **18** the act or an instance of reciprocation or repayment (esp. in **in return for**). **19** a recurrence or reappearance. **20** an official report, esp. of the financial condition of a company. **21a** a form (a **tax return**) on which a statement of one's taxable income is made. **21b** the statement itself. **22** (*often pl*) a statement of the votes counted at an election. **23** an answer or reply. **24** *Brit.* short for **return ticket. 25** *Archit.* a part of a

building that forms an angle with the façade. **26** *Law.* a report by a bailiff or other officer on the outcome of a formal document such as a writ, summons, etc. **27** *Cards.* a lead of a card in the suit that one's partner has previously led. **28** *Ball games.* the act of playing or throwing a ball, etc., back. **29 by return (of post).** *Brit.* by the next post back to the sender. **30 many happy returns (of the day).** a conventional birthday greeting. ◆ *adj* **31** of, relating to, or characterized by a return: *a return visit.* **32** denoting a second, reciprocal occasion: *a return match.* ORIG C14: from OF *retorner;* see RE-, TURN
▸ **re'turnable** *adj*

return crease *n Cricket.* one of two lines marked at right-angles to each bowling crease, from inside which a bowler must deliver the ball.

returned serviceman *n Austral. & NZ.* a serviceman who has served abroad. Also (Austral. and Canad.): **returned man.**

returner (rɪ'tɜːnə) *n* **1** a person or thing that returns. **2** a person who goes back to work after a break, esp. a woman who has had children.

returning officer *n* (in Britain, Canada, Australia, etc.) an official in charge of conducting an election in a constituency, etc.

return ticket *n Brit., Austral., & NZ.* a ticket entitling a passenger to travel to his or her destination and back.

retuse (rɪ'tjuːs) *adj Bot.* having a rounded apex and a central depression. ORIG C18: from L *retundere* to make blunt, from RE- + *tundere* to pound

Retz ★ (*French* rɛ) *n* **Gilles de.** See (Gilles de) **Rais.**

Reuben ★ ('ruːbɪn) *n Old Testament.* **1** the eldest son of Jacob and Leah: one of the 12 patriarchs of Israel (Genesis 29:30). **2** the Israelite tribe descended from him. **3** the territory of this tribe, lying to the northeast of the Dead Sea. Douay spelling: **Ruben.**

reunify (riː'juːnɪˌfaɪ) *vb* **reunifies, reunifying, reunified.** (*tr*) to bring together again (something, esp. a country previously divided).
▸ **ˌreunifi'cation** *n*

reunion (riː'juːnjən) *n* **1** the act of coming together again. **2** the state or condition of having been brought together again. **3** a gathering of relatives, friends, or former associates.

Réunion ★ (riː'juːnjən; *French* reynjɔ̃) *n* an island in the Indian Ocean, in the Mascarene Islands: an overseas region of France, having been in French possession since 1642. Capital: Saint-Denis. Pop.: 714 000 (1999 est.). Area: 2510 sq. km (970 sq. miles).

reunite (ˌriːjuː'naɪt) *vb* **reunites, reuniting, reunited.** to bring or come together again.
▸ **ˌreu'nitable** *adj*

Reus ★ (*Spanish* rɛus) *n* a city in NE Spain, northwest of Tarragona: became commercially important after the establishment of an English colony (about 1750). Pop.: 86 864 (1991).

Reuter ★ ('rɔɪtə) *n* Baron **Paul Julius von** (paul 'juːlius fɔn). original name *Israel Beer Josaphat.* 1816–99, German telegrapher, who founded a news agency in London (1851).

Reutlingen ★ (*German* 'rɔytlɪŋən) *n* a city in SW Germany, in Baden-Württemberg: founded in the 11th century; an Imperial free city from 1240 until 1802; textile industry. Pop.: 108 565 (1996 est.).

rev (rɛv) *Inf.* ◆ *n* **1** revolution per minute. ◆ *vb* **revs, revving, revved. 2** (often foll. by *up*) to increase the speed of revolution of (an engine).

rev. *abbrev. for:* **1** revenue. **2** reverse(d). **3** review. **4** revise(d). **5** revision. **6** revolution. **7** revolving.

Rev. *abbrev. for:* **1** *Bible.* Revelation (of Saint John the Divine). **2** Reverend.

Reval ★ ('reːval) *n* the German name for **Tallinn.**

revalue (riː'væljuː) *or US* **revaluate** *vb* **revalues, revaluing, revalued** *or US* **revaluates, revaluating, revaluated. 1** to adjust the exchange value of (a currency), esp. upwards. Cf. **devalue. 2** (*tr*) to make a fresh valuation of.
▸ **reˌvalu'ation** *n*

revamp (riː'væmp) *vb* (*tr*) **1** to patch up or renovate; repair or restore. ◆ *n* **2** something that has been renovated or revamped. **3** the act or process of revamping. ORIG C19: from RE- + VAMP[2]

revanchism (rɪ'væntʃɪzəm) *n* **1** a foreign policy aimed at revenge or the regaining of lost territories. **2** support for such a policy. ORIG C20: from F *revanche* REVENGE
▸ **re'vanchist** *n, adj*

rev counter *n Brit.* an informal name for **tachometer.**

Revd *abbrev. for* Reverend.

reveal (rɪ'viːl) *vb* (*tr*) **1** (*may take a clause as object or an infinitive*) to disclose (a secret); divulge. **2** to expose to view or show (something concealed). **3** (of God) to disclose (divine truths). ◆ *n* **4** *Archit.* the vertical side of an opening in a wall, esp. the side of a window or door between the frame and the front of the wall. ORIG C14: from OF *reveler,* from L *revēlāre* to unveil, from RE- + *vēlum* a VEIL
▸ **re'vealable** *adj* ▸ **re'vealer** *n* ▸ **re'vealment** *n*

revealed religion *n* **1** religion based on the revelation by God to man of ideas that he would not have arrived at by reason alone. **2** religion in which the existence of God depends on revelation.

revealing (rɪ'viːlɪŋ) *adj* **1** of significance or import: *a very revealing experience.* **2** showing more of the body than is usual: *a revealing costume.*
▸ **re'vealingly** *adv*

reveille (rɪ'vælɪ) *n* **1** a signal, given by a bugle, drum, etc., to awaken soldiers or sailors in the morning. **2** the hour at which this takes place. ORIG C17: from F *réveillez!* awake! from RE- + OF *esveillier* to be wakeful, ult. from L *vigilāre* to keep watch

revel ('rɛv°l) *vb* **revels, revelling, revelled** *or US* **revels, reveling, reveled.** (*intr*) **1** (foll. by *in*) to take pleasure or wallow: *to revel in success.* **2** to take part in noisy festivities; make merry. ◆ *n* **3** (*often pl*) an occasion of noisy merrymaking. ORIG C14: from OF *reveler* to be merry, noisy, from L *rebellāre* to revolt
▸ **'reveller** *n*

revelation (ˌrɛvə'leɪʃən) *n* **1** the act or process of disclosing something previously secret or obscure, esp. something true. **2** a fact disclosed or revealed, esp. in a dramatic or surprising way. **3** *Christianity.* God's disclosure of his own nature and his purpose for mankind. ORIG C14: from Church L *revēlātiō,* from L *revēlāre* to REVEAL
▸ **ˌreve'latory** *or* **ˌreve'lational** *adj*

Revelation (ˌrɛvə'leɪʃən) *n* (*popularly, often pl*) the last book of the New Testament, containing visionary descriptions of heaven, and of the end of the world. Also called: the **Apocalypse,** the **Revelation of Saint John the Divine.**

revelationist (ˌrɛvə'leɪʃənɪst) *n* a person who believes that God has revealed certain truths to man.

revelry ('rɛv°lrɪ) *n, pl* **revelries.** noisy or unrestrained merrymaking.

revenant ('rɛvɪnənt) *n* something, esp. a ghost, that returns. ORIG C19: from F: ghost, from *revenir,* from L *revenīre,* from RE- + *venīre* to come

revenge (rɪ'vɛndʒ) *n* **1** the act of retaliating for wrongs or injury received; vengeance. **2** something done as a means of vengeance. **3** the desire to take vengeance. **4** a return match, regarded as a loser's opportunity to even the score. ◆ *vb* **revenges, revenging, revenged.** (*tr*) **5** to inflict equivalent injury or damage for (injury received). **6** to take vengeance for (oneself or another); avenge. ORIG C14: from OF *revenger,* from LL *revindicāre,* from RE- + *vindicāre* to VINDICATE
▸ **re'venger** *n* ▸ **re'venging** *adj* ▸ **re'vengingly** *adv*

revengeful (rɪ'vɛndʒfʊl) *adj* full of or characterized by desire for vengeance; vindictive.
▸ **re'vengefully** *adv* ▸ **re'vengefulness** *n*

revenue ('rɛvɪˌnjuː) *n* **1** the income accruing from taxation to a government. **2a** a government department responsible for the collection of government revenue. **2b** (*as modifier*): *revenue men.* **3** the gross income from a business enterprise, investment, etc. **4** a particular item of income. **5** a source of income. ORIG C16: from OF, from *revenir* to return, from L *revenīre;* see REVENANT

revenue cutter *n* a small lightly armed boat used to enforce customs regulations and catch smugglers.

reverb (rɪ'vɜːb) *n* an electronic device that creates artificial acoustics.

reverberate (rɪ'vɜːbəˌreɪt) *vb* **reverberates, reverberating, reverberated.** **1** (*intr*) to resound or re-echo. **2** to reflect or be reflected many times. **3** (*intr*) to rebound or recoil. **4** (*intr*) (of the flame or heat in a reverberatory furnace) to be deflected onto the metal or ore on the hearth. **5** (*tr*) to heat, melt, or refine (a metal or ore) in a reverberatory furnace. ORIG C16: from L *reverberāre,* from RE- + *verberāre* to beat, from *verber* a lash
▸ **re'verberantly** *adv* ▸ **reˌverber'ation** *n* ▸ **re'verberative** *adj* ▸ **re'verbeˌrator** *n* ▸ **re'verberatory** *adj*

reverberation time *n* a measure of the acoustic properties of a room, equal to the time taken for a sound to fall in intensity by 60 decibels. It is usually measured in seconds.

reverberatory furnace *n* a metallurgical furnace having a curved roof that deflects heat onto the charge so that the fuel is not in direct contact with the ore.

revere (rɪ'vɪə) *vb* **reveres, revering, revered.** (*tr*) to be in awe of and respect deeply; venerate. ORIG C17: from L *reverēri,* from RE- + *verērī* to fear, be in awe of

Revere ★ (rɪ'vɪə) *n* **Paul.** 1735–1818, American patriot and silversmith, known for his night ride on April 18, 1775, to warn the Massachusetts colonists that British troops were coming.

reverence ('rɛvərəns) *n* **1** a feeling or attitude of profound respect, usually reserved for the sacred or divine. **2** an outward manifestation of this feeling, esp. a bow or act of obeisance. **3** the state of being revered or commanding profound respect. ◆ *vb* **reverences, reverencing, reverenced.** **4** (*tr*) to revere or venerate.

Reverence ('rɛvərəns) *n* (preceded by *Your* or *His*) a title sometimes used to address or refer to a Roman Catholic priest.

reverend ('rɛvərənd) *adj* **1** worthy of reverence. **2** relating to or designating a clergyman. ◆ *n* **3** *Inf.* a clergyman. ORIG C15: from L *reverendus* fit to be revered

Reverend ('rɛvərənd) *adj* a title of respect for a clergyman. Abbrev.: **Rev., Revd.**

> **USAGE NOTE** *Reverend* with a surname alone (*Reverend Smith*), as a term of address (*"Yes, Reverend"*), or in the greeting of a letter (*Dear Rev. Mr Smith*) are all generally considered to be wrong usage. Preferred are (*the*) *Reverend John Smith* or *Reverend Mr Smith* and *Dear Mr Smith.*

reverent ('rɛvərənt, 'rɛvrənt) *adj* feeling, expressing, or characterized by reverence. ORIG C14: from L *reverēns* respectful
▸ **'reverently** *adv*

reverential (ˌrɛvə'rɛnʃəl) *adj* resulting from or showing reverence.
▸ **ˌrever'entially** *adv*

reverie ('rɛvərɪ) *n* **1** an act or state of absent-minded daydreaming: *to fall into a reverie.* **2** a piece of instrumental music suggestive of a daydream. **3** *Arch.* a fanciful or visionary notion; daydream. ORIG C14: from OF *resverie* wildness, from *resver* to behave wildly, from ?

revers (rɪ'vɪə) *n, pl* **revers** (-'vɪəz). (*usually pl*) the turned-back lining of part of a garment, esp. of a lapel or cuff. ORIG C19: from F, lit.: REVERSE

reversal (rɪ'vɜːsᵊl) *n* **1** the act or an instance of reversing. **2** a change for the worse; reverse. **3** the state of being reversed. **4** the annulment of a judicial decision, esp. by an appeal court.

reverse (rɪ'vɜːs) *vb* **reverses, reversing, reversed.** (*mainly tr*) **1** to turn or set in an opposite direction, order, or position. **2** to change into something different or contrary; alter completely: *reverse one's policy.* **3** (*also intr*) to move or cause to move backwards or in an opposite direction: *to reverse a car.* **4** to run (machinery, etc.) in the opposite direction to normal. **5** to turn inside out. **6** *Law.* to revoke or set aside (a judgment, decree, etc.); annul. **7 reverse the charge(s).** to make a telephone call at the recipient's expense. ◆ *n* **8** the opposite or contrary of something. **9** the back or rear side of something. **10** a change to an opposite position, state, or direction. **11** a change for the worse; setback or defeat. **12a** the mechanism or gears by which machinery, a vehicle, etc., can be made to reverse its direction. **12b** (*as modifier*): *reverse gear.* **13** the side of a coin bearing a secondary design. **14a** printed matter in which normally black or coloured areas, esp. lettering, appear white, and vice versa. **14b** (*as modifier*): *reverse plates.* **15 in reverse.** in an opposite or backward direction. **16 the reverse of.** emphatically not; not at all: *he was the reverse of polite when I called.* ◆ *adj* **17** opposite or contrary in direction, position, order, nature, etc.; turned backwards. **18** back to front; inverted. **19** operating or moving in a manner contrary to that which is usual. **20** denoting or relating to a mirror image. ORIG C14: from OF, from L *reversus,* from *revertere* to turn back
▸ **re'versely** *adv* ▸ **re'verser** *n*

reverse-charge *adj* (*prenominal*) (of a telephone call) made at the recipient's expense.

reverse osmosis *n* a technique for purifying water, in which pressure is applied to force liquid through a semipermeable membrane in the opposite direction to that in normal osmosis.

reverse takeover *n Finance.* the purchase of a larger company by a smaller company, esp. of a public company by a private company.

reverse transcriptase (træn'skrɪpteɪz) *n* an enzyme present in retroviruses that copies RNA into DNA, thus reversing the usual flow of genetic information in which DNA is copied into RNA.

reverse video *n Computing.* highlighting by reversing the colours of normal characters and background on a visual display unit.

reversible (rɪ'vɜːsɪbᵊl) *adj* **1** capable of being reversed: *a reversible decision.* **2** capable of returning to an original condition. **3** *Chem., physics.* capable of assuming or producing either of two possible states and changing from one to the other: *a reversible reaction.* **4** (of a fabric or garment) woven, printed, or finished so that either side may be used as the outer side. ◆ *n* **5** a reversible garment, esp. a coat.
▸ **reˌversi'bility** *n* ▸ **re'versibly** *adv*

reversing lights *pl n* lights on the rear of a motor vehicle that go on when the vehicle is being reversed.

reversion (rɪ'vɜːʃən) *n* **1** a return to an earlier condition, practice, or belief; act of reverting. **2** *Biol.* the return of individuals, organs, etc., to a more primitive condition or type. **3** *Property law.* **3a** an interest in an estate that reverts to the grantor or his or her heirs at the end of a period, esp. at the end of the life of a grantee. **3b** an estate so reverting. **3c** the right to succeed to such an estate. **4** the benefit payable on the death of a life-insurance policyholder.
▸ **re'versionary** *or* **re'versional** *adj*

reversionary bonus *n Insurance.* a bonus added to the sum payable on death or at the maturity of a with-profits assurance policy.

revert (rɪ'vɜːt) *vb* (*intr*; foll. by *to*). **1** to go back to a former practice, condition, belief, etc.: *he reverted to his old wicked ways.* **2** to take up again or come back to a former topic. **3** *Biol.* (of individuals, organs, etc.) to return to a more primitive, earlier, or simpler condition or type. **4** *Property law.* (of an estate or interest in land) to return to its former owner or his or her heirs. **5 revert to type.** to resume characteristics that were thought to have disappeared. ORIG C13: from L *revertere,* from RE- + *vertere* to turn
▸ **re'verter** *n* ▸ **re'vertible** *adj*

> **USAGE NOTE** Since *back* is part of the meaning of *revert,* it is better not to say that someone *reverts back* to a certain type of behaviour.

revet (rɪ'vɛt) *vb* **revets, revetting, revetted.** to face (a wall or embankment) with stones. ORIG C19: from F *revêt,* from OF *revestir* to reclothe; see REVETMENT

revetment (rɪ'vɛtmənt) *n* **1** a facing of stones, sandbags, etc., to protect a wall, embankment, or earthworks. **2** another name for **retaining wall.** ORIG C18: from F *revêtement,* lit.: a reclothing, from *revêtir;* ult. from L RE- + *vestīre* to clothe

review (rɪ'vjuː) *vb* (*mainly tr*) **1** to look at or examine again: *to review a situation.* **2** to look back upon (a period of time, sequence of events, etc.); remember: *he reviewed his achievements with pride.* **3** to inspect, esp. formally or officially: *the general reviewed his troops.* **4** *Law.* to re-examine (a decision) judicially. **5** to write a critical assessment of (a book, film, play, concert, etc.), esp. as a profession. ◆ *n* **6** Also called: **reviewal.** the act or an instance of reviewing. **7** a general survey or report: *a review of the political situation.* **8** a critical assessment of a book, film, play, concert, etc., esp. one printed in a newspaper or periodical. **9** a publication containing such articles. **10** a second consideration; re-examination. **11** a retrospective survey. **12** a formal or official inspection. **13** a US and Canad. word for **revision** (sense 2). **14** *Law.* judicial re-examination of a case, esp. by a superior court. **15** a less common spelling of **revue.** ORIG C16: from F, from *revoir* to see again, from L RE- + *vidēre* to see
▸ **re'viewer** *n*

revile (rɪ'vaɪl) *vb* **reviles, reviling, reviled.** to use abusive or scornful language against (someone or something). ORIG C14: from OF *reviler,* from RE- + *vil* VILE
▸ **re'vilement** *n* ▸ **re'viler** *n*

revise (rɪ'vaɪz) *vb* **revises, revising, revised. 1** (*tr*) to change or amend: *to revise one's opinion.* **2** *Brit.* to reread (a subject or notes on it) so as to memorize it, esp. for an examination. **3** (*tr*) to prepare a new version or edition of (a previously printed work). ◆ *n* **4** the act, process, or result of revising; revision. ORIG C16: from L *revīsere,* from RE- + *vīsere* to inspect, from *vidēre* to see
▸ **re'visal** *n* ▸ **re'viser** *n*

Revised Standard Version *n* a revision by American scholars of the American Standard Version of the Bible. The New Testament was published in 1946 and the entire Bible in 1953.

Revised Version *n* a revision of the Authorized Version of the Bible by two committees of British scholars, the New Testament being published in 1881 and the Old in 1885.

revision (rɪ'vɪʒən) *n* **1** the act or process of revising. **2** *Brit.* the process of rereading a subject or notes on it, esp. for an examination. **3** a corrected or new version of a book, article, etc.
▸ **re'visionary** *adj*

revisionism (rɪ'vɪʒəˌnɪzəm) *n* **1** (*sometimes cap.*) **1a** a moderate, nonrevolutionary version of Marxism developed in Germany around 1900. **1b** (in Marxist-Leninist ideology) any dangerous departure from the true interpretation of Marx's teachings. **2** the advocacy of revision of some political theory, etc.
▸ **re'visionist** *n, adj*

revisory (rɪ'vaɪzərɪ) *adj* of, relating to, or having the power of revision.

revitalize *or* **revitalise** (riː'vaɪtəˌlaɪz) *vb* **revitalizes, revitalizing, revitalized** *or* **revitalises, revitalising, revitalised.** (*tr*) to restore vitality or animation to.

revival (rɪ'vaɪvəl) *n* **1** the act or an instance of reviving or the state of being revived. **2** an instance of returning to life or consciousness; restoration of vigour or vitality. **3** a renewed use, acceptance of, or interest in (past customs, styles, etc.): *the Gothic revival.* **4** a new production of a play that has not been recently performed. **5** a reawakening of faith. **6** an evangelistic meeting or meetings intended to effect such a reawakening in those present.

revivalism (rɪ'vaɪvəˌlɪzəm) *n* **1** a movement that seeks to reawaken faith. **2** the tendency or desire to revive former customs, styles, etc.
▸ **re'vivalist** *n* ▸ **reˌvival'istic** *adj*

revive (rɪ'vaɪv) *vb* **revives, reviving, revived. 1** to bring or be brought back to life, consciousness, or strength: *revived by a drop of whisky.* **2** to give or assume new vitality; flourish again or cause to flourish again. **3** to make or become operative or active again: *the youth movement was revived.* **4** to bring or come back to mind. **5** (*tr*) *Theatre.* to mount a new production of (an old play). ORIG C15: from OF *revivre* to live again, from L *revīvere,* from RE- + *vīvere* to live
▸ **re'vivable** *adj* ▸ **reˌviva'bility** *n* ▸ **re'viver** *n* ▸ **re'viving** *adj*

revivify (riː'vɪvɪˌfaɪ) *vb* **revivifies, revivifying, revivified.** (*tr*) to give new life or spirit to.
▸ **reˌvivifi'cation** *n*

revocable ('rɛvəkəbəl) *or* **revokable** (rɪ'vəʊkəbəl) *adj* capable of being revoked.
▸ **ˌrevoca'bility** *or* **reˌvoka'bility** *n* ▸ **'revocably** *or* **re'vokably** *adv*

revocation (ˌrɛvə'keɪʃən) *n* **1** the act of revoking or state of being revoked. **2a** the cancellation or annulment of a legal instrument. **2b** the withdrawal of an offer, power of attorney, etc.
▸ **revocatory** ('rɛvəkətərɪ, -trɪ) *adj*

revoice (riː'vɔɪs) *vb* **revoices, revoicing, revoiced.** (*tr*) **1** to utter again; echo. **2** to adjust the design of (an organ pipe or wind instrument) as after disuse or to conform with modern pitch.

revoke (rɪ'vəʊk) *vb* **revokes, revoking, revoked. 1** (*tr*) to take back or withdraw; cancel; rescind. **2** (*intr*) *Cards.* to break a rule by failing to follow suit when able to do so. ◆ *n* **3** *Cards.* the act of revoking. ORIG C14: from L *revocāre* to call back, withdraw, from RE- + *vocāre* to call
▸ **re'voker** *n*

revolt (rɪ'vəʊlt) *n* **1** a rebellion or uprising against authority. **2 in revolt.** in the process or state of rebelling. ◆ *vb* **3** (*intr*) to rise up in rebellion against authority. **4** (*usually passive*) to feel or cause to feel revulsion, disgust, or abhorrence. ORIG C16: from F *révolter,* from OIt. *rivoltare* to overturn, ult. from L *revolvere* to roll back

revolting (rɪ'vəʊltɪŋ) *adj* **1** causing revulsion; nauseating, disgusting, or repulsive. **2** *Inf.* unpleasant or nasty.
▸ **re'voltingly** *adv*

revolute ('rɛvəˌluːt) *adj* (esp. of the margins of a leaf) rolled backwards and downwards. ORIG C18: from L *revolūtus* rolled back; see REVOLVE

revolution (ˌrɛvə'luːʃən) *n* **1** the overthrow or repudiation of a regime or political system by the governed. **2** (in Marxist theory) the inevitable, violent transition from one system of production in a society to the next. **3** a far-reaching and drastic change, esp. in ideas, methods, etc. **4a** movement in or as if in a circle. **4b** one complete turn in such a circle: *33 revolutions per minute.* **5a** the orbital motion of one body, such as a planet, around another. **5b** one complete turn in such motion. **6** a cycle of successive events or changes. ORIG C14: via OF from LL *revolūtiō,* from L *revolvere* to REVOLVE

revolutionary (ˌrɛvə'luːʃənərɪ) *n, pl* **revolutionaries. 1** a person who advocates or engages in revolution. ◆ *adj* **2** relating to or characteristic of a revolution. **3** advocating or engaged in revolution. **4** radically new or different: *a revolutionary method of making plastics.*

Revolutionary (ˌrɛvə'luːʃənərɪ) *adj* **1** *Chiefly US.* of or relating to the War of American Independence (1775–83). **2** of or relating to any of various other Revolutions, esp. the **Russian Revolution** (1917) or the **French Revolution** (1789).

revolutionist (ˌrɛvə'luːʃənɪst) *n* **1** a less common word for a **revolutionary.** ◆ *adj* **2** of or relating to revolution or revolutionaries.

revolutionize *or* **revolutionise** (ˌrɛvə'luːʃəˌnaɪz) *vb* **revolutionizes, revolutionizing, revolutionized** *or* **revolutionises, revolutionising, revolutionised.** (*tr*) **1** to bring about a radical change in: *science has revolutionized civilization.* **2** to inspire or infect with revolutionary ideas: *they revolutionized the common soldiers.* **3** to cause a revolution in (a country, etc.).
▸ **ˌrevo'lutionˌizer** *or* **ˌrevo'lutionˌiser** *n*

revolve (rɪ'vɒlv) *vb* **revolves, revolving, revolved. 1** to move or cause to move around a centre or axis; rotate. **2** (*intr*) to occur periodically or in cycles. **3** to consider or be considered. **4** (*intr;* foll. by *around* or *about*) to be centred or focused (upon): *Juliet's thoughts revolved around Romeo.* ◆ *n* **5** *Theatre.* a circular section of a stage that can be rotated by electric power to provide a scene change. ORIG C14: from L *revolvere,* from RE- + *volvere* to roll, wind
▸ **re'volvable** *adj*

revolver (rɪ'vɒlvə) *n* a pistol having a revolving multichambered cylinder that allows several shots to be discharged without reloading.

revolving (rɪ'vɒlvɪŋ) *adj* **1** moving round a central axis: *revolving door.* **2** (of a fund) constantly added to from income from its investments to offset outgoing payments. **3** (of a letter of credit, loan, etc.) available to be repeatedly drawn on by the beneficiary provided that a specified amount is never exceeded.

revue (rɪ'vjuː) *n* a light entertainment consisting of topical sketches, songs, dancing, etc. ORIG C20: from F; see REVIEW

revulsion (rɪ'vʌlʃən) *n* **1** a sudden violent reaction in feeling, esp. one of extreme loathing. **2** the act or an instance of drawing back or recoiling from something. **3** the diversion of disease from one part of the body to another by cupping, counterirritants, etc. ORIG C16: from L *revulsiō* a pulling away, from *revellere,* from RE- + *vellere* to pull, tear

revulsive (rɪ'vʌlsɪv) *adj* **1** of or causing revulsion. ◆ *n* **2** *Med.* a counterirritant.
▸ **re'vulsively** *adv*

reward (rɪ'wɔːd) *n* **1** something given in return for a deed or service rendered. **2** a sum of money offered, esp. for help in finding a criminal or for the return of lost or stolen property. **3** profit or return. **4** something received in return for good or evil; deserts. ◆ *vb* **5** (*tr*) to give something to (someone), esp. in gratitude for (a service rendered); recompense. ORIG C14: from OF *rewarder,* from RE- + *warder* to care for, guard, of Gmc origin
▸ **re'wardless** *adj*

reward claim *n Austral. history.* a claim granted to a miner who discovered gold in a new area.

rewarding (rɪ'wɔːdɪŋ) *adj* giving personal satisfaction; gratifying.

rewa-rewa ('reɪwə'reɪwə) *n* a tall tree of New Zealand, yielding reddish timber. ORIG C19: from Maori

rewind *vb* (riː'waɪnd), **rewinds, rewinding, rewound. 1** (*tr*) to wind back, esp. a film or tape onto the original reel. ◆ *n* ('riːˌwaɪnd, riː'waɪnd). **2** something rewound. **3** the act of rewinding.
▸ **re'winder** *n*

rewire (riː'waɪə) *vb* **rewires, rewiring, rewired.** (*tr*) to provide (a house, engine, etc.) with new wiring.
▸ **re'wirable** *adj*

reword (riː'wɜːd) *vb* (*tr*) to alter the wording of; express differently.

rework (riː'wɜːk) *vb* (*tr*) **1** to use again in altered form. **2** to rewrite or revise. **3** to reprocess for use again.

rewrite *vb* (riː'raɪt), **rewrites, rewriting, rewrote, rewritten.** (*tr*) **1** to write (material) again, esp. changing the words or form. ◆ *n* ('riːˌraɪt). **2** *Computing.* to return (data) to a store when it has been erased during reading. **3** something rewritten.

Rex (rɛks) *n* king: part of the official title of a king, now used chiefly in documents, legal proceedings, on coins, etc. Cf. **Regina**[1]. ORIG L

Rexine ('rɛksiːn) *n Trademark.* a form of artificial leather.

Reye's syndrome (raɪz, reɪz) *n* a rare metabolic disease in children that can be fatal, involving damage to the brain, liver, and kidneys. ORIG C20: after R.D.K. *Reye* (1912–78), Austral. paediatrician

Reykjavik ★ ('reɪkjəˌviːk) *n* the capital and chief port of Iceland, situated in the southwest: its buildings are heated by natural hot water. Pop.: 105 487 (1996 est.).

Reynard *or* **Renard** ('rɛnəd, 'rɛnɑːd) *n* a name for a fox, used in fables, etc.

Reynaud ★ (*French* rɛno) *n* **Paul** (pɔl). 1878–1966, French statesman: premier during the defeat of France by Germany (1940); later imprisoned by the Germans.

Reynolds ★ ('rɛnəldz) *n* **1 Albert.** born 1935, Irish politician: prime minister of the Republic of Ireland (1994–96). **2** Sir **Joshua.** 1723–92, British portrait painter; first president of the Royal Academy (1768).

Reynosa ★ (*Spanish* re'nosa) *n* a city in E Mexico, in Tamaulipas state on the Rio Grande. Pop.: 265 663 (1990).

RF *abbrev. for* radio frequency.

RFC *abbrev. for:* **1** Royal Flying Corps. **2** Rugby Football Club.

RGN (in Britain) *abbrev. for* Registered General Nurse.

RGS *abbrev. for* Royal Geographical Society.

rh *or* **RH** *abbrev. for* right hand.

Rh 1 *the chemical symbol for* rhodium. ◆ **2** *abbrev. for* rhesus (esp. in **Rh factor**).

RHA *abbrev. for:* **1** Regional Health Authority. **2** Royal Horse Artillery.

rhabdomancy ('ræbdəˌmænsɪ) *n* divination for water or mineral ore by means of a rod or wand. ORIG C17: via LL from LGk *rhabdomanteia,* from Gk *rhabdos* rod + *manteia* divination
▸ **'rhabdoˌmantist** *or* **'rhabdoˌmancer** *n*

rhachis ('reɪkɪs) *n, pl* **rhachises** *or* **rhachides** ('rækɪˌdiːz, 'reɪ-). a variant spelling of **rachis.**

Rhadamanthus *or* **Rhadamanthys** ★ (ˌrædə'mænθəs) *n Greek myth.* one of the judges of the dead in the underworld.
▸ **ˌRhada'manthine** *adj*

Rhaetia ★ ('riːʃɪə) *n* an Alpine province of ancient Rome including parts of present-day Tyrol and E Switzerland.
▸ **'Rhaetian** *adj, n*

Rhaetian Alps ★ *pl n* a section of the central Alps along E Switzerland's borders with Austria and Italy. Highest peak: Piz Bernina, 4049 m (13 284 ft).

rhapsodic (ræp'sɒdɪk) *adj* **1** of or like a rhapsody. **2** lyrical or romantic.

rhapsodize *or* **rhapsodise** ('ræpsəˌdaɪz) *vb* **rhapsodizes, rhapsodizing, rhapsodized** *or* **rhapsodises, rhapsodising, rhapsodised. 1** to speak or write (something) with extravagant enthusiasm. **2** (*intr*) to recite or write rhapsodies.
▸ **'rhapsodist** *n*

rhapsody ('ræpsədɪ) *n, pl* **rhapsodies. 1** *Music.* a composition free in structure and highly emotional in character. **2** an expression of ecstatic enthusiasm. **3** (in ancient Greece) an epic poem or part of an epic recited by a rhapsodist. **4** a literary work composed in an intense or exalted style. **5** rapturous delight or ecstasy. ORIG C16: via L from Gk *rhapsōidia,* from *rhaptein* to sew together + *ōidē* song

rhatany ('rætənɪ) *n, pl* **rhatanies. 1** either of two South American leguminous shrubs that have thick fleshy roots. **2** the dried roots used as an astringent. ◆ Also called: **krameria.** ORIG C19: from NL *rhatānia,* ult. from Quechua *ratánya*

rhea (rɪə) *n* either of two large fast-running flightless birds inhabiting the open plains of S South America. They are similar to but smaller than the ostrich. ORIG C19: NL; arbitrarily after RHEA

Rhea ★ ('rɪə) *n Greek myth.* a Titaness, wife of Cronus and mother of several of the gods, including Zeus: a fertility goddess. Roman counterpart: **Ops.**

Rhea Silvia *or* **Rea Silvia** ★ ('sɪlvɪə) *n Roman myth.* the mother of Romulus and Remus by Mars. See also **Ilia.**

rhebuck *or* **rhebok** ('riːbʌk) *n, pl* **rhebucks, rhebuck** *or* **rheboks, rhebok.** an antelope of southern Africa, having woolly brownish-grey hair. ORIG C18: Afrik., from Du. *reebok* ROEBUCK

Rhee ★ (riː) *n* **Syngman** ('sɪŋmən). 1875–1965, Korean statesman, leader of the campaign for independence from Japan; first president of South Korea (1948–60).

Rheims ★ (riːmz; *French* rɛ̃s) *n* a variant spelling of **Reims.**

Rhein ★ (rain) *n* the German name for the **Rhine.**

Rheinland ★ ('rainlant) *n* the German name for the **Rhineland.**

Rheinland-Pfalz ★ ('raɪnlant'pfalts) *n* the German name for **Rhineland-Palatinate.**

Rhenish ('rɛnɪʃ, 'riː-) *adj* **1** of or relating to the River Rhine or the lands adjacent to it. ◆ *n* **2** another word for **hock**[2].

rhenium ('riːnɪəm) *n* a dense silvery-white metallic element that has a high melting point. Symbol: Re; atomic

★ people and places

no.: 75; atomic wt.: 186.2. ORIG C19: NL, from *Rhēnus* the Rhine

rheo- *combining form.* indicating stream, flow, or current: *rheostat.* ORIG from Gk *rheos* stream, anything flowing, from *rhein* to flow

rheology (rɪˈɒlədʒɪ) *n* the branch of physics concerned with the flow and change of shape of matter, esp. the viscosity of liquids.
▸ **rheological** (ˌriːəˈlɒdʒɪkᵊl) *adj* ▸ **rheˈologist** *n*

rheostat (ˈrɪəˌstæt) *n* a variable resistance, usually a coil of wire with a terminal at one end and a sliding contact that moves along the coil to tap off the current.
▸ **ˌrheoˈstatic** *adj*

Rhesus ★ (ˈriːsəs) *n Greek myth.* a king of Thrace, who arrived in the tenth year of the Trojan War to aid Troy. Odysseus and Diomedes stole his horses because an oracle had said that if they drank from the River Xanthus, Troy would not fall.

rhesus baby (ˈriːsəs) *n* a baby suffering from haemolytic disease at birth as its red blood cells (which are Rh positive) have been attacked in the womb by antibodies from its Rh negative mother. ORIG C20: see RH FACTOR

rhesus factor *n* See **Rh factor.**

rhesus monkey *n* a macaque monkey of S Asia. ORIG C19: NL, arbitrarily from Gk *Rhesos,* mythical Thracian king

rhetoric (ˈrɛtərɪk) *n* **1** the study of the technique of using language effectively. **2** the art of using speech to persuade, influence, or please; oratory. **3** excessive ornamentation and contrivance in spoken or written discourse; bombast. **4** speech or discourse that pretends to significance but lacks true meaning: *mere rhetoric.* ORIG C14: via L from Gk *rhētorikē* (*tekhnē*) (the art of) rhetoric, from *rhētōr* teacher of rhetoric, orator

rhetorical (rɪˈtɒrɪkᵊl) *adj* **1** concerned with effect or style rather than content or meaning; bombastic. **2** of or relating to rhetoric or oratory.
▸ **rheˈtorically** *adv*

rhetorical question *n* a question to which no answer is required: used esp. for dramatic effect. An example is *Who knows?* (with the implication *Nobody knows*).

rhetorician (ˌrɛtəˈrɪʃən) *n* **1** a teacher of rhetoric. **2** a stylish or eloquent writer or speaker. **3** a pompous or extravagant speaker.

rheum (ruːm) *n* a watery discharge from the eyes or nose. ORIG C14: from OF *reume,* ult. from Gk *rheuma* bodily humour, stream, from *rhein* to flow
▸ **ˈrheumy** *adj*

rheumatic (ruːˈmætɪk) *adj* **1** of, relating to, or afflicted with rheumatism. ◆ *n* **2** a person afflicted with rheumatism. ORIG C14: ult. from Gk *rheumatikos,* from *rheuma* a flow; see RHEUM
▸ **rheuˈmatically** *adv*

rheumatic fever *n* a disease characterized by inflammation and pain in the joints.

rheumatics (ruːˈmætɪks) *n* (*functioning as sing*) *Inf.* rheumatism.

rheumatism (ˈruːməˌtɪzəm) *n* any painful disorder of joints, muscles, or connective tissue. ORIG C17: from L *rheumatismus* catarrh, from Gk *rheumatismos;* see RHEUM

rheumatoid (ˈruːməˌtɔɪd) *adj* (of symptoms) resembling rheumatism.

rheumatoid arthritis *n* a chronic disease characterized by inflammation and swelling of joints (esp. in the hands, wrists, knees, and feet), muscle weakness, and fatigue.

rheumatology (ˌruːməˈtɒlədʒɪ) *n* the study of rheumatic diseases.
▸ **rheumatological** (ˌruːmətəˈlɒdʒɪkᵊl) *adj*

Rh factor *n* an antigen commonly found in human blood: the terms **Rh positive** and **Rh negative** are used to indicate its presence or absence. It may cause a haemolytic reaction, esp. during pregnancy or following transfusion of blood that does not contain this antigen. Full name: **rhesus factor.** ORIG after the rhesus monkey, in which it was first discovered

rhinal (ˈraɪnᵊl) *adj* of or relating to the nose.

Rhine ★ (raɪn) *n* a river in central and W Europe, rising in SE Switzerland: flows through Lake Constance north through W Germany and west through the Netherlands to the North Sea. Length: about 1320 km (820 miles). Dutch name: **Rijn.** French name: **Rhin** (rɛ̃). German name: **Rhein.**

Rhineland ★ (ˈraɪnˌlænd, -lənd) *n* the region of W Germany surrounding the Rhine. German name: **Rheinland.**

Rhineland-Palatinate ★ *n* a state of W Germany: formed in 1946 from the S part of the Prussian Rhine province, the Palatinate, and parts of Rhine-Hesse and Hesse-Nassau; part of West Germany until 1990: agriculture and tourism are important. Capital: Mainz. Pop.: 3 983 300 (1996 est.). Area: 19 832 sq. km (7657 sq. miles). German name: **Rheinland-Pfalz.**

Rhine Palatinate ★ *n* See **Palatinate.**

rhinestone (ˈraɪnˌstəʊn) *n* an imitation gem made of paste. ORIG C19: translation of F *caillou du Rhin,* referring to Strasbourg, where such gems were made

Rhine wine (raɪn) *n* any wine produced along the Rhine, characteristically a white table wine.

rhinitis (raɪˈnaɪtɪs) *n* inflammation of the mucous membrane that lines the nose.
▸ **rhinitic** (raɪˈnɪtɪk) *adj*

rhino[1] (ˈraɪnəʊ) *n, pl* **rhinos** *or* **rhino.** short for **rhinoceros.**

rhino[2] (ˈraɪnəʊ) *n Brit.* a slang word for **money.** ORIG C17: from ?

rhino- *or before a vowel* **rhin-** *combining form.* the nose: *rhinology.* ORIG from Gk *rhis, rhin*

rhinoceros (raɪˈnɒsərəs, -ˈnɒsrəs) *n, pl* **rhinoceroses** *or* **rhinoceros.** any of several mammals constituting a family of SE Asia and Africa and having either one horn on the nose, like the **Indian rhinoceros,** or two horns, like the African **white rhinoceros.** They have a very thick skin and a massive body. ORIG C13: via L from Gk *rhinokerōs,* from *rhis* nose + *keras* horn
▸ **rhinocerotic** (ˌraɪnəʊsɪˈrɒtɪk) *adj*

rhinology (raɪˈnɒlədʒɪ) *n* the branch of medical science concerned with the nose.
▸ **rhinological** (ˌraɪnᵊˈlɒdʒɪkᵊl) *adj* ▸ **rhiˈnologist** *n*

rhinoplasty (ˈraɪnəʊˌplæstɪ) *n* plastic surgery of the nose.
▸ **ˌrhinoˈplastic** *adj*

rhinoscopy (raɪˈnɒskəpɪ) *n Med.* examination of the nasal passages, esp. with a special instrument called a **rhinoscope** (ˈraɪnəʊˌskəʊp).

rhizo- *or before a vowel* **rhiz-** *combining form.* root: *rhizocarpous.* ORIG from Gk *rhiza*

rhizocarpous (ˌraɪzəʊˈkɑːpəs) *adj* **1** (of plants) producing subterranean flowers and fruit. **2** (of plants) having perennial roots but stems and leaves that wither.

rhizoid (ˈraɪzɔɪd) *n* any of various hairlike structures that function as roots in mosses, ferns, and fungi.
▸ **rhiˈzoidal** *adj*

rhizome (ˈraɪzəʊm) *n* a thick horizontal underground stem whose buds develop into new plants. Also called: **rootstock, rootstalk.** ORIG C19: from NL *rhizoma,* from Gk, from *rhiza* a root
▸ **rhizomatous** (raɪˈzɒmətəs, -ˈzəʊ-) *adj*

rhizopod (ˈraɪzəʊˌpɒd) *n* **1** any of various protozoans characterized by naked protoplasmic processes (pseudopodia). ◆ *adj* **2** of, relating to, or belonging to rhizopods.

rho (rəʊ) *n, pl* **rhos.** the 17th letter in the Greek alphabet (Ρ, ρ).

rhodamine (ˈrəʊdəˌmiːn, -mɪn) *n* any one of a group of synthetic red or pink basic dyestuffs used for wool and silk. ORIG C20: from RHODO- + AMINE

Rhode Island ★ (rəʊd) *n* a state of the northeastern US, bordering on the Atlantic: the smallest state in the US; mainly low-lying and undulating, with an indented coastline in the east and uplands in the northwest. Capital: Providence. Pop.: 988 480 (1998 est.). Area: 2717 sq. km (1049 sq. miles). Abbrevs.: **R.I.** or (with zip code) **RI**

Rhode Island Red *n* a breed of domestic fowl, originating in America, characterized by a dark reddish-brown plumage and the production of brown eggs.

Rhodes[1] ★ *n* (rəʊdz) **1** a Greek island in the SE Aegean Sea, about 16 km (10 miles) off the Turkish coast: the largest of the Dodecanese and the most easterly island in the Aegean. Capital: Rhodes. Pop.: 41 000 (latest est.). Area: 1400 sq. km (540 sq. miles). **2** a port on this island, in the NE: founded in 408 B.C.; of great commercial and political importance in the 3rd century B.C.; suffered several earthquakes, notably in 225, when the Colossus was destroyed. Pop.: 40 656 (1981). ◆ Ancient Greek name: **Rhodos.** Modern Greek name: **Ródhos.**

Rhodes[2] ★ (rəʊdz) *n* **1 Cecil John.** 1853–1902, British colonial financier and statesman in South Africa; as prime minister of the Cape Colony (1890–96), he helped to extend British territory. He established the annual Rhodes scholarships. **2 Gary.** born 1960, British chef and presenter of television cookery programmes.

Rhodesia ★ (rəʊ'di:ʃə, -zɪə) *n* a former name (1964–79) for **Zimbabwe.**
▸ **Rho'desian** *adj, n*

Rhodesia and Nyasaland ★ *n* **Federation of.** a federation consisting of Northern Rhodesia, Southern Rhodesia, and Nyasaland, which existed from 1953 to 1963.

Rhodesian man *n* a type of early man, occurring in Africa in late Pleistocene times and resembling Neanderthal man.

Rhodes scholarship (rəʊdz) *n* one of 72 scholarships founded by Cecil Rhodes, awarded annually to Commonwealth and US students to study at Oxford University.
▸ **Rhodes scholar** *n*

Rhodian ('rəʊdɪən) *adj* **1** of or relating to the island of Rhodes. ◆ *n* **2** a native or inhabitant of Rhodes.

rhodium ('rəʊdɪəm) *n* a hard silvery-white element of the platinum metal group. Used as an alloying agent to harden platinum and palladium. Symbol: Rh; atomic no.: 45; atomic wt.: 102.90. ORIG C19: NL, from Gk *rhodon* rose, from the pink colour of its compounds

rhodo- *or before a vowel* **rhod-** *combining form.* rose or rose-coloured: *rhododendron; rhodolite.* ORIG from Gk *rhodon* rose

rhodochrosite (ˌrəʊdəʊ'krəʊsaɪt) *n* a pink, grey, or brown mineral that consists of manganese carbonate in hexagonal crystalline form. Formula: $MnCO_3$. ORIG C19: from Gk *rhodokhrōs,* from *rhodon* rose + *khrōs* colour

rhododendron (ˌrəʊdə'dɛndrən) *n* any of various shrubs native to S Asia but widely cultivated in N temperate regions. They are mostly evergreen and have clusters of showy red, purple, pink, or white flowers. ORIG C17: from L: oleander, from Gk, from *rhodon* rose + *dendron* tree

rhodolite ('rɒdəˌlaɪt) *n* a pale violet or red variety of garnet, used as a gemstone.

rhodonite ('rɒdəˌnaɪt) *n* a brownish translucent mineral consisting of manganese silicate in crystalline form with calcium, iron, or magnesium sometimes replacing the manganese. It is used as an ornamental stone, glaze, and pigment. ORIG C19: from G *Rhodonit,* from Gk *rhodon* rose + -ITE[1]

Rhodope Mountains ★ ('rɒdəpɪ, rɒ'dəʊ-) *pl n* a mountain range in SE Europe, in the Balkan Peninsula extending along the border between Bulgaria and Greece. Highest peak: Golyam Perelik (Bulgaria), 2191 m (7188 ft).

rhodopsin (rəʊ'dɒpsɪn) *n* a red pigment in the rods of the retina in vertebrates. Also called: **visual purple.** See also **iodopsin.** ORIG C20: from RHODO- + Gk *opsis* sight + -IN

Rhodos ★ ('rɔðɔs) *n* the Ancient Greek name for **Rhodes**[1].

rhomb (rɒm) *n* another name for **rhombus.**

rhombencephalon (ˌrɒmbɛn'sɛfəˌlɒn) *n* the part of the brain that develops from the posterior portion of the embryonic neural tube. Nontechnical name: **hindbrain.** ORIG C20: from RHOMBUS + ENCEPHALON

rhombic aerial *n* a directional travelling-wave aerial, usually horizontal, consisting of two conductors forming a rhombus.

rhombohedral (ˌrɒmbəʊ'hi:drəl) *adj* **1** of or relating to a rhombohedron. **2** *Crystallog.* another term for **trigonal** (sense 2).

rhombohedron (ˌrɒmbəʊ'hi:drən) *n, pl* **rhombohedrons** *or* **rhombohedra** (-drə). a six-sided prism whose sides are parallelograms. ORIG C19: from RHOMBUS + -HEDRON

rhomboid ('rɒmbɔɪd) *n* **1** a parallelogram having adjacent sides of unequal length. ◆ *adj also* **rhom'boidal.** **2** having such a shape. ORIG C16: from LL, from Gk *rhomboeidēs* shaped like a RHOMBUS

rhombus ('rɒmbəs) *n, pl* **rhombuses** *or* **rhombi** (-baɪ). an oblique-angled parallelogram having four equal sides. Also called: **rhomb.** ORIG C16: from Gk *rhombos* something that spins; rel. to *rhembein* to whirl
▸ **'rhombic** *adj*

rhonchus ('rɒŋkəs) *n, pl* **rhonchi** (-kaɪ). a rattling or whistling respiratory sound resembling snoring, caused by secretions in the trachea or bronchi. ORIG C19: from L, from Gk *rhenkhos* snoring

Rhondda ★ ('rɒndə) *n* an urbanized region in S Wales, on two branches of the **Rhondda Valley**: developed into a major coal-mining centre after 1807 and grew to a population of 167 900 in 1924: the last mine closed in 1990. Pop.: 59 947 (1991).

Rhondda Cynon Taff ★ ('kʌnən tæf) *n* a county borough in S Wales, created in 1996. Pop.: 232 581 (1996 est.). Area: 558 sq. km (215 sq. miles).

Rhône ★ (rəʊn) *n* **1** a river in W Europe, rising in S Switzerland in the **Rhône glacier** and flowing to Lake Geneva, then into France through gorges between the Alps and Jura and south to its delta on the Gulf of Lions: important esp. for hydroelectricity and for wine production along its valley. Length: 812 km (505 miles). **2** a department of E central France, in the Rhône-Alpes region. Capital: Lyons. Pop.: 1 558 869 (1994 est.). Area: 3233 sq. km (1261 sq. miles).

Rhône-Alpes ★ (*French* ronalp) *n* a region of E France: mainly mountainous, rising to the edge of the Massif Central in the west and the French Alps in the east; drained by the Rivers Rhône, Saône, and Isère.

RHS *abbrev. for:* **1** Royal Historical Society. **2** Royal Horticultural Society. **3** Royal Humane Society.

rhubarb ('ru:bɑ:b) *n* **1** any of several temperate and subtropical plants, esp. **common garden rhubarb,** which has long green and red acid-tasting edible leafstalks, usually eaten sweetened and cooked. **2** the leafstalks of this plant. **3** a related plant of central Asia, having a bitter-tasting underground stem that can be dried and used as a laxative or astringent. **4** *US & Canad. sl.* a heated discussion or quarrel. ◆ *interj, n, vb* **5** the noise made by actors to simulate conversation, esp. by repeating the word *rhubarb.* ORIG C14: from OF *reubarbe,* from Med. L *reubarbum,* prob. var. of *rha barbarum,* from *rha* rhubarb (from Gk, ?from *Rha,* ancient name of the Volga) + L *barbarus* barbarian

rhumb (rʌm) *n* short for **rhumb line.**

rhumba ('rʌmbə, 'rum-) *n, pl* **rhumbas.** a variant spelling of **rumba.**

rhumb line *n* **1** an imaginary line on the surface of a sphere that intersects all meridians at the same angle. **2** the course navigated by a vessel or aircraft that maintains a uniform compass heading. ORIG C16: from OSp. *rumbo,* apparently from MDu. *ruum* space, ship's hold, infl. by RHOMBUS

rhyme *or (arch.)* **rime** (raɪm) *n* **1** identity of the terminal sounds in lines of verse or in words. **2** a word that is identical to another in its terminal sound: *"while" is a rhyme for "mile".* **3** a piece of poetry, esp. having corresponding sounds at the ends of the lines. **4 rhyme or reason.** sense, logic, or meaning. ◆ *vb* **rhymes, rhyming, rhymed** *or* **rimes, riming, rimed.** **5** to use (a word) or (of a word) to be used so as to form a rhyme. **6** to render (a subject) into rhyme. **7** to compose (verse) in a metrical structure. ◆ See also **eye rhyme.** ORIG C12: from OF *rime,* ult. from OHG *rīm* a number; spelling infl. by RHYTHM

rhymester, rimester ('raɪmstə), **rhymer,** *or* **rimer** *n* a poet, esp. one considered to be mediocre; poetaster or versifier.

rhyming slang *n* slang in which a word is replaced by another word or phrase that rhymes with it; e.g. *apples and pears* meaning *stairs.*

rhyolite ('raɪəˌlaɪt) *n* a fine-grained igneous rock consisting of quartz, feldspars, and mica or amphibole. ORIG C19: *rhyo-* from Gk *rhuax* a stream of lava + -LITE
▸ **rhyolitic** (ˌraɪə'lɪtɪk) *adj*

Rhys ★ (riːs) *n* **Jean (Ella Gwendolen Rees Williams).** ?1890–1979, British writer, born in Dominica. Her novels include *Wide Sargasso Sea* (1966).

rhythm ('rɪðəm) *n* **1a** the arrangement of the durations of and accents on the notes of a melody, usually laid out into regular groups (**bars**) of beats. **1b** any specific arrangement of such groupings; time: *quadruple rhythm.* **2** (in poetry) **2a** the arrangement of words into a sequence of stressed and unstressed or long and short syllables. **2b** any specific such arrangement; metre. **3** (in painting, sculpture, etc.) a harmonious sequence or pattern of masses alternating with voids, of light alternating with shade, of alternating colours, etc. **4** any sequence of regularly recurring functions or events, such as certain physiological functions of the body. ORIG C16: from L *rhythmus,* from Gk *rhuthmos;* rel. to *rhein* to flow

rhythm and blues *n* (*functioning as sing*) any of various kinds of popular music derived from or influenced by the blues. Abbrev.: **R & B.**

rhythmic ('rɪðmɪk) *or* **rhythmical** ('rɪðmɪkᵊl) *adj* of, relating to, or characterized by rhythm, as in movement or sound; metrical, periodic, or regularly recurring.
▸ **'rhythmically** *adv* ▸ **rhythmicity** (rɪð'mɪsɪtɪ) *n*

rhythm method *n* a method of contraception by restricting sexual intercourse to those days in a woman's menstrual cycle on which conception is considered least likely to occur.

rhythm section *n* those instruments in a band or group (usually piano, double bass, and drums) whose prime function is to supply the rhythm.

RI *abbrev. for:* **1** Regina et Imperatrix. ORIG L: Queen and Empress **2** Rex et Imperator. ORIG L: King and Emperor **3** Royal Institution. **4** religious instruction.

ria (rɪə) *n* a long narrow inlet of the seacoast, being a former valley that was submerged by the sea. ORIG C19: from Sp., from *rio* river

Rialto ★ (rɪ'æltəʊ) *n* an island in Venice, Italy, linked with San Marco Island by the **Rialto Bridge** (1590) over the Grand Canal: the business centre of medieval and renaissance Venice.

riata *or* **reata** (rɪ'ɑːtə) *n South & West US.* a lariat or lasso. ORIG C19: from American Sp., from Sp. *reatar* to tie together again, from RE- + *atar* to tie, from L *aptāre* to fit

rib[1] (rɪb) *n* **1** any of the 24 elastic arches of bone that together form the chest wall in man. All are attached behind to the thoracic part of the spinal column. **2** the corresponding bone in other vertebrates. **3** a cut of meat including one or more ribs. **4** a part or element similar in function or appearance to a rib, esp. a structural member or a ridge. **5** a structural member in a wing that extends from the leading edge to the trailing edge. **6** a projecting moulding or band on the underside of a vault or ceiling. **7** one of a series of raised rows in knitted fabric. **8** a raised ornamental line on the spine of a book where the stitching runs across it. **9** any of the transverse stiffening timbers or joists forming the frame of a ship's hull. **10** any of the larger veins of a leaf. **11** a vein of ore in rock. **12** a projecting ridge of a mountain; spur. ◆ *vb* **ribs, ribbing, ribbed.** (*tr*) **13** to furnish or support with a rib or ribs. **14** to mark with or form into ribs or ridges. **15** to knit plain and purl stitches alternately in order to make raised rows in (knitting). ORIG OE *ribb;* rel. to OHG *rippi,* ON *rif* REEF[1]
▸ **'ribless** *adj*

rib[2] (rɪb) *vb* **ribs, ribbing, ribbed.** (*tr*) *Inf.* to tease or ridicule. ORIG C20: short for *rib-tickle* (vb)

RIBA *abbrev. for* Royal Institute of British Architects.

ribald ('rɪbᵊld) *adj* **1** coarse, obscene, or licentious, usually in a humorous or mocking way. ◆ *n* **2** a ribald person. ORIG C13: from OF *ribauld,* from *riber* to live licentiously, of Gmc origin

ribaldry ('rɪbᵊldrɪ) *n* ribald language or behaviour.

riband *or* **ribband** ('rɪbənd) *n* a ribbon, esp. one awarded for some achievement. ORIG C14: var. of RIBBON

Ribbentrop ★ (*German* 'rɪbəntrɔp) *n* **Joachim von** ('joːaxɪm fɔn). 1893–1946, German Nazi politician: foreign minister (1938–45), hanged as a war criminal at Nuremberg.

ribbing ('rɪbɪŋ) *n* **1** a framework or structure of ribs. **2** a pattern of ribs in woven or knitted material. **3** *Inf.* teasing.

Ribble ★ ('rɪbᵊl) *n* a river in NW England, flowing south and west through Lancashire to the Irish Sea. Length: 121 km (75 miles).

ribbon ('rɪbᵊn) *n* **1** a narrow strip of fine material, esp. silk, used for trimming, tying, etc. **2** something resembling a ribbon; a long strip. **3** a long thin flexible band of metal used as a graduated measure, spring, etc. **4** a long narrow strip of ink-impregnated cloth for making the impression of type characters on paper in a typewriter, etc. **5** (*pl*) ragged strips or shreds (esp. in **torn to ribbons**). **6** a small strip of coloured cloth signifying membership of an order or award of military decoration, prize, etc. **7** a small, usually looped, strip of coloured cloth worn to signify support for a charity or cause: *a red AIDS ribbon.* ◆ *vb* (*tr*) **8** to adorn with a ribbon or ribbons. **9** to mark with narrow ribbon-like marks. ORIG C14 *ryban,* from OF *riban,* apparently of Gmc origin

ribbon development *n Brit.* the building of houses in a continuous row along a main road.

ribbonfish ('rɪbᵊnˌfɪʃ) *n, pl* **ribbonfish** *or* **ribbonfishes.** any of various soft-finned deep-sea fishes that have an elongated compressed body.

ribbonwood ('rɪbᵊnˌwʊd) *n* a small evergreen malvaceous tree of New Zealand. Its wood is used in furniture making. Also: **lacebark.**

ribcage ('rɪbˌkeɪdʒ) *n* the bony structure of the ribs and their connective tissue that encloses the lungs, heart, etc.

Ribeirão Prêto ★ (*Portuguese* riβəi'rɐ̃u 'pretu) *n* a city in SE Brazil, in São Paulo state. Pop.: 416 186 (1991).

Ribera ★ (*Spanish* ri'βera) *n* **José de** (xo'se de) also called *Jusepe de Ribera,* Italian nickname *Lo Spagnoletto* (The Little Spaniard). 1591–1652, Spanish artist, living in Italy.

riboflavin *or* **riboflavine** (ˌraɪbəʊ'fleɪvɪn) *n* a vitamin of the B complex that occurs in green vegetables, milk, fish, egg yolk, liver, and kidney: used as a yellow or orange food colouring (**E 101**). Also called: **vitamin B_2.** ORIG C20: from RIBOSE + FLAVIN

ribonuclease (ˌraɪbəʊ'njuːklɪˌeɪz) *n* any of a group of enzymes that catalyse the hydrolysis of RNA. ORIG C20: from RIBONUCLE(IC ACID) + -ASE

ribonucleic acid (ˌraɪbəʊnjuː'kliːɪk, -'kleɪ-) *n* the full name of **RNA.** ORIG C20: from RIBO(SE) + NUCLEIC ACID

ribose ('raɪbəʊz, -bəʊs) *n* a sugar that occurs in RNA and riboflavin. ORIG C20: changed from *arabinose,* from (GUM) ARAB(IC) + -IN+ -OSE[2]

ribosomal RNA (ˌraɪbə'səʊməl) *n* a type of RNA thought to form the component of ribosomes on which the translation of messenger RNA into protein chains is accomplished.

ribosome ('raɪbəˌsəʊm) *n* any of numerous minute particles in the cytoplasm of cells that contain RNA and protein and are the site of protein synthesis. ORIG C20: from RIBO(NUCLEIC ACID) + -SOME[3]
▸ **ˌribo'somal** *adj*

rib-tickler *n* a very amusing joke or story.
▸ **'rib-ˌtickling** *adj*

ribwort ('rɪbˌwɜːt) *n* a Eurasian plant that has lancelike ribbed leaves. Also called: **ribgrass.** See also **plantain**[1].

Ricardo ★ (rɪ'kɑːdəʊ) *n* **David.** 1772–1823, British economist. His main work is *Principles of Political Economy and Taxation* (1817).
▸ **Ri'cardian** *adj, n*

Riccio ★ ('rɪtsɪəʊ) *n* a variant of **Rizzio.**

rice (raɪs) *n* **1** an erect grass that grows in warm climates on wet ground and has yellow oblong edible grains that become white when polished. **2** the grain of this plant. ◆ *vb* **rices, ricing, riced. 3** (*tr*) *US & Canad.* to sieve (potatoes or other vegetables) to a coarse mashed consistency. ORIG C13 *rys,* via F, It., & L from Gk *orūza,* of Oriental origin

Rice ★ (raɪs) *n* **Elmer,** original name *Elmer Reizenstein.* 1892–1967, US dramatist. His plays include *Street Scene* (1929).

rice bowl *n* **1** a small bowl used for eating rice. **2** a fertile rice-producing region.

rice paper *n* **1** a thin edible paper made from the straw of rice, on which macaroons and similar cakes are baked. **2** a thin delicate Chinese paper made from the **rice-paper plant**, the pith of which is pared and flattened into sheets.

ricercare (ˌriːtʃəˈkɑːreɪ) *or* **ricercar** (ˈriːtʃəˌkɑː) *n, pl* **ricercari** (-ˈkɑːriː) *or* **ricercars.** (in music of the 16th and 17th centuries) **1** an elaborate polyphonic composition making extensive use of contrapuntal imitation and usually very slow in tempo. **2** an instructive composition to illustrate instrumental technique; étude. ORIG It., lit.: to seek again

rich (rɪtʃ) *adj* **1a** well supplied with wealth, property, etc.; owning much. **1b** (*as collective n; preceded by the*): *the rich.* **2** (when *postpositive,* usually foll. by *in*) having an abundance of natural resources, minerals, etc.: *a land rich in metals.* **3** producing abundantly; fertile: *rich soil.* **4** (when *postpositive,* foll. by *in* or *with*) well supplied (with desirable qualities); abundant (in): *a country rich with cultural interest.* **5** of great worth or quality: *a rich collection of antiques.* **6** luxuriant or prolific: *a rich growth of weeds.* **7** expensively elegant, elaborate, or fine; costly: *a rich display.* **8** (of food) having a large proportion of flavoursome or fatty ingredients. **9** having a full-bodied flavour: *a rich ruby port.* **10** (of a smell) pungent or fragrant. **11** (of colour) intense or vivid; deep: *a rich red.* **12** (of sound or a voice) full, mellow, or resonant. **13** (of a fuel-air mixture) containing a relatively high proportion of fuel. **14** very amusing or ridiculous: *a rich joke.* ◆ *n* **15** See **riches.** ORIG OE *rīce* (orig. of persons: great, mighty), of Gmc origin, ult. from Celtic

Rich ★ (rɪtʃ) *n* **Buddy,** real name *Bernard Rich.* 1917–87, US jazz drummer and band leader.

Richard ★ (ˈrɪtʃəd) *n* Sir **Cliff,** real name *Harry Rodger Webb.* born 1940, British pop singer. Film musicals include *Summer Holiday* (1962).

Richard I ★ *n* nicknamed *Cœur de Lion* or *the Lion-Heart.* 1157–99, king of England (1189–99); a leader of the third crusade (joining it in 1191). On his way home, he was captured in Austria (1192) and held to ransom. After a brief return to England (1194), he spent the rest of his life in France.

Richard II ★ *n* 1367–1400, king of England (1377–99); forced to abdicate in favour of Henry Bolingbroke, who became Henry IV.

Richard III ★ *n* 1452–85, king of England (1483–85), notorious as the suspected murderer of his two young nephews in the Tower of London; killed at the battle of Bosworth.

Richards ★ (ˈrɪtʃədz) *n* **1 I**(**vor**) **A**(**rmstrong**). 1893–1979, British critic and linguist, who, with C. K. Ogden, wrote *The Meaning of Meaning* (1923) and devised Basic English. **2** Sir **Gordon.** 1904–86, British jockey. **3** Sir (**Isaac**) **Viv**(**ian Alexander**). born 1952, West Indian cricketer; captain of the West Indies (1985–91).

Richardson ★ (ˈrɪtʃədsən) *n* **1 Henry Handel.** pen name of *Ethel Florence Lindesay Richardson,* 1870–1946, Australian novelist; author of the trilogy *The Fortunes of Richard Mahony* (1917–29). **2** Sir **Owen Willans.** 1879–1959, British physicist; a pioneer in atomic physics: Nobel prize for physics 1928. **3** Sir **Ralph** (**David**). 1902–83, British actor. **4 Samuel.** 1689–1761, British novelist. His novels include *Pamela* (1740) and *Clarissa* (1747).

Richelieu ★ (ˈrɪʃəˌljɜː; *French* riʃəljø) *n* **Armand Jean du Plessis** (armɑ̃ ʒɑ̃ dy plɛsi). 1585–1642, French statesman and cardinal, principal minister to Louis XIII and virtual ruler of France (1624–42).

Richelieu River ★ *n* a river in E Canada, in S Quebec, rising in Lake Champlain and flowing north to the St Lawrence River. Length: 338 km (210 miles).

riches (ˈrɪtʃɪz) *pl n* wealth; an abundance of money, valuable possessions, or property.

Richler ★ (ˈrɪʃlə) *n* **Mordecai.** born 1931, Canadian novelist. His novels include *Joshua Now and Then* (1981) and *Barney's Version* (1997).

richly (ˈrɪtʃlɪ) *adv* **1** in a rich or elaborate manner: *a richly decorated carving.* **2** fully and appropriately: *he was richly rewarded.*

Richmond ★ (ˈrɪtʃmənd) *n* **1** a borough of Greater London, on the River Thames: formed in 1965 by the amalgamation of Barnes, Richmond, and Twickenham; site of Hampton Court Palace and the Royal Botanic Gardens at Kew. Pop.: 172 000 (1994 est.). Area: 55 sq. km (21 sq. miles). Official name: **Richmond-upon-Thames. 2** a town in N England, in North Yorkshire: Norman castle. Pop.: 7862 (1991). **3** a port in E Virginia, the state capital, at the falls of the James River: developed after the establishment of a trading post (1637); scene of the Virginia Conventions of 1774 and 1775; Confederate capital in the American Civil War. Pop.: 201 108 (1994 est.). **4** a county of SW New York City: coextensive with Staten Island borough; consists of Staten Island and several smaller islands.

richness (ˈrɪtʃnɪs) *n* **1** the state or quality of being rich. **2** *Ecology.* the number of individuals of a species in a given area.

Richter ★ *n* **1** (ˈrɪktə). **Burton.** born 1931, US physicist; shared Nobel prize for physics (1976), for discovery of the J/psi particle. **2** (*German* ˈrɪçtər). **Johann Friedrich** (joˈhan ˈfriːdrɪç), wrote under the name *Jean Paul.* 1763–1825, German novelist. His works include *Titan* (1800–03). **3** (*Russian* ˈrixtɪr). **Sviatoslav** (svɪtaˈslaf). 1915–97, Ukrainian pianist.

Richter scale (ˈrɪxtə) *n* a scale for expressing the magnitude of an earthquake, ranging from 0 to over 8. ORIG C20: after Charles *Richter* (1900–85), US seismologist

Richthofen ★ (*German* ˈrɪçthoːfən) *n* Baron **Manfred von** (ˈmanfreːt fɔn), nickname *the Red Baron.* 1892–1918, German aviator; commander during World War I of the 11th Chasing Squadron (**Richthofen's Flying Circus**); shot down after 80 victories.

rick[1] (rɪk) *n* **1** a large stack of hay, corn, etc., built in a regular-shaped pile, esp. with a thatched top. ◆ *vb* **2** (*tr*) to stack into ricks. ORIG OE *hrēac*

rick[2] (rɪk) *n* **1** a wrench or sprain, as of the back. ◆ *vb* **2** (*tr*) to wrench or sprain (a joint, a limb, the back, etc.). ORIG C18: var. of *wrick*

rickets (ˈrɪkɪts) *n* (*functioning as sing or pl*) a disease mainly of children, characterized by softening of developing bone, and hence bow legs, caused by a deficiency of vitamin D. ORIG C17: from ?

rickettsia (rɪˈkɛtsɪə) *n, pl* **rickettsiae** (-sɪˌiː) *or* **rickettsias.** any of a group of parasitic microorganisms, that live in the tissues of ticks, mites, etc., and cause disease when transmitted to man. ORIG C20: after Howard T. *Ricketts* (1871–1910), US pathologist
▸ **rickˈettsial** *adj*

rickettsial disease *n* any of several acute infectious diseases, such as typhus, caused by ticks, mites, or body lice infected with rickettsiae.

rickety (ˈrɪkɪtɪ) *adj* **1** (of a structure, piece of furniture, etc.) likely to collapse or break. **2** feeble. **3** resembling or afflicted with rickets. ORIG C17: from RICKETS
▸ **ˈricketiness** *n*

rickrack *or* **ricrac** (ˈrɪkˌræk) *n* a zigzag braid used for trimming. ORIG C20: reduplication of RACK[1]

rickshaw (ˈrɪkʃɔː) *or* **ricksha** (ˈrɪkʃə) *n* **1** Also called: **jinrikisha.** a small two-wheeled passenger vehicle drawn by one or two men, used in parts of Asia. **2** Also called: **trishaw.** a similar vehicle with three wheels, propelled by a man pedalling as on a tricycle. ORIG C19: shortened from JINRIKISHA

ricochet ('rɪkəˌʃeɪ, 'rɪkəˌʃɛt) *vb* **ricochets** (-ˌʃeɪz), **ricocheting** (-ˌʃeɪɪŋ), **ricocheted** (-ˌʃeɪd) *or* **ricochets** (-ˌʃɛts), **ricochetting** (-ˌʃɛtɪŋ), **ricochetted** (-ˌʃɛtɪd). **1** (*intr*) (esp. of a bullet) to rebound from a surface, usually with a whining or zipping sound. ◆ *n* **2** the motion or sound of a rebounding object, esp. a bullet. **3** an object that ricochets. ORIG C18: from F

ricotta (rɪ'kɒtə) *n* a soft white unsalted cheese made from sheep's milk. ORIG It., from L *recocta* recooked, from *recoquere,* from RE- + *coquere* to COOK

RICS *abbrev. for* Royal Institution of Chartered Surveyors.

rictus ('rɪktəs) *n, pl* **rictus** *or* **rictuses. 1** the gap or cleft of an open mouth or beak. **2** a fixed or unnatural grin or grimace as in horror or death. ORIG C18: from L, from *ringī* to gape
▸ **'rictal** *adj*

rid (rɪd) *vb* **rids, ridding, rid** *or* **ridded.** (*tr*) **1** (foll. by *of*) to relieve from something disagreeable or undesirable; make free (of). **2 get rid of.** to relieve or free oneself of (something unpleasant or undesirable). ORIG C13 (meaning: to clear land): from ON *rythja*

riddance ('rɪdᵊns) *n* the act of getting rid of something; removal (esp. in **good riddance**).

ridden ('rɪdᵊn) *vb* **1** the past participle of **ride.** ◆ *adj* **2** (*in combination*) afflicted or dominated by something specified: *disease-ridden.*

riddle[1] ('rɪdᵊl) *n* **1** a question, puzzle, or verse so phrased that ingenuity is required for elucidation of the answer or meaning. **2** a person or thing that puzzles, perplexes, or confuses. ◆ *vb* **riddles, riddling, riddled. 3** to solve, explain, or interpret (a riddle). **4** (*intr*) to speak in riddles. ORIG OE *rǣdelle, rǣdelse,* from *rǣd* counsel
▸ **'riddler** *n*

riddle[2] ('rɪdᵊl) *vb* **riddles, riddling, riddled.** (*tr*) **1** (usually foll. by *with*) to pierce or perforate with numerous holes: *riddled with bullets.* **2** to put through a sieve; sift. ◆ *n* **3** a sieve, esp. a coarse one used for sand, grain, etc. ORIG OE *hriddel* a sieve
▸ **'riddler** *n*

ride (raɪd) *vb* **rides, riding, rode, ridden. 1** to sit on and control the movements of (a horse or other animal). **2** (*tr*) to sit on and propel (a bicycle or similar vehicle). **3** (*intr;* often foll. by *on* or *in*) to be carried along or travel on or in a vehicle: *she rides to work on the bus.* **4** (*tr*) to travel over or traverse: *they rode the countryside in search of shelter.* **5** (*tr*) to take part in by riding: *to ride a race.* **6** to travel through or be carried across (sea, sky, etc.): *the small boat rode the waves; the moon was riding high.* **7** (*tr*) *US & Canad.* to cause to be carried: *to ride someone out of town.* **8** (*intr*) to be supported as if floating: *the candidate rode to victory on his new policies.* **9** (*intr*) (of a vessel) to lie at anchor. **10** (*tr*) (of a vessel) to be attached to (an anchor). **11** (*tr*) **11a** *Sl.* to have sexual intercourse with (someone). **11b** (of a male animal) to copulate with; mount. **12** (*tr; usually passive*) to tyrannize over or dominate: *ridden by fear.* **13** (*tr*) *Inf.* to persecute, esp. by constant or petty criticism: *don't ride me so hard.* **14** (*intr*) *Inf.* to continue undisturbed: *let it ride.* **15** (*tr*) to endure successfully; ride out. **16** (*tr*) to yield slightly to (a punch, etc.) to lessen its impact. **17** (*intr;* often foll. by *on*) (of a bet) to remain placed: *let your winnings ride on the same number.* **18 ride again.** *Inf.* to return to a former activity or scene. **19 ride for a fall.** to act in such a way as to invite disaster. **20 riding high.** confident, popular, and successful. ◆ *n* **21** a journey or outing on horseback or in a vehicle. **22** a path specially made for riding on horseback. **23** transport in a vehicle; lift: *can you give me a ride to the station?* **24** a device or structure, such as a roller coaster at a fairground, in which people ride for pleasure or entertainment. **25** *Sl.* an act of sexual intercourse. **26** *Sl.* a partner in sexual intercourse. **27 take for a ride.** *Inf.* **27a** to cheat, swindle, or deceive. **27b** to take (someone) away in a car and murder him. ORIG OE *rīdan*
▸ **'ridable** *or* **'rideable** *adj*

ride out *vb* (*tr, adv*) to endure successfully; survive (esp. in **ride out the storm**).

rider ('raɪdə) *n* **1** a person or thing that rides. **2** an additional clause, amendment, or stipulation added to a document, esp. (in Britain) a legislative bill at its third reading. **3** *Brit.* a statement made by a jury in addition to its verdict, such as a recommendation for mercy. **4** any of various objects or devices resting on or strengthening something else.
▸ **'riderless** *adj*

ride up *vb* (*intr, adv*) to work away from the proper position: *her new skirt rode up.*

ridge (rɪdʒ) *n* **1** a long narrow raised land formation with sloping sides. **2** any long narrow raised strip or elevation, as on a fabric or in ploughed land. **3** *Anat.* any elongated raised margin or border on a bone, tissue, etc. **4a** the top of a roof at the junction of two sloping sides. **4b** (*as modifier*)*: a ridge tile.* **5** *Meteorol.* an elongated area of high pressure, esp. an extension of an anticyclone. Cf. **trough** (sense 4). ◆ *vb* **ridges, ridging, ridged. 6** to form into a ridge or ridges. ORIG OE *hrycg*
▸ **'ridgeˌlike** *adj* ▸ **'ridgy** *adj*

ridgepole ('rɪdʒˌpəʊl) *n* **1** a timber along the ridge of a roof, to which the rafters are attached. **2** the horizontal pole at the apex of a tent.

ridgeway ('rɪdʒˌweɪ) *n Brit.* a road or track along a ridge, esp. one of great antiquity.

ridgy-didge ('rɪdʒɪˌdɪdʒ) *adj Austral. inf.* genuine; correct: *a full, ridgy-didge Aussie bloke.*

ridicule ('rɪdɪˌkjuːl) *n* **1** language or behaviour intended to humiliate or mock. ◆ *vb* **ridicules, ridiculing, ridiculed. 2** (*tr*) to make fun of or mock. ORIG C17: from F, from L *rīdiculus,* from *rīdēre* to laugh

ridiculous (rɪ'dɪkjʊləs) *adj* worthy of or exciting ridicule; absurd, preposterous, laughable, or contemptible. ORIG C16: from L *rīdiculōsus,* from *rīdēre* to laugh
▸ **ri'diculousness** *n*

riding[1] ('raɪdɪŋ) *n* **1a** the art or practice of horsemanship. **1b** (*as modifier*)*: a riding school.* **2** a track for riding.

riding[2] ('raɪdɪŋ) *n* **1** (*cap. when part of a name*) any of the three former administrative divisions of Yorkshire: **North Riding, East Riding,** and **West Riding. 2** (in Canada) a parliamentary constituency. ORIG from OE *thriding,* from ON *thrithjungr* a third

riding crop *n* a short whip with a handle at one end for opening gates.

riding lamp *or* **light** *n* a light on a boat or ship showing that it is at anchor.

Ridley ★ ('rɪdlɪ) *n* **Nicholas.** ?1500–55, English bishop; burnt at the stake for refusing to disavow his Protestant beliefs when Mary I became queen.

Riefenstahl ★ (*German* 'riːfənʃtaːl) *n* **Leni** ('leːni). born 1902, German photographer and film director, known for her Nazi propaganda films.

Riemann ★ (*German* 'riːman) *n* **Georg Friedrich Bernhard** ('geːɔrk 'friːdrɪç 'bɛrnhart). 1826–66, German mathematician whose non-Euclidean geometry was used by Einstein.
▸ **Rie'mannian** *adj*

riempie ('rɪmpɪ) *n S. African.* a leather thong or lace used mainly to make chair seats. ORIG C19: Afrik., dim. of *riem,* from Du.: RIM

riesling ('riːzlɪŋ, 'raɪz-) *n* **1** a white wine from the Rhine valley in Germany and from certain districts in other countries. **2** the grape used to make this wine. ORIG C19: from G, from earlier *Rüssling,* from ?

rife (raɪf) *adj* (*postpositive*) **1** of widespread occurrence; current. **2** very plentiful; abundant. **3** (foll. by *with*) abounding (in): *a garden rife with weeds.* ORIG OE *rīfe*
▸ **'rifely** *adv* ▸ **'rifeness** *n*

riff (rɪf) *Jazz, rock.* ◆ *n* **1** an ostinato played over changing harmonies. ◆ *vb* **2** (*intr*) to play riffs. ORIG C20: prob. altered from REFRAIN[2]

riffle ('rɪfᵊl) *vb* **riffles, riffling, riffled. 1** (when *intr,* often foll. by *through*) to flick rapidly through (pages of a book, etc.). **2** to shuffle (cards) by halving the pack and flicking the corners together. **3** to cause or form a ripple on water. ◆ *n* **4** *US & Canad.* **4a** a rapid in a stream. **4b** a rocky shoal causing a rapid. **4c** a ripple on water. **5** *Mining.* a contrivance on the bottom of a sluice, containing grooves for trapping particles of gold. **6** the act or an instance of riffling. ORIG C18: prob. from RUFFLE[1], infl. by RIPPLE[1]

riffraff (ˈrɪfˌræf) *n* (*sometimes functioning as pl*) worthless people, esp. collectively; rabble. ORIG C15 *rif and raf*, from OF *rif et raf*; rel. to *rifler* to plunder, and *rafle* a sweeping up

rifle[1] (ˈraɪfᵊl) *n* **1a** a firearm having a long barrel with a spirally grooved interior, which imparts to the bullet spinning motion and thus greater accuracy over a longer range. **1b** (*as modifier*): *rifle fire*. **2** (formerly) a large cannon with a rifled bore. **3** one of the grooves in a rifled bore. **4** (*pl*) **4a** a unit of soldiers equipped with rifles. **4b** (*cap. when part of a name*): *the King's Own Rifles*. ◆ *vb* **rifles, rifling, rifled.** (*tr*) **5** to make spiral grooves inside the barrel of (a gun). ORIG C18: from OF *rifler* to scratch; rel. to Low G *rifeln* from *riefe* groove

rifle[2] (ˈraɪfᵊl) *vb* **rifles, rifling, rifled.** (*tr*) **1** to search (a house, safe, etc.) and steal from it; ransack. **2** to steal and carry off: *to rifle goods*. ORIG C14: from OF *rifler* to plunder, scratch, of Gmc origin
▸ **ˈrifler** *n*

riflebird (ˈraɪfᵊlˌbɜːd) *n* any of various Australian birds of paradise whose plumage has a metallic sheen.

rifleman (ˈraɪfᵊlmən) *n, pl* **riflemen. 1** a person skilled in the use of a rifle, esp. a soldier. **2** a wren of New Zealand.

rifle range *n* an area used for target practice with rifles.

rifling (ˈraɪflɪŋ) *n* **1** the cutting of spiral grooves on the inside of a firearm's barrel. **2** the series of grooves so cut.

rift (rɪft) *n* **1** a gap or space made by cleaving or splitting. **2** *Geol.* a fault produced by tension on either side of the fault plane. **3** a gap between two cloud masses; break or chink. **4** a break in friendly relations between people, nations, etc. ◆ *vb* **5** to burst or cause to burst open; split. ORIG C13: from ON

rift valley *n* a long narrow valley resulting from the subsidence of land between two faults.

rig (rɪg) *vb* **rigs, rigging, rigged.** (*tr*) **1** *Naut.* to equip (a vessel, mast, etc.) with (sails, rigging, etc.). **2** *Naut.* to set up or prepare ready for use. **3** to put the components of (an aircraft, etc.) into their correct positions. **4** to manipulate in a fraudulent manner, esp. for profit: *to rig prices*. ◆ *n* **5** *Naut.* the distinctive arrangement of the sails, masts, etc., of a vessel. **6** the installation used in drilling for and exploiting natural gas and oil deposits: *an oil rig*. **7** apparatus or equipment. **8** *Chiefly US & Canad.* an articulated lorry. ◆ See also **rig out, rig up.** ORIG C15: of Scand. origin; rel. to Norwegian *rigga* to wrap

Riga ★ (ˈriːgə) *n* the capital of Latvia, on the **Gulf of Riga** at the mouth of the Western Dvina: a major trading centre of the Baltic since Viking times. Pop.: 826 100 (1996 est.).

rigadoon (ˌrɪgəˈduːn) *n* **1** an old Provençal couple dance, light and graceful, in lively duple time. **2** a piece of music composed for or in the rhythm of this dance. ORIG C17: from F, allegedly after *Rigaud*, a dancing master at Marseilles

rigamarole (ˈrɪgəməˌrəʊl) *n* a variant of **rigmarole.**

-rigged *adj* (*in combination*) (of a sailing vessel) having a rig of a certain kind: *ketch-rigged; schooner-rigged*.

rigger (ˈrɪgə) *n* **1** a workman who rigs vessels, etc. **2** *Rowing.* a bracket on a boat to support a projecting rowlock. **3** a person skilled in the use of pulleys, cranes, etc.

rigging (ˈrɪgɪŋ) *n* **1** the shrouds, stays, etc., of a vessel. **2** the bracing wires, struts, and lines of a biplane, etc. **3** any form of lifting gear.

right (raɪt) *adj* **1** in accordance with accepted standards of moral or legal behaviour, justice, etc.: *right conduct*. **2** correct or true: *the right answer*. **3** appropriate, suitable, or proper: *the right man for the job*. **4** most favourable or convenient: *the right time to act*. **5** in a satisfactory condition: *things are right again now*. **6** indicating or designating the correct time: *the clock is right*. **7** correct in opinion or judgment. **8** sound in mind or body. **9** (*usually prenominal*) of, designating, or located near the side of something or someone that faces east when the front is turned towards the north. **10** (*usually prenominal*) worn on a right hand, foot, etc. **11** (*sometimes cap.*) of, designating, belonging to, or relating to the political or intellectual right (see sense 36). **12** (*sometimes cap.*) conservative: *the right wing of the party*. **13** *Geom.* **13a** formed by or containing a line or plane perpendicular to another line or plane. **13b** having the axis perpendicular to the base: *a right circular cone*. **13c** straight: *a right line*. **14** relating to or designating the side of cloth worn or facing outwards. **15 in one's right mind.** sane. **16 she'll be right.** *Austral. & NZ inf.* that's all right; not to worry. **17 the right side of. 17a** in favour with: *you'd better stay on the right side of him*. **17b** younger than: *she's still on the right side of fifty*. **18 too right.** *Austral. & NZ inf.* an exclamation of agreement. ◆ *adv* **19** in accordance with correctness or truth: *to guess right*. **20** in the appropriate manner: *do it right next time!* **21** in a straight line: *right to the top*. **22** in the direction of the east from the point of view of a person or thing facing north. **23** absolutely or completely: *he went right through the floor*. **24** all the way: *the bus goes right into town*. **25** without delay: *I'll be right over*. **26** exactly or precisely: *right here*. **27** in a manner consistent with a legal or moral code: *do right by me*. **28** in accordance with propriety; fittingly: *it serves you right*. **29** to good or favourable advantage: *it all came out right in the end*. **30** (esp. in religious titles) most or very: *right reverend*. **31 right, left, and centre.** on all sides. ◆ *n* **32** any claim, title, etc., that is morally just or legally granted as allowable or due to a person: *I know my rights*. **33** anything that accords with the principles of legal or moral justice. **34** the fact or state of being in accordance with reason, truth, or accepted standards (esp. in **in the right**) **35** the right side, direction, position, area, or part: *the right of the army*. **36** (*often cap.* and preceded by *the*) the supporters or advocates of social, political, or economic conservatism or reaction. **37** *Boxing.* **37a** a punch with the right hand. **37b** the right hand. **38** (*often pl*) *Finance.* the privilege of a company's shareholders to subscribe for new issues of the company's shares on advantageous terms. **39 by right** (*or* **rights**). properly: *by rights you should be in bed*. **40 in one's own right.** having a claim or title oneself rather than through marriage or other connection. **41 to rights.** consistent with justice or orderly arrangement: *he put the matter to rights*. ◆ *vb* (*mainly tr*) **42** (*also intr*) to restore to or attain a normal, esp. an upright, position: *the raft righted in a few seconds*. **43** to make (something) accord with truth or facts. **44** to restore to an orderly state or condition. **45** to compensate for or redress (esp. in **right a wrong**). ◆ *interj* **46** an expression of agreement or compliance. ORIG OE *riht, reoht*
▸ **ˈrightable** *adj* ▸ **ˈrighter** *n* ▸ **ˈrightness** *n*

right about *n* **1** a turn executed through 180°. ◆ *adj, adv* **2** in the opposite direction.

right angle *n* **1** the angle between radii of a circle that cut off on the circumference an arc equal in length to one quarter of the circumference; an angle of 90° or $\pi/2$ radians. **2 at right angles.** perpendicular or perpendicularly.
▸ **ˈright-ˌangled** *adj*

right-angled triangle *n* a triangle one angle of which is a right angle. US and Canad. name: **right triangle.**

right ascension *n Astron.* the angular distance measured eastwards along the celestial equator from the vernal equinox to the point at which the celestial equator intersects a great circle passing through the celestial pole and the heavenly object in question.

right away *adv* without delay.

righteous (ˈraɪtʃəs) *adj* **1a** characterized by, proceeding from, or in accordance with accepted standards of morality or uprightness: *a righteous man*. **1b** (*as collective n; preceded by the*): *the righteous*. **2** morally justifiable or right: *righteous indignation*. ORIG OE *rīhtwīs*, from RIGHT + WISE[2]
▸ **ˈrighteously** *adv* ▸ **ˈrighteousness** *n*

rightful (ˈraɪtfʊl) *adj* **1** in accordance with what is right. **2** (*prenominal*) having a legally or morally just claim: *the rightful owner*. **3** (*prenominal*) held by virtue of a legal or just claim: *my rightful property*.
▸ **ˈrightfully** *adv*

right-hand *adj* (*prenominal*) **1** of, located on, or moving towards the right: *a right-hand bend*. **2** for use by the right hand. **3 right-hand man.** one's most valuable assistant.

right-handed *adj* **1** using the right hand with greater skill or ease than the left. **2** performed with the right

hand. **3** made for use by the right hand. **4** turning from left to right.
▸ ˌ**right-ˈhandedness** *n*

rightist (ˈraɪtɪst) *adj* **1** of, tending towards, or relating to the political right or its principles. ◆ *n* **2** a person who supports or belongs to the political right.
▸ ˈ**rightism** *n*

rightly (ˈraɪtlɪ) *adv* **1** in accordance with the true facts. **2** in accordance with principles of justice or morality. **3** with good reason: *he was rightly annoyed with her.* **4** properly or suitably. **5** (*used with a negative*) *Inf.* with certainty (usually in **I don't rightly know**).

right-minded *adj* holding opinions or principles that accord with what is right or with the opinions of the speaker.

righto *or* **right oh** (ˈraɪtˈəʊ) *sentence substitute. Brit. inf.* an expression of agreement or compliance.

right off *adv* immediately; right away.

right of way *n, pl* **rights of way. 1** the right of one vehicle or vessel to take precedence over another, as laid down by law or custom. **2a** the legal right of someone to pass over another's land, acquired by grant or by long usage. **2b** the path used by this right. **3** *US.* the strip of land over which a power line, road, etc., extends.

right-on *adj Inf.* modern, trendy, and socially aware or relevant: *right-on green politics.*

Right Reverend *adj* (in Britain) a title of respect for an Anglican or Roman Catholic bishop.

rights issue *n Stock Exchange.* an issue of new shares offered by a company to its existing shareholders on favourable terms.

rightsize (ˈraɪtˌsaɪz) *vb* to restructure (an organization) to cut costs and improve effectiveness without ruthlessly downsizing.

right-thinking (ˈraɪtˌθɪŋkɪŋ) *adj* possessing reasonable and generally acceptable opinions.

rightward (ˈraɪtwəd) *adj* **1** situated on or directed towards the right. ◆ *adv* **2** a variant of **rightwards.**

rightwards (ˈraɪtwədz) *or* **rightward** *adv* towards or on the right.

right whale *n* a large whalebone whale which is grey or black, has a large head and no dorsal fin, and is hunted as a source of whalebone and oil. See also **bowhead.** ORIG C19: ? because it was *right* for hunting

right wing *n* **1** (*often cap.*) the conservative faction of an assembly, party, etc. **2** the part of an army or field of battle on the right from the point of view of one facing the enemy. **3a** the right-hand side of the field of play from the point of view of a team facing its opponent's goal. **3b** a player positioned in this area in any of various games. ◆ *adj* **right-wing. 4** of, belonging to, or relating to the right wing.
▸ ˈ**right-ˈwinger** *n*

Rigi ★ (ˈriːgɪ) *n* a mountain in the Alps of N central Switzerland, between Lakes Lucerne, Zug, and Lauerz.

rigid (ˈrɪdʒɪd) *adj* **1** physically inflexible or stiff: *a rigid piece of plastic.* **2** rigorously strict: *rigid rules.* ORIG C16: from L *rigidus,* from *rigēre* to be stiff
▸ **riˈgidity** *n* ▸ ˈ**rigidly** *adv*

rigidify (rɪˈdʒɪdɪˌfaɪ) *vb* **rigidifies, rigidifying, rigidified.** to make or become rigid.

rigmarole (ˈrɪgməˌrəʊl) *or* **rigamarole** *n* **1** any long complicated procedure. **2** a set of incoherent or pointless statements. ORIG C18: from earlier *ragman roll* a list, prob. a roll used in a medieval game, wherein characters were described in verse, beginning with *Ragemon le bon* Ragman the good

rigor (ˈraɪgɔː, ˈrɪgə) *n* **1** *Med.* a sudden feeling of chilliness, often accompanied by shivering: it sometimes precedes a fever. **2** (ˈrɪgə). *Pathol.* rigidity of a muscle. **3** a state of rigidity assumed in reaction to shock. ORIG see RIGOUR

rigor mortis (ˈrɪgə ˈmɔːtɪs) *n Pathol.* the stiffness of joints and muscular rigidity of a dead body. ORIG C19: L, lit.: rigidity of death

rigorous (ˈrɪgərəs) *adj* **1** harsh, strict, or severe: *rigorous discipline.* **2** severely accurate: *rigorous book-keeping.* **3** (esp. of weather) extreme or harsh. **4** *Maths, logic.* (of a proof) making the validity of each step explicit.
▸ ˈ**rigorously** *adv*

rigour *or US* **rigor** (ˈrɪgə) *n* **1** harsh but just treatment or action. **2** a severe or cruel circumstance: *the rigours of famine.* **3** strictness, harshness, or severity of character. **4** strictness in judgment or conduct. ORIG C14: from L *rigor*

rig out *vb* **1** (*tr, adv;* often foll. by *with*) to equip or fit out (with): *his car is rigged out with gadgets.* **2** to dress or be dressed: *rigged out smartly.* ◆ *n* **rigout. 3** *Inf.* a person's clothing or costume, esp. a bizarre outfit.

rig up *vb* (*tr, adv*) to erect or construct, esp. as a temporary measure: *cameras were rigged up.*

Rig-Veda (rɪgˈveɪdə) *n* a compilation of Hindu poems dating from 2000 B.C. or earlier. ORIG C18: from Sansk. *rigveda,* from *ric* song of praise + VEDA

Rijeka ★ (rɪˈɛkə; *Serbo-Croat* riˈjɛka) *n* a port in NW Croatia: an ancient town, changing hands many times before passing to Yugoslavia in 1947 and to Croatia in 1991. Pop.: 167 964 (1991). Italian name: **Fiume.**

Rijksmuseum ★ (ˈraɪxsmjuːˌzɪəm) *n* a museum in Amsterdam housing the national art collection of the Netherlands.

Rijn ★ (rɛjn) *n* the Dutch name for the **Rhine.**

Rijswijk ★ (ˈraɪsvaɪk; *Dutch* ˈrɛjswɛjk) *n* a town in the SW Netherlands, in South Holland province on the SE outskirts of The Hague: scene of the signing (1697) of the **Treaty of Rijswijk,** ending the War of the Grand Alliance. Pop.: 48 000 (1991). English name: **Ryswick.**

rile (raɪl) *vb* **riles, riling, riled.** (*tr*) **1** to annoy or anger. **2** *US & Canad.* to agitate (water, etc.). ORIG C19: var. of ROIL

Riley ★ (ˈraɪlɪ) *n* **Bridget** (**Louise**). born 1931, British painter, best known for her black-and-white op art paintings of the 1960s.

Rilke ★ (*German* ˈrɪlkə) *n* **Rainer Maria** (ˈrainər maˈriːa). 1875–1926, Austro-German poet, born in Prague. Author of the *Duino Elegies* (1922) and *Sonnets to Orpheus* (1923).

rill (rɪl) *n* **1** a brook or stream. **2** a channel or gulley, such as one formed during soil erosion. **3** Also: **rille.** one of many winding cracks on the moon. ORIG C15: from Low G *rille*

rim (rɪm) *n* **1** the raised edge of an object, esp. of something more or less circular such as a cup or crater. **2** the peripheral part of a wheel, to which the tyre is attached. **3** *Basketball.* the hoop from which the net is suspended. ◆ *vb* **rims, rimming, rimmed.** (*tr*) **4** to put a rim on (a pot, cup, wheel, etc.). **5** *Sl.* to lick, kiss, or suck the anus of (one's sexual partner). ORIG OE *rima*

Rimbaud ★ (*French* rɛ̃bo) *n* **Arthur** (artyr). 1854–91, French poet, whose work includes *A Season in Hell* (1873) and *Illuminations* (published 1884).

rime[1] (raɪm) *n* **1** frost formed by the freezing of water droplets in fog onto solid objects. ◆ *vb* **rimes, riming, rimed. 2** (*tr*) to cover with rime or something resembling rime. ORIG OE *hrīm*

rime[2] (raɪm) *n, vb* **rimes, riming, rimed.** an archaic spelling of **rhyme.**

rim-fire *adj* **1** (of a cartridge) having the primer in the rim of the base. **2** (of a firearm) adapted for such cartridges.

Rimini ★ (ˈrɪmɪnɪ) *n* a port and resort in NE Italy, in Emilia-Romagna on the N Adriatic coast. Pop.: 129 598 (1996 est.). Ancient name: **Ariminum.**

rimose (raɪˈməʊs, -ˈməʊz) *adj* (esp. of plant parts) having the surface marked by a network of cracks. ORIG C18: from L *rīmōsus,* from *rīma* a split

Rimsky-Korsakov ★ (ˈrɪmskɪˈkɔːsəkɒf; *Russian* ˈrimskij ˈkɔrsəkəf) *n* **Nikolai Andreyevich** (nikaˈlaj anˈdrjejɪvitʃ). 1844–1908, Russian composer; noted for such works as the suite *Scheherazade* (1888).

rimu (ˈriːmuː) *n* a New Zealand tree. Also called: **red pine.** ORIG from Maori

rimy (ˈraɪmɪ) *adj* **rimier, rimiest.** coated with rime.

rind (raɪnd) *n* **1** a hard outer layer or skin on bacon, cheese, etc. **2** the outer layer of a fruit or of the spore-producing body of certain fungi. **3** the outer layer of the bark of a tree. ORIG OE *rinde*

rinderpest ('rɪndə,pɛst) *n* an acute contagious viral disease of cattle, characterized by severe inflammation of the intestinal tract and diarrhoea. ORIG C19: from G *Rinderpest* cattle pest

ring[1] (rɪŋ) *n* **1** a circular band of a precious metal often set with gems and worn upon the finger as an adornment or as a token of engagement or marriage. **2** any object or mark that is circular in shape. **3** a circular path or course: *to run around in a ring.* **4** a group of people or things standing or arranged so as to form a circle: *a ring of spectators.* **5** an enclosed space, usually circular in shape, where circus acts are performed. **6** a square raised platform, marked off by ropes, in which contestants box or wrestle. **7 the ring.** the sport of boxing. **8 throw one's hat in the ring.** to announce one's intention to be a candidate or contestant. **9** a group of people usually operating illegally and covertly: *a drug ring; a paedophile ring.* **10** (esp. at country fairs) an enclosure where horses, cattle, and other livestock are paraded and auctioned. **11** an area reserved for betting at a racecourse. **12** a circular strip of bark cut from a tree or branch. **13** a single turn in a spiral. **14** *Geom.* the area of space lying between two concentric circles. **15** *Maths.* a set that is subject to two binary operations, addition and multiplication, such that the set is a commutative group under addition and is closed under multiplication, this latter operation being associative. **16** *Bot.* short for **annual ring. 17** *Chem.* a closed loop of atoms in a molecule. **18** *Astron.* any of the thin circular bands of small bodies orbiting a giant planet, esp. Saturn. **19 run rings round.** *Inf.* to outclass completely. ◆ *vb* **rings, ringing, ringed.** (*tr*) **20** to surround with, or as if with, or form a ring. **21** to mark a bird with a ring or clip for subsequent identification. **22** to fit a ring in the nose of (a bull, etc.) so that it can be led easily. **23** to ringbark. ORIG OE *hring*
▸ **ringed** *adj*

ring[2] (rɪŋ) *vb* **rings, ringing, rang, rung. 1** to emit or cause to emit a resonant sound, characteristic of certain metals when struck. **2** to cause (a bell, etc.) to emit a ringing sound by striking it once or repeatedly or (of a bell) to emit such a sound. **3a** (*tr*) to cause (a large bell) to emit a ringing sound by pulling on a rope attached to a wheel on which the bell swings back and forth, being sounded by a clapper inside it. **3b** (*intr*) (of a bell) to sound by being swung in this way. **4** (*intr*) (of a building, place, etc.) to be filled with sound: *the church rang with singing.* **5** (*intr;* foll. by *for*) to call by means of a bell, etc.: *to ring for the butler.* **6** Also: **ring up.** *Chiefly Brit.* to call (a person) by telephone. **7** (*tr*) to strike or tap (a coin) in order to assess its genuineness by the sound produced. **8** *Sl.* to change the identity of (a stolen vehicle) by using the licence plate, serial number, etc., of another, usually disused, vehicle. **9** (*intr*) (of the ears) to have or give the sensation of humming or ringing. **10 ring a bell.** to bring something to the mind or memory: *that rings a bell.* **11 ring down the curtain. 11a** to lower the curtain at the end of a theatrical performance. **11b** (foll. by *on*) to put an end (to). **12 ring false.** to give the impression of being false. **13 ring true.** to give the impression of being true. ◆ *n* **14** the act of or a sound made by ringing. **15** a sound produced by or suggestive of a bell. **16** any resonant or metallic sound: *the ring of trumpets.* **17** *Inf., chiefly Brit.* a telephone call. **18** the complete set of bells in a tower or belfry: *a ring of eight bells.* **19** an inherent quality or characteristic: his words had the ring of sincerity. ◆ See also **ring in, ring off,** etc. ORIG OE *hringan*

> **USAGE NOTE** *Rang* and *sang* are the correct forms of the past tenses of *ring* and *sing*, although *rung* and *sung* are still heard informally and dialectally: *he rung* (*rang*) *the bell.*

ringbark ('rɪŋ,bɑːk) *vb* (*tr*) to kill (a tree) by cutting away a strip of bark from around the trunk.

ring binder *n* a loose-leaf binder with metal rings that can be opened to insert perforated paper.

ringbolt ('rɪŋ,bəʊlt) *n* a bolt with a ring fitted through an eye attached to the bolt head.

ringdove ('rɪŋ,dʌv) *n* **1** another name for **wood pigeon. 2** an Old World turtledove, having a black neck band.

ringed plover *n* a European shorebird with a greyish-brown back, white underparts, a black throat band, and orange legs.

ringer ('rɪŋə) *n* **1** a person or thing that rings a bell, etc. **2** Also called: **dead ringer.** *Sl.* a person or thing that is almost identical to another. **3** *Sl.* a stolen vehicle the identity of which has been changed by the use of the licence plate, serial number, etc., of another, usually disused, vehicle. **4** *Chiefly US.* a contestant, esp. a horse, entered in a competition under false representations of identity, record, or ability. **5** *Austral.* a stockman; station hand. **6** *Austral.* the fastest shearer in a shed. **7** *Austral. inf.* the fastest or best at anything. **8** a quoit thrown so as to encircle a peg. **9** such a throw.

ring-fence *vb* **1** to assign (money, a grant, fund, etc.) to one particular purpose, so as to restrict its use: *to ring-fence a financial allowance.* **2** to oblige (a person or organization) to use money for a particular purpose: *to ring-fence a local authority.* ◆ *n* **ring fence. 3** an agreement, contract, etc., in which the use of money is restricted to a particular purpose.

ring finger *n* the third finger, esp. of the left hand, on which a wedding ring is worn.

ring in *vb* (*adv*) **1** (*intr*) *Chiefly Brit.* to report to someone by telephone. **2** (*tr*) to accompany the arrival of with bells (esp. in **ring in the new year**). ◆ *n* **ring-in. 3** *Austral. & NZ inf.* a person or thing that is not normally a member of a particular group; outsider.

ringing tone *n Brit.* a sequence of pairs of tones heard by the dialler on a telephone when the number dialled is ringing. Cf. **engaged tone, dialling tone.**

ringleader ('rɪŋ,liːdə) *n* a person who leads others in unlawful or mischievous activity.

ringlet ('rɪŋlɪt) *n* **1** a lock of hair hanging down in a spiral curl. **2** a butterfly that occurs in S Europe and has dark brown wings marked with small black-and-white eyespots.
▸ **'ringleted** *adj*

ring main *n* a domestic electrical supply in which outlet sockets are connected to the mains supply through a continuous closed circuit (**ring circuit**).

ringmaster ('rɪŋ,mɑːstə) *n* the master of ceremonies in a circus.

ring-necked *adj* (of animals, esp. birds and snakes) having a band of distinctive colour around the neck.

ring-necked pheasant *n* a common pheasant originating in Asia. The male has a bright plumage with a band of white around the neck and the female is mottled brown.

ring off *vb* (*intr, adv*) *Chiefly Brit.* to terminate a telephone conversation by replacing the receiver; hang up.

ring out *vb* (*adv*) **1** (*tr*) to accompany the departure of with bells (esp. in **ring out the old year**). **2** (*intr*) to send forth a loud resounding noise.

ring ouzel *n* a European thrush common in rocky areas. The male has a blackish plumage and the female is brown.

ring road *n* a main road that bypasses a town or town centre. US names: **belt, beltway.**

ringside ('rɪŋ,saɪd) *n* **1** the row of seats nearest a boxing or wrestling ring. **2a** any place affording a close uninterrupted view. **2b** (*as modifier*): *a ringside seat.*

ringtail ('rɪŋ,teɪl) *n Austral.* any of several tree-living phalangers having curling prehensile tails used to grasp branches while climbing.

ring up *vb* (*adv*) **1** *Chiefly Brit.* to make a telephone call (to). **2** (*tr*) to record on a cash register. **3 ring up the curtain. 3a** to begin a theatrical performance. **3b** (often foll. by *on*) to make a start (on).

ringworm ('rɪŋ,wɜːm) *n* any of various fungal infections of the skin or nails, often appearing as itching circular patches. Also called: **tinea.**

rink (rɪŋk) *n* **1** an expanse of ice for skating on, esp. one that is artificially prepared and under cover. **2** an area for roller-skating on. **3** a building or enclosure for ice-skating or roller-skating. **4** *Bowls.* a strip of the green on which a game is played. **5** *Curling.* the strip of ice on which the game is played. **6** (in bowls and curling) the players on one side in a game. ORIG C14 (Scots): from OF *renc* row

rinkhals (ˈrɪŋkˌhæls) *or* **ringhals** (ˈrɪŋgˌhæls) *n, pl* **rinkhals, rinkhalses, ringhals** *or* **ringhalses.** a venomous snake of southern Africa, which can spit venom over 2 m (7 ft). ORIG Afrik., lit.: ring neck

rink rat *n Canad. sl.* a youth who helps with odd chores around an ice-hockey rink in return for free admission to games, etc.

rinse (rɪns) *vb* **rinses, rinsing, rinsed.** (*tr*) **1** to remove soap from (clothes, etc.) by applying clean water in the final stage in washing. **2** to wash lightly, esp. without using soap. **3** to give a light tint to (hair). ◆ *n* **4** the act or an instance of rinsing. **5** *Hairdressing.* a liquid preparation put on the hair when wet to give a tint to it: *a blue rinse.* ORIG C14: from OF *rincer,* from L *recens* fresh
▸ **ˈrinser** *n*

Rio Branco ★ (*Portuguese* ˈriu ˈbrəŋku) *n* **1** a city in W Brazil, capital of Acre state. Pop.: 167 457 (1991). **2** a river in Brazil, flowing south to the Rio Negro. Length: 644 km (400 miles).

Río Bravo ★ (ˈrio ˈbraβo) *n* the Mexican name for the **Rio Grande.**

Rio de Janeiro (ˈriːəʊ də dʒəˈnɪərəʊ) *or* **Rio** ★ *n* **1** a port in SE Brazil, on Guanabara Bay: the country's chief port and its capital from 1763 to 1960; backed by mountains, notably Sugar Loaf Mountain; founded by the French in 1555 and taken by the Portuguese in 1567. Pop. (urban area): 9 888 000 (1995). **2** a state of E Brazil. Capital: Rio de Janeiro. Pop.: 13 406 308 (1996). Area: 42 911 sq. km (16 568 sq. miles).

Río de la Plata ★ (ˈriːəʊ də lɑː ˈplɑːtə) *n* See **Plata.**

Río de Oro ★ (*Spanish* ˈrio ðe ˈoro) *n* a former region of W Africa: comprised the S part of the Spanish Sahara (now Western Sahara).

Rio Grande ★ *n* **1** (ˈriːəʊ ˈgrænd, ˈgrændɪ). a river in North America, rising in SW Colorado and flowing southeast to the Gulf of Mexico, forming the border between the US and Mexico. Length: about 3030 km (1885 miles). Mexican name: **Río Bravo. 2** (*Portuguese* ˈriu ˈgrəndi). a port in SE Brazil, in SE Rio Grande do Sul state: serves as the port for Pôrto Alegre. Pop.: 157 608 (1991).

Rio Grande do Norte ★ (*Portuguese* ˈriu ˈgrəndi do ˈnɔrti) *n* a state of NE Brazil, on the Atlantic: much of it is semiarid plateau. Capital: Natal. Pop.: 2 558 660 (1996). Area: 53 014 sq. km (20 469 sq. miles).

Rio Grande do Sul ★ (*Portuguese* ˈriu ˈgrəndi du ˈsul) *n* a state of S Brazil, on the Atlantic. Capital: Pôrto Alegre. Pop.: 9 634 688 (1996). Area: 282 183 sq. km (108 951 sq. miles).

rioja (rɪˈəʊxə) *n* a red or white wine, with a distinctive vanilla bouquet and flavour, produced around the Ebro river in central N Spain. ORIG C20: from *La Rioja,* the area where it is produced

Río Negro ★ (ˈriːəʊ ˈneɪgrəʊ, ˈnɛg-; *Spanish* ˈrio ˈneɣro) *n* See **Negro**[2].

riot (ˈraɪət) *n* **1a** a disturbance made by an unruly mob or (in law) three or more persons. **1b** (*as modifier*): *a riot shield.* **2** unrestrained revelry. **3** an occasion of boisterous merriment. **4** *Sl.* a person who occasions boisterous merriment. **5** a dazzling display: *a riot of colour.* **6** *Hunting.* the indiscriminate following of any scent by hounds. **7** *Arch.* wanton lasciviousness. **8 run riot. 8a** to behave without restraint. **8b** (of plants) to grow profusely. ◆ *vb* **9** (*intr*) to take part in a riot. **10** (*intr*) to indulge in unrestrained revelry. **11** (*tr;* foll. by *away*) to spend (time or money) in wanton or loose living. ORIG C13: from OF *riote* dispute, from *ruihoter* to quarrel, prob. from *ruir* to make a commotion, from L *rugīre* to roar
▸ **ˈrioter** *n*

Riot Act *n* **1** *Criminal law.* (formerly, in England) a statute of 1715 by which persons committing a riot had to disperse within an hour of the reading of the act by a magistrate. **2 read the riot act to.** to warn or reprimand severely.

riotous (ˈraɪətəs) *adj* **1** proceeding from or of the nature of riots or rioting. **2** characterized by wanton revelry: *riotous living.* **3** characterized by unrestrained merriment: *riotous laughter.*
▸ **ˈriotously** *adv* ▸ **ˈriotousness** *n*

riot shield *n* (in Britain) a shield used by police controlling crowds.

rip[1] (rɪp) *vb* **rips, ripping, ripped. 1** to tear or be torn violently or roughly. **2** (*tr;* foll. by *off* or *out*) to remove hastily or roughly. **3** (*intr*) *Inf.* to move violently or precipitously. **4** (*intr;* foll. by *into*) *Inf.* to pour violent abuse (on). **5** (*tr*) to saw or split (wood) in the direction of the grain. **6 let rip.** to act or speak without restraint. ◆ *n* **7** a tear or split. **8** short for **ripsaw.** ◆ See also **rip off.** ORIG C15: ?from Flemish *rippen*

rip[2] (rɪp) *n* short for **riptide.** ORIG C18: ?from RIP[1]

rip[3] (rɪp) *n Inf., arch.* **1** a debauched person. **2** an old worn-out horse. ORIG C18: ?from *rep,* shortened from REPROBATE

RIP *abbrev. for* requiescat *or* requiescant in pace. ORIG L: may he, she, *or* they rest in peace

riparian (raɪˈpɛərɪən) *adj* **1** of, inhabiting, or situated on the bank of a river. **2** denoting or relating to the legal rights of the owner of land on a river bank, such as fishing. ◆ *n* **3** *Property law.* a person who owns land on a river bank. ORIG C19: from L, from *rīpa* river bank

ripcord (ˈrɪpˌkɔːd) *n* **1** a cord that when pulled opens a parachute from its pack. **2** a cord on the gas bag of a balloon that when pulled enables gas to escape and the balloon to descend.

ripe (raɪp) *adj* **1** (of fruit, grain, etc.) mature and ready to be eaten or used. **2** mature enough to be eaten or used: *ripe cheese.* **3** fully developed in mind or body. **4** resembling ripe fruit, esp. in redness or fullness: *a ripe complexion.* **5** (*postpositive;* foll. by *for*) ready or eager (to undertake or undergo an action). **6** (*postpositive;* foll. by *for*) suitable: *the time is not yet ripe.* **7** mature in judgment or knowledge. **8** advanced but healthy (esp. in **a ripe old age**). **9** *Sl.* **9a** complete; thorough. **9b** excessive; exorbitant. **10** *Sl.* slightly indecent; risqué. ORIG OE *rīpe*
▸ **ˈripely** *adv* ▸ **ˈripeness** *n*

ripen (ˈraɪpᵊn) *vb* to make or become ripe.

ripieno (ˌrɪpɪˈeɪnəʊ) *n, pl* **ripieni** (-niː) *or* **ripienos.** *Music.* a supplementary instrument or player. ORIG It.

rip off *vb* (*tr*) **1** to tear roughly (from). **2** (*adv*) *Sl.* to steal from or cheat (someone). ◆ *n* **rip-off. 3** *Sl.* a grossly overpriced article. **4** *Sl.* the act of stealing or cheating.

Ripon ★ (ˈrɪpᵊn) *n* a city in N England, in North Yorkshire: cathedral (12th–16th centuries). Pop.: 13 806 (1991 est.).

riposte (rɪˈpɒst, rɪˈpəʊst) *n* **1** a swift sharp reply in speech or action. **2** *Fencing.* a counterattack made immediately after a successful parry. ◆ *vb* **ripostes, riposting, riposted. 3** (*intr*) to make a riposte. ORIG C18: from F, from It., from *rispondere* to reply

ripper (ˈrɪpə) *n* **1** a person or thing that rips. **2** a murderer who dissects or mutilates the victim's body. **3** *Inf., chiefly Austral. & NZ.* a fine or excellent person or thing.

ripping (ˈrɪpɪŋ) *adj Arch. Brit. sl.* excellent; splendid.
▸ **ˈrippingly** *adv*

ripple[1] (ˈrɪpᵊl) *n* **1** a slight wave or undulation on the surface of water. **2** a small wave or undulation in fabric, hair, etc. **3** a sound reminiscent of water flowing quietly in ripples: *a ripple of laughter.* **4** *Electronics.* an oscillation of small amplitude superimposed on a steady value. **5** *US & Canad.* another word for **riffle** (sense 4). ◆ *vb* **ripples, rippling, rippled. 6** (*intr*) to form ripples or flow with an undulating motion. **7** (*tr*) to stir up (water) so as to form ripples. **8** (*tr*) to make ripple marks. **9** (*intr*) (of sounds) to rise and fall gently. ORIG C17: ?from RIP[1]
▸ **ˈrippler** *n* ▸ **ˈrippling** *or* **ˈripply** *adj*

ripple[2] (ˈrɪpᵊl) *n* **1** a special kind of comb designed to separate the seed from the stalks in flax or hemp. ◆ *vb* **ripples, rippling, rippled. 2** (*tr*) to comb with this tool. ORIG C14: of Gmc origin
▸ **ˈrippler** *n*

★ people and places

ripple effect *n* the repercussions of an event or situation experienced far beyond its immediate location.

ripple mark *n* one of a series of small wavy ridges of sand formed by waves on a beach, by a current in a sandy riverbed, or by wind on land: sometimes found fossilized on bedding planes of sedimentary rock.

rip-roaring *adj Inf.* characterized by excitement, intensity, or boisterous behaviour.

ripsaw ('rɪpˌsɔː) *n* a handsaw for cutting along the grain of timber.

ripsnorter ('rɪpˌsnɔːtə) *n Sl.* a person or thing noted for intensity or excellence.
▸ **'ripˌsnorting** *adj*

riptide ('rɪpˌtaɪd) *n* **1** Also called: **rip**. a stretch of turbulent water in the sea, caused by the meeting of currents. **2** Also called: **rip current**. a strong current, esp. one flowing outwards from the shore.

rise (raɪz) *vb* **rises, rising, rose, risen** ('rɪzᵊn). (*mainly intr*) **1** to get up from a lying, sitting, kneeling, or prone position. **2** to get out of bed, esp. to begin one's day: *he always rises early.* **3** to move from a lower to a higher position or place. **4** to ascend or appear above the horizon: *the sun is rising.* **5** to increase in height or level: *the water rose above the normal level.* **6** to attain higher rank, status, or reputation: *he will rise in the world.* **7** to be built or erected: *those blocks of flats are rising fast.* **8** to appear: *new troubles rose to afflict her.* **9** to increase in strength, degree, etc.: *the wind is rising.* **10** to increase in amount or value: *house prices are always rising.* **11** to swell up: *dough rises.* **12** to become erect, stiff, or rigid: *the hairs on his neck rose in fear.* **13** (of one's stomach or gorge) to manifest nausea. **14** to revolt: *the people rose against their oppressors.* **15** to slope upwards: *the ground rises beyond the lake.* **16** to be resurrected. **17** to originate: *that river rises in the mountains.* **18** (of a session of a court, legislative assembly, etc.) to come to an end. **19** *Angling.* (of fish) to come to the surface of the water. **20** (often foll. by *to*) *Inf.* to respond (to teasing, etc.). ◆ *n* **21** the act or an instance of rising. **22** an increase in height. **23** an increase in rank, status, or position. **24** an increase in amount, cost, or value. **25** an increase in degree or intensity. **26** *Brit.* an increase in salary or wages. US and Canad. word: **raise. 27** the vertical height of a step or of a flight of stairs. **28** the vertical height of a roof above the walls or columns. **29** *Angling.* the act or instance of fish coming to the surface of the water to take flies, etc. **30** the beginning, origin, or source. **31** a piece of rising ground; incline. **32 get** *or* **take a rise out of.** *Sl.* to provoke an angry or petulant reaction from. **33 give rise to.** to cause the development of. ORIG OE *rīsan*

riser ('raɪzə) *n* **1** a person who rises, esp. from bed: *an early riser.* **2** the vertical part of a stair. **3** a vertical pipe, esp. one within a building.

rise to *vb* (*intr, prep*) to respond adequately to (the demands of something, esp. a testing challenge).

risibility (ˌrɪzɪ'bɪlɪtɪ) *n, pl* **risibilities**. **1** a tendency to laugh. **2** hilarity; laughter.

risible ('rɪzɪbᵊl) *adj* **1** having a tendency to laugh. **2** causing laughter; ridiculous. ORIG C16: from LL *rīsibilis,* from L *rīdēre* to laugh
▸ **'risibly** *adv*

rising ('raɪzɪŋ) *n* **1** a rebellion; revolt. **2** the leaven used to make dough rise in baking. ◆ *adj* (*prenominal*) **3** increasing in rank, status, or reputation: *a rising young politician.* **4** growing up to adulthood: *the rising generation.* ◆ *adv* **5** *Inf.* approaching: *he's rising 50.*

rising damp *n* capillary movement of moisture from the ground into the walls of buildings, resulting in damage up to a level of 3 feet.

rising trot *n* a horse's trot in which the rider rises from the saddle every second beat.

risk (rɪsk) *n* **1** the possibility of incurring misfortune or loss. **2** *Insurance.* **2a** chance of a loss or other event on which a claim may be filed. **2b** the type of such an event, such as fire or theft. **2c** the amount of the claim should such an event occur. **2d** a person or thing considered with respect to the characteristics that may cause an insured event to occur. **3 at risk.** vulnerable. **4 take** *or* **run a risk.** to proceed in an action without regard to the possibility of danger involved. ◆ *vb* (*tr*) **5** to expose to danger or loss. **6** to act in spite of the possibility of (injury or loss): *to risk a fall in climbing.* ORIG C17: from F, from It., from *rischiare* to be in peril, from Gk *rhiza* cliff (from the hazards of sailing along rocky coasts)

risk capital *n Chiefly Brit.* capital invested in an issue of ordinary shares, esp. of a speculative enterprise. Also called: **venture capital.**

risk factor *n Med.* a factor, such as a habit or an environmental condition, that predisposes an individual to develop a particular disease.

risky ('rɪskɪ) *adj* **riskier, riskiest**. involving danger.
▸ **'riskily** *adv* ▸ **'riskiness** *n*

risotto (rɪ'zɒtəʊ) *n, pl* **risottos**. a dish of rice cooked in stock and served variously with tomatoes, cheese, chicken, etc. ORIG C19: from It., from *riso* RICE

risqué ('rɪskeɪ) *adj* bordering on impropriety or indecency: *a risqué joke.* ORIG C19: from F *risquer* to hazard, RISK

rissole ('rɪsəʊl) *n* a mixture of minced cooked meat coated in egg and breadcrumbs and fried. ORIG C18: from F, prob. ult. from L *russus* red

risus sardonicus ('riːsəs sɑː'dɒnɪkəs) *n Pathol.* fixed contraction of the facial muscles resulting in a peculiar distorted grin, caused esp. by tetanus. Also called: **trismus cynicus** ('trɪzməs 'sɪnɪkəs). ORIG C17: NL, lit.: sardonic laugh

rit. *Music. abbrev. for:* **1** ritardando. **2** ritenuto.

Ritalin ('rɪtəlɪn) *n Trademark.* a preparation of methylphenidate, a drug related to amphetamine, used to treat attention deficit disorder in children.

ritardando (ˌrɪtɑː'dændəʊ) *adj, adv* another term for **rallentando.** Abbrev.: **rit.** ORIG C19: from It., from *ritardare* to slow down

Ritchie ★ ('rɪtʃɪ) *n* **Guy (Stuart)**. born 1968, British film director and screenwriter; his films include *Lock, Stock and Two Smoking Barrels* (1998) and *Snatch* (2000); he married Madonna in 2000.

rite (raɪt) *n* **1** a formal act prescribed or customary in religious ceremonies: *the rite of baptism.* **2** a particular body of such acts, esp. of a particular Christian Church: *the Latin rite.* **3** a Christian Church: *the Greek rite.* ORIG C14: from L *rītus* religious ceremony

ritenuto (ˌrɪtə'nuːtəʊ) *adj, adv Music.* **1** held back momentarily. **2** Abbrev.: **rit.** another term for **rallentando.** ORIG C19: from It., from L *retinēre* to hold back

rite of passage *n* a ceremony performed in some cultures at times when an individual changes his status, as at puberty and marriage.

ritornello (ˌrɪtə'nɛləʊ) *n, pl* **ritornellos** *or* **ritornelli** (-liː). *Music.* a short piece of instrumental music interpolated in a song. ORIG It., lit.: a little return

ritual ('rɪtjʊəl) *n* **1** the prescribed or established form of a religious or other ceremony. **2** such prescribed forms in general or collectively. **3** stereotyped activity or behaviour. **4** any formal act, institution, or procedure that is followed consistently: *the ritual of the law.* ◆ *adj* **5** of or characteristic of religious, social, or other rituals. ORIG C16: from L *rītuālis,* from *rītus* RITE
▸ **'ritually** *adv*

ritualism ('rɪtjʊəˌlɪzəm) *n* **1** exaggerated emphasis on the importance of rites and ceremonies. **2** the study of rites and ceremonies, esp. magical or religious ones.
▸ **'ritualist** *n* ▸ **ˌritual'istic** *adj* ▸ **ˌritual'istically** *adv*

ritualize *or* **ritualise** ('rɪtjʊəˌlaɪz) *vb* **ritualizes, ritualizing, ritualized** *or* **ritualises, ritualising, ritualised. 1** (*intr*) to engage in ritualism or devise rituals. **2** (*tr*) to make (something) into a ritual.

ritzy ('rɪtsɪ) *adj* **ritzier, ritziest.** *Sl.* luxurious or elegant. ORIG C20: after the hotels established by César *Ritz* (1850–1918), Swiss hotelier
▸ **'ritzily** *adv* ▸ **'ritziness** *n*

rival ('raɪvᵊl) *n* **1a** a person, organization, team, etc., that competes with another for the same object or in the same field. **1b** (*as modifier*): *rival suitors.* **2** a person or thing that is considered the equal of another: *she is without rival in the field of physics.* ◆ *vb* **rivals, rivalling, rivalled** *or US* **rivals, rivaling, rivaled.** (*tr*) **3** to be the equal or near equal of: *an empire that rivalled Rome.* **4** to try to equal or surpass. ORIG C16: from L *rīvalis,* lit.: one who shares the same brook, from *rīvus* a brook

rivalry (ˈraɪvəlrɪ) *n, pl* **rivalries. 1** the act of rivalling. **2** the state of being a rival or rivals.

rive (raɪv) *vb* **rives, riving, rived; rived** *or* **riven** (ˈrɪvᵊn). (*usually passive*) **1** to split asunder: *a tree riven by lightning.* **2** to tear apart: *riven to shreds.* ORIG C13: from ON *rīfa*

river (ˈrɪvə) *n* **1a** a large natural stream of fresh water flowing along a definite course, usually into the sea, being fed by tributary streams. **1b** (*as modifier*): *river traffic.* **1c** (*in combination*): *riverside; riverbed.* Related adjs.: **fluvial, potamic. 2** any abundant stream or flow: *a river of blood.* ORIG C13: from OF, from L *rīpārius* of a river bank, from *rīpa* bank
▸ ˈ**riverless** *adj*

Rivera ★ (*Spanish* riˈβera) *n* **Diego** (ˈdjeɣo). 1886–1957, Mexican painter, noted for his monumental murals.

riverine (ˈrɪvəˌraɪn) *adj* **1** of, like, relating to, or produced by a river. **2** located or dwelling near a river; riparian.

Rivers ★ (ˈrɪvəz) *n* a state of S Nigeria, in the Niger River Delta on the Gulf of Guinea. Capital: Port Harcourt. Pop.: 4 454 337 (1995 est.). Area: 21 850 sq. km (8436 sq. miles).

Riverside ★ (ˈrɪvəˌsaɪd) *n* a city in SW California. Pop.: 211 000 (1989).

rivet (ˈrɪvɪt) *n* **1** a short metal pin for fastening two or more pieces together, having a head at one end, the other end being hammered flat after being passed through holes in the pieces. ◆ *vb* **rivets, riveting, riveted.** (*tr*) **2** to join by riveting. **3** to hammer in order to form into a head. **4** (*often passive*) to cause to be fixed, as in fascinated attention, horror, etc.: *to be riveted to the spot.* ORIG C14: from OF, from *river* to fasten, from ?
▸ ˈ**riveter** *n* ▸ ˈ**riveting** *adj*

riviera (ˌrɪvɪˈɛərə) *n* a coastal region reminiscent of the Riviera.

Riviera ★ (ˌrɪvɪˈɛərə) *n* the Mediterranean coastal region between Cannes, France, and La Spezia, Italy: contains some of Europe's most popular resorts. ORIG C18: from It. lit.: shore, ult. from L *rīpa* bank, shore

rivière (ˌrɪvɪˈɛə) *n* a necklace the diamonds or other precious stones of which gradually increase in size up to a large centre stone. ORIG C19: from F: brook, RIVER

rivulet (ˈrɪvjʊlɪt) *n* a small stream. ORIG C16: from It. *rivoletto,* from L *rīvulus,* from *rīvus* stream

Riyadh ★ (rɪˈjɑːd) *n* the joint capital (with Mecca) of Saudi Arabia, situated in a central oasis: the largest city in the country. Pop.: 1 800 000 (1991 est.).

riyal (rɪˈjɑːl) *n* the standard monetary and currency unit of Saudi Arabia or Yemen. ORIG from Ar. *riyāl,* from Sp. *real*

Rizal[1] ★ (*Spanish* riˈθal) *n* another name for **Pasay.**

Rizal[2] ★ (*Spanish* riˈθal) *n* **Jose** (xoˈse). 1861–96, Philippine nationalist, executed by the Spanish during the Philippine revolution.

Rizzio (ˈrɪtsɪəʊ) *or* **Riccio** ★ *n* **David.** ?1533–66, Italian musician who became the secretary of Mary, Queen of Scots; murdered at the instigation of a group of nobles.

RL *abbrev. for* **1** Rugby League. **2** real life; used esp. in e-mails, text messages, etc.

rly *abbrev. for* railway.

rm *abbrev. for:* **1** ream. **2** room.

RM *abbrev. for:* **1** Royal Mail. **2** Royal Marines. **3** (in Canada) Rural Municipality.

RMA *abbrev. for* Royal Military Academy (Sandhurst).

rms *abbrev. for* root mean square.

Rn *the chemical symbol for* radon.

RN *abbrev. for:* **1** (in Canada) Registered Nurse. **2** Royal Navy.

RNA *n Biochem.* ribonucleic acid; any of a group of nucleic acids, present in all living cells, that play an essential role in the synthesis of proteins.

RNAS *abbrev. for:* **1** Royal Naval Air Service(s). **2** Royal Naval Air Station.

RNIB (in Britain) *abbrev. for* Royal National Institute for the Blind.

RNID (in Britain) *abbrev. for* Royal National Institute for Deaf People.

RNLI *abbrev. for* Royal National Lifeboat Institution.

RNZAF *abbrev. for* Royal New Zealand Air Force.

RNZN *abbrev. for* Royal New Zealand Navy.

roach[1] (rəʊtʃ) *n, pl* **roaches** *or* **roach.** a European freshwater food fish having a deep compressed body and reddish ventral and tail fins. ORIG C14: from OF *roche,* from ?

roach[2] (rəʊtʃ) *n* **1** short for **cockroach. 2** *Sl.* the butt of a cannabis cigarette.

roach[3] (rəʊtʃ) *n Naut.* the curve at the foot of a square sail. ORIG C18: from ?

roach clip *n Sl.* a small clip resembling tweezers, used to hold the butt of a cannabis cigarette, in order to avoid burning one's fingers.

road (rəʊd) *n* **1a** an open way, usually surfaced with tarmac or concrete, providing passage from one place to another. **1b** (*as modifier*): *road traffic; a road sign.* **1c** (*in combination*): *the roadside.* **2a** a street. **2b** (*cap. when part of a name*): *London Road.* **3** *Brit.* one of the tracks of a railway. **4** a way, path, or course: *the road to fame.* **5** (*often pl*) *Naut.* Also called: **roadstead.** a partly sheltered anchorage. **6** a drift or tunnel in a mine, esp. a level one. **7 hit the road.** *Sl.* to start or resume travelling. **8 one for the road.** *Inf.* a last alcoholic drink before leaving. **9 on the road. 9a** travelling about; on tour. **9b** leading a wandering life. **10 take (to) the road.** to begin a journey or tour. ORIG OE *rād;* rel. to *rīdan* to RIDE
▸ ˈ**roadless** *adj*

road allowance *n Canad.* land reserved by the government to be used for public roads.

roadblock (ˈrəʊdˌblɒk) *n* a barrier set up across a road by the police or military, in order to stop a fugitive, inspect traffic, etc.

road-fund licence *n Brit.* a paper disc showing that the tax in respect of a motor vehicle has been paid. ORIG C20: from the former *road fund* for the maintenance of public highways

road hog *n Inf.* a selfish or aggressive driver.

roadholding (ˈrəʊdˌhəʊldɪŋ) *n* the extent to which a motor vehicle is stable and does not skid, esp. on sharp bends or wet roads.

roadhouse (ˈrəʊdˌhaʊs) *n* a pub, restaurant, etc., that is situated at the side of a road.

road hump *n* the official name for **sleeping policeman.**

roadie (ˈrəʊdɪ) *n Inf.* a person who transports and sets up equipment for a band or group. ORIG C20: shortened from *road manager*

road metal *n* crushed rock, broken stone, etc., used to construct a road.

road movie *n* a genre of film in which the chief character takes to the road, esp. to escape the law, his own past, etc.

road pricing *n* the practice of charging motorists for using certain stretches of road, in order to reduce congestion.

road rage *n* aggressive behaviour by a motorist in response to the actions of another road user.

roadroller (ˈrəʊdˌrəʊlə) *n* a motor vehicle with heavy rollers for compressing road surfaces during roadmaking.

road show *n* **1** *Radio.* **1a** a live programme, usually with some audience participation, transmitted from a radio van taking a particular show on the road. **1b** the personnel and equipment needed for such a show. **2** a group of entertainers on tour. **3** any occasion when an organization attracts publicity while touring or visiting: *the royal road show.*

roadstead (ˈrəʊdˌsted) *n Naut.* another word for **road** (sense 5).

roadster (ˈrəʊdstə) *n* **1** an open car, esp. one seating only two. **2** a kind of bicycle.

road tax *n* a tax paid, usually annually, on motor vehicles in use on the roads.

road test *n* **1** a test to ensure that a vehicle is roadworthy, esp. after repair or servicing, by driving it on roads. **2** a test of something in actual use. ◆ *vb* **road-test.** (*tr*) **3** to test (a vehicle, etc.) in this way.

road train *n Austral.* a truck pulling one or more large trailers, esp. on western roads.

roadway ('rəʊdˌweɪ) *n* **1** the surface of a road. **2** the part of a road that is used by vehicles.

roadwork ('rəʊdˌwɜːk) *n* sports training by running along roads.

roadworks ('rəʊdˌwɜːks) *pl n* repairs to a road or cable under a road, esp. when forming an obstruction to traffic.

roadworthy ('rəʊdˌwɜːðɪ) *adj* (of a motor vehicle) mechanically sound; fit for use on the roads.
▸ **'roadˌworthiness** *n*

roam (rəʊm) *vb* **1** to travel or walk about with no fixed purpose or direction. ◆ *n* **2** the act of roaming. ORIG C13: from ?
▸ **'roamer** *n*

roan (rəʊn) *adj* **1** (of a horse) having a bay (**red roan**), chestnut (**strawberry roan**), or black (**blue roan**) coat sprinkled with white hairs. ◆ *n* **2** a horse having such a coat. **3** a soft sheepskin leather used in bookbinding, etc. ORIG C16: from OF, from Sp. *roano,* prob. from Gothic *rauths* red

Roanoke Island ★ ('rəʊəˌnəʊk) *n* an island off the coast of North Carolina: site of the first attempted English settlement in America. Length: 19 km (12 miles). Average width: 5 km (3 miles).

roar (rɔː) *vb* (*mainly intr*) **1** (of lions and other animals) to utter characteristic loud growling cries. **2** (*also tr*) (of people) to utter (something) with a loud deep cry, as in anger or triumph. **3** to laugh in a loud hearty unrestrained manner. **4** (of horses) to breathe with laboured rasping sounds. **5** (of the wind, waves, etc.) to blow or break loudly and violently, as during a storm. **6** (of a fire) to burn fiercely with a roaring sound. **7** (*tr*) to bring (oneself) into a certain condition by roaring: *to roar oneself hoarse.* ◆ *n* **8** a loud deep cry, uttered by a person or crowd, esp. in anger or triumph. **9** a prolonged loud cry of certain animals, esp. lions. **10** any similar noise made by a fire, the wind, waves, an engine, etc. ORIG OE *rārian*
▸ **'roarer** *n*

roaring ('rɔːrɪŋ) *adj* **1** *Inf.* very brisk and profitable (esp. in **a roaring trade**). ◆ *adv* **2** noisily or boisterously (esp. in **roaring drunk**). ◆ *n* **3** a loud prolonged cry.
▸ **'roaringly** *adv*

roast (rəʊst) *vb* (*mainly tr*) **1** to cook (meat or other food) by dry heat, usually with added fat and esp. in an oven. **2** to brown or dry (coffee, etc.) by exposure to heat. **3** *Metallurgy.* to heat (an ore) in order to produce a concentrate that is easier to smelt. **4** to heat (oneself or something) to an extreme degree, as when sunbathing, etc. **5** (*intr*) to be excessively and uncomfortably hot. **6** (*tr*) *Inf.* to criticize severely. ◆ *n* **7** something that has been roasted, esp. meat. ORIG C13: from OF *rostir,* of Gmc origin
▸ **'roaster** *n*

roasting ('rəʊstɪŋ) *Inf.* ◆ *adj* **1** extremely hot. ◆ *n* **2** severe criticism.

rob (rɒb) *vb* **robs, robbing, robbed. 1** to take something from (someone) illegally, as by force. **2** (*tr*) to plunder (a house, etc.). **3** (*tr*) to deprive unjustly: *to be robbed of an opportunity.* ORIG C13: from OF *rober,* of Gmc origin
▸ **'robber** *n*

Robbe-Grillet ★ (*French* rɔbgrijɛ) *n* **Alain** (alɛ̃). born 1922, French novelist; his novels include *Jealousy* (1957).

Robben Island ★ ('rɒbᵊn) *n* a small island in South Africa, 11 km (7 miles) off the Cape Peninsula: formerly used by the South African government to house political prisoners.

robbery ('rɒbərɪ) *n, pl* **robberies. 1** *Criminal law.* the stealing of property from a person by using or threatening to use force. **2** the act or an instance of robbing.

Robbia ★ ('rəʊbɪə; *Italian* 'robbja) *n* **1 Andrea della** (an'drɛːa 'dɛlla). 1435–1525, Florentine sculptor. **2** his uncle, **Luca della** ('luːka 'dɛlla). ?1400–82, Florentine sculptor.

Robbins ★ ('rɒbɪnz) *n* **Jerome.** 1918–98, US ballet dancer and choreographer; noted for his choreography of *West Side Story* (1957).

robe (rəʊb) *n* **1** any loose flowing garment, esp. the official vestment of a peer, judge, or academic. **2** a dressing gown or bathrobe. ◆ *vb* **robes, robing, robed. 3** to put a robe, etc., on (oneself or someone else). ORIG C13: from OF; of Gmc origin

Robert I ★ ('rɒbət) *n* known as *Robert the Bruce.* 1274–1329, king of Scotland (1306–29): he defeated the English army of Edward II at Bannockburn (1314) and gained recognition of Scotland's independence (1328).

Robert II ★ *n* 1316–90, king of Scotland (1371–90).

Robert III ★ *n* ?1337–1406, king of Scotland (1390–1406), son of Robert II.

Roberts ★ ('rɒbəts) *n* **1 Frederick Sleigh,** 1st Earl. 1832–1914, British field marshal. He was awarded the Victoria Cross (1858) for his service during the Indian Mutiny and was commander in chief (1899–1900) in the second Boer War. **2 Julia.** born 1967, US actress born in Smyrna, Georgia. Her films include *Pretty Woman* (1990), *Notting Hill* (1999), and *Erin Brockovich* (2000).

Robeson ★ ('rəʊbsən) *n* **Paul.** 1898–1976, US bass singer and actor.

Robespierre ★ ('rəʊbzpjɛə; *French* rɔbzpjɛr) *n* **Maximilien François Marie Isidore de** (maksimiljɛ̃ frɑ̃swa mari izidɔr də). 1758–94, French revolutionary and Jacobin leader: established the Reign of Terror: executed in the coup d'état of Thermidor (1794).

Robey ★ ('rəʊbɪ) *n* Sir **George**, original name *George Edward Wade*, known as *the prime minister of mirth.* 1869–1954, British music-hall comedian, who also appeared in films.

robin ('rɒbɪn) *n* **1** Also called: **robin redbreast.** a small Old World songbird related to the thrushes. The adult has a brown back, orange-red breast and face, and grey underparts. **2** a North American thrush similar to but larger than the Old World robin. ORIG C16: arbitrary use of name *Robin*

Robin Goodfellow ★ ('rɒbɪn 'gʊdˌfɛləʊ) *n* another name for **puck**[2].

Robin Hood ★ *n* a legendary English outlaw, who lived in Sherwood Forest (in the reign of Richard I) and robbed the rich to give to the poor.

robinia (rə'bɪnɪə) *n* any tree of the leguminous genus *Robinia,* esp. the locust tree.

Robinson ★ ('rɒbɪnsən) *n* **1 Anne (Josephine)**. born 1944, British journalist and broadcaster: presenter of the television quiz show *The Weakest Link* (from 2000). **2 Edward G.**, real name *Emanuel Goldenberg.* 1893–1973, US film actor, born in Romania. His films include *Little Caesar* (1930) and *All My Sons* (1948). **3 Edwin Arlington.** 1869–1935, US poet. **4 (William) Heath.** 1872–1944, British illustrator, noted for his drawings of fantastic machines. **5 John (Arthur Thomas)**. 1919–83, British theologian; Bishop of Woolwich (1959–69); author of *Honest to God* (1963). **6 Mary.** born 1944, Irish stateswoman; president of the Republic of Ireland (1990–97); UN High Commissioner for Human Rights (1997–2001). **7 Smokey,** real name *William Robinson.* born 1940, US Motown singer and songwriter. **8 "Sugar" Ray,** real name *Walker Smith.* 1921–89, US boxer, five-times world middleweight champion.

Robinson Crusoe ★ *n* the hero of Daniel Defoe's novel *Robinson Crusoe* (1719), who survived being shipwrecked on a desert island. See also **Selkirk**.

roborant ('rəʊbərənt, 'rɒb-) *adj* **1** tending to fortify or increase strength. ◆ *n* **2** a drug or agent that increases strength. ORIG C17: from L *roborāre* to strengthen, from *rōbur* an oak

robot ('rəʊbɒt) *n* **1** any automated machine programmed to perform specific mechanical functions in the manner of a human. **2** (*modifier*) automatic: *a robot pilot.* **3** a person who works or behaves like a machine. **4** *S. African.* a set of traffic lights. ORIG C20: (used in *R.U.R.,* a play by Karel ČAPEK) from Czech *robota* work
▸ **ro'botic** *adj* ▸ **'robot-ˌlike** *adj*

★ people and places

robot bomb *n* another name for the **V-1**.

robot dancing *or* **robotic dancing** (rəʊˈbɒtɪk) *n* a dance of the 1980s, characterized by jerky, mechanical movements. Also called: **robotics**.

robotics (rəʊˈbɒtɪks) *n* (*functioning as sing*) **1** the science or technology of designing, building, and using robots. **2** another name for **robot dancing**.

Rob Roy ★ (ˈrɒb ˈrɔɪ) *n* real name *Robert Macgregor*. 1671–1734, Scottish outlaw.

Robson[1] ★ (ˈrɒbsən) *n* **Mount**. a mountain in SW Canada, in E British Columbia: the highest peak in the Canadian Rockies. Height: 3954 m (12 972 ft).

Robson[2] ★ (ˈrɒbsən) *n* **1 Bobby**, full name *Robert William*. born 1933, English footballer and manager of England (1982–90). **2 Bryan**. born 1957, English footballer and manager: captain of England (1982–90). **3** Dame **Flora**. 1902–84, British actress.

robust (rəʊˈbʌst, ˈrəʊbʌst) *adj* **1** strong in constitution. **2** sturdily built: *a robust shelter*. **3** requiring or suited to physical strength: *a robust sport*. **4** (esp. of wines) having a full-bodied flavour. **5** rough or boisterous. **6** (of thought, intellect, etc.) straightforward. ORIG C16: from L *rōbustus*, from *rōbur* an oak, strength
▸ **roˈbustly** *adv*

robusta (rəʊˈbʌstə) *n* **1** a species of coffee tree, *Coffea canephora*. **2** coffee or coffee beans obtained from this plant. ORIG from L *rōbustus* robust

robustious (rəʊˈbʌstʃəs) *adj Arch.* **1** rough; boisterous. **2** strong, robust, or stout.
▸ **roˈbustiously** *adv* ▸ **roˈbustiousness** *n*

robustness (rəʊˈbʌstnɪs) *n* **1** the quality of being robust. **2** *Computing*. the ability of a computer system to cope with errors during execution.

roc (rɒk) *n* (in Arabian legend) a bird of enormous size and power. ORIG C16: from Ar., from Persian *rukh*

ROC *abbrev. for* Royal Observer Corps.

Roca ★ (ˈrəʊkə) *n* **Cape**. a cape in SW central Portugal, near Lisbon: the westernmost point of continental Europe.

rocaille (rɒˈkaɪ) *n* decorative rock or shell work, esp. as ornamentation in a rococo fountain, grotto, or interior. ORIG from F, from *roc* ROCK[1]

rocambole (ˈrɒkəmˌbəʊl) *n* a variety of alliaceous plant whose garlic-like bulb is used for seasoning. ORIG C17: from F, from G *Rockenbolle*, lit.: distaff bulb (with reference to its shape)

Rocard ★ (*French* rɔkaːr) *n* **Michel**. born 1930, French politician: prime minister (1988–91).

Rochdale ★ (ˈrɒtʃˌdeɪl) *n* **1** a town in NW England, in Greater Manchester: former centre of textile industry. Pop.: 94 313 (1991). **2** a unitary authority in NW England, in Greater Manchester. Pop.: 207 100 (1996 est.). Area: 159 sq. km (61 sq. miles).

Rochelle salt (rɒˈʃɛl) *n* a white crystalline double salt used in Seidlitz powder. Formula: $KNaC_4H_4O_6.4H_2O$. ORIG C18: after LA ROCHELLE

roche moutonnée (rəʊʃ ˌmuːtəˈneɪ) *n, pl* **roches moutonnées** (rəʊʃ ˌmuːtəˈneɪz). a rounded mass of rock smoothed and striated by ice that has flowed over it. ORIG C19: F, lit.: fleecy rock, from *mouton* sheep

Rochester[1] ★ (ˈrɒtʃɪstə) *n* **1** a city in SE England, in Kent on the River Medway: with Chatham and Gillingham forms the conurbation of the Medway towns. Pop.: 23 971 (1991). **2** a city in the US, in NW New York State, on Lake Ontario. Pop.: 231 170 (1994 est.).

Rochester[2] ★ (ˈrɒtʃɪstə) *n* **2nd Earl of**, title of *John Wilmot*. 1647–80, English poet, wit, and libertine. His poems include satires, love lyrics, and bawdy verse.

rochet (ˈrɒtʃɪt) *n* a white surplice with tight sleeves, worn by bishops, abbots, and certain other Church dignitaries. ORIG C14: from OF, from *roc* coat, of Gmc origin

rock[1] (rɒk) *n* **1** *Geol.* any aggregate of minerals that makes up part of the earth's crust. It may be unconsolidated, such as a sand, clay, or mud, or consolidated, such as granite, limestone, or coal. **2** any hard mass of consolidated mineral matter, such as a boulder. **3** *US, Canad., & Austral.* a stone. **4** a person or thing suggesting a rock, esp. in being dependable, unchanging, or providing firm foundation. **5** *Brit.* a hard sweet, typically a long brightly coloured peppermint-flavoured stick, sold esp. in holiday resorts. **6** *Sl.* a jewel, esp. a diamond. **7** *Sl.* another name for **crack** (sense 28). **8 on the rocks**. **8a** in a state of ruin or destitution. **8b** (of drinks, esp. whisky) served with ice. ORIG C14: from OF *roche*, from ?

rock[2] (rɒk) *vb* **1** to move or cause to move from side to side or backwards and forwards. **2** to reel or sway or cause (someone) to reel or sway, as with a violent shock or emotion. **3** (*tr*) to shake or move (something) violently. **4** (*intr*) to dance in the rock-and-roll style. ◆ *n* **5** a rocking motion. **6** short for **rock and roll**. **7** Also called: **rock music**. any of various styles of pop music having a heavy beat, derived from rock and roll. ORIG OE *roccian*

Rock ★ (rɒk) *n* **the**. an informal name for **Gibraltar**.

rockabilly (ˈrɒkəˌbɪlɪ) *n* a fast, spare style of White rock music which originated in the mid-1950s in the US South. ORIG C20: from ROCK (AND ROLL) + (HILL)BILLY

Rockall ★ (ˈrɒkɔːl) *n* an uninhabited British island in the N Atlantic, 354 km (220 miles) W of the Outer Hebrides. Area: 0.07 ha (0.18 acres).

rock and roll *or* **rock'n'roll** *n* **1a** a type of pop music originating in the 1950s as a blend of rhythm and blues and country and western. **1b** (*as modifier*): *the rock-and-roll era*. **2** dancing performed to such music, with exaggerated body movements stressing the beat. ◆ *vb* **3** (*intr*) to perform this dance.
▸ **rock and roller** *or* **rock'n'roller** *n*

rock bass (bæs) *n* an eastern North American freshwater food fish, related to the sunfish family.

rock bottom *n* **a** the lowest possible level. **b** (*as modifier*): *rock-bottom prices*.

rock-bound *adj* hemmed in or encircled by rocks. Also (poetic): **rock-girt**.

rock cake *n* a small cake containing dried fruit and spice, with a rough surface supposed to resemble a rock.

rock crystal *n* a pure transparent colourless quartz, used in electronic and optical equipment.

rock dove *or* **pigeon** *n* a common dove from which domestic and feral pigeons are descended.

Rockefeller ★ (ˈrɒkəˌfɛlə) *n* **1 John D**(**avison**). 1839–1937, US industrialist and philanthropist. **2** his son, **John D**(**avison**). 1874–1960, US philanthropist. **3** his son, **Nelson** (**Aldrich**). 1908–79, US politician; governor of New York State (1958–74); vice president (1974–76).

rocker (ˈrɒkə) *n* **1** any of various devices that transmit or operate with a rocking motion. See also **rocker arm**. **2** another word for **rocking chair**. **3** either of two curved supports on the legs of a chair on which it may rock. **4a** an ice skate with a curved blade. **4b** the curve itself. **5** a rock-music performer, fan, or song. **6** *Brit.* an adherent of a youth movement rooted in the 1950s, characterized by motorcycle trappings. **7 off one's rocker**. *Sl.* crazy.

rocker arm *n* a lever that rocks about a pivot, esp. a lever in an internal-combustion engine that transmits the motion of a pushrod or cam to a valve.

rockery (ˈrɒkərɪ) *n, pl* **rockeries**. a garden constructed with rocks, esp. one where alpine plants are grown.

rocket[1] (ˈrɒkɪt) *n* **1** a self-propelling device, esp. a cylinder containing a mixture of solid explosives, used as a firework, distress signal, etc. **2a** any vehicle that carries its own fuel and oxidant to burn in a rocket engine, esp. one used to carry a spacecraft, etc. **2b** (*as modifier*): *rocket launcher*. **3** *Brit. & NZ inf.* a severe reprimand (esp. in **get a rocket**). ◆ *vb* **rockets, rocketing, rocketed**. **4** (*tr*) to propel (a missile, spacecraft, etc.) by means of a rocket. **5** (*intr;* foll. by *off, away,* etc.) to move off at high speed. **6** (*intr*) to rise rapidly: *he rocketed to the top*. ORIG C17: from OF, from It. *rochetto*, dim. of *rocca* distaff, of Gmc origin

rocket[2] (ˈrɒkɪt) *n* any of several plants of the mustard family, typically having yellowish flowers, such as **London rocket** and **yellow rocket**. See also **arugula, wall rocket**. ORIG C16: from F *roquette*, from It. *rochetta*, from L *ērūca* hairy plant

★ people and places

rocket engine *n* a reaction engine in which a fuel and oxidizer are burnt in a combustion chamber, the products of combustion expanding through a nozzle and producing thrust.

rocket scientist *n* a person of considerable intelligence and ability (esp. in the phrase **not exactly a rocket scientist**).
▸ **rocket science** *n*

rocketry ('rɒkɪtrɪ) *n* the science and technology of the design, operation, maintenance, and launching of rockets.

rockfish ('rɒkˌfɪʃ) *n, pl* **rockfish** *or* **rockfishes. 1** any of various fishes that live among rocks, such as the goby, bass, etc. **2** *Brit.* any of several coarse fishes when used as food, esp. the dogfish or wolffish.

Rockford ★ ('rɒkfəd) *n* a city in N Illinois, on the Rock River. Pop.: 143 263 (1994 est.).

rock garden *n* a garden featuring rocks or rockeries.

Rockhampton ★ (rɒk'hæmptən, -'hæmtən) *n* a port in Australia, in E Queensland on the Fitzroy River. Pop.: 65 868 (1993).

Rockies ★ ('rɒkɪz) *pl n* another name for the **Rocky Mountains.**

rocking chair *n* a chair set on curving supports so that the sitter may rock backwards and forwards.

Rockingham ★ ('rɒkɪŋəm) *n* **Marquess of,** title of *Charles Watson-Wentworth.* 1730–82, British statesman and opposition leader, whose supporters were known as the **Rockingham Whigs**; prime minister (1765–66; 1782).

rocking horse *n* a toy horse mounted on a pair of rockers on which a child can rock to and fro in a seesaw movement.

rocking stone *n* a boulder so delicately poised that it can be rocked.

rockling ('rɒklɪŋ) *n, pl* **rocklings** *or* **rockling.** a small gadoid fish which has an elongated body with barbels around the mouth and occurs mainly in the North Atlantic Ocean. ORIG C17: from ROCK[1] + -LING[1]

rock lobster *n* another name for the **spiny lobster.**

rock melon *n US, Austral., & NZ.* another name for **cantaloupe.**

rock pigeon *n* another name for **rock dove.**

rock plant *n* any plant that grows on rocks or in rocky ground.

rock rabbit *n S. African.* another name for **dassie.** See **hyrax.**

rockrose ('rɒkˌrəʊz) *n* any of various shrubs or herbaceous plants cultivated for their yellow-white or reddish roselike flowers.

rock salmon *n Brit.* a former term for **rockfish** (sense 2).

rock salt *n* another name for **halite.**

rock snake *or* **python** *n* any large Australasian python of the genus *Liasis.*

rock tripe *n Canad.* any of various edible lichens that grow on rocks and are used in the North as a survival food.

Rockwell ★ ('rɒkˌwɛl, -wəl) *n* **Norman.** 1894–1978, US illustrator.

rock wool *n* another name for **mineral wool.**

rocky[1] ('rɒkɪ) *adj* **rockier, rockiest. 1** consisting of or abounding in rocks: *a rocky shore.* **2** unyielding: *rocky determination.* **3** hard like rock: *rocky muscles.*
▸ **'rockiness** *n*

rocky[2] ('rɒkɪ) *adj* **rockier, rockiest. 1** weak or unstable. **2** *Inf.* (of a person) dizzy; nauseated.
▸ **'rockily** *adv* ▸ **'rockiness** *n*

Rocky Mountains *or* **Rockies** ★ *pl n* the chief mountain system of W North America, extending from British Columbia to New Mexico: forms the Continental Divide. Highest peak: Mount Elbert, 4399 m (14 431 ft). Mount McKinley (6194 m (20 320 ft)), in the Alaska Range, is not strictly part of the Rocky Mountains.

Rocky Mountain spotted fever *n* an acute rickettsial disease characterized by high fever, chills, pain in muscles and joints, etc. It is caused by the bite of an infected tick.

rococo (rə'kəʊkəʊ) *n* (*often cap.*) **1** a style of architecture and decoration that originated in France in the early 18th century, characterized by elaborate but graceful ornamentation. **2** an 18th-century style of music characterized by prettiness and extreme use of ornamentation. **3** any florid or excessively ornamental style. ◆ *adj* **4** denoting, being in, or relating to the rococo. **5** florid or excessively elaborate. ORIG C19: from F, from ROCAILLE, from *roc* ROCK[1]

rod (rɒd) *n* **1** a slim cylinder of metal, wood, etc. **2** a switch or bundle of switches used to administer corporal punishment. **3** any of various staffs of insignia or office. **4** power, esp. of a tyrannical kind: *a dictator's iron rod.* **5** a straight slender shoot, stem, or cane of a woody plant. **6** See **fishing rod. 7** Also called: **pole, perch. 7a** a unit of length equal to 5½ yards. **7b** a unit of square measure equal to 30¼ square yards. **8** *Surveying.* another name (esp. US) for **staff**[1] (sense 8). **9** Also called: **retinal rod.** any of the elongated cylindrical cells in the retina of the eye, which are sensitive to dim light but not to colour. **10** any rod-shaped bacterium. **11** *US.* a slang name for **pistol. 12** short for **hot rod.** ORIG OE *rodd*
▸ **'rodˌlike** *adj*

Rodchenko ★ (rɒd'tʃɛŋkəʊ) *n* **Alexander** (**Mikhailovich**). 1891–1956, Soviet painter, sculptor, designer, and photographer, noted for his abstract geometrical style: a member of the constructivist movement.

rode (rəʊd) *vb* the past tense of **ride.**

rodent ('rəʊdᵊnt) *n* **a** any of the relatively small placental mammals having constantly growing incisor teeth specialized for gnawing. The group includes rats, mice, squirrels, etc. **b** (*as modifier*): *rodent characteristics.* ORIG C19: from L *rōdere* to gnaw
▸ **'rodent-ˌlike** *adj*

rodent ulcer *n* a slow-growing malignant tumour on the face, usually occurring at the edge of the eyelids, lips, or nostrils.

rodeo ('rəʊdɪˌəʊ) *n, pl* **rodeos.** *Chiefly US & Canad.* **1** a display of the skills of cowboys, including bareback riding. **2** the rounding up of cattle for branding, etc. **3** an enclosure for cattle that have been rounded up. ORIG C19: from Sp., from *rodear* to go around, from *rueda* a wheel, from L *rota*

Roderic ★ ('rɒdərɪk) *n* See **Rory O'Connor.**

Rodgers ★ ('rɒdʒəz) *n* **Richard.** 1902–79, US composer of musical comedies, including *Pal Joey* (1940; with Lorenz Hart) and *Oklahoma!* (1943; with Oscar Hammerstein II).

Ródhos ★ ('rɔðɔs) *n* transliteration of the Modern Greek name for **Rhodes.**

Rodin ★ (*French* rɔdɛ̃) *n* **Auguste** (ogyst). 1840–1917, French sculptor. His works include *The Kiss* (1886) and *The Thinker* (1905).

Rodney ★ ('rɒdnɪ) *n* **George Brydges,** 1st Baron Rodney. 1719–92, British admiral: captured Martinique (1762): defeated the Spanish at Cape St Vincent (1780) and the French off Dominica (1782), restoring British superiority in the Caribbean.

rodomontade (ˌrɒdəmɒn'teɪd, -'tɑːd) *Literary.* ◆ *n* **1a** boastful words or behaviour. **1b** (*as modifier*): *rodomontade behaviour.* ◆ *vb* **rodomontades, rodomontading, rodomontaded. 2** (*intr*) to boast or rant. ORIG C17: from F, from It. *rodomonte* a boaster, from *Rodomonte,* the name of a braggart king of Algiers in epic poems

Rodrigo ★ (*Spanish* rɔ'ðriγo) *n* **Joaquín** (xwa'kin). 1902–99, Spanish composer. His works include *Concierto de Aranjuez* (1940) for guitar and orchestra.

roe[1] (rəʊ) *n* **1** Also called: **hard roe.** the ovary of a female fish filled with mature eggs. **2** Also called: **soft roe.** the testis of a male fish filled with mature sperm. ORIG C15: from MDu. *roge,* from OHG *roga*

roe[2] (rəʊ) *n, pl* **roes** *or* **roe.** short for **roe deer.** ORIG OE *rā(ha)*

Roe (rəʊ) *n* **Richard.** *Law.* (formerly) the defendant in a fictitious action, Doe versus Roe, to test a point of law. See also **Doe.**

roebuck (ˈrəʊˌbʌk) *n, pl* **roebucks** *or* **roebuck**. the male of the roe deer.

roe deer *n* a small graceful deer of woodlands of Europe and Asia. The antlers are small and the summer coat is reddish-brown.

Roeg ★ (rəʊg) *n* **Nic(olas)**. born 1928, British film director and cinematographer. Films include *Walkabout* (1970), *Don't Look Now* (1972), and *Heart of Darkness* (1994).

roentgen *or* **röntgen** (ˈrɒntgən, -tjən, ˈrɛnt-) *n* a unit of dose of electromagnetic radiation equal to the dose that will produce in air a charge of 0.258×10^{-3} coulomb on all ions of one sign. ORIG C19: after W. K. ROENTGEN

Roentgen *or* **Röntgen ★** (ˈrɒntgən, -tjən, ˈrɛnt-; *German* ˈrœntgən) *n* **Wilhelm Konrad** (ˈvɪlhɛlm ˈkɔnraːt). 1845–1923, German physicist, who discovered X-rays: Nobel prize for physics 1901.

roentgen ray *n* a former name for **X-ray**.

Roeselare ★ (ˈruːsəlaːrə) *n* the Flemish name for **Roulers**.

Roethke ★ (ˈrɛtkə) *n* **Theodore**. 1908–63, US poet, whose books include *The Far Field* (1964).

rogation (rəʊˈgeɪʃən) *n* (*usually pl*) *Christianity*. a solemn supplication, esp. in a form of ceremony prescribed by the Church. ORIG C14: from L *rogātiō*, from *rogāre* to ask, make supplication

Rogation Days *pl n* April 25 (the **Major Rogation**) and the Monday, Tuesday, and Wednesday before Ascension Day, observed by Christians as days of solemn supplication and marked by processions and special prayers.

roger (ˈrɒdʒə) *interj* **1** (used in signalling, telecommunications, etc.) message received and understood. **2** an expression of agreement. ◆ *vb* **3** *Taboo sl.* (of a man) to copulate (with). ORIG C20: from the name *Roger*, representing *R* for *received*

Rogers ★ (ˈrɒdʒəz) *n* **1 Ginger**, real name *Virginia McMath*. 1911–95, US dancer and film actress, who partnered Fred Astaire. **2 Richard**, Baron Rogers of Riverside. born 1933, British architect. His works include the Pompidou Centre in Paris (1971–77; with Renzo Piano), the Lloyd's building in London (1986), and the Millennium Dome in Greenwich, London. **3 William Penn Adair**, known as *Will*. 1879–1935, US actor and humorist.

Roget ★ (ˈrɒʒeɪ) *n* **Peter Mark**. 1779–1869, British physician, who on retirement devised a *Thesaurus of English Words and Phrases* (1852).

rogue (rəʊg) *n* **1** a dishonest or unprincipled person, esp. a man. **2** *Often jocular.* a mischievous or wayward person, often a child. **3** a crop plant which is inferior, diseased, or of a different, unwanted variety. **4a** any inferior or defective specimen. **4b** (*as modifier*): *rogue heroin.* **5** *Arch.* a vagrant. **6a** an animal of vicious character that leads a solitary life. **6b** (*as modifier*): *a rogue elephant.* ◆ *vb* **rogues, roguing, rogued. 7** (*tr*) to rid (a field or crop) of plants that are inferior, diseased, etc. ORIG C16: from ?

roguery (ˈrəʊgərɪ) *n, pl* **rogueries. 1** behaviour characteristic of a rogue. **2** a roguish or mischievous act.

rogues' gallery *n* **1** a collection of photographs of known criminals kept by the police for identification purposes. **2** a group of undesirable people.

roguish (ˈrəʊgɪʃ) *adj* **1** dishonest or unprincipled. **2** mischievous.

▸ **ˈroguishly** *adv*

roil (rɔɪl) *vb* **1** (*tr*) to make (a liquid) cloudy or turbid by stirring up dregs or sediment. **2** (*intr*) (esp. of a liquid) to be agitated. **3** (*intr*) *Dialect.* to be noisy. **4** (*tr*) *Now rare.* another word for **rile** (sense 1). ORIG C16: from ?

roister (ˈrɔɪstə) *vb* (*intr*) **1** to engage in noisy or unrestrained merrymaking. **2** to brag, bluster, or swagger. ORIG C16: from OF *rustre* lout, from *ruste* uncouth, from L *rusticus* rural

▸ **ˈroisterer** *n* ▸ **ˈroisterous** *adj* ▸ **ˈroisterously** *adv*

Roland ★ (ˈrəʊlənd) *n* **1** the greatest of the legendary 12 peers or paladins (of whom Oliver was another) in attendance on Charlemagne. **2 a Roland for an Oliver**. an effective retort or retaliation.

role *or* **rôle** (rəʊl) *n* **1** a part or character in a play, film, etc., to be played by an actor or actress. **2** *Psychol.* the part played by a person in a particular social setting, influenced by his expectation of what is appropriate. **3** usual function: *what is his role in the organization?* ORIG C17: from F *rôle* ROLL, an actor's script

role model *n* a person regarded by others, esp. younger people, as a good example to follow.

role-playing *n Psychol.* activity in which a person imitates, consciously or unconsciously, a role uncharacteristic of himself. See also **psychodrama**.

Rolf (rɒlf) *or* **Rolf the Ganger ★** *n* other names for **Rollo**.

Rolfe ★ (rɒlf) *n* **Frederick William**, also known as *Baron Corvo*. 1860–1913, British novelist. His best-known work is *Hadrian the Seventh* (1904).

roll (rəʊl) *vb* **1** to move or cause to move along by turning over and over. **2** to move or cause to move along on wheels or rollers. **3** to flow or cause to flow onwards in an undulating movement. **4** (*intr*) (of animals, etc.) to turn onto the back and kick. **5** (*intr*) to extend in undulations: *the hills roll down to the sea.* **6** (*intr;* usually foll. by *around*) to move or occur in cycles. **7** (*intr*) (of a planet, the moon, etc.) to revolve in an orbit. **8** (*intr;* foll. by *on, by,* etc.) to pass or elapse: *the years roll by.* **9** to rotate or cause to rotate wholly or partially: *to roll one's eyes.* **10** to curl, cause to curl, or admit of being curled, so as to form a ball, tube, or cylinder. **11** to make or form by shaping into a ball, tube, or cylinder: *to roll a cigarette.* **12** (often foll. by *out*) to spread or cause to spread out flat or smooth under or as if under a roller: *to roll pastry.* **13** to emit or utter with a deep prolonged reverberating sound: *the thunder rolled continuously.* **14** to trill or cause to be trilled: *to roll one's r's.* **15** (*intr*) (of a vessel, aircraft, rocket, etc.) to turn from side to side around the longitudinal axis. **16** to cause (an aircraft) to execute a roll or (of an aircraft) to execute a roll (sense 34). **17** (*intr*) to walk with a swaying gait, as when drunk. **18** *Chiefly US.* to throw (dice). **19** (*intr*) to operate or begin to operate: *the presses rolled.* **20** (*intr*) *Inf.* to make progress: *let the good times roll.* **21** (*tr*) *Inf., chiefly US & NZ.* to rob (a helpless person). ◆ *n* **22** the act or an instance of rolling. **23** anything rolled up in a cylindrical form: *a roll of newspaper.* **24** an official list or register, esp. of names: *an electoral roll.* **25** a rounded mass: *rolls of flesh.* **26** a cylinder used to flatten something; roller. **27** a small cake of bread for one person. **28** a flat pastry or cake rolled up with a meat (**sausage roll**), jam (**jam roll**), or other filling. **29** a swell or undulation on a surface: *the roll of the hills.* **30** a swaying, rolling, or unsteady movement or gait. **31** a deep prolonged reverberating sound: *the roll of thunder.* **32** a trilling sound; trill. **33** a very rapid beating of the sticks on a drum. **34** a flight manoeuvre in which an aircraft makes one complete rotation about its longitudinal axis without loss of height or change in direction. **35** *Sl.* an act of sexual intercourse or petting (esp. in **a roll in the hay**). **36** *US sl.* an amount of money, esp. a wad of paper money. **37 on a roll**. *Sl.* experiencing continued good luck or success. **38 strike off the roll(s)**. **38a** to expel from membership. **38b** to debar (a solicitor) from practising, usually because of dishonesty. ◆ See also **roll in, roll on,** etc. ORIG C14 *rollen*, from OF *roler*, from L *rotulus*, dim. of *rota* a wheel

Rolland ★ (*French* rɔlɑ̃) *n* **Romain** (rɔmɛ̃). 1866–1944, French writer, noted for his novels about a musical genius, *Jean-Christophe* (1904–12): Nobel prize for literature 1915.

rollbar (ˈrəʊlˌbɑː) *n* a bar that reinforces the frame of a car used for racing, rallying, etc., to protect the driver if the car should turn over.

roll call *n* the reading aloud of an official list of names, those present responding when their names are read out.

rolled gold *n* a metal, such as brass, coated with a thin layer of gold. Also (US): **filled gold**.

rolled-steel joist *n* a steel beam, esp. one with a cross section in the form of a letter *H* or *I*. Abbrev.: **RSJ**.

roller (ˈrəʊlə) *n* **1** a cylinder having an absorbent surface and a handle, used for spreading paint. **2** Also called: **garden roller**. a heavy cast-iron cylinder on an axle to which a handle is attached; used for flattening lawns. **3** a long heavy wave of the sea, advancing towards the shore. **4** a hardened cylinder of precision-ground steel that forms one of the rolling components of a roller bearing or of a linked driving chain. **5** a cylinder fitted on pivots, used to enable heavy objects to be easily moved. **6** *Printing.* a cylinder, usually of hard rubber, used to ink a plate before impression. **7** any of various other cylindrical devices that rotate about a cylinder, used for any of various purposes. **8** a small cylinder onto which a woman's hair may be rolled to make it curl. **9** *Med.* a bandage consisting of a long strip of muslin rolled tightly into a cylindrical form before application. **10** any of various Old World birds, such as the **European roller**, that have a blue, green, and brown plumage, a slightly hooked bill, and an erratic flight. **11** (*often cap.*) a variety of tumbler pigeon. **12** a person or thing that rolls. **13** short for **steamroller**.

rollerball ('rəʊlə,bɔːl) *n* a pen having a small moving nylon, plastic, or metal ball as a writing point.

roller bearing *n* a bearing in which a shaft runs on a number of hardened-steel rollers held within a cage.

Rollerblade ('rəʊlə,bleɪd) *n Trademark.* a type of roller skate in which the wheels are set in a single straight line under the boot.

roller chain *n Engineering.* a chain for transmitting power in which each link consists of two free-moving rollers held in position by pins connected to sideplates.

roller coaster *n* another term for **big dipper**.

roller derby *n* a race on roller skates, esp. one involving aggressive tactics.

roller skate *n* **1** a device having straps for fastening to a shoe and four small wheels that enable the wearer to glide swiftly over a floor. ◆ *vb* **roller-skate, roller-skates, roller-skating, roller-skated. 2** (*intr*) to move on roller skates.
▸ **roller skater** *n*

roller towel *n* **1** a towel with the two ends sewn together, hung on a roller. **2** a towel wound inside a roller enabling a clean section to be pulled out when needed.

rollick ('rɒlɪk) *vb* **1** (*intr*) to behave in a carefree or boisterous manner. ◆ *n* **2** a boisterous or carefree escapade. ORIG C19: Scot. dialect, prob. from ROMP + FROLIC

rollicking[1] ('rɒlɪkɪŋ) *adj* boisterously carefree. ORIG C19: from ROLLICK

rollicking[2] ('rɒlɪkɪŋ) *n Brit. inf.* a very severe telling-off. ORIG C20: from ROLLICK (vb) (in former sense: to be angry, make a fuss); ? infl. by BOLLOCKING

roll in *vb* (*mainly intr*) **1** (*adv*) to arrive in abundance or in large numbers. **2** (*adv*) *Inf.* to arrive at one's destination. **3 be rolling in.** (*prep*) *Sl.* to abound or luxuriate in (wealth, money, etc.).

rolling ('rəʊlɪŋ) *adj* **1** having gentle rising and falling slopes: *rolling country.* **2** progressing by stages or by occurrences in different places in succession: *a rolling strike.* **3** subject to regular review and updating: *a rolling plan for overseas development.* **4** reverberating: *rolling thunder.* **5** *Sl.* extremely rich. **6** that may be turned up or down: *a rolling hat brim.* ◆ *adv* **7** *Sl.* swaying or staggering (in **rolling drunk**).

rolling launch *n Marketing.* the process of introducing a product onto a market gradually. Cf. **roll out** (sense 3).

rolling mill *n* **1** a mill or factory where ingots of heated metal are passed between rollers to produce sheets or bars of a required cross section and form. **2** a machine having rollers that may be used for this purpose.

rolling pin *n* a cylinder with handles at both ends used for rolling dough, pastry, etc., out flat.

rolling stock *n* the wheeled vehicles collectively used on a railway, including the locomotives, coaches, etc.

rolling stone *n* a restless or wandering person.

Rolling Stones ★ *pl n* **the.** British rock band (formed 1962): comprising Mick Jagger, Keith Richards (born 1943; guitar, vocals), Bill Jones (1942–69; guitar), Charlie Watts (born 1941; drums), Bill Wyman (born 1936; bass guitar), and subsequently Mick Taylor (born 1948; guitar; with the band 1969–74) and Ron Wood (born 1947; guitar; with the band from 1975). See also (Michael Philip) **Jagger**.

Rollins ★ ('rɒlɪnz) *n* **Sonny,** original name *Theodore Walter Rollins.* born 1930, US jazz tenor saxophonist.

rollmop ('rəʊl,mɒp) *n* a herring fillet rolled, usually around onion slices, and pickled in spiced vinegar. ORIG C20: from G *Rollmops,* from *rollen* to ROLL + *Mops* pug dog

rollneck ('rəʊl,nɛk) *adj* **1** (of a garment) having a high neck that may be rolled over. ◆ *n* **2** a rollneck sweater or other garment.

Rollo ★ ('rɒləʊ) *n* ?860–?930 A.D., Norse war leader who received from Charles the Simple a fief that formed the basis of the duchy of Normandy. Also called: **Rolf, Rolf the Ganger.**

roll of honour *n* a list of those who have died in war for their country.

roll on *vb* **1** *Brit.* used to express the wish that an eagerly anticipated event or date will come quickly: *roll on Saturday.* ◆ *adj* **roll-on. 2** (of a deodorant, etc.) dispensed by means of a revolving ball fitted into the neck of the container. ◆ *n* **roll-on. 3** a woman's foundation garment, made of elasticized material and having no fastenings.

roll-on/roll-off *adj* denoting a cargo ship or ferry designed so that vehicles can be driven on and off.

roll out *vb* (*tr, adv*) **1** to cause (pastry) to become flatter and thinner by pressure with a rolling pin. **2** to show (a new type of aircraft) to the public for the first time. **3** to launch (a new film, product, etc.) in a series of successive waves, as over the whole country. ◆ *n* **roll-out. 4** a presentation to the public of a new aircraft, product, etc.; a launch.

roll over *vb* (*adv*) **1** (*intr*) to overturn. **2** (*intr*) (of an animal, esp. a dog) to lie on its back while kicking its legs in the air. **3** (*intr*) to capitulate. **4** (*tr*) to allow (a loan, prize, etc.) to continue in force for a further period. ◆ *n* **rollover. 5** an instance of such continuance of a loan, prize, etc.

roll-top desk *n* a desk having a slatted wooden panel that can be pulled down over the writing surface when not in use.

roll up *vb* (*adv*) **1** to form or cause to form a cylindrical shape. **2** (*tr*) to wrap (an object) round on itself or on an axis: *to roll up a map.* **3** (*intr*) *Inf.* to arrive, esp. in a vehicle. **4** (*intr*) to proceed or develop. **5** (*intr*) *Austral.* to assemble; congregate. ◆ *n* **roll-up. 6** *Brit. inf.* a cigarette made by hand from loose tobacco and cigarette papers. **7** *Austral.* the number attending a meeting, etc.

Rolodex ('rəʊlə,dɛks) *n Trademark, chiefly US.* a small file for holding names, addresses, and telephone numbers, consisting of cards attached horizontally to a rotatable central cylinder.

roly-poly ('rəʊlɪ'pəʊlɪ) *adj* **1** plump, buxom, or rotund. ◆ *n, pl* **roly-polies. 2** *Brit.* a strip of suet pastry spread with jam, fruit, or a savoury mixture, rolled up, and baked or steamed. ORIG C17: apparently by reduplication from *roly,* from ROLL

ROM (rɒm) *n Computing. acronym for* read only memory: a storage device that holds data permanently and cannot be altered by the programmer.

rom. *Printing. abbrev. for* roman (type).

Rom. *abbrev. for:* **1** Roman. **2** Romance (languages). **3** Romania(n). **4** *Bible.* Romans.

Roma ★ ('roːma) *n* the Italian name for **Rome**.

Romagna ★ (*Italian* ro'maɲɲa) *n* an area of N Italy: part of the Papal States up to 1860.

Romaic (rəʊ'meɪɪk) *Obs.* ◆ *n* **1** the modern Greek vernacular. ◆ *adj* **2** of or relating to Greek. ORIG C19: from Gk *Rhōmaikos* Roman, with reference to the Eastern Roman Empire

Romains ★ (*French* rɔmɛ̃) *n* **Jules** (ʒyl). pseudonym of *Louis Farigoule.* 1885–1972, French writer. His works include the novel *Men of Good Will* (1932–46).

roman ('rəʊmən) *adj* **1** of, relating to, or denoting a vertical style of printing type: the usual form of type for most printed matter. Cf. **italic.** ◆ *n* **2** roman type. ORIG C16: so called because the style of letters is that used in ancient Roman inscriptions

Roman ('rəʊmən) *adj* **1** of or relating to Rome or its inhabitants in ancient or modern times. **2** of or relating to

★ people and places

Roman Catholicism or the Roman Catholic Church. ◆ *n* **3** a citizen or inhabitant of ancient or modern Rome.

roman à clef *French.* (rɔmɑ̃ a kle) *n, pl* ***romans à clef*** (rɔmɑ̃ a kle). a novel in which real people are depicted under fictitious names. ORIG lit.: novel with a key

Roman alphabet *n* the alphabet evolved by the ancient Romans for the writing of Latin, derived ultimately from the Phoenicians. The alphabet serves for writing most of the languages of W Europe.

Roman blind *n* a window blind consisting of a length of material which, when drawn up, gathers into horizontal folds from the bottom.

Roman candle *n* a firework that produces a continuous shower of sparks punctuated by coloured balls of fire. ORIG C19: it originated in Italy

Roman Catholic *adj* **1** of or relating to the Roman Catholic Church. ◆ *n* **2** a member of this Church. ◆ Often shortened to **Catholic.**
▸ **Roman Catholicism** *n*

Roman Catholic Church *n* the Christian Church over which the pope presides, with administrative headquarters in the Vatican. Also called: **Catholic Church, Church of Rome.**

romance *n* (rəˈmæns, ˈrəʊmæns). **1** a love affair. **2** love, esp. romantic love idealized for its purity or beauty. **3** a spirit of or inclination for adventure or mystery. **4** a mysterious, exciting, sentimental, or nostalgic quality, esp. one associated with a place. **5** a narrative in verse or prose, written in a vernacular language in the Middle Ages, dealing with adventures of chivalrous heroes. **6** any similar narrative work dealing with events and characters remote from ordinary life. **7** a story, novel, film, etc., dealing with love, usually in an idealized or sentimental way. **8** an extravagant, absurd, or fantastic account. **9** a lyrical song or short instrumental composition having a simple melody. ◆ *vb* (rəˈmæns), **romances, romancing, romanced. 10** (*intr*) to tell, invent, or write extravagant or romantic fictions. **11** (*intr*) to tell extravagant or improbable lies. **12** (*intr*) to have romantic thoughts. **13** (*intr*) (of a couple) to indulge in romantic behaviour. **14** (*tr*) to be romantically involved with. ORIG C13: *romauns,* from OF *romans,* ult. from L *Rōmānicus* Roman
▸ **roˈmancer** *n*

Romance (rəˈmæns, ˈrəʊmæns) *adj* **1** denoting, relating to, or belonging to the languages derived from Latin, including Italian, Spanish, Portuguese, French, and Romanian. **2** denoting a word borrowed from a Romance language. ◆ *n* **3** this group of languages.

Roman Empire *n* **1** the territories ruled by ancient Rome. At its height the Roman Empire included W and S Europe, N Africa, and SW Asia. In 395 A.D. it was divided into the **Eastern Roman Empire,** whose capital was Byzantium, and the **Western Roman Empire,** whose capital was Rome. **2** the government of Rome and its dominions by the emperors from 27 B.C. **3** the Byzantine Empire. **4** the Holy Roman Empire.

Romanesque (ˌrəʊməˈnɛsk) *adj* **1** denoting or having the style of architecture used in W and S Europe from the 9th to the 12th century, characterized by the rounded arch and massive-masonry wall construction. **2** denoting a corresponding style in painting, sculpture, etc. ORIG C18: see ROMAN, -ESQUE

Roman holiday *n* entertainment or pleasure that depends on the suffering of others. ORIG C19: from Byron's poem *Childe Harold* (IV, 141)

Romania (rəʊˈmeɪnɪə), **Rumania,** *or* **Roumania** ★ *n* a republic in SE Europe, bordering on the Black Sea: united in 1861; became independent in 1878; Communist government set up in 1945; became a socialist republic in 1965; a more democratic regime was installed after a revolution in 1989. It consists chiefly of a great central arc of the Carpathian Mountains and Transylvanian Alps, with the plains of Walachia, Moldavia, and Dobriya on the south and east and the Pannonian Plain in the west. Official language: Romanian. Religion: Christian (Romanian Orthodox) majority. Currency: leu. Capital: Bucharest. Pop.: 22 405 000 (1999 est.). Area: 237 500 sq. km (91 699 sq. miles).

Romanian (rəʊˈmeɪnɪən), **Rumanian,** *or* **Roumanian** *n* **1** the official language of Romania. **2** a native, citizen, or inhabitant of Romania. ◆ *adj* **3** relating to, denoting, or characteristic of Romania, its people, or their language.

Romanic (rəʊˈmænɪk) *adj* another word for **Roman** or **Romance.**

Romanism (ˈrəʊməˌnɪzəm) *n* Roman Catholicism, esp. when regarded as excessively or superstitiously ritualistic.
▸ **ˈRomanist** *n*

Romanize *or* **Romanise** (ˈrəʊməˌnaɪz) *vb* **Romanizes, Romanizing, Romanized** *or* **Romanises, Romanising, Romanised. 1** (*tr*) to impart a Roman Catholic character to (a ceremony, etc.). **2** (*intr*) to be converted to Roman Catholicism. **3** (*tr*) to transcribe (a language) into the Roman alphabet.
▸ **ˌRomaniˈzation** *or* **ˌRomaniˈsation** *n*

Roman law *n* the system of jurisprudence of ancient Rome, codified under Justinian and forming the basis of many modern legal systems.

Roman nose *n* a nose having a high prominent bridge.

Roman numerals *pl n* the letters used by the Romans for the representation of cardinal numbers, still used occasionally today. The integers are represented by the following letters: I (= 1), V (= 5), X (= 10), L (= 50), C (= 100), D (= 500), and M (= 1000). VI = 6 (V + I) but IV = 4 (V − I).

Romano ★ (*Italian* roˈmaːno) *n* See **Giulio Romano.**

Romanov ★ (ˈrəʊmənɒf; *Russian* raˈmanəf) *n* any of the Russian imperial dynasty that ruled from the crowning (1613) of Mikhail Fyodorovich to the abdication (1917) of Nicholas II during the February Revolution.

Romansch *or* **Romansh** (rəʊˈmænʃ) *n* a group of Romance dialects spoken in the Swiss canton of Grisons; an official language of Switzerland since 1938. ORIG C17: from Romansch, lit.: Romance language

romantic (rəʊˈmæntɪk) *adj* **1** of, relating to, imbued with, or characterized by romance. **2** evoking or given to thoughts and feelings of love, esp. idealized or sentimental love: *a romantic setting.* **3** impractical, visionary, or idealistic: *a romantic scheme.* **4** *Often euphemistic.* imaginary or fictitious: *a romantic account of one's war service.* **5** (*often cap.*) of or relating to a movement in European art, music, and literature in the late 18th and early 19th centuries, characterized by an emphasis on feeling and content rather than order and form. ◆ *n* **6** a person who is romantic, as in being idealistic, amorous, or soulful. **7** a person whose tastes in art, literature, etc., lie mainly in romanticism. **8** (*often cap.*) a poet, composer, etc., of the romantic period or whose main inspiration is romanticism. ORIG C17: from F, from obs. *romant* story, romance, from OF *romans* ROMANCE
▸ **roˈmantically** *adv*

romanticism (rəʊˈmæntɪˌsɪzəm) *n* **1** (*often cap.*) the theory, practice, and style of the romantic art, music, and literature of the late 18th and early 19th centuries, usually opposed to classicism. **2** romantic attitudes, ideals, or qualities.
▸ **roˈmanticist** *n*

romanticize *or* **romanticise** (rəʊˈmæntɪˌsaɪz) *vb* **romanticizes, romanticizing, romanticized** *or* **romanticises, romanticising, romanticised. 1** (*intr*) to think or act in a romantic way. **2** (*tr*) to interpret according to romantic precepts. **3** to make or become romantic, as in style.
▸ **roˌmanticiˈzation** *or* **roˌmanticiˈsation** *n*

Romany *or* **Romani** (ˈrɒmənɪ, ˈrəʊ-) *n* **1a** (*pl* **Romanies** *or* **Romanis**) another name for a **Gypsy. 1b** (*as modifier*): *Romany customs.* **2** the language of the Gypsies, belonging to the Indic branch of the Indo-European family. ORIG C19: from Romany *romani* (adj) Gypsy, ult. from Sansk. *domba* man of a low caste of musicians, of Dravidian origin

romanza (rəʊˈmænzə) *n* a short instrumental piece of songlike character. ORIG It.

romaunt (rəˈmɔːnt) *n Arch.* a verse romance. ORIG C16: from OF; see ROMANTIC

Romberg ★ (ˈrɒmbɜːg) *n* **Sigmund.** 1887–1951, Hungarian-born US composer of such operettas as *The Student Prince* (1924) and *The Desert Song* (1926).

Rome ★ (rəum) *n* **1** the capital of Italy, on the River Tiber: includes the independent state of the Vatican City; traditionally founded by Romulus on the Palatine Hill in 753 B.C., later spreading to six other hills east of the Tiber; capital of the Roman Empire; a great cultural and artistic centre, esp. during the Renaissance. Pop.: 2 654 187 (1996 est.). Italian name: **Roma. 2** the Roman Empire. **3** the Roman Catholic Church or Roman Catholicism.

Romeo ('rəumɪəu) *n, pl* **Romeos.** an ardent male lover. ORIG after the hero of Shakespeare's *Romeo and Juliet* (1594)

Romish ('rəumɪʃ) *adj Usually derog.* of or resembling Roman Catholic beliefs or practices.

Rommel ★ (*German* 'rɔməl) *n* **Erwin** ('ɛrvi:n), nicknamed *the Desert Fox*. 1891–1944, German field marshal, noted for his leadership of the Afrika Corps (1941–42); committed suicide after the failure of the officers' plot against Hitler.

Romney ★ ('rɒmnɪ, 'rʌm-) *n* **George.** 1734–1802, British portrait painter.

Romney Marsh ★ ('rɒmnɪ, 'rʌm-) *n* a marshy area of SE England, on the Kent coast between New Romney and Rye: includes Dungeness.

romp (rɒmp) *vb* (*intr*) **1** to play or run about wildly, boisterously, or joyfully. **2 romp home** (*or* **in**). to win a race, etc., easily. ◆ *n* **3** a noisy or boisterous game or prank. **4** an instance of sexual activity between two or more people that is entered into light-heartedly and without emotional commitment: *naked sex romps*. **5** *Arch.* a playful or boisterous child, esp. a girl. **6** an easy victory. ORIG C18: prob. var. of RAMP, from OF *ramper* to crawl, climb

rompers ('rɒmpəz) *pl n* **1** a one-piece baby garment consisting of trousers and a bib with straps. **2** *NZ old-fashioned.* a type of costume worn by schoolgirls for games and gymnastics.

Romulus ★ ('rɒmjʊləs) *n Roman myth.* the founder of Rome, suckled with his twin brother Remus by a she-wolf after they were abandoned in infancy. Their parents were Rhea Silvia and Mars. Romulus later killed Remus in an argument over the new city.

Roncesvalles ★ ('rɒnsəˌvælz; *Spanish* rɔnθez'βaʎes) *n* a village in N Spain, in the Pyrenees: a nearby pass was the scene of the defeat of Charlemagne and death of Roland in 778. French name: **Roncevaux** (rɔ̃svo).

rondavel (ˌrɒn'dɑ:vəl) *n S. African.* a circular, often thatched, building with a conical roof. ORIG from ?

rondeau ('rɒndəu) *n, pl* **rondeaux** (-dəu, -dəuz). a poem consisting of 13 or 10 lines with two rhymes and having the opening words of the first line used as an unrhymed refrain. ORIG C16: from OF, from *rondel* a little round, from *rond* ROUND

rondel ('rɒnd°l) *n* a rondeau consisting of three stanzas of 13 or 14 lines with a two-line refrain appearing twice or three times. ORIG C14: from OF, lit.: a little circle, from *rond* ROUND

rondo ('rɒndəu) *n, pl* **rondos.** a piece of music in which a refrain is repeated between episodes: often constitutes the form of the last movement of a sonata or concerto. ORIG C18: from It., from F RONDEAU

Rondônia ★ (*Portuguese* rõ'donja) *n* a state of W Brazil: consists chiefly of tropical rainforest; a centre of the Amazon rubber boom until about 1912. Capital: Pôrto Velho. Pop.: 1 229 306 (1996). Area: 243 043 sq. km (93 839 sq. miles). Former name (until 1956): **Guaporé.**

rone (rəun) *or* **ronepipe** *n Scot.* a drainpipe for carrying rainwater from a roof. ORIG C19: from ?

Ronsard ★ (*French* rɔ̃sar) *n* **Pierre de** (pjɛr də). 1524–85, French poet, foremost of the *Pléiade*.

röntgen ('rɒntgən, -tjən, 'rɛnt-) *n* a variant spelling of **roentgen.**

Röntgen ★ ('rɒntgən, -tjən, 'rɛnt-; *German* 'rœntgən) *n* a variant spelling of (Wilhelm Konrad) **Roentgen.**

roo (ru:) *n Austral. inf.* a kangaroo.

roo bars *pl n Austral.* another name for **bull bars.**

rood (ru:d) *n* **1a** a crucifix, esp. one set on a beam or screen at the entrance to the chancel of a church. **1b** (*as modifier*): *rood screen.* **2** the Cross on which Christ was crucified. **3** a unit of area equal to one quarter of an acre or 0.10117 hectare. **4** a unit of area equal to 40 square rods. ORIG OE *rōd*

Roodepoort-Maraisburg ★ ('ru:dəˌpʊət mə'reɪsbɜ:g) *n* an industrial city in NE South Africa on the Witwatersrand. Pop.: 162 632 (1991).

roof (ru:f) *n, pl* **roofs** (ru:fs, ru:vz). **1a** a structure that covers or forms the top of a building. **1b** (*in combination*): *the rooftop.* **1c** (*as modifier*): *a roof garden.* **2** the top covering of a vehicle, oven, or other structure: *the roof of a car.* **3** *Anat.* any structure that covers an organ or part: *the roof of the mouth.* **4** a highest or topmost point or part: *Mount Everest is the roof of the world.* **5** a house or other shelter: *a poor man's roof.* **6 hit** (*or* **raise** *or* **go through**) **the roof.** *Inf.* to get extremely angry. ◆ *vb* **7** (*tr*) to provide or cover with a roof or rooflike part. ORIG OE *hrōf*
▸ **'roofer** *n* ▸ **'roofless** *adj*

roof garden *n* a garden on a flat roof of a building.

roofie ('ru:fɪ) *n* a tablet of flunitrazepam used as an illegal drug, often in combination with alcohol or other drugs. ORIG C20: from *Rophy*, street name for *Rohypnol*, a tradename for flunitrazepam

roofing ('ru:fɪŋ) *n* **1** material used to construct a roof. **2** the act of constructing a roof.

roof rack *n* a rack attached to the roof of a motor vehicle for carrying luggage, skis, etc.

rooftree ('ru:fˌtri:) *n* another name for **ridgepole.**

rooibos ('rɔɪˌbɒs, 'rʊɪˌbɒs) *n* any of various South African trees with red leaves. ORIG from Afrik. *rooi* red + *bos* bush

rooibos tea *n S. African.* a tealike drink made from the leaves of the rooibos.

rooikat ('rɔɪˌkæt, 'rʊɪˌkæt) *n* a South African lynx. ORIG from Afrik. *rooi* red + *kat* cat

rooinek ('rɔɪˌnɛk, 'rʊɪˌnɛk) *n S. African.* a contemptuous name for an **Englishman.** ORIG C19: Afrik., lit.: red neck

rook[1] (rʊk) *n* **1** a large Eurasian passerine bird, with a black plumage and a whitish base to its bill. **2** *Sl.* a swindler or cheat, esp. one who cheats at cards. ◆ *vb* **3** (*tr*) *Sl.* to overcharge, swindle, or cheat. ORIG OE *hrōc*

rook[2] (rʊk) *n* a chesspiece that may move any number of unoccupied squares in a straight line, horizontally or vertically. Also called: **castle.** ORIG C14: from OF *rok*, ult. from Ar. *rukhkh*

rookery ('rʊkərɪ) *n, pl* **rookeries. 1** a group of nesting rooks. **2** a clump of trees containing rooks' nests. **3a** a breeding ground or communal living area of certain other birds or mammals, esp. penguins or seals. **3b** a colony of any such creatures. **4** *Arch.* an overcrowded slum.

rookie ('rʊkɪ) *n Inf.* a newcomer, esp. a raw recruit in the army. ORIG C20: changed from RECRUIT

room (ru:m, rʊm) *n* **1** space or extent, esp. unoccupied or unobstructed space for a particular purpose: *is there room to pass?* **2** an area within a building enclosed by a floor, a ceiling, and walls or partitions. **3** (*functioning as sing or pl*) the people present in a room: *the whole room was laughing.* **4** (foll. by *for*) opportunity or scope: *room for manoeuvre.* **5** (*pl*) a part of a house, hotel, etc., that is rented out as separate accommodation: *living in dingy rooms in Dalry.* ◆ *vb* **6** (*intr*) to occupy or share a room or lodging: *where does he room?* ORIG OE *rūm*
▸ **'roomer** *n*

roomful ('ru:mˌfʊl, 'rʊm-) *n, pl* **roomfuls.** a number or quantity sufficient to fill a room: *a roomful of furniture.*

rooming house *n US & Canad.* a house having self-contained furnished rooms or flats for renting.

roommate ('ru:mˌmeɪt, 'rʊm-) *n* a person with whom one shares a room or lodging.

room service *n* service in a hotel providing meals, drinks, etc., in guests' rooms.

roomy ('ru:mɪ, 'rʊmɪ) *adj* **roomier, roomiest.** spacious.
▸ **'roomily** *adv* ▸ **'roominess** *n*

Roosevelt ★ ('rəuzəˌvɛlt) *n* **1** (**Anna**) **Eleanor.** 1884–1962, US writer and diplomat: delegate to the United Nations

(1945–52). **2** her husband, **Franklin Delano** ('dɛlənəʊ), known as *FDR*. 1882–1945, 32nd president of the US (1933–45); elected four times. He instituted major reforms (the **New Deal**) and was a forceful leader during World War II. **3 Theodore.** 1858–1919, 26th president of the US (1901–09). He negotiated the right to build the Panama Canal (1903); Nobel peace prize (1906), for mediating in the Russo-Japanese war.

roost (ruːst) *n* **1** a place, perch, branch, etc., where birds, esp. domestic fowl, rest or sleep. **2** a temporary place to rest or stay. ◆ *vb* **3** (*intr*) to rest or sleep on a roost. **4** (*intr*) to settle down or stay. **5 come home to roost.** to have unfavourable repercussions. ORIG OE *hrōst*

Roost (ruːst) *n* **the.** a powerful current caused by conflicting tides around the Shetland and Orkney Islands. ORIG C16: from ON *röst*

rooster ('ruːstə) *n Chiefly US & Canad.* the male of the domestic fowl; a cock.

root[1] (ruːt) *n* **1a** the organ of a higher plant that anchors the rest of the plant in the ground and absorbs water and mineral salts from the soil. **1b** (loosely) any of the branches of such an organ. **2** any plant part, such as a tuber, that is similar to a root in function or appearance. **3a** the essential part or nature of something: *your analysis strikes at the root of the problem.* **3b** (*as modifier*): *the root cause of the problem.* **4** *Anat.* the embedded portion of a tooth, nail, hair, etc. **5** origin or derivation. **6** (*pl*) a person's sense of belonging in a community, place, etc., esp. the one in which he was born or brought up. **7** *Bible.* a descendant. **8** *Linguistics.* the form of a word that remains after removal of all affixes. **9** *Maths.* a quantity that when multiplied by itself a certain number of times equals a given quantity: *3 is a cube root of 27.* **10** Also called: **solution.** *Maths.* a number that when substituted for the variable satisfies a given equation. **11** *Music.* (in harmony) the note forming the foundation of a chord. **12** *Austral. & NZ sl.* sexual intercourse. **13 root and branch.** (*adv*) entirely; utterly. ◆ Related adj: **radical.** ◆ *vb* **14** (*intr*) Also: **take root.** to establish a root and begin to grow. **15** (*intr*) Also: **take root.** to become established, embedded, or effective. **16** (*tr*) to embed with or as if with a root or roots. **17** *Austral. & NZ sl.* to have sexual intercourse (with). ◆ See also **root out, roots.** ORIG OE *rōt*, from ON
▸ **'rooter** *n* ▸ **'root,like** *adj* ▸ **'rooty** *adj* ▸ **'rootiness** *n*

root[2] (ruːt) *vb* (*intr*) **1** (of a pig) to burrow in or dig up the earth in search of food, using the snout. **2** (foll. by *about, around, in*, etc.) *Inf.* to search vigorously but unsystematically. ORIG C16: changed (through infl. of ROOT[1]) from earlier *wroot*, from OE *wrōtan;* rel. to OE *wrōt* snout
▸ **'rooter** *n*

root[3] (ruːt) *vb* (*intr;* usually foll. by *for*) *Inf.* to give support to (a contestant, team, etc.), as by cheering. ORIG C19: ? var. of Scot. *rout* to make a loud noise, from ON *rauta* to roar

root beer *n US & Canad.* an effervescent drink made from extracts of various roots and herbs.

root canal *n* the passage in the root of a tooth through which its nerves and blood vessels enter the pulp cavity.

root-canal therapy *n* another name for **root treatment.**

root climber *n* any of various climbing plants, such as the ivy, that adhere to a supporting structure by means of small roots growing from the side of the stem.

root crop *n* a crop, as of turnips or beets, cultivated for the food value of its roots.

rooted ('ruːtɪd) *adj* **1** having roots. **2** deeply felt: *rooted objections.*

root ginger *n* the raw underground stem of the ginger plant used finely chopped or grated, esp. in Chinese dishes.

root hair *n* any of the hollow hairlike outgrowths of the outer cells of a root, just behind the tip, that absorb water and salts from the soil.

rooting compound *n Horticulture.* a substance, usually a powder, containing auxins in which plant cuttings are dipped in order to promote root growth.

rootle ('ruːtᵊl) *vb* **rootles, rootling, rootled.** (*intr*) *Brit.* another word for **root**[2].

rootless ('ruːtlɪs) *adj* having no roots, esp. (of a person) having no ties with a particular place.

rootlet ('ruːtlɪt) *n* a small root.

root mean square *n* the square root of the average of the squares of a set of numbers or quantities: *the root mean square of* 1, 2, *and* 4 *is* $\sqrt{[(1^2 + 2^2 + 4^2)/3]} = \sqrt{7}$. Abbrev.: **rms.**

root nodule *n* a swelling on the root of a leguminous plant, such as clover, that contains bacteria capable of nitrogen fixation.

root out *vb* (*tr, adv*) to remove or eliminate completely: *we must root out inefficiency.*

roots (ruːts) *adj* (of popular music) going back to the origins of a style, esp. in being genuine and unpretentious: *roots rock.*
▸ **'rootsy** *adj*

rootserver ('ruːt,sɜːvə) *n* any of a small number of important large servers on the Internet that match addresses at the top-domain level.

roots music *n* **1** another name for **world music. 2** reggae, esp. when regarded as authentic and uncommercialized.

rootstock ('ruːt,stɒk) *n* **1** another name for **rhizome. 2** another name for **stock** (sense 7). **3** *Biol.* a basic structure from which offshoots have developed.

root treatment *n Dentistry.* a procedure, used for treating an abscess at the tip of the root of a tooth, in which the pulp is removed and a filling (**root filling**) inserted in the root canal. Also called: **root-canal therapy.**

ropable *or* **ropeable** ('rəʊpəbᵊl) *adj* **1** capable of being roped. **2** *Austral. & NZ inf.* **2a** angry. **2b** wild or intractable: *a ropable beast.*

rope (rəʊp) *n* **1a** a fairly thick cord made of intertwined hemp or other fibres or of wire or other strong material. **1b** (*as modifier*): *a rope ladder.* **2** a row of objects fastened to form a line: *a rope of pearls.* **3** a quantity of material wound in the form of a cord. **4** a filament or strand, esp. of something viscous or glutinous: *a rope of slime.* **5 give (someone) enough** (*or* **plenty of**) **rope to hang himself** (*or* **herself**). to allow (someone) to accomplish his or her own downfall by his or her own foolish acts. **6 know the ropes.** to have a thorough understanding of a particular sphere of activity. **7 on the ropes. 7a** *Boxing.* driven against the ropes enclosing the ring by an opponent's attack. **7b** in a hopeless position. **8 the rope. 8a** a rope halter used for hanging. **8b** death by hanging. ◆ *vb* **ropes, roping, roped. 9** (*tr*) to bind or fasten with or as if with a rope. **10** (*tr;* usually foll. by *off*) to enclose or divide by means of a rope. **11** (when *intr*, foll. by *up*) *Mountaineering.* to tie (climbers) together with a rope. ORIG OE *rāp*

rope in *vb* (*tr, adv*) **1** *Brit.* to persuade to take part in some activity. **2** *US & Canad.* to trick or entice into some activity.

rope's end *n* a short piece of rope, esp. as formerly used for flogging sailors.

ropewalk ('rəʊp,wɔːk) *n* a long narrow usually covered path or shed where ropes are made.

ropey *or* **ropy** ('rəʊpɪ) *adj* **ropier, ropiest. 1** *Brit. inf.* **1a** inferior. **1b** slightly unwell. **2** (of a viscous or sticky substance) forming strands. **3** resembling a rope.
▸ **'ropily** *adv* ▸ **'ropiness** *n*

Roquefort ('rɒkfɔː) *n* a blue-veined cheese with a strong flavour, made from ewe's and goat's milk. ORIG C19: after *Roquefort*, village in S France

roquet ('rəʊkɪ) *Croquet.* ◆ *vb* **roquets** (-kɪz), **roqueting** (-kɪɪŋ), **roqueted** (-kɪd). **1** to drive one's ball against (another person's ball) in order to be allowed to croquet. ◆ *n* **2** the act of roqueting. ORIG C19: var. of CROQUET

Roraima ★ (*Portuguese* rɔ'raima) *n* a state of N Brazil: chiefly rainforest. Capital: Boa Vista. Pop.: 247 131 (1996). Area: 230 104 sq. km (89 740 sq. miles).

ro-ro ('rəʊrəʊ) *adj acronym for* roll-on/roll-off.

rorqual ('rɔːkwəl) *n* any of several whalebone whales that have a dorsal fin and a series of grooves along the throat and chest. Also called: **finback.** ORIG C19: from F, from Norwegian *rörhval*, from ON *reytharhvalr*, from *reythr* (from *rauthr* red) + *hvalr* whale

Rorschach test ('rɔːʃɑːk) *n Psychol.* a personality test consisting of a number of unstructured inkblots presented for interpretation. ORIG C20: after Hermann *Rorschach* (1884–1922), Swiss psychiatrist

rort (rɔːt) *Austral. inf.* ◆ *n* **1** a rowdy party or celebration. **2** a fraud; deception. ◆ *vb* (*tr*) **3** to take unfair advantage of (something): *our voting system can be rorted.* ORIG C20: back formation from E dialect *rorty* (in the sense: good, splendid)
▸ **'rorty** *adj*

Rory O'Connor ★ (ˌrɔːrɪ əʊ'kɒnə) *n* Also called *Roderic.* ?1116–98, king of Connaught and last High King of Ireland.

Rosa[1] ★ ('rəʊzə; *Italian* 'rɔːza) *n* **Monte** ('mɒntɪ; *Italian* 'monte). a mountain between Italy and Switzerland: the highest in the Pennine Alps. Height: 4634 m (15 204 ft).

Rosa[2] ★ (*Italian* 'rɔːza) *n* **Salvator** ('salvatɔr). 1615–73, Italian artist, noted esp. for his romantic landscapes.

rosace ('rəʊzeɪs) *n* **1** another name for **rose window.** **2** another name for **rosette.** ORIG C19: from F, from L *rosāceus* ROSACEOUS

rosaceous (rəʊ'zeɪʃəs) *adj* **1** of or belonging to the Rosaceae, a family of plants typically having white, yellow, pink, or red five-petalled flowers. The family includes the rose, strawberry, blackberry, and many fruit trees. **2** like a rose, esp., rose-coloured. ORIG C18: from L *rosāceus* composed of roses, from *rosa* ROSE[1]

rosarian (rəʊ'zɛərɪən) *n* a person who cultivates roses, esp. professionally.

Rosario ★ (rəʊ'sɑːrɪəʊ; *Spanish* rɔ'sarjo) *n* an inland port in E Argentina, on the Paraná River: the second largest city in the country; industrial centre. Pop.: 1 157 372 (1992 est.).

rosarium (rəʊ'zɛərɪəm) *n, pl* **rosariums** *or* **rosaria** (-'zɛərɪə). a rose garden. ORIG C19: NL

rosary ('rəʊzərɪ) *n, pl* **rosaries.** **1** *RC Church.* **1a** a series of prayers counted on a string of beads, usually five or 15 decades of Aves, each decade beginning with a Paternoster and ending with a Gloria. **1b** a string of 55 or 165 beads used to count these prayers as they are recited. **2** (in other religions) a similar string of beads used in praying. **3** an archaic word for a **garland** (of flowers, etc.). ORIG C14: from L *rosārium* rose garden, from *rosārius* of roses, from *rosa* ROSE[1]

Roscius ★ ('rɒskɪəs, -sɪəs) *n* **1** full name *Quintus Roscius Gallus.* died 62 B.C., Roman actor. **2** any actor.
▸ **'Roscian** *adj*

Roscommon ★ (rɒs'kɒmən) *n* an inland county of N central Republic of Ireland, in Connacht: economy based on cattle and sheep farming. County town: Roscommon. Pop.: 52 000 (1996). Area: 2463 sq. km (951 sq. miles).

rose[1] (rəʊz) *n* **1a** a shrub or climbing plant having prickly stems, compound leaves, and fragrant flowers. **1b** (*in combination*): *rosebush.* **2** the flower of any of these plants. **3** any of various similar plants, such as the Christmas rose. **4a** a purplish-pink colour. **4b** (*as adj*): *rose paint.* **5** a rose, or a representation of one, as the national emblem of England. **6a** a cut for a gemstone, having a hemispherical faceted crown and a flat base. **6b** a gem so cut. **7** a perforated cap fitted to a watering can or hose, causing the water to issue in a spray. **8** a design or decoration shaped like a rose; rosette. **9** Also called: **ceiling rose.** *Electrical engineering.* a circular boss attached to a ceiling through which the flexible lead of an electric-light fitting passes. **10** *History.* See **red rose, white rose.** **11 bed of roses.** a situation of comfort or ease. **12 under the rose.** in secret; privately; sub rosa. ◆ *vb* **roses, rosing, rosed.** **13** (*tr*) to make rose-coloured; cause to blush or redden. ORIG OE, from L *rosa,* prob. from Gk *rhodon* rose
▸ **'roseˌlike** *adj*

rose[2] (rəʊz) *vb* the past tense of **rise.**

rosé ('rəʊzeɪ) *n* any pink wine, made either by removing the skins of red grapes after only a little colour has been extracted or by mixing red and white wines. ORIG C19: from F, lit.: pink, from L *rosa* ROSE[1]

roseate ('rəʊzɪˌeɪt) *adj* **1** of the colour rose or pink. **2** excessively or idealistically optimistic.

rosebay ('rəʊzˌbeɪ) *n* **1** any of several rhododendrons. **2** **rosebay willowherb.** a perennial plant that has spikes of deep pink flowers and is widespread in N temperate regions. **3** another name for **oleander.**

Rosebery ★ ('rəʊzbərɪ, -brɪ) *n* **Earl of,** title of *Archibald Philip Primrose.* 1847–1929, British statesman; Liberal prime minister (1894–95).

rosebud ('rəʊzˌbʌd) *n* **1** the bud of a rose. **2** *Literary.* a pretty young woman.

rose campion *n* a European plant widely cultivated for its pink flowers. Its stems and leaves are covered with white woolly down. Also called: **dusty miller.**

rose chafer *or* **beetle** *n* a British beetle that has a greenish-golden body with a metallic lustre and feeds on plants.

rose-coloured *adj* **1** of the colour rose; rosy. **2** Also: **rose-tinted.** excessively optimistic. **3 see through rose-coloured** *or* **rose-tinted glasses** (*or* **spectacles**). to view in an excessively optimistic light.

rose-cut *adj* (of a gemstone) cut with a hemispherical faceted crown and a flat base.

rosehip ('rəʊzˌhɪp) *n* the berry-like fruit of a rose plant.

rosella (rəʊ'zɛlə) *n* any of various Australian parrots. ORIG C19: prob. alteration of *Rose-hiller,* after *Rose Hill,* Parramatta, near Sydney

rosemary ('rəʊzmərɪ) *n, pl* **rosemaries.** an aromatic European shrub widely cultivated for its grey-green evergreen leaves, which are used in cookery and in the manufacture of perfumes. It is the traditional flower of remembrance. ORIG C15: earlier *rosmarine,* from L *rōs* dew + *marīnus* marine; modern form infl. by folk etymology, as if ROSE[1] + *Mary*

Rosenberg ★ ('rəʊzənˌbɜːg) *n* **1 Alfred.** 1893–1946, German Nazi politician and writer, who devised much of the racial ideology of Nazism: hanged for war crimes. **2 Isaac.** 1890–1918, British poet and painter, best known for his poems of World War I: died in action. **3 Julius.** 1918–53, US spy, who, with his wife **Ethel** (1914–53), was executed for passing information about nuclear weapons to the Russians.

rose of Sharon ('ʃærən) *n* a creeping shrub native to SE Europe but widely cultivated, having large yellow flowers. Also called: **Aaron's beard.**

roseola (rəʊ'ziːələ) *n Pathol.* any red skin rash, esp. **roseola infantum,** a rash in young children. ORIG C19: from NL, dim. of L *roseus* rosy
▸ **ro'seolar** *adj*

rosery ('rəʊzərɪ) *n, pl* **roseries.** a bed or garden of roses.

Rosetta ★ (rəʊ'zɛtə) *n* a town in N Egypt, in the Nile delta. Pop.: 52 014 (1986). Egyptian name: **Rashid.**

Rosetta stone *n* a basalt slab discovered in 1799 at Rosetta, dating to the reign of Ptolemy V (196 B.C.) and carved with parallel inscriptions in hieroglyphics, Egyptian demotic, and Greek, which provided the key to the decipherment of ancient Egyptian texts.

rosette (rəʊ'zɛt) *n* **1** a decoration resembling a rose, esp. an arrangement of ribbons in a rose-shaped design worn as a badge or presented as a prize. **2** another name for **rose window.** **3** *Bot.* a circular cluster of leaves growing from the base of a stem. ORIG C18: from OF: a little ROSE[1]

rose-water *n* **1** scented water made by the distillation of rose petals or by impregnation with oil of roses. **2** (*modifier*) elegant or delicate, esp. excessively so.

rose window *n* a circular window, esp. one that has ornamental tracery radiating from the centre to form a symmetrical roselike pattern. Also called: **wheel window, rosette.**

rosewood ('rəʊzˌwʊd) *n* the hard dark wood of any of various tropical trees. It has a roselike scent and is used in cabinetwork.

Rosh Hashanah *or* **Rosh Hashana** ('rɒʃ hə'ʃɑːnə; *Hebrew* 'rɔʃ haʃa'na) *n* the Jewish New Year festival, celebrated on the first and second of Tishri. ORIG from Heb., lit.: beginning of the year, from *rōsh* head + *hash-shānāh* year

Rosicrucian (ˌrəʊzɪ'kruːʃən) *n* **1** a member of a society professing esoteric religious doctrines, venerating the rose and Cross as symbols of Christ's Resurrection and Redemption, and claiming various occult powers. ◆ *adj* **2** of or designating the Rosicrucians or Rosicrucianism. ORIG C17: from L *Rosa Crucis* Rose of the Cross, translation of the G name Christian *Rosenkreuz,* supposed founder of the society

rosin ('rɒzɪn) *n* **1** Also called: **colophony.** a translucent brittle amber substance produced in the distillation of crude turpentine oleoresin and used esp. in making varnishes, printing inks, and sealing waxes and for treating the bows of stringed instruments. **2** (not in technical usage) another name for **resin** (sense 1). ◆ *vb* **3** (*tr*) to treat or coat with rosin. ORIG C14: var. of RESIN
▸ **'rosiny** *adj*

Roskilde ★ (*Danish* 'rɔskilə) *n* a city in Denmark, on NE Sjælland west of Copenhagen: capital of Denmark from the 10th century to 1443; scene of the signing (1658) of the **Peace of Roskilde** between Denmark and Sweden. Pop.: 49 080 (1990).

ROSPA ('rɒspə) *n* (in Britain) *acronym for* Royal Society for the Prevention of Accidents.

Ross ★ (rɒs) *n* **1 Diana.** born 1944, US Motown singer. **2** Sir **James Clark.** 1800–62, British naval officer and explorer, who located the north magnetic pole (1831) and discovered the Ross Sea (1839–43). **3** his uncle, Sir **John.** 1777–1856, Scottish naval officer and Arctic explorer. **4** Sir **Ronald.** 1857–1932, British bacteriologist, who discovered the transmission of malaria by mosquitoes: Nobel prize for physiology or medicine 1902.

Ross and Cromarty ★ ('krɒmətɪ) *n* a historic county of N Scotland, including the island of Lewis and many islets: now part of Highland and Western Isles council areas.

Ross Dependency ★ *n* a section of Antarctica administered by New Zealand: includes the coastal regions of Victoria Land and King Edward VII Land, the Ross Sea and islands, and the Ross Ice Shelf. Area: about 414 400 sq. km (160 000 sq. miles).

Rossellini ★ (ˌrɒsə'li:nɪ) *n* **Roberto.** 1906–77, Italian film director. His films include *Rome, Open City* (1945) and *L'Amore* (1948).

Rossetti ★ (rɒ'zɛtɪ) *n* **1 Christina Georgina.** 1830–94, British poet. **2** her brother, **Dante Gabriel.** 1828–82, British poet and painter: a leader of the Pre-Raphaelites.

Rossini ★ (rɒ'si:nɪ) *n* **Gioacchino Antonio** (*Italian* dʒoak'ki:no an'tɔ:njo). 1792–1868, Italian composer, esp. of operas, such as *The Barber of Seville* (1816) and *William Tell* (1829).

Ross Island ★ *n* an island in the W Ross Sea: contains the active volcano Mount Erebus.

Rossiya ★ (ra'si:jə) *n* transliteration of the Russian name for **Russia.**

Ross Sea ★ *n* a large arm of the S Pacific in Antarctica, incorporating the Ross Ice Shelf and lying between Victoria Land and the Edward VII Peninsula.

Rostand ★ (*French* rɔstɑ̃) *n* **Edmond** (ɛdmɔ̃). 1868–1918, French playwright and poet; noted for his drama *Cyrano de Bergerac* (1897).

roster ('rɒstə) *n* **1** a list or register, esp. one showing the order of people enrolled for duty. ◆ *vb* **2** (*tr*) to place on a roster. ORIG C18: from Du. *rooster* grating or list (the lined paper looking like a grid)

Rostock ★ ('rɒstɒk) *n* a port in NE Germany, on the Warnow estuary 13 km (8 miles) from the Baltic and its outport, Warnemünde: formerly the chief port of East Germany; university (1419). Pop.: 227 535 (1996 est.).

Rostov *or* **Rostov-on-Don** ★ ('rɒstɒv) *n* a port in S Russia, on the River Don 48 km (30 miles) from the Sea of Azov: industrial centre. Pop.: 1 026 000 (1995 est.).

Rostropovich ★ (ˌrɒstrə'pəuvɪtʃ; *Russian* rəstra'pɔvitʃ) *n* **Mstislav Leopoldovich** ('mɪstɪslɑ:v; *Russian* msti'slaf lea'pɔldavitʃ). born 1927, Soviet cellist and conductor; became a US citizen in 1978.

rostrum ('rɒstrəm) *n, pl* **rostrums** *or* **rostra** (-trə). **1** any platform on which public speakers stand to address an audience. **2** a platform in front of an orchestra on which the conductor stands. **3** another word for **ram** (sense 5). **4** the prow of an ancient Roman ship. **5** *Biol., zool.* a beak or beaklike part. ORIG C16: from L *rōstrum* beak, ship's prow, from *rōdere* to nibble, gnaw; in pl, *rōstra* orator's platform, because this platform in the Roman forum was adorned with the prows of captured ships
▸ **'rostral** *adj*

rosy ('rəuzɪ) *adj* **rosier, rosiest. 1** of the colour rose or pink. **2** having a healthy pink complexion: *rosy cheeks.* **3** optimistic, esp. excessively so: *a rosy view of social improvements.* **4** resembling or abounding in roses.
▸ **'rosily** *adv* ▸ **'rosiness** *n*

rot (rɒt) *vb* **rots, rotting, rotted. 1** to decay or cause to decay as a result of bacterial or fungal action. **2** (*intr;* usually foll. by *off* or *away*) to crumble (off) or break (away), as from decay or long use. **3** (*intr*) to become weak or depressed through inertia, confinement, etc.; languish: *rotting in prison.* **4** to become or cause to become morally degenerate. ◆ *n* **5** the process of rotting or the state of being rotten. **6** something decomposed. Related adj: **putrid. 7** short for **dry rot. 8** *Pathol.* any putrefactive decomposition of tissues. **9** a condition in plants characterized by decay of tissues, caused by bacteria, fungi, etc. **10** *Vet. science.* a contagious fungal disease of sheep. **11** (*also interj*) nonsense; rubbish. ORIG OE *rotian* (vb); rel. to ON, *rotna;* C13 (n), from ON

rota ('rəutə) *n Chiefly Brit.* a register of names showing the order in which people take their turn to perform certain duties. ORIG C17: from L: a wheel

Rota ('rəutə) *n RC Church.* the supreme ecclesiastical tribunal.

rotachute ('rəutəˌʃu:t) *n* a device serving the same purpose as a parachute, in which the canopy is replaced by freely revolving rotor blades, used for the delivery of stores or recovery of missiles.

rotaplane ('rəutəˌpleɪn) *n* an aircraft that derives its lift from freely revolving rotor blades.

rotary ('rəutərɪ) *adj* **1** operating by rotation. **2** turning; revolving. ◆ *n, pl* **rotaries. 3** a part of a machine that rotates about an axis. **4** *US & Canad.* another term for **roundabout** (sense 2). ORIG C18: from Med. L *rotārius,* from L *rota* wheel

Rotary Club *n* any of the local clubs that form **Rotary International,** an international association of professional and businessmen founded in the US in 1905 to promote community service.
▸ **Rotarian** (rəu'tɛərɪən) *n, adj*

rotary engine *n* **1** an internal-combustion engine having radial cylinders that rotate about a fixed crankshaft. **2** an engine, such as a turbine or wankel engine, in which power is transmitted directly to rotating components.

rotary plough *or* **tiller** *n* an implement with a series of blades mounted on a power-driven shaft which rotates so as to break up soil.

rotary press *n* a machine for printing from a revolving cylindrical forme, usually onto a continuous strip of paper.

rotary table *n* a chain or gear-driven unit, mounted in the derrick floor which rotates the drill pipe and bit.

rotate *vb* (rəu'teɪt), **rotates, rotating, rotated. 1** to turn or cause to turn around an axis; revolve or spin. **2** to follow or cause to follow a set sequence. **3** to replace (one set of personnel) with another. ◆ *adj* ('rəuteɪt). **4** *Bot.* designating a corolla the petals of which radiate like the spokes of a wheel.
▸ **ro'tatable** *adj*

rotation (rəu'teɪʃən) *n* **1** the act of rotating; rotary motion. **2** a regular cycle of events in a set order or sequence. **3** a planned sequence of cropping according to which the crops grown in successive seasons on the same land are varied so as to make a balanced demand on its resources of fertility. **4** the spinning motion of a body, such as a planet, about an internal axis. **5** *Maths.* **5a** a circular motion of a configuration about a given point, without a change in shape. **5b** a transformation in

which the coordinate axes are rotated by a fixed angle about the origin.
▸ **ro'tational** *adj*

rotator (rəʊ'teɪtə) *n* **1** a person, device, or part that rotates or causes rotation. **2** *Anat.* any of various muscles that revolve a part on its axis.

rotatory ('rəʊtətərɪ, -trɪ) *or* (*less commonly*) **rotative** *adj* of, possessing, or causing rotation.
▸ **'rotatorily** *adv*

Rotavator ('rəʊtəˌveɪtə) *n Trademark.* a mechanical cultivator with rotary blades. ORIG C20: from ROTA(RY) + (CULTI)VATOR
▸ **'RotaˌVate** *vb* (*tr*)

rote (rəʊt) *n* **1** a habitual or mechanical routine or procedure. **2 by rote.** by repetition; by heart (often in **learn by rote**). ORIG C14: from ?

rotenone ('rəʊtɪˌnəʊn) *n* a white odourless crystalline substance extracted from the roots of derris: a powerful insecticide. ORIG C20: from Japanese *rōten* derris + -ONE

rotgut ('rɒtˌgʌt) *n Facetious sl.* alcoholic drink, esp. spirits, of inferior quality.

Roth ★ (rɒθ) *n* **Philip.** born 1933, US novelist. His works include *Portnoy's Complaint* (1969) and *I Married a Communist* (1998).

Rotherham ★ ('rɒðərəm) *n* **1** an industrial town in N England, in South Yorkshire. Pop.: 121 380 (1991). **2** a unitary authority in N England, in South Yorkshire. Pop.: 255 300 (1996 est.). Area: 283 sq. km (109 sq. miles).

Rothermere ★ ('rɒðəˌmɪə) *n* **Viscount.** title of *Harold Sidney Harmsworth.* 1868–1940, British newspaper magnate.

Rothesay ★ ('rɒθsɪ) *n* a town in SW Scotland, on the E coast of Bute Island. Pop.: 5264 (1991).

Rothko ★ ('rɒθkəʊ) *n* **Mark.** 1903–70, US expressionist painter, born in Russia.

Rothschild ★ ('rɒθtʃaɪld, 'rɒθs-) *n* a powerful family of European Jewish bankers, prominent members of which were: **1 Lionel Nathan,** Baron de Rothschild. 1809–79, British banker and first Jewish member of Parliament. **2** his grandfather **Meyer Amschel** ('maɪər 'amʃəl). 1743–1812, German financier and founder of the Rothschild bank. **3** his son, **Nathan Meyer,** Baron de Rothschild. 1777–1836, British banker, born in Germany.

rotifer ('rəʊtɪfə) *n* a minute aquatic multicellular invertebrate having a ciliated wheel-like organ used in feeding and locomotion: common constituents of freshwater plankton. Also called: **wheel animalcule.** ORIG C18: from NL *Rotifera,* from L *rota* wheel + *ferre* to bear
▸ **rotiferal** (rəʊ'tɪfərəl) *or* **ro'tiferous** *adj*

rotisserie (rəʊ'tɪsərɪ) *n* **1** a rotating spit on which meat, poultry, etc., can be cooked. **2** a shop or restaurant where meat is roasted to order. ORIG C19: from F, from OF *rostir* to ROAST

rotogravure (ˌrəʊtəʊgrə'vjʊə) *n* **1** a printing process using cylinders with many small holes, from which ink is transferred to a moving web of paper, etc., in a rotary press. **2** printed material produced in this way, esp. magazines. ORIG C20: from L *rota* wheel + GRAVURE

rotor ('rəʊtə) *n* **1** the rotating member of a machine or device, such as the revolving arm of the distributor of an internal-combustion engine. **2** a rotating device having radiating blades projecting from a hub which produces thrust to lift and propel a helicopter. ORIG C20: shortened form of ROTATOR

Rotorua ★ (ˌrəʊtə'ruːə) *n* a city in New Zealand, on North Island at the SW end of Lake Rotorua: centre of forestry; noted for hydrothermal activity. Pop.: 54 700 (1994).

rotten ('rɒtᵊn) *adj* **1** decomposing, decaying, or putrid. **2** breaking up, esp. through age or hard use: *rotten ironwork.* **3** morally corrupt. **4** disloyal or treacherous. **5** *Inf.* unpleasant: *rotten weather.* **6** *Inf.* unsatisfactory or poor: *rotten workmanship.* **7** *Inf.* miserably unwell. **8** *Inf.* distressed and embarrassed: *I felt rotten breaking the bad news to him.* ◆ *adv Inf.* **9** extremely; very much: *men fancy her rotten.* ORIG C13: from ON *rottin;* rel. to OE *rotian* to ROT
▸ **'rottenly** *adv* ▸ **'rottenness** *n*

rotten borough *n* (before the Reform Act of 1832) any of certain English parliamentary constituencies with few or no electors.

rottenstone ('rɒtᵊnˌstəʊn) *n* a much-weathered limestone, rich in silica: used in powdered form for polishing metal.

rotter ('rɒtə) *n Sl., chiefly Brit.* a worthless, unpleasant, or despicable person.

Rotterdam ★ ('rɒtəˌdæm) *n* a port in the SW Netherlands, in South Holland province: the second largest city of the Netherlands and one of the world's largest ports; oil refineries, shipbuilding yards, etc. Pop.: 599 414 (1995).

Rottweiler ('rɒtˌwaɪlə, -ˌvaɪlə) *n* **1** a breed of large dog with a smooth black and tan coat, noted for strength and aggression. **2** (*often not cap.*) **2a** an aggressive and unscrupulous person. **2b** (*as modifier*): *rottweiler politics.* ORIG G, from *Rottweil,* town in Swabia where the breed originated

rotund (rəʊ'tʌnd) *adj* **1** rounded or spherical in shape. **2** plump. **3** sonorous or grandiloquent. ORIG C18: from L *rotundus* round, from *rota* wheel
▸ **ro'tundity** *n* ▸ **ro'tundly** *adv*

rotunda (rəʊ'tʌndə) *n* a circular building or room, esp. one that has a dome. ORIG C17: from It. *rotonda,* from L *rotundus* round, from *rota* a wheel

Rouault ★ (ruː'əʊ; *French* rwo) *n* **Georges** (ʒɔrʒ). 1871–1958, French expressionist artist.

Roubaix ★ (*French* rubɛ) *n* a city in N France near the Belgian border: forms, with Tourcoing, a large industrial conurbation. Pop.: 97 746 (1990).

Roubiliac *or* **Roubillac** ★ (rubijak) *n* **Louis-François** (lwifrɑ̃swa). ?1695–1762, French sculptor: lived chiefly in England.

rouble *or* **ruble** ('ruːbᵊl) *n* the standard monetary unit of Belarus, Russia, and Tajikistan. ORIG C16: from Russian *rubl* silver bar, from ORussian *rublĭ* bar, block of wood, from *rubiti* to cut up

roué ('ruːeɪ) *n* a debauched or lecherous man; rake. ORIG C19: from F, lit.: one broken on the wheel; with reference to the fate deserved by a debauchee

Rouen ★ (*French* rwɑ̃) *n* a city in N France, on the River Seine: the chief river port of France; became capital of the duchy of Normandy in 912; scene of the burning of Joan of Arc (1431); university (1964). Pop.: 105 470 (1990).

rouge (ruːʒ) *n* **1** a red powder or cream, used as a cosmetic for adding redness to the cheeks. **2** short for **jeweller's rouge.** ◆ *vb* **rouges, rouging, rouged. 3** (*tr*) to apply rouge to. ORIG C18: F: red, from L *rubeus*

rouge et noir ('ruːʒ eɪ 'nwɑː) *n* a card game in which the players put their stakes on any of two red and two black diamond-shaped spots marked on the table. ORIG F, lit.: red and black

Rouget de Lisle ★ (*French* ruʒɛ də lil) *n* **Claude Joseph** (klod ʒozɛf). 1760–1836, French army officer: composer of the *Marseillaise* (1792).

rough (rʌf) *adj* **1** (of a surface) not smooth; uneven or irregular. **2** (of ground) covered with scrub, boulders, etc. **3** denoting or taking place on uncultivated ground: *rough grazing.* **4** shaggy or hairy. **5** turbulent: *a rough sea.* **6** (of performance or motion) uneven; irregular: *a rough engine.* **7** (of behaviour or character) rude, coarse, or violent. **8** harsh or sharp: *rough words.* **9** *Inf.* severe or unpleasant: *a rough lesson.* **10** (of work, etc.) requiring physical rather than mental effort. **11** *Inf.* ill: *he felt rough after an evening of heavy drinking.* **12** unfair: *rough luck.* **13** harsh or grating to the ear. **14** without refinement, luxury, etc. **15** not perfected in any detail; rudimentary: *rough workmanship; rough justice.* **16** not prepared or dressed: *rough gemstones.* **17** (of a guess, etc.) approximate. **18** having the sound of *h;* aspirated. **19 rough on.** *Inf., chiefly Brit.* **19a** severe towards. **19b** unfortunate for (a person). **20 the rough side of one's tongue.** harsh words; a

rebuke. ♦ *n* **21** rough ground. **22** a sketch or preliminary piece of artwork. **23** unfinished or crude state (esp. in **in the rough**). **24 the rough.** *Golf.* the part of the course bordering the fairways where the grass is untrimmed. **25** *Inf.* a violent person; thug. **26** the unpleasant side of something (esp. in **take the rough with the smooth**). ♦ *adv* **27** roughly. **28 sleep rough.** to spend the night in the open; be without shelter. ♦ *vb (tr)* **29** to make rough; roughen. **30** (foll. by *out, in,* etc.) to prepare (a sketch, report, etc.) in preliminary form. **31 rough it.** *Inf.* to live without the usual comforts of life. ♦ See also **rough up.** ORIG OE *rūh*
▸ **'roughly** *adv* ▸ **'roughness** *n*

roughage ('rʌfɪdʒ) *n* **1** the coarse indigestible constituents of food, which provide bulk to the diet and aid digestion. **2** any rough material.

rough-and-ready *adj* **1** crude, unpolished, or hastily prepared, but sufficient for the purpose. **2** (of a person) without formality or refinement.

rough-and-tumble *n* **1** a fight or scuffle without rules. ♦ *adj* **2** characterized by disorderliness and disregard for rules.

rough breathing *n* (in Greek) the sign (῾) placed over an initial letter, indicating that (in ancient Greek) it was pronounced with an *h*.

roughcast ('rʌf,kɑːst) *n* **1** a mixture of plaster and small stones used to cover the surface of an external wall. **2** any rough or preliminary form, model, etc. ♦ *adj* **3** covered with roughcast. ♦ *vb* **roughcasts, roughcasting, roughcast. 4** to apply roughcast to (a wall, etc.). **5** to prepare in rough.
▸ **'rough,caster** *n*

rough-cut *n* a first basic edited version of a film with the scenes in sequence and the soundtrack synchronized.

rough diamond *n* **1** an unpolished diamond. **2** an intrinsically trustworthy or good person with uncouth manners or dress.

rough-dry *adj* **1** (of clothes or linen) dried ready for pressing. ♦ *vb* **rough-dries, rough-drying, rough-dried. 2** *(tr)* to dry (clothes, etc.) without ironing them.

roughen ('rʌfᵊn) *vb* to make or become rough.

rough-hew *vb* **rough-hews, rough-hewing, rough-hewed; rough-hewed** *or* **rough-hewn.** *(tr)* to cut or shape roughly without finishing the surface.

roughhouse ('rʌf,haʊs) *n Sl.* rough, disorderly, or noisy behaviour.

roughish ('rʌfɪʃ) *adj* somewhat rough.

rough music *n* (formerly) a loud cacophony created with tin pans, drums, etc., esp. as a protest or demonstration of indignation outside someone's house.

roughneck ('rʌf,nɛk) *n Sl.* **1** a rough or violent person; thug. **2** a worker in an oil-drilling operation.

rough puff pastry *n* a rich flaky pastry.

roughrider ('rʌf,raɪdə) *n* a rider of wild or unbroken horses.

roughshod ('rʌf,ʃɒd) *adj* **1** (of a horse) shod with rough-bottomed shoes to prevent sliding. ♦ *adv* **2 ride roughshod over.** to domineer over or act with complete disregard for.

rough stuff *n Inf.* violence.

rough trade *n Sl.* (in homosexual use) a tough or violent sexual partner, esp. one casually picked up.

rough up *vb (tr, adv)* **1** *Inf.* to treat violently; beat up. **2** to cause (feathers, hair, etc.) to stand up by rubbing against the grain.

roulade (ruː'lɑːd) *n* **1** something cooked in the shape of a roll, esp. a slice of meat. **2** an elaborate run in vocal music. ORIG C18: from F, lit.: a rolling, from *rouler* to ROLL

Roulers ★ (ruː'lɛəz; *French* rulɛrs) *n* a city in NW Belgium, in West Flanders province. Pop.: 53 617 (1995 est.). Flemish name: **Roeselare.**

roulette (ruː'lɛt) *n* **1** a gambling game in which a ball is dropped onto a spinning horizontal wheel divided into numbered slots, with players betting on the slot into which the ball will fall. **2** a toothed wheel for making a line of perforations. **3** a curve generated by a point on one curve rolling on another. ♦ *vb* **roulettes, rouletting, rouletted.** *(tr)* **4** to use a roulette on (something), as in engraving, making stationery, etc. ORIG C18: from F, from *rouelle,* dim. of *roue* a wheel, from L *rota*

Roumania ★ (rʊ'meɪnɪə) *n* a variant of **Romania.**
▸ **Rou'manian** *adj, n*

round (raʊnd) *adj* **1** having a flat circular shape, as a hoop. **2** having the shape of a ball. **3** curved; not angular. **4** involving or using circular motion. **5** *(prenominal)* complete: *a round dozen.* **6** *Maths.* **6a** forming or expressed by a whole number, with no fraction. **6b** expressed to the nearest ten, hundred, or thousand: *in round figures.* **7** (of a sum of money) considerable. **8** fully depicted or developed, as a character in a book. **9** full and plump: *round cheeks.* **10** (of sound) full and sonorous. **11** (of pace) brisk; lively. **12** *(prenominal)* (of speech) candid; unmodified: *a round assertion.* **13** (of a vowel) pronounced with rounded lips. ♦ *n* **14** a round shape or object. **15 in the round. 15a** in full detail. **15b** *Theatre.* with the audience all round the stage. **16** a session, as of a negotiation: *a round of talks.* **17** a series: *a giddy round of parties.* **18 the daily round.** the usual activities of one's day. **19** a stage of a competition: *he was eliminated in the first round.* **20** *(often pl)* a series of calls: *a milkman's round.* **21** a playing of all the holes on a golf course. **22** a single turn of play by each player, as in a card game. **23** one of a number of periods in a boxing, wrestling, or other match. **24** a single discharge by a gun. **25** a bullet or other charge of ammunition. **26** a number of drinks bought at one time for a group of people. **27a** a single slice of bread. **27b** a sandwich made from two slices of bread. **28** a general outburst of applause, etc. **29** movement in a circle. **30** *Music.* a part song in which the voices follow each other at equal intervals at the same pitch. **31** a sequence of bells rung in order of treble to tenor. **32** a cut of beef from the thigh. **33 go** *or* **make the rounds. 33a** to go from place to place, as in making social calls. **33b** (of information, rumour, etc.) to be passed around, so as to be generally known. ♦ *prep* **34** surrounding, encircling, or enclosing: *a band round her head.* **35** on all or most sides of: *to look round one.* **36** on or outside the circumference or perimeter of. **37** from place to place in: *driving round Ireland.* **38** reached by making a partial circuit about: *the shop round the corner.* **39** revolving round (a centre or axis): *the earth's motion round its axis.* ♦ *adv* **40** on all or most sides. **41** on or outside the circumference or perimeter: *the racing track is two miles round.* **42** to all members of a group: *pass the food round.* **43** in rotation or revolution: *the wheels turn round.* **44** by a circuitous route: *the road to the farm goes round by the pond.* **45** to a specific place: *she came round to see me.* **46 all year round.** throughout the year. ♦ *vb* **47** to make or become round. **48** *(tr)* to encircle; surround. **49** to move or cause to move with turning motion: *to round a bend.* **50** *(tr)* **50a** to pronounce (a speech sound) with rounded lips. **50b** to purse (the lips). ♦ See also **round down, round off,** etc. ORIG C13: from OF *ront,* from L *rotundus* round, from *rota* a wheel
▸ **'roundish** *adj* ▸ **'roundness** *n*

USAGE NOTE See at **around.**

roundabout ('raʊndə,baʊt) *n* **1** *Brit.* a revolving circular platform provided with wooden animals, seats, etc., on which people ride for amusement; merry-go-round. **2** a road junction in which traffic streams circulate around a central island. US and Canad. name: **traffic circle.** ♦ *adj* **3** indirect; devious. ♦ *adv, prep* **round about. 4** on all sides: *spectators standing round about.* **5** approximately: *at round about 5 o'clock.*

round dance *n* **1** a dance in which the dancers form a circle. **2** a ballroom dance, such as the waltz, in which couples revolve.

round down *vb (tr, adv)* to lower (a number) to the nearest whole number or ten, hundred, or thousand below it.

rounded ('raʊndɪd) *adj* **1** round or curved. **2** mature or complete. **3** (of the lips) pursed. **4** (of a speech sound) articulated with rounded lips.

roundel ('raʊndᵊl) *n* **1** a form of rondeau consisting of three stanzas each of three lines with a refrain after the first and the third. **2** a circular identifying mark in national colours on military aircraft. **3** a small circular window, medallion, etc. **4** a round plate of armour used to protect the armpit. **5** another word for **roundelay.** ORIG C13: from OF *rondel;* see RONDEL

roundelay ('raʊndɪˌleɪ) *n* **1** Also called: **roundel.** a slow medieval dance performed in a circle. **2** a song in which a line or phrase is repeated as a refrain. ORIG C16: from OF *rondelet* a little rondel, from *rondel;* also infl. by LAY[4]

rounders ('raʊndəz) *n (functioning as sing) Brit.* a ball game in which players run between posts after hitting the ball, scoring a **rounder** if they run round all four before the ball is retrieved.

Roundhead ('raʊndˌhɛd) *n English history.* a supporter of Parliament against Charles I during the Civil War. ORIG referring to their short-cut hair

roundhouse ('raʊnd,haʊs) *n* **1** *US & Canad.* a building in which railway locomotives are serviced, radial tracks being fed by a central turntable. **2** *US boxing sl.* a swinging punch or style of punching. **3** an obsolete word for **jail. 4** *Obs.* a cabin on the quarterdeck of a sailing ship.

rounding ('raʊndɪŋ) *n Computing.* a process in which a number is approximated as the closest number that can be expressed using the number of bits or digits available.

roundly ('raʊndlɪ) *adv* **1** frankly, bluntly, or thoroughly: *to be roundly criticized.* **2** in a round manner or so as to be round.

round off *vb (tr, adv)* **1** (often foll. by *with*) to complete, esp. agreeably: *we rounded off the evening with a brandy.* **2** to make less jagged.

round on *vb (intr, prep)* to attack or reply to (someone) with sudden irritation or anger.

round robin *n* **1** a petition or protest having the signatures in a circle to disguise the order of signing. **2** a tournament in which each player plays against every other player.

round-shouldered *adj* denoting a faulty posture characterized by drooping shoulders and a slight forward bending of the back.

roundsman ('raʊndzmən) *n, pl* **roundsmen. 1** *Brit.* a person who makes rounds, as for inspection or to deliver goods. **2** *Austral. & NZ.* a reporter covering a particular district or topic.

round table *n* **a** a meeting of parties or people on equal terms for discussion. **b** *(as modifier): a round-table conference.*

Round Table *n* **the. 1** (in Arthurian legend) the circular table of King Arthur, enabling his knights to sit around it without any having precedence. **2** Arthur and his knights collectively. **3** one of an organization of clubs of young business and professional men who meet in order to further charitable work.

round-the-clock *adj (or as adv* **round the clock**) throughout the day and night.

round tower *n* a freestanding circular stone belfry built in Ireland from the 10th century beside a monastery and used as a place of refuge.

round trip *n* a trip to a place and back again, esp. returning by a different route.

roundtripping ('raʊnd,trɪpɪŋ) *n Finance.* a form of trading in which a company borrows a sum of money from one source and takes advantage of a short-term rise in interest rates to make a profit by lending it to another.

round up *vb (tr, adv)* **1** to gather together: *to round ponies up.* **2** to raise (a number) to the nearest whole number or ten, hundred, or thousand above it. ◆ *n* **roundup. 3** the act of gathering together livestock, esp. cattle, so that they may be branded, counted, or sold. **4** any similar act of bringing together: *a roundup of today's news.*

roundworm ('raʊnd,wɜːm) *n* a nematode worm that is a common intestinal parasite of man and pigs.

roup (raʊp) *Scot. & N English dialect.* ◆ *vb (tr)* **1** to sell by auction. ◆ *n* **2** an auction. ORIG C16 (orig.: to shout): of Scand. origin

rouse (raʊz) *vb* **rouses, rousing, roused. 1** to bring (oneself or another person) out of sleep, etc., or (of a person) to come to consciousness in this way. **2** *(tr)* to provoke: *to rouse someone's anger.* **3 rouse oneself.** to become energetic. **4** to start or cause to start from cover: *to rouse game birds.* **5** *(intr;* foll. by *on) Austral.* to scold or rebuke. ORIG C15 (in sense of hawks ruffling their feathers): from ?
▸ **'rouser** *n*

rouseabout ('raʊzəˌbaʊt) *n* **1** Also called: **rousie.** *Austral. & NZ.* an unskilled labourer in a shearing shed. **2** a variant of **roustabout** (sense 1).

rousing ('raʊzɪŋ) *adj* tending to excite; lively or vigorous: *a rousing chorus.*
▸ **'rousingly** *adv*

Rousseau ★ *(French* ruso) *n* **1 Henri** (ɑ̃ri), known as *le Douanier.* 1844–1910, French painter, noted for such works as *Sleeping Gypsy* (1897) and *Jungle with a Lion* (1904–06). **2 Jean Jacques** (ʒɑ̃ ʒak). 1712–78, French philosopher and writer, born in Switzerland. His works include *Émile* (1762) and *Confessions* (1782). **3 Théodore** (teɔdɔr). 1812–67, French landscape painter.

Roussillon ★ *(French* rusijɔ̃) *n* a former province of S France: united with Aragon in 1172; passed to the French crown in 1659; now forms part of the region of Languedoc-Roussillon.

roust (raʊst) *vb (tr;* often foll. by *out)* to rout or stir, as out of bed. ORIG C17: ?from ROUSE

roustabout ('raʊstəˌbaʊt) *n* **1** an unskilled labourer, esp. on an oil rig. **2** *Austral. & NZ.* a variant of **rouseabout** (sense 1).

rout[1] (raʊt) *n* **1** an overwhelming defeat. **2** a disorderly retreat. **3** a noisy rabble. **4** *Law.* a group of three or more people proceeding to commit an illegal act. **5** *Arch.* a large party or social gathering. ◆ *vb* **6** *(tr)* to defeat and cause to flee in confusion. ORIG C13: from Anglo-Norman *rute,* from OF: disorderly band, from L *ruptus,* from *rumpere* to burst

rout[2] (raʊt) *vb* **1** to dig over or turn up (something), esp. (of an animal) with the snout; root. **2** *(tr;* usually foll. by *out* or *up)* to find by searching. **3** *(tr;* usually foll. by *out)* to drive out: *they routed him out of bed at midnight.* **4** *(tr;* often foll. by *out)* to hollow or gouge out. **5** *(intr)* to search, poke, or rummage. ORIG C16: var. of ROOT[2]

route (ruːt) *n* **1** the choice of roads taken to get to a place. **2** a regular journey travelled. **3** *(cap.) US.* a main road between cities: *Route 66.* ◆ *vb* **routes, routeing, routed.** *(tr)* **4** to plan the route of; send by a particular route. ORIG C13: from OF *rute,* from Vulgar L *rupta via* (unattested), lit.: a broken (established) way, from L *ruptus,* from *rumpere* to break

USAGE NOTE When adding *-ing* to the verb, it is preferable to retain the *e* in order to distinguish it from *routing,* deriving from *rout*[1], 'to defeat' or *rout*[2], 'to dig, rummage': *...the routeing of buses from the city centre to the suburbs.* The spelling *routing* in this sense is, however, sometimes found, especially in American English.

routemarch ('ruːtˌmɑːtʃ) *n* **1** *Mil.* a long training march. **2** *Inf.* any long exhausting walk.

router ('raʊtə) *n* any of various tools or machines for hollowing out, cutting grooves, etc.

routine (ruː'tiːn) *n* **1** a usual or regular method of procedure, esp. one that is unvarying. **2** *Computing.* a program or part of a program performing a specific function: *an input routine.* **3** a set sequence of dance steps. **4** *Inf.* a hackneyed or insincere speech. ◆ *adj* **5** relating to or characteristic of routine. ORIG C17: from OF, from *route* a customary way, ROUTE
▸ **rou'tinely** *adv*

roux (ruː) *n* a mixture of equal amounts of fat and flour, heated, blended, and used as a basis for sauces. ORIG F: brownish, from L *russus* RUSSET

rove[1] (rəʊv) *vb* **roves, roving, roved. 1** to wander about (a place) with no fixed direction; roam. **2** *(intr)* (of the eyes) to look around; wander. ◆ *n* **3** the act of roving. ORIG

C15 *roven* (in archery) to shoot at a target chosen at random (C16: to wander, stray), from ON

rove[2] (rəʊv) *vb* **roves, roving, roved. 1** (*tr*) to pull out and twist (fibres of wool, cotton, etc.) lightly, as before spinning. ♦ *n* **2** wool, cotton, etc., thus prepared. ORIG C18: from ?

rove[3] (rəʊv) *vb* a past tense and past participle of **reeve**[2].

rover[1] ('rəʊvə) *n* **1** a person who roves. **2** *Archery.* a mark selected at random for use as a target. **3** *Australian Rules football.* a player without a fixed position who, with the ruckmen, forms the ruck. ORIG C15: from ROVE[1]

rover[2] ('rəʊvə) *n* a pirate or pirate ship. ORIG C14: prob. from MDu. or MLow G, from *roven* to rob

Rover *or* **Rover Scout** ('rəʊvə) *n Brit.* the former name for **Venture Scout.**

roving commission *n* authority or power given in a general area, without precisely defined terms of reference.

row[1] (rəʊ) *n* **1** an arrangement of persons or things in a line: *a row of chairs.* **2** *Chiefly Brit.* a street, esp. a narrow one lined with identical houses. **3** a line of seats, as in a cinema, theatre, etc. **4** *Maths.* a horizontal linear arrangement of numbers, quantities, or terms. **5** a horizontal rank of squares on a chessboard or draughtboard. **6 a hard row to hoe.** a difficult task or assignment. **7 in a row.** in succession; one after the other: *he won two gold medals in a row.* ORIG OE *rāw, rǣw*

row[2] (rəʊ) *vb* **1** to propel (a boat) by using oars. **2** (*tr*) to carry (people, goods, etc.) in a rowing boat. **3** to be propelled by means of (oars or oarsmen). **4** (*intr*) to take part in the racing of rowing boats as a sport. **5** (*tr*) to race against in a boat propelled by oars: *Oxford row Cambridge every year.* ♦ *n* **6** an act, instance, period, or distance of rowing. **7** an excursion in a rowing boat. ORIG OE *rōwan*
► **'rower** *n*

row[3] (raʊ) *n* **1** a noisy quarrel. **2** a noisy disturbance: *we couldn't hear the music for the row next door.* **3** a reprimand. ♦ *vb* **4** (*intr;* often foll. by *with*) to quarrel noisily. **5** (*tr*) *Arch.* to reprimand. ORIG C18: from ?

rowan ('rəʊən, 'raʊ-) *n* another name for the (European) **mountain ash.** ORIG C16: of Scand. origin

rowdy ('raʊdɪ) *adj* **rowdier, rowdiest. 1** tending to create noisy disturbances; rough, loud, or disorderly: *a rowdy gang of football supporters.* ♦ *n, pl* **rowdies. 2** a person who behaves in such a fashion. ORIG C19: orig. US sl., ? rel. to ROW[3]
► **'rowdily** *adv* ► **'rowdiness** *or* **'rowdyism** *n*

Rowe ★ (rəʊ) *n* **Nicholas.** 1674–1718, English dramatist; poet laureate (1715–18). His plays include *Tamerlane* (1702) and *The Fair Penitent* (1703).

rowel ('raʊəl) *n* **1** a small spiked wheel attached to a spur. **2** *Vet. science.* a piece of leather inserted under the skin of a horse to cause a discharge. ♦ *vb* **rowels, rowelling, rowelled** *or US* **rowels, roweling, roweled.** (*tr*) **3** to goad (a horse) using a rowel. **4** *Vet. science.* to insert a rowel in (the skin of a horse) to cause a discharge. ORIG C14: from OF *roel* a little wheel, from *roe* a wheel, from L *rota*

rowing boat ('rəʊɪŋ) *n Chiefly Brit.* a small pleasure boat propelled by one or more pairs of oars. Usual US and Canad. word: **rowboat.**

rowing machine ('rəʊɪŋ) *n* a device with oars and a sliding seat, resembling a sculling boat, used to provide exercise.

Rowlandson ★ ('rəʊləndsᵊn) *n* **Thomas.** 1756–1827, British caricaturist.

Rowley ★ ('rəʊlɪ, 'raʊ-) *n* **Thomas.** ?1586–?1642, English dramatist, who collaborated with John Ford and Thomas Dekker on *The Witch of Edmonton* (1621) and with Thomas Middleton on *The Changeling* (1622).

Rowling ★ ('rəʊlɪŋ) *n* **J(oanne) K(athleen).** born 1965, British novelist: author of a bestselling series of children's books featuring a boy wizard, Harry Potter, which began with *The Philosopher's Stone* (1997).

rowlock ★ ('rɒlək) *n* a swivelling device attached to the gunwale of a boat that holds an oar in place. Usual US and Canad. word: **oarlock.**

Roxas y Acuña ★ (*Spanish* 'roxas i a'kuɲa) *n* **Manuel** (ma'nwel). 1892–1948, Philippine statesman; first president of the Republic of the Philippines (1946–48).

Roxburghshire ★ ('rɒksbərəʃɪə, -ʃə) *n* a historic county of SE Scotland, now part of Scottish Borders.

royal ('rɔɪəl) *adj* **1** of, relating to, or befitting a king, queen, or other monarch; regal. **2** (*prenominal; often cap.*) established by, chartered by, under the patronage of, or in the service of royalty: *the Royal Society of St George.* **3** being a member of a royal family. **4** above the usual or normal in standing, size, quality, etc. **5** *Inf.* unusually good or impressive; first-rate. **6** *Naut.* just above the topgallant (in **royal mast**). ♦ *n* **7** (*sometimes cap.*) a member of a royal family. **8** Also: **royal stag.** a stag with antlers having 12 or more branches. **9** *Naut.* a sail set next above the topgallant, on a royal mast. **10** a size of printing paper, 20 by 25 inches. ORIG C14: from OF *roial,* from L *rēgālis* fit for a king, from *rēx* king; cf. REGAL
► **'royally** *adv*

Royal Academy *n* a society founded by George III in 1768 to foster a national school of painting, sculpture, and design in England. Full name: **Royal Academy of Arts.**

Royal Air Force *n* the air force of Great Britain. Abbrev.: **RAF.**

Royal and Ancient Club *n* **the.** a golf club, headquarters of the sport's ruling body, based in St Andrews, Scotland. Abbrev.: **R&A.**

royal assent *n Brit. & Canad.* the formal signing of an act of Parliament by the sovereign, by which it becomes law.

royal blue *n* **a** a deep blue colour. **b** (*as adj*): *a royal-blue carpet.*

Royal Commission *n* (in Britain and Canada) a body set up by the monarch on the recommendation of the prime minister to gather information about the operation of existing laws or to investigate any social, educational, or other matter.

royal fern *n* a fern of damp regions, having large fronds up to 2 metres (7 feet) in height.

royal flush *n Poker.* a hand made up of the five top honours of a suit.

royalist ('rɔɪəlɪst) *n* **1** a supporter of a monarch or monarchy, esp. during the English Civil War. **2** *Inf.* an extreme reactionary: *an economic royalist.* ♦ *adj* **3** of or relating to royalists.
► **'royalism** *n*

royal jelly *n* a substance secreted by the pharyngeal glands of worker bees and fed to all larvae when very young and to larvae destined to become queens throughout their development.

Royal Leamington Spa ★ *n* the official name of **Leamington Spa.**

Royal Marines *pl n Brit.* a corps of soldiers specially trained in amphibious warfare. Abbrev.: **RM.**

Royal Mint *n* a British organization having the sole right to manufacture coins since the 16th century. In 1968 it moved from London to Llantrisant in Wales.

Royal National Theatre ★ *n* a theatre complex in London, on the S bank of the Thames (opened 1976). The prefix Royal was added in 1988. It houses the Royal National Theatre Company.

Royal Navy *n* the navy of Great Britain. Abbrev.: **RN.**

royal palm *n* any of several palm trees of tropical America, having a tall trunk with a tuft of feathery pinnate leaves.

royal standard *n* a flag bearing the arms of the British sovereign, flown only when she or he is present.

royal tennis *n* another name for **real tennis.**

royalty ('rɔɪəltɪ) *n, pl* **royalties. 1** the rank, power, or position of a king or queen. **2a** royal persons collectively. **2b** a person who belongs to a royal family. **3** any quality characteristic of a monarch. **4** a percentage of the revenue from the sale of a book, performance of a theatrical work, use of a patented invention or of land, etc., paid to the author, inventor, or proprietor.

royal warrant *n* an authorization to a tradesman to supply goods to a royal household.

Royce ★ (rɔɪs) *n* Sir (**Frederick**) **Henry.** 1863–1933, British car designer, who with C. S. Rolls (1877–1910) founded Rolls-Royce Ltd.

rozzer (ˈrɒzə) *n Sl.* a policeman. ORIG C19: from ?

RPG *abbrev. for* report program generator: a business-oriented computer programming language.

RPI (in Britain) *abbrev. for* retail price index.

rpm *abbrev. for:* **1** resale price maintenance. **2** revolutions per minute.

RPV *abbrev. for* remotely piloted vehicle.

RR *abbrev. for:* **1** Right Reverend. **2** *Canad. & US.* rural route.

-rrhagia *n combining form.* (in pathology) an abnormal discharge: *menorrhagia.* ORIG from Gk *-rrhagia* a bursting forth, from *rhēgnunai* to burst

-rrhoea *or esp. US* **-rrhea** *n combining form.* (in pathology) a flow: *diarrhoea.* ORIG from NL, from Gk *-rrhoia,* from *rhein* to flow

r-RNA *abbrev. for* ribosomal RNA.

RRP *abbrev. for* recommended retail price.

Rs *symbol for* rupees.

RS (in Britain) *abbrev. for* Royal Society.

RSA *abbrev. for:* **1** Republic of South Africa. **2** (in New Zealand) Returned Services Association. **3** Royal Scottish Academician. **4** Royal Scottish Academy. **5** Royal Society of Arts.

RSFSR (formerly) *abbrev. for* Russian Soviet Federative Socialist Republic.

RSI *abbrev. for* repetitive strain injury.

RSL (in Australia) *abbrev. for* Returned Services League.

RSM *abbrev. for:* **1** regimental sergeant major. **2** Royal School of Music. **3** Royal Society of Medicine.

RSNZ *abbrev. for* Royal Society of New Zealand.

RSPB (in Britain) *abbrev. for* Royal Society for the Protection of Birds.

RSPCA (in Britain and Australia) *abbrev. for* Royal Society for the Prevention of Cruelty to Animals.

RSV *abbrev. for* Revised Standard Version (of the Bible).

RSVP *abbrev. for* répondez s'il vous plaît. ORIG F: please reply

rt *abbrev. for* right.

RTE *abbrev. for* Radio Telefis Éireann. ORIG Irish Gaelic: Irish Radio and Television

Rt Hon. *abbrev. for* Right Honourable.

Ru *the chemical symbol for* ruthenium.

RU *abbrev. for* Rugby Union.

Ruanda-Urundi ★ (rʊˈændaʊˈrʊndɪ) *n* a former territory of central Africa: part of German East Africa from 1890; a League of Nations mandate under Belgian administration from 1919; a United Nations trusteeship from 1946; divided into the independent states of Rwanda and Burundi in 1962.

rub (rʌb) *vb* **rubs, rubbing, rubbed. 1** to apply pressure and friction to (something) with a backward and forward motion. **2** to move (something) with pressure along, over, or against (a surface). **3** to chafe or fray. **4** (*tr*) to bring into a certain condition by rubbing: *rub it clean.* **5** (*tr*) to spread with pressure, esp. in order to cause to be absorbed: *she rubbed ointment into his back.* **6** (*tr*) to mix (fat) into flour with the fingertips, as in making pastry. **7** (foll. by *off, out, away,* etc.) to remove or be removed by rubbing: *the mark would not rub off the chair.* **8** (*intr*) *Bowls.* (of a bowl) to be slowed or deflected by an uneven patch on the green. **9** (*tr;* often foll. by *together*) to move against each other with pressure and friction (esp. in **rub one's hands,** often a sign of glee, keen anticipation, or satisfaction, and **rub noses,** a greeting among Eskimos). **10 rub (up) the wrong way.** to arouse anger in; annoy. ◆ *n* **11** the act of rubbing. **12** (preceded by *the*) an obstacle or difficulty (esp. in **there's the rub**). **13** something that hurts the feelings or annoys; cut; rebuke. **14** *Bowls.* an uneven patch in the green. ◆ See also **rub along, rub down,** etc. ORIG C15: ?from Low G *rubben,* from ?

Rub' al Khali ★ (ˈrʊb æl ˈkɑːlɪ) *n* a desert in S Arabia, mainly in Saudi Arabia, extending southeast from Nejd to Hadramaut and northeast from Yemen to the United Arab Emirates. Area: about 777 000 sq. km (300 000 sq. miles). English names: **Great Sandy Desert, Empty Quarter.** Also called: **Ar Rimal, Dahna.**

rub along *vb* (*intr, adv*) *Brit.* **1** to continue in spite of difficulties. **2** to maintain an amicable relationship; not quarrel.

rubato (ruːˈbɑːtəʊ) *Music.* ◆ *n, pl* **rubatos. 1** flexibility of tempo in performance. ◆ *adj, adv* **2** to be played with a flexible tempo. ORIG C19: from It. *tempo rubato,* lit.: stolen time, from *rubare* to ROB

rubber[1] (ˈrʌbə) *n* **1** Also called: **India rubber, gum elastic, caoutchouc.** a cream to dark brown elastic material obtained by coagulating and drying the latex from certain plants, esp. the rubber tree. **2** any of a large variety of elastomers produced from natural rubber or by synthetic means. **3** *Chiefly Brit.* a piece of rubber used for erasing something written; eraser. **4** a cloth, pad, etc., used for polishing. **5** a person who rubs something in order to smooth, polish, or massage. **6** (*often pl*) *Chiefly US & Canad.* a rubberized waterproof overshoe. **7** *Sl.* a condom. **8** (*modifier*) made of or producing rubber: *a rubber ball; a rubber factory.* ORIG C17: from RUB + -ER[1]; the tree was so named because its product was used for rubbing out writing
▸ **ˈrubbery** *adj*

rubber[2] (ˈrʌbə) *n* **1** *Bridge, whist, etc.* **1a** a match of three games. **1b** the deal that wins such a match. **2** a series of matches or games in any of various sports. ORIG C16: from ?

rubber band *n* a continuous loop of thin rubber, used to hold papers, etc., together. Also called: **elastic band.**

rubber cement *n* any of a number of adhesives made by dissolving rubber in a solvent such as benzene.

rubberize *or* **rubberise** (ˈrʌbəˌraɪz) *vb* **rubberizes, rubberizing, rubberized** *or* **rubberises, rubberising, rubberised.** (*tr*) to coat or impregnate with rubber.

rubberneck (ˈrʌbəˌnɛk) *Sl.* ◆ *n* **1** a person who stares or gapes inquisitively. **2** a sightseer or tourist. ◆ *vb* **3** (*intr*) to stare in a naive or foolish manner.

rubber plant *n* **1** a plant with glossy leathery leaves that grows as a tall tree in India and Malaya but is cultivated as a house plant in Europe and North America. **2** any of several tropical trees, the sap of which yields crude rubber.

rubber stamp *n* **1** a device used for imprinting dates, etc., on forms, invoices, etc. **2** automatic authorization of a payment, proposal, etc. **3** a person who makes such automatic authorizations; a cipher or person of little account. ◆ *vb* **rubber-stamp.** (*tr*) **4** to imprint (forms, invoices, etc.) with a rubber stamp. **5** *Inf.* to approve automatically.

rubber tree *n* a tropical American tree cultivated throughout the tropics, esp. in Malaya, for the latex of its stem, which is the major source of commercial rubber.

rubbing (ˈrʌbɪŋ) *n* an impression taken of an incised or raised surface by laying paper over it and rubbing with wax, graphite, etc.

rubbing alcohol *n* denatured alcohol used in massage, as an antiseptic, etc.

rubbish (ˈrʌbɪʃ) *n* **1** worthless, useless, or unwanted matter. **2** discarded or waste matter; refuse. **3** foolish words or speech; nonsense. ◆ *vb* **4** (*tr*) *Inf.* to criticize; attack verbally. ORIG C14 *robys,* from ?
▸ **ˈrubbishy** *adj*

rubble (ˈrʌbᵊl) *n* **1** fragments of broken stones, bricks, etc. **2** debris from ruined buildings. **3** Also called: **rubblework.** masonry constructed of broken pieces of rock, stone, etc. ORIG C14 *robyl;* ? rel. to RUBBISH, or to ME *rubben* to rub
▸ **ˈrubbly** *adj*

Rubbra ★ (ˈrʌbrə) *n* (**Charles**) **Edmund.** 1901–86, British composer; his works include 11 symphonies and a piano concerto.

rubby *or* **rubbie** (ˈrʌbɪ) *n, pl* **rubbies.** *Canad. sl.* **1** rubbing alcohol, esp. when mixed with cheap wine for drinking.

★ people and places

2 a person who drinks such mixtures, esp. a derelict alcoholic.

rub down *vb* (*adv*) **1** to dry or clean (a horse, athlete, oneself, etc.) vigorously, esp. after exercise. **2** to make or become smooth by rubbing. **3** (*tr*) to prepare (a surface) for painting by rubbing it with sandpaper. ◆ *n* **rubdown.** **4** the act of rubbing down.

rube (ru:b) *n US sl.* an unsophisticated countryman. ORIG C20: prob. from the name *Reuben*

rubella (ru:'bɛlə) *n* a mild contagious viral disease, somewhat similar to measles, characterized by cough, sore throat, and skin rash. Also called: **German measles.** ORIG C19: from NL, from L *rubellus* reddish, from *rubeus* red

rubellite ('ru:bɪˌlaɪt, ru:'bɛl-) *n* a red transparent variety of tourmaline, used as a gemstone. ORIG C18: from L *rubellus* reddish

Rubens ★ ('ru:bɪnz) *n* Sir **Peter Paul.** 1577–1640, Flemish painter, appointed (1609) painter to Archduke Albert of Austria and knighted by Charles I of England in 1629. His works include *Descent from the Cross* (1611–14) and *The Rape of the Sabines* (1635).

rubeola (ru:'bi:ələ) *n* the technical name for **measles.** ORIG C17: from NL, from L *rubeus* reddish

Rubicon ★ ('ru:bɪkən) *n* **1** a stream in N Italy: in ancient times the boundary between Italy and Cisalpine Gaul. By leading his army across it and marching on Rome in 49 B.C., Julius Caesar committed himself to civil war with the senatorial party. **2** (*sometimes not cap.*) a point of no return. **3** a penalty in piquet by which the score of a player who fails to reach 100 points in six hands is added to his opponent's. **4 cross** (*or* **pass**) **the Rubicon.** to commit oneself irrevocably to some course of action.

rubicund ('ru:bɪkənd) *adj* of a reddish colour; ruddy; rosy. ORIG C16: from L *rubicundus*, from *rubēre* to be ruddy, from *ruber* red
▸ **rubicundity** (ˌru:bɪ'kʌndɪtɪ) *n*

rubidium (ru:'bɪdɪəm) *n* a soft highly reactive radioactive element of the alkali metal group. It is used in electronic valves, photocells, and special glass. Symbol: Rb; atomic no.: 37; atomic wt.: 85.47; half-life of ^{87}Rb: 5×10^{11} years. ORIG C19: from NL, from L *rubidus* dark red, with reference to the two red lines in its spectrum
▸ **ru'bidic** *adj*

rubidium-strontium dating *n* a technique for determining the age of minerals based on the occurrence in natural rubidium of a fixed amount of the radioisotope ^{87}Rb which decays to the stable strontium isotope ^{87}Sr with a half-life of 5×10^{11} years.

rubiginous (ru:'bɪdʒɪnəs) *adj* rust-coloured. ORIG C17: from L *rūbīginōsus*, from *rūbīgō* rust, from *ruber* red

rub in *vb* (*tr, adv*) **1** to spread with pressure, esp. in order to cause to be absorbed. **2 rub it in.** *Inf.* to harp on something distasteful to a person.

Rubinstein ★ ('ru:bɪnˌstaɪn) *n* **1 Anton Grigorevich** (*Russian* an'tɔn gri'gɔrjɪvitʃ). 1829–94, Russian composer and pianist. **2 Artur** (*Polish* 'artur). 1886–1982, US pianist, born in Poland.

ruble ('ru:bᵊl) *n* a variant spelling of **rouble.**

rub off *vb* **1** to remove or be removed by rubbing. **2** (*intr; often foll. by on or onto*) to have an effect through close association or contact: *her crude manners have rubbed off on you.*

rub out *vb* (*tr, adv*) **1** to remove or be removed with a rubber. **2** *US sl.* to murder.

rubric ('ru:brɪk) *n* **1** a title, heading, or initial letter in a book, manuscript, or section of a legal code, esp. one printed or painted in red ink or in some similarly distinguishing manner. **2** a set of rules of conduct or procedure. **3** a set of directions for the conduct of Christian church services, often printed in red in a prayer book or missal. ORIG C15 *rubrike* red ochre, red lettering, from L *rubrīca* (*terra*) red (earth), ruddle, from *ruber* red
▸ **'rubrical** *adj* ▸ **'rubrically** *adv*

ruby ('ru:bɪ) *n, pl* **rubies.** **1** a deep red transparent precious variety of corundum: used as a gemstone, in lasers, and for bearings and rollers in watchmaking. **2a** the deep-red colour of a ruby. **2b** (*as adj*): *ruby lips.* **3a** something resembling, made of, or containing a ruby. **3b** (*as modifier*): *a ruby necklace.* **4** (*modifier*) denoting a fortieth anniversary: *our ruby wedding.* ORIG C14: from OF *rubi*, from L *rubeus*, from *ruber* red

RUC *abbrev. for* Royal Ulster Constabulary.

ruche (ru:ʃ) *n* a strip of pleated or frilled lawn, lace, etc., used to decorate blouses, dresses, etc. ORIG C19: from F, lit.: beehive, from Med. L *rūsca* bark of a tree, of Celtic origin

ruching ('ru:ʃɪŋ) *n* **1** material used for a ruche. **2** a ruche or ruches collectively.

ruck[1] (rʌk) *n* **1** a large number or quantity; mass, esp. of undistinguished people or things. **2** (in a race) a group of competitors who are well behind the leaders. **3** *Rugby.* a loose scrum that forms around the ball when it is on the ground. **4** *Australian Rules football.* the three players who do not have fixed positions but follow the ball closely. ◆ *vb* **5** (*intr*) *Rugby.* to try to win the ball by mauling and scrummaging. ORIG C13 (meaning "heap of firewood"): ?from ON

ruck[2] (rʌk) *n* **1** a wrinkle, crease, or fold. ◆ *vb* **2** (usually foll. by *up*) to become or make wrinkled, creased, or puckered. ORIG C18: of Scand. origin; rel. to ON *hrukka*

ruckman ('rʌkmən) *n, pl* **ruckmen.** *Australian Rules football.* either of two players who, with the rover, form the ruck.

ruck-rover *n Australian Rules football.* a player playing a role midway between that of the rover and the ruckmen.

rucksack ('rʌkˌsæk) *n* a large bag, usually having two straps, carried on the back and often used by climbers, campers, etc. Also called: **backpack.** ORIG C19: from G, lit.: back sack

ruction ('rʌkʃən) *n Inf.* **1** an uproar; noisy or quarrelsome disturbance. **2** (*pl*) an unpleasant row; trouble. ORIG C19: ? changed from INSURRECTION

rudaceous (ru:'deɪʃəs) *adj* (of conglomerate, breccia, and similar rocks) composed of coarse-grained material. ORIG C20: from L *rudis* coarse, rough + -ACEOUS

Ruda Śląska ★ ('ru:də 'ʃlɒnskə) *n* a town in SW Poland: coalmining. Pop.: 166 600 (1995 est.).

rudbeckia (rʌd'bɛkɪə) *n* any of a genus of North American plants of the composite family, cultivated for their showy flowers, which have golden-yellow rays and green or black conical centres. See also **black-eyed Susan.** ORIG C18: NL, after Olaus *Rudbeck* (1630–1702), Swedish botanist

rudd (rʌd) *n* a European freshwater fish, having a compressed dark greenish body and reddish ventral and tail fins. ORIG C17: prob. from dialect *rud* red colour, from OE *rudu* redness

Rudd ★ (rʌd) *n* **Steele,** pen name of *Arthur Hoey Davis*, 1868–1935, Australian author. His works include *On Our Selection* (1899).

rudder ('rʌdə) *n* **1** *Naut.* a pivoted vertical vane that projects into the water at the stern and can be used to steer a vessel. **2** a vertical control surface attached to the rear of the fin used to steer an aircraft. **3** anything that guides or directs. ORIG OE *rōther*
▸ **'rudderless** *adj*

rudderpost ('rʌdəˌpəʊst) *n Naut.* **1** a postlike member at the forward edge of a rudder. **2** the part of the stern frame of a vessel to which a rudder is fitted.

ruddle ('rʌdᵊl), **raddle,** *or* **reddle** *n* **1** a red ochre, used esp. to mark sheep. ◆ *vb* **ruddles, ruddling, ruddled.** **2** (*tr*) to mark (sheep) with ruddle. ORIG C16: dim. formed from OE *rudu* redness; see RUDD

ruddy ('rʌdɪ) *adj* **ruddier, ruddiest.** **1** (of the complexion) having a healthy reddish colour. **2** coloured red or pink: *a ruddy sky.* ◆ *adv, adj Inf., chiefly Brit.* **3** (intensifier) bloody; damned: *a ruddy fool.* ORIG OE *rudig*, from *rudu* redness
▸ **'ruddily** *adv* ▸ **'ruddiness** *n*

rude (ru:d) *adj* **1** insulting or uncivil; discourteous; impolite. **2** lacking refinement; coarse or uncouth. **3** vulgar or obscene: *a rude joke.* **4** unexpected and unpleasant: *a rude awakening.* **5** roughly or crudely made: *we made a rude shelter on the island.* **6** rough or harsh in sound, appear-

ance, or behaviour. **7** humble or lowly. **8** (*prenominal*) robust or sturdy: *in rude health.* **9** (*prenominal*) approximate or imprecise: *a rude estimate.* ORIG C14: via OF from L *rudis* coarse, unformed
▸ **'rudely** *adv* ▸ **'rudeness** *or* (*inf.*) **'rudery** *n*

ruderal ('ru:dərəl) *n* **1** a plant that grows on waste ground. ◆ *adj* **2** growing in waste places. ORIG C19: from NL *rūderālis,* from L *rūdus* rubble

rudiment ('ru:dɪmənt) *n* **1** (*often pl*) the first principles or elementary stages of a subject. **2** (*often pl*) a partially developed version of something. **3** *Biol.* an organ or part in an embryonic or vestigial state. ORIG C16: from L *rudīmentum* a beginning, from *rudis* unformed

rudimentary (ˌru:dɪ'mɛntərɪ, -trɪ) *or* **rudimental** *adj* **1** basic; fundamental. **2** incompletely developed; vestigial: *rudimentary leaves.*
▸ **ˌrudi'mentarily** *or* (*less commonly*) **ˌrudi'mentally** *adv*

rudish ('ru:dɪʃ) *adj* somewhat rude.

Rudolf ★ ('ru:dɒlf) *n* **Lake.** the former name (until 1979) of (Lake) **Turkana.**

Rudolf I *or* **Rudolph I** ★ ('ru:dɒlf) *n* 1218–91, king of Germany (1273–91): founder of the Hapsburg dynasty.

rue[1] (ru:) *vb* **rues, ruing, rued. 1** to feel sorrow, remorse, or regret for (one's own wrongdoing, past events, etc.). ◆ *n* **2** *Arch.* sorrow, pity, or regret. ORIG OE *hrēowan*
▸ **'ruer** *n*

rue[2] (ru:) *n* an aromatic Eurasian shrub with small yellow flowers and evergreen leaves which yield an acrid volatile oil, formerly used medicinally as a narcotic and stimulant. Archaic name: **herb of grace.** ORIG C14: from OF, from L *rūta,* from Gk *rhutē*

rueful ('ru:fʊl) *adj* **1** feeling or expressing sorrow or regret: *a rueful face.* **2** inspiring sorrow or pity.
▸ **'ruefully** *adv* ▸ **'ruefulness** *n*

ruff[1] (rʌf) *n* **1** a circular pleated or fluted collar of lawn, muslin, etc., worn by both men and women in the 16th and 17th centuries. **2** a natural growth of long or coloured hair or feathers around the necks of certain animals or birds. **3** an Old World shore bird of the sandpiper family, the male of which has a large erectile ruff of feathers in the breeding season. ORIG C16: back formation from RUFFLE[1]
▸ **'ruffˌlike** *adj*

ruff[2] (rʌf) *Cards.* ◆ *n, vb* **1** another word for **trump**[1] (senses 1, 4). ◆ *n* **2** an old card game similar to whist. ORIG C16: from OF *roffle;* ? changed from It. *trionfa* TRUMP[1]

ruffe *or* **ruff** (rʌf) *n* a European freshwater teleost fish of the perch family, having a single spiny dorsal fin. ORIG C15: ? alteration of ROUGH (referring to its scales)

ruffian ('rʌfɪən) *n* a violent or lawless person; hoodlum. ORIG C16: from OF *rufien,* from It. *ruffiano* pander
▸ **'ruffianism** *n* ▸ **'ruffianly** *adj*

ruffle[1] ('rʌfᵊl) *vb* **ruffles, ruffling, ruffled. 1** to make, be, or become irregular or rumpled: *a breeze ruffling the water.* **2** to annoy, irritate, or be annoyed or irritated. **3** (*tr*) to make into a ruffle; pleat. **4** (of a bird) to erect (its feathers) in anger, display, etc. **5** (*tr*) to flick (cards, pages, etc.) rapidly. ◆ *n* **6** an irregular or disturbed surface. **7** a strip of pleated material used as a trim. **8** *Zool.* another name for **ruff**[1] (sense 2). **9** annoyance or irritation. ORIG C13: of Gmc origin; cf. MLow G *ruffelen* to crumple, ON *hrufla* to scratch

ruffle[2] ('rʌfᵊl) *n* **1** a low continuous drumbeat. ◆ *vb* **ruffles, ruffling, ruffled. 2** (*tr*) to beat (a drum) with a low repetitive beat. ORIG C18: from earlier *ruff,* imit.

rufous ('ru:fəs) *adj* reddish-brown. ORIG C18: from L *rūfus*

rufty-tufty (ˌrʌftɪ 'tʌftɪ) *adj Sl.* rugged in appearance or manner.

rug (rʌg) *n* **1** a floor covering, smaller than a carpet and made of thick wool or of other material, such as an animal skin. **2** *Chiefly Brit.* a blanket, esp. one used for travellers. **3** *Sl.* a wig. **4 pull the rug out from under.** to betray, expose, or leave defenceless. ORIG C16: of Scand. origin

ruga ('ru:gə) *n, pl* **rugae** (-dʒi:). (*usually pl*) *Anat.* a fold, wrinkle, or crease. ORIG C18: L

rugby *or* **rugby football** ('rʌgbɪ) *n* **1** a form of football played with an oval ball in which the handling and carrying of the ball is permitted. Also called: **rugger.** See also **rugby league, rugby union. 2** *Canad.* another name for **Canadian football.** ORIG after the public school at *Rugby,* where it was first played

Rugby ★ ('rʌgbɪ) *n* a town in central England, in E Warwickshire: famous public school, founded in 1567. Pop.: 61 106 (1991).
▸ **'Rugbeian** *adj, n*

rugby league *n* a form of rugby football played between teams of 13 players.

rugby union *n* a form of rugby football played between teams of 15 players.

rugged ('rʌgɪd) *adj* **1** having an uneven or jagged surface. **2** rocky or steep: *rugged scenery.* **3** (of the face) strong-featured or furrowed. **4** rough, severe, or stern in character. **5** without refinement or culture; rude: *rugged manners.* **6** involving hardship; harsh: *he leads a rugged life in the mountains.* **7** difficult or hard: *a rugged test.* **8** (of equipment, machines, etc.) designed to withstand rough treatment or use in rough conditions. **9** *Chiefly US & Canad.* sturdy or strong; robust. ORIG C14: from ON
▸ **'ruggedly** *adv* ▸ **'ruggedness** *n*

rugger ('rʌgə) *n Chiefly Brit.* an informal name for **rugby.**

rugose ('ru:gəʊs, -gəʊz) *adj* wrinkled: *rugose leaves.* ORIG C18: from L *rūgōsus,* from *rūga* wrinkle
▸ **'rugosely** *adv* ▸ **rugosity** (ru:'gɒsɪtɪ) *n*

rug rat *n US & Canad. inf.* a young child not yet walking.

Ruhr ★ (rʊə; *German* ru:r) *n* the chief coalmining and industrial region of Germany: in North Rhine-Westphalia around the valley of the **River Ruhr,** a tributary of the Rhine 235 km (146 miles) long. German name: **Ruhrgebiet** ('ru:rgəˌbi:t).

ruin ('ru:ɪn) *n* **1** a destroyed or decayed building or town. **2** the state of being destroyed or decayed. **3** loss of wealth, position, etc., or something that causes such loss; downfall. **4** something that is severely damaged: *his life was a ruin.* **5** a person who has suffered a downfall, bankruptcy, etc. **6** *Arch.* loss of her virginity by a woman outside marriage. ◆ *vb* **7** (*tr*) to bring to ruin; destroy. **8** (*tr*) to injure or spoil: *the town has been ruined with tower blocks.* **9** (*intr*) *Arch. or poetic.* to fall into ruins; collapse. **10** (*tr*) *Arch.* to seduce and abandon (a woman). ORIG C14: from OF *ruine,* from L *ruīna* a falling down, from *ruere* to fall violently

ruination (ˌru:ɪ'neɪʃən) *n* **1** the act of ruining or the state of being ruined. **2** something that causes ruin.

ruinous ('ru:ɪnəs) *adj* causing, tending to cause, or characterized by ruin or destruction.
▸ **'ruinously** *adv* ▸ **'ruinousness** *n*

Ruisdael *or* **Ruysdael** ★ ('ri:zdɑ:l, -deɪl, 'raɪz-; *Dutch* 'rœizda:l) *n* **Jacob van** ('ja:kɔp van). ?1628–82, Dutch landscape painter.

rule (ru:l) *n* **1** an authoritative regulation or direction concerning method or procedure, as for a court of law, legislative body, game, or other activity: *judges' rules; play according to the rules.* **2** the exercise of governmental authority or control: *the rule of Caesar.* **3** the period of time in which a monarch or government has power: *his rule lasted 100 days.* **4** a customary form or procedure: *he made a morning swim his rule.* **5** (usually preceded by *the*) the common order of things: *violence was the rule rather than the exception.* **6** a prescribed method or procedure for solving a mathematical problem. **7** any of various devices with a straight edge for guiding or measuring; ruler: *a carpenter's rule.* **8** *Printing.* **8a** a printed or drawn character in the form of a long thin line. **8b** another name for **dash**[1] (sense 12): *en rule; em rule.* **8c** a strip of metal used to print such a line. **9** *Christianity.* a systematic body of prescriptions followed by members of a religious order. **10** *Law.* an order by a court or judge. **11 as a rule.** normally or ordinarily. ◆ *vb* **rules, ruling, ruled. 12** to exercise governing or controlling authority over (a people, political unit, individual, etc.). **13** (when *tr, often takes a clause as object*) to decide authoritatively; decree: *the chairman ruled against the proposal.* **14** (*tr*) to mark with straight parallel lines or one straight line. **15** (*tr*) to restrain or control. **16** (*intr*) to be customary or prevalent:

chaos rules in this school. **17** (*intr*) to be pre-eminent or superior: *football rules in the field of sport.* **18 rule the roost** (*or* **roast**). to be pre-eminent; be in charge. ORIG C13: from OF *riule,* from L *rēgula* a straight edge
▸ **'rulable** *adj*

rule of three *n* a mathematical rule asserting that the value of one unknown quantity in a proportion is found by multiplying the denominator of each ratio by the numerator of the other.

rule of thumb *n* **a** a rough and practical approach, based on experience, rather than theory. **b** (*as modifier*): *a rule-of-thumb decision.*

rule out *vb* (*tr, adv*) **1** to dismiss from consideration. **2** to make impossible; preclude.

ruler ('ru:lə) *n* **1** a person who rules or commands. **2** Also called: **rule.** a strip of wood, metal, or other material, having straight edges, used for measuring and drawing straight lines.

Rules (ru:lz) *pl n* **1** short for **Australian Rules** (football). **2 the Rules.** *English history.* the neighbourhood around certain prisons in which trusted prisoners were allowed to live under specified restrictions.

ruling ('ru:lɪŋ) *n* **1** a decision of someone in authority, such as a judge. **2** one or more parallel ruled lines. ◆ *adj* **3** controlling or exercising authority. **4** predominant.

rum[1] (rʌm) *n* spirit made from sugar cane. ORIG C17: ? shortened from C16 *rumbullion,* from ?

rum[2] (rʌm) *adj* **rummer, rummest.** *Brit. sl.* strange; peculiar; odd. ORIG C19: ?from Romany *rom* man
▸ **'rumly** *adv* ▸ **'rumness** *n*

Rumania ★ (ru'meɪnɪə) *n* a variant of **Romania.**
▸ **Ru'manian** *adj, n*

rumba *or* **rhumba** ('rʌmbə, 'rʊm-) *n* **1** a rhythmic and syncopated Cuban dance in duple time. **2** a ballroom dance derived from this. **3** a piece of music composed for or in the rhythm of this dance. ORIG C20: from Sp.: lavish display, from ?

rumble ('rʌmb^{ə}l) *vb* **rumbles, rumbling, rumbled. 1** to make or cause to make a deep resonant sound: *thunder rumbled in the sky.* **2** (*intr*) to move with such a sound: *the train rumbled along.* **3** (*tr*) to utter with a rumbling sound: *he rumbled an order.* **4** (*tr*) *Brit. sl.* to find out about (someone or something): *the police rumbled their plans.* **5** (*intr*) *US sl.* to be involved in a gang fight. ◆ *n* **6** a deep resonant sound. **7** a widespread murmur of discontent. **8** *US, Canad., & NZ sl.* a gang fight. ORIG C14: ?from MDu. *rummelen*
▸ **'rumbler** *n* ▸ **'rumbling** *adj*

rumble seat *n* a folding outside seat at the rear of some early cars; dicky.

rumbustious (rʌm'bʌstʃəs) *adj* boisterous or unruly. ORIG C18: prob. var. of ROBUSTIOUS
▸ **rum'bustiously** *adv* ▸ **rum'bustiousness** *n*

rumen ('ru:mɛn) *n, pl* **rumens** *or* **rumina** (-mɪnə). the first compartment of the stomach of ruminants, in which food is partly digested before being regurgitated as cud. ORIG C18: from L: gullet

Rumford ★ ('rʌmfəd) *n* **Count.** See (Benjamin) **Thompson.**

ruminant ('ru:mɪnənt) *n* **1** any of a suborder of artiodactyl mammals which chew the cud and have a stomach of four compartments. The suborder includes deer, antelopes, cattle, sheep, and goats. **2** any other animal that chews the cud, such as a camel. ◆ *adj* **3** of, relating to, or belonging to this suborder. **4** (of members of this suborder and related animals, such as camels) chewing the cud; ruminating. **5** meditating or contemplating in a slow quiet way.

ruminate ('ru:mɪˌneɪt) *vb* **ruminates, ruminating, ruminated. 1** (of ruminants) to chew (the cud). **2** (when *intr,* often foll. by *upon, on,* etc.) to meditate or ponder (upon). ORIG C16: from L *rūmināre* to chew the cud, from RUMEN
▸ **ˌrumi'nation** *n* ▸ **'ruminative** *adj* ▸ **'ruminatively** *adv*
▸ **'rumiˌnator** *n*

rummage ('rʌmɪdʒ) *vb* **rummages, rummaging, rummaged. 1** (when *intr,* often foll. by *through*) to search (through) while looking for something, often causing disorder. ◆ *n* **2** an act of rummaging. **3** a jumble of articles. ORIG C14 (in the sense: to pack a cargo): from OF *arrumage,* from *arrumer* to stow in a ship's hold, prob. of Gmc origin
▸ **'rummager** *n*

rummage sale *n* **1** the US and Canad. term for **jumble sale. 2** *US.* a sale of unclaimed property.

rummer ('rʌmə) *n* a drinking glass having an ovoid bowl on a short stem. ORIG C17: from Du. *roemer* a glass for drinking toasts, from *roemen* to praise

rummy ('rʌmɪ) *or* **rum** *n* a card game based on collecting sets and sequences. ORIG C20: ?from RUM[2]

rumour *or US* **rumor** ('ru:mə) *n* **1a** information, often a mixture of truth and untruth, passed around verbally. **1b** (*in combination*): *a rumourmonger.* **2** gossip or hearsay. ◆ *vb* **3** (*tr; usually passive*) to pass around or circulate in the form of a rumour: *it is rumoured that the Queen is coming.* ORIG C14: via OF from L *rūmor* common talk

rump (rʌmp) *n* **1** the hindquarters of a mammal, not including the legs. **2** the rear part of a bird's back, nearest to the tail. **3** a person's buttocks. **4** Also called: **rump steak.** a cut of beef from behind the loin. **5** an inferior remnant. ORIG C15: from ON
▸ **'rumpless** *adj*

Rumpelstiltskin ★ (ˌrʌmp^{ə}l'stɪltskɪn) *n* a dwarf in a German folktale who aids the king's bride on condition that she give him her first child or guess the dwarf's name. She guesses correctly and in his rage he destroys himself.

rumple ('rʌmp^{ə}l) *vb* **rumples, rumpling, rumpled. 1** to make or become crumpled or dishevelled. ◆ *n* **2** a wrinkle, fold, or crease. ORIG C17: from MDu. *rompelen;* rel. to OE *gerumpen* wrinkled
▸ **'rumply** *adj*

Rump Parliament *or* **the Rump** *n English history.* the remainder of the Long Parliament after Pride's Purge. It sat from 1648–53.

rumpus ('rʌmpəs) *n, pl* **rumpuses.** a noisy, confused, or disruptive commotion. ORIG C18: from ?

rumpus room *n* a room used for noisy activities, such as parties or children's games.

rumpy-pumpy ('rʌmpɪ'pʌmpɪ) *n Inf.* sexual intercourse.

run (rʌn) *vb* **runs, running, ran, run. 1** (*intr*) **1a** (of a two-legged creature) to move on foot at a rapid pace so that both feet are off the ground for part of each stride. **1b** (of a four-legged creature) to move at a rapid gait. **2** (*tr*) to pass over (a distance, route, etc.) in running: *to run a mile.* **3** (*intr*) to run in or finish a race as specified, esp. in a particular position: *John is running third.* **4** (*tr*) to perform as by running: *to run an errand.* **5** (*intr*) to flee; run away. **6** (*tr*) to bring into a specified state by running: *to run oneself to a standstill.* **7** (*tr*) to track down or hunt (an animal): *to run a fox to earth.* **8** (*tr*) to set (animals) loose on (a field or tract of land) so as to graze freely: *he ran stock on that pasture last year.* **9** (*intr;* often foll. by *over, round,* or *up*) to make a short trip or brief visit: *I'll run over this afternoon.* **10** (*intr*) to move quickly and easily on wheels by rolling, or in any of certain other ways: *a sledge running over snow.* **11** to move or cause to move with a specified result: *to run a ship aground; run into a tree.* **12** (often foll. by *over*) to move or pass or cause to move or pass quickly: *to run one's eyes over a page.* **13** (*tr;* foll. by *into, out of, through,* etc.) to force, thrust, or drive: *she ran a needle into her finger.* **14** (*tr*) to drive or maintain and operate (a vehicle). **15** (*tr*) to give a lift to (someone) in a vehicle: *he ran her to the station.* **16** to ply or cause to ply between places on a route: *the bus runs from Piccadilly to Golders Green.* **17** to function or cause to function: *the engine is running smoothly.* **18** (*tr*) to manage: *to run a company.* **19** to extend or continue or cause to extend or continue in a particular direction, for a particular duration or distance, etc.: *the road runs north; the play ran for two years.* **20** (*intr*) *Law.* to have legal force or effect: *the house lease runs for two more years.* **21** (*tr*) to be subjected to, be affected by, or incur: *to run a risk; run a temperature.* **22** (*intr;* often foll. by *to*) to be characterized (by); tend or incline: *to run to fat.* **23** (*intr*) to recur persistently or be inherent: *red hair runs in my family.* **24** to cause or allow (liquids) to flow or (of liquids) to flow: *the well has run dry.* **25** (*intr*) to melt and flow: *the wax grew hot and began to run.* **26** *Metallurgy.* **26a** to melt or fuse. **26b** (*tr*) to cast (molten metal): *to run lead into ingots.* **27** (*intr*) (of waves, tides, rivers, etc.) to rise high, surge, or be at a specified height: *a high sea was running that night.* **28** (*intr*) to be diffused: *the colours in my dress ran when I washed it.* **29** (*intr*) (of stitches) to unravel or come undone or (of a garment) to have stitches unravel or come undone. **30** (*intr*) (of growing creepers, etc.) to trail, spread, or climb: *ivy running over a cottage wall.* **31** (*intr*) to spread or circulate quickly: *a rumour ran through the town.* **32** (*intr*) to be stated or reported: *his story runs as follows.* **33** to publish or print or be published or printed in a newspaper, magazine, etc.: *they ran his story in the next issue.* **34** (often foll. by *for*) *Chiefly US & Canad.* to be a candidate or present as a candidate for political or other office: *Jones is running for president.* **35** (*tr*) to get past or through: *to run a blockade.* **36** (*tr*) to deal in (arms, etc.), esp. by importing illegally: *he runs guns for the rebels.* **37** *Naut.* to sail (a vessel, esp. a sailing vessel) or (of such a vessel) to be sailed with the wind coming from astern. **38** (*intr*) (of fish) to migrate upstream from the sea, esp. in order to spawn. **39** (*tr*) *Cricket.* to score (a run or number of runs) by hitting the ball and running between the wickets. **40** (*tr*) *Billiards, etc.* to make (a number of successful shots) in sequence. **41** (*tr*) *Golf.* to hit (the ball) so that it rolls along the ground. **42** (*tr*) *Bridge.* to cash (all one's winning cards in a long suit) successively. ◆ *n* **43** an act, instance, or period of running. **44** a gait, pace, or motion faster than a walk: *she went off at a run.* **45** a distance covered by running or a period of running: *a run of ten miles.* **46** an instance or period of travelling in a vehicle, esp. for pleasure: *to go for a run in the car.* **47** free and unrestricted access: *we had the run of the house.* **48a** a period of time during which a machine, computer, etc., operates. **48b** the amount of work performed in such a period. **49** a continuous or sustained period: *a run of good luck.* **50** a continuous sequence of performances: *the play had a good run.* **51** *Cards.* a sequence of winning cards in one suit: *a run of spades.* **52** tendency or trend: *the run of the market.* **53** type, class, or category: *the usual run of graduates.* **54** (usually foll. by *on*) a continuous and urgent demand: *a run on the dollar.* **55** a series of unravelled stitches, esp. in tights; ladder. **56** the characteristic pattern or direction of something: *the run of the grain on wood.* **57a** a period during which water or other liquid flows. **57b** the amount of such a flow. **58** a pipe, channel, etc., through which water or other liquid flows. **59** *US.* a small stream. **60** a steeply inclined course, esp. a snow-covered one used for skiing. **61** an enclosure for domestic fowls or other animals: *a chicken run.* **62** (esp. in Australia and New Zealand) a tract of land for grazing livestock. **63** the migration of fish upstream in order to spawn. **64** *Mil.* **64a** a mission in a warplane. **64b** Also called: **bombing run.** an approach by a bomber to a target. **65** the movement of an aircraft along the ground during takeoff or landing. **66** *Music.* a rapid scalelike passage of notes. **67** *Cricket.* a score of one, normally achieved by both batsmen running from one end of the wicket to the other after one of them has hit the ball. **68** *Baseball.* an instance of a batter touching all four bases safely, thereby scoring. **69** *Golf.* the distance that a ball rolls after hitting the ground. **70 a run for (one's) money.** *Inf.* **70a** a close competition. **70b** pleasure derived from an activity. **71 in the long run.** as the eventual outcome of a series of events, etc. **72 in the short run.** as the immediate outcome of a series of events, etc. **73 on the run. 73a** escaping from arrest; fugitive. **73b** in rapid flight; retreating: *the enemy is on the run.* **73c** hurrying from place to place. **74 the runs.** *Sl.* diarrhoea. ◆ See also **runabout, run across,** etc. ORIG OE *runnen,* p.p. of *(ge)rinnan*

runabout (ˈrʌnəˌbaut) *n* **1** a small light vehicle or aeroplane. ◆ *vb* **run about. 2** (*intr, adv*) to move busily from place to place.

run across *vb* (*intr, prep*) to meet unexpectedly; encounter by chance.

run along *vb* (*intr, adv*) (often said patronizingly) to go away; leave.

run around *Inf.* ◆ *vb* (*intr, adv*) **1** (often foll. by *with*) to associate habitually (with). **2** to behave in a fickle or promiscuous manner. ◆ *n* **run-around. 3** deceitful or evasive treatment of a person (esp. in **give** *or* **get the run-around**).

run away *vb* (*intr, adv*) **1** to take flight; escape. **2** to go away; depart. **3** (of a horse) to gallop away uncontrollably. **4 run away with. 4a** to abscond or elope with: *he ran away with his boss's daughter.* **4b** to make off with; steal. **4c** to escape from the control of: *his enthusiasm ran away with him.* **4d** to win easily or be assured of victory in (a competition): *he ran away with the race.* ◆ *n* **runaway. 5a** a person or animal that runs away. **5b** (*as modifier*): *a runaway horse.* **6** the act or an instance of running away. **7** (*modifier*) rising rapidly, as prices: *runaway inflation.* **8** (*modifier*) (of a race, victory, etc.) easily won.

runcible spoon (ˈrʌnsɪbᵊl) *n* a forklike utensil with two broad prongs and one sharp curved prong. ORIG *runcible* coined by Edward Lear, in a nonsense poem (1871)

Runcorn ★ (ˈrʌŋˌkɔːn) *n* a town in NW England, in N Cheshire on the Manchester Ship Canal: port and industrial centre; designated a new town in 1964. Pop.: 64 154 (1991).

run down *vb* (*mainly adv*) **1** to allow (an engine, etc.) to lose power gradually and cease to function or (of an engine, etc.) to do this. **2** to decline or reduce in number or size: *the firm ran down its sales force.* **3** (*tr; usually passive*) to tire, sap the strength of, or exhaust: *he was thoroughly run down.* **4** (*tr*) to criticize adversely; decry. **5** (*tr*) to hit and knock to the ground with a moving vehicle. **6** (*tr*) *Naut.* to collide with and cause to sink. **7** (*tr*) to pursue and find or capture: *to run down a fugitive.* **8** (*tr*) to read swiftly or perfunctorily: *he ran down their list of complaints.* ◆ *adj* **run-down. 9** tired; exhausted. **10** worn-out, shabby, or dilapidated. ◆ *n* **rundown. 11** a brief review, résumé, or summary. **12** the process of a mechanism coming gradually to a standstill after the power is removed. **13** a reduction in number or size.

Rundstedt ★ (ˈrundstɛt; *German* ˈruntʃtɛt) *n* **Karl Rudolf Gerd von** (karl ˈruːdɔlf gɛrt fɔn). 1875–1953, German field marshal; commanded the conquest of Poland and France and the Western Front (1942–44); led the Ardennes counteroffensive (Dec. 1944).

rune (ruːn) *n* **1** any of the characters of an ancient Germanic alphabet, in use, esp. in Scandinavia, from the 3rd century A.D. to the end of the Middle Ages. **2** any obscure piece of writing using mysterious symbols. **3** a kind of Finnish poem or a stanza in such a poem. ORIG OE *rūn,* from ON *rūn* secret
▸ **ˈrunic** *adj*

rung[1] (rʌŋ) *n* **1** one of the bars or rods that form the steps of a ladder. **2** a crosspiece between the legs of a chair, etc. **3** *Naut.* a spoke on a ship's wheel or a handle projecting from the periphery. ORIG OE *hrung*
▸ **ˈrungless** *adj*

rung[2] (rʌŋ) *vb* the past participle of **ring**[2].

> **USAGE NOTE** See at **ring**[2].

run in *vb* (*adv*) **1** to run (an engine) gently, usually when it is new. **2** (*tr*) to insert or include. **3** (*intr*) (of an aircraft) to approach a point or target. **4** (*tr*) *Inf.* to take into custody; arrest. ◆ *n* **run-in. 5** *Inf.* an argument or quarrel. **6** an approach to the end of an event, etc.: *the run-in for the championship.* **7** *Printing.* matter inserted in an existing paragraph.

run into *vb* (*prep, mainly intr*) **1** (*also tr*) to collide with or cause to collide with: *her car ran into a tree.* **2** to encounter unexpectedly. **3** (*also tr*) to be beset by: *the project ran into financial difficulties.* **4** to extend to; be of the order of: *debts running into thousands.*

runnel (ˈrʌnᵊl) *n Literary.* a small stream. ORIG C16: from OE *rynele;* rel. to RUN

runner (ˈrʌnə) *n* **1** a person who runs, esp. an athlete. **2** a messenger for a bank, etc. **3** a person engaged in the solicitation of business. **4** a person on the run; fugitive. **5a** a person or vessel engaged in smuggling. **5b** (*in combination*): *a gunrunner.* **6** a person who operates, manages, or controls something. **7a** either of the strips of metal or wood on which a sledge runs. **7b** the blade of an ice skate. **8** a roller or guide for a sliding component. **9** *Bot.* **9a** Also called: **stolon.** a slender horizontal stem, as of the strawberry, that grows along the surface of the soil and propagates by producing roots and shoots at the nodes or tip. **9b** a plant that propagates in this way. **10** a strip of lace, linen, etc., placed across a table or dressing table for protection and decoration. **11** another word for **rocker** (on a rocking chair). **12 do a runner.** *Sl.* to run away in order to escape trouble or to avoid paying for something.

runner bean *n* another name for **scarlet runner.**

runner-up *n, pl* **runners-up.** a contestant finishing a race or competition in second place.

running ('rʌnɪŋ) *adj* **1** maintained continuously; incessant: *running commentary.* **2** (*postpositive*) without interruption; consecutive: *he lectured for two hours running.* **3** denoting or relating to the scheduled operation of a public vehicle: *the running time of a train.* **4** accomplished at a run: *a running jump.* **5** moving or slipping easily, as a rope or a knot. **6** (of a wound, etc.) discharging pus. **7** prevalent; current: *running prices.* **8** repeated or continuous: *a running design.* **9** (of plants, plant stems, etc.) creeping along the ground. **10** flowing: *running water.* **11** (of handwriting) having the letters run together. ◆ *n* **12** management or organization: *the running of a company.* **13** operation or maintenance: *the running of a machine.* **14** competition or competitive situation (in **in the running, out of the running**). **15 make the running.** to set the pace in a competition or race.

running board *n* a footboard along the side of a vehicle, esp. an early motorcar.

running head *or* **title** *n Printing.* a heading printed at the top of every page of a book.

running light *n Naut.* one of several lights displayed by vessels operating at night.

running mate *n* **1** *US.* a candidate for the subordinate of two linked positions, esp. a candidate for the vice-presidency. **2** a horse that pairs another in a team.

running repairs *pl n* repairs that do not, or do not greatly, interrupt operations.

runny ('rʌnɪ) *adj* **runnier, runniest. 1** tending to flow; liquid. **2** (of the nose) exuding mucus.

Runnymede ★ ('rʌnɪˌmiːd) *n* a meadow on the S bank of the Thames near Windsor, where King John met his rebellious barons in 1215 and acceded to Magna Carta.

run off *vb* (*adv*) **1** (*intr*) to depart in haste. **2** (*tr*) to produce quickly, as copies on a duplicating machine. **3** to drain (liquid) or (of liquid) to be drained. **4** (*tr*) to decide (a race) by a run-off. **5 run off with. 5a** to steal; purloin. **5b** to elope with. ◆ *n* **run-off. 6** an extra race, contest, election, etc., to decide the winner after a tie. **7** *NZ.* grazing land for store cattle. **8** that portion of rainfall that runs into streams as surface water rather than being absorbed by the soil. **9** the overflow of a liquid from a container.

run-of-the-mill *adj* ordinary, average, or undistinguished in quality, character, or nature.

run on *vb* (*adv*) **1** (*intr*) to continue without interruption. **2** to write with linked-up characters. **3** *Printing.* to compose text matter without indentation or paragraphing. ◆ *n* **run-on. 4** *Printing.* **4a** text matter composed without indenting. **4b** an additional quantity required in excess of the originally stated amount, whilst the job is being produced. **5a** a word added at the end of a dictionary entry whose meaning can be easily inferred from the definition of the headword. **5b** (*as modifier*): *a run-on entry.*

run out *vb* (*adv*) **1** (*intr;* often foll. by *of*) to exhaust (a supply of something) or (of a supply) to become exhausted. **2 run out on.** *Inf.* to desert or abandon. **3** (*tr*) *Cricket.* to dismiss (a running batsman) by breaking the wicket with the ball, or with the ball in the hand, while he or she is out of his or her ground. ◆ *n* **run-out. 4** *Cricket.* dismissal of a batsman by running him or her out.

run over *vb* **1** (*tr, adv*) to knock down (a person) with a moving vehicle. **2** (*intr*) to overflow the capacity of (a container). **3** (*intr, prep*) to examine hastily or make a rapid survey of. **4** (*intr, prep*) to exceed (a limit): *we've run over our time.*

runt (rʌnt) *n* **1** the smallest and weakest young animal in a litter, esp. the smallest piglet in a litter. **2** *Derog.* an undersized or inferior person. **3** a large pigeon, originally bred for eating. ORIG C16: from ?
▸ **'runtish** *or* **'runty** *adj* ▸ **'runtiness** *n*

run through *vb* **1** (*tr, adv*) to transfix with a sword or other weapon. **2** (*intr, prep*) to exhaust (money) by wasteful spending. **3** (*intr, prep*) to practise or rehearse: *let's run through the plan.* **4** (*intr, prep*) to examine hastily. ◆ *n* **run-through. 5** a practice or rehearsal. **6** a brief survey.

run time *n Computing.* the time during which a computer program is executed.

run to *vb* (*intr, prep*) to be sufficient for: *my income doesn't run to luxuries.*

run up *vb* (*tr, adv*) **1** to amass; incur: *to run up debts.* **2** to make by sewing together quickly. **3** to hoist: *to run up a flag.* ◆ *n* **run-up. 4** an approach run by an athlete for the long jump, pole vault, etc. **5** a preliminary or preparatory period: *the run-up to the election.*

runway ('rʌnˌweɪ) *n* **1** a hard level roadway from which aircraft take off and on which they land. **2** *Forestry, US & Canad.* a chute for sliding logs down. **3** *Chiefly US.* a narrow ramp extending from the stage into the audience in a theatre, etc. esp. as used by models in a fashion show.

Runyon ★ ('rʌnjən) *n* **(Alfred) Damon** ('deɪmən). 1884–1946, US writer, noted for his short stories, such as *Guys and Dolls* (1932), about Broadway characters.

rupee (ruː'piː) *n* the standard monetary unit of India, Mauritius, Nepal, Pakistan, the Seychelles, and Sri Lanka. ORIG C17: from Hindi *rupaīyā,* from Sansk. *rūpya* coined silver, from *rūpa* shape, beauty

Rupert ★ ('ruːpət) *n* **Prince.** 1619–82, German-born nephew of Charles I: Royalist general during the Civil War (until 1646) and commander of the Royalist fleet (1648–50).

Rupert's Land ★ *n* (formerly, in Canada) the territories granted by Charles II to the Hudson's Bay Company in 1670 and ceded to the Canadian Government in 1870, comprising all the land watered by rivers flowing into Hudson Bay.

rupiah (ruː'piːə) *n, pl* **rupiah** *or* **rupiahs.** the standard monetary unit of Indonesia. ORIG from Hindi: RUPEE

rupture ('rʌptʃə) *n* **1** the act of breaking or bursting or the state of being broken or burst. **2** a breach of peaceful or friendly relations. **3** *Pathol.* **3a** the breaking or tearing of a bodily structure or part. **3b** another word for **hernia.** ◆ *vb* **ruptures, rupturing, ruptured. 4** to break or burst. **5** to affect or be affected with a rupture or hernia. **6** to undergo or cause to undergo a breach in relations or friendship. ORIG C15: from L *ruptūra,* from *rumpere* to burst forth
▸ **'rupturable** *adj*

rural ('rʊərəl) *adj* **1** of, relating to, or characteristic of the country or country life. **2** living in the country. **3** of, relating to, or associated with farming. ◆ Cf. **urban.** ORIG C15: via OF from L *rūrālis,* from *rūs* the country
▸ **'ruralism** *n* ▸ **'ruralist** *n* ▸ **ru'rality** *n* ▸ **'rurally** *adv*

rural dean *n Chiefly Brit.* a clergyman having authority over a group of parishes.

rural district *n* (formerly) a rural division of a county.

ruralize *or* **ruralise** ('rʊərəˌlaɪz) *vb* **ruralizes, ruralizing, ruralized** *or* **ruralises, ruralising, ruralised. 1** (*tr*) to make rural in character, appearance, etc. **2** (*intr*) to go into the country to live.
▸ **ˌrurali'zation** *or* **ˌrurali'sation** *n*

rural route *n US & Canad.* a mail service or route in a rural area, the mail being delivered by car or van.

Rurik *or* **Ryurik** ★ ('rʊərɪk) *n* died 879. Varangian (Scandinavian Viking) leader who founded the Russian monarchy. He gained control over Novgorod (?862) and his dynasty, the **Rurikids,** ruled until 1598.

Ruritania ★ (ˌrʊərɪ'teɪnɪə, -njə) *n* **1** an imaginary kingdom of central Europe: setting of several novels by Anthony Hope, esp. *The Prisoner of Zenda* (1894). **2** any setting of adventure, romance, and intrigue.
▸ **ˌRuri'tanian** *adj, n*

Rus. *abbrev. for* Russia(n).

ruse (ruːz) *n* an action intended to mislead, deceive, or trick; stratagem. ORIG C15: from OF: trick, esp. to evade capture, from *ruser* to retreat, from L *recūsāre* to refuse

Ruse ★ ('ruːseɪ) *n* a city in NE Bulgaria, on the River Danube: the chief river port and one of the largest industrial centres in Bulgaria. Pop.: 168 051 (1996 est.).

rush[1] (rʌʃ) *vb* **1** to hurry or cause to hurry; hasten. **2** (*tr*) to make a sudden attack upon (a fortress, position, person, etc.). **3** (when *intr*, often foll. by *at*, *in*, or *into*) to proceed or approach in a reckless manner. **4 rush one's fences.** to proceed with precipitate haste. **5** (*intr*) to come, flow, swell, etc., quickly or suddenly: *tears rushed to her eyes.* **6** (*tr*) *Sl.* to cheat, esp. by grossly overcharging. **7** (*tr*) *US & Canad.* to make a concerted effort to secure the agreement, participation, etc., of (a person). **8** (*intr*) *American football.* to gain ground by running forwards with the ball. ◆ *n* **9** the act or condition of rushing. **10** a sudden surge towards someone or something: *a gold rush.* **11** a sudden surge of sensation, esp. from a drug. **12** a sudden demand. ◆ *adj* (*prenominal*) **13** requiring speed or urgency: *a rush job.* **14** characterized by much movement, business, etc.: *a rush period.* ORIG C14 *ruschen*, from OF *ruser* to put to flight, from L *recūsāre* to refuse
▸ **'rusher** *n*

rush[2] (rʌʃ) *n* **1** an annual or perennial plant growing in wet places and typically having grasslike cylindrical leaves and small green or brown flowers. **2** something valueless; a trifle; straw: *not worth a rush.* **3** short for **rush light.** ORIG OE *risce*, *rysce*
▸ **'rush,like** *adj* ▸ **'rushy** *adj*

Rushdie ★ ('rʊʃdɪ) *n* (**Ahmed**) **Salman** ('sælmən). born 1947, British writer, born in India. His novels include *The Satanic Verses* (1988), which some Muslims regard as blasphemous. He was forced into hiding (1989) after Ayatollah Khomeini called for his death in a fatwa; in 1998 the Iranian government withdrew its official support for the fatwa.

rushes ('rʌʃɪz) *pl n* (*sometimes sing*) (in film-making) the initial prints of a scene or scenes before editing, usually prepared daily.

rush hour *n* a period at the beginning and end of the working day when large numbers of people are travelling to or from work.

rush light *or* **candle** *n* a narrow candle, formerly in use, made of the pith of various types of rush dipped in tallow.

Rushmore ★ ('rʌʃmɔː) *n* **Mount.** a mountain in W South Dakota, in the Black Hills: a national memorial, with the faces of Washington, Lincoln, Jefferson, and Roosevelt carved into its side by Gutzon Borglum between 1927 and 1941. Height: 1841 m (6040 ft).

rusk (rʌsk) *n* a light bread dough, sweet or plain, baked twice until it is brown, hard, and crisp: often given to babies. ORIG C16: from Sp. or Port. *rosca* screw, bread shaped in a twist, from ?

Rusk ★ (rʌsk) *n* (**David**) **Dean.** 1909–94, US statesman: secretary of state (1961–69). He defended US military involvement in Vietnam.

Ruskin ★ ('rʌskɪn) *n* **John.** 1819–1900, British critic and social reformer. His works include *The Stones of Venice* (1851–53) and *Time and Tide* (1867).

Russ. *abbrev. for* Russia(n).

Russell ★ ('rʌsᵊl) *n* **1 Bertrand** (**Arthur William**), 3rd Earl Russell. 1872–1970, British philosopher and mathematician. His books include *Principia Mathematica* (1910–13; with A. N. Whitehead), and *An Enquiry into Meaning and Truth* (1940): Nobel prize for literature 1950. **2 George William**, pen name *Æ.* 1867–1935, Irish poet and journalist. **3 John**, 1st Earl Russell. 1792–1878, British statesman; prime minister (1846–52; 1865–66). **4 Ken.** born 1927, film director. His films include *Women in Love* (1969) and *Valentino* (1977).

russet ('rʌsɪt) *n* **1** brown with a yellowish or reddish tinge. **2** a rough homespun fabric, reddish-brown in colour, formerly in use for clothing. **3** any of various apples with rough brownish-red skins. ◆ *adj* **4** *Arch.* simple; homely; rustic: *a russet life.* **5** of the colour russet: *russet hair.* ORIG C13: from Anglo-Norman, from OF *rosset*, from *rous*, from L *russus*; rel. to L *ruber* red
▸ **'russety** *adj*

Russia ★ ('rʌʃə) *n* **1** the largest country in the world, covering N Eurasia and bordering on the Pacific and Arctic Oceans and the Baltic, Black, and Caspian Seas: ranges from arctic to subtropical in climate and includes tundra, forests, steppes, and arable land. Originating from the principality of Muscovy in the 17th century, it expanded to become the Russian Empire: became the Communist Russian Soviet Federative Socialist Republic after the overthrow of the tsar in 1917; merged with neighbouring Soviet Republics to form the Soviet Union in 1922; became an independent state following the disintegration of the Soviet Union in 1991. Official language: Russian. Religion: nonreligious and Christian (Russian Orthodox). Currency: rouble. Capital: Moscow. Pop.: 146 394 000 (1999 est.). Area: 17 074 984 sq. km (6 592 658 sq. miles). Also called: **Russian Federation. 2** another name for the **Russian Empire. 3** (formerly) another name for the **Soviet Union. 4** (formerly) another name for the **Russian Soviet Federative Socialist Republic.** ◆ Russian name: **Rossiya.**

Russia leather *n* a smooth dyed leather made from calfskin and scented with birch tar oil, originally produced in Russia.

Russian ('rʌʃən) *n* **1** the official language of Russia, and of the former Soviet Union: an Indo-European language belonging to the East Slavonic branch. **2** a native or inhabitant of Russia. ◆ *adj* **3** of, relating to, or characteristic of Russia, its people, or their language.

Russian doll *n* a hollow wooden figure, usually representing a Russian peasant woman, that comes apart to reveal a similar smaller figure, which itself contains another, and so on.

Russian Empire *n* the tsarist empire in Asia and E Europe, overthrown by the Russian Revolution of 1917.

Russian Federation ★ *n* See **Russia.**

Russianize *or* **Russianise** ('rʌʃə,naɪz) *vb* **Russianizes, Russianizing, Russianized** *or* **Russianises, Russianising, Russianised.** to make or become Russian in style, etc.
▸ **,Russiani'zation** *or* **,Russiani'sation** *n*

Russian roulette *n* **1** an act of bravado in which each person in turn spins the cylinder of a revolver loaded with only one cartridge and presses the trigger with the barrel against his own head. **2** any foolish or potentially suicidal undertaking.

Russian salad *n* a salad of cold diced cooked vegetables mixed with mayonnaise and pickles.

Russian Soviet Federative Socialist Republic ★ *n* (formerly) the largest administrative division of the Soviet Union. Abbrev.: **RSFSR.**

Russian Turkestan ★ *n* See **Turkestan.**

Russian Zone ★ *n* another name for the **Soviet Zone.**

Russo- ('rʌsəʊ) *combining form.* Russia or Russian: *Russo-Japanese.*

rust (rʌst) *n* **1** a reddish-brown oxide coating formed on iron or steel by the action of oxygen and moisture. **2** Also called: **rust fungus.** *Plant pathol.* **2a** any of a group of fungi which are parasitic on cereal plants, conifers, etc. **2b** any of various plant diseases characterized by reddish-brown discoloration of the leaves and stem, esp. that caused by the rust fungi. **3a** a strong brown colour, sometimes with a reddish or yellowish tinge. **3b** (*as adj*): *a rust carpet.* **4** any corrosive or debilitating influence, esp. lack of use. ◆ *vb* **5** to become or cause to become coated with a layer of rust. **6** to deteriorate or cause to deteriorate through some debilitating influence or lack of use: *he allowed his talent to rust over the years.* ORIG OE *rūst*
▸ **'rustless** *adj*

rust belt *n* an area where heavy industry is in decline, esp. in the Midwest of the US.

rustic ('rʌstɪk) *adj* **1** of, characteristic of, or living in the country; rural. **2** having qualities ascribed to country life or people; simple; unsophisticated: *rustic pleasures.* **3** crude, awkward, or uncouth. **4** made of untrimmed branches: *a rustic seat.* **5** (of masonry, etc.) having a rusticated finish. ◆ *n* **6** a person who comes from or lives in the country. **7** an unsophisticated, simple, or clownish person from the country. **8** Also called: **rusticwork.** brick

or stone having a rough finish. ORIG C16: from OF *rustique,* from L *rūsticus,* from *rūs* the country
▸ **'rustically** *adv* ▸ **rusticity** (rʌ'stɪsɪtɪ) *n*

rusticate ('rʌstɪˌkeɪt) *vb* **rusticates, rusticating, rusticated. 1** to banish or retire to the country. **2** to make or become rustic in style, etc. **3** (*tr*) *Architect.* to finish (an exterior wall) with large blocks of masonry separated by deep joints. **4** (*tr*) *Brit.* to send down from university for a specified time as a punishment. ORIG C17: from L *rūsticārī,* from *rūs* the country
▸ **ˌrusti'cation** *n* ▸ **'rustiˌcator** *n*

rusticated ('rʌstɪˌkeɪtɪd) *or* **rusticating** ('rʌstɪˌkeɪtɪŋ) *n* (in New Zealand) a wide type of weatherboarding used in older houses.

rustle[1] ('rʌsᵊl) *vb* **rustles, rustling, rustled. 1** to make or cause to make a low crisp whispering or rubbing sound, as of dry leaves or paper. **2** to move with such a sound. ◆ *n* **3** such a sound or sounds. ORIG OE *hrūxlian*

rustle[2] ('rʌsᵊl) *vb* **rustles, rustling, rustled. 1** *Chiefly US & Canad.* to steal (cattle, horses, etc.). **2** *Inf., US & Canad.* to move swiftly and energetically. ORIG C19: prob. special use of RUSTLE[1] (in the sense: to move with a quiet sound)
▸ **'rustler** *n*

rustle up *vb* (*tr, adv*) *Inf.* **1** to prepare (a meal, etc.) rapidly, esp. at short notice. **2** to forage for and obtain.

rustproof ('rʌstˌpruːf) *adj* treated against rusting.

rusty ('rʌstɪ) *adj* **rustier, rustiest. 1** covered with, affected by, or consisting of rust: *a rusty machine.* **2** of the colour rust. **3** discoloured by age: *a rusty coat.* **4** (of the voice) tending to croak. **5** old-fashioned in appearance: *a rusty old gentleman.* **6** impaired in skill or knowledge by inaction or neglect. **7** (of plants) affected by the rust fungus.
▸ **'rustily** *adv* ▸ **'rustiness** *n*

rut[1] (rʌt) *n* **1** a groove or furrow in a soft road, caused by wheels. **2** a narrow or predictable way of life; dreary or undeviating routine (esp. in **in a rut**). ◆ *vb* **ruts, rutting, rutted. 3** (*tr*) to make a rut in. ORIG C16: prob. from F *route* road

rut[2] (rʌt) *n* **1** a recurrent period of sexual excitement and reproductive activity in certain male ruminants. ◆ *vb* **ruts, rutting, rutted. 2** (*intr*) (of male ruminants) to be in a period of sexual excitement and activity. ORIG C15: from OF *rut* noise, roar, from L *rugītus,* from *rugīre* to roar

rutabaga (ˌruːtə'beɪgə) *n* the US and Canad. name for **swede.** ORIG C18: from Swedish dialect *rotabagge,* lit.: root bag

rutaceous (ruː'teɪʃəs) *adj* of, relating to, or belonging to a family of tropical and temperate flowering plants many of which have aromatic leaves. The family includes rue, citrus trees, and dittany. ORIG C19: from NL *Rutaceae,* from L *rūta* RUE[2]

ruth (ruːθ) *n Arch.* **1** pity; compassion. **2** repentance; remorse. ORIG C12: from *rewen* to RUE[1]

Ruth ★ (ruːθ) *n* **1** *Old Testament.* **1a** a Moabite woman, who married a Hebrew and on his death remained with her mother-in-law Naomi, later becoming the wife of Boaz. **1b** the book in which these events are recounted. **2** **George Herman,** nicknamed *Babe.* 1895–1948, US baseball player.

Ruthenia ★ (ruː'θiːnɪə) *n* a region of E Europe on the south side of the Carpathian Mountains: belonged to Hungary from the 14th century, to Czechoslovakia from 1918 to 1939, and to the Soviet Union from 1945 to 1991; now forms the Transcarpathian Region of Ukraine. Also called: **Carpatho-Ukraine.**

ruthenium (ruː'θiːnɪəm) *n* a hard brittle white element of the platinum metal group. It is used to harden platinum and palladium. Symbol: Ru; atomic no.: 44; atomic wt.: 101.07. ORIG C19: from Med. L *Ruthenia* Russia, where it was discovered

rutherford ('rʌðəfəd) *n* a former unit of activity equal to the quantity of a radioactive nuclide required to produce one million disintegrations per second. Abbrev.: **rd.** ORIG C20: after E. RUTHERFORD

Rutherford ★ ('rʌðəfəd) *n* **Ernest,** 1st Baron Rutherford. 1871–1937, British physicist, born in New Zealand, who discovered the atomic nucleus (1909). Nobel prize for chemistry 1908.

rutherfordium (ˌrʌðə'fɔːdɪəm) *n* the US name for the element with the atomic no. 104. Soviet name **kurchatovium.** Symbol: Rf ORIG C20: after E. RUTHERFORD

ruthful ('ruːθfʊl) *adj Arch.* full of or causing sorrow or pity.
▸ **'ruthfully** *adv* ▸ **'ruthfulness** *n*

ruthless ('ruːθlɪs) *adj* feeling or showing no mercy; hardhearted.
▸ **'ruthlessly** *adv* ▸ **'ruthlessness** *n*

rutile ('ruːtaɪl) *n* a mineral consisting of titanium(IV) oxide (TiO_2) in tetragonal crystalline form. It is an important source of titanium. ORIG C19: via F from G *Rutil,* from L *rutilus* red, glowing

Rutland ★ ('rʌtlənd) *n* a historic inland county of central England. It became part of Leicestershire in 1974; reinstated as a unitary authority in 1997: mainly agricultural. Administrative centre: Oakham. Pop.: 34 600 (1996 est.). Area: 394 sq. km (152 sq. miles).

ruttish ('rʌtɪʃ) *adj* **1** (of an animal) in a condition of rut. **2** lascivious or salacious.
▸ **'ruttishly** *adv* ▸ **'ruttishness** *n*

rutty ('rʌtɪ) *adj* **ruttier, ruttiest.** full of ruts or holes: *a rutty track.*
▸ **'ruttily** *adv* ▸ **'ruttiness** *n*

Ruwenzori ★ (ˌruːwɛn'zɔːrɪ) *n* a mountain range in central Africa, on the border between Uganda and the Democratic Republic of Congo and between Lakes Edward and Albert: generally thought to be Ptolemy's "Mountains of the Moon". Highest peak: Mount Stanley, 5109 m (16 763 ft).

Ruysdael ★ ('riːzdɑːl, -deɪl, 'raɪz-; *Dutch* 'rœizdaːl) *n* a variant spelling of **Ruisdael.**

Ruyter ★ ('raɪtə; *Dutch* 'rœitər) *n* **Michiel Adriaanszoon de** (miː'xiːl ˌaːdri'aːnsun də). 1607–76, Dutch admiral, noted for his prevention of an Anglo-French invasion.

RV *abbrev. for:* **1** *Chiefly US.* recreational vehicle. **2** Revised Version (of the Bible).

Rwanda ★ (ru'ændə) *n* a republic in central Africa: part of German East Africa from 1899 until 1917, when Belgium took over the administration; became a republic in 1961 after the successful Hutu revolt against the Tutsi (1959); Tutsis from Uganda invaded in 1990; civil war broke out again in 1994. Official languages: Rwanda, French, and English. Religion: Roman Catholic, African Protestant, Muslim, and animist. Currency: Rwanda franc. Capital: Kigali. Pop.: 8 155 000 (1999 est.). Area: 26 338 sq. km (10 169 sq. miles). Former name (until 1962): **Ruanda.**
▸ **R'wandan** *adj*

-ry *suffix forming nouns.* a variant of **-ery:** *dentistry.*

Ryazan ★ (*Russian* rɪ'zanj) *n* a city in W central Russia: capital of a medieval principality; oil refineries and engineering industries. Pop.: 536 000 (1995 est.).

Rybinsk ★ (*Russian* 'ribinsk) *n* a city in W central Russia, on the River Volga: an important river port, terminal of the Mariinsk Waterway (between Saint Petersburg and the Volga) at the SE end of the **Rybinsk Reservoir** (area 4700 sq. km (1800 sq. miles)). Pop 248 000 (1995 est.). Former names: (from the Revolution until 1957) **Shcherbakov,** (1984–91) **Andropov.**

Rydal ★ ('raɪdᵊl) *n* a village in NW England, in Cumbria on **Rydal Water** (a small lake). **Rydal Mount,** home of Wordsworth from 1813 to 1850, is situated here.

Ryder ★ ('raɪdə) *n* **Susan** (known as *Sue*), Baroness Ryder of Warsaw. 1923–2000, British philanthropist; founder of the Sue Ryder Foundation for the Sick and Disabled: married to Leonard Cheshire.

Ryder Cup *n* **the.** the trophy awarded in a professional golfing competition between teams representing Europe and the US. ORIG C20: after Samuel *Ryder* (1859–1936), Brit. businessman and golf patron

rye (raɪ) *n* **1** a tall hardy widely cultivated annual grass having bristly flower spikes and light brown grain. **2** the grain of this grass, used in making flour and whisky, and as a livestock food. **3** Also called: (esp. US): **rye whiskey.** whisky distilled from rye. **4** *US.* short for **rye bread.** ORIG OE *ryge*

Rye ★ (raɪ) *n* a resort in SE England, in East Sussex: one of the Cinque ports. Pop.: 3708 (1991).

rye bread *n* any of various breads made entirely or partly from rye flour, often with caraway seeds.

rye-grass *n* any of various grasses native to Europe, N Africa, and Asia, and widely cultivated as forage crops. They have flattened flower spikes and hairless leaves.

Ryle ★ (raɪl) *n* **1 Gilbert.** 1900–76, British philosopher; noted for his *Concept of Mind* (1949). **2** Sir **Martin.** 1918–84, British radio astronomer; Astronomer Royal (1972–82); shared Nobel prize for physics 1974.

Ryswick ★ (ˈrɪzwɪk) *n* the English name for **Rijswijk.**

Ryukyu Islands ★ (rɪˈuːkjuː) *pl n* a chain of 55 islands in the W Pacific, extending almost 650 km (400 miles) from S Japan to N Taiwan: an ancient kingdom, under Chinese rule from the late 14th century, Japanese supremacy from 1879 to 1945, and US control from 1945 to 1972; now part of Japan again. They are subject to frequent typhoons. Chief town: Naha City (on Okinawa). Pop.: 1 273 508 (1995). Area: 2196 sq. km (849 sq. miles).

Ryurik ★ (ˈrʊərɪk) *n* a variant spelling of **Rurik.**

Ss

s *or* **S** (ɛs) *n, pl* **s's, S's,** *or* **Ss. 1** the 19th letter of the English alphabet. **2** a speech sound represented by this letter, either voiceless, as in *sit,* or voiced, as in *dogs.* **3a** something shaped like an S. **3b** (*in combination*)*: an S-bend in a road.*

s *symbol for* second (of time).

S *symbol for:* **1** small. **2** Society. **3** South. **4** *Chem.* sulphur. **5** *Physics.* **5a** entropy. **5b** siemens. **5c** strangeness. **6** *Currency.* Schilling.

s. *abbrev. for:* **1** shilling. **2** singular. **3** son. **4** succeeded.

s. *or* **S.** *Music. abbrev. for* soprano.

S. *abbrev. for:* **1** sabbath. **2** (*pl* **SS**) Saint. **3** Saturday. **4** Saxon. **5** school. **6** September. **7** Signor. **8** Sunday.

-s[1] *or* **-es** *suffix.* forming the plural of most nouns: *boys; boxes.* ORIG from OE *-as,* pl. nominative and accusative ending of some masc nouns

-s[2] *or* **-es** *suffix.* forming the third person singular present indicative tense of verbs: *he runs.* ORIG from OE (northern dialect) *-es, -s,* orig. the ending of the second person singular

-'s *suffix.* **1** forming the possessive singular of nouns and some pronouns: *man's; one's.* **2** forming the possessive plural of nouns whose plurals do not end in *-s: children's.* (The possessive plural of nouns ending in *s* and of some singular nouns is formed by the addition of an apostrophe after the final *s: girls'; for goodness' sake.*) **3** forming the plural of numbers, letters, or symbols: *20's.* **4** *Inf.* contraction of *is* or *has: it's gone.* **5** *Inf.* contraction of *us* with *let: let's.* **6** *Inf.* contraction of *does* in some questions: *what's he do?* ORIG senses 1, 2: assimilated contraction from ME *-es,* from OE, masc and neuter genitive sing; sense 3, equivalent to -s[1]

SA *abbrev. for:* **1** Salvation Army. **2** South Africa. **3** South America. **4** South Australia. **5** *Sturmabteilung:* the Nazi terrorist militia.

Saadi ★ (sɑːˈdiː) *n* a variant spelling of **Sadi.**

Saar ★ (sɑː; *German* zaːr) *n* **1** a river in W Europe, rising in the Vosges Mountains and flowing north to the Moselle River in Germany. Length: 246 km (153 miles). French name: **Sarre. 2 the Saar.** another name for **Saarland.**

Saarbrücken ★ (*German* zaːrˈbrykən) *n* an industrial city in W Germany, capital of Saarland state, on the Saar River. Pop.: 187 032 (1996 est.).

Saarinen ★ (ˈsɑːrɪnən) *n* **Eero** (ˈeɪrəʊ). 1910–61, US architect, born in Finland.

Saarland ★ (*German* ˈzaːrlant) *n* a state of W Germany: formed in 1919; under League of Nations administration until 1935; occupied by France (1945–57); part of West Germany (1957–90): contains rich coal deposits and is a major industrial region. Capital: Saarbrücken. Pop.: 1 083 100 (1996 est.). Area: 2567 sq. km (991 sq. miles).

Saba ★ (ˈsɑːbə) *n* **1** an island in the NE Caribbean, in the Netherlands Antilles. Pop.: 1197 (1994 est.). Area: 13 sq. km (5 sq. miles). **2** another name for **Sheba**[1] (sense 1).

Sabadell ★ (*Spanish* saβaˈðel) *n* a town in NE Spain, near Barcelona: textile manufacturing. Pop.: 189 006 (1994 est.).

sabadilla (ˌsæbəˈdɪlə) *n* **1** a tropical American liliaceous plant. **2** the bitter brown seeds of this plant, which contain the alkaloid veratrine used in insecticides. ORIG C19: from Sp. *cebadilla,* dim. of *cebada* barley, from L *cibāre* to feed, from *cibus* food

Sabaean *or* **Sabean** (səˈbiːən) *n* **1** an inhabitant or native of ancient Saba. **2** the ancient Semitic language of Saba. ♦ *adj* **3** of or relating to ancient Saba, its inhabitants, or their language. ORIG C16: from L *Sabaeus,* from Gk *Sabaios* belonging to Saba (Sheba)

Sabah ★ (ˈsɑːbɑː) *n* a state of Malaysia, occupying N Borneo and offshore islands in the South China and Sulu Seas: became a British protectorate in 1888; gained independence and joined Malaysia in 1963. Capital: Kota Kinabalu. Pop.: 1 472 700 (1993 est.). Area: 76 522 sq. km (29 545 sq. miles). Former name (until 1963): **North Borneo.**

Sabatier ★ (*French* sabatje) *n* **Paul** (pɔl). 1854–1941, French chemist: shared the Nobel prize for chemistry (1912) for his organic hydrogenation process.

sabbat (ˈsæbæt, -ət) *n* another word for **Sabbath** (sense 4).

Sabbatarian (ˌsæbəˈtɛərɪən) *n* **1** a person advocating the strict religious observance of Sunday. **2** a person who observes Saturday as the Sabbath. ♦ *adj* **3** of the Sabbath or its observance. ORIG C17: from LL *sabbatārius* a Sabbath-keeper
▸ ˌ**Sabbaˈtarianism** *n*

Sabbath (ˈsæbəθ) *n* **1** the seventh day of the week, Saturday, devoted to worship and rest from work in Judaism and in certain Christian Churches. **2** Sunday, observed by Christians as the day of worship and rest. **3** (*not cap.*) a period of rest. **4** Also called: **sabbat, witches' Sabbath.** a midnight meeting for practitioners of witchcraft or devil worship. ORIG OE *sabbat,* from L, from Gk *sabbaton,* from Heb., from *shābath* to rest

sabbatical (səˈbætɪkᵊl) *adj* **1** denoting a period of leave granted to university staff, teachers, etc., esp. originally every seventh year: *a sabbatical year.* ♦ *n* **2** any sabbatical period. ORIG C16: from Gk *sabbatikos;* see SABBATH

Sabbatical (səˈbætɪkᵊl) *adj* of, relating to, or appropriate to the Sabbath as a day of rest and religious observance.

SABC *abbrev. for* South African Broadcasting Corporation.

saber (ˈseɪbə) *n, vb* the US spelling of **sabre.**

sabin (ˈsæbɪn, ˈseɪ-) *n Physics.* a unit of acoustic absorption. ORIG C20: introduced by Wallace C. *Sabine* (1868–1919), US physicist

Sabin ★ (ˈseɪbɪn) *n* **Albert Bruce.** 1906–93, US microbiologist, born in Poland. He developed the oral **Sabin vaccine** (1955) against poliomyelitis.

Sabine (ˈsæbaɪn) *n* **1** a member of an ancient people who lived in central Italy. ♦ *adj* **2** of or relating to this people or their language.

sabkha (ˈsæbxə, -kə) *n* a flat coastal plain with a salt crust, common in Arabia. ORIG C19: from Ar.

sable (ˈseɪbᵊl) *n, pl* **sables** *or* **sable. 1** a marten of N Asian forests, with dark brown luxuriant fur. **2a** the highly valued fur of this animal. **2b** (*as modifier*)*: a sable coat.* **3** **American sable.** the brown, slightly less valuable fur of the American marten. **4** a dark brown to yellowish-brown colour. ♦ *adj* **5** of the colour of sable fur. **6** black; dark. **7** (*usually postpositive*) *Heraldry.* of the colour black. ORIG C15: from OF, from OHG *zobel,* of Slavic origin

Sable ★ (ˈseɪbᵊl) *n* **Cape. 1** a cape at the S tip of Florida: the southernmost point of continental US. **2** the southernmost point of Nova Scotia, Canada.

sable antelope *n* a large black E African antelope with long backward-curving horns.

sabot (ˈsæbəʊ) *n* **1** a shoe made from a single block of wood. **2** a shoe with a wooden sole and a leather or cloth upper. **3** *Austral.* a small sailing boat with a shortened bow. ORIG C17: from F, prob. from OF *savate* an old shoe, also infl. by *bot* BOOT[1]

sabotage (ˈsæbəˌtɑːʒ) *n* **1** the deliberate destruction, disruption, or damage of equipment, a public service, etc., as by enemy agents, dissatisfied employees, etc. **2** any similar action. ♦ *vb* **sabotages, sabotaging, sabotaged. 3** (*tr*) to destroy or disrupt, esp. by secret means. ORIG C20: from F, from *saboter* to spoil through clumsiness (lit.: to clatter in sabots)

★ people and places

saboteur (ˌsæbəˈtɜː) *n* a person who commits sabotage. ORIG C20: from F

sabra (ˈsɑːbrə) *n* a native-born Israeli Jew. ORIG from Heb. *Sabēr* prickly pear, common plant in the coastal areas of the country

sabre *or US* **saber** (ˈseɪbə) *n* **1** a stout single-edged cavalry sword, having a curved blade. **2** a sword used in fencing, having a narrow V-shaped blade. ◆ *vb* **sabres, sabring, sabred** *or US* **sabers, sabering, sabered. 3** (*tr*) to injure or kill with a sabre. ORIG C17: via F from G (dialect) *Sabel,* from MHG *sebel,* ?from Magyar *száblya*

sabre-rattling *n, adj Inf.* seeking to intimidate by an aggressive display of military power.

sabre-toothed tiger *or* **cat** *n* any of various extinct felines with long curved upper canine teeth.

sac (sæk) *n* a pouch, bag, or pouchlike part in an animal or plant. ORIG C18: from F, from L *saccus;* see SACK[1]
▸ **saccate** (ˈsækɪt, -eɪt) *adj* ▸ **ˈsacˌlike** *adj*

saccharide (ˈsækəˌraɪd) *n* any sugar or other carbohydrate, esp. a simple sugar.

saccharimeter (ˌsækəˈrɪmɪtə) *n* any instrument for measuring the strength of sugar solutions.
▸ **ˌsacchaˈrimetry** *n*

saccharin (ˈsækərɪn) *n* a very sweet white crystalline slightly soluble powder used as a nonfattening sweetener. ORIG C19: from SACCHARO- + -IN

saccharine (ˈsækəˌriːn) *adj* **1** excessively sweet; sugary: *a saccharine smile.* **2** of the nature of or containing sugar or saccharin.

saccharo- *or before a vowel* **sacchar-** *combining form.* sugar. ORIG via L from Gk *sakkharon,* ult. from Sansk. *śarkarā* sugar

saccharose (ˈsækəˌrəʊz, -ˌrəʊs) *n* a technical name for **sugar** (sense 1).

saccule (ˈsækjuːl) *or* **sacculus** (ˈsækjʊləs) *n* **1** a small sac. **2** the smaller of the two parts of the membranous labyrinth of the internal ear. Cf. **utricle.** ORIG C19: from L *sacculus* dim. of *saccus* SACK[1]

sacerdotal (ˌsæsəˈdəʊtᵊl) *adj* of, relating to, or characteristic of priests. ORIG C14: from L *sacerdōtālis,* from *sacerdōs* priest, from *sacer* sacred
▸ **ˌsacerˈdotaˌlism** *n* ▸ **ˌsacerˈdotally** *adv*

sachem (ˈseɪtʃəm) *n* **1** *US.* a leader of a political party or organization. **2** another name for **sagamore.** ORIG C17: from Amerind *săchim* chief

sachet (ˈsæʃeɪ) *n* **1** a small sealed envelope, usually made of plastic, for containing shampoo, etc. **2a** a small soft bag containing perfumed powder, placed in drawers to scent clothing. **2b** the powder contained in such a bag. ORIG C19: from OF: a little bag, from *sac* bag; see SACK[1]

Sachs ★ (*German* zaks) *n* **1 Hans** (hans). 1494–1576, German master shoemaker and Meistersinger, portrayed by Wagner in *Die Meistersinger von Nürnberg.* **2 Nelly** (**Leonie**). 1891–1970, German Jewish poet and dramatist, who escaped from Nazi Germany and settled in Sweden. Nobel prize for literature (1966) with Shmuel Yosef Agnon.

Sachsen ★ (ˈzaksən) *n* the German name for **Saxony.**

sack[1] (sæk) *n* **1** a large bag made of coarse cloth, thick paper, etc., used as a container. **2** Also called: **sackful.** the amount contained in a sack. **3a** a woman's loose tube-shaped dress. **3b** Also called: **sacque** (sæk). a woman's full loose hip-length jacket. **4 the sack.** *Inf.* dismissal from employment. **5** a slang word for **bed. 6 hit the sack.** *Sl.* to go to bed. ◆ *vb* (*tr*) **7** *Inf.* to dismiss from employment. **8** to put into a sack or sacks. ORIG OE *sacc,* from L *saccus* bag, from Gk *sakkos*
▸ **ˈsackˌlike** *adj*

sack[2] (sæk) *n* **1** the plundering of a place by an army or mob. **2** *American football.* a tackle on a quarterback that brings him or her down before he or she has passed the ball. ◆ *vb* (*tr*) **3** to plunder and partially destroy (a place). **4** *American football.* to tackle and bring down (a quarterback) before he or she has passed the ball. ORIG C16: from F *mettre à sac,* lit.: to put (loot) in a sack, from L *saccus* SACK[1]
▸ **ˈsacker** *n*

sack[3] (sæk) *n Arch. except in trademarks.* any dry white wine from SW Europe. ORIG C16 *wyne seck,* from F *vin sec* dry wine, from L *siccus* dry

sackbut (ˈsækˌbʌt) *n* a medieval form of trombone. ORIG C16: from F *saqueboute,* from OF *saquer* to pull + *bouter* to push

sackcloth (ˈsækˌklɒθ) *n* **1** coarse cloth such as sacking. **2** garments made of such cloth, worn formerly to indicate mourning. **3 sackcloth and ashes.** a public display of extreme grief.

sacking (ˈsækɪŋ) *n* coarse cloth used for making sacks, woven from flax, hemp, jute, etc.

sack race *n* a race in which the competitors' legs and often bodies are enclosed in sacks.

Sackville ★ (ˈsækvɪl) *n* **Thomas,** 1st Earl of Dorset. 1536–1608, English poet, dramatist, and statesman.

Sackville-West ★ *n* **Victoria** (**Mary**), known as *Vita.* 1892–1962, British writer, noted for the poem *The Land* (1931) and the novel *The Edwardians* (1930). Married to Harold Nicolson.

sacral[1] (ˈseɪkrəl) *adj* of or associated with sacred rites. ORIG C19: from L *sacrum* sacred object

sacral[2] (ˈseɪkrəl) *adj* of or relating to the sacrum. ORIG C18: from NL *sacrālis* of the SACRUM

sacrament (ˈsækrəmənt) *n* **1** an outward sign combined with a prescribed form of words and regarded as conferring grace upon those who receive it. The Protestant sacraments are baptism and the Lord's Supper. In the Roman Catholic and Eastern Churches they are baptism, penance, confirmation, the Eucharist, holy orders, matrimony, and the anointing of the sick (formerly extreme unction). **2** (*often cap.*) the Eucharist. **3** the consecrated elements of the Eucharist, esp. the bread. **4** something regarded as possessing a sacred significance. **5** a pledge. ORIG C12: from Church L *sacrāmentum* vow, from L *sacrāre* to consecrate

sacramental (ˌsækrəˈmɛntᵊl) *adj* **1** of or having the nature of a sacrament. ◆ *n* **2** *RC Church.* a sacrament-like ritual action, such as the sign of the cross or the use of holy water.
▸ **ˌsacraˈmentaˌlism** *n* ▸ **sacramentality** (ˌsækrəmɛnˈtælɪtɪ) *n*

Sacramento ★ (ˌsækrəˈmɛntəʊ) *n* **1** an inland port in N central California, capital of the state at the confluence of the American and Sacramento Rivers: became a boom town in the gold rush of the 1850s. Pop.: 374 964 (1994 est.). **2** a river in N California, flowing generally south to San Francisco Bay. Length: 615 km (382 miles).

sacrarium (sæˈkrɛərɪəm) *n, pl* **sacraria** (-ˈkrɛərɪə). **1** the sanctuary of a church. **2** *RC Church.* a place near the altar of a church where materials used in the sacred rites are deposited or poured away. ORIG C18: from L, from *sacer* sacred

sacred (ˈseɪkrɪd) *adj* **1** exclusively devoted to a deity or to some religious ceremony or use. **2** worthy of or regarded with reverence and awe. **3** connected with or intended for religious use: *sacred music.* **4 sacred to.** dedicated to. ORIG C14: from L *sacrāre* to set apart as holy, from *sacer* holy
▸ **ˈsacredly** *adv* ▸ **ˈsacredness** *n*

sacred cow *n Inf.* a person, custom, etc., held to be beyond criticism. ORIG alluding to the Hindu belief that cattle are sacred

sacred mushroom *n* **1** any of various hallucinogenic mushrooms that have been eaten in rituals in various parts of the world. **2** a mescal button, used in a similar way.

sacrifice (ˈsækrɪˌfaɪs) *n* **1** a surrender of something of value as a means of gaining something more desirable or of preventing some evil. **2** a ritual killing of a person or animal with the intention of propitiating or pleasing a deity. **3** a symbolic offering of something to a deity. **4** the person, animal, or object killed or offered. **5** loss entailed by giving up or selling something at less than its value. **6** *Chess.* the act or an instance of sacrificing a piece. ◆ *vb* **sacrifices, sacrificing, sacrificed. 7** to make a sacrifice (of). **8** *Chess.* to permit or force one's opponent to capture a piece freely, as in playing a gambit: *he sacrificed his queen and checkmated his opponent on the next move.*

ORIG C13: via OF from L *sacrificium,* from *sacer* holy + *facere* to make
▸ **'sacri,ficer** *n*

sacrificial (,sækrɪ'fɪʃəl) *adj* used in or connected with a sacrifice.
▸ **,sacri'ficially** *adv*

sacrilege ('sækrɪlɪdʒ) *n* **1** the misuse or desecration of anything regarded as sacred or as worthy of extreme respect. **2** the act or an instance of taking anything sacred for secular use. ORIG C13: from OF, from L, from *sacrilegus* temple-robber, from *sacra* sacred things + *legere* to take
▸ **sacrilegist** (,sækrɪ'li:dʒɪst) *n*

sacrilegious (,sækrɪ'lɪdʒəs) *adj* **1** of, relating to, or involving sacrilege. **2** guilty of sacrilege.
▸ **,sacri'legiously** *adv*

sacring bell ('seɪkrɪŋ) *n Chiefly RC Church.* a small bell rung at the elevation of the Host and chalice during Mass.

sacristan ('sækrɪstən) *or* **sacrist** ('sækrɪst, 'seɪ-) *n* **1** a person who has charge of the contents of a church. **2** a less common word for **sexton.** ORIG C14: from Med. L *sacristānus,* ult. from L *sacer* holy

sacristy ('sækrɪstɪ) *n, pl* **sacristies.** a room attached to a church or chapel where the sacred vessels, vestments, etc., are kept. ORIG C17: from Med. L *sacristia;* see SACRISTAN

sacroiliac (,seɪkrəʊ'ɪlɪ,æk) *Anat.* ◆ *adj* **1** of or relating to the sacrum and ilium or their articulation. ◆ *n* **2** the joint where these bones meet.

sacrosanct ('sækrəʊ,sæŋkt) *adj* very sacred or holy. ORIG C17: from L *sacrōsanctus* made holy by sacred rite, from *sacer* holy + *sanctus,* from *sancīre* to hallow
▸ **,sacro'sanctity** *n*

sacrum ('seɪkrəm) *n, pl* **sacra** (-krə). the large wedge-shaped bone, consisting of five fused vertebrae, in the lower part of the back. ORIG C18: from L *os sacrum* holy bone, because it was used in sacrifices, from *sacer* holy

sad (sæd) *adj* **sadder, saddest. 1** feeling sorrow; unhappy. **2** causing, suggestive, or expressive of such feelings: *a sad story.* **3** unfortunate; shabby: *her clothes were in a sad state.* **4** *Brit. inf.* ludicrously contemptible; pathetic: *a sad, boring little wimp.* ORIG OE *sæd* weary
▸ **'sadly** *adv* ▸ **'sadness** *n*

SAD *abbrev. for* seasonal affective disorder.

Sadat ★ (sə'dæt) *n* **(Mohammed) Anwar El** ('ænwɑ: ɛl). 1918–81, Egyptian statesman: president of Egypt (1970–81): shared Nobel peace prize (1978) with Begin: assassinated.

sadden ('sædᵊn) *vb* to make or become sad.

saddle ('sædᵊl) *n* **1** a seat for a rider, usually made of leather, placed on a horse's back and secured with a girth under the belly. **2** a similar seat on a bicycle, tractor, etc. **3** a back pad forming part of the harness of a packhorse. **4** anything that resembles a saddle in shape, position, or function. **5** a cut of meat, esp. mutton, consisting of both loins. **6** the part of a horse or similar animal on which a saddle is placed. **7** the part of the back of a domestic chicken that is nearest to the tail. **8** another word for **col** (sense 1). **9 in the saddle.** in a position of control. ◆ *vb* **saddles, saddling, saddled. 10** (sometimes foll. by *up*) to put a saddle on (a horse). **11** (*intr*) to mount into the saddle. **12** (*tr*) to burden: *I didn't ask to be saddled with this job.* ORIG OE *sadol, sædel*
▸ **'saddle-,like** *adj*

saddleback ('sædᵊl,bæk) *n* a marking resembling a saddle on the backs of various animals.
▸ **'saddle-,backed** *adj*

saddlebag ('sædᵊl,bæg) *n* a pouch or small bag attached to the saddle of a horse, bicycle, etc.

saddlebill ('sædᵊl,bɪl) *n* a large black-and-white stork of tropical Africa, having a heavy red bill with a black band around the middle. Also called: **jabiru.**

saddlebow ('sædᵊl,bəʊ) *n* the pommel of a saddle.

saddlecloth ('sædᵊl,klɒθ) *n* a light cloth put under a horse's saddle, so as to prevent rubbing.

saddle horse *n* a lightweight horse kept for riding only.

saddler ('sædlə) *n* a person who makes, deals in, or repairs saddles and other leather equipment for horses.

saddle roof *n* a roof that has a ridge and two gables.

saddlery ('sædlərɪ) *n, pl* **saddleries. 1** saddles, harness, and other leather equipment for horses collectively. **2** the business, work, or place of work of a saddler.

saddle soap *n* a soft soap containing neat's-foot oil used to preserve and clean leather.

saddletree ('sædᵊl,tri:) *n* the frame of a saddle.

saddo ('sædəʊ) *n, pl* **saddos, saddoes.** *Brit. sl.* a socially inadequate or pathetic person. ORIG C20: from SAD (sense 4) + -O

Sadducee ('sædjʊ,si:) *n Judaism.* a member of an ancient Jewish sect that was opposed to the Pharisees, denying the resurrection of the dead and the validity of oral tradition. ORIG OE *saddūcēas,* via L & Gk from LHeb. *sāddūqi,* prob. from *Sadoq* Zadok, high priest and supposed founder of the sect
▸ **,Saddu'cean** *adj*

Sade ★ (sɑ:d) *n* Comte **Donatien Alphonse François de** (*French* dɔnasjɛ̃ alfɔ̃s frɑ̃swa də), known as the *Marquis de Sade.* 1740–1814, French soldier and writer, whose exposition of sexual perversion gave rise to the term sadism.

sadhu *or* **saddhu** ('sɑ:du:) *n* a Hindu wandering holy man. ORIG Sansk., from *sādhu* good

Sadi *or* **Saadi** ★ (sɑ:'di:) *n* original name *Sheikh Muslih Addin.* ?1184–1292, Persian poet. His best-known works are *Gulistān* (Flower Garden) and *Būstān* (Tree Garden), long moralistic poems in prose and verse.

sadiron ('sæd,aɪən) *n* a heavy iron, pointed at both ends for pressing clothes. ORIG C19: from SAD (in the obs. sense: heavy) + IRON

sadism ('seɪdɪzəm) *n* the gaining of pleasure or sexual gratification from the infliction of pain and mental suffering on another person. Cf. **masochism.** ORIG C19: from F, after the Marquis de SADE
▸ **'sadist** *n* ▸ **sadistic** (sə'dɪstɪk) *adj* ▸ **sa'distically** *adv*

Sadler's Wells ★ ('sædləz wɛlz) *n* (*functioning as sing*) a theatre in London. Renovated (1931) by Lilian Bayliss, it became the home of the Sadler's Wells Opera Company and the Sadler's Wells Ballet (now the Royal Ballet). ORIG named after the medicinal *wells* on the site and its owner Thomas *Sadler,* who founded the original theatre on the site

sadomasochism (,seɪdəʊ'mæsə,kɪzəm) *n* **1** the combination of sadistic and masochistic elements in one person. **2** sexual practice in which one partner adopts a sadistic role and the other a masochistic one.
▸ **,sadomaso'chistic** *adj*

Sadowa ★ ('sɑ:dəʊvə) *n* a village in the W Czech Republic, in NE Bohemia: scene of the decisive battle of the Austro-Prussian war (1866) in which the Austrians were defeated by the Prussians. Czech name: **Sadová** ('sadɔva:).

SADS *abbrev. for* sudden adult death syndrome.

s.a.e. *abbrev. for* stamped addressed envelope.

safari (sə'fɑ:rɪ) *n, pl* **safaris. 1** an overland journey or hunting expedition, esp. in Africa. **2** the people, animals, etc., that go on the expedition. ORIG C19: from Swahili: journey, from Ar., from *safara* to travel

safari park *n* an enclosed park in which lions and other wild animals are kept uncaged in the open and can be viewed by the public from cars, etc.

safari suit *n* an outfit made of tough cotton, denim, etc., consisting of a bush jacket with matching trousers, shorts, or skirt.

safe (seɪf) *adj* **1** affording security or protection from harm: *a safe place.* **2** (*postpositive*) free from danger: *you'll be safe here.* **3** secure from risk: *a safe investment.* **4** worthy of trust: *a safe companion.* **5** tending to avoid controversy or risk: *a safe player.* **6** not dangerous: *water safe to drink.* **7 on the safe side.** as a precaution. ◆ *adv* **8** in a safe condition: *the children are safe in bed now.* **9 play safe.** to act in a way least likely to cause danger, controversy, or defeat. ◆ *n* **10** a strong container, usually of metal and provided with a secure lock, for storing money or valuables. **11** a small cupboard-like container for storing food. ORIG C13: from OF *salf,* from L *salvus*
▸ **'safely** *adv* ▸ **'safeness** *n*

safe-breaker *n* a person who breaks open and robs safes. Also called: **safe-cracker.**

safe-conduct *n* **1** a document giving official permission to travel through a region, esp. in time of war. **2** the protection afforded by such a document.

safe-deposit *or* **safety-deposit** *n* **a** a place with facilities for the safe storage of money. **b** (*as modifier*): *a safe-deposit box.*

safeguard ('seɪf,gɑːd) *n* **1** a person or thing that ensures protection against danger, injury, etc. **2** a safe-conduct. ◆ *vb* **3** (*tr*) to protect.

safe house *n* a place used secretly by undercover agents, terrorists, etc., as a refuge.

safekeeping ('seɪf'kiːpɪŋ) *n* the act of keeping or state of being kept in safety.

safe period *n Inf.* the period during the menstrual cycle when conception is considered least likely to occur.

safe seat *n* a Parliamentary seat that at an election is sure to be held by the same party as held it before.

safe sex *n* sexual intercourse using physical protection, such as a condom, or nonpenetrative methods to prevent the spread of such diseases as AIDS.

safety ('seɪftɪ) *n, pl* **safeties. 1** the quality of being safe. **2** freedom from danger or risk of injury. **3** a contrivance designed to prevent injury. **4** *American football.* Also called: **safetyman.** either of two players who defend the area furthest back in the field.

safety belt *n* **1** another name for **seat belt** (sense 1). **2** a belt or strap worn by a person working at a great height to prevent him from falling.

safety curtain *n* a curtain made of fireproof material that can be lowered to separate the auditorium and stage in a theatre to prevent the spread of a fire.

safety factor *n* the ratio of the breaking stress of a material to the calculated maximum stress in use. Also called: **factor of safety.**

safety glass *n* glass that if broken will not shatter.

Safety Islands ★ *pl n* a group of three small French islands in the Atlantic, off the coast of French Guiana. French name: **Îles du Salut.**

safety lamp *n* an oil-burning miner's lamp in which the flame is surrounded by a metal gauze to prevent it from igniting combustible gas.

safety match *n* a match that will light only when struck against a specially prepared surface.

safety net *n* **1** a net used in a circus to catch high-wire and trapeze artistes if they fall. **2** any means of protection from hardship or loss.

safety pin *n* a spring wire clasp with a covering catch, made so as to shield the point when closed.

safety razor *n* a razor with a guard over the blade or blades to prevent deep cuts.

safety valve *n* **1** a valve in a pressure vessel that allows fluid to escape at excess pressure. **2** a harmless outlet for emotion, etc.

saffian ('sæfɪən) *n* leather tanned with sumach and usually dyed a bright colour. ORIG C16: via Russian & Turkish from Persian *sakhtiyān* goatskin, from *sakht* hard

safflower ('sæflaʊə) *n* **1** a thistle-like Eurasian annual plant having large heads of orange-yellow flowers and yielding a dye and an oil used in paints, medicines, etc. **2** a red dye used for cotton and for colouring foods and cosmetics. ORIG C16: via Du. *saffloer* or G *safflor* from OF *saffleur*

saffron ('sæfrən) *n* **1** an Old World crocus having purple or white flowers with orange stigmas. **2** the dried stigmas of this plant, used to flavour or colour food. **3 meadow saffron.** another name for **autumn crocus. 4a** an orange to orange-yellow colour. **4b** (*as adj*): *a saffron dress.* ORIG C13: from OF *safran,* from Med. L *safranum,* from Ar. *za'farān*

Safi ★ (*French* safi) *n* a port in W Morocco, 170 km (105 miles) northwest of Marrakech, to which it is the nearest port. Pop.: 278 000 (1993 est.).

Safid Rud ★ (sæ'fiːd 'ruːd) *n* a river in N Iran, flowing northeast to a delta on the Caspian Sea. Length: about 785 km (490 miles).

S.Afr. *abbrev. for* South Africa(n).

safranine *or* **safranin** ★ ('sæfrənɪn) *n* any of a class of azine dyes used for textiles. ORIG C19: from F *safran* SAFFRON + -INE[2]

sag (sæg) *vb* **sags, sagging, sagged.** (*mainly intr*) **1** (*also tr*) to sink or cause to sink in parts, as under weight or pressure: *the bed sags in the middle.* **2** to fall in value: *prices sagged to a new low.* **3** to hang unevenly. **4** (of courage, etc.) to weaken. ◆ *n* **5** the act or an instance of sagging: *a sag in profits.* **6** *Naut.* the extent to which a vessel's keel sags at the centre. ORIG C15: from ON
▸ **'saggy** *adj*

saga ('sɑːgə) *n* **1** any of several medieval prose narratives written in Iceland and recounting the exploits of a hero or a family. **2** any similar heroic narrative. **3** a series of novels about several generations or members of a family. **4** *Inf.* a series of events or a story stretching over a long period. ORIG C18: from ON: a narrative

sagacious (sə'geɪʃəs) *adj* having or showing sagacity; wise. ORIG C17: from L *sagāx,* from *sāgīre* to be astute
▸ **sa'gaciously** *adv*

sagacity (sə'gæsɪtɪ) *n* foresight, discernment, or keen perception; ability to make good judgments.

sagamore ('sægə,mɔː) *n* (among some North American Indians) a chief or eminent man. ORIG C17: from Amerind *sāgimau,* lit.: he overcomes

Sagan ★ *n* **1** ('seɪgən) **Carl Edward.** 1934–96, US astronomer, who won a Pulitzer prize for *The Dragons of Eden: Speculations on the Evolution of Human Intelligence* (1978). He became well known as the presenter of the television series *Cosmos* (1980). **2** (*French* sagɑ̃) **Françoise** (frɑ̃swaz), original name *Françoise Quoirez.* born 1935, French writer, best-known for the novels *Bonjour Tristesse* (1954) and *Aimez-vous Brahms?* (1959).

sage[1] ★ (seɪdʒ) *n* **1** a man revered for his profound wisdom. ◆ *adj* **2** profoundly wise or prudent. ORIG C13: from OF, from L *sapere* to be sensible
▸ **'sagely** *adv* ▸ **'sageness** *n*

sage[2] (seɪdʒ) *n* **1** a perennial Mediterranean plant having grey-green leaves and purple, blue, or white flowers. **2** the leaves of this plant, used in cooking for flavouring. **3** short for **sagebrush.** ORIG C14: from OF *saulge,* from L *salvia,* from *salvus* in good health (from its curative properties)

sagebrush ('seɪdʒ,brʌʃ) *n* any of a genus of aromatic plants of W North America, having silver-green leaves and large clusters of small white flowers.

saggar *or* **sagger** ('sægə) *n* a clay box in which ceramic wares are placed during firing. ORIG C17: ? alteration of SAFEGUARD

Saghalien ★ (sə'gɑːljən) *n* a variant of **Sakhalin.**

sagittal suture ('sædʒɪtᵊl) *n* a serrated line on the top of the skull that marks the junction of the two parietal bones.

Sagittarius (,sædʒɪ'tɛərɪəs) *n, Latin genitive* **Sagittarii** (,sædʒɪ'tɛərɪ,aɪ). **1** *Astron.* a S constellation. **2** Also called: the **Archer.** *Astrol.* the ninth sign of the zodiac. The sun is in this sign between Nov. 22 and Dec. 21. ORIG C14: from L: an archer, from *sagitta* an arrow
▸ **Sagittarian** (,sædʒɪ'tɛərɪən) *adj*

sagittate ('sædʒɪ,teɪt) *adj* (esp. of leaves) shaped like the head of an arrow. ORIG C18: from NL *sagittātus,* from L *sagitta* arrow

sago ('seɪgəʊ) *n* a starchy cereal obtained from the powdered pith of a palm (**sago palm**), used for puddings and as a thickening agent. ORIG C16: from Malay *sāgū*

saguaro (sə'gwɑːrəʊ) *n, pl* **saguaros.** a giant cactus of desert regions of Arizona, S California, and Mexico. ORIG Mexican Sp., var. of *sahuaro,* an Indian name

Saguenay ★ (,sægə'neɪ) *n* a river in SE Canada in S Quebec, rising as the Péribonca River on the central plateau and flowing south, then east to the St Lawrence. Length: 764 km (475 miles).

Sagunto ★ (*Spanish* sa'γunto) *n* an industrial town in E Spain, near Valencia: allied to Rome and made a heroic resistance to the Carthaginian attack led by Hannibal (219–218 B.C.). Pop.: 57 359 (1989). Ancient name: **Saguntum** (sə'guːntəm).

Sahara ★ (sə'hɑːrə) *n* a desert in N Africa, extending from the Atlantic to the Red Sea and from the Mediterranean to central Mali, Niger, Chad, and the Sudan: the largest desert in the world, occupying over a quarter of Africa; rises to over 3300 m (11 000 ft) in the central mountain system of the Ahaggar and Tibesti massifs; large reserves of iron ore, oil, and natural gas. Area: 9 100 000 sq. km (3 500 000 sq. miles). Average annual rainfall: less than 254 mm (10 in.). Highest recorded temperature: 58°C (136.4°F).
▸ **Sa'haran** *n, adj*

sahib ('sɑːhɪb) *n* (in India) a form of address placed after a man's name, used as a mark of respect. ORIG C17: from Urdu, from Ar. *çāhib*, lit.: friend

said[1] (sɛd) *adj* **1** (*prenominal*) (in contracts, etc.) aforesaid. ◆ *vb* **2** the past tense and past participle of **say**.

said[2] ('sɑːɪd) *n* a variant of **sayyid**.

Saida ★ ('sɑːɪdə) *n* a port in SW Lebanon, on the Mediterranean: on the site of ancient Sidon; terminal of the Trans-Arabian pipeline from Saudi Arabia. Pop.: 100 000 (1991 est.).

saiga ('saɪgə) *n* either of two species of antelope of the plains of central Asia, having a slightly elongated nose. ORIG C19: from Russian

Saigon ★ (saɪ'gɒn) *n* the former name (until 1976) of **Ho Chi Minh City**.

sail (seɪl) *n* **1** an area of fabric, usually Terylene or nylon (formerly canvas), with fittings for holding it in any suitable position to catch the wind, used for propelling certain kinds of vessels, esp. over water. **2** a voyage on such a vessel: *a sail down the river.* **3** a vessel with sails or such vessels collectively: *to travel by sail.* **4** a ship's sails collectively. **5** something resembling a sail in shape, position, or function, such as the part of a windmill that is turned by the wind. **6 in sail.** having the sail set. **7 make sail. 7a** to run up the sail or to run up more sail. **7b** to begin a voyage. **8 set sail. 8a** to embark on a voyage by ship. **8b** to hoist sail. **9 under sail. 9a** with sail hoisted. **9b** under way. ◆ *vb* (*mainly intr*) **10** to travel in a boat or ship: *we sailed to Le Havre.* **11** to begin a voyage: *we sail at 5 o'clock.* **12** (of a vessel) to move over the water. **13** (*tr*) to manoeuvre or navigate a vessel: *he sailed the schooner up the channel.* **14** (*tr*) to sail over: *she sailed the Atlantic single-handed.* **15** (often foll. by *over, through,* etc.) to move fast or effortlessly: *we sailed through customs.* **16** to move along smoothly; glide. **17** (often foll. by *in* or *into*) *Inf.* **17a** to begin (something) with vigour. **17b** to make an attack (on) violently. ORIG OE *segl*
▸ **'sailable** *adj* ▸ **'sailless** *adj*

sailboard ('seɪlˌbɔːd) *n* the craft used for windsurfing, consisting of a moulded board to which a mast bearing a single sail is attached.

sailboarding ('seɪlˌbɔːdɪŋ) *n* another name for **windsurfing**.

sailcloth ('seɪlˌklɒθ) *n* **1** any of various fabrics from which sails are made. **2** a canvas-like cloth used for clothing, etc.

sailer ('seɪlə) *n* a vessel, with specified sailing characteristics: *a good sailer.*

sailfish ('seɪlˌfɪʃ) *n, pl* **sailfish** *or* **sailfishes. 1** any of several large game fishes of warm and tropical seas. They have an elongated upper jaw and a long sail-like dorsal fin. **2** another name for **basking shark**.

sailing ship *n* a large sailing vessel.

sailor ('seɪlə) *n* **1** any member of a ship's crew, esp. one below the rank of officer. **2** a person who sails, esp. with reference to the likelihood of his becoming seasick: *a good sailor.*

sailplane ('seɪlˌpleɪn) *n* a high-performance glider.

sainfoin ('sænfɔɪn) *n* a Eurasian perennial plant, widely grown as a forage crop, having pale pink flowers and curved pods. ORIG C17: from F, from Med. L *sānum faenum* wholesome hay, referring to its former use as a medicine

saint (seɪnt; *unstressed* sənt) *n* **1** a person who after death is formally recognized by a Christian Church as having attained a specially exalted place in heaven and the right to veneration. **2** a person of exceptional holiness. **3** (*pl*) *Bible.* the collective body of those who are righteous in God's sight. ◆ *vb* **4** (*tr*) to recognize formally as a saint. ORIG C12: from OF, from L *sanctus* holy, from *sancīre* to hallow
▸ **'sainthood** *n* ▸ **'saintlike** *adj*

Saint Agnes' Eve *n, usually abbreviated to* **St Agnes' Eve.** the night of Jan. 20, when according to tradition a woman can discover the identity of her future husband by performing certain rites.

Saint Albans ★ ('ɔːlbənz) *n, usually abbreviated to* **St Albans.** a city in SE England, in W Hertfordshire: founded in 948 A.D. around the Benedictine abbey first built in Saxon times on the site of the martyrdom (about 303 A.D.) of St Alban; present abbey built in 1077; Roman ruins. Pop.: 80 376 (1991). Latin name: **Verulamium.**

Saint Andrews ★ *n, usually abbreviated to* **St Andrews.** a city in E Scotland, in Fife on the North Sea: the oldest university in Scotland (1411); famous golf links. Pop.: 11 136 (1991).

Saint Andrew's Cross *n, usually abbreviated to* **St Andrew's Cross. 1** a diagonal cross with equal arms. **2** a white diagonal cross on a blue ground.

Saint Anthony's fire *n, usually abbreviated to* **St Anthony's fire.** *Pathol.* another name for **ergotism** or **erysipelas.**

Saint Augustine ★ ('ɔːgəsˌtiːn) *n, usually abbreviated to* **St Augustine.** a resort in NE Florida, on the Intracoastal Waterway: the oldest town in North America (1565); the northernmost outpost of the Spanish colonial empire for over 200 years. Pop.: 11 692 (1990).

Saint Austell ★ ('ɔːstəl) *n, usually abbreviated to* **St Austell.** a town in SW England, in S Cornwall on **St Austell Bay** (an inlet of the English Channel): china clay industry; administratively part of St Austell with Fowey since 1968. Pop. (with Fowey): 21 622 (1991).

Saint Bernard *n, usually abbreviated to* **St Bernard.** a large breed of dog with a dense red-and-white coat, formerly used as a rescue dog in mountainous areas.

Saint Bernard Pass ★ *n, usually abbreviated to* **St Bernard Pass.** either of two passes over the Alps: the **Great St Bernard Pass,** 2472 m (8110 ft) high, east of Mont Blanc between Italy and Switzerland, or the **Little St Bernard Pass,** 2157 m (7077 ft) high, south of Mont Blanc between Italy and France.

Saint-Brieuc ★ (*French* sɛ̃briø) *n, usually abbreviated to* **St-Brieuc.** a market town in NW France, near the N coast of Brittany. Pop.: 47 370 (1990).

Saint Catharines ★ *n, usually abbreviated to* **St Catharines.** an industrial city in S central Canada, in S Ontario on the Welland Canal. Pop.: 129 300 (1991).

Saint Christopher ★ *n, usually abbreviated to* **St Christopher.** another name for **Saint Kitts.**

Saint Christopher-Nevis ★ *n, usually abbreviated to* **St Christopher-Nevis.** the official name of **Saint Kitts-Nevis.**

Saint Clair ★ (klɛə) *n, usually abbreviated to* **St Clair. Lake.** a lake between SE Michigan and Ontario: linked with Lake Huron by the **St Clair River** and with Lake Erie by the Detroit River. Area: 1191 sq. km (460 sq. miles).

Saint-Cloud ★ (*French* sɛ̃klu) *n, usually abbreviated to* **St-Cloud.** a residential suburb of Paris: former royal palace; Sèvres porcelain factory. Pop.: 28 670 (1990).

Saint Croix ★ (krɔɪ) *n, usually abbreviated to* **St Croix.** an island in the Caribbean, the largest of the Virgin Islands of the US: purchased by the US in 1917. Chief town: Christiansted. Pop.: 50 139 (1990). Area: 207 sq. km (80 sq. miles). Also called: **Santa Cruz** ('sæntə 'kruːz).

Saint Croix River ★ *n, usually abbreviated to* **St Croix River.** a river on the border between the northeast US and SE Canada, flowing from the Chiputneticook Lakes to Passamaquoddy Bay, forming the border between Maine, US, and New Brunswick, Canada. Length: 121 km (75 miles).

Saint David's ★ *n, usually abbreviated to* **St David's.** a town in SW Wales, in Pembrokeshire: its cathedral was a place of pilgrimage in medieval times. Pop.: 1627 (1991).

Saint-Denis ★ (*French* sɛ̃dni) *n, usually abbreviated to* **St-Denis. 1** a town in N France, on the Seine: 12th-century Gothic abbey church, containing the tombs of many French monarchs; an industrial suburb of Paris. Pop.: 89 988 (1990). **2** the capital of the French overseas region of Réunion, a port on the N coast. Pop.: 207 158 (1995).

Sainte-Beuve ★ (*French* sɛ̃tbœv) *n* **Charles Augustin** (ʃarl ogystɛ̃). 1804–69, French critic, best known for his collections of essays *Port Royal* (1840–59) and *Les Causeries du Lundi* (1851–62).

sainted ('seɪntɪd) *adj* **1** canonized. **2** like a saint in character or nature. **3** hallowed or holy.

Sainte Foy ★ (seɪnt 'fɔɪ, sənt) *n, usually abbreviated to* **Ste Foy.** a SW suburb of Quebec, on the St Lawrence River. Pop.: 71 133 (1991).

Saint Elias Mountains ★ *pl n, usually abbreviated to* **St Elias Mountains.** a mountain range between SE Alaska and the SW Yukon, Canada. Highest peak: Mount Logan, 6050 m (19 850 ft).

Saint Elmo's fire ('ɛlməʊz) *n, usually abbreviated to* **St Elmo's fire.** (not in technical usage) a luminous region that sometimes appears around church spires, the masts of ships, etc.

Saint-Étienne ★ (*French* sɛ̃tetjɛn) *n, usually abbreviated to* **St-Étienne.** a town in E central France: a major producer of textiles and armaments. Pop.: 201 569 (1990).

Saint-Exupéry ★ (*French* sɛ̃tɛgzyperi) *n* **Antoine de** (ɑ̃twan də). 1900–44, French novelist and aviator. His novels include *Vol de nuit* (1931): he also wrote the fairy tale *Le petit prince* (1943).

Saint Gall ★ (*French* sɛ̃ gal) *n, usually abbreviated to* **St Gall. 1** a canton of NE Switzerland. Capital: St Gall. Pop.: 440 744 (1995 est.). Area: 2012 sq. km (777 sq. miles). **2** a town in NE Switzerland, capital of St Gall canton: an important educational centre in the Middle Ages. Pop.: 75 541 (1994). German name: **Sankt Gallen** (zaŋkt 'galən).

Saint George's ★ *n, usually abbreviated to* **St George's.** the capital of Grenada, a port in the southwest. Pop.: 4621 (1991).

Saint George's Channel ★ *n, usually abbreviated to* **St George's Channel.** a strait between Wales and Ireland, linking the Irish Sea with the Atlantic. Length: about 160 km (100 miles). Width: up to 145 km (90 miles).

Saint Gotthard ★ ('gɒtəd) *n, usually abbreviated to* **St Gotthard. 1** a range of the Lepontine Alps in SE central Switzerland. **2** a pass over the St Gotthard mountains, in S Switzerland. Height: 2114 m (6935 ft).

Saint Helena ★ (ˌsɛntɪ'liːnə) *n, usually abbreviated to* **St Helena.** a volcanic island in the SE Atlantic, forming (with its dependencies Tristan da Cunha and Ascension) a United Kingdom overseas territory: discovered by the Portuguese in 1502 and annexed by England in 1651; scene of Napoleon's exile and death. Capital: Jamestown. Pop.: 5700 (1992). Area: 122 sq. km (47 sq. miles).

Saint Helens ★ *n, usually abbreviated to* **St Helens. 1** a town in NW England, in Merseyside: glass industry. Pop.: 106 293 (1991). **2** a unitary authority in NW England, in Merseyside. Pop.: 179 500 (1996 est.). Area: 130 sq. km (50 sq. miles.) **3 Mount.** a volcanic peak in S Washington state; it erupted in 1980 after lying dormant from 1857.

Saint Helier ★ ('hɛlɪə) *n, usually abbreviated to* **St Helier.** a market town and resort in the Channel Islands, on the S coast of Jersey. Pop.: 28 123 (1991).

Saint James's Palace ★ *n, usually abbreviated to* **St James's Palace.** a palace in Pall Mall, London: residence of British monarchs from 1697 to 1837.

Saint John ★ *n* **1** a port in E Canada, at the mouth of the St John River: the largest city in New Brunswick. Pop.: 90 457 (1991). **2** an island in the Caribbean, in the Virgin Islands of the US. Pop.: 3504 (1990). Area: 49 sq. km (19 sq. miles). **3 Lake.** a lake in Canada, in S Quebec: drained by the Saguenay River. Area: 971 sq. km (375 sq. miles). **4** a river in E North America, rising in Maine, US, and flowing northeast to New Brunswick, Canada, then generally southeast to the Bay of Fundy. Length: 673 km (418 miles). ◆ Abbrev. (for senses 2–4): **St John.**

Saint-John Perse ★ ('sɪndʒən 'pɜːs) *n* See (Saint-John) **Perse.**

Saint John's ★ *n, usually abbreviated to* **St John's. 1** a port in Canada, capital of Newfoundland, on the E coast of the Avalon Peninsula. Pop.: 95 770 (1991). **2** the capital of Antigua and Barbuda: a port on the NW coast of the island of Antigua. Pop.: 21 514 (1991).

Saint John's wort *n, usually abbreviated to* **St John's wort. 1** any of various shrubs or perennial herbaceous plants of a genus having yellow flowers. **2** a herbal remedy made from a species of this plant, used to treat mild depression. ◆ See also **hypericum.**

Saint-Just ★ (*French* sɛ̃ʒyst) *n* **Louis Antoine Léon de** (lwi ɑ̃twan leɔ̃ də). 1767–94, French Revolutionary leader and orator. A member of the Committee of Public Safety (1793–94), he was guillotined with Robespierre.

Saint Kilda ★ ('kɪldə) *n, usually abbreviated to* **St Kilda. 1** a group of volcanic islands in the Atlantic, in the Outer Hebrides: uninhabited since 1930; bird sanctuary. **2** the main island of this group. Also called: **Hirta.**

Saint Kitts ★ (kɪts) *n, usually abbreviated to* **St Kitts.** an island in the E Caribbean, in the Leeward Islands: part of the state of St Kitts-Nevis. Capital: Basseterre. Pop.: 40 618 (1991). Area: 168 sq. km (65 sq. miles). Also called: **Saint Christopher.**

Saint Kitts-Nevis ★ *n, usually abbreviated to* **St Kitts-Nevis.** an independent state in the E Caribbean, in the Caribbean; comprises the two islands of St Kitts and Nevis: with the island of Anguilla formed a colony (1882–1967) and a British associated state (1967–83); Anguilla formally separated from the group in 1983; gained full independence in 1983 as a member of the Commonwealth. Official language: English. Religion: Protestant majority. Currency: Eastern Caribbean dollar. Capital: Basseterre. Pop.: 42 800 (1999 est.). Area: 262 sq. km (101 sq. miles).

Saint Laurent ★ (*French* sɛ̃ lɔrɑ̃) *n, usually abbreviated to* **St Laurent.** a W suburb of Montreal, Canada. Pop.: 72 402 (1991).

Saint-Laurent ★ (*French* sɛ̃lɔrɑ̃) *n* **Yves** (iv), full name *Yves-Mathieu.* born 1936, French couturier: popularized trousers for women for all occasions.

Saint Lawrence ★ *n, usually abbreviated to* **St Lawrence. 1** a river in SE Canada, flowing northeast from Lake Ontario, forming part of the border between Canada and the US, to the Gulf of St Lawrence: commercially one of the most important rivers in the world as the easternmost link of the St Lawrence Seaway. Length: 1207 km (750 miles). Width at mouth: 145 km (90 miles). **2 Gulf of.** a deep arm of the Atlantic off the E coast of Canada between Newfoundland and the mainland coasts of Quebec, New Brunswick, and Nova Scotia.

Saint Lawrence Seaway ★ *n, usually abbreviated to* **St Lawrence Seaway.** an inland waterway of North America, passing through the Great Lakes, the St Lawrence River, and connecting canals and locks: one of the most important waterways in the world. Length: 3993 km (2480 miles).

Saint Leger ('lɛdʒə) *n, usually abbreviated to* **St Leger. the.** an annual horse race run at Doncaster, England, since 1776.

Saint Leonard ★ ('lɛnəd) *n, usually abbreviated to* **St Leonard.** a N suburb of Montreal, Canada. Pop.: 82 200 (latest est.).

Saint-Lô ★ (*French* sɛ̃lo) *n, usually abbreviated to* **St-Lô.** a market town in NW France: a Calvinist stronghold in the 16th century. Pop.: 22 819 (1990).

Saint Louis ★ ('luɪs) *n, usually abbreviated to* **St Louis.** a port in E Missouri, on the Mississippi River near its confluence with the Missouri: the largest city in the state; university; major industrial centre. Pop.: 368 215 (1994 est.).

Saint-Louis ★ (*French* sɛ̃lwi) *n, usually abbreviated to* **St-Louis.** a port in NW Senegal, on an island at the mouth of the Senegal River: the first French settlement in W Africa (1689); capital of Senegal until 1958. Pop.: 179 000 (1995 est.).

Saint Lucia ★ ('luːʃə) *n, usually abbreviated to* **St Lucia.** an island state in the Caribbean, in the Windward Islands group of the Lesser Antilles: a volcanic island; gained self-government in 1967 as a British Associated State; attained full independence within the Commonwealth in 1979. Official language: English. Religion: Roman Catholic majority. Currency: Eastern Caribbean dollar. Capital: Castries. Pop.: 155 000 (1999 est.). Area: 616 sq. km (238 sq. miles).

saintly ('seɪntlɪ) *adj* like, relating to, or suitable for a saint.
▸ **'saintlily** *adv* ▸ **'saintliness** *n*

Saint Martin ★ *n, usually abbreviated to* **St Martin.** an island in the E Caribbean, in the Leeward Islands: administratively divided since 1648, the north belonging to France (as a dependency of Guadeloupe) and the south belonging to the Netherlands (as part of the Netherlands Antilles); salt industry. Pop.: (French) 28 518 (1990); (Dutch) 37 256 (1994 est.). Areas: (French) 52 sq. km (20 sq. miles); (Dutch) 33 sq. km (13 sq. miles). Dutch name: **Sint Maarten.**

Saint-Maur-des-Fossés ★ (*French* sɛ̃mɔrdefose) *n, usually abbreviated to* **St-Maur-des-Fossés.** a town in N France, on the River Marne: a residential suburb of SE Paris. Pop.: 77 492 (1990).

Saint-Mihiel ★ (*French* sɛ̃mjɛl) *n, usually abbreviated to* **St-Mihiel.** a village in NE France, on the River Meuse: site of a battle in World War I, in which the American army launched its first offensive in France.

Saint Moritz ★ (mə'rɪts) *n, usually abbreviated to* **St Moritz.** a village in E Switzerland, in Graubünden canton in the Upper Engadine, at an altitude of 1856 m (6089 ft): sports and tourist centre. Pop.: 5335 (1990 est.).

Saint-Nazaire ★ (*French* sɛ̃nazɛr) *n, usually abbreviated to* **St-Nazaire.** a port in NW France, at the mouth of the River Loire: German submarine base in World War II; shipbuilding. Pop.: 64 812 (1990).

Saint-Ouen ★ (*French* sɛ̃twɛ̃) *n, usually abbreviated to* **St-Ouen.** a town in N France, on the Seine: an industrial suburb of Paris; famous flea market. Pop.: 42 611 (1990).

Saint Paul ★ *n, usually abbreviated to* **St Paul.** a port in SE Minnesota, capital of the state, at the head of navigation of the Mississippi: now contiguous with Minneapolis (the Twin Cities). Pop.: 262 071 (1994 est.).

saintpaulia (sənt'pɔːlɪə) *n* another name for **African violet.** ORIG C20: NL, after Baron W. von *Saint Paul,* G soldier (died 1910), who discovered it

Saint Paul's ★ *n, usually abbreviated to* **St Paul's.** a cathedral in central London, built between 1675 and 1710 to replace an earlier cathedral destroyed during the Great Fire (1666): regarded as Wren's masterpiece.

Saint Peter's ★ *n, usually abbreviated to* **St Peter's.** the basilica of the Vatican City, built between 1506 and 1615 to replace an earlier church: the largest church in the world, 188 m (615 ft) long, and chief pilgrimage centre of Europe; designed by many architects, notably Bramante, Raphael, Sangallo, Michelangelo, and Bernini.

Saint Petersburg ★ ('piːtəzˌbɜːg) *n, usually abbreviated to* **St Petersburg. 1** a city and port in NW Russia, on the Gulf of Finland at the mouth of the Neva River: founded by Peter the Great in 1703 and built on low-lying marshes subject to frequent flooding; capital of Russia from 1712 to 1918; a cultural and educational centre, with a university (1819); a major industrial centre, with engineering, shipbuilding, chemical, textile, and printing industries. Pop.: 4 838 500 (1995 est.). Former names: **Petrograd** (1914–24), **Leningrad** (1924–91). **2** a city and resort in W Florida, on Tampa Bay. Pop.: 238 585 (1994 est.).

Saint Pierre ★ (*French* sɛ̃ pjɛr) *n, usually abbreviated to* **St Pierre.** a former town on the coast of the French island of Martinique, destroyed by the eruption of Mont Pelée in 1902.

Saint Pierre and Miquelon ★ (ˌmɪkə'lɒn; *French* miklɔ̃) *n, usually abbreviated to* **St Pierre and Miquelon.** an archipelago in the Atlantic, just off the S coast of Newfoundland: administratively an overseas department of France and the only remaining French possession in North America; consists of the islands of St Pierre, with most of the population, and Miquelon, about ten times as large; fishing industries. Capital: St Pierre. Pop.: 6392 (1990). Area: 242 sq. km (94 sq. miles).

Saint Pölten ★ ('pɜːltən) *n* See **Sankt Pölten.**

Saint-Quentin ★ (*French* sɛ̃kɑ̃tɛ̃) *n, usually abbreviated to* **St-Quentin.** a town in N France, on the River Somme: textile industry. Pop.: 62 085 (1990).

Saint-Saëns ★ (*French* sɛ̃sɑ̃s) *n* (**Charles**) **Camille** (kamij). 1835–1921, French composer. His works include the opera *Samson and Delilah* (1877), the suite *Carnival of Animals* (1886), five symphonies, and five piano concertos.

saint's day *n Christianity.* a day in the church calendar commemorating a saint.

Saint-Simon ★ (*French* sɛ̃simɔ̃) *n* **1 Comte de** (kɔ̃t də), title of *Claude Henri de Rouvroy.* 1760–1825, French social philosopher, generally regarded as the founder of French socialism. He thought society should be reorganized along industrial lines and that scientists should be the new spiritual leaders. His most important work is *Nouveau Christianisme* (1825). **2 Duc de** (dyk də), title of *Louis de Rouvroy.* 1675–1755, French soldier, statesman, and writer: his *Mémoires* are an outstanding account of the period 1694–1723, during the reigns of Louis XIV and Louis XV.

Saint Thomas ★ *n, usually abbreviated to* **St Thomas. 1** an island in the E Caribbean, in the Virgin Islands of the US. Capital: Charlotte Amalie. Pop.: 48 166 (1990). Area: 83 sq. km (28 sq. miles). **2** the former name (1921–37) of **Charlotte Amalie.**

Saint Vincent ★ *n, usually abbreviated to* **St Vincent. 1 Cape.** a headland at the SW extremity of Portugal: scene of several important naval battles, notably in 1797, when the British defeated the French and Spanish. **2 Gulf.** a shallow inlet of SE Australia, to the east of the Yorke Peninsula: salt industry.

Saint Vincent and the Grenadines ★ *n, usually abbreviated to* **St Vincent and the Grenadines.** an island state in the Caribbean, in the Windward Islands of the Lesser Antilles: comprises the island of St Vincent and the Northern Grenadines; formerly a British associated state (1969–79); gained full independence in 1979 as a member of the Commonwealth. Official language: English. Religion: Christian majority. Currency: East Caribbean dollar. Capital: Kingstown. Pop.: 113 000 (1999 est.). Area: 389 sq. km (150 sq. miles).

Saint Vitus's dance ('vaɪtəsɪz) *n, usually abbreviated to* **St Vitus's dance.** *Pathol.* a nontechnical name for **Sydenham's chorea.**

Saipan ★ (saɪ'pæn) *n* an island in the W Pacific, in the S central Mariana Islands: administrative centre of the US Trust Territory of the Pacific Islands; captured by the Americans and used as a leading air base until the end of World War II; administered by the US since 1946. Pop.: 38 896 (1990). Area: 180 sq. km (70 sq. miles).

Saïs ★ ('seɪɪs) *n* (in ancient Egypt) a city in the W Nile delta; the royal capital of the 24th dynasty (about 730–715 B.C.) and the 26th dynasty (about 664–525 B.C.).
▸ **Saite** ('seɪaɪt) *n* ▸ **Saitic** (seɪ'ɪtɪk) *adj*

saith (sɛθ) *vb* (used with *he, she,* or *it*) *Arch.* a form of the present tense of **say.**

saithe (seɪθ) *n Brit.* another name for **coalfish.** ORIG C19: from ON

Sakai ★ (sɑː'kaɪ) *n* a port in S Japan, on S Honshu on Osaka Bay: a major port in the 16th century; an industrial satellite of Osaka. Pop.: 802 965 (1995).

sake[1] (seɪk) *n* **1** benefit or interest (esp. in **for** (**someone's** *or* **one's own**) **sake**). **2** the purpose of obtaining or achieving (esp. in **for the sake of** (**something**)). **3** used in various exclamations of impatience, urgency, etc.: *for heaven's sake.* ORIG C13 (in the phrase *for the sake of,* prob. from legal usage): from OE *sacu* lawsuit (hence, a cause)

sake[2], **saké,** *or* **saki** ('sækɪ) *n* a Japanese alcoholic drink made from fermented rice. ORIG C17: from Japanese

saker ('seɪkə) *n* a large falcon of E Europe and Asia. ORIG C14 *sagre,* from OF *sacre,* from Ar. *saqr*

Sakhalin (*Russian* səxa'lin) *or* **Saghalien** ★ *n* an island in the Sea of Okhotsk, off the SE coast of Russia north of Japan: fishing, forestry, and mineral resources (coal and petroleum). Capital: Yuzhno-Sakhalinsk. Pop.: 673 000 (1995 est.). Area: 76 000 sq. km (29 300 sq. miles). Japanese name (1905–24): **Karafuto.**

Sakha Republic ★ (*Russian* 'saxa) *n* an administrative division in E Russia, in NE Siberia on the Arctic Ocean. Capital: Yakutsk. Pop.: 663 000 (1996 est.). Area: 3 103 200 sq. km (1 197 760 sq. miles). Former names: **Yakut Republic, Yakutia.**

Sakharov ★ (*Russian* za'xarəf) *n* **Andrei** (an'drjej). 1921–89, Soviet nuclear physicist and human-rights campaigner: Nobel peace prize 1975.

saki ('sɑːkɪ) *n* **1** any of several small mostly arboreal New World monkeys having a long bushy tail. **2** another name for **sake**[2]. ORIG sense 1: C20: F, from Tupi *saqi*

Saki ★ ('sɑːkɪ) *n* pen name of (Hector Hugh) **Munro.**

sal (sæl) *n* a pharmacological term for **salt** (sense 3). ORIG L

salaam (sə'lɑːm) *n* **1** a Muslim salutation consisting of a deep bow with the right palm on the forehead. **2** a salutation signifying peace. ◆ *vb* **3** to make a salaam (to). ORIG C17: from Ar. *salām* peace, from *assalām 'alaikum* peace be to you

salable ('seɪləb[ə]l) *adj* the US spelling of **saleable.**

salacious (sə'leɪʃəs) *adj* **1** having an excessive interest in sex. **2** (of books, etc.) erotic, bawdy, or lewd. ORIG C17: from L *salax* fond of leaping, from *salīre* to leap
▸ **sa'laciously** *adv* ▸ **sa'laciousness** *or* **salacity** (sə'læsɪtɪ) *n*

salad ('sæləd) *n* **1** a dish of raw vegetables, such as lettuce, tomatoes, etc., served as a separate course with cold meat, eggs, etc., or as part of a main course. **2** any dish of cold vegetables or fruit served with a dressing: *potato salad.* **3** any green vegetable or herb used in such a dish. ORIG C15: from OF *salade,* from OProvençal *salada,* from *salar* to season with salt, from L *sal* salt

salad days *pl n* a period of youth and inexperience.

salad dressing *n* a sauce for salad, such as oil and vinegar or mayonnaise.

salade niçoise (sæ'lɑːd niː'swɑːz) *n* a cold dish consisting of a variety of ingredients, usually including hard-boiled eggs, anchovy fillets, olives, tomatoes, and sometimes tuna fish. ORIG C20: from F, lit.: salad of or from NICE

Saladin ★ ('sælədɪn) *n* Arabic name *Salah-ed-Din Yusuf ibn-Ayyub.* ?1137–93, sultan of Egypt and Syria. He defeated the Crusaders near Tiberias (1187) and captured Acre, Jerusalem, and Ashkelon. He fought against Richard I of England and Philip II of France during the Third Crusade (1189–92).

Salado ★ (*Spanish* sa'laðo) *n* **1** a river in N Argentina, rising in the Andes as the Juramento and flowing southeast to the Paraná River. Length: 2012 km (1250 miles). **2** a river in W Argentina, rising near the Chilean border as the Desaguadero and flowing south to the Colorado River. Length: about 1365 km (850 miles).

Salamanca ★ (*Spanish* sala'maŋka) *n* a city in W Spain: a leading cultural centre of Europe till the end of the 16th century; market town. Pop.: 167 382 (1991).

salamander ('sælə͵mændə) *n* **1** any of various amphibians of central and S Europe. They have an elongated body, and only return to water to breed. **2** *Chiefly US & Canad.* any amphibian with a tail, as the newt. **3** a mythical reptilian creature supposed to live in fire. **4** an elemental fire-inhabiting being. ORIG C14: from OF *salamandre,* from L *salamandra,* from Gk

Salambria ★ (sə'læmbrɪə, ͵sɑːlɑːm'brɪə) *n* a river in N Greece, in Thessaly, rising in the Pindus Mountains and flowing southeast and east to the Gulf of Salonika. Length: about 200 km (125 miles). Ancient name: **Peneus.** Modern Greek name: **Piniós.**

salami (sə'lɑːmɪ) *n* a highly seasoned type of sausage, usually flavoured with garlic. ORIG C19: from It., pl of *salame,* from Vulgar L *salāre* (unattested) to salt, from L *sal* salt

Salamis ★ ('sæləmɪs) *n* an island in the Saronic Gulf, Greece: scene of the naval battle in 480 B.C., in which the Greeks defeated the Persians. Pop.: 20 000 (latest est.). Area: 95 sq. km (37 sq. miles).

sal ammoniac *n* another name for **ammonium chloride.**

salaried ('sælərɪd) *adj* earning or yielding a salary: *a salaried worker; salaried employment.*

salary ('sælərɪ) *n, pl* **salaries. 1** a fixed payment made by an employer, often monthly, for professional or office work. Cf. **wage.** ◆ *vb* **salaries, salarying, salaried. 2** (*tr*) to pay a salary to. ORIG C14: from Anglo-Norman *salarie,* from L *salārium* the sum given to Roman soldiers to buy salt, from *sal* salt

Salazar ★ (*Portuguese* sələ'zar) *n* **Antonio de Oliveira** (ən'tɔnju 'də: oli'vəjrə). 1889–1970, Portuguese statesman; dictator (1932–68).

salchow ('sælkəʊ) *n Figure skating.* a jump from the inner backward edge of one foot with one, two, or three full turns in the air, returning to the outer backward edge of the opposite foot. ORIG C20: after Ulrich *Salchow* (1877–1949), Swedish figure skater, who originated it

Salduba ★ (sæl'duːbə, 'sældəbə) *n* the pre-Roman (Celtiberian) name for **Zaragoza.**

sale (seɪl) *n* **1** the exchange of goods, property, or services for an agreed sum of money or credit. **2** the amount sold. **3** the opportunity to sell: *there was no sale for luxuries.* **4a** an event at which goods are sold at reduced prices, usually to clear old stocks. **4b** (*as modifier*): *sale bargains.* **5** an auction. ORIG OE *sala,* from ON *sala*

Sale ★ (seɪl) *n* **1** a town in NW England, in Greater Manchester: a residential suburb of Manchester. Pop.: 56 052 (1991). **2** a city in SE Australia, in SE Victoria: centre of an agricultural region. Pop.: 13 858 (1991).

Salé ★ (*French* sale) *n* a port in NW Morocco, on the Atlantic adjoining Rabat. Pop.: 521 000 (1993 est.).

saleable *or US* **salable** ('seɪləb[ə]l) *adj* fit for selling or capable of being sold.
▸ **͵salea'bility** *or US* **͵sala'bility** *n*

Salem ★ ('seɪləm) *n* **1** a city in S India, in Tamil Nadu: textile industries. Pop.: 366 712 (1991). **2** a city in NE Massachusetts, on the Atlantic: scene of the execution of 19 witches after the witch hunts of 1692. Pop.: 38 091 (1990). **3** a city in the NW US, the state capital of Oregon. Pop.: 115 912 (1994 est.). **4** an Old Testament name for **Jerusalem.** (Genesis 14:18; Psalms 76:2).

sale of work *n* a sale of articles, often handmade, the proceeds of which benefit a charity or charities.

sale or return *n* an arrangement by which a retailer pays only for goods sold, returning those that are unsold.

Salerno ★ (*Italian* sa'lɛrno) *n* a port in SW Italy, in Campania on the **Gulf of Salerno:** first medical school of medieval Europe. Pop.: 143 863 (1996 est.).

saleroom ('seɪl͵ruːm, -͵rʊm) *n Chiefly Brit.* a room where objects are displayed for sale, esp. by auction.

salesclerk ('seɪlz͵klɜːk) *n US & Canad.* a shop assistant.

salesman ('seɪlzmən) *n, pl* **salesmen. 1** Also called: **saleswoman** (*fem*), **salesgirl** (*fem*), *or* **salesperson.** a person who sells merchandise or services in a shop. **2** short for **travelling salesman.**

salesmanship ('seɪlzmənʃɪp) *n* **1** the technique of, skill, or ability in selling. **2** the work of a salesman.

sales pitch *or* **talk** *n* an argument or other persuasion used in selling.

sales resistance *n* opposition of potential customers to selling, esp. aggressive selling.

sales tax *n* a tax levied on retail sales receipts and added to selling prices by retailers.

sales trader *n Stock Exchange.* a person employed by a market maker, or his or her firm, to find clients.

Salford ★ ('sɔːlfəd, 'sɒl-) *n* **1** a city in NW England in Greater Manchester, on the Manchester Ship Canal: a major centre of the cotton industry in the 19th century; extensive docks; seat of The University of Salford (1967).

Pop.: 79 755 (1991). **2** a unitary authority in NW England, in Greater Manchester. Pop.: 229 200 (1996 est.). Area: 97 sq. km (37 sq. miles).

Salian ('seɪlɪən) *adj* **1** denoting or relating to a group of Franks (the **Salii**) who settled in the Netherlands in the 4th century A.D. ◆ *n* **2** a member of this group.

salicin ('sælɪsɪn) *n* a crystalline water-soluble glucoside obtained from the bark of poplar trees and used as a medical analgesic. ORIG C19: from F, from L *salix* willow

Salic law ('sælɪk) *n History.* **1** the code of laws of the Salian Franks and other Germanic tribes. **2** a law excluding women from succession to the throne in certain countries, such as France.

salicylate (sə'lɪsɪˌleɪt) *n* any salt or ester of salicylic acid.

salicylic acid (ˌsælɪ'sɪlɪk) *n* a white crystalline substance with a sweet taste and bitter aftertaste, used in the manufacture of aspirin, and as a fungicide. ORIG C19: *salicyl* (from F, from L *salix* a willow + -YL) + -IC

salient ('seɪlɪənt) *adj* **1** conspicuous or striking: *a salient feature.* **2** projecting outwards at an angle of less than 180°. **3** (esp. of animals) leaping. ◆ *n* **4** *Mil.* a projection of the forward line into enemy-held territory. **5** a salient angle. ORIG C16: from L *salīre* to leap
▸ **'salience** *or* **'saliency** *n* ▸ **'saliently** *adv*

salientian (ˌseɪlɪ'ɛnʃɪən) *n* **1** any of an order of vertebrates with no tail and long hind legs adapted for hopping, as the frog or the toad. ◆ *adj* **2** of or belonging to this order. ORIG C19: from NL *Salientia,* lit.: leapers, from L *salīre* to leap

Salieri ★ (*Italian* sa'ljɛːri) *n* **Antonio** (an'tɔːnjo). 1750–1825, Italian composer and conductor, who worked in Vienna (from 1766). The suggestion that he poisoned Mozart has no foundation.

salina (sə'laɪnə) *n* a salt marsh or lake. ORIG C17: from Sp., from Med. L: salt pit, from LL *salīnus* SALINE

saline ('seɪlaɪn) *adj* **1** of, consisting of, or containing common salt: *a saline taste.* **2** *Med.* of or relating to a saline. **3** of, consisting of, or containing any chemical salt, esp. sodium chloride. ◆ *n* **4** *Med.* a solution of sodium chloride and water. ORIG C15: from LL *salīnus,* from L *sal* salt
▸ **salinity** (sə'lɪnɪtɪ) *n*

Salinger ★ ('sælɪndʒə) *n* **J(erome) D(avid).** born 1919, US writer, noted for his novel *The Catcher in the Rye* (1951). In 1997 he published *Hapworth 16, 1924,* his first novel for 34 years.

salinometer (ˌsælɪ'nɒmɪtə) *n* a hydrometer for determining the amount of salt in a solution.
▸ **ˌsali'nometry** *n*

Salisbury[1] ★ ('sɔːlzbərɪ, -brɪ) *n* **1** the former name (until 1982) of **Harare. 2** a city in S Australia: an industrial suburb of N Adelaide. Pop.: 89 000 (latest est.). **3** a city in S England, in SE Wiltshire: nearby Old Sarum was the site of an Early Iron Age hill fort; its cathedral (1220–58) has the highest spire in England. Pop.: 39 268 (1991). Ancient name: **Sarum.** Official name: **New Sarum.**

Salisbury[2] ★ ('sɔːlzbərɪ, -brɪ) *n* **Robert Gascoyne Cecil** ('gæskɔɪn), 3rd Marquess of Salisbury. 1830–1903, British statesman; Conservative prime minister (1885–86; 1886–92; 1895–1902).

Salisbury Plain ★ *n* an open chalk plateau in S England, in Wiltshire: site of Stonehenge; military training area. Average height: 120 m (400 ft).

saliva (sə'laɪvə) *n* the secretion of salivary glands, consisting of a clear usually slightly acid aqueous fluid of variable composition. ORIG C17: from L, from ?
▸ **salivary** (sə'laɪvərɪ) *adj*

salivary gland *n* any of the glands in mammals that secrete saliva.

salivate ('sælɪˌveɪt) *vb* **salivates, salivating, salivated. 1** (*intr*) to secrete saliva, esp. an excessive amount. **2** (*tr*) to cause (an animal, etc.) to produce saliva, as by the administration of mercury.
▸ **ˌsali'vation** *n*

Salk ★ (sɔːlk) *n* **Jonas Edward.** 1914–95, US virologist: developed the injectable **Salk vaccine** against poliomyelitis (1954).

sallee *or* **sally** ('sælɪ) *n Austral.* **1** a SE Australian eucalyptus tree with pale grey bark. **2** any of various acacia trees. ORIG prob. from Abor.

sallow[1] ('sæləʊ) *adj* **1** (esp. of human skin) of an unhealthy pale or yellowish colour. ◆ *vb* **2** (*tr*) to make sallow. ORIG OE *salu*
▸ **'sallowish** *adj* ▸ **'sallowness** *n*

sallow[2] ('sæləʊ) *n* **1** any of several small willow trees, esp. the common sallow, which has large catkins that appear before the leaves. **2** a twig or the wood of any of these trees. ORIG OE *sealh*
▸ **'sallowy** *adj*

Sallust ★ ('sæləst) *n* full name *Gaius Sallustius Crispus.* 86–?34 B.C., Roman historian and statesman.

sally ('sælɪ) *n, pl* **sallies. 1** a sudden sortie, esp. by troops. **2** a sudden outburst or emergence into action or expression. **3** an excursion. **4** a jocular retort. ◆ *vb* **sallies, sallying, sallied.** (*intr*) **5** to make a sudden violent sortie. **6** (often foll. by *forth*) to go out on an expedition, etc. **7** to come or set out in an energetic manner. **8** to rush out suddenly. ORIG C16: from OF *saillie,* from *saillir* to dash forwards, from L *salīre* to leap

Sally Lunn (lʌn) *n* a flat round cake made from a sweet yeast dough. ORIG C19: said to be after an 18th-century E baker who invented it

salmagundi (ˌsælmə'gʌndɪ) *n* **1** a mixed salad dish of cooked meats, eggs, beetroot, etc., popular in 18th-century England. **2** a miscellany. ORIG C17: from F *salmigondis,* ?from It. *salami conditi* pickled salami

salmon ('sæmən) *n, pl* **salmons** *or* **salmon. 1** a soft-finned fish of the Atlantic and the Pacific, which is an important food fish. Salmon occur in cold and temperate waters and many species migrate to fresh water to spawn. **2** *Austral.* any of several unrelated fish. ORIG C13: from OF *saumon,* from L *salmō*
▸ **'salmoˌnoid** *adj*

salmonella (ˌsælmə'nɛlə) *n, pl* **salmonellae** (-ˌliː). any of a genus of rod-shaped aerobic bacteria including many species which cause food poisoning. ORIG C19: NL, after Daniel E. *Salmon* (1850–1914), US veterinary surgeon

salmon ladder *n* a series of steps designed to enable salmon to move upstream to their breeding grounds.

Salome ★ (sə'ləʊmɪ) *n New Testament.* the daughter of Herodias, at whose instigation she beguiled Herod by her seductive dancing into giving her the head of John the Baptist.

salon ('sælɒn) *n* **1** a room in a large house in which guests are received. **2** an assembly of guests in a fashionable household, esp. a gathering of major literary, artistic, and political figures. **3** a commercial establishment in which hairdressers, etc., carry on their businesses. **4a** a hall for exhibiting works of art. **4b** such an exhibition, esp. one showing the work of living artists. ORIG C18: from F, from It. *salone,* augmented form of *sala* hall, of Gmc origin

Salonika *or* **Salonica** ★ (sə'lɒnɪkə) *n* the English name for **Thessaloníki.**

saloon (sə'luːn) *n* **1** Also called: **saloon bar.** *Brit.* another word for **lounge** (sense 5). **2** a large public room on a passenger ship. **3** any large public room used for a purpose: *a dancing saloon.* **4** *Chiefly US & Canad.* a place where alcoholic drink is sold and consumed. **5** a closed two-door or four-door car with four to six seats. US, Canad., and NZ name: **sedan.** ORIG C18: from F SALON

Salop ★ ('sæləp) *n* a former name (1974–80) of **Shropshire.**
▸ **Salopian** (sə'ləʊpjən) *n, adj*

salopettes (ˌsælə'pɛts) *pl n* a garment worn for skiing, consisting of quilted trousers held up by shoulder straps. ORIG C20: from F

salpiglossis (ˌsælpɪ'glɒsɪs) *n* any of a genus of plants, some species of which are cultivated for their bright funnel-shaped flowers. ORIG C19: NL, from Gk *salpinx* trumpet + *glōssa* tongue

salpinx ('sælpɪŋks) *n, pl* **salpinges** (sæl'pɪndʒiːz). *Anat.* an-

other name for **Fallopian tube** or **Eustachian tube.** ORIG C19: from Gk: trumpet
▸ **salpingectomy** (ˌsælpɪnˈdʒɛktəmɪ) *n* ▸ **salpingitis** (ˌsælpɪnˈdʒaɪtɪs) *n*

salsa (ˈsælsə) *n* **1** a type of Latin American big-band dance music. **2** a dance performed to this. **3** *Cookery.* a spicy Mexican tomato-based sauce. ORIG C20: from Sp.: sauce

salsify (ˈsælsɪfɪ) *n, pl* **salsifies. 1** Also called: **oyster plant, vegetable oyster.** a Mediterranean plant having grasslike leaves, purple flower heads, and a long white edible taproot. **2** the root of this plant, which tastes of oysters and is eaten as a vegetable. ORIG C17: from F, from It. *sassefrica,* from LL, from L *saxum* rock + *fricāre* to rub

sal soda *n* the crystalline decahydrate of sodium carbonate, $Na_2CO_3.10H_2O$.

salt (sɔːlt) *n* **1** a white powder or colourless crystalline solid, consisting mainly of sodium chloride and used for seasoning and preserving food. **2** (*modifier*) preserved in, flooded with, containing, or growing in salt or salty water: *salt pork.* **3** *Chem.* any of a class of crystalline solid compounds that are formed from, or can be regarded as formed from, an acid and a base. **4** liveliness or pungency: *his wit added salt to the discussion.* **5** dry or laconic wit. **6** an experienced sailor. **7** short for **saltcellar. 8 rub salt into someone's wounds.** to make someone's pain, shame, etc., even worse. **9 salt of the earth.** a person or group of people regarded as the finest of their kind. **10 with a grain** (*or* **pinch**) **of salt.** with reservations. **11 worth one's salt.** worthy of one's pay. ◆ *vb* (*tr*) **12** to season or preserve with salt. **13** to scatter salt over (an iced road, etc.) to melt the ice. **14** to add zest to. **15** (often foll. by *down* or *away*) to preserve or cure with salt. **16** *Chem.* to treat with salt. **17** to give a false appearance of value to, esp. to introduce valuable ore fraudulently into (a mine, sample, etc.). ◆ *adj* **18** not sour, sweet, or bitter; salty. ◆ See also **salt away, salts.** ORIG OE *sealt*
▸ **ˈsaltˌlike** *adj* ▸ **ˈsaltness** *n*

SALT (sɔːlt) *n acronym for* Strategic Arms Limitation Talks *or* Treaty.

Salta ★ (*Spanish* ˈsalta) *n* a city in NW Argentina: thermal springs. Pop.: 370 904 (1991).

saltation (sælˈteɪʃən) *n* **1** *Biol.* an abrupt variation in the appearance of an organism, species, etc. **2** *Geol.* the leaping movement of sand or soil particles carried in water or by the wind. **3** a sudden abrupt movement. ORIG C17: from L *saltātiō* a dance, from *saltāre* to leap about
▸ **saltatorial** (ˌsæltəˈtɔːrɪəl) *or* **ˈsaltatory** *adj*

salt away *or* (*less commonly*) **down** *vb* (*tr, adv*) to hoard or save (money, valuables, etc.).

saltbush (ˈsɔːltˌbʊʃ) *n* any of certain shrubs that grow in alkaline desert regions.

salt cake *n* an impure form of sodium sulphate used in the manufacture of detergents, glass, and ceramic glazes.

saltcellar (ˈsɔːltˌsɛlə) *n* **1** a small container for salt used at the table. **2** *Brit. inf.* either of the two hollows formed above the collarbones. ORIG changed (through infl. of cellar) from C15 *salt saler; saler* from OF *saliere* container for salt, from L *salārius* belonging to salt, from *sal* salt

salt dome *or* **plug** *n* a domelike structure of stratified rocks containing a central core of salt.

salted (ˈsɔːltɪd) *adj* seasoned, preserved, or treated with salt.

salt flat *n* a flat expanse of salt left by the total evaporation of a body of water.

saltigrade (ˈsæltɪˌgreɪd) *adj* (of animals) adapted for moving in a series of jumps. ORIG C19: from NL *Saltigradae,* name formerly applied to jumping spiders, from L *saltus* a leap + *gradī* to move

Saltillo ★ (*Spanish* salˈtiʎo) *n* a city in N Mexico, capital of Coahuila state: resort and commercial centre of a mining region. Pop.: 420 947 (1990).

saltings (ˈsɔːltɪŋz) *pl n* meadow land or marsh that is periodically flooded by sea water.

saltire *or* **saltier** (ˈsɔːlˌtaɪə) *n Heraldry.* an ordinary consisting of a diagonal cross on a shield. ORIG C14 *sawturoure,* from OF *sauteour* cross-shaped barricade, from *saulter* to jump, from L *saltāre*

Salt Lake City ★ *n* a city in N central Utah, near the Great Salt Lake at an altitude of 1330 m (4300 ft): state capital; founded in 1847 by the Mormons as world capital of the Mormon Church; University of Utah (1850). Pop.: 171 849 (1994 est.).

salt lick *n* **1** a place where wild animals go to lick salt deposits. **2** a block of salt given to domestic animals to lick. **3** *Austral. & NZ.* a soluble cake of minerals used to supplement the diet of farm animals.

Salto ★ (*Spanish* ˈsalto) *n* a port in NW Uruguay, on the Uruguay River: Uruguay's second largest city. Pop.: 77 400 (1985).

saltpan (ˈsɔːltˌpæn) *n* a shallow basin, usually in a desert region, containing salt, gypsum, etc., that was deposited from an evaporated salt lake.

saltpetre *or US* **saltpeter** (ˌsɔːltˈpiːtə) *n* **1** another name for **potassium nitrate. 2** short for **Chile saltpetre.** ORIG C16: from OF *salpetre,* from L *sal petrae* salt of rock

salt pork *n* pork, esp. taken from the back and belly, that has been cured with salt.

salts (sɔːlts) *pl n* **1** *Med.* any of various mineral salts, such as magnesium sulphate, for use as a cathartic. **2** short for **smelling salts. 3 like a dose of salts.** *Inf.* very quickly.

saltus (ˈsæltəs) *n, pl* **saltuses.** a break in the continuity of a sequence. ORIG L: a leap

saltwater (ˈsɔːltˌwɔːtə) *adj* of or inhabiting salt water, esp. the sea: *saltwater fishes.*

saltworks (ˈsɔːltˌwɜːks) *n* (*functioning as sing*) a building or factory where salt is produced.

saltwort (ˈsɔːltˌwɜːt) *n* any of various plants, of beaches and salt marshes, having prickly leaves, striped stems, and small green flowers. Also called: **glasswort, kali.**

salty (ˈsɔːltɪ) *adj* **saltier, saltiest. 1** of, tasting of, or containing salt. **2** (esp. of humour) sharp. **3** relating to life at sea.
▸ **ˈsaltiness** *n*

salubrious (səˈluːbrɪəs) *adj* conducive or favourable to health. ORIG C16: from L, from *salūs* health
▸ **saˈlubriously** *adv* ▸ **saˈlubrity** *n*

Saluki (səˈluːkɪ) *n* a tall breed of hound with a smooth coat and long fringes on the ears and tail. ORIG C19: from Ar. *salūqī* of Saluq, an ancient Arabian city

salutary (ˈsæljutərɪ) *adj* **1** promoting or intended to promote an improvement: *a salutary warning.* **2** promoting or intended to promote health. ORIG C15: from L *salūtāris* wholesome, from *salūs* safety
▸ **ˈsalutarily** *adv*

salutation (ˌsæljuˈteɪʃən) *n* **1** an act, phrase, gesture, etc., that serves as a greeting. **2** a form of words used as an opening to a speech or letter, such as *Dear Sir.* ORIG C14: from L *salūtātiō,* from *salūtāre* to greet; see SALUTE

salutatory (səˈluːtətərɪ) *adj* of, relating to, or resembling a salutation.
▸ **saˈlutatorily** *adv*

salute (səˈluːt) *vb* **salutes, saluting, saluted. 1** (*tr*) to address or welcome with friendly words or gestures of respect, such as bowing. **2** (*tr*) to acknowledge with praise: *we salute your gallantry.* **3** *Mil.* to pay formal respect, as by raising the right arm. ◆ *n* **4** the act of saluting. **5** a formal military gesture of respect. ORIG C14: from L *salūtāre* to greet, from *salūs* wellbeing
▸ **saˈluter** *n*

salvable (ˈsælvəbᵊl) *adj* capable of or suitable for being saved or salvaged. ORIG C17: from LL *salvāre* to save, from *salvus* safe

Salvador ★ (ˈsælvəˌdɔː; *Portuguese* salvaˈdor) *n* a port in E Brazil, capital of Bahia state: founded in 1549 as capital of the Portuguese colony, which it remained until 1763; a major centre of the African slave trade in colonial times. Pop.: 2 070 296 (1991). Former name: **Bahia.** Official name: **São Salvador da Bahia de Todos os Santos** (sãu salvaˈdor ˈdəː baˈia ˈdəː ˈtoːduʃ uʃ ˈsəntuʃ).
▸ **ˌSalvaˈdorian** *n, adj*

salvage (ˈsælvɪdʒ) *n* **1** the act, process, or business of rescuing vessels or their cargoes from loss at sea. **2a** the act of saving any goods or property in danger of damage or

destruction. **2b** (*as modifier*): *a salvage operation.* **3** the goods or property so saved. **4** compensation paid for the salvage of a vessel or its cargo. **5** the proceeds from the sale of salvaged goods. ◆ *vb* **salvages, salvaging, salvaged.** (*tr*) **6** to save or rescue (goods or property) from fire, shipwreck, etc. **7** to gain (something beneficial) from a failure. ORIG C17: from OF, from Med. L *salvāgium,* from *salvāre* to SAVE[1]
▸ **'salvageable** *adj* ▸ **'salvager** *n*

salvation (sæl'veɪʃən) *n* **1** the act of preserving or the state of being preserved from harm. **2** a person or thing that is the means of preserving from harm. **3** *Christianity.* deliverance by redemption from the power of sin. ORIG C13: from OF, from LL *salvātiō,* from L *salvātus* saved, from *salvāre* to SAVE[1]

Salvation Army *n* a Christian body founded in 1865 by William Booth and organized on quasi-military lines for evangelism and social work among the poor.

salvationist (sæl'veɪʃənɪst) *n* **1** a member of an evangelical sect emphasizing the doctrine of salvation. **2** (*often cap.*) a member of the Salvation Army.

salve (sælv, sɑːv) *n* **1** an ointment for wounds, etc. **2** anything that heals or soothes. ◆ *vb* **salves, salving, salved.** (*tr*) **3** to apply salve to (a wound, etc.). **4** to soothe, comfort, or appease. ORIG OE *sealf*

salver ('sælvə) *n* a tray, esp. one of silver, on which food, letters, visiting cards, etc., are presented. ORIG C17: from F *salve,* from Sp. *salva* tray from which the king's taster sampled food, from L *salvāre* to SAVE[1]

salvia ('sælvɪə) *n* any of a genus of herbaceous plants or small shrubs, such as the sage, grown for their medicinal or culinary properties or for ornament. ORIG C19: from L: SAGE[2]

salvo ('sælvəʊ) *n, pl* **salvos** *or* **salvoes. 1** a discharge of fire from weapons in unison, esp. on a ceremonial occasion. **2** concentrated fire from many weapons, as in a naval battle. **3** an outburst, as of applause. ORIG C17: from It. *salva,* from OF *salve,* from L *salvē!* greetings!, ult. from *salvus* safe

Salvo ('sælvəʊ) *n, pl* **Salvos.** *Austral. sl.* a member of the Salvation Army.

sal volatile (vɒ'lætɪlɪ) *n* a solution of ammonium carbonate in alcohol and aqueous ammonia, used as smelling salts. Also called: **spirits of ammonia.** ORIG C17: from NL: volatile salt

Salween ★ ('sælwiːn) *n* a river in SW Asia, rising in the Tibetan Plateau and flowing east and south through SW China and Myanmar to the Gulf of Martaban. Length: 2400 km (1500 miles).

Salzburg ★ ('sæltsbɜːg; *German* 'zaltsbʊrk) *n* **1** a city in W Austria, capital of Salzburg province: 7th-century Benedictine abbey; a centre of music since the Middle Ages and birthplace of Mozart; tourist centre. Pop.: 143 978 (1991). **2** a state of W Austria. Pop.: 513 853 (1998 est.). Area: 7154 sq. km (2762 sq. miles).

Salzgitter ★ (*German* zalts'gɪtər) *n* an industrial city in central Germany, in SE Lower Saxony. Pop.: 117 713 (1996 est.).

SAM (sæm) *n acronym for* surface-to-air missile.

Sam. *Bible. abbrev. for* Samuel.

S.Am. *abbrev. for* South America(n).

Samar ★ ('sɑːmə) *n* an island in the E central Philippines, separated from S Luzon by the San Bernardino Strait. Capital: Catbalogan. Pop.: 1 300 000 (latest est.). Area: 13 080 sq. km (5050 sq. miles).

samara (sə'mɑːrə, 'sæmərə) *n* a dry winged one-seeded fruit: occurs in the ash, maple, etc. Also called: **key fruit.** ORIG C16: from NL, from L: seed of an elm

Samara ★ (*Russian* sa'marə) *n* a port in SW Russia, on the River Volga: centre of an important industrial complex; oil refining. Pop.: 1 184 000 (1995 est.). Former name (1935–91): **Kuibyshev** *or* **Kuybyshev.**

Samarang ★ (sə'mɑːrɑːŋ) *n* a variant spelling of **Semarang.**

Samaria ★ (sə'mɛərɪə) *n* **1** the region of ancient Palestine that extended from Judaea to Galilee and from the Mediterranean to the River Jordan; the N kingdom of Israel. **2** the capital of this kingdom; constructed northwest of Shechem in the 9th century B.C.

Samaritan (sə'mærɪtən) *n* **1** a native or inhabitant of Samaria. **2** short for **Good Samaritan. 3** (in the UK) a member of a voluntary organization (**the Samaritans**) that offers counselling to people in despair, esp. by telephone.

samarium (sə'mɛərɪəm) *n* a silvery metallic element of the lanthanide series used in carbon-arc lighting, as a doping agent in laser crystals, and as a neutron-absorber. Symbol: Sm; atomic no.: 62; atomic wt.: 150.35. ORIG C19: from NL, from mineral, *samarskite,* after Col. von *Samarski,* 19th-century Russian inspector of mines + -IUM

Samarkand ★ ('sæmə,kænd; *Russian* səmar'kant) *n* a city in E Uzbekistan: under Tamerlane it became the chief economic and cultural centre of central Asia, on trade routes from China and India (the "silk road"). Pop.: 368 000 (1996). Ancient name: **Maracanda.**

samba ('sæmbə) *n, pl* **sambas. 1** a modern ballroom dance from Brazil in bouncy duple time. **2** a piece of music composed for or in the rhythm of this dance. ◆ *vb* **sambas, sambaing, sambaed. 3** (*intr*) to perform such a dance. ORIG Port., of African origin

sambar *or* **sambur** ('sæmbə) *n, pl* **sambars, sambar** *or* **samburs, sambur.** a S Asian deer with three-tined antlers. ORIG C17: from Hindi, from Sansk. *śambarra,* from ?

Sambre ★ (*French* sɑ̃brə) *n* a river in W Europe, rising in N France and flowing east into Belgium to join the Meuse at Namur. Length: 190 km (118 miles).

Sam Browne belt (,sæm 'braʊn) *n* a military officer's wide belt supported by a strap passing from the left side of the belt over the right shoulder. ORIG C20: after Sir *Samuel J. Browne* (1824–1901), British general, who devised it

same (seɪm) *adj* (usually preceded by *the*) **1** being the very one: *she is wearing the same hat.* **2a** being the one previously referred to. **2b** (*as n*): *a note received about same.* **3a** identical in kind, quantity, etc.: *two girls of the same age.* **3b** (*as n*): *we'd like the same.* **4** unchanged in character or nature: *his attitude is the same as ever.* **5 all the same. 5a** Also: **just the same.** nevertheless; yet. **5b** immaterial: *it's all the same to me.* ◆ *adv* **6** in an identical manner. ORIG C12: from ON *samr*
▸ **'sameness** *n*

> **USAGE NOTE** The use of *same* as in *if you send us your order for the materials, we will deliver same tomorrow* is common in business and official English. In general English, however, this use of the word is best avoided, as it may sound rather stilted: *may I borrow your book? I will return it* (not *same*) *tomorrow.*

samfoo ('sæmfuː) *n* a style of dress worn by Chinese women, consisting of a waisted blouse and trousers. ORIG from Chinese *sam* dress + *foo* trousers

Sami ('sɑːmɪ) *n* **1** (*pl* **Sami** *or* **Samis**) a member of the indigenous people of Lapland. **2** the language of this people, belonging to the Finno-Ugric family. ◆ *adj* **3** of or relating to this people or their language.

> **USAGE NOTE** The indigenous people of Lapland prefer to be called *Sami,* although Lapp is still in widespread use.

Samian ('seɪmɪən) *adj* **1** of or relating to Samos, an island in the Aegean, or its inhabitants. ◆ *n* **2** a native or inhabitant of Samos.

Samian ware *n* a fine earthenware pottery, reddish-brown or black in colour, found in large quantities on Roman sites. ORIG C19: after the island of SAMOS, source of a reddish earth similar to that from which the pottery was made

samisen ('sæmɪ,sen) *n* a Japanese plucked stringed instrument with a long neck and a rectangular soundbox. ORIG Japanese, from Chinese *san-hsien,* from *san* three + *hsien* string

samite ('sæmaɪt) *n* a heavy fabric of silk, often woven with gold or silver threads, used in the Middle Ages. ORIG C13: from OF *samit,* from Med. L *examitum,* from Gk, from *hexamitos* having six threads

samizdat (*Russian* səmiz'dat) *n* (formerly, in the Soviet Union) **a** a system of clandestine printing and distribution of banned literature. **b** (*as modifier*): *a samizdat publication.* ORIG from Russian

Samnium ★ ('sæmnɪəm) *n* an ancient country of central Italy inhabited by Oscan-speaking Samnites: corresponds to the present-day regions of Abruzzi, Molise, and part of Campania.

Samoa ★ (sə'məʊə) *n* an independent state occupying four inhabited islands and five uninhabited islands in the S Pacific archipelago of the Samoa Islands: established as a League of Nations mandate under New Zealand administration in 1920 and a UN trusteeship in 1946; gained independence as Western Samoa in 1962: a member of the Commonwealth: changed its name to Samoa in 1997. Languages: Samoan and English. Religion: Christian. Currency: tala. Capital: Apia. Pop.: 177 000 (1999 est.). Area: 2841 sq. km (1097 sq. miles). Former name (1962–97): **Western Samoa.**
▸ **Sa'moan** *adj, n*

Samoa Islands ★ *pl n* a group of islands in the S Pacific, northeast of Fiji: an independent kingdom until the mid 19th century, when it was divided administratively into **American Samoa** (in the east) and **German Samoa** (in the west); the latter was mandated to New Zealand in 1919 and gained full independence in 1962 as Western Samoa (now called **Samoa**). Area: 3038 sq. km (1173 sq. miles).

Samos ★ ('seɪmɒs) *n* an island in the E Aegean Sea, off the SW coast of Turkey: a leading commercial centre of ancient Greece. Pop.: 41 965 (1991). Area: 492 sq. km (190 sq. miles).

samosa (sə'məʊsə) *n, pl* **samosas** *or* **samosa.** (in Indian cookery) a small, fried, triangular spiced meat or vegetable pasty. ORIG C20: from Hindi

Samothrace ★ ('sæməˌθreɪs) *n* a Greek island in the NE Aegean Sea: mountainous. Pop.: 4000 (latest est.).

samovar ('sæməˌvɑː) *n* (esp. in Russia) a metal urn for making tea, in which the water is usually heated by an inner container. ORIG C19: from Russian, from *samo-* self + *varit'* to boil

Samoyed (ˌsæmə'jɛd) *n* **1** (*pl* **Samoyed** *or* **Samoyeds**) a member of a group of peoples who live chiefly in the area of the N Urals: related to the Finns. **2** the languages of these peoples. **3** (sə'mɔɪɛd) a white or cream breed of dog having a dense coat and a tightly curled tail. ORIG C17: from Russian *Samoed*

samp (sæmp) *n S. African.* crushed maize used for porridge. ORIG from Amerind *nasaump* softened by water

sampan ('sæmpæn) *n* a small skiff, widely used in the Orient, that is propelled by oars. ORIG C17: from Chinese, from *san* three + *pan* board

samphire ('sæmˌfaɪə) *n* **1** an umbelliferous plant of Eurasian coasts, having fleshy divided leaves and clusters of small white flowers. **2 golden samphire.** a Eurasian coastal plant with fleshy leaves and yellow flower heads. **3 marsh samphire.** another name for **glasswort** (sense 1). **4** any of several other plants of coastal areas. ORIG C16 *sampiere,* from F *herbe de Saint Pierre* Saint Peter's herb

sample ('sɑːmpᵊl) *n* **1a** a small part of anything, intended as representative of the whole. **1b** (*as modifier*): *a sample bottle.* **2** Also called: **sampling.** *Statistics.* a set of individuals or items selected from a population and analysed to test hypotheses about or yield estimates of the population. ◆ *vb* **samples, sampling, sampled. 3** (*tr*) to take a sample or samples of. **4** *Music.* **4a** to take a short extract from (one record) and mix it into a different backing track. **4b** to record (a sound) and feed it into a computerized synthesizer so that it can be reproduced at any pitch. ORIG C13: from OF *essample,* from L *exemplum* EXAMPLE

sampler ('sɑːmplə) *n* **1** a person who takes samples. **2** a piece of embroidery done to show the embroiderer's skill in using many different stitches. **3** *Music.* a piece of electronic equipment used for sampling. **4** a recording comprising a collection of tracks from other albums, to stimulate interest in the featured products.

sampling ('sɑːmplɪŋ) *n* **1** the process of selecting a random sample. **2** a variant of **sample** (sense 2). **3** *Music.* the process of taking a short extract from a record and mixing it into a different backing track.

sampling distribution *n Statistics.* the distribution of a random, experimentally obtained sample.

Sampras ★ ('sæmˌpræs) *n* **Pete.** born 1971, US tennis player: US singles champion (1990; 1993; 1995; 1996); Wimbledon singles champion (1993; 1994; 1995; 1997; 1998; 1999; 2000).

Samson ★ ('sæmsən) *n* **1** a judge of Israel, who performed feats of strength until he was betrayed by his mistress Delilah (Judges 13–16). **2** any man of outstanding physical strength.

Samsun ★ (*Turkish* 'samsun) *n* a port in N Turkey, on the Black Sea. Pop.: 326 900 (1994 est.). Ancient name: **Amisus** (ə'miːsəs).

Samuel ★ ('sæmjʊəl) *n Old Testament.* **1** a Hebrew prophet, seer, and judge, who anointed the first two kings of the Israelites (I Samuel 1–3; 8–15). **2** either of the two books named after him, **I** and **II Samuel.**

samurai ('sæmʊˌraɪ) *n, pl* **samurai. 1** the Japanese warrior caste from the 11th to the 19th centuries. **2** a member of this aristocratic caste. ORIG C19: from Japanese

samurai bond *n Finance.* a bond issued in Japan and denominated in yen, available for purchase by nonresidents of Japan. Cf. **shogun bond.**

San ★ (sɑːn) *n* a river in E central Europe, rising in W Ukraine and flowing northwest across SE Poland to the Vistula River. Length: about 450 km (280 miles).

San'a *or* **Sanaa** ★ (sɑː'nɑː) *n* the administrative capital of Yemen, on the central plateau at an altitude of 2350 m (7700 ft). Pop.: 972 000 (1995 est.).

San Antonio ★ (sæn æn'təʊnɪˌəʊ) *n* a city in S Texas: site of the Alamo; the leading town in Texas until about 1930. Pop.: 998 905 (1994 est.).
▸ **San Antonian** *adj, n*

sanative ('sænətɪv) *adj, n* a less common word for **curative.** ORIG C15: from Med. L *sānātīvus,* from L *sānāre* to heal, from *sānus* healthy

sanatorium (ˌsænə'tɔːrɪəm) *or US* **sanitarium** *n, pl* **sanatoriums** *or* **sanatoria** (-rɪə). **1** an institution for the medical care and recuperation of persons who are chronically ill. **2** *Brit.* a room as in a boarding school where sick pupils may receive treatment. ORIG C19: from NL, from L *sānāre* to heal

San Bernardino ★ (sæn ˌbɜːnə'diːnəʊ) *n* a city in SE California: founded in 1851 by Mormons from Salt Lake City. Pop.: 181 718 (1994 est.).

San Bernardino Pass ★ *n* a pass over the Lepontine Alps in SE Switzerland. Highest point: 2062 m (6766 ft).

San Blas ★ ('sɑːn 'blɑːs) *n* **1 Isthmus of.** the narrowest part of the Isthmus of Panama. Width: about 50 km (30 miles). **2 Gulf of.** an inlet of the Caribbean on the N coast of Panama.

San Cristóbal ★ (*Spanish* saŋ kri'stoβal) *n* **1** Also called: **Chatham Island.** an island in the Pacific, in the Galápagos Islands. Area: 505 sq. km (195 sq. miles). **2** a city in SW Venezuela: founded in 1561 by Spanish conquistadores. Pop.: 220 675 (1990).

sanctified ('sæŋktɪˌfaɪd) *adj* **1** consecrated or made holy. **2** sanctimonious.

sanctify ('sæŋktɪˌfaɪ) *vb* **sanctifies, sanctifying, sanctified.** (*tr*) **1** to make holy. **2** to free from sin. **3** to sanction (an action or practice) as religiously binding: *to sanctify a marriage.* **4** to declare or render (something) productive of or conducive to holiness or grace. ORIG C14: from LL *sanctificāre,* from L *sanctus* holy + *facere* to make
▸ **ˌsanctifi'cation** *n* ▸ **'sanctiˌfier** *n*

sanctimonious (ˌsæŋktɪ'məʊnɪəs) *adj* affecting piety or making a display of holiness. ORIG C17: from L *sanctimonia* sanctity, from *sanctus* holy
▸ **ˌsancti'moniously** *adv* ▸ **ˌsancti'moniousness** *or* **'sanctimony** *n*

sanction ('sæŋkʃən) *n* **1** authorization. **2** aid or encour-

★ people and places

agement. **3** something, such as an ethical principle, that imparts binding force to a rule, oath, etc. **4** the penalty laid down in a law for contravention of its provisions. **5** (*often pl*) a coercive measure, esp. one taken by one or more states against another guilty of violating international law. ◆ *vb* (*tr*) **6** to give authority to. **7** to confirm. ORIG C16: from L *sanctiō* the establishment of an inviolable decree, from *sancīre* to decree

sanctitude (ˈsæŋktɪˌtjuːd) *n* saintliness; holiness.

sanctity (ˈsæŋktɪtɪ) *n, pl* **sanctities. 1** the condition of being sanctified; holiness. **2** anything regarded as sanctified or holy. **3** the condition of being inviolable: *the sanctity of marriage.* ORIG C14: from OF *saincteté,* from L *sanctitās,* from *sanctus* holy

sanctuary (ˈsæŋktjʊərɪ) *n, pl* **sanctuaries. 1** a holy place. **2** a consecrated building or shrine. **3** *Old Testament.* **3a** the Israelite temple at Jerusalem. **3b** the tabernacle in which the Ark was enshrined. **4** the chancel, or that part of a sacred building surrounding the main altar. **5a** a sacred building where fugitives were formerly entitled to immunity from arrest or execution. **5b** the immunity so afforded. **6** a place of refuge. **7** a place, protected by law, where animals can live and breed without interference. ORIG C14: from OF *saintuarie,* from LL *sanctuārium* repository for holy things, from L *sanctus* holy

sanctuary lamp *n Christianity.* a lamp, usually red, placed in a prominent position in the sanctuary of a church, which, when lit, indicates the presence of the Blessed Sacrament.

sanctum (ˈsæŋktəm) *n, pl* **sanctums** *or* **sancta** (-tə). **1** a sacred or holy place. **2** a room or place of total privacy. ORIG C16: from L, from *sanctus* holy

sanctum sanctorum (sæŋkˈtɔːrəm) *n* **1** *Bible.* another term for the **holy of holies. 2** *Often facetious.* an especially private place. ORIG C14: from L, lit.: holy of holies, rendering Heb. *qōdesh haqqodāshīm*

Sanctus (ˈsæŋktəs) *n* **1** *Liturgy.* the hymn that occurs immediately after the preface in the celebration of the Eucharist. **2** a musical setting of this. ORIG C14: from the hymn, *Sanctus sanctus sanctus* Holy, holy, holy, from L *sancīre* to consecrate

Sanctus bell *n Chiefly RC Church.* a bell rung as the opening words of the Sanctus are pronounced.

sand (sænd) *n* **1** loose material consisting of rock or mineral grains, esp. rounded grains of quartz. **2** (*often pl*) a sandy area, esp. on the seashore or in a desert. **3a** a greyish-yellow colour. **3b** (*as adj*): *sand upholstery.* **4** the grains of sandlike material in an hourglass. **5** *US inf.* courage. **6 the sands are running out.** there is not much time left before the end. ◆ *vb* **7** (*tr*) to smooth or polish the surface of with sandpaper or sand. **8** (*tr*) to sprinkle or cover with or as if with sand. **9** to fill or cause to fill with sand: *the channel sanded up.* ORIG OE
▸ **ˈsand,like** *adj*

Sand ★ (*French* sɑ̃d) *n* **George** (ʒɔrʒ), pen name of *Amandine Aurore Lucie Dupin.* 1804–76, French novelist, author of such novels as *La Mare au diable* (1846): a champion of women's independence.

Sandage ★ (ˈsændɪdʒ) *n* **Allan Rex.** born 1926, US astronomer, who discovered the first quasar (1961).

Sandakan ★ (sɑːnˈdɑːkɑːn) *n* a port in Malaysia, on the NE coast of Sabah: capital (until 1947) of North Borneo. Pop.: 223 432 (1991).

sandal (ˈsændᵊl) *n* **1** a light shoe consisting of a sole held on the foot by thongs, straps, etc. **2** a strap passing over the instep or around the ankle to keep a low shoe on the foot. **3** another name for **sandalwood.** ORIG C14: from L *sandalium,* from Gk, from *sandalon* sandal
▸ **ˈsandalled** *adj*

sandalwood (ˈsændᵊlˌwʊd) *or* **sandal** *n* **1** any of a genus of evergreen trees, esp. the **white sandalwood,** of S Asia and Australia, having hard light-coloured heartwood. **2** the wood of any of these trees, which is used for carving, is burned as incense, and yields an aromatic oil used in perfumery. **3** any of various similar trees or their wood, esp. a leguminous tree of SE Asia having dark red wood used as a dye. ORIG C14 *sandal,* from Med. L, from LGk *sandanon,* from Sansk. *candana* sandalwood

Sandalwood Island ★ *n* the former name for **Sumba.**

sandarac *or* **sandarach** (ˈsændəˌræk) *n* **1** a pinaceous tree of NW Africa, having hard fragrant dark wood. **2** a brittle pale yellow transparent resin obtained from the bark of this tree and used in making varnish and incense. ORIG C16 *sandaracha,* from L *sandaraca* red pigment, from Gk *sandarakē*

sandbag (ˈsændˌbæg) *n* **1** a sack filled with sand used for protection against gunfire, floodwater, etc., or as ballast in a balloon, etc. **2** a bag filled with sand and used as a weapon. ◆ *vb* **sandbags, sandbagging, sandbagged.** (*tr*) **3** to protect or strengthen with sandbags. **4** to hit with or as if with a sandbag. **5** *Finance.* to obstruct (an unwelcome takeover bid) by having prolonged talks in the hope that a more acceptable bidder will come forward.
▸ **ˈsand,bagger** *n*

sandbank (ˈsændˌbæŋk) *n* a bank of sand in a sea or river, that may be exposed at low tide.

sand bar *n* a ridge of sand in a river or sea, built up by the action of tides, currents, etc., and often exposed at low tide.

sandblast (ˈsændˌblɑːst) *n* **1** a jet of sand blown from a nozzle under air or steam pressure. ◆ *vb* **2** (*tr*) to clean or decorate (a surface) with a sandblast.
▸ **ˈsand,blaster** *n*

sand-blind *adj* not completely blind. Cf. **stone-blind.** ORIG C15: changed (through infl. of SAND) from OE *samblind* (unattested), from *sam-* half, + BLIND
▸ **ˈsand-ˌblindness** *n*

sandbox (ˈsændˌbɒks) *n* **1** a container on a railway locomotive from which sand is released onto the rails to assist the traction. **2** a container of sand for small children to play in.

sandboy (ˈsændˌbɔɪ) *n* **happy** (*or* **jolly**) **as a sandboy.** very happy; high-spirited.

Sandburg ★ (ˈsændbɜːg, ˈsænbɜːg) *n* **Carl.** 1878–1967, US writer, noted for his free verse.

sand castle *n* a mass of sand moulded into a castle-like shape, esp. by a child on the beach.

sand eel *or* **lance** *n* a silvery eel-like marine spiny-finned fish found burrowing in sand or shingle. Popular name: **launce.**

sander (ˈsændə) *n* **1** a power-driven tool for smoothing surfaces by rubbing with an abrasive disc. **2** a person who uses such a device.

sanderling (ˈsændəlɪŋ) *n* a small sandpiper that frequents sandy shores. ORIG C17: ?from SAND + OE *erthling, eorthling* inhabitant of earth

Sanderson ★ (ˈsændəsᵊn) *n* **Tessa.** born 1956, British javelin-thrower.

sand flea *n* another name for the **chigoe** or **sand hopper.**

sandfly (ˈsændˌflaɪ) *n, pl* **sandflies. 1** any of various small mothlike dipterous flies: the bloodsucking females transmit diseases including leishmaniasis. **2** any of various similar flies.

sandgrouse (ˈsændˌgraʊs) *n* a bird of dry regions of the Old World, having very short feet, a short bill, and long pointed wings and tail.

sand hopper *n* any of various small hopping crustaceans, common in intertidal regions of seashores. Also called: **beach flea, sand flea.**

Sandhurst ★ (ˈsændˌhɜːst) *n* a village in S England, in Berkshire: seat of the Royal Military Academy for the training of officer cadets in the British Army. Pop.: 19 153 (1991).

San Diego ★ (ˌsæn dɪˈeɪgəʊ) *n* a port in S California, on the Pacific: naval base; two universities. Pop.: 1 151 977 (1994 est.).

sandman (ˈsændˌmæn) *n, pl* **sandmen.** (in folklore) a magical person supposed to put children to sleep by sprinkling sand in their eyes.

sand martin *n* a small brown European songbird with white underparts: it nests in tunnels bored in sand, river banks, etc.

sandpaper (ˈsændˌpeɪpə) *n* **1** a strong paper coated with sand or other abrasive material for smoothing and polishing. ◆ *vb* **2** (*tr*) to polish or grind (a surface) with or as if with sandpaper.

sandpiper (ˈsænd,paɪpə) *n* **1** any of numerous N hemisphere shore birds having a long slender bill and legs and cryptic plumage. **2** any other bird of the family which includes snipes and woodcocks.

sandpit (ˈsænd,pɪt) *n* **1** a shallow pit or container holding sand for children to play in. **2** a pit from which sand is extracted.

Sandringham ★ (ˈsændrɪŋəm) *n* a village in E England, in Norfolk near the E shore of the Wash: site of **Sandringham House**, a residence of the royal family.

Sandrocottus ★ (,sændrəʊˈkɒtəs) *n* the Greek name of **Chandragupta**.

sandshoe (ˈsænd,ʃuː) *n* a light canvas shoe with a rubber sole.

sandstone (ˈsænd,stəʊn) *n* any of a group of common sedimentary rocks consisting of sand grains consolidated with such materials as quartz, haematite, and clay minerals.

sandstorm (ˈsænd,stɔːm) *n* a strong wind that whips up clouds of sand, esp. in a desert.

sand trap *n* another name (esp. US) for **bunker** (sense 2).

sand viper *n* a S European viper having a yellowish-brown coloration with a zigzag pattern along the back.

Sandwell ★ (ˈsændwɛl) *n* a unitary authority in central England, in the West Midlands. Pop.: 292 200 (1996 est.). Area: 86 sq. km (33 sq. miles).

sandwich (ˈsænwɪdʒ, -wɪtʃ) *n* **1** two or more slices of bread, usually buttered, with a filling of meat, cheese, etc. **2** anything that resembles a sandwich in arrangement. ◆ *vb* (*tr*) **3** to insert tightly between two other things. **4** to put into a sandwich. **5** to place between two dissimilar things. ORIG C18: after 4th Earl of *Sandwich* (1718–92), who ate sandwiches rather than leave the gambling table for meals

sandwich board *n* one of two connected boards that are hung over the shoulders in front of and behind a person to display advertisements.

sandwich course *n* any of several courses consisting of alternate periods of study and industrial work.

Sandwich Islands ★ *pl n* the former name of **Hawaii**.

sandwich man *n* a man who carries sandwich boards.

sandwort (ˈsænd,wɜːt) *n* **1** any of various plants which grow in dense tufts on sandy soil and have white or pink solitary flowers. **2** any of various related plants.

sandy (ˈsændɪ) *adj* **sandier, sandiest. 1** consisting of, containing, or covered with sand. **2** (esp. of hair) reddish-yellow. **3** resembling sand in texture.
▸ **ˈsandiness** *n*

sand yacht *n* a wheeled boat with sails, built to be propelled over sand by the wind.

sandy blight *n Austral. inf.* any inflammation and irritation of the eye.

sane (seɪn) *adj* **1** free from mental disturbance. **2** having or showing reason or sound sense. ORIG C17: from L *sānus* healthy
▸ **ˈsanely** *adv* ▸ **ˈsaneness** *n*

San Fernando ★ (*Spanish* san fɛrˈnando) *n* **1** a port in Trinidad and Tobago, in SW Trinidad, on the Gulf of Paria: the second-largest town in the country. Pop.: 30 100 (1990). **2** an inland port in W Venezuela, on the Apure River. Pop.: 84 179 (1990 est.). Official name: **San Fernando de Apure**. **3** a port in SW Spain, on the Isla de León SE of Cádiz; site of an arsenal (founded 1790) and of the most southerly observatory in Europe. Pop.: 85 191 (1991).

Sanforized *or* **Sanforised** (ˈsænfə,raɪzd) *adj Trademark.* (of a fabric) preshrunk using a patented process.

San Francisco ★ (,sæn frænˈsɪskəʊ) *n* a port in W California, situated around the Golden Gate: developed rapidly during the California gold rush; a major commercial centre and one of the world's finest harbours. Pop.: 734 676 (1994 est.).
▸ **San Franciscan** *n, adj*

San Francisco Bay ★ *n* an inlet of the Pacific in W California, linked with the open sea by the Golden Gate strait. Length: about 80 km (50 miles). Greatest width: 19 km (12 miles).

sang (sæŋ) *vb* the past tense of **sing**.

USAGE NOTE See at **ring**[2].

Sanger ★ (ˈsæŋə) *n* **1 Frederick**. born 1918, British biochemist, who determined the structure of insulin: awarded two Nobel prizes for chemistry (1958; 1980). **2 Margaret (Higgins)**. 1883–1966, US leader of the birth-control movement.

sang-froid (*French* sɑ̃frwa) *n* composure; self-possession. ORIG C18: from F, lit.: cold blood

sangoma (sæŋˈɡəʊmə) *n, pl* **sangomas**. *S. African.* a witch doctor. ORIG from Bantu

Sangraal (sæŋˈɡreɪl), **Sangrail**, *or* **Sangreal** (ˈsæŋɡrɪəl) *n* another name for the **Holy Grail**.

Sangre de Cristo Mountains ★ (ˈsæŋɡrɪ də ˈkrɪstəʊ) *pl n* a mountain range in S Colorado and N New Mexico: part of the Rocky Mountains. Highest peak: Blanca Peak, 4364 m (14 317 ft).

sangria (sæŋˈɡriːə) *n* a Spanish drink of red wine, sugar, and orange or lemon juice, sometimes laced with brandy. ORIG Sp.: a bleeding

sanguinary (ˈsæŋɡwɪnərɪ) *adj* **1** accompanied by much bloodshed. **2** bloodthirsty. **3** consisting of or stained with blood. ORIG C17: from L *sanguinārius*
▸ **ˈsanguinarily** *adv* ▸ **ˈsanguinariness** *n*

sanguine (ˈsæŋɡwɪn) *adj* **1** cheerful and confident; optimistic. **2** (esp. of the complexion) ruddy in appearance. **3** blood-red. ◆ *n* **4** a red pencil containing ferric oxide, used in drawing. ORIG C14: from L *sanguineus* bloody, from *sanguis* blood
▸ **ˈsanguinely** *adv* ▸ **ˈsanguineness** *n*

sanguineous (sæŋˈɡwɪnɪəs) *adj* **1** of, containing, or associated with blood. **2** a less common word for **sanguine**.
▸ **sanˈguineousness** *n*

Sanhedrin (ˈsænɪdrɪn) *n Judaism.* the supreme judicial, ecclesiastical, and administrative council of the Jews in New Testament times. ORIG C16: from LHeb., from Gk *sunedrion* council, from *sun-* SYN- + *hedra* seat

sanies (ˈseɪnɪ,iːz) *n Pathol.* a thin greenish foul-smelling discharge from a wound, ulcer, etc., containing pus and blood. ORIG C16: from L, from ?

San Ildefonso ★ (*Spanish* san ildeˈfɔnso) *n* a town in central Spain, near Segovia: site of the 18th-century summer palace of the kings of Spain. Also called: **La Granja**.

sanitarium (,sænɪˈtɛərɪəm) *n, pl* **sanitariums** *or* **sanitaria** (-rɪə). the US word for **sanatorium**. ORIG C19: from L *sānitās* health

sanitary (ˈsænɪtərɪ) *adj* **1** of or relating to health and measures for the protection of health. **2** free from dirt, germs, etc.; hygienic. ORIG C19: from F *sanitaire*, from L *sānitās* health
▸ **sanitarian** (,sænɪˈtɛərɪən) *n* ▸ **ˈsanitariness** *n*

sanitary engineering *n* the branch of civil engineering associated with the supply of water, disposal of sewage, and other public health services.
▸ **sanitary engineer** *n*

sanitary towel *or esp. US* **napkin** *n* an absorbent pad worn externally by women during menstruation to absorb the menstrual flow.

sanitation (,sænɪˈteɪʃən) *n* the study and use of practical measures for the preservation of public health.

sanitize *or* **sanitise** (ˈsænɪ,taɪz) *vb* **sanitizes, sanitizing, sanitized** *or* **sanitises, sanitising, sanitised.** (*tr*) **1** *Chiefly US & Canad.* to make hygienic, as by sterilizing. **2** to omit unpleasant details from (a news report, document, etc.) to make it more palatable to the recipients.
▸ **,sanitiˈzation** *or* **,sanitiˈsation** *n*

sanity (ˈsænɪtɪ) *n* **1** the state of being sane. **2** good sense or soundness of judgment. ORIG C15: from L *sānitās* health, from *sānus* healthy

San Jose ★ (,sæn həʊˈzeɪ) *n* a city in W central California: a leading world centre of the fruit drying and canning industry. Pop.: 816 884 (1994 est.).

San José ★ (*Spanish* saŋ xo'se) *n* the capital of Costa Rica, on the central plateau: a major centre of coffee production in the mid-19th century; University of Costa Rica (1843). Pop.: 329 154 (1997 est.).

San Juan ★ (*Spanish* saŋ 'xwan) *n* **1** the capital and chief port of Puerto Rico, on the NE coast; University of Puerto Rico; manufacturing centre. Pop.: 433 705 (1996 est.). **2** a city in W Argentina: almost completely destroyed by an earthquake in 1944. Pop.: 352 691 (1991).

San Juan Bautista ★ (*Spanish* saŋ 'xwan bau'tista) *n* the former name of **Villahermosa**.

San Juan Islands ★ (sæn 'wɑːn, 'hwɑːn) *pl n* a group of islands between NW Washington, US, and SE Vancouver Island, Canada: administratively part of Washington.

San Juan Mountains ★ *pl n* a mountain range in SW Colorado and N New Mexico: part of the Rocky Mountains. Highest peak: Uncompahgre Peak, 4363 m (14 314 ft).

sank (sæŋk) *vb* the past tense of **sink**.

Sankey ★ ('sæŋkɪ) *n* **Ira David.** 1840–1908, US evangelist and hymnodist.

Sankt Pölten ★ (*German* zaŋkt 'pœltən) *n, usually abbreviated to* **St Pölten.** a city in NE Austria, the capital of Lower Austria. Pop.: 50 026 (1991).

San Luis Potosí ★ (*Spanish* san 'lwis poto'si) *n* **1** a state of central Mexico: mainly high plateau; economy based on mining (esp. silver) and agriculture. Capital: San Luis Potosí. Pop.: 2 247 042 (1997 est.). Area: 62 849 sq. km (24 266 sq. miles). **2** an industrial city in central Mexico, capital of San Luis Potosí state, at an altitude of 1850 m (6000 ft). Pop.: 488 238 (1990).

San Marino ★ (ˌsæn mə'riːnəʊ) *n* a republic in S central Europe in the Apennines, forming an enclave in Italy: the smallest republic in Europe, according to tradition founded by St Marinus in the 4th century. Official language: Italian. Religion: Roman Catholic. Currency: lira. Capital: San Marino. Pop.: 26 500 (1999 est.). Area: 62 sq. km (24 sq. miles).
▸ **San Marinese** (ˌsæn ˌmærɪ'niːz) *or* **Sammarinese** (səˌmærɪ'niːz) *adj, n*

San Martín ★ (*Spanish* san mar'tin) *n* **José de** (xo'se de). 1778–1850, South American patriot, who played an important part in gaining independence for Argentina, Chile, and Peru. He was protector of Peru (1821–22).

Sanmicheli ★ (*Italian* sanmi'kɛːli) *n* **Michele** (mi'kɛːle). ?1484–1559, Italian mannerist architect.

San Pedro Sula ★ (*Spanish* san 'peðro 'sula) *n* a city in NW Honduras: the country's chief industrial centre. Pop.: 383 900 (1995 est.).

San Remo ★ (*Italian* san 'rɛːmo) *n* a port and resort in NW Italy, in Liguria on the slopes of the Maritime Alps; flower market. Pop.: 60 800 (1995 est.).

sans (sænz) *prep* an archaic word for **without.** ORIG C13: from OF *sanz,* from L *sine* without, but prob. also infl. by L *absentiā* in the absence of

Sans. *or* **Sansk.** *abbrev. for* Sanskrit.

San Salvador ★ (sæn 'sælvəˌdɔː; *Spanish* san salβa'ðor) *n* the capital of El Salvador, situated in the SW central part: became capital in 1841; ruined by earthquakes in 1854 and 1873; university (1841). Pop.: 422 570 (1992).

San Salvador Island ★ *n* an island in the central Bahamas: the first land in the New World seen by Christopher Columbus (1492). Area: 156 sq. km (60 sq. miles). Also called: **Watling Island.**

sans-culotte (ˌsænzkjʊ'lɒt) *n* **1** (during the French Revolution) **1a** (originally) a revolutionary of the poorer class. **1b** (later) any revolutionary. **2** any revolutionary extremist. ORIG C18: from F, lit.: without knee breeches, because the revolutionaries wore pantaloons or trousers rather than knee breeches

San Sebastián ★ (ˌsæn sə'bæstjən; *Spanish* san seβas'tjan) *n* a port and resort in N Spain on the Bay of Biscay: former summer residence of the Spanish court. Pop.: 169 933 (1991).

sansevieria (ˌsænsɪ'vɪərɪə) *n* any of a genus of herbaceous perennial plants of Old World tropical regions: some are cultivated as house plants for their bayonet-like leaves; others yield a useful fibre. ORIG NL, after Raimondo di Sangro (1710–71), It. scholar and prince of *San Severo*

Sanskrit ('sænskrɪt) *n* an ancient language of India. It is the oldest recorded member of the Indic branch of the Indo-European family of languages. Although it is used only for religious purposes, it is one of the official languages of India. ORIG C17: from Sansk. *samskrta* perfected, lit.: put together
▸ **San'skritic** *adj*

sans serif *or* **sanserif** (sæn'sɛrɪf) *n* a style of printer's typeface in which the characters have no serifs.

San Stefano ★ (ˌsæn stɪ'fɑːnəʊ) *n* a village in NW Turkey, near Istanbul on the Sea of Marmara: scene of the signing (1878) of the treaty ending the Russo-Turkish War. Turkish name: **Yeşilköy.**

Santa ★ ('sæntə) *n Inf.* short for **Santa Claus.**

Santa Ana ★ *n* **1** (*Spanish* 'santa 'ana). a city in NW El Salvador: the second largest city in the country; coffee-processing industry. Pop.: 202 337 (1992). **2** ('sæntə 'ænə). a city in SW California: commercial and processing centre of a rich agricultural region. Pop.: 290 827 (1994 est.).

Santa Anna *or* **Santa Ana** ★ (*Spanish* 'santa 'ana) *n* **Antonio López de** (a'tonjo 'lopeθ de). ?1795–1876, Mexican general, revolutionary, and president (1833–36, 1841–?45, 1847–48, 1853–55).

Santa Catalina ★ ('sæntə ˌkætᵊ'liːnə) *n* an island in the Pacific, off the coast of SW California: part of Los Angeles county: resort. Area: 181 sq. km (70 sq. miles). Also called: **Catalina Island.**

Santa Catarina ★ (*Portuguese* 'santə kətə'rinə) *n* a state of S Brazil, on the Atlantic: consists chiefly of the Great Escarpment. Capital: Florianópolis. Pop.: 4 875 244 (1996). Area: 95 985 sq. km (37 060 sq. miles).

Santa Clara ★ (*Spanish* 'santa 'klara) *n* a city in W central Cuba: sugar and tobacco industries. Pop.: 205 400 (1994 est.).

Santa Claus ★ ('sæntə ˌklɔːz) *n* the legendary patron saint of children, commonly identified with Saint Nicholas. Often shortened to **Santa.** Also called: **Father Christmas.**

Santa Cruz ★ ('sæntə 'kruːz; *Spanish* 'santa 'kruθ) *n* **1** a province of S Argentina, on the Atlantic: consists of a large part of Patagonia, with the forested foothills of the Andes in the west. Capital: Río Gallegos. Pop.: 180 115 (1995 est.). Area: 243 940 sq. km (94 186 sq. miles). **2** a city in E Bolivia: the second largest town in Bolivia. Pop.: 767 260 (1993 est.). **3** another name for **Saint Croix.**

Santa Cruz de Tenerife ★ ('sæntə 'kruːz də ˌtɛnə'riːf; *Spanish* 'santa 'kruθ de tene'rife) *n* a port and resort in the W Canary Islands, on NE Tenerife: oil refinery. Pop.: 211 389 (1986).

Santa Fe ★ *n* **1** ('sæntə 'feɪ). a city in N central New Mexico, capital of the state: one of the oldest European settlements in North America, founded in 1610 as the capital of the Kingdom of New Mexico; developed trade with the US by the Santa Fe Trail in the early 19th century. Pop.: 62 514 (1994 est.). **2** (*Spanish* 'santa 'fe). an inland port in E Argentina, on the Salado River: University of the Littoral (1920). Pop.: 406 388 (1991).
▸ **'Santa 'Fean** *adj, n*

Santa Gertrudis ('sæntə gə'truːdɪs) *n* one of a breed of red beef cattle developed in Texas.

Santa Isabel ★ (*Spanish* 'santa isa'βel) *n* the former name (until 1973) of **Malabo.**

Santa Maria ★ *n* **1** (*Portuguese* 'səntə ma'ria) a city in S Brazil, in Rio Grande do Sul state. Pop.: 193 294 (1991). **2** (*Spanish* 'santa ma'ria) an active volcano in SW Guatemala. Height: 3768 m (12 362 ft).

Santa Marta ★ (*Spanish* 'santa 'marta) *n* a port in NW Colombia, on the Caribbean: the oldest city in Colombia, founded in 1525; terminus of the Atlantic railway from Bogotá (opened 1961). Pop.: 309 372 (1995 est.).

Santa Maura ★ ('santa 'maura) *n* the Italian name for **Levkás.**

Santander ★ (*Spanish* santan'dɛr) *n* a port and resort in N Spain, on an inlet of the Bay of Biscay: noted for its prehistoric collection from nearby caves; shipyards and an oil refinery. Pop.: 194 822 (1994 est.).

Santarém ★ (*Portuguese* sənta'rə̃j) *n* a port in N Brazil, in Pará state where the Tapajós River flows into the Amazon. Pop.: 168 153 (1991).

Santa Rosa de Copán ★ (*Spanish* 'santa 'rɔsa de ko'pan) *n* a village in W Honduras: noted for the ruined Mayan city of Copán, which lies to the west.

Santayana ★ (ˌsæntɪ'ænə) *n* **George.** 1863–1952, US philosopher, poet, and critic, born in Spain. His works include *The Life of Reason* (1905–06) and *The Realms of Being* (1927–40).

Santee ★ (sæn'tiː) *n* a river in SE central South Carolina, formed by the union of the Congaree and Wateree Rivers: flows southeast to the Atlantic; part of the **Santee-Wateree-Catawba River System,** an inland waterway 866 km (538 miles) long. Length: 230 km (143 miles).

Santer ★ ('sæntə) *n* **Jacques.** born 1937, Luxembourg politician; prime minister of Luxembourg (1984–95); president of the European Commission (1994–99).

Santiago ★ (ˌsæntɪ'ɑːgəʊ; *Spanish* san'tjaɣo) *n* **1** the capital of Chile, at the foot of the Andes: commercial and industrial centre; two universities. Pop.: 5 076 808 (1995 est.). Official name: **Santiago de Chile** (de 'tʃile). **2** a city in the N Dominican Republic. Pop.: 364 859 (1993). Official name: **Santiago de los Caballeros** (de los kaβa'ʎeros).

Santiago de Compostela ★ (*Spanish* de kɔmpɔs'tela) *n* a city in NW Spain: place of pilgrimage since the 9th century and the most visited (after Jerusalem and Rome) in the Middle Ages; cathedral built over the tomb of the apostle St James. Pop.: 87 472 (1991). Latin name: **Campus Stellae** ('kæmpəs 'stɛliː).

Santiago de Cuba ★ (*Spanish* de 'kuβa) *n* a port in SE Cuba, on **Santiago Bay** (a large inlet of the Caribbean): capital of Cuba until 1589; university (1947); industrial centre. Pop.: 440 084 (1994 est.).

Santiago del Estero ★ (*Spanish* del es'tero) *n* a city in N Argentina: the oldest continuous settlement in Argentina, founded in 1553 by Spaniards from Peru. Pop.: 263 471 (1991).

Santo Domingo ★ ('sæntəʊ də'mɪŋgəʊ; *Spanish* 'santo ðo'miŋgo) *n* **1** the capital and chief port of the Dominican Republic, on the S coast: the oldest continuous European settlement in the Americas, founded in 1496; university (1538). Pop. (capital district): 2 138 262 (1993). Former name (1936–61): **Ciudad Trujillo. 2** the former name (until 1844) of the **Dominican Republic. 3** another name (esp. in colonial times) for **Hispaniola.**

santonica (sæn'tɒnɪkə) *n* **1** an oriental wormwood plant. **2** the dried flower heads of this plant, formerly used as a vermifuge. ◆ Also called: **wormseed.** ORIG C17: NL, from LL *herba santonica* herb of the *Santones* (prob. wormwood), from L *Santonī* a people of Aquitania

santonin ('sæntənɪn) *n* a white crystalline soluble substance extracted from the dried flower heads of santonica and used in medicine as an anthelmintic. ORIG C19: from SANTONICA + -IN

Santos ★ (*Portuguese* 'səntuʃ) *n* a port in S Brazil, in São Paulo state: the world's leading coffee port. Pop.: 415 554 (1991).

São Francisco ★ (*Portuguese* sə̃u frə̃'sisku) *n* a river in E Brazil, rising in SW Minas Gerais state and flowing northeast, then southeast to the Atlantic northeast of Aracajú. Length: 3200 km (1990 miles).

São Luís (*Portuguese* sə̃u 'lwis) *or* **São Luíz** ★ ('lwiʃ) *n* a port in NE Brazil, capital of Maranhão state, on the W coast of São Luís Island: founded in 1612 by the French and taken by the Portuguese in 1615. Pop.: 164 334 (1991).

São Miguel ★ (*Portuguese* sə̃u mi'ɣɛl) *n* an island in the E Azores: the largest of the group. Pop.: 126 388 (1991 est.). Area: 854 sq. km (333 sq. miles).

Saône ★ (*French* son) *n* a river in E France, rising in Lorraine and flowing generally south to join the Rhône at Lyon, as its chief tributary: canalized for 375 km (233 miles) above Lyon; linked by canals with the Rhine, Marne, Seine, and Loire Rivers. Length: 480 km (298 miles).

Saône-et-Loire ★ (*French* sonelwar) *n* a department of central France, in Burgundy region. Capital: Mâcon. Pop.: 555 348 (1994 est.). Area: 8627 sq. km (3365 sq. miles).

São Paulo ★ (*Portuguese* sə̃u 'paulu) *n* **1** a state of SE Brazil: consists chiefly of tableland draining west into the Paraná River. Capital: São Paulo. Pop.: 34 119 110 (1996). Area: 247 239 sq. km (95 459 sq. miles). **2** a city in S Brazil, capital of São Paulo state: the largest city and industrial centre in Brazil, with one of the busiest airports in the world; three universities; rapidly expanding population. Pop.: 25 000 (1874); 2 017 025 (1950); 9 393 753 (1991).

Saorstat Eireann ★ ('sɛəstɑːt 'ɛərən) *n* the Gaelic name for the **Irish Free State.**

São Salvador ★ (*Portuguese* sə̃u salva'dor) *n* short for **São Salvador da Bahia de Todos os Santos,** the official name for **Salvador.**

São Tomé e Principe ★ (*Portuguese* sə̃u tu'mɛ 'ɛː 'prĩːsipə) *n* a republic in the Gulf of Guinea, off the W coast of Africa, on the Equator: consists of the islands of Principe and São Tomé; colonized by the Portuguese in the late 15th century; became independent in 1975. Official language: Portuguese. Religion: Roman Catholic majority. Currency: dobra. Capital: São Tomé. Pop.: 140 000 (1999 est.). Area: 1001 sq. km (386 sq. miles).

sap[1] (sæp) *n* **1** a solution of mineral salts, sugars, etc., that circulates in a plant. **2** any vital body fluid. **3** energy; vigour. **4** *Sl.* a gullible person. **5** another name for **sapwood.** ◆ *vb* **saps, sapping, sapped.** (*tr*) **6** to drain of sap. ORIG OE *sæp*

sap[2] (sæp) *n* **1** a deep and narrow trench used to approach or undermine an enemy position. ◆ *vb* **saps, sapping, sapped. 2** to undermine (a fortification, etc.) by digging saps. **3** (*tr*) to weaken. ORIG C16 *zappe,* from It. *zappa* spade, from ?

sapele (sə'piːlɪ) *n* **1** any of various W African trees yielding a hard timber resembling mahogany. **2** the timber of such a tree, used to make furniture. ORIG C20: West African name

sapid ('sæpɪd) *adj* **1** having a pleasant taste. **2** agreeable or engaging. ORIG C17: from L *sapidus,* from *sapere* to taste
▸ **sapidity** (sə'pɪdɪtɪ) *n*

sapient ('seɪpɪənt) *adj Often used ironically.* wise or sagacious. ORIG C15: from L *sapere* to taste
▸ **'sapience** *n* ▸ **'sapiently** *adv*

sapiential (ˌseɪpɪ'ɛnʃəl) *adj* showing, having, or providing wisdom.

sapling ('sæplɪŋ) *n* **1** a young tree. **2** *Literary.* a youth.

sapodilla (ˌsæpə'dɪlə) *n* **1** a large tropical American evergreen tree, the latex of which yields chicle. **2** Also called: **sapodilla plum.** the edible brown rough-skinned fruit of this tree. ORIG C17: from Sp. *zapotillo,* dim. of *zapote* sapodilla fruit, from Nahuatl *tsapotl*

saponaceous (ˌsæpəʊ'neɪʃəs) *adj* resembling soap. ORIG C18: from NL, from L *sāpō* soap

saponify (sə'pɒnɪˌfaɪ) *vb* **saponifies, saponifying, saponified.** *Chem.* **1** to undergo or cause to undergo a process in which a fat is converted into a soap by treatment with alkali. **2** to undergo or cause to undergo a reaction in which an ester is hydrolysed to an acid and an alcohol as a result of treatment with an alkali. ORIG C19: from F *saponifier,* from L *sāpō* soap
▸ **saˌponifi'cation** *n*

saponin ('sæpənɪn) *n* any of a group of plant glycosides with a steroid structure that foam when shaken and are used in detergents. ORIG C19: from F *saponine,* from L *sāpō* soap

sappanwood *or* **sapanwood** ('sæpənˌwʊd) *n* **1** a small tree of S Asia producing wood that yields a red dye.

2 the wood of this tree. ORIG C16: *sapan,* via Du. from Malay *sapang*

sapper ('sæpə) *n* **1** a soldier who digs trenches, etc. **2** (in the British Army) a private of the Royal Engineers.

Sapper ★ ('sæpə) *n* real name *Herman Cyril McNeile.* 1888–1937, British novelist, author of the popular thriller *Bulldog Drummond* (1920) and its sequels.

Sapphic ('sæfɪk) *adj* **1** *Prosody.* denoting a metre associated with Sappho. **2** of or relating to Sappho or her poetry. **3** lesbian. ◆ *n* **4** *Prosody.* a verse, line, or stanza written in the Sapphic form of classical lyric poetry.

Sapphira ★ (sæ'faɪrə) *n New Testament.* the wife of Ananias, who together with her husband was struck dead for fraudulently concealing their wealth from the Church (Acts 5).

sapphire ('sæfaɪə) *n* **1a** any precious corundum gemstone that is not red, esp. the highly valued transparent blue variety. **1b** (*as modifier*): *a sapphire ring.* **2a** the blue colour of sapphire. **2b** (*as adj*): *sapphire eyes.* **3** (*modifier*) denoting a forty-fifth anniversary: *our sapphire wedding.* ORIG C13 *safir,* from OF, from L *sapphīrus,* from Gk *sappheiros,* ?from Sansk. *śanipriya,* lit.: beloved of the planet Saturn

Sappho ★ ('sæfəʊ) *n* 6th century B.C., Greek lyric poetess of Lesbos.

Sapporo ★ ('sɑːpəʊˌrəʊ) *n* a city in N Japan, on W Hokkaido: commercial centre; university (1918). Pop.: 1 756 968 (1995).

sappy ('sæpɪ) *adj* **sappier, sappiest. 1** (of plants) full of sap. **2** full of energy or vitality.

sapro- *or before a vowel* **sapr-** *combining form.* indicating dead or decaying matter: *saprogenic.* ORIG from Gk *sapros* rotten

saprogenic (ˌsæprəʊ'dʒɛnɪk) *or* **saprogenous** (sæ'prɒdʒɪnəs) *adj* **1** producing or resulting from decay. **2** growing on decaying matter.

saprophyte ('sæprəʊˌfaɪt) *n* any plant that lives and feeds on dead organic matter.
▸ **saprophytic** (ˌsæprəʊ'fɪtɪk) *adj*

saprotroph ('sæprəʊtrəʊf) *n* any organism, esp. a fungus or bacterium, that lives and feeds on dead organic matter. Also called: **saprobe, saprobiont.**
▸ **saprotrophic** (ˌsæprəʊ'trəʊfɪk) *adj* ▸ **ˌsapro'trophically** *adv*

saprozoic (ˌsæprəʊ'zəʊɪk) *adj* (of animals or plants) feeding on dead organic matter.

sapsucker ('sæpˌsʌkə) *n* either of two North American woodpeckers that have white wing patches and feed on the sap from trees.

sapwood ('sæpˌwʊd) *n* the soft wood, just beneath the bark in tree trunks, that consists of living tissue.

Sar. *abbrev. for* Sardinia(n).

sarabande *or* **saraband** ★ ('særəˌbænd) *n* **1** a decorous 17th-century courtly dance. **2** a piece of music composed for or in the rhythm of this dance, in slow triple time. ORIG C17: from F *sarabande,* from Sp. *zarabanda,* from ?

Saracen ('særəsᵊn) *n* **1** *History.* a member of one of the nomadic Arabic tribes, esp. of the Syrian desert. **2a** a Muslim, esp. one who opposed the crusades. **2b** (in later use) any Arab. ◆ *adj* **3** of or relating to Arabs of either of these periods, regions, or types. ORIG C13: from OF *Sarrazin,* from LL *Saracēnus,* from LGk *Sarakēnos,* ?from Ar. *sharq* sunrise
▸ **Saracenic** (ˌsærə'sɛnɪk) *adj*

Saragossa ★ (ˌsærə'gɒsə) *n* the English name for **Zaragoza.**

Sarah ★ ('sɛərə) *n Old Testament.* the wife of Abraham and mother of Isaac (Genesis 17:15–22).

Sarajevo (ˌsærə'jeɪvəʊ; *Serbo-Croat* 'sarajɛvɔ) *or* **Serajevo** ★ *n* the capital of Bosnia-Herzegovina: developed as a Turkish town in the 15th century; capital of the Turkish and Austro-Hungarian administrations in 1850 and 1878 respectively; scene of the assassination of Archduke Franz Ferdinand in 1914, precipitating World War I; besieged by Bosnian Serbs (1992–95). Pop.: 525 980 (1991).

Saransk ★ (*Russian* sa'ransk) *n* a city in W central Russia, capital of the Mordovian Republic: university (1957). Pop.: 320 000 (1995 est.).

Saratov ★ (*Russian* sa'ratəf) *n* an industrial city in W Russia, on the River Volga: university (1919). Pop.: 895 000 (1995 est.).

Sarawak ★ (sə'rɑːwək) *n* a state of Malaysia, on the NW coast of Borneo on the South China Sea: granted to Sir James Brooke by the Sultan of Brunei in 1841 as a reward for helping quell a revolt; mainly agricultural. Capital: Kuching. Pop.: 1 642 771 (1991). Area: about 121 400 sq. km (48 250 sq. miles).

sarcasm ('sɑːkæzəm) *n* **1** mocking or ironic language intended to convey scorn or insult. **2** the use or tone of such language. ORIG C16: from LL *sarcasmus,* from Gk, from *sarkazein* to rend the flesh, from *sarx* flesh

sarcastic (sɑː'kæstɪk) *adj* **1** characterized by sarcasm. **2** given to the use of sarcasm.
▸ **sar'castically** *adv*

sarcenet *or* **sarsenet** ('sɑːsnɪt) *n* a fine soft silk fabric used for clothing, ribbons, etc. ORIG C15: from OF *sarzinet,* from *Sarrazin* SARACEN

sarco- *or before a vowel* **sarc-** *combining form.* indicating flesh: *sarcoma.* ORIG from Gk *sark-, sarx* flesh

sarcocarp ('sɑːkəʊˌkɑːp) *n Bot.* the fleshy mesocarp of such fruits as the peach or plum.

sarcoma (sɑː'kəʊmə) *n, pl* **sarcomata** (-mətə) *or* **sarcomas.** *Pathol.* a usually malignant tumour arising from connective tissue. ORIG C17: via NL from Gk *sarkōma* fleshy growth
▸ **sar'comatous** *adj*

sarcomatosis (sɑːˌkəʊmə'təʊsɪs) *n Pathol.* a condition characterized by the development of several sarcomas at various bodily sites. ORIG C19: see SARCOMA, -OSIS

sarcophagus (sɑː'kɒfəgəs) *n, pl* **sarcophagi** (-ˌgaɪ) *or* **sarcophaguses.** a stone or marble coffin or tomb, esp. one bearing sculpture or inscriptions. ORIG C17: via L from Gk *sarkophagos* flesh-devouring; from the type of stone used, which was believed to destroy the flesh of corpses

sarcoplasm ('sɑːkəʊˌplæzəm) *n* the cytoplasm of a muscle fibre.
▸ **ˌsarco'plasmic** *adj*

sarcous ('sɑːkəs) *adj* (of tissue) muscular or fleshy. ORIG C19: from Gk *sarx* flesh

sard (sɑːd) *or* **sardius** ('sɑːdɪəs) *n* an orange, red, or brown variety of chalcedony, used as a gemstone. Also called: **sardine.** ORIG C14: from L *sarda,* from Gk *sardios* stone from Sardis

sardar *or* **sirdar** (sə'dɑː) *n* (in India) **1** a title used before the name of Sikh men. **2** a leader. ORIG Hindi, from Persian

Sardegna ★ (sar'deɲɲa) *n* the Italian name for **Sardinia.**

sardine[1] (sɑː'diːn) *n, pl* **sardines** *or* **sardine. 1** any of various small food fishes of the herring family, esp. a young pilchard. **2 like sardines.** very closely crowded together. ORIG C15: via OF from L *sardīna,* dim. of *sarda* a fish suitable for pickling

sardine[2] ('sɑːdiːn) *n* another name for **sard.** ORIG C14: from LL *sardinus,* from Gk *sardinos lithos* Sardian stone, from *Sardeis* Sardis

Sardinia ★ (sɑː'dɪnɪə) *n* the second largest island in the Mediterranean: forms, with offshore islands, an administrative region of Italy; ceded to Savoy by Austria in 1720 in exchange for Sicily and formed the Kingdom of Sardinia with Piedmont; became part of Italy in 1861. Capital: Cagliari. Pop.: 1 660 701 (1996 est.). Area: 24 089 sq. km (9301 sq. miles). Italian name: **Sardegna.**

Sardinian (sɑː'dɪnɪən) *adj* **1** of or relating to Sardinia, its inhabitants, or their language. ◆ *n* **2** a native or inhabitant of Sardinia. **3** the spoken language of Sardinia, sometimes regarded as a dialect of Italian but containing many loan words from Spanish.

Sardis ('sɑːdɪs) *or* **Sardes** ★ ('sɑːdiːz) *n* an ancient city of W Asia Minor: capital of Lydia.

sardonic (sɑː'dɒnɪk) *adj* characterized by irony, mockery, or derision. ORIG C17: from F, from L, from Gk

sardonios derisive, lit.: of Sardinia, alteration of Homeric *sardanios* scornful (laughter or smile)
▸ **sar'donically** *adv* ▸ **sar'donicism** *n*

sardonyx ('sɑːdənɪks) *n* a variety of chalcedony with alternating reddish-brown and white parallel bands. ORIG C14: via L from Gk *sardonux,* ?from *sardion* SARD + *onux* nail

Sardou ★ (*French* sardu) *n* **Victorien** (viktɔrjɛ̃). 1831–1908, French dramatist. His plays include *La Tosca* (1887), the source of Puccini's opera.

Sargasso Sea ★ *n* a calm area of the N Atlantic, between the Caribbean and the Azores, where there is an abundance of sargassum.

sargassum (sɑː'gæsəm) *n* a floating brown seaweed having ribbon-like fronds containing air sacs, esp. abundant in the Sargasso Sea. ORIG C16: from Port. *sargaço* from ?

sarge (sɑːdʒ) *n Inf.* sergeant.

Sargent ★ ('sɑːdʒənt) *n* **1** Sir **(Harold) Malcolm (Watts)**. 1895–1967, British conductor. **2 John Singer.** 1856–1925, US painter; in London from 1885.

Sargeson ★ ('sɑːdʒəsᵊn) *n* **Frank.** 1903–82, New Zealand writer. His work includes the collection *That Summer and Other Stories* (1946).

Sargodha ★ (sɑː'gəʊdə) *n* a city in NE Pakistan: grain market. Pop.: 294 000 (latest est.).

Sargon II ★ ('sɑːgɒn) *n* died 705 B.C., king of Assyria (722–705).

sari *or* **saree** ('sɑːrɪ) *n, pl* **saris** *or* **sarees.** the traditional dress of women of India, Pakistan, etc., consisting of a very long piece of cloth swathed around the body. ORIG C18: from Hindi *sārī,* from Sansk. *śāṭī*

Sark ★ (sɑːk) *n* an island in the English Channel in the Channel Islands, consisting of **Great Sark** and **Little Sark,** connected by an isthmus: ruled by a hereditary seigneur or dame. Pop.: 550 (1986 est.). Area: 5 sq. km (2 sq. miles). French name: **Sercq.**

Sarka ★ ('zɑːkə) *n* a variant spelling of **Zarqa.**

sarking ('sɑːkɪŋ) *n Scot., northern English, & NZ.* flat planking supporting the roof cladding of a building. ORIG C15 in England: from Scot. *sark* shirt

sarky ('sɑːkɪ) *adj* **sarkier, sarkiest.** *Brit. inf.* sarcastic.

Sarmatia ★ (sɑː'meɪʃɪə) *n* the ancient name of a region of present-day Poland, Belarus, and SW Russia, between the Volga and Vistula Rivers.
▸ **Sar'matian** *n, adj* ▸ **Sarmatic** (sɑː'mætɪk) *adj*

sarmentose (sɑː'mɛntəʊs) *or* **sarmentous** (sɑː'mɛntəs) *adj* (of plants such as the strawberry) having stems in the form of runners. ORIG C18: from L *sarmentōsus* full of twigs, from *sarmentum* brushwood, from *sarpere* to prune

sarmie ('sɑːmɪ) *n S. African children's sl.* a sandwich. ORIG C20: from SARNIE

Sarnen ★ (*German* 'zarnən) *n* a town in central Switzerland, capital of Obwalden demicanton: resort. Pop.: 7200 (1980).

Sarnia ★ ('sɑːnɪə) *n* an inland port in S central Canada, in SW Ontario at the S end of Lake Huron: oil refineries. Pop.: 74 376 (1991).

sarnie ('sɑːnɪ) *n Brit. inf.* a sandwich. ORIG C20: prob. from N or dialect pronunciation of first syllable of *sandwich*

sarod (sæ'rəʊd) *n* an Indian stringed musical instrument that may be played with a bow or plucked. ORIG C19: from Hindi

sarong (sə'rɒŋ) *n* **1** a garment worn by men and women in the Malay Archipelago, Sri Lanka, etc., consisting of a long piece of cloth tucked around the waist or under the armpits. **2** a western adaptation of this garment, worn by women as beachwear. ORIG C19: from Malay, lit.: sheath

Saronic Gulf ★ (sə'rɒnɪk) *n* an inlet of the Aegean on the SE coast of Greece. Length: about 80 km (50 miles). Width: about 48 km (30 miles). Also called: (Gulf of) **Aegina.**

saros ('seɪrɒs) *n* a cycle of about 18 years 11 days (6585.32 days) in which eclipses of the sun and moon occur in the same sequence. ORIG C19: from Gk, from Babylonian *šāru* 3600 (years); modern use apparently based on mistaken interpretation of *šāru* as a period of 18½ years

Saros ★ ('sɑːrɒs) *n* **Gulf of.** an inlet of the Aegean in NW Turkey, north of the Gallipoli Peninsula. Length: 59 km (37 miles). Width: 35 km (22 miles).

Sarpedon ★ (sɑː'piːdɒn) *n Greek myth.* a son of Zeus and Laodameia, or perhaps Europa, and king of Lycia. He was slain by Patroclus while fighting on behalf of the Trojans.

Sarraute ★ (*French* sarot) *n* **Nathalie** (natali). 1900–99, French novelist, noted for *Portrait of a Man Unknown* (1947): later works include *Ici* (1995).

Sarre ★ (sar) *n* the French name for the **Saar.**

sarrusophone (sə'ruːzəˌfəʊn) *n* a wind instrument resembling the oboe but made of brass. ORIG C19: after *Sarrus,* F bandmaster, who invented it (1856)

sarsaparilla (ˌsɑːsəpə'rɪlə) *n* **1** any of a genus of tropical American prickly climbing plants having large aromatic roots and heart-shaped leaves. **2** the dried roots of any of these plants, formerly used as a medicine. **3** a nonalcoholic drink prepared from these roots. ORIG C16: from Sp. *sarzaparrilla,* from *zarza* a bramble + *-parrilla,* from *parra* a climbing plant

sarsen ('sɑːsᵊn) *n* **1** *Geol.* a boulder of silicified sandstone, probably of Tertiary age. **2** such a stone used in a megalithic monument. ◆ Also called: **greywether.** ORIG C17: prob. a var. of SARACEN

sarsenet ('sɑːsnɪt) *n* a variant spelling of **sarcenet.**

Sarthe ★ (*French* sart) *n* a department of NW France, in Pays de la Loire region. Capital: Le Mans. Pop.: 520 615 (1994 est.). Area: 6245 sq. km (2436 sq. miles).

Sarto ★ (*Italian* 'sarto) *n* **Andrea del** (an'drɛːa del). 1486–1531, Florentine painter. His works include *The Nativity of the Virgin* (1514).

sartorial (sɑː'tɔːrɪəl) *adj* **1** of or relating to a tailor or to tailoring. **2** *Anat.* of the sartorius. ORIG C19: from LL *sartōrius* from L *sartor* a patcher, from *sarcīre* to patch
▸ **sar'torially** *adv*

sartorius (sɑː'tɔːrɪəs) *n, pl* **sartorii** (-'tɔːrɪˌaɪ). *Anat.* a long ribbon-shaped muscle that aids in flexing the knee. ORIG C18: NL, from *sartorius musculus,* lit.: tailor's muscle, because it is used when one sits in the cross-legged position in which tailors traditionally sat while sewing

Sartre ★ (*French* sartrə) *n* **Jean-Paul** (ʒɑ̃pɔl). 1905–80, French philosopher, novelist, and dramatist; exponent of existentialism. His works include the essay *Being and Nothingness* (1943), the novel *Nausea* (1938), and the play *Huis clos* (1944).

Sarum ★ ('sɛərəm) *n* the ancient name of **Salisbury**[1] (sense 3).

Sarum use *n* the distinctive local rite or system of rites used at Salisbury cathedral in late medieval times.

SAS *abbrev. for* Special Air Service.

Sasebo ★ ('sɑːsəˌbəʊ) *n* a port in SW Japan, on NW Kyushu on Omura Bay: naval base. Pop.: 244 879 (1995).

saser ('seɪzə) *n* a device for amplifying ultrasound, working on a similar principle to a laser. ORIG C20: *s(ound) a(mplification by) s(timulated) e(mission of) r(adiation)*

sash[1] (sæʃ) *n* a long piece of ribbon, etc., worn around the waist or over one shoulder, as a symbol of rank. ORIG C16: from Ar. *shāsh* muslin

sash[2] (sæʃ) *n* **1** a frame that contains the panes of a window or door. **2** a complete frame together with panes of glass. ◆ *vb* **3** (*tr*) to furnish with a sash, sashes, or sash windows. ORIG C17: orig. pl *sashes,* var. of *shashes,* from CHASSIS

sashay (sæ'ʃeɪ) *vb* (*intr*) *Inf., chiefly US & Canad.* **1** to move, walk, or glide along casually. **2** to move or walk in a showy way; parade. ORIG C19: from an alteration of *chassé,* a gliding dance step

sash cord *n* a strong cord connecting a sash weight to a sliding sash.

sashimi ('sæʃɪmɪ) *n* a Japanese dish of thin fillets of raw fish. ORIG C19: from Japanese *sashi* pierce + *mi* flesh

sash saw *n* a small tenon saw used for cutting sashes.

sash weight *n* a weight used to counterbalance the weight of a sliding sash in a sash window and thus hold it in position at any height.

sash window *n* a window consisting of two sashes placed one above the other so that they can be slid past each other.

Saskatchewan ★ (sæs'kætʃɪwən) *n* **1** a province of W Canada: consists of Canadian Shield in the north and open prairie in the south; economy based chiefly on agriculture and mineral resources. Capital: Regina. Pop.: 1 028 137 (1999 est.). Area: 651 900 sq. km (251 700 sq. miles). Abbrevs.: **Sask., SK. 2** a river in W Canada, formed by the confluence of the North and South Saskatchewan Rivers: flows east to Lake Winnipeg. Length: 596 km (370 miles).
▸ **Saskatchewanian** (sæsˌkætʃə'wɒnɪən) *n, adj*

Saskatoon ★ (ˌsæskə'tuːn) *n* a city in W Canada, in S Saskatchewan on the South Saskatchewan River: oil refining; university (1907). Pop.: 186 058 (1991).

sasquatch ('sæsˌkwætʃ) *n* (in Canadian folklore) in British Columbia, a hairy beast or manlike monster said to leave huge footprints. ORIG from Amerind

sass (sæs) *US & Canad. inf.* ◆ *n* **1** impudent talk or behaviour. ◆ *vb* (*intr*) **2** to talk or answer back in such a way. ORIG C20: back formation from SASSY

sassaby ('sæsəbɪ) *n, pl* **sassabies.** an African antelope of grasslands and semideserts, having angular curved horns. ORIG C19: from Bantu *tshêsêbê*

sassafras ('sæsəˌfræs) *n* **1** an aromatic deciduous tree of North America, having three-lobed leaves and dark blue fruits. **2** the aromatic dried root bark of this tree, used as a flavouring, and yielding **sassafras oil. 3** *Austral.* any of several unrelated trees having a similar fragrant bark. ORIG C16: from Sp. *sasafras,* from ?

Sassari ★ (*Italian* 'sassari) *n* a city in NW Sardinia, Italy: the second-largest city on the island; university (1565). Pop.: 121 639 (1996 est.).

Sassenach ('sæsəˌnæx) *n Scot. & occasionally Irish.* an English person or Lowland Scot. ORIG C18: from Gaelic *Sassunach,* from LL *saxonēs* Saxons

Sassoon ★ (sæ'suːn) *n* **Siegfried (Lorraine)**. 1886–1967, British poet and writer, best known for his poems of World War I. He also wrote a semiautobiographical trilogy *The Memoirs of George Sherston* (1928–36).

sassy ('sæsɪ) *adj* **sassier, sassiest.** *US & Canad. inf.* insolent; impertinent. ORIG C19: var. of SAUCY
▸ **'sassily** *adv* ▸ **'sassiness** *n*

sat (sæt) *vb* the past tense and past participle of **sit.**

Sat. *abbrev. for:* **1** Saturday. **2** Saturn.

Satan ('seɪtᵊn) *n* the devil, adversary of God, and tempter of mankind: sometimes identified with Lucifer (Luke 4:5–8). ORIG OE, from LL, from Gk, from Heb.: plotter, from *sātan* to plot against

satanic (sə'tænɪk) *adj* **1** of or relating to Satan. **2** supremely evil or wicked.
▸ **sa'tanically** *adv*

Satanism ('seɪtᵊˌnɪzəm) *n* **1** the worship of Satan. **2** a form of such worship which includes blasphemous parodies of Christian prayers, etc. **3** a satanic disposition.
▸ **'Satanist** *n, adj*

SATB *abbrev. for* soprano, alto, tenor, bass: a combination of voices in choral music.

satchel ('sætʃəl) *n* a rectangular bag, usually made of leather or cloth and provided with a shoulder strap, used for carrying school books. ORIG C14: from OF *sachel,* from LL *saccellus,* from L *saccus* SACK[1]
▸ **'satchelled** *adj*

sate[1] (seɪt) *vb* **sates, sating, sated.** (*tr*) **1** to satisfy (a desire or appetite) fully. **2** to supply beyond capacity or desire. ORIG OE *sadian*

sate[2] (sæt, seɪt) *vb Arch.* a past tense and past participle of **sit.**

sateen (sæ'tiːn) *n* a glossy linen or cotton fabric that resembles satin. ORIG C19: changed from SATIN, on the model of VELVETEEN

satellite ('sætᵊˌlaɪt) *n* **1** a celestial body orbiting around a planet or star: *the earth is a satellite of the sun.* **2** a man-made device orbiting around the earth, moon, or another planet transmitting to earth scientific information or used for communication. **3** a country or political unit under the domination of a foreign power. **4** a subordinate area that is dependent upon a larger adjacent town. **5** (*modifier*) subordinate to or dependent upon another: *a satellite nation.* **6** (*modifier*) of, used in, or relating to the transmission of television signals from a satellite to the house: *a satellite dish aerial.* ORIG C16: from L *satelles* an attendant, prob. of Etruscan origin

satiable ('seɪʃɪəbᵊl) *adj* capable of being satiated.
▸ **ˌsatia'bility** *n* ▸ **'satiably** *adv*

satiate ('seɪʃɪˌeɪt) *vb* **satiates, satiating, satiated.** (*tr*) **1** to fill or supply beyond capacity or desire. **2** to supply to capacity. ORIG C16: from L *satiāre* to satisfy, from *satis* enough
▸ **ˌsati'ation** *n*

Satie ★ (*French* sati) *n* **Erik (Alfred Leslie)** (erik). 1866–1925, French composer. His music includes piano pieces and several ballets.

satiety (sə'taɪɪtɪ) *n* the state of being satiated. ORIG C16: from L *satietās,* from *satis* enough

satin ('sætɪn) *n* **1** a fabric of silk, rayon, etc., closely woven to show much of the warp, giving a smooth glossy appearance. **2** (*modifier*) like satin in texture: *a satin finish.* ORIG C14: via OF from Ar. *zaitūnī,* Ar. rendering of Chinese *Tseutung* (now *Tsinkiang*), port from which the cloth was prob. first exported
▸ **'satiny** *adj*

satinet *or* **satinette** (ˌsætɪ'nɛt) *n* a thin satin or satin-like fabric. ORIG C18: from F: small satin

satinflower ('sætɪnˌflaʊə) *n* another name for **greater stitchwort** (see **stitchwort**).

satinwood ('sætɪnˌwʊd) *n* **1** a tree that occurs in the East Indies and has hard wood with a satiny texture. **2** the wood of this tree, used in veneering, marquetry, etc.

satire ('sætaɪə) *n* **1** a novel, play, etc., in which topical issues, folly, or evil are held up to scorn by means of ridicule. **2** the genre constituted by such works. **3** the use of ridicule, irony, etc., to create such an effect. ORIG C16: from L *satira* a mixture, from *satur* sated, from *satis* enough

satirical (sə'tɪrɪkᵊl) *or* **satiric** *adj* **1** of, relating to, or containing satire. **2** given to the use of satire.
▸ **sa'tirically** *adv*

satirist ('sætərɪst) *n* **1** a person who writes satire. **2** a person given to the use of satire.

satirize *or* **satirise** ('sætəˌraɪz) *vb* **satirizes, satirizing, satirized** *or* **satirises, satirising, satirised.** to deride (a person or thing) by means of satire.
▸ **ˌsatiri'zation** *or* **ˌsatiri'sation** *n*

satisfaction (ˌsætɪs'fækʃən) *n* **1** the act of satisfying or state of being satisfied. **2** the fulfilment of a desire. **3** the pleasure obtained from such fulfilment. **4** a source of fulfilment. **5** compensation for a wrong done or received. **6** *RC Church, Church of England.* the performance of a penance. **7** *Christianity.* the atonement for sin by the death of Christ.

satisfactory (ˌsætɪs'fæktərɪ) *adj* **1** adequate or suitable; acceptable. **2** giving satisfaction. **3** constituting or involving atonement or expiation for sin.
▸ **ˌsatis'factorily** *adv*

satisfice ('sætɪsˌfaɪs) *vb* **satisfices, satisficing, satisficed. 1** (*intr*) to act in such a way as to satisfy the minimum requirements for achieving a particular result. **2** (*tr*) *Obs.* to satisfy. ORIG C16: altered from SATISFY
▸ **'satisˌficer** *n*

satisficing behaviour *n Econ.* the form of behaviour demonstrated by firms who seek satisfactory profits and satisfactory growth rather than maximum profits.

satisfy ('sætɪsˌfaɪ) *vb* **satisfies, satisfying, satisfied.** (*mainly tr*) **1** (*also intr*) to fulfil the desires or needs of (a person). **2** to provide amply for (a need or desire). **3** to convince. **4** to dispel (a doubt). **5** to make reparation to or for. **6** to discharge or pay off (a debt) to (a creditor). **7** to fulfil the

requirements of; comply with: *you must satisfy the terms of your lease.* **8** *Maths, logic.* to fulfil the conditions of (a theorem, assumption, etc.); to yield a truth by substitution of the given value. ORIG C15: from OF *satisfier,* from L *satisfacere,* from *satis* enough + *facere* to make
▸ **'satis,fiable** *adj* ▸ **'satis,fying** *adj* ▸ **'satis,fyingly** *adv*

Sato Eisaku ★ ('sɑːtəʊ 'aɪsɑːˌkuː) *n* 1901–75, Japanese statesman: prime minister (1964–72): shared the Nobel peace prize (1974) for opposing the proliferation of nuclear weapons.

satori (sə'tɔːrɪ) *n Zen Buddhism.* a state of sudden intuitive enlightenment. ORIG from Japanese

satrap ('sætræp) *n* **1** (in ancient Persia) a provincial governor. **2** a subordinate ruler. ORIG C14: from L *satrapa,* from Gk *satrapēs,* from OPersian *khshathrapāvan,* lit.: protector of the land

satrapy ('sætrəpɪ) *n, pl* **satrapies.** the province, office, or period of rule of a satrap.

SATs (sæts) *pl n Brit. education. acronym for* standard assessment tasks: see **assessment tests.**

satsuma (sæt'suːmə) *n* **1** a small citrus tree cultivated, esp. in Japan, for its edible fruit. **2** the fruit of this tree, which has easily separable segments. ORIG from SATSUMA

Satsuma ★ ('sætsʊˌmɑː) *n* a former province of SW Japan, on S Kyushu: famous for its porcelain.

saturable ('sætʃərəbᵊl) *adj Chem.* capable of being saturated.
▸ **ˌsatura'bility** *n*

saturate *vb* ('sætʃəˌreɪt), **saturates, saturating, saturated. 1** to fill, soak, or imbue totally. **2** to make (a chemical compound, solution, etc.) saturated or (of a compound, etc.) to become saturated. **3** (*tr*) *Mil.* to bomb or shell heavily. ◆ *adj* ('sætʃərɪt, -ˌreɪt). **4** saturated. ORIG C16: from L *saturāre,* from *satur* sated, from *satis* enough

saturated ('sætʃəˌreɪtɪd) *adj* **1** (of a solution or solvent) containing the maximum amount of solute that can normally be dissolved at a given temperature and pressure. **2** (of a chemical compound) containing no multiple bonds: *a saturated hydrocarbon.* **3** (of a fat) containing a high proportion of fatty acids having single bonds. **4** (of a vapour) containing the maximum amount of gaseous material at a given temperature and pressure.

saturation (ˌsætʃə'reɪʃən) *n* **1** the act of saturating or the state of being saturated. **2** *Chem.* the state of a chemical compound, solution, or vapour when it is saturated. **3** *Meteorol.* the state of the atmosphere when it can hold no more water vapour at its particular temperature and pressure. **4** the attribute of a colour that enables an observer to judge its proportion of pure chromatic colour. **5** the level beyond which demand for a product or service is not expected to rise. ◆ *modifier.* **6** denoting the maximum possible intensity of coverage of an area: *saturation bombing.*

saturation point *n* the point at which no more can be absorbed, accommodated, used, etc.

Saturday ('sætədɪ) *n* the seventh and last day of the week: the Jewish Sabbath. ORIG OE *sæternes dæg,* translation of L *Sāturnī diēs* day of Saturn

Saturn[1] ★ ('sætɜːn) *n* the Roman god of agriculture and vegetation. Greek counterpart: **Cronus.**

Saturn[2] ('sætɜːn) *n* **1** the sixth planet from the sun, around which revolve planar concentric rings (**Saturn's rings**) consisting of small frozen particles. **2** the alchemical name for **lead**[2].
▸ **Saturnian** (sæ'tɜːnɪən) *adj*

Saturnalia (ˌsætə'neɪlɪə) *n, pl* **Saturnalia** *or* **Saturnalias. 1** an ancient Roman festival celebrated in December: renowned for its general merrymaking. **2** (*sometimes not cap.*) a period or occasion of wild revelry. ORIG C16: from L *Sāturnālis* relating to SATURN[1]
▸ **ˌSatur'nalian** *adj*

saturnine ('sætəˌnaɪn) *adj* **1** having a gloomy temperament. **2** *Arch.* **2a** of or relating to lead. **2b** having lead poisoning. ORIG C15: from F *saturnin,* from Med. L *sāturnīnus* (unattested), from L *Sāturnus* Saturn, from the gloomy influence attributed to the planet Saturn
▸ **'satur,ninely** *adv*

satyagraha ('sɔːtjɑːgrɔːhɑː) *n* the policy of nonviolent resistance adopted by Mahatma Gandhi to oppose British rule in India. ORIG via Hindi from Sansk., lit.: insistence on truth, from *satya* truth + *agraha* fervour

satyr ('sætə) *n* **1** *Greek myth.* one of a class of sylvan deities, represented as goatlike men who drank and danced in the train of Dionysus and chased the nymphs. **2** a man who has strong sexual desires. **3** any of various butterflies, having dark wings often marked with eyespots. ORIG C14: from L *satyrus,* from Gk *saturos*
▸ **satyric** (sə'tɪrɪk) *adj*

satyriasis (ˌsætɪ'raɪəsɪs) *n* a neurotic compulsion in men to have sexual intercourse with many women without being able to have lasting relationships with them. ORIG C17: via NL from Gk *saturiasis*

sauce (sɔːs) *n* **1** any liquid or semiliquid preparation eaten with food to enhance its flavour. **2** anything that adds piquancy. **3** *US & Canad.* stewed fruit. **4** *Inf.* impudent language or behaviour. ◆ *vb* **sauces, saucing, sauced.** (*tr*) **5** to prepare (food) with sauce. **6** to add zest to. **7** *Inf.* to be saucy to. ORIG C14: via OF from L *salsus* salted, from *sal* salt

saucepan ('sɔːspən) *n* a metal or enamel pan with a long handle and often a lid, used for cooking food.

saucer ('sɔːsə) *n* **1** a small round dish on which a cup is set. **2** any similar dish. ORIG C14: from OF *saussier* container for SAUCE
▸ **'saucerful** *n*

saucy ('sɔːsɪ) *adj* **saucier, sauciest. 1** impertinent. **2** pert; jaunty: *a saucy hat.*
▸ **'saucily** *adv* ▸ **'sauciness** *n*

Saud ★ (saud) *n* full name *Saud ibn Abdul-Aziz.* 1902–69, king of Saudi Arabia (1953–64); son of Ibn Saud. He was deposed by his brother Faisal.

Saudi Arabia ★ ('sɔːdɪ, 'saʊ-) *n* a kingdom in SW Asia, occupying most of the Arabian peninsula between the Persian Gulf and the Red Sea: founded in 1932 by Ibn Saud, who united Hejaz and Nejd; consists mostly of desert plateau; large reserves of petroleum and natural gas. Official language: Arabic. Official religion: (Sunni) Muslim. Currency: riyal. Capital: Riyadh (royal), Jidda (administrative). Pop.: 21 505 000 (1999 est.). Area: 2 260 353 sq. km (872 722 sq. miles).
▸ **Saudi** *or* **Saudi Arabian** *adj, n*

sauerkraut ('saʊəˌkraʊt) *n* finely shredded cabbage which has been fermented in brine. ORIG G, from *sauer* sour + *Kraut* cabbage

sauger ('sɔːgə) *n* a small North American pikeperch with a spotted dorsal fin: valued as a food and game fish. ORIG C19: from ?

Saul ★ (sɔːl) *n* **1** *Old Testament.* the first king of Israel (?1020–1000 B.C.). He led Israel successfully against the Philistines, but became afflicted with madness and died by his own hand; succeeded by David. **2** *New Testament.* the name borne by Paul prior to his conversion (Acts 9: 1–30).

sault (suː) *n Canad.* a waterfall or rapids. ORIG C17: from Canad. F, from F *saut* a leap

Sault Sainte Marie ★ ('suː seɪnt mə'riː) *n, usually abbreviated to* **Sault Ste Marie. 1** an inland port in central Canada, in Ontario on the St Mary's River, which links Lake Superior and Lake Huron, opposite Sault Ste Marie, Michigan: canal by-passing the rapids completed in 1895. Pop.: 81 476 (1991). **2** an inland port in NE Michigan, opposite Sault Ste Marie, Ontario: canal around the rapids completed in 1855, enlarged and divided in 1896 and 1919 (popularly called **Soo Canals**). Pop.: 14 689 (1990).

sauna ('sɔːnə) *n* **1** an invigorating bath originating in Finland in which the bather is subjected to hot steam, usually followed by a cold plunge. **2** the place in which such a bath is taken. ORIG C20: from Finnish

Saunders ★ ('sɔːndəz) *n* Dame **Cicely.** born 1918, British philanthropist: founder of the modern hospice movement. Her books include *Living with Dying* (1983).

saunter ('sɔːntə) *vb* **1** (*intr*) to walk in a casual manner; stroll. ◆ *n* **2** a leisurely pace or stroll. ORIG C17 (meaning: to wander aimlessly), C15 (to muse): from ?
▸ **'saunterer** *n*

-saur *or* **-saurus** *n combining form.* lizard: *dinosaur.* ORIG from NL *saurus*

saurian ('sɔːrɪən) *adj* **1** of or resembling a lizard. ◆ *n* **2** a former name for **lizard.** ORIG C15: from NL *Sauria,* from Gk *sauros*

saury ('sɔːrɪ) *n, pl* **sauries.** a fish of tropical and temperate seas, having an elongated body and long toothed jaws. Also called: **skipper.** ORIG C18: ?from LL *saurus,* from ?

sausage ('sɒsɪdʒ) *n* **1** finely minced meat, esp. pork or beef, mixed with fat, cereal, and seasonings (**sausage meat**), and packed into a tube-shaped edible casing. **2** *Scot.* sausage meat. **3** an object shaped like a sausage. **4 not a sausage.** nothing at all. ORIG C15: from OF *saussiche,* from LL *salsīcia,* from L *salsus* salted; see SAUCE

sausage dog *n* an informal name for **dachshund.**

sausage roll *n Brit.* a roll of sausage meat in pastry.

Saussure ★ (*French* sosyr) *n* **Ferdinand de** (fɛrdinɑ̃ də). 1857–1913, Swiss linguist, who pioneered structuralism in linguistics.
▸ **Saus'surean** *adj, n*

sauté ('səuteɪ) *vb* **sautés, sautéing** *or* **sautéeing, sautéed. 1** to fry (food) quickly in a little fat. ◆ *n* **2** a dish of sautéed food, esp. meat that is browned and then cooked in a sauce. ◆ *adj* **3** sautéed until lightly brown: *sauté potatoes.* ORIG C19: from F: tossed, from *sauter* to jump, from L, from *salīre* to spring

Sauvignon Blanc ('səuvɪnjɒn blɒŋk) *n* **1** a white grape grown in the Bordeaux and Loire regions of France and in New Zealand and elsewhere. **2** any of various white wines made from this grape.

Sava ('sɑːvə) *or* **Save** ★ (sɑːv) *n* a river in SE Europe, rising in NW Slovenia and flowing east and south to the Danube at Belgrade. Length: 940 km (584 miles).

savage ('sævɪdʒ) *adj* **1** wild; untamed: *savage beasts.* **2** ferocious in temper: *a savage dog.* **3** uncivilized; crude: *savage behaviour.* **4** (of peoples) nonliterate or primitive: *a savage tribe.* **5** (of terrain) rugged and uncultivated. ◆ *n* **6** a member of a nonliterate society, esp. one regarded as primitive. **7** a fierce or vicious person or animal. ◆ *vb* **savages, savaging, savaged.** (*tr*) **8** to criticize violently. **9** to attack ferociously and wound. ORIG C13: from OF *sauvage,* from L *silvāticus* belonging to a wood, from *silva* a wood
▸ **'savagely** *adv* ▸ **'savageness** *n*

Savage ★ ('sævɪdʒ) *n* **Michael Joseph.** 1872–1940, New Zealand statesman; prime minister (1935-40).

Savage Island ★ *n* another name for **Niue.**

savagery ('sævɪdʒrɪ) *n, pl* **savageries. 1** an uncivilized condition. **2** a savage act or nature. **3** savages collectively.

Savaii ★ (sɑː'vaiː) *n* the largest island in Samoa: mountainous and volcanic. Pop.: 44 930 (1986). Area: 1174 sq. km (662 sq. miles).

savanna *or* **savannah** (sə'vænə) *n* open grasslands, usually with scattered bushes or trees, characteristic of much of tropical Africa. ORIG C16: from Sp. *zavana,* from Amerind *zabana*

Savannah ★ (sə'vænə) *n* **1** a port in E Georgia, near the mouth of the Savannah River: port of departure of the *Savannah* for Liverpool (1819), the first steamship to cross the Atlantic. Pop.: 140 597 (1994 est.). **2** a river in the southeastern US, formed by the confluence of the Tugaloo and Seneca Rivers in NW South Carolina: flows southeast to the Atlantic. Length: 505 km (314 miles).

savant ('sævənt) *n* a man of great learning; sage. ORIG C18: from F, from *savoir* to know, from L *sapere* to be wise
▸ **'savante** *fem n*

savate (sə'væt) *n* a form of boxing in which blows may be delivered with the feet as well as the hands. ORIG C19: from F, lit.: old worn-out shoe

save[1] (seɪv) *vb* **saves, saving, saved. 1** (*tr*) to rescue, preserve, or guard (a person or thing) from danger or harm. **2** to avoid the spending, waste, or loss of (money, possessions, etc.). **3** (*tr*) to deliver from sin; redeem. **4** (often foll. by *up*) to set aside or reserve (money, goods, etc.) for future use. **5** (*tr*) to treat with care so as to avoid or lessen wear or degeneration. **6** (*tr*) to prevent the necessity for; obviate the trouble of. **7** (*tr*) *Soccer, hockey, etc.* to prevent (a goal) by stopping (a struck ball or puck). ◆ *n* **8** *Soccer, hockey, etc.* the act of saving a goal. **9** *Computing.* an instruction to write information from the memory onto a tape or disk. ORIG C13: from OF *salver,* via LL from L *salvus* safe
▸ **'savable** *or* **'saveable** *adj* ▸ **'saver** *n*

save[2] (seɪv) *Arch.* ◆ *prep* **1** (often foll. by *for*) Also: **saving.** with the exception of. ◆ *conj* **2** but. ORIG C13 *sauf,* from OF, from L *salvō,* from *salvus* safe

save as you earn *n* (in Britain) a savings scheme operated by the government, in which monthly contributions earn tax-free interest. Abbrev.: **SAYE.**

saveloy ('sævɪˌlɔɪ) *n* a smoked sausage made from salted pork, coloured red with saltpetre. ORIG C19: prob. via F from It. *cervellato,* from *cervello* brain, from L, from *cerebrum* brain

Savery ★ ('seɪvərɪ) *n* **Thomas.** ?1650–1715, English engineer, who built (1698) the first practical steam engine, used to pump water from mines.

savin *or* **savine** ('sævɪn) *n* **1** a small spreading juniper bush of Europe, N Asia, and North America. **2** the oil derived from the shoots and leaves of this plant, formerly used in medicine to treat rheumatism, etc. ORIG C14: from OF *savine,* from L *herba Sabīna* the Sabine plant

saving ('seɪvɪŋ) *adj* **1** tending to save or preserve. **2** redeeming or compensating (esp. in **saving grace**). **3** thrifty or economical. **4** *Law.* denoting or relating to an exception or reservation: *a saving clause in an agreement.* ◆ *n* **5** preservation or redemption. **6** economy or avoidance of waste. **7** reduction in cost or expenditure. **8** anything saved. **9** (*pl*) money saved for future use. ◆ *prep* **10** with the exception of. ◆ *conj* **11** except.
▸ **'savingly** *adv*

savings bank *n* a bank that accepts the savings of depositors and pays interest on them.

savings ratio *n Econ.* the ratio of personal savings to disposable income, esp. using the difference between national figures for disposable income and consumer spending as a measure of savings.

saviour *or US* **savior** ('seɪvjə) *n* a person who rescues another person or a thing from danger or harm. ORIG C13 *saveour,* from OF, from Church L *Salvātor* the Saviour

Saviour *or US* **Savior** ('seɪvjə) *n Christianity.* Jesus Christ regarded as the saviour of men from sin.

Savoie ★ (*French* savwa) *n* **1** a department of E France, in Rhône-Alpes region. Capital: Chambéry. Pop.: 365 392 (1994 est.). Area: 6188 sq. km (2413 sq. miles). **2** the French name for **Savoy**[1].

savoir-faire ('sævwɑː'fɛə) *n* the ability to do the right thing in any situation. ORIG F, lit.: a knowing how to do

Savona ★ (*Italian* sa'voːna) *n* a port in NW Italy, in Liguria on the Mediterranean: an important centre of the Italian iron and steel industry. Pop.: 69 806 (1990).

Savonarola ★ (*Italian* savona'rɔːla) *n* **Girolamo** (dʒi'rɔːlamo). 1452–98, Italian religious and political reformer. When the Medici were expelled from Florence (1494) he instituted a puritanical republic but lost the citizens' support after being excommunicated (1497); hanged as a heretic.

savory ('seɪvərɪ) *n, pl* **savories. 1** any of numerous aromatic plants, including the **winter savory** and **summer savory,** of the Mediterranean region, having narrow leaves and white, pink, or purple flowers. **2** the leaves of any of these plants, used as a potherb. ORIG C14: prob. from OE *sætherie,* from L *saturēia,* from ?

savour *or US* **savor** ('seɪvə) *n* **1** the quality in a substance that is perceived by the sense of taste or smell. **2** a specific taste or smell: *the savour of lime.* **3** a slight but distinctive quality or trace. **4** the power to excite interest: *the savour of wit has been lost.* ◆ *vb* **5** (*intr;* often foll. by *of*) to possess the taste or smell (of). **6** (*intr;* often foll. by *of*) to have a suggestion (of). **7** (*tr*) to season. **8** (*tr*) to taste or smell, esp. appreciatively. **9** (*tr*) to relish or enjoy. ORIG C13: from OF *savour,* from L *sapor* taste, from *sapere* to taste
▸ **'savourless** *or US* **'savorless** *adj*

savoury *or US* **savory** ('seɪvərɪ) *adj* **1** attractive to the sense of taste or smell. **2** salty or spicy: *a savoury dish.* **3** pleasant. **4** respectable. ◆ *n, pl* **savouries** *or US* **savories. 5** *Chiefly Brit.* a savoury dish served as an hors d'oeuvre or dessert. ORIG C13 *savure,* from OF, from *savourer* to SAVOUR
▸ **'savouriness** *or US* **'savoriness** *n*

savoy (sə'vɔɪ) *n* a cultivated variety of cabbage having a compact head and wrinkled leaves. ORIG C16: after the SAVOY region

Savoy[1] ★ (sə'vɔɪ) *n* an area of SE France, bordering on Italy, mainly in the Savoy Alps: a duchy in the late Middle Ages and part of the Kingdom of Sardinia from 1720 to 1860, when it became part of France. French name: **Savoie.**

Savoy[2] ★ (sə'vɔɪ) *n* a noble family of Italy that ruled over the duchy of Savoy and became the royal house of Italy (1861–1946): the oldest reigning dynasty in Europe before the dissolution of the Italian monarchy.

Savoy Alps ★ *pl n* a range of the Alps in SE France. Highest peak: Mont Blanc, 4807 m (15 772 ft).

Savoyard (sə'vɔɪɑːd; *French* savwajar) *n* **1** a native of Savoy. **2** the dialect of French spoken in Savoy. ◆ *adj* **3** of or relating to Savoy, its inhabitants, or their dialect.

savvy ('sævɪ) *Sl.* ◆ *vb* **savvies, savvying, savvied. 1** to understand or get the sense of (an idea, etc.). ◆ *n* **2** comprehension. ◆ *adj* **savvier, savviest. 3** *Chiefly US.* shrewd. ORIG C18: corruption of Sp. *sabe* (*usted*) (you) know, from *saber* to know, from L *sapere* to be wise

saw[1] (sɔː) *n* **1** any of various hand tools for cutting wood, metal, etc., having a blade with teeth along one edge. **2** any of various machines or devices for cutting by use of a toothed blade, such as a power-driven toothed band of metal. ◆ *vb* **saws, sawing, sawed; sawed** *or* **sawn. 3** to cut with a saw. **4** to form by sawing. **5** to cut as if wielding a saw: *to saw the air.* **6** to move (an object) from side to side as if moving a saw. ORIG OE *sagu:* rel. to L *secare* to cut
▸ **'sawer** *n* ▸ **'saw,like** *adj*

saw[2] (sɔː) *vb* the past tense of **see**[1].

saw[3] (sɔː) *n* a wise saying, maxim, or proverb. ORIG OE *sagu* a saying

sawbones ('sɔː,bəunz) *n, pl* **sawbones** *or* **sawboneses.** *Sl.* a surgeon or doctor.

sawdust ('sɔː,dʌst) *n* particles of wood formed by sawing.

sawfish ('sɔː,fɪʃ) *n, pl* **sawfish** *or* **sawfishes.** a sharklike ray of subtropical coastal waters, having a serrated bladelike mouth.

sawfly ('sɔː,flaɪ) *n, pl* **sawflies.** any of various hymenopterous insects, the females of which have a sawlike ovipositor.

sawhorse ('sɔː,hɔːs) *n* a stand for timber during sawing.

sawmill ('sɔː,mɪl) *n* an industrial establishment where timber is sawn into planks, etc.

sawn (sɔːn) *vb* a past participle of **saw**[1].

sawn-off *or esp. US* **sawed-off** *adj* (*prenominal*) (of a shotgun) having the barrel cut short, mainly to facilitate concealment of the weapon.

saw-off *n Canad. sl.* **1** a compromise. **2** a deadlocked situation.

saw set *n* a tool used for setting the teeth of a saw, consisting of a clamp used to bend each tooth at a slight angle to the plane of the saw, alternate teeth being bent in the same direction.

sawyer ('sɔːjə) *n* a person who saws timber for a living. ORIG C14 *sawier,* from SAW[1] + *-ier,* var. of -ER[1]

sax (sæks) *n Inf.* short for **saxophone.**

Sax. *abbrev. for:* **1** Saxon. **2** Saxony.

Saxe[1] ★ (saks) *n* the French name for **Saxony.**

Saxe[2] ★ (*French* saks) *n* **Hermann Maurice** (ɛrman mɔris), comte de Saxe. 1696–1750, French marshal in the War of the Austrian Succession (1740–48).

saxe blue (sæks) *n* **a** a light greyish-blue colour. **b** (*as adj*): *a saxe-blue dress.* ORIG C19: from F *Saxe* Saxony, source of a dye of this colour

Saxe-Coburg-Gotha ★ (sæks'kəubɜːg'gəuθə) *n* the ruling house of the former German duchy of Saxe-Coburg-Gotha (until 1918) and the name of the British royal family (1901–17) through Prince Albert.

saxhorn ('sæks,hɔːn) *n* a valved brass instrument used chiefly in brass and military bands, having a tube of conical bore. It resembles the tuba. ORIG C19: after Adolphe *Sax* (see SAXOPHONE), who invented it (1845)

saxicolous (sæk'sɪkələs) *adj* living on or among rocks: *saxicolous plants.* Also: **saxicole** ('sæksɪ,kəul), **saxatile** ('sæksə,taɪl). ORIG C19: from NL *saxicolus,* from L *saxum* rock + *colere* to dwell

saxifrage ('sæksɪ,freɪdʒ) *n* a plant having small white, yellow, purple, or pink flowers. ORIG C15: from LL *saxifraga,* lit.: rock-breaker, from L *saxum* rock + *frangere* to break

Saxo Grammaticus ★ ('sæksəu grə'mætɪkəs) *n* ?1150–?1220, Danish chronicler, noted for his *Gesta Danorum,* a partly legendary history of Denmark, which contains the Hamlet (Amleth) legend.

Saxon ('sæksən) *n* **1** a member of a West Germanic people who raided and settled parts of S Britain in the fifth and sixth centuries A.D. **2** a native or inhabitant of Saxony. **3a** the Low German dialect of Saxony. **3b** any of the West Germanic dialects spoken by the ancient Saxons. ◆ *adj* **4** of or characteristic of the ancient Saxons, the Anglo-Saxons, or their descendants. **5** of or characteristic of Saxony, its inhabitants, or their Low German dialect. ORIG C13 (replacing OE *Seaxe*): via OF from LL *Saxon-, Saxo,* from Gk; of Gmc origin

Saxony ★ ('sæksənɪ) *n* **1** a state in E Germany, formerly part of East Germany. Pop.: 4 557 200 (1996 est.). **2** a former duchy and electorate in SE and central Germany, whose territory changed greatly over the centuries. **3** (in the early Middle Ages) any territory inhabited or ruled by Saxons. ◆ Cf. **Saxony-Anhalt, Lower Saxony.** German name: **Sachsen.** French name: **Saxe.**

Saxony-Anhalt ★ ('sæksənɪ'ænhælt) *n* a state of E Germany: created in 1947 from the state of Anhalt and those parts of Prussia formerly ruled by the duchy of Saxony: part of East Germany until 1990. Pop.: 2 731 500 (1996 est.).

saxophone ('sæksə,fəun) *n* a keyed single-reed wind instrument of mellow tone colour, used mainly in jazz and dance music. Often shortened to **sax.** ORIG C19: after Adolphe *Sax* (1814–94), Belgian musical-instrument maker, who invented it (1846)
▸ **saxophonic** (,sæksə'fɒnɪk) *adj* ▸ **saxophonist** (sæk'sɒfənɪst) *n*

say (seɪ) *vb* **says, saying, said.** (*mainly tr*) **1** to speak, pronounce, or utter. **2** (*also intr*) to express (an idea, etc.) in words; tell. **3** (*also intr; may take a clause as object*) to state (an opinion, fact, etc.) positively. **4** to recite: *to say grace.* **5** (*may take a clause as object*) to report or allege: *they say we shall have rain today.* **6** (*may take a clause as object*) to suppose: *let us say that he is lying.* **7** (*may take a clause as object*) to convey by means of artistic expression. **8** to make a case for: *there is much to be said for it.* **9 go without saying.** to be so obvious as to need no explanation. **10 I say!** *Inf., chiefly Brit.* an exclamation of surprise. **11 not to say.** even. **12 that is to say.** in other words. **13 to say the least.** at the very least. ◆ *adv* **14** approximately: *there were, say, 20 people present.* **15** for example: *choose a number, say, four.* ◆ *n* **16** the right or chance to speak: *let him have his say.* **17** authority, esp. to influence a decision: *he has a lot of say.* **18** a statement of opinion: *you've had your say.* ◆ *interj* **19** *US & Canad. inf.* an exclamation to attract attention or express surprise. ORIG OE *secgan*
▸ **'sayer** *n*

Sayan Mountains ★ (sɑː'jæn) *pl n* a mountain range in S central Russia, in S Siberia. Highest peak: Munku-Sardyk, 3437 m (11 457 ft).

SAYE (in Britain) *abbrev. for* save as you earn.

Sayers ★ ('seɪəz) *n* **Dorothy L(eigh).** 1893–1957, British detective-story writer.

saying ('seɪɪŋ) *n* a maxim, adage, or proverb.

say-so *n Inf.* **1** an arbitrary assertion. **2** an authoritative decision. **3** the authority to make a final decision.

sayyid ('saɪɪd) *or* **said** *n* **1** a Muslim claiming descent from Mohammed's grandson Husain. **2** a Muslim honorary title. ORIG C17: from Ar.: lord

Sb *the chemical symbol for* antimony. ORIG from NL *stibium*

SBU *abbrev. for* strategic business unit: a division within an organization responsible for marketing its own range of products.

sc *Printing. abbrev. for* small capitals.

Sc *the chemical symbol for* scandium.

SC *abbrev. for:* **1** *NZ.* School Certificate. **2** Signal Corps. **3** *Canad.* Social Credit.

sc. *abbrev. for:* **1** scale. **2** scene. **3** science. **4** scilicet. **5** screw. **6** scruple (unit of weight).

scab (skæb) *n* **1** the dried crusty surface of a healing skin wound or sore. **2** a contagious disease of sheep resembling mange, caused by a mite. **3** a fungal disease of plants characterized by crusty spots on the fruits, leaves, etc. **4** *Derog.* **4a** Also called: **blackleg.** a person who refuses to support a trade union's actions, esp. strikes. **4b** (*as modifier*): *scab labour.* **5** a despicable person. ◆ *vb* **scabs, scabbing, scabbed.** (*intr*) **6** to become covered with a scab. **7** to replace a striking worker. ORIG OE *sceabb*

scabbard ('skæbəd) *n* a holder for a bladed weapon such as a sword or bayonet. ORIG C13 *scauberc,* from Norman F *escaubers,* (pl) of Gmc origin

scabby ('skæbɪ) *adj* **scabbier, scabbiest. 1** *Pathol.* having an area of the skin covered with scabs. **2** *Pathol.* having scabies. **3** *Inf.* despicable.
▸ **'scabbily** *adv* ▸ **'scabbiness** *n*

scabies ('skeɪbiːz) *n* a contagious skin infection caused by a mite, characterized by intense itching and inflammation. ORIG C15: from L: scurf, from *scabere* to scratch

scabious[1] ('skeɪbɪəs) *adj* **1** having or covered with scabs. **2** of, relating to, or resembling scabies. ORIG C17: from L *scabiōsus,* from SCABIES

scabious[2] ('skeɪbɪəs) *n* any of a genus of plants of the Mediterranean region, having blue, red, or whitish dome-shaped flower heads. ORIG C14: from Med. L *scabiōsa herba* the scabies plant, referring to its use in treating scabies

scabrous ('skeɪbrəs) *adj* **1** roughened because of small projections. **2** indecent or salacious: *scabrous humour.* **3** difficult to deal with. ORIG C17: from L *scaber* rough
▸ **'scabrously** *adv*

scad (skæd) *n, pl* **scad** *or* **scads.** any of various marine fishes having a deeply forked tail, such as the large mackerel. ORIG C17: from ?

scads (skædz) *pl n Inf.* a large amount or number. ORIG C19: from ?

Scafell Pike ★ (skɔː'fɛl) *n* a mountain in NW England, in Cumbria in the Lake District: the highest peak in England. Height: 978 m (3209 ft).

scaffold ('skæfəld) *n* **1** a temporary framework that is used to support workmen and materials during the erection, repair, etc., of a building. **2** a raised wooden platform on which plays are performed, tobacco, etc., is dried, or (esp. formerly) criminals are executed. ◆ *vb* (*tr*) **3** to provide with a scaffold. **4** to support by means of a scaffold. ORIG C14: from OF *eschaffaut,* from Vulgar L *catafalicum* (unattested)
▸ **'scaffolder** *n*

scaffolding ('skæfəldɪŋ) *n* **1** a scaffold or system of scaffolds. **2** the building materials used to make scaffolds.

Scala ★ ('skaːla) *n* **La.** See **La Scala.**

scalable ('skeɪləbᵊl) *adj* capable of being climbed.
▸ **'scalableness** *n* ▸ **'scalably** *adv*

scalar ('skeɪlə) *n* **1** a quantity, such as time or temperature, that has magnitude but not direction. **2** *Maths.* an element of a field associated with a vector space. ◆ *adj* **3** having magnitude but not direction. ORIG C17 (meaning: resembling a ladder): from L *scālāris,* from *scāla* ladder

scalar product *n* the product of two vectors to form a scalar, whose value is the product of the magnitudes of the vectors and the cosine of the angle between them. Also called: **dot product.**

scalawag ('skælə,wæg) *n* a variant of **scallywag.**

scald[1] (skɔːld) *vb* **1** to burn or be burnt with or as if with hot liquid or steam. **2** (*tr*) to subject to the action of boiling water, esp. so as to sterilize. **3** (*tr*) to heat (a liquid) almost to boiling point. **4** to plunge (tomatoes, etc.) into boiling water in order to skin them more easily. ◆ *n* **5** the act or result of scalding. **6** an abnormal condition in plants, caused by exposure to excessive sunlight, gases, etc. ORIG C13: via OF from LL *excaldāre* to wash in warm water, from *calida* (*aqua*) warm (water), from *calēre* to be warm
▸ **'scalder** *n*

scald[2] (skɔːld) *n* a variant spelling of **skald.**

scaldfish ('skɔːld,fɪʃ, 'skɑːld-) *n, pl* **scaldfish** *or* **scaldfishes.** a small European flatfish, covered with large fragile scales.

scale[1] (skeɪl) *n* **1** any of the numerous plates, made of various substances, covering the bodies of fishes. **2a** any of the horny or chitinous plates covering a part or the entire body of certain reptiles and mammals. **2b** any of the numerous minute structures covering the wings of lepidoptera. **3** a thin flat piece or flake. **4** a thin flake of dead epidermis shed from the skin. **5** a specialized leaf or bract, esp. the protective covering of a bud or the dry membranous bract of a catkin. **6** See **scale insect. 7** any oxide formed on a metal when heated. **8** tartar formed on the teeth. **9** another name for **limescale.** ◆ *vb* **scales, scaling, scaled. 10** (*tr*) to remove the scales or coating from. **11** to peel off or cause to peel off in flakes or scales. **12** (*intr*) to shed scales. **13** to cover or become covered with scales, incrustation, etc. ORIG C14: from OF *escale,* of Gmc origin

scale[2] (skeɪl) *n* **1** (*often pl*) a machine or device for weighing. **2** one of the pans of a balance. **3 tip the scales. 3a** to exercise a decisive influence. **3b** (foll. by *at*) to amount in weight (to). ◆ *vb* **scales, scaling, scaled.** (*tr*) **4** to weigh with or as if with scales. ORIG C13: from ON *skāl* bowl

scale[3] (skeɪl) *n* **1** a sequence of marks either at regular intervals, or representing equal steps, used as a reference in making measurements. **2** a measuring instrument having such a scale. **3a** the ratio between the size of something real and that of a representation of it. **3b** (*as modifier*): *a scale model.* **4** a line, numerical ratio, etc., for showing this ratio. **5** a progressive or graduated table of things, wages, etc.: *a wage scale for carpenters.* **6** an established standard. **7** a relative degree or extent: *he entertained on a grand scale.* **8** *Music.* a group of notes taken in ascending or descending order, esp. within the compass of one octave. **9** *Maths.* the notation of a given number system: *the decimal scale.* ◆ *vb* **scales, scaling, scaled. 10** to climb to the top of (a height) by or as if by a ladder. **11** (*tr*) to make or draw (a model, etc.) according to a particular ratio of proportionate reduction. **12** (*tr; usually foll. by up* or *down*) to increase or reduce proportionately in size, etc. **13** (*intr*) *Austral. inf.* to ride on public transport without paying a fare. ORIG C15: via It. from L *scāla* ladder

scaleboard ('skeɪl,bɔːd) *n* a very thin piece of board, used for backing a picture, etc.

scale insect *n* a small insect which typically lives and feeds on plants and secretes a protective scale around itself. Many species are pests.

scalene ('skeɪliːn) *adj* **1** *Maths.* (of a triangle) having all sides of unequal length. **2** *Anat.* of or relating to any of the scalenus muscles. ORIG C17: from LL *scalēnus* with unequal sides, from Gk *skalēnos*

scalenus (skə'liːnəs) *n, pl* **scaleni** (-naɪ). *Anat.* any one of the three muscles situated on each side of the neck extending from the cervical vertebrae to the first or second pair of ribs. ORIG C18: from NL; see SCALENE

scaling ladder *n* a ladder used to climb high walls, esp. one used formerly to enter a besieged town, fortress, etc.

scallion ('skæljən) *n* any of various onions, such as the spring onion, that have a small bulb and long leaves and are eaten in salads. ORIG C14: from Anglo-F *scalun,* from

L *Ascalōnia (caepa)* Ascalonian (onion), from *Ascalo* Ascalon, a Palestinian port

scallop ('skɒləp, 'skæl-) *n* **1** any of various marine bivalves having a fluted fan-shaped shell. **2** the edible adductor muscle of certain of these molluscs. **3** either of the shell valves of any of these molluscs. **4** a scallop shell in which fish, esp. shellfish, is cooked and served. **5** one of a series of curves along an edge. **6** the shape of a scallop shell used as the badge of a pilgrim, esp. in the Middle Ages. **7** *Chiefly Austral.* a potato cake fried in batter. ◆ *vb* **8** *(tr)* to decorate (an edge) with scallops. **9** to bake (food) in a scallop shell or similar dish. ORIG C14: from OF *escalope* shell, of Gmc origin
▸ **'scalloper** *n* ▸ **'scalloping** *n*

scally ('skælɪ) *n, pl* **scallies.** *Northwest English dialect.* a rascal; rogue. ORIG C20: from SCALLYWAG

scallywag ('skælɪˌwæg) *n Inf.* a scamp; rascal. ◆ Also: **scalawag, scallawag.** ORIG C19: (orig. undersized animal): from ?

scalp (skælp) *n* **1** *Anat.* the skin and subcutaneous tissue covering the top of the head. **2** *Hist.* (among North American Indians) a part of this removed as a trophy from a slain enemy. **3** a trophy or token signifying conquest. **4** *Scot. dialect.* a projection of bare rock from vegetation. ◆ *vb (tr)* **5** to cut the scalp from. **6** *Inf., chiefly US.* to purchase and resell (securities) quickly so as to make several small profits. **7** *Inf.* to buy (tickets) cheaply and resell at an inflated price. ORIG C13: prob. from ON
▸ **'scalper** *n*

scalpel ('skælpᵊl) *n* a surgical knife with a short thin blade. ORIG C18: from L *scalpellum,* from *scalper* a knife, from *scalpere* to scrape

scaly ('skeɪlɪ) *adj* **scalier, scaliest. 1** resembling or covered in scales. **2** peeling off in scales.
▸ **'scaliness** *n*

scaly anteater *n* another name for **pangolin.**

Scamander ★ (skə'mændə) *n* the ancient name for the **Menderes** (sense 2).

scamp[1] (skæmp) *n* **1** an idle mischievous person. **2** a mischievous child. ORIG C18: from *scamp* (vb) to be a highway robber, prob. from MDu. *schampen* to decamp, from OF *escamper,* from L *campus* field
▸ **'scampish** *adj*

scamp[2] (skæmp) *vb* a less common word for **skimp.**
▸ **'scamper** *n*

scamper ('skæmpə) *vb* **1** *(intr)* to run about playfully. **2** (often foll. by *through*) to hurry through (a place, task, etc.). ◆ *n* **3** the act of scampering. ORIG C17: prob. from *scamp* (vb); see SCAMP[1]

scampi ('skæmpɪ) *n* *(usually functioning as sing)* large prawns, usually eaten fried in breadcrumbs. ORIG It.: pl of *scampo* shrimp, from ?

scan (skæn) *vb* **scans, scanning, scanned. 1** *(tr)* to scrutinize minutely. **2** *(tr)* to glance at quickly. **3** *(tr) Prosody.* to read or analyse (verse) according to the rules of metre and versification. **4** *(intr) Prosody.* to conform to the rules of metre and versification. **5** *(tr) Electronics.* to move a beam of light, electrons, etc., in a predetermined pattern over (a surface or region) to obtain information, esp. to reproduce a television image. **6** *(tr)* to examine data stored on (magnetic tape, etc.), usually in order to retrieve information. **7** to examine or search (a prescribed region) by systematically varying the direction of a radar or sonar beam. **8** *Med.* to obtain an image of (a part of the body) by means of a scanner. ◆ *n* **9** the act or an instance of scanning. **10** *Med.* **10a** the examination of a part of the body by means of a scanner: *a brain scan; an ultrasound scan.* **10b** the image produced by a scanner. ORIG C14: from LL *scandere* to scan (verse), from L: to climb
▸ **'scannable** *adj*

Scand. *or* **Scan.** *abbrev. for* Scandinavia(n).

scandal ('skændᵊl) *n* **1** a disgraceful action or event: *his negligence was a scandal.* **2** censure or outrage arising from an action or event. **3** a person whose conduct causes reproach or disgrace. **4** malicious talk, esp. gossip. **5** *Law.* a libellous action or statement. ORIG C16: from LL *scandalum* stumbling block, from Gk *skandalon* a trap
▸ **'scandalous** *adj* ▸ **'scandalously** *adv*

scandalize *or* **scandalise** ('skændəˌlaɪz) *vb* **scandalizes, scandalizing, scandalized** *or* **scandalises, scandalising, scandalised.** *(tr)* to shock, as by improper behaviour.
▸ **ˌscandali'zation** *or* **ˌscandali'sation** *n*

scandalmonger ('skændᵊlˌmʌŋgə) *n* a person who spreads or enjoys scandal, gossip, etc.

Scandinavia ★ (ˌskændɪ'neɪvɪə) *n* **1** Also called: **the Scandinavian Peninsula.** the peninsula of N Europe occupied by Norway and Sweden. **2** the countries of N Europe, esp. considered as a cultural unit and including Norway, Sweden, Denmark, and often Finland, Iceland, and the Faeroe Islands.
▸ **ˌScandi'navian** *adj, n*

scandium ('skændɪəm) *n* a rare silvery-white metallic element occurring in minute quantities in numerous minerals. Symbol: Sc; atomic no.: 21; atomic wt.: 44.96. ORIG C19: from NL, from L *Scandia* Scandinavia, where discovered

scanner ('skænə) *n* **1** a person or thing that scans. **2** a device, usually electronic, used to measure or sample the distribution of some quantity or condition in a particular system, region, or area. **3** an aerial or similar device designed to transmit or receive signals, esp. radar signals, inside a given solid angle of space. **4** any device used in medical diagnosis to obtain an image of an internal organ or part. **5** short for **optical scanner.**

scanning electron microscope *n* a type of electron microscope that produces a three-dimensional image.

scansion ('skænʃən) *n* the analysis of the metrical structure of verse. ORIG C17: from L: climbing up, from *scandere* to climb

scant (skænt) *adj* **1** scarcely sufficient: *he paid her scant attention.* **2** *(prenominal)* bare: *a scant ten inches.* **3** *(postpositive;* foll. by *of)* having a short supply (of). ◆ *vb (tr)* **4** to limit in size or quantity. **5** to provide with a limited supply of. **6** to treat in an inadequate manner. ◆ *adv* **7** scarcely; barely. ORIG C14: from ON *skamt,* from *skammr* short
▸ **'scantly** *adv*

scantling ('skæntlɪŋ) *n* **1** a piece of sawn timber, such as a rafter, that has a small cross section. **2** the dimensions of a piece of building material or the structural parts of a ship or aircraft. **3** a building stone. **4** a small quantity or amount. ORIG C16: changed (through infl. of SCANT & -LING[1]) from earlier *scantillon* a carpenter's gauge, from OF *escantillon,* ult. from L *scandere* to climb

scanty ('skæntɪ) *adj* **scantier, scantiest. 1** limited; barely enough. **2** inadequate. **3** lacking fullness.
▸ **'scantily** *adv* ▸ **'scantiness** *n*

Scapa Flow ★ ('skæpə) *n* an extensive landlocked anchorage off the N coast of Scotland, in the Orkney Islands: major British naval base in both World Wars. Length: about 24 km (15 miles). Width: 13 km (8 miles).

scape *or* **'scape** (skeɪp) *vb* **scapes, scaping, scaped,** *n* an archaic word for **escape.**

-scape *suffix forming nouns.* indicating a scene or view of something: *seascape.* ORIG from LANDSCAPE

scapegoat ('skeɪpˌgəʊt) *n* **1** a person made to bear the blame for others. **2** *Bible.* a goat symbolically laden with the sins of the Israelites and sent into the wilderness. ◆ *vb* **3** *(tr)* to make a scapegoat of. ORIG C16: from ESCAPE + GOAT, coined by William Tyndale to translate Biblical Heb. *azāzēl* (prob.) goat for Azazel, mistakenly thought to mean "goat that escapes"

scapegrace ('skeɪpˌgreɪs) *n* a mischievous person. ORIG C19: from SCAPE + GRACE, alluding to a person who lacks God's grace

scaphoid ('skæfɔɪd) *adj Anat.* an obsolete word for **navicular.** ORIG C18: via NL from Gk *skaphoeidēs,* from *skaphē* boat

scapula ('skæpjʊlə) *n, pl* **scapulae** (-liː) *or* **scapulas.** either of two large flat triangular bones, one on each side of the back part of the shoulder in man. Nontechnical name: **shoulder blade.** ORIG C16: from LL: shoulder

scapular ('skæpjʊlə) *adj* **1** *Anat.* of or relating to the scapula. ◆ *n* **2** part of the monastic habit worn by members of many Christian religious orders, consisting of a piece of woollen cloth worn over the shoulders, and hanging down to the ankles. **3** two small rectangular pieces of cloth joined by tapes passing over the shoulders and worn in token of affiliation to a religious order. **4** any of the small feathers of a bird that lie along the shoulder. ♦ Also called (for senses 2 and 3): **scapulary.**

scar[1] (skɑː) *n* **1** any mark left on the skin or other tissue following the healing of a wound, etc. **2** a permanent change in a person's character resulting from emotional distress. **3** the mark on a plant indicating the former point of attachment of a part. **4** a mark of damage. ♦ *vb* **scars, scarring, scarred. 5** to mark or become marked with a scar. **6** (*intr*) to heal leaving a scar. ORIG C14: via LL from Gk *eskhara* scab

scar[2] (skɑː) *n* a bare craggy rock formation. ORIG C14: from ON *sker* low reef

scarab (ˈskærəb) *n* **1** any scarabaeid beetle, esp. the **sacred scarab**, regarded by the ancient Egyptians as divine. **2** the scarab as represented on amulets, etc. ORIG C16: from L *scarabaeus*

scarabaeid (ˌskærəˈbiːɪd) *n* **1** any of a family of beetles including the sacred scarab and other dung beetles, the chafers, and rhinoceros beetles. ♦ *adj* **2** of or belonging to this family. ORIG C19: from NL

Scaramouch (ˈskærəˌmuːʃ) *n* a stock character who appears as a boastful coward in commedia dell'arte. ORIG C17: via F from It. *Scaramuccia*, from *scaramuccia* a SKIRMISH

Scarborough ★ (ˈskɑːbrə) *n* a fishing port and resort in NE England, in North Yorkshire on the North Sea: developed as a spa after 1660; ruined 12th-century castle. Pop.: 38 809 (1991).

scarce (skɛəs) *adj* **1** rarely encountered. **2** insufficient to meet the demand. **3 make oneself scarce.** *Inf.* to go away. ♦ *adv* **4** *Arch. or literary.* scarcely. ORIG C13: from OF *scars*, from Vulgar L *excarpsus* (unattested) plucked out, from L *excerpere* to select

▸ **ˈscarceness** *n*

scarcely (ˈskɛəslɪ) *adv* **1** hardly at all. **2** *Often used ironically.* probably or definitely not: *that is scarcely justification for your actions.*

> **USAGE NOTE** Since *scarcely*, *hardly*, and *barely* already have negative force, it is unnecessary to use another negative word with them: *he had hardly had* (not *he hadn't hardly had*) *time to think; there was scarcely any* (not *scarcely no*) *bread left.* When *scarcely*, *hardly*, and *barely* are used at the beginning of a sentence, as in *Scarcely had I arrived...*, the following clause should be introduced by *when*: *Scarcely had I arrived when I was asked to chair a meeting.* The word *before* is quite often used instead, and this would generally be considered correct. However, use of the word *than*, though increasingly common, is still thought by many to be incorrect. See also at **sooner.**

scarcity (ˈskɛəsɪtɪ) *n, pl* **scarcities. 1** inadequate supply. **2** rarity or infrequent occurrence.

scare (skɛə) *vb* **scares, scaring, scared. 1** to fill or be filled with fear or alarm. **2** (*tr*; often foll. by *away* or *off*) to drive (away) by frightening. **3** (*tr*; foll. by *up*) *US & Canad. inf.* **3a** to produce (a meal) quickly from whatever is available. **3b** to manage to find (something) quickly or with difficulty: *brewers need to scare up more sales.* ♦ *n* **4** a sudden attack of fear or alarm. **5** a period of general fear or alarm. ♦ *adj* **6** causing (needless) fear or alarm: *a scare story.* ORIG C12: from ON *skirra*

▸ **ˈscarer** *n*

scarecrow (ˈskɛəˌkrəʊ) *n* **1** an object, usually in the shape of a man, made out of sticks and old clothes to scare birds away from crops. **2** a person or thing that appears frightening. **3** *Inf.* an untidy-looking person.

scaremonger (ˈskɛəˌmʌŋgə) *n* a person who delights in spreading rumours of disaster.

▸ **ˈscareˌmongering** *n*

scarf[1] (skɑːf) *n, pl* **scarves** *or* **scarfs.** a rectangular, triangular, or long narrow piece of cloth worn around the head, neck, or shoulders for warmth or decoration. ORIG C16: from ?

scarf[2] (skɑːf) *n, pl* **scarfs. 1** Also called: **scarf joint, scarfed joint.** a lapped joint between two pieces of timber made by notching the ends and strapping or gluing the two pieces together. **2** the end of a piece of timber shaped to form such a joint. **3** *Whaling.* an incision made along a whale before stripping off the blubber. ♦ *vb* (*tr*) **4** to join (two pieces of timber) by means of a scarf. **5** to make a scarf on (a piece of timber). **6** to cut a scarf in (a whale). ORIG C14: prob. from ON

Scarfe ★ (skɑːf) *n* **Gerald.** born 1936, British cartoonist, famous for his scathing caricatures of politicians and celebrities.

scarfskin (ˈskɑːfˌskɪn) *n* the outermost layer of the skin; epidermis or cuticle. ORIG C17: from SCARF[1] (in the sense: an outer covering)

Scargill ★ (ˈskɑːgɪl) *n* **Arthur.** born 1941, British trade-union leader; president of the National Union of Mineworkers (from 1982). He led the miners in a long and bitter strike (1984–85) against pit closures, but was unable to stop the closures.

scarify (ˈskɛərɪˌfaɪ, ˈskærɪ-) *vb* **scarifies, scarifying, scarified.** (*tr*) **1** *Surgery.* to make tiny punctures or superficial incisions in (the skin or other tissue), as for inoculating. **2** *Agriculture.* to break up and loosen (soil) to a shallow depth. **3** to wound with harsh criticism. ORIG C15: via OF from L *scarīfāre* to scratch open, from Gk *skariphasthai* to draw, from *skariphos* a pencil

▸ **ˌscarifiˈcation** *n* ▸ **ˈscariˌfier** *n*

scarlatina (ˌskɑːləˈtiːnə) *n* the technical name for **scarlet fever.** ORIG C19: from NL, from It. *scarlattina*, dim. of *scarlatto* scarlet

Scarlatti ★ (skɑːˈlætɪ) *n* **1 Alessandro** (alesˈsandro). ?1659–1725, Italian composer; regarded as the founder of modern opera. **2** his son, (**Giuseppe**) **Domenico** (doˈmeːniko). 1685–1757, Italian composer, who wrote over 550 sonatas for harpsichord.

scarlet (ˈskɑːlɪt) *n* **1** a vivid orange-red colour. **2** cloth or clothing of this colour. ♦ *adj* **3** of the colour scarlet. **4** sinful or immoral. ORIG C13: from OF *escarlate* fine cloth, from ?

scarlet fever *n* an acute communicable disease characterized by fever, strawberry-coloured tongue, and a rash starting on the neck and chest and spreading to the abdomen and limbs. Technical name: **scarlatina.**

scarlet letter *n* (esp. among US Puritans) a scarlet letter *A* formerly worn by a person convicted of adultery.

scarlet pimpernel *n* a plant, related to the primrose, having small red, purple, or white star-shaped flowers that close in bad weather. Also called: **shepherd's** (or **poor man's**) **weatherglass.**

scarlet runner *n* a climbing perennial bean plant of South America, having scarlet flowers: widely cultivated for its long green edible pods containing edible seeds. Also: **runner bean.**

scarlet woman *n* **1** a sinful woman described in the Bible (Rev. 17), interpreted as a symbol of pagan Rome or of the Roman Catholic Church. **2** any sexually promiscuous woman.

scarp (skɑːp) *n* **1** a steep slope, esp. one formed by erosion or faulting. **2** *Fortifications.* the side of a ditch cut nearest to a rampart. ♦ *vb* **3** (*tr; often passive*) to wear or cut so as to form a steep slope. ORIG C16: from It. *scarpa*

scarper (ˈskɑːpə) *Brit. sl.* ♦ *vb* **1** (*intr*) to depart in haste. ♦ *n* **2** a hasty departure. ORIG from ?

Scarron ★ (*French* skarɔ̃) *n* **Paul** (pɔl). 1610–60, French dramatist and novelist, noted for his novel *Le Roman comique* (1651–57).

Scart *or* **SCART** (skɑːt) *n Electronics.* **a** a 21-pin plug-and-socket system which carries picture, sound, and other signals, used especially in home entertainment systems. **b** (*as modifier*): *a Scart cable.* ORIG C20: after Syndicat des Constructeurs des Appareils Radiorécepteurs et Téléviseurs, the company that designed it

scarves (skɑːvz) *n* a plural of **scarf**[1].

scary (ˈskɛərɪ) *adj* **scarier, scariest.** *Inf.* **1** causing fear or alarm. **2** timid.

scat[1] (skæt) *vb* **scats, scatting, scatted.** (*intr; usually imperative*) *Inf.* to go away in haste. ORIG C19: ?from a hiss + *cat*, used to frighten away cats

scat[2] (skæt) *n* **1** a type of jazz singing characterized by improvised vocal sounds instead of words. ◆ *vb* **scats, scatting, scatted. 2** (*intr*) to sing jazz in this way. ORIG C20: ? imit.

scathe (skeɪð) *vb* **scathes, scathing, scathed.** (*tr*) **1** *Rare.* to attack with severe criticism. **2** *Arch. or dialect.* to injure. ◆ *n* **3** *Arch. or dialect.* harm. ORIG OE *sceatha*

scathing (ˈskeɪðɪŋ) *adj* **1** harshly critical; scornful. **2** damaging.
▸ **ˈscathingly** *adv*

scatology (skæˈtɒlədʒɪ) *n* **1** the scientific study of excrement, esp. in medicine and in palaeontology. **2** obscenity or preoccupation with obscenity, esp. in the form of references to excrement. ORIG C19: from Gk *skat-* excrement + -LOGY
▸ **scatological** (ˌskætəˈlɒdʒɪkᵊl) *adj*

scatter (ˈskætə) *vb* **1** (*tr*) to throw about in various directions. **2** to separate and move or cause to separate and move in various directions. **3** to deviate or cause to deviate in many directions, as in the refraction of light. ◆ *n* **4** the act of scattering. **5** a substance or a number of objects scattered about. ORIG C13: prob. a var. of SHATTER
▸ **ˈscatterer** *n*

scatterbrain (ˈskætəˌbreɪn) *n* a person who is incapable of serious thought or concentration.
▸ **ˈscatterˌbrained** *adj*

scatter diagram *n Statistics.* a representation by a Cartesian graph of the correlation between two quantities, such as height and weight.

scattering (ˈskætərɪŋ) *n* **1** a small amount. **2** *Physics.* the process in which particles, atoms, etc., are deflected as a result of collision.

scatty (ˈskætɪ) *adj* **scattier, scattiest.** *Brit. inf.* **1** empty-headed or thoughtless. **2** distracted (esp. in **drive someone scatty**). ORIG C20: from SCATTERBRAINED
▸ **ˈscattily** *adv* ▸ **ˈscattiness** *n*

scaup *or* **scaup duck** (skɔːp) *n* either of two diving ducks, the **greater scaup** or the **lesser scaup**, of Europe and America, having a black-and-white plumage in the male. ORIG C16: Scot. var. of SCALP

scavenge (ˈskævɪndʒ) *vb* **scavenges, scavenging, scavenged. 1** to search for (anything usable) among discarded material. **2** (*tr*) to purify (a molten metal) by bubbling a suitable gas through it. **3** to clean up filth from (streets, etc.).

scavenger (ˈskævɪndʒə) *n* **1** a person who collects things discarded by others. **2** any animal that feeds on decaying organic matter. **3** a person employed to clean the streets. ORIG C16: from Anglo-Norman *scawager*, from OF *escauwage* examination, from *escauwer* to scrutinize, of Gmc origin
▸ **ˈscavengery** *n*

ScD *abbrev. for* Doctor of Science.

SCE (in Scotland) *abbrev. for* Scottish Certificate of Education: either of two public examinations in specific subjects taken as school-leaving qualifications or as qualifying examinations for entry into a university, college, etc.

scena (ˈʃeɪnə) *n, pl* **scene** (-ˌneɪ). a solo vocal piece of dramatic style and large scope, esp. in opera. ORIG C19: It., from L *scēna* scene

scenario (sɪˈnɑːrɪˌəʊ) *n, pl* **scenarios. 1** a summary of the plot of a play, etc., including information about its characters, scenes, etc. **2** a predicted sequence of events. ORIG C19: via It. from L *scēnārium*, from *scēna*; see SCENE

scene (siːn) *n* **1** the place where an action or event, real or imaginary, occurs. **2** the setting for the action of a play, novel, etc. **3** an incident or situation, real or imaginary, esp. as described or represented. **4a** a subdivision of an act of a play, in which the setting is fixed. **4b** a single event, esp. a significant one, in a play. **5** *Films.* a shot or series of shots that constitutes a unit of the action. **6** the backcloths, etc., for a play or film set. **7** the prospect of a place, landscape, etc. **8** a display of emotion. **9** *Inf.* the environment for a specific activity: *the fashion scene.* **10** *Inf.* interest or chosen occupation: *classical music is not my scene.* **11** *Rare.* the stage. **12 behind the scenes.** out of public view. ORIG C16: from L *scēna* theatrical stage, from Gk *skēnē* tent, stage

scene dock *or* **bay** *n* a place in a theatre where scenery is stored, usually near the stage.

scenery (ˈsiːnərɪ) *n, pl* **sceneries. 1** the natural features of a landscape. **2** *Theatre.* the painted backcloths, etc., used to represent a location in a theatre or studio. ORIG C18: from It. SCENARIO

scenic (ˈsiːnɪk) *adj* **1** of or relating to natural scenery. **2** having beautiful natural scenery: *a scenic drive.* **3** of or relating to the stage or stage scenery. **4** (in painting, etc.) representing a scene.
▸ **ˈscenically** *adv*

scenic railway *n* a miniature railway used for amusement in a park, zoo, etc.

scenic reserve *n NZ.* an area of natural beauty, set aside for public recreation.

scent (sɛnt) *n* **1** a distinctive smell, esp. a pleasant one. **2** a smell left in passing, by which a person or animal may be traced. **3** a trail, clue, or guide. **4** an instinctive ability for detecting. **5** another word (esp. Brit.) for **perfume.** ◆ *vb* **6** (*tr*) to recognize by or as if by the smell. **7** (*tr*) to have a suspicion of: *I scent foul play.* **8** (*tr*) to fill with odour or fragrance. **9** (*intr*) (of hounds, etc.) to hunt by the sense of smell. **10** to smell (at): *the dog scented the air.* ORIG C14: from OF *sentir* to sense, from L *sentīre* to feel
▸ **ˈscented** *adj*

sceptic *or arch. & US* **skeptic** (ˈskɛptɪk) *n* **1** a person who habitually doubts the authenticity of accepted beliefs. **2** a person who mistrusts people, ideas, etc., in general. **3** a person who doubts the truth of religion. ORIG C16: from L *scepticus*, from Gk *skeptikos* one who reflects upon, from *skeptesthai* to consider
▸ **ˈsceptical** *or arch. & US* **ˈskeptical** *adj* ▸ **ˈsceptically** *or arch. & US* **ˈskeptically** *adv* ▸ **ˈscepticism** *or arch. & US* **ˈskepticism** *n*

Sceptic *or arch. & US* **Skeptic** (ˈskɛptɪk) *n* **1** a member of one of the ancient Greek schools of philosophy, esp. that of Pyrrho, who believed that real knowledge of things is impossible. ◆ *adj* **2** of or relating to the Sceptics.
▸ **ˈScepticism** *or arch. & US* **ˈSkepticism** *n*

sceptre *or US* **scepter** (ˈsɛptə) *n* **1** a ceremonial staff held by a monarch as the symbol of authority. **2** imperial authority; sovereignty. ORIG C13: from OF *sceptre*, from L, from Gk *skeptron* staff
▸ **ˈsceptred** *or US* **ˈsceptered** *adj*

Schaerbeek ★ (*Flemish* ˈsxaːrbeːk) *n* a city in central Belgium: an industrial suburb of Brussels. Pop.: 102 417 (1992 est.).

Schaffhausen ★ (*German* ʃaːfˈhauzən) *n* **1** a small canton of N Switzerland. Pop.: 73 894 (1995 est.). Area: 298 sq. km (115 sq. miles). **2** a town in N Switzerland, capital of Schaffhausen canton, on the Rhine. Pop.: 70 000 (latest est.). French name: **Schaffhouse.**

Schama ★ (ˈʃɑːmə) *n* **Simon.** born 1945, British historian and art historian, whose books include *Citizens* (1989) and *Rembrandt's Eyes* (1999); noted esp. for his television series *A History of Britain* (2000).

Schaumburg-Lippe ★ (*German* ˈʃaumburkˈlɪpə) *n* a former state of NW Germany, between Westphalia and Hanover: part of Lower Saxony since 1946.

schedule (ˈʃɛdjuːl; *also, esp. US* ˈskɛdʒʊəl) *n* **1** a plan of procedure for a project. **2** a list of items: *a schedule of fixed prices.* **3** a list of times; timetable. **4** a list of tasks to be performed, esp. within a set period. **5** *Law.* a list or inventory. ◆ *vb* **schedules, scheduling, scheduled.** (*tr*) **6** to make a schedule of or place in a schedule. **7** to plan to occur at a certain time. ORIG C14: earlier *cedule, sedule* via OF from LL *schedula* small piece of paper, from L *scheda* sheet of paper

scheduled castes *pl n* certain classes in Indian society officially granted special concessions. See **Harijan.**

scheduled territories *pl n* **the.** another name for **sterling area.**

Scheele ★ (*Swedish* 'ʃeːlə) *n* **Karl Wilhelm** (kɑːrl 'vilhɛlm). 1742–86, Swedish chemist, who discovered oxygen.

scheelite ('ʃiːlaɪt) *n* a white, brownish, or greenish mineral, usually fluorescent, consisting of calcium tungstate with some tungsten often replaced by molybdenum. It is an important source of tungsten. ORIG C19: from G *Scheelit,* after K. W. SCHEELE

Scheldt ★ (ʃɛlt, skɛlt) *n* a river in W Europe, rising in NE France and flowing north and northeast through W Belgium to Antwerp, then northwest to the North Sea in the SW Netherlands. Length: 435 km (270 miles). Flemish and Dutch name: **Schelde** ('sxɛldɛ). French name: **Escaut.**

Schelling ★ (*German* 'ʃɛlɪŋ) *n* **Friedrich Wilhelm Joseph von** ('friːdrɪç 'vɪlhɛlm 'joːzɛf fɔn). 1775–1854, German philosopher. His works include *System of Transcendental Idealism* (1800).
▸ **Schellingian** (ʃɛ'lɪŋɪən) *adj*

schema ('skiːmə) *n, pl* **schemata** (-mətə). **1** a plan, diagram, or scheme. **2** (in the philosophy of Kant) a rule or principle that enables the understanding to unify experience. **3** *Logic.* **3a** a syllogistic figure. **3b** a representation of the form of an inference. ORIG C19: from Gk: form

schematic (skɪ'mætɪk) *adj* **1** of or relating to the nature of a diagram, plan, or schema. ◆ *n* **2** a schematic diagram, esp. of an electrical circuit, etc.
▸ **sche'matically** *adv*

schematize *or* **schematise** ('skiːməˌtaɪz) *vb* **schematizes, schematizing, schematized** *or* **schematises, schematising, schematised.** (*tr*) to form into or arrange in a scheme.
▸ **'schemaˌtism** *n* ▸ **ˌschemati'zation** *or* **ˌschemati'sation** *n*

scheme (skiːm) *n* **1** a systematic plan for a course of action. **2** a systematic arrangement of parts. **3** a secret plot. **4** a chart, diagram, or outline. **5** an astrological diagram giving the aspects of celestial bodies. **6** *Chiefly Brit.* a plan formally adopted by a commercial enterprise or governmental body, as for pensions, etc. **7** Short for **housing scheme.** ◆ *vb* **schemes, scheming, schemed. 8** (*tr*) to devise a system for. **9** to form intrigues (for) in an underhand manner. ORIG C16: from L *schema,* from Gk *skhēma* form
▸ **'schemer** *n*

scheming ('skiːmɪŋ) *adj* **1** given to making plots; cunning. ◆ *n* **2** intrigues.

Schengen Convention *or* **Agreement** ('ʃɛŋən) *n* an agreement, signed in 1985, but not implemented until 1995, to abolish border controls within Europe: thirteen countries had acceded by 1995; the UK is not a signatory.

scherzando (skɛə'tsændəʊ) *Music.* ◆ *adj, adv* **1** to be performed in a light-hearted manner. ◆ *n, pl* **scherzandi** (-diː) *or* **scherzandos. 2** a movement, passage, etc., directed to be performed in this way. ORIG It., lit.: joking; see SCHERZO

scherzo ('skɛətsəʊ) *n, pl* **scherzos** *or* **scherzi** (-tsiː). a brisk lively movement, developed from the minuet, with a contrastive middle section (a trio). ORIG It.: joke, of Gmc origin

Schiaparelli ★ (*Italian* skjapa'rɛlli) *n* **1 Elsa** ('elsa). 1896–1973, Italian couturière. **2 Giovanni Virginio** (dʒo'vanni vir'dʒiːnjo). 1835–1910, Italian astronomer, who discovered the asteroid Hesperia (1861).

Schick test (ʃɪk) *n Med.* a skin test to determine immunity to diphtheria. ORIG C20: after Bela *Schick* (1877–1967), US paediatrician

Schiedam ★ (*Dutch* sxiː'dɑm) *n* a port in the SW Netherlands, in South Holland province west of Rotterdam: gin distilleries. Pop.: 72 515 (1994).

Schiele ★ (*German* 'ʃiːlə) *n* **Egon** ('eːgɔn). 1890–1918, Austrian expressionist painter.

Schiller ★ (*German* 'ʃɪlər) *n* **Johann Christoph Friedrich von** (jo'han 'krɪstɔf 'friːdrɪç fɔn). 1759–1805, German writer. His plays include the trilogy *Wallenstein* (1800) and *Maria Stuart* (1800).

schilling ('ʃɪlɪŋ) *n* the standard monetary unit of Austria. ORIG C18: from G: SHILLING

schism ('skɪzəm, 'sɪz-) *n* **1** the division of a group into opposing factions. **2** the factions so formed. **3** division within or separation from an established Church, not necessarily involving differences in doctrine. ORIG C14: from Church L *schisma,* from Gk *skhisma* a cleft, from *skhizein* to split

schismatic (skɪz'mætɪk, sɪz-) *or* **schismatical** *adj* **1** of or promoting schism. ◆ *n* **2** a person who causes schism or belongs to a schismatic faction.
▸ **schis'matically** *adv*

schist (ʃɪst) *n* any metamorphic rock that can be split into thin layers. ORIG C18: from F *schiste,* from L *lapis schistos* stone that may be split, from Gk *skhizein* to split
▸ **'schistose** *adj*

schistosome ('ʃɪstəˌsəʊm) *n* any of a genus of blood flukes which cause disease in man and domestic animals. Also called: **bilharzia.** ORIG C19: from NL *Schistosoma;* see SCHIST, -SOME[3]

schistosomiasis (ˌʃɪstəsəʊ'maɪəsɪs) *n* a disease caused by infestation of the body with schistosomes. Also called: **bilharziasis.**

schizanthus (skɪz'ænθəs) *n* a flowering annual plant, native to Chile, that has finely divided leaves. ORIG C19: NL from Gk *skhizein* to cut + *anthos* flower

schizo ('skɪtsəʊ) *Offens.* ◆ *adj* **1** schizophrenic. ◆ *n, pl* **schizos. 2** a schizophrenic person.

schizo- *or before a vowel* **schiz-** *combining form.* indicating a cleavage, split, or division: *schizophrenia.* ORIG from Gk *skhizein* to split

schizocarp ('skɪzəˌkɑːp) *n Bot.* a dry fruit that splits into two or more one-seeded portions at maturity.
▸ **ˌschizo'carpous** *adj*

schizoid ('skɪtsɔɪd) *adj* **1** *Psychol.* denoting a personality disorder characterized by extreme shyness and oversensitivity. **2** *Inf.* characterized by conflicting or contradictory ideas, attitudes, etc. ◆ *n* **3** a person who has a schizoid personality.

schizomycete (ˌskɪtsəʊmaɪ'siːt) *n* any microscopic organism of the class *Schizomycetes,* which includes the bacteria.

schizophrenia (ˌskɪtsəʊ'friːnɪə) *n* **1** any of a group of psychotic disorders characterized by progressive deterioration of the personality, withdrawal from reality, hallucinations, emotional instability, etc. **2** *Inf.* behaviour that seems to be motivated by contradictory or conflicting principles. ORIG C20: from SCHIZO- + Gk *phrēn* mind
▸ **ˌschizo'phrenic** *adj, n*

schizothymia (ˌskɪtsəʊ'θaɪmɪə) *n Psychiatry.* the condition of being schizoid or introverted. It encompasses elements of schizophrenia. ORIG C20: NL, from SCHIZO- + *-thymia,* from Gk *thumos* spirit
▸ **ˌschizo'thymic** *adj*

Schlegel ★ (*German* 'ʃleːgəl) *n* **1 August Wilhelm von** ('august 'vɪlhɛlm fɔn). 1767–1845, German romantic critic and scholar, noted particularly for his translations of Shakespeare. **2** his brother, **Friedrich von** ('friːdrɪç fɔn). 1772–1829, German philosopher and critic; a founder of the romantic movement in Germany.

Schlesien ★ ('ʃleːziən) *n* the German name for **Silesia.**

Schlesinger ★ ('ʃlɛsɪndʒə) *n* **John** (**Richard**). born 1926, British film and theatre director. Films include *Billy Liar* (1963), *Midnight Cowboy* (1969), and *Eye for an Eye* (1995).

Schleswig ★ (*German* 'ʃleːsvɪç) *n* **1** a fishing port in N Germany, in Schleswig-Holstein state: on an inlet of the Baltic; formerly in West Germany. Pop.: 30 000 (1985 est.). **2** a former duchy, in the S Jutland Peninsula: annexed by Prussia in 1864; N part returned to Denmark after a plebiscite in 1920; S part forms part of the German state of Schleswig-Holstein. Danish name: **Slesvig.**

Schleswig-Holstein ★ (*German* 'ʃleːsvɪç'hɔlʃtain) *n* a state of N Germany, formerly in West Germany: drained chiefly by the River Elbe; mainly agricultural. Capital:

Kiel. Pop.: 2 730 600 (1996 est.). Area: 15 658 sq. km (6045 sq. miles).

Schlick ★ (*German* ʃlɪk) *n* **Moritz** ('mo:rɪts). 1882–1936, German philosopher, working in Austria, who founded (1924) the Vienna Circle to develop the doctrine of logical positivism.

Schlieffen ★ (*German* 'ʃli:fən) *n* **Alfred** ('alfre:t), Count von Schlieffen. 1833–1913, German field marshal, who devised the **Schlieffen Plan** (1905) to ensure German victory over a Franco-Russian alliance by holding off Russia and swiftly defeating France by a flanking movement. A modified version was unsuccessfully used in World War I (1914).

Schliemann ★ (*German* 'ʃli:man) *n* **Heinrich** ('hainrɪç). 1822–90, German archaeologist, who discovered the nine superimposed cities of Troy (1871–90) and excavated Mycenae (1876).

schlieren ('ʃlɪərən) *n* **1** *Physics.* visible streaks produced in a transparent fluid as a result of variations in the fluid's density. **2** streaks or platelike masses of mineral in a rock mass. ORIG G, pl of *Schliere* streak

schmaltz *or* **schmalz** (ʃmælts, ʃmɔ:lts) *n* excessive sentimentality. ORIG C20: from G (*Schmalz*) & Yiddish: melted fat, from OHG *smalz*
▸ **'schmaltzy** *or* **'schmalzy** *adj*

Schmidt ★ (ʃmɪt) *n* **Helmut (Heinrich Waldemar)** ('hɛlmu:t). born 1918, German Social Democrat statesman; chancellor of West Germany (1974–82).

Schmidt telescope *or* **camera** (ʃmɪt) *n* a catadioptric telescope designed to produce a very sharp image of a large area of sky in one photographic exposure. ORIG C20: after B. V. *Schmidt* (1879–1935), Estonian-born G inventor

Schnabel ★ ('ʃnɑ:bᵊl) *n* **Artur** ('artur). 1882–1951, US pianist, born in Austria.

schnapper ('ʃnæpə) *n* a variant spelling of **snapper** (senses 1, 2).

schnapps *or* **schnaps** (ʃnæps) *n* **1** a Dutch spirit distilled from potatoes. **2** (in Germany) any strong spirit. ORIG C19: from G *Schnaps,* from *schnappen* to SNAP

schnauzer ('ʃnaʊtsə) *n* a wire-haired breed of dog of the terrier type, originally from Germany, with a greyish coat. ORIG C19: from G *Schnauze* snout

Schnittke ★ ('ʃnɪtkə) *n* **Alfred.** 1934–98, Russian composer: his works include four symphonies, four violin concertos, choral, chamber, and film music.

schnitzel ('ʃnɪtsəl) *n* a thin slice of meat, esp. veal. ORIG G: cutlet, from *schnitzen* to carve, *schnitzeln* to whittle

schnorkel ('ʃnɔ:kᵊl) *n, vb* **schnorkels, schnorkelling, schnorkelled.** a less common variant of **snorkel.**

schnozzle ('ʃnɒzᵊl) *n Chiefly US.* a slang word for **nose.** ORIG alteration of Yiddish *shnoitsl,* from G *Schnauze* snout

Schoenberg *or* **Schönberg ★** ('ʃɜ:nbɜ:g; *German* 'ʃø.nbɛrk) *n* **Arnold** ('arnɔlt). 1874–1951, Austrian composer, in the US after 1933, who developed the twelve-tone technique. His works include the song cycle *Pierrot Lunaire* (1912) and the unfinished opera *Moses and Aaron.*

scholar ('skɒlə) *n* **1** a learned person, esp. in the humanities. **2** a person, esp. a child, who studies; pupil. **3** a student receiving a scholarship. **4** *S. African.* a school pupil. ORIG C14: from OF *escoler,* via LL from L *schola* SCHOOL[1]
▸ **'scholarly** *adj* ▸ **'scholarliness** *n*

scholarship ('skɒləʃɪp) *n* **1** academic achievement; learning. **2a** financial aid provided for a scholar because of academic merit. **2b** the position of a student who gains this financial aid. **2c** (*as modifier*): *a scholarship student.* **3** the qualities of a scholar.

scholastic (skə'læstɪk) *adj* **1** of or befitting schools, scholars, or education. **2** pedantic or precise. **3** (*often cap.*) characteristic of or relating to the medieval Schoolmen. ◆ *n* **4** a student or pupil. **5** a person who is given to logical subtleties. **6** (*often cap.*) a disciple or adherent of scholasticism; Schoolman. **7** a Jesuit student who is undergoing a period of probation prior to commencing his theological studies. ORIG C16: via L from Gk *skholastikos* devoted to learning, ult. from *skholē* SCHOOL[1]
▸ **scho'lastically** *adv*

scholasticism (skə'læstɪˌsɪzəm) *n* (*sometimes cap.*) the system of philosophy, theology, and teaching that dominated medieval western Europe and was based on the writings of the Church Fathers and Aristotle.

scholiast ('skəʊlɪˌæst) *n* a medieval annotator, esp. of classical texts. ORIG C16: from LGk, ult. from Gk *skholē* school
▸ **ˌscholi'astic** *adj*

Schönberg ★ ('ʃɜ:nbɜ:g; *German* 'ʃø:nbɛrk) *n* See **Schoenberg.**

Schongauer ★ (*German* 'ʃo:ngauər) *n* **Martin** ('marti:n). ?1445–91, German painter.

school[1] (sku:l) *n* **1a** an institution or building at which children and young people receive education. **1b** (*as modifier*): *school day.* **1c** (*in combination*): *schoolwork.* **2** any educational institution or building. **3** a faculty or department specializing in a particular subject: *a law school.* **4** the staff and pupils of a school. **5** the period of instruction in a school or one session of this: *he stayed after school to do extra work.* **6** a place or sphere of activity that instructs: *the school of hard knocks.* **7** a body of people or pupils adhering to a certain set of principles, doctrines, or methods. **8** a group of artists, writers, etc., linked by the same style, teachers, or aims. **9** a style of life: *a gentleman of the old school.* **10** *Inf.* a group assembled for a common purpose, esp. gambling or drinking. ◆ *vb* (*tr*) **11** to train or educate in or as in a school. **12** to discipline or control. ORIG OE *scōl,* from L *schola* school, from Gk *skholē* leisure spent in the pursuit of knowledge

school[2] (sku:l) *n* **1** a group of fish or other aquatic animals that swim together. ◆ *vb* **2** (*intr*) to form such a group. ORIG OE *scolu* SHOAL[2]

school board *n* **1** *English History.* an elected board of ratepayers who provided elementary schools (**board schools**). **2** (in the US and Canada) a local board of education.

schoolboy ('sku:lˌbɔɪ) *or* (*fem*) **schoolgirl** *n* a child attending school.

schoolhouse ('sku:lˌhaʊs) *n* **1** a building used as a school. **2** a house attached to a school.

schoolie ('sku:lɪ) *n Austral. sl.* **1** a schoolteacher. **2** a high school student.

schooling ('sku:lɪŋ) *n* **1** education, esp. when received at school. **2** the process of teaching or being taught in a school. **3** the training of an animal, esp. of a horse for dressage.

schoolman ('sku:lmən) *n, pl* **schoolmen.** (*sometimes cap.*) a scholar versed in the learning of the **Schoolmen**, the masters in the universities of the Middle Ages who were versed in scholasticism.

schoolmarm ('sku:lˌmɑ:m) *n Inf.* **1** a woman schoolteacher. **2** any woman considered to be prim or old-fashioned.
▸ **'schoolˌmarmish** *adj*

schoolmaster ('sku:lˌmɑ:stə) *or* (*fem*) **schoolmistress** *n* **1** a person who teaches in or runs a school. **2** a person or thing that acts as an instructor.

schoolmate ('sku:lˌmeɪt) *or* **schoolfellow** *n* a companion at school; fellow pupil.

school of arts *n Austral.* a public building in a small town: orig. one used for adult education.

Schools (sku:lz) *pl n* **1** **the Schools.** the medieval Schoolmen collectively. **2** (at Oxford University) **2a** the University building in which examinations are held. **2b** *Inf.* the Second Public Examination for the degree of Bachelor of Arts.

schoolteacher ('sku:lˌti:tʃə) *n* a person who teaches in a school.
▸ **'schoolˌteaching** *n*

school year *n* **1** a twelve-month period, usually of three terms, during which pupils remain in the same class. **2** the time during this period when the school is open.

schooner ('sku:nə) *n* **1** a sailing vessel with at least two masts, with all lower sails rigged fore-and-aft, and with the main mast stepped aft. **2** *Brit.* a large glass for sherry. **3** *US, Canad., Austral., & NZ.* a large glass for beer. ORIG C18: from ?

Schopenhauer ★ (*German* 'ʃoːpənhauər) *n* **Arthur** ('artʊr). 1788–1860, German philosopher, noted for his *The World as Will and Idea* (1819).
▸ **Schopenhauerian** (ˌʃəupən'hauərɪən) *adj* ▸ **'Schopenˌhauerˌism** *n*

schottische (ʃɒ'tiːʃ) *n* **1** a 19th-century German dance resembling a slow polka. **2** a piece of music composed for or in the manner of this dance. ORIG C19: from G *der schottische Tanz* the Scottish dance

Schottky effect ('ʃɒtkɪ) *n Physics.* a reduction in the energy required to remove an electron from a solid surface in a vacuum when an electric field is applied to the surface. ORIG C20: after W. *Schottky* (1886–1976), G physicist

Schouten Islands ★ ('ʃautᵊn) *pl n* a group of islands in the Pacific, off the N coast of Irian Jaya. Pop.: 25 487 (1966). Area: 3185 sq. km (1230 sq. miles).

Schreiner ★ ('ʃraɪnə) *n* **Olive** (**Emilie Albertina**). 1855–1920, South African novelist and feminist writer, whose works include the autobiographical *The Story of an African Farm* (1883).

Schrödinger ★ (*German* 'ʃrøːdɪŋər) *n* **Erwin** ('ɛrviːn). 1887–1961, Austrian physicist, who discovered the **Schrödinger wave equation**: shared the Nobel prize for physics 1933.

Schubert ★ ('ʃuːbət) *n* **Franz** (**Peter**) (*German* frants). 1797–1828, Austrian composer; his many songs include the cycles *Die Winterreise* (1827); other works include symphonies and much piano and chamber music.

Schumacher ★ (*German* 'ʃuːmaxər) *n* **1 Ernst Friedrich** (ɛrnst 'friːdrɪç). 1911–77, British economist, born in Germany, noted for his book *Small is Beautiful* (1973). **2 Michael.** born 1969, German motor-racing driver.

Schuman ★ *n* **1** (*French* ʃuman). **Robert** (rɔbɛr). 1886–1963, French statesman; prime minister (1947–48). **2** ('ʃuːmən). **William** (**Howard**). 1910–91, US composer.

Schumann ★ ('ʃuːmən) *n* **1 Elisabeth** (*German* e'liːzabɛt). 1885–1952, German lieder singer. **2 Robert Alexander** (*German* 'roːbɛrt alɛ'ksandər). 1810–56, German composer, noted for his piano music, such as *Carneval* (1835), his songs, and four symphonies.

schuss (ʃʊs) *Skiing.* ◆ *n* **1** a straight high-speed downhill run. ◆ *vb* **2** (*intr*) to perform a schuss. ORIG G: SHOT[1]

Schütz ★ (*German* ʃyts) *n* **Heinrich** ('hainrɪç). 1585–1672, German composer, esp. of church music and madrigals.

schwa *or* **shwa** (ʃwɑː) *n* **1** a central vowel represented in the International Phonetic Alphabet by (ə). The sound occurs in unstressed syllables in English, as in *around* and *sofa.* **2** the symbol (ə) used to represent this sound. ORIG C19: via G from Heb. *shewā,* a diacritic indicating lack of a vowel sound

Schwaben ★ ('ʃvaːbən) *n* the German name for **Swabia.**

Schwarzkopf ★ *n* **1** (*German* 'ʃvartskɔpf). **Elisabeth** (e'liːzabɛt). born 1915, Austro-British soprano, born in Germany. **2** ('ʃwɔːtsˌkɒpf). **Norman,** nicknamed *Stormin' Norman.* born 1934, US general: victorious commander-in-chief of the US-led forces in the Gulf War (1991).

Schwarzwald ★ ('ʃvartsvalt) *n* the German name for the **Black Forest.**

Schweinfurt ★ (*German* 'ʃvainfʊrt) *n* a city in central Germany, in N Bavaria on the River Main. Pop.: 54 520 (1991).

Schweitzer ★ ('ʃwaɪtsə, 'ʃvaɪt-) *n* **Albert.** 1875–1965, Franco-German physician, theologian, and organist, born in Alsace. He devoted most of his life after 1913 to a mission at Lambaréné, Gabon: Nobel peace prize 1952.

Schweiz ★ (ʃvaits) *n* the German name for **Switzerland.**

Schwerin ★ (*German* ʃve'riːn) *n* a city in N Germany, in Mecklenburg-West Pomerania on **Lake Schwerin.** Pop.: 114 688 (1996 est.).

Schwitters ★ (*German* 'ʃvɪtərs) *n* **Kurt** (kʊrt). 1887–1948, German Dadaist painter and poet.

Schwyz ★ (*German* ʃviːts) *n* **1** a canton of central Switzerland: played an important part in the formation of the Swiss confederation, to which it gave its name. Capital: Schwyz. Pop.: 120 576 (1995 est.). Area: 908 sq. km (351 sq. miles). **2** a town in E central Switzerland, capital of Schwyz canton: tourism. Pop.: 12 740 (1990).

sci. *abbrev. for:* **1** science. **2** scientific.

sciatic (saɪ'ætɪk) *adj* **1** *Anat.* of or relating to the hip or the hipbone. **2** of or afflicted with sciatica. ORIG C16: from F, from LL, from L *ischiadicus* relating to pain in the hip, from Gk, from *iskhia* hip-joint

sciatica (saɪ'ætɪkə) *n* a form of neuralgia characterized by intense pain along the body's longest nerve (**sciatic nerve**), extending from the back of the thigh down to the calf of the leg. ORIG C15: from LL *sciatica;* see SCIATIC

science ('saɪəns) *n* **1** the systematic study of the nature and behaviour of the material and physical universe, based on observation, experiment, and measurement. **2** the knowledge so obtained or the practice of obtaining it. **3** any particular branch of this knowledge: *the applied sciences.* **4** any body of knowledge organized in a systematic manner. **5** skill or technique. **6** *Arch.* knowledge. ORIG C14: via OF from L *scientia* knowledge, from *scīre* to know

science fiction *n* **a** a literary genre that makes imaginative use of scientific knowledge. **b** (*as modifier*): *a science-fiction writer.*

Science Museum *n* a museum in London, originating from 1852 and given its present name and site in 1899: contains collections relating to the history of science, technology, and industry.

science park *n* an area where scientific research and commercial development are carried on in cooperation.

scienter (saɪ'ɛntə) *adv Law.* knowingly; wilfully. ORIG from L

sciential (saɪ'ɛnʃəl) *adj* **1** of or relating to science. **2** skilful or knowledgeable.

scientific (ˌsaɪən'tɪfɪk) *adj* **1** (*prenominal*) of, derived from, or used in science: *scientific equipment.* **2** (*prenominal*) occupied in science: *scientific manpower.* **3** conforming with the methods used in science.
▸ **ˌscien'tifically** *adv*

scientism ('saɪənˌtɪzəm) *n* **1** the application of the scientific method. **2** the uncritical application of scientific methods to inappropriate fields of study.
▸ **ˌscien'tistic** *adj*

scientist ('saɪəntɪst) *n* a person who studies or practises any of the sciences or who uses scientific methods.

Scientology (ˌsaɪən'tɒlədʒɪ) *n Trademark.* the philosophy of the Church of Scientology, a nondenominational movement founded in the US in the 1950s, which emphasizes self-knowledge as a means of realizing full spiritual potential. ORIG C20: from L *scient(ia)* SCIENCE + -LOGY
▸ **ˌScien'tologist** *n*

sci-fi ('saɪ'faɪ) *n* short for **science fiction.**

scilicet ('sɪlɪˌsɛt) *adv* namely: used esp. in explaining an obscure text or supplying a missing word. ORIG L: from *scīre licet* it is permitted to know

scilla ('sɪlə) *n* any of a genus of liliaceous plants having small bell-shaped flowers. See also **squill** (sense 3). ORIG C19: via L from Gk *skilla*

Scilly Isles, Scilly Islands ('sɪlɪ), *or* **Scillies** ★ ('sɪlɪz) *pl n* a group of about 140 small islands (only five inhabited) off the extreme SW coast of England; tourist centre. Capital: Hugh Town. Pop.: 2900 (1991). Area: 16 sq. km (6 sq. miles).
▸ **Scillonian** (sɪ'ləunɪən) *adj, n*

scimitar ('sɪmɪtə) *n* an oriental sword with a curved blade broadening towards the point. ORIG C16: from OIt., prob. from Persian *shimshīr,* from ?

scintigraphy (ˌsɪn'tɪgrəfɪ) *n Med.* a diagnostic technique using a radioactive tracer and scintillation counter for producing pictures (**scintigrams**) of internal parts of the body. ORIG C20: from SCINTI(LLATION) + -GRAPHY

scintilla (sɪn'tɪlə) *n* a minute amount; hint, trace, or particle. ORIG C17: from L: a spark

scintillate ('sɪntɪˌleɪt) *vb* **scintillates, scintillating, scintillated.** (*mainly intr*) **1** (*also tr*) to give off (sparks); sparkle. **2** to be animated or brilliant. **3** *Physics.* to give off flashes of light as a result of the impact of photons. ORIG C17: from L *scintillāre,* from *scintilla* a spark
▸ **'scintillant** *adj* ▸ **'scintilˌlating** *adj*

scintillation (ˌsɪntɪˈleɪʃən) *n* **1** the act of scintillating. **2** a spark or flash. **3** the twinkling of stars. **4** *Physics.* a flash of light produced when a material scintillates.

scintillation counter *n* an instrument for detecting and measuring the intensity of high-energy radiation. It consists of a phosphor with which particles collide producing flashes of light that are converted into pulses of electric current that are counted by electronic equipment.

sciolism (ˈsaɪəˌlɪzəm) *n Rare.* the practice of opinionating on subjects of which one has only superficial knowledge. ORIG C19: from LL *sciolus* someone with a smattering of knowledge, from L *scīre* to know
▸ **ˈsciolist** *n* ▸ **ˌscioˈlistic** *adj*

scion (ˈsaɪən) *n* **1** a descendant or young member of a family. **2** a shoot of a plant used to form a graft. ORIG C14: from OF *cion,* of Gmc origin

Scipio ★ (ˈskɪpɪˌəʊ, ˈsɪpɪˌəʊ) *n* **1** full name *Publius Cornelius Scipio Africanus Major.* 237–183 B.C., Roman general. He commanded the Roman invasion of Carthage in the Second Punic War, defeating Hannibal at Zama (202). **2** his grandson by adoption, full name *Publius Cornelius Scipio Aemilianus Africanus Minor.* ?185–129 B.C., Roman statesman and general; commanded an army in the last Punic War and destroyed Carthage (146).

scirrhus (ˈsɪrəs) *n, pl* **scirrhi** (-raɪ) *or* **scirrhuses.** *Pathol.* a firm cancerous growth composed of fibrous tissues. ORIG C17: from NL, from L *scirros,* from Gk, from *skiros* hard
▸ **scirrhoid** (ˈsɪrɔɪd) *adj*

scission (ˈsɪʃən) *n* the act or an instance of cutting, splitting, or dividing. ORIG C15: from LL *scissiō,* from *scindere* to split

scissor (ˈsɪzə) *vb* to cut (an object) with scissors.

scissors (ˈsɪzəz) *pl n* **1** Also called: **pair of scissors.** a cutting instrument used for cloth, hair, etc., having two crossed pivoted blades that cut by a shearing action. **2** a wrestling hold in which the legs are wrapped round the opponent's body or head and squeezed. **3** any gymnastic feat in which the legs cross and uncross in a scissor-like movement. ORIG C14 *sisoures,* from OF *cisoires,* from Vulgar L *cīsōria* (unattested), ult. from L *caedere* to cut

scissors kick *n* a type of swimming kick in which one leg is moved forward and the other bent back and they are then brought together again in a scissor-like action.

sciurine (ˈsaɪjʊrɪn, -ˌraɪn) *adj* of or belonging to a family of rodents inhabiting most parts of the world except Australia and southern South America: includes squirrels, marmots, and chipmunks. ORIG C19: from L *sciūrus,* from Gk *skiouros* squirrel, from *skia* a shadow + *oura* a tail

sclera (ˈsklɪərə) *n* the firm white fibrous membrane that forms the outer covering of the eyeball. Also called: **sclerotic.** ORIG C19: from NL, from Gk *sklēros* hard
▸ **scleˈritis** *n*

sclerenchyma (sklɪəˈrɛŋkɪmə) *n* a supporting tissue in plants consisting of dead cells with very thick lignified walls. ORIG C19: from SCLERO- + PARENCHYMA

sclero- *or before a vowel* **scler-** *combining form.* **1** indicating hardness: *sclerosis.* **2** of the sclera: *sclerotomy.* ORIG from Gk *sklēros* hard

scleroderma (ˌsklɪərəʊˈdɜːmə) *or* **sclerodermia** (ˌsklɪərəʊˈdɜːmɪə) *n* a chronic disease common among women, characterized by thickening and hardening of the skin.

scleroma (sklɪəˈrəʊmə) *n, pl* **scleromata** (-mətə). *Pathol.* any small area of abnormally hard tissue, esp. in a mucous membrane. ORIG C17: from NL, from Gk, from *sklēroun* to harden, from *sklēros* hard

scleroprotein (ˌsklɪərəʊˈprəʊtiːn) *n* any of a group of insoluble stable proteins such as keratin that occur in skeletal and connective tissues. Also called: **albuminoid.**

sclerosis (sklɪəˈrəʊsɪs) *n, pl* **scleroses** (-siːz). **1** *Pathol.* a hardening or thickening of organs, tissues, or vessels from inflammation, degeneration, or (esp. on the inner walls of arteries) deposition of fatty plaques. **2** the hardening of a plant cell wall or tissue. ORIG C14: via Med. L from Gk *sklērōsis* a hardening

sclerotic (sklɪəˈrɒtɪk) *adj* **1** of or relating to the sclera. **2** of, relating to, or having sclerosis. ◆ *n* **3** another name for **sclera.** ORIG C16: from Med. L *sclērōticus,* from Gk; see SCLEROMA

sclerous (ˈsklɪərəs) *adj Anat., pathol.* hard; bony; indurated. ORIG C19: from Gk *sklēros* hard

SCM (in Britain) *abbrev. for:* **1** State Certified Midwife. **2** Student Christian Movement.

scoff[1] (skɒf) *vb* **1** (*intr;* often foll. by *at*) to speak contemptuously (about); mock. **2** (*tr*) *Obs.* to regard with derision. ◆ *n* **3** an expression of derision. **4** an object of derision. ORIG C14: prob. from ON
▸ **ˈscoffer** *n* ▸ **ˈscoffing** *adj, n*

scoff[2] (skɒf) *Inf., chiefly Brit.* ◆ *vb* **1** to eat (food) fast and greedily. ◆ *n* **2** food or rations. ORIG C19: var. of *scaff* food

Scofield ★ (ˈskəʊfiːld) *n* **(David) Paul.** born 1922, English stage and film actor.

scold (skəʊld) *vb* **1** to find fault with or reprimand (a person) harshly. **2** (*intr*) to use harsh or abusive language. ◆ *n* **3** a person, esp. a woman, who constantly finds fault. ORIG C13: from ON SKALD
▸ **ˈscolder** *n* ▸ **ˈscolding** *n*

scoliosis (ˌskɒlɪˈəʊsɪs) *n Pathol.* an abnormal lateral curvature of the spine. ORIG C18: from NL, from Gk: a curving, from *skolios* bent
▸ **scoliotic** (ˌskɒlɪˈɒtɪk) *adj*

scollop (ˈskɒləp) *n, vb* a variant spelling of **scallop.**

scombroid (ˈskɒmbrɔɪd) *adj* **1** of, relating to, or belonging to the *Scombroidea,* a suborder of marine spiny-finned fishes having a forked powerful tail: includes the mackerels, tunnies, and sailfish. ◆ *n* **2** any fish belonging to the suborder *Scombroidea.* ORIG C19: from Gk *skombros* a mackerel; see -OID

sconce[1] (skɒns) *n* **1** a bracket fixed to a wall for holding candles or lights. **2** a flat candlestick with a handle. ORIG C14: from OF *esconse* hiding place, lantern, or from LL *sconsa,* from *absconsa* dark lantern

sconce[2] (skɒns) *n* a small protective fortification, such as an earthwork. ORIG C16: from Du. *schans,* from MHG *schanze* bundle of brushwood

scone (skɒn, skəʊn) *n* a light plain doughy cake made from flour with very little fat, cooked in an oven or (esp. originally) on a griddle. ORIG C16: Scot., ?from MDu. *schoonbrot* fine bread

Scone ★ (skuːn) *n* a parish in E Scotland near Perth, consisting of the two villages of New Scone and Old Scone, formerly the site of the Pictish capital and the stone upon which medieval Scottish kings were crowned. The stone was removed to Westminster Abbey by Edward I in 1296: it was returned to Scotland in 1996 and placed in Edinburgh Castle. Scone Palace was rebuilt in the neogothic style in the 19th century.

scoop (skuːp) *n* **1** a utensil used as a shovel or ladle, esp. a small shovel with deep sides and a short handle, used for taking up flour, etc. **2** a utensil with a long handle and round bowl used for dispensing liquids, etc. **3** anything that resembles a scoop in action, such as the bucket on a dredge. **4** a utensil used for serving mashed potatoes, ice cream, etc. **5** a spoonlike surgical instrument for extracting foreign matter, etc., from the body. **6** the quantity taken up by a scoop. **7** the act of scooping, dredging, etc. **8** a hollow cavity. **9** *Sl.* a large quick gain, as of money. **10** a news story reported in one newspaper before all the others. ◆ *vb* (*mainly tr*) **11** (often foll. by *up*) to take up and remove (an object or substance) with or as if with a scoop. **12** (often foll. by *out*) to hollow out with or as if with a scoop. **13** to win (a prize, award, or large amount of money). **14** to beat (rival newspapers) in uncovering a news item. ORIG C14: via MDu. *schōpe* from Gmc
▸ **ˈscooper** *n* ▸ **ˈscoopˌful** *n*

scoot (skuːt) *vb* **1** to go or cause to go quickly or hastily; dart or cause to dart off or away. ◆ *n* **2** the act of scooting. ORIG C19 (US): from ?

scooter (ˈskuːtə) *n* **1** a child's vehicle consisting of a low footboard on wheels, steered by handlebars. **2** See **motor scooter.**

Scopas ★ ('skəupəs) *n* 4th century B.C., Greek sculptor and architect.

scope (skəup) *n* **1** opportunity for exercising the faculties or abilities. **2** range of view or grasp. **3** the area covered by an activity, topic, etc.: *the scope of his thesis was vast.* **4** *Naut.* slack left in an anchor cable. **5** *Logic.* the part of a formula that follows a quantifier or an operator. **6** *Inf.* short for **telescope, microscope, oscilloscope,** etc. **7** *Arch.* purpose. ORIG C16: from It. *scopo* goal, from L *scopus,* from Gk *skopos* target

-scope *n combining form.* indicating an instrument for observing or detecting: *microscope.* ORIG from NL *-scopium,* from Gk *-skopion,* from *skopein* to look at
▸ **-scopic** *adj combining form.*

scopolamine (skə'pɒlə,mi:n) *n* a colourless viscous liquid alkaloid extracted from certain plants, such as henbane: used in preventing travel sickness and as a sedative and truth serum. Also called: **hyoscine.** ORIG C20: *scopol-* from NL *scopolia Japonica* Japanese belladonna (from which the alkaloid is extracted), after G. A. *Scopoli* (1723–88), It. naturalist, + AMINE

Scopus ★ ('skəupəs) *n* **Mount.** a mountain in central Israel, east of Jerusalem: a N extension of the Mount of Olives; site of the Hebrew University (1925). Height: 834 m (2736 ft).

-scopy *n combining form.* indicating a viewing or observation: *microscopy.* ORIG from Gk *-skopia,* from *skopein* to look at

scorbutic (skɔ:'bju:tɪk) *adj* of or having scurvy. ORIG C17: from NL *scorbūticus,* from Med. L *scorbūtus,* prob. of Gmc origin
▸ **scor'butically** *adv*

scorch (skɔ:tʃ) *vb* **1** to burn or become burnt, esp. so as to affect the colour, taste, etc. **2** to wither or parch or cause to wither from exposure to heat. **3** (*intr*) *Inf.* to be very hot: *it is scorching outside.* **4** (*tr*) *Inf.* to criticize harshly. ◆ *n* **5** a slight burn. **6** a mark caused by the application of too great heat. **7** *Horticulture.* a mark on fruit, etc., caused by pests or insecticides. ORIG C15: prob. from ON *skorpna* to shrivel up
▸ **'scorching** *adj*

scorched earth policy *n* **1** the policy in warfare of removing or destroying everything that might be useful to an invading enemy. **2** *Business.* a manoeuvre by a company expecting an unwelcome takeover bid in which apparent profitability is greatly reduced by a reversible operation, such as borrowing at an exorbitant interest rate.

scorcher ('skɔ:tʃə) *n* **1** a person or thing that scorches. **2** something caustic. **3** *Inf.* a very hot day. **4** *Brit. inf.* something remarkable.

score (skɔ:) *n* **1** a numerical record of a competitive game or match. **2** the total number of points made by a side or individual in a game. **3** the act of scoring, esp. a point or points. **4 the score.** *Inf.* the actual situation. **5** a group or set of twenty: *three score years and ten.* **6** (*usually pl;* foll. by *of*) lots: *I have scores of things to do.* **7** *Music.* **7a** the printed form of a composition in which the instrumental or vocal parts appear on separate staves vertically arranged on large pages (**full score**) or in a condensed version, usually for piano (**short score**) or voices and piano (**vocal score**). **7b** the incidental music for a film or play. **7c** the songs, music, etc., for a stage or film musical. **8** a mark or notch, esp. one made in keeping a tally. **9** an account of amounts due. **10** an amount recorded as due. **11** a reason: *the book was rejected on the score of length.* **12** a grievance. **13a** a line marking a division or boundary. **13b** (*as modifier*): *score line.* **14 over the score.** *Inf.* excessive; unfair. **15 settle** *or* **pay off a score. 15a** to avenge a wrong. **15b** to repay a debt. ◆ *vb* **scores, scoring, scored. 16** to gain (a point or points) in a game or contest. **17** (*tr*) to make a total score of. **18** to keep a record of the score (of). **19** (*tr*) to be worth (a certain amount) in a game. **20** (*tr*) to record by making notches in. **21** to make (cuts, lines, etc.) in or on. **22** (*intr*) *Sl.* to obtain something desired, esp. to purchase an illegal drug. **23** (*intr*) *Sl.* (of men) to be successful in seducing a person. **24** (*tr*) **24a** to arrange (a piece of music) for specific instruments or voices. **24b** to write the music for (a film, play, etc.). **25** to achieve (success or an advantage): *your idea scored with the boss.* ORIG OE *scora*
▸ **'scorer** *n*

scoreboard ('skɔ:,bɔ:d) *n Sport, etc.* a board for displaying the score of a game or match.

scorecard ('skɔ:,kɑ:d) *n* **1** a card on which scores are recorded, as in golf. **2** a card identifying the players in a sports match, esp. cricket.

score off *vb* (*intr, prep*) to gain an advantage at someone else's expense.

scoria ('skɔ:rɪə) *n, pl* **scoriae** (-rɪ,i:). **1** a mass of solidified lava containing many cavities. **2** refuse obtained from smelted ore. ORIG C17: from L: dross, from Gk *skōria,* from *skōr* excrement

scorify ('skɔ:rɪ,faɪ) *vb* **scorifies, scorifying, scorified.** to remove (impurities) from metals by forming scoria.
▸ **,scorifi'cation** *n* ▸ **'scori,fier** *n*

scoring ('skɔ:rɪŋ) *n* another name for **orchestration** (see **orchestrate**).

scorn (skɔ:n) *n* **1** open contempt for a person or thing. **2** an object of contempt or derision. ◆ *vb* **3** to treat with contempt or derision. **4** (*tr*) to reject with contempt. ORIG C12 *schornen,* from OF *escharnir,* of Gmc origin
▸ **'scorner** *n* ▸ **'scornful** *adj* ▸ **'scornfully** *adv*

Scorpio ('skɔ:pɪ,əu) *n* **1** Also called: **Scorpius.** *Astron.* a large S constellation. **2** Also called: the **Scorpion.** *Astrol.* the eighth sign of the zodiac. The sun is in this sign between about Oct. 23 and Nov. 21. ORIG L: SCORPION

scorpion ('skɔ:pɪən) *n* **1** an arachnid of warm dry regions, having a segmented body with a long tail terminating in a venomous sting. **2 false scorpion.** a small nonvenomous arachnid that superficially resembles the scorpion but lacks the long tail. **3** *Bible.* a barbed scourge (I Kings 12:11). ORIG C13: via OF from L *scorpiō,* from Gk *skorpios,* from ?

Scorpion ('skɔ:pɪən) *n* **the.** the constellation Scorpio, the eighth sign of the zodiac.

scorpion fish *n* any of a genus of fish of temperate and tropical seas, having venomous spines on the dorsal and anal fins.

Scorsese ★ (skɔ:'seɪzɪ) *n* **Martin.** born 1942, US film director, whose films include *Taxi Driver* (1976), *Casino* (1995), *Kundun* (1998), and the controversial *The Last Temptation of Christ* (1988).

Scot (skɒt) *n* **1** a native or inhabitant of Scotland. **2** a member of a tribe of Celtic raiders from the north of Ireland who eventually settled in N Britain during the 5th and 6th centuries.

Scot. *abbrev. for:* **1** Scotch (whisky). **2** Scotland. **3** Scottish.

scot and lot *n Brit. history.* a municipal tax paid by burgesses that came to be regarded as a qualification for the borough franchise in parliamentary elections. ORIG C13 *scot* tax, from Gmc

scotch[1] (skɒtʃ) *vb* (*tr*) **1** to put an end to; crush: *bad weather scotched our plans.* **2** *Obs.* to cut or score. ◆ *n* **3** *Arch.* a gash. **4** a line marked down, as for hopscotch. ORIG C15: from ?

scotch[2] (skɒtʃ) *vb* **1** (*tr*) to block, prop, or prevent from moving with or as if with a wedge. ◆ *n* **2** a block or wedge to prevent motion. ORIG C17: from ?

Scotch[1] (skɒtʃ) *adj* **1** another word for **Scottish.** ◆ *n* **2** the Scots or their language.

> **USAGE NOTE** In the north of England and in Scotland, *Scotch* is not used outside fixed expressions such as *Scotch whisky, Scotch broth,* etc. The use of *Scotch* for *Scots* or *Scottish* is otherwise felt to be incorrect, especially when applied to people.

Scotch[2] (skɒtʃ) *n* whisky distilled from fermented malted barley and made in Scotland. Also called: **Scotch whisky.**

Scotch broth *n Brit.* a thick soup made from mutton or beef stock, vegetables, and pearl barley.

Scotch egg *n Brit.* a hard-boiled egg enclosed in a layer of sausage meat, covered in egg and crumbs, and fried.

Scotchman ('skɒtʃmən) *or (fem)* **Scotchwoman** *n, pl* **Scotchmen** *or* **Scotchwomen.** (*regarded as bad usage by the Scots*) another word for **Scotsman** or **Scotswoman.**

Scotch mist *n* **1** a heavy wet mist. **2** drizzle.

Scotch snap *n Music.* a rhythmic pattern consisting of a short note followed by a long one. Also called: **Scotch catch.**

Scotch terrier *n* another name for **Scottish terrier.**

scoter ('skəʊtə) *n, pl* **scoters** *or* **scoter.** a sea duck of northern regions. The male plumage is black with white patches around the head and eyes. ORIG C17: from ?

scot-free *adv, adj* (*predicative*) without harm, loss, or penalty. ORIG C16: see SCOT AND LOT

Scotland ★ ('skɒtlənd) *n* a country that is part of the United Kingdom, occupying the north of Great Britain: the English and Scottish thrones were united under one monarch in 1603 and the parliaments in 1707. The establishment of a separate Scottish parliament was approved in a referendum in 1997. It consists of the Highlands in the north, the central Lowlands, and hilly uplands in the south; has a deeply indented coastline, about 800 offshore islands (mostly in the west), and many lochs. Capital: Edinburgh. Pop.: 4 998 567 (1991). Area: 78 768 sq. km (30 412 sq. miles).

Scotland Yard *n* the headquarters of the police force of metropolitan London. Official name: **New Scotland Yard.**

scotoma (skɒ'təʊmə) *n, pl* **scotomas** *or* **scotomata** (-mətə). **1** *Pathol.* a blind spot. **2** *Psychol.* a mental blind spot. ORIG C16: via Med. L from Gk *skotōma* giddiness, from *skotoun* to make dark, from *skotos* darkness

Scots (skɒts) *adj* **1** of or characteristic of Scotland, its people, their English dialects, or their Gaelic language. ◆ *n* **2** any of the English dialects spoken or written in Scotland.

Scotsman ('skɒtsmən) *or (fem)* **Scotswoman** *n, pl* **Scotsmen** *or* **Scotswomen.** a native or inhabitant of Scotland.

Scots pine *or* **Scotch pine** *n* **1** a coniferous tree of Europe and W and N Asia, having blue-green needle-like leaves and brown cones with a small prickle on each scale. **2** the wood of this tree.

Scott ★ (skɒt) *n* **1** Sir **George Gilbert.** 1811–78, British Gothic-Revival architect, who designed the Albert Memorial (1863) and St Pancras Station (1865). **2** his grandson, Sir **Giles Gilbert.** 1880–1960, British architect, who designed the Anglican cathedral in Liverpool (1904–78). **3 Paul** (**Mark**). 1920–78, British novelist, noted for his "Raj Quartet": *The Jewel in the Crown* (1966), *The Day of the Scorpion* (1968), *The Towers of Silence* (1972), and *A Division of the Spoils* (1975). **4** Sir **Peter** (**Markham**). 1909–89, British wildlife artist and conservationist. He founded (1946) the Slimbridge waterfowl refuge in Gloucestershire. **5 Robert Falcon.** 1868–1912, British naval officer who commanded two Antarctic expeditions (1901–04; 1910–12), reaching the South Pole on Jan. 18, 1912, shortly after Amundsen; he and his party died on the return journey. **6** Sir **Walter.** 1771–1832, Scottish novelist, best known for his "Waverley" novels, including *Waverley* (1814), *The Heart of Midlothian* (1818), and *Redgauntlet* (1824).

Scotticism ('skɒtɪˌsɪzəm) *n* a Scottish idiom, word, etc.

Scottie *or* **Scotty** ('skɒtɪ) *n, pl* **Scotties. 1** See **Scottish terrier. 2** *Inf.* a Scotsman.

Scottish ('skɒtɪʃ) *adj* of, relating to, or characteristic of Scotland, its people, their Gaelic language, or their English dialects.

Scottish Borders ★ *n* a council area in SE Scotland, on the English border. Administrative centre: Newtown St Boswells. Pop.: 106 100 (1996 est.). Area: 4734 sq. km (1827 sq. miles).

Scottish Certificate of Education *n* See **SCE.**

Scottish Gaelic *n* the Goidelic language of the Celts of Scotland, used esp. in the Highlands and Western Isles.

Scottish National Party *n* a political party advocating the independence of Scotland. Abbrev.: **SNP.**

Scottish terrier *n* a small but sturdy long-haired breed of terrier, usually with a black coat.

Scotus ★ ('skəʊtəs) *n* See **Duns Scotus.**

scoundrel ('skaʊndrəl) *n* a worthless or villainous person. ORIG C16: from ?

scour[1] ('skaʊə) *vb* **1** to clean or polish (a surface) by washing and rubbing. **2** to remove dirt from or have the dirt removed from. **3** (*tr*) to clear (a channel) by the force of water. **4** (*tr*) to remove by or as if by rubbing. **5** (*tr*) to cause (livestock) to purge their bowels. ◆ *n* **6** the act of scouring. **7** the place scoured, esp. by running water. **8** something that scours, such as a cleansing agent. **9** (*often pl*) prolonged diarrhoea in livestock, esp. cattle. ORIG C13: via MLow G *schüren,* from OF *escurer,* from LL *excūrāre* to cleanse, from *cūrāre;* see CURE
▸ **'scourer** *n*

scour[2] ('skaʊə) *vb* **1** to range over (territory), as in making a search. **2** to move swiftly or energetically over (territory). ORIG C14: from ON *skūr*

scourge (skɜːdʒ) *n* **1** a person who harasses or causes destruction. **2** a means of inflicting punishment or suffering. **3** a whip used for inflicting punishment or torture. ◆ *vb* **scourges, scourging, scourged.** (*tr*) **4** to whip. **5** to punish severely. ORIG C13: from Anglo-F, from OF *escorgier* (unattested) to lash, from *es-* EX-[1] + L *corrigia* whip
▸ **'scourger** *n*

scourings ('skaʊərɪŋz) *pl n* **1** the residue left after cleaning grain. **2** residue that remains after scouring.

scouse (skaʊs) *n Liverpool dialect.* a stew made from leftover meat. ORIG C19: shortened from LOBSCOUSE

Scouse (skaʊs) *Brit. inf.* ◆ *n* **1** Also: **Scouser.** a person who comes from Liverpool. **2** the dialect spoken by such a person. ◆ *adj* **3** of or from Liverpool. ORIG C20: from SCOUSE

scout[1] (skaʊt) *n* **1** a person, ship, or aircraft sent out to gain information. **2** *Mil.* a person or unit despatched to reconnoitre the position of the enemy, etc. **3** the act or an instance of scouting. **4** (esp. at Oxford University) a college servant. **5** *Inf.* a fellow. ◆ *vb* **6** to examine or observe (anything) in order to obtain information. **7** (*tr; sometimes foll. by out* or *up*) to seek. **8** (*intr; foll. by about* or *around*) to go in search (for). ORIG C14: from OF *ascouter* to listen to, from L *auscultāre* to AUSCULTATE
▸ **'scouter** *n*

scout[2] (skaʊt) *vb* to reject (a person, etc.) with contempt. ORIG C17: from ON *skūta* derision

Scout (skaʊt) *n* (*sometimes not cap.*) a boy or (in some countries) a girl who is a member of a worldwide movement (the **Scout Association**) founded as the Boy Scouts in England in 1908 by Lord Baden-Powell.
▸ **'Scouting** *n*

Scouter ('skaʊtə) *n* the leader of a troop of Scouts. Also called (esp. formerly): **Scoutmaster.**

scow (skaʊ) *n* an unpowered barge used for freight, etc.; lighter. ORIG C18: via Du. *schouw* from Low G *schalde*

scowl (skaʊl) *vb* **1** (*intr*) to contract the brows in a threatening or angry manner. ◆ *n* **2** a gloomy or threatening expression. ORIG C14: prob. from ON
▸ **'scowler** *n*

SCPS (in Britain) *abbrev. for* Society of Civil and Public Servants.

scrabble ('skræbᵊl) *vb* **scrabbles, scrabbling, scrabbled. 1** (*intr; often foll. by about* or *at*) to scrape (at) or grope (for), as with hands or claws. **2** to struggle (with). **3** (*intr; often foll. by for*) to struggle to gain possession. **4** to scribble. ◆ *n* **5** the act or an instance of scrabbling. **6** a scribble. **7** a disorderly struggle. ORIG C16: from MDu. *shrabbelen,* frequentative of *shrabben* to scrape
▸ **'scrabbler** *n*

Scrabble ('skræbᵊl) *n Trademark.* a game in which words are formed by placing lettered tiles in a pattern similar to a crossword puzzle.

scrag (skræg) *n* **1** a thin or scrawny person or animal. **2** the lean end of a neck of veal or mutton. **3** *Inf.* the neck of a human being. ◆ *vb* **scrags, scragging, scragged. 4** (*tr*) *Inf.* to wring the neck of. ORIG C16: ? var. of CRAG

scraggly ('skræglɪ) *adj* **scragglier, scraggliest.** *Chiefly US.* untidy or irregular.

scraggy ('skrægɪ) *adj* **scraggier, scraggiest. 1** lean or scrawny. **2** rough; unkempt.
▸ **'scraggily** *adv* ▸ **'scragginess** *n*

scram[1] (skræm) *vb* **scrams, scramming, scrammed.** (*intr; often imperative*) *Inf.* to go away hastily. ORIG C20: from SCRAMBLE

scram[2] (skræm) *n* **1** an emergency shutdown of a nuclear reactor. ◆ *vb* **scrams, scramming, scrammed. 2** (of a nuclear reactor) to shut down or be shut down in an emergency. ORIG C20: ?from SCRAM[1]

scramble ('skræmbᵊl) *vb* **scrambles, scrambling, scrambled. 1** (*intr*) to climb or crawl, esp. by using the hands to aid movement. **2** to proceed hurriedly or in a disorderly fashion. **3** (*intr; often foll. by for*) to compete with others, esp. in a disordered manner. **4** (*intr; foll. by through*) to deal with hurriedly. **5** (*tr*) to throw together in a haphazard manner. **6** (*tr*) to collect in a hurried or disorganized manner. **7** (*tr*) to cook (eggs that have been whisked up with milk) in a pan containing a little melted butter. **8** *Mil.* to order (a crew or aircraft) to take off immediately or (of a crew or aircraft) to take off immediately. **9** (*tr*) to render (speech) unintelligible during transmission by means of an electronic scrambler. ◆ *n* **10** the act of scrambling. **11** a climb or trek over difficult ground. **12** a disorderly struggle, esp. to gain possession. **13** *Mil.* an immediate preparation for action, as of crew, aircraft, etc. **14** *Brit.* a motorcycle rally in which competitors race across rough open ground. ORIG C16: blend of SCRABBLE & RAMP

scrambler ('skræmblə) *n* an electronic device that renders speech unintelligible during transmission, by altering frequencies.

Scranton ★ ('skræntən) *n* an industrial city in NE Pennsylvania: university (1988). Pop.: 77 964 (1994 est.).

scrap[1] (skræp) *n* **1** a small piece of something larger; fragment. **2** an extract from something written. **3a** waste material or used articles, esp. metal, often collected and reprocessed. **3b** (*as modifier*): *scrap iron.* **4** (*pl*) pieces of discarded food. ◆ *vb* **scraps, scrapping, scrapped.** (*tr*) **5** to discard as useless. ORIG C14: from ON *skrap*

scrap[2] (skræp) *Inf.* ◆ *n* **1** a fight or argument. ◆ *vb* **scraps, scrapping, scrapped. 2** (*intr*) to quarrel or fight. ORIG C17: ?from SCRAPE

scrapbook ('skræpˌbʊk) *n* a book or album of blank pages in which to mount newspaper cuttings, pictures, etc.

scrape (skreɪp) *vb* **scrapes, scraping, scraped. 1** to move (a rough or sharp object) across (a surface), esp. to smooth or clean. **2** (*tr; often foll. by away or off*) to remove (a layer) by rubbing. **3** to produce a harsh or grating sound by rubbing against (a surface, etc.). **4** (*tr*) to injure or damage by rough contact: *to scrape one's knee.* **5** (*intr*) to be very economical (esp. in **scrimp and scrape**). **6** (*intr*) to draw the foot backwards in making a bow. **7 scrape acquaintance with.** to contrive an acquaintance with. ◆ *n* **8** the act of scraping. **9** a scraped place. **10** a harsh or grating sound. **11** *Inf.* an awkward or embarrassing predicament. **12** *Inf.* a conflict or struggle. ORIG OE *scrapian*
▸ **'scraper** *n*

scraperboard ('skreɪpəˌbɔːd) *n* thin card covered with a layer of china clay and a top layer of Indian ink, which can be scraped away with a special tool to leave a white line.

scrape through *vb* (*adv*) **1** (*intr*) to manage or survive with difficulty. **2** to succeed in with difficulty or by a narrow margin.

scrape together *or* **up** *vb* (*tr, adv*) to collect with difficulty: *to scrape together money for a new car.*

scrapheap ('skræpˌhiːp) *n* **1** a pile of discarded material. **2 on the scrapheap.** (of people or things) having outlived their usefulness.

scrappy ('skræpɪ) *adj* **scrappier, scrappiest.** fragmentary; disjointed.
▸ **'scrappily** *adv*

scratch (skrætʃ) *vb* **1** to mark or cut (the surface of something) with a rough or sharp instrument. **2** (often foll. by *at, out, off,* etc.) to scrape (the surface of something), as with claws, nails, etc. **3** to scrape (the surface of the skin) with the nails, as to relieve itching. **4** to chafe or irritate (a surface, esp. the skin). **5** to make or cause to make a grating sound. **6** (*tr; sometimes foll. by out*) to erase by or as if by scraping. **7** (*tr*) to write or draw awkwardly. **8** (*intr; sometimes foll. by along*) to earn a living, manage, etc., with difficulty. **9** to withdraw (an entry) from a race, (US) election, etc. ◆ *n* **10** the act of scratching. **11** a slight injury. **12** a mark made by scratching. **13** a slight grating sound. **14** (in a handicap sport) a competitor or the status of a competitor who has no allowance. **15a** the line from which competitors start in a race. **15b** (formerly) a line drawn on the floor of a prize ring at which the contestants stood to begin fighting. **16** *Billiards, etc.* a lucky shot. **17 from scratch.** *Inf.* from the very beginning. **18 up to scratch.** (*usually used with a negative*) *Inf.* up to standard. ◆ *adj* **19** *Sport.* (of a team) assembled hastily. **20** (in a handicap sport) with no allowance or penalty. **21** *Inf.* rough or haphazard. ORIG C15: via OF *escrater* from Gmc
▸ **'scratcher** *n* ▸ **'scratchy** *adj*

scratchcard ('skrætʒˌkɑːd) *n* a ticket that reveals whether or not the holder is eligible for a prize when the surface is removed by scratching.

scratch file *n Computing.* a temporary store for use during the execution of a program.

scratching ('skrætʃɪŋ) *n* a percussive effect obtained by rotating a gramophone record manually: a disc-jockey and dub technique.

scratch pad *n* **1** *Chiefly US & Canad.* a notebook, esp. one with detachable leaves. **2** *Computing.* a small semiconductor memory for temporary storage.

scratch video *n* the recycling of images from films or television to make collages.

scrawl (skrɔːl) *vb* **1** to write or draw (words, etc.) carelessly or hastily. ◆ *n* **2** careless or scribbled writing or drawing. ORIG C17: ? a blend of SPRAWL & CRAWL[1]
▸ **'scrawly** *adj*

scrawny ('skrɔːnɪ) *adj* **scrawnier, scrawniest. 1** very thin and bony. **2** meagre or stunted. ORIG C19: var. of dialect *scranny*
▸ **'scrawnily** *adv* ▸ **'scrawniness** *n*

scream (skriːm) *vb* **1** to utter or emit (a sharp piercing cry or similar sound), esp. as of fear, pain, etc. **2** (*intr*) to laugh wildly. **3** (*intr*) to speak, shout, or behave in a wild manner. **4** (*tr*) to bring (oneself) into a specified state by screaming: *she screamed herself hoarse.* **5** (*intr*) to be extremely conspicuous: *these orange curtains scream; you need something more restful.* ◆ *n* **6** a sharp piercing cry or sound, esp. one denoting fear or pain. **7** *Inf.* a person or thing that causes great amusement. ORIG C13: from Gmc

screamer ('skriːmə) *n* **1** a person or thing that screams. **2** a goose-like aquatic bird, such as the **crested screamer** of tropical and subtropical South America. **3** *Inf.* (in printing) an exclamation mark. **4** someone or something that raises screams of laughter or astonishment. **5** *US & Canad. sl.* a sensational headline. **6** *Austral. sl.* a person or thing that is excellent of its kind.

scree (skriː) *n* an accumulation of rock fragments at the foot of a cliff or hillside, often forming a sloping heap. ORIG OE *scrīthan* to slip; rel. to ON *skrītha* to slide

screech[1] (skriːtʃ) *n* **1** a shrill or high-pitched sound or cry. ◆ *vb* **2** to utter with or produce a screech. ORIG C16: var. of earlier *scritch*, imit.
▸ **'screecher** *n* ▸ **'screechy** *adj*

screech[2] (skriːtʃ) *n Canad. sl.* (esp. in Newfoundland) a dark rum. ORIG ?from SCREECH[1]

screech owl *n* **1** *Brit.* another name for **barn owl. 2** a small North American owl having a reddish-brown or grey plumage.

screed (skriːd) *n* **1** a long or prolonged speech or piece of writing. **2** a strip of wood, plaster, or metal placed on a surface to act as a guide to the thickness of the cement or plaster coat to be applied. **3** a mixture of cement, sand, and water applied to a concrete slab, etc., to give a smooth surface finish. ORIG C14: prob. var. of OE *scrēade* shred

screen (skri:n) *n* **1** a light movable frame, panel, or partition serving to shelter, divide, hide, etc. **2** anything that serves to shelter, protect, or conceal. **3** a frame containing a mesh that is placed over a window to keep out insects. **4** a decorated partition, esp. in a church around the choir. **5** a sieve. **6** the wide end of a cathode-ray tube, esp. in a television set, on which a visible image is formed. **7** a white or silvered surface, placed in front of a projector to receive the enlarged image of a film or of slides. **8 the screen.** the film industry or films collectively. **9** *Photog.* a plate of ground glass in some types of camera on which the image of a subject is focused. **10** men or ships deployed around and ahead of a larger military formation to warn of attack. **11** *Electronics.* See **screen grid.** ◆ *vb* (*tr*) **12** (sometimes foll. by *off*) to shelter, protect, or conceal. **13** to sieve or sort. **14** to test or check (an individual or group) so as to determine suitability for a task, etc. **15** to examine for the presence of a disease, weapons, etc. **16** to provide with a screen or screens. **17** to project (a film) onto a screen, esp. for public viewing. ORIG C15: from OF *escren* (F *écran*)
▸ **'screenable** *adj* ▸ **'screener** *n* ▸ **'screenful** *n*

screen grid *n Electronics.* an electrode placed between the control grid and anode of a valve which acts as an electrostatic shield, thus increasing the stability of the device. Sometimes shortened to **screen.**

screenings ('skri:nɪŋz) *pl n* refuse separated by sifting.

screening test *n* a simple test performed on a large number of people to identify those who have or are likely to develop a specified disease.

screenplay ('skri:nˌpleɪ) *n* the script for a film, including instructions for sets and camera work.

screen process *n* a method of printing using a fine mesh of silk, nylon, etc., treated with an impermeable coating except in the areas through which ink is subsequently forced onto the paper behind. Also called: **silk-screen printing.**

screensaver ('skri:nseɪvə) *n Computing.* a computer program that reduces screen damage resulting from an unchanging display, when the computer is switched on but not in use, by blanking the screen or generating moving patterns, pictures, etc.

screenwriter ('skri:nˌraɪtə) *n* a person who writes screenplays.

screw (skru:) *n* **1** a device used for fastening materials together, consisting of a threaded shank that has a slotted head by which it may be rotated so as to cut its own thread. **2** Also called: **screw-bolt.** a threaded cylindrical rod that engages with a similarly threaded cylindrical hole. **3** a thread in a cylindrical hole corresponding with that on the screw with which it is designed to engage. **4** anything resembling a screw in shape or spiral form. **5** a twisting movement of or resembling that of a screw. **6** Also called: **screw-back.** *Billiards, etc.* a stroke in which the cue ball moves backward after striking the object ball. **7** another name for **propeller** (sense 1). **8** *Sl.* a prison guard. **9** *Brit. sl.* salary, wages, or earnings. **10** *Brit.* a small amount of salt, tobacco, etc., in a twist of paper. **11** *Sl.* a person who is mean with money. **12** *Sl.* an old or worthless horse. **13** (*often pl*) *Sl.* force or compulsion (esp. in **put the screws on**). **14** *Taboo sl.* sexual intercourse. **15 have a screw loose.** *Inf.* to be insane. ◆ *vb* **16** (*tr*) to rotate (a screw or bolt) so as to drive it into or draw it out of a material. **17** (*tr*) to cut a screw thread in (a rod or hole) with a tap or die or on a lathe. **18** to turn or cause to turn in the manner of a screw. **19** (*tr*) to attach or fasten with a screw or screws. **20** (*tr*) *Inf.* to take advantage of; cheat. **21** (*tr;* often foll. by *up*) *Inf.* to distort or contort: *he screwed his face into a scowl.* **22** (*tr;* often foll. by *from* or *out of*) *Inf.* to coerce or force out of; extort. **23** *Taboo sl.* to have sexual intercourse (with). **24** (*tr*) *Sl.* to burgle. **25 have one's head screwed on the right way.** *Inf.* to be sensible. ◆ See also **screw up.** ORIG C15: from F *escroe,* from Med. L *scrōfa* screw, from L: sow, presumably because the thread of the screw is like the spiral of the sow's tail
▸ **'screwer** *n*

screwball ('skru:ˌbɔ:l) *Sl., chiefly US & Canad.* ◆ *n* **1** an odd or eccentric person. ◆ *adj* **2** odd; eccentric.

screwdriver ('skru:ˌdraɪvə) *n* **1** a tool used for turning screws, usually having a steel shank with a flattened square-cut tip that fits into a slot in the head of the screw. **2** an alcoholic beverage consisting of orange juice and vodka.

screwed (skru:d) *adj* **1** fastened by a screw or screws. **2** having spiral grooves like a screw. **3** twisted or distorted. **4** *Brit. sl.* drunk.

screw eye *n* a wood screw with its shank bent into a ring.

screw pine *n* any of various tropical Old World plants having a spiral mass of pineapple-like leaves and conelike fruits.

screw propeller *n* an early form of ship's propeller in which an Archimedes' screw is used to produce thrust by accelerating a flow of water.

screw top *n* **1** a bottle top that screws onto the bottle, allowing the bottle to be resealed after use. **2** a bottle with such a top.
▸ **'screw-ˌtop** *adj*

screw up *vb* (*tr, adv*) **1** to twist out of shape or distort. **2** to summon up: *to screw up one's courage.* **3** (*also intr*) *Inf.* to mishandle or bungle.

screwy ('skru:ɪ) *adj* **screwier, screwiest.** *Inf.* odd, crazy, or eccentric.

Scriabin ★ ('skrɪəbɪn; *Russian* 'skrjabin) *n* **Aleksandr Nikolayevich** (alɪk'sandr nika'lajɪvitʃ). 1872–1915, Russian composer, who wrote many piano works; his orchestral compositions include *Prometheus* (1911).

scribble ('skrɪbᵊl) *vb* **scribbles, scribbling, scribbled. 1** to write or draw in a hasty or illegible manner. **2** to make meaningless or illegible marks (on). **3** *Derog. or facetious.* to write poetry, novels, etc. ◆ *n* **4** hasty careless writing or drawing. **5** meaningless or illegible marks. ORIG C15: from Med. L *scrībillāre* to write hastily, from L *scrībere* to write
▸ **'scribbler** *n* ▸ **'scribbly** *adj*

scribbly gum *n Austral.* a eucalypt with smooth white bark, marked with random patterns made by wood-boring insects.

scribe (skraɪb) *n* **1** a person who copies documents, esp. a person who made handwritten copies before the invention of printing. **2** a clerk or public copyist. **3** *Bible.* a recognized scholar and teacher of the Jewish Law. ◆ *vb* **scribes, scribing, scribed. 4** to score a line on (a surface) with a pointed instrument, as in metalworking. ORIG (in the senses: writer, etc.) C14: from L *scrība* clerk, from *scrībere* to write; C17 (vb): ?from INSCRIBE
▸ **'scribal** *adj*

Scribe ★ (*French* skrib) *n* **Augustin Eugène** (ogystɛ̃ øʒɛn). 1791–1861, French writer of comedies and libretti for light opera.

scriber ('skraɪbə) *n* a pointed steel tool used to score materials as a guide to cutting, etc. Also called: **scribe.**

scrim (skrɪm) *n* a fine open-weave fabric, used in upholstery, lining, building, and in the theatre to create the illusion of a solid wall. ORIG C18: from ?

scrimmage ('skrɪmɪdʒ) *n* **1** a rough or disorderly struggle. **2** *American football.* the clash of opposing linemen at every down. ◆ *vb* **scrimmages, scrimmaging, scrimmaged. 3** (*intr*) to engage in a scrimmage. **4** (*tr*) to put (the ball) into a scrimmage. ORIG C15: from earlier *scrimish,* var. of SKIRMISH
▸ **'scrimmager** *n*

scrimp (skrɪmp) *vb* **1** (when *intr,* sometimes foll. by *on*) to be very sparing in the use (of) (esp. in **scrimp and save**). **2** (*tr*) to treat meanly: *he is scrimping his children.* ORIG C18: Scot., from ?
▸ **'scrimpy** *adj* ▸ **'scrimpiness** *n*

scrimshank ('skrɪmˌʃæŋk) *vb* (*intr*) *Brit. mil. sl.* to shirk work. ORIG C19: from ?

scrimshaw ('skrɪmˌʃɔ:) *n* **1** the art of decorating or carving shells, bone, ivory, etc., done by sailors as a leisure activity. **2** an article or articles made in this manner. ORIG C19: from ?

scrip[1] (skrɪp) *n* **1** a written certificate, list, etc. **2** a small scrap, esp. of paper with writing on it. **3** *Finance.* **3a** a certificate representing a claim to part of a share of stock. **3b** the shares issued by a company (**scrip** or **bonus issue**) without charge and distributed among existing shareholders. ORIG C18: in some senses, prob. from SCRIPT; otherwise, short for *subscription receipt*

scrip[2] (skrɪp) *or* **script** *n Inf.* a medical prescription. ORIG C20: from PRESCRIPTION

script (skrɪpt) *n* **1** handwriting as distinguished from print. **2** the letters, characters, or figures used in writing by hand. **3** any system or style of writing. **4** written copy for the use of performers in films and plays. **5** *Law.* an original or principal document. **6** an answer paper in an examination. **7** another word for **scrip**[2]. ◆ *vb* **8** (*tr*) to write a script for. ORIG C14: from L *scriptum* something written, from *scrībere* to write

Script. *abbrev. for* Scripture(s).

scriptorium (skrɪp'tɔːrɪəm) *n, pl* **scriptoriums** *or* **scriptoria** (-rɪə). a room, esp. in a monastery, set apart for the copying of manuscripts. ORIG from Med. L

scripture ('skrɪptʃə) *n* a sacred, solemn, or authoritative book or piece of writing. ORIG C13: from L *scriptūra* written material, from *scrībere* to write
▸ **'scriptural** *adj*

Scripture ('skrɪptʃə) *n* **1** Also called: **Holy Scripture, Holy Writ, the Scriptures.** *Christianity.* the Old and New Testaments. **2** any book or body of writings, esp. when regarded as sacred by a particular religious group.

scriptwriter ('skrɪpt,raɪtə) *n* a person who prepares scripts, esp. for a film.
▸ **'script,writing** *n*

scrivener ('skrɪvnə) *n Arch.* **1** a person who writes out deeds, etc. **2** a notary. ORIG C14: from *scrivein* clerk, from OF *escrivain,* ult. from L *scrība* SCRIBE

scrod (skrɒd) *n US.* a young cod or haddock. ORIG C19: ? from obs. Du. *schrood,* from MDu. *schrode* SHRED (n); the name perhaps refers to the method of preparing the fish for cooking

scrofula ('skrɒfjʊlə) *n Pathol.* (*no longer in technical use*) tuberculosis of the lymphatic glands. Also called (formerly): (the) **king's evil.** ORIG C14: from Med. L, from LL *scrōfulae* swollen glands in the neck, lit.: little sows (sows were thought to be particularly prone to the disease), from L *scrōfa* sow
▸ **'scrofulous** *adj*

scroggin ('skrɒgɪn) *n NZ inf.* a home-made high-calorie sweetmeat eaten by people walking in the bush.

scroll (skrəʊl) *n* **1** a roll of parchment, etc., usually inscribed with writing. **2** an ancient book in the form of a roll of parchment, papyrus, etc. **3** a decorative carving or moulding resembling a scroll. ◆ *vb* **4** (*tr*) to saw into scrolls. **5** to roll up like a scroll. **6** *Computing.* to move (text) on a screen in order to view a section that cannot be fitted into a single display. ORIG C15 *scrowle,* from *scrowe,* from OF *escroe* scrap of parchment, but also infl. by ROLL

scroll saw *n* a saw with a narrow blade for cutting intricate ornamental curves in wood.

scrollwork ('skrəʊl,wɜːk) *n* ornamental work in scroll-like patterns.

Scrooge (skruːdʒ) *n* a mean or miserly person. ORIG C19: after a character in Dickens' story *A Christmas Carol* (1843)

scrophulariaceous (,skrɒfjʊ,lɛərɪ'eɪʃəs) *adj* of or belonging to the *Scrophulariaceae,* a family of plants including figwort, snapdragon, foxglove, and mullein. ORIG C19: from NL (*herba*) *scrophularia* scrofula (plant), from the use of such plants in treating scrofula

scrotum ('skrəʊtəm) *n, pl* **scrota** (-tə) *or* **scrotums.** the pouch of skin containing the testes in most mammals. ORIG C16: from L
▸ **'scrotal** *adj*

scrounge (skraʊndʒ) *vb* **scrounges, scrounging, scrounged.** *Inf.* **1** (when *intr,* sometimes foll. by *around*) to search in order to acquire (something) without cost. **2** to obtain or seek to obtain (something) by begging. ORIG C20: var. of dialect *scrunge* to steal, from ?
▸ **'scrounger** *n*

scrub[1] (skrʌb) *vb* **scrubs, scrubbing, scrubbed. 1** to rub (a surface, etc.) hard, with or as if with a brush, soap, and water, in order to clean it. **2** to remove (dirt) by rubbing, esp. with a brush and water. **3** (*intr;* foll. by *up*) (of a surgeon) to wash the hands and arms thoroughly before operating. **4** (*tr*) to purify (a gas) by removing impurities. **5** (*tr*) *Inf.* to delete or cancel. ◆ *n* **6** the act of or an instance of scrubbing. ORIG C14: from MLow G *schrubben,* or MDu. *schrobben*

scrub[2] (skrʌb) *n* **1a** vegetation consisting of stunted trees, bushes, and other plants growing in an arid area. **1b** (*as modifier*): *scrub vegetation.* **2** an area of arid land covered with such vegetation. **3a** an animal of inferior breeding or condition. **3b** (*as modifier*): *a scrub bull.* **4** a small person. **5** anything stunted or inferior. **6** *Sport, US & Canad.* a player not in the first team. **7 the scrub.** *Austral. inf.* a remote or uncivilized place. ◆ *adj* (*prenominal*) **8** small or inferior. **9** *Sport, US.* **9a** (of a player) not in the first team. **9b** (of a team) composed of such players. ORIG C16: var. of SHRUB[1]

scrubber ('skrʌbə) *n* **1** a person or thing that scrubs. **2** an apparatus for purifying a gas. **3** *Derog. sl.* a promiscuous woman.

scrubby ('skrʌbɪ) *adj* **scrubbier, scrubbiest. 1** covered with or consisting of scrub. **2** (of trees, etc.) stunted in growth. **3** *Brit. inf.* messy.

scrubland ('skrʌb,lænd) *n* an area of scrub vegetation.

scrub turkey *n* another term for **megapode.**

scrub typhus *n* a disease characterized by severe headache, skin rash, chills, and swelling of the lymph nodes, caused by the bite of mites infected with a microorganism: occurs mainly in Asia and Australia.

scruff[1] (skrʌf) *n* the nape of the neck (esp. in **by the scruff of the neck**). ORIG C18: var. of *scuft,* ?from ON *skoft* hair

scruff[2] (skrʌf) *n Inf.* **1** an untidy scruffy person. **2** a disreputable person; ruffian.

scruffy ('skrʌfɪ) *adj* **scruffier, scruffiest.** unkempt or shabby.

scrum (skrʌm) *n* **1** *Rugby.* the act or method of restarting play when the two opposing packs of forwards group together with heads down and arms interlocked and push to gain ground while the scrum half throws the ball in and the hookers attempt to scoop it out to their own team. **2** *Inf.* a disorderly struggle. ◆ *vb* **scrums, scrumming, scrummed. 3** (*intr;* usually foll. by *down*) *Rugby.* to form a scrum. ORIG C19: from SCRUMMAGE

scrum half *n Rugby.* **1** a player who puts in the ball at scrums and tries to get it away to his three-quarter backs. **2** this position in a team.

scrummage ('skrʌmɪdʒ) *n, vb* **scrummages, scrummaging, scrummaged. 1** *Rugby.* another word for **scrum. 2** a variant of **scrimmage.** ORIG C19: var. of SCRIMMAGE

scrump (skrʌmp) *vb Dialect.* to steal (apples) from an orchard or garden. ORIG var. of SCRIMP

scrumptious ('skrʌmpʃəs) *adj Inf.* very pleasing; delicious. ORIG C19: prob. changed from SUMPTUOUS
▸ **'scrumptiously** *adv*

scrumpy ('skrʌmpɪ) *n* a rough dry cider, brewed esp. in the West Country of England. ORIG from *scrump,* var. of SCRIMP (in obs. sense: withered), referring to the apples used

scrunch (skrʌntʃ) *vb* **1** to crumple or crunch or to be crumpled or crunched. ◆ *n* **2** the act or sound of scrunching. ORIG C19: var. of CRUNCH

scrunchie ('skrʌntʃɪ) *n* a loop of elastic covered loosely with fabric, used to hold the hair in a ponytail.

scruple ('skruːp°l) *n* **1** (*often pl*) a doubt or hesitation as to what is morally right in a certain situation. **2** *Arch.* a very small amount. **3** a unit of weight equal to 20 grains (1.296 grams). ◆ *vb* **scruples, scrupling, scrupled. 4** (*obs. when tr*) to have doubts (about), esp. from a moral compunction. ORIG C16: from L *scrūpulus* a small weight, from *scrūpus* rough stone

scrupulous ('skruːpjʊləs) *adj* **1** characterized by careful

observation of what is morally right. **2** very careful or precise. ORIG C15: from L *scrūpulōsus* punctilious
▸ **'scrupulously** *adv* ▸ **'scrupulousness** *n*

scrutineer (ˌskruːtɪ'nɪə) *n* a person who examines, esp. one who scrutinizes the conduct of an election poll.

scrutinize *or* **scrutinise** ('skruːtɪˌnaɪz) *vb* **scrutinizes, scrutinizing, scrutinized** *or* **scrutinises, scrutinising, scrutinised.** (*tr*) to examine carefully or in minute detail.
▸ **'scrutiˌnizer** *or* **'scrutiˌniser** *n*

scrutiny ('skruːtɪnɪ) *n, pl* **scrutinies. 1** close or minute examination. **2** a searching look. **3** (in the early Christian Church) a formal testing that catechumens had to undergo before being baptized. ORIG C15: from LL *scrūtinium* an investigation, from *scrūtārī* to search (orig. referring to rag-and-bone men), from *scrūta* rubbish

scry (skraɪ) *vb* **scries, scrying, scried.** (*intr*) to divine, esp. by crystal gazing. ORIG C16: from DESCRY

scuba ('skjuːbə) *n* an apparatus used in skin diving, consisting of a cylinder or cylinders containing compressed air attached to a breathing apparatus. ORIG C20: from the initials of *self-contained underwater breathing apparatus*

scud (skʌd) *vb* **scuds, scudding, scudded.** (*intr*) **1** (esp. of clouds) to move along swiftly and smoothly. **2** *Naut.* to run before a gale. ◆ *n* **3** the act of scudding. **4a** a formation of low ragged clouds driven by a strong wind beneath rain-bearing clouds. **4b** a sudden shower or gust of wind. ORIG C16: prob. of Scand. origin

scuff (skʌf) *vb* **1** to drag (the feet) while walking. **2** to scratch (a surface) or (of a surface) to become scratched. **3** (*tr*) *US.* to poke at (something) with the foot. ◆ *n* **4** the act or sound of scuffing. **5** a rubbed place caused by scuffing. **6** a backless slipper. ORIG C19: prob. imit.

scuffle ('skʌfᵊl) *vb* **scuffles, scuffling, scuffled.** (*intr*) **1** to fight in a disorderly manner. **2** to move by shuffling. ◆ *n* **3** a disorderly struggle. **4** the sound made by scuffling. ORIG C16: of Scand. origin; cf. Swedish *skuff, skuffa* to push

scull (skʌl) *n* **1** a single oar moved from side to side over the stern of a boat to propel it. **2** one of a pair of short-handled oars, both of which are pulled by one oarsman. **3** a racing shell propelled by an oarsman or oarsmen pulling two oars. **4** an act, instance, period, or distance of sculling. ◆ *vb* **5** to propel (a boat) with a scull. ORIG C14: from ?
▸ **'sculler** *n*

scullery ('skʌlərɪ) *n, pl* **sculleries.** *Chiefly Brit.* a small room or part of a kitchen where washing-up, vegetable preparation, etc., is done. ORIG C15: from Anglo-Norman *squillerie,* from OF, from *escuele* a bowl, from L *scutella,* from *scutra* a flat tray

Scullin ★ ('skʌlɪn) *n* **James Henry.** 1876–1953, Australian statesman; prime minister of Australia (1929–31).

scullion ('skʌljən) *n* **1** a mean or despicable person. **2** *Arch.* a servant employed to work in a kitchen. ORIG C15: from OF *escouillon* cleaning cloth, from *escouve* a broom, from L *scōpa* a broom, twig

sculpt (skʌlpt) *vb* **1** a variant of **sculpture. 2** (*intr*) to practise sculpture. ◆ Also: **sculp.** ORIG C19: from F *sculpter,* from L *sculpere* to carve

sculptor ('skʌlptə) *or* (*fem*) **sculptress** *n* a person who practises sculpture.

sculpture ('skʌlptʃə) *n* **1** the art of making figures or designs in relief or the round by carving wood, moulding plaster, etc., or casting metals, etc. **2** works or a work made in this way. **3** ridges or indentations as on a shell, formed by natural processes. ◆ *vb* **sculptures, sculpturing, sculptured.** (*mainly tr*) **4** (*also intr*) to carve, cast, or fashion (stone, bronze, etc.) three-dimensionally. **5** to portray (a person, etc.) by means of sculpture. **6** to form in the manner of sculpture. **7** to decorate with sculpture. ORIG C14: from L *sculptūra* a carving
▸ **'sculptural** *adj*

sculpturesque (ˌskʌlptʃə'rɛsk) *adj* resembling sculpture.
▸ **ˌsculptur'esquely** *adv*

scum (skʌm) *n* **1** a layer of impure matter that forms on the surface of a liquid, often as the result of boiling or fermentation. **2** the greenish film of algae and similar vegetation surface of a stagnant pond. **3** the skin of oxides or impurities on the surface of a molten metal. **4** waste matter. **5** a worthless person or group of people. ◆ *vb* **scums, scumming, scummed. 6** (*tr*) to remove scum from. **7** (*intr*) *Rare.* to form a layer of or become covered with scum. ORIG C13: of Gmc origin
▸ **'scummy** *adj*

scumbag ('skʌmˌbæg) *n Sl* an offensive or despicable person. ORIG C20: ?from earlier US sense: condom, from US slang *scum* semen + bag

scumble ('skʌmbᵊl) *vb* **scumbles, scumbling, scumbled. 1** (in painting and drawing) to soften or blend (an outline or colour) with an upper coat of opaque colour, applied very thinly. **2** to produce an effect of broken colour on doors, panelling, etc., by exposing coats of paint below the top coat. ◆ *n* **3** the upper layer of colour applied in this way. ORIG C18: prob. from SCUM

scuncheon ('skʌntʃən) *n* the inner part of a door jamb or window frame. ORIG C15: from OF *escoinson,* from *coin* angle

scungy ('skʌndʒɪ) *adj* **scungier, scungiest.** *Austral. & NZ sl.* miserable; sordid; dirty. ORIG C20: from ?

scunner ('skʌnə) *Dialect, chiefly Scot.* ◆ *vb* **1** (*intr*) to feel aversion. **2** (*tr*) to produce a feeling of aversion in. ◆ *n* **3** a strong aversion (often in **take a scunner**). **4** an object of dislike; nuisance. ORIG C14: from Scot. *skunner,* from ?

Scunthorpe ★ ('skʌnˌθɔːp) *n* a town in E England, in North Lincolnshire: developed rapidly after the discovery of local iron ore (1871); iron and steel industries have declined. Pop.: 75 982 (1991).

scup (skʌp) *n* a common fish of American coastal regions of the Atlantic. ORIG C19: from Amerind *mishcup,* from *mishe* big + *kuppe* close together; from the form of the scales

scupper[1] ('skʌpə) *n Naut.* a drain or spout allowing water on the deck of a vessel to flow overboard. ORIG C15 *skopper,* from ?

scupper[2] ('skʌpə) *vb* (*tr*) *Brit. sl.* **1** to overwhelm, ruin, or disable. **2** to sink (one's ship) deliberately. ORIG C19: from ?

scurf (skɜːf) *n* **1** another name for **dandruff. 2** flaky or scaly matter adhering to or peeling off a surface. ORIG OE *scurf*
▸ **'scurfy** *adj*

scurrilous ('skʌrɪləs) *adj* **1** grossly or obscenely abusive or defamatory. **2** characterized by gross or obscene humour. ORIG C16: from L *scurrīlis* derisive, from *scurra* buffoon
▸ **scurrility** (skə'rɪlɪtɪ) *n* ▸ **'scurrilously** *adv*

scurry ('skʌrɪ) *vb* **scurries, scurrying, scurried. 1** to move about hurriedly. **2** (*intr*) to whirl about. ◆ *n, pl* **scurries. 3** the act or sound of scurrying. **4** a brisk light whirling movement, as of snow. ORIG C19: prob. from *hurry-scurry,* from HURRY

scurvy ('skɜːvɪ) *n* **1** a disease caused by a lack of vitamin C, characterized by anaemia, spongy gums, and bleeding beneath the skin. ◆ *adj* **scurvier, scurviest. 2** mean or despicable. ORIG C16: see SCURF
▸ **'scurvily** *adv* ▸ **'scurviness** *n*

scurvy grass *n* any of various plants of Europe and North America, formerly used to treat scurvy.

scut (skʌt) *n* the short tail of animals such as the deer and rabbit. ORIG C15: prob. from ON

scutage ('skjuːtɪdʒ) *n* (in feudal society) a payment sometimes exacted by a lord from his vassal in lieu of military service. ORIG C15: from Med. L *scūtāgium,* lit.: shield dues, from L *scūtum* a shield

Scutari ★ *n* **1** ('skuːtərɪ, skuː'tɑːrɪ). the former name of **Üsküdar. 2** (sku'tari). the Italian name for **Shkodër.**

scutate ('skjuːteɪt) *adj* **1** (of animals) covered with large bony or horny plates. **2** *Bot.* shaped like a round shield. ORIG C19: from L *scūtātus* armed with a shield, from *scūtum* a shield

scutcheon ('skʌtʃən) *n* **1** a variant of **escutcheon. 2** any rounded or shield-shaped structure.

scutch grass (skʌtʃ) *n* another name for **couch grass.** ORIG var. of COUCH GRASS

scute (skjuːt) *n Zool.* a horny plate that makes up part of the exoskeleton in armadillos, turtles, etc. ORIG C14 (the name of a F coin; C19 in zoological sense): from L *scūtum* shield

scutellum (skjuːˈtɛləm) *n, pl* **scutella** (-lə). *Biol.* **1** the last of three plates into which an insect's thorax is divided. **2** one of the scales on the tarsus of a bird's leg. **3** the cotyledon of a developing grass seed. ORIG C18: from NL: a little shield, from L *scūtum* a shield
▸ **scutellate** (ˈskjuːtɪˌleɪt, -lɪt) *adj*

scutter (ˈskʌtə) *vb, n Brit. inf.* scurry. ORIG C18: prob. from SCUTTLE[2], with -ER[1] as in SCATTER

scuttle[1] (ˈskʌtᵊl) *n* **1** See **coal scuttle. 2** *Dialect, chiefly Brit.* a shallow basket, esp. for carrying vegetables. **3** the part of a motorcar body lying immediately behind the bonnet. ORIG OE *scutel* trencher, from L *scutella* bowl, dim. of *scutra* platter

scuttle[2] (ˈskʌtᵊl) *vb* **scuttles, scuttling, scuttled. 1** (*intr*) to run or move about with short hasty steps. ◆ *n* **2** a hurried pace or run. ORIG C15: ?from SCUD, infl. by SHUTTLE

scuttle[3] (ˈskʌtᵊl) *vb* **scuttles, scuttling, scuttled.** (*tr*) **1** *Naut.* to cause (a vessel) to sink by opening the seacocks or making holes in the bottom. **2** to give up (hopes, plans, etc.). ◆ *n* **3** *Naut.* a small hatch or its cover. ORIG C15 (n): via OF from Sp. *escotilla* a small opening, from *escote* opening in a piece of cloth, from *escotar* to cut out

scuttlebutt (ˈskʌtᵊlˌbʌt) *n Naut.* **1** a drinking fountain. **2** (formerly) a cask of drinking water aboard a ship. **3** *Chiefly US sl.* gossip.

scutum (ˈskjuːtəm) *n, pl* **scuta** (-tə). **1** the middle of three plates into which an insect's thorax is divided. **2** another word for **scute.** ORIG L: shield

scuzzy (ˈskʌzɪ) *adj* **scuzzier, scuzziest.** *Sl., chiefly US.* unkempt, dirty, or squalid. ORIG C20: ?from *disgusting* or ?from blend of *scum* & *fuzz*

Scylla ★ (ˈsɪlə) *n* **1** *Greek myth.* a sea nymph transformed into a sea monster believed to drown sailors navigating the Strait of Messina. Cf. **Charybdis. 2 between Scylla and Charybdis.** in a predicament in which avoidance of either of two dangers means exposure to the other.

Scyros ★ (ˈskirɔs) *n* a variant spelling of **Skyros.**

scythe (saɪð) *n* **1** a long-handled implement for cutting grass, etc., having a curved sharpened blade that moves in a plane parallel to the ground. ◆ *vb* **scythes, scything, scythed. 2** (*tr*) to cut (grass, etc.) with a scythe. ORIG OE *sigthe*

Scythia ★ (ˈsɪðɪə) *n* an ancient region of SE Europe and Asia, north of the Black Sea: now part of Ukraine.
▸ **ˈScythian** *adj, n*

SD *abbrev. for:* **1** South Dakota. **2** Also: **sd.** *Statistics.* standard deviation.

S. Dak. *abbrev. for* South Dakota.

SDI *abbrev. for* Strategic Defense Initiative. See **Star Wars.**

SDLP *abbrev. for* Social Democratic and Labour Party.

SDP *abbrev. for* Social Democratic Party.

SDRs *Finance. abbrev. for* special drawing rights.

Se *the chemical symbol for* selenium.

SE *symbol for* southeast(ern).

sea ★ (siː) *n* **1a** (usually preceded by *the*) the mass of salt water on the earth's surface as differentiated from the land. Related adjs.: **marine, maritime. 1b** (*as modifier*): *sea air.* **2** (*cap. when part of place name*) **2a** one of the smaller areas of ocean: *the Irish Sea.* **2b** a large inland area of water: *the Caspian Sea.* **3** turbulence or swell: *heavy seas.* **4** (*cap. when part of a name*) *Astron.* any of many huge dry plains on the surface of the moon: *Sea of Serenity.* See also **mare[2]. 5** anything resembling the sea in size or apparent limitlessness. **6 at sea. 6a** on the ocean. **6b** in a state of confusion. **7 go to sea.** to become a sailor. **8 put (out) to sea.** to embark on a sea voyage. ORIG OE *sǣ*

sea anchor *n Naut.* any device, such as a bucket, dragged in the water to keep a vessel heading into the wind or reduce drifting.

sea anemone *n* any of various coelenterates having a polypoid body with oral rings of tentacles.

sea bag *n* a canvas bag used by a seaman for his belongings.

sea bass (bæs) *n* any of various American coastal fishes having an elongated body with a long spiny dorsal fin almost divided into two.

sea bird *n* a bird such as a gull, that lives on the sea.

seaboard (ˈsiːˌbɔːd) *n* land bordering on the sea.

Seaborg ★ (ˈsiːbɔːg) *n* **Glenn Theodore.** 1912–99, US chemist. With E. M. McMillan, he discovered several transuranic elements: shared the Nobel prize for chemistry 1951.

seaborgium (ˈsiːbɔːgɪəm) *n* a synthetic transuranic element, synthesized and identified in 1974. Symbol: Sg; atomic no.: 106. ORIG C20: after Glenn SEABORG

seaborne (ˈsiːˌbɔːn) *adj* **1** carried on or by the sea. **2** transported by ship.

sea bream *n* a fish of European seas, valued as a food fish.

sea breeze *n* a wind blowing from the sea to the land, esp. during the day when the land surface is warmer.

SEAC (ˈsiːæk) *n* (in Britain) *acronym for* School Examination and Assessment Council.

sea change *n* a seemingly magical change. ORIG from Ariel's song "Full Fathom Five" in *The Tempest* (1611)

seacoast (ˈsiːˌkəʊst) *n* land bordering on the sea; a coast.

seacock (ˈsiːˌkɒk) *n Naut.* a valve in the hull of a vessel below the water line for admitting sea water or for pumping out bilge water.

sea cow *n* **1** a dugong or manatee. **2** an archaic name for the **walrus.**

sea cucumber *n* an echinoderm having an elongated body covered with a leathery skin and a cluster of tentacles at the oral end.

sea dog *n* an experienced or old sailor.

sea eagle *n* any of various fish-eating eagles of coastal areas, esp. the **European sea eagle,** having a brown plumage and white tail.

seafarer (ˈsiːˌfɛərə) *n* **1** a traveller who goes by sea. **2** a sailor.

seafaring (ˈsiːˌfɛərɪŋ) *adj* (*prenominal*) **1** travelling by sea. **2** working as a sailor. ◆ *n* **3** the act of travelling by sea. **4** the work of a sailor.

seafood (ˈsiːˌfuːd) *n* edible saltwater fish or shellfish.

seafront (ˈsiːˌfrʌnt) *n* a built-up area facing the sea.

sea-girt *adj Literary.* surrounded by the sea.

seagoing (ˈsiːˌgəʊɪŋ) *adj* intended for or used at sea.

sea green *n* **a** a moderate green colour, sometimes with a bluish or yellowish tinge. **b** (*as adj*): *a sea-green carpet.*

sea gull *n* **1** a popular name for the **gull** (the bird). **2** *NZ inf.* a casual dock worker.

sea holly *n* a European plant of sandy shores, having bluish-green stems and blue flowers.

sea horse *n* **1** a marine teleost fish of temperate and tropical waters, having a bony-plated body, a prehensile tail, and a horselike head and swimming in an upright position. **2** an archaic name for the **walrus. 3** a fabled sea creature with the tail of a fish and the front parts of a horse.

sea-island cotton *n* **1** a cotton plant of the Sea Islands, off the Florida coast, widely cultivated for its fine long fibres. **2** the fibre of this plant or the material woven from it.

Sea Islands ★ *pl n* a chain of islands in the Atlantic off the coasts of South Carolina, Georgia, and Florida.

sea kale *n* a European coastal plant with broad fleshy leaves and white flowers: cultivated for its edible asparagus-like shoots. Cf. **kale.**

seal[1] (siːl) *n* **1** a device impressed on a piece of wax, etc., fixed to a letter, etc., as a mark of authentication. **2** a stamp, ring, etc., engraved with a device to form such an impression. **3** a substance, esp. wax, so placed over an envelope, etc., that it must be broken before the object can be opened or used. **4** any substance or device used to close or fasten tightly. **5** a small amount of water contained in the trap of a drain to prevent the passage of

foul smells. **6** anything that gives a pledge or confirmation. **7** a token; sign: *seal of death.* **8** a decorative stamp sold in aid of charity. **9** *RC Church.* Also called: **seal of confession.** the obligation never to reveal anything said in confession. **10** **set one's seal on** (*or* **to**). **10a** to mark with one's sign or seal. **10b** to endorse. ◆ *vb* (*tr*) **11** to affix a seal to, as proof of authenticity, etc. **12** to stamp with or as if with a seal. **13** to approve or authorize. **14** (sometimes foll. by *up*) to close or secure with or as if with a seal: *to seal one's lips.* **15** (foll. by *off*) to enclose (a place) with a fence, etc. **16** to decide irrevocably. **17** to close tightly so as to render airtight or watertight. **18** to subject (the outside of meat, etc.) to fierce heat so as to retain the juices during cooking. **19** to paint (a porous material) with a nonporous coating. **20** *Austral.* to cover (a road) with bitumen, asphalt, tarmac, etc. ORIG C13 *seel,* from OF, from L *sigillum* little figure, from *signum* a sign
▸ **'sealable** *adj*

seal[2] (siːl) *n* **1** a fish-eating mammal with four flippers which is aquatic but comes on shore to breed. **2** sealskin. ◆ *vb* **3** (*intr*) to hunt for seals. ORIG OE *seolh*
▸ **'sealer** *n* ▸ **'seal-ˌlike** *adj*

sea lane *n* an established route for ships.

sealant ('siːlənt) *n* **1** any substance, such as wax, used for sealing documents, bottles, etc. **2** any of a number of substances used for stopping leaks, waterproofing wood, etc.

sea lavender *n* any of various plants found on temperate salt marshes, having spikes of white, pink, or mauve flowers.

sealed-beam *adj* (esp. of a car headlight) having a lens and prefocused reflector sealed in the lamp vacuum.

sealed road *n Austral. & NZ.* a road surfaced with bitumen or some other hard material.

sea legs *pl n Inf.* **1** the ability to maintain one's balance on board ship. **2** the ability to resist seasickness.

sea level *n* the level of the surface of the sea with respect to the land, taken to be the mean level between high and low tide.

sea lily *n* any of various echinoderms in which the body consists of a long stalk bearing a central disc with delicate radiating arms.

sealing wax *n* a hard material made of shellac, turpentine, and pigment that softens when heated.

sea lion *n* any of various large eared seals, such as the **Californian sea lion,** of the N Pacific, often used as a performing animal.

Sea Lord *n* (in Britain) either of the two serving naval officers (**First** and **Second Sea Lords**) who sit on the admiralty board of the Ministry of Defence.

seal ring *n* another term for **signet ring.**

sealskin ('siːlˌskɪn) *n* **a** the skin or pelt of a fur seal, esp. when dressed with the outer hair removed and the underfur dyed dark brown. **b** (*as modifier*): *a sealskin coat.*

Sealyham terrier ('siːlɪəm) *n* a short-legged wire-haired breed of terrier with a medium-length white coat. ORIG C19: after *Sealyham,* village in S Wales

seam (siːm) *n* **1** the line along which pieces of fabric, etc., are joined, esp. by stitching. **2** a ridge or line made by joining two edges. **3** a stratum of coal, ore, etc. **4** a linear indentation, such as a wrinkle or scar. **5** (*modifier*) *Cricket.* of or relating to a style of bowling in which the bowler utilizes the stitched seam round the ball in order to make it swing in flight and after touching the ground: *a seam bowler.* **6** **bursting at the seams.** full to overflowing. ◆ *vb* **7** (*tr*) to join or sew together by or as if by a seam. **8** to mark or become marked with or as if with a seam or wrinkle. ORIG OE

seaman ('siːmən) *n, pl* **seamen. 1** a naval rating trained in seamanship. **2** a man who serves as a sailor. **3** a person skilled in seamanship.
▸ **'seamanly** *adj, adv* ▸ **'seaman-ˌlike** *adj*

seamanship ('siːmənʃɪp) *n* skill in and knowledge of the work of navigating, maintaining, and operating a vessel.

Seami ★ (siː'ɑːmɪ) *n* a variant spelling of **Zeami.**

sea mile *n* a unit of distance used in navigation, defined as the length of one minute of arc, measured along the meridian, in the latitude of the position. Its actual length varies slightly with latitude, but is about 1853 metres (6080 feet). See also **nautical mile.**

seamless ('siːmlɪs) *adj* **1** (of a garment) having no seams. **2** continuous or flowing: *seamless output; a seamless performance.*

sea mouse *n* any of various large worms having a broad flattened body covered dorsally with a dense mat of iridescent hairlike setae.

seamstress ('sɛmstrɪs) *or* (*rarely*) **sempstress** ('sɛmpstrɪs) *n* a woman who sews and makes clothes, esp. professionally.

seamy ('siːmɪ) *adj* **seamier, seamiest.** showing the least pleasant aspect; sordid.
▸ **'seaminess** *n*

Seanad Éireann ('ʃænəð 'eːrən) *n* (in the Republic of Ireland) the upper chamber of parliament. ORIG from Irish, lit.: senate of Ireland

seance *or* **séance** ('seɪɑ̃ns) *n* a meeting at which spiritualists attempt to receive messages from the spirits of the dead. ORIG C19: from F, lit.: a sitting, from OF *seoir* to sit, from L *sedēre*

sea otter *n* a large marine otter of N Pacific coasts, formerly hunted for its thick brown fur.

sea pink *n* another name for **thrift** (the plant).

seaplane ('siːˌpleɪn) *n* any aircraft that lands on and takes off from water.

seaport ('siːˌpɔːt) *n* **1** a port or harbour accessible to seagoing vessels. **2** a town or city located at such a place.

SEAQ ('siːˌæk) *n acronym for* Stock Exchange Automated Quotations: an electronic system that collects and displays information needed to trade in equities.

sear (sɪə) *vb* (*tr*) **1** to scorch or burn the surface of. **2** to brand with a hot iron. **3** to cause to wither. **4** *Rare.* to make unfeeling. ◆ *adj* **5** *Poetic.* dried up. ORIG OE *sēarian* to become withered, from *sēar* withered

search (sɜːtʃ) *vb* **1** to look through (a place, etc.) thoroughly in order to find someone or something. **2** (*tr*) to examine (a person) for concealed objects. **3** to look at or examine (something) closely: *to search one's conscience.* **4** (*tr;* foll. by *out*) to discover by investigation. **5** *Surgery.* to probe (a wound, etc.). **6** *Computing.* to review (a file) to locate specific information. **7** *Arch.* to penetrate. **8** **search me.** *Inf.* I don't know. ◆ *n* **9** the act or an instance of searching. **10** the examination of a vessel by the right of search. **11** **right of search.** *International law.* the right possessed by the warships of a belligerent state to search merchant vessels to ascertain whether ship or cargo is liable to seizure. ORIG C14: from OF *cerchier,* from LL *circāre* to go around, from L *circus* circle
▸ **'searchable** *adj* ▸ **'searcher** *n*

search engine *n Computing.* a service provided on the Internet that carries out searches and locates information on the Internet.

searching ('sɜːtʃɪŋ) *adj* keenly penetrating: *a searching look.*
▸ **'searchingly** *adv*

searchlight ('sɜːtʃˌlaɪt) *n* **1** a device that projects a powerful beam of light in a particular direction. **2** the beam of light produced by such a device.

search party *n* a group of people taking part in an organized search, as for a lost, missing, or wanted person.

search warrant *n* a written order issued by a justice of the peace authorizing a constable to enter and search premises for stolen goods, etc.

Searle ★ (sɜːl) *n* **Ronald** (**William Fordham**). born 1920, British cartoonist, best known as the creator of the schoolgirls of St Trinian's.

seascape ('siːˌskeɪp) *n* a sketch, etc., of the sea.

sea scorpion *n* any of various northern marine fishes having a tapering body and a large head covered with bony plates and spines.

Sea Scout *n* a Scout belonging to any of a number of Scout troops whose main activities are canoeing, sailing, etc.

sea serpent *n* a huge legendary creature of the sea resembling a snake or dragon.

sea shanty *n* another name for **shanty**[2].

seashell ('siːˌʃɛl) *n* the empty shell of a marine mollusc.

seashore ('siːˌʃɔː) *n* **1** land bordering on the sea. **2** *Law.* the land between the marks of high and low water.

seasick ('siːˌsɪk) *adj* suffering from nausea and dizziness caused by the motion of a ship at sea.
▸ **'sea,sickness** *n*

seaside ('siːˌsaɪd) *n* **a** any area bordering on the sea, esp. one regarded as a resort. **b** (*as modifier*): *a seaside hotel.*

sea snail *n* a small spiny-finned fish of cold seas, having a soft scaleless tadpole-shaped body with the pelvic fins fused into a sucker.

sea snake *n* a venomous snake of tropical seas that swims by means of a laterally compressed oarlike tail.

season ('siːzᵊn) *n* **1** one of the four equal periods into which the year is divided by the equinoxes and solstices. These periods (spring, summer, autumn, and winter) have characteristic weather conditions, and occur at opposite times of the year in the N and S hemispheres. **2** a period of the year characterized by particular conditions or activities: *the rainy season.* **3** the period during which any particular species of animal, bird, or fish is legally permitted to be caught or killed: *open season on red deer.* **4** a period during which a particular entertainment, sport, etc., takes place: *the football season.* **5** any definite or indefinite period. **6** any of the major periods into which the ecclesiastical calendar is divided, such as Lent or Easter. **7** fitting or proper time. **8 in good season.** early enough. **9 in season. 9a** (of game) permitted to be killed. **9b** (of fresh food) readily available. **9c** Also: **in** *or* **on heat.** (of some female mammals) sexually receptive. **9d** appropriate. ◆ *vb* **10** (*tr*) to add herbs, salt, pepper, or spice to (food). **11** (*tr*) to add zest to. **12** (in the preparation of timber) to undergo or cause to undergo drying. **13** (*tr; usually passive*) to make or become experienced: *seasoned troops.* **14** (*tr*) to mitigate or temper. ORIG C13: from OF *seson,* from L *satiō* a sowing, from *serere* to sow
▸ **'seasoned** *adj* ▸ **'seasoner** *n*

seasonable ('siːzənəbᵊl) *adj* **1** suitable for the season: *a seasonable Christmas snow scene.* **2** taking place at the appropriate time.
▸ **'seasonableness** *n* ▸ **'seasonably** *adv*

seasonal ('siːzənᵊl) *adj* of, relating to, or occurring at a certain season or seasons of the year: *seasonal labour.*
▸ **'seasonally** *adv*

seasonal affective disorder *n* a state of depression sometimes experienced by people in winter, thought to be related to lack of sunlight. Abbrev.: **SAD.**

seasoning ('siːzənɪŋ) *n* **1** something that enhances the flavour of food, such as salt or herbs. **2** another term (not now in technical usage) for **drying.**

season ticket *n* a ticket for a series of events, number of journeys, etc., within a limited time, usually obtained at a reduced rate.

sea squirt *n* a minute primitive marine animal, most of which are sedentary, having a saclike body with openings through which water enters and leaves.

sea swallow *n* a popular name for **tern.**

seat (siːt) *n* **1** a piece of furniture designed for sitting on, such as a chair or sofa. **2** the part of a chair, bench, etc., on which one sits. **3** a place to sit, esp. one that requires a ticket: *I have two seats for the film tonight.* **4** the buttocks. **5** the part of a garment covering the buttocks. **6** the part or area serving as the base of an object. **7** the part or surface on which the base of an object rests. **8** the place or centre in which something is located: *a seat of government.* **9** a place of abode, esp. a country mansion. **10** a membership or the right to membership in a legislative or similar body. **11** *Chiefly Brit.* a parliamentary constituency. **12** the manner in which a rider sits on a horse. ◆ *vb* **13** (*tr*) to bring to or place on a seat. **14** (*tr*) to provide with seats. **15** (*tr; often passive*) to place or centre: *the ministry is seated in the capital.* **16** (*tr*) to set firmly in place. **17** (*tr*) to fix or install in a position of power. **18** (*intr*) (of garments) to sag in the area covering the buttocks: *your skirt has seated badly.* ORIG OE *gesete*

seat belt *n* **1** Also called: **safety belt.** a belt or strap worn in a vehicle to restrain forward motion in the event of a collision. **2** a similar belt or strap worn in an aircraft at takeoff and landing.

seating ('siːtɪŋ) *n* **1** the act of providing with a seat or seats. **2a** the provision of seats, as in a theatre, etc. **2b** (*as modifier*): *seating arrangements.* **3** material used for covering seats. **4** a surface on which a part, such as a valve, is supported.

Seaton Valley ★ ('siːtᵊn) *n* a region in NE England, in SE Northumberland: consists of a group of former coal-mining villages. Pop.: 45 000 (latest est.).

sea trout *n* a silvery marine variety of the brown trout that migrates to fresh water to spawn.

Seattle ★ (sɪ'ætᵊl) *n* a port in W Washington, on the isthmus between Lake Washington and Puget Sound: the largest city in the state and chief commercial centre of the Northwest; two universities. Pop.: 520 947 (1994 est.).

sea urchin *n* any echinoderm such as the **edible sea urchin,** having a globular body enclosed in a rigid spiny test and occurring in shallow marine waters.

sea vegetables *pl n* edible seaweed.

sea wall *n* a wall or embankment built to prevent encroachment or erosion by the sea.

seaward ('siːwəd) *adv* **1** Also called: **seawards.** towards the sea. ◆ *adj* **2** directed or moving towards the sea. **3** (esp. of a wind) coming from the sea.

seaway ('siːˌweɪ) *n* **1** a waterway giving access to an inland port. **2** a vessel's progress. **3** a route across the sea.

seaweed ('siːˌwiːd) *n* any of numerous multicellular marine algae that grow on the seashore, in salt marshes, in brackish water, or submerged in the ocean.

seaworthy ('siːˌwɜːðɪ) *adj* in a fit condition or ready for a sea voyage.
▸ **'sea,worthiness** *n*

sebaceous (sɪ'beɪʃəs) *adj* **1** of or resembling sebum, fat, or tallow. **2** secreting fat. ORIG C18: from LL *sēbāceus,* from SEBUM

sebaceous glands *pl n* the small glands in the skin that secrete sebum into hair follicles and onto most of the body surface except the soles of the feet and the palms of the hands.

Sebastian ★ (sɪ'bæstjən) *n* **Saint.** died ?288 A.D., Christian martyr. According to tradition, he was first shot with arrows and then beaten to death. Feast day: Jan. 20.

Sebastopol ★ (sɪ'bæstəpəl) *n* the English name for **Sevastopol.**

seborrhoea *or esp. US* **seborrhea** (ˌsɛbə'rɪə) *n* a disease of the sebaceous glands characterized by excessive secretion of sebum.

sebum ('siːbəm) *n* the oily secretion of the sebaceous glands that acts as a lubricant for the hair and skin and provides some protection against bacteria. ORIG C19: from NL, from L: tallow

sec[1] (sɛk) *adj* **1** (of wines) dry. **2** (of champagne) of medium sweetness. ORIG C19: from F, from L *siccus*

sec[2] (sɛk) *n Inf.* short for **second**[2]: *wait a sec.*

sec[3] (sɛk) *abbrev. for* secant.

SEC *abbrev. for* Securities and Exchange Commission.

sec. *abbrev. for:* **1** second (of time). **2** secondary. **3** secretary. **4** section. **5** sector.

secant ('siːkənt) *n* **1** (of an angle) a trigonometric function that in a right-angled triangle is the ratio of the length of the hypotenuse to that of the adjacent side; the reciprocal of cosine. Abbrev.: **sec. 2** a line that intersects a curve. ORIG C16: from L *secāre* to cut

secateurs ('sɛkətəz) *pl n Chiefly Brit.* a small pair of shears for pruning, having a pair of pivoted handles and usually a single cutting blade that closes against a flat surface. ORIG C19: pl of F *sécateur,* from L *secāre* to cut

secede (sɪ'siːd) *vb* **secedes, seceding, seceded.** (*intr; often foll. by from*) (of a person, section, etc.) to make a formal withdrawal of membership, as from a political alliance, etc. ORIG C18: from L *sēcēdere* to withdraw, from *sē-* apart + *cēdere* to go
▸ **se'ceder** *n*

secession (sɪ'sɛʃən) *n* **1** the act of seceding. **2** (*often cap.*) *Chiefly US.* the withdrawal in 1860–61 of 11 Southern states from the Union to form the Confederacy, precipitating the American Civil War. ORIG C17: from L *sēcessiō* a withdrawing, from *sēcēdere* to SECEDE
▸ **se'cession,ism** *n* ▸ **se'cessionist** *n, adj*

sech (ʃɛk, sɛtʃ, 'sɛk'eɪtʃ) *n* hyperbolic secant.

seclude (sɪ'klu:d) *vb* **secludes, secluding, secluded.** (*tr*) **1** to remove from contact with others. **2** to shut off or screen from view. ORIG C15: from L *sēclūdere* to shut off, from *sē-* + *claudere* to imprison

secluded (sɪ'klu:dɪd) *adj* **1** kept apart from the company of others: *a secluded life.* **2** private.
▸ **se'cludedly** *adv* ▸ **se'cludedness** *n*

seclusion (sɪ'klu:ʒən) *n* **1** the act of secluding or the state of being secluded. **2** a secluded place. ORIG C17: from Med. L *sēclūsiō;* see SECLUDE

second[1] ('sɛkənd) *adj* (*usually prenominal*) **1a** coming directly after the first in numbering or counting order, position, time, etc.; being the ordinal number of *two:* often written 2nd. **1b** (*as n*): *the second in line.* **2** graded or ranked between the first and third levels. **3** alternate: *every second Thursday.* **4** extra: *a second opportunity.* **5** resembling a person or event from an earlier period of history: *a second Wagner.* **6** of lower quality; inferior. **7** denoting the lowest but one forward ratio of a gearbox in a motor vehicle. **8** *Music.* denoting a musical part, voice, or instrument subordinate to or lower in pitch than another (the first): *the second tenors.* **9 at second hand.** by hearsay. ◆ *n* **10** *Brit. education.* an honours degree of the second class, usually further divided into an upper and lower designation. Full term: **second-class honours degree. 11** the lowest but one forward ratio of a gearbox in a motor vehicle. **12** (in boxing, duelling, etc.) an attendant who looks after a competitor. **13** a speech seconding a motion or the person making it. **14** *Music.* the interval between one note and another lying next above or below it in the diatonic scale. **15** (*pl*) goods of inferior quality. **16** (*pl*) *Inf.* a second helping of food. **17** (*pl*) the second course of a meal. ◆ *vb* (*tr*) **18** to give aid or backing to. **19** (in boxing, etc.) to act as second to (a competitor). **20** to express formal support for (a motion already proposed). ◆ *adv* **21** Also: **secondly.** in the second place. ◆ *sentence connector.* **22** Also: **secondly.** as the second point. ORIG C13: via OF from L *secundus* coming next in order, from *sequī* to follow
▸ **'seconder** *n*

second[2] ('sɛkənd) *n* **1a** 1/60 of a minute of time. **1b** the basic SI unit of time: the duration of 9 192 631 770 periods of radiation corresponding to the transition between two hyperfine levels of the ground state of caesium-133. Symbol: s **2** 1/60 of a minute of angle. Symbol: ″ **3** a very short period of time. ORIG C14: from OF, from Med. L *pars minūta secunda* the second small part (a minute being the first small part of an hour); see SECOND[1]

second[3] (sɪ'kɒnd) *vb* (*tr*) *Brit.* **1** to transfer (an employee) temporarily to another branch, etc. **2** *Mil.* to transfer (an officer) to another post. ORIG C19: from F *en second* in second rank (or position)
▸ **se'condment** *n*

secondary ('sɛkəndərɪ) *adj* **1** one grade or step after the first. **2** derived from or depending on what is primary or first: *a secondary source.* **3** below the first in rank, importance, etc. **4** (*prenominal*) of or relating to the education of young people between the ages of 11 and 18: *secondary education.* **5** (of the flight feathers of a bird's wing) growing from the ulna. **6a** being the part of an electric circuit, such as a transformer or induction coil, in which a current is induced by a changing current in a neighbouring coil: *a secondary coil.* **6b** (of a current) flowing in such a circuit. **7** *Chem.* **7a** (of an amine) containing the group NH. **7b** (of a salt) derived from a tribasic acid by replacement of two acidic hydrogen atoms with metal atoms. ◆ *n, pl* **secondaries. 8** a person or thing that is secondary. **9** a subordinate, deputy, or inferior. **10** a secondary coil, winding, inductance, or current in an electric circuit. **11** *Ornithol.* any of the flight feathers that grow from the ulna of a bird's wing. **12** *Astron.* a celestial body that orbits around a specified primary body: *the moon is the secondary of the earth.* **13** *American football.* **13a** (usually preceded by *the*) cornerbacks and safeties collectively. **13b** their area in the field. **14** short for **secondary colour.**
▸ **'secondarily** *adv* ▸ **'secondariness** *n*

secondary cell *n* an electric cell that can be recharged and can therefore be used to store electrical energy in the form of chemical energy.

secondary colour *n* a colour formed by mixing two primary colours.

secondary emission *n Physics.* the emission of electrons (**secondary electrons**) from a solid as a result of bombardment with a beam of electrons, ions, or metastable atoms.

secondary picketing *n* the picketing by striking workers of a factory, distribution outlet, etc., that supplies goods to or distributes goods from their employer.

secondary sexual characteristic *n* any of various features distinguishing individuals of different sex but not directly concerned in reproduction. Examples are the antlers of a stag and the beard of a man.

second ballot *n* an electoral procedure in which, after a first ballot, candidates at the bottom of the poll are eliminated and another ballot is held among the remaining candidates.

second-best *adj* **1** next to the best. **2 come off second best.** *Inf.* to be worsted by someone. ◆ *n* **3 second best.** an inferior alternative.

second chamber *n* the upper house of a bicameral legislative assembly.

second childhood *n* dotage; senility (esp. in **in his, her,** etc., **second childhood**).

second class *n* **1** the class or grade next in value, quality, etc., to the first. ◆ *adj* (**second-class** *when prenominal*). **2** of the class or grade next to the best in quality, etc. **3** shoddy or inferior. **4** of or denoting the class of accommodation in a hotel or on a train, etc., lower in quality and price than first class. **5** (in Britain) of mail that is processed more slowly than first-class mail. **6** *Education.* See **second**[1] (sense 10). ◆ *adv* **7** by second-class mail, transport, etc.

second-class citizen *n* a person whose rights and opportunities are treated as less important than those of other people in the same society.

Second Coming *n* the prophesied return of Christ to earth at the Last Judgment.

second cousin *n* the child of a first cousin of either of one's parents.

second-degree burn *n Pathol.* a burn in which blisters appear on the skin.

seconde (sɪ'kɒnd) *n* the second of eight positions from which a parry or attack can be made in fencing. ORIG C18: from F *seconde parade* the second parry

Second Empire *n* the style of furniture and decoration of the Second Empire in France (1852–70), reviving the Empire style, but with fussier ornamentation.

second fiddle *n Inf.* **1a** the second violin in a string quartet or an orchestra. **1b** the musical part assigned to such an instrument. **2** a person who has a secondary status.

second floor *n Brit.* the storey of a building immediately above the first and two floors up from the ground. US and Canad. term: **third floor.**

second generation *n* **1** offspring of parents born in a given country. **2** (*modifier*) of a refined stage of development in manufacture: *a second-generation robot.*

second growth *n* natural regrowth of a forest after fire, cutting, etc.

second hand *n* a pointer on the face of a timepiece that indicates the seconds.

second-hand *adj* **1** previously owned or used. **2** not from an original source or experience. **3** dealing in or selling goods that are not new: *a second-hand car dealer.* ◆ *adv* **4** from a source of previously owned or used goods: *he prefers to buy second-hand.* **5** not directly: *he got the news second-hand.*

second language *n* **1** a language other than the mother tongue used for business transactions, teaching, debate, etc. **2** a language that is officially recognized in a country, other than the main national language.

second lieutenant *n* an officer holding the lowest commissioned rank in the armed forces of certain nations.

secondly (ˈsɛkəndlɪ) *adv* another word for **second**[1], usually used to precede the second item in a list of topics.

second nature *n* a habit, characteristic, etc., long practised or acquired so as to seem innate.

second person *n* a grammatical category of pronouns and verbs used when referring to or describing the individual or individuals being addressed.

second-rate *adj* **1** not of the highest quality; mediocre. **2** second in importance, etc.

second reading *n* the second presentation of a bill in a legislative assembly, as to approve its general principles (in Britain), or to discuss a committee's report on it (in the US).

second sight *n* the alleged ability to foresee the future, see actions taking place elsewhere, etc.
▸ **ˈsecond-ˈsighted** *adj*

second string *n* **1** *Chiefly Brit.* an alternative course of action, etc., intended to come into use should the first fail (esp. in **a second string to one's bow**). **2** *Chiefly US & Canad.* a substitute or reserve player or team.

second thought *n* (*usually pl*) a revised opinion or idea on a matter already considered.

second wind (wɪnd) *n* **1** the return of the ability to breathe at a comfortable rate, esp. following a period of exertion. **2** renewed ability to continue in an effort.

secrecy (ˈsiːkrɪsɪ) *n, pl* **secrecies. 1** the state or quality of being secret. **2** the state of keeping something secret. **3** the ability or tendency to keep things secret.

secret (ˈsiːkrɪt) *adj* **1** kept hidden or separate from the knowledge of others. Related adj: **cryptic. 2** known only to initiates: *a secret password.* **3** hidden from general view or use: *a secret garden.* **4** able or tending to keep things private or to oneself. **5** operating without the knowledge of outsiders: *a secret society.* ◆ *n* **6** something kept or to be kept hidden. **7** something unrevealed; a mystery. **8** an underlying explanation, reason, etc.: *the secret of success.* **9** a method, plan, etc., known only to initiates. **10** *Liturgy.* a prayer said by the celebrant of the Mass after the offertory and before the preface. ORIG C14: via OF from L *sēcrētus* concealed, from *sēcernere* to sift
▸ **ˈsecretly** *adv*

secret agent *n* a person employed in espionage.

secretaire (ˌsɛkrɪˈtɛə) *n* an enclosed writing desk, usually having an upper cabinet section. ORIG C19: from F; see SECRETARY

secretariat (ˌsɛkrɪˈtɛərɪət) *n* **1a** an office responsible for the secretarial, clerical, and administrative affairs of a legislative body or international organization. **1b** the staff of such an office. **2** a body of secretaries. **3** a secretary's place of work; office. **4** the position of a secretary. ORIG C19: via F from Med. L *sēcrētāriātus,* from *sēcrētārius* SECRETARY

secretary (ˈsɛkrətrɪ) *n, pl* **secretaries. 1** a person who handles correspondence, keeps records, and does general clerical work for an individual, organization, etc. **2** the official manager of the day-to-day business of a society or board. **3** (in Britain) a senior civil servant who assists a government minister. **4** (in the US) the head of a government administrative department. **5** (in Britain) See **secretary of state. 6** Another name for **secretaire.** ORIG C14: from Med. L *sēcrētārius,* from L *sēcrētum* something hidden; see SECRET
▸ **secretarial** (ˌsɛkrɪˈtɛərɪəl) *adj* ▸ **ˈsecretaryship** *n*

secretary bird *n* a large African long-legged bird of prey having a crest and tail of long feathers and feeding chiefly on snakes.

secretary-general *n, pl* **secretaries-general.** a chief administrative official, as of the United Nations.

secretary of state *n* **1** (in Britain) the head of any of several government departments. **2** (in the US) the head of the government department in charge of foreign affairs (**State Department**).

secrete[1] (sɪˈkriːt) *vb* **secretes, secreting, secreted.** (of a cell, organ, etc.) to synthesize and release (a secretion). ORIG C18: back formation from SECRETION
▸ **seˈcretor** *n* ▸ **seˈcretory** *adj*

secrete[2] (sɪˈkriːt) *vb* **secretes, secreting, secreted.** (*tr*) to put in a hiding place. ORIG C18: var. of obs. *secret* to hide away

secretion (sɪˈkriːʃən) *n* **1** a substance that is released from a cell, esp. a glandular cell. **2** the process involved in producing and releasing such a substance from the cell. ORIG C17: from Med. L *sēcrētiō,* from L: a separation

secretive (ˈsiːkrɪtɪv) *adj* inclined to secrecy.
▸ **ˈsecretively** *adv* ▸ **ˈsecretiveness** *n*

secretory (sɪˈkriːtərɪ) *adj* of, relating to, or producing a secretion: *secretory function.*

secret police *n* a police force that operates relatively secretly to check subversion or political dissent.

secret service *n* a government agency or department that conducts intelligence or counterintelligence operations.

sect (sɛkt) *n* **1** a subdivision of a larger religious group (esp. the Christian Church as a whole) the members of which have to some extent diverged from the rest by developing deviating beliefs, practices, etc. **2** *Often disparaging.* **2a** a schismatic religious body. **2b** a religious group regarded as extreme or heretical. **3** a group of people with a common interest, doctrine, etc. ORIG C14: from L *secta* faction, from *sequī* to follow

-sect *vb combining form.* to cut or divide, esp. into a specified number of parts: *trisect.* ORIG from L *sectus* cut, from *secāre* to cut

sectarian (sɛkˈtɛərɪən) *adj* **1** of, relating to, or characteristic of sects or sectaries. **2** adhering to a particular sect, faction, or doctrine. **3** narrow-minded, esp. as a result of adherence to a particular sect. ◆ *n* **4** a member of a sect or faction, esp. one who is intolerant towards other sects, etc.
▸ **secˈtarianˌism** *n*

sectary (ˈsɛktərɪ) *n, pl* **sectaries. 1** a member of a sect, esp. a religous sect. **2** a member of a Nonconformist denomination, esp. one that is small. ORIG C16: from Med. L *sectārius,* from L *secta* SECT

section (ˈsɛkʃən) *n* **1** a part cut off or separated from the main body of something. **2** a part or subdivision of a piece of writing, book, etc.: *the sports section of the newspaper.* **3** one of several component parts. **4** a distinct part of a country, community, etc. **5** *US & Canad.* an area one mile square. **6** *NZ.* a plot of land for building, esp. in a suburban area. **7** the section of a railway track that is controlled by a particular signal box. **8** the act or process of cutting or separating by cutting. **9** a representation of an object cut by an imaginary vertical plane so as to show its construction and interior. **10** *Geom.* a plane surface formed by cutting through a solid. **11** a thin slice of biological tissue, etc., prepared for examination by microscope. **12** a segment of an orange or other citrus fruit. **13** a small military formation. **14** *Austral. & NZ.* a fare stage on a bus, tram, etc. **15** *Music.* **15a** an extended division of a composition or movement: *the development section.* **15b** a division in an orchestra, band, etc., containing instruments belonging to the same class: *the brass section.* **16** Also called: **signature, gathering.** a folded printing sheet or sheets ready for gathering and binding. **17 on section.** *NZ.* (of a trainee teacher) working under supervision in a school. ◆ *vb* (*tr*) **18** to cut or divide into sections. **19** to cut through so as to reveal a section. **20** (in drawing, esp. mechanical drawing) to shade so as to indicate sections. **21** *Brit.* to commit (someone) to a psychiatric hospital under the terms of a certain section of the Mental Health Act. ORIG C16: from L *sectiō,* from *secāre* to cut

sectional (ˈsɛkʃənᵊl) *adj* **1** composed of several sections. **2** of or relating to a section. **3** of or concerned with a particular group within a community, esp. to the exclusion of others.
▸ **ˈsectionaˌlize** *or* **ˈsectionaˌlise** *vb* (*tr*) ▸ **ˈsectionally** *adv*

sectionalism ('sɛkʃənəˌlɪzəm) *n* excessive or narrow-minded concern for local or regional interests.
▸ **'sectionalist** *n, adj*

sector ('sɛktə) *n* **1** a part or subdivision, esp. of a society or an economy: *the private sector.* **2** *Geom.* either portion of a circle included between two radii and an arc. **3** a measuring instrument consisting of two graduated arms hinged at one end. **4** a part or subdivision of an area of military operations. **5** *Computing.* the smallest addressable portion of the track on a magnetic tape, disk, or drum store. ORIG C16: from LL: sector, from L: a cutter, from *secāre* to cut
▸ **'sectoral** *adj*

sectorial (sɛk'tɔːrɪəl) *adj* **1** of or relating to a sector. **2** *Zool.* adapted for cutting: *the sectorial teeth of carnivores.*

secular ('sɛkjulə) *adj* **1** of or relating to worldly as opposed to sacred things. **2** not concerned with or related to religion. **3** not within the control of the Church. **4** (of an education, etc.) having no particular religious affinities. **5** (of clerics) not bound by religious vows to a monastic or other order. **6** occurring or appearing once in an age or century. **7** lasting for a long time. **8** *Astron.* occurring slowly over a long period of time. ◆ *n* **9** a member of the secular clergy. ORIG C13: from OF *seculer,* from LL *saeculāris* temporal, from L: concerning an age, from *saeculum* an age
▸ **secularity** (ˌsɛkju'lærɪtɪ) *n* ▸ **'secularly** *adv*

secularism ('sɛkjuləˌrɪzəm) *n* **1** *Philosophy.* a doctrine that rejects religion, esp. in ethics. **2** the attitude that religion should have no place in civil affairs.
▸ **'secularist** *n, adj*

secularize *or* **secularise** ('sɛkjuləˌraɪz) *vb* **secularizes, secularizing, secularized** *or* **secularises, secularising, secularised.** (*tr*) **1** to change from religious or sacred to secular functions, etc. **2** to dispense from allegiance to a religious order. **3** *Law.* to transfer (property) from ecclesiastical to civil possession or use.
▸ **ˌsecularі'zation** *or* **ˌsecularі'sation** *n*

secund (sɪ'kʌnd) *adj Bot.* having parts arranged on or turned to one side of the axis. ORIG C18: from L *secundus* following, from *sequī* to follow

Secunderabad ★ (sə'kʌndərəˌbæd, -ˌbɑːd) *n* a former town in S central India, in N Andra Pradesh: one of the largest British military stations in India: now part of Hyderabad city.

secure (sɪ'kjuə) *adj* **1** free from danger, damage, etc. **2** free from fear, care, etc. **3** in safe custody. **4** not likely to fail, become loose, etc. **5** able to be relied on: *a secure investment.* **6** *Arch.* overconfident. ◆ *vb* **secures, securing, secured. 7** (*tr*) to obtain: *I will secure some good seats.* **8** (when *intr,* often foll. by *against*) to make or become free from danger, fear, etc. **9** (*tr*) to make fast or firm. **10** (when *intr,* often foll. by *against*) to make or become certain: *this plan will secure your happiness.* **11** (*tr*) to assure (a creditor) of payment, as by giving security. **12** (*tr*) to make (a military position) safe from attack. **13** *Naut.* to make (a vessel or its contents) safe or ready by battening down hatches, etc. ORIG C16: from L *sēcūrus* free from care
▸ **se'curable** *adj* ▸ **se'curely** *adv* ▸ **se'curement** *n* ▸ **se'curer** *n*

Securities and Investment Board *n* a British regulatory body set up in 1986 to oversee London's financial markets, each of which has its own self-regulatory organization. Abbrev.: **SIB.**

securitization *or* **securitisation** (sɪˌkjuərɪtaɪ'zeɪʃən) *n Finance.* the use of such securities as eurobonds to enable investors to lend directly to borrowers with a minimum of risk but without using banks as intermediaries.

security (sɪ'kjuərɪtɪ) *n, pl* **securities. 1** the state of being secure. **2** assured freedom from poverty or want: *he needs the security of a permanent job.* **3** a person or thing that secures, guarantees, etc. **4** precautions taken to ensure against theft, espionage, etc. **5** (*often pl*) **5a** a certificate of creditorship or property carrying the right to receive interest or dividend, such as shares or bonds. **5b** the financial asset represented by such a certificate. **6** the specific asset that a creditor can claim in the event of default on an obligation. **7** something given or pledged to secure the fulfilment of a promise or obligation. **8** the protection of data to ensure that only authorised personnel have access to computer files.

security blanket *n* **1** a policy of temporary secrecy by police or those in charge of security, in order to protect a person, place, etc., threatened with danger, from further risk. **2** a baby's blanket, soft toy, etc., to which a baby or young child becomes very attached, using it as a comforter. **3** *Inf.* anything used or thought of as providing reassurance.

Security Council *n* an organ of the United Nations established to maintain world peace.

security guard *n* someone employed to protect buildings, people, etc., and to collect and deliver large sums of money.

security risk *n* a person deemed to be a threat to state security in that he or she could be open to pressure, have subversive political beliefs, etc.

secy. *or* **sec'y.** *abbrev. for* secretary.

sedan (sɪ'dæn) *n* **1** *US, Canad., & NZ.* a saloon car. **2** short for **sedan chair.** ORIG C17: from ?

Sedan ★ (*French* sədɑ̃; *English* sɪ'dæn) *n* a town in NE France, on the River Meuse: passed to France in 1642; a Protestant stronghold (16th–17th centuries); scene of a French defeat (1870) during the Franco-Prussian War and of a battle (1940) in World War II, which began the German invasion of France. Pop.: 22 400 (1990).

sedan chair *n* a closed chair for one passenger, carried on poles by two bearers, commonly used in the 17th and 18th centuries.

sedate[1] (sɪ'deɪt) *adj* **1** habitually calm and composed in manner. **2** sober or decorous. ORIG C17: from L *sēdāre* to soothe
▸ **se'dately** *adv* ▸ **se'dateness** *n*

sedate[2] (sɪ'deɪt) *vb* **sedates, sedating, sedated.** (*tr*) to administer a sedative to. ORIG C20: back formation from SEDATIVE

sedation (sɪ'deɪʃən) *n* **1** a state of calm or reduced nervous activity. **2** the administration of a sedative.

sedative ('sɛdətɪv) *adj* **1** having a soothing or calming effect. **2** of or relating to sedation. ◆ *n* **3** *Med.* a sedative drug or agent. ORIG C15: from Med. L *sēdātīvus,* from L *sēdātus* assuaged; see SEDATE[1]

Seddon ★ ('sɛdᵊn) *n* **Richard John,** known as *King Dick.* 1845–1906, New Zealand statesman, born in England; prime minister (1893–1906).

sedentary ('sɛdᵊntərɪ) *adj* **1** characterized by or requiring a sitting position: *sedentary work.* **2** tending to sit about without taking much exercise. **3** (of animals) moving about very little. **4** (of birds) not migratory. ORIG C16: from L *sedentārius,* from *sedēre* to sit
▸ **'sedentarily** *adv* ▸ **'sedentariness** *n*

Seder ('seɪdə) *n Judaism.* a ceremonial meal on the first night or first two nights of Passover. ORIG from Heb. *sēdher* order

sedge (sɛdʒ) *n* a grasslike plant growing on wet ground and having rhizomes, triangular stems, and minute flowers in spikelets. ORIG OE *secg*
▸ **'sedgy** *adj*

Sedgemoor ★ ('sɛdʒˌmuə) *n* a plain in SW England, in central Somerset: scene of the defeat (1685) of the Duke of Monmouth.

sedge warbler *n* a European songbird of reed beds and swampy areas, having a streaked brownish plumage with white eye stripes.

Sedgwick ★ ('sɛdʒwɪk) *n* **Adam.** 1785–1873, British geologist, who helped to establish the geological time scale.

sedilia (sɛ'daɪlɪə) *n* (*functioning as sing*) the group of three seats, each called a **sedile** (sɛ'daɪlɪ) on the south side of a sanctuary where the celebrant and ministers sit during High Mass. ORIG C18: from L, from *sedīle* a chair, from *sedēre* to sit

sediment ('sɛdɪmənt) *n* **1** matter that settles to the bottom of a liquid. **2** material that has been deposited from water, ice, or wind. ORIG C16: from L *sedimentum* a settling, from *sedēre* to sit
▸ **ˌsedimen'tation** *n*

sedimentary (ˌsɛdɪˈmɛntərɪ) *adj* **1** characteristic of, resembling, or containing sediment. **2** (of rocks) formed by the accumulation of mineral and organic fragments that have been deposited by water, ice, or wind.
▸ **ˌsediˈmentarily** *adv*

sedimentation tank *n* a tank into which sewage is passed to allow suspended solid matter to separate out.

sedition (sɪˈdɪʃən) *n* **1** speech or behaviour directed against the peace of a state. **2** an offence that tends to undermine the authority of a state. **3** an incitement to public disorder. ORIG C14: from L *sēditiō* discord, from *sēd-* apart + *itiō* a going, from *īre* to go
▸ **seˈditionary** *n, adj*

seditious (sɪˈdɪʃəs) *adj* **1** of, like, or causing sedition. **2** inclined to or taking part in sedition.

seduce (sɪˈdjuːs) *vb* **seduces, seducing, seduced.** (*tr*) **1** to persuade to engage in sexual intercourse. **2** to lead astray, as from the right action. **3** to win over, attract, or lure. ORIG C15: from L *sēdūcere* to lead apart
▸ **seˈducible** *adj*

seducer (sɪˈdjuːsə) *or (fem)* **seductress** (sɪˈdʌktrɪs) *n* a person who entices, allures, or seduces, esp. one who entices another to engage in sexual intercourse.

seduction (sɪˈdʌkʃən) *n* **1** the act of seducing or the state of being seduced. **2** a means of seduction.

seductive (sɪˈdʌktɪv) *adj* tending to seduce or capable of seducing; enticing; alluring.
▸ **seˈductively** *adv* ▸ **seˈductiveness** *n*

sedulous (ˈsɛdjʊləs) *adj* assiduous; diligent. ORIG C16: from L *sēdulus*, from ?
▸ **sedulity** (sɪˈdjuːlɪtɪ) *or* **ˈsedulousness** *n* ▸ **ˈsedulously** *adv*

sedum (ˈsiːdəm) *n* a rock plant having thick fleshy leaves and clusters of white, yellow, or pink flowers. ORIG C15: from L: houseleek

see[1] (siː) *vb* **sees, seeing, saw, seen. 1** to perceive with the eyes. **2** (when *tr, may take a clause as object*) to understand: *I explained the problem but he could not see it.* **3** (*tr*) to perceive with any or all of the senses: *I hate to see you so unhappy.* **4** (*tr; may take a clause as object*) to foresee: *I can see what will happen if you don't help.* **5** (when *tr, may take a clause as object*) to ascertain or find out (a fact): *see who is at the door.* **6** (when *tr, takes a clause as object;* when *intr,* foll. by *to*) to make sure (of something) or take care (of something): *see that he gets to bed early.* **7** (when *tr, may take a clause as object*) to consider, deliberate, or decide: *see if you can come next week.* **8** (*tr*) to have experience of: *he had seen much unhappiness in his life.* **9** (*tr*) to allow to be in a specified condition: *I cannot stand by and see a child in pain.* **10** (*tr*) to be characterized by: *this period of history has seen much unrest.* **11** (*tr*) to meet or pay a visit to: *to see one's solicitor.* **12** (*tr*) to receive: *the Prime Minister will see the deputation now.* **13** (*tr*) to frequent the company of: *she is seeing a married man.* **14** (*tr*) to accompany: *I saw her to the door.* **15** (*tr*) to refer to or look up: *for further information see the appendix.* **16** (in gambling, esp. in poker) to match (another player's bet) or match the bet of (another player) by staking an equal sum. **17 as far as I can see.** to the best of my judgment. **18 see fit.** (*takes an infinitive*) to consider proper, etc.: *I don't see fit to allow her to come here.* **19 see (someone) hanged** *or* **damned first.** *Inf.* to refuse absolutely to do what one has been asked. **20 see you, see you later,** *or* **be seeing you.** an expression of farewell. ◆ See also **see about, see into,** etc. ORIG OE *sēon*

see[2] (siː) *n* the diocese of a bishop, or the place within it where his or her cathedral is situated. ORIG C13: from OF *sed*, from L *sēdēs* a seat

see about *vb* (*intr, prep*) **1** to take care of: *he couldn't see about the matter because he was ill.* **2** to investigate: *to see about a new car.*

Seebeck effect (ˈsiːbɛk) *n* the phenomenon in which a current is produced in a circuit containing two or more different metals when the junctions between the metals are maintained at different temperatures. Also called: **thermoelectric effect.** ORIG C19: after Thomas *Seebeck* (1770–1831), G physicist

seed (siːd) *n* **1** *Bot.* a mature fertilized plant ovule, consisting of an embryo and its food store surrounded by a protective seed coat (testa). Related adj: **seminal. 2** the small hard seedlike fruit of plants such as wheat. **3** any propagative part of a plant, such as a tuber, spore, or bulb. **4** the source, beginning, or germ of anything: *the seeds of revolt.* **5** *Chiefly Bible.* descendants: *the seed of Abraham.* **6** an archaic term for **sperm** or **semen. 7** *Sport.* a seeded player. **8** *Chem.* a small crystal added to a supersaturated solution to induce crystallization. **9 go** *or* **run to seed. 9a** (of plants) to produce and shed seeds. **9b** to lose vigour, usefulness, etc. ◆ *vb* **10** to plant (seeds, grain, etc.) in (soil): *we seeded this field with oats.* **11** (*intr*) (of plants) to form or shed seeds. **12** (*tr*) to remove the seeds from (fruit, etc.). **13** (*tr*) *Chem.* to add a small crystal to (a supersaturated solution) in order to cause crystallization. **14** (*tr*) to scatter certain substances, such as silver iodide, in (clouds) in order to cause rain. **15** (*tr*) to arrange (the draw of a tournament) so that outstanding teams or players will not meet in the early rounds. ORIG OE *sǣd*
▸ **ˈseeder** *n* ▸ **ˈseedless** *adj*

seedbed (ˈsiːdˌbɛd) *n* **1** a plot of land in which seedlings are grown before being transplanted. **2** the place where something develops.

seedcake (ˈsiːdˌkeɪk) *n* a sweet cake flavoured with caraway seeds and lemon rind or essence.

seed capital *n Finance.* a small amount of capital required to finance the research necessary to produce a business plan for a new company.

seed coral *n* small pieces of coral used in jewellery, etc.

seed corn *n* **1** the good quality ears or kernels of corn that are used as seed. **2** assets that are expected to provide future benefits.

seed leaf *n* the nontechnical name for **cotyledon.**

seedling (ˈsiːdlɪŋ) *n* a plant produced from a seed, esp. a very young plant.

seed money *n* money used for the establishment of an enterprise.

seed oyster *n* a young oyster, esp. a cultivated oyster, ready for transplantation.

seed pearl *n* a tiny pearl weighing less than a quarter of a grain.

seed pod *n* a carpel or pistil enclosing the seeds of a plant, esp. a flowering plant.

seed potato *n* a potato tuber used for planting.

seed vessel *n Bot.* a dry fruit, such as a capsule.

seedy (ˈsiːdɪ) *adj* **seedier, seediest. 1** shabby in appearance: *seedy clothes.* **2** (of a plant) at the stage of producing seeds. **3** *Inf.* not physically fit.
▸ **ˈseedily** *adv* ▸ **ˈseediness** *n*

Seeger ★ (ˈsiːgə) *n* **Pete.** born 1919, US folk singer and songwriter, noted for his protest songs, which include "Where Have all the Flowers Gone?" (1961) and "If I Had a Hammer" (1962).

seeing (ˈsiːɪŋ) *n* **1** the sense or faculty of sight. **2** *Astron.* the condition of the atmosphere with respect to observation of stars, planets, etc. ◆ *conj* **3** (*subordinating;* often foll. by *that*) in light of the fact (that).

> **USAGE NOTE** The use of *seeing as how* as in *seeing as (how) the bus is always late, I don't need to hurry* is generally thought to be incorrect or nonstandard.

see into *vb* (*intr, prep*) to discover the true nature of: *I can't see into your thoughts.*

seek (siːk) *vb* **seeks, seeking, sought.** (*mainly tr*) **1** (when *intr,* often foll. by *for* or *after*) to try to find by searching: *to seek a solution.* **2** (*also intr*) to try to obtain or acquire: *to seek happiness.* **3** to attempt (to do something): *I'm only seeking to help.* **4** (*also intr*) to inquire about or request (something). **5** to resort to: *to seek the garden for peace.* ORIG OE *sēcan*
▸ **ˈseeker** *n*

seek out *vb* (*tr, adv*) to search hard for and find a specific person or thing: *she sought out her friend from amongst the crowd.*

Seeland ★ ('ze:lant) *n* the German name for **Sjælland.**

seem (si:m) *vb* (*may take an infinitive*) **1** (*copula*) to appear to the mind or eye; look: *the car seems to be running well.* **2** to appear to be: *there seems no need for all this nonsense.* **3** used to diminish the force of a following infinitive to be polite, more noncommittal, etc.: *I can't seem to get through to you.* ORIG C12: ?from ON *soma* to beseem, from *sœmr* befitting

USAGE NOTE See at **like.**

seeming ('si:mɪŋ) *adj* **1** (*prenominal*) apparent but not actual or genuine. ◆ *n* **2** outward or false appearance.
▸ **'seemingly** *adv*

seemly ('si:mlɪ) *adj* **seemlier, seemliest. 1** proper or fitting. **2** *Obs.* pleasing in appearance. ◆ *adv* **3** *Arch.* decorously. ORIG C13: from ON *sœmiligr,* from *sœmr* befitting

seen (si:n) *vb* the past participle of **see**[1].

see off *vb* (*tr, adv*) **1** to be present at the departure of (a person making a journey). **2** *Inf.* to cause to leave or depart, esp. by force.

seep (si:p) *vb* **1** (*intr*) to pass gradually or leak as if through small openings. ◆ *n* **2** a small spring or place where water, oil, etc., has oozed through the ground. ORIG OE *sīpian*
▸ **'seepage** *n*

seer[1] (sɪə) *n* **1** a person who can supposedly see into the future. **2** a person who professes supernatural powers. **3** a person who sees.

seer[2] (sɪə) *n* a varying unit of weight used in India, usually about two pounds or one kilogram. ORIG from Hindi

seersucker ('sɪəˌsʌkə) *n* a light cotton, linen, or other fabric with a crinkled surface and often striped. ORIG C18: from Hindi *śīrśakar,* from Persian *shīr o shakkar,* lit.: milk and sugar

seesaw ('si:ˌsɔ:) *n* **1** a plank balanced in the middle so that two people seated on the ends can ride up and down by pushing on the ground with their feet. **2** the pastime of riding up and down on a seesaw. **3** an up-and-down or back-and-forth movement. ◆ *vb* **4** (*intr*) to move up and down or back and forth in such a manner. ORIG C17: reduplication of SAW[1], alluding to the movement from side to side, as in sawing

seethe (si:ð) *vb* **seethes, seething, seethed. 1** (*intr*) to boil or to foam as if boiling. **2** (*intr*) to be in a state of extreme agitation, esp. through anger. **3** (*tr*) to soak in liquid. **4** (*tr*) *Arch.* to cook by boiling. ORIG OE *sēothan*
▸ **'seething** *adj* ▸ **'seethingly** *adv*

see through *vb* **1** (*tr*) to help out in time of need or trouble. **2** (*tr, adv*) to remain with until the end or completion: *let's see the job through.* **3** (*intr, prep*) to perceive the true nature of: *I can see through your evasion.* ◆ *adj* **see-through. 4** partly or wholly transparent or translucent, esp. (of clothes) in a titillating way.

Seferis ★ (sə'fɛərɪs) *n* **George.** pen name of *Georgios Seferiades.* 1900–71, Greek poet and diplomat: Nobel prize for literature 1963.

Sefton ★ ('sɛftᵊn) *n* a unitary authority in NW England, in Merseyside. Pop.: 289 700 (1996 est.). Area: 150 sq. km (58 sq. miles).

segment *n* ('sɛgmənt). **1** *Maths.* **1a** a part of a line or curve between two points. **1b** a part of a plane or solid figure cut off by an intersecting line, plane, or planes. **2** one of several parts or sections into which an object is divided. **3** *Zool.* any of the parts into which the body or appendages of an annelid or arthropod are divided. **4** *Linguistics.* a speech sound considered in isolation. ◆ *vb* (sɛg'mɛnt). **5** to cut or divide (a whole object) into segments. ORIG C16: from L *segmentum,* from *secāre* to cut
▸ **seg'mental** *adj* ▸ **'segmentary** *adj*

segmentation (ˌsɛgmɛn'teɪʃən) *n* **1** the act or an instance of dividing into segments. **2** *Embryol.* another name for **cleavage** (sense 4).

Segovia[1] ★ (sɪ'gəʊvɪə; *Spanish* se'ɣoβja) *n* a town in central Spain: site of a Roman aqueduct, still in use, and the fortified palace of the kings of Castile (the Alcázar). Pop.: 58 060 (1991).

Segovia[2] ★ (sɪ'gəʊvɪə; *Spanish* se'ɣoβja) *n* **Andrés** (an'dres), Marquis of Salobreña. 1893–1987, Spanish classical guitarist.

Segrè ★ (sə'greɪ) *n* **Emilio** (ɪ'mi:lɪəʊ). 1905–89, US physicist, born in Italy, who was the first to produce an artificial element. He shared the Nobel prize for physics (1959) with Owen Chamberlain for their discovery (1955) of the antiproton.

segregate ('sɛgrɪˌgeɪt) *vb* **segregates, segregating, segregated. 1** to set or be set apart from others or from the main group. **2** (*tr*) to impose segregation on (a racial or minority group). **3** *Genetics.* to undergo or cause to undergo segregation. ORIG C16: from L *sēgregāre,* from *sē-* apart + *grex* a flock
▸ **'segreˌgative** *adj* ▸ **'segreˌgator** *n*

segregation (ˌsɛgrɪ'geɪʃən) *n* **1** the act of segregating or state of being segregated. **2** *Sociol.* the practice or policy of creating separate facilities within the same society for the use of a particular group. **3** *Genetics.* the separation at meiosis of the two members of any pair of alleles into separate gametes.
▸ **ˌsegre'gational** *adj* ▸ **ˌsegre'gationist** *n*

segue ('seɪgwɪ) *vb* **segues, segueing, segued.** (*intr*) **1** (often foll. by *into*) to proceed from one piece of music to another without a break. ◆ *n* **2** the practice or an instance of segueing. ORIG from It: follows, from *seguire* to follow, from L *sequī*

seguidilla (ˌsɛgɪ'di:ljə) *n* **1** a Spanish dance in a fast triple rhythm. **2** a piece of music composed for or in the rhythm of this dance. ORIG Sp.: a little dance, from *seguida* a dance, from *seguir* to follow, from L *sequī*

seiche (seɪʃ) *n* a tide-like movement of a body of water caused by barometric pressure, earth tremors, etc. ORIG C19: from Swiss F, from ?

Seidlitz powder *or* **powders** ('sɛdlɪts) *n* a laxative consisting of two powders, tartaric acid and a mixture of sodium bicarbonate and Rochelle salt. ORIG C19: after *Seidlitz,* a village in Bohemia with mineral springs having similar laxative effects

seif dune (seɪf) *n* (in deserts, esp. the Sahara) a long ridge of blown sand, often several miles long. ORIG *seif,* from Ar.: sword, from the shape of the dune

seigneur (sɛ'njɜ:; *French* sɛɲœr) *n* a feudal lord, esp. in France and New France. ORIG C16: from OF, from Vulgar L *senior,* from L: an elderly man; see SENIOR
▸ **sei'gneurial** *adj*

seigneury ('seɪnjərɪ) *n, pl* **seigneuries.** the estate of a seigneur.

seignior ('seɪnjə) *n* **1** a less common name for a **seigneur. 2** (in England) the lord of a seigniory. ORIG C14: from Anglo-F *segnour*
▸ **seigniorial** (seɪ'njɔ:rɪəl) *adj*

seigniory ('seɪnjərɪ) *or* **signory** ('si:njərɪ) *n, pl* **seigniories** *or* **seignories. 1** less common names for a **seigneury. 2** (in England) the fee or manor of a seignior; a feudal domain. **3** the authority of a seignior.

seine (seɪn) *n* **1** a large fishing net that hangs vertically in the water by means of floats at the top and weights at the bottom. ◆ *vb* **seines, seining, seined. 2** to catch (fish) using this net. ORIG OE *segne,* from L *sagēna,* from Gk *sagēnē*

Seine ★ (seɪn; *French* sɛn) *n* a river in N France, rising on the Plateau de Langres and flowing northwest through Paris to the English Channel: the second longest river in France, linked by canal with the Rivers Somme, Scheldt, Meuse, Rhine, Saône, and Loire. Length: 776 km (482 miles).

Seine-et-Marne ★ (*French* sɛnemarn) *n* a department of N central France, in Île-de-France region. Capital: Melun. Pop.: 1 171 313 (1994 est.). Area: 5931 sq. km (2313 sq. miles).

Seine-Maritime ★ (*French* sɛnmaritim) *n* a department of N France, in Haute-Normandie region. Capital: Rouen. Pop.: 1 239 973 (1994 est.). Area: 6342 sq. km (2473 sq. miles).

Seine-Saint-Denis ★ (*French* sɛnsɛ̃dni) *n* a department of N central France, in Île-de-France region. Capital: Bobigny. Pop.: 1 404 430 (1994 est.). Area: 236 sq. km (92 sq. miles).

seise *or US* **seize** (siːz) *vb* **seises, seising, seised** *or US* **seizes, seizing, seized.** to put into legal possession of (property, etc.).
▸ **'seiser** *n*

seisin *or US* **seizin** ('siːzɪn) *n Property law.* feudal possession of an estate in land. ORIG C13: from OF *seisine,* from *seisir* to SEIZE

seismic ('saɪzmɪk) *adj* relating to or caused by earthquakes or artificially produced earth tremors.

seismo- *or before a vowel* **seism-** *combining form.* earthquake: *seismology.* ORIG from Gk *seismos*

seismograph ('saɪzmə,grɑːf) *n* an instrument that registers and records earthquakes. A **seismogram** is the record from such an instrument.
▸ **seismographic** (,saɪzmə'græfɪk) *adj* ▸ **seismographer** (saɪz'mɒgrəfə) *n* ▸ **seis'mography** *n*

seismology (saɪz'mɒlədʒɪ) *n* the branch of geology concerned with the study of earthquakes.
▸ **seismologic** (,saɪzmə'lɒdʒɪk) *or* **,seismo'logical** *adj* ▸ **,seismo'logically** *adv* ▸ **seis'mologist** *n*

seize[1] (siːz) *vb* **seizes, seizing, seized.** (*mainly tr*) **1** (also *intr,* foll. by *on*) to take hold of quickly; grab. **2** (sometimes foll. by *on* or *upon*) to grasp mentally, esp. rapidly: *she immediately seized his idea.* **3** to take mental possession of: *alarm seized the crowd.* **4** to take possession of rapidly and forcibly: *the thief seized the woman's purse.* **5** to take legal possession of. **6** to take by force or capture: *the army seized the undefended town.* **7** to take immediate advantage of: *to seize an opportunity.* **8** *Naut.* to bind (two ropes together). **9** (*intr;* often foll. by *up*) (of mechanical parts) to become jammed, esp. because of excessive heat. ORIG C13 *saisen,* from OF *saisir,* from Med. L *sacīre* to position, of Gmc origin
▸ **'seizable** *adj*

seize[2] (siːz) *vb* **seizes, seizing, seized.** the US spelling of **seise.**

seizure ('siːʒə) *n* **1** the act or an instance of seizing or the state of being seized. **2** *Pathol.* a sudden manifestation or recurrence of a disease, such as an epileptic convulsion.

Sekondi ★ (,sekən'diː) *n* a port in SW Ghana, 8 km (5 miles) northeast of Takoradi: linked administratively with Takoradi in 1946. Pop. (with Takoradi): 103 600 (1988 est.).

selachian (sɪ'leɪkɪən) *adj* of or belonging to a large subclass of cartilaginous fishes including the sharks, rays, dogfish, and skates. ORIG C19: from NL *Selachii,* from Gk *selakhē* a shark

Selangor ★ (sə'læŋə) *n* a state of Peninsular Malaysia, on the Strait of Malacca: established as a British protectorate in 1874, became a Federated Malay State in 1896 and part of Malaysia in 1946; tin producer. Capital: Shah Alam. Pop.: 2 297 159 (1991). Area: 8203 sq. km (3167 sq. miles).

Selby ★ ('sɛlbɪ) *n* an inland port in N England, in N Yorkshire, on the River Ouse: centre for a major coalfield since 1983: agricultural products. Pop.: 15 292 (1991).

seldom ('sɛldəm) *adv* rarely. ORIG OE *seldon*

select (sɪ'lɛkt) *vb* **1** to choose (someone or something) in preference to another or others. ◆ *adj also* **selected. 2** chosen in preference to others. **3** of particular quality. **4** limited as to membership or entry: *a select gathering.* ◆ *n Austral. history.* **5** a piece of land acquired by a free-selector. **6** the process of free-selection. ORIG C16: from L *sēligere* to sort, from *sē-* apart + *legere* to choose
▸ **se'lectness** *n* ▸ **se'lector** *n*

select committee *n* (in Britain) a small committee of members of parliament, set up to investigate and report on a specified matter.

selection (sɪ'lɛkʃən) *n* **1** the act or an instance of selecting or the state of being selected. **2** a thing or number of things that have been selected. **3** a range from which something may be selected: *a good selection of clothes.* **4** *Biol.* the process by which certain organisms or characters are reproduced and perpetuated in the species in preference to others.

selective (sɪ'lɛktɪv) *adj* **1** of or characterized by selection. **2** tending to choose carefully or characterized by careful choice. **3** *Electronics.* occurring at or operating at a particular frequency or band of frequencies.
▸ **se'lectively** *adv*

selectivity (sɪ,lɛk'tɪvɪtɪ) *n* **1** the state or quality of being selective. **2** the degree to which a radio receiver, etc., can respond to the frequency of a desired signal.

Selene ★ (sɪ'liːnɪ) *n* the Greek goddess of the moon. Roman counterpart: **Luna.**

selenite ('sɛlɪ,naɪt) *n* a colourless glassy variety of gypsum.

selenium (sɪ'liːnɪəm) *n* a nonmetallic element that exists in several allotropic forms. The common form is a grey crystalline solid that is photoconductive, photovoltaic, and semiconducting: used in photocells, solar cells, and in xerography. Symbol: Se; atomic no.: 34; atomic wt.: 78.96. ORIG C19: from NL, from Gk *selēnē* moon; by analogy to TELLURIUM (from L *tellus* earth)

seleno- *or before a vowel* **selen-** *combining form.* denoting the moon: *selenography.* ORIG from Gk *selēnē* moon

selenography (,siːlɪ'nɒgrəfɪ) *n* the branch of astronomy concerned with the description and mapping of the surface features of the moon.
▸ **,sele'nographer** *n* ▸ **selenographic** (sɪ,liːnəʊ'græfɪk) *adj*

Seles ★ ('sɛlɛʃ, -lɛz) *n* **Monica.** born 1973, US tennis player, born in Yugoslavia.

Seleucia ★ (sɪ'luːʃɪə) *n* **1** an ancient city in Mesopotamia, on the River Tigris: founded by Seleucus Nicator in 312 B.C.; became the chief city of the Seleucid empire; sacked by the Romans around 162 A.D. **2** an ancient city in SE Asia Minor, on the River Calycadnus (modern Goksu Nehri): captured by the Turks in the 13th century; site of present-day Silifke (Turkey). Official name: **Seleucia Tracheotis** (,trækɪ'əʊtɪs) or **Trachea** (trə'kɪə). **3** an ancient port in Syria, on the River Orontes: the port of Antioch, of military importance during the wars between the Ptolemies and Seleucids; largely destroyed by earthquake in 526; site of present-day Samandağ (Turkey). Official name: **Seleucia Pieria** (paɪ'iːrɪə).

Seleucus I ★ (sɪ'luːkəs) *n* surname *Nicator.* ?358–280 B.C., Macedonian general under Alexander the Great, who founded the Seleucid kingdom.

self (sɛlf) *n, pl* **selves. 1** the distinct individuality or identity of a person or thing. **2** a person's typical bodily make-up or personal characteristics: *she's looking her old self again.* **3** one's own welfare or interests: *he only thinks of self.* **4** an individual's consciousness of his or her own identity or being. **5** a bird, animal, etc., that is a single colour throughout. ◆ *pron* **6** *Not standard.* myself, yourself, etc.: *seats for self and wife.* ◆ *adj* **7** of the same colour or material. **8** *Obs.* the same. ORIG OE *seolf*

self- *combining form.* **1** of oneself or itself: *self-defence.* **2** by, to, in, due to, for, or from the self: *self-employed; self-respect.* **3** automatic or automatically: *self-propelled.*

self-abnegation *n* the denial of one's own interests in favour of the interests of others.

self-absorption *n* **1** preoccupation with oneself to the exclusion of others. **2** *Physics.* the process in which some of the radiation emitted by a material is absorbed by the material itself.

self-abuse *n* **1** disparagement or misuse of one's own abilities, etc. **2** a censorious term for **masturbation.**

self-acting *adj* not requiring an external influence or control to function; automatic.

self-addressed *adj* **1** addressed for return to the sender. **2** directed to oneself: *a self-addressed remark.*

self-aggrandizement *n* the act of increasing one's own power, importance, etc.
▸ **,self-ag'gran,dizing** *adj*

self-appointed *adj* having assumed authority without the agreement of others: *a self-appointed critic.*

self-assertion *n* the act or an instance of putting forward one's own opinions, etc., esp. in an aggressive or conceited manner.
▸ **,self-as'serting** *adj* ▸ **,self-as'sertive** *adj*

★ people and places

self-assurance *n* confidence in the validity, value, etc., of one's own ideas, opinions, etc.
► ˌ**self-as'sured** *adj* ► ˌ**self-as'suredly** *adv*

self-centred *adj* totally preoccupied with one's own concerns.
► ˌ**self-'centredness** *n*

self-certification *n* (in Britain) a formal assertion by a worker to his or her employer that absence from work for up to seven days was due to sickness.

self-coloured *adj* **1** having only a single and uniform colour: *a self-coloured dress.* **2** (of cloth, etc.) having the natural or original colour.

self-command *n* another term for **self-control.**

self-confessed *adj* according to one's own testimony or admission: *a self-confessed liar.*

self-confidence *n* confidence in one's own powers, judgment, etc.
► ˌ**self-'confident** *adj* ► ˌ**self-'confidently** *adv*

self-conscious *adj* **1** unduly aware of oneself as the object of the attention of others. **2** conscious of one's existence.
► ˌ**self-'consciously** *adv* ► ˌ**self-'consciousness** *n*

self-contained *adj* **1** containing within itself all parts necessary for completeness. **2** (of a flat) having its own kitchen, bathroom, and lavatory not shared by others. **3** able or tending to keep one's feelings, thoughts, etc., to oneself.
► ˌ**self-con'tainedness** *n*

self-contradictory *adj Logic.* (of a proposition) both asserting and denying a given proposition.

self-control *n* the ability to exercise restraint or control over one's feelings, emotions, reactions, etc.
► ˌ**self-con'trolled** *adj*

self-deception *or* **self-deceit** *n* the act or an instance of deceiving oneself.
► ˌ**self-de'ceptive** *adj*

self-defence *n* **1** the act of defending oneself, one's actions, ideas, etc. **2** boxing as a means of defending the person (esp. in **noble art of self-defence**). **3** *Law.* the right to defend one's person, family, or property against attack or threat of attack.
► ˌ**self-de'fensive** *adj*

self-denial *n* the denial or sacrifice of one's own desires.
► ˌ**self-de'nying** *adj*

self-deprecating *or* **self-depreciating** *adj* having a tendency to disparage oneself.

self-determination *n* **1** the ability to make a decision for oneself without influence from outside. **2** the right of a nation or people to determine its own form of government.
► ˌ**self-de'termined** *adj* ► ˌ**self-de'termining** *adj*

self-discipline *n* the act of disciplining or power to discipline one's own feelings, desires, etc.
► ˌ**self-'disciplined** *adj*

self-drive *adj* denoting or relating to a hired car that is driven by the hirer.

self-educated *adj* **1** educated through one's own efforts without formal instruction. **2** educated at one's own expense.

self-effacement *n* the act of making oneself, one's actions, etc., inconspicuous, esp. because of timidity.
► ˌ**self-ef'facing** *adj*

self-employed *adj* earning one's living in one's own business or through freelance work, rather than as the employee of another.
► ˌ**self-em'ployment** *n*

self-esteem *n* **1** respect for or a favourable opinion of oneself. **2** an unduly high opinion of oneself.

self-evident *adj* containing its own evidence or proof without need of further demonstration.
► ˌ**self-'evidence** *n* ► ˌ**self-'evidently** *adv*

self-existent *adj Philosophy.* existing independently of any other being or cause.

self-explanatory *adj* understandable without explanation; self-evident.

self-expression *n* the expression of one's own personality, feelings, etc., as in painting or poetry.
► ˌ**self-ex'pressive** *adj*

self-government *n* **1** the government of a country, nation, etc., by its own people. **2** the state of being self-controlled.
► ˌ**self-'governed** *adj* ► ˌ**self-'governing** *adj*

selfheal ('sɛlfˌhiːl) *n* **1** a low-growing European herbaceous plant with tightly clustered violet-blue flowers and reputedly having healing powers. **2** any of several other plants thought to have healing powers.

self-help *n* **1** the act or state of providing the means to help oneself without relying on the assistance of others. **2a** the practice of solving one's problems by joining or forming a group designed to help those suffering from a particular problem. **2b** (*as modifier*): *a self-help group.*

self-image *n* one's own idea of oneself or sense of one's worth.

self-important *adj* having or showing an unduly high opinion of one's own abilities, importance, etc.
► ˌ**self-im'portantly** *adv* ► ˌ**self-im'portance** *n*

self-improvement *n* the improvement of one's status, position, education, etc., by one's own efforts.

self-induced *adj* **1** induced or brought on by oneself or itself. **2** *Electronics.* produced by self-induction.

self-induction *n* the production of an electromotive force in a circuit when the magnetic flux linked with the circuit changes as a result of a change in current in the same circuit.

self-indulgent *adj* tending to indulge one's own desires, etc.
► ˌ**self-in'dulgence** *n*

self-interest *n* **1** one's personal interest or advantage. **2** the act or an instance of pursuing one's own interest.
► ˌ**self-'interested** *adj*

selfish ('sɛlfɪʃ) *adj* **1** chiefly concerned with one's own interest, advantage, etc., esp. to the exclusion of the interests of others. **2** relating to or characterized by self-interest.
► **'selfishly** *adv* ► **'selfishness** *n*

self-justification *n* the act or an instance of justifying or providing excuses for one's own behaviour, etc.

selfless ('sɛlflɪs) *adj* having little concern for one's own interests.
► **'selflessly** *adv* ► **'selflessness** *n*

self-loading *adj* (of a firearm) utilizing some of the force of the explosion to eject the empty shell and replace it with a new one.
► ˌ**self-'loader** *n*

self-love *n* the instinct to seek one's own well-being or to further one's own interest.

self-made *adj* **1** having achieved wealth, status, etc., by one's own efforts. **2** made by oneself.

self-opinionated *adj* **1** having an unduly high regard for oneself or one's own opinions. **2** clinging stubbornly to one's own opinions.

self-pity *n* the act or state of pitying oneself, esp. in an exaggerated or self-indulgent manner.
► ˌ**self-'pitying** *adj* ► ˌ**self-'pityingly** *adv*

self-pollination *n* the transfer of pollen from the anthers to the stigma of the same flower.
► ˌ**self-'polliˌnated** *adj*

self-possessed *adj* having control of one's emotions, etc.
► ˌ**self-pos'session** *n*

self-preservation *n* the preservation of oneself from danger or injury.

self-pronouncing *adj* (in a phonetic transcription) of or denoting a word that, except for marks of stress, keeps the letters of its ordinary orthography to represent its pronunciation.

self-propelled *adj* (of a vehicle) provided with its own source of tractive power rather than requiring an external means of propulsion.
► ˌ**self-pro'pelling** *adj*

self-raising *adj* (of flour) having a raising agent, such as baking powder, already added.

self-realization *n* the realization or fulfilment of one's own potential or abilities.

self-regard *n* **1** concern for one's own interest. **2** proper esteem for oneself.

self-regulating organization *n* one of several British organizations set up in 1986 under the auspices of the Securities and Investment Board to regulate the activities of London investment markets. Abbrev.: **SRO.**

self-reliance *n* reliance on one's own abilities, decisions, etc.
▸ **ˌself-reˈliant** *adj*

self-reproach *n* the act of finding fault with or blaming oneself.
▸ **ˌself-reˈproachful** *adj*

self-respect *n* a proper sense of one's own dignity and integrity.
▸ **ˌself-reˈspecting** *adj*

self-restraint *n* restraint imposed by oneself on one's own feelings, desires, etc.

self-righteous *adj* having an exaggerated awareness of one's own virtuousness.
▸ **ˌself-ˈrighteously** *adv* ▸ **ˌself-ˈrighteousness** *n*

self-rule *n* another term for **self-government** (sense 1).

self-sacrifice *n* the sacrifice of one's own desires, etc., for the sake of duty or for the well-being of others.
▸ **ˌself-ˈsacriˌficing** *adj*

selfsame (ˈsɛlfˌseɪm) *adj* (*prenominal*) the very same.

self-satisfied *adj* having or showing a complacent satisfaction with oneself, one's own actions, behaviour, etc.
▸ **ˌself-ˌsatisˈfaction** *n*

self-sealing *adj* (esp. of an envelope) designed to become sealed with the application of pressure only.

self-seeking *n* **1** the act or an instance of seeking one's own profit or interest. ◆ *adj* **2** having or showing an exclusive preoccupation with one's own profit or interest: *a self-seeking attitude.*
▸ **ˌself-ˈseeker** *n*

self-service *adj* **1** of or denoting a shop, restaurant, petrol station, etc., where the customer serves himself. ◆ *n* **2** the practice of serving oneself, as in a shop, etc.

self-serving *adj* habitually seeking one's own advantage, esp. at the expense of others.

self-sown *adj* (of plants) growing from seed dispersed by any means other than by the agency of man or animals. Also: **self-seeded.**

self-starter *n* **1** an electric motor used to start an internal-combustion engine. **2** the switch that operates this motor. **3** a person who is strongly motivated and shows initiative, esp. at work.

self-styled *adj* (*prenominal*) claiming to be of a specified nature, quality, profession, etc.: *a self-styled expert.*

self-sufficient *or* **self-sufficing** *adj* **1** able to provide for or support oneself without the help of others. **2** *Rare.* having undue confidence in oneself.
▸ **ˌself-sufˈficiency** *n* ▸ **ˌself-sufˈficiently** *adv*

self-supporting *adj* **1** able to support or maintain oneself without the help of others. **2** able to stand up or hold firm without support, props, attachments, etc.

self-tender *n* an offer by a company to buy back some or all of its shares from its shareholders, esp. as a protection against an unwelcome takeover bid.

self-will *n* stubborn adherence to one's own will, desires, etc., esp. at the expense of others.
▸ **ˌself-ˈwilled** *adj*

self-winding *adj* (of a wrist watch) having a mechanism in which a rotating or oscillating weight rewinds the mainspring.

Seljuk (sɛlˈdʒuːk) *n* **1** a member of any of the pre-Ottoman Turkish dynasties ruling over large parts of Asia in the 11th, 12th, and 13th centuries A.D. ◆ *adj* **2** of or relating to these dynasties. ORIG C19: from Turkish

Selkirk ★ (ˈsɛlˌkɜːk) *n* **Alexander**, original name *Alexander Selcraig.* 1676–1721, Scottish sailor, who was marooned on one of the islets of Juan Fernández and is regarded as the prototype of Defoe's Robinson Crusoe.

Selkirk Mountains ★ *pl n* a mountain range in SW Canada, in SE British Columbia. Highest peak: Mount Sir Sandford, 3533 m (11 590 ft).

Selkirkshire ★ (ˈsɛlkɜːkˌʃɪə, -ʃə) *n* a historic county of SE Scotland, now part of Scottish Borders.

sell (sɛl) *vb* **sells, selling, sold. 1** to dispose of or transfer or be disposed of or transferred to a purchaser in exchange for money or other consideration. **2** to deal in (objects, property, etc.): *he sells used cars.* **3** (*tr*) to give up or surrender for a price or reward: *to sell one's honour.* **4** to promote or facilitate the sale of (objects, property, etc.): *publicity sells many products.* **5** to gain acceptance of: *to sell an idea.* **6** (*intr*) to be in demand on the market: *these dresses sell well.* **7** (*tr*) *Inf.* to deceive. **8 sell down the river.** *Inf.* to betray. **9 sell oneself. 9a** to convince someone else of one's potential or worth. **9b** to give up one's moral standards, etc. **10 sell short. 10a** *Inf.* to belittle. **10b** *Finance.* to sell securities or goods without owning them in anticipation of buying them before delivery at a lower price. ◆ *n* **11** the act or an instance of selling: *a soft sell.* **12** *Inf.* a hoax or deception. ◆ See also **sell off, sell out,** etc. ORIG OE *sellan* to lend, deliver
▸ **ˈsellable** *adj* ▸ **ˈseller** *n*

Sellafield ★ (ˈsɛləˌfiːld) *n* the site of an atomic power station and nuclear reprocessing plant in NW England, in W Cumbria. Former name: **Windscale.**

sell-by date *n* **1** a date printed on the packaging of perishable goods, indicating the date after which the goods should not be offered for sale. **2 past one's sell-by date.** *Inf.* beyond one's prime.

Sellers ★ (ˈsɛləz) *n* **Peter.** 1925–80, British actor, noted for his part in *The Goon Show* (BBC Radio, 1952–60). His films include *I'm All Right, Jack* (1959), *The Pink Panther* (1963), and *Being There* (1979).

selling race *or* **plate** *n* a horse race in which the winner must be offered for sale at auction.

sell off *vb* (*tr, adv*) to sell (remaining or unprofitable items), esp. at low prices.

Sellotape (ˈsɛləˌteɪp) *n* **1** *Trademark.* a type of transparent adhesive tape. ◆ *vb* **Sellotapes, Sellotaping, Sellotaped.** (*tr*) **2** to seal or stick using adhesive tape.

sell out *vb* (*adv*) **1** Also (*chiefly Brit.*): **sell up.** to dispose of (something) completely by selling. **2** (*tr*) *Inf.* to betray. **3** (*intr*) *Inf.* to abandon one's principles, standards, etc. ◆ *n* **sellout. 4** *Inf.* a performance for which all tickets are sold. **5** a commercial success. **6** *Inf.* a betrayal.

sell-through *adj* **1** (of prerecorded video cassettes) sold without first being available for hire only. ◆ *n* **2** the sale of prerecorded video cassettes in this way.

sell up *vb* (*adv*) *Chiefly Brit.* **1** (*tr*) to sell all (the possessions) of (a bankrupt debtor) in order to discharge his debts. **2** (*intr*) to sell a business.

selsyn (ˈsɛlsɪn) *n* another name for **synchro.** ORIG from SEL(F-) + SYN(CHRONOUS)

Seltzer (ˈsɛltsə) *n* **1** a natural effervescent water with a high content of minerals. **2** a similar synthetic water, used as a beverage. ORIG C18: changed from G *Selterser Wasser* water from (*Nieder*) *Selters,* district where mineral springs are located, near Wiesbaden, Germany

selva (ˈsɛlvə) *n* **1** dense equatorial forest, esp. in the Amazon basin, characterized by tall broad-leaved evergreen trees. **2** a tract of such forest. ORIG C19: from Sp. & Port., from L *silva* forest

selvage *or* **selvedge** (ˈsɛlvɪdʒ) *n* **1** the finished nonfraying edge of a length of woven fabric. **2** a similar strip of material allowed in fabricating a metal or plastic article. ORIG C15: from SELF + EDGE
▸ **ˈselvaged** *adj*

selves (sɛlvz) *n* **a** the plural of **self. b** (*in combination*): *ourselves, yourselves, themselves.*

Sem. *abbrev. for:* **1** Seminary. **2** Semitic.

semantic (sɪˈmæntɪk) *adj* **1** of or relating to the meanings of different words or symbols. **2** of or relating to se-

★ people and places

mantics. ORIG C19: from Gk *sēmantikos* having significance, from *sēmainein* to signify, from *sēma* a sign
▸ **se'mantically** *adv*

semantics (sɪ'mæntɪks) *n* (*functioning as sing*) **1** the branch of linguistics that deals with the study of meaning. **2** the study of the relationships between signs and symbols and what they represent. **3** *Logic.* the principles that determine the truth-values of the formulas in a logical system.
▸ **se'manticist** *n*

semaphore ('sɛmə,fɔː) *n* **1** an apparatus for conveying information by means of visual signals, as with flags, etc. **2** a system of signalling by holding a flag in each hand and moving the arms to designated positions for each letter of the alphabet. ◆ *vb* **semaphores, semaphoring, semaphored. 3** to signal (information) by means of semaphore. ORIG C19: via F, from Gk *sēma* a signal + -PHORE
▸ **semaphoric** (,sɛmə'fɒrɪk) *adj*

Semarang *or* **Samarang** ★ (sə'mɑːrɑːŋ) *n* a port in S Indonesia, in N Java on the Java Sea. Pop.: 1 366 500 (1995 est.).

semasiology (sɪ,meɪsɪ'ɒlədʒɪ) *n* another name for **semantics.** ORIG C19: from Gk *sēmasia* meaning, from *sēmainein* to signify + -LOGY

sematic (sɪ'mætɪk) *adj* (of the conspicuous coloration of certain animals) acting as a warning. ORIG C19: from Gk *sēma* a sign

semblance ('sɛmbləns) *n* **1** outward appearance, esp. without any inner substance. **2** a resemblance. ORIG C13: from OF, from *sembler* to seem, from L *simulāre* to imitate, from *similis* like

Semele ★ ('sɛmɪlɪ) *n Greek myth.* mother of Dionysus by Zeus.

sememe ('siːmiːm) *n Linguistics.* the meaning of a morpheme. ORIG C20 (coined in 1933 by L. Bloomfield, US linguist): from Gk *sēma* a sign + -EME

semen ('siːmɛn) *n* **1** the thick whitish fluid containing spermatozoa that is ejaculated from the male genital tract. **2** another name for **sperm**[1]. ORIG C14: from L: seed

Semeru *or* **Semeroe** ★ (sə'mɛruː) *n* a volcano in Indonesia: the highest peak in Java. Height: 3676 m (12 060 ft).

semester (sɪ'mɛstə) *n* **1** *Chiefly US & Canad.* either of two divisions of the academic year. **2** (in German universities) a session of six months. ORIG C19: via G from L *sēmestris* half-yearly, from *sex* six + *mensis* a month

semi ('sɛmɪ) *n, pl* **semis.** *Inf.* **1** *Brit.* short for **semidetached (house). 2** short for **semifinal.**

semi- *prefix* **1** half: *semicircle.* **2** partially, partly, or almost: *semiprofessional.* **3** occurring twice in a specified period of time: *semiweekly.* ORIG from L

semiannual (,sɛmɪ'ænjʊəl) *adj* **1** occurring every half-year. **2** lasting for half a year.
▸ **,semi'annually** *adv*

semiarid (,sɛmɪ'ærɪd) *adj* characterized by scanty rainfall and scrubby vegetation, often occurring in continental interiors.

semiautomatic (,sɛmɪ,ɔːtə'mætɪk) *adj* **1** partly automatic. **2** (of a firearm) self-loading but firing only one shot at each pull of the trigger. ◆ *n* **3** a semiautomatic firearm.
▸ **,semi,auto'matically** *adv*

semibreve ('sɛmɪ,briːv) *n Music.* a note, now the longest in common use, having a time value that may be divided by any power of 2 to give all other notes. Usual US and Canad. name: **whole note.**

semicircle ('sɛmɪ,sɜːkᵊl) *n* **1a** one half of a circle. **1b** half the circumference of a circle. **2** anything having the shape or form of half a circle.
▸ **semicircular** (,sɛmɪ'sɜːkjʊlə) *adj*

semicircular canal *n Anat.* any of the three looped fluid-filled membranous tubes, at right angles to one another, that comprise the labyrinth of the ear.

semicolon (,sɛmɪ'kəʊlən) *n* the punctuation mark ; used to indicate a pause intermediate in value or length between that of a comma and that of a full stop.

semiconductor (,sɛmɪkən'dʌktə) *n* **1** a substance, such as germanium or silicon, that has an electrical conductivity that increases with temperature. **2a** a device, such as a transistor or integrated circuit, that depends on the properties of such a substance. **2b** (*as modifier*): *a semiconductor diode.*

semiconscious (,sɛmɪ'kɒnʃəs) *adj* not fully conscious.
▸ **,semi'consciously** *adv* ▸ **,semi'consciousness** *n*

semidetached (,sɛmɪdɪ'tætʃt) *adj* **a** (of a building) joined to another building on one side by a common wall. **b** (*as n*): *they live in a semidetached.*

semifinal (,sɛmɪ'faɪnᵊl) *n* **a** the round before the final in a competition. **b** (*as modifier*): *the semifinal draw.*
▸ **,semi'finalist** *n*

semifluid (,sɛmɪ'fluːɪd) *adj* **1** having properties between those of a liquid and those of a solid. ◆ *n* **2** a substance that has such properties because of high viscosity: *tar is a semifluid.* ◆ Also: **semiliquid.**

semiliterate (,sɛmɪ'lɪtərɪt) *adj* **1** hardly able to read or write. **2** able to read but not to write.

semilunar (,sɛmɪ'luːnə) *adj* shaped like a crescent or half-moon.

semilunar valve *n Anat.* either of two crescent-shaped valves, one in the aorta and one in the pulmonary artery, that prevent regurgitation of blood into the heart.

seminal ('sɛmɪnəl) *adj* **1** potentially capable of development. **2** highly original and important. **3** rudimentary or unformed. **4** of or relating to semen: *seminal fluid.* **5** *Biol.* of or relating to seed. ORIG C14: from LL *sēminālis* belonging to seed, from L *sēmen* seed
▸ **'seminally** *adv*

seminar ('sɛmɪ,nɑː) *n* **1** a small group of students meeting regularly under the guidance of a tutor, professor, etc. **2** one such meeting or the place in which it is held. **3** a higher course for postgraduates. **4** any group or meeting for holding discussions or exchanging information. ORIG C19: via G from L *sēminārium* SEMINARY

seminary ('sɛmɪnərɪ) *n, pl* **seminaries. 1** an academy for the training of priests, etc. **2** *Arch.* a private secondary school, esp. for girls. ORIG C15: from L *sēminārium* a nursery garden, from *sēmen* seed
▸ **,semi'narial** *adj* ▸ **seminarian** (,sɛmɪ'nɛərɪən) *n*

seminiferous (,sɛmɪ'nɪfərəs) *adj* **1** containing, conveying, or producing semen. **2** (of plants) bearing or producing seeds.

seminoma (,sɛmɪ'nəʊmə) *n, pl* **seminomas** *or* **seminomata** (-mətə). a malignant tumour of the testicle. ORIG C20: from F *seminome,* from L *sēmen* seed

semiotics (,sɛmɪ'ɒtɪks) *n* (*functioning as sing*) **1** the study of signs and symbols, esp. the relations between written or spoken signs and their referents in the physical world or the world of ideas. **2** the scientific study of the symptoms of disease. ◆ Also called: **semiology.** ORIG from Gk *sēmeiōtikos,* from *sēmeion* a sign
▸ **,semi'otic** *adj*

Semipalatinsk ★ (*Russian* sɪmipa'latinsk) *n* a city in NE Kazakhstan, on the Irtysh River. Pop.: 320 200 (1995 est.).

semipermeable (,sɛmɪ'pɜːmɪəbᵊl) *adj* (esp. of a cell membrane) selectively permeable.
▸ **,semi,permea'bility** *n*

semiprecious (,sɛmɪ'prɛʃəs) *adj* (of certain stones) having less value than a precious stone.

semiprofessional (,sɛmɪprə'fɛʃənᵊl) *adj* **1** (of a person) engaged in an activity or sport part-time but for pay. **2** (of an activity or sport) engaged in by semiprofessional people. **3** of or relating to a person whose activities are professional in some respects. ◆ *n* **4** a semiprofessional person.
▸ **,semipro'fessionally** *adv*

semiquaver ('sɛmɪ,kweɪvə) *n Music.* a note having the time value of one-sixteenth of a semibreve. Usual US and Canad. name: **sixteenth note.**

Semiramis ★ (sɛ'mɪrəmɪs) *n* the legendary founder of Babylon and wife of Ninus, king of Assyria, which she ruled with great skill after his death.

semirigid (,sɛmɪ'rɪdʒɪd) *adj* **1** partly but not wholly rigid. **2** (of an airship) maintaining shape by means of a main supporting keel and internal gas pressure.

semiskilled (ˌsɛmɪˈskɪld) *adj* partly skilled or trained but not sufficiently so to perform specialized work.

semisolid (ˌsɛmɪˈsɒlɪd) *adj* having a viscosity and rigidity intermediate between that of a solid and a liquid.

semisolus (ˌsɛmɪˈsəʊləs) *n* an advertisement that appears on the same page as another advertisement but not adjacent to it.

semisweet (ˈsɛmɪˌswiːt) *adj* (of biscuits, etc.) slightly sweetened.

Semite (ˈsiːmaɪt) *n* a member of the group of peoples who speak a Semitic language, including the Jews and Arabs as well as the ancient Babylonians, Assyrians, and Phoenicians. ORIG C19: from NL *sēmīta* descendant of Shem, via Gk *Sēm*, from Heb. SHEM

Semitic (sɪˈmɪtɪk) *n* **1** a branch or subfamily of the Afro-Asiatic family of languages that includes Arabic, Hebrew, Aramaic, and such ancient languages as Phoenician. ◆ *adj* **2** denoting or belonging to this group of languages. **3** denoting or characteristic of any of the peoples speaking a Semitic language, esp. the Jews or the Arabs. **4** another word for **Jewish**.

semitone (ˈsɛmɪˌtəʊn) *n* an interval denoting the pitch difference between certain adjacent degrees of the diatonic scale (**diatonic semitone**) or between one note and its sharpened or flattened equivalent (**chromatic semitone**); minor second. Also called (US and Canad.): **half step.** Cf. **whole tone.**
▸ **semitonic** (ˌsɛmɪˈtɒnɪk) *adj*

semitrailer (ˌsɛmɪˈtreɪlə) *n* a type of trailer or articulated lorry that has wheels only at the rear, the front end being supported by the towing vehicle.

semitropical (ˌsɛmɪˈtrɒpɪkᵊl) *adj* partly tropical.
▸ **ˌsemiˈtropics** *pl n*

semivowel (ˈsɛmɪˌvaʊəl) *n Phonetics.* a vowel-like sound that acts like a consonant. In English and many other languages the chief semivowels are (w) in *well* and (j), represented as *y*, in *yell*. Also called: **glide.**

semiyearly (ˌsɛmɪˈjɪəlɪ) *adj* another word for **semiannual.**

Semmelweis ★ (ˈzɛməlˌvaɪs) *n* **Ignaz Philipp** (ˈɪgnaːts ˈfiːlɪp). 1818–65, Hungarian obstetrician, who discovered the cause of puerperal infection and pioneered the use of antiseptics.

semolina (ˌsɛməˈliːnə) *n* the large hard grains of wheat left after flour has been bolted, used for puddings, soups, etc. ORIG C18: from It. *semolino*, dim. of *semola* bran, from L *simila* very fine wheat flour

Sempach ★ (*German* ˈzɛmpax) *n* a village in central Switzerland, in Lucerne canton on **Lake Sempach:** scene of the victory (1386) of the Swiss over the Hapsburgs.

sempervivum (ˌsɛmpəˈvaɪvəm) *n* any of a genus of hardy perennials including the houseleek. ORIG C16 (used of the houseleek, adopted C18 by Linnaeus (1707–78), Swedish botanist, for the genus): L, from *sempervivus* ever-living

sempiternal (ˌsɛmpɪˈtɜːnᵊl) *adj Literary.* everlasting; eternal. ORIG C15: from OF, from LL *sempiternālis*, from L, from *semper* always + *aeternus* ETERNAL
▸ **ˌsempiˈternally** *adv*

semplice (ˈsɛmplɪtʃɪ) *adj, adv Music.* to be performed in a simple manner. ORIG It.: simple, from L *simplex*

sempre (ˈsɛmprɪ) *adv Music.* (preceding a tempo or dynamic marking) always; consistently. It is used to indicate that a specified volume, tempo, etc., is to be sustained throughout a piece or passage. ORIG It.: always, from L *semper*

sempstress (ˈsɛmpstrɪs) *n* a rare word for **seamstress.**

Semtex (ˈsɛmtɛks) *n* a pliable plastic explosive. ORIG orig. a trade name

SEN (in Britain) *abbrev. for:* **1** (formerly) State Enrolled Nurse. **2** special educational needs: needs arising from any of a wide range of problems that affect a pupil's normal educational development and for which special provisions are made.

Sen. *or* **sen.** *abbrev. for:* **1** senate. **2** senator. **3** senior.

senate (ˈsɛnɪt) *n* **1** any legislative body considered to resemble a Senate. **2** the main governing body at some universities. ORIG C13: from L *senātus* council of the elders, from *senex* an old man

Senate (ˈsɛnɪt) *n* (*sometimes not cap.*) **1** the upper chamber of the legislatures of the US, Canada, Australia, and many other countries. **2** the legislative council of ancient Rome.

senator (ˈsɛnətə) *n* **1** (*often cap.*) a member of a Senate or senate. **2** any legislator.
▸ **senatorial** (ˌsɛnəˈtɔːrɪəl) *adj*

send (sɛnd) *vb* **sends, sending, sent. 1** (*tr*) to cause or order (a person or thing) to be taken, directed, or transmitted to another place: *to send a letter.* **2** (when *intr*, foll. by *for;* when *tr, takes an infinitive*) to dispatch a request or command (for something or to do something): *he sent for a bottle of wine.* **3** (*tr*) to direct or cause to go to a place or point: *his blow sent the champion to the floor.* **4** (*tr*) to bring to a state or condition: *this noise will send me mad.* **5** (*tr;* often foll. by *forth, out,* etc.) to cause to issue: *his cooking sent forth a lovely smell.* **6** (*tr*) to cause to happen or come: *misery sent by fate.* **7** to transmit (a message) by radio. **8** (*tr*) *Sl.* to move to excitement or rapture: *this music really sends me.* ◆ *n* **9** another word for **swash** (sense 4). ORIG OE *sendan*
▸ **ˈsendable** *adj* ▸ **ˈsender** *n*

Sendai ★ (sɛnˈdaɪ) *n* a city in central Japan, on NE Honshu: university (1907). Pop.: 971 263 (1995).

send down *vb* (*tr, adv*) **1** *Brit.* to expel from a university. **2** *Inf.* to send to prison.

sendoff (ˈsɛndˌɒf) *n Inf.* **1** a demonstration of good wishes to a person about to set off on a journey, etc. ◆ *vb* **send off.** (*tr, adv*) **2** to cause to depart. **3** *Soccer, rugby, etc.* (of the referee) to dismiss (a player) from the field of play for some offence. **4** *Inf.* to give a sendoff to.

send up *vb* (*tr, adv*) **1** *Sl.* to send to prison. **2** *Brit. inf.* to make fun of, esp. by doing an imitation or parody of. ◆ *n* **send-up. 3** *Brit. inf.* a parody or imitation.

Seneca ★ (ˈsɛnɪkə) *n* **1 Lucius Annaeus** (ˈluːsɪəs əˈniːəs), called *the Younger*. ?4 B.C.–65 A.D., Roman philosopher, statesman, and dramatist; tutor and adviser to Nero, in whose murder he was implicated; committed suicide. **2** his father, **Marcus** (ˈmɑːkəs) *or* **Lucius Annaeus,** called *the Elder* or *the Rhetorician*. ?55 B.C.–?39 A.D., Roman writer.

Senegal ★ (ˌsɛnɪˈgɔːl) *n* a republic in West Africa, on the Atlantic: made part of French West Africa in 1895; became fully independent in 1960; mostly low-lying, with semidesert in the north and tropical forest in the southwest. Official language: French. Religion: Muslim majority. Currency: franc. Capital: Dakar. Pop.: 10 052 000 (1999 est.). Area: 197 160 sq. km (76 124 sq. miles).
▸ **Senegalese** (ˌsɛnɪgəˈliːz) *adj, n*

Senegambia ★ (ˌsɛnəˈgæmbɪə) *n* a region of W Africa, between the Senegal and Gambia Rivers: now mostly in Senegal.

Senegambia Confederation *n* an economic and political union (1982–89) between Senegal and The Gambia.

senescent (sɪˈnɛsᵊnt) *adj* **1** growing old. **2** characteristic of old age. ORIG C17: from L *senēscere* to grow old, from *senex* old
▸ **seˈnescence** *n*

seneschal (ˈsɛnɪʃəl) *n* **1** a steward of the household of a medieval prince or nobleman. **2** *Brit.* a cathedral official. ORIG C14: from OF, from Med. L *siniscalcus,* of Gmc origin

Senghor ★ (*French* sɑ̃gɔr) *n* **Léopold Sédar** (leɔpɔl sedar). born 1906, Senegalese statesman and writer; president of Senegal (1960–80).

senile (ˈsiːnaɪl) *adj* **1** of or characteristic of old age. **2** mentally or physically weak or infirm on account of old age. ORIG C17: from L *senīlis,* from *senex* an old man
▸ **senility** (sɪˈnɪlɪtɪ) *n*

senile dementia *n* dementia starting in old age with no clear physical cause.

senior (ˈsiːnjə) *adj* **1** higher in rank or length of service. **2** older in years: *senior citizens.* **3** of or relating to maturity or old age: *senior privileges.* **4** *Education.* **4a** of or designating more advanced or older pupils. **4b** of or relating to a secondary school. **4c** *US.* denoting a student in the last year of school or university. ◆ *n* **5** a senior person. **6** a senior pupil, student, etc. ORIG C14: from L: older, from *senex* old

Senior ('siːnjə) *adj Chiefly US.* being the older: used to distinguish the father from the son: *Charles Parker, Senior.* Abbrevs.: **Sr., Sen.**

senior aircraftman *n* a rank in the Royal Air Force comparable to that of a private in the army, though not the lowest rank in the Royal Air Force.

senior citizen *n* an old age pensioner.

senior common room *n* (in British universities, colleges, etc.) a common room for the use of academic staff.

seniority (ˌsiːnɪ'ɒrɪtɪ) *n, pl* **seniorities. 1** the state of being senior. **2** precedence in rank, etc., due to senior status.

senior service *n Brit.* the Royal Navy.

Senlac ★ ('sɛnlæk) *n* a hill in Sussex: site of the Battle of Hastings in 1066.

senna ('sɛnə) *n* **1** any of a genus of tropical plants having typically yellow flowers and long pods. **2 senna leaf.** the dried leaflets of any of these plants, used as a cathartic and laxative. **3 senna pods.** the dried fruits of any of these plants, used as a cathartic and laxative. ORIG C16: via NL from Ar. *sanā*

Senna ★ ('sɛnə) *n* **Ayrton** ('ɛətən). 1960–94, Brazilian racing driver: world champion (1988, 1990, 1991).

Sennacherib ★ (sɛ'nækərɪb) *n* died 681 B.C., king of Assyria (705–681); son of Sargon II. He defeated Babylon and rebuilt Nineveh.

Sennar ★ ('sɛnɑː, sɛ'nɑː) *n* **1** a region of the E Sudan, between the White Nile and the Blue Nile: a kingdom from the 16th to 19th centuries. **2** a town in this region, on the Blue Nile: the nearby **Sennar Dam** (1925) supplies irrigation water to Gezira. Pop.: 8000 (latest est.).

sennight *or* **se'nnight** ('sɛnaɪt) *n* an archaic word for **week.** ORIG OE *seofan nihte;* see SEVEN, NIGHT

señor (sɛ'njɔː; *Spanish* se'ɲor) *n, pl* **señors** *or* **señores** (*Spanish* -'ɲores). a Spaniard: a title of address equivalent to *Mr* when placed before a name or *sir* when used alone. ORIG Sp., from L *senior* an older man, SENIOR

señora (sɛ'njɔːrə; *Spanish* se'ɲora) *n, pl* **señoras** (-rəz; *Spanish* -ras). a married Spanish woman: a title of address equivalent to *Mrs* when placed before a name or *madam* when used alone.

señorita (ˌsɛnjɔː'riːtə; *Spanish* ˌseɲo'rita) *n, pl* **señoritas** (-təz; *Spanish* -tas). an unmarried Spanish woman: title of address equivalent to *Miss* when placed before a name or *madam* or *miss* when used alone.

sensation (sɛn'seɪʃən) *n* **1** the power of perceiving through the senses. **2** a physical experience resulting from the stimulation of one of the sense organs. **3** a general feeling or awareness: *a sensation of fear.* **4** a state of widespread public excitement. *his announcement caused a sensation.* **5** anything that causes such a state: *your speech was a sensation.* ORIG C17: from Med. L, from LL *sensātus* endowed with SENSE

sensational (sɛn'seɪʃənᵊl) *adj* **1** causing or intended to cause intense feelings, esp. of curiosity, horror, etc.: *sensational disclosures in the press.* **2** *Inf.* extremely good: *a sensational skater.* **3** of or relating to the faculty of sensation.
▸ **sen'sationally** *adv*

sensationalism (sɛn'seɪʃənᵊˌlɪzəm) *n* **1** the use of sensational language, etc., to arouse an intense emotional response. **2** such sensational matter itself. **3** *Philosophy.* the doctrine that knowledge cannot go beyond the analysis of experience.
▸ **sen'sationalist** *n* ▸ **senˌsational'istic** *adj*

sensationalize *or* **sensationalise** (sɛn'seɪʃənᵊˌlaɪz) *vb* **sensationalizes, sensationalizing, sensationalized** *or* **sensationalises, sensationalising, sensationalised.** (*tr*) to cause (events, esp. in newspaper reports) to seem more vivid, shocking, etc., than they really are.

sense (sɛns) *n* **1** any of the faculties by which the mind receives information about the external world or the state of the body. The five traditional senses are sight, hearing, touch, taste, and smell. **2** the ability to perceive. **3** a feeling perceived through one of the senses: *a sense of warmth.* **4** a mental perception or awareness: *a sense of happiness.* **5** moral discernment: *a sense of right and wrong.* **6** (*sometimes pl*) sound practical judgment or intelligence. **7** reason or purpose: *what is the sense of going out?* **8** meaning: *what is the sense of this proverb?* **9** specific meaning; definition: *in what sense are you using the word?* **10** an opinion or consensus. **11** *Maths.* one of two opposite directions in which a vector can operate. **12 make sense.** to be understandable. **13 take leave of one's senses.** *Inf.* to go mad. ◆ *vb* **senses, sensing, sensed.** (*tr*) **14** to perceive through one or more of the senses. **15** to apprehend or detect without or in advance of the evidence of the senses. **16** to understand. **17** *Computing.* **17a** to test or locate the position of (a part of computer hardware). **17b** to read (data). ORIG C14: from L *sēnsus,* from *sentīre* to feel

sense datum *n* a unit of sensation, such as a sharp pain, detached both from any information it may convey and from its putative source in the external world.

senseless ('sɛnslɪs) *adj* **1** foolish: *a senseless plan.* **2** lacking in feeling; unconscious. **3** lacking in perception.
▸ **'senselessly** *adv* ▸ **'senselessness** *n*

sense organ *n* a structure in animals that is specialized for receiving external or internal stimuli and transmitting them in the form of nervous impulses to the brain.

sensibility (ˌsɛnsɪ'bɪlɪtɪ) *n, pl* **sensibilities. 1** the ability to perceive or feel. **2** (*often pl*) the capacity for responding to emotion, etc. **3** (*often pl*) the capacity for responding to aesthetic stimuli. **4** discernment; awareness. **5** (*usually pl*) emotional or moral feelings: *cruelty offends most people's sensibilities.*

sensible ('sɛnsɪbᵊl) *adj* **1** having or showing good sense or judgment. **2** (of clothing) serviceable; practical. **3** having the capacity for sensation; sensitive. **4** capable of being apprehended by the senses. **5** perceptible to the mind. **6** (sometimes foll. by *of*) having perception; aware: *sensible of your kindness.* **7** readily perceived: *a sensible difference.* ORIG C14: from OF, from LL *sēnsibilis,* from L *sentīre* to sense
▸ **'sensibleness** *n* ▸ **'sensibly** *adv*

sensitive ('sɛnsɪtɪv) *adj* **1** having the power of sensation. **2** responsive to or aware of feelings, moods, etc. **3** easily irritated; delicate. **4** affected by external conditions or stimuli. **5** easily offended. **6** of or relating to the senses or the power of sensation. **7** capable of registering small differences or changes in amounts, etc.: *a sensitive instrument.* **8** *Photog.* responding readily to light: *a sensitive emulsion.* **9** *Chiefly US.* connected with matters affecting national security. **10** (of a stock market or prices) quickly responsive to external influences. ORIG C14: from Med. L *sēnsitīvus,* from L *sentīre* to feel
▸ **'sensitively** *adv* ▸ **ˌsensi'tivity** *n*

sensitive plant *n* a tropical American mimosa plant, the leaflets and stems of which fold if touched.

sensitize *or* **sensitise** ('sɛnsɪˌtaɪz) *vb* **sensitizes, sensitizing, sensitized** *or* **sensitises, sensitising, sensitised. 1** to make or become sensitive. **2** (*tr*) to render (an individual) sensitive to a drug, etc. **3** (*tr*) *Photog.* to make (a material) sensitive to light by coating it with a photographic emulsion often containing special chemicals, such as dyes.
▸ **ˌsensiti'zation** *or* **ˌsensiti'sation** *n* ▸ **'sensiˌtizer** *or* **'sensiˌtiser** *n*

sensitometer (ˌsɛnsɪ'tɒmɪtə) *n* an instrument for measuring the sensitivity to light of a photographic material over a range of exposures.

sensor ('sɛnsə) *n* anything, such as a photoelectric cell, that receives a signal or stimulus and responds to it. ORIG C19: from L *sēnsus* perceived, from *sentīre* to observe

sensorimotor (ˌsɛnsərɪ'məʊtə) *or* **sensomotor** (ˌsɛnsə'məʊtə) *adj* of or relating to both the sensory and motor functions of an organism or to the nerves controlling them.

sensorium (sɛn'sɔːrɪəm) *n, pl* **sensoriums** *or* **sensoria** (-rɪə). **1** the area of the brain considered responsible for receiving and integrating sensations from the outside world. **2** *Physiol.* the entire sensory and intellectual apparatus of the body. ORIG C17: from LL, from L *sēnsus* felt, from *sentīre* to perceive

sensory ('sɛnsərɪ) *adj* of or relating to the senses or the power of sensation. ORIG C18: from L *sensōrius,* from *sentīre* to feel

sensual ('sɛnsjʊəl) *adj* **1** of or relating to any of the senses or sense organs; bodily. **2** strongly or unduly inclined to gratification of the senses. **3** tending to arouse the bodily appetites, esp. the sexual appetite. ORIG C15: from LL *sensuālis,* from L *sēnsus* SENSE
▸ **'sensually** *adv*

sensualism ('sɛnsjʊəˌlɪzəm) *n* **1** the quality or state of being sensual. **2** the doctrine that the ability to gratify the senses is the only criterion of goodness.

sensuality (ˌsɛnsjʊ'ælɪtɪ) *n, pl* **sensualities. 1** the quality or state of being sensual. **2** excessive indulgence in sensual pleasures.
▸ **sensualist** ('sɛnsjʊəlɪst) *n*

sensuous ('sɛnsjʊəs) *adj* **1** aesthetically pleasing to the senses. **2** appreciative of qualities perceived by the senses. **3** of or derived from the senses. ORIG C17, but not common until C19: apparently coined by Milton to avoid the sexual overtones of SENSUAL
▸ **'sensuously** *adv* ▸ **'sensuousness** *n*

sent (sɛnt) *vb* the past tense and past participle of **send.**

sentence ('sentəns) *n* **1** a sequence of words capable of standing alone to make an assertion, ask a question, or give a command, usually consisting of a subject and a predicate. **2** the judgment formally pronounced upon a person convicted in criminal proceedings, esp. the decision as to what punishment is to be imposed. **3** *Music.* a passage or division of a piece of music, usually consisting of two or more contrasting musical phrases and ending in a cadence. **4** *Arch.* a proverb, maxim, or aphorism. ◆ *vb* **sentences, sentencing, sentenced. 5** (*tr*) to pronounce sentence on (a convicted person) in a court of law. ORIG C13: via OF from L *sententia* a way of thinking, from *sentīre* to feel
▸ **sentential** (sɛn'tɛnʃəl) *adj*

sentence connector *n* a word or phrase that introduces a clause or sentence and serves as a transition between it and a previous clause or sentence, as for example *also* in *I'm buying eggs and also I'm looking for a dessert for tonight.*

sentence substitute *n* a word or phrase, esp. one traditionally classified as an adverb, that is used in place of a finite sentence, such as *yes, no, certainly,* and *never.*

sententious (sɛn'tɛnʃəs) *adj* **1** characterized by or full of aphorisms or axioms. **2** constantly using aphorisms, etc. **3** tending to indulge in pompous moralizing. ORIG C15: from L *sententiōsus* full of meaning, from *sententia;* see SENTENCE
▸ **sen'tentiously** *adv* ▸ **sen'tentiousness** *n*

sentient ('sɛnʃənt, 'sɛntɪənt) *adj* **1** having the power of sense perception or sensation; conscious. ◆ *n* **2** *Rare.* a sentient person or thing. ORIG C17: from L *sentiēns* feeling, from *sentīre* to perceive
▸ **sentience** ('sɛnʃəns) *n*

sentiment ('sɛntɪmənt) *n* **1** susceptibility to tender or romantic emotion: *she has too much sentiment to be successful.* **2** (*often pl*) a thought, opinion, or attitude. **3** exaggerated or mawkish feeling or emotion. **4** an expression of response to deep feeling, esp. in art. **5** a feeling or awareness: *a sentiment of pity.* **6** a mental attitude determined by feeling: *there is a strong revolutionary sentiment in his country.* **7** a feeling conveyed, or intended to be conveyed, in words. ORIG C17: from Med. L *sentīmentum,* from L *sentīre* to feel

sentimental (ˌsɛntɪ'mɛntᵊl) *adj* **1** tending to indulge the emotions excessively. **2** making a direct appeal to the emotions, esp. to romantic feelings. **3** relating to or characterized by sentiment.
▸ **ˌsenti'mentaˌlism** *n* ▸ **ˌsenti'mentalist** *n* ▸ **ˌsenti'mentally** *adv*

sentimentality (ˌsɛntɪmɛn'tælɪtɪ) *n, pl* **sentimentalities. 1** the state, quality, or an instance of being sentimental. **2** an act, statement, etc., that is sentimental.

sentimentalize *or* **sentimentalise** (ˌsɛntɪ'mɛntᵊˌlaɪz) *vb* **sentimentalizes, sentimentalizing, sentimentalized** *or* **sentimentalises, sentimentalising, sentimentalised.** to make sentimental or behave sentimentally.
▸ **ˌsentiˌmentali'zation** *or* **ˌsentiˌmentali'sation** *n*

sentimental value *n* the value of an article in terms of its sentimental associations for a particular person.

sentinel ('sɛntɪnᵊl) *n* **1** a person, such as a sentry, assigned to keep guard. ◆ *vb* **sentinels, sentinelling, sentinelled** *or US* **sentinels, sentineling, sentineled.** (*tr*) **2** to guard as a sentinel. **3** to post as a sentinel. ORIG C16: from OF *sentinelle,* from OIt., from *sentina* watchfulness, from *sentire* to notice, from L

sentry ('sɛntrɪ) *n, pl* **sentries.** a soldier who guards or prevents unauthorized access to a place, etc. ORIG C17: ? shortened from obs. *centrinel,* C16 var. of SENTINEL

sentry box *n* a small shelter with an open front in which a sentry may stand to be sheltered from the weather.

senza ('sɛntsɑː) *prep Music.* omitting. ORIG It.

Seoul ★ (səʊl) *n* the capital of South Korea, in the west on the Han River: capital of Korea from 1392 to 1910, then seat of the Japanese administration until 1945; became capital of South Korea in 1948; cultural and educational centre. Pop.: 10 229 262 (1995). Also called: **Kyongsong.** Japanese name: **Keijo.**

Sep. *abbrev. for:* **1** September. **2** Septuagint.

sepal ('sɛpᵊl) *n* any of the separate parts of the calyx of a flower. ORIG C19: from NL *sepalum: sep-* from Gk *skepē* a covering + *-alum,* from NL *petalum* PETAL

-sepalous *adj combining form.* having sepals of a specified type or number: *polysepalous.*
▸ **-sepaly** *n combining form.*

separable ('sɛpərəbᵊl) *adj* able to be separated, divided, or parted.
▸ **ˌsepara'bility** *or* **'separableness** *n* ▸ **'separably** *adv*

separate *vb* ('sɛpəˌreɪt), **separates, separating, separated. 1** (*tr*) to act as a barrier between: *a range of mountains separates the two countries.* **2** to part or be parted from a mass or group. **3** (*tr*) to discriminate between: *to separate the men from the boys.* **4** to divide or be divided into component parts. **5** to sever or be severed. **6** (*intr*) (of a married couple) to cease living together. ◆ *adj* ('sɛprɪt, 'sɛpərɪt). **7** existing or considered independently: *a separate problem.* **8** disunited or apart. **9** set apart from the main body or mass. **10** distinct, individual, or particular. **11** solitary or withdrawn. ORIG C15: from L *sēparāre,* from *sē-* apart + *parāre* to obtain
▸ **'separately** *adv* ▸ **'separateness** *n* ▸ **'separative** *adj* ▸ **'sepaˌrator** *n*

separates ('sɛprɪts, 'sɛpərɪts) *pl n* women's outer garments that only cover part of the body; skirts, blouses, jackets, trousers, etc.

separate school *n* **1** (in certain Canadian provinces) a school for a large religious minority financed by provincial grants in addition to the education tax. **2** a Roman Catholic school.

separation (ˌsɛpə'reɪʃən) *n* **1** the act of separating or state of being separated. **2** the place or line where a separation is made. **3** a gap that separates. **4** *Family law.* the cessation of cohabitation between a man and wife, either by mutual agreement or under a decree of a court.

separatist ('sɛpərətɪst) *n* **a** a person who advocates secession from an organization, federation, union, etc. **b** (*as modifier*): *a separatist movement.*
▸ **'separaˌtism** *n*

Sephardi (sɪ'fɑːdiː) *n, pl* **Sephardim** (-dɪm). *Judaism.* **1** a Jew of Spanish, Portuguese, or North African descent. **2** the pronunciation of Hebrew used by these Jews, and of Modern Hebrew as spoken in Israel. ◆ Cf. **Ashkenazi.** ORIG C19: from LHeb., from Heb. *sepharad* a region mentioned in Obadiah 20, thought to have been Spain
▸ **Se'phardic** *adj*

sepia ('siːpɪə) *n* **1** a dark reddish-brown pigment obtained from the inky secretion of the cuttlefish. **2** a brownish tone imparted to a photograph, esp. an early one. **3** a brownish-grey to dark yellowish-brown colour. **4** a drawing or photograph in sepia. ◆ *adj* **5** of the colour sepia or done in sepia: *a sepia print.* ORIG C16: from L: a cuttlefish, from Gk

sepoy ('si:pɔɪ) *n* (formerly) an Indian soldier in the service of the British. ORIG C18: from Port. *sipaio,* from Urdu *sipāhī,* from Persian: horseman, from *sipāh* army

seppuku (sɛ'pu:ku:) *n* another word for **hara-kiri.** ORIG from Japanese, from Chinese *ch'ieh* to cut + *fu* bowels

sepsis ('sɛpsɪs) *n* the presence of pus-forming bacteria in the body. ORIG C19: via NL from Gk *sēpsis* a rotting

sept (sɛpt) *n* **1** *Anthropol.* a clan that believes itself to be descended from a common ancestor. **2** a branch of a tribe, esp. in Ireland or Scotland. ORIG C16: ? a var. of SECT

Sept. *abbrev. for:* **1** September. **2** Septuagint.

septa ('sɛptə) *n* the plural of **septum.**

septal ('sɛptəl) *adj* of or relating to a septum.

September (sɛp'tɛmbə) *n* the ninth month of the year, consisting of 30 days. ORIG OE, from L: the seventh (month) according to the original calendar of ancient Rome, from *septem* seven

septenary ('sɛptɪnərɪ) *adj* **1** of or relating to the number seven. **2** forming a group of seven. ◆ *n, pl* **septenaries. 3** the number seven. **4** a group of seven things. **5** a period of seven years. ORIG C16: from L *septēnārius,* from *septēnī* seven each, from *septem* seven

septennial (sɛp'tɛnɪəl) *adj* **1** occurring every seven years. **2** relating to or lasting seven years. ORIG C17: from L, from *septem* seven + *annus* a year

septet (sɛp'tɛt) *n* **1** *Music.* a group of seven singers or instrumentalists or a piece of music composed for such a group. **2** a group of seven people or things. ORIG C19: from G, from L *septem* seven

septic ('sɛptɪk) *adj* **1** of or caused by sepsis. **2** of or caused by putrefaction. ◆ *n* **3** *Austral. & NZ inf.* short for **septic tank.** ORIG C17: from L *sēpticus,* from Gk, from *sēptos* decayed, from *sēpein* to make rotten
▸ **'septically** *adv* ▸ **septicity** (sɛp'tɪsɪtɪ) *n*

septicaemia *or US* **septicemia** (ˌsɛptɪ'si:mɪə) *n* any of various diseases caused by microorganisms in the blood. Nontechnical name: **blood poisoning.** ORIG C19: from NL, from Gk *sēptik(os)* SEPTIC + -AEMIA
▸ **ˌsepti'caemic** *or US* **ˌsepti'cemic** *adj*

septic tank *n* a tank, usually below ground, for containing sewage to be decomposed by anaerobic bacteria. Also called (Austral.): **septic system.**

septillion (sɛp'tɪljən) *n, pl* **septillions** *or* **septillion. 1** (in Britain, France, and Germany) the number represented as one followed by 42 zeros (10^{42}). **2** (in the US and Canada) the number represented as one followed by 24 zeros (10^{24}). Brit. word: **quadrillion.** ORIG C17: from F, from *sept* seven + *-illion,* on the model of *million*
▸ **sep'tillionth** *adj, n*

septime ('sɛpti:m) *n* the seventh of eight basic positions from which a parry or attack can be made in fencing. ORIG C19: from L *septimus* seventh, from *septem* seven

septuagenarian (ˌsɛptjuədʒɪ'nɛərɪən) *n* **1** a person who is from 70 to 79 years old. ◆ *adj* **2** being between 70 and 79 years old. **3** of or relating to a septuagenarian. ORIG C18: from L, from *septuāgintā* seventy

Septuagesima (ˌsɛptjuə'dʒɛsɪmə) *n* the third Sunday before Lent. ORIG C14: from Church L *septuāgēsima* (*dīes*) the seventieth (day)

Septuagint ('sɛptjuəˌdʒɪnt) *n* the principal Greek version of the Old Testament, including the Apocrypha, believed to have been translated by 70 or 72 scholars. ORIG C16: from L *septuāgintā* seventy

septum ('sɛptəm) *n, pl* **septa.** *Biol., anat.* a dividing partition between two tissues or cavities. ORIG C18: from L *saeptum* wall, from *saepīre* to enclose

septuple ('sɛptjʊpᵊl) *adj* **1** seven times as much or as many. **2** consisting of seven parts or members. ◆ *vb* **septuples, septupling, septupled. 3** (*tr*) to multiply by seven. ORIG C17: from LL *septuplus,* from *septem* seven
▸ **septuplicate** (sɛp'tju:plɪkɪt) *n, adj*

sepulchral (sɪ'pʌlkrəl) *adj* **1** suggestive of a tomb; gloomy. **2** of or relating to a sepulchre.
▸ **se'pulchrally** *adv*

sepulchre *or US* **sepulcher** ('sɛpəlkə) *n* **1** a burial vault, tomb, or grave. **2** Also called: **Easter sepulchre.** an alcove in some churches in which the Eucharistic elements were kept from Good Friday until Easter. ◆ *vb* **sepulchres, sepulchring, sepulchred** *or US* **sepulchers, sepulchering, sepulchered. 3** (*tr*) to bury in a sepulchre. ORIG C12: from OF *sépulcre,* from L *sepulcrum,* from *sepelīre* to bury

sepulture ('sɛpəltʃə) *n* the act of placing in a sepulchre. ORIG C13: via OF from L *sepultūra,* from *sepultus* buried, from *sepelīre* to bury

seq. *abbrev. for:* **1** sequel. **2** sequens. ORIG L: the following (one)

sequel ('si:kwəl) *n* **1** anything that follows from something else. **2** a consequence. **3** a novel, play, etc., that continues a previously related story. ORIG C15: from LL *sequēla,* from L *sequī* to follow

sequela (sɪ'kwi:lə) *n, pl* **sequelae** (-li:). (*often pl*) *Med.* **1** any abnormal bodily condition or disease arising from a pre-existing disease. **2** any complication of a disease. ORIG C18: from L: SEQUEL

sequence ('si:kwəns) *n* **1** an arrangement of two or more things in a successive order. **2** the successive order of two or more things: *chronological sequence.* **3** an action or event that follows another or others. **4a** *Cards.* a set of three or more consecutive cards, usually of the same suit. **4b** *Bridge.* a set of two or more consecutive cards. **5** *Music.* an arrangement of notes or chords repeated several times at different pitches. **6** *Maths.* an ordered set of numbers or other mathematical entities in one-to-one correspondence with the integers 1 to *n* **7** a section of a film constituting a single continuous uninterrupted episode. **8** *Biochem.* the unique order of amino acids in a protein or of nucleotides in DNA or RNA. ◆ *vb* (*tr*) **9** to arrange in a sequence. ORIG C14: from Med. L *sequentia* that which follows, from L *sequī* to follow

sequence of tenses *n Grammar.* the sequence according to which the tense of a subordinate verb in a sentence is determined by the tense of the principal verb, as in *I believe he is lying, I believed he was lying,* etc.

sequencing ('si:kwənsɪŋ) *n Biochem.* the procedure of determining the order of amino acids in the polypeptide chain of a protein (**protein sequencing**) or of nucleotides in a DNA section comprising a gene (**gene sequencing**).

sequent ('si:kwənt) *adj* **1** following in order or succession. **2** following as a result. ◆ *n* **3** something that follows. ORIG C16: from L *sequēns,* from *sequī* to follow
▸ **'sequently** *adv*

sequential (sɪ'kwɛnʃəl) *adj* **1** characterized by or having a regular sequence. **2** another word for **sequent.**
▸ **sequentiality** (sɪˌkwɛnʃɪ'ælɪtɪ) *n* ▸ **se'quentially** *adv*

sequential access *n* a method of reading data from a computer file by reading through the file from the beginning.

sequester (sɪ'kwɛstə) *vb* (*tr*) **1** to remove or separate. **2** (*usually passive*) to retire into seclusion. **3** *Law.* to take (property) temporarily out of the possession of its owner, esp. until creditors are satisfied or a court order is complied with. **4** *International law.* to appropriate (enemy property). ORIG C14: from LL *sequestrāre* to surrender for safekeeping, from L *sequester* a trustee

sequestrate (sɪ'kwɛstreɪt) *vb* **sequestrates, sequestrating, sequestrated.** (*tr*) *Law.* a variant of **sequester** (sense 3). ORIG C16: from LL *sequestrāre* to SEQUESTER
▸ **sequestrator** ('si:kwɛsˌtreɪtə) *n*

sequestration (ˌsi:kwɛ'streɪʃən) *n* **1** the act of sequestering or state of being sequestered. **2** *Law.* the sequestering of property. **3** *Chem.* the effective removal of ions from a solution by coordination with another type of ion or molecule to form complexes.

sequestrum (sɪ'kwɛstrəm) *n, pl* **sequestra** (-trə). *Pathol.* a detached piece of dead bone that often migrates to a wound, etc. ORIG C19: from NL, from L: something deposited
▸ **se'questral** *adj*

sequin ('si:kwɪn) *n* **1** a small piece of shiny often coloured metal foil, usually round, used to decorate garments, etc. **2** a gold coin formerly minted in Italy. ORIG

C17: via F from It. *zecchino,* from *zecca* mint, from Ar. *sikkah* die for striking coins
▸ **'sequined** *adj*

sequoia (sɪ'kwɔɪə) *n* either of two giant Californian coniferous trees, the **redwood,** or the **big tree** or **giant sequoia.** ORIG C19: NL, after *Sequoya,* known also as George Guess, (?1770–1843), American Indian scholar and leader

Sequoia National Park ★ *n* a national park in central California, in the Sierra Nevada Mountains: established in 1890 to protect groves of giant sequoias, some of which are about 4000 years old. Area: 1556 sq. km (601 sq. miles).

sérac ('sɛræk) *n* a pinnacle of ice among crevasses on a glacier, usually on a steep slope. ORIG C19: from Swiss F: a variety of white cheese (hence the ice that resembles it), from Med. L *serācium,* from L *serum* whey

seraglio (sɛ'rɑːlɪˌəʊ) *or* **serail** (sə'raɪ) *n, pl* **seraglios** *or* **serails. 1** the harem of a Muslim house or palace. **2** a sultan's palace, esp. in the former Turkish empire. ORIG C16: from It. *serraglio* animal cage, from Med. L *serrāculum* bolt, from L *sera* a door bar; associated also with Turkish *seray* palace

Serajevo ★ (*Serbo-Croat* 'sɛrajɛvɔ) *n* a variant of **Sarajevo.**

Seram *or* **Ceram** ★ (sɪ'ræm) *n* an island in Indonesia, in the Moluccas, separated from New Guinea by the **Ceram Sea:** mountainous and densely forested. Area: 17 150 sq. km (6622 sq. miles). Also called: **Serang** (sə'ræŋ).

serape (sə'rɑːpɪ) *n* **1** a blanket-like shawl, often of brightly coloured wool, worn by men in Latin America. **2** a large shawl worn around the shoulders by women as a fashion garment. ORIG C19: Mexican Sp.

seraph ('sɛrəf) *n, pl* **seraphs** *or* **seraphim** (-əfɪm). *Theol.* a member of the highest order of angels in the celestial hierarchies, often depicted as the winged head of a child. ORIG C17: back formation from pl *seraphim,* via LL from Heb.
▸ **seraphic** (sɪ'ræfɪk) *adj*

Serapis ★ ('sɛrəpɪs) *n* a Graeco-Egyptian god combining attributes of Apis and Osiris.

Serb (sɜːb) *n, adj* another word for **Serbian.** ORIG C19: from Serbian *Srb*

Serb. *abbrev. for* Serbia(n).

Serbia ★ ('sɜːbɪə) *n* a constituent republic of Yugoslavia: declared a kingdom in 1882; precipitated World War I by the conflict with Austria; became part of the Kingdom of the Serbs, Croats, and Slovenes (later called Yugoslavia) in 1918; remained united with Montenegro to form the Federal Republic of Yugoslavia when the other constituent republics became independent in 1991–92. Capital: Belgrade. Pop.: 5 806 000 (1995 est.). Area: 88 361 sq. km (34 109 sq. miles). Former name: **Servia.** Serbian name: **Srbija.**

Serbian ('sɜːbɪən) *adj* **1** of, relating to, or characteristic of Serbia, its people, or their dialect of Serbo-Croat. ◆ *n* **2** the dialect of Serbo-Croat spoken in Serbia. **3** a native or inhabitant of Serbia.

Serbo-Croat *or* **Serbo-Croatian** ('sɜːbəʊ-) *n* **1** the language of the Serbs and the Croats. The Serbian dialect is usually written in the Cyrillic alphabet, the Croatian in Roman. ◆ *adj* **2** of or relating to this language.

SERC (in Britain) *abbrev. for* Science and Engineering Research Council.

Sercq ★ (sɛrk) *n* the French name for **Sark.**

sere[1] (sɪə) *adj* **1** *Arch.* dried up. ◆ *vb* **seres, sering, sered,** *n* **2** a rare spelling of **sear.** ORIG OE *sēar*

sere[2] (sɪə) *n* the series of changes occurring in the ecological succession of a community. ORIG C20: from SERIES

Seremban ★ (sə'rɛmbən) *n* a town in Peninsular Malaysia, capital of Negri Sembilan state. Pop.: 182 584 (1991).

serenade (ˌsɛrɪ'neɪd) *n* **1** a piece of music characteristically played outside the house of a woman. **2** a piece of music suggestive of this. **3** an extended composition in several movements similar to the modern suite. ◆ *vb* **serenades, serenading, serenaded. 4** (*tr*) to play a serenade for (someone). **5** (*intr*) to play a serenade. ORIG C17: from F *sérénade,* from It. *serenata,* from *sereno* peaceful, from L *serēnus;* also infl. in meaning by It. *sera* evening, from L *sērus* late
▸ **ˌsere'nader** *n*

serendipity (ˌsɛrən'dɪpɪtɪ) *n* the faculty of making fortunate discoveries by accident. ORIG C18: coined by Horace Walpole, from the Persian fairytale *The Three Princes of Serendip,* in which the heroes possess this gift
▸ **ˌseren'dipitous** *adj*

serene (sɪ'riːn) *adj* **1** peaceful or tranquil; calm. **2** clear or bright: *a serene sky.* **3** (*often cap.*) honoured: *His Serene Highness.* ORIG C16: from L *serēnus*
▸ **se'renely** *adv* ▸ **serenity** (sɪ'rɛnɪtɪ) *n*

serf (sɜːf) *n* (esp. in medieval Europe) an unfree person, esp. one bound to the land. ORIG C15: from OF, from L *servus* a slave
▸ **'serfdom** *or* **'serfhood** *n*

serge (sɜːdʒ) *n* **1** a twill-weave woollen or worsted fabric used for clothing. **2** a similar twilled cotton, silk, or rayon fabric. ORIG C14: from OF *sarge,* from Vulgar L *sārica* (unattested), from L *sēricum,* from Gk *sērikon* silk, ult. from *sēr* silkworm

sergeant ('sɑːdʒənt) *n* **1** a noncommissioned officer in certain armies, air forces, and marine corps, usually ranking immediately above a corporal. **2a** (in Britain) a police officer ranking between constable and inspector. **2b** (in the US) a police officer ranking below a captain. **3** a court or municipal officer who has ceremonial duties. ◆ Also: **serjeant.** ORIG C12: from OF *sergent,* from L *serviēns,* lit.: serving, from *servīre* to SERVE

sergeant at arms *n* an officer of a legislative or fraternal body responsible for maintaining internal order. Also: **sergeant, serjeant at arms.**

Sergeant Baker ('beɪkə) *n* a large brightly coloured Australian sea fish.

sergeant major *n* the chief administrative noncommissioned officer of a military headquarters. See also **warrant officer.**

Sergipe ★ (*Portuguese* ser'ʒipi) *n* a state of NE Brazil: the smallest Brazilian state; a centre of resistance to Dutch conquest (17th century). Capital: Aracajú. Pop.: 1 624 020 (1996). Area: 13 672 sq. km (8492 sq. miles).

Sergt *abbrev. for* Sergeant.

serial ('sɪərɪəl) *n* **1** a novel, film, etc., presented in instalments at regular intervals. **2** a publication, regularly issued and consecutively numbered. ◆ *adj* **3** of or resembling a series. **4** published or presented as a serial. **5** of or relating to such publication or presentation. **6** *Computing.* of or operating on items of information, etc., in the order in which they occur. **7** of or using the techniques of serialism. ORIG C19: from NL *seriālis,* from L *seriēs* SERIES
▸ **'serially** *adv*

serialism ('sɪərɪəˌlɪzəm) *n* (in 20th-century music) the use of a sequence of notes in a definite order as a thematic basis for a composition. See also **twelve-tone.**

serialize *or* **serialise** ('sɪərɪəˌlaɪz) *vb* **serializes, serializing, serialized** *or* **serialises, serialising, serialised.** (*tr*) to publish or present in the form of a serial.
▸ **ˌseriali'zation** *or* **ˌseriali'sation** *n*

serial killer *n* a person who carries out a series of murders, selecting victims at random or according to a perverse pattern.

serial monogamy *n* the practice of having a number of long-term monogamous romantic or sexual relationships or marriages in succession.

serial number *n* any of the consecutive numbers assigned to machines, tools, books, etc.

seriate ('sɪərɪɪt) *adj* forming a series.

seriatim (ˌsɪərɪ'ætɪm) *adv* one after another in order. ORIG C17: from Med. L, from L *seriēs* SERIES

sericeous (sɪ'rɪʃəs) *adj Bot.* **1** covered with a layer of small silky hairs: *a sericeous leaf.* **2** silky. ORIG C18: from LL *sēriceus* silken, from L *sēricus;* see SERGE

sericulture ('sɛrɪˌkʌltʃə) *n* the rearing of silkworms for the production of raw silk. ORIG C19: via F; *seri-* from L *sēricum* silk, ult. from Gk *sēr* a silkworm
▸ **ˌseri'cultural** *adj* ▸ **ˌseri'culturist** *n*

series ('sɪəri:z) *n, pl* **series.** **1** a group or succession of related things, usually arranged in order. **2** a set of radio or television programmes having the same characters but different stories. **3** a set of books having the same format, related content, etc., published by one firm. **4** a set of stamps, coins, etc., issued at a particular time. **5** *Maths.* the sum of a finite or infinite sequence of numbers or quantities. **6** *Electronics.* an arrangement of two or more components connected in a circuit so that the same current flows in turn through each of them (esp. in **in series**). Cf. **parallel** (sense 10). **7** *Geol.* a stratigraphical unit that represents the rocks formed during an epoch. ORIG C17: from L: a row, from *serere* to link

series-wound ('sɪəri:z,waʊnd) *adj* (of a motor or generator) having the field and armature circuits connected in series.

serif ('sɛrɪf) *n Printing.* a small line at the extremities of a main stroke in a type character. ORIG C19: ?from Du. *schreef* dash, prob. of Gmc origin

serigraph ('sɛrɪ,grɑ:f) *n* a colour print made by an adaptation of the silk-screen process. ORIG C19: from *seri-*, from L *sēricum* silk + -GRAPH
▸ **serigraphy** (sə'rɪgrəfɪ) *n*

serin ('sɛrɪn) *n* any of various small yellow-and-brown finches of parts of Europe. ORIG C16: from F, ?from OProvençal *sirena* a bee-eater, from L *sīrēn*, a kind of bird, from SIREN

seringa (sə'rɪŋgə) *n* **1** any of a Brazilian genus of trees that yield rubber. **2** a deciduous tree of southern Africa with a graceful shape. ORIG C18: from Port., var. of SYRINGA

Seringapatam ★ (sə,rɪŋgəpə'tæm) *n* a small town in S India, in Karnataka on **Seringapatam Island** in the Cauvery River: capital of Mysore from 1610 to 1799, when it was besieged and captured by the British. Pop.: 21 902 (1991 est.).

seriocomic (,sɪərɪəʊ'kɒmɪk) *adj* mixing serious and comic elements.
▸ **,serio'comically** *adv*

serious ('sɪərɪəs) *adj* **1** grave in nature or disposition: *a serious person.* **2** marked by deep feeling; sincere: *is he serious or joking?* **3** concerned with important matters: *a serious conversation.* **4** requiring effort or concentration: *a serious book.* **5** giving rise to fear or anxiety: *a serious illness.* **6** *Inf.* worthy of regard because of substantial quantity or quality: *serious money; serious wine.* **7** *Inf.* extreme or remarkable: *a serious haircut.* ORIG C15: from LL *sēriōsus*, from L *sērius*
▸ **'seriousness** *n*

seriously ('sɪərɪəslɪ) *adv* **1** in a serious manner or to a serious degree. **2** *Inf.* extremely or remarkably: *seriously tall.*

serjeant ('sɑ:dʒənt) *n* a variant spelling of **sergeant.**

serjeant at law *n* (formerly, in England) a barrister of a special rank. Also: **serjeant, sergeant at law, sergeant.**

sermon ('sɜ:mən) *n* **1a** an address of religious instruction or exhortation, often based on a passage from the Bible, esp. one delivered during a church service. **1b** a written version of such an address. **2** a serious speech, esp. one administering reproof. ORIG C12: via OF from L *sermō* discourse, prob. from *serere* to join together

sermonize *or* **sermonise** ('sɜ:mə,naɪz) *vb* **sermonizes, sermonizing, sermonized** *or* **sermonises, sermonising, sermonised.** to address (a person or audience) as if delivering a sermon.
▸ **'sermon,izer** *or* **'sermon,iser** *n*

Sermon on the Mount *n Bible.* a major discourse delivered by Christ, including the Beatitudes and the Lord's Prayer (Matthew 5–7).

sero- *combining form.* indicating a serum: *serology.*

seroconvert (,sɪərəʊkən'vɜ:t) *vb* (*intr*) (of an individual) to produce antibodies specific to, and in response to the presence in the blood of, a particular antigen, such as a virus or vaccine.
▸ **,serocon'version** *n*

serology (sɪ'rɒlədʒɪ) *n* the branch of science concerned with serums.
▸ **serologic** (,sɪərə'lɒdʒɪk) *or* **,sero'logical** *adj*

seropositive (,sɪərəʊ'pɒzɪtɪv) *adj* (of a person whose blood has been tested for a specific disease, such as AIDS) showing a serological reaction indicating the presence of the disease.

serotine ('sɛrə,taɪn) *adj* **1** *Biol.* produced, flowering, or developing late in the season. ◆ *n* **2** a reddish-coloured European insectivorous bat. ORIG C16: from L *sērōtinus* late, from *sērus* late; applied to the bat because it flies late in the evening

serotonin (,sɛrə'təʊnɪn) *n* a compound that occurs in the brain, intestines, and blood platelets and induces vasoconstriction.

serous ('sɪərəs) *adj* of, producing, or containing serum. ORIG C16: from L *serōsus*
▸ **serosity** (sɪ'rɒsɪtɪ) *n*

serous fluid *n* a thin watery fluid found in many body cavities.

serous membrane *n* any of the smooth moist delicate membranes, such as the pleura, that line the closed cavities of the body.

serow ('sɛrəʊ) *n* either of two antelopes of mountainous regions of S and SE Asia, having a dark coat and conical backward-pointing horns. ORIG C19: from native name *să-ro* Tibetan goat

Seroxat ('se,rɒksæt) *n Trademark.* a drug that prolongs the action of serotin in the brain; used to treat depression and social anxiety.

serpent ('sɜ:pənt) *n* **1** a literary word for **snake. 2** *Bible.* a manifestation of Satan as a guileful tempter (Genesis 3:1–5). **3** a sly or unscrupulous person. **4** an obsolete wind instrument resembling a snake in shape. ORIG C14: via OF from L *serpēns* a creeping thing, from *serpere* to creep

serpentine[1] ('sɜ:pən,taɪn) *adj* **1** of, relating to, or resembling a serpent. **2** twisting; winding. ORIG C14: from LL *serpentīmus*, from *serpēns* SERPENT

serpentine[2] ('sɜ:pən,taɪn) *n* any of several secondary minerals, consisting of hydrated magnesium silicate, that are green to brown in colour and greasy to the touch. ORIG C15 *serpentyn*, from Med. L *serpentīnum* SERPENTINE[1]; referring to the snakelike patterns of these minerals

serpigo (sɜ:'paɪgəʊ) *n Pathol.* any progressive skin eruption, such as ringworm or herpes. ORIG C14: from Med. L, from L *serpere* to creep

SERPS *or* **Serps** (sɜ:ps) *n* (in Britain) *acronym for* state earnings-related pension scheme.

serrate *adj* ('sɛrɪt, -eɪt). **1** (of leaves) having a margin of forward pointing teeth. **2** having a notched or sawlike edge. ◆ *vb* (sɛ'reɪt), **serrates, serrating, serrated. 3** (*tr*) to make serrate. ORIG C17: from L *serrātus* saw-shaped, from *serra* a saw
▸ **ser'rated** *adj*

serration (sɛ'reɪʃən) *n* **1** the state or condition of being serrated. **2** a row of toothlike projections on an edge. **3** a single notch.

serried ('sɛrɪd) *adj* in close or compact formation: *serried ranks of troops.* ORIG C17: from OF *serré* close-packed, from *serrer* to shut up

serriform ('sɛrɪ,fɔ:m) *adj Biol.* resembling a notched or sawlike edge. ORIG *serri-*, from L *serra* saw

serrulate ('sɛrʊ,leɪt, -lɪt) *adj* (esp. of leaves) minutely serrate. ORIG C18: from NL *serrulātus*, from L *serrula* dim. of *serra* a saw
▸ **,serru'lation** *n*

Sertorius ★ (sɜ:'tɔ:rɪəs) *n* **Quintus** ('kwɪntəs). ?123–72 B.C., Roman soldier who led an insurrection in Spain against Sulla; assassinated.

serum ('sɪərəm) *n, pl* **serums** *or* **sera** (-rə). **1** Also called: **blood serum.** blood plasma from which the clotting factors have been removed. **2** antitoxin obtained from the blood serum of immunized animals. **3** *Physiol., zool.* clear watery fluid, esp. that exuded by serous membranes. **4** a less common word for **whey.** ORIG C17: from L: whey

serum albumin *n* a form of albumin that is the most abundant protein constituent of blood plasma.

serum hepatitis *n* a former name for **hepatitis B.**

serum sickness *n* an allergic reaction, such as vomiting, skin rash, etc., that sometimes follows injection of a foreign serum.

serval (ˈsɜːvᵊl) *n, pl* **servals** *or* **serval.** a slender feline mammal of the African bush, having an orange-brown coat with black spots. ORIG C18: via F from LL *cervālis* staglike, from L *cervus* a stag

servant (ˈsɜːvᵊnt) *n* **1** a person employed to work for another, esp. one who performs household duties. **2** See **public servant.** ORIG C13: via OF from *servant* serving, from *servir* to SERVE

serve (sɜːv) *vb* **serves, serving, served. 1** to be in the service of (a person). **2** to render or be of service to (a person, cause, etc.); help. **3** to attend to (customers) in a shop, etc. **4** (*tr*) to provide (guests, etc.) with food, drink, etc.: *she served her guests with cocktails.* **5** to distribute or provide (food, etc.) for guests, etc.: *do you serve coffee?* **6** (*tr;* sometimes foll. by *up*) to present (food, etc.) in a specified manner: *peaches served with cream.* **7** (*tr*) to provide with a regular supply of. **8** (*tr*) to work actively for: *to serve the government.* **9** (*tr*) to pay homage to: *to serve God.* **10** to suit: *this will serve my purpose.* **11** (*intr; may take an infinitive*) to function: *this wood will serve to build a fire.* **12** to go through (a period of service, enlistment, etc.). **13** (*intr*) (of weather, conditions, etc.) to be suitable. **14** (*tr*) Also: **service.** (of a male animal) to copulate with (a female animal). **15** *Tennis, squash, etc.* to put (the ball) into play. **16** (*tr*) to deliver (a legal document) to (a person). **17** (*tr*) *Naut.* to bind (a rope, etc.) with fine cord to protect it from chafing, etc. **18 serve (a person) right.** *Inf.* to pay (a person) back, esp. for wrongful or foolish treatment or behaviour. ◆ *n* **19** *Tennis, squash, etc.* short for **service. 20** *Austral. inf.* hostile or critical remarks. ORIG C13: from OF *servir,* from L *servīre,* from *servus* a slave
▸ ˈ**servable** *or* ˈ**serveable** *adj*

server (ˈsɜːvə) *n* **1** a person who serves. **2** *RC Church.* a person who assists the priest at Mass. **3** something that is used in serving food and drink. **4** the player who serves in racket games. **5** *Computing.* a computer or program that supplies data or resources to other machines on a network.

Servetus ★ (sɜːˈviːtəs) *n* **Michael,** Spanish name *Miguel Serveto.* 1511–53, Spanish theologian and physician. He was burnt at the stake by order of Calvin for denying the doctrine of the Trinity and the divinity of Christ.

Servia ★ (ˈsɜːvɪə) *n* the former name of **Serbia.**
▸ ˈ**Servian** *adj, n*

service (ˈsɜːvɪs) *n* **1** an act of help or assistance. **2** an organized system of labour and material aids used to supply the needs of the public: *telephone service.* **3** the supply, installation, or maintenance of goods carried out by a dealer. **4** the state of availability for use by the public (esp. in **into** *or* **out of service**). **5** a periodic overhaul made on a car, etc. **6** the act or manner of serving guests, customers, etc., in a shop, hotel, etc. **7** a department of public employment and its employees: *civil service.* **8** employment in or performance of work for another: *in the service of his firm.* **9a** one of the branches of the armed forces. **9b** (*as modifier*): *service life.* **10** the state or duties of a domestic servant (esp. in **in service**). **11** the act or manner of serving food. **12** a set of dishes, cups, etc., for use at table. **13** public worship carried out according to certain prescribed forms: *divine service.* **14** the prescribed form according to which a specific kind of religious ceremony is to be carried out: *the burial service.* **15** *Tennis, squash, etc.* **15a** the act, manner, or right of serving a ball. **15b** the game in which a particular player serves: *he has lost his service.* **16** the serving of a writ, summons, etc., upon a person. **17** (of male animals) the act of mating. **18** (*modifier*) of or for the use of servants or employees. **19** (*modifier*) serving the public rather than producing goods: *service industry.* ◆ *vb* **services, servicing, serviced.** (*tr*) **20** to provide service or services to. **21** to make fit for use. **22** to supply with assistance. **23** to overhaul (a car, machine, etc.). **24** (of a male animal) to mate with (a female). **25** *Brit.* to meet interest on (debt). ◆ See also **services.** ORIG C12 *servise,* from OF, from L *servitium* condition of a slave, from *servus* a slave

serviceable (ˈsɜːvɪsəbᵊl) *adj* **1** capable of or ready for service. **2** capable of giving good service.
▸ ˌ**serviceaˈbility** *n* ▸ ˈ**serviceably** *adv*

service area *n* a place on a motorway providing garage services, restaurants, toilet facilities, etc.

service car *n NZ.* a bus operating on a long-distance route.

service charge *n* a percentage of a bill, as at a hotel, added to the total to pay for service.

service contract *n* a contract between an employer and a senior employee, esp. a director, executive, etc.

service flat *n Brit.* a flat in which domestic services are provided by the management. Also called (esp. Austral.): **serviced flat.**

serviceman (ˈsɜːvɪsmən) *n, pl* **servicemen. 1** a person who serves in the armed services of a country. **2** a man employed to service and maintain equipment.
▸ ˈ**serviceˌwoman** *fem n*

service road *n Brit.* a narrow road running parallel to a main road and providing access to houses, shops, etc., situated along its length.

services (ˈsɜːvɪsɪz) *pl n* **1** work performed for remuneration. **2** (usually preceded by *the*) the armed forces. **3** (*sometimes sing*) *Econ.* commodities, such as banking, that are mainly intangible and usually consumed concurrently with their production. **4** a system of providing the public with gas, water, etc.

service station *n* a place that supplies fuel, oil, etc., for motor vehicles and often carries out repairs, servicing, etc.

service tree *n* **1** Also called: **sorb.** a Eurasian rosaceous tree, cultivated for its white flowers and brown edible apple-like fruits. **2 wild service tree.** a similar and related Eurasian tree. ORIG *service* from OE *syrfe,* from Vulgar L *sorbea* (unattested), from L *sorbus* sorb

serviette (ˌsɜːvɪˈɛt) *n Brit. & Canad.* a small square of cloth or paper used while eating to protect the clothes, etc. ORIG C15: from OF, from *servir* to SERVE; on the model of OUBLIETTE

servile (ˈsɜːvaɪl) *adj* **1** obsequious or fawning in attitude or behaviour. **2** of or suitable for a slave. **3** existing in or relating to a state of slavery. **4** (when *postpositive,* foll. by *to*) submitting or obedient. ORIG C14: from L *servīlis,* from *servus* slave
▸ **servility** (sɜːˈvɪlɪtɪ) *n*

serving (ˈsɜːvɪŋ) *n* a portion or helping of food or drink.

servitor (ˈsɜːvɪtə) *n Arch.* a person who serves another. ORIG C14: from OF, from LL, from L *servīre* to SERVE

servitude (ˈsɜːvɪˌtjuːd) *n* **1** the state or condition of a slave. **2** the state or condition of being subjected to or dominated by a person or thing. **3** *Law.* a burden attaching to an estate for the benefit of an adjoining estate or of some definite person. See also **easement.** ORIG C15: via OF from L *servitūdō,* from *servus* a slave

servo (ˈsɜːvəʊ) *adj* **1** (*prenominal*) of or activated by a servomechanism: *servo brakes.* ◆ *n, pl* **servos. 2** *Inf.* short for **servomechanism.** ORIG from *servomotor* from F, from L *servus* slave + F *moteur* motor

servomechanism (ˈsɜːvəʊˌmɛkəˌnɪzəm) *n* a mechanical or electromechanical system for control of the position or speed of an output transducer.

servomotor (ˈsɜːvəʊˌməʊtə) *n* any motor that supplies power to a servomechanism.

servqual (ˈsɜːvˌkwɒl) *n Marketing.* the provision of high-quality products by an organization backed by a high level of service for consumers. ORIG C20: from SERV(ICE) + QUAL(ITY)

sesame (ˈsɛsəmɪ) *n* **1** a tropical herbaceous plant of the East Indies, cultivated, esp. in India, for its small oval seeds. **2** the seeds of this plant, used in flavouring bread and yielding an edible oil (**benne oil** or **gingili**). ORIG C15: from L *sēsamum,* from Gk *sēsamon, sēsamē,* of Semitic origin

sesamoid (ˈsɛsəˌmɔɪd) *adj Anat.* **1** of or relating to various small bones formed in tendons, such as the patella. **2** of or relating to any of various small cartilages, esp. those of the nose. ORIG C17: from L *sēsamoīdēs* like sesame (seed), from Gk

sesh (sɛʃ) *n Sl.* short for **session.**

★ people and places

Sesostris I ★ (sɛˈsɒstrɪs) *n* 20th century B.C., king of Egypt of the 12th dynasty. He conquered Nubia and brought ancient Egypt to the height of its prosperity.

sesqui- *prefix* **1** indicating one and a half: *sesquicentennial.* **2** (in a chemical compound) indicating a ratio of two to three. ORIG from L, contraction of SEMI- + *as* AS[2] + *-que* and

sesquicentennial (ˌsɛskwɪsɛnˈtɛnɪəl) *adj* **1** of a period of 150 years. ◆ *n* **2** a period of 150 years. **3** a 150th anniversary or its celebration.
▸ **ˌsesquicenˈtennially** *adv*

sessile (ˈsɛsaɪl) *adj* **1** (of flowers or leaves) having no stalk. **2** (of animals such as the barnacle) permanently attached. ORIG C18: from L *sēssilis* concerning sitting, from *sedēre* to sit
▸ **sessility** (sɛˈsɪlɪtɪ) *n*

sessile oak *n* another name for the **durmast.**

session (ˈsɛʃən) *n* **1** the meeting of a court, legislature, judicial body, etc., for the execution of its function or the transaction of business. **2** a single continuous meeting of such a body. **3** a series or period of such meetings. **4** *Education.* **4a** the time during which classes are held. **4b** a school or university year. **5** *Presbyterian Church.* the body presiding over a local congregation and consisting of the minister and elders. **6** a meeting of a group of musicians to record in a studio. **7** any period devoted to an activity. ORIG C14: from L *sessiō* a sitting, from *sedēre* to sit
▸ **ˈsessional** *adj*

Sessions ★ (ˈsɛʃənz) *n* **Roger (Huntington).** 1896–1985, US composer.

sesterce (ˈsɛstəs) *or* **sestertius** (sɛˈstɜːtɪəs) *n* a silver or, later, bronze coin of ancient Rome worth a quarter of a denarius. ORIG C16: from L *sēstertius* a coin worth two and a half asses, from *sēmis* half + *tertius* a third

sestet (sɛˈstɛt) *n* **1** *Prosody.* the last six lines of a sonnet. **2** another word for **sextet** (sense 1). ORIG C19: from It., from *sesto* sixth, from L, from *sex* six

sestina (sɛˈstiːnə) *n* an elaborate verse form of Italian origin in which the six final words of the lines in the first stanza are repeated in a different order in each of the remaining five stanzas. ORIG C19: from It., from *sesto* sixth, from L *sextus*

Sestos ★ (ˈsɛstɒs) *n* a ruined town in NW Turkey, at the narrowest point of the Dardanelles: N terminus of the bridge of boats built by Xerxes in 481 B.C. for the crossing of his armies of invasion.

set[1] (sɛt) *vb* **sets, setting, set.** (*mainly tr*) **1** to put or place in position or into a specified state or condition: *to set someone free.* **2** (*also intr;* foll. by *to* or *on*) to put or be put (to); apply or be applied: *he set fire to the house.* **3** to put into order or readiness for use: *to set the table for dinner.* **4** (*also intr*) to put, form, or be formed into a jelled, firm, or rigid state: *the jelly set in three hours.* **5** (*also intr*) to put or be put into a position that will restore a normal state: *to set a broken bone.* **6** to adjust (a clock or other instrument) to a position. **7** to establish: *we have set the date for our wedding.* **8** to prescribe (an undertaking, course of study, etc.): *the examiners have set "Paradise Lost".* **9** to arrange in a particular fashion, esp. an attractive one: *she set her hair.* **10** Also: **set to music.** to provide music for (a poem or other text to be sung). **11** Also: **set up.** *Printing.* to arrange or produce (type, film, etc.) from (text or copy). **12** to arrange (a stage, television studio, etc.) with scenery and props. **13** to describe (a scene or the background to a literary work, etc.) in words: *his novel is set in Russia.* **14** to present as a model of good or bad behaviour (esp. in **set an example**). **15** (foll. by *on* or *by*) to value (something) at a specified price or estimation of worth: *he set a high price on his services.* **16** (*also intr*) to give or be given a particular direction: *his course was set to the East.* **17** (*also intr*) to rig (a sail) or (of a sail) to be rigged so as to catch the wind. **18** (*intr*) (of the sun, moon, etc.) to disappear beneath the horizon. **19** to leave (dough, etc.) in one place so that it may prove. **20** to sink (the head of a nail) below the surface surrounding it by using a nail set. **21** *Computing.* to give (a binary circuit) the value 1. **22** (of plants) to produce (fruits, seeds, etc.) after pollination or (of fruits or seeds) to develop after pollination. **23** to plant (seeds, seedlings, etc.). **24** to place (a hen) on (eggs) for the purpose of incubation. **25** (*intr*) (of a gun dog) to turn in the direction of game. **26** *Bridge.* to defeat (one's opponents) in their attempt to make a contract. **27** a dialect word for **sit.** ◆ *n* **28** the act of setting or the state of being set. **29** a condition of firmness or hardness. **30** bearing, carriage, or posture: *the set of a gun dog when pointing.* **31** the scenery and other props used in a dramatic production, film, etc. **32** Also called: **set width.** *Printing.* **32a** the width of the body of a piece of type. **32b** the width of the lines of type in a page or column. **33** *Psychol.* a temporary bias disposing an organism to react to a stimulus in one way rather than in others. **34** a seedling, cutting, or similar part that is ready for planting: *onion sets.* **35** a variant spelling of **sett.** ◆ *adj* **36** fixed or established by authority or agreement: *set hours of work.* **37** (*usually postpositive*) rigid or inflexible: *she is set in her ways.* **38** unmoving; fixed: *a set expression on his face.* **39** conventional, artificial, or stereotyped: *she made her apology in set phrases.* **40** (*postpositive;* foll. by *on* or *upon*) resolute in intention: *he is set upon marrying.* **41** (of a book, etc.) prescribed for students' preparation for an examination. ◆ See also **set about, set against,** etc. ORIG OE *settan,* causative of *sittan* to SIT

set[2] (sɛt) *n* **1** a number of objects or people grouped or belonging together, often having certain features or characteristics in common: *a set of coins.* **2** a group of people who associate together, etc.: *he's part of the jet set.* **3** *Maths.* a collection of numbers, objects, etc., that are treated as an entity: {3, the moon} is the set the two members of which are the number 3 and the moon. **4** any apparatus that receives or transmits television or radio signals. **5** *Tennis, squash, etc.* one of the units of a match, in tennis, one in which one player or pair of players must win at least six games: *Hingis lost the first set.* **6a** the number of couples required for a formation dance. **6b** a series of figures that make up a formation dance. **7a** a band's or performer's concert repertoire on a given occasion: *the set included no new songs.* **7b** a continuous performance: *the Who played two sets.* **8 make a dead set at. 8a** to attack by arguing or ridiculing. **8b** (of a woman) to try to gain the affections of (a man). ◆ *vb* **sets, setting, set. 9** (*intr*) (in square and country dancing) to perform a sequence of steps while facing towards another dancer. **10** (*usually tr*) to divide into sets: *in this school we set our older pupils for English.* ORIG C14 (in the obs. sense: a religious sect): from OF *sette,* from L *secta* SECT; later sense infl. by the verb SET[1]

seta (ˈsiːtə) *n, pl* **setae** (-tiː). (in invertebrates and plants) any bristle or bristle-like appendage. ORIG C18: from L
▸ **setaceous** (sɪˈteɪʃəs) *adj*

set about *vb* (*intr, prep*) **1** to start or begin. **2** to attack physically or verbally.

set against *vb* (*tr, prep*) **1** to balance or compare. **2** to cause to be unfriendly to.

set aside *vb* (*tr, adv*) **1** to reserve for a special purpose. **2** to discard or quash. ◆ *n* **set-aside. 3a** (in the European Union) a scheme in which a proportion of farmland is taken out of production in order to reduce surpluses or maintain or increase prices of a specific crop. **3b** (*as modifier*): *set-aside land.*

set back *vb* (*tr, adv*) **1** to hinder; impede. **2** *Inf.* to cost (a person) a specified amount. ◆ *n* **setback. 3** anything that serves to hinder or impede. **4** a recession in the upper part of a high building. **5** a steplike shelf where a wall is reduced in thickness.

set down *vb* (*tr, adv*) **1** to record. **2** to judge or regard: *he set him down as an idiot.* **3** (foll. by *to*) to attribute: *his attitude was set down to his illness.* **4** to rebuke. **5** to snub. **6** *Brit.* to allow (passengers) to alight from a bus, etc.

set forth *vb* (*adv*) *Formal or arch.* **1** (*tr*) to state, express, or utter. **2** (*intr*) to start out on a journey.

Seth ★ (sɛθ) *n Old Testament.* Adam's third son, given by God in place of the murdered Abel (Genesis 4:25).

SETI (ˈsɛtɪ) *n acronym for* Search for Extraterrestrial Intelligence; a scientific programme attempting, by radio transmissions, to make contact with beings from other planets.

setiferous (sɪˈtɪfərəs) *or* **setigerous** (sɪˈtɪdʒərəs) *adj Biol.* bearing bristles. ORIG C19: see SETA, -FEROUS, -GEROUS

set in *vb (intr, adv)* **1** to become established: *the winter has set in.* **2** (of wind) to blow or (of current) to move towards shore. ♦ *adj* **set-in.** **3** (of a part) made separately and then added to a larger whole: *a set-in sleeve.*

setline ('sɛt,laɪn) *n* any of various types of fishing line that consist of a long suspended line having shorter hooked and baited lines attached.

set off *vb (adv)* **1** *(intr)* to embark on a journey. **2** *(tr)* to cause (a person) to act or do something, such as laugh. **3** *(tr)* to cause to explode. **4** *(tr)* to act as a foil or contrast to: *that brooch sets your dress off well.* **5** *(tr) Accounting.* to cancel a credit on (one account) against a debit on another. ♦ *n* **setoff.** **6** anything that serves as a counterbalance. **7** anything that serves to contrast with or enhance something else; foil. **8** a cross claim brought by a debtor that partly offsets the creditor's claim.

set-off *n Printing.* a fault in which ink is transferred from a heavily inked or undried printed sheet to the sheet next to it in a pile.

set on *vb* **1** *(prep)* Also: **set upon.** to attack or cause to attack: *they set the dogs on him.* **2** *(tr, adv)* to instigate or incite; urge.

Seton ★ ('siːtᵊn) *n* **Ernest Thompson.** 1860–1946, US author and illustrator of animal books, born in England.

Seto Naikai ★ ('sɛtəu 'naɪkaɪ) *n* transliteration of the Japanese name for the **Inland Sea.**

setose ('siːtəus) *adj Biol.* covered with setae; bristly. ORIG C17: from L *saetōsus,* from *saeta* a bristle

set out *vb (adv, mainly tr)* **1** to present, arrange, or display. **2** to give a full account of: *he set out the matter in full.* **3** to plan or lay out (a garden, etc.). **4** *(intr)* to begin or embark on an undertaking, esp. a journey.

set piece *n* **1** a work of literature, music, etc., often having a conventional or prescribed theme, intended to create an impressive effect. **2** a display of fireworks. **3** *Sport.* a rehearsed team manoeuvre usually attempted at a restart of play.

setscrew ('sɛt,skruː) *n* a screw that fits into the boss or hub of a wheel, coupling, cam, etc., and prevents motion of the part relative to the shaft on which it is mounted.

set square *n* a thin flat piece of plastic, metal, etc., in the shape of a right-angled triangle, used in technical drawing.

sett *or* **set** (sɛt) *n* **1** a small rectangular paving block made of stone. **2** the burrow of a badger. **3a** a square in a pattern of tartan. **3b** the pattern itself. ORIG C19: var. of SET[1] (n)

settee (sɛ'tiː) *n* a seat, for two or more people, with a back and usually with arms. ORIG C18: changed from SETTLE[2]

setter ('sɛtə) *n* any of various breeds of large long-haired gun dog trained to point out game by standing rigid.

set theory *n Maths.* the branch of mathematics concerned with the properties and interrelationships of sets.

setting ('sɛtɪŋ) *n* **1** the surroundings in which something is set. **2** the scenery, properties, or background used to create the location for a stage play, film, etc. **3** *Music.* a composition consisting of a certain text and music arranged for it. **4** the metal mounting and surround of a gem. **5** the tableware, cutlery, etc., for a single place at table. **6** any of a set of points on a scale or dial that can be selected to control the speed, temperature, etc., at which a machine operates.

settle[1] ('sɛtᵊl) *vb* **settles, settling, settled.** **1** *(tr)* to put in order: *he settled his affairs before he died.* **2** to arrange or be arranged in a fixed or comfortable position: *he settled himself by the fire.* **3** *(intr)* to come to rest or a halt: *a bird settled on the hedge.* **4** to take up or cause to take up residence: *the family settled in the country.* **5** to establish or become established in a way of life, job, etc. **6** *(tr)* to migrate to and form a community; colonize. **7** to make or become quiet, calm, or stable. **8** to cause (sediment) to sink to the bottom, as in a liquid, or (of sediment) to sink thus. **9** to subside or cause to subside: *the dust settled.* **10** (sometimes foll. by *up*) to pay off or account for (a bill, debt, etc.). **11** *(tr)* to decide or dispose of: *to settle an argument.* **12** *(intr;* often foll. by *on* or *upon)* to agree or fix: *to settle upon a plan.* **13** *(tr;* usually foll. by *on* or *upon)* to secure (title, property, etc.) to a person: *he settled his property on his wife.* **14** to determine (a legal dispute, etc.) by agreement of the parties without resort to court action (esp. in **settle out of court**). ORIG OE *setlan*
▸ **'settleable** *adj*

settle[2] ('sɛtᵊl) *n* a seat, for two or more people, usually made of wood with a high back and arms, and sometimes having a storage space in the boxlike seat. ORIG OE *setl*

settle down *vb (adv, mainly intr)* **1** *(also tr)* to make or become quiet and orderly. **2** (often foll. by *to*) to apply oneself diligently: *please settle down to work.* **3** to adopt an orderly and routine way of life, esp. after marriage.

settle for *vb (intr, prep)* to accept or agree to in spite of dispute or dissatisfaction.

settlement ('sɛtᵊlmənt) *n* **1** the act or state of settling or being settled. **2** the establishment of a new region; colonization. **3** a place newly settled; colony. **4** a community formed by members of a group, esp. of a religious sect. **5** a public building used to provide educational and general welfare facilities for persons living in deprived areas. **6** a subsidence of all or part of a structure. **7a** the payment of an outstanding account, invoice, charge, etc. **7b** *(as modifier): settlement day.* **8** an agreement reached in matters of finance, business, etc. **9** *Law.* **9a** a conveyance, usually to trustees, of property to be enjoyed by several persons in succession. **9b** the deed conveying such property.

settler ('sɛtlə) *n* a person who settles in a new country or a colony.

settlings ('sɛtlɪŋz) *pl n* any matter that has settled at the bottom of a liquid.

set to *vb (intr, adv)* **1** to begin working. **2** to start fighting. ♦ *n* **set-to.** **3** *Inf.* a brief disagreement or fight.

set-top box *n* a device that converts the signals from a digital television broadcast into a form which can be viewed on a standard analogue television set.

Setúbal ★ (*Portuguese* sə'tuβal) *n* a port in SW Portugal, on **Setúbal Bay** south of Lisbon: an earthquake in 1755 destroyed most of the old town. Pop.: 83 550 (1991).

set up *vb (adv, mainly tr)* **1** *(also intr)* to put into a position of power, etc. **2** *(also intr)* to begin or enable (someone) to begin (a new venture), as by acquiring or providing means, etc. **3** to build or construct: *to set up a shed.* **4** to raise or produce: *to set up a wail.* **5** to advance or propose: *to set up a theory.* **6** to restore the health of: *the sea air will set you up again.* **7** to establish (a record). **8** *Inf.* to cause (a person) to be blamed, accused, etc. ♦ *n* **setup.** **9** *Inf.* the way in which anything is organized or arranged. **10** *Sl.* an event the result of which is prearranged: *it's a setup.* **11** a prepared arrangement of materials, machines, etc., for a job or undertaking. ♦ *adj* **set-up.** **12** physically well-built.

Seurat ★ (*French* sœra) *n* **Georges** (ʒɔrʒ). 1859–91, French painter. He developed the pointillist technique, as in *Dimanche à la Grande-Jatte* (1886).

Sevan ★ (sɛ'vɑːn) *n* **Lake.** a lake in Armenia, at an altitude of 1914 m (6279 ft). Area: 1417 sq. km (547 sq. miles).

Sevastopol ★ (*Russian* sɪvas'tɔpəlj) *n* a port, naval base, and resort in S Ukraine, on the Black Sea: captured and destroyed by British, French, and Turkish forces after a siege of 11 months (1854–55) during the Crimean War; taken by the Germans after a siege of 8 months (1942) during World War II. Pop.: 365 000 (1996 est.). English name: **Sebastopol.**

seven ('sɛvᵊn) *n* **1** the cardinal number that is the sum of six and one and is a prime number. **2** a numeral, 7, VII, etc., representing this number. **3** the amount or quantity that is one greater than six. **4** anything representing, represented by, or consisting of seven units, such as a playing card with seven symbols on it. **5** Also called: **seven o'clock.** seven hours after noon or midnight. ♦ *determiner* **6a** amounting to seven: *seven swans a-swimming.* **6b** *(as pron): you've eaten seven already.* ♦ See also **sevens.** ORIG OE *seofon*

Seven against Thebes ★ *pl n Greek myth.* the seven members of an expedition undertaken to regain for

Polynices, a son of Oedipus, his share in the throne of Thebes from his usurping brother Eteocles. The seven are usually listed as Polynices, Adrastus, Amphiaraus, Capaneus, Hippomedon, Tydeus, and Parthenopaeus. The campaign failed and the warring brothers killed each other in single combat before the Theban walls. See also **Adrastus.**

seven deadly sins *pl n* a fuller name for the **deadly sins.**

sevenfold ('sɛvᵊn,fəʊld) *adj* **1** equal to or having seven times as many or as much. **2** composed of seven parts. ◆ *adv* **3** by or up to seven times as many or as much.

Seven Hills of Rome ★ *pl n* the hills on which the ancient city of Rome was built: the Palatine, Capitoline, Quirinal, Caelian, Aventine, Esquiline, and Viminal.

sevens ('sɛvᵊnz) *n* (*functioning as sing*) a rugby union match or competition played with seven players on each side.

seven seas *pl n* the oceans of the world considered as the N and S Pacific, the N and S Atlantic, and the Arctic, Antarctic, and Indian Oceans.

seven-segment display *n* an arrangement of seven bars forming a square figure of eight, used in electronic displays of alphanumeric characters: any letter or figure can be represented by illuminating selected bars.

Seven Sleepers ★ *pl n* seven Christian youths from Ephesus who were walled up in a cave by the Emperor Decius in 250 A.D. and, according to legend, slept for 187 years.

seventeen ('sɛvᵊn'tiːn) *n* **1** the cardinal number that is the sum of ten and seven and is a prime number. **2** a numeral, 17, XVII, etc., representing this number. **3** the amount or quantity that is seven more than ten. **4** something represented by, representing, or consisting of 17 units. ◆ *determiner* **5a** amounting to seventeen: *seventeen attempts.* **5b** (*as pron*): *seventeen were sold.* ORIG OE *seofontīene*
▸ **'seven'teenth** *adj, n*

seventh ('sɛvᵊnθ) *adj* **1** (*usually prenominal*) **1a** coming after the sixth and before the eighth in numbering, position, etc.; being the ordinal number of *seven:* often written 7th. **1b** (*as n*): *she left on the seventh.* ◆ *n* **2a** one of seven equal parts of an object, quantity, measurement, etc. **2b** (*as modifier*): *a seventh part.* **3** the fraction equal to one divided by seven (1/7). **4** *Music.* **4a** the interval between one note and another seven notes away from it in a diatonic scale. **4b** one of two notes constituting such an interval in relation to the other. ◆ *adv* **5** Also: **seventhly.** after the sixth person, event, etc.

Seventh-Day Adventist *n* a member of that branch of the Adventists which constituted itself as a separate body after the expected Second Coming of Christ failed to be realized in 1844. They believe that Christ's coming is imminent and observe Saturday instead of Sunday as their Sabbath.

seventh heaven *n* **1** the final state of eternal bliss. **2** a state of supreme happiness.

seventy ('sɛvᵊntɪ) *n, pl* **seventies. 1** the cardinal number that is the product of ten and seven. **2** a numeral, 70, LXX, etc., representing this number. **3** (*pl*) the numbers 70–79, esp. the 70th to the 79th year of a person's life or of a particular century. **4** the amount or quantity that is seven times as big as ten. **5** something represented by, representing, or consisting of 70 units. ◆ *determiner* **6a** amounting to seventy: *the seventy varieties of fabric.* **6b** (*as pron*): *to invite seventy to the wedding.* ORIG OE *seofontig*
▸ **'seventieth** *adj, n*

Seven Wonders of the World *pl n* the seven structures considered by ancient and medieval scholars to be the most wondrous of the ancient world. The list varies, but generally consists of the Pyramids of Egypt, the Hanging Gardens of Babylon, Phidias' statue of Zeus at Olympia, the temple of Artemis at Ephesus, the mausoleum of Halicarnassus, the Colossus of Rhodes, and the Pharos (or lighthouse) of Alexandria.

Seven Years' War *n* the war (1756–63) of Britain and Prussia, who emerged in the ascendant, against France and Austria, resulting from commercial and colonial rivalry between Britain and France and from the conflict in Germany between Prussia and Austria.

sever ('sɛvə) *vb* **1** to put or be put apart. **2** to divide or be divided into parts. **3** (*tr*) to break off or dissolve (a tie, relationship, etc.). ORIG C14 *severen,* from OF, from L *sēparāre* to SEPARATE
▸ **'severable** *adj*

several ('sɛvrəl) *determiner* **1a** more than a few: *several people objected.* **1b** (*as pronoun; functioning as pl*): *several of them know.* ◆ *adj* **2** (*prenominal*) various; separate: *the members with their several occupations.* **3** (*prenominal*) distinct; different: *three several times.* **4** *Law.* capable of being dealt with separately. ORIG C15: via Anglo-F from Med. L *sēparālis,* from L *sēpār,* from *sēparāre* to SEPARATE

severally ('sɛvrəlɪ) *adv* **1** separately or distinctly. **2** each in turn.

severalty ('sɛvrəltɪ) *n, pl* **severalties. 1** the state of being several or separate. **2** (usually preceded by *in*) *Property law.* the tenure of property, esp. land, in a person's own right.

severance ('sɛvərəns) *n* **1** the act of severing or state of being severed. **2** a separation. **3** *Law.* the division into separate parts of a joint estate, contract, etc.

severance pay *n* compensation paid by a firm to employees for loss of employment.

severe (sɪ'vɪə) *adj* **1** rigorous or harsh in the treatment of others: *a severe parent.* **2** serious in appearance or manner. **3** critical or dangerous: *a severe illness.* **4** causing discomfort by its harshness: *severe weather.* **5** strictly restrained in appearance: *a severe way of dressing.* **6** hard to perform or accomplish: *a severe test.* ORIG C16: from L *sevērus*
▸ **se'verely** *adv* ▸ **severity** (sɪ'vɛrɪtɪ) *n*

Severn ★ ('sɛvᵊn) *n* **1** a river in E Wales and W England, rising in Powys and flowing northeast and east into England, then south to the Bristol Channel. Length: about 290 km (180 miles). **2** a river in SE central Canada, in Ontario, flowing northeast to Hudson Bay. Length: about 676 km (420 miles).

Severnaya Zemlya ★ (*Russian* 'sjevɪrnəjə zɪm'lja) *n* an archipelago in the Arctic Ocean off the coast of N central Russia.

Severus ★ (sɪ'vɪərəs) *n* **Lucius Septimius** (sɛp'tɪmɪəs). 146–211 A.D., Roman soldier and emperor (193–211). He waged war successfully against the Parthians (197–202) and spent his last years in Britain (208–11).

Seveso ★ (sə'veɪzəʊ) *n* a town in N Italy, near Milan: evacuated in 1976 after contamination by a poisonous cloud of dioxin gas released from a factory.

Sévigné ★ (*French* seviɲe) *n* **Marquise de,** title of *Marie de Rabutin-Chantal.* 1626–96, French writer, whose correspondence with her daughter provides an account of society during the reign of Louis XIV.

Seville ★ (sə'vɪl) *n* a port in SW Spain, on the Guadalquivir River: chief town of S Spain under the Vandals and Visigoths (5th–8th centuries); centre of Spanish colonial trade (16th–17th centuries); tourist centre. Pop.: 714 148 (1991). Ancient name: **Hispalis.** Spanish name: **Sevilla** (se'βiʎa).

Seville orange *n* **1** an orange tree of tropical and semitropical regions: grown for its bitter fruit, which is used to make marmalade. **2** the fruit of this tree.

Sèvres (*French* sɛvrə) *n* porcelain ware manufactured at Sèvres, near Paris, from 1756, characterized by the use of clear colours and elaborate decorative detail.

sew (səʊ) *vb* **sews, sewing, sewed; sewn** *or* **sewed. 1** to join or decorate (pieces of fabric, etc.) by means of a thread repeatedly passed through with a needle. **2** (*tr; often foll. by on or up*) to attach, fasten, or close by sewing. **3** (*tr*) to make (a garment, etc.) by sewing. ◆ See also **sew up.** ORIG OE *sēowan*

sewage ('suːɪdʒ) *n* waste matter from domestic or industrial establishments that is carried away in sewers or drains. ORIG C19: back formation from SEWER[1]

sewage farm *n* a place where sewage is treated, esp. for use as manure.

Seward ★ ('sjuːəd) *n* **William Henry.** 1801–72, US statesman; secretary of state (1861–69); an opponent of slavery, he was also responsible for the purchase of Alaska (1867).

Seward Peninsula ★ *n* a peninsula of W Alaska, on the Bering Strait. Length: about 290 km (180 miles).

Sewell ★ ('su:əl) *n* **Henry.** 1807–79, New Zealand statesman, born in England: first prime minister of New Zealand (1856).

sewer[1] (suə) *n* **1** a drain or pipe, esp. one that is underground, used to carry away surface water or sewage. ◆ *vb* **2** (*tr*) to provide with sewers. ORIG C15: from OF, from *essever* to drain, from Vulgar L *exaquāre* (unattested), from L EX-[1] + *aqua* water

sewer[2] ('səuə) *n* a person or thing that sews.

sewerage ('suərɪdʒ) *n* **1** an arrangement of sewers. **2** the removal of surface water or sewage by means of sewers. **3** another word for **sewage.**

sewing ('səuɪŋ) *n* **a** a piece of cloth, etc., that is sewn or to be sewn. **b** (*as modifier*): *sewing basket.*

sewing machine *n* any machine designed to sew material. It is now usually driven by electric motor but is sometimes operated by a foot treadle or by hand.

sewn (səun) *vb* a past participle of **sew.**

sew up *vb* (*tr, adv*) **1** to fasten or mend completely by sewing. **2** *US.* to acquire sole use or control of. **3** *Inf.* to complete or negotiate successfully: *to sew up a deal.*

sex (sɛks) *n* **1** the sum of the characteristics that distinguish organisms on the basis of their reproductive function. **2** either of the two categories, male or female, into which organisms are placed on this basis. **3** short for **sexual intercourse. 4** feelings or behaviour resulting from the urge to gratify the sexual instinct. **5** sexual matters in general. ◆ *modifier.* **6** of or concerning sexual matters: *sex education.* **7** based on or arising from the difference between the sexes: *sex discrimination.* ◆ *vb* **8** (*tr*) to ascertain the sex of. ORIG C14: from L *sexus*

sex- *combining form.* six: *sexcentenary.* ORIG from L

sexagenarian (ˌsɛksədʒɪ'nɛərɪən) *n* **1** a person from 60 to 69 years old. ◆ *adj* **2** being from 60 to 69 years old. **3** of or relating to a sexagenarian. ORIG C18: from L, from *sexāgēnī* sixty each, from *sexāgintā* sixty

Sexagesima (ˌsɛksə'dʒɛsɪmə) *n* the second Sunday before Lent. ORIG C16: from L: sixtieth, from *sexāgintā* sixty

sexagesimal (ˌsɛksə'dʒɛsɪməl) *adj* **1** relating to or based on the number 60: *sexagesimal measurement of angles.* ◆ *n* **2** a fraction in which the denominator is some power of 60.

sex-and-shopping *adj* (*prenomial*) (of a novel) belonging to a genre of novel in which the central character, a woman, has a number of sexual encounters, and the author mentions the name of many upmarket products.

sex appeal *n* the quality or power of attracting the opposite sex.

sexcentenary (ˌsɛksɛn'ti:nərɪ) *adj* **1** of or relating to 600 or a period of 600 years. **2** of or celebrating a 600th anniversary. ◆ *n, pl* **sexcentenaries. 3** a 600th anniversary or its celebration. ORIG C18: from L *sexcentēnī* six hundred each

sex chromosome *n* either of the chromosomes determining the sex of animals.

sexed (sɛkst) *adj* **1** (*in combination*) having a specified degree of sexuality: *undersexed.* **2** of, relating to, or having sexual differentiation.

sex hormone *n* an animal hormone affecting development and growth of reproductive organs and related parts.

sexism ('sɛksɪzəm) *n* discrimination on the basis of sex, esp. the oppression of women by men.
▸ **'sexist** *n, adj*

sexless ('sɛkslɪs) *adj* **1** having or showing no sexual differentiation. **2** having no sexual desires. **3** sexually unattractive.

sex linkage *n Genetics.* the condition in which a gene is located on a sex chromosome so that the character controlled by the gene is associated with either of the sexes.
▸ **'sex-ˌlinked** *adj*

sex object *n* someone, esp. a woman, regarded only from the point of view of someone else's sexual desires.

sexology (sɛk'sɒlədʒɪ) *n* the study of sexual behaviour in human beings.
▸ **sex'ologist** *n* ▸ **sexological** (ˌsɛksə'lɒdʒɪkəl) *adj*

sexpartite (sɛks'pɑ:taɪt) *adj* **1** (esp. of vaults, arches, etc.) divided into or composed of six parts. **2** involving six participants.

sex shop *n* a shop selling aids to sexual activity, pornographic material, etc.

sext (sɛkst) *n Chiefly RC Church.* the fourth of the seven canonical hours of the divine office or the prayers prescribed for it. ORIG C15: from Church L *sexta hōra* the sixth hour

sextan ('sɛkstən) *adj* (of a fever) marked by paroxysms that recur every fifth day. ORIG C17: from Med. L *sextana* (*febris*) (fever) of the sixth (day)

sextant ('sɛkstənt) *n* **1** an instrument used in navigation and consisting of a telescope through which a sighting of a heavenly body is taken, with protractors for determining its angular distance above the horizon. **2** a sixth part of a circle. ORIG C17: from L *sextāns* one sixth of a unit

sextet *or* **sextette** (sɛks'tɛt) *n* **1** *Music.* a group of six singers or instrumentalists or a piece of music composed for such a group. **2** a group of six people or things. ORIG C19: var. of SESTET

sextillion (sɛks'tɪljən) *n, pl* **sextillions** *or* **sextillion. 1** (in Britain, France, and Germany) the number represented as one followed by 36 zeros (10^{36}). **2** (in the US and Canada) the number represented as one followed by 21 zeros (10^{21}). ORIG C17: from F, from SEX- + *-illion,* on the model of SEPTILLION

sexto ('sɛkstəu) *n, pl* **sextos** another word for **sixmo.**

sexton ('sɛkstən) *n* a person employed to act as caretaker of a church and often also as a bell-ringer, grave-digger, etc. ORIG C14: from OF, from Med. L *sacristānus* SACRISTAN

sextuple ('sɛkstjupəl) *n* **1** a quantity or number six times as great as another. ◆ *adj* **2** six times as much or as many. **3** consisting of six parts or members. ORIG C17: L *sextus* sixth + *-uple,* as in QUADRUPLE

sextuplet ('sɛkstjuplɪt) *n* **1** one of six offspring at one birth. **2** a group of six. **3** *Music.* a group of six notes played in a time value of four.

sexual ('sɛksjuəl) *adj* **1** of or characterized by sex. **2** (of reproduction) characterized by the union of male and female gametes. Cf. **asexual** (sense 2). ORIG C17: from LL *sexuālis*
▸ **sexuality** (ˌsɛksju'ælɪtɪ) *n* ▸ **'sexually** *adv*

sexual harassment *n* the persistent unwelcome directing of sexual remarks and looks, and unnecessary physical contact, at a person, usually a woman, esp. in the work place.

sexual intercourse *n* the sexual act in which the male's erect penis is inserted into the female's vagina; copulation; coitus.

sexually transmitted disease *n* any of various diseases, such as syphilis or gonorrhoea, transmitted by sexual intercourse. Also called: **venereal disease.**

sexual selection *n* an evolutionary process in animals, in which selection by females of males with certain characters results in the preservation of these characters in the species.

sex up *vb* (*tr, adv*) *Inf.* to make (something) more interesting or exciting: *the BBC decided to sex up the book's title.*

sex worker *n* a prostitute.

sexy ('sɛksɪ) *adj* **sexier, sexiest.** *Inf.* **1** provoking or intended to provoke sexual interest: *a sexy dress.* **2** feeling sexual interest; aroused. **3** interesting, exciting, or trendy: *a sexy project; a sexy new car.*
▸ **'sexily** *adv* ▸ **'sexiness** *n*

Seychelles ★ (seɪ'ʃɛl, -'ʃɛlz) *pl n* a group of volcanic islands in the W Indian Ocean: taken by the British from the French in 1744: became an independent republic within the Commonwealth in 1976, incorporating the British Indian Ocean Territory islands of Aldabra,

Farquhar and Desroches. Languages: Creole, English, and French. Religion: Roman Catholic majority. Currency: rupee. Capital: Victoria. Pop.: 80 000 (1999 est.). Area: 455 sq. km (176 sq. miles).

Seyhan ★ (seɪˈhɑːn) *n* another name for **Adana**.

Seymour ★ (ˈsiːmɔː) *n* **Jane.** ?1509–37, third wife of Henry VIII of England; mother of Edward VI.

sf *or* **sfz** *Music. abbrev. for* sforzando.

SF *or* **sf** *abbrev. for* science fiction.

SFA *abbrev. for:* **1** Scottish Football Association. **2** sweet Fanny Adams. See **fanny adams.**

Sfax ★ (sfæks) *n* a port in E Tunisia, on the Gulf of Gabès: the second largest town in Tunisia; commercial centre of a phosphate region. Pop.: 230 900 (1994).

SFO *abbrev. for* Serious Fraud Office: the department of the British government which investigates cases of serious financial fraud.

Sforza ★ (*Italian* ˈsfɔrtsa) *n* **1** Count **Carlo** (ˈkarlo). 1873–1952, Italian statesman; leader of the anti-Fascist opposition. **2 Francesco** (franˈtʃesko). 1401–66, duke of Milan (1450–66). **3** his father **Giacomuzzo** (dʒakoˈmuttso) or **Muzio** (ˈmuttsjo), original name *Attendolo.* 1369–1424, Italian condottiere and founder of the dynasty that ruled Milan (1450–1535). **4 Lodovico** (lodoˈviːko), called *the Moor.* 1451–1508, duke of Milan (1494–1500), but effective ruler from 1480; patron of Leonardo da Vinci.

sforzando (sfɔːˈtsɑːndəʊ) *or* **sforzato** (sfɔːˈtsɑːtəʊ) *Music.* ◆ *adj, adv* **1** to be played with strong initial attack. Abbrevs.: **sf, sfz.** ◆ *n* **2** a symbol, mark, etc., indicating this. ORIG C19: from It., from *sforzare* to force, from Vulgar L *fortiāre* (unattested) to FORCE

SG *abbrev. for* solicitor general.

sgd *abbrev. for* signed.

S. Glam *abbrev. for* South Glamorgan.

SGML *abbrev. for* standard generalized mark-up language: an international standard for defining the structure and formatting of electronic texts.

sgraffito ★ (sgræˈfiːtəʊ) *n, pl* **sgraffiti** (-tɪ). **1** a technique in mural or ceramic decoration in which the top layer of glaze, plaster, etc., is incised with a design to reveal parts of the ground. **2** such a decoration. ORIG C18: from It., from *sgraffire* to scratch

's Gravenhage ★ (sxraːvənˈhaːxə) *n* the Dutch name for (The) **Hague.**

Sgt *abbrev. for* Sergeant.

sh (*spelling pron* ʃʃʃ) *interj* an exclamation to request silence or quiet.

sh. *abbrev. for:* **1** *Stock Exchange.* share. **2** sheep. **3** *Bookbinding.* sheet.

Shaanxi (ˈʃænˈʃiː) *or* **Shensi** ★ *n* a province of NW China: one of the earliest centres of Chinese civilization; largely mountainous. Capital: Xi An. Pop.: 35 700 000 (1997 est.). Area: 195 800 sq. km (75 598 sq. miles).

Shaba ★ (ˈʃɑːbə) *n* a region of the SE Democratic Republic of Congo: site of secessionist movement during the 1960s and declared itself independent again in 1993: important for hydroelectric power and rich mineral resources (copper and tin ore). Area: 496 964 sq. km (191 878 sq. miles). Former name (until 1972): **Katanga.**

shabby (ˈʃæbɪ) *adj* **shabbier, shabbiest. 1** threadbare or dilapidated in appearance. **2** wearing worn and dirty clothes. **3** mean or unworthy: *shabby treatment.* **4** dirty or squalid. ORIG C17: from OE *sceabb* scab
▸ ˈ**shabbily** *adv* ▸ ˈ**shabbiness** *n*

Shache (ˈʃæˈtʃeɪ), **Soche,** *or* **So-ch'e** ★ *n* a town in W China, in the W Xinjiang Uygur AR: a centre of the caravan trade between China, India, and Transcaspian areas. Also called: **Yarkand.**

shack (ʃæk) *n* **1** a roughly built hut. ◆ *vb* **2** See **shack up.** ORIG C19: ?from dialect *shackly* ramshackle, from dialect *shack* to shake

shackle (ˈʃækᵊl) *n* **1** (*often pl*) a metal ring or fastening, usually part of a pair used to secure a person's wrists or ankles. **2** (*often pl*) anything that confines or restricts freedom. **3** a U-shaped bracket, the open end of which is closed by a bolt (**shackle pin**), used for securing ropes, chains, etc. ◆ *vb* **shackles, shackling, shackled.** (*tr*) **4** to confine with or as if with shackles. **5** to fasten or connect with a shackle. ORIG OE *sceacel*
▸ ˈ**shackler** *n*

Shackleton ★ (ˈʃækəltən) *n* Sir **Ernest Henry.** 1874–1922, British explorer. He commanded three expeditions to the Antarctic (1907–09; 1914–17; 1921–22), during which the south magnetic pole was located (1909).

shack-shack *n Caribbean.* **1** the dried pod of a tree, esp. of the flamboyant tree, which rattles in the wind. **2** a pair of maracas made from dried coconut shells or gourds containing stones or seeds. **3** a child's rattle. ORIG from *sheke-sheke,* the Yoruban name for the flamboyant tree

shack up *vb* (*intr, adv;* usually foll. by *with*) *Sl.* to live, esp. with a lover.

shad (ʃæd) *n, pl* **shad** *or* **shads.** any of various herring-like food fishes that migrate from the sea to fresh water to spawn. ORIG OE *sceadd*

Shadbolt ★ (ˈʃædˌbəʊlt) *n* **Maurice.** born 1932, New Zealand novelist.

shaddock (ˈʃædək) *n* another name for **pomelo** (sense 1). ORIG C17: after Captain *Shaddock,* who brought its seed from the East Indies to Jamaica in 1696

shade (ʃeɪd) *n* **1** relative darkness produced by the blocking out of light. **2** a place made relatively darker or cooler than other areas by the blocking of light, esp. sunlight. **3** a position of relative obscurity. **4** something used to provide a shield or protection from a direct source of light, such as a lampshade. **5** a darker area indicated in a painting, drawing, etc., by shading. **6** a colour that varies slightly from a standard colour: *a darker shade of green.* **7** a slight amount: *a shade of difference.* **8** *Literary.* a ghost. ◆ *vb* **shades, shading, shaded.** (*mainly tr*) **9** to screen or protect from heat, light, view, etc. **10** to make darker or dimmer. **11** to represent (a darker area) in (a painting, etc.), by means of hatching, etc. **12** (*also intr*) to change or cause to change slightly. **13** to lower (a price) slightly. ORIG OE *sceadu*
▸ ˈ**shadeless** *adj*

shades (ʃeɪdz) *pl n* **1** gathering darkness at nightfall. **2** *Sl.* sunglasses. **3** (*often cap.;* preceded by *the*) a literary term for **Hades. 4** (foll. by *of*) undertones: *shades of my father!*

shading (ˈʃeɪdɪŋ) *n* the graded areas of tone, lines, dots, etc., indicating light and dark in a painting or drawing.

shadoof (ʃəˈduːf) *n* a mechanism for raising water, consisting of a pivoted pole with a bucket at one end and a counterweight at the other, esp. as used in Egypt. ORIG C19: from Egyptian Ar.

shadow (ˈʃædəʊ) *n* **1** a dark image or shape cast on a surface by the interception of light rays by an opaque body. **2** an area of relative darkness. **3** the dark portions of a picture. **4** a hint or faint semblance: *beyond a shadow of a doubt.* **5** a remnant or vestige: *a shadow of one's past self.* **6** a reflection. **7** a threatening influence: *a shadow over one's happiness.* **8** a spectre. **9** an inseparable companion. **10** a person who trails another in secret, such as a detective. **11** *Med.* a dark area on an X-ray film representing an opaque structure or part. **12** (in Jungian psychology) the archetype that represents man's animal ancestors. **13** *Arch.* shelter. **14** (*modifier*) *Brit.* designating a member or members of the main opposition party in Parliament who would hold ministerial office if their party were in power: *shadow cabinet.* ◆ *vb* (*tr*) **15** to cast a shadow over. **16** to make dark or gloomy. **17** to shade from light. **18** to follow or trail secretly. **19** (often foll. by *forth*) to represent vaguely. ORIG OE *sceadwe,* oblique case of *sceadu* shade
▸ ˈ**shadower** *n*

shadow-box *vb* (*intr*) *Boxing.* to practise blows and footwork against an imaginary opponent.
▸ ˈ**shadow-**ˌ**boxing** *n*

shadowgraph (ˈʃædəʊˌgrɑːf) *n* **1** a silhouette made by casting a shadow on a lighted surface. **2** another name for **radiograph.**

shadow play *n* a theatrical entertainment using shadows thrown by puppets or actors onto a lighted screen.

shadow price *n Econ.* the calculated price of a good or service for which no market price exists.

shadowy (ˈʃædəʊɪ) *adj* **1** dark; shady. **2** resembling a shadow in faintness. **3** illusory or imaginary. **4** mysterious or secretive: *a shadowy underworld figure.*
▸ **ˈshadowiness** *n*

Shadrach ★ (ˈʃædræk, ˈʃeɪ-) *n Old Testament.* one of Daniel's three companions, who, together with Meshach and Abednego, was miraculously saved from destruction in Nebuchadnezzar's fiery furnace (Daniel 3:12–30).

shady (ˈʃeɪdɪ) *adj* **shadier, shadiest. 1** shaded. **2** affording or casting a shade. **3** quiet or concealed. **4** *Inf.* questionable as to honesty or legality.
▸ **ˈshadily** *adv* ▸ **ˈshadiness** *n*

SHAEF (ʃeɪf) (in WWII) *n acronym for* Supreme Headquarters Allied Expeditionary Forces.

Shaffer ★ (ˈʃæfə) *n* Sir **Peter.** born 1926, British dramatist. His plays include *The Royal Hunt of the Sun* (1964), *Equus* (1973), and *Amadeus* (1979).

shaft (ʃɑːft) *n* **1** the long narrow pole that forms the body of a spear, arrow, etc. **2** something directed at a person in the manner of a missile. **3** a ray or streak, esp. of light. **4** a rod or pole forming the handle of a hammer, golf club, etc. **5** a revolving rod that transmits motion or power. **6** one of the two wooden poles by which an animal is harnessed to a vehicle. **7** *Anat.* the middle part of a long bone. **8** the middle part of a column or pier, between the base and the capital. **9** *Archit.* a column that supports a vaulting rib, sometimes one of a set. **10** a vertical passageway through a building, as for a lift. **11** a vertical passageway into a mine. **12** *Ornithol.* the central rib of a feather. **13** an archaic or literary word for **arrow.** ◆ *vb* **14** *US & Canad. sl.* to trick or cheat. ORIG OE *sceaft*

Shaftesbury ★ (ˈʃɑːftsbərɪ, -brɪ) *n* **1 1st Earl of,** title of *Anthony Ashley Cooper.* 1621–83, English statesman, a major figure in the Whig opposition to Charles II. **2 7th Earl of,** title of *Anthony Ashley Cooper.* 1801–85, British evangelical churchman and social reformer.

shag¹ (ʃæg) *n* **1** a matted tangle, esp. of hair, etc. **2** a napped fabric, usually a rough wool. **3** shredded coarse tobacco. ORIG OE *sceacga*

shag² (ʃæg) *n* another name for the **green cormorant** (*Phalacrocorax aristotelis*). ORIG C16: special use of SHAG¹, with reference to its crest

shag³ (ʃæg) *Brit. sl.* ◆ *vb* **shags, shagging, shagged. 1** *Taboo.* to have sexual intercourse with (a person). **2** (*tr;* often foll. by *out; usually passive*) to exhaust. ◆ *n* **3** *Taboo.* an act of sexual intercourse. ORIG C20: from ?

shaggy (ˈʃægɪ) *adj* **shaggier, shaggiest. 1** having or covered with rough unkempt fur, hair, wool, etc.: *a shaggy dog.* **2** rough or unkempt.
▸ **ˈshaggily** *adv* ▸ **ˈshagginess** *n*

shaggy dog story *n Inf.* a long rambling joke ending in a deliberate anticlimax, such as a pointless punch line.

shagreen (ʃæˈgriːn) *n* **1** the rough skin of certain sharks and rays, used as an abrasive. **2** a rough grainy leather made from certain animal hides. ORIG C17: from F *chagrin,* from Turkish *çagri* rump

shah (ʃɑː) *n* a ruler of certain Middle Eastern countries, esp. (formerly) Iran. ORIG C16: from Persian: king
▸ **ˈshahdom** *n*

Shah Jahan ★ (dʒəˈhɑːn) *n* 1592–1666, Mogul emperor (1628–58), who created the Taj Mahal and the Pearl Mosque at Agra.

Shahjahanpur ★ (ˌʃɑːdʒəˌhɑːnˈpʊə) *n* a city in N India, in central Uttar Pradesh: founded in 1647 in the reign of Shah Jahan. Pop.: 237 713 (1991).

Shah of Iran ★ (ʃɑː) *n* See (Mohammed Reza) **Pahlavi¹.**

Shaka *or* **Chaka ★** (ˈʃaka) *n* died 1828, Zulu military leader, who founded the Zulu Empire in southern Africa.

shake (ʃeɪk) *vb* **shakes, shaking, shook, shaken. 1** to move or cause to move up and down or back and forth with short quick movements. **2** to sway or totter or cause to sway or totter. **3** to clasp or grasp (the hand) of (a person) in greeting, agreement, etc.: *he shook John's hand.* **4 shake hands.** to clasp hands in greeting, agreement, etc. **5 shake on it.** *Inf.* to shake hands in agreement, reconciliation, etc. **6** to bring or come to a specified condition by or as if by shaking: *he shook free and ran.* **7** (*tr*) to wave or brandish: *he shook his sword.* **8** (*tr;* often foll. by *up*) to rouse or agitate. **9** (*tr*) to shock, disturb, or upset: *he was shaken by the news.* **10** (*tr*) to undermine or weaken: *the crisis shook his faith.* **11** to mix (dice) by rattling in a cup or the hand before throwing. **12** *Austral. old-fashioned sl.* to steal. **13** (*tr*) *US & Canad. inf.* to get rid of. **14** *Music.* to perform a trill on (a note). **15 shake in one's shoes.** to tremble with fear or apprehension. **16 shake one's head.** to indicate disagreement or disapproval by moving the head from side to side. ◆ *n* **17** the act or an instance of shaking. **18** a tremor or vibration. **19 the shakes.** *Inf.* a state of uncontrollable trembling or a condition that causes it, such as a fever. **20** *Inf.* a very short period of time: *in half a shake.* **21** a fissure or crack in timber or rock. **22** an instance of shaking dice before casting. **23** *Music.* another word for **trill** (sense 1). **24** an informal name for **earthquake. 25** short for **milk shake. 26 no great shakes.** *Inf.* of no great merit or value. ◆ See also **shake down, shake off, shake up.** ORIG OE *sceacan*
▸ **ˈshakable** *or* **ˈshakeable** *adj*

shake down *vb* (*adv*) **1** to fall or settle or cause to fall or settle by shaking. **2** (*tr*) *US sl.* to extort money from, esp. by blackmail. **3** (*tr*) *Inf., chiefly US.* to submit (a vessel, etc.) to a shakedown test. **4** (*intr*) to go to bed, esp. to a makeshift bed. ◆ *n* **shakedown. 5** *US sl.* a swindle or act of extortion. **6** a makeshift bed, esp. of straw, blankets, etc. **7** *Inf., chiefly US.* **7a** a voyage to test the performance of a ship or aircraft or to familiarize the crew with their duties. **7b** (*as modifier*): *a shakedown run.*

shake off *vb* (*adv*) **1** to remove or be removed with or as if with a quick movement: *she shook off her depression.* **2** (*tr*) to escape from; elude: *they shook off the police.*

shaker (ˈʃeɪkə) *n* **1** a person or thing that shakes. **2** a container from which a condiment is shaken. **3** a container in which the ingredients of alcoholic drinks are shaken together.

Shakers (ˈʃeɪkəz) *pl n* **the.** an American millenarian sect, founded in 1747 as an offshoot of the Quakers, given to ecstatic shaking and practising common ownership of property.

Shakespeare ★ (ˈʃeɪkspɪə) *n* **William.** 1564–1616, English dramatist and poet. He was born and died at Stratford-upon-Avon but spent most of his life as an actor and playwright in London. His plays with approximate dates of composition are: *Henry VI, Parts I–III* (1590); *Richard III* (1592); *The Comedy of Errors* (1592); *Titus Andronicus* (1593); *The Taming of the Shrew* (1593); *The Two Gentlemen of Verona* (1594); *Love's Labour's Lost* (1594); *Romeo and Juliet* (1594); *Richard II* (1595); *A Midsummer Night's Dream* (1595); *King John* (1596); *The Merchant of Venice* (1596); *Henry IV, Parts I–II* (1597); *Much Ado about Nothing* (1598); *Henry V* (1598); *Julius Caesar* (1599); *As You Like It* (1599); *Twelfth Night* (1599); *Hamlet* (1600); *The Merry Wives of Windsor* (1600); *Troilus and Cressida* (1601); *All's Well that ends Well* (1602); *Measure for Measure* (1604); *Othello* (1604); *King Lear* (1605); *Macbeth* (1605); *Antony and Cleopatra* (1606); *Coriolanus* (1607); *Timon of Athens* (1607); *Pericles* (1608); *Cymbeline* (1609); *The Winter's Tale* (1610); *The Tempest* (1611); and, possibly in collaboration with John Fletcher, *Two Noble Kinsmen* (1612) and *Henry VIII* (1612). His *Sonnets,* variously addressed to a fair young man and a dark lady, were published in 1609.

Shakespearean *or* **Shakespearian** (ʃeɪkˈspɪərɪən) *adj* **1** of, relating to, or characteristic of Shakespeare or his works. ◆ *n* **2** a student of or specialist in Shakespeare's works.

Shakespearean sonnet *n* a sonnet form developed in 16th-century England and employed by Shakespeare, having the rhyme scheme a b a b c d c d e f e f g g.

shake up *vb* (*tr, adv*) **1** to shake in order to mix. **2** to reorganize drastically. **3** to stir. **4** to restore the shape of (a pillow, etc.). **5** *Inf.* to shock mentally or physically. ◆ *n* **shake-up. 6** *Inf.* a radical reorganization.

Shakhty ★ (*Russian* ˈʃaxtɪ) *n* an industrial city in W Russia: the chief town of the E Donets Basin. Pop.: 230 000 (1995 est.).

shako ('ʃækəʊ) *n, pl* **shakos** *or* **shakoes.** a tall usually cylindrical military headdress, having a plume and often a peak. ORIG C19: via F from Hungarian *csákó*, from MHG *zacke* a sharp point

shaky ('ʃeɪkɪ) *adj* **shakier, shakiest. 1** tending to shake or tremble. **2** liable to prove defective. **3** uncertain or questionable: *your arguments are very shaky.*
▸ '**shakily** *adv* ▸ '**shakiness** *n*

shale (ʃeɪl) *n* a dark fine-grained sedimentary rock formed by compression of successive layers of clay. ORIG OE *scealu* shell
▸ '**shaly** *adj*

shale oil *n* an oil distilled from shales and used as fuel.

shall (ʃæl; *unstressed* ʃəl) *vb past* **should.** (takes an infinitive without *to* or an implied infinitive) used as an auxiliary: **1** (esp. with *I* or *we* as subject) to make the future tense: *we shall see you tomorrow.* Cf. **will**[1] (sense 1). **2** (with *you, he, she, it, they,* or a noun as subject) **2a** to indicate determination on the part of the speaker, as in issuing a threat: *you shall pay for this!* **2b** to indicate compulsion, now esp. in official documents. **2c** to indicate certainty or inevitability: *our day shall come.* **3** (*with any noun or pronoun as subject, esp. in conditional clauses or clauses expressing doubt*) to indicate nonspecific futurity: *I don't think I shall ever see her again.* ORIG OE *sceal*

USAGE NOTE The usual rule given for the use of *shall* and *will* is that where the meaning is one of an action in the future, *shall* is used with *I* and *we* and *will* with all other subjects: *I shall go tomorrow; they will be there now.* Where the meaning involves command, obligation, or determination, the reverse is true: *it shall be done; I will definitely go.* However, *shall* has largely been ousted in favour of *will*, which has become the commonest form of the future with all subjects.

shallop ('ʃæləp) *n* a light boat used for rowing in shallow water. ORIG C16: from F *chaloupe*, from Du. *sloep* sloop

shallot (ʃə'lɒt) *n* **1** an alliaceous plant cultivated for its edible bulb. **2** the bulb of this plant, which divides into small sections and is used in cooking for flavouring. ORIG C17: from OF, from *eschaloigne*, from L *Ascalōnia caepa* Ascalonian onion, from *Ascalon*, a Palestinian town

shallow ('ʃæləʊ) *adj* **1** having little depth. **2** lacking intellectual or mental depth or subtlety. ◆ *n* **3** (*often pl*) a shallow place in a body of water. ◆ *vb* **4** to make or become shallow. ORIG C15: rel. to OE *sceald* shallow
▸ '**shallowly** *adv* ▸ '**shallowness** *n*

shalom aleichem *Hebrew.* (ʃa'lɔm a'lexɛm) *sentence substitute.* peace be to you: used by Jews as a greeting or farewell. Often shortened to **shalom.**

shalt (ʃælt) *vb Arch. or dialect.* (used with the pronoun *thou*) a singular form of the present tense (indicative mood) of **shall.**

shalwar ('ʃæwɑː) *pl n* loose-fitting trousers tapering to a narrow fit around the ankles, worn in the Indian subcontinent, often with a kameez. ORIG from Urdu and Persian *shalwār*

sham (ʃæm) *n* **1** anything that is not what it appears to be. **2** something false or fictitious that purports to be genuine. **3** a person who pretends to be something other than he or she is. ◆ *adj* **4** counterfeit or false. ◆ *vb* **shams, shamming, shammed. 5** to assume the appearance of (something); counterfeit: *to sham illness.* ORIG C17: ? a N English dialect var. of SHAME

shaman ('ʃæmən) *n* **1** a priest of shamanism. **2** a medicine man of a similar religion, esp. among certain tribes of North American Indians. ORIG C17: from Russian *shaman*, ult. from Sansk. *śrama* religious exercise

shamanism ('ʃæməˌnɪzəm) *n* **1** the religion of certain peoples of northern Asia, based on the belief that the world is pervaded by good and evil spirits who can be influenced or controlled only by the shamans. **2** any similar religion involving forms of spiritualism.
▸ '**shamanist** *n, adj*

Shamash ★ ('ʃɑːmæʃ) *n* the sun god of Assyria and Babylonia. ORIG from Akkadian: sun

shamateur ('ʃæmətə) *n* a sportsperson who is officially an amateur but accepts payment. ORIG C20: from SHAM + AMATEUR

shamble ('ʃæmbᵊl) *vb* **shambles, shambling, shambled. 1** (*intr*) to walk or move along in an awkward or unsteady way. ◆ *n* **2** an awkward or unsteady walk. ORIG C17: from *shamble* (adj) ungainly, ?from *shamble legs* legs resembling those of a meat vendor's table; see SHAMBLES
▸ '**shambling** *adj, n*

shambles ('ʃæmbᵊlz) *n* (*functioning as sing or pl*) **1** a place of great disorder: *the room was a shambles after the party.* **2** a place where animals are brought to be slaughtered. **3** any place of slaughter or carnage. ORIG C14 *shamble* table used by meat vendors, from OE *sceamel* stool, from LL *scamellum* a small bench, from L *scamnum* stool

shambolic (ʃæm'bɒlɪk) *adj Inf.* completely disorganized; chaotic. ORIG C20: from SHAMBLES

shame (ʃeɪm) *n* **1** a painful emotion resulting from an awareness of having done something dishonourable, unworthy, etc. **2** capacity to feel such an emotion. **3** ignominy or disgrace. **4** a person or thing that causes this. **5** an occasion for regret, disappointment, etc.: *it's a shame you can't come with us.* **6 put to shame. 6a** to disgrace. **6b** to surpass totally. ◆ *vb* **shames, shaming, shamed.** (*tr*) **7** to cause to feel shame. **8** to bring shame on. **9** (often foll. by *into*) to compel through a sense of shame. **10 name and shame.** See **name** (sense 8). ◆ *interj* **11** *S. African inf.* **11a** an expression of sympathy. **11b** an expression of pleasure or endearment. ORIG OE *scamu*
▸ '**shamable** *or* '**shameable** *adj*

shamefaced ('ʃeɪmˌfeɪst) *adj* **1** bashful or modest. **2** showing a sense of shame. ORIG C16: alteration of earlier *shamefast*, from OE *sceamfaest*
▸ **shamefacedly** (ˌʃeɪm'feɪsɪdlɪ) *adv*

shameful ('ʃeɪmfʊl) *adj* causing or deserving shame.
▸ '**shamefully** *adv* ▸ '**shamefulness** *n*

shameless ('ʃeɪmlɪs) *adj* **1** having no sense of shame. **2** without decency or modesty.
▸ '**shamelessly** *adv* ▸ '**shamelessness** *n*

Shamir ★ (ʃæ'mɪə) *n* **Yitzhak** ('jɪtʒæk). born 1915, Israeli statesman, born in Poland: prime minister (1983–84; 1986–92).

shammy ('ʃæmɪ) *n, pl* **shammies.** *Inf.* another word for **chamois** (sense 3). Also called: **shammy leather.** ORIG C18: variant of CHAMOIS

Shamo ★ ('ʃɑː'məʊ) *n* transliteration of the Chinese name for the **Gobi.**

shampoo (ʃæm'puː) *n* **1** a preparation of soap or detergent to wash the hair. **2** a similar preparation for washing carpets, etc. **3** the process of shampooing. ◆ *vb* **shampoos, shampooing, shampooed.** (*tr*) **4** to wash (the hair, etc.) with such a preparation. ORIG C18: from Hindi, from *chāmpnā* to knead

shamrock ('ʃæmˌrɒk) *n* a plant having leaves divided into three leaflets: the national emblem of Ireland. ORIG C16: from Irish Gaelic *seamrōg*, dim. of *seamar* clover

shamus ('ʃɑːməs, 'ʃeɪ-) *n, pl* **shamuses.** *US sl.* a police or private detective. ORIG prob. from *shammes* caretaker of a synagogue, infl. by Irish *Séamas* James

Shandong ('ʃæn'dʌŋ) *or* **Shantung** ★ *n* a province of NE China, on the Yellow Sea and the Gulf of Chihli: part of the earliest organized state of China (1520–1030 B.C.); consists chiefly of the fertile plain of the lower Yellow River, with mountains over 1500 m (5000 ft) high in the centre. Capital: Jinan. Pop.: 87 850 000 (1997 est.). Area: 153 300 sq. km (59 189 sq. miles).

shandy ('ʃændɪ) *n, pl* **shandies.** an alcoholic drink made of beer and ginger beer or lemonade. ORIG C19: from ?

Shang ★ (ʃæŋ) *n* **1** the dynasty ruling in China from about the 18th to the 12th centuries B.C. ◆ *adj* **2** of or relating to the pottery produced during the Shang dynasty.

shanghai (ˈʃæŋhaɪ, ʃæŋˈhaɪ) *Sl.* ◆ *vb* **shanghais, shanghaiing, shanghaied.** (*tr*) **1** to kidnap (a man or seaman) for enforced service at sea. **2** to force or trick (someone) into doing something, etc. **3** *Austral. & NZ.* to shoot with a catapult. ◆ *n* **4** *Austral. & NZ.* a catapult. ORIG C19: from the city of SHANGHAI; from the forceful methods formerly used to collect crews for voyages to the Orient

Shanghai ★ (ʃæŋˈhaɪ) *n* a port in E China, in SE Jiangsu near the estuary of the Yangtze: the largest city in China and one of the largest ports in the world; a major cultural and industrial centre, with two universities. Pop.: 14 570 000 (1997 est.).

Shangri-la (ˌʃæŋgrɪˈlɑː) *n* a remote or imaginary utopia. ORIG C20: from the name of an imaginary valley in the Himalayas, from *Lost Horizon* (1933), a novel by James Hilton

shank (ʃæŋk) *n* **1** *Anat.* the shin. **2** the corresponding part of the leg in vertebrates other than man. **3** a cut of meat from the top part of an animal's shank. **4** the main part of a tool, between the working part and the handle. **5** the part of a bolt between the thread and the head. **6** the ring or stem on the back of some buttons. **7** the stem or long narrow part of a key, hook, spoon handle, nail, etc. **8** the band of a ring as distinguished from the setting. **9** the part of a shoe connecting the wide part of the sole with the heel. **10** *Printing.* the body of a piece of type. ◆ *vb* **11** (*intr*) (of fruits, roots, etc.) to show disease symptoms, esp. discoloration. **12** (*tr*) *Golf.* to mishit (the ball) with the foot of the shaft. ORIG OE *scanca*

Shankar ★ (ˈʃæŋkɑː) *n* **Ravi** (ˈrɑːviː). born 1920, Indian sitarist.

Shankaracharya (ˈʃʌŋkərɑːˈtʃɑːrjə) *or* **Shankara** ★ (ˈʃʌŋkərə) *n* 9th century A.D., Hindu philosopher and teacher; chief exponent of Vedanta philosophy.

Shankly ★ (ˈʃæŋklɪ) *n* **Bill.** 1913–81, Scottish footballer and manager of Liverpool FC (1959–74).

shanks's pony *or US* **shanks's mare** (ˈʃæŋksɪz) *n Inf.* one's own legs as a means of transportation.

Shannon[1] ★ (ˈʃænən) *n* a river in the Republic of Ireland, rising in NW Co. Cavan and flowing south to the Atlantic by an estuary 113 km (70 miles) long: the longest river in the Republic of Ireland. Length: 260 km (161 miles).

Shannon[2] ★ (ˈʃænən) *n* **Claude** (**Elwood**). born 1916, US mathematician, who was responsible for the development of information theory.

shanny (ˈʃænɪ) *n, pl* **shannies.** a European blenny of rocky coastal waters. ORIG C19: from ?

Shansi ★ (ˈʃænˈsiː) *n* a variant transliteration of the Chinese name for **Shanxi.**

Shan State ★ (ʃɑːn, ʃæn) *n* an administrative division of E Myanmar: formed in 1947 from the joining of the Federation of Shan States with the Wa States; consists of the **Shan plateau,** crossed by forested mountain ranges reaching over 2100 m (7000 ft). Pop.: 4 416 000 (1994 est.). Area: 149 743 sq. km (57 816 sq. miles).

shan't (ʃɑːnt) *contraction of* shall not.

Shantou *or* **Shantow** ★ (ˈʃænˈtaʊ) *n* a port in SE China, in E Guangdong near the mouth of the Han River: became a treaty port in 1869. Pop.: 578 630 (1990 est.). Also called: **Swatow.**

shantung (ˌʃænˈtʌŋ) *n* **1** a heavy silk fabric with a knobbly surface. **2** a cotton or rayon imitation of this. ORIG C19: after SHANTUNG

Shantung ★ (ʃænˈtʌŋ) *n* a variant transliteration of the Chinese name for **Shandong.**

shanty[1] (ˈʃæntɪ) *n, pl* **shanties. 1** a ramshackle hut; crude dwelling. **2** *Austral.* a public house, esp. an unlicensed one. ORIG C19: from Canad. F *chantier* cabin built in a lumber camp, from OF *gantier* GANTRY

shanty[2] (ˈʃæntɪ) *or* **chanty** *n, pl* **shanties** *or* **chanties.** a song originally sung by sailors, esp. a rhythmic one forming an accompaniment to work. ORIG C19: from F *chanter* to sing; see CHANT

shantytown (ˈʃæntɪˌtaʊn) *n* a town or section of a town or city inhabited by very poor people living in shanties.

Shanxi *or* **Shansi** ★ (ˈʃænˈʃiː) *n* a province of N China: China's richest coal reserves and much heavy industry. Capital: Taiyuan. Pop.: 31 410 000 (1997 est.). Area: 157 099 sq. km (60 656 sq. miles).

shape (ʃeɪp) *n* **1** the outward form of an object defined by outline. **2** the figure or outline of the body of a person. **3** a phantom. **4** organized or definite form: *my plans are taking shape.* **5** the form that anything assumes. **6** pattern; mould. **7** condition or state of efficiency: *to be in good shape.* **8 out of shape. 8a** in bad physical condition. **8b** bent, twisted, or deformed. **9 take shape.** to assume a definite form. ◆ *vb* **shapes, shaping, shaped. 10** (when *intr,* often foll. by *into* or *up*) to receive or cause to receive shape or form. **11** (*tr*) to mould into a particular pattern or form. **12** (*tr*) to plan, devise, or prepare: *to shape a plan of action.* ◆ See also **shape up.** ORIG OE *gesceap,* lit.: that which is created, from *scieppan* to create
▸ **ˈshapable** *or* **ˈshapeable** *adj* ▸ **ˈshaper** *n*

SHAPE (ʃeɪp) *n acronym for* Supreme Headquarters Allied Powers Europe.

-shaped (ʃeɪpt) *adj combining form.* having the shape of: *an L-shaped room; a pear-shaped figure.*

shapeless (ˈʃeɪplɪs) *adj* **1** having no definite shape or form: *a shapeless mass.* **2** lacking a symmetrical or aesthetically pleasing shape: *a shapeless figure.*
▸ **ˈshapelessness** *n*

shapely (ˈʃeɪplɪ) *adj* **shapelier, shapeliest.** (esp. of a woman's body or legs) pleasing or attractive in shape.
▸ **ˈshapeliness** *n*

shape up *vb* (*intr, adv*) *Inf.* **1** to proceed or develop satisfactorily. **2** to develop a definite or proper form.

shard (ʃɑːd) *or* **sherd** *n* **1** a broken piece or fragment of a brittle substance, esp. of pottery. **2** *Zool.* a tough sheath, scale, or shell, esp. the elytra of a beetle. ORIG OE *sceard*

share[1] (ʃɛə) *n* **1** a part or portion of something owned or contributed by a person or group. **2** (*often pl*) any of the equal parts, usually of low par value, into which the capital stock of a company is divided. **3 go shares.** *Inf.* to share (something) with another or others. ◆ *vb* **shares, sharing, shared. 4** (*tr;* often foll. by *out*) to divide or apportion, esp. equally. **5** (when *intr,* often foll. by *in*) to receive or contribute a portion of: *we can share the cost of the petrol.* **6** to join with another or others in the use of (something): *can I share your umbrella?* ORIG OE *scearu*
▸ **ˈsharable** *or* **ˈshareable** *adj* ▸ **ˈsharer** *n*

share[2] (ʃɛə) *n* short for **ploughshare.** ORIG OE *scear*

sharecrop (ˈʃɛəˌkrɒp) *vb* **sharecrops, sharecropping, sharecropped.** *Chiefly US.* to cultivate (farmland) as a sharecropper.

sharecropper (ˈʃɛəˌkrɒpə) *n Chiefly US.* a farmer, esp. a tenant farmer, who pays over a proportion of a crop or crops as rent.

shared ownership *n* (in Britain) a form of house purchase whereby the purchaser buys a proportion of the dwelling, usually from a local authority or housing association, and rents the rest.

share-farmer *n Chiefly Austral.* a farmer who pays a fee to another in return for use of land to raise crops, etc.

shareholder (ˈʃɛəˌhəʊldə) *n* the owner of one or more shares in a company.

share index *n* an index showing the movement of share prices. See **FT Index.**

share-milker *n* (in New Zealand) a person who lives on a dairy farm and milks the farmer's herd in return for an agreed share of the profits.

share option *n* a scheme giving employees an option to buy shares in the company for which they work at a favourable price or discount.

share premium *n Brit.* the excess of the amount actually subscribed for an issue of corporate capital over its par value.

share shop *n* a stockbroker, bank, or other financial intermediary that handles the buying and selling of shares for members of the public, esp. during a privatization issue.

shareware (ˈʃɛəˌwɛə) *n Computing.* software available to all users without the need for a licence and for which a token fee is requested.

Shari ★ ('ʃɑːrɪ) *n* a variant spelling of **Chari** (the river).

sharia *or* **sheria** (ʃəˈriːə) *n* the body of doctrines that regulate the lives of those who profess Islam. ORIG Ar.

sharif (ʃæˈriːf) *n* a variant transliteration of **sherif**.

shark[1] (ʃɑːk) *n* any of various usually ferocious fishes, with a long body, two dorsal fins, and rows of sharp teeth. ORIG C16: from ?
▸ ˈ**shark**ˌ**like** *adj*

shark[2] (ʃɑːk) *n* a person who preys on or victimizes others, esp. by swindling or extortion. ORIG C18: prob. from G *Schurke* rogue

shark repellent *pl n* **1** any of various substances used by divers to deter shark attack. **2** (*pl*) *Finance.* another name for **porcupine provisions.**

sharkskin ('ʃɑːkˌskɪn) *n* a smooth glossy fabric of acetate rayon, used for sportswear, etc.

shark watcher *n Inf.* a business consultant who assists companies in identifying and preventing unwelcome takeover bids.

Sharon[1] ★ ('ʃærən) *n* **Plain of.** a plain in W Israel, between the Mediterranean and the hills of Samaria, extending from Haifa to Tel Aviv.

Sharon[2] ★ (ʃæˈrɒn) *n* **Ariel** ('ærɪəl). born 1928, Israeli politician and soldier; prime minister from 2001.

sharon fruit ('ʃærən) *n* another name for **persimmon** (sense 2).

sharp (ʃɑːp) *adj* **1** having a keen edge suitable for cutting. **2** having an edge or point. **3** involving a sudden change, esp. in direction: *a sharp bend.* **4** moving, acting, or reacting quickly, etc.: *sharp reflexes.* **5** clearly defined. **6** mentally acute; keen-witted; attentive. **7** sly or artful: *sharp practice.* **8** bitter or harsh: *sharp words.* **9** shrill or penetrating: *a sharp cry.* **10** having an acrid taste. **11** keen; biting: *a sharp wind.* **12** *Music.* **12a** (*immediately postpositive*) denoting a note that has been raised in pitch by one chromatic semitone: *F sharp.* **12b** (of an instrument, voice, etc.) out of tune by being too high in pitch. Cf. **flat**[1] (sense 20). **13** *Inf.* **13a** stylish. **13b** too smart. **14 at the sharp end.** involved in the most competitive or difficult aspect of any activity. ◆ *adv* **15** in a sharp manner. **16** exactly: *six o'clock sharp.* **17** *Music.* **17a** higher than a standard pitch. **17b** out of tune by being too high in pitch: *she sings sharp.* Cf. **flat**[1] (sense 25). ◆ *n* **18** *Music.* **18a** an accidental that raises the pitch of a note by one chromatic semitone. Usual symbol: ♯ **18b** a note affected by this accidental. Cf. **flat**[1] (sense 31). **19** a thin needle with a sharp point. **20** *Inf.* a sharper. ◆ *vb* **21** (*tr*) *Music.* the usual US and Canad. word for **sharpen.** ORIG OE *scearp*
▸ ˈ**sharply** *adv* ▸ ˈ**sharpness** *n*

Sharp ★ (ʃɑːp) *n* **Cecil (James).** 1859–1924, British musician, best known for collecting, editing, and publishing English folk songs.

sharpbender ('ʃɑːpˌbɛndə) *n Inf.* an organization that has been underperforming its competitors but suddenly becomes more successful, often as a result of new management or changes in its business strategy. ORIG C20: from the sharp upward bend in its sales or profits

sharpen ('ʃɑːpᵊn) *vb* **1** to make or become sharp or sharper. **2** *Music.* to raise the pitch of (a note), esp. by one semitone.
▸ ˈ**sharpener** *n*

sharper ('ʃɑːpə) *n* a person who cheats or swindles; fraud.

Sharpeville ★ ('ʃɑːpvɪl) *n* a town in E South Africa: scene of riots in 1960, when 69 demonstrators died, in 1984, and in 1985, when 19 died.

sharpish ('ʃɑːpɪʃ) *adj* **1** rather sharp. ◆ *adv* **2** *Inf.* quickly; fairly sharply: *quick sharpish.*

sharp-set *adj* **1** set to give an acute cutting angle. **2** keenly hungry. **3** keen or eager.

sharpshooter ('ʃɑːpˌʃuːtə) *n* an expert marksman.
▸ ˈ**sharp**ˌ**shooting** *n*

sharp-tongued *adj* bitter or critical in speech; sarcastic.

sharp-witted *adj* having or showing a keen intelligence; perceptive.
▸ ˌ**sharp-**ˈ**wittedly** *adv* ▸ ˌ**sharp-**ˈ**wittedness** *n*

Shasta daisy ('ʃæstə) *n* a plant widely cultivated for its large white daisy-like flowers.

shastra ('ʃɑːstrə), **shaster** ('ʃɑːstə), *or* **sastra** ('ʃɑːstrə) *n* any of the sacred writings of Hinduism. ORIG C17: from Sansk. *śāstra,* from *śās* to teach

shat (ʃæt) *vb Taboo.* a past tense and past participle of **shit.**

Shatt-al-Arab ★ (ˈʃætælˈærəb) *n* a river in SE Iraq, formed by the confluence of the Tigris and Euphrates Rivers: flows southeast as part of the border between Iraq and Iran to the Persian Gulf. Length: 193 km (120 miles).

shatter ('ʃætə) *vb* **1** to break or be broken into many small pieces. **2** (*tr*) to impair or destroy: *his nerves were shattered by the torture.* **3** (*tr*) to dumbfound or thoroughly upset: *she was shattered by the news.* **4** (*tr*) *Inf.* to cause to be tired out or exhausted. ORIG C12: ? obscurely rel. to SCATTER
▸ ˈ**shattered** *adj* ▸ ˈ**shattering** *adj* ▸ ˈ**shatteringly** *adv*

shatterproof ('ʃætəˌpruːf) *adj* designed to resist shattering.

shave (ʃeɪv) *vb* **shaves, shaving, shaved; shaved** *or* **shaven.** (*mainly tr*) **1** (*also intr*) to remove (the beard, hair, etc.) from (the face, head, or body) by scraping the skin with a razor. **2** to cut or trim very closely. **3** to reduce to shavings. **4** to remove thin slices from (wood, etc.) with a sharp cutting tool. **5** to touch or graze in passing. **6** *Inf.* to reduce (a price) by a slight amount. ◆ *n* **7** the act or an instance of shaving. **8** any tool for scraping. **9** a thin slice or shaving. ORIG OE *sceafan*
▸ ˈ**shavable** *or* ˈ**shaveable** *adj*

shaveling ('ʃeɪvlɪŋ) *n Arch.* **1** *Derog.* a priest or clergyman with a shaven head. **2** a young fellow; youth.

shaven ('ʃeɪvᵊn) *adj* **a** closely shaved or tonsured. **b** (*in combination*): *clean-shaven.*

shaver ('ʃeɪvə) *n* **1** a person or thing that shaves. **2** Also called: **electric razor, electric shaver.** an electrically powered implement for shaving, having rotating blades behind a fine metal comb. **3** *Inf.* a youngster, esp. a young boy.

Shavian ('ʃeɪvɪən) *adj* **1** of or like George Bernard Shaw (1856–1950), Irish dramatist, his works, ideas, etc. ◆ *n* **2** an admirer of Shaw or his works.

shaving ('ʃeɪvɪŋ) *n* **1** a thin paring or slice, esp. of wood, that has been shaved from something. ◆ *modifier.* **2** used when shaving the face, etc.: *shaving cream.*

Shavuot *or* **Shabuoth** (ʃəˈvuːəs, -əʊs; *Hebrew* ʃavuːˈɔt) *n* the Hebrew name for **Pentecost** (sense 2). ORIG from Heb. *shābhūʻōth,* pl of *shābhūaʻ* week

Shaw ★ (ʃɔː) *n* **1 George Bernard,** often known as *GBS.* 1856–1950, Irish dramatist and critic, in England from 1876. His plays include *Arms and the Man* (1894), *Man and Superman* (1903), *Pygmalion* (1913), *Back to Methuselah* (1921), and *St Joan* (1923): Nobel prize for literature 1925. **2 Richard Norman.** 1831–1912, British architect. **3 Thomas Edward.** the name assumed by (T. E.) **Lawrence** after 1927.

shawl (ʃɔːl) *n* a piece of fabric or knitted or crocheted material worn around the shoulders by women or wrapped around a baby. ORIG C17: from Persian *shāl*

shawm (ʃɔːm) *n Music.* a medieval form of the oboe with a conical bore and flaring bell. ORIG C14 *shalmye,* from OF *chalemie,* ult. from L *calamus* a reed, from Gk *kalamos*

shay (ʃeɪ) *n* a dialect word for **chaise.** ORIG C18: back formation from CHAISE, mistaken for pl

Shcheglovsk ★ (*Russian* ʃtʃɪgˈlɔfsk) *n* the former name (until 1932) of **Kemerovo.**

Shcherbakov ★ (*Russian* ʃtʃɪrbaˈkɔf) *n* the former name (from the Revolution until 1957) of **Rybinsk.**

she (ʃiː) *pron* (*subjective*) **1** refers to a female person or animal: *she is a doctor.* **2** refers to things personified as feminine, such as cars, ships, and nations. **3** *Austral. & NZ.* a pronoun often used instead of *it,* as in **she'll be right** (it will be all right). ◆ *n* **4a** a female person or animal. **4b** (*in combination*): *she-cat.* ORIG OE *sīe,* accusative of *sēo,* fem. demonstrative pron

shea (ʃɪə) *n* **1** a tropical African tree with oily seeds. **2 shea butter.** the white butter-like fat obtained from the seeds of this plant and used as food, etc. ORIG C18: from W African *si*

sheading ('ʃi:dɪŋ) *n* any of the six subdivisions of the Isle of Man. ORIG var. of *shedding*

sheaf (ʃi:f) *n, pl* **sheaves. 1** a bundle of reaped but unthreshed corn tied with one or two bonds. **2** a bundle of objects tied together. **3** the arrows contained in a quiver. ◆ *vb* **4** (*tr*) to bind or tie into a sheaf. ORIG OE *sceaf*

shear (ʃɪə) *vb* **shears, shearing, sheared** *or* (*arch., Austral., & NZ*) *sometimes* **shore; sheared** *or* **shorn. 1** (*tr*) to remove (the fleece or hair) of (sheep, etc.) by cutting or clipping. **2** to cut or cut through (something) with shears or a sharp instrument. **3** *Engineering.* to cause (a part, member, etc.) to deform or fracture or (of a part, etc.) to deform or fracture as a result of excess torsion. **4** (*tr;* often foll. by *of*) to strip or divest: *to shear someone of his power.* **5** (when *intr,* foll. by *through*) to move through (something) by or as if by cutting. ◆ *n* **6** the act, process, or an instance of shearing. **7** a shearing of a sheep or flock of sheep: *a sheep of two shears.* **8** a form of deformation or fracture in which parallel planes in a body slide over one another. **9** *Physics.* the deformation of a body, part, etc., expressed as the lateral displacement between two points in parallel planes divided by the distance between the planes. **10** either one of the blades of a pair of shears, scissors, etc. ◆ See also **shears.** ORIG OE *sceran*
▸ **'shearer** *n*

shearling ('ʃɪəlɪŋ) *n* **1** a young sheep after its first shearing. **2** the skin of such an animal.

shear pin *n* an easily replaceable pin in a machine designed to break and stop the machine if the stress becomes too great.

shears (ʃɪəz) *pl n* **1a** large scissors, as for cutting cloth, jointing poultry, etc. **1b** a large scissor-like and usually hand-held cutting tool with flat blades, as for cutting hedges. **2** any of various analogous cutting implements.

shearwater ('ʃɪəˌwɔ:tə) *n* any of several oceanic birds specialized for an aerial or aquatic existence.

sheatfish ('ʃi:tˌfɪʃ) *n, pl* **sheatfish** *or* **sheatfishes.** another name for **European catfish** (see **silurid** (sense 1)). ORIG C16: var. of *sheathfish;* ? infl. by G *Schaid* sheatfish

sheath (ʃi:θ) *n, pl* **sheaths** (ʃi:ðz). **1** a case or covering for the blade of a knife, sword, etc. **2** any similar close-fitting case. **3** *Biol.* an enclosing or protective structure. **4** the protective covering on an electric cable. **5** a figure-hugging dress with a narrow tapering skirt. **6** another name for **condom.** ORIG OE *scēath*

sheathe (ʃi:ð) *vb* **sheathes, sheathing, sheathed.** (*tr*) **1** to insert (a knife, sword, etc.) into a sheath. **2** (esp. of cats) to retract (the claws). **3** to surface with or encase in a sheath or sheathing.

sheathing ('ʃi:ðɪŋ) *n* **1** any material used as an outer layer, as on a ship's hull. **2** boarding, etc., used to cover a timber frame.

sheath knife *n* a knife carried in or protected by a sheath.

sheave[1] (ʃi:v) *vb* **sheaves, sheaving, sheaved.** (*tr*) to gather or bind into sheaves.

sheave[2] (ʃi:v) *n* a wheel with a grooved rim, esp. one used as a pulley. ORIG C14: of Gmc origin

sheaves (ʃi:vz) *n* the plural of **sheaf.**

Sheba[1] ★ ('ʃi:bə) *n* **1** Also called: **Saba.** the ancient kingdom of the Sabeans: a rich trading nation dealing in gold, spices, and precious stones (I Kings 10). **2** the region inhabited by this nation, located in the SW corner of the Arabian peninsula: modern Yemen.

Sheba[2] ★ ('ʃi:bə) *n* **Queen of.** *Old Testament.* a queen of the Sabeans, who visited Solomon (I Kings 10:1–13).

shebang (ʃɪ'bæŋ) *n Sl., chiefly US & Canad.* a situation or affair (esp. in **the whole shebang**). ORIG C19: from ?

shebeen *or* **shebean** (ʃə'bi:n) *n* **1** *Irish, Scot., & S. African.* a place where alcoholic drink is sold illegally. **2** (in Ireland) alcohol, esp. home-distilled whiskey, sold without a licence. **3** (in South Africa) a place where Black African men engage in social drinking. ORIG C18: from Irish Gaelic *sībīn* beer of poor quality

shebeen king *or* (*fem*) **shebeen queen** *n* (in South Africa) the proprietor of a shebeen.

Shechem ★ ('ʃɛkəm, -ɛm) *n* the ancient name of **Nablus.**

shed[1] (ʃɛd) *n* **1** a small building or lean-to of light construction, used for storage, shelter, etc. **2** a large roofed structure, esp. one with open sides, used for storage, repairing locomotives, etc. **3** *Austral. & NZ.* the building in which sheep are shorn. ORIG OE *sced;* prob. var. of *scead* shelter

shed[2] (ʃɛd) *vb* **sheds, shedding, shed.** (*mainly tr*) **1** to pour forth or cause to pour forth: *to shed tears.* **2 shed light on** *or* **upon.** to clarify (a problem, etc.). **3** to cast off or lose: *the snake shed its skin.* **4** (of a lorry) to drop (its load) on the road by accident. **5** to repel: *this coat sheds water.* **6** to separate or divide a group of sheep: *a good dog can shed his sheep in minutes.* **7** *Dialect.* to make a parting in (the hair). ◆ *n* **8** short for **watershed. 9** the action of separating or dividing a group of sheep: *the old dog was better at the shed than the young one.* ORIG OE *sceadan*
▸ **'shedable** *or* **'sheddable** *adj*

she'd (ʃi:d) *contraction of* she had *or* she would.

shedder ('ʃɛdə) *n* **1** a person or thing that sheds. **2** an animal, such as a llama, snake, or lobster, that moults.

shed hand *n Chiefly Austral.* an unskilled worker in a sheepshearing shed.

shed out *vb* (*tr, adv*) *NZ.* to separate off (sheep that have lambed) and move them to better pasture.

sheen (ʃi:n) *n* **1** a gleaming or glistening brightness; lustre. **2** *Poetic.* splendid clothing. ◆ *adj* **3** *Rare.* beautiful. ORIG OE *sciene*
▸ **'sheeny** *adj*

sheep (ʃi:p) *n, pl* **sheep. 1** any of a genus of ruminant mammals having transversely ribbed horns and a narrow face. **2 Barbary sheep.** another name for **aoudad. 3** a meek or timid person. **4 separate the sheep from the goats.** to pick out the members of a group who are superior in some respects. ORIG OE *sceap*
▸ **'sheepˌlike** *adj*

sheepcote ('ʃi:pˌkəʊt) *n Chiefly Brit.* another word for **sheepfold.**

sheep-dip *n* **1** any of several liquid disinfectants and insecticides in which sheep are immersed. **2** a deep trough containing such a liquid.

sheepdog ('ʃi:pˌdɒg) *n* **1** a dog used for herding sheep. **2** any of various breeds of dog reared originally for herding sheep. See **Old English sheepdog, Shetland sheepdog.**

sheepdog trial *n* (*often pl*) a competition in which sheepdogs are tested in their tasks.

sheepfold ('ʃi:pˌfəʊld) *n* a pen or enclosure for sheep.

sheepish ('ʃi:pɪʃ) *adj* **1** abashed or embarrassed, esp. through looking foolish. **2** resembling a sheep in timidity.
▸ **'sheepishly** *adv* ▸ **'sheepishness** *n*

sheepo ('ʃi:pəʊ) *n, pl* **sheepos.** *NZ.* a person employed to bring sheep to the catching pen in a shearing shed.

sheep's eyes *pl n Old-fashioned.* amorous or inviting glances.

sheepshank ('ʃi:pˌʃæŋk) *n* a knot made in a rope to shorten it temporarily.

sheepskin ('ʃi:pˌskɪn) *n* **a** the skin of a sheep, esp. when used for clothing, etc. **b** (*as modifier*): *a sheepskin coat.*

sheepwalk ('ʃi:pˌwɔ:k) *n Chiefly Brit.* a tract of land for grazing sheep.

sheer[1] (ʃɪə) *adj* **1** perpendicular; very steep: *a sheer cliff.* **2** (of textiles) so fine as to be transparent. **3** (*prenominal*) absolute: *sheer folly.* **4** *Obs.* bright. ◆ *adv* **5** steeply. **6** completely or absolutely. ORIG OE *scīr*
▸ **'sheerly** *adv* ▸ **'sheerness** *n*

sheer[2] (ʃɪə) *vb* (foll. by *off* or *away* (*from*)). **1** to deviate or cause to deviate from a course. **2** (*intr*) to avoid an unpleasant person, thing, topic, etc. ◆ *n* **3** *Naut.* the position of a vessel relative to its mooring. ORIG C17: ? var. of SHEAR

sheerlegs *or* **shearlegs** ('ʃɪəˌlɛgz) *n* (*functioning as sing*) a device for lifting weights consisting of two spars lashed together at the upper ends from which a lifting tackle is suspended. Also called: **shears.** ORIG C19: var. of *shear legs*

★ people and places

Sheerness ★ (ˌʃɪəˈnɛs) *n* a port and resort in SE England, in N Kent at the junction of the Medway estuary and the Thames: administratively part of Queenborough in Sheppey since 1968.

sheet[1] (ʃiːt) *n* **1** a large rectangular piece of cloth, generally one of a pair used as inner bedclothes. **2a** a thin piece of a substance such as paper or glass, usually rectangular in form. **2b** (*as modifier*): *sheet iron.* **3** a broad continuous surface: *a sheet of water.* **4** a newspaper, esp. a tabloid. **5** a piece of printed paper to be folded into a section for a book. ◆ *vb* **6** (*tr*) to provide with, cover, or wrap in a sheet. ORIG OE *sciete*

sheet[2] (ʃiːt) *n Naut.* a line or rope for controlling the position of a sail relative to the wind. ORIG OE *scēata* corner of a sail

sheet anchor *n* **1** *Naut.* a large strong anchor for use in emergency. **2** a person or thing to be relied on in an emergency. ORIG C17: from earlier *shute anker,* from *shoot* (obs.) the sheet of a sail

sheet bend *n* a knot used esp. for joining ropes of different sizes.

sheeting (ˈʃiːtɪŋ) *n* fabric from which sheets are made.

sheet lightning *n* lightning that appears as a broad sheet, caused by the reflection of more distant lightning.

sheet metal *n* metal in the form of a sheet, the thickness being intermediate between that of plate and that of foil.

sheet music *n* **1** the printed or written copy of a short composition or piece. **2** music in its written or printed form.

Sheffield ★ (ˈʃɛfiːld) *n* **1** a city in N England, in South Yorkshire on the River Don: important centre of steel manufacture and of the cutlery industry; seat of The University of Sheffield (1905) and Sheffield Hallam University (1992). Pop.: 431 607 (1991). **2** a unitary authority in N England, in South Yorkshire. Pop.: 530 400 (1996 est.). Area: 368 sq. km (142 sq. miles).

sheikh *or* **sheik** (ʃeɪk) *n* (in Muslim countries) **a** the head of an Arab tribe, village, etc. **b** a religious leader. ORIG C16: from Ar. *shaykh* old man
▸ **ˈsheikhdom** *or* **ˈsheikdom** *n*

sheila (ˈʃiːlə) *n Austral. & NZ old-fashioned.* an informal word for **girl** or **woman.** ORIG C19: from the girl's name *Sheila*

shekel (ˈʃɛkəl) *n* **1** the standard monetary unit of modern Israel, divided into 100 agorot. **2** any of several former coins and units of weight of the Near East. **3** (*often pl*) *Inf.* any coin or money. ORIG C16: from Heb. *sheqel*

Shelburne ★ (ˈʃɛlbɜːn) *n* **2nd Earl of,** title of *William Petty Fitzmaurice,* also called (from 1784) *1st Marquess of Lansdowne.* 1737–1805, British statesman; prime minister (1782–83).

shelduck (ˈʃɛlˌdʌk) *or* (*masc*) **sheldrake** (ˈʃɛlˌdreɪk) *n, pl* **shelducks, shelduck** *or* **sheldrakes, sheldrake.** any of various large usually brightly coloured gooselike ducks of the Old World. ORIG C14: *shel,* prob. from dialect *sheld* pied

shelf (ʃɛlf) *n, pl* **shelves. 1** a thin flat plank of wood, metal, etc., fixed horizontally against a wall, etc., for the purpose of supporting objects. **2** something resembling this in shape or function. **3** the objects placed on a shelf: *a shelf of books.* **4** a projecting layer of ice, rock, etc., on land or in the sea. **5** See **off the shelf. 6 on the shelf.** put aside or abandoned; used esp. of unmarried women considered to be past the age of marriage. ORIG OE *scylfe* ship's deck
▸ **ˈshelfˌlike** *adj*

shelf life *n* the length of time a packaged food, etc., will last without deteriorating.

shell (ʃɛl) *n* **1** the protective outer layer of an egg, esp. a bird's egg. **2** the hard outer covering of many molluscs. **3** any other hard outer layer, such as the exoskeleton of many arthropods. **4** the hard outer layer of some fruits, esp. of nuts. **5** any hard outer case. **6** a hollow artillery projectile filled with explosive primed to explode either during flight or on impact. **7** a small-arms cartridge. **8** a pyrotechnic cartridge designed to explode in the air. **9** *Rowing.* a very light narrow racing boat. **10** the external structure of a building, esp. one that is unfinished. **11** *Physics.* **11a** a class of electron orbits in an atom in which the electrons have the same principal quantum number and little difference in their energy levels. **11b** an analogous energy state of nucleons in certain theories (**shell models**) of the structure of the atomic nucleus. **12 come** (*or* **bring**) **out of one's shell.** to become (or help to become) less shy and reserved. ◆ *vb* **13** to divest or be divested of a shell, husk, etc. **14** to separate or be separated from an ear, husk, etc. **15** (*tr*) to bombard with artillery shells. ◆ See also **shell out.** ORIG OE *sciell*
▸ **ˈshell-less** *adj* ▸ **ˈshell-ˌlike** *adj* ▸ **ˈshelly** *adj*

she'll (ʃiːl; *unstressed* ʃɪl) *contraction of* she will *or* she shall.

shellac (ʃəˈlæk, ˈʃɛlæk) *n* **1** a yellowish resin secreted by the lac insect, esp. a commercial preparation of this used in varnishes, polishes, etc. **2** Also called: **shellac varnish.** a varnish made by dissolving shellac in ethanol or a similar solvent. ◆ *vb* **shellacs, shellacking, shellacked.** (*tr*) **3** to coat (an article) with a shellac varnish. ORIG **C18:** SHELL + LAC[1], translation of F *laque en écailles,* lit.: lac in scales, that is, in thin plates

shellback (ˈʃɛlˌbæk) *n* an experienced or old sailor.

shell company *n Business.* **1** a near-defunct company, esp. one with a stock-exchange listing, used as a vehicle for a thriving company. **2** a company that has ceased to trade but retains its registration and is sold for a small sum to enable its new owners to avoid the cost and trouble of registering a new company.

Shelley ★ (ˈʃɛlɪ) *n* **1 Mary Wollstonecraft** (**Godwin**) (ˈwʊlstənˌkrɑːft). 1797–1851, British writer; author of *Frankenstein* (1818); the daughter of William Godwin and Mary Wollstonecraft, she eloped with Percy Bysshe Shelley. **2 Percy Bysshe** (bɪʃ). 1792–1822, British Romantic poet. His works include *Queen Mab* (1813) and the verse drama *Prometheus Unbound* (1820): shorter lyrics include the odes *To the West Wind* and *To a Skylark* (both 1820). He was drowned off Leghorn.

shellfire (ˈʃɛlˌfaɪə) *n* the firing of artillery shells.

shellfish (ˈʃɛlˌfɪʃ) *n, pl* **shellfish** *or* **shellfishes.** any aquatic invertebrate having a shell or shell-like carapace, esp. such an animal used as human food. Examples are crustaceans such as crabs and lobsters and molluscs such as oysters.

shell out *vb* (*adv*) *Inf.* to pay out or hand over (money).

shell program *n Computing.* a basic low-cost computer program that provides a framework within which the user can develop the program to suit his personal requirements.

shellproof (ˈʃɛlˌpruːf) *adj* designed, intended, or able to resist shellfire.

shell shock *n* loss of sight, etc., resulting from psychological strain during prolonged engagement in warfare.
▸ **ˈshell-ˌshocked** *adj*

shell suit *n* a lightweight tracksuit consisting of an inner cotton layer covered by a waterproof nylon layer.

Shelta (ˈʃɛltə) *n* a secret language used by some itinerant tinkers in Ireland and parts of Britain, based on Gaelic. ORIG C19: from earlier *sheldrū,* ? an arbitrary alteration of OIrish *bēlre* speech

shelter (ˈʃɛltə) *n* **1** something that provides cover or protection, as from weather or danger. **2** the protection afforded by such a cover. **3** the state of being sheltered. ◆ *vb* **4** (*tr*) to provide with or protect by a shelter. **5** (*intr*) to take cover, as from rain. **6** (*tr*) to act as a shelter for. ORIG C16: from ?
▸ **ˈshelterer** *n*

sheltered (ˈʃɛltəd) *adj* **1** protected from wind or weather. **2** protected from outside influences: *a sheltered upbringing.* **3** specially designed to provide a safe environment for the elderly, handicapped, or disabled: *sheltered housing.*

sheltie *or* **shelty** (ˈʃɛltɪ) *n, pl* **shelties.** another name for **Shetland pony** or **Shetland sheepdog.** ORIG C17: prob. from Orkney dialect *sjalti,* from ON *Hjalti* Shetlander, from *Hjaltland* Shetland

shelve[1] (ʃɛlv) *vb* **shelves, shelving, shelved.** (*tr*) **1** to place on a shelf. **2** to provide with shelves. **3** to put aside or post-

pone from consideration. **4** to dismiss or cause to retire. ORIG C16: from *shelves*, pl of SHELF
▸ **'shelver** *n*

shelve[2] (ʃɛlv) *vb* **shelves, shelving, shelved.** (*intr*) to slope away gradually. ORIG C16: from ?

shelves (ʃɛlvz) *n* the plural of **shelf.**

shelving ('ʃɛlvɪŋ) *n* **1** material for making shelves. **2** a set of shelves; shelves collectively.

Shem ★ (ʃɛm) *n Old Testament.* the eldest of Noah's three sons (Genesis 10:21). Douay spelling: **Sem** (sɛm).

shemozzle (ʃɪ'mɒzᵊl) *n Inf.* a noisy confusion or dispute; uproar. ORIG C19: ?from Yiddish *shlimazl* misfortune

shenanigan (ʃɪ'nænɪgən) *n Inf.* **1** (*usually pl*) roguishness; mischief. **2** an act of treachery; deception. ORIG C19: from ?

Shensi ★ ('ʃɛn'siː) *n* a variant transliteration of the Chinese name for **Shaanxi.**

Shenyang ★ ('ʃɛn'jæŋ) *n* a walled city in NE China in S Manchuria, capital of Liaoning province: capital of the Manchu dynasty from 1644–1912; seized by the Japanese in 1931. Pop.: 4 540 000 (1991 est.). Former name: **Mukden.**

she-oak *n* any of various Australian trees of the genus *Casuarina*. See **casuarina.** ORIG C18: *she* (in the sense: inferior) + OAK

Sheol ('ʃiːəʊl, -ɒl) *n Bible.* **1** the abode of the dead. **2** (*often not cap.*) hell. ORIG C16: from Heb. *shĕ'ōl*

Shepard ★ ('ʃɛpəd) *n* **1 Alan Bartlett, Jr.** 1923–98, US naval officer; first US astronaut in space (1961). **2 Sam,** original name *Samuel Shepard Rogers.* born 1943, US dramatist, film actor, and director.

shepherd ('ʃɛpəd) *n* **1** a person employed to tend sheep. Fem. equivalent: **shepherdess. 2** a person, such as a clergyman, who watches over a group of people. ◆ *vb* (*tr*) **3** to guide or watch over in the manner of a shepherd. **4** *Australian Rules, rugby, etc.* to prevent opponents from tackling (a member of one's own team) by blocking their path: illegal in rugby.

shepherd dog *n* another term for **sheepdog** (sense 1).

shepherd's pie *n Brit. & Canad.* a baked dish of minced meat covered with mashed potato.

shepherd's-purse *n* a plant having small white flowers and flattened triangular seed pods.

shepherd's weatherglass *n Brit.* another name for the **scarlet pimpernel.**

Sheppey ★ ('ʃɛpɪ) *n* **Isle of.** an island in SE England, off the N coast of Kent in the Thames estuary: separated from the mainland by **The Swale,** a narrow channel. Chief towns: Sheerness, Minster. Pop.: 32 000 (latest est.). Area: 80 sq. km (30 sq. miles).

Sheraton[1] ★ ('ʃɛrətən) *n* **Thomas.** 1751–1806, British furniture maker, author of the influential *Cabinet-Maker and Upholsterer's Drawing Book* (1791).

Sheraton[2] ('ʃɛrətən) *adj* denoting furniture made by or in the style of Thomas Sheraton, characterized by lightness, elegance, and the extensive use of inlay.

sherbet ('ʃɜːbət) *n* **1** a fruit-flavoured slightly effervescent powder, eaten as a sweet or used to make a drink. **2** another word (esp. US and Canad.) for **sorbet** (sense 1). **3** *Austral. sl.* beer. **4** a cooling Oriental drink of sweetened fruit juice. ORIG C17: from Turkish, from Persian, from Ar. *sharbah* drink, from *shariba* to drink

Sherborne ★ ('ʃɛːbɔːn) *n* a town in S England in Dorset: noted for its medieval abbey, ruined medieval castle, and **Sherborne Castle,** a mansion built by Sir Walter Raleigh in 1594. Pop.: 7606 (1991).

Sherbrooke ★ ('ʃɜːˌbrʊk) *n* a city in E Canada, in S Quebec: industrial and commercial centre. Pop.: 76 429 (1991).

sherd (ʃɜːd) *n* a variant of **shard.**

Sheridan ★ ('ʃɛrɪdən) *n* **1 Philip Henry.** 1831–88, American Union cavalry commander in the Civil War. He forced Lee's surrender to Grant (1865). **2 Richard Brinsley** ('brɪnzlɪ). 1751–1816, Irish dramatist and politician, noted for his comedies *The Rivals* (1775), *School for Scandal* (1777), and *The Critic* (1779).

sherif *or* **shereef** (ʃɛ'riːf) *or* **sharif** *n Islam.* **1** a descendant of Mohammed through his daughter Fatima. **2** an honorific title accorded to any Muslim ruler. ORIG C16: from Ar. *sharīf* noble

sheriff ('ʃɛrɪf) *n* **1** (in the US) the chief elected law-enforcement officer in a county. **2** (in Canada) a municipal official who enforces court orders, escorts convicted criminals to prison, etc. **3** (in England and Wales) the chief executive officer of the Crown in a county, having chiefly ceremonial duties. **4** (in Scotland) a judge in any of the sheriff courts. **5** (in New Zealand) an officer of the High Court. ORIG OE *scīrgerēfa,* from *scīr* SHIRE + *gerēfa* REEVE[1]
▸ **'sheriffdom** *n*

sheriff court *n* (in Scotland) a court having jurisdiction to try all but the most serious crimes and to deal with most civil actions.

Sherman ★ ('ʃɜːmən) *n* **William Tecumseh** (tɪ'kʌmsə). 1820–91, American Union commander during the Civil War. He led the victorious march through Georgia (1864).

Sherpa ('ʃɜːpə) *n, pl* **Sherpas** *or* **Sherpa.** a member of a people of Mongolian origin living on the southern slopes of the Himalayas in Nepal, noted as mountaineers.

Sherrington ★ ('ʃɛrɪŋtən) *n* Sir **Charles Scott.** 1857–1952, British physiologist, noted for his work on reflex action: shared the Nobel prize for physiology or medicine 1932.

sherry ('ʃɛrɪ) *n, pl* **sherries.** a fortified wine, originally only from the Jerez region of southern Spain. ORIG C16: from earlier *sherris* (assumed to be pl), from Sp. *Xeres,* now *Jerez*

's Hertogenbosch ★ (*Dutch* shɛrtoːxən'bɔs) *n* a city in the S Netherlands, capital of North Brabant province: birthplace of Hieronymus Bosch. Pop.: 95 448 (1994). Also called: **Den Bosch.** French name: **Bois-le-Duc.**

sherwani (ʃɛə'wɑːnɪ) *n* a long coat closed up to the neck, worn by men in India. ORIG Hindi

Sherwood ★ ('ʃɜːˌwʊd) *n* **Robert Emmet.** 1896–1955, US dramatist. His plays include *The Petrified Forest* (1935) and *There Shall be no Night* (1940).

Sherwood Forest ★ *n* an ancient forest in central England, in Nottinghamshire: formerly a royal hunting ground and much more extensive; famous as the home of Robin Hood.

she's (ʃiːz) *contraction of* she is *or* she has.

Shetland *or* **Shetland Islands** ★ ('ʃɛtlənd) *pl n* a group of about 100 islands (fewer than 20 inhabited), off the N coast of Scotland, which constitute an island authority of Scotland: a Norse dependency from the 8th century until 1472; noted for the breeding of Shetland ponies, knitwear manufacturing, and fishing; oil-related industries. Administrative centre: Lerwick. Pop.: 23 020 (1996 est.). Area: 1426 sq. km (550 sq. miles). Official name (until 1974): **Zetland.**

Shetland pony *n* a very small sturdy breed of pony with a long shaggy mane and tail. Also called: **sheltie.**

Shetland sheepdog *n* a small dog similar in appearance to a collie. Also called: **sheltie.**

Shevardnadze ★ (ˌʃɛvəd'nɑːdzə) *n* **Eduard (Amvrosiyevich).** born 1928, Georgian statesman; Soviet minister of foreign affairs (1985–91 and from 1991), who played an important part in arms negotiations with the US; president of Georgia from 1992.

shew (ʃəʊ) *vb* **shews, shewing, shewed; shewn** *or* **shewed.** an archaic spelling of **show.**

shewbread *or* **showbread** ('ʃəʊˌbrɛd) *n Bible.* the loaves of bread placed every Sabbath on the table beside the altar of incense in the tabernacle or temple of ancient Israel.

SHF *or* **shf** *Radio. abbrev. for* superhigh frequency.

Shiah *or* **Shia** ('ʃiːə) *n* **1** one of the two main branches of Islam (the other being the Sunni), now mainly in Iran, which regards Mohammed's cousin Ali and his successors as the true imams. ◆ *adj* **2** designating or characteristic of this sect or its beliefs and practices. ORIG C17: from Ar. *shī'ah* sect, from *shā'a* to follow

shiatsu (ʃiː'ætsuː) *n* a type of massage in which pressure is applied to the same points of the body as in acupuncture. Also called: **acupressure.** ORIG Japanese from Chinese *chǐ* finger + *yā* pressure

shibboleth ('ʃɪbəˌlɛθ) *n* **1** a slogan or catch phrase, usually considered outworn, characteristic of a particular party or sect. **2** a custom, phrase, or use of language that acts as a test of belonging to, or as a stumbling block to joining a particular social class, profession, etc. ORIG C14: from Heb., lit.: ear of grain; the word is used in the Old Testament by the Gileadites as a test word for the Ephraimites, who could not pronounce the sound *sh*

shickered ('ʃɪkəd) *adj Austral. & NZ old-fashioned sl.* drunk; intoxicated. ORIG via Yiddish from Heb.

shied (ʃaɪd) *vb* the past tense and past participle of **shy**[1] and **shy**[2].

shield (ʃiːld) *n* **1** any protection used to intercept blows, missiles, etc., such as a tough piece of armour carried on the arm. **2** any similar protective device. **3** *Heraldry.* a pointed stylized shield used for displaying armorial bearings. **4** anything that resembles a shield in shape, such as a prize in a sports competition. **5** *Physics.* a structure of concrete, lead, etc., placed around a nuclear reactor. **6** a broad stable plateau of ancient Precambrian rocks forming the rigid nucleus of a particular continent. **7 the shield.** *NZ.* the Bledisloe Shield, a trophy competed for by provincial rugby teams. ◆ *vb* **8** (*tr*) to protect, hide, or conceal (something) from danger or harm. ORIG OE *scield*
▸ **'shieldˌlike** *adj*

Shield (ʃiːld) *n* **the.** *Canad.* another term for the **Canadian Shield.**

shield match *n* **1** *Austral.* a cricket match for the Sheffield Shield. **2** *NZ.* a rugby match for the Ranfurly Shield.

shield volcano *n* a broad volcano built up from the repeated nonexplosive eruption of basalt to form a low dome or shield, usually having a large caldera at the summit.

shieling ('ʃiːlɪŋ) *or* **shiel** (ʃiːl) *n Chiefly Scot.* **1** a temporary shelter used by people tending cattle on high or remote ground. **2** pasture land for the grazing of cattle in summer. ORIG C16: from earlier *shiel,* from ME *shale* hut, from ?

shier ('ʃaɪə) *adj* a comparative of **shy**[1].

shiest ('ʃaɪɪst) *adj* a superlative of **shy**[1].

shift (ʃɪft) *vb* **1** to move or cause to move from one place or position to another. **2** (*tr*) to change for another or others. **3** to change (gear) in a motor vehicle. **4** (*intr*) (of a sound or set of sounds) to alter in a systematic way. **5** (*intr*) to provide for one's needs (esp. in **shift for oneself**). **6** to remove or be removed, esp. with difficulty: *no detergent can shift these stains.* **7** (*intr*) *Sl.* to move quickly. **8** (*tr*) *Computing.* to move (bits held in a store location) to the left or right. ◆ *n* **9** the act or an instance of shifting. **10** a group of workers who work for a specific period. **11** the period of time worked by such a group. **12** an expedient, contrivance, or artifice. **13** an underskirt or dress with little shaping. ORIG OE *sciftan*
▸ **'shifter** *n*

shiftless ('ʃɪftlɪs) *adj* lacking in ambition or initiative.
▸ **'shiftlessness** *n*

shifty ('ʃɪftɪ) *adj* **shiftier, shiftiest. 1** given to evasions. **2** furtive in character or appearance.
▸ **'shiftily** *adv* ▸ **'shiftiness** *n*

shigella (ʃɪ'gɛlə) *n* any of a genus of rod-shaped bacteria, some species of which cause dysentery. ORIG C20: after K. *Shiga* (1870–1957), Japanese bacteriologist, who discovered them

Shiite ('ʃiːaɪt) *or* **Shiah** *Islam.* ◆ *n* **1** an adherent of Shiah. ◆ *adj* **2** of or relating to Shiah.
▸ **Shiism** ('ʃiːɪzəm) *n* ▸ **Shiitic** (ʃiː'ɪtɪk) *adj*

Shijiazhuang ('ʃiːdʒɑː'dʒwæŋ), **Shihchiachuang,** *or* **Shihkiachwang** ★ (ˌʃiːtʃjɑː'tʃwæŋ) *n* a city in NE China, capital of Hebei province: textile manufacturing. Pop.: 1 320 000 (1991 est.).

Shikoku ★ ('ʃiːkəʊˌkuː) *n* the smallest of the four main islands of Japan, separated from Honshu by the Inland Sea: mostly forested and mountainous. Pop.: 4 183 000 (1995). Area: 17 759 sq. km (6857 sq. miles).

shillelagh *or* **shillala** (ʃə'leɪlə, -lɪ) *n* (in Ireland) a stout club or cudgel. ORIG C18: from Irish Gaelic *sail* cudgel + *éille* leash, thong

shilling ('ʃɪlɪŋ) *n* **1** a former British or Australian silver or cupronickel coin worth one twentieth of a pound, not minted in Britain since 1970. Abbrevs.: **s., sh. 2** the standard monetary unit of Kenya, Somalia, Tanzania, and Uganda. ORIG OE *scilling*

Shillong ★ (ʃɪ'lɒŋ) *n* a city in NE India, capital of Meghalaya: situated on the **Shillong Plateau** at an altitude of 1520 m (4987 ft); destroyed by earthquake in 1897 and rebuilt. Pop.: 131 719 (1991).

shillyshally ('ʃɪlɪˌʃælɪ) *Inf.* ◆ *vb* **shillyshallies, shillyshallying, shillyshallied. 1** (*intr*) to be indecisive, esp. over unimportant matters. ◆ *adv* **2** in an indecisive manner. ◆ *adj* **3** indecisive or hesitant. ◆ *n, pl* **shillyshallies. 4** vacillation. ORIG C18: from *shill I shall I,* by reduplication of *shall I*
▸ **'shillyˌshallier** *n*

Shiloh ★ ('ʃaɪləʊ) *n* a town in central ancient Palestine, in Canaan on the E slope of Mount Ephraim: keeping place of the tabernacle and the ark; destroyed by the Philistines.

shily ('ʃaɪlɪ) *adv* a less common spelling of **shyly.** See **shy**[1].

shim (ʃɪm) *n* **1** a thin washer or strip often used with a number of similar washers or strips to adjust a clearance for gears, etc. ◆ *vb* **shims, shimming, shimmed. 2** (*tr*) to modify clearance on (a gear, etc.) by use of shims. ORIG C18: from ?

shimmer ('ʃɪmə) *vb* **1** (*intr*) to shine with a glistening or tremulous light. ◆ *n* **2** a faint, glistening, or tremulous light. ORIG OE *scimerian*
▸ **'shimmering** *or* **'shimmery** *adj*

shimmy ('ʃɪmɪ) *n, pl* **shimmies. 1** an American ragtime dance with much shaking of the hips and shoulders. **2** abnormal wobbling motion in a motor vehicle, esp. in the front wheels or steering. ◆ *vb* **shimmies, shimmying, shimmied.** (*intr*) **3** to dance the shimmy. **4** to vibrate or wobble. ORIG C19: changed from CHEMISE, mistaken for pl

Shimonoseki ★ (ˌʃɪmənəʊ'sɛkɪ) *n* a port in SW Japan, on SW Honshu: scene of the peace treaty (1895) ending the Sino-Japanese War; a heavy industrial centre. Pop.: 259 791 (1995).

shin (ʃɪn) *n* **1** the front part of the lower leg. **2** the front edge of the tibia. **3** *Chiefly Brit.* a cut of beef, the lower foreleg. ◆ *vb* **shins, shinning, shinned. 4** (when *intr,* often foll. by *up*) to climb (a pole, tree, etc.) by gripping with the hands or arms and the legs and hauling oneself up. **5** (*tr*) to kick (a person) in the shins. ORIG OE *scinu*

Shinar ★ ('ʃaɪnə) *n Old Testament.* the southern part of the valley of the Tigris and Euphrates, often identified with Sumer; Babylonia.

shinbone ('ʃɪnˌbəʊn) *n* the nontechnical name for **tibia** (sense 1).

shindig ('ʃɪnˌdɪg) *or* **shindy** ('ʃɪndɪ) *n, pl* **shindigs** *or* **shindies.** *Sl.* **1** a noisy party, dance, etc. **2** a quarrel or commotion. ORIG C19: var. of SHINTY

shine (ʃaɪn) *vb* **shines, shining, shone. 1** (*intr*) to emit light. **2** (*intr*) to glow or be bright with reflected light. **3** (*tr*) to direct the light of (a lamp, etc.): *he shone the torch in my eyes.* **4** (*tr; p.t. & p.p.* **shined**) to cause to gleam by polishing: *to shine shoes.* **5** (*intr*) to excel: *she shines at tennis.* **6** (*intr*) to appear clearly. ◆ *n* **7** the state or quality of shining; sheen; lustre. **8** *Inf.* a liking or fancy (esp. in **take a shine to**). ORIG OE *scīnan*

shiner ('ʃaɪnə) *n* **1** something that shines, such as a polishing device. **2** any of numerous small North American freshwater cyprinid fishes. **3** *Inf.* a black eye. **4** *NZ. old-fashioned inf.* a tramp.

shingle[1] ('ʃɪŋgᵊl) *n* **1** a thin rectangular tile, esp. one made of wood, that is laid with others in overlapping rows to cover a roof or a wall. **2** a woman's short-cropped hairstyle. **3** *US & Canad.* a small signboard fixed outside the office of a doctor, lawyer, etc. ◆ *vb* **shingles, shingling, shingled.** (*tr*) **4** to cover (a roof or a wall) with shingles. **5** to cut (the hair) in a short-cropped style. ORIG C12

scingle, from LL *scindula* a split piece of wood, from L *scindere* to split
▸ **'shingler** *n*

shingle[2] (ˈʃɪŋgᵊl) *n* **1** coarse gravel, esp. the pebbles found on beaches. **2** a place or area strewn with shingle. ORIG C16: of Scand. origin
▸ **'shingly** *adj*

shingles (ˈʃɪŋgᵊlz) *n* (*functioning as sing*) an acute viral disease characterized by inflammation, pain, and skin eruptions along the course of affected nerves. Technical names: **herpes zoster, zoster.** ORIG C14: from Med. L *cingulum* girdle, rendering Gk *zōnē* zone

shinny (ˈʃɪnɪ) *n Canad.* a kind of hockey either played on ice with skates, or without skates on the street without nets. ORIG C20: from SHIN

Shinto (ˈʃɪntəʊ) *n* the indigenous religion of Japan, incorporating the worship of a number of ethnic divinities. ORIG C18: from Japanese: the way of the gods, from Chinese *shên* gods + *tao* way
▸ **'Shintoism** *n* ▸ **'Shintoist** *n, adj*

shinty (ˈʃɪntɪ) *n* **1** a game resembling hockey played with a ball and sticks curved at the lower end. **2** (*pl* **shinties**) the stick used in this game. ORIG C17: ? from Scot. Gaelic *sinteag* a pace, bound

shiny (ˈʃaɪnɪ) *adj* **shinier, shiniest. 1** glossy or polished; bright. **2** (of clothes or material) worn to a smooth and glossy state, as by continual rubbing.
▸ **'shininess** *n*

ship (ʃɪp) *n* **1** a vessel propelled by engines or sails for navigating on the water, esp. a large vessel. **2** *Naut.* a large sailing vessel with three or more square-rigged masts. **3** the crew of a ship. **4** short for **airship** or **spaceship. 5 when one's ship comes in** (*or* **home**). when one has become successful. ◆ *vb* **ships, shipping, shipped. 6** to place, transport, or travel on any conveyance, esp. aboard a ship. **7** (*tr*) *Naut.* to take (water) over the side. **8** to bring or go aboard a vessel: *to ship oars.* **9** (*tr;* often foll. by *off*) *Inf.* to send away: *they shipped the children off to boarding school.* **10** (*intr*) to engage to serve aboard a ship: *I shipped aboard a Liverpool liner.* ORIG OE *scip*
▸ **'shippable** *adj*

-ship *suffix forming nouns.* **1** indicating state or condition: *fellowship.* **2** indicating rank, office, or position: *lordship.* **3** indicating craft or skill: *scholarship.* ORIG OE *-scipe*

shipboard (ˈʃɪpˌbɔːd) *n* (*modifier*) taking place, used, or intended for use aboard a ship: *a shipboard encounter.*

shipbuilder (ˈʃɪpˌbɪldə) *n* a person or business engaged in building ships.
▸ **'shipˌbuilding** *n*

ship chandler *n* a person or business dealing in supplies for ships.
▸ **ship chandlery** *n*

Shipka Pass ★ (ˈʃɪpkə) *n* a pass over the Balkan Mountains in central Bulgaria: scene of a bloody Turkish defeat in the Russo-Turkish War (1877–78). Height: 1334 m (4376 ft).

shipload (ˈʃɪpˌləʊd) *n* the quantity carried by a ship.

shipmaster (ˈʃɪpˌmɑːstə) *n* the master or captain of a ship.

shipmate (ˈʃɪpˌmeɪt) *n* a sailor who serves on the same ship as another.

shipment (ˈʃɪpmənt) *n* **1a** goods shipped together as part of the same lot: *a shipment of grain.* **1b** (*as modifier*): *a shipment schedule.* **2** the act of shipping cargo.

ship money *n English history.* a tax levied to finance the fitting out of warships: abolished 1640.

ship of the line *n Naut.* (formerly) a warship large enough to fight in the first line of battle.

shipowner (ˈʃɪpˌəʊnə) *n* a person who owns or has shares in a ship or ships.

shipper (ˈʃɪpə) *n* a person or company in the business of shipping freight.

shipping (ˈʃɪpɪŋ) *n* **1a** the business of transporting freight, esp. by ship. **1b** (*as modifier*): *a shipping magnate; shipping line.* **2** ships collectively: *there is a lot of shipping in the Channel.*

ship's biscuit *n* another name for **hardtack.**

shipshape (ˈʃɪpˌʃeɪp) *adj* **1** neat; orderly. ◆ *adv* **2** in a neat and orderly manner.

shipworm (ˈʃɪpˌwɜːm) *n* any of a genus of wormlike marine bivalve molluscs that bore into wooden piers, ships, etc., by means of drill-like shell valves.

shipwreck (ˈʃɪpˌrɛk) *n* **1** the partial or total destruction of a ship at sea. **2** a wrecked ship or part of such a ship. **3** ruin or destruction: *the shipwreck of all my hopes.* ◆ *vb* (*tr*) **4** to wreck or destroy (a ship). **5** to bring to ruin or destruction. ORIG OE *scipwræc,* from SHIP + *wræc* something driven by the sea

shipwright (ˈʃɪpˌraɪt) *n* an artisan skilled in one or more of the tasks required to build vessels.

shipyard (ˈʃɪpˌjɑːd) *n* a place or facility for the building, maintenance, and repair of ships.

shiralee (ˌʃɪrəˈliː) *n Austral. sl.* a swagman's bundle. ORIG from ?

Shiraz[1] ★ (ʃɪəˈrɑːz) *n* a city in SW Iran, at an altitude of 1585 m (5200 ft): an important Muslim cultural centre in the 14th century; university (1948); noted for fine carpets. Pop.: 1 042 801 (1994 est.).

Shiraz[2] (ʃɪəˈrɑːz) *n* the Austral. name for **Syrah.** ORIG from SHIRAZ[1], where the wine supposedly originated

shire (ˈʃaɪə) *n* **1a** one of the British counties. **1b** (*in combination*): *Yorkshire.* **2** (in Australia) a rural district having its own local council. **3** See **shire horse. 4 the Shires.** the Midland counties of England, famous for hunting, etc. ORIG OE *scīr* office

Shiré ★ (ˈʃɪəreɪ) *n* a river in E central Africa, flowing from Lake Malawi through Malawi and Mozambique to the Zambezi. Length: 596 km (370 miles).

Shiré Highlands ★ *pl n* an upland area of S Malawi. Average height: 900 m (3000 ft).

shire horse *n* a large heavy breed of carthorse with long hair on the fetlocks.

shirk (ʃɜːk) *vb* **1** to avoid discharging (work, a duty, etc.); evade. ◆ *n also* **shirker. 2** a person who shirks. ORIG C17: prob. from G *Schurke* rogue

shirr (ʃɜː) *vb* **1** to gather (fabric) into two or more parallel rows to decorate a dress, blouse, etc., often using elastic thread. **2** (*tr*) to bake (eggs) out of their shells. ◆ *n also* **shirring. 3** a series of gathered rows decorating a dress, blouse, etc. ORIG C19: from ?

shirt (ʃɜːt) *n* **1** a garment worn on the upper part of the body, esp. by men, usually having a collar and sleeves and buttoning up the front. **2** short for **nightshirt. 3 keep your shirt on.** *Inf.* refrain from losing your temper. **4 put** *or* **lose one's shirt on.** *Inf.* to bet or lose all one has on (a horse, etc.). ORIG OE *scyrte*

shirting (ˈʃɜːtɪŋ) *n* fabric used in making men's shirts.

shirt-lifter *n Derog. sl.* a male homosexual.

shirtsleeve (ˈʃɜːtˌsliːv) *n* **1** the sleeve of a shirt. **2 in one's shirtsleeves.** not wearing a jacket.

shirt-tail *n* the part of a shirt that extends below the waist.

shirtwaister (ˈʃɜːtˌweɪstə) *or US* **shirtwaist** *n* a woman's dress with a tailored bodice resembling a shirt.

shirty (ˈʃɜːtɪ) *adj* **shirtier, shirtiest.** *Sl., chiefly Brit.* bad-tempered or annoyed. ORIG C19: ? based on such phrases as *to get someone's shirt out* to annoy someone
▸ **'shirtily** *adv*

shish kebab (ʃiːʃ kəˈbæb) *n* a dish consisting of small pieces of meat and vegetables threaded onto skewers and grilled. ORIG from Turkish *şiş kebab,* from *şiş* skewer; see KEBAB

shit (ʃɪt) *Taboo.* ◆ *vb* **shits, shitting; shitted, shit,** *or* **shat. 1** to defecate. **2** (usually foll. by *on*) *Sl.* to give the worst possible treatment (to). ◆ *n* **3** faeces; excrement. **4** an act of defecation. **5** *Sl.* rubbish; nonsense. **6** *Sl.* an obnoxious or worthless person. ◆ *interj* **7** *Sl.* an exclamation expressing anger, disgust, etc. ORIG OE *scite* (unattested) dung, *scītan* to defecate, of Gmc origin
▸ **'shitty** *adj*

Shittim ★ (ˈʃɪtɪm) *n Old Testament.* the site to the east of the Jordan and northeast of the Dead Sea where the Israelites encamped before crossing the Jordan (Numbers 25:1–9).

shiv (ʃɪv) *n* a variant of **chiv.**

Shiva ★ (ˈʃiːvə, ˈʃɪvə) *n* a variant spelling of **Siva.**

shivaree (ˌʃɪvəˈriː) *n* a variant spelling (esp. US and Canad.) of **charivari.**

shiver[1] (ˈʃɪvə) *vb (intr)* **1** to shake or tremble, as from cold or fear. ◆ *n* **2** the act of shivering; a tremulous motion. **3 the shivers.** an attack of shivering, esp. through fear or illness. ORIG C13 *chiveren,* ? var. of *chevelen* to chatter (used of teeth), from OE *ceafl* jowl
▸ **ˈshiverer** *n* ▸ **ˈshivering** *n, adj* ▸ **ˈshivery** *adj*

shiver[2] (ˈʃɪvə) *vb* **1** to break or cause to break into fragments. ◆ *n* **2** a splintered piece. ORIG C13: of Gmc origin

Shizuoka ★ (ˌʃiːzuːˈəʊkə) *n* a city in central Japan, on S Honshu: a centre for green tea; university (1949). Pop.: 474 089 (1995).

Shkodër ★ (*Albanian* ˈʃkodər) *n* a market town in NW Albania, on **Lake Shkodër**: an Illyrian capital in the first millennium B.C. Pop.: 83 700 (1991 est.). Italian name: **Scutari.**

shoal[1] (ʃəʊl) *n* **1** a stretch of shallow water. **2** a sandbank or rocky area, esp. one that is visible at low water. ◆ *vb* **3** to make or become shallow. **4** *(intr) Naut.* to sail into shallower water. ◆ *adj also* **shoaly. 5** a less common word for **shallow.** ORIG OE *sceald* shallow

shoal[2] (ʃəʊl) *n* **1** a large group of fish. **2** a large group of people or things. ◆ *vb* **3** *(intr)* to collect together in such a group. ORIG OE *scolu*

shock[1] (ʃɒk) *vb* **1** to experience or cause to experience extreme horror, disgust, surprise, etc.: *the atrocities shocked us.* **2** to cause a state of shock in (a person). **3** to come or cause to come into violent contact. ◆ *n* **4** a sudden and violent jarring blow or impact. **5** something that causes a sudden and violent disturbance in the emotions. **6** *Pathol.* a state of bodily collapse, as from severe bleeding, burns, fright, etc. **7** Also: **electric shock.** pain and muscular spasm as the physical reaction to an electric current passing through the body. ORIG C16: from OF *choc,* from *choquier* to make violent contact with, of Gmc origin
▸ **ˈshockable** *adj* ▸ **ˌshockaˈbility** *n*

shock[2] (ʃɒk) *n* **1** a number of sheaves set on end in a field to dry. **2** a pile or stack of unthreshed corn. ◆ *vb* **3** *(tr)* to set up (sheaves) in shocks. ORIG C14: prob. of Gmc origin

shock[3] (ʃɒk) *n* a thick bushy mass, esp. of hair. ORIG C19: ?from SHOCK[2]

shock absorber *n* any device designed to absorb mechanical shock, esp. one fitted to a motor vehicle to damp the recoil of the road springs.

shocker (ˈʃɒkə) *n Inf.* **1** a person or thing that shocks. **2** a sensational novel, film, or play.

shockheaded (ˈʃɒkˌhɛdɪd) *adj* having a head of bushy or tousled hair.

shock-horror *adj Facetious.* (esp. of newspaper headlines) sensationalistic: *shock-horror stories about the British diet.*

shocking (ˈʃɒkɪŋ) *adj* **1** causing shock, horror, or disgust. **2 shocking pink. 2a** of a garish shade of pink. **2b** *(as n): dressed in shocking pink.* **3** *Inf.* very bad or terrible: *shocking weather.*
▸ **ˈshockingly** *adv*

Shockley ★ (ˈʃɒklɪ) *n* **William Bradfield.** 1910–89, US physicist, born in Britain, who shared the Nobel prize for physics (1956) with John Bardeen and Walter Brattain for developing the transistor. He also held controversial views on the connection between race and intelligence.

shockproof (ˈʃɒkˌpruːf) *adj* capable of absorbing shock without damage.

shock therapy *or* **treatment** *n* the treatment of certain psychotic conditions by injecting drugs or by passing an electric current through the brain (**electroconvulsive therapy**) to produce convulsions or coma.

shock troops *pl n* soldiers specially trained and equipped to carry out an assault.

shock wave *n* a region across which there is a rapid pressure, temperature, and density rise caused by a body moving supersonically in a gas or by a detonation. See also **sonic boom.**

shod (ʃɒd) *vb* the past participle of **shoe.**

shoddy (ˈʃɒdɪ) *adj* **shoddier, shoddiest. 1** imitating something of better quality. **2** of poor quality. ◆ *n, pl* **shoddies. 3** a yarn or fabric made from wool waste or clippings. **4** anything of inferior quality that is designed to simulate superior quality. ORIG C19: from ?
▸ **ˈshoddily** *adv* ▸ **ˈshoddiness** *n*

shoe (ʃuː) *n* **1a** one of a matching pair of coverings shaped to fit the foot, esp. one ending below the ankle, having an upper of leather, plastic, etc., on a sole and heel of heavier material. **1b** *(as modifier): shoe cleaner.* **2** anything resembling a shoe in shape, function, position, etc., such as a horseshoe. **3** a band of metal or wood on the bottom of the runner of a sledge. **4** *Engineering.* a lining to protect from wear: see **brake shoe. 5 be in (a person's) shoes.** *Inf.* to be in (another person's) situation. ◆ *vb* **shoes, shoeing, shod.** *(tr)* **6** to furnish with shoes. **7** to fit (a horse) with horseshoes. **8** to furnish with a hard cover, such as a metal plate, for protection against friction or bruising. ORIG OE *scōh*

shoeblack (ˈʃuːˌblæk) *n* (esp. formerly) a person who shines boots and shoes.

shoehorn (ˈʃuːˌhɔːn) *n* **1** a smooth curved implement of horn, metal, plastic, etc., inserted at the heel of a shoe to ease the foot into it. ◆ *vb (tr)* **2** to cram (people or things) into a small space.

shoelace (ˈʃuːˌleɪs) *n* a cord for fastening shoes.

shoe leather *n* **1** leather used to make shoes. **2 save shoe leather.** to avoid wearing out shoes, as by taking a bus rather than walking.

shoemaker (ˈʃuːˌmeɪkə) *n* a person who makes or repairs shoes or boots.
▸ **ˈshoeˌmaking** *n*

shoer (ˈʃuːə) *n Rare.* a person who shoes horses; farrier.

shoeshine (ˈʃuːˌʃaɪn) *n* the act or an instance of polishing a pair of shoes.

shoestring (ˈʃuːˌstrɪŋ) *n* **1** another word for **shoelace. 2** *Inf.* a very small or petty amount of money (esp. in **on a shoestring**).

shoetree (ˈʃuːˌtriː) *n* a wooden or metal form inserted into a shoe or boot to stretch it or preserve its shape.

shofar *or* **shophar** (*Hebrew* ʃɔˈfar) *n, pl* **shofars, shophars** *or* **shofroth, shophroth** (*Hebrew* -ˈfrɔt). *Judaism.* a ram's horn sounded on certain religious occasions. ORIG from Heb. *shōphār* ram's horn

shogun (ˈʃəʊˌguːn) *n Japanese history.* (from about 1192 to 1867) any of a line of hereditary military dictators who relegated the emperors to a position of purely theoretical supremacy. ORIG C17: from Japanese, from Chinese *chiang chün* general, from *chiang* to lead + *chün* army
▸ **ˈshogunate** *n*

shogun bond *n* a bond sold on the Japanese market by a foreign institution and denominated in a foreign currency. Cf. **samurai bond.**

Sholapur ★ (ˈʃəʊləˌpʊə) *n* a city in SW India, in S Maharashtra: major textile centre. Pop.: 604 215 (1991).

Sholem Aleichem ★ (ˈʃɒləm ɑːˈleɪçɛm) *n* See (Sholem) **Aleichem.**

Sholokhov ★ (*Russian* ˈʃɔləxəf) *n* **Mikhail Aleksandrovich** (mixaˈil alɪkˈsandrəvitʃ). 1905–84, Soviet author, noted for *And Quiet Flows the Don* (1934) and *The Don Flows Home to the Sea* (1940): Nobel prize for literature 1965.

shone (ʃɒn; *US* ʃəʊn) *vb* a past tense and past participle of **shine.**

shoo (ʃuː) *sentence substitute.* **1** go away!: used to drive away unwanted or annoying people, animals, etc. ◆ *vb* **shoos, shooing, shooed. 2** *(tr)* to drive away by or as if by crying "shoo". **3** *(intr)* to cry "shoo". ORIG C15: imit.

shoo-in *n* **1** a person or thing that is certain to win or succeed. **2** a match or contest that is easy to win.

shook[1] (ʃʊk) *n* **1** a set of parts ready for assembly, esp. of a barrel. **2** a group of sheaves piled together on end; shock. ORIG C18: from ?

shook[2] (ʃuk) *vb* the past tense of **shake.**

shoon (ʃu:n) *n Dialect, chiefly Scot.* a plural of **shoe.**

shoot (ʃu:t) *vb* **shoots, shooting, shot. 1** (*tr*) to hit, wound, damage, or kill with a missile discharged from a weapon. **2** to discharge (a missile or missiles) from a weapon. **3** to fire (a weapon) or (of a weapon) to be fired. **4** to send out or be sent out as if from a weapon: *he shot questions at her.* **5** (*intr*) to move very rapidly. **6** (*tr*) to slide or push into or out of a fastening: *to shoot a bolt.* **7** to emit (a ray of light) or (of a ray of light) to be emitted. **8** (*tr*) to go or pass quickly over or through: *to shoot rapids.* **9** (*intr*) to hunt game with a gun for sport. **10** (*tr*) to pass over (an area) in hunting game. **11** (*intr*) (of a plant) to produce (buds, branches, etc.). **12** to photograph or record (a sequence, etc.). **13** (*tr; usually passive*) to variegate or streak, as with colour. **14** *Soccer, hockey, etc.* to hit or propel (the ball, etc.) towards the goal. **15** (*tr*) *Sport, chiefly US & Canad.* to score (strokes, etc.): *he shot 72 on the first round.* **16** (*tr*) to measure the altitude of (a celestial body). **17** (often foll. by *up*) *Sl.* to inject (someone, esp. oneself) with (a drug, esp. heroin). **18 shoot a line.** *Sl.* **18a** to boast. **18b** to tell a lie. **19 shoot oneself in the foot.** *Inf.* to damage one's own cause inadvertently. ◆ *n* **20** the act of shooting. **21** the action or motion of something that is shot. **22** the first aerial part of a plant to develop from a germinating seed. **23** any new growth of a plant, such as a bud, etc. **24** *Chiefly Brit.* a meeting or party organized for hunting game with guns. **25** an area where game can be hunted with guns. **26** a steep descent in a stream; rapid. **27** *Inf.* a photographic assignment **28 the whole shoot.** *Sl.* everything. ◆ *interj* **29** *US & Canad.* an exclamation expressing disbelief, scepticism, disappointment, etc. ◆ See also **shoot down, shoot through.** ORIG OE *sceōtan*

shoot down *vb* (*tr, adv*) **1** to shoot callously. **2** to defeat or disprove: *he shot down her argument.*

shoot-'em-up *or* **shoot-em-up** *n Inf.* **1** a type of computer game, the object of which is to shoot as many enemies, targets, etc. as possible. **2** a fast-moving film involving many gunfights, battles, etc.

shooter ('ʃu:tə) *n* **1** a person or thing that shoots. **2** *Sl.* a gun.

shooting box *n* a small country house providing accommodation for a shooting party. Also called: **shooting lodge.**

shooting brake *n Brit.* another name for **estate car.**

shooting star *n Inf.* a meteor.

shooting stick *n* a device that resembles a walking stick, having a spike at one end and a folding seat at the other.

shoot through *vb* (*intr, adv*) *Austral. inf.* to leave; go away.

shop (ʃɒp) *n* **1** a place, esp. a small building, for the retail sale of goods and services. **2** an act or instance of shopping. **3** a place for the performance of a specified type of work; workshop. **4 all over the shop.** *Inf.* **4a** in disarray: *his papers were all over the shop.* **4b** in every direction: *I've searched for it all over the shop.* **5 shut up shop. 5a** to close business at the end of the day or permanently. **5b** to become defensive or inactive. **6 talk shop.** *Inf.* to discuss one's business, profession, etc., esp. on a social occasion. ◆ *vb* **shops, shopping, shopped. 7** (*intr;* often foll. by *for*) to visit a shop or shops in search of (goods) with the intention of buying them. **8** (*tr*) *Sl., chiefly Brit.* to inform on (someone), esp. to the police. ORIG OE *sceoppa* stall
▸ **'shopping** *n*

shop around *vb* (*intr, adv*) *Inf.* **1** to visit a number of shops or stores to compare goods and prices. **2** to consider a number of possibilities before making a choice.

shop assistant *n* a person who serves in a shop.

shop floor *n* **1** the part of a factory housing the machines and men directly involved in production. **2** workers, esp. factory workers organized in a union.

shopkeeper ('ʃɒpˌki:pə) *n* a person who owns or manages a shop or small store.
▸ **'shopˌkeeping** *n*

shoplifter ('ʃɒpˌlɪftə) *n* a customer who steals goods from a shop.
▸ **'shopˌlifting** *n*

★ people and places

shopper ('ʃɒpə) *n* **1** a person who buys goods in a shop. **2** a bag for shopping.

shopping centre *n* **1** a purpose-built complex of stores, restaurants, etc. **2** the area of a town where most of the shops are situated.

shopping mall *n* a large enclosed shopping centre.

shopping plaza *n Chiefly US & Canad.* a shopping centre, esp. a small group of stores built as a strip.

shopsoiled ('ʃɒpˌsɔɪld) *adj* worn, faded, etc., from being displayed in a shop or store.

shop steward *n* an elected representative of the union workers in a shop, factory, etc.

shoptalk ('ʃɒpˌtɔ:k) *n* conversation concerning one's work, esp. when carried on outside business hours.

shopwalker ('ʃɒpˌwɔ:kə) *n Brit.* a person employed by a departmental store to supervise sales personnel, assist customers, etc.

shoran ('ʃɔ:ræn) *n* a short-range radar system by which an aircraft, ship, etc., can accurately determine its position. ORIG C20: *sho(rt-)ra(nge) n(avigation)*

shore[1] (ʃɔ:) *n* **1** the land along the edge of a sea, lake, or wide river. Related adj: **littoral. 2a** land, as opposed to water. **2b** (*as modifier*): *shore duty.* **3** *Law.* the tract of coastland lying between the ordinary marks of high and low water. **4** (*often pl*) a country: *his native shores.* ORIG C14: prob. from MLow G, MDu. *schōre*

shore[2] (ʃɔ:) *n* **1** a prop or beam used to support a wall, building, etc. ◆ *vb* **shores, shoring, shored. 2** (*tr;* often foll. by *up*) to make safe with or as if with a shore. ORIG C15: from MDu. *schōre*
▸ **'shoring** *n*

shore[3] (ʃɔ:) *vb Arch., Austral., & NZ.* a past tense of **shear.**

shore bird *n* any of various birds that live close to water, esp. plovers, sandpipers, etc. Also called (Brit.): **wader.**

shore leave *n Naval.* **1** permission to go ashore. **2** time spent ashore during leave.

shoreless ('ʃɔ:lɪs) *adj* **1** without a shore suitable for landing. **2** *Poetic.* boundless; vast.

shoreline ('ʃɔ:ˌlaɪn) *n* the edge of a body of water.

shoreward ('ʃɔ:wəd) *adj* **1** near or facing the shore. ◆ *adv also* **shorewards. 2** towards the shore.

shorn (ʃɔ:n) *vb* a past participle of **shear.**

short (ʃɔ:t) *adj* **1** of little length; not long. **2** of little height; not tall. **3** of limited duration. **4** deficient: *the number of places laid at the table was short by four.* **5** (*postpositive;* often foll. by *of* or *on*) lacking (in) or needful (of): *I'm always short of money.* **6** concise; succinct. **7** (of drinks) consisting chiefly of a spirit, such as whisky. **8** *Cricket.* (of a fielding position) near the batsman: *short leg.* **9** lacking in the power of retentiveness: *a short memory.* **10** abrupt to the point of rudeness: *the salesgirl was very short with him.* **11** (of betting odds) almost even. **12** *Finance.* **12a** not possessing the securities or commodities that have been sold under contract and therefore obliged to make a purchase before the delivery date. **12b** of or relating to such sales, which depend on falling prices for profit. **13** *Phonetics.* **13a** denoting a vowel of relatively brief temporal duration. **13b** (in popular usage) denoting the qualities of the five English vowels represented orthographically in the words *pat, pet, pit, pot, put,* and *putt.* **14** *Prosody.* **14a** denoting a vowel that is phonetically short or a syllable containing such a vowel. **14b** (of a vowel or syllable in verse) not carrying emphasis or accent. **15** (of pastry) crumbly in texture. **16 in short supply.** scarce. **17 short and sweet.** unexpectedly brief. **18 short for.** an abbreviation for. ◆ *adv* **19** abruptly: *to stop short.* **20** briefly or concisely. **21** rudely or curtly. **22** *Finance.* without possessing the securities or commodities at the time of their contractual sale: *to sell short.* **23 caught** *or* **taken short.** having a sudden need to urinate or defecate. **24 go short.** not to have a sufficient amount, etc. **25 short of.** except: *nothing short of a miracle can save him now.* ◆ *n* **26** anything that is short. **27** a drink of spirits. **28** *Phonetics, prosody.* a short vowel or syllable. **29** *Finance.* **29a** a short contract or sale. **29b** a short seller. **30** a short film, usually of a factual nature. **31** See **short circuit. 32 for short.** *Inf.* as a shortened form: *he is called J.R. for short.* **33 in**

short. 33a as a summary. **33b** in a few words. ◆ *vb* **34** See **short circuit** (sense 2). ◆ See also **shorts.** ORIG OE *scort*
▸ **'shortness** *n*

short-acting *adj* (of a drug) quickly effective, but requiring regularly repeated doses for long-term treatment. Cf. **intermediate-acting, long-acting.**

shortage ('ʃɔːtɪdʒ) *n* a deficiency or lack in the amount needed, expected, or due; deficit.

shortbread ('ʃɔːtˌbrɛd) *n* a rich crumbly biscuit made with a large proportion of butter.

shortcake ('ʃɔːtˌkeɪk) *n* **1** shortbread. **2** a dessert made of layers of biscuit or cake filled with fruit and cream.

short-change *vb* **short-changes, short-changing, short-changed.** *(tr)* **1** to give less than correct change to. **2** *Sl.* to treat unfairly or dishonestly, esp. by giving less than is expected or deserved.

short circuit *n* **1** a faulty or accidental connection between two points of different potential in an electric circuit, establishing a path of low resistance through which an excessive current can flow. ◆ *vb* **short-circuit. 2** to develop or cause to develop a short circuit. **3** *(tr)* to bypass (a procedure, etc.). **4** *(tr)* to hinder or frustrate (plans, etc.). ◆ Sometimes (for senses 1, 2) shortened to **short.**

shortcoming ('ʃɔːtˌkʌmɪŋ) *n* a failing, defect, or deficiency.

short corner *n Hockey.* another name for **penalty corner.**

short covering *n* the purchase of securities or commodities by a short seller to meet delivery requirements.

shortcrust pastry ('ʃɔːtˌkrʌst) *n* a basic type of pastry that has a crisp but crumbly texture. Also: **short pastry.**

short cut *n* **1** a route that is shorter than the usual one. **2** a means of saving time or effort. ◆ *vb* **short-cut, short-cuts, short-cutting, short-cut. 3** *(intr)* to use a short cut.

short-dated *adj* (of a gilt-edged security) having less than five years to run before redemption. Cf. **medium-dated, long-dated.**

short-day *adj* (of plants) able to flower only if exposed to short periods of daylight, each followed by a long dark period. Cf. **long-day.**

shorten ('ʃɔːtᵊn) *vb* **1** to make or become short or shorter. **2** *(tr) Naut.* to reduce the area of (sail). **3** *(tr)* to make (pastry, etc.) short, by adding fat. **4** *Gambling.* to cause (the odds) to lessen or (of odds) to become less.

shortening ('ʃɔːtᵊnɪŋ) *n* butter or other fat, used in a dough, etc., to make the mixture short.

Shorter Catechism *n Chiefly Presbyterian Church.* the more widely used of two catechisms of religious instruction drawn up in 1647.

shortfall ('ʃɔːtˌfɔːl) *n* **1** failure to meet a goal or a requirement. **2** the amount of such a failure.

shorthand ('ʃɔːtˌhænd) *n* **a** a system of rapid handwriting employing simple strokes and other symbols to represent words or phrases. **b** *(as modifier): a shorthand typist.*

short-handed *adj* **1** lacking the usual or necessary number of assistants, workers, etc. **2** *Sport, US & Canad.* with less than the full complement of players.

shorthand typist *n Brit.* a person skilled in the use of shorthand and in typing. US and Canad. name: **stenographer.**

short head *n Horse racing.* a distance shorter than the length of a horse's head.

shorthorn ('ʃɔːtˌhɔːn) *n* a short-horned breed of cattle with several regional varieties.

shortie *or* **shorty** ('ʃɔːtɪ) *n, pl* **shorties.** *Inf.* **a** a person or thing that is extremely short. **b** *(as modifier): a shortie nightdress.*

short list *Chiefly Brit.* ◆ *n* **1** Also called (Scot.): **short leet.** a list of suitable applicants for a job, post, etc., from which the successful candidate will be selected. ◆ *vb* **short-list.** *(tr)* **2** to put (someone) on a short list.

short-lived *adj* living or lasting only for a short time.

shortly ('ʃɔːtlɪ) *adv* **1** in a short time; soon. **2** briefly. **3** in a curt or rude manner.

short-order *adj Chiefly US.* of or connected with food that is easily and quickly prepared.

short-range *adj* of small or limited extent in time or distance: *a short-range forecast.*

shorts (ʃɔːts) *pl n* **1** trousers reaching the top of the thigh or partway to the knee, worn by both sexes for sport, etc. **2** *Chiefly US & Canad.* men's underpants that usually reach mid-thigh. **3** short-dated gilt-edged securities. **4** short-term bonds. **5** securities or commodities that have been sold short. **6** a livestock feed containing a large proportion of bran and wheat germ.

short shrift *n* **1** brief and unsympathetic treatment. **2** (formerly) a brief period allowed to a condemned prisoner to make confession. **3 make short shrift of.** to dispose of quickly.

short-sighted *adj* **1** relating to or suffering from myopia. **2** lacking foresight: *a short-sighted plan.*
▸ **ˌshort-'sightedly** *adv* ▸ **ˌshort-'sightedness** *n*

short-spoken *adj* tending to be abrupt in speech.

short story *n* a prose narrative of shorter length than the novel.

short-tempered *adj* easily moved to anger.

short-term *adj* **1** of, for, or extending over a limited period. **2** *Finance.* extending over, maturing within, or required within a short period of time, usually twelve months: *short-term credit; short-term capital.*

short-termism (-'tɜːmɪzəm) *n* the tendency to focus attention on short-term gains, often at the expense of long-term success or stability.

short time *n* the state or condition of working less than the normal working week, esp. because of a business recession.

short ton *n* the full name for **ton**[1] (sense 2).

short-waisted *adj* unusually short from the shoulders to the waist.

short wave *n* **a** a radio wave with a wavelength in the range 10–100 metres. **b** *(as modifier): a short-wave broadcast.*

short-winded *adj* **1** tending to run out of breath, esp. after exertion. **2** (of speech or writing) terse or abrupt.

Shostakovich ★ (ˌʃɒstə'kəʊvɪtʃ; *Russian* ʃəsta'kɔvitʃ) *n* **Dmitri Dmitriyevich** ('dmitrij 'dmitrijɪvitʃ). 1906–75, Soviet composer, noted esp. for his 15 symphonies and his chamber music.

shot[1] (ʃɒt) *n* **1** the act or an instance of discharging a projectile. **2** *(pl* **shot***)* a solid missile, such as an iron ball or a lead pellet, discharged from a firearm. **3a** small round pellets of lead collectively, as used in cartridges. **3b** metal in the form of coarse powder or small pellets. **4** the distance that a discharged projectile travels or is capable of travelling. **5** a person who shoots, esp. with regard to his or her ability: *he is a good shot.* **6** *Inf.* an attempt. **7** *Inf.* a guess. **8** any act of throwing or hitting something, as in certain sports. **9** the launching of a rocket, etc., esp. to a specified destination: *a moon shot.* **10a** a single photograph. **10b** a length of film taken by a single camera without breaks. **11** *Inf.* an injection, as of a vaccine or narcotic drug. **12** *Inf.* a glass of alcoholic drink, esp. spirits. **13** *Sport.* a heavy metal ball used in the shot put. **14 call the shots.** *Sl.* to have control over an organization, etc. **15 have a shot at.** *Inf.* to attempt. **16 like a shot.** very quickly, esp. willingly. **17 shot in the arm.** *Inf.* anything that regenerates, increases confidence or efficiency, etc. **18 shot in the dark.** a wild guess. ORIG OE *scot*

shot[2] (ʃɒt) *vb* **1** the past tense and past participle of **shoot.** ◆ *adj* **2** (of textiles) woven to give a changing colour effect: *shot silk.* **3** streaked with colour.

shotgun ('ʃɒtˌgʌn) *n* **1** a shoulder firearm with unrifled bore used mainly for hunting small game. **2** *American football.* an offensive formation in which the quarterback lines up for a snap unusually far behind the line of scrimmage. ◆ *adj* **3** *Chiefly US.* involving coercion or duress: *a shotgun merger.*

shotgun wedding *n Inf.* a wedding into which one or both partners are coerced, usually because the woman is pregnant.

shot put *n* an athletic event in which contestants hurl or put a heavy metal ball or shot as far as possible.
▸ **'shot-ˌputter** *n*

shotten ('ʃɒtᵊn) *adj* **1** (of fish, esp. herring) having recently spawned. **2** *Arch.* worthless. ORIG C15: from obs. p.p. of SHOOT

shot tower *n* a building formerly used in the production of shot, in which molten lead was graded and dropped from a great height into water, thus cooling it and forming the shot.

should (ʃʊd) *vb* the past tense of **shall**: used as an auxiliary verb to indicate that an action is considered by the speaker to be obligatory (*you should go*) or to form the subjunctive mood with *I* or *we* (*I should like to see you*). ORIG OE *sceold*

> **USAGE NOTE** The use of *should of* instead of *should have* in phrases such as *I should of known better* is nonstandard, and should be avoided in writing.

shoulder ('ʃəʊldə) *n* **1** the part of the vertebrate body where the arm or a corresponding forelimb joins the trunk. **2** the joint at the junction of the forelimb with the pectoral girdle. **3** a cut of meat including the upper part of the foreleg. **4** *Printing.* the flat surface of a piece of type from which the face rises. **5** the part of a garment that covers the shoulder. **6** anything that resembles a shoulder in shape or position. **7** the strip of unpaved land that borders a road. **8 a shoulder to cry on.** a person one turns to for sympathy with one's troubles. **9 give (someone) the cold shoulder.** *Inf.* **9a** to treat in a cold manner; snub. **9b** to ignore or shun. **10 put one's shoulder to the wheel.** *Inf.* to work very hard. **11 rub shoulders with.** *Inf.* to mix with socially or associate with. **12 shoulder to shoulder.** **12a** side by side. **12b** in a corporate effort. ◆ *vb* **13** (*tr*) to bear or carry (a burden, etc.) as if on one's shoulders. **14** to push (something) with or as if with the shoulder. **15** (*tr*) to lift or carry on the shoulders. **16 shoulder arms.** *Mil.* to bring the rifle vertically close to the right side with the muzzle uppermost. ORIG OE *sculdor*

shoulder blade *n* the nontechnical name for **scapula**.

shoulder strap *n* a strap over the shoulders, as to hold up a garment or to support a bag, etc.

shouldn't ('ʃʊdᵊnt) *contraction of* should not.

shouldst (ʃʊdst) *or* **shouldest** ('ʃʊdɪst) *vb Arch. or dialect.* (used with the pronoun *thou*) a form of the past tense of **shall**.

shout (ʃaʊt) *n* **1** a loud cry, esp. to convey emotion or a command. **2** *Inf.* **2a** a round, esp. of drinks. **2b** one's turn to buy a round of drinks. ◆ *vb* **3** to utter (something) in a loud cry. **4** (*intr*) to make a loud noise. **5** (*tr*) *Austral. & NZ inf.* to treat (someone or a group of people) to (something, esp. a round of drinks). ORIG C14: prob. from ON *skūta* taunt
▸ **'shouter** *n*

shout down *vb* (*tr, adv*) to drown, overwhelm, or silence by talking loudly.

shove (ʃʌv) *vb* **shoves, shoving, shoved. 1** to give a thrust or push to (a person or thing). **2** (*tr*) to give a violent push to. **3** (*intr*) to push one's way roughly. **4** (*tr*) *Inf.* to put (something) somewhere: *shove it in the bin.* ◆ *n* **5** the act or an instance of shoving. ◆ See also **shove off.** ORIG OE *scūfan*
▸ **'shover** *n*

shove-halfpenny *n Brit.* a game in which players try to propel coins, originally old halfpennies, with the hand into lined sections of a wooden board.

shovel ('ʃʌvᵊl) *n* **1** an instrument for lifting or scooping loose material, such as earth, coal, etc., consisting of a curved blade or a scoop attached to a handle. **2** any machine or part resembling a shovel in action. **3** Also called: **shovelful.** the amount that can be contained in a shovel. ◆ *vb* **shovels, shovelling, shovelled** *or US* **shovels, shoveling, shoveled. 4** to lift (earth, etc.) with a shovel. **5** (*tr*) to clear or dig (a path) with or as if with a shovel. **6** (*tr*) to gather, load, or unload in a hurried or careless way. ORIG OE *scofl*
▸ **'shoveller** *or US* **'shoveler** *n*

shoveler ('ʃʌvələ) *n* a duck of ponds and marshes, having a spoon-shaped bill, a blue patch on each wing, and in the male a green head, white breast, and reddish-brown body.

shovelhead ('ʃʌvᵊl,hɛd) *n* a common shark of the Atlantic and Pacific Oceans, having a shovel-shaped head.

shove off *vb* (*intr, adv; often imperative*) **1** to move from the shore in a boat. **2** *Inf.* to go away; depart.

show (ʃəʊ) *vb* **shows, showing, showed; shown** *or* **showed. 1** to make, be, or become visible or noticeable: *to show one's dislike.* **2** (*tr*) to exhibit: *he showed me a picture.* **3** (*tr*) to indicate or explain; prove: *to show that the earth moves round the sun.* **4** (*tr*) to present (oneself or itself) in a specific character: *to show oneself to be trustworthy.* **5** (*tr;* foll. by *how* and an infinitive) to instruct by demonstration: *show me how to swim.* **6** (*tr*) to indicate: *a barometer shows changes in the weather.* **7** (*tr*) to grant or bestow: *to show favour to someone.* **8** (*intr*) to appear: *to show to advantage.* **9** to exhibit, display, or offer (goods, etc.) for sale: *three artists were showing at the gallery.* **10** (*tr*) to allege, as in a legal document: *to show cause.* **11** to present (a film, etc.) or (of a play, etc.) to be presented, as at a theatre or cinema. **12** (*tr*) to guide or escort: *please show me to my room.* **13 show in** *or* **out.** to conduct a person into or out of a room or building by opening the door for him or her. **14** (*intr*) *Inf.* to arrive. ◆ *n* **15** a display or exhibition. **16** a public spectacle. **17** an ostentatious display. **18** a theatrical or other entertainment. **19** a trace or indication. **20** *Obstetrics.* a discharge of blood at the onset of labour. **21** *US, Austral., & NZ inf.* a chance (esp. in **give someone a show**). **22** *Sl., chiefly Brit.* a thing or affair (esp. in **good show, bad show,** etc.). **23 for show.** in order to attract attention. **24 run the show.** *Inf.* to take charge of or manage an affair, business, etc. **25 steal the show.** *Inf.* to be looked upon as the most interesting, popular, etc., esp. unexpectedly. ◆ See also **show off, show up.** ORIG OE *scēawian*

showboat ('ʃəʊ,bəʊt) *n* **1** a paddle-wheel river steamer with a theatre and a repertory company. ◆ *vb* **2** (*intr*) to perform or behave in a showy flamboyant way.

showbread ('ʃəʊ,brɛd) *n* a variant spelling of **shewbread.**

show business *n* the entertainment industry, including theatre, films, television, and radio. Informal term: **show biz.**

show card *n Commerce.* a card containing a tradesman's advertisement; poster.

showcase ('ʃəʊ,keɪs) *n* **1** a glass case used to display objects in a museum or shop. **2** a setting in which anything may be displayed to best advantage. ◆ *vb* **showcases, showcasing, showcased. 3** (*tr*) to display or exhibit.

show day *n* (in Australia) a public holiday in a state on the date of its annual agricultural and industrial show.

showdown ('ʃəʊ,daʊn) *n* **1** *Inf.* an action that brings matters to a head or acts as a conclusion. **2** *Poker.* the exposing of the cards in the players' hands at the end of the game.

shower[1] ('ʃaʊə) *n* **1** a brief period of rain, hail, sleet, or snow. **2** a sudden abundant fall or downpour, as of tears, sparks, or light. **3** a rush: *a shower of praise.* **4a** a kind of bath in which a person stands upright and is sprayed with water from a nozzle. **4b** the room, booth, etc., containing such a bath. Full name: **shower bath. 5** *Brit. sl.* a derogatory term applied to a person or group. **6** *US, Canad., Austral., & NZ.* a party held to honour and present gifts to a person, as to a prospective bride. **7** a large number of particles formed by the collision of a cosmic-ray particle with a particle in the atmosphere. **8** *NZ.* a light fabric put over a tea table to protect the food from flies, etc. ◆ *vb* **9** (*tr*) to sprinkle or spray with or as if with a shower. **10** (often with *it* as subject) to fall or cause to fall in the form of a shower. **11** (*tr*) to give (gifts, etc.) in abundance or present (a person) with (gifts, etc.): *they showered gifts on him.* **12** (*intr*) to take a shower. ORIG OE *scūr*
▸ **'showery** *adj*

shower[2] ('ʃəʊə) *n* a person or thing that shows.

showgirl ('ʃəʊ,gɜːl) *n* a girl who appears in variety shows, nightclub acts, etc.

show house *n* a house on a newly built estate that is decorated and furnished for prospective buyers to view.

showing ('ʃəʊɪŋ) *n* **1** a presentation, exhibition, or display. **2** manner of presentation.

showjumping (ˈʃəʊˌdʒʌmpɪŋ) *n* the riding of horses in competitions to demonstrate skill in jumping over or between various obstacles.
▸ ˈ**show-ˌjumper** *n*

showman (ˈʃəʊmən) *n, pl* **showmen. 1** a person who presents or produces a theatrical show, etc. **2** a person skilled at presenting anything in an effective manner.
▸ ˈ**showmanship** *n*

shown (ʃəʊn) *vb* a past participle of **show.**

show off *vb* (*adv*) **1** (*tr*) to exhibit or display so as to invite admiration. **2** (*intr*) *Inf.* to behave in such a manner as to make an impression. ◆ *n* **show-off. 3** *Inf.* a person who makes a vain display of himself or herself.

showpiece (ˈʃəʊˌpiːs) *n* **1** anything displayed or exhibited. **2** anything prized as a very fine example of its type.

showplace (ˈʃəʊˌpleɪs) *n* a place exhibited or visited for its beauty, historic interest, etc.

showroom (ˈʃəʊˌruːm, -ˌrʊm) *n* a room in which goods for sale, such as cars, are on display.

show up *vb* (*adv*) **1** to reveal or be revealed clearly. **2** (*tr*) to expose or reveal the faults or defects of by comparison. **3** (*tr*) *Inf.* to put to shame; embarrass. **4** (*intr*) *Inf.* to appear or arrive.

showy (ˈʃəʊɪ) *adj* **showier, showiest. 1** gaudy or ostentatious. **2** making an imposing display.
▸ ˈ**showily** *adv* ▸ ˈ**showiness** *n*

shrank (ʃræŋk) *vb* a past tense of **shrink.**

shrapnel (ˈʃræpnᵊl) *n* **1** a projectile containing a number of small pellets or bullets exploded before impact. **2** fragments from this type of shell. ORIG C19: after H. *Shrapnel* (1761–1842), E army officer, who invented it

shred (ʃrɛd) *n* **1** a long narrow strip or fragment torn or cut off. **2** a very small piece or amount. ◆ *vb* **shreds, shredding, shredded** *or* **shred. 3** (*tr*) to tear or cut into shreds. ORIG OE *scread*
▸ ˈ**shredder** *n*

Shreveport ★ (ˈʃriːvˌpɔːt) *n* a city in NW Louisiana, on the Red River: centre of an oil and natural-gas region. Pop.: 196 982 (1994 est.).

shrew (ʃruː) *n* **1** Also called: **shrewmouse.** a small mouselike long-snouted insectivorous mammal. **2** a bad-tempered or mean-spirited woman. ORIG OE *scrēawa*

shrewd (ʃruːd) *adj* **1** astute and penetrating, often with regard to business. **2** artful: *a shrewd politician.* **3** *Obs.* piercing: *a shrewd wind.* ORIG C14: from *shrew* (obs. vb) to curse, from SHREW
▸ ˈ**shrewdly** *adv* ▸ ˈ**shrewdness** *n*

shrewish (ˈʃruːɪʃ) *adj* (esp. of a woman) bad-tempered and nagging.

Shrewsbury ★ (ˈʃrəʊzbərɪ, -brɪ, ˈʃruːz-) *n* a town in W central England, administrative centre of Shropshire, on the River Severn: strategically situated near the Welsh border; market town. Pop.: 90 900 (1991).

shriek (ʃriːk) *n* **1** a shrill and piercing cry. ◆ *vb* **2** to produce or utter (words, sounds, etc.) in a shrill piercing tone. ORIG C16: prob. from ON *skrækja* to screech
▸ ˈ**shrieker** *n*

shrieval (ˈʃriːvᵊl) *adj* of or relating to a sheriff.

shrievalty (ˈʃriːvəltɪ) *n, pl* **shrievalties. 1** the office or term of office of a sheriff. **2** the jurisdiction of a sheriff. ORIG C16: from arch. *shrieve* sheriff, on the model of *mayoralty*

shrift (ʃrɪft) *n Arch.* the act or an instance of shriving or being shriven. See also **short shrift.** ORIG OE *scrift,* from L *scriptum* SCRIPT

shrike (ʃraɪk) *n* an Old World songbird having a heavy hooked bill and feeding on smaller animals which it sometimes impales on thorns, etc. Also called: **butcherbird.** ORIG OE *scrīc* thrush

shrill (ʃrɪl) *adj* **1** sharp and high-pitched in quality. **2** emitting a sharp high-pitched sound. ◆ *vb* **3** to utter (words, sounds, etc.) in a shrill tone. ORIG C14: prob. from OE *scralletan*
▸ ˈ**shrillness** *n* ▸ ˈ**shrilly** *adv*

shrimp (ʃrɪmp) *n* **1** any of a genus of chiefly marine decapod crustaceans having a slender flattened body with a long tail and a single pair of pincers. **2** *Inf.* a diminutive person, esp. a child. ◆ *vb* **3** (*intr*) to fish for shrimps. ORIG C14: prob. of Gmc origin
▸ ˈ**shrimper** *n*

shrine (ʃraɪn) *n* **1** a place of worship hallowed by association with a sacred person or object. **2** a container for sacred relics. **3** the tomb of a saint or other holy person. **4** a place or site venerated for its association with a famous person or event. **5** *RC Church.* a building, alcove, or shelf arranged as a setting for a statue, picture, etc., of Christ, the Virgin Mary, or a saint. ◆ *vb* **shrines, shrining, shrined. 6** short for **enshrine.** ORIG OE *scrīn,* from L *scrīnium* bookcase
▸ ˈ**shrineˌlike** *adj*

shrink (ʃrɪŋk) *vb* **shrinks, shrinking; shrank** *or* **shrunk; shrunk** *or* **shrunken. 1** to contract or cause to contract as from wetness, heat, cold, etc. **2** to become or cause to become smaller in size. **3** (*intr;* often foll. by *from*) **3a** to recoil or withdraw: *to shrink from the sight of blood.* **3b** to feel great reluctance (at). ◆ *n* **4** the act or an instance of shrinking. **5** a slang word for **psychiatrist.** ORIG OE *scrincan*
▸ ˈ**shrinkable** *adj* ▸ ˈ**shrinker** *n* ▸ ˈ**shrinking** *adj*

shrinkage (ˈʃrɪŋkɪdʒ) *n* **1** the act or fact of shrinking. **2** the amount by which anything decreases in size, value, weight, etc. **3** *Commerce.* the loss of merchandise through shoplifting or damage.

shrinking violet *n Inf.* a shy person.

shrink-wrap *vb* **shrink-wraps, shrink-wrapping, shrink-wrapped.** (*tr*) to package a product in a flexible plastic wrapping designed to shrink about its contours to protect and seal it.

shrive (ʃraɪv) *vb* **shrives, shriving; shrove** *or* **shrived; shriven** (ˈʃrɪvᵊn) *or* **shrived.** *Chiefly RC Church.* **1** to hear the confession of (a penitent). **2** (*tr*) to impose a penance upon (a penitent) and grant him or her absolution. **3** (*intr*) to confess one's sins to a priest in order to obtain forgiveness. ORIG OE *scrīfan,* from L *scrībere* to write
▸ ˈ**shriver** *n*

shrivel (ˈʃrɪvᵊl) *vb* **shrivels, shrivelling, shrivelled** *or US* **shrivels, shriveling, shriveled. 1** to make or become shrunken and withered. **2** to lose or cause to lose vitality. ORIG C16: prob. of Scand. origin

Shropshire ★ (ˈʃrɒpˌʃɪə, -ʃə) *n* a county of W central England: mainly agricultural. In 1998 the area around Telford became an independent unitary authority, Telford and Wrekin. Administrative centre: Shrewsbury. Pop. (excluding Telford and Wrekin): 227 100 (1996 est.). Area (excluding Telford and Wrekin): 3201 sq. km (1236 sq. miles).

shroud (ʃraʊd) *n* **1** a garment or piece of cloth used to wrap a dead body. **2** anything that envelops like a garment: *a shroud of mist.* **3** a protective covering for a piece of equipment. **4** *Astronautics.* a streamlined protective covering used to protect the payload during a rocket-powered launch. **5** *Naut.* one of a pattern of ropes or cables used to stay a mast. ◆ *vb* (*tr*) **6** to wrap in a shroud. **7** to cover, envelop, or hide. ORIG OE *scrūd* garment
▸ ˈ**shroudless** *adj*

shrove (ʃrəʊv) *vb* a past tense of **shrive.**

Shrovetide (ˈʃrəʊvˌtaɪd) *n* the Sunday, Monday, and Tuesday before Ash Wednesday, formerly a time when confessions were made for Lent.

shrub[1] (ʃrʌb) *n* a woody perennial plant, smaller than a tree, with several major branches arising from near the base of the main stem. ORIG OE *scrybb*
▸ ˈ**shrubˌlike** *adj*

shrub[2] (ʃrʌb) *n* a mixed drink of rum, fruit juice, sugar, and spice. ORIG C18: from Ar. *sharāb,* var. of *shurb* drink; see SHERBET

shrubbery (ˈʃrʌbərɪ) *n, pl* **shrubberies. 1** a place where a number of shrubs are planted. **2** shrubs collectively.

shrubby (ˈʃrʌbɪ) *adj* **shrubbier, shrubbiest. 1** consisting of, planted with, or abounding in shrubs. **2** resembling a shrub.
▸ ˈ**shrubbiness** *n*

shrug (ʃrʌg) *vb* **shrugs, shrugging, shrugged. 1** to draw up and drop (the shoulders) abruptly in a gesture expressing indifference, ignorance, etc. ◆ *n* **2** the gesture so made. ORIG C14: from ?

shrug off *vb (tr, adv)* **1** to minimize the importance of; dismiss. **2** to get rid of.

shrunk (ʃrʌŋk) *vb* a past participle and past tense of **shrink**.

shrunken (ˈʃrʌŋkᵊn) *vb* **1** a past participle of **shrink**. ◆ *adj* **2** *(usually prenominal)* reduced in size.

shtoom (ʃtum) *adj Sl.* silent, dumb (esp. in **keep shtoom**). ORIG from Yiddish, from G *stumm* silent

shuck (ʃʌk) *n* **1** the outer covering of something, such as the husk of a grain of maize, a pea pod, or an oyster shell. ◆ *vb (tr)* **2** to remove the shucks from. ORIG C17: US dialect, from ?
▸ ˈ**shucker** *n*

shucks (ʃʌks) *interj US & Canad. inf.* an exclamation of disappointment, annoyance, etc.

shudder (ˈʃʌdə) *vb* **1** *(intr)* to shake or tremble suddenly and violently, as from horror, fear, aversion, etc. ◆ *n* **2** a convulsive shiver. ORIG C18: from MLow G *schōderen*
▸ ˈ**shuddering** *adj* ▸ ˈ**shudderingly** *adv* ▸ ˈ**shuddery** *adj*

shuffle (ˈʃʌfᵊl) *vb* **shuffles, shuffling, shuffled. 1** to walk or move (the feet) with a slow dragging motion. **2** to change the position of (something), esp. in order to deceive others. **3** *(tr)* to mix together in a careless manner: *he shuffled the papers nervously*. **4** to mix up (cards in a pack) to change their order. **5** *(intr)* to behave in an evasive or underhand manner. **6** (when *intr*, often foll. by *into* or *out of*) to move or cause to move clumsily: *he shuffled out of the door*. ◆ *n* **7** the act or an instance of shuffling. **8** a rearrangement: *a Cabinet shuffle*. **9** a dance or dance step with short dragging movements of the feet. ORIG C16: prob. from Low G *schüffeln*
▸ ˈ**shuffler** *n*

shuffleboard (ˈʃʌfᵊlˌbɔːd) *n* a game in which players push wooden or plastic discs with a long cue towards numbered scoring sections marked on a floor, esp. a ship's deck.

shuffle off *vb (tr, adv)* to thrust off or put aside: *shuffle off responsibility*.

shuffle play *n* a facility on a compact disc player that selects tracks at random from a number of compact discs.

shufty *or* **shufti** (ˈʃuftɪ, ˈʃʌftɪ) *n, pl* **shufties**. *Brit. sl.* a look; peep. ORIG C20: from Ar.

Shufu *or* **Sufu** ★ (ˈʃuːˈfuː) *n* transliteration of the Chinese name for **Kashi**.

shun (ʃʌn) *vb* **shuns, shunning, shunned.** *(tr)* to avoid deliberately. ORIG OE *scunian*, from ?

shunt (ʃʌnt) *vb* **1** to turn or cause to turn to one side. **2** *Railways.* to transfer (rolling stock) from track to track. **3** *Electronics.* to divert or be diverted through a shunt. **4** *(tr)* to evade by putting off onto someone else. ◆ *n* **5** the act or an instance of shunting. **6** a railway point. **7** *Electronics.* a low-resistance conductor connected in parallel across a part of a circuit to provide an alternative path for a known fraction of the current. **8** *Med.* a channel that bypasses the normal circulation of the blood. **9** *Brit. inf.* a collision that occurs when a vehicle runs into the back of the vehicle in front. ORIG C13: ?from *shunen* to SHUN

shunt-wound (ˈʃʌntˌwaund) *adj Electrical engineering.* (of a motor or generator) having the field and armature circuits connected in parallel.

shush (ʃuʃ) *interj* **1** be quiet! hush! ◆ *vb* **2** to silence or calm (someone) by or as if by saying "shush". ORIG C20: reduplication of SH, infl. by HUSH

Shushan ★ (ˈʃuːʃæn) *n* the Biblical name for **Susa**.

shut (ʃʌt) *vb* **shuts, shutting, shut. 1** to move (something) so as to cover an aperture: *to shut a door*. **2** to close (something) by bringing together the parts: *to shut a book*. **3** *(tr;* often foll. by *up)* to close or lock the doors of: *to shut up a house*. **4** *(tr;* foll. by *in, out,* etc.) to confine, enclose, or exclude. **5** *(tr)* to prevent (a business, etc.) from operating. **6 shut the door on. 6a** to refuse to think about. **6b** to render impossible. ◆ *adj* **7** closed or fastened. ◆ *n* **8** the act or time of shutting. ◆ See also **shutdown, shut-off,** etc. ORIG OE *scyttan*

shutdown (ˈʃʌtˌdaun) *n* **1a** the closing of a factory, shop, etc. **1b** *(as modifier): shutdown costs*. ◆ *vb* **shut down.** *(adv)* **2** to cease or cause to cease operation. **3** *(tr)* to close by lowering.

Shute ★ (ʃuːt) *n* **Nevil,** real name *Nevil Shute Norway*. 1899–1960, British novelist, in Australia after World War II: noted for his novels *A Town like Alice* (1950) and *On the Beach* (1957).

shuteye (ˈʃʌtˌaɪ) *n* a slang term for **sleep**.

shut-in *n Chiefly US.* **a** a person confined indoors by illness. **b** *(as modifier): a shut-in patient*.

shut-off *n* **1** a device that shuts something off, esp. a machine control. **2** a stoppage or cessation. ◆ *vb* **shut off.** *(tr, adv)* **3** to stem the flow of. **4** to block off the passage through. **5** to isolate or separate.

shutout (ˈʃʌtˌaut) *n* **1** a less common word for a **lockout. 2** *Sport.* a match in which the opposition does not score. ◆ *vb* **shut out.** *(tr, adv)* **3** to keep out or exclude. **4** to conceal from sight: *we planted trees to shut out the view of the road*.

shutter (ˈʃʌtə) *n* **1** a hinged doorlike cover, often louvred and usually one of a pair, for closing off a window. **2 put up the shutters.** to close business at the end of the day or permanently. **3** *Photog.* an opaque shield in a camera that, when tripped, admits light to expose the film or plate for a predetermined period, usually a fraction of a second. **4** *Music.* one of the louvred covers over the mouths of organ pipes, operated by the swell pedal. **5** a person or thing that shuts. ◆ *vb (tr)* **6** to close with a shutter or shutters. **7** to equip with a shutter or shutters.

shuttering (ˈʃʌtərɪŋ) *n* another word (esp. Brit.) for **formwork**.

shuttle (ˈʃʌtᵊl) *n* **1** a bobbin-like device used in weaving for passing the weft thread between the warp threads. **2** a small bobbin-like device used to hold the thread in a sewing machine, etc. **3a** a bus, train, aircraft, etc., that plies between two points. **3b** short for **space shuttle. 4a** the movement between various countries of a diplomat in order to negotiate with rulers who refuse to meet each other. **4b** *(as modifier): shuttle diplomacy*. **5** *Badminton, etc.* short for **shuttlecock**. ◆ *vb* **shuttles, shuttling, shuttled. 6** to move or cause to move by or as if by a shuttle. ORIG OE *scytel* bolt

shuttlecock (ˈʃʌtᵊlˌkɒk) *n* **1** a light cone consisting of a cork stub with feathered flights, struck to and fro in badminton and battledore. **2** anything moved to and fro, as in an argument.

shut up *vb (adv)* **1** *(tr)* to prevent all access to. **2** *(tr)* to confine or imprison. **3** *Inf.* to cease to talk or make a noise or cause to cease to talk or make a noise: often used in commands.

shwa (ʃwɑː) *n* a variant spelling of **schwa**.

shy[1] (ʃaɪ) *adj* **shyer, shyest** *or* **shier, shiest. 1** not at ease in the company of others. **2** easily frightened; timid. **3** (often foll. by *of*) watchful or wary. **4** (foll. by *of*) *Inf., chiefly US & Canad.* short (of). **5** *(in combination)* showing reluctance or disinclination: *workshy*. ◆ *vb* **shies, shying, shied.** *(intr)* **6** to move suddenly, as from fear: *the horse shied at the snake in the road*. **7** (usually foll. by *off* or *away*) to draw back. ◆ *n, pl* **shies. 8** a sudden movement, as from fear. ORIG OE *sceoh*
▸ ˈ**shyer** *n* ▸ ˈ**shyly** *adv* ▸ ˈ**shyness** *n*

shy[2] (ʃaɪ) *vb* **shies, shying, shied. 1** to throw (something) with a sideways motion. ◆ *n, pl* **shies. 2** a quick throw. **3** *Inf.* a gibe. **4** *Inf.* an attempt. ORIG C18: of Gmc origin
▸ ˈ**shyer** *n*

Shylock (ˈʃaɪˌlɒk) *n* a heartless or demanding creditor. ORIG C19: after *Shylock*, the heartless usurer in Shakespeare's *The Merchant of Venice* (1596)

shyster (ˈʃaɪstə) *n Sl., chiefly US.* a person, esp. a lawyer or politician, who uses discreditable methods. ORIG C19: prob. based on *Scheuster*, a disreputable 19th-cent. New York lawyer

si (siː) *n Music.* the syllable used in the fixed system of solmization for the note B. ORIG C14: see GAMUT

Si[1] (ʃiː) *or* **Si Kiang** ★ *n* a variant transliteration of the Chinese name for the **Xi**.

Si[2] *the chemical symbol for* silicon.

SI **1** *symbol for* Système International (d'Unités). See **SI unit. 2** *NZ abbrev. for* South Island.

sial ★ ('saɪəl) *n* the silicon-rich and aluminium-rich rocks of the earth's continental upper crust. ORIG C20: *si(licon)* + *al(uminium)*
▸ **sialic** (saɪ'ælɪk) *adj*

Sialkot ★ (sɪ'ælkɒt) *n* a city in NE Pakistan: shrine of Guru Nanak. Pop.: 296 000 (1981).

Siam ★ (saɪ'æm, 'saɪæm) *n* **1** the former name (until 1939 and 1945–49) of **Thailand. 2 Gulf of.** an arm of the South China Sea between the Malay Peninsula and Indochina.

siamang ('saɪəˌmæŋ) *n* a large black gibbon of Sumatra and the Malay Peninsula, having the second and third toes united. ORIG C19: from Malay

Siamese (ˌsaɪə'miːz) *n, pl* **Siamese. 1** See **Siamese cat.** ◆ *adj* **2** characteristic of, relating to, or being a Siamese twin. ◆ *adj, n, pl* **Siamese. 3** another word for **Thai.**

Siamese cat *n* a short-haired breed of cat with a tapering tail, blue eyes, and dark ears, mask, tail, and paws.

Siamese fighting fish *n* a brightly coloured labyrinth fish of Thailand and Malaysia: the males are very pugnacious.

Siamese twins *pl n* (*not in technical usage*) another name for **conjoined twins.**

Sian ★ (ʃjɑːn) *n* a variant transliteration of the Chinese name for **Xi An.**

Siang ★ (ʃjɑːŋ) *n* a variant transliteration of the Chinese name for the **Xiang.**

Siangtan ★ ('ʃjɑːŋ'tɑːn) *n* a variant transliteration of the Chinese name for **Xiangtan.**

sib (sɪb) *n* **1** a blood relative. **2** kinsmen collectively; kindred. ORIG OE *sibb*

SIB (in Britain) *abbrev. for* Securities and Investments Board: a body that regulates financial dealings in the City of London.

Sib. *abbrev. for* Siberia(n).

Sibelius ★ (sɪ'beɪlɪəs) *n* **Jean** (ʒan). 1865–1957, Finnish composer, noted for his seven symphonies, his symphonic poems, such as *Finlandia* (1900), and his violin concerto (1905).

Siberia ★ (saɪ'bɪərɪə) *n* a vast region of Russia and N Kazakhstan: extends from the Ural Mountains to the Pacific and from the Arctic Ocean to the borders with China and Mongolia; colonized rapidly after the building of the Trans-Siberian Railway. Area: 13 807 037 sq. km (5 330 896 sq. miles).
▸ **Si'berian** *n, adj*

sibilant ('sɪbɪlənt) *adj* **1** *Phonetics.* relating to or denoting the consonants (s, z, ʃ, ʒ), all pronounced with a characteristic hissing sound. **2** having a hissing sound. ◆ *n* **3** a sibilant consonant. ORIG C17: from L *sībilāre* to hiss, imit.
▸ **'sibilance** *or* **'sibilancy** *n* ▸ **'sibilantly** *adv*

sibilate ('sɪbɪˌleɪt) *vb* **sibilates, sibilating, sibilated.** to pronounce or utter (words or speech) with a hissing sound.
▸ **ˌsibi'lation** *n*

Sibiu ★ (*Romanian* si'biu) *n* an industrial town in W central Romania: originally a Roman city, refounded by German colonists in the 12th century. Pop.: 168 619 (1993 est.). German name: **Hermannstadt.** Hungarian name: **Nagyszeben.**

sibling ('sɪblɪŋ) *n* **a** a person's brother or sister. **b** (*as modifier*): *sibling rivalry.* ORIG C19: specialized modern use of OE *sibling* relative, from SIB

sibyl ('sɪbɪl) *n* **1** (in ancient Greece and Rome) any of a number of women believed to be oracles or prophetesses. **2** a witch, fortune-teller, or sorceress. ORIG C13: ult. from Gk *Sibulla,* from ?
▸ **sibylline** ('sɪbɪˌlaɪn) *adj*

sic[1] (sɪk) *adv* so or thus: inserted in brackets in a text to indicate that an odd or questionable reading is what was actually written or printed. ORIG L

sic[2] (sɪk) *vb* **sics, sicking, sicked.** (*tr*) **1** to attack: used only in commands, as to a dog. **2** to urge (a dog) to attack. ORIG C19: dialect var. of SEEK

Sic. *abbrev. for:* **1** Sicilian. **2** Sicily.

Sica ★ (*Italian* 'siːka) *n* **Vittorio de.** See (Vittorio) **de Sica.**

siccative ('sɪkətɪv) *n* a substance added to a liquid to promote drying: used in paints and some medicines. ORIG C16: from LL *siccātīvus,* from L *siccāre* to dry up, from *siccus* dry

Sichuan ('sɪ'tʃwɑːn) *or* **Szechwan** ★ *n* a province of SW China: the most populous administrative division in the country, esp. in the central Red Basin, where it is crossed by three main tributaries of the Yangtze. Capital: Chengdu. Pop.: 84 300 000 (1997 est.). Area: about 569 800 sq. km (220 000 sq. miles).

Sicilia ★ (si'tʃiːlja) *n* the Latin and Italian name for **Sicily.**

siciliano (ˌsiːtʃiː'ljɑːnəʊ) *n, pl* **sicilianos. 1** an old dance in six-beat or twelve-beat time. **2** a piece of music composed for or in the rhythm of this dance. ORIG It.

Sicily ★ ('sɪsɪlɪ) *n* the largest island in the Mediterranean, separated from the tip of SW Italy by the Strait of Messina: administratively an autonomous region of Italy; settled by Phoenicians, Greeks, and Carthaginians before the Roman conquest of 241 B.C.; under Normans (12th–13th centuries); formed the **Kingdom of the Two Sicilies** with Naples in 1815; mountainous and volcanic. Capital: Palermo. Pop.: 5 094 735 (1996 est.). Area: 25 460 sq. km (9830 sq. miles). Latin names: **Sicilia, Trinacria.** Italian name: **Sicilia.**
▸ **Sicilian** (sɪ'sɪlɪən) *adj, n*

sick[1] (sɪk) *adj* **1** inclined or likely to vomit. **2a** suffering from ill health. **2b** (*as collective n;* preceded by *the*): *the sick.* **3a** of or used by people who are unwell: *sick benefits.* **3b** (*in combination*): *a sickroom.* **4** deeply affected with a mental or spiritual feeling akin to physical sickness: *sick at heart.* **5** mentally or spiritually disturbed. **6** *Inf.* delighting in or catering for the macabre: *sick humour.* **7** Also: **sick and tired.** (often foll. by *of*) *Inf.* disgusted or weary: *I am sick of his everlasting laughter.* **8** (often foll. by *for*) weary with longing: *I am sick for my own country.* **9** pallid or sickly. **10** not in working order. ◆ *n, vb* **11** an informal word for **vomit.** ORIG OE *sēoc*
▸ **'sickish** *adj*

sick[2] (sɪk) *vb* a variant spelling of **sic**[2].

sickbay ('sɪkˌbeɪ) *n* a room for the treatment of the sick or injured, as on board a ship or at a boarding school.

sick building syndrome *n* a group of symptoms, such as headaches, eye irritation, and lethargy, that may be experienced by workers in offices that are totally air-conditioned.

sicken ('sɪkən) *vb* **1** to make or become nauseated or disgusted. **2** (*intr;* often foll. by *for*) to show symptoms (of an illness).
▸ **'sickener** *n*

sickening ('sɪkənɪŋ) *adj* **1** causing sickness or revulsion. **2** *Inf.* extremely annoying.
▸ **'sickeningly** *adv*

Sickert ★ ('sɪkət) *n* **Walter Richard.** 1860–1942, British impressionist painter.

sick headache *n* **1** a headache accompanied by nausea. **2** a nontechnical name for **migraine.**

sickie ('sɪkɪ) *n Inf.* a day of sick leave from work. ORIG C20: from SICK[1] + -IE

sickle ('sɪkᵊl) *n* an implement for cutting grass, corn, etc., having a curved blade and a short handle. ORIG OE *sicol,* from L *sēcula*

sick leave *n* leave of absence from work through illness.

sicklebill ('sɪkᵊlˌbɪl) *n* any of various birds having a markedly curved bill, such as certain hummingbirds and birds of paradise.

sickle-cell anaemia *n* a hereditary form of anaemia occurring mainly in Black populations, in which a large number of red blood cells become sickle-shaped.

sick list *n* **1** a list of the sick, esp. in the army or navy. **2 on the sick list.** ill.

sickly ('sɪklɪ) *adj* **sicklier, sickliest. 1** disposed to frequent ailments; not healthy; weak. **2** of or caused by sickness. **3** (of a smell, taste, etc.) causing revulsion or nausea. **4** (of

light or colour) faint or feeble. **5** mawkish; insipid. ◆ *adv* **6** in a sick or sickly manner.
▸ **'sickliness** *n*

sick-making *adj Inf.* galling; sickening.

sickness ('sɪknɪs) *n* **1** an illness or disease. **2** nausea or queasiness. **3** the state or an instance of being sick.

sick pay *n* wages paid to an employee while he or she is on sick leave.

sic transit gloria mundi *Latin.* ('sɪk 'trænsɪt 'glɔːrɪˌɑː 'mʊndiː) thus passes the glory of the world.

Sicyon ★ ('sɪsɪˌɒn, 'sɪsɪən) *n* an ancient city in S Greece, in the NE Peloponnese near Corinth: declined after 146 B.C.

sidalcea (sɪ'dælsɪə) *n* any of a genus of hardy perennial plants with pink flowers. Also called **Greek mallow.** ORIG from NL

Siddhartha ★ (sɪ'dɑːtə) *n* the personal name of the **Buddha.**

Siddons ★ ('sɪdᵊnz) *n* **Sarah.** 1755–1831, British tragedienne.

side (saɪd) *n* **1** a line or surface that borders anything. **2** *Geom.* **2a** any line segment forming part of the perimeter of a plane geometric figure. **2b** another name for **face** (sense 13). **3** either of two parts into which an object, surface, area, etc., can be divided: *the right side and the left side.* **4** either of the two surfaces of a flat object: *the right and wrong side of the cloth.* **5** a surface or part of an object that extends vertically: *the side of a cliff.* **6** either half of a human or animal body, esp. the area around the waist: *I have a pain in my side.* **7** the area immediately next to a person or thing: *he stood at her side.* **8** a district, point, or direction within an area identified by reference to a central point: *the south side of the city.* **9** the area at the edge of a room, road, etc. **10** aspect or part: *look on the bright side.* **11** one of two or more contesting factions, teams, etc. **12** a page in an essay, etc. **13** a position, opinion, etc., held in opposition to another in a dispute. **14** line of descent: *he gets his brains from his mother's side.* **15** *Inf.* a television channel. **16** *Billiards, etc.* spin imparted to a ball by striking it off-centre with the cue. **17** *Brit. sl.* insolence or pretentiousness: *to put on side.* **18 on one side.** set apart from the rest, as provision for emergencies, etc. **19 on the side. 19a** apart from or in addition to the main object. **19b** as a sideline. **19c** *US.* as a side dish. **20 take sides.** to support one group, opinion, etc., as against another. ◆ *adj* **21** being on one side; lateral. **22** from or viewed as if from one side. **23** directed towards one side. **24** subordinate or incidental: *side road.* ◆ *vb* **sides, siding, sided. 25** (*intr;* usually foll. by *with*) to support or associate oneself (with a faction, interest, etc.). ORIG OE *sīde*

side arms *pl n* weapons carried on the person, by belt or holster, such as a sword, pistol, etc.

sideband ('saɪdˌbænd) *n* the frequency band either above (**upper sideband**) or below (**lower sideband**) the carrier frequency, within which fall the components produced by modulation of a carrier wave.

sideboard ('saɪdˌbɔːd) *n* a piece of furniture intended to stand at the side of a dining room, with drawers, cupboards, and shelves to hold silver, china, linen, etc.

sideboards ('saɪdˌbɔːdz) *pl n* another term for **sideburns.**

sideburns ('saɪdˌbɜːnz) *pl n* a man's whiskers grown down either side of the face in front of the ears. Also called: **sideboards, side whiskers,** (*Austral.*) **sidelevers.**

sidecar ('saɪdˌkɑː) *n* a small car attached on one side to a motorcycle, the other side being supported by a single wheel.

side chain *n Chem.* a group of atoms bound to an atom, usually a carbon atom, that forms part of a larger chain or ring in a molecule.

-sided *adj* (*in combination*) having a side or sides as specified: *three-sided; many-sided.*

side deal *n* a transaction between two people for their private benefit, which is subsidiary to a contract negotiated by them on behalf of the organizations they represent.

side dish *n* a portion of food served in addition to the main dish.

side drum *n* a small double-headed drum carried at the side with snares that produce a rattling effect.

side effect *n* **1** any unwanted nontherapeutic effect caused by a drug. **2** any secondary effect, esp. an undesirable one.

side-foot *Soccer.* ◆ *n* **1** a shot or pass played with the side of the foot. ◆ *vb* **2** (*tr*) to strike (a ball) with the side of the foot.

sidekick ('saɪdˌkɪk) *n Inf.* a close friend or follower who accompanies another on adventures, etc.

sidelight ('saɪdˌlaɪt) *n* **1** light coming from the side. **2** a side window. **3** either of the two navigational running lights used by vessels at night, a red light on the port and a green on the starboard. **4** *Brit.* either of two small lights on the front of a motor vehicle. **5** additional or incidental information.

sideline ('saɪdˌlaɪn) *n* **1** *Sport.* a line that marks the side boundary of a playing area. **2** a subsidiary interest or source of income. **3** an auxiliary business activity or line of merchandise. ◆ *vb* **sidelines, sidelining, sidelined. 4** (*tr*) *Chiefly US & Canad.* to prevent (a player) from taking part in a game.

sidelines ('saɪdˌlaɪnz) *pl n* **1** *Sport.* the area immediately outside the playing area, where substitute players sit. **2** the peripheral areas of any region, organization, etc.

sidelong ('saɪdˌlɒŋ) *adj* (*prenominal*) **1** directed or inclining to one side. **2** indirect or oblique. ◆ *adv* **3** from the side; obliquely.

sidereal (saɪ'dɪərɪəl) *adj* **1** of or involving the stars. **2** determined with reference to one or more stars: *the sidereal day.* ORIG C17: from L *sīdereus,* from *sīdus* a star
▸ **si'dereally** *adv*

sidereal day *n* See **day** (sense 5).

sidereal period *n Astron.* the period of revolution of a body about another with respect to one or more stars.

sidereal time *n* time based upon the rotation of the earth with respect to a particular star, the **sidereal day** being the unit of measurement.

sidereal year *n* See **year** (sense 5).

siderite ('saɪdəˌraɪt) *n* **1** a pale yellow to brownish-black mineral consisting chiefly of iron(II) carbonate. It occurs mainly in ore veins and sedimentary rocks and is an important source of iron. Formula: $FeCO_3$. **2** a meteorite consisting principally of metallic iron.

sidero- *or before a vowel* **sider-** *combining form.* indicating iron: *siderolite.* ORIG from Gk *sidēros*

siderolite ('saɪdərəˌlaɪt) *n* a meteorite consisting of a mixture of iron, nickel, and such ferromagnesian minerals as olivine.

siderosis (ˌsaɪdə'rəʊsɪs) *n* a lung disease caused by breathing in fine particles of iron or other metallic dust.

siderostat ('saɪdərəʊˌstæt) *n* an astronomical instrument consisting of a plane mirror rotated by a clock mechanism about two axes so that light from a celestial body, esp. the sun, is reflected along a constant direction for a long period of time. ORIG C19: from *sidero-,* from L *sidus* a star + -STAT

side-saddle *n* **1** a riding saddle originally designed for women riders in skirts who sit with both legs on the near side of the horse. ◆ *adv* **2** on or as if on a side-saddle.

sideshow ('saɪdˌʃəʊ) *n* **1** a small show or entertainment offered in conjunction with a larger attraction, as at a circus or fair. **2** a subordinate event or incident.

sideslip ('saɪdˌslɪp) *n* **1** a sideways skid, as of a motor vehicle. ◆ *vb* **sideslips, sideslipping, sideslipped. 2** another name for **slip**[1] (sense 11).

sidesman ('saɪdzmən) *n, pl* **sidesmen.** *Church of England.* a man elected to help the parish church-warden.

side-splitting *adj* **1** producing great mirth. **2** (of laughter) uproarious or very hearty.

sidestep ('saɪdˌstɛp) *vb* **sidesteps, sidestepping, sidestepped. 1** to step aside from or out of the way of (something). **2** (*tr*) to dodge or circumvent. ◆ *n* **side step. 3** a movement to one side, as in dancing, boxing, etc.
▸ **'sideˌstepper** *n*

sidestroke ('saɪdˌstrəʊk) *n* a type of swimming stroke in which the swimmer lies sideways in the water making a scissors kick with his or her legs.

sideswipe ('saɪdˌswaɪp) *n* **1** a glancing blow or hit along or from the side. **2** an unexpected criticism of someone or something while discussing another subject. ◆ *vb* **sideswipes, sideswiping, sideswiped. 3** to strike (someone) with a glancing blow from the side.
▸ **'sideˌswiper** *n*

sidetrack ('saɪdˌtræk) *vb* **1** to distract or be distracted from a main subject or topic. ◆ *n* **2** *US & Canad.* a railway siding. **3** a digression.

side-valve engine *n* a type of internal-combustion engine in which the inlet and exhaust valves are in the cylinder block at the side of the pistons.

sidewalk ('saɪdˌwɔːk) *n* the US and Canad. word for **pavement.**

sidewall ('saɪdˌwɔːl) *n* either of the sides of a pneumatic tyre between the tread and the rim.

sideward ('saɪdwəd) *adj* **1** directed or moving towards one side. ◆ *adv also* **sidewards. 2** towards one side.

sideways ('saɪdˌweɪz) *adv* **1** moving, facing, or inclining towards one side. **2** from one side; obliquely. **3** with one side forward. ◆ *adj (prenominal)* **4** moving or directed to or from one side. **5** towards or from one side.

side whiskers *pl n* another name for **sideburns.**

sidewinder ('saɪdˌwaɪndə) *n* **1** a North American rattlesnake that moves forwards by a sideways looping motion. **2** *Boxing, US.* a heavy swinging blow from the side.

Sidi-bel-Abbès ★ (*French* sidibɛlabɛs) *n* a city in NW Algeria: headquarters of the Foreign Legion until Algerian independence (1962). Pop.: 152 778 (1987).

siding ('saɪdɪŋ) *n* **1** a short stretch of railway track connected to a main line, used for storing rolling stock. **2** a short railway line giving access to the main line for freight from a factory, etc. **3** *US & Canad.* material attached to the outside of a building to make it weatherproof.

sidle ('saɪdᵊl) *vb* **sidles, sidling, sidled.** *(intr)* **1** to move in a furtive or stealthy manner. **2** to move along sideways. ORIG C17: back formation from obs. *sideling* sideways

Sidmouth ★ ('sɪdməθ) *n* **1st Viscount.** See (Henry) **Addington.**

Sidney *or* **Sydney** ★ ('sɪdnɪ) *n* Sir **Philip.** 1554–86, English poet, courtier, and soldier. His works include the romance *Arcadia* (1590) and the sonnet sequence *Astrophel and Stella* (1591).

Sidon ★ ('saɪdᵊn) *n* the chief city of ancient Phoenicia: founded in the third millennium B.C.; wealthy through trade and the making of glass and purple dyes; now the Lebanese city of Saïda.
▸ **Sidonian** (saɪ'dəʊnɪən) *adj, n*

Sidra ★ ('sɪdrə) *n* **Gulf of.** a wide inlet of the Mediterranean on the N coast of Libya.

SIDS *abbrev.* for sudden infant death syndrome. See **cot death.**

Siegbahn ★ ('siːgbɑːn) *n* **1 Kai** (kaɪ). born 1918, Swedish physicist who worked on electron spectroscopy: Nobel prize for physics 1981. **2** his father, **Karl Manne Georg** (kɑːrl 'manə 'jeːɔrj). 1886–1978, Swedish physicist: Nobel prize for physics (1924) for his work on X-ray spectroscopy.

siege (siːdʒ) *n* **1a** the offensive operations carried out to capture a fortified place by surrounding it and deploying weapons against it. **1b** *(as modifier): siege warfare.* **2** a persistent attempt to gain something. **3** *Obs.* a seat or throne. **4 lay siege to. 4a** to besiege. **4b** to importune. ORIG C13: from OF *sege* a seat, from Vulgar L *sēdicāre* (unattested) to sit down, from L *sedēre*

siege mentality *n* a state of mind in which a person believes that he or she is being constantly oppressed or attacked.

Siegen ★ ('ziːgən) *n* a city in NW Germany, in North Rhine-Westphalia: manufacturing centre: birthplace of Rubens. Pop.: 111 398 (1996 est.).

Siegfried ★ ('siːgfriːd; *German* 'ziːkfriːt) *n German myth.* a German prince, the son of Sigmund and husband of Kriemhild, who, in the *Nibelungenlied,* assumes possession of the treasure of the Nibelungs by slaying the dragon that guards it, wins Brunhild for King Gunther, and is eventually killed by Hagen. Norse equivalent: **Sigurd.**

siemens ('siːmənz) *n, pl* **siemens.** the derived SI unit of electrical conductance equal to 1 reciprocal ohm. Symbol: S Formerly called: **mho.**

Siemens ★ ('siːmənz) *n* **1 Ernst Werner von** (ɛrnst 'vɛrnər fɔn). 1816–92, German engineer. His inventions include the self-excited dynamo and electrolytic refining. **2** his brother, Sir **William,** original name *Karl Wilhelm Siemens.* 1823–83, British engineer, born in Germany, who invented the open-hearth steel furnace.

Siena ★ (sɪ'ɛnə; *Italian* 'sjɛːna) *n* a walled city in central Italy, in Tuscany: founded by the Etruscans; important artistic centre (13th–14th centuries); university (13th century). Pop.: 58 278 (1990).

Sienkiewicz ★ (*Polish* ʃɛŋ'kjɛvitʃ) *n* **Henryk** ('xɛnrik). 1846–1916, Polish novelist. His works include *Quo Vadis?* (1896) and the war trilogy *With Fire and Sword* (1884): Nobel prize for literature 1905.

sienna (sɪ'ɛnə) *n* **1** a natural earth containing ferric oxide used as a yellowish-brown pigment when untreated (**raw sienna**) or a reddish-brown pigment when roasted (**burnt sienna**). **2** the colour of this pigment. ORIG C18: from It. *terra di Siena* earth of SIENA

sierra (sɪ'ɛərə) *n* a range of mountains with jagged peaks, esp. in Spain or America. ORIG C17: from Sp., lit.: saw, from L *serra*
▸ **si'erran** *adj*

Sierra Leone ★ (sɪ'ɛərə lɪ'əʊnɪ, lɪ'əʊn) *n* a republic in W Africa, on the Atlantic: became a British colony in 1808 and gained independence (within the Commonwealth) in 1961; declared a republic in 1971; became a one-party state in 1978; multiparty democracy restored in 1991 but civil unrest followed: consists of coastal swamps rising to a plateau in the east. Official language: English. Religion: Muslim majority and animist. Currency: leone. Capital: Freetown. Pop.: 4 717 000 (1999 est.). Area: 71 740 sq. km (27 699 sq. miles).
▸ **Sierra Leonean** *adj, n*

Sierra Madre ★ (*Spanish* 'sjɛrra 'maðre) *n (functioning as sing)* the main mountain system of Mexico, extending for 2500 km (1500 miles) southeast from the N border: consists of the **Sierra Madre Oriental** in the east, the **Sierra Madre Occidental** in the west, and the **Sierra Madre del Sur** in the south. Highest peak: Citlaltépetl, 5699 m (18 698 ft).

Sierra Morena ★ (*Spanish* 'sjɛrra mo'rena) *n (functioning as sing)* a mountain range in SW Spain, between the Guadiana and Guadalquivir Rivers. Highest peak: Estrella, 1299 m (4262 ft).

Sierra Nevada ★ *n (functioning as sing)* **1** (sɪ'ɛərə nɪ'vɑːdə). a mountain range in E California, parallel to the Coast Ranges. Highest peak: Mount Whitney, 4418 m (14 495 ft). **2** (*Spanish* 'sjɛrra ne'βaða). a mountain range in SE Spain, mostly in Granada and Almería provinces. Highest peak: Cerro de Mulhacén, 3478 m (11 411 ft).

siesta (sɪ'ɛstə) *n* a rest or nap, usually taken in the early afternoon, as in hot countries. ORIG C17: from Sp., from L *sexta hōra* the sixth hour, i.e. noon

sieve (sɪv) *n* **1** a device for separating lumps from powdered material, straining liquids, etc., consisting of a container with a mesh or perforated bottom through which the material is shaken or poured. ◆ *vb* **sieves, sieving, sieved. 2** to pass or cause to pass through a sieve. **3** *(tr; often foll. by out)* to separate or remove (lumps, materials, etc.) by use of a sieve. ORIG OE *sife*
▸ **'sieveˌlike** *adj*

Sieyès ★ (*French* sjejɛs) *n* **Emmanuel Joseph** (ɛmanɥɛl ʒozɛf), called *Abbé Sieyès.* 1748–1836, French statesman and churchman, prominent during the Revolution. He was instrumental in bringing Napoleon I to power (1799).

sift (sɪft) *vb* **1** *(tr)* to sieve (sand, flour, etc.) in order to remove the coarser particles. **2** to scatter (something) over a surface through a sieve. **3** *(tr)* to separate with or as if

with a sieve. **4** (*tr*) to examine minutely: *to sift evidence.* **5** (*intr*) to move as if through a sieve. ORIG OE *siftan*
▸ **'sifter** *n*

siftings ('sɪftɪŋz) *pl n* material or particles separated out by or as if by a sieve.

sigh (saɪ) *vb* **1** (*intr*) to draw in and exhale audibly a deep breath as an expression of weariness, relief, etc. **2** (*intr*) to make a sound resembling this. **3** (*intr; often foll. by for*) to yearn, long, or pine. **4** (*tr*) to utter or express with sighing. ◆ *n* **5** the act or sound of sighing. ORIG OE *sīcan,* from ?
▸ **'sigher** *n*

sight (saɪt) *n* **1** the power or faculty of seeing; vision. Related adj: **visual. 2** the act or an instance of seeing. **3** the range of vision: *within sight of land.* **4** point of view; judgment: *in his sight she could do no wrong.* **5** a glimpse or view (esp. in **catch** *or* **lose sight of**). **6** anything that is seen. **7** (*often pl*) anything worth seeing: *the sights of London.* **8** *Inf.* anything unpleasant or undesirable to see: *his room was a sight!* **9** any of various devices or instruments used to assist the eye in making alignments or directional observations, esp. such a device used in aiming a gun. **10** an observation or alignment made with such a device. **11 a sight.** *Inf.* a great deal: *she's a sight too good for him.* **12 a sight for sore eyes.** a person or thing that one is pleased or relieved to see. **13 at** *or* **on sight. 13a** as soon as seen. **13b** on presentation: *a bill payable at sight.* **14 know by sight.** to be familiar with the appearance of without having personal acquaintance. **15 not by a long sight.** *Inf.* on no account. **16 set one's sights on.** to have (a specified goal) in mind. **17 sight unseen.** without having seen the object at issue: *to buy a car sight unseen.* ◆ *vb* **18** (*tr*) to see, view, or glimpse. **19** (*tr*) **19a** to furnish with a sight or sights. **19b** to adjust the sight of. **20** to aim (a firearm) using the sight. ORIG OE *sihth*
▸ **'sightable** *adj*

sighted ('saɪtɪd) *adj* **1** not blind. **2** (*in combination*) having sight of a specified kind: *short-sighted.*

sighting ('saɪtɪŋ) *n* **1** an occasion on which something is seen, esp. something rare or unusual. **2** another name for **sight** (sense 10).

sighting shot *n* an experimental shot made to assist gunmen in setting their sights.

sightless ('saɪtlɪs) *adj* **1** blind. **2** invisible.
▸ **'sightlessly** *adv* ▸ **'sightlessness** *n*

sightly ('saɪtlɪ) *adj* **sightlier, sightliest.** pleasing or attractive to see.
▸ **'sightliness** *n*

sight-read ('saɪt,ri:d) *vb* **sight-reads, sight-reading, sight-read** (-,rɛd). to sing or play (music in a printed or written form) without previous preparation.
▸ **'sight-,reader** *n* ▸ **'sight-,reading** *n*

sightscreen ('saɪt,skri:n) *n Cricket.* a large white screen placed near the boundary behind the bowler to help the batsman see the ball.

sightsee ('saɪt,si:) *vb* **sightsees, sightseeing, sightsaw, sightseen.** to visit the famous or interesting sights of (a place).
▸ **'sight,seeing** *n* ▸ **'sight,seer** *n*

Sigismund ★ ('sɪgɪsmənd) *n* 1368–1437, king of Hungary (1387–1437) and of Bohemia (1419–37); Holy Roman Emperor (1411–37).

sigla ('sɪglə) *n* the list of symbols used in a book, usually collected together as part of the preliminaries. ORIG L: pl of *siglum,* dim. of *signum* sign

sigma ('sɪgmə) *n* **1** the 18th letter in the Greek alphabet (Σ, σ, or, when final, ς), a consonant, transliterated as *S.* **2** *Maths.* the symbol Σ, indicating summation of the numbers of quantities indicated. ORIG C17: from Gk

sigma notation *n* an algebraic notation in which a capital Greek sigma (Σ) is used to indicate that all values of the expression following the sigma are to be added together (usually for values of a variable between specified limits).

sigmoid ('sɪgmɔɪd) *or* **sigmoidal** *adj* **1** shaped like the letter S. **2** of or relating to the sigmoid flexure of the large intestine. ORIG C17: from Gk *sigmoeidēs* sigma-shaped

sigmoid flexure *n* the S-shaped bend in the final portion of the large intestine.

Sigmund ★ ('sɪgmənd, 'si:gmund; *German* 'zi:kmunt) *n* **1** *Norse myth.* the father of the hero Sigurd. **2** Also called: **Siegmund** (*German* 'zi:kmunt). *German myth.* king of the Netherlands, father of Siegfried.

sign (saɪn) *n* **1** something that indicates a fact, condition, etc., that is not immediately or outwardly observable. **2** an action or gesture intended to convey information, a command, etc. **3a** a board, placard, etc., displayed in public and intended to inform, warn, etc. **3b** (*as modifier*): *a sign painter.* **4** an arbitrary mark or device that stands for a word, phrase, etc. **5** *Maths, logic.* **5a** any symbol used to indicate an operation: *a plus sign.* **5b** the positivity or negativity of a number, expression, etc. **6** an indication or vestige: *the house showed no signs of being occupied.* **7** a portentous or significant event. **8** the scent or spoor of an animal. **9** *Med.* any objective evidence of the presence of a disease or disorder. **10** *Astrol.* See **sign of the zodiac.** ◆ *vb* **11** to write (one's name) as a signature to (a document, etc.) in attestation, confirmation, etc. **12** (*intr; often foll. by to*) to make a sign. **13** to engage or be engaged by written agreement, as a player for a team, etc. **14** (*tr*) to outline in gestures a sign over, esp. the sign of the cross. **15** (*tr*) to indicate by or as if by a sign; betoken. ◆ See also **sign away, sign in,** etc. ORIG C13: from OF, from L *signum* a sign
▸ **'signable** *adj* ▸ **'signer** *n*

Signac ★ (*French* siɲak) *n* **Paul** (pɔl). 1863–1935, French painter.

signal ('sɪgnᵊl) *n* **1** any sign, gesture, etc., that serves to communicate information. **2** anything that acts as an incitement to action: *the rise in prices was a signal for rebellion.* **3a** a variable parameter, such as a current or electromagnetic wave, by which information is conveyed through an electronic circuit, etc. **3b** the information so conveyed. **3c** (*as modifier*): *a signal generator.* ◆ *adj* **4** distinguished or conspicuous. **5** used to give or act as a signal. ◆ *vb* **signals, signalling, signalled** *or US* **signals, signaling, signaled. 6** to communicate (a message, etc.) to (a person). ORIG C16: from OF *seignal,* from Med. L *signāle,* from L *signum* sign
▸ **'signaller** *or US* **'signaler** *n*

signal box *n* **1** a building containing signal levers for all the railway lines in its section. **2** a control point for a large area of a railway system.

signalize *or* **signalise** ('sɪgnə,laɪz) *vb* **signalizes, signalizing, signalized** *or* **signalises, signalising, signalised.** (*tr*) **1** to make noteworthy. **2** to point out carefully.

signally ('sɪgnəlɪ) *adv* conspicuously or especially.

signalman ('sɪgnᵊlmən) *n, pl* **signalmen.** a railway employee in charge of the signals and points within a section.

signal-to-noise ratio *n* the ratio of one parameter, such as power of a wanted signal, to the same parameter of the noise at a specified point in an electronic circuit, etc.

signatory ('sɪgnətərɪ, -trɪ) *n, pl* **signatories. 1** a person who has signed a document such as a treaty or an organization, state, etc., on whose behalf such a document has been signed. ◆ *adj* **2** having signed a document, treaty, etc. ORIG C17: from L *signātōrius* concerning sealing, from *signāre* to seal, from *signum* a mark

signature ('sɪgnɪtʃə) *n* **1** the name of a person or a mark or sign representing his or her name. **2** the act of signing one's name. **3a** a distinctive mark, characteristic, etc., that identifies a person or thing. **3b** (*as modifier*): *a signature fragrance.* **4** *Music.* See **key signature, time signature. 5** *Printing.* **5a** a sheet of paper printed with several pages that upon folding will become a section or sections of a book. **5b** such a sheet so folded. **5c** a mark, esp. a letter, printed on the first page of a signature. ORIG C16: from OF, from Med. L *signātūra,* from L *signāre* to sign

signature tune *n Brit.* a melody used to introduce or identify a television or radio programme, a performer, etc.

sign away *vb* (*tr, adv*) to dispose of by or as if by signing a document.

★ people and places

signboard ('saɪnˌbɔːd) *n* a board carrying a sign or notice, esp. one used to advertise a product, event, etc.

signet ('sɪgnɪt) *n* **1** a small seal, esp. one as part of a finger ring. **2** a seal used to stamp or authenticate documents. **3** the impression made by such a seal. ORIG C14: from Med. L *signētum* a little seal, from L *signum* a sign

signet ring *n* a finger ring bearing a signet.

significance (sɪg'nɪfɪkəns) *n* **1** consequence or importance. **2** something expressed or intended. **3** the state or quality of being significant. **4** *Statistics.* a measure of the confidence that can be placed in a result as not being merely a matter of chance.

significant (sɪg'nɪfɪkənt) *adj* **1** having or expressing a meaning. **2** having a covert or implied meaning. **3** important or momentous. **4** *Statistics.* of or relating to a difference between a result derived from a hypothesis and its observed value that is too large to be attributed to chance. ORIG C16: from L *significāre* to SIGNIFY
▸ **sig'nificantly** *adv*

significant figures *pl n* **1** the figures of a number that express a magnitude to a specified degree of accuracy: *3.141 59 to four significant figures is 3.142.* **2** the number of such figures: *3.142 has four significant figures.*

significant other *n US inf.* a spouse or lover.

signification (ˌsɪgnɪfɪ'keɪʃən) *n* **1** meaning or sense. **2** the act of signifying.

signify ('sɪgnɪˌfaɪ) *vb* **signifies, signifying, signified.** (when *tr, may take a clause as object*) **1** (*tr*) to indicate or suggest. **2** (*tr*) to imply or portend: *the clouds signified the coming storm.* **3** (*tr*) to stand as a symbol, sign, etc. (for). **4** (*intr*) to be important. ORIG C13: from OF, from L *significāre*, from *signum* a mark + *facere* to make
▸ **sig'nificative** *adj* ▸ **'signiˌfier** *n*

sign in *vb* (*adv*) **1** to sign or cause to sign a register, as at a hotel, club, etc. **2** to make or become a member, as of a club.

signing ('saɪnɪŋ) *n* a specific set of manual signs used to communicate with deaf people.

sign language *n* any system of communication by manual signs or gestures, such as one used by deaf people.

sign off *vb* (*adv*) **1** (*intr*) to announce the end of a radio or television programme, esp. at the end of a day. **2** (*tr*) (of a doctor) to declare (someone) unfit for work, because of illness. **3** (*intr*) *Brit.* to terminate one's claim to social security benefits.

sign of the zodiac *n* any of the 12 equal areas into which the zodiac can be divided, named after the 12 zodiacal constellations. In astrology, it is thought that a person's attitudes to life can be correlated with the sign in which the sun lay at the moment of their birth. Also called: **sign, star sign, sun sign.**

sign on *vb* (*adv*) **1** (*tr*) to hire or employ. **2** (*intr*) to commit oneself to a job, activity, etc. **3** (*intr*) *Brit.* to claim social security benefits.

signor *or* **signior** ('siːnjɔː; *Italian* siɲ'ɲor) *n, pl* **signors** *or* **signori** (*Italian* -'ɲori). an Italian man: usually used before a name as a title equivalent to *Mr.*

signora (siːn'jɔːrə; *Italian* siɲ'ɲora) *n, pl* **signoras** *or* **signore** (*Italian* -re). a married Italian woman: a title of address equivalent to *Mrs* when placed before a name or *madam* when used alone. ORIG It., fem of SIGNORE

signore (siːn'jɔːreɪ; *Italian* siɲ'ɲore) *n, pl* **signori** (-rɪ; *Italian* -ri). an Italian man: a title of respect equivalent to *sir* when used alone. ORIG It., ult. from L *senior* an elder, from *senex* an old man

Signorelli ★ (*Italian* siɲɲo'rɛlli) *n* **Luca** ('luːka). ?1441–1523, Italian painter.

Signoret ★ (*French* siɲɔrɛ) *n* **Simone** (simɔn), original name *Simone Kaminker.* 1921–85, French actress, whose films include *La Ronde* (1950) and *Ship of Fools* (1965): married to the actor and singer Yves Montand (1921–91).

signorina (ˌsiːnjɔː'riːnə; *Italian* siɲɲo'rina) *n, pl* **signorinas** *or* **signorine** (*Italian* -ne). an unmarried Italian woman: a title of address equivalent to *Miss* when placed before a name or *madam* or *miss* when used alone. ORIG It., dim. of SIGNORA

signory ('siːnjərɪ) *n, pl* **signories.** a variant spelling of **seigniory.**

sign out *vb* (*adv*) to sign (one's name) to indicate that one is leaving a place: *he signed out for the evening.*

signpost ('saɪnˌpəʊst) *n* **1** a post bearing a sign that shows the way, as at a roadside. **2** something that serves as a clue or indication. ◆ *vb* (*tr; usually passive*) **3** to mark with signposts. **4** to indicate direction towards.

sign up *vb* (*adv*) to enlist or cause to enlist, as for military service.

Sigurd ★ ('sɪgʊəd; *German* 'ziːgʊrt) *n Norse myth.* a hero who killed the dragon Fafnir to gain the treasure of Andvari, won Brynhild for Gunnar by deception, and then was killed by her when she discovered the fraud. His wife was Gudrun. German counterpart: **Siegfried.**

Sihanouk ★ ('sɪənʊk) *n* King **Norodom** (ˌnɒrə'dɒm). born 1922, Cambodian statesman; king of Cambodia (1941–55 and from 1993); prime minister (1955–60); head of state (1960–70, 1975–76); head of the transitional government (1991–93).

sika ('siːkə) *n* a Japanese forest-dwelling deer, now introduced into Britain, having a brown coat and a large white patch on the rump. ORIG from Japanese *shika*

Sikang ★ ('ʃiː'kæŋ) *n* a former province of W China: established in 1928 from part of W Sichuan and E Tibet; dissolved in 1955.

Sikh (siːk) *n* **1** a member of an Indian religion that separated from Hinduism and was founded in the 16th century, that teaches monotheism and rejects the authority of the Vedas. ◆ *adj* **2** of or relating to the Sikhs or their religious beliefs. ORIG C18: from Hindi, lit.: disciple, from Sansk. *śiksati* he studies
▸ **'SikhˌIsm** *n*

Si Kiang ★ ('ʃiː 'kjæŋ, kaɪ'æŋ) *n* See **Xi.**

Siking ★ ('siː'kɪŋ) *n* a former name for **Xi An.**

Sikkim ★ ('sɪkɪm) *n* a state of NE India: under British control (1861–1947); became an Indian protectorate in 1950 and an Indian state in 1975; lies in the Himalayas, rising to 8600 m (28 216 ft) at Kanchenjunga in the north. Capital: Gangtok. Pop.: 444 000 (1994 est.). Area: 7096 sq. km (2740 sq. miles).
▸ **ˌSikki'mese** *adj, n*

Sikorski ★ (sɪ'kɔːskɪ) *n* **Władysław** ('vlædɪˌslæf). 1881–1943, Polish general and statesman: prime minister (1922–23) and prime minister of the Polish government in exile during World War II: died in an air crash.

Sikorsky ★ (sɪ'kɔːskɪ) *n* **Igor.** 1889–1972, US aeronautical engineer, born in Russia. He designed the first successful helicopter (1939).

silage ('saɪlɪdʒ) *n* any crop harvested while green for fodder and kept succulent by partial fermentation in a silo. Also called: **ensilage.** ORIG C19: alteration (infl. by SILO) of ENSILAGE

sild (sɪld) *n* any of various small young herrings, esp. when prepared and canned in Norway. ORIG Norwegian

silence ('saɪləns) *n* **1** the state or quality of being silent. **2** the absence of sound or noise. **3** refusal or failure to speak, etc., when expected: *his silence on their promotion was alarming.* **4** a period of time without noise. **5** oblivion or obscurity. ◆ *vb* **silences, silencing, silenced.** (*tr*) **6** to bring to silence. **7** to put a stop to: *to silence all complaint.*

silencer ('saɪlənsə) *n* **1** any device designed to reduce noise, esp. the device in the exhaust system of a motor vehicle. US and Canad. name: **muffler. 2** a device fitted to the muzzle of a firearm to deaden the report. **3** a person or thing that silences.

silene (saɪ'liːnɪ) *n* any of a genus of plants with pink or white flowers and slender leaves. ORIG C18: NL, from L

silent ('saɪlənt) *adj* **1** characterized by an absence or near absence of noise or sound: *a silent house.* **2** tending to speak very little or not at all. **3** unable to speak. **4** failing to speak, communicate, etc., when expected: *the witness chose to remain silent.* **5** not spoken or expressed. **6** (of a letter) used in the orthography of a word but no longer pronounced in that word: *the "k" in "know" is silent.* **7** de-

noting a film that has no accompanying soundtrack. ORIG C16: from L *silēns*, from *silēre* to be quiet
▸ **'silently** *adv* ▸ **'silentness** *n*

silent cop *n Austral. sl.* a small raised hemispherical marker in the middle of a crossroads.

silent majority *n* a presumed moderate majority of the citizens who are too passive to make their views known.

Silenus ★ (saɪ'li:nəs; 'sileɪnəs) *n Greek myth.* **1** chief of the satyrs and foster father to Dionysus. **2** *pl* **Sileni** (saɪ'li:naɪ; 'sileɪni:). (*often not cap.*) one of a class of woodland deities, closely similar to the satyrs.

Silesia ★ (saɪ'li:ʃɪə) *n* a region of central Europe around the upper and middle Oder valley: mostly annexed by Prussia in 1742 but became almost wholly Polish in 1945; rich coal and iron-ore deposits. Polish name: **Śląsk.** Czech name: **Slezsko.** German name: **Schlesien.**
▸ **Si'lesian** *adj, n*

silex ('saɪlɛks) *n* a type of heat-resistant glass made from fused quartz. ORIG C16: from L: hard stone

silhouette (ˌsɪlu:'ɛt) *n* **1** the outline of a solid figure as cast by its shadow. **2** an outline drawing filled in with black, often a profile portrait cut out of black paper and mounted on a light ground. ◆ *vb* **silhouettes, silhouetting, silhouetted. 3** (*tr*) to cause to appear in silhouette. ORIG C18: after Étienne de *Silhouette* (1709–67), F politician

silica ('sɪlɪkə) *n* the dioxide of silicon (SiO_2), occurring naturally as quartz. It is a refractory insoluble material used in the manufacture of glass, ceramics, and abrasives. ORIG C19: NL, from L *silex* hard stone

silica gel *n* an amorphous form of silica capable of absorbing large quantities of water: used esp. in drying gases and oils.

silicate ('sɪlɪkɪt, -ˌkeɪt) *n* a salt or ester that can be regarded as derived from silicic acid. Silicates constitute a large proportion of the earth's minerals and are present in cement and glass.

siliceous *or* **silicious** (sɪ'lɪʃəs) *adj* **1** of, relating to, or containing silica: *a siliceous clay.* **2** (of plants) growing in soil rich in silica.

silicic (sɪ'lɪsɪk) *adj* of or containing silicon or an acid obtained from silicon.

silicic acid *n* a white gelatinous substance obtained by adding an acid to a solution of sodium silicate. It is best regarded as hydrated silica.

silicify (sɪ'lɪsɪˌfaɪ) *vb* **silicifies, silicifying, silicified.** to convert or be converted into silica: *silicified wood.*
▸ **siˌlicifi'cation** *n*

silicon ('sɪlɪkən) *n* **a** a brittle metalloid element that exists in two allotropic forms; occurs principally in sand, quartz, granite, feldspar, and clay. It is usually a grey crystalline solid but is also found as a brown amorphous powder. It is used in transistors, solar cells, and alloys. Its compounds are widely used in glass manufacture and the building industry. Symbol: Si; atomic no.: 14; atomic wt.: 28.09. **b** (*modifier; sometimes cap.*) denoting an area of a country that contains much high-technology industry. ORIG C19: from SILICA, on the model of *boron, carbon*

silicon carbide *n* an extremely hard bluish-black insoluble crystalline substance produced by heating carbon with sand at a high temperature and used as an abrasive and refractory material. Very pure crystals are used as semiconductors. Formula: SiC.

silicon chip *n* another term for **chip** (sense 7).

silicon-controlled rectifier *n* a semiconductor rectifier whose forward current between two electrodes, the anode and cathode, is initiated by means of a signal applied to a third electrode, the gate. The current subsequently becomes independent of the signal. Also called: **thyristor.**

silicone ('sɪlɪˌkəʊn) *n Chem.* **a** any of a large class of polymeric synthetic materials that usually have resistance to temperature, water, and chemicals, and good insulating and lubricating properties, making them suitable for wide use as oils, water repellents, resins, etc. **b** (*as modifier*): *silicone rubber.*

Silicon Valley ★ *n* **1** an industrial strip in W California, extending S of San Francisco, in which the US information technology industry is concentrated. **2** any area in which industries associated with information technology are concentrated.

silicosis (ˌsɪlɪ'kəʊsɪs) *n Pathol.* a form of pneumoconiosis caused by breathing in tiny particles of silica, quartz, or slate, and characterized by shortness of breath.

siliqua (sɪ'li:kwə, 'sɪlɪkwə) *or* **silique** (sɪ'li:k, 'sɪlɪk) *n, pl* **siliquae** (-'li:kwi:), **siliquas,** *or* **siliques.** the long dry dehiscent fruit of cruciferous plants, such as the wallflower. ORIG C18: via F from L *siliqua* a pod
▸ **siliquose** ('sɪlɪˌkwəʊs) *or* **siliquous** ('sɪlɪkwəs) *adj*

silk (sɪlk) *n* **1** the very fine soft lustrous fibre produced by a silkworm to make its cocoon. **2a** thread or fabric made from this fibre. **2b** (*as modifier*): *a silk dress.* **3** a garment made of this. **4** a very fine fibre produced by a spider to build its web, nest, or cocoon. **5** the tuft of long fine styles on an ear of maize. **6** *Brit.* **6a** the gown worn by a Queen's (or King's) Counsel. **6b** *Inf.* a Queen's (or King's) Counsel. **6c take silk.** to become a Queen's (or King's) Counsel. ORIG OE *sioluc;* ult. from Chinese *ssŭ* silk
▸ **'silkˌlike** *adj*

silk cotton *n* another name for **kapok.**

silk-cotton tree *n* any of a genus of tropical trees having seeds covered with silky hairs from which kapok is obtained. Also called: **kapok tree.**

silken ('sɪlkən) *adj* **1** made of silk. **2** resembling silk in smoothness or gloss. **3** dressed in silk. **4** soft and delicate.

silk hat *n* a man's top hat covered with silk.

silkworm ('sɪlkˌwɜ:m) *n* **1** the larva of the Chinese moth that feeds on the leaves of the mulberry tree: widely cultivated as a source of silk. **2** any of various similar or related larvae.

silky ('sɪlkɪ) *adj* **silkier, silkiest. 1** resembling silk in texture; glossy. **2** made of silk. **3** (of a voice, manner, etc.) suave; smooth. **4** *Bot.* covered with long fine soft hairs: *silky leaves.*
▸ **'silkily** *adv* ▸ **'silkiness** *n*

silky oak *n* any of an Australian genus of trees having divided leaves and showy clusters of orange, red, or white flowers: cultivated in the tropics as shade trees.

sill (sɪl) *n* **1** a shelf at the bottom of a window inside a room. **2** a horizontal piece along the outside lower member of a window, that throws water clear of the wall below. **3** the lower horizontal member of a window or door frame. **4** a horizontal member placed on top of a foundation wall in order to carry a timber framework. **5** a mass of igneous rock, situated between two layers of older sedimentary rock. ORIG OE *syll*

sillabub ('sɪləˌbʌb) *n* a variant spelling of **syllabub.**

Sillanpää ★ (*Finnish* 'sillɑmpæ:) *n* **Frans Eemil** (frans 'e:mil). 1888–1964, Finnish writer, noted for his novels *Meek Heritage* (1919) and *The Maid Silja* (1931): Nobel prize for literature 1939.

Sillitoe ★ ('sɪlɪtəʊ) *n* **Alan.** born 1928, British novelist. His works include *The Loneliness of the Long Distance Runner* (1959).

silly ('sɪlɪ) *adj* **sillier, silliest. 1** lacking in good sense; absurd. **2** frivolous, trivial, or superficial. **3** feeble-minded. **4** dazed, as from a blow. ◆ *n* **5** (*modifier*) *Cricket.* (of a fielding position) near the batsman's wicket: *silly mid-on.* **6** (*pl* **sillies**) Also called: **silly-billy.** *Inf.* a foolish person. ORIG C15 (in the sense: pitiable, hence the later senses: foolish): from OE *sælig* (unattested) happy, from *sæl* happiness
▸ **'silliness** *n*

silly season *n Brit.* a period, usually during the summer months, when journalists fill space reporting on frivolous events and activities.

silo ('saɪləʊ) *n, pl* **silos. 1** a pit, trench, or tower, often cylindrical in shape, in which silage is made and stored. **2** an underground position in which missile systems are sited for protection. ORIG C19: from Sp., ? of Celtic origin

Siloam ★ (saɪ'ləʊəm, sɪ-) *n Bible.* a pool in Jerusalem where Jesus cured a man of his blindness (John 9).

Silone ★ (*Italian* si'lo:ne) *n* **Ignazio** (iɲ'ɲattsjo). 1900–78,

Italian writer, noted for his novels *Fontamara* (1933) and *Bread and Wine* (1937).

silt (sɪlt) *n* **1** a fine deposit of mud, clay, etc., esp. one in a river or lake. ◆ *vb* **2** (usually foll. by *up*) to fill or become filled with silt; choke. ORIG C15: from ON
▸ **sil'tation** *n* ▸ **'silty** *adj*

Silurian (saɪ'lʊərɪən) *adj* **1** of or formed in the third period of the Palaeozoic era, during which fishes first appeared. ◆ *n* **2 the.** the Silurian period or rock system. ORIG C19: from *Silures,* a Welsh tribe who opposed the Romans

silurid (saɪ'lʊərɪd) *n* **1** any freshwater teleost fish of the family Siluridae, such as the **European catfish**, which has an elongated body, naked skin, and a long anal fin. ◆ *adj* **2** of, relating to, or belonging to the family Siluridae. ORIG C19: from L *silūrus,* from Gk *silouros* a river fish

silva ('sɪlvə) *n* a variant spelling of **sylva.**

silvan ('sɪlvən) *adj, n* a variant spelling of **sylvan.**

Silvanus *or* **Sylvanus** ★ (sɪl'veɪnəs) *n Roman myth.* the Roman god of woodlands, fields, and flocks. Greek counterpart: **Pan.** ORIG L: from *silva* woodland

silver ('sɪlvə) *n* **1a** a ductile malleable brilliant greyish-white element having the highest electrical and thermal conductivity of any metal. It occurs free and in argentite and other ores: used in jewellery, tableware, coinage, electrical contacts, and electroplating. Symbol: Ag; atomic no.: 47; atomic wt.: 107.870. **1b** (*as modifier*): *a silver coin.* Related adj: **argent. 2** coin made of, or having the appearance of, this metal. **3** cutlery, whether made of silver or not. **4** any household articles made of silver. **5** short for **silver medal. 6a** a brilliant or light greyish-white colour. **6b** (*as adj*): *silver hair.* ◆ *adj* **7** well-articulated: *silver speech.* **8** (*prenominal*) denoting the 25th in a series: *a silver wedding anniversary.* ◆ *vb* **9** (*tr*) to coat with silver or a silvery substance: *to silver a spoon.* **10** to become or cause to become silvery in colour. ORIG OE *siolfor*
▸ **'silvering** *n*

silver age *n* **1** (in Greek and Roman mythology) the second of the world's major epochs, inferior to the preceding golden age. **2** the postclassical period of Latin literature, occupying the early part of the Roman imperial era.

silver beet *n* an Australian and New Zealand variety of beet, cultivated for its edible leaves with white stems.

silver bell *n* any of various deciduous trees of North America and China, having white bell-shaped flowers. Also called: **snowdrop tree.**

silver birch *n* a tree of N temperate regions of the Old World, having silvery-white peeling bark.

silver bromide *n* a yellowish powder that darkens when exposed to light: used in making photographic emulsions. Formula: AgBr.

silver chloride *n* a white powder that darkens on exposure to light: used in making photographic emulsions and papers. Formula: AgCl.

silver disc *n* (in Britain) an album certified to have sold 60 000 copies or a single certified to have sold 200 000 copies.

silver-eye *n Austral. & NZ.* another name for **waxeye** or **white-eye.**

silver fern *n NZ.* **1** another name for **ponga. 2** a formalized spray of fern leaf, silver on a black background: the symbol of New Zealand sporting teams.

silver fir *n* any of various fir trees the leaves of which have a silvery undersurface.

silverfish ('sɪlvə,fɪʃ) *n, pl* **silverfish** *or* **silverfishes. 1** a silver variety of the goldfish. **2** any of various other silvery fishes, such as the moonfish. **3** any of various small primitive wingless insects that have long antennae and tail appendages and occur in buildings, feeding on food scraps, book-bindings, etc.

silver fox *n* **1** an American red fox in a colour phase in which the fur is black with long silver-tipped hairs. **2** the valuable fur or pelt of this animal.

silver-gilt *n* silver covered with a thin film of gold.

silver iodide *n* a yellow powder that darkens on exposure to light: used in photography and artificial rainmaking. Formula: AgI.

silver lining *n* a hopeful aspect of an otherwise desperate or unhappy situation (esp. in the phrase **every cloud has a silver lining**).

silver medal *n* a medal of silver awarded to a competitor who comes second in a contest or race.

silver nitrate *n* a white crystalline soluble poisonous substance used in making photographic emulsions and as a medical antiseptic and astringent. Formula: $AgNO_3$.

silver plate *n* **1** a thin layer of silver deposited on a base metal. **2** articles, esp. tableware, made of silver plate. ◆ *vb* **silver-plate, silver-plates, silver-plating, silver-plated. 3** (*tr*) to coat (a metal, object, etc.) with silver, as by electroplating.

silver screen *n* **the.** *Inf.* **1** films collectively or the film industry. **2** the screen onto which films are projected.

silver service *n* (in restaurants) a style of serving food using a spoon and fork in one hand like a pair of tongs.

silverside ('sɪlvə,saɪd) *n* **1** *Brit. & NZ.* a cut of beef below the aitchbone and above the leg. **2** a small marine or freshwater teleost fish related to the grey mullets.

silversmith ('sɪlvə,smɪθ) *n* a craftsman who makes or repairs articles of silver.
▸ **'silver,smithing** *n*

silver thaw *n Canad.* **1** a freezing rainstorm. **2** another name for **glitter** (sense 7).

silverware ('sɪlvə,wɛə) *n* articles, esp. tableware, made of or plated with silver.

silverweed ('sɪlvə,wiːd) *n* **1** a rosaceous perennial creeping plant with silvery pinnate leaves and yellow flowers. **2** any of various twining shrubs of SE Asia and Australia, having silvery leaves and showy purple flowers.

silvery ('sɪlvərɪ) *adj* **1** of or having the appearance of silver: *the silvery moon.* **2** containing or covered with silver. **3** having a clear ringing sound.
▸ **'silveriness** *n*

silviculture ('sɪlvɪ,kʌltʃə) *n* the branch of forestry that is concerned with the cultivation of trees. ORIG C20: *silvi-,* from L *silva* woodland + CULTURE
▸ **,silvi'cultural** *adj* ▸ **,silvi'culturist** *n*

sim (sɪm) *n* a computer game that simulates an activity, such as playing a sport or flying an aircraft.

sima ('saɪmə) *n* **1** the silicon-rich and magnesium-rich rocks of the earth's oceanic crust. **2** the earth's continental lower crust. ORIG C20: from SI(LICA) + MA(GNESIA)

Simbirsk ★ (*Russian* sim'birsk) *n* a city in W central Russia, on the River Volga: birthplace of Lenin (V. I. Ulyanov). Pop.: 678 000 (1995 est.). Former name (1924–91): **Ulyanovsk.**

Simenon ★ ('sɪmənɒn; *French* simnɔ̃) *n* **Georges** (ʒɔrʒ). 1903–89, Belgian writer, who wrote over two hundred novels, including a detective series featuring Maigret.

Simeon ★ ('sɪmɪən) *n* **1a** *Old Testament.* the second son of Jacob and Leah. **1b** the tribe descended from him. **1c** the territory once occupied by this tribe in the extreme south of the land of Canaan. **2** *New Testament.* a devout Jew, who recognized the infant Jesus as the Messiah and uttered the canticle *Nunc Dimittis* over him in the Temple (Luke 2:25–35).

Simeon Stylites ★ (staɪ'laɪtiːz) *n* **Saint.** ?390–459 A.D., Syrian monk, first of the ascetics who lived on pillars. Feast day: Jan. 5 or Sept. 1.

Simferopol ★ (*Russian* simfɪ'rɔpəlj) *n* a city in S Ukraine, on the S Crimean Peninsula: a Scythian town in the 1st century B.C.; seized by the Russians in 1736. Pop.: 348 000 (1996 est.).

simian ('sɪmɪən) *adj* **1** of or resembling a monkey or ape. ◆ *n* **2** a monkey or ape. ORIG C17: from L *sīmia* an ape, prob. from Gk *sīmos* flat-nosed

similar ('sɪmɪlə) *adj* **1** showing resemblance in qualities, characteristics, or appearance. **2** *Geom.* (of two or more figures) having corresponding angles equal and all cor-

responding sides in the same ratio. ORIG C17: from OF, from L *similis*
▸ **similarity** (ˌsɪmɪˈlærɪtɪ) *n* ▸ **ˈsimilarly** *adv*

> **USAGE NOTE** *As* should not be used after *similar*: *Wilson held a similar position to Jones* (not *a similar position as Jones*); *the system is similar to the one in France* (not *similar as in France*).

simile (ˈsɪmɪlɪ) *n* a figure of speech that expresses the resemblance of one thing to another of a different category, usually introduced by *as* or *like*. Cf. **metaphor.** ORIG C14: from L *simile* something similar, from *similis* like

similitude (sɪˈmɪlɪˌtjuːd) *n* **1** likeness. **2** a thing or sometimes a person that is like or the counterpart of another. **3** *Arch.* a simile or parable. ORIG C14: from L *similitūdō,* from *similis* like

Simla ★ (ˈsɪmlə) *n* a city in N India, capital of Himachal Pradesh state: summer capital of India (1865–1939); hill resort and health centre. Pop.: 109 860 (1991).

simmer (ˈsɪmə) *vb* **1** to cook (food) gently at or just below the boiling point. **2** (*intr*) to be about to break out in rage or excitement. ◆ *n* **3** the act, sound, or state of simmering. ORIG C17: ? imit.

simmer down *vb* (*adv*) **1** (*intr*) *Inf.* to grow calmer, as after intense rage. **2** (*tr*) to reduce the volume of (a liquid) by boiling slowly.

simnel cake (ˈsɪmnᵊl) *n Brit.* a fruit cake covered with a layer of marzipan, traditionally eaten during Lent or at Easter. ORIG C13 *simenel,* from OF, from L *simila* fine flour, prob. of Semitic origin

Simon ★ (ˈsaɪmən) *n* **1** the original name of (Saint) **Peter. 2** *New Testament.* **2a** See **Simon Zelotes. 2b** a relative of Jesus, who may have been identical with Simon Zelotes (Matthew 13:55). **2c** Also called: **Simon the Tanner.** a Christian of Joppa with whom Peter stayed (Acts of the Apostles 9:43). **3 John (Allsebrook),** 1st Viscount Simon. 1873–1954, British statesman and lawyer. He was Liberal home secretary (1915–16) and, as a leader of the National Liberals, foreign secretary (1931–35), home secretary (1935–37), Chancellor of the Exchequer (1937–40), Lord Chancellor (1940–45). **4 (Marvin) Neil.** born 1927, US dramatist and librettist: his plays include *Barefoot in the Park* (1963) and *London Suite* (1995). **5 Paul.** born 1942, US pop singer and songwriter. His albums include: with Art Garfunkel (born 1941), *Bridge over Troubled Water* (1970); and, solo, *Graceland* (1986).

Simonides ★ (saɪˈmɒnɪˌdiːz) *n* ?556–?468 B.C., Greek lyric poet and epigrammatist, noted for his odes to victory.

Simon Magus ★ *n New Testament.* a Samaritan sorcerer, probably from Gitta, of the 1st century A.D. After being converted to Christianity, he tried to buy miraculous powers from the apostles (Acts of the Apostles 8:9–24). He is also identified as the founder of a Gnostic sect.

Simon Peter ★ *n New Testament.* the full name of the apostle Peter, a combination of his original name and the name given him by Christ (Matthew 16:17–18).

simon-pure (ˈsaɪmən-) *adj Rare.* real; authentic. ORIG C19: from *the real Simon Pure,* a character in the play *A Bold Stroke for a Wife* (1717) by Susannah Centlivre (1669–1723), who is impersonated by another character in some scenes

simony (ˈsaɪmənɪ) *n Christianity.* the practice, now usually regarded as a sin, of buying or selling spiritual or Church benefits such as pardons, relics, etc. ORIG C13: from OF *simonie,* from LL *sīmōnia,* from SIMON MAGUS

Simon Zelotes ★ (zɪˈləʊtiːz) *n* **Saint.** one of the 12 apostles, who had probably belonged to the Zealot party before becoming a Christian (Luke 6:15). Owing to a misinterpretation of two similar Aramaic words he is also, but mistakenly, called *the Canaanite* (Matthew 10:4). Feast day: Oct. 28 or May 10.

simoom (sɪˈmuːm) *or* **simoon** (sɪˈmuːn) *n* a strong suffocating sand-laden wind of the deserts of Arabia and North Africa. ORIG from Ar. *samūm* poisonous, from Aramaic *sammā* poison

simpatico (sɪmˈpɑːtɪˌkəʊ) *adj Inf.* **1** pleasant or congenial. **2** of similar mind or temperament. ORIG It.: from *simpatia* SYMPATHY

simper (ˈsɪmpə) *vb* **1** (*intr*) to smile coyly, affectedly, or in a silly self-conscious way. **2** (*tr*) to utter (something) in such a manner. ◆ *n* **3** a simpering smile; smirk. ORIG C16: prob. from Du. *simper* affected
▸ **ˈsimpering** *adj* ▸ **ˈsimperingly** *adv*

simple (ˈsɪmpᵊl) *adj* **1** easy to understand or do: *a simple problem.* **2** plain; unadorned: *a simple dress.* **3** not combined or complex: *a simple mechanism.* **4** unaffected or unpretentious: *despite his fame, he remained a simple man.* **5** sincere; frank: *her simple explanation was readily accepted.* **6** of humble condition or rank: *the peasant was of simple birth.* **7** feeble-minded. **8** (*prenominal*) without additions or modifications: *the witness told the simple truth.* **9** (*prenominal*) straightforward: *a simple case of mumps.* **10** *Chem.* (of a substance) consisting of only one chemical compound. **11** *Maths.* (of an equation) containing variables to the first power only. **12** *Biol.* **12a** not divided into parts: *a simple leaf.* **12b** formed from only one ovary: *simple fruit.* **13** *Music.* relating to or denoting a time where the number of beats per bar may be two, three, or four. ◆ *n Arch.* **14** a simpleton. **15** a plant having medicinal properties. ORIG C13: via OF from L *simplex* plain
▸ **simplicity** (sɪmˈplɪsɪtɪ) *n*

simple fraction *n* a fraction in which the numerator and denominator are both integers. Also called: **common fraction, vulgar fraction.**

simple fracture *n* a fracture in which the broken bone does not pierce the skin.

simple harmonic motion *n* a form of periodic motion of a particle, etc., in which the acceleration is always directed towards some equilibrium point and is proportional to the displacement from this point. Abbrev.: **SHM.**

simple-hearted *adj* free from deceit; frank.

simple interest *n* interest paid on the principal alone. Cf. **compound interest.**

simple machine *n* a simple device for altering the magnitude or direction of a force. The six basic types are the lever, wheel and axle, pulley, screw, wedge, and inclined plane.

simple-minded *adj* **1** stupid; foolish; feeble-minded. **2** unsophisticated; artless.
▸ **ˌsimple-ˈmindedly** *adv* ▸ **ˌsimple-ˈmindedness** *n*

simple sentence *n* a sentence consisting of a single main clause.

simpleton (ˈsɪmpᵊltən) *n* a foolish or ignorant person.

simplify (ˈsɪmplɪˌfaɪ) *vb* **simplifies, simplifying, simplified.** (*tr*) **1** to make less complicated or easier. **2** *Maths.* to reduce (an equation, fraction, etc.) to its simplest form. ORIG C17: via F from Med. L *simplificāre,* from L *simplus* simple + *facere* to make
▸ **ˌsimplifiˈcation** *n*

simplistic (sɪmˈplɪstɪk) *adj* **1** characterized by extreme simplicity. **2** making unrealistically simple judgments or analyses.
▸ **ˈsimplism** *n* ▸ **simˈplistically** *adv*

> **USAGE NOTE** Since *simplistic* already has 'too' as part of its meaning, some people object to something being referred to as *too simplistic* or *oversimplistic,* and it is best to avoid such uses in serious writing.

Simplon Pass ★ (ˈsɪmplɒn) *n* a pass over the Lepontine Alps in S Switzerland, between Brig (Switzerland) and Iselle (Italy). Height: 2009 m (6590 ft).

simply (ˈsɪmplɪ) *adv* **1** in a simple manner. **2** merely. **3** absolutely; altogether: *a simply wonderful holiday.* **4** (*sentence modifier*) frankly.

Simpson ★ (ˈsɪmpsᵊn, ˈsɪmsᵊn) *n* **1** Sir **James Young.** 1811–70, Scottish obstetrician, who pioneered the use of chloroform as an anaesthetic. **2 Wallis (Warfield).** See **Edward VIII.**

Simpson Desert ★ *n* an uninhabited arid region in

central Australia, mainly in the Northern Territory. Area: about 145 000 sq. km (56 000 sq. miles).

simulacrum (ˌsɪmjʊˈleɪkrəm) *n, pl* **simulacra** (-krə). *Arch.* **1** any image or representation of something. **2** a superficial likeness. ORIG C16: from L: likeness, from *simulāre* to imitate, from *similis* like

simulate *vb* (ˈsɪmjʊˌleɪt), **simulates, simulating, simulated.** (*tr*) **1** to make a pretence of: *to simulate anxiety.* **2** to reproduce the conditions of (a situation, etc.), as in carrying out an experiment: *to simulate weightlessness.* **3** to have the appearance of. ◆ *adj* (ˈsɪmjʊlɪt, -ˌleɪt). **4** *Arch.* assumed. ORIG C17: from L *simulāre* to copy, from *similis* like
▸ **ˌsimuˈlation** *n* ▸ **ˈsimulative** *adj*

simulated (ˈsɪmjʊˌleɪtɪd) *adj* **1** (of fur, leather, pearls, etc.) being an imitation of the genuine article, usually made from cheaper material. **2** (of actions, emotions, etc.) imitated; feigned.

simulator (ˈsɪmjʊˌleɪtə) *n* **1** any device that simulates specific conditions for the purposes of research or operator training: *space simulator.* **2** a person who simulates.

simulcast (ˈsɪməlˌkɑːst) *vb* **1** (*tr*) to broadcast (a programme, etc.) simultaneously on radio and television. ◆ *n* **2** a programme, etc., so broadcast. ORIG C20: from SIMUL(TANEOUS) + (BROAD)CAST

simultaneous (ˌsɪməlˈteɪnɪəs) *adj* occurring, existing, or operating at the same time. ORIG C17: on the model of INSTANTANEOUS from L *simul* at the same time
▸ **ˌsimulˈtaneously** *adv* ▸ **ˌsimulˈtaneousness** *or* **simultaneity** (ˌsɪməltəˈniːɪtɪ) *n*

simultaneous equations *pl n* a set of equations that are all satisfied by the same values of the variables, the number of variables being equal to the number of equations.

sin[1] (sɪn) *n* **1a** transgression of God's known will or any principle or law regarded as embodying this. **1b** the condition of estrangement from God arising from such transgression. **2** any serious offence, as against a religious or moral principle. **3** any offence against a principle or standard. **4** **live in sin.** *Inf.* (of an unmarried couple) to live together. ◆ *vb* **sins, sinning, sinned.** (*intr*) **5** to commit a sin. **6** (usually foll. by *against*) to commit an offence (against a person, etc.). ORIG OE *synn*
▸ **ˈsinner** *n*

sin[2] (saɪn) *Maths. abbrev. for* sine.

SIN (in Canada) *abbrev. for* Social Insurance Number.

Sinai ★ (ˈsaɪnaɪ) *n* **1** a mountainous peninsula of NE Egypt at the N end of the Red Sea, between the Gulf of Suez and the Gulf of Aqaba: occupied by Israel in 1967; fully restored by 1982. **2** **Mount.** the mountain where Moses received the Law from God (Exodus 19–20): often identified as Jebel Musa, sometimes as Jebel Serbal, both on the S Sinai Peninsula.
▸ **Sinaitic** (ˌsaɪnɪˈɪtɪk) *or* **Sinaic** (sɪˈneɪɪk) *adj*

Sinaloa ★ (ˌsiːnəˈləʊə, ˌsɪn-; *Spanish* sinaˈloa) *n* a state of W Mexico. Capital: Culiacán. Pop.: 2 509 142 (1997 est.). Area: 58 092 sq. km (22 425 sq. miles).

sinanthropus (sɪnˈænθrəpəs) *n* a primitive apelike man of the genus *Sinanthropus,* now considered a subspecies of *Homo erectus.* ORIG C20: from NL, from LL *Sīnae* the Chinese + *-anthropus,* from Gk *anthrōpos* man

Sinatra ★ (sɪˈnɑːtrə) *n* **Frank,** full name *Francis Albert Sinatra.* 1915–98, US popular singer and film actor. His recordings include "My Way" (1969).

sin bin *n* **1** *Sl.* (in ice hockey, etc.) an area off the field of play where a player who has committed a foul can be sent to sit for a specified period. **2** *Inf.* a separate unit for disruptive schoolchildren.

since (sɪns) *prep* **1** during or throughout the period of time after: *since May it has only rained once.* ◆ *conj* (*subordinating*) **2** (sometimes preceded by *ever*) continuously from or starting from the time when. **3** seeing that; because. ◆ *adv* **4** since that time: *I haven't seen him since.* ORIG OE *sīththan,* lit.: after that

USAGE NOTE See at **ago.**

sincere (sɪnˈsɪə) *adj* **1** not hypocritical or deceitful; genuine: *sincere regret.* **2** *Arch.* pure; unmixed. ORIG C16: from L *sincērus*
▸ **sinˈcerely** *adv* ▸ **sincerity** (sɪnˈsɛrɪtɪ) *or* **sinˈcereness** *n*

sinciput (ˈsɪnsɪˌpʌt) *n, pl* **sinciputs** *or* **sincipita** (sɪnˈsɪpɪtə). *Anat.* the forward upper part of the skull. ORIG C16: from L: half a head, from SEMI- + *caput* head
▸ **sinˈcipital** *adj*

Sinclair ★ (sɪŋˈklɛə, ˈsɪŋklɛə) *n* **Upton** (**Beall**). 1878–1968, US novelist, noted for *The Jungle* (1906) and his series *World's End* (1940–53).

Sind ★ (sɪnd) *n* a province of SE Pakistan, mainly in the lower Indus valley: formerly a province of British India; became a province of Pakistan in 1947; divided in 1955 between Hyderabad and Khairpur; reunited as a province in 1970. Capital: Karachi. Pop.: 21 682 000 (1985 est.). Area: 140 914 sq. km (54 407 sq. miles).

sine[1] (saɪn) *n* (of an angle) a trigonometric function that in a right-angled triangle is the ratio of the length of the opposite side to that of the hypotenuse. ORIG C16: from L *sinus* a bend; in NL, *sinus* was mistaken as a translation of Ar. *jiba* sine (from Sansk. *jīva,* lit.: bowstring) because of confusion with Ar. *jaib* curve

sine[2] (ˈsaɪnɪ) *prep* (esp. in Latin phrases or legal terms) lacking; without.

sinecure (ˈsaɪnɪˌkjʊə) *n* **1** a paid office or post involving minimal duties. **2** a Church benefice to which no spiritual charge is attached. ORIG C17: from Med. L (*beneficium*) *sine cūrā* (benefice) without cure (of souls), from L *sine* without + *cūra* cure
▸ **ˈsineˌcurism** *n* ▸ **ˈsineˌcurist** *n*

sine curve (saɪn) *n* a curve of the equation $y = \sin x$. Also called: **sinusoid.**

sine die *Latin.* (ˈsaɪnɪ ˈdaɪɪ) *adv, adj* without a day fixed. ORIG lit.: without a day

sine qua non *Latin.* (ˈsaɪnɪ kweɪ ˈnɒn) *n* an essential requirement. ORIG lit.: without which not

sinew (ˈsɪnjuː) *n* **1** *Anat.* another name for **tendon.** **2** (*often pl*) **2a** a source of strength or power. **2b** a literary word for **muscle.** ORIG OE *sionu*
▸ **ˈsinewless** *adj*

sine wave (saɪn) *n* any oscillation, such as an alternating current, whose waveform is that of a sine curve.

sinewy (ˈsɪnjʊɪ) *adj* **1** consisting of or resembling a tendon or tendons. **2** muscular. **3** (esp. of language, style, etc.) forceful. **4** (of meat, etc.) tough.
▸ **ˈsinewiness** *n*

sinfonia (ˌsɪnfəˈnɪə) *n, pl* **sinfonie** (-ˈniːeɪ) *or* **sinfonias.** **1** another word for **symphony** (senses 2, 3). **2** (*cap. when part of a name*) a symphony orchestra. ORIG It.

sinfonietta (ˌsɪnfənˈjɛtə) *n* **1** a short or light symphony. **2** (*cap. when part of a name*) a small symphony orchestra. ORIG It.: a little symphony

sinful (ˈsɪnfʊl) *adj* **1** having committed or tending to commit sin: *a sinful person.* **2** characterized by or being a sin: *a sinful act.*
▸ **ˈsinfully** *adv* ▸ **ˈsinfulness** *n*

sing (sɪŋ) *vb* **sings, singing, sang, sung.** **1** to produce or articulate (sounds, words, a song, etc.) with musical intonation. **2** (when *intr,* often foll. by *to*) to perform (a song) to the accompaniment (of): *to sing to a guitar.* **3** (*intr;* foll. by *of*) to tell a story in song (about): *I sing of a maiden.* **4** (*intr*) to perform songs for a living. **5** (*intr*) (esp. of certain birds and insects) to utter calls or sounds reminiscent of music. **6** (when *intr,* usually foll. by *of*) to tell (something), esp. in verse: *the poet who sings of the war.* **7** (*intr*) to make a whining, ringing, or whistling sound: *the arrow sang past his ear.* **8** (*intr*) (of the ears) to experience a continuous ringing. **9** (*tr*) to bring to a given state by singing: *to sing a child to sleep.* **10** (*intr*) *Sl., chiefly US.* to confess or act as an informer. ◆ *n* **11** *Inf.* an act or performance of singing. ◆ See also **sing out.** ORIG OE *singan*
▸ **ˈsingable** *adj* ▸ **ˈsinger** *n* ▸ **ˈsinging** *adj, n*

USAGE NOTE See at **ring**[2].

sing. *abbrev. for* singular.

Singapore ★ (ˌsɪŋəˈpɔː, ˌsɪŋgə-) *n* **1** a republic in SE Asia, occupying one main island and about 58 small islands at the S end of the Malay Peninsula: established as a British trading post in 1819 and became part of the Straits Settlements in 1826; occupied by the Japanese (1942–45); a British colony from 1946, becoming self-governing in 1959; part of the Federation of Malaysia from 1963 to 1965, when it became an independent republic (within the Commonwealth). Official languages: Chinese, Malay, English, and Tamil. Religion: Buddhist, Taoist, traditional beliefs, and Muslim. Currency: Singapore dollar. Capital: Singapore. Pop.: 3 225 000 (1999 est.). Area: 648 sq. km (250 sq. miles). **2** the capital of the republic of Singapore: a major international port. Pop.: 3 104 000 (1997 est.).
▸ **ˌSingaˈporean** *adj, n*

singe (sɪndʒ) *vb* **singes, singeing, singed. 1** to burn or be burnt superficially; scorch: *to singe one's clothes.* **2** (*tr*) to burn the ends of (hair, etc.). **3** (*tr*) to expose (a carcass) to flame to remove bristles or hair. ◆ *n* **4** a superficial burn. ORIG OE *sengan*

Singer ★ (ˈsɪŋə) *n* **1 Isaac Bashevis.** 1904–91, US writer of Yiddish novels, born in Poland. His works include *The Family Moskrat* (1950) and *The King of the Fields* (1989): Nobel prize for literature 1978. **2 Isaac Merrit.** 1811–75, US inventor, who originated a chain-stitch sewing machine (1852).

Singh (sɪŋ) *n* a title assumed by a Sikh when he becomes a full member of the community. ORIG from Hindi, from Sansk. *sinhá* a lion

Singhalese (ˌsɪŋəˈliːz) *n, pl* **Singhaleses** *or* **Singhalese,** *adj* a variant spelling of **Sinhalese.**

singing telegram *n* **a** a service by which a person is employed to present greetings or congratulations by singing. **b** the greetings or congratulations presented thus.

single (ˈsɪŋgᵊl) *adj* (*usually prenominal*) **1** existing alone; solitary: *upon the hill stood a single tower.* **2** distinct from other things. **3** composed of one part. **4** designed or sufficient for one user: *a single bed.* **5** (*also postpositive*) unmarried. **6** connected with the condition of being unmarried: *he led a single life.* **7** (esp. of combat) involving two individuals. **8** even one: *there wasn't a single person on the beach.* **9** (of a flower) having only one set or whorl of petals. **10** single-minded: *a single devotion to duty.* **11** *Rare.* honest or sincere. ◆ *n* **12** something forming one individual unit. **13** (*often pl*) **13a** an unmarried person. **13b** (*as modifier*): *singles bar.* **14** a gramophone record, CD, or cassette with a short recording, usually of pop music, on it. **15** *Cricket.* a hit from which one run is scored. **16a** *Brit.* a pound note. **16b** *US & Canad.* a dollar note. **17** See **single ticket.** ◆ *vb* **singles, singling, singled. 18** (*tr; usually foll. by out*) to select from a group of people or things: *he singled him out for special mention.* ◆ See also **singles.** ORIG C14: from OF *sengle,* from L *singulus* individual
▸ **ˈsingleness** *n*

single-acting *adj* (of a reciprocating engine or pump) having a piston or pistons pressurized on one side only.

single-breasted *adj* (of a garment) having the fronts overlapping only slightly and with one row of fastenings.

single cream *n* cream having a low fat content that does not thicken with beating.

single-decker *n Brit. inf.* a bus with only one passenger deck.

single-end *n Scot.* a dwelling consisting of a single room.

single entry *n* **a** a book-keeping system in which transactions are entered in one account only. **b** (*as modifier*): *a single-entry account.*

single file *n* a line of persons, animals, or things ranged one behind the other.

single-foot *n* **1** a rapid showy gait of a horse in which each foot strikes the ground separately. ◆ *vb* **2** to move or cause to move at this gait.

single-handed *adj, adv* **1** unaided or working alone: *a single-handed crossing of the Atlantic.* **2** having or operated by one hand or one person only.
▸ **ˌsingle-ˈhandedly** *adv* ▸ **ˌsingle-ˈhandedness** *n*

single-lens reflex *n* See **reflex camera.**

single-minded *adj* having but one aim or purpose; dedicated.
▸ **ˌsingle-ˈmindedly** *adv* ▸ **ˌsingle-ˈmindedness** *n*

single-parent family *n* a household consisting of at least one dependent child and the mother or father, the other parent being dead or permanently absent. Also called: **one-parent family.**

singles (ˈsɪŋgᵊlz) *pl n Tennis, etc.* a match played with one person on each side.

singles bar *n* a bar or club that is a social meeting place for single people.

single-sex *adj* (of schools, etc.) admitting members of one sex only.

single sideband transmission *n* a method of transmitting radio waves in which either the upper or the lower sideband is transmitted, the carrier being either wholly or partially suppressed.

singlestick (ˈsɪŋgᵊlˌstɪk) *n* **1** a wooden stick used instead of a sword for fencing. **2** fencing with such a stick. **3** any short heavy stick.

singlet (ˈsɪŋglɪt) *n* **1** a sleeveless undergarment covering the body from the shoulders to the hips. **2** a garment worn with shorts by athletes, boxers, etc. ORIG C18: from SINGLE, on the model of *doublet*

single ticket *n Brit.* a ticket entitling a passenger to travel only to his or her destination, without returning.

singleton (ˈsɪŋgᵊltən) *n* **1** *Bridge, etc.* an original holding of one card only in a suit. **2** a single object, etc., distinguished from a pair or group. **3** *Maths.* a set containing only one member. **4** a person who is neither married nor in a relationship. ORIG C19: from SINGLE, on the model of SIMPLETON

single-track *adj* **1** (of a railway) having only a single pair of lines, so that trains can travel in only one direction at a time. **2** (of a road) only wide enough for one vehicle.

Single Transferable Vote *n* (*modifier*) of or relating to a system of voting in which voters list the candidates in order of preference. Abbrev.: **STV.** See **proportional representation.**

singletree (ˈsɪŋgᵊlˌtriː) *n US & Austral.* another word for **swingletree.**

singly (ˈsɪŋglɪ) *adv* **1** one at a time; one by one. **2** apart from others; separately; alone.

sing out *vb* (*tr, adv*) to call out in a loud voice; shout.

singsong (ˈsɪŋˌsɒŋ) *n* **1** an accent or intonation that is characterized by an alternately rising and falling rhythm, such as in a person's voice. **2** *Brit.* an informal session of singing, esp. of popular songs. ◆ *adj* **3** having a monotonous rhythm: *a singsong accent.*

singular (ˈsɪŋgjʊlə) *adj* **1** remarkable; extraordinary: *a singular feat.* **2** unusual; odd: *a singular character.* **3** unique. **4** denoting a word or an inflected form of a word indicating that one referent is being referred to or described. **5** *Logic.* (of a proposition) referring to a specific thing or person. ◆ *n* **6** *Grammar.* **6a** the singular number. **6b** a singular form of a word. ORIG C14: from L *singulāris* single
▸ **ˈsingularly** *adv*

singularity (ˌsɪŋgjʊˈlærɪtɪ) *n, pl* **singularities. 1** the state or quality of being singular. **2** something distinguishing a person or thing from others. **3** something unusual. **4** *Maths.* a point at which a function is not differentiable although it is differentiable in a neighbourhood of that point. **5** *Astron.* a hypothetical point in space-time at which matter is infinitely compressed to infinitesimal volume.

singularize *or* **singularise** (ˈsɪŋgjʊləˌraɪz) *vb* **singularizes, singularizing, singularized** *or* **singularises, singularising, singularised.** (*tr*) **1** to make (a word, etc.) singular. **2** to make conspicuous.
▸ **ˌsingulariˈzation** *or* **ˌsingulariˈsation** *n*

singultus (sɪŋ'gʌltəs) *n, pl* **singultuses.** a technical name for **hiccup.** ORIG C18: from L, lit.: a sob

sinh (ʃaɪn, sɪnʃ) *n* hyperbolic sine. ORIG C20: from SIN(E)[1] + H(YPERBOLIC)

Sinhailien ★ ('ʃɪn'haɪ'ljɛn) *n* a variant transliteration of the Chinese name for **Lianyungang.**

Sinhalese (ˌsɪnhə'li:z) *or* **Singhalese** *n* **1** (*pl* **Sinhaleses** *or* **Sinhalese**) a member of a people living chiefly in Sri Lanka, where they constitute the majority of the population. **2** the language of this people: the official language of Sri Lanka. ♦ *adj* **3** of or relating to this people or their language.

Sining ★ ('ʃi:'nɪŋ) *n* variant transliteration of the Chinese name for **Xining.**

sinister ('sɪnɪstə) *adj* **1** threatening or suggesting evil or harm: *a sinister glance.* **2** evil or treacherous. **3** (*usually postpositive*) *Heraldry.* of, on, or starting from the left side from the bearer's point of view. **4** *Arch.* located on the left side. ORIG C15: from L *sinister* on the left-hand side, considered by Roman augurs to be the unlucky one
▸ **'sinisterly** *adv* ▸ **'sinisterness** *n*

sinistral ('sɪnɪstrəl) *adj* **1** of or located on the left side, esp. the left side of the body. **2** a technical term for **left-handed. 3** (of the shells of certain molluscs) coiling in a clockwise direction from the apex.
▸ **'sinistrally** *adv*

sinistrorse ('sɪnɪˌstrɔ:s, ˌsɪnɪ'strɔ:s) *adj* (of some climbing plants) growing upwards in a spiral from right to left. ORIG C19: from L *sinistrōrsus* turned towards the left, from *sinister* on the left + *vertere* to turn
▸ **ˌsinis'trorsal** *adj*

Sinitic (sɪ'nɪtɪk) *n* **1** a branch of the Sino-Tibetan family of languages, consisting of the various dialects of Chinese. ♦ *adj* **2** belonging to this group of languages.

sink (sɪŋk) *vb* **sinks, sinking, sank; sunk** *or* **sunken. 1** to descend or cause to descend, esp. beneath the surface of a liquid. **2** (*intr*) to appear to move down towards or descend below the horizon. **3** (*intr*) to slope downwards. **4** (*intr; often foll. by in or into*) to pass into a specified lower state or condition: *to sink into apathy.* **5** to make or become lower in volume, pitch, etc. **6** to make or become lower in value, price, etc. **7** (*intr*) to become weaker in health, strength, etc. **8** (*intr*) to seep or penetrate. **9** (*tr*) to dig, cut, drill, bore, or excavate (a hole, shaft, etc.). **10** (*tr*) to drive into the ground: *to sink a stake.* **11** (*tr; usually foll. by in or into*) **11a** to invest (money). **11b** to lose (money) in an unwise investment. **12** (*tr*) to pay (a debt). **13** (*intr*) to become hollow: *his cheeks had sunk during his illness.* **14** (*tr*) to hit or propel (a ball) into a hole, pocket, etc.: *he sank a 15-foot putt.* **15** (*tr*) *Brit. inf.* to drink, esp. quickly: *he sank three pints in half an hour.* **16 sink or swim.** to take risks where the alternatives are loss or success. ♦ *n* **17** a fixed basin, esp. in a kitchen, made of stone, metal, etc., used for washing. **18** a place of vice or corruption. **19** an area of ground below that of the surrounding land, where water collects. **20** *Physics.* a device by which energy is removed from a system: *a heat sink.* ♦ *adj* **21** *Inf.* (of a housing estate or school) deprived or having low standards of achievement. ORIG OE *sincan*
▸ **'sinkable** *adj*

sinker ('sɪŋkə) *n* **1** a weight attached to a fishing line, net, etc., to cause it to sink in water. **2** a person who sinks shafts, etc.

sinkhole ('sɪŋkˌhəʊl) *n* **1** Also called (esp. in Britain): **swallow hole.** a depression in the ground surface, esp. in limestone, where a surface stream disappears underground. **2** a place into which foul matter runs.

Sinkiang-Uighur Autonomous Region ★ ('sɪn'kjæŋ'wi:gʊə) *n* a variant transliteration of the Chinese name for the **Xinjiang Uygur Autonomous Region.**

sink in *vb* (*intr, adv*) to enter or penetrate the mind: *eventually the news sank in.*

sinking ('sɪŋkɪŋ) *n* **a** a feeling in the stomach caused by hunger or uneasiness. **b** (*as modifier*): *a sinking feeling.*

sinking fund *n* a fund accumulated out of a business enterprise's earnings or a government's revenue and invested to repay a long-term debt.

sinless ('sɪnlɪs) *adj* free from sin or guilt; pure.
▸ **'sinlessly** *adv* ▸ **'sinlessness** *n*

Sinn Féin ('ʃɪn 'fe:n) *n* an Irish republican political movement founded about 1905 and linked to the revolutionary Irish Republican Army. ORIG C20: from Irish Gaelic: we ourselves
▸ **'Sinn 'Féiner** *n* ▸ **'Sinn 'Féinism** *n*

Sino- *combining form.* Chinese: *Sino-Tibetan; Sinology.* ORIG from F, from LL *Sīnae* the Chinese, from LGk, from Ar. *Sīn* China, prob. from Chinese *Ch'in*

Sinology (saɪ'nɒlədʒɪ) *n* the study of Chinese history, language, culture, etc.
▸ **Sinological** (ˌsaɪnə'lɒdʒɪkᵊl) *adj* ▸ **Si'nologist** *n* ▸ **Sinologue** ('saɪnəˌlɒg) *n*

Sino-Tibetan ('saɪnəʊ-) *n* **1** a family of languages that includes most of the languages of China, as well as Tibetan, Burmese, and possibly Thai. ♦ *adj* **2** belonging or relating to this family of languages.

sinsemilla (ˌsɪnsə'mi:ljə) *n* **1** a type of marijuana with a very high narcotic content. **2** the plant from which it is obtained, a strain of *Cannabis sativa.* ORIG C20: from American Sp., lit.: without seed

sinter ('sɪntə) *n* **1** a whitish porous incrustation, usually consisting of silica, that is deposited from hot springs. **2** the product of a sintering process. ♦ *vb* **3** (*tr*) to form large particles, lumps, or masses from (metal powders) by heating or pressure or both. ORIG C18: from G *Sinter* CINDER

Sint Maarten ★ (sɪnt 'ma:rtə) *n* the Dutch name for **Saint Martin.**

Sintra ★ ('sɪntrə) *n* a town in central Portugal, near Lisbon, in the Sintra mountains: noted for its castles and palaces and the beauty of its setting: tourism. Former name: **Cintra.**

sinuate ('sɪnjʊɪt, -ˌeɪt) *adj* **1** Also: **sinuous.** (of leaves) having a strongly waved margin. **2** another word for **sinuous.** ORIG C17: from L *sinuātus* curved
▸ **'sinuately** *adv*

Sinŭiju ★ (sɪˌnu:ɪ'dʒu:) *n* a port in North Korea, on the Yalu River opposite Andong, China: developed by the Japanese during their occupation (1910–45); industrial centre. Pop.: 289 000 (1987 est.).

sinuous ('sɪnjʊəs) *adj* **1** full of turns or curves. **2** devious; not straightforward. **3** supple. ORIG C16: from L *sinuōsus* winding, from *sinus* a curve
▸ **'sinuously** *adv* ▸ **sinuosity** (ˌsɪnjʊ'ɒsɪtɪ) *n*

sinus ('saɪnəs) *n, pl* **sinuses. 1** *Anat.* **1a** any bodily cavity or hollow space. **1b** a large channel for venous blood, esp. between the brain and the skull. **1c** any of the air cavities in the cranial bones. **2** *Pathol.* a passage leading to a cavity containing pus. ORIG C16: from L: a curve

sinusitis (ˌsaɪnə'saɪtɪs) *n* inflammation of the membrane lining a sinus, esp. a nasal sinus.

sinusoid ('saɪnəˌsɔɪd) *n* **1** any of the irregular terminal blood vessels that replace capillaries in certain organs, such as the liver, heart, spleen, and pancreas. **2** another name for **sine curve.** ♦ *adj* **3** resembling a sinus. ORIG C19: from F *sinusoïde.* See SINUS, -OID

sinusoidal projection *n* an equal-area map projection on which all parallels are straight lines and all except the prime meridian are sine curves, often used to show tropical latitudes.

Sion ★ *n* **1** (*French* sjɔ̃). a town in SW Switzerland, capital of Valais canton, on the River Rhône. Pop.: 24 538 (1990). Latin name: **Sedunum. 2** ('saɪən). a variant of **Zion.**

Siouan ('su:ən) *n* a family of North American Indian languages, including Sioux.

Sioux (su:) *n* **1** (*pl* **Sioux** (su:, su:z)). a member of a group of North American Indian peoples. **2** any of the languages of the Sioux. ORIG from F, shortened from *Nadowessioux*

sip (sɪp) *vb* **sips, sipping, sipped. 1** to drink (a liquid) by taking small mouthfuls. ♦ *n* **2** a small quantity of a liquid taken into the mouth and swallowed. **3** an act of sipping. ORIG C14: prob. from Low G *sippen*
▸ **'sipper** *n*

siphon *or* **syphon** ('saɪfᵊn) *n* **1** a tube placed with one end at a certain level in a vessel of liquid and the other

end outside the vessel below this level, so that atmospheric pressure forces the liquid through the tube and out of the vessel. **2** See **soda siphon. 3** *Zool.* any of various tubular organs in different aquatic animals, such as molluscs, through which water passes. ◆ *vb* **4** (often foll. by *off*) to draw off through or as if through a siphon. ORIG C17: from L *sīphō,* from Gk *siphōn*
▸ **'siphonal** *or* **siphonic** (saɪ'fɒnɪk) *adj*

siphon bottle *n* another name (esp. US) for **soda siphon.**

siphonophore ('saɪfənəˌfɔː) *n* any of an order of marine colonial hydrozoans, including the Portuguese man-of-war. ORIG C19: from NL, from Gk *siphōnophoros* tube-bearing

Siple ★ ('saɪpᵊl) *n* **Mount.** a mountain in Antarctica, on the coast of Byrd Land. Height: 3100 m (10 171 ft).

sippet ('sɪpɪt) *n* a small piece of something, esp. a piece of toast or fried bread eaten with soup or gravy. ORIG C16: used as dim. of SOP

sir (sɜː) *n* **1** a formal or polite term of address for a man. **2** *Arch.* a gentleman of high social status. ORIG C13: var. of SIRE

Sir (sɜː) *n* **1** a title of honour placed before the name of a knight or baronet: *Sir Walter Raleigh.* **2** *Arch.* a title placed before the name of a figure from ancient history.

Siracusa ★ (sira'kuːza) *n* the Italian name for **Syracuse.**

Siraj-ud-daula ★ (sɪ'rɑːdʒʊd'daʊlə) *n* ?1728–57, Indian leader who became the Great Mogul's deputy in Bengal (1756); opponent of English colonization. He captured Calcutta (1756) from the English and many of his prisoners suffocated in a crowded room that became known as the Black Hole of Calcutta. He was defeated (1757) by a group of Indian nobles in alliance with Robert Clive.

sirdar ('sɜːdɑː) *n* **1** a general or military leader in Pakistan and India. **2** (formerly) the title of the British commander in chief of the Egyptian Army. **3** a variant of **sardar.** ORIG from Hindi *sardār,* from Persian, from *sar* head + *dār* possession

sire ('saɪə) *n* **1** a male parent, esp. of a horse or other domestic animal. **2** a respectful term of address, now used only in addressing a male monarch. ◆ *vb* **sires, siring, sired. 3** (*tr*) (esp. of a domestic animal) to father. ORIG C13: from OF, from L *senior* an elder, from *senex* an old man

siren ('saɪərən) *n* **1** a device for emitting a loud wailing sound, esp. as a warning or signal, consisting of a rotating perforated metal drum through which air or steam is passed under pressure. **2** (*sometimes cap.*) *Greek myth.* one of several sea nymphs whose singing was believed to lure sailors to destruction on the rocks the nymphs inhabited. **3** a woman considered to be dangerously alluring or seductive. **4** an aquatic eel-like salamander of North America, having external gills, no hind limbs, and reduced forelimbs. ORIG C14: from OF *sereine,* from L *sīrēn,* from Gk *seirēn*

sirenian (saɪ'riːnɪən) *adj* **1** of or belonging to the *Sirenia,* an order of aquatic herbivorous placental mammals having forelimbs modified as paddles and a horizontally flattened tail: contains only the dugong and manatees. ◆ *n* **2** an animal belonging to this order; sea cow.

Siret ★ (sɪ'rɛt) *n* a river in SE Europe, rising in Ukraine and flowing southeast through E Romania to the Danube. Length: about 450 km (280 miles).

Sirius ('sɪrɪəs) *n* the brightest star in the sky, lying in the constellation Canis Major. Also called: the **Dog Star.** ORIG C14: via L from Gk *Seirios,* from ?

sirloin ('sɜːˌlɔɪn) *n* a prime cut of beef from the loin, esp. the upper part. ORIG C16 *surloyn,* from OF *surlonge,* from *sur* above + *longe,* from *loigne* LOIN

sirocco (sɪ'rɒkəʊ) *n, pl* **siroccos.** a hot oppressive and often dusty wind usually occurring in spring, beginning in N Africa and reaching S Europe. ORIG C17: from It., from Ar. *sharq* east wind

sironize *or* **sironise** ('saɪrəˌnaɪz) *vb* **sironizes, sironizing, sironized** *or* **sironises, sironising, sironised.** (*tr*) *Austral.* to treat (a woollen fabric) chemically to prevent it wrinkling after being washed. ORIG C20: from (C)SIRO + *-n-* + -IZE

siroset ('saɪrəʊˌsɛt) *adj Austral.* of or relating to the chemical treatment of woollen fabrics to give a permanent-press effect, or a garment so treated.

sirrah ('sɪrə) *n Arch.* a contemptuous term used in addressing a man or boy. ORIG C16: prob. var. of SIRE

sirree (sə'riː) *interj* (*sometimes cap.*) *US inf.* an exclamation used with *yes* or *no.*

sirup ('sɪrəp) *n US.* a less common spelling of **syrup.**

sis[1] (sɪs) *n Inf.* short for **sister.**

sis[2] (sɪs) *interj S. African inf.* an exclamation of disgust. ORIG Afrik.

SIS (in Britain) *abbrev. for* Secret Intelligence Service. Also called: **MI6.**

sisal ('saɪsᵊl) *n* **1** a Mexican agave plant cultivated for its large fleshy leaves, which yield a stiff fibre used for making rope. **2** the fibre of this plant. ◆ Also called: **sisal hemp.** ORIG C19: from Mexican Sp., after *Sisal,* a port in Yucatán, Mexico

Sisera ★ ('sɪsərə) *n* a defeated leader of the Canaanites, who was assassinated by Jael (Judges 4:17–21).

siskin ('sɪskɪn) *n* **1** a yellow-and-black Eurasian finch. **2** **pine siskin.** a North American finch, having a streaked yellowish-brown plumage. ORIG C16: from MDu. *sīseken,* from MLow G *sīsek*

Sisley ★ ('sɪslɪ; *French* sislɛ) *n* **Alfred** (alfrɛd). 1839–99, French painter, esp. of landscapes; one of the originators of impressionism.

sissy *or* **cissy** ('sɪsɪ) *n, pl* **sissies. 1** an effeminate, weak, or cowardly boy or man. ◆ *adj* **2** effeminate, weak, or cowardly.

sister ('sɪstə) *n* **1** a female person having the same parents as another person. **2** a female person who belongs to the same group, trade union, etc., as another or others. **3** a senior nurse. **4** *Chiefly RC Church.* a nun or a title given to a nun. **5** a woman fellow member of a religious body. **6** (*modifier*) belonging to the same class, fleet, etc., as another or others: *a sister ship.* **7** (*modifier*) *Biol.* denoting any of the cells or cell components formed by division of a parent cell or cell component: *sister nuclei.* ORIG OE *sweostor*

sisterhood ('sɪstəˌhʊd) *n* **1** the state of being related as a sister or sisters. **2** a religious body or society of sisters.

sister-in-law *n, pl* **sisters-in-law. 1** the sister of one's husband or wife. **2** the wife of one's brother.

sisterly ('sɪstəlɪ) *adj* of or suitable to a sister, esp. in showing kindness.
▸ **'sisterliness** *n*

Sistine Chapel ★ ('sɪstaɪn, -tiːn) *n* the chapel of the pope in the Vatican at Rome, built for Sixtus IV and decorated with frescoes by Michelangelo and others. ORIG Sistine, from It. *Sistino* relating to *Sisto* Sixtus (Pope Sixtus IV)

sistrum ('sɪstrəm) *n, pl* **sistra** (-trə). a musical instrument of ancient Egypt consisting of a metal rattle. ORIG C14: via L from Gk *seistron,* from *seiein* to shake

Sisyphean (ˌsɪsɪ'fiːən) *adj* **1** relating to Sisyphus. **2** actually or seemingly endless and futile.

Sisyphus ★ ('sɪsɪfəs) *n Greek myth.* a king of Corinth, punished in Hades for his misdeeds by eternally having to roll a heavy stone up a hill: every time he approached the top, the stone escaped his grasp and rolled to the bottom.

sit (sɪt) *vb* **sits, sitting, sat.** (*mainly intr*) **1** (*also tr;* when *intr,* often foll. by *down, in,* or *on*) to adopt a posture in which the body is supported on the buttocks and the torso is more or less upright: *to sit on a chair.* **2** (*tr*) to cause to adopt such a posture. **3** (of an animal) to adopt or rest in a posture with the hindquarters lowered to the ground. **4** (of a bird) to perch or roost. **5** (of a hen or other bird) to cover eggs to hatch them. **6** to be situated or located. **7** (of the wind) to blow from the direction specified. **8** to adopt and maintain a posture for one's portrait to be painted, etc. **9** to occupy or be entitled to a seat in some official capacity, as a judge, etc. **10** (of a deliberative body) to be in session. **11** to remain inactive or unused: *his car sat in the garage.* **12** (of a garment) to fit or hang as specified: *that dress sits well on you.* **13** to weigh, rest, or lie as specified: *greatness sits easily on him.* **14** (*tr*) *Chiefly Brit.* to take (an examination): *he's sitting his bar finals.* **15** (usually foll. by *for*) *Chiefly Brit.* to be a candidate (for a qualification): *he's sitting for a BA.* **16** (*intr; in combination*) to look after a specified person or thing for someone else: *granny-sit.* **17** (*tr*) to have seating capacity for. **18 sit tight.** *Inf.* **18a** to wait patiently. **18b** to maintain one's stand, opinion, etc., firmly. ◆ See also **sit back, sit down,** etc. ORIG OE *sittan*

sitar (sɪ'tɑː) *n* a stringed musical instrument, esp. of India, having a long neck, a rounded body, and movable frets. ORIG from Hindi *sitār,* lit.: three-stringed
▸ **si'tarist** *n*

sit back *vb* (*intr, adv*) to relax, as when action should be taken: *many people just sit back and ignore the problems of today.*

sitcom ('sɪtˌkɒm) *n* an informal term for **situation comedy.**

sit down *vb* (*adv*) **1** to adopt or cause (oneself or another) to adopt a sitting posture. **2** (*intr; foll. by under*) to suffer (insults, etc.) without protests or resistance. ◆ *n* **sit-down. 3** a form of civil disobedience in which demonstrators sit down in a public place. **4** See **sit-down strike.** ◆ *adj* **sit-down. 5** (of a meal, etc.) eaten while sitting down at a table.

sit-down strike *n* a strike in which workers refuse to leave their place of employment until a settlement is reached.

site (saɪt) *n* **1a** the piece of land where something was, is, or is intended to be located: *a building site.* **1b** (*as modifier*): *site office.* **2** *Computing.* an Internet location where information relating to a specific subject or group of subjects can be accessed. ◆ *vb* **sites, siting, sited. 3** (*tr*) to locate or install (something) in a specific place. ORIG C14: from L *situs* situation, from *sinere* to be placed

sith (sɪθ) *adv, conj, prep* an archaic word for **since.** ORIG OE *siththa*

sit-in *n* **1** a form of civil disobedience in which demonstrators occupy seats in a public place and refuse to move. **2** another term for **sit-down strike.** ◆ *vb* **sit in.** (*intr, adv*) **3** (often foll. by *for*) to deputize (for). **4** (foll. by *on*) to take part (in) as a visitor or guest. **5** to organize or take part in a sit-in.

Sitka ★ ('sɪtkə) *n* a town in SE Alaska, in the Alexander Archipelago on W Baranof Island: capital of Russian America (1804–67) and of Alaska (1867–1906). Pop.: 8588 (1990).

sitkamer ('sɪtˌkɑːmə) *n S. African.* a sitting room. ORIG from Afrik.

sitka spruce ('sɪtkə) *n* a tall North American spruce tree having yellowish-green needle-like leaves. ORIG from SITKA

sit on *vb* (*intr, prep*) **1** to be a member of (a committee, etc.). **2** *Inf.* to suppress. **3** *Inf.* to check or rebuke.

sit out *vb* (*tr, adv*) **1** to endure to the end: *I sat out the play although it was terrible.* **2** to remain seated throughout (a dance, etc.).

Sitsang ★ ('siː'tsæŋ) *n* a Chinese name for **Tibet.**

sitter ('sɪtə) *n* **1** a person or animal that sits. **2** a person who is posing for his or her portrait to be painted, etc. **3** a broody hen that is sitting on its eggs to hatch them. **4** (*in combination*) a person who looks after a specified person or thing for someone else: *flat-sitter.* **5** *US.* short for **babysitter. 6** anyone, other than the medium, taking part in a seance. **7** anything that is extremely easy, such as an easy catch in cricket.

Sitter ★ ('sɪtə) *n* **Willem de** ('wɪləm də). 1872–1934, Dutch astronomer, who calculated the size of the universe and conceived of it as expanding.

sitting ('sɪtɪŋ) *n* **1** a continuous period of being seated: *I read his novel at one sitting.* **2** such a period in a restaurant, canteen, etc.: *dinner will be served in two sittings.* **3** the act or period of posing for one's portrait to be painted, etc. **4** a meeting, esp. of an official body, to conduct business. **5** the incubation period of a bird's eggs during which the mother sits on them. ◆ *adj* **6** in office: *a sitting councillor.* **7** seated: *in a sitting position.*

Sitting Bull ★ *n* Indian name *Tatanka Yotanka* ?1831–90, American Indian chief of the Teton Dakota Sioux. Resisting White encroachment on his people's hunting grounds, he led the Sioux tribes against the US Army in the Sioux War (1876–77). The hunger of the Sioux, whose food came from the diminishing buffalo, forced his surrender (1881).

sitting duck *n Inf.* a person or thing in a defenceless or vulnerable position. Also called: **sitting target.**

sitting room *n* a room in a private house or flat used for relaxation and entertainment of guests.

sitting tenant *n* a tenant occupying a house, flat, etc.

situate ('sɪtjʊˌeɪt) *vb* **situates, situating, situated. 1** (*tr; often passive*) to place. ◆ *adj* **2** (now used esp. in legal contexts) situated. ORIG C16: from LL *situāre* to position, from L *situs* a SITE

situation (ˌsɪtjʊ'eɪʃən) *n* **1** physical placement, esp. with regard to the surroundings. **2a** state of affairs. **2b** a complex or critical state of affairs in a novel, play, etc. **3** social or financial status, position, or circumstances. **4** a position of employment.
▸ ˌ**situ'ational** *adj*

> **USAGE NOTE** *Situation* is often used in contexts in which it is redundant or imprecise. Typical examples are: *the company is in a crisis situation* or *people in a job situation.* In neither example does *situation* add to the meaning and should be left out.

situation comedy *n* (on television or radio) a comedy series involving the same characters in various day-to-day situations which are developed as separate stories for each episode. Also called: **sitcom.**

sit up *vb* (*adv*) **1** to raise (oneself or another) from a recumbent to an upright posture. **2** (*intr*) to remain out of bed and awake, esp. until a late hour. **3** (*intr*) *Inf.* to become suddenly interested: *devaluation of the dollar made the money market sit up.* ◆ *n* **sit-up. 4** a physical exercise in which the body is brought into a sitting position from one of lying on the back. Also called: **trunk curl.**

Sitwell ★ ('sɪtwəl) *n* **1** Dame **Edith.** 1887–1964, British poet, noted for her collection *Façade* (1922). **2** her brother, Sir **Osbert.** 1892–1969, British writer, best known for his autobiographical books. **3** his brother, Sir **Sacheverell** (sə'ʃɛvərəl). 1897–1988, British writer on art, architecture, and travel.

sitz bath (sɪts, zɪts) *n* a bath in which the buttocks and hips are immersed in hot water. ORIG half translation of G *Sitzbad,* from *Sitz* seat + *Bad* bath

SI unit *n* any of the units adopted for international use under the Système International d'Unités, now employed for all scientific and most technical purposes. There are seven fundamental units: the metre, kilogram, second, ampere, kelvin, candela, and mole; and two supplementary units: the radian and the steradian. All other units are derived by multiplication or division of these units.

Siva ('siːvə) *n Hinduism.* the destroyer, one of the three chief divinities of the later Hindu pantheon. ORIG from Sansk. *Śiva,* lit.: the auspicious (one)
▸ **'Sivaˌism** *n*

Sivas ★ (*Turkish* 'sivɑs) *n* a city in central Turkey, at an altitude of 1347 m (4420 ft): one of the chief cities in Asia Minor in ancient times; scene of the national congress (1919) leading to the revolution that established modern Turkey. Pop.: 240 100 (1994 est.).

six (sɪks) *n* **1** the cardinal number that is the sum of five and one. **2** a numeral, 6, VI, etc., representing this number. **3** something representing, represented by, or consisting of six units, such as a playing card with six symbols on it. **4** Also: **six o'clock.** six hours after noon or midnight. **5** *Cricket.* **5a** a stroke from which the ball crosses the boundary without bouncing. **5b** the six runs scored for such a stroke. **6** a division of a Brownie Guide or Cub Scout pack. **7 at sixes and sevens. 7a** in disagreement. **7b** in a state of confusion. **8 knock (someone) for six.** *Inf.* to upset or overwhelm (someone) completely. **9 six of one and half a dozen of the other.** a situation in which the alternatives are considered equivalent. ◆ *determiner* **10a** amounting to six: *six nations.* **10b** *(as pron): set the table for six.* ORIG OE *siex*

Six (*French* sis) *n* **Les** (le). a group of six young composers in France, who from about 1916 formed a temporary association. Its members were Darius Milhaud, Arthur Honegger, Francis Poulenc, Georges Auric, Louis Durey, and Germaine Tailleferre.

Six Counties ★ *pl n* the counties of Northern Ireland.

sixer ('sɪksə) *n* the leader of a group of six Cub Scouts or Brownie Guides.

sixfold ('sɪks,fəʊld) *adj* **1** equal to or having six times as many or as much. **2** composed of six parts. ◆ *adv* **3** by or up to six times as many or as much.

sixmo ('sɪksməʊ) *n, pl* **sixmos.** a book size resulting from folding a sheet of paper into six leaves or twelve pages, each one sixth the size of the sheet. Often written: **6mo, 6°**. Also called: **sexto.**

Six Nations ★ *pl n* (in North America) the Indian confederacy of the Cayugas, Mohawks, Oneidas, Onondagas, Senecas, and Tuscaroras. Also called: **Iroquois.** See also **Five Nations.**

six-pack *n Inf.* **1** a package containing six units, esp. six cans of beer. **2** a highly developed set of abdominal muscles in a man.

sixpence ('sɪkspəns) *n* (formerly) a small British cupronickel coin with a face value of six old pennies, worth 2½ pence.

six-shooter *n US inf.* a revolver with six chambers. Also called: **six-gun.**

sixte (sɪkst) *n* the sixth of eight basic positions from which a parry or attack can be made in fencing. ORIG from F: (the) sixth (parrying position), from L *sextus* sixth

sixteen ('sɪks'ti:n) *n* **1** the cardinal number that is the sum of ten and six. **2** a numeral, 16, XVI, etc., representing this number. **3** something represented by, representing, or consisting of 16 units. ◆ *determiner* **4a** amounting to sixteen: *sixteen tons.* **4b** *(as pron): sixteen are known to the police.* ORIG OE *sextyne*
▸ **'six'teenth** *adj, n*

sixteenmo ('sɪks'ti:nməʊ) *n, pl* **sixteenmos.** a book size resulting from folding a sheet of paper into 16 leaves or 32 pages. Often written: **16mo, 16°**. Also called: **sextodecimo.**

sixteenth note *n* the usual US and Canad. name for **semiquaver.**

sixth (sɪksθ) *adj* **1** *(usually prenominal)* **1a** coming after the fifth and before the seventh in numbering, position, time, etc.; being the ordinal number of *six:* often written 6th. **1b** *(as n): the sixth to go.* ◆ *n* **2a** one of six parts of an object, quantity, measurement, etc. **2b** *(as modifier): a sixth part.* **3** the fraction equal to one divided by six (1/6). **4** *Music.* **4a** the interval between one note and another six notes away from it in the diatonic scale. **4b** one of two notes constituting such an interval in relation to the other. ◆ *adv* **5** Also: **sixthly.** after the fifth person, position, etc. ◆ *sentence connector.* **6** Also: **sixthly.** as the sixth point.

sixth form *n* (in England and Wales) **a** the most senior level in a secondary school to which pupils, usually above the legal leaving age, may proceed to take A levels, retake GCSEs, etc. **b** *(as modifier): a sixth-form college.*
▸ **'sixth-,former** *n*

sixth sense *n* any supposed means of perception, such as intuition, other than the five senses of sight, hearing, touch, taste, and smell.

Sixtus V ★ ('sɪkstəs) *n* original name *Felice Peretti.* 1520–90, Italian ecclesiastic; pope (1585–90).

sixty ('sɪkstɪ) *n, pl* **sixties. 1** the cardinal number that is the product of ten and six. **2** a numeral, 60, LX, etc., representing sixty. **3** something represented by, representing, or consisting of 60 units. ◆ *determiner* **4a** amounting to sixty: *sixty soldiers.* **4b** *(as pron): sixty are dead.* ORIG OE *sixtig*
▸ **'sixtieth** *adj, n*

sixty-fourmo (,sɪkstɪ'fɔ:məʊ) *n, pl* **sixty-fourmos.** a book size resulting from folding a sheet of paper into 64 leaves or 128 pages, each one sixty-fourth the size of the sheet. Often written **64mo, 64°**.

sixty-fourth note *n* the usual US and Canad. name for **hemidemisemiquaver.**

sixty-nine *n* another term for **soixante-neuf.**

sizable *or* **sizeable** ('saɪzəbᵊl) *adj* quite large.
▸ **'sizably** *or* **'sizeably** *adv*

size[1] (saɪz) *n* **1** the dimensions, amount, or extent of something. **2** large dimensions, etc. **3** one of a series of graduated measurements, as of clothing: *she takes size 4 shoes.* **4** *Inf.* state of affairs as summarized: *he's bankrupt, that's the size of it.* ◆ *vb* **sizes, sizing, sized. 5** to sort according to size. **6** *(tr)* to cut to a particular size or sizes. ORIG C13: from OF *sise,* shortened from *assise* ASSIZE
▸ **'sizer** *n*

size[2] (saɪz) *n* **1** Also called: **sizing.** a thin gelatinous mixture, made from glue, clay, or wax, that is used as a sealer on paper or plaster surfaces. ◆ *vb* **sizes, sizing, sized. 2** *(tr)* to treat or coat (a surface) with size. ORIG C15: ?from OF *sise;* see SIZE[1]

sized (saɪzd) *adj* of a specified size: *medium-sized.*

size up *vb (adv)* **1** *(tr) Inf.* to make an assessment of (a person, problem, etc.). **2** to conform to or make so as to conform to certain specifications of dimension.

sizzle ('sɪzᵊl) *vb* **sizzles, sizzling, sizzled.** *(intr)* **1** to make the hissing sound characteristic of frying fat. **2** *Inf.* to be very hot. **3** *Inf.* to be very angry. ◆ *n* **4** a hissing sound. ORIG C17: imit.
▸ **'sizzler** *n* ▸ **'sizzling** *adj*

SJ *abbrev. for* Society of Jesus.

SJA *abbrev. for* Saint John's Ambulance (Brigade *or* Association).

Sjælland ★ (*Danish* 'sjɛlan) *n* the Danish name for **Zealand.**

sjambok ('ʃæmbʌk) *n* (in South Africa) a heavy whip of rhinoceros or hippopotamus hide. ORIG C19: from Afrik., ult. from Urdu *chābuk* horsewhip

SK *abbrev. for* Saskatchewan.

ska ★ (skɑ:) *n* a type of West Indian pop music: a precursor of reggae. ORIG C20: from ?

skaapsteker ('skɑ:p,stɪəkə) *n* any of several back-fanged venomous South African snakes. ORIG from Afrik. *skaap* sheep + *steek* to pierce

Skagen ★ ('skɑ:gən) *n* **Cape.** another name for the **Skaw.**

Skagerrak ★ ('skægə,ræk) *n* an arm of the North Sea between Denmark and Norway, merging with the Kattegat in the southeast.

skald *or* **scald** (skɔ:ld) *n* (in ancient Scandinavia) a bard or minstrel. ORIG from ON, from ?
▸ **'skaldic** *or* **'scaldic** *adj*

Skara Brae ★ ('skærə) *n* a neolithic village in NE Scotland, in the Orkney Islands: one of Europe's most perfectly preserved Stone Age villages, buried by a sand dune until uncovered by a storm in 1850.

skat (skæt) *n* a three-handed card game using 32 cards, popular in German-speaking communities. ORIG C19: from G, from It. *scarto* played cards, from *scartare* to discard, from L *charta* CARD[1]

skate[1] (skeɪt) *n* **1** See **roller skate, ice skate. 2** the steel blade or runner of an ice skate. **3** such a blade fitted with straps for fastening to a shoe. **4 get one's skates on.** to hurry. ◆ *vb* **skates, skating, skated.** *(intr)* **5** to glide swiftly on skates. **6** to slide smoothly over a surface. **7 skate on thin ice.** to place oneself in a dangerous situation. ORIG C17: via Du. from OF *éschasse* stilt, prob. of Gmc origin
▸ **'skater** *n*

skate[2] (skeɪt) *n, pl* **skate** *or* **skates.** any of a family of large rays of temperate and tropical seas, having two dorsal fins, a short spineless tail, and a long snout. ORIG C14: from ON *skata*

skateboard ('skeɪt,bɔ:d) *n* **1** a board mounted on roller-skate wheels, usually ridden while standing up. ◆ *vb* **2** *(intr)* to ride on a skateboard.
▸ **'skate,boarder** *n* ▸ **'skate,boarding** *n*

skate over *vb (intr, prep)* **1** to cross on or as if on skates. **2** to avoid dealing with (a matter) fully.

Skaw ★ (skɔː) *n* **the.** a cape at the N tip of Denmark. Also called: (Cape) **Skagen.**

skean-dhu (ˌskiːən'duː) *n* a dirk worn in the stocking as part of Highland dress. ORIG C19: from Gaelic *sgian dubh* black knife

skedaddle (skɪ'dædᵊl) *Inf.* ◆ *vb* **skedaddles, skedaddling, skedaddled. 1** (*intr*) to run off hastily. ◆ *n* **2** a hasty retreat. ORIG C19: from ?

skeet (skiːt) *n* a form of clay-pigeon shooting in which targets are hurled from two traps at varying speeds and angles. ORIG C20: changed from ON *skeyti* a thrown object, from *skjōta* to shoot

skein (skeɪn) *n* **1** a length of yarn, etc., wound in a long coil. **2** something resembling this, such as a lock of hair. **3** a flock of geese flying. ORIG C15: from OF *escaigne,* from ?

skeleton ('skɛlɪtən) *n* **1** a hard framework consisting of inorganic material that supports and protects the soft parts of an animal's body: may be internal, as in vertebrates, or external, as in arthropods. **2** *Inf.* a very thin emaciated person or animal. **3** the essential framework of any structure, such as a building or leaf. **4** an outline consisting of bare essentials: *the skeleton of a novel.* **5** (*modifier*) reduced to a minimum: *a skeleton staff.* **6 skeleton in the cupboard** *or US & Canad.* **closet.** a scandalous fact or event in the past that is kept secret. ORIG C16: via NL from Gk: something desiccated, from *skellein* to dry up
▸ **'skeletal** *or* **'skeleton-ˌlike** *adj*

skeletonize *or* **skeletonise** ('skɛlɪtəˌnaɪz) *vb* **skeletonizes, skeletonizing, skeletonized** *or* **skeletonises, skeletonising, skeletonised.** (*tr*) **1** to reduce to a minimum framework or outline. **2** to create the essential framework of.

skeleton key *n* a key with the serrated edge filed down so that it can open numerous locks. Also called: **passkey.**

skelm ('skɛlᵊm) *n S. African inf.* a villain or crook. ORIG Afrik.

Skelmersdale ★ ('skɛlməzˌdeɪl) *n* a town in NW England, in Lancashire: designated a new town in 1962. Pop.: 42 104 (1991).

Skelton ★ ('skɛltən) *n* **John.** ?1460–1529, English poet, noted for his colloquial speech rhythms.
▸ **Skeltonic** (skɛl'tɒnɪk) *adj*

skep (skɛp) *n* **1** a beehive, esp. one constructed of straw. **2** *Now chiefly dialect.* a large basket of wickerwork or straw. ORIG OE *sceppe*

skeptic ('skɛptɪk) *n, adj* an archaic and the usual US spelling of **sceptic.**

skerrick ('skɛrɪk) *n US, Austral., & NZ.* a small fragment or amount (esp. in **not a skerrick**). ORIG C20: N English dialect, prob. of Scand. origin

skerry ('skɛrɪ) *n, pl* **skerries.** *Chiefly Scot.* **1** a small rocky island. **2** a reef. ORIG C17: Orkney dialect, from ON *sker* scar (rock formation)

sketch (skɛtʃ) *n* **1** a rapid drawing or painting. **2** a brief usually descriptive essay or other literary composition. **3** a short play, often comic, forming part of a revue. **4** a short evocative piece of instrumental music. **5** any brief outline. ◆ *vb* **6** to make a rough drawing (of). **7** (*tr; often foll. by out*) to make a brief description of. ORIG C17: from Du. *schets,* via It. from L *schedius* hastily made, from Gk *skhedios* unprepared
▸ **'sketcher** *n*

sketchbook ('skɛtʃˌbʊk) *n* **1** a book of plain paper containing sketches or for making sketches in. **2** a book of literary sketches.

sketchy ('skɛtʃɪ) *adj* **sketchier, sketchiest. 1** existing only in outline. **2** superficial or slight.
▸ **'sketchily** *adv* ▸ **'sketchiness** *n*

skew (skjuː) *adj* **1** placed in or turning into an oblique position or course. **2** *Machinery.* having a component that is at an angle to the main axis of an assembly: *a skew bevel gear.* **3** *Maths.* composed of or being elements that are neither parallel nor intersecting. **4** (of a statistical distribution) not having equal probabilities above and below the mean. **5** distorted or biased. ◆ *n* **6** an oblique, slanting, or indirect course or position. ◆ *vb* **7** to take or cause to take an oblique course or direction. **8** (*intr*) to look sideways. **9** (*tr*) to distort. ORIG C14: from OF *escuer* to shun, of Gmc origin
▸ **'skewness** *n*

skewback ('skjuːˌbæk) *n Archit.* the sloping surface on both sides of a segmental arch that takes the thrust.

skewbald ('skjuːˌbɔːld) *adj* **1** marked or spotted in white and any colour except black. ◆ *n* **2** a horse with this marking. ORIG C17: see SKEW, PIEBALD

skewer (skjʊə) *n* **1** a long pin for holding meat in position while being cooked, etc. **2** a similar pin having some other function. ◆ *vb* **3** (*tr*) to drive a skewer through or fasten with a skewer. ORIG C17: prob. from dialect *skiver*

skewwhiff ('skjuː'wɪf) *adj* (*postpositive*) *Brit. inf.* not straight. ORIG C18: prob. infl. by ASKEW

ski (skiː) *n, pl* **skis** *or* **ski. 1a** one of a pair of wood, metal, or plastic runners that are used for gliding over snow. **1b** (*as modifier*): *a ski boot.* **2** a water-ski. ◆ *vb* **skis, skiing; skied** *or* **ski'd. 3** (*intr*) to travel on skis. ORIG C19: from Norwegian, from ON *skith* snowshoes
▸ **'skier** *n* ▸ **'skiing** *n*

skibob ('skiːbɒb) *n* a vehicle made of two short skis, the forward one having a steering handle and the rear one supporting a low seat, for gliding down snow slopes.
▸ **'skibobber** *n*

skid (skɪd) *vb* **skids, skidding, skidded. 1** to cause (a vehicle) to slide sideways or (of a vehicle) to slide sideways while in motion, esp. out of control. **2** (*intr*) to slide without revolving, as the wheel of a moving vehicle after sudden braking. ◆ *n* **3** an instance of sliding, esp. sideways. **4** a support on which heavy objects may be stored and moved short distances by sliding. **5** a shoe or drag used to apply pressure to the metal rim of a wheel to act as a brake. ORIG C17: ? of Scand. origin

Skidoo ('skɪduː) *n Canad., trademark.* another name for **snowmobile.**

skid row (rəʊ) *or* **skid road** *n Sl., chiefly US & Canad.* a dilapidated section of a city inhabited by vagrants, etc.

skied[1] (skaɪd) *vb* the past tense and past participle of **sky.**

skied[2] (skiːd) *vb* a past tense and past participle of **ski.**

Skien ★ (*Norwegian* 'ʃeːən) *n* a port in S Norway, on the **Skien River:** one of the oldest towns in Norway; timber industry. Pop.: 47 870 (1990).

skiff (skɪf) *n* a small narrow boat. ORIG C18: from F *esquif,* from OIt. *schifo* a boat, of Gmc origin

skiffle ('skɪfᵊl) *n* a style of popular music of the 1950s, played chiefly on guitars and improvised percussion instruments. ORIG C20: from ?

skijoring (skiː'dʒɔːrɪŋ, -'jɔːrɪŋ) *n* a sport in which a skier is pulled over snow or ice, usually by a horse. ORIG Norwegian *skikjöring,* lit.: ski-driving
▸ **ski'jorer** *n*

ski jump *n* **1** a high ramp overhanging a slope from which skiers compete to make the longest jump. ◆ *vb* **ski-jump. 2** (*intr*) to perform a ski jump.
▸ **ski jumper** *n*

Skikda ★ ('skɪkdɑː) *n* a port in NE Algeria, on an inlet of the Mediterranean: founded by the French in 1838 on the site of a Roman city. Pop.: 128 747 (1987). Former name: **Philippeville.**

skilful *or US* **skillful** ('skɪlfʊl) *adj* **1** possessing or displaying accomplishment or skill. **2** involving or requiring accomplishment or skill.
▸ **'skilfully** *or US* **'skillfully** *adv*

ski lift *n* any device for carrying skiers up a slope, such as a chairlift.

skill (skɪl) *n* **1** special ability in a sport, etc., esp. ability acquired by training. **2** something, esp. a trade or technique, requiring special training or manual proficiency. ORIG C12: from ON *skil* distinction
▸ **'skill-less** *or* **'skilless** *adj*

skilled (skɪld) *adj* **1** demonstrating accomplishment or special training. **2** (*prenominal*) involving skill or special training: *a skilled job.*

skillet ('skɪlɪt) *n* **1** a small frying pan. **2** *Chiefly Brit.* a saucepan. ORIG C15: prob. from *skele* bucket, from ON

skilly ('skɪlɪ) *n Chiefly Brit.* a thin soup or gruel. ORIG C19: from *skilligallee,* from ?

skim (skɪm) *vb* **skims, skimming, skimmed. 1** (*tr*) to remove floating material from the surface of (a liquid), as with a spoon. **2** to glide smoothly or lightly over (a surface). **3** (*tr*) to throw (something) in a path over a surface, so as to bounce: *to skim stones over water.* **4** (when *intr,* usually foll. by *through*) to read (a book) in a superficial manner. ◆ *n* **5** the act or process of skimming. **6** material skimmed off a liquid, esp. off milk. **7** any thin layer covering a surface. ORIG C15 *skimmen,* prob. from *scumen* to skim

skimboarding *n* a water sport similar to surfing but using a shorter board, which is rounded at both ends. Also called: **skimming.**

skimmed milk *n* milk from which the cream has been removed. Also called: **skim milk.**

skimmer ('skɪmə) *n* **1** a person or thing that skims. **2** any of several mainly tropical coastal aquatic birds having a bill with an elongated lower mandible for skimming food from the surface of the water. **3** a flat perforated spoon used for skimming fat from liquids.

skimmia ('skɪmɪə) *n* any of a genus of rutaceous shrubs grown for their ornamental red berries and evergreen foliage. ORIG C18: NL from Japanese (*mijama-*) *shikimi,* a native name of the plant

skimming ('skɪmɪŋ) *n* another word for **skimboarding.**

skimp (skɪmp) *vb* **1** to be extremely sparing or supply (someone) sparingly. **2** to perform (work, etc.) carelessly or with inadequate materials. ORIG C17: ? a combination of SCANT & SCRIMP

skimpy ('skɪmpɪ) *adj* **skimpier, skimpiest. 1** made of too little material. **2** excessively thrifty; mean.
▸ **'skimpily** *adv* ▸ **'skimpiness** *n*

skin (skɪn) *n* **1** the tissue forming the outer covering of the vertebrate body: it consists of two layers, the outermost of which may be covered with hair, scales, feathers, etc. **2** a person's complexion: *a fair skin.* **3** any similar covering in a plant or lower animal. **4** any coating or film, such as one that forms on the surface of a liquid. **5** the outer covering of a fur-bearing animal, dressed and finished with the hair on. **6** a container made from animal skin. **7** the outer covering surface of a vessel, rocket, etc. **8** a person's skin regarded as his or her life: *to save one's skin.* **9** (*often pl*) *Inf.* (in jazz or pop use) a drum. **10** *Inf.* short for **skinhead. 11 by the skin of one's teeth.** only just. **12 get under one's skin.** *Inf.* to irritate. **13 no skin off one's nose.** *Inf.* not a matter that affects one adversely. **14 skin and bone.** extremely thin. **15 thick** (*or* **thin**) **skin.** an insensitive (*or* sensitive) nature. ◆ *vb* **skins, skinning, skinned. 16** (*tr*) to remove the outer covering from (fruit, etc.). **17** (*tr*) to scrape a small piece of skin from (a part of oneself) in falling, etc.: *he skinned his knee.* **18** (often foll. by *over*) to cover (something) with skin or a skinlike substance or (of something) to be covered in this way. **19** (*tr*) *Sl.* to swindle. ◆ *adj* **20** of or for the skin: *skin cream.* ORIG OE *scinn*
▸ **'skinless** *adj* ▸ **'skin,like** *adj*

skin-deep *adj* **1** superficial; shallow. ◆ *adv* **2** superficially.

skin diving *n* the sport or activity of diving and underwater swimming without wearing a diver's costume.
▸ **'skin-,diver** *n*

skin flick *n Sl.* a film containing much nudity and explicit sex for sensational purposes.

skinflint ('skɪn,flɪnt) *n* an ungenerous or niggardly person. ORIG C18: referring to a person so avaricious that he would skin (swindle) a flint

skinful ('skɪn,fʊl) *n, pl* **skinfuls.** *Sl.* sufficient alcoholic drink to make one drunk.

skin graft *n* a piece of skin removed from one part of the body and surgically grafted at the site of a severe burn or similar injury.

skinhead ('skɪn,hɛd) *n* **1** a member of a group of White youths, noted for their cropped hair, aggressive behaviour, and overt racism. **2** a closely cropped hairstyle.

skink (skɪŋk) *n* any of a family of lizards commonest in tropical Africa and Asia, having an elongated body covered with smooth scales. ORIG C16: from L *scincus* a lizard, from Gk *skinkos*

skinned (skɪnd) *adj* **1** stripped of the skin. **2a** having a skin as specified. **2b** (*in combination*): *thick-skinned.*

Skinner ★ ('skɪnə) *n* **B(urrhus) F(rederic).** 1904–90, US behavioural psychologist.

skinny ('skɪnɪ) *adj* **skinnier, skinniest. 1** lacking in flesh; thin. **2** consisting of or resembling skin.

skint (skɪnt) *adj* (*usually postpositive*) *Brit. sl.* without money. ORIG var. of *skinned,* p.p. of SKIN

skin test *n Med.* any test to determine immunity to a disease or hypersensitivity by introducing a small amount of the test substance beneath the skin.

skintight ('skɪn'taɪt) *adj* (of garments) fitting tightly over the body; clinging.

skip[1] (skɪp) *vb* **skips, skipping, skipped. 1** (when *intr,* often foll. by *over, into,* etc.) to spring or move lightly, esp. to move by hopping from one foot to the other. **2** (*intr*) to jump over a skipping-rope. **3** to cause (a stone, etc.) to skim over a surface or (of a stone) to move in this way. **4** to omit (intervening matter): *he skipped a chapter of the book.* **5** (*intr;* foll. by *through*) *Inf.* to read or deal with quickly or superficially. **6 skip it!** *Inf.* it doesn't matter! **7** (*tr*) *Inf.* to miss deliberately: *to skip school.* **8** (*tr*) *Inf., chiefly US & Canad.* to leave (a place) in haste: *to skip town.* ◆ *n* **9** a skipping movement or gait. **10** the act of passing over or omitting. ORIG C13: prob. from ON

skip[2] (skɪp) *n, vb* **skips, skipping, skipped.** *Inf.* short for **skipper**[1].

skip[3] (skɪp) *n* **1** a large open container for transporting building materials, etc. **2** a cage used as a lift in mines, etc. ORIG C19: var. of SKEP

ski pants *pl n* stretch trousers, worn for skiing or as a fashion garment, kept taut by a strap under the foot.

skip distance *n* the shortest distance between a transmitter and a receiver that will permit reception of radio waves of a specified frequency by one reflection from the ionosphere.

skipjack ('skɪp,dʒæk) *n, pl* **skipjack** *or* **skipjacks. 1** Also called: **skipjack tuna.** an important food fish that has a striped abdomen and occurs in all tropical seas. **2 black skipjack.** a small spotted tuna of Indo-Pacific seas.

skiplane ('ski:,pleɪn) *n* an aircraft fitted with skis to enable it to land on and take off from snow.

skipper[1] ('skɪpə) *n* **1** the captain of any vessel. **2** the captain of an aircraft. **3** a leader, as of a sporting team. ◆ *vb* **4** to act as skipper (of). ORIG C14: from MLow G, MDu. *schipper* shipper

skipper[2] ('skɪpə) *n* **1** a person or thing that skips. **2** a small butterfly having a hairy mothlike body and erratic darting flight.

skipping ('skɪpɪŋ) *n* the act of jumping over a rope that is held either by the person jumping or by two other people, as a game or for exercise.

skipping-rope *n Brit.* a cord, usually having handles at each end, that is held in the hands and swung round and down so that the holder or others can jump over it.

Skipton ★ ('skɪptən) *n* a market town in N England, in North Yorkshire: 11th-century castle. Pop.: 13 583 (1991).

skip-tooth saw *n* a saw with alternate teeth absent.

skip zone *n* a region surrounding a broadcasting station that cannot receive transmissions either directly or by reflection off the ionosphere.

skirl (skɜ:l) *Scot. & N English dialect.* ◆ *vb* **1** (*intr*) (esp. of bagpipes) to emit a shrill sound. ◆ *n* **2** the sound of bagpipes. ORIG C14: prob. from ON

skirmish ('skɜ:mɪʃ) *n* **1** a minor short-lived military engagement. **2** any brisk clash or encounter. ◆ *vb* **3** (*intr; often foll. by with*) to engage in a skirmish. ORIG C14: from OF *eskirmir,* of Gmc origin
▸ **'skirmisher** *n*

Skíros ★ ('skirɔs) *n* transliteration of the Modern Greek name for **Skyros.**

skirt (skɜ:t) *n* **1** a garment hanging from the waist, worn chiefly by women and girls. **2** the part of a dress below the waist. **3** Also called: **apron.** a circular flap, as round the base of a hovercraft. **4** the flaps on a saddle. **5** *Brit.* a cut

of beef from the flank. **6** (*often pl*) an outlying area. **7 bit of skirt.** *Sl.* a girl or woman. ◆ *vb* **8** (*tr*) to form the edge of. **9** (*tr*) to provide with a border. **10** (when *intr*, foll. by *around, along,* etc.) to pass (by) or be situated (near) the outer edge of (an area, etc.). **11** (*tr*) to avoid (a difficulty, etc.): *he skirted the issue.* **12** *Chiefly Austral. & NZ.* to trim the ragged edges from (a fleece). ORIG C13: from ON *skyrta* shirt
▸ **'skirted** *adj*

skirting ('skɜːtɪŋ) *n* **1** a border, esp. of wood or tiles, fixed round the base of an interior wall to protect it. **2** material used for skirts.

skirting board *n* a skirting made of wood.

skirtings ('skɜːtɪŋz) *pl n* ragged edges trimmed from the fleece of a sheep.

ski stick *or* **pole** *n* a stick, usually with a metal point, used by skiers to gain momentum and maintain balance.

skit (skɪt) *n* **1** a brief satirical theatrical sketch. **2** a short satirical piece of writing. ORIG C18: rel. to earlier verb *skit* to move rapidly, hence to score a satirical hit, prob. of Scand. origin

skite[1] (skaɪt) *Scot. dialect.* ◆ *vb* **skites, skiting, skited. 1** (*intr*) to slide or slip, as on ice. **2** (*tr*) to strike with a sharp blow. ◆ *n* **3** an instance of slipping or sliding. **4** a sharp blow. ORIG C18: from ?

skite[2] (skaɪt) *Austral. & NZ inf.* ◆ *vb* **skites, skiting, skited.** (*intr*) **1** to boast. ◆ *n* **2** boastful talk. **3** a person who boasts. ORIG C19: from Scot. & N English dialect

ski tow *n* a device for pulling skiers uphill, usually a motor-driven rope grasped by the skier while riding on his skis.

skitter ('skɪtə) *vb* **1** (*intr;* often foll. by *off*) to move or run rapidly or lightly. **2** to skim or cause to skim lightly and rapidly. **3** (*intr*) *Angling.* to draw a bait lightly over the surface of water. ORIG C19: prob. from dialect *skite* to dash about

skittish ('skɪtɪʃ) *adj* **1** playful, lively, or frivolous. **2** difficult to handle or predict. ORIG C15: prob. from ON
▸ **'skittishly** *adv* ▸ **'skittishness** *n*

skittle ('skɪtᵊl) *n* **1** a wooden or plastic pin, typically widest just above the base. **2** (*pl; functioning as sing*) Also called (esp. US): **ninepins.** a bowling game in which players knock over as many skittles as possible by rolling a wooden ball at them. ORIG C17: from ?

skive[1] (skaɪv) *vb* **skives, skiving, skived.** (*tr*) to shave or remove the surface of (leather). ORIG C19: of Scand. origin, from *skifa*
▸ **'skiver** *n*

skive[2] (skaɪv) *vb* **skives, skiving, skived.** (when *intr*, often foll. by *off*) *Brit. inf.* to evade (work or responsibility). ORIG C20: from ?
▸ **'skiver** *n*

skivvy[1] ('skɪvɪ) *n, pl* **skivvies. 1** *Chiefly Brit., often contemptuous.* a servant, esp. a female; drudge. ◆ *vb* **skivvies, skivvying, skivvied. 2** (*intr*) *Brit.* to work as a skivvy. ORIG C20: from ?

skivvy[2] ('skɪvɪ) *n, pl* **skivvies.** *Austral. & NZ.* a lightweight sweater-like garment with long sleeves and a polo neck. ORIG from ?

skol (skɒl) *or* **skoal** (skəʊl) *sentence substitute* good health! (a drinking toast). ORIG C16: from Danish *skaal* bowl, of Scand. origin, from *skal*

skookum ('skuːkəm) *adj W Canad.* large or big. ORIG from Chinook Jargon

Skopje ★ ('skɔːpjɛ) *n* the capital of (the Former Yugoslav Republic of) Macedonia, on the Vardar River: became capital of Serbia in 1346 and of Macedonia in 1945; suffered a severe earthquake in 1963. Pop.: 41 280 (1994). Serbo-Croat name: **Skoplje** ('skɔpljɛ). Turkish name (1392–1913): **Üsküb.**

Skryabin ★ ('skrɪəbɪn; *Russian* 'skrjabin) *n* a variant spelling of **Scriabin.**

Skt, Skt., Skr, *or* **Skr.** *abbrev. for* Sanskrit.

skua ('skjuːə) *n* any of various predatory aquatic gull-like birds having a dark plumage and long tail. ORIG C17: from NL, from Faeroese *skūgvur,* of Scand. origin, from *skūfr*

skulduggery *or US* **skullduggery** (skʌl'dʌgərɪ) *n Inf.* underhand dealing; trickery. ORIG C18: from earlier Scot. *sculduddery,* from ?

skulk (skʌlk) *vb* (*intr*) **1** to move stealthily so as to avoid notice. **2** to lie in hiding; lurk. **3** to shirk duty or evade responsibilities. ◆ *n* **4** a person who skulks. **5** *Obs.* a pack of foxes. ORIG C13: from ON
▸ **'skulker** *n*

skull (skʌl) *n* **1** the bony skeleton of the head of vertebrates. **2** *Often derog.* the head regarded as the mind or intelligence: *to have a dense skull.* **3** a picture of a skull used to represent death or danger. ORIG C13: from ON

skull and crossbones *n* a picture of the human skull above two crossed thighbones, formerly on the pirate flag, now used as a warning of danger or death.

skullcap ('skʌl,kæp) *n* **1** a rounded brimless hat fitting the crown of the head. **2** the top part of the skull. **3** any of a genus of perennial plants, that have helmet-shaped flowers.

skunk (skʌŋk) *n, pl* **skunks** *or* **skunk. 1** any of various American mammals having a black-and-white coat and bushy tail: they eject an unpleasant-smelling fluid from the anal gland when attacked. **2** *Inf.* a despicable person. ORIG C17: of Amerind origin

skunk cabbage *n* a low-growing fetid aroid swamp plant of E North America, having broad leaves and minute flowers enclosed in a greenish spathe.

sky (skaɪ) *n, pl* **skies. 1** (*sometimes pl*) the apparently dome-shaped expanse extending upwards from the horizon that is blue or grey during the day and black at night. **2** outer space, as seen from the earth. **3** (*often pl*) weather, as described by the appearance of the upper air: *sunny skies.* **4** heaven. **5** *Inf.* the highest level of attainment: *the sky's the limit.* **6 to the skies.** extravagantly. ◆ *vb* **skies, skying, skied. 7** *Rowing.* to lift (the blade of an oar) too high before a stroke. **8** (*tr*) *Inf.* to hit (a ball) high in the air. ORIG C13: from ON *skȳ*

sky blue *n, adj* (of) a light or pale blue colour.

skydiving ('skaɪ,daɪvɪŋ) *n* the sport of parachute jumping, in which participants perform manoeuvres before opening the parachute.
▸ **'sky,dive** *vb* **'sky,dives, 'sky,diving, 'sky,dived** *or US* **'sky,dove; 'sky,dived** ▸ **'sky,diver** *n*

Skye ★ (skaɪ) *n* a mountainous island off the NW coast of Scotland, the largest island of the Inner Hebrides: tourist centre. Chief town: Portree. Pop.: 7500 (latest est.). Area: 1735 sq. km (670 sq. miles).

Skye terrier *n* a short-legged long-bodied breed of terrier with long wiry hair and erect ears.

sky-high *adj, adv* **1** at or to an unprecedented level: *prices rocketed sky-high.* ◆ *adv* **2** high into the air. **3 blow sky-high.** to destroy.

skyjack ('skaɪ,dʒæk) *vb* (*tr*) to hijack (an aircraft). ORIG C20: from SKY + HIJACK

skylark ('skaɪ,lɑːk) *n* **1** an Old World lark, noted for singing while hovering at a great height. ◆ *vb* **2** (*intr*) *Inf.* to romp or play jokes.

skylight ('skaɪ,laɪt) *n* a window placed in a roof or ceiling to admit daylight. Also called: **fanlight.**

skyline ('skaɪ,laɪn) *n* **1** the line at which the earth and sky appear to meet. **2** the outline of buildings, trees, etc., seen against the sky.

sky pilot *n Sl.* a clergyman, esp. a chaplain.

skyrocket ('skaɪ,rɒkɪt) *n* **1** another word for **rocket[1]** (sense 1). ◆ *vb* **2** (*intr*) *Inf.* to rise rapidly, as in price.

Skyros *or* **Scyros** ★ ('skiːrɒs) *n* a Greek island in the Aegean, the largest island in the N Sporades. Pop.: 3000 (latest est.). Area: 199 sq. km (77 sq. miles). Modern Greek name: **Skíros.**

skysail ('skaɪ,seɪl) *n Naut.* a square sail set above the royal on a square-rigger.

skyscraper ('skaɪ,skreɪpə) *n* a tall multistorey building.

skyward ('skaɪwəd) *adj* **1** directed or moving towards the sky. ◆ *adv* **2** Also: **skywards.** towards the sky.

skywriting ('skaɪˌraɪtɪŋ) *n* **1** the forming of words in the sky by the release of smoke or vapour from an aircraft. **2** the words so formed.
▸ **'skyˌwriter** *n*

slab (slæb) *n* **1** a broad flat thick piece of wood, stone, or other material. **2** a thick slice of cake, etc. **3** any of the outside parts of a log that are sawn off while the log is being made into planks. **4** *Austral. & NZ.* **4a** a rough-hewn wooden plank. **4b** (*as modifier*): *a slab hut.* **5** *Inf., chiefly Brit.* an operating or mortuary table. **6** *Austral. inf.* a pack of 24 cans, esp. of beer. ◆ *vb* **slabs, slabbing, slabbed.** (*tr*) **7** to cut or make into a slab or slabs. **8** to saw slabs from (a log). ORIG C13: from ?

slack¹ (slæk) *adj* **1** not tight, tense, or taut. **2** negligent or careless. **3** (esp. of water, etc.) moving slowly. **4** (of trade, etc.) not busy. **5** *Phonetics.* another term for **lax** (sense 4). ◆ *adv* **6** in a slack manner. ◆ *n* **7** a part of a rope, etc., that is slack: *take in the slack.* **8** a period of decreased activity. ◆ *vb* **9** to neglect (one's duty, etc.). **10** (often foll. by *off*) to loosen. ◆ See also **slacks.** ORIG OE *slæc, sleac*
▸ **'slackly** *adv* ▸ **'slackness** *n*

slack² (slæk) *n* small pieces of coal with a high ash content. ORIG C15: prob. from MLow G *slecke*

slacken ('slækən) *vb* (often foll. by *off*) **1** to make or become looser. **2** to make or become slower, less intense, etc.

slacker ('slækə) *n* a person who evades work or duty; shirker.

slacks (slæks) *pl n* informal trousers worn by both sexes.

slack water *n* the period of still water around the turn of the tide, esp. at low tide.

slag (slæg) *n* **1** Also called: **cinder.** the fused material formed during the smelting or refining of metals. It usually consists of a mixture of silicates with calcium, phosphorus, sulphur, etc. **2** the mass of rough fragments of rock derived from volcanic lava. **3** a mixture of shale, clay, coal dust, etc., produced during coal mining. **4** *Brit. sl.* a coarse or dissipated woman or girl. ◆ *vb* **slags, slagging, slagged. 5** to convert into or become slag. **6** (*tr; sometimes foll. by off*) *Sl.* to make disparaging comments about; slander. ORIG C16: from MLow G *slagge,* ?from *slagen* to slay
▸ **'slagging** *n* ▸ **'slaggy** *adj*

slag heap *n* a hillock of waste matter from coal mining, etc.

slain (sleɪn) *vb* the past participle of **slay.**

slake (sleɪk) *vb* **slakes, slaking, slaked. 1** (*tr*) *Literary.* to satisfy (thirst, desire, etc.). **2** (*tr*) *Poetic.* to cool or refresh. **3** to undergo or cause to undergo the process in which lime reacts with water to produce calcium hydroxide. ORIG OE *slacian,* from *slæc* SLACK¹
▸ **'slakable** *or* **'slakeable** *adj*

slaked lime *n* another name for **calcium hydroxide.**

slalom ('slɑːləm) *n Skiing, canoeing, etc.* a race over a winding course marked by artificial obstacles. ORIG Norwegian, from *slad* sloping + *lom* path

slam¹ (slæm) *vb* **slams, slamming, slammed. 1** to cause (a door or window) to close noisily or (of a door, etc.) to close in this way. **2** (*tr*) to throw (something) down violently. **3** (*tr*) *Sl.* to criticize harshly. **4** (*intr;* usually foll. by *into* or *out of*) *Inf.* to go (into or out of a room, etc.) in violent haste or anger. **5** (*tr*) to strike with violent force. **6** (*tr*) *Inf.* to defeat easily. ◆ *n* **7** the act or noise of slamming. ORIG C17: of Scand. origin

slam² (slæm) *n* **a** the winning of all (**grand slam**) or all but one (**little** *or* **small slam**) of the 13 tricks at bridge or whist. **b** the bid to do so in bridge. ORIG C17: from ?

slam³ (slæm) *n* a poetry contest in which entrants compete with each other by reciting their work and are awarded points by the audience. ORIG C20: from ?

slam-dance *vb* **slam-dances, slam-dancing, slam-danced.** (*intr*) to hurl oneself repeatedly into or through a crowd at a rock-music concert.

slammer ('slæmə) *n* **the.** *Sl.* prison.

slander ('slɑːndə) *n* **1** *Law.* **1a** defamation in some transient form, as by spoken words, gestures, etc. **1b** a slanderous statement, etc. **2** any defamatory words spoken about a person. ◆ *vb* **3** to utter or circulate slander (about). ORIG C13: via Anglo-F from OF *escandle,* from LL *scandalum* a cause of offence; see SCANDAL
▸ **'slanderer** *n* ▸ **'slanderous** *adj*

slang (slæŋ) *n* **1a** vocabulary, idiom, etc., that is not appropriate to the standard form of a language or to formal contexts and may be restricted as to social status or distribution. **1b** (*as modifier*): *a slang word.* ◆ *vb* **2** to abuse (someone) with vituperative language. ORIG C18: from ?
▸ **'slangy** *adj* ▸ **'slangily** *adv* ▸ **'slanginess** *n*

slant (slɑːnt) *vb* **1** to incline or be inclined at an oblique or sloping angle. **2** (*tr*) to write or present (news, etc.) with a bias. **3** (*intr;* foll. by *towards*) (of a person's opinions) to be biased. ◆ *n* **4** an inclined or oblique line or direction. **5** a way of looking at something. **6** a bias or opinion, as in an article. **7 on a** (*or* **the**) **slant.** sloping. ◆ *adj* **8** oblique; sloping. ORIG C17: short for ASLANT, prob. of Scand. origin
▸ **'slanting** *adj*

slantwise ('slɑːntˌwaɪz) *or* **slantways** *adv, adj* (*prenominal*) in a slanting or oblique direction.

slap (slæp) *n* **1** a sharp blow or smack, as with the open hand, something flat, etc. **2** the sound made by or as if by such a blow. **3** (**a bit of**) **slap and tickle.** *Brit. inf.* sexual play. **4 a slap in the face.** an insult or rebuff. **5 a slap on the back.** congratulation. ◆ *vb* **slaps, slapping, slapped. 6** (*tr*) to strike (a person or thing) sharply, as with the open hand or something flat. **7** (*tr*) to bring down (the hand, etc.) sharply. **8** (when *intr,* usually foll. by *against*) to strike (something) with or as if with a slap. **9** (*tr*) *Inf., chiefly Brit.* to apply in large quantities, haphazardly, etc.: *she slapped butter on the bread.* **10 slap on the back.** to congratulate. ◆ *adv Inf.* **11** exactly: *slap on time.* **12** forcibly or abruptly: *to fall slap on the floor.* ORIG C17: from Low G *slapp,* G *Schlappe,* imit.

slapdash ('slæpˌdæʃ) *adv* **1** in a careless, hasty, or haphazard manner. ◆ *adj* **2** careless, hasty, or haphazard. ◆ *n* **3** slapdash activity or work.

slap-happy *adj* **slap-happier, slap-happiest.** *Inf.* **1** cheerfully irresponsible or careless. **2** dazed or giddy from or as if from repeated blows.

slaphead ('slæpˌhɛd) *n Derog. sl.* a bald person. ORIG C20: from ?

slapstick ('slæpˌstɪk) *n* **1a** comedy characterized by horseplay and physical action. **1b** (*as modifier*): *slapstick humour.* **2** a pair of paddles formerly used in pantomime to strike a blow with a loud sound but without injury.

slap-up *adj* (*prenominal*) *Brit. inf.* (esp. of meals) lavish; excellent; first-class.

slash (slæʃ) *vb* (*tr*) **1** to cut or lay about (a person or thing) with sharp sweeping strokes, as with a sword, etc. **2** to lash with a whip. **3** to make large gashes in: *to slash tyres.* **4** to reduce (prices, etc.) drastically. **5** to criticize harshly. **6** to slit (the outer fabric of a garment) so that the lining material is revealed. **7** to clear (scrub or undergrowth) by cutting. ◆ *n* **8** a sharp sweeping stroke, as with a sword or whip. **9** a cut or rent made by such a stroke. **10** a decorative slit in a garment revealing the lining material. **11** *US & Canad.* littered wood chips that remain after trees have been cut down. **12** another name for **solidus. 13** *Brit. sl.* the act of urinating. ORIG C14 *slaschen,* ?from OF *esclachier* to break

slasher ('slæʃə) *n* **1** a person or thing that slashes. **2** *Austral. & NZ.* a tool or machine used for cutting scrub or undergrowth in the bush.

slasher movie *n Sl.* a film in which victims, usually women, are slashed with knives, razors, etc. Also called: **stalk-and-slash movie.**

slashing ('slæʃɪŋ) *adj* aggressively or harshly critical (esp. in **slashing attack**).

Śląsk ★ (ʃlɔ̃sk) *n* the Polish name for **Silesia.**

slat (slæt) *n* **1** a narrow thin strip of wood or metal, as used in a Venetian blind, etc. **2** a movable or fixed aerofoil attached to the leading edge of an aircraft wing to increase lift. ORIG C14: from OF *esclat* splinter, from *esclater* to shatter

slate¹ (sleɪt) *n* **1a** a compact fine-grained metamorphic

rock that can be split into thin layers and is used as a roofing and paving material. **1b** (*as modifier*): *a slate tile.* **2** a roofing tile of slate. **3** (formerly) a writing tablet of slate. **4** a dark grey colour. **5** *Chiefly US & Canad.* a list of candidates in an election. **6 clean slate.** a record without dishonour. **7 have a slate loose.** *Brit. & Irish inf.* to be eccentric or crazy. **8 on the slate.** *Brit. inf.* on credit. ◆ *vb* **slates, slating, slated.** (*tr*) **9** to cover (a roof) with slates. **10** *Chiefly US.* to enter (a person's name) on a list, esp. on a political slate. ◆ *adj* **11** of the colour slate. ORIG C14: from OF *esclate,* from *esclat* a fragment
▸ **'slaty** *adj*

slate[2] (sleɪt) *vb* **slates, slating, slated.** (*tr*) *Inf., chiefly Brit.* to criticize harshly. ORIG C19: prob. from SLATE[1]
▸ **'slating** *n*

slater ('sleɪtə) *n* **1** a person trained in laying roof slates. **2** another name for **woodlouse.**

slather ('slɑːðə) *n* **1** (*usually pl*) *Inf., chiefly US & Canad.* a large quantity. **2 open slather.** *Austral. & NZ sl.* a free-for-all. ORIG C19: from ?

slattern ('slætən) *n* a slovenly woman or girl. ORIG C17: prob. from *slattering,* from dialect *slatter* to slop
▸ **'slatternly** *adj* ▸ **'slatternliness** *n*

slaughter ('slɔːtə) *n* **1** the killing of animals, esp. for food. **2** the savage killing of a person. **3** the indiscriminate or brutal killing of large numbers of people, as in war. ◆ *vb* (*tr*) **4** to kill (animals), esp. for food. **5** to kill in a brutal manner. **6** to kill indiscriminately or in large numbers. **7** to defeat resoundingly. ORIG OE *sleaht*
▸ **'slaughterer** *n* ▸ **'slaughterous** *adj*

slaughterhouse ('slɔːtəˌhaʊs) *n* a place where animals are butchered for food; abattoir.

Slav (slɑːv) *n* a member of any of the peoples of E Europe or NW Asia who speak a Slavonic language. ORIG C14: from Med. L *Sclāvus* a captive Slav; see SLAVE

slave (sleɪv) *n* **1** a person legally owned by another and having no freedom of action or right to property. **2** a person who is forced to work for another against his or her will. **3** a person under the domination of another person or some habit or influence. **4** a drudge. **5** a device that is controlled by or that duplicates the action of another similar device. ◆ *vb* **slaves, slaving, slaved. 6** (*intr;* often foll. by *away*) to work like a slave. ORIG C13: via OF from Med. L *Sclāvus* a Slav, one held in bondage (the Slavonic races were frequently conquered in the Middle Ages), from LGk *Sklabos* a Slav

Slave Coast ★ *n* the coast of W Africa between the Volta River and Mount Cameroon, chiefly along the Bight of Benin: the main source of African slaves (16th–19th centuries).

slave cylinder *n* a small cylinder containing a piston that operates the brake shoes or pads in hydraulic brakes or the working part in any other hydraulically operated system.

slave-driver *n* **1** (esp. formerly) a person forcing slaves to work. **2** an employer who demands excessively hard work from his or her employees.

slaveholder ('sleɪvˌhəʊldə) *n* a person who owns slaves.
▸ **'slaveˌholding** *n*

slaver[1] ('sleɪvə) *n* **1** an owner of or dealer in slaves. **2** another name for **slave ship.**

slaver[2] ('slævə) *vb* (*intr*) **1** to dribble saliva. **2** (often foll. by *over*) **2a** to fawn or drool (over someone). **2b** to show great desire (for). ◆ *n* **3** saliva dribbling from the mouth. **4** *Inf.* drivel. ORIG C14: prob. from Low Du.
▸ **'slaverer** *n*

Slave River ★ *n* a river in W Canada, in the Northwest Territories and NE Alberta, flowing from Lake Athabaska northwest to Great Slave Lake. Length: about 420 km (260 miles). Also called: **Great Slave River.**

slavery ('sleɪvərɪ) *n* **1** the state or condition of being a slave. **2** the subjection of a person to another person, esp. in being forced into work. **3** the condition of being subject to some influence or habit. **4** work done in harsh conditions for low pay.

slave ship *n* a ship used to transport slaves, esp. formerly from Africa to the New World.

Slave State *n US history.* any of the 15 Southern states in which slavery was legal until the Civil War.

slave trade *n* the business of trading in slaves, esp. the transportation of Black Africans to America from the 16th to 19th centuries.
▸ **'slave-ˌtrader** *n* ▸ **'slave-ˌtrading** *n*

slavey ('sleɪvɪ) *n Brit. inf.* a female general servant.

Slavic ('slɑːvɪk) *n, adj* another word (esp. US) for **Slavonic.**

slavish ('sleɪvɪʃ) *adj* **1** of or befitting a slave. **2** being or resembling a slave. **3** unoriginal; imitative.
▸ **'slavishly** *adv*

Slavkov ★ ('slafkɔf) *n* the Czech name for **Austerlitz.**

Slavonia ★ (slə'vəʊnɪə) *n* a region of Croatia, mainly between the Drava and Sava Rivers.
▸ **Sla'vonian** *adj, n*

Slavonic (slə'vɒnɪk) *or esp. US* **Slavic** *n* **1** a branch of the Indo-European family of languages, usually divided into three subbranches: **South Slavonic** (including Bulgarian), **East Slavonic** (including Russian), and **West Slavonic** (including Polish and Czech). ◆ *adj* **2** of or relating to this group of languages. **3** of or relating to the people who speak these languages.

slaw (slɔː) *n Chiefly US & Canad.* short for **coleslaw.** ORIG C19: from Danish *sla,* short for *salade* SALAD

slay (sleɪ) *vb* **slays, slaying, slew, slain.** (*tr*) **1** *Arch. or literary.* to kill, esp. violently. **2** *Sl.* to impress (someone of the opposite sex). ORIG OE *slēan*
▸ **'slayer** *n*

SLCM *abbrev. for* sea-launched cruise missile: a type of cruise missile that can be launched from either a submarine or a surface ship.

SLD *abbrev. for* Social and Liberal Democrats.

sleaze (sliːz) *n Inf.* **1** sleaziness. **2** dishonest, disreputable, or immoral behaviour, esp. of public officials or employees: *political sleaze.*

sleazy ('sliːzɪ) *adj* **sleazier, sleaziest. 1** disreputable: *a sleazy nightclub.* **2** flimsy, as cloth. ORIG C17: from ?
▸ **'sleazily** *adv* ▸ **'sleaziness** *n*

sledge[1] (slɛdʒ) *or esp. US & Canad.* **sled** (slɛd) *n* **1** Also called: **sleigh.** a vehicle mounted on runners, drawn by horses or dogs, for transporting people or goods, esp. over snow. **2** a light wooden frame used, esp. by children, for sliding over snow. ◆ *vb* **sledges, sledging, sledged. 3** to convey, travel, or go by sledge. ORIG C17: from MDu. *sleedse;* C14 *sled,* from MLow G, from ON *slethi*
▸ **'sledger** *n*

sledge[2] (slɛdʒ) *n* short for **sledgehammer.**

sledge[3] (slɛdʒ) *vb* **sledges, sledging, sledged.** (*tr*) *Austral.* to bait (an opponent, esp. a batsman in cricket) in order to upset his or her concentration. ORIG from ?

sledgehammer ('slɛdʒˌhæmə) *n* **1** a large heavy hammer with a long handle used with both hands for heavy work such as breaking rocks, etc. **2** (*modifier*) resembling the action of a sledgehammer in power, etc.: *a sledgehammer blow.* ORIG C15: *sledge,* from OE *slecg* a large hammer

sleek (sliːk) *adj* **1** smooth and shiny. **2** polished in speech or behaviour. **3** (of an animal or bird) having a shiny healthy coat or feathers. **4** (of a person) having a prosperous appearance. ◆ *vb* (*tr*) **5** to make smooth and glossy, as by grooming, etc. **6** (usually foll. by *over*) to gloss (over). ORIG C16: var. of SLICK
▸ **'sleekly** *adv* ▸ **'sleekness** *n* ▸ **'sleeky** *adj*

sleep (sliːp) *n* **1** a periodic state of physiological rest during which consciousness is suspended. **2** *Bot.* the nontechnical name for **nyctitropism. 3** a period spent sleeping. **4** a state of quiescence or dormancy. **5** a poetic word for **death.** ◆ *vb* **sleeps, sleeping, slept. 6** (*intr*) to be in or as in the state of sleep. **7** (*intr*) (of plants) to show nyctitropism. **8** (*intr*) to be inactive or quiescent. **9** (*tr*) to have sleeping accommodation for (a certain number): *the boat could sleep six.* **10** (*tr;* foll. by *away*) to pass (time) sleeping. **11** (*intr*) *Poetic.* to be dead. **12 sleep on it.** to give (something) extended consideration, esp. overnight. ◆ See also **sleep around, sleep in,** etc. ORIG OE *slǣpan*

★ people and places

sleep around *vb* (*intr, adv*) *Inf.* to be sexually promiscuous.

sleeper ('sli:pə) *n* **1** a person, animal, or thing that sleeps. **2** a railway sleeping car or compartment. **3** *Brit.* one of the blocks supporting the rails on a railway track. **4** a heavy timber beam, esp. one that is laid horizontally on the ground. **5** *Chiefly Brit.* a small plain gold circle worn in a pierced ear lobe to prevent the hole from closing up. **6** *Inf.* a person or thing that achieves unexpected success after an initial period of obscurity. **7** a spy planted in advance for future use.

sleep in *vb* (*intr, adv*) **1** *Brit.* to sleep longer than usual. **2** to sleep at the place of one's employment.

sleeping bag *n* a large well-padded bag designed for sleeping in, esp. outdoors.

sleeping car *n* a railway carriage fitted with compartments containing bunks for people to sleep in.

sleeping partner *n* a partner in a business who does not play an active role. Also called: **silent partner.**

sleeping pill *n* a pill or tablet containing a sedative drug, such as a barbiturate, used to induce sleep.

sleeping policeman *n* a bump built across a road to deter motorists from speeding. Official name: **road hump.**

sleeping sickness *n* **1** Also called: **African sleeping sickness.** an African disease transmitted by the bite of the tsetse fly, characterized by fever and sluggishness. **2** Also called: **sleepy sickness.** an epidemic viral form of encephalitis characterized by extreme drowsiness. Technical name: **encephalitis lethargica.**

sleepless ('sli:plɪs) *adj* **1** without sleep or rest: *a sleepless journey.* **2** unable to sleep. **3** always alert. **4** *Chiefly poetic.* always active or moving.
▸ **'sleeplessly** *adv* ▸ **'sleeplessness** *n*

sleep off *vb* (*tr, adv*) *Inf.* to lose by sleeping: *to sleep off a hangover.*

sleep out *vb* (*intr, adv*) **1** (esp. of a tramp) to sleep in the open air. **2** to sleep away from the place of one's employment. ◆ *n* **sleep-out. 3** *Austral.* an area of a veranda partitioned off so that it may be used as a bedroom. **4** *NZ.* a small building for sleeping that is separate from the rest of a house.

sleepover ('sli:pˌəuvə) *n Inf.* an instance of spending the night at someone else's home.

sleepwalk ('sli:pˌwɔ:k) *vb* (*intr*) to walk while asleep.
▸ **'sleepˌwalker** *n* ▸ **'sleepˌwalking** *n, adj*

sleep with *vb* (*intr, prep*) to have sexual intercourse and (usually) spend the night with. Also: **sleep together.**

sleepy ('sli:pɪ) *adj* **sleepier, sleepiest. 1** inclined to or needing sleep. **2** characterized by or exhibiting drowsiness, etc. **3** conducive to sleep. **4** without activity or bustle: *a sleepy town.*
▸ **'sleepily** *adv* ▸ **'sleepiness** *n*

sleet (sli:t) *n* **1** partly melted falling snow or hail or (esp. US) partly frozen rain. **2** *Chiefly US.* the thin coat of ice that forms when sleet or rain freezes on cold surfaces. ◆ *vb* **3** (*intr*) to fall as sleet. ORIG C13: of Gmc origin
▸ **'sleety** *adj*

sleeve (sli:v) *n* **1** the part of a garment covering the arm. **2** a tubular piece that is shrunk into a cylindrical bore to reduce its bore or to line it with a different material. **3** a tube fitted externally over two cylindrical parts in order to join them. **4** a flat cardboard container to protect a gramophone record. US name: **jacket. 5** (**have a few tricks**) **up one's sleeve.** (to have options, etc.) secretly ready. **6 roll up one's sleeves.** to prepare oneself for work, a fight, etc. ◆ *vb* **sleeves, sleeving, sleeved. 7** (*tr*) to provide with a sleeve or sleeves. ORIG OE *slīf, slēf*
▸ **'sleeveless** *adj* ▸ **'sleeveˌlike** *adj*

sleeve board *n* a small ironing board for pressing sleeves, fitted onto an ironing board or table.

sleeving ('sli:vɪŋ) *n Electronics, chiefly Brit.* tubular flexible insulation into which bare wire can be inserted.

sleigh (sleɪ) *n* **1** another name for **sledge**[1] (sense 1). ◆ *vb* **2** (*intr*) to travel by sleigh. ORIG C18: from Du. *slee,* var. of *slede* SLEDGE[1]

sleight (slaɪt) *n Arch.* **1** skill; dexterity. **2** a trick or stratagem. **3** cunning. ORIG C14: from ON *slægth,* from *slægr* SLY

sleight of hand *n* **1** manual dexterity used in performing conjuring tricks. **2** the performance of such tricks.

slender ('slɛndə) *adj* **1** of small width relative to length or height. **2** (esp. of a person's figure) slim and well-formed. **3** small or inadequate in amount, size, etc.: *slender resources.* **4** (of hopes, etc.) feeble. **5** very small: *a slender margin.* ORIG C14 *slendre,* from ?
▸ **'slenderly** *adv* ▸ **'slenderness** *n*

slenderize *or* **slenderise** ('slɛndəˌraɪz) *vb* **slenderizes, slenderizing, slenderized** *or* **slenderises, slenderising, slenderised.** *Chiefly US & Canad.* to make or become slender.

slept (slɛpt) *vb* the past tense and past participle of **sleep.**

Slesvig ★ ('sle:svi) *n* the Danish name for **Schleswig.**

sleuth (slu:θ) *n* **1** an informal word for **detective. 2** short for **sleuthhound** (sense 1). ◆ *vb* **3** (*tr*) to track or follow. ORIG C19: short for *sleuthhound,* from C12 *sleuth* trail, from ON *sloth*

sleuthhound ('slu:θˌhaund) *n* **1** a dog trained to track people, esp. a bloodhound. **2** an informal word for **detective.**

S level *n Brit.* the Special level of a subject taken for the General Certificate of Education: usually taken at the same time as A levels as an additional qualification.

slew[1] (slu:) *vb* the past tense of **slay.**

slew[2] *or esp. US* **slue** (slu:) *vb* **1** to twist or be twisted sideways, esp. awkwardly. **2** *Naut.* to cause (a mast) to rotate in its step or (of a mast) to rotate in its step. ◆ *n* **3** the act of slewing. ORIG C18: from ?

slew[3] (slu:) *n* a variant spelling (esp. US) of **slough**[1] (sense 2).

slew[4] *or* **slue** (slu:) *n Inf., chiefly US & Canad.* a great number. ORIG C20: from Irish Gaelic *sluagh*

Slezsko ★ ('slɛskɔ) *n* the Czech name for **Silesia.**

slice (slaɪs) *n* **1** a thin flat piece cut from something having bulk: *a slice of pork.* **2** a share or portion: *a slice of the company's revenue.* **3** any of various utensils having a broad flat blade and resembling a spatula. **4** (in golf, tennis, etc.) **4a** the flight of a ball that travels obliquely. **4b** the action of hitting such a shot. **4c** the shot so hit. ◆ *vb* **slices, slicing, sliced. 5** to divide or cut (something) into parts or slices. **6** (when *intr,* usually foll. by *through*) to cut in a clean and effortless manner. **7** (when *intr,* foll. by *into* or *through*) to move or go (through something) like a knife. **8** (usually foll. by *off, from, away,* etc.) to cut or be cut (from) a larger piece. **9** (*tr*) to remove by use of a slicing implement. **10** to hit (a ball) with a slice. ORIG C14: from OF *esclice* a piece split off, from *esclicier* to splinter
▸ **'sliceable** *adj* ▸ **'slicer** *n*

slick (slɪk) *adj* **1** flattering and glib: *a slick salesman.* **2** adroitly devised or executed: *a slick show.* **3** *Inf., chiefly US & Canad.* shrewd; sly. **4** *Inf.* superficially attractive: *a slick publication.* **5** *Chiefly US & Canad.* slippery. ◆ *n* **6** a slippery area, esp. a patch of oil floating on water. ◆ *vb* (*tr*) **7** *Chiefly US & Canad.* to make smooth or sleek. ORIG C14: prob. from ON
▸ **'slickly** *adv* ▸ **'slickness** *n*

slicker ('slɪkə) *n* **1** *Inf.* a sly or untrustworthy person (esp. in **city slicker**). **2** *US & Canad.* a shiny raincoat, esp. an oilskin.

slide (slaɪd) *vb* **slides, sliding, slid** (slɪd); **slid** *or* **slidden** ('slɪdᵊn). **1** to move or cause to move smoothly along a surface in continual contact with it: *doors that slide open.* **2** (*intr*) to lose grip or balance: *he slid on his back.* **3** (*intr;* usually foll. by *into, out of, away from,* etc.) to pass or move unobtrusively: *she slid into the room.* **4** (*intr;* usually foll. by *into*) to go (into a specified condition) by degrees, etc.: *he slid into loose living.* **5** (foll. by *in, into,* etc.) to move (an object) unobtrusively or (of an object) to move in this way: *he slid the gun into his pocket.* **6 let slide.** to allow to deteriorate: *to let things slide.* ◆ *n* **7** the act or an instance of sliding. **8** a smooth surface, as of ice or mud, for sliding on. **9** a construction incorporating an inclined smooth slope for sliding down in playgrounds, etc. **10** a small glass plate on which specimens are mounted for

microscopical study. **11** Also called: **diapositive, transparency.** a positive photograph on a transparent base, mounted in a frame, that can be viewed by means of a slide projector. **12** Also called: **hair slide.** *Chiefly Brit.* an ornamental clip to hold hair in place. **13** *Machinery.* a sliding part or member. **14** *Music.* a portamento. **15** *Music.* the sliding curved tube of a trombone that is moved in or out. **16** *Music* **16a** a tube placed over a finger held against the frets of a guitar to produce a portamento. **16b** the style of guitar playing using a slide. **17** *Geol.* **17a** the downward movement of a large mass of earth, rocks, etc. **17b** the mass of material involved in this descent. See also **landslide.** ORIG OE *slīdan*
▸ **'slidable** *adj* ▸ **'slider** *n*

slide over *vb (intr, prep)* **1** to cross as if by sliding. **2** to avoid dealing with (a matter) fully.

slide rule *n* a mechanical calculating device consisting of two strips, one sliding along a central groove in the other, each strip graduated in two or more logarithmic scales of numbers, trigonometric functions, etc.

sliding scale *n* a variable scale according to which specified wages, prices, etc., fluctuate in response to changes in some other factor.

slier ('slaɪə) *adj* a comparative of **sly.**

sliest ('slaɪɪst) *adj* a superlative of **sly.**

slight (slaɪt) *adj* **1** small in quantity or extent. **2** of small importance. **3** slim and delicate. **4** lacking in strength or substance. ◆ *vb (tr)* **5** to show disregard for (someone); snub. **6** to treat as unimportant or trifling. **7** *US.* to devote inadequate attention to (work, duties, etc.). ◆ *n* **8** an act or omission indicating supercilious neglect. ORIG C13: from ON *slēttr* smooth
▸ **'slightingly** *adv* ▸ **'slightly** *adv* ▸ **'slightness** *n*

Sligo ★ ('slaɪgəʊ) *n* **1** a county of NW Republic of Ireland, on the Atlantic: has a deeply indented low-lying coast; livestock and dairy farming. County town: Sligo. Pop.: 56 000 (1996). Area: 1795 sq. km (693 sq. miles). **2** a port in NW Republic of Ireland, county town of Co. Sligo on **Sligo Bay.** Pop.: 17 300 (1991).

slily ('slaɪlɪ) *adv* a variant spelling of **slyly.**

slim (slɪm) *adj* **slimmer, slimmest. 1** small in width relative to height or length. **2** poor; meagre: *slim chances of success.* ◆ *vb* **3** to make or become slim, esp. by diets and exercise. **4** *(tr)* to reduce in size: *the workforce was slimmed.* ORIG C17: from Du.: crafty, from MDu. *slimp* slanting
▸ **'slimmer** *n* ▸ **'slimming** *n* ▸ **'slimness** *n*

Slim[1] (slɪm) *n* the E African name for **AIDS.** ORIG from its wasting effects

Slim[2] ★ (slɪm) *n* **William Joseph,** 1st Viscount. 1891–1970, British field marshal, who commanded (1943–45) the 14th Army in recapturing Burma from the Japanese; governor general of Australia (1953–60).

slim down *vb (adv)* **1** to make or become slim, esp. intentionally. **2** to make (an organization) more efficient or (of an organization) to become more efficient, esp. by cutting staff. ◆ *n* **slimdown. 3** an instance of an organization slimming down.

slime (slaɪm) *n* **1** soft thin runny mud or filth. **2** any moist viscous fluid, esp. when noxious or unpleasant. **3** a mucous substance produced by various organisms, such as fish, slugs, and fungi. ◆ *vb* **slimes, sliming, slimed.** *(tr)* **4** to cover with slime. ORIG OE *slīm*

slimline ('slɪm,laɪn) *adj* slim or conducive to slimness.

slimy ('slaɪmɪ) *adj* **slimier, slimiest. 1** characterized by, covered with, secreting, or resembling slime. **2** offensive or repulsive. **3** *Chiefly Brit.* characterized by servility.

sling[1] (slɪŋ) *n* **1** a simple weapon consisting of a loop of leather, etc., in which a stone is whirled and then let fly. **2** a rope or strap by which something may be secured or lifted. **3** *Med.* a wide piece of cloth suspended from the neck for supporting an injured hand or arm. **4** a loop or band attached to an object for carrying. **5** the act of slinging. ◆ *vb* **slings, slinging, slung. 6** *(tr)* to hurl with or as if with a sling. **7** to attach a sling or slings to (a load, etc.). **8** *(tr)* to carry or hang loosely from or as if from a sling: *to sling washing from the line.* **9** *(tr) Inf.* to throw. ORIG C13: ?from ON
▸ **'slinger** *n*

sling[2] (slɪŋ) *n* a mixed drink with a spirit base, usually sweetened. ORIG C19: from ?

slingback ('slɪŋ,bæk) *n* a shoe with a strap instead of a full covering for the heel.

sling off *vb (intr, adv; often foll. by at) Austral. & NZ inf.* to mock; deride; jeer (at).

slingshot ('slɪŋ,ʃɒt) *n* **1** the US and Canad. name for **catapult** (sense 1). **2** another name for **sling**[1] (sense 1).

slink (slɪŋk) *vb* **slinks, slinking, slunk. 1** *(intr)* to move or act in a furtive manner from or as if from fear, guilt, etc. **2** *(intr)* to move in a sinuous alluring manner. **3** *(tr)* (of animals, esp. cows) to give birth to prematurely. ◆ *n* **4** an animal, esp. a calf, born prematurely. ORIG OE *slincan*

slinky ('slɪŋkɪ) *adj* **slinkier, slinkiest.** *Inf.* **1** moving in a sinuously graceful or provocative way. **2** (of clothes) figure-hugging.
▸ **'slinkily** *adv* ▸ **'slinkiness** *n*

slip[1] (slɪp) *vb* **slips, slipping, slipped. 1** to move or cause to move smoothly and easily. **2** *(tr)* to place, insert, or convey quickly or stealthily. **3** *(tr)* to put on or take off easily or quickly: *to slip on a sweater.* **4** *(intr)* to lose balance and slide unexpectedly: *he slipped on the ice.* **5** to let loose or be let loose. **6** to be released from (something). **7** *(tr)* to let go (mooring or anchor lines) over the side. **8** (when *intr,* often foll. by *from* or *out of*) to pass out of (the mind or memory). **9** *(intr)* to move or pass swiftly or unperceived: *to slip quietly out of the room.* **10** *(intr;* sometimes foll. by *up)* to make a mistake. **11** Also: **sideslip.** to cause (an aircraft) to slide sideways or (of an aircraft) to slide sideways. **12** *(intr)* to decline in health, mental ability, etc. **13** *(intr)* (of an intervertebral disc) to become displaced from the normal position. **14** *(tr)* to dislocate (a bone). **15** (of animals) to give birth to (offspring) prematurely. **16** *(tr)* to pass (a stitch) from one needle to another without knitting it. **17a** *(tr)* to operate (the clutch of a motor vehicle) so that it partially disengages. **17b** *(intr)* (of the clutch of a motor vehicle) to fail to engage, esp. as a result of wear. **18 let slip. 18a** to allow to escape. **18b** to say unintentionally. ◆ *n* **19** the act or an instance of slipping. **20** a mistake or oversight: *a slip of the pen.* **21** a moral lapse or failing. **22** a woman's sleeveless undergarment, worn as a lining for a dress. **23** a pillowcase. **24** See **slipway. 25** *Cricket.* **25a** the position of the fielder who stands a little way behind and to the offside of the wicketkeeper. **25b** the fielder himself or herself. **26** the relative movement of rocks along a fault plane. **27** *Metallurgy, crystallog.* the deformation of a metallic crystal caused when one part glides over another part along a plane. **28** a landslide. **29** the deviation of a propeller from its helical path through a fluid. **30** another name for **sideslip** (sense 1). **31 give someone the slip.** to elude or escape from someone. ◆ See also **slip up.** ORIG C13: from MLow G or Du. *slippen*
▸ **'slipless** *adj*

slip[2] (slɪp) *n* **1** a narrow piece; strip. **2** a small piece of paper: *a receipt slip.* **3** a part of a plant that, when detached from the parent, will grow into a new plant; cutting. **4** a young slender person: *a slip of a child.* **5** *Printing.* **5a** a long galley. **5b** a galley proof. ◆ *vb* **slips, slipping, slipped. 6** *(tr)* to detach (portions of stem, etc.) from (a plant) for propagation. ORIG C15: prob. from MLow G, MDu. *slippe* to cut, strip

slip[3] (slɪp) *n* clay mixed with water to a creamy consistency, used for decorating or patching a ceramic piece. ORIG OE *slyppe* slime

slipcase ('slɪp,keɪs) *n* a protective case for a book or set of books that is open at one end so that only the spines of the books are visible.

slipcover ('slɪp,kʌvə) *n US & Canad.* **1** a loose cover. **2** a book jacket; dust cover.

slipe (slaɪp) *n NZ.* **a** wool removed from the pelt of a slaughtered sheep by immersion in a chemical bath. **b** *(as modifier): slipe wool.* ORIG C14 in England: from *slype* to strip, skin

slipknot ('slɪp,nɒt) *n* **1** Also called: **running knot.** a nooselike knot tied so that it will slip along the rope round which it is made. **2** a knot that can be easily untied by pulling one free end.

slip-on *adj* **1** (of a garment or shoe) made so as to be easily and quickly put on or taken off. ◆ *n* **2** a slip-on garment or shoe.

slipover ('slɪpˌəuvə) *adj* **1** of or denoting a garment that can be put on easily over the head. ◆ *n* **2** such a garment, esp. a sleeveless pullover.

slippage ('slɪpɪdʒ) *n* **1** the act or an instance of slipping. **2** the amount of slipping or the extent to which slipping occurs. **3a** an instance of not reaching a target, etc. **3b** the extent of this.

slipped disc *n Pathol.* a herniated intervertebral disc, often resulting in pain because of pressure on the spinal nerves.

slipper ('slɪpə) *n* **1** a light shoe of some soft material, for wearing around the house. **2** a woman's evening shoe. ◆ *vb* **3** (*tr*) *Inf.* to hit or beat with a slipper.
▸ **'slippered** *adj*

slipper bath *n* a bath in the shape of a slipper, with a covered end.

slipperwort ('slɪpəˌwɜːt) *n* another name for **calceolaria.**

slippery ('slɪpərɪ, -prɪ) *adj* **1** causing or tending to cause objects to slip: *a slippery road.* **2** liable to slip from the grasp, etc. **3** not to be relied upon: *a slippery character.* **4** (esp. of a situation) unstable. ORIG C16: prob. coined by Coverdale to translate G *schlipfferig* in Luther's Bible (Psalm 35:6)
▸ **'slipperiness** *n*

slippery elm *n* **1** a North American tree, having notched winged fruits and a mucilaginous inner bark. **2** the bark of this tree, used medicinally as a demulcent. ◆ Also called: **red elm.**

slippy ('slɪpɪ) *adj* **slippier, slippiest. 1** *Inf. or dialect.* another word for **slippery** (senses 1, 2). **2** *Brit. inf.* alert; quick.
▸ **'slippiness** *n*

slip rail *n Austral. & NZ.* a rail in a fence that can be slipped out of place to make an opening.

slip road *n Brit.* a short road connecting a motorway to another road.

slipshod ('slɪpˌʃɒd) *adj* **1** (of an action) negligent; careless. **2** (of a person's appearance) slovenly; down-at-heel. ORIG C16: from SLIP[1] + SHOD

slipstream ('slɪpˌstriːm) *n* Also called: **airstream. a** the stream of air forced backwards by an aircraft propeller. **b** a stream of air behind any moving object.

slip up *Inf.* ◆ *vb* (*intr, adv*) **1** to make a blunder or mistake. ◆ *n* **slip-up. 2** a mistake or mishap.

slipware ('slɪpˌwɛə) *n* pottery that has been decorated with slip and glazed.

slipway ('slɪpˌweɪ) *n* **1** the sloping area in a shipyard, containing the ways. **2** the ways on which a vessel is launched.

slit (slɪt) *vb* **slits, slitting, slit.** (*tr*) **1** to make a straight long incision in. **2** to cut into strips lengthwise. ◆ *n* **3** a long narrow cut. **4** a long narrow opening. ORIG OE *slītan* to slice
▸ **'slitter** *n*

slither ('slɪðə) *vb* **1** to move or slide or cause to move or slide unsteadily, as on a slippery surface. **2** (*intr*) to travel with a sliding motion. ◆ *n* **3** a slithering motion. ORIG OE *slidrian,* from *slīdan* to slide
▸ **'slithery** *adj*

slit trench *n Mil.* a narrow trench dug for the protection of a small number of people.

sliver ('slɪvə) *n* **1** a thin piece that is cut or broken off lengthwise. **2** a loose fibre obtained by carding. ◆ *vb* **3** to divide or be divided into splinters. **4** (*tr*) to form (wool, etc.) into slivers. ORIG C14: from *sliven* to split

Sloan ★ (sləun) *n* **John.** 1871–1951, US painter, a leading member of the Ash Can School.

Sloane Ranger (sləun) *n* (in Britain) *Inf.* a young upper-class person having a home in London and in the country, characterized as wearing expensive informal clothes. Also called: **Sloane.** ORIG C20: pun on *Sloane* Square, London, and *Lone Ranger,* television cowboy character

★ people and places

slob (slɒb) *n* **1** *Inf.* a slovenly, unattractive, and lazy person. **2** *Irish.* mire. ORIG C19: from Irish Gaelic *slab* mud
▸ **'slobbish** *adj*

slobber ('slɒbə) *or* **slabber** *vb* **1** to dribble (saliva, food, etc.) from the mouth. **2** (*intr*) to speak or write mawkishly. **3** (*tr*) to smear with matter dribbling from the mouth. ◆ *n* **4** liquid or saliva spilt from the mouth. **5** maudlin language or behaviour. ORIG C15: from MLow G, MDu. *slubberen*
▸ **'slobberer** *or* **'slabberer** *n* ▸ **'slobbery** *or* **'slabbery** *adj*

sloe (sləu) *n* **1** the small sour blue-black fruit of the blackthorn. **2** another name for **blackthorn.** ORIG OE *slāh*

sloe-eyed *adj* having dark slanted or almond-shaped eyes.

sloe gin *n* gin flavoured with sloe juice.

slog (slɒg) *vb* **slogs, slogging, slogged. 1** to hit with heavy blows, as in boxing. **2** (*intr*) to work hard; toil. **3** (*intr;* foll. by *down, up, along,* etc.) to move with difficulty. **4** *Cricket.* to take large swipes at the ball. ◆ *n* **5** a tiring walk. **6** long exhausting work. **7** a heavy blow or swipe. ORIG C19: from ?
▸ **'slogger** *n*

slogan ('sləugən) *n* **1** a distinctive or topical phrase used in politics, advertising, etc. **2** *Scot. history.* a Highland battle cry. ORIG C16: from Gaelic *sluagh-ghairm* war cry

sloop (sluːp) *n* a single-masted sailing vessel, rigged fore-and-aft. ORIG C17: from Du. *sloep*

sloot (sluːt) *n S. African.* a ditch for irrigation or drainage. ORIG from Afrik., from Du. *sluit, sluis* SLUICE

slop[1] (slɒp) *vb* **slops, slopping, slopped. 1** (when *intr,* often foll. by *about*) to cause (liquid) to splash or spill or (of liquid) to splash or spill. **2** (*intr;* foll. by *along, through,* etc.) to tramp (through) mud or slush. **3** (*tr*) to feed slop or swill to: *to slop the pigs.* **4** (*tr*) to ladle or serve, esp. clumsily. **5** (*intr;* foll. by *over*) *Inf., chiefly US & Canad.* to be unpleasantly effusive. ◆ *n* **6** a puddle of spilt liquid. **7** (*pl*) wet feed, esp. for pigs, made from kitchen waste, etc. **8** (*pl*) waste food or liquid refuse. **9** (*often pl*) *Inf.* liquid or semiliquid food of low quality. **10** soft mud, snow, etc. ORIG C14: prob. from OE *-sloppe* in *cūsloppe* COWSLIP

slop[2] (slɒp) *n* **1** (*pl*) sailors' clothing and bedding issued from a ship's stores. **2** any loose article of clothing, esp. a smock. **3** (*pl*) shoddy manufactured clothing. ORIG OE *oferslop* surplice

slop basin *n* a bowl or basin into which the dregs from teacups are emptied at the table.

slope (sləup) *vb* **slopes, sloping, sloped. 1** to lie or cause to lie at a slanting or oblique angle. **2** (*intr*) (esp. of natural features) to follow an inclined course: *many paths sloped down the hillside.* **3** (*intr;* foll. by *off, away,* etc.) to go furtively. **4** (*tr*) *Mil.* (formerly) to hold (a rifle) in the slope position. ◆ *n* **5** an inclined portion of ground. **6** (*pl*) hills or foothills. **7** any inclined surface or line. **8** the degree or amount of such inclination. **9** *Maths.* (of a line) the tangent of the angle between the line and another line parallel to the *x*-axis. **10** (formerly) the position adopted for military drill when the rifle is rested on the shoulder. ORIG C15: short for *aslope,* ?from the p.p. of OE *āslūpan* to slip away
▸ **'sloper** *n* ▸ **'sloping** *adj*

slop out *vb* (*intr, adv*) (of prisoners) to empty chamber pots and collect water for washing.

sloppy ('slɒpɪ) *adj* **sloppier, sloppiest. 1** (esp. of the ground, etc.) wet; slushy. **2** *Inf.* careless; untidy. **3** *Inf.* mawkishly sentimental. **4** (of food or drink) watery and unappetizing. **5** splashed with slops. **6** (of clothes) loose; baggy.
▸ **'sloppily** *adv* ▸ **'sloppiness** *n*

slosh (slɒʃ) *n* **1** watery mud, snow, etc. **2** *Brit. sl.* a heavy blow. **3** the sound of splashing liquid. ◆ *vb* **4** (*tr;* foll. by *around, on, in,* etc.) *Inf.* to throw or pour (liquid). **5** (when *intr,* often foll. by *about* or *around*) *Inf.* **5a** to shake or stir (something) in a liquid. **5b** (of a person) to splash (around) in water, etc. **6** (*tr*) *Brit. sl.* to deal a heavy blow to. **7** (usually foll. by *about* or *around*) *Inf.* to shake (a container of liquid) or (of liquid within a container) to be shaken. ORIG C19: var. of SLUSH, infl. by SLOP[1]
▸ **'sloshy** *adj*

sloshed (slɒʃt) *adj Chiefly Brit. sl.* drunk.

slot[1] (slɒt) *n* **1** an elongated aperture or groove, such as one in a vending machine for inserting a coin. **2** *Inf.* a place in a series or scheme. ◆ *vb* **slots, slotting, slotted. 3** (*tr*) to furnish with a slot or slots. **4** (usually foll. by *in* or *into*) to fit or adjust in a slot. **5** *Inf.* to situate or be situated in a series. ORIG C13: from OF *esclot* the depression of the breastbone, from ?
▸ **'slotter** *n*

slot[2] (slɒt) *n* the trail of an animal, esp. a deer. ORIG C16: from OF *esclot* horse's hoofprint, prob. of Scand. origin

sloth (sləʊθ) *n* **1** any of a family of shaggy-coated arboreal edentate mammals, such as the three-toed sloth or ai or the two-toed sloth or unau, of Central and South America. They are slow-moving, hanging upside down by their long arms and feeding on vegetation. **2** reluctance to exert oneself. ORIG OE *slǣwth,* from *slǣw,* var. of *slāw* slow

sloth bear *n* a bear of forests of S India and Sri Lanka, having an elongated snout specialized for feeding on termites.

slothful ('sləʊθfʊl) *adj* lazy; indolent.
▸ **'slothfully** *adv* ▸ **'slothfulness** *n*

slot machine *n* a machine, esp. one for gambling, activated by placing a coin in a slot.

slouch (slaʊtʃ) *vb* **1** (*intr*) to sit or stand with a drooping bearing. **2** (*intr*) to walk or move with an awkward slovenly gait. **3** (*tr*) to cause (the shoulders) to droop. ◆ *n* **4** a drooping carriage. **5** (*usually used in negative constructions*) *Inf.* an incompetent or slovenly person: *he's no slouch at football.* ORIG C16: from ?
▸ **'slouching** *adj*

slouch hat *n* any soft hat with a brim that can be pulled down over the ears, esp. an Australian army hat with the left side of the brim turned up.

slough[1] (slaʊ) *n* **1** a hollow filled with mud; bog. **2** (slu:) Also: **slew** (esp. US), **slue.** *North American.* a large hole where water collects or a marshy inlet. **3** despair or degradation. ORIG OE *slōh*
▸ **'sloughy** *adj*

slough[2] (slʌf) *n* **1** any outer covering that is shed, such as the dead outer layer of the skin of a snake, the cellular debris in a wound, etc. ◆ *vb* **2** (often foll. by *off*) to shed (a skin, etc.) or (of a skin, etc.) to be shed. ORIG C13: of Gmc origin
▸ **'sloughy** *adj*

Slough ★ (slaʊ) *n* **1** an industrial town in SE central England, in NE Berkshire. Pop.: 108 000 (1998 est.). **2** a unitary authority in SE England, in NE Berkshire. Pop.: 110 500 (1996 est.). Area: 28 sq. km (11 sq. miles).

slough off (slʌf) *vb* (*tr, adv*) to cast off (cares, etc.).

Slovak ('sləʊvæk) *adj* **1** of or characteristic of Slovakia, its people, or their language. ◆ *n* **2** the official language of Slovakia. Slovak is closely related to Czech; they are mutually intelligible. **3** a native or inhabitant of Slovakia.

Slovakia ★ (sləʊ'vækɪə) *n* a country in central Europe: part of Hungary from the 11th century until 1918, when it united with Bohemia and Moravia to form Czechoslovakia; it became independent in 1993. Official language: Slovak. Religion: Roman Catholic majority. Currency: koruna. Capital: Bratislava. Pop.: 5 398 000 (1999 est.). Area: 49 036 sq. km (18 940 sq. miles).
▸ **Slo'vakian** *adj, n*

sloven ('slʌvᵊn) *n* a person who is habitually negligent in appearance, hygiene, or work. ORIG C15: prob. rel. to Flemish *sloef* dirty, Du. *slof* negligent

Slovene (sləʊ'vi:n) *adj* **1** Also **Slovenian.** of or characteristic of Slovenia, its people, or their language. ◆ *n* **2** Also **Slovenian.** the official language of Slovenia. **3** a native or inhabitant of Slovenia.

Slovenia ★ (sləʊ'vi:nɪə) *n* a republic in S central Europe: settled by the Slovenes in the 6th century; joined Yugoslavia in 1918 and became an autonomous republic in 1946; declared independence in 1991 (internationally recognized in 1992): rises over 2800 m (9000 ft) in the Julian Alps. Official language: Slovene. Religion: Roman Catholic majority. Currency: tolar. Capital: Ljubljana. Pop.: 1 977 000 (1999 est.). Area: 20 251 sq. km (7819 sq. miles).

slovenly ('slʌvənlɪ) *adj* **1** frequently or habitually unclean or untidy. **2** negligent and careless: *slovenly manners.* ◆ *adv* **3** in a negligent or slovenly manner.
▸ **'slovenliness** *n*

slow (sləʊ) *adj* **1** performed or occurring during a comparatively long interval of time. **2** lasting a comparatively long time: *a slow journey.* **3** characterized by lack of speed: *a slow walker.* **4** (*prenominal*) adapted to or productive of slow movement: *the slow lane of a motorway.* **5** (of a clock, etc.) indicating a time earlier than the correct time. **6** not readily responsive to stimulation: *a slow mind.* **7** dull or uninteresting: *the play was very slow.* **8** not easily aroused: *a slow temperament.* **9** lacking promptness or immediacy: *a slow answer.* **10** unwilling to perform an action or enter into a state: *slow to anger.* **11** behind the times. **12** (of trade, etc.) unproductive; slack. **13** (of a fire) burning weakly. **14** (of an oven) cool. **15** *Photog.* requiring a relatively long time of exposure to produce a given density: *a slow lens.* **16** *Sport.* (of a court, track, etc.) tending to reduce the speed of the ball or the competitors. **17** *Cricket.* (of a bowler, etc.) delivering the ball slowly, usually with spin. ◆ *adv* **18** in a manner characterized by lack of speed; slowly. ◆ *vb* **19** (often foll. by *up, down,* etc.) to decrease or cause to decrease in speed, efficiency, etc. ORIG OE *slāw* sluggish
▸ **'slowly** *adv* ▸ **'slowness** *n*

slowcoach ('sləʊˌkəʊtʃ) *n Brit. inf.* a person who moves or works slowly. US and Canad. equivalent: **slowpoke.**

slow handclap *n Brit.* slow rhythmic clapping, esp. used by an audience to indicate dissatisfaction or impatience.

slow march *n Mil.* a march in **slow time,** usually 65 or 75 paces to the minute.

slow match *or* **fuse** *n* a match or fuse that burns slowly without flame.

slow-mo *or* **slo-mo** ('sləʊˌməʊ) *n, adj Inf.* short for **slow motion** *or* **slow-motion.**

slow motion *n* **1** *Films, television, etc.* action that is made to appear slower than normal by passing the film through the camera at a faster rate or by replaying a video recording more slowly. ◆ *adj* **slow-motion. 2** of or relating to such action. **3** moving or functioning at considerably less than usual speed.

slow virus *n* a type of virus that is present in the body for a long time before it becomes active or infectious.

slowworm ('sləʊˌwɜ:m) *n* a Eurasian legless lizard with a brownish-grey snakelike body. Also called: **blindworm.**

SLR *abbrev. for* single-lens reflex: see **reflex camera.**

SLSC *Austral. abbrev. for* Surf Life Saving Club.

slub (slʌb) *n* **1** a lump in yarn or fabric, often made intentionally to give a knobbly effect. **2** a loosely twisted roll of fibre prepared for spinning. ◆ *vb* **slubs, slubbing, slubbed. 3** (*tr*) to draw out and twist (a sliver of fibre). ◆ *adj* **4** (of material) having an irregular appearance. ORIG C18: from ?

sludge (slʌdʒ) *n* **1** soft mud, snow, etc. **2** any deposit or sediment. **3** a surface layer of ice that is not frozen solid but has a slushy appearance. **4** (in sewage disposal) the solid constituents of sewage that are removed for purification. ORIG C17: prob. rel. to SLUSH
▸ **'sludgy** *adj*

slue[1] (slu:) *n, vb* **slues, sluing, slued.** a variant spelling (esp. US) of **slew**[2].

slue[2] (slu:) *n* a variant spelling of **slough**[1] (sense 2).

slug[1] (slʌg) *n* **1** any of various terrestrial gastropod molluscs in which the body is elongated and the shell is absent or very much reduced. **2** any of various other invertebrates having a soft slimy body, esp. the larvae of certain sawflies. ORIG C15 (in the sense: a slow person or animal): prob. from ON

slug[2] (slʌg) *n* **1** an fps unit of mass; the mass that will acquire an acceleration of 1 foot per second per second when acted upon by a force of 1 pound. **2** *Metallurgy.* a metal blank from which small forgings are worked. **3** a bullet. **4** *Chiefly US & Canad.* a metal token for use in slot

★ people and places

machines, etc. **5** *Printing.* **5a** a thick strip of type metal that is used for spacing. **5b** a metal strip containing a line of characters as produced by a Linotype machine. **6** a draught of a drink, esp. an alcoholic one. ORIG C17 (bullet), C19 (printing): ?from SLUG[1], with allusion to the shape of the animal

slug[3] (slʌg) *vb* **slugs, slugging, slugged. 1** *Chiefly US & Canad.* to hit very hard and solidly. **2** (*tr*) *Austral. & NZ inf.* to charge (someone) an exorbitant price. ◆ *n* **3** *US & Canad.* a heavy blow. **4** *Austral. & NZ inf.* an exorbitant price. ORIG C19: ?from SLUG[2] (bullet)

sluggard (ˈslʌgəd) *n* **1** a person who is habitually indolent. ◆ *adj* **2** lazy. ORIG C14 *slogarde*
▸ **ˈsluggardly** *adj*

sluggish (ˈslʌgɪʃ) *adj* **1** lacking energy; inactive. **2** functioning at below normal rate or level. **3** exhibiting poor response to stimulation.
▸ **ˈsluggishly** *adv* ▸ **ˈsluggishness** *n*

sluice (sluːs) *n* **1** Also called: **sluiceway.** a channel that carries a rapid current of water, esp. one that has a sluicegate to control the flow. **2** the body of water controlled by a sluicegate. **3** See **sluicegate. 4** *Mining.* an inclined trough for washing ore. **5** an artificial channel through which logs can be floated. ◆ *vb* **sluices, sluicing, sluiced. 6** (*tr*) to draw out or drain (water, etc.) from (a pond, etc.) by means of a sluice. **7** (*tr*) to wash or irrigate with a stream of water. **8** (*tr*) *Mining.* to wash in a sluice. **9** (*tr*) to send (logs, etc.) down a sluice. **10** (*intr; often foll. by away or out*) (of water, etc.) to run or flow from or as if from a sluice. **11** (*tr*) to provide with a sluice. ORIG C14: from OF *escluse,* from LL *exclūsa aqua* water shut out, from L *exclūdere* to shut out
▸ **ˈsluiceˌlike** *adj*

sluicegate (ˈsluːsˌgeɪt) *n* a valve or gate fitted to a sluice to control the rate of flow of water. See also **floodgate** (sense 1).

slum (slʌm) *n* **1** a squalid overcrowded house, etc. **2** (*often pl*) a squalid section of a city, characterized by inferior living conditions. **3** (*modifier*) of or characteristic of slums: *slum conditions.* ◆ *vb* **slums, slumming, slummed.** (*intr*) **4** to visit slums, esp. for curiosity. **5** Also: **slum it.** to suffer conditions below those to which one is accustomed. ORIG C19: orig. sl., from ?
▸ **ˈslummy** *adj*

slumber (ˈslʌmbə) *vb* **1** (*intr*) to sleep, esp. peacefully. **2** (*intr*) to be quiescent or dormant. **3** (*tr; foll. by away*) to spend (time) sleeping. ◆ *n* **4** (*sometimes pl*) sleep. **5** a dormant or quiescent state. ORIG OE *slūma* sleep (n)
▸ **ˈslumberer** *n* ▸ **ˈslumbering** *adj*

slumberous (ˈslʌmbərəs) *or* **slumbrous** *adj Chiefly poetic.* **1** sleepy; drowsy. **2** inducing sleep.
▸ **ˈslumberously** *adv* ▸ **ˈslumberousness** *n*

slump (slʌmp) *vb* (*intr*) **1** to sink or fall heavily and suddenly. **2** to relax ungracefully. **3** (of business activity, etc.) to decline suddenly. **4** (of health, interest, etc.) to deteriorate or decline suddenly. ◆ *n* **5** a sudden or marked decline or failure, as in progress or achievement. **6** a decline in commercial activity, prices, etc.; depression. **7** the act of slumping. ORIG C17: prob. of Scand. origin

slung (slʌŋ) *vb* the past tense and past participle of **sling**[1].

slunk (slʌŋk) *vb* the past tense and past participle of **slink.**

slur (slɜː) *vb* **slurs, slurring, slurred.** (*mainly tr*) **1** (often foll. by *over*) to treat superficially, hastily, or without due deliberation. **2** (*also intr*) to pronounce or utter (words, etc.) indistinctly. **3** to speak disparagingly of. **4** *Music.* to execute (a melodic interval of two or more notes) smoothly, as in legato performance. ◆ *n* **5** an indistinct sound or utterance. **6** a slighting remark. **7** a stain or disgrace, as upon one's reputation. **8** *Music.* **8a** a performance or execution of a melodic interval of two or more notes in a part. **8b** the curved line (⌒ or ⌣) indicating this. ORIG C15: prob. from MLow G

slurp (slɜːp) *Inf.* ◆ *vb* **1** to eat or drink (something) noisily. ◆ *n* **2** a sound produced in this way. ORIG C17: from MDu. *slorpen* to sip

slurry (ˈslʌrɪ) *n, pl* **slurries.** a suspension of solid particles in a liquid, as in a mixture of cement, coal dust, manure, meat, etc. with water. ORIG C15 *slory*

slush (slʌʃ) *n* **1** any watery muddy substance, esp. melting snow. **2** *Inf.* sloppily sentimental language. ◆ *vb* **3** (*intr; often foll. by along*) to make one's way through or as if through slush. ORIG C17: rel. to Danish *slus* sleet, Norwegian *slusk* slops
▸ **ˈslushy** *adj* ▸ **ˈslushiness** *n*

slush fund *n* a fund for financing political or commercial corruption.

slushy (ˈslʌʃɪ) *adj* **slushier, slushiest.** of, resembling, or consisting of slush.
▸ **ˈslushiness** *n*

slut (slʌt) *n* **1** a dirty slatternly woman. **2** an immoral woman. ORIG C14: from ?
▸ **ˈsluttish** *adj* ▸ **ˈsluttishness** *n*

Sluter ★ (*Dutch* ˈslyːtər) *n* **Claus** (klaus). ?1345–1406, Dutch sculptor, working in Burgundy. He is best known for the portal sculptures and the *Well of Moses* in the Carthusian monastery at Champnol.

sly (slaɪ) *adj* **slyer, slyest** *or* **slier, sliest. 1** crafty; artful: *a sly dodge.* **2** insidious; furtive: *a sly manner.* **3** roguish: *sly humour.* ◆ *n* **4 on the sly.** in a secretive manner. ORIG C12: from ON *slǣgr* clever, lit.: able to strike, from *slā* to slay
▸ **ˈslyly** *or* **ˈslily** *adv* ▸ **ˈslyness** *n*

slype (slaɪp) *n* a covered passage in a church that connects the transept to the chapterhouse. ORIG C19: prob. from MFlemish *slijpen* to slip

Sm *the chemical symbol for* samarium.

SM *abbrev. for* **1** sergeant major. **2** sadomasochism.

smack[1] (smæk) *n* **1** a smell or flavour that is distinctive though faint. **2** a distinctive trace: *the smack of corruption.* **3** a small quantity, esp. a taste. **4** a slang word for **heroin.** ◆ *vb* (*intr; foll. by of*) **5** to have the characteristic smell or flavour (of something): *to smack of the sea.* **6** to have an element suggestive (of something): *his speeches smacked of bigotry.* ORIG OE *smæc*

smack[2] (smæk) *vb* **1** (*tr*) to strike or slap smartly, with or as if with the open hand. **2** to strike or send forcibly or loudly or to be struck or sent forcibly or loudly. **3** to open and close (the lips) loudly, esp. to show pleasure. ◆ *n* **4** a sharp resounding slap or blow with something flat, or the sound of such a blow. **5** a loud kiss. **6** a sharp sound made by the lips, as in enjoyment. **7 have a smack at.** *Inf., chiefly Brit.* to attempt. **8 smack in the eye.** *Inf., chiefly Brit.* a snub or setback. ◆ *adv Inf.* **9** directly; squarely. **10** sharply and unexpectedly. ORIG C16: from MLow G or MDu. *smacken,* prob. imit.

smack[3] (smæk) *n* a sailing vessel, usually sloop-rigged, used in coasting and fishing along the British coast. ORIG C17: from Low G *smack* or Du. *smak,* from ?

smacker (ˈsmækə) *n Sl.* **1** a loud kiss; smack. **2** a pound note or dollar bill.

smackhead (ˈsmækˌhɛd) *n Brit. sl.* a person who is addicted to heroin.

small (smɔːl) *adj* **1** limited in size, number, importance, etc. **2** of little importance or on a minor scale: *a small business.* **3** lacking in moral or mental breadth or depth: *a small mind.* **4** modest or humble: *small beginnings.* **5** of low or inferior status, esp. socially. **6 feel small.** to be humiliated. **7** (of a child or animal) young; not mature. **8** unimportant; trivial: *a small matter.* **9** of or designating the ordinary modern minuscule letter used in printing and cursive writing. **10** lacking great strength or force: *a small effort.* **11** in fine particles: *small gravel.* ◆ *adv* **12** into small pieces: *cut it small.* **13** in a small or soft manner. ◆ *n* **14** (often preceded by *the*) an object, person, or group considered to be small: *the small or the large?* **15** a small slender part, esp. of the back. **16** (*pl*) *Inf., chiefly Brit.* items of personal laundry, such as underwear. ORIG OE *smæl*
▸ **ˈsmallish** *adj* ▸ **ˈsmallness** *n*

small arms *pl n* portable firearms of relatively small calibre.

small beer *n Inf., chiefly Brit.* people or things of no importance.

★ people and places

small change *n* **1** coins, esp. those of low value. **2** a person or thing that is not outstanding or important.

small circle *n* a circular section of a sphere that does not contain the centre of the sphere.

small claims court *n Brit. & Canad.* a local court with jurisdiction to try civil actions involving small claims.

small fry *pl n* **1** people or things regarded as unimportant. **2** young children. **3** young or small fishes.

small goods *pl n Austral. & NZ.* meats bought from a delicatessen, such as sausages.

smallholding ('smɔːlˌhəʊldɪŋ) *n* a holding of agricultural land smaller than a small farm.
► **'smallˌholder** *n*

small hours *pl n* **the.** the early hours of the morning, after midnight and before dawn.

small intestine *n* the longest part of the alimentary canal, in which digestion is completed. Cf. **large intestine.**

small-minded *adj* narrow-minded; intolerant.
► **ˌsmall-'mindedly** *adv* ► **ˌsmall-'mindedness** *n*

smallpox ('smɔːlˌpɒks) *n* a highly contagious viral disease characterized by high fever and a rash changing to pustules, which dry up and form scabs that are cast off, leaving pitted depressions. Technical name: **variola.**

small print *n* matter in a contract, etc., printed in small type, esp. when considered to be a trap for the unwary.

small-scale *adj* **1** of limited size or scope. **2** (of a map, model, etc.) giving a relatively small representation of something.

small screen *n* an informal name for **television.**

small slam *n Bridge.* another name for **little slam.**

small talk *n* light conversation for social occasions.

small-time *adj Inf.* insignificant; minor: *a small-time criminal.*
► **'small-'timer** *n*

smalt (smɔːlt) *n* **1** a type of silica glass coloured deep blue with cobalt oxide. **2** a pigment made by crushing this glass, used in colouring enamels. ORIG C16: via F from It. *smalto* coloured glass, of Gmc origin

smarm (smɑːm) *vb Brit. inf.* **1** (*tr;* often foll. by *down*) to flatten (the hair, etc.) with grease. **2** (when *intr,* foll. by *up to*) to ingratiate oneself (with). ORIG C19: from ?

smarmy ('smɑːmɪ) *adj* **smarmier, smarmiest.** *Brit. inf.* obsequiously flattering or unpleasantly suave.
► **'smarmily** *adv* ► **'smarminess** *n*

smart (smɑːt) *adj* **1** astute, as in business. **2** quick, witty, and often impertinent in speech: *a smart talker.* **3** fashionable; chic: *a smart hotel.* **4** well-kept; neat. **5** causing a sharp stinging pain. **6** vigorous or brisk. **7** (of systems) operating as if by human intelligence by using automatic computer control. **8** (of a weapon, etc.) containing a device which enables it to be guided to its target: *smart bombs.* ◆ *vb* (*mainly intr*) **9** to feel, cause, or be the source of a sharp stinging physical pain or keen mental distress: *he smarted under their abuse.* **10** (often foll. by *for*) to suffer a harsh penalty. ◆ *n* **11** a stinging pain or feeling. ◆ *adv* **12** in a smart manner. ◆ See also **smarts.** ORIG OE *smeortan*
► **'smartly** *adv* ► **'smartness** *n*

Smart ★ (smɑːt) *n* **Christopher.** 1722–71, British poet, author of *A Song to David* (1763) and *Jubilate Agno* (written 1758–63, published 1939). He was confined (1756–63) for religious mania and died in a debtors' prison.

smart aleck ('ælɪk) *n Inf.* **a** an irritatingly oversmart person. **b** (*as modifier*): *a smart-aleck remark.* ORIG C19: from *Aleck, Alec,* short for *Alexander*
► **'smart-ˌalecky** *adj*

smart card *n* a plastic card with integrated circuits used for storing and processing computer data. Also called: **laser card, intelligent card.**

smart drug *n* any of various drugs that are claimed to improve the intelligence or memory of the person taking them.

smarten ('smɑːtᵊn) *vb* (usually foll. by *up*) **1** (*intr*) to make oneself neater. **2** (*tr*) to make quicker or livelier.

smart money *n* **1** money bet or invested by experienced gamblers or investors. **2** money paid in order to extricate oneself from an unpleasant situation or agreement, esp. from military service. **3** *Law.* damages awarded to a plaintiff where the wrong was aggravated by fraud, malice, etc.

smarts (smɑːts) *pl n Sl., chiefly US.* know-how, intelligence, or wits: *street smarts.*

smart set *n* (*functioning as sing or pl*) fashionable people considered as a group.

smash (smæʃ) *vb* **1** to break into pieces violently and usually noisily. **2** (when *intr,* foll. by *against, through, into,* etc.) to throw or crash (against) vigorously, causing shattering: *he smashed the equipment.* **3** (*tr*) to hit forcefully and suddenly. **4** (*tr*) *Tennis, etc.* to hit (the ball) fast and powerfully, esp. with an overhead stroke. **5** (*tr*) to defeat (persons, theories, etc.). **6** to make or become bankrupt. **7** (*intr*) to collide violently; crash. ◆ *n* **8** an act, instance, or sound of smashing or the state of being smashed. **9** a violent collision, esp. of vehicles. **10** a total failure or collapse, as of a business. **11** *Tennis, etc.* a fast and powerful overhead stroke. **12** *Inf.* **12a** something having popular success. **12b** (*in combination*): *smash-hit.* ◆ *adv* **13** with a smash. ◆ See also **smash-up.** ORIG C18: prob. from SM(ACK[2] + M)ASH
► **'smashable** *adj*

smash-and-grab *adj Inf.* of or relating to a robbery in which a shop window is broken and the contents removed.

smashed (smæʃt) *adj Sl.* drunk or under the influence of a drug.

smasher ('smæʃə) *n Inf., chiefly Brit.* a person or thing that is very attractive or outstanding.

smashing ('smæʃɪŋ) *adj Inf., chiefly Brit.* excellent or first-rate: *we had a smashing time.*

smash-up *Inf.* ◆ *n* **1** a bad collision, esp of cars. ◆ *vb* **smash up. 2** (*tr, adv*) to damage to the point of complete destruction: *they smashed the place up.*

smatter ('smætə) *n* **1** a smattering. ◆ *vb* **2** (*tr*) *Arch.* to dabble in. ORIG C14 (in the sense: to prattle): from ?
► **'smatterer** *n*

smattering ('smætərɪŋ) *n* **1** a slight or superficial knowledge. **2** a small amount.

smear (smɪə) *vb* (*mainly tr*) **1** to bedaub or cover with oil, grease, etc. **2** to rub over or apply thickly. **3** to rub so as to produce a smudge. **4** to slander. **5** (*intr*) to be or become smeared or dirtied. ◆ *n* **6** a dirty mark or smudge. **7a** a slanderous attack. **7b** (*as modifier*): *smear tactics.* **8** a preparation of blood, secretions, etc., smeared onto a glass slide for examination under a microscope. ORIG OE *smeoru* (n)
► **'smeary** *adj* ► **'smearily** *adv* ► **'smeariness** *n*

smear test *n Med.* another name for **Pap test.**

smectic ('smɛktɪk) *adj Chem.* (of a substance) existing in or having a mesomorphic state in which the molecules are oriented in layers. ORIG C17: via L from Gk *smēktikos,* from *smekhein* to wash; from the soaplike consistency of a smectic substance

smegma ('smɛgmə) *n Physiol.* a whitish sebaceous secretion that accumulates beneath the prepuce. ORIG C19: via L from Gk *smēgma* detergent, from *smekhein* to wash

smell (smɛl) *vb* **smells, smelling, smelt** *or* **smelled. 1** (*tr*) to perceive the scent of (a substance) by means of the olfactory nerves. **2** (*copula*) to have a specified smell: *the curry smells very spicy.* **3** (*intr;* often foll. by *of*) to emit an odour (of): *the park smells of flowers.* **4** (*intr*) to emit an unpleasant odour. **5** (*tr;* often foll. by *out*) to detect through shrewdness or instinct. **6** (*intr*) to have or use the sense of smell; sniff. **7** (*intr;* foll. by *of*) to give indications (of): *he smells of money.* **8** (*intr;* foll. by *around, about,* etc.) to search, investigate, or pry. **9** (*copula*) to be or seem to be untrustworthy. ◆ *n* **10** that sense (olfaction) by which scents or odours are perceived. Related adj: **olfactory. 11** anything detected by the sense of smell. **12** a trace or indication. **13** the act or an instance of smelling. ORIG C12: from ?
► **'smeller** *n*

smelling salts *pl n* a pungent preparation containing crystals of ammonium carbonate that has a stimulant action when sniffed in cases of faintness, headache, etc.

★ people and places

smelly ('smɛlɪ) *adj* **smellier, smelliest.** having a strong or nasty smell.
▸ '**smelliness** *n*

smelt[1] (smɛlt) *vb* (*tr*) to extract (a metal) from (an ore) by heating. ORIG C15: from MLow G, MDu. *smelten*

smelt[2] (smɛlt) *n, pl* **smelt** *or* **smelts.** a marine or freshwater salmonoid food fish having a long silvery body and occurring in temperate and cold northern waters. ORIG OE *smylt*

smelt[3] (smɛlt) *vb* a past tense and past participle of **smell.**

smelter ('smɛltə) *n* **1** a person engaged in smelting. **2** Also called: **smeltery.** an industrial plant in which smelting is carried out.

Smetana ★ (*Czech* 'smɛtana) *n* **Bedřich** ('bɛdrʒix). 1824–84, Czech composer, founder of his country's national school of music. His works include *My Fatherland* (1874–79), a cycle of six symphonic poems, and the opera *The Bartered Bride* (1866).

smew (smjuː) *n* a merganser of N Europe and Asia, having a male plumage of white with black markings. ORIG C17: from ?

smidgen *or* **smidgin** ('smɪdʒən) *n Inf., chiefly US.* a very small amount. ORIG C20: from ?

smilax ('smaɪlæks) *n* **1** any of a genus of climbing shrubs having slightly lobed leaves, small greenish or yellow flowers, and berry-like fruits: includes the sarsaparilla plant and greenbrier. **2** a fragile, much branched vine of southern Africa: cultivated for its glossy green foliage. ORIG C17: via L from Gk: bindweed

smile (smaɪl) *n* **1** a facial expression characterized by an upturning of the corners of the mouth, usually showing amusement, friendliness, etc. **2** favour or blessing: *the smile of fortune.* ◆ *vb* **smiles, smiling, smiled. 3** (*intr*) to wear or assume a smile. **4** (*intr;* foll. by *at*) **4a** to look (at) with a kindly expression. **4b** to look derisively (at). **4c** to bear (troubles, etc.) patiently. **5** (*intr;* foll. by *on* or *upon*) to show approval. **6** (*tr*) to express by means of a smile: *she smiled a welcome.* **7** (*tr;* often foll. by *away*) to drive away or change by smiling. **8 come up smiling.** to recover cheerfully from misfortune. ORIG C13: prob. from ON
▸ '**smiler** *n* ▸ '**smiling** *adj* ▸ '**smilingly** *adv*

Smiles ★ (smaɪlz) *n* **Samuel.** 1812–1904, British writer: author of the didactic work *Self-Help* (1859).

smiley ('smaɪlɪ) *adj* **1** given to smiling; cheerful. **2** depicting a smile: *a smiley badge.* ◆ *n* **3** any of a group of symbols depicting a smile, or other facial expression, used in electronic mail.

smirch (smɜːtʃ) *vb* (*tr*) **1** to dirty; soil. ◆ *n* **2** the act of smirching or state of being smirched. **3** a smear or stain. ORIG C15 *smorchen,* from ?

smirk (smɜːk) *n* **1** a smile expressing scorn, smugness, etc., rather than pleasure. ◆ *vb* **2** (*intr*) to give such a smile. **3** (*tr*) to express with such a smile. ORIG OE *smearcian*
▸ '**smirker** *n* ▸ '**smirking** *adj* ▸ '**smirkingly** *adv*

smite (smaɪt) *vb* **smites, smiting, smote; smitten** *or* **smit** (smɪt). (*mainly tr*) *Now arch. in most senses.* **1** to strike with a heavy blow. **2** to damage with or as if with blows. **3** to affect severely: *smitten with flu.* **4** to afflict in order to punish. **5** (*intr;* foll. by *on*) to strike forcibly or abruptly: *the sun smote down on him.* ORIG OE *smītan*
▸ '**smiter** *n*

smith (smɪθ) *n* **1a** a person who works in metal. **1b** (*in combination*): *a silversmith.* **2** See **blacksmith.** ORIG OE

Smith ★ (smɪθ) *n* **1 Adam.** 1723–90, Scottish economist and philosopher, whose *The Wealth of Nations* (1776) advocated free trade. **2 Bessie,** known as *Empress of the Blues.* 1894–1937, US blues singer. **3 F. E.** See (1st Earl of) **Birkenhead. 4 Ian (Douglas).** born 1919, Zimbabwean statesman; prime minister of Rhodesia (1964–79). He declared independence from Britain unilaterally (1965). **5 John.** ?1580–1631, English explorer, who helped found the North American colony of Jamestown, Virginia. **6 John.** 1938–94, British Labour politician; leader of the Labour Party (1992–94). **7 Joseph.** 1805–44, US religious leader; founder of the Mormon Church. **8** Dame **Maggie.** born 1934, British actress. Her films include *The Prime of Miss Jean Brodie* (1969), *The Lonely Passion of Judith Hearne* (1988), and *The Secret Garden* (1993). **9 Stevie,** real name *Florence Margaret Smith.* 1902–71, British poet. Her poems include 'A Good Time was had by All' (1937) and 'Not Waving but Drowning' (1957). **10 Sydney.** 1771–1845, British clergyman and writer, noted for *The Letters of Peter Plymley* (1807–08), advocating Catholic emancipation. **11 William.** 1769–1839, British geologist, who founded the science of stratigraphy. **12 Zadie** ('zeɪdɪ). born 1975, British novelist, author of *White Teeth* (2000).

smithereens (ˌsmɪðəˈriːnz) *pl n* little shattered pieces or fragments. ORIG C19: from Irish Gaelic *smidirīn,* from *smiodar*

smithery ('smɪθərɪ) *n, pl* **smitheries. 1** the trade or craft of a blacksmith. **2** a rare word for **smithy.**

Smithson ★ ('smɪθsən) *n* **James.** original name *James Lewes Macie.* 1765–1829, British chemist, who left a bequest to found the Smithsonian Institution, Washington DC.

smithy ('smɪðɪ) *n, pl* **smithies.** a place in which metal, usually iron or steel, is worked by heating and hammering; forge. ORIG OE *smiththe*

smitten ('smɪtᵊn) *vb* **1** a past participle of **smite.** ◆ *adj* **2** (*postpositive*) affected by love (for).

smock (smɒk) *n* **1** any loose protective garment, worn by artists, laboratory technicians, etc. **2** a woman's loose blouselike garment, reaching to below the waist, worn over slacks, etc. **3** Also called: **smock frock.** a loose protective overgarment decorated with smocking, worn formerly esp. by farm workers. **4** *Arch.* a woman's loose undergarment. ◆ *vb* **5** to ornament (a garment) with smocking. ORIG OE *smocc*
▸ '**smockˌlike** *adj*

smocking ('smɒkɪŋ) *n* ornamental needlework used to gather and stitch material in a honeycomb pattern so that the part below the gathers hangs in even folds.

smog (smɒg) *n* a mixture of smoke, fog, and chemical fumes. ORIG C20: from SM(OKE + F)OG[1]
▸ '**smoggy** *adj*

smoke (sməʊk) *n* **1** the product of combustion, consisting of fine particles of carbon carried by hot gases and air. **2** any cloud of fine particles suspended in a gas. **3a** the act of smoking tobacco, esp. as a cigarette. **3b** the duration of smoking such substances. **4** *Inf.* a cigarette or cigar. **5** something with no concrete or lasting substance: *everything turned to smoke.* **6** a thing or condition that obscures. **7 go** *or* **end up in smoke. 7a** to come to nothing. **7b** to burn up vigorously. **7c** to flare up in anger. ◆ *vb* **smokes, smoking, smoked. 8** (*intr*) to emit smoke or the like, sometimes excessively or in the wrong place. **9** to draw in on (a burning cigarette, etc.) and exhale the smoke. **10** (*tr*) to bring (oneself) into a specified state by smoking. **11** (*tr*) to subject or expose to smoke. **12** (*tr*) to cure (meat, fish, etc.) by treating with smoke. **13** (*tr*) to fumigate or purify the air of (rooms, etc.). **14** (*tr*) to darken (glass, etc.) by exposure to smoke. ◆ See also **smoke out.** ORIG OE *smoca* (n)
▸ '**smokable** *or* '**smokeable** *adj*

Smoke (sməʊk) *n* **the.** short for the **Big Smoke.**

smoke and mirrors *n* irrelevant or misleading information serving to obscure the truth of a situation. ORIG C20: reference to the use of smoke and mirrors in conjuring illusions

smoke-dried *adj* (of fish, etc.) cured in smoke.

smoked rubber *n* a type of crude natural rubber in the form of brown sheets obtained by coagulating latex with an acid, rolling it into sheets, and drying over open wood fires. It is the main raw material for natural rubber products.

smokeho ('sməʊkəʊ) *n* a variant spelling of **smoko.**

smokehouse ('sməʊkˌhaʊs) *n* a building or special construction for curing meat, fish, etc., by smoking.

smokeless ('sməʊklɪs) *adj* having or producing little or no smoke: *smokeless fuel.*

smokeless zone *n* an area where only smokeless fuels are permitted to be used.

smoke out *vb* (*tr, adv*) **1** to subject to smoke in order to drive out of hiding. **2** to bring into the open: *they smoked out the plot.*

smoker ('sməʊkə) *n* **1** a person who habitually smokes tobacco. **2** Also called: **smoking compartment**. a compartment of a train where smoking is permitted. **3** an informal social gathering, as at a club.

smoke screen *n* **1** *Mil.* a cloud of smoke produced to obscure movements. **2** something said or done in order to hide the truth.

smokestack ('sməʊkˌstæk) *n* a tall chimney that conveys smoke into the air.

smokestack industry *n Inf.* any of the traditional British industries, esp. heavy engineering or manufacturing, as opposed to such modern industries as electronics.

smoking jacket *n* (formerly) a man's comfortable jacket of velvet, etc., closed by a tie belt or fastenings, worn at home.

smoko *or* **smokeho** ('sməʊkəʊ) *n, pl* **smokos** *or* **smokehos**. *Austral. & NZ inf.* **1** a short break from work for tea, a cigarette, etc. **2** refreshment taken during this break.

smoky ('sməʊkɪ) *adj* **smokier, smokiest**. **1** emitting or resembling smoke. **2** emitting smoke excessively or in the wrong place: *a smoky fireplace.* **3** having the flavour of having been cured by smoking. **4** made dirty or hazy by smoke: *a smoky atmosphere.*
▸ **'smokily** *adv* ▸ **'smokiness** *n*

Smoky Mountains ★ *pl n* See **Great Smoky Mountains**.

smolder ('sməʊldə) *vb, n* the US spelling of **smoulder**.

Smolensk ★ (*Russian* smaˈljɛnsk; *English* 'smɒlɛnsk) *n* a city in W Russia, on the Dnieper River: a major commercial centre in medieval times; scene of severe fighting (1941 and 1943) in World War II. Pop.: 353 000 (1995 est.).

Smollett ★ ('smɒlɪt) *n* **Tobias George**. 1721–71, Scottish novelist, whose satires include *Roderick Random* (1748) and *Humphry Clinker* (1771).

smolt (sməʊlt) *n* a young salmon at the stage when it migrates from fresh water to the sea. ORIG C14: Scot., from ?

smooch (smuːtʃ) *Sl.* ◆ *vb* (*intr*) **1** Also (Austral. and NZ): **smoodge, smooge**. (of two people) to kiss and cuddle. **2** *Brit.* to dance very slowly and amorously with one's arms around another person or (of two people) to dance together in such a way. ◆ *n* **3** the act of smooching. ORIG C20: var. of dialect *smouch*, imit.

smoodge *or* **smooge** (smuːdʒ) *vb* **smoodges, smoodging, smoodged** *or* **smooges, smooging, smooged**. (*intr*) *Austral. & NZ.* **1** another word for **smooch** (sense 1). **2** to seek to ingratiate oneself.

smooth (smuːð) *adj* **1** without bends or irregularities. **2** silky to the touch: *smooth velvet.* **3** lacking roughness of surface; flat. **4** tranquil or unruffled: *smooth temper.* **5** lacking obstructions or difficulties. **6a** suave or persuasive, esp. as suggestive of insincerity. **6b** (*in combination*): *smooth-tongued.* **7** (of the skin) free from hair. **8** of uniform consistency: *smooth batter.* **9** free from jolts: *smooth driving.* **10** not harsh or astringent: *a smooth wine.* **11** having all projections worn away: *smooth tyres.* **12** *Phonetics.* without preliminary aspiration. **13** *Physics.* (of a plane, etc.) regarded as being frictionless. ◆ *adv* **14** in a calm or even manner. ◆ *vb* (*mainly tr*) **15** (*also intr;* often foll. by *down*) to make or become flattened or without roughness. **16** (often foll. by *out* or *away*) to take or rub (away) in order to make smooth: *she smoothed out the creases in her dress.* **17** to make calm; soothe. **18** to make easier: *smooth his path.* ◆ *n* **19** the smooth part of something. **20** the act of smoothing. **21** *Tennis, etc.* the side of a racket on which the binding strings form a continuous line. ◆ See also **smooth over**. ORIG OE *smōth*
▸ **'smoother** *n* ▸ **'smoothly** *adv* ▸ **'smoothness** *n*

smoothbore ('smuːðˌbɔː) *n* (*modifier*) (of a firearm) having an unrifled bore: *a smoothbore shotgun.*
▸ **'smoothˌbored** *adj*

smooth breathing *n* (in Greek) the sign (ʼ) placed over an initial vowel, indicating that (in ancient Greek) it was not pronounced with an *h*.

smoothen ('smuːðən) *vb* to make or become smooth.

smooth hound *n* any of several small sharks of North Atlantic coastal regions.

smoothie *or* **smoothy** ('smuːðɪ) *n, pl* **smoothies**. **1** *Sl., usually derog.* a person, esp. a man, who is suave or slick, esp. in speech, dress, or manner. **2** a smooth thick drink made from puréed fresh fruit and yoghurt, ice cream, or milk.

smoothing iron *n* a former name for **iron** (sense 3).

smooth muscle *n* muscle that is capable of slow rhythmic involuntary contractions: occurs in the walls of the blood vessels, etc.

smooth over *vb* (*tr*) to ease or gloss over: *to smooth over a difficulty.*

smooth snake *n* any of several slender nonvenomous European snakes having very smooth scales and a reddish-brown coloration.

smooth-spoken *adj* speaking or spoken in a gently persuasive or competent manner.

smooth-tongued *adj* suave or persuasive in speech.

smorgasbord ('smɔːɡəsˌbɔːd) *n* a variety of cold or hot savoury dishes served in Scandinavia as hors d'oeuvres or as a buffet meal. ORIG Swedish, from *smörgås* sandwich + *bord* table

smote (sməʊt) *vb* the past tense of **smite**.

smother ('smʌðə) *vb* **1** to suffocate or stifle by cutting off or being cut off from the air. **2** (*tr*) to surround (with) or envelop (in): *he smothered her with love.* **3** (*tr*) to extinguish (a fire) by covering so as to cut it off from the air. **4** to be or cause to be suppressed or stifled: *smother a giggle.* **5** (*tr*) to cook or serve (food) thickly covered with sauce, etc. ◆ *n* **6** anything, such as a cloud of smoke, that stifles. **7** a profusion or turmoil. ORIG OE *smorian* to suffocate
▸ **'smothery** *adj*

smothered mate *n Chess.* checkmate given by a knight when the king is prevented from moving by surrounding men.

smoulder *or US* **smolder** ('sməʊldə) *vb* (*intr*) **1** to burn slowly without flame, usually emitting smoke. **2** (esp. of anger, etc.) to exist in a suppressed state. **3** to have strong repressed feelings, esp. anger. ◆ *n* **4** a smouldering fire. ORIG C14: from *smolder* (n), from ?

SMP *abbrev. for* statutory maternity pay.

SMS *abbrev. for* short message system; used for sending data to mobile phones, etc.

smudge (smʌdʒ) *vb* **smudges, smudging, smudged**. **1** to smear or soil or cause to do so. **2** (*tr*) *Chiefly US & Canad.* to fill (an area) with smoke in order to drive insects away. ◆ *n* **3** a smear or dirty mark. **4** a blurred form or area: *that smudge in the distance is a quarry.* **5** *Chiefly US & Canad.* a smoky fire for driving insects away or protecting plants from frost. ORIG C15: from ?
▸ **'smudgy** *adj* ▸ **'smudgily** *adv* ▸ **'smudginess** *n*

smug (smʌg) *adj* **smugger, smuggest**. excessively self-satisfied or complacent. ORIG C16: of Gmc origin
▸ **'smugly** *adv* ▸ **'smugness** *n*

smuggle ('smʌgᵊl) *vb* **smuggles, smuggling, smuggled**. **1** to import or export (prohibited or dutiable goods) secretly. **2** (*tr;* often foll. by *into* or *out of*) to bring or take secretly, as against the law or rules. ORIG C17: from Low G *smukkelen* & Du. *smokkelen*, ?from OE *smūgen* to creep
▸ **'smuggler** *n* ▸ **'smuggling** *n*

smut (smʌt) *n* **1** a small dark smudge or stain, esp. one caused by soot. **2** a speck of soot or dirt. **3** something obscene or indecent. **4a** any of various fungal diseases of flowering plants, esp. cereals, in which black sooty masses of spores cover the affected parts. **4b** any parasitic fungus that causes such a disease. ◆ *vb* **smuts, smutting, smutted**. **5** to mark or become marked or smudged, as with soot. **6** to affect (grain, etc.) or (of grain) to be affected with smut. ORIG OE *smitte;* associated with SMUDGE, SMUTCH
▸ **'smutty** *adj* ▸ **'smuttily** *adv* ▸ **'smuttiness** *n*

smutch (smʌtʃ) *vb* **1** (*tr*) to smudge; mark. ◆ *n* **2** a mark; smudge. **3** soot; dirt. ORIG C16: prob. from MHG *smutzen* to soil
▸ **'smutchy** *adj*

Smuts ★ (smʌts) *n* **Jan Christiaan** (jan 'kristiˌan). 1870–1950, South African statesman; prime minister (1919–24;

1939–48). After fighting for the Boers in the Boer War, he advocated Anglo-Boer reconciliation and served the Allies in World Wars I and II.

Smyrna ★ (ˈsmɜːnə) *n* an ancient city on the W coast of Asia Minor: a major trading centre in the ancient world; a centre of early Christianity. Modern name: **Izmir.**

Sn *the chemical symbol for* tin. ORIG from NL *stannum*

snack (snæk) *n* **1** a light quick meal eaten between or in place of main meals. **2** a sip or bite. ◆ *vb* **3** (*intr*) to eat a snack. ORIG C15: prob. from MDu. *snacken,* var. of *snappen* to snap

snack bar *n* a place where light meals or snacks can be obtained, often with a self-service system.

snaffle (ˈsnæfᵊl) *n* **1** Also called: **snaffle bit.** a simple jointed bit for a horse. ◆ *vb* **snaffles, snaffling, snaffled.** (*tr*) **2** *Brit. inf.* to steal or take for oneself. **3** to equip or control with a snaffle. ORIG C16: from ?

snafu (snæˈfuː) *Sl., chiefly mil.* ◆ *n* **1** confusion or chaos regarded as the normal state. ◆ *adj* **2** (*postpositive*) confused or muddled up, as usual. ◆ *vb* **snafus, snafuing, snafued. 3** (*tr*) *US & Canad.* to throw into chaos. ORIG C20: from *s(ituation) n(ormal): a(ll) f(ucked) u(p)*

snag[1] (snæg) *n* **1** a difficulty or disadvantage: *the snag is that I have nothing suitable to wear.* **2** a sharp protuberance, such as a tree stump. **3** a small loop or hole in a fabric caused by a sharp object. **4** *Chiefly US & Canad.* a tree stump in a riverbed that is dangerous to navigation. **5** *US & Canad.* a standing dead tree, esp. one used as a perch by an eagle. ◆ *vb* **snags, snagging, snagged. 6** (*tr*) to hinder or impede. **7** (*tr*) to tear or catch (fabric). **8** (*intr*) to develop a snag. **9** (*intr*) *Chiefly US & Canad.* (of a boat) to strike a snag. **10** (*tr*) *Chiefly US & Canad.* to clear (a stretch of water) of snags. **11** (*tr*) *US.* to seize (an opportunity, etc.). ORIG C16: of Scand. origin
▸ **ˈsnaggy** *adj*

snag[2] (snæg) *n* (*usually pl*) *Austral. sl.* a sausage. ORIG from ?

snaggletooth (ˈsnægᵊlˌtuːθ) *n, pl* **snaggleteeth.** a tooth that is broken or projecting.

snail (sneɪl) *n* **1** any of numerous terrestrial or freshwater gastropod molluscs with a spirally coiled shell, esp. the **garden snail. 2** any other gastropod with a spirally coiled shell, such as a whelk. **3** a slow-moving person or animal. ORIG OE *snægl*
▸ **ˈsnail-ˌlike** *adj*

snail mail *Inf. n* **1** the conventional postal system, as opposed to electronic mail. ◆ *vb* **snail-mail. 2** (*tr*) to send by the conventional postal system, rather than by electronic mail. ORIG C20: so named because of the relative slowness of the conventional postal system

snail's pace *n* a very slow speed or rate.

snake (sneɪk) *n* **1** a reptile having a scaly cylindrical limbless body, fused eyelids, and a jaw modified for swallowing large prey: includes venomous forms such as cobras and rattlesnakes, large nonvenomous constrictors (boas and pythons), and small harmless types such as the grass snake. **2** Also: **snake in the grass.** a deceitful or treacherous person. **3** anything resembling a snake in appearance or action. **4** (in the European Union) a group of currencies, any one of which can only fluctuate within narrow limits, but each can fluctuate more against other currencies. **5** a tool in the form of a long flexible wire for unblocking drains. ◆ *vb* **snakes, snaking, snaked. 6** (*intr*) to glide or move like a snake. **7** (*tr*) to move in or follow (a sinuous course). ORIG OE *snaca*
▸ **ˈsnakeˌlike** *adj*

snakebird (ˈsneɪkˌbɜːd) *n* another name for **darter** (the bird).

snakebite (ˈsneɪkˌbaɪt) *n* **1** a bite inflicted by a snake, esp. a venomous one. **2** a drink of cider and lager.

snake charmer *n* an entertainer, esp. in Asia, who charms or appears to charm snakes by playing music.

Snake River ★ *n* a river in the northwestern US, rising in NW Wyoming and flowing west through Idaho, turning north as part of the border between Idaho and Oregon, and flowing west to the Columbia River near Pasco, Washington. Length: 1670 km (1038 miles).

snakeroot (ˈsneɪkˌruːt) *n* **1** any of various North American plants the roots or rhizomes of which have been used as a remedy for snakebite. **2** the rhizome or root of any such plant.

snakes and ladders *n* (*functioning as sing*) a board game in which players move counters along a series of squares according to throws of a dice. A ladder provides a short cut to a square nearer the finish and a snake obliges a player to return to a square nearer the start.

snake's head *n* a European fritillary plant of damp meadows, having purple-and-white flowers.

snakeskin (ˈsneɪkˌskɪn) *n* the skin of a snake, esp. when made into a leather valued for handbags, shoes, etc.

snaky (ˈsneɪkɪ) *adj* **snakier, snakiest. 1** of or like a snake. **2** treacherous or insidious. **3** infested with snakes. **4** *Austral. & NZ sl.* angry or bad-tempered.
▸ **ˈsnakily** *adv* ▸ **ˈsnakiness** *n*

snap (snæp) *vb* **snaps, snapping, snapped. 1** to break or cause to break suddenly, esp. with a sharp sound. **2** to make or cause to make a sudden sharp cracking sound. **3** (*intr*) to give way or collapse suddenly, esp. from strain. **4** to move, close, etc., or cause to move, close, etc., with a sudden sharp sound. **5** to move or cause to move in a sudden or abrupt way. **6** (*intr;* often foll. by *at* or *up*) to seize something suddenly or quickly. **7** (when *intr,* often foll. by *at*) to bite at (something) bringing the jaws rapidly together. **8** to speak (words) sharply or abruptly. **9** to take a snapshot of (something). **10** (*tr*) *American football.* to put (the ball) into play by sending it back from the line of scrimmage. **11 snap one's fingers at.** *Inf.* **11a** to dismiss with contempt. **11b** to defy. **12 snap out of it.** *Inf.* to recover quickly, esp. from depression or anger. ◆ *n* **13** the act of breaking suddenly or the sound produced by a sudden breakage. **14** a sudden sharp sound, esp. of bursting, popping, or cracking. **15** a catch, clasp, or fastener that operates with a snapping sound. **16** a sudden grab or bite. **17** a thin crisp biscuit: *ginger snaps.* **18** *Inf.* See **snapshot. 19** *Inf.* vigour, liveliness, or energy. **20** *Inf.* a task or job that is easy or profitable to do. **21** a short spell or period, esp. of cold weather. **22** *Brit.* a card game in which the word *snap* is called when two cards of equal value are turned up on the separate piles dealt by each player. **23** *American football.* the start of each play when the centre passes the ball back from the line of scrimmage to a teammate. **24** (*modifier*) done on the spur of the moment: *a snap decision.* **25** (*modifier*) closed or fastened with a snap. ◆ *adv* **26** with a snap. ◆ *interj* **27a** *Cards.* the word called while playing snap. **27b** an exclamation used to draw attention to the similarity of two things. ◆ See also **snap up.** ORIG C15: from MLow G or MDu. *snappen* to seize
▸ **ˈsnapless** *adj* ▸ **ˈsnappingly** *adv*

snapdragon (ˈsnæpˌdrægən) *n* any of several plants of the genus *Antirrhinum* having spikes of showy white, yellow, pink, red, or purplish flowers. Also called: **antirrhinum.**

snap fastener *n* another name for **press stud.**

snapper (ˈsnæpə) *n, pl* **snapper** *or* **snappers. 1** any large sharp-toothed percoid food fish of warm and tropical coastal regions. See also **red snapper. 2** a food fish of Australia and New Zealand that has a pinkish body covered with blue spots. **3** another name for the **snapping turtle. 4** a person or thing that snaps. ◆ Also (for sense 1, 2): **schnapper.**

snapping turtle *n* any large aggressive North American river turtle having powerful hooked jaws and a rough shell. Also called: **snapper.**

snappy (ˈsnæpɪ) *adj* **snappier, snappiest. 1** Also: **snappish.** apt to speak sharply or irritably. **2** Also: **snappish.** apt to snap or bite. **3** crackling in sound: *a snappy fire.* **4** brisk, sharp, or chilly: *a snappy pace.* **5** smart and fashionable: *a snappy dresser.* **6 make it snappy.** *Sl.* hurry up!
▸ **ˈsnappily** *adv* ▸ **ˈsnappiness** *n*

snap ring *n Mountaineering.* another name for **karabiner.**

snapshot (ˈsnæpˌʃɒt) *n* an informal photograph taken with a simple camera. Often shortened to **snap.**

snap shot *n Sport.* a sudden, fast shot at goal.

snap up *vb* (*tr, adv*) **1** to avail oneself of eagerly and quickly: *she snapped up the bargains.* **2** to interrupt abruptly.

snare[1] (snɛə) *n* **1** a device for trapping birds or small animals, esp. a flexible loop that is drawn tight around the prey. **2** a surgical instrument for removing certain tumours, consisting of a wire loop that may be drawn tight around their base to sever them. **3** anything that traps or entangles someone or something unawares. ◆ *vb* **snares, snaring, snared.** (*tr*) **4** to catch (birds or small animals) with a snare. **5** to catch or trap in or as if in a snare. ORIG OE *sneare*
▸ **'snarer** *n*

snare[2] (snɛə) *n Music.* a set of gut strings wound with wire fitted against the lower drumhead of a snare drum. They produce a rattling sound when the drum is beaten. ORIG C17: from MDu. *snaer* or MLow G *snare* string

snare drum *n Music.* a cylindrical drum with two drumheads, the upper of which is struck and the lower fitted with a snare. See **snare**[2].

snarl[1] (snɑːl) *vb* **1** (*intr*) (of an animal) to growl viciously, baring the teeth. **2** to speak or express (something) viciously. ◆ *n* **3** a vicious growl or facial expression. **4** the act of snarling. ORIG C16: of Gmc origin
▸ **'snarler** *n* ▸ **'snarling** *adj* ▸ **'snarly** *adj*

snarl[2] (snɑːl) *n* **1** a tangled mass of thread, hair, etc. **2** a complicated or confused state or situation. **3** a knot in wood. ◆ *vb* **4** (often foll. by *up*) to be, become, or make tangled or complicated. **5** (*tr;* often foll. by *up*) to confuse mentally. **6** (*tr*) to emboss (metal) by hammering on a tool held against the under surface. ORIG C14: from ON
▸ **'snarler** *n* ▸ **'snarly** *adj*

snarl-up *n Inf., chiefly Brit.* a confusion, obstruction, or tangle, esp. a traffic jam.

snatch (snætʃ) *vb* **1** (*tr*) to seize or grasp (something) suddenly or peremptorily: *he snatched the chocolate.* **2** (*intr;* usually foll. by *at*) to seize or attempt to seize suddenly. **3** (*tr*) to take hurriedly: *to snatch some sleep.* **4** (*tr*) to remove suddenly: *she snatched her hand away.* **5** (*tr*) to gain, win, or rescue, esp. narrowly: *they snatched victory in the closing seconds.* ◆ *n* **6** an act of snatching. **7** a fragment or incomplete part: *snatches of conversation.* **8** a brief spell: *snatches of time off.* **9** *Weightlifting.* a lift in which the weight is raised in one quick motion from the floor to an overhead position. **10** *Sl., chiefly US.* an act of kidnapping. **11** *Brit. sl.* a robbery: *a diamond snatch.* ORIG C13 *snacchen*
▸ **'snatcher** *n*

snatchy ('snætʃɪ) *adj* **snatchier, snatchiest.** disconnected or spasmodic.
▸ **'snatchily** *adv*

snazzy ('snæzɪ) *adj* **snazzier, snazziest.** *Inf.* (esp. of clothes) stylishly and often flashily attractive. ORIG C20: ?from SN(APPY + J)AZZY
▸ **'snazzily** *adv* ▸ **'snazziness** *n*

sneak (sniːk) *vb* **1** (*intr;* often foll. by *along, off, in,* etc.) to move furtively. **2** (*intr*) to behave in a cowardly or underhand manner. **3** (*tr*) to bring, take, or put stealthily. **4** (*intr*) *Inf., chiefly Brit.* to tell tales (esp. in schools). **5** (*tr*) *Inf.* to steal. **6** (*intr;* foll. by *off, out, away,* etc.) *Inf.* to leave unobtrusively. ◆ *n* **7** a person who acts in an underhand or cowardly manner, esp. as an informer. **8a** a stealthy act. **8b** (*as modifier*): *a sneak attack.* ORIG OE *snīcan* to creep
▸ **'sneaky** *adj* ▸ **'sneakily** *adv* ▸ **'sneakiness** *n*

sneakers ('sniːkəz) *pl n Chiefly US & Canad.* canvas shoes with rubber soles worn informally.

sneaking ('sniːkɪŋ) *adj* **1** acting in a furtive or cowardly way. **2** secret: *a sneaking desire to marry a millionaire.* **3** slight but nagging (esp. in **a sneaking suspicion**).
▸ **'sneakingly** *adv*

sneak thief *n* a person who steals paltry articles from premises, which he or she enters through open doors, windows, etc.

sneer (snɪə) *n* **1** a facial expression of scorn or contempt, typically with the upper lip curled. **2** a scornful or contemptuous remark or utterance. ◆ *vb* **3** (*intr*) to assume a facial expression of scorn or contempt. **4** to say or utter (something) in a scornful manner. ORIG C16: ?from Low Du.
▸ **'sneerer** *n* ▸ **'sneering** *adj, n*

sneeze (sniːz) *vb* **sneezes, sneezing, sneezed. 1** (*intr*) to expel air from the nose involuntarily, esp. as the result of irritation of the nasal mucous membrane. ◆ *n* **2** the act or sound of sneezing. ORIG OE *fnēosan* (unattested)
▸ **'sneezer** *n* ▸ **'sneezy** *adj*

sneeze at *vb* (*intr, prep;* usually with a negative) *Inf.* to dismiss lightly: *his offer is not to be sneezed at.*

sneezewood ('sniːzˌwʊd) *n* **1** a South African tree. **2** its exceptionally hard wood, used for furniture, gateposts and railway sleepers.

sneezewort ('sniːzˌwɜːt) *n* a Eurasian plant having daisy-like flowers and long grey-green leaves, which cause sneezing when powdered.

snick (snɪk) *n* **1** a small cut; notch. **2** *Cricket.* **2a** a glancing blow off the edge of the bat. **2b** the ball so hit. ◆ *vb* (*tr*) **3** to cut a small corner or notch in (material, etc.). **4** *Cricket.* to hit (the ball) with a snick. ORIG C18: prob. of Scand. origin

snicker ('snɪkə) *n, vb* **1** another word (esp. US and Canad.) for **snigger.** ◆ *vb* **2** (*intr*) (of a horse) to whinny. ORIG C17: prob. imit.

Snickometer (snɪ'kɒmɪtə) *n Trademark, cricket.* a device, employed by TV commentators, that uses a microphone close to the stumps to determine whether or not a batsman has made contact with the ball. ORIG C20: from SNICK (sense 4) + -METER

snide (snaɪd) *adj* **1** Also: **snidey** ('snaɪdɪ). (of a remark, etc.) maliciously derogatory. **2** counterfeit. ◆ *n* **3** *Sl.* sham jewellery. ORIG C19: from ?
▸ **'snidely** *adv* ▸ **'snideness** *n*

sniff (snɪf) *vb* **1** to inhale through the nose, usually in short rapid audible inspirations, as for clearing a congested nasal passage or for taking a drug. **2** (when *intr,* often foll. by *at*) to perceive or attempt to perceive (a smell) by inhaling through the nose. ◆ *n* **3** the act or sound of sniffing. **4** a smell perceived by sniffing, esp. a faint scent. ◆ See also **sniff at, sniff out.** ORIG C14: prob. rel. to *snivelen* to snivel
▸ **'sniffer** *n* ▸ **'sniffing** *n, adj*

sniff at *vb* (*intr, prep*) to express contempt or dislike for.

sniffer dog *n* a police dog trained to detect drugs or explosives by smell.

sniffle ('snɪfᵊl) *vb* **sniffles, sniffling, sniffled. 1** (*intr*) to breathe audibly through the nose, as when the nasal passages are congested. ◆ *n* **2** the act, sound, or an instance of sniffling.
▸ **'sniffler** *n* ▸ **'sniffly** *adj*

sniffles ('snɪfᵊlz) *or* **snuffles** *pl n Inf.* **the.** a cold in the head.

sniff out *vb* (*tr, adv*) to detect through shrewdness or instinct.

sniffy ('snɪfɪ) *adj* **sniffier, sniffiest.** *Inf.* contemptuous or disdainful.
▸ **'sniffily** *adv* ▸ **'sniffiness** *n*

snifter ('snɪftə) *n* **1** a pear-shaped glass with a bowl that narrows towards the top so that the aroma of brandy or a liqueur is retained. **2** *Inf.* a small quantity of alcoholic drink. ORIG C19: ?from dialect *snifter* to sniff, ? of Scand. origin

snig (snɪg) *vb* **snigs, snigging, snigged.** (*tr*) *NZ.* to drag (a felled log) by a chain or cable. ORIG from E dialect

snigger ('snɪgə) *n* **1** a sly or disrespectful laugh, esp. one partly stifled. ◆ *vb* (*intr*) **2** to utter such a laugh. ORIG C18: var. of SNICKER
▸ **'sniggering** *n, adj*

snigging chain *n Austral. & NZ.* a chain attached to a log when being hauled out of the bush.

snip (snɪp) *vb* **snips, snipping, snipped. 1** to cut or clip with a small quick stroke or a succession of small quick strokes, esp. with scissors or shears. ◆ *n* **2** the act of snipping. **3** the sound of scissors or shears closing. **4** Also called: **snipping.** a small piece of anything. **5** a small cut made by snipping. **6** *Chiefly Brit.* an informal word for **bargain. 7**

Inf. something easily done; cinch. ◆ See also **snips**[1]. ORIG C16: from Low G, Du. *snippen*

snipe (snaɪp) *n, pl* **snipe** *or* **snipes. 1** any of a genus of birds, such as the common snipe, of marshes and river banks, having a long straight bill. **2** a shot, esp. a gunshot, fired from a place of concealment. ◆ *vb* **snipes, sniping, sniped. 3** (when *intr,* often foll. by *at*) to attack (a person or persons) with a rifle from a place of concealment. **4** (*intr;* often foll. by *at*) to criticize a person or persons from a position of security. **5** (*intr*) to hunt or shoot snipe. ORIG C14: from ON *snīpa*
▸ **ˈsniper** *n*

snipefish (ˈsnaɪpˌfɪʃ) *n, pl* **snipefish** *or* **snipefishes.** a teleost fish of tropical and temperate seas, having a deep body, long snout, and a single long dorsal fin. Also called: **bellows fish.**

snippet (ˈsnɪpɪt) *n* a small scrap or fragment of fabric, news, etc.
▸ **ˈsnippetiness** *n* ▸ **ˈsnippety** *adj*

snips[1] (snɪps) *pl n* a small pair of shears used for cutting sheet metal.

snips[2] (snɪps) *pl n Biochemistry inf.* differences in single pairs of purine and pyrimidine bases in the nucleotides of DNA that occur between individuals and comprise the most common type of variation in the human genome. Analysis of snips is important in the identification of genes responsible for disease. ORIG C20: from *s(ingle) n(ucleot)i(de) p(olymorphism)s*

snitch (snɪtʃ) *Sl.* ◆ *vb* **1** (*tr*) to steal; take, esp. in an underhand way. **2** (*intr*) to act as an informer. ◆ *n* **3** an informer. **4** the nose. ORIG C17: from ?

snitchy (ˈsnɪtʃɪ) *adj* **snitchier, snitchiest.** *NZ inf.* bad-tempered or irritable.

snivel (ˈsnɪv^{ə}l) *vb* **snivels, snivelling, snivelled** *or US* **snivels, sniveling, sniveled. 1** (*intr*) to sniffle as a sign of distress. **2** to utter (something) tearfully; whine. **3** (*intr*) to have a runny nose. ◆ *n* **4** an instance of snivelling. ORIG C14 *snivelen*
▸ **ˈsniveller** *n* ▸ **ˈsnivelling** *adj, n*

snob (snɒb) *n* **1a** a person who strives to associate with those of higher social status and who behaves condescendingly to others. **1b** (*as modifier*): *snob appeal.* **2** a person having similar pretensions with regard to his or her tastes, etc.: *an intellectual snob.* ORIG C18 (in the sense: shoemaker; hence, C19: a person who flatters those of higher station, etc.): from ?
▸ **ˈsnobbery** *n* ▸ **ˈsnobbish** *adj* ▸ **ˈsnobbishly** *adv*

SNOBOL (ˈsnəubɒl) *n* String Oriented Symbolic Language: a computer-programming language for handling strings of symbols.

Sno-Cat (ˈsnəuˌkæt) *n Trademark.* a type of snowmobile.

snoek (snʊk) *n* a South African edible marine fish. ORIG Afrik., from Du. *snoek* pike

snoep (snʊp) *adj S. African inf.* mean or tight-fisted. ORIG Afrik., lit.: greedy

snog (snɒg) *Brit. sl.* ◆ *vb* **snogs, snogging, snogged. 1** to kiss and cuddle (someone). ◆ *n* **2** the act of kissing and cuddling. ORIG from ?

snood (snuːd) *n* **1** a pouchlike hat, often of net, loosely holding a woman's hair at the back. **2** a headband, esp. one formerly worn by young unmarried women in Scotland. ORIG OE *snōd;* from ?

snook[1] (snuːk) *n, pl* **snook** *or* **snooks. 1** any of a genus of large game fishes of tropical American marine and fresh waters. **2** *Austral.* the sea pike. ORIG C17: from Du. *snoek* pike

snook[2] (snuːk) *n Brit.* a rude gesture, made by putting one thumb to the nose with the fingers of the hand outstretched (esp. in **cock a snook**). ORIG C19: from ?

snooker (ˈsnuːkə) *n* **1** a game played on a billiard table with 15 red balls, six balls of other colours, and a white cue ball. The object is to pot the balls in a certain order. **2** a shot in which the cue ball is left in a position such that another ball blocks the target ball. ◆ *vb* (*tr*) **3** to leave (an opponent) in an unfavourable position by playing a snooker. **4** to place (someone) in a difficult situation. **5** (*often passive*) to thwart; defeat. ORIG C19: from ?

snoop (snuːp) *Inf.* ◆ *vb* **1** (*intr;* often foll. by *about* or *around*) to pry into the private business of others. ◆ *n* **2** a person who pries into the business of others. **3** an act or instance of snooping. ORIG C19: from Du. *snoepen* to eat furtively
▸ **ˈsnooper** *n* ▸ **ˈsnoopy** *adj*

snooperscope (ˈsnuːpəˌskəup) *n Mil., US.* an instrument that enables the user to see objects in the dark by illuminating the object with infrared radiation.

snoot (snuːt) *n Sl.* the nose. ORIG C20: var. of SNOUT

snooty (ˈsnuːtɪ) *adj* **snootier, snootiest.** *Inf.* **1** aloof or supercilious. **2** snobbish: *a snooty restaurant.*
▸ **ˈsnootily** *adv* ▸ **ˈsnootiness** *n*

snooze (snuːz) *Inf.* ◆ *vb* **snoozes, snoozing, snoozed. 1** (*intr*) to take a brief light sleep. ◆ *n* **2** a nap. ORIG C18: from ?
▸ **ˈsnoozer** *n* ▸ **ˈsnoozy** *adj*

snore (snɔː) *vb* **snores, snoring, snored. 1** (*intr*) to breathe through the mouth and nose while asleep with snorting sounds caused by the soft palate vibrating. ◆ *n* **2** the act or sound of snoring. ORIG C14: imit.
▸ **ˈsnorer** *n*

snorkel (ˈsnɔːk^{ə}l) *n* **1** a device allowing a swimmer to breathe while face down on the surface of the water, consisting of a bent tube fitting into the mouth and projecting above the surface. **2** (on a submarine) a retractable vertical device containing air-intake and exhaust pipes for the engines and general ventilation. ◆ *vb* **snorkels, snorkelling, snorkelled** *or US* **snorkels, snorkeling, snorkeled. 3** (*intr*) to swim with a snorkel. ORIG C20: from G *Schnorchel*

Snorri Sturluson ★ (ˈsnɔːrɪ ˈstɜːləs^{ə}n) *n* 1179–1241, Icelandic historian and poet; author of *Younger* or *Prose Edda* (?1222) and the *Heimskringla* sagas of the Norwegian kings.

snort (snɔːt) *vb* **1** (*intr*) to exhale forcibly through the nostrils, making a characteristic noise. **2** (*intr*) (of a person) to express contempt or annoyance by such an exhalation. **3** (*tr*) to utter in a contemptuous or annoyed manner. **4** *Sl.* to inhale (a powdered drug) through the nostrils. ◆ *n* **5** a forcible exhalation of air through the nostrils, esp. (of persons) as a noise of contempt. **6** *Sl.* an instance of snorting a drug. ORIG C14 *snorten*
▸ **ˈsnorting** *n, adj* ▸ **ˈsnortingly** *adv*

snorter (ˈsnɔːtə) *n* **1** a person or animal that snorts. **2** *Brit. sl.* something outstandingly impressive or difficult.

snot (snɒt) *n* (*usually considered vulgar*) **1** nasal mucus or discharge. **2** *Sl.* a contemptible person. ORIG OE *gesnot*

snotty (ˈsnɒtɪ) *adj* **snottier, snottiest.** (*considered vulgar*) **1** dirty with nasal discharge. **2** *Sl.* contemptible; nasty. **3** snobbish; conceited.
▸ **ˈsnottily** *adv* ▸ **ˈsnottiness** *n*

snout (snaut) *n* **1** the part of the head of a vertebrate, esp. a mammal, consisting of the nose, jaws, and surrounding region. **2** the corresponding part of the head of such insects as weevils. **3** anything projecting like a snout, such as a nozzle. **4** *Sl.* a person's nose. **5** *Brit. sl.* a cigarette or tobacco. **6** *Sl.* an informer. ORIG C13: of Gmc origin
▸ **ˈsnouted** *adj* ▸ **ˈsnoutless** *adj* ▸ **ˈsnoutˌlike** *adj*

snout beetle *n* another name for **weevil.**

snow (snəu) *n* **1** precipitation from clouds in the form of flakes of ice crystals formed in the upper atmosphere. **2** a layer of snowflakes on the ground. **3** a fall of such precipitation. **4** anything resembling snow in whiteness, softness, etc. **5** the random pattern of white spots on a television or radar screen, occurring when the signal is weak. **6** *Sl.* cocaine. ◆ *vb* **7** (*intr,* with *it* as subject) to be the case that snow is falling. **8** (*tr;* usually passive, foll. by *over, under, in,* or *up*) to cover or confine with a heavy fall of snow. **9** (often with *it* as subject) to fall or cause to fall as or like snow. **10** (*tr*) *US & Canad. sl.* to overwhelm with elaborate often insincere talk. **11 be snowed under.** to be overwhelmed, esp. with paperwork. ORIG OE *snāw*
▸ **ˈsnowless** *adj* ▸ **ˈsnowˌlike** *adj*

Snow ★ (snəu) *n* **C**(**harles**) **P**(**ercy**), Baron. 1905–80, British novelist and physicist. His novels include the series *Strangers and Brothers* (1949–70).

snowball (ˈsnəuˌbɔːl) *n* **1** snow pressed into a ball for throwing, as in play. **2** a drink made of advocaat and lemonade. ◆ *vb* **3** (*intr*) to increase rapidly in size, importance, etc. **4** (*tr*) to throw snowballs at.

snowball tree *n* any of several shrubs of the genus *Viburnum,* with spherical clusters of white or pinkish flowers.

snowberry ('snəubərɪ) *n, pl* **snowberries. 1** a shrub cultivated for its small pink flowers and white berries. **2** Also called: **waxberry.** any of the berries of such a plant.

snow-blind *adj* having temporarily impaired vision because of the intense reflection of sunlight from snow.
▸ **snow blindness** *n*

snowblower ('snəuˌbləuə) *n* a snow-clearing machine that draws the snow in and blows it away.

snowboard ('snəuˌbɔːd) *n* a shaped board, resembling a skateboard without wheels, on which a person can stand to slide across snow. ORIG C20: on the model of SURFBOARD
▸ **'snowˌboarding** *n*

snowbound ('snəuˌbaund) *adj* confined to one place by heavy falls or drifts of snow; snowed in.

snow bunting *n* a bunting of northern and arctic regions, having a white plumage with dark markings on the wings, back, and tail.

snowcap ('snəuˌkæp) *n* a cap of snow, as on top of a mountain.
▸ **'snowˌcapped** *adj*

Snowdon ★ ('snəudᵊn) *n* a mountain in NW Wales, in Gwynedd: the highest peak in Wales. Height: 1085 m (3560 ft).

Snowdonia ★ (snəu'dəunɪə) *n* **1** a massif in NW Wales, in Gwynedd, the highest peak being Snowdon. **2** a national park in NW Wales, in Gwynedd and Conwy: includes the Snowdonia massif in the north. Area: 2189 sq. km (845 sq. miles).

snowdrift ('snəuˌdrɪft) *n* a bank of deep snow driven together by the wind.

snowdrop ('snəuˌdrɒp) *n* a Eurasian plant having drooping white bell-shaped flowers that bloom in early spring.

snowfall ('snəuˌfɔːl) *n* **1** a fall of snow. **2** *Meteorol.* the amount of snow received in a specified place and time.

snow fence *n* a lath-and-wire fence put up in winter beside windy roads to prevent snowdrifts.

snowfield ('snəuˌfiːld) *n* a large area of permanent snow.

snowflake ('snəuˌfleɪk) *n* **1** one of the mass of small thin delicate arrangements of ice crystals that fall as snow. **2** any of various European plants that have white nodding bell-shaped flowers.

snow goose *n* a North American goose having a white plumage with black wing tips.

snow gum *n* any of several eucalypts of mountainous regions of SE Australia.

snow-in-summer *n* a plant of SE Europe and Asia having white flowers and downy stems and leaves: cultivated as a rock plant.

snow leopard *n* a large feline mammal of mountainous regions of central Asia, closely related to the leopard but having a long pale brown coat marked with black rosettes.

snow lily *n Canad.* another name for **dogtooth violet.**

snow line *n* the altitudinal or latitudinal limit of permanent snow.

snowman ('snəuˌmæn) *n, pl* **snowmen.** a figure resembling a man, made of packed snow.

snowmobile ('snəuməˌbiːl) *n* a motor vehicle for travelling on snow, esp. one with caterpillar tracks and front skis.

snowplough *or esp. US* **snowplow** ('snəuˌplau) *n* an implement or vehicle for clearing away snow.

snowshoe ('snəuˌʃuː) *n* **1** a device to facilitate walking on snow, esp. a racket-shaped frame with a network of thongs stretched across it. ◆ *vb* **snowshoes, snowshoeing, snowshoed. 2** (*intr*) to walk or go using snowshoes.
▸ **'snowˌshoer** *n*

snowstorm ('snəuˌstɔːm) *n* a storm with heavy snow.

snow tyre *n* a motor-vehicle tyre with deep treads to give improved grip on snow and ice.

snow-white *adj* **1** white as snow. **2** pure as white snow.

snowy ('snəuɪ) *adj* **snowier, snowiest. 1** covered with or abounding in snow: *snowy hills.* **2** characterized by snow: *snowy weather.* **3** resembling snow in whiteness, purity, etc.
▸ **'snowily** *adv* ▸ **'snowiness** *n*

Snowy Mountains ★ *pl n* a mountain range in SE Australia, part of the Australian Alps: famous hydroelectric scheme. Also called (Austral. informal): **the Snowy, the Snowies.**
▸ **Snowy Mountain** *adj*

snowy owl *n* a large owl of tundra regions, having a white plumage flecked with brown.

Snowy River ★ *n* a river in SE Australia, rising in SE New South Wales: waters diverted through a system of dams and tunnels across the watershed into the Murray and Murrumbidgee Rivers for hydroelectric power and to provide water for irrigation. Length: 426 km (265 miles).

SNP *abbrev. for* Scottish National Party.

Snr *or* **snr** *abbrev. for* senior.

snub (snʌb) *vb* **snubs, snubbing, snubbed.** (*tr*) **1** to insult (someone) deliberately. **2** to stop or check the motion of (a boat, horse, etc.) by taking turns of a rope around a post. ◆ *n* **3** a deliberately insulting act or remark. **4** *Naut.* an elastic shock absorber attached to a mooring line. ◆ *adj* **5** short and blunt. See also **snub-nosed.** ORIG C14: from ON *snubba* to scold
▸ **'snubber** *n* ▸ **'snubby** *adj*

snub-nosed *adj* **1** having a short turned-up nose. **2** (of a pistol) having an extremely short barrel.

snuff[1] (snʌf) *vb* **1** (*tr*) to inhale through the nose. **2** (when *intr,* often foll. by *at*) (esp. of an animal) to examine by sniffing. ◆ *n* **3** an act or the sound of snuffing. ORIG C16: prob. from MDu. *snuffen* to snuffle, ult. imit.
▸ **'snuffer** *n*

snuff[2] (snʌf) *n* **1** finely powdered tobacco, esp. for sniffing up the nostrils. **2** a small amount of this. **3 up to snuff.** *Inf.* **3a** in good health or in good condition. **3b** *Chiefly Brit.* not easily deceived. ◆ *vb* **4** (*intr*) to use or inhale snuff. ORIG C17: from Du. *snuf,* shortened from *snuftabale,* lit.: tobacco for snuffing

snuff[3] (snʌf) *vb* (*tr*) **1** (often foll. by *out*) to extinguish (a light from a candle). **2** to cut off the charred part of (the wick of a candle, etc.). **3** (usually foll. by *out*) *Inf.* to put an end to. **4 snuff it.** *Brit. inf.* to die. ◆ *n* **5** the burned portion of the wick of a candle. ORIG C14 *snoffe,* from ?

snuffbox ('snʌfˌbɒks) *n* a container, often of elaborate ornamental design, for holding small quantities of snuff.

snuff-dipping *n* the practice of absorbing nicotine by holding in one's mouth, between the cheek and the gum, a small amount of tobacco.

snuffer ('snʌfə) *n* **1** a cone-shaped implement for extinguishing candles. **2** (*pl*) an instrument resembling a pair of scissors for trimming the wick or extinguishing the flame of a candle.

snuffle ('snʌfᵊl) *vb* **snuffles, snuffling, snuffled. 1** (*intr*) to breathe noisily or with difficulty. **2** to say or speak in a nasal tone. **3** (*intr*) to snivel. ◆ *n* **4** an act or the sound of snuffling. **5** a nasal voice. **6 the snuffles.** a condition characterized by snuffling. ORIG C16: from Low G or Du. *snuffelen*
▸ **'snuffly** *adj*

snuff movie *or* **film** *n Sl.* a pornographic film in which an unsuspecting actress or actor is murdered as the climax of the film.

snuffy ('snʌfɪ) *adj* **snuffier, snuffiest. 1** of or resembling snuff. **2** covered with or smelling of snuff. **3** disagreeable.
▸ **'snuffiness** *n*

snug (snʌg) *adj* **snugger, snuggest. 1** comfortably warm and well protected; cosy: *the children were snug in bed.* **2** small but comfortable: *a snug cottage.* **3** well ordered; compact: *a snug boat.* **4** sheltered and secure: *a snug anchorage.* **5** fitting closely and comfortably. **6** offering safe conceal-

ment. ◆ *n* **7** (in Britain and Ireland) one of the bars in certain pubs, offering intimate seating for only a few persons. ◆ *vb* **snugs, snugging, snugged. 8** to make or become comfortable and warm. ORIG C16 (in the sense: prepared for storms (used of a ship)) from O Icelandic *snöggr* short-haired, from Swedish *snygg* tidy
▸ **'snugly** *adv* ▸ **'snugness** *n*

snuggery ('snʌgərɪ) *n, pl* **snuggeries. 1** a cosy and comfortable place or room. **2** another name for **snug** (sense 7).

snuggle ('snʌgᵊl) *vb* **snuggles, snuggling, snuggled. 1** (usually *intr;* usually foll. by *down, up,* or *together*) to nestle into or draw close to (somebody or something) for warmth or from affection. ◆ *n* **2** the act of snuggling. ORIG C17: frequentative of SNUG (vb)

so[1] (səʊ) *adv* **1** (foll. by an adjective or adverb and a correlative clause often introduced by *that*) to such an extent: *the river is so dirty that it smells.* **2** (*used with a negative;* it replaces the first *as* in an equative comparison) to the same extent as: *she is not so old as you.* **3** (intensifier): *it's so lovely.* **4** in the state or manner expressed or implied: *they're happy and will remain so.* **5** (*not used with a negative;* foll. by an auxiliary verb or *do, have,* or *be* used as main verbs) also: *I can speak Spanish and so can you.* **6** *Dialect.* indeed: used to contradict a negative statement: *"you didn't phone her." "I did so!"* **7** *Arch.* provided that. **8 and so on** *or* **forth.** and continuing similarly. **9 or so.** approximately: *fifty or so people came to see me.* **10 so be it.** used to express agreement or resignation. **11 so much. 11a** a certain degree or amount (of). **11b** a lot (of): *it's just so much nonsense.* **12 so much for. 12a** no more can or need be said about. **12b** used to express contempt for something that has failed. ◆ *conj* (*subordinating;* often foll. by *that*) **13** in order (that): *to die so that you might live.* **14** with the consequence (that): *he was late home, so that there was trouble.* **15 so as.** (*takes an infinitive*) in order (to): *to diet so as to lose weight.* ◆ *sentence connector.* **16** in consequence: *she wasn't needed, so she left.* **17** thereupon: *and so we ended up in France.* **18 so what!** *Inf.* what importance does that have? ◆ *pron* **19** used to substitute for a clause or sentence, which may be understood: *you'll stop because I said so.* ◆ *adj* **20** (used with *is, was,* etc.) factual: *it can't be so.* ◆ *interj* **21** an exclamation of surprise, etc. ORIG OE *swā*

so[2] (səʊ) *n Music.* a variant spelling of **soh.**

So. *abbrev. for* south(ern).

soak (səʊk) *vb* **1** to make, become, or be thoroughly wet or saturated, esp. by immersion in a liquid. **2** (when *intr,* usually foll. by *in* or *into*) (of a liquid) to penetrate or permeate. **3** (*tr;* usually foll. by *in* or *up*) (of a permeable solid) to take in (a liquid) by absorption: *the earth soaks up rainwater.* **4** (*tr;* foll. by *out* or *out of*) to remove by immersion in a liquid: *she soaked the stains out of the dress.* **5** *Inf.* to drink excessively or make or become drunk. **6** (*tr*) *Sl.* to overcharge. ◆ *n* **7** the act of immersing in a liquid or the period of immersion. **8** the liquid in which something may be soaked. **9** *Austral.* a natural depression holding rainwater, esp. just beneath the surface of the ground. **10** *Sl.* a person who drinks to excess. ORIG OE *sōcian* to cook
▸ **'soaker** *n* ▸ **'soaking** *n, adj* ▸ **'soakingly** *adv*

soakaway ('səʊkə,weɪ) *n* a pit filled with rubble, etc., into which waste water drains.

so-and-so *n, pl* **so-and-sos.** *Inf.* **1** a person whose name is forgotten or ignored. **2** *Euphemistic.* a person or thing regarded as unpleasant: *which so-and-so broke my razor?*

Soane ★ (səʊn) *n* Sir **John.** 1753–1837, British architect. His work includes Dulwich College Art Gallery (1811–14) and his own house in Lincoln's Inn Fields, London (1812–13), which is now the Sir John Soane Museum.

soap (səʊp) *n* **1** a cleaning agent made by reacting animal or vegetable fats or oils with potassium or sodium hydroxide. Soaps act by emulsifying grease and lowering the surface tension of water, so that it more readily penetrates open materials such as textiles. **2** any metallic salt of a fatty acid, such as palmitic or stearic acid. **3** *Sl.* flattery or persuasive talk (esp. in **soft soap**). **4** *Inf.* short for **soap opera. 5 no soap.** *Sl.* not possible. ◆ *vb* (*tr*) **6** to apply soap to. **7** (often foll. by *up*) *Sl.* to flatter. ORIG OE *sāpe*
▸ **'soapless** *adj* ▸ **'soap,like** *adj*

soapberry ('səʊp,berɪ) *n, pl* **soapberries. 1** any of various chiefly tropical American trees having pulpy fruit containing saponin. **2** the fruit of any of these trees.

soapbox ('səʊp,bɒks) *n* **1** a box or crate for packing soap. **2** a crate used as a platform for speech-making. **3** a child's home-made racing cart.

soap opera *n* a serialized drama, usually dealing with domestic themes, broadcast on radio or television. Often shortened to **soap.** ORIG C20: so called because manufacturers of soap were typical sponsors

soapstone ('səʊp,stəʊn) *n* a massive compact soft variety of talc, used for making table tops, hearths, ornaments, etc. Also called: **steatite.**

soapsuds ('səʊp,sʌdz) *pl n* foam or lather made from soap.
▸ **'soap,sudsy** *adj*

soapwort ('səʊp,wɜːt) *n* a Eurasian plant having rounded clusters of fragrant pink or white flowers and leaves that were formerly used as a soap substitute. Also called: **bouncing Bet.**

soapy ('səʊpɪ) *adj* **soapier, soapiest. 1** containing or covered with soap: *soapy water.* **2** resembling or characteristic of soap. **3** *Sl.* flattering.
▸ **'soapily** *adv* ▸ **'soapiness** *n*

soar (sɔː) *vb* (*intr*) **1** to rise or fly upwards into the air. **2** (of a bird, aircraft, etc.) to glide while maintaining altitude by the use of ascending air currents. **3** to rise or increase in volume, size, etc.: *soaring prices.* ORIG C14: from OF *essorer,* from Vulgar L *exaurāre* (unattested) to expose to the breezes, from L EX-[1] + *aura* breeze
▸ **'soarer** *n* ▸ **'soaring** *n, adj* ▸ **'soaringly** *adv*

Soares ★ (*Portuguese* 'swarɪʃ) *n* **Mário** ('mərju). born 1924, Portuguese statesman; prime minister (1976–77; 1978–80; 1983–86); president (1986–96).

sob (sɒb) *vb* **sobs, sobbing, sobbed. 1** (*intr*) to weep with convulsive gasps. **2** (*tr*) to utter with sobs. **3** to cause (oneself) to be in a specified state by sobbing: *to sob oneself to sleep.* ◆ *n* **4** a convulsive gasp made in weeping. ORIG C12: prob. from Low G
▸ **'sobbing** *n, adj*

soba ('səʊbə) *n* (in Japanese cookery) noodles made from buckwheat flour. ORIG Japanese

sober ('səʊbə) *adj* **1** not drunk. **2** not given to excessive indulgence in drink or any other activity. **3** sedate and rational: *a sober attitude to a problem.* **4** (of colours) plain and dull or subdued. **5** free from exaggeration or speculation: *he told us the sober truth.* ◆ *vb* **6** (usually foll. by *up*) to make or become less intoxicated. ORIG C14 *sobre,* from OF, from L *sōbrius*
▸ **'sobering** *n, adj* ▸ **'soberly** *adv*

Sobers ★ ('səʊbəz) *n* Sir **Garfield St Auburn,** known as *Gary.* born 1936, West Indian cricketer.

sobriety (səʊ'braɪətɪ) *n* **1** the state or quality of being sober. **2** the quality of refraining from excess. **3** the quality of being serious or sedate.

sobriquet *or* **soubriquet** ('səʊbrɪ,keɪ) *n* a humorous epithet, assumed name, or nickname. ORIG C17: from F *soubriquet,* from ?

sob story *n* a tale of personal distress intended to arouse sympathy.

Soc. *or* **soc.** *abbrev. for:* **1** socialist. **2** society.

soca ('səʊkə) *n* a mixture of soul and calypso music typical of the E Caribbean. ORIG C20: a blend of *soul* + *calypso*

socage ('sɒkɪdʒ) *n English legal history.* the tenure of land by certain services, esp. of an agricultural nature. ORIG C14: from Anglo-F, from *soc* SOKE

so-called *adj* **a** (*prenominal*) designated or styled by the name or word mentioned, esp. (in the speaker's opinion) incorrectly: *a so-called genius.* **b** (also used parenthetically after a noun): *these experts, so-called, are no help.*

soccer ('sɒkə) *n* **a** a game in which two teams of eleven players try to kick or head a ball into their opponents' goal, only the goalkeeper on either side being allowed to touch the ball with his hands and arms, except in the case of throw-ins. **b** (*as modifier*): *a soccer player.* ◆ Also called: **Association Football.** ORIG C19: from *Assoc(iation Football)* + -ER[1]

socceroo (ˌsɒkəˈruː) *n, pl* **socceroos.** *Austral. sl.* a member of the Australian national soccer team. ORIG C20: from SOCCER + (KANGAR)OO

Soche *or* **So-ch'e** ★ (ˈsəʊˈtʃɛ) *n* a variant transliteration of the Chinese name for **Shache.**

Sochi ★ (*Russian* ˈsɔtʃi) *n* a city and resort in SW Russia, in the Krasnodar Territory on the Black Sea: hot mineral springs. Pop.: 355 000 (1995 est.).

sociable (ˈsəʊʃəbᵊl) *adj* **1** friendly or companionable. **2** (of an occasion) providing the opportunity for friendliness and conviviality. ◆ *n* **3** *Chiefly US.* a social. **4** a type of open carriage with two seats facing each other. ORIG C16: via F from L, from *sociāre* to unite, from *socius* an associate
▸ ˌ**sociaˈbility** *n* ▸ ˈ**sociably** *adv*

social (ˈsəʊʃəl) *adj* **1** living or preferring to live in a community rather than alone. **2** denoting or relating to human society or any of its subdivisions. **3** of or characteristic of the behaviour and interaction of persons forming groups. **4** relating to or having the purpose of promoting companionship, communal activities, etc.: *a social club.* **5** relating to or engaged in social services: *a social worker.* **6** relating to or considered appropriate to a certain class of society. **7** (esp. of certain species of insects) living together in organized colonies: *social bees.* **8** (of plant species) growing in clumps. ◆ *n* **9** an informal gathering, esp. of an organized group. ORIG C16: from L *sociālis* companionable, from *socius* a comrade
▸ ˈ**socially** *adv*

Social and Liberal Democrats *pl n* (in Britain) a political party formed in 1988 by the merging of the Liberal Party and part of the Social Democratic Party; in 1989 it changed its name to the Liberal Democrats.

social anthropology *n* the branch of anthropology that deals with cultural and social phenomena such as kinship systems or beliefs.

Social Chapter *n* the section of the **Maastricht Treaty** concerning working conditions, consultation of workers, employment rights, and social security.

Social Charter *n* a declaration of the rights, minimum wages, maximum hours, etc., of workers in the European Union, codified in the Maastricht Treaty (1992).

social climber *n* a person who seeks advancement to a higher social class, esp. by obsequious behaviour.
▸ **social climbing** *n*

social contract *or* **compact** *n* (in the theories of Locke, Hobbes, Rousseau, and others) an agreement, entered into by individuals, that results in the formation of the state, the prime motive being the desire for protection, which entails the surrender of some personal liberties.

Social Credit *n* **1** (esp. in Canada) a right-wing Populist political party, movement, or doctrine. **2** **Social Credit League.** (in New Zealand) a middle-of-the-road political party, in favour of free enterprise. **3** **Social Credit Rally.** (in Canada) a political party formed in 1963 from a splinter group of the Social Credit Party.

social democrat *n* **1** any socialist who believes in the gradual transformation of capitalism into democratic socialism. **2** (*usually cap.*) a member of a Social Democratic Party.
▸ **social democracy** *n*

Social Democratic and Labour Party *n* a Northern Irish political party, which advocates peaceful union with the Republic of Ireland. Abbrev.: **SDLP.**

Social Democratic Party *n* **1** (in Britain, 1981–90) a political party founded by ex-members of the Labour Party. It formed an alliance with the Liberal Party and continued in a reduced form after many members left to join the Social and Liberal Democrats in 1988. **2** one of the two major political parties in Germany, favouring gradual reform. **3** any of the parties in many other countries similar to that of Germany.

social engineering *n* the manipulation of the social position and function of individuals in order to manage change in a society.

social fund *n* (in Britain) a social security fund from which loans or payments may be made to people in cases of extreme need.

social inclusion *n Sociol.* the provision of certain rights, such as employment, health care, adequate housing, education, etc., to all individuals and groups in society.

social insurance *n* government insurance providing coverage for the unemployed, the injured, the old, etc.: usually financed by contributions from employers and employees.

Social Insurance Number *n Canad.* an identification number issued to individuals by the government in connection with income tax and social insurance.

socialism (ˈsəʊʃəˌlɪzəm) *n* **1** an economic theory or system in which the means of production, distribution, and exchange are owned by the community collectively, usually through the state. Cf. **capitalism. 2** any of various social or political theories or movements in which the common welfare is to be achieved through the establishment of a socialist economic system. **3** (in Leninist theory) a transitional stage in the development of a society from capitalism to communism: characterized by the distribution of income according to work rather than need.

socialist (ˈsəʊʃəlɪst) *n* **1** a supporter or advocate of socialism or any party promoting socialism (**socialist party**). ◆ *adj* **2** of, implementing, or relating to socialism. **3** (*sometimes cap.*) of or relating to socialists or a socialist party.
▸ ˌ**sociaˈlistic** *adj*

Socialist International *n* an international association of largely anti-Communist Social Democratic Parties founded in Frankfurt in 1951.

socialist realism *n* (in Communist countries, esp. formerly) the doctrine that art, literature, etc., should present an idealized portrayal of reality, which glorifies the achievements of the Communist Party.

socialite (ˈsəʊʃəˌlaɪt) *n* a person who is or seeks to be prominent in fashionable society.

sociality (ˌsəʊʃɪˈælɪtɪ) *n, pl* **socialities. 1** the tendency of groups and persons to develop social links and live in communities. **2** the quality or state of being social.

socialize *or* **socialise** (ˈsəʊʃəˌlaɪz) *vb* **socializes, socializing, socialized** *or* **socialises, socialising, socialised. 1** (*intr*) to behave in a friendly or sociable manner. **2** (*tr*) to prepare for life in society. **3** (*tr*) *Chiefly US.* to alter or create so as to be in accordance with socialist principles.

social market *n* **a** an economic system in which industry and commerce are run by private enterprise within limits set by the government to ensure equality of opportunity and social and environmental responsibility. **b** (*as modifier*): *a social-market economy.*

social realism *n* **1** the use of realist art, literature, etc., as a medium for social or political comment. **2** another name for **socialist realism.**

social science *n* **1** the study of society and of the relationship of individual members within society, including economics, history, political science, psychology, anthropology, and sociology. **2** any of these subjects studied individually.
▸ **social scientist** *n*

social secretary *n* **1** a member of an organization who arranges its social events. **2** a personal secretary who deals with private correspondence, etc.

social security *n* **1** public provision for the economic welfare of the aged, unemployed, etc., esp. through pensions and other monetary assistance. **2** (*often cap.*) a government programme designed to provide such assistance.

social services *pl n* welfare activities organized by the state or a local authority and carried out by trained personnel.

social studies *n* (*functioning as sing*) the study of how people live and organize themselves in society, embracing geography, history, economics, and other subjects.

social welfare *n* **1** social services provided by a state for the benefit of its citizens. **2** (*caps.*) (in New Zealand) a government department concerned with pensions and benefits for the elderly, the sick, etc.

social work *n* any of various social services designed to alleviate the conditions of the poor and aged and to increase the welfare of children.
▸ **social worker** *n*

societal (səˈsaɪətᵊl) *adj* of or relating to society, esp. human society.
▸ **soˈcietally** *adv*

societal marketing *n* **1** marketing that takes into account society's long-term welfare. **2** the marketing of a social or charitable cause, such as an anti-apartheid campaign.

society (səˈsaɪətɪ) *n, pl* **societies. 1** the totality of social relationships among organized groups of human beings or animals. **2** a system of human organizations generating distinctive cultural patterns and institutions. **3** such a system with reference to its mode of social and economic organization or its dominant class: *middle-class society.* **4** those with whom one has companionship. **5** an organized group of people associated for some specific purpose or on account of some common interest: *a learned society.* **6a** the privileged class of people in a community, esp. as considered superior or fashionable. **6b** (*as modifier*): *a society woman.* **7** the social life and intercourse of such people: *to enter society.* **8** companionship: *I enjoy her society.* **9** *Ecology.* a small community of plants within a larger association. ORIG C16: via OF *societé* from L *societās,* from *socius* a comrade

Society Islands ★ *pl n* a group of islands in the S Pacific: administratively part of French Polynesia; consists of the Windward Islands and the Leeward Islands; became a French protectorate in 1843 and a colony in 1880. Pop.: 162 573 (1988). Area: 1595 sq. km (616 sq. miles).

Society of Jesus *n* the religious order of the Jesuits, founded by Ignatius Loyola.

socio- *combining form.* denoting social or society: *socioeconomic; sociopolitical; sociology.*

sociobiology (ˌsəʊsɪəʊbaɪˈɒlədʒɪ) *n* the study of social behaviour in animals and humans.
▸ **ˌsociobiˈologist** *n*

socioeconomic (ˌsəʊsɪəʊˌiːkəˈnɒmɪk, -ˌɛkə-) *adj* of, relating to, or involving both economic and social factors.
▸ **ˌsocioˌecoˈnomically** *adv*

sociolinguistics (ˌsəʊsɪəʊlɪŋˈgwɪstɪks) *n* (*functioning as sing*) the study of language in relation to its social context.
▸ **ˌsocioˈlinguist** *n*

sociology (ˌsəʊsɪˈɒlədʒɪ) *n* the study of the development, organization, functioning, and classification of human societies.
▸ **sociological** (ˌsəʊsɪəˈlɒdʒɪkᵊl) *adj* ▸ **ˌsociˈologist** *n*

sociometry (ˌsəʊsɪˈɒmɪtrɪ) *n* the study of sociological relationships within groups.
▸ **sociometric** (ˌsəʊsɪəˈmɛtrɪk) *adj* ▸ **ˌsociˈometrist** *n*

sociopath (ˈsəʊsɪəˌpæθ) *n Psychiatry.* another term for **psychopath.**
▸ **ˌsocioˈpathic** *adj* ▸ **sociopathy** (ˌsəʊsɪˈɒpəθɪ) *n*

sociopolitical (ˌsəʊsɪəʊpəˈlɪtɪkᵊl) *adj* of or involving both political and social factors.

sock¹ (sɒk) *n* **1** a cloth covering for the foot, reaching to between the ankle and knee and worn inside a shoe. **2** an insole put in a shoe, as to make it fit better. **3** a light shoe worn by actors in ancient Greek and Roman comedy. **4** **pull one's socks up.** *Brit. inf.* to make a determined effort, esp. to improve one's behaviour or performance. **5** **put a sock in it.** *Brit. sl.* be quiet! ORIG OE *socc* a light shoe, from L *soccus,* from Gk *sukkhos*

sock² (sɒk) *Sl.* ◆ *vb* **1** (*usually tr*) to hit with force. **2** **sock it to.** *Sl.* to make a forceful impression on. ◆ *n* **3** a forceful blow. ORIG C17: from ?

socket (ˈsɒkɪt) *n* **1** a device into which an electric plug can be inserted in order to make a connection in a circuit. **2** *Chiefly Brit.* such a device mounted on a wall and connected to the electricity supply; power point. **3** a part with an opening or hollow into which some other part can be fitted. **4** *Anat.* **4a** a bony hollow into which a part or structure fits: *an eye socket.* **4b** the receptacle of a ball-and-socket joint. ◆ *vb* **5** (*tr*) to furnish with or place into a socket. ORIG C13: from Anglo-Norman *soket* a little ploughshare, from *soc,* of Celtic origin

socket set *n* a set of tools consisting of a handle into which various interchangeable heads can be fitted.

sockeye (ˈsɒkˌaɪ) *n* a Pacific salmon having red flesh and valued as a food fish. Also called: **red salmon.** ORIG by folk etymology from *sukkegh,* of Amerind origin

socle (ˈsəʊkᵊl) *n* another name for **plinth** (sense 1). ORIG C18: via F from It. *zoccolo,* from L *socculus* a little shoe, from *soccus* a SOCK[1]

Socotra, Sokotra, *or* **Suqutra** ★ (səˈkəʊtrə) *n* an island in the Indian Ocean, about 240 km (150 miles) off Cape Guardafui, Somalia: administratively part of Yemen. Area: 3100 sq. km (1200 sq. miles).

Socrates ★ (ˈsɒkrəˌtiːz) *n* ?470–399 B.C., Athenian philosopher; his beliefs that virtue is based on knowledge, attained by a dialectical process, are known through the writings of his pupils Plato and Xenophon. He was condemned to death for impiety and corruption of youth (399) and died by drinking hemlock.

Socratic (sɒˈkrætɪk) *adj* **1** of or relating to Socrates, his methods, etc. ◆ *n* **2** a person who follows the teachings of Socrates.
▸ **Soˈcratically** *adv* ▸ **Soˈcratiˌcism** *n* ▸ **Socratist** (ˈsɒkrətɪst) *n*

Socratic irony *n Philosophy.* a means by which the feigned ignorance of a questioner leads the person answering to expose his own ignorance.

Socratic method *n Philosophy.* the method of instruction by question and answer used by Socrates in order to elicit from his pupils truths he considered to be implicitly known by all rational beings.

sod¹ (sɒd) *n* **1** a piece of grass-covered surface soil held together by the roots of the grass; turf. **2** *Poetic.* the ground. ◆ *vb* **sods, sodding, sodded. 3** (*tr*) to cover with sods. ORIG C15: from Low G

sod² (sɒd) *Sl., chiefly Brit.* ◆ *n* **1** a person considered to be obnoxious. **2** a jocular word for a **person. 3** **sod all.** *Sl.* nothing. ◆ *interj* **4** **sod it.** a strong exclamation of annoyance. See also **sod off.** ORIG C19: shortened from SODOMITE
▸ **ˈsodding** *adj*

soda (ˈsəʊdə) *n* **1** any of a number of simple inorganic compounds of sodium, such as sodium carbonate (**washing soda**), sodium bicarbonate (**baking soda**), and sodium hydroxide (**caustic soda**). **2** See **soda water. 3** *US & Canad.* a fizzy drink. ORIG C16: from Med. L, from *sodanum* barilla, a plant that was burned to obtain a type of sodium carbonate, ?from Ar.

soda ash *n* the anhydrous commercial form of sodium carbonate.

soda bread *n* a type of bread leavened with sodium bicarbonate combined with milk and cream of tartar.

soda fountain *n US & Canad.* **1** a counter that serves drinks, snacks, etc. **2** an apparatus dispensing soda water.

sodality (səʊˈdælɪtɪ) *n, pl* **sodalities. 1** *RC Church.* a religious society. **2** fellowship. ORIG C16: from L *sodālitās* fellowship, from *sodālis* a comrade

sodamide (ˈsəʊdəˌmaɪd) *n* a white crystalline compound used as a dehydrating agent and in making sodium cyanide. Formula: $NaNH_2$.

soda siphon *n* a sealed bottle containing and dispensing soda water. The water is forced up a tube reaching to the bottom of the bottle by the pressure of gas above the water.

soda water *n* an effervescent beverage made by charging water with carbon dioxide under pressure. Sometimes shortened to **soda.**

sodden (ˈsɒdᵊn) *adj* **1** completely saturated. **2a** dulled, esp. by excessive drinking. **2b** (*in combination*): *a drink-sodden mind.* **3** doughy, as bread is when improperly cooked. ◆ *vb* **4** to make or become sodden. ORIG C13 *soden,* p.p. of SEETHE
▸ **ˈsoddenness** *n*

Soddy ★ ('sɒdɪ) *n* **Frederick.** 1877–1956, British chemist, who discovered isotopes: Nobel prize for chemistry 1921.

sodium ('səʊdɪəm) *n* **a** a very reactive soft silvery-white element of the alkali metal group occurring principally in common salt, Chile saltpetre, and cryolite. It is used in the production of chemicals, in metallurgy, and, alloyed with potassium, as a cooling medium in nuclear reactors. Symbol: Na; atomic no.: 11; atomic wt.: 22.99. **b** (*as modifier*): *sodium light.* ORIG C19: NL, from SODA + -IUM

sodium amytal *n* another name for **Amytal.**

sodium benzoate *n* a white crystalline soluble compound used in preserving food (**E 211**), as an antiseptic, and in making dyes.

sodium bicarbonate *n* a white crystalline soluble compound used in effervescent drinks, baking powders, fire-extinguishers, and in medicine as an antacid; sodium hydrogen carbonate. Formula: $NaHCO_3$. Systematic name: **sodium hydrogencarbonate.** Also called: **bicarbonate of soda, baking soda.**

sodium carbonate *n* a colourless or white odourless soluble crystalline compound used in the manufacture of glass, ceramics, soap, and paper, and as a cleansing agent. Formula: Na_2CO_3.

sodium chlorate *n* a colourless crystalline soluble compound used as a bleaching agent, antiseptic, and weedkiller. Formula: $NaClO_3$.

sodium chloride *n* common table salt; a soluble colourless crystalline compound widely used as a seasoning and preservative for food and in the manufacture of chemicals, glass, and soap. Formula: NaCl. Also called: **salt.**

sodium cyanide *n* a white odourless crystalline soluble poisonous compound used for extracting gold and silver from their ores and for case-hardening steel. Formula: NaCN.

sodium glutamate ('gluːtəˌmeɪt) *n* another name for **monosodium glutamate.**

sodium hydrogencarbonate *n* the systematic name for **sodium bicarbonate.**

sodium hydroxide *n* a white strongly alkaline solid used in the manufacture of rayon, paper, aluminium, soap, and sodium compounds. Formula: NaOH. Also called: **caustic soda.**

sodium hyposulphite *n* another name (not in technical usage) for **sodium thiosulphate.**

sodium lamp *n* another name for **sodium-vapour lamp.**

sodium nitrate *n* a white crystalline soluble solid compound used in matches, explosives, and rocket propellants, as a fertilizer, and as a curing salt for preserving food (**E 251**). Formula: $NaNO_3$.

Sodium Pentothal *n Trademark.* another name for **thiopentone sodium.**

sodium silicate *n* **1** Also called: **soluble glass.** See **water glass. 2** any sodium salt of a silicic acid.

sodium sulphate *n* a solid white substance used in making glass, detergents, and pulp. Formula: Na_2SO_4. See **salt cake** and **Glauber's salt.**

sodium thiosulphate *n* a white soluble substance used in photography as a fixer to dissolve unchanged silver halides and also to remove excess chlorine from chlorinated water. Formula: $Na_2S_2O_3$. Also called (not in technical usage): **sodium hyposulphite, hypo.**

sodium-vapour lamp *n* a type of electric lamp consisting of a glass tube containing neon and sodium vapour at low pressure through which an electric current is passed to give an orange light: used in street lighting.

sod off *Brit. taboo sl.* ◆ *interj* **1** a forceful expression of dismissal. ◆ *vb* **sods, sodding, sodded. 2** (*intr, adv*) to go away.

Sodom ★ ('sɒdəm) *n* **1** *Old Testament.* a city destroyed by God for its wickedness that, with Gomorrah, traditionally typifies depravity (Genesis 19:24). **2** this city as representing homosexuality. **3** any place notorious for depravity.

sodomite ('sɒdəˌmaɪt) *n* a person who practises sodomy.

sodomize *or* **sodomise** ('sɒdəˌmaɪz) *vb* **sodomizes, sodomizing, sodomized** *or* **sodomises, sodomising, sodomised.** (*tr*) to have anal intercourse with (a person).

sodomy ('sɒdəmɪ) *n* anal intercourse committed by a man with another man or a woman. ORIG C13: via OF *sodomie* from L (Vulgate) *Sodoma* Sodom

Sod's law (sɒdz) *n Inf.* a facetious precept stating that if something can go wrong or turn out inconveniently it will.

Soekarno ★ (suːˈkɑːnəʊ) *n* a variant spelling of (Achmed) **Sukarno.**

Soemba ★ ('suːmbə) *n* a variant spelling of **Sumba.**

Soembawa ★ (suːmˈbɑːwə) *n* a variant spelling of **Sumbawa.**

Soenda Islands ★ ('suːndə) *pl n* a variant spelling of **Sunda Islands.**

Soenda Strait ★ *n* a variant spelling of **Sunda Strait.**

Soerabaja ★ (ˌsʊərəˈbaɪə) *n* a variant spelling of **Surabaya.**

soever (səʊˈɛvə) *adv* in any way at all: used to emphasize or make less precise a word or phrase, usually in combination with *what, where, when, how,* etc., or else separated by intervening words. Cf. **whatsoever.**

sofa ('səʊfə) *n* an upholstered seat with back and arms for two or more people. ORIG C17 (in the sense: dais upholstered as a seat): from Ar. *suffah*

soffit ('sɒfɪt) *n* the underside of a part of a building or a structural component, such as an arch, beam, stair, etc. ORIG C17: via F from It. *soffitto,* from L *suffixus* something fixed underneath, from *suffigere,* from *sub-* under + *figere* to fasten

Sofia ★ ('səʊfɪə) *n* the capital of Bulgaria, in the west: colonized by the Romans in 29 A.D.; became capital of Bulgaria in 1879; university (1880). Pop.: 1 116 823 (1996 est.). Ancient name: **Serdica.** Bulgarian name: **Sofiya** ('sɔfiˌja).

S. of Sol. *Bible. abbrev. for* Song of Solomon.

soft (sɒft) *adj* **1** easy to dent, work, or cut without shattering; malleable. **2** not hard; giving little or no resistance to pressure or weight. **3** fine, light, smooth, or fluffy to the touch. **4** gentle; tranquil. **5** (of music, sounds, etc.) low and pleasing. **6** (of light, colour, etc.) not excessively bright or harsh. **7** (of a breeze, climate, etc.) temperate, mild, or pleasant. **8** slightly blurred; not sharply outlined: *soft focus.* **9** (of a diet) consisting of easily digestible foods. **10** kind or lenient, often excessively so. **11** easy to influence or impose upon. **12** prepared to compromise; not doctrinaire: *the soft left.* **13** *Inf.* feeble or silly; simple (often in **soft in the head**). **14** unable to endure hardship, esp. through pampering. **15** physically out of condition; flabby: *soft muscles.* **16** loving; tender: *soft words.* **17** *Inf.* requiring little exertion; easy: *a soft job.* **18** *Chem.* (of water) relatively free of mineral salts and therefore easily able to make soap lather. **19** (of a drug such as cannabis) nonaddictive. **20** *Phonetics.* (not in technical usage) denoting the consonants *c* and *g* in English when they are pronounced as palatal or alveolar fricatives or affricates (s, dʒ, ʃ, ð, tʃ) before *e* and *i,* rather than as velar stops (k, g). **21** *Finance, chiefly US.* (of prices, a market, etc.) unstable and tending to decline. **22** (of currency) in relatively little demand, esp. because of a weak balance of payments situation. **23** (of radiation, such as X-rays and ultraviolet radiation) having low energy and not capable of deep penetration of materials. **24** related to the performance of nonspecific generalized tasks: *soft skills such as customer services and office support.* **25 soft on** *or* **about. 25a** gentle, sympathetic, or lenient towards. **25b** feeling affection or infatuation for. ◆ *adv* **26** in a soft manner: *to speak soft.* ◆ *n* **27** a soft object, part, or piece. **28** *Inf.* See **softie.** ◆ *sentence substitute. Arch.* **29** quiet! **30** wait! ORIG OE *sōfte*

▸ **'softly** *adv* ▸ **'softness** *n*

softa ('sɒftə) *n* a Muslim student of divinity and jurisprudence, esp. in Turkey. ORIG C17: from Turkish, from Persian *sōkhtah* aflame (with love of learning)

softball ('sɒft,bɔ:l) *n* a variation of baseball using a larger softer ball, pitched underhand.

soft ball *n Cookery.* a term used for sugar syrup boiled to a consistency at which it may be rubbed into balls after dipping in cold water.

soft-boiled *adj* (of an egg) boiled for a short time so that the yolk is still soft.

soft coal *n* another name for **bituminous coal.**

soft commodities *pl n* nonmetal commodities, such as cocoa, sugar, and grains, bought and sold on a futures market. Also called: **softs.**

soft-core *adj* (of pornography) suggestive and titillating through not being totally explicit.

soft-cover *adj* a less common word for **paperback.**

soft drink *n* a nonalcoholic drink.

soften ('sɒfᵊn) *vb* **1** to make or become soft or softer. **2** to make or become more gentle.
▸ '**softener** *n*

softening of the brain *n* an abnormal softening of the tissues of the cerebrum characterized by mental impairment.

soft-focus lens *n Photog.* a lens designed to produce an image that is slightly out of focus: typically used for portrait work.

soft furnishings *pl n Brit.* curtains, hangings, rugs, etc.

soft goods *pl n* textile fabrics and related merchandise. Also called (US and Canad.): **dry goods.**

soft-headed *adj* **1** *Inf.* feeble-minded; stupid; simple. **2** (of a stick or hammer for playing a percussion instrument) having a soft head.
▸ ,**soft-'headedness** *n*

softhearted (,sɒft'hɑ:tɪd) *adj* easily moved to pity.
▸ ,**soft'heartedly** *adv* ▸ ,**soft'heartedness** *n*

softie *or* **softy** ('sɒftɪ) *n, pl* **softies.** *Inf.* a person who is sentimental, weakly foolish, or lacking in physical endurance.

soft landing *n* **1** a landing by a spacecraft on the moon or a planet at a sufficiently low velocity for the equipment or occupants to remain unharmed. **2** a painless resolution of a problem, esp. an economic problem. Cf. **hard landing.**

soft option *n* in a number of choices, the one involving the least difficulty or exertion.

soft palate *n* the posterior fleshy portion of the roof of the mouth.

soft paste *n* **a** artificial porcelain made from clay, bone ash, etc. **b** (*as modifier*): *softpaste porcelain.*

soft-pedal *vb* **soft-pedals, soft-pedalling, soft-pedalled** *or US* **soft-pedals, soft-pedaling, soft-pedaled.** (*tr*) **1** to mute the tone of (a piano) by depressing the soft pedal. **2** *Inf.* to make (something, esp. something unpleasant) less obvious by deliberately failing to emphasize or allude to it. ◆ *n* **soft pedal. 3** a foot-operated lever on a piano, the left one of two, that either moves the whole action closer to the strings so that the hammers strike with less force or causes fewer of the strings to sound.

soft porn *n Inf.* soft-core pornography.

softs (sɒfts) *pl n* another name for **soft commodities.**

soft sell *n* a method of selling based on indirect suggestion or inducement.

soft shoulder *or* **verge** *n* a soft edge along the side of a road that is unsuitable for vehicles to drive on.

soft soap *n* **1** *Med.* Also called: **green soap.** a soft or liquid alkaline soap used in treating certain skin disorders. **2** *Inf.* flattering, persuasive, or cajoling talk. ◆ *vb* **soft-soap. 3** *Inf.* to use such talk on (a person).

soft-spoken *adj* **1** speaking or said with a soft gentle voice. **2** able to persuade or impress by glibness of tongue.

soft spot *n* a sentimental fondness (esp. in **have a soft spot for**).

soft touch *n Inf.* a person easily persuaded or imposed on, esp. to lend money.

software ('sɒft,wɛə) *n Computing.* the programs that can be used with a particular computer system. Cf. **hardware** (sense 2).

softwood ('sɒft,wʊd) *n* **1** the open-grained wood of any of numerous coniferous trees, such as pine and cedar. **2** any tree yielding this wood.

SOGAT ('səʊgæt) *n* (formerly, in Britain) *acronym for* Society of Graphical and Allied Trades.

Sogdiana ★ (,sɒgdɪ'ɑ:nə) *n* a region of ancient central Asia. Its chief city was Samarkand.
▸ '**Sogdian** *adj, n*

soggy ('sɒgɪ) *adj* **soggier, soggiest. 1** soaked with liquid. **2** (of bread, pastry, etc.) moist and heavy. **3** *Inf.* lacking in spirit or positiveness. ORIG C18: prob. from dialect *sog* marsh, from ?
▸ '**soggily** *adv* ▸ '**sogginess** *n*

soh *or* **so** (səʊ) *n Music.* (in tonic sol-fa) the name used for the fifth note or dominant of any scale. ORIG C14: later variant of *sol*; see GAMUT

Soho ★ ('səʊhəʊ) *n* a district of central London, in the City of Westminster: a foreign quarter since the late 17th century, now chiefly known for restaurants, nightclubs, striptease clubs, etc.

soi-disant *French.* (swadizɑ̃) *adj* so-called; self-styled. ORIG lit.: calling oneself

soigné *or* (*fem*) **soignée** ('swɑ:njeɪ) *adj* well-groomed; elegant. ORIG F, from *soigner* to take good care of, of Gmc origin

soil[1] (sɔɪl) *n* **1** the top layer of the land surface of the earth that is composed of disintegrated rock particles, humus, water, and air. **2** a type of this material having specific characteristics: *loamy soil.* **3** land, country, or region: *one's native soil.* **4 the soil.** life and work on a farm; land: *he belonged to the soil.* **5** any place or thing encouraging growth or development. ORIG C14: from Anglo-Norman, from L *solium* a seat, but confused with L *solum* the ground

soil[2] (sɔɪl) *vb* **1** to make or become dirty or stained. **2** (*tr*) to pollute with sin or disgrace; sully; defile. ◆ *n* **3** the state or result of soiling. **4** refuse, manure, or excrement. ORIG C13: from OF *soillier* to defile, from *soil* pigsty, prob. from L *sūs* a swine

soil[3] (sɔɪl) *vb* (*tr*) to feed (livestock) green fodder to fatten or purge them. ORIG C17: ?from obs. vb (C16) *soil* to manure, from SOIL[2] (n)

soil pipe *n* a pipe that conveys sewage or waste water from a toilet, etc., to a soil drain or sewer.

soiree ('swɑ:reɪ) *n* an evening party or gathering, usually at a private house, esp. where guests listen to, play, or dance to music. ORIG C19: from F, from OF *soir* evening, from L *sērum* a late time, from *sērus* late

Soissons ★ (*French* swasɔ̃) *n* a city in N France, on the Aisne River: has Roman remains and an 11th-century abbey. Pop.: 32 144 (1990).

soixante-neuf *French.* (swasɑ̃tnœf) *n* a sexual activity in which two people simultaneously stimulate each other's genitalia with their mouths. Also called: **sixty-nine.** ORIG lit.: sixty-nine, from the position adopted by the participants

sojourn ('sɒdʒɜ:n, 'sʌdʒ-) *n* **1** a temporary stay. ◆ *vb* **2** (*intr*) to stay or reside temporarily. ORIG C13: from OF *sojorner,* from Vulgar L *subdiurnāre* (unattested) to spend a day, from L *sub-* during + LL *diurnum* day
▸ '**sojourner** *n*

soke (səʊk) *n English legal history.* **1** the right to hold a local court. **2** the territory under the jurisdiction of a particular court. ORIG C14: from Med. L *sōca,* from OE *sōcn* a seeking

Sokoto ★ ('səʊkə,təʊ) *n* **1** a state of NW Nigeria. Capital: Sokoto. Pop.: 4 911 118 (1995 est.). Area: 65 735 sq. km (25 380 sq. miles). **2** a town in NW Nigeria, capital of Sokoto state: capital of the Fulah Empire in the 19th century; Muslim place of pilgrimage. Pop.: 185 500 (1992 est.).

Sokotra ★ (sə'kəʊtrə) *n* a variant spelling of **Socotra.**

sol[1] (sɒl) *n Music.* the syllable used in the fixed system of solmization for the note G. ORIG C14: see GAMUT

sol[2] (sɒl) *n* a colloid that has a continuous liquid phase, esp. one in which a solid is suspended in a liquid. ORIG C20: shortened from SOLUTION

Sol ★ (sɒl) *n* **1** the Roman god personifying the sun. **2** a poetic word for the **sun**.

sol. *abbrev. for:* **1** soluble. **2** solution.

Sol. *abbrev. for:* **1** Also: **Solr.** solicitor. **2** *Bible.* Solomon.

sola *Latin.* ★ (ˈsəʊlə) *adj* the feminine form of ***solus***.

solace (ˈsɒlɪs) *n* **1** comfort in misery, disappointment, etc. **2** something that gives comfort or consolation. ◆ *vb* **solaces, solacing, solaced.** (*tr*) **3** to give comfort or cheer to (a person) in time of sorrow, distress, etc. **4** to alleviate (sorrow, misery, etc.). ORIG C13: from OF *solas,* from L *sōlātium* comfort, from *sōlārī* to console
▸ ˈ**solacer** *n*

solan *or* **solan goose** (ˈsəʊlən) *n* an archaic name for the **gannet**. ORIG C15 *soland,* from ON

solanaceous (ˌsɒləˈneɪʃəs) *adj* of or relating to the Solanaceae, a family of plants having typically tubular flowers, protruding anthers, and often poisonous or narcotic properties: includes the potato, tobacco, and several nightshades. ORIG C19: from NL *Sōlānāceae,* from L *sōlānum* nightshade

solanum (səʊˈleɪnəm) *n* any tree, shrub, or herbaceous plant of the mainly tropical solanaceous genus *Solanum:* includes the potato and certain nightshades. ORIG C16: from L: nightshade

solar (ˈsəʊlə) *adj* **1** of or relating to the sun. **2** operating by or utilizing the energy of the sun: *solar cell.* **3** *Astron.* determined from the motion of the earth relative to the sun: *solar year.* **4** *Astrol.* subject to the influence of the sun. ORIG C15: from L *sōlāris,* from *sōl* the sun

solar cell *n* a cell that produces electricity from the sun's rays, used esp. in spacecraft.

solar constant *n* the rate at which the sun's energy is received per unit area at the top of the earth's atmosphere when the sun is at its mean distance from the earth and atmospheric absorption has been corrected for.

solar day *n* See under **day** (sense 6).

solar energy *n* energy obtained from solar power.

solar flare *n* a brief powerful eruption of intense high-energy radiation from the sun's surface, associated with sunspots and causing radio and magnetic disturbances on earth.

solarium (səʊˈlɛərɪəm) *n, pl* **solariums** *or* **solaria** (-ˈlɛərɪə) **1** a room built largely of glass to afford exposure to the sun. **2** a bed equipped with ultraviolet lights used for acquiring an artificial suntan. **3** an establishment offering such facilities. ORIG C19: from L: a terrace, from *sōl* sun

solar month *n* See under **month** (sense 4).

solar plexus *n* **1** *Anat.* the network of nerves situated behind the stomach that supply the abdominal organs. **2** (not in technical usage) the part of the stomach beneath the diaphragm; pit of the stomach. ORIG C18: referring to resemblance between the radial network of nerves & ganglia & the rays of the sun

solar power *n* radiation from the sun used to heat a fluid or to generate electricity using solar cells.

solar system *n* the system containing the sun and the bodies held in its gravitational field, including the planets (Mercury, Venus, earth, Mars, Jupiter, Saturn, Uranus, Neptune, Pluto), the asteroids, and comets.

solar wind (wɪnd) *n* the stream of charged particles, such as protons, emitted by the sun at high velocities, its intensity increasing during periods of solar activity.

solar year *n* See under **year** (sense 4).

solatium (səʊˈleɪʃɪəm) *n, pl* **solatia** (-ʃɪə). *Law, chiefly US & Scot.* compensation awarded for injury to the feelings as distinct from physical suffering and pecuniary loss. ORIG C19: from L: see SOLACE

sold (səʊld) *vb* **1** the past tense and past participle of **sell**. ◆ *adj* **2 sold on.** *Sl.* uncritically attached to or enthusiastic about.

solder (ˈsɒldə; *US* ˈsɒdər) *n* **1** an alloy used for joining two metal surfaces by melting the alloy so that it forms a thin layer between the surfaces. **2** something that joins things together firmly; a bond. ◆ *vb* **3** to join or mend or be joined or mended with or as if with solder. ORIG C14: via OF from L *solidāre* to strengthen, from *solidus* solid
▸ ˈ**solderable** *adj* ▸ ˈ**solderer** *n*

soldering iron *n* a hand tool consisting of a handle fixed to a copper tip that is heated and used to melt and apply solder.

soldier (ˈsəʊldʒə) *n* **1a** a person who serves or has served in an army. **1b** Also called: **common soldier.** a noncommissioned member of an army as opposed to a commissioned officer. **2** a person who works diligently for a cause. **3** *Zool.* an individual in a colony of social insects, esp. ants, that has powerful jaws adapted for defending the colony, crushing food, etc. ◆ *vb* **4** (*intr*) to serve as a soldier. ORIG C13: from OF *soudier,* from *soude* (army) pay, from LL *solidus* a gold coin, from L: firm
▸ ˈ**soldierly** *adj*

soldier of fortune *n* a man who seeks money or adventure as a soldier; mercenary.

soldier on *vb* (*intr, adv*) to persist in one's efforts in spite of difficulties, pressure, etc.

soldiery (ˈsəʊldʒərɪ) *n, pl* **soldieries. 1** soldiers collectively. **2** a group of soldiers. **3** the profession of being a soldier.

sole[1] (səʊl) *adj* **1** (*prenominal*) being the only one; only. **2** (*prenominal*) of or relating to one individual or group and no other: *sole rights.* **3** *Law.* having no wife or husband. **4** an archaic word for **solitary**. ORIG C14: from OF *soule,* from L *sōlus* alone
▸ ˈ**soleness** *n*

sole[2] (səʊl) *n* **1** the underside of the foot. **2** the underside of a shoe. **3a** the bottom of a furrow. **3b** the bottom of a plough. **4** the underside of a golf-club head. ◆ *vb* **soles, soling, soled.** (*tr*) **5** to provide (a shoe) with a sole. ORIG C14: via OF from L *solea* sandal

sole[3] (səʊl) *n, pl* **sole** *or* **soles.** any of various tongue-shaped flatfishes, esp. the **European sole:** most common in warm seas and highly valued as food fishes. ORIG C14: via OF from Vulgar L *sola* (unattested), from L *solea* a sandal (from the fish's shape)

solecism (ˈsɒlɪˌsɪzəm) *n* **1a** the nonstandard use of a grammatical construction. **1b** any mistake, incongruity, or absurdity. **2** a violation of good manners. ORIG C16: from L *soloecismus,* from Gk, from *soloikos* speaking incorrectly, from *Soloi* an Athenian colony of Cilicia where the inhabitants spoke a corrupt form of Greek
▸ ˈ**solecist** *n* ▸ ˌ**soleˈcistic** *adj* ▸ ˌ**soleˈcistically** *adv*

solely (ˈsəʊllɪ) *adv* **1** only; completely. **2** without others; singly. **3** for one thing only.

solemn (ˈsɒləm) *adj* **1** characterized or marked by seriousness or sincerity: *a solemn vow.* **2** characterized by pomp, ceremony, or formality. **3** serious, glum, or pompous. **4** inspiring awe: *a solemn occasion.* **5** performed with religious ceremony. **6** gloomy or sombre: *solemn colours.* ORIG C14: from OF *solempne,* from L *sōllemnis* appointed, ?from *sollus* whole
▸ ˈ**solemnly** *adv* ▸ ˈ**solemnness** *or* ˈ**solemness** *n*

solemnify (səˈlɛmnɪˌfaɪ) *vb* **solemnifies, solemnifying, solemnified.** (*tr*) to make serious or grave.
▸ **soˌlemnifiˈcation** *n*

solemnity (səˈlɛmnɪtɪ) *n, pl* **solemnities. 1** the state or quality of being solemn. **2** (*often pl*) solemn ceremony, observance, etc. **3** *Law.* a formality necessary to validate a deed, contract, etc.

solemnize *or* **solemnise** (ˈsɒləmˌnaɪz) *vb* **solemnizes, solemnizing, solemnized** *or* **solemnises, solemnising, solemnised.** (*tr*) **1** to celebrate or observe with rites or formal ceremonies, as a religious occasion. **2** to celebrate or perform the ceremony of (marriage). **3** to make solemn or serious. **4** to perform or hold (ceremonies, etc.) in due manner.
▸ ˌ**solemniˈzation** *or* ˌ**solemniˈsation** *n* ▸ ˈ**solemˌnizer** *or* ˈ**solemˌniser** *n*

solenodon (səˈlɛnədən) *n* either of two rare shrewlike nocturnal mammals of the Caribbean having a long hairless tail and an elongated snout. ORIG C19: from NL, from L *sōlēn* sea mussel (from Gk: pipe) + Gk *odōn* tooth

solenoid (ˈsəʊlɪˌnɔɪd) *n* **1** a coil of wire, usually cylindri-

cal, in which a magnetic field is set up by passing a current through it. **2** a coil of wire, partially surrounding an iron core, that is made to move inside the coil by the magnetic field set up by a current: used to convert electrical to mechanical energy, as in the operation of a switch. ORIG C19: from F *solénoïde,* from Gk *sōlēn* a tube
▸ **ˌsoleˈnoidal** *adj*

Solent ★ (ˈsəʊlənt) *n* **the.** a strait of the English Channel between the coast of Hampshire (on the English mainland) and the Isle of Wight. Width: up to 6 km (4 miles).

Soleure ★ (sɔlœr) *n* the French name for **Solothurn.**

sol-fa (ˈsɒlˈfɑː) *n* **1** short for **tonic sol-fa.** ◆ *vb* **sol-fas, sol-faing, sol-faed. 2** *US.* to use tonic sol-fa syllables in singing (a tune). ORIG C16: see GAMUT

solfatara (ˌsɒlfəˈtɑːrə) *n* a volcanic vent emitting only sulphurous gases and water vapour or sometimes hot mud. ORIG C18: from It.: a sulphurous volcano near Naples, from *solfo* sulphur

solfeggio (sɒlˈfɛdʒɪəʊ) *or* **solfège** (sɒlˈfɛʒ) *n, pl* **solfeggi** (-ˈfɛdʒiː), **solfeggios,** *or* **solfèges.** *Music.* **1** a voice exercise in which runs, scales, etc., are sung to the same syllable or syllables. **2** solmization, esp. the French or Italian system, in which the names correspond to the notes of the scale of C major. ORIG C18: from It. *solfeggiare* to use the syllables sol-fa; see GAMUT

soli (ˈsəʊlɪ) *adj, adv Music.* (of a piece or passage) (to be performed) by or with soloists.

solicit (səˈlɪsɪt) *vb* **solicits, soliciting, solicited. 1** (when *intr,* foll. by *for*) to make a request, application, etc., to (a person for business, support, etc.). **2** to accost (a person) with an offer of sexual relations in return for money. **3** to provoke or incite (a person) to do something wrong or illegal. ORIG C15: from OF *solliciter* to disturb, from L *sollicitāre* to harass, from *sollus* whole + *ciēre* to excite
▸ **soˌliciˈtation** *n*

solicitor (səˈlɪsɪtə) *n* **1** (in Britain) a lawyer who advises clients on matters of law, draws up legal documents, prepares cases for barristers, etc. **2** (in the US) an officer responsible for the legal affairs of a town, city, etc. **3** a person who solicits.
▸ **soˈlicitorˌship** *n*

Solicitor General *n, pl* **Solicitors General. 1** (in Britain) the law officer of the Crown ranking next to the Attorney General (in Scotland to the Lord Advocate) and acting as his assistant. **2** (in New Zealand) the government's chief lawyer.

solicitous (səˈlɪsɪtəs) *adj* **1** showing consideration, concern, attention, etc. **2** keenly anxious or willing; eager. ORIG C16: from L *sollicitus* anxious; see SOLICIT
▸ **soˈlicitousness** *n*

solicitude (səˈlɪsɪˌtjuːd) *n* **1** the state or quality of being solicitous. **2** (*often pl*) something that causes anxiety or concern. **3** anxiety or concern.

solid (ˈsɒlɪd) *adj* **1** of, concerned with, or being a substance in a physical state in which it resists changes in size and shape. Cf. **gas** (sense 1), **liquid** (sense 1). **2** consisting of matter all through. **3** of the same substance all through: *solid rock.* **4** sound; proved or provable: *solid facts.* **5** reliable or sensible; upstanding: *a solid citizen.* **6** firm, strong, compact, or substantial: *a solid table; solid ground.* **7** (of a meal or food) substantial. **8** (*often postpositive*) without interruption or respite: *solid bombardment.* **9** financially sound or solvent: *a solid institution.* **10** strongly linked or consolidated: *a solid relationship.* **11 solid for.** unanimously in favour of. **12** *Geom.* having or relating to three dimensions. **13** (of a word composed of two or more elements) written or printed as a single word without a hyphen. **14** *Printing.* with no space or leads between lines of type. **15** (of a writer, work, etc.) adequate; sensible. **16** of or having a single uniform colour or tone. **17** *Austral.* excessively severe or unreasonable. ◆ *n* **18** *Geom.* **18a** a closed surface in three-dimensional space. **18b** such a surface together with the volume enclosed by it. **19** a solid substance, such as wood, iron, or diamond. **20** (*pl*) solid food, as opposed to liquid: *babies are messy eaters when they start on solids.* ORIG C14: from OF *solide,* from L *solidus* firm
▸ **solidity** (səˈlɪdɪtɪ) *n* ▸ **ˈsolidly** *adv* ▸ **ˈsolidness** *n*

solidago (ˌsɒlɪˈdeɪɡəʊ) *n, pl* **solidagos.** any plant of a chiefly American genus, which includes the goldenrods. ORIG C18: via NL from Med. L *soldago* a plant reputed to have healing properties, from *soldāre* to strengthen, from L *solidāre,* from *solidus* solid

solid angle *n* an area subtended in three dimensions by lines intersecting at a point on a sphere whose radius is the distance to the point. See also **steradian.**

solidarity (ˌsɒlɪˈdærɪtɪ) *n, pl* **solidarities.** unity of interests, sympathies, etc., as among members of the same class.

solid fuel *n* **1** a fuel, such as coal or coke, that is a solid rather than an oil or gas. **2** Also called: **solid propellant.** a rocket fuel that is a solid rather than a liquid or a gas.

solid geometry *n* the branch of geometry concerned with three-dimensional geometric figures.

solidify (səˈlɪdɪˌfaɪ) *vb* **solidifies, solidifying, solidified. 1** to make or become solid or hard. **2** to make or become strong, united, determined, etc.
▸ **soˌlidifiˈcation** *n* ▸ **soˈlidiˌfier** *n*

solid-state *n* (*modifier*) **1** (of an electronic device) activated by a semiconductor component in which current flow is through solid material rather than in a vacuum. **2** of, concerned with, characteristic of, or consisting of solid matter.

solid-state physics *n* (*functioning as sing*) the branch of physics concerned with the properties of solids, such as superconductivity, photoconductivity, and ferromagnetism.

solidus (ˈsɒlɪdəs) *n, pl* **solidi** (-ˌdaɪ). **1** Also called: **diagonal, oblique, separatrix, shilling mark, slash, stroke, virgule.** a short oblique stroke used in text to separate items of information, such as days, months, and years in dates (*18/7/80*), alternative words (*and/or*), numerator from denominator in fractions (*55/103*), etc. **2** a gold coin of the Byzantine empire. ORIG C14: from LL *solidus* (*nummus*) a gold coin (from *solidus* solid); in Med. L, *solidus* referred to a shilling and was indicated by a long *s,* which ult. became the virgule

solifluction *or* **solifluxion** (ˈsɒlɪˌflʌkʃən, ˈsəʊlɪ-) *n* slow downhill movement of soil, saturated with meltwater, over a permanently frozen subsoil in tundra regions. ORIG C20: from L *solum* soil + *fluctio* act of flowing

Solihull ★ (ˌsəʊlɪˈhʌl) *n* **1** a town in central England, in the S West Midlands near Birmingham: mainly residential. Pop.: 94 531 (1991). **2** a unitary authority in central England, in the West Midlands. Pop.: 203 900 (1996 est.). Area 180 sq. km (70 sq. miles).

soliloquize *or* **soliloquise** (səˈlɪləˌkwaɪz) *vb* **soliloquizes, soliloquizing, soliloquized** *or* **soliloquises, soliloquising, soliloquised.** (*intr*) to utter a soliloquy.
▸ **soˈliloquist** *n* ▸ **soˈliloˌquizer** *or* **soˈliloˌquiser** *n*

soliloquy (səˈlɪləkwɪ) *n, pl* **soliloquies. 1** the act of speaking alone or to oneself, esp. as a theatrical device. **2** a speech in a play that is spoken in soliloquy. ORIG C17: via LL *sōliloquium,* from L *sōlus* sole + *loquī* to speak

> **USAGE NOTE** *Soliloquy* is sometimes wrongly used where *monologue* is meant. Both words refer to a long speech by one person, but a *monologue* can be addressed to other people, whereas in a *soliloquy* the speaker is always talking to himself or herself.

Soliman ★ (ˈsɒlɪmən) *n* a variant spelling of **Suleiman I.**

Solimões ★ (suliˈmõəʃ) *n* **the.** the Brazilian name for the Amazon from the Peruvian border to the Rio Negro.

Solingen ★ (*German* ˈzoːlɪŋən) *n* a city in W Germany, in North Rhine-Westphalia: a major European centre of the cutlery industry. Pop.: 165 735 (1996 est.).

solipsism (ˈsɒlɪpˌsɪzəm) *n Philosophy.* the extreme form of scepticism which denies the possibility of any knowledge other than of one's own existence. ORIG C19: from L *sōlus* alone + *ipse* self
▸ **ˈsolipsist** *n, adj* ▸ **ˌsolipˈsistic** *adj*

solitaire (ˈsɒlɪˌtɛə, ˌsɒlɪˈtɛə) *n* **1** Also called: **pegboard.** a game played by one person, esp. one involving moving and taking pegs in a pegboard with the object of being left with only one. **2** the US name for **patience** (the card game). **3** a gem, esp. a diamond, set alone in a ring. **4** any of several extinct birds related to the dodo. **5** any of several dull grey North American songbirds. ORIG C18: from OF: SOLITARY

solitary ('sɒlɪtərɪ, -trɪ) *adj* **1** following or enjoying a life of solitude: *a solitary disposition.* **2** experienced or performed alone: *a solitary walk.* **3** (of a place) unfrequented. **4** (*prenominal*) single; sole: *a solitary cloud.* **5** having few companions; lonely. **6** (of animals) not living in organized colonies or large groups: *solitary bees.* **7** (of flowers) growing singly. ◆ *n, pl* **solitaries. 8** a person who lives in seclusion; hermit. **9** *Inf.* short for **solitary confinement.** ORIG C14: from L *sōlitārius,* from *sōlus* SOLE[1]
▸ '**solitarily** *adv* ▸ '**solitariness** *n*

solitary confinement *n* isolation imposed on a prisoner, as by confinement in a special cell.

solitude ('sɒlɪˌtjuːd) *n* **1** the state of being solitary or secluded. **2** *Poetic.* a solitary place. ORIG C14: from L *sōlitūdō,* from *sōlus* alone, SOLE[1]
▸ ˌ**soli'tudinous** *adj*

solmization *or* **solmisation** (ˌsɒlmɪ'zeɪʃən) *n Music.* a system of naming the notes of a scale by syllables instead of letters, which assigns the names *ut* (or *do*), *re, mi, fa, sol, la, si* (or *ti*) to the degrees of the major scale of C (**fixed system**) or (excluding the syllables *ut* and *si*) to the major scale in any key (**movable system**). See also **tonic sol-fa.** ORIG C18: from F *solmisation,* from *solmiser* to use the sol-fa syllables, from SOL[1] + MI

solo ('səʊləʊ) *n, pl* **solos. 1** (*pl* **solos** *or* **soli** (-liː)). a musical composition for one performer with or without accompaniment. **2** any of various card games in which each person plays on his or her own, such as solo whist. **3** a flight in which an aircraft pilot is unaccompanied. **4a** any performance carried out by an individual without assistance. **4b** (*as modifier*): *a solo attempt.* ◆ *adj* **5** *Music.* unaccompanied: *a sonata for cello solo.* ◆ *adv* **6** by oneself; alone: *to fly solo.* ◆ *vb* **7** (*intr*) to operate an aircraft alone. ORIG C17: via It. from L *sōlus* alone
▸ **soloist** ('səʊləʊɪst) *n*

Solomon ★ ('sɒləmən) *n* 10th century B.C., king of Israel, son of David and Bathsheba, credited with great wisdom.
▸ **Solomonic** (ˌsɒlə'mɒnɪk) *or* **Solomonian** (ˌsɒlə'məʊnɪən) *adj*

Solomon Islands ★ *pl n* an independent state in the SW Pacific comprising an archipelago extending for almost 1450 km (900 miles) in a northwest–southeast direction: the northernmost islands of the archipelago (Buka and Bougainville) form part of Papua New Guinea; the main islands are Guadalcanal, Malaita, San Cristobal, New Georgia, Santa Isabel, and Choiseul: a member of the Commonwealth. Official language: English. Religion: Christian majority. Currency: Solomon Islands dollar. Capital: Honiara. Pop.: 442 000 (1999 est.). Area: 29 785 sq. km (11 500 sq. miles).

Solomon's seal *n* **1** another name for **Star of David. 2** any of several plants of N temperate regions, having greenish or yellow paired flowers, long narrow waxy leaves, and prominent leaf scars. ORIG C16: translation of Med. L *sigillum Solomonis,* ?from resemblance of the leaf scars to seals

Solon ★ ('səʊlən) *n* ?638–?559 B.C., Athenian statesman, who introduced economic, political, and legal reforms.
▸ **Solonian** (səʊ'ləʊnɪən) *or* **Solonic** (səʊ'lɒnɪk) *adj*

so long *sentence substitute.* **1** *Inf.* farewell; goodbye. ◆ *adv* **2** *S. African sl.* for the time being; meanwhile.

Solothurn ★ (*German* 'zoːloturn) *n* **1** a canton of NW Switzerland. Capital: Solothurn. Pop.: 237 338 (1995 est.). Area: 793 sq. km (306 sq. miles). **2** a town in NW Switzerland, capital of Solothurn canton, on the Aare River. Pop.: 15 480 (1990 est.). ◆ French name: **Soleure.**

solo whist *n* a version of whist for four players acting independently, each of whom may bid to win or lose a fixed number of tricks.

solstice ('sɒlstɪs) *n* **1** either the shortest day of the year (**winter solstice**) or the longest day of the year (**summer solstice**). **2** either of the two points on the ecliptic at which the sun is overhead at the tropic of Cancer or Capricorn at the summer and winter solstices. ORIG C13: via OF from L *sōlstitium,* lit.: the (apparent) standing still of the sun, from *sōl* sun + *sistere* to stand still
▸ **solstitial** (sɒl'stɪʃəl) *adj*

Solti ★ ('ʃɒltɪ) *n* Sir **Georg** ('geːɔrk). 1912–97, British conductor, born in Hungary.

soluble ('sɒljubᵊl) *adj* **1** (of a substance) capable of being dissolved, esp. easily dissolved. **2** capable of being solved or answered. ORIG C14: from LL *solūbilis,* from L *solvere* to dissolve
▸ ˌ**solu'bility** *n* ▸ '**solubly** *adv*

solus ('səʊləs) *adj* **1** alone; separate. **2** of or denoting the position of an advertising poster or press advertisement that is separated from competing advertisements: *a solus position.* **3** of or denoting a retail outlet, such as a petrol station, that sells the products of one company exclusively: *a solus site.* **4** (*fem* **sola**) alone; by oneself (formerly used in stage directions). ORIG C17: from L *sōlus* alone

solute ('sɒljuːt) *n* **1** the substance in a solution that is dissolved. ◆ *adj* **2** *Bot.* loose or unattached; free. ORIG C16: from L *solūtus* free, from *solvere* to release

solution (sə'luːʃən) *n* **1** a homogeneous mixture of two or more substances in which the molecules or atoms of the substances are completely dispersed. **2** the act or process of forming a solution. **3** the state of being dissolved (esp. in **in solution**). **4** a mixture of substances in which one or more components are present as small particles with colloidal dimension: *a colloidal solution.* **5** a specific answer to or way of answering a problem. **6** the act or process of solving a problem. **7** *Maths.* **7a** the unique set of values that yield a true statement when substituted for the variables in an equation. **7b** a member of a set of assignments of values to variables under which a given statement is satisfied; a member of a solution set. ORIG C14: from L *solūtiō* an unloosing, from *solūtus;* see SOLUTE

solution set *n* another name for **truth set.**

Solutrean (sə'luːtrɪən) *adj* of or relating to an Upper Palaeolithic culture of Europe. ORIG C19: after *Solutré,* village in central France where traces of this culture were orig. found

solvation (sɒl'veɪʃən) *n* the process in which there is some chemical association between the molecules of a solute and those of the solvent.

Solvay process ('sɒlveɪ) *n* an industrial process for manufacturing sodium carbonate. Carbon dioxide is passed into a solution of sodium chloride saturated with ammonia. Sodium bicarbonate is precipitated and heated to form the carbonate. ORIG C19: after Ernest *Solvay* (1838–1922), Belgian chemist who invented it

solve (sɒlv) *vb* **solves, solving, solved.** (*tr*) **1** to find the explanation for or solution to (a mystery, problem, etc.). **2** *Maths.* **2a** to work out the answer to (a problem). **2b** to obtain the roots of (an equation). ORIG C15: from L *solvere* to loosen
▸ '**solvable** *adj*

solvent ('sɒlvənt) *adj* **1** capable of meeting financial obligations. **2** (of a substance, esp. a liquid) capable of dissolving another substance. ◆ *n* **3** a liquid capable of dissolving another substance. **4** something that solves. ORIG C17: from L *solvēns* releasing, from *solvere* to free
▸ '**solvency** *n*

solvent abuse *n* the deliberate inhaling of intoxicating fumes given off by certain solvents.

Solway Firth ★ ('sɒlweɪ) *n* an inlet of the Irish Sea between SW Scotland and NW England. Length: about 56 km (35 miles).

Solyman ★ ('sɒlɪmən) *n* a variant spelling of **Suleiman I.**

Solzhenitsyn ★ (*Russian* səlʒə'nitsin; ˌsɒlʒə'nɪtsɪn) *n* **Alexander Isayevich** (alɪk'sandr i'sajɪvitʃ). born 1918, Russian novelist. His books include *One Day in the Life of Ivan Denisovich* (1962), *Cancer Ward* (1968), and *The Gulag Archipelago* (1974). Critical of the Soviet regime, he was imprisoned (1945–53), exiled to Siberia (1953–56), and deported to the West (1974). He returned to Russia in 1994. Nobel prize for literature 1970.

Som. *abbrev. for* Somerset.

soma[1] ★ ('səumə) *n, pl* **somata** (-mətə) *or* **somas.** the body of an organism, as distinct from the germ cells. ORIG C19: via NL from Gk *sōma* the body

soma[2] ('səumə) *n* an intoxicating plant juice drink used in Vedic rituals. ORIG from Sansk.

Somali (səu'mɑːlɪ) *n* **1** (*pl* **Somalis** *or* **Somali**) a member of a tall dark-skinned people inhabiting Somalia. **2** the Cushitic language of this people. ◆ *adj* **3** of, relating to, or characteristic of Somalia, the Somalis, or their language.

Somalia ★ (səu'mɑːlɪə) *n* a republic in NE Africa, on the Indian Ocean and the Gulf of Aden: the north became a British protectorate in 1884; the east and south were established as an Italian protectorate in 1889; gained independence and united as the Somali Republic in 1960. In 1991 the former British Somaliland region in the north unilaterally declared itself independent but this was not officially recognized. Factional fighting has continued. Official languages: Arabic and Somali. Official religion: (Sunni) Muslim. Currency: Somali shilling. Capital: Mogadishu. Pop.: 7 141 000 (1999 est.). Area: 637 541 sq. km (246 154 sq. miles).
▸ **So'malian** *adj, n*

Somaliland ★ (səu'mɑːlɪˌlænd) *n* a former region of E Africa, between the equator and the Gulf of Aden: includes Somalia, Djibouti, and SE Ethiopia.

somatic (səu'mætɪk) *adj* **1** of or relating to the soma: *somatic cells.* **2** of or relating to an animal body or body wall as distinct from the viscera, limbs, and head. **3** of or relating to the human body as distinct from the mind: *a somatic disease.* ORIG C18: from Gk *sōmatikos* concerning the body, from *sōma* the body
▸ **so'matically** *adv*

somato- *or before a vowel* **somat-** *combining form.* body: *somatotype.* ORIG from Gk *sōma, sōmat-* body

somatogenic (səˌmætəu'dʒɛnɪk) *adj Med.* originating in the cells of the body: of organic, rather than mental, origin: *a somatogenic disorder.*

somatotype ('səumətəˌtaɪp) *n* a type or classification of physique or body build. See **endomorph, mesomorph, ectomorph.**

sombre *or US* **somber** ('sɒmbə) *adj* **1** dismal; melancholy: *a sombre mood.* **2** dim, gloomy, or shadowy. **3** (of colour, clothes, etc.) sober, dull, or dark. ORIG C18: from F, from Vulgar L *subumbrāre* (unattested) to shade, from L *sub* beneath + *umbra* shade
▸ **'sombrely** *or US* **'somberly** *adv* ▸ **'sombreness** *or US* **'somberness** *n* ▸ **sombrous** ('sɒmbrəs) *adj*

sombrero (sɒm'brɛərəu) *n, pl* **sombreros.** a hat with a wide brim, as worn in Mexico. ORIG C16: from Sp., from *sombrero de sol* shade from the sun

some (sʌm; *unstressed* səm) *determiner* **1a** (a) certain unknown or unspecified: *some people never learn.* **1b** (*as pron; functioning as sing or pl*): *some can teach and others can't.* **2a** an unknown or unspecified quantity or amount of: *there's some rice on the table; he owns some horses.* **2b** (*as pron; functioning as sing or pl*): *we'll buy some.* **3a** a considerable number or amount of: *he lived some years afterwards.* **3b** a little: *show him some respect.* **4** (*usually stressed*) *Inf.* an impressive or remarkable: *that was some game!* ◆ *adv* **5** about; approximately: *some thirty pounds.* **6** a certain amount (more) (in **some more** and (*inf.*) **and then some**). **7** *US, not standard.* to a certain degree or extent: *I like him some.* ORIG OE *sum*

-some[1] *suffix forming adjectives.* characterized by; tending to: *awesome; tiresome.* ORIG OE *-sum*

-some[2] *suffix forming nouns.* indicating a group of a specified number of members: *threesome.* ORIG OE *sum,* special use of SOME (determiner)

-some[3] (-səum) *n combining form.* a body: *chromosome.* ORIG from Gk *sōma* body

somebody ('sʌmbədɪ) *pron* **1** some person; someone. ◆ *n, pl* **somebodies. 2** a person of great importance: *he is somebody in this town.*

> **USAGE NOTE** See at **everyone.**

someday ('sʌmˌdeɪ) *adv* at some unspecified time in the (distant) future.

somehow ('sʌmˌhau) *adv* **1** in some unspecified way. **2** Also: **somehow or other.** by any means that are necessary.

someone ('sʌmˌwʌn, -wən) *pron* some person; somebody.

> **USAGE NOTE** See at **everyone.**

someplace ('sʌmˌpleɪs) *adv US & Canad. inf.* in, at, or to some unspecified place or region.

somersault *or* **summersault** ('sʌməˌsɔːlt) *n* **1a** a forward roll in which the head is placed on the ground and the trunk and legs are turned over it. **1b** a similar roll in a backward direction. **2** an acrobatic feat in which either of these rolls is performed in midair, as in diving or gymnastics. **3** a complete reversal of opinion, policy, etc. ◆ *vb* **4** (*intr*) to perform a somersault. ORIG C16: from OF *soubresault,* prob. from OProvençal *sobresaut,* from *sobre* over (from L *super*) + *saut* a jump, leap (from L *saltus*)

Somerset[1] ★ ('sʌməsɪt, -ˌsɛt) *n* a county of SW England, on the Bristol Channel; includes the unitary authorities of North Somerset and Bath and North East Somerset. The Mendip Hills lie in the north and Exmoor in the west; mainly agricultural (esp. dairying and fruit). Administrative centre: Taunton. Pop. (excluding North Somerset and Bath and North East Somerset): 482 700 (1996 est.). Area (excluding North Somerset and Bath and North East Somerset): 3452 sq. km (1332 sq. miles).

Somerset[2] ★ ('sʌməsɛt) *n* **1st Duke of,** title of *Edward Seymour.* ?1500–52, English statesman, protector of England (1547–49) during Edward VI's minority. He defeated the Scots (1547) and furthered the Protestant Reformation: executed.

something ('sʌmθɪŋ) *pron* **1** an unspecified or unknown thing; some thing: *take something warm with you.* **2 something or other.** one unspecified thing or an alternative thing. **3** an unspecified or unknown amount: *something less than a hundred.* **4** an impressive or important person, thing, or event: *isn't that something?* ◆ *adv* **5** to some degree; a little; somewhat: *to look something like me.* **6** (foll. by an *adj*) *Inf.* (intensifier): *it hurts something awful.* **7 something else.** *Sl., chiefly US.* a remarkable person or thing.

-something *n combining form.* **a** a person whose age can be approximately expressed by a specified decade. **b** (*as modifier*): *the thirtysomething market.* ORIG C20: from the US television series *thirtysomething*

sometime ('sʌmˌtaɪm) *adv* **1** at some unspecified point of time. ◆ *adj* **2** (*prenominal*) having been at one time; former: *the sometime President.*

> **USAGE NOTE** *Sometime* as a single word should only be used to refer to an unspecified point in time. When referring to a considerable length of time, you should use *some time.* Compare: *it was some time after, that the rose garden was planted,* i.e. after a considerable period of time, with *it was sometime after, that the rose garden was planted,* i.e. at some unspecified point after the move, but not necessarily a long time after.

sometimes ('sʌmˌtaɪmz) *adv* **1** now and then; from time to time. **2** *Obs.* formerly; sometime.

someway ('sʌmˌweɪ) *adv* in some unspecified manner.

somewhat ('sʌmˌwɒt) *adv* (*not used with a negative*) rather; a bit: *she found it somewhat odd.*

somewhere ('sʌmˌwɛə) *adv* **1** in, to, or at some unknown or unspecified place or point: *somewhere in England; somewhere between 3 and 4 o'clock.* **2 get somewhere.** *Inf.* to make progress.

Somme ★ (*French* sɔm) *n* **1** a department of N France, in Picardy region. Capital: Amiens. Pop.: 552 398 (1994 est.). Area: 6277 sq. km (2448 sq. miles). **2** a river in N France, rising in Aisne department and flowing west to Amiens, then northwest to the English Channel: scene of heavy fighting in World War I. Length: 245 km (152 miles).

sommelier (ˈsʌməlˌjeɪ) *n* a wine waiter. ORIG F: butler, via OF from OProvençal *saumalier* pack-animal driver, from LL *sagma* a packsaddle, from Gk

somnambulate (sɒmˈnæmbjʊˌleɪt) *vb* **somnambulates, somnambulating, somnambulated.** (*intr*) to walk while asleep. ORIG C19: from L *somnus* sleep + *ambulāre* to walk
▸ **somˈnambulance** *n* ▸ **somˈnambulant** *adj, n* ▸ **somˌnambuˈlation** *n* ▸ **somˈnambuˌlator** *n*

somnambulism (sɒmˈnæmbjʊˌlɪzəm) *n* a condition characterized by walking while asleep or in a hypnotic trance. Also called: **noctambulism.**
▸ **somˈnambulist** *n*

somniferous (sɒmˈnɪfərəs) *or* **somnific** *adj Rare.* tending to induce sleep.

somnolent (ˈsɒmnələnt) *adj* **1** drowsy; sleepy. **2** causing drowsiness. ORIG C15: from L *somnus* sleep
▸ **ˈsomnolence** *or* **ˈsomnolency** *n* ▸ **ˈsomnolently** *adv*

Somnus ★ (ˈsɒmnəs) *n* the Roman god of sleep. Greek counterpart: **Hypnos.**

son (sʌn) *n* **1** a male offspring; a boy or man in relation to his parents. **2** a male descendant. **3** (*often cap.*) a familiar term of address for a boy or man. **4** a male from a certain country, environment, etc.: *a son of the circus.* ◆ Related adj: **filial.** ORIG OE *sunu*
▸ **ˈsonless** *adj*

Son (sʌn) *n Christianity.* the second person of the Trinity, Jesus Christ.

sonant (ˈsəʊnənt) *adj* **1** *Phonetics.* denoting a voiced sound capable of forming a syllable or syllable nucleus. **2** inherently possessing, exhibiting, or producing a sound. **3** *Rare.* resonant; sounding. ◆ *n* **4** *Phonetics.* a voiced sound belonging to the class of frictionless continuants or nasals (l, r, m, n, ŋ) considered from the point of view of being a vowel and, in this capacity, able to form a syllable or syllable nucleus. ORIG C19: from L *sonāns* sounding, from *sonāre* to make a noise, resound
▸ **ˈsonance** *n*

sonar (ˈsəʊnɑː) *n* a communication and position-finding device used in underwater navigation and target detection using echolocation. ORIG C20: from *so(und) na(vigation and) r(anging)*

sonata (səˈnɑːtə) *n* **1** an instrumental composition, usually in three or more movements, for piano alone (**piano sonata**) or for any other instrument with or without piano accompaniment (**violin sonata, cello sonata,** etc.). See also **sonata form. 2** a one-movement keyboard composition of the baroque period. ORIG C17: from It., from *sonare* to sound, from L

sonata form *n* a musical structure consisting of an expanded ternary form whose three sections (exposition, development, and recapitulation), followed by a coda, are characteristic of the first movement in a sonata, symphony, string quartet, concerto, etc.

sondage (sɒnˈdɑːʒ) *n, pl* **sondages** (-ˈdɑːʒɪz, -ˈdɑːʒ). *Archaeol.* a deep trial trench for inspecting stratigraphy. ORIG C20: from F: a sounding, from *sonder* to sound

sonde (sɒnd) *n* a rocket, balloon, or probe used for observing in the upper atmosphere. ORIG C20: from F: plummet, plumb line; see SOUND[3]

Sondheim ★ (ˈsɒndhaɪm) *n* **Stephen** (**Joshua**). born 1930, US songwriter. He wrote the lyrics for *West Side Story* (1957), the score for *Company* (1971), and both for *Into the Woods* (1987).

sone (səʊn) *n* a unit of loudness equal to 40 phons. ORIG C20: from L *sonus* a sound

son et lumière (ˈsɒn eɪ ˈluːmɪˌɛə) *n* an entertainment staged at night at a famous building, historical site, etc., whereby the history of the location is presented by means of lighting effects, sound effects, and narration. ORIG F, lit.: sound and light

song (sɒŋ) *n* **1a** a piece of music, usually employing a verbal text, composed for the voice, esp. one intended for performance by a soloist. **1b** the whole repertory of such pieces. **1c** (*as modifier*): *a song book.* **2** poetical composition; poetry. **3** the characteristic tuneful call or sound made by certain birds or insects. **4** the act or process of singing: *they raised their voices in song.* **5 for a song.** at a bargain price. **6 on song.** *Brit. inf.* performing at peak efficiency or ability. ORIG OE *sang*

Song ★ (sʊŋ) *n* the Pinyin transliteration of the Chinese name for **Sung.**

song and dance *n Inf.* **1** *Brit.* a fuss, esp. one that is unnecessary. **2** *US & Canad.* a long or elaborate story or explanation.

songbird (ˈsɒŋˌbɜːd) *n* **1** any of a suborder of passerine birds having highly developed vocal organs and, in most, a musical call. **2** any bird having a musical call.

song cycle *n* any of several groups of songs written during and after the Romantic period, each series relating a story or grouped around a central motif.

Songhua ★ (ˈsʌŋˈwɑː) *n* a river in NE China, rising in SE Jilin province and flowing north and northeast to the Amur River near Tongjiang: the chief river of Manchuria and largest tributary of the Amur; frozen from November to April. Length: over 1300 km (800 miles). Also called: **Sungari.**

Song Koi *or* **Song Coi** ★ (ˈsɒŋ ˈkɔɪ) *n* transliteration of the Vietnamese name for the **Red River** (sense 3).

songololo (ˌsɒŋgɒˈlɒlɒ) *n, pl* **songololos.** *S. African.* a millipede. ORIG from Nguni, from *ukusonga* to roll up

songster (ˈsɒŋstə) *n* **1** a singer or poet. **2** a singing bird; songbird.
▸ **ˈsongstress** *fem n*

song thrush *n* a common Old World thrush with a spotted breast, noted for its song.

songwriter (ˈsɒŋˌraɪtə) *n* a person who composes songs in a popular idiom.

sonic (ˈsɒnɪk) *adj* **1** of, involving, or producing sound. **2** having a speed about equal to that of sound in air. ORIG C20: from L *sonus* sound

sonic barrier *n* another name for **sound barrier.**

sonic boom *n* a loud explosive sound caused by the shock wave of an aircraft, etc., travelling at supersonic speed.

sonic depth finder *n* an instrument for detecting the depth of water or of a submerged object by means of sound waves; Fathometer.

sonics (ˈsɒnɪks) *n* (*functioning as sing*) *Physics.* the study of mechanical vibrations in matter.

son-in-law *n, pl* **sons-in-law.** the husband of one's daughter.

sonnet (ˈsɒnɪt) *Prosody.* ◆ *n* **1** a verse form consisting of 14 lines in iambic pentameter with a fixed rhyme scheme, usually divided into octave and sestet or, in the English form, into three quatrains and a couplet. ◆ *vb* **2** (*intr*) to compose sonnets. **3** (*tr*) to celebrate in a sonnet. ORIG C16: via It. from OProvençal *sonet* a little poem, from *son* song, from L *sonus* a sound

sonneteer (ˌsɒnɪˈtɪə) *n* a writer of sonnets.

sonny (ˈsʌnɪ) *n, pl* **sonnies.** *Often patronizing.* a familiar term of address to a boy or man.

sonobuoy (ˈsəʊnəˌbɔɪ) *n* a buoy equipped to detect underwater noises and transmit them by radio. ORIG SONIC + BUOY

Son of Man ★ *n Bible.* a title of Jesus Christ.

sonoluminescence (ˌsəʊnəʊˌluːmɪˈnɛsəns) *n* luminescence produced by ultrasound.

Sonora ★ (*Spanish* soˈnora) *n* a state of NW Mexico, on the Gulf of California: consists of a narrow coastal plain rising inland to the Sierra Madre Occidental; an important mining area in colonial times. Capital: Hermosillo. Pop.: 2 183 108 (1997 est.). Area: 184 934 sq. km (71 403 sq. miles).

sonorant (ˈsɒnərənt) *n Phonetics.* **1** one of the frictionless continuants or nasals (l, r, m, n, ŋ) having consonantal or vocalic functions depending on its situation within the syllable. **2** either of the two consonants represented in English orthography by *w* or *y* and regarded as either consonantal or vocalic articulations of the vowels (iː) and (uː).

sonorous (səˈnɔːrəs, ˈsɒnərəs) *adj* **1** producing or capable

of producing sound. **2** (of language, sound, etc.) deep or resonant. **3** (esp. of speech) high-flown; grandiloquent. ORIG C17: from L *sonōrus* loud, from *sonor* a noise
▸ **sonority** (səˈnɒrɪtɪ) *n* ▸ **soˈnorously** *adv* ▸ **soˈnorousness** *n*

sonsy *or* **sonsie** (ˈsɒnsɪ) *adj* **sonsier, sonsiest.** *Scot., Irish, & English dialect.* **1** plump; buxom. **2** cheerful; good-natured. **3** lucky. ORIG C16: from Gaelic *sonas* good fortune

Sontag ★ (ˈsɒntæg) *n* **Susan.** born 1933, US intellectual and essayist, noted esp. for her writings on modern culture. Her works include "Notes on Camp" (1964), *On Photography* (1977), *Illness as Metaphor* (1979), and *The Volcano Lover* (1992).

Soo Canals ★ (suː) *pl n* **the.** the two ship canals linking Lakes Superior and Huron. There is a canal on the Canadian and on the US side of the rapids of the St Mary's River. See also **Sault Sainte Marie.**

Soochow ★ (ˈsuːˈtʃaʊ) *n* a variant transliteration of the Chinese name for **Suzhou.**

sook (sʊk) *n* **1** *SW English dialect.* a baby. **2** *Derog.* a coward. ORIG ?from OE *sūcan* to suck, infl. by Welsh *swci swead* tame

sool (suːl) *vb* (*tr*) *Austral. & NZ sl.* **1** to incite (esp. a dog) to attack. **2** to attack.
▸ **ˈsooler** *n*

soon (suːn) *adv* **1** in or after a short time; in a little while; before long. **2 as soon as.** at the very moment that: *as soon as she saw him.* **3 as soon ... as.** used to indicate that the second alternative is not preferable to the first: *I'd just as soon go by train as drive.* ORIG OE *sōna*

sooner (ˈsuːnə) *adv* **1** the comparative of **soon:** *he came sooner than I thought.* **2** rather; in preference: *I'd sooner die than give up.* **3 no sooner ... than.** immediately after or when: *no sooner had he got home than the rain stopped.* **4 sooner or later.** eventually; inevitably.

> **USAGE NOTE** *When* is sometimes used instead of *than* after *no sooner*, but this use is generally regarded as incorrect: *no sooner had he arrived than* (not *when*) *the telephone rang.*

Soong *or* **Song** ★ (sʊŋ) *n* an influential Chinese family, notably **Soong Ch'ing-ling** (1890–1981), who married **Sun Yat-sen** and became a vice-chairman of the People's Republic of China (1959); and **Soong Mei-ling** (born 1898), who married **Chiang Kai-shek.**

soot (sʊt) *n* **1** finely divided carbon deposited from flames during the incomplete combustion of organic substances such as coal. ◆ *vb* **2** (*tr*) to cover with soot. ORIG OE *sōt*

sooth (suːθ) *Arch. or poetic.* ◆ *n* **1** truth or reality (esp. in **in sooth**). ◆ *adj* **2** true or real. ORIG OE *sōth*

soothe (suːð) *vb* **soothes, soothing, soothed. 1** (*tr*) to make calm or tranquil. **2** (*tr*) to relieve or assuage (pain, longing, etc.). **3** (*intr*) to bring tranquillity or relief. ORIG C16 (in the sense: to mollify): from OE *sōthian* to prove
▸ **ˈsoother** *n* ▸ **ˈsoothing** *adj* ▸ **ˈsoothingly** *adv* ▸ **ˈsoothingness** *n*

soothsayer (ˈsuːθˌseɪə) *n* a seer or prophet.

sooty (ˈsʊtɪ) *adj* **sootier, sootiest. 1** covered with soot. **2** resembling or consisting of soot.
▸ **ˈsootily** *adv* ▸ **ˈsootiness** *n*

sop (sɒp) *n* **1** (*often pl*) food soaked in a liquid before being eaten. **2** a concession, bribe, etc., given to placate or mollify: *a sop to one's feelings.* **3** *Inf.* a stupid or weak person. ◆ *vb* **sops, sopping, sopped. 4** (*tr*) to dip or soak (food) in liquid. **5** (when *intr*, often foll. by *in*) to soak or be soaked. **6** (*tr*; often foll. by *up*) to mop or absorb (liquid) as with a sponge. ORIG OE *sopp*

SOP *abbrev. for* standard operating procedure.

sop. *abbrev. for* soprano.

Soper ★ (ˈsəʊpə) *n* **Donald (Oliver),** Baron. 1903–98, British Methodist minister and publicist, noted esp. for his pacifist convictions.

Sophia ★ (səʊˈfaɪə) *n* 1630–1714, electress of Hanover (1658–1714), in whom the Act of Settlement (1701) vested the English Crown. She was a granddaughter of James I of England and her son became George I of Great Britain and Ireland.

sophism (ˈsɒfɪzəm) *n* an instance of sophistry. Cf. **paralogism.** ORIG C14: from L *sophisma,* from Gk: ingenious trick, from *sophizesthai* to use clever deceit, from *sophos* wise

sophist (ˈsɒfɪst) *n* **1** a person who uses clever or quibbling but unsound arguments. **2** one of the pre-Socratic philosophers who were prepared to enter into debate on any subject however specious. ORIG C16: from L *sophista,* from Gk *sophistēs* a wise man, from *sophizesthai* to act craftily

sophistic (səˈfɪstɪk) *or* **sophistical** *adj* **1** of or relating to sophists or sophistry. **2** consisting of sophisms or sophistry; specious.
▸ **soˈphistically** *adv*

sophisticate *vb* (səˈfɪstɪˌkeɪt), **sophisticates, sophisticating, sophisticated. 1** (*tr*) to make (someone) less natural or innocent, as by education. **2** to pervert or corrupt (an argument, etc.) by sophistry. **3** (*tr*) to make more complex or refined. **4** *Rare.* to falsify (a text, etc.) by alterations. ◆ *n* (səˈfɪstɪˌkeɪt, -kɪt). **5** a sophisticated person. ORIG C14: from Med. L *sophisticāre,* from L *sophisticus* sophistic
▸ **soˌphistiˈcation** *n* ▸ **soˈphistiˌcator** *n*

sophisticated (səˈfɪstɪˌkeɪtɪd) *adj* **1** having refined or cultured tastes and habits. **2** appealing to sophisticates: *a sophisticated restaurant.* **3** unduly refined or cultured. **4** pretentiously or superficially wise. **5** (of machines, methods, etc.) complex and refined.

sophistry (ˈsɒfɪstrɪ) *n, pl* **sophistries. 1a** a method of argument that is seemingly plausible though actually invalid and misleading. **1b** the art of using such arguments. **2** subtle but unsound or fallacious reasoning. **3** an instance of this.

Sophocles ★ (ˈsɒfəˌkliːz) *n* ?496–406 B.C., Greek dramatist; author of seven extant tragedies, including *Oedipus Rex, Electra,* and *Oedipus at Colonus.*
▸ **Sophoclean** (ˌsɒfəˈkliːən) *adj*

sophomore (ˈsɒfəˌmɔː) *n Chiefly US & Canad.* a second-year student at a secondary (high) school or college. ORIG C17: ?from earlier *sophumer,* from *sophum,* var. of SOPHISM, + -ER[1]

Sophy *or* **Sophi** (ˈsəʊfɪ) *n, pl* **Sophies.** (formerly) a title of the Persian monarchs. ORIG C16: from L *sophī* wise men, from Gk *sophos* wise

-sophy *n combining form.* indicating knowledge or an intellectual system: *philosophy.* ORIG from Gk, from *sophia* wisdom, from *sophos* wise
▸ **-sophic** *or* **-sophical** *adj combining form.*

soporific (ˌsɒpəˈrɪfɪk) *adj also* (*arch.*) **ˌsoporˈiferous. 1** inducing sleep. **2** drowsy; sleepy. ◆ *n* **3** a drug or other agent that induces sleep. ORIG C17: from F, from L *sopor* sleep + -FIC

sopping (ˈsɒpɪŋ) *adj* completely soaked; wet through. Also: **sopping wet.**

soppy (ˈsɒpɪ) *adj* **soppier, soppiest. 1** wet or soggy. **2** *Brit. inf.* silly or sentimental. **3 soppy on.** *Brit. inf.* foolishly charmed or affected by.
▸ **ˈsoppily** *adv* ▸ **ˈsoppiness** *n*

sopranino (ˌsɒprəˈniːnəʊ) *n, pl* **sopraninos. a** the instrument with the highest possible pitch in a family of instruments. **b** (*as modifier*): *a sopranino recorder.* ORIG It., dim. of SOPRANO

soprano (səˈprɑːnəʊ) *n, pl* **sopranos** *or* **soprani** (-ˈprɑːniː). **1** the highest adult female voice. **2** the voice of a young boy before puberty. **3** a singer with such a voice. **4** the highest part of a piece of harmony. **5a** the highest or second highest instrument in a family of instruments. **5b** (*as modifier*): *a soprano saxophone.* ◆ See also **treble.** ORIG C18: from It., from *sopra* above, from L *suprā*

soprano clef *n* the clef that establishes middle C as being on the bottom line of the staff.

Sopwith ★ (ˈsɒpwɪθ) *n* Sir **Thomas Octave Murdoch.** 1888–1989, British aircraft designer, who built the Sopwith

Camel biplane used during World War I. He was chairman (1935–63) of the Hawker Siddeley Group, which developed the Hurricane fighter and Lancaster bomber.

Sorata ★ (*Spanish* so'rata) *n* **Mount.** a mountain in W Bolivia, in the Andes: the highest mountain in the Cordillera Real, with two peaks, Ancohuma, 6550 m (21 490 ft), and Illampu, 6485 m (21 276 ft).

sorb (sɔːb) *n* **1** another name for **service tree. 2** any of various related trees, esp. the mountain ash. **3** Also called: **sorb apple.** the fruit of any of these trees. ORIG C16: from L *sorbus*

sorbefacient (ˌsɔːbɪ'feɪʃənt) *adj* **1** inducing absorption. ♦ *n* **2** a sorbefacient drug. ORIG C19: from L *sorbē(re)* to absorb + -FACIENT

sorbet ('sɔːbeɪ, -bɪt) *n* **1** a water ice made from fruit juice, egg whites, etc. **2** a US word for **sherbet** (sense 1). ORIG C16: from F, from OIt. *sorbetto,* from Turkish *şerbet,* from Ar. *sharbah* a drink

sorbic acid ('sɔːbɪk) *n* a white crystalline carboxylic acid found in berries of the mountain ash and used to inhibit the growth of moulds and as an additive (**E 200**) for certain synthetic coatings. ORIG C19: from SORB (the tree), from its discovery in berries of the mountain ash

sorbitol ('sɔːbɪˌtɒl) *n* a white crystalline alcohol, found in certain fruits and berries and manufactured by the catalytic hydrogenation of sucrose: used as a sweetener (**E 420**) and in the manufacture of ascorbic acid and synthetic resins. ORIG C19: from SORB + -ITOL

Sorbonne ★ (*French* sɔrbɔn) *n* **the.** a part of the University of Paris containing the faculties of science and literature: founded in 1253 by Robert de Sorbon as a theological college; given to the university in 1808.

sorbo rubber ('sɔːbəʊ) *n Brit.* a spongy form of rubber. ORIG C20: from ABSORB

sorcerer ('sɔːsərə) *or* (*fem*) **sorceress** ('sɔːsərɪs) *n* a person who seeks to control and use magic powers; a wizard or magician. ORIG C16: from OF *sorcier,* from Vulgar L *sortiārius* (unattested) caster of lots, from L *sors* lot

sorcery ('sɔːsərɪ) *n, pl* **sorceries.** the art, practices, or spells of magic, esp. black magic. ORIG C13: from OF *sorcerie,* from *sorcier* SORCERER

sordid ('sɔːdɪd) *adj* **1** dirty, foul, or squalid. **2** degraded; vile; base. **3** selfish and grasping: *sordid avarice.* ORIG C16: from L *sordidus,* from *sordēre* to be dirty
▸ **'sordidly** *adv* ▸ **'sordidness** *n*

sordino (sɔː'diːnəʊ) *n, pl* **sordini** (-niː). **1** a mute for a stringed or brass musical instrument. **2** any of the dampers in a piano. **3 con sordino** *or* **sordini.** a musical direction to play with a mute. **4 senza sordino** *or* **sordini.** a musical direction to remove or play without the mute or (on the piano) with the sustaining pedal pressed down. ORIG It.: from *sordo* deaf, from L *surdus*

sore (sɔː) *adj* **1** (esp. of a wound, injury, etc.) painfully sensitive; tender. **2** causing annoyance: *a sore point.* **3** resentful; irked. **4** urgent; pressing: *in sore need.* **5** (*postpositive*) grieved; distressed. **6** causing grief or sorrow. ♦ *n* **7** a painful or sensitive wound, injury, etc. **8** any cause of distress or vexation. ♦ *adv* **9** *Arch.* direly; sorely (now only in such phrases as **sore afraid**). ORIG OE *sār*
▸ **'soreness** *n*

sorehead ('sɔːˌhɛd) *n Inf., chiefly US & Canad.* a peevish or disgruntled person.

sorely ('sɔːlɪ) *adv* **1** painfully or grievously: *sorely wounded.* **2** pressingly or greatly: *to be sorely taxed.*

sorghum ('sɔːgəm) *n* any grass of the Old World genus *Sorghum,* having glossy seeds: cultivated for grain, hay, and as a source of syrup. ORIG C16: from NL, from It. *sorgo,* prob. from Vulgar L *Syricum grānum* (unattested) Syrian grain

Sorocaba ★ (*Portuguese* soro'kaba) *n* a city in S Brazil, in São Paulo state: industrial centre. Pop.: 348 952 (1991).

soroptimist (sə'rɒptɪmɪst) *n* a member of Soroptimist International, an organization of clubs for professional and executive businesswomen.

sororal (sə'rɔːrəl) *adj* of or relating to a sister or sisters. ORIG C17: from L *soror* sister

sorority (sə'rɒrɪtɪ) *n, pl* **sororities.** *Chiefly US.* a social club or society for university women. ORIG C16: from Med. L *sorōritās,* from L *soror* sister

sorption ('sɔːpʃən) *n* the process in which one substance takes up or holds another; adsorption or absorption. ORIG C20: back formation from ABSORPTION, ADSORPTION

sorrel[1] ('sɒrəl) *n* **1a** a light brown to brownish-orange colour. **1b** (*as adj*): *a sorrel carpet.* **2** a horse of this colour. ORIG C15: from OF *sorel,* from *sor* a reddish brown, of Gmc origin

sorrel[2] ('sɒrəl) *n* **1** any of several plants of Eurasia and North America, having acid-tasting leaves used in salads and sauces. **2** short for **wood sorrel.** ORIG C14: from OF *surele,* from *sur* sour, of Gmc origin

Sorrento ★ (sə'rɛntəʊ; *Italian* sor'rɛnto) *n* a port in SW Italy, in Campania on a mountainous peninsula between the Bay of Naples and the Gulf of Salerno: a resort since Roman times. Pop.: 17 500 (1990).

sorrow ('sɒrəʊ) *n* **1** the feeling of sadness, grief, or regret associated with loss, bereavement, sympathy for another's suffering, etc. **2** a particular cause or source of this. **3** Also called: **sorrowing.** the outward expression of grief or sadness. ♦ *vb* **4** (*intr*) to mourn or grieve. ORIG OE *sorg*
▸ **'sorrowful** *adj* ▸ **'sorrowfully** *adv* ▸ **'sorrowfulness** *n*

sorry ('sɒrɪ) *adj* **sorrier, sorriest. 1** (*usually postpositive;* often foll. by *for*) feeling or expressing pity, sympathy, grief, or regret: *I feel sorry for him.* **2** pitiful, wretched, or deplorable: *a sorry sight.* **3** poor; paltry: *a sorry excuse.* **4** affected by sorrow; sad. **5** causing sorrow or sadness. ♦ *interj* **6** an exclamation expressing apology. ORIG OE *sārig*
▸ **'sorrily** *adv* ▸ **'sorriness** *n*

sort (sɔːt) *n* **1** a class, group, kind, etc., as distinguished by some common quality or characteristic. **2** *Inf.* a type of character, nature, etc.: *he's a good sort.* **3** *Austral. sl.* a person, esp. a girl. **4** a more or less definable or adequate example: *it's a sort of review.* **5** (*often pl*) *Printing.* any of the individual characters making up a fount of type. **6** *Arch.* manner; way: *in this sort we struggled home.* **7 after a sort.** to some extent. **8 of sorts** *or* **of a sort. 8a** of an inferior kind. **8b** of an indefinite kind. **9 out of sorts.** not in normal good health, temper, etc. **10 sort of.** in some way or other; as it were; rather. ♦ *vb* **11** (*tr*) to arrange according to class, type, etc. **12** (*tr*) to put (something) into working order. **13** to arrange (computer information) by machine in an order convenient to the user. **14** (*intr*) *Arch.* to agree; accord. ORIG C14: from OF, from Med. L *sors* kind, from L: fate
▸ **'sortable** *adj* ▸ **'sorter** *n*

USAGE NOTE See at **kind**[2].

sortie ('sɔːtɪ) *n* **1a** (of troops, etc.) the act of attacking from a contained or besieged position. **1b** the troops doing this. **2** an operational flight made by one aircraft. **3** a short or relatively short return trip. ♦ *vb* **sorties, sortieing, sortied. 4** (*intr*) to make a sortie. ORIG C17: from F: a going out, from *sortir* to go out

sortilege ('sɔːtɪlɪdʒ) *n* the act or practice of divination by drawing lots. ORIG C14: via OF from Med. L *sortilegium,* from L *sortilegus* a soothsayer, from *sors* fate + *legere* to select

sort out *vb* (*tr, adv*) **1** to find a solution to (a problem, etc.), esp. to make clear or tidy: *to sort out the mess.* **2** to take or separate, as from a larger group: *to sort out the likely ones.* **3** to organize into an orderly and disciplined group. **4** *Inf.* to beat or punish.

SOS *n* **1** an internationally recognized distress signal in which the letters SOS are repeatedly spelt out, as by radiotelegraphy: used esp. by ships and aircraft. **2** a message broadcast in an emergency for people otherwise unobtainable. **3** *Inf.* a call for help.

sosatie (sə'sɑːtɪ) *n S. African.* curried meat on skewers. ORIG from Afrik., from Du.

Sosnowiec ★ (*Polish* sɔs'nɔvjɛts) *n* an industrial town in S Poland. Pop.: 248 900 (1995 est.).

so-so *Inf.* ◆ *adj* **1** (*postpositive*) neither good nor bad. ◆ *adv* **2** in an average or indifferent manner.

sostenuto (ˌsɒstəˈnuːtəʊ) *adj, adv Music.* to be performed in a smooth sustained manner. ORIG C18: from It., from *sostenere* to sustain, from L *sustinēre*

sot (sɒt) *n* **1** a habitual or chronic drunkard. **2** a person stupefied by or as if by drink. ORIG OE, from Med. L *sottus*
▸ ˈ**sottish** *adj*

soteriology (sɒˌtɪərɪˈɒlədʒɪ) *n Christian theol.* the doctrine of salvation. ORIG C19: from Gk *sōtēria* deliverance (from *sōtēr* a saviour) + -LOGY

Soto ★ (ˈsəʊtəʊ; *Spanish* ˈsoto) *n* See (Hernando) **De Soto.**

sotto voce (ˈsɒtəʊ ˈvəʊtʃɪ) *adv* in an undertone. ORIG C18: from It.: under (one's) voice

sou (suː) *n* **1** a former French coin of low denomination. **2** a very small amount of money: *I haven't a sou.* ORIG C19: from F, from OF *sol,* from L: SOLIDUS

soubrette (suːˈbrɛt) *n* **1** a minor female role in comedy, often that of a pert lady's maid. **2** any pert or flirtatious girl. ORIG C18: from F: maidservant, from Provençal, from *soubret* conceited, from *soubra* to exceed, from L *superāre* to surmount

soubriquet (ˈsəʊbrɪˌkeɪ) *n* a variant spelling of **sobriquet.**

Soudan ★ (sudɑ̃) *n* the French name for the **Sudan.**

soufflé (ˈsuːfleɪ) *n* **1** a light fluffy dish made with beaten egg whites combined with cheese, fish, etc. **2** a similar sweet or savoury cold dish, set with gelatine. ◆ *adj also* **souffléed. 3** made light and puffy, as by beating and cooking. ORIG C19: from F, from *souffler* to blow, from L *sufflāre*

Soufrière ★ (*French* sufrjɛr) *n* **1** a volcano in the Caribbean, on N St Vincent: erupted in 1902, killing about 2000 people. Height: 1234 m (4048 ft). **2** a volcano in the Caribbean, on S Montserrat: the highest point on the island: erupted in 1997 killing 19 people and destroying the island's capital. Height: 915 m (3002 ft). **3** a volcano in the Caribbean, on Guadeloupe. Height: 1484 m (4869 ft).

sough (saʊ) *vb* **1** (*intr*) (esp. of the wind) to make a sighing sound. ◆ *n* **2** a soft continuous murmuring sound. ORIG OE *swōgan* to resound

sought (sɔːt) *vb* the past tense and past participle of **seek.**

souk (suːk) *n* an open-air marketplace in Muslim countries, esp. North Africa and the Middle East. ORIG from Ar.

soukous (ˈsuːkʊs) *n* a style of African popular music that originated in Zaïre (now the Democratic Republic of Congo), characterized by syncopated rhythms and intricate contrasting guitar melodies. ORIG C20: ? from F *secouer* to shake

soul (səʊl) *n* **1** the spirit or immaterial part of man, the seat of human personality, intellect, will, and emotions: regarded as an entity that survives the body after death. **2** *Christianity.* the spiritual part of a person, capable of redemption from sin through divine grace. **3** the essential part or fundamental nature of anything. **4** a person's feelings or moral nature. **5a** Also called: **soul music.** a type of Black music resulting from the addition of jazz, gospel, and pop elements to the urban blues style. **5b** (*as modifier*): *a soul singer.* **6** (*modifier*) of or relating to Black Americans and their culture: *soul food.* **7** nobility of spirit or temperament: *a man of great soul.* **8** an inspiring or leading figure, as of a movement. **9** a person regarded as typifying some characteristic or quality: *the soul of discretion.* **10** a person; individual: *an honest soul.* **11 upon my soul!** an exclamation of surprise. ORIG OE *sāwol*

soul-destroying *adj* (of an occupation, situation, etc.) unremittingly monotonous.

soul food *n Inf.* food, such as chitterlings, yams, etc., traditionally eaten by African-Americans.

soulful (ˈsəʊlfʊl) *adj* expressing profound thoughts or feelings.
▸ ˈ**soulfully** *adv* ▸ ˈ**soulfulness** *n*

soulless (ˈsəʊllɪs) *adj* **1** lacking humanizing qualities or influences; mechanical: *soulless work.* **2** (of a person) lacking in sensitivity or nobility.
▸ ˈ**soullessness** *n*

★ people and places

soul mate *n* a person for whom one has a deep affinity, esp. a lover, wife, husband, etc.

soul-searching *n* **1** deep or critical examination of one's motives, actions, beliefs, etc. ◆ *adj* **2** displaying the characteristics of this.

sound[1] (saʊnd) *n* **1a** a periodic disturbance in the pressure or density of a fluid or in the elastic strain of a solid, produced by a vibrating object. It travels as longitudinal waves. **1b** (*as modifier*): *a sound wave.* **2** the sensation produced by such a periodic disturbance in the organs of hearing. **3** anything that can be heard. **4** (*modifier*) of or relating to radio as distinguished from television: *sound broadcasting.* **5** a particular instance or type of sound: *the sound of running water.* **6** volume or quality of sound: *a radio with poor sound.* **7** the area or distance over which something can be heard: *within the sound of Big Ben.* **8** impression or implication: *I don't like the sound of that.* **9** (*often pl*) *Sl.* music, esp. rock, jazz, or pop. ◆ *vb* **10** to cause (an instrument, etc.) to make a sound or (of an instrument, etc.) to emit a sound. **11** to announce or be announced by a sound: *to sound the alarm.* **12** (*intr*) (of a sound) to be heard. **13** (*intr*) to resonate with a certain quality or intensity: *to sound loud.* **14** (*copula*) to give the impression of being as specified: *to sound reasonable.* **15** (*tr*) to pronounce distinctly or audibly: *to sound one's consonants.* ORIG C13: from OF *soner* to make a sound, from L *sonāre,* from *sonus* a sound
▸ ˈ**soundable** *adj*

sound[2] (saʊnd) *adj* **1** free from damage, injury, decay, etc. **2** firm; substantial: *a sound basis.* **3** financially safe or stable: *a sound investment.* **4** showing good judgment or reasoning; wise: *sound advice.* **5** valid, logical, or justifiable: *a sound argument.* **6** holding approved beliefs; ethically correct; honest. **7** (of sleep) deep; peaceful; unbroken. **8** thorough: *a sound examination.* ◆ *adv* **9** soundly; deeply: now archaic except when applied to sleep. ORIG OE *sund*
▸ ˈ**soundly** *adv* ▸ ˈ**soundness** *n*

sound[3] (saʊnd) *vb* **1** to measure the depth of (a well, the sea, etc.) by plumb line, sonar, etc. **2** to seek to discover (someone's views, etc.), as by questioning. **3** (*intr*) (of a whale, etc.) to dive downwards swiftly and deeply. **4** *Med.* **4a** to probe or explore (a bodily cavity or passage) by means of a sound. **4b** to examine (a patient) by means of percussion and auscultation. ◆ *n* **5** *Med.* an instrument for insertion into a bodily cavity or passage to dilate strictures, dislodge foreign material, etc. ◆ See also **sound out.** ORIG C14: from OF *sonder,* from *sonde* sounding line, prob. of Gmc origin
▸ ˈ**sounder** *n*

sound[4] (saʊnd) *n* **1** a relatively narrow channel between two larger areas of sea or between an island and the mainland. **2** an inlet or deep bay of the sea. **3** the air bladder of a fish. ORIG OE *sund* swimming, narrow sea

Sound ★ (saʊnd) *n* **the.** a strait between SW Sweden and Sjælland (Denmark), linking the Kattegat with the Baltic: busy shipping lane. Length: 113 km (70 miles). Narrowest point: 5 km (3 miles). Swedish and Danish name: **Øresund.**

soundalike (ˈsaʊndəˌlaɪk) *n* **a** a person or thing that sounds like another, often well-known, person or thing. **b** (*as modifier*): *a soundalike band.*

sound barrier *n* (not in technical usage) a hypothetical barrier to flight at or above the speed of sound, when a sudden large increase in drag occurs. Also called: **sonic barrier.**

sound bite *n* a short pithy sentence or phrase extracted from a longer speech for use on radio or television.

soundbox (ˈsaʊndˌbɒks) *n* the resonating chamber of the hollow body of a violin, guitar, etc.

sound effect *n* any sound artificially produced, reproduced from a recording, etc., to create a theatrical effect, as in plays, films, etc.

sounding[1] (ˈsaʊndɪŋ) *adj* **1** resounding; resonant. **2** having an imposing sound and little content; pompous: *sounding phrases.*

sounding[2] (ˈsaʊndɪŋ) *n* **1** (*sometimes pl*) the act or process of measuring depth of water or examining the bottom of a river, lake, etc., as with a sounding line. **2** an observation or measurement of atmospheric conditions, as made using a sonde. **3** (*often pl*) measurements taken by sounding. **4** (*pl*) a place where a sounding line will reach the bottom, esp. less than 100 fathoms in depth.

sounding board *n* **1** Also called: **soundboard.** a thin wooden board in a violin, piano, etc., serving to amplify the vibrations produced by the strings passing across it. **2** Also called: **soundboard.** a thin screen suspended over a pulpit, stage, etc., to reflect sound towards an audience. **3** a person, group, experiment, etc., used to test a new idea, policy, etc.

sounding line *n* a line marked off to indicate its length and having a **sounding lead** at one end. It is dropped over the side of a vessel to determine the depth of the water.

soundless ('saʊndlɪs) *adj* extremely still or silent.
▸ **'soundlessness** *n*

sound out *vb* (*tr, adv*) to question (someone) in order to discover (opinions, facts, etc.).

soundpost ('saʊnd,pəʊst) *n Music.* a small wooden post in guitars, violins, etc., that joins the front to the back and helps support the bridge.

soundproof ('saʊnd,pru:f) *adj* **1** not penetrable by sound. ◆ *vb* **2** (*tr*) to render soundproof.

sound spectrograph *n* an electronic instrument that produces a record (**sound spectrogram**) of the frequencies and intensities of the components of a sound.

sound system *n* **1** any system of sounds, as in the speech of a language. **2** integrated equipment for producing amplified sound, as in a hi-fi or mobile disco, or as a public-address system on stage.

soundtrack ('saʊnd,træk) *n* **1** the recorded sound accompaniment to a film. **2** a narrow strip along the side of a spool of film, which carries the sound accompaniment.

sound wave *n* a wave that propagates sound.

Souness ★ ('su:nɪs) *n* **Graeme.** born 1953, Scottish football player and manager.

soup (su:p) *n* **1** a liquid food made by boiling or simmering meat, fish, vegetables, etc. **2** *Inf.* a photographic developer. **3** *Inf.* anything resembling soup, esp. thick fog. **4** a slang name for **nitroglycerine. 5 in the soup.** *Sl.* in trouble or difficulties. ORIG C17: from OF *soupe,* from LL *suppa,* of Gmc origin
▸ **'soupy** *adj*

soupçon *French.* (supsɔ̃) *n* a slight amount; dash. ORIG C18: from F, ult. from L *suspicio* SUSPICION

Souphanouvong ★ (,su:fænu:'vɒŋ) *n* **Prince.** 1902–95, Laotian statesman; president of Laos (1975–86).

soup kitchen *n* **1** a place or mobile stall where food and drink, esp. soup, is served to destitute people. **2** *Mil.* a mobile kitchen.

soup plate *n* a deep plate with a wide rim, used esp. for drinking soup.

soup up *vb* (*tr, adv*) *Sl.* to modify the engine of (a car or motorcycle) in order to increase its power. Also: **hot up,** (esp. US and Canad.) **hop up.**

sour ('saʊə) *adj* **1** having or denoting a sharp biting taste like that of lemon juice or vinegar. **2** made acid or bad, as in the case of milk, by the action of microorganisms. **3** having a rancid or unwholesome smell. **4** (of a person's temperament) sullen, morose, or disagreeable. **5** (esp. of the weather) harsh and unpleasant. **6** disagreeable; distasteful: *a sour experience.* **7** (of land, etc.) lacking in fertility, esp. due to excessive acidity. **8** (of petrol, gas, etc.) containing a relatively large amount of sulphur compounds. **9 go** *or* **turn sour.** to become unfavourable or inharmonious: *his marriage went sour.* ◆ *n* **10** something sour. **11** *Chiefly US.* an iced drink usually made with spirits, lemon juice, and ice: *a whiskey sour.* **12** an acid used in bleaching clothes or in curing skins. ◆ *vb* **13** to make or become sour. ORIG OE *sūr*
▸ **'sourish** *adj* ▸ **'sourly** *adv* ▸ **'sourness** *n*

Sour ★ (sʊə) *n* a variant spelling of **Sur.**

source (sɔ:s) *n* **1** the point or place from which something originates. **2a** a spring that forms the starting point of a stream. **2b** the area where the headwaters of a river rise. **3** a person, group, etc., that creates, issues, or originates something: *the source of a complaint.* **4a** any person, book, organization, etc., from which information, evidence, etc., is obtained. **4b** (*as modifier*): *source material.* **5** anything, such as a story or work of art, that provides a model or inspiration for a later work. **6 at source.** at the point of origin. ◆ *vb* **sources, sourcing, sourced.** (*tr*) **7** to establish an originator or source of (a product, etc.). **8** (foll. by *from*) to originate from. ORIG C14: from OF *sors,* from *sourdre* to spring forth, from L *surgere* to rise

source program *n* an original computer program written by a programmer that is converted into the equivalent object program, written in machine language.

sour cherry *n* **1** a Eurasian tree with white flowers: cultivated for its tart red fruits. **2** the fruit.

sour cream *n* cream soured by lactic acid bacteria, used in making salads, dips, etc.

sourdough ('saʊə,dəʊ) *Dialect.* ◆ *adj* **1** (of bread) made with fermented dough used as leaven. ◆ *n* **2** (in the Western US, Canada, and Alaska) an old-time prospector or pioneer.

sour gourd *n* **1** a large tree of N Australia, having gourdlike fruit. **2** the acid-tasting fruit. **3** the fruit of the baobab tree.

sour grapes *n* (*functioning as sing*) the attitude of affecting to despise something because one cannot have it oneself.

sourpuss ('saʊə,pʊs) *n Inf.* a person who is habitually gloomy or sullen.

sourveld ('saʊə,fɛlt) *n* (in South Africa) a type of grazing characterized by long coarse grass. ORIG from Afrik. *suur* sour + *veld* grassland

Sousa ★ ('su:zə) *n* **John Philip.** 1854–1932, US composer of military marches, such as *The Stars and Stripes Forever* (1897).

sousaphone ('su:zə,fəʊn) *n* a large tuba that encircles the player's body and has a bell facing forwards. ORIG C20: after J. P. SOUSA
▸ **'sousa,phonist** *n*

souse (saʊs) *vb* **souses, sousing, soused. 1** to plunge (something) into water or other liquid. **2** to drench or be drenched. **3** (*tr*) to pour or dash (liquid) over (a person or thing). **4** to steep or cook (food) in a marinade. **5** (*tr*) *Sl.* to make drunk. ◆ *n* **6** the liquid used in pickling. **7** the act or process of sousing. **8** *Sl.* a drunkard. ORIG C14: from OF *sous,* of Gmc origin

Sousse (su:s), **Susa,** *or* **Susah** ★ *n* a port in E Tunisia, on the Mediterranean: founded by the Phoenicians in the 9th century B.C. Pop.: 125 000 (1994). Ancient name: **Hadrumetum** (,hædrə'mi:təm).

soutane (su:'tæn) *n RC Church.* a priest's cassock. ORIG C19: from F, from OIt. *sottana,* from Med. L *subtanus* (adj) (worn) beneath, from L *subtus* below

souterrain ('su:tə,reɪn) *n Archaeol.* an underground chamber or passage. ORIG C18: from F

south (saʊθ) *n* **1** one of the four cardinal points of the compass, at 180° from north and 90° clockwise from east and anticlockwise from west. **2** the direction along a meridian towards the South Pole. **3 the south.** (*often cap.*) any area lying in or towards the south. **4** (*usually cap.*) *Cards.* the player or position corresponding to south on the compass. ◆ *adj* **5** in, towards, or facing the south. **6** (esp. of the wind) from the south. ◆ *adv* **7** in, to, or towards the south. ORIG OE *sūth*

South (saʊθ) *n* **the. 1** the southern part of England, generally regarded as lying to the south of an imaginary line between the Wash and the Severn. **2** (in the US) **2a** the states south of the Mason-Dixon Line that formed the Confederacy during the Civil War. **2b** the Confederacy itself. **3** the countries of the world that are not economically and technically advanced. ◆ *adj* **4** of or denoting the southern part of a specified country, area, etc.

South Africa ★ *n* **Republic of.** a republic occupying the southernmost part of the African continent: the Dutch Cape Colony (1652) was acquired by Britain in 1806 and British victory in the Boer War resulted in the formation

of the Union of South Africa in 1910, which became a republic in 1961; implementation of the apartheid system began in 1948 and was abolished, following an intense civil rights campaign, in 1993 with multiracial elections held in 1994; a member of the Commonwealth, it withdrew in 1961 because of opposition to apartheid but was re-admitted in 1994: mainly plateau with mountains in the south and east. Mineral production includes gold, diamonds, coal, and copper. Official languages: Afrikaans; English; Ndebele, Pedi; South Sotho; Swazi; Tsonga; Tswana; Venda; Xhosa; Zulu. Religion: chiefly Christian. Currency: rand. Capitals: Cape Town (legislative), Pretoria (administrative), Bloemfontein (judicial). Pop.: 43 426 000 (1999 est.). Area: 1 221 044 sq. km (471 445 sq. miles). Former name (1910–61): **Union of South Africa.**
▸ **South African** *adj, n*

South America ★ *n* the fourth largest of the continents, bordering on the Caribbean in the north, the Pacific in the west, and the Atlantic in the east and joined to Central America by the Isthmus of Panama. It is dominated by the Andes Mountains, which extend over 7250 km (4500 miles) and include many volcanoes; ranges from dense tropical jungle, desert, and temperate plains to the cold wet windswept region of Tierra del Fuego. It comprises chiefly developing countries undergoing great changes. Pop.: 317 846 000 (1996). Area: 17 816 600 sq. km (6 879 000 sq. miles).
▸ **South American** *adj, n*

Southampton ★ (sauθ'æmptən, -'hæmp-) *n* **1** a port in S England, in Hampshire on **Southampton Water** (an inlet of the English Channel): chief English passenger port; seat of The University of Southampton (1952); shipyards and oil refinery. Pop.: 210 138 (1991). **2** a unitary authority in S England, in Hampshire. Pop.: 214 900 (1996 est.). Area: 49 sq. km (19 sq. miles).

Southampton Island ★ *n* an island in N Canada, in the Northwest Territories at the entrance to Hudson Bay: inhabited chiefly by Inuit. Area: 49 470 sq. km (19 100 sq. miles).

South Arabia ★ *n* **Federation of.** the former name (1959–67) of **South Yemen** (excluding Aden).
▸ **South Arabian** *adj, n*

South Australia ★ *n* a state of S central Australia, on the Great Australian Bight: generally arid, with the Great Victoria Desert in the west central part, the Lake Eyre basin in the northeast, and the Flinders Ranges, Murray River basin, and salt lakes in the southeast. Capital: Adelaide. Pop.: 1 427 936 (1996). Area: 984 395 sq. km (380 070 sq. miles).
▸ **South Australian** *adj, n*

South Ayrshire ★ *n* a council area of SW Scotland. Administrative centre: Ayr. Pop.: 114 440 (1999 est.). Area: 1202 sq. km (464 sq. miles).

South Bend ★ *n* a city in the US, N Indiana: university (1842). Pop.: 105 092 (1994 est.).

southbound ('sauθˌbaund) *adj* going or leading towards the south.

south by east *n* **1** one point on the compass east of south. ◆ *adj, adv* **2** in, from, or towards this direction.

south by west *n* **1** one point on the compass west of south. ◆ *adj, adv* **2** in, from, or towards this direction.

South Carolina ★ *n* a state of the southeastern US, on the Atlantic: the first state to secede from the Union in 1860; consists largely of low-lying coastal plains, rising in the northwest to the Blue Ridge Mountains; the largest US textile producer. Capital: Columbia. Pop.: 3 835 962 (1998 est.). Area: 78 282 sq. km (30 225 sq. miles). Abbrev. (and zip code): **SC**
▸ **South Carolinian** *adj, n*

South China Sea ★ *n* part of the Pacific surrounded by SE China, Vietnam, the Malay Peninsula, Borneo, and the Philippines.

Southcott ★ ('sauθkɒt) *n* **Joanna.** 1750–1814, British religious fanatic, who claimed that she would give birth to the second Messiah.

South Dakota ★ *n* a state of the western US: lies mostly in the Great Plains; the chief US producer of gold and beryl. Capital: Pierre. Pop.: 738 171 (1998 est.). Area: 196 723 sq. km (75 955 sq. miles). Abbrevs.: **S. Dak.** or (with zip code) **SD**
▸ **South Dakotan** *adj, n*

Southdown ('sauθˌdaun) *n* an English breed of sheep with short wool and a greyish-brown face and legs. ORIG C18: so called because it was originally bred on the SOUTH DOWNS

South Downs ★ *pl n* a range of low hills in S England, extending from E Hampshire to East Sussex.

southeast (ˌsauθ'iːst; *Naut.* ˌsau'iːst) *n* **1** the point of the compass or the direction midway between south and east. **2** (*often cap.*; usually preceded by *the*) any area lying in or towards this direction. ◆ *adj also* **southeastern. 3** (*sometimes cap.*) of or denoting the southeastern part of a specified country, area, etc. **4** in, towards, or facing the southeast. **5** (esp. of the wind) from the southeast. ◆ *adv* **6** in, to, or towards the southeast.
▸ **ˌsouth'easternmost** *adj*

Southeast ★ (ˌsauθ'iːst) *n* (usually preceded by *the*) the southeastern part of Britain, esp. the London area.

Southeast Asia ★ *n* a region including Brunei, Cambodia, Indonesia, Laos, Malaysia, Myanmar, the Philippines, Thailand, and Vietnam.
▸ **Southeast Asian** *adj, n*

southeast by east *n* **1** one point on the compass north of southeast. ◆ *adj, adv* **2** in, from, or towards this direction.

southeast by south *n* **1** one point on the compass south of southeast. ◆ *adj, adv* **2** in, from, or towards this direction.

southeaster (ˌsauθ'iːstə; *Naut.* ˌsau'iːstə) *n* a strong wind or storm from the southeast.

southeasterly (ˌsauθ'iːstəlɪ; *Naut.* ˌsau'iːstəlɪ) *adj, adv* **1** in, towards, or (esp. of the wind) from the southeast. ◆ *n, pl* **southeasterlies. 2** a strong wind or storm from the southeast.

southeastward (ˌsauθ'iːstwəd; *Naut.* ˌsau'iːstwəd) *adj* **1** towards or (esp. of a wind) from the southeast. ◆ *n* **2** a direction towards or area in the southeast. ◆ *adv* **3** Also: **southeastwards.** towards the southeast.

Southend-on-Sea ★ (ˌsauθ'ɛnd-) *n* **1** a town in SE England, in SE Essex, on the Thames estuary: one of England's largest resorts, extending for about 11 km (7 miles) along the coast. Pop.: 158 517 (1991). **2** a unitary authority in SE England, in SE Essex. Pop.: 175 500 (1997 est.). Area: 42 sq. km (16 sq. miles).

souther ('sauðə) *n* a strong wind or storm from the south.

southerly ('sʌðəlɪ) *adj* **1** of or situated in the south. ◆ *adv, adj* **2** towards the south. **3** from the south. ◆ *n, pl* **southerlies. 4** a wind from the south.
▸ **'southerliness** *n*

southern ('sʌðən) *adj* **1** in or towards the south. **2** (of a wind, etc.) coming from the south. **3** native to or inhabiting the south.
▸ **'southernˌmost** *adj*

Southern ('sʌðən) *adj* of, relating to, or characteristic of the south of a particular region or country.

Southern Alps ★ *pl n* a mountain range in New Zealand, on South Island: the highest range in Australasia. Highest peak: Mount Cook, 3764 m (12 349 ft).

Southern Cross *n* a small constellation in the S hemisphere whose four brightest stars form a cross. It is represented on the national flags of Australia and New Zealand.

Southerner ('sʌðənə) *n* (*sometimes not cap.*) a native or inhabitant of the south of any specified region, esp. the South of England or the Southern states of the US.

southern hemisphere *n* (*often caps.*) that half of the earth lying south of the equator.

Southern Ireland ★ *n* See **Ireland**[1] (sense 2).

southern lights *pl n* another name for **aurora australis.**

Southern Ocean ★ *n* another name for the **Antarctic Ocean.**

Southern Rhodesia ★ *n* the former name (until 1964) of **Zimbabwe**.
▸ **Southern Rhodesian** *adj, n*

Southern Uplands ★ *pl n* a hilly region extending across S Scotland: includes the Lowther, Moorfoot, and Lammermuir hills.

Southey ★ ('sauðɪ, 'sʌðɪ) *n* **Robert**. 1774–1843, British poet; poet laureate (1813–43).

South Georgia ★ *n* an island in the S Atlantic, about 1300 km (800 miles) southeast of the Falkland Islands; a United Kingdom overseas territory. Area: 3755 sq. km (1450 sq. miles).
▸ **South Georgian** *adj*

South Glamorgan ★ *n* a former county of S Wales, created in 1974 and replaced by two county boroughs in 1996.

South Gloucestershire ★ *n* a unitary authority of SW England, in Gloucestershire. Pop.: 235 100 (1996 est.). Area: 510 sq. km (197 sq. miles).

South Holland ★ *n* a province of the SW Netherlands, on the North Sea: lying mostly below sea level, it has a coastal strip of dunes and is drained chiefly by distributaries of the Rhine, with large areas of reclaimed land; the most densely populated province in the country, intensively cultivated and industrialized. Capital: The Hague. Pop.: 3 344 700 (1997 est.). Area: 3196 sq. km (1234 sq. miles). Dutch name: **Zuidholland**.

southing ('sauðɪŋ) *n* **1** *Navigation*. movement, deviation, or distance covered in a southerly direction. **2** *Astron*. a south or negative declination.

South Island ★ *n* **the**. the largest island of New Zealand, separated from the North Island by Cook Strait. Pop.: 926 350 (1996). Area: 153 947 sq. km (59 439 sq. miles).

South Korea ★ *n* a republic in NE Asia: established as a republic in 1948; invaded by North Korea and Chinese Communists in 1950 but division remained unchanged at the end of the war (1953); includes over 3000 islands; rapid industrialization. Language: Korean. Religions: Buddhist, Christian, Confucianist, Shamanist, and Chondokyo. Currency: won. Capital: Seoul. Pop.: 46 858 000 (1999 est.). Area: 98 477 sq. km (38 022 sq. miles). Korean name: **Hanguk**.
▸ **South Korean** *adj, n*

South Lanarkshire ★ *n* a council area of S Scotland. Administrative centre: Hamilton. Pop.: 307 450 (1996 est.). Area: 1771 sq. km (684 sq. miles).

South Orkney Islands ★ *pl n* a group of islands in the S Atlantic, southeast of Cape Horn: formerly a dependency of the Falkland Islands; part of British Antarctic Territory since 1962. Area: 621 sq. km (240 sq. miles).

South Ossetia ★ (ə'si:ʃən) *n* an administrative division of Georgia, on the S slopes of the Caucasus Mountains. Capital: Tskhinvali. Pop.: 99 800 (1990). Area: 3900 sq. km (1500 sq. miles). Official name: **Tskhinvali**.

southpaw ('sauθ,pɔ:) *Inf*. ◆ *n* **1** a left-handed boxer. **2** any left-handed person. ◆ *adj* **3** of or relating to a southpaw.

South Pole ★ *n* **1** the southernmost point on the earth's axis, at the latitude of 90°S. **2** *Astron*. the point of intersection of the earth's extended axis and the southern half of the celestial sphere. **3** (*usually not caps*.) the south-seeking pole of a freely suspended magnet.

Southport ★ ('sauθ,pɔ:t) *n* a town and resort in NW England, in Merseyside on the Irish Sea. Pop.: 90 959 (1991).

South Saskatchewan ★ *n* a river in S central Canada, rising in S Alberta and flowing east and northeast to join the North Saskatchewan River, forming the Saskatchewan River. Length: 1392 km (865 miles).

South Sea Bubble *n Brit. history*. the financial crash that occurred in 1720 after the **South Sea Company** had taken over the national debt in return for a monopoly of trade with the South Seas, causing feverish speculation in their stocks.

South Sea Islands ★ *pl n* the islands in the S Pacific.

South Seas ★ *pl n* the seas south of the equator.

South Shetland Islands ★ *pl n* a group of islands in the S Atlantic, north of the Antarctic Peninsula: formerly a dependency of the Falkland Islands; part of British Antarctic Territory since 1962. Area: 4662 sq. km (1800 sq. miles).

South Shields ★ *n* a port in NE England, in Tyne and Wear on the Tyne estuary opposite North Shields. Pop.: 83 704 (1991).

south-southeast *n* **1** the point on the compass or the direction midway between southeast and south. ◆ *adj, adv* **2** in, from, or towards this direction.

south-southwest *n* **1** the point on the compass or the direction midway between south and southwest. ◆ *adj, adv* **2** in, from, or towards this direction.

South Tyneside ★ *n* a unitary authority of NE England, in Tyne and Wear. Pop.: 156 100 (1996 est.). Area: 64 sq. km (25 sq. miles).

South Tyrol *or* **Tirol** ★ *n* a former part of the Austrian state of Tyrol: ceded to Italy in 1919, becoming the Bolzano and Trento provinces of the Trentino-Alto Adige Autonomous Region. Area: 14 037 sq. km (5420 sq. miles).

South Vietnam ★ *n* a former republic (1955–76) occupying the S of present-day Vietnam, on the South China Sea and the Gulf of Siam.
▸ **South Vietnamese** *adj, n*

southward ('sauθwəd; *Naut*. 'sʌðəd) *adj* **1** situated, directed, or moving towards the south. ◆ *n* **2** the southward part, direction, etc. ◆ *adv* **3** Also: **southwards**. towards the south.

Southwark ★ ('sʌðək) *n* a borough of S central Greater London, on the River Thames: site of the Globe Theatre; docks and warehouses. Pop.: 228 800 (1994 est.). Area: 29 sq. km (11 sq. miles).

Southwell ★ ('sauθwɛl) *n* **Saint Robert**. ?1561–95, English poet and Roman Catholic martyr, who was imprisoned, tortured, and executed for his Jesuit activities. His best known poem is "The Burning Babe".

southwest (,sauθ'wɛst; *Naut*. ,sau'wɛst) *n* **1** the point of the compass or the direction midway between west and south. **2** (*often cap*.; usually preceded by *the*) any area lying in or towards this direction. ◆ *adj also* **southwestern**. **3** (*sometimes cap*.) of or denoting the southwestern part of a specified country, area, etc.: *southwest Italy*. **4** in or towards the southwest. **5** (esp. of the wind) from the southwest. ◆ *adv* **6** in, to, or towards the southwest.
▸ **,south'westernmost** *adj*

Southwest ★ (,sauθ'wɛst) *n* (usually preceded by *the*) the southwestern part of Britain, esp. Cornwall, Devon, and Somerset.

South West Africa ★ *n* another name for **Namibia**.

southwest by south *n* **1** one point on the compass south of southwest. ◆ *adj, adv* **2** in, from, or towards this direction.

southwest by west *n* **1** one point on the compass north of southwest. ◆ *adj, adv* **2** in, from, or towards this direction.

southwester (,sauθ'wɛstə; *Naut*. ,sau'wɛstə) *n* a strong wind or storm from the southwest.

southwesterly (,sauθ'wɛstəlɪ; *Naut*. ,sau'wɛstəlɪ) *adj, adv* **1** in, towards, or (esp. of a wind) from the southwest. ◆ *n, pl* **southwesterlies**. **2** a wind or storm from the southwest.

southwestward (,sauθ'wɛstwəd; *Naut*. ,sau'wɛstwəd) *adj* **1** from or towards the southwest. ◆ *adv* **2** Also: **southwestwards**. towards the southwest. ◆ *n* **3** a direction towards or area in the southwest.

South Yemen ★ *n* a former republic (1967–90) in SW Arabia, on the Gulf of Aden: now part of Yemen. Official name: **People's Democratic Republic of Yemen**. Name from 1963 to 1967 (excluding Aden): Federation of **South Arabia**. See also **Yemen, North Yemen**.

South Yorkshire ★ *n* a metropolitan county of N England, administered since 1986 by the unitary authorities of Barnsley, Doncaster, Sheffield, and Rotherham. Area: 1560 sq. km (602 sq. miles).

★ people and places

Soutine ★ (*French* sutin) *n* **Chaim** ('xaɪɪm). 1893–1943, French expressionist painter, born in Russia.

souvenir (ˌsuːvəˈnɪə, ˈsuːvəˌnɪə) *n* **1** an object that recalls a certain place, occasion, or person; memento. **2** *Rare.* a thing recalled. ◆ *vb* **3** (*tr*) *Austral.* & *NZ. sl.* to steal or keep for one's own use; purloin. ORIG C18: from F, from (*se*) *souvenir* to remember, from L *subvenīre* to come to mind

sou'wester (sauˈwɛstə) *n* a waterproof hat having a very broad rim behind, worn esp. by seamen. ORIG C19: a contraction of SOUTHWESTER

sovereign (ˈsɒvrɪn) *n* **1** a person exercising supreme authority, esp. a monarch. **2** a former British gold coin worth one pound sterling. ◆ *adj* **3** supreme in rank or authority: *a sovereign lord.* **4** excellent or outstanding: *a sovereign remedy.* **5** of or relating to a sovereign. **6** independent of outside authority: *a sovereign state.* ORIG C13: from OF *soverain,* from Vulgar L *superānus* (unattested), from L *super* above; also infl. by REIGN
▸ ˈ**sovereignly** *adv*

sovereigntist (ˈsɒvrəntɪst) (in Canada) ◆ *n* **1** a supporter of sovereignty association. ◆ *adj* **2** supporting sovereignty association.

sovereignty (ˈsɒvrəntɪ) *n, pl* **sovereignties. 1** supreme and unrestricted power, as of a state. **2** the position, dominion, or authority of a sovereign. **3** an independent state.

sovereignty association *n* (in Canada) a proposed arrangement by which Quebec would become independent but would maintain a formal association with Canada.

Sovetsk ★ (*Russian* saˈvjetsk) *n* a town in W Russia, in the Kaliningrad Region on the Neman River: scene of the signing of the treaty (1807) between Napoleon I and Tsar Alexander I; passed from East Prussia to the Soviet Union in 1945 and to Russia in 1991. Former name (until 1945): **Tilsit.**

soviet (ˈsəuvɪət, ˈsɒv-) *n* **1** (in the former Soviet Union) an elected government council at the local, regional, and national levels, culminating in the Supreme Soviet. ◆ *adj* **2** of or relating to a soviet. ORIG C20: from Russian *sovyet* council, from ORussian sŭvětŭ
▸ ˈ**savieˌtism** *n*

Soviet (ˈsəuvɪət, ˈsɒv-) *adj* of or relating to the former Soviet Union, its people, or its government.

Soviet Central Asia ★ *n* (formerly) the region of the Soviet Union now occupied by Kazakhstan, Kyrgyzstan, Tajikistan, Turkmenistan, and Uzbekistan. Also called: **Russian Turkestan, West Turkestan.**

sovietize *or* **sovietise** (ˈsəuvɪɪˌtaɪz, ˈsɒv-) *vb* **sovietizes, sovietizing, sovietized** *or* **sovietises, sovietising, sovietised.** (*tr*) (*often cap.*) **1** to bring (a country, person, etc.) under Soviet control or influence. **2** to cause (a country) to conform to the Soviet model in its social, political, and economic structure.
▸ ˌ**sovietiˈzation** *or* ˌ**sovietiˈsation** *n*

Soviet Russia ★ *n* (formerly) another name for the **Russian Soviet Federative Socialist Republic** or the **Soviet Union.**

Soviets (ˈsəuvɪəts, ˈsɒv-) *pl n* the people or government of the former Soviet Union.

Soviet Union ★ *n* a former federal republic in E Europe and central and N Asia: established in 1922 as a Communist state, following the revolution of 1917; dissolved at the end of 1991, following the collapse of Communist Party rule earlier in that year and the declarations of independence by many of the constituent republics. Area: 22 402 202 sq. km (8 649 489 sq. miles). Official name: **Union of Soviet Socialist Republics.** Also called: **Russia, Soviet Russia.** Abbrev.: **USSR.**

Soviet Zone ★ *n* that part of Germany occupied by the Soviet forces in 1945–49: transformed into the German Democratic Republic in 1949–50. Also called: **Russian Zone.**

sow[1] (səu) *vb* **sows, sowing, sowed; sown** *or* **sowed. 1** to scatter or place (seed, a crop, etc.) in or on (a piece of ground, field, etc.) so that it may grow: *to sow wheat; to sow a strip of land.* **2** (*tr*) to implant or introduce: *to sow a doubt in someone's mind.* ORIG OE *sāwan*
▸ ˈ**sower** *n*

sow[2] (sau) *n* **1** a female adult pig. **2** the female of certain other animals, such as the mink. **3** *Metallurgy.* **3a** the channels for leading molten metal to the moulds in casting pig iron. **3b** iron that has solidified in these channels. ORIG OE *sugu*

Soweto ★ (səˈwɛtəu, -ˈweɪtəu) *n* a contiguous group of Black African townships southwest of Johannesburg, South Africa: the largest purely Black African urban settlement in southern Africa: scene of riots (1976) following protests against the use of Afrikaans in schools for Black African children. Area: 62 sq. km (24 sq. miles). Pop.: 596 632 (1991). ORIG C20: from *so(uth) we(st) to(wnship)*

sown (səun) *vb* a past participle of **sow**[1].

sow thistle (sau) *n* any of various plants of an Old World genus, having milky juice, prickly leaves, and heads of yellow flowers.

soya bean (ˈsɔɪə) *or US & Canad.* **soybean** (ˈsɔɪˌbiːn) *n* **1** an Asian bean plant cultivated for its nutritious seeds, for forage, and to improve the soil. **2** the seed, used as food, forage, and as the source of an oil. ORIG C17 *soya,* via Du. from Japanese *shōyu,* from Chinese *chiang yu,* from *chiang* paste + *yu* sauce

Soyinka ★ (sɔˈjɪŋkə) *n* **Wole** (ˈwoːle). born 1934, Nigerian writer. His works include the play *Kongi's Harvest* (1966), the novel *The Interpreters* (1965), and the essays collected in *The Burden of Memory, the Muse of Forgiveness* (1999). Nobel prize for literature 1986.

soy sauce (sɔɪ) *n* a salty dark brown sauce made from fermented soya beans, used esp. in Chinese cookery. Also called: **soya sauce.**

sozzled (ˈsɒzəld) *adj* an informal word for **drunk.** ORIG C19: ?from obs. *sozzle* stupor

SP *abbrev. for* starting price.

sp. *abbrev. for:* **1** special. **2** (*pl* **spp.**) species. **3** specific. **4** specimen. **5** spelling.

Sp. *abbrev. for:* **1** Spain. **2** Spaniard. **3** Spanish.

spa (spɑː) *n* a mineral spring or a place or resort where such a spring is found. ORIG C17: after SPA

Spa ★ (spɑː) *n* a town in E Belgium, in Liège province: a resort with medicinal mineral springs (discovered in the 14th century). Pop.: 10 140 (1991).

Spaak ★ (spɑːk) *n* **Paul Henri** (pɔl ɑ̃ri). 1899–1972, Belgian statesman, socialist prime minister (1937–38); president of the consultative assembly of the Council of Europe (1949–51) and secretary-general of NATO (1957–61).

space (speɪs) *n* **1** the unlimited three-dimensional expanse in which all material objects are located. Related adj: **spatial. 2** an interval of distance or time between two points, objects, or events. **3** a blank portion or area. **4a** unoccupied area or room: *there is no space for a table.* **4b** (*in combination*): *space-saving.* Related adj: **spacious. 5a** the region beyond the earth's atmosphere containing other planets, stars, galaxies, etc.; universe. **5b** (*as modifier*): *a space probe.* **6** a seat or place, as on a train, aircraft, etc. **7** *Printing.* a piece of metal, less than type-high, used to separate letters or words. **8** *Music.* any of the gaps between the lines that make up the staff. **9** Also called: **spacing.** *Telegraphy.* the period of time that separates characters in Morse code. ◆ *vb* **spaces, spacing, spaced.** (*tr*) **10** to place or arrange at intervals or with spaces between. **11** to divide into or by spaces: *to space one's time evenly.* **12** *Printing.* to separate (letters, words, or lines) by the insertion of spaces. ORIG C13: from OF *espace,* from L *spatium*
▸ ˈ**spacer** *n*

space age *n* **1** the period in which the exploration of space has become possible. ◆ *adj* **space-age. 2** (*usually prenominal*) futuristic or ultramodern.

space-bar *n* a horizontal bar on a typewriter that is depressed in order to leave a space between words, letters, etc.

space capsule *n* a vehicle, sometimes carrying people

or animals, designed to obtain scientific information from space, planets, etc., and be recovered on returning to earth.

spacecraft ('speɪsˌkrɑːft) *n* a manned or unmanned vehicle designed to orbit the earth or travel to celestial objects.

spaced out *adj Sl.* intoxicated through or as if through taking a drug. Often shortened to **spaced.**

space heater *n* a heater used to warm the air in an enclosed area, such as a room.

Space Invaders *n Trademark.* a video or computer game, the object of which is to destroy attacking alien spacecraft.

spaceman ('speɪsˌmæn) *or* (*fem*) **spacewoman** *n, pl* **spacemen** *or* (*fem*) **spacewomen.** a person who travels in outer space.

space platform *n* another name for **space station.**

spaceport ('speɪsˌpɔːt) *n* a base equipped to launch, maintain, and test spacecraft.

space probe *n* a vehicle, such as a satellite, equipped to obtain scientific information, normally transmitted back to earth by radio, about a planet, conditions in space, etc.

spaceship ('speɪsˌʃɪp) *n* a manned spacecraft.

space shuttle *n* any of a series of reusable US space vehicles (*Columbia, Challenger* (exploded 1986), *Discovery, Atlantis, Endeavor*) that can be launched into earth orbit transporting astronauts and equipment for a period of observation, research, etc., before re-entry and an unpowered landing on a runway; the first operational flight was in 1982.

space station *n* any large manned artificial satellite designed to orbit the earth during a long period of time thus providing a base for scientific research in space and a construction site, launch pad, and docking arrangements for spacecraft.

spacesuit ('speɪsˌsuːt, -ˌsjuːt) *n* a sealed and pressurized suit worn by astronauts providing an artificial atmosphere, acceptable temperature, radiocommunication link, and protection from radiation.

space-time *or* **space-time continuum** *n Physics.* the four-dimensional continuum having three spatial coordinates and one time coordinate that together completely specify the location of a particle or an event.

spacewalk ('speɪsˌwɔːk) *n* **1** the act or an instance of floating and manoeuvring in space, outside but attached by a lifeline to a spacecraft. Technical name: **extravehicular activity.** ◆ *vb* **2** (*intr*) to engage in this activity.

spacey ('speɪsɪ) *adj* **spacier, spaciest.** *Sl.* vague and dreamy, as if under the influence of drugs. ORIG C20: SPACE + -EY

spacial ('speɪʃəl) *adj* a variant spelling of **spatial.**

spacing ('speɪsɪŋ) *n* **1** the arrangement of letters, words, spaces, etc., on a page. **2** the arrangement of objects in a space.

spacious ('speɪʃəs) *adj* having a large capacity or area.
▸ **'spaciously** *adv* ▸ **'spaciousness** *n*

SPAD (spæd) *n acronym for* signal passed at danger: an incident in which a train goes through a red light.

spade[1] (speɪd) *n* **1** a tool for digging, typically consisting of a flat rectangular steel blade attached to a long wooden handle. **2** something resembling a spade. **3** a cutting tool for stripping the blubber from a whale or skin from a carcass. **4 call a spade a spade.** to speak plainly and frankly. ◆ *vb* **spades, spading, spaded. 5** (*tr*) to use a spade on. ORIG OE *spadu*
▸ **'spader** *n*

spade[2] (speɪd) *n* **1a** the black symbol on a playing card resembling a heart-shaped leaf with a stem. **1b** a card with one or more of these symbols or (*when pl*) the suit of cards so marked, usually the highest ranking of the four. **2** a derogatory word for a **Black**[1]. **3 in spades.** *Inf.* in an extreme or emphatic way. ORIG C16: from It. *spada* sword, used as an emblem on playing cards, from L *spatha,* from Gk *spathē* blade

spadework ('speɪdˌwɜːk) *n* dull or routine preparatory work.

spadix ('speɪdɪks) *n, pl* **spadices** (speɪ'daɪsiːz). a spike of small flowers on a fleshy stem, the whole being enclosed in a spathe. ORIG C18: from L: pulled-off branch of a palm, with its fruit, from Gk: torn-off frond

spaghetti (spə'gɛtɪ) *n* pasta in the form of long strings. ORIG C19: from It.: little cords, from *spago* a cord

spaghetti junction *n* a junction, usually between motorways, in which there are a large number of intersecting roads used by a large volume of high-speed traffic. ORIG C20: from the nickname given to the Gravelly Hill Interchange, Birmingham, where the M6, A38M, A38, and A5127 intersect

spaghetti western *n* a cowboy film made in Europe, esp. by an Italian director.

spahi *or* **spahee** ('spɑːhiː, 'spɑːiː) *n, pl* **spahis** *or* **spahees. 1** (formerly) an irregular cavalryman in the Turkish army. **2** (formerly) a member of a body of native Algerian cavalry in the French army. ORIG C16: from OF, from Turkish *sipahi,* from Persian *sipāhī* soldier

Spain ★ (speɪn) *n* a kingdom of SW Europe, occupying the Iberian peninsula between the Mediterranean and the Atlantic: a leading European power in the 16th century, with many overseas possessions, esp. in the New World; became a republic in 1931; under the fascist dictatorship of Franco following the Civil War (1936–39) until his death in 1975; a member of the European Union. It consists chiefly of a central plateau (the Meseta), with the Pyrenees and the Cantabrian Mountains in the north and the Sierra Nevada in the south. Official languages: Castilian Spanish, with Catalan, Galician, and Basque official regional languages. Religion: Roman Catholic. Currency: peseta and euro. Capital: Madrid. Pop.: 40 017 000 (1999 est.). Area: 504 748 sq. km (194 883 sq. miles). Spanish name: **España.**

spake (speɪk) *vb Arch.* a past tense of **speak.**

Spalato ★ ('spaːlato) *n* the Italian name for **Split.**

Spalding ★ ('spɔːldɪŋ) *n* a town in E England, in S Lincolnshire: noted for its bulbfields. Pop.: 18 731 (1991).

spam (spæm) *Computing sl.* ◆ *vb* **spams, spamming, spammed. 1** to send unsolicited electronic mail simultaneously to a number of newsgroups on the Internet. ◆ *n* **2** unsolicited electronic mail sent in this way. ORIG C20: from the repeated use of the word *Spam* in a popular sketch from the Brit. television show *Monty Python's Flying Circus,* first broadcast in 1969

Spam (spæm) *n Trademark.* a kind of tinned luncheon meat, made largely from pork.

span[1] (spæn) *n* **1** the interval, space, or distance between two points, such as the ends of a bridge or arch. **2** the complete duration or extent: *the span of his life.* **3** *Psychol.* the amount of material that can be processed in a single mental act: *span of attention.* **4** short for **wingspan. 5** a unit of length based on the width of an expanded hand, usually taken as nine inches. ◆ *vb* **spans, spanning, spanned.** (*tr*) **6** to stretch or extend across, over, or around. **7** to provide with something that spans: *to span a river with a bridge.* **8** to measure or cover, esp. with the extended hand. ORIG OE *spann*

span[2] (spæn) *n* a team of horses or oxen, esp. two matched animals. ORIG C16 (in the sense: yoke): from MDu.: something stretched, from *spannen* to stretch

span[3] (spæn) *vb Arch. or dialect.* a past tense of **spin.**

Span. *abbrev. for* Spanish.

spandrel *or* **spandril** ('spændrəl) *n Archit.* **1** an approximately triangular surface bounded by the outer curve of an arch and the adjacent wall. **2** the surface area between two adjacent arches and the horizontal cornice above them. ORIG C15 *spaundrell,* from Anglo-F *spaundre,* from OF *spandre* to spread

spangle ('spæŋgᵊl) *n* **1** a small thin piece of metal or other shiny material used as a decoration, esp. on clothes; sequin. **2** any glittering or shiny spot or object. ◆ *vb* **spangles, spangling, spangled. 3** (*intr*) to glitter or shine with or like spangles. **4** (*tr*) to cover with spangles. ORIG C15: dim. of *spange,* ?from MDu.: clasp
▸ **'spangly** *adj*

★ people and places

Spaniard ('spænjəd) *n* a native or inhabitant of Spain.

spaniel ('spænjəl) *n* **1** any of several breeds of gundog with long drooping ears and a silky coat. **2** an obsequiously devoted person. ORIG C14: from OF *espaigneul* Spanish (dog), from OProvençal *espanhol,* ult. from L *Hispāniolus* Spanish

Spanish ('spænɪʃ) *n* **1** the official language of Spain, Mexico, and most countries of South and Central America except Brazil. Spanish is an Indo-European language belonging to the Romance group. **2 the Spanish.** (*functioning as pl*) the natives, citizens, or inhabitants of Spain. ◆ *adj* **3** of or relating to the Spanish language or its speakers. **4** of or relating to Spain or Spaniards.

Spanish America ★ *n* the parts of America colonized by Spaniards and now chiefly Spanish-speaking: includes most of South and Central America, Mexico, and much of the Caribbean.

Spanish-American *adj* **1** of or relating to any of the Spanish-speaking countries or peoples of the Americas. ◆ *n* **2** a native or inhabitant of Spanish America. **3** a Spanish-speaking person in the US.

Spanish customs *or* **practices** *pl n Inf.* irregular practices among a group of workers to gain increased financial allowances, reduced working hours, etc.

Spanish fly *n* **1** a European blister beetle, the dried body of which yields cantharides. **2** another name for **cantharides.**

Spanish Guinea ★ *n* the former name (until 1964) of **Equatorial Guinea.**

Spanish guitar *n* the classic form of the guitar; a six-stringed instrument with a waisted body and a central sound hole.

Spanish Main ★ *n* **1** the mainland of Spanish America, esp. the N coast of South America. **2** the Caribbean Sea, the S part of which in colonial times was the haunt of pirates.

Spanish Morocco ★ *n* a former Spanish colony on the N coast of Morocco: part of the kingdom of Morocco since 1956.
▸ **Spanish Moroccan** *adj, n*

Spanish moss *n* **1** an epiphytic plant growing in tropical and subtropical regions as long bluish-grey strands suspended from the branches of trees. **2** a tropical lichen growing as long trailing green threads from the branches of trees.

Spanish omelette *n* an omelette containing green peppers, onions, tomato, etc.

Spanish rice *n* rice cooked with tomatoes, onions, green peppers, etc.

Spanish Sahara ★ *n* the former name (until 1975) of **Western Sahara.**

Spanish West Africa ★ *n* a former overseas territory of Spain in NW Africa: divided in 1958 into the overseas provinces of Ifni and Spanish Sahara.
▸ **Spanish West African** *adj, n*

spank[1] (spæŋk) *vb* **1** (*tr*) to slap with the open hand, esp. on the buttocks. ◆ *n* **2** one or a series of these slaps. ORIG C18: prob. imit.

spank[2] (spæŋk) *vb* (*intr*) to go at a quick and lively pace. ORIG C19: back formation from SPANKING[2]

spanker ('spæŋkə) *n* **1** a person or thing that spanks. **2** *Naut.* a fore-and-aft sail or a mast that is aftermost in a sailing vessel. **3** *Inf.* something outstandingly fine or large.

spanking[1] ('spæŋkɪŋ) *n* a series of spanks, usually as a punishment for children.

spanking[2] ('spæŋkɪŋ) *adj* (*prenominal*) **1** *Inf.* outstandingly fine, smart, large, etc. **2** quick and energetic. **3** (esp. of a breeze) fresh and brisk.

spanner ('spænə) *n* **1** a steel hand tool with jaws or a hole, designed to grip a nut or bolt head. **2 spanner in the works.** *Brit. inf.* an impediment or annoyance. ORIG C17: from G, from *spannen* to stretch

span roof *n* a roof consisting of two equal sloping sides.

spanspek (ˌspæn'spɛk) *n S. African.* the sweet melon. ORIG C19: possibly from Afrik.: literally, Spanish bacon

spar[1] (spɑː) *n* **1** any piece of nautical gear resembling a pole and used as a mast, boom, gaff, etc. **2** a principal supporting structural member of an aerofoil that runs from tip to tip or root to tip. ORIG C13: from ON *sperra* beam

spar[2] (spɑː) *vb* **spars, sparring, sparred.** (*intr*) **1** *Boxing & martial arts.* to box using light blows, as in training. **2** to dispute or argue. **3** (of gamecocks, etc.) to fight with the feet or spurs. ◆ *n* **4** an unaggressive fight. **5** an argument or wrangle. ORIG OE, ? from SPUR

spar[3] (spɑː) *n* any of various minerals, such as feldspar, that are light-coloured, crystalline, and easily cleavable. ORIG C16: from MLow G *spar*

sparaxis (spər'æksɪs) *n* a South African plant of the iris family, having lacerated spathes and showy flowers. ORIG C19: NL, from Gk, from *sparassō* to tear

spare (spɛə) *vb* **spares, sparing, spared. 1** (*tr*) to refrain from killing, punishing, or injuring. **2** (*tr*) to release or relieve, as from pain, suffering, etc. **3** (*tr*) to refrain from using: *spare the rod, spoil the child.* **4** (*tr*) to be able to afford or give: *I can't spare the time.* **5** (*usually passive*) (esp. of Providence) to allow to survive: *I'll see you next year if we are spared.* **6** (*intr*) *Now rare.* to act or live frugally. **7 not spare oneself.** to exert oneself to the full. **8 to spare.** more than is required: *two minutes to spare.* ◆ *adj* **9** (*often immediately postpositive*) in excess of what is needed; additional. **10** able to be used when needed: *a spare part.* **11** (of a person) thin and lean. **12** scanty or meagre. **13** (*postpositive*) *Brit. sl.* upset, angry, or distracted (esp. in **go spare**). ◆ *n* **14** a duplicate kept as a replacement in case of damage or loss. **15** a spare tyre. **16** *Tenpin bowling.* **16a** the act of knocking down all the pins with the two bowls of a single frame. **16b** the score thus made. ORIG OE *sparian* to refrain from injuring
▸ **'sparely** *adv* ▸ **'spareness** *n* ▸ **'sparer** *n*

spare-part surgery *n* surgical replacement of defective or damaged organs by transplant or insertion of artficial devices.

sparerib (ˌspɛə'rɪb) *n* a cut of pork ribs with most of the meat trimmed off.

spare tyre *n* **1** an additional tyre carried by a motor vehicle in case of puncture. **2** *Brit. sl.* a deposit of fat just above the waist.

sparing ('spɛərɪŋ) *adj* **1** (sometimes foll. by *of*) economical or frugal (with). **2** scanty; meagre. **3** merciful or lenient.
▸ **'sparingly** *adv* ▸ **'sparingness** *n*

spark[1] (spɑːk) *n* **1** a fiery particle thrown out or left by burning material or caused by the friction of two hard surfaces. **2a** a momentary flash of light accompanied by a sharp crackling noise, produced by a sudden electrical discharge through the air or some other insulating medium between two points. **2b** the electrical discharge itself. **2c** (*as modifier*): *a spark gap.* **3** anything that serves to animate or kindle. **4** a trace or hint: *a spark of interest.* **5** vivacity, enthusiasm, or humour. **6** a small piece of diamond, as used in cutting glass. ◆ *vb* **7** (*intr*) to give off sparks. **8** (*intr*) (of the sparking plug or ignition system of an internal-combustion engine) to produce a spark. **9** (*tr; often foll. by off*) to kindle or animate. ◆ See also **sparks.** ORIG OE *spearca*

spark[2] (spɑːk) *n* **1** *Rare.* a fashionable or gallant young man. **2 bright spark.** *Brit., usually ironic.* a person who appears clever or witty. ORIG C16 (in the sense: beautiful or witty woman): ? of Scand. origin
▸ **'sparkish** *adj*

Spark ★ (spɑːk) *n* Dame **Muriel.** born 1918, British novelist; her works include *Memento Mori* (1959), *The Prime of Miss Jean Brodie* (1961), and *Reality and Dreams* (1996).

spark gap *n* the space between two electrodes across which a spark can jump.

sparking plug *n* a device screwed into the cylinder head of an internal-combustion engine to ignite the explosive mixture by means of an electric spark. Also called: **spark plug.**

sparkle ('spɑːkᵊl) *vb* **sparkles, sparkling, sparkled. 1** to issue or reflect or cause to issue or reflect bright points of light. **2** (*intr*) (of wine, mineral water, etc.) to effervesce.

3 (*intr*) to be vivacious or witty. ◆ *n* 4 a point of light, spark, or gleam. 5 vivacity or wit. ORIG C12 *sparklen,* frequentative of *sparken* to SPARK[1]

sparkler ('spɑːklə) *n* 1 a type of firework that throws out sparks. 2 *Inf.* a sparkling gem.

sparkling wine *n* a wine made effervescent by carbon dioxide gas added artificially or produced naturally by secondary fermentation.

spark plug *n* another name for **sparking plug.**

sparks (spɑːks) *n* (*functioning as sing*) *Inf.* 1 an electrician. 2 a radio officer, esp. on a ship.

sparky ('spɑːkɪ) *adj* **sparkier, sparkiest.** lively, vivacious, spirited.

sparring partner ('spɑːrɪŋ) *n* 1 a person who practises with a boxer during training. 2 a person with whom one has friendly arguments.

sparrow ('spærəʊ) *n* 1 any of various weaverbirds, esp. the house sparrow, having a brown or grey plumage and feeding on seeds or insects. 2 *US & Canad.* any of various North American finches, such as the chipping sparrow, that have a dullish streaked plumage. ◆ See also **hedge sparrow, tree sparrow.** ORIG OE *spearwa*

sparrowgrass ('spærəʊˌgrɑːs) *n* a dialect or popular name for **asparagus.**

sparrowhawk ('spærəʊˌhɔːk) *n* any of several small hawks of Eurasia and N Africa that prey on smaller birds.

sparrow hawk *n* a very small North American falcon, closely related to the kestrels.

sparse (spɑːs) *adj* scattered or scanty; not dense. ORIG C18: from L *sparsus,* from *spargere* to scatter
▸ **'sparsely** *adv* ▸ **'sparseness** *or* **'sparsity** *n*

Sparta ★ ('spɑːtə) *n* an ancient Greek city in the S Peloponnese, famous for the discipline and military prowess of its citizens and for their austere way of life.

Spartacus ★ ('spɑːtəkəs) *n* died 71 B.C., Thracian slave, who led an unsuccessful revolt of gladiators against Rome (73–71 B.C.).

Spartan ('spɑːtᵊn) *adj* 1 of or relating to Sparta or its citizens. 2 (*sometimes not cap.*) very strict or austere: *a Spartan upbringing.* 3 (*sometimes not cap.*) possessing courage and resolve. ◆ *n* 4 a citizen of Sparta. 5 (*sometimes not cap.*) a disciplined or brave person.

spasm ('spæzəm) *n* 1 an involuntary muscular contraction, esp. one resulting in cramp or convulsion. 2 a sudden burst of activity, emotion, etc. ORIG C14: from L *spasmus,* from Gk *spasmos* a cramp, from *span* to tear

spasmodic (spæz'mɒdɪk) *or* (*rarely*) **spasmodical** *adj* 1 taking place in sudden brief spells. 2 of or characterized by spasms. ORIG C17: NL, from Gk *spasmos* SPASM
▸ **spas'modically** *adv*

Spassky ★ ('spæskɪ; *Russian* 'spaskij) *n* **Boris** (ba'ris). born 1937, Russian chess player; world champion (1969–72).

spastic ('spæstɪk) *n* 1 a person who is affected by spasms or convulsions, esp. one who has cerebral palsy. 2 *Offens. sl.* a clumsy, incapable, or incompetent person. ◆ *adj* 3 affected by or resembling spasms. 4 *Offens. sl.* clumsy, incapable, or incompetent. ORIG C18: from L *spasticus,* from Gk, from *spasmos* SPASM
▸ **'spastically** *adv* ▸ **spas'ticity** (spæs'tɪsɪtɪ) *n*

spat[1] (spæt) *n* 1 *Now rare.* a slap or smack. 2 a slight quarrel. ◆ *vb* **spats, spatting, spatted.** 3 *Rare.* to slap (someone). 4 (*intr*) *US, Canad., & NZ.* to have a slight quarrel. ORIG C19: prob. imit.

spat[2] (spæt) *vb* a past tense and past participle of **spit**[1].

spat[3] (spæt) *n* another name for **gaiter** (sense 2). ORIG C19: short for SPATTERDASH

spat[4] (spæt) *n* 1 a larval oyster or similar bivalve mollusc. 2 such oysters or other molluscs collectively. ORIG C17: from Anglo-Norman *spat*

spatchcock ('spætʃˌkɒk) *n* 1 a chicken or game bird split down the back and grilled. ◆ *vb* (*tr*) 2 to interpolate (words, a story, etc.) into a sentence, narrative, etc., esp. inappropriately. ORIG C18: ? var. of *spitchcock* eel when prepared & cooked

spate (speɪt) *n* 1 a fast flow, rush, or outpouring: *a spate of words.* 2 *Chiefly Brit.* a sudden flood: *the rivers were in spate.* 3 *Chiefly Brit.* a sudden heavy downpour. ORIG C15 (Scot. & N English): from ?

spathe (speɪð) *n* a large bract that encloses the inflorescence of several members of the lily family. ORIG C18: from L *spatha,* from Gk *spathē* a blade
▸ **spathaceous** (spə'θeɪʃəs) *adj*

spathic ('spæθɪk) *or* **spathose** ('spæθəʊs) *adj* (of minerals) resembling spar, esp. in having good cleavage. ORIG C18: from G *Spat* SPAR[3]

spatial *or* **spacial** ('speɪʃəl) *adj* 1 of or relating to space. 2 existing or happening in space.
▸ **spatiality** (ˌspeɪʃɪ'ælɪtɪ) *n* ▸ **'spatially** *adv*

spatiotemporal (ˌspeɪʃɪəʊ'tɛmpərəl) *adj* 1 of or existing in both space and time. 2 of or concerned with space-time.
▸ **ˌspatio'temporally** *adv*

spatter ('spætə) *vb* 1 to scatter or splash (a substance, esp. a liquid) or (of a substance) to splash (something) in scattered drops: *to spatter mud on the car; mud spattered in her face.* 2 (*tr*) to sprinkle, cover, or spot (with a liquid). 3 (*tr*) to slander or defame. 4 (*intr*) to shower or rain down: *bullets spattered around them.* ◆ *n* 5 the sound of spattering. 6 something spattered, such as a spot or splash. 7 the act or an instance of spattering. ORIG C16: imit.

spatterdash ('spætəˌdæʃ) *n* 1 *US.* another name for **roughcast.** 2 (*pl*) long leather leggings worn in the 18th century, as to protect from mud when riding. ORIG C17: see SPATTER, DASH[1]

spatula ('spætjʊlə) *n* a utensil with a broad flat blade, used for lifting, spreading, or stirring foods, etc. ORIG C16: from L: a broad piece, from *spatha* a flat wooden implement; see SPATHE
▸ **'spatular** *adj*

spatulate ('spætjʊlɪt) *adj* 1 shaped like a spatula; having thickened rounded ends: *spatulate fingers.* 2 Also: **spathulate.** *Bot.* having a narrow base and a broad rounded apex.

spavin ('spævɪn) *n* enlargement of the hock of a horse by a bony growth (**bony spavin**) or distension of the ligament (**bog spavin**), often resulting in lameness. ORIG C15: from OF *espavin,* from ?
▸ **'spavined** *adj*

spawn (spɔːn) *n* 1 the mass of eggs deposited by fish, amphibians, or molluscs. 2 *Often derog.* offspring, product, or yield. 3 *Bot.* the nontechnical name for **mycelium.** ◆ *vb* 4 (of fish, amphibians, etc.) to produce or deposit (eggs). 5 *Often derog.* (of people) to produce (offspring). 6 (*tr*) to produce or engender. ORIG C14: from Anglo-Norman *espaundre,* from OF *spandre* to spread out
▸ **'spawner** *n*

spay (speɪ) *vb* (*tr*) to remove the ovaries from (a female animal). ORIG C15: from OF *espeer* to cut with the sword, from *espee* sword, from L *spatha*

SPCK (in Britain) *abbrev. for* Society for Promoting Christian Knowledge.

speak (spiːk) *vb* **speaks, speaking, spoke, spoken.** 1 to make (verbal utterances); utter (words). 2 to communicate or express (something) in or as if in words. 3 (*intr*) to deliver a speech, discourse, etc. 4 (*tr*) to know how to talk in (a language or dialect): *he does not speak German.* 5 (*intr*) to make a characteristic sound: *the clock spoke.* 6 (*intr*) (of hounds used in hunting) to give tongue; bark. 7 (*tr*) *Naut.* to hail and communicate with (another vessel) at sea. 8 (*intr*) (of a musical instrument) to produce a sound. 9 **on speaking terms.** on good terms; friendly. 10 **so to speak.** in a manner of speaking; as it were. 11 **speak one's mind.** to express one's opinions frankly and plainly. 12 **to speak of.** of a significant or worthwhile nature: *no support to speak of.* ◆ See also **speak for, speak out, speak to.** ORIG OE *specan*
▸ **'speakable** *adj*

speakeasy ('spiːkˌiːzɪ) *n, pl* **speakeasies.** *US.* a place where alcoholic drink was sold illicitly during Prohibition.

speaker ('spiːkə) *n* 1 a person who speaks, esp. at a formal occasion. 2 See **loudspeaker.**
▸ **'speakership** *n*

Speaker ('spi:kə) *n* the presiding officer in any of numerous legislative bodies.

speak for *vb* (*intr, prep*) **1** to speak as a representative of (other people). **2 speak for itself.** to be so evident that no further comment is necessary. **3 speak for yourself.** *Inf.* (used as an imperative) do not presume that other people agree with you.

speaking ('spi:kɪŋ) *adj* **1** (*prenominal*) eloquent, impressive, or striking. **2a** able to speak. **2b** (*in combination*) able to speak a particular language: *French-speaking.*

speaking clock *n Brit.* a telephone service that gives a verbal statement of the time.

speaking in tongues *n* another term for **gift of tongues.**

speaking tube *n* a tube for conveying a person's voice from one room or building to another.

speak out *or* **up** *vb* (*intr, adv*) **1** to state one's beliefs, objections, etc., bravely and firmly. **2** to speak more loudly and clearly.

speak to *vb* (*intr, prep*) **1** to address (a person). **2** to reprimand. **3** *Formal.* to give evidence of or comments on (a subject).

spear[1] (spɪə) *n* **1** a weapon consisting of a long shaft with a sharp pointed end of metal, stone, or wood that may be thrown or thrust. **2** a similar implement used to catch fish. **3** another name for **spearman.** ♦ *vb* **4** to pierce (something) with or as if with a spear. ORIG OE *spere*

spear[2] (spɪə) *n* a shoot, stalk, or blade, as of grass. ORIG C16: prob. var. of SPIRE[1], infl. by SPEAR[1]

spear grass *n* **1** Also called: **wild Spaniard.** a New Zealand grass with sharp leaves that grows on mountains. **2** any of various other grasses with sharp stiff blades or seeds.

spear gun *n* a device for shooting spears underwater.

spearhead ('spɪəˌhɛd) *n* **1** the pointed head of a spear. **2** the leading force in a military attack. **3** any person or thing that leads or initiates an attack, campaign, etc. ♦ *vb* **4** (*tr*) to lead or initiate (an attack, campaign, etc.).

spearman ('spɪəmən) *n, pl* **spearmen.** a soldier armed with a spear.

spearmint ('spɪəmɪnt) *n* a purple-flowered mint plant of Europe, with leaves that yield an oil used for flavouring.

Spears ★ ('spɪəz) *n* **Britney** ('brɪtnɪ). born 1981, US pop singer; records include the single "Baby One More Time" (1998) and the album *Oops!...I Did It Again* (2000).

spec (spɛk) *n* **1 on spec.** *Inf.* as a speculation or gamble: *all the tickets were sold so I went to the theatre on spec.* ♦ *adj* **2** (*prenominal*) *Austral. & NZ inf.* speculative: *a spec developer.*

spec. *abbrev. for:* **1** special. **2** specification. **3** speculation.

special ('spɛʃəl) *adj* **1** distinguished from, set apart from, or excelling others of its kind. **2** (*prenominal*) designed or reserved for a particular purpose. **3** not usual or commonplace. **4** (*prenominal*) particular or primary: *his special interest was music.* **5** of or relating to the education of handicapped children: *a special school.* ♦ *n* **6** a special person or thing, such as an extra edition of a newspaper or a train reserved for a particular purpose. **7** a dish or meal given prominence, esp. at a low price, in a café, etc. **8** short for **special constable. 9** *US, Canad., Austral., & NZ inf.* an item in a store advertised at a reduce price. ♦ *vb* **specials, specialling, specialled.** (*tr*) **10** (of a nurse) to give (a gravely ill patient) constant individual care. **11** *NZ inf.* to advertise and sell (an item) at a reduced price. ORIG C13: from OF *especial,* from L *speciālis* individual, special, from *speciēs* appearance
► **'specially** *adv* ► **'specialness** *n*

Special Branch *n* (in Britain) the department of the police force that is concerned with political security.

special clearing *n Banking.* (in Britain) the clearing of a cheque through a bank in less than the usual three days, for an additional charge.

special constable *n* a person recruited for temporary or occasional police duties, esp. in time of emergency.

special delivery *n* the delivery of a piece of mail outside the time of a scheduled delivery.

special drawing rights *pl n* (*sometimes caps.*) the reserve assets of the International Monetary Fund on which member nations may draw.

special effects *pl n Films.* techniques used in the production of scenes that cannot be achieved by normal techniques.

specialist ('spɛʃəlɪst) *n* a person who specializes in a particular activity, field of research, etc.
► **'specialˌism** *n* ► **ˌspecial'istic** *adj*

speciality (ˌspɛʃɪ'ælɪtɪ) *or esp. US & Canad.* **specialty** *n, pl* **specialities** *or esp. US & Canad.* **specialties. 1** a special interest or skill. **2a** a service or product specialized in, as at a restaurant. **2b** (*as modifier*): *a speciality dish.* **3** a special feature or characteristic.

specialize *or* **specialise** ('spɛʃəˌlaɪz) *vb* **specializes, specializing, specialized** *or* **specialises, specialising, specialised. 1** (*intr*) to train in or devote oneself to a particular area of study, occupation, or activity. **2** (*usually passive*) to cause (organisms or parts) to develop in a way most suited to a particular environment or way of life or (of organisms, etc.) to develop in this way. **3** (*tr*) to modify for a special use or purpose.
► **ˌspeciali'zation** *or* **ˌspeciali'sation** *n*

special licence *n Brit.* a licence permitting a marriage to take place by waiving the usual legal conditions.

special pleading *n Law.* **1** a pleading that alleges new facts that offset those put forward by the other side rather than directly admitting or denying those facts. **2** a pleading that emphasizes the favourable aspects of a case while omitting the unfavourable.

special school *n Brit.* a school for children who are unable to benefit from ordinary schooling because they have learning difficulties, physical or mental handicaps, etc.

special team *n American football.* any of several predetermined permutations of the players within a team that play in situations, such as kickoffs and attempts at field goals, where the standard offensive and defensive formations are not appropriate.

specialty ('spɛʃəltɪ) *n, pl* **specialties. 1** *Law.* a formal contract or obligation expressed in a deed. **2** a variant (esp. US and Canad.) of **speciality.**

speciation (ˌspi:ʃɪ'eɪʃən) *n* the evolutionary development of a biological species.

specie ('spi:ʃi:) *n* **1** coin money, as distinguished from bullion or paper money. **2 in specie. 2a** (of money) in coin. **2b** in kind. ORIG C16: from L *in speciē* in kind

species ('spi:ʃi:z; *Latin* 'spi:ʃɪˌi:z) *n, pl* **species. 1** *Biol.* **1a** any of the taxonomic groups into which a genus is divided, the members of which are capable of interbreeding. Abbrev.: **sp. 1b** the animals of such a group. **1c** any group of related animals or plants not necessarily of this taxonomic rank. **2** (*modifier*) denoting a plant that is a natural member of a species rather than a hybrid or cultivar: *a species clematis.* **3** *Logic.* a group of objects or individuals, all sharing common attributes, that forms a subdivision of a genus. **4** a kind, sort, or variety: *a species of treachery.* **5** *Chiefly RC Church.* the outward form of the bread and wine in the Eucharist. **6** *Obs.* an outward appearance or form. ORIG C16: from L: appearance, from *specere* to look

specif. *abbrev. for* specifically.

specific (spɪ'sɪfɪk) *adj* **1** explicit, particular, or definite. **2** relating to a specified or particular thing: *a specific treatment for arthritis.* **3** of or relating to a biological species. **4** (of a disease) caused by a particular pathogenic agent. **5** *Physics.* **5a** characteristic of a property of a substance, esp. in relation to the same property of a standard reference substance: *specific gravity.* **5b** characteristic of a property of a substance per unit mass, length, area, etc.: *specific heat.* **5c** (of an extensive physical quantity) divided by mass: *specific volume.* **6** denoting a tariff levied at a fixed sum per unit of weight, quantity, volume, etc., irrespective of value. ♦ *n* **7** (*sometimes pl*) a designated quality, thing, etc. **8** *Med.* any drug used to treat a particular disease. ORIG C17: from Med. L *specificus,* from L SPECIES
► **spe'cifically** *adv* ► **specificity** (ˌspɛsɪ'fɪsɪtɪ) *n*

specification (ˌspɛsɪfɪ'keɪʃən) *n* **1** the act or an instance of specifying. **2** (in patent law) a written statement accompanying an application for a patent that describes the nature of an invention. **3** a detailed description of the criteria for the constituents, construction, appearance, performance, etc., of a material, apparatus, etc., or of the standard of workmanship required in its manufacture. **4** an item, detail, etc., specified.

specific charge *n Physics.* the charge-to-mass ratio of an elementary particle.

specific gravity *n* the ratio of the density of a substance to that of water.

specific heat capacity *n* the heat required to raise unit mass of a substance by unit temperature interval under specified conditions, such as constant pressure. Also called: **specific heat.**

specific humidity *n* the mass of water vapour in a sample of moist air divided by the mass of the sample.

specific volume *n Physics.* the volume of matter per unit mass.

specify ('spɛsɪˌfaɪ) *vb* **specifies, specifying, specified.** (*tr; may take a clause as object*) **1** to refer to or state specifically. **2** to state as a condition. **3** to state or include in the specification of. ORIG C13: from Med. L *specificāre* to describe
▸ **'speciˌfiable** *adj* ▸ **specificative** ('spɛsɪfɪˌkeɪtɪv) *adj*

specimen ('spɛsɪmɪn) *n* **1a** an individual, object, or part regarded as typical of its group or class. **1b** (*as modifier*): *a specimen page.* **2** *Med.* a sample of tissue, blood, urine, etc., taken for diagnostic examination or evaluation. **3** the whole or a part of an organism, plant, rock, etc., collected and preserved as an example of its class, species, etc. **4** *Inf., often derog.* a person. ORIG C17: from L: mark, proof, from *specere* to look at

specious ('spiːʃəs) *adj* **1** apparently correct or true, but actually wrong or false. **2** deceptively attractive in appearance. ORIG C14 (orig.: fair): from L *speciōsus* plausible, from *speciēs* outward appearance, from *specere* to look at
▸ **'speciously** *adv* ▸ **speciosity** (ˌspiːʃɪ'ɒsɪtɪ) *or* **'speciousness** *n*

speck (spɛk) *n* **1** a very small mark or spot. **2** a small or tiny piece of something. ◆ *vb* **3** (*tr*) to mark with specks or spots. ORIG OE *specca*

speckle ('spɛkᵊl) *n* **1** a small mark usually of a contrasting colour, as on the skin, eggs, etc. ◆ *vb* **speckles, speckling, speckled. 2** (*tr*) to mark with or as if with speckles. ORIG C15: from MDu. *spekkel*
▸ **'speckled** *adj*

specs (spɛks) *pl n Inf.* short for **spectacles.**

spectacle ('spɛktəkᵊl) *n* **1** a public display or performance, esp. a showy or ceremonial one. **2** a thing or person seen, esp. an unusual or ridiculous one: *he makes a spectacle of himself.* **3** a strange or interesting object or phenomenon. ORIG C14: via OF from L *spectaculum* a show, from *spectāre* to watch, from *specere* to look at

spectacles ('spɛktəkᵊlz) *pl n* a pair of glasses for correcting defective vision. Often (informal) shortened to **specs.**
▸ **'spectacled** *adj*

spectacular (spɛk'tækjʊlə) *adj* **1** of or resembling a spectacle; impressive, grand, or dramatic. **2** unusually marked or great: *a spectacular increase.* ◆ *n* **3** a lavishly produced performance.
▸ **spec'tacularly** *adv*

spectate (spɛk'teɪt) *vb* **spectates, spectating, spectated.** (*intr*) to be a spectator; watch. ORIG C20: back formation from SPECTATOR

spectator (spɛk'teɪtə) *n* a person viewing anything; onlooker; observer. ORIG C16: from L, from *spectāre* to watch; see SPECTACLE

spectator sport *n* a sport that attracts more people as spectators than as participants.

Spector ★ ('spɛktə) *n* **Phil.** born 1940, US record producer and songwriter, noted for the densely orchestrated "Wall of Sound" in his work with groups such as the Ronettes and the Crystals.

spectra ('spɛktrə) *n* the plural of **spectrum.**

spectral ('spɛktrəl) *adj* **1** of or like a spectre. **2** of or relating to a spectrum.
▸ **spectrality** (spɛk'trælɪtɪ) *n* ▸ **'spectrally** *adv*

spectral type *or* **class** *n* any of various groups into which stars are classified according to characteristic spectral lines and bands.

spectre *or US* **specter** ('spɛktə) *n* **1** a ghost; phantom; apparition. **2** an unpleasant or menacing mental image: *the spectre of redundancy.* ORIG C17: from L *spectrum,* from *specere* to look at

spectro- *combining form.* indicating a spectrum: *spectrogram.*

spectrograph ('spɛktrəʊˌgrɑːf) *n* a spectroscope or spectrometer that produces a photographic record (**spectrogram**) of a spectrum. See also **sound spectrograph.**
▸ **ˌspectro'graphic** *adj* ▸ **ˌspectro'graphically** *adv* ▸ **spectrography** (spɛk'trɒgrəfɪ) *n*

spectroheliograph (ˌspɛktrəʊ'hiːlɪəˌgrɑːf) *n* an instrument used to take a photograph (**spectroheliogram**) of the sun in light of a particular wavelength, usually that of calcium or hydrogen, to show the distribution of the element over the surface and in the atmosphere.
▸ **ˌspectroˌhelio'graphic** *adj*

spectrometer (spɛk'trɒmɪtə) *n* any instrument for producing a spectrum, esp. one in which wavelength, energy, intensity, etc., can be measured. See also **mass spectrometer.**
▸ **spectrometric** (ˌspɛktrəʊ'mɛtrɪk) *adj* ▸ **spec'trometry** *n*

spectrophotometer (ˌspɛktrəʊfəʊ'tɒmɪtə) *n* an instrument for producing or recording a spectrum and measuring the photometric intensity of each wavelength present.
▸ **spectrophotometric** (ˌspɛktrəʊˌfəʊtə'mɛtrɪk) *adj*
▸ **ˌspectropho'tometry** *n*

spectroscope ('spɛktrəˌskəʊp) *n* any of a number of instruments for dispersing electromagnetic radiation and thus forming or recording a spectrum.
▸ **spectroscopic** (ˌspɛktrə'skɒpɪk) *or* **ˌspectro'scopical** *adj*

spectroscopy (spɛk'trɒskəpɪ) *n* the science and practice of using spectrometers and spectroscopes and of analysing spectra.
▸ **spec'troscopist** *n*

spectrum ('spɛktrəm) *n, pl* **spectra. 1** the distribution of colours produced when white light is dispersed by a prism or diffraction grating. There is a continuous change in wavelength from red, the longest wavelength, to violet, the shortest. Seven colours are usually distinguished: violet, indigo, blue, green, yellow, orange, and red. **2** the whole range of electromagnetic radiation with respect to its wavelength or frequency. **3** any particular distribution of electromagnetic radiation often showing lines or bands characteristic of the substance emitting the radiation or absorbing it. **4** any similar distribution or record of the energies, velocities, masses, etc., of atoms, ions, electrons, etc.: *a mass spectrum.* **5** any range or scale, as of capabilities, emotions, or moods. **6** another name for an **afterimage.** ORIG C17: from L: image, from *spectāre* to observe, from *specere* to look at

spectrum analysis *n* the analysis of a spectrum to determine the properties of its source.

specular ('spɛkjʊlə) *adj* **1** of, relating to, or having the properties of a mirror. **2** of or relating to a speculum. ORIG C16: from L *speculāris,* from *speculum* a mirror, from *specere* to look at

speculate ('spɛkjʊˌleɪt) *vb* **speculates, speculating, speculated. 1** (when *tr, takes a clause as object*) to conjecture without knowing the complete facts. **2** (*intr*) to buy or sell securities, property, etc., in the hope of deriving capital gains. **3** (*intr*) to risk loss for the possibility of considerable gain. **4** (*intr*) *NZ.* in rugby football, to make an emergency undirected forward kick at the ball. ORIG C16: from L *speculārī* to spy out, from *specula* a watchtower, from *specere* to look at

speculation (ˌspɛkjʊ'leɪʃən) *n* **1** the act or an instance of speculating. **2** a supposition, theory, or opinion arrived at through speculating. **3** investment involving high risk but also possible high profits.
▸ **'speculative** *adj*

speculator ('spɛkjʊˌleɪtə) *n* **1** a person who speculates. **2** *NZ rugby.* an undirected kick of the ball.

speculum ('spɛkjʊləm) *n, pl* **specula** (-lə) *or* **speculums. 1** a mirror, esp. one made of polished metal for use in a telescope, etc. **2** *Med.* an instrument for dilating a bodily cavity or passage to permit examination of its interior. **3** a patch of distinctive colour on the wing of a bird. ORIG C16: from L: mirror, from *specere* to look at

sped (spɛd) *vb* a past tense and past participle of **speed**.

speech (spiːtʃ) *n* **1a** the act or faculty of speaking. **1b** (*as modifier*): *speech therapy.* **2** that which is spoken; utterance. **3** a talk or address delivered to an audience. **4** a person's characteristic manner of speaking. **5** a national or regional language or dialect. **6** *Linguistics.* another word for **parole.** ORIG OE *spēc*

speech day *n Brit.* (in schools) an annual day on which prizes are presented, speeches are made by guest speakers, etc.

speechify (ˈspiːtʃɪˌfaɪ) *vb* **speechifies, speechifying, speechified.** (*intr*) **1** to make a speech or speeches. **2** to talk pompously and boringly.
▸ **ˈspeechiˌfier** *n*

speechless (ˈspiːtʃlɪs) *adj* **1** not able to speak. **2** temporarily deprived of speech. **3** not expressed or able to be expressed in words: *speechless fear.*
▸ **ˈspeechlessly** *adv* ▸ **ˈspeechlessness** *n*

speed (spiːd) *n* **1** the act or quality of acting or moving fast; rapidity. **2** the rate at which something moves, is done, or acts. **3** *Physics.* **3a** a scalar measure of the rate of movement of a body expressed either as the distance travelled divided by the time taken (**average speed**) or the rate of change of position with respect to time at a particular point (**instantaneous speed**). **3b** another word for **velocity** (sense 2). **4** a rate of rotation, usually expressed in revolutions per unit time. **5a** a gear ratio in a motor vehicle, bicycle, etc. **5b** (*in combination*): *a three-speed gear.* **6** *Photog.* a numerical expression of the sensitivity to light of a particular type of film, paper, or plate. See also **ISO rating.** **7** *Photog.* a measure of the ability of a lens to pass light from an object to the image position. **8** a slang word for **amphetamine.** **9** *Arch.* prosperity or success. **10 at speed.** quickly. ◆ *vb* **speeds, speeding; sped** *or* **speeded. 11** to move or go or cause to move or go quickly. **12** (*intr*) to drive (a motor vehicle) at a high speed, esp. above legal limits. **13** (*tr*) to help further the success or completion of. **14** (*intr*) *Sl.* to take or be under the influence of amphetamines. **15** (*intr*) to operate or run at a high speed. **16** *Arch.* **16a** (*intr*) to prosper or succeed. **16b** (*tr*) to wish success to. ◆ See also **speed up.** ORIG OE *spēd* (orig. in the sense: success)
▸ **ˈspeeder** *n*

speedball (ˈspiːdˌbɔːl) *n Sl.* a mixture of heroin with amphetamine or cocaine.

speedboat (ˈspiːdˌbəʊt) *n* a high-speed motorboat.

speed chess *n* a form of chess in which each player's game is limited to a total stipulated time, usually half an hour; the first player to exceed the time limit loses.

speed limit *n* the maximum permitted speed at which a vehicle may travel on certain roads.

speedo (ˈspiːdəʊ) *n, pl* **speedos.** an informal name for **speedometer.**

speed of light *n* the speed at which electromagnetic radiation travels in a vacuum; 2.997 924 58 × 10^8 metres per second exactly. Symbol: *c* Also called (not in technical usage): **velocity of light.**

speedometer (spɪˈdɒmɪtə) *n* a device fitted to a vehicle to measure and display the speed of travel. See also **mileometer.**

speed up *vb* (*adv*) **1** to increase or cause to increase in speed or rate; accelerate. ◆ *n* **speed-up. 2** an instance of this; acceleration.

> **USAGE NOTE** The past tense and past participle of *speed up* is *speeded up* not *sped up.*

speedway (ˈspiːdˌweɪ) *n* **1** the sport of racing on light powerful motorcycles round cinder tracks. **2** the track or stadium where such races are held. **3** *US & Canad.* **3a** a racetrack for cars. **3b** a road on which fast driving is allowed.

speedwell (ˈspiːdˌwɛl) *n* any of various temperate plants, such as the **common speedwell** and the **germander speedwell,** having small blue or pinkish-white flowers.

speedy (ˈspiːdɪ) *adj* **speedier, speediest. 1** characterized by speed. **2** done or decided without delay.
▸ **ˈspeedily** *adv* ▸ **ˈspeediness** *n*

spek (spɛk) *n S. African.* bacon. ORIG from Afrik., from Du.

speleology *or* **spelaeology** (ˌspiːlɪˈɒlədʒɪ) *n* **1** the scientific study of caves. **2** the sport or pastime of exploring caves. ORIG C19: from L *spēlaeum* cave
▸ **speleological** *or* **spelaeological** (ˌspiːlɪəˈlɒdʒɪkᵊl) *adj*
▸ **ˌspeleˈologist** *or* **ˌspelaeˈologist** *n*

spell[1] (spɛl) *vb* **spells, spelling; spelt** *or* **spelled. 1** to write or name in correct order the letters that comprise the conventionally accepted form of (a word). **2** (*tr*) (of letters) to go to make up the conventionally established form of (a word) when arranged correctly: *d-o-g spells dog.* **3** (*tr*) to indicate or signify: *such actions spell disaster.* ◆ See also **spell out.** ORIG C13: from OF *espeller,* of Gmc origin
▸ **ˈspellable** *adj*

spell[2] (spɛl) *n* **1** a verbal formula considered as having magical force. **2** any influence that can control the mind or character; fascination. **3** a state induced as by the pronouncing of a spell; trance: *to break the spell.* **4 under a spell.** held in or as if in a spell. ORIG OE *spell* speech

spell[3] (spɛl) *n* **1** an indeterminate, usually short, period of time: *a spell of cold weather.* **2** a period or tour of duty after which one person or group relieves another. **3** *Scot., Austral., & NZ.* a period or interval of rest. ◆ *vb* **4** (*tr*) to take over from (a person) for an interval of time; relieve temporarily. ORIG OE *spelian* to take the place of, from ?

spellbind (ˈspɛlˌbaɪnd) *vb* **spellbinds, spellbinding, spellbound.** (*tr*) to cause to be spellbound; entrance or enthral.
▸ **ˈspellˌbinder** *n*

spellbound (ˈspɛlˌbaʊnd) *adj* having one's attention held as though one is bound by a spell.

spellchecker (ˈspɛlˌtʃɛkə) *n Computing.* a program that highlights any word in a word-processed document that is not recognized as being correctly spelt.

speller (ˈspɛlə) *n* **1** a person who spells words in the manner specified: *a bad speller.* **2** a book designed to teach or improve spelling.

spelling (ˈspɛlɪŋ) *n* **1** the act or process of writing words by using the letters conventionally accepted for their formation; orthography. **2** the art or study of orthography. **3** the way in which a word is spelt. **4** the ability of a person to spell.

spelling bee *n* a contest in which players are required to spell words.

spell out *vb* (*tr, adv*) **1** to make clear, distinct, or explicit; clarify in detail: *let me spell out the implications.* **2** to read laboriously or with difficulty, working out each word letter by letter. **3** to discern by study; puzzle out.

spelt[1] (spɛlt) *vb* a past tense and past participle of **spell**[1].

spelt[2] (spɛlt) *n* a species of wheat that was formerly much cultivated and was used to develop present-day cultivated wheats. ORIG OE

spelter (ˈspɛltə) *n* impure zinc. ORIG C17: prob. from MDu. *speauter,* from ?

spelunker (spɪˈlʌŋkə) *n* a person whose hobby is the exploration of caves. ORIG C20: from L *spēlunca,* from Gk *spēlunx* a cave
▸ **speˈlunking** *n*

Spence ★ (spɛns) *n* Sir **Basil** (**Unwin**). 1907–76, British architect, born in India; designed Coventry Cathedral (1951).

spencer[1] (ˈspɛnsə) *n* **1** a short fitted coat or jacket. **2** a woman's knitted vest. ORIG C18: after Earl *Spencer* (1758–1834)

spencer[2] (ˈspɛnsə) *n Naut.* a large loose-footed gaffsail on a square-rigger or barque. ORIG C19: ?from a proper name

Spencer ★ (ˈspɛnsə) *n* **1 Herbert.** 1820–1903, British philosopher, who applied evolutionary theory to the study of society. **2** Sir **Stanley.** 1891–1959, British painter, noted for his paintings of Christ in a contemporary British setting.

Spencer Gulf ★ *n* an inlet of the Indian Ocean in S Australia, between the Eyre and Yorke Peninsulas. Length: about 320 km (200 miles). Greatest width: about 145 km (90 miles).

spend (spɛnd) *vb* **spends, spending, spent. 1** to pay out (money, wealth, etc.). **2** (*tr*) to concentrate (time, effort, etc.) upon an object, activity, etc. **3** (*tr*) to pass (time) in a specific way, place, etc. **4** (*tr*) to use up completely: *the hurricane spent its force.* **5** (*tr*) to give up (one's blood, life, etc.) in a cause. ORIG OE *spendan,* from L *expendere;* infl. also by OF *despendre* to spend; see EXPEND, DISPENSE
▸ **ˈspendable** *adj* ▸ **ˈspender** *n*

Spender ★ (ˈspɛndə) *n* Sir **Stephen.** 1909–95, British poet; coeditor of *Horizon* (1939–41) and of *Encounter* (1953–67).

spendthrift (ˈspɛndˌθrɪft) *n* **1** a person who spends money in an extravagant manner. ◆ *adj* **2** (*usually prenominal*) of or like a spendthrift.

Spengler ★ (ˈspɛŋlə; *German* ˈʃpɛŋlər) *n* **Oswald** (ˈɔsvalt). 1880–1936, German philosopher, noted for *The Decline of the West* (1918–22).

Spenser ★ (ˈspɛnsə) *n* **Edmund.** ?1552–99, English poet celebrated for the allegorical *The Faerie Queene* (1590; 1596). His other verse includes the collection of eclogues *The Shepheardes Calendar* (1579).

Spenserian (spɛnˈsɪərɪən) *adj* **1** relating to or characteristic of Edmund Spenser or his poetry. ◆ *n* **2** a student or imitator of Edmund Spenser.

Spenserian stanza *n Prosody.* the stanza form used by the poet Spenser in his poem *The Faerie Queene,* consisting of eight lines in iambic pentameter and a concluding Alexandrine, rhyming a b a b b c b c c.

spent (spɛnt) *vb* **1** the past tense and past participle of **spend.** ◆ *adj* **2** used up or exhausted; consumed. **3** (of a fish) exhausted by spawning.

sperm¹ (spɜːm) *n, pl* **sperms** *or* **sperm. 1** another name for **semen. 2** a male reproductive cell; male gamete. ORIG C14: from LL *sperma,* from Gk

sperm² (spɜːm) *n* short for **sperm whale, spermaceti,** or **sperm oil.**

-sperm *n combining form.* (in botany) a seed: *gymnosperm.*
▸ **-spermous** *or* **-spermal** *adj combining form.*

spermaceti (ˌspɜːməˈsɛtɪ, -ˈsiːtɪ) *n* a white waxy substance obtained from oil from the head of the sperm whale. ORIG C15: from Med. L *sperma cētī* whale's sperm, from *sperma* SPERM¹ + L *cētus* whale, from Gk *kētos*

spermatic (spɜːˈmætɪk), **spermic** (ˈspɜːmɪk), *or* **spermous** (ˈspɜːməs) *adj* **1** of or relating to spermatozoa: *spermatic fluid.* **2** of or relating to the testis: *the spermatic artery.* ORIG C16: from LL *spermaticus,* from Gk *spermatikos* concerning seed, from *sperma* seed
▸ **sperˈmatically** *adv*

spermatid (ˈspɜːmətɪd) *n Zool.* any of four immature male gametes that are formed from a spermatocyte, each of which develops into a spermatozoon.

spermato-, spermo- *or before a vowel* **spermat-, sperm-** *combining form.* **1** indicating sperm: *spermatozoon.* **2** indicating seed: *spermatophyte.* ORIG from Gk *sperma, spermat-* seed

spermatocyte (ˈspɜːmətəʊˌsaɪt) *n* an immature male germ cell.

spermatogenesis (ˌspɜːmətəʊˈdʒɛnɪsɪs) *n* the formation and maturation of spermatozoa in the testis.
▸ **spermatogenetic** (ˌspɜːmətəʊdʒɪˈnɛtɪk) *adj*

spermatogonium (ˌspɜːmətəˈgəʊnɪəm) *n, pl* **spermatogonia** (-nɪə). *Zool.* an immature male germ cell that divides to form many spermatocytes.

spermatophyte (ˈspɜːmətəʊˌfaɪt) *or* **spermophyte** *n* (in traditional classifications) any seed-bearing plant. Former name: **phanerogam.**
▸ **spermatophytic** (ˌspɜːmətəʊˈfɪtɪk) *adj*

spermatozoon (ˌspɜːmətəʊˈzəʊɒn) *n, pl* **spermatozoa** (-ˈzəʊə). any of the male reproductive cells released in the semen during ejaculation. Also called: **sperm, zoosperm.**
▸ **ˌspermatoˈzoal, ˌspermatoˈzoan,** *or* **ˌspermatoˈzoic** *adj*

spermicide (ˈspɜːmɪˌsaɪd) *n* any agent that kills spermatozoa.
▸ **ˌspermiˈcidal** *adj*

sperm oil *n* an oil obtained from the head of the sperm whale, used as a lubricant.

spermous (ˈspɜːməs) *adj* **1** of or relating to the sperm whale or its products. **2** another word for **spermatic.**

sperm whale *n* a large toothed whale, having a square-shaped head and hunted for sperm oil, spermaceti, and ambergris. Also called: **cachalot.** ORIG C19: short for SPERMACETI *whale*

spew (spjuː) *vb* **1** to eject (the contents of the stomach) involuntarily through the mouth; vomit. **2** to spit (spittle, phlegm, etc.) out of the mouth. **3** (usually foll. by *out*) to send or be sent out in a stream: *flames spewed out.* ◆ *n* **4** something ejected from the mouth. ◆ Also (archaic): **spue.** ORIG OE *spīwan*
▸ **ˈspewer** *n*

Spey ★ (speɪ) *n* a river in E Scotland, flowing generally northeast through the Grampian Mountains to the Moray Firth: salmon fishing. Length: 172 km (107 miles).

Speyer ★ (*German* ˈʃpaiər) *n* a port in SW Germany, in Rhineland-Palatinate on the Rhine: the scene of 50 imperial diets. Pop.: 47 450 (1991). English name: **Spires.**

SPF *abbrev. for* sun protection factor: an indicator of how effectively a lotion, cosmetic, etc., protects the skin from the harmful rays of the sun.

sp. gr. *abbrev. for* specific gravity.

sphagnum (ˈsfægnəm) *n* any moss of the genus *Sphagnum,* of temperate bogs: layers of these mosses decay to form peat. Also called: **peat moss, bog moss.** ORIG C18: from NL, from Gk *sphagnos* a variety of moss
▸ **ˈsphagnous** *adj*

sphairee (sfaɪriː) *n Austral.* a game resembling tennis played with wooden bats and a perforated plastic ball. ORIG from Gk *sphaira* a ball

sphalerite (ˈsfæləˌraɪt, ˈsfeɪlə-) *n* a yellow to brownish-black mineral consisting mainly of zinc sulphide in cubic crystalline form: the chief source of zinc. Formula: ZnS. Also called: **zinc blende.** ORIG C19: from Gk *sphaleros* deceitful, from *sphallein* to cause to stumble

sphene (sfiːn) *n* a brown, yellow, green, or grey lustrous mineral consisting of calcium titanium silicate in monoclinic crystalline form. Also called: **titanite.** ORIG C19: from F *sphène,* from Gk *sphēn* a wedge, alluding to its crystals

sphenoid (ˈsfiːnɔɪd) *adj also* **sphenoidal. 1** wedge-shaped. **2** of or relating to the sphenoid bone. ◆ *n* **3** See **sphenoid bone.**

sphenoid bone *n* the large butterfly-shaped compound bone at the base of the skull.

sphere (sfɪə) *n* **1** *Maths.* **1a** a three-dimensional closed surface such that every point on the surface is equidistant from a given point, the centre. **1b** the solid figure bounded by this surface or the space enclosed by it. **2** any object having approximately this shape; a globe. **3** the night sky considered as a vaulted roof; firmament. **4** any heavenly object such as a planet, natural satellite, or star. **5** (in the Ptolemaic or Copernican systems of astronomy) one of a series of revolving hollow globes, arranged concentrically, on whose transparent surfaces the sun, the moon, the planets, and fixed stars were thought to be set. **6** a particular field of activity; environment. **7** a social class or stratum of society. ◆ *vb* **spheres, sphering, sphered.** (*tr*) *Chiefly poetic.* **8** to surround or encircle. **9** to place aloft or in the heavens. ORIG C14: from LL *sphēra,* from L *sphaera* globe, from Gk *sphaira*
▸ **ˈspheral** *adj*

-sphere *n combining form.* **1** having the shape or form of a sphere: *bathysphere.* **2** indicating a spherelike enveloping mass: *atmosphere.*
▸ **-spheric** *adj combining form.*

spherical (ˈsfɛrɪkᵊl) *or* **spheric** *adj* **1** shaped like a sphere. **2** of or relating to a sphere: *spherical geometry.* **3** *Geom.* formed on the surface of or inside a sphere: *a spherical triangle.* **4a** of or relating to heavenly bodies. **4b**

of or relating to the spheres of the Ptolemaic or the Copernican system.
▸ **'spherically** *adv* ▸ **'sphericalness** *n*

spherical aberration *n Physics.* a defect of optical systems that arises when light striking a mirror or lens near its edge is focused at different points on the axis to the light striking near the centre. The effect occurs when the mirror or lens has spherical surfaces.

spherical angle *n* an angle formed at the intersection of two great circles of a sphere.

spherical coordinates *pl n* three coordinates that define the location of a point in space in terms of its radius vector, *r,* the angle, θ, which this vector makes with one axis, and the angle, ϕ, which the plane of this vector makes with a mutually perpendicular axis.

spherical trigonometry *n* the branch of trigonometry concerned with the measurement of the angles and sides of spherical triangles.

spheroid ('sfɪərɔɪd) *n* **1** another name for **ellipsoid of revolution.** ◆ *adj* **2** shaped like but not exactly a sphere.
▸ **spher'oidal** *adj* ▸ **,spheroid'icity** *n*

spherometer (sfɪə'rɒmɪtə) *n* an instrument for measuring the curvature of a surface.

spherule ('sfɛru:l) *n* a very small sphere. ORIG C17: from LL *sphaerula*
▸ **'spherular** *adj*

spherulite ('sfɛru,laɪt) *n* any of several spherical masses of radiating needle-like crystals of one or more minerals occurring in rocks such as obsidian.
▸ **spherulitic** (,sfɛru'lɪtɪk) *adj*

sphincter ('sfɪŋktə) *n Anat.* a ring of muscle surrounding the opening of a hollow organ or body and contracting to close it. ORIG C16: from LL, from Gk *sphinktēr,* from *sphingein* to grip tightly
▸ **'sphincteral** *adj*

sphinx (sfɪŋks) *n, pl* **sphinxes** *or* **sphinges** ('sfɪndʒi:z). **1** any of a number of huge stone statues built by the ancient Egyptians, having the body of a lion and the head of a man. **2** an inscrutable person.

Sphinx ★ (sfɪŋks) *n* **the. 1** *Greek myth.* a monster with a woman's head and a lion's body. She lay outside Thebes, asking travellers a riddle and killing them when they failed to answer it. Oedipus answered the riddle and the Sphinx then killed herself. **2** the huge statue of a sphinx near the pyramids at El Gîza in Egypt. ORIG C16: via L from Gk, apparently from *sphingein* to hold fast

sphragistics (sfrə'dʒɪstɪks) *n* (*functioning as sing*) the study of seals and signet rings. ORIG C19: from Gk *sphragistikos,* from *sphragizein* to seal, from *sphragis* a seal
▸ **sphra'gistic** *adj*

sphygmo- *or before a vowel* **sphygm-** *combining form.* indicating the pulse: *sphygmograph.* ORIG from Gk *sphugmos* pulsation, from *sphuzein* to throb

sphygmograph ('sfɪgməu,grɑ:f) *n Med.* an instrument for making a recording (**sphygmogram**) of variations in blood pressure and pulse.
▸ **sphygmographic** (,sfɪgməu'græfɪk) *adj* ▸ **sphygmography** (sfɪg'mɒgrəfɪ) *n*

sphygmomanometer (,sfɪgməumə'nɒmɪtə) *n Med.* an instrument for measuring arterial blood pressure.

spicate ('spaɪkeɪt) *adj Bot.* having, arranged in, or relating to spikes: *a spicate inflorescence.* ORIG C17: from L *spīcātus* having spikes, from *spīca* a point

spiccato (spɪ'kɑ:təu) *Music.* ◆ *n* **1** a style of playing a bowed stringed instrument in which the bow bounces lightly off the strings. ◆ *adj, adv* **2** (to be played) in this manner. ORIG It.: detached

spice (spaɪs) *n* **1a** any of a variety of aromatic vegetable substances, such as ginger, cinnamon, or nutmeg, used as flavourings. **1b** these substances collectively. **2** something that represents or introduces zest, charm, or gusto. **3** *Rare.* a small amount. ◆ *vb* **spices, spicing, spiced.** (*tr*) **4** to prepare or flavour (food) with spices. **5** to introduce charm or zest into. ORIG C13: from OF *espice,* from LL *speciēs* (pl) spices, from L *speciēs* (sing) kind; also associated with LL *spīcea* (unattested) fragrant herb, from L *spīceus* having spikes of foliage

spicebush ('spaɪs,bʊʃ) *n* a North American shrub having aromatic leaves and bark.

Spice Islands ★ *pl n* the former name of the **Moluccas.**

spick-and-span *or* **spic-and-span** ('spɪkən'spæn) *adj* **1** extremely neat and clean. **2** new and fresh. ORIG C17: shortened from *spick-and-span-new,* from obs. *spick* spike + *span-new,* from ON *spānnȳr* absolutely new

spicule ('spɪkju:l) *n* **1** Also called: **spiculum.** a small slender pointed structure or crystal, esp. any of the calcareous or siliceous elements of the skeleton of sponges, corals, etc. **2** *Astron.* a spiked ejection of hot gas above the sun's surface. ORIG C18: from L *spiculum* small, sharp point
▸ **spiculate** ('spɪkju,leɪt, -lɪt) *adj*

spicy ('spaɪsɪ) *adj* **spicier, spiciest. 1** seasoned with or containing spice. **2** highly flavoured; pungent. **3** *Inf.* suggestive of scandal or sensation.
▸ **'spicily** *adv* ▸ **'spiciness** *n*

spider ('spaɪdə) *n* **1** any of various predatory silk-producing arachnids, having four pairs of legs and a rounded unsegmented body. **2** any of various similar or related arachnids. **3** any implement or tool having the shape of a spider. **4** any part of a machine having a number of radiating spokes, tines, or arms. **5** Also called: **octopus.** *Brit.* a cluster of elastic straps fastened at a central point and used to hold a load on a car rack, motorcycle, etc. **6** *Snooker, etc.* a rest having long legs, used to raise the cue above the level of the height of the ball. **7** *Computing.* a program that is capable of performing sophisticated recursive searches on the Internet. ORIG OE *spīthra*
▸ **'spidery** *adj*

spider crab *n* any of various crabs having a small triangular body and very long legs.

spiderman ('spaɪdə,mæn) *n, pl* **spidermen.** *Inf., chiefly Brit.* a person who erects the steel structure of a building.

spider mite *n* any of various plant-feeding mites, esp. the **red spider mite,** which is a serious orchard pest.

spider monkey *n* **1** any of several arboreal New World monkeys of Central and South America, having very long legs, a long prehensile tail, and a small head. **2** **woolly spider monkey.** a rare related monkey of SE Brazil.

spider plant *n* a house plant having long narrow leaves with a light central stripe.

spiderwort ('spaɪdə,wɜ:t) *n* **1** any of various American plants having blue, purplish, or pink flowers and widely grown as house plants. See also **tradescantia. 2** any of various similar or related plants.

spiel (ʃpi:l) *n* **1** glib plausible talk, associated esp. with salesmen. ◆ *vb* **2** (*intr*) to deliver a prepared spiel. **3** (*tr;* usually foll. by *off*) to recite (a prepared oration). ORIG C19: from G *Spiel* play
▸ **'spieler** *n*

Spielberg ★ ('spi:lbɜ:g) *n* **Steven.** born 1947, US film director, noted for such films as *Jaws* (1975), *Close Encounters of the Third Kind* (1977), *E.T.* (1982), *Schindler's List* (1993), and *Saving Private Ryan* (1998).

spier ('spaɪə) *n Arch.* a person who spies or scouts.

spiffing ('spɪfɪŋ) *adj Brit. sl., old-fashioned.* excellent; splendid. ORIG C19: prob. from dialect *spiff* spruce, smart

spiffy ('spɪfɪ) *adj* **spiffier, spiffiest.** *US & Canad. sl.* smart; stylish. ORIG C19: from dialect *spiff* smartly dressed
▸ **'spiffily** *adv*

spigot ('spɪgət) *n* **1** a stopper for the vent hole of a cask. **2** a tap, usually of wood, fitted to a cask. **3** a US name for **tap**[2] (sense 1). **4** a short projection on one component designed to fit into a hole on another, esp. the male part of a joint between two pipes. ORIG C14: prob. from OProvençal *espiga* a head of grain, from L *spīca* a point

spike[1] (spaɪk) *n* **1** a sharp point. **2** any sharp-pointed object, esp. one made of metal. **3** a long metal nail. **4** (*pl*) shoes with metal projections on the sole and heel for greater traction, as used by athletes. **5** *Brit. sl.* another word for **dosshouse.** ◆ *vb* **spikes, spiking, spiked.** (*tr*) **6** to secure or supply with or as with spikes. **7** to render ineffective or block the intentions of; thwart. **8** to impale on a spike. **9** to add alcohol to (a drink). **10** *Volleyball.* to hit (a

ball) sharply downwards with an overarm motion from the front of one's own court into the opposing court. **11** (formerly) to render (a cannon) ineffective by blocking its vent with a spike. **12 spike (someone's) guns.** to thwart (someone's) purpose. ORIG C13 *spyk*
▸ **'spiky** *adj*

spike[2] (spaɪk) *n Bot.* **1** an inflorescence consisting of a raceme of sessile flowers. **2** an ear of wheat, etc. ORIG C14: from L *spīca* ear of corn

spikelet ('spaɪklɪt) *n Bot.* a small spike, esp. the inflorescence of most grasses and sedges.

spikenard ('spaɪknɑːd, 'spaɪkə,nɑːd) *n* **1** an aromatic Indian plant, having rose-purple flowers. **2** an aromatic ointment obtained from this plant. **3** any of various similar or related plants. **4** a North American plant having small green flowers and an aromatic root. ◆ Also called (for senses 1, 2): **nard.** ORIG C14: from Med. L *spīca nardī;* see SPIKE[2], NARD

spile (spaɪl) *n* **1** a heavy timber stake or pile. **2** *US.* a spout for tapping sap from the sugar maple tree. **3** a plug or spigot. ◆ *vb* **spiles, spiling, spiled.** (*tr*) **4** to provide or support with a spile. **5** *US.* to tap (a tree) with a spile. ORIG C16: prob. from MDu. *spile* peg

spill[1] (spɪl) *vb* **spills, spilling; spilt** *or* **spilled.** (*mainly tr*) **1** (when *intr,* usually foll. by *from, out of,* etc.) to fall or cause to fall from or as from a container, esp. unintentionally. **2** to disgorge (contents, occupants, etc.) or (of contents, occupants, etc.) to be disgorged. **3** to shed (blood). **4** Also: **spill the beans.** *Inf.* to divulge something confidential. **5** *Naut.* to let (wind) escape from a sail or (of the wind) to escape from a sail. ◆ *n* **6** *Inf.* a fall or tumble. **7** short for **spillway. 8** a spilling of liquid, etc., or the amount spilt. **9** *Austral.* the declaring of several political jobs vacant when one higher up becomes so. ORIG OE *spillan* to destroy
▸ **'spillage** *n* ▸ **'spiller** *n*

spill[2] (spɪl) *n* a splinter of wood or strip of twisted paper with which pipes, fires, etc., are lit. ORIG C13: of Gmc origin

Spillane ★ (spɪ'leɪn) *n* **Mickey,** original name *Frank Morrison Spillane.* born 1918, US detective-story writer, best known for his books featuring the detective Mike Hammer, for example *I, the Jury* (1947).

spillikin, spilikin ('spɪlɪkɪn), *or* **spellican** ('spɛlɪkən) *n* a thin strip of wood, cardboard, or plastic, esp. one used in spillikins.

spillikins ('spɪlɪkɪnz) *n* (*functioning as sing*) *Brit.* a game in which players try to pick each spillikin from a heap without moving any of the others. Also called: **jackstraws.**

spill over *vb* **1** (*intr, adv*) to overflow or be forced out of an area, container, etc. ◆ *n* **spillover.** *Chiefly US & Canad.* **2** the act of spilling over. **3** the excess part of something.

spillway ('spɪl,weɪ) *n* a channel that carries away surplus water, as from a dam.

spilt (spɪlt) *vb* a past tense and past participle of **spill**[1].

spin (spɪn) *vb* **spins, spinning, spun. 1** to rotate or cause to rotate rapidly, as on an axis. **2a** to draw out and twist (natural fibres, as of silk or cotton) into a long continuous thread. **2b** to make such a thread or filament from (synthetic resins, etc.), usually by forcing through a nozzle. **3** (of spiders, silkworms, etc.) to form (webs, cocoons, etc.) from a silky fibre exuded from the body. **4** (*tr*) to shape (metal) into a rounded form on a lathe. **5** (*tr*) *Inf.* to tell (a tale, story, etc.) by drawing it out at great length (esp. in **spin a yarn**). **6** to bowl, pitch, hit, or kick (a ball) so that it rotates in the air and changes direction or speed on bouncing, or (of a ball) to be projected in this way. **7** (*intr*) (of wheels) to revolve rapidly without causing propulsion. **8** to cause (an aircraft) to dive in a spiral descent or (of an aircraft) to dive in a spiral descent. **9** (*intr;* foll. by *along*) to drive or travel swiftly. **10** (*tr*) Also: **spin-dry.** to rotate (clothes) in a washing machine in order to extract surplus water. **11** (*intr*) to reel or grow dizzy, as from turning around: *my head is spinning.* **12** (*intr*) to fish by drawing a revolving lure through the water. **13** (*intr*) *Inf.* to present news or information in a way that creates a favourable impression. ◆ *n* **14** a swift rotating motion; instance of spinning. **15** *Physics.* **15a** the intrinsic angular momentum of an elementary particle or atomic nucleus. **15b** a quantum number determining values of this angular momentum. **16** a condition of loss of control of an aircraft or an intentional flight manoeuvre in which the aircraft performs a continuous spiral descent. **17** a spinning motion imparted to a ball, etc. **18** *Inf.* a short or fast drive, ride, etc., esp. in a car, for pleasure. **19** *Inf.* the practice of presenting news or information in a way that creates a favourable impression. **20** *Austral. & NZ inf.* a period of a specified kind of fortune: *a bad spin.* **21 flat spin.** *Inf., chiefly Brit.* a state of agitation or confusion. **22 on the spin.** *Inf.* one after another: *they have lost two finals on the spin.* ◆ See also **spin out.** ORIG OE *spinnan*

spina bifida ('spaɪnə 'bɪfɪdə) *n* a congenital condition in which the meninges of the spinal cord protrude through a gap in the backbone, sometimes causing enlargement of the skull and paralysis. ORIG NL; see SPINE, BIFID

spinach ('spɪnɪdʒ, -ɪtʃ) *n* **1** an annual plant cultivated for its dark green edible leaves. **2** the leaves, eaten as a vegetable. ORIG C16: from OF *espinache,* from OSp., from Ar. *isfānākh,* from Persian

spinal ('spaɪnᵊl) *adj* **1** of or relating to the spine or the spinal cord. ◆ *n* **2** short for **spinal anaesthesia.**
▸ **'spinally** *adv*

spinal anaesthesia *n* **1** anaesthesia of the lower half of the body produced by injecting an anaesthetic beneath the arachnoid membrane. Cf. **epidural** (sense 2). **2** loss of sensation in part of the body as the result of injury of the spinal cord.

spinal canal *n* the passage through the spinal column that contains the spinal cord.

spinal column *n* a series of contiguous or interconnecting bony or cartilaginous segments that surround and protect the spinal cord. Also called: **spine, vertebral column.** Nontechnical name: **backbone.**

spinal cord *n* the thick cord of nerve tissue within the spinal canal, which together with the brain forms the central nervous system.

spin bowler *n* another name for **spinner** (sense 2b).

spindle ('spɪndᵊl) *n* **1** a rod or stick that has a notch in the top, used to draw out natural fibres for spinning into thread, and a long narrow body around which the thread is wound when spun. **2** one of the thin rods or pins bearing bobbins upon which spun thread is wound in a spinning machine. **3** any of various parts in the form of a rod, esp. a rotating rod that acts as an axle, etc. **4** a piece of wood that has been turned, such as a table leg. **5** a small square metal shaft that passes through the lock of a door and to which the door knobs or handles are fixed. **6** *Biol.* a spindle-shaped structure formed in a cell during mitosis or meiosis which draws the duplicated chromosomes apart during cell division. **7** a device consisting of a sharp upright spike on a pedestal on which bills, order forms, etc., are impaled. ◆ *vb* **spindles, spindling, spindled. 8** (*tr*) to form into a spindle or equip with spindles. **9** (*intr*) *Rare.* (of a plant, stem, shoot, etc.) to grow rapidly and become elongated and thin. ORIG OE *spinel*

spindlelegs ('spɪndᵊl,lɛgz) *or* **spindleshanks** *n* **1** (*functioning as pl*) long thin legs. **2** (*functioning as sing*) a person who has such legs.

spindle tree *n* any of various shrubs or trees of Europe and W Asia, typically having red fruits and yielding a hard wood formerly used in making spindles.

spindly ('spɪndlɪ) *adj* **spindlier, spindliest.** tall, slender, and frail; attenuated.

spin doctor *n Inf.* a person who provides a favourable slant to an item of news, potentially unpopular policy, etc., esp. on behalf of a political personality or party. ORIG C20: from the spin given to a ball in various sports to make it go in the desired direction

spindrift ('spɪn,drɪft) *n* spray blown up from the sea. Also: **spoondrift.** ORIG C16: Scot. var. of *spoondrift,* from *spoon* to scud + DRIFT

spin-dry *vb* **spin-dries, spin-drying, spin-dried.** (*tr*) to extract

★ people and places

water from (wet washing) by spinning in a washing machine or spin-dryer.

spin-dryer *n* a device that extracts water from clothes, etc., by spinning them in a perforated drum.

spine (spaɪn) *n* **1** the spinal column. **2** the sharply pointed tip or outgrowth of a leaf, stem, etc. **3** *Zool.* a hard pointed process or structure, such as the quill of a porcupine. **4** the back of a book, record sleeve, etc. **5** a ridge, esp. of a hill. **6** strength of endurance, will, etc. **7** anything resembling the spinal column in function or importance; main support or feature. ORIG C14: from OF *espine* spine, from L *spīna* thorn, backbone
▸ **spined** *adj*

spine-chiller *n* a book, film, etc., that arouses terror.
▸ **'spine-ˌchilling** *adj*

spinel (spɪ'nɛl) *n* any of a group of hard glassy minerals of variable colour consisting of oxides of aluminium, magnesium, iron, zinc, or manganese: used as gemstones. ORIG C16: from F *spinelle,* from It. *spinella,* dim. of *spina* a thorn, from L; so called from the shape of the crystals

spineless ('spaɪnlɪs) *adj* **1** lacking a backbone. **2** having no spiny processes: *spineless stems.* **3** lacking character, resolution, or courage.
▸ **'spinelessly** *adv* ▸ **'spinelessness** *n*

spinet (spɪ'nɛt, 'spɪnɪt) *n* a small type of harpsichord having one manual. ORIG C17: from It. *spinetta,* ? from Giovanni *Spinetti,* 16th-cent. It. maker of musical instruments & its supposed inventor

spinifex ('spɪnɪˌfɛks) *n* **1** any of various Australian grasses having pointed leaves and spiny seed heads. **2** Also called: **porcupine grass.** *Austral.* any of various coarse spiny-leaved inland grasses. ORIG C19: from NL, from L *spīna* a thorn + *-fex* maker, from *facere* to make

spinnaker ('spɪnəkə; *Naut.* 'spæŋkə) *n* a large light triangular racing sail set from the foremast of a yacht. ORIG C19: prob. from SPIN + (MO)NIKER, but traditionally from *Sphinx,* the yacht that first adopted this type of sail

spinner ('spɪnə) *n* **1** a person or thing that spins. **2** *Cricket.* **2a** a ball that is bowled with a spinning motion. **2b** a bowler who specializes in bowling such balls. **3** a streamlined fairing that fits over the hub of an aircraft propeller. **4** a fishing lure with a fin or wing that revolves.

spinneret ('spɪnəˌrɛt) *n* **1** any of several organs in spiders and certain insects through which silk threads are exuded. **2** a finely perforated dispenser through which a liquid is extruded in the production of synthetic fibres.

spinney ('spɪnɪ) *n Chiefly Brit.* a small wood or copse. ORIG C16: from OF *espinei,* from *espine* thorn, from L *spīna*

spinning ('spɪnɪŋ) *n* **1** the act or process of spinning. **2** the act or technique of casting and drawing a revolving lure through the water so as to imitate a live fish, etc. **3** indoor cycling performed on a static bike while watching a simulated bike ride and listening to music.

spinning jenny *n* an early type of spinning frame with several spindles, invented in 1764.

spinning wheel *n* a wheel-like machine for spinning at home, having one hand- or foot-operated spindle.

spin-off *n* **1** any product or development derived incidentally from the application of existing knowledge or enterprise. **2** a book, film, or television series derived from a similar successful book, film, or television series.

spinose ('spaɪnəʊs, spaɪ'nəʊs) *adj* (esp. of plants) bearing many spines. ORIG C17: from L *spīnōsus* prickly, from *spīna* a thorn

spin out *vb* (*tr, adv*) **1** to extend or protract (a story, etc.) by including superfluous detail. **2** to spend or pass (time). **3** to contrive to cause (money, etc.) to last as long as possible.

Spinoza ★ (spɪ'nəʊzə) *n* **Baruch** (bə'ruːk). 1632–77, Dutch pantheistic rationalist philosopher. His chief work is *The Ethics* (1677).

spinster ('spɪnstə) *n* **1** an unmarried woman. **2** a woman regarded as being beyond the age of marriage. **3** (formerly) a woman who spins thread for her living. ORIG C14 (in the sense: a person, esp. a woman, whose occupation is spinning; C17: a woman still unmarried): from SPIN + -STER
▸ **'spinsterˌhood** *n* ▸ **'spinsterish** *adj*

spiny ('spaɪnɪ) *adj* **spinier, spiniest. 1** (of animals) having or covered with quills or spines. **2** (of plants) covered with spines; thorny. **3** troublesome; puzzling.
▸ **'spininess** *n*

spiny anteater *n* another name for **echidna.**

spiny-finned *adj* (of certain fishes) having fins that are supported by stiff bony spines.

spiny lobster *n* any of various large edible marine decapod crustaceans having a very tough spiny carapace. Also called: **rock lobster, crawfish, langouste.**

spiracle ('spaɪərəkᵊl, 'spaɪrə-) *n* **1** any of several paired apertures in the cuticle of an insect, by which air enters and leaves the trachea. **2** a small paired rudimentary gill slit in skates, rays, and related fishes. **3** any similar respiratory aperture, such as the blowhole in whales. ORIG C14 (orig.: breath): from L *spīrăculum* vent, from *spīrāre* to breathe
▸ **spiracular** (spɪ'rækjʊlə) *adj* ▸ **spi'raculate** *adj*

spiraea *or esp. US* **spirea** (spaɪ'rɪə) *n* any of various rosaceous plants having sprays of small white or pink flowers. See also **meadowsweet** (sense 2). ORIG C17: via L from Gk *speiraia,* from *speira* SPIRE[2]

spiral ('spaɪərəl) *n* **1** *Geom.* one of several plane curves formed by a point winding about a fixed point at an ever-increasing distance from it. **2** a curve that lies on a cylinder or cone, at a constant angle to the line segments making up the surface; helix. **3** something that pursues a winding, usually upward, course or that displays a twisting form or shape. **4** a flight manoeuvre in which an aircraft descends describing a helix of comparatively large radius with the angle of attack within the normal flight range. **5** *Econ.* a continuous upward or downward movement in economic activity or prices, caused by interaction between prices, wages, demand, and production. ◆ *adj* **6** having the shape of a spiral. ◆ *vb* **spirals, spiralling, spiralled** *or US* **spirals, spiraling, spiraled. 7** to assume or cause to assume a spiral course or shape. **8** (*intr*) to increase or decrease with steady acceleration: *prices continue to spiral.* ORIG C16: via F from Med. L *spīrālis,* from L *spīra* a coil; see SPIRE[2]
▸ **'spirally** *adv*

spiral galaxy *n* a galaxy consisting of an ellipsoidal nucleus of old stars from opposite sides of which arms, containing younger stars, spiral outwards around the nucleus.

spirant ('spaɪrənt) *adj* **1** *Phonetics.* another word for **fricative.** ◆ *n* **2** a fricative consonant. ORIG C19: from L *spīrāns* breathing, from *spīrāre* to breathe

spire[1] ('spaɪə) *n* **1** Also called: **steeple.** a tall structure that tapers upwards to a point, esp. one on a tower or roof or one that forms the upper part of a steeple. **2** a slender tapering shoot or stem, such as a blade of grass. **3** the apical part of any tapering formation; summit. ◆ *vb* **spires, spiring, spired. 4** (*intr*) to assume the shape of a spire; point up. **5** (*tr*) to furnish with a spire or spires. ORIG OE *spīr* blade
▸ **'spiry** *adj*

spire[2] ('spaɪə) *n* **1** any of the coils or turns in a spiral structure. **2** the apical part of a spiral shell. ORIG C16: from L *spīra* a coil, from Gk *speira*

Spires ★ ('spaɪəz) *n* the English name for **Speyer.**

spirillum (spaɪ'rɪləm) *n, pl* **spirilla** (-lə). **1** any bacterium having a curved or spirally twisted rodlike body. **2** any bacterium of the genus *Spirillum,* such as *S. minus,* which causes ratbite fever. ORIG C19: from NL, lit.: a little coil, from *spīra* a coil

spirit[1] ('spɪrɪt) *n* **1** the force or principle of life that animates the body of living things. **2** temperament or disposition: *truculent in spirit.* **3** liveliness; mettle: *they set to it with spirit.* **4** the fundamental, emotional, and activating principle of a person; will: *the experience broke his spirit.* **5** a sense of loyalty or dedication: *team spirit.* **6** the prevailing element; feeling: *a spirit of joy pervaded the atmosphere.* **7** state of mind or mood; attitude: *he did it in the wrong spirit.* **8** (*pl*) an emotional state, esp. with regard to exaltation or dejection: *in high spirits.* **9** a person characterized by some activity, quality, or disposition: *a leading spirit of the movement.* **10** the deeper more significant meaning as

opposed to a pedantic interpretation: *the spirit of the law.* **11** a person's intangible being as contrasted with his physical presence: *I shall be with you in spirit.* **12a** an incorporeal being, esp. the soul of a dead person. **12b** (*as modifier*): *spirit world.* ◆ *vb* (*tr*) **13** (usually foll. by *away* or *off*) to carry off mysteriously or secretly. **14** (often foll. by *up*) to impart animation or determination to. ORIG C13: from OF *esperit,* from L *spīritus* breath, spirit
▸ **'spiritless** *adj*

spirit² ('spɪrɪt) *n* **1** (*often pl*) any distilled alcoholic liquor, such as whisky or gin. **2** *Chem.* **2a** an aqueous solution of ethanol, esp. one obtained by distillation. **2b** the active principle or essence of a substance, extracted as a liquid, esp. by distillation. **3** *Pharmacol.* a solution of a volatile substance, esp. a volatile oil, in alcohol. **4** *Alchemy.* any of the four substances sulphur, mercury, sal ammoniac, or arsenic. ORIG C14: special use of SPIRIT¹, name applied to alchemical substances (as in sense 4), hence extended to distilled liquids

Spirit ('spɪrɪt) *n* **the. a** another name for the **Holy Spirit. b** God, esp. when regarded as transcending material limitations.

spirited ('spɪrɪtɪd) *adj* **1** displaying animation, vigour, or liveliness. **2** (*in combination*) characterized by mood, temper, or disposition as specified: *high-spirited; public-spirited.*
▸ **'spiritedly** *adv* ▸ **'spiritedness** *n*

spirit gum *n* a glue made from gum dissolved in ether used to affix a false beard, etc.

spiritism ('spɪrɪˌtɪzəm) *n* a less common word for **spiritualism.**
▸ **'spiritist** *n* ▸ **ˌspirit'istic** *adj*

spirit lamp *n* a lamp that burns methylated or other spirits instead of oil.

spirit level *n* a device for setting horizontal surfaces, consisting of a block of material in which a sealed tube partially filled with liquid is set so that the air bubble rests between two marks on the tube when the block is horizontal.

spiritous ('spɪrɪtəs) *adj* a variant of **spirituous.**

spirits of ammonia *n* (*functioning as sing or pl*) another name for **sal volatile.**

spirits of hartshorn *n* (*functioning as sing or pl*) a solution of ammonia gas in water. See **ammonium hydroxide.** Also called: **aqueous ammonia.**

spirits of salt *n* (*functioning as sing or pl*) a solution of hydrochloric acid in water.

spiritual ('spɪrɪtjʊəl) *adj* **1** relating to the spirit or soul and not to physical nature or matter; intangible. **2** of or relating to sacred things, the Church, religion, etc. **3** standing in a relationship based on communication between souls or minds: *a spiritual father.* **4** having a mind or emotions of a high and delicately refined quality. ◆ *n* **5** Also called: **Negro spiritual.** a type of religious song originating among Black slaves in the American South. **6** (*often pl*) the sphere of religious, spiritual, or ecclesiastical matters, or such matters in themselves.
▸ **ˌspiritu'ality** *n* ▸ **'spiritually** *adv*

spiritualism ('spɪrɪtjʊəˌlɪzəm) *n* **1** the belief that the disembodied spirits of the dead, surviving in another world, can communicate with the living in this world, esp. through mediums. **2** the doctrines and practices associated with this belief. **3** *Philosophy.* the belief that because reality is to some extent immaterial it is therefore spiritual. **4** any doctrine that prefers the spiritual to the material.
▸ **'spiritualist** *n*

spiritualize *or* **spiritualise** ('spɪrɪtjʊəˌlaɪz) *vb* **spiritualizes, spiritualizing, spiritualized** *or* **spiritualises, spiritualising, spiritualised.** (*tr*) to make spiritual or infuse with spiritual content.
▸ **ˌspirituali'zation** *or* **ˌspirituali'sation** *n* ▸ **'spiritualˌizer** *or* **'spiritualˌiser** *n*

spirituel (ˌspɪrɪtjʊ'ɛl) *adj* having a refined and lively mind or wit. Also (fem): **spirituelle.** ORIG C17: from F

spirituous ('spɪrɪtjʊəs) *adj* **1** characterized by or containing alcohol. **2** (of a drink) being a spirit.
▸ **spirituosity** (ˌspɪrɪtjʊ'ɒsɪtɪ) *or* **'spirituousness** *n*

spirochaete *or US* **spirochete** ('spaɪrəʊˌkiːt) *n* any of a group of spirally coiled rodlike bacteria that includes the causative agent of syphilis. ORIG C19: from NL, from *spiro-,* from L *spira,* from Gk *speira* a coil + *chaeta,* from Gk *khaitē* long hair

spirograph ('spaɪrəˌgrɑːf) *n Med.* an instrument for recording the movements of breathing. ORIG C20: NL, from *spiro-,* from L *spīrāre* to breathe + -GRAPH
▸ **ˌspiro'graphic** *adj*

spirogyra (ˌspaɪrə'dʒaɪrə) *n* any of various green freshwater multicellular algae containing spirally coiled chloroplasts. ORIG C20: from NL, from *spiro-,* from L *spīra,* from Gk *speira* a coil + Gk *guros* a circle

spirt (spɜːt) *n* a variant spelling of **spurt.**

spiry ('spaɪərɪ) *adj Poetic.* of spiral form; helical.

spit¹ (spɪt) *vb* **spits, spitting, spat** *or* **spit. 1** (*intr*) to expel saliva from the mouth; expectorate. **2** (*intr*) *Inf.* to show disdain or hatred by spitting. **3** (of a fire, hot fat, etc.) to eject (sparks, etc.) violently and with an explosive sound. **4** (*intr*) to rain very lightly. **5** (*tr;* often foll. by *out*) to eject or discharge (something) from the mouth: *he spat the food out.* **6** (*tr;* often foll. by *out*) to utter (short sharp words or syllables), esp. in a violent manner. **7 spit it out!** *Brit. inf.* a command given to someone to speak forthwith. ◆ *n* **8** another name for **spittle. 9** a light or brief fall of rain, snow, etc. **10** the act or an instance of spitting. **11** *Inf., chiefly Brit.* another word for **spitting image.** ORIG OE *spittan*
▸ **'spitter** *n*

spit² (spɪt) *n* **1** a pointed rod on which meat is skewered and roasted before or over an open fire. **2** Also called: **rotisserie, rotating spit.** a similar device fitted onto a cooker. **3** an elongated often hooked strip of sand or shingle projecting from a shore. ◆ *vb* **spits, spitting, spitted. 4** (*tr*) to impale on or transfix with or as if with a spit. ORIG OE *spitu*

spit and polish *n Inf.* punctilious attention to neatness, discipline, etc., esp. in the armed forces.

spite (spaɪt) *n* **1** maliciousness; venomous ill will. **2** an instance of such malice; grudge. **3 in spite of.** (*prep*) in defiance of; regardless of; notwithstanding. ◆ *vb* **spites, spiting, spited.** (*tr*) **4** to annoy in order to vent spite. ORIG C13: var. of DESPITE
▸ **'spiteful** *adj*

spitfire ('spɪtˌfaɪə) *n* a person given to outbursts of spiteful temper, esp. a woman or girl.

Spithead ★ (ˌspɪt'hɛd) *n* an extensive anchorage between the mainland of England and the Isle of Wight, off Portsmouth.

Spitsbergen ★ ('spɪtsˌbɜːgən) *n* another name for **Svalbard.**

spitting image *n Inf.* a person who bears a strong physical resemblance to another. Also called: **spit, spit and image.** ORIG C19: modification of *spit and image,* from SPIT¹ (as in *the very spit of* the exact likeness of)

spitting snake *n* another name for the **rinkhals.**

spittle ('spɪtᵊl) *n* **1** the fluid secreted in the mouth; saliva. **2** Also called: **cuckoo spit, frog spit.** the frothy substance secreted on plants by the larvae of certain froghoppers. ORIG OE *spǣtl* saliva

spittoon (spɪ'tuːn) *n* a receptacle for spittle, usually in a public place.

spitz (spɪts) *n* any of various breeds of dog characterized by a stocky build, a pointed muzzle, erect ears, and a tightly-curled tail. ORIG C19: from G *Spitz,* from *spitz* pointed

Spitz ★ (spɪts) *n* **Mark.** born 1950, US swimmer, who won seven gold medals at the 1972 Olympic Games.

spiv (spɪv) *n Brit. sl.* a person who makes a living by underhand dealings or swindling; black marketeer. ORIG C20: back formation from dialect *spiving* smart
▸ **'spivvy** *adj*

splake (spleɪk) *n* a type of hybrid trout bred by Canadian zoologists. ORIG from *sp(eckled)* + *lake (trout)*

splanchnic ('splæŋknɪk) *adj* of or relating to the viscera: *a splanchnic nerve.* ORIG C17: from NL *splanchnicus,* from Gk, from *splankhna* the entrails

★ people and places

splash (splæʃ) *vb* **1** to scatter (liquid) about in blobs; spatter. **2** to descend or cause to descend upon in scattered blobs: *he splashed his jacket; rain splashed against the window.* **3** to make (one's way) by or as if by splashing: *he splashed through the puddle.* **4** (*tr*) to print (a story or photograph) prominently in a newspaper. ◆ *n* **5** an instance or sound of splashing. **6** an amount splashed. **7** a mark or patch created by or as if by splashing. **8** *Inf.* an extravagant display, usually for effect (esp. in **make a splash**). **9** a small amount of soda water, etc., added to an alcoholic drink. ORIG C18: alteration of PLASH
▸ 'splashy *adj*

splashdown ('splæʃˌdaʊn) *n* **1** the controlled landing of a spacecraft on water at the end of a space flight. **2** the time scheduled for this event. ◆ *vb* **splash down. 3** (*intr, adv*) (of a spacecraft) to make a splashdown.

splat[1] (splæt) *n* a wet slapping sound. ORIG C19: imit.

splat[2] (splæt) *n* a wide flat piece of wood, esp. one that is the upright central part of a chair back. ORIG C19: ? rel. to OE *splātan* to split

splatter ('splætə) *vb* **1** to splash with small blobs. ◆ *n* **2** a splash of liquid, mud, etc.

splatter movie *n Sl.* a film in which the main feature is the graphic and gory murder of numerous victims.

splay (spleɪ) *adj* **1** spread out; broad and flat. **2** turned outwards in an awkward manner. ◆ *vb* **3** to spread out; turn out or expand. ◆ *n* **4** a surface of a wall that forms an oblique angle to the main flat surfaces, esp. at a doorway or window opening. ORIG C14: short for DISPLAY

splayfoot ('spleɪˌfʊt) *n, pl* **splayfeet.** *Pathol.* another word for **flatfoot.**
▸ 'splayˌfooted *adj*

spleen (spliːn) *n* **1** a spongy highly vascular organ situated near the stomach in man. It forms lymphocytes, produces antibodies, and filters bacteria and foreign particles from the blood. **2** the corresponding organ in other animals. **3** spitefulness or ill humour: *to vent one's spleen.* **4** *Arch.* the organ in the human body considered to be the seat of the emotions. **5** *Arch.* another word for **melancholy.** ORIG C13: from OF *esplen,* from L *splēn,* from Gk
▸ 'spleenish *or* 'spleeny *adj*

spleenwort ('spliːnˌwɜːt) *n* any of various ferns that often grow on walls.

splendent ('splɛndənt) *adj Arch.* **1** shining brightly; lustrous: *a splendent sun.* **2** famous; illustrious. ORIG C15: from L *splendēns* brilliant, from *splendēre* to shine

splendid ('splɛndɪd) *adj* **1** brilliant or fine, esp. in appearance. **2** characterized by magnificence. **3** glorious or illustrious: *a splendid reputation.* **4** brightly gleaming; radiant: *splendid colours.* **5** very good or satisfactory: *a splendid time.* ORIG C17: from L *splendidus,* from *splendēre* to shine
▸ 'splendidly *adv* ▸ 'splendidness *n*

splendiferous (splɛn'dɪfərəs) *adj Facetious.* grand; splendid: *a really splendiferous meal.* ORIG C15: from Med. L *splendiferus,* from L *splendor* radiance + *ferre* to bring

splendour *or US* **splendor** ('splɛndə) *n* **1** the state or quality of being splendid. **2 sun in splendour.** *Heraldry.* a representation of the sun with rays and a human face.

splenetic (splɪ'nɛtɪk) *adj* **1** of or relating to the spleen. **2** spiteful or irritable; peevish. ◆ *n* **3** a spiteful or irritable person.
▸ sple'netically *adv*

splenic ('splɛnɪk, 'spliː-) *adj* **1** of, relating to, or in the spleen. **2** having a disease or disorder of the spleen.

splenius ('spliːnɪəs) *n, pl* **splenii** (-nɪˌaɪ). either of two muscles at the back of the neck that rotate, flex, and extend the head and neck. ORIG C18: via NL from Gk *splēnion* a plaster
▸ 'splenial *adj*

splenomegaly (ˌspliːnəʊ'mɛgəlɪ) *n* abnormal enlargement of the spleen. ORIG C20: NL, from Gk *splēn* spleen + *megal-,* stem of *megas* big

splice (splaɪs) *vb* **splices, splicing, spliced.** (*tr*) **1** to join (two ropes) by intertwining the strands. **2** to join up the trimmed ends of (two pieces of wire, film, etc.) with solder or an adhesive material. **3** to join (timbers) by overlapping and binding or bolting the ends together. **4** (*passive*) *Inf.* to enter into marriage: *the couple got spliced.* **5 splice the mainbrace.** *Naut. hist.* to issue and partake of an extra allocation of alcoholic spirits. ◆ *n* **6** a join made by splicing. **7** the place where such a join occurs. **8** the wedge-shaped end of a cricket-bat handle that fits into the blade. ORIG C16: prob. from MDu. *splissen*
▸ 'splicer *n*

spline (splaɪn) *n* **1** any one of a series of narrow keys formed longitudinally around a shaft that fit into corresponding grooves in a mating part: used to prevent movement between two parts, esp. in transmitting torque. **2** a long narrow strip of wood, metal, etc.; slat. **3** a thin narrow strip made of wood, metal, or plastic fitted into a groove in the edge of a board, tile, etc., to connect it to another. ◆ *vb* **splines, splining, splined. 4** (*tr*) to provide (a shaft, part, etc.) with splines. ORIG C18: East Anglian dialect; ? rel. to OE *splin* spindle

splint (splɪnt) *n* **1** a rigid support for restricting movement of an injured part, esp. a broken bone. **2** a thin sliver of wood, esp. one used to light cigars, a fire, etc. **3** a thin strip of wood woven with others to form a chair seat, basket, etc. **4** *Vet. science.* a bony enlargement of the cannon bone of a horse. ◆ *vb* **5** to apply a splint to (a broken arm, etc.). ORIG C13: from MLow G *splinte*

splinter ('splɪntə) *n* **1** a small thin sharp piece of wood, glass, etc., broken off from a whole. **2** a metal fragment from a shell, bomb, etc., thrown out during an explosion. ◆ *vb* **3** to reduce or be reduced to sharp fragments. **4** to break or be broken off in small sharp fragments. ORIG C14: from MDu. *splinter;* see SPLINT
▸ 'splintery *adj*

splinter group *n* a number of members of an organization, political party, etc., who split from the main body and form an independent association of their own.

split (splɪt) *vb* **splits, splitting, split. 1** to break or cause to break, esp. forcibly, by cleaving into separate pieces, often into two roughly equal pieces. **2** to separate or be separated from a whole: *he split a piece of wood from the block.* **3** to separate or be separated into factions, usually through discord. **4** (often foll. by *up*) to separate or cause to separate through a disagreement. **5** (when *tr,* often foll. by *up*) to divide or be divided among two or more persons: *split up the pie among us.* **6** *Sl.* to depart; leave: *let's split.* **7** (*tr*) to separate (something) into its components by interposing something else: *to split a word with hyphens.* **8** (*intr;* usually foll. by *on*) *Sl.* to betray; inform: *he split on me to the cops.* **9** (*tr*) *US politics.* to mark (a ballot, etc.) so as to vote for the candidates of more than one party: *he split the ticket.* **10 split one's sides.** to laugh very heartily. ◆ *n* **11** the act or process of splitting. **12** a gap or rift caused or a piece removed by the process of splitting. **13** a breach or schism in a group or the faction resulting from such a breach. **14** a dessert of sliced fruit and ice cream, covered with whipped cream, nuts, etc.: *banana split.* **15** See **Devonshire split. 16** *Tenpin bowling.* a formation of the pins after the first bowl in which there is a large gap between two pins or groups of pins. **17** *Inf.* an arrangement or process of dividing up loot or money. ◆ *adj* **18** having been split; divided: *split logs.* **19** having a split or splits: *hair with split ends.* ◆ See also **splits, split up.** ORIG C16: from MDu. *splitten* to cleave
▸ 'splitter *n*

Split ★ (*Serbo-Croat* split) *n* a port and resort in W Croatia on the Adriatic: became part of Yugoslavia in 1918 after Austrian rule since 1797: remains of the palace of Diocletian (295–305). Pop.: 200 459 (1991). Italian name: **Spalato.**

split infinitive *n* (in English grammar) an infinitive used with another word between *to* and the verb itself, as in *to really finish it.*

USAGE NOTE The often quoted 'rule' against placing an adverb between *to* and its verb seems to be honoured more in the breach than the observance. Although it is true that a split infinitive may result in a clumsy sentence (*he decided to firmly and definitively deal with the problem*), this is not enough to justify the absolute condemnation that this practice has attracted in some circles. Indeed, very often the most natural position for the adverb is between *to* and the verb (*he decided to really try next time*) and to change it would result in an artificial and awkward construction (*he decided really to try next time*). And one of the most well known catchphrases of the time enshrines the split infinitive: 'to boldly go where no man has gone before'. Many people therefore maintain that the split infinitive is not in itself a grammatical error, but a matter of style. Nevertheless, many writers prefer to avoid it in formal written English, since readers with a more traditional point of view are likely to view this type of construction as incorrect.

split-level *adj* (of a house, room, etc.) having the floor level of one part about half a storey above the floor level of an adjoining part.

split pea *n* a pea dried and split and used in soups, pease pudding, or as a vegetable.

split personality *n* **1** the tendency to change rapidly in mood or temperament. **2** a nontechnical term for **multiple personality.**

split pin *n* a metal pin made by bending double a wire, often of hemispherical section, so that it can be passed through a hole in a nut, shaft, etc., to secure another part by bending back the ends of the wire.

split ring *n* a steel ring having two helical turns, often used as a key ring.

splits (splɪts) *n* (*functioning as sing*) (in gymnastics, etc.) the act of sinking to the floor to achieve a sitting position in which both legs are straight, pointing in opposite directions, and at right angles to the body.

split-screen technique *n* a cinematic device by which two or more complete images are projected simultaneously onto separate parts of the screen. Also called: **split screen.**

split second *n* **1** an extremely small period of time; instant. ◆ *adj* **split-second.** (*prenominal*) **2** made or arrived at in an extremely short time: *a split-second decision.* **3** depending upon minute precision: *split-second timing.*

split shift *n* a work period divided into two parts that are separated by an interval longer than a normal rest period.

splitting ('splɪtɪŋ) *adj* **1** (of a headache) intolerably painful; acute. **2** (of the head) assailed by an overpowering unbearable pain.

split up *vb* (*adv*) **1** (*tr*) to separate out into parts; divide. **2** (*intr*) to become parted through disagreement: *they split up after years of marriage.* **3** to break down or be capable of being broken down into constituent parts. ◆ *n* **split-up. 4** the act or an instance of separating.

splodge (splɒdʒ) *n* **1** a large irregular spot or blot. ◆ *vb* **splodges, splodging, splodged. 2** (*tr*) to mark (something) with such a blot or blots. ORIG C19: alteration of earlier SPLOTCH
▸ **'splodgy** *adj*

splotch (splɒtʃ) *n, vb* the usual US word for **splodge.** ORIG C17: ? a blend of SPOT + BLOTCH
▸ **'splotchy** *adj*

splurge (splɜːdʒ) *n* **1** an ostentatious display, esp. of wealth. **2** a bout of unrestrained extravagance. ◆ *vb* **splurges, splurging, splurged. 3** (often foll. by *out*) to spend (money) extravagantly. ORIG C19: from ?

splutter ('splʌtə) *vb* **1** to spit out (saliva, food particles, etc.) from the mouth in an explosive manner, as through choking or laughing. **2** to utter (words) with spitting sounds, as through rage or choking. **3** to eject or be ejected in an explosive manner: *sparks spluttered from the fire.* **4** (*tr*) to bespatter (a person) with tiny particles explosively ejected. ◆ *n* **5** the process or noise of spluttering. **6** spluttering incoherent speech. **7** anything ejected through spluttering. ORIG C17: var. of SPUTTER, infl. by SPLASH
▸ **'splutterer** *n*

Spock ★ (spɒk) *n* **Benjamin,** known as *Dr Spock.* 1903–98, US paediatrician, who wrote the permissive *The Common Sense Book of Baby and Child Care* (1946).

spode (spəud) *n* (*sometimes cap.*) china or porcelain manufactured by Josiah Spode (1754–1827), English potter, or his company.

spoil (spɔɪl) *vb* **spoils, spoiling, spoilt** *or* **spoiled. 1** (*tr*) to cause damage to (something), in regard to its value, beauty, usefulness, etc. **2** (*tr*) to weaken the character of (a child) by complying unrestrainedly with its desires. **3** (*intr*) (of perishable substances) to become unfit for consumption or use. **4** (*intr*) *Sport.* to disrupt the play or style of an opponent, as to prevent him from settling into a rhythm. **5** *Arch.* to strip (a person or place) of (property) by force. **6 be spoiling for.** to have an aggressive desire for (a fight, etc.). ◆ *n* **7** waste material thrown up by an excavation. **8** any treasure accumulated by a person. **9** *Obs.* the act of plundering. ◆ See also **spoils.** ORIG C13: from OF *espoillier,* from L *spoliāre* to strip, from *spolium* booty

spoilage ('spɔɪlɪdʒ) *n* **1** the act or an instance of spoiling or the state or condition of being spoilt. **2** an amount of material that has been wasted by being spoilt: *considerable spoilage.*

spoiler ('spɔɪlə) *n* **1** a plunderer or robber. **2** a person or thing that causes spoilage or corruption. **3** a device fitted to an aircraft wing to increase drag and reduce lift. **4** a similar device fitted to a car. **5** *Sport.* a competitor who adopts spoiling tactics. **6** a magazine, newspaper, etc., produced specifically to coincide with the production of a rival magazine, newspaper, etc., in order to divert public interest and reduce its sales.

spoils (spɔɪlz) *pl n* **1** (*sometimes sing*) valuables seized by violence, esp. in war. **2** *Chiefly US.* the rewards and benefits of public office regarded as plunder for the winning party or candidate. See also **spoils system.**

spoilsport ('spɔɪlˌspɔːt) *n Inf.* a person who spoils the pleasure of other people.

spoils system *n Chiefly US.* the practice of filling appointive public offices with friends and supporters of the ruling political party.

spoilt (spɔɪlt) *vb* a past tense and past participle of **spoil.**

Spokane ★ (spəu'kæn) *n* a city in E Washington: commercial centre of an agricultural region. Pop.: 192 781 (1994 est.).

spoke[1] (spəuk) *vb* **1** the past tense of **speak. 2** *Arch. or dialect.* a past participle of **speak.**

spoke[2] (spəuk) *n* **1** a radial member of a wheel, joining the hub to the rim. **2** a radial projection from the rim of a wheel, as in a ship's wheel. **3** a rung of a ladder. **4 put a spoke in someone's wheel.** *Brit.* to thwart someone's plans. ◆ *vb* **spokes, spoking, spoked. 5** (*tr*) to equip with or as if with spokes. ORIG OE *spaca*

spoken ('spəukən) *vb* **1** the past participle of **speak.** ◆ *adj* **2** uttered in speech. **3** (*in combination*) having speech as specified: *soft-spoken.* **4 spoken for.** engaged or reserved.

spokeshave ('spəukˌʃeɪv) *n* a small plane with two handles, one on each side of its blade, used for shaping or smoothing cylindrical wooden surfaces, such as spokes.

spokesman ('spəuksmən), **spokesperson** ('spəuksˌpɜːsᵊn), *or* **spokeswoman** ('spəuksˌwumən) *n, pl* **spokesmen, spokespersons** *or* **spokespeople,** *or* **spokeswomen.** a person authorized to speak on behalf of another person or group.

spoliation (ˌspəulɪ'eɪʃən) *n* **1** the act or an instance of despoiling or plundering. **2** the authorized plundering of neutral vessels on the seas by a belligerent state in time of war. **3** *Law.* the material alteration of a document so as to render it invalid. **4** *English ecclesiastical law.* the taking of the fruits of a benefice by a person not entitled to them. ORIG C14: from L *spoliātiō,* from *spoliāre* to SPOIL
▸ **spoliatory** ('spəulɪətərɪ, -trɪ) *adj*

spondee ('spɒndiː) *n Prosody.* a metrical foot consisting

of two long syllables (– –). ORIG C14: from OF *spondée*, from L *spondēus*, from Gk, from *spondē* ritual libation; from use of spondee in the music for such ceremonies
▸ **spondaic** (spɒn'deɪɪk) *adj*

spondylitis (ˌspɒndɪ'laɪtɪs) *n* inflammation of the vertebrae. ORIG C19: from NL, from Gk *spondulos* vertebra; see -ITIS

sponge (spʌndʒ) *n* **1** any of various multicellular typically marine animals, usually occurring in complex sessile colonies, in which the porous body is supported by a fibrous, calcareous, or siliceous skeletal framework. **2** a piece of the light porous highly absorbent elastic skeleton of certain sponges, used in bathing, cleaning, etc. **3** any of a number of light porous elastic materials resembling a sponge. **4** another word for **sponger** (sense 1). **5** *Inf.* a person who indulges in heavy drinking. **6** leavened dough, esp. before kneading. **7** See **sponge cake**. **8** Also called: **sponge pudding**. *Brit.* a light steamed or baked spongy pudding. **9** porous metal capable of absorbing large quantities of gas: *platinum sponge*. **10** a rub with a sponge. **11 throw in the sponge** (*or* **towel**). See **throw in** (sense 3). ◆ *vb* **sponges, sponging, sponged. 12** (*tr;* often foll. by *off* or *down*) to clean (something) by wiping or rubbing with a damp or wet sponge. **13** (*tr;* usually foll. by *off, away, out,* etc.) to remove (marks, etc.) by rubbing with a damp or wet sponge or cloth. **14** (when *tr*, often foll. by *up*) to absorb (liquids, esp. when spilt) in the manner of a sponge. **15** (*intr*) to go collecting sponges. **16** (foll. by *off*) to get (something) from someone by presuming on his or her generosity: *to sponge a meal off someone.* **17** (foll. by *off* or *on*) to obtain one's subsistence, etc., unjustifiably (from): *he sponges off his friends.* ORIG OE, from L *spongia*, from Gk
▸ **'spongy** *adj*

sponge bag *n* a small waterproof bag made of plastic, etc., that holds toilet articles, used esp. when travelling.

sponge bath *n* a washing of the body with a wet sponge or cloth, without immersion in water.

sponge cake *n* a light porous cake, made of eggs, sugar, flour, and flavourings, without any fat.

sponger ('spʌndʒə) *n* **1** *Inf.* a person who lives off other people by continually taking advantage of their generosity; parasite or scrounger. **2** a person or ship employed in collecting sponges.

spongiform ('spʌndʒɪˌfɔːm) *adj* **1** resembling a sponge in appearance, esp. in having many holes. **2** denoting diseases characterized by this appearance of affected tissues.

sponsion ('spɒnʃən) *n* **1** the act or process of becoming surety; sponsorship. **2** (*often pl*) *International law.* an unauthorized agreement made by a public officer, requiring ratification by his or her government. **3** any act or promise, esp. one made on behalf of someone else. ORIG C17: from L *sponsiō*, from *spondēre* to pledge

sponson ('spɒnsən) *n* **1** *Naval.* an outboard support for a gun, etc. **2** a structural projection from the side of a paddle steamer for supporting a paddle wheel. **3** a float or flotation chamber along the gunwale of a boat or ship. **4** a structural unit attached to a helicopter fuselage by struts, housing the landing gear and flotation bags. ORIG C19: ?from EXPANSION

sponsor ('spɒnsə) *n* **1** a person or group that promotes either another person or group in an activity or the activity itself, either for profit or for charity. **2** *Chiefly US & Canad.* a person or business firm that pays the costs of a radio or television programme in return for advertising time. **3** a legislator who presents and supports a bill, motion, etc. **4** Also called: **godparent. 4a** an authorized witness who makes the required promises on behalf of a person to be baptized and thereafter assumes responsibility for his Christian upbringing. **4b** a person who presents a candidate for confirmation. ◆ *vb* **5** (*tr*) to act as a sponsor for. ORIG C17: from L, from *spondēre* to promise solemnly
▸ **sponsorial** (spɒn'sɔːrɪəl) *adj* ▸ **'sponsorˌship** *n*

sponsored ('spɒnsəd) *adj* denoting an activity organized to raise money for a charity in which sponsors agree to donate money on completion of the activity by participants.

spontaneity (ˌspɒntə'niːɪtɪ, -'neɪ-) *n, pl* **spontaneities. 1** the state or quality of being spontaneous. **2** (*often pl*) the exhibiting of spontaneous actions, impulses, or behaviour.

spontaneous (spɒn'teɪnɪəs) *adj* **1** occurring, produced, or performed through natural processes without external influence. **2** arising from an unforced personal impulse; voluntary; unpremeditated. **3** (of plants) growing naturally; indigenous. ORIG C17: from LL *spontāneus*, from L *sponte* voluntarily
▸ **spon'taneously** *adv* ▸ **spon'taneousness** *n*

spontaneous combustion *n* the ignition of a substance or body as a result of internal oxidation processes, without the application of an external source of heat.

spontaneous generation *n* another name for **abiogenesis**.

spoof (spuːf) *Inf.* ◆ *n* **1** a mildly satirical mockery or parody; lampoon. **2** a good-humoured deception or trick. ◆ *vb* **3** to indulge in a spoof of (a person or thing). ORIG C19: coined by A. Roberts (1852–1933), E comedian
▸ **'spoofer** *n*

spook (spuːk) *Inf.* ◆ *n* **1** a ghost. **2** *US & Canad.* a spy. **3** a strange or frightening person. ◆ *vb* (*tr*) *US & Canad.* **4** to frighten: *to spook horses; to spook a person.* **5** (of a ghost) to haunt. ORIG C19: Du. *spook*, from MLow G *spōk* ghost
▸ **'spooky** *adj*

spool (spuːl) *n* **1** a device around which magnetic tape, film, cotton, etc., can be wound, with plates at top and bottom to prevent it from slipping off. **2** anything round which other materials, esp. thread, are wound. ◆ *vb* **3** (sometimes foll. by *up*) to wind or be wound onto a spool. ORIG C14: of Gmc origin

spoon (spuːn) *n* **1** a utensil having a shallow concave part, usually elliptical in shape, attached to a handle, used in eating or serving food, stirring, etc. **2** Also called: **spoonbait**. an angling lure consisting of a bright piece of metal which swivels on a trace to which are attached a hook or hooks. **3** *Golf.* a former name for a No. 3 wood. **4 be born with a silver spoon in one's mouth.** to inherit wealth or social standing. **5** *Rowing.* a type of oar blade that is curved at the edges and tip. ◆ *vb* **6** (*tr*) to scoop up or transfer (food, liquid, etc.) from one container to another with or as if with a spoon. **7** (*intr*) *Old-fashioned sl.* to kiss and cuddle. **8** *Sport.* to hit (a ball) with a weak lifting motion, as in golf, cricket, etc. ORIG OE *spōn* splinter

spoonbill ('spuːnˌbɪl) *n* any of several wading birds of warm regions, having a long horizontally flattened bill.

spoondrift ('spuːnˌdrɪft) *n* a less common spelling of **spindrift**.

spoonerism ('spuːnəˌrɪzəm) *n* the transposition of the initial consonants or consonant clusters of a pair of words, often resulting in an amusing ambiguity, such as *hush my brat* for *brush my hat.* ORIG C20: after W. A. *Spooner* (1844–1930), E clergyman renowned for this

spoon-feed *vb* **spoon-feeds, spoon-feeding, spoon-fed.** (*tr*) **1** to feed with a spoon. **2** to overindulge or spoil. **3** to provide (a person) with ready-made opinions, judgments, etc.

spoonful ('spuːnˌfʊl) *n, pl* **spoonfuls. 1** the amount that a spoon is able to hold. **2** a small quantity.

spoony *or* **spooney** ('spuːnɪ) *Inf., old-fashioned.* ◆ *adj* **spoonier, spooniest. 1** foolishly or stupidly amorous. ◆ *n, pl* **spoonies. 2** a fool or silly person, esp. one in love.

spoor (spʊə, spɔː) *n* **1** the trail of an animal or person, esp. as discernible to the eye. ◆ *vb* **2** to track (an animal) by following its trail. ORIG C19: from Afrik., from MDu. *spor;* rel. to OE *spor* track

Sporades ★ ('spɒrəˌdiːz) *pl n* two groups of Greek islands in the Aegean: the **Northern Sporades**, lying northeast of Euboea, and the **Southern Sporades**, which include the Dodecanese and lie off the SW coast of Turkey.

sporadic (spə'rædɪk) *adj* **1** occurring at irregular points in time; intermittent: *sporadic firing.* **2** scattered; isolated: *a sporadic disease.* ORIG C17: from Med. L *sporadicus*, from Gk, from *sporas* scattered
▸ **spo'radically** *adv*

sporangium (spə'rændʒɪəm) *n, pl* **sporangia** (-dʒɪə). any

organ, esp. in fungi, in which asexual spores are produced. ORIG C19: from NL, from SPORO- + Gk *angeion* receptacle
▸ **spo'rangial** *adj*

spore (spɔː) *n* **1** a reproductive body, produced by bacteria, fungi, some protozoans and many plants, that develops into a new individual. A **sexual spore** is formed after the fusion of gametes and an **asexual spore** is the result of asexual reproduction. **2** a germ cell, seed, dormant bacterium, or similar body. ◆ *vb* **spores, sporing, spored. 3** (*intr*) to produce, carry, or release spores. ORIG C19: from NL *spora,* from Gk: a sowing; rel. to Gk *speirein* to sow

spore case *n* the nontechnical name for **sporangium.**

sporo- *or before a vowel* **spor-** *combining form.* spore: *sporophyte.* ORIG from NL *spora*

sporogenesis (ˌspɔːrəʊ'dʒɛnɪsɪs, ˌspɒ-) *n* the process of spore formation in plants and animals.
▸ **sporogenous** (spɔː'rɒdʒɪnəs, spɒ-) *adj*

sporogonium (ˌspɔːrəʊ'gəʊnɪəm, ˌspɒ-) *n, pl* **sporogonia** (-nɪə). a structure in mosses and liverworts consisting of a spore-bearing capsule on a short stalk that arises from the parent plant.

sporophyll *or* **sporophyl** ('spɔːrəʊfɪl, 'spɒ-) *n* a leaf in mosses, ferns, and related plants that bears the sporangia.

sporophyte ('spɔːrəʊˌfaɪt, 'spɒ-) *n* the diploid form of plants that have alternation of generations. It produces asexual spores.
▸ **sporophytic** (ˌspɔːrə'fɪtɪk, ˌspɒ-) *adj*

-sporous *adj combining form.* (in botany) having a specified type or number of spores.

sporozoan (ˌspɔːrə'zəʊən, ˌspɒ-) *n* **1** any parasitic protozoan of a phylum that includes the malaria parasite. ◆ *adj* **2** of or relating to the sporozoans.

sporran ('spɒrən) *n* a large pouch, usually of fur, worn hanging from a belt in front of the kilt in Scottish Highland dress. ORIG C19: from Scot. Gaelic *sporan* purse

sport (spɔːt) *n* **1** an individual or group activity pursued for exercise or pleasure, often taking a competitive form. **2** such activities considered collectively. **3** any pastime indulged in for pleasure. **4** the pleasure derived from a pastime, esp. hunting, shooting, or fishing. **5** playful or good-humoured joking: *to say a thing in sport.* **6** derisive mockery or the object of such mockery: *to make sport of someone.* **7** someone or something that is controlled by external influences: *the sport of fate.* **8** *Inf.* (sometimes qualified by *good, bad,* etc.) a person who reacts cheerfully in the face of adversity, esp. a good loser. **9** *Inf.* a person noted for being scrupulously fair and abiding by the rules of a game. **10** *Inf.* a person who leads a merry existence, esp. a gambler: *he's a bit of a sport.* **11** *Austral. & NZ inf.* a form of address used esp. between males. **12** *Biol.* **12a** an animal or plant that differs conspicuously from other organisms of the same species, usually because of a mutation. **12b** an anomalous characteristic of such an organism. ◆ *vb* **13** (*tr*) *Inf.* to wear or display in an ostentatious or proud manner: *she was sporting a new hat.* **14** (*intr*) to skip about or frolic happily. **15** to amuse (oneself), esp. in outdoor physical recreation. **16** (*intr;* often foll. by *with*) *Arch.* to make fun (of). **17** (*intr*) *Biol.* to produce or undergo a mutation. ◆ See also **sports.** ORIG C15 *sporten,* var. of *disporten* to DISPORT
▸ **'sporter** *n* ▸ **'sportful** *adj* ▸ **'sportfully** *adv*
▸ **'sportfulness** *n*

sporting ('spɔːtɪŋ) *adj* **1** (*prenominal*) of, relating to, or used or engaged in a sport or sports. **2** relating or conforming to sportsmanship; fair. **3** of or relating to gambling. **4** willing to take a risk.
▸ **'sportingly** *adv*

sportive ('spɔːtɪv) *adj* **1** playful or joyous. **2** done in jest rather than seriously.
▸ **'sportively** *adv* ▸ **'sportiveness** *n*

sports (spɔːts) *n* **1** (*modifier*) relating to, concerned with, or used in sports: *sports equipment.* **2** Also called: **sports day.** *Brit.* a meeting held at a school or college for competitions in various athletic events.

sports car *n* a production car designed for speed and manoeuvrability, having a low body and usually seating only two persons.

sportscast ('spɔːtsˌkɑːst) *n US.* a broadcast consisting of sports news.
▸ **'sportsˌcaster** *n*

sports jacket *n* a man's informal jacket, made esp. of tweed. Also called (US, Austral., and NZ): **sports coat.**

sportsman ('spɔːtsmən) *n, pl* **sportsmen. 1** a man who takes part in sports, esp. of the outdoor type. **2** a person who exhibits fairness, generosity, observance of the rules, and good humour when losing.
▸ **'sportsman-ˌlike** *or* **'sportsmanly** *adj* ▸ **'sportsmanˌship** *n*

sports medicine *n* the branch of medicine concerned with injuries sustained through sport.

sportswear ('spɔːtsˌwɛə) *n* clothes worn for sport or outdoor leisure wear.

sportswoman ('spɔːtsˌwʊmən) *n, pl* **sportswomen.** a woman who takes part in sports, esp. of the outdoor type.

sport utility vehicle *or* **sports utility vehicle** *n Chiefly US.* a powerful four-wheel drive vehicle suitable for rough terrain. Sometimes shortened to **sport utility** *or* **sports utility.** Abbrev.: **SUV.**

sporty ('spɔːtɪ) *adj* **sportier, sportiest. 1** (of a person) fond of sport or outdoor activities. **2** (of clothes) having the appearance of sportswear. **3** (of a car) having the performance or appearance of a sports car.
▸ **'sportily** *adv* ▸ **'sportiness** *n*

sporule ('spɒruːl) *n* a very small spore. ORIG C19: from NL *sporula*

spot (spɒt) *n* **1** a small mark on a surface, such as a circular patch or stain, differing in colour or texture from its surroundings. **2** a location: *this is the exact spot.* **3** a blemish of the skin, esp. a pimple or one occurring through some disease. **4** a blemish on the character of a person; moral flaw. **5** *Inf.* a place of entertainment: *a night spot.* **6** *Inf., chiefly Brit.* a small quantity or amount: *a spot of lunch.* **7** *Inf.* an awkward situation: *that puts me in a spot.* **8** a short period between regular television or radio programmes that is used for advertising. **9** a position or length of time in a show assigned to a specific performer. **10** short for **spotlight. 11** (in billiards) **11a** Also called: **spot ball.** the white ball that is distinguished from the plain by a mark or spot. **11b** the player using this ball. **12** *Billiards, snooker, etc.* one of the marked places where the ball is placed. **13** (*modifier*) **13a** denoting or relating to goods, currencies, or securities available for immediate delivery and payment: *spot goods.* See also **spot price. 13b** involving immediate cash payment: *spot sales.* **14 change one's spots.** (*used mainly in negative constructions*) to reform one's character. **15 high spot.** an outstanding event: *the high spot of the holiday.* **16 knock spots off.** to outstrip or outdo with ease. **17 on the spot. 17a** immediately. **17b** at the place in question. **17c** in the best position to deal with a situation. **17d** in an awkward predicament. **17e** (*as modifier*): *our on-the-spot reporter.* **18 tight spot.** a serious, difficult, or dangerous situation. **19 weak spot. 19a** some aspect of a character or situation that is susceptible to criticism. **19b** a flaw in a person's knowledge. ◆ *vb* **spots, spotting, spotted. 20** (*tr*) to observe or perceive suddenly; discern. **21** to put stains or spots upon (something). **22** (*intr*) (of some fabrics) to be susceptible to spotting by or as if by water: *silk spots easily.* **23** *Billiards.* to place (a ball) on one of the spots. **24** to look out for and note (trains, talent, etc.). **25** (*intr*) to rain slightly; spit. ORIG C12 (in the sense: moral blemish): from G
▸ **'spotless** *adj* ▸ **'spotlessly** *adv* ▸ **'spotlessness** *n*

spot check *n* **1** a quick random examination. **2** a check made without prior warning. ◆ *vb* **spot-check. 3** (*tr*) to perform a spot check on.

spot height *n* a mark on a map indicating the height of a hill, mountain, etc.

spotlight ('spɒtˌlaɪt) *n* **1** a powerful light focused so as to illuminate a small area. **2 the.** the focus of attention. ◆ *vb* **spotlights, spotlighting, spotlit** *or* **spotlighted.** (*tr*) **3** to direct a spotlight on. **4** to focus attention on.

spot-on *adj Brit. inf.* absolutely correct; very accurate.

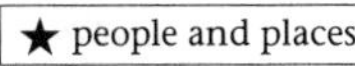

spot price *n* the price of goods, currencies, or securities that are offered for immediate delivery and payment.

spotted ('spɒtɪd) *adj* **1** characterized by spots or marks, esp. in having a pattern of spots. **2** stained or blemished; soiled or bespattered.

spotted dick *or* **dog** *n Brit.* a steamed or boiled suet pudding containing dried fruit and shaped into a roll.

spotted fever *n* any of various severe febrile diseases characterized by small irregular spots on the skin.

spotted gum *n* **1** an Australian eucalyptus tree. **2** the wood of this tree, used for shipbuilding, sleepers, etc.

spotter ('spɒtə) *n* **1a** a person or thing that watches or observes. **1b** (*as modifier*): *a spotter plane.* **2** a person who makes a hobby of watching for and noting numbers or types of trains, buses, etc.: *a train spotter.* **3** *Mil.* a person who advises adjustment of fire on a target by observations. **4** a person, esp. one engaged in civil defence, who watches for enemy aircraft.

spottie ('spɒtɪ) *n NZ.* a young deer of up to three months of age.

spotty ('spɒtɪ) *adj* **spottier, spottiest. 1** abounding in or characterized by spots or marks, esp. on the skin. **2** not consistent or uniform; irregular or uneven.
▸ **'spottily** *adv* ▸ **'spottiness** *n*

spot-weld *vb* **1** (*tr*) to join (two pieces of metal) by small circular welds by means of heat, usually electrically generated, and pressure. ◆ *n* **2** a weld so formed.
▸ **'spot-ˌwelder** *n*

spousal ('spaʊzᵊl) *n* **1** (*often pl*) **1a** the marriage ceremony. **1b** a wedding. ◆ *adj* **2** of or relating to marriage.
▸ **'spousally** *adv*

spouse *n* (spaʊs, spaʊz). **1** a person's partner in marriage. Related adj: **spousal.** ◆ *vb* (spaʊz, spaʊs), **spouses, spousing, spoused. 2** (*tr*) *Obs.* to marry. ORIG C12: from OF *spus* (masc), *spuse* (fem), from L *sponsus, sponsa* betrothed man or woman, from *spondēre* to promise solemnly

spout (spaʊt) *vb* **1** to discharge (a liquid) in a continuous jet or in spurts, esp. through a narrow gap or under pressure, or (of a liquid) to gush thus. **2** (of a whale, etc.) to discharge air through the blowhole in a spray at the surface of the water. **3** *Inf.* to utter (a stream of words) on a subject. ◆ *n* **4** a tube, pipe, chute, etc., allowing the passage or pouring of liquids, grain, etc. **5** a continuous stream or jet of liquid. **6** short for **waterspout. 7 up the spout.** *Sl.* **7a** ruined or lost: *any hope of rescue is right up the spout.* **7b** pregnant. ORIG C14: ?from MDu. *spouten,* from ON *spyta* to spit
▸ **'spouter** *n*

spouting ('spaʊtɪŋ) *n NZ.* **a** a rainwater downpipe on the exterior of a building. **b** such pipes collectively.

SPQR *abbrev. for* Senatus Populusque Romanus. ORIG L: the Senate and People of Rome

sprag (spræg) *n* **1** a chock or steel bar used to prevent a vehicle from running backwards on an incline. **2** a support or post used in mining. ORIG C19: from ?

sprain (spreɪn) *vb* **1** (*tr*) to injure (a joint) by a sudden twisting or wrenching of its ligaments. ◆ *n* **2** the injury, characterized by swelling and temporary disability. ORIG C17: from ?

sprang (spræŋ) *vb* a past tense of **spring.**

sprat (spræt) *n* **1** Also called: **brisling.** a small marine food fish of the herring family. **2** any of various small or young herrings. ORIG C16: var. of OE *sprott*

sprawl (sprɔːl) *vb* **1** (*intr*) to sit or lie in an ungainly manner with one's limbs spread out. **2** to fall down or knock down with the limbs spread out in an ungainly way. **3** to spread out or cause to spread out in a straggling fashion: *his handwriting sprawled all over the paper.* ◆ *n* **4** the act or an instance of sprawling. **5** a sprawling posture or arrangement of items. **6a** the urban area formed by the expansion of a town or city into surrounding countryside: *the urban sprawl.* **6b** the process by which this has happened. ORIG OE *spreawlian*
▸ **'sprawling** *or* **'sprawly** *adj*

spray[1] (spreɪ) *n* **1** fine particles of a liquid. **2a** a liquid, such as perfume, paint, etc., designed to be discharged from an aerosol or atomizer: *hair spray.* **2b** the aerosol or atomizer itself. **3** a quantity of small objects flying through the air: *a spray of bullets.* ◆ *vb* **4** to scatter (liquid) in the form of fine particles. **5** to discharge (a liquid) from an aerosol or atomizer. **6** (*tr*) to treat or bombard with a spray: *to spray the lawn.* ORIG C17: from MDu. *sprāien*
▸ **'sprayer** *n*

spray[2] (spreɪ) *n* **1** a single slender shoot, twig, or branch that bears buds, leaves, flowers, or berries. **2** an ornament or floral design like this. ORIG C13: of Gmc origin

spray gun *n* a device that sprays a fluid in a finely divided form by atomizing it in an air jet.

spread (sprɛd) *vb* **spreads, spreading, spread. 1** to extend or unfold or be extended or unfolded to the fullest width: *she spread the map.* **2** to extend or cause to extend over a larger expanse: *the milk spread all over the floor; the political unrest spread over several years.* **3** to apply or be applied in a coating: *butter does not spread very well when cold.* **4** to distribute or be distributed over an area or region. **5** to display or be displayed in its fullest extent: *the landscape spread before us.* **6** (*tr*) to prepare (a table) for a meal. **7** (*tr*) to lay out (a meal) on a table. **8** to send or be sent out in all directions; disseminate or be disseminated: *someone was spreading rumours; the disease spread quickly.* **9** (of rails, wires, etc.) to force or be forced apart. **10** to increase the breadth of (a part), esp. to flatten the head of a rivet by pressing, hammering, or forging. **11** (*tr*) *Agriculture.* **11a** to lay out (hay) in a relatively thin layer to dry. **11b** to scatter (seed, manure, etc.) over an area. **12** (*tr; often foll. by around*) *Inf.* to make (oneself) agreeable to a large number of people. ◆ *n* **13** the act or process of spreading; diffusion, dispersion, expansion, etc. **14** *Inf.* the wingspan of an aircraft. **15** an extent of space or time; stretch: *a spread of 50 years.* **16** *Inf., chiefly US & Canad.* a ranch or large tract of land. **17** the limit of something fully extended: *the spread of a bird's wings.* **18** a covering for a table or bed. **19** *Inf.* a large meal or feast, esp. when it is laid out on a table. **20** a food which can be spread on bread, etc.: *salmon spread.* **21** two facing pages in a book or other publication. **22** a widening of the hips and waist: *middle-age spread.* ◆ *adj* **23** extended or stretched out, esp. to the fullest extent. ORIG OE *sprǣdan*
▸ **'spreadable** *adj* ▸ **'spreader** *n*

spread betting *n* a form of gambling in which stakes are placed not on the results of contests but on the number of points scored, etc. Winnings and losses are calculated according to the accuracy or inaccuracy of the prediction.

spread eagle *n* **1** the representation of an eagle with outstretched wings, used as an emblem of the US. **2** an acrobatic skating figure.

spread-eagle *adj also* **spread-eagled. 1** lying or standing with arms and legs outstretched. ◆ *vb* **spread-eagles, spread-eagling, spread-eagled. 2** to assume or cause to assume the shape of a spread eagle. **3** (*intr*) *Skating.* to execute a spread eagle.

spreadsheet ('sprɛdˌʃiːt) *n* a computer program that allows easy entry and manipulation of figures, equations, and text: used esp. for financial planning.

sprechgesang (*German* 'ʃprɛçgəzaŋ) *n Music.* a type of vocalization between singing and recitation. ORIG C20: from G *Sprechgesang,* lit.: speaking-song

spree (spriː) *n* **1** a session of considerable overindulgence, esp. in drinking, squandering money, etc. **2** a romp. ORIG C19: ? changed from Scot. *spreath* plundered cattle, ult. from L *praeda* booty

sprig (sprɪg) *n* **1** a shoot, twig, or sprout of a tree, shrub, etc.; spray. **2** an ornamental device resembling a spray of leaves or flowers. **3** Also called: **dowel pin.** a small wire nail without a head. **4** *Inf., rare.* a youth. **5** *Inf., rare.* a person considered as the descendant of an established family, social class, etc. **6** *NZ.* another word for **stud**[1] (sense 5). ◆ *vb* **sprigs, sprigging, sprigged.** (*tr*) **7** to fasten or secure with sprigs. **8** to ornament (fabric, etc.) with a design of sprigs. ORIG C15: prob. of Gmc origin
▸ **'sprigger** *n* ▸ **'spriggy** *adj*

sprightly ('spraɪtlɪ) *adj* **sprightlier, sprightliest. 1** full of vitality; lively and active. ◆ *adv* **2** *Obs.* in an active or lively manner. ORIG C16: from *spright,* var. of SPRITE + -LY[1]
▸ **'sprightliness** *n*

spring (sprɪŋ) *vb* **springs, springing, sprang** *or* **sprung; sprung. 1** to move or cause to move suddenly upwards or forwards in a single motion. **2** to release or be released from a forced position by elastic force: *the bolt sprang back.* **3** (*tr*) to leap or jump over. **4** (*intr*) to come or arise suddenly. **5** (*intr*) (of a part of a mechanism, etc.) to jump out of place. **6** to make (wood, etc.) warped or split or (of wood, etc.) to become warped or split. **7** to happen or cause to happen unexpectedly: *to spring a surprise.* **8** (*intr;* usually foll. by *from*) to originate; be descended: *the idea sprang from a chance meeting; he sprang from peasant stock.* **9** (*intr;* often foll. by *up*) to come into being or appear suddenly: *factories springing up.* **10** (*tr*) (of a gundog) to rouse (game) from cover. **11** (*intr*) (of game or quarry) to start or rise suddenly from cover. **12** to explode (a mine) or (of a mine) to explode. **13** (*tr*) to provide with a spring or springs. **14** (*tr*) *Inf.* to arrange the escape of (someone) from prison. **15** (*intr*) *Arch. or poetic.* (of daylight or dawn) to begin to appear. ◆ *n* **16** the act or an instance of springing. **17** a leap, jump, or bound. **18a** the quality of resilience; elasticity. **18b** (*as modifier*): *spring steel.* **19** the act or an instance of moving rapidly back from a position of tension. **20a** a natural outflow of ground water, as forming the source of a stream. **20b** (*as modifier*): *spring water.* **21a** a device, such as a coil or strip of steel, that stores potential energy when it is compressed, stretched, or bent and releases it when the restraining force is removed. **21b** (*as modifier*): *a spring mattress.* **22** a structural defect such as a warp or bend. **23a** (*sometimes cap.*) the season of the year between winter and summer, astronomically from the March equinox to the June solstice in the N hemisphere and from the September equinox to the December solstice in the S hemisphere. **23b** (*as modifier*): *spring showers.* Related adj: **vernal. 24** the earliest or freshest time of something. **25** a source or origin. **26** Also called: **spring line.** *Naut.* a mooring line, usually one of a pair that cross amidships. ORIG OE *springan*
▸ **'springless** *adj* ▸ **'spring,like** *adj*

spring balance *or esp. US* **spring scale** *n* a device in which an object to be weighed is attached to the end of a helical spring, the extension of which indicates the weight of the object on a calibrated scale.

springboard ('sprɪŋ,bɔːd) *n* **1** a flexible board, usually projecting low over the water, used for diving. **2** a similar board used for gaining height or momentum in gymnastics. **3** *Austral. & NZ.* a board inserted into the trunk of a tree at some height above the ground on which a lumberjack stands to chop down the tree. **4** anything that serves as a point of departure or initiation.

springbok ('sprɪŋ,bʌk) *n, pl* **springbok** *or* **springboks.** an antelope of semidesert regions of southern Africa, which moves in leaps. ORIG C18: from Afrik., from Du. *springen* to spring + *bok* goat

Springbok ('sprɪŋ,bʌk, -,bɒk) *n* a person who has represented South Africa in a national sports team.

spring chicken *n* **1** *Chiefly US.* a young chicken, tender for cooking, esp. one from two to ten months old. **2 he** *or* **she is no spring chicken.** *Inf.* he or she is no longer young.

spring-clean *vb* **1** to clean (a house) thoroughly: traditionally at the end of winter. ◆ *n* **2** an instance of this.
▸ **,spring-'cleaning** *n*

springe (sprɪndʒ) *n* **1** a snare set to catch small wild animals or birds and consisting of a loop attached to a bent twig or branch under tension. ◆ *vb* **springes, springeing, springed. 2** (*tr*) to catch (animals or birds) with this. ORIG C13: rel. to OE *springan* to spring

springer ('sprɪŋə) *n* **1** a person or thing that springs. **2** short for **springer spaniel. 3** *Archit.* **3a** the first and lowest stone of an arch. **3b** the impost of an arch.

springer spaniel *n* either of two breeds of spaniel with a slightly domed head and ears of medium length.

Springfield ★ ('sprɪŋ,fiːld) *n* **1** a city in S Massachusetts, on the Connecticut River: the site of the US arsenal and armoury (1794–1968), which developed the Springfield and Garand rifles. Pop.: 149 164 (1994 est.). **2** a city in SW Missouri. Pop.: 149 727 (1994 est.). **3** a city in central Illinois, capital of the state: the home and burial place of Abraham Lincoln. Pop.: 105 938 (1994 est.).

springhaas ('sprɪŋ,hɑːs) *n, pl* **springhaas** *or* **springhase** (-,hɑːzə). a small S and E African nocturnal kangaroo-like rodent. ORIG from Afrik.: spring hare

springing ('sprɪŋɪŋ) *n Archit.* the level where an arch or vault rises from a support.

spring lock *n* a type of lock having a spring-loaded bolt, a key being required only to unlock it.

spring onion *n* an immature form of the onion, widely cultivated for its tiny bulb and long green leaves which are eaten in salads, etc. Also called: **scallion.**

spring roll *n* a Chinese dish consisting of a savoury mixture rolled up in a thin pancake and fried.

Springs ★ (sprɪŋz) *n* a city in E South Africa: developed around a coal mine established in 1885 and later became a major world gold-mining centre, now with uranium extraction. Pop.: 68 235 (1985).

Springsteen ★ ('sprɪŋ,stiːn) *n* **Bruce.** born 1949, US rock singer, songwriter, and guitarist. His albums with the E Street Band include *Born to Run* (1975), *Darkness on the Edge of Town* (1978), and *Born in the USA* (1984).

springtail ('sprɪŋ,teɪl) *n* any of various primitive wingless insects having a forked springing organ.

spring tide *n* **1** either of the two tides that occur at or just after new moon and full moon: the greatest rise and fall in tidal level. Cf. **neap tide. 2** any great rush or flood.

springtime ('sprɪŋ,taɪm) *n* **1** Also called: **springtide.** the season of spring. **2** the earliest, usually the most attractive, period of the existence of something.

springy ('sprɪŋɪ) *adj* **springier, springiest. 1** possessing or characterized by resilience or bounce. **2** (of a place) having many springs of water.
▸ **'springily** *adv* ▸ **'springiness** *n*

sprinkle ('sprɪŋkᵊl) *vb* **sprinkles, sprinkling, sprinkled. 1** to scatter (liquid, powder, etc.) in tiny particles or droplets over (something). **2** (*tr*) to distribute over (something): *the field was sprinkled with flowers.* **3** (*intr*) to drizzle slightly. ◆ *n* **4** the act or an instance of sprinkling or a quantity that is sprinkled. **5** a slight drizzle. ORIG C14: prob. from MDu. *sprenkelen*
▸ **'sprinkler** *n*

sprinkler system *n* a fire-extinguishing system that releases water from overhead nozzles opened automatically by a temperature rise.

sprinkling ('sprɪŋklɪŋ) *n* a small quantity or amount: *a sprinkling of common sense.*

sprint (sprɪnt) *n* **1** *Athletics.* a short race run at top speed. **2** a fast finishing speed at the end of a longer race, as in running or cycling, etc. **3** any quick run. ◆ *vb* **4** (*intr*) to go at top speed, as in running, cycling, etc. ORIG C16: of Scand. origin
▸ **'sprinter** *n*

sprit (sprɪt) *n Naut.* a light spar pivoted at the mast and crossing a fore-and-aft quadrilateral sail diagonally to the peak. ORIG OE *spreot*

sprite (spraɪt) *n* **1** (in folklore) a nimble elflike creature, esp. one associated with water. **2** a small dainty person. ORIG C13: from OF *esprit,* from L *spīritus* SPIRIT[1]

spritsail ('sprɪt,seɪl; *Naut.* 'sprɪtsəl) *n Naut.* a sail mounted on a sprit or bowsprit.

spritzer ('sprɪtsə) *n* a drink, usually white wine, with soda water added. ORIG from G *spritzen* to splash

sprocket ('sprɒkɪt) *n* **1** Also called: **sprocket wheel.** a relatively thin wheel having teeth projecting radially from the rim, esp. one that drives or is driven by a chain. **2** an individual tooth on such a wheel. **3** a cylindrical wheel with teeth on one or both rims for pulling film through a camera or projector. ORIG C16: from ?

sprog (sprɒg) *n Sl.* **1** a child; baby. **2** (esp. in RAF) a new recruit.

sprout (spraʊt) *vb* **1** (of a plant, seed, etc.) to produce (new leaves, shoots, etc.). **2** (*intr;* often foll. by *up*) to begin to grow or develop. ◆ *n* **3** a new shoot or bud. **4** something that grows like a sprout. **5** See **Brussels sprout.** ORIG OE *sprūtan*

spruce[1] (spruːs) *n* **1** any coniferous tree of a N temperate genus, cultivated for timber and for ornament. They grow in a pyramidal shape and have needle-like leaves and light-coloured wood. See also **Norway spruce.** **2** the wood of any of these trees. ORIG C17: short for *Spruce fir,* from C14 *Spruce* Prussia, changed from *Pruce,* via OF from L *Prussia*

spruce[2] (spru:s) *adj* neat, smart, and trim. ORIG C16: ?from *Spruce leather,* a fashionable leather imported from Prussia; see SPRUCE[1]
► **'sprucely** *adv* ► **'spruceness** *n*

spruce beer *n* an alcoholic drink made of fermented molasses flavoured with spruce twigs and cones.

spruce up *vb* **spruces, sprucing, spruced.** (*adv*) to make (oneself, a person, or thing) smart and neat.

sprue[1] (spru:) *n* **1** a vertical channel in a mould through which plastic or molten metal is introduced or out of which it flows when the mould is filled. **2** plastic or metal that solidifies in a sprue. ORIG C19: from ?

sprue[2] (spru:) *n* a chronic disease, esp. of tropical climates, characterized by diarrhoea and emaciation. ORIG C19: from Du. *spruw*

spruik ('spru:ɪk) *vb* (*intr*) *Austral. sl.* to describe or hold forth like a salesman; spiel or advertise loudly. ORIG C20: from ?
► **'spruiker** *n*

spruit (spreɪt) *n S. African.* a small tributary stream or watercourse. ORIG Afrik. *sprint* offshoot, tributary

sprung (sprʌŋ) *vb* a past tense and past participle of **spring.**

sprung rhythm *n Prosody.* a type of poetic rhythm characterized by metrical feet of irregular composition, each having one strongly stressed syllable, often the first, and an indefinite number of unstressed syllables.

spry (spraɪ) *adj* **spryer, spryest** *or* **sprier, spriest.** active and brisk; nimble. ORIG C18: ? of Scand. origin
► **'spryly** *adv* ► **'spryness** *n*

spud (spʌd) *n* **1** an informal word for **potato. 2** a narrow-bladed spade for cutting roots, digging up weeds, etc. ◆ *vb* **spuds, spudding, spudded. 3** (*tr*) to eradicate (weeds) with a spud. **4** (*intr*) to drill the first foot of an oil well. ORIG C15 *spudde* short knife, from ?; applied later to a digging tool, & hence to a potato

Spud Island ★ *n* a slang name for **Prince Edward Island.**

spue (spju:) *vb* **spues, spuing, spued.** an archaic spelling of **spew.**
► **'spuer** *n*

spume (spju:m) *n* **1** foam or surf, esp. on the sea; froth. ◆ *vb* **spumes, spuming, spumed. 2** (*intr*) to foam or froth. ORIG C14: from OF *espume,* from L *spūma*
► **'spumous** *or* **'spumy** *adj*

spun (spʌn) *vb* **1** the past tense and past participle of **spin.** ◆ *adj* **2** formed or manufactured by spinning: *spun gold; spun glass.*

spunk (spʌŋk) *n* **1** *Inf.* courage or spirit. **2** *Brit. taboo sl.* semen. **3** touchwood or tinder. ORIG C16 (in the sense: a spark): from Scot. Gaelic *spong* tinder, sponge, from L *spongia* sponge
► **'spunky** *adj* ► **'spunkily** *adv*

spun silk *n* shiny yarn or fabric made from silk waste.

spur (spɜ:) *n* **1** a pointed device or sharp spiked wheel fixed to the heel of a rider's boot to enable him to urge his horse on. **2** anything serving to urge or encourage. **3** a sharp horny projection from the leg in male birds, such as the domestic cock. **4** a pointed process in any of various animals. **5** a tubular extension at the base of the corolla in flowers such as larkspur. **6** a short or stunted branch of a tree. **7** a ridge projecting laterally from a mountain or mountain range. **8** another name for **groyne. 9** Also called: **spur track.** a railway branch line or siding. **10** a short side road leading off a main road. **11** a sharp cutting instrument attached to the leg of a gamecock. **12 on the spur of the moment.** on impulse. **13 win one's spurs. 13a** to prove one's ability; gain distinction. **13b** *History.* to earn a knighthood. ◆ *vb* **spurs, spurring, spurred. 14** (*tr*) to goad or urge with or as if with spurs. **15** (*intr*) to go or ride quickly; press on. **16** (*tr*) to provide with a spur or spurs. ORIG OE *spura*

spurge (spɜ:dʒ) *n* any of various plants that have milky sap and small flowers typically surrounded by conspicuous bracts. ORIG C14: from OF *espurge,* from *espurgier* to purge, from L *expurgāre* to cleanse

spur gear *or* **wheel** *n* a gear having involuted teeth either straight or helically cut on a cylindrical surface.

spurious ('spjʊərɪəs) *adj* **1** not genuine or real. **2** (of a plant part or organ) resembling another part in appearance only; false: *a spurious fruit.* **3** *Rare.* illegitimate. ORIG C17: from L *spurius* of illegitimate birth
► **'spuriously** *adv* ► **'spuriousness** *n*

spurn (spɜ:n) *vb* **1** to reject (a person or thing) with contempt. **2** (when *intr,* often foll. by *against*) *Arch.* to kick (at). ◆ *n* **3** an instance of spurning. **4** *Arch.* a kick or thrust. ORIG OE *spurnan*
► **'spurner** *n*

spurt *or* **spirt** (spɜ:t) *vb* **1** to gush or cause to gush forth in a sudden stream or jet. **2** (*intr*) to make a sudden effort. ◆ *n* **3** a sudden stream or jet. **4** a short burst of activity, speed, or energy. ORIG C16: ? rel. to MHG *sprützen* to squirt

Sputnik ('spʊtnɪk, 'spʌt-) *n* any of a series of Soviet artificial satellites, **Sputnik 1** (launched in 1957) being the first man-made satellite to orbit the earth. ORIG C20: from Russian, lit.: fellow traveller, from *s-* with + *put* path + *-nik,* suffix indicating agent

sputter ('spʌtə) *vb* **1** another word for **splutter** (senses 1–3). **2** *Physics.* **2a** to undergo or cause to undergo a process in which atoms of a solid are removed from its surface by the impact of high-energy ions. **2b** to coat (a metal) onto (a solid surface) by this process. ◆ *n* **3** the process or noise of sputtering. **4** incoherent stammering speech. **5** something ejected while sputtering. ORIG C16: from Du. *sputteren,* imit.
► **'sputterer** *n*

sputum ('spju:təm) *n, pl* **sputa** (-tə). saliva ejected from the mouth, esp. mixed with mucus. ORIG C17: from L: spittle, from *spuere* to spit out

spy (spaɪ) *n, pl* **spies. 1** a person employed by a state or institution to obtain secret information from rival countries, organizations, companies, etc. **2** a person who keeps secret watch on others. **3** *Obs.* a close view. ◆ *vb* **spies, spying, spied. 4** (*intr;* usually foll. by *on*) to keep a secret or furtive watch (on). **5** (*intr*) to engage in espionage. **6** (*tr*) to catch sight of; descry. ORIG C13 *spien,* from OF *espier,* of Gmc origin

spyglass ('spaɪ,glɑ:s) *n* a small telescope.

spy out *vb* (*tr, adv*) **1** to discover by careful observation. **2** to make a close scrutiny of.

sq. *abbrev. for:* **1** sequence. **2** square. **3** (*pl* **sqq.**) the following one. ORIG from L *sequens*

Sq. *abbrev. for:* **1** Squadron. **2** Square.

SQL *abbrev. for* structured query language: a computer programming language used for database management.

squab (skwɒb) *n, pl* **squabs** *or* **squab. 1** a young unfledged bird, esp. a pigeon. **2** a short fat person. **3a** a well-stuffed bolster or cushion. **3b** a sofa. ◆ *adj* **4** (of birds) unfledged. **5** short and fat. ORIG C17: prob. of Gmc origin
► **'squabby** *adj*

squabble ('skwɒbᵊl) *vb* **squabbles, squabbling, squabbled. 1** (*intr*) to quarrel over a small matter. ◆ *n* **2** a petty quarrel. ORIG C17: prob. of Scand. origin
► **'squabbler** *n*

squad (skwɒd) *n* **1** the smallest military formation, typically a dozen soldiers, esp. a drill formation. **2** any small group of people engaged in a common pursuit. **3** *Sport.* a number of players from which a team is to be selected. ORIG C17: from OF *esquade,* from OSp. *escuadra,* from *escuadrar* to SQUARE, from the square formations used

squaddie *or* **squaddy** ('skwɒdɪ) *n, pl* **squaddies.** *Brit. sl.* a private soldier. ORIG C20: from SQUAD

squadron ('skwɒdrən) *n* **1** a subdivision of a naval fleet detached for a particular task. **2** a cavalry unit comprising two or more troops. **3** the basic tactical and administrative air force unit comprising two or more flights. ORIG C16: from It. *squadrone* soldiers drawn up in square formation, from *squadro* square

squadron leader *n* an officer holding commissioned

★ people and places

rank, between flight lieutenant and wing commander in the air forces of Britain and certain other countries.

squalamine (ˈskweɪləˌmiːn) *n* a steroid derivative found in sharks; it has antibiotic properties and inhibits cell division and may be useful in cancer and AIDS treatments. ORIG C20: from NL *squalus*, genus name of the shark

squalene (ˈskweɪˌliːn) *n Biochemistry.* a terpene first found in the liver of sharks but also present in the livers of most higher animals. ORIG C20: from NL *squalus*, genus name of the shark

squalid (ˈskwɒlɪd) *adj* **1** dirty and repulsive, esp. as a result of neglect or poverty. **2** sordid. ORIG C16: from L *squālidus*, from *squālēre* to be stiff with dirt
▸ **squaˈlidity** *or* **ˈsqualidness** *n* ▸ **ˈsqualidly** *adv*

squall[1] (skwɔːl) *n* **1** a sudden strong wind or brief turbulent storm. **2** any sudden commotion. ◆ *vb* **3** (*intr*) to blow in a squall. ORIG C18: ? a special use of SQUALL[2]
▸ **ˈsqually** *adj*

squall[2] (skwɔːl) *vb* **1** (*intr*) to cry noisily; yell. ◆ *n* **2** a shrill or noisy yell or howl. ORIG C17: prob. of Scand. origin
▸ **ˈsqualler** *n*

squalor (ˈskwɒlə) *n* the condition or quality of being squalid; disgusting filth. ORIG C17: from L

squama (ˈskweɪmə) *n, pl* **squamae** (-miː). *Biol.* a scale or scalelike structure. ORIG C18: from L
▸ **squamate** (ˈskweɪmeɪt) *adj* ▸ **squaˈmation** *n*
▸ **ˈsquamose** *or* **ˈsquamous** *adj*

squander (ˈskwɒndə) *vb* (*tr*) to spend wastefully or extravagantly; dissipate. ORIG C16: from ?
▸ **ˈsquanderer** *n*

square (skwɛə) *n* **1** a plane geometric figure having four equal sides and four right angles. **2** any object, part, or arrangement having this or a similar shape. **3** an open area in a town, sometimes including the surrounding buildings, which may form a square. **4** *Maths.* the product of two equal factors; the second power: *9 is the square of 3, written* 3^2. **5** an instrument having two strips of wood, metal, etc., set in the shape of a T or L, used for constructing or testing right angles. **6** *Cricket.* the closely-cut area in the middle of a ground on which wickets are prepared. **7** *Inf.* a person who is old-fashioned in views, customs, appearance, etc. **8** *Obs.* a standard, pattern, or rule. **9 back to square one.** indicating a return to the starting point because of failure, lack of progress, etc. **10 on the square. 10a** at right angles. **10b** *Inf.* honestly and openly. **11 out of square. 11a** not at right angles or not having a right angle. **11b** not in order or agreement. ◆ *adj* **12** being a square in shape or section. **13** having or forming one or more right angles or being at right angles to something. **14a** (*prenominal*) denoting a measure of area of any shape: *a circle of four square feet.* **14b** (*immediately postpositive*) denoting a square having a specified length on each side: *a board four feet square.* **15** fair and honest (esp. in **a square deal**). **16** straight, even, or level: *a square surface.* **17** *Cricket.* at right angles to the wicket: *square leg.* **18** *Soccer, hockey, etc.* in a straight line across the pitch: *a square pass.* **19** *Naut.* (of the sails of a square-rigged ship) set at right angles to the keel. **20** *Inf.* old-fashioned. **21** stocky or sturdy: *square shoulders.* **22** (*postpositive*) having no remaining debts or accounts to be settled. **23** (*prenominal*) unequivocal or straightforward: *a square contradiction.* **24** (*postpositive*) neat and tidy. **25** *Maths.* (of a matrix) having the same number of rows and columns. **26 all square.** on equal terms; even in score. **27 square peg** (**in a round hole**). *Inf.* a person or thing that is a misfit. ◆ *vb* **squares, squaring, squared.** (*mainly tr*) **28** to make into a square or similar shape. **29** *Maths.* to raise (a number or quantity) to the second power. **30** to test or adjust for deviation with respect to a right angle, plane surface, etc. **31** (sometimes foll. by *off*) to divide into squares. **32** to position so as to be rectangular, straight, or level: *to square the shoulders.* **33** (sometimes foll. by *up*) to settle (debts, accounts, etc.). **34** to level (the score) in a game, etc. **35** (*also intr;* often foll. by *with*) to agree or cause to agree: *your ideas don't square with mine.* **36** to arrange (something) or come to an arrangement with (someone) as by bribery. **37 square the circle.** to attempt the impossible (in reference to the insoluble problem of constructing a square having exactly the same area as a given circle). ◆ *adv* **38** in order to be square. **39** at right angles. **40** *Soccer, hockey, etc.* in a straight line across the pitch: *to pass the ball square.* **41** *Inf.* squarely. ◆ See also **square away, square off, square up.** ORIG C13: from OF *esquare*, from Vulgar L *exquadra* (unattested), from L *quadrāre* to make square
▸ **ˈsquareness** *n* ▸ **ˈsquarer** *n*

square away *vb* (*adv*) **1** to set the sails of (a square-rigged ship) at right angles to the keel. **2** (*tr*) *US & Canad.* to make neat and tidy.

square-bashing *n Brit. mil. sl.* drill on a barracks square.

square bracket *n* **1** either of a pair of characters [ ], used to enclose a section of writing or printing to separate it from the main text. **2** Also called: **bracket.** either of these characters used as a sign of aggregation in mathematical or logical expressions.

square dance *n* **1** any of various formation dances in which the couples form squares. ◆ *vb* **square-dance, square-dances, square-dancing, square-danced. 2** (*intr*) to perform such a dance.
▸ **ˈsquare-ˌdancer** *n*

square knot *n* another name for **reef knot.**

square leg *n Cricket.* **1** a fielding position on the on side approximately at right angles to the batsman. **2** a person who fields in this position.

squarely (ˈskwɛəlɪ) *adv* **1** in a direct way; straight: *he hit me squarely on the nose.* **2** in an honest, frank, and just manner. **3** at right angles.

square meal *n* a substantial meal consisting of enough to satisfy.

square measure *n* a unit or system of units for measuring areas.

square number *n* an integer, such as 1, 4, 9, or 16, that is the square of an integer.

square off *vb* (*intr, adv*) to assume a posture of offence or defence, as in boxing.

square of opposition *n Logic.* the diagrammatic representation of the relationships between the four types of proposition found in the syllogism.

square-rigged *adj Naut.* rigged with square sails. See **square sail.**

square root *n* a number or quantity that when multiplied by itself gives a given number or quantity: *the square roots of 4 are 2 and –2.*

square sail *n Naut.* a rectangular or square sail set on a horizontal yard rigged more or less at right angles to the keel.

square shooter *n Inf., chiefly US.* an honest or frank person.
▸ **square shooting** *adj*

square up *vb* (*adv*) **1** to pay or settle (bills, debts, etc.). **2** *Inf.* to arrange or be arranged satisfactorily. **3** (*intr;* foll. by *to*) to prepare to be confronted (with), esp. courageously. **4** (*tr;* foll. by *to*) to adopt a position of readiness to fight (an opponent). **5** *Scot.* to tidy up.

squarrose (ˈskwærəʊz, ˈskwɒ-) *adj* **1** *Biol.* having a rough surface, caused by projecting hairs, scales, etc. **2** *Bot.* having or relating to overlapping parts that are pointed or recurved. ORIG C18: from L *squarrōsus* scabby

squash[1] (skwɒʃ) *vb* **1** to press or squeeze or be pressed or squeezed in or down so as to crush, distort, or pulp. **2** (*tr*) to suppress or overcome. **3** (*tr*) to humiliate or crush (a person), esp. with a disconcerting retort. **4** (*intr*) to make a sucking, splashing, or squelching sound. **5** (often foll. by *in* or *into*) to enter or insert in a confined space. ◆ *n* **6** *Brit.* a still drink made from fruit juice or fruit syrup diluted with water. **7** a crush, esp. of people in a confined space. **8** something squashed. **9** the act or sound of squashing or the state of being squashed. **10** Also called: **squash rackets.** a game for two or four players played in an enclosed court with a small rubber ball and light long-handled rackets. **11** Also called: **squash tennis.** a similar game played with larger rackets and a larger pneumatic ball. ORIG C16: from OF *esquasser*, from Vulgar L *exquassāre* (unattested), from L EX-[1] + *quassāre* to shatter
▸ **ˈsquasher** *n*

squash² (skwɒʃ) *n, pl* **squashes** *or* **squash.** *US & Canad.* **1** any of various marrow-like plants, the fruits of which have a hard rind surrounding edible flesh. **2** the fruit, eaten as a vegetable. ORIG C17: of Amerind origin, from *askutasquash,* lit.: green vegetable eaten green

squashy (ˈskwɒʃɪ) *adj* **squashier, squashiest. 1** easily squashed; pulpy: *a squashy peach.* **2** soft and wet; marshy: *squashy ground.*
▸ ˈ**squashily** *adv* ▸ ˈ**squashiness** *n*

squat (skwɒt) *vb* **squats, squatting, squatted.** (*intr*) **1** to rest in a crouching position with the knees bent and the weight on the feet. **2** to crouch down, esp. in order to hide. **3** *Law.* to occupy land or property to which the occupant has no legal title. ◆ *adj* **4** Also: **squatty.** short and broad. ◆ *n* **5** a squatting position. **6** a house occupied by squatters. ORIG C13: from OF *esquater,* from *es-* EX-¹ + *catir* to press together, from Vulgar L *coactīre* (unattested), from L *cōgere* to compress
▸ ˈ**squatly** *adv* ▸ ˈ**squatness** *n*

squatter (ˈskwɒtə) *n* **1** a person who occupies property or land to which he or she has no legal title. **2** (in Australia) **2a** a grazier with extensive holdings. **2b** *History.* a person occupying land as tenant of the Crown. **3** (in New Zealand) a 19th-century settler who took up large acreage on a crown lease.

squat thrust *n* an exercise in which the hands are kept on the floor with the arms held straight while the legs are straightened out behind and quickly drawn in towards the body again.

squattocracy (skwɒˈtɒkrəsɪ) *n Austral.* squatters collectively, regarded as rich and influential. See **squatter** (sense 2a). ORIG C19: from SQUATTER + -CRACY

squaw (skwɔː) *n* **1** *Offens.* a North American Indian woman. **2** *Sl., usually facetious.* a woman or wife. ORIG C17: of Amerind origin

squawk (skwɔːk) *n* **1** a loud raucous cry; screech. **2** *Inf.* a loud complaint. ◆ *vb* **3** to utter (with) a squawk. **4** (*intr*) *Inf.* to complain loudly. ORIG C19: imit.
▸ ˈ**squawker** *n*

squaw man *n Derog.* a White man married to a North American Indian woman.

squeak (skwiːk) *n* **1** a short shrill cry or high-pitched sound. **2** *Inf.* an escape (esp. in **narrow squeak, near squeak**). **3** *Inf.* (*usually used with a negative*) a word; a slight sound. ◆ *vb* **4** to make or cause to make a squeak. **5** (*intr; usually foll. by through or by*) to pass with only a narrow margin: *to squeak through an examination.* **6** (*intr*) *Inf.* to confess information about oneself or another. **7** (*tr*) to utter with a squeak. ORIG C17: prob. of Scand. origin
▸ ˈ**squeaky** *adj* ▸ ˈ**squeakily** *adv* ▸ ˈ**squeakiness** *n*

squeaky-clean *adj* **1** (of hair) washed so clean that wet strands squeak when rubbed. **2** completely clean. **3** *Inf., derog.* (of a person) cultivating a virtuous and wholesome image.

squeal (skwiːl) *n* **1** a high shrill yelp, as of pain. **2** a screaming sound. ◆ *vb* **3** to utter (with) a squeal. **4** (*intr*) *Sl.* to confess information about another. **5** (*intr*) *Inf., chiefly Brit.* to complain loudly. ORIG C13 *squelen,* imit.
▸ ˈ**squealer** *n*

squeamish (ˈskwiːmɪʃ) *adj* **1** easily sickened or nauseated. **2** easily shocked; prudish. **3** easily frightened: *squeamish about spiders.* ORIG C15: from Anglo-F *escoymous,* from ?
▸ ˈ**squeamishly** *adv* ▸ ˈ**squeamishness** *n*

squeegee (ˈskwiːdʒiː) *n* **1** an implement with a rubber blade used for wiping away surplus water from a surface, such as a windowpane. **2** any of various similar devices used in photography for pressing water out of wet prints or negatives or for squeezing prints onto a glazing surface. ◆ *vb* **squeegees, squeegeeing, squeegeed. 3** to remove (liquid) from (something) by use of a squeegee. ORIG C19: prob. imit., infl. by SQUEEZE

squeeze (skwiːz) *vb* **squeezes, squeezing, squeezed.** (*mainly tr*) **1** to grip or press firmly, esp. so as to crush or distort. **2** to crush or press (something) so as to extract (a liquid): *to squeeze juice from an orange; to squeeze an orange.* **3** to apply gentle pressure to, as in affection or reassurance: *he squeezed her hand.* **4** to push or force in a confined space: *to squeeze six lettuces into one box; to squeeze through a crowd.* **5** to hug closely. **6** to oppress with exacting demands, such as excessive taxes. **7** to exert pressure on (someone) in order to extort (something): *to squeeze money out of a victim by blackmail.* **8** *Bridge, whist.* to lead a card that forces (opponents) to discard potentially winning cards. ◆ *n* **9** the act or an instance of squeezing or of being squeezed. **10** a hug or handclasp. **11** a crush of people in a confined space. **12** *Chiefly Brit.* a condition of restricted credit imposed by a government to counteract price inflation. **13** an amount extracted by squeezing: *a squeeze of lemon juice.* **14** *Inf.* pressure brought to bear in order to extort something (esp. in **put the squeeze on**). **15** *Commerce.* any action taken by a trader or traders on a market that forces buyers to make purchases and prices to rise. **16** Also called: **squeeze play.** *Bridge, whist.* a manoeuvre that forces opponents to discard potentially winning cards. ORIG C16: from ME *queysen* to press, from OE *cwӯsan*
▸ ˈ**squeezable** *adj* ▸ ˈ**squeezer** *n*

squelch (skwɛltʃ) *vb* **1** (*intr*) to walk laboriously through soft wet material or with wet shoes, making a sucking noise. **2** (*intr*) to make such a noise. **3** (*tr*) to crush completely; squash. **4** (*tr*) *Inf.* to silence, as by a crushing retort. ◆ *n* **5** a squelching sound. **6** something that has been squelched. **7** *Inf.* a crushing remark. ORIG C17: imit.
▸ ˈ**squelcher** *n* ▸ ˈ**squelchy** *adj*

squib (skwɪb) *n* **1** a firework that burns with a hissing noise and culminates in a small explosion. **2** a short witty attack; lampoon. **3 damp squib.** something intended but failing to impress. ◆ *vb* **squibs, squibbing, squibbed. 4** (*intr*) to sound, move, or explode like a squib. **5** (*intr*) to let off or shoot a squib. **6** to write a squib against (someone). ORIG C16: prob. imit. of a light explosion

squid (skwɪd) *n, pl* **squid** *or* **squids.** any of various ten-limbed pelagic cephalopod molluscs of most seas, having a torpedo-shaped body ranging from about 10 centimetres to 16.5 metres long. See also **cuttlefish.** ORIG C17: from ?

squiffy (ˈskwɪfɪ) *adj* **squiffier, squiffiest.** *Brit. inf.* slightly drunk. ORIG C19: from ?

squiggle (ˈskwɪgᵊl) *n* **1** a mark or movement in the form of a wavy line; curlicue. **2** an illegible scrawl. ◆ *vb* **squiggles, squiggling, squiggled. 3** (*intr*) to wriggle. **4** (*intr*) to form or draw squiggles. **5** (*tr*) to make into squiggles. ORIG C19: ? a blend of SQUIRM + WIGGLE
▸ ˈ**squiggler** *n* ▸ ˈ**squiggly** *adj*

squilgee (ˈskwɪldʒiː) *n* a variant spelling of **squeegee.** ORIG C19: ?from SQUEEGEE, infl. by SQUELCH

squill (skwɪl) *n* **1** Also called: **sea squill.** a Mediterranean plant of the lily family. **2** any of various related Old World plants. **3** Also called: **scilla.** the bulb of the sea squill, which is sliced, dried, and used medicinally, as an expectorant. ORIG C14: from L *squilla* sea onion, from Gk *skilla,* from ?

squinch (skwɪntʃ) *n* a small arch, corbelling, etc., across an internal corner of a tower, used to support a spire, etc. Also called: **squinch arch.** ORIG C15: from obs. *scunch,* from ME *sconcheon,* from OF *escoinson,* from *es-* EX-¹ + *coin* corner

squint (skwɪnt) *vb* **1** (*usually intr*) to cross or partly close (the eyes). **2** (*intr*) to have a squint. **3** (*intr*) to look or glance sideways or askance. ◆ *n* **4** the nontechnical name for **strabismus. 5** the act or an instance of squinting; glimpse. **6** a narrow oblique opening in a wall or pillar of a church to permit a view of the main altar from a side aisle or transept. **7** *Inf.* a quick look; glance. ◆ *adj* **8** having a squint. **9** *Inf.* askew; crooked. ORIG C14: short for ASQUINT
▸ ˈ**squinter** *n* ▸ ˈ**squinty** *adj*

squire (ˈskwaɪə) *n* **1** a country gentleman in England, esp. the main landowner in a rural community. **2** *Feudal history.* a young man of noble birth, who attended upon a knight. **3** *Rare.* a man who courts or escorts a woman. **4** *Inf., chiefly Brit.* a term of address used by one man to another. ◆ *vb* **squires, squiring, squired. 5** (*tr*) (of a man) to escort (a woman). ORIG C13: from OF *esquier;* see ESQUIRE

squirearchy *or* **squirarchy** (ˈskwaɪəˌrɑːkɪ) *n, pl* **squire-**

archies *or* **squirarchies.** **1** government by squires. **2** squires collectively, esp. as a political or social force.
▸ **squire'archal, squir'archal** *or* **squire'archical, squir'archical** *adj*

squireen (skwaɪ'ri:n) *or* **squireling** ('skwaɪəlɪŋ) *n Rare.* a petty squire. ORIG C19: from SQUIRE + *-een,* Anglo-Irish dim. suffix

squirm (skwɜ:m) *vb* (*intr*) **1** to move with a wriggling motion; writhe. **2** to feel deep mental discomfort, guilt, embarrassment, etc. ◆ *n* **3** a squirming movement. ORIG C17: imit. (? infl. by WORM)
▸ **'squirmer** *n* ▸ **'squirmy** *adj*

squirrel ('skwɪrəl) *n, pl* **squirrels** *or* **squirrel.** **1** any of various arboreal rodents having a bushy tail and feeding on nuts, seeds, etc. **2** any of various related rodents, such as a ground squirrel or a marmot. **3** the fur of such an animal. **4** *Inf.* a person who hoards things. ◆ *vb* **squirrels, squirrelling, squirrelled** *or US* **squirrels, squirreling, squirreled.** **5** (*tr*; usually foll. by *away*) *Inf.* to store for future use; hoard. ORIG C14: from OF *esquireul,* from LL *sciūrus,* from Gk *skiouros,* from *skia* shadow + *oura* tail

squirrel cage *n* **1** a cage consisting of a cylindrical framework that is made to rotate by a small animal running inside the framework. **2** a repetitive purposeless task, way of life, etc. **3** Also called: **squirrel-cage motor.** *Electrical engineering.* the rotor of an induction motor with a cylindrical winding having copper bars around the periphery parallel to the axis.

squirt (skwɜ:t) *vb* **1** to force (a liquid) or (of a liquid) to be forced out of a narrow opening. **2** (*tr*) to cover or spatter with liquid so ejected. ◆ *n* **3** a jet or amount of liquid so ejected. **4** the act or an instance of squirting. **5** an instrument used for squirting. **6** *Inf.* **6a** a person regarded as insignificant or contemptible. **6b** a short person. ORIG C15: imit.
▸ **'squirter** *n*

squirting cucumber *n* a hairy plant of the Mediterranean region, having a fruit that discharges seeds explosively when ripe.

squish (skwɪʃ) *vb* **1** (*tr*) to crush, esp. so as to make a soft splashing noise. **2** (*intr*) (of mud, etc.) to make a splashing noise. ◆ *n* **3** a soft squashing sound. ORIG C17: imit.
▸ **'squishy** *adj*

squit (skwɪt) *n Brit. sl.* **1** an insignificant person. **2** nonsense. ORIG C19: var. of SQUIRT

squiz (skwɪz) *n, pl* **squizzes.** *Austral. & NZ sl.* a look or glance, esp. an inquisitive one. ORIG C20: ? blend of SQUINT + QUIZ

sr *Maths. abbrev. for* steradian.

Sr *abbrev. for:* **1** (after a name) senior. **2** Señor. **3** Sir. **4** Sister (religious). **5** *the chemical symbol for* strontium.

Sra *abbrev. for* Señora.

Srbija ★ ('sərbija) *n* the Serbian name for **Serbia.**

SRC (in Britain) *abbrev. for* Science Research Council.

Sri Lanka ★ (ˌsri: 'læŋkə) *n* a republic in S Asia, occupying the island of Ceylon: settled by the Sinhalese from S India in about 550 B.C.; became a British colony 1802; gained independence in 1948, becoming a republic within the Commonwealth in 1972. Exports include tea, cocoa, cinnamon, and copra. Official languages: Sinhalese and Tamil; English is also widely spoken. Religion: Hinayana Buddhist majority. Currency: Sri Lanka rupee. Capital: Colombo (administrative), Sri Jayewardenepura Kotte (legislative). Pop.: 18 940 000 (1999 est.). Area: 65 610 sq. km (25 332 sq. miles). Official name (since 1978): **Democratic Socialist Republic of Sri Lanka.** Former name (until 1972): **Ceylon.**
▸ **Sri Lankan** *adj, n*

Srinagar ★ (sri:'nʌgə) *n* a city in N India, the summer capital of the state of Jammu and Kashmir, at an altitude of 1600 m (5250 ft) on the Jhelum River: seat of the University of Jammu and Kashmir (1948). Pop.: 586 038 (1991).

SRN (formerly, in Britain) *abbrev. for* State Registered Nurse.

SRO *abbrev. for:* **1** standing room only. **2** (in Britain) Statutory Rules and Orders. **3** self-regulatory organization.

Srta *abbrev. for* Señorita.

SS *abbrev. for:* **1** Saints. **2** a paramilitary organization within the Nazi party that provided Hitler's bodyguard, security forces, concentration-camp guards, etc. ORIG G *Schutzstaffel* protection squad **3** steamship.

SSE *symbol for* south-southeast.

ssp. (*pl* **sspp.**) *Biol. abbrev. for* subspecies.

SSR (formerly) *abbrev. for* Soviet Socialist Republic.

SSRC (formerly in Britain) *abbrev. for* Social Science Research Council.

SST *abbrev. for* supersonic transport.

SSW *symbol for* south-southwest.

St *abbrev. for:* **1** Saint (all entries that are usually preceded by *St* are in this dictionary listed alphabetically under **Saint**). **2** statute. **3** Strait. **4** Street.

st. *abbrev. for:* **1** stanza. **2** statute. **3** stone. **4** *Cricket.* stumped by.

s.t. *abbrev. for* short ton.

-st *suffix.* a variant of **-est**[2].

Sta (in the names of places or churches) *abbrev. for* Saint (female). ORIG It. *Santa*

stab (stæb) *vb* **stabs, stabbing, stabbed.** **1** (*tr*) to pierce or injure with a sharp pointed instrument. **2** (*tr*) (of a sharp pointed instrument) to pierce or wound. **3** (when *intr,* often foll. by *at*) to make a thrust (at); jab. **4** (*tr*) to inflict with a sharp pain. **5** **stab in the back.** **5a** (*vb*) to damage the reputation of (a person, esp. a friend) in a surreptitious way. **5b** (*n*) a treacherous action or remark that causes the downfall of or injury to a person. ◆ *n* **6** the act or an instance of stabbing. **7** an injury or rift made by stabbing. **8** a sudden sensation, esp. an unpleasant one: *a stab of pity.* **9** *Inf.* an attempt (esp. in **make a stab at**). ORIG C14: from *stabbe* stab wound
▸ **'stabber** *n*

Stabat Mater ('stɑ:bæt 'mɑ:tə) *n* **1** *RC Church.* a Latin hymn commemorating the sorrows of the Virgin Mary at the crucifixion. **2** a musical setting of this hymn. ORIG from opening words, lit.: the mother was standing

stabile ('steɪbaɪl) *n* **1** *Arts.* a stationary abstract construction, usually of wire, metal, wood, etc. ◆ *adj* **2** fixed; stable. **3** resistant to chemical change. ORIG C18: from L *stabilis*

stability (stə'bɪlɪtɪ) *n, pl* **stabilities.** **1** the quality of being stable. **2** the ability of an aircraft to resume its original flight path after inadvertent displacement.

stabilize *or* **stabilise** ('steɪbɪˌlaɪz) *vb* **stabilizes, stabilizing, stabilized** *or* **stabilises, stabilising, stabilised.** **1** to make or become stable or more stable. **2** to keep or be kept stable. **3** (*tr*) to put or keep (an aircraft, vessel, etc.) in equilibrium by one or more special devices or (of an aircraft, etc.) to become stable.
▸ **ˌstabili'zation** *or* **ˌstabili'sation** *n*

stabilizer *or* **stabiliser** ('steɪbɪˌlaɪzə) *n* **1** any device for stabilizing an aircraft. **2** a substance added to something to maintain it in a stable or unchanging state, such as an additive that preserves the texture of food. **3** *Naut.* **3a** a system of pairs of fins projecting from the hull of a ship and controllable to counteract roll. **3b** See **gyrostabilizer.** **4** either of a pair of small wheels fitted to the back wheel of a bicycle to help a beginner to maintain balance. **5** *Econ.* a measure, such as progressive taxation, interest-rate control, or unemployment benefit, used to restrict swings in prices, employment, production, etc., in a free economy. **6** a person or thing that stabilizes.

stable[1] ('steɪbəl) *n* **1** a building, usually consisting of stalls, for the lodging of horses or other livestock. **2** the animals lodged in such a building, collectively. **3a** the racehorses belonging to a particular establishment or owner. **3b** the establishment itself. **3c** (*as modifier*): *stable companion.* **4** *Inf.* a source of training, such as a school, theatre, etc.: *the two athletes were out of the same stable.* **5** a number of people considered as a source of a particular talent: *a stable of writers.* **6** (*modifier*) of, relating to, or suitable for a stable: *stable door.* ◆ *vb* **stables, stabling, stabled.** **7** to put, keep, or be kept in a stable. ORIG C13: from OF *estable* cowshed, from L *stabulum* shed, from *stāre* to stand

stable² (ˈsteɪbᵊl) *adj* **1** steady in position or balance; firm. **2** lasting: *a stable relationship.* **3** steadfast or firm of purpose. **4** (of an elementary particle, etc.) not undergoing decay; not radioactive. **5** (of a chemical compound) not readily partaking in a chemical change. ORIG C13: from OF *estable,* from L *stabilis* steady, from *stāre* to stand
▸ **ˈstableness** *n* ▸ **ˈstably** *adv*

stableboy (ˈsteɪbᵊlˌbɔɪ), **stablegirl** (ˈsteɪbᵊlˌgɜl), *or* **stableman** (ˈsteɪbᵊlˌmæn, -mən) *n, pl* **stableboys, stablegirls,** *or* **stablemen.** a boy, girl, or man who works in a stable.

stable door *n* a door with an upper and lower leaf that may be opened separately. US and Canad. equivalent: **Dutch door.**

Stableford (ˈsteɪbᵊlfəd) *n Golf.* **a** a scoring system in which points are awarded according to the number of strokes taken at each hole, whereby a hole completed in one stroke over par counts as one point, a hole completed in level par counts as two points, etc. **b** (*as modifier*): *a Stableford competition.* ◆ Cf. **match play, stroke play.** ORIG C20: after its inventor Dr Frank *Stableford* (1870–1959), E amateur golfer

stable lad *n* a person who looks after the horses in a racing stable.

stabling (ˈsteɪblɪŋ) *n* stable buildings or accommodation.

stablish (ˈstæblɪʃ) *vb* an archaic variant of **establish.**

Stabroek ★ (*Dutch* ˈsta:bru:k) *n* the former name (until 1812) of **Georgetown** (sense 1).

staccato (stəˈkɑ:təʊ) *adj* **1** *Music.* (of notes) short, clipped, and separate. **2** characterized by short abrupt sounds, as in speech: *a staccato command.* ◆ *adv* **3** (esp. used as a musical direction) in a staccato manner. ORIG C18: from It., from *staccare* to detach, shortened from *distaccare*

stachys (ˈstækɪs) *n* any plant of the herbaceous genus *Stachys.* See also **woundwort.** ORIG C16: from L, from Gk: ear of corn

stack (stæk) *n* **1** an ordered pile or heap. **2** a large orderly pile of hay, straw, etc., for storage in the open air. **3** (*often pl*) compactly spaced bookshelves, used to house collections of books in an area usually prohibited to library users. **4** a number of aircraft circling an airport at different altitudes, awaiting their signal to land. **5** a large amount. **6** *Mil.* a pile of rifles or muskets in the shape of a cone. **7** *Brit.* a measure of coal or wood equal to 108 cubic feet. **8** See **chimney stack, smokestack. 9** a vertical pipe, such as the funnel of a ship or the soil pipe attached to the side of a building. **10** a high column of rock, esp. one isolated from the mainland by the erosive action of the sea. **11** an area in a computer memory for temporary storage. ◆ *vb* (*tr*) **12** to place in a stack; pile. **13** to load or fill up with piles of something: *to stack a lorry with bricks.* **14** to control a number of aircraft waiting to land at an airport so that each flies at a different altitude. **15 stack the cards.** to prearrange the order of a pack of cards secretly so as to cheat. ORIG C13: from ON *stakkr* haystack, of Gmc origin
▸ **ˈstackable** *adj* ▸ **ˈstacker** *n*

stacked (stækt) *adj Sl.* a variant of **well-stacked.**

stadholder *or* **stadtholder** (ˈstædˌhəʊldə) *n* **1** the chief magistrate of the former Dutch republic or any of its provinces (from about 1580 to 1802). **2** a viceroy or governor of a province. ORIG C16: from Du. *stad houder,* from *stad* city + *houder* holder

stadia¹ (ˈsteɪdɪə) *n* **1** measurement of distance using a telescopic surveying instrument and a graduated staff calibrated to correspond with the distance from the observer. **2** the two parallel cross hairs or **stadia hairs** in the eyepiece of the instrument used. **3** the staff used. ORIG C19: prob. from STADIA²

stadia² (ˈsteɪdɪə) *n* a plural of **stadium.**

stadium (ˈsteɪdɪəm) *n, pl* **stadiums** *or* **stadia. 1** a sports arena with tiered seats for spectators. **2** (in ancient Greece) a course for races, usually located between two hills providing slopes for tiers of seats. **3** an ancient Greek measure of length equivalent to about 607 feet or 184 metres. ORIG C16: via L from Gk *stadion,* changed from *spadion* racecourse, from *spān* to pull; infl. by Gk *stadios* steady

Staël ★ (*French* stal) *n* **Madame de.** full name *Baronne Anne Louise Germaine* (née *Necker*) *de Staël-Holstein.* 1766–1817, French writer, whose works, esp. *De l'Allemagne* (1810), anticipated French romanticism.

staff¹ (stɑ:f) *n, pl* **staffs** *for senses 1–4;* **staffs** *or* **staves** *for senses 5–9.* **1** a group of people employed by a company, individual, etc., for executive, clerical, sales work, etc. **2** (*modifier*) attached to or provided for the staff of an establishment: *a staff doctor.* **3** the body of teachers or lecturers of an educational institution. **4** *Mil.* the officers appointed to assist a commander, service, or central headquarters organization. **5** a stick with some special use, such as a walking stick or an emblem of authority. **6** something that sustains or supports: *bread is the staff of life.* **7** a pole on which a flag is hung. **8** *Chiefly Brit.* a graduated rod used in surveying, esp. for sighting to with a levelling instrument. **9** Also called: **stave.** *Music.* **9a** the system of horizontal lines grouped into sets of five (four in plainsong) upon which music is written. The spaces between them are employed in conjunction with a clef in order to give a graphic indication of pitch. **9b** any set of five lines in this system together with its clef: *the treble staff.* ◆ *vb* **10** (*tr*) to provide with a staff. ORIG OE *stæf*

staff² (stɑ:f) *n US.* a mixture of plaster and hair used to cover the external surface of temporary structures and for decoration. ORIG C19: from ?

Staffa ★ (ˈstæfə) *n* an island in W Scotland, in the Inner Hebrides west of Mull: site of Fingal's Cave.

staff corporal *n* a noncommissioned rank in the British Army above that of staff sergeant and below that of warrant officer.

staff nurse *n* a qualified nurse ranking immediately below a sister.

staff officer *n* a commissioned officer serving on the staff of a commander, service, or central headquarters.

Stafford¹ ★ (ˈstæfəd) *n* a market town in central England, administrative centre of Staffordshire. Pop.: 61 885 (1991).

Stafford² ★ (ˈstæfəd) *n* Sir **Edward William.** 1819–1901, New Zealand statesman, born in Scotland: prime minister (1856–61; 1865–69; 1872).

Staffordshire ★ (ˈstæfədˌʃɪə, -ʃə) *n* a county of central England, includes the unitary authority of Stoke-on-Trent: coalfields lie in the east and south and the Pennine uplands in the north; important in the history of industry, coal and iron having been worked at least since the 13th century. Administrative centre: Stafford. Pop. (excluding Stoke-on-Trent unitary authority): 801 300 (1996 est.). Area (excluding Stoke-on-Trent unitary authority): 2716 sq. km (1049 sq. miles).

Staffordshire bull terrier *n* a breed of smooth-coated terrier with a stocky frame and generally a pied or brindled coat.

Staffs. (stæfs) *abbrev. for* Staffordshire.

staff sergeant ★ *n Mil.* **1** *Brit.* a noncommissioned officer holding a rank between sergeant and warrant officer and employed on administrative duties. **2** *US.* a noncommissioned officer who ranks: **2a** (in the Army) above sergeant and below sergeant first class. **2b** (in the Air Force) above airman first class and below technical sergeant. **2c** (in the Marine Corps) above sergeant and below gunnery sergeant.

stag (stæg) *n* **1** the adult male of a deer. **2** a man unaccompanied by a woman at a social gathering. **3** *Stock Exchange, Brit.* a speculator who applies for shares in a new issue in anticipation of a rise in its price and thus a quick profit on resale. **4** (*modifier*) (of a social gathering) attended by men only. ◆ *adv* **5** without a female escort. ◆ *vb* **stags, stagging, stagged.** (*tr*) **6** *Stock Exchange.* to apply for (shares in a new issue) with the intention of selling them for a quick profit when trading commences. ORIG OE *stagga* (unattested); rel. to ON *steggr* male bird

stag beetle *n* any of various beetles, the males of which have large branched mandibles.

stage (steɪdʒ) *n* **1** a distinct step or period of development, growth, or progress. **2** a raised area or platform. **3**

the platform in a theatre where actors perform. **4 the.** the theatre as a profession. **5** any scene regarded as a setting for an event or action. **6** a portion of a journey or a stopping place after such a portion. **7** short for **stagecoach. 8** *Brit.* a division of a bus route for which there is a fixed fare. **9** one of the separate propulsion units of a rocket that can be jettisoned when it has burnt out. **10** a small stratigraphical unit; a subdivision of a rock series or system. **11** the platform on a microscope on which the specimen is mounted for examination. **12** *Electronics.* a part of a complex circuit, esp. a transistor with the associated elements required to amplify a signal in an amplifier. **13 by** *or* **in easy stages.** not hurriedly: *he learned French by easy stages.* ◆ *vb* **stages, staging, staged.** (*tr*) **14** to perform (a play), esp. on a stage: *to stage "Hamlet".* **15** to set the action of (a play) in a particular time or place. **16** to plan, organize, and carry out (an event). ORIG C13: from OF *estage* position, from Vulgar L *staticum* (unattested), from L *stāre* to stand

stagecoach ('steɪdʒˌkəʊtʃ) *n* a large four-wheeled horse-drawn vehicle formerly used to carry passengers, mail, etc., on a regular route.

stagecraft ('steɪdʒˌkrɑːft) *n* skill in or the art of writing or staging plays.

stage direction *n* an instruction to an actor or director, written into the script of a play.

stage door *n* a door at a theatre leading backstage.

stage fright *n* nervousness or panic that may beset a person about to appear in front of an audience.

stagehand ('steɪdʒˌhænd) *n* a person who sets the stage, moves props, etc., in a theatrical production.

stage left *n* the part of the stage to the left of a performer facing the audience.

stage-manage *vb* **stage-manages, stage-managing, stage-managed. 1** to work as stage manager (for a play, etc.). **2** (*tr*) to arrange, present, or supervise from behind the scenes.

stage manager *n* a person who supervises the stage arrangements of a theatrical production.

stager ('steɪdʒə) *n* **1** a person of experience; veteran (esp. in **old stager**). **2** an archaic word for **actor.**

stage right *n* the part of the stage to the right of a performer facing the audience.

stage-struck *adj* infatuated with the glamour of theatrical life, esp. with the desire to act.

stage whisper *n* **1** a loud whisper from one actor to another onstage intended to be heard by the audience. **2** any loud whisper that is intended to be overheard.

stagflation (stæg'fleɪʃən) *n* a situation in which inflation is combined with stagnant or falling output and employment. ORIG C20: blend of *stagnation* + *inflation*

stagger ('stægə) *vb* **1** (*usually intr*) to walk or cause to walk unsteadily as if about to fall. **2** (*tr*) to astound or overwhelm, as with shock: *I am staggered by his ruthlessness.* **3** (*tr*) to place or arrange in alternating or overlapping positions or time periods to prevent confusion or congestion: *a staggered junction; to stagger holidays.* **4** (*intr*) to falter or hesitate: *his courage staggered in the face of the battle.* ◆ *n* **5** the act or an instance of staggering. ORIG C13: from dialect *stacker,* from ON *staka* to push
▸ **'staggerer** *n* ▸ **'staggering** *adj* ▸ **'staggeringly** *adv*

staggered directorships *pl n Business.* a defence against unwelcome takeover bids in which a company resolves that its directors should serve staggered terms of office and that no director can be removed from office without just cause, thus preventing a bidder from controlling the board for some years.

staggers ('stægəz) *n* (*functioning as sing or pl*) **1** a form of vertigo associated with decompression sickness. **2** Also called: **blind staggers.** a disease of horses and some other domestic animals characterized by a swaying unsteady gait, caused by infection or lesions of the central nervous system.

staging ('steɪdʒɪŋ) *n* any temporary structure used in the process of building, esp. the horizontal platforms supported by scaffolding.

staging area *n* a checkpoint or regrouping area for military formations in transit.

staging post *n* a place where a journey is usually broken, esp. a stopover on a flight.

Stagira ★ (stə'dʒaɪrə) *n* an ancient city on the coast of Chalcidice in Macedonia: the birthplace of Aristotle.

stagnant ('stægnənt) *adj* **1** (of water, etc.) standing still; without flow or current. **2** brackish and foul from standing still. **3** stale, sluggish, or dull from inaction. **4** not growing or developing; static. ORIG C17: from L *stagnāns,* from *stagnāre* to be stagnant, from *stagnum* a pool
▸ **'stagnancy** *n*

stagnate (stæg'neɪt) *vb* **stagnates, stagnating, stagnated.** (*intr*) to be or become stagnant.
▸ **stag'nation** *n*

stag night *or* **party** *n* a party for men only, esp. one held for a man just before he is married.

stagy *or US* **stagey** ('steɪdʒɪ) *adj* **stagier, stagiest.** excessively theatrical or dramatic.
▸ **'stagily** *adv* ▸ **'staginess** *n*

staid (steɪd) *adj* of a settled, sedate, and steady character. ORIG C16: obs. p.p. of STAY[1]
▸ **'staidly** *adv* ▸ **'staidness** *n*

stain (steɪn) *vb* (*mainly tr*) **1** to mark or discolour with patches of something that dirties. **2** to dye with a penetrating dyestuff or pigment. **3** to bring disgrace or shame on: *to stain one's honour.* **4** to colour (specimens) for microscopic study by treatment with a dye or similar reagent. **5** (*intr*) to produce indelible marks or discoloration: *does ink stain?* ◆ *n* **6** a spot, mark, or discoloration. **7** a moral taint; blemish or slur. **8** a dye or similar reagent, used to colour specimens for microscopic study. **9** a solution or liquid used to penetrate the surface of a material, esp. wood, and impart a rich colour without covering up the surface or grain. **10** any dye used to colour textiles and hides. ORIG C14 *steynen* (vb), shortened from *disteynen* to remove colour from, from OF *desteindre* to discolour, ult. from L *tingere* to tinge
▸ **'stainable** *adj* ▸ **ˌstaina'bility** *n* ▸ **'stainer** *n*

stained glass *n* **a** glass that has been coloured, as by fusing with a film of metallic oxide or burning pigment into the surface. **b** (*as modifier*): *a stained-glass window.*

Stainer ★ ('steɪnə) *n* Sir **John.** 1840–1901, British composer and organist, noted for his sacred music, esp. the oratorio *The Crucifixion* (1887).

Staines ★ (steɪnz) *n* a town in SE England, in N Surrey on the River Thames. Pop.: 51 167 (1991).

stainless ('steɪnlɪs) *adj* **1** resistant to discoloration, esp. that resulting from corrosion; rust-resistant: *stainless steel.* **2** having no blemish: *stainless reputation.*
▸ **'stainlessly** *adv*

stainless steel *n* **a** a type of steel resistant to corrosion as a result of the presence of large amounts of chromium. **b** (*as modifier*): *stainless-steel cutlery.*

stair (stɛə) *n* **1** one of a flight of stairs. **2** a series of steps: *a narrow stair.* ◆ See also **stairs.** ORIG OE *stæger*

staircase ('stɛəˌkeɪs) *n* a flight of stairs, its supporting framework, and, usually, a handrail or banisters.

stairs (stɛəz) *pl n* **1** a flight of steps leading from one storey or level to another, esp. indoors. **2 below stairs.** *Brit.* in the servants' quarters.

stairway ('stɛəˌweɪ) *n* a means of access consisting of stairs; staircase or flight of steps.

stairwell ('stɛəˌwɛl) *n* a vertical shaft or opening that contains a staircase.

stake[1] (steɪk) *n* **1** a stick or metal bar driven into the ground as a marker, part of a fence, support for a plant, etc. **2** one of a number of vertical posts that fit into sockets around a flat truck or railway wagon to hold the load in place. **3** a method or the practice of executing a person by binding him or her to a stake in the centre of a pile of wood that is then set on fire. **4 pull up stakes.** to leave one's home or resting place and move on. ◆ *vb* **stakes, staking, staked.** (*tr*) **5** to tie, fasten, or tether with or to a stake. **6** (often foll. by *out* or *off*) to fence or surround with stakes. **7** (often foll. by *out*) to lay (a claim) to land, rights, etc. **8** to support with a stake. ORIG OE *staca* pin

stake[2] (steɪk) *n* **1** the money or valuables that a player must hazard in order to buy into a gambling game or make a bet. **2** an interest, often financial, held in something: *a stake in the company's future.* **3** (*often pl*) the money that a player has available for gambling. **4** (*often pl*) a prize in a race, etc., esp. one made up of contributions from contestants or owners. **5** (*pl*) a horse race in which all owners of competing horses contribute to the prize. **6** *US & Canad. inf.* short for **grubstake. 7 at stake.** at risk: *lives are at stake.* **8 raise the stakes. 8a** to increase the amount of money or valuables hazarded in a gambling game. **8b** to increase the costs, risks, or considerations involved in taking an action or reaching a conclusion. ◆ *vb* **stakes, staking, staked.** (*tr*) **9** to hazard (money, etc.) on a result. **10** to invest in or support with money, etc.: *to stake a business.* ORIG C16: from ?

Staked Plain ★ *n* another name for the **Llano Estacado.**

stakeholder ('steɪk,həʊldə) *n* **1** a person or group owning a significant percentage of a company's shares. **2** a person or group not owning shares in an enterprise but affected by or having an interest in its operations, such as the employees, customers, local community, etc. ◆ *adj* **3** of or relating to policies intended to allow people to participate in and benefit from decisions made by enterprises in which they have a stake: *a stakeholder economy.*
▸ **'stake,holding** *n, adj*

stakeholder pension *n* (in Britain) a flexible pension scheme with low charges, in which contributors can stop and restart payments and switch schemes to another fund without paying a penalty.

stakeout ('steɪkaʊt) *Chiefly US & Canad. sl.* ◆ *n* **1** a police surveillance. **2** an area or house kept under such surveillance. ◆ *vb* **stake out. 3** (*tr, adv*) to keep under surveillance.

Stakhanovism (stæ'kænə,vɪzəm) *n* (in the former Soviet Union) a system designed to raise production by offering incentives to efficient workers. ORIG C20: after A. G. *Stakhanov* (1906–77), Soviet miner, the worker first awarded benefits under the system in 1935
▸ **Sta'khanov,ite** *n, adj*

stalactite ('stæləkˌtaɪt) *n* a cylindrical mass of calcium carbonate hanging from the roof of a limestone cave: formed by precipitation from continually dripping water. Cf. **stalagmite.** ORIG C17: from NL *stalactites,* from Gk *stalaktos* dripping, from *stalassein* to drip
▸ **stalactiform** (stə'læktɪ,fɔːm) *adj* ▸ **stalactitic** (,stælək'tɪtɪk) *or* ,**stalac'titical** *adj*

stalag ('stælæg) *n* a German prisoner-of-war camp in World War II, esp. for men from the ranks. ORIG short for *Stammlager* base camp

stalagmite ('stæləg,maɪt) *n* a cylindrical mass of calcium carbonate projecting upwards from the floor of a limestone cave: formed by precipitation from continually dripping water. Cf. **stalactite.** ORIG C17: from NL *stalagmites,* from Gk *stalagmos* dripping; rel. to Gk *stalassein* to drip
▸ **stalagmitic** (,stæləg'mɪtɪk) *or* ,**stalag'mitical** *adj*

stale[1] (steɪl) *adj* **1** (esp. of food) hard, musty, or dry from being kept too long. **2** (of beer, etc.) flat and tasteless from being kept open too long. **3** (of air) stagnant; foul. **4** uninteresting from overuse: *stale clichés.* **5** no longer new: *stale news.* **6** lacking in energy or ideas through overwork or lack of variety. **7** *Banking.* (of a cheque) not negotiable by a bank as a result of not having been presented within six months of being written. **8** *Law.* (of a claim, etc.) having lost its effectiveness or force, as by failure to act or by the lapse of time. ◆ *vb* **stales, staling, staled. 9** to make or become stale. ORIG C13 (orig. applied to liquor in the sense: well matured): prob. from OF *estale* (unattested) motionless, of Frankish origin
▸ **'staleness** *n*

stale[2] (steɪl) *vb* **stales, staling, staled. 1** (*intr*) (of livestock) to urinate. ◆ *n* **2** the urine of horses or cattle. ORIG C15: ?from OF *estaler* to stand in one position

stale bull *n Business.* a dealer or speculator who holds unsold commodities after a rise in market prices but who cannot trade because there are no buyers at the new levels and because his financial commitments prevent him from making further purchases.

stalemate ('steɪl,meɪt) *n* **1** a chess position in which any of a player's possible moves would place his king in check: in this position the game ends in a draw. **2** a situation in which two opposing forces find that further action is impossible or futile; deadlock. ◆ *vb* **stalemates, stalemating, stalemated. 3** (*tr*) to subject to a stalemate. ORIG C18: from obs. *stale,* from OF *estal* STALL[1] + (CHECK)MATE

Stalin[1] ★ ('stɑːlɪn) *n* **1** Also called: **Stalino.** a former name (from after the Revolution until 1961) of **Donetsk. 2** the former name (1950–61) of **Braşov. 3** the former name (1949–56) of **Varna.**

Stalin[2] ★ ('stɑːlɪn) *n* **Joseph.** original name *Iosif Vissarionovich Dzhugashvili.* 1879–1953, Soviet leader; general secretary of the Communist Party of the Soviet Union (1922–53). He succeeded Lenin and created a totalitarian state, crushing all opposition, esp. in the purges of 1934–37. He instigated rapid industrialization and the collectivization of agriculture and established the Soviet Union as a world power.

Stalinabad ★ (*Russian* stəlina'bat) *n* the former name (1929–61) of **Dushanbe.**

Stalingrad ★ ('stɑːlɪn,græd; *Russian* stəlin'grat) *n* the former name (1925–61) of **Volgograd.**

Stalinism ('stɑːlɪ,nɪzəm) *n* the theory and form of government associated with Joseph Stalin: a variant of Marxism-Leninism characterized by totalitarianism, rigid bureaucracy, and loyalty to the state.
▸ **'Stalinist** *n, adj*

Stalinogrod ★ (*Polish* stali'nɔgrɔt) *n* the former name (1953–56) for **Katowice.**

Stalin Peak ★ *n* a former name for **Kommunizma Peak.**

Stalinsk ★ (*Russian* 'stalinsk) *n* the former name (1932–61) of **Novokuznetsk.**

stalk[1] (stɔːk) *n* **1** the main stem of a herbaceous plant. **2** any of various subsidiary plant stems, such as a leafstalk or flower stalk. **3** a slender supporting structure in animals such as crinoids and barnacles. **4** any long slender supporting shaft or column. ORIG C14: prob. dim. from OE *stalu* upright piece of wood
▸ **stalked** *adj* ▸ **'stalk,like** *adj*

stalk[2] (stɔːk) *vb* **1** to follow or approach (game, prey, etc.) stealthily and quietly. **2** to pursue persistently and, sometimes, attack (a person with whom one is obsessed, often a celebrity). **3** to spread over (a place) in a menacing or grim manner: *fever stalked the camp.* **4** (*intr*) to walk in a haughty, stiff, or threatening way. **5** to search (a piece of land) for prey. ◆ *n* **6** the act of stalking. **7** a stiff or threatening stride. ORIG OE *bestealcian* to walk stealthily
▸ **'stalker** *n*

stalk-and-slash movie *n* another name for **slasher movie.**

stalking-horse *n* **1** a horse or an imitation one used by a hunter to hide behind while stalking. **2** something serving as a means of concealing plans; pretext. **3** a candidate put forward to divide the opposition or mask the candidacy of another person for whom the stalking-horse would then withdraw.

stalky ('stɔːkɪ) *adj* **stalkier, stalkiest. 1** like a stalk; slender and tall. **2** having or abounding in stalks.
▸ **'stalkily** *adv* ▸ **'stalkiness** *n*

stall[1] (stɔːl) *n* **1a** a compartment in a stable or shed for a single animal. **1b** another name for **stable**[1] (sense 1). **2** a small often temporary stand or booth for the sale of goods. **3** (in a church) **3a** one of a row of seats usually divided by armrests or a small screen, for the choir or clergy. **3b** a pen. **4** an instance of an engine stalling. **5** a condition of an aircraft in flight in which a reduction in speed or an increase in the aircraft's angle of attack causes a sudden loss of lift resulting in a downward plunge. **6** any small room or compartment. **7** *Brit.* **7a** a seat in a theatre or cinema, usually fixed to the floor. **7b** (*pl*) the area of seats on the ground floor of a theatre or cinema nearest to the stage or screen. **8** a tubelike covering for a finger. **9** (*pl*) short for **starting stalls.** ◆ *vb* **10** to cause (a motor vehicle or its engine) to stop, usually by incorrect use of the clutch or incorrect adjustment of the fuel mixture, or (of an engine or motor vehicle) to stop, usually for these reasons. **11** to cause (an aircraft) to go into a stall or (of an aircraft) to go into a stall. **12** to stick or cause to stick fast, as in mud or snow. **13** (*tr*) to confine (an animal) in a stall. ORIG OE *steall* a place for standing

stall² (stɔːl) *vb* **1** to employ delaying tactics towards (someone); be evasive. ◆ *n* **2** an evasive move; pretext. ORIG C16: from Anglo-F *estale* bird used as a decoy, infl. by STALL¹

stall-feed *vb* **stall-feeds, stall-feeding, stall-fed.** (*tr*) to keep and feed (an animal) in a stall, esp. as an intensive method of fattening it for slaughter.

stallholder (ˈstɔːlˌhəʊldə) *n* a person who sells goods at a market stall.

stallion (ˈstæljən) *n* an uncastrated male horse, esp. one used for breeding. ORIG C14 *staloun,* from OF *estalon,* of Gmc origin

stalwart (ˈstɔːlwət) *adj* **1** strong and sturdy; robust. **2** solid, dependable, and courageous. **3** resolute and firm. ◆ *n* **4** a stalwart person, esp. a supporter. ORIG OE *stǣlwirthe* serviceable, from *stǣl,* from *stathol* support + *wierthe* WORTH
▸ ˈ**stalwartly** *adv* ▸ ˈ**stalwartness** *n*

Stambul *or* **Stamboul** ★ (stæmˈbuːl) *n* the old part of Istanbul, Turkey, south of the Golden Horn: the site of ancient Byzantium; sometimes used as a name for the whole city.

stamen (ˈsteɪmɛn) *n, pl* **stamens** *or* **stamina.** the male reproductive organ of a flower, consisting of a stalk (filament) bearing an anther in which pollen is produced. ORIG C17: from L: the warp in an upright loom, from *stāre* to stand
▸ **staminiferous** (ˌstæmɪˈnɪfərəs) *adj*

Stamford ★ (ˈstæmfəd) *n* a city in SW Connecticut, on Long Island Sound: major chemical research laboratories. Pop.: 107 199 (1994 est.).

Stamford Bridge ★ *n* a village in N England, east of York: site of a battle (1066) in which King Harold of England defeated his brother Tostig and King Harald Hardrada of Norway, three weeks before the Battle of Hastings.

stamina¹ (ˈstæmɪnə) *n* enduring energy, strength, and resilience. ORIG C19: identical with STAMINA², from L *stāmen* thread, hence the threads of life spun out by the Fates, hence energy, etc.

stamina² (ˈstæmɪnə) *n* a plural of **stamen.**

staminate (ˈstæmɪnɪt, -ˌneɪt) *adj* (of plants) having stamens, esp. having stamens but no carpels; male.

stammer (ˈstæmə) *vb* **1** to speak or say (something) in a hesitant way, esp. as a result of a speech disorder or through fear, stress, etc. ◆ *n* **2** a speech disorder characterized by involuntary repetitions and hesitations. ORIG OE *stamerian*
▸ ˈ**stammerer** *n* ▸ ˈ**stammering** *n, adj*

stamp (stæmp) *vb* **1** (when *intr,* often foll. by *on*) to bring (the foot) down heavily (on the ground, etc.). **2** (*intr*) to walk with heavy or noisy footsteps. **3** (*intr;* foll. by *on*) to repress or extinguish: *he stamped on criticism.* **4** (*tr*) to impress or mark (a device or sign) on (something). **5** to mark (something) with an official seal or device: *to stamp a passport.* **6** (*tr*) to fix or impress permanently: *the date was stamped on her memory.* **7** (*tr*) to affix a postage stamp to. **8** (*tr*) to distinguish or reveal: *that behaviour stamps him as a cheat.* **9** to pound or crush (ores, etc.). ◆ *n* **10** the act or an instance of stamping. **11a** See **postage stamp. 11b** a mark applied to postage stamps for cancellation. **12** a similar piece of gummed paper used for commercial or trading purposes. **13** a block, die, etc., used for imprinting a design or device. **14** a design, device, or mark that has been stamped. **15** a characteristic feature or trait; hallmark: *the stamp of authenticity.* **16** a piece of gummed paper or other mark applied to official documents to indicate payment, validity, ownership, etc. **17** *Brit. inf.* a national insurance contribution, formerly recorded by means of a stamp on an official card. **18** type or class: *men of his stamp.* **19** an instrument or machine for crushing or pounding ores, etc., or the pestle in such a device. ◆ See also **stamp out.** ORIG OE *stampe*
▸ ˈ**stamper** *n*

stamp duty *or* **tax** *n* a tax on legal documents, publications, etc., the payment of which is certified by the attaching or impressing of official stamps.

stampede (stæmˈpiːd) *n* **1** an impulsive headlong rush of startled cattle or horses. **2** headlong rush of a crowd. **3** any sudden large-scale action, such as a rush of people to support a candidate. **4** *W US & Canad.* a rodeo event featuring fairground and social elements. ◆ *vb* **stampedes, stampeding, stampeded. 5** to run away or cause to run away in a stampede. ORIG C19: from American Sp. *estampida,* from Sp.: a din, from *estampar* to stamp, of Gmc origin
▸ stamˈ**peder** *n*

stamping ground *n* a habitual or favourite meeting or gathering place.

stamp mill *n* a machine for crushing ore.

stamp out *vb* (*tr, adv*) **1** to put out or extinguish by stamping: *to stamp out a fire.* **2** to suppress by force: *to stamp out a rebellion.*

stance (stæns, stɑːns) *n* **1** the manner and position in which a person or animal stands. **2** *Sport.* the posture assumed when about to play the ball, as in golf, cricket, etc. **3** emotional or intellectual attitude: *a leftist stance.* **4** *Chiefly Scot.* a place where a vehicle waits: *taxi stance.* ORIG C16: via F from It. *stanza* place for standing, from L *stāns,* from *stāre* to stand

stanch (stɑːntʃ) *vb* a variant of **staunch².**

stanchion (ˈstɑːnʃən) *n* **1** any vertical pole, beam, rod, etc., used as a support. ◆ *vb* **2** (*tr*) to provide or support with a stanchion or stanchions. ORIG C15: from OF *estanchon,* from *estance,* from Vulgar L *stantia* (unattested) a standing, from L *stāre* to stand

stand (stænd) *vb* **stands, standing, stood.** (*mainly intr*) **1** (*also tr*) to be or cause to be in an erect or upright position. **2** to rise to, assume, or maintain an upright position. **3** (*copula*) to have a specified height when standing: *to stand six feet tall.* **4** to be situated or located: *the house stands in the square.* **5** to be in a specified state or condition: *to stand in awe of someone.* **6** to adopt or remain in a resolute position or attitude. **7** (*may take an infinitive*) to be in a specified position: *I stand to lose money in this venture.* **8** to remain in force or continue in effect: *my orders stand.* **9** to come to a stop or halt, esp. temporarily. **10** (of water, etc.) to collect and remain without flowing. **11** (often foll. by *at*) (of a score, account, etc.) to indicate the specified position: *the score stands at 20 to 1.* **12** (*also tr;* when *intr,* foll. by *for*) to tolerate or bear: *I won't stand for your nonsense; I can't stand spiders.* **13** (*tr*) to resist; survive: *to stand the test of time.* **14** (*tr*) to submit to: *to stand trial.* **15** (often foll. by *for*) *Chiefly Brit.* to be or become a candidate: *stand for Parliament.* **16** to navigate in a specified direction: *we were standing for Madeira.* **17** (of a gun dog) to point at game. **18** to halt, esp. to give action, repel attack, or disrupt an enemy advance when retreating. **19** (*tr*) *Inf.* to bear the cost of; pay for: *to stand someone a drink.* **20 stand a chance.** to have a hope or likelihood of winning, succeeding, etc. **21 stand fast.** to maintain one's position firmly. **22 stand one's ground.** to maintain a stance or position in the face of opposition. **23 stand still. 23a** to remain motionless. **23b** (foll. by *for*) *US.* to tolerate: *I won't stand still for your threats.* **24 stand to (someone).** *Irish inf.* to be useful to (someone): *your knowledge of English will stand to you.* ◆ *n* **25** the act or an instance of standing. **26** an opinion, esp. a resolutely held one: *he took a stand on capital punishment.* **27** a halt or standstill. **28** a place where a person or thing stands. **29** *Austral. & NZ.* **29a** a position on the floor of a shearing shed allocated to one shearer. **29b** the shearer's equipment. **30** a structure on which people can sit or stand. **31** a frame or rack on which such articles as coats and hats may be hung. **32** a small table or piece of furniture where articles may be placed or stored: *a music stand.* **33** a supporting framework, esp. for a tool or instrument. **34** a stall, booth, or counter from which goods may be sold. **35** a halt to give action, etc., esp. during a retreat and having some duration or success. **36** *Cricket.* an extended period at the wicket by two batsmen. **37** a growth of plants in a particular area, esp. trees in a forest or a crop in a field. **38** a stop made by a touring theatrical company, pop group, etc., to give a performance (esp. in **one-night stand**). **39** (of a gun dog) the act of pointing at game. ◆ See also **stand by, stand down,** etc. ORIG OE *standan* ▸ **'stander** *n*

standard ('stændəd) *n* **1** an accepted or approved example of something against which others are judged or measured. **2** (*often pl*) a principle of propriety, honesty, and integrity. **3** a level of excellence or quality. **4** any distinctive flag or device, etc., as of a nation, sovereign, or special cause, etc., or the colours of a cavalry regiment. **5** a flag or emblem formerly used to show the central or rallying point of an army in battle. **6** the commodity or commodities in which is stated the value of a basic monetary unit: *the gold standard; the silver standard.* **7** an authorized model of a unit of measure or weight. **8** a unit of board measure equal to 1980 board feet. **9** (in coinage) the prescribed proportion by weight of precious metal and base metal that each coin must contain. **10** an upright pole or beam, esp. one used as a support. **11a** a piece of furniture consisting of an upright pole or beam on a base or support. **11b** (*as modifier*): *a standard lamp.* **12a** a plant, esp. a fruit tree, that is trained so that it has an upright stem free of branches. **12b** (*as modifier*): *a standard cherry.* **13** a song or piece of music that has remained popular for many years. **14** a form or grade in an elementary school. ◆ *adj* **15** of the usual, regularized, medium, or accepted kind: *a standard size.* **16** of recognized authority, competence, or excellence: *the standard work on Greece.* **17** denoting or characterized by idiom, vocabulary, etc., that is regarded as correct and acceptable by educated native speakers. **18** *Brit.* (formerly) (of eggs) of a size that is smaller than *large* and larger than *medium.* ORIG C12: from OF *estandart* gathering place, flag to mark such a place, prob. of Gmc origin

standard assessment tasks *pl n Brit. education.* the formal name for assessment tests. Acronym: **SATs.**

standard-bearer *n* **1** a man who carries a standard. **2** a leader of a cause or party.

standard cell *n* a voltaic cell producing a constant and accurately known electromotive force that can be used to calibrate voltage-measuring instruments.

standard cost *n* the predetermined budgeted cost of a manufacturing process against which actual costs are compared.

standard deviation *n Statistics.* a measure of dispersion obtained by extracting the square root of the mean of the squared deviations of the observed values from their mean in a frequency distribution.

standard error of the mean *n Statistics.* the standard deviation of the distribution of means of samples chosen from a larger population; equal to the standard deviation of the whole population divided by the square root of the sample size.

standard function *n Computing.* a subprogram provided by a translator that carries out a task, for example the computation of a mathematical function, such as sine, square root, etc.

standard gauge *n* **1** a railway track with a distance of 4 ft. 8½ in. (1.435 m) between the lines; used on most railways. ◆ *adj* **standard-gauge** *or* **standard-gauged. 2** of, relating to, or denoting a railway with a standard gauge.

Standard Grade *n* (in Scotland) an examination designed to test skills and the application of knowledge, which replaced O grade.

standardize *or* **standardise** ('stændəˌdaɪz) *vb* **standardizes, standardizing, standardized** *or* **standardises, standardising, standardised. 1** to make or become standard. **2** (*tr*) to test by or compare with a standard.
▸ **ˌstandardiˈzation** *or* **ˌstandardiˈsation** *n* ▸ **ˈstandardˌizer** *or* **ˈstandardˌiser** *n*

standard model *n Physics.* a theory of fundamental interactions in which the electromagnetic, weak, and strong interactions are described in terms of the exchange of virtual particles.

standard of living *n* a level of subsistence or material welfare of a community, class, or person.

standard time *n* the official local time of a region or country determined by the distance from Greenwich of a line of longitude passing through the area.

stand by *vb* (*intr*) **1** (*adv*) to be available and ready to act if needed. **2** (*adv*) to be present as an onlooker or without taking any action: *he stood by at the accident.* **3** (*prep*) to be faithful to: *to stand by one's principles.* ◆ *n* **stand-by. 4a** a person or thing that is ready for use or can be relied on in an emergency. **4b** (*as modifier*): *stand-by provisions.* **5 on stand-by.** in a state of readiness for action or use. ◆ *adj* **stand-by. 6** not booked in advance but awaiting or subject to availability: *a stand-by ticket.*

stand down *vb* (*adv*) **1** (*intr*) to resign or withdraw, esp. in favour of another. **2** (*intr*) to leave the witness box in a court of law after giving evidence. **3** *Chiefly Brit.* to go or be taken off duty.

stand for *vb* (*intr, prep*) **1** to represent or mean. **2** *Chiefly Brit.* to be or become a candidate for. **3** to support or recommend. **4** *Inf.* to tolerate or bear: *he won't stand for it.*

stand in *vb* **1** (*intr, adv;* usually foll. by *for*) to act as a substitute. **2 stand (someone) in good stead.** to be of benefit or advantage to (someone). ◆ *n* **stand-in. 3a** a person or thing that serves as a substitute. **3b** (*as modifier*): *a stand-in teacher.* **4** a person who substitutes for an actor during intervals of waiting or in dangerous stunts.

standing ('stændɪŋ) *n* **1** social or financial position, status, or reputation: *a man of some standing.* **2** length of existence, experience, etc. **3** (*modifier*) used to stand in or on: *standing room.* ◆ *adj* **4** *Athletics.* **4a** (of the start of a race) begun from a standing position. **4b** (of a jump, leap, etc.) performed from a stationary position without a run-up. **5** (*prenominal*) permanent, fixed, or lasting. **6** (*prenominal*) still or stagnant: *a standing pond.* **7** *Printing.* (of type) set and stored for future use.

standing army *n* a permanent army of paid soldiers maintained by a nation.

standing order *n* **1** Also called: **banker's order.** an instruction to a bank by a depositor to pay a stated sum at regular intervals. Cf. **direct debit. 2** a rule or order governing the procedure, conduct, etc., of an organization. **3** *Mil.* one of a number of orders which have long-term validity.

standing rigging *n* the stays, shrouds, and other more or less fixed, though adjustable, ropes that support the masts of a sailing vessel.

standing wave *n Physics.* a wave that has unchanging amplitude at each point along its axis. Also called: **stationary wave.**

Standish ★ ('stændɪʃ) *n* **Myles** (or **Miles**). ?1584–1656, English military leader of the Pilgrim Fathers at Plymouth, New England.

standoff ('stændˌɒf) *n* **1** *US & Canad.* the act or an instance of standing off or apart. **2** a deadlock or stalemate. **3** *Rugby.* short for **stand-off half.** ◆ *vb* **stand off.** (*adv*) **4** (*intr*) to navigate a vessel so as to avoid the shore, an obstruction, etc. **5** (*tr*) to keep or cause to keep at a distance. **6** (*intr*) to reach a deadlock or stalemate. **7** (*tr*) to dismiss (workers), esp. temporarily.

stand-off half *n Rugby.* **1** a player who acts as a link between his or her scrum half and three-quarter backs. **2** this position. ◆ Also called: **fly half.**

standoffish (ˌstændˈɒfɪʃ) *adj* reserved, haughty, or aloof.
▸ **ˌstandˈoffishness** *n*

stand on *vb* (*intr*) **1** (*adv*) to continue to navigate a vessel on the same heading. **2** (*prep*) to insist on: *to stand on ceremony.*

stand out *vb* (*intr, adv*) **1** to be distinctive or conspicuous. **2** to refuse to agree or comply: *they stood out for a better price.* **3** to protrude or project. **4** to navigate a vessel away from a port, harbour, etc. ◆ *n* **standout. 5** *Inf.* **5a** a person or thing that is distinctive or outstanding. **5b** (*as modifier*): *the standout track from the album.*

stand over *vb* (*tr, prep*) **1** to supervise closely. **2** *Austral. & NZ inf.* to threaten or intimidate.

standover man ('stænd,əuvə) *n Austral.* a person who extorts money by intimidation.

standpipe ('stænd,paɪp) *n* **1** a vertical pipe, open at the upper end, attached to a pipeline or tank serving to limit the pressure head to that of the height of the pipe. **2** a temporary freshwater outlet installed in a street when household water supplies are cut off.

standpoint ('stænd,pɔɪnt) *n* a physical or mental position from which things are viewed.

standstill ('stænd,stɪl) *n* a complete cessation of movement; halt: *come to a standstill.*

stand to *vb* **1** *(adv) Mil.* to assume positions or cause to assume positions to resist a possible attack. **2 stand to reason.** to conform with the dictates of reason: *it stands to reason.*

stand up *vb (adv)* **1** *(intr)* to rise to the feet. **2** *(intr)* to resist or withstand wear, criticism, etc. **3** *(tr) Inf.* to fail to keep an appointment with, esp. intentionally. **4 stand up for.** to support, side with, or defend. **5 stand up to. 5a** to confront or resist courageously. **5b** to withstand or endure (wear, criticism, etc.). ◆ *adj* **stand-up.** *(prenominal)* **6** having or being in an erect position: *a stand-up collar.* **7** done, taken, etc., while standing: *a stand-up meal.* **8** (of comedy or a comedian) performed or performing solo. ◆ *n* **stand-up. 9** a stand-up comedian. **10** stand-up comedy.

Stanford ★ ('stænfəd) *n* Sir **Charles (Villiers).** 1852–1924, Anglo-Irish composer and conductor: noted esp. for his church music, oratorios, and cantatas.

Stanford-Binet test (-bɪ'neɪ) *n Psychol.* a revision, esp. for US use, of the Binet-Simon scale designed to measure mental ability by comparing the performance of an individual with the average performance for his age group. See also **Binet-Simon scale, intelligence test.** ORIG C20: after *Stanford University,* California, & Alfred *Binet* (1857–1911), F psychologist

stanhope ('stænəp) *n* a light one-seater carriage with two or four wheels. ORIG C18: after Fitzroy *Stanhope* (1787–1864), E clergyman for whom it was first built

Stanislavsky *or* **Stanislavski** ★ (,stænɪ'slævskɪ; *Russian* stəni'slafskij) *n* **Konstantin** (kənstan'tin). 1863–1938, Russian actor, cofounder of the Moscow Art Theatre (1897) and creator of the Method theory of acting.

Stanisław *(Polish* sta'niswaf) *or* **Stanislaus** ★ ('stænɪslaus) *n* **Saint.** 1030–79, the patron saint of Poland. As Bishop of Cracow (1072–79) he excommunicated King Bolesław II, who arranged his murder. Feast day: May 11.

stank (stæŋk) *vb* a past tense of **stink.**

Stanley[1] ★ ('stænlɪ) *n* **1** the capital of the Falkland Islands, in NE East Falkland Island: scene of fighting in the Falklands War of 1982. Pop.: 1557 (1991). **2** a town in NE England, in N Durham. Pop.: 18 905 (1991). **3 Mount.** a mountain in central Africa, between Uganda and the Democratic Republic of Congo: the highest peak of the Ruwenzori range. Height: 5109 m (16 763 ft). Congolese name: **Ngaliema Mountain.**

Stanley[2] ★ ('stænlɪ) *n* Sir **Henry Morton.** 1841–1904, British explorer, who led an expedition to Africa in search of Livingstone, whom he found on Nov. 10, 1871. He led three further expeditions in Africa (1874–77; 1879–84; 1887–89).

Stanley Falls ★ *pl n* the former name of **Boyoma Falls.**

Stanley knife *n Trademark.* a type of knife used for carpet fitting, etc., consisting of a thick hollow metal handle with a short, very sharp, replaceable blade inserted in one end. ORIG C19: after F. T. *Stanley,* US businessman and founder of the Stanley Rule and Level Company

Stanley Pool ★ *n* a lake between the Democratic Republic of Congo and Congo-Brazzaville, formed by a widening of the River Congo. Area: 829 sq. km (320 sq. miles). Congolese name: **Pool Malebo.**

Stanleyville ★ ('stænlɪ,vɪl) *n* the former name (until 1966) of **Kisangani.**

stann- *combining form.* denoting tin: *stannite.* ORIG from LL *stannum* tin

Stannaries ★ ('stænərɪz) *n (sometimes functioning as sing)* **the.** a former tin-mining district of Devon and Cornwall, under the jurisdiction of special courts.

stannary ('stænərɪ) *n, pl* **stannaries.** a place or region where tin is mined or worked. ORIG C15: from Med. L *stannāria,* from LL *stannum* tin

stannic ('stænɪk) *adj* of or containing tin, esp. in the tetravalent state; designating a tin(IV) compound. ORIG C18: from LL *stannum* tin

stannite ('stænaɪt) *n* a grey metallic mineral that consists of a sulphide of tin, copper, and iron and is a source of tin. Formula: Cu_2FeSnS_4. ORIG C19: from LL *stannum* tin + -ITE[1]

stannous ('stænəs) *adj* of or containing tin, esp. in the divalent state; designating a tin(II) compound.

Stanovoi Range *or* **Stanovoy Range** ★ *(Russian* stəna'vɔj) *n* a mountain range in SE Russia: forms part of the watershed between rivers flowing to the Arctic and the Pacific. Highest peak: Mount Skalisty, 2482 m (8143 ft).

Stans ★ *(German* ʃtans) *n* a town in central Switzerland, capital of Nidwalden demicanton, 11 km (7 miles) southeast of Lucerne: tourist centre. Pop.: 5700 (latest est.).

stanza ('stænzə) *n* **1** *Prosody.* a fixed number of verse lines arranged in a definite metrical pattern, forming a unit of a poem. **2** *US & Austral.* a half or a quarter in a football match. ORIG C16: from It.: halting place, from Vulgar L *stantia* (unattested) station, from L *stāre* to stand
▸ **'stanzaed** *adj* ▸ **stanzaic** (stæn'zeɪɪk) *adj*

stapelia (stə'piːlɪə) *n* any of various fleshy cactus-like leafless African plants having large fetid flowers. ORIG C18: from NL, after J. B. van *Stapel* (died 1636), Du. botanist

stapes ('steɪpiːz) *n, pl* **stapes** *or* **stapedes** (stæ'piːdiːz). the stirrup-shaped bone that is the innermost of three small bones in the middle ear of mammals. Nontechnical name: **stirrup bone.** Cf. **incus, malleus.** ORIG C17: via NL from Med. L, ? var. of *stapeda* stirrup, infl. by L *stāre* to stand + *pēs* a foot

staphylo- *combining form.* **1** uvula: *staphyloplasty.* **2** resembling a bunch of grapes: *staphylococcus.* ORIG from Gk *staphulē* bunch of grapes, uvula

staphylococcus (,stæfɪləu'kɒkəs) *n, pl* **staphylococci** (-'kɒkaɪ, -'kɒkiː). any spherical Gram-positive bacterium of the genus *Staphylococcus,* typically occurring in clusters and causing boils, infection in wounds, and septicaemia. Often shortened to **staph.**
▸ **,staphylo'coccal** *adj*

staphyloplasty ('stæfɪləu,plæstɪ) *n* plastic surgery or surgical repair involving the soft palate or the uvula.
▸ **,staphylo'plastic** *adj*

staple[1] ('steɪpᵊl) *n* **1** a short length of thin wire bent into a square U-shape, used to fasten papers, cloth, etc. **2** a short length of stiff wire formed into a U-shape with pointed ends, used for holding a hasp to a post, securing electric cables, etc. ◆ *vb* **staples, stapling, stapled. 3** *(tr)* to secure (papers, wire, etc.) with staples. ORIG OE *stapol* prop, of Gmc origin
▸ **'stapler** *n*

staple[2] ('steɪpᵊl) *adj* **1** of prime importance; principal: *staple foods.* **2** (of a commodity) forming a predominant element in the product, consumption, or trade of a nation, region, etc. ◆ *n* **3** a staple commodity. **4** a main constituent; integral part. **5** *Chiefly US & Canad.* a principal raw material produced or grown in a region. **6** the fibre of wool, cotton, etc., graded as to length and degree of fineness. ◆ *vb* **staples, stapling, stapled. 7** *(tr)* to arrange or sort (wool, cotton, etc.) according to length and fineness. ORIG C15: from MDu. *stapel* warehouse

staple gun *n* a mechanism that fixes staples to a surface.

star (stɑː) *n* **1** any of a vast number of celestial objects visible in the clear night sky as points of light. **2a** a hot gaseous mass, such as the sun, that radiates energy, esp. as light and infrared radiation, and in some cases as ultraviolet, radio waves, and X-rays. **2b** *(as modifier): a star catalogue.* Related adjs.: **astral, sidereal, stellar. 3** *Astrol.* **3a** a celestial body, esp. a planet, supposed to influence events, personalities, etc. **3b** *(pl)* another name for **horo-**

scope (sense 1). **4** an emblem shaped like a conventionalized star, often used as a symbol of rank, an award, etc. **5** a small white blaze on the forehead of an animal, esp. a horse. **6a** a distinguished or glamorous celebrity, often from the entertainment world. **6b** (*as modifier*): *star quality.* **7** another word for **asterisk. 8 see stars.** to see or seem to see bright moving pinpoints of light, as from a blow on the head, increased blood pressure, etc. ◆ *vb* **stars, starring, starred. 9** (*tr*) to mark or decorate with a star or stars. **10** to feature or be featured as a star: *"Greed" starred Erich von Stroheim; Olivier starred in "Hamlet".* ORIG OE *steorra*

▸ **'starless** *adj* ▸ **'star,like** *adj*

Stara Zagora ★ (*Bulgarian* 'stara za'gɔra) *n* a city in central Bulgaria: ceded to Bulgaria by Turkey in 1877. Pop.: 149 666 (1996 est.).

starboard ('stɑːbəd, -ˌbɔːd) *n* **1** the right side of an aeroplane or vessel when facing the nose or bow. Cf. **port**[2] (sense 1). ◆ *adj* **2** relating to or on the starboard. ◆ *vb* **3** to turn or be turned towards the starboard. ORIG OE *stēorbord,* lit.: steering side, from *stēor* steering paddle + *bord* side; from the fact that boats were formerly steered by a paddle held over the right-hand side

starburst ('stɑːˌbɜːst) *n* **1** a pattern of rays or lines radiating from a light source. **2** *Photog.* a lens attachment which produces a starburst effect.

starch (stɑːtʃ) *n* **1** a polysaccharide composed of glucose units that occurs widely in plant tissues in the form of storage granules. **2** a starch obtained from potatoes and some grain: it is fine white powder that, in solution with water, is used to stiffen fabric. **3** any food containing a large amount of starch, such as rice and potatoes. **4** stiff or pompous formality. ◆ *vb* **5** (*tr*) to stiffen with or soak in starch. ORIG OE *stercan* (unattested except by the p.p. *sterced*) to stiffen

▸ **'starcher** *n*

Star Chamber *n* **1** *English history.* the Privy Council sitting as a court of equity; abolished 1641. **2** (*sometimes not caps.*) any arbitrary tribunal dispensing summary justice. **3** (*sometimes not caps.*) (in Britain, in a Conservative government) a group of senior ministers who make the final decision on the public spending of each government department.

starch-reduced *adj* (of food, esp. bread) having the starch content reduced, as in proprietary slimming products.

starchy ('stɑːtʃɪ) *adj* **starchier, starchiest. 1** of or containing starch. **2** extremely formal, stiff, or conventional: *a starchy manner.* **3** stiffened with starch.

▸ **'starchily** *adv* ▸ **'starchiness** *n*

star connection *n* a connection used in a polyphase electrical device or system of devices in which the windings each have one end connected to a common junction, the **star point,** and the other end to a separate terminal.

star-crossed *adj* dogged by ill luck; destined to misfortune.

stardom ('stɑːdəm) *n* **1** the fame and prestige of being a star in films, sport, etc. **2** the world of celebrities.

stardust ('stɑːˌdʌst) *n* **1** a large number of distant stars appearing to the observer as a cloud of dust. **2** a dreamy romantic or sentimental quality or feeling.

stare (stɛə) *vb* **stares, staring, stared. 1** (*intr*) (often foll. by *at*) to look or gaze fixedly, often with hostility or rudeness. **2** (*intr*) to stand out as obvious; glare. **3 stare one in the face.** to be glaringly obvious or imminent. ◆ *n* **4** the act or an instance of staring. ORIG OE *starian*

▸ **'starer** *n*

starfish ('stɑːˌfɪʃ) *n, pl* **starfish** *or* **starfishes.** any of various echinoderms, typically having a flattened body covered with a flexible test and five arms radiating from a central disc.

star fruit *n* another name for **carambola.**

stargaze ('stɑːˌgeɪz) *vb* **stargazes, stargazing, stargazed.** (*intr*) **1** to observe the stars. **2** to daydream.

▸ **'star,gazer** *n* ▸ **'star,gazing** *n, adj*

stark (stɑːk) *adj* **1** (*usually prenominal*) devoid of any elaboration; blunt: *the stark facts.* **2** grim; desolate: *a stark landscape.* **3** (*usually prenominal*) utter; absolute: *stark folly.* **4** *Arch.* severe; violent. **5** *Arch. or poetic.* rigid, as in death (esp. in **stiff and stark, stark dead**). **6** short for **stark-naked.** ◆ *adv* **7** completely: *stark mad.* **8** *Rare.* starkly. ORIG OE *stearc* stiff

▸ **'starkly** *adv* ▸ **'starkness** *n*

Stark ★ *n* **1** (stɑːk). Dame **Freya** (**Madeline**) ('freɪə). 1893–1993, British traveller and writer. **2** (*German* ʃtark). **Johannes** (jo'hanəs). 1874–1957, German physicist, who discovered the splitting of spectrum lines in a strong electrostatic field (**Stark effect,** 1913): Nobel prize for physics 1919.

stark-naked *adj* completely naked. Informal word (*postpositive*): **starkers.** ORIG C13 *stert naket,* lit.: tail naked; *stert,* from OE *steort* tail

starlet ('stɑːlɪt) *n* **1** a young actress who is projected as a potential star. **2** a small star.

starlight ('stɑːˌlaɪt) *n* **1** the light emanating from the stars. ◆ *adj also* **starlighted. 2** of or like starlight. **3** Also: **starlit** ('stɑːˌlɪt). illuminated by starlight.

starling ('stɑːlɪŋ) *n* any gregarious passerine songbird of an Old World family, esp. the **common starling,** which has a blackish iridescent plumage and a short tail. ORIG OE *stærlinc,* from *stær* starling + *-line* -LING[1]

star-of-Bethlehem *n* **1** Also: **starflower.** a Eurasian liliaceous plant having narrow leaves and starlike white flowers. **2** any of several similar and related plants.

Star of David *n* an emblem symbolizing Judaism and consisting of a six-pointed star formed by superimposing one inverted equilateral triangle upon another of equal size.

Starr ★ (stɑː) *n* **1** (**Myra**) **Belle.** 1848–89, US outlaw, a famous rustler of horses and cattle. **2 Ringo,** original name *Richard Starkey.* born 1940, British rock musician; drummer (1962–70) with the Beatles.

starry ('stɑːrɪ) *adj* **starrier, starriest. 1** filled, covered with, or illuminated by stars. **2** of, like, or relating to a star or stars.

▸ **'starriness** *n*

starry-eyed *adj* given to naive wishes, judgments, etc.; full of unsophisticated optimism.

Stars and Stripes *n* (*functioning as sing*) **the.** the national flag of the United States of America, consisting of 50 white stars representing the present states on a blue field and seven red and six white horizontal stripes representing the original states. Also called: the **Star-Spangled Banner.**

star sapphire *n* a sapphire showing a starlike figure in reflected light because of its crystalline structure.

star sign *n* another name for **sign of the zodiac.**

Star-Spangled Banner *n* **the. 1** the national anthem of the United States of America. **2** another term for the **Stars and Stripes.**

star stream *n* one of two main streams of stars that, because of the rotation of the Milky Way, appear to move in opposite directions.

star-studded *adj* featuring a large proportion of well-known performers: *a star-studded cast.*

start (stɑːt) *vb* **1** to begin or cause to begin (something or to do something); come or cause to come into being, operation, etc.: *he started a quarrel; they started to work.* **2** (when *intr,* sometimes foll. by *on*) to make or cause to make a beginning of (a process, series of actions, etc.): *they started on the project.* **3** (sometimes foll. by *up*) to set or be set in motion: *he started up the machine.* **4** (*intr*) to make a sudden involuntary movement, as from fright; jump. **5** (*intr;* sometimes foll. by *up, away,* etc.) to spring or jump suddenly from a position or place. **6** to establish or be established; set up: *to start a business.* **7** (*tr*) to support (someone) in the first part of a venture, career, etc. **8** to work or cause to work loose. **9** to enter or be entered in a race. **10** (*intr*) to flow violently from a source: *wine started from a hole in the cask.* **11** (*tr*) to rouse (game) from a hiding place, lair, etc. **12** (*intr*) (esp. of eyes) to bulge; pop. **13** (*intr*) *Brit. inf.* to commence quarrelling or causing a disturbance. **14 to start with.** in the first place. ◆ *n* **15** the beginning or first part of a journey, series of actions or operations, etc. **16** the place or time of starting, as of a race or performance. **17** a signal to proceed, as in a race. **18** a lead or advantage, either in time or distance, in a competitive activity: *he had an hour's start on me.* **19** a slight involuntary movement, as through fright, surprise, etc.: *she gave a start as I entered.* **20** an opportunity to enter a career, undertake a project, etc. **21** *Inf.* a surprising incident. **22** **for a start.** in the first place. ◆ See also **start in, start off,** etc. ORIG OE *styrtan*

starter (ˈstɑːtə) *n* **1** Also called: **self-starter.** a device for starting an internal-combustion engine, usually consisting of a powerful electric motor that engages with the flywheel. **2** a person who supervises and signals the start of a race. **3** a competitor who starts in a race or contest. **4** *Inf., chiefly Austral.* an acceptable or practicable proposition, plan, idea, etc. **5** *Chiefly Brit.* the first course of a meal. **6** (*modifier*) designed to be used by a novice: *a starter kit.* **7** **for starters.** *Sl.* in the first place. **8** **under starter's orders. 8a** (of horses in a race) awaiting the start signal. **8b** (of a person) eager or ready to begin.

starter home *n* a compact flat or house marketed by price and size specifications to suit the requirements of first-time home buyers.

start in *vb* (*adv*) to undertake (something or doing something); commence or begin.

starting block *n* one of a pair of adjustable devices with pads or blocks against which a sprinter braces his feet in crouch starts.

starting gate *n* **1** a movable barrier so placed on the starting line of a racecourse that the raising of it releases all the contestants simultaneously. **2** the US name for **starting stalls.**

starting grid *n Motor racing.* a marked section of the track at the start where the cars line up according to their times in practice, the fastest occupying the front position.

starting price *n* (esp. in horse racing) the latest odds offered by bookmakers at the start of a race.

starting stalls *pl n Brit.* a line of stalls in which horses are enclosed at the start of a race and from which they are released by the simultaneous springing open of retaining barriers at the front of each stall.

startle (ˈstɑːtᵊl) *vb* **startles, startling, startled.** to be or cause to be surprised or frightened, esp. so as to start involuntarily. ORIG OE *steartlian* to stumble
▸ **ˈstartler** *n* ▸ **ˈstartling** *adj*

start off *vb* (*adv*) **1** (*intr*) to set out on a journey. **2** to be or make the first step in (an activity); initiate: *he started the show off with a lively song.* **3** (*tr*) to cause (a person) to act or do something, such as to laugh, to tell stories, etc.

start on *vb* (*intr, prep*) *Brit. inf.* to pick a quarrel with; upbraid.

start out *vb* (*intr, adv*) **1** to set out on a journey. **2** to take the first steps, as in life, one's career, etc.: *he started out as a salesman.* **3** to take the first actions in an activity in a particular way or with a specified aim: *they started out wanting a house, but eventually bought a flat.*

start up *vb* (*adv*) **1** to come or cause to come into being for the first time; originate. **2** (*intr*) to spring or jump suddenly. **3** to set in or go into motion, activity, etc.: *he started up the engine.* ◆ *n* **start-up. 4a** a recently launched project or business enterprise. **4b** (*as modifier*): *start-up grants; an Internet start-up company.*

starve (stɑːv) *vb* **starves, starving, starved. 1** to die or cause to die from lack of food. **2** to deprive (a person or animal) or (of a person, etc.) to be deprived of food. **3** (*intr*) *Inf.* to be very hungry. **4** (foll. by *of* or *for*) to deprive or be deprived (of something), esp. so as to cause suffering or malfunctioning: *the engine was starved of fuel.* **5** (*tr*; foll. by *into*) to bring (to) a specified condition by starving: *to starve someone into submission.* **6** *Arch. or dialect.* to be or cause to be extremely cold. ORIG OE *steorfan* to die
▸ **starˈvation** *n*

starveling (ˈstɑːvlɪŋ) *Arch.* ◆ *n* **1a** a starving or poorly fed person, animal, etc. **1b** (*as modifier*): *a starveling child.* ◆ *adj* **2** insufficient; meagre; scant.

Star Wars *n* (*functioning as sing*) (in the US) a proposed system of artificial satellites armed with lasers to destroy enemy missiles in space. ORIG C20: popularly named after the science-fiction film *Star Wars* (1977)

starwort (ˈstɑːˌwɜːt) *n* **1** any of several plants with star-shaped flowers, esp. the stitchwort. **2** any of several aquatic plants having a star-shaped rosette of floating leaves.

stash (stæʃ) *vb* **1** (*tr;* often foll. by *away*) *Inf.* to put or store (money, valuables, etc.) in a secret place, as for safekeeping. ◆ *n* **2** *Inf., chiefly US & Canad.* a secret store or the place where this is hidden. **3** *Sl.* drugs kept for personal consumption. ORIG C20: from ?

stasis (ˈsteɪsɪs) *n* **1** *Pathol.* a stagnation in the normal flow of bodily fluids, such as the blood or urine. **2** a state or condition in which there is no action or progress. ORIG C18: via NL from Gk: a standing, from *histanai* to cause to stand

-stat *n combining form.* indicating a device that causes something to remain stationary or constant: *thermostat.* ORIG from Gk *-statēs,* from *histanai* to cause to stand

state (steɪt) *n* **1** the condition of a person, thing, etc., with regard to main attributes. **2** the structure or form of something: *a solid state.* **3** any mode of existence. **4** position in life or society; estate. **5** ceremonious style, as befitting wealth or dignity: *to live in state.* **6** a sovereign political power or community. **7** the territory occupied by such a community. **8** the sphere of power in such a community: *affairs of state.* **9** (*often cap.*) one of a number of areas or communities having their own governments and forming a federation under a sovereign government, as in the US. **10** (*often cap.*) the body politic of a particular sovereign power, esp. as contrasted with a rival authority such as the Church. **11** *Obs.* a class or order; estate. **12** *Inf.* a nervous, upset, or excited condition (esp. in **in a state**). **13** **lie in state.** (of a body) to be placed on public view before burial. **14** **state of affairs.** a situation; circumstances or condition. ◆ *modifier.* **15** controlled or financed by a state: *state university.* **16** of, relating to, or concerning the State: *State trial.* **17** involving ceremony or concerned with a ceremonious occasion: *state visit.* ◆ *vb* **states, stating, stated.** (*tr; may take a clause as object*) **18** to articulate in words; utter. **19** to declare formally or publicly. ORIG C13: from OF *estat,* from L *status* a standing, from *stāre* to stand
▸ **ˈstatable** *or* **ˈstateable** *adj* ▸ **ˈstatehood** *n*

state bank *n* (in the US) a commercial bank incorporated under a State charter and not required to be a member of the Federal Reserve System.

statecraft (ˈsteɪtˌkrɑːft) *n* the art of conducting public affairs; statesmanship.

state duma *n* another name for **duma** (sense 3).

state house *n NZ.* a house built by the government and rented to a **state tenant.** Brit. equivalent: **council house.**

Statehouse (ˈsteɪtˌhaʊs) *n* (in the US) the building which houses a state legislature.

stateless (ˈsteɪtlɪs) *adj* **1** without nationality: *stateless persons.* **2** without a state or states.
▸ **ˈstatelessness** *n*

stately (ˈsteɪtlɪ) *adj* **statelier, stateliest. 1** characterized by a graceful, dignified, and imposing appearance or manner. ◆ *adv* **2** in a stately manner.
▸ **ˈstateliness** *n*

stately home *n Brit.* a large mansion, esp. one open to the public.

statement (ˈsteɪtmənt) *n* **1** the act of stating. **2** something that is stated, esp. a formal prepared announcement or reply. **3** *Law.* a declaration of matters of fact. **4** an account containing a summary of bills or invoices and displaying the total amount due. **5** an account prepared by a bank for a client, usually at regular intervals, to show all credits and debits and the balance at the end of the period. **6** a computer instruction written in a source language, such as FORTRAN, which is converted into one or more machine-code instructions by a compiler. **7** *Logic.* the content of a sentence that affirms or denies something and may be true or false. **8** *Brit. education.* a legally binding account of the provisions that will be made to meet the needs of a pupil with special educational needs. ◆ *vb* (*tr; usually passive*) **9** to supply a legally binding account of the provisions that will be made to meet the needs of (a pupil with special educational needs).

statement of attainment *n Brit. education.* a programme of specific objectives that pupils should achieve within their own levels of attainment in a particular subject.

statement of claim *n Law.* (in England) the first pleading made by the plaintiff in a High Court action.

Staten Island ★ ('stætᵊn) *n* an island in SE New York State, in New York Harbor: a borough of New York city; heavy industry. Pop.: 378 977 (1990). Area: 155 sq. km (60 sq. miles).

state of the art *n* **1** the level of knowledge and development achieved in a technique, science, etc., esp. at present. ◆ *adj* **state-of-the-art.** (*prenominal*) **2** the most recent and therefore considered the best; up-to-the-minute: *a state-of-the-art amplifier.*

State Registered Nurse *n* (formerly, in Britain) a nurse who had extensive training and was qualified to perform all nursing services. See **Registered General Nurse.**

stateroom ('steɪtˌruːm, -ˌrʊm) *n* **1** a private cabin or room on a ship, train, etc. **2** *Chiefly Brit.* a large room in a palace or other building for use on state occasions.

States ★ (steɪts) *n* (*functioning as sing or pl*) **the.** an informal name for the **United States of America.**

state school *n* any school maintained by the state, in which education is free.

stateside ('steɪtˌsaɪd) *adj, adv* (*sometimes cap.*) *US.* of, in, to, or towards the US.

statesman ('steɪtsmən) *n, pl* **statesmen. 1** a political leader whose wisdom, integrity, etc., win great respect. **2** a person active and influential in the formulation of high government policy.
▸ **'statesman-ˌlike** *or* **'statesmanly** *adj* ▸ **'statesmanship** *n*
▸ **'statesˌwoman** *fem n*

state socialism *n* a variant of socialism in which the power of the state is employed for the purpose of creating an egalitarian society by means of public control of major industries, banks, etc.
▸ **state socialist** *n*

state trooper *n US.* a state policeman.

static ('stætɪk) *adj also* **statical. 1** not active or moving; stationary. **2** (of a weight, force, or pressure) acting but causing no movement. **3** of or concerned with forces that do not produce movement. **4** relating to or causing stationary electric charges; electrostatic. **5** of or relating to interference in the reception of radio or television transmissions. **6** of or concerned with statics. **7** *Computing.* (of a memory) not needing its contents refreshed periodically. ◆ *n* **8** random hissing or crackling or a speckled picture caused by interference in the reception of radio or television transmissions. **9** electric sparks or crackling produced by friction. ORIG C16: from NL *staticus,* from Gk *statikos* causing to stand, from *histanai* to stand
▸ **'statically** *adv*

statice ('stætɪsɪ) *n* another name for **sea lavender.**

static electricity *n* electricity that is not dynamic or flowing as a current.

statics ('stætɪks) *n* (*functioning as sing*) the branch of mechanics concerned with the forces that produce a state of equilibrium in a system.

station ('steɪʃən) *n* **1** the place or position at which a thing or person stands. **2a** a place along a route or line at which a bus, train, etc., stops for fuel or to pick up or let off passengers or goods, esp. one with ancillary buildings and services. **2b** (*as modifier*): *a station buffet.* **3a** the headquarters or local offices of an organization such as the police or fire services. **3b** (*as modifier*): *a station sergeant.* See **police station, fire station. 4** a building, depot, etc., with special equipment for some particular purpose: *power station; petrol station.* **5** *Mil.* a place of duty: *an action station.* **6** *Navy.* **6a** a location to which a ship or fleet is assigned for duty. **6b** an assigned location for a member of a ship's crew. **7** a television or radio channel. **8** a position or standing, as in a particular society or organization. **9** the type of one's occupation; calling. **10** (in British India) a place where the British district officials or garrison officers resided. **11** *Biol.* the habitat occupied by a particular animal or plant. **12** *Austral. & NZ.* a large sheep or cattle farm. **13** (*sometimes cap.*) *RC Church.* **13a** one of the stations of the Cross. **13b** any of the churches (**station churches**) in Rome used as points of assembly for religious processions and ceremonies on particular days (**station days**). ◆ *vb* **14** (*tr*) to place in or assign to a station. ORIG C14: via OF from L *statiō* a standing still, from *stāre* to stand

stationary ('steɪʃənərɪ) *adj* **1** not moving; standing still. **2** not able to be moved. **3** showing no change: *the doctors said his condition was stationary.* **4** tending to remain in one place. ORIG C15: from L *statiōnārius,* from *statiō* STATION

> **USAGE NOTE** This word, which is always an adjective, is occasionally wrongly used where paper products are meant: *in the stationery* (not *stationary*) *cupboard.*

stationary orbit *n Astronautics.* a synchronous orbit lying in or approximately in the plane of the equator.

stationary wave *n* another name for **standing wave.**

stationer ('steɪʃənə) *n* a person who sells stationery or a shop where stationery is sold. ORIG C14: from Med. L *stationarius* a person having a regular station, hence a shopkeeper (esp. a bookseller) as distinguished from an itinerant tradesman; see STATION

stationery ('steɪʃənərɪ) *n* any writing materials, such as paper, envelopes, pens, ink, rulers, etc.

> **USAGE NOTE** See at **stationary.**

station house *n Chiefly US.* a house that is situated by or serves as a station, esp. as a police or fire station.

stationmaster ('steɪʃənˌmɑːstə) *n* the senior official in charge of a railway station.

Stations of the Cross *pl n RC Church.* **1** a series of 14 crosses, often accompanied by 14 pictures or carvings, arranged around the walls of a church, to commemorate 14 stages in Christ's journey to Calvary. **2** a devotion of 14 prayers relating to each of these stages.

station wagon *n* another name (less common in Britain) for **estate car.**

statism ('steɪtɪzəm) *n* the theory or practice of concentrating economic and political power in the state.
▸ **'statist** *n*

statistic (stə'tɪstɪk) *n* a datum capable of exact numerical representation, such as the correlation coefficient of two series or the standard deviation of a sample.
▸ **sta'tistical** *adj* ▸ **sta'tistically** *adv* ▸ **statistician** (ˌstætɪ'stɪʃən) *n*

statistical mechanics *n* (*functioning as sing*) the study of the properties of physical systems as predicted by the statistical behaviour of their constituent particles.

statistics (stə'tɪstɪks) *n* **1** (*functioning as sing*) a science concerned with the collection, classification, and interpretation of quantitative data and with the application of probability theory to the analysis and estimation of population parameters. **2** the quantitative data themselves. ORIG C18 (orig. "science dealing with facts of a state"): via G *Statistik,* from NL *statisticus* concerning state affairs, from L *status* STATE

Statius ★ ('steɪʃɪəs) *n* **Publius Papinius** ('pʌblɪəs pə'pɪnɪəs). ?45–96 A.D., Roman poet.

stator ('steɪtə) *n* the stationary part of a rotary machine or device, esp. of a motor or generator. ORIG C20: from L: one who stands (by), from *stāre* to stand

statoscope ('stætəˌskəʊp) *n* a very sensitive form of aneroid barometer used to detect and measure small variations in atmospheric pressure, such as one used in an aircraft to indicate small changes in altitude.

statuary ('stætjʊərɪ) *n* **1** statues collectively. **2** the art of making statues. ♦ *adj* **3** of or for statues. ORIG C16: from L *statuārius*

statue ('stætjuː) *n* a wooden, stone, metal, plaster, or other sculpture of a human or animal figure, usually life-size or larger. ORIG C14: via OF from L *statua,* from *statuere* to set up; cf. STATUTE

statuesque (ˌstætjʊ'ɛsk) *adj* like a statue, esp. in possessing great formal beauty or dignity.
▸ **ˌstatu'esquely** *adv* ▸ **ˌstatu'esqueness** *n*

statuette (ˌstætjʊ'ɛt) *n* a small statue.

stature ('stætʃə) *n* **1** height, esp. of a person or animal when standing. **2** the degree of development of a person: *the stature of a champion.* **3** intellectual or moral greatness: *a man of stature.* ORIG C13: via OF from L *statūra,* from *stāre* to stand

status ('steɪtəs) *n, pl* **statuses. 1** a social or professional position, condition, or standing. **2** the relative position or standing of a person or thing. **3** a high position or standing: *he has acquired a new status in that job.* **4** the legal standing or condition of a person. **5** a state of affairs. ORIG C17: from L: posture, from *stāre* to stand

status Indian *n* (in Canada) a registered member of an Indian band who is recognized by the federal government as having specific rights and privileges.

status quo (kwəʊ) *n* (usually preceded by *the*) the existing state of affairs. ORIG lit.: the state in which

status symbol *n* a possession which is regarded as proof of the owner's social position, wealth, prestige, etc.

statute ('stætjuːt) *n* **1a** an enactment of a legislative body expressed in a formal document. **1b** this document. **2** a permanent rule made by a body or institution. ORIG C13: from OF *estatut,* from LL *statūtum,* from L *statuere* to set up, decree, ult. from *stāre* to stand

statute book *n Chiefly Brit.* a register of enactments passed by the legislative body of a state: *not on the statute book.*

statute law *n* **1** a law enacted by a legislative body. **2** a particular example of this. ♦ Cf. **common law, equity.**

statute mile *n* a legal or formal name for **mile** (sense 1).

statute of limitations *n* a legislative enactment prescribing the period of time within which proceedings must be instituted to enforce a right or bring an action at law.

statutory ('stætjʊtərɪ, -trɪ) *adj* **1** of, relating to, or having the nature of a statute. **2** prescribed or authorized by statute. **3** (of an offence) **3a** recognized by statute. **3b** subject to a punishment or penalty prescribed by statute.
▸ **'statutorily** *adv*

statutory order *n* a statute that applies further legislation to an existing act.

Stauffenberg ★ (*German* 'ʃtaufənbɛrk) *n* **Claus** (klaus), Graf von. 1907–44, German army officer, who tried to assassinate Hitler (1944). He and his fellow conspirators were executed.

staunch[1] (stɔːntʃ) *adj* **1** loyal, firm, and dependable: *a staunch supporter.* **2** solid or substantial in construction. **3** *Rare.* (of a ship, etc.) watertight; seaworthy. ORIG C15 (orig.: watertight): from OF *estanche,* from *estanchier* to STANCH
▸ **'staunchly** *adv* ▸ **'staunchness** *n*

staunch[2] (stɔːntʃ) *or* **stanch** (stɑːntʃ) *vb* **1** to stem the flow of (a liquid, esp. blood) or (of a liquid) to stop flowing. **2** to prevent the flow of a liquid, esp. blood, from (a hole, wound, etc.). ORIG C14: from OF *estanchier,* from Vulgar L *stanticāre* (unattested) to cause to stand, from L *stāre* to halt
▸ **'staunchable** *or* **'stanchable** *adj* ▸ **'stauncher** *or* **'stancher** *n*

Stavanger ★ (*Norwegian* sta'vaŋər) *n* a port in SW Norway: canning and shipbuilding industries. Pop.: 105 573 (1997 est.).

stave (steɪv) *n* **1** any one of a number of long strips of wood joined together to form a barrel, bucket, boat hull, etc. **2** any of various bars, slats, or rods, usually of wood, such as a rung of a ladder. **3** any stick, staff, etc. **4** a stanza or verse of a poem. **5** *Music.* **5a** *Brit.* an individual group of five lines and four spaces used in staff notation. **5b** another word for **staff**[1] (sense 9). ♦ *vb* **staves, staving, staved** *or* **stove. 6** (often foll. by *in*) to break or crush (the staves of a boat, barrel, etc.) or (of the staves of a boat) to be broken or crushed. **7** (*tr;* usually foll. by *in*) to burst or force (a hole in something). **8** (*tr*) to provide (a ladder, chair, etc.) with staves. ORIG C14: back formation from *staves,* pl. of STAFF[1]

stave off *vb* (*tr, adv*) to avert or hold off, esp. temporarily: *to stave off hunger.*

staves (steɪvz) *n* a plural of **staff**[1] or **stave.**

stavesacre ('steɪvzˌeɪkə) *n* **1** a Eurasian ranunculaceous plant having poisonous seeds. **2** the seeds, which have strong emetic and cathartic properties. ORIG C14 *staphisagre,* from L *staphis agria,* from Gk, from *staphis* raisin + *agria* wild

Stavropol ★ (*Russian* 'stavrəpəlj) *n* **1** a city in SW Russia: founded as a fortress in 1777. Pop.: 342 000 (1995 est.). Former name (1940–44): **Voroshilovsk. 2** the former name (until 1964) of **Togliatti.**

stay[1] (steɪ) *vb* **1** (*intr*) to continue or remain in a certain place, position, etc.: *to stay outside.* **2** (*copula*) to continue to be; remain: *to stay awake.* **3** (*intr;* often foll. by *at*) to reside temporarily: *to stay at a hotel.* **4** (*tr*) to remain for a specified period: *to stay the weekend.* **5** (*intr*) *Scot. & S. African.* to reside permanently or habitually; live. **6** *Arch.* to stop or cause to stop. **7** (*intr*) to wait, pause, or tarry. **8** (*tr*) to delay or hinder. **9** (*tr*) **9a** to discontinue or suspend (a judicial proceeding). **9b** to hold in abeyance or restrain from enforcing (an order, decree, etc.). **10** to endure (something testing or difficult, such as a race): *stay the course.* **11** (*tr*) to hold back or restrain: *to stay one's anger.* **12** (*tr*) to satisfy or appease (an appetite, etc.) temporarily. ♦ *n* **13** the act of staying or sojourning in a place or the period during which one stays. **14** the act of stopping or restraining or state of being stopped, etc. **15** the suspension of a judicial proceeding, etc.: *stay of execution.* ORIG C15 *staien,* from Anglo-F *estaier* to stay, from OF *ester* to stay, from L *stāre* to stand
▸ **'stayer** *n*

stay[2] (steɪ) *n* **1** anything that supports or steadies, such as a prop or buttress. **2** a thin strip of metal, plastic, bone, etc., used to stiffen corsets, etc. See also **stays** (sense 1). ♦ *vb* (*tr*) *Arch.* **3** (often foll. by *up*) to prop or hold. **4** (often foll. by *up*) to comfort or sustain. **5** (foll. by *on* or *upon*) to cause to rely or depend. ORIG C16: from OF *estaye,* of Gmc origin

stay[3] (steɪ) *n* a rope, cable, or chain, usually one of a set, used for bracing uprights, such as masts, funnels, flagpoles, chimneys, etc.; guy. ♦ See also **stays** (senses 2, 3). ORIG OE *stæg*

stay-at-home *adj* **1** (of a person) enjoying a quiet, settled, and unadventurous use of leisure. ♦ *n* **2** a stay-at-home person.

staying power *n* endurance; stamina.

stays (steɪz) *pl n* **1** old-fashioned corsets with bones in them. **2** a position of a sailing vessel relative to the wind so that the sails are luffing or aback. **3 miss** *or* **refuse stays.** (of a sailing vessel) to fail to come about.

staysail ('steɪˌseɪl; *Naut.* 'steɪsᵊl) *n* an auxiliary sail, often triangular, set on a stay.

STD *abbrev. for:* **1** Doctor of Sacred Theology. **2** sexually transmitted disease. **3** subscriber trunk dialling.

STD code *n Brit.* a code of four or more digits, other than those comprising a subscriber's local telephone number, that determines the routing of a call. ORIG C20: *s*(*ubscriber*) *t*(*runk*) *d*(*ialling*)

Ste *abbrev. for* Saint (female). ORIG F *Sainte*

stead (stɛd) *n* **1** (preceded by *in*) *Rare.* the place, function, or position that should be taken by another: *to come in someone's stead.* **2 stand** (**someone**) **in good stead.** to be useful or of good service to (someone). ♦ *vb* **3** (*tr*) *Arch.* to help or benefit. ORIG OE *stede*

Stead ★ (stɛd) *n* **Christina** (**Ellen**). 1902–83, Australian novelist. Her works include *The Man who Loved Children* (1940).

steadfast *or* **stedfast** ('stɛdfəst, -ˌfɑːst) *adj* **1** (esp. of a

person's gaze) fixed in intensity or direction; steady. **2** unwavering or determined in purpose, loyalty, etc.: *steadfast resolve.*
▸ **'steadfastly** *or* **'stedfastly** *adv* ▸ **'steadfastness** *or* **'stedfastness** *n*

steading ('stɛdɪŋ) *n* another name for **farmstead.**

steady ('stɛdɪ) *adj* **steadier, steadiest. 1** not able to be moved or disturbed easily; stable. **2** free from fluctuation. **3** not easily excited; imperturbable. **4** staid; sober. **5** regular; habitual: *a steady drinker.* **6** continuous: *a steady flow.* **7** *Naut.* (of a vessel) keeping upright, as in heavy seas. ◆ *vb* **steadies, steadying, steadied. 8** to make or become steady. ◆ *adv* **9** in a steady manner. **10 go steady.** *Inf.* to date one person regularly. ◆ *n, pl* **steadies. 11** *Inf.* one's regular boyfriend or girlfriend. ◆ *interj* **12** *Naut.* an order to the helmsman to stay on a steady course. **13** a warning to keep calm, be careful, etc. **14** *Brit.* a command to get set to start, as in a race: *ready, steady, go!* ORIG C16: from STEAD + -Y[1]
▸ **'steadily** *adv* ▸ **'steadiness** *n* ▸ **'steadying** *adj*

steady state *n Physics.* the condition of a system when some or all of the quantities describing it are independent of time but not necessarily in thermodynamic or chemical equilibrium.

steady-state theory *n* a theory postulating that the universe exists throughout time in a steady state such that the average density of matter does not vary with distance or time. Matter is continuously created in the space left by the receding stars and galaxies of the expanding universe. Cf. **big-bang theory.**

steak (steɪk) *n* **1** See **beefsteak. 2** any of various cuts of beef, for braising, stewing, etc. **3** a thick slice of pork, veal, cod, salmon, etc. **4** minced meat prepared in the same way as steak: *hamburger steak.* ORIG C15: from ON *steik* roast

steakhouse ('steɪk,haus) *n* a restaurant that has steaks as its speciality.

steak tartare (tɑː'tɑː) *or* **tartar** *n* raw minced steak, mixed with onion, seasonings, and raw egg. Also called: **tartare steak, tartar steak.**

steal (stiːl) *vb* **steals, stealing, stole, stolen. 1** to take (something) from someone, etc., without permission or unlawfully, esp. in a secret manner. **2** (*tr*) to obtain surreptitiously. **3** (*tr*) to appropriate (ideas, etc.) without acknowledgment, as in plagiarism. **4** to move or convey stealthily: *they stole along the corridor.* **5** (*intr*) to pass unnoticed: *the hours stole by.* **6** (*tr*) to win or gain by strategy or luck, as in various sports: *to steal a few yards.* ◆ *n Inf.* **7** the act of stealing. **8** something stolen or acquired easily or at little cost. ORIG OE *stelan*
▸ **'stealer** *n*

stealth (stɛlθ) *n* **1** the act or characteristic of moving with extreme care and quietness, esp. so as to avoid detection. **2** cunning or underhand procedure or dealing. ORIG C13 *stelthe;* see STEAL, -TH[1]
▸ **'stealthy** *adj*

Stealth (stɛlθ) *n* (*modifier*) *Inf.* denoting or referring to technology that aims to reduce the radar, thermal, and acoustic recognizability of aircraft and missiles.

Stealth bomber *or* **plane** *n* a type of US military aircraft using advanced technology to render it virtually undetectable to sight, radar, or infrared sensors. Also called: **B-2.**

stealth tax *n* an indirect tax, such as a tax on fuel or pension plans, esp. one of which people are unaware or one that is felt to be unfair.

steam (stiːm) *n* **1** the gas or vapour into which water is changed when boiled. **2** the mist formed when such gas or vapour condenses in the atmosphere. **3** any vaporous exhalation. **4** *Inf.* power, energy, or speed. **5 get up steam. 5a** (of a ship, etc.) to work up a sufficient head of steam in a boiler to drive an engine. **5b** *Inf.* to go quickly. **6 let off steam.** *Inf.* to release pent-up energy, feelings, etc. **7 under one's own steam.** without the assistance of others. **8** (*modifier*) driven, operated, heated, powered, etc., by steam: *a steam radiator.* **9** (*modifier*) treated by steam: *steam-ironed.* **10** (*modifier*) *Humorous.* old-fashioned; outmoded: *steam radio.* ◆ *vb* **11** to emit or be emitted as steam. **12** (*intr*) to generate steam, as a boiler, etc. **13** (*intr*) to move or travel by steam power, as a ship, etc. **14** (*intr*) *Inf.* to proceed quickly and sometimes forcefully. **15** to cook or be cooked in steam. **16** (*tr*) to treat with steam or apply steam to, as in cleaning, pressing clothes, etc. ◆ See also **steam up.** ORIG OE

steam bath *n* **1** a room or enclosure that can be filled with steam in which people bathe to induce sweating and refresh or cleanse themselves. **2** an act of taking such a bath.

steamboat ('stiːm,bəut) *n* a boat powered by a steam engine.

steam boiler *n* a vessel in which water is boiled to generate steam.

steam engine *n* an engine that uses steam to produce mechanical work, esp. one in which steam from a boiler is expanded in a cylinder to drive a reciprocating piston.

steamer ('stiːmə) *n* **1** a boat or ship driven by steam engines. **2** a vessel used to cook food by steam. **3** *Austral. sl.* a rough clash between sports teams.

steaming ('stiːmɪŋ) *adj* **1** very hot. **2** *Inf.* angry. **3** *Sl.* drunk. ◆ *n* **4** *Inf.* robbery, esp. of passengers in a railway carriage or bus, by a large gang of armed youths.

steam iron *n* an electric iron that emits steam from channels in the iron face to facilitate pressing and ironing, the steam being produced from water contained within the iron.

steam jacket *n Engineering.* a jacket containing steam that surrounds and heats a cylinder.

steam organ *n* a type of organ powered by steam, once common at fairgrounds, played either by a keyboard or by a moving punched card. US name: **calliope.**

steam point *n* the temperature at which the maximum vapour pressure of water is equal to one atmosphere (1.01325×10^5 N/m^2). It has the value of 100° on the Celsius scale.

steam reforming *n Chem.* a process in which methane from natural gas is heated, with steam, usually with a catalyst, to produce a mixture of carbon monoxide and hydrogen used in organic synthesis and as a fuel.

steamroller ('stiːm,rəulə) *n* **1a** a steam-powered vehicle with heavy rollers used for compressing road surfaces during road-making. **1b** another word for **roadroller. 2a** an overpowering force or person that overcomes all opposition. **2b** (*as modifier*): *steamroller tactics.* ◆ *vb* **3** (*tr*) to crush (opposition, etc.) by overpowering force.

steamship ('stiːm,ʃɪp) *n* a ship powered by one or more steam engines.

steam shovel *n* a steam-driven mechanical excavator.

steam turbine *n* a turbine driven by steam.

steam up *vb* (*adv*) **1** to cover (windows, etc.) or (of windows, etc.) to become covered with a film of condensed steam. **2** (*tr; usually passive*) *Sl.* to excite or make angry: *he's all steamed up about the delay.*

steamy ('stiːmɪ) *adj* **steamier, steamiest. 1** of, resembling, full of, or covered with steam. **2** *Inf.* lustful or erotic: *steamy nightlife.*
▸ **'steaminess** *n*

steapsin (stɪ'æpsɪn) *n Biochem.* a pancreatic lipase. ORIG C19: from Gk *stear* fat + PEPSIN

stearic (stɪ'ærɪk) *adj* **1** of or relating to suet or fat. **2** of, consisting of, containing, or derived from stearic acid.

stearic acid *n* a colourless odourless insoluble waxy carboxylic acid used for making candles and suppositories. Formula: $CH_3(CH_2)_{16}COOH$. Systematic name: **octadecanoic acid.**

stearin *or* **stearine** ('stɪərɪn) *n* **1** Also called: **tristearin.** a colourless crystalline ester of glycerol and stearic acid, present in fats and used in soap and candles. **2** another name for **stearic acid. 3** fat in its solid form. ORIG C19: from F *stéarine,* from Gk *stear* fat + -IN

steatite ('stɪə,taɪt) *n* another name for **soapstone.** ORIG C18: from L *steatītēs,* from Gk *stear* fat + -ITE[1]
▸ **steatitic** (,stɪə'tɪtɪk) *adj*

steato- *combining form.* denoting fat. ORIG from Gk *stear, steat-* fat, tallow

steatolysis (ˌstɪəˈtɒlɪsɪs) *n Physiol.* **1** the digestive process whereby fats are emulsified and then hydrolysed to fatty acids and glycerine. **2** the breaking down of fat.

steatopygia (ˌstɪətəʊˈpɪdʒɪə, -ˈpaɪ-) *or* **steatopyga** (ˌstɪətəʊˈpaɪgə) *n* excessive fatness of the buttocks. ORIG C19: from NL, from STEATO- + Gk *pugē* the buttocks
▸ **ˌsteatoˈpygic** *or* **steatopygous** (ˌstɪəˈtɒpɪgəs) *adj*

Stębark ★ (ˈstɛmbark) *n* the Polish name for **Tannenberg**.

stedfast (ˈstɛdfəst, -ˌfɑːst) *adj* a less common spelling of **steadfast**.

steed (stiːd) *n Arch. or literary.* a horse, esp. one that is spirited or swift. ORIG OE *stēda* stallion

steel (stiːl) *n* **1a** any of various alloys based on iron containing carbon and often small quantities of other elements such as sulphur, manganese, chromium, and nickel. Steels exhibit a variety of properties, such as strength, malleability, etc., depending on their composition and the way they have been treated. **1b** (*as modifier*): *steel girders*. See also **stainless steel**. **2** something that is made of steel. **3** a steel stiffener in a corset, etc. **4** a ridged steel rod used for sharpening knives. **5** the quality of hardness, esp. with regard to a person's character or attitudes. **6** *Canad.* a railway track or line. **7 cold steel.** bladed weapons. ◆ *vb* (*tr*) **8** to fit, plate, edge, or point with steel. **9** to make hard and unfeeling: *he steeled his heart against her sorrow; he steeled himself for the blow.* ORIG OE *stēli*
▸ **ˈsteely** *adj* ▸ **ˈsteeliness** *n*

Steel ★ (stiːl) *n* **David** (**Martin Scott**), Baron. born 1938, British politician; leader of the Liberal Party (1976–88); speaker of the Scottish Parliament from 1999.

steel band *n Music.* a type of band, popular in the Caribbean Islands, consisting mainly of percussion instruments made from oil drums, hammered or embossed to obtain different notes.

steel blue *n* **a** a dark bluish-grey colour. **b** (*as adj*): *steel-blue eyes.*

Steele ★ (stiːl) *n* Sir **Richard.** 1672–1729, British essayist and dramatist, born in Ireland.

steel engraving *n* **a** a method or art of engraving (letters, etc.) on a steel plate. **b** a print made from such a plate.

steel grey *n* **a** a dark grey colour, usually slightly purple. **b** (*as adj*): *a steel-grey suit.*

steelhead (ˈstiːlˌhɛd) *n, pl* **steelheads** *or* **steelhead.** a silvery North Pacific variety of the rainbow trout.

steelpan (ˈstiːlˌpæn) *n* a metal percussion instrument made from the bottom of an oil drum, hammered or embossed to obtain different notes.

steel wool *n* a tangled or woven mass of fine steel fibres, used for cleaning or polishing.

steelworks (ˈstiːlˌwɜːks) *n* (*functioning as sing or pl*) a plant in which steel is made from iron ore and rolled or forged into bars, sheets, etc.
▸ **ˈsteelˌworker** *n*

steelyard (ˈstiːlˌjɑːd) *n* a portable balance consisting of a pivoted bar with two unequal arms. The load is suspended from the shorter one and the bar is returned to the horizontal by sliding a weight along the longer, graduated arm.

Steen ★ (steɪn) *n* **Jan** (jɑn). 1626–79, Dutch genre painter.

steenbok (ˈstiːnˌbɒk) *n, pl* **steenboks** *or* **steenbok.** a small antelope of central and southern Africa, having a reddish-brown coat and straight horns. ORIG C18: from Afrik., from Du. *steen* stone + *bok* BUCK[1]

steenbras (ˈstiːnˌbrɑːs) *n S. African.* a variety of edible marine fish. ORIG Afrik., from Du. *steen* stone + *brasen* bream

steep[1] (stiːp) *adj* **1a** having or being a slope or gradient approaching the perpendicular. **1b** (*as n*): *the steep.* **2** *Inf.* (of a fee, price, demand, etc.) unduly high; unreasonable (esp. in **that's a bit steep**). **3** *Inf.* excessively demanding or ambitious: *a steep task.* **4** *Brit. inf.* (of a statement) extreme or far-fetched. ORIG OE *steap*
▸ **ˈsteeply** *adv* ▸ **ˈsteepness** *n*

steep[2] (stiːp) *vb* **1** to soak or be soaked in a liquid in order to soften, cleanse, extract an element, etc. **2** (*tr; usually passive*) to saturate; imbue: *steeped in ideology.* ◆ *n* **3** an instance or the process of steeping or the condition of being steeped. **4** a liquid or solution used for the purpose of steeping something. ORIG OE *stēpan*
▸ **ˈsteeper** *n*

steepen (ˈstiːp^{ə}n) *vb* to become or cause to become steep or steeper.

steeple (ˈstiːp^{ə}l) *n* **1** a tall ornamental tower that forms the superstructure of a church, temple, etc. **2** such a tower with the spire above it. **3** any spire or pointed structure. ORIG OE *stēpel*
▸ **ˈsteepled** *adj*

steeplechase (ˈstiːp^{ə}lˌtʃeɪs) *n* **1** a horse race over a course equipped with obstacles to be jumped. **2** a track race in which the runners have to leap hurdles, a water jump, etc. **3** *Arch.* **3a** a horse race across a stretch of open countryside including obstacles to be jumped. **3b** a rare word for **point-to-point.** ◆ *vb* **steeplechases, steeplechasing, steeplechased. 4** (*intr*) to take part in a steeplechase.
▸ **ˈsteepleˌchaser** *n* ▸ **ˈsteepleˌchasing** *n*

steeplejack (ˈstiːp^{ə}lˌdʒæk) *n* a person trained and skilled in the construction and repair of steeples, chimneys, etc.

steer[1] (stɪə) *vb* **1** to direct the course of (a vehicle or vessel) with a steering wheel, rudder, etc. **2** (*tr*) to guide with tuition: *his teachers steered him through his exams.* **3** (*tr*) to direct the movements or course of (a person, conversation, etc.). **4** to pursue (a specified course). **5** (*intr*) (of a vessel, vehicle, etc.) to admit of being guided in a specified fashion: *this boat does not steer properly.* **6 steer clear of.** to keep away from; shun. ◆ *n* **7** *Chiefly US.* guidance; information (esp. in **a bum steer**). ORIG OE *stieran*
▸ **ˈsteerable** *adj* ▸ **ˈsteerer** *n*

steer[2] (stɪə) *n* a castrated male ox or bull; bullock. ORIG OE *stēor*

steerage (ˈstɪərɪdʒ) *n* **1** the cheapest accommodation on a passenger ship, originally the compartments containing steering apparatus. **2** an instance or the practice of steering and its effect on a vessel or vehicle.

steerageway (ˈstɪərɪdʒˌweɪ) *n Naut.* enough forward movement to allow a vessel to be steered.

steering committee *n* a committee set up to prepare and arrange topics to be discussed, the order of business, etc., for a legislative assembly or other body.

steering wheel *n* a wheel turned by the driver of a motor vehicle, ship, etc., when he wishes to change direction.

steersman (ˈstɪəzmən) *n, pl* **steersmen.** the helmsman of a vessel.

Stefansson ★ (ˈstɛfənsən) *n* **Vilhjalmur** (ˈvɪlˌhjaʊmɛr) 1879–1962, Canadian explorer, noted for his books on the Inuit.

Steffens ★ (ˈstɛfənz) *n* (**Joseph**) **Lincoln.** 1866–1936, US political analyst, known for his exposure of political corruption.

stegosaur (ˈstɛgəˌsɔː) *or* **stegosaurus** (ˌstɛgəˈsɔːrəs) *n* any of various quadrupedal herbivorous dinosaurs of Jurassic and early Cretaceous times, having an armour of bony plates. ORIG C19: from Gk *stegos* roof + -SAUR

Steier ★ (*German* ˈʃtaiər) *n* a variant spelling of **Steyr.**

Steiermark ★ (ˈʃtaiərˌmark) *n* the German name for **Styria.**

stein (staɪn) *n* an earthenware beer mug, esp. of a German design. ORIG from G *Stein,* lit.: stone

Stein ★ *n* **1** (staɪn). **Gertrude.** 1874–1946, US writer, resident in Paris (1903–1946). Her works include *The Autobiography of Alice B. Toklas* (1933). **2** (*German* ʃtain). **Heinrich Friedrich Carl** (ˈhainrɪç ˈfriːdrɪç karl), Baron. 1757–1831, Prussian statesman; a leader of the European coalition against Napoleon (1813–15).

Steinbeck ★ (ˈstaɪnbɛk) *n* **John** (**Ernst**). 1902–68, US writer, noted for his novel *The Grapes of Wrath* (1939): Nobel prize for literature 1962.

steinbok (ˈstaɪnˌbɒk) *n, pl* **steinboks** *or* **steinbok.** a variant of **steenbok.**

Steiner ★ (ˈstaɪnə; *German* ˈʃtainər) *n* **Rudolf** (ˈruːdɔlf). 1861–1925, Austrian philosopher, founder of anthroposophy. He was particularly influential in education. See also **anthroposophy.**

Steinitz ★ ('staɪnɪts; *German* 'ʃtainɪts) *n* **Wilhelm** ('vɪlhɛlm). 1836–1900, US chess player, born in Prague; world champion (1866–94).

Steinway ★ ('staɪnweɪ) *n* **Henry** (**Engelhard**), original name *Heinrich Engelhardt Steinweg.* 1797–1871, US piano maker, born in Germany.

stele ('sti:lɪ, sti:l) *n, pl* **stelae** ('sti:li:) *or* **steles. 1** an upright stone slab or column decorated with figures or inscriptions, common in prehistoric times. **2** a prepared vertical surface that has a commemorative inscription or design, esp. one on the face of a building. **3** the conducting tissue of the stems and roots of plants, which is in the form of a cylinder. ♦ Also called (for senses 1, 2): **stela.** ORIG C19: from Gk *stēlē*
▸ **'stelar** *adj*

stellar ('stɛlə) *adj* **1** of, relating to, or resembling a star or stars. **2** of or relating to star entertainers. **3** *Inf.* outstanding or immense: *companies are registering stellar profits.* ORIG C17: from LL *stellāris,* from L *stella* star

stellar evolution *n Astron.* the sequence of changes that occurs in a star as it ages.

stellate ('stɛlɪt, -eɪt) *or* **stellated** *adj* resembling a star in shape; radiating from the centre: *a stellate arrangement of petals.* ORIG C16: from L *stellātus* starry, from *stellāre* to stud with stars, from *stella* a star
▸ **'stellately** *adv*

stellular ('stɛljʊlə) *adj* **1** displaying or abounding in small stars: *a stellular pattern.* **2** resembling a little star or little stars. ORIG C18: from LL *stellula,* dim. of L *stella* star
▸ **'stellularly** *adv*

stem[1] (stɛm) *n* **1** the main axis of a plant, which bears the leaves, axillary buds, and flowers and contains a hollow cylinder of vascular tissue. **2** any similar subsidiary structure in such plants that bears a flower, fruit, or leaf. **3** a corresponding structure in algae and fungi. **4** any long slender part, such as the hollow part of a tobacco pipe between the bit and the bowl. **5** the main line of descent or branch of a family. **6** any shank or cylindrical pin or rod, such as the pin that carries the winding knob on a watch. **7** *Linguistics.* the form of a word that remains after removal of all inflectional affixes. **8** the main, usually vertical, stroke of a letter or of a musical note such as a minim. **9a** the main upright timber or structure at the bow of a vessel. **9b** the very forward end of a vessel (esp. in **from stem to stern**). ♦ *vb* **stems, stemming, stemmed. 10** (*intr; usually foll. by from*) to be derived; originate. **11** (*tr*) to make headway against (a tide, wind, etc.). **12** (*tr*) to remove or disengage the stem or stems from. ORIG OE *stemn*
▸ **'stem,like** *adj*

stem[2] (stɛm) *vb* **stems, stemming, stemmed. 1** (*tr*) to restrain or stop (the flow of something) by or as if by damming up. **2** (*tr*) to pack tightly or stop up. **3** *Skiing.* to manoeuvre (a ski or skis), as in performing a stem. ♦ *n* **4** *Skiing.* a technique in which the heel of one ski or both skis is forced outwards from the direction of movement in order to slow down or turn. ORIG C15 *stemmen,* from ON *stemma*

stem cell *n Histology.* an undifferentiated cell that gives rise to specialized cells, such as blood cells.

stem ginger *n* choice pieces of the underground stem of the ginger plant which are crystallized or preserved in syrup and eaten as a sweetmeat.

stemma ('stɛmə) *n* a family tree; pedigree. ORIG C19: via L from Gk *stema* garland, wreath, from *stephein* to crown, wreathe

stemmed (stɛmd) *adj* **1a** having a stem. **1b** (*in combination*): *a long-stemmed glass.* **2** having had the stem or stems removed.

stem turn *n Skiing.* a turn in which the heel of one ski is stemmed and the other ski is brought parallel. Also called: **stem.**

stench (stɛntʃ) *n* a strong and extremely offensive odour; stink. ORIG OE *stenc*

stencil ('stensəl) *n* **1** a device for applying a design, characters, etc., to a surface, consisting of a thin sheet of plastic, metal, etc., in which the design or characters have been cut so that ink or paint can be applied through the incisions onto the surface. **2** a design or characters produced in this way. ♦ *vb* **stencils, stencilling, stencilled** *or US* **stencils, stenciling, stenciled.** (*tr*) **3** to mark (a surface) with a stencil. **4** to produce (characters or a design) with a stencil. ORIG C14 *stanselen* to decorate with bright colours, from OF *estenceler,* from *estencele* a spark, from L *scintilla*

Stendhal ★ (*French* stɛ̃dal) *n* original name *Marie Henri Beyle.* 1783–1842, French writer. His two chief novels are *Le Rouge et le noir* (1830) and *La Chartreuse de Parme* (1839).

Sten gun (stɛn) *n* a light 9mm sub-machine-gun formerly used in the British Army. ORIG C20: from *S* & *T* (initials of Shepherd & Turpin, the inventors) + *-en,* as in BREN GUN

steno- *or before a vowel* **sten-** *combining form.* indicating narrowness or contraction: *stenography; stenosis.* ORIG from Gk *stenos* narrow

stenograph ('stɛnə,grɑ:f) *n* **1** any of various keyboard machines for writing in shorthand. **2** any character used in shorthand. ♦ *vb* **3** (*tr*) to record (minutes, letters, etc.) in shorthand.

stenographer (stə'nɒgrəfə) *n* the US & Canad. name for **shorthand typist.**

stenography (stə'nɒgrəfɪ) *n* **1** the act or process of writing in shorthand by hand or machine. **2** matter written in shorthand.
▸ **stenographic** (,stɛnə'græfɪk) *adj*

stenosis (stɪ'nəʊsɪs) *n, pl* **stenoses** (-si:z). *Pathol.* an abnormal narrowing of a bodily canal or passage. ORIG C19: via NL from Gk *stenōsis,* ult. from *stenos* narrow
▸ **stenotic** (stɪ'nɒtɪk) *adj*

Stenotype ('stɛnə,taɪp) *n* **1** *Trademark.* a machine with a keyboard for recording speeches, etc., in a phonetic shorthand. **2** any machine resembling this. **3** the phonetic symbol typed in one stroke of such a machine.

stenotypy ('stɛnə,taɪpɪ) *n* a form of shorthand in which alphabetic combinations are used to represent groups of sounds or short common words.
▸ **'steno,typist** *n*

Stentor ★ ('stɛntɔ:) *n* **1** *Greek myth.* a Greek herald with a powerful voice who died after he lost a shouting contest with Hermes, herald of the gods. **2** (*not cap.*) any person with an unusually loud voice.

stentorian (stɛn'tɔ:rɪən) *adj* (of the voice, etc.) uncommonly loud: *stentorian tones.* ORIG C17: after STENTOR

step (stɛp) *n* **1** the act of raising the foot and setting it down again in coordination with the transference of the weight of the body. **2** the distance or space covered by such a motion. **3** the sound made by such a movement. **4** the impression made by such movement of the foot; footprint. **5** the manner of walking or moving the feet; gait: *a proud step.* **6** a sequence of foot movements that make up a particular dance or part of a dance: *the steps of the waltz.* **7** any of several paces or rhythmic movements in marching, dancing, etc.: *the goose step.* **8** (*pl*) a course followed by a person in walking or as walking: *they followed in their leader's steps.* **9** one of a sequence of separate consecutive stages in the progression towards some goal. **10** a rank or grade in a series or scale. **11** an object or device that offers support for the foot when ascending or descending. **12** (*pl*) a flight of stairs, esp. out of doors. **13** (*pl*) another name for **stepladder. 14** a very short easily walked distance: *it is only a step.* **15** *Music.* a melodic interval of a second. **16** an offset or change in the level of a surface similar to the step of a stair. **17** a strong block or frame bolted onto the keel of a vessel and fitted to receive the base of a mast. **18** a ledge cut in mining or quarrying excavations. **19 break step.** to cease to march in step. **20 in step. 20a** marching, dancing, etc., in conformity with a specified pace or moving in unison with others. **20b** *Inf.* in agreement or harmony. **21 keep step.** to remain walking, marching, dancing, etc., in unison or in a specified rhythm. **22 out of step. 22a** not moving in conformity with a specified pace or in accordance with others. **22b** *Inf.* not in agreement; out of harmony. **23 step by step.** with care and deliberation; gradually. **24 take steps.**

to undertake measures (to do something). **25 watch one's step. 25a** *Inf.* to conduct oneself with caution and good behaviour. **25b** to walk or move carefully. ◆ *vb* **steps, stepping, stepped. 26** (*intr*) to move by raising the foot and then setting it down in a different position, transferring the weight of the body to this foot and repeating the process with the other foot. **27** (*intr; often foll. by in, out,* etc.) to move or go on foot, esp. for a short distance: *step this way.* **28** (*intr*) *Inf., chiefly US.* to move, often in an attractive graceful manner, as in dancing: *he can really step around.* **29** (*intr;* usually foll. by *on* or *upon*) to place or press the foot; tread: *to step on the accelerator.* **30** (*intr;* usually foll. by *into*) to enter (into a situation) apparently with ease: *she stepped into a life of luxury.* **31** (*tr*) to walk or take (a number of paces, etc.): *to step ten paces.* **32** (*tr*) to perform the steps of: *they step the tango well.* **33** (*tr*) to set or place (the foot). **34** (*tr;* usually foll. by *off* or *out*) to measure (some distance of ground) by stepping. **35** (*tr*) to arrange in or supply with a series of steps so as to avoid coincidence or symmetry. **36** (*tr*) to raise (a mast) and fit it into its step. ◆ See also **step down, step in,** etc. ORIG OE *stepe, stæpe*
▸ **'step,like** *adj*

Step (stɛp) *n* **a** a set of aerobic exercises designed to improve the cardiovascular system, which consists of stepping on and off a special box of adjustable height. **b** (*as modifer*): *Step aerobics.*

step- *combining form.* indicating relationship through the previous marriage of a spouse or parent: *stepson; stepfather.* ORIG OE *stēop-*

stepbrother ('stɛp,brʌðə) *n* a son of one's stepmother or stepfather by a union with someone other than one's father or mother.

stepchild ('stɛp,tʃaɪld) *n, pl* **stepchildren.** a stepson or stepdaughter.

stepdaughter ('stɛp,dɔ:tə) *n* a daughter of one's husband or wife by a former union.

step down *vb* (*adv*) **1** (*tr*) to reduce gradually. **2** (*intr*) *Inf.* to resign or abdicate (from a position). **3** (*intr*) *Inf.* to assume an inferior or less senior position. ◆ *adj* **step-down.** (*prenominal*) **4** (of a transformer) reducing a high voltage to a lower voltage. Cf. **step-up** (sense 3). ◆ *n* **step-down. 5** *Inf.* a decrease in quantity or size.

stepfather ('stɛp,fɑ:ðə) *n* a man who has married one's mother after the death or divorce of one's father.

stephanotis (,stɛfə'nəutɪs) *n* any of various climbing shrubs of Madagascar and Malaya, cultivated for their fragrant white waxy flowers. ORIG C19: via NL from Gk: fit for a crown, from *stephanos* a crown

Stephen ★ ('sti:vᵊn) *n* **1** ?1097–1154, king of England (1135–54); grandson of William the Conqueror. He seized the throne on the death of Henry I, causing civil war with Henry's daughter Matilda. He eventually recognized her son (later Henry II) as his successor. **2 Saint.** died ?35 A.D., the first Christian martyr. Feast day: Dec. 26 or 27. **3 Saint,** Hungarian name *István.* ?975–1038 A.D., first king of Hungary as Stephen I (997–1038). Feast day: Aug. 16. **4** Sir **Leslie.** 1832–1904, British biographer and first editor of the *Dictionary of National Biography;* father of Virginia Woolf.

Stephenson ★ ('sti:vənsən) *n* **1 George.** 1781–1848, British inventor of the first successful steam locomotive (1814); constructed the first railway to carry passengers, the Stockton and Darlington Railway (opened 1825). **2** his son, **Robert.** 1803–59, British engineer, noted for his construction of locomotives, railway bridges, and viaducts.

step in *vb* **1** (*intr, adv*) *Inf.* to intervene or involve oneself. ◆ *adj* **step-in. 2** (*prenominal*) (of garments, etc.) put on by being stepped into; without fastenings. **3** (of a ski binding) engaging automatically when the boot is positioned on the ski. ◆ *n* **step-in. 4** (*often pl*) a step-in garment, esp. underwear.

stepladder ('stɛp,lædə) *n* a folding portable ladder that is made of broad flat steps fixed to a supporting frame hinged at the top to another supporting frame.

stepmother ('stɛp,mʌðə) *n* a woman who has married one's father after the death or divorce of one's mother.

step on *vb* (*intr, prep*) **1** to place or press the foot on. **2** *Inf.* to behave harshly or contemptuously towards. **3 step on it.** *Inf.* to go more quickly; hurry up.

step out *vb* (*intr, adv*) **1** to go outside or leave a room, etc., esp. briefly. **2** to begin to walk more quickly and take longer strides. **3** *US & Canad. inf.* to withdraw from involvement.

step-parent ('stɛp,pɛərənt) *n* a stepfather or stepmother.
▸ **'step-,parenting** *n*

steppe (stɛp) *n* (*often pl*) an extensive grassy plain usually without trees. ORIG C17: from ORussian *step* lowland

stepper ('stɛpə) *n* a person who or animal that steps, esp. a horse or a dancer.

Steppes ★ (stɛps) *pl n* **the. 1** the huge grasslands of Eurasia, chiefly in Ukraine and Russia. **2** another name for **Kyrgyz Steppe.**

stepping stone *n* **1** one of a series of stones acting as footrests for crossing streams, marshes, etc. **2** a circumstance that assists progress towards some goal.

stepsister ('stɛp,sɪstə) *n* a daughter of one's stepmother or stepfather by a union with someone other than one's father or mother.

stepson ('stɛp,sʌn) *n* a son of one's husband or wife by a former union.

step up *vb* (*adv*) *Inf.* **1** (*tr*) to increase or raise by stages; accelerate. **2** (*intr*) to make progress or effect an advancement; be promoted. ◆ *adj* **step-up.** (*prenominal*) **3** (of a transformer) increasing a low voltage to a higher voltage. Cf. **step-down** (sense 4). ◆ *n* **step-up. 4** *Inf.* an increment in quantity, size, etc.

-ster *suffix forming nouns.* **1** indicating a person who is engaged in a certain activity: *prankster; songster.* **2** indicating a person associated with or being something specified: *mobster; youngster.* ORIG OE *-estre*

steradian (stə'reɪdɪən) *n* an SI unit of solid angle; the angle that, having its vertex in the centre of a sphere, cuts off an area of the surface of the sphere equal to the square of the length of the radius. Symbol: sr ORIG C19: from STEREO- + RADIAN

stercoraceous (,stɜ:kə'reɪʃəs) *adj* of, relating to, or consisting of dung or excrement. ORIG C18: from L *stercus* dung + -ACEOUS

stere (stɪə) *n* a unit used to measure volumes of stacked timber equal to one cubic metre (35.315 cubic feet). ORIG C18: from F *stère,* from Gk *stereos* solid

stereo ('stɛrɪəu, 'stɪər-) *adj* **1** short for **stereophonic** or **stereoscopic.** ◆ *n, pl* **stereos. 2** stereophonic sound: *to broadcast in stereo.* **3** a stereophonic record player, tape recorder, etc. **4** *Photog.* **4a** stereoscopic photography. **4b** a stereoscopic photograph. **5** *Printing.* short for **stereotype.** ORIG C20: shortened form

stereo- *or sometimes before a vowel* **stere-** *combining form.* indicating three-dimensional quality or solidity: *stereoscope.* ORIG from Gk *stereos* solid

stereochemistry (,stɛrɪəu'kɛmɪstrɪ, ,stɪər-) *n* the study of the spatial arrangement of atoms in molecules and its effect on chemical properties.

stereograph ('stɛrɪə,grɑ:f, 'stɪər-) *n* two almost identical pictures, or one special picture, that when viewed through special glasses or a stereoscope form a single three-dimensional image. Also called: **stereogram.**

stereoisomer (,stɛrɪəu'aɪsəmə, ,stɪər-) *n Chem.* an isomer that exhibits stereoisomerism.

stereoisomerism (,stɛrɪəuaɪ'sɒmə,rɪzəm, ,stɪər-) *n Chem.* isomerism caused by differences in the spatial arrangement of atoms in molecules.

stereophonic (,stɛrɪə'fɒnɪk, ,stɪər-) *adj* (of a system for recording, reproducing, or broadcasting sound) using two or more separate microphones to feed two or more loudspeakers through separate channels in order to give a spatial effect to the sound. Often shortened to **stereo.**
▸ **,stereo'phonically** *adv* ▸ **stereophony** (,stɛrɪ'ɒfənɪ, ,stɪər-) *n*

stereoscope ('stɛrɪə,skəup, 'stɪər-) *n* an optical instrument for viewing two-dimensional pictures, giving an illusion of depth and relief. It has a binocular eyepiece

through which two slightly different pictures of an object are viewed, one with each eye.
▸ **stereoscopic** (ˌstɛrɪəˈskɒpɪk, ˌstɪər-) *adj*

stereoscopy (ˌstɛrɪˈɒskəpɪ, ˌstɪər-) *n* **1** the viewing or appearance of objects in or as if in three dimensions. **2** the study and use of the stereoscope.
▸ **ˌstereˈoscopist** *n*

stereospecific (ˌstɛrɪəʊspɪˈsɪfɪk, ˌstɪər-) *adj Chem.* relating to or having fixed position in space, as in the spatial arrangements of atoms in certain polymers.

stereotype (ˈstɛrɪəˌtaɪp, ˈstɪər-) *n* **1a** a method of producing cast-metal printing plates from a mould made from a forme of type. **1b** the plate so made. **2** another word for **stereotypy**. **3** an idea, convention, etc., that has grown stale through fixed usage. **4** a standardized image or conception of a type of person, etc. ◆ *vb* **stereotypes, stereotyping, stereotyped.** (*tr*) **5a** to make a stereotype of. **5b** to print from a stereotype. **6** to impart a fixed usage or convention to.
▸ **ˈstereoˌtyper** *or* **ˈstereoˌtypist** *n*

stereotyped (ˈstɛrɪəˌtaɪpt, ˈstɪər-) *adj* **1** lacking originality or individuality; conventional; trite. **2** reproduced from or on a stereotype printing plate.

stereotypy (ˈstɛrɪəˌtaɪpɪ, ˈstɪər-) *n* **1** the act or process of making stereotype printing plates. **2** a tendency to think or act in rigid, repetitive, and often meaningless patterns.

stereovision (ˈstɛrɪəʊˌvɪʒən, ˈstɪər-) *n* the perception or exhibition of three-dimensional objects in three dimensions.

steric (ˈstɛrɪk, ˈstɪər-) *or* **sterical** *adj Chem.* of or caused by the spatial arrangement of atoms in a molecule. ORIG C19: from STEREO- + -IC

sterile (ˈstɛraɪl) *adj* **1** unable to produce offspring; permanently infertile. **2** free from living, esp. pathogenic, microorganisms. **3** (of plants or their parts) not producing or bearing seeds, fruit, spores, stamens, or pistils. **4** lacking inspiration or vitality; fruitless. ORIG C16: from L *sterilis*
▸ **ˈsterilely** *adv* ▸ **sterility** (stɛˈrɪlɪtɪ) *n*

sterilize *or* **sterilise** (ˈstɛrɪˌlaɪz) *vb* **sterilizes, sterilizing, sterilized** *or* **sterilises, sterilising, sterilised.** (*tr*) to render sterile; make infertile or barren.
▸ **ˌsteriliˈzation** *or* **ˌsteriliˈsation** *n* ▸ **ˈsteriˌlizer** *or* **ˈsteriˌliser** *n*

sterling (ˈstɜːlɪŋ) *n* **1a** British money: *pound sterling.* **1b** (*as modifier*): *sterling reserves.* **2** the official standard of purity of British coins. **3a** short for **sterling silver. 3b** (*as modifier*): *a sterling bracelet.* **4** an article or articles manufactured from sterling silver. ◆ *adj* **5** (*prenominal*) genuine and reliable: first-class: *sterling quality.* ORIG C13: prob. from OE *steorra* star + -LING[1]; referring to a small star on early Norman pennies

sterling area *n* a group of countries that use sterling as a medium of international payments. Also called: **scheduled territories.**

sterling silver *n* **1** an alloy containing not less than 92.5 per cent of silver. **2** sterling-silver articles collectively.

Sterlitamak ★ (*Russian* stjerlitəˈmak) *n* an industrial city in W Russia, in the Bashkir Republic. Pop.: 259 000 (1995 est.).

stern[1] (stɜːn) *adj* **1** showing uncompromising or inflexible resolve; firm or authoritarian. **2** lacking leniency or clemency. **3** relentless; unyielding: *the stern demands of parenthood.* **4** having an austere or forbidding appearance or nature. ORIG OE *styrne*
▸ **ˈsternly** *adv* ▸ **ˈsternness** *n*

stern[2] (stɜːn) *n* **1** the rear or after part of a vessel, opposite the bow or stem. **2** the rear part of any object. ◆ *adj* **3** relating to or located at the stern. ORIG C13: from ON *stjōrn* steering

Stern ★ (stɜːn) *n* **Isaac.** born 1920, US violinist, born in Russia.

Sternberg ★ (ˈstɜːnˌbɜːg, ˈʃtɜːn-) *n* See (Joseph) **von Sternberg.**

Sterne ★ (stɜːn) *n* **Laurence.** 1713–68, British novelist, born in Ireland, author of *The Life and Opinions of Tristram Shandy, Gentleman* (1759–67).

sternforemost (ˈstɜːnˈfɔːməʊst) *adv Naut.* backwards.

sternmost (ˈstɜːnˌməʊst) *adj Naut.* **1** farthest to the stern; aftmost. **2** nearest the stern.

sternpost (ˈstɜːnˌpəʊst) *n Naut.* the main upright timber or structure at the stern of a vessel.

stern sheets *pl n Naut.* the part of an open boat near the stern.

sternum (ˈstɜːnəm) *n, pl* **sterna** (-nə) *or* **sternums. 1** (in man) a long flat vertical bone in front of the thorax, to which are attached the collarbone and the first seven pairs of ribs. Nontechnical name: **breastbone. 2** the corresponding part in many other vertebrates. ORIG C17: via NL from Gk *sternon* breastbone
▸ **ˈsternal** *adj*

sternutation (ˌstɜːnjʊˈteɪʃən) *n* a sneeze or the act of sneezing. ORIG C16: from LL *sternūtāre* to sneeze, from *sternuere* to sputter (of a light)

sternutator (ˈstɜːnjʊˌteɪtə) *n* a substance that causes sneezing, coughing, and tears; used in chemical warfare.
▸ **sternutatory** (stɜːˈnjuːtətərɪ, -trɪ) *adj, n*

sternwards (ˈstɜːnwədz) *or* **sternward** *adv Naut.* towards the stern; astern.

sternway (ˈstɜːnˌweɪ) *n Naut.* movement of a vessel sternforemost.

stern-wheeler *n* a vessel, esp. a river boat, propelled by a large paddle wheel at the stern.

steroid (ˈstɪərɔɪd, ˈstɛr-) *n Biochem.* any of a large group of organic compounds containing a characteristic chemical ring system, including sterols, bile acids, many hormones, and the D vitamins. ORIG C20: from STEROL + -OID
▸ **steˈroidal** *adj*

sterol (ˈstɛrɒl) *n Biochem.* any of a group of natural steroid alcohols, such as cholesterol and ergosterol, that are waxy insoluble substances. ORIG C20: shortened from CHOLESTEROL, ERGOSTEROL, etc.

stertorous (ˈstɜːtərəs) *adj* **1** marked by heavy snoring. **2** breathing in this way. ORIG C19: from L *stertere* to snore
▸ **ˈstertorously** *adv* ▸ **ˈstertorousness** *n*

stet (stɛt) *n* **1** a word or mark indicating that certain deleted typeset or written matter is to be retained. ◆ *vb* **stets, stetting, stetted. 2** (*tr*) to mark (matter) thus. ORIG L, lit.: let it stand

stethoscope (ˈstɛθəˌskəʊp) *n Med.* an instrument for listening to the sounds made within the body, typically consisting of a hollow disc that transmits the sound through hollow tubes to earpieces. ORIG C19: from F, from Gk *stēthos* breast + -SCOPE
▸ **stethoscopic** (ˌstɛθəˈskɒpɪk) *adj* ▸ **stethoscopy** (stɛˈθɒskəpɪ) *n*

Stetson (ˈstɛtsᵊn) *n Trademark.* a type of felt hat with a broad brim and high crown, worn mainly by cowboys. ORIG C20: after John *Stetson* (1830–1906), US hat-maker

Stettin ★ (ʃtɛˈtiːn) *n* the German name for **Szczecin.**

stevedore (ˈstiːvɪˌdɔː) *n* **1** a person employed to load or unload ships. ◆ *vb* **stevedores, stevedoring, stevedored. 2** to load or unload (a ship, ship's cargo, etc.). ORIG C18: from Sp. *estibador* a packer, from *estibar* to load (a ship), from L *stīpāre* to pack full

Stevenage ★ (ˈstiːvənɪdʒ) *n* a town in SE England, in N Hertfordshire on the Great North Road: developed chiefly as the first of the new towns (1946). Pop.: 76 064 (1991).

Stevenson ★ (ˈstiːvənsən) *n* **1 Adlai Ewing** (ˈædleɪ ˈjuːɪŋ). 1900–68, US statesman: twice defeated as Democratic presidential candidate (1952; 1956); US delegate at the United Nations (1961–65). **2 Robert Louis** (**Balfour**). 1850–94, Scottish writer: his novels include *Treasure Island* (1883), *Kidnapped* (1886), and *The Master of Ballantrae* (1889).

stew[1] (stjuː) *n* **1a** a dish of meat, fish, or other food, cooked by stewing. **1b** (*as modifier*): *stew pot.* **2** *Inf.* a difficult or worrying situation or a troubled state (esp. in **in a stew**). **3** a heterogeneous mixture: *a stew of people of every race.* **4** (*usually pl*) *Arch.* a brothel. ◆ *vb* **5** to cook or cause to cook by long slow simmering. **6** (*intr*) *Inf.* to be troubled or agitated. **7** (*intr*) *Inf.* to be oppressed with heat or crowding. **8** to cause (tea) to become bitter or (of tea) to become bitter through infusing for too long. **9 stew in one's own juice.** to suffer unaided the consequences of one's actions. ORIG C14 *stuen* to take a very hot bath, from OF *estuver,* from Vulgar L *extūfāre* (unattested), from EX-[1] + (unattested) *tūfus* vapour, from Gk *tuphos*

stew² (stjuː) *n Brit.* **1** a fishpond or fishtank. **2** an artificial oyster bed. ORIG C14: from OF *estui,* from *estoier* to confine, ult. from L *studium* STUDY

steward (stjʊəd) *n* **1** a person who administers the property, house, finances, etc., of another. **2** a person who manages the eating arrangements, staff, or service at a club, hotel, etc. **3** a waiter on a ship or aircraft. **4** a mess attendant in a naval mess. **5** a person who helps to supervise some event or proceedings in an official capacity. **6** short for **shop steward.** ◆ *vb* **7** to act or serve as a steward (of something). ORIG OE *stigweard,* from *stig* hall + *weard* WARD
▸ **'stewardship** *n*

stewardess ('stjʊədɪs, ˌstjʊə'dɛs) *n* a woman steward on an aircraft or ship.

Stewart ★ ('stjʊət) *n* **1** the usual spelling for the royal house of **Stuart** before the reign of Mary Queen of Scots (Mary Stuart). **2 Jackie,** full name *John Young Stewart.* born 1939, Scottish motor-racing driver: world champion 1969, 1971, and 1973. **3 James** (**Maitland**). 1908–97, US film actor: films include *The Philadelphia Story* (1940) and *Shenandoah* (1965). **4 Rod.** born 1945, British rock singer: vocalist with the Faces (1969–75). His albums include *Every Picture Tells a Story* (1971).

Stewart Island ★ *n* the third largest island of New Zealand, in the SW Pacific off the S tip of South Island. Pop.: 450 (1989 est.). Area: 1735 sq. km (670 sq. miles).

stewed (stjuːd) *adj* **1** (of meat, fish, etc.) cooked by stewing. **2** *Brit.* (of tea) bitter through having been left to infuse for too long. **3** a slang word for **drunk** (sense 1).

Steyr *or* **Steier** ★ (*German* 'ʃtaiər) *n* an industrial city in N central Austria, in Upper Austria. Pop.: 39 542 (1991).

stg *abbrev. for* sterling.

sthenic ('sθɛnɪk) *adj* abounding in energy or bodily strength; active or strong. ORIG C18: from NL *sthenicus,* from Gk *sthenos* force, on the model of *asthenic*

Stheno ★ ('sθiːnəʊ, 'sθɛnəʊ) *n Greek myth.* one of the three Gorgons.

stibine ('stɪbaɪn) *n* **1** a colourless poisonous gas with an offensive odour: made by the action of hydrochloric acid on an alloy of antimony and zinc. **2** any one of a class of stibine derivatives in which one or more hydrogen atoms have been replaced by organic groups. ORIG C19: from L *stibium* antimony + -INE[2]

stibnite ('stɪbnaɪt) *n* a soft greyish mineral consisting of antimony sulphide in crystalline form: the chief ore of antimony. ORIG C19: from obs. *stibine* stibnite + -ITE[1]

-stichous *adj combining form.* having a certain number of rows. ORIG from LL *-stichus,* from Gk *-stikhos,* from *stikhos* row

stick¹ (stɪk) *n* **1** a small thin branch of a tree. **2a** any long thin piece of wood. **2b** such a piece of wood having a characteristic shape for a special purpose: *a walking stick; a hockey stick.* **2c** a baton, wand, staff, or rod. **3** an object or piece shaped like a stick: *a stick of celery.* **4** In full: **control stick.** the lever by which a pilot controls the movements of an aircraft. **5** *Inf.* the lever used to change gear in a motor vehicle. **6** *Naut.* a mast or yard. **7a** a group of bombs arranged to fall at intervals across a target. **7b** a number of paratroops jumping in sequence. **8** *Sl.* **8a** verbal abuse, criticism: *I got some stick for that blunder.* **8b** physical power, force (esp. in **give it some stick**). **9** (*usually pl*) a piece of furniture: *these few sticks are all I have.* **10** (*pl*) *Inf.* a rural area considered remote or backward (esp. in **in the sticks**). **11** (*pl*) *Hockey.* a declaration made by the umpire if a player's stick is above the shoulders. **12** (*pl*) goalposts. **13** *Inf.* a dull boring person. **14** (usually preceded by *old*) *Inf.* a familiar name for a person: *not a bad old stick.* **15** punishment; beating. **16 in a cleft stick.** in a difficult position. **17 wrong end of the stick.** a complete misunderstanding of a situation, explanation, etc. ◆ *vb* **sticks, sticking, sticked. 18** to support (a plant) with sticks; stake. ORIG OE *sticca*

stick² (stɪk) *vb* **sticks, sticking, stuck. 1** (*tr*) to pierce or stab with or as if with something pointed. **2** to thrust or push (a sharp or pointed object) or (of a sharp or pointed object) to be pushed into or through another object. **3** (*tr*) to fasten in position by pushing or forcing a point into something: *to stick a peg in a hole.* **4** (*tr*) to fasten in position by or as if by pins, nails, etc.: *to stick a picture on the wall.* **5** (*tr*) to transfix or impale on a pointed object. **6** (*tr*) to cover with objects piercing or set in the surface. **7** (when *intr*, foll. by *out, up, through,* etc.) to put forward or be put forward; protrude or cause to protrude: *to stick one's head out.* **8** (*tr*) *Inf.* to place or put in a specified position: *stick your coat on this chair.* **9** to fasten or be fastened by or as if by an adhesive substance: *stick the pages together; they won't stick.* **10** (*tr*) *Inf.* to cause to become sticky. **11** (when *tr, usually passive*) to come or cause to come to a standstill: *stuck in a traffic jam; the wheels stuck.* **12** (*intr*) to remain for a long time: *the memory sticks in my mind.* **13** (*tr*) *Sl., chiefly Brit.* to tolerate; abide: *I can't stick that man.* **14** (*intr*) to be reluctant. **15** (*tr; usually passive*) *Inf.* to cause to be at a loss; baffle or puzzle: *I was totally stuck for an answer.* **16** (*tr*) *Sl.* to force or impose something unpleasant on: *they stuck me with the bill.* **17** (*tr*) to kill by piercing or stabbing. **18 stick to the ribs.** *Inf.* (of food) to be hearty and satisfying. ◆ *n* **19** the state or condition of adhering. **20** *Inf.* a substance causing adhesion. **21** *Obs.* something that causes delay or stoppage. ◆ See also **stick around, stick by,** etc. ORIG OE *stician*

stick around *or* **about** *vb* (*intr, adv*) *Inf.* to remain in a place, esp. awaiting something.

stick by *vb* (*intr, prep*) to remain faithful to; adhere to.

sticker ('stɪkə) *n* **1** an adhesive label, poster, or paper. **2** a person or thing that sticks. **3** a persevering or industrious person. **4** something prickly, such as a thorn, that clings to one's clothing, etc. **5** *Inf.* something that perplexes. **6** *Inf.* a knife used for stabbing or piercing.

stick fighting *n Caribbean.* a form of combat between two trained fighters, each of whom uses a stick, held with both hands at the midpoint, to hit the opponent's head and body.

stickhandle ('stɪkˌhændᵊl) *vb* **stickhandles, stickhandling, stickhandled.** *Ice hockey.* to manoeuvre (the puck) deftly.

sticking plaster *n* a thin cloth with an adhesive substance on one side, used for covering slight or superficial wounds.

stick insect *n* any of various mostly tropical insects that have an elongated cylindrical body and long legs and resemble twigs.

stick-in-the-mud *n Inf.* a conservative person who lacks initiative or imagination.

stickle ('stɪkᵊl) *vb* **stickles, stickling, stickled.** (*intr*) **1** to dispute stubbornly, esp. about minor points. **2** to refuse to agree or concur, esp. by making petty stipulations. ORIG C16 *stightle* (in the sense: to arbitrate): frequentative of OE *stihtan* to arrange

stickleback ('stɪkᵊlˌbæk) *n* any of various small fishes that have a series of spines along the back and occur in cold and temperate northern regions. ORIG C15: from OE *stickel* prick, sting + BACK

stickler ('stɪklə) *n* **1** (usually foll. by *for*) a person who makes insistent demands: *a stickler for accuracy.* **2** a problem or puzzle.

stick out *vb* (*adv*) **1** to project or cause to project. **2** (*tr*) *Inf.* to endure (something disagreeable) (esp. in **stick it out**). **3 stick out a mile** *or* **like a sore thumb.** *Inf.* to be extremely obvious. **4 stick out for.** to insist on (a demand), refusing to yield until it is met.

stick shift *n US & Canad.* **1a** a manually operated transmission system in a motor vehicle. **1b** a motor vehicle having manual transmission. **2** a gear lever.

stick to *vb* (*prep, mainly intr*) **1** (*also tr*) to adhere or cause to adhere to. **2** to continue constantly at. **3** to remain faithful to. **4** not to move or digress from: *the speaker stuck closely to his subject.* **5 stick to someone's fingers.** *Inf.* to be stolen by someone.

stick-up *n* **1** *Sl., chiefly US.* a robbery at gunpoint; hold-up. ◆ *vb* **stick up.** (*adv*) **2** (*tr*) *Sl., chiefly US.* to rob, esp. at gunpoint. **3** (*intr;* foll. by *for*) *Inf.* to support or defend: *stick up for oneself.*

sticky ('stɪkɪ) *adj* **stickier, stickiest. 1** covered or daubed with an adhesive or viscous substance: *sticky fingers.* **2** having the property of sticking to a surface. **3** (of weather or atmosphere) warm and humid; muggy. **4** *Inf.* difficult, awkward, or painful: *a sticky business.* **5** (of a website) encouraging users to stay on the website or to visit it repeatedly. ◆ *vb* **stickies, stickying, stickied. 6** (*tr*) *Inf.* to make sticky.
▸ **'stickily** *adv* ▸ **'stickiness** *n*

stickybeak ('stɪkɪˌbiːk) *Austral. & NZ inf.* ◆ *n* **1** an inquisitive person. ◆ *vb* **2** (*intr*) to pry.

sticky end *n Inf.* an unpleasant finish or death (esp. in **come to** *or* **meet a sticky end**).

sticky wicket *n* **1** a cricket pitch that is rapidly being dried by the sun after rain and is particularly conducive to spin. **2** *Inf.* a difficult or awkward situation.

Stieglitz ★ ('stiːglɪts) *n* **Alfred.** 1864–1946, US photographer, whose work helped to develop photography as an art: among his best photographs are those of his wife, Georgia O'Keeffe.

stiff (stɪf) *adj* **1** not easily bent; rigid; inflexible. **2** not working or moving easily or smoothly: *a stiff handle.* **3** difficult to accept in its severity or harshness: *a stiff punishment.* **4** moving with pain or difficulty; not supple: *a stiff neck.* **5** difficult; arduous: *a stiff climb.* **6** unrelaxed or awkward; formal. **7** firmer than liquid in consistency; thick or viscous. **8** powerful; strong: *a stiff breeze; a stiff drink.* **9** excessively high: *a stiff price.* **10** lacking grace or attractiveness. **11** stubborn or stubbornly maintained: *a stiff fight.* **12** *Obs.* tightly stretched; taut. **13** *Sl.* intoxicated. **14 stiff with.** *Inf.* amply provided with. ◆ *n* **15** *Sl.* a corpse. **16** *Sl.* anything thought to be a loser or a failure; flop. ◆ *adv* **17** completely or utterly: *bored stiff; frozen stiff.* ◆ *vb* **18** (*intr*) *Sl.* to fail: *the film stiffed.* **19** (*tr*) *Sl., chiefly US.* to cheat or swindle. ORIG OE *stīf*
▸ **'stiffish** *adj* ▸ **'stiffly** *adv* ▸ **'stiffness** *n*

stiffen ('stɪfᵊn) *vb* **1** to make or become stiff or stiffer. **2** (*intr*) to become suddenly tense or unyielding.
▸ **'stiffener** *n*

stiff-necked *adj* haughtily stubborn or obstinate.

stifle ('staɪfᵊl) *vb* **stifles, stifling, stifled. 1** (*tr*) to smother or suppress: *stifle a cough.* **2** to feel or cause to feel discomfort and difficulty in breathing. **3** to prevent or be prevented from breathing so as to cause death. **4** (*tr*) to crush or stamp out. ORIG C14: var. of *stuflen,* prob. from OF *estouffer* to smother

stigma ('stɪgmə) *n, pl* **stigmas** *or* **stigmata** ('stɪgmətə, stɪg'mɑːtə). **1** a distinguishing mark of social disgrace: *the stigma of having been in prison.* **2** a small scar or mark such as a birthmark. **3** *Pathol.* any mark on the skin, such as one characteristic of a specific disease. **4** *Bot.* the terminal part of the ovary, at the end of the style, where deposited pollen enters the gynoecium. **5** *Zool.* **5a** a pigmented eyespot in some invertebrates. **5b** the spiracle of an insect. **6** *Arch.* a mark branded on the skin. **7** (*pl*) *Christianity.* marks resembling the wounds of the crucified Christ, believed to appear on the bodies of certain individuals. ORIG C16: via L from Gk: brand, from *stizein* to tattoo

stigmatic (stɪg'mætɪk) *adj* **1** relating to or having a stigma or stigmata. **2** another word for **anastigmatic.** ◆ *n also* **stigmatist** ('stɪgmətɪst). **3** *Chiefly RC Church.* a person marked with the stigmata.

stigmatism ('stɪgməˌtɪzəm) *n* **1** *Physics.* the state or condition of being anastigmatic. **2** *Pathol.* the condition resulting from or characterized by stigmata.

stigmatize *or* **stigmatise** ('stɪgməˌtaɪz) *vb* **stigmatizes, stigmatizing, stigmatized** *or* **stigmatises, stigmatising, stigmatised.** (*tr*) **1** to mark out or describe (as something bad). **2** to mark with a stigma or stigmata.
▸ **ˌstigmati'zation** *or* **ˌstigmati'sation** *n* ▸ **'stigmaˌtizer** *or* **'stigmaˌtiser** *n*

stilbene ('stɪlbiːn) *n* a colourless or slightly yellow crystalline unsaturated hydrocarbon used in the manufacture of dyes. ORIG C19: from Gk *stilbos* glittering + -ENE

stilboestrol *or US* **stilbestrol** (stɪl'biːstrəl) *n* a synthetic hormone having derivatives with oestrogenic properties. Also called: **diethylstilboestrol.** ORIG C20: from STILBENE + OESTRUS + -OL[1]

stile[1] (staɪl) *n* **1** a set of steps or rungs in a wall or fence to allow people, but not animals, to pass over. **2** short for **turnstile.** ORIG OE *stigel*

stile[2] (staɪl) *n* a vertical framing member in a door, window frame, etc. ORIG C17: prob. from Du. *stijl* pillar, ult. from L *stilus* writing instrument

stiletto (stɪ'lɛtəʊ) *n, pl* **stilettos. 1** a small dagger with a slender tapered blade. **2** a sharply pointed tool used to make holes in leather, cloth, etc. **3** Also called: **spike heel, stiletto heel.** a very high heel on a woman's shoe, tapering to a very narrow tip. ◆ *vb* **stilettoes, stilettoeing, stilettoed. 4** (*tr*) to stab with a stiletto. ORIG C17: from It., from *stilo* a dagger, from L *stilus* a stake, pen

Stilicho ★ ('stɪlɪkəʊ) *n* **Flavius** ('fleɪvɪəs). ?365–408 A.D., Roman general and statesman, born a Vandal: effective ruler of the Western Roman Empire (395–408).

still[1] (stɪl) *adj* **1** (*usually predicative*) motionless; stationary. **2** undisturbed or tranquil; silent and calm. **3** not sparkling or effervescent. **4** gentle or quiet; subdued. **5** *Obs.* (of a child) dead at birth. ◆ *adv* **6** continuing now or in the future as in the past: *do you still love me?* **7** up to this or that time; yet: *I still don't know your name.* **8** (often used with a comparative) even or yet: *still more insults.* **9** quietly or without movement: *sit still.* **10** *Poetic & dialect.* always. ◆ *n* **11** *Poetic.* silence or tranquillity: *the still of the night.* **12a** a still photograph, esp. of a scene from a film. **12b** (*as modifier*): *a still camera.* ◆ *vb* **13** to make or become still, quiet, or calm. **14** (*tr*) to allay or relieve: *her fears were stilled.* ◆ *sentence connector.* **15** even then; nevertheless: *he is rich but he is still not happy.* ORIG OE *stille*
▸ **'stillness** *n*

still[2] (stɪl) *n* an apparatus for carrying out distillation, used esp. in the manufacture of spirits. ORIG C16: from OF *stiller* to drip, from L *stillāre,* from *stilla* a drip

stillage ('stɪlɪdʒ) *n* **1** a frame or stand for keeping things off the ground, such as casks in a brewery. **2** a container in which goods, machinery, etc., are transported. ORIG C16: prob. from Du. *stillagie* frame, scaffold, from *stellen* to stand; see -AGE

stillborn ('stɪlˌbɔːn) *adj* **1** (of a fetus) dead at birth. **2** (of an idea, plan, etc.) fruitless; abortive; unsuccessful.
▸ **'stillˌbirth** *n*

still life *n, pl* **still lifes. 1a** a painting or drawing of inanimate objects, such as fruit, flowers, etc. **1b** (*as modifier*): *a still-life painting.* **2** the genre of such paintings.

still room *n Brit.* **1** a room in which distilling is carried out. **2** a pantry or storeroom, as in a large house.

Stillson wrench ('stɪlsᵊn) *n Trademark.* a large wrench having adjustable jaws that tighten as the pressure on the handle is increased.

stilly *adv* ('stɪllɪ). **1** *Arch. or literary.* quietly or calmly. ◆ *adj* ('stɪlɪ). **2** *Poetic.* still, quiet, or calm.

stilt (stɪlt) *n* **1** either of a pair of two long poles with footrests on which a person stands and walks, as used by circus clowns. **2** a long post or column that is used with others to support a building above ground level. **3** any of several shore birds similar to the avocets but having a straight bill. ◆ *vb* **4** (*tr*) to raise or place on or as if on stilts. ORIG C14 (in the sense: crutch, handle of a plough): rel. to Low G *stilte* pole

stilted ('stɪltɪd) *adj* **1** (of speech, writing, etc.) formal, pompous, or bombastic. **2** not flowing continuously or naturally: *stilted conversation.* **3** *Archit.* (of an arch) having vertical piers between the impost and the springing.
▸ **'stiltedly** *adv* ▸ **'stiltedness** *n*

Stilton ('stɪltən) *n Trademark.* either of two rich cheeses, blue-veined (**blue Stilton**) or white (**white Stilton**), both very strong in flavour. ORIG C18: named after *Stilton,* Cambridgeshire, where it was orig. sold

Stilwell ★ ('stɪlwɛl) *n* **Joseph W(arren),** known as *Vinegar Joe.* 1883–1946, US general, who was (1941–44) Chiang Kai-shek's chief of staff and commander of all US forces in China, Burma, and India.

stimulant ('stɪmjʊlənt) *n* **1** a drug or similar substance that increases physiological activity, esp. of a particular organ. **2** any stimulating agent or thing. ◆ *adj* **3** stimulating. ORIG C18: from L *stimulāns* goading, from *stimulāre* to urge on

stimulate ('stɪmjʊˌleɪt) *vb* **stimulates, stimulating, stimulated. 1** (*tr*) to arouse or quicken the activity or senses of. **2** (*tr*) *Physiol.* to excite (a nerve, organ, etc.) with a stimulus. **3** (*intr*) to act as a stimulant or stimulus. ORIG C16: from L *stimulāre*
▸ **'stimuˌlating** *adj* ▸ **ˌstimu'lation** *n* ▸ **'stimulative** *adj, n* ▸ **'stimuˌlator** *n*

stimulus ('stɪmjʊləs) *n, pl* **stimuli** (-ˌlaɪ, -ˌliː). **1** something that stimulates or acts as an incentive. **2** any drug, agent, electrical impulse, or other factor able to cause a response in an organism. ORIG C17: from L: a cattle goad

sting (stɪŋ) *vb* **stings, stinging, stung. 1** (of certain animals and plants) to inflict a wound on (an organism) by the injection of poison. **2** to feel or cause to feel a sharp mental or physical pain. **3** (*tr*) to goad or incite (esp. in **sting into action**). **4** (*tr*) *Inf.* to cheat, esp. by overcharging. ◆ *n* **5** a skin wound caused by the poison injected by certain insects or plants. **6** pain caused by or as if by the sting of a plant or animal. **7** a mental pain or pang: *a sting of conscience.* **8** a sharp pointed organ, such as the ovipositor of a wasp, by which poison can be injected. **9** the ability to sting: *a sharp sting in his criticism.* **10** something as painful or swift of action as a sting: *the sting of death.* **11** a sharp stimulus or incitement. **12** *Sl.* a swindle or fraud. **13** *Sl.* a police trap, esp. one whereby a person is enticed into committing a crime for which he is then arrested. ORIG OE *stingan*
▸ **'stinger** *n* ▸ **'stinging** *adj*

stinging nettle *n* See **nettle** (sense 1).

stingray ('stɪŋˌreɪ) *n* any of various rays having a whiplike tail bearing a serrated venomous spine capable of inflicting painful weals.

stingy[1] ('stɪndʒɪ) *adj* **stingier, stingiest. 1** unwilling to spend or give. **2** insufficient or scanty. ORIG C17 (? in the sense: ill-tempered): ?from *stinge,* dialect var. of STING
▸ **'stingily** *adv* ▸ **'stinginess** *n*

stingy[2] ('stɪŋɪ) *adj* **stingier, stingiest.** *Inf.* stinging or capable of stinging.

stink (stɪŋk) *n* **1** a strong foul smell; stench. **2** *Sl.* a great deal of trouble (esp. in **make** *or* **raise a stink**). **3 like stink.** intensely; furiously. ◆ *vb* **stinks, stinking, stank** *or* **stunk; stunk.** (*mainly intr*) **4** to emit a foul smell. **5** *Sl.* to be thoroughly bad or abhorrent: *this town stinks.* **6** *Inf.* to have a very bad reputation: *his name stinks.* **7** to be of poor quality. **8** (foll. by *of* or *with*) *Sl.* to have or appear to have an excessive amount (of money). **9** (*tr;* usually foll. by *up*) *Inf.* to cause to stink. ◆ See also **stink out.** ORIG OE *stincan*
▸ **'stinky** *adj*

stink bomb *n* a small glass globe used by practical jokers: it releases a liquid with an offensive smell when broken.

stinker ('stɪŋkə) *n* **1** a person or thing that stinks. **2** *Sl.* a difficult or very unpleasant person or thing. **3** *Sl.* something of very poor quality. **4** *Inf.* any of several fulmars or related birds that feed on carrion.

stinkhorn ('stɪŋkˌhɔːn) *n* any of various fungi having an unpleasant odour.

stinking ('stɪŋkɪŋ) *adj* **1** having a foul smell. **2** *Inf.* unpleasant or disgusting. **3** (*postpositive*) *Sl.* very drunk. **4 cry stinking fish.** to decry something, esp. one's own products. ◆ *adv* **5** *Inf.* (intensifier, expressing contempt): *stinking rich.*
▸ **'stinkingly** *adv* ▸ **'stinkingness** *n*

stinko ('stɪŋkəʊ) *adj* (*postpositive*) *Sl.* drunk.

stink out *vb* (*tr, adv*) **1** to drive out or away by a foul smell. **2** *Brit.* to cause to stink: *the smell of orange peel stinks out the room.*

stinkweed ('stɪŋkˌwiːd) *n* **1** Also called: **wall mustard.** a cruciferous plant, naturalized in Britain and S and central Europe, having pale yellow flowers and a disagreeable smell when bruised. **2** any of various other ill-smelling plants.

stinkwood ('stɪŋkˌwʊd) *n* **1** any of various trees having offensive-smelling wood, esp. a southern African lauraceous tree yielding a hard wood used for furniture. **2** the heavy durable wood of any of these trees.

stint[1] (stɪnt) *vb* **1** to be frugal or miserly towards (someone) with (something). **2** *Arch.* to stop or check (something). ◆ *n* **3** an allotted or fixed amount of work. **4** a limitation or check. ORIG OE *styntan* to blunt
▸ **'stinter** *n*

stint[2] (stɪnt) *n* any of various small sandpipers of a chiefly northern genus. ORIG OE

stipe (staɪp) *n* **1** a stalk in plants that bears reproductive structures, esp. the stalk bearing the cap of a mushroom. **2** the stalk that bears the leaflets of a fern or the thallus of a seaweed. **3** *Zool.* any stalklike part; stipes. ORIG C18: via F from L *stīpes* tree trunk

stipel ('staɪpᵊl) *n* a small paired leaflike structure at the base of certain leaflets; secondary stipule. ORIG C19: via NL from L *stipula,* dim. of *stīpes* a log
▸ **stipellate** (staɪ'pɛlɪt, -eɪt) *adj*

stipend ('staɪpɛnd) *n* a fixed or regular amount of money paid as a salary or allowance, as to a clergyman. ORIG C15: from OF *stipende,* from L *stīpendium* tax, from *stips* a contribution + *pendere* to pay out

stipendiary (staɪ'pɛndɪərɪ) *adj* **1** receiving or working for regular pay: *a stipendiary magistrate.* **2** paid for by a stipend. ◆ *n, pl* **stipendiaries. 3** a person who receives regular payment. ORIG C16: from L *stīpendiārius* concerning tribute, from *stīpendium* STIPEND

stipes ('staɪpiːz) *n, pl* **stipites** ('stɪpɪˌtiːz). *Zool.* **1** the second maxillary segment in insects and crustaceans. **2** the eyestalk of a crab or similar crustacean. **3** any similar stemlike structure. ORIG C18: from L; see STIPE
▸ **stipiform** ('staɪpɪˌfɔːm) *or* **stipitiform** ('stɪpɪtɪˌfɔːm) *adj*

stipple ('stɪpᵊl) *vb* **stipples, stippling, stippled.** (*tr*) **1** to draw, engrave, or paint using dots or flecks. **2** to apply paint, powder, etc., to (something) with many light dabs. ◆ *n also* **stippling. 3** the technique of stippling or a picture produced by or using stippling. ORIG C18: from Du. *stippelen,* from *stippen* to prick, from *stip* point
▸ **'stippler** *n*

stipulate ('stɪpjʊˌleɪt) *vb* **stipulates, stipulating, stipulated. 1** (*tr; may take a clause as object*) to specify, often as a condition of an agreement. **2** (*intr;* foll. by *for*) to insist (on) as a term of an agreement. **3** (*tr; may take a clause as object*) to guarantee or promise. ORIG C17: from L *stipulārī,* prob. from OL *stipulus* firm
▸ **ˌstipu'lation** *n* ▸ **'stipuˌlator** *n*

stipule ('stɪpjuːl) *n* a small paired usually leaflike outgrowth occurring at the base of a leaf or its stalk. ORIG C18: from L; see STIPE
▸ **stipular** ('stɪpjʊlə) *adj*

stir[1] (stɜː) *vb* **stirs, stirring, stirred. 1** to move an implement such as a spoon around in (a liquid) so as to mix up the constituents. **2** to change or cause to change position; disturb or be disturbed. **3** (*intr;* often foll. by *from*) to venture or depart (from one's usual or preferred place). **4** (*intr*) to be active after a rest; be up and about. **5** (*tr*) to excite or stimulate, esp. emotionally. **6** to move (oneself) briskly or vigorously; exert (oneself). **7** (*tr*) to rouse or awaken: *to stir someone from sleep; to stir memories.* **8** (when *tr,* foll. by *up*) to cause or incite others to cause (trouble, arguments, etc.). **9 stir one's stumps.** to move or become active. ◆ *n* **10** the act or an instance of stirring or the state of being stirred. **11** a strong reaction, esp. of excitement: *his publication caused a stir.* **12** a slight movement. ◆ See also **stir up.** ORIG OE *styrian*

stir[2] (stɜː) *n* **1** a slang word for **prison:** *in stir.* **2 stir-crazy.** *Sl., chiefly US & Canad.* mentally disturbed as a result of being in prison. ORIG C19: from ?

Stir. *abbrev. for* Stirlingshire.

stir-fry ★ *vb* **stir-fries, stir-frying, stir-fried. 1** to cook (chopped meat, vegetables, etc.) rapidly by stirring them in a wok or frying pan over a high heat. ◆ *n, pl* **stir-fries. 2** a dish cooked in this way.

stirk (stɜːk) *n* **1** a heifer of 6 to 12 months old. **2** a yearling heifer or bullock. ORIG OE *stierc*

Stirling ★ ('stɜːlɪŋ) *n* **1** a town in central Scotland, on the River Forth: its castle was a regular residence of many Scottish monarchs between the 12th century and 1603. Pop.: 30 515 (1991). **2** a council area of central Scotland. Administrative centre: Stirling. Pop.: 82 750 (1996 est.). Area: 2173 sq. km (839 sq. miles).

Stirlingshire ★ ('stɜːlɪŋˌʃɪə, -ʃə) *n* a historic county of central Scotland, now mostly part of Stirling and Falkirk council areas with a small part included in East Dunbartonshire.

stirps (stɜːps) *n, pl* **stirpes** ('stɜːpiːz). **1** *Genealogy.* a line of descendants from an ancestor. **2** *Bot.* a race or variety. ORIG C17: from L: root, family origin

stirrer ('stɜːrə) *n* **1** a person or thing that stirs. **2** *Inf.* a person who deliberately causes trouble. **3** *Austral. & NZ inf.* a political activist or agitator.

stirring ('stɜːrɪŋ) *adj* **1** exciting the emotions; stimulating. **2** active, lively, or busy.
► **'stirringly** *adv*

stirrup ('stɪrəp) *n* **1** Also called: **stirrup iron.** either of two metal loops on a riding saddle, with a flat footpiece through which a rider puts his foot for support. They are attached to the saddle by **stirrup leathers. 2** a U-shaped support or clamp. **3** *Naut.* one of a set of ropes fastened to a yard at one end and having a thimble at the other through which a footrope is reeved for support. ORIG OE *stigrāp,* from *stīg* step + *rāp* rope

stirrup cup *n* a cup containing an alcoholic drink offered to a horseman ready to ride away.

stirrup pump *n* a hand-operated pump, the base of the cylinder of which is placed in a bucket of water: used in fighting fires.

stir up *vb (tr, adv)* to set in motion; instigate: *he stirred up trouble.*

stitch (stɪtʃ) *n* **1** a link made by drawing a thread through material by means of a needle. **2** a loop of yarn formed around an implement used in knitting, crocheting, etc. **3** a particular method of stitching or shape of stitch. **4** a sharp spasmodic pain in the side resulting from running or exercising. **5** *(usually used with a negative) Inf.* the least fragment of clothing: *he wasn't wearing a stitch.* **6** *Agriculture.* the ridge between two furrows. **7 drop a stitch.** to allow a loop of wool to fall off a knitting needle accidentally while knitting. **8 in stitches.** *Inf.* laughing uncontrollably. ◆ *vb* **9** *(tr)* to sew, fasten, etc., with stitches. **10** *(intr)* to be engaged in sewing. **11** *(tr)* to bind together (the leaves of a book, pamphlet, etc.) with wire staples or thread. ◆ *n, vb* **12** an informal word for **suture** (senses 1b, 5). ORIG OE *stice* sting
► **'stitcher** *n*

stitch up *vb (tr, adv)* **1** to join or mend by means of stitches or sutures. **2** *Sl.* **2a** to incriminate (someone) on a false charge by manufacturing evidence. **2b** to betray, cheat, or defraud. **3** *Sl.* to prearrange (something) in a clandestine manner. ◆ *n* **stitch-up. 4** *Sl.* a matter that has been prearranged clandestinely.

stitchwort ('stɪtʃˌwɜːt) *n* any of several low-growing N temperate herbaceous plants having small white star-shaped flowers.

stiver ('staɪvə) *n* **1** a former Dutch coin worth one twentieth of a guilder. **2** a small amount, esp. of money. ORIG C16: from Du. *stuiver*

St John ★ ('sɪndʒən) *n* **Henry.** See (1st Viscount) **Bolingbroke.**

stoa ('stəʊə) *n, pl* **stoae** ('stəʊiː) *or* **stoas.** a covered walk that has a colonnade on one or both sides, esp. as in ancient Greece. ORIG C17: from Gk

stoat (stəʊt) *n* a small Eurasian mammal, closely related to the weasels, having a brown coat and a black-tipped tail: in the northern parts of its range it has a white winter coat and is then known as an ermine. ORIG C15: from ?

stochastic (stɒ'kæstɪk) *adj* **1** *Statistics.* **1a** (of a random variable) having a probability distribution, usually with finite variance. **1b** (of a process) involving a random variable the successive values of which are not independent. **1c** (of a matrix) square with non-negative elements that add to unity in each row. **2** *Rare.* involving conjecture. ORIG C17: from Gk *stokhastikos* capable of guessing, from *stokhazesthai* to aim at, conjecture, from *stokhos* a target

stock (stɒk) *n* **1a** *(sometimes pl)* the total goods or raw material kept on the premises of a shop or business. **1b** *(as modifier): a stock book.* **2** a supply of something stored for future use. **3** *Finance.* **3a** the capital raised by a company through the issue and subscription of shares entitling their holders to dividends, partial ownership, and usually voting rights. **3b** the proportion of such capital held by an individual shareholder. **3c** the shares of a specified company or industry. **4** standing or status. **5a** farm animals, such as cattle and sheep, bred and kept for their meat, skins, etc. **5b** *(as modifier): stock farming.* **6** the trunk or main stem of a tree or other plant. **7** *Horticulture.* **7a** a rooted plant into which a scion is inserted during grafting. **7b** a plant or stem from which cuttings are taken. **8** the original type from which a particular race, family, group, etc., is derived. **9** a race, breed, or variety of animals or plants. **10** *(often pl)* a small pen in which a single animal can be confined. **11** a line of descent. **12** any of the major subdivisions of the human species; race or ethnic group. **13** the part of a rifle, etc., into which the barrel is set: held by the firer against the shoulder. **14** the handle of something, such as a whip or fishing rod. **15** the main body of a tool, such as the block of a plane. **16** short for **diestock, gunstock,** or **rolling stock. 17** (formerly) the part of a plough to which the irons and handles were attached. **18** the main upright part of a supporting structure. **19** a liquid or broth in which meat, fish, bones, or vegetables have been simmered for a long time. **20** film material before exposure and processing. **21** Also called: **gillyflower.** any of several cruciferous plants such as **evening** or **night-scented stock**, of the Mediterranean region: cultivated for their brightly coloured flowers. **22 Virginian stock.** a similar and related North American plant. **23** a long usually white neckcloth wrapped around the neck, worn in the 18th century and as part of modern riding dress. **24a** the repertoire of plays available to a repertory company. **24b** *(as modifier): a stock play.* **25** a log or block of wood. **26** See **laughing stock. 27 in stock. 27a** stored on the premises or available for sale or use. **27b** supplied with goods of a specified kind. **28 out of stock. 28a** not immediately available for sale or use. **28b** not having goods of a specified kind immediately available. **29 take stock. 29a** to make an inventory. **29b** to make a general appraisal, esp. of prospects, resources, etc. **30 take stock in.** to attach importance to. ◆ *adj* **31** staple; standard: *stock sizes in clothes.* **32** *(prenominal)* being a cliché; hackneyed: *a stock phrase.* ◆ *vb* **33** *(tr)* to keep (goods) for sale. **34** *(intr; usually foll. by up or up on)* to obtain a store of (something) for future use or sale: *to stock up on beer.* **35** *(tr)* to supply with live animals, fish, etc.: *to stock a farm.* **36** *(intr)* (of a plant) to put forth new shoots. **37** *(tr) Obs.* to punish by putting in the stocks. ◆ See also **stocks.** ORIG OE *stocc* trunk (of a tree), stem, stick (the various senses developed from these meanings, as trunk of a tree, hence line of descent; structures made of timber; a store of timber or other goods for future use, hence an aggregate of goods, animals, etc.)
► **'stocker** *n*

stockade (stɒ'keɪd) *n* **1** an enclosure or barrier of stakes and timbers. ◆ *vb* **stockades, stockading, stockaded. 2** *(tr)* to surround with a stockade. ORIG C17: from Sp. *estacada,* from *estaca* a stake, of Gmc origin

stockbreeder ('stɒkˌbriːdə) *n* a person who breeds or rears livestock as an occupation.
► **'stockˌbreeding** *n*

stockbroker ('stɒkˌbrəʊkə) *n* a person who buys and sells securities on a commission basis for customers.
► **'stockˌbrokerage** *or* **'stockˌbroking** *n*

stockbroker belt *n Brit. inf.* the area outside a city, esp. London, in which rich commuters live.

stock car *n* **1** a car, usually a production saloon, strengthened and modified for a form of racing in which the cars often collide. **2** *US & Canad.* a railway wagon for carrying livestock.

stock dove *n* a European dove, smaller than the wood pigeon and having a grey plumage.

stock exchange *n* **1a** a highly organized market facilitating the purchase and sale of securities and operated by professional stockbrokers and market makers according to fixed rules. **1b** a place where securities are regularly traded. **1c** (*as modifier*): *a stock-exchange operator; stock-exchange prices*. **2** the prices or trading activity of a stock exchange: *the stock exchange fell heavily today*. ◆ Also called: **stock market.**

stockfish (ˈstɒkˌfɪʃ) *n, pl* **stockfish** *or* **stockfishes.** fish cured by splitting and drying in the air.

Stockhausen ★ (*German* ˈʃtɔkhauzən) *n* **Karlheinz** (karlˈhaints). born 1928, German composer. His avant-garde works include *Gruppen* (1959) for three orchestras and *Stimmung* (1968) for six vocalists.

stockholder (ˈstɒkˌhəʊldə) *n* **1** an owner of corporate capital stock. **2** *Austral.* a person who keeps livestock.
▸ ˈ**stockˌholding** *n*

Stockholm ★ (ˈstɒkhəʊm; *Swedish* ˈstɔkhɔlm) *n* the capital of Sweden, a port in the E central part at the outflow of Lake Mälar into the Baltic: situated partly on the mainland and partly on islands; traditionally founded about 1250; university (1877). Pop.: 711 119 (1996 est.).

stockhorse (ˈstɒkˌhɔːs) *n Austral.* a stockman's horse.

stockinet (ˌstɒkɪˈnɛt) *n* a machine-knitted elastic fabric used, esp. formerly, for stockings, underwear, etc. ORIG C19: ?from earlier *stocking-net*

stocking (ˈstɒkɪŋ) *n* **1** one of a pair of close-fitting garments made of knitted yarn to cover the foot and part or all of the leg. **2** something resembling this in position, function, etc. **3 in (one's) stocking** *or* **stockinged feet.** wearing stockings or socks but no shoes. ORIG C16: from dialect *stock* stocking + -ING[1]
▸ ˈ**stockinged** *adj*

stocking cap *n* a conical knitted cap, often with a tassel.

stocking filler *n Brit.* a present of a size suitable for inclusion in a Christmas stocking.

stock in trade *n* **1** goods in stock necessary for carrying on a business. **2** anything constantly used by someone as a part of his or her profession, occupation, or trade: *friendliness is the salesman's stock in trade.*

stockist (ˈstɒkɪst) *n Commerce, Brit.* a dealer who undertakes to maintain stocks of a specified product at or above a certain minimum in return for favourable buying terms granted by the manufacturer of the product.

stockjobber (ˈstɒkˌdʒɒbə) *n* **1** *Brit.* (formerly) a wholesale dealer on a stock exchange who sold securities to brokers without transacting directly with the public. See **market maker. 2** *US, disparaging.* a stockbroker, esp. one dealing in worthless securities.
▸ ˈ**stockˌjobbery** *or* ˈ**stockˌjobbing** *n*

stockman (ˈstɒkmən, -ˌmæn) *n, pl* **stockmen. 1a** a man engaged in the rearing or care of farm livestock, esp. cattle. **1b** an owner of cattle or other livestock. **2** *US & Canad.* a man employed in a warehouse or stockroom.

stock market *n* another name for **stock exchange.**

stockpile (ˈstɒkˌpaɪl) *vb* **stockpiles, stockpiling, stockpiled. 1** to acquire and store a large quantity of (something). ◆ *n* **2** a large store or supply accumulated for future use.
▸ ˈ**stockˌpiler** *n*

Stockport ★ (ˈstɒkˌpɔːt) *n* **1** a town in NW England, in Greater Manchester: an early textile centre and scene of several labour disturbances in the early 19th century. Pop.: 132 813 (1991). **2** a unitary authority in NW England, in Greater Manchester. Pop.: 290 567 (1997 est.). Area: 126 sq. km (49 sq. miles).

stockpot (ˈstɒkˌpɒt) *n Chiefly Brit.* a pot in which stock for soup, etc., is made or kept.

stockroom (ˈstɒkˌruːm, -ˌrʊm) *n* a room in which a stock of goods is kept, as in a shop or factory.

stock route *n Austral. & NZ.* a route designated for droving sheep or cattle.

stocks (stɒks) *pl n* **1** *History.* an instrument of punishment consisting of a heavy wooden frame with holes in which the feet, hands, or head of an offender were locked. **2** a frame used to support a boat while under construction. **3** *Naut.* a vertical post or shaft at the forward edge of a rudder, extended upwards for attachment to the steering controls. **4 on the stocks.** in preparation or under construction.

stock-still *adv* absolutely still; motionless.

stocktaking (ˈstɒkˌteɪkɪŋ) *n* **1** the examination, counting, and valuing of goods on hand in a shop or business. **2** a reassessment of one's current situation, progress, prospects, etc.

Stockton[1] ★ (ˈstɒktən) *n* an inland port in central California, on the San Joaquin River: seat of the University of the Pacific (1851). Pop.: 222 633 (1994 est.).

Stockton[2] ★ (ˈstɒktən) *n* **1st Earl of.** title of (Maurice Harold) **Macmillan.**

Stockton-on-Tees ★ *n* **1** a port in NE England, on the River Tees: industrial centre, famous for the **Stockton-Darlington Railway** (1825), the first passenger-carrying railway in the world. Pop.: 82 800 (1996 est.). **2** a unitary authority in NE England, in Co. Durham. Pop.: 179 000 (1996 est.). Area: 195 sq. km (75 sq. miles).

stock watering *n Business.* the creation of more new shares in a company than is justified by its assets.

stock whip *n* a whip with a long lash and a short handle, used to herd cattle, etc.

stocky (ˈstɒkɪ) *adj* **stockier, stockiest.** (usually of a person) thickset; sturdy.
▸ ˈ**stockily** *adv* ▸ ˈ**stockiness** *n*

stockyard (ˈstɒkˌjɑːd) *n* a large yard with pens or covered buildings where farm animals are assembled, sold, etc.

stodge (stɒdʒ) *Inf.* ◆ *n* **1** heavy filling starchy food. **2** a dull person or subject. ◆ *vb* **stodges, stodging, stodged. 3** to stuff (oneself or another) with food. ORIG C17: ? blend of STUFF + *podge*, from *podgy* fat

stodgy (ˈstɒdʒɪ) *adj* **stodgier, stodgiest. 1** (of food) heavy or uninteresting. **2** excessively formal and conventional. ORIG C19: from STODGE
▸ ˈ**stodgily** *adv* ▸ ˈ**stodginess** *n*

stoep (stuːp) *n S. African.* a veranda. ORIG from Afrik., from Du.

stoic (ˈstəʊɪk) *n* **1** a person who maintains stoical qualities. ◆ *adj* **2** a variant of **stoical.**

Stoic (ˈstəʊɪk) *n* **1** a member of the ancient Greek school of philosophy founded by Zeno, holding that virtue and happiness can be attained only by submission to destiny and the natural law. ◆ *adj* **2** of or relating to the doctrines of the Stoics. ORIG C16: via L from Gk *stōikos*, from *stoa*, the porch in Athens where Zeno taught

stoical (ˈstəʊɪkᵊl) *adj* characterized by impassivity or resignation.
▸ ˈ**stoically** *adv*

stoichiometry *or* **stoicheiometry** (ˌstɔɪkɪˈɒmɪtrɪ) *n* the branch of chemistry concerned with the proportions in which elements are combined in compounds and the quantitative relationships between reactants and products in chemical reactions. ORIG C19: from Gk *stoikheion* element + -METRY
▸ ˌ**stoichioˈmetric** *or* ˌ**stoicheioˈmetric** *adj*

stoicism (ˈstəʊɪˌsɪzəm) *n* **1** indifference to pleasure and pain. **2** (*cap.*) the philosophy of the Stoics.

stoke (stəʊk) *vb* **stokes, stoking, stoked. 1** to feed, stir, and tend (a fire, furnace, etc.). **2** (*tr*) to tend the furnace of; act as a stoker for. ORIG C17: back formation from STOKER

stokehold (ˈstəʊkˌhəʊld) *n Naut.* **1** a coal bunker for a ship's furnace. **2** the hold for a ship's boilers; fire room.

stokehole (ˈstəʊkˌhəʊl) *n* **1** another word for **stokehold. 2** a hole in a furnace through which it is stoked.

Stoke-on-Trent ★ (stəʊk-) *n* **1** a city in central England, in N Staffordshire on the River Trent: a major centre of the pottery industry; seat of Staffordshire University (1992). Pop.: 266 543 (1991). **2** a unitary authority in central England, in N Staffordshire. Pop.: 254 400 (1996 est.). Area: 93 sq. km (36 sq. miles).

stoker (ˈstəʊkə) *n* a person employed to tend a furnace, as on a steamship. ORIG C17: from Du., from *stoken* to stoke

Stoker ★ (ˈstəʊkə) *n* **Bram,** original name *Abraham Stoker.* 1847–1912, Irish novelist, author of *Dracula* (1897).

stoke up *vb* (*adv*) **1** to feed and tend (a fire, etc.) with fuel. **2** (*intr*) to fill oneself with food.

Stokowski ★ (stəˈkɒfskɪ) *n* **Leopold.** 1887–1977, US conductor, born in Britain.

STOL (stɒl) *n* **1** a system in which an aircraft can take off and land in a short distance. **2** an aircraft using this system. Cf. **VTOL** ORIG C20: *s(hort) t(ake)o(ff and) l(anding)*

stole[1] (stəʊl) *vb* the past tense of **steal.**

stole[2] (stəʊl) *n* **1** a long scarf or shawl, worn by women. **2** a long narrow scarf worn by various officiating clergymen. ORIG OE *stole,* from L *stola,* from Gk *stolē* clothing

stolen (ˈstəʊlən) *vb* the past participle of **steal.**

stolen generation *n Austral.* Aboriginal children removed from their families and placed in institutions or fostered by White families.

stolid (ˈstɒlɪd) *adj* showing little or no emotion or interest. ORIG C17: from L *stolidus* dull
▸ **stolidity** (stɒˈlɪdɪtɪ) *or* **ˈstolidness** *n* ▸ **ˈstolidly** *adv*

stolon (ˈstəʊlən) *n* **1** another name for **runner** (sense 9). **2** a branching structure in lower animals, esp. the anchoring rootlike part of colonial organisms. ORIG C17: from L *stolō* shoot
▸ **stoloniferous** (ˌstəʊləˈnɪfərəs) *adj*

Stolypin ★ (*Russian* staˈljipin) *n* **Petr Arkadievich** (pjɔtr arˈkadijɪvitʃ). 1863–1911, Russian conservative statesman: prime minister (1906–11). He instituted agrarian reforms but was ruthless in suppressing rebellion: assassinated.

stoma (ˈstəʊmə) *n, pl* **stomata. 1** *Bot.* an epidermal pore in plant leaves, that controls the passage of gases into and out of a plant. **2** *Zool., anat.* a mouth or mouthlike part. **3** *Surgery.* an artificial opening made in a tubular organ, esp. the colon or ileum. See **colostomy, ileostomy.** ORIG C17: via NL from Gk: mouth

stomach (ˈstʌmək) *n* **1** (in vertebrates) the enlarged muscular saclike part of the alimentary canal in which food is stored until it has been partially digested. Related adj: **gastric. 2** the corresponding organ in invertebrates. **3** the abdominal region. **4** desire, appetite, or inclination: *I have no stomach for arguments.* ◆ *vb* (*tr; used mainly in negative constructions*) **5** to tolerate; bear: *I can't stomach his bragging.* **6** to eat or digest: *he cannot stomach oysters.* ORIG C14: from OF *stomaque,* from L *stomachus,* from Gk *stomakhos,* from *stoma* mouth

stomachache (ˈstʌməkˌeɪk) *n* pain in the stomach, as from acute indigestion. Also called: **stomach upset, upset stomach.**

stomacher (ˈstʌməkə) *n* a decorative V-shaped panel of stiff material worn over the chest and stomach by men and women in the 16th century, later only by women.

stomachic (stəˈmækɪk) *adj also* **stomachical. 1** stimulating gastric activity. **2** of or relating to the stomach. ◆ *n* **3** a stomachic medicine.

stomach pump *n Med.* a suction device for removing stomach contents by a tube inserted through the mouth.

stomata (ˈstəʊmətə, ˈstɒm-, stəʊˈmɑːtə) *n* the plural of **stoma.**

stomatitis (ˌstəʊməˈtaɪtɪs, ˌstɒm-) *n* inflammation of the mouth.
▸ **stomatitic** (ˌstəʊməˈtɪtɪk, ˌstɒm-) *adj*

stomato- *or before a vowel* **stomat-** *combining form.* indicating the mouth or a mouthlike part: *stomatology.* ORIG from Gk *stoma, stomat-*

stomatology (ˌstəʊməˈtɒlədʒɪ) *n* the branch of medicine concerned with the mouth.
▸ **stomatological** (ˌstəʊmətəˈlɒdʒɪkᵊl) *adj*

-stome *n combining form.* indicating a mouth or opening resembling a mouth: *peristome.* ORIG from Gk *stoma* mouth, & *stomion* little mouth

-stomous *adj combining form.* having a specified type of mouth.

stomp (stɒmp) *vb* **1** (*intr*) to tread or stamp heavily. ◆ *n* **2** a rhythmic stamping jazz dance. ORIG var. of STAMP
▸ **ˈstomper** *n*

stompie (ˈstɒmpɪ) *n S. African sl.* **1** a cigarette butt. **2** a short man. ORIG Afrik. *stomp* stamp

-stomy *n combining form.* indicating a surgical operation performed to make an artificial opening into or for a specified part: *cytostomy.* ORIG from Gk *-stomia,* from *stoma* mouth

stone (stəʊn) *n* **1** the hard compact nonmetallic material of which rocks are made. **2** a small lump of rock; pebble. **3** short for **gemstone. 4a** a piece of rock designed or shaped for some particular purpose. **4b** (*in combination*): *gravestone; millstone.* **5a** something that resembles a stone. **5b** (*in combination*): *hailstone.* **6** the woody central part of such fruits as the peach and plum, that contains the seed; endocarp. **7** any similar hard part of a fruit, such as the stony seed of a date. **8** (*pl* **stone**) *Brit.* a unit of weight, used esp. to express human body weight, equal to 14 pounds or 6.350 kilograms. **9** Also called: **granite.** the rounded heavy mass of granite or iron used in the game of curling. **10** *Pathol.* a nontechnical name for **calculus. 11** *Printing.* a table with a very flat iron or stone surface upon which pages are composed. **12** (*modifier*) relating to or made of stone: *a stone house.* **13** (*modifier*) made of stoneware: *a stone jar.* **14 cast a stone** (**at**). cast aspersions (upon). **15 heart of stone.** an obdurate or unemotional nature. **16 leave no stone unturned.** to do everything possible to achieve an end. ◆ *vb* **stones, stoning, stoned.** (*tr*) **17** to throw stones at, esp. to kill. **18** to remove the stones from. **19** to furnish or provide with stones. ORIG OE *stān*
▸ **ˈstoner** *n*

Stone ★ (stəʊn) *n* **1 Oliver.** born 1946, US film director: his films include *Platoon* (1986), *JFK* (1991), and *U-Turn* (1998). **2 Sharon.** born 1958, US film actress: her films include *Casino* (1995) and *Sphere* (1998).

stone- *prefix* very, completely: *stone-blind, stone-cold.* ORIG from STONE in sense of "like a stone"

Stone Age *n* **1** a period in human culture identified by the use of stone implements. ◆ *modifier.* **Stone-Age. 2** (*sometimes not caps.*) of or relating to this period.

stone-blind *adj* completely blind. Cf. **sand-blind.**

stonechat (ˈstəʊnˌtʃæt) *n* an Old World songbird having a black plumage with a reddish-brown breast. ORIG C18: from its cry, which sounds like clattering pebbles

stone-cold *adj* **1** completely cold. **2 stone-cold sober.** completely sober.

stonecrop (ˈstəʊnˌkrɒp) *n* any of various N temperate plants having fleshy leaves and typically red, yellow, or white flowers.

stone curlew *n* any of several brownish shore birds having a large head and eyes. Also called: **thick-knee.**

stonecutter (ˈstəʊnˌkʌtə) *n* **1** a person who is skilled in cutting and carving stone. **2** a machine used to dress stone.
▸ **ˈstoneˌcutting** *n*

stoned (stəʊnd) *adj Sl.* under the influence of drugs or alcohol.

stone-deaf *adj* completely deaf.

stonefish (ˈstəʊnˌfɪʃ) *n, pl* **stonefish** *or* **stonefishes.** a venomous tropical marine fish that resembles a piece of rock on the seabed.

stonefly (ˈstəʊnˌflaɪ) *n, pl* **stoneflies.** any of various insects, in which the larvae are aquatic, living beneath stones.

stone fruit *n* the nontechnical name for **drupe.**

Stonehenge ★ (ˌstəʊnˈhɛndʒ) *n* a prehistoric ruin in S England, in Wiltshire on Salisbury Plain: constructed over the period of roughly 2500–1500 B.C.; one of the most important megalithic monuments in Europe; believed to have had religious and astronomical purposes.

stonemason (ˈstəʊnˌmeɪsᵊn) *n* a person who is skilled in preparing stone for building.
▸ **ˈstoneˌmasonry** *n*

stone pine *n* a pine tree with a short bole and radiating branches forming an umbrella shape.

Stones ★ (stəʊnz) *pl n* **the.** See **Rolling Stones.**

stone's throw *n* a short distance.

★ people and places

stonewall (ˌstəʊnˈwɔːl) *vb* **1** (*intr*) *Cricket.* (of a batsman) to play defensively. **2** to obstruct (an investigation, etc.), esp. by giving uncommunicative answers to questioning. **3** to obstruct or hinder (parliamentary business).
▸ **ˌstoneˈwaller** *n*

stoneware (ˈstəʊnˌwɛə) *n* **1** a hard opaque pottery, fired at a very high temperature. ◆ *adj* **2** made of stoneware.

stonewashed (ˈstəʊnˌwɒʃt) *adj* (of clothes or fabric) given a worn faded look by being subjected to the abrasive action of many small pieces of pumice.

stonework (ˈstəʊnˌwɜːk) *n* **1** any structure or part of a building made of stone. **2** the process of dressing or setting stones.
▸ **ˈstoneˌworker** *n*

stonkered (ˈstɒŋkəd) *adj Sl.* completely exhausted or beaten. ORIG C20: from *stonker* to beat, from ?

stony *or* **stoney** (ˈstəʊnɪ) *adj* **stonier, stoniest. 1** of or resembling stone. **2** abounding in stone or stones. **3** unfeeling or obdurate. **4** short for **stony-broke.**
▸ **ˈstonily** *adv* ▸ **ˈstoniness** *n*

stony-broke *adj Brit. sl.* completely without money; penniless.

stony-hearted *adj* unfeeling; hardhearted.
▸ **ˌstony-ˈheartedness** *n*

stood (stʊd) *vb* the past tense and past participle of **stand.**

stooge (stuːdʒ) *n* **1** an actor who feeds lines to a comedian or acts as his or her butt. **2** *Sl.* someone who is taken advantage of by another. ◆ *vb* **stooges, stooging, stooged. 3** (*intr*) *Sl.* to act as a stooge. ORIG C20: from ?

stook (stuːk) *n* **1** a number of sheaves set upright in a field to dry with their heads together. ◆ *vb* **2** (*tr*) to set up (sheaves) in stooks. ORIG C15: var. of *stouk,* of Gmc origin
▸ **ˈstooker** *n*

stool (stuːl) *n* **1** a backless seat or footrest consisting of a small flat piece of wood, etc., resting on three or four legs, a pedestal, etc. **2** a rootstock or base of a plant from which shoots, etc., are produced. **3** a cluster of shoots growing from such a base. **4** *Chiefly US.* a decoy used in hunting. **5** waste matter evacuated from the bowels. **6** a lavatory seat. **7** (in W Africa, esp. Ghana) a chief's throne. **8 fall between two stools. 8a** to fail through vacillation between two alternatives. **8b** to be in an unsatisfactory situation through not belonging to either of two categories or groups. ◆ *vb* (*intr*) **9** (of a plant) to send up shoots from the base of the stem, rootstock, etc. **10** to lure wildfowl with a decoy. ORIG OE *stōl*

stool ball *n* a game resembling cricket, still played by girls and women in Sussex, England.

stool pigeon *n* **1** an informer for the police. **2** *Sl.* a person acting as a decoy. ORIG C19: from use of pigeon fixed to a stool as a decoy

stoop[1] (stuːp) *vb* (*mainly intr*) **1** (*also tr*) to bend (the body) forward and downward. **2** to carry oneself with head and shoulders habitually bent forward. **3** (often foll. by *to*) to abase or degrade oneself. **4** (often foll. by *to*) to condescend; deign. **5** (of a bird of prey) to swoop down. ◆ *n* **6** the act, position, or characteristic of stooping. **7** a lowering from a position of dignity or superiority. **8** a downward swoop, esp. of a bird of prey. ORIG OE *stūpan*
▸ **ˈstooping** *adj*

stoop[2] (stuːp) *n US.* an open porch or small platform with steps leading up to it at the entrance to a building. ORIG C18: from Du. *stoep,* of Gmc origin

stop (stɒp) *vb* **stops, stopping, stopped. 1** to cease from doing or being (something); discontinue. **2** to cause (something moving) to halt or (of something moving) to come to a halt. **3** (*tr*) to prevent the continuance or completion of. **4** (*tr;* often foll. by *from*) to prevent or restrain: *to stop George from fighting.* **5** (*tr*) to keep back: *to stop supplies.* **6** (*tr*) to intercept or hinder in transit: *to stop a letter.* **7** (*tr;* often foll. by *up*) to block or plug, esp. so as to close: *to stop up a pipe.* **8** (*tr;* often foll. by *up*) to fill a hole or opening in: *to stop up a wall.* **9** (*tr*) to staunch or stem: *to stop a wound.* **10** (*tr*) to instruct a bank not to honour (a cheque). **11** (*tr*) to deduct (money) from pay. **12** (*tr*) *Brit.* to provide with punctuation. **13** (*tr*) *Boxing.* to beat (an opponent) by a knockout. **14** (*tr*) *Inf.* to receive (a blow, hit, etc.). **15** (*intr*) to stay or rest: *we stopped at the Robinsons'.* **16** (*tr*) *Rare.* to defeat, beat, or kill. **17** (*tr*) *Music.* **17a** to alter the vibrating length of (a string on a violin, guitar, etc.) by pressing down on it at some point with the finger. **17b** to alter the vibrating length of an air column in a wind instrument by closing (a finger hole, etc.). **17c** to produce (a note) in this manner. **18** *Bridge.* to have a protecting card or winner in (a suit in which one's opponents are strong). **19 stop at nothing.** to be prepared to do anything; be unscrupulous or ruthless. ◆ *n* **20** an arrest of movement or progress. **21** the act of stopping or the state of being stopped. **22** a place where something halts or pauses: *a bus stop.* **23** a stay in or as if in the course of a journey. **24** the act or an instance of blocking or obstructing. **25** a plug or stopper. **26** a block, screw, etc., that prevents, limits, or terminates the motion of a mechanism or moving part. **27** *Brit.* a punctuation mark, esp. a full stop. **28** *Music.* **28a** the act of stopping the string, finger hole, etc., of an instrument. **28b** a set of organ pipes or harpsichord strings that may be allowed to sound as a group by muffling or silencing all other such sets. **28c** a knob, lever, or handle on an organ, etc., that is operated to allow sets of pipes to sound. **28d** an analogous device on a harpsichord or other instrument with variable registers, such as an electronic instrument. **29 pull out all the stops. 29a** to play at full volume. **29b** to spare no effort. **30** Also called: **stop consonant.** *Phonetics.* any of a class of consonants articulated by first making a complete closure at some point of the vocal tract and then releasing it abruptly with audible plosion. **31** Also called: **f-stop.** *Photog.* **31a** a setting of the aperture of a camera lens, calibrated to the corresponding f-number. **31b** another name for **diaphragm** (sense 4). **32** Also called: **stopper.** *Bridge.* a protecting card or winner in a suit in which one's opponents are strong. ◆ See also **stop off, stop out, stopover.** ORIG C14: from OE *stoppian* (unattested), as in *forstoppian* to plug the ear, ult. from LL *stuppāre* to stop with tow, from L *stuppa* tow, from Gk *stuppē*
▸ **ˈstoppable** *adj*

stopbank (ˈstɒpbæŋk) *n NZ.* an embankment to prevent flooding.

stop bath *n* a weakly acidic solution used to stop the action of a developer on a film, plate, or paper before the material is immersed in fixer.

stopcock (ˈstɒpˌkɒk) *n* a valve used to control or stop the flow of a fluid in a pipe.

stope (stəʊp) *n* **1** a steplike excavation made in a mine to extract ore. ◆ *vb* **stopes, stoping, stoped. 2** to mine (ore, etc.) in stopes. ORIG C18: prob. from Low G *stope*

Stopes ★ (stəʊps) *n* **Marie Carmichael.** 1880–1958, British pioneer of birth control, who established the first clinic in Britain (1921).

stopgap (ˈstɒpˌgæp) *n* **a** a temporary substitute. **b** (*as modifier*): *a stopgap programme.*

stop-go *adj Brit.* (of economic policy) characterized by deliberate alternate expansion and contraction of aggregate demand in an effort to curb inflation and eliminate balance-of-payments deficits, and yet maintain full employment.

stoplight (ˈstɒpˌlaɪt) *n* **1** a red light on a traffic signal indicating that vehicles or pedestrians coming towards it should stop. **2** another word for **brake light.**

stop-loss *adj Business.* of or relating to an order to a broker in a commodity or security market to close an open position at a specified price in order to limit any loss.

stop off *vb also* **stop in,** (esp. US) **stop by. 1** (*intr, adv;* often foll. by *at*) to halt and call somewhere, as on a visit or errand, esp. en route to another place. ◆ *n* **stopoff. 2a** a break in a journey. **2b** (*as modifier*): *stopoff point.*

stop out *vb* (*adv*) **1** (*tr*) to cover (part of the area) of a piece of cloth, printing plate, etc., to prevent it from being dyed, etched, etc. **2** (*intr*) to remain out of a house, esp. overnight.

stopover (ˈstɒpˌəʊvə) *n* **1** a stopping place on a journey. ◆ *vb* **stop over. 2** (*intr, adv*) to make a stopover.

stoppage (ˈstɒpɪdʒ) *n* **1** the act of stopping or the state of being stopped. **2** something that stops or blocks. **3** a deduction of money, as from pay. **4** an organized cessation of work, as during a strike.

stoppage time *n Soccer, rugby, etc.* another name for **injury time.**

Stoppard ★ ('stɒpɑːd) *n* Sir **Tom**, original name *Thomas Straussler.* born 1937, British playwright, born in Czechoslovakia: his works include *Rosencrantz and Guildenstern are Dead* (1967), *Jumpers* (1972), and *Invention of Love* (1997).

stopped (stɒpt) *adj* (of a pipe, esp. an organ pipe) closed at one end and thus sounding an octave lower than an open pipe of the same length.

stopper ('stɒpə) *n* **1** Also called: **stopple.** a plug or bung for closing a bottle, pipe, duct, etc. **2** a person or thing that stops or puts an end to something. **3** *Bridge.* another name for **stop** (sense 32). ◆ *vb* **4** (*tr*) Also: **stopple.** to close or fit with a stopper.

stopping ('stɒpɪŋ) *n* **1** *Brit. inf.* a dental filling. ◆ *adj* **2** *Chiefly Brit.* making many stops in a journey: *a stopping train.*

stop press *n Brit.* **1** news items inserted into a newspaper after the printing has been started. **2** the space regularly left blank for this.

stopwatch ('stɒpˌwɒtʃ) *n* a type of watch used for timing sporting events, etc., accurately, having a device for stopping the hands instantly.

storage ('stɔːrɪdʒ) *n* **1** the act of storing or the state of being stored. **2** space or an area reserved for storing. **3** a charge made for storing. **4** *Computing.* **4a** the act or process of storing information in a computer memory or on a disk, etc. **4b** (*as modifier*): *storage capacity.*

storage battery *n* another name (esp. US) for **accumulator** (sense 1).

storage capacity *n* the maximum number of bits, bytes, words, etc., that can be held in a memory system such as that of a computer or of the brain.

storage device *n* a piece of computer equipment, such as a magnetic tape, disk, drum, etc., in or on which information can be stored.

storage heater *n* an electric device capable of accumulating and radiating heat generated by off-peak electricity.

storax ('stɔːræks) *n* **1** any of numerous trees or shrubs of tropical and subtropical regions, having drooping showy white flowers. **2** a vanilla-scented solid resin obtained from one of these trees, formerly used as incense and in perfumery and medicine. **3** a liquid aromatic balsam obtained from liquidambar trees and used in perfumery and medicine. ORIG C14: via LL from Gk *sturax*

store (stɔː) *vb* **stores, storing, stored. 1** (*tr*) to keep, set aside, or accumulate for future use. **2** (*tr*) to place in a warehouse, depository, etc., for safekeeping. **3** (*tr*) to supply, provide, or stock. **4** (*intr*) to be put into storage. **5** *Computing.* to enter or retain (information) in a storage device. ◆ *n* **6a** an establishment for the retail sale of goods and services. **6b** (*in combination*): *storefront.* **7** a large supply or stock kept for future use. **8** short for **department store. 9a** a storage place such as a warehouse or depository. **9b** (*in combination*): *storeman.* **10** the state of being stored (esp. in **in store**). **11** a large amount or quantity. **12** *Computers, chiefly Brit.* another name for **memory** (sense 7). **13 in store.** forthcoming or imminent. **14 lay, put,** *or* **set store by.** to value or reckon as important. ◆ *adj* **15** (of cattle, sheep, etc.) bought lean to be fattened up for market. ◆ See also **stores.** ORIG C13: from OF *estor,* from *estorer* to restore, from L *instaurāre* to refresh
▸ **'storable** *adj*

Store Bælt ★ ('sdoːrə 'bɛld) *n* the Danish name for the **Great Belt.**

store card *n* another name for **charge card.**

storehouse ('stɔːˌhaʊs) *n* a place where things are stored.

storekeeper ('stɔːˌkiːpə) *n* a manager, owner, or keeper of a store.
▸ **'storeˌkeeping** *n*

store of value *n Econ.* the function of money that enables goods and services to be paid for a considerable time after they have been acquired.

storeroom ('stɔːˌruːm, -ˌrʊm) *n* **1** a room in which things are stored. **2** room for storing.

stores (stɔːz) *pl n* supply or stock of something, esp. essentials, for a specific purpose.

storey *or esp. US* **story** ('stɔːrɪ) *n, pl* **storeys** *or* **stories. 1** a floor or level of a building. **2** a set of rooms on one level. ORIG C14: from Anglo-L *historia,* picture, from L: narrative, prob. from the pictures on medieval windows

Storey ★ ('stɔːrɪ) *n* **David** (**Malcolm**). born 1933, British novelist and dramatist. His works include the novel *This Sporting Life* (1960) and the plays *Home* (1970) and *Stages* (1992).

storeyed *or US* **storied** ('stɔːrɪd) *adj* **a** having a storey or storeys. **b** (*in combination*): *a two-storeyed house.*

storied ('stɔːrɪd) *adj* **1** recorded in history or in a story. **2** decorated with narrative scenes.

stork (stɔːk) *n* any of a family of large wading birds, chiefly of warm regions of the Old World, having very long legs and a long stout pointed bill, and typically having a white-and-black plumage. ORIG OE *storc*

storksbill ('stɔːksˌbɪl) *n* a plant related to the geranium, having pink or reddish-purple flowers and fruits with a beaklike process.

storm (stɔːm) *n* **1a** a violent weather condition of strong winds, rain, hail, thunder, lightning, blowing sand, snow, etc. **1b** (*as modifier*): *storm cloud.* **1c** (*in combination*): *stormproof.* **2** *Meteorol.* a wind of force 10 on the Beaufort scale, reaching speeds of 55 to 63 mph. **3** a strong or violent reaction: *a storm of protest.* **4** a direct assault on a stronghold. **5** a heavy discharge or rain, as of bullets or missiles. **6** short for **storm window. 7 storm in a teacup.** *Brit.* a violent fuss or disturbance over a trivial matter. **8 take by storm. 8a** to capture or overrun by a violent assault. **8b** to overwhelm and enthral. ◆ *vb* **9** to attack or capture (something) suddenly and violently. **10** (*intr*) to be vociferously angry. **11** (*intr*) to move or rush violently or angrily. **12** (*intr;* with *it* as subject) to rain, hail, or snow hard and be very windy, often with thunder and lightning. ORIG OE

stormbound ('stɔːmˌbaʊnd) *adj* detained or harassed by storms.

storm centre *n* **1** the centre of a cyclonic storm, etc., where pressure is lowest. **2** the centre of any disturbance or trouble.

storm cloud *n* **1** a heavy dark cloud presaging rain or a storm. **2** a herald of disturbance, anger, etc.: *the storm clouds of war.*

storm-cock *n* another name for **mistle thrush.**

storm cone *n Brit.* a canvas cone hoisted as a warning of high winds.

storm door *n* an additional door outside an ordinary door, providing extra insulation against wind, cold, rain, etc.

storming ('stɔːmɪŋ) *adj Inf.* characterized by or displaying dynamism, speed, and energy: *a storming performance.*

storm lantern *n* another name for **hurricane lamp.**

Stormont ★ ('stɔːmənt) *n* a suburb of Belfast: site of Parliament House (1928–30), formerly the seat of the parliament of Northern Ireland (1922–72) and (from 1998) seat of the Northern Ireland Assembly; Stormont House, formerly the residence of the prime minister of Northern Ireland; and Stormont Castle.

storm trooper *n* **1** a member of the Nazi SA. **2** a member of a force of shock troops.

storm window *n* **1** an additional window fitted outside an ordinary window to provide insulation against wind, cold, rain, etc. **2** a type of dormer window.

stormy ('stɔːmɪ) *adj* **stormier, stormiest. 1** characterized by storms. **2** involving or characterized by violent disturbance or emotional outburst.
▸ **'stormily** *adv* ▸ **'storminess** *n*

stormy petrel *n* **1** Also called: **storm petrel.** any of various small petrels typically having dark plumage and paler underparts. **2** a person who brings or portends trouble.

Stornoway ★ ('stɔːnəˌweɪ) *n* a port in NW Scotland, on the E coast of Lewis in the Outer Hebrides, administrative centre of the Western Isles. Pop.: 5975 (1991).

Storting *or* **Storthing** ('stɔːtɪŋ) *n* the parliament of Norway. ORIG C19: Norwegian, from *stor* great + *thing* assembly

story[1] ('stɔːrɪ) *n, pl* **stories.** **1** a narration of a chain of events told or written in prose or verse. **2** Also called: **short story.** a piece of fiction, briefer and usually less detailed than a novel. **3** Also called: **story line.** the plot of a book, film, etc. **4** an event that could be the subject of a narrative. **5** a report or statement on a matter or event. **6** the event or material for such a report. **7** *Inf.* a lie, fib, or untruth. **8 cut** (*or* **make**) **a long story short.** to leave out details in a narration. **9 the same old story.** *Inf.* the familiar or regular course of events. **10 the story goes.** it is commonly said or believed. ◆ *vb* **stories, storying, storied.** (*tr*) **11** to decorate (a pot, wall, etc.) with scenes from history or legends. ORIG C13: from Anglo-F *estorie,* from L *historia;* see HISTORY

story[2] ('stɔːrɪ) *n, pl* **stories.** another spelling (esp. US) of **storey.**

storyboard ('stɔːrɪˌbɔːd) *n* (in films, television, etc.) a series of sketches or photographs showing the sequence of shots or images planned for a film.

storybook ('stɔːrɪˌbʊk) *n* **1** a book containing stories, esp. for children. ◆ *adj* **2** unreal or fantastic: *a storybook world.*

storyteller ('stɔːrɪˌtɛlə) *n* **1** a person who tells stories. **2** *Inf.* a liar.
▸ **'story,telling** *n*

Stoss ★ (*German* ʃtoːs) *n* **Viet** (faɪət). ?1445–1533, German Gothic sculptor and woodcarver. His masterpiece is the high altar in the Church of St Mary, Cracow (1477–89).

stoup *or* **stoop** (stuːp) *n* **1** a small basin for holy water. **2** *Dialect.* a bucket or cup. ORIG C14 (in the sense: bucket): from ON

Stour ★ ('staʊə) *n* any of several rivers in England, including the Great Stour in Kent.

Stourbridge ★ ('staʊəˌbrɪdʒ) *n* an industrial town in W central England, in the West Midlands. Pop.: 55 624 (1991).

stoush (staʊʃ) *Austral. & NZ sl.* ◆ *vb* **1** (*tr*) to hit or punch. ◆ *n* **2** fighting, violence, or a fight. ORIG C19: from ?

stout (staʊt) *adj* **1** solidly built or corpulent. **2** (*prenominal*) resolute or valiant: *stout fellow.* **3** strong, substantial, and robust. **4 a stout heart.** courage; resolution. ◆ *n* **5** strong porter highly flavoured with malt. ORIG C14: from OF *estout* bold, of Gmc origin
▸ **'stoutly** *adv* ▸ **'stoutness** *n*

Stout ★ (staʊt) *n* Sir **Robert.** 1844–1930, New Zealand statesman, born in Scotland: prime minister of New Zealand (1884–87).

stouthearted (ˌstaʊt'hɑːtɪd) *adj* valiant; brave.
▸ **ˌstout'heartedly** *adv* ▸ **ˌstout'heartedness** *n*

stove[1] (stəʊv) *n* **1** another word for **cooker** (sense 1). **2** any heating apparatus, such as a kiln. ORIG OE *stofa* bathroom

stove[2] (stəʊv) *vb* a past tense and past participle of **stave.**

stove enamel *n* a type of enamel made heatproof by treatment in a stove.

stovepipe ('stəʊvˌpaɪp) *n* **1** a pipe that serves as a flue to a stove. **2** Also called: **stovepipe hat.** a man's tall silk hat.

stow (stəʊ) *vb* (*tr*) **1** (often foll. by *away*) to pack or store. **2** to fill by packing. **3** *Naut.* to pack or put away (cargo, sails, etc.). **4** to have enough room for. **5** (*usually imperative*) *Brit. sl.* to cease from: *stow your noise!* ORIG OE *stōwian* to keep, from *stōw* a place

Stow ★ (stəʊ) *n* **John.** 1525–1605, English antiquary, noted for his *Survey of London and Westminster* (1598; 1603).

stowage ('stəʊɪdʒ) *n* **1** space, room, or a charge for stowing goods. **2** the act or an instance of stowing or the state of being stowed. **3** something that is stowed.

stowaway ('stəʊəˌweɪ) *n* **1** a person who hides aboard a vehicle, ship, or aircraft in order to gain free passage. ◆ *vb* **stow away.** **2** (*intr, adv*) to travel in such a way.

Stowe ★ (stəʊ) *n* **Harriet Elizabeth Beecher.** 1811–96, US writer, whose bestselling novel *Uncle Tom's Cabin* (1852) contributed to the antislavery cause.

STP *abbrev. for:* **1** Professor of Sacred Theology. ORIG from L: *Sanctae Theologiae Professor* **2** *Trademark.* scientifically treated petroleum: an oil substitute promising renewed power for an internal-combustion engine. **3** standard temperature and pressure. ◆ *n* **4** a synthetic hallucinogenic drug related to mescaline. ORIG from humorous reference to the extra power resulting from scientifically treated petroleum

Strabane ★ (strə'bæn) *n* a district of W Northern Ireland, bordering the Irish Republic: agriculture, textiles. Administrative centre: Strabane. Pop.: 36 141 (1991). Area: 862 sq. km (333 sq. miles).

strabismus (strə'bɪzməs) *n* abnormal alignment of one or both eyes, characterized by a turning inwards or outwards from the nose: caused by paralysis of an eye muscle, etc. Also called: **squint.** ORIG C17: via NL from Gk *strabismos,* from *strabizein* to squint, from *strabos* cross-eyed
▸ **stra'bismal, stra'bismic,** *or* **stra'bismical** *adj*

Strabo ★ ('streɪbəʊ) *n* ?63 B.C.–?23 A.D., Greek geographer and historian, noted for his *Geographica.*

Strachey ★ ('streɪtʃɪ) *n* (**Giles**) **Lytton.** 1880–1932, British biographer, best known for *Eminent Victorians* (1918) and *Queen Victoria* (1921).

straddle ('stræd°l) *vb* **straddles, straddling, straddled.** **1** (*tr*) to have one leg, part, or support on each side of. **2** (*tr*) *US & Canad. inf.* to be in favour of both sides of (something). **3** (*intr*) to stand, walk, or sit with the legs apart. **4** (*tr*) to spread (the legs) apart. **5** *Gunnery.* to fire a number of shots slightly beyond and slightly short of (a target) to determine the correct range. **6** (*intr*) (in poker, of the second player after the dealer) to double the ante before looking at one's cards. ◆ *n* **7** the act or position of straddling. **8** a noncommittal attitude or stand. **9** *Business.* a contract or option permitting its purchaser either to sell or buy securities or commodities within a specified period of time at specified prices. **10** *Athletics.* a high-jumping technique in which the body is parallel with the bar and the legs straddle it at the highest point of the jump. **11** (in poker) the stake put up after the ante in poker by the second player after the dealer. ORIG C16: from obs. *strad-* (OE *strode*), past stem of STRIDE
▸ **'straddler** *n*

Stradivari ★ (ˌstrædɪ'vɑːrɪ) *n* **Antonio** (an'tɔːnjo). ?1644–1737, Italian violin, viola, and cello maker.

Stradivarius (ˌstrædɪ'veərɪəs) *n* any of a number of violins manufactured by Antonio Stradivari or his family. Often shortened to (informal) **Strad.**

strafe (streɪf, strɑːf) *vb* **strafes, strafing, strafed.** (*tr*) **1** to machine-gun (troops, etc.) from the air. **2** *Sl.* to punish harshly. ◆ *n* **3** an act or instance of strafing. ORIG C20: from G *strafen* to punish
▸ **'strafer** *n*

Strafford ★ ('stræfəd) *n* **Thomas Wentworth,** Earl of. 1593–1641, English statesman. Lord deputy of Ireland (1632–39) and a chief adviser to Charles I, he was impeached by Parliament and executed.

straggle ('stræg°l) *vb* **straggles, straggling, straggled.** (*intr*) **1** to go, come, or spread in a rambling or irregular way. **2** to linger behind or wander from a main line or part. ORIG C14: from ?
▸ **'straggler** *n* ▸ **'straggly** *adj*

straight (streɪt) *adj* **1** not curved or crooked; continuing in the same direction without deviating. **2** straightforward, outright, or candid: *a straight rejection.* **3** even, level, or upright. **4** in keeping with the facts; accurate. **5** honest, respectable, or reliable. **6** accurate or logical: *straight reasoning.* **7** continuous; uninterrupted. **8** (esp. of an alcoholic drink) undiluted; neat. **9** not crisp, kinked, or curly: *straight hair.* **10** correctly arranged; orderly. **11**

(of a play, acting style, etc.) straightforward or serious. **12** *Boxing.* (of a blow) delivered with an unbent arm: *a straight left.* **13** (of the cylinders of an internal-combustion engine) in line, rather than in a V-formation or in some other arrangement: *a straight eight.* **14** a slang word for **heterosexual. 15** *Inf.* no longer owing or being owed something: *if you buy the next round we'll be straight.* **16** *Sl.* conventional in views, customs, appearance, etc. **17** *Sl.* not using narcotics. ♦ *adv* **18** in a straight line or direct course. **19** immediately; at once: *he came straight back.* **20** in an even, level, or upright position. **21** without cheating, lying, or unreliability: *tell it to me straight.* **22** continuously; uninterruptedly. **23** (often foll. by *out*) frankly; candidly: *he told me straight out.* **24 go straight.** *Inf.* to reform after having been dishonest or a criminal. ♦ *n* **25** the state of being straight. **26** a straight line, form, part, or position. **27** *Brit.* a straight part of a racetrack. **28** *Poker.* **28a** five cards that are in sequence irrespective of suit. **28b** a hand containing such a sequence. **28c** (*as modifier*): *a straight flush.* **29** *Sl.* a conventional person. **30** *Sl.* a heterosexual person. **31** *Sl.* a cigarette containing only tobacco, without marijuana, etc. ORIG C14: from p.p. of OE *streccan* to stretch
▸ **'straightly** *adv* ▸ **'straightness** *n*

straight and narrow *n Inf.* the proper, honest, and moral path of behaviour.

straight angle *n* an angle of 180°.

straightaway *adv* (ˌstreɪtəˈweɪ). *also* **straight away. 1** at once. ♦ *n* (ˈstreɪtəˌweɪ). **2** the US word for **straight** (sense 27).

straight chair *n* a straight-backed side chair.

straightedge (ˈstreɪtˌɛdʒ) *n* a stiff strip of wood or metal with one edge straight, used for ruling and testing straight lines.

straighten (ˈstreɪtᵊn) *vb* (sometimes foll. by *up* or *out*) **1** to make or become straight. **2** (*tr*) to make neat or tidy.
▸ **'straightener** *n*

straighten out *vb* (*adv*) **1** to make or become less complicated or confused. **2** *US & Canad.* to reform or become reformed.

straight face *n* a serious facial expression, esp. one that conceals the impulse to laugh.
▸ **'straight-'faced** *adj*

straight fight *n* a contest between two candidates only.

straight flush *n* (in poker) five consecutive cards of the same suit.

straightforward (ˌstreɪtˈfɔːwəd) *adj* **1** (of a person) honest, frank, or simple. **2** *Chiefly Brit.* (of a task, etc.) simple; easy. ♦ *adv, adj* **3** in a straight course.
▸ **ˌstraight'forwardly** *adv* ▸ **ˌstraight'forwardness** *n*

straightjacket (ˈstreɪtˌdʒækɪt) *n* a less common spelling of **straitjacket.**

straight-laced *adj* a variant spelling of **strait-laced.**

straight man *n* a subsidiary actor who acts as stooge to a comedian.

straight-out *adj US inf.* **1** complete; thoroughgoing. **2** frank or honest.

straight razor *n* another name for **cut-throat** (sense 2).

straightway (ˈstreɪtˌweɪ) *adv Arch.* at once.

strain[1] (streɪn) *vb* **1** to draw or be drawn taut; stretch tight. **2** to exert, tax, or use (resources) to the utmost extent. **3** to injure or damage or be injured or damaged by overexertion: *he strained himself.* **4** to deform or be deformed as a result of a stress. **5** (*intr*) to make intense or violent efforts; strive. **6** to subject or be subjected to mental tension or stress. **7** to pour or pass (a substance) or (of a substance) to be poured or passed through a sieve, filter, or strainer. **8** (*tr*) to draw off or remove (one part of a substance or mixture from another) by or as if by filtering. **9** (*tr*) to clasp tightly; hug. **10** (*intr;* foll. by *at*) to push, pull, or work with violent exertion (upon). ♦ *n* **11** the act or an instance of straining. **12** the damage resulting from excessive exertion. **13** an intense physical or mental effort. **14** (*often pl*) *Music.* a theme, melody, or tune. **15** a great demand on the emotions, resources, etc. **16** a way of speaking; tone of voice: *don't go on in that strain.* **17** tension or tiredness resulting from overwork, worry, etc.; stress. **18** *Physics.* the change in dimension of a body under load expressed as the ratio of the total deflection or change in dimension to the original unloaded dimension. ORIG C13: from OF *estreindre* to press together, from L *stringere* to bind tightly

strain[2] (streɪn) *n* **1** the main body of descendants from one ancestor. **2** a group of organisms within a species or variety, distinguished by one or more minor characteristics. **3** a variety of bacterium or fungus, esp. one used for a culture. **4** a streak; trace. **5** *Arch.* a kind, type, or sort. ORIG OE *strēon*

strained (streɪnd) *adj* **1** (of an action, expression, etc.) not natural or spontaneous. **2** (of an atmosphere, relationship, etc.) not relaxed; tense.

strainer (ˈstreɪnə) *n* **1** a sieve used for straining sauces, vegetables, tea, etc. **2** a gauze or simple filter used to strain liquids.

strait (streɪt) *n* **1** (*often pl*) a narrow channel of the sea linking two larger areas of sea. **2** (*often pl*) a position of acute difficulty (often in **in dire** *or* **desperate straits**). **3** *Arch.* a narrow place or passage. ♦ *adj* **4** *Arch.* (of spaces, etc.) affording little room. ORIG C13: from OF *estreit* narrow, from L *strictus* constricted, from *stringere* to bind tightly
▸ **'straitly** *adv* ▸ **'straitness** *n*

straiten (ˈstreɪtᵊn) *vb* **1** (*tr; usually passive*) to embarrass or distress, esp. financially. **2** (*tr*) to limit, confine, or restrict. **3** *Arch.* to make or become narrow.

straitjacket (ˈstreɪtˌdʒækɪt) *n* **1** Also: **straightjacket.** a jacket made of strong canvas material with long sleeves for binding the arms of violent prisoners or mental patients. **2** a restriction or limitation. ♦ *vb* **3** (*tr*) to confine in or as if in a straitjacket.

strait-laced *or* **straight-laced** *adj* prudish or puritanical.

Straits Settlements ★ (streɪts) *n* (*functioning as sing*) (formerly) a British crown colony of SE Asia that included Singapore, Penang, Malacca, Labuan, and some smaller islands.

strake (streɪk) *n* **1a** a curved metal plate forming part of the metal rim on a wooden wheel. **1b** any metal plate let into a rubber tyre. **2** Also called: **streak.** *Naut.* one of a continuous range of planks or plates forming the side of a vessel. ORIG C14: rel. to OE *streccan* to stretch

Stralsund ★ (*German* ˈʃtraːlzʊnt) *n* a port in NE Germany, on a strait of the Baltic: one of the leading towns of the Hanseatic League. Pop.: 71 620 (1991).

stramonium (strəˈməʊnɪəm) *n* **1** a preparation of the dried leaves and flowers of the thorn apple, containing hyoscyamine and used as a drug to treat nervous disorders. **2** another name for **thorn apple** (sense 1). ORIG C17: from NL, from ?

strand[1] (strænd) *vb* **1** to leave or drive (ships, fish, etc.) aground or ashore or (of ships, etc.) to be left or driven ashore. **2** (*tr; usually passive*) to leave helpless, as without transport, money, etc. ♦ *n* **3** *Chiefly poetic.* a shore or beach. ORIG OE

strand[2] (strænd) *n* **1** a set of or one of the individual fibres or threads of string, wire, etc., that form a rope, cable, etc. **2** a single length of string, hair, wool, wire, etc. **3** a string of pearls or beads. **4** a constituent element of something. ♦ *vb* **5** (*tr*) to form (a rope, cable, etc.) by winding strands together. ORIG C15: from ?

Strand ★ (strænd) *n* **the.** a street in W central London, parallel to the Thames: famous for its hotels and theatres.

strange (streɪndʒ) *adj* **1** odd, unusual, or extraordinary; peculiar. **2** not known, seen, or experienced before; unfamiliar. **3** not easily explained. **4** (usually foll. by *to*) inexperienced (in) or unaccustomed (to): *strange to a task.* **5** not of one's own kind, locality, etc.; alien; foreign. **6** shy; distant; reserved. **7 strange to say.** it is unusual or surprising (that). **8** *Physics.* **8a** denoting a particular flavour of quark. **8b** denoting or relating to a hypothetical form of matter composed of such quarks: *strange matter; a strange star.* ♦ *adv* **9** *Not standard.* in a strange manner. ORIG C13: from OF *estrange,* from L *extrāneus* foreign; see EXTRANEOUS
▸ **'strangely** *adv*

strangeness ('streɪndʒnɪs) *n* **1** the state or quality of being strange. **2** *Physics.* a property of certain elementary particles characterized by a quantum number (**strangeness number**) conserved in strong but not in weak interactions.

stranger ('streɪndʒə) *n* **1** any person whom one does not know. **2** a person who is new to a particular locality, from another region, town, etc. **3** a guest or visitor. **4** (foll. by *to*) a person who is unfamiliar (with) or new (to) something: *he is no stranger to computing.*

strangle ('stræŋgᵊl) *vb* **strangles, strangling, strangled.** (*tr*) **1** to kill by compressing the windpipe; throttle. **2** to prevent or inhibit the growth or development of: *to strangle originality.* **3** to suppress (an utterance) by or as if by swallowing suddenly: *to strangle a cry.* ◆ See also **strangles.** ORIG C13: via OF, ult. from Gk *strangalē* a halter
▸ **'strangler** *n*

stranglehold ('stræŋgᵊl,həʊld) *n* **1** a wrestling hold in which a wrestler's arms are pressed against his opponent's windpipe. **2** complete power or control over a person or situation.

strangles ('stræŋgᵊlz) *n* (*functioning as sing*) an acute infectious bacterial disease of horses, characterized by inflammation of the respiratory tract. Also called: **equine distemper.**

strangulate ('stræŋgjʊ,leɪt) *vb* **strangulates, strangulating, strangulated.** (*tr*) **1** to constrict (a hollow organ, vessel, etc.) so as to stop the flow of air, blood, etc., through it. **2** another word for **strangle.**
▸ **,strangu'lation** *n*

strangury ('stræŋgjʊrɪ) *n Pathol.* painful excretion of urine, drop by drop. ORIG C14: from L *strangūria,* from Gk, from *stranx* a drop squeezed out + *ouron* urine

Stranraer ★ (stræn'rɑː) *n* a market town in SW Scotland, in W Dumfries and Galloway: fishing port with a ferry service to Northern Ireland. Pop.: 11 348 (1991).

strap (stræp) *n* **1** a long strip of leather or similar material, for binding trunks, baggage, etc. **2** a strip of leather or similar material used for carrying, lifting, or holding. **3** a loop of leather, rubber, etc., suspended from the roof in a bus or train for standing passengers to hold on to. **4** a razor strop. **5** short for **shoulder strap. 6** *Business.* a triple option on a security or commodity consisting of one put option and two call options at the same price and for the same period. Cf. **strip**[2] (sense 4). **7** *Irish, derog. sl.* a shameless or promiscuous woman. **8 the strap.** a beating with a strap as a punishment. ◆ *vb* **straps, strapping, strapped.** (*tr*) **9** to tie or bind with a strap. **10** to beat with a strap. **11** to sharpen with a strap or strop. ORIG C16: var. of STROP

straphanger ('stræp,hæŋə) *n Inf.* a passenger in a bus, train, etc., who has to travel standing, esp. holding on to a strap.
▸ **'strap,hanging** *n*

strapping ('stræpɪŋ) *adj* (*prenominal*) tall and sturdy. ORIG C17: from STRAP (in the arch. sense: to work vigorously)

strapwork ('stræp,wɜːk) *n Archit.* decorative work resembling interlacing straps.

Strasbourg ★ (*French* strasbur; *English* 'stræzbɜːg) *n* a city in NE France, on the Rhine: the chief French inland port; under German rule (1870–1918); university (1567); seat of the Council of Europe and of the European Parliament. Pop.: 255 937 (1990). German name: **Strassburg** ('ʃtraːsbʊrk).

strata ('strɑːtə) *n* a plural of **stratum.**

> **USAGE NOTE** *Strata* is sometimes wrongly used as a singular noun: *this stratum* (not *strata*) *of society is often disregarded.*

stratagem ('strætɪdʒəm) *n* a plan or trick, esp. to deceive an enemy. ORIG C15: ult. from Gk *stratēgos* a general, from *stratos* an army + *agein* to lead

strategic (strə'tiːdʒɪk) *or* **strategical** *adj* **1** of or characteristic of strategy. **2** important to strategy. **3** (of weapons, esp. missiles) directed against an enemy's homeland rather than used on a battlefield. Cf. **tactical.**
▸ **stra'tegically** *adv*

strategics (strə'tiːdʒɪks) *n* (*functioning as sing*) strategy, esp. in a military sense.

strategist ('strætɪdʒɪst) *n* a specialist or expert in strategy.

strategy ('strætɪdʒɪ) *n, pl* **strategies. 1** the art or science of the planning and conduct of a war. **2** a particular long-term plan for success, esp. in politics, business, etc. **3** a plan or stratagem. ORIG C17: from F *stratégie,* from Gk *stratēgia* function of a general; see STRATAGEM

Stratford-on-Avon *or* **Stratford-upon-Avon** ★ ('strætfəd-) *n* a market town in central England, in SW Warwickshire on the River Avon: the birthplace and burial place of William Shakespeare and home of the Royal Shakespeare Company; tourist centre. Pop.: 22 231 (1991).

strath (stræθ) *n Scot.* a flat river valley. ORIG C16: from Scot. & Irish Gaelic *srath*

Strathclyde Region ★ (stræθ'klaɪd) *n* a former local government region in W Scotland, formed in 1975 and replaced in 1996 by twelve council areas: Glasgow, Renfrewshire, East Renfrewshire, Inverclyde, North Lanarkshire, South Lanarkshire, Argyll and Bute, East Dunbartonshire, West Dunbartonshire, North Ayrshire, South Ayrshire, and East Ayrshire.

strathspey (stræθ'speɪ) *n* **1** a Scottish dance with gliding steps, slower than a reel. **2** a piece of music composed for or in the rhythm of this dance. ORIG after *Strathspey,* valley of the river Spey

strati- *combining form.* indicating stratum or strata: *stratigraphy.*

straticulate (strə'tɪkjʊlɪt, -,leɪt) *adj* (of a rock formation) composed of very thin even strata. ORIG C19: from NL *strāticulum* (unattested), dim. of L *strātum* something strewn; see STRATUS
▸ **stra,ticu'lation** *n*

stratify ('strætɪ,faɪ) *vb* **stratifies, stratifying, stratified. 1** to form or be formed in layers or strata. **2** *Sociol.* to divide (a society) into status groups or (of a society) to develop such groups. ORIG C17: from F *stratifier,* from NL *stratificāre,* from L STRATUM
▸ **,stratifi'cation** *n* ▸ **'strati,fied** *adj*

stratigraphy (strə'tɪgrəfɪ) *n* **1** the study of the composition, relative positions, etc., of rock strata in order to determine their geological history. **2** *Archaeol.* a vertical section through the earth showing the relative positions of the human artefacts and therefore the chronology of successive levels of occupation.
▸ **stratigraphic** (,strætɪ'græfɪk) *or* **,strati'graphical** *adj*

stratocumulus (,strætəʊ'kjuːmjʊləs) *n, pl* **stratocumuli** (-,laɪ). *Meteorol.* a uniform stretch of cloud containing dark grey globular masses.

stratopause ('strætə,pɔːz) *n Meteorol.* the transitional zone of maximum temperature between the stratosphere and the mesosphere.

stratosphere ('strætə,sfɪə) *n* the atmospheric layer lying between the troposphere and the mesosphere, in which temperature generally increases with height.
▸ **stratospheric** (,strætə'sfɛrɪk) *or* **,strato'spherical** *adj*

stratum ('strɑːtəm) *n, pl* **strata** *or* **stratums. 1** (*usually pl*) any of the distinct layers into which sedimentary rocks are divided. **2** *Biol.* a single layer of tissue or cells. **3** a layer of any material, esp. one of several parallel layers. **4** a layer of ocean or atmosphere either naturally or arbitrarily demarcated. **5** a level of a social hierarchy. ORIG C16: via NL from L: something strewn, from *sternere* to scatter
▸ **'stratal** *adj*

> **USAGE NOTE** See at **strata.**

stratus ('streɪtəs) *n, pl* **strati** (-taɪ). a grey layer cloud. ORIG C19: via NL from L: strewn, from *sternere* to extend

Straus ★ (straʊs) *n* **Oscar** (ɔskar). 1870–1954, French composer, born in Austria, noted for such operettas as *Waltz Dream* (1907) and *The Chocolate Soldier* (1908).

Strauss ★ (straʊs; *German* ʃtraʊs) *n* **1 David Friedrich** ('daːfɪt 'friːdrɪç). 1808–74, German Protestant theologian, noted for his *Life of Jesus* (1835–36). **2 Johann** (jo-

'han). 1804–49, Austrian composer, noted for his waltzes. **3** his son, **Johann,** called the *Waltz King.* 1825–99, Austrian composer, whose works include *The Blue Danube Waltz* (1867) and the operetta *Die Fledermaus* (1874). **4 Richard** ('rɪçart). 1864–1949, German composer, noted esp. for his symphonic poems, including *Till Eulenspiegel* (1895), his operas, such as *Der Rosenkavalier* (1911), and his *Four Last Songs* (1948).

Stravinsky ★ (*Russian* stra'vinskij) *n* **Igor Fyodorovich** ('igərj 'fjɔdərəvitʃ). 1882–1971, US composer, born in Russia. He created ballet scores, such as *The Firebird* (1910), *Petrushka* (1911), and *The Rite of Spring* (1913), for Diaghilev. Later works include *Requiem Canticles* (1966).

straw (strɔː) *n* **1a** stalks of threshed grain, esp. of wheat, rye, oats, or barley, used in plaiting hats, baskets, etc., or as fodder. **1b** (*as modifier*): *a straw hat.* **2** a single dry or ripened stalk, esp. of a grass. **3** a long thin hollow paper or plastic tube, used for sucking up liquids into the mouth. **4** (*usually used with a negative*) anything of little value or importance: *I wouldn't give a straw for our chances.* **5** a measure or remedy that one turns to in desperation (esp. in **clutch** *or* **grasp at a straw** *or* **straws**). **6a** a pale yellow colour. **6b** (*as adj*): *straw hair.* **7 draw the short straw.** to be the person to whom an unpleasant task falls. **8 straw in the wind.** a hint or indication. **9 the last straw.** a small incident, setback, etc., that coming after others proves insufferable. ORIG OE *streaw*
▸ '**strawy** *adj*

Straw ★ (strɔː) *n* **Jack**, full name *John Whitaker Straw.* born 1946, British Labour politician; Home Secretary from 1997.

strawberry ('strɔːbərɪ, -brɪ) *n, pl* **strawberries. 1** any of various low-growing rosaceous plants which have red edible fruits and spread by runners. **2a** the fruit of any of these plants, consisting of a sweet fleshy receptacle bearing small seedlike parts (the true fruits). **2b** (*as modifier*): *strawberry ice cream.* **3a** a purplish-red colour. **3b** (*as adj*): *strawberry shoes.* ORIG OE *streawberige;* ?from the strawlike appearance of the runners

strawberry blonde *adj* **1** (of hair) reddish blonde. ◆ *n* **2** a woman with such hair.

strawberry mark *n* a soft vascular red birthmark. Also called: **strawberry.**

strawberry tomato *n* **1** a tropical annual plant having bell-shaped whitish-yellow flowers and small edible round yellow berries. **2** the fruit of this plant, eaten fresh or made into preserves or pickles. ◆ Also called: **Cape gooseberry.**

strawberry tree *n* a S European evergreen tree having white or pink flowers and red strawberry-like berries. See also **arbutus.**

strawboard ('strɔːˌbɔːd) *n* a board made of compressed straw and adhesive.

strawflower ('strɔːˌflaʊə) *n* an Australian plant in which the coloured bracts retain their colour when the plant is dried. See also **immortelle.**

straw man *n Chiefly US.* **1** a figure of a man made from straw. **2** a person of little substance. **3** a person used as a cover for some dubious plan or enterprise.

straw poll *or esp. US, Canad., & NZ.* **vote** *n* an unofficial poll or vote taken to determine the opinion of a group or the public on some issue.

Strawson ★ ('strɔːsən) *n* Sir **Peter** (**Frederick**). born 1919, British philosopher. His early work deals with the relationship between language and logic, his later work with metaphysics. His books include *The Bounds of Sense* (1966) and *Freedom and Resentment* (1974).

strawweight ('strɔːˌweɪt) *n* **a** a professional boxer weighing not more than 47.6 kg (105 pounds). **b** (*as modifier*): *the strawweight title.* ◆ Also called: **mini-flyweight.**

stray (streɪ) *vb* (*intr*) **1** to wander away, as from the correct path or from a given area. **2** to wander haphazardly. **3** to digress from the point, lose concentration, etc. **4** to deviate from certain moral standards. ◆ *n* **5a** a domestic animal, fowl, etc., that has wandered away from its place of keeping and is lost. **5b** (*as modifier*): *stray dogs.* **6** a lost or homeless person, esp. a child: *waifs and strays.* **7** an occurrence, specimen, etc., that is out of place or outside the usual pattern. ◆ *adj* **8** scattered, random, or haphazard. ORIG C14: from OF *estraier,* from Vulgar L *estragāre* (unattested), from L *extrā-* outside + *vagāri* to roam
▸ '**strayer** *n*

Strayhorn ★ ('streɪˌhɔːn) *n* **Billy**, full name *William Strayhorn.* 1915–67, US jazz composer and pianist, noted esp. for his association (1939–67) with Duke Ellington.

strays (streɪz) *pl n* **1** Also called: **stray capacitance.** *Electronics.* undesired capacitance in equipment. **2** another word for **static** (sense 8).

streak (striːk) *n* **1** a long thin mark, stripe, or trace of some contrasting colour. **2** (of lightning) a sudden flash. **3** an element or trace, as of some quality or characteristic. **4** a strip, vein, or layer. **5** a short stretch or run, esp. of good or bad luck. **6** *Inf.* an act or the practice of running naked through a public place. ◆ *vb* **7** (*tr*) to mark or daub with a streak or streaks. **8** (*intr*) to form streaks or become streaked. **9** (*intr*) to move rapidly in a straight line. **10** (*intr*) *Inf.* to run naked through a public place in order to shock or amuse. ORIG OE *strica*
▸ **streaked** *adj* ▸ '**streaker** *n* ▸ '**streakˌlike** *adj*

streaky ('striːkɪ) *adj* **streakier, streakiest. 1** marked with streaks. **2** occurring in streaks. **3** (of bacon) having alternate layers of meat and fat. **4** of varying or uneven quality.
▸ '**streakiness** *n*

stream (striːm) *n* **1** a small river; brook. **2** any steady flow of water or other fluid. **3** something that resembles a stream in moving continuously in a line or particular direction. **4** a rapid or unbroken flow of speech, etc.: *a stream of abuse.* **5** *Brit., Austral., & NZ.* any of several parallel classes of schoolchildren, or divisions of children within a class, grouped together because of similar ability. **6 go** (*or* **drift**) **with the stream.** to conform to the accepted standards. **7 on** (*or* **off**) **stream. 7a** (of an industrial plant, manufacturing process, etc.) in (*or* not in) operation or production. **7b** available (*or* not available) or in existence (*or* not in existence). ◆ *vb* **8** to emit or be emitted in a continuous flow: *his nose streamed blood.* **9** (*intr*) to move in unbroken succession, as a crowd of people, vehicles, etc. **10** (*intr*) to float freely or with a waving motion: *bunting streamed in the wind.* **11** (*tr*) to unfurl (a flag, etc.). **12** *Brit. education.* to group or divide (children) in streams. ORIG OE
▸ '**streamlet** *n*

streamer ('striːmə) *n* **1** a long narrow flag or part of a flag. **2** a long narrow coiled ribbon of coloured paper that becomes unrolled when tossed. **3** a stream of light, esp. one appearing in some forms of the aurora. **4** *Journalism.* a large heavy headline printed across the width of a page. **5** *Computing.* another word for **tape streamer.**

streamline ('striːmˌlaɪn) *n* **1** a contour on a body that offers the minimum resistance to a gas or liquid flowing around it. ◆ *vb* **streamlines, streamlining, streamlined. 2** (*tr*) to make streamlined.

streamlined ('striːmˌlaɪnd) *adj* **1** offering or designed to offer the minimum resistance to the flow of a gas or liquid. **2** made more efficient, esp. by simplifying.

stream of consciousness *n* **1** *Psychol.* the continuous flow of ideas, thoughts, and feelings forming the content of an individual's consciousness. **2** a literary technique that reveals the flow of thoughts and feelings of characters through long passages of soliloquy.

streamy ('striːmɪ) *adj* **streamier, streamiest.** *Chiefly poetic.* **1** (of an area, land, etc.) having many streams. **2** flowing or streaming.

Streep ★ (striːp) *n* **Meryl**, original name *Mary Louise Streep.* born 1949, US actress. Her films include *Kramer vs Kramer* (1979), *The French Lieutenant's Woman* (1981), *Sophie's Choice* (1982), *Out of Africa* (1986), and *Dancing at Lughnasa* (1998).

street (striːt) *n* **1a** a public road that is usually lined with buildings, esp. in a town: *Oxford Street.* **1b** (*as modifier*): *a street directory.* **2** the buildings lining a street. **3** the part of the road between the pavements, used by vehicles. **4** the people living, working, etc., in a particular street. **5** (*modifier*) of or relating to the urban counterculture. **6 on the streets. 6a** earning a living as a prostitute. **6b** homeless. **7**

(right) up one's street. *Inf.* (just) what one knows or likes best. **8 streets ahead of.** *Inf.* superior to, more advanced than, etc. **9 streets apart.** *Inf.* markedly different. ORIG OE *strǣt,* from L *via strāta* paved way (*strāta,* from *strātus,* p.p. of *sternere* to stretch out)

street Arab *n Literary & old-fashioned.* a homeless child, esp. one who survives by begging and stealing; urchin.

streetcar (ˈstriːtˌkɑː) *n* the usual US and Canad. name for **tram** (sense 1).

street credibility *n* a command of the style, knowledge, etc., associated with urban counter-culture. Often shortened to **street cred.**
▸ ˌ**street-ˈcredible** *adj*

street cry *n* (*often pl*) the cry of a street hawker.

street furniture *n* pieces of equipment, such as street lights and pillar boxes, placed in the street for the benefit of the public.

street value *n* the monetary worth of a commodity, usually an illicit one, considered as the price it would fetch when sold to the ultimate user.

streetwalker (ˈstriːtˌwɔːkə) *n* a prostitute who solicits on the streets.
▸ ˈ**streetˌwalking** *n, adj*

streetwise (ˈstriːtˌwaɪz) *adj* adept at surviving in an urban, poor, and often criminal environment.

Streicher ★ (*German* ˈʃtraɪçər) *n* **Julius** (ˈjuːlius). 1885–1946, German Nazi journalist and politician, who spread anti-Semitic propaganda as editor of *Der Stürmer* (1923–45). He was hanged as a war criminal.

Streisand ★ (ˈstraɪsænd) *n* **Barbra.** born 1942, US singer, film actress, and film director: her films as an actress include *Funny Girl* (1968), *A Star is Born* (1976), and as actress and director *Yentl* (1983) and *The Mirror has Two Faces* (1996).

strelitzia (strɛˈlɪtsɪə) *n* any of various southern African perennial herbaceous plants, cultivated for their showy flowers: includes the bird-of-paradise flower. ORIG C18: after Charlotte of Mecklenburg-*Strelitz* (1744–1818), queen of Great Britain & Ireland

strength (strɛŋθ) *n* **1** the state or quality of being physically or mentally strong. **2** the ability to withstand or exert great force, stress, or pressure. **3** something regarded as beneficial or a source of power: *their chief strength is technology.* **4** potency, as of a drink, drug, etc. **5** power to convince; cogency: *the strength of an argument.* **6** degree of intensity or concentration of colour, light, sound, flavour, etc. **7** the full or part of the full complement as specified: *at full strength; below strength.* **8 from strength to strength.** with ever-increasing success. **9 in strength.** in large numbers. **10 on the strength of.** on the basis of or relying upon. **11 the strength of.** *Austral. & NZ inf.* the essential facts about. ORIG OE *strengthu*

strengthen (ˈstrɛŋθən) *vb* to make or become stronger.
▸ ˈ**strengthener** *n*

strenuous (ˈstrɛnjʊəs) *adj* **1** requiring or involving the use of great energy or effort. **2** characterized by great activity, effort, or endeavour. ORIG C16: from L *strēnuus* brisk
▸ ˈ**strenuously** *adv* ▸ ˈ**strenuousness** *n*

strep (strɛp) *n Inf.* short for **streptococcus.**

strepitoso (ˌstrɛpɪˈtəʊsəʊ) *adv Music.* boisterously. ORIG It.

strepto- *combining form.* **1** indicating a shape resembling a twisted chain: *streptococcus.* **2** indicating streptococcus. ORIG from Gk *streptos* twisted, from *strephein* to twist

streptocarpus (ˌstrɛptəʊˈkɑːpəs) *n* any of various mostly African plants having spirally-twisted capsules. ORIG C19: from NL, from Gk *streptos* twisted + *karpos* fruit

streptococcus (ˌstrɛptəʊˈkɒkəs) *n, pl* **streptococci** (-ˈkɒkaɪ, -ˈkɒkiː, -ˈkɒksiː). any spherical bacterium of the genus *Strepto-coccus,* typically occurring in chains and including many pathogenic species. Often shortened to **strep.**
▸ **streptococcal** (ˌstrɛptəʊˈkɒkᵊl) *or* **streptococcic** (ˌstrɛptəʊˈkɒksɪk) *adj*

streptomycin (ˌstrɛptəʊˈmaɪsɪn) *n* an antibiotic obtained from the bacterium *Streptomyces griseus:* used in the treatment of tuberculosis and other bacterial infections.

streptothricin (ˌstrɛptəʊˈθraɪsɪn) *n* an antibiotic produced by the bacterium *Streptomyces lavendulae.*

Stresemann ★ (*German* ˈʃtreːzəman) *n* **Gustav.** 1878–1929, German statesman; chancellor (1923) and foreign minister (1923–29) of the Weimar Republic. He gained (1926) Germany's admission to the League of Nations and shared the Nobel peace prize (1926) with Aristide Briand.

stress (strɛs) *n* **1** special emphasis or significance. **2** mental, emotional, or physical strain or tension. **3** emphasis placed upon a syllable by pronouncing it more loudly than those that surround it. **4** such emphasis as part of a rhythm in music or poetry. **5** a syllable so emphasized. **6** *Physics.* **6a** force or a system of forces producing deformation or strain. **6b** the force acting per unit area. ◆ *vb* (*tr*) **7** to give emphasis or prominence to. **8** to pronounce (a word or syllable) more loudly than those that surround it. **9** to subject to stress. ORIG C14 *stresse,* shortened from DISTRESS
▸ ˈ**stressful** *adj*

-stress *suffix forming nouns.* indicating a woman who performs or is engaged in a certain activity: *songstress; seamstress.* ORIG from -ST(E)R + -ESS

stretch (strɛtʃ) *vb* **1** to draw out or extend or be drawn out or extended in length, area, etc. **2** to extend or be extended to an undue degree, esp. so as to distort or lengthen permanently. **3** to extend (the limbs, body, etc.). **4** (*tr*) to reach or suspend (a rope, etc.) from one place to another. **5** (*tr*) to draw tight; tighten. **6** (often foll. by *out, forward,* etc.) to reach or hold (out); extend. **7** (*intr;* usually foll. by *over*) to extend in time: *the course stretched over three months.* **8** (*intr;* foll. by *for, over,* etc.) (of a region, etc.) to extend in length or area. **9** (*intr*) (esp. of a garment) to be capable of expanding, as to a larger size: *socks that will stretch.* **10** (*tr*) to put a great strain upon or extend to the limit. **11** to injure (a muscle, tendon, etc.) by means of a strain or sprain. **12** (*tr;* often foll. by *out*) to make do with (limited resources): *to stretch one's budget.* **13** (*tr*) *Inf.* to expand or elaborate (a story, etc.) beyond what is credible or acceptable. **14** (*tr; often passive*) to extend, as to the limit of one's abilities or talents. **15** *Arch. or sl.* to hang or be hanged by the neck. **16 stretch a point. 16a** to make a concession or exception not usually made. **16b** to exaggerate. ◆ *n* **17** the act of stretching or state of being stretched. **18** a large or continuous expanse or distance: *a stretch of water.* **19** extent in time, length, area, etc. **20a** capacity for being stretched, as in some garments. **20b** (*as modifier*): *stretch pants.* **21** the section or sections of a racecourse that are straight, esp. the final section leading to the finishing line. **22** *Sl.* a term of imprisonment. **23 at a stretch.** *Chiefly Brit.* **23a** with some difficulty; by making a special effort. **23b** if really necessary or in extreme circumstances. **23c** at one time: *he sometimes read for hours at a stretch.* ORIG OE *streccan*
▸ ˈ**stretchable** *adj* ▸ ˌ**stretchaˈbility** *n*

stretcher (ˈstrɛtʃə) *n* **1** a device for transporting the ill, wounded, or dead, consisting of a frame covered by canvas or other material. **2** a strengthening often decorative member joining the legs of a chair, table, etc. **3** the wooden frame on which canvas is stretched and fixed for oil painting. **4** a tie beam or brace used in a structural framework. **5** a brick or stone laid horizontally with its length parallel to the length of a wall. **6** *Rowing.* a fixed board across a boat on which a rower braces his or her feet. **7** *Austral. & NZ.* a camp bed. ◆ *vb* (*tr*) **8** to transport (a sick or injured person) on a stretcher.

stretcher-bearer *n* a person who helps to carry a stretcher, esp. in wartime.

stretch limo *n Inf.* a limousine that has been lengthened to provide extra seating accommodation and more legroom. In full: **stretch limousine.**

stretchmarks (ˈstrɛtʃˌmɑːks) *pl n* marks that remain visible on the abdomen after its distension in pregnancy.

stretchy (ˈstrɛtʃɪ) *adj* **stretchier, stretchiest.** characterized by elasticity.
▸ ˈ**stretchiness** *n*

Stretford ★ (ˈstrɛtfəd) *n* an industrial town in NW England, in Trafford, in Greater Manchester. Pop.: 43 953 (1991).

stretto (ˈstrɛtəʊ) *n, pl* **strettos** *or* **stretti** (-tiː). **1** (in a fugue) the close overlapping of two parts or voices, the second one entering before the first has completed its statement. **2** Also called: **stretta**. a concluding passage, played at a faster speed than earlier material. ORIG C17: from It., from L *strictus* tightly bound; see STRICT

strew (stru:) *vb* **strews, strewing, strewed; strewn** *or* **strewed.** to spread or scatter or be spread or scattered, as over a surface or area. ORIG OE *streowian*
▸ **'strewer** *n*

strewth (stru:θ) *interj* an expression of surprise or dismay. ORIG C19: alteration of *God's truth*

stria ('straɪə) *n, pl* **striae** ('straɪi:). (*often pl*) **1** Also called: **striation.** *Geol.* any of the parallel scratches or grooves on the surface of a rock over which a glacier has flowed or on the surface of a crystal. **2** *Biol., anat.* a narrow band of colour or a ridge, groove, or similar linear mark. **3** *Archit.* a narrow channel, such as a flute on the shaft of a column. ORIG C16: from L: a groove

striate *adj* ('straɪɪt), *also* **striated. 1** marked with striae; striped. ◆ *vb* ('straɪeɪt), **striates, striating, striated. 2** (*tr*) to mark with striae. ORIG C17: from L *striāre* to make grooves

striation (straɪ'eɪʃən) *n* **1** an arrangement or pattern of striae. **2** the condition of being striate. **3** another word for **stria** (sense 1).

stricken ('strɪkən) *adj* **1** laid low, as by disease or sickness. **2** deeply affected, as by grief, love, etc. **3** *Arch.* wounded or injured. **4 stricken in years.** made feeble by age. ORIG C14: p.p. of STRIKE
▸ **'strickenly** *adv*

strict (strɪkt) *adj* **1** adhering closely to specified rules, ordinances, etc. **2** complied with or enforced stringently; rigorous: *a strict code of conduct.* **3** severely correct in attention to conduct or morality: *a strict teacher.* **4** (of a punishment, etc.) harsh; severe. **5** (*prenominal*) complete; absolute: *strict secrecy.* ORIG C16: from L *strictus,* from *stringere* to draw tight
▸ **'strictly** *adv* ▸ **'strictness** *n*

strict implication *n Logic.* a form of implication in which the proposition "if A then B" is true only when B is deducible from A.

stricture ('strɪktʃə) *n* **1** a severe criticism; censure. **2** *Pathol.* an abnormal constriction of a tubular organ or part. ORIG C14: from L *strictūra* contraction; see STRICT
▸ **'strictured** *adj*

stride (straɪd) *n* **1** a long step or pace. **2** the space measured by such a step. **3** a striding gait. **4** an act of forward movement by an animal. **5** progress or development (esp. in **make rapid strides**). **6** a regular pace or rate of progress: *to get into one's stride; to be put off one's stride.* **7** Also: **stride piano.** *Jazz.* a piano style characterized by single bass notes on the first and third beats and chords on the second and fourth. **8** (*pl*) *Inf., chiefly Austral. & NZ.* men's trousers. **9 take (something) in one's stride.** to do (something) without difficulty or effort. ◆ *vb* **strides, striding, strode, stridden** ('strɪdᵊn). **10** (*intr*) to walk with long regular or measured paces, as in haste, etc. **11** (*tr*) to cover or traverse by striding: *he strode thirty miles.* **12** (often foll. by *over, across,* etc.) to cross (over a space, obstacle, etc.) with a stride. **13** *Arch. or poetic.* to straddle or bestride. ORIG OE *strīdan*
▸ **'strider** *n*

strident ('straɪdᵊnt) *adj* **1** (of a shout, voice, etc.) loud or harsh. **2** urgent, clamorous, or vociferous: *strident demands.* ORIG C17: from L *strīdēns,* from *strīdēre* to make a grating sound
▸ **'stridence** *or* **'stridency** *n* ▸ **'stridently** *adv*

stridor ('straɪdɔ:) *n* **1** *Pathol.* a high-pitched whistling sound made during respiration, caused by obstruction of the air passages. **2** *Chiefly literary.* a harsh or shrill sound. ORIG C17: from L; see STRIDENT

stridulate ('strɪdjʊˌleɪt) *vb* **stridulates, stridulating, stridulated.** (*intr*) (of insects such as the cricket) to produce sounds by rubbing one part of the body against another. ORIG C19: back formation from *stridulation,* from L *strīdulus* creaking, from *strīdēre* to make a harsh noise
▸ **ˌstriduˈlation** *n* ▸ **'striduˌlator** *n*

stridulous ('strɪdjʊləs) *or* **stridulant** *adj* **1** making a harsh, shrill, or grating noise. **2** *Pathol.* of, relating to, or characterized by stridor.
▸ **'stridulousness** *or* **'stridulance** *n*

strife (straɪf) *n* **1** angry or violent struggle; conflict. **2** rivalry or contention, esp. of a bitter kind. **3** *Austral. & NZ inf.* trouble or discord of any kind. **4** *Arch.* striving. ORIG C13: from OF *estrif,* prob. from *estriver* to STRIVE

strigil ('strɪdʒɪl) *n* a curved blade used by the ancient Romans and Greeks to scrape the body after bathing. ORIG C16: from L *strigilis,* from *stringere* to graze

strigose ('straɪgəʊs) *adj* **1** *Bot.* bearing stiff hairs or bristles. **2** *Zool.* marked with fine closely set grooves or ridges. ORIG C18: via NL *strigōsus,* from *striga* a bristle, from L: grain cut down

strike (straɪk) *vb* **strikes, striking, struck. 1** to deliver (a blow or stroke) to (a person). **2** to come or cause to come into sudden or violent contact (with). **3** (*tr*) to make an attack on. **4** to produce (fire, sparks, etc.) or (of fire, sparks, etc.) to be produced by ignition. **5** to cause (a match) to light by friction or (of a match) to be lighted. **6** to press (the key of a piano, organ, etc.) or to sound (a specific note) in this or a similar way. **7** to indicate (a specific time) by the sound of a hammer striking a bell or by any other percussive sound. **8** (of a venomous snake) to cause injury by biting. **9** (*tr*) to affect or cause to affect deeply, suddenly, or radically: *her appearance struck him as strange.* **10** (*past participle* **struck** *or* **stricken**) (*tr; passive;* usually foll. by *with*) to render incapable or nearly so: *stricken with grief.* **11** (*tr*) to enter the mind of: *it struck me that he had become very quiet.* **12** (*past participle* **struck** *or* **stricken**) to render: *struck dumb.* **13** (*tr*) to be perceived by; catch: *the glint of metal struck his eye.* **14** to arrive at or come upon (something), esp. suddenly or unexpectedly: *to strike the path for home; to strike upon a solution.* **15** (*intr;* sometimes foll. by *out*) to set (out) or proceed, esp. upon a new course: *to strike out for the coast.* **16** (*tr; usually passive*) to afflict with a disease, esp. unexpectedly: *he was struck with polio.* **17** (*tr*) to discover or come upon a source of (ore, petroleum, etc.). **18** (*tr*) (of a plant) to produce or send down (a root or roots). **19** (*tr*) to take apart or pack up; break (esp. in **strike camp**). **20** (*tr*) to take down or dismantle (a stage set, etc.). **21** (*tr*) *Naut.* **21a** to lower or remove (a specified piece of gear). **21b** to haul down or dip (a flag, sail, etc.) in salute or in surrender. **22** to attack (an objective). **23** to impale the hook in the mouth of (a fish) by suddenly tightening or jerking the line after the bait has been taken. **24** (*tr*) to form or impress (a coin, metal, etc.) by or as if by stamping. **25** to level (a surface) by use of a flat board. **26** (*tr*) to assume or take up (an attitude, posture, etc.). **27** (*intr*) (of workers in a factory, etc.) to cease work collectively as a protest against working conditions, low pay, etc. **28** (*tr*) to reach by agreement: *to strike a bargain.* **29** (*tr*) to form (a jury, esp. a special jury) by cancelling certain names among those nominated for jury service until only the requisite number remains. **30 strike home. 30a** to deliver an effective blow. **30b** to achieve the intended effect. **31 strike it rich.** *Inf.* **31a** to discover an extensive deposit of a mineral, petroleum, etc. **31b** to have an unexpected financial success. ◆ *n* **32** an act or instance of striking. **33** a cessation of work, as a protest against working conditions or low pay: *on strike.* **34** a military attack, esp. an air attack on a surface target: *air strike.* **35** *Baseball.* a pitched ball judged good but missed or not swung at, three of which cause a batter to be out. **36** Also called: **ten-strike.** *Tenpin bowling.* **36a** the act or an instance of knocking down all the pins with the first bowl of a single frame. **36b** the score thus made. **37** a sound made by striking. **38** the mechanism that makes a clock strike. **39** the discovery of a source of ore, petroleum, etc. **40** the horizontal direction of a fault, rock stratum, etc. **41** *Angling.* the act or an instance of striking. **42** *Inf.* an unexpected or complete success, esp. one that brings financial gain. **43 take strike.** *Cricket.* (of a batsman) to prepare to play a ball delivered by the bowler. ◆ See also **strike down, strike off,** etc. ORIG OE *strīcan*

strikebound ('straɪkˌbaʊnd) *adj* (of a factory, etc.) closed or made inoperative by a strike.

strikebreaker ('straɪkˌbreɪkə) *n* a person who tries to

make a strike ineffectual by working or by taking the place of those on strike.
▸ **'strike,breaking** *n, adj*

strike down *vb (tr, adv)* to cause to die, esp. suddenly: *he was struck down in his prime.*

strike off *vb (tr)* **1** to remove or erase from (a list, record, etc.) by or as if by a stroke of the pen. **2** *(adv)* to cut off or separate by or as if by a blow: *she was struck off from the inheritance.*

strike out *vb (adv)* **1** *(tr)* to remove or erase. **2** *(intr)* to start out or begin: *to strike out on one's own.* **3** *Baseball.* to put out or be put out on strikes. **4** *(intr) US inf.* to fail utterly.

strike pay *n* money paid to strikers from the funds of a trade union.

striker ('straɪkə) *n* **1** a person who is on strike. **2** the hammer in a timepiece that rings a bell or alarm. **3** any part in a mechanical device that strikes something, such as the firing pin of a gun. **4** *Soccer, inf.* an attacking player, esp. one who generally positions himself or herself near the opponent's goal in the hope of scoring. **5** *Cricket.* the batsman who is about to play a ball.

strike up *vb (adv)* **1** (of a band, orchestra, etc.) to begin to play or sing **2** *(tr)* to bring about; cause to begin: *to strike up a friendship.*

striking ('straɪkɪŋ) *adj* **1** attracting attention; fine; impressive: *a striking beauty.* **2** conspicuous; noticeable: *a striking difference.*
▸ **'strikingly** *adv* ▸ **'strikingness** *n*

striking circle *n Hockey.* the semicircular area in front of each goal, which an attacking player must have entered before scoring a goal.

Strimmer ('strɪmə) *n Trademark.* an electrical tool for trimming the edges of lawns.

Strimon ★ ('strimɔn) *n* a transliteration of the Greek name for the **Struma**.

Strindberg ★ ('strɪndbɜːg; *Swedish* 'strɪndbærj) *n* **August** ('august). 1849–1912, Swedish dramatist and novelist, whose plays include *The Father* (1887), *Miss Julie* (1888), and *The Ghost Sonata* (1907).

Strine (straɪn) *n* a humorous transliteration of Australian pronunciation, as in *Gloria Soame* for *glorious home.* ORIG C20: a jocular rendering of the Australian pronunciation of *Australian*

string (strɪŋ) *n* **1** a thin length of cord, twine, fibre, or similar material used for tying, hanging, binding, etc. **2** a group of objects threaded on a single strand: *a string of beads.* **3** a series or succession of things, events, etc.: *a string of oaths.* **4** a number, chain, or group of similar things, animals, etc., owned by or associated with one person or body: *a string of girlfriends.* **5** a tough fibre or cord in a plant. **6** *Music.* a tightly stretched wire, cord, etc., found on stringed instruments, such as the violin, guitar, and piano. **7** short for **bowstring. 8** *Archit.* short for **string course** or **stringer** (sense 1). **9** *(pl; usually preceded by the)* **9a** violins, violas, cellos, and double basses collectively. **9b** the section of a symphony orchestra constituted by such instruments. **10** a group of characters that can be treated as a unit by a computer program. **11** *Physics.* a one-dimensional entity postulated to be a fundamental component of matter in some theories of particle physics. See also **cosmic string. 12** *(pl)* complications or conditions (esp. in **no strings attached**). **13** *(modifier)* composed of stringlike strands woven in a large mesh: *a string bag; a string vest.* **14 first (second,** etc.**) string.** a person or thing regarded as a primary (secondary, etc.) source of strength. **15 keep on a string.** to have control or a hold over (a person), esp. emotionally. **16 pull strings.** *Inf.* to exert power or influence, esp. secretly or unofficially. **17 pull the strings.** to have real or ultimate control of something. ◆ *vb* **strings, stringing, strung. 18** *(tr)* to provide with a string or strings. **19** *(tr)* to suspend or stretch from one point to another. **20** *(tr)* to thread on a string. **21** *(tr)* to form or extend in a line or series. **22** (foll. by *out*) to space or spread out at intervals. **23** *(tr; usually foll. by up) Inf.* to kill (a person) by hanging. **24** *(tr)* to remove the stringy parts from (vegetables, esp. beans). **25** *(intr)* (esp. of viscous liquids) to become stringy or ropey. **26** *(tr;* often foll. by *up)* to cause to be tense or nervous. ORIG OE *streng*
▸ **'string,like** *adj*

string along *vb (adv) Inf.* **1** *(intr;* often foll. by *with)* to agree or appear to be in agreement (with). **2** *(intr;* often foll. by *with)* to accompany. **3** to deceive or hoax, esp. in order to gain time.

stringboard ('strɪŋ,bɔːd) *n* a skirting that covers the ends of the steps in a staircase. Also called: **stringer.**

string course *n Archit.* an ornamental projecting band or continuous moulding along a wall. Also called: **cordon.**

stringed (strɪŋd) *adj* (of musical instruments) having or provided with strings.

stringendo (strɪn'dʒɛndəʊ) *adj, adv Music.* to be performed with increasing speed. ORIG It., from *stringere* to compress, from L: to draw tight

stringent ('strɪndʒənt) *adj* **1** requiring strict attention to rules, procedure, detail, etc. **2** *Finance.* characterized by or causing a shortage of credit, loan capital, etc. ORIG C17: from L *stringere* to bind
▸ **'stringency** *n* ▸ **'stringently** *adv*

stringer ('strɪŋə) *n* **1** *Archit.* **1a** a long horizontal beam that is used for structural purposes. **1b** another name for **stringboard. 2** *Naut.* a longitudinal structural brace for strengthening the hull of a vessel. **3** a journalist retained by a newspaper or news service on a part-time basis to cover a particular town or area.

stringhalt ('strɪŋ,hɔːlt) *n Vet. science.* a sudden spasmodic lifting of the hind leg of a horse. Also called: **springhalt.** ORIG C16: prob. STRING + HALT[2]

stringpiece ('strɪŋ,piːs) *n* a long horizontal timber beam used to strengthen or support a framework.

string quartet *n Music.* **1** an instrumental ensemble consisting of two violins, one viola, and one cello. **2** a piece of music for such a group.

string tie *n* a very narrow tie.

stringy ('strɪŋɪ) *adj* **stringier, stringiest. 1** made of strings or resembling strings. **2** (of meat, etc.) fibrous. **3** (of a person's build) wiry; sinewy. **4** (of liquids) forming in strings.
▸ **'stringily** *adv* ▸ **'stringiness** *n*

stringy-bark *n Austral.* any of several eucalyptus trees having fibrous bark.

strip[1] (strɪp) *vb* **strips, stripping, stripped. 1** to take or pull (the covering, clothes, etc.) off (oneself, another person, or thing). **2** *(intr)* **2a** to remove all one's clothes. **2b** to perform a striptease. **3** *(tr)* to denude or empty completely. **4** *(tr)* to deprive: *he was stripped of his pride.* **5** *(tr)* to rob or plunder. **6** *(tr)* to remove (paint, etc.) from (a surface, furniture, etc.): *stripped pine.* **7** *(tr)* to pull out the old coat of hair from (dogs of certain long- and wire-haired breeds). **8a** to remove the leaves from the stalks of (tobacco, etc.). **8b** to separate the leaves from the stems of (tobacco, etc.). **9** *(tr) Agriculture.* to draw the last milk from (a cow). **10** to dismantle (an engine, mechanism, etc.). **11** to tear off or break (the thread) from (a screw, bolt, etc.) or (the teeth) from (a gear). **12** (often foll. by *down)* to remove the accessories from (a motor vehicle): *his car was stripped down.* ◆ *n* **13** the act or an instance of undressing or of performing a striptease. ORIG OE *bestriepan* to plunder

strip[2] (strɪp) *n* **1** a relatively long, flat, narrow piece of something. **2** short for **airstrip. 3** the clothes worn by the members of a team, esp. a football team. **4** *Business.* a triple option on a security or commodity consisting of one call option and two put options at the same price and for the same period. Cf. **strap** (sense 6). **5 tear (someone) off a strip.** *Inf.* to rebuke (someone) angrily. ◆ *vb* **strips, stripping, stripped. 6** to cut or divide into strips. ORIG C15: from MDu. *strīpe* STRIPE[1]

strip cartoon *n* a sequence of drawings in a newspaper, magazine, etc., relating a humorous story or an adventure. Also called: **comic strip.**

strip club *n* a small club in which striptease performances take place.

stripe[1] (straɪp) *n* **1** a relatively long band of colour or tex-

ture that differs from the surrounding material or background. **2** a fabric having such bands. **3** a strip, band, or chevron worn on a uniform, etc., esp. to indicate rank. **4** *Chiefly US & Canad.* kind; type: *a man of a certain stripe.* ◆ *vb* **stripes, striping, striped. 5** (*tr*) to mark with stripes. ORIG C17: prob. from MDu. *strīpe*
▸ **striped** *adj*

stripe[2] (straɪp) *n* a stroke from a whip, rod, cane, etc. ORIG C15: ?from MLow G *strippe*

striped muscle *n* a type of contractile tissue that is marked by transverse striations. Also called: **striated muscle.**

strip lighting *n* electric lighting by means of long glass tubes that are fluorescent lamps or that contain long filaments.

stripling ('strɪplɪŋ) *n* a lad. ORIG C13: from STRIP[2] + -LING[1]

strip mining *n* another term (esp. US) for **opencast mining.**

stripper ('strɪpə) *n* **1** a striptease artiste. **2** a person or thing that strips. **3** a device or substance for removing paint, varnish, etc.

strip-search *vb* **1** (*tr*) (of police, customs officials, etc.) to strip (a prisoner or suspect) naked to search him or her for contraband, narcotics, etc. ◆ *n* **2** a search that involves stripping a person naked.
▸ **'strip-ˌsearching** *n*

striptease ('strɪpˌti:z) *n* **a** a form of erotic entertainment in which a person gradually undresses to music. **b** (*as modifier*): *a striptease club.*
▸ **'stripˌteaser** *n*

stripy *or* **stripey** ('straɪpɪ) *adj* **stripier, stripiest.** marked by or with stripes; striped.

strive (straɪv) *vb* **strives, striving, strove, striven** ('strɪvᵊn). **1** (*may take a clause as object or an infinitive*) to make a great and tenacious effort. **2** (*intr*) to fight; contend. ORIG C13: from OF *estriver,* of Gmc origin
▸ **'striver** *n*

strobe (strəʊb) *n* short for **strobe lighting** or **stroboscope.**

strobe lighting *n* **1** a high-intensity flashing beam of light produced by rapid electrical discharges in a tube or by a perforated disc rotating in front of an intense light source. **2** the use of or the apparatus for producing such light. Sometimes shortened to **strobe.**

strobilus ('strəʊbɪləs) *or* **strobile** ('strəʊbaɪl) *n, pl* **strobiluses, strobili** (-bɪlaɪ), *or* **strobiles.** *Bot.* the technical name for **cone** (sense 3). ORIG C18: via LL from Gk *strobilos* a fir cone

stroboscope ('strəʊbəˌskəʊp) *n* **1** an instrument producing an intense flashing light, the frequency of which can be synchronized with some multiple of the frequency of rotation, vibration, or operation of an object, etc., making it appear stationary. Sometimes shortened to **strobe. 2** a similar device synchronized with the shutter of a camera so that a series of still photographs can be taken of a moving object. ORIG C19: from *strobo-,* from Gk *strobos* a whirling + -SCOPE
▸ **stroboscopic** (ˌstrəʊbə'skɒpɪk) *or* **ˌstrobo'scopical** *adj*
▸ **ˌstrobo'scopically** *adv*

strode (strəʊd) *vb* the past tense of **stride.**

Stroessner ★ ('ʃtræsnər) *n* **Alfredo.** born 1912, Paraguayan soldier and politician; president (1954–89): deposed in a military coup.

stroganoff ('strɒgəˌnɒf) *n* a dish of sliced beef cooked with onions and mushrooms, served in a sour-cream sauce. Also called: **beef stroganoff.** ORIG C19: after Count *Stroganoff,* 19th-century Russian diplomat

Stroheim ★ ('strəʊˌhaɪm, 'ʃtrəʊ-) *n* See (Erich) **von Stroheim.**

stroke (strəʊk) *n* **1** the act or an instance of striking; a blow, knock, or hit. **2** a sudden action, movement, or occurrence: *a stroke of luck.* **3** a brilliant or inspired act or feat: *a stroke of genius.* **4** *Pathol.* apoplexy; rupture of a blood vessel in the brain resulting in loss of consciousness, often followed by paralysis, or embolism or thrombosis affecting a cerebral vessel. **5a** the striking of a clock. **5b** the hour registered by this: *on the stroke of three.* **6** a mark made by a writing implement. **7** another name for **solidus** (sense 1), used esp. when dictating or reading aloud. **8** a light touch or caress, as with the fingers. **9** a pulsation, esp. of the heart. **10** a single complete movement or one of a series of complete movements. **11** *Sport.* the act or manner of striking the ball with a club, bat, etc. **12** any one of the repeated movements used by a swimmer. **13** a manner of swimming, esp. one of several named styles such as the crawl. **14a** any one of a series of linear movements of a reciprocating part, such as a piston. **14b** the distance travelled by such a part from one end of its movement to the other. **15** a single pull on an oar or oars in rowing. **16** manner or style of rowing. **17** the oarsman who sits nearest the stern of a shell, facing the cox, and sets the rate of rowing. **18 a stroke (of work).** (*usually used with a negative*) a small amount of work. **19 at a stroke.** with one action. **20 off one's stroke.** performing or working less well than usual. **21 on the stroke.** punctually. ◆ *vb* **strokes, stroking, stroked. 22** (*tr*) to touch, brush, etc. lightly or gently. **23** (*tr*) to mark a line or a stroke on or through. **24** to act as the stroke of (a racing shell). **25** (*tr*) *Sport.* to strike (a ball) with a smooth swinging blow. ORIG OE *strācian*

stroke play *n Golf.* **a** scoring by counting the strokes taken. **b** (*as modifier*): *a strokeplay tournament.* ◆ Also called: **medal play.** Cf. **match play, Stableford.**

stroll (strəʊl) *vb* **1** to walk about in a leisurely manner. **2** (*intr*) to wander about. ◆ *n* **3** a leisurely walk. ORIG C17: prob. from dialect G *strollen,* from ?

stroller ('strəʊlə) *n* the usual US, Canad., and Austral. word for **pushchair.**

stroma ('strəʊmə) *n, pl* **stromata** (-mətə). *Biol.* **1** the dense colourless framework of a chloroplast and certain cells. **2** the fibrous connective tissue forming the matrix of the mammalian ovary and testis. **3** a dense mass of hyphae that is produced by certain fungi and gives rise to spore-producing bodies. ORIG C19: via NL from LL: a mattress, from Gk
▸ **stromatic** (strəʊ'mætɪk) *or* **'stromatous** *adj*

Stromboli ★ ('strɒmbəlɪ) *n* an island in the Tyrrhenian Sea, in the Lipari Islands off the N coast of Sicily: famous for its active volcano, 927 m (3040 ft) high.

Strombolian (strɒm'bəʊlɪən) *adj* relating to or denoting a type of volcanic eruption characterized by repeated small explosions caused by gas escaping through lava.

strong (strɒŋ) *adj* **stronger** ('strɒŋgə), **strongest** ('strɒŋgɪst). **1** involving or possessing strength. **2** solid or robust; not easily broken or injured. **3** resolute or morally firm. **4** intense in quality; not faint or feeble: *a strong voice; a strong smell.* **5** easily defensible; incontestable or formidable. **6** concentrated; not weak or diluted. **7a** (*postpositive*) containing or having a specified number: *a navy 40 000 strong.* **7b** (*in combination*): *a 40 000-strong navy.* **8** having an unpleasantly powerful taste or smell. **9** having an extreme or drastic effect: *strong discipline.* **10** emphatic or immoderate: *strong language.* **11** convincing, effective, or cogent. **12** (of a colour) having a high degree of saturation or purity; produced by a concentrated quantity of colouring agent. **13** *Grammar.* **13a** of or denoting a class of verbs, in certain languages including the Germanic languages, whose conjugation shows vowel gradation, as *sing, sang, sung.* **13b** belonging to any part-of-speech class, in various languages, whose inflections follow the less regular of two possible patterns. Cf. **weak** (sense 10). **14** (of a wind, current, etc.) moving fast. **15** (of a syllable) accented or stressed. **16** (of an industry, etc.) firm in price or characterized by firm or increasing prices. **17** (of certain acids and bases) producing high concentrations of hydrogen or hydroxide ions in aqueous solution. **18 have a strong stomach.** not to be prone to nausea. ◆ *adv* **19** *Inf.* in a strong way; effectively: *going strong.* **20 come on strong.** to make a forceful or exaggerated impression. ORIG OE *strang*
▸ **'strongly** *adv* ▸ **'strongness** *n*

strong-arm *Inf.* ◆ *n* **1** (*modifier*) of or involving physical force or violence: *strong-arm tactics.* ◆ *vb* **2** (*tr*) to show violence towards.

strongbox ('strɒŋˌbɒks) *n* a box or safe in which valuables are locked for safety.

strong breeze *n Meteorol.* a wind of force 6 on the Beaufort scale, reaching speeds of 25 to 31 mph.

strong drink *n* alcoholic drink.

strong-eye dog *n NZ.* See **eye dog.**

strong gale *n Meteorol.* a wind of force 9 on the Beaufort scale, reaching speeds of 47 to 54 mph.

stronghold ('strɒŋˌhəʊld) *n* **1** a defensible place; fortress. **2** a major centre or area of predominance.

strong interaction *or* **force** *n Physics.* an interaction between elementary particles responsible for the forces between nucleons in the nucleus. Also called: **strong nuclear interaction** *or* **force.** See **interaction** (sense 2). Cf. **weak interaction.**

strong-minded *adj* having strength of mind; firm, resolute, and determined.
▸ **ˌstrong-ˈmindedly** *adv* ▸ **ˌstrong-ˈmindedness** *n*

strong point *n* something at which one excels; forte.

strongroom ('strɒŋˌruːm, -ˌrʊm) *n* a specially designed room in which valuables are locked for safety.

strong-willed *adj* having strength of will.

strontium ('strɒntɪəm) *n* a soft silvery-white element of the alkaline earth group of metals. The radioisotope **strontium-90,** with a half-life of 28.1 years, is used in nuclear power sources and is a hazardous nuclear fallout product. Symbol: Sr; atomic no.: 38; atomic wt.: 87.62. ORIG C19: from NL, after *Strontian,* in the Highlands of Scotland, where discovered

strontium unit *n* a unit expressing the concentration of strontium-90 in an organic medium, such as soil, bone, etc., relative to the concentration of calcium in the medium.

strop (strɒp) *n* **1** a leather strap or an abrasive strip for sharpening razors. **2** a rope or metal band around a block or deadeye for support. ◆ *vb* **strops, stropping, stropped. 3** (*tr*) to sharpen (a razor, etc.) on a strop. ORIG C14 (in nautical use: a strip of rope): via MLow G or MDu. *strop,* ult. from L *stroppus,* from Gk *strophos* cord

strophanthin (strəʊ'fænθɪn) *n* a toxic glycoside or mixture of glycosides obtained from the ripe seeds of certain species of strophanthus. ORIG C19: NL, from STROPHANTH(US) + -IN

strophanthus (strəʊ'fænθəs) *n* **1** any of various small trees or shrubs of tropical Africa and Asia, having strap-shaped twisted petals. **2** the seeds of any of these plants. ORIG C19: NL, from Gk *strophos* twisted cord + *anthos* flower

strophe ('strəʊfɪ) *n Prosody.* (in ancient Greek drama) **a** the first of two movements made by a chorus during the performance of a choral ode. **b** the first part of a choral ode sung during this movement. ◆ See **antistrophe, epode.** ORIG C17: from Gk: a verse, lit.: a turning, from *strephein* to twist
▸ **strophic** ('strɒfɪk, 'strəʊ-) *adj*

stroppy ('strɒpɪ) *adj* **stroppier, stroppiest.** *Brit. inf.* angry or awkward. ORIG C20: changed & shortened from OBSTREPEROUS
▸ **'stroppily** *adv* ▸ **'stroppiness** *n*

strove (strəʊv) *vb* the past tense of **strive.**

strow (strəʊ) *vb* **strows, strowing, strowed; strown** *or* **strowed.** an archaic variant of **strew.**

struck (strʌk) *vb* **1** the past tense and past participle of **strike.** ◆ *adj* **2** *Chiefly US & Canad.* (of an industry, factory, etc.) shut down or otherwise affected by a labour strike.

structural ('strʌktʃərəl) *adj* **1** of, relating to, or having structure or a structure. **2** of, relating to, or forming part of the structure of a building. **3** of or relating to the structure of the earth's crust. **4** of or relating to the structure of organisms. **5** *Chem.* of or involving the arrangement of atoms in molecules.
▸ **'structurally** *adv*

structural formula *n* a chemical formula showing the composition and structure of a molecule.

structuralism ('strʌktʃərəˌlɪzəm) *n* **1** an approach to social sciences and to literature in terms of oppositions, contrasts, and hierarchical structures, esp. as they might reflect universal mental characteristics or organizing principles. **2** an approach to linguistics that analyses and describes the structure of language, as distinguished from its comparative and historical aspects.
▸ **'structuralist** *n, adj*

structural linguistics *n* (*functioning as sing*) a descriptive approach to an analysis of language on the basis of its structure as reflected by irreducible units of phonological, morphological, and semantic features.

structural unemployment *n Econ.* unemployment resulting from changes in the structure of an industry as a result of changes in either technology or taste.

structure ('strʌktʃə) *n* **1** a complex construction or entity. **2** the arrangement and interrelationship of parts in a construction. **3** the manner of construction or organization. **4** *Chem.* the arrangement of atoms in a molecule of a chemical compound. **5** *Geol.* the way in which a mineral, rock, etc., is made up of its component parts. ◆ *vb* **structures, structuring, structured.** (*tr*) **6** to impart a structure to. ORIG C15: from L *structūra,* from *struere* to build

structured interview *n Marketing.* an interview in which the respondent answers only "yes", "no", or "don't know".

strudel ('struːdəl) *n* a thin sheet of filled dough rolled up and baked: *apple strudel.* ORIG G, from MHG *strodel* whirlpool, from the way the pastry is rolled

struggle ('strʌgᵊl) *vb* **struggles, struggling, struggled.** (*intr*) **1** (usually foll. by *for* or *against; may take an infinitive*) to exert strength, energy, and force; work or strive. **2** to move about strenuously so as to escape from something confining. **3** to contend, battle, or fight. **4** to go or progress with difficulty. ◆ *n* **5** a laboured or strenuous exertion or effort. **6** a fight or battle. **7** the act of struggling. **8 the struggle.** *S. African.* the concerted opposition to apartheid. ORIG C14: from ?
▸ **'struggling** *adj*

strum (strʌm) *vb* **strums, strumming, strummed. 1** to sound (the strings of a guitar, etc.) with a downward or upward sweep of the thumb or of a plectrum. **2** to play (chords, a tune, etc.) in this way. ORIG C18: prob. imit.
▸ **'strummer** *n*

struma ('struːmə) *n, pl* **strumae** (-miː). **1** an abnormal enlargement of the thyroid gland; goitre. **2** *Bot.* a swelling, esp. at the base of a moss capsule. **3** another word for **scrofula.** ORIG C16: from L: scrofulous tumour, from *struere* to heap up
▸ **strumous** ('struːməs) *or* **strumose** ('struːməʊs) *adj*

Struma ★ ('struːmə) *n* a river in S Europe, rising in SW Bulgaria near Sofia and flowing generally southeast through Greece to the Aegean. Length: 362 km (225 miles). Greek names: **Strimon, Strymon.**

strumpet ('strʌmpɪt) *n Arch.* a prostitute or promiscuous woman. ORIG C14: from ?

strung (strʌŋ) *vb* **1** a past tense and past participle of **string.** ◆ *adj* **2a** (of a piano, etc.) provided with strings. **2b** (*in combination*): *gut-strung.* **3 highly strung.** very nervous or volatile in character.

strung up *adj* (*postpositive*) *Inf.* tense or nervous.

strut (strʌt) *vb* **struts, strutting, strutted. 1** (*intr*) to walk in a pompous manner; swagger. **2** (*tr*) to support or provide with struts. ◆ *n* **3** a structural member, esp. as part of a framework. **4** an affected, proud, or stiff walk. ORIG C14 *strouten* (in the sense: swell, stand out; C16: to walk stiffly), from OE *strūtian* to stand stiffly
▸ **'strutter** *n* ▸ **'strutting** *adj* ▸ **'struttingly** *adv*

struthious ('struːθɪəs) *adj* **1** (of birds) related to or resembling the ostrich. **2** of, relating to, or designating all flightless birds. ORIG C18: from LL *strūthiō,* from Gk *strouthiōn,* from *strouthos* ostrich

Struve ★ ('struːvə) *n* **Otto.** 1897–1963, US astronomer, born in Russia, noted for his work in stellar spectroscopy and his discovery (1937) of interstellar hydrogen.

strychnine ('strɪkniːn) *n* a white crystalline very poisonous alkaloid, obtained from the plant nux vomica: formerly used in small quantities as a stimulant. ORIG C19: via F from NL *Strychnos,* from Gk *strukhnos* nightshade

Strymon ★ ('straɪmən) *n* transliteration of the Greek name for the **Struma.**

Stuart ★ ('stjuət) *n* **1** the royal house that ruled in Scotland from 1371 to 1714 and in England from 1603 to 1714. See also **Stewart** (sense 1). **2 Charles Edward,** called *the Young Pretender* or *Bonnie Prince Charlie.* 1720–88, pretender to the British throne. He led the Jacobite Rebellion (1745–46) in an attempt to re-establish the Stuart succession. **3** his father, **James Francis Edward,** called *the Old Pretender.* 1688–1766, pretender to the British throne; son of James II (James VII of Scotland) and his second wife, Mary of Modena. He made two unsuccessful attempts to realize his claim to the throne (1708; 1715). **4 Mary.** See **Mary, Queen of Scots.**

stub (stʌb) *n* **1** a short piece remaining after something has been cut, removed, etc.: *a cigar stub.* **2** the residual piece or section of a receipt, ticket, cheque, etc. **3** the usual US and Canad. word for **counterfoil. 4** any short projection or blunted end. **5** the stump of a tree or plant. ♦ *vb* **stubs, stubbing, stubbed.** (*tr*) **6** to strike (one's toe, foot, etc.) painfully against a hard surface. **7** (usually foll. by *out*) to put (out a cigarette or cigar) by pressing the end against a surface. **8** to clear (land) of stubs. **9** to dig up (the roots) of (a tree or bush). ORIG OE *stubb*

stub axle *n* a short axle that carries one of the front steered wheels of a motor vehicle.

stubble ('stʌbᵊl) *n* **1a** the stubs of stalks left in a field where a crop has been harvested. **1b** (*as modifier*): *a stubble field.* **2** any bristly growth. ORIG C13: from OF *estuble,* from L *stupula,* var. of *stipula* stalk
▸ **'stubbled** *or* **'stubbly** *adj*

stubble-jumper *n Canad. sl.* a prairie grain farmer.

stubborn ('stʌbᵊn) *adj* **1** refusing to comply, agree, or give in. **2** difficult to handle, treat, or overcome. **3** persistent and dogged. ORIG C14 *stoborne,* from ?
▸ **'stubbornly** *adv* ▸ **'stubbornness** *n*

Stubbs ★ (stʌbz) *n* **George.** 1724–1806, British painter, esp. of horses.

stubby ('stʌbɪ) *adj* **stubbier, stubbiest. 1** short and broad; stumpy or thickset. **2** bristling and stiff. ♦ *n* **3** *Austral. sl.* Also: **stubbie.** a small bottle of beer.
▸ **'stubbily** *adv* ▸ **'stubbiness** *n*

stucco ('stʌkəʊ) *n, pl* **stuccoes** *or* **stuccos. 1** a weather-resistant mixture of dehydrated lime, powdered marble, and glue, used in decorative mouldings on buildings. **2** any of various types of cement or plaster used for coating outside walls. **3** Also called: **stuccowork.** decorative work moulded in stucco. ♦ *vb* **stuccoes** *or* **stuccos, stuccoing, stuccoed. 4** (*tr*) to apply stucco to. ORIG C16: from It., of Gmc origin

stuck (stʌk) *vb* **1** the past tense and past participle of **stick**[2]. ♦ *adj* **2** *Inf.* baffled or nonplussed. **3** (foll. by *on*) *Sl.* keen (on) or infatuated (with). **4 get stuck in** *or* **into.** *Inf.* **4a** to perform (a task) with determination. **4b** to attack (a person).

stuck-up *adj Inf.* conceited, arrogant, or snobbish.
▸ **'stuck-'upness** *n*

stud[1] (stʌd) *n* **1** a large-headed nail or other projection protruding from a surface, usually as decoration. **2** a type of fastener consisting of two discs at either end of a short shank, used to fasten shirtfronts, collars, etc. **3** a vertical member used with others to construct the framework of a wall. **4** the crossbar in the centre of a link of a heavy chain. **5** one of a number of rounded projections on the sole of a boot or shoe to give better grip, as on a football boot. ♦ *vb* **studs, studding, studded.** (*tr*) **6** to provide, ornament, or make with studs. **7** to dot or cover (with): *the park was studded with daisies.* **8** to provide or support (a wall, partition, etc.) with studs. ORIG OE *studu*

stud[2] (stʌd) *n* **1** a group of pedigree animals, esp. horses, kept for breeding purposes. **2** any male animal kept principally for breeding purposes, esp. a stallion. **3** a farm or stable where a stud is kept. **4** the state or condition of being kept for breeding purposes: *at stud; put to stud.* **5** (*modifier*) of or relating to such animals or the place where they are kept: *a stud farm; a stud horse.* **6** *Sl.* a virile or sexually active man. **7** short for **stud poker.** ORIG OE *stōd*

studbook ('stʌd,bʊk) *n* a written record of the pedigree of a purebred stock, esp. of racehorses.

studding ('stʌdɪŋ) *n* **1** studs collectively, esp. as used to form a wall or partition. **2** material used to form or serve as studs.

studdingsail ('stʌdɪŋ,seɪl; *Naut.* 'stʌnsᵊl) *n Naut.* a light auxiliary sail set outboard on spars on either side of a square sail. Also called: **stunsail, stuns'l.** ORIG C16: *studding,* ?from MLow G, MDu. *stōtinge,* from *stōten* to thrust

student ('stju:dᵊnt) *n* **1a** a person following a course of study, as in a school, college, university, etc. **1b** (*as modifier*): *student teacher.* **2** a person who makes a thorough study of a subject. ORIG C15: from L *studēns* diligent, from *studēre* to be zealous

Student's t *n* a statistic often used to test the hypothesis that a random sample of normally distributed observations has a given mean. ORIG after *Student,* pen name of W. S. Gosset (1876–1937), Brit. mathematician

studenty ('stju:dᵊntɪ) *adj Inf., sometimes derog.* denoting or exhibiting the characteristics believed typical of an undergraduate student.

studhorse ('stʌd,hɔ:s) *n* another word for **stallion.**

studied ('stʌdɪd) *adj* carefully practised, designed, or premeditated: *a studied reply.*
▸ **'studiedly** *adv* ▸ **'studiedness** *n*

studio ('stju:dɪəʊ) *n, pl* **studios. 1** a room in which an artist, photographer, or musician works. **2** a room used to record television or radio programmes, make films, etc. **3** (*pl*) the premises of a radio, television, or film company. ORIG C19: from It., lit.: study, from L *studium* diligence

studio couch *n* an upholstered couch, usually backless, convertible into a double bed.

studio flat *n* a flat with one main room.

studious ('stju:dɪəs) *adj* **1** given to study. **2** of a serious, thoughtful, and hard-working character. **3** showing deliberation, care, or precision. ORIG C14: from L *studiōsus* devoted to, from *studium* assiduity
▸ **'studiously** *adv* ▸ **'studiousness** *n*

stud poker *n* a variety of poker in which the first card is dealt face down before each player and the next four are dealt face up (**five-card stud**) or in which the first two cards and the last card are dealt face down and the intervening four cards are dealt face up (**seven-card stud**).

study ('stʌdɪ) *vb* **studies, studying, studied. 1** to apply the mind to the learning or understanding of (a subject), esp. by reading. **2** (*tr*) to investigate or examine, as by observation, research, etc. **3** (*tr*) to look at minutely; scrutinize. **4** (*tr*) to give much careful or critical thought to. **5** to take a course in (a subject), as at a college. **6** (*tr*) to try to memorize: *to study a part for a play.* **7** (*intr*) to meditate or contemplate; reflect. ♦ *n, pl* **studies. 8a** the act or process of studying. **8b** (*as modifier*): *study group.* **9** a room used for studying, reading, writing, etc. **10** (*often pl*) work relating to a particular discipline: *environmental studies.* **11** an investigation and analysis of a subject, institution etc. **12** a product of studying, such as a written paper or book. **13** a drawing, sculpture, etc., executed for practice or in preparation for another work. **14** a musical composition intended to develop one aspect of performing technique. **15** *Inf.* **in a brown study.** in a reverie or daydream. ORIG C13: from OF *estudie,* from L *studium* zeal, from *studēre* to be diligent

stuff (stʌf) *vb* (*mainly tr*) **1** to pack or fill completely; cram. **2** (*intr*) to eat large quantities. **3** to force, shove, or squeeze: *to stuff money into a pocket.* **4** to fill (food such as poultry or tomatoes) with a stuffing. **5** to fill (an animal's skin) with material so as to restore the shape of the live animal. **6** *Taboo sl.* to have sexual intercourse with (a woman). **7** *US & Canad.* to fill (a ballot box) with fraudulent votes. **8** *Sl.* to ruin, frustrate, or defeat. ♦ *n* **9** the raw material or fabric of something. **10** woollen cloth or fabric. **11** any general or unspecified substance or accumulation of objects. **12** stupid or worthless actions, speech, etc. **13** subject matter, skill, etc.: *he knows his stuff.* **14** a slang word for **money. 15** *Sl.* a drug, esp. cannabis. **16** *Inf.* **do one's stuff.** to do what is expected of one. **17 that's the stuff.** that is what is needed. **18** *Brit. sl.* a girl or woman

considered sexually (esp. in **bit of stuff**). ORIG C14: from OF *estoffe,* from *estoffer* to furnish, of Gmc origin
▸ **'stuffer** *n*

stuffed (stʌft) *adj* **1** filled with something, esp. (of poultry and other food) filled with stuffing. **2** (foll. by *up*) having the nasal passages blocked with mucus. **3 get stuffed!** *Brit. taboo sl.* an exclamation of contemptuous anger or annoyance against another person.

stuffed shirt *n Inf.* a pompous person.

stuff gown *n Brit.* a woollen gown worn by a barrister who has not taken silk.

stuffing ('stʌfɪŋ) *n* **1** the material with which something is stuffed. **2** a mixture of ingredients with which poultry, meat, etc., is stuffed before cooking. **3 knock the stuffing out of (someone)**. to defeat (someone) utterly.

stuffing box *n* a small chamber in which packing is compressed around a reciprocating or rotating rod or shaft to form a seal.

stuffy ('stʌfɪ) *adj* **stuffier, stuffiest. 1** lacking fresh air. **2** excessively dull, staid, or conventional. **3** (of the nasal passages) blocked with mucus.
▸ **'stuffily** *adv* ▸ **'stuffiness** *n*

stultify ('stʌltɪˌfaɪ) *vb* **stultifies, stultifying, stultified.** (*tr*) **1** to make useless, futile, or ineffectual, esp. by routine. **2** to cause to appear absurd or inconsistent. ORIG C18: from L *stultus* stupid + *facere* to make
▸ **ˌstultifiˈcation** *n* ▸ **'stultiˌfier** *n*

stum (stʌm) (in wine-making) ◆ *n* **1** a less common word for **must**[2]. **2** partly fermented wine added to fermented wine as a preservative. ◆ *vb* **stums, stumming, stummed. 3** to preserve (wine) by adding stum. ORIG C17: from Du. *stom* dumb

stumble ('stʌmbᵊl) *vb* **stumbles, stumbling, stumbled.** (*intr*) **1** to trip or fall while walking or running. **2** to walk in an awkward, unsteady, or unsure way. **3** to make mistakes or hesitate in speech or actions. **4** (foll. by *across* or *upon*) to come (across) by accident. ◆ *n* **5** a false step, trip, or blunder. **6** the act of stumbling. ORIG C14: rel. to Norwegian *stumla,* Danish dialect *stumle*
▸ **'stumbler** *n* ▸ **'stumbling** *adj* ▸ **'stumblingly** *adv*

stumbling block *n* any impediment or obstacle.

stumer ('stjuːmə) *n* **1** *Sl.* a forgery or cheat. **2** *Irish dialect.* a poor bargain. **3** *Scot.* a stupid person. **4 come a stumer.** *Austral. sl.* to crash financially. ORIG from ?

stump (stʌmp) *n* **1** the base of a tree trunk left standing after the tree has been felled or has fallen. **2** the part of something, such as a tooth, limb, or blade, that remains after a larger part has been removed. **3** (*often pl*) *Inf., facetious.* a leg (esp. in **stir one's stumps**). **4** *Cricket.* any of three upright wooden sticks that, with two bails laid across them, form a wicket (the **stumps**). **5** Also called: **tortillon.** a short sharply-pointed stick of cork or rolled paper or leather, used in drawing and shading. **6** a heavy tread or the sound of heavy footsteps. **7** a platform used by an orator when addressing a meeting. ◆ *vb* **8** (*tr*) to stop, confuse, or puzzle. **9** (*intr*) to plod or trudge heavily. **10** (*tr*) *Cricket.* to dismiss (a batsman) by breaking his wicket with the ball or with the ball in the hand while he is out of his crease. **11** *Chiefly US & Canad.* to campaign or canvass (an area), esp. by political speech-making. ORIG C14: from MLow G *stump*
▸ **'stumper** *n*

stump up *vb* (*adv*) *Brit. inf.* to give (the money required).

stumpy ('stʌmpɪ) *adj* **stumpier, stumpiest. 1** short and thickset like a stump; stubby. **2** full of stumps.
▸ **'stumpiness** *n*

stun (stʌn) *vb* **stuns, stunning, stunned.** (*tr*) **1** to render unconscious, as by a heavy blow or fall. **2** to shock or overwhelm. **3** to surprise or astound. ◆ *n* **4** the state or effect of being stunned. ORIG C13 *stunen,* from OF *estoner* to daze, ult. from L EX-[1] + *tonāre* to thunder

stung (stʌŋ) *vb* the past tense and past participle of **sting.**

stunk (stʌŋk) *vb* a past tense and past participle of **stink.**

stunner ('stʌnə) *n Inf.* a person or thing of great beauty, quality, size, etc.

stunning ('stʌnɪŋ) *adj Inf.* very attractive, impressive, astonishing, etc.
▸ **'stunningly** *adv*

stunsail *or* **stuns'l** ('stʌnsᵊl) *n* another word for **studdingsail.**

stunt[1] (stʌnt) *vb* **1** (*tr*) to prevent or impede (the growth or development) of (a plant, animal, etc.). ◆ *n* **2** the act or an instance of stunting. **3** a person, animal, or plant that has been stunted. ORIG C17 (as vb: to check the growth of): ?from C15 *stont* of short duration, from OE *stunt* foolish; sense prob. infl. by ON *stuttr* dwarfed
▸ **'stunted** *adj* ▸ **'stuntedness** *n*

stunt[2] (stʌnt) *n* **1** a feat of daring or skill. **2a** an acrobatic or dangerous piece of action in a film, etc. **2b** (*as modifier*)*: a stunt man.* **3** anything spectacular or unusual done for attention. ◆ *vb* **4** (*intr*) to perform a stunt or stunts. ORIG C19: US student slang, from ?

stupa ('stuːpə) *n* a domed edifice housing Buddhist or Jain relics. ORIG C19: from Sansk.: dome

stupe (stjuːp) *n Med.* a hot damp cloth, usually sprinkled with an irritant, applied to the body to relieve pain by counterirritation. ORIG C14: from L *stuppa* flax, from Gk *stuppē*

stupefacient (ˌstjuːpɪˈfeɪʃɪənt) *n* **1** a drug that causes stupor. ◆ *adj* **2** of, relating to, or designating this type of drug. ORIG C17: from L *stupefaciēns,* from *stupēre* to be stunned + *facere* to make

stupefaction (ˌstjuːpɪˈfækʃən) *n* **1** astonishment. **2** the act of stupefying or the state of being stupefied.

stupefy ('stjuːpɪˌfaɪ) *vb* **stupefies, stupefying, stupefied.** (*tr*) **1** to render insensitive or lethargic. **2** to confuse or astound. ORIG C16: from OF *stupefier,* from L *stupefacere;* see STUPEFACIENT
▸ **'stupeˌfying** *adj*

stupendous (stjuːˈpɛndəs) *adj* astounding, wonderful, huge, etc. ORIG C17: from L *stupēre* to be amazed
▸ **stuˈpendously** *adv* ▸ **stuˈpendousness** *n*

stupid ('stjuːpɪd) *adj* **1** lacking in common sense, perception, or intelligence. **2** (*usually postpositive*) dazed or stupefied: *stupid from lack of sleep.* **3** slow-witted. **4** trivial, silly, or frivolous. ◆ *n* **5** *Inf.* a stupid person. ORIG C16: from F *stupide,* from L *stupidus* silly, from *stupēre* to be amazed
▸ **stuˈpidity** *or* **'stupidness** *n*

stupor ('stjuːpə) *n* **1** a state of unconsciousness. **2** mental dullness; torpor. ORIG C17: from L, from *stupēre* to be aghast
▸ **'stuporous** *adj*

sturdy ('stɜːdɪ) *adj* **sturdier, sturdiest. 1** healthy, strong, and vigorous. **2** strongly built; stalwart. ORIG C13 (in the sense: rash, harsh): from OF *estordi* dazed, from *estordir* to stun
▸ **'sturdily** *adv* ▸ **'sturdiness** *n*

sturgeon ('stɜːdʒən) *n* any of various primitive bony fishes of temperate waters of the N hemisphere, having an elongated snout and rows of spines along the body. ORIG C13: from OF *estourgeon,* of Gmc origin

Sturt ★ (stɜːt) *n* **Charles.** 1795–1869, British explorer, who led three expeditions (1828–29; 1829; 1844–45) into the Australian interior, discovering the Darling River (1828).

Sturt's desert pea (stɜːts) *n* another name for **desert pea.**

stutter ('stʌtə) *vb* **1** to speak (a word, phrase, etc.) with recurring repetition of consonants, esp. initial ones. **2** to make (an abrupt sound) repeatedly: *the gun stuttered.* ◆ *n* **3** the act or habit of stuttering. **4** a stuttering sound. ORIG C16
▸ **'stutterer** *n* ▸ **'stuttering** *n, adj* ▸ **'stutteringly** *adv*

Stuttgart ★ (*German* 'ʃtutgart) *n* an industrial city in W Germany, capital of Baden-Württemberg state, on the River Neckar: developed around a stud farm (*Stuotgarten*) of the Counts of Württemberg. Pop.: 585 604 (1996 est.).

Stuyvesant ★ ('staɪvɪsᵊnt) *n* **Peter.** ?1610–72, Dutch colonial administrator of New Netherland (later New York) (1646–64).

sty (staɪ) *n, pl* **sties. 1** a pen in which pigs are housed. **2** any filthy or corrupt place. ◆ *vb* **sties, stying, stied. 3** to enclose or be enclosed in a sty. ORIG OE *stig*

stye *or* **sty** (staɪ) *n, pl* **styes** *or* **sties.** inflammation of a sebaceous gland of the eyelid. ORIG C15 *styanye* (mistaken as *sty on eye*), from OE *stīgend* rising, hence swelling, + *ye* eye

Stygian ('stɪdʒɪən) *adj* **1** of or relating to the Styx. **2** *Chiefly literary.* dark, gloomy, or hellish. ORIG C16: from L *Stygius,* from Gk *Stugios,* from *Stux* STYX

style (staɪl) *n* **1** a form of appearance, design, or production; type or make. **2** the way in which something is done: *good style.* **3** the manner in which something is expressed or performed, considered as separate from its intrinsic content, meaning, etc. **4** a distinctive, formal, or characteristic manner of expression in words, music, painting, etc. **5** elegance or refinement of manners, dress, etc. **6** prevailing fashion in dress, looks, etc. **7** a fashionable or ostentatious mode of existence: *to live in style.* **8** the particular mode of orthography, punctuation, design, etc., followed in a book, journal, etc., or in a printing or publishing house. **9** *Chiefly Brit.* the distinguishing title or form of address of a person or firm. **10** *Bot.* the long slender extension of the ovary, bearing the stigma. **11** a method of expressing or calculating dates. See **Old Style, New Style. 12** another word for **stylus** (sense 1). **13** the arm of a sundial. ◆ *vb* **styles, styling, styled.** (*mainly tr*) **14** to design, shape, or tailor: *to style hair.* **15** to adapt or make suitable for. **16** to make consistent or correct according to a printing or publishing style. **17** to name or call; designate: *to style a man a fool.* ORIG C13: from L *stylus, stilus* writing implement, hence characteristics of the writing, style
▸ **'stylar** *adj* ▸ **'styler** *n*

stylebook ('staɪlˌbʊk) *n* a book containing rules and examples of punctuation, typography, etc., for the use of writers, editors, and printers.

stylet ('staɪlɪt) *n Surgery.* **1** a wire for insertion into a catheter, etc., to maintain its rigidity during passage. **2** a slender probe. ORIG C17: from F *stilet,* from OIt. STILETTO; infl. by L *stylus* style

styling mousse *n* a light foamy substance applied to the hair before styling in order to retain the style.

stylish ('staɪlɪʃ) *adj* having style; smart; fashionable.
▸ **'stylishly** *adv* ▸ **'stylishness** *n*

stylist ('staɪlɪst) *n* **1** a person who performs, writes, or acts with attention to style. **2** a designer of clothes, décor, etc. **3** a hairdresser who styles hair.

stylistic (staɪ'lɪstɪk) *adj* of or relating to style, esp. artistic or literary style.
▸ **sty'listically** *adv*

stylite ('staɪlaɪt) *n Christianity.* one of a class of recluses who in ancient times lived on the top of high pillars. ORIG C17: from LGk *stulitēs,* from Gk *stulos* a pillar
▸ **stylitic** (staɪ'lɪtɪk) *adj*

stylize *or* **stylise** ('staɪlaɪz) *vb* **stylizes, stylizing, stylized** *or* **stylises, stylising, stylised.** (*tr*) to give a conventional or established stylistic form to.
▸ **ˌstyli'zation** *or* **ˌstyli'sation** *n*

stylo- *or before a vowel* **styl-** *combining form.* **1** (in biology) a style. **2** indicating a column or point: *stylobate; stylograph.* ORIG from Gk *stulos* column

stylobate ('staɪləˌbeɪt) *n* a continuous horizontal course of masonry that supports a colonnade. ORIG C17: from L *stylobatēs,* from Gk *stulos* pillar + *-batēs,* from *bainein* to walk

stylograph ('staɪləˌgrɑːf) *n* a fountain pen having a fine hollow tube as the writing point instead of a nib. ORIG C19: from STYL(US) + -GRAPH

styloid ('staɪlɔɪd) *adj* **1** resembling a stylus. **2** *Anat.* of or relating to a projecting process of the temporal bone. ORIG C18: from NL *styloides,* from Gk *stuloeidēs* like a stylus; infl. by Gk *stulos* pillar

stylops ('staɪlɒps) *n, pl* **stylopes** (-ləˌpiːz). any of various insects living as a parasite in other insects, esp. bees and wasps. ORIG C19: NL, from Gk, from *stulos* a pillar + *ōps* an eye, from the fact that the male has stalked eyes

stylus ('staɪləs) *n, pl* **styli** (-laɪ) *or* **styluses. 1** Also called: **style.** a pointed instrument for engraving, drawing, or writing. **2** a tool used in ancient times for writing on wax tablets, which was pointed at one end and blunt at the other for erasing. **3** Also called: **needle.** a device attached to the cartridge in the pick-up arm of a record player that rests in the groove in the record, transmitting the vibrations to the sensing device in the cartridge. ORIG C18: from L, var. of *stilus* writing implement

stymie *or* **stymy** ('staɪmɪ) *vb* **stymies, stymieing** *or* **stymying, stymied.** (*tr; often passive*) **1** to hinder or thwart. **2** *Golf.* (formerly) to impede with a stymie. ◆ *n, pl* **stymies. 3** *Golf.* (formerly) a situation in which an opponent's ball is blocking the line between the hole and the ball about to be played. **4** a situation of obstruction. ORIG C19: from ?

styptic ('stɪptɪk) *adj* **1** contracting the blood vessels or tissues. ◆ *n* **2** a styptic drug. ORIG C14: via LL, from Gk *stuptikos* capable of contracting, from *stuphein* to contract

styrene ('staɪriːn) *n* a colourless oily volatile flammable liquid made from ethylene and benzene. It readily polymerizes and is used in making synthetic plastics and rubbers. Formula: $C_6H_5CH:CH_2$. Systematic name: **phenylethene.** ORIG C20: from Gk *sturax* tree of the genus *Styrax* + -ENE

Styria ★ ('stɪərɪə) *n* a mountainous state of SE Austria: rich mineral resources. Capital: Graz. Pop.: 1 204 904 (1998 est.). Area: 16 384 sq. km (6326 sq. miles). German name: **Steiermark.**

Styrofoam ('staɪrəˌfəʊm) *n Trademark.* (*sometimes not cap.*) a light form of expanded polystyrene. ORIG C20: from POLYSTYRENE + FOAM

Styx ★ (stɪks) *n Greek myth.* a river in Hades across which Charon ferried the souls of the dead. ORIG from Gk *Stux;* related to *stugein* to hate

suable ('sjuːəbᵊl) *adj* liable to be sued in a court.
▸ **ˌsua'bility** *n*

Suakin ★ ('suːɑːkɪn) *n* a port in the NE Sudan, on the Red Sea: formerly the chief port of the African Red Sea; now obstructed by a coral reef. Pop.: 6000 (latest est.).

suasion ('sweɪʒən) *n* a rare word for **persuasion.** ORIG C14: from L *suāsiō,* from *suādēre* to PERSUADE
▸ **'suasive** *adj*

suave (swɑːv) *adj* (esp. of a man) displaying smoothness and sophistication in manner; urbane. ORIG C16: from L *suāvis* sweet
▸ **'suavely** *adv* ▸ **suavity** ('swɑːvɪtɪ) *or* **'suaveness** *n*

sub (sʌb) *n* **1** short for several words beginning with *sub-,* such as **subeditor, submarine, subordinate, subscription,** and **substitute. 2** *Brit. inf.* an advance payment of wages or salary. Formal term: **subsistence allowance.** ◆ *vb* **subs, subbing, subbed. 3** (*intr*) to serve or act as a substitute. **4** *Brit. inf.* to grant or receive (an advance payment of wages or salary). **5** (*tr*) *Inf.* short for **subedit.**

sub. *abbrev. for:* **1** subeditor. **2** *Music.* subito. **3** subscription. **4** substitute.

sub- *prefix* **1** situated under or beneath: *subterranean.* **2** secondary in rank; subordinate: *subeditor.* **3** falling short of; less than or imperfectly: *subarctic; subhuman.* **4** forming a subdivision or subordinate part: *subcommittee.* **5** (in chemistry) **5a** indicating that a compound contains a relatively small proportion of a specified element: *suboxide.* **5b** indicating that a salt is basic salt: *subacetate.* ORIG from L *sub*

subacid (sʌb'æsɪd) *adj* (esp. of some fruits) moderately acid or sour.
▸ **subacidity** (ˌsʌbə'sɪdɪtɪ) *or* **sub'acidness** *n*

subadar *or* **subahdar** ('suːbəˌdɑː) *n* (formerly) the chief native officer of a company of Indian soldiers in the British service. ORIG C17: via Urdu from Persian, from *sūba* province + *-dār* holding

subalpine (sʌb'ælpaɪn) *adj* **1** situated in or relating to the regions at the foot of mountains. **2** (of plants) growing below the tree line in mountainous regions.

subaltern ('sʌbᵊltən) *n* **1** a commissioned officer below the rank of captain in certain armies, esp. the British.

◆ *adj* **2** of inferior position or rank. **3** *Logic.* (of a proposition) particular, esp. in relation to a universal of the same quality. ORIG C16: from LL *subalternus,* from L SUB- + *alternus* alternate, from *alter* the other

subalternation (ˌsʌbɔːltəˈneɪʃən) *n Logic.* the relation between a universal and a particular proposition of the same quality where the universal proposition implies the particular proposition.

subantarctic (ˌsʌbæntˈɑːktɪk) *adj* of or relating to latitudes immediately north of the Antarctic Circle.

subaqua (ˌsʌbˈækwə) *adj* of or relating to underwater sport: *subaqua swimming.*

subaqueous (sʌbˈeɪkwɪəs, -ˈækwɪ-) *adj* occurring, formed, or used under water.

subarctic (sʌbˈɑːktɪk) *adj* of or relating to latitudes immediately south of the Arctic Circle.

subatomic (ˌsʌbəˈtɒmɪk) *adj* **1** of, relating to, or being a particle making up an atom or a process occurring within atoms. **2** having dimensions smaller than atomic dimensions.

subbasement (ˈsʌbˌbeɪsmənt) *n* a storey of a building beneath the main basement.

subclass (ˈsʌbˌklɑːs) *n* **1** a principal subdivision of a class. **2** *Biol.* a taxonomic group that is a subdivision of a class. **3** *Maths.* another name for **subset.**

subclavian (sʌbˈkleɪvɪən) *adj Anat.* (of an artery, vein, etc.) below the clavicle. ORIG C17: from NL *subclāvius,* from L SUB- + *clavis* key

subclinical (sʌbˈklɪnɪkᵊl) *adj Med.* of or relating to the stage in the course of a disease before the symptoms are first noted.
▸ **subˈclinically** *adv*

subconscious (sʌbˈkɒnʃəs) *adj* **1** acting or existing without one's awareness. ◆ *n* **2** *Psychol.* that part of the mind on the fringe of consciousness which contains material it is possible to become aware of by redirecting attention.
▸ **subˈconsciously** *adv* ▸ **subˈconsciousness** *n*

subcontinent (sʌbˈkɒntɪnənt) *n* a large land mass that is a distinct part of a continent, such as India is of Asia.
▸ **subcontinental** (ˌsʌbkɒntɪˈnɛntᵊl) *adj*

subcontract *n* (sʌbˈkɒntrækt). **1** a subordinate contract under which the supply of materials, labour, etc., is let out to someone other than a party to the main contract. ◆ *vb* (ˌsʌbkənˈtrækt). **2** (*intr;* often foll. by *for*) to enter into or make a subcontract. **3** (*tr*) to let out (work) on a subcontract.
▸ **ˌsubconˈtractor** *n*

subcontrary (sʌbˈkɒntrərɪ) *Logic.* ◆ *adj* **1** (of a pair of propositions) related such that they cannot both be false at once, although they may be true together. ◆ *n, pl* **subcontraries. 2** a statement which cannot be false when a given statement is false.

subcritical (sʌbˈkrɪtɪkᵊl) *adj Physics.* (of a nuclear reaction, power station, etc.) having or involving a chain reaction that is not self-sustaining; not yet critical.

subculture (ˈsʌbˌkʌltʃə) *n* a subdivision of a national culture or an enclave within it with a distinct integrated network of behaviour, beliefs, and attitudes.
▸ **subˈcultural** *adj*

subcutaneous (ˌsʌbkjuːˈteɪnɪəs) *adj Med.* situated, used, or introduced beneath the skin.
▸ **ˌsubcuˈtaneously** *adv*

subdeacon (ˌsʌbˈdiːkən) *n Chiefly RC Church.* **1** a cleric who assists at High Mass. **2** (formerly) a person ordained to the lowest of the major orders.
▸ **subdeaconate** (sʌbˈdiːkənɪt) *n*

subdivide (ˌsʌbdɪˈvaɪd, ˈsʌbdɪˌvaɪd) *vb* **subdivides, subdividing, subdivided.** to divide (something) resulting from an earlier division.
▸ **ˈsubdiˌvision** *n*

subdominant (sʌbˈdɒmɪnənt) *Music.* ◆ *n* **1** the fourth degree of a major or minor scale. **2** a key or chord based on this. ◆ *adj* **3** of or relating to the subdominant.

subdue (səbˈdjuː) *vb* **subdues, subduing, subdued.** (*tr*) **1** to establish ascendancy over by force. **2** to overcome and bring under control, as by intimidation or persuasion. **3** to hold in check or repress (feelings, etc.). **4** to render less intense or less conspicuous. ORIG C14 *sobdue,* from OF *soduire* to mislead, from L *subdūcere* to remove; infl. by L *subdere* to subject
▸ **subˈduable** *adj* ▸ **subˈdual** *n*

subdued (səbˈdjuːd) *adj* **1** cowed, passive, or shy. **2** gentle or quiet: *a subdued whisper.* **3** (of colours, lighting, etc.) not harsh or bright.

subdural (sʌbˈdjʊərəl) *adj Anat.* between the dura mater and the arachnoid: *subdural haematoma.*

subedit (sʌbˈɛdɪt) *vb* **subedits, subediting, subedited.** to edit and correct (written or printed material).

subeditor (sʌbˈɛdɪtə) *n* a person who checks and edits copy, esp. on a newspaper.

subequatorial (sʌbˌɛkwəˈtɔːrɪəl) *adj* in or characteristic of regions immediately north or south of equatorial regions.

suberose (ˈsjuːbəˌrəʊs), **subereous** (sjuːˈbɛrɪəs), *or* **suberic** (sjuːˈbɛrɪk) *adj Bot.* relating to, resembling, or consisting of cork; corky. ORIG C19: from L *sūber* cork + -OSE[1]

subfamily (ˈsʌbˌfæmɪlɪ) *n, pl* **subfamilies. 1** *Biol.* a taxonomic group that is a subdivision of a family. **2** a subdivision of a family of languages.

subfusc (ˈsʌbfʌsk) *adj* **1** devoid of brightness or appeal; drab, dull, or dark. ◆ *n* **2** (at Oxford University) formal academic dress. ORIG C18: from L *subfuscus* dusky, from *fuscus* dark

subgenus (ˈsʌbˌdʒiːnəs, -ˌdʒɛn-) *n, pl* **subgenera** (-ˈdʒɛnərə) *or* **subgenuses.** *Biol.* a subdivision of a genus that is of higher rank than a species.
▸ **subgeneric** (ˌsʌbdʒəˈnɛrɪk) *adj*

subheading (ˈsʌbˌhɛdɪŋ) *or* **subhead** *n* **1** the heading or title of a subdivision or subsection of a printed work. **2** a division subordinate to a main heading or title.

subhuman (sʌbˈhjuːmən) *adj* **1** of or designating animals below man (*Homo sapiens*) in evolutionary development. **2** less than human.

subindex (sʌbˈɪndɛks) *n, pl* **subindices** (-dɪˌsiːz) *or* **subindexes.** another word for **subscript** (sense 2).

subitize *or* **subitise** (ˈsʌbɪˌtaɪz) *vb* **subitizes, subitizing, subitized** *or* **subitises, subitising, subitised.** *Psychol.* to perceive the number of (a group of items) at a glance and without counting: *the maximum number of items that can be subitized is about five.* ORIG C20: from L *subitus* sudden + -IZE

subito (ˈsuːbɪˌtəʊ) *adv Music.* suddenly; immediately. ORIG C18: via It. from L: suddenly, from *subitus* sudden, from *subīre* to approach

subj. *abbrev. for:* **1** subject. **2** subjective(ly). **3** subjunctive.

subjacent (sʌbˈdʒeɪsᵊnt) *adj* **1** forming a foundation; underlying. **2** lower than. ORIG C16: from L *subjacēre* to lie close, be under
▸ **subˈjacency** *n* ▸ **subˈjacently** *adv*

subject *n* (ˈsʌbdʒɪkt). **1** the predominant theme or topic, as of a book, discussion, etc. **2** any branch of learning considered as a course of study. **3** *Grammar, logic.* a word, phrase, etc., about which something is predicated or stated in a sentence; for example, *the cat* in the sentence *The cat catches mice.* **4** a person or thing that undergoes experiment, treatment, etc. **5** a person under the rule of a monarch, government, etc. **6** an object, figure, scene, etc., as portrayed by an artist or photographer. **7** *Philosophy.* **7a** that which thinks or feels as opposed to the object of thinking and feeling; the self or the mind. **7b** a substance as opposed to its attributes. **8** Also called: **theme.** *Music.* the principal motif of a fugue, the basis from which the musical material is derived in a sonata-form movement, or the recurrent figure in a rondo. **9** *Logic.* the term of a proposition about which something is asserted. **10** an originating motive. **11 change the subject.** to select a new topic of conversation. ◆ *adj* (ˈsʌbdʒɪkt). (*usually postpositive;* foll. by *to*) **12** being under the power or sovereignty of a ruler, government, etc.: *subject peoples.* **13** showing a tendency (towards): *a child subject to indiscipline.* **14** exposed or vulnerable: *subject to ribaldry.* **15** conditional upon: *the results are subject to correction.* ◆ *adv* (ˈsʌbdʒɪkt). **16 subject to.** (*prep*) under the condition that: *we accept, subject to her agreement.*

◆ *vb* (səbˈdʒɛkt). (*tr*) **17** (foll. by *to*) to cause to undergo: *they subjected him to torture.* **18** (*often passive;* foll. by *to*) to expose or render vulnerable or liable (to some experience): *he was subjected to great danger.* **19** (foll. by *to*) to bring under the control or authority (of): *to subject a soldier to discipline.* **20** *Rare.* to present for consideration; submit. ORIG C14: from L *subjectus* brought under, from *subicere* to place under, from SUB- + *jacere* to throw
▸ **subˈjectable** *adj* ▸ **subˈjection** *n*

subjective (səbˈdʒɛktɪv) *adj* **1** of, proceeding from, or relating to the mind of the thinking subject and not the nature of the object being considered. **2** of, relating to, or emanating from a person's emotions, prejudices, etc. **3** relating to the inherent nature of a person or thing; essential. **4** existing only as perceived and not as a thing in itself. **5** *Med.* (of a symptom, condition, etc.) experienced only by the patient and incapable of being recognized or studied by anyone else. **6** *Grammar.* denoting a case of nouns and pronouns, esp. in languages having only two cases, that identifies the subject of a finite verb and (in formal use in English) is selected for predicate complements, as in *It is I.* ◆ *n* **7** *Grammar.* **7a** the subjective case. **7b** a subjective word or speech element. Cf. **objective.**
▸ **subˈjectively** *adv* ▸ **ˌsubjecˈtivity** *or* **subˈjectiveness** *n*

subjectivism (səbˈdʒɛktɪˌvɪzəm) *n Philosophy.* the doctrine that there are no absolute moral values but that these are variable in the same way that taste is.
▸ **subˈjectivist** *n*

subjoin (sʌbˈdʒɔɪn) *vb* (*tr*) to add or attach at the end of something spoken, written, etc. ORIG C16: from F *subjoindre,* from L *subjungere* to add to, from *sub-* in addition + *jungere* to join
▸ **subˈjoinder** *n*

sub judice (ˈdʒuːdɪsɪ) *adj* (*usually postpositive*) before a court of law or a judge; under judicial consideration. ORIG L

subjugate (ˈsʌbdʒʊˌgeɪt) *vb* **subjugates, subjugating, subjugated.** (*tr*) **1** to bring into subjection. **2** to make subservient or submissive. ORIG C15: from LL *subjugāre* to subdue, from L SUB- + *jugum* yoke
▸ **ˈsubjugable** *adj* ▸ **ˌsubjuˈgation** *n* ▸ **ˈsubjuˌgator** *n*

subjunctive (səbˈdʒʌŋktɪv) *Grammar.* ◆ *adj* **1** denoting a mood of verbs used when the content of the clause is being doubted, supposed, feared true, etc., rather than being asserted. In the following sentence, *were* is in the subjunctive: *I'd think seriously about it if I were you.* Cf. **indicative.** ◆ *n* **2a** the subjunctive mood. **2b** a verb in this mood. ORIG C16: via LL *subjunctīvus,* from L *subjungere* to SUBJOIN
▸ **subˈjunctively** *adv*

sublease *n* (ˈsʌbˌliːs). **1** a lease of property made by a lessee or tenant of that property. ◆ *vb* (sʌbˈliːs), **subleases, subleasing, subleased. 2** to grant a sublease of (property); sublet. **3** (*tr*) to obtain or hold by sublease.
▸ **sublessee** (ˌsʌblɛˈsiː) *n* ▸ **sublessor** (ˌsʌblɛˈsɔː) *n*

sublet (sʌbˈlɛt) *vb* **sublets, subletting, sublet. 1** to grant a sublease of (property). **2** to let out (work, etc.) under a subcontract.

sublieutenant (ˌsʌbləˈtɛnənt) *n* the most junior commissioned officer in the Royal Navy and certain other navies.
▸ **ˌsublieuˈtenancy** *n*

sublimate (ˈsʌblɪˌmeɪt) *vb* **sublimates, sublimating, sublimated. 1** *Psychol.* to direct the energy of (a primitive impulse) into activities that are socially more acceptable. **2** (*tr*) to make purer; refine. ◆ *n* **3** *Chem.* the material obtained when a substance is sublimed. ORIG C16: from L *sublīmāre* to elevate, from *sublīmis* lofty; see SUBLIME
▸ **ˌsubliˈmation** *n*

sublime (səˈblaɪm) *adj* **1** of high moral, intellectual, or spiritual value; noble; exalted. **2** inspiring deep veneration or awe. **3** unparalleled; supreme. **4** *Poetic.* of proud bearing or aspect. **5** *Arch.* raised up. ◆ *n* **the sublime. 6** something that is sublime. **7** the ultimate degree or perfect example: *the sublime of folly.* ◆ *vb* **sublimes, subliming, sublimed. 8** (*tr*) to make higher or purer. **9** to change or cause to change directly from a solid to a vapour or gas without first melting. **10** to undergo or cause to undergo this process followed by a reverse change directly from a vapour to a solid: *to sublime iodine onto glass.* ORIG C14: from L *sublīmis* lofty, ?from *sub-* up to + *līmen* lintel
▸ **subˈlimely** *adv* ▸ **sublimity** (səˈblɪmɪtɪ) *n*

subliminal (sʌbˈlɪmɪnᵊl) *adj* **1** resulting from processes of which the individual is not aware. **2** (of stimuli) less than the minimum intensity or duration required to elicit a response. ORIG C19: from L *sub-* below + *līmen* threshold
▸ **subˈliminally** *adv*

subliminal advertising *n* advertising on film or television that employs subliminal images to influence the viewer unconsciously.

sublingual (sʌbˈlɪŋgwəl) *adj Anat.* situated beneath the tongue.

sublunary (sʌbˈluːnərɪ) *adj* **1** between the moon and the earth. **2** of or relating to the earth. ORIG C16: via LL, from L SUB- + *lūna* moon

sub-machine-gun *n* a portable automatic or semiautomatic light gun with a short barrel, designed to be fired from the hip or shoulder.

submarginal (sʌbˈmɑːdʒɪnᵊl) *adj* **1** below the minimum requirements. **2** (of land) infertile and unprofitable.
▸ **subˈmarginally** *adv*

submarine (ˈsʌbməˌriːn, ˌsʌbməˈriːn) *n* **1** a vessel, esp. a warship, capable of operating below the surface of the sea. **2** (*modifier*) **2a** of or relating to a submarine: *a submarine captain.* **2b** below the surface of the sea: *a submarine cable.*
▸ **submariner** (sʌbˈmærɪnə) *n*

submaxillary gland (ˌsʌbmækˈsɪlərɪ) *n* (in mammals) either of a pair of salivary glands situated on each side behind the lower jaw.

submediant (sʌbˈmiːdɪənt) *Music.* ◆ *n* **1** the sixth degree of a major or minor scale. **2** a key or chord based on this. ◆ *adj* **3** of or relating to the submediant.

submerge (səbˈmɜːdʒ) *or* **submerse** (səbˈmɜːs) *vb* **submerges, submerging, submerged** *or* **submerses, submersing, submersed. 1** to plunge, sink, or dive or cause to plunge, sink, or dive below the surface of water, etc. **2** (*tr*) to cover with water or other liquid. **3** (*tr*) to hide; suppress. **4** (*tr*) to overwhelm, as with work, etc. ORIG C17: from L *submergere*
▸ **subˈmergence** *or* **subˈmersion** *n*

submersible (səbˈmɜːsɪbᵊl) *or* **submergible** (səbˈmɜːdʒɪbᵊl) *adj* **1** able to be submerged. **2** capable of operating under water, etc. ◆ *n* **3** a vessel designed to operate under water for short periods. **4** a submarine designed and equipped to carry out work below the level that divers can work.
▸ **subˌmersiˈbility** *or* **subˌmergiˈbility** *n*

subminiature (sʌbˈmɪnɪətʃə) *adj* smaller than miniature.

subminiature camera *n* a pocket-sized camera, usually using 16 millimetre film.

submission (səbˈmɪʃən) *n* **1** an act or instance of submitting. **2** something submitted; a proposal, etc. **3** the quality or condition of being submissive. **4** the act of referring a document, etc., for the consideration of someone else.

submissive (səbˈmɪsɪv) *adj* of, tending towards, or indicating submission, humility, or servility.
▸ **subˈmissively** *adv* ▸ **subˈmissiveness** *n*

submit (səbˈmɪt) *vb* **submits, submitting, submitted. 1** (*often* foll. by *to*) to yield (oneself), as to the will of another person, a superior force, etc. **2** (foll. by *to*) to subject or be voluntarily subjected (to analysis, treatment, etc.). **3** (*tr; often* foll. by *to*) to refer (something to someone) for judgment or consideration. **4** (*tr; may take a clause as object*) to state, contend, or propose deferentially. **5** (*intr; often* foll. by *to*) to defer or accede (to the decision, etc., of another). ORIG C14: from L *submittere* to place under
▸ **subˈmittable** *or* **subˈmissible** *adj* ▸ **subˈmittal** *n* ▸ **subˈmitter** *n*

submultiple (sʌbˈmʌltɪpᵊl) *n* **1** a number that can be divided into another number an integral number of times without a remainder: *three is a submultiple of nine.* ◆ *adj* **2** being a submultiple of a quantity or number.

subnormal (sʌb'nɔːməl) *adj* **1** less than the normal. **2** having a low intelligence. ◆ *n* **3** a subnormal person.
▸ **subnormality** (ˌsʌbnɔː'mælɪtɪ) *n*

subnuclear (sʌb'njuːklɪə) *adj* in or smaller than the nucleus of an atom.

suborbital (sʌb'ɔːbɪtᵊl) *adj* **1** (of a rocket, missile, etc.) having a flight path that is less than an orbit of the earth or other celestial body. **2** *Anat.* situated beneath the orbit of the eye.

suborder ('sʌbˌɔːdə) *n Biol.* a subdivision of an order.
▸ **sub'ordinal** *adj*

subordinate *adj* (sə'bɔːdɪnɪt). **1** of lesser order or importance. **2** under the authority or control of another: *a subordinate functionary.* ◆ *n* (sə'bɔːdɪnɪt). **3** a person or thing that is subordinate. ◆ *vb* (sə'bɔːdɪˌneɪt), **subordinates, subordinating, subordinated.** (*tr;* usually foll. by *to*) **4** to put in a lower rank or position (than). **5** to make subservient: *to subordinate mind to heart.* ORIG C15: from Med. L *subordināre,* from L SUB- + *ordō* rank
▸ **sub'ordinately** *adv* ▸ **subˌordi'nation** *n* ▸ **sub'ordinative** *adj*

subordinate clause *n Grammar.* a clause with an adjectival, adverbial, or nominal function, rather than one that functions as a separate sentence in its own right.

subordinating conjunction *n* a conjunction that introduces subordinate clauses, such as *if, because, although,* and *until.*

suborn (sə'bɔːn) *vb* (*tr*) **1** to bribe, incite, or instigate (a person) to commit a wrongful act. **2** *Law.* to induce (a witness) to commit perjury. ORIG C16: from L *subornāre,* from *sub-* secretly + *ornāre* to furnish
▸ **subornation** (ˌsʌbɔː'neɪʃən) *n* ▸ **subornative** (sʌ'bɔːnətɪv) *adj* ▸ **sub'orner** *n*

Subotica ★ (*Serbo-Croat* 'subɔtitsa) *n* a town in NE Yugoslavia, in Serbia near the border with Hungary: agricultural and industrial centre. Pop.: 100 386 (1991). Hungarian name: **Szabadka.**

suboxide (sʌb'ɒksaɪd) *n* an oxide of an element containing less oxygen than the common oxide formed by the element: *carbon suboxide,* C_2O_3.

subplot ('sʌbˌplɒt) *n* a subordinate or auxiliary plot in a novel, play, film, etc.

subpoena (səb'piːnə) *n* **1** a writ issued by a court of justice requiring a person to appear before the court at a specified time. ◆ *vb* **subpoenas, subpoenaing, subpoenaed. 2** (*tr*) to serve with a subpoena. ORIG C15: from L: under penalty

subrogate ('sʌbrəˌgeɪt) *vb* **subrogates, subrogating, subrogated.** (*tr*) *Law.* to put (one person or thing) in the place of another in respect of a right or claim. ORIG C16: from L *subrogāre,* from *sub-* in place of + *rogāre* to ask
▸ **ˌsubro'gation** *n*

sub rosa ('rəʊzə) *adv* in secret. ORIG L, lit.: under the rose; from use of the rose in ancient times as a token of secrecy

subroutine ('sʌbruːˌtiːn) *n* a section of a computer program that is stored only once but can be used at several different points in the program. Also called: **procedure.**

sub-Saharan *adj* in, of, or relating to Africa south of the Sahara desert.

subscribe (səb'skraɪb) *vb* **subscribes, subscribing, subscribed. 1** (usually foll. by *to*) to pay or promise to pay (money) as a contribution (to a fund, for a magazine, etc.), esp. at regular intervals. **2** to sign (one's name, etc.) at the end of a document. **3** (*intr;* foll. by *to*) to give support or approval: *to subscribe to the theory of reincarnation.* ORIG C15: from L *subscrībere* to write underneath
▸ **sub'scriber** *n*

subscriber trunk dialling *n Brit.* a service by which telephone subscribers can obtain trunk calls by dialling direct without the aid of an operator. Abbrev.: **STD.**

subscript ('sʌbskrɪpt) *Printing.* ◆ *adj* **1** (of a character) written or printed below the base line. Cf. **superscript.** ◆ *n* **2** Also called: **subindex.** a subscript character.

subscription (səb'skrɪpʃən) *n* **1** a payment or promise of payment for consecutive issues of a magazine, newspaper, book, etc., over a specified period of time. **2a** the advance purchase of tickets for a series of concerts, etc. **2b** (*as modifier*): *a subscription concert.* **3** money paid or promised, as to a charity, or the fund raised in this way. **4** an offer to buy shares or bonds issued by a company. **5** the act of signing one's name to a document, etc. **6** a signature or other appendage attached to the bottom of a document, etc. **7** agreement or acceptance expressed by or as if by signing one's name. **8** a signed document, statement, etc. **9** *Chiefly Brit.* the membership dues or fees paid to a society or club. **10** an advance order for a new product. **11a** the sale of books, etc., prior to publishing. **11b** (*as modifier*): *a subscription edition.*
▸ **sub'scriptive** *adj* ▸ **sub'scriptively** *adv*

subsequence ('sʌbsɪkwəns) *n* **1** the fact or state of being subsequent. **2** a subsequent incident or occurrence.

subsequent ('sʌbsɪkwənt) *adj* occurring after; succeeding. ORIG C15: from L *subsequēns* following on, from *subsequī,* from *sub-* near + *sequī* to follow
▸ **'subsequently** *adv* ▸ **'subsequentness** *n*

subserve (səb'sɜːv) *vb* **subserves, subserving, subserved.** (*tr*) to be helpful or useful to. ORIG C17: from L *subservīre* to be subject to, from SUB- + *servīre* to serve

subservient (səb'sɜːvɪənt) *adj* **1** obsequious. **2** serving as a means to an end. **3** a less common word for **subordinate** (sense 2). ORIG C17: from L *subserviēns* complying with, from *subservīre* to SUBSERVE
▸ **sub'serviently** *adv* ▸ **sub'servience** *or* **sub'serviency** *n*

subset ('sʌbˌsɛt) *n* a mathematical set contained within a larger set.

subshrub ('sʌbˌʃrʌb) *n* a small bushy plant that is woody except for the tips of the branches.

subside (səb'saɪd) *vb* **subsides, subsiding, subsided.** (*intr*) **1** to become less loud, excited, violent, etc.; abate. **2** to sink or fall to a lower level. **3** (of the surface of the earth, etc.) to cave in; collapse. **4** (of sediment, etc.) to sink or descend to the bottom; settle. ORIG C17: from L *subsīdere* to settle down
▸ **sub'sider** *n*

subsidence (səb'saɪdᵊns, 'sʌbsɪdᵊns) *n* **1** the act or process of subsiding or the condition of having subsided. **2** *Geol.* the gradual sinking of landforms to a lower level.

subsidiarity (səbˌsɪdɪ'ærɪtɪ) *n* the principle of devolving political decisions to the lowest practical level.

subsidiary (səb'sɪdɪərɪ) *adj* **1** serving to aid or supplement; auxiliary. **2** of lesser importance; subordinate. ◆ *n, pl* **subsidiaries. 3** a subsidiary person or thing. **4** Also called: **subsidiary company.** a company with at least half of its capital stock owned by another company. ORIG C16: from L *subsidiārius* supporting, from *subsidium* SUBSIDY
▸ **sub'sidiarily** *adv* ▸ **sub'sidiariness** *n*

subsidize *or* **subsidise** ('sʌbsɪˌdaɪz) *vb* **subsidizes, subsidizing, subsidized** *or* **subsidises, subsidising, subsidised.** (*tr*) **1** to aid or support with a subsidy. **2** to obtain the aid of by means of a subsidy.
▸ **ˌsubsidi'zation** *or* **ˌsubsidi'sation** *n* ▸ **'subsiˌdizer** *or* **'subsiˌdiser** *n*

subsidy ('sʌbsɪdɪ) *n, pl* **subsidies. 1** a financial aid supplied by a government, as to industry, for public welfare, the balance of payments, etc. **2** *English history.* a financial grant made originally for special purposes by Parliament to the Crown. **3** any monetary aid, grant, or contribution. ORIG C14: from Anglo-Norman *subsidie,* from L *subsidium* assistance, from *subsidēre* to remain, from *sub-* down + *sedēre* to sit

subsist (səb'sɪst) *vb* (*mainly intr*) **1** (often foll. by *on*) to be sustained; manage to live: *to subsist on milk.* **2** to continue in existence. **3** (foll. by *in*) to lie or reside by virtue (of); consist. **4** (*tr*) *Obs.* to provide with support. ORIG C16: from L *subsistere* to stand firm
▸ **sub'sistent** *adj*

subsistence (səb'sɪstəns) *n* **1** the means by which one maintains life. **2** the act or condition of subsisting.

subsistence farming *n* a type of farming in which most of the produce (**subsistence crop**) is consumed by the farmer and his family.

subsistence level *n* a standard of living barely adequate to support life.

★ people and places

subsistence wage *n* the lowest wage upon which a worker and his or her family can survive.

subsoil ('sʌbˌsɔɪl) *n* **1** Also called: **undersoil.** the layer of soil beneath the surface soil and overlying the bedrock. ◆ *vb* **2** (*tr*) to plough (land) to a depth so as to break up the subsoil.

subsonic (sʌb'sɒnɪk) *adj* being, having, or travelling at a velocity below that of sound.

subspecies ('sʌbˌspiːʃiːz) *n, pl* **subspecies.** *Biol.* a subdivision of a species: usually occurs because of isolation within a species.

substance ('sʌbstəns) *n* **1** the tangible basic matter of which a thing consists. **2** a specific type of matter, esp. a homogeneous material with definite or fairly definite chemical composition. **3** the essence, meaning, etc., of a discourse, thought, or written article. **4** solid or meaningful quality: *an education of substance.* **5** material density or body: *free space has no substance.* **6** material possessions or wealth: *a man of substance.* **7** *Philosophy.* the supposed immaterial substratum of anything that can receive modifications and in which attributes and accidents inhere. **8 in substance.** with regard to the salient points. ORIG C13: via OF from L *substantia,* from *substāre,* from SUB- + *stāre* to stand

substandard (sʌb'stændəd) *adj* **1** below an established or required standard. **2** another word for **nonstandard.**

substantial (səb'stænʃəl) *adj* **1** of a considerable size or value: *substantial funds.* **2** worthwhile; important; telling: *a substantial reform.* **3** having wealth or importance: *a substantial member of the community.* **4** (of food or a meal) sufficient and nourishing. **5** solid or strong: *a substantial door.* **6** real; actual; true: *substantial evidence.* **7** of or relating to the basic or fundamental substance or aspects of a thing. ◆ *n* **8** (*often pl*) *Rare.* an essential or important element.
▸ **substantiality** (səbˌstænʃɪ'ælɪtɪ) *or* **sub'stantialness** *n*
▸ **sub'stantially** *adv*

substantialism (səb'stænʃəˌlɪzəm) *n Philosophy.* the doctrine that a substantial reality underlies phenomena.
▸ **sub'stantialist** *n*

substantiate (səb'stænʃɪˌeɪt) *vb* **substantiates, substantiating, substantiated.** (*tr*) **1** to establish as valid or genuine. **2** to give form or real existence to. ORIG C17: from NL *substantiāre,* from L *substantia* SUBSTANCE
▸ **subˌstanti'ation** *n*

substantive ('sʌbstəntɪv) *n* **1** *Grammar.* a noun or pronoun used in place of a noun. ◆ *adj* **2** of, relating to, containing, or being the essential element of a thing. **3** having independent function, resources, or existence. **4** of substantial quantity. **5** solid in foundation or basis. **6** *Grammar.* denoting, relating to, or standing in place of a noun. **7** (səb'stæntɪv). (of a dye or colour) staining the material directly without use of a mordant. ORIG C15: from LL *substantīvus,* from L *substāre* to stand beneath
▸ **substantival** (ˌsʌbstən'taɪvᵊl) *adj* ▸ **ˌsubstan'tivally** *adv*
▸ **'substantively** *adv*

substantive rank *n* a permanent rank in the armed services.

substation ('sʌbˌsteɪʃən) *n* **1** a subsidiary station. **2** an installation at which electrical energy is received from one or more power stations for conversion from alternating to direct current, stepping down the voltage, or switching before distribution by a low-tension network.

substituent (sʌb'stɪtjuənt) *n* **1** *Chem.* an atom or group that replaces another atom or group in a molecule or can be regarded as replacing an atom in a parent compound. ◆ *adj* **2** substituted or substitutable. ORIG C19: from L *substituere* to SUBSTITUTE

substitute ('sʌbstɪˌtjuːt) *vb* **substitutes, substituting, substituted.** **1** (often foll. by *for*) to serve or cause to serve in place of another person or thing. **2** *Chem.* to replace (an atom or group in a molecule) with (another atom or group). ◆ *n* **3a** a person or thing that serves in place of another, such as a player in a game who takes the place of an injured colleague. **3b** (*as modifier*): *a substitute goalkeeper.* ORIG C16: from L *substituere,* from *sub-* in place of + *statuere* to set up
▸ **ˌsubsti'tutable** *adj* ▸ **'substiˌtutive** *adj*

★ people and places

USAGE NOTE Although *substitute* and *replace* have the same meaning, the structures they are used in are different. You replace A *with* B, while you substitute B *for* A. Accordingly, *he replaced the worn tyre with a new one,* and *he substituted a new tyre for the worn one* are both correct ways of saying the same thing.

substitution (ˌsʌbstɪ'tjuːʃən) *n* **1** the act of substituting or state of being substituted. **2** something or someone substituted.

substrate ('sʌbstreɪt) *n* **1** *Biochem.* the substance upon which an enzyme acts. **2** another word for **substratum.**

substratum (sʌb'strɑːtəm, -'streɪ-) *n, pl* **substrata** (-'strɑːtə, -'streɪtə). **1** any layer or stratum lying underneath another. **2** a basis or foundation; groundwork. ORIG C17: from NL, from L *substrātus* strewn beneath, from *substernere* to spread under
▸ **sub'strative** *or* **sub'stratal** *adj*

substructure ('sʌbˌstrʌktʃə) *n* **1** a structure, pattern, etc., that forms the basis of anything. **2** a structure forming a foundation or framework for a building or other construction.
▸ **sub'structural** *adj*

subsume (səb'sjuːm) *vb* **subsumes, subsuming, subsumed.** (*tr*) **1** to incorporate (an idea, case, etc.) under a comprehensive or inclusive classification. **2** to consider (an instance of something) as part of a general rule. ORIG C16: from NL *subsumere,* from L SUB- + *sumere* to take
▸ **sub'sumable** *adj* ▸ **subsumption** (səb'sʌmpʃən) *n*

subtemperate (sʌb'tɛmpərɪt) *adj* of or relating to the colder temperate regions.

subtenant (sʌb'tɛnənt) *n* a person who rents or leases property from a tenant.
▸ **sub'tenancy** *n*

subtend (səb'tɛnd) *vb* (*tr*) **1** *Geom.* to be opposite to and delimit (an angle or side). **2** (of a bract, stem, etc.) to have (a bud or similar part) growing in its axil. ORIG C16: from L *subtendere* to extend beneath

subterfuge ('sʌbtəˌfjuːdʒ) *n* a stratagem employed to conceal something, evade an argument, etc. ORIG C16: from LL *subterfugium,* from L *subterfugere* to escape by stealth, from *subter* secretly + *fugere* to flee

subterminal (sʌb'tɜːmɪnᵊl) *adj* almost at an end.

subterranean (ˌsʌbtə'reɪnɪən) *adj* **1** Also: **subterraneous, subterrestrial.** situated, living, or operating below the surface of the earth. **2** existing or operating in concealment. ORIG C17: from L *subterrāneus,* from SUB- + *terra* earth
▸ **ˌsubter'raneanly** *or* **ˌsubter'raneously** *adv*

subtext ('sʌbˌtɛkst) *n* **1** an underlying theme in a piece of writing. **2** a message which is not stated directly but can be inferred.

subtile ('sʌtᵊl) *adj* a rare spelling of **subtle.**
▸ **'subtilely** *adv* ▸ **subtility** (sʌb'tɪlɪtɪ) *or* **'subtileness** *n*
▸ **'subtilty** *n*

subtilize *or* **subtilise** ('sʌtɪˌlaɪz) *vb* **subtilizes, subtilizing, subtilized** *or* **subtilises, subtilising, subtilised.** **1** (*tr*) to bring to a purer state; refine. **2** to debate subtly. **3** (*tr*) to make (the mind, etc.) keener.
▸ **ˌsubtili'zation** *or* **ˌsubtili'sation** *n*

subtitle ('sʌbˌtaɪtᵊl) *n* **1** an additional subordinate title given to a literary or other work. **2** (*often pl*) **2a** text superimposed on a film or television broadcast, either a translation of foreign dialogue or as an aid for the hard of hearing. **2b** Also called: **caption.** explanatory text on a silent film. ◆ *vb* **subtitles, subtitling, subtitled.** **3** (*tr; usually passive*) to provide a subtitle for.

subtle ('sʌtᵊl) *adj* **1** not immediately obvious or comprehensible. **2** difficult to detect or analyse, often through being delicate or highly refined: *a subtle scent.* **3** showing or making or capable of showing or making fine distinctions of meaning. **4** marked by or requiring mental acuteness or ingenuity; discriminating. **5** delicate or faint: *a subtle shade.* **6** cunning or wily: *a subtle rogue.* **7** op-

erating or executed in secret: *a subtle intrigue.* ORIG C14: from OF *soutil,* from L *subtīlis* finely woven
▸ **'subtleness** *n* ▸ **'subtly** *adv*

subtlety ('sʌtᵊltɪ) *n, pl* **subtleties. 1** the state or quality of being subtle; delicacy. **2** a fine distinction. **3** something subtle.

subtonic (sʌb'tɒnɪk) *n Music.* the seventh degree of a major or minor scale.

subtotal (sʌb'təʊtᵊl, 'sʌbˌtəʊtᵊl) *n* **1** the total made up by a column of figures, etc., forming part of the total made up by a larger column. ◆ *vb* **subtotals, subtotalling, subtotalled** *or US* **subtotals, subtotaling, subtotaled. 2** to work out a subtotal for (a column, etc.).

subtract (səb'trækt) *vb* **1** to calculate the difference between (two numbers or quantities) by subtraction. **2** to remove (a part of a thing, quantity, etc.) from the whole. ORIG C16: from L *subtractus* withdrawn, from *subtrahere* to draw away from beneath
▸ **sub'tracter** *n* ▸ **sub'tractive** *adj*

subtraction (səb'trækʃən) *n* **1** the act or process of subtracting. **2** a mathematical operation in which the difference between two numbers or quantities is calculated.

subtrahend ('sʌbtrəˌhɛnd) *n* the number to be subtracted from another number (the **minuend**). ORIG C17: from L *subtrahendus,* from *subtrahere* to SUBTRACT

subtropics (sʌb'trɒpɪks) *pl n* the region lying between the tropics and temperate lands.
▸ **sub'tropical** *adj*

subulate ('su:bjəlɪt, -ˌleɪt) *adj* (esp. of plant parts) tapering to a point; awl-shaped. ORIG C18: from NL *subulatus* like an awl, from L *sūbula* awl

suburb ('sʌbɜ:b) *n* a residential district situated on the outskirts of a city or town. ORIG C14: from L *suburbium,* from *sub-* close to + *urbs* a city

suburban (sə'bɜ:bᵊn) *adj* **1** of, in, or inhabiting a suburb or the suburbs. **2** characteristic of a suburb or the suburbs. **3** *Mildly derog.* narrow or unadventurous in outlook.
▸ **su'burbanˌite** *n* ▸ **su'burbanˌize** *or* **su'burbanˌise** *vb (tr)*

suburbia (sə'bɜ:bɪə) *n* **1** suburbs or the people living in them considered as an identifiable community or class in society. **2** the life, customs, etc., of suburbanites.

subvention (səb'vɛnʃən) *n* **1** a grant, aid, or subsidy, as from a government. **2** *Sport.* a fee paid indirectly to a supposedly amateur athlete for appearing at a meeting. ORIG C15: from LL *subventiō* assistance, from L *subvenīre,* from *sub-* under + *venīre* to come

subversion (səb'vɜ:ʃən) *n* **1** the act or an instance of subverting a legally constituted government, institution, etc. **2** the state of being subverted; destruction or ruin. ORIG C14: from LL *subversiō* destruction, from L *subvertere* to overturn

subversive (səb'vɜ:sɪv) *adj* **1** liable to subvert or overthrow a government, legally constituted institution, etc. ◆ *n* **2** a person engaged in subversive activities, etc.
▸ **sub'versively** *adv* ▸ **sub'versiveness** *n*

subvert (səb'vɜ:t) *vb (tr)* **1** to bring about the complete downfall or ruin of (something existing by a system of law, etc.). **2** to undermine the moral principles of (a person, etc.). ORIG C14: from L *subvertere* to overturn
▸ **sub'verter** *n*

subway ('sʌbˌweɪ) *n* **1** *Brit.* an underground tunnel enabling pedestrians to cross a road, railway, etc. **2** an underground tunnel for traffic, power supplies, etc. **3** an underground railway.

succedaneum (ˌsʌksɪ'deɪnɪəm) *n, pl* **succedanea** (-nɪə). something that is used as a substitute, esp. any medical drug or agent that may be taken or prescribed in place of another. ORIG C17: from L *succēdāneus* following after; see SUCCEED
▸ **ˌsucce'daneous** *adj*

succeed (sək'si:d) *vb* **1** *(intr)* to accomplish an aim, esp. in the manner desired. **2** *(intr)* to happen in the manner desired: *the plan succeeded.* **3** *(intr)* to acquit oneself satisfactorily or do well, as in a specified field. **4** (when *intr,* often foll. by *to*) to come next in order (after someone or something). **5** (when *intr,* often foll. by *to*) to take over an office, post, etc. (from a person). **6** *(intr;* usually foll. by *to)* to come into possession (of property, etc.); inherit. **7** *(intr)* to have a result according to a specified manner: *the plan succeeded badly.* ORIG C15: from L *succēdere* to follow after
▸ **suc'ceeder** *n* ▸ **suc'ceedingly** *adv*

success (sək'sɛs) *n* **1** the favourable outcome of something attempted. **2** the attainment of wealth, fame, etc. **3** an action, performance, etc., that is characterized by success. **4** a person or thing that is successful. ORIG C16: from L *successus* an outcome; see SUCCEED

successful (sək'sɛsful) *adj* **1** having succeeded in one's endeavours. **2** marked by a favourable outcome. **3** having obtained fame, wealth, etc.
▸ **suc'cessfully** *adv* ▸ **suc'cessfulness** *n*

succession (sək'sɛʃən) *n* **1** the act or an instance of one person or thing following another. **2** a number of people or things following one another in order. **3** the act, process, or right by which one person succeeds to the office, etc., of another. **4** the order that determines how one person or thing follows another. **5** a line of descent to a title, etc. **6 in succession.** in a manner such that one thing is followed uninterruptedly by another. ORIG C14: from L *successio;* see SUCCEED
▸ **suc'cessional** *adj*

successive (sək'sɛsɪv) *adj* **1** following another without interruption. **2** of or involving succession: *a successive process.*
▸ **suc'cessively** *adv* ▸ **suc'cessiveness** *n*

successor (sək'sɛsə) *n* a person or thing that follows, esp. a person who succeeds another.

succinct (sək'sɪŋkt) *adj* marked by brevity and clarity; concise. ORIG C15: from L *succinctus* girt about, from *succingere* to gird from below
▸ **suc'cinctly** *adv* ▸ **suc'cinctness** *n*

succinic acid (sʌk'sɪnɪk) *n* a colourless odourless water-soluble acid found in plant and animal tissues, deriving from amber. Formula: $HOOC(CH_2)_2COOH$. Systematic name: **butanedioic acid.** ORIG C19: from L *succinum* amber

succotash ('sʌkəˌtæʃ) *n US & Canad.* a mixture of cooked sweet corn kernels and lima beans, served as a vegetable. ORIG C18: of Amerind origin, from *msiquatash,* lit.: broken pieces

succour *or US* **succor** ('sʌkə) *n* **1** help or assistance, esp. in time of difficulty. **2** a person or thing that provides help. ◆ *vb* **3** *(tr)* to give aid to. ORIG C13: from OF *sucurir,* from L *succurrere* to hurry to help

succubus ('sʌkjubəs) *n, pl* **succubi** (-ˌbaɪ). **1** Also called: **succuba.** a female demon fabled to have sexual intercourse with sleeping men. Cf. **incubus. 2** any evil demon. ORIG C16: from Med. L, from LL *succuba* harlot, from L *succubāre* to lie beneath

succulent ('sʌkjulənt) *adj* **1** juicy. **2** (of plants) having thick fleshy leaves or stems. ◆ *n* **3** a plant that can exist in arid conditions by using water stored in its fleshy tissues. ORIG C17: from L *succulentus,* from *sūcus* juice
▸ **'succulence** *or* **'succulency** *n* ▸ **'succulently** *adv*

succumb (sə'kʌm) *vb (intr;* often foll. by *to)* **1** to give way to the force (of) or desire (for). **2** to be fatally overwhelmed (by disease, etc.); die (of). ORIG C15: from L *succumbere* to be overcome, from SUB- + *-cumbere,* from *cubāre* to lie down

succursal (sʌ'kɜ:sᵊl) *adj* **1** (esp. of a religious establishment) subsidiary. ◆ *n* **2** a subsidiary establishment. ORIG C19: from F, from Med. L *succursus,* from L *succurrere* to SUCCOUR

such (sʌtʃ) (often foll. by a corresponding subordinate clause introduced by *that* or *as*) ◆ *determiner* **1a** of the sort specified or understood: *such books.* **1b** *(as pronoun): such is life; robbers, rapists, and such.* **2** so great; so much: *such a help.* **3 as such. 3a** in the capacity previously specified or understood: *a judge as such hasn't so much power.* **3b** in itself or themselves: *intelligence as such can't guarantee success.* **4 such and such.** specific, but not known or named: *at such and such a time.* **5 such as. 5a** for example: *animals, such as tigers.* **5b** of a similar kind as; like: *people such as your friend.* **5c** of the (usually small) amount, etc.: *the food, such as there was, was excellent.* **6 such that.** so that: used to express purpose or result: *power such that it was effortless.* ◆ *adv* **7** (intensifier): *such a nice person.* ORIG OE *swilc*

suchlike (ˈsʌtʃˌlaɪk) *adj* **1** (*prenominal*) of such a kind; similar: *John, Ken, and other suchlike idiots.* ◆ *n* **2** such or similar persons or things: *hyenas, jackals, and suchlike.*

Su-chou ★ (ˈsuːˈtʃaʊ) *n* a variant transliteration of the Chinese name for **Suzhou.**

Süchow ★ (ˈʃuːˈtʃaʊ) *n* a variant transliteration of the Chinese name for **Xuzhou.**

suck (sʌk) *vb* **1** to draw (a liquid or other substance) into the mouth by creating a partial vacuum in the mouth. **2** to draw in (fluid, etc.) by or as if by a similar action: *plants suck moisture from the soil.* **3** to drink milk from (a mother's breast); suckle. **4** (*tr*) to extract fluid content from (a solid food): *to suck a lemon.* **5** (*tr*) to take into the mouth and moisten, dissolve, or roll around with the tongue: *to suck one's thumb.* **6** (*tr;* often foll. by *down, in,* etc.) to draw by using irresistible force. **7** (*intr*) (of a pump) to draw in air because of a low supply level or leaking valves, etc. **8** (*tr*) to assimilate or acquire (knowledge, comfort, etc.). **9** (*intr*) *Sl.* to be contemptible or disgusting. ◆ *n* **10** the act or an instance of sucking. **11** something that is sucked, esp. milk from the mother's breast. **12 give suck to.** to give (a baby or young animal) milk from the breast or udder. **13** an attracting or sucking force. **14** a sound caused by sucking. ◆ See also **suck in, sucks, suck up to.** ORIG OE *sūcan*

sucker (ˈsʌkə) *n* **1** a person or thing that sucks. **2** *Sl.* a person who is easily deceived or swindled. **3** *Sl.* a person who cannot resist the attractions of a particular type of person or thing: *he's a sucker for blondes.* **4** a young animal that is not yet weaned. **5** *Zool.* an organ specialized for sucking or adhering. **6** a cup-shaped device, generally made of rubber, that may be attached to articles allowing them to adhere to a surface by suction. **7** *Bot.* **7a** a strong shoot that arises in a mature plant from a root, rhizome, or the base of the main stem. **7b** a short branch of a parasitic plant that absorbs nutrients from the host. **8** a pipe or tube through which a fluid is drawn by suction. **9** any of various small mainly North American cyprinoid fishes having a large sucking mouth. **10** any of certain fishes that have sucking discs, esp. the sea snail. **11** a piston in a suction pump or the valve in such a piston. ◆ *vb* **12** (*tr*) to strip the suckers from (a plant). **13** (*intr*) (of a plant) to produce suckers.

suck in *vb* (*adv*) **1** (*tr*) to attract by using an inexorable force, inducement, etc. **2** to draw in (one's breath) sharply.

suckle (ˈsʌkᵊl) *vb* **suckles, suckling, suckled. 1** to give (a baby or young animal) milk from the breast or (of a baby, etc.) to suck milk from the breast. **2** (*tr*) to bring up; nurture. ORIG C15: prob. back formation from SUCKLING
▸ ˈ**suckler** *n*

suckling (ˈsʌklɪŋ) *n* **1** an infant or young animal that is still taking milk from the mother. **2** a very young child. ORIG C15: see SUCK, -LING[1]

Suckling ★ (ˈsʌklɪŋ) *n* Sir **John.** 1609–42, English Cavalier poet and dramatist.

sucks (sʌks) *interj Sl.* **1** an expression of disappointment. **2** an exclamation of defiance or derision (esp. in **yah boo sucks to you**).

suck up to *vb* (*intr, adv + prep*) *Inf.* to flatter for one's own profit; toady.

sucrase (ˈsjuːkreɪz) *n* another name for **invertase.** ORIG C19: from F *sucre* sugar + -ASE

sucre (*Spanish* ˈsukre) *n* the former (until 2000) standard monetary unit of Ecuador. ORIG C19: after Antonio José de SUCRE

Sucre[1] ★ (*Spanish* ˈsukre) *n* the legal capital of Bolivia, in the south central part of the country in the E Andes: university (1624). Pop.: 144 994 (1993 est.). Former name (until 1839): **Chuquisaca.**

Sucre[2] ★ (*Spanish* ˈsukre) *n* **Antonio José de** (anˈtonjo xoˈse de). 1795–1830, South American liberator, born in Venezuela, who assisted Bolivar in the colonial revolt against Spain; first president of Bolivia (1826–28).

sucrose (ˈsjuːkrəʊz, -krəʊs) *n* the technical name for **sugar** (sense 1). ORIG C19: F *sucre* sugar + -OSE[2]

suction (ˈsʌkʃən) *n* **1** the act or process of sucking. **2** the force produced by a pressure difference, as the force holding a sucker onto a surface. **3** the act or process of producing such a force. ORIG C17: from LL *suctiō* a sucking, from L *sūgere* to suck
▸ ˈ**suctional** *adj*

suction pump *n* a pump for raising water or a similar fluid by suction. It usually consists of a cylinder containing a piston fitted with a flap valve.

suctorial (sʌkˈtɔːrɪəl) *adj* **1** specialized for sucking or adhering. **2** relating to or possessing suckers or suction. ORIG C19: from NL *suctōrius,* from L *sūgere* to suck

Sudan ★ (suːˈdɑːn, -ˈdæn) *n* **the. 1** a republic in NE Africa, on the Red Sea: the largest country in Africa; conquered by Mehemet Ali of Egypt (1820–22) and made an Anglo-Egyptian condominium in 1899 after joint forces defeated the Mahdist revolt; became a republic in 1956; civil war has been waged between separatists, in the mainly Christian south, and the government since independence, apart from a period of peace (1972–83). It consists mainly of a plateau, with the Nubian Desert in the north. Official language: Arabic. Official religion: Muslim; there are large Christian and animist minorities. Currency: Sudanese dinar. Capital: Khartoum. Pop.: 34 476 000 (1999 est.). Area: 2 505 805 sq. km (967 491 sq. miles). Former name (1899–1956): **Anglo-Egyptian Sudan.** French name: **Soudan. 2** a region stretching across Africa south of the Sahara and north of the tropical zone: inhabited chiefly by Negroid tribes rather than Arabs.
▸ **Sudanese** (ˌsuːdᵊˈniːz) *adj, n*

sudarium (sjuˈdɛərɪəm) *n, pl* **sudaria** (-ˈdɛərɪə). another word for **sudatorium.** ORIG C17: from L, from *sūdāre* to sweat

sudatorium (ˌsjuːdəˈtɔːrɪəm) *or* **sudatory** *n, pl* **sudatoria** (-ˈtɔːrɪə) *or* **sudatories.** a room, esp. in a Roman bathhouse, where sweating is induced by heat. ORIG C18: from L, from *sūdāre* to sweat

sudatory (ˈsjuːdətərɪ, -trɪ) *adj* **1** relating to or producing sweating. ◆ *n, pl* **sudatories. 2** a sudatory agent. **3** another word for **sudatorium.**

Sudbury ★ (ˈsʌdbərɪ, -brɪ) *n* a city in central Canada, in Ontario: a major nickel-mining centre. Pop.: 92 884 (1991).

sudd (sʌd) *n* floating masses of reeds and weeds that occur on the White Nile and obstruct navigation. ORIG C19: from Ar., lit.: obstruction

sudden (ˈsʌdᵊn) *adj* **1** occurring or performed quickly and without warning. **2** marked by haste; abrupt. **3** *Rare.* rash; precipitate. ◆ *n* **4** *Arch.* an abrupt occurrence (in **on a sudden**). **5 all of a sudden.** without warning; unexpectedly. ORIG C13: via F from LL *subitāneus,* from L *subitus* unexpected, from *subīre* to happen unexpectedly, from *sub-* secretly + *īre* to go
▸ ˈ**suddenly** *adv* ▸ ˈ**suddenness** *n*

sudden adult death syndrome *n* the unexpected death of a young adult, usually due to undetected inherited heart disease. Also called: **sudden death syndrome, sudden cardiac death.** Abbrevs: **SADS, SDS, SCD.**

sudden death *n* **1** (in sports, etc.) an extra game or contest to decide the winner of a tied competition. **2** an unexpected or quick death.

sudden infant death syndrome *n* a technical name for **cot death.** Abbrev.: **SIDS.**

Sudetenland ★ (suːˈdeɪtᵊnˌlænd) *n* a mountainous region of the N Czech Republic: part of Czechoslovakia (1919–38; 1945–93); occupied by Germany (1938–45). Also called: **the Sudeten.**

Sudetes (suːˈdiːtiːz) *or* **Sudeten Mountains** ★ *pl n* a mountain range in E central Europe, along the N border of the Czech Republic, extending into Germany and Poland: rich in minerals, esp. coal. Highest peak: Schneekoppe, 1603 m (5259 ft).

sudor (ˈsjuːdɔː) *n* a technical name for **sweat.** ORIG L
▸ **sudoral** (ˈsjuːdərəl) *adj*

sudoriferous (ˌsjuːdəˈrɪfərəs) *adj* producing or conveying sweat. Also: ˌ**sudoˈriparous.** ORIG C16: via NL from SUDOR + L *ferre* to bear
▸ ˌ**sudorˈiferousness** *n*

sudorific (ˌsjuːdəˈrɪfɪk) *adj* **1** producing or causing sweating. ◆ *n* **2** a sudorific agent. ORIG C17: from NL *sūdōrificus,* from SUDOR + L *facere* to make

suds (sʌdz) *pl n* **1** the bubbles on the surface of water in which soap, detergents, etc., have been dissolved; lather. **2** soapy water. ORIG C16: prob. from MDu. *sudse* marsh
▸ **ˈsudsy** *adj*

sue (sjuː, suː) *vb* **sues, suing, sued. 1** to institute legal proceedings (against). **2** to make suppliant requests of (someone for something). ORIG C13: from OF *sivre,* from L *sequī* to follow
▸ **ˈsuer** *n*

Sue ★ (*French* sy) *n* **Eugène** (øʒɛn). original name *Marie-Joseph Sue.* 1804–57, French novelist, whose works include *Les mystères de Paris* (1842–43) and *Le juif errant* (1844–45).

suede (sweɪd) *n* **a** a leather with a fine velvet-like nap on the flesh side, produced by abrasive action. **b** (*as modifier*): *a suede coat.* ORIG C19: from F *gants de Suède,* lit.: gloves from Sweden

suet (ˈsuːɪt, ˈsjuːɪt) *n* a hard waxy fat around the kidneys and loins in sheep, cattle, etc., used in cooking and making tallow. ORIG C14: from OF *seu,* from L *sēbum*
▸ **ˈsuety** *adj*

Suetonius ★ (swiːˈtəʊnɪəs) *n* full name *Gaius Suetonius Tranquillus.* 75–150 A.D., Roman biographer and historian, whose chief works were *Concerning Illustrious Men* and *The Lives of the Caesars* (from Julius Caesar to Domitian).

suet pudding *n Brit.* any of a variety of puddings made with suet and steamed or boiled.

Suez ★ (ˈsuːɪz) *n* **1** a port in NE Egypt, at the head of the Gulf of Suez at the S end of the Suez Canal: an ancient trading site and a major naval station under the Ottoman Empire; port of departure for pilgrims to Mecca; oil-refining centre. It suffered severely in the Arab–Israeli conflicts of 1967 and 1973. Pop.: 388 000 (1992 est.). **2 Isthmus of.** a strip of land in NE Egypt, between the Mediterranean and the Red Sea: links Africa and Asia and is crossed by the Suez Canal. **3 Gulf of.** the NW arm of the Red Sea: linked with the Mediterranean by the Suez Canal.

Suez Canal ★ *n* a sea-level canal in NE Egypt, crossing the Isthmus of Suez and linking the Mediterranean with the Red Sea: built (1854–69) by de Lesseps with French and Egyptian capital; nationalized in 1956 by the Egyptians. Length: 163 km (101 miles).

Suff. *abbrev. for:* **1** Suffolk. **2** Suffragan.

suffer ★ (ˈsʌfə) *vb* **1** to undergo or be subjected to (pain, punishment, etc.). **2** (*tr*) to undergo or experience (anything): *to suffer a change of management.* **3** (*intr*) to be set at a disadvantage: *this author suffers in translation.* **4** (*tr*) *Arch.* to tolerate; permit (someone to do something): *suffer the little children to come unto me.* **5 suffer from. 5a** to be ill with, esp. recurrently. **5b** to be given to: *he suffers from a tendency to exaggerate.* ORIG C13: from OF *soffrir,* from L *sufferre,* from SUB- + *ferre* to bear
▸ **ˈsufferer** *n* ▸ **ˈsuffering** *n*

sufferable (ˈsʌfərəbᵊl, ˈsʌfrə-) *adj* able to be tolerated or suffered; endurable.

sufferance (ˈsʌfərəns, ˈsʌfrəns) *n* **1** tolerance arising from failure to prohibit; tacit permission. **2** capacity to endure pain, injury, etc. **3** the state or condition of suffering. **4 on sufferance.** tolerated with reluctance. ORIG C13: via OF from LL *sufferentia* endurance, from L *sufferre* to SUFFER

suffice (səˈfaɪs) *vb* **suffices, sufficing, sufficed. 1** to be adequate or satisfactory for (something). **2 suffice it to say that.** (*takes a clause as object*) let us say no more than that; I shall just say that. ORIG C14: from OF *suffire,* from L *sufficere* from *sub-* below + *facere* to make

sufficiency (səˈfɪʃənsɪ) *n, pl* **sufficiencies. 1** the quality or condition of being sufficient. **2** an adequate amount. **3** *Arch.* efficiency.

sufficient (səˈfɪʃənt) *adj* **1** enough to meet a need or purpose; adequate. **2** *Logic.* (of a condition) assuring the truth of a statement; requiring but not necessarily caused by some other state of affairs. Cf. **necessary** (sense 3b). **3** *Arch.* competent; capable. ◆ *n* **4** a sufficient quantity. ORIG C14: from L *sufficiens* supplying the needs of, from *sufficere* to SUFFICE
▸ **sufˈficiently** *adv*

suffix *n* (ˈsʌfɪks). **1** *Grammar.* an affix that follows the stem to which it is attached, as for example *-s* and *-ness* in *dogs* and *softness.* Cf. **prefix** (sense 1). **2** anything added at the end of something else. ◆ *vb* (ˈsʌfɪks, səˈfɪks). **3** (*tr*) *Grammar.* to add (a morpheme) as a suffix to a word. ORIG C18: from NL *suffixum,* from L *suffixus* fastened below, from *suffigere* to fasten below

suffocate (ˈsʌfəˌkeɪt) *vb* **suffocates, suffocating, suffocated. 1** to kill or be killed by the deprivation of oxygen, as by obstruction of the air passage. **2** to block the air passages or have the air passages blocked. **3** to feel or cause to feel discomfort from heat and lack of air. ORIG C16: from L *suffōcāre,* from SUB- + *faucēs* throat
▸ **ˈsuffoˌcating** *adj* ▸ **ˌsuffoˈcation** *n*

Suffolk ★ (ˈsʌfək) *n* a county of SE England, on the North Sea: its coast is flat and marshy, indented by broad tidal estuaries. Administrative centre: Ipswich. Pop.: 661 600 (1996 est.). Area: 3800 sq. km (1467 sq. miles).

Suffolk punch *n* a breed of draught horse with a chestnut coat and short legs.

suffragan (ˈsʌfrəgən) *adj* **1a** (of any bishop of a diocese) subordinate to and assisting his superior archbishop or metropolitan. **1b** (of any assistant bishop) assisting the bishop of his diocese but having no ordinary jurisdiction in that diocese. ◆ *n* **2** a suffragan bishop. ORIG C14: from Med. L *suffragāneus,* from *suffrāgium* assistance, from L: suffrage
▸ **ˈsuffraganship** *n*

suffrage (ˈsʌfrɪdʒ) *n* **1** the right to vote, esp. in public elections; franchise. **2** the exercise of such a right; casting a vote. **3** a short intercessory prayer. ORIG C14: from L *suffrāgium*

suffragette (ˌsʌfrəˈdʒɛt) *n* a female advocate of the extension of the franchise to women, esp. a militant one, as in Britain at the beginning of the 20th century. ORIG C20: from SUFFRAG(E) + -ETTE

suffragist (ˈsʌfrədʒɪst) *n* an advocate of the extension of the franchise, esp. to women.
▸ **ˈsuffragism** *n*

suffruticose (səˈfruːtɪˌkəʊz) *adj* (of a plant) having a permanent woody base and herbaceous branches. ORIG C18: from NL *suffruticōsus,* from L SUB- + *frutex* shrub

suffuse (səˈfjuːz) *vb* **suffuses, suffusing, suffused.** (*tr; usually passive*) to spread or flood through or over (something). ORIG C16: from L *suffūsus* overspread with, from *suffundere,* from SUB- + *fundere* to pour
▸ **suffusion** (səˈfjuːʒən) *n* ▸ **sufˈfusive** *adj*

Sufi (ˈsuːfɪ) *n, pl* **Sufis.** an adherent of any of various Muslim mystical orders or teachings, which emphasize the direct personal experience of God. ORIG C17: from Ar. *ṣūfīy,* lit.: (man) of wool; prob. from the ascetic's woollen garments
▸ **ˈSufic** *adj* ▸ **ˈSufism** *n*

Sufu ★ (ˈʃuːˈfuː) *n* a variant spelling of **Shufu.**

sugar (ˈʃʊgə) *n* **1** Also called: **sucrose, saccharose.** a white crystalline sweet carbohydrate, a disaccharide, found in many plants: used esp. as a sweetening agent in food and drinks. Related adj: **saccharine. 2** any of a class of simple water-soluble carbohydrates, such as sucrose, lactose, and fructose. **3** *Inf., chiefly US & Canad.* a term of affection, esp. for one's sweetheart. ◆ *vb* **4** (*tr*) to add sugar to; make sweet. **5** (*tr*) to cover or sprinkle with sugar. **6** (*intr*) to produce sugar. **7 sugar the pill** *or* **medicine.** to make something unpleasant more agreeable by adding something pleasant. ORIG C13 *suker,* from OF *çucre,* from Med. L *zuccārum,* ult. from Sansk. *śarkarā*
▸ **ˈsugared** *adj*

sugar beet *n* a variety of beet cultivated for its white roots from which sugar is obtained.

sugar candy *n* **1** Also called: **rock candy.** large crystals of sugar formed by suspending strings in a strong sugar solution that hardens on the strings, used chiefly for sweetening coffee. **2** *Chiefly US.* confectionery; sweets.

sugar cane *n* a coarse perennial grass of Old World

tropical regions, having tall stout canes that yield sugar: cultivated chiefly in the Caribbean and the southern US.

sugar-coat *vb (tr)* **1** to coat or cover with sugar. **2** to cause to appear more attractive.

sugar diabetes *n* an informal name for **diabetes mellitus** (see **diabetes**).

sugar glider *n* a common Australian phalanger that glides from tree to tree feeding on insects and nectar.

sugaring off *n Canad.* the boiling down of maple sap to produce sugar, traditionally a social event in early spring.

sugar loaf *n* **1** a large conical mass of hard refined sugar. **2** something resembling this.

Sugar Loaf Mountain ★ *n* a mountain in SE Brazil, in Rio de Janeiro on Guanabara Bay. Height: 390 m (1280 ft). Portuguese name: **Pão de Açúcar**.

sugar maple *n* a North American maple tree, grown as a source of sugar, which is extracted from the sap, and for its hard wood.

sugar of lead (lɛd) *n* another name for **lead acetate**.

sugarplum (ˈʃʊɡəˌplʌm) *n* a crystallized plum.

sugary (ˈʃʊɡərɪ) *adj* **1** of, like, or containing sugar. **2** excessively sweet. **3** deceptively pleasant; insincere.
▸ **ˈsugariness** *n*

Suger ★ (suːˈʒɛa) *n* 1081–1151, French ecclesiastic and statesman, who acted as adviser to Louis VI and regent (1147–49) to Louis VII. As abbot of Saint-Denis (1122–51) he influenced the development of Gothic architecture.

suggest (səˈdʒɛst) *vb (tr; may take a clause as object)* **1** to put forward (a plan, idea, etc.) for consideration: *I suggest Smith for the post; a plan suggested itself.* **2** to evoke (a person, thing, etc.) in the mind by the association of ideas: *that painting suggests home to me.* **3** to give an indirect or vague hint of: *his face always suggests his peace of mind.* ORIG C16: from L *suggerere* to bring up
▸ **sugˈgester** *n*

suggestible (səˈdʒɛstɪbᵊl) *adj* **1** easily influenced by ideas provided by other persons. **2** characteristic of something that can be suggested.
▸ **sugˌgestiˈbility** *n*

suggestion (səˈdʒɛstʃən) *n* **1** something that is suggested. **2** a hint or indication: *a suggestion of the odour of violets.* **3** *Psychol.* the process whereby the mere presentation of an idea to a receptive individual leads to the acceptance of that idea. See also **autosuggestion**.

suggestive (səˈdʒɛstɪv) *adj* **1** *(postpositive;* foll. by *of)* conveying a hint (of something). **2** tending to suggest something improper or indecent.
▸ **sugˈgestively** *adv* ▸ **sugˈgestiveness** *n*

Suharto ★ (sʊˈhɑːtəʊ) *n* born 1921, Indonesian general and statesman; president (1968–98).

suicidal (ˌsuːɪˈsaɪdᵊl, ˌsjuː-) *adj* **1** involving, indicating, or tending towards suicide. **2** liable to result in suicide: *a suicidal attempt.* **3** liable to destroy one's own interests or prospects; dangerously rash.
▸ **ˌsuiˈcidally** *adv*

suicide (ˈsuːɪˌsaɪd, ˈsjuː-) *n* **1** the act or an instance of killing oneself intentionally. **2** the self-inflicted ruin of one's own prospects or interests: *a merger would be financial suicide.* **3** a person who kills himself or herself intentionally. **4** *(modifier)* reckless; extremely dangerous: *a suicide mission.* **5** *(modifier)* (of an action) undertaken or (of a person) undertaking an action in the knowledge that it will result in the death of the person performing it in order that maximum damage may be inflicted: *suicide bomber.* ORIG C17: from NL *suīcīdium,* from L *suī* of oneself + *-cīdium,* from *caedere* to kill

sui generis (ˌsuːaɪ ˈdʒɛnərɪs) *adj* unique. ORIG L, lit.: of its own kind

suint (ˈsuːɪnt, swɪnt) *n* a water-soluble substance found in the fleece of sheep, formed from dried perspiration. ORIG C18: from F *suer* to sweat, from L *sūdāre*

Suisse ★ (sɥis) *n* the French name for **Switzerland**.

suit (suːt, sjuːt) *n* **1** any set of clothes of the same or similar material designed to be worn together, now usually (for men) a jacket with matching trousers or (for women) a jacket with matching or contrasting skirt or trousers. **2** *(in combination)* any outfit worn for a specific purpose: *a spacesuit.* **3** any set of items, such as parts of personal armour. **4** any of the four sets of 13 cards in a pack of playing cards, being spades, hearts, diamonds, and clubs. **5** a civil proceeding; lawsuit. **6** the act or process of suing in a court of law. **7** a petition or appeal made to a person of superior rank or status or the act of making such a petition. **8** a man's courting of a woman. **9** *Sl.* an executive, manager, or bureaucrat, esp. one considered faceless or dull. **10 follow suit. 10a** to play a card of the same suit as the card played immediately before it. **10b** to act in the same way as someone else. **11 strong** *or* **strongest suit**. something that one excels in. ◆ *vb* **12** to make or be fit or appropriate for: *that dress suits your figure.* **13** to meet the requirements or standards (of). **14** to be agreeable or acceptable to (someone). **15 suit oneself**. to pursue one's own intentions without reference to others. ORIG C13: from OF *sieute* set of things, from *sivre* to follow

suitable (ˈsuːtəbᵊl, ˈsjuːt-) *adj* appropriate; proper; fit.
▸ **ˌsuitaˈbility** *or* **ˈsuitableness** *n* ▸ **ˈsuitably** *adv*

suitcase (ˈsuːtˌkeɪs, ˈsjuːt-) *n* a portable rectangular travelling case for clothing, etc.

suite (swiːt) *n* **1** a series of items intended to be used together; set. **2** a set of connected rooms in a hotel. **3** a matching set of furniture, esp. of two armchairs and a settee. **4** a number of attendants or followers. **5** *Music.* **5a** an instrumental composition consisting of several movements in the same key based on or derived from dance rhythms, esp. in the baroque period. **5b** an instrumental composition in several movements less closely connected than a sonata. ORIG C17: from F, from OF *sieute;* see SUIT

suiting (ˈsuːtɪŋ, ˈsjuːt-) *n* a fabric used for suits.

suitor (ˈsuːtə, ˈsjuːt-) *n* **1** a man who courts a woman; wooer. **2** *Law.* a person who brings a suit in a court of law; plaintiff. ORIG C13: from Anglo-Norman *suter,* from L *secūtor* follower, from *sequī* to follow

Suiyüan ★ (ˈswiːˈyɑːn) *n* a former province in N China: now part of the Inner Mongolian Autonomous Region.

Sukarnapura ★ (sʊˌkɑːnəˈpʊərə) *n* a former name of **Jayapura**.

Sukarno *or* **Soekarno** ★ (suːˈkɑːnəʊ) *n* **Achmed** (ˈɑːkmɛd). 1901–70, Indonesian statesman; first president of the Republic of Indonesia (1945–67).

Sukarno Peak ★ *n* a former name of (Mount) **Jaya**.

Sukhumi ★ (*Russian* suˈxumi) *n* a port and resort in W Georgia, on the Black Sea: site of an ancient Greek colony. Pop.: 112 000 (1994 est.).

sukiyaki (ˌsuːkɪˈjɑːkɪ) *n* a Japanese dish consisting of very thinly sliced beef or other meat, vegetables, and seasonings cooked together quickly, usually at the table. ORIG from Japanese

Sukkoth *or* **Succoth** (ˈsʊkəʊt, -kəʊθ; *Hebrew* suːˈkɔt) *n* an eight-day Jewish harvest festival beginning on Tishri 15, which commemorates the period when the Israelites lived in the wilderness. Also called: **Feast of Tabernacles**. ORIG from Heb., lit.: tabernacles

Sulawesi ★ (ˌsuːləˈweɪsɪ) *n* an island in E Indonesia: mountainous and forested, with volcanoes and hot springs. Pop.: 12 520 711 (1990). Area (including adjacent islands): 229 108 sq. km (88 440 sq. miles). Also called: **Celebes**.

sulcate (ˈsʌlkeɪt) *adj Biol.* marked with longitudinal parallel grooves. ORIG C18: via L *sulcātus* from *sulcāre* to plough, from *sulcus* a furrow

sulcus (ˈsʌlkəs) *n, pl* **sulci** (-saɪ). **1** a linear groove, furrow, or slight depression. **2** any of the narrow grooves on the surface of the brain that mark the cerebral convolutions. ORIG C17: from L

Suleiman I (ˌsuːlɪˈmɑːn, -leɪ-), **Soliman,** *or* **Solyman** ★ *n* called *the Magnificent.* ?1495–1566, sultan of the Ottoman Empire (1520–66), noted for his military power and cultural achievements.

sulf- *combining form.* a US variant of **sulph-**.

★ people and places

sulfur ('sʌlfə) *n* the US spelling of **sulphur.**

sulk (sʌlk) *vb* **1** (*intr*) to be silent and resentful because of a wrong done to one; brood sullenly: *the child sulked after being slapped.* ◆ *n* **2** (*often pl*) a state or mood of feeling resentful or sullen: *he's in a sulk; he's got the sulks.* **3** Also: **sulker.** a person who sulks. ORIG C18: ? back formation from SULKY[1]

sulky[1] ('sʌlkɪ) *adj* **sulkier, sulkiest. 1** sullen, withdrawn, or moody, through or as if through resentment. **2** dull or dismal: *sulky weather.* ORIG C18: ?from obs. *sulke* sluggish
► **'sulkily** *adv* ► **'sulkiness** *n*

sulky[2] ('sʌlkɪ) *n, pl* **sulkies.** a light two-wheeled vehicle for one person, usually drawn by one horse. ORIG C18: from SULKY[1]

Sulla ★ ('sʌlə) *n* full name *Lucius Cornelius Sulla Felix.* 138–78 B.C., Roman general and dictator (82–79).

sullage ('sʌlɪdʒ) *n* **1** filth or waste, esp. sewage. **2** sediment deposited by running water. ORIG C16: ?from F *souiller* to sully

sullen ('sʌlən) *adj* **1** unwilling to talk or be sociable; sulky; morose. **2** sombre; gloomy: *a sullen day.* ◆ *n* **3** (*pl*) *Arch.* a sullen mood. ORIG C16: ?from Anglo-F *solain* (unattested), ult. rel. to L *sōlus* alone
► **'sullenly** *adv* ► **'sullenness** *n*

Sullivan ★ ('sʌlɪvᵊn) *n* **1** Sir **Arthur (Seymour).** 1842–1900, British composer of such operettas as *H.M.S. Pinafore* (1878) and *The Mikado* (1885), with W. S. Gilbert as librettist. **2 Louis (Henri).** 1856–1924, US pioneer of modern architecture.

Sullom Voe ★ ('sʌləm vəʊ) *n* a deep coastal inlet in the Shetland Islands, on the N coast of Mainland. It is used for the storage and transshipment of oil.

sully ('sʌlɪ) *vb* **sullies, sullying, sullied.** (*tr*) to stain or tarnish (a reputation, etc.) or (of a reputation) to become stained or tarnished. ORIG C16: prob. from F *souiller* to soil

Sully ★ ('sʌlɪ; *French* sylli) *n* **Maximilien de Béthune** (maksimiljɛ̃ də betyn), Duc de Sully. 1559–1641, French statesman; minister of Henry IV.

Sully-Prudhomme ★ (*French* sylli prydɔm) *n* **René François Armand** (rəne frɑ̃swa armɑ̃). 1839–1907, French poet: Nobel prize for literature 1901.

sulph- *or US* **sulf-** *combining form.* containing sulphur: *sulphate.*

sulpha *or US* **sulfa drug** ('sʌlfə) *n* any of a group of sulphonamides that inhibit the activity of bacteria and are used to treat bacterial infections.

sulphadiazine *or US* **sulfadiazine** (ˌsʌlfə'daɪəˌziːn) *n* an important sulpha drug used chiefly in combination with an antibiotic. ORIG from SULPH- + DIAZ(O) + -INE[2]

sulphanilamide *or US* **sulfanilamide** (ˌsʌlfə'nɪləˌmaɪd) *n* a white crystalline compound formerly used in the treatment of bacterial infections. ORIG from SULPH- + ANIL(INE) + AMIDE

sulphate *or US* **sulfate** ('sʌlfeɪt) *n* **1** any salt or ester of sulphuric acid. ◆ *vb* **sulphates, sulphating, sulphated** *or US* **sulfates, sulfating, sulfated. 2** (*tr*) to treat with a sulphate or convert into a sulphate. **3** to undergo or cause to undergo the formation of a layer of lead sulphate on the plates of an accumulator. ORIG C18: from NL *sulfātum*
► **sul'phation** *or US* **sul'fation** *n*

sulphide *or US* **sulfide** ('sʌlfaɪd) *n* a compound of sulphur with a more electropositive element.

sulphite *or US* **sulfite** ('sʌlfaɪt) *n* any salt or ester of sulphurous acid.
► **sulphitic** *or US* **sulfitic** (sʌl'fɪtɪk) *adj*

sulphonamide *or US* **sulfonamide** (sʌl'fɒnəˌmaɪd) *n* any of a class of organic compounds that are amides of sulphonic acids containing the group $-SO_2NH_2$ or a group derived from this. An important class of sulphonamides are the sulpha drugs.

sulphone *or US* **sulfone** ('sʌlfəʊn) *n* any of a class of organic compounds containing the divalent group SO_2 linked to two other organic groups.

sulphonic *or US* **sulfonic acid** (sʌl'fɒnɪk) *n* any of a large group of strong organic acids that contain the group $-SO_2OH$ and are used in the manufacture of dyes and drugs.

sulphonmethane *or US* **sulfonmethane** (ˌsʌlfɒn'miːθeɪn) *n* a colourless crystalline compound used medicinally as a hypnotic. Formula: $C_7H_{16}O_4S_2$.

sulphur *or US* **sulfur** ('sʌlfə) *n* **a** an allotropic nonmetallic element, occurring free in volcanic regions and in combined state in gypsum, pyrite, and galena. It is used in the production of sulphuric acid, in the vulcanization of rubber, and in fungicides. Symbol: S; atomic no.: 16; atomic wt.: 32.066. **b** (*as modifier*): *sulphur springs.* ORIG C14 *soufre,* from OF, from L *sulfur*
► **sulphuric** *or US* **sulfuric** (sʌl'fjʊərɪk) *adj*

sulphurate *or US* **sulfurate** ('sʌlfjʊˌreɪt) *vb* **sulphurates, sulphurating, sulphurated.** (*tr*) to combine or treat with sulphur or a sulphur compound.
► ˌ**sulphu'ration** *or US* ˌ**sulfu'ration** *n*

sulphur-bottom *n* another name for **blue whale.**

sulphur dioxide *n* a colourless soluble pungent gas. It is both an oxidizing and a reducing agent and is used in the manufacture of sulphuric acid, the preservation of foodstuffs (**E 220**), bleaching, and disinfecting. Formula: SO_2. Systematic name: **sulphur(IV) oxide.**

sulphureous *or US* **sulfureous** (sʌl'fjʊərɪəs) *adj* **1** another word for **sulphurous** (sense 1). **2** of the yellow colour of sulphur.

sulphuretted *or US* **sulfureted hydrogen** ('sʌlfjʊˌrɛtɪd) *n* another name for **hydrogen sulphide.**

sulphuric acid *n* a colourless dense oily corrosive liquid used in accumulators and in the manufacture of fertilizers, dyes, and explosives. Formula: H_2SO_4. Systematic name: **tetraoxosulphuric(VI) acid.**

sulphurize, sulphurise, *or US* **sulfurize** ('sʌlfjʊˌraɪz) *vb* **sulphurizes, sulphurizing, sulphurized, sulphurises, sulphurising, sulphurised** *or US* **sulfurizes, sulfurizing, sulfurized.** (*tr*) to combine or treat with sulphur or a sulphur compound.
► ˌ**sulphuri'zation,** ˌ**sulphuri'sation,** *or US* ˌ**sulfuri'zation** *n*

sulphurous *or US* **sulfurous** ('sʌlfərəs) *adj* **1** Also: **sulphureous.** of, relating to, or resembling sulphur: *a sulphurous colour.* **2** (sʌl'fjʊərəs). of or containing sulphur with an oxidation state of 4: *sulphurous acid.* **3** of or relating to hellfire. **4** hot-tempered.
► **'sulphurously** *or US* **'sulfurously** *adv* ► **'sulphurousness** *or US* **'sulfurousness** *n*

sulphurous acid *n* an unstable acid produced when sulphur dioxide dissolves in water: used as a preservative for food and a bleaching agent. Formula: H_2SO_3. Systematic name: **sulphuric(IV) acid.**

sulphur trioxide *n* a colourless reactive fuming solid that forms sulphuric acid with water. Formula: SO_3. Systematic name: **sulphur(VI) oxide.**

sultan ('sʌltən) *n* **1** the sovereign of a Muslim country, esp. of the former Ottoman Empire. **2** a small domestic fowl with a white crest and heavily feathered legs and feet: originated in Turkey. ORIG C16: from Med. L *sultānus,* from Ar. *sultān* rule, from Aramaic *salita* to rule

sultana (sʌl'tɑːnə) *n* **1a** the dried fruit of a small white seedless grape, originally produced in SW Asia; seedless raisin. **1b** the grape itself. **2** Also called: **sultaness.** a wife, concubine, or female relative of a sultan. **3** a mistress; concubine. ORIG C16: from It., fem of *sultano* SULTAN

sultanate ('sʌltəˌneɪt) *n* **1** the territory or a country ruled by a sultan. **2** the office, rank, or jurisdiction of a sultan.

sultry ('sʌltrɪ) *adj* **sultrier, sultriest. 1** (of weather or climate) oppressively hot and humid. **2** characterized by or emitting oppressive heat. **3** displaying or suggesting passion; sensual: *sultry eyes.* ORIG C16: from obs. *sulter* to swelter + -Y[1]
► **'sultrily** *adv* ► **'sultriness** *n*

Sulu Archipelago ★ ('suːluː) *n* a chain of over 500 islands in the SW Philippines, separating the Sulu Sea from the Celebes Sea: formerly a sultanate, ceded to the Philippines in 1940. Capital: Jolo. Pop.: 555 239 (1980). Area: 2686 sq. km (1037 sq. miles).

Sulu Sea ★ *n* part of the W Pacific between Borneo and the central Philippines.

sum (sʌm) *n* **1** the result of the addition of numbers, quantities, objects, etc. **2** one or more columns or rows of numbers to be added, subtracted, multiplied, or divided. **3** *Maths.* the limit of the first *n* terms of a converging infinite series as *n* tends to infinity. **4** a quantity, esp. of money: *he borrows enormous sums.* **5** the essence or gist of a matter (esp. in **in sum, in sum and substance**). **6** a less common word for **summary. 7** (*modifier*) complete or final (esp. in **sum total**). ◆ *vb* **sums, summing, summed. 8** (often foll. by *up*) to add or form a total of (something). **9** (*tr*) to calculate the sum of (the terms in a sequence). ◆ See also **sum up.** ORIG C13 *summe,* from OF, from L *summa* the top, sum, from *summus* highest, from *super* above

sumach *or US* **sumac** (ˈsuːmæk, ˈʃuː-) *n* **1** any of various temperate or subtropical shrubs or small trees, having compound leaves and red hairy fruits. See also **poison sumach. 2** a preparation of powdered leaves of certain species of sumach, used in dyeing and tanning. **3** the wood of any of these plants. ORIG C14: via OF from Ar. *summāq*

Sumatra ★ (sʊˈmɑːtrə) *n* a mountainous island in W Indonesia, in the Greater Sunda Islands, separated from the Malay Peninsula by the Strait of Malacca: Dutch control began in the 16th century; joined Indonesia in 1945. Pop.: 22 706 200 (1995 est.). Area: 473 606 sq. km (182 821 sq. miles).
▸ **Suˈmatran** *adj, n*

Sumba *or* **Soemba** ★ (ˈsuːmbə) *n* an island in Indonesia, in the Lesser Sunda Islands, separated from Flores by the **Sumba Strait:** formerly important for sandalwood exports. Pop.: 355 073 (1995 est.). Area: 11 153 sq. km (4306 sq. miles). Former name: **Sandalwood Island.**

Sumbawa *or* **Soembawa** ★ (suːmˈbɑːwə) *n* a mountainous island in Indonesia, in the Lesser Sunda Islands, between Lombok and Flores Islands. Pop.: 373 000 (1990 est.). Area: 14 750 sq. km (5695 sq. miles).

Sumer ★ (ˈsuːmə) *n* the S region of Babylonia; seat of a civilization of city-states that reached its height in the 3rd millennium B.C.

Sumerian (suːˈmɪərɪən, -ˈmɛər-) *n* **1** a member of a people who established a civilization in Sumer during the 4th millennium B.C. **2** the extinct language of this people. ◆ *adj* **3** of or relating to ancient Sumer, its inhabitants, or their language or civilization.

summa cum laude (ˈsʊmɑː kʊm ˈlaʊdeɪ) *adv, adj Chiefly US.* with the utmost praise: the highest designation for achievement in examinations. In Britain it is sometimes used to designate a first-class honours degree. ORIG from L

summarize *or* **summarise** (ˈsʌməˌraɪz) *vb* **summarizes, summarizing, summarized** *or* **summarises, summarising, summarised.** (*tr*) to make or be a summary of; express concisely.
▸ **ˌsummariˈzation** *or* **ˌsummariˈsation** *n* ▸ **ˈsummaˌrizer, ˈsummaˌriser,** *or* **ˈsummarist** *n*

summary (ˈsʌmərɪ) *n, pl* **summaries. 1** a brief account giving the main points of something. ◆ *adj* (*usually prenominal*). **2** performed arbitrarily and quickly, without formality: *a summary execution.* **3** (of legal proceedings) short and free from the complexities and delays of a full trial. **4 summary jurisdiction.** the right a court has to adjudicate immediately upon some matter. **5** giving the gist or essence. ORIG C15: from L *summārium,* from *summa* SUM
▸ **ˈsummarily** *adv* ▸ **ˈsummariness** *n*

summary offence *n* an offence that is triable in a magistrates' court.

summation (sʌˈmeɪʃən) *n* **1** the act or process of determining a sum; addition. **2** the result of such an act or process. **3** a summary. **4** *US law.* the concluding statements made by opposing counsel in a case before a court. ORIG C18: from Med. L *summātiō,* from *summāre* to total, from L *summa* SUM
▸ **sumˈmational** *adj* ▸ **ˈsummative** *adj*

summative assessment *n Brit. education.* general assessment of a pupil's achievements over a range of subjects by means of a combined appraisal of formative assessments.

summer (ˈsʌmə) *n* **1** (*sometimes cap.*) **1a** the warmest season of the year, between spring and autumn, astronomically from the June solstice to the September equinox in the N hemisphere and at the opposite time of year in the S hemisphere. **1b** (*as modifier*): *summer flowers.* Related adj: **aestival. 2** the period of hot weather associated with the summer. **3** a time of blossoming, greatest happiness, etc. **4** *Chiefly poetic.* a year represented by this season: *a child of nine summers.* ◆ *vb* **5** (*intr*) to spend the summer (at a place). **6** (*tr*) to keep or feed (farm animals) during the summer: *they summered their cattle on the mountain slopes.* ORIG OE *sumor*
▸ **ˈsummerly** *adj* ▸ **ˈsummery** *adj*

summerhouse (ˈsʌməˌhaʊs) *n* a small building in a garden or park, used for shade or recreation in the summer.

summer pudding *n Brit.* a pudding made by filling a bread-lined basin with a purée of fruit.

summersault (ˈsʌməˌsɔːlt) *n, vb* a variant spelling of **somersault.**

summer school *n* a school, academic course, etc., held during the summer.

summer solstice *n* **1** the time at which the sun is at its northernmost point in the sky (southernmost point in the S hemisphere). It occurs about June 21 (December 22 in the S hemisphere). **2** *Astron.* the point on the celestial sphere, opposite the **winter solstice,** at which the ecliptic is furthest north from the celestial equator.

summertime (ˈsʌməˌtaɪm) *n* the period or season of summer.

summer time *n Brit.* any daylight-saving time, esp. British Summer Time.

summerweight (ˈsʌməˌweɪt) *adj* (of clothes) suitable in weight for wear in the summer.

summing-up *n* **1** a review or summary of the main points of an argument, speech, etc. **2** concluding statements made by a judge to the jury before they retire to consider their verdict.

summit (ˈsʌmɪt) *n* **1** the highest point or part, esp. of a mountain; top. **2** the highest possible degree or state; peak or climax: *the summit of ambition.* **3** the highest level, importance, or rank: *a meeting at the summit.* **4a** a meeting of chiefs of governments or other high officials. **4b** (*as modifier*): *a summit conference.* ORIG C15: from OF *somet,* dim. of *som,* from L *summum;* see SUM

summon (ˈsʌmən) *vb* (*tr*) **1** to order to come; send for, esp. to attend court, by issuing a summons. **2** to order or instruct (to do something) or call (to something): *the bell summoned them to their work.* **3** to call upon to meet or convene. **4** (often foll. by *up*) to muster or gather (one's strength, courage, etc.). **5** *Arch.* to call upon to surrender. ORIG C13: from L *summonēre* to give a discreet reminder, from *monēre* to advise

summons (ˈsʌmənz) *n, pl* **summonses. 1** a call, signal, or order to do something, esp. to attend at a specified place or time. **2a** an official order requiring a person to attend court, either to answer a charge or to give evidence. **2b** the writ making such an order. **3** a call or command given to the members of an assembly to convene a meeting. ◆ *vb* **4** to take out a summons against (a person). ORIG C13: from OF *somonse,* from *somondre* to SUMMON

summum bonum *Latin.* (ˈsʊmʊm ˈbɒnʊm) *n* the principle of goodness in which all moral values are included or from which they are derived; highest or supreme good.

sumo (ˈsuːməʊ) *n* the national style of wrestling of Japan, in which two contestants of great height and weight attempt to force each other to touch the ground with any part of the body except the soles of the feet or to step out of the ring. ORIG from Japanese *sumō*

sump (sʌmp) *n* **1** a receptacle, as in the crankcase of an internal-combustion engine, into which liquids, esp. lubricants, can drain to form a reservoir. **2** another name for **cesspool** (sense 1). **3** *Mining.* a depression at the bottom of a shaft where water collects. ORIG C17: from MDu. *somp* marsh

sumpter (ˈsʌmptə) *n Arch.* a packhorse, mule, or other beast of burden. ORIG C14: from OF *sometier* driver of a baggage horse, from Vulgar L *sagmatārius* (unattested), from LL *sagma* packsaddle

sumptuary (ˈsʌmptjʊərɪ) *adj* relating to or controlling expenditure or extravagance. ORIG C17: from L *sumptuārius* concerning expense, from *sumptus* expense, from *sūmere* to spend

sumptuous ('sʌmptjuəs) *adj* **1** expensive or extravagant: *sumptuous costumes.* **2** magnificent; splendid: *a sumptuous scene.* ORIG C16: from OF *somptueux,* from L *sumptuōsus* costly, from *sumptus;* see SUMPTUARY
▸ **'sumptuously** *adv* ▸ **'sumptuousness** *n*

Sumter ★ ('sʌmtə) *n* See **Fort Sumter.**

sum up *vb* (*adv*) **1** to summarize (the main points of an argument, etc.). **2** (*tr*) to form a quick opinion of: *I summed him up in five minutes.*

Sumy ★ (*Russian* 'sumi) *n* a city in NE Ukraine, on the River Pysol: site of early Slav settlements. Pop.: 304 000 (1996 est.).

sun (sʌn) *n* **1** the star that is the source of heat and light for the planets in the solar system. Related adj: **solar. 2** any star around which a planetary system revolves. **3** the sun as it appears at a particular time or place: *the winter sun.* **4** the radiant energy, esp. heat and light, received from the sun; sunshine. **5** a person or thing considered as a source of radiant warmth, glory, etc. **6** a pictorial representation of the sun, often depicted with a human face. **7** *Poetic.* a year or a day. **8** *Poetic.* a climate. **9** *Arch.* sunrise or sunset (esp. in **from sun to sun**). **10 catch the sun.** to become slightly sunburnt. **11 place in the sun.** a prominent or favourable position. **12 take** *or* **shoot the sun.** *Naut.* to measure the altitude of the sun in order to determine latitude. **13 touch of the sun.** slight sunstroke. **14 under** *or* **beneath the sun.** on earth; at all: *nobody under the sun eats more than you.* ◆ *vb* **suns, sunning, sunned. 15** to expose (oneself) to the sunshine. **16** (*tr*) to expose to the sunshine in order to warm, etc. ORIG OE *sunne*

Sun. *abbrev. for* Sunday.

sunbaked ('sʌn,beɪkt) *adj* **1** (esp. of roads, etc.) dried or cracked by the sun's heat. **2** baked hard by the heat of the sun: *sunbaked bricks.*

sun bath *n* the exposure of the body to the rays of the sun or a sun lamp, esp. in order to get a suntan.

sunbathe ('sʌn,beɪð) *vb* **sunbathes, sunbathing, sunbathed.** (*intr*) to bask in the sunshine, esp. in order to get a suntan.
▸ **'sun,bather** *n*

sunbeam ('sʌn,biːm) *n* a beam, ray, or stream of sunlight.
▸ **'sun,beamed** *or* **'sun,beamy** *adj*

Sunbelt ★ ('sʌn,bɛlt) *n* the southern states of the USA.

sunbird ('sʌn,bɜːd) *n* any of various small songbirds of tropical regions of the Old World, esp. Africa, having a long slender curved bill and a bright plumage in the males.

sunblock ('sʌn,blɒk) *n* another name for **sunscreen.**

sunbonnet ('sʌn,bɒnɪt) *n* a hat that shades the face and neck from the sun, esp. one of cotton with a projecting brim, now worn esp. by babies.

sunburn ('sʌn,bɜːn) *n* **1** inflammation of the skin caused by overexposure to the sun. **2** another word for **suntan.**
▸ **'sun,burnt** *or* **'sun,burned** *adj*

sunburst ('sʌn,bɜːst) *n* **1** a burst of sunshine, as through a break in the clouds. **2** a pattern or design resembling that of the sun. **3** a jewelled brooch with this pattern.

Sunbury-on-Thames ★ ('sʌnbərɪ, -brɪ) *n* a town in SE England, in N Surrey. Pop.: 27 392 (1991).

sun-cured *adj* cured or preserved by exposure to the sun.

sundae ('sʌndɪ, -deɪ) *n* ice cream topped with a sweet sauce, nuts, whipped cream, etc. ORIG C20: from ?

Sunda Islands ('sʌndə) *or* **Soenda Islands ★** *pl n* a chain of islands in the Malay Archipelago, consisting of the **Greater Sunda Islands** (chiefly Sumatra, Java, Borneo, and Sulawesi) and **Nusa Tenggara** (formerly the Lesser Sunda Islands).

Sunda Strait *or* **Soenda Strait ★** *n* a strait between Sumatra and Java, linking the Java Sea with the Indian Ocean. Narrowest point: about 26 km (16 miles).

Sunday ('sʌndɪ) *n* the first day of the week and the Christian day of worship. ORIG OE *sunnandæg,* translation of L *diēs sōlis* day of the sun, translation of Gk *hēmera hēliou*

Sunday best *n* one's best clothes, esp. regarded as those most suitable for churchgoing.

Sunday school *n* **1a** a school for the religious instruction of children on Sundays, usually held in a church hall. **1b** (*as modifier*): *a Sunday-school outing.* **2** the members of such a school.

sunder ('sʌndə) *Arch. or literary.* ◆ *vb* **1** to break or cause to break apart or in pieces. ◆ *n* **2 in sunder.** into pieces; apart. ORIG OE *sundrian*

Sunderland ★ ('sʌndələnd) *n* **1** a port in NE England, in Tyne and Wear at the mouth of the River Wear: shipbuilding and marine engineering; seat of the University of Sunderland (1992). Pop.: 183 310 (1991). **2** a unitary authority in NE England, in Tyne and Wear. Pop.: 294 300 (1996 est.). Area: 138 sq. km (53 sq. miles).

sundew ('sʌn,djuː) *n* any of several bog plants having leaves covered with sticky hairs that trap and digest insects. ORIG C16: translation of L *ros solis*

sundial ('sʌn,daɪəl) *n* a device indicating the time during the hours of sunlight by means of a stationary arm (the **gnomon**) that casts a shadow onto a plate or surface marked in hours.

sun disc *n* a disc symbolizing the sun, esp. one flanked by two serpents and the extended wings of a vulture: a religious figure in ancient Egypt.

sundog ('sʌn,dɒg) *n* another word for **parhelion.**

sundown ('sʌn,daʊn) *n* another name for **sunset.**

sundowner ('sʌn,daʊnə) *n* **1** *Austral. sl.* a tramp, esp. one who seeks food and lodging at sundown when it is too late to work. **2** *Inf., chiefly Brit.* an alcoholic drink taken at sunset.

sundress ('sʌn,drɛs) *n* a dress for hot weather that exposes the shoulders, arms, and back.

sun-dried *adj* dried or preserved by exposure to the sun.

sundry ('sʌndrɪ) *determiner* **1** several or various; miscellaneous. ◆ *pron* **2 all and sundry.** everybody, individually and collectively. ◆ *n, pl* **sundries. 3** (*pl*) miscellaneous unspecified items. **4** the Austral. term for **extra** (sense 6). ORIG OE *syndrig* separate

Sundsvall ★ (*Swedish* 'sundsval) *n* a port in E Sweden, on the Gulf of Bothnia: icebound in winter; cellulose industries. Pop.: 94 815 (1994).

sunfast ('sʌn,fɑːst) *adj Chiefly US & Canad.* not fading in sunlight.

sunfish ('sʌn,fɪʃ) *n, pl* **sunfish** *or* **sunfishes. 1** any of various large fishes of temperate and tropical seas, esp. one which has a large rounded compressed body, long pointed dorsal and anal fins, and a fringelike tail fin. **2** any of various small predatory North American freshwater percoid fishes, typically having a compressed brightly coloured body.

sunflower ('sʌn,flaʊə) *n* **1** any of several American plants having very tall thick stems, large flower heads with yellow rays, and seeds used as food, esp. for poultry. See also **Jerusalem artichoke. 2 sunflower seed oil.** the oil extracted from sunflower seeds, used as a salad oil, in margarine, etc.

sung (sʌŋ) *vb* **1** the past participle of **sing.** ◆ *adj* **2** produced by singing: *a sung syllable.*

USAGE NOTE See at **ring**[2].

Sung *or* **Song ★** (sʊŋ) *n* an imperial dynasty of China (960–1279 A.D.), notable for its art, literature, and philosophy.

Sungari ★ ('sʊŋgərɪ) *n* another name for the **Songhua.**

Sungkiang ★ ('sʊŋ'kjæŋ, -kaɪ'æŋ) *n* a former province of NE China: now part of the Inner Mongolian AR.

sunglass ('sʌn,glɑːs) *n* another name for **burning glass.**

sunglasses ('sʌn,glɑːsɪz) *pl n* glasses with darkened or polarizing lenses that protect the eyes from the sun's glare.

sun-god *n* **1** the sun considered as a personal deity. **2** a deity associated with the sun or controlling its movements.

sunk (sʌŋk) *vb* **1** a past participle of **sink**. ◆ *adj* **2** *Inf.* with all hopes dashed; ruined.

sunken ('sʌŋkən) *vb* **1** a past participle of **sink**. ◆ *adj* **2** unhealthily hollow: *sunken cheeks*. **3** situated at a lower level than the surrounding or usual one: *a sunken bath*. **4** situated under water; submerged. **5** depressed; low: *sunken spirits*.

sunk fence *n* another name for **ha-ha**[2].

Sun King ★ *n* **the.** an epithet of **Louis XIV**.

sun lamp *n* **1** a lamp that generates ultraviolet rays, used for obtaining an artificial suntan, for muscular therapy, etc. **2** a lamp used in film studios, etc., to give an intense beam of light by means of parabolic mirrors.

sunless ('sʌnlɪs) *adj* **1** without sun or sunshine. **2** gloomy; depressing.
▸ **'sunlessly** *adv*

sunlight ('sʌnlaɪt) *n* **1** the light emanating from the sun. **2** an area or the time characterized by sunshine.
▸ **'sunlit** *adj*

sun lounge *or US* **sun parlor** *n* a room with large windows positioned to receive as much sunlight as possible.

Sunna ('sʌnə) *n* the body of traditional Islamic law accepted by most orthodox Muslims as based on the words and acts of Mohammed. ORIG C18: from Ar. *sunnah* rule

Sunni ('sʌnɪ) *n* **1** one of the two main branches of orthodox Islam (the other being the Shiah), consisting of those who acknowledge the authority of the Sunna. **2** (*pl* **Sunnis** *or* **Sunni**) a less common word for **Sunnite**.

Sunnite ('sʌnaɪt) *n* an adherent of the Sunni.

sunny ('sʌnɪ) *adj* **sunnier, sunniest. 1** full of or exposed to sunlight. **2** radiating good humour. **3** of or resembling the sun.
▸ **'sunnily** *adv* ▸ **'sunniness** *n*

sunrise ('sʌnˌraɪz) *n* **1** the daily appearance of the sun above the horizon. **2** the atmospheric phenomena accompanying this appearance. **3** Also called (esp. US): **sunup.** the time at which the sun rises at a particular locality.

sunrise industry *n* any of the high-technology industries, such as electronics, that hold promise of future development.

sunroof ('sʌnˌru:f) *or* **sunshine roof** *n* a panel, often translucent, that may be opened in the roof of a car.

sunscreen ('sʌnˌskri:n) *n* a cream or lotion applied to exposed skin to protect it from harmful ultraviolet radiation from the sun. Also called: **sunblock.**

sunset ('sʌnˌsɛt) *n* **1** the daily disappearance of the sun below the horizon. **2** the atmospheric phenomena accompanying this disappearance. **3** Also called: **sundown.** the time at which the sun sets at a particular locality. **4** the final stage or closing period, as of a person's life.

sunshade ('sʌnˌʃeɪd) *n* a device, esp. a parasol or awning, serving to shade from the sun.

sunshine ('sʌnˌʃaɪn) *n* **1** the light received directly from the sun. **2** the warmth from the sun. **3** a sunny area. **4** a light-hearted or ironic term of address.
▸ **'sunˌshiny** *adj*

sun sign *n* another name for **sign of the zodiac.**

sunspot ('sʌnˌspɒt) *n* **1** any of the dark cool patches that appear on the surface of the sun and last about a week. **2** *Inf.* a sunny holiday resort. **3** *Austral.* a small cancerous spot produced by overexposure to the sun.

sunstroke ('sʌnˌstrəʊk) *n* heatstroke caused by prolonged exposure to intensely hot sunlight.

sunsuit ('sʌnˌsu:t, -ˌsju:t) *n* a child's outfit consisting of a brief top and shorts or skirt.

suntan ('sʌnˌtæn) *n* **a** a brownish colouring of the skin caused by the formation of the pigment melanin within the skin on exposure to the ultraviolet rays of the sun or a sun lamp. Often shortened to **tan. b** (*as modifier*): *suntan oil*.
▸ **'sunˌtanned** *adj*

suntrap ('sʌnˌtræp) *n* a very sunny sheltered place.

sunward ('sʌnwəd) *adj* **1** directed or moving towards the sun. ◆ *adv* **2** Also: **sunwards.** towards the sun.

Sun Yat-sen ★ ('sʊn 'jɑ:t'sɛn) *n* 1866–1925, Chinese statesman, who was instrumental in the overthrow of the Manchu dynasty and was the first president of the Republic of China (1911). He reorganized the Kuomintang.

Suomi ★ ('suɔmi) *n* the Finnish name for **Finland.**

sup[1] (sʌp) *vb* **sups, supping, supped.** (*intr*) *Arch.* to have supper. ORIG C13: from OF *soper*

sup[2] (sʌp) *vb* **sups, supping, supped. 1** to partake of (liquid) by swallowing a little at a time. **2** *Scot. & N English dialect.* to drink. ◆ *n* **3** a sip. ORIG OE *sūpan*

sup. *abbrev. for:* **1** above. ORIG from L *supra* **2** superior. **3** *Grammar.* superlative. **4** supplement. **5** supplementary. **6** supply.

super (su:pə) *adj* **1** *Inf.* outstanding; exceptional. ◆ *n* **2** petrol with a high octane rating. **3** *Inf.* a supervisor. **4** *Austral. & NZ inf.* superannuation benefits. **5** *Austral & NZ inf.* superphosphate. ◆ *interj* **6** *Brit. inf.* an enthusiastic expression of approval. ORIG from L: above

super. *abbrev. for:* **1** superfine. **2** superior.

super- *prefix* **1** placed above or over: *superscript*. **2** surpassing others; outstanding: *superstar*. **3** of greater size, extent, quality, etc.: *supermarket*. **4** beyond a standard or norm: *supersonic*. **5** indicating that a chemical compound contains a specified element in a higher proportion than usual: *superphosphate*. ORIG from L *super* above

superable ('su:pərəbᵊl) *adj* able to be surmounted or overcome. ORIG C17: from L *superābilis*, from *superāre* to overcome
▸ **ˌsupera'bility** *or* **'superableness** *n* ▸ **'superably** *adv*

superannuate (ˌsu:pər'ænjʊˌeɪt) *vb* **superannuates, superannuating, superannuated.** (*tr*) **1** to pension off. **2** to discard as obsolete or old-fashioned.

superannuated (ˌsu:pər'ænjʊˌeɪtɪd) *adj* **1** discharged, esp. with a pension, owing to age or illness. **2** too old to serve usefully. **3** obsolete. ORIG C17: from Med. L *superannātus* aged more than one year, from L SUPER- + *annus* a year

superannuation (ˌsu:pərˌænjʊ'eɪʃən) *n* **1a** the amount deducted regularly from employees' incomes in a contributory pension scheme. **1b** the pension finally paid. **2** the act or process of superannuating or the condition of being superannuated.

superb (sʊ'pɜ:b, sjʊ-) *adj* **1** surpassingly good; excellent. **2** majestic or imposing. **3** magnificently rich; luxurious. ORIG C16: from OF *superbe*, from L *superbus* distinguished, from *super* above
▸ **su'perbly** *adv* ▸ **su'perbness** *n*

Super Bowl *n American football.* the championship game held annually between the best team of the American Football Conference and that of the National Football Conference.

superbug ('su:pəˌbʌg) *n Inf.* an infective microorganism that has become resistant to antibiotics.

supercalender (ˌsu:pə'kæləndə) *n* **1** a calender that gives a high gloss to paper. ◆ *vb* **2** (*tr*) to finish (paper) in this way.
▸ **ˌsuper'calendered** *adj*

supercargo (ˌsu:pə'kɑ:gəʊ) *n, pl* **supercargoes.** an officer on a merchant ship who supervises commercial matters and is in charge of the cargo. ORIG C17: changed from Sp. *sobrecargo*, from *sobre* over + *cargo* CARGO

supercharge ('su:pəˌtʃɑ:dʒ) *vb* **supercharges, supercharging, supercharged.** (*tr*) **1** to increase the intake pressure of (an internal-combustion engine) with a supercharger; boost. **2** to charge (the atmosphere, a remark, etc.) with an excess amount of (tension, emotion, etc.). **3** to apply pressure to (a fluid); pressurize.

supercharger ('su:pəˌtʃɑ:dʒə) *n* a device that increases the mass of air drawn into an internal-combustion engine by raising the intake pressure. Also called: **blower, booster.**

superciliary (ˌsu:pə'sɪlɪərɪ) *adj* over the eyebrow or a corresponding region in lower animals. ORIG C18: from NL *superciliaris*, from L, from SUPER- + *cilium* eyelid

★ people and places

supercilious (ˌsuːpəˈsɪlɪəs) *adj* displaying arrogant pride, scorn, or indifference. ORIG C16: from L, from *supercilium* eyebrow
► ˌ**superˈciliously** *adv* ► ˌ**superˈciliousness** *n*

superclass (ˈsuːpəˌklɑːs) *n* a taxonomic group that is a subdivision of a subphylum.

supercolumnar (ˌsuːpəkəˈlʌmnə) *adj Archit.* **1** having one colonnade above another. **2** placed above a colonnade or a column.
► ˌ**supercolˌumniˈation** *n*

superconductivity (ˌsuːpəˌkɒndʌkˈtɪvɪtɪ) *n Physics.* the property of certain substances that have no electrical resistance. In metals it occurs at very low temperatures; higher-temperature superconductivity occurs in some ceramic materials.
► **superconduction** (ˌsuːpəkənˈdʌkʃən) *n* ► ˌ**superconˈductive** *or* ˌ**superconˈducting** *adj* ► ˌ**superconˈductor** *n*

supercontinent (ˈsuːpəˌkɒntɪnənt) *n* a great landmass thought to have existed in the geological past and to have split into smaller landmasses, which drifted and formed the present continents.

supercool (ˌsuːpəˈkuːl) *vb Chem.* to cool or be cooled without freezing or crystallization to a temperature below that at which freezing or crystallization should occur.

supercritical (ˌsuːpəˈkrɪtɪkᵊl) *adj* **1** *Physics.* (of a fluid) brought to a temperature and pressure higher than its critical temperature and pressure, so that its physical and chemical properties change. **2** *Nuclear physics.* of or containing more than the critical mass.

superdense theory (ˌsuːpəˈdɛns) *n Astron.* another name for the **big-bang theory**.

super-duper (ˈsuːpəˈduːpə) *adj Inf.* extremely pleasing, impressive, etc.: often used as an exclamation.

superego (ˌsuːpərˈiːgəʊ, -ˈɛgəʊ) *n, pl* **superegos.** *Psychoanal.* that part of the unconscious mind that acts as a conscience for the ego.

superelevation (ˌsuːpərˌɛlɪˈveɪʃən) *n* **1** another name for **bank**[2] (sense 8). **2** the difference between the heights of the sides of a road or railway track on a bend.

supereminent (ˌsuːpərˈɛmɪnənt) *adj* of distinction, dignity, or rank superior to that of others; pre-eminent.
► ˌ**superˈeminence** *n* ► ˌ**superˈeminently** *adv*

supererogation (ˌsuːpərˌɛrəˈgeɪʃən) *n* **1** the performance of work in excess of that required or expected. **2** *RC Church.* supererogatory prayers, devotions, etc.

supererogatory (ˌsuːpərɛˈrɒgətərɪ, -trɪ) *adj* **1** performed to an extent exceeding that required or expected. **2** exceeding what is needed; superfluous. **3** *RC Church.* of or relating to prayers, good works, etc., performed over and above those prescribed as obligatory. ORIG C16: from Med. L *superērogātōrius,* from L *supererogāre* to spend over and above

superfamily (ˈsuːpəˌfæmɪlɪ) *n, pl* **superfamilies. 1** *Biol.* a subdivision of a suborder. **2** any analogous group, such as a group of related languages.

superfecundation (ˌsuːpəˌfiːkənˈdeɪʃən) *n Physiol.* the fertilization of two or more ova, produced during the same menstrual cycle, by sperm ejaculated during two or more acts of sexual intercourse.

superfetation (ˌsuːpəfiːˈteɪʃən) *n Physiol.* the presence in the uterus of two fetuses developing from ova fertilized at different times. ORIG C17 *superfetate,* from L *superfētāre* to fertilize when already pregnant, from *fētus* offspring

superficial (ˌsuːpəˈfɪʃəl) *adj* **1** of, near, or forming the surface: *superficial bruising.* **2** displaying a lack of thoroughness or care: *a superficial inspection.* **3** only outwardly apparent rather than genuine or actual: *the similarity was merely superficial.* **4** of little substance or significance: *superficial differences.* **5** lacking profundity: *the film's plot was quite superficial.* **6** (of measurements) involving only the surface area. ORIG C14: from LL *superficiālis* of the surface, from L SUPERFICIES
► **superficiality** (ˌsuːpəˌfɪʃɪˈælɪtɪ) *n* ► ˌ**superˈficially** *adv*

superficies (ˌsuːpəˈfɪʃiːz) *n, pl* **superficies. 1** a surface or outer face. **2** the outward form of a thing. ORIG C16: from L: upper side

superfine (ˌsuːpəˈfaɪn) *adj* **1** of exceptional fineness or quality. **2** excessively refined.
► ˌ**superˈfineness** *n*

superfix (ˈsuːpəˌfɪks) *n Linguistics.* a type of feature distinguishing the meaning or grammatical function of one word or phrase from that of another, as stress does for example between the noun *conduct* and the verb *conduct.*

superfluid (ˌsuːpəˈfluːɪd) *n* **1** *Physics.* a fluid in a state characterized by a very low viscosity, high thermal conductivity, high capillarity, etc. The only known example is that of liquid helium at temperatures close to absolute zero. ◆ *adj* **2** being or relating to a superfluid.
► ˌ**superfluˈidity** *n*

superfluity (ˌsuːpəˈfluːɪtɪ) *n* **1** the condition of being superfluous. **2** a quantity or thing that is in excess of what is needed. **3** a thing that is not needed. ORIG C14: from OF *superfluité,* via LL from L *superfluus* SUPERFLUOUS

superfluous (suːˈpɜːflʊəs) *adj* **1** exceeding what is sufficient or required. **2** not necessary or relevant; uncalled for. ORIG C15: from L *superfluus* overflowing, from *fluere* to flow
► **suˈperfluously** *adv* ► **suˈperfluousness** *n*

Super-G *n Skiing.* a type of slalom in which the course is shorter than in a standard slalom and the obstacles are farther apart than in a giant slalom. ORIG C20: from SUPER- + G(IANT)

supergiant (ˈsuːpəˌdʒaɪənt) *n* any of a class of extremely bright stars which have expanded to a large diameter and are eventually likely to explode as supernovas.

superglue (ˈsuːpəˌgluː) *n* any of various adhesives that quickly make an exceptionally strong bond.

supergrass (ˈsuːpəˌgrɑːs) *n* an informer whose information implicates a large number of people.

supergravity (ˌsuːpəˈgrævɪtɪ) *n Physics.* any of various theories in which supersymmetry is applied to the theory of gravitation.

superheat (ˌsuːpəˈhiːt) *vb (tr)* **1** to heat (a vapour, esp. steam) to a temperature above its saturation point for a given pressure. **2** to heat (a liquid) to a temperature above its boiling point without boiling occurring. **3** to heat excessively; overheat.
► ˌ**superˈheater** *n*

superheavy (ˌsuːpəˈhɛvɪ) *adj Physics.* denoting or relating to elements of high atomic number (above 109) postulated to exist with special stability as a consequence of the shell model of the nucleus.

superheavyweight (ˌsuːpəˈhɛvɪˌweɪt) *n* an amateur boxer weighing more than 91 kg.

superheterodyne receiver (ˌsuːpəˈhɛtərəˌdaɪn) *n* a radio receiver that combines two radio-frequency signals by heterodyne action, to produce a signal above the audible frequency limit. Sometimes shortened to **superhet.** ORIG C20: from SUPER(SONIC) + HETERODYNE

superhigh frequency (ˈsuːpəˌhaɪ) *n* a radio-frequency band or radio frequency lying between 30 000 and 3000 megahertz.

superhuman (ˌsuːpəˈhjuːmən) *adj* **1** having powers above and beyond those of mankind. **2** exceeding normal human ability or experience.
► ˌ**superˈhumanly** *adv*

superimpose (ˌsuːpərɪmˈpəʊz) *vb* **superimposes, superimposing, superimposed.** *(tr)* **1** to set or place on or over something else. **2** (usually foll. by *on* or *upon*) to add (to).
► ˌ**superˌimpoˈsition** *n*

superinduce (ˌsuːpərɪnˈdjuːs) *vb* **superinduces, superinducing, superinduced.** *(tr)* to introduce as an additional feature, factor, etc.
► **superinduction** (ˌsuːpərɪnˈdʌkʃən) *n*

superintend (ˌsuːpərɪnˈtɛnd) *vb* to undertake the direction or supervision (of); manage. ORIG C17: from Church L *superintendere,* from L SUPER- + *intendere* to give attention to
► ˌ**superinˈtendence** *n*

superintendent (ˌsuːpərɪnˈtɛndənt) *n* **1** a person who

directs and manages an organization, office, etc. **2** (in Britain) a senior police officer higher in rank than an inspector but lower than a chief superintendent. **3** (in the US) the head of a police department. **4** *Chiefly US & Canad.* a caretaker, esp. of a block of apartments. ◆ *adj* **5** of or relating to supervision; superintending. ORIG C16: from Church L *superintendens* overseeing
▸ **ˌsuperinˈtendency** *n*

superior (suːˈpɪərɪə) *adj* **1** greater in quality, quantity, etc. **2** of high or extraordinary worth, merit, etc. **3** higher in rank or status. **4** displaying a conscious sense of being above or better than others; supercilious. **5** (*often postpositive;* foll. by *to*) not susceptible (to) or influenced (by). **6** placed higher up; further from the base. **7** *Astron.* (of a planet) having an orbit further from the sun than the orbit of the earth. **8** (of a plant ovary) situated above the calyx and other floral parts. **9** *Printing.* (of a character) written or printed above the line; superscript. ◆ *n* **10** a person or thing of greater rank or quality. **11** *Printing.* a character set in a superior position. **12** (*often cap.*) the head of a community in a religious order. ORIG C14: from L, from *superus* placed above, from *super* above
▸ **suˈperioress** *fem n* ▸ **superiority** (suːˌpɪərɪˈɒrɪtɪ) *n*

USAGE NOTE *Superior* should not be used with *than*: *he is a better* (not *a superior*) *poet than his brother; his poetry is superior to* (not *than*) *his brother's.*

Superior ★ (suːˈpɪərɪə, sjuː-) *n* **Lake.** a lake in the N central US and S Canada: one of the largest freshwater lakes in the world and westernmost of the Great Lakes. Area: 82 362 sq. km (31 800 sq. miles).

superior court *n* **1** (in England) a higher court not subject to control by any other court except by way of appeal. See also **Supreme Court of Judicature. 2** (in several states of the US) a court of general jurisdiction ranking above the inferior courts and below courts of last resort.

superiority complex *n Inf.* an inflated estimate of one's own merit, usually manifested in arrogance.

superior planet *n* any of the six planets (Mars, Jupiter, Saturn, Uranus, Neptune, and Pluto) whose orbit lies outside that of the earth.

superl. *abbrev. for* superlative.

superlative (suːˈpɜːlətɪv) *adj* **1** of outstanding quality, degree, etc.; supreme. **2** *Grammar.* denoting the form of an adjective or adverb that expresses the highest or a very high degree of quality. In English this is usually marked by the suffix *-est* or the word *most,* as in *loudest* or *most loudly.* **3** (of language or style) excessive; exaggerated. ◆ *n* **4** a thing that excels all others or is of the highest quality. **5** *Grammar.* the superlative form of an adjective or adverb. **6** the highest degree; peak. ORIG C14: from OF *superlatif,* via LL from L *superlātus* extravagant, from *superferre* to carry beyond
▸ **suˈperlatively** *adv* ▸ **suˈperlativeness** *n*

superlunar (ˌsuːpəˈluːnə) *adj* beyond the moon; celestial.
▸ **ˌsuperˈlunary** *adj*

superman (ˈsuːpəˌmæn) *n, pl* **supermen. 1** (in the philosophy of Nietzsche) an ideal man who would rise above good and evil and who represents the goal of human evolution. **2** any man of apparently superhuman powers.

supermarket (ˈsuːpəˌmɑːkɪt) *n* a large self-service store selling food and household supplies.

supermembrane (ˌsuːpəˈmɛmbreɪn) *n Physics.* a type of membrane postulated in certain theories of elementary particles that involve supersymmetry.

supermodel (ˈsuːpəˌmɒdᵊl) *n* a very successful and well-known photographic or catwalk model.

supermundane (ˌsuːpəˈmʌndeɪn) *adj* elevated above earthly things.

supernal (suːˈpɜːnᵊl, sjuː-) *adj Literary.* **1** divine; celestial. **2** of, from above, or from the sky. ORIG C15: from Med. L *supernālis,* from L *supernus* that is on high, from *super* above
▸ **suˈpernally** *adv*

supernatant (ˌsuːpəˈneɪtᵊnt) *adj* **1** floating on the surface or over something. **2** *Chem.* (of a liquid) lying above a sediment or precipitate. ORIG C17: from L *supernatāre* to float, from SUPER- + *natāre* to swim
▸ **ˌsupernaˈtation** *n*

supernatural (ˌsuːpəˈnætʃərəl) *adj* **1** of or relating to things that cannot be explained according to natural laws. **2** of or caused as if by a god; miraculous. **3** of or involving occult beings. **4** exceeding the ordinary; abnormal. ◆ *n* **5 the supernatural.** supernatural forces, occurrences, and beings collectively.
▸ **ˌsuperˈnaturally** *adv* ▸ **ˌsuperˈnaturalness** *n*

supernaturalism (ˌsuːpəˈnætʃərəlɪzəm) *n* **1** the quality or condition of being supernatural. **2** belief in supernatural forces or agencies as producing effects in this world.
▸ **ˌsuperˈnaturalist** *n, adj* ▸ **ˌsuperˌnaturalˈistic** *adj*

supernormal (ˌsuːpəˈnɔːməl) *adj* greatly exceeding the normal.
▸ **supernormality** (ˌsuːpənɔːˈmælɪtɪ) *n* ▸ **ˌsuperˈnormally** *adv*

supernova (ˌsuːpəˈnəʊvə) *n, pl* **supernovae** (-viː) *or* **supernovas.** a star that explodes owing to instabilities following the exhaustion of its nuclear fuel, becoming for a few days up to one hundred million times brighter than the sun. Cf. **nova.**

supernumerary (ˌsuːpəˈnjuːmərərɪ) *adj* **1** exceeding a regular or proper number; extra. **2** functioning as a substitute or assistant with regard to a regular body or staff. ◆ *n, pl* **supernumeraries. 3** a person or thing that exceeds the required or regular number. **4** a substitute or assistant. **5** an actor who has no lines, esp. a nonprofessional one. ORIG C17: from LL *supernumerārius,* from L SUPER- + *numerus* number

supernurse (ˈsuːpəˌnɜːs) *n* (in Britain) an experienced senior nurse on an elevated salary who is responsible for running clinics and managing nursing teams.

superorder (ˈsuːpərˌɔːdə) *n Biol.* a subdivision of a subclass.

superordinate (ˌsuːpərˈɔːdɪnɪt) *adj* **1** of higher status or condition. ◆ *n* **2** a person or thing that is superordinate. **3** a word the meaning of which includes the meaning of another word or words: *"red" is the superordinate of "scarlet" and "crimson".*

superphosphate (ˌsuːpəˈfɒsfeɪt) *n* **1** a mixture of the diacid calcium salt of orthophosphoric acid with calcium sulphate and small quantities of other phosphates: used as a fertilizer. **2** a salt of phosphoric acid formed by incompletely replacing its acidic hydrogen atoms.

superpose (ˌsuːpəˈpəʊz) *vb* **superposes, superposing, superposed.** (*tr*) *Geom.* to transpose (the coordinates of one geometric figure) to coincide with those of another. ORIG C19: from F *superposer,* from L *superpōnere,* from *pōnere* to place

superposition (ˌsuːpəpəˈzɪʃən) *n* **1** the act of superposing or state of being superposed. **2** *Geol.* the principle that in any sequence of sedimentary rocks that has not been disturbed the lowest strata are the oldest.

superpower (ˈsuːpəˌpaʊə) *n* **1** an extremely powerful state, such as the US. **2** extremely high power, esp. electrical or mechanical.
▸ **ˈsuperˌpowered** *adj*

supersaturated (ˌsuːpəˈsætʃəˌreɪtɪd) *adj* **1** (of a solution) containing more solute than a saturated solution. **2** (of a vapour) containing more material than a saturated vapour.
▸ **ˌsuperˌsatuˈration** *n*

superscribe (ˌsuːpəˈskraɪb) *vb* **superscribes, superscribing, superscribed.** (*tr*) to write (an inscription, name, etc.) above, on top of, or outside. ORIG C16: from L *superscrībere,* from *scrībere* to write
▸ **superscription** (ˌsuːpəˈskrɪpʃən) *n*

superscript (ˈsuːpəˌskrɪpt) *Printing.* ◆ *adj* **1** (of a character) written or printed above the line; superior. Cf. **subscript.** ◆ *n* **2** a superscript or superior character. ORIG C16: from L *superscriptus*

supersede (ˌsuːpəˈsiːd) *vb* **supersedes, superseding, superseded.** (*tr*) **1** to take the place of (something old-fashioned or less appropriate); supplant. **2** to replace in

★ people and places

function, office, etc.; succeed. **3** to discard or set aside or cause to be set aside as obsolete or inferior. ORIG C15: via OF from L *supersedēre* to sit above
▸ **ˌsuper'sedence** *n* ▸ **supersedure** (ˌsu:pə'si:dʒə) *n* ▸ **supersession** (ˌsu:pə'sɛʃən) *n*

supersex ('su:pəˌsɛks) *n Genetics.* a sterile organism in which the ratio between the sex chromosomes is disturbed.

supersonic (ˌsu:pə'sɒnɪk) *adj* being, having, or capable of a velocity in excess of the velocity of sound.
▸ **ˌsuper'sonically** *adv*

supersonics (ˌsu:pə'sɒnɪks) *n* (*functioning as sing*) **1** the study of supersonic motion. **2** a less common name for **ultrasonics.**

superstar ('su:pəˌstɑ:) *n* an extremely popular film star, pop star, etc.
▸ **'superˌstardom** *n*

superstition (ˌsu:pə'stɪʃən) *n* **1** irrational belief usually founded on ignorance or fear and characterized by obsessive reverence for omens, charms, etc. **2** a notion, act, or ritual that derives from such belief. **3** any irrational belief, esp. with regard to the unknown. ORIG C15: from L *superstitiō*, from *superstāre* to stand still by something (as in amazement)

superstitious (ˌsu:pə'stɪʃəs) *adj* **1** disposed to believe in superstition. **2** of or relating to superstition.
▸ **ˌsuper'stitiously** *adv* ▸ **ˌsuper'stitiousness** *n*

superstore ('su:pəˌstɔ:) *n* a large supermarket.

superstratum (ˌsu:pə'strɑ:təm, -'streɪ-) *n, pl* **superstrata** (-tə) *or* **superstratums.** *Geol.* a layer or stratum overlying another layer or similar structure.

superstring ('su:pəˌstrɪŋ) *n Physics.* a type of string postulated in certain theories of elementary particles that involve supersymmetry.

superstructure ('su:pəˌstrʌktʃə) *n* **1** the part of a building above its foundation. **2** any structure or concept erected on something else. **3** *Naut.* any structure above the main deck of a ship with sides flush with the sides of the hull. **4** the part of a bridge supported by the piers and abutments.
▸ **'superˌstructural** *adj*

supersymmetry (ˌsu:pə'sɪmɪtrɪ) *n Physics.* a symmetry of elementary particles having a higher order than that in the standard model, postulated to encompass the behaviour of both bosons and fermions.

supertanker ('su:pəˌtæŋkə) *n* a large fast tanker of more than 275 000 tons capacity.

supertax ('su:pəˌtæks) *n* a tax levied in addition to the basic tax, esp. on incomes above a certain level.

supertonic (ˌsu:pə'tɒnɪk) *n Music.* **1** the second degree of a major or minor scale. **2** a key or chord based on this.

supervene (ˌsu:pə'vi:n) *vb* **supervenes, supervening, supervened.** (*intr*) **1** to follow closely; ensue. **2** to occur as an unexpected or extraneous development. ORIG C17: from L *supervenīre* to come upon
▸ **ˌsuper'venience** *or* **supervention** (ˌsu:pə'vɛnʃən) *n*
▸ **ˌsuper'venient** *adj*

supervise ('su:pəˌvaɪz) *vb* **supervises, supervising, supervised.** (*tr*) **1** to direct or oversee the performance or operation of. **2** to watch over so as to maintain order, etc. ORIG C16: from Med. L *supervidēre*, from L SUPER- + *vidēre* to see
▸ **supervision** (ˌsu:pə'vɪʒən) *n*

supervisor ('su:pəˌvaɪzə) *n* **1** a person who manages or supervises. **2** a foreman or forewoman. **3** (in some British universities) a tutor supervising the work, esp. research work, of a student. **4** (in some US schools) an administrator running a department of teachers.
▸ **'superˌvisorship** *n* ▸ **'superˌvisory** *adj*

supinate ('su:pɪˌneɪt, 'sju:-) *vb* **supinates, supinating, supinated.** to turn (the hand and forearm) so that the palm faces up or forwards. ORIG C19: from L *supīnāre* to lay on the back, from *supīnus* supine
▸ **ˌsupi'nation** *n*

supine *adj* (su:'paɪn, sju:-; 'su:paɪn, 'sju:-). **1** lying or resting on the back with the face, palm, etc., upwards. **2** displaying no interest or animation; lethargic. ◆ *n* ('su:paɪn, 'sju:-). **3** *Grammar.* a noun form derived from a verb in Latin, often used to express purpose with verbs of motion. ORIG C15: from L *supīnus* rel. to *sub* under, up; (in grammatical sense) from L *verbum supīnum* supine word (from ?)
▸ **su'pinely** *adv* ▸ **su'pineness** *n*

supp. *or* **suppl.** *abbrev. for* supplement(ary).

supper ('sʌpə) *n* **1** an evening meal, esp. a light one. **2** an evening social event featuring a supper. **3 sing for one's supper.** to obtain something by performing a service. ORIG C13: from OF *soper*
▸ **'supperless** *adj*

Suppiluliumas I ★ (ˌsʌpɪlʌlɪ'u:məs) *n* king of the Hittites (?1375–?1335 B.C.); founder of the Hittite empire.

supplant (sə'plɑ:nt) *vb* (*tr*) to take the place of, often by trickery or force. ORIG C13: via OF from L *supplantāre* to trip up, from *sub-* from below + *planta* sole of the foot
▸ **sup'planter** *n*

supple ('sʌp^{ə}l) *adj* **1** bending easily without damage. **2** capable of or showing easy or graceful movement; lithe. **3** mentally flexible; responding readily. **4** disposed to agree, sometimes to the point of servility. ◆ *vb* **supples, suppling, suppled. 5** *Rare.* to make or become supple. ORIG C13: from OF *souple*, from L *supplex* bowed
▸ **'suppleness** *n*

supplejack ('sʌp^{ə}lˌdʒæk) *n* **1** a North American twining woody vine that has greenish-white flowers and purple fruits. **2** a bush plant of New Zealand having tough climbing vines. **3** a tropical American woody vine having strong supple wood. **4** any of various other vines with strong supple stems. **5** *US.* a walking stick made from the wood of the tropical supplejack.

supplement *n* ('sʌplɪmənt). **1** an addition designed to complete, make up for a deficiency, etc. **2** a section appended to a publication to supply further information, correct errors, etc. **3** a magazine or section inserted into a newspaper or periodical, such as one issued every week. **4** *Geom.* **4a** either of a pair of angles whose sum is 180°. **4b** an arc of a circle that when added to another arc forms a semicircle. ◆ *vb* ('sʌplɪˌmɛnt). **5** (*tr*) to provide a supplement to, esp. in order to remedy a deficiency. ORIG C14: from L *supplēmentum*, from *supplēre* to SUPPLY
▸ **ˌsupplemen'tation** *n*

supplementary (ˌsʌplɪ'mɛntərɪ) *adj* **1** Also (*less commonly*): **supplemental** (ˌsʌplə'mɛnt^{ə}l). forming or acting as a supplement. ◆ *n, pl* **supplementaries. 2** a person or thing that is a supplement.
▸ **ˌsupple'mentarily** *or* (*less commonly*) **ˌsupple'mentally** *adv*

supplementary angle *n* either of two angles whose sum is 180°. Cf. **complementary angle.**

suppliant ('sʌplɪənt) *adj* **1** expressing entreaty or supplication. ◆ *n, adj* **2** another word for **supplicant.** ORIG C15: from F *supplier* to beseech, from L *supplicāre* to kneel in entreaty
▸ **'suppliantly** *adv*

supplicant ('sʌplɪkənt) *or* **suppliant** *n* **1** a person who supplicates. ◆ *adj* **2** entreating humbly; supplicating. ORIG C16: from L *supplicāns* beseeching

supplicate ('sʌplɪˌkeɪt) *vb* **supplicates, supplicating, supplicated. 1** to make a humble request to (someone); plead. **2** (*tr*) to ask for or seek humbly. ORIG C15: from L *supplicāre* to beg on one's knees
▸ **ˌsuppli'cation** *n* ▸ **'suppliˌcatory** *adj*

supply[1] (sə'plaɪ) *vb* **supplies, supplying, supplied. 1** (*tr;* often foll. by *with*) to furnish with something required. **2** (*tr;* often foll. by *to* or *for*) to make available or provide (something desired or lacking): *to supply books to the library.* **3** (*tr*) to provide for adequately; satisfy: *who will supply their needs?* **4** to serve as a substitute, usually temporary, in (another's position, etc.): *there are no clergymen to supply the pulpit.* **5** (*tr*) *Brit.* to fill (a vacancy, position, etc.). ◆ *n, pl* **supplies. 6a** the act of providing or something provided. **6b** (*as modifier*): *a supply dump.* **7** (*often pl*) an amount available for use; stock. **8** (*pl*) food, equipment, etc., needed for a campaign or trip. **9** *Econ.* **9a** willingness and ability to offer goods and services for sale. **9b** the amount of a commodity that producers are willing and able to offer for sale at a specified price. Cf.

demand (sense 9). **10** *Mil.* **10a** the management and disposal of food and equipment. **10b** (*as modifier*): *supply routes.* **11** (*often pl*) a grant of money voted by a legislature for government expenses. **12** (in Parliament and similar legislatures) the money voted annually for the expenses of the civil service and armed forces. **13a** a person who acts as a temporary substitute. **13b** (*as modifier*): *a supply vicar.* **14** a source of electricity, gas, etc. ORIG C14: from OF *souppleier,* from L *supplēre* to complete, from *sub-* up + *plēre* to fill
▸ **sup'pliable** *adj* ▸ **sup'plier** *n*

supply[2] ('sʌplɪ) *or* **supplely** ('sʌpᵊlɪ) *adv* in a supple manner.

supply-side economics (səˈplaɪ-) *n* (*functioning as sing*) a school of economic thought that emphasizes the importance to a strong economy of policies that remove impediments to supply.

support (səˈpɔːt) *vb* (*tr*) **1** to carry the weight of. **2** to bear (pressure, weight, etc.). **3** to provide the necessities of life for (a family, person, etc.). **4** to tend to establish (a theory, statement, etc.) by providing new facts. **5** to speak in favour of (a motion). **6** to give aid or courage to. **7** to give approval to (a cause, principle, etc.); subscribe to. **8** to endure with forbearance: *I will no longer support bad behaviour.* **9** to give strength to; maintain: *to support a business.* **10** (in a concert) to perform earlier than (the main attraction). **11** *Films, theatre.* **11a** to play a subordinate role to. **11b** to accompany (the feature) in a film programme. **12** to act or perform (a role or character). ◆ *n* **13** the act of supporting or the condition of being supported. **14** a thing that bears the weight or part of the weight of a construction. **15** a person who or thing that furnishes aid. **16** the means of maintenance of a family, person, etc. **17** a band or entertainer not topping the bill. **18** (often preceded by *the*) an actor or group of actors playing subordinate roles. **19** *Med.* an appliance worn to ease the strain on an injured bodily structure or part. **20** Also: **athletic support**. a more formal term for **jockstrap**. ORIG C14: from OF *supporter,* from L *supportāre* to bring, from *sub-* up + *portāre* to carry
▸ **sup'portable** *adj* ▸ **sup'portive** *adj*

supporter (səˈpɔːtə) *n* **1** a person who or thing that acts as a support. **2** a person who backs a sports team, politician, etc. **3** a garment or device worn to ease the strain on or restrict the movement of a bodily structure or part. **4** *Heraldry.* a figure or beast in a coat of arms depicted as holding up the shield.

supporting (səˈpɔːtɪŋ) *adj* **1** (of a role) being a fairly important but not leading part. **2** (of an actor or actress) playing a supporting role.

suppose (səˈpəuz) *vb* **supposes, supposing, supposed.** (*tr; may take a clause as object*) **1** to presume (something) to be true without certain knowledge: *I suppose he meant to kill her.* **2** to consider as a possible suggestion for the sake of discussion, etc.: *suppose that he wins.* **3** (of theories, etc.) to imply the inference or assumption (of): *your policy supposes full employment.* ORIG C14: from OF *supposer,* from Med. L *suppōnere,* from L: to substitute, from SUB- + *pōnere* to put
▸ **sup'posable** *adj* ▸ **sup'poser** *n*

supposed (səˈpəuzd, -ˈpəuzɪd) *adj* **1** (*prenominal*) presumed to be true without certain knowledge. **2** (*prenominal*) believed to be true on slight grounds; highly doubtful. **3** (səˈpəuzd). (*postpositive; foll. by to*) expected or obliged (to): *I'm supposed to be there.* **4** (səˈpəuzd). (*postpositive; used in negative; foll. by to*) expected or obliged not (to): *you're not supposed to walk on the grass.*
▸ **supposedly** (səˈpəuzɪdlɪ) *adv*

supposition (ˌsʌpəˈzɪʃən) *n* **1** the act of supposing. **2** a fact, theory, etc., that is supposed.
▸ ˌ**suppo'sitional** *adj* ▸ ˌ**suppo'sitionally** *adv*

suppositious (ˌsʌpəˈzɪʃəs) *adj* deduced from supposition; hypothetical.
▸ ˌ**suppo'sitiously** *adv* ▸ ˌ**suppo'sitiousness** *n*

supposititious (səˌpɒzɪˈtɪʃəs) *adj* substituted with intent to mislead or deceive.
▸ **supˌposi'titiously** *adv* ▸ **supˌposi'titiousness** *n*

suppositive (səˈpɒzɪtɪv) *adj* **1** of, involving, or arising out of supposition. **2** *Grammar.* denoting a conjunction introducing a clause expressing a supposition, as for example *if, supposing,* or *provided that.* ◆ *n* **3** *Grammar.* a suppositive conjunction.
▸ **sup'positively** *adv*

suppository (səˈpɒzɪtərɪ, -trɪ) *n, pl* **suppositories.** *Med.* a solid medication for insertion into the vagina, rectum, or urethra, where it melts and releases the active substance. ORIG C14: from Med. L *suppositōrium,* from L *suppositus* placed beneath

suppress (səˈprɛs) *vb* (*tr*) **1** to put an end to; prohibit. **2** to hold in check; restrain: *I was obliged to suppress a smile.* **3** to withhold from circulation or publication: *to suppress seditious pamphlets.* **4** to stop the activities of; crush: *to suppress a rebellion.* **5** *Electronics.* **5a** to reduce or eliminate (unwanted oscillations) in a circuit. **5b** to eliminate (a particular frequency or frequencies) in a signal. **6** *Psychiatry.* to resist consciously (an idea or a desire entering one's mind). ORIG C14: from L *suppressus* held down, from *supprimere* to restrain, from *sub-* down + *premere* to press
▸ **sup'pressible** *adj* ▸ **sup'pressive** *adj* ▸ **sup'presser** *n*

suppressant (səˈprɛsənt) *adj* **1** tending to suppress or restrain an action or condition. ◆ *n* **2** a suppressant drug or agent: *a cough suppressant.*

suppression (səˈprɛʃən) *n* **1** the act or process of suppressing or the condition of being suppressed. **2** *Psychiatry.* the conscious avoidance of unpleasant thoughts.

suppressor (səˈprɛsə) *n* **1** a person or thing that suppresses. **2** a device fitted to an electrical appliance to suppress unwanted electrical interference to audiovisual signals.

suppurate (ˈsʌpjuˌreɪt) *vb* **suppurates, suppurating, suppurated.** (*intr*) *Pathol.* (of a wound, sore, etc.) to discharge pus; fester. ORIG C16: from L *suppūrāre,* from SUB- + *pūs* pus
▸ ˌ**suppu'ration** *n* ▸ **'suppurative** *adj*

supra- *prefix* over, above, beyond, or greater than: *supranational.* ORIG from L *suprā* above

supraliminal (ˌsuːprəˈlɪmɪnᵊl, ˌsjuː-) *adj* of or relating to any stimulus that is above the threshold of sensory awareness.
▸ ˌ**supra'liminally** *adv*

supramolecular (ˌsuːprəməˈlɛkjulə, ˌsjuː-) *adj* **1** more complex than a molecule. **2** consisting of more than one molecule.

supranational (ˌsuːprəˈnæʃnᵊl, ˌsjuː-) *adj* beyond the authority or jurisdiction of one national government: *the supranational institutions of the EU.*
▸ ˌ**supra'nationalism** *n*

supraorbital (ˌsuːprəˈɔːbɪtᵊl, ˌsjuː-) *adj Anat.* situated above the orbit.

suprarenal (ˌsuːprəˈriːnᵊl, ˌsjuː-) *adj Anat.* situated above a kidney.

suprarenal gland *n* another name for **adrenal gland.**

supremacist (suˈprɛməsɪst, sju-) *n* **1** a person who promotes or advocates the supremacy of any particular group. ◆ *adj* **2** characterized by belief in the supremacy of any particular group.
▸ **su'premacism** *or* **su'prematism** *n*

supremacy (suˈprɛməsɪ, sju-) *n* **1** supreme power; authority. **2** the quality or condition of being supreme.

supreme (suˈpriːm, sju-) *adj* **1** of highest status or power. **2** (*usually prenominal*) of highest quality, importance, etc. **3** greatest in degree; extreme: *supreme folly.* **4** (*prenominal*) final or last, ultimate: *the supreme judgment.* ORIG C16: from L *suprēmus* highest, from *superus* that is above, from *super* above
▸ **su'premely** *adv*

Supreme Being *n* God.

Supreme Court *n* (in the US) **1** the highest Federal court. **2** (in many states) the highest state court.

Supreme Court of Judicature *n* (in England) a court formed in 1873 by the amalgamation of several superior courts into two divisions, the High Court of Justice and the Court of Appeal.

supreme sacrifice *n* **the.** the sacrifice of one's life.

Supreme Soviet *n* (in the former Soviet Union) **1** the bicameral legislature, comprising the **Soviet of the Union** and the **Soviet of the Nationalities. 2** a similar legislature in each former Soviet republic.

supremo (sʊ'priːməʊ, sjʊ-) *n, pl* **supremos.** *Brit. inf.* a person in overall authority. ORIG C20: from SUPREME

Supt *or* **supt** *abbrev. for* superintendent.

Suqutra ★ (sə'kəʊtrə) *n* a variant spelling of **Socotra.**

Sur *or* **Sour** ★ (sʊə) *n* transliteration of the Arabic name for **Tyre.**

sur-[1] *prefix* over; above; beyond: *surcharge; surrealism.* Cf. **super-.** ORIG from OF, from L SUPER-

sur-[2] *prefix* a variant of **sub-** before *r*: *surrogate.*

sura ('sʊərə) *n* any of the 114 chapters of the Koran. ORIG C17: from Ar. *sūrah* section

Surabaya, Surabaja, *or* **Soerabaja** ★ (ˌsʊərə'baɪə) *n* a port in Indonesia, on E Java on the **Surabaya Strait:** the country's second port and chief naval base; university (1954); fishing and ship-building industries; oil refinery. Pop.: 2 701 300 (1995 est.).

surah ('sʊərə) *n* a twill-weave fabric of silk or rayon. ORIG C19: from F pronunciation of *Surat,* a port in W India where orig. made

Surakarta ★ (ˌsʊərə'kɑːtə) *n* a town in Indonesia, on central Java: textile manufacturing. Pop.: 516 500 (1995 est.).

sural ('sjʊərəl) *adj Anat.* of or relating to the calf of the leg. ORIG C17: via NL from L *sūra* calf

Surat ★ (sʊ'ræt, 'sʊərət) *n* a port in W India, in W Gujarat: a major port in the 17th century; textile manufacturing. Pop.: 1 498 817 (1991).

surbase ('sɜːˌbeɪs) *n* the uppermost part, such as a moulding, of a pedestal, base, or skirting.

surcease (sɜː'siːs) *Arch.* ◆ *n* **1** cessation or intermission. ◆ *vb* **surceases, surceasing, surceased. 2** to desist from (some action). **3** to cease or cause to cease. ORIG C16: from earlier *sursesen,* from OF *surseoir,* from L *supersedēre* to sit above

surcharge *n* ('sɜːˌtʃɑːdʒ). **1** a charge in addition to the usual payment, tax, etc. **2** an excessive sum charged, esp. when unlawful. **3** an extra and usually excessive burden or supply. **4** an overprint that alters the face value of a postage stamp. ◆ *vb* (sɜː'tʃɑːdʒ, 'sɜːˌtʃɑːdʒ), **surcharges, surcharging, surcharged.** (*tr*) **5** to charge an additional sum, tax, etc. **6** to overcharge (a person) for something. **7** to put an extra physical burden upon; overload. **8** to fill to excess; overwhelm. **9** *Law.* to insert credits that have been omitted in (an account). **10** to overprint a surcharge on (a stamp).

surcingle ('sɜːˌsɪŋgᵊl) *n* a girth for a horse which goes around the body, used esp. with a racing saddle. ORIG C14: from OF *surcengle,* from *sur-* over + *cengle* a belt, from L *cingulum*

surcoat ('sɜːˌkəʊt) *n* **1** a tunic, often embroidered with heraldic arms, worn by a knight over his armour during the Middle Ages. **2** (formerly) an outer coat or other garment.

surculose ('sɜːkjʊˌləʊs) *adj* (of a plant) bearing suckers. ORIG C19: from L *surculōsus* woody, from *surculus* twig, from *sūrus* a branch

surd (sɜːd) *n* **1** *Maths.* a number containing an irrational root, such as $2\sqrt{3}$; irrational number. **2** *Phonetics.* a voiceless consonant, such as (t). ◆ *adj* **3** of or relating to a surd. ORIG C16: from L *surdus* muffled

sure (ʃʊə, ʃɔː) *adj* **1** (sometimes foll. by *of*) free from hesitancy or uncertainty (with regard to a belief, conviction, etc.): *we are sure of the accuracy of the data; I am sure that he is lying.* **2** (foll. by *of*) having no doubt, as of the occurrence of a future state or event: *sure of success.* **3** always effective; unfailing: *a sure remedy.* **4** reliable in indication or accuracy: *a sure criterion.* **5** (of persons) worthy of trust or confidence: *a sure friend.* **6** not open to doubt: *sure proof.* **7** admitting of no vacillation or doubt: *he is sure in his beliefs.* **8** bound to be or occur; inevitable: *victory is sure.* **9** (*postpositive*) bound inevitably (to be or do something); certain: *she is sure to be there.* **10** physically secure or dependable: *a sure footing.* **11 be sure.** (*usually imperative or dependent imperative; takes a clause as object or an infinitive,* sometimes with *to* replaced by *and*) to be careful or certain: *be sure and shut the door; be sure to shut the door.* **12 for sure.** without a doubt; surely. **13 make sure. 13a** (*takes a clause as object*) to make certain; ensure. **13b** (foll. by *of*) to establish or confirm power or possession (over). **14 sure enough.** *Inf.* as might have been confidently expected; definitely: often used as a sentence substitute. **15 to be sure. 15a** without doubt; certainly. **15b** it has to be acknowledged; admittedly. ◆ *adv* **16** (*sentence modifier*) *US & Canad. inf.* without question; certainly. ◆ *sentence substitute.* **17** *US & Canad. inf.* willingly; yes. ORIG C14: from OF *seur,* from L *sēcūrus* SECURE
▸ **'sureness** *n*

sure-fire *adj* (*usually prenominal*) *Inf.* certain to succeed or meet expectations; assured.

sure-footed *adj* **1** unlikely to fall, slip, or stumble. **2** not likely to err or fall.
▸ **ˌsure-'footedly** *adv* ▸ **ˌsure-'footedness** *n*

surely ('ʃʊəlɪ, 'ʃɔː-) *adv* **1** without doubt; assuredly. **2** without fail; inexorably (esp. in **slowly but surely**). **3** (*sentence modifier*) am I not right in thinking that?; I am sure that: *surely you don't mean it?* **4** *Rare.* in a sure manner. **5** *Arch.* safely; securely. ◆ *sentence substitute.* **6** *Chiefly US & Canad.* willingly; yes.

sure thing *Inf.* ◆ *sentence substitute.* **1** *Chiefly US.* used to express enthusiastic assent. ◆ *n* **2** something guaranteed to be successful.

surety ('ʃʊətɪ, 'ʃʊərɪtɪ) *n, pl* **sureties. 1** a person who assumes legal responsibility for another's debt or obligation and himself becomes liable if the other defaults. **2** security given against loss or damage or as a guarantee that an obligation will be met. **3** *Obs.* the quality or condition of being sure. **4 stand surety.** to act as a surety. ORIG C14: from OF *seurte,* from L *sēcūritās* security
▸ **'suretyship** *n*

surf (sɜːf) *n* **1** waves breaking on the shore or on a reef. **2** foam caused by the breaking of waves. ◆ *vb* (*intr*) **3** to take part in surfing. **4** to move rapidly and easily through a particular medium: *surfing the Internet.* **5** *Inf.* to be carried on top of something: *that guy's surfing the audience.* ORIG C17: prob. var. of SOUGH

surface ('sɜːfɪs) *n* **1a** the exterior face of an object or one such face. **1b** (*as modifier*): *surface gloss.* **2** the area or size of such a face. **3** material resembling such a face, with length and width but without depth. **4a** the superficial appearance as opposed to the real nature. **4b** (*as modifier*): *a surface resemblance.* **5** *Geom.* **5a** the complete boundary of a solid figure. **5b** a continuous two-dimensional configuration. **6a** the uppermost level of the land or sea. **6b** (*as modifier*): *surface transportation.* **7 come to the surface.** to emerge; become apparent. **8 on the surface.** to all appearances. ◆ *vb* **surfaces, surfacing, surfaced. 9** to rise or cause to rise to or as if to the surface (of water, etc.). **10** (*tr*) to treat the surface of, as by polishing, smoothing, etc. **11** (*tr*) to furnish with a surface. **12** (*intr*) to become apparent; emerge. **13** (*intr*) *Inf.* **13a** to wake up. **13b** to get up. ORIG C17: from F, from *sur* on + *face* FACE
▸ **'surfacer** *n*

surface-active *adj* (of a substance, esp. a detergent) capable of lowering the surface tension of a liquid. See also **surfactant.**

surface mail *n* mail transported by land or sea. Cf. **airmail.**

surface structure *n Generative grammar.* a representation of a string of words or morphemes as they occur in a sentence, together with labels and brackets that represent syntactic structure. Cf. **deep structure.**

surface tension *n* **1** a property of liquids caused by intermolecular forces near the surface leading to the apparent presence of a surface film and to capillarity, etc. **2** a measure of this.

surface-to-air *adj* of or relating to a missile launched from the surface of the earth against airborne targets.

surfactant (sɜː'fæktənt) *n* **1** Also called: **surface-active agent.** a substance, such as a detergent, that can reduce the surface tension of a liquid and thus allow it to foam or penetrate solids; a wetting agent. ◆ *adj* **2** having the properties of a surfactant. ORIG C20: *surf(ace)-act(ive) a(ge)nt*

surfboard ('sɜːfˌbɔːd) *n* a long narrow board used in surfing.

surfboat ('sɜːfˌbəʊt) *n* a boat with a high bow and stern and flotation chambers, equipped for use in rough surf.

surfcasting ('sɜːfˌkɑːstɪŋ) *n* fishing from the shore by casting into the surf.
▸ **'surfˌcaster** *n*

surfeit ('sɜːfɪt) *n* **1** (usually foll. by *of*) an excessive amount. **2** overindulgence, esp. in eating or drinking. **3** disgust, nausea, etc., caused by such overindulgence. ◆ *vb* **4** (*tr*) to supply or feed excessively; satiate. **5** (*intr*) *Arch.* to eat, drink, or be supplied to excess. ORIG C13: from F *sourfait,* from *sourfaire* to overdo, from SUR-[1] + *faire,* from L *facere* to do

surfie ('sɜːfɪ) *n Austral. & NZ sl.* a young person whose main interest in life is surfing.

surfing ('sɜːfɪŋ) *n* the sport of riding towards shore on the crest of a wave by standing or lying on a surfboard.
▸ **'surfer** *or* **'surfˌrider** *n*

surf mat *n Austral. inf.* a small inflatable rubber mattress used to ride on waves.

surg. *abbrev. for:* **1** surgeon. **2** surgery. **3** surgical.

surge (sɜːdʒ) *n* **1** a strong rush or sweep; sudden increase: *a surge of anger.* **2** the rolling swell of the sea. **3** a heavy rolling motion or sound: *the surge of the trumpets.* **4** an undulating rolling surface, as of hills. **5** a billowing cloud or volume. **6** *Naut.* a temporary release or slackening of a rope or cable. **7** a large momentary increase in the voltage or current in an electric circuit. **8** an instability or unevenness in the power output of an engine. ◆ *vb* **surges, surging, surged. 9** (*intr*) (of waves, the sea, etc.) to rise or roll with a heavy swelling motion. **10** (*intr*) to move like a heavy sea. **11** *Naut.* to slacken or temporarily release (a rope or cable) from a capstan or (of a rope, etc.) to be slackened or released and slip back. **12** (*intr*) (of an electric current or voltage) to undergo a large momentary increase. **13** (*tr*) *Rare.* to cause to move in or as if in a wave or waves. ORIG C15: from L *surgere* to rise, from *sub-* up + *regere* to lead
▸ **'surger** *n*

surgeon ('sɜːdʒən) *n* **1** a medical practitioner who specializes in surgery. **2** a medical officer in the Royal Navy. ORIG C14: from Anglo-Norman *surgien,* from OF *cirurgien;* see SURGERY

surgeonfish ('sɜːdʒənˌfɪʃ) *n, pl* **surgeonfish** *or* **surgeonfishes.** any of various tropical marine spiny-finned fishes, having a compressed brightly coloured body with knife-like spines at the base of the tail.

surgeon general *n, pl* **surgeons general. 1** (esp. in the British and US armies and navies) the senior officer of the medical service. **2** the head of the US public health service.

surgery ('sɜːdʒərɪ) *n, pl* **surgeries. 1** the branch of medicine concerned with manual or operative procedures, esp. incision into the body. **2** the performance of such procedures by a surgeon. **3** *Brit.* a place where, or time when, a doctor, dentist, etc., can be consulted. **4** *Brit.* an occasion when an MP, lawyer, etc., is available for consultation. **5** *US & Canad.* an operating theatre. ORIG C14: via OF from L *chirurgia,* from Gk *kheirurgia,* from *kheir* hand + *ergon* work

surgical ('sɜːdʒɪkᵊl) *adj* of, relating to, involving, or used in surgery.
▸ **'surgically** *adv*

surgical boot *n* a specially designed boot or shoe that compensates for deformities of the foot or leg.

surgical spirit *n* methylated spirit used medically for sterilizing.

Suribachi ★ (ˌsʊərɪ'bɑːtʃɪ) *n* **Mount.** a volcanic hill in the Volcano Islands, on Iwo Jima: site of a US victory (1945) over the Japanese in World War II.

suricate ('sjʊərɪˌkeɪt) *n* another name for **slender-tailed meerkat** (see **meerkat**). ORIG C18: from F *surikate,* prob. from a native South African word

Surinam ★ (ˌsʊərɪ'næm) *n* a republic in NE South America, on the Atlantic: became a self-governing part of the Netherlands in 1954 and fully independent in 1975. Official language: Dutch; English is also widely spoken. Religion: Hindu, Christian, and Muslim. Currency: guilder. Capital: Paramaribo. Pop.: 415 000 (1999 est.). Area: 163 820 sq. km (63 251 sq. miles). Former names: **Dutch Guiana, Netherlands Guiana.**

surly ('sɜːlɪ) *adj* **surlier, surliest. 1** sullenly ill-tempered or rude. **2** (of an animal) ill-tempered or refractory. ORIG C16: from obs. *sirly* haughty
▸ **'surlily** *adv* ▸ **'surliness** *n*

surmise *vb* (sɜː'maɪz), **surmises, surmising, surmised. 1** (when *tr, may take a clause as object*) to infer (something) from incomplete or uncertain evidence. ◆ *n* (sɜː'maɪz, 'sɜːmaɪz). **2** an idea inferred from inconclusive evidence. ORIG C15: from OF, from *surmettre* to accuse, from L *supermittere* to throw over
▸ **surmisedly** (sɜː'maɪzɪdlɪ) *adv*

surmount (sɜː'maʊnt) *vb* (*tr*) **1** to prevail over; overcome. **2** to ascend and cross to the opposite side of. **3** to lie on top of or rise above. **4** to put something on top of or above. ORIG C14: from OF *surmonter,* from SUR-[1] + *monter* to mount
▸ **sur'mountable** *adj*

surname ('sɜːˌneɪm) *n* **1** Also called: **last name, second name.** a family name as opposed to a first or Christian name. **2** (formerly) a descriptive epithet attached to a person's name to denote a personal characteristic, profession, etc.; nickname. ◆ *vb* **surnames, surnaming, surnamed. 3** (*tr*) to furnish with or call by a surname.
▸ **'surˌnamer** *n*

surpass (sɜː'pɑːs) *vb* (*tr*) **1** to be greater than in degree, extent, etc. **2** to be superior to in achievement or excellence. **3** to overstep the limit or range of: *the theory surpasses my comprehension.* ORIG C16: from F *surpasser,* from SUR-[1] + *passer* to PASS
▸ **sur'passable** *adj*

surpassing (sɜː'pɑːsɪŋ) *adj* **1** exceptional; extraordinary. ◆ *adv* **2** *Obs. or poetic.* (intensifier): *surpassing fair.*
▸ **sur'passingly** *adv*

surplice ('sɜːplɪs) *n* a loose wide-sleeved liturgical vestment of linen, reaching to the knees, worn over the cassock by clergymen, choristers, and acolytes. ORIG C13: from OF *sourpelis,* from Med. L *superpellīcium,* from SUPER- + *pellīcium* coat made of skins, from L *pellis* a skin

surplus ('sɜːpləs) *n, pl* **surpluses. 1** a quantity or amount in excess of what is required. **2** *Accounting.* **2a** an excess of total assets over total liabilities. **2b** an excess of actual net assets over the nominal value of capital stock. **2c** an excess of revenues over expenditures. **3** *Econ.* **3a** an excess of government revenues over expenditures. **3b** an excess of receipts over payments on the balance of payments. ◆ *adj* **4** being in excess; extra. ORIG C14: from OF, from Med. L *superplūs,* from L SUPER- + *plūs* more

surprise (sə'praɪz) *vb* **surprises, surprising, surprised.** (*tr*) **1** to cause to feel amazement or wonder. **2** to encounter or discover unexpectedly or suddenly. **3** to capture or assault suddenly and without warning. **4** to present with something unexpected, such as a gift. **5** (foll. by *into*) to provoke (someone) to unintended action by a trick, etc. **6** (often foll. by *from*) to elicit by unexpected behaviour or by a trick: *to surprise information from a prisoner.* ◆ *n* **7** the act or an instance of surprising; the act of taking unawares. **8** a sudden or unexpected event, gift, etc. **9** the feeling or condition of being surprised; astonishment. **10** (*modifier*) causing, characterized by, or relying upon surprise: *a surprise move.* **11 take by surprise. 11a** to come upon suddenly and without warning. **11b** to capture unexpectedly or catch unprepared. **11c** to astonish; amaze. ORIG C15: from OF, from *surprendre* to overtake, from SUR-[1] + L *prehendere* to grasp
▸ **sur'prisal** *n* ▸ **sur'prised** *adj* ▸ **surprisedly** (sə'praɪzɪdlɪ) *adv*

surprising (sə'praɪzɪŋ) *adj* causing surprise; unexpected or amazing.
▸ **sur'prisingly** *adv*

surra ('sʊərə) *n* a tropical febrile disease of cattle, horses, camels, and dogs. ORIG from Marathi, a language of India

★ people and places

surrealism (səˈrɪəˌlɪzəm) *n* (*sometimes cap.*) a movement in art and literature in the 1920s, which developed esp. from Dada, characterized by the evocative juxtaposition of incongruous images in order to include unconscious and dream elements. ORIG C20: from F *surréalisme*, from SUR-[1] + *réalisme* realism
▸ **surˈreal** *adj* ▸ **surˈrealist** *n, adj* ▸ **surˌrealˈistic** *adj*

surrebutter (ˌsɜːrɪˈbʌtə) *n Law.* (in pleading) the plaintiff's reply to the defendant's rebutter.
▸ **ˌsurreˈbuttal** *n*

surrejoinder (ˌsɜːrɪˈdʒɔɪndə) *n Law.* (in pleading) the plaintiff's reply to the defendant's rejoinder.

surrender (səˈrɛndə) *vb* **1** (*tr*) to relinquish to another under duress or on demand: *to surrender a city*. **2** (*tr*) to relinquish or forego (an office, position, etc.), esp. as a voluntary concession to another: *he surrendered his place to a lady*. **3** to give (oneself) up physically, as to an enemy. **4** to allow (oneself) to yield, as to a temptation, influence, etc. **5** (*tr*) to give up (hope, etc.). **6** (*tr*) *Law.* to give up or restore (an estate), esp. to give up a lease before expiration of the term. **7 surrender to bail.** to present oneself at court at the appointed time after having been on bail. ◆ *n* **8** the act or instance of surrendering. **9** *Insurance.* the voluntary discontinuation of a life policy by its holder in return for a consideration (the **surrender value**). **10** *Law.* **10a** the yielding up or restoring of an estate, esp. the giving up of a lease before its term has expired. **10b** the giving up to the appropriate authority of a fugitive from justice. **10c** the act of surrendering or being surrendered to bail. **10d** the deed by which a legal surrender is effected. ORIG C15: from OF *surrendre* to yield

surreptitious (ˌsʌrəpˈtɪʃəs) *adj* **1** done, acquired, etc., in secret or by improper means. **2** operating by stealth. ORIG C15: from L *surreptīcius* furtive, from *surripere* to steal, from *sub-* secretly + *rapere* to snatch
▸ **ˌsurrepˈtitiously** *adv* ▸ **ˌsurrepˈtitiousness** *n*

surrey (ˈsʌrɪ) *n* a light four-wheeled horse-drawn carriage having two or four seats. ORIG C19: from *Surrey cart*, after SURREY[1] where orig. made

Surrey[1] ★ (ˈsʌrɪ) *n* a county of SE England, on the River Thames: urban in the northeast; crossed from east to west by the North Downs and drained by tributaries of the Thames. Administrative centre: Kingston upon Thames. Pop.: 1 047 100 (1996 est.). Area: 1679 sq. km (648 sq. miles).

Surrey[2] ★ (ˈsʌrɪ) *n* **Earl of,** title of *Henry Howard*. ?1517–47, English courtier and poet; one of the first in England to write sonnets. He was beheaded for high treason.

surrogate *n* (ˈsʌrəgɪt). **1** a person or thing acting as a substitute. **2** *Chiefly Brit.* a deputy, such as a clergyman appointed to deputize for a bishop in granting marriage licences. **3** (in some US states) a judge with jurisdiction over the probate of wills, etc. **4** (*modifier*) of, relating to, or acting as a surrogate: *a surrogate pleasure*. ◆ *vb* (ˈsʌrəˌgeɪt), **surrogates, surrogating, surrogated.** (*tr*) **5** to put in another's position as a deputy, substitute, etc. ORIG C17: from L *surrogāre* to substitute
▸ **ˈsurrogateship** *n* ▸ **ˌsurroˈgation** *n*

surrogate motherhood *or* **surrogacy** (ˈsʌrəgəsɪ) *n* the role of a woman who bears a child on behalf of a childless couple, either by artificial insemination or implantation of an embryo.
▸ **surrogate mother** *n*

surround (səˈraʊnd) *vb* (*tr*) **1** to encircle or enclose or cause to be encircled or enclosed. **2** to deploy forces on all sides of (a place or military formation), so preventing access or retreat. **3** to exist around: *the people who surround her*. ◆ *n* **4** *Chiefly Brit.* a border, esp. the area of uncovered floor between the walls of a room and the carpet or around an opening or panel. **5** *Chiefly US.* **5a** a method of capturing wild beasts by encircling the area in which they are believed to be. **5b** the area so encircled. ORIG C15 *surrounden* to overflow, from OF *suronder*, from LL, from L SUPER- + *undāre* to abound, from *unda* a wave
▸ **surˈrounding** *adj*

surroundings (səˈraʊndɪŋz) *pl n* the conditions, scenery, etc., around a person, place, or thing; environment.

sursum corda (ˈsɜːsəm ˈkɔːdə) *n* **1** *RC Church.* a Latin versicle meaning *Lift up your hearts*, said by the priest at Mass. **2** a cry of exhortation, hope, etc.

surtax (ˈsɜːˌtæks) *n* **1** a tax, usually highly progressive, levied on the amount by which a person's income exceeds a specific level. **2** an additional tax on something that has already been taxed. ◆ *vb* **3** (*tr*) to assess for liability to surtax; charge with an extra tax.

Surtees ★ (ˈsɜːtiːz) *n* **1 John.** born 1934, British racing motorcyclist and motor-racing driver; motorcycling world champion (1956, 1958–60) and world champion motor-racing driver (1964). **2 Robert Smith.** 1803–64, British journalist and novelist, who satirized the sporting life of the English gentry in such works as *Jorrocks's Jaunts and Jollities* (1838).

surtitles (ˈsɜːˌtaɪtᵊlz) *pl n* brief translations of the text of an opera or play that is being sung or spoken in a foreign language, projected above the stage.

surtout (ˈsɜːtuː) *n* a man's overcoat resembling a frock coat, popular in the late 19th century. ORIG C17: from F, from *sur* over + *tout* all

surveillance (sɜːˈveɪləns) *n* close observation or supervision over a person, group, etc., esp. one in custody or under suspicion. ORIG C19: from F, from *surveiller* to watch over, from SUR-[1] + *veiller* to keep watch (from L *vigilāre*; see VIGIL)
▸ **surˈveillant** *adj, n*

survey *vb* (sɜːˈveɪ, ˈsɜːveɪ). **1** (*tr*) to view or consider in a comprehensive or general way. **2** (*tr*) to examine carefully, in order to or as if to appraise condition and value. **3** to plot a detailed map of (an area of land) by measuring or calculating distances and height. **4** *Brit.* to inspect a building to determine its condition and value. **5** to examine a vessel thoroughly in order to determine its seaworthiness. **6** (*tr*) to run a statistical survey on (incomes, opinions, etc.). ◆ *n* (ˈsɜːveɪ). **7** a comprehensive or general view. **8** a critical, detailed, and formal inspection. **9** *Brit.* an inspection of a building to determine its condition and value. **10** a report incorporating the results of such an inspection. **11a** a body of surveyors. **11b** an area surveyed. ORIG C15: from F *surveoir*, from SUR-[1] + *veoir* to see, from L *vidēre*

surveying (sɜːˈveɪɪŋ) *n* **1** the study or practice of making surveys of land. **2** the setting out on the ground of the positions of proposed construction or engineering works.

surveyor (sɜːˈveɪə) *n* **1** a person whose occupation is to survey land or buildings. See also **quantity surveyor. 2** *Chiefly Brit.* a person concerned with the official inspection of something for purposes of measurement and valuation. **3** a person who carries out surveys, esp. of ships (**marine surveyor**) to determine seaworthiness, etc. **4** a customs official. **5** *Arch.* a supervisor.
▸ **surˈveyorship** *n*

surveyor's measure *n* the system of measurement based on the **surveyor's chain** (66 feet) as a unit.

survival (səˈvaɪvᵊl) *n* **1** a person or thing that survives, such as a custom. **2a** the act or fact of surviving or condition of having survived. **2b** (*as modifier*): *survival kit*.

survival bag *n* a large plastic bag carried by climbers for use in an emergency as protection against exposure.

survivalist (səˈvaɪvəlɪst) *n Chiefly US.* **a** a person who believes in ensuring his or her personal survival of a catastrophic event by arming himself or herself and often by living in the wild. **b** (*as modifier*): *survivalist weapons*.
▸ **surˈvivalˌism** *n*

survival of the fittest *n* a popular term for **natural selection.**

survive (səˈvaɪv) *vb* **survives, surviving, survived. 1** (*tr*) to live after the death of (another). **2** to continue in existence or use after (a passage of time, adversity, etc.). **3** *Inf.* to endure (something): *I don't know how I survive such an awful job*. ORIG C15: from OF *sourvivre*, from L *supervīvere*, from SUPER- + *vīvere* to live
▸ **surˈvivor** *n*

sus (sʌs) *Brit. sl.* ◆ *n* **1** short for **suspicion,** with reference to former police powers (**sus laws**) of detaining for questioning, searching, etc., any person suspected of criminal intent: *he was picked up on sus.* ◆ *vb* **susses, sussing, sussed.** **2** a variant spelling of **suss** (sense 2).

Susa ★ ('suːsə) *n* an ancient city north of the Persian Gulf: capital of Elam and of the Persian Empire; flourished as a Greek polis under the Seleucids and Parthians. Biblical name: **Shushan.**

Susah *or* **Susa** ★ ('suːzə) *n* other names for **Sousse.**

Susanna ★ (suː'zænə) *n Apocrypha.* **1** the wife of Joachim, who was condemned to death for adultery because of a false accusation, but saved by Daniel's sagacity. **2** the book of the Apocrypha containing this story.

susceptance (sə'sɛptəns) *n Physics.* the imaginary component of the admittance. ORIG C19: from *suscept(ibility)* + -ANCE

susceptibility (səˌsɛptə'bɪlɪtɪ) *n, pl* **susceptibilities. 1** the quality or condition of being susceptible. **2** the ability or tendency to be impressed by emotional feelings. **3** (*pl*) emotional sensibilities; feelings. **4** *Physics.* **4a** Also called: **electric susceptibility.** (of a dielectric) the amount by which the relative permittivity differs from unity. **4b** Also called: **magnetic susceptibility.** (of a magnetic medium) the amount by which the relative permeability differs from unity.

susceptible (sə'sɛptəbᵊl) *adj* **1** (*postpositive;* foll. by *of* or *to*) yielding readily (to); capable (of): *hypotheses susceptible of refutation; susceptible to control.* **2** (*postpositive;* foll. by *to*) liable to be afflicted (by): *susceptible to colds.* **3** easily impressed emotionally. ORIG C17: from LL *susceptibilis,* from L *suscipere* to take up
▸ **sus'ceptibly** *adv*

sushi ('suːʃɪ) *n* a Japanese dish consisting of small cakes of cold rice with a topping, esp. of raw fish. ORIG Japanese

suslik ('sʌslɪk) *or* **souslik** *n* a central Eurasian ground squirrel having large eyes and small ears. ORIG from Russian

suspect *vb* (sə'spɛkt). **1** (*tr*) to believe guilty of a specified offence without proof. **2** (*tr*) to think false, questionable, etc.: *she suspected his sincerity.* **3** (*tr; may take a clause as object*) to surmise to be the case; think probable: *to suspect fraud.* **4** (*intr*) to have suspicion. ◆ *n* ('sʌspɛkt). **5** a person under suspicion. ◆ *adj* ('sʌspɛkt). **6** causing or open to suspicion. ORIG C14: from L *suspicere* to mistrust, from SUB- + *specere* to look

suspend (sə'spɛnd) *vb* **1** (*tr*) to hang from above. **2** (*tr; passive*) to cause to remain floating or hanging: *a cloud of smoke was suspended over the town.* **3** (*tr*) to render inoperative or cause to cease, esp. temporarily. **4** (*tr*) to hold in abeyance; postpone action on. **5** (*tr*) to debar temporarily from privilege, office, etc., as a punishment. **6** (*tr*) *Chem.* to cause (particles) to be held in suspension in a fluid. **7** (*tr*) *Music.* to continue (a note) until the next chord is sounded, with which it usually forms a dissonance. See **suspension** (sense 11). **8** (*intr*) to cease payment, as from incapacity to meet financial obligations. ORIG C13: from L *suspendere* from SUB- + *pendere* to hang
▸ **sus'pendible** *or* **sus'pensible** *adj* ▸ **susˌpendi'bility** *n*

suspended animation *n* a temporary cessation of the vital functions, as by freezing an organism.

suspended sentence *n* a sentence of imprisonment that is not served by an offender unless he commits a further offence during its currency.

suspender (sə'spɛndə) *n* **1** (*often pl*) *Brit.* **1a** an elastic strap attached to a belt or corset having a fastener at the end, for holding up women's stockings. **1b** a similar fastener attached to a garter worn by men in order to support socks. **2** (*pl*) the US and Canad. name for **braces. 3** a person or thing that suspends, such as one of the vertical cables in a suspension bridge.

suspender belt *n* a belt with suspenders hanging from it to hold up women's stockings.

suspense (sə'spɛns) *n* **1** the condition of being insecure or uncertain. **2** mental uncertainty; anxiety: *their father's illness kept them in a state of suspense.* **3** excitement felt at the approach of the climax: *a play of terrifying suspense.* **4** the condition of being suspended. ORIG C15: from Med. L *suspensum* delay, from L *suspendere* to hang up
▸ **sus'penseful** *adj*

suspense account *n Book-keeping.* an account in which entries are made until determination of their proper disposition.

suspension (sə'spɛnʃən) *n* **1** an interruption or temporary revocation: *the suspension of a law.* **2** a temporary debarment, as from position, privilege, etc. **3** a deferment, esp. of a decision, judgment, etc. **4** *Law.* a postponement of execution of a sentence or the deferring of a judgment, etc. **5** cessation of payment of business debts, esp. as a result of insolvency. **6** the act of suspending or the state of being suspended. **7** a system of springs, shock absorbers, etc., that supports the body of a wheeled or tracked vehicle and insulates it from shocks transmitted by the wheels. **8** a device or structure, usually a wire or spring, that serves to suspend or support something, such as the pendulum of a clock. **9** *Chem.* a dispersion of fine solid or liquid particles in a fluid, the particles being supported by buoyancy. See also **colloid. 10** the process by which eroded particles of rock are transported in a river. **11** *Music.* one or more notes of a chord that are prolonged until a subsequent chord is sounded, usually to form a dissonance.

suspension bridge *n* a bridge suspended from cables or chains that hang between two towers and are anchored at both ends.

suspensive (sə'spɛnsɪv) *adj* **1** having the power of deferment; effecting suspension. **2** causing, characterized by, or relating to suspense.
▸ **sus'pensively** *adv* ▸ **sus'pensiveness** *n*

suspensory (sə'spɛnsərɪ) *n, pl* **suspensories. 1** Also called: **suspensor.** *Anat.* a ligament or muscle that holds a structure or part in position. **2** *Med.* a bandage, sling, etc., for supporting a dependent part. ◆ *adj* **3** suspending or supporting. **4** *Anat.* (of a ligament or muscle) supporting or holding a structure or part in position.

suspicion (sə'spɪʃən) *n* **1** the act or an instance of suspecting; belief without sure proof, esp. that something is wrong. **2** the feeling of mistrust of a person who suspects. **3** the state of being suspected: *to be shielded from suspicion.* **4** a slight trace. **5 above suspicion.** in such a position that no guilt may be thought or implied, esp. through having an unblemished reputation. **6 on suspicion.** as a suspect. **7 under suspicion.** regarded with distrust. ORIG C14: from OF *sospeçon,* from L *suspīciō* distrust, from *suspicere;* see SUSPECT
▸ **sus'picional** *adj*

suspicious (sə'spɪʃəs) *adj* **1** exciting or liable to excite suspicion; questionable. **2** disposed to suspect something wrong. **3** indicative or expressive of suspicion.
▸ **sus'piciously** *adv* ▸ **sus'piciousness** *n*

Susquehanna ★ (ˌsʌskwɪ'hænə) *n* a river in the eastern US, rising in Otsego Lake and flowing generally south to Chesapeake Bay at Havre de Grace: the longest river in the eastern US. Length: 714 km (444 miles).

suss (sʌs) *Inf.* ◆ *vb* (*tr*) **1** (often foll. by *out*) to attempt to work out (a situation, person's character, etc.), esp. using one's intuition. **2** Also: **sus.** to become aware of; suspect (esp. in **suss it**). ◆ *n* **3** sharpness of mind; social astuteness. ORIG C20: shortened from SUSPECT

sussed (sʌst) *adj Brit. inf.* well-informed; aware.

Sussex ★ ('sʌsɪks) *n* **1** (until 1974) a county of SE England, now divided into the separate counties of East Sussex and West Sussex. **2** (in Anglo-Saxon England) the kingdom of the South Saxons, which became a shire of the kingdom of Wessex in the early 9th century A.D. **3** a breed of red beef cattle originally from Sussex. **4** a heavy and long-established breed of domestic fowl used principally as a table bird.

sustain (sə'steɪn) *vb* (*tr*) **1** to hold up under; withstand: *to sustain great provocation.* **2** to undergo (an injury, loss, etc.); suffer: *to sustain a broken arm.* **3** to maintain or prolong: *to sustain a discussion.* **4** to support physically from below. **5** to provide for or give support to, esp. by supplying necessities: *to sustain one's family.* **6** to keep up the vitality or courage of. **7** to uphold or affirm the justice or validity of: *to sustain a decision.* **8** to establish the truth of; confirm. ◆ *n* **9** *Music.* the prolongation of a note, by playing technique or electronics. ORIG C13: via OF from L *sustinēre* to hold up

▸ **sus'tained** *adj* ▸ **sustainedly** (sə'steɪnɪdlɪ) *adv* ▸ **sus'tainer** *n* ▸ **sus'taining** *adj* ▸ **sus'tainment** *n*

sustainable (sə'steɪnəbᵊl) *adj* **1** capable of being sustained. **2** (of economic development, energy sources, etc.) capable of being maintained at a steady level without exhausting natural resources or causing severe ecological damage: *sustainable development.*

sustaining pedal *n Music.* a foot-operated lever on a piano that keeps the dampers raised from the strings when keys are released, allowing them to continue to vibrate.

sustenance ('sʌstənəns) *n* **1** means of sustaining health or life; nourishment. **2** means of maintenance; livelihood. **3** Also: **sustention** (sə'stɛnʃən). the act or process of sustaining or the quality of being sustained. ORIG C13: from OF *sostenance,* from *sustenir* to SUSTAIN

sustentation (ˌsʌstɛn'teɪʃən) *n* a less common word for **sustenance.** ORIG C14: from L *sustentātio,* from *sustentāre,* frequentative of *sustinēre* to SUSTAIN

susurrate ('sjuːsəˌreɪt) *vb* **susurrates, susurrating, susurrated.** (*intr*) *Literary.* to make a soft rustling sound; whisper; murmur. ORIG C17: from L *susurrāre* to whisper
▸ ˌ**susur'ration** *or* **susurrus** (sjuː'sʌrəs) *n*

Sutcliffe ★ ('sʌtˌklɪf) *n* **Herbert.** 1894–1978, English cricketer, who played for Yorkshire.

Suth. *abbrev. for* Sutherland.

Sutherland[1] ★ ('sʌðələnd) *n* (until 1975) a county of N Scotland, now part of Highland.

Sutherland[2] ★ ('sʌðələnd) *n* **1 Graham.** 1903–80, British artist, noted for his tapestry *Christ in Majesty* (1962) in Coventry Cathedral. **2** Dame **Joan,** known as *La Stupenda.* born 1926, Australian soprano.

Sutherland Falls ★ *n* a waterfall in New Zealand, on SW South Island. Height: 580 m (1904 ft).

Sutlej ★ ('sʌtlɪdʒ) *n* a river in S Asia, rising in SW Tibet and flowing west through the Himalayas: crosses Himachal Pradesh and the Punjab (India), enters Pakistan, and joins the Chenab west of Bahawalpur: the longest of the five rivers of the Punjab. Length: 1368 km (850 miles).

sutler ('sʌtlə) *n* (formerly) a merchant who accompanied an army in order to sell provisions to the soldiers. ORIG C16: from obs. Du. *soeteler,* ult. from MHG *sudelen* to do dirty work

sutra ('suːtrə) *n* **1** *Hinduism.* Sanskrit sayings or collections of sayings on Vedic doctrine dating from about 200 A.D. onwards. **2** (*modifier*) *Hinduism.* **2a** of or relating to the last of the Vedic literary periods, from about 500 to 100 B.C.: *the sutra period.* **2b** of or relating to the sutras or compilations of sutras of about 200 A.D. onwards. **3** *Buddhism.* collections of dialogues and discourses of classic Mahayana Buddhism dating from the 2nd to the 6th century A.D. ORIG C19: from Sansk.: list of rules

suttee (sʌ'tiː, 'sʌtiː) *n* **1** the former Hindu custom whereby a widow burnt herself to death on her husband's funeral pyre. **2** a widow performing this. ORIG C18: from Sansk. *satī* virtuous woman, from *sat* good
▸ **sut'teeism** *n*

Sutton ★ ('sʌtᵊn) *n* a borough of S Greater London. Pop.: 173 400 (1994 est.). Area: 43 sq. km (17 sq. miles).

Sutton Coldfield ★ ('kəʊldˌfiːld) *n* a town in central England, in Birmingham, in the N West Midlands. Pop.: 86 494 (1981).

Sutton-in-Ashfield ★ (-'æʃˌfiːld) *n* a market town in N central England, in W Nottinghamshire. Pop.: 37 890 (1991).

suture ('suːtʃə) *n* **1** *Surgery.* **1a** catgut, silk thread, or wire used to stitch together two bodily surfaces. **1b** the surgical seam formed after stitching. **2** *Anat.* a type of immovable joint, esp. between the bones of the skull (**cranial suture**). **3** a seam or joining, as in sewing. **4** *Zool.* a line of junction in a mollusc shell. ◆ *vb* **sutures, suturing, sutured. 5** (*tr*) *Surgery.* to join (the edges of a wound, etc.) by means of sutures. ORIG C16: from L *sūtūra,* from *suere* to sew
▸ **'sutural** *adj*

Suu Kyi ★ *n* **Aung San.** See **Aung San Suu Kyi.**

SUV *abbrev. for* sport (*or* sports) utility vehicle.

Suva ★ ('suːvə) *n* the capital and chief port of Fiji, on the SE coast of Viti Levu. Pop.: 167 421 (1996).

Suvorov ★ (*Russian* su'vɔrəf) *n* **Aleksandr Vasilyevich** (alɪk'sandr va'siljɪvitʃ). 1729–1800, Russian field marshal, who fought successfully against the Turks (1787–91), the Poles (1794), and the French in Italy (1798–99).

Suwannee (sʊ'wɒnɪ) *or* **Swanee** ★ *n* a river in the southeastern US, rising in SE Georgia and flowing across Florida to the Gulf of Mexico at **Suwannee Sound.** Length: about 400 km (250 miles).

suzerain ('suːzəˌreɪn) *n* **1a** a state or sovereign exercising some degree of dominion over a dependent state, usually controlling its foreign affairs. **1b** (*as modifier*): *a suzerain power.* **2a** a feudal overlord. **2b** (*as modifier*): *suzerain lord.* ORIG C19: from F, from *sus* above (from L *sursum* turned upwards) + *-erain,* as in *souverain* sovereign

suzerainty ('suːzərəntɪ) *n, pl* **suzerainties. 1** the position, power, or dignity of a suzerain. **2** the relationship between suzerain and subject.

Suzhou ('suː'dʒəʊ), **Su-chou,** *or* **Soochow** ★ *n* a city in E China, in S Jiangsu on the Grand Canal: noted for its gardens; produces chiefly silk. Pop.: 706 459 (1990 est.). Also called: **Wuhsien.**

sv *abbrev. for:* **1** sailing vessel. **2** side valve. **3** sub verbo *or* voce. ORIG L: under the word *or* voice

Svalbard ★ (*Norwegian* 'svaːlbar) *n* a Norwegian archipelago in the Arctic Ocean, about 650 km (400 miles) north of Norway: consists of the main group (Spitsbergen, North East Land, Edge Island, Barents Island, and Prince Charles Foreland) and a number of outlying islands; sovereignty long disputed but granted to Norway in 1920; coal mining. Administrative centre: Longyearbyen. Area: 62 050 sq. km (23 958 sq. miles). Also called: **Spitsbergen.**

svelte (svɛlt, sfɛlt) *adj* attractively or gracefully slim; slender. ORIG C19: from F, from It. *svelto,* from *svellere* to pull out, from L *ēvellere*

Svengali (svɛn'gɑːlɪ) *n* a person who controls another's mind, usually with sinister intentions. ORIG after a character in George Du Maurier's novel *Trilby* (1894)

Sverdlovsk ★ (*Russian* svɪr'dlɔfsk) *n* the former name (1924–91) for **Yekaterinburg.**

Sverige ★ ('sværjə) *n* the Swedish name for **Sweden.**

Svevo ★ (*Italian* 'zvɛːvo) *n* **Italo** ('iːtalo), original name *Ettore Schnitz.* 1861–1928, Italian novelist and short-story writer, best known for the novel *Confessions of Zeno* (1923).

Svizzera ★ ('zvittsera) *n* the Italian name for **Switzerland.**

Svizzra ★ ('zvitsra) *n* the Romansch name for **Switzerland.**

SW 1 *symbol for* southwest(ern). **2** *abbrev. for* short wave.

Sw. *abbrev. for.* **1** Sweden. **2** Swedish.

swab (swɒb) *n* **1** *Med.* **1a** a small piece of cotton, gauze, etc., for use in applying medication, cleansing a wound, or obtaining a specimen of a secretion, etc. **1b** the specimen so obtained. **2** a mop for cleaning floors, decks, etc. **3** a brush used to clean a firearm's bore. **4** *Sl.* an uncouth or worthless fellow. ◆ *vb* **swabs, swabbing, swabbed. 5** (*tr*) to clean or medicate with or as if with a swab. **6** (*tr;* foll. by *up*) to take up with a swab. ORIG C16: prob. from MDu. *swabbe* mop
▸ **'swabber** *n*

Swabia ★ ('sweɪbɪə) *n* a region and former duchy (from the 10th century to 1313) of S Germany: now in Baden-Württemberg and Bavaria; part of West Germany until 1990. German name: **Schwaben** ('ʃvaːbᵊn).
▸ **'Swabian** *adj, n*

swaddle ('swɒdᵊl) *vb* **swaddles, swaddling, swaddled.** (*tr*) **1** to wind a bandage round. **2** to wrap (a baby) in swaddling clothes. **3** to restrain as if by wrapping with bandages; smother. ◆ *n* **4** *Chiefly US.* swaddling clothes. ORIG C15: from OE *swæthel* swaddling clothes

swaddling clothes *pl n* **1** long strips of linen or other cloth formerly wrapped round a newly born baby. **2** restrictions or supervision imposed on the immature.

swaddy *or* **swaddie** ('swɒdɪ) *n Brit. sl., old-fashioned.* a soldier. ORIG C19: from E dialect *swad* country bumpkin, soldier

swag (swæg) *n* **1** *Sl.* property obtained by theft or other illicit means. **2** *Sl.* goods; valuables. **3** an ornamental festoon of fruit, flowers, or drapery or a representation of this. **4** a swaying movement; lurch. **5** *Austral. & NZ inf.* a swagman's pack containing personal belongings, etc. **6** **swags of.** *Austral. & NZ inf.* lots of. ◆ *vb* **swags, swagging, swagged. 7** *Chiefly Brit.* to lurch or sag or cause to lurch or sag. **8** (*tr*) to adorn or arrange with swags. ORIG C17: ? of Scand. origin

swage (sweɪdʒ) *n* **1** a shaped tool or die used in forming cold metal by hammering, pressing, etc. ◆ *vb* **swages, swaging, swaged. 2** (*tr*) to form (metal) with a swage. ORIG C19: from F *souage,* from ?
▸ **'swager** *n*

swage block *n* an iron block with holes, grooves, etc., to assist in the cold-working of metal.

swagger ('swægə) *vb* **1** (*intr*) to walk or behave in an arrogant manner. **2** (*intr;* often foll. by *about*) to brag loudly. ◆ *n* **3** an arrogant gait or manner. ◆ *adj* **4** *Brit. inf., rare.* elegantly fashionable. ORIG C16: prob. from SWAG
▸ **'swaggerer** *n* ▸ **'swaggering** *adj* ▸ **'swaggeringly** *adv*

swagger stick *or esp. Brit.* **swagger cane** *n* a short cane or stick carried on occasion mainly by army officers.

swaggie ('swægɪ) *n Austral. sl.* short for **swagman.**

swagman ('swæg,mæn, -mən) *n, pl* **swagmen.** *Austral. & NZ inf.* a tramp or vagrant worker who carries his possessions on his back. Also called: **swaggie.**

Swahili (swɑː'hiːlɪ) *n* **1** a language of E Africa that is an official language of Kenya and Tanzania and is widely used as a lingua franca throughout E and central Africa. Also called: **Kiswahili. 2** (*pl* **Swahilis** *or* **Swahili**) a member of a people speaking this language, living chiefly in Zanzibar. Also called: **Mswahili** (*pl* **Waswahili**). ◆ *adj* **3** of or relating to the Swahilis or their language. ORIG C19: from Ar. *sawāhil* coasts
▸ **Swa'hilian** *adj*

swain (sweɪn) *n Arch. or poetic.* **1** a male lover or admirer. **2** a country youth. ORIG OE *swān* swineherd

swallow[1] ('swɒləʊ) *vb* (*mainly tr*) **1** to pass (food, drink, etc.) through the mouth to the stomach by means of the muscular action of the oesophagus. **2** (often foll. by *up*) to engulf or destroy as if by ingestion. **3** *Inf.* to believe gullibly: *he will never swallow such an excuse.* **4** to refrain from uttering or manifesting: *to swallow one's disappointment.* **5** to endure without retaliation. **6** to enunciate (words, etc.) indistinctly; mutter. **7** (often foll. by *down*) to eat or drink reluctantly. **8** (*intr*) to perform or simulate the act of swallowing, as in gulping. ◆ *n* **9** the act of swallowing. **10** the amount swallowed at any single time; mouthful. **11** *Rare.* another word for **throat** or **gullet.** ORIG OE *swelgan*
▸ **'swallowable** *adj* ▸ **'swallower** *n*

swallow[2] ('swɒləʊ) *n* any of various passerine songbirds having long pointed wings, a forked tail, short legs, and a rapid flight. ORIG OE *swealwe*

swallow dive *n* a type of dive in which the diver arches back while in the air, keeping his legs straight and together and his arms outstretched, finally entering the water headfirst. US and Canad. equivalent: **swan dive.**

swallow hole *n Chiefly Brit.* another word for **sinkhole** (sense 1).

swallowtail ('swɒləʊ,teɪl) *n* **1** any of various butterflies of Europe, having a tail-like extension of each hind wing. **2** the forked tail of a swallow or similar bird. **3** short for **swallow-tailed coat.**
▸ **'swallow-,tailed** *adj*

swallow-tailed coat *n* another name for **tail coat.**

swam (swæm) *vb* the past tense of **swim.**

swami ('swɑːmɪ) *n, pl* **swamies** *or* **swamis.** (in India) a title of respect for a Hindu saint or religious teacher. ORIG C18: from Hindi *svāmī,* from Sansk. *svāmin* master, from *sva* one's own

swamp (swɒmp) *n* **1** permanently waterlogged ground that is usually overgrown and sometimes partly forested. Cf. **marsh.** ◆ *vb* **2** to drench or submerge or be drenched or submerged. **3** *Naut.* to cause (a boat) to sink or fill with water or (of a boat) to sink or fill with water. **4** to overburden or overwhelm or be overburdened or overwhelmed, as by excess work or great numbers. **5** (*tr*) to render helpless. ORIG C17: prob. from MDu. *somp*
▸ **'swampy** *adj*

swamp boat *n* a shallow-draught boat powered by an aeroplane engine mounted on a raised structure for use in swamps. Also called: **airboat.**

swamp cypress *n* a North American deciduous coniferous tree that grows in swamps. Also called: **bald cypress.**

swamp fever *n* **1** Also called: **equine infectious anaemia.** a viral disease of horses. **2** *US.* another name for **malaria.**

swampland ('swɒmp,lænd) *n* a permanently waterlogged area; marshland.

swan (swɒn) *n* **1** any of various large aquatic birds having a long neck and usually a white plumage. **2** *Rare, literary.* **2a** a poet. **2b** (*cap. when part of a title or epithet*): *the Swan of Avon* (Shakespeare). ◆ *vb* **swans, swanning, swanned. 3** (*intr;* usually foll. by *around* or *about*) *Inf.* to wander idly. ORIG OE
▸ **'swan,like** *adj*

Swan[1] ★ (swɒn) *n* a river in SW Western Australia, rising as the Avon northeast of Narrogin and flowing northwest and west to the Indian Ocean below Perth. Length: about 240 km (150 miles).

Swan[2] ★ (swɒn) *n* Sir **Joseph Wilson.** 1828–1914, British physicist and chemist, who developed the incandescent electric light (1880).

swan dive *n* the US and Canad. name for **swallow dive.**

Swanee ★ ('swɒnɪ) *n* a variant spelling of **Suwannee.**

swank (swæŋk) *Inf.* ◆ *vb* **1** (*intr*) to show off or swagger. ◆ *n* **2** Also called: **swankpot.** *Brit.* a swaggering or conceited person. **3** *Chiefly US.* showy elegance or style. **4** swagger; ostentation. ◆ *adj* **5** another word (esp. US) for **swanky.** ORIG C19: ?from MHG *swanken* to sway

swanky ('swæŋkɪ) *adj* **swankier, swankiest.** *Inf.* **1** expensive and showy; stylish: *a swanky hotel.* **2** boastful or conceited.
▸ **'swankily** *adv* ▸ **'swankiness** *n*

swan neck *n* a tube, rail, etc., curved like a swan's neck.

swannery ('swɒnərɪ) *n, pl* **swanneries.** a place where swans are kept and bred.

swan's-down *n* **1** the fine soft down feathers of a swan, used to trim powder puffs, clothes, etc. **2** a thick soft fabric of wool with silk, cotton, or rayon, used for infants' clothing, etc. **3** a cotton fabric with a heavy nap.

Swansea ★ ('swɒnzɪ) *n* **1** a port in S Wales, on an inlet of the Bristol Channel (**Swansea Bay**); a metallurgical and oil-refining centre; university (1920). Pop.: 171 038 (1991). **2** a county of S Wales, on the Bristol Channel; created in 1996 from part of West Glamorgan. Administrative centre: Swansea. Pop.: 230 600 (1996 est.). Area: 378 sq. km (146 sq. miles).

swan song *n* **1** the last act, publication, etc., of a person before retirement or death. **2** the song that a dying swan is said to sing.

swan-upping *n Brit.* **1** the practice or action of marking nicks in swans' beaks as a sign of ownership. **2** the annual swan-upping of royal cygnets on the River Thames.

swap *or* **swop** (swɒp) *vb* **swaps, swapping, swapped** *or* **swops, swopping, swopped. 1** to trade or exchange (something or someone) for another. ◆ *n* **2** an exchange. **3** something that is exchanged. **4** *Finance.* Also called: **swap option, swaption.** a contract in which the parties to it exchange liabilities on outstanding debts, often exchanging fixed-interest-rate for floating-rate debts (**debt swap**), either as a means of debt management or in trading (**swap trading**). ORIG C14 (in the sense: to shake hands on a bargain, strike): prob. imit.
▸ **'swapper** *or* **'swopper** *n*

SWAPO *or* **Swapo** ('swɑːpəʊ) *n acronym for* South-West Africa People's Organization.

swaption ('swɒpʃən) *n* another name for **swap** (sense 4).

swaraj (swəˈrɑːdʒ) *n* (in British India) self-government; independence. ORIG C20: from Sansk. *svarāj*, from *sva* self + *rājya* rule
▸ **swaˈrajism** *n* ▸ **swaˈrajist** *n, adj*

sward (swɔːd) *n* **1** turf or grass or a stretch of turf or grass. ◆ *vb* **2** to cover or become covered with grass. ORIG OE *sweard* skin

swarf (swɔːf, swɑːf) *n* **1** material removed by cutting or grinding tools in the machining of metals, stone, etc. **2** radioactive metal waste from a nuclear power station. **3** small fragments of disintegrating spacecraft orbiting the earth. ORIG C16: of Scand. origin

swarm[1] (swɔːm) *n* **1** a group of bees, led by a queen, that has left the parent hive to start a new colony. **2** a large mass of small animals, esp. insects. **3** a throng or mass, esp. when moving or in turmoil. ◆ *vb* **4** (*intr*) (of small animals, esp. bees) to move in or form a swarm. **5** (*intr*) to congregate, move about or proceed in large numbers. **6** (when *intr*, often foll. by *with*) to overrun or be overrun (with): *swarming with rats*. **7** (*tr*) to cause to swarm. ORIG OE *swearm*

swarm[2] (swɔːm) *vb* (when *intr*, usually foll. by *up*) to climb (a ladder, etc.) by gripping with the hands and feet: *the boys swarmed up the rigging*. ORIG C16: from ?

swart (swɔːt) *or* **swarth** (swɔːθ) *adj Arch. or dialect*. swarthy. ORIG OE *sweart*

swarthy (ˈswɔːðɪ) *adj* **swarthier, swarthiest.** dark-hued or dark-complexioned. ORIG C16: from obs. *swarty*
▸ **ˈswarthily** *adv* ▸ **ˈswarthiness** *n*

swash (swɒʃ) *vb* **1** (*intr*) (esp. of water or things in water) to wash or move with noisy splashing. **2** (*tr*) to dash (a liquid, esp. water) against or upon. **3** (*intr*) *Arch.* to swagger. ◆ *n* **4** Also called: **send.** the dashing movement or sound of water, as of waves on a beach. **5** Also called: **swash channel.** a channel of moving water cutting through or running behind a sandbank. **6** *Arch.* swagger or bluster. ORIG C16: prob. imit.

swashbuckler (ˈswɒʃˌbʌklə) *n* **1** a swaggering or flamboyant adventurer. **2** a film, book, play, etc., depicting excitement and adventure, esp. in a historical setting. ORIG C16: from SWASH (in archaic sense: to make the noise of a sword striking a shield) + BUCKLER
▸ **ˈswashˌbuckling** *adj*

swash letter *n Printing.* a decorative letter, esp. an ornamental italic capital. ORIG C17: from *aswash* aslant

swastika (ˈswɒstɪkə) *n* **1** a primitive religious symbol or ornament in the shape of a Greek cross, usually having the ends of the arms bent at right angles. **2** this symbol with clockwise arms, the emblem of Nazi Germany. ORIG C19: from Sansk. *svastika*, from *svasti* prosperity; from belief that it brings good luck

swat (swɒt) *vb* **swats, swatting, swatted.** (*tr*) **1** to strike or hit sharply: *to swat a fly*. ◆ *n* **2** a sharp or violent blow. ◆ Also: **swot.** ORIG C17: N English dialect & US var. of SQUAT
▸ **ˈswatter** *n*

Swat ★ (swɒt) *n* **1** a former princely state of NW India: passed to Pakistan in 1947. **2** a river in Pakistan, rising in the north and flowing south to the Kabul River north of Peshawar. Length: about 640 km (400 miles).

swatch (swɒtʃ) *n* **1** a sample of cloth or other material. **2** a number of such samples, usually fastened together in book form. ORIG C16: Scot. & N English, from ?

swath (swɔːθ) *or* **swathe** (sweɪð) *n, pl* **swaths** (swɔːðz) *or* **swathes. 1** the width of one sweep of a scythe or of the blade of a mowing machine. **2** the strip cut by these in one course. **3** the quantity of cut grass, hay, etc., left in one such course. **4** a long narrow strip or belt. ORIG OE *swæth*

swathe (sweɪð) *vb* **swathes, swathing, swathed.** (*tr*) **1** to bandage (a wound, limb, etc.), esp. completely. **2** to wrap a band, garment, etc., around, esp. so as to cover completely; swaddle. **3** to envelop. ◆ *n* **4** a bandage or wrapping. **5** a variant spelling of **swath.** ORIG OE *swathian*

Swatow ★ (ˈswɒˈtaʊ) *n* a variant transliteration of the Chinese name for **Shantou.**

sway (sweɪ) *vb* **1** (*usually intr*) to swing or cause to swing to and fro: *the door swayed in the wind*. **2** (*usually intr*) to lean or incline or cause to lean or incline to one side or in different directions in turn. **3** (*usually intr*) to vacillate or cause to vacillate between two or more opinions. **4** to be influenced or swerve or influence or cause to swerve to or from a purpose or opinion. **5** *Arch. or poetic.* to rule or wield power (over). ◆ *n* **6** control; power. **7** a swinging or leaning movement. **8** *Arch.* dominion; governing authority. **9 hold sway.** to be master; reign. ORIG C16: prob. from ON *sveigja* to bend

sway-back *n* an abnormal sagging or concavity of the spine in horses.
▸ **ˈsway-ˌbacked** *adj*

Swaziland ★ (ˈswɑːzɪˌlænd) *n* a kingdom in southern Africa: made a protectorate of the Transvaal by Britain in 1894; gained independence in 1968; a member of the Commonwealth. Official languages: Swazi and English. Religion: Christian majority, traditional beliefs. Currency: lilangeni (*pl* emalangeni). Capital: Mbabane (administrative); Lobamba (legislative). Pop.: 985 000 (1999 est.). Area: 17 363 sq. km (6704 sq. miles).

Swazi Territory ★ *n* the former name of **KaNgwane.**

swear (swɛə) *vb* **swears, swearing, swore, sworn. 1** to declare or affirm (a statement) as true, esp. by invoking a deity, etc., as witness. **2** (foll. by *by*) **2a** to invoke (a deity, etc.) by name as a witness or guarantee to an oath. **2b** to trust implicitly; have complete confidence (in). **3** (*intr;* often foll. by *at*) to curse, blaspheme, or use swearwords. **4** (when *tr, may take a clause as object or an infinitive*) to promise solemnly on oath; vow. **5** (*tr*) to assert or affirm with great emphasis or earnestness. **6** (*intr*) to give evidence or make any statement or solemn declaration on oath. **7** to take an oath in order to add force or solemnity to (a statement or declaration). ◆ *n* **8** a period of swearing. ORIG OE *swerian*
▸ **ˈswearer** *n*

swear in *vb* (*tr, adv*) to administer an oath to (a person) on his or her assuming office, entering the witness box to give evidence, etc.

swear off *vb* (*intr, prep*) to promise to abstain from something: *to swear off drink*.

swearword (ˈswɛəˌwɜːd) *n* a socially taboo word of a profane, obscene, or insulting character.

sweat (swɛt) *n* **1** the secretion from the sweat glands, esp. when profuse and visible, as during strenuous activity, from excessive heat, etc.; perspiration. **2** the act or process of secreting this fluid. **3** the act of inducing the exudation of moisture. **4** drops of moisture given forth or gathered on the surface of something. **5** *Inf.* a state or condition of worry or eagerness (esp. in **in a sweat**). **6** *Sl.* drudgery or hard labour: *mowing lawns is a real sweat!* **7** *Sl., chiefly Brit.* a soldier, esp. one who is old and experienced. **8 no sweat!** *Sl.* an expression conveying consent or assurance. ◆ *vb* **sweats, sweating, sweat** *or* **sweated. 9** to secrete (sweat) through the pores of the skin, esp. profusely; perspire. **10** (*tr*) to make wet or stain with perspiration. **11** to give forth or cause to give forth (moisture) in droplets: *the maple sweats sap*. **12** (*intr*) to collect and condense moisture on an outer surface: *a glass of beer sweating*. **13** (*intr*) (of a liquid) to pass through a porous surface in droplets. **14** (of tobacco leaves, hay, etc.) to exude moisture and, sometimes, begin to ferment or to cause (tobacco leaves, etc.) to exude moisture. **15** (*tr*) to heat (food, esp. vegetables) slowly in butter in a tightly closed saucepan. **16** (*tr*) to join (pieces of metal) by pressing together and heating. **17** (*tr*) to heat (solder) until it melts. **18** (*tr*) to heat (partially fused metal) to extract an easily fusible constituent. **19** *Inf.* to suffer anxiety, impatience, or distress. **20** *Inf.* to overwork or be overworked. **21** (*tr*) *Inf.* to employ at very low wages and under bad conditions. **22** (*tr*) *Inf.* to extort, esp. by torture: *to sweat information out of a captive*. **23** (*intr*) *Inf.* to suffer punishment: *you'll sweat for this!* **24 sweat blood.** *Inf.* **24a** to work very hard. **24b** to be filled with anxiety or impatience. ◆ See also **sweat off, sweat out, sweats.** ORIG OE *swætan* to sweat, from *swāt* sweat

sweatband (ˈswɛtˌbænd) *n* **1** a band of material set in a hat or cap to protect it from sweat. **2** a piece of cloth tied around the forehead to keep sweat out of the eyes or around the wrist to keep the hands dry, as in sports.

sweated ('swɛtɪd) *adj* **1** made by exploited labour: *sweated goods.* **2** (of workers, etc.) forced to work in poor conditions for low pay.

sweater ('swɛtə) *n* **1** a garment made of knitted or crocheted material covering the upper part of the body, esp. a heavy one worn for warmth. **2** a person or thing that sweats. **3** an employer who overworks and underpays his or her employees.

sweat gland *n* any of the coiled tubular subcutaneous glands that secrete sweat.

sweating sickness *n* an acute infectious febrile disease that was widespread in Europe during the late 15th century, characterized by profuse sweating.

sweat off *or* **away** *vb (tr, adv) Inf.* to get rid of (weight) by strenuous exercise or sweating.

sweat out *vb (tr, adv)* **1** to cure or lessen the effects of (a cold, respiratory infection, etc.) by sweating. **2** *Inf.* to endure (hardships) for a time (often in **sweat it out**). **3 sweat one's guts out.** *Inf.* to work extremely hard.

sweat pants *pl n* loose thick cotton trousers with elasticated ankles and an elasticated or drawstring waist, worn esp. by athletes warming up or training.

sweats (swɛts) *pl n* sweatshirts and sweat-suit trousers: *jeans and sweats.*

sweatshirt ('swɛt,ʃɜːt) *n* a long-sleeved knitted cotton sweater worn by athletes, etc.

sweatshop ('swɛt,ʃɒp) *n* a workshop where employees work long hours under bad conditions for low wages.

sweat suit *n* a suit worn by athletes for training comprising knitted cotton trousers and a light cotton sweater.

sweaty ('swɛtɪ) *adj* **sweatier, sweatiest. 1** covered with perspiration; sweating. **2** smelling of or like sweat. **3** causing sweat.
► **'sweatily** *adv* ► **'sweatiness** *n*

swede (swiːd) *n* **1** a Eurasian plant cultivated for its bulbous edible root, which is used as a vegetable and as cattle fodder. **2** the root of this plant. ◆ Also called: **Swedish turnip.** ORIG C19: so called after being introduced into Scotland from Sweden in the 18th century

Swede (swiːd) *n* a native, citizen, or inhabitant of Sweden.

Sweden ★ ('swiːdᵊn) *n* a kingdom in NW Europe, occupying the E part of the Scandinavian Peninsula, on the Gulf of Bothnia and the Baltic: first united during the Viking period (8th–11th centuries); a member of the European Union. About 50 per cent of the total area is forest and 9 per cent lakes. Exports include timber, pulp, paper, iron ore, and steel. Official language: Swedish. Official religion: Church of Sweden (Lutheran Christian). Currency: krona. Capital: Stockholm. Pop.: 8 859 000 (1999 est.). Area: 449 793 sq. km (173 665 sq. miles). Swedish name: **Sverige.**

Swedenborg ★ ('swiːdᵊn,bɔːg; *Swedish* 'sveːdənbɔrj) *n* **Emanuel** (e'manuel). original surname *Svedberg.* 1688–1772, Swedish scientist and theologian.

Swedish ('swiːdɪʃ) *adj* **1** of, relating to, or characteristic of Sweden, its people, or their language. ◆ *n* **2** the official language of Sweden.

Sweelinck ★ (*Dutch* 'sweːlɪŋk) *n* **Jan Pieterszoon** (jɑn 'piːtər,zoːn). 1562–1621, Dutch composer, noted for his organ works.

sweep (swiːp) *vb* **sweeps, sweeping, swept. 1** to clean or clear (a space, chimney, etc.) with a brush, broom, etc. **2** (often foll. by *up*) to remove or collect (dirt, rubbish, etc.) with a brush, broom, etc. **3** to move in a smooth or continuous manner, esp. quickly or forcibly: *cars swept along the road.* **4** to move in a proud or dignified fashion: *she swept past.* **5** to spread or pass rapidly across, through, or along (a region, area, etc.): *the news swept through the town.* **6** (*tr*) to direct (the gaze, line of fire, etc.) over; survey. **7** (*tr;* foll. by *away* or *off*) to overwhelm emotionally: *she was swept away by his charm.* **8** to brush or lightly touch (a surface, etc.): *the dress swept along the ground.* **9** (*tr;* often foll. by *away*) to convey, clear, or abolish, esp. with strong or continuous movements: *the sea swept the sandcastle away; secondary modern schools were swept away.* **10** (*intr*) to extend gracefully or majestically, esp. in a wide circle: *the plains sweep down to the sea.* **11** to search (a body of water) for mines, etc., by dragging. **12** (*tr*) to win overwhelmingly, esp. in an election: *Labour swept the country.* **13** (*tr*) to propel (a boat) with sweeps. **14 sweep the board. 14a** (in gambling) to win all the cards or money. **14b** to win every event or prize in a contest. **15 sweep (something) under the carpet.** to conceal (something, esp. a problem) in the hope that it will be overlooked by others. ◆ *n* **16** the act or an instance of sweeping; removal by or as if by a brush or broom. **17** a swift or steady movement, esp. in an arc. **18** the distance, arc, etc., through which something, such as a pendulum, moves. **19** a wide expanse or scope: *the sweep of the plains.* **20** any curving line or contour. **21** short for **sweepstake. 22a** a long oar used on an open boat. **22b** *Austral.* a person steering a surf boat with such an oar at the stern. **23** any of the sails of a windmill. **24** *Electronics.* a steady horizontal or circular movement of an electron beam across or around the fluorescent screen of a cathode-ray tube. **25** a curving driveway. **26** *Chiefly Brit.* See **chimney sweep. 27** another name for **swipe** (sense 6). **28 clean sweep. 28a** an overwhelming victory or success. **28b** a complete change; purge: *to make a clean sweep.* ORIG C13 *swepen*
► **'sweepy** *adj*

sweeper ('swiːpə) *n* **1** a person employed to sweep, such as a roadsweeper. **2** any device for sweeping: *a carpet sweeper.* **3** *Inf., soccer.* a player who supports the main defenders, as by intercepting loose balls, etc.

sweep hand *n Horology.* a long hand that registers seconds or fractions of seconds on the perimeter of the dial.

sweeping ('swiːpɪŋ) *adj* **1** comprehensive and wide-ranging: *sweeping reforms.* **2** indiscriminate or without reservations: *sweeping statements.* **3** decisive or overwhelming: *a sweeping victory.* **4** taking in a wide area: *a sweeping glance.* **5** driving steadily onwards, esp. over a large area: *a sweeping attack.*
► **'sweepingly** *adv* ► **'sweepingness** *n*

sweep-saw *n* a saw with a thin blade that can be used for cutting curved shapes.

sweepstake ('swiːp,steɪk) *or esp. US* **sweepstakes** *n* **1a** a lottery in which the stakes of the participants constitute the prize. **1b** the prize itself. **2** any event involving such a lottery, esp. a horse race. ◆ Often shortened to **sweep.** ORIG C15: orig. referring to someone who *sweeps* or takes all the stakes in a game

sweet (swiːt) *adj* **1** having or denoting a pleasant taste like that of sugar. **2** agreeable to the senses or the mind: *sweet music.* **3** having pleasant manners; gentle: *a sweet child.* **4** (of wine, etc.) having a relatively high sugar content; not dry. **5** (of foods) not decaying or rancid: *sweet milk.* **6** not salty: *sweet water.* **7** free from unpleasant odours: *sweet air.* **8** containing no corrosive substances: *sweet soil.* **9** (of petrol) containing no sulphur compounds. **10** sentimental or unrealistic. **11** *Jazz.* performed with a regular beat, with the emphasis on clearly outlined melody and little improvisation. **12** *Arch.* respected; dear (used in polite forms of address): *sweet sir.* **13** smooth and precise; perfectly executed: *a sweet shot.* **14 at one's own sweet will.** as it suits oneself alone. **15 keep (someone) sweet.** to ingratiate oneself in order to ensure cooperation. **16 sweet on.** fond of or infatuated with. ◆ *adv* **17** *Inf.* in a sweet manner. ◆ *n* **18** a sweet taste or smell; sweetness in general. **19** (*often pl*) *Brit.* any of numerous kinds of confectionery consisting wholly or partly of sugar, esp. of sugar boiled and crystallized (**boiled sweets**). **20** *Brit.* any sweet dish served as a dessert. **21** dear; sweetheart (used as a form of address). **22** anything that is sweet. **23** (*often pl*) a pleasurable experience, state, etc.: *the sweets of success.* ORIG OE *swēte*
► **'sweetish** *adj* ► **'sweetly** *adv* ► **'sweetness** *n*

Sweet ★ (swiːt) *n* **Henry.** 1845–1912, British philologist; a pioneer of modern phonetics. His books include *A History of English Sounds* (1874).

sweet alyssum *n* a Mediterranean plant having clusters of small fragrant white or violet flowers. See also **alyssum.**

sweet-and-sour *adj* (of food) cooked in a sauce made from sugar and vinegar and other ingredients.

sweet bay *n* a small tree of SE North America, belonging to the magnolia family and having large fragrant white flowers. Sometimes shortened to **bay**.

sweetbread ('swi:tˌbrɛd) *n* the pancreas or the thymus gland of an animal, used for food. ORIG C16: SWEET + BREAD, ? from OE *brǣd* meat

sweetbrier ('swi:tˌbraɪə) *n* a Eurasian rose having a tall bristly stem, fragrant leaves, and single pink flowers. Also called: **eglantine**.

sweet cherry *n* either of two types of cherry tree that are cultivated for their edible sweet fruit.

sweet chestnut *n* See **chestnut** (sense 1).

sweet cicely ('sɪsəlɪ) *n* **1** Also called: **myrrh**. an aromatic European plant, having compound leaves and clusters of small white flowers. **2** the leaves, formerly used in cookery for their flavour of aniseed. **3** any of various related plants of Asia and America, having aromatic roots.

sweet corn *n* **1** a variety of maize whose kernels are rich in sugar and eaten as a vegetable when young. **2** the unripe ears of maize, esp. the sweet kernels removed from the cob, cooked as a vegetable.

sweeten ('swi:tᵊn) *vb* (*mainly tr*) **1** (*also intr*) to make or become sweet or sweeter. **2** to mollify or soften (a person). **3** to make more agreeable. **4** (*also intr*) *Chem.* to free or be freed from unpleasant odours, acidic or corrosive substances, or the like.

sweetener ('swi:tᵊnə) *n* **1** a sweetening agent, esp. one that does not contain sugar. **2** *Inf.* a bribe. **3** *Inf.* a financial inducement.

sweetening ('swi:tᵊnɪŋ) *n* something that sweetens.

sweet flag *n* an aroid marsh plant, having swordlike leaves, small greenish flowers, and aromatic roots. Also called: **calamus**.

sweet gale *n* a shrub of northern swamp regions, having yellow catkin-like flowers and aromatic leaves. Also called: **bog myrtle**. Often shortened to **gale**.

sweet gum *n* **1** a North American liquidambar tree, having prickly spherical fruit clusters and fragrant sap: the wood (called **satin walnut**) is used to make furniture. **2** the sap of this tree. ♦ Also called: **red gum**.

sweetheart ('swi:tˌhɑ:t) *n* **1** a person loved by another. **2** *Inf.* a lovable, generous, or obliging person. **3** a term of endearment.

sweetheart agreement *n Austral. inf.* an industrial agreement on pay and conditions concluded without resort to arbitration.

sweetie ('swi:tɪ) *n Inf.* **1** sweetheart; darling: used as a term of endearment. **2** *Brit.* another word for **sweet** (sense 19). **3** *Chiefly Brit.* an endearing person. **4** a large seedless variety of grapefruit that has a green-to-yellow rind and juicy sweet pulp.

sweeting ('swi:tɪŋ) *n* **1** a variety of sweet apple. **2** an archaic word for **sweetheart**.

sweet marjoram *n* another name for **marjoram** (sense 1).

sweetmeat ('swi:tˌmi:t) *n* a sweetened delicacy, such as a preserve, sweet, or, formerly, a cake or pastry.

sweet pea *n* a climbing plant of S Europe, widely cultivated for its butterfly-shaped fragrant flowers of delicate pastel colours.

sweet pepper *n* **1** a pepper plant with large bell-shaped fruits that are eaten unripe (**green pepper**) or ripe (**red pepper**). **2** the fruit of this plant.

sweet potato *n* **1** a twining plant of tropical America, cultivated in the tropics for its edible fleshy yellow root. **2** the root of this plant.

sweet shop *n Chiefly Brit.* a shop solely or largely selling sweets, esp. boiled sweets.

sweetsop ('swi:tˌsɒp) *n* **1** a small West Indian tree, having yellowish-green fruit. **2** the fruit, which has a sweet edible pulp. ♦ Also called: **custard apple**.

sweet spot *n Sport.* the centre area of a racket, golf club, etc., from which the cleanest shots are made.

sweet-talk *Inf.* ♦ *vb* **1** to coax, flatter, or cajole (someone). ♦ *n* **sweet talk**. **2** cajolery; coaxing.

sweet tooth *n* a strong liking for sweet foods.

sweetveld ('swi:tˌfɛlt) *n* (in South Africa) a type of grazing characterized by high-quality grass. ORIG pron. from Afrik. *soetveld*

sweet william ('wɪljəm) *n* a widely cultivated Eurasian plant with flat clusters of white, pink, red, or purple flowers.

swell (swɛl) *vb* **swells, swelling, swelled; swollen** *or* **swelled**. **1** to grow or cause to grow in size, esp. as a result of internal pressure. **2** to expand or cause to expand at a particular point or above the surrounding level; protrude. **3** to grow or cause to grow in size, amount, intensity, or degree: *the party is swelling with new recruits.* **4** to puff or be puffed up with pride or another emotion. **5** (*intr*) (of seas or lakes) to rise in waves. **6** (*intr*) to well up or overflow. **7** (*tr*) to make (a musical phrase) increase gradually in volume and then diminish. ♦ *n* **8a** the undulating movement of the surface of the open sea. **8b** a succession of waves or a single large wave. **9** a swelling or being swollen; expansion. **10** an increase in quantity or degree; inflation. **11** a bulge; protuberance. **12** a gentle hill. **13** *Inf.* a person very fashionably dressed. **14** *Inf.* a man of high social or political standing. **15** *Music.* a crescendo followed by an immediate diminuendo. **16** Also called: **swell organ**. *Music.* **16a** a set of pipes on an organ housed in a box (**swell box**) fitted with a shutter operated by a pedal, which can be opened or closed to control the volume. **16b** the manual on an organ controlling this. ♦ *adj* **17** *Inf.* stylish or grand. **18** *Sl.* excellent; first-class. ORIG OE *swellan*

swelled head *or* **swollen head** *n Inf.* an inflated view of one's own worth, often caused by sudden success.
▸ **swelled-headed, swell-headed**, *or* **swollen-headed** *adj*

swelling ('swɛlɪŋ) *n* **1** the act of expansion or inflation. **2** the state of being or becoming swollen. **3** a swollen or inflated part or area. **4** an abnormal enlargement of a bodily structure or part, esp. as the result of injury. ♦ Related adj: **tumescent**.

swelter ('swɛltə) *vb* **1** (*intr*) to suffer under oppressive heat, esp. to perspire and feel faint. **2** (*tr*) *Rare.* to cause to suffer under oppressive heat. ♦ *n* **3** a sweltering condition (esp. in **in a swelter**). **4** oppressive humid heat. ORIG C15 *swelten*, from OE *sweltan* to die

sweltering ('swɛltərɪŋ) *adj* oppressively hot and humid: *a sweltering day.*
▸ **'swelteringly** *adv*

swept (swɛpt) *vb* the past tense and past participle of **sweep**.

sweptback ('swɛptˌbæk) *adj* (of an aircraft wing) inclined backwards towards the rear of the fuselage.

sweptwing ('swɛptˌwɪŋ) *adj* (of an aircraft, etc.) having wings swept (usually) backwards.

swerve (swɜ:v) *vb* **swerves, swerving, swerved**. **1** to turn or cause to turn aside, usually sharply or suddenly, from a course. ♦ *n* **2** the act, instance, or degree of swerving. ORIG OE *sweorfan* to scour
▸ **'swervable** *adj* ▸ **'swerver** *n* ▸ **'swerving** *adj*

Sweyn ★ (sweɪn) *n* known as *Sweyn Forkbeard.* died 1014, king of Denmark (?986–1014). He conquered England, forcing Ethelred II to flee (1013); father of Canute.

SWG *abbrev. for* Standard Wire Gauge; a notation for the diameters of metal rods or thickness of metal sheet ranging from 16 mm to 0.02 mm or from 0.5 inch to 0.001 inch.

swift (swɪft) *adj* **1** moving or able to move quickly; fast. **2** occurring or performed quickly or suddenly; instant. **3** (*postpositive;* foll. by *to*) prompt to act or respond: *swift to take revenge.* ♦ *adv* **4a** swiftly or quickly. **4b** (*in combination*): *swift-moving.* ♦ *n* **5** any of various insectivorous birds of the Old World. They have long narrow wings and spend most of the time on the wing. **6** any of certain North American lizards of the iguana family that can run very rapidly. **7** the main cylinder in a carding machine. **8** an expanding circular frame used to hold skeins of silk, wool, etc. ORIG OE, from *swīfan* to turn
▸ **'swiftly** *adv* ▸ **'swiftness** *n*

Swift ★ (swɪft) *n* **1 Graham Colin.** born 1949, British novelist: his books include *Last Orders* (1996). **2 Jonathan.** 1667–1745, Anglo-Irish satirist and churchman, who became dean of St Patrick's, Dublin, in 1713. His works include *Gulliver's Travels* (1726).

swiftlet ('swɪftlɪt) *n* any of various small swifts of an Asian genus that often live in caves and use echolocation.

swig (swɪg) *Inf.* ◆ *n* **1** a large swallow or deep drink, esp. from a bottle. ◆ *vb* **swigs, swigging, swigged. 2** to drink (some liquid) deeply, esp. from a bottle. ORIG C16: from ?
▸ **'swigger** *n*

swill (swɪl) *vb* **1** to drink large quantities of (liquid, esp. alcoholic drink); guzzle. **2** (*tr;* often foll. by *out*) *Chiefly Brit.* to drench or rinse in large amounts of water. **3** (*tr*) to feed swill to (pigs, etc.). ◆ *n* **4** wet feed, esp. for pigs, consisting of kitchen waste, skimmed milk, etc. **5** refuse, esp. from a kitchen. **6** a deep drink, esp. beer. **7** any liquid mess. **8** the act of swilling. ORIG OE *swilian* to wash out
▸ **'swiller** *n*

swim (swɪm) *vb* **swims, swimming, swam, swum. 1** (*intr*) to move along in water by means of movements of the body, esp. the arms and legs, or (in the case of fish) tail and fins. **2** (*tr*) to cover (a distance or stretch of water) in this way. **3** (*tr*) to compete in (a race) in this way. **4** (*intr*) to be supported by and on a liquid; float. **5** (*tr*) to use (a particular stroke) in swimming. **6** (*intr*) to move smoothly, usually through air or over a surface. **7** (*intr*) to reel or seem to reel: *my head swam; the room swam around me.* **8** (*intr;* often foll. by *in* or *with*) to be covered or flooded with water or other liquid. **9** (*intr;* often foll. by *in*) to be liberally supplied (with): *he's swimming in money.* **10** (*tr*) to cause to float or swim. **11 swim with** (*or* **against**) **the stream** *or* **tide.** to conform to (or resist) prevailing opinion. ◆ *n* **12** the act, an instance, or period of swimming. **13** any graceful gliding motion. **14** a condition of dizziness; swoon. **15** a pool in a river good for fishing. **16 in the swim.** *Inf.* fashionable or active in social or political activities. ORIG OE *swimman*
▸ **'swimmable** *adj* ▸ **'swimmer** *n* ▸ **'swimming** *n, adj*

swim bladder *n Ichthyol.* another name for **air bladder** (sense 1).

swimmeret ('swɪmə,rɛt) *n* any of the small paired appendages on the abdomen of crustaceans, used chiefly in locomotion.

swimming bath *n* (*often pl*) an indoor swimming pool.

swimming costume *or* **bathing costume** *n Chiefly Brit.* any garment worn for swimming or sunbathing, such as a woman's one-piece garment covering most of the torso but not the limbs.

swimmingly ('swɪmɪŋlɪ) *adv* successfully, effortlessly, or well (esp. in **go swimmingly**).

swimming pool *n* an artificial pool for swimming.

swimsuit ('swɪm,su:t, -,sju:t) *n* a woman's one-piece swimming garment that leaves the arms and legs bare.

Swinburne ★ ('swɪn,bɜ:n) *n* **Algernon Charles.** 1837–1909, British poet and critic.

swindle ('swɪnd°l) *vb* **swindles, swindling, swindled. 1** to cheat (someone) of money, etc.; defraud. **2** (*tr*) to obtain (money, etc.) by fraud. ◆ *n* **3** a fraudulent scheme or transaction. ORIG C18: back formation from G *Schwindler,* from *schwindeln,* from OHG *swintilōn,* from *swintan* to disappear
▸ **'swindler** *n*

swindle sheet *n* a slang term for **expense account.**

Swindon ★ ('swɪndən) *n* **1** a town in S England, in NE Wiltshire: railway workshops. Pop.: 145 236 (1991). **2** a unitary authority in S England, in NE Wiltshire. Pop.: 174 600 (1996 est.). Area: 230 sq. km (89 sq. miles).

swine (swaɪn) *n* **1** (*pl* **swine** *or* **swines**). a coarse or contemptible person. **2** (*pl* **swine**). another name for a **pig.** ORIG OE *swīn*
▸ **'swinish** *adj* ▸ **'swinishly** *adv* ▸ **'swinishness** *n*

swine fever *n* an infectious viral disease of pigs, characterized by fever and diarrhoea.

swineherd ('swaɪn,hɜ:d) *n Arch.* a person who looks after pigs.

swing (swɪŋ) *vb* **swings, swinging, swung. 1** to move or cause to move rhythmically to and fro, as a free-hanging object; sway. **2** (*intr*) to move, walk, etc., with a relaxed and swaying motion. **3** to pivot or cause to pivot, as on a hinge. **4** to move or cause to move in a curve: *the car swung around the bend.* **5** to move or cause to move by suspending or being suspended. **6** to hang or be hung so as to be able to turn freely. **7** (*intr*) *Sl.* to be hanged: *he'll swing for it.* **8** to alter or cause to alter habits, a course, etc. **9** (*tr*) *Inf.* to influence or manipulate successfully: *I hope he can swing the deal.* **10** (*tr;* foll. by *up*) to raise or hoist, esp. in a sweeping motion. **11** (*intr;* often foll. by *at*) to hit out or strike (at), esp. with a sweeping motion. **12** (*tr*) to wave (a weapon, etc.) in a sweeping motion; flourish. **13** to arrange or play (music) with the rhythmically flexible and compulsive quality associated with jazz. **14** (*intr*) (of popular music, esp. jazz, or of the musicians who play it) to have this quality. **15** *Sl.* to be lively and modern. **16** (*intr*) *Cricket.* to bowl (a ball) with swing or (of a ball) to move with a swing. **17 swing the lead.** *Inf.* to malinger or make up excuses. ◆ *n* **18** the act or manner of swinging or the distance covered while swinging: *a wide swing.* **19** a sweeping stroke or blow. **20** *Boxing.* a wide punch from the side similar to but longer than a hook. **21** *Cricket.* the lateral movement of a bowled ball through the air. **22** any free-swaying motion. **23** any curving movement; sweep. **24** something that swings or is swung, esp. a suspended seat on which a person may swing back and forth. **25** a kind of popular dance music influenced by jazz, usually played by big bands and originating in the 1930s. **26** *Prosody.* a steady distinct rhythm or cadence in prose or verse. **27** *Inf.* the normal round or pace: *the swing of things.* **28a** a fluctuation, as in some business activity, voting pattern, etc. **28b** (*modifier*) able to bring about a swing in a voting pattern. **29** *Canad.* (in the North) a train of freight sleighs or canoes. **30** *Chiefly US.* a circular tour. **31 go with a swing.** to go well; be successful. **32 in full swing.** at the height of activity. **33 swings and roundabouts.** equal advantages and disadvantages. ORIG OE *swingan*

swingboat ('swɪŋ,bəʊt) *n* a piece of fairground equipment consisting of a boat-shaped carriage for swinging in.

swing bridge *n* a low bridge that can be rotated about a vertical axis to permit the passage of ships, etc.

swinge (swɪndʒ) *vb* **swinges, swingeing** *or* **swinging, swinged.** (*tr*) *Arch.* to beat, flog, or punish. ORIG OE *swengan*

swingeing ('swɪndʒɪŋ) *adj Chiefly Brit.* punishing; severe.

swinger ('swɪŋə) *n Sl.* **1** a person regarded as being modern and lively. **2** a person who swaps sexual partners in a group, esp. habitually.
▸ **'swinging** *adj* ▸ **'swingingly** *adv*

swingle ('swɪŋg°l) *n* **1** a flat-bladed wooden instrument used for beating and scraping flax or hemp to remove coarse matter from it. ◆ *vb* **swingles, swingling, swingled. 2** (*tr*) to use a swingle on. ORIG OE *swingel* stroke

swingletree ('swɪŋg°l,tri:) *n* a crossbar in a horse's harness to which the ends of the traces are attached. Also called: **whippletree.**

swing shift *n US & Canad. inf.* the usual US and Canad. term for **back shift.**

swing-wing *adj* **1** of or relating to a variable-geometry aircraft. ◆ *n* **2a** such an aircraft. **2b** either of the two wings of such an aircraft.

swipe (swaɪp) *vb* **swipes, swiping, swiped. 1** (when *intr,* usually foll. by *at*) *Inf.* to hit hard with a sweeping blow. **2** (*tr*) *Sl.* to steal. **3** (*tr*) to pass a machine-readable card, such as a credit card, debit card, etc., through a machine that electronically interprets the information encoded on it, usu. in a magnetic strip. ◆ *n* **4** *Inf.* a hard blow. **5** an unexpected criticism of someone or something while discussing another subject. **6** Also called: **sweep.** a type of lever for raising and lowering a weight, such as a bucket in a well. ORIG C19: ? rel. to SWEEP

swirl (swɜ:l) *vb* **1** to turn or cause to turn in a twisting

spinning fashion. **2** (*intr*) to be dizzy; swim: *my head was swirling.* ◆ *n* **3** a whirling or spinning motion, esp. in water. **4** a whorl; curl. **5** the act of swirling or stirring. **6** dizzy confusion or disorder. ORIG C15: prob. from Du. *zwirrelen*
▸ **'swirling** *adj* ▸ **'swirly** *adj*

swish (swɪʃ) *vb* **1** to move with or make or cause to move with or make a whistling or hissing sound. **2** (*intr*) (esp. of fabrics) to rustle. **3** (*tr*) *Sl., now rare.* to whip; flog. **4** (*tr; foll. by off*) to cut with a swishing blow. ◆ *n* **5** a hissing or rustling sound or movement. **6** a rod for flogging or a blow from this. ◆ *adj* **7** *Inf., chiefly Brit.* fashionable; smart. ORIG C18: imit.
▸ **'swishy** *adj*

Swiss (swɪs) *adj* **1** of, relating to, or characteristic of Switzerland, its inhabitants, or their dialects of German, French, and Italian. ◆ *n, pl* **Swiss. 2** a native, inhabitant, or citizen of Switzerland.

Swiss chard *n* another name for **chard.**

Swiss cheese plant *n* See **monstera.**

swiss roll *n* a sponge cake spread with jam, cream, or some other filling, and rolled up.

switch (swɪtʃ) *n* **1** a mechanical, electrical, or electronic device for opening or closing a circuit or for diverting a current from one part of a circuit to another. **2** a swift and usually sudden shift or change. **3** an exchange or swap. **4** a flexible rod or twig, used esp. for punishment. **5** the sharp movement or blow of such an instrument. **6** a tress of false hair used to give added length or bulk to a woman's own hair-style. **7** the tassel-like tip of the tail of cattle and certain other animals. **8** any of various card games in which the suit is changed during play. **9** *US & Canad.* a railway siding. **10** *US & Canad.* a railway point. **11** *Austral. inf.* short for **switchboard** (sense 1). ◆ *vb* **12** to shift, change, turn aside, or change the direction of (something). **13** to exchange (places); replace (something by something else). **14** *Chiefly US & Canad.* to transfer (rolling stock) from one railway track to another. **15** (*tr*) to cause (an electric current) to start or stop flowing or to change its path by operating a switch. **16** (*tr*) to lash or whip with or as if with a switch. ◆ See also **switch off, switch on.** ORIG C16: ?from MDu. *swijch* twig
▸ **'switcher** *n*

switchback ('swɪtʃˌbæk) *n* **1** a mountain road, railway, or track which rises and falls sharply many times or a sharp rise and fall on such a road, railway, or track. **2** another word (esp. Brit.) for **big dipper.**

switchblade *or* **switchblade knife** ('swɪtʃˌbleɪd) *n* another name (esp. US and Canad.) for **flick knife.**

switchboard ('swɪtʃˌbɔːd) *n* **1** an installation in a telephone exchange, office, etc., at which the interconnection of telephone lines is manually controlled. **2** an assembly of switchgear for the control of power supplies in an installation or building.

switched-on *adj Inf.* well-informed or aware of what is up to date.

switchgear ('swɪtʃˌgɪə) *n Electrical engineering.* any of several devices used for opening and closing electric circuits, esp. those that pass high currents.

switchman ('swɪtʃmən) *n, pl* **switchmen.** the US and Canad. name for **pointsman.**

switch off *vb* (*adv*) **1** to cause (a device) to stop operating as by moving a switch, knob, etc. **2** *Inf.* to cease to interest or be interested; make or become bored, alienated, etc.

switch on *vb* (*adv*) **1** to cause (a device) to operate as by moving a switch, knob, or lever. **2** (*tr*) *Inf.* to produce (charm, tears, etc.) suddenly or automatically. **3** (*tr*) *Inf.* (now dated) to make up-to-date, esp. in outlook, dress, etc.

swither ('swɪðə) *Scot.* ◆ *vb* (*intr*) **1** to hesitate; vacillate; be perplexed. ◆ *n* **2** hesitation; perplexity; agitation. ORIG C16: from ?

Swithin *or* **Swithun** ★ ('swɪðɪn, 'swɪθ-) *n* **Saint.** died 862 A.D., English ecclesiastic: bishop of Winchester (?852–862). Feast day: July 15.

Switz. *or* **Swit.** *abbrev. for* Switzerland.

Switzer ('swɪtsə) *n* a less common word for **Swiss.** ORIG C16: from MHG, from *Swīz* Switzerland

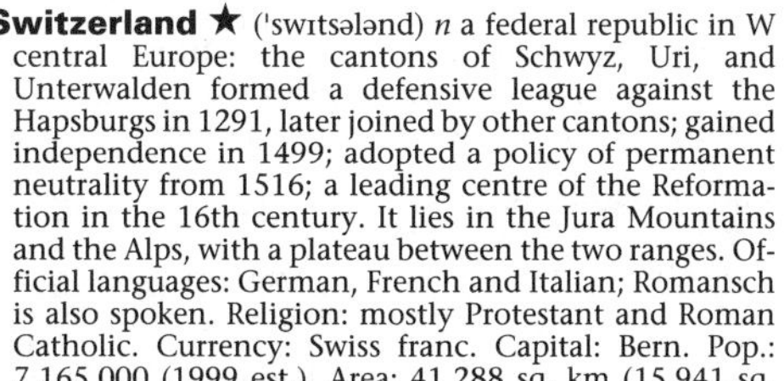

Switzerland ★ ('swɪtsələnd) *n* a federal republic in W central Europe: the cantons of Schwyz, Uri, and Unterwalden formed a defensive league against the Hapsburgs in 1291, later joined by other cantons; gained independence in 1499; adopted a policy of permanent neutrality from 1516; a leading centre of the Reformation in the 16th century. It lies in the Jura Mountains and the Alps, with a plateau between the two ranges. Official languages: German, French and Italian; Romansch is also spoken. Religion: mostly Protestant and Roman Catholic. Currency: Swiss franc. Capital: Bern. Pop.: 7 165 000 (1999 est.). Area: 41 288 sq. km (15 941 sq. miles). German name: **Schweiz.** French name: **Suisse.** Italian name: **Svizzera.** Romansch name: **Svizzra.** Latin name: **Helvetia** (hɛl'viːʃə).

swivel ('swɪvᵊl) *n* **1** a coupling device which allows an attached object to turn freely. **2** such a device made of two parts which turn independently, such as a compound link of a chain. **3a** a pivot on which is mounted a gun that may be swung horizontally from side to side. **3b** Also called: **swivel gun.** the gun itself. ◆ *vb* **swivels, swivelling, swivelled** *or US* **swivels, swiveling, swiveled. 4** to turn or swing on or as if on a pivot. **5** (*tr*) to provide with, secure by, or support with a swivel. ORIG C14: from OE *swīfan* to turn

swivel chair *n* a chair, the seat of which is joined to the legs by a swivel and which thus may be spun round.

swivel pin *n* another name for **kingpin** (sense 2).

swiz *or* **swizz** (swɪz) *n Brit. inf.* a swindle or disappointment; swizzle.

swizzle ('swɪzᵊl) *n* **1** an alcoholic drink containing gin or rum. **2** *Brit. inf.* a swiz. ◆ *vb* **swizzles, swizzling, swizzled. 3** (*tr*) to stir a swizzle stick in (a drink). **4** *Brit. inf.* to swindle; cheat. ORIG C19: from ?

swizzle stick *n* a small rod used to agitate an effervescent drink to facilitate the escape of carbon dioxide.

swob (swɒb) *n, vb* **swobs, swobbing, swobbed.** a less common word for **swab.**

swollen ('swəʊlən) *vb* **1** a past participle of **swell.** ◆ *adj* **2** tumid or enlarged as by swelling. **3** turgid or bombastic.
▸ **'swollenness** *n*

swoon (swuːn) *vb* (*intr*) **1** a literary word for **faint. 2** to become ecstatic. ◆ *n* **3** an instance of fainting. ◆ Also (archaic or dialect): **swound** (swaʊnd). ORIG OE *geswōgen* insensible, p.p. of *swōgan* (unattested except in compounds) suffocate
▸ **'swooning** *adj*

swoop (swuːp) *vb* **1** (*intr; usually foll. by down, on,* or *upon*) to sweep or pounce suddenly. **2** (*tr; often foll. by up, away,* or *off*) to seize or scoop suddenly. ◆ *n* **3** the act of swooping. **4** a swift descent. ORIG OE *swāpan* to sweep

swoosh (swʊʃ) *vb* **1** to make or cause to make a rustling or swirling sound, esp. when moving or pouring out. ◆ *n* **2** a swirling or rustling sound or movement. ORIG C20: imit.

swop (swɒp) *vb* **swops, swopping, swopped,** *n* a variant spelling of **swap.**

sword (sɔːd) *n* **1** a thrusting, striking, or cutting weapon with a long blade having one or two cutting edges, a hilt, and usually a crosspiece or guard. **2** such a weapon worn on ceremonial occasions as a symbol of authority. **3** something resembling a sword, such as the snout of a swordfish. **4 the sword. 4a** violence or power, esp. military power. **4b** death; destruction: *to put to the sword.* ORIG OE *sweord*

swordbearer ('sɔːdˌbɛərə) *n* an official who carries a ceremonial sword.

sword dance *n* a dance in which the performers dance nimbly over swords on the ground or brandish them in the air.
▸ **sword dancer** *n* ▸ **sword dancing** *n*

swordfish ('sɔːdˌfɪʃ) *n, pl* **swordfish** *or* **swordfishes.** a large fish with a very long upper jaw: valued as a food and game fish.

★ people and places

sword grass *n* any of various grasses and other plants having sword-shaped sharp leaves.

sword knot *n* a loop on the hilt of a sword by which it was attached to the wrist, now purely decorative.

sword lily *n* another name for **gladiolus.**

Sword of Damocles *n* a closely impending disaster. ORIG see DAMOCLES

swordplay ('sɔːdˌpleɪ) *n* **1** the action or art of fighting with a sword. **2** verbal sparring.

swordsman ('sɔːdzmən) *n, pl* **swordsmen.** one who uses or is skilled in the use of a sword.
▸ **'swordsmanship** *n*

swordstick ('sɔːdˌstɪk) *n* a hollow walking stick containing a short sword or dagger.

swordtail ('sɔːdˌteɪl) *n* any of several small freshwater fishes of Central America having a long swordlike tail.

swore (swɔː) *vb* the past tense of **swear.**

sworn (swɔːn) *vb* **1** the past participle of **swear.** ◆ *adj* **2** bound, pledged, or made inveterate, by or as if by an oath: *a sworn statement; he was sworn to God.*

swot[1] (swɒt) *Brit. inf.* ◆ *vb* **swots, swotting, swotted. 1** (often foll. by *up*) to study (a subject) intensively, as for an examination; cram. ◆ *n* **2** Also called: **swotter.** a person who works or studies hard. **3** hard work or grind. ◆ Also: **swat.** ORIG C19: var. of SWEAT (n)

swot[2] (swɒt) *vb* **swots, swotting, swotted,** *n* a variant of **swat.**

SWOT (swɒt) *n acronym for* strengths, weaknesses, opportunities, and threats: an analysis of a product made before it is marketed.

swounds *or* **'swounds** (zwaʊndz, zaʊndz) *interj Arch.* less common spellings of **zounds.**

swum (swʌm) *vb* the past participle of **swim.**

swung (swʌŋ) *vb* the past tense and past participle of **swing.**

swy (swaɪ) *n Austral.* another name for **two-up.** ORIG C20: from G *zwei* two

Sybaris ★ ('sɪbərɪs) *n* a Greek colony in S Italy, on the Gulf of Taranto: notorious for its luxurious living, founded about 720 B.C. and sacked in 510.
▸ **'Sybarite** *n* ▸ **Sybaritic** (ˌsɪbə'rɪtɪk) *adj*

sybarite ('sɪbəˌraɪt) *n* **1** (*sometimes cap.*) a devotee of luxury and the sensual vices. ◆ *adj* **2** luxurious; sensuous. ORIG C16: from L *Sybarīta,* from Gk *Subaritēs* inhabitant of SYBARIS
▸ **sybaritic** (ˌsɪbə'rɪtɪk) *adj* ▸ **ˌsyba'ritically** *adv*
▸ **'sybaritism** *n*

sycamore ('sɪkəˌmɔː) *n* **1** a Eurasian maple tree, naturalized in Britain and North America, having five-lobed leaves and two-winged fruits. **2** *US & Canad.* an American plane tree. See **plane tree. 3** a tree of N Africa and W Asia, having an edible figlike fruit. ORIG C14: from OF *sicamor,* from L *sȳcomorus,* from Gk, from *sukon* fig + *moron* mulberry

syconium (saɪ'kəʊnɪəm) *n, pl* **syconia** (-nɪə). *Bot.* the fleshy fruit of the fig, consisting of an enlarged receptacle. ORIG C19: from NL, from Gk *sukon* fig

sycophant ('sɪkəfənt) *n* a person who uses flattery to win favour from individuals wielding influence; toady. ORIG C16: from L *sȳcophanta,* from Gk *sukophantēs,* lit.: person showing a fig, apparently referring to the fig sign used in accusation, from *sukon* fig + *phainein* to show; sense prob. developed from "accuser" to "informer, flatterer"
▸ **'sycophancy** *n* ▸ **sycophantic** (ˌsɪkə'fæntɪk) *adj*
▸ **ˌsyco'phantically** *adv*

sycosis (saɪ'kəʊsɪs) *n* chronic inflammation of the hair follicles, esp. those of the beard. ORIG C16: via NL from Gk *sukōsis,* from *sukon* fig

Sydenham's chorea ('sɪdᵊnəmz) *n* a form of chorea affecting children, often associated with rheumatic fever. Nontechnical name: **Saint Vitus's dance.** ORIG after T. *Sydenham* (1624–89), E physician

Sydney[1] ★ ('sɪdnɪ) *n* **1** a port in SE Australia, capital of New South Wales, on an inlet of the S Pacific: the largest city in Australia and the first British settlement, established as a penal colony in 1788; developed rapidly after 1820 with the discovery of gold in its hinterland; large wool market; three universities. Pop.: 3 772 700 (1995 est.). **2** a port in SE Canada, in Nova Scotia on NE Cape Breton Island: capital of Cape Breton Island until 1820, when the island united administratively with Nova Scotia. Pop.: 26 063 (1991).

Sydney[2] ★ ('sɪdnɪ) *n* a variant spelling of (Sir Philip) **Sidney.**

Syene ★ (saɪ'iːnɪ) *n* transliteration of the Ancient Greek name for **Aswan.**

syenite ('saɪəˌnaɪt) *n* a light-coloured coarse-grained igneous rock consisting of feldspars with hornblende. ORIG C18: from F, from L *syēnītēs lapis* stone from *Syene* (Aswan), where orig. quarried
▸ **syenitic** (ˌsaɪə'nɪtɪk) *adj*

Syktyvkar ★ (*Russian* siktif'kar) *n* a city in NW Russia, capital of the Komi Republic: timber industry. Pop.: 229 000 (1995 est.).

syllabary ('sɪləbərɪ) *n, pl* **syllabaries. 1** a table or list of syllables. **2** a set of symbols used in certain writing systems, such as one used for Japanese, in which each symbol represents a spoken syllable. ORIG C16: from NL *syllabārium,* from L *syllaba* SYLLABLE

syllabi ('sɪləˌbaɪ) *n* a plural of **syllabus.**

syllabic (sɪ'læbɪk) *adj* **1** of or relating to syllables or the division of a word into syllables. **2** denoting a kind of verse line based on a specific number of syllables rather than being regulated by stresses or quantities. **3** (of a consonant) constituting a syllable. ◆ *n* **4** a syllabic consonant.
▸ **syl'labically** *adv*

syllabify (sɪ'læbɪˌfaɪ) *or* **syllabicate** *vb* **syllabifies, syllabifying, syllabified** *or* **syllabicates, syllabicating, syllabicated.** (*tr*) to divide (a word) into its constituent syllables.
▸ **sylˌlabifi'cation** *or* **sylˌlabi'cation** *n*

syllable ('sɪləbᵊl) *n* **1** a combination or set of one or more units of sound in a language that must consist of a sonorous element (a sonant or vowel) and may or may not contain less sonorous elements (consonants or semivowels) flanking it: for example "paper" has two syllables. **2** (in the writing systems of certain languages, esp. ancient ones) a symbol or set of symbols standing for a syllable. **3** the least mention: *don't breathe a syllable of it.* **4 in words of one syllable.** simply; bluntly. ◆ *vb* **syllables, syllabling, syllabled. 5** to pronounce syllables of (a text); articulate. **6** (*tr*) to write down in syllables. ORIG C14: via OF from L *syllaba,* from Gk *sullabē,* from *sullambanein* to collect together

syllabub *or* **sillabub** ('sɪləˌbʌb) *n* **1** a spiced drink made of milk with rum, port, brandy, or wine, often hot. **2** *Brit.* a cold dessert made from milk or cream beaten with sugar, wine, and lemon juice. ORIG C16: from ?

syllabus ('sɪləbəs) *n, pl* **syllabuses** *or* **syllabi** (-ˌbaɪ). **1** an outline of a course of studies, text, etc. **2** *Brit., Austral., & NZ.* **2a** the subjects studied for a particular course. **2b** a list of these subjects. ORIG C17: from LL, erroneously from L *sittybus* parchment strip giving title and author, from Gk *sittuba*

syllepsis (sɪ'lɛpsɪs) *n, pl* **syllepses** (-siːz). **1** (in grammar or rhetoric) the use of a single sentence construction in which a verb, adjective, etc., is made to cover two syntactical functions, as *have* in *she and they have promised to come.* **2** another word for **zeugma.** ORIG C16: from LL, from Gk *sullēpsis,* from *sul-* SYN- + *lēpsis,* from *lambanein* to take
▸ **syl'leptic** *adj* ▸ **syl'leptically** *adv*

syllogism ('sɪləˌdʒɪzəm) *n* **1** a deductive inference consisting of two premises and a conclusion, all of which are categorical propositions. The subject of the conclusion is the **minor term** and its predicate the **major term;** the **middle term** occurs in both premises but not the conclusion. There are 256 such arguments but only 24 are valid. *Some men are mortal; some men are angelic; so some mortals are angelic* is invalid, while *some temples are in ruins; all ruins are fascinating; so some temples are fascinating* is valid. Here *fascinating, in ruins,* and *temples* are respectively major, middle, and minor terms. **2** a piece of deductive reasoning from the general to the particular. ORIG C14:

via L from Gk *sullogismos,* from *sullogizesthai* to reckon together, from *logos* a discourse
▸ ˌ**syllo'gistic** *adj* ▸ **'sylloˌgize** *or* **'sylloˌgise** *vb*

sylph (sɪlf) *n* **1** a slender graceful girl or young woman. **2** any of a class of imaginary beings assumed to inhabit the air. ORIG C17: from NL *sylphus,* prob. coined from L *silva* wood + Gk *numphē* nymph
▸ **'sylphˌlike** *adj*

sylva *or* **silva** ('sɪlvə) *n, pl* **sylvas** *or* **sylvae** (-viː). the trees growing in a particular region. ORIG C17: from L *silva* a wood

sylvan *or* **silvan** ('sɪlvən) *Chiefly poetic.* ◆ *adj* **1** of or consisting of woods or forests. **2** in woods or forests. **3** idyllically rural or rustic. ◆ *n* **4** an inhabitant of the woods, esp. a spirit. ORIG C16: from L *silvānus,* from *silva* forest

sylvanite ('sɪlvəˌnaɪt) *n* a silver-white mineral consisting of a compound of tellurium with gold and silver in the form of elongated crystals. ORIG C18: from (TRAN)SYLVAN(IA) + -ITE[1], with reference to the region where first found

Sylvanus ★ (sɪl'veɪnəs) *n* a variant spelling of **Silvanus.**

Sylvester II ★ (sɪl'vɛstə) *n* original name *Gerbert of Aurillac. c.* 940–1003 A.D., French ecclesiastic and scholar; pope (999–1003): noted for his achievements in mathematics and astronomy.

sylviculture ('sɪlvɪˌkʌltʃə) *n* a variant spelling of **silviculture.**

sym- *prefix* a variant of **syn-** before *b, p,* and *m.*

symbiont ('sɪmbɪˌɒnt) *n* an organism living in a state of symbiosis. ORIG C19: from Gk *sumbioun* to live together, from *bioun* to live
▸ ˌ**symbi'ontic** *adj* ▸ ˌ**symbi'ontically** *adv*

symbiosis (ˌsɪmbɪ'əʊsɪs) *n* **1** a close association of two interdependent animal or plant species. **2** a similar relationship between persons or groups. ORIG C19: via NL from Gk: a living together
▸ ˌ**symbi'otic** *adj*

symbol ('sɪmbᵊl) *n* **1** something that represents or stands for something else, usually by convention or association, esp. a material object used to represent something abstract. **2** an object, person, etc., used in a literary work, film, etc., to stand for or suggest something else with which it is associated. **3** a letter, figure, or sign used in mathematics, music, etc., to represent a quantity, phenomenon, operation, function, etc. ◆ *vb* **symbols, symbolling, symbolled** *or US* **symbols, symboling, symboled. 4** (*tr*) another word for **symbolize.** ORIG C15: from Church L *symbolum,* from Gk *sumbolon* sign, from *sumballein* to throw together, from SYN- + *ballein* to throw

symbolic (sɪm'bɒlɪk) *or* **symbolical** *adj* **1** of or relating to a symbol or symbols. **2** serving as a symbol. **3** characterized by the use of symbols or symbolism.
▸ **sym'bolically** *adv*

symbolic logic *n* another name for **formal logic.**

symbolism ('sɪmbəˌlɪzəm) *n* **1** the representation of something in symbolic form or the attribution of symbolic character to something. **2** a system of symbols or symbolic representation. **3** a symbolic significance or quality. **4** (*often cap.*) a late 19th-century movement in art that sought to express mystical or abstract ideas through the symbolic use of images.

symbolist ('sɪmbəlɪst) *n* **1** a person who uses or can interpret symbols, esp. as a means to revealing aspects of truth and reality. **2** an artist or writer who practises symbolism in his or her work. **3** (*usually cap.*) a writer associated with the symbolist movement. **4** (*often cap.*) an artist associated with the symbolist movement. ◆ *adj* **5** of, relating to, or characterizing symbolism or symbolists.
▸ ˌ**symbol'istic** *adj* ▸ ˌ**symbol'istically** *adv*

symbolist movement *n* (*usually cap.*) a movement beginning in French and Belgian poetry towards the end of the 19th century with Mallarmé, Valéry, Verlaine, Rimbaud, and others, and seeking to express states of mind rather than objective reality by the power of words and images to suggest as well as denote.

symbolize *or* **symbolise** ('sɪmbəˌlaɪz) *vb* **symbolizes, symbolizing, symbolized** *or* **symbolises, symbolising, symbolised. 1** (*tr*) to serve as or be a symbol of. **2** (*tr; usually foll. by by*) to represent by a symbol or symbols. **3** (*intr*) to use symbols. **4** (*tr*) to treat or regard as symbolic.
▸ ˌ**symboli'zation** *or* ˌ**symboli'sation** *n*

symbol retailer *n* any member of a voluntary group of independent retailers, often using a common name or symbol, formed to obtain better prices from wholesalers or manufacturers in competition with supermarket chains. Also called: **voluntary retailer.**

symmetrical (sɪ'mɛtrɪkᵊl) *adj* possessing or displaying symmetry.

symmetry ('sɪmɪtrɪ) *n, pl* **symmetries. 1** similarity, correspondence, or balance among systems or parts of a system. **2** *Maths.* an exact correspondence in position or form about a given point, line, or plane. **3** beauty or harmony of form based on a proportionate arrangement of parts. ORIG C16: from L *symmetria,* from Gk *summetria* proportion, from SYN- + *metron* measure

Symonds ★ ('sɪməndz) *n* **John Addington** ('ædɪŋtən). 1840–93, British writer, noted for his *Renaissance in Italy* (1875–86) and for studies of homosexuality.

Symons ★ ('saɪmənz) *n* **Arthur.** 1865–1945, British poet and critic, who helped to introduce the French symbolists to England.

sympathectomy (ˌsɪmpə'θɛktəmɪ) *n, pl* **sympathectomies.** the surgical excision or chemical destruction (**chemical sympathectomy**) of one or more parts of the sympathetic nervous system. ORIG C20: from SYMPATHETIC + -ECTOMY

sympathetic (ˌsɪmpə'θɛtɪk) *adj* **1** characterized by, feeling, or showing sympathy; understanding. **2** in accord with the subject's personality or mood; congenial: *a sympathetic atmosphere.* **3** (when *postpositive,* often foll. by *to* or *towards*) showing agreement (with) or favour (towards). **4** *Anat., physiol.* of or relating to the division of the autonomic nervous system that acts in opposition to the parasympathetic system accelerating the heartbeat, dilating the bronchi, inhibiting the smooth muscles of the digestive tract, etc. Cf. **parasympathetic. 5** relating to vibrations occurring as a result of similar vibrations in a neighbouring body: *sympathetic strings on a sitar.*
▸ ˌ**sympa'thetically** *adv*

sympathetic magic *n* a type of magic in which it is sought to produce a large-scale effect, often at a distance, by performing some small-scale ceremony resembling it, such as the pouring of water on an altar to induce rainfall.

sympathize *or* **sympathise** ('sɪmpəˌθaɪz) *vb* **sympathizes, sympathizing, sympathized** *or* **sympathises, sympathising, sympathised.** (*intr;* often foll. by *with*) **1** to feel or express compassion or sympathy (for); commiserate: *he sympathized with my troubles.* **2** to share or understand the sentiments or ideas (of); be in sympathy (with).
▸ **'sympaˌthizer** *or* **'sympaˌthiser** *n*

sympatholytic (ˌsɪmpəθəʊ'lɪtɪk) *Med.* ◆ *adj* **1a** inhibiting or antagonistic to nerve impulses of the sympathetic nervous system. **1b** of or relating to such inhibition. ◆ *n* **2** a sympatholytic drug. Cf. **sympathomimetic.** ORIG C20: from SYMPATH(ETIC) + -LYTIC

sympathomimetic (ˌsɪmpəθəʊmɪ'mɛtɪk) *Med.* ◆ *adj* **1** causing a physiological effect similar to that produced by stimulation of the sympathetic nervous system. ◆ *n* **2** a sympathomimetic drug. Cf. **sympatholytic.** ORIG C20: from SYMPATH(ETIC) + MIMETIC

sympathy ('sɪmpəθɪ) *n, pl* **sympathies. 1** the sharing of another's emotions, esp. of sorrow or anguish; compassion. **2** affinity or harmony, usually of feelings or interests, between persons or things: *to be in sympathy with someone.* **3** mutual affection or understanding arising from such a relationship. **4** the condition of a physical system or body when its behaviour is similar or corresponds to that of a different system that influences it, such as the vibration of sympathetic strings. **5** (*sometimes pl*) a feeling of loyalty, support, or accord, as for an idea, cause, etc. **6** *Physiol.* the relationship between two organs or parts whereby a change in one affects the other. ORIG C16: from L *sympathīa,* from Gk, from *sumpathēs,* from SYN- + *pathos* suffering

sympathy strike *n* a strike organized in support of another strike or cause. Also called: **sympathetic strike.**

symphonic poem *n Music.* an extended orchestral composition, originated by Liszt, based on nonmusical material, such as a work of literature or folk tale. Also called: **tone poem.**

symphony ('sɪmfənɪ) *n, pl* **symphonies. 1** an extended large-scale orchestral composition, usually with several movements, at least one of which is in sonata form. **2** a piece of instrumental music in up to three very short movements, used as an overture to or interlude in a baroque opera. **3** any purely orchestral movement in a vocal work, such as a cantata or oratorio. **4** short for **symphony orchestra. 5** anything distinguished by a harmonious composition: *the picture was a symphony of green.* **6** *Arch.* harmony in general; concord. ORIG C13: from OF *symphonie,* from L *symphōnia* concord, from Gk, from SYN- + *phōnē* sound
▸ **symphonic** (sɪm'fɒnɪk) *adj* ▸ **sym'phonically** *adv*

symphony orchestra *n Music.* an orchestra capable of performing symphonies, esp. a large orchestra comprising strings, brass, woodwind, harp and percussion.

symphysis ('sɪmfɪsɪs) *n, pl* **symphyses** (-ˌsiːz). **1** *Anat., bot.* a growing together of parts or structures, such as two bony surfaces joined by an intermediate layer of fibrous cartilage. **2** a line marking this growing together. **3** *Pathol.* an abnormal adhesion of two or more parts or structures. ORIG C16: via NL from Gk *sumphusis,* from *sumphuein,* from SYN- + *phuein* to grow
▸ **symphysial** *or* **symphyseal** (sɪm'fɪzɪəl) *adj*

sympodium (sɪm'pəʊdɪəm) *n, pl* **sympodia** (-dɪə). the main axis of growth in the grapevine and similar plants: a number of lateral branches that arise from just behind the apex of the main stem, which ceases to grow. ORIG C19: from NL, from SYN- + Gk *podion* a little foot
▸ **sym'podial** *adj* ▸ **sym'podially** *adv*

symposium (sɪm'pəʊzɪəm) *n, pl* **symposiums** *or* **symposia** (-zɪə). **1** a conference or meeting for the discussion of some subject, esp. an academic topic or social problem. **2** a collection of scholarly contributions on a given subject. **3** (in classical Greece) a drinking party with intellectual conversation, music, etc. ORIG C16: via L from Gk *symposion,* from *sumpinein* to drink together

symptom ('sɪmptəm) *n* **1** *Med.* any sensation or change in bodily function experienced by a patient that is associated with a particular disease. **2** any phenomenon or circumstance accompanying something and regarded as evidence of its existence; indication. ORIG C16: from LL *symptōma,* from Gk *sumptōma* chance, from *sumpiptein* to occur, from SYN- + *piptein* to fall

symptomatic (ˌsɪmptə'mætɪk) *adj* **1** (often foll. by *of*) being a symptom; indicative: *symptomatic of insanity.* **2** of, relating to, or according to symptoms: *a symptomatic analysis.*
▸ **ˌsympto'matically** *adv*

symptomatology (ˌsɪmptəmə'tɒlədʒɪ) *n* the branch of medicine concerned with the study and classification of the symptoms of disease.

syn. *abbrev. for* synonym(ous).

syn- *prefix* **1** with or together: *synecology.* **2** fusion: *syngamy.* ORIG from Gk *sun* together

synaeresis (sɪ'nɪərɪsɪs) *n* a variant spelling of **syneresis.**

synaesthesia *or US* **synesthesia** (ˌsɪniːs'θiːzɪə) *n* **1** *Physiol.* a sensation experienced in a part of the body other than the part stimulated. **2** *Psychol.* the subjective sensation of a sense other than the one being stimulated. ORIG C19: from NL, from SYN- + *-esthesia,* from Gk *aisthēsis* sensation
▸ **synaesthetic** *or US* **synesthetic** (ˌsɪniːs'θetɪk) *adj*

synagogue ('sɪnəˌgɒg) *n* **1a** a building for Jewish religious services and religious instruction. **1b** (*as modifier*): *synagogue services.* **2** a congregation of Jews who assemble for worship or religious study. **3** the religion of Judaism as organized in such congregations. ORIG C12: from OF, from LL *synagōga,* from Gk *sunagōgē* a gathering, from *sunagein* to bring together
▸ **synagogical** (ˌsɪnə'gɒdʒɪkᵊl) *or* **synagogal** ('sɪnəˌgɒgᵊl) *adj*

synapse ('saɪnæps) *n* the point at which a nerve impulse is relayed from the terminal portion of an axon to the dendrites of an adjacent neuron.

synapsis (sɪ'næpsɪs) *n, pl* **synapses** (-siːz). **1** *Cytology.* the association in pairs of homologous chromosomes at the start of meiosis. **2** another word for **synapse.** ORIG C19: from NL, from Gk *sunapsis* junction, from *sunaptein* to join together
▸ **synaptic** (sɪ'næptɪk) *adj* ▸ **syn'aptically** *adv*

synarthrosis (ˌsɪnɑː'θrəʊsɪs) *n, pl* **synarthroses** (-siːz). *Anat.* any of various joints which lack a synovial cavity and are virtually immovable; a fixed joint. ORIG C16: via NL from Gk *sunarthrōsis,* from *sunarthrousthai* to be connected by joints, from *sun-* SYN- + *arthron* a joint
▸ **ˌsynar'throdial** *adj*

sync *or* **synch** (sɪŋk) *Films, television, computing.* ◆ *vb* **1** an informal word for **synchronize.** ◆ *n* **2** an informal word for **synchronization** (esp. in **in** *or* **out of sync**).

syncarp ('sɪnkɑːp) *n Bot.* a fleshy multiple fruit, formed from two or more carpels of one flower or the aggregated fruits of several flowers. ORIG C19: from NL *syncarpium,* from SYN- + Gk *karpos* fruit

syncarpous (sɪn'kɑːpəs) *adj* **1** (of the ovaries of certain flowering plants) consisting of united carpels. **2** of or relating to a syncarp.

synchro ('sɪŋkrəʊ) *n, pl* **synchros. 1** Also called: **selsyn.** any of a number of electrical devices in which the angular position of a rotating part is transformed into a voltage, or vice versa. **2** short for **synchronized swimming.**

synchro- *combining form.* indicating synchronization: *synchromesh.*

synchrocyclotron (ˌsɪŋkrəʊ'saɪkləˌtrɒn) *n* a cyclotron in which the frequency of the electric field is modulated to allow for relativistic effects at high velocities and thus produce higher energies.

synchromesh ('sɪŋkrəʊˌmɛʃ) *adj* **1** (of a gearbox, etc.) having a system of clutches that synchronizes the speeds of the driving and driven members before engagement to avoid shock in gear changing and to reduce noise and wear. ◆ *n* **2** a gear system having these features. ORIG C20: shortened from *synchronized mesh*

synchronic (sɪn'krɒnɪk) *adj* **1** concerned with the events or phenomena at a particular period without considering historical antecedents: *synchronic linguistics.* Cf. **diachronic. 2** synchronous.
▸ **syn'chronically** *adv* ▸ **synchronicity** (ˌsɪnkrə'nɪsɪtɪ) *n*

synchronicity (ˌsɪŋkrə'nɪsɪtɪ) *n* an apparently meaningful coincidence in time of two or more similar or identical events that are causally unrelated. ORIG C20: coined by Carl Jung from SYNCHRONIC + -ITY

synchronism ('sɪŋkrəˌnɪzəm) *n* **1** the quality or condition of being synchronous. **2** a chronological list of historical persons and events, arranged to show parallel or synchronous occurrence. **3** the representation in a work of art of one or more incidents that occurred at separate times. ORIG C16: from Gk *sunkhronismos*
▸ **ˌsynchro'nistic** *or* **ˌsynchro'nistical** *adj* ▸ **ˌsynchro'nistically** *adv*

synchronize *or* **synchronise** ('sɪŋkrəˌnaɪz) *vb* **synchronizes, synchronizing, synchronized** *or* **synchronises, synchronising, synchronised. 1** (when *intr,* usually foll. by *with*) to occur or recur or cause to occur or recur at the same time or in unison. **2** to indicate or cause to indicate the same time: *synchronize your watches.* **3** (*tr*) *Films.* to establish (the picture and soundtrack records) in their correct relative position. **4** (*tr*) to designate (events) as simultaneous.
▸ **ˌsynchroni'zation** *or* **ˌsynchroni'sation** *n* ▸ **'synchroˌnizer** *or* **'synchroˌniser** *n*

synchronized swimming *n* a sport in which swimmers move in patterns in time to music. Sometimes shortened to **synchro** *or* **synchro swimming.**

synchronous ('sɪŋkrənəs) *adj* **1** occurring at the same time. **2** *Physics.* (of periodic phenomena, such as voltages) having the same frequency and phase. **3** occurring or recurring exactly together and at the same rate. ORIG C17: from LL *synchronus,* from Gk *sunkhronos,* from SYN- + *khronos* time
▸ **'synchronously** *adv* ▸ **'synchronousness** *n*

synchronous machine *n* an electrical machine whose rotating speed is proportional to the frequency of the alternating-current supply and independent of the load.

synchronous motor *n* an alternating-current motor that runs at a speed that is equal to or is a multiple of the frequency of the supply.

synchrony ('sɪŋkrənɪ) *n* the state of being synchronous; simultaneity.

synchrotron ('sɪŋkrəˌtrɒn) *n* a particle accelerator having an electric field of fixed frequency and a changing magnetic field. ORIG C20: from SYNCHRO- + (ELEC)TRON

syncline ('sɪŋklaɪn) *n* a downward fold of stratified rock in which the strata slope towards a vertical axis. ORIG C19: from SYN- + Gk *klīnein* to lean
▸ **syn'clinal** *adj*

Syncom ('sɪnˌkɒm) *n* a communications satellite in stationary orbit. ORIG C20: from *syn(chronous) com(munication)*

syncopate ('sɪŋkəˌpeɪt) *vb* **syncopates, syncopating, syncopated.** (*tr*) **1** *Music.* to modify or treat (a beat, rhythm, note, etc.) by syncopation. **2** to shorten (a word) by omitting sounds or letters from the middle. ORIG C17: from Med. L *syncopāre* to omit a letter or syllable, from LL *syncopa* SYNCOPE
▸ **'syncoˌpator** *n*

syncopation (ˌsɪŋkə'peɪʃən) *n* **1** *Music.* **1a** the displacement of the usual rhythmic accent away from a strong beat onto a weak beat. **1b** a note, beat, rhythm, etc., produced by syncopation. **2** another word for **syncope** (sense 2).

syncope ('sɪŋkəpɪ) *n* **1** a technical word for a **faint. 2** the omission of sounds or letters from the middle of a word. ORIG C16: from LL *syncopa,* from Gk *sunkopē* a cutting off, from SYN- + *koptein* to cut
▸ **syncopic** (sɪŋ'kɒpɪk) *or* **'syncopal** *adj*

syncretism ('sɪŋkrɪˌtɪzəm) *n* **1** the tendency to syncretize. **2** the historical tendency of languages to reduce their use of inflection, as in the development of Old English into Modern English. ORIG C17: from NL *syncrētismus,* from Gk *sunkrētismos* alliance of Cretans, from *sunkrētizein* to join forces (in the manner of the Cretan towns), from SYN- + *Krēs* a Cretan
▸ **syncretic** (sɪŋ'krɛtɪk) *or* ˌ**syncre'tistic** *adj* ▸ **'syncretist** *n*

syncretize *or* **syncretise** ('sɪŋkrɪˌtaɪz) *vb* **syncretizes, syncretizing, syncretized** *or* **syncretises, syncretising, syncretised.** to attempt to combine the characteristic teachings, beliefs, or practices of (differing systems of religion or philosophy).
▸ ˌ**syncreti'zation** *or* ˌ**syncreti'sation** *n*

syndactyl (sɪn'dæktɪl) *adj* **1** (of certain animals) having two or more digits growing fused together. ◆ *n* **2** an animal with this arrangement of digits.
▸ **syn'dactylism** *n*

syndesmosis (ˌsɪndɛs'məʊsɪs) *n, pl* **syndesmoses** (-siːz). *Anat.* a type of joint in which the articulating bones are held together by a ligament of connective tissue. ORIG C18: NL, from Gk *sundein* to bind together
▸ **syndesmotic** (ˌsɪndɛs'mɒtɪk) *adj*

syndetic (sɪn'dɛtɪk) *adj* denoting a grammatical construction in which two clauses are connected by a conjunction. ORIG C17: from Gk *sundetikos,* from *sundetos* bound together
▸ **syndesis** (sɪn'diːsɪs) *n* ▸ **syn'detically** *adv*

syndic ('sɪndɪk) *n* **1** *Brit.* a business agent of some universities or other bodies. **2** (in several countries) a government administrator or magistrate with varying powers. ORIG C17: via OF from LL *syndicus,* from Gk *sundikos* defendant's advocate, from SYN- + *dikē* justice
▸ **'syndical** *adj*

syndicalism ('sɪndɪkəˌlɪzəm) *n* **1** a revolutionary movement and theory advocating seizure of the means of production and distribution by syndicates of workers, esp. by a general strike. **2** an economic system resulting from such action.
▸ **'syndical** *adj* ▸ **'syndicalist** *adj, n* ▸ ˌ**syndical'istic** *adj*

syndicate *n* ('sɪndɪkɪt). **1** an association of business enterprises or individuals organized to undertake a joint project. **2** a news agency that sells articles, photographs, etc., to a number of newspapers for simultaneous publication. **3** any association formed to carry out an enterprise of common interest to its members. **4** a board of syndics or the office of syndic. ◆ *vb* ('sɪndɪˌkeɪt) **syndicates, syndicating, syndicated. 5** (*tr*) to sell (articles, photographs, etc.) to several newspapers for simultaneous publication. **6** (*tr*) *US.* to sell (a programme or programmes) to several local commercial stations. **7** to form a syndicate of (people). ORIG C17: from OF *syndicat* office of a SYNDIC
▸ ˌ**syndi'cation** *n*

syndicated research *n Marketing.* a large-scale marketing research project undertaken without being commissioned and subsequently offered to interested parties.

syndrome ('sɪndrəʊm) *n* **1** *Med.* any combination of signs and symptoms that are indicative of a particular disease or disorder. **2** a symptom, characteristic, or set of symptoms or characteristics indicating the existence of a condition, problem, etc. ORIG C16: via NL from Gk *sundromē,* lit.: a running together, from SYN- + *dramein* to run
▸ **syndromic** (sɪn'drɒmɪk) *adj*

syne *or* **syn** (saɪn) *adv, prep, conj* a Scottish word for **since.** ORIG C14: prob. rel. to OE *sīth* since

synecdoche (sɪn'ɛkdəkɪ) *n* a figure of speech in which a part is substituted for a whole or a whole for a part, as in *50 head of cattle* for *50 cows,* or *the army* for *a soldier.* ORIG C14: via L from Gk *sunekdokhē,* from SYN- + *ekdokhē* interpretation, from *dekhesthai* to accept
▸ **synecdochic** (ˌsɪnɛk'dɒkɪk) *or* ˌ**synec'dochical** *adj*

synecious (sɪ'niːʃəs) *adj* a variant spelling of **synoecious.**

synecology (ˌsɪnɪ'kɒlədʒɪ) *n* the ecological study of communities of plants and animals.
▸ **synecologic** (sɪnˌɛkə'lɒdʒɪk) *or* **synˌeco'logical** *adj*
▸ **synˌeco'logically** *adv*

syneresis *or* **synaeresis** (sɪ'nɪərɪsɪs) *n* **1** *Chem.* the process in which a gel contracts on standing and exudes liquid, as in the separation of whey in cheese-making. **2** the contraction of two vowels into a diphthong. ORIG C16: via LL from Gk *sunairesis* a shortening, from *sunairein* to draw together, from SYN- + *hairein* to take

synergism ('sɪnəˌdʒɪzəm, sɪ'nɜː-) *n* **1** Also called: **synergy.** the working together of two or more drugs, muscles, etc., to produce an effect greater than the sum of their individual effects. **2** another name for **synergy** (sense 1). ORIG C18: from NL *synergismus,* from Gk *sunergos,* from SYN- + *ergon* work
▸ ˌ**syner'getic** *adj* ▸ **'synergist** *n, adj*

synergy ('sɪnədʒɪ) *n, pl* **synergies. 1** Also called: **synergism.** the potential ability of individual organizations or groups to be more successful or productive as a result of a merger. **2** another name for **synergism** (sense 1). ORIG C19: from NL *synergia,* from Gk *sunergos;* see SYNERGISM
▸ **sy'nergic** *adj*

synesis ('sɪnɪsɪs) *n* a grammatical construction in which the inflection or form of a word is conditioned by the meaning rather than the syntax, as for example the plural form *have* with the singular noun *group* in the sentence *the group have already assembled.* ORIG via NL from Gk *sunesis* union, from *sunienai* to bring together, from SYN- + *hienai* to send

synesthesia (ˌsɪniːs'θiːzɪə) *n* the usual US spelling of **synaesthesia.**

syngamy ('sɪŋgəmɪ) *or* **syngenesis** (sɪn'dʒɛnɪsɪs) *n* reproduction involving the fusion of a male and female haploid gamete. Also called: **sexual reproduction.**
▸ **syngamic** (sɪŋ'gæmɪk) *or* **syngamous** ('sɪŋgəməs) *adj*

Synge ★ (sɪŋ) *n* **John Millington.** 1871–1909, Irish playwright. His plays, marked by vivid colloquial Irish speech, include *Riders to the Sea* (1904) and *The Playboy of the Western World,* produced amidst uproar at the Abbey Theatre, Dublin, in 1907.

synod ('sɪnəd, 'sɪnɒd) *n* **1** a special ecclesiastical council, esp. of a diocese, formally convened to discuss ecclesiastical affairs. **2** *Rare.* any council, esp. for discussion. ORIG C14: from LL *synodus,* from Gk SYN- + *hodos* a way
▸ **'synodal** *adj*

synodic (sɪˈnɒdɪk) *adj* relating to or involving a conjunction or two successive conjunctions of the same star, planet, or satellite.

synodic month *n* See **month** (sense 6).

synoecious *or* **synecious** (sɪˈniːʃəs) *adj* (of plants) having male and female organs on the same flower or structure. ORIG C19: SYN- + *-oecious,* from Gk *oikion* dim. of *oikos* house

synonym (ˈsɪnənɪm) *n* **1** a word that means the same or nearly the same as another word, such as *bucket* and *pail.* **2** a word or phrase used as another name for something, such as *Hellene* for a *Greek.*
▸ **ˌsynoˈnymic** *or* **ˌsynoˈnymical** *adj* ▸ **ˌsynoˈnymity** *n*

synonymous (sɪˈnɒnɪməs) *adj* **1** (often foll. by *with*) being a synonym (of). **2** (*postpositive;* foll. by *with*) closely associated (with) or suggestive (of): *his name was synonymous with greed.*
▸ **synˈonymously** *adv* ▸ **synˈonymousness** *n*

synonymy (sɪˈnɒnɪmɪ) *n, pl* **synonymies. 1** the study of synonyms. **2** the character of being synonymous; equivalence. **3** a list or collection of synonyms, esp. one in which their meanings are discriminated.

synopsis (sɪˈnɒpsɪs) *n, pl* **synopses** (-siːz). a brief review of a subject; summary. ORIG C17: via LL from Gk *sunopsis,* from SYN- + *opsis* view

synopsize *or* **synopsise** (sɪˈnɒpsaɪz) *vb* **synopsizes, synopsizing, synopsized** *or* **synopsises, synopsising, synopsised.** (*tr*) **1** *US.* variants of **epitomize. 2** *US & Canad.* to make a synopsis of.

synoptic (sɪˈnɒptɪk) *adj* **1** of or relating to a synopsis. **2** (*often cap.*) *Bible.* **2a** (of the Gospels of Matthew, Mark, and Luke) presenting the narrative of Christ's life, ministry, etc., from a point of view held in common by all three, and with close similarities in content, order, etc. **2b** of or relating to these three Gospels. **3** *Meteorol.* concerned with the distribution of meteorological conditions over a wide area at a given time: *a synoptic chart.* ◆ *n* **4** (*often cap.*) *Bible.* **4a** any of the three synoptic Gospels. **4b** any of the authors of these. ORIG C18: from Gk *sunoptikos*
▸ **synˈoptically** *adv* ▸ **synˈoptist** *n*

synovia (saɪˈnəʊvɪə, sɪ-) *n* a transparent viscid lubricating fluid, secreted by the membrane lining joints, tendon sheaths, etc. ORIG C17: from NL, prob. from SYN- + L *ōvum* egg
▸ **synˈovial** *adj*

synovitis (ˌsaɪnəʊˈvaɪtɪs, ˌsɪn-) *n* inflammation of the membrane surrounding a joint.
▸ **synovitic** (ˌsaɪnəʊˈvɪtɪk, ˌsɪn-) *adj*

synroc (ˈsɪnˌrɒk) *n* a titanium-ceramic substance that can incorporate nuclear waste in its crystals. ORIG from *syn(thetic)* + *roc(k)*

syntactics (sɪnˈtæktɪks) *n* (*functioning as sing*) the branch of semiotics that deals with the formal properties of symbol systems; proof theory.

syntagma (sɪnˈtægmə) *or* **syntagm** (ˈsɪnˌtæm) *n, pl* **syntagmata** (-ˈtægmətə) *or* **syntagms. 1** a word or phrase forming a syntactic unit. **2** a systematic collection of statements or propositions. ORIG C17: from LL, from Gk, from *suntassein* to put in order; see SYNTAX
▸ **ˌsyntagˈmatic** *adj*

syntax (ˈsɪntæks) *n* **1** the branch of linguistics that deals with the grammatical arrangement of words and morphemes in sentences. **2** the totality of facts about the grammatical arrangement of words in a language. **3** a systematic statement of the rules governing the grammatical arrangement of words and morphemes in a language. **4** a systematic statement of the rules governing the properly formed formulas of a logical system. ORIG C17: from LL *syntaxis,* from Gk *suntaxis,* from *suntassein* to put in order, from SYN- + *tassein* to arrange
▸ **synˈtactic** *or* **synˈtactical** *adj* ▸ **synˈtactically** *adv*

synth (sɪnθ) *n* short for **synthesizer.**

synthesis (ˈsɪnθɪsɪs) *n, pl* **syntheses** (-ˌsiːz). **1** the process of combining objects or ideas into a complex whole. **2** the combination or whole produced by such a process. **3** the process of producing a compound by a chemical reaction or series of reactions, usually from simpler starting materials. **4** *Linguistics.* the use of inflections rather than word order and function words to express the syntactic relations in a language. ORIG C17: via L from Gk *sunthesis,* from *suntithenai* to put together, from SYN- + *tithenai* to place
▸ **ˈsynthesist** *n*

synthesis gas *n Chem.* **1** a mixture of carbon dioxide, carbon monoxide, and hydrogen formerly made by reacting water gas with steam to enrich the proportion of hydrogen in the synthesis of ammonia. **2** a similar mixture of gases made by steam reforming natural gas, used for synthesizing organic chemicals and as a fuel.

synthesize (ˈsɪnθɪˌsaɪz), **synthetize,** *or* **synthesise, synthetise** *vb* **synthesizes, synthesizing, synthesized; synthetizes, synthetizing, synthetized** *or* **synthesises, synthesising, synthesised; synthetises, synthetising, synthetised. 1** to combine or cause to combine into a whole. **2** (*tr*) to produce by synthesis.
▸ **ˌsynthesiˈzation, ˌsynthetiˈzation** *or* **ˌsynthesiˈsation, ˌsynthetiˈsation** *n*

synthesizer (ˈsɪnθɪˌsaɪzə) *n* **1** an electronic musical instrument, usually operated by means of a keyboard, in which sounds are produced by oscillators, filters, and amplifiers. **2** a person or thing that synthesizes.

synthetic (sɪnˈθɛtɪk) *adj also* **synthetical. 1** (of a substance or material) made artificially by chemical reaction. **2** not genuine; insincere: *synthetic compassion.* **3** denoting languages, such as Latin, whose morphology is characterized by synthesis. **4** *Philosophy.* **4a** (of a proposition) having a truth-value that is not determined solely by virtue of the meanings of the words, as in *all men are arrogant.* **4b** contingent. ◆ *n* **5** a synthetic substance or material. ORIG C17: from NL *syntheticus,* from Gk *sunthetikos* expert in putting together, from *suntithenai* to put together; see SYNTHESIS
▸ **synˈthetically** *adv*

syphilis (ˈsɪfɪlɪs) *n* a sexually transmitted disease caused by infection with the microorganism *Treponema pallidum:* characterized by an ulcerating chancre, usually on the genitals and progressing through the lymphatic system to nearly all tissues of the body, producing serious clinical manifestations. ORIG C18: from NL *Syphilis* (*sive Morbus Gallicus*) "Syphilis (or the French disease)", title of a poem (1530) by G. Fracastoro, It. physician and poet, in which a shepherd *Syphilus* is portrayed as the first victim of the disease
▸ **syphilitic** (ˌsɪfɪˈlɪtɪk) *adj* ▸ **ˈsyphiˌloid** *adj*

syphon (ˈsaɪfᵊn) *n, vb* a variant spelling of **siphon.**

Syr. *abbrev. for:* **1** Syria. **2** Syriac. **3** Syrian.

Syracuse ★ *n* **1** (ˈsaɪrəˌkjuːz). a port in SW Italy, in SE Sicily on the Ionian Sea: founded in 734 B.C. by Greeks from Corinth and taken by the Romans in 212 B.C., after a siege of three years. Pop.: 127 448 (1996 est.). Italian name: **Siracusa. 2** (ˈsɪrəˌkjuːs). a city in central New York State, on Lake Onondaga: site of the capital of the Iroquois Indian federation. Pop.: 159 895 (1994 est.).

Syrah (ˈsaɪrə) **1** a red grape grown in France and Australia, used, often in a blend, for making wine. **2** any of various wines made from this grape. ◆ Australian name: **Shiraz.** ORIG from SHIRAZ[1], the city in Iran where the wine supposedly originated

Syr Darya ★ (*Russian* si darjˈja) *n* a river in central Asia, formed from two headstreams rising in the Tian Shan: flows generally west to the Aral Sea: the longest river in central Asia. Length: (from the source of the Naryn) 2900 km (1800 miles). Ancient name: **Jaxartes.**

Syria ★ (ˈsɪrɪə) *n* **1** a republic in W Asia, on the Mediterranean: ruled by the Ottoman Turks (1516–1918); made a French mandate in 1920; became independent in 1944; joined Egypt in the United Arab Republic (1958–61). Official language: Arabic. Religion: Muslim majority. Currency: Syrian pound. Capital: Damascus. Pop.: 15 727 000 (1999 est.). Area: 185 180 sq. km (71 498 sq. miles). **2** (formerly) the region between the Mediterranean, the Euphrates, the Taurus, and the Arabian Desert.

Syriac (ˈsɪrɪˌæk) *n* a dialect of Aramaic spoken in Syria until about the 13th century A.D.

Syrian (ˈsɪrɪən) *adj* **1** of or relating to Syria, its people, or their dialect of Arabic. ◆ *n* **2** a native or inhabitant of Syria.

syringa (sɪˈrɪŋɡə) *n* another name for **mock orange** (sense 1) or **lilac** (sense 1). ORIG C17: from NL, from Gk *surinx* tube, from use of its hollow stems for pipes

syringe (ˈsɪrɪndʒ, sɪˈrɪndʒ) *n* **1** *Med.* a hypodermic syringe or a rubber ball with a slender nozzle, for use in withdrawing or injecting fluids, cleaning wounds, etc. **2** any similar device for injecting, spraying, or extracting liquids by means of pressure or suction. ◆ *vb* **syringes, syringing, syringed. 3** (*tr*) to cleanse, inject, or spray with a syringe. ORIG C15: from LL, from L: SYRINX

syringomyelia (səˌrɪŋɡəʊmaɪˈiːlɪə) *n* a chronic progressive disease of the spinal cord in which cavities form in the grey matter: characterized by loss of the sense of pain and temperature. ORIG C19: *syringo-*, from Gk: SYRINX + *-myelia* from Gk *muelos* marrow
▸ **syringomyelic** (səˌrɪŋɡəʊmaɪˈɛlɪk) *adj*

syrinx (ˈsɪrɪŋks) *n, pl* **syringes** (sɪˈrɪndʒiːz) *or* **syrinxes. 1** the vocal organ of a bird, situated in the lower part of the trachea. **2** (in classical Greek music) a panpipe or set of panpipes. ORIG C17: via L from Gk *surinx* pipe
▸ **syringeal** (sɪˈrɪndʒɪəl) *adj*

Syrinx ★ (ˈsɪrɪŋks) *n Greek myth.* a nymph who was changed into a reed to save her from the amorous pursuit of Pan. From this reed Pan then fashioned his musical pipes.

syrup (ˈsɪrəp) *n* **1** a solution of sugar dissolved in water and often flavoured with fruit juice: used for sweetening fruit, etc. **2** any of various thick sweet liquids prepared for cooking or table use from molasses, sugars, etc. **3** *Inf.* cloying sentimentality. **4** a liquid medicine containing a sugar solution for flavouring or preservation. ◆ Also: **sirup.** ORIG C15: from Med. L *syrupus,* from Ar. *sharāb* a drink, from *shariba* to drink
▸ **ˈsyrupy** *adj*

syssarcosis (ˌsɪsɑːˈkəʊsɪs) *n, pl* **syssarcoses** (-siːz). *Anat.* the union or articulation of bones by muscle. ORIG C17: from NL, from Gk *sussarkōsis,* from *sus-* SYN- + *sarkoun* to become fleshy, from *sarx* flesh
▸ **syssarcotic** (ˌsɪsɑːˈkɒtɪk) *adj*

systaltic (sɪˈstæltɪk) *adj* (esp. of the action of the heart) of, relating to, or characterized by alternate contractions and dilations; pulsating. ORIG C17: from LL *systalticus,* from Gk, from *sustellein* to contract, from SYN- + *stellein* to place

system (ˈsɪstəm) *n* **1** a group or combination of interrelated, interdependent, or interacting elements forming a collective entity; a methodical or coordinated assemblage of parts, facts, etc. **2** any scheme of classification or arrangement. **3** a network of communications, transportation, or distribution. **4** a method or complex of methods: *he has a perfect system at roulette.* **5** orderliness; an ordered manner. **6 the system.** (*often cap.*) society seen as an environment exploiting, restricting, and repressing individuals. **7** an organism considered as a functioning entity. **8** any of various bodily parts or structures that are anatomically or physiologically related: *the digestive system.* **9** one's physiological or psychological constitution: *get it out of your system.* **10** any assembly of electronic, mechanical, etc., components with interdependent functions, usually forming a self-contained unit: *a brake system.* **11** a group of celestial bodies that are associated as a result of natural laws, esp. gravitational attraction: *the solar system.* **12** a point of view or doctrine used to interpret a branch of knowledge. **13** *Mineralogy.* one of a group of divisions into which crystals may be placed on the basis of the lengths and inclinations of their axes. **14** *Geol.* a stratigraphical unit for the rock strata formed during a period of geological time. ORIG C17: from F, from LL *systēma,* from Gk *sustēma,* from SYN- + *histanai* to cause to stand

systematic (ˌsɪstɪˈmætɪk) *adj* **1** characterized by the use of order and planning; methodical: *a systematic administrator.* **2** comprising or resembling a system: *systematic theology.* **3** Also: **systematical.** *Biol.* of or relating to taxonomic classification.
▸ **ˌsystemˈatically** *adv* ▸ **ˈsystemaˌtism** *n* ▸ **ˈsystematist** *n*

systematics (ˌsɪstɪˈmætɪks) *n* (*functioning as sing*) the study of systems and the principles of classification and nomenclature.

systematize (ˈsɪstɪməˌtaɪz), **systemize** *or* **systematise, systemise** *vb* **systematizes, systematizing, systematized; systemizes, systemizing, systemized** *or* **systematises, systematising, systematised; systemises, systemising, systemised.** (*tr*) to arrange in a system.
▸ **ˌsystematiˈzation, ˌsystematiˈsation** *or* **ˌsystemiˈzation, ˌsystemiˈsation** *n* ▸ **ˈsystemaˌtizer, ˈsystemaˌtiser** *or* **ˈsysteˌmizer, ˈsysteˌmiser** *n*

system building *n* a method of building in which prefabricated components are used to speed the construction of buildings.
▸ **ˌsystem ˈbuilt** *adj*

Système International d'Unités (*French* sistɛm ɛ̃tɛrnasjɔnal dynite) *n* the International System of units. See **SI unit.**

systemic (sɪˈstɛmɪk, -ˈstiː-) *adj* **1** another word for **systematic** (senses 1, 2). **2** *Physiol.* (of a poison, disease, etc.) affecting the entire body. **3** (of an insecticide, fungicide, etc.) designed to be absorbed by a plant into its tissues. ◆ *n* **4** a systemic insecticide, fungicide, etc.
▸ **sysˈtemically** *adv*

systems analysis *n* the analysis of the requirements of a task and the expression of these in a form that permits the assembly of computer hardware and software to perform the task.
▸ **systems analyst** *n*

systems engineering *n* the branch of engineering, based on systems analysis and information theory, concerned with the design of integrated systems.

systole (ˈsɪstəlɪ) *n* contraction of the heart, during which blood is pumped into the aorta and the arteries. Cf. **diastole.** ORIG C16: via LL from Gk *sustolē,* from *sustellein* to contract; see SYSTALTIC
▸ **systolic** (sɪˈstɒlɪk) *adj*

Syzran ★ (*Russian* ˈsizrənj) *n* a port in W central Russia, in Samara Region on the Volga River: oil refining. Pop.: 177 000 (1995 est.).

syzygy (ˈsɪzɪdʒɪ) *n, pl* **syzygies. 1** either of the two positions (conjunction or opposition) of a celestial body when sun, earth, and the body lie in a straight line: *the moon is at syzygy when full.* **2** *Rare.* any pair, usually of opposites. ORIG C17: from LL, from Gk *suzugia,* from *suzugos* yoked together, from SYN- + *zugon* a yoke
▸ **syzygial** (sɪˈzɪdʒɪəl), **syzygetic** (ˌsɪzɪˈdʒɛtɪk), *or* **syzygal** (ˈsɪzɪɡᵊl) *adj* ▸ **ˌsyzyˈgetically** *adv*

Szabadka ★ (ˈsɔbɔtkɔ) *n* the Hungarian name for **Subotica.**

Szczecin ★ (*Polish* ˈʃtʃɛtʃin) *n* a port in NW Poland, on the River Oder: the busiest Polish port and leading coal exporter; shipbuilding. Pop.: 419 600 (1995 est.). German name: **Stettin.**

Szechwan ★ (ˈseɪˈtʃwɑːn) *n* a variant transliteration of the Chinese name for **Sichuan.**

Szeged ★ (*Hungarian* ˈsɛɡɛd) *n* an industrial city in S Hungary, on the Tisza River. Pop.: 167 000 (1996).

Szell ★ (sɛl) *n* **George.** 1897–1970, US conductor, born in Hungary.

Szent-Györgyi ★ (ˈsɛntdjørdji) *n* **Albert (von Nagyrapolt).** 1893–1986, US biochemist, born in Hungary, who isolated ascorbic acid and identified it as vitamin C. Nobel prize for physiology or medicine 1937.

Szilard ★ (ˈsɪlɑːd) *n* **Leo.** 1898–1964, US physicist, born in Hungary, who worked on the atomic bomb during World War II.

Szombathely ★ (*Hungarian* ˈsombɔthɛj) *n* a city in W Hungary: site of the Roman capital of Pannonia. Pop.: 84 000 (1995 est.).

Szymanowski ★ (*Polish* ʃimaˈnɔfski) *n* **Karol** (ˈkarɔl). 1882–1937, Polish composer, whose works include the opera *King Roger* (1926), two violin concertos, symphonies, piano music, and songs.

Tt

t *or* **T** (tiː) *n, pl* **t's, T's,** *or* **Ts. 1** the 20th letter of the English alphabet. **2** a speech sound represented by this letter. **3** something shaped like a T. **4 to a T.** in every detail; perfectly.

t *symbol for:* **1** *Statistics.* distribution. **2** tonne(s). **3** troy (weight).

T *symbol for:* **1** absolute temperature. **2** surface tension. **3** tera-. **4** tesla. **5** *Chem.* tritium. **6** *Biochem.* thymine.

t. *abbrev. for:* **1** *Commerce.* tare. **2** teaspoon(ful). **3** temperature. **4** *Music.* tempo. **5** *Music.* Also: **T.** tenor. **6** *Grammar.* tense. **7** ton(s). **8** transitive.

't *contraction of* it.

ta (tɑː) *interj Brit. inf.* thank you. ORIG C18: imit. of baby talk

Ta *the chemical symbol for* tantalum.

TA (in Britain) *abbrev. for* Territorial Army (now superseded by **TAVR**).

taal (tɑːl) *n S. African* language: usually, by implication, Afrikaans. ORIG Afrik. from Du.

Taal ★ (tɑː'ɑːl) *n* an active volcano in the Philippines, on S Luzon on an island in the centre of **Lake Taal.** Height: 300 m (984 ft). Area of lake: 243 sq. km (94 sq. miles).

tab[1] (tæb) *n* **1** a small flap of material, esp. one on a garment for decoration or for fastening to a button. **2** any similar flap, such as a piece of paper attached to a file for identification. **3** *Brit. mil.* the insignia on the collar of a staff officer. **4** *Chiefly US & Canad.* a bill, esp. for a meal or drinks. **5 keep tabs on.** *Inf.* to keep a watchful eye on. ◆ *vb* **tabs, tabbing, tabbed. 6** (*tr*) to supply with a tab or tabs. ORIG C17: from ?

tab[2] (tæb) *n* short for **tabulator** or **tablet.**

TAB *abbrev. for:* **1** *Austral. & NZ.* Totalizator Agency Board. **2** typhoid-paratyphoid A and B (vaccine).

tabard ('tæbəd) *n* a sleeveless or short-sleeved jacket, esp. one worn by a herald, bearing a coat of arms, or by a knight over his armour. ORIG C13: from OF *tabart,* from ?

tabaret ('tæbərɪt) *n* a hard-wearing fabric of silk or similar cloth with stripes of satin or moire, used esp. for upholstery. ORIG C19: ? from TABBY[1]

Tabasco[1] (tə'bæskəʊ) *n Trademark.* a very hot red sauce made from matured capsicums.

Tabasco[2] ★ (*Spanish* ta'βasko) *n* a state in SE Mexico, on the Gulf of Campeche: mostly flat and marshy with extensive jungles; hot and humid climate. Capital: Villahermosa. Pop.: 1 817 703 (1997 est.). Area: 24 661 sq. km (9520 sq. miles).

tabby[1] ('tæbɪ) *n* a fabric with a watered pattern, esp. silk or taffeta. ORIG C17: from OF *tabis* silk cloth, from Ar. *al-'attabiya,* lit.: the quarter of (Prince) 'Attab, the part of Baghdad where the fabric was first made

tabby[2] ('tæbɪ) *adj* **1** (esp. of cats) brindled with dark stripes or wavy markings on a lighter background. **2** having a wavy or striped pattern, particularly in colours of grey and brown. ◆ *n, pl* **tabbies. 3** a tabby cat. **4** any female domestic cat. ORIG C17: from *Tabby,* pet form of the girl's name *Tabitha,* prob. infl. by TABBY[1]

tabernacle ('tæbəˌnækəl) *n* **1** (*often cap.*) *Old Testament.* **1a** the portable sanctuary in which the ancient Israelites carried the Ark of the Covenant. **1b** the Jewish Temple. **2** any place of worship that is not called a church. **3** *RC Church.* a receptacle in which the Blessed Sacrament is kept. **4** *Chiefly RC Church.* a canopied niche. **5** *Naut.* a strong framework for holding the foot of a mast, allowing it to be swung down to pass under low bridges, etc. ORIG C13: from L *tabernāculum* a tent, from *taberna* a hut
▸ ˌ**taber'nacular** *adj*

tabes ('teɪbiːz) *n, pl* **tabes. 1** a wasting of a bodily organ or part. **2** short for **tabes dorsalis.** ORIG C17: from L: a wasting away
▸ **tabetic** (tə'bɛtɪk) *adj*

tabescent (tə'bɛsənt) *adj* **1** progressively emaciating; wasting away. **2** of, relating to, or having tabes. ORIG C19: from L *tābēscere,* from TABES
▸ **ta'bescence** *n*

tabes dorsalis (dɔː'sɑːlɪs) *n* a form of late syphilis that attacks the spinal cord causing degeneration of the nerve fibres, paralysis of the leg muscles, acute abdominal pain, etc. ORIG NL, lit.: tabes of the back

tabla ('tʌblə, 'tɑːblɑː) *n* a musical instrument of India consisting of a pair of drums whose pitches can be varied. ORIG Hindu, from Ar. *tabla* drum

tablature ('tæblətʃə) *n Music.* any of a number of forms of musical notation, esp. for playing the lute, consisting of letters and signs indicating rhythm and fingering. ORIG C16: from F, ult. from L *tabulātum* wooden floor, from *tabula* a plank

table ('teɪbəl) *n* **1** a flat horizontal slab or board, usually supported by one or more legs. **2a** such a slab or board on which food is served. **2b** (*as modifier*): *table linen.* **3** food as served in a particular household, etc.: *a good table.* **4** such a piece of furniture specially designed for any of various purposes: *a bird table.* **5a** a company of persons assembled for a meal, game, etc. **5b** (*as modifier*): *table talk.* **6** any flat or level area, such as a plateau. **7** a rectangular panel set below or above the face of a wall. **8** *Archit.* another name for **string course. 9** any of various flat surfaces, as an upper horizontal facet of a cut gem. **10** *Music.* the sounding board of a violin, guitar, etc. **11a** an arrangement of words, numbers, or signs, usually in parallel columns. **11b** See **multiplication table. 12** a tablet on which laws were inscribed by the ancient Romans, the Hebrews, etc. **13 turn the tables.** to cause a complete reversal of circumstances. **14 under the table. 14a** (**under-the-table** *when prenominal*) done illicitly and secretly. **14b** *Sl.* drunk. ◆ *vb* **tables, tabling, tabled.** (*tr*) **15** to place on a table. **16** *Brit.* to submit (a bill, etc.) for consideration by a legislative body. **17** *US.* to suspend discussion of (a bill, etc.) indefinitely. **18** to enter in or form into a list. ORIG C12: via OF from L *tabula* a writing tablet

tableau ('tæbləʊ) *n, pl* **tableaux** (-ləʊ, -ləʊz) *or* **tableaus. 1** See ***tableau vivant.*** **2** a pause on stage when all the performers briefly freeze in position. **3** any dramatic group or scene. ORIG C17: from F, from OF *tablel* a picture, dim. of TABLE

tableau vivant *French.* (tablo vivɑ̃) *n, pl* ***tableaux vivants*** (tablo vivɑ̃). a representation of a scene by a person or group posed silent and motionless. ORIG C19, lit.: living picture

Table Bay ★ *n* the large bay on which Cape Town is situated, on the SW coast of South Africa.

tablecloth ('teɪbəlˌklɒθ) *n* a cloth for covering the top of a table, esp. during meals.

table d'hôte ('tɑːbəl 'dəʊt) *adj* **1** (of a meal) consisting of a set number of courses with limited choice of dishes offered at a fixed price. Cf. **à la carte.** ◆ *n, pl* **tables d'hôte** ('tɑːbəlz 'dəʊt). **2** a table d'hôte meal or menu. ORIG C17: from F, lit.: the host's table

tableland ('teɪbəlˌlænd) *n* flat elevated land.

table licence *n* a licence authorizing the sale of alcoholic drinks with meals only.

Table Mountain ★ *n* a mountain in SW South Africa, overlooking Cape Town and Table Bay: flat-topped and steep-sided. Height: 1087 m (3567 ft).

tablespoon ('teɪbəlˌspuːn) *n* **1** a spoon, larger than a dessertspoon, used for serving food, etc. **2** Also called: **tablespoonful.** the amount contained in such a spoon. **3** a unit of capacity used in cooking, etc., equal to half a fluid ounce.

tablet ('tæblɪt) *n* **1** a pill made of a compressed medicinal substance. **2** a flattish cake of some substance, such as soap. **3** a slab of stone, wood, etc., esp. one used for inscriptions. **4a** a rigid sheet, as of bark, etc., used for similar purposes. **4b** (*often pl*) a set of these fastened together. **5** a pad of writing paper. **6** *Scot.* a sweet made from butter, sugar, and condensed milk, usually shaped into flat oblong cakes. ORIG C14: from OF *tablete* a little table, from L *tabula* a board

table tennis *n* a miniature form of tennis played on a table with bats and a hollow ball.

table-turning *n* the movement of a table attributed by spiritualists to the power of spirits.

tableware ('teɪbᵊl,wɛə) *n* articles such as dishes, plates, knives, forks, etc., used at meals.

tabloid ('tæblɔɪd) *n* **1** a newspaper with pages about 30 cm (12 inches) by 40 cm (16 inches), usually with many photographs and a concise and often sensational style. **2** (*modifier*) designed to appeal to a mass audience or readership; sensationalist: *the tabloid press; tabloid television.* ORIG C20: from earlier *Tabloid,* a trademark for a medicine in tablet form

taboo *or* **tabu** (tə'bu:) *adj* **1** forbidden or disapproved of: *taboo words.* **2** (in Polynesia) marked off as sacred and forbidden. ◆ *n, pl* **taboos** *or* **tabus. 3** any prohibition resulting from social or other conventions. **4** ritual restriction or prohibition, esp. of something that is considered holy or unclean. ◆ *vb* **5** (*tr*) to place under a taboo. ORIG C18: from Tongan *tapu*

tabor *or* **tabour** ('teɪbə) *n* a small drum used esp. in the Middle Ages, struck with one hand while the other held a pipe. ORIG C13: from OF *tabour,* ?from Persian *tabīr*

Tabor ★ ('teɪbə) *n* **Mount.** a mountain in N Israel, near Nazareth: traditionally regarded as the mountain where the Transfiguration took place. Height: 588 m (1929 ft).

taboret *or* **tabouret** ('tæbərɪt) *n* **1** a low stool. **2** a frame for stretching out cloth while it is being embroidered. **3** a small tabor. ORIG C17: from F *tabouret,* dim. of TABOR

Tabriz ★ (tæ'bri:z) *n* a city in NW Iran: an ancient city, situated in a volcanic region of hot springs; university (1947); carpet manufacturing. Pop.: 1 166 203 (1994 est.). Ancient name: **Tauris** ('tɔ:rɪs).

tabular ('tæbjulə) *adj* **1** arranged in systematic or table form. **2** calculated from or by means of a table. **3** like a table in form; flat. ORIG C17: from L *tabulāris* concerning boards, from *tabula* a board
▸ **'tabularly** *adv*

tabula rasa ('tæbjulə 'rɑ:sə) *n, pl* **tabulae rasae** ('tæbjuli: 'rɑ:si:). **1** the mind in its uninformed original state. **2** an opportunity for a fresh start; clean slate. ORIG L: a scraped tablet

tabulate *vb* ('tæbju,leɪt), **tabulates, tabulating, tabulated.** (*tr*) **1** to set out, arrange, or write in tabular form. **2** to form or cut with a flat surface. ◆ *adj* ('tæbjulɪt, -,leɪt). **3** having a flat surface. ORIG C18: from L *tabula* a board
▸ **'tabulable** *adj* ▸ **,tabu'lation** *n*

tabulator ('tæbju,leɪtə) *n* **1** a device for setting the stops that locate the column margins on a typewriter. **2** *Computing.* a machine that reads data from one medium, such as punched cards, producing lists, tabulations, or totals.

tacamahac ('tækəmə,hæk) *or* **tacmahack** *n* **1** any of several strong-smelling resinous gums used in ointments, incense, etc. **2** any tree yielding this resin. ORIG C16: from Sp. *tacamahaca,* from Nahuatl *tecomahca* aromatic resin

tacet ('teɪsɛt, 'tæs-) *vb* (*intr*) (on a musical score) a direction indicating that a particular instrument or singer does not take part. ORIG C18: from L: it is silent, from *tacēre* to be quiet

tacheometer (,tækɪ'ɒmɪtə) *or* **tachymeter** *n* *Surveying.* a type of theodolite designed for the rapid measurement of distances, elevations, and directions.
▸ **,tache'ometry** *n*

tachisme ('tɑ:ʃɪzəm) *n* a type of action painting in which haphazard dabs and blots of colour are treated as a means of unconscious expression. ORIG C20: F, from *tache* stain

tachistoscope (tæ'kɪstə,skəʊp) *n* an instrument for displaying visual images for very brief intervals, usually a fraction of a second. ORIG C20: from Gk *takhistos* swiftest + -SCOPE
▸ **tachistoscopic** (tæ,kɪstə'skɒpɪk) *adj*

tacho- *combining form.* speed: *tachograph; tachometer.* ORIG from Gk *takhos*

tachograph ('tækə,grɑ:f) *n* a tachometer that produces a record (**tachogram**) of its readings, esp. a device for recording the speed of and distance covered by a vehicle. Often shortened to **tacho.**

tachometer (tæ'kɒmɪtə) *n* any device for measuring speed, esp. the rate of revolution of a shaft. Tachometers are often fitted to cars to indicate the number of revolutions per minute of the engine.
▸ **ta'chometry** *n*

tachy- *or* **tacheo-** *combining form.* swift or accelerated: *tachyon.* ORIG from Gk *takhus* swift

tachycardia (,tækɪ'kɑ:dɪə) *n* abnormally rapid beating of the heart.

tachygraphy (tæ'kɪgrəfɪ) *n* shorthand, esp. as used in ancient Rome or Greece.

tachymeter (tæ'kɪmɪtə) *n* another name for **tacheometer.**

tachyon ('tækɪ,ɒn) *n* *Physics.* a hypothetical elementary particle capable of travelling faster than the velocity of light. ORIG C20: from TACHY- + -ON

tachyphylaxis (,tækɪfɪ'læksɪs) *n* very rapid development of tolerance or immunity to the effects of a drug. ORIG NL, from TACHY- + *phylaxis* on the model of *prophylaxis;* see PROPHYLACTIC

tacit ('tæsɪt) *adj* implied or inferred without direct expression; understood: *a tacit agreement.* ORIG C17: from L *tacitus,* p.p. of *tacēre* to be silent
▸ **'tacitly** *adv*

taciturn ('tæsɪ,tɜ:n) *adj* habitually silent, reserved, or uncommunicative. ORIG C18: from L *taciturnus,* from *tacēre* to be silent
▸ **,taci'turnity** *n* ▸ **'taci,turnly** *adv*

Tacitus ★ ('tæsɪtəs) *n* **Publius Cornelius** ('pʌblɪəs kɔ:'ni:ljəs). ?55–?120 A.D., Roman historian. His works include the *Histories* and the *Annals.*

tack[1] (tæk) *n* **1** a short sharp-pointed nail, with a large flat head. **2** *Brit.* a long loose temporary stitch used in dressmaking, etc. **3** See **tailor's-tack. 4** a temporary fastening. **5** stickiness. **6** *Naut.* the heading of a vessel sailing to windward, stated in terms of the side of the sail against which the wind is pressing. **7** *Naut.* **7a** a course sailed with the wind blowing from forward of the beam. **7b** one such course or a zigzag pattern of such courses. **8** *Naut.* **8a** a sheet for controlling the weather clew of a course. **8b** the weather clew itself. **9** *Naut.* the forward lower clew of a fore-and-aft sail. **10** a course of action or policy. **11 on the wrong tack.** under a false impression. ◆ *vb* **12** (*tr*) to secure by a tack or tacks. **13** *Brit.* to sew (something) with long loose temporary stitches. **14** (*tr*) to attach or append. **15** *Naut.* to change the heading of (a sailing vessel) to the opposite tack. **16** *Naut.* to steer (a sailing vessel) on alternate tacks. **17** (*intr*) *Naut.* (of a sailing vessel) to proceed on a different tack or to alternate tacks. **18** (*intr*) to follow a zigzag route; keep changing one's course of action. ORIG C14 *tak* fastening, nail
▸ **'tacker** *n*

tack[2] (tæk) *n* riding harness for horses, such as saddles, bridles, etc. ORIG C20: shortened from TACKLE

tack hammer *n* a light hammer for driving tacks.

tackies *or* **takkies** ('tækɪz) *pl n, sing* **tacky.** *S. African inf.* tennis shoes or plimsolls. ORIG C20: prob. from TACKY[1], from their nonslip rubber soles

tackle ('tækᵊl) *n* **1** an arrangement of ropes and pulleys designed to lift heavy weights. **2** the equipment required for a particular occupation, etc. **3** *Naut.* the halyards and other running rigging aboard a vessel. **4** *Sport.* a physical challenge to an opponent, as to prevent him or her progress. **5** *American football.* a defensive lineman. ◆ *vb* **tack-**

les, tackling, tackled. **6** (*tr*) to undertake (a task, etc.). **7** (*tr*) to confront (esp. an opponent) with a difficult proposition. **8** *Sport.* to challenge (an opponent) with a tackle. ORIG C13: rel. to MLow G *takel* ship's rigging
▸ **'tackler** *n*

tack rag *n Building trades.* a cotton cloth impregnated with an oil, used to remove dust from a surface prior to painting.

tacky[1] ('tækɪ) *adj* **tackier, tackiest.** slightly sticky or adhesive. ORIG C18: from TACK[1] (in the sense: stickiness)
▸ **'tackily** *adv* ▸ **'tackiness** *n*

tacky[2] ('tækɪ) *adj* **tackier, tackiest.** *Inf.* **1** shabby or shoddy. **2** ostentatious and vulgar. **3** *US.* (of a person) dowdy; seedy. ORIG C19: from dialect *tacky* an inferior horse, from ?
▸ **'tackiness** *n*

Tacna-Arica ★ (*Spanish* 'taknaa'rika) *n* a coastal desert region of W South America, long disputed by Chile and Peru: divided in 1929 into the Peruvian department of Tacna and the Chilean department of Arica.

tacnode ('tæk,nəʊd) *n* another name for **osculation** (sense 1). ORIG C19: from L *tactus* touch (from *tangere* to touch) + NODE

Tacoma ★ (tə'kəʊmə) *n* a port in W Washington, on Puget Sound: industrial centre. Pop.: 183 060 (1994 est.).

tact (tækt) *n* **1** a sense of what is fitting and considerate in dealing with others, so as to avoid giving offence. **2** skill in handling difficult situations; diplomacy. ORIG C17: from L *tactus* a touching, from *tangere* to touch
▸ **'tactful** *adj* ▸ **'tactfulness** *n* ▸ **'tactless** *adj* ▸ **'tactlessness** *n*

tactic ('tæktɪk) *n* a piece of tactics; tactical move. See also **tactics.**

-tactic *adj combining form.* having a specified kind of pattern or arrangement or having an orientation determined by a specified force: *syndiotactic; phototactic.* ORIG from Gk *taktikos* relating to order; see TACTICS

tactical ('tæktɪkᵊl) *adj* **1** of, relating to, or employing tactics: *a tactical error.* **2** (of missiles, bombing, etc.) for use in or supporting limited military operations; short-range. **3** skilful, adroit, or diplomatic.
▸ **'tactically** *adv*

tactical voting *n* (in an election) the practice of casting one's vote not for the party of one's choice but for the second strongest contender in a constituency in order to defeat the likeliest winner.

tactics ('tæktɪks) *pl n* **1** (*functioning as sing*) *Mil.* the art and science of the detailed direction and control of movement of forces in battle to achieve an aim or task. **2** the manoeuvres used to achieve an aim or task. **3** plans followed to achieve a particular short-term aim. ORIG C17: from NL *tactica,* from Gk, from *taktikos* concerning arrangement, from *taktos* arranged (for battle), from *tassein* to arrange
▸ **tac'tician** *n*

tactile ('tæktaɪl) *adj* **1** of, relating to, affecting, or having a sense of touch. **2** *Now rare.* tangible. ORIG C17: from L *tactilis,* from *tangere* to touch
▸ **tactility** (tæk'tɪlɪtɪ) *n*

Tadmor ★ ('tædmɔː) *n* the biblical name for **Palmyra.**

tadpole ('tæd,pəʊl) *n* the aquatic larva of frogs, toads, etc., which develops from a limbless tailed form with external gills into a form with internal gills, limbs, and a reduced tail. ORIG C15 *taddepol,* from *tadde* toad + *pol* head

Tadzhik ★ *n* a variant spelling of **Tajik.**

Tadzhikistan ★ *n* a variant spelling of **Tajikistan.**

taedium vitae ('tiːdɪəm 'viːtaɪ, 'vaɪtiː) *n* the feeling that life is boring and dull. ORIG L, lit.: weariness of life

Taegu ★ (tɛ'guː) *n* a city in SE South Korea: textile and agricultural trading centre. Pop.: 2 449 139 (1995).

Taejon ★ (tɛ'dʒɒn) *n* a city in W South Korea: market centre of an agricultural region. Pop.: 1 272 143 (1995).

tae kwon do ('taɪ 'kwɒn 'dəʊ, 'teɪ) *n* a Korean martial art that resembles karate. ORIG C20: Korean *tae* kick + *kwon* fist + *do* way, method

tael (teɪl) *n* **1** a unit of weight, used in the Far East. **2** (formerly) a Chinese monetary unit. ORIG C16: from Port., from Malay *tahil* weight, ?from Sansk.

ta'en (teɪn) *vb* a Scot. or poetic contraction of **taken.**

taenia *or US* **tenia** ('tiːnɪə) *n, pl* **taeniae** *or US* **teniae** (-nɪ,iː). **1** (in ancient Greece) a headband. **2** *Archit.* the fillet between the architrave and frieze of a Doric entablature. **3** *Anat.* any bandlike structure or part. **4** any of a genus of tapeworms. ORIG C16: via L from Gk *tainia* narrow strip

taeniasis *or US* **teniasis** (tiː'naɪəsɪs) *n Pathol.* infestation with tapeworms of the genus *Taenia.*

taffeta ('tæfɪtə) *n* a thin crisp lustrous plain-weave fabric of silk, etc., used esp. for women's clothes. ORIG C14: from Med. L *taffata,* from Persian *tāftah* spun, from *tāftan* to spin

taffrail ('tæf,reɪl) *n Naut.* a rail at the stern of a vessel. ORIG C19: changed from earlier *tafferel,* from Du. *taffereel* panel (hence applied to the part of a vessel decorated with carved panels), from *tafel* table

Taffy ('tæfɪ) *n, pl* **Taffies.** a slang word or nickname for a **Welshman.** ORIG C17: from the supposed Welsh pronunciation of *Davy* (from *David,* Welsh *Dafydd*), a common Welsh Christian name

tafia *or* **taffia** ('tæfɪə) *n* a type of rum, esp. from Guyana or the Caribbean. ORIG C18: from F, from West Indian Creole, prob. from RATAFIA

Tafilelt (tæ'fiːlɛlt) *or* **Tafilalet** ★ (,tæfɪ'lɑːlɛt) *n* an oasis in SE Morocco, the largest in the Sahara. Area: about 1300 sq. km (500 sq. miles).

Taft ★ (tæft) *n* **William Howard.** 1857–1930, US statesman; 27th president of the US (1909–13).

tag[1] (tæg) *n* **1** a piece of paper, leather, etc., for attaching to something as a mark or label: *a price tag.* **2** Also called: **electronic tag.** an electronic device worn by an offender serving a noncustodial sentence, which monitors the offender's whereabouts by means of a link to a central computer through the telephone system. **3** a small piece of material hanging from a part or piece. **4** a point of metal, etc., at the end of a cord or lace. **5** an epithet or verbal appendage, the refrain of a song, the moral of a fable, etc. **6** a brief quotation. **7** an ornamental flourish. **8** the tip of an animal's tail. **9** a matted lock of wool or hair. **10** *Sl.* a graffito consisting of a nickname or personal symbol. ◆ *vb* **tags, tagging, tagged.** (*mainly tr*) **11** to mark with a tag. **12** to monitor the whereabouts of (an offender) by means of an electronic tag. **13** to add or append as a tag. **14** to supply (prose or blank verse) with rhymes. **15** (*intr; usually foll. by on or along*) to trail (behind). **16** to name or call (someone something). **17** to cut the tags of wool or hair from (an animal). ORIG C15: from ?

tag[2] (tæg) *n* **1** Also called: **tig.** a children's game in which one player chases the others in an attempt to catch one of them who will then become the chaser. **2** the act of tagging one's partner in tag wrestling. **3** (*modifier*) denoting a wrestling contest between two teams of two wrestlers, in which only one from each team may be in the ring at one time. The contestant outside the ring may change places with his team-mate inside the ring after touching his hand. ◆ *vb* **tags, tagging, tagged.** (*tr*) **4** to catch (another child) in the game of tag. **5** (in tag wrestling) to touch the hand of (one's partner). ORIG C18: ?from TAG[1]

Tagalog (tə'gɑːlɒg) *n* **1** (*pl* **Tagalogs** *or* **Tagalog**) a member of a people of the Philippines. **2** the language of this people. ◆ *adj* **3** of or relating to this people or their language.

Taganrog ★ (*Russian* təgan'rɔk) *n* a port in SW Russia, on the **Gulf of Taganrog** (an inlet of the Sea of Azov): founded in 1698 as a naval base and fortress by Peter the Great: industrial centre. Pop.: 292 000 (1995 est.).

tag end *n* **1** the last part of something. **2** a loose end of cloth, thread, etc.

tagetes (tæ'dʒiːtiːz) *n, pl* **tagetes.** any of a genus of plants with yellow or orange flowers, including the French and African marigolds. ORIG from NL, from *Tages,* an Etruscan god

tagliatelle (ˌtæljəˈtɛlɪ) *n* a form of pasta made in narrow strips. ORIG It., from *tagliare* to cut

tag line *n* **1** an amusing or memorable phrase designed to catch attention in an advert. **2** another name for **punch line.**

Tagore ★ (təˈgɔː) *n* **Rabindranath** (rəˈbiːndrəˌnɑːt). 1861–1941, Indian poet and philosopher. His works include *Gitanjali* (1910; 1912): Nobel prize for literature 1913.

Tagus ★ (ˈteɪgəs) *n* a river in SW Europe, rising in E central Spain and flowing west to the border with Portugal, then southwest to the Atlantic at Lisbon: the longest river of the Iberian Peninsula. Length: 1007 km (626 miles). Portuguese name: **Tejo.** Spanish name: **Tajo.**

Tahiti ★ (təˈhiːtɪ) *n* an island in the S Pacific, in the Windward group of the Society Islands: the largest and most important island in French Polynesia; became a French protectorate in 1842 and a colony in 1880. Capital: Papeete. Pop.: 115 820 (1988). Area: 1005 sq. km (388 sq. miles).
▸ **Tahitian** (təˈhiːtɪən, təˈhiːʃɪən) *adj, n*

Tahoe ★ (ˈtɑːhəʊ, ˈteɪ-) *n* **Lake.** a lake between E California and W Nevada, in the Sierra Nevada Mountains at an altitude of 1899 m (6229 ft). Area: about 520 sq. km (200 sq. miles).

tahr *or* **thar** (tɑː) *n* any of several goatlike mammals of S and SW Asia, having a shaggy coat and curved horns. ORIG from Nepali *thār*

tahsil (təˈsiːl) *n* an administrative division in certain states in India. ORIG Urdu, from Ar.: collection

Tai (taɪ) *adj, n* a variant spelling of **Thai.**

taiaha (ˈtaɪəˌhɑː) *n NZ.* a carved weapon in the form of a staff, now used in Maori ceremonial oratory. ORIG from Maori

t'ai chi ch'uan (ˈtaɪ dʒiː ˈtʃwɑːn) *n* a Chinese system of callisthenics characterized by coordinated and rhythmic movements. Often shortened to **t'ai chi** (ˈtaɪ ˈdʒiː). ORIG Chinese, lit.: great art of boxing

Taichung *or* **T'ai-chung** ★ (ˈtaɪˈtʃʊŋ) *n* a city in W Taiwan (Republic of China): commercial centre of an agricultural region. Pop.: 857 590 (1996 est.).

taiga (ˈtaɪgɑː) *n* the coniferous forests extending across much of subarctic North America and Eurasia. ORIG from Russian, of Turkic origin

taihoa (ˈtaɪhəʊə) *sentence substitute. NZ.* hold on! no hurry! ORIG Maori

tail[1] (teɪl) *n* **1** the rear part of the vertebrate body that contains an elongation of the vertebral column, esp. forming a flexible appendage. **2** anything resembling such an appendage; the bottom, lowest, or rear part. **3** the last part or parts: *the tail of the storm.* **4** the rear part of an aircraft including the fin, tailplane, and control surfaces. **5** *Astron.* the luminous stream of gas and dust particles driven from the head of a comet when close to the sun. **6** the rear portion of a bomb, rocket, missile, etc., usually fitted with guiding or stabilizing vanes. **7** a line of people or things. **8** a long braid or tress of hair: *a pigtail.* **9** a final short line in a stanza. **10** *Inf.* a person employed to follow and spy upon another. **11** an informal word for **buttocks.** **12** *Taboo sl.* **12a** the female genitals. **12b** a woman considered sexually (esp. in **piece of tail, bit of tail**). **13** the foot of a page. **14** the lower end of a pool or part of a stream. **15** *Inf.* the course or track of a fleeing person or animal. **16** (*modifier*) coming from or situated in the rear: *a tail wind.* **17 turn tail.** to run away; escape. **18 with one's tail between one's legs.** in a state of utter defeat or confusion. ◆ *vb* **19** to form or cause to form the tail. **20** to remove the tail of (an animal). **21** (*tr*) to remove the stalk of. **22** (*tr*) to connect (objects, ideas, etc.) together by or as if by the tail. **23** (*tr*) *Inf.* to follow stealthily. **24** (*intr*) (of a vessel) to assume a specified position, as when at a mooring. **25** to build the end of (a brick, joist, etc.) into a wall or (of a brick, etc.) to have one end built into a wall. ◆ See also **tail off, tail out, tails.** ORIG OE *tægel*
▸ **ˈtailless** *adj*

tail[2] (teɪl) *Law.* ◆ *n* **1** the limitation of an estate or interest to a person and the heirs of his body. ◆ *adj* **2** (*immediately postpositive*) limited in this way. ORIG C15: from OF *taille* a division; see TAILOR
▸ **ˈtailless** *adj*

tailback (ˈteɪlˌbæk) *n* a queue of traffic stretching back from an obstruction.

tailboard (ˈteɪlˌbɔːd) *n* a board at the rear of a lorry, etc., that can be removed or let down.

tail coat *n* **1** a man's black coat having a horizontal cut over the hips and a tapering tail with a vertical slit up to the waist. **2** a cutaway frock coat, part of morning dress.

tail covert *n* any of the covert feathers of a bird covering the bases of the tail feathers.

tail end *n* the last, endmost, or final part.

tailgate (ˈteɪlˌgeɪt) *n* **1** another name for **tailboard.** **2** a door at the rear of a hatchback vehicle. ◆ *vb* **tailgates, tailgating, tailgated.** **3** to drive very close behind (a vehicle).
▸ **ˈtailˌgater** *n*

tail gate *n* a gate that is used to control the flow of water at the lower end of a lock.

tailing (ˈteɪlɪŋ) *n* the part of a beam, rafter, projecting brick, etc., embedded in a wall.

tailings (ˈteɪlɪŋz) *pl n* waste left over after certain processes, such as from an ore-crushing plant or in milling grain.

tail-light (ˈteɪlˌlaɪt) *or* **tail lamp** *n* other names for **rear light.**

tail off *or* **away** *vb* (*adv; usually intr*) to decrease or cause to decrease in quantity, degree, etc., esp. gradually.

tailor (ˈteɪlə) *n* **1** a person who makes, repairs, or alters outer garments, esp. menswear. Related adj: **sartorial.** **2** a voracious and active marine food fish of Australia. ◆ *vb* **3** to cut or style (material, etc.) to satisfy certain requirements. **4** (*tr*) to adapt so as to make suitable. **5** (*intr*) to work as a tailor. ORIG C13: from Anglo-Norman *taillour,* from OF *taillier* to cut, from L *tālea* a cutting
▸ **ˈtailored** *adj*

tailorbird (ˈteɪləˌbɜːd) *n* any of several tropical Asian warblers that build nests by sewing together large leaves using plant fibres.

tailor-made *adj* **1** made by a tailor to fit exactly. **2** perfectly meeting a particular purpose. ◆ *n* **3** a tailor-made garment. **4** *Inf.* a factory-made cigarette.

tailor's chalk *n* pipeclay used by tailors and dressmakers to mark seams, darts, etc., on material.

tailor's-tack *n* one of a series of loose looped stitches used to transfer markings for seams, darts, etc., from a paper pattern to material.

tail out *vb* (*tr, adv*) *NZ.* to guide (timber) as it emerges from a circular saw.

tailpiece (ˈteɪlˌpiːs) *n* **1** an extension or appendage that lengthens or completes something. **2** a decorative design at the foot of a page or end of a chapter. **3** *Music.* a piece of wood to which the strings of a violin, etc., are attached at their lower end. **4** a short beam or rafter that has one end embedded in a wall.

tailpipe (ˈteɪlˌpaɪp) *n* a pipe from which exhaust gases are discharged, esp. the terminal pipe of the exhaust system of a motor vehicle.

tailplane (ˈteɪlˌpleɪn) *n* a small horizontal wing at the tail of an aircraft to provide longitudinal stability. Also called (esp. US): **horizontal stabilizer.**

tailrace (ˈteɪlˌreɪs) *n* a channel that carries water away from a water wheel, turbine, etc.

tail rotor *n* a small propeller fitted to the rear of a helicopter to counteract the torque reaction of the main rotor and thus prevent the body of the helicopter from rotating in an opposite direction.

tails (teɪlz) *pl n* **1** an informal name for **tail coat.** ◆ *interj, adv* **2** with the reverse side of a coin uppermost.

tailskid (ˈteɪlˌskɪd) *n* **1** a runner under the tail of an aircraft. **2** a rear-wheel skid of a motor vehicle.

tailspin (ˈteɪlˌspɪn) *n* **1** *Aeronautics.* another name for **spin** (sense 16). **2** *Inf.* a state of confusion or panic.

tailstock (ˈteɪlˌstɒk) *n* a casting that slides on the bed of a lathe and is locked in position to support the free end of a workpiece.

tailwind ('teɪlˌwɪnd) *n* a wind blowing in the same direction as the course of an aircraft or ship.

Taimyr Peninsula ★ (*Russian* taj'mir) *n* a large peninsula of the N central Soviet Union, between the Kara Sea and the Laptev Sea. Also: **Taymyr Peninsula.**

Tainan *or* **T'ai-nan** ★ ('taɪ'næn) *n* a city in SW Taiwan (Republic of China): an early centre of Chinese emigration from the mainland; largest city and capital of the island (1638–1885); Chengkung University. Pop.: 707 658 (1996 est.).

Taínaron ★ ('tɛnarɔn) *n* transliteration of the Modern Greek name for (Cape) **Matapan.**

Taino ('taɪnəʊ) *n* **1** (*pl* **Tainos** *or* **Taino**) a member of an extinct American Indian people of the West Indies. **2** the language of this people.

taint (teɪnt) *vb* **1** to affect or be affected by pollution or contamination. **2** to tarnish (someone's reputation, etc.). ◆ *n* **3** a defect or flaw. **4** a trace of contamination or infection. ORIG C14: (infl. by *attaint* infected, from ATTAIN) from OF *teindre* to dye, from L *tingere*
► **'taintless** *adj*

taipan ('taɪˌpæn) *n* a large highly venomous Australian snake. ORIG C20: from Abor.

Taipei *or* **T'ai-pei** ★ ('taɪ'peɪ) *n* the capital of Taiwan (Republic of China), at the N tip of the island: became capital in 1885; industrial centre; two universities. Pop.: 2 626 138 (1996 est.).

Taisho (taɪ'ʃəʊ) *n* **1** the period of Japanese history and artistic style associated with the reign of Emperor Yoshihito (1912–26). **2** the throne name of Yoshihito (1879–1926), emperor of Japan (1912–26).

Taiwan ★ ('taɪ'wɑːn) *n* **1** an island in SE Asia between the East China Sea and the South China Sea, off the SE coast of the People's Republic of China: the principal territory of the Republic of China. Pop.: 22 024 000 (1999 est.). Former name: **Formosa. 2** another name for the Republic of **China** (sense 2).
► **ˌTaiwan'ese** *adj, n*

Taiwan Strait ★ *n* another name for **Formosa Strait.**

Taiyuan *or* **T'ai-yüan** ★ ('taɪjuː'ɑːn) *n* a city in N China, capital of Shanxi: founded before 450 A.D.; an industrial centre, surrounded by China's largest reserves of high-grade bituminous coal. Pop.: 1 500 000 (1991 est.).

Ta'izz ★ (tæ'ɪz, teɪ'iːz) *n* a town in SW Yemen, formerly in North Yemen: agricultural trading centre. Pop.: 178 043 (1995 est.).

taj (tɑːdʒ) *n* a tall conical cap worn as a mark of distinction by Muslims. ORIG via Ar. from Persian: crown

Tajik *or* **Tadzhik** ★ ('tɑːdʒɪk, tɑː'dʒiːk) *n* **1** a member of a Muslim people of Tajikistan. **2** the language of this people.

Tajikistan *or* **Tadzhikistan** ★ (tɑːˌdʒɪkɪ'stɑːn) *n* a republic in central Asia: under Uzbek rule from the 15th century until taken by Russia in the 1860s; a Soviet republic from 1929 until gaining independence in 1991; mountainous. Language: Tajik. Religion: nonreligious and Muslim. Currency: rouble. Capital: Dushanbe. Pop.: 6 213 000 (1999 est.). Area: 143 100 sq. km (55 240 sq. miles).

Taj Mahal ★ ('tɑːdʒ mə'hɑːl) *n* a marble mausoleum in central India, in Agra: built (1632–43) by the emperor Shah Jahan in memory of his wife. ORIG Urdu, lit.: crown of buildings

Tajo ★ ('taxo) *n* the Spanish name for the **Tagus.**

takahe ('tɑːkəˌhiː) *n* a rare flightless New Zealand rail. Also called: **notornis.** ORIG from Maori

Takamatsu ★ (ˌtækə'mætsuː) *n* a port in SW Japan, on NE Shikoku on the Inland Sea. Pop.: 330 997 (1995).

Takao ★ (tæ'kaʊ) *n* the Japanese name for **Gaoxiong.**

take (teɪk) *vb* **takes, taking, took, taken.** (*mainly tr*) **1** (*also intr*) to gain possession of (something) by force or effort. **2** to appropriate or steal. **3** to receive or accept into a relationship with oneself: *to take a wife.* **4** to pay for or buy. **5** to rent or lease. **6** to obtain by regular payment. **7** to win. **8** to obtain or derive from a source. **9** to assume the obligations of: *to take office.* **10** to endure, esp. with fortitude: *to take punishment.* **11** to adopt as a symbol of duty, etc.: *to take the veil.* **12** to receive in a specified way: *she took the news very well.* **13** to adopt as one's own: *to take someone's part in a quarrel.* **14** to receive and make use of: *to take advice.* **15** to receive into the body, as by eating, inhaling, etc. **16** to eat, drink, etc., esp. habitually. **17** to have or be engaged in for one's benefit or use: *to take a rest.* **18** to work at or study: *to take economics at college.* **19** to make, do, or perform (an action). **20** to make use of: *to take an opportunity.* **21** to put into effect: *to take measures.* **22** (*also intr*) to make a photograph of or admit of being photographed. **23** to act or perform. **24** to write down or copy: *to take notes.* **25** to experience or feel: *to take offence.* **26** to consider or regard: *I take him to be honest.* **27** to accept as valid: *I take your point.* **28** to hold or maintain in the mind: *his father took a dim view of his career.* **29** to deal or contend with. **30** to use as a particular case: *take hotels for example.* **31** (*intr;* often foll. by *from*) to diminish or detract: *the actor's bad performance took from the effect of the play.* **32** to confront successfully: *the horse took the jump at the third attempt.* **33** (*intr*) to have or produce the intended effect: *her vaccination took.* **34** (*intr*) (of plants, etc.) to start growing successfully. **35** to aim or direct: *he took a swipe at his opponent.* **36** to deal a blow to in a specified place. **37** *Arch.* to have sexual intercourse with (a woman). **38** to remove from a place. **39** to carry along or have in one's possession. **40** to convey or transport. **41** to use as a means of transport: *I shall take the bus.* **42** to conduct or lead. **43** to escort or accompany. **44** to bring or deliver to a state, position, etc.: *his ability took him to the forefront.* **45** to seek: *to take cover.* **46** to ascertain by measuring, etc.: *to take a pulse.* **47** (*intr*) (of a mechanism) to catch or engage (a part). **48** to put an end to: *she took her own life.* **49** to come upon unexpectedly. **50** to contract: *he took a chill.* **51** to affect or attack: *the fever took him one night.* **52** (*copula*) to become suddenly or be rendered (ill): *he was taken sick.* **53** (*also intr*) to absorb or become absorbed by something: *to take a polish.* **54** (*usually passive*) to charm: *she was very taken with the puppy.* **55** (*intr*) to be or become popular; win favour. **56** to require: *that task will take all your time.* **57** to subtract or deduct. **58** to hold: *the suitcase won't take all your clothes.* **59** to quote or copy. **60** to proceed to occupy: *to take a seat.* **61** (often foll. by *to*) to use or employ: *to take steps to ascertain the answer.* **62** to win or capture (a trick, piece, etc.). **63** *Sl.* to cheat, deceive, or victimize. **64 take five** (*or* **ten**). *Inf., chiefly US & Canad.* to take a break of five (or ten) minutes. **65 take it. 65a** to assume; believe. **65b** *Inf.* to stand up to or endure criticism, harsh treatment, etc. **66 take one's time.** to use as much time as is needed. **67 take (someone's) name in vain. 67a** to use a name, esp. of God, disrespectfully or irreverently. **67b** *Jocular.* to say (someone's) name. **68 take upon oneself.** to assume the right to do or responsibility for something. ◆ *n* **69** the act of taking. **70** the number of quarry killed or captured. **71** *Inf., chiefly US.* the amount of anything taken, esp. money. **72** *Films, music.* **72a** one of a series of recordings from which the best will be selected. **72b** the process of taking one such recording. **72c** a scene photographed without interruption. **73** *Inf., chiefly US.* a version or interpretation: *Cronenberg's harsh take on the sci-fi story.* ◆ See also **take after, take against,** etc. ORIG OE *tacan*
► **'takable** *or* **'takeable** *adj* ► **'taker** *n*

take after *vb* (*intr, prep*) to resemble in appearance, character, behaviour, etc.

take against *vb* (*intr, prep*) to start to dislike, esp. without good reason.

take apart *vb* (*tr, adv*) **1** to separate (something) into component parts. **2** to criticize severely.

take away *vb* (*tr, adv*) **1** to subtract: *take away four from nine to leave five.* ◆ *prep* **2** minus: *nine take away four is five.* ◆ *adj* **takeaway.** *Brit., Austral., & NZ.* **3** sold for consumption away from the premises: *a takeaway meal.* **4** selling food for consumption away from the premises: *a takeaway Indian restaurant.* ◆ *n* **takeaway.** *Brit., Austral., & NZ.* **5** a shop or restaurant that sells such food. **6** a meal bought at such a shop or restaurant: *we'll have a Chinese* *takeaway tonight.* ◆ Scot. word (for senses 3–6): **carry out.** US and Canad. word (for senses 3–6): **takeout.**

take back *vb (adv, mainly tr)* **1** to retract or withdraw (something said, promised, etc.). **2** to regain possession of. **3** to return for exchange. **4** to accept (someone) back (into one's home, affections, etc.). **5** to remind one of the past: *that tune really takes me back.* **6** *(also intr) Printing.* to move (copy) to the previous line.

take down *vb (tr, adv)* **1** to record in writing. **2** to dismantle or tear down. **3** to lower or reduce in power, arrogance, etc. (esp. in **take down a peg**). ◆ *adj* **take-down. 4** made or intended to be disassembled.

take for *vb (tr, prep) Inf.* to consider or suppose to be, esp. mistakenly: *the fake coins were taken for genuine; who do you take me for?*

take-home pay *n* the remainder of one's pay after all income tax and other compulsory deductions have been made.

take in *vb (tr, adv)* **1** to understand. **2** to include. **3** to receive into one's house in exchange for payment: *to take in lodgers.* **4** to make (clothing, etc.) smaller by altering seams. **5** *Inf.* to cheat or deceive. **6** *US.* to go to: *let's take in a movie tonight.*

taken ('teɪkən) *vb* **1** the past participle of **take.** ◆ *adj* **2** *(postpositive;* foll. by *with)* enthusiastically impressed (by); infatuated (with).

take off *vb (adv)* **1** *(tr)* to remove (a garment). **2** *(intr)* (of an aircraft) to become airborne. **3** *Inf.* to set out or cause to set out on a journey: *they took off for Spain.* **4** *(tr)* (of a disease) to kill. **5** *(tr) Inf.* to mimic. **6** *(intr) Inf.* to become successful or popular. ◆ *n* **takeoff. 7** the act or process of making an aircraft airborne. **8** the stage of a country's economic development when rapid and sustained economic growth is first achieved. **9** *Inf.* an act of mimicry.

take on *vb (adv, mainly tr)* **1** to employ or hire. **2** to assume or acquire: *his voice took on a plaintive note.* **3** to agree to do; undertake. **4** to compete against; fight. **5** *(intr) Inf.* to exhibit great emotion, esp. grief.

take out *vb (tr, adv)* **1** to extract or remove. **2** to obtain or secure (a licence, patent, etc.). **3** to go out with; escort. **4** *Bridge.* to bid a different suit from (one's partner) in order to rescue him or her from a difficult contract. **5** *Sl.* to kill or destroy. **6** *Austral. inf.* to win, esp. in sport. **7 take it** *or* **a lot out of.** *Inf.* to sap the energy or vitality of. **8 take out on.** *Inf.* to vent (anger, etc.) on. **9 take someone out of himself** (*or* **herself**). *Inf.* to make someone forget his or her anxieties, problems, etc. ◆ *adj* **takeout. 10** *Bridge.* of or designating a conventional informatory bid, asking one's partner to bid another suit. ◆ *adj, n* **takeout. 11** the US and Canad. word for **takeaway** (senses 3–6).

take over *vb (adv)* **1** to assume the control or management of. **2** *Printing.* to move (copy) to the next line. ◆ *n* **takeover. 3** the act of seizing or assuming power, control, etc.

take to *vb (intr, prep)* **1** to make for; flee to: *to take to the hills.* **2** to form a liking for. **3** to have recourse to: *to take to the bottle.*

take up *vb (adv, mainly tr)* **1** to adopt the study, practice, or activity of: *to take up gardening.* **2** to shorten (a garment). **3** to pay off (a note, mortgage, etc.). **4** to agree to or accept (an invitation, etc.). **5** to pursue further or resume (something): *he took up French where he left off.* **6** to absorb (a liquid). **7** to act as a patron to. **8** to occupy or fill (space or time). **9** to interrupt, esp. in order to contradict or criticize. **10** *Austral. & NZ.* to occupy and break in (uncultivated land): *he took up some hundreds of acres in the back country.* **11 take up on. 11a** to argue with (someone): *can I take you up on two points in your talk?* **11b** to accept what is offered by (someone): *let me take you up on your invitation.* **12 take up with. 12a** to discuss with (someone); refer to. **12b** *(intr)* to begin to keep company or associate with. ◆ *n* **take-up. 13a** the claiming of something, esp. a state benefit. **13b** *(as modifier)*: *take-up rate.*

takin ('tɑːkiːn) *n* a massive bovid mammal of S Asia, having a shaggy coat, short legs, and horns. ORIG C19: from Tibetan native name

taking ('teɪkɪŋ) *adj* **1** charming, fascinating, or intriguing. **2** *Inf.* infectious; catching. ◆ *n* **3** something taken. **4** *(pl)* receipts; earnings.
▸ **'takingly** *adv* ▸ **'takingness** *n*

Takoradi ★ (ˌtɑːkə'rɑːdɪ) *n* the chief port of Ghana, in the southwest on the Gulf of Guinea: modern harbour opened in 1928. Pop. (with Sekondi): 103 600 (1988 est.).

talapoin ('tæləˌpɔɪn) *n* **1** a small W African monkey. **2** (in Myanmar and Thailand) a Buddhist monk. ORIG C16: from F, lit.: Buddhist monk, from Port. *talapão;* orig. jocular, from the appearance of the monkey

talaria (tə'lɛərɪə) *pl n Greek myth.* winged sandals. ORIG C16: from L, from *tālāris* belonging to the ankle, from *tālus* ankle

Talavera de la Reina ★ (*Spanish* tala'βera ðe la 'reina) *n* a walled town in central Spain, on the Tagus River: scene of the defeat of the French by British and Spanish forces (1809) during the Peninsular War; agricultural processing centre. Pop.: 68 640 (1991).

Talbot ★ ('tɒlbət) *n* (**William Henry**) **Fox.** 1800–77, British pioneer of photography.

talc (tælk) *n also* **talcum. 1** See **talcum powder. 2** a soft mineral, consisting of magnesium silicate, used in the manufacture of ceramics and paints and as a filler in talcum powder, etc. ◆ *vb* **talcs, talcking, talcked** *or* **talcs, talcing, talced. 3** *(tr)* to apply talc to. ORIG C16: from Med. L *talcum,* from Ar. *talq* mica, from Persian *talk*
▸ **'talcose** *or* **'talcous** *adj*

Talca ★ (*Spanish* 'talka) *n* a city in central Chile: scene of the declaration of Chilean independence (1818). Pop.: 169 448 (1995 est.).

Talcahuano ★ (*Spanish* talka'wano) *n* a port in S central Chile, near Concepción on an inlet of the Pacific: oil refinery. Pop.: 260 915 (1995 est.).

talcum powder ('tælkəm) *n* a powder made of purified talc, usually scented, used for perfuming the body and for absorbing excess moisture. Often shortened to **talcum** or **talc.**

tale (teɪl) *n* **1** a report, narrative, or story. **2** one of a group of short stories. **3a** a malicious or meddlesome rumour or piece of gossip. **3b** *(in combination)*: *talebearer; taleteller.* **4** a fictitious or false statement. **5 tell tales. 5a** to tell fanciful lies. **5b** to report malicious stories, trivial complaints, etc., esp. to someone in authority. **6 tell a tale.** to reveal something important. **7 tell its own tale.** to be self-evident. **8** *Arch.* a number; amount. ORIG OE *talu* list

talent ('tælənt) *n* **1** innate ability, aptitude, or faculty; above average ability: *a talent for cooking; a child with talent.* **2** a person or persons possessing such ability. **3** any of various ancient units of weight and money. **4** *Inf.* members of the opposite sex collectively: *the local talent.* ORIG OE *talente,* from L *talenta,* pl. of *talentum* sum of money, from Gk *talanton* unit of money; in Med. L the sense was extended to ability through the infl. of the parable of the talents (Matthew 25:14–30)
▸ **'talented** *adj*

talent scout *n* a person whose occupation is the search for talented sportsmen, performers, etc., for engagements as professionals.

tales ('teɪliːz) *n Law.* **1** *(functioning as pl)* a group of persons summoned to fill vacancies on a jury panel. **2** *(functioning as sing)* the writ summoning such jurors. ORIG C15: from Med. L *tālēs dē circumstantibus* such men from among the bystanders, from L *tālis* such
▸ **'talesman** *n*

Taliban *or* **Taleban** ('tælɪˌbæn) *n* a militant fundamentalist Islamic organization in Afghanistan. ORIG C20: from Ar. *tāliban* seekers

Taliesin ★ (ˌtælɪ'ɛsɪn) *n* 6th century A.D., Welsh bard; reputed author of the *Book of Taliesin.*

taligrade ('tælɪˌgreɪd) *adj* (of mammals) walking on the outer side of the foot. ORIG C20: from NL, from L *tālus* ankle, heel + -GRADE

talion ('tælɪən) *n* the system or legal principle of making the punishment correspond to the crime; retaliation. ORIG C15: via OF from L *tāliō,* from *tālis* such

talipes ('tælɪˌpiːz) *n* **1** a congenital deformity of the foot by which it is twisted in any of various positions. **2** a technical name for **club foot.** ORIG C19: NL, from L *tālus* ankle + *pēs* foot

talipot *or* **talipot palm** ('tælɪˌpɒt) *n* a palm tree of the East Indies, having large leaves that are used for fans, thatching houses, etc. ORIG C17: from Bengali: palm leaf, from Sansk. *tālī* fan palm + *pattra* leaf

talisman ('tælɪzmən) *n, pl* **talismans. 1** a stone or other small object, usually inscribed or carved, believed to protect the wearer from evil influences. **2** anything thought to have magical or protective powers. ORIG C17: via F or Sp. from Ar. *tilsam,* from Med. Gk *telesma* ritual, from Gk: consecration, from *telein* to perform a rite, complete
▸ **talismanic** (ˌtælɪz'mænɪk) *adj*

talk (tɔːk) *vb* **1** (*intr;* often foll. by *to* or *with*) to express one's thoughts, feelings, or desires by means of words (to). **2** (*intr*) to communicate by other means: *lovers talk with their eyes.* **3** (*intr;* usually foll. by *about*) to exchange ideas or opinions (about). **4** (*intr*) to articulate words. **5** (*tr*) to give voice to; utter: *to talk rubbish.* **6** (*tr*) to discuss: *to talk business.* **7** (*intr*) to reveal information. **8** (*tr*) to know how to communicate in (a language or idiom): *he talks English.* **9** (*intr*) to spread rumours or gossip. **10** (*intr*) to make sounds suggestive of talking. **11** (*intr*) to be effective or persuasive: *money talks.* **12 now you're talking.** *Inf.* at last you're saying something agreeable. **13 talk big.** to boast. **14 you can talk.** *Inf.* **14a** you don't have to worry about doing a particular thing yourself. **14b** Also: **you can't talk.** you yourself are guilty of offending in the very matter you are upholding or decrying. ◆ *n* **15** a speech or lecture. **16** an exchange of ideas or thoughts. **17** idle chatter, gossip, or rumour. **18** a subject of conversation; theme. **19** (*often pl*) a conference, discussion, or negotiation. **20** a specific manner of speaking: *children's talk.* ◆ See also **talk about, talk back,** etc. ORIG C13 *talkien*
▸ **'talker** *n*

talk about *vb* (*intr, prep*) **1** to discuss. **2** used informally and often ironically to add emphasis to a statement: *all his plays have such ridiculous plots – talk about good drama!*

talkative ('tɔːkətɪv) *adj* given to talking a great deal.
▸ **'talkatively** *adv* ▸ **'talkativeness** *n*

talk back *vb* (*intr, adv*) **1** to answer boldly or impudently. **2** *NZ.* to conduct a telephone dialogue for immediate transmission over the air. ◆ *n* **talkback. 3** *Television, radio.* a system of telephone links enabling spoken directions to be given during the production of a programme. **4** *NZ.* a broadcast telephone dialogue.

talk down *vb* (*adv*) **1** (*intr;* often foll. by *to*) to behave (towards) in a superior manner. **2** (*tr*) to override (a person) by continuous or loud talking. **3** (*tr*) to give instructions to (an aircraft) by radio to enable it to land.

talkie ('tɔːkɪ) *n Inf.* an early film with a soundtrack. Full name: **talking picture.**

Talking Book *n Trademark.* a recording of a book, designed to be used by blind people.

talking head *n* (on television) a person, shown only from the shoulders up, who speaks without illustrative material.

talking-to *n Inf.* a session of criticism, as of a subordinate by a person in authority.

talk into *vb* (*tr, prep*) to persuade to by talking: *I talked him into buying the house.*

talk out *vb* (*tr, adv*) **1** to resolve or eliminate by talking. **2** *Brit.* to block (a bill, etc.) in a legislative body by lengthy discussion. **3 talk out of.** to dissuade from by talking.

talk round *vb* **1** (*tr, adv*) Also: **talk over.** to persuade to one's opinion. **2** (*intr, prep*) to discuss (a subject), esp. without coming to a conclusion.

talk shop *vb* to talk about one's profession, esp. at a social occasion.

talk show *n* another name for **chat show.**

tall (tɔːl) *adj* **1** of more than average height. **2** (*postpositive*) having a specified height: *five feet tall.* ORIG C14 (in the sense: big, comely, valiant)
▸ **'tallness** *n*

tallage ('tælɪdʒ) *n English history.* **a** a tax levied by kings on Crown lands and royal towns. **b** a toll levied by a lord upon his tenants or by a feudal lord upon his vassals. ORIG C13: from OF *taillage,* from *taillier* to cut; see TAILOR

Tallahassee ★ (ˌtælə'hæsɪ) *n* a city in N Florida, capital of the state: two universities. Pop.: 133 718 (1994 est.).

tallboy ('tɔːlˌbɔɪ) *n* **1** a high chest of drawers made in two sections placed one on top of the other. **2** a fitting on the top of a chimney to prevent downdraughts.

Talleyrand-Périgord ★ ('tælɪˌrænd'pɛrɪgɔː; *French* talɛrɑ̃-perigɔr) *n* **Charles Maurice** (ʃarl mɔris). 1754–1838, French statesman; foreign minister (1797–1807; 1814–15).

Tallinn *or* **Tallin** ★ ('tælɪn) *n* the capital of Estonia, on the Gulf of Finland: founded by the Danes in 1219; naval base. Pop.: 427 500 (1996 est.). German name: **Reval.**

Tallis ★ ('tælɪs) *n* **Thomas.** ?1505–85, English composer; noted for his Anglican liturgical music.

tallith ('tælɪθ) *n* a shawl with fringed corners worn by Jewish males, esp. during religious services. ORIG C17: from Heb. *tallīt*

tall order *n Inf.* a difficult or unreasonable request.

tallow ('tæləʊ) *n* **1** a fatty substance extracted chiefly from the suet of sheep and cattle: used for making soap, candles, food, etc. ◆ *vb* **2** (*tr*) to cover or smear with tallow. ORIG OE *tælg,* a dye
▸ **'tallowy** *adj*

tallowwood ('tæləʊˌwʊd) *n Austral.* a tall eucalyptus tree having soft fibrous bark and a greasy timber.

tall poppy *n Austral. inf.* a prominent or highly paid person.

tall poppy syndrome *n Austral. inf.* a tendency to disparage any person who has achieved great prominence or wealth.

tall ship *n* any square-rigged sailing ship.

tall story *n Inf.* an exaggerated or incredible account.

tally ('tælɪ) *vb* **tallies, tallying, tallied. 1** (*intr*) to correspond one with the other: *the two stories don't tally.* **2** (*tr*) to supply with an identifying tag. **3** (*intr*) to keep score. **4** (*tr*) *Obs.* to record or mark. ◆ *n, pl* **tallies. 5** any record of debit, credit, the score in a game, etc. **6** *Austral. & NZ.* the number of sheep shorn in a specified period. **7** an identifying label or mark. **8** a counterpart or duplicate of something. **9** a stick used (esp. formerly) as a record of the amount of a debt according to the notches cut in it. **10** a notch or mark made on such a stick. **11** a mark used to represent a certain number in counting. ORIG C15: from Med. L *tālea,* from L: cutting

tally clerk *n Austral. & NZ.* a person, esp. on a wharf or in an airport, who checks the count of goods being loaded or unloaded.

tally-ho (ˌtælɪ'həʊ) *interj* **1** the cry of a participant at a hunt when the quarry is sighted. ◆ *n, pl* **tally-hos. 2** an instance of crying tally-ho. **3** another name for a **four-in-hand** (sense 1). ◆ *vb* **tally-hos, tally-hoing, tally-hoed** *or* **tally-ho'd. 4** (*intr*) to make the cry of tally-ho. ORIG C18: ?from F *taïaut* cry used in hunting

tallyman ('tælɪmən) *n, pl* **tallymen. 1** a scorekeeper or recorder. **2** *Dialect.* a travelling salesman for a firm specializing in hire-purchase.
▸ **'tallyˌwoman** *fem n*

Talmud ('tælmʊd) *n Judaism.* the primary source of Jewish religious law, consisting of the Mishnah and the Gemara. ORIG C16: from Heb. *talmūdh,* lit.: instruction, from *lāmadh* to learn
▸ **Tal'mudic** *or* **Tal'mudical** *adj* ▸ **'Talmudism** *n* ▸ **'Talmudist** *n*

talon ('tælən) *n* **1** a sharply hooked claw, esp. of a bird of prey. **2** anything resembling this. **3** the part of a lock that the key presses on when it is turned. **4** *Piquet, etc.* the pile of cards left after the deal. **5** *Archit.* another name for **ogee. 6** *Stock Exchange.* a printed slip attached to some bearer bonds to enable the holder to apply for a new sheet of coupons. ORIG C14: from OF: heel, from L *tālus*
▸ **'taloned** *adj*

Talos ★ ('teɪlɒs) *n Greek myth.* the nephew and apprentice of Daedalus, who surpassed his uncle as an inventor and was killed by him out of jealousy.

talus[1] ('teɪləs) *n, pl* **tali** (-laɪ). the bone of the ankle that articulates with the leg bones to form the ankle joint; anklebone. ORIG C18: from L: ankle

talus[2] ('teɪləs) *n, pl* **taluses. 1** *Geol.* another name for **scree. 2** *Fortifications.* the sloping side of a wall. ORIG C17: from F, from L *talūtium* slope, ? of Iberian origin

tam (tæm) *n* short for **tam-o'-shanter.**

tamale (tə'mɑːlɪ) *n* a Mexican dish made of minced meat mixed with crushed maize and seasonings, wrapped in maize husks and steamed. ORIG C19: erroneously for *tamal,* from Mexican Sp., from Nahuatl *tamalli*

tamandua (ˌtæmən'dʊə) *n* a small arboreal mammal of Central and South America, having a tubular mouth specialized for feeding on termites. Also called: **lesser anteater.** ORIG C17: via Port. from Tupi: ant trapper, from *taixi* ant + *mondê* to catch

tamarack ('tæməˌræk) *n* **1** any of several North American larches. **2** the wood of any of these trees. ORIG C19: of Amerind origin

tamari (tə'mɑːrɪ) *n* a Japanese variety of soy sauce. ORIG Japanese

tamarillo (ˌtæmə'rɪləʊ) *n, pl* **tamarillos.** another name for **tree tomato.**

tamarin ('tæmərɪn) *n* any of numerous small monkeys of South and Central American forests; similar to the marmosets. ORIG C18: via F, of Amerind origin

tamarind ('tæmərɪnd) *n* **1** a tropical evergreen tree having yellow flowers and brown pods. **2** the fruit of this tree, used as a food and to make beverages and medicines. **3** the wood of this tree. ORIG C16: from Med. L *tamarindus,* ult. from Ar. *tamr hindī* Indian date

tamarisk ('tæmərɪsk) *n* any of a genus of trees and shrubs of the Mediterranean region and S and SE Asia, having scalelike leaves, slender branches, and feathery flower clusters. ORIG C15: from LL *tamariscus,* from L *tamarix*

Tamatave ★ (*French* tamatav) *n* the former name (until 1979) of **Toamasina.**

Tamaulipas ★ (*Spanish* tamau'lipas) *n* a state of NE Mexico, on the Gulf of Mexico. Capital: Ciudad Victoria. Pop.: 2 628 839 (1997 est.). Area: 79 829 sq. km (30 822 sq. miles).

Tambo ★ ('tæmbəʊ) *n* **Oliver.** 1917–93, South African politician; president (1977–91) of the African National Congress.

Tambora ★ ('tæmbəˌrɑː) *n* a volcano in Indonesia, on N Sumbawa: violent eruption of 1815 reduced its height from about 4000 m (13 000 ft) to 2850 m (9400 ft).

tambour ('tæmbʊə) *n* **1** *Real Tennis.* the sloping buttress on one side of the receiver's end of the court. **2** a small embroidery frame, consisting of two hoops over which the fabric is stretched while being worked. **3** embroidered work done on such a frame. **4** a sliding door on desks, cabinets, etc., made of thin strips of wood glued onto a canvas backing. **5** *Archit.* a wall that is circular in plan, esp. one that supports a dome or one that is surrounded by a colonnade. **6** a drum. ◆ *vb* **7** to embroider on a tambour. ORIG C15: from F, from *tabour* TABOR

tamboura (tæm'bʊərə) *n* a stringed instrument with a long neck used in Indian music to provide a drone. ORIG from Persian *tanbūr,* from Ar. *tunbūr*

tambourin ('tæmbʊrɪn) *n* **1** an 18th-century Provençal folk dance. **2** a piece of music composed for or in the rhythm of this dance. **3** a small drum. ORIG C18: from F: a little drum

tambourine (ˌtæmbə'riːn) *n Music.* a percussion instrument consisting of a single drumhead of skin stretched over a circular wooden frame hung with pairs of metal discs that jingle when it is struck or shaken. ORIG C16: from MFlemish *tamborijn* a little drum, from OF: TAMBOURIN

▸ ˌ**tambou'rinist** *n*

Tambov ★ (*Russian* tam'bɔf) *n* an industrial city in W Russia: founded in 1636 as a Muscovite fort. Pop.: 316 000 (1995 est.).

Tamburlaine ★ ('tæmbəˌleɪn) *n* a variant of **Tamerlane.**

tame (teɪm) *adj* **1** changed by man from a wild state into a domesticated or cultivated condition. **2** (of animals) not fearful of human contact. **3** meek or submissive. **4** flat, insipid, or uninspiring. ◆ *vb* **tames, taming, tamed.** (*tr*) **5** to make tame; domesticate. **6** to break the spirit of, subdue, or curb. **7** to tone down, soften, or mitigate. ORIG OE *tam*

▸ **'tamable** *or* **'tameable** *adj* ▸ **'tamely** *adv* ▸ **'tameness** *n* ▸ **'tamer** *n*

Tamerlane ('tæməˌleɪn) *or* **Tamburlaine** ★ *n* Turkic name *Timur* (tiː'mʊə). ?1336–1405, Mongol conqueror; ruler of Samarkand (1369–1405): died while invading China.

Tameside ★ ('teɪmˌsaɪd) *n* a unitary authority of NW England, in Greater Manchester. Pop.: 220 700 (1996 est.). Area: 103 sq. km (40 sq. miles).

Tamil ('tæmɪl) *n* **1** (*pl* **Tamils** *or* **Tamil**) a member of a mixed Dravidian and Caucasoid people of S India and Sri Lanka. **2** the language of this people. ◆ *adj* **3** of or relating to this people or their language.

Tamil Nadu ★ ('tæmɪl nɑː'duː) *n* a state of SE India, on the Coromandel Coast: reorganized in 1956 and 1960 and made smaller; consists of a coastal plain backed by hills, including the Nilgiri Hills in the west. Capital: Madras. Pop.: 58 840 000 (1994 est.). Area: 130 058 sq. km (50 216 sq. miles). Former name (until 1968): **Madras.**

Tammerfors ★ (tamər'fɔrs) *n* the Swedish name for **Tampere.**

tammy[1] ('tæmɪ) *n, pl* **tammies.** another word for **tam-o'-shanter.**

tammy[2] ('tæmɪ) *n, pl* **tammies.** (esp. formerly) a woollen cloth used for straining sauces, soups, etc. ORIG C18: changed from F *tamis,* ? of Celtic origin

tam-o'-shanter (ˌtæmə'ʃæntə) *n* a Scottish brimless wool or cloth cap with a bobble in the centre. ORIG C19: after the hero of Burns's poem *Tam o' Shanter* (1790)

tamoxifen (tə'mɒksɪˌfen) *n* a drug that antagonizes the action of oestrogen and is used to treat breast cancer and some types of infertility in women. ORIG C20: from T(RANS-) + AM(INE) + OXY-[2] + PHEN(OL)

tamp (tæmp) *vb* (*tr*) **1** to force or pack down firmly by repeated blows. **2** to pack sand, earth, etc., into (a drill hole) over an explosive. ORIG C17: prob. back formation from *tampin* (obs. var. of TAMPION), taken as a present participle *tamping*

Tampa ★ ('tæmpə) *n* a port and resort in W Florida, on **Tampa Bay** (an arm of the Gulf of Mexico): two universities. Pop.: 285 523 (1994 est.).

tamper[1] ('tæmpə) *vb* (*intr*) **1** (usually foll. by *with*) to interfere or meddle. **2** to use bribery or blackmail. **3** (usually foll. by *with*) to attempt to influence, esp. by bribery. ORIG C16: alteration of TEMPER (vb)

▸ **'tamperer** *n*

tamper[2] ('tæmpə) *n* **1** a person or thing that tamps, esp. an instrument for packing down tobacco in a pipe. **2** a casing around the core of a nuclear weapon to increase its efficiency by reflecting neutrons and delaying the expansion.

Tampere ★ (*Finnish* 'tampɛrɛ) *n* a city in SW Finland: the second largest town in Finland; textile manufacturing. Pop.: 182 742 (1996 est.). Swedish name: **Tammerfors.**

Tampico ★ (*Spanish* tam'piko) *n* a port and resort in E Mexico, in Tamaulipas on the Pánuco River: oil refining. Pop.: 272 690 (1990).

tampion ('tæmpɪən) *or* **tompion** *n* a plug placed in a gun's muzzle when the gun is not in use. ORIG C15: from F: TAMPON

tampon ('tæmpɒn) *n* **1** a plug of lint, cotton wool, etc., inserted into a wound or body cavity to stop the flow of blood, absorb secretions, etc. ◆ *vb* **2** (*tr*) to plug (a wound, etc.) with a tampon. ORIG C19: via F from OF *tapon* a little plug, of Gmc origin

▸ **tamponage** ('tæmpənɪdʒ) *n*

tam-tam *n* another name for **gong** (sense 1). ORIG from Hindi; see TOM-TOM

Tamworth ★ ('tæmwəθ) *n* **1** a market town in W central England, in SE Staffordshire. Pop.: 68 440 (1991). **2** a city in SE Australia, in E central New South Wales: industrial centre of an agricultural region. Pop.: 34 000 (latest est.).

tan[1] (tæn) *n* **1** the brown colour produced by the skin after exposure to ultraviolet rays, esp. those of the sun. **2** a yellowish-brown colour. **3** short for **tanbark.** ◆ *vb* **tans, tanning, tanned. 4** to go brown or cause to go brown after exposure to ultraviolet rays. **5** to convert (a skin or hide) into leather by treating it with a tanning agent. **6** (*tr*) *Sl.* to beat or flog. ◆ *adj* **tanner, tannest. 7** of the colour tan. ORIG OE *tannian* (unattested as infinitive, attested as *getanned,* p.p.), from Med. L *tannāre,* from *tannum* tanbark, ? of Celtic origin
▸ **'tannable** *adj* ▸ **'tannish** *adj*

tan[2] (tæn) *abbrev. for* tangent (sense 2).

Tana ★ ('tɑːnə) *n* **1 Lake.** Also called: (Lake) **Tsana.** a lake in NW Ethiopia, on a plateau 1800 m (6000 ft) high: the largest lake of Ethiopia; source of the Blue Nile. Area: 3673 sq. km (1418 sq. miles). **2** a river in E Kenya, rising in the Aberdare Range and flowing in a wide curve east to the Indian Ocean: the longest river in Kenya. Length: 708 km (440 miles). **3** a river in NE Norway, flowing generally northeast as part of the border between Norway and Finland to the Arctic Ocean by Tana Fjord. Length: about 320 km (200 miles). Finnish name: **Teno.**

tanager ('tænədʒə) *n* any of a family of American songbirds having a short thick bill and, in the male, a brilliantly coloured plumage. ORIG C19: from NL *tanagra,* based on Amerind *tangara*

Tanagra ★ ('tænəgrə) *n* a town in ancient Boeotia, famous for terracotta figurines of the same name, first discovered in its necropolis.

Tanana ★ ('tænənɑː) *n* a river in central Alaska, rising in the Wrangell Mountains and flowing northwest to the Yukon River. Length: about 765 km (475 miles).

Tananarive ★ (*French* tananariv) *n* the former name of **Antananarivo.**

tanbark ('tæn,bɑːk) *n* the bark of certain trees, esp. the oak, used as a source of tannin.

Tancred ★ ('tæŋkrɪd) *n* died 1112, Norman hero of the First Crusade, who played a prominent part in the capture of Jerusalem (1099).

tandem ('tændəm) *n* **1** a bicycle with two sets of pedals and two saddles, arranged one behind the other for two riders. **2** a two-wheeled carriage drawn by two horses harnessed one behind the other. **3** a team of two horses so harnessed. **4** any arrangement of two things in which one is placed behind the other. **5 in tandem.** together or in conjunction. ◆ *adj* **6** *Brit.* used as, used in, or routed through an intermediate automatic telephone exchange. ◆ *adv* **7** one behind the other. ORIG C18: whimsical use of L *tandem* at length, to indicate a long vehicle

Tandjungpriok *or* **Tanjungpriok** ★ (,tændʒʊŋ'priːɒk) *n* a port in Indonesia, on the NW coast of Java adjoining the capital, Jakarta: a major shipping and distributing centre for the whole archipelago.

tandoori (tæn'dʊərɪ) *n* an Indian method of cooking meat or vegetables on a spit in a clay oven. ORIG from Urdu, from *tandoor* an oven

tang (tæŋ) *n* **1** a strong taste or flavour. **2** a pungent or characteristic smell. **3** a trace, touch, or hint of something. **4** the pointed end of a tool, such as a chisel, file, knife, etc., which is fitted into a handle, shaft, or stock. ORIG C14: from ON *tangi* point

Tang ★ (tæŋ) *n* the imperial dynasty of China from 618–907 A.D.

Tanga ★ ('tæŋgə) *n* a port in N Tanzania, on the Indian Ocean: Tanzania's second port. Pop.: 187 155 (1988).

Tanganyika ★ (,tæŋgə'njiːkə) *n* **1** a former state in E Africa: became part of German East Africa in 1884; ceded to Britain as a League of Nations mandate in 1919 and as a UN trust territory in 1946; gained independence in 1961 and united with Zanzibar in 1964 as the United Republic of Tanzania. **2 Lake.** a lake in central Africa between Tanzania and the Democratic Republic of Congo, bordering also on Burundi and Zambia, in the Great Rift Valley: the longest freshwater lake in the world. Area: 32 893 sq. km (12 700 sq. miles). Length: 676 km (420 miles).
▸ **,Tangan'yikan** *adj, n*

tangata whenua ('tɑːŋɑːtɑː 'fɛnuːɑː) *n NZ.* **1** the original settlers of New Zealand who came from Polynesia by canoe. **2** the descendants of these people. ORIG Maori, lit.: people of the land

Tange ★ ('tæŋgə) *n* **Kenzo.** born 1913, Japanese architect. His buildings include the Kurashiki city hall (1960) and St Mary's Cathedral in Tokyo (1962–64).

tangent ('tændʒənt) *n* **1** a geometric line, curve, plane, or curved surface that touches another curve or surface at one point but does not intersect it. **2** (of an angle) a trigonometric function that in a right-angled triangle is the ratio of the length of the opposite side to that of the adjacent side; the ratio of sine to cosine. Abbrev.: **tan. 3** *Music.* a small piece of metal that strikes the string of a clavichord. **4 on** *or* **at a tangent.** on a completely different or divergent course, esp. of thought. ◆ *adj* **5a** of or involving a tangent. **5b** touching at a single point. **6** touching. ORIG C16: from L *līnea tangēns* the touching line, from *tangere* to touch
▸ **'tangency** *n*

tangent galvanometer *n* a galvanometer having a vertical coil of wire with a horizontal magnetic needle at its centre. The current to be measured is passed through the coil and produces a proportional magnetic field which deflects the needle.

tangential (tæn'dʒenʃəl) *adj* **1** of, being, or in the direction of a tangent. **2** *Astron.* (of velocity) in a direction perpendicular to the line of sight of a celestial object. **3** of superficial relevance only; digressive.
▸ **tan,genti'ality** *n* ▸ **tan'gentially** *adv*

tangerine (,tændʒə'riːn) *n* **1** an Asian citrus tree cultivated for its small orange-like fruits. **2** the fruit of this tree, having sweet spicy flesh. **3a** a reddish-orange colour. **3b** (*as adj*): *a tangerine door.* ORIG C19: from TANGIER

tangi ('tæŋiː) *n NZ.* **1** a Maori funeral ceremony. **2** *Inf.* a lamentation.

tangible ('tændʒɪbᵊl) *adj* **1** capable of being touched or felt. **2** capable of being clearly grasped by the mind. **3** having a physical existence: *tangible assets.* ORIG C16: from LL *tangibilis,* from L *tangere* to touch
▸ **,tangi'bility** *or* **'tangibleness** *n* ▸ **'tangibly** *adv*

Tangier ★ (tæn'dʒɪə) *n* a port in N Morocco, on the Strait of Gibraltar: a Phoenician trading post in the 15th century B.C.; a neutral international zone (1923–56); made the summer capital of Morocco and a free port in 1962; commercial and financial centre. Pop.: 307 000 (1993 est.).
▸ **,Tange'rine** *n, adj*

tangle ('tæŋgᵊl) *n* **1** a confused or complicated mass of hairs, lines, fibres, etc., knotted or coiled together. **2** a complicated problem, condition, or situation. ◆ *vb* **tangles, tangling, tangled. 3** to become or cause to become twisted together in a confused mass. **4** (*intr;* often foll. by *with*) to come into conflict; contend. **5** (*tr*) to involve in matters which hinder or confuse. **6** (*tr*) to ensnare or trap, as in a net. ORIG C14 *tangilen,* var. of *tagilen,* prob. from ON
▸ **'tangled** *or* **'tangly** *adj*

tango ('tæŋgəʊ) *n, pl* **tangos. 1** a Latin-American dance characterized by long gliding steps and sudden pauses. **2** a piece of music composed for or in the rhythm of this dance. ◆ *vb* **tangoes, tangoing, tangoed. 3** (*intr*) to perform this dance. ORIG C20: from American Sp., prob. of Niger-Congo origin

tangram ('tæŋgræm) *n* a Chinese puzzle in which a square, cut into a parallelogram, a square, and five triangles, is formed into figures. ORIG C19: ?from Chinese *t'ang* Chinese + -GRAM

Tangshan ★ ('tæŋ'ʃæn) *n* an industrial city in NE China, in Hebei province. Pop.: 1 500 000 (1991 est.).

Tanguy ★ (*French* tɑ̃gi) *n* **Yves** (iv). 1900–55, US surrealist painter, born in France.

tangy ('tæŋɪ) *adj* **tangier, tangiest.** having a pungent, fresh, or briny flavour or aroma.

tanh (θæn, tænʃ) *n* hyperbolic tangent; a hyperbolic function that is the ratio of sinh to cosh. ORIG C20: from TAN(GENT) + H(YPERBOLIC)

Tanis ★ ('teɪnɪs) *n* an ancient city located in the E part of the Nile delta: abandoned after the 6th century B.C.; at one time the capital of Egypt. Biblical name: **Zoan.**

taniwha ('tʌniːfɑː, 'tænəwɑː) *n NZ.* a legendary Maori monster that lives in rivers and lakes. ORIG Maori

Tanjore ★ (tæn'dʒɔː) *n* the former name of **Thanjavur.**

Tanjungpriok ★ (ˌtændʒʊŋ'priːɒk) *n* a variant spelling of **Tandjungpriok.**

tank (tæŋk) *n* **1** a large container or reservoir for liquids or gases. **2** an armoured combat vehicle moving on tracks and armed with guns, etc. **3** *Brit. or US dialect.* a reservoir, lake, or pond. **4** *Sl., chiefly US.* a jail. **5** Also called: **tankful.** the quantity contained in a tank. **6** *Austral.* a reservoir formed by excavation and damming. ◆ *vb* **7** (*tr*) to put or keep in a tank. **8** *Sl.* to defeat heavily. ◆ See also **tank up.** ORIG C17: from Gujarati (a language of W India) *tānkh* artificial lake, but infl. also by Port. *tanque,* from *estanque* pond, ult. from Vulgar L *stanticāre* (unattested) to block

tanka ('tɑːŋkə) *n, pl* **tankas** *or* **tanka.** a Japanese verse form consisting of five lines, the first and third having five syllables, the others seven. ORIG C19: from Japanese, from *tan* short + *ka* verse

tankage ('tæŋkɪdʒ) *n* **1** the capacity or contents of a tank or tanks. **2** the act of storing in a tank or tanks, or a fee charged for this. **3** *Agriculture.* **3a** fertilizer consisting of the dried and ground residues of animal carcasses. **3b** a protein supplement feed for livestock.

tankard ('tæŋkəd) *n* a large one-handled drinking vessel sometimes fitted with a hinged lid. ORIG C14

tank engine *or* **locomotive** *n* a steam locomotive that carries its water supply in tanks mounted around its boiler.

tanker ('tæŋkə) *n* a ship, lorry, or aeroplane designed to carry liquid in bulk, such as oil.

tank farming *n* another name for **hydroponics.**
▸ **tank farmer** *n*

tank top *n* a sleeveless upper garment with wide shoulder straps and a low neck. ORIG C20: after *tank suits,* one-piece bathing costumes of the 1920s worn in tanks or swimming pools

tank up *vb* (*adv*) *Chiefly Brit.* **1** to fill the tank of (a vehicle) with petrol. **2** *Sl.* to imbibe or cause to imbibe a large quantity of alcoholic drink.

tank wagon *or esp. US & Canad.* **tank car** *n* a form of railway wagon carrying a tank for the transport of liquids.

Tannenberg ★ (*German* 'tanənbɛrk) *n* a village in N Poland, formerly in East Prussia: site of a decisive defeat of the Teutonic Knights by the Poles in 1410 and of a decisive German victory over the Russians in 1914. Polish name: **Stębark.**

tanner[1] ('tænə) *n* a person who tans skins and hides.

tanner[2] ('tænə) *n Brit.* an informal word for **sixpence.** ORIG C19: from ?

tannery ('tænərɪ) *n, pl* **tanneries.** a place or building where skins and hides are tanned.

Tannhäuser ★ ('tænˌhɔɪzə) *n* 13th-century German minnesinger, identified with a legendary knight. The legend forms the basis of an opera by Wagner.

tannic ('tænɪk) *adj* of, relating to, containing, or produced from tan, tannin, or tannic acid.

tannie ('tʌnɪ) *n S. African.* a title of respect used to refer to an elderly woman. ORIG Afrik., lit.: aunt

tannin ('tænɪn) *n* any of a class of yellowish compounds found in many plants and used as tanning agents, mordants, medical astringents, etc. Also called: **tannic acid.** ORIG C19: from F *tanin,* from TAN[1]

Tannoy ('tænɔɪ) *n Trademark.* a type of public-address system.

Tans (tænz) *pl n* **the.** *Irish inf.* short for the **Black and Tans.**

tansy ('tænzɪ) *n, pl* **tansies.** any of numerous plants having yellow flowers in flat-topped clusters and formerly used in medicine and for seasoning. ORIG C15: from OF *tanesie,* from Med. L *athanasia* (from its alleged power to prolong life) from Gk: immortality

Tanta ★ ('tæntə) *n* a city in N Egypt, on the Nile delta: noted for its Muslim festivals. Pop.: 380 000 (1992 est.).

tantalite ('tæntəˌlaɪt) *n* a heavy brownish mineral: it occurs in coarse granite and is an ore of tantalum. ORIG C19: from TANTALUM + -ITE[1]

tantalize *or* **tantalise** ('tæntəˌlaɪz) *vb* **tantalizes, tantalizing, tantalized** *or* **tantalises, tantalising, tantalised.** (*tr*) to tease or make frustrated, as by tormenting with the sight of something desired but inaccessible. ORIG C16: from TANTALUS
▸ **ˌtantaliˈzation** *or* **ˌtantaliˈsation** *n* ▸ **ˈtantaˌlizing** *or* **ˈtantaˌlising** *adj* ▸ **ˈtantaˌlizingly** *or* **ˈtantaˌlisingly** *adv*

tantalum ('tæntələm) *n* a hard greyish-white metallic element: used in electrolytic rectifiers and in alloys to increase hardness and chemical resistance, esp. in surgical instruments. Symbol: Ta; atomic no.: 73; atomic wt.: 180.95. ORIG C19: after TANTALUS, from the metal's incapacity to absorb acids

tantalus ('tæntələs) *n Brit.* a case in which bottles may be locked with their contents tantalizingly visible.

Tantalus ★ ('tæntələs) *n Greek myth.* a king, the father of Pelops, punished in Hades for his misdeeds by having to stand in water that recedes when he tries to drink it and under fruit that moves away as he reaches for it.

tantamount ('tæntəˌmaʊnt) *adj* (*postpositive;* foll. by *to*) as good (as); equivalent in effect (to). ORIG C17: from Anglo-F *tant amunter* to amount to as much

tantara ('tæntərə, tæn'tɑːrə) *n* a fanfare or blast, as on a trumpet or horn. ORIG C16: from L *taratantara,* imit. of the sound of the tuba

tantivy (tæn'tɪvɪ) *adv* **1** at full speed; rapidly. ◆ *n, pl* **tantivies,** *sentence substitute.* **2** a hunting cry, esp. at full gallop. ORIG C17: ? imit. of galloping hooves

tant mieux *French.* (tɑ̃ mjø) so much the better.

tanto ('tæntəʊ) *adv Music.* too much; excessively. ORIG It.

tant pis *French.* (tɑ̃ pi) so much the worse.

Tantrism ('tæntrɪzəm) *n* **1** a movement within Hinduism combining magical and mystical elements and with sacred writings of its own (**the Tantra**). **2** a similar movement within Buddhism. ORIG C18: from Sansk. *tantra,* lit.: warp, hence doctrine
▸ **ˈTantric** *adj* ▸ **ˈTantrist** *n*

tantrum ('tæntrəm) *n* (*often pl*) a childish fit of rage; outburst of bad temper. ORIG C18: from ?

Tan-tung ★ ('tæn'tʊŋ) *n* a variant transliteration of the Chinese name for **Andong.**

Tanzania ★ (ˌtænzə'nɪə) *n* a republic in E Africa, on the Indian Ocean: formed by the union of the independent states of Tanganyika and Zanzibar in 1964; a member of the Commonwealth. Exports include coffee, tea, sisal, and cotton. Official languages: Swahili and English. Religions: Christian, Muslim, and animist. Currency: Tanzanian shilling. Capital: Dodoma. Pop.: 31 271 000 (1999 est.). Area: 945 203 sq. km (364 943 sq. miles).
▸ **ˌTanzaˈnian** *adj, n*

Tao (taʊ) *n* (in the philosophy of Taoism) **1** that in virtue of which all things happen or exist. **2** the rational basis of human conduct. **3** the course of life and its relation to eternal truth. ORIG Chinese, lit.: path, way

Taoiseach ('tiːʃæx) *n* the prime mininster of the Irish Republic. ORIG from Irish, lit.: leader

Taoism ('taʊɪzəm) *n* a system of religion and philosophy based on the teachings of Lao Zi and advocating a simple honest life and noninterference with the course of natural events.
▸ **ˈTaoist** *n, adj* ▸ **ˌTaoˈistic** *adj*

taonga (tɑ'ɔŋgə) *n NZ.* anything highly prized. ORIG Maori

tap[1] (tæp) *vb* **taps, tapping, tapped. 1** to strike (something) lightly and usually repeatedly. **2** (*tr*) to produce by striking in this way: *to tap a rhythm.* **3** (*tr*) to strike lightly with (something): *to tap one's finger on the desk.* **4** (*intr*) to walk with a tapping sound. **5** (*tr*) to attach reinforcing pieces to (the toe or heel of a shoe). ◆ *n* **6** a light blow or knock, or the sound made by it. **7** the metal piece attached to the toe or heel of a shoe used for tap-dancing. **8** short for **tap-dancing.** ◆ See also **taps.** ORIG C13 *tappen,* prob. from OF *taper,* of Gmc origin

tap[2] (tæp) *n* **1** a valve by which a fluid flow from a pipe can be controlled. US names: **faucet, spigot. 2** a stopper to plug a cask or barrel. **3** a particular quality of alcoholic drink, esp. when contained in casks: *an excellent tap.* **4** *Brit.* short for **taproom. 5** the withdrawal of fluid from a bodily cavity. **6** a tool for cutting female screw threads. **7** *Electronics, chiefly US & Canad.* a connection made at some point between the end terminals of an inductor, resistor, etc. Usual Brit. name: **tapping. 8** *Stock Exchange.* **8a** an issue of a government security released slowly onto the market when its market price reaches a predetermined level. **8b** (*as modifier*): *tap stock; tap issue.* **9** a concealed listening or recording device connected to a telephone or telegraph wire. **10 on tap. 10a** *Inf.* ready for use. **10b** (of drinks) on draught. ◆ *vb* **taps, tapping, tapped.** (*tr*) **11** to furnish with a tap. **12** to draw off with or as if with a tap. **13** to cut into (a tree) and draw off sap from it. **14** *Brit. inf.* **14a** to ask (someone) for money: *he tapped me for a fiver.* **14b** to obtain (money) from someone. **15** to connect a tap to (a telephone or telegraph wire). **16** to make a connection to (a pipe, drain, etc.). **17** to cut a female screw thread in (an object or material) by use of a tap. **18** *Inf.* (of a sports team or an employer) to make an illicit attempt to recruit (a player or employee bound by an existing contract). ORIG OE *tæppa*
▸ **'tapper** *n*

tapa ('tɑ:pə) *n* **1** the inner bark of the paper mulberry. **2** a cloth made from this in the Pacific islands. ORIG C19: from native Polynesian name

Tapajós ★ (*Portuguese* tapa'ʒɔs) *n* a river in N Brazil, rising in N central Mato Grosso and flowing northeast to the Amazon. Length: about 800 km (500 miles).

tapas ('tæpəs) *pl n* **a** light snacks or appetizers, usually eaten with drinks. **b** (*as modifier*): *a tapas bar.* ORIG from Sp. *tapa* cover, lid

tap dance *n* **1** a step dance in which the performer wears shoes equipped with taps that make a rhythmic sound on the stage as he dances. ◆ *vb* **tap-dance, tap-dances, tap-dancing, tap-danced.** (*intr*) **2** to perform a tap dance.
▸ **'tap-ˌdancer** *n* ▸ **'tap-ˌdancing** *n*

tape (teɪp) *n* **1** a long thin strip of cotton, linen, etc., used for binding, fastening, etc. **2** a long narrow strip of paper, metal, etc. **3** a string stretched across the track at the end of a race course. **4** See **magnetic tape, ticker tape, paper tape, tape recording.** ◆ *vb* **tapes, taping, taped.** (*mainly tr*) **5** (*also intr*) Also: **tape record.** to record (speech, music, etc.). **6** to furnish with tapes. **7** to bind, measure, secure, or wrap with tape. **8** (*usually passive*) *Brit. inf.* to take stock of (a person or situation). ORIG OE *tæppe*
▸ **'tapeˌlike** *adj* ▸ **'taper** *n*

tape deck *n* **1** a tape recording unit in a hi-fi system. **2** the platform supporting the spools, cassettes, or cartridges of a tape recorder, incorporating the motor and the playback, recording, and erasing heads.

tape machine *n* **1** another word for **tape recorder. 2** a telegraphic device that records current stock quotations electronically or on ticker tape. US equivalent: **ticker.**

tape measure *n* a tape or length of metal marked off in inches, centimetres, etc., used for measuring. Also called (esp. US): **tapeline.**

tapenade ('tæpənɑ:d) *n* a savoury paste made from capers, olives, and anchovies, with olive oil and lemon juice. ORIG C20: F, from Provençal *tapéo* capers

taper ('teɪpə) *vb* **1** to become or cause to become narrower towards one end. **2** (often foll. by *off*) to become or cause to become smaller or less significant. ◆ *n* **3** a thin candle. **4** a thin wooden or waxed strip for transferring a flame; spill. **5** a narrowing. **6** any feeble light. ORIG OE *tapor,* prob. from L *papȳrus* papyrus (from its use as a wick)
▸ **'taperer** *n* ▸ **'tapering** *adj*

tape recorder *n* an electrical device used for recording sounds on magnetic tape and usually also for reproducing them.

tape recording *n* **1** the act of recording on magnetic tape. **2** the magnetized tape used for this. **3** the speech, music, etc., so recorded.

tape streamer *n Computing.* an electromechanical device that enables data to be copied byte by byte from a hard disk onto magnetic tape for security or storage.

tapestry ('tæpɪstrɪ) *n, pl* **tapestries. 1** a heavy woven fabric, often in the form of a picture, used for wall hangings, furnishings, etc. **2** another word for **needlepoint** (sense 1). **3** a colourful and complicated situation: *the rich tapestry of life.* ORIG C15: from OF *tapisserie* carpeting, from OF *tapiz;* see TAPIS
▸ **'tapestried** *adj*

tapeworm ('teɪpˌwɜ:m) *n* any of a class of parasitic ribbon-like flatworms. The adults inhabit the intestines of vertebrates.

taphole ('tæpˌhəʊl) *n* a hole in a furnace for running off molten metal or slag.

taphouse ('tæpˌhaʊs) *n Now rare.* an inn.

tapioca (ˌtæpɪ'əʊkə) *n* a beadlike starch obtained from cassava root, used in cooking as a thickening agent, esp. in puddings. ORIG C18: via Port. from Tupi *tipioca* pressed-out juice, from *tipi* residue + *ok* to squeeze out

tapir ('teɪpə) *n, pl* **tapirs** *or* **tapir.** any of various mammals of South and Central America and SE Asia, having an elongated snout, three-toed hind legs, and four-toed forelegs. ORIG C18: from Tupi *tapiira*

tapis ('tæpi:) *n, pl* **tapis. 1** tapestry or carpeting, esp. as formerly used to cover a table. **2 on the tapis.** currently under consideration. ORIG C17: from F, from OF *tapiz,* from Gk *tapētion* rug, from *tapēs* carpet

tappet ('tæpɪt) *n* a mechanical part that reciprocates to receive or transmit intermittent motion. ORIG C18: from TAP[1] + -ET

taproom ('tæpˌru:m, -ˌrʊm) *n* a bar, as in a hotel or pub.

taproot ('tæpˌru:t) *n* the main root of plants such as the dandelion, which grows vertically downwards and bears smaller lateral roots.

taps (tæps) *n* (*functioning as sing*) **1** *Chiefly US.* **1a** (in army camps, etc.) a signal given on a bugle, drum, etc., indicating that lights are to be put out. **1b** any similar signal, as at a military funeral. **2** (in the Guide movement) a closing song sung at an evening camp fire or at the end of a meeting.

tapster ('tæpstə) *n* **1** *Rare.* a barman. **2** (in W Africa) a man who taps palm trees. ORIG OE *tæppestre,* fem. of *tæppere,* from *tappian* to TAP[2]

tap water *n* water drawn off through taps from pipes in a house, as distinguished from distilled water, mineral water, etc.

tar[1] (tɑ:) *n* **1** any of various dark viscid substances obtained by the destructive distillation of organic matter such as coal, wood, or peat. **2** another name for **coal tar.** ◆ *vb* **tars, tarring, tarred.** (*tr*) **3** to coat with tar. **4 tar and feather.** to punish by smearing tar and feathers over (someone). **5 tarred with the same brush.** regarded as having the same faults. ORIG OE *teoru*
▸ **'tarry** *adj* ▸ **'tarriness** *n*

tar[2] (tɑ:) *n* an informal word for **seaman.** ORIG C17: short for TARPAULIN

Tara ★ ('tærə, 'tɑ:rə) *n* a village in Co. Meath near Dublin, by the **Hill of Tara**, the historic seat of the ancient Irish kings.

Tarabulus el Gharb ★ (tə'rɑ:bələs ɛl 'gɑ:b) *n* transliteration of the Arabic name for **Tripoli** (Libya).

Tarabulus esh Sham ★ (tə'rɑ:bələs ɛʃ 'ʃæm) *n* transliteration of the Arabic name for **Tripoli** (Lebanon).

taradiddle ('tærəˌdɪdᵊl) *n* a variant spelling of **tarradiddle.**

tarakihi *or* **terakihi** ('tærəˌki:hi:) *n, pl* **tarakihis.** a common edible sea fish of New Zealand waters. ORIG from Maori

taramasalata (ˌtærəməsə'lɑ:tə) *n* a creamy pale pink paté, made from the roe of grey mullet or smoked cod and served as an hors d'oeuvre. ORIG C20: from Mod. Gk, from *tarama* cod's roe

tarantass (ˌtɑːrən'tæs) *n* a four-wheeled Russian carriage without springs. ORIG C19: from Russian *tarantas*

tarantella (ˌtærən'tɛlə) *n* **1** a peasant dance from S Italy. **2** a piece of music composed for or in the rhythm of this dance. ORIG C18: from It., from TARANTO

tarantism ('tærənˌtɪzəm) *n* a nervous disorder marked by uncontrollable bodily movement, widespread in S Italy during the 15th to 17th centuries: popularly thought to be caused by the bite of a tarantula. ORIG C17: from NL *tarantismus,* from TARANTO

Taranto ★ (tə'ræntəʊ; *Italian* 'taːranto) *n* a port in SE Italy, in Apulia on the **Gulf of Taranto** (an inlet of the Ionian Sea): the chief city of Magna Graecia; taken by the Romans in 272 B.C. Pop.: 212 650 (1996 est.). Latin name: **Tarentum.**

tarantula (tə'ræntjʊlə) *n, pl* **tarantulas** *or* **tarantulae** (-ˌliː). **1** any of various large hairy spiders of tropical America. **2** a large hairy spider of S Europe. ORIG C16: from Med. L, from OIt. *tarantola,* from TARANTO

Tarawa ★ (tə'rɑːwə) *n* an atoll in Kiribati, occupying a chain of islets surrounding a lagoon in the W central Pacific: the capital of Kiribati, Bairiki, is on this atoll. Pop.: 29 028 (1990).

taraxacum (tə'ræksəkəm) *n* **1** any of a genus of perennial plants of the composite family, such as the dandelion. **2** the dried root of the dandelion, used as a laxative, diuretic, and tonic. ORIG C18: from Med. L, from Ar. *tarakhshaqūn* wild chicory, ? of Persian origin

Tarbes ★ (*French* tarb) *n* a town in SW France: noted for the breeding of Anglo-Arab horses. Pop.: 50 228 (1990).

tarboosh (tɑː'buːʃ) *n* a felt or cloth brimless cap, usually red and often with a silk tassel, worn by Muslim men. ORIG C18: from Ar. *tarbūsh*

tarboy ('tɑːˌbɔɪ) *n Austral. inf.* a boy who applies tar to the skin of sheep cut during shearing.

Tardenoisian (ˌtɑːdə'nɔɪzɪən) *adj* of or referring to a Mesolithic culture characterized by small flint instruments. ORIG C20: after *Tardenois,* France, where implements were found

tardigrade ('tɑːdɪˌgreɪd) *n* any of various minute aquatic segmented eight-legged invertebrates occurring in soil, ditches, etc. Popular name: **water bear.** ORIG C17: via L *tardigradus,* from *tardus* sluggish + *gradī* to walk

tardy ('tɑːdɪ) *adj* **tardier, tardiest. 1** occurring later than expected. **2** slow in progress, growth, etc. ORIG C15: from OF *tardif,* from L *tardus* slow
▸ **'tardily** *adv* ▸ **'tardiness** *n*

tare[1] (tɛə) *n* **1** any of various vetch plants of Eurasia and N Africa. **2** the seed of any of these plants. **3** *Bible.* a weed, thought to be the darnel. ORIG C14: from ?

tare[2] (tɛə) *n* **1** the weight of the wrapping or container in which goods are packed. **2** a deduction from gross weight to compensate for this. **3** the weight of an unladen vehicle. ◆ *vb* **tares, taring, tared. 4** (*tr*) to weigh (a package, etc.) in order to calculate the amount of tare. ORIG C15: from OF: waste, from Med. L *tara,* from Ar. *tarhah* something discarded, from *taraha* to reject

Tarentum ★ (tə'rɛntəm) *n* the Latin name of **Taranto.**

targe (tɑːdʒ) *n* an archaic word for **shield.** ORIG C13: from OF, of Gmc origin

target ('tɑːgɪt) *n* **1a** an object or area at which an archer or marksman aims, usually a round flat surface marked with concentric rings. **1b** (*as modifier*): *target practice.* **2a** any point or area aimed at. **2b** (*as modifier*): *target area; target company.* **3** a fixed goal or objective. **4** a person or thing at which an action or remark is directed or the object of a person's feelings. **5** a joint of lamb consisting of the breast and neck. **6** (formerly) a small round shield. **7** *Physics, electronics.* **7a** a substance subjected to bombardment by electrons or other particles, or to irradiation. **7b** an electrode in a television camera tube whose surface is scanned by the electron beam. **8** *Electronics.* an object detected by the reflection of a radar or sonar signal, etc. ◆ *vb* **targets, targeting, targeted.** (*tr*) **9** to make a target of. **10** to direct or aim: *to target benefits at those most in need.* ORIG C14: from OF *targette* a little shield, from OF TARGE

tariff ('tærɪf) *n* **1a** a tax levied by a government on imports or occasionally exports. **1b** a system or list of such taxes. **2** any schedule of prices, fees, fares, etc. **3** *Chiefly Brit.* **3a** a method of charging for the supply of services such as gas and electricity. **3b** a schedule of such charges. **4** *Chiefly Brit.* a bill of fare with prices listed; menu. ◆ *vb* (*tr*) **5** to set a tariff on. **6** to price according to a schedule of tariffs. ORIG C16: from It. *tariffa,* from Ar. *ta'rīfa* to inform

tariff office *n Insurance.* a company whose premiums are based on a tariff agreed with other insurance companies.

Tarim ★ ('tɑː'riːm) *n* a river in NW China, in Xinjiang Uygur AR: flows east along the N edge of the Taklimakan Shama desert, dividing repeatedly and forming lakes among the dunes, finally disappearing in the Lop Nor depression; the chief river of Xinjiang Uygur AR; drains the great **Tarim Basin** between the Tian Shan and Kunlun mountain systems of central Asia, an area of about 906 500 sq. km (350 000 sq. miles). Length: 2190 km (1360 miles).

Tarkington ★ ('tɑːkɪŋtən) *n* (**Newton**) **Booth.** 1869–1946, US novelist. His works include *Monsieur Beaucaire* (1900) and *The Magnificent Ambersons* (1918).

Tarkovsky ★ (tɑː'kɒfskɪ) *n* **Andrei** (*Russian* an'drjej). 1932–86, Soviet film director, whose films include *Andrei Rublev* (1966) and *The Sacrifice* (1986).

tarlatan ('tɑːlətən) *n* an open-weave cotton fabric, used for stiffening garments. ORIG C18: from F *tarlatane,* var. of *tarnatane* type of muslin, ? of Indian origin

Tarmac ('tɑːmæk) *n* **1** *Trademark.* (*often not cap.*) a paving material that consists of crushed stone rolled and bound with a mixture of tar and bitumen, esp. as used for a road, airport runway, etc. Full name: **Tarmacadam** (ˌtɑːmə'kædəm). See also **macadam.** ◆ *vb* **Tarmacs, Tarmacking, Tarmacked.** (*tr*) **2** (*usually not cap.*) to apply Tarmac to.

tarn (tɑːn) *n* a small mountain lake or pool. ORIG C14: from ON

Tarn ★ (*French* tarn) *n* **1** a department of S France, in Midi-Pyrénées region. Capital: Albi. Pop.: 341 954 (1994 est.). Area: 5780 sq. km (2254 sq. miles). **2** a river in SW France, rising in the Massif Central and flowing generally west to the Garonne River. Length: 375 km (233 miles).

tarnation (tɑː'neɪʃən) *n* a euphemism for **damnation.**

Tarn-et-Garonne ★ (*French* tarnegarɔn) *n* a department of SW France, in Midi-Pyrénées region. Capital: Montauban. Pop.: 204 732 (1994 est.). Area: 3731 sq. km (1455 sq. miles).

tarnish ('tɑːnɪʃ) *vb* **1** to lose or cause to lose the shine, esp. by exposure to air or moisture resulting in surface oxidation; discolour. **2** to stain or become stained; taint. ◆ *n* **3** a tarnished condition, surface, or film. ORIG C16: from OF *ternir* to make dull, from *terne* lustreless of Gmc origin
▸ **'tarnishable** *adj*

Tarnopol ★ (tar'nɔpɔl) *n* the Polish name for **Ternopol.**

Tarnów ★ (*Polish* 'tarnuf) *n* an industrial city in SE Poland. Pop.: 121 600 (1995 est.).

taro ('tɑːrəʊ) *n, pl* **taros. 1** a plant cultivated in the tropics for its large edible rootstock. **2** the rootstock of this plant. ◆ Also called: **eddo.** ORIG C18: from Tahitian & Maori

tarot ('tærəʊ) *n* **1** one of a special pack of cards, now used mainly for fortune-telling. **2** a card in a tarot pack with distinctive symbolic design. ◆ *adj* **3** relating to tarot cards. ORIG C16: from F, from OIt. *tarocco,* from ?

tarpan ('tɑːpæn) *n* a European wild horse, now extinct. ORIG from Tatar

tarpaulin (tɑː'pɔːlɪn) *n* **1** a heavy waterproof fabric made of canvas or similar material coated with tar, wax, or paint. **2** a sheet of this fabric. **3** a hat made of or covered with this fabric, esp. a sailor's hat. **4** a rare word for **seaman.** ORIG C17: prob. from TAR[1] + PALL[1] + -ING[1]

Tarpeia ★ (tɑːˈpiːə) *n* (in Roman legend) a vestal virgin, who betrayed Rome to the Sabines and was killed by them when she requested a reward.

Tarpeian Rock ★ (tɑːˈpiːən) *n* (in ancient Rome) a cliff on the Capitoline hill from which traitors were hurled.

tarpon (ˈtɑːpən) *n, pl* **tarpons** *or* **tarpon.** a large silvery game fish of warm oceans. ORIG C17: ?from Du. *tarpoen,* from ?

Tarquin ★ (ˈtɑːkwɪn) *n* **1** Latin name *Lucius Tarquinius Priscus.* fifth legendary king of Rome (616–578 B.C.). **2** Latin name *Lucius Tarquinius Superbus.* seventh and last legendary king of Rome (534–510 B.C.).

tarradiddle (ˈtærəˌdɪdᵊl) *n* **1** a trifling lie. **2** nonsense; twaddle. ORIG C18: from ?

tarragon (ˈtærəgən) *n* **1** an aromatic plant of the Old World, having leaves which are used as seasoning. **2** the leaves of this plant. ORIG C16: from OF *targon,* from Med. L *tarcon,* ? ult. from Gk *drakontion* adderwort

Tarragona ★ (*Spanish* tarraˈɣona) *n* a port in NE Spain, on the Mediterranean: one of the richest seaports of the Roman Empire; destroyed by the Moors (714). Pop.: 110 003 (1994 est.). Latin name: **Tarraco** (təˈrɑːkəʊ).

Tarrant ★ (ˈtærənt) *n* **Chris(topher).** born 1946, British broadcaster; presenter of the television quiz show *Who Wants to be a Millionaire?* from 1998.

Tarrasa ★ (*Spanish* taˈrrasa) *n* a city in NE Spain: textile centre. Pop.: 161 428 (1994 est.).

tarry (ˈtærɪ) *vb* **tarries, tarrying, tarried. 1** (*intr*) to delay; linger. **2** (*intr*) to remain temporarily or briefly. **3** (*intr*) to wait or stay. **4** (*tr*) *Arch. or poetic.* to await. ORIG C14 *tarien,* from ?
▸ **ˈtarrier** *n*

tarsal (ˈtɑːsᵊl) *adj* **1** of the tarsus or tarsi. ◆ *n* **2** a tarsal bone.

tarseal (ˈtɑːˌsiːl) *n NZ.* **1** the bitumen surface of a road. **2 the tarseal.** the main highway.

Tarshish ★ (ˈtɑːʃɪʃ) *n Old Testament.* an ancient port, mentioned in I Kings 10:22, situated in Spain or in one of the Phoenician colonies in Sardinia.

tarsia (ˈtɑːsɪə) *n* another term for **intarsia.** ORIG C17: from It., from Ar. *tarsiʿ*

tarsier (ˈtɑːsɪə) *n* any of several nocturnal arboreal primates of Indonesia and the Philippines, having huge eyes, long hind legs, and digits ending in pads to facilitate climbing. ORIG C18: from F, from *tarse* the flat of the foot; see TARSUS

tarsus (ˈtɑːsəs) *n, pl* **tarsi** (-saɪ). **1** the bones of the ankle and heel, collectively. **2** the corresponding part in other mammals and in amphibians and reptiles. **3** the connective tissue supporting the free edge of each eyelid. **4** the part of an insect's leg that lies distal to the tibia. ORIG C17: from NL, from Gk *tarsos* flat surface, instep

Tarsus ★ (ˈtɑːsəs) *n* **1** a city in SE Turkey, on the Tarsus River: site of ruins of ancient Tarsus, capital of Cilicia, and birthplace of St Paul. Pop.: 225 000 (1994 est.). **2** a river in SE Turkey, in Cilicia, rising in the Taurus Mountains and flowing south past Tarsus to the Mediterranean. Ancient name: **Cydnus.** Length: 153 km (95 miles).

tart[1] (tɑːt) *n* a pastry case with a filling of fruit, custard, etc. ORIG C14: from OF *tarte,* from ?

tart[2] (tɑːt) *adj* **1** (of a flavour, etc.) sour; acid. **2** cutting; sharp: *a tart remark.* ORIG OE *teart* rough
▸ **ˈtartly** *adv* ▸ **ˈtartness** *n*

tart[3] (tɑːt) *n Inf.* a promiscuous woman, esp. a prostitute. See also **tart up.** ORIG C19: shortened from SWEETHEART
▸ **ˈtarty** *adj*

tartan (ˈtɑːtᵊn) *n* **1a** a design of straight lines, crossing at right angles to give a chequered appearance, esp. the design or designs associated with each Scottish clan. **1b** (*as modifier*): *a tartan kilt.* **2** a fabric or garment with this design. ORIG C16: ?from OF *tertaine* linsey-woolsey, from OSp. *tiritaña* a fine silk fabric, from *tiritar* to rustle
▸ **ˈtartaned** *adj*

tartar[1] (ˈtɑːtə) *n* **1** a hard deposit on the teeth, consisting of food, cellular debris, and mineral salts. **2** a brownish-red substance consisting mainly of potassium hydrogen tartrate, deposited during the fermentation of wine. ORIG C14: from Med. L *tartarum,* from Med. Gk *tartaron*

tartar[2] (ˈtɑːtə) *n* (*sometimes cap.*) a fearsome or formidable person. ORIG C16: special use of TARTAR

Tartar (ˈtɑːtə) *n, adj* a variant spelling of **Tatar.**

Tartarean (tɑːˈteərɪən) *adj Literary.* of or relating to Tartarus; infernal.

tartar emetic *n* antimony potassium tartrate, a poisonous, crystalline salt used as a mordant and in medicine.

tartaric (tɑːˈtærɪk) *adj* of, containing, or derived from tartar or tartaric acid.

tartaric acid *n* a colourless crystalline acid which is found in many fruits: used as a food additive (**E334**) in soft drinks, confectionery, and baking powders, and in tanning and photography. Formula: $(CHOH)_2(COOH)_2$. Systematic name: **2,3-dihydroxybutanedioic acid.**

tartar sauce *n* a mayonnaise sauce mixed with hard-boiled egg yolks, chopped herbs, capers, etc. ORIG from F *sauce tartare,* from TARTAR

Tartarus ★ (ˈtɑːtərəs) *n Greek myth.* **1** an abyss under Hades where the Titans were imprisoned. **2** a part of Hades reserved for evildoers. **3** the underworld; Hades. **4** a primordial god who became the father of the monster Typhon. ORIG C16: from L, from Gk *Tartaros,* of obscure origin

Tartary ★ (ˈtɑːtərɪ) *n* a variant spelling of **Tatary.**

tartlet (ˈtɑːtlɪt) *n Brit.* an individual pastry case with a sweet or savoury filling.

tartrate (ˈtɑːtreɪt) *n* any salt or ester of tartaric acid.

tartrated (ˈtɑːtreɪtɪd) *adj* being in the form of a tartrate.

tartrazine (ˈtɑːtrəˌziːn, -zɪn) *n* an azo dye that produces a yellow colour: used as a food additive (**E102**), in drugs, and to dye textiles.

Tartu ★ (*Russian* ˈtartu) *n* a city in Estonia; university (1632). Pop.: 103 400 (1996 est.). Former name (11th century until 1918): **Yurev.** German name: **Dorpat.**

tart up *vb* (*tr; adv*) *Brit. inf.* **1** to dress and make (oneself) up in a provocative or promiscuous way. **2** to decorate or improve the appearance of: *to tart up a bar.*

tarwhine (ˈtɑːˌwaɪn) *n* any of various Australian marine food fishes, esp. the sea bream. ORIG ?from Abor.

Tarzan (ˈtɑːzən) *n* (*sometimes not cap.*) *Inf., often ironical.* a man with great physical strength, agility, and virility. ORIG C20: after the hero of stories by E. R. BURROUGHS

Tas. *abbrev. for* Tasmania.

Tashkent ★ (*Russian* taʃˈkjent) *n* the capital of Uzbekistan: one of the oldest cities in central Asia; taken by the Russians in 1865; cotton textile manufacturing. Pop.: 2 106 000 (1994 est.).

tasimeter (təˈsɪmɪtə) *n* a device for measuring small temperature changes. It depends on the changes of pressure resulting from expanding or contracting solids. ORIG C19 *tasi-,* from Gk *tasis* tension + -METER
▸ **tasimetric** (ˌtæsɪˈmɛtrɪk) *adj* ▸ **taˈsimetry** *n*

task (tɑːsk) *n* **1** a specific piece of work required to be done. **2** an unpleasant or difficult job or duty. **3** any piece of work. **4 take to task.** to criticize or reprove. ◆ *vb* (*tr*) **5** to assign a task to. **6** to subject to severe strain; tax. ORIG C13: from OF *tasche,* from Med. L *tasca,* from *taxa* tax, from L *taxāre* to TAX

task force *n* **1** a temporary grouping of military units formed to undertake a specific mission. **2** any organization set up to carry out a continuing task.

taskmaster (ˈtɑːskˌmɑːstə) *n* a person, discipline, etc., that enforces work, esp. hard or continuous work.
▸ **ˈtaskˌmistress** *fem n*

taskwork (ˈtɑːskˌwɜːk) *n* **1** hard or unpleasant work. **2** a rare word for **piecework.**

Tasman ★ (ˈtæzmən) *n* **Abel Janszoon** (ˈabəl ˈjansuːn). 1603–59, Dutch navigator, who discovered Tasmania, New Zealand, and the Tonga and Fiji Islands (1642–43).

Tasmania ★ (tæzˈmeɪnɪə) *n* an island in the S Pacific, south of mainland Australia: forms, with offshore islands, the smallest state of Australia; discovered by the Dutch explorer Tasman in 1642; used as a penal colony by the British (1803–53); mostly forested and mountainous. Capital: Hobart. Pop.: 459 659 (1996). Area: 68 332

sq. km (26 383 sq. miles). Former name (1642–1855): **Van Diemen's Land.**
▸ **Tas'manian** *adj, n*

Tasmanian devil *n* a small ferocious carnivorous marsupial of Tasmania.

Tasmanian tiger *or* **wolf** *n* other names for **thylacine.**

Tasman Sea ★ *n* the part of the Pacific between SE Australia and NW New Zealand.

tass (tæs) *or* **tassie** ('tæsɪ) *n Scot. & N English dialect.* **1** a cup or glass. **2** its contents. ORIG C15: from OF *tasse* cup, from Ar. *tassah* basin, from Persian *tast*

Tass (tæs) *n* (formerly) the principal news agency of the Soviet Union: replaced in 1992 by Itar Tass. ORIG *T(elegrafnoye) a(gentstvo) S(ovetskogo) S(oyuza)* Telegraphic Agency of the Soviet Union

tassel ('tæsᵊl) *n* **1** a tuft of loose threads secured by a knot or knob, used to decorate soft furnishings, clothes, etc. **2** anything resembling this, esp. the tuft of stamens at the tip of a maize inflorescence. ◆ *vb* **tassels, tasselling, tasselled** *or US* **tassels, tasseling, tasseled. 3** (*tr*) to adorn with tassels. **4** (*intr*) (of maize) to produce stamens in a tuft. ORIG C13: from OF, from Vulgar L *tassellus* (unattested), changed from L *taxillus* a small die

Tassie *or* **Tassy** ★ ('tæzɪ) *n, Austral. inf.* **1** Tasmania. **2** (*pl* **Tassies**) a native or inhabitant of Tasmania.

Tasso ★ (*Italian* 'tasso) *n* **Torquato** (tor'kwa:to). 1544–95, Italian poet.

taste (teɪst) *n* **1** the sense by which the qualities and flavour of a substance are distinguished by the taste buds. **2** the sensation experienced by means of the taste buds. **3** the act of tasting. **4** a small amount eaten, drunk, or tried on the tongue. **5** a brief experience of something: *a taste of the whip.* **6** a preference or liking for something. **7** the ability to make discerning judgments about aesthetic, artistic, and intellectual matters. **8** judgment of aesthetic or social matters according to a generally accepted standard: *bad taste.* **9** discretion; delicacy: *that remark lacks taste.* ◆ *vb* **tastes, tasting, tasted. 10** to distinguish the taste of (a substance) by means of the taste buds. **11** (*usually tr*) to take a small amount of (a food, liquid, etc.) into the mouth, esp. in order to test the quality. **12** (often foll. by *of*) to have a specific flavour or taste. **13** (when *intr*, usually foll. by *of*) to have an experience of (something): *to taste success.* **14** (*tr*) an archaic word for **enjoy.** ORIG C13: from OF *taster,* ult. from L *taxāre* to appraise
▸ **'tastable** *adj*

taste bud *n* any of the elevated sensory organs on the surface of the tongue, by means of which the sensation of taste is experienced.

tasteful ('teɪstfʊl) *adj* indicating good taste: *a tasteful design.*
▸ **'tastefully** *adv* ▸ **'tastefulness** *n*

tasteless ('teɪstlɪs) *adj* **1** lacking in flavour; insipid. **2** lacking social or aesthetic taste.
▸ **'tastelessly** *adv* ▸ **'tastelessness** *n*

taster ('teɪstə) *n* **1** a person who samples food or drink for quality. **2** any device used in tasting or sampling. **3** a person employed, esp. formerly, to taste food and drink prepared for a king, etc., to test for poison. **4** a sample or preview of a product, experience, etc., intended to stimulate interest in the product, experience, etc., itself: *the single serves as a taster for the band's new album.*

-tastic *adj combining form. Jocular.* denoting excellence in a specified area: *the funtastic theme park; their poptastic new single.* ORIG C20: from (FAN)TASTIC

tasty ('teɪstɪ) *adj* **tastier, tastiest. 1** having a pleasant flavour. **2** *Brit. inf.* skilful or impressive: *she was a bit tasty with a cutlass.*
▸ **'tastily** *adv* ▸ **'tastiness** *n*

tat[1] (tæt) *vb* **tats, tatting, tatted.** to make (something) by tatting. ORIG C19: from ?

tat[2] (tæt) *n* **1** tatty articles or a tatty condition. **2** tasteless articles. **3** a tangled mass. ORIG C20: back formation from TATTY

tat[3] (tæt) *n* See **tit for tat.**

ta-ta (tæ'tɑ:) *sentence substitute. Brit. inf.* goodbye; farewell. ORIG C19: from ?

Tatar *or* **Tartar** ('tɑ:tə) *n* **1a** a member of a Mongoloid people who established a powerful state in central Asia in the 13th century. **1b** a descendant of this people, now scattered throughout Russia and N central Asia. **2** any of the Turkic languages spoken by the present-day Tatars. ◆ *adj* **3** of or relating to the Tatars. ORIG C14: from OF *Tartare,* from Med. L *Tartarus* (associated with L *Tartarus* the underworld), from Persian *Tātār*
▸ **Tatarian** (tɑ:'tɛərɪən), **Tar'tarian** *or* **Tataric** (tɑ:'tærɪk), **Tar'taric** *adj*

Tatar Republic ★ *n* a constituent republic of W Russia, around the confluence of the Volga and Kama Rivers. Capital: Kazan. Pop.: 3 760 000 (1996 est.). Area: 68 000 sq. km (26 250 sq. miles).

Tatar Strait ★ *n* an arm of the Pacific between the mainland of SE Russia and Sakhalin Island, linking the Sea of Japan with the Sea of Okhotsk. Length: about 560 km (350 miles). Also called: **Gulf of Tatary.**

Tatary *or* **Tartary** ★ ('tɑ:tərɪ) *n* **1** a historical region (with indefinite boundaries) in E Europe and Asia, inhabited by Bulgars until overrun by the Tatars in the mid-13th century: extended as far east as the Pacific under Genghis Khan. **2 Gulf of.** another name for the **Tatar Strait.**

Tate ★ (teɪt) *n* **1** Sir **Henry.** 1819–99, British sugar refiner and philanthropist; founder of the Tate Gallery (Tate Britain). **2** (**John Orley**) **Allen.** 1899–1979, US poet and critic.

Tate Gallery ★ *n* either of two art galleries in London, **Tate Britain**, built in 1897, and **Tate Modern**, built 1999–2000.

tater ('teɪtə) *n* a dialect word for **potato.**

Tati ★ (*French* tati) *n* **Jacques** (ʒak), real name *Jacques Tatischeff.* 1908–82, French actor, creator of the character Monsieur Hulot.

tatouay ('tætʊˌeɪ) *n* a large armadillo of South America. ORIG C16: from Sp. *tatuay,* from Guarani, from *tatu* armadillo + *ai* worthless (because inedible)

Tatra Mountains ★ ('tɑ:trə, 'tæt-) *pl n* a mountain range along the border between Slovakia and Poland, extending for about 64 km (40 miles): the highest range of the central Carpathians. Highest peak: Gerlachovka, 2663 m (8737 ft). Also called: **High Tatra.**

TATT *abbrev. for* tired all the time: used to describe a set of symptoms often reported to doctors by patients.

tatter ('tætə) *vb* **1** to make or become ragged or worn to shreds. ◆ *n* **2** a torn or ragged piece, esp. of material. ORIG C14: from ON

tatterdemalion (ˌtætədɪ'meɪljən) *n Rare.* a person dressed in ragged clothes. ORIG C17: from TATTER + *-demalion,* from ?

tattersall ('tætəˌsɔ:l) *n* a fabric having stripes or bars in a checked or squared pattern. ORIG C19: after *Tattersall's,* a horse market in London founded by Richard *Tattersall* (died 1795), Brit. horseman; the horse blankets at the market orig. had this pattern

Tattersall's ('tætəˌsɔ:lz) *n Austral.* **1** Also called (inf.): **Tatt's.** a lottery now based in Melbourne. **2** a name used for sportsmen's clubs. ORIG after *Tattersall's* horse market; see TATTERSALL

tatting ('tætɪŋ) *n* **1** an intricate type of lace made by looping a thread of cotton or linen by means of a hand shuttle. **2** the act or work of producing this. ORIG C19: from ?

tattle ('tætᵊl) *vb* **tattles, tattling, tattled. 1** (*intr*) to gossip about another's personal matters. **2** (*tr*) to reveal by gossiping. **3** (*intr*) to talk idly; chat. ◆ *n* **4** the act or an instance of tattling. **5** a scandalmonger; gossip. ORIG C15 (in the sense: to stammer, hesitate): from MDu. *tatelen* to prate, imit.
▸ **'tattler** *n*

tattletale ('tætᵊlˌteɪl) *Chiefly US & Canad. n* **1** a scandalmonger or gossip. **2** another word for **telltale** (sense 1).

tattoo[1] (tæ'tu:) *n, pl* **tattoos. 1** (formerly) a signal by drum or bugle ordering the military to return to their quarters. **2** a military display or pageant. **3** any similar beating on a drum, etc. ORIG C17: from Du. *taptoe,* from *tap toe!* turn off the taps! from *tap* tap of a barrel + *toe* to shut

tattoo[2] (tæ'tu:) *vb* **tattoos, tattooing, tattooed. 1** to make (pictures or designs) on (the skin) by pricking and staining with indelible colours. ◆ *n, pl* **tattoos. 2** a design made by this process. **3** the practice of tattooing. ORIG C18: from Tahitian *tatau*
▸ **tat'tooer** *or* **tat'tooist** *n*

tatty ('tætɪ) *adj* **tattier, tattiest.** *Chiefly Brit.* worn out, shabby, or unkempt. ORIG C16: of Scot. origin
▸ **'tattily** *adv* ▸ **'tattiness** *n*

Tatum ★ ('teɪtəm) *n* **Art**, full name *Arthur Tatum*. 1910–56, US jazz pianist.

tau (tɔ:, taʊ) *n* the 19th letter in the Greek alphabet (Τ or τ). ORIG C13: from Gk

tau cross *n* a cross shaped like the Greek letter tau. Also called: **Saint Anthony's cross.**

taught (tɔ:t) *vb* the past tense and past participle of **teach**.

taunt (tɔ:nt) *vb* (*tr*) **1** to provoke or deride with mockery, contempt, or criticism. **2** to tease; tantalize. ◆ *n* **3** a jeering remark. ORIG C16: from F *tant pour tant* like for like
▸ **'taunting** *adj*

Taunton ★ ('tɔ:ntən) *n* a market town in SW England, administrative centre of Somerset: scene of Judge Jeffreys' "Bloody Assize" (1685) after the Battle of Sedgemoor. Pop.: 55 855 (1991).

tau particle *n Physics.* a type of elementary particle classified as a lepton.

taupe (təʊp) *n* **a** a brownish-grey colour. **b** (*as adj*): *a taupe coat.* ORIG C20: from F, lit.: mole, from L *talpa*

Taupo ★ ('taʊpəʊ) *n* **Lake.** a lake in New Zealand, on central North Island: the largest lake of New Zealand. Area: 616 sq. km (238 sq. miles).

Tauranga ★ (taʊ'ræŋə) *n* a port in New Zealand, on NE North Island on the Bay of Plenty: exports dairy produce, meat, and timber. Pop.: 76 100 (1994).

taurine ('tɔ:raɪn) *adj* of or resembling a bull. ORIG C17: from L *taurīnus,* from *taurus* a bull

tauromachy (tɔ:'rɒməkɪ) *n* the art or act of bullfighting. ORIG C19: Gk *tauromakhia,* from *tauros* bull + *makhē* fight

Taurus ('tɔ:rəs) *n* **1** *Astron.* a constellation in the N hemisphere. **2** *Astrol.* Also called: the **Bull.** the second sign of the zodiac. The sun is in this sign between about April 20 and May 20. ORIG C14: from L: bull

Taurus Mountains ★ *pl n* a mountain range in S Turkey, parallel to the Mediterranean coast: crossed by the Cilician Gates; continued in the northeast by the Anti-Taurus range. Highest peak: Kaldi Dağ, 3734 m (12 251 ft).

taut (tɔ:t) *adj* **1** tightly stretched; tense. **2** showing nervous strain; stressed. **3** *Chiefly naut.* in good order; neat. ORIG C14 *tought*
▸ **'tautly** *adv* ▸ **'tautness** *n*

tauten ('tɔ:tən) *vb* to make or become taut.

tauto- *or before a vowel* **taut-** *combining form.* identical or same: *tautology.* ORIG from Gk *tauto,* from *to auto*

tautog (tɔ:'tɒg) *n* a large dark-coloured food fish of the North American coast of the Atlantic Ocean. ORIG C17: from Narraganset *tautauog,* pl. of *tautau* sheepshead

tautology (tɔ:'tɒlədʒɪ) *n, pl* **tautologies. 1** the use of words that merely repeat elements of the meaning already conveyed, as in *Will these supplies be adequate enough?* in place of *Will these supplies be adequate?* **2** *Logic.* a statement that is always true, as in *either the sun is out or the sun is not out.* ORIG C16: from LL *tautologia,* from Gk, from *tautologos*
▸ **tautological** (ˌtɔ:tə'lɒdʒɪkəl) *or* **tau'tologous** *adj*

tautomerism (tɔ:'tɒməˌrɪzəm) *n* the ability of certain chemical compounds to exist as a mixture of two interconvertible isomers in equilibrium. ORIG C19: from TAUTO- + ISOMERISM
▸ **tautomer** ('tɔ:təmə) *n* ▸ **tautomeric** (ˌtɔ:tə'mɛrɪk) *adj*

tautonym ('tɔ:tənɪm) *n Biol.* a taxonomic name in which the generic and specific components are the same, as in *Rattus rattus* (black rat).
▸ **ˌtauto'nymic** *or* **tautonymous** (tɔ:'tɒnəməs) *adj* ▸ **tau'tonymy** *n*

Tavener ★ ('tævənə) *n* Sir **John** (**Kenneth**). born 1944, British composer, whose works include the cantata *The Whale* (1966), the opera *Thérèse* (1979), and the choral work *The Last Discourse* (1998).

tavern ('tævən) *n* **1** a less common word for **pub. 2** *US, E Canad., & NZ.* a place licensed for the sale and consumption of alcoholic drink. ORIG C13: from OF *taverne,* from L *taberna* hut

taverna (tə'vɜ:nə) *n* **1** (in Greece) a guesthouse that has its own bar. **2** a Greek restaurant. ORIG C20: Mod. Gk, from L *taberna*

Taverner ★ ('tævənə) *n* **John.** ?1495–1545, English composer, esp. of church music.

TAVR *abbrev. for* Territorial and Army Volunteer Reserve.

taw[1] (tɔ:) *n* **1** a large marble used for shooting. **2** a game of marbles. **3** the line from which the players shoot in marbles. **4 back to taws.** *Austral. inf.* back to the beginning. ORIG C18: from ?

taw[2] (tɔ:) *vb* (*tr*) to convert (skins) into leather by treatment with alum and salt rather than by normal tanning processes. ORIG OE *tawian*
▸ **'tawer** *n*

tawa ('tɑ:wə) *n* a New Zealand timber tree with edible berries. ORIG from Maori

tawdry ('tɔ:drɪ) *adj* **tawdrier, tawdriest.** cheap, showy, and of poor quality: *tawdry jewellery.* ORIG C16 *tawdry lace,* shortened & altered from *Seynt Audries lace,* finery sold at the fair of St *Audrey* (Etheldrida), 7th-century queen of Northumbria
▸ **'tawdrily** *adv* ▸ **'tawdriness** *n*

tawny ('tɔ:nɪ) *n* **a** a light brown to brownish-orange colour. **b** (*as adj*): *tawny port.* ORIG C14: from OF *tané,* from *taner* to tan
▸ **'tawniness** *n*

tawny owl *n* a European owl having a reddish-brown plumage and a round head.

tawse *or* **taws** (tɔ:z) *n Chiefly Scot.* a leather strap having one end cut into thongs, formerly used as an instrument of punishment by a schoolteacher. ORIG C16: prob. pl of obs. *taw* strip of leather; see TAW[2]

tax (tæks) *n* **1** a compulsory financial contribution imposed by a government to raise revenue, levied on income or property, on the prices of goods and services, etc. **2** a heavy demand on something; strain. ◆ *vb* (*tr*) **3** to levy a tax on (persons, companies, etc.). **4** to make heavy demands on; strain. **5** to accuse or blame. **6** *Law.* to determine (the amount legally chargeable or allowable to a party to a legal action): *to tax costs.* **7** *Sl.* to demand money or goods from (someone) with menaces. ORIG C13: from OF *taxer,* from L *taxāre* to appraise, from *tangere* to touch
▸ **'taxable** *adj* ▸ **'taxer** *n*

taxation (tæk'seɪʃən) *n* **1** the act or principle of levying taxes or the condition of being taxed. **2a** an amount assessed as tax. **2b** a tax rate. **3** revenue from taxes.
▸ **tax'ational** *adj*

tax avoidance *n* reduction or minimization of tax liability by lawful methods.

tax-deductible *adj* legally deductible from income or wealth before tax assessment.

tax disc *n* a paper disc displayed on the windscreen of a motor vehicle showing that the tax due on it has been paid.

taxeme ('tæksi:m) *n Linguistics.* any element of speech that may differentiate one utterance from another with a different meaning, such as the occurrence of a particular phoneme, the presence of a certain intonation, or a distinctive word order. ORIG C20: from Gk *taxis* order, arrangement + -EME
▸ **tax'emic** *adj*

tax evasion *n* reduction or minimization of tax liability by illegal methods.

tax exile *n* a person having a high income who chooses to live abroad so as to avoid paying high taxes.

tax haven *n* a country or state having a lower rate of taxation than elsewhere.

tax holiday *n* a period during which tax concessions are made for some reason; examples include an export incentive or an incentive to start a new business given by

★ people and places

some governments, in which a company is excused all or part of its tax liability.

taxi ('tæksɪ) *n, pl* **taxis** *or* **taxies. 1** Also called: **cab, taxicab.** a car, usually fitted with a taximeter, that may be hired, along with its driver, to carry passengers to any specified destination. ◆ *vb* **taxis** *or* **taxies, taxiing** *or* **taxying, taxied. 2** to cause (an aircraft) to move along the ground, esp. before takeoff and after landing, or (of an aircraft) to move along the ground in this way. **3** (*intr*) to travel in a taxi. ORIG C20: shortened from *taximeter cab*

taxidermy ('tæksɪˌdɜːmɪ) *n* the art or process of preparing, stuffing, and mounting animal skins so that they have a lifelike appearance. ORIG C19: from Gk *taxis* arrangement + *-dermy,* from Gk *derma* skin
▸ **ˌtaxi'dermal** *or* **ˌtaxi'dermic** *adj* ▸ **'taxiˌdermist** *n*

taximeter ('tæksɪˌmiːtə) *n* a meter fitted to a taxi to register the fare, based on the length of the journey. ORIG C19: from F *taximètre;* see TAX, -METER

taxing ('tæksɪŋ) *adj* demanding, onerous, and wearing.
▸ **'taxingly** *adv*

taxi rank *n* a place where taxis wait to be hired.

taxis ('tæksɪs) *n* **1** the movement of an organism in response to an external stimulus. **2** *Surgery.* the repositioning of a displaced part by manual manipulation only. ORIG C18: via NL from Gk: arrangement, from *tassein* to place in order

-taxis *or* **-taxy** *n combining form.* **1** indicating movement towards or away from a specified stimulus: *thermotaxis.* **2** order or arrangement: *phyllotaxis.* ORIG from NL, from Gk *taxis* order
▸ **-tactic** *or* **-taxic** *adj combining form.*

taxiway ('tæksɪˌweɪ) *n* a marked path along which aircraft taxi to or from a runway, parking area, etc.

tax loss *n* a loss sustained by a company that can be set against future profits for tax purposes.

taxman ('tæksˌmæn) *n, pl* **-men. 1** a collector of taxes. **2** *Inf.* a tax-collecting body personified: *he was convicted of conspiring to cheat the taxman of five million pounds.*

taxon ('tæksɒn) *n, pl* **taxa** ('tæksə). *Biol.* any taxonomic group or rank. ORIG C20: back formation from TAXONOMY

taxonomy (tæk'sɒnəmɪ) *n* **1** the branch of biology concerned with the classification of organisms into groups based on similarities of structure, origin, etc. **2** the science or practice of classification. ORIG C19: from F *taxonomie,* from Gk *taxis* order + -NOMY
▸ **taxonomic** (ˌtæksə'nɒmɪk) *or* **ˌtaxo'nomical** *adj* ▸ **ˌtaxo'nomically** *adv* ▸ **tax'onomist** *n*

taxpayer ('tæksˌpeɪə) *n* a person or organization that pays taxes.

tax relief *n* remission of income tax due on a proportion of income earned.

tax return *n* a declaration of personal income used as a basis for assessing an individual's liability for taxation.

tax shelter *n* a form into which business activities may be organized to minimize taxation.

-taxy *n combining form.* a variant of **-taxis.**

Tay ★ (teɪ) *n* **1 Firth of.** the estuary of the River Tay on the North Sea coast of Scotland. Length: 40 km (25 miles). **2** a river in central Scotland, flowing northeast through Loch Tay, then southeast to the Firth of Tay: the longest river in Scotland; noted for salmon fishing. Length: 193 km (120 miles). **3 Loch.** a lake in central Scotland, in Stirling council area. Length: 23 km (14 miles).

Taylor ★ ('teɪlə) *n* **1 A(lan) J(ohn) P(ercivale).** 1906–90, British historian; his works include *The Origins of the Second World War* (1961). **2 Brook.** 1685–1731, English mathematician, who laid the foundations of differential calculus. **3** Dame **Elizabeth.** born 1932, US film actress, born in England: films include *Cat on a Hot Tin Roof* (1958) and *Who's Afraid of Virginia Woolf?* (1966). **4 Zachary.** 1784–1850, 12th president of the US (1849–50); hero of the Mexican War.

Taymyr Peninsula ★ (taɪ'mɪə) *n* a variant spelling of **Taimyr Peninsula.**

Tay-Sachs disease (ˌteɪ'sæks) *n* an inherited disorder, caused by a faulty recessive gene, in which lipids accumulate in the brain, leading to mental retardation and blindness. ORIG C20: after W. *Tay* (1843–1927), Brit. physician, and B. *Sachs* (1858–1944), US neurologist

Tayside Region ★ ('teɪˌsaɪd) *n* (until 1996) a local government region in E Scotland: replaced by the council areas of Angus, City of Dundee, and Perth and Kinross.

tazza ('tætsə) *n* a wine cup with a shallow bowl and a circular foot. ORIG C19: from It., prob. from Ar. *tassah* bowl

Tb *the chemical symbol for* terbium.

TB *abbrev. for:* **1** torpedo boat. **2** Also: **tb.** tuberculosis.

T-bar *n* **1** a T-shaped wrench for use with a socket. **2** a T-shaped bar on a ski tow which skiers hold on to while being pulled up slopes.

tbc *or* **TBC** *abbrev. for* to be confirmed.

Tbilisi ★ (dbɪ'liːsɪ) *n* the capital of Georgia, on the Kura River: founded in 458; taken by the Russians in 1801; university (1918); a major industrial centre. Pop.: 1 253 100 (1994 est.). Russian name: **Tiflis.**

T-bone steak *n* a large choice steak cut from the sirloin of beef, containing a T-shaped bone.

tbs. *or* **tbsp.** *abbrev. for* tablespoon(ful).

TBT *abbrev. for* tri-*n*-butyl tin: a biocide used in marine paints to prevent fouling.

Tc *the chemical symbol for* technetium.

T-cell *n* a type of lymphocyte that matures in the thymus gland and is responsible for killing cells infected by a virus. Also called: **T-lymphocyte.**

Tchad ★ (tʃad) *n* the French name for **Chad.**

Tchaikovsky ★ (tʃaɪ'kɒfskɪ; *Russian* tʃɪj'kɔfskij) *n* **Pyotr Ilyich** (pjɔtr ilj'jitʃ). 1840–93, Russian composer. His works include six symphonies, three piano concertos, a violin concerto, ballets, and operas.

t.d.c. *abbrev. for* top dead-centre.

t distribution *n* See **Student's t.**

te *or* **ti** (tiː) *n Music.* (in tonic sol-fa) the syllable used for the seventh note or subtonic of any scale. ORIG later variant of *si;* see GAMUT

Te *the chemical symbol for* tellurium.

tea (tiː) *n* **1** an evergreen shrub of tropical and subtropical Asia, having white fragrant flowers: family *Theaceae.* **2a** the dried leaves of this shrub, used to make a beverage by infusion in boiling water. **2b** such a beverage, served hot or iced. **3a** any of various similar plants or any plants that are used to make a tealike beverage. **3b** any such beverage. **4** *Chiefly Brit.* **4a** Also called: **afternoon tea.** a light meal eaten in mid-afternoon, usually consisting of tea and cakes, etc. **4b** Also called: **high tea.** afternoon tea that also includes a light cooked dish. **5** *Brit., Austral., & NZ.* the main evening meal. **6** *US & Canad. dated sl.* marijuana. **7 tea and sympathy.** *Inf.* a caring attitude, esp. to someone in trouble. ORIG C17: from Chinese (Amoy) *t'e,* from Ancient Chinese *d'a*

tea bag *n* a small bag containing tea leaves, infused in boiling water to make tea.

tea ball *n Chiefly US.* a perforated metal ball filled with tea leaves and used to make tea.

tea break *n* a short rest period during working hours during which tea, coffee, etc., is drunk.

teacake ('tiːˌkeɪk) *n Brit.* a flat bun, usually eaten toasted and buttered.

teach (tiːtʃ) *vb* **teaches, teaching, taught. 1** (*tr; may take a clause as object or an infinitive;* often foll. by *how*) to help to learn; tell or show (how). **2** to give instruction or lessons in (a subject) to (a person or animal). **3** (*tr; may take a clause as object or an infinitive*) to cause to learn or understand: *experience taught him that he could not be a journalist.* ORIG OE *tǣcan*
▸ **'teachable** *adj*

teacher ('tiːtʃə) *n* a person whose occupation is teaching others, esp. children.

teach-in *n* an informal conference, esp. on a topical subject, usually held at a university or college and involving a panel of visiting speakers, lecturers, students, etc.

teaching ('tiːtʃɪŋ) *n* **1** the art or profession of a teacher. **2** (*sometimes pl*) something taught; precept. **3** (*modifier*) denoting a person or institution that teaches: *a teaching hospital.* **4** (*modifier*) used in teaching: *teaching aids.*

teaching machine *n* a machine that presents information and questions to the user, registers the answers, and indicates whether these are correct or acceptable.

tea cloth *n* another name for **tea towel.**

tea cosy *n* a covering for a teapot to keep the contents hot.

teacup ('tiːˌkʌp) *n* **1** a cup out of which tea may be drunk. **2** Also called: **teacupful.** the amount a teacup will hold, about four fluid ounces.

tea dance *n* a dance held in the afternoon at which tea is served.

teahouse ('tiːˌhaʊs) *n* a restaurant, esp. in Japan or China, where tea and light refreshments are served.

teak (tiːk) *n* **1** a large tree of the East Indies. **2** the hard resinous yellowish-brown wood of this tree, used for furniture making, etc. ORIG C17: from Port. *teca,* from Malayalam *tēkka*

teakettle ('tiːˌkɛtᵊl) *n* a kettle for boiling water to make tea.

teal (tiːl) *n, pl* **teals** *or* **teal. 1** any of various small freshwater ducks that are related to the mallard. **2** a greenish-blue colour. ORIG C14

tea lady *n* a woman employed in a factory, office, etc., to make tea during a tea break.

tea leaf *n* **1** the dried leaf of the tea shrub, used to make tea. **2** (*usually pl*) shredded parts of these leaves, esp. after infusion.

team (tiːm) *n* (*sometimes functioning as pl*) **1** a group of people organized to work together. **2** a group of players forming one of the sides in a sporting contest. **3** two or more animals working together, as to pull a vehicle. **4** such animals and the vehicle. ◆ *vb* **5** (when *intr,* often foll. by *up*) to make or cause to make a team. **6** (*tr*) *US & Canad.* to drag or transport in or by a team. **7** (*intr*) *US & Canad.* to drive a team. ORIG OE *team* offspring

tea-maker *n* a spoon with a perforated cover used to infuse tea in a cup of boiling water.

team-mate *n* a fellow member of a team.

team spirit *n* willingness to cooperate as part of a team.

teamster ('tiːmstə) *n* **1** a driver of a team of horses. **2** *US & Canad.* the driver of a lorry.

team teaching *n* a system whereby two or more teachers pool their skills, knowledge, etc., to teach combined classes.

teamwork ('tiːmˌwɜːk) *n* **1** the cooperative work done by a team. **2** the ability to work efficiently as a team.

teapot ('tiːˌpɒt) *n* a container with a lid, spout, and handle, in which tea is made and from which it is served.

teapoy ('tiːpɔɪ) *n* a small table with a tripod base. ORIG C19: from Hindi *tipāī,* from Sansk. *tri* three + *pāda* foot

tear[1] (tɪə) *n* **1** a drop of the secretion of the lacrimal glands. See **tears. 2** something shaped like a hanging drop: *a tear of amber.* ◆ Also called: **teardrop.** ORIG OE *tēar*
▸ **'tearless** *adj*

tear[2] (tɛə) *vb* **tears, tearing, tore, torn. 1** to cause to come apart or to come apart; rip. **2** (*tr*) to make (a hole or split) in (something). **3** (*intr;* often foll. by *along*) to hurry or rush. **4** (*tr;* usually foll. by *away* or *from*) to remove or take by force. **5** (when *intr,* often foll. by *at*) to cause pain, distress, or anguish (to). **6 tear one's hair.** *Inf.* to be angry, frustrated, very worried, etc. ◆ *n* **7** a hole, cut, or split. **8** the act of tearing. ◆ See also **tear away, tear down,** etc. ORIG OE *teran*
▸ **'tearable** *adj* ▸ **'tearer** *n*

tear away (tɛə) *vb* **1** (*tr, adv*) to persuade (oneself or someone else) to leave. ◆ *n* **tearaway. 2** *Brit.* a reckless impetuous unruly person.

tear down (tɛə) *vb* (*tr, adv*) to destroy or demolish: *to tear down an argument.*

tear duct (tɪə) *n* a short tube in the inner corner of the eyelid through which tears drain into the nose. Technical name: **lacrimal duct.**

tearful ('tɪəfʊl) *adj* **1** crying or about to cry. **2** tending to produce tears; sad.
▸ **'tearfully** *adv* ▸ **'tearfulness** *n*

tear gas (tɪə) *n* a gas that makes the eyes smart and water, causing temporary blindness; used in warfare and to control riots.

tearing ('tɛərɪŋ) *adj* violent or furious (esp. in **tearing hurry** *or* **rush**).

tear into (tɛə) *vb* (*intr, prep*) *Inf.* to attack vigorously and damagingly.

tear-jerker ('tɪəˌdʒɜːkə) *n Inf.* an excessively sentimental film, play, book, etc.

tearoom ('tiːˌruːm, -ˌrʊm) *n Brit.* a restaurant where tea and light refreshments are served. Also called: **teashop.**

tea rose *n* any of several varieties of hybrid rose that have pink or yellow flowers with a scent resembling that of tea.

tears (tɪəz) *pl n* **1** the clear salty solution secreted by the lacrimal glands that lubricates and cleanses the surface of the eyeball. **2** a state of intense frustration (esp. in **bored to tears**). **3 in tears.** weeping.

tear sheet (tɛə) *n* a page in a newspaper or periodical that is cut or perforated so that it can be easily torn out.

teary ('tɪərɪ) *adj* **tearier, teariest. 1** characterized by, covered with, or secreting tears. **2** given to weeping; tearful.
▸ **'tearily** *adv* ▸ **'teariness** *n*

tease (tiːz) *vb* **teases, teasing, teased. 1** to annoy (someone) by deliberately offering something with the intention of delaying or withdrawing the offer. **2** to vex (someone) maliciously or playfully. **3** (*tr*) to separate the fibres of; comb; card. **4** (*tr*) to raise the nap of (a fabric) with a teasel. **5** another word (esp. US and Canad.) for **backcomb. 6** (*tr*) to loosen or pull apart (biological tissues, etc.). ◆ *n* **7** a person or thing that teases. **8** the act of teasing. ◆ See also **tease out.** ORIG OE *tǣsan*
▸ **'teasing** *adj* ▸ **'teasingly** *adv*

teasel, teazel, *or* **teazle** ('tiːzᵊl) *n* **1** any of various plants (esp. the **fuller's teasel**) of Eurasia and N Africa, having prickly leaves and prickly heads of yellow or purple flowers. **2a** the dried flower head of the fuller's teasel, used for teasing. **2b** any implement used for the same purpose. ◆ *vb* **teasels, teaselling, teaselled** *or US* **teasels, teaseling, teaseled. 3** (*tr*) to tease (a fabric). ORIG OE *tǣsel*
▸ **'teaseller** *n*

tease out *vb* (*tr, adv*) to extract (information) with difficulty.

teaser ('tiːzə) *n* **1** a person who teases. **2** a difficult question. **3** a preliminary advertisement in a campaign that attracts attention by making people curious to know what product is being advertised.

tea service *or* **set** *n* the china or pottery articles used in serving tea, including a teapot, cups, saucers, etc.

teashop ('tiːˌʃɒp) *n Brit.* another name for **tearoom.**

teaspoon ('tiːˌspuːn) *n* **1** a small spoon used for stirring tea, etc. **2** Also called: **teaspoonful** the amount contained in such a spoon. **3** a unit of capacity used in cooking, medicine, etc., equal to about 5 ml.

teat (tiːt) *n* **1a** the nipple of a mammary gland. **1b** (in cows, etc.) any of the projections from the udder. **2** something resembling a teat such as the rubber mouthpiece of a feeding bottle. ORIG C13: from OF *tete,* of Gmc origin

tea towel *or* **cloth** *n* a towel for drying dishes, etc. US name: **dishtowel.**

tea tree *n* any of various trees of Australia and New Zealand that yield an oil used as an antiseptic.

tea trolley *n Brit.* a trolley from which tea is served.

tebi- ('tɛbɪ) *combining form. Computing.* denoting 2^{40}: *tebibyte.* Symbol: Ti ORIG C20: from TE(RA-) + BI(NARY)

TEC (tɛk) *n acronym for* Training and Enterprise Council. See **Training Agency.**

tech (tɛk) *n Inf.* a technical college.

tech. *abbrev. for:* **1** technical. **2** technology.

techie *or* **techy** ('tɛkɪ) *Inf.* ◆ *n, pl* **techies. 1** a person who is skilled in the use of technological devices, such as computers. ◆ *adj* **2** of, relating to, or skilled in the use of such devices.

technetium (tɛk'niːʃɪəm) *n* a silvery-grey metallic element, artificially produced by bombardment of molybdenum by deuterons. The radioisotope **technetium-99m** is used in radiotherapy. Symbol: Tc; atomic no.: 43; half-life of most stable isotope, ^{97}Tc: 2.6 × 10^6 years. ORIG C20: NL, from Gk *tekhnētos* manmade, from *tekhnasthai* to devise artificially, from *tekhnē* skill

technic *n* **1** (tɛk'niːk). another word for **technique. 2** ('tɛknɪk). another word for **technics.** ORIG C17: from L *technicus,* from Gk *tekhnikos,* from *tekhnē* skill

technical ('tɛknɪkᵊl) *adj* **1** of or specializing in industrial, practical, or mechanical arts and applied sciences. **2** skilled in practical arts rather than abstract thinking. **3** relating to a particular field of activity: *the technical jargon of linguistics.* **4** existing by virtue of a strict application of the rules or a strict interpretation of the wording: *a technical loophole in the law.* **5** of or showing technique: *technical brilliance.*
▸ **'technically** *adv* ▸ **'technicalness** *n*

technical college *n Brit.* an institution for further education that provides courses in technology, art, secretarial skills, agriculture, etc.

technical drawing *n* the study and practice of the basic techniques of draughtsmanship, as employed in mechanical drawing, architecture, etc.

technicality (ˌtɛknɪ'kælɪtɪ) *n, pl* **technicalities. 1** a petty formal point arising from a strict interpretation of rules, etc. **2** the state or quality of being technical. **3** technical methods and vocabulary.

technical knockout *n Boxing.* a judgment of a knockout given when a boxer is in the referee's opinion too badly beaten to continue without risk of serious injury.

technician (tɛk'nɪʃən) *n* **1** a person skilled in mechanical or industrial techniques or in a particular technical field. **2** a person employed in a laboratory, etc., to do mechanical and practical work. **3** a person having specific artistic or mechanical skill, esp. if lacking flair.

Technicolor ('tɛknɪˌkʌlə) *n Trademark.* the process of producing colour film by means of superimposing synchronized films of the same scene, each of which has a different colour filter.

technics ('tɛknɪks) *n* (*functioning as sing*) the study or theory of industry and industrial arts; technology.

technikon ('tɛknɪˌkɒn) *n S. African.* a technical college.

technique (tɛk'niːk) *n* **1** a practical method, skill, or art applied to a particular task. **2** proficiency in a practical or mechanical skill. **3** special facility; knack. ORIG C19: from F, from *technique* (adj): see TECHNIC

techno ('tɛknəʊ) *n* a type of fast disco music, using electronic sounds and having a strong technological influence.

techno- *combining form.* **1** craft or art: *technology; technography.* **2** technological or technical: *technocracy.* ORIG from Gk *tekhnē* skill

technocracy (tɛk'nɒkrəsɪ) *n, pl* **technocracies.** government by scientists, engineers, and other such experts.
▸ **technocrat** ('tɛknəˌkræt) *n* ▸ **ˌtechno'cratic** *adj*

technology (tɛk'nɒlədʒɪ) *n, pl* **technologies. 1** the application of practical or mechanical sciences to industry or commerce. **2** the methods, theory, and practices governing such application. **3** the total knowledge and skills available to any human society. ORIG C17: from Gk *tekhnologia* systematic treatment, from *tekhnē* skill
▸ **technological** (ˌtɛknə'lɒdʒɪkᵊl) *adj* ▸ **tech'nologist** *n*

technophile ('tɛknəʊˌfaɪl) *n* **1** a person who is enthusiastic about technology. ◆ *adj* **2** enthusiastic about technology.

technophobe ('tɛknəʊˌfəʊb) *n* **1** someone who fears the effects of technological development on society or the environment. **2** someone who is afraid of using technological devices, such as computers.
▸ **ˌtechno'phobic** *adj*

techy[1] ('tɛkɪ) *n, pl* **techies,** *adj* a variant spelling of **techie.**

techy[2] ('tɛtʃɪ) *adj* **techier, techiest.** a variant spelling of **tetchy.**
▸ **'techily** *adv* ▸ **'techiness** *n*

tectonic (tɛk'tɒnɪk) *adj* **1** denoting or relating to building. **2** *Geol.* **2a** (of landforms, etc.) resulting from distortion of the earth's crust due to forces within it. **2b** (of processes, movements, etc.) occurring within the earth's crust and causing structural deformation. ORIG C17: from LL *tectonicus,* from Gk *tektonikos* belonging to carpentry, from *tektōn* a builder

tectonics (tɛk'tɒnɪks) *n* (*functioning as sing*) **1** the art and science of construction or building. **2** the study of the processes by which the earth's surface has attained its present structure.

tectrix ('tɛktrɪks) *n, pl* **tectrices** ('tɛktrɪˌsiːz). (*usually pl*) *Ornithol.* another name for **covert** (sense 5). ORIG C19: NL, from L *tector* plasterer, from *tegere* to cover
▸ **tectricial** (tɛk'trɪʃəl) *adj*

Tecumseh ★ (tɪ'kʌmsə) *n* ?1768–1813, American Indian chief of the Shawnee tribe; killed fighting for the British in the War of 1812.

ted[1] (tɛd) *vb* **teds, tedding, tedded.** to shake out (hay), so as to dry it. ORIG C15: from ON *tethja*

ted[2] (tɛd) *n Inf.* short for **teddy boy.**

tedder ('tɛdə) *n* **1** a machine equipped with a series of small rotating forks for tedding hay. **2** a person who teds.

Tedder ★ ('tɛdə) *n* **Arthur William,** 1st Baron Tedder of Glenguin. 1890–1967, British marshal of the Royal Air Force; deputy commander of the Allied Expeditionary Force (1944–45).

teddy ('tɛdɪ) *n, pl* **teddies.** a woman's one-piece undergarment, incorporating a chemise top and panties.

teddy bear *n* a stuffed toy bear. Often shortened to **teddy.** ORIG C20: from *Teddy,* from *Theodore,* after Theodore ROOSEVELT, well known as a hunter of bears

teddy boy *n* **1** (in Britain, esp. in the mid-1950s) one of a cult of youths who wore mock Edwardian fashions. **2** any tough or delinquent youth. ORIG C20: from *Teddy,* from *Edward,* referring to the Edwardian dress

Te Deum (ˌtiː 'diːəm) *n* **1** an ancient Latin hymn in rhythmic prose. **2** a musical setting of this hymn. **3** a service of thanksgiving in which the recital of this hymn forms a central part. ORIG from the L canticle beginning *Tē Deum laudāmus,* lit.: Thee, God, we praise

tedious ('tiːdɪəs) *adj* causing fatigue or tedium; monotonous.
▸ **'tediousness** *n*

tedium ('tiːdɪəm) *n* the state of being bored or the quality of being boring; monotony. ORIG C17: from L *taedium,* from *taedēre* to weary

tee[1] (tiː) *n* **1** a pipe fitting in the form of a letter T, used to join three pipes. **2** a metal section with a cross section in the form of a letter T.

tee[2] (tiː) *Golf.* ◆ *n* **1** an area from which the first stroke of a hole is made. **2** a support for a golf ball, usually a small wooden or plastic peg, used when teeing off or in long grass, etc. ◆ *vb* **tees, teeing, teed. 3** (when *intr,* often foll. by *up*) to position (the ball) ready for striking, on or as if on a tee. ◆ See also **tee off.** ORIG C17 *teaz,* from ?

tee[3] (tiː) *n* a mark used as a target in certain games such as curling and quoits. ORIG C18: ?from T-shaped marks, which may have orig. been used in curling

tee-hee *or* **te-hee** ('tiː'hiː) *interj* **1** an exclamation of laughter, esp. when mocking. ◆ *n* **2** a chuckle. ◆ *vb* **tee-hees, tee-heeing, tee-heed** *or* **te-hees, te-heeing, te-heed. 3** (*intr*) to snigger or laugh, esp. derisively. ORIG C14: imit.

teem[1] (tiːm) *vb* (*intr;* usually foll. by *with*) to be prolific or abundant (in). ORIG OE *tēman* to produce offspring; rel. to West Saxon *tīeman;* see TEAM

teem[2] (tiːm) *vb* **1** (*intr;* often foll. by *down* or *with rain*) to pour in torrents. **2** (*tr*) to pour or empty out. ORIG C15 *temen* to empty, from ON *tœma*

teen (tiːn) *adj Inf.* another word for **teenage.**

teenage ('tiːnˌeɪdʒ) *adj* (*prenominal*) of or relating to the

★ people and places

time in a person's life between the ages of 13 and 19. Also: **teenaged.**

teenager ('ti:nˌeɪdʒə) *n* a person between the ages of 13 and 19 inclusive.

teens (ti:nz) *pl n* **1** the years of a person's life between the ages of 13 and 19 inclusive. **2** all the numbers that end in *-teen.*

teeny ('ti:nɪ) *adj* **teenier, teeniest.** *Inf.* extremely small; tiny. Also: **teeny-weeny** ('ti:nɪ'wi:nɪ) *or* **teensy-weensy** ('ti:nzɪ'wi:nzɪ). ORIG C19: var. of TINY

teenybopper ('ti:nɪˌbɒpə) *n Sl.* a young teenager, usually a girl, who avidly follows fashions in clothes and pop music. ORIG C20: *teeny,* from teenage + *-bopper;* see BOP

tee off *vb (adv)* **1** *Golf.* to strike (the ball) from a tee. **2** *Inf.* to begin; start.

teepee ('ti:pi:) *n* a variant spelling of **tepee.**

Tees ★ (ti:z) *n* a river in N England, rising in the N Pennines and flowing southeast and east to the North Sea at Middlesbrough. Length: 113 km (70 miles).

tee shirt *n* a variant of **T-shirt.**

Teesside ★ ('ti:zˌsaɪd) *n* the industrial region around the lower Tees valley and estuary: a county borough, containing Middlesbrough, from 1968 to 1974.

teeter ('ti:tə) *vb* **1** to move or cause to move unsteadily; wobble. ◆ *n, vb* **2** another word for **seesaw.** ORIG C19: from ME *titeren*

teeth (ti:θ) *n* **1** the plural of **tooth. 2** the most violent part: *the teeth of the gale.* **3** the power to produce a desired effect: *that law has no teeth.* **4 get one's teeth into.** to become engrossed in. **5 in the teeth of.** in direct opposition to; against. **6 to the teeth.** to the greatest possible degree: *armed to the teeth.* **7 show one's teeth.** to threaten.

teethe (ti:ð) *vb* **teethes, teething, teethed.** *(intr)* to cut one's baby (deciduous) teeth.

teething ring *n* a hard ring on which babies may bite while teething.

teething troubles *pl n* the problems that arise during the initial stages of a project, etc.

teetotal (ti:'təʊtᵊl) *adj* **1** of or practising abstinence from alcoholic drink. **2** *Dialect.* complete. ORIG C19: allegedly coined in 1833 by Richard Turner, E advocate of total abstinence from alcohol; prob. from TOTAL, with emphatic reduplication
▸ **tee'totaller** *n* ▸ **tee'totalism** *n*

teetotum (ti:'təʊtəm) *n Arch.* a spinning top bearing letters of the alphabet on its four sides. ORIG C18: from *T totum,* from *T* initial on one of the faces + *totum* the name of the toy, from L *tōtum* the whole

teff (tɛf) *n* an annual grass of NE Africa, grown for its grain. ORIG C18: from Amharic *tēf*

TEFL ('tɛfᵊl) *acronym for* Teaching (of) English as a Foreign Language.

Teflon ('tɛflɒn) *n* a trademark for **polytetrafluoroethylene.**

teg (tɛg) *n* **1** a two-year-old sheep. **2** the fleece of a two-year-old sheep. ORIG C16: from ?

tegmen ('tɛgmən) *n, pl* **tegmina** (-mənə). **1** either of the leathery forewings of the cockroach and related insects. **2** the delicate inner covering of a seed. **3** any similar covering or layer. ORIG C19: from L: a cover, from *tegere* to cover
▸ **'tegminal** *adj*

Tegucigalpa ★ (*Spanish* teγuθi'γalpa) *n* the capital of Honduras, in the south on the Choluteca River: founded about 1579; university (1847). Pop.: 813 900 (1995 est.).

tegument ('tɛgjʊmənt) *n* a less common word for **integument.** ORIG C15: from L *tegumentum* a covering, from *tegere* to cover

te-hee (ti:'hi:) *interj, n, vb* a variant of **tee-hee.**

Tehran *or* **Teheran** ★ (tɛə'rɑ:n, -'ræn) *n* the capital of Iran, at the foot of the Elburz Mountains: built on the site of the ancient capital Ray, destroyed by Mongols in 1220; became capital in the 1790s; three universities. Pop.: 11 000 000 (1994 est.).

Tehuantepec ★ (tə'wɑ:ntəˌpɛk) *n* **Isthmus of.** the narrowest part of S Mexico, with the Bay of Campeche on the north coast and the **Gulf of Tehuantepec** (an inlet of the Pacific) on the south coast.

Teide *or* **Teyde** ★ (*Spanish* 'tɛiðe) *n* **Pico de** ('piko de). a volcanic mountain in the Canary Islands, on Tenerife. Height: 3718 m (12 198 ft).

te igitur *Latin.* (teɪ 'ɪgɪˌtʊə; *English* teɪ 'ɪdʒɪtʊə) *n RC Church.* the first prayer of the canon of the Mass, which begins *Te igitur clementissime Pater* (Thee, therefore, most merciful Father).

Teilhard de Chardin ★ (*French* tɛjar də ʃardɛ̃) *n* **Pierre** (pjɛr). 1881–1955, French Jesuit priest and palaeontologist, noted for his *The Phenomenon of Man* (1938–40).

Tejo ★ ('təʒu) *n* the Portuguese name for the **Tagus.**

Te Kanawa ★ (teɪ 'kɑ:nəwə) *n* Dame **Kiri** ('kɪrɪ). born 1944, New Zealand soprano.

tektite ('tɛktaɪt) *n* a small dark glassy object found in several areas around the world, thought to be a product of meteorite impact. ORIG C20: from Gk *tēktos* molten

tel. *abbrev. for:* **1** telegram. **2** telegraph(ic). **3** telephone.

tel- *combining form.* a variant of **tele-** and **telo-** before a vowel.

telaesthesia *or US* **telesthesia** (ˌtɛlɪs'θi:zɪə) *n* the alleged perception of events that are beyond the normal range of perceptual processes.
▸ **telaesthetic** *or US* **telesthetic** (ˌtɛlɪs'θɛtɪk) *adj*

telamon ('tɛləmən) *n, pl* **telamones** (ˌtɛlə'məʊni:z) *or* **telamons.** a column in the form of a male figure, used to support an entablature. ORIG C18: via L from Gk, from *tlēnai* to bear

Telamon ★ ('tɛləmən, -ˌmɒn) *n Greek myth.* a king of Salamis; brother of Peleus and father of Teucer and Ajax.

Telanaipura ★ (ˌtɛlənaɪ'pʊərə) *n* another name for **Jambi.**

telangiectasis (tɪˌlændʒɪ'ɛktəsɪs) *or* **telangiectasia** (tɪˌlændʒɪɛk'teɪzɪə) *n, pl* **telangiectases** (-ˌsi:z). *Pathol.* an abnormal dilation of the capillaries or terminal arteries producing blotched red spots, esp. on the face or thighs. ORIG C19: NL, from Gk *telos* end + *angeion* vessel + *ektasis* dilation
▸ **telangiectatic** (tɪˌlændʒɪɛk'tætɪk) *adj*

Tel Aviv ★ ('tɛl ə'vi:v) *n* a city in W Israel, on the Mediterranean: the largest city and chief financial centre in Israel; incorporated the city of Jaffa in 1950; university (1953): the capital of Israel in international law. Pop.: 355 900 (1996 est.). Official name: **Tel Aviv-Jaffa** ('tɛl ə'vi:v'dʒæfə).

tele- *combining form.* **1** at or over a distance; distant: *telescope; telekinesis.* **2** television: *telecast.* **3** by means of or via telephone or television: *telesales.* ORIG from Gk *tele* far

telecast ('tɛləˌkɑ:st) *vb* **telecasts, telecasting, telecast** *or* **telecasted. 1** to broadcast by television. ◆ *n* **2** a television broadcast.
▸ **'teleˌcaster** *n*

telecom ('tɛlɪˌkɒm) *or* **telecoms** ('tɛlɪˌkɒmz) *n (functioning as sing)* short for **telecommunications.**

telecommunications (ˌtɛlɪkəˌmju:nɪ'keɪʃənz) *n (functioning as sing)* the science and technology of communications by telephony, radio, television, etc.

telecommuting (ˌtɛlɪkə'mju:tɪŋ) *n* another name for **teleworking.**
▸ **ˌtelecom'muter** *n*

teledu ('tɛlɪˌdu:) *n* a badger of SE Asia and Indonesia, having dark brown hair with a white stripe along the back and producing a fetid secretion when attacked. ORIG C19: from Malay

telegenic (ˌtɛlɪ'dʒɛnɪk) *adj* having or showing a pleasant television image. ORIG C20: from TELE(VISION) + (PHOTO)-GENIC
▸ **ˌtele'genically** *adv*

telegnosis (ˌtɛlə'nəʊsɪs, ˌtɛləg-) *n* knowledge about distant events alleged to have been obtained without the use of any normal sensory mechanism. ORIG C20: from TELE- + *-gnosis,* from Gk *gnōsis* knowledge

Telegonus ★ (tɪ'lɛgənəs) *n Greek myth.* a son of Odysseus

★ people and places

and Circe, who sought his father and mistakenly killed him, later marrying Odysseus' widow Penelope.

telegony (tɪ'lɛgənɪ) *n Genetics.* the supposed influence of a previous sire on offspring borne by a female to other sires.
▸ **telegonic** (ˌtɛlɪ'gɒnɪk) *or* **te'legonous** *adj*

telegram ('tɛlɪˌgræm) *n* a communication transmitted by telegraph.

telegraph ('tɛlɪˌgrɑːf) *n* **1a** a device, system, or process by which information can be transmitted over a distance, esp. using radio signals or coded electrical signals sent along a transmission line. **1b** (*as modifier*): *telegraph pole.* ◆ *vb* **2** to send a telegram to (a person or place); wire. **3** (*tr*) to transmit or send by telegraph. **4** (*tr*) to give advance notice of (anything), esp. unintentionally. **5** (*tr*) *Canad. inf.* to cast (votes) illegally by impersonating registered voters.
▸ **telegraphist** (tɪ'lɛgrəˌfɪst) *or* **telegrapher** (tɪ'lɛgrəfə) *n* ▸ ˌ**tele'graphic** *adj*

telegraph plant *n* a small tropical Asian shrub having small leaflets that turn in various directions during the day and droop at night.

telegraphy (tɪ'lɛgrəfɪ) *n* **1** a system of telecommunications involving any process providing reproduction at a distance of written, printed, or pictorial matter. **2** the skill or process of operating a telegraph.

Telegu ('tɛləˌguː) *n, adj* a variant spelling of **Telugu**.

telekinesis (ˌtɛlɪkaɪ'niːsɪs) *n* **1** the movement of a body caused by thought or willpower without the application of a physical force. **2** the ability to cause such movement.
▸ **telekinetic** (ˌtɛlɪkɪ'nɛtɪk) *adj*

Telemachus ★ (tɪ'lɛməkəs) *n Greek myth.* the son of Odysseus and Penelope, who helped his father slay his mother's suitors.

Telemann ★ (*German* 'teːləman) *n* **Georg Philipp** ('geːɔrk 'fiːlɪp). 1681–1767, German composer.

telemark ('tɛlɪˌmɑːk) *n Skiing.* a turn in which one ski is placed far forward of the other and turned gradually inwards. ORIG C20: after *Telemark,* county in Norway

telemarketing ('tɛlɪˌmɑːkɪtɪŋ) *n* another name for **telesales**.
▸ **'teleˌmarketer** *n*

telemedicine ('tɛlɪˌmɛdɪsɪn, -ˌmɛdsɪn) *n* the treatment of disease or injury by consultation with a specialist in a distant place, esp. by means of a computer or satellite link.

Telemessage ('tɛlɪˌmɛsɪdʒ) *n Trademark.* a message sent by telephone or telex and delivered in printed form.

telemeter (tɪ'lɛmɪtə) *n* **1** any device for recording or measuring a distant event and transmitting the data to a receiver. **2** any device used to measure a distance without directly comparing it with a measuring rod, etc. ◆ *vb* **3** (*tr*) to obtain and transmit (data) from a distant source.
▸ **telemetric** (ˌtɛlɪ'mɛtrɪk) *adj*

telemetry (tɪ'lɛmɪtrɪ) *n* **1** the use of radio waves, telephone lines, etc., to transmit the readings of measuring instruments to a device on which the readings can be indicated or recorded. **2** the measurement of linear distance using a tellurometer.

telencephalon (ˌtɛlɛn'sɛfəˌlɒn) *n* the cerebrum together with related parts of the hypothalamus and the third ventricle.
▸ **telencephalic** ('tɛlɛnsɪ'fælɪk) *adj*

teleology (ˌtɛlɪ'ɒlədʒɪ, ˌtiːlɪ-) *n* **1** *Philosophy.* **1a** the doctrine that there is evidence of purpose or design in the universe, and esp. that this provides proof of the existence of a Designer. **1b** the belief that certain phenomena are best explained in terms of purpose rather than cause. **2** *Biol.* the belief that natural phenomena have a predetermined purpose and are not determined by mechanical laws. ORIG C18: from NL *teleologia,* from Gk *telos* end + -LOGY
▸ **teleological** (ˌtɛlɪə'lɒdʒɪkᵊl, ˌtiːlɪ-) *adj* ▸ ˌ**tele'ologist** *n*

teleost ('tɛlɪˌɒst, 'tiːlɪ-) *n* any of a subclass of bony fishes having rayed fins and a swim bladder, as herrings, carps, eels, cod, perches, etc. ORIG C19: from NL *teleosteī* (pl) creatures having complete skeletons, from Gk *teleos* complete + *osteon* bone

telepathy (tɪ'lɛpəθɪ) *n* the communication between people of thoughts, feelings, etc., involving mechanisms that cannot be understood in terms of known scientific laws.
▸ **telepathic** (ˌtɛlɪ'pæθɪk) *adj* ▸ **te'lepathist** *n* ▸ **te'lepaˌthize** *or* ▸ **te'lepaˌthise** *vb* (*intr*)

telephone ('tɛlɪˌfəʊn) *n* **1** an electrical device for transmitting speech, consisting of a microphone and receiver mounted on a handset. **2a** a worldwide system of communications using telephones. The microphone in one telephone converts sound waves into electrical signals that are transmitted along a telephone wire or by radio to one or more distant sets. **2b** (*as modifier*): *a telephone exchange.* ◆ *vb* **3** to call or talk to (a person) by telephone. **4** to transmit (a message, etc.) by telephone.
▸ **'teleˌphoner** *n* ▸ **telephonic** (ˌtɛlɪ'fɒnɪk) *adj*

telephone banking *n* a facility enabling customers to make use of banking services, such as oral payment instructions, account movements, raising loans, etc., over the telephone rather than by personal visit.

telephone box *n* an enclosure from which a paid telephone call can be made. Also called: **telephone kiosk, telephone booth.**

telephone directory *n* a book listing the names, addresses, and telephone numbers of subscribers in a particular area.

telephone number *n* **1** a set of figures identifying the telephone of a particular subscriber, and used in making connections to that telephone. **2** (*pl*) extremely large numbers, esp. in reference to salaries or prices.

telephone selling *n* another name for **telesales**.

telephonist (tɪ'lɛfənɪst) *n Brit.* a person who operates a telephone switchboard. Also called (esp. US): **telephone operator.**

telephony (tɪ'lɛfənɪ) *n* a system of telecommunications for the transmission of speech or other sounds.

telephotography (ˌtɛlɪfə'tɒgrəfɪ) *n* the process or technique of photographing distant objects using a telephoto lens.

telephoto lens ('tɛlɪˌfəʊtəʊ) *n* a compound camera lens in which the focal length is greater than that of a simple lens and thus produces a magnified image of a distant object.

teleprinter ('tɛlɪˌprɪntə) *n* **1** a telegraph apparatus consisting of a keyboard transmitter, which converts a typed message into coded pulses for transmission along a wire or cable, and a printing receiver, which converts incoming signals and prints out the message. US name: **teletypewriter.** **2** a network of such devices: no longer widely used. **3** a similar device used for direct input/output of data into a computer at a distant location.

Teleprompter ('tɛlɪˌprɒmptə) *n Trademark.* a device for displaying a television script so that the speaker can read it while appearing to look at the camera.

Teleran ('tɛləˌræn) *n Trademark.* an electronic navigational aid in which the image of a ground-based radar system is televised to aircraft. ORIG C20: from *Tele(vision) R(adar) A(ir) N(avigation)*

telesales ('tɛlɪˌseɪlz) *n* (*functioning as sing*) the selling or attempted selling of a particular commodity or service by a salesperson who makes his or her initial approach by telephone. Also called: **telemarketing, telephone selling.**

telescope ('tɛlɪˌskəʊp) *n* **1** an optical instrument for making distant objects appear closer by use of a combination of lenses (**refracting telescope**) or lenses and curved mirrors (**reflecting telescope**). **2** any instrument, such as a radio telescope, for collecting, focusing, and detecting electromagnetic radiation from space. ◆ *vb* **telescopes, telescoping, telescoped.** **3** to crush together or be crushed together, as in a collision. **4** to fit together like a set of cylinders that slide into one another, thus allowing extension and shortening. **5** to make or become smaller or shorter. ORIG C17: from It. *telescopio* or NL *telescopium,* lit.: far-seeing instrument

telescopic (ˌtɛlɪˈskɒpɪk) *adj* **1** of or relating to a telescope. **2** seen through or obtained by means of a telescope. **3** visible only with a telescope. **4** able to see far. **5** having parts that telescope.
▸ ˌ**teleˈscopically** *adv*

telescopic sight *n* a telescope mounted on a rifle, etc., used for sighting.

telescopy (tɪˈlɛskəpɪ) *n* the branch of astronomy concerned with the use and design of telescopes.

telespectroscope (ˌtɛlɪˈspɛktrəˌskəʊp) *n* a combination of a telescope and a spectroscope, used for spectroscopic analysis of radiation from stars and other celestial bodies.

telestereoscope (ˌtɛlɪˈstɪərɪəˌskəʊp, -ˈstɛrɪə-) *n* an optical instrument for obtaining stereoscopic images of distant objects.

telestich (tɪˈlɛstɪk, ˈtɛlɪˌstɪk) *n* a short poem in which the last letters of each successive line form a word. ORIG C17: from Gk *telos* end + *stikhos* row

Teletext (ˈtɛlɪˌtɛkst) *n Trademark.* a form of Videotex in which information is broadcast by a television station and received on an adapted television set. **Ceefax** is provided by the BBC and **Oracle** by ITV.

telethon (ˈtɛlɪˌθɒn) *n* a lengthy television programme to raise charity funds, etc. ORIG C20: from TELE- + MARATHON

Teletype (ˈtɛlɪˌtaɪp) *n* **1** *Trademark.* a type of teleprinter. **2** (*sometimes not cap.*) a network of such devices. ◆ *vb* **Teletypes, Teletyping, Teletyped. 3** (*sometimes not cap.*) to transmit (a message) by Teletype.

teletypewriter (ˌtɛlɪˈtaɪpˌraɪtə, ˈtɛlɪˌtaɪp-) *n* a US name for **teleprinter.**

televangelist (ˌtɛlɪˈvændʒəlɪst) *n US.* an evangelical preacher who appears regularly on television, preaching the gospel and appealing for donations from viewers. ORIG C20: from TELE(VISION + E)VANGELIST

televise (ˈtɛlɪˌvaɪz) *vb* **televises, televising, televised. 1** to put on television. **2** (*tr*) to transmit by television.

television (ˈtɛlɪˌvɪʒən) *n* **1** the system or process of producing on a distant screen a series of transient visible images, usually with an accompanying sound signal. Electrical signals, converted from optical images by a camera tube, are transmitted by radio waves or by cable and reconverted into optical images by means of a television tube inside a television set. **2** Also called: **television set.** a device designed to receive and convert incoming electrical signals into a series of visible images on a screen together with accompanying sound. **3** the content, etc., of television programmes. **4** the occupation or profession concerned with any aspect of the broadcasting of television programmes. **5** (*modifier*) of, relating to, or used in the transmission or reception of video and audio UHF or VHF radio signals: *a television transmitter.* ◆ Abbrev.: **TV.**

television tube *n* a cathode-ray tube designed for the reproduction of television pictures. Sometimes shortened to **tube.**

televisual (ˌtɛlɪˈvɪʒʊəl, -zjʊ-) *adj* relating to or suitable for production on television.
▸ ˌ**teleˈvisually** *adv*

teleworking (ˈtɛlɪˌwɜːkɪŋ) *n* the use of home computers, telephones, etc., to enable a person to work from home while maintaining contact with colleagues, customers, or a central office. Also called: **telecommuting.**
▸ ˈ**teleˌworker** *n*

telex (ˈtɛlɛks) *n* **1** an international telegraph service in which teleprinters are rented out to subscribers. **2** a teleprinter used in such a service. **3** a message transmitted or received by telex. ◆ *vb* **4** to transmit (a message) to (a person, etc.) by telex. ORIG C20: from *tel(eprinter) ex(change)*

Telford[1] ★ (ˈtɛlfəd) *n* a town in W central England, in Shropshire: designated a new town in 1963. Pop.: 119 340 (1991).

Telford[2] ★ (ˈtɛlfəd) *n* **Thomas.** 1757–1834, Scottish civil engineer, noted for the Menai suspension bridge (1825).

Telford and Wrekin ★ *n* a unitary authority in W central England, in Shropshire. Pop.: 144 200 (1996 est.). Area: 289 sq. km (112 sq. miles).

Telidon (ˈtɛlɪˌdɒn) *n Trademark.* a Canadian interactive viewdata service.

tell[1] (tɛl) *vb* **tells, telling, told. 1** (when *tr, may take a clause as object*) to let know or notify. **2** (*tr*) to order or instruct. **3** (when *intr,* usually foll. by *of*) to give an account or narration (of). **4** (*tr*) to communicate by words: *tell lies.* **5** (*tr*) to make known: *to tell fortunes.* **6** (*intr;* often foll. by *of*) to serve as an indication: *her blush told of her embarrassment.* **7** (*tr;* used with *can,* etc.; *may take a clause as object*) to discover or discern: *I can tell what is wrong.* **8** (*tr;* used with *can,* etc.) to distinguish or discriminate: *he couldn't tell chalk from cheese.* **9** (*intr*) to have or produce an impact, effect, or strain: *every step told on his bruised feet.* **10** (*intr;* sometimes foll. by *on*) *Inf.* to reveal secrets or gossip (about). **11** (*tr*) to assure: *I tell you, I've had enough!* **12** (*tr*) to count (votes). **13 tell the time.** to read the time from a clock. **14 you're telling me.** *Sl.* I know that very well. ◆ See also **tell apart, tell off.** ORIG OE *tellan*
▸ ˈ**tellable** *adj*

tell[2] (tɛl) *n* a large mound resulting from the accumulation of rubbish on a long-settled site, esp. in the Middle East. ORIG C19: from Ar. *tall*

Tell ★ (tɛl) *n* **William,** German name *Wilhelm Tell.* legendary Swiss patriot, who shot an apple from his son's head on the order of an Austrian governor.

tell apart *vb* (*tr, adv*) to distinguish between.

Tell el Amarna ★ (ˈtɛl ɛl əˈmɑːnə) *n* a group of ruins and rock tombs in Upper Egypt, on the Nile below Asyut: site of the capital of Amenhotep IV, built about 1375 B.C.; excavated from 1891 onwards.

teller (ˈtɛlə) *n* **1** a bank cashier. **2** a person appointed to count votes. **3** a person who tells; narrator.

Teller ★ (ˈtɛlə) *n* **Edward.** born 1908, US nuclear physicist, born in Hungary: contributed to the development of the hydrogen bomb (1952).

telling (ˈtɛlɪŋ) *adj* **1** having a marked effect or impact. **2** revealing.
▸ ˈ**tellingly** *adv*

tell off *vb* (*tr, adv*) **1** *Inf.* to reprimand; scold. **2** to count and select for duty.

telltale (ˈtɛlˌteɪl) *n* **1** a person who tells tales about others. **2a** an outward indication of something concealed. **2b** (*as modifier*): *a telltale paw mark.* **3** a device used to monitor a process, machine, etc.

tellurian (tɛˈlʊərɪən) *adj* **1** of the earth. ◆ *n* **2** (esp. in science fiction) an inhabitant of the earth. ORIG C19: from L *tellūs* the earth

telluric[1] (tɛˈlʊərɪk) *adj* of or originating on or in the earth or soil; terrestrial. ORIG C19: from L *tellūs* the earth

telluric[2] (tɛˈlʊərɪk) *adj* of or containing tellurium, esp. in a high valence state. ORIG C20: from TELLUR(IUM) + -IC

tellurion *or* **tellurian** (tɛˈlʊərɪən) *n* an instrument that shows how day and night, etc., result from the earth's rotation on its axis, etc. ORIG C19: from L *tellūs* the earth

tellurium (tɛˈlʊərɪəm) *n* a brittle silvery-white nonmetallic element. Symbol: Te; atomic no.: 52; atomic wt.: 127.60. ORIG C19: NL, from L *tellūs* the earth, by analogy with URANIUM

tellurometer (ˌtɛljʊˈrɒmɪtə) *n Surveying.* an electronic instrument for measuring distances by the transmission of radio waves. ORIG C20: from L *tellūs* the earth + -METER

Tellus ★ (ˈtɛləs) *n* the Roman goddess of the earth; protectress of marriage, fertility, and the dead.

telly (ˈtɛlɪ) *n, pl* **tellies.** *Inf., chiefly Brit.* short for **television.**

telo- *or before a vowel* **tel-** *combining form.* **1** complete; final; perfect. **2** end; at the end. ORIG from Gk *telos* end

telpherage (ˈtɛlfərɪdʒ) *n* an overhead transport system in which an electrically driven truck runs along a rail or cable, the load being suspended in a car beneath. Also called: **telpher.** ORIG C19: changed from *telephore,* from TELE- + -PHORE + -AGE

telson (ˈtɛlsən) *n* the last segment or an appendage on the last segment of the body of crustaceans and arachnids. ORIG C19: from Gk: a boundary

★ people and places

Telugu *or* **Telegu** ('tɛlə,guː) *n* **1** a language of SE India, belonging to the Dravidian family of languages. **2** (*pl* **Telugus** *or* **Telugu**) a member of the people who speak this language. ◆ *adj* **3** of or relating to this people or their language.

Telukbetung *or* **Teloekbetoeng** ★ (tə,lʊkbə'tʊŋ) *n* a port in Indonesia, in S Sumatra on the Sunda Strait. Pop.: 285 000 (latest est.).

Tema ★ ('tiːmə) *n* a port in SE Ghana on the Atlantic: new harbour opened in 1962; oil-refining. Pop.: 110 000 (1988 est.).

temazepam (tə'mæzə,pæm) *n* a sedative in the form of a gel-like capsule, which is taken orally or melted and injected by drug users.

Témbi ★ ('tɛmbiː) *n* transliteration of the Modern Greek name for **Tempe**.

temblor ('tɛmblə, -blɔː) *n, pl* **temblors** *or* **temblores** (tɛm'blɔːreɪz). *Chiefly US.* an earthquake or earth tremor. ORIG C19: American Sp., from Sp. *temblar* to shake, tremble

temerity (tɪ'mɛrɪtɪ) *n* rashness or boldness. ORIG C15: from L *temeritās* accident, from *temere* at random
▸ **temerarious** (,tɛmə'rɛərɪəs) *adj*

Temesvár ★ ('tɛmɛʃvaːr) *n* the Hungarian name for **Timişoara**.

temp (tɛmp) *Inf.* ◆ *n* **1** a person, esp. a typist or other office worker, employed on a temporary basis. ◆ *vb* (*intr*) **2** to work as a temp.

temp. *abbrev. for:* **1** temperature. **2** temporary. **3** tempore. ORIG L: in the time of

Tempe ★ ('tɛmpɪ) *n* **Vale of.** a wooded valley in E Greece, in Thessaly between the mountains Olympus and Ossa. Modern Greek name: **Témbi**.

temper ('tɛmpə) *n* **1** a frame of mind; mood or humour. **2** a sudden outburst of anger. **3** a tendency to exhibit anger; irritability. **4** a mental condition of moderation and calm (esp. in **keep one's temper** *or* **lose one's temper**). **5** the degree of hardness, elasticity, etc., of a metal. ◆ *vb* (*tr*) **6** to make more acceptable or suitable by adding something else; moderate: *he tempered his criticism with sympathy.* **7** to reduce the brittleness of (a hardened metal) by reheating it and allowing it to cool. **8** *Music.* **8a** to adjust the frequency differences between the notes of a scale on (a keyboard instrument). **8b** to make such an adjustment to the pitches of notes in (a scale). ORIG OE *temprian* to mingle, from L *temperāre* to mix, prob. from *tempus* time
▸ **'temperable** *adj* ▸ **'temperer** *n*

tempera ('tɛmpərə) *n* **1** a painting medium for powdered pigments, consisting usually of egg yolk and water. **2a** any emulsion used as a painting medium, with casein, glue, wax, etc., as a base. **2b** the paint made from this. **3** the technique of painting with tempera. ORIG C19: from It. *pingere a tempera* painting in tempera, from *temperare* to mingle; see TEMPER

temperament ('tɛmpərəmənt) *n* **1** a person's character, disposition, and tendencies. **2** excitability, moodiness, or anger. **3** the characteristic way an individual behaves, esp. towards other people. **4a** an adjustment made to the frequency differences between notes on a keyboard instrument to allow modulation to other keys. **4b** any of several systems of such adjustment, esp. **equal temperament**, a system giving a scale based on an octave divided into twelve exactly equal semitones. **5** *Obs.* the characteristic way an individual behaves, viewed as the result of the influence of the four humours. ORIG C15: from L *temperāmentum* a mixing in proportion, from *temperāre* to TEMPER

temperamental (,tɛmpərə'mɛntᵊl) *adj* **1** easily upset or irritated; excitable. **2** of or caused by temperament. **3** *Inf.* working erratically and inconsistently; unreliable.
▸ **,tempera'mentally** *adv*

temperance ('tɛmpərəns) *n* **1** restraint or moderation, esp. in yielding to one's appetites or desires. **2** abstinence from alcoholic drink. ORIG C14: from L *temperantia,* from *temperāre* to regulate

temperate ('tɛmpərɪt) *adj* **1** having a climate intermediate between tropical and polar; moderate or mild in temperature. **2** mild in quality or character; exhibiting temperance. ORIG C14: from L *temperātus*
▸ **'temperately** *adv* ▸ **'temperateness** *n*

Temperate Zone *n* those parts of the earth's surface lying between the Arctic Circle and the tropic of Cancer and between the Antarctic Circle and the tropic of Capricorn.

temperature ('tɛmprɪtʃə) *n* **1** the degree of hotness of a body, substance, or medium, esp. as measured on a scale that has one or more fixed reference points. **2** *Inf.* a body temperature in excess of the normal. ORIG C16 (orig.: a mingling): from L *temperātūra* proportion, from *temperāre* to TEMPER

temperature gradient *n* the rate of change in temperature in a given direction.

temperature-humidity index *n* an index of the effect on human comfort of temperature and humidity levels, 65 being the highest comfortable level.

tempered ('tɛmpəd) *adj* **1** *Music.* adjusted in accordance with a system of temperament. **2** (*in combination*) having a temper or temperament as specified: *ill-tempered.*

tempest ('tɛmpɪst) *n* **1** *Chiefly literary.* a violent wind or storm. **2** a violent commotion, uproar, or disturbance. ORIG C13: from OF *tempeste,* from L *tempestās* storm, from *tempus* time

tempestuous (tɛm'pɛstjʊəs) *adj* **1** of or relating to a tempest. **2** violent or stormy.
▸ **tem'pestuously** *adv* ▸ **tem'pestuousness** *n*

tempi ('tɛmpiː) *n* (in musical senses) the plural of **tempo**.

Templar ('tɛmplə) *n* **1** a member of a military order (**Knights of the Temple of Solomon**) founded by Crusaders in Jerusalem around 1118; suppressed in 1312. **2** (*sometimes not cap.*) *Brit.* a lawyer who has chambers in the Temple in London. ORIG C13: from Med. L *templārius* of the TEMPLE; applied to the order because their house adjoined the site of the Temple of Solomon

template *or* **templet** ('tɛmplɪt) *n* **1** a gauge or pattern, cut out in wood or metal, used in woodwork, etc., to help shape something accurately. **2** a pattern cut out in card or plastic, used to reproduce shapes. **3** a short beam that is used to spread a load, as over a doorway. **4** *Biochem.* the molecular structure of a compound that serves as a pattern for the production of another compound. ORIG C17 *templet* (later spelling infl. by PLATE), prob. from F, dim. of TEMPLE[3]

temple[1] ('tɛmpᵊl) *n* **1** a building or place dedicated to the worship of a deity or deities. **2** a Mormon church. **3** *US.* another name for a **synagogue**. **4** a Christian church. **5** any place or object regarded as a shrine where God makes himself present. **6** a building regarded as the focus of an activity, interest, or practice: *a temple of the arts.* ORIG OE *tempel,* from L *templum*

temple[2] ('tɛmpᵊl) *n* the region on each side of the head in front of the ear and above the cheek bone. ORIG C14: from OF *temple,* from L *tempora* the temples, from *tempus* temple of the head

temple[3] ('tɛmpᵊl) *n* the part of a loom that keeps the cloth being woven stretched to the correct width. ORIG C15: from F, from L *templum* a small timber

Temple[1] ★ ('tɛmpəl) *n* **1** a building in London that belonged to the Templars: it now houses two law societies. **2** any of three buildings erected by the Jews in ancient Jerusalem for the worship of Jehovah.

Temple[2] ★ ('tɛmpəl) *n* **1 Shirley,** married name *Shirley Temple Black.* born 1928, US child film star and (later) politician. She was US ambassador to Ghana (1974–76) and to Czechoslovakia (1989–92). **2** Sir **William.** 1628–99, English diplomat. He negotiated the Triple Alliance (1668) and the marriage of William of Orange to Mary II. **3 William.** 1881–1944, British prelate and advocate of social reform; archbishop of Canterbury (1942–44).

Temple of Artemis ★ *n* the large temple at Ephesus, on the W coast of Asia Minor: one of the Seven Wonders of the World.

tempo ('tɛmpəʊ) *n, pl* **tempos** *or* **tempi** (-piː). **1** the speed at which a piece of music is meant to be played. **2** rate or pace. ORIG C18: from It., from L *tempus* time

temporal[1] (ˈtɛmpərəl) *adj* **1** of or relating to time. **2** of secular as opposed to spiritual or religious affairs. **3** lasting for a relatively short time. **4** *Grammar.* of or relating to tense or the linguistic expression of time. ORIG C14: from L *temporālis,* from *tempus* time
▸ ˈ**temporally** *adv*

temporal[2] (ˈtɛmpərəl) *adj Anat.* of or near the temple or temples. ORIG C16: from LL *temporālis* belonging to the temples; see TEMPLE[2]

temporal bone *n* either of two compound bones forming the sides of the skull.

temporality (ˌtɛmpəˈrælɪtɪ) *n, pl* **temporalities. 1** the state or quality of being temporal. **2** something temporal. **3** (*often pl*) a secular possession or revenue belonging to a Church.

temporal lobe *n* the laterally protruding portion of each cerebral hemisphere, situated below the parietal lobe and associated with sound perception and interpretation.

temporary (ˈtɛmpərərɪ) *adj* **1** not permanent; provisional. **2** lasting only a short time. ◆ *n, pl* **temporaries. 3** a person employed on a temporary basis. ORIG C16: from L *temporārius,* from *tempus* time
▸ ˈ**temporarily** *adv* ▸ ˈ**temporariness** *n*

temporize *or* **temporise** (ˈtɛmpəˌraɪz) *vb* **temporizes, temporizing, temporized** *or* **temporises, temporising, temporised.** (*intr*) **1** to delay, act evasively, or protract a negotiation, etc., esp. in order to gain time or effect a compromise. **2** to adapt oneself to the circumstances, as by temporary or apparent agreement. ORIG C16: from F *temporiser,* from Med. L *temporizāre,* from L *tempus* time
▸ ˌ**temporiˈzation** *or* ˌ**temporiˈsation** *n* ▸ ˈ**tempoˌrizer** *or* ˈ**tempoˌriser** *n*

tempt (tɛmpt) *vb* (*tr*) **1** to entice to do something, esp. something morally wrong or unwise. **2** to allure or attract. **3** to give rise to a desire in (someone) to do something; dispose. **4** to risk provoking (esp. in **tempt fate**). ORIG C13: from OF *tempter,* from L *temptāre* to test
▸ ˈ**temptable** *adj* ▸ ˈ**tempter** *n* ▸ ˈ**temptress** *fem n*

temptation (tɛmpˈteɪʃən) *n* **1** the act of tempting or the state of being tempted. **2** a person or thing that tempts.

tempting (ˈtɛmptɪŋ) *adj* attractive or inviting: *a tempting meal.*
▸ ˈ**temptingly** *adv*

tempus fugit *Latin.* (ˈtɛmpəs ˈfjuːdʒɪt) time flies.

Temuco ★ (*Spanish* teˈmuko) *n* a city in S Chile: agricultural trading centre. Pop.: 239 340 (1995 est.).

ten (tɛn) *n* **1** the cardinal number that is the sum of nine and one. It is the base of the decimal number system and the base of the common logarithm. **2** a numeral, 10, X, etc., representing this number. **3** something representing or consisting of ten units. **4** Also called: **ten o'clock.** ten hours after noon or midnight. ◆ *determiner* **5** amounting to ten. ◆ Related adj: **decimal.** ORIG OE *tēn*

ten. *Music. abbrev. for:* **1** tenor. **2** tenuto.

tenable (ˈtɛnəbᵊl) *adj* able to be upheld, believed, maintained, or defended. ORIG C16: from OF, from *tenir* to hold, from L *tenēre*
▸ ˌ**tenaˈbility** *or* ˈ**tenableness** *n* ▸ ˈ**tenably** *adv*

tenace (ˈtɛneɪs) *n Bridge, whist.* a holding of two nonconsecutive high cards of a suit, such as the ace and queen. ORIG C17: from F, from Sp. *tenaza* forceps, ult. from L *tenāx* holding fast, from *tenēre* to hold

tenacious (tɪˈneɪʃəs) *adj* **1** holding firmly: *a tenacious grip.* **2** retentive: *a tenacious memory.* **3** stubborn or persistent. **4** holding together firmly; cohesive. **5** tending to stick or adhere. ORIG C16: from L *tenāx,* from *tenēre* to hold
▸ **teˈnaciously** *adv* ▸ **teˈnaciousness** *or* **tenacity** (tɪˈnæsɪtɪ) *n*

tenaculum (tɪˈnækjʊləm) *n, pl* **tenacula** (-lə). a hooked surgical instrument for grasping and holding parts. ORIG C17: from LL, from L *tenēre* to hold

tenancy (ˈtɛnənsɪ) *n, pl* **tenancies. 1** the temporary possession or holding by a tenant of lands or property owned by another. **2** the period of holding or occupying such property. **3** the period of holding office, a position, etc.

tenant (ˈtɛnənt) *n* **1** a person who holds, occupies, or possesses land or property, esp. from a landlord. **2** a person who has the use of a house, etc., subject to the payment of rent. **3** any holder or occupant. ◆ *vb* **4** (*tr*) to hold as a tenant. ORIG C14: from OF, lit.: (one who is) holding, from *tenir* to hold, from L *tenēre*
▸ ˈ**tenantable** *adj* ▸ ˈ**tenantless** *adj*

tenant farmer *n* a person who farms land rented from another, the rent usually taking the form of crops or livestock.

tenantry (ˈtɛnəntrɪ) *n* **1** tenants collectively. **2** the status or condition of being a tenant.

tench (tɛntʃ) *n* a European freshwater game fish of the carp family. ORIG C14: from OF *tenche,* from LL *tinca*

Ten Commandments *pl n* **the.** *Old Testament.* the commandments summarizing the basic obligations of man towards God and his fellow men, delivered to Moses on Mount Sinai engraved on two tables of stone (Exodus 20:1–17).

tend[1] (tɛnd) *vb* (when *intr,* usually foll. by *to* or *towards*) **1** (when *tr, takes an infinitive*) to have a general disposition (to do something); be inclined: *children tend to prefer sweets to meat.* **2** (*intr*) to have or be an influence (towards a specific result). **3** (*intr*) to go or move (in a particular direction): *to tend to the south.* ORIG C14: from OF *tendre,* from L *tendere* to stretch

tend[2] (tɛnd) *vb* **1** (*tr*) to care for. **2** (when *intr,* often foll. by *on* or *to*) to attend (to). **3** (*tr*) to handle or control. **4** (*intr;* often foll. by *to*) *Inf., chiefly US & Canad.* to pay attention. ORIG C14: var. of ATTEND

tendency (ˈtɛndənsɪ) *n, pl* **tendencies. 1** (often foll. by *to*) an inclination, predisposition, propensity, or leaning. **2** the general course, purport, or drift of something, esp. a written work. ORIG C17: from Med. L *tendentia,* from L *tendere* to TEND[1]

tendentious *or* **tendencious** (tɛnˈdɛnʃəs) *adj* having or showing an intentional tendency or bias, esp. a controversial one. ORIG C20: from TENDENCY
▸ **tenˈdentiously** *or* **tenˈdenciously** *adv* ▸ **tenˈdentiousness** *or* **tenˈdenciousness** *n*

tender[1] (ˈtɛndə) *adj* **1** easily broken, cut, or crushed; soft. **2** easily damaged; vulnerable or sensitive: *at a tender age.* **3** having or expressing warm feelings. **4** kind or sympathetic: *a tender heart.* **5** arousing warm feelings; touching. **6** gentle and delicate: *a tender breeze.* **7** requiring care in handling: *a tender question.* **8** painful or sore. **9** sensitive to moral or spiritual feelings. **10** (*postpositive;* foll. by *of*) protective: *tender of one's emotions.* ORIG C13: from OF *tendre,* from L *tener* delicate
▸ ˈ**tenderly** *adv* ▸ ˈ**tenderness** *n*

tender[2] (ˈtɛndə) *vb* **1** (*tr*) to give, present, or offer: *to tender a bid.* **2** (*intr;* foll. by *for*) to make a formal offer or estimate (for a job or contract). **3** (*tr*) *Law.* to offer (money or goods) in settlement of a debt or claim. ◆ *n* **4** the act or an instance of tendering; offer. **5** a formal offer to supply specified goods or services at a stated cost or rate. **6** something, esp. money, used as an official medium of payment: *legal tender.* ORIG C16: from Anglo-F *tendre,* from L *tendere* to extend
▸ ˈ**tenderer** *n*

tender[3] (ˈtɛndə) *n* **1** a small boat towed or carried by a ship. **2** a vehicle drawn behind a steam locomotive to carry the fuel and water. **3** a person who tends. ORIG C15: var. of *attender*

tenderfoot (ˈtɛndəˌfʊt) *n, pl* **tenderfoots** *or* **tenderfeet. 1** a newcomer, esp. to the mines or ranches of the southwestern US. **2** (formerly) a beginner in the Scouts or Guides.

tenderhearted (ˌtɛndəˈhɑːtɪd) *adj* having a compassionate, kindly, or sensitive disposition.

tenderize *or* **tenderise** (ˈtɛndəˌraɪz) *vb* **tenderizes, tenderizing, tenderized** *or* **tenderises, tenderising, tenderised.** (*tr*) to make (meat) tender, as by pounding it or adding a substance to break down the fibres.
▸ ˌ**tenderiˈzation** *or* ˌ**tenderiˈsation** *n* ▸ ˈ**tenderˌizer** *or* ˈ**tenderˌiser** *n*

tenderloin (ˈtɛndəˌlɔɪn) *n* a tender cut of pork or other meat from between the sirloin and ribs.

tendon (ˈtɛndən) *n* a cord or band of tough tissue that attaches a muscle to a bone or some other part; sinew. ORIG C16: from Med. L *tendō,* from L *tendere* to stretch

tendril (ˈtɛndrɪl) *n* a threadlike leaf or stem that attaches climbing plants to a support by twining or adhering. ORIG C16: ?from OF *tendron* tendril (confused with OF *tendron* bud), from Med. L *tendō* TENDON

tenebrism (ˈtɛnəˌbrɪzəm) *n* (*sometimes cap.*) a school, style, or method of painting, adopted chiefly by 17th-century Spanish and Neapolitan painters, characterized by large areas of dark colours, usually relieved with a shaft of light.
▸ **ˈtenebrist** *n, adj*

tenebrous (ˈtɛnəbrəs) *or* **tenebrious** (təˈnɛbrɪəs) *adj* gloomy, shadowy, or dark. ORIG C15: from L *tenebrōsus* from *tenebrae* darkness

Tenedos ★ (ˈtɛnɪˌdɒs) *n* an island in the NE Aegean, near the entrance to the Dardanelles: in Greek legend the base of the Greek fleet during the siege of Troy. Modern Turkish name: **Bozcaada.**

tenement (ˈtɛnəmənt) *n* **1** Also called: **tenement building.** a large building divided into rooms or flats. **2** a dwelling place or residence. **3** *Chiefly Brit.* a room or flat for rent. **4** *Property law.* any form of permanent property, such as land, dwellings, offices, etc. ORIG C14: from Med. L *tenementum,* from L *tenēre* to hold
▸ **tenemental** (ˌtɛnəˈmɛntᵊl) *adj*

Tenerife ★ (ˌtɛnəˈriːf; *Spanish* teneˈrife) *n* a Spanish island in the Atlantic, off the NW coast of Africa: the largest of the Canary Islands; volcanic and mountainous; tourism and agriculture. Capital: Santa Cruz. Pop.: 560 000 (latest est.). Area: 2058 sq. km (795 sq. miles).

tenesmus (tɪˈnɛzməs) *n* an ineffective painful straining to empty the bowels or bladder. ORIG C16: from Med. L, from L *tēnesmos,* from Gk, from *teinein* to strain
▸ **teˈnesmic** *adj*

tenet (ˈtɛnɪt, ˈtiːnɪt) *n* a belief, opinion, or dogma. ORIG C17: from L, lit.: he (it) holds, from *tenēre* to hold

tenfold (ˈtɛnˌfəʊld) *adj* **1** equal to or having 10 times as many or as much. **2** composed of 10 parts. ◆ *adv* **3** by or up to 10 times as many or as much.

ten-gallon hat *n* (in the US) a cowboy's broad-brimmed felt hat with a very high crown.

Teng Hsiao-ping ★ (ˈtɛŋ sjaʊ ˈpɪŋ) *n* a variant transliteration of the Chinese name for **Deng Xiaoping.**

Tengri Khan ★ (ˈtɛŋgrɪ ˈkɑːn) *n* a mountain in central Asia, on the border between Kyrgyzstan and the Xinjiang Uygur Autonomous Region of W China. Height: 6995 m (22 951 ft).

Tengri Nor ★ (ˈtɛŋgrɪ ˈnɔː) *n* another name for **Nam Co.**

Ten Gurus ★ *pl n* the ten leaders of the Sikh religion, from its founder Guru Nanak (1469–1539) to Guru Govind Singh (1666–1708).

Teniers ★ (ˈtɛnɪəz) *n* **David** (ˈdɑːvɪt), called *the Elder,* 1582–1649, and his son **David,** called *the Younger,* 1610–90, Flemish painters.

tenner (ˈtɛnə) *n Inf.* **1** *Brit.* **1a** a ten-pound note. **1b** the sum of ten pounds. **2** *US.* a ten-dollar bill.

Tennessee ★ (ˌtɛnɪˈsiː) *n* **1** a state of the E central US: consists of a lowland plain in the west, rising to the Appalachians and the Cumberland Plateau in the east. Capital: Nashville. Pop.: 5 430 621 (1998 est.). Area: 109 412 sq. km (42 244 sq. miles). Abbrevs.: **Tenn.** or (with zip code) **TN** **2** a river in the E central US, flowing southwest from E Tennessee into N Alabama, then west and north to the Ohio River at Paducah: the longest tributary of the Ohio; includes a series of dams and reservoirs under the Tennessee Valley Authority. Length: 1049 km (652 miles).
▸ **ˌTennesˈsean** *adj, n*

Tenniel ★ (ˈtɛnjəl) *n* Sir **John.** 1820–1914, British illustrator of Lewis Carroll's *Alice* books and political cartoonist in *Punch.*

tennis (ˈtɛnɪs) *n* **a** a racket game played between two players or pairs of players who hit a ball to and fro over a net on a rectangular court of grass, asphalt, clay, etc. See also **lawn tennis, real tennis, table tennis. b** (*as modifier*): *tennis court; tennis racket.* ORIG C14: prob. from Anglo-F *tenetz* hold (imperative), from OF *tenir* to hold, from L *tenēre*

tennis elbow *n* inflammation of the elbow caused by exertion in playing tennis, etc.

tennis shoe *n* a rubber-soled canvas shoe tied with laces.

Tennyson ★ (ˈtɛnɪsᵊn) *n* **Alfred,** Lord Tennyson. 1809–92, British poet; poet laureate (1850–92). His poems include *The Lady of Shalott* (1832) and *Idylls of the King* (1859).
▸ **Tennysonian** (ˌtɛnɪˈsəʊnɪən) *adj, n*

Teno ★ (ˈtɛnɔ) *n* the Finnish name for **Tana** (sense 3).

teno- *or before a vowel* **ten-** *combining form.* tendon: *tenosynovitis.* ORIG from Gk *tenōn*

Tenochtitlán ★ (tɛˌnɔːtʃtiːˈtlɑːn) *n* an ancient city and capital of the Aztec empire on the present site of Mexico City; razed by Cortés in 1521.

tenon (ˈtɛnən) *n* **1** the projecting end of a piece of wood formed to fit into a corresponding mortise in another piece. ◆ *vb* (*tr*) **2** to form a tenon on (a piece of wood). **3** to join with a tenon and mortise. ORIG C15: from OF, from *tenir* to hold, from L *tenēre*
▸ **ˈtenoner** *n*

tenon saw *n* a small fine-toothed saw with a strong back, used esp. for cutting tenons.

tenor (ˈtɛnə) *n* **1** *Music.* **1a** the male voice intermediate between alto and baritone. **1b** a singer with such a voice. **1c** a saxophone, horn, etc., intermediate between the alto and baritone or bass. **2** general drift of thought; purpose. **3** a settled course of progress. **4** *Arch.* general tendency. **5** *Finance.* the time required for a bill of exchange or promissory note to become due for payment. **6** *Law.* **6a** the exact words of a deed, etc. **6b** an exact copy. ORIG C13 (orig.: general sense): from OF *tenour,* from L *tenor* a holding to a course, from *tenēre* to hold; musical sense via It. *tenore,* referring to the voice part that was continuous, that is, to which the melody was assigned

tenor clef *n* the clef that establishes middle C as being on the fourth line of the staff.

tenorrhaphy (tɪˈnɒrəfɪ) *n, pl* **tenorrhaphies.** *Surgery.* the union of torn or divided tendons by means of sutures. ORIG C19: from TENO- + Gk *raphē* a sewing

tenosynovitis (ˈtɛnəʊˌsaɪnəʊˈvaɪtɪs) *n* painful swelling and inflammation of tendons, usually of the wrist, often the result of repetitive movements such as typing.

tenotomy (təˈnɒtəmɪ) *n, pl* **tenotomies.** surgical division of a tendon.
▸ **teˈnotomist** *n*

tenpin bowling (ˈtɛnˌpɪn) *n* a bowling game in which bowls are rolled down a lane to knock over the ten target pins. Also called (esp. US and Canad.): **tenpins.**

tenrec (ˈtɛnrɛk) *n* any of a family of small mammals of Madagascar resembling hedgehogs or shrews. ORIG C18: via F from Malagasy *tràndraka*

tense[1] (tɛns) *adj* **1** stretched or stressed tightly; taut or rigid. **2** under mental or emotional strain. **3** producing mental or emotional strain: *a tense day.* **4** *Phonetics.* Also: **narrow.** pronounced with considerable muscular effort, as the vowel (iː) in "beam". ◆ *vb* **tenses, tensing, tensed.** (often foll. by *up*) **5** to make or become tense. ORIG C17: from L *tensus* taut, from *tendere* to stretch
▸ **ˈtensely** *adv* ▸ **ˈtenseness** *n*

tense[2] (tɛns) *n Grammar.* a category of the verb or verbal inflections, such as present, past, and future, that expresses the temporal relations between what is reported in a sentence and the time of its utterance. ORIG C14: from OF *tens* time, from L *tempus*
▸ **ˈtenseless** *adj*

tense logic *n Logic.* the study of temporal relations between propositions, usually pursued by considering the logical properties of symbols representing the tenses of natural languages.

tensile (ˈtɛnsaɪl) *adj* **1** of or relating to tension. **2** suffi-

ciently ductile to be stretched or drawn out. ORIG C17: from NL *tensilis,* from L *tendere* to stretch
▸ **tensility** (tɛnˈsɪlɪtɪ) *or* **ˈtensileness** *n*

tensile strength *n* a measure of the ability of a material to withstand a longitudinal stress, expressed as the greatest stress that the material can stand without breaking.

tensimeter (tɛnˈsɪmɪtə) *n* a device that measures differences in vapour pressures. ORIG C20: from TENSI(ON) + -METER

tensiometer (ˌtɛnsɪˈɒmɪtə) *n* **1** an instrument for measuring the tensile strength of a wire, beam, etc. **2** an instrument used to compare the vapour pressures of two liquids. **3** an instrument for measuring the surface tension of a liquid. **4** an instrument for measuring the moisture content of soil.

tension (ˈtɛnʃən) *n* **1** the act of stretching or the state or degree of being stretched. **2** mental or emotional strain; stress. **3** a situation or condition of hostility, suspense, or uneasiness. **4** *Physics.* a force that tends to produce an elongation of a body or structure. **5** *Physics.* voltage, electromotive force, or potential difference. **6** a device for regulating the tension in a part, string, thread, etc., as in a sewing machine. **7** the degree of tightness or looseness with which a person knits. ORIG C16: from L *tensiō,* from *tendere* to strain
▸ **ˈtensional** *adj* ▸ **ˈtensionless** *adj*

tensor (ˈtɛnsə, -sɔː) *n* **1** *Anat.* any muscle that can cause a part to become firm or tense. **2** *Maths.* a set of components, functions of the coordinates of any point in space, that transform linearly between coordinate systems. ORIG C18: from NL, lit.: a stretcher
▸ **tensorial** (tɛnˈsɔːrɪəl) *adj*

tent (tɛnt) *n* **1** a portable shelter of canvas, plastic, etc., supported on poles and fastened to the ground by pegs and ropes. **2** something resembling this in function or shape. ◆ *vb* **3** (*intr*) to camp in a tent. **4** (*tr*) to cover with or as if with a tent or tents. **5** (*tr*) to provide with a tent as shelter. ORIG C13: from OF *tente,* from L *tentōrium* something stretched out, from *tendere* to stretch
▸ **ˈtentage** *n* ▸ **ˈtented** *adj*

tentacle (ˈtɛntəkᵊl) *n* **1** any of various elongated flexible organs that occur near the mouth in many invertebrates and are used for feeding, grasping, etc. **2** any of the hairs on the leaf of an insectivorous plant that are used to capture prey. **3** something resembling a tentacle, esp. in its ability to reach out or grasp. ORIG C18: from NL *tentāculum,* from L *tentāre,* var. of *temptāre* to feel
▸ **ˈtentacled** *adj* ▸ **tentacular** (tɛnˈtækjʊlə) *adj*

tentation (tɛnˈteɪʃən) *n* a method of achieving the correct adjustment of a mechanical device by a series of trials. ORIG C14: from L *tentātiō,* variant of *temptātiō* TEMPTATION

tentative (ˈtɛntətɪv) *adj* **1** provisional or experimental. **2** hesitant, uncertain, or cautious. ORIG C16: from Med. L *tentātīvus,* from L *tentāre* to test
▸ **ˈtentatively** *adv* ▸ **ˈtentativeness** *n*

tenter (ˈtɛntə) *n* **1** a frame on which cloth is stretched in order that it may retain its shape while drying. **2** a person who stretches cloth on a tenter. ◆ *vb* **3** (*tr*) to stretch (cloth) on a tenter. ORIG C14: from Med. L *tentōrium,* from L *tentus* stretched, from *tendere* to stretch

tenterhook (ˈtɛntəˌhʊk) *n* **1** one of a series of hooks used to hold cloth on a tenter. **2 on tenterhooks.** in a state of tension or suspense.

tenth (tɛnθ) *adj* **1** (*usually prenominal*) **1a** coming after the ninth in numbering, position, etc.; being the ordinal number of *ten:* often written 10th. **1b** (*as n*)*: see you on the tenth.* ◆ *n* **2a** one of 10 equal parts of something. **2b** (*as modifier*)*: a tenth part.* **3** the fraction equal to one divided by ten (1/10). ◆ *adv* **4** Also: **tenthly.** after the ninth person, position, event, etc. ORIG C12 *tenthe,* from OE *tēotha*

tent stitch *n* another term for **petit point.** ORIG C17: from ?

tenuis (ˈtɛnjʊɪs) *n, pl* **tenues** (ˈtɛnjʊˌiːz). (in classical Greek) a voiceless stop (k, p, t). ORIG C17: from L: thin

tenuous (ˈtɛnjʊəs) *adj* **1** insignificant or flimsy: *a tenuous argument.* **2** slim, fine, or delicate: *a tenuous thread.* **3** diluted or rarefied in consistency or density: *a tenuous fluid.* ORIG C16: from L *tenuis*
▸ **tenuity** (tɛˈnjuːɪtɪ) *or* **ˈtenuousness** *n* ▸ **ˈtenuously** *adv*

tenure (ˈtɛnjʊə, ˈtɛnjə) *n* **1** the possession or holding of an office or position. **2** the length of time an office, position, etc., lasts. **3** *Chiefly US & Canad.* the improved security status of a person after having been in the employ of the same company or institution for a specified period. **4** the right to permanent employment until retirement, esp. for teachers, etc. **5a** the holding of property, esp. realty, in return for services rendered, etc. **5b** the duration of such holding. ORIG C15: from OF, from Med. L *tenitūra,* ult. from L *tenēre* to hold
▸ **tenˈurial** *adj*

tenuto (tɪˈnjuːtəʊ) *adj, adv Music.* (of a note) to be held for or beyond its full time value. ORIG from It., lit.: held, from *tenere* to hold, from L *tenēre*

Tenzing Norgay ★ (ˈtɛnsɪŋ ˈnɔːgeɪ) *n* 1914–86, Nepalese mountaineer. With Sir Edmund Hillary, he was the first to reach the summit of Mount Everest (1953).

teocalli (ˌtiːəʊˈkælɪ) *n, pl* **teocallis.** any of various truncated pyramids built by the Aztecs as bases for their temples. ORIG C17: from Nahuatl, from *teotl* god + *calli* house

tepee *or* **teepee** (ˈtiːpiː) *n* a cone-shaped tent of animal skins used by American Indians. ORIG C19: from Siouan *tīpī,* from *ti* to dwell + *pi* used for

tephra (ˈtɛfrə) *n Chiefly US.* solid matter ejected during a volcanic eruption. ORIG C20: Gk, lit.: ashes

Tepic ★ (*Spanish* teˈpik) *n* a city in W central Mexico, capital of Nayarit state: agricultural, trading and processing centre. Pop.: 206 967 (1990).

tepid (ˈtɛpɪd) *adj* **1** slightly warm; lukewarm. **2** relatively unenthusiastic or apathetic. ORIG C14: from L *tepidus,* from *tepēre* to be lukewarm
▸ **tepidity** (tɛˈpɪdɪtɪ) *or* **ˈtepidness** *n* ▸ **ˈtepidly** *adv*

tequila (tɪˈkiːlə) *n* **1** a spirit that is distilled in Mexico from an agave plant and forms the basis of many mixed drinks. **2** the plant from which this drink is made. ORIG C19: from Mexican Sp., from *Tequila,* region of Mexico

ter. *abbrev. for:* **1** terrace. **2** territory.

ter- *combining form.* three, third, or three times. ORIG from L *ter* thrice

tera- *prefix* **1** denoting 10^{12}: *terameter.* **2** Also: **tebi-.** denoting 2^{40}: *terabyte.* ◆ Symbol: T ORIG from Gk *teras* monster

USAGE NOTE See at **kilo-.**

Terai ★ (təˈraɪ) *n* **1** (in India) a belt of marshy land at the foot of mountains, esp. at the foot of the Himalayas in Uttar Pradesh. **2** a felt hat with a wide brim worn in subtropical regions.

terat- *or* **terato-** *combining form.* indicating a monster or something abnormal: *teratism.* ORIG from Gk *terat-, teras* monster, prodigy

teratism (ˈtɛrəˌtɪzəm) *n* a malformed animal or human, esp. in the fetal stage; monster.

teratogen (ˈtɛrətədʒən, tɪˈrætə-) *n* any substance, organism, or process that causes malformations in a fetus. Teratogens include certain drugs (such as thalidomide), infections (such as German measles), and ionizing radiation.
▸ **ˌteratoˈgenic** *adj*

teratoid (ˈtɛrəˌtɔɪd) *adj Biol.* resembling a monster.

teratology (ˌtɛrəˈtɒlədʒɪ) *n* **1** the branch of medical science concerned with the development of physical abnormalities during the fetal or early embryonic stage. **2** the branch of biology concerned with the structure, development, etc., of monsters. **3** a collection of tales about mythical or fantastic creatures, monsters, etc.
▸ **ˌteraˈtologist** *n*

teratoma (ˌtɛrəˈtəʊmə) *n, pl* **teratomata** (-mətə) *or* **teratomas.** a tumour composed of tissue foreign to the site of growth.

terbium (ˈtɜːbɪəm) *n* a soft malleable silvery-grey ele-

ment of the lanthanide series of metals. Symbol: Tb; atomic no.: 65; atomic wt.: 158.925. ORIG C19: from NL, after *Ytterby,* Sweden, village where discovered
▸ **'terbic** *adj*

terbium metal *n Chem.* any of a group of related lanthanides, including terbium, europium, and gadolinium.

Ter Borch *or* **Terborch** ★ (*Dutch* tɛr 'bɔrx) *n* **Gerard** ('xe:rɑrt). 1617–81, Dutch genre and portrait painter.

terce (tɜ:s) *or* **tierce** *n Chiefly RC Church.* the third of the seven canonical hours, originally fixed at the third hour of the day, about 9 a.m. ORIG C14: var. of TIERCE

Terceira ★ (*Portuguese* tər'səirə) *n* an island in the N Atlantic, in the Azores: NATO military air base. Pop.: 60 000 (latest est.). Area: 397 sq. km (153 sq. miles).

tercel ('tɜ:sᵊl) *or* **tiercel** *n* a male falcon or hawk, esp. as used in falconry. ORIG C14: from OF, from Vulgar L *tertiolus* (unattested), from L *tertius* third, from the tradition that only one egg in three hatched a male chick

tercentenary (ˌtɜ:sɛn'ti:nərɪ) *or* **tercentennial** *adj* **1** of a period of 300 years. **2** of a 300th anniversary. ◆ *n, pl* **tercentenaries** *or* **tercentennials. 3** an anniversary of 300 years.

tercet ('tɜ:sɪt, tɜ:'sɛt) *n* a group of three lines of verse that rhyme together or are connected by rhyme with adjacent groups of three lines. ORIG C16: from F, from It. *terzetto,* dim. of *terzo* third, from L *tertius*

terebene ('tɛrəˌbi:n) *n* a mixture of hydrocarbons prepared from oil of turpentine and sulphuric acid, used to make paints and varnishes and medicinally as an expectorant and antiseptic. ORIG C19: from TEREB(INTH) + -ENE

terebinth ('tɛrɪbɪnθ) *n* a small Mediterranean tree that yields a turpentine. ORIG C14: from L *terebinthus,* from Gk *terebinthos* turpentine tree

terebinthine (ˌtɛrɪ'bɪnθaɪn) *adj* **1** of or relating to terebinth or related plants. **2** of, consisting of, or resembling turpentine.

teredo (tɛ'ri:dəʊ) *n, pl* **teredos** *or* **teredines** (-dɪˌni:z). any of a genus of marine bivalve molluscs. See **shipworm.** ORIG C17: via L from Gk *terēdōn* wood-boring worm

Terence ★ ('tɛrəns) *n* Latin name *Publius Terentius Afer.* ?190–159 B.C., Roman dramatist.

Terengganu (tɛrɛŋ'gɑ:nu:) *n* a variant spelling of **Trengganu.**

Teresa *or* **Theresa** ★ (tə'ri:zə; *Spanish* te'resa) *n* **1 Saint,** known as *Teresa of Avila.* 1515–82, Spanish nun, who reformed the Carmelite order. Her writings include *The Way to Perfection.* Feast day: Oct. 15. **2 Mother,** original name *Agnes Gonxha Bojaxhiu.* 1910–97, Indian Roman Catholic missionary, born in Skopje, now in the Former Yugoslav Republic of Macedonia, of Albanian parents: noted for her relief work in Calcutta; Nobel peace prize 1979. ◆ See also **Thérèse de Lisieux.**

Tereshkova ★ (*Russian* tɪrɪʃ'kɔvə) *n* **Valentina Vladimirovna** (vəlɪn'tinə vla'dimirəvnə). born 1937, Soviet cosmonaut; first woman in space (1963).

Teresina ★ (*Portuguese* tere'zina) *n* an inland port in NE Brazil, capital of Piauí state, on the Parnaíba River: chief commercial centre of the Parnaíba valley. Pop.: 556 073 (1991). Former name: **Therezina.**

terete ('tɛri:t) *adj* (esp. of plant parts) cylindrical and tapering. ORIG C17: from L *teres* smooth, from *terere* to rub

tergiversate ('tɜ:dʒɪvəˌseɪt) *vb* **tergiversates, tergiversating, tergiversated.** (*intr*) **1** to change sides or loyalties. **2** to be evasive or ambiguous. ORIG C17: from L *tergiversārī* to turn one's back, from *tergum* back + *vertere* to turn
▸ **ˌtergiver'sation** *n* ▸ **'tergiverˌsator** *n*

tergum ('tɜ:gəm) *n, pl* **terga** (-gə). a cuticular plate covering the dorsal surface of a body segment of an arthropod. ORIG C19: from L: the back
▸ **'tergal** *adj*

term (tɜ:m) *n* **1** a name, expression, or word used for some particular thing, esp. in a specialized field of knowledge: *a medical term.* **2** any word or expression. **3** a limited period of time: *a prison term.* **4** any of the divisions of the academic year during which a school, college, etc., is in session. **5** a point in time determined for an event or for the end of a period. **6** the period at which childbirth is imminent. **7** *Law.* **7a** an estate or interest in land limited to run for a specified period. **7b** the duration of an estate, etc. **7c** (formerly) a period of time during which sessions of courts of law are held. **7d** time allowed to a debtor to settle. **8** *Maths.* any distinct quantity making up a fraction or proportion, or contained in a polynominal, sequence, series, etc. **9** *Logic.* **9a** the word or phrase that forms either the subject or predicate of a proposition. **9b** a name or variable, as opposed to a predicate. **9c** any of the three subjects or predicates occurring in a syllogism. **10** *Archit.* a sculptured post, esp. one in the form of an armless bust or an animal on the top of a square pillar. ◆ *vb* **11** (*tr*) to designate; call: *he was termed a thief.* ◆ See also **terms.** ORIG C13: from OF *terme,* from L *terminus* end
▸ **'termly** *adj, adv*

> **USAGE NOTE** Many people object to the use of *in terms of* as an all-purpose preposition replacing phrases such as 'as regards', 'about', and so forth in a context such as the following: *in terms of trends in smoking habits, there is good news.* They would maintain that in strict usage it should be used to specify a relationship, as in: *obesity is defined in terms of body mass index, which involves a bit of cumbersome maths.* Nevertheless, despite objections, it is very commonly used as a link word, particularly in speech.

termagant ('tɜ:məgənt) *n* a shrewish woman; scold. ORIG C13: from earlier *Tervagaunt,* from OF *Tervagan,* from It. *Trivigante;* after an arrogant character in medieval mystery plays who was supposed to be a Muslim deity

-termer *n* (*in combination*) a person serving a specified length of time in prison: *a short-termer.*

terminable ('tɜ:mɪnəbᵊl) *adj* **1** able to be terminated. **2** terminating after a specific period or event.
▸ **ˌtermina'bility** *or* **'terminableness** *n* ▸ **'terminably** *adv*

terminal ('tɜ:mɪnᵊl) *adj* **1** of, being, or situated at an end, terminus, or boundary. **2** of or occurring after or in a term: *terminal examinations.* **3** (of a disease) terminating in death. **4** *Inf.* extreme: *terminal boredom.* **5** of or relating to the storage or delivery of freight at a warehouse. ◆ *n* **6** a terminating point, part, or place. **7a** a point at which current enters or leaves an electrical device, such as a battery or a circuit. **7b** a conductor by which current enters or leaves at such a point. **8** *Computing.* a device having input/output links with a computer. **9** *Archit.* **9a** an ornamental carving at the end of a structure. **9b** another name for **term** (sense 10). **10a** a point or station at the end of the line of a railway or at an airport, serving as an important access point for passengers or freight. **10b** a less common name for **terminus** (sense 2). **11** a reception and departure building at the terminus of a bus, sea, or air transport route. **12** a site where raw material is unloaded and processed, esp. an onshore installation designed to receive offshore oil or gas. ORIG C15: from L *terminālis,* from *terminus* end
▸ **'terminally** *adv*

terminal market *n* a commodity market in a trading centre rather than at a producing centre.

terminal velocity *n* **1** the constant maximum velocity reached by a body falling under gravity through a fluid, esp. the atmosphere. **2** the velocity of a missile or projectile when it reaches its target. **3** the maximum velocity attained by a rocket, missile, or shell flying in a parabolic flight path. **4** the maximum velocity that an aircraft can attain.

terminate ('tɜ:mɪˌneɪt) *vb* **terminates, terminating, terminated.** (when *intr,* often foll. by *in* or *with*) to form, be, or put an end (to); conclude. ORIG C16: from L *terminātus* limited, from *termināre* to set boundaries, from *terminus* end
▸ **'terminative** *adj* ▸ **'termiˌnator** *n*

termination (ˌtɜ:mɪ'neɪʃən) *n* **1** the act of terminating or the state of being terminated. **2** something that terminates. **3** a final result.

terminator seed *n* a seed that produces sterile plants, used in some genetically modified crops so that a new supply of seeds has to be bought every year.

terminology (ˌtɜːmɪˈnɒlədʒɪ) *n, pl* **terminologies. 1** the body of specialized words relating to a particular subject. **2** the study of terms. ORIG C19: from Med. L *terminus* term from L: end
▸ **terminological** (ˌtɜːmɪnəˈlɒdʒɪkᵊl) *adj* ▸ ˌ**termiˈnologist** *n*

term insurance *n* life assurance, usually low in cost and offering no cash value, that provides for the payment of a specified sum of money only if the insured dies within a stipulated time.

terminus (ˈtɜːmɪnəs) *n, pl* **termini** (-naɪ) *or* **terminuses. 1** the last or final part or point. **2** either end of a railway, bus route, etc., or a station or town at such a point. **3** a goal aimed for. **4** a boundary or boundary marker. **5** *Archit.* another name for **term** (sense 10). ORIG C16: from L: end

Terminus ★ (ˈtɜːmɪnəs) *n* the Roman god of boundaries.

terminus ad quem *Latin.* (ˈtɜːmɪˌnʊs æd ˈkwɛm) *n* the aim or terminal point. ORIG lit.: the end to which

terminus a quo *Latin.* (ˈtɜːmɪˌnʊs ɑː ˈkwəʊ) *n* the starting point; beginning. ORIG lit.: the end from which

termitarium (ˌtɜːmɪˈtɛərɪəm) *n, pl* **termitaria** (-ɪə). the nest of a termite colony. ORIG C20: from TERMITE + -ARIUM

termite (ˈtɜːmaɪt) *n* any of an order of whitish antlike social insects of warm and tropical regions. Some species feed on wood, causing damage to buildings, trees, etc. ORIG C18: from NL *termitēs* white ants, pl of *termes,* from L: a woodworm
▸ **termitic** (tɜːˈmɪtɪk) *adj*

termless (ˈtɜːmlɪs) *adj* **1** without limit or boundary. **2** unconditional. **3** an archaic word for **indescribable.**

termor *or* **termer** (ˈtɜːmə) *n Property law.* a person who holds an estate for a term of years or until he or she dies.

terms (tɜːmz) *pl n* **1** (usually specified prenominally) the actual language or mode of presentation used: *he described the project in loose terms.* **2** conditions of an agreement. **3** a sum of money paid for a service. **4** (usually preceded by *on*) mutual relationship or standing: *they are on affectionate terms.* **5 bring to terms.** to cause to agree or submit. **6 come to terms.** to reach acceptance or agreement. **7 in terms of.** as expressed by; regarding: *in terms of money he was no better off.*

terms of trade *pl n Economics, Brit.* the ratio of export prices to import prices.

tern (tɜːn) *n* any of several aquatic birds related to the gulls, having a forked tail, long narrow wings, and a typically black-and-white plumage. ORIG C18: from ON *therna*

ternary (ˈtɜːnərɪ) *adj* **1** consisting of three or groups of three. **2** *Maths.* (of a number system) to the base three. ORIG C14: from L *ternārius,* from *ternī* three each

ternary form *n* a musical structure consisting of two contrasting sections followed by a repetition of the first; the form *aba.*

ternate (ˈtɜːnɪt, -neɪt) *adj* **1** (esp. of a leaf) consisting of three leaflets or other parts. **2** (esp. of plants) having groups of three members. ORIG C18: from NL *ternātus,* from Med. L *ternāre* to increase threefold
▸ ˈ**ternately** *adv*

terne (tɜːn) *n* **1** an alloy of lead containing tin and antimony. **2** Also called: **terne plate.** steel plate coated with this alloy. ORIG C16: ?from F *terne* dull, from OF *ternir* to TARNISH

Terni ★ (*Italian* ˈtɛrni) *n* an industrial city in central Italy, in Umbria: site of waterfalls created in Roman times. Pop.: 108 435 (1996 est.).

Ternopol ★ (*Russian* tɪrˈnɔpəlj) *n* a town in W Ukraine: formerly under Polish rule. Pop.: 235 000 (1996 est.). Polish name: **Tarnopol.**

terotechnology (ˌtɪərəʊtɛkˈnɒlədʒɪ, tɛr-) *n* a branch of technology that utilizes management, financial, and engineering expertise in the installation, efficient operation, and maintenance of equipment and machinery. ORIG C20: from Gk *tērein* to care for + TECHNOLOGY

terpene (ˈtɜːpiːn) *n* any one of a class of unsaturated hydrocarbons, such as pinene and the carotenes, that are found in the essential oils of many plants, esp. conifers. ORIG C19: *terp-* from obs. *terpentine* turpentine + -ENE

terpineol (tɜːˈpɪnɪˌɒl) *n* a terpene alcohol with an odour of lilac, existing in three isomeric forms that occur in several essential oils. ORIG C20: from TERPENE + -INE[2] + -OL[1]

Terpsichore ★ (tɜːpˈsɪkərɪ) *n* the Muse of the dance and of choral song. ORIG C18: via L from Gk, from *terpsikhoros* delighting in the dance, from *terpein* to delight + *khoros* dance

Terpsichorean (ˌtɜːpsɪkəˈrɪən, -ˈkɔːrɪən) *Often used facetiously.* ◆ *adj also* **Terpsichoreal. 1** of or relating to dancing. ◆ *n* **2** a dancer.

terra (ˈtɛrə) *n* (in legal contexts) earth or land. ORIG from L

terra alba (ˈælbə) *n* **1** a white finely powdered form of gypsum, used to make paints, paper, etc. **2** any of various other white earthy substances, such as kaolin, pipeclay, and magnesia. ORIG from L, lit.: white earth

terrace (ˈtɛrəs) *n* **1** a horizontal flat area of ground, often one of a series in a slope. **2a** a row of houses, usually identical and having common dividing walls, or the street onto which they face. **2b** (*cap. when part of a street name*)*: Grosvenor Terrace.* **3** a paved area alongside a building, serving partly as a garden. **4** a balcony or patio. **5** the flat roof of a house built in a Spanish or Oriental style. **6** a flat area bounded by a short steep slope formed by the down-cutting of a river or by erosion. **7** (*usually pl*) unroofed tiers around a football pitch on which the spectators stand. ◆ *vb* **terraces, terracing, terraced. 8** (*tr*) to make into or provide with a terrace or terraces. ORIG C16: from OF *terrasse,* from OProvençal *terrassa* pile of earth, from *terra* earth, from L

terraced house *n Brit.* a house that is part of a terrace. US and Canad. name: **row house.**

terracing (ˈtɛrəsɪŋ) *n* **1** a series of terraces, esp. one dividing a slope into a steplike system of flat narrow fields. **2** the act of making a terrace or terraces. **3** another name for **terrace** (sense 7).

terra cotta (ˈkɒtə) *n* **1** a hard unglazed brownish-red earthenware, or the clay from which it is made. **2** something made of terra cotta, such as a sculpture. **3** a strong reddish-brown to brownish-orange colour. ORIG C18: from It., lit.: baked earth
▸ ˈ**terra-**ˈ**cotta** *adj*

terra firma (ˈfɜːmə) *n* the solid earth; firm ground. ORIG C17: from L

terrain (təˈreɪn) *n* a piece of ground, esp. with reference to its physical character or military potential: *a rocky terrain.* ORIG C18: from F, ult. from L *terrēnum* ground, from *terra* earth

terra incognita *Latin.* (ˈtɛrə ɪnˈkɒgnɪtə) *n* an unexplored or unknown land, region, or area.

Terramycin (ˌtɛrəˈmaɪsɪn) *n Trademark.* a broad-spectrum antibiotic used in treating various infections.

terrapin (ˈtɛrəpɪn) *n* any of various web-footed reptiles that live on land and in fresh water and feed on small aquatic animals. Also called: **water tortoise.** ORIG C17: of Amerind origin

terrarium (tɛˈrɛərɪəm) *n, pl* **terrariums** *or* **terraria** (-ˈrɛərɪə). **1** an enclosure for small land animals. **2** a glass container, often a globe, in which plants are grown. ORIG C19: NL, from L *terra* earth

terra sigillata (ˌsɪdʒɪˈlɑːtə) *n* **1** a reddish-brown clayey earth found on the Aegean island of Lemnos: formerly used as an astringent and in the making of earthenware pottery. **2** any similar earth resembling this. **3** earthenware pottery made from this or a similar earth, esp. Samian ware. ORIG from L: sealed earth

terrazzo (tɛˈrætsəʊ) *n, pl* **terrazzos.** a floor made by setting marble chips into a layer of mortar and polishing the surface. ORIG C20: from It.: TERRACE

terrene (tɛˈriːn) *adj* **1** of the earth; worldly; mundane. **2**

Rare. of earth; earthy. ◆ *n* **3** a land. **4** a rare word for **earth.** ORIG C14: from Anglo-Norman, from L *terrēnus,* from *terra* earth

terreplein ('tɛəˌpleɪn) *n* the top of a rampart where guns are placed behind the parapet. ORIG C16: from F, from Med. L *terrā plēnus* filled with earth

terrestrial (tə'rɛstrɪəl) *adj* **1** of the earth. **2** of the land as opposed to the sea or air. **3** (of animals and plants) living or growing on the land. **4** earthly, worldly, or mundane. **5** *Television.* denoting or using signals sent over the earth's surface from a transmitter on land, rather than by satellite. ◆ *n* **6** an inhabitant of the earth. ORIG C15: from L *terrestris,* from *terra* earth
▸ **ter'restrially** *adv* ▸ **ter'restrialness** *n*

terrestrial telescope *n* a telescope for use on earth rather than for making astronomical observations. Such telescopes contain an additional lens or prism system to produce an erect image.

terret ('tɛrɪt) *n* **1** either of the two rings on a harness through which the reins are passed. **2** the ring on a dog's collar for attaching the lead. ORIG C15: var. of *toret,* from OF, dim. of *tor* loop

terre-verte ('tɛəˌvɜːt) *n* **1** a greyish-green pigment used in paints. It is made from a mineral found in greensand and similar rocks. ◆ *adj* **2** of a greyish-green colour. ORIG C17: from F, lit.: green earth

terrible ('tɛrəbᵊl) *adj* **1** very serious or extreme. **2** *Inf.* of poor quality; unpleasant or bad. **3** causing terror. **4** causing awe. ORIG C15: from L *terribilis,* from *terrēre* to terrify
▸ **'terribleness** *n* ▸ **'terribly** *adv*

terricolous (tɛ'rɪkələs) *adj* living on or in the soil. ORIG C19: from L *terricola,* from *terra* earth + *colere* to inhabit

terrier[1] ('tɛrɪə) *n* any of several usually small, active, and short-bodied breeds of dog, originally trained to hunt animals living underground. ORIG C15: from OF *chien terrier* earth dog, from Med. L *terrārius* belonging to the earth, from L *terra* earth

terrier[2] ('tɛrɪə) *n English legal history.* a register or survey of land. ORIG C15: from OF, from Med. L *terrārius* of the land, from L *terra* land

terrific (tə'rɪfɪk) *adj* **1** very great or intense. **2** *Inf.* very good; excellent. **3** very frightening. ORIG C17: from L *terrificus,* from *terrēre* to frighten
▸ **ter'rifically** *adv*

terrify ('tɛrɪˌfaɪ) *vb* **terrifies, terrifying, terrified.** (*tr*) to inspire fear or dread in; frighten greatly. ORIG C16: from L *terrificāre,* from *terrēre* to alarm + *facere* to cause
▸ **'terriˌfying** *adj* ▸ **'terriˌfyingly** *adv*

terrigenous (tɛ'rɪdʒɪnəs) *adj* **1** of or produced by the earth. **2** (of geological deposits) formed in the sea from material derived from the land by erosion. ORIG C17: from L *terrigenus,* from *terra* earth + *gignere* to beget

terrine (tɛ'riːn) *n* **1** an oval earthenware cooking dish with a tightly fitting lid used for pâtés, etc. **2** the food cooked or served in such a dish, esp. pâté. ORIG C18: earlier form of TUREEN

territorial (ˌtɛrɪ'tɔːrɪəl) *adj* **1** of or relating to a territory or territories. **2** restricted to or owned by a particular territory. **3** local or regional. **4** *Zool.* establishing and defending a territory. **5** pertaining to a territorial army, providing a reserve of trained men for use in emergency.
▸ **ˌterriˌtori'ality** *n* ▸ **ˌterri'torially** *adv*

Territorial (ˌtɛrɪ'tɔːrɪəl) *n* a member of a Territorial Army.

Territorial Army *n* (in Britain) a standing reserve army originally organized between 1907 and 1908. Full name: **Territorial and Volunteer Reserve.**

Territorial Council *n* (in Canada) an elected body responsible for local government in the Northwest Territories or the Yukon.

territorial waters *pl n* the waters over which a nation exercises jurisdiction and control.

territory ('tɛrɪtərɪ) *n, pl* **territories. 1** any tract of land; district. **2** the geographical domain under the jurisdiction of a political unit, esp. of a sovereign state. **3** the district for which an agent, etc., is responsible. **4** an area inhabited and defended by an animal or a pair of animals. **5** an area of knowledge. **6** (in football, hockey, etc.) the area defended by a team. **7** (*often cap.*) a region of a country, esp. of a federal state, that enjoys less autonomy and a lower status than most constituent parts of the state. **8** (*often cap.*) a protectorate or other dependency of a country. ORIG C15: from L *territōrium* land surrounding a town, from *terra* land

terror ('tɛrə) *n* **1** great fear, panic, or dread. **2** a person or thing that inspires great dread. **3** *Inf.* a troublesome person or thing, esp. a child. **4** terrorism. ORIG C14: from OF *terreur,* from L *terror,* from *terrēre* to frighten
▸ **'terrorful** *adj* ▸ **'terrorless** *adj*

terrorism ('tɛrəˌrɪzəm) *n* **1** the systematic use of violence and intimidation to achieve some goal. **2** the act of terrorizing. **3** the state of being terrorized.
▸ **'terrorist** *n, adj*

terrorize *or* **terrorise** ('tɛrəˌraɪz) *vb* **terrorizes, terrorizing, terrorized** *or* **terrorises, terrorising, terrorised.** (*tr*) **1** to coerce or control by violence, fear, threats, etc. **2** to inspire with dread; terrify.
▸ **ˌterrori'zation** *or* **ˌterrori'sation** *n* ▸ **'terrorˌizer** *or* **'terrorˌiser** *n*

terror-stricken *or* **terror-struck** *adj* in a state of terror.

terry ('tɛrɪ) *n, pl* **terries. 1** an uncut loop in the pile of towelling or a similar fabric. **2** a fabric with such a pile. ORIG C18: ? var. of TERRET

Terry ★ ('tɛrɪ) *n* Dame **Ellen.** 1847–1928, British actress.

terse (tɜːs) *adj* **1** neatly brief and concise. **2** curt; abrupt. ORIG C17: from L *tersus* precise, from *tergēre* to polish
▸ **'tersely** *adv* ▸ **'terseness** *n*

tertial ('tɜːʃəl) *adj, n* another word for **tertiary** (senses 5, 6). ORIG C19: from L *tertius* third, from *ter* thrice, from *trēs* three

tertian ('tɜːʃən) *adj* **1** (of a fever) occurring every other day. ◆ *n* **2** a tertian fever. ORIG C14: from L *febris tertiāna* fever occurring every third day, from *tertius* third

tertiary ('tɜːʃərɪ) *adj* **1** third in degree, order, etc. **2** (of an industry) involving services as opposed to extraction or manufacture, such as transport, finance, etc. **3** *RC Church.* of or relating to a Third Order. **4** *Chem.* **4a** (of an organic compound) having a functional group attached to a carbon atom that is attached to three other groups. **4b** (of an amine) having three organic groups attached to a nitrogen atom. **4c** (of a salt) derived from a tribasic acid by replacement of all its acidic hydrogen atoms with metal atoms or electropositive groups. **5** *Ornithol., rare.* of or designating any of the small flight feathers attached to the part of the humerus nearest to the body. ◆ *n, pl* **tertiaries. 6** *Ornithol., rare.* any of the tertiary feathers. **7** *RC Church.* a member of a Third Order. ORIG C16: from L *tertiārius* containing one third, from *tertius* third

Tertiary ('tɜːʃərɪ) *adj* **1** of, denoting, or formed in the first period of the Cenozoic era. ◆ *n* **2 the.** the Tertiary period or rock system.

tertiary college *n Brit.* a college system incorporating the secondary school sixth form and vocational courses.

tertiary colour *n* a colour formed by mixing two secondary colours.

tertium quid ('tɜːtɪəm) *n* an unknown or indefinite thing related in some way to two known or definite things, but distinct from both. ORIG C18: from LL, rendering Gk *triton ti* some third thing

Tertullian ★ (tɜː'tʌlɪən) *n* Latin name *Quintus Septimius Florens Tertullianus.* ?160–?220 A.D., Carthaginian Christian theologian.

Teruel ★ (*Spanish* te'rwɛl) *n* a city in E central Spain: 15th-century cathedral; scene of fierce fighting during the Spanish Civil War. Pop.: 31 000 (1991).

tervalent (tɜː'veɪlənt) *adj Chem.* another word for **trivalent.**
▸ **ter'valency** *n*

Terylene ('tɛrɪˌliːn) *n Trademark.* a synthetic polyester fibre or fabric. US name (trademark): **Dacron.**

terza rima ('tɛətsə 'riːmə) *n, pl* **terze rime** ('tɛətseɪ 'riːmeɪ). a verse form consisting of a series of tercets in which the middle line of one tercet rhymes with the first and third lines of the next. ORIG C19: from It., lit.: third rhyme

TESL ('tɛsᵊl) *acronym for* Teaching (of) English as a Second Language.

tesla ('tɛslə) *n* the derived SI unit of magnetic flux density equal to a flux of 1 weber in an area of 1 square metre. Symbol: T ORIG C20: after Nikola TESLA

Tesla ★ ('tɛslə) *n* **Nikola** ('nɪkələ). 1857–1943, US electrical engineer, born in Smiljan, now in Croatia. His inventions include a transformer, generators, and dynamos.

tesla coil *n* a step-up transformer with an air core, used for producing high voltages at high frequencies.

TESSA *or* **Tessa** ('tɛsə) *n* (in Britain) *acronym for* Tax Exempt Special Savings Account; a former (available 1991–99) tax-free savings scheme.

tessellate ('tɛsɪˌleɪt) *vb* **tessellates, tessellating, tessellated. 1** (*tr*) to construct, pave, or inlay with a mosaic of small tiles. **2** (*intr*) (of identical shapes) to fit together exactly. ORIG C18: from L *tessellātus* checked, from *tessella* small stone cube, from TESSERA

tessera ('tɛsərə) *n, pl* **tesserae** (-səˌriː). **1** a small square tile of stone, glass, etc., used in mosaics. **2** a die, tally, etc., used in classical times, made of bone or wood. ORIG C17: from L, from Ionic Gk *tesseres* four
▸ **'tesseral** *adj*

Tessin ★ (tɛ'siːn) *n* the German name for **Ticino**.

tessitura (ˌtɛsɪ'tʊərə) *n Music.* the general pitch level of a piece of vocal music. ORIG It.: texture, from L *textura;* see TEXTURE

test[1] (tɛst) *vb* **1** to ascertain (the worth, capability, or endurance) of (a person or thing) by subjection to certain examinations, etc.; try. **2** (often foll. by *for*) to carry out an examination on (a substance, material, or system) to indicate the presence of a substance or the possession of a property: *to test food for arsenic.* **3** (*tr*) to put under severe strain: *the long delay tested my patience.* **4** (*intr*) to achieve a specified result in a test: *he tested positive for the AIDS virus.* ◆ *n* **5** a method, practice, or examination designed to test a person or thing. **6** a series of questions or problems designed to test a specific skill or knowledge. **7** a standard of judgment; criterion. **8a** a chemical reaction or physical procedure for testing a substance, material, etc. **8b** a chemical reagent used in such a procedure. **8c** the result of the procedure or the evidence gained from it. **9** *Sport.* See **test match. 10** *Arch.* a declaration of truth, loyalty, etc. **11** (*modifier*) performed as a test: *test drive.* ORIG C14 (in the sense: vessel used in treating metals): from L *testum* earthen vessel
▸ **'testable** *adj* ▸ **'testing** *adj*

test[2] (tɛst) *n* the hard outer covering of certain invertebrates and tunicates. ORIG C19: from L *testa* shell

testa ('tɛstə) *n, pl* **testae** (-tiː). the hard outer layer of a seed. ORIG C18: from L: shell

testaceous (tɛ'steɪʃəs) *adj Biol.* **1** of or possessing a test or testa. **2** of the reddish-brown colour of terra cotta. ORIG C17: from L *testācens,* from TESTA

testament ('tɛstəmənt) *n* **1** *Law.* a will (esp. in **last will and testament**). **2** a proof, attestation, or tribute. **3a** a covenant instituted between God and man. **3b** a copy of either the Old or the New Testament, or of the complete Bible. ORIG C14: from L *testamentum* a will, from *testārī* to bear witness, from *testis* a witness
▸ **ˌtesta'mental** *adj* ▸ **ˌtesta'mentary** *adj*

Testament ('tɛstəmənt) *n* **1** either of the two main parts of the Bible; the Old Testament or the New Testament. **2** the New Testament as distinct from the Old.

testate ('tɛsteɪt, 'tɛstɪt) *adj* **1** having left a legally valid will at death. ◆ *n* **2** a person who dies testate. ORIG C15: from L *testārī* to make a will; see TESTAMENT
▸ **testacy** ('tɛstəsɪ) *n*

testator (tɛ'steɪtə) *or* (*fem*) **testatrix** (tɛ'steɪtrɪks) *n* a person who makes a will, esp. one who dies testate. ORIG C15: from Anglo-F *testatour,* from LL *testātor,* from L *testārī* to make a will

test ban *n* an agreement among nations to forgo tests of nuclear weapons.

★ people and places

test-bed *n Engineering.* an area used for testing machinery, etc., under working conditions.

test card *or* **pattern** *n* a complex pattern used to test the characteristics of a television transmission system.

test case *n* a legal action that serves as a precedent in deciding similar succeeding cases.

test-drive *vb* **test-drives, test-driving, test-drove, test-driven.** (*tr*) to drive (a car or other motor vehicle) for a limited period in order to assess it.

tester[1] ('tɛstə) *n* a person or thing that tests.

tester[2] ('tɛstə) *n* a canopy over a bed. ORIG C14: from Med. L *testerium,* from LL *testa* a skull, from L: shell

testes ('tɛstiːz) *n* the plural of **testis.**

testicle ('tɛstɪkᵊl) *n* either of the two male reproductive glands, in most mammals enclosed within the scrotum, that produce spermatozoa. ORIG C15: from L *testiculus,* dim. of *testis*
▸ **testicular** (tɛ'stɪkjʊlə) *adj*

testiculate (tɛ'stɪkjʊlɪt) *adj Bot.* having an oval shape: *the testiculate tubers of certain orchids.* ORIG C18: from LL *testiculātus;* see TESTICLE

testify ('tɛstɪˌfaɪ) *vb* **testifies, testifying, testified. 1** (when *tr, may take a clause as object*) to state (something) formally as a declaration of fact. **2** *Law.* to declare or give (evidence) under oath, esp. in court. **3** (when *intr,* often foll. by *to*) to be evidence (of); serve as witness (to). **4** (*tr*) to declare or acknowledge openly. ORIG C14: from L *testificārī,* from *testis* witness
▸ **ˌtestifi'cation** *n* ▸ **'testiˌfier** *n*

testimonial (ˌtɛstɪ'məʊnɪəl) *n* **1a** a recommendation of the character, ability, etc., of a person or of the quality of a product or service. **1b** (*as modifier*): *testimonial advertising.* **2** a formal statement of truth or fact. **3** a tribute given for services or achievements. **4** a sports match to raise money for a particular player. ◆ *adj* **5** of or relating to a testimony or testimonial.

> **USAGE NOTE** *Testimonial* is sometimes wrongly used where *testimony* is meant: *his re-election is a testimony* (not *a testimonial*) *to his popularity with his constituents.*

testimony ('tɛstɪmənɪ) *n, pl* **testimonies. 1** a declaration of truth or fact. **2** *Law.* evidence given by a witness, esp. in court under oath. **3** evidence testifying to something: *her success was a testimony to her good luck.* **4** *Old Testament.* the Ten Commandments. ORIG C15: from L *testimōnium,* from *testis* witness

testis ('tɛstɪs) *n, pl* **testes.** another word for **testicle.** ORIG C17: from L, lit.: witness (to masculinity)

test match *n* (in various sports, esp. cricket) an international match, esp. one of a series.

testosterone (tɛ'stɒstəˌrəʊn) *n* a potent steroid hormone secreted mainly by the testes. ORIG C20: from TESTIS + STEROL + -ONE

test paper *n* **1** *Chem.* paper impregnated with an indicator for use in chemical tests. **2a** the question sheet of a test. **2b** the paper completed by a test candidate.

test pilot *n* a pilot who flies aircraft of new design to test their performance in the air.

test tube *n* **1** a cylindrical round-bottomed glass tube open at one end: used in scientific experiments. **2** (*modifier*) made synthetically in, or as if in, a test tube: *a test-tube product.*

test-tube baby *n* **1** a fetus that has developed from an ovum fertilized in an artificial womb. **2** a baby conceived by artificial insemination.

testudinal (tɛ'stjuːdɪnᵊl) *adj* of or resembling a tortoise. ORIG C19: from L TESTUDO

testudo (tɛ'stjuːdəʊ) *n, pl* **testudines** (-dɪˌniːz). a form of shelter used by the ancient Roman Army as protection against attack from above, consisting of a mobile arched structure or of overlapping shields held by the soldiers over their heads. ORIG C17: from L: a tortoise, from *testa* a shell

testy ('tɛstɪ) *adj* **testier, testiest.** irritable or touchy. ORIG

C14: from Anglo-Norman *testif* headstrong, from OF *teste* head, from LL *testa* skull, from L: shell
▸ **'testily** *adv* ▸ **'testiness** *n*

tetanus ('tɛtənəs) *n* **1** Also called: **lockjaw.** an acute infectious disease in which sustained muscular spasm, contraction, and convulsion are caused by the release of toxins from a bacterium. **2** *Physiol.* any tense contraction of a muscle. ORIG C16: via L from Gk *tetanos,* ult. from *teinein* to stretch
▸ **'tetanal** *adj* ▸ **'teta,noid** *adj*

tetany ('tɛtənɪ) *n* an abnormal increase in the excitability of nerves and muscles caused by a deficiency of parathyroid secretion. ORIG C19: from F; see TETANUS

tetchy ('tɛtʃɪ) *adj* **tetchier, tetchiest.** being or inclined to be cross, irritable, or touchy. ORIG C16: prob. from obs. *tetch* defect, from OF *tache* spot, of Gmc origin
▸ **'tetchily** *adv* ▸ **'tetchiness** *n*

tête-à-tête (ˌteɪtɑ'teɪt) *n, pl* **tête-à-têtes** *or* **tête-à-tête. 1a** a private conversation between two people. **1b** *(as modifier): a tête-à-tête conversation.* **2** a small sofa for two people, esp. one that is S-shaped in plan so that the sitters are almost face to face. ◆ *adv* **3** intimately; in private. ORIG C17: from F, lit.: head to head

tête-bêche (tɛt'bɛʃ) *adj Philately.* (of an unseparated pair of stamps) printed so that one is inverted in relation to the other. ORIG C19: from F, from *tête* head + *bêche,* from obs. *béchevet* double-headed (orig. of a bed)

tether ('tɛðə) *n* **1** a rope, chain, etc., by which an animal is tied to a particular spot. **2** the range of one's endurance, etc. **3 at the end of one's tether.** distressed or exasperated to the limit of one's endurance. ◆ *vb* **4** *(tr)* to tie with or as if with a tether. ORIG C14: from ON *tjothr*

Tethys[1] ★ ('ti:θɪs, 'tɛθ-) *n Greek myth.* a Titaness and sea goddess, wife of Oceanus.

Tethys[2] ★ ('ti:θɪs, 'tɛθ-) *n* the sea that lay between the two ancient supercontinents, Laurasia and Gondwanaland, and which can be regarded as the predecessor of today's smaller Mediterranean.

Teton Range ★ ('ti:tᵊn) *n* a mountain range in the N central US, mainly in NW Wyoming. Highest peak: Grand Teton, 4196 m (13 766 ft).

tetra- *or before a vowel* **tetr-** *combining form.* four: *tetrameter.* ORIG from Gk

tetrabasic (ˌtɛtrə'beɪsɪk) *adj* (of an acid) containing four replaceable hydrogen atoms.
▸ **tetrabasicity** (ˌtɛtrəbeɪ'sɪsɪtɪ) *n*

tetrachloromethane ('tɛtrəklɔ:rəʊˌmi:θeɪn) *n* the systematic name for **carbon tetrachloride.**

tetrachord ('tɛtrəˌkɔ:d) *n Music.* any of several groups of four notes in descending order, in which the first and last notes form a perfect fourth. ORIG C17: from Gk *tetrakhordos* four-stringed
▸ **ˌtetra'chordal** *adj*

tetracyclic (ˌtɛtrə'saɪklɪk) *adj Chem.* containing four rings in its molecular structure.

tetracycline (ˌtɛtrə'saɪklaɪn, -klɪn) *n* an antibiotic synthesized from chlortetracycline or derived from a bacterium. ORIG C20: from TETRA- + CYCL(IC) + -INE[2]

tetrad ('tɛtræd) *n* a group or series of four. ORIG C17: from Gk *tetras,* from *tettares* four

tetraethyl lead (ˌtɛtrə'i:θaɪl lɛd) *n* a colourless oily insoluble liquid used in petrol to prevent knocking. Systematic name: **lead tetraethyl.**

tetrafluoroethene ('tɛtrəˌflʊərəʊ'ɛθi:n) *n Chem.* a dense colourless gas that is polymerized to make polytetrafluorethene (PTFE). Formula: F_2C:CF_2. Also called: **tetrafluoroethylene.** ORIG C20: from TETRA- + FLUORO- + ETHENE

tetragon ('tɛtrəˌgɒn) *n* a less common name for **quadrilateral** (sense 2). ORIG C17: from Gk *tetragōnon*

tetragonal (tɛ'trægənᵊl) *adj* **1** *Crystallog.* relating or belonging to the crystal system characterized by three mutually perpendicular axes of which only two are equal. **2** of or shaped like a quadrilateral.
▸ **te'tragonally** *adv*

Tetragrammaton (ˌtɛtrə'græmətᵊn) *n Bible.* the Hebrew name for God consisting of the four consonants Y H V H (or Y H W H). It is usually transliterated as *Jehovah* or *Yahweh.* Sometimes shortened to **Tetragram.** ORIG C14: from Gk, from *tetragrammatos* having four letters

tetrahedron (ˌtɛtrə'hi:drən) *n, pl* **tetrahedrons** *or* **tetrahedra** (-drə). a solid figure having four triangular plane faces. A **regular tetrahedron** has faces that are equilateral triangles. ORIG C16: from NL, from LGk *tetraedron*
▸ **ˌtetra'hedral** *adj*

tetralogy (tɛ'trælədʒɪ) *n, pl* **tetralogies.** a series of four related works, as in drama or opera. ORIG C17: from Gk *tetralogia*

tetramerous (tɛ'træmərəs) *adj Biol.* having or consisting of four parts. ORIG C19: from NL *tetramerus,* from Gk *tetramerēs*

tetrameter (tɛ'træmɪtə) *n Prosody.* **1** a line of verse consisting of four metrical feet. **2** a verse composed of such lines.

tetraplegia (ˌtɛtrə'pli:dʒɪə) *n* another name for **quadriplegia.**
▸ **ˌtetra'plegic** *adj*

tetraploid ('tɛtrəˌplɔɪd) *Genetics.* ◆ *adj* **1** having four times the haploid number of chromosomes in the nucleus. ◆ *n* **2** a tetraploid organism, nucleus, or cell.

tetrapod ('tɛtrəˌpɒd) *n* **1** any vertebrate that has four limbs. **2** a device consisting of four arms radiating from a central point: three arms form a supporting tripod and the fourth is vertical.

tetrapterous (tɛ'træptərəs) *adj* having four wings. ORIG C19: from NL *tetrapterus,* from Gk *tetrapteros,* from TETRA- + *pteron* wing

tetrarch ('tɛtrɑ:k) *n* **1** the ruler of one fourth of a country. **2** a subordinate ruler. **3** any of four joint rulers. ORIG C14: from Gk *tetrarkhēs;* see TETRA-, -ARCH
▸ **tetrarchate** (tɛ'trɑ:ˌkeɪt, -kɪt) *n* ▸ **te'trarchic** *adj* ▸ **'tetrarchy** *n*

tetrastich ('tɛtrəˌstɪk) *n* a poem, stanza, or strophe that consists of four lines. ORIG C16: via L from Gk *tetrastikhon,* from TETRA- + *stikhos* row
▸ **tetrastichic** (ˌtɛtrə'stɪkɪk) *or* **tetrastichal** (tɛ'træstɪkᵊl) *adj*

tetravalent (ˌtɛtrə'veɪlənt) *adj Chem.* **1** having a valency of four. **2** Also: **quadrivalent.** having four valencies.
▸ **ˌtetra'valency** *n*

Tetrazzini ★ (*Italian* tetrat'tsi:ni) *n* **Luisa** (lu'i:za). 1871–1940, Italian soprano.

tetrode ('tɛtrəʊd) *n* an electronic valve having four electrodes.

tetroxide (tɛ'trɒksaɪd) *n* any oxide that contains four oxygen atoms per molecule.

tetryl ('tɛtrɪl) *n* a yellow crystalline explosive solid, trinitrophenylmethylnitramine, used in detonators.

Tetuán ★ (tɛ'twɑ:n) *n* a city in N Morocco: capital of Spanish Morocco (1912–56). Pop.: 272 000 (1993 est.).

Tetzel *or* **Tezel** ★ ('tɛtsᵊl) *n* **Johann** (jo'han). ?1465–1519, German Dominican monk. His preaching on papal indulgences provoked Luther's 95 theses at Wittenberg (1517).

Teucer ★ ('tju:sə) *n Greek myth.* **1** a Cretan leader, who founded Troy. **2** a son of Telamon and Hesione, who distinguished himself by his archery on the side of the Greeks in the Trojan War.

Teucrian ('tju:krɪən) *n, adj* another word for **Trojan.**

Teut. *abbrev. for* Teuton(ic).

Teutoburger Wald ★ (*German* 'tɔytobʊrgər valt) *n* a low wooded mountain range in N Germany.

Teuton ('tju:tən) *n* **1** a member of an ancient Germanic people from Jutland who migrated to S Gaul in the 2nd century B.C. **2** a member of any people speaking a Germanic language, esp. a German. ◆ *adj* **3** Teutonic. ORIG C18: from L *Teutonī* the Teutons, of Gmc origin

Teutonic (tju:'tɒnɪk) *adj* **1** characteristic of or relating to the German people. **2** of the ancient Teutons. **3** (not used in linguistics) of or relating to the Germanic languages.

Tevere ★ ('te:vere) *n* the Italian name for the **Tiber.**

Tewkesbury ★ ('tju:ksbərɪ, -brɪ) *n* a town in W England, in N Gloucestershire at the confluence of the

Rivers Severn and Avon: scene of a decisive battle (1471) of the Wars of the Roses in which the Yorkists defeated the Lancastrians; 12th-century abbey. Pop.: 9488 (1991).

Tex. *abbrev. for:* **1** Texan. **2** Texas.

Texas ★ ('tɛksəs) *n* a state of the southwestern US, on the Gulf of Mexico: the second largest state; part of Mexico from 1821 to 1836, when it was declared an independent republic; joined the US in 1845; consists chiefly of a plain, with a wide flat coastal belt rising up to the semiarid Sacramento and Davis Mountains of the southwest; a major producer of cotton, rice, and livestock; the chief US producer of oil and gas; a leading world supplier of sulphur. Capital: Austin. Pop.: 19 759 614 (1998 est.). Area: 678 927 sq. km (262 134 sq. miles). Abbrevs.: **Tex.** or (with zip code) **TX**
▸ **'Texan** *n, adj*

Tex-Mex ('tɛks,mɛks) *adj* of, relating to, or denoting the Texan version of something Mexican, such as music, food, or language.

text (tɛkst) *n* **1** the main body of a printed or written work as distinct from commentary, notes, illustrations, etc. **2** the words of something printed, written, or displayed on a visual display unit. **3** the original exact wording of a work as distinct from a revision or translation. **4** a short passage of the Bible used as a starting point for a sermon. **5** the topic or subject of a discussion or work. **6** short for **textbook**. **7** any novel, play, etc., prescribed as part of a course of study. ORIG C14: from Med. L *textus* version, from L *textus* texture, from *texere* to compose

textbook ('tɛkst,bʊk) *n* a book used as a standard source of information on a particular subject.
▸ **'text,bookish** *adj*

textile ('tɛkstaɪl) *n* **1** any fabric or cloth, esp. woven. **2** raw material suitable to be made into cloth. ◆ *adj* **3** of or relating to fabrics. ORIG C17: from L *textilis* woven, from *texere* to weave

text message *n* **1** a message sent in text form, esp. by means of a mobile phone. **2** a message appearing on a computer screen.
▸ **text messaging** *n*

textual ('tɛkstjʊəl) *adj* **1** of or relating to a text or texts. **2** based on a text.
▸ **'textually** *adv*

textual criticism *n* **1** the scholarly study of manuscripts, esp. of the Bible, in an effort to establish the original text. **2** literary criticism emphasizing a close analysis of the text.

textualism ('tɛkstjʊə,lɪzəm) *n* **1** doctrinaire adherence to a text, esp. of the Bible. **2** textual criticism, esp. of the Bible.
▸ **'textualist** *n, adj*

texture ('tɛkstʃə) *n* **1** the surface of a material, esp. as perceived by the sense of touch. **2** the structure, appearance, and feel of a woven fabric. **3** the general structure and disposition of the constituent parts of something: *the texture of a cake.* **4** the distinctive character or quality of something: *the texture of life in America.* ◆ *vb* **textures, texturing, textured. 5** (*tr*) to give a distinctive texture to. ORIG C15: from L *textūra* web, from *texere* to weave
▸ **'textural** *adj* ▸ **'texturally** *adv*

Teyde ★ (*Spanish* 'teiðe) *n* a variant spelling of **Teide**.

Tezel ('tɛtsᵊl) *n* a variant spelling of (Johann) **Tetzel**.

TGAT ('tiːgæt) *n* (in Britain) *acronym for* Task Group on Assessment and Testing: a group that advises on assessment and testing within the National Curriculum.

TGV (,tiːdʒiː'viː, *French* teʒeve) (in France) *abbrev. for* train à grande vitesse: a high-speed passenger train.

TGWU (in Britain) *abbrev. for* Transport and General Workers' Union.

Th *the chemical symbol for* thorium.

Th. *abbrev. for* Thursday.

-th[1] *suffix forming nouns.* **1** (*from verbs*) indicating an action or its consequence: *growth.* **2** (*from adjectives*) indicating a quality: *width.* ORIG from OE *-thu, -tho*

-th[2] *or* **-eth** *suffix.* forming ordinal numbers: *fourth; thousandth.* ORIG from OE *-(o)tha, -(o)the*

Thabana-Ntlenyana ★ (tɑː'bɑːnəᵊn'tleɪnjənə) *n* a mountain in Lesotho: the highest peak of the Drakensberg Mountains. Height: 3482 m (11 425 ft). Also called: **Thadentsonyane, Thabantshonyana.**

Thackeray ★ ('θækərɪ) *n* **William Makepeace.** 1811–63, British novelist, born in India. His novels include *Vanity Fair* (1848), *Pendennis* (1850), and *The Newcomes* (1855).

Thaddeus *or* **Thadeus** ★ ('θædɪəs) *n New Testament.* one of the 12 apostles (Matthew 10:3; Mark 3:18), traditionally identified with Jude.

Thadentsonyane ★ (,tɑːdən'tsɒnjənə) *n* another name for **Thabana-Ntlenyana**.

Thai (taɪ) *adj* **1** of Thailand, its people, or their language. ◆ *n* **2** (*pl* **Thais** *or* **Thai**) a native or inhabitant of Thailand. **3** the language of Thailand, sometimes classified as belonging to the Sino-Tibetan family.

Thailand ★ ('taɪ,lænd) *n* a kingdom in SE Asia, on the Andaman Sea and the Gulf of Siam: united as a kingdom in 1350 and became a major SE Asian power; consists chiefly of a central plain around the Chao Phraya river system, mountains rising over 2400 m (8000 ft) in the northwest, and rainforest the length of the S peninsula. Official language: Thai. Official religion: (Hinayana) Buddhist. Currency: baht. Capital: Bangkok. Pop.: 61 806 000 (1999 est.). Area: 513 998 sq. km (198 455 sq. miles). Former name (until 1939 and 1945–49): **Siam.**

Thaïs ★ ('θeɪɪs) *n* 4th-century B.C. Athenian courtesan; mistress of Alexander the Great.

thalamus ('θæləməs) *n, pl* **thalami** (-,maɪ). **1** either of the two contiguous egg-shaped masses of grey matter at the base of the brain. **2** both of these masses considered as a functional unit. **3** the receptacle or torus of a flower. ORIG C18: from L, from Gk *thalamos* inner room
▸ **thalamic** (θə'læmɪk) *adj*

thalassaemia *or US* **thalassemia** (,θælə'siːmɪə) *n* a hereditary disease resulting from defects in the synthesis of the red blood pigment haemoglobin. ORIG NL, from Gk *thalassa* sea + -AEMIA, it being esp. prevalent round the eastern Mediterranean

thalassic (θə'læsɪk) *adj* of or relating to the sea, esp. to small or inland seas. ORIG C19: from F *thalassique,* from Gk *thalassa* sea

thaler ('tɑːlə) *n, pl* **thaler** *or* **thalers.** a former German, Austrian, or Swiss silver coin. ORIG from G; see DOLLAR

Thales ★ ('θeɪliːz) *n* ?624–?546 B.C., Greek philosopher, mathematician, and astronomer, born in Miletus. He held that water was the origin of all things and he predicted the solar eclipse of May 28, 585 B.C.

Thalia ★ (θə'laɪə) *n Greek myth.* **1** the Muse of comedy and pastoral poetry. **2** one of the three Graces, the others are Aglaia and Euphrosyne. ORIG C17: via L from Gk, from *thaleia* blooming

thalidomide (θə'lɪdə,maɪd) *n* **a** a drug formerly used as a sedative and hypnotic but withdrawn from use when found to cause abnormalities in developing fetuses. **b** (*as modifier*): *a thalidomide baby.* ORIG C20: from *thali(mi)do-(glutari)mide*

thallium ('θælɪəm) *n* a soft malleable highly toxic white metallic element. Symbol: Tl; atomic no.: 81; atomic wt.: 204.37. ORIG C19: from NL, from Gk *thallos* a green shoot; from the green line in its spectrum

thallus ('θæləs) *n, pl* **thalli** ('θælaɪ) *or* **thalluses.** the undifferentiated vegetative body of algae, fungi, and lichens. ORIG C19: from L, from Gk *thallos* green shoot, from *thallein* to bloom
▸ **'thalloid** *adj*

thalweg *or* **talweg** ('tɑːlvɛg) *n Geog., rare.* **1** the longitudinal outline of a riverbed from source to mouth. **2** the line of steepest descent from any point on the land surface. ORIG C19: from G *Thal* or *Tal* valley + *Weg* way

Thames ★ *n* **1** (tɛmz). a river in S England, rising in the Cotswolds and flowing east through London to the North Sea by a large estuary. Length: 346 km (215 miles). Ancient name: **Tamesis** ('tæməsɪs). **2** (teɪmz, θeɪmz). a river in SE Canada, in Ontario, flowing south to London, then southwest to Lake St Clair. Length: 217 km (135 miles).

than (ðæn; *unstressed* ðən) *conj* (*coordinating*), *prep* **1** used to introduce the second element of a comparison, the first element of which expresses difference: *shorter than you.* **2** used after adverbs such as *rather* or *sooner* to introduce a rejected alternative in an expression of preference: *rather than be imprisoned, I shall die.* ORIG OE *thanne*

> **USAGE NOTE** In formal English, *than* is usually regarded as a conjunction governing an unexpressed verb: *he does it far better than I (do).* Which pronoun to use therefore depends on whether it is the subject or object of the unexpressed verb: *she likes him more than I (like him); she likes him more than (she likes) me.* However, in ordinary speech and writing *than* is usually treated as a preposition and is followed by the object form of a pronoun: *my brother is younger than me.*

thanatology (ˌθænəˈtɒlədʒɪ) *n* the scientific study of death and its related phenomena. ORIG C19: from Gk *thanatos* death + -LOGY

thanatopsis (ˌθænəˈtɒpsɪs) *n* a meditation on death, as in a poem. ORIG C19: from Gk *thanatos* death + *opsis* a view

Thanatos ★ (ˈθænəˌtɒs) *n* the Greek personification of death: son of Nyx, goddess of night. Roman counterpart: **Mors.** Cf. **Eros.**
▸ **Thanatotic** (ˌθænəˈtɒtɪk) *adj*

thane or (*less commonly*) **thegn** (θeɪn) *n* **1** (in Anglo-Saxon England) a member of an aristocratic class who held land from the king or from another nobleman in return for certain services. **2** (in medieval Scotland) a person of rank holding land from the king. ORIG OE *thegn*
▸ **thanage** (ˈθeɪnɪdʒ) *n*

Thanet ★ (ˈθænɪt) *n* **Isle of.** an island in SE England, in NE Kent, separated from the mainland by two branches of the River Stour: scene of many Norse invasions. Area: 109 sq. km (42 sq. miles).

Thanjavur ★ (ˌtʌndʒəˈvʊə) *n* a city in SE India, in E Tamil Nadu: headquarters of the earliest Protestant missions in India. Pop.: 202 013 (1991). Former name: **Tanjore.**

thank (θæŋk) *vb* (*tr*) **1** to convey feelings of gratitude to. **2** to hold responsible: *he has his creditors to thank for his bankruptcy.* ORIG OE *thancian*

thankful (ˈθæŋkfʊl) *adj* grateful and appreciative.
▸ **ˈthankfully** *adv* ▸ **ˈthankfulness** *n*

> **USAGE NOTE** Some people object to the use of *thankfully* to qualify a complete statement, as in *that conflict is, thankfully, over.* However, this use is now very well established, and far more common than e.g. *she drew some smoke in thankfully and settled herself more comfortably on her chair.*

thankless (ˈθæŋklɪs) *adj* **1** receiving no thanks or appreciation. **2** ungrateful.
▸ **ˈthanklessly** *adv* ▸ **ˈthanklessness** *n*

thanks (θæŋks) *pl n* **1** an expression of appreciation or gratitude. **2 thanks to.** because of: *thanks to him we lost the match.* ◆ *interj* **3** *Inf.* an exclamation expressing gratitude.

thanksgiving (ˈθæŋksˌgɪvɪŋ; *US* θæŋksˈgɪv-) *n* **1** the act of giving thanks. **2** a formal public expression of thanks to God.

Thanksgiving Day *n* an annual day of holiday celebrated in thanksgiving to God on the fourth Thursday of November in the United States, and on the second Monday of October in Canada. Often shortened to **Thanksgiving.**

Thapsus ★ (ˈθæpsəs) *n* an ancient town near Carthage in North Africa: site of Caesar's victory over Pompey in 46 B.C.

thar (tɑː) *n* a variant spelling of **tahr.**

Thar Desert ★ (tɑː) *n* a desert in NW India, mainly in NW Rajasthan state and extending into Pakistan. Area: over 260 000 sq. km (100 000 sq. miles). Also called: **Indian Desert, Great Indian Desert.**

Thásos ★ (ˈθæsɒs) *n* a Greek island in the N Aegean: colonized by Greeks from Paros in the 7th century B.C. as a gold-mining centre; under Turkish rule (1455–1912). Pop.: 13 110 (1981). Area: 379 sq. km (146 sq. miles).

that (ðæt; *unstressed* ðət) *determiner* (*used before a sing n*) **1a** used preceding a noun that has been mentioned or is understood: *that idea of yours.* **1b** (*as pronoun*): *don't eat that.* **2a** used preceding a noun that denotes something more remote or removed: *that building over there is for sale.* **2b** (*as pronoun*): *that is John and this is his wife.* **3** used to refer to something that is familiar: *that old chap from across the street.* **4 and** (**all**) **that.** *Inf.* everything connected with the subject mentioned: *he knows a lot about building and that.* **5 at that.** (*completive-intensive*) additionally, all things considered, or nevertheless: *I might decide to go at that.* **6 like that. 6a** effortlessly: *he gave me the answer just like that.* **6b** of such a nature, character, etc.: *he paid for all our tickets — he's like that.* **7 that is. 7a** to be precise. **7b** in other words. **7c** for example. **8 that's that.** there is no more to be done, discussed, etc. ◆ *conj* (*subordinating*) **9** used to introduce a noun clause: *I believe that you'll come.* **10** used to introduce: **10a** a clause of purpose: *they fought that others might have peace.* **10b** a clause of result: *he laughed so hard that he cried.* **10c** a clause after an understood sentence expressing desire, indignation, or amazement: *oh, that I had never lived!* ◆ *adv* **11** used to reinforce the specification of a precise degree already mentioned: *go just that fast and you should be safe.* **12** Also: **all that.** (*usually used with a negative*) *Inf.* (intensifier): *he wasn't that upset at the news.* **13** *Dialect.* (intensifier): *the cat was that weak after the fight.* ◆ *pron* **14** used to introduce a restrictive relative clause: *the book that we want.* **15** used to introduce a clause with the verb *to be* to emphasize the extent to which the preceding noun is applicable: *genius that she is, she outwitted the computer.* ORIG OE *thæt*

> **USAGE NOTE** Precise writers maintain a distinction between *that* and *which*. In *the book that is on the table is mine*, the clause *that is on the table* is used to distinguish one particular book (the one on the table) from another or others (which may be anywhere, but not on the table). In *the book, which is on the table, is mine*, the *which* clause is merely descriptive or incidental. The more formal the level of language, the more important it is to preserve the distinction between the two relative pronouns; but in informal or colloquial language they are often used interchangeably.

thatch (θætʃ) *n* **1a** Also called: **thatching.** a roofing material that consists of straw, reed, etc. **1b** a roof made of such a material. **2** anything resembling this, such as the hair of the head. **3** Also called: **thatch palm.** any of various palms with leaves suitable for thatching. ◆ *vb* **4** to cover with thatch. ORIG OE *theccan* to cover
▸ **ˈthatcher** *n*

Thatcher ★ (ˈθætʃə) *n* **Margaret** (**Hilda**), Baroness (née *Roberts*). born 1925, British stateswoman; leader of the Conservative Party (1975–90); prime minister (1979–90).

Thatcherism (ˈθætʃəˌrɪzəm) *n* the policies of monetarism, privatization, and self-help promoted by Margaret Thatcher.
▸ **ˈThatcherˌite** *n, adj*

thaumatology (ˌθɔːməˈtɒlədʒɪ) *n* the study of or a treatise on miracles. ORIG C19: from Gk *thaumato-* combining form of *thauma* a wonder, marvel + -LOGY

thaumatrope (ˈθɔːməˌtrəʊp) *n* a toy in which partial pictures on the two sides of a card appear to merge when the card is twirled rapidly. ORIG C19: from Gk *thaumato-* (see THAUMATOLOGY) + -TROPE
▸ **thaumatropical** (ˌθɔːməˈtrɒpɪkᵊl) *adj*

thaumaturge (ˈθɔːməˌtɜːdʒ) *n Rare.* a performer of miracles; magician. ORIG C18: from Med. L *thaumaturgus*, from Gk *thaumatourgos* miracle-working
▸ **ˌthaumaˈturgic** *adj* ▸ **ˈthaumaˌturgy** *n*

thaw (θɔː) *vb* **1** to melt or cause to melt: *the snow thawed.* **2** to become or cause to become unfrozen; defrost. **3** (*intr*) to be the case that the ice or snow is melting: *it's thawing fast.* **4** (*intr*) to become more relaxed or friendly. ◆ *n* **5** the act or process of thawing. **6** a spell of relatively warm weather, causing snow or ice to melt. **7** an increase in relaxation or friendliness. ORIG OE *thawian*

ThD *abbrev. for* Doctor of Theology.

the[1] (*stressed or emphatic* ðiː; *unstressed before a consonant* ðə; *unstressed before a vowel* ðɪ) *determiner* (*article*) **1** used preceding a noun that has been previously specified: *the pain should disappear soon.* Cf. **a**[1]. **2** used to indicate a particular person, object, etc.: *ask the man standing outside.* Cf. **a**[1]. **3** used preceding certain nouns associated with one's culture, society, or community: *to go to the doctor; to listen to the news.* **4** used preceding present participles and adjectives when they function as nouns: *the singing is awful.* **5** used preceding titles and certain uniquely specific or proper nouns: *the United States; the Chairman.* **6** used preceding a qualifying adjective or noun in certain names or titles: *Edward the First.* **7** used preceding a noun to make it refer to its class generically: *the white seal is hunted for its fur.* **8** used instead of *my, your, her,* etc., with parts of the body: *take me by the hand.* **9** (usually stressed) the best, only, or most remarkable: *Harry's is* the *club in this town.* **10** used with proper nouns when qualified: *written by the young Hardy.* **11** another word for **per**: *fifty pence the pound.* **12** *Often facetious or derog.* my; our: *the wife goes out on Thursdays.* **13** used preceding a unit of time in phrases or titles indicating an outstanding person, event, etc.: *housewife of the year.* ORIG ME, from OE *thē*, a demonstrative adjective that later superseded *sē* (masculine singular) and *sēo, sio* (feminine singular)

the[2] (ðə, ðɪ) *adv* **1** (often foll. by *for*) used before comparative adjectives or adverbs for emphasis: *she looks the happier for her trip.* **2** used correlatively before each of two comparative adjectives or adverbs to indicate equality: *the sooner you come, the better; the more I see you, the more I love you.* ORIG OE *thī, thȳ*

theanthropism (θiːˈænθrəˌpɪzəm) *n* **1** the ascription of human traits or characteristics to a god or gods. **2** *Christian theol.* the doctrine of the union of the divine and human natures in the single person of Christ. ORIG C19: from Ecclesiastical Gk *theanthrōpos* (from *theos* god + *anthrōpos* man) + -ISM
▸ **theanthropic** (ˌθiːænˈθrɒpɪk) *adj*

thearchy (ˈθiːɑːkɪ) *n, pl* **thearchies.** rule or government by God or gods; theocracy. ORIG C17: from Church Gk *thearkhia;* see THEO-, -ARCHY

theatre *or US* **theater** (ˈθɪətə) *n* **1** a building designed for the performance of plays, operas, etc. **2** a large room or hall, usually with a raised platform and tiered seats for an audience. **3** a room in a hospital equipped for surgical operations. **4** plays regarded collectively as a form of art. **5 the theatre.** the world of actors, theatrical companies, etc. **6** a setting for dramatic or important events. **7** writing that is suitable for dramatic presentation: *a good piece of theatre.* **8** *US & Austral.* the usual word for **cinema** (sense 1). **9** a major area of military activity. **10** a circular or semicircular open-air building with tiers of seats. ORIG C14: from L *theātrum,* from Gk *theatron* place for viewing, from *theasthai* to look at

theatre-in-the-round *n, pl* **theatres-in-the-round.** a theatre with seats arranged around a central acting area.

theatre of cruelty *n* a type of theatre that seeks to communicate a sense of pain, suffering, and evil, using gesture, movement, sound, and symbolism rather than language.

theatre of the absurd *n* drama in which normal conventions and dramatic structure are modified in order to present life as irrational.

theatrical (θɪˈætrɪkᵊl) *adj* **1** of or relating to the theatre or dramatic performances. **2** exaggerated and affected in manner or behaviour; histrionic.
▸ **theˌatriˈcality** *or* **theˈatricalness** *n* ▸ **theˈatrically** *adv*

theatricals (θɪˈætrɪkᵊlz) *pl n* dramatic performances, esp. as given by amateurs.

theatrics (θɪˈætrɪks) *n* (*functioning as sing*) **1** the art of staging plays. **2** exaggerated mannerisms or displays of emotions.

Thebaid ★ (ˈθiːbeɪɪd, -bɪ-) *n* the territory around ancient Thebes in Egypt, or sometimes around Thebes in Greece.

thebaine (ˈθiːbəˌiːn) *n* a poisonous white crystalline alkaloid, extracted from opium. ORIG C19: from NL *thebaia* opium of Thebes (with reference to Egypt as a chief source of opium) + -INE[2]

Thebes ★ (θiːbz) *n* **1** (in ancient Greece) the chief city of Boeotia, destroyed by Alexander the Great (336 B.C.). **2** (in ancient Egypt) a city on the Nile: at various times capital of Upper Egypt or of the entire country.
▸ **Thebaic** (θɪˈbeɪɪk) *adj* ▸ **ˈTheban** *adj, n*

theca (ˈθiːkə) *n, pl* **thecae** (-siː). **1** *Bot.* an enclosing organ, cell, or spore case. **2** *Zool.* a hard outer covering, such as the container of a coral polyp. ORIG C17: from L *thēca,* from Gk *thēkē* case
▸ **ˈthecate** *adj*

thecodont (ˈθiːkəˌdɒnt) *adj* **1** (of mammals and certain reptiles) having teeth that grow in sockets. **2** of or relating to teeth of this type. ◆ *n* **3** any of various extinct reptiles of Triassic times, having teeth set in sockets: they gave rise to the dinosaurs, crocodiles, pterodactyls, and birds. ORIG C20: NL *Thecodontia,* from Gk *thēkē* case + -ODONT

thé dansant *French.* (te dɑ̃sɑ̃) *n, pl* **thés dansant** (te dɑ̃sɑ̃). a dance held while afternoon tea is served, popular in the 1920s and 1930s. ORIG lit.: dancing tea

thee (ðiː) *pron* **1** the objective form of **thou**[1]. **2** (*subjective*) *Rare.* refers to the person addressed: used mainly by members of the Society of Friends. ORIG OE *thē*

theft (θɛft) *n* **1** the dishonest taking of property belonging to another person with the intention of depriving the owner permanently of its possession. **2** *Rare.* something stolen. ORIG OE *thēofth*

thegn (θeɪn) *n* a less common variant of **thane.**

Theiler ★ (ˈtaɪlə) *n* **Max.** 1899–1972, US virologist, born in South Africa: Nobel prize for physiology or medicine (1951) for developing a vaccine against yellow fever.

theine (ˈθiːiːn, -ɪn) *n* caffeine, esp. when present in tea. ORIG C19: from NL *thea* tea + -INE[2]

their (ðɛə) *determiner* **1** of or associated in some way with them: *their own clothes; she tried to combat their mocking her.* **2** belonging to or associated with people in general: *in many countries they wash their clothes in the river.* **3** belonging to or associated with an indefinite antecedent such as *one, whoever,* or *anybody: everyone should bring their own lunch.* ORIG C12: from ON *theira*

USAGE NOTE See at **they.**

theirs (ðɛəz) *pron* **1** something or someone belonging to or associated with them: *theirs is difficult.* **2** something or someone belonging to or associated with an indefinite antecedent such as *one, whoever,* or *anybody: everyone thinks theirs is best.* **3 of theirs.** belonging to or associated with them.

theism (ˈθiːɪzəm) *n* **1** the belief in one God as the creator and ruler of the universe. **2** the belief in the existence of a God or gods. ORIG C17: from Gk *theos* god + -ISM
▸ **ˈtheist** *n, adj* ▸ **theˈistic** *or* **theˈistical** *adj*

them (ðɛm; *unstressed* ðəm) *pron* **1** (*objective*) refers to things or people other than the speaker or people addressed: *I'll kill them; what happened to them?* ◆ *determiner* **2** a nonstandard word for **those:** *three of them oranges.* ORIG OE *thǣm,* infl. by ON *theim*

USAGE NOTE See at **me**[1], **they.**

thematic apperception test *n Psychol.* a projective test in which drawings of interacting people are shown and the person being tested is asked to make up a story about them.

theme (θiːm) *n* **1** an idea or topic expanded in a discourse, discussion, etc. **2** (in literature, music, art, etc.) a unifying idea, image, or motif, repeated or developed

throughout a work. **3** *Music.* a group of notes forming a recognizable melodic unit, often used as the basis of the musical material in a composition. **4** a short essay, esp. one set as an exercise for a student. **5** *Grammar.* another word for **root**[1] (sense 8) or **stem**[1] (sense 7). **6** (*modifier*) planned or designed round one unifying subject, image, etc.: *a theme holiday.* ◆ *vb* **themes, theming, themed.** (*tr*) **7** to design, decorate, etc., in accordance with a theme. ORIG C13: from L *thema,* from Gk: deposit, from *tithenai* to lay down
▸ **thematic** (θɪ'mætɪk) *adj*

theme park *n* an area planned as a leisure attraction, in which all the displays, buildings, activities, etc., are based on one subject.

theme song *n* **1** a melody used, esp. in a film score, to set a mood, introduce a character, etc. **2** another term for **signature tune.**

Themis ★ ('θi:mɪs) *n Greek myth.* a goddess of order and justice.

Themistocles ★ (θə'mɪstə,kli:z) *n* ?527–?460 B.C., Athenian statesman, who led the Athenians in their victory against the Persians at Salamis (480): ostracized in 470.

themselves (ðəm'sɛlvz) *pron* **1a** the reflexive form of *they* or *them.* **1b** (intensifier): *the team themselves voted on it.* **2** (*preceded by a copula*) their normal or usual selves: *they don't seem themselves any more.* **3** Also: **themself.** *Not standard.* a reflexive form of an indefinite antecedent such as *one, whoever,* or *anybody: everyone has to look after themselves.*

then (ðɛn) *adv* **1** at that time; over that period of time. **2** (*sentence modifier*) in that case; that being so: *then why don't you ask her? go on then, take it.* ◆ *sentence connector.* **3** after that; with that: *then John left the room.* ◆ *n* **4** that time: *from then on.* ◆ *adj* **5** (*prenominal*) existing, functioning, etc., at that time: *the then prime minister.* ORIG OE *thenne*

thenar ('θi:nɑ:) *n* **1** the palm of the hand. **2** the fleshy area of the palm at the base of the thumb. ORIG C17: via NL from Gk

thence (ðɛns) *adv* **1** from that place. **2** Also: **thenceforth** ('ðɛns'fɔ:θ). from that time or event; thereafter. **3** therefore. ORIG C13 *thannes,* from *thanne,* from OE *thanon*

thenceforward ('ðɛns'fɔ:wəd) *or* **thenceforwards** *adv* from that time or place on.

theo- *or before a vowel* **the-** *combining form.* indicating God or gods: *theology.* ORIG from Gk *theos* god

theobromine (,θi:əʊ'brəʊmi:n, -mɪn) *n* a white crystalline alkaloid that occurs in tea and cacao: used to treat coronary heart disease and headaches. ORIG C18: from NL *theobroma* genus of trees, lit.: food of the gods

theocentric (,θɪə'sɛntrɪk) *adj Theol.* having God as the focal point of attention.

theocracy (θɪ'ɒkrəsɪ) *n, pl* **theocracies. 1** government by a deity or by a priesthood. **2** a community under such government.
▸ **'theo,crat** *n* ▸ **,theo'cratic** *adj*

theocrasy (θɪ'ɒkrəsɪ) *n* **1** a mingling into one of deities or divine attributes previously regarded as distinct. **2** the union of the soul with God in mysticism. ORIG C19: from Gk *theokrasia,* from THEO- + *-krasia* from *krasis* a blending

Theocritus ★ (θɪ'ɒkrɪtəs) *n* ?310–?250 B.C., Greek poet, born in Syracuse.
▸ **The'ocritan** *or* **Theocritean** (θɪ,ɒkrɪ'ti:ən) *adj, n*

theodicy (θɪ'ɒdɪsɪ) *n, pl* **theodicies.** the branch of theology concerned with defending the attributes of God against objections resulting from the existence of physical and moral evil. ORIG C18: coined by Leibnitz in F as *théodicée,* from THEO- + Gk *dikē* justice
▸ **the,odi'cean** *adj*

theodolite (θɪ'ɒdə,laɪt) *n* a surveying instrument for measuring horizontal and vertical angles, consisting of a small tripod-mounted telescope. Also called (in the US and Canada): **transit.** ORIG C16: from NL *theodolitus,* from ?
▸ **theodolitic** (θɪ,ɒdə'lɪtɪk) *adj*

Theodora ★ (,θɪə'dɔ:rə) *n* ?500–548 A.D., Byzantine empress; wife and counsellor of Justinian I.

Theodorakis ★ (*Greek* θεɔðɔ'rakis) *n* **Mikis** ('mikis). born 1925, Greek composer: he wrote the music for the film *Zorba the Greek* (1965) and was imprisoned (1967–70) for opposing the military government.

Theodoric *or* **Theoderic** ★ (θɪ'ɒdərɪk) *n* called *the Great.* ?454–526 A.D., king and founder of the Ostrogothic kingdom.

Theodosius I ★ (,θɪə'dəʊsɪəs) *n* called *the Great.* ?346–395 A.D., Roman emperor of the Eastern Roman Empire (379–95) and of the Western Roman Empire (392–95).

theogony (θɪ'ɒgənɪ) *n, pl* **theogonies. 1** the origin and descent of the gods. **2** an account of this. ORIG C17: from Gk *theogonia*
▸ **theogonic** (,θɪə'gɒnɪk) *adj* ▸ **the'ogonist** *n*

theol. *abbrev. for:* **1** theologian. **2** theological. **3** theology.

theologian (,θɪə'ləʊdʒɪən) *n* a person versed in or engaged in the study of theology.

theological (,θɪə'lɒdʒɪkᵊl) *adj* of, relating to, or based on theology.
▸ **,theo'logically** *adv*

theological virtues *pl n* those virtues that are infused into man by a special grace of God, specifically faith, hope, and charity.

theologize *or* **theologise** (θɪ'ɒlə,dʒaɪz) *vb* **theologizes, theologizing, theologized** *or* **theologises, theologising, theologised. 1** (*intr*) to speculate upon theological subjects or engage in theological study or discussion. **2** (*tr*) to render theological or treat from a theological point of view.
▸ **the,ologi'zation** *or* **the,ologi'sation** *n* ▸ **the'olo,gizer** *or* **the'olo,giser** *n*

theology (θɪ'ɒlədʒɪ) *n, pl* **theologies. 1** the systematic study of the existence and nature of the divine and its relationship to other beings. **2** the systematic study of Christian revelation concerning God's nature and purpose. **3** a specific system, form, or branch of this study. ORIG C14: from LL *theologia,* from L
▸ **the'ologist** *n*

theomachy (θɪ'ɒməkɪ) *n, pl* **theomachies.** a battle among the gods or against them. ORIG C16: from Gk *theomakhia,* from THEO- + *makhē* battle

theomancy ('θi:əʊ,mænsɪ) *n* divination or prophecy by an oracle or by people directly inspired by a god.

theomania (,θɪə'meɪnɪə) *n* religious madness, esp. when it takes the form of believing oneself to be a god.
▸ **,theo'mani,ac** *n*

theophany (θɪ'ɒfənɪ) *n, pl* **theophanies.** a visible manifestation of a deity to man. ORIG C17: from LL *theophania,* from LGk, from THEO- + *phainein* to show
▸ **theophanic** (,θɪə'fænɪk) *adj*

Theophrastus ★ (,θɪə'fræstəs) *n* ?372–?287 B.C., Greek Peripatetic philosopher.

theophylline (,θɪə'fɪli:n, -ɪn) *n* a white crystalline alkaloid that is an isomer of theobromine: it occurs in plants such as tea. ORIG C19: from THEO(BROMINE) + PHYLLO- + -INE[2]

theorem ('θɪərəm) *n* a statement or formula that can be deduced from the axioms of a formal system by means of its rules of inference. ORIG C16: from LL *theōrēma,* from Gk: something to be viewed, from *theōrein* to view
▸ **theorematic** (,θɪərə'mætɪk) *or* **theoremic** (,θɪə'rɛmɪk) *adj*

theoretical (,θɪə'rɛtɪkᵊl) *or* **theoretic** *adj* **1** of or based on theory. **2** lacking practical application or actual existence; hypothetical. **3** using or dealing in theory; impractical.
▸ **,theo'retically** *adv*

theoretician (,θɪərɪ'tɪʃən) *n* a student or user of the theory rather than the practical aspects of a subject.

theoretics (,θɪə'rɛtɪks) *n* (*functioning as sing or pl*) the theory of a particular subject.

theorize *or* **theorise** ('θɪə,raɪz) *vb* **theorizes, theorizing, theorized** *or* **theorises, theorising, theorised.** (*intr*) to produce or use theories; speculate.
▸ **'theorist** *n* ▸ **,theori'zation** *or* **,theori'sation** *n* ▸ **'theo,rizer** *or* **'theo,riser** *n*

theory ('θɪərɪ) *n, pl* **theories. 1** a system of rules, procedures, and assumptions used to produce a result. **2** abstract knowledge or reasoning. **3** a conjectural view or idea: *I have a theory about that.* **4** an ideal or hypothetical situation (esp. in **in theory**). **5** a set of hypotheses related by logical or mathematical arguments to explain a wide variety of connected phenomena in general terms: *the theory of relativity.* **6** a nontechnical name for **hypothesis.** ORIG C16: from LL *theōria,* from Gk: a sight, from *theōrein* to gaze upon

theory of games *n* a mathematical theory concerned with the optimum choice of strategy in situations involving a conflict of interest. Also called: **game theory.**

theosophy (θɪ'ɒsəfɪ) *n* **1** any of various religious or philosophical systems claiming to be based on or to express an intuitive insight into the divine nature. **2** the system of beliefs of the Theosophical Society founded in 1875, claiming to be derived from the sacred writings of Brahmanism and Buddhism. ORIG C17: from Med. L *theosophia,* from LGk; see THEO-, -SOPHY
▸ **theosophical** (ˌθɪə'sɒfɪkᵊl) *or* ˌ**theo'sophic** *adj* ▸ **the'osophist** *n*

Thera ★ ('θɪərə) *n* a Greek island in the Aegean Sea, in the Cyclades: site of a Minoan settlement and of the volcano that ended Minoan civilization on Crete. Pop.: 7000 (latest est.). Also called: **Santoríni.** Modern Greek name: **Thíra.**

therapeutic (ˌθɛrə'pjuːtɪk) *adj* **1** of or relating to the treatment of disease; curative. **2** serving or performed to maintain health: *therapeutic abortion.* ORIG C17: from NL *therapeuticus,* from Gk, from *therapeuein* to minister to, from *theraps* an attendant
▸ ˌ**thera'peutically** *adv*

therapeutics (ˌθɛrə'pjuːtɪks) *n* (*functioning as sing*) the branch of medicine concerned with the treatment of disease.

therapy ('θɛrəpɪ) *n, pl* **therapies. a** the treatment of physical, mental, or social disorders or disease. **b** (*in combination*): *physiotherapy.* ORIG C19: from NL *therapia,* from Gk *therapeia* attendance; see THERAPEUTIC
▸ '**therapist** *n*

Theravada (ˌθɛrə'vɑːdə) *n* the southern school of Buddhism, the name preferred by Hinayana Buddhists. ORIG from Pali: doctrine of the elders

there (ðɛə) *adv* **1** in, at, or to that place, point, case, or respect: *we never go there; I agree with you there.* ◆ *pron* **2** used as a grammatical subject with some verbs, esp. *be,* when the true subject follows the verb: *there is a girl in that office.* ◆ *adj* **3** (*postpositive*) who or which is in that place or position: *that boy there did it.* **4 all there.** (*predicative*) of normal intelligence. **5 so there.** an exclamation that usually follows a declaration of refusal or defiance. **6 there you are. 6a** an expression used when handing a person something requested or desired. **6b** an exclamation of triumph. ◆ *n* **7** that place: *near there.* ◆ *interj* **8** an expression of sympathy, as in consoling a child: *there, there, dear.* ORIG OE *thǣr*

> **USAGE NOTE** In correct usage, the verb should agree with the subject in such constructions as *there is a man waiting* and *there are several people waiting.* However, where the subject is compound, it is common in speech to use a singular verb, as in *there's a police car and an ambulance outside.*

thereabouts ('ðɛərəˌbaʊts) *or US* **thereabout** *adv* near that place, time, amount, etc.

thereafter (ˌðɛər'ɑːftə) *adv* from that time on or after that time.

thereat (ˌðɛər'æt) *adv Rare.* **1** at that point or time. **2** for that reason.

thereby (ˌðɛə'baɪ, 'ðɛəˌbaɪ) *adv* **1** by that means; because of that. **2** *Arch.* thereabouts.

therefor (ˌðɛə'fɔː) *adv Arch.* for this, that, or it.

therefore ('ðɛəˌfɔː) *sentence connector.* **1** thus; hence: *those people have their umbrellas up; therefore, it must be raining.* **2** consequently; as a result.

therefrom (ˌðɛə'frɒm) *adv Arch.* from that or there: *the roads that lead therefrom.*

therein (ˌðɛər'ɪn) *adv Formal or law.* in or into that place, thing, etc.

thereinto (ˌðɛər'ɪntuː) *adv Formal or law.* into that place, circumstance, etc.

thereof (ˌðɛər'ɒv) *adv Formal or law.* **1** of or concerning that or it. **2** from or because of that.

thereon (ˌðɛər'ɒn) *adv Arch.* thereupon.

Theresa ★ (tə'riːzə; *Spanish* te'resa) *n* See (Saint) **Teresa.**

Thérèse de Lisieux ★ (*French* terɛz də lizjø) *n* **Saint,** known as *the Little Flower of Jesus.* 1873–97, French Carmelite nun, noted for her autobiography, *The Story of a Soul* (1897). Feast day: Oct. 3.

thereto (ˌðɛə'tuː) *adv* **1** *Formal or law.* to that or it. **2** *Obs.* in addition to that.

theretofore (ˌðɛətʊ'fɔː) *adv Formal or law.* before that time; previous to that.

thereunder (ˌðɛər'ʌndə) *adv Formal or law.* **1** (in documents, etc.) below that or it; subsequently in that; thereafter. **2** under the terms or authority of that.

thereupon (ˌðɛərə'pɒn) *adv* **1** immediately after that; at that point. **2** *Formal or law.* upon that thing, point, subject, etc.

therewith (ˌðɛə'wɪθ, -'wɪð) *or* **therewithal** *adv* **1** *Formal or law.* with or in addition to that. **2** a less common word for **thereupon** (sense 1). **3** *Arch.* by means of or on account of that.

Therezina ★ (*Portuguese* tere'zina) *n* the former name of **Teresina.**

therianthropic (ˌθɪərɪən'θrɒpɪk) *adj* **1** (of certain mythical creatures or deities) having a partly animal, partly human form. **2** of or relating to such creatures or deities. ORIG C19: from Gk *thērion* wild animal + *anthrōpos* man
▸ **therianthropism** (ˌθɪərɪ'ænθrəˌpɪzəm) *n*

theriomorphic (ˌθɪərɪəʊ'mɔːfɪk) *adj* (esp. of a deity) possessing or depicted in the form of a beast. ORIG C19: from Gk *thēriomorphos,* from *thērion* wild animal + *morphē* shape

therm (θɜːm) *n Brit.* a unit of heat equal to 100 000 British thermal units. One therm is equal to $1.055\ 056 \times 10^8$ joules. ORIG C19: from Gk *thermē* heat

thermae ('θɜːmiː) *pl n* public baths or hot springs, esp. in ancient Greece or Rome. ORIG C17: from L, from Gk *thermai,* pl. of *thermē* heat

thermal ('θɜːməl) *adj* **1** Also: **thermic.** of, caused by, or generating heat. **2** hot or warm: *thermal baths.* **3** (of garments) specially made so as to have exceptional heat-retaining qualities: *thermal underwear.* ◆ *n* **4** a column of rising air caused by local unequal heating of the land surface, and used by gliders and birds to gain height. **5** (*pl*) thermal garments, esp. underclothes.
▸ '**thermally** *adv*

thermal barrier *n* an obstacle to flight at very high speeds as a result of the heating effect of air friction. Also called: **heat barrier.**

thermal conductivity *n* a measure of the ability of a substance to conduct heat.

thermal efficiency *n* the ratio of the work done by a heat engine to the energy supplied to it.

thermal equator *n* an imaginary line round the earth running through the point on each meridian with the highest average temperature.

thermal imaging *n* the technique of producing images of people or objects by using the infrared radiation that they emit or reflect.
▸ **thermal image** *n*

thermalize *or* **thermalise** ('θɜːməˌlaɪz) *vb* **thermalizes, thermalizing, thermalized** *or* **thermalises, thermalising, thermalised.** *Physics.* to undergo or cause to undergo a process in which neutrons lose energy in a moderator and become thermal neutrons.
▸ ˌ**thermali'zation** *or* ˌ**thermali'sation** *n*

thermal neutrons *pl n* slow neutrons that are approximately in thermal equilibrium with a moderator.

thermal reactor *n* a nuclear reactor in which most of the fission is caused by thermal neutrons.

thermal shock *n* a fluctuation in temperature causing stress in a material. It often results in fracture, esp. in brittle materials such as ceramics.

thermion ('θɜːmɪən) *n Physics*. an electron or ion emitted by a body at high temperature.

thermionic (ˌθɜːmɪ'ɒnɪk) *adj* of, relating to, or operated by electrons emitted from materials at high temperatures: *a thermionic valve*.

thermionic current *n* an electric current produced between two electrodes as a result of electrons emitted by thermionic emission.

thermionic emission *n* the emission of electrons from very hot solids or liquids.

thermionics (ˌθɜːmɪ'ɒnɪks) *n* (*functioning as sing*) the branch of electronics concerned with the emission of electrons by hot bodies and with devices based on this effect.

thermionic valve *or esp. US & Canad.* **tube** *n* an electronic valve in which electrons are emitted from a heated rather than a cold cathode.

thermistor (θɜː'mɪstə) *n* a semiconductor device having a resistance that decreases rapidly with an increase in temperature. It is used for temperature measurement and control. ORIG C20: from THERMO- + (RES)ISTOR

Thermit ('θɜːmɪt) *or* **Thermite** ('θɜːmaɪt) *n Trademark*. a mixture of aluminium powder and a metal oxide, which when ignited produces great heat: used for welding and in incendiary bombs.

thermo- *or before a vowel* **therm-** *combining form*. related to, caused by, or measuring heat: *thermodynamics; thermophile*. ORIG from Gk *thermos* hot, *thermē* heat

thermobarograph (ˌθɜːməʊ'bærəˌgrɑːf) *n* a device that simultaneously records the temperature and pressure of the atmosphere.

thermobarometer (ˌθɜːməʊbə'rɒmɪtə) *n* an apparatus that provides an accurate measurement of pressure by observation of the change in the boiling point of a fluid.

thermochemistry (ˌθɜːməʊ'kɛmɪstrɪ) *n* the branch of chemistry concerned with the study and measurement of the heat evolved or absorbed during chemical reactions.
▸ **ˌthermo'chemical** *adj* ▸ **ˌthermo'chemist** *n*

thermochromism (ˌθɜːməɔ'krəʊmɪzəm) *n* a phenomenon in which certain dyes made from liquid crystals change colour reversibly when their temperature is changed.
▸ **'thermoˌchromy** *n* ▸ **ˌthermo'chromic** *adj*

thermocline ('θɜːməʊˌklaɪn) *n* a temperature gradient in a thermally stratified body of water, such as a lake.

thermocouple ('θɜːməʊˌkʌpᵊl) *n* **1** a device for measuring temperature consisting of a pair of wires of different metals or semiconductors joined at both ends. One junction is at the temperature to be measured, the second at a fixed temperature. The electromotive force generated depends upon the temperature difference. **2** a similar device with only one junction between two dissimilar metals or semiconductors.

thermodynamic (ˌθɜːməʊdaɪ'næmɪk) *or* **thermodynamical** *adj* **1** of or concerned with thermodynamics. **2** determined by or obeying the laws of thermodynamics.

thermodynamic equilibrium *n* the condition of a system in which the quantities that specify its properties, such as pressure, temperature, etc., all remain unchanged.

thermodynamics (ˌθɜːməʊdaɪ'næmɪks) *n* (*functioning as sing*) the branch of physical science concerned with the interrelationship and interconversion of different forms of energy.

thermodynamic temperature *n* temperature defined in terms of the laws of thermodynamics rather than of the properties of a real material: expressed in kelvins.

thermoelectric (ˌθɜːməʊɪ'lɛktrɪk) *or* **thermoelectrical** *adj* **1** of, relating to, used in, or operated by the conversion of heat energy to electrical energy. **2** of, relating to, used in, or operated by the conversion of electrical energy.

thermoelectric effect *n* another name for the **Seebeck effect**.

thermoelectricity (ˌθɜːməʊɪlɛk'trɪsɪtɪ) *n* **1** electricity generated by a thermocouple. **2** the study of the relationship between heat and electrical energy.

thermoelectron (ˌθɜːməʊɪ'lɛktrɒn) *n* an electron emitted at high temperature, as in a thermionic valve.

thermogenesis (ˌθɜːməʊ'dʒɛnɪsɪs) *n* the production of heat by metabolic processes.
▸ **ˌthermo'genic** *adj*

thermogram ('θɜːməʊˌgræm) *n* **1** *Med.* a picture produced by thermography, using film sensitive to infrared radiation. **2** the record produced by a thermograph.

thermograph ('θɜːməʊˌgrɑːf, -ˌgræf) *n* a type of thermometer that produces a continuous record of a fluctuating temperature.

thermography (θɜː'mɒgrəfɪ) *n* **1** any writing, printing, or recording process involving the use of heat. **2** *Med.* the measurement and recording of heat produced by a part of the body: used in the diagnosis of tumours, esp. of the breast (**mammothermography**), which have increased blood supply and therefore generate more heat than normal tissue. See also **thermogram**.
▸ **ther'mographer** *n* ▸ **thermographic** (ˌθɜːməʊ'græfɪk) *adj*

thermojunction (ˌθɜːməʊ'dʒʌŋkʃən) *n* a point of electrical contact between two dissimilar metals across which a voltage appears, the magnitude of which depends on the temperature of the contact and the nature of the metals.

thermolabile (ˌθɜːməʊ'leɪbɪl) *adj* easily decomposed or subject to a loss of characteristic properties by the action of heat.

thermoluminescence (ˌθɜːməʊˌluːmɪ'nɛsəns) *n* phosphorescence of certain materials or objects as a result of heating.

thermolysis (θɜː'mɒlɪsɪs) *n* **1** *Physiol.* loss of heat from the body. **2** the dissociation of a substance as a result of heating.
▸ **thermolytic** (ˌθɜːməʊ'lɪtɪk) *adj*

thermomagnetic (ˌθɜːməʊmæg'nɛtɪk) *adj* of or concerned with the relationship between heat and magnetism, esp. the change in temperature of a body when it is magnetized or demagnetized.

thermometer (θə'mɒmɪtə) *n* an instrument used to measure temperature, esp. one in which a thin column of liquid, such as mercury, expands and contracts within a graduated sealed tube.
▸ **ther'mometry** *n*

thermonuclear (ˌθɜːməʊ'njuːklɪə) *adj* **1** involving nuclear fusion. **2** involving thermonuclear weapons.

thermonuclear reaction *n* a nuclear fusion reaction occurring at a very high temperature: responsible for the energy produced in the sun, nuclear weapons, and fusion reactors.

thermophile ('θɜːməʊˌfaɪl) *or* **thermophil** ('θɜːməʊˌfɪl) *n* **1** an organism, esp. a bacterium or plant, that thrives under warm conditions. ◆ *adj* **2** thriving under warm conditions.
▸ **ˌthermo'philic** *adj*

thermopile ('θɜːməʊˌpaɪl) *n* an instrument for detecting and measuring heat radiation or for generating a thermoelectric current. It consists of a number of thermocouple junctions.

thermoplastic (ˌθɜːməʊ'plæstɪk) *adj* **1** (of a material, esp. a synthetic plastic) becoming soft when heated and rehardening on cooling without appreciable change of properties. ◆ *n* **2** a synthetic plastic or resin, such as polystyrene, with these properties.

Thermopylae ★ (θɜː'mɒpɪˌliː) *n* (in ancient Greece) a narrow pass between the mountains and the sea linking Locris and Thessaly: scene of a famous battle (480 B.C.) in which an outnumbered Greek army delayed the advance of the Persians in their attempt to conquer Greece.

Thermos *or* **Thermos flask** ('θɜːməs) *n Trademark.* a type of stoppered vacuum flask used to preserve the temperature of its contents.

thermosetting (ˌθɜːməʊ'sɛtɪŋ) *adj* (of a material, esp. a synthetic plastic) hardening permanently after one application of heat and pressure.

thermosiphon (ˌθɜːməʊ'saɪfən) *n* a system in which a coolant is circulated by convection caused by a difference in density between the hot and cold portions of the liquid.

thermosphere ('θɜːməˌsfɪə) *n* an atmospheric layer lying between the mesosphere and the exosphere.

thermostable (ˌθɜːməʊ'steɪbᵊl) *adj* capable of withstanding moderate heat without loss of characteristic properties.

thermostat ('θɜːməˌstæt) *n* **1** a device that maintains a system at a constant temperature. **2** a device that sets off a sprinkler, etc., at a certain temperature.
▸ **ˌthermo'static** *adj* ▸ **ˌthermo'statically** *adv*

thermostatics (ˌθɜːmə'stætɪks) *n* (*functioning as sing*) the branch of science concerned with thermal equilibrium.

thermotaxis (ˌθɜːməʊ'tæksɪs) *n* the directional movement of an organism in response to the stimulus of heat.
▸ **ˌthermo'taxic** *adj*

thermotropism (ˌθɜːməʊ'trəʊpɪzəm) *n* the directional growth of a plant in response to the stimulus of heat.
▸ **ˌthermo'tropic** *adj*

-thermy *n combining form.* indicating heat: *diathermy.* ORIG from NL *-thermia,* from Gk *thermē*
▸ **-thermic** *or* **-thermal** *adj combining form.*

theroid ('θɪərɔɪd) *adj* of, relating to, or resembling a beast. ORIG C19: from Gk *thēroeidēs,* from *thēr* wild animal; see -OID

Theroux ★ (θə'ruː) *n* **Paul** (**Edward**). born 1941, US writer. His novels include *The Mosquito Coast* (1981) and *My Other Life* (1996); travel writings include *The Great Railway Bazaar* (1975).

Thersites ★ (θə'saɪtiːz) *n* the ugliest and most evil-tongued fighter on the Greek side in the Trojan War, killed by Achilles.

thesaurus (θɪ'sɔːrəs) *n, pl* **thesauruses** *or* **thesauri** (-raɪ). **1** a book containing systematized lists of synonyms and related words. **2** a dictionary of selected words or topics. **3** *Rare.* a treasury. ORIG C18: from L, Gk: TREASURE

these (ðiːz) *determiner* **a** the form of **this** used before a plural noun: *these men.* **b** (*as pronoun*): *I don't much care for these.*

Theseus ★ ('θiːsɪəs) *n Greek myth.* a hero of Attica, noted for slaying the Minotaur and conquering the Amazons.
▸ **Thesean** (θɪ'siːən) *adj*

Thesiger ★ ('θɛsɪdʒə) *n* **Wilfred** (**Patrick**). born 1910, British writer, whose books include *Arabian Sands* (1958) and *My Kenya Days* (1994).

thesis ('θiːsɪs) *n, pl* **theses** (-siːz). **1** a dissertation resulting from original research, esp. when submitted for a degree or diploma. **2** a doctrine maintained in argument. **3** a subject for a discussion or essay. **4** an unproved statement put forward as a premise in an argument. ORIG C16: via LL from Gk: a placing, from *tithenai* to place

Thespian ('θɛspɪən) *adj* **1** of or relating to Thespis. **2** (*usually not cap.*) of or relating to drama and the theatre; dramatic. ◆ *n* (*usually not cap.*) **3** *Often facetious.* an actor or actress.

Thespis ★ ('θɛspɪs) *n* 6th century B.C., Greek poet, regarded as the founder of tragic drama.

Thess. *Bible. abbrev. for* Thessalonians.

Thessalonian (ˌθɛsə'ləʊnɪən) *adj* **1** of or relating to ancient Thessalonica (modern Salonika). ◆ *n* **2** an inhabitant of ancient Thessalonica.

Thessaloníki ★ (*Greek* θɛsalɔ'niki) *n* a port in NE Greece, in central Macedonia at the head of the **Gulf of Salonika** (an inlet of the Aegean): capital of the Roman province of Macedonia; university (1926). Pop.: 377 951 (1991). Latin name: **Thessalonica** (ˌθɛsə'lɒnɪkə). English name: **Salonika** or **Salonica**.

Thessaly ★ ('θɛsəlɪ) *n* a region of E Central Greece, on the Aegean: an extensive fertile plain, edged with mountains. Pop.: 734 846 (1991). Area: 14 037 sq. km (5418 sq. miles). Modern Greek name: **Thessalía** (ˌθɛsa'lja).
▸ **Thessalian** (θɛ'seɪlɪən) *adj, n*

theta ('θiːtə) *n* the eighth letter of the Greek alphabet (Θ, θ). ORIG C17: from Gk

Thetford Mines ★ ('θɛtfəd) *n* a city in SE Canada, in S Quebec: asbestos industry. Pop.: 17 273 (1991).

Thetis ★ ('θiːtɪs) *n* one of the Nereids and mother of Achilles by Peleus.

theurgy ('θiːˌɜːdʒɪ) *n, pl* **theurgies. 1** the intervention of a divine or supernatural agency in the affairs of man. **2** beneficent magic as taught by Egyptian Neoplatonists. ORIG C16: from LL *theūrgia,* from LGk *theourgia* the practice of magic, from *theo-* THEO- + *-urgia,* from *ergon* work
▸ **the'urgic** *or* **the'urgical** *adj* ▸ **'theurgist** *n*

thew (θjuː) *n* **1** muscle, esp. if strong or well-developed. **2** (*pl*) muscular strength. ORIG OE *thēaw*
▸ **'thewless** *adj* ▸ **'thewy** *adj*

they (ðeɪ) *pron* (*subjective*) **1** refers to people or things other than the speaker or people addressed: *they fight among themselves.* **2** refers to people in general: *in Australia they have Christmas in the summer.* **3** refers to an indefinite antecedent such as *one, whoever,* or *anybody: if anyone objects, they can go.* ORIG C12 *thei* from ON *their,* masc. nominative pl, equivalent to OE *thā*

USAGE NOTE It was formerly considered correct to use *he, him,* or *his* after pronouns such as *everyone, no-one, anyone,* or *someone* as in *everyone did his best.* Nowadays it is probably more common to use *they, them,* or *their,* in order to avoid referring specifically to one gender, and this use has become acceptable in all but the most formal contexts: *everyone did their best.*

they'd (ðeɪd) *contraction of* they would *or* they had.

they'll (ðeɪl) *contraction of* they will *or* they shall.

they're (ðɛə, 'ðeɪə) *contraction of* they are.

they've (ðeɪv) *contraction of* they have.

thi- *combining form.* a variant of **thio-**.

thiamine ('θaɪəˌmiːn, -mɪn) *or* **thiamin** ('θaɪəmɪn) *n* a white crystalline vitamin that occurs in the outer coat of rice and other grains. It forms part of the vitamin B complex: deficiency leads to nervous disorders and to the disease beriberi. Also called: **vitamin B_1, aneurin.** ORIG C20: THIO- + (VIT)AMIN

thiazine ('θaɪəˌziːn, -ˌzaɪn) *n* any of a group of organic compounds containing a ring system composed of four carbon atoms, a sulphur atom, and a nitrogen atom.

thiazole ('θaɪəˌzəʊl) *n* **1** a colourless liquid that contains a ring system composed of three carbon atoms, a sulphur atom, and a nitrogen atom. **2** any of a group of compounds derived from this substance that are used in dyes.

thick (θɪk) *adj* **1** of relatively great extent from one surface to the other: *a thick slice of bread.* **2a** (*postpositive*) of specific fatness: *ten centimetres thick.* **2b** (*in combination*): *a six-inch-thick wall.* **3** having a dense consistency: *thick soup.* **4** abundantly covered or filled: *a piano thick with dust.* **5** impenetrable; dense: *a thick fog.* **6** stupid, slow, or insensitive. **7** throaty or badly articulated: *a voice thick with emotion.* **8** (of accents, etc.) pronounced. **9** *Inf.* very friendly (esp. in **thick as thieves**). **10 a bit thick.** *Brit.* unfair or excessive. ◆ *adv* **11** in order to produce something thick: *to slice bread thick.* **12** profusely; in quick succession (esp. in **thick and fast**). **13 lay it on thick.** *Inf.* **13a** to exaggerate a story, etc. **13b** to flatter excessively. ◆ *n* **14** a thick piece or part. **15 the thick.** the busiest or most intense part. **16 through thick and thin.** in good times and bad. ORIG OE *thicce*
▸ **'thickish** *adj* ▸ **'thickly** *adv*

thicken ('θɪkən) *vb* **1** to make or become thick or thicker. **2** (*intr*) to become more involved: *the plot thickened.*
▸ **'thickener** *n*

★ people and places

thickening ('θɪkənɪŋ) *n* **1** something added to a liquid to thicken it. **2** a thickened part or piece.

thicket ('θɪkɪt) *n* a dense growth of small trees, shrubs, and similar plants. ORIG OE *thiccet*

thickhead ('θɪk,hɛd) *n* **1** a stupid or ignorant person; fool. **2** any of a family of Australian and SE Asian songbirds.
▸ ,**thick'headed** *adj*

thickie *or* **thicky** ('θɪkɪ) *n, pl* **thickies.** *Brit. sl.* a variant of **thicko.**

thick-knee *n* another name for **stone curlew.**

thickness ('θɪknɪs) *n* **1** the state or quality of being thick. **2** the dimension through an object, as opposed to length or width. **3** a layer.

thicko ('θɪkəʊ) *n, pl* **thickos** *or* **thickoes.** *Brit. sl.* a slow-witted unintelligent person. Also: **thickie, thicky.**

thickset (,θɪk'sɛt) *adj* **1** stocky in build; sturdy. **2** densely planted or placed. ◆ *n* **3** a rare word for **thicket.**

thick-skinned *adj* insensitive to criticism or hints; not easily upset or affected.

thick-witted *or* **thick-skulled** *adj* stupid, dull, or slow to learn.
▸ ,**thick-'wittedly** *adv* ▸ ,**thick-'wittedness** *n*

thief (θi:f) *n, pl* **thieves** (θi:vz). a person who steals something from another. ORIG OE *thēof*
▸ '**thievish** *adj*

Thiers ★ (*French* tjɛr) *n* **Louis Adolphe** (lwi adɔlf). 1797–1877, French statesman, who became first president of the Third Republic (1871–73).

thieve (θi:v) *vb* **thieves, thieving, thieved.** to steal (someone's possessions). ORIG OE *thēofian,* from *thēof* thief
▸ '**thievery** *n* ▸ '**thieving** *adj*

thigh (θaɪ) *n* **1** the part of the leg between the hip and the knee in man. **2** the corresponding part in other vertebrates and insects. ◆ Related adj: **femoral.** ORIG OE *thēh*

thighbone ('θaɪ,bəʊn) *n* a nontechnical name for the **femur.**

thimble ('θɪmbᵊl) *n* **1** a cap of metal, plastic, etc., used to protect the end of the finger when sewing. **2** any small metal cap resembling this. **3** *Naut.* a loop of metal having a groove at its outer edge for a rope or cable. ORIG OE *thȳmel* thumbstall, from *thūma* thumb

thimbleful ('θɪmbᵊl,fʊl) *n* a very small amount, esp. of a liquid.

thimblerig ('θɪmbᵊl,rɪg) *n* a game in which the operator rapidly moves about three inverted thimbles, often with sleight of hand, one of which conceals a token, the other player betting on which thimble the token is under. ORIG C19: from THIMBLE + RIG (in obs. sense meaning a trick, scheme)
▸ '**thimble,rigger** *n*

Thimbu ('θɪmbu:) *or* **Thimphu** ★ ('θɪmfu:) *n* the capital of Bhutan, in the west in the foothills of the E Himalayas: became the official capital in 1962. Pop.: 30 340 (1993 est.).

thin (θɪn) *adj* **thinner, thinnest. 1** of relatively small extent from one side or surface to the other. **2** slim or lean. **3** sparsely placed; meagre: *thin hair.* **4** of low density: *a thin liquid.* **5** weak; poor: *a thin disguise.* **6 thin on the ground.** few in number; scarce. ◆ *adv* **7** in order to produce something thin: *to cut bread thin.* ◆ *vb* **thins, thinning, thinned. 8** to make or become thin or sparse. ORIG OE *thynne*
▸ '**thinly** *adv* ▸ '**thinness** *n*

thine (ðaɪn) *determiner Arch.* **a** (*preceding a vowel*) of or associated with you (thou): *thine eyes.* **b** (*as pronoun*): *thine is the greatest burden.* ORIG OE *thīn*

thin-film *adj* (of an electronic component, etc.) composed of one or more extremely thin layers of metal, semiconductor, etc.

thing (θɪŋ) *n* **1** an object, fact, affair, circumstance, or concept considered as being a separate entity. **2** any inanimate object. **3** an object or entity that cannot or need not be precisely named. **4** *Inf.* a person or animal: *you poor thing.* **5** an event or act. **6** a thought or statement. **7** *Law.* property. **8** a device, means, or instrument. **9** (*often pl*) a possession, article of clothing, etc. **10** *Inf.* a preoccupation or obsession (esp. in **have a thing about**). **11** an activity or mode of behaviour satisfying to one's personality (esp. in **do one's (own) thing**). **12 make a thing of.** exaggerate the importance of. **13 the thing.** the latest fashion. ORIG OE *thing* assembly

thing-in-itself *n* (in the philosophy of Immanuel Kant) reality regarded apart from human knowledge and perception.

thingumabob *or* **thingamabob** ('θɪŋəmə,bɒb) *n Inf.* a person or thing the name of which is unknown, temporarily forgotten, or deliberately overlooked. Also: **thingumajig, thingamajig,** *or* **thingummy.** ORIG C18: from THING, with humorous suffix

think (θɪŋk) *vb* **thinks, thinking, thought. 1** (*tr; may take a clause as object*) to consider, judge, or believe: *he thinks my ideas impractical.* **2** (*intr;* often foll. by *about*) to exercise the mind as in order to make a decision; ponder. **3** (*intr*) to be capable of conscious thought: *man is the only animal that thinks.* **4** to remember; recollect. **5** (*intr;* foll. by *of*) to make the mental choice (of): *think of a number.* **6** (*may take a clause as object or an infinitive*) **6a** to expect; suppose. **6b** to be considerate enough (to do something): *he did not think to thank them.* **7** (*intr*) to focus the attention on being: *think big.* **8 think twice.** to consider carefully before deciding. ◆ *n* **9** *Inf.* a careful, open-minded assessment. **10** (*modifier*) *Inf.* characterized by or involving thinkers, thinking, or thought. ◆ See also **think over, think up.** ORIG OE *thencan*
▸ '**thinkable** *adj* ▸ '**thinker** *n*

thinking ('θɪŋkɪŋ) *n* **1** opinion or judgment. **2** the process of thought. ◆ *adj* **3** (*prenominal*) using or capable of using intelligent thought: *thinking people.* **4 put on one's thinking cap.** to ponder a matter or problem.

think over *vb* (*tr, adv*) to ponder or consider.

think-tank *n Inf.* a group of specialists commissioned to undertake intensive study and research into specified problems.

think up *vb* (*tr, adv*) to invent or devise.

thinner ('θɪnə) *n* (*often pl, functioning as sing*) a solvent, such as turpentine, added to paint or varnish to dilute it, reduce its opacity or viscosity, or increase its penetration.

thin-skinned *adj* sensitive to criticism or hints; easily upset or affected.

thio- *or before a vowel* **thi-** *combining form.* sulphur, esp. denoting the replacement of an oxygen atom with a sulphur atom: *thiol; thiosulphate.* ORIG from Gk *theion* sulphur

thiol ('θaɪɒl) *n* any of a class of sulphur-containing organic compounds with the formula RSH, where R is an organic group.

thionine ('θaɪəʊ,ni:n, -,naɪn) *or* **thionin** ('θaɪənɪn) *n* **1** a crystalline derivative of thiazine used as a violet dye to stain microscope specimens. **2** any of a class of related dyes. ORIG C19: by shortening, from *ergothioneine*

thiopentone sodium (,θaɪəʊ'pɛntəʊn) *or* **thiopental sodium** (,θaɪəʊ'pɛntæl) *n* a barbiturate drug used as an intravenous general anaesthetic. Also called: **Sodium Pentothal.**

thiophen ('θaɪəʊ,fɛn) *or* **thiophene** ('θaɪəʊ,fi:n) *n* a colourless liquid heterocyclic compound found in the benzene fraction of coal tar and manufactured from butane and sulphur.

thiosulphate (,θaɪəʊ'sʌlfeɪt) *n* any salt of thiosulphuric acid.

thiosulphuric acid (,θaɪəʊsʌl'fjʊərɪk) *n* an unstable acid known only in solutions and in the form of its salts. Formula: $H_2S_2O_3$.

thiouracil (,θaɪəʊ'jʊərəsɪl) *n* a white crystalline water-insoluble substance with an intensely bitter taste, used in medicine to treat hyperthyroidism. ORIG from THIO- + *uracil* (URO- + AC(ETIC) + -IL(E))

thiourea (,θaɪəʊ'jʊərɪə) *n* a white crystalline substance used in photographic fixing, rubber vulcanization, and the manufacture of synthetic resins.

third (θɜ:d) *adj* (*usually prenominal*) **1a** coming after the second in numbering, position, etc.; being the ordinal

number of *three:* often written 3rd. **1b** (*as n*): *the third got a prize.* **2** rated, graded, or ranked below the second level. **3** denoting the third from lowest forward ratio of a gearbox in a motor vehicle. ◆ *n* **4a** one of three equal parts of an object, quantity, etc. **4b** (*as modifier*): *a third part.* **5** the fraction equal to one divided by three (1/3). **6** the forward ratio above second of a gearbox in a motor vehicle. **7a** the interval between one note and another three notes away from it counting inclusively along the diatonic scale. **7b** one of two notes constituting such an interval in relation to the other. **8** *Brit.* an honours degree of the third and usually the lowest class. Full term: **third class honours degree.** ◆ *adv* **9** Also: **thirdly.** in the third place. ORIG OE *thirda,* var. of *thridda;* rel. to OFrisian *thredda,* OSaxon *thriddio*
▸ **'thirdly** *adv*

Third Age *n* **the.** old age, esp. when viewed as a period of opportunity for learning something new or for other new developments: *University of the Third Age.*

third class *n* **1** the class or grade next in value, quality, etc., to the second. ◆ *adj* (**third-class** *when prenominal*). **2** of the class or grade next in value, quality, etc., to the second. ◆ *adv* **3** by third-class transport, etc.

third degree *n Inf.* torture or bullying, esp. used to extort confessions or information.

third-degree burn *n Pathol.* the most severe type of burn, involving the destruction of both epidermis and dermis.

third dimension *n* the dimension of depth by which a solid object may be distinguished from a two-dimensional drawing or picture of it.

third eyelid *n* another name for **nictitating membrane.**

Third International *n* another name for **Comintern.**

third-line forcing *n* the deprecated practice of forcing a buyer to purchase a supply of a product that he does not want as a condition of supplying him with the product he does want.

third man *n Cricket.* **a** a fielding position on the off side near the boundary behind the batsman's wicket. **b** a fielder in this position.

Third Market *n Stock Exchange.* a new small market designed to meet the needs of young growing British companies for raising capital.

Third Order *n RC Church.* a religious society of laymen affiliated to one of the religious orders and following a mitigated form of religious rule.

third party *n* **1** a person who is involved by chance or only incidentally in a legal proceeding, agreement, or other transaction. ◆ *adj* **2** *Insurance.* providing protection against liability caused by accidental injury or death of other persons.

third person *n* a grammatical category of pronouns and verbs used when referring to objects or individuals other than the speaker or his addressee or addressees.

third-rate *adj* mediocre or inferior.

third reading *n* (in a legislative assembly) **1** *Brit.* the process of discussing the committee's report on a bill. **2** *US.* the final consideration of a bill.

Third Way *n* **a** a political ideology that seeks to combine egalitarian and individualist policies, and elements of socialism and capitalism. **b** (*as modifier*): *Third-Way government.*

Third World *n* the less economically and industrially advanced countries of Africa, Asia, and Latin America collectively. Also called: **developing world.**

Thirlmere ★ ('θɜːlmɪə) *n* a lake in NW England, in Cumbria in the Lake District: provides part of Manchester's water supply. Length: 6 km (4 miles).

thirst (θɜːst) *n* **1** a craving to drink, accompanied by a feeling of dryness in the mouth and throat. **2** an eager longing, craving, or yearning. ◆ *vb* (*intr*) **3** to feel a thirst. ORIG OE *thyrstan, from thurst*

thirsty ('θɜːstɪ) *adj* **thirstier, thirstiest. 1** feeling a desire to drink. **2** dry; arid. **3** (foll. by *for*) feeling an eager desire. **4** causing thirst.
▸ **'thirstily** *adv* ▸ **'thirstiness** *n*

thirteen ('θɜː'tiːn) *n* **1** the cardinal number that is the sum of ten and three and is a prime number. **2** a numeral, 13, XIII, etc., representing this number. **3** something representing or consisting of 13 units. ◆ *determiner* **4a** amounting to thirteen. **4b** (*as pronoun*): *thirteen of them fell.* ORIG OE *threotēne*
▸ **'thir'teenth** *adj, n*

thirteenth chord *n* a chord much used in jazz and pop, consisting of a major or minor triad upon which are superimposed the seventh, ninth, eleventh, and thirteenth above the root. Often shortened to **thirteenth.**

thirty ('θɜːtɪ) *n, pl* **thirties. 1** the cardinal number that is the product of ten and three. **2** a numeral, 30, XXX, etc., representing this number. **3** (*pl*) the numbers 30-39, esp. the 30th to the 39th year of a person's life or of a century. **4** the amount or quantity that is three times as big as ten. **5** something representing or consisting of 30 units. ◆ *determiner* **6a** amounting to thirty. **6b** (*as pronoun*): *thirty are broken.* ORIG OE *thrītig*
▸ **'thirtieth** *adj, n*

Thirty-nine Articles *pl n* a set of formulas defining the doctrinal position of the Church of England, drawn up in the 16th century.

thirty-second note *n* the usual US and Canad. name for **demisemiquaver.**

thirty-twomo (ˌθɜːtɪ'tuːməʊ) *n, pl* **thirty-twomos.** a book size resulting from folding a sheet of paper into 32 leaves or 64 pages.

this (ðɪs) *determiner* (*used before a sing n*) **1a** used preceding a noun referring to something or someone that is closer: *look at this picture.* **1b** (*as pronoun*): *take this.* **2a** used preceding a noun that has just been mentioned or is understood: *this plan of yours won't work.* **2b** (*as pronoun*): *I first saw this on Sunday.* **3a** used to refer to something about to be said, read, etc.: *consider this argument.* **3b** (*as pronoun*): *listen to this.* **4a** the present or immediate: *this time you'll know better.* **4b** (*as pronoun*): *before this, I was mistaken.* **5** *Inf.* an emphatic form of **a** or **the**[1]: *I saw this big brown bear.* **6 this and that.** various unspecified and trivial actions, matters, objects, etc. **7 with** (*or* **at**) **this.** after this. ◆ *adv* **8** used with adjectives and adverbs to specify a precise degree that is about to be mentioned: *go just this fast and you'll be safe.* ORIG OE *thēs, thēos, this* (masc, fem, neuter sing)

Thisbe ★ ('θɪzbɪ) *n* See **Pyramus and Thisbe.**

thistle ('θɪsᵊl) *n* **1** any of a genus of plants of the composite family, having prickly-edged leaves, dense flower heads, and feathery hairs on the seeds: the national emblem of Scotland. **2** any of various similar or related plants. ORIG OE *thīstel*
▸ **'thistly** *adj*

thistledown ('θɪsᵊlˌdaʊn) *n* the mass of feathery plumed seeds produced by a thistle.

thither ('ðɪðə) *or* **thitherward** *adv Obs. or formal.* to or towards that place; in that direction. ORIG OE *thider,* var. of *thæder,* infl. by *hider* hither

thitherto (ˌðɪðə'tuː, 'ðɪðəˌtuː) *adv Obs. or formal.* until that time.

thixotropic (ˌθɪksə'trɒpɪk) *adj* (of fluids and gels) having a reduced viscosity when stress is applied, as when stirred: *thixotropic paints.* ORIG C20: from Gk *thixis* the act of touching + -TROPIC
▸ **thixotropy** (θɪk'sɒtrəpɪ) *n* ▸ **thixotrope** ('θɪksəˌtrəʊp) *n*

tho' *or* **tho** (ðəʊ) *conj, adv US or poetic.* a variant spelling of **though.**

thole[1] (θəʊl) *or* **tholepin** ('θəʊlˌpɪn) *n* a wooden pin or one of a pair, set upright in the gunwales of a rowing boat to serve as a fulcrum in rowing. ORIG OE *tholl*

thole[2] (θəʊl) *vb* **tholes, tholing, tholed. 1** (*tr*) *Scot. & N English dialect.* to put up with; bear. **2** an archaic word for **suffer.** ORIG OE *tholian*

tholos ('θəʊlɒs) *n, pl* **tholoi** (-lɔɪ). a dry-stone beehive-shaped tomb associated with the Mycenaean culture of Greece from the 16th to the 12th centuries B.C. ORIG C17: from Gk

Thomas ★ ('tɒməs) *n* **1 Saint.** Also called: **doubting Thomas.** one of the twelve apostles, who refused to believe in Christ's resurrection until he had seen his wounds (John 20:24–29). Feast day: July 3 or Dec. 21 or Oct. 6. **2** (*French* tɔma). **Ambroise** (ɑ̃brwaz). 1811–96, French composer of light operas, including *Mignon* (1866). **3 Dylan** (**Marlais**) ('dɪlən). 1914–53, Welsh poet, whose works include the play *Under Milk Wood* (1954). **4** (**Philip**) **Edward**, pen name *Edward Eastaway*. 1878–1917, British poet; killed in World War I.

Thomas à Kempis ★ *n* See (Thomas à) **Kempis.**

Thomas Becket ★ *n* **Saint.** See (Saint Thomas) **Becket.**

Thomas of Woodstock ★ *n* 1355–97, youngest son of Edward III, who led opposition to his nephew Richard II (1386–89); died in prison.

Thomism ('təʊmɪzəm) *n* the system of philosophy and theology developed by Saint Thomas Aquinas in the 13th century.

Thompson ★ ('tɒmpsən, 'tɒmsən) *n* **1 Benjamin,** Count Rumford. 1753–1814, Anglo-American physicist, noted for his work on heat. **2 Daley.** born 1958, British athlete: Olympic decathlon champion (1980, 1984). **3 Emma.** born 1959, British actress: her films include *Howards End* (1991) and *The Winter Guest* (1997). **4 Francis.** 1859–1907, British poet, noted for his poem *The Hound of Heaven* (1893).

Thompson sub-machine-gun *n Trademark.* a .45 calibre sub-machine-gun. ORIG C20: after John T. *Thompson* (1860–1940), US Army officer, its co-inventor

Thomson ★ ('tɒmsən) *n* **1** Sir **George Paget,** son of Joseph John Thomson. 1892–1975, British physicist, who discovered (1927) electron diffraction: shared the Nobel prize for physics (1937). **2** Sir **Joseph John.** 1856–1940, British physicist, who discovered the electron (1897): Nobel prize for physics 1906. **3 Roy,** 1st Baron Thomson of Fleet. 1894–1976, British newspaper proprietor, born in Canada. **4 Virgil.** 1896–1989, US composer. His works include two operas, a cello concerto, and film music. **5** Sir **William.** See (1st Baron) **Kelvin.**

-thon *suffix forming nouns.* indicating a large-scale event or operation of a specified kind: *telethon.* ORIG C20: on the pattern of MARATHON

Thonburi ★ (ˌtɒnbʊ'riː) *n* a city in central Thailand, part of Bangkok Metropolis on the Chao Phraya River; the national capital (1767–82).

thong (θɒŋ) *n* **1** a thin strip of leather or other material. **2** a whip or whiplash, esp. one made of leather. **3** *US, Canad., & Austral.* the usual name for **flip-flop** (sense 5). ORIG OE *thwang*

Thor ★ (θɔː) *n Norse myth.* the god of thunder, depicted as wielding a hammer, emblematic of the thunderbolt. ORIG OE *Thōr,* from ON *thōrr* THUNDER

thoracic (θɔː'ræsɪk) *adj* of, near, or relating to the thorax.

thoracic duct *n* the major duct of the lymphatic system, beginning below the diaphragm and ascending in front of the spinal column to the base of the neck.

thoraco- *or before a vowel* **thorac-** *combining form.* thorax: *thoracotomy.*

thoracoplasty ('θɔːrəkəʊˌplæstɪ) *n, pl* **thoracoplasties. 1** plastic surgery of the thorax. **2** surgical removal of several ribs or a part of them to permit the collapse of a diseased lung.

thorax ('θɔːræks) *n, pl* **thoraxes** *or* **thoraces** ('θɔːrəˌsiːz, θɔː'reɪsiːz). **1** the part of the human body enclosed by the ribs. **2** the corresponding part in other vertebrates. **3** the part of an insect's body between the head and abdomen. ORIG C16: via L from Gk *thōrax* breastplate, chest

Thoreau ★ ('θɔːrəʊ, θɔː'rəʊ) *n* **Henry David.** 1817–62, US writer, noted esp. for *Walden, or Life in the Woods* (1854) and *Civil Disobedience* (1849).

thorium ('θɔːrɪəm) *n* a silvery-white radioactive metallic element. It is used in electronic equipment and as a nuclear power source. Symbol: Th; atomic no.: 90; atomic wt.: 232.04. ORIG C19: NL, THOR + -IUM
▸ **'thoric** *adj*

thorium dioxide *n* a white powder used in incandescent mantles. Also called: **thoria.**

thorium series *n* a radioactive series that starts with thorium-232 and ends with lead-208.

thorn (θɔːn) *n* **1** a sharp pointed woody extension of a stem or leaf. Cf. **prickle** (sense 1). **2** any of various trees or shrubs having thorns, esp. the hawthorn. **3** a Germanic character of runic origin (þ) used in Icelandic to represent the sound of *th,* as in *thin, bath.* **4** this same character as used in Old and Middle English to represent this sound. **5** a source of irritation (esp. in **a thorn in one's side** *or* **flesh**). ORIG OE
▸ **'thornless** *adj*

Thorn ★ (*German* tɔrn) *n* the German name for **Toruń.**

thorn apple *n* **1** a poisonous plant of the N hemisphere, having white funnel-shaped flowers and spiny fruits. US name: **jimson weed. 2** the fruit of certain types of hawthorn.

thornbill ('θɔːnˌbɪl) *n* **1** any of various South American hummingbirds having a thornlike bill. **2** Also called: **thornbill warbler.** any of various Australasian wrens. **3** any of various other birds with thornlike bills.

Thorndike ★ ('θɔːnˌdaɪk) *n* **1 Edward Lee.** 1874–1949, US psychologist. **2** Dame **Sybil.** 1882–1976, British actress.

thorny ('θɔːnɪ) *adj* **thornier, thorniest. 1** bearing or covered with thorns. **2** difficult or unpleasant. **3** sharp.
▸ **'thornily** *adv* ▸ **'thorniness** *n*

thoron ('θɔːrɒn) *n* a radioisotope of radon that is a decay product of thorium. Symbol: Tn or ^{220}Rn; atomic no.: 86; half-life: 54.5s. ORIG C20: from THORIUM + -ON

thorough ('θʌrə) *adj* **1** carried out completely and carefully. **2** (*prenominal*) utter: *a thorough bore.* **3** painstakingly careful. ORIG OE *thurh*
▸ **'thoroughly** *adv* ▸ **'thoroughness** *n*

thorough bass (beɪs) *n* a bass part underlying a piece of concerted music. Also called: **basso continuo, continuo.** See also **figured bass.**

thoroughbred ('θʌrəˌbrɛd) *adj* **1** purebred. ◆ *n* **2** a pedigree animal; purebred. **3** a person regarded as being of good breeding.

Thoroughbred ('θʌrəˌbrɛd) *n* a British breed of horse the ancestry of which can be traced to English mares and Arab sires.

thoroughfare ('θʌrəˌfɛə) *n* **1** a road from one place to another, esp. a main road. **2** way through, access, or passage: *no thoroughfare.*

thoroughgoing ('θʌrəˌgəʊɪŋ) *adj* **1** extremely thorough. **2** (*usually prenominal*) absolute; complete: *thoroughgoing incompetence.*

thoroughpaced ('θʌrəˌpeɪst) *adj* **1** (of a horse) showing performing ability in all paces. **2** thoroughgoing.

thorp *or* **thorpe** (θɔːp) *n Obs. except in place names.* a small village. ORIG OE

Thorpe ★ (θɔːp) *n* **Jeremy.** born 1929, British politician; leader of the Liberal party (1967–76).

Thorshavn ★ (*Danish* 'tɔːrshaun) *n* the capital of the Faeroe Islands, a port on the northernmost island. Pop.: 15 272 (1996 est.).

Thorvaldsen *or* **Thorwaldsen** ★ (*Danish* 'tɔrvalsən) *n* **Bertel** ('bertəl). 1770–1884, Danish neoclassical sculptor.

those (ðəʊz) *determiner* the form of **that** used before a plural noun. ORIG OE *thās,* pl. of THIS

Thoth ★ (θəʊθ, təʊt) *n* (in Egyptian mythology) a moon deity, scribe of the gods and protector of learning and the arts.

thou[1] (ðaʊ) *pron* (*subjective*) **1** *Arch. or dialect.* refers to the person addressed: used mainly in familiar address. **2** (*usually cap.*) refers to God when addressed in prayer, etc. ORIG OE *thū*

thou[2] (θaʊ) *n, pl* **thous** *or* **thou. 1** one thousandth of an inch. **2** *Inf.* short for **thousand.**

though (ðəʊ) *conj* (*subordinating*) **1** (sometimes preceded by *even*) despite the fact that: *though he tries hard, he always fails.* ◆ *adv* **2** nevertheless; however: *he can't dance; he sings well, though.* ORIG OE *theah*

thought (θɔːt) *vb* **1** the past tense and past participle of **think.** ◆ *n* **2** the act or process of thinking. **3** a concept, opinion, or idea. **4** ideas typical of a particular time or place: *German thought in the 19th century.* **5** application of mental attention; consideration. **6** purpose or intention: *I have no thought of giving up.* **7** expectation: *no thought of reward.* **8** a small amount; trifle: *you could be a thought more enthusiastic.* **9** kindness or regard. ORIG OE *thōht*

thoughtful (ˈθɔːtfʊl) *adj* **1** considerate in the treatment of other people. **2** showing careful thought. **3** pensive; reflective.
▸ **ˈthoughtfully** *adv* ▸ **ˈthoughtfulness** *n*

thoughtless (ˈθɔːtlɪs) *adj* **1** inconsiderate. **2** having or showing lack of thought.
▸ **ˈthoughtlessly** *adv* ▸ **ˈthoughtlessness** *n*

thought-out *adj* conceived and developed by careful thought: *a well thought-out scheme.*

thought transference *n Psychol.* another name for **telepathy.**

thousand (ˈθaʊzənd) *n* **1** the cardinal number that is the product of 10 and 100. **2** a numeral, 1000, 10^3, M, etc., representing this number. **3** (*often pl*) a very large but unspecified number, amount, or quantity. **4** something representing or consisting of 1000 units. ◆ *determiner* **5a** amounting to a thousand. **5b** (*as pronoun*): *a thousand is hardly enough.* ◆ Related adj: **millenary.** ORIG OE *thūsend*
▸ **ˈthousandth** *adj, n*

Thousand Guineas *n* (*functioning as sing*), usually written **1,000 Guineas.** an annual horse race, restricted to fillies, run at Newmarket in England since 1814.

Thousand Island dressing *n* a salad dressing made from mayonnaise with ketchup, chopped gherkins, etc.

Thousand Islands ★ *pl n* a group of about 1500 islands on the border between the US and Canada, in the upper St Lawrence River: administratively divided between the US and Canada.
▸ **Thousand Island** *adj*

Thrace ★ (θreɪs) *n* **1** an ancient country in the E Balkan Peninsula: successively under the Persians, Macedonians, and Romans. **2** a region of SE Europe, corresponding to the S part of the ancient country: divided by the Maritsa River into **Western Thrace** (Greece) and **Eastern Thrace** (Turkey).

Thracian (ˈθreɪʃɪən) *n* **1** a member of an ancient Indo-European people who lived in Thrace. **2** the ancient language spoken by this people. ◆ *adj* **3** of or relating to Thrace, its inhabitants, or the extinct Thracian language.

thrall (θrɔːl) *n* **1** Also: **thraldom** *or US* **thralldom** (ˈθrɔːldəm). the state or condition of being in the power of another person. **2** a person who is in such a state. **3** a person totally subject to some need, desire, appetite, etc. ◆ *vb* **4** (*tr*) to enslave or dominate. ORIG OE *thrǣl* slave

thrash (θræʃ) *vb* **1** (*tr*) to beat soundly, as with a whip or stick. **2** (*tr*) to defeat totally; overwhelm. **3** (*intr*) to beat or plunge about in a wild manner. **4** to sail (a boat) against the wind or tide or (of a boat) to sail in this way. **5** another word for **thresh.** ◆ *n* **6** the act of thrashing; beating. **7** *Inf.* a party. ◆ See also **thrash out.** ORIG OE *threscan*

thrasher[1] (ˈθræʃə) *n* another name for **thresher** (the shark).

thrasher[2] (ˈθræʃə) *n* any of various brown thrushlike American songbirds.

thrashing (ˈθræʃɪŋ) *n* a physical assault; flogging.

thrash metal *n* a type of very fast very loud rock music that combines elements of heavy metal and punk rock. Often shortened to **thrash.**

thrash out *vb* (*tr, adv*) to discuss fully or vehemently, esp. in order to come to an agreement.

thrasonical (θrəˈsɒnɪkəl) *adj Rare.* bragging; boastful. ORIG C16: from L *Thrasō* name of boastful soldier in *Eunuchus,* a play by Terence, from Gk *Thrasōn,* from *thrasus* forceful
▸ **thraˈsonically** *adv*

thrawn (θrɔːn) *adj Scot. & N English dialect.* **1** crooked or twisted. **2** stubborn; perverse. ORIG N English dialect, var. of *thrown,* from OE *thrāwan* to twist about, throw

thread (θrɛd) *n* **1** a fine strand, filament, or fibre of some material. **2** a fine cord of twisted filaments, esp. of cotton, used in sewing, etc. **3** any of the filaments of which a spider's web is made. **4** any fine line, stream, mark, or piece. **5** the helical ridge on a screw, bolt, nut, etc. **6** a very thin seam of coal or vein of ore. **7** something acting as the continuous link or theme of a whole: *the thread of the story.* **8** the course of an individual's life believed in Greek mythology to be spun, measured, and cut by the Fates. ◆ *vb* **9** (*tr*) to pass (thread, film, tape, etc.) through (something). **10** (*tr*) to string on a thread: *she threaded the beads.* **11** to make (one's way) through or over (something). **12** (*tr*) to produce a screw thread. **13** (*tr*) to pervade: *hysteria threaded his account.* **14** (*intr*) (of boiling syrup) to form a fine thread when poured from a spoon. ◆ See also **threads.** ORIG OE *thrǣd*
▸ **ˈthreader** *n* ▸ **ˈthreadˌlike** *adj*

threadbare (ˈθrɛdˌbɛə) *adj* **1** (of cloth, clothing, etc.) having the nap worn off so that the threads are exposed; worn out. **2** meagre or poor. **3** hackneyed: *a threadbare argument.* **4** wearing threadbare clothes; shabby.

thread mark *n* a mark put into paper money to prevent counterfeiting, consisting of a pattern of silk fibres.

Threadneedle Street ★ (ˌθrɛdˈniːdəl, ˈθrɛdˌniːdəl) *n* a street in the City of London famous for its banks, including the Bank of England, known as **The Old Lady of Threadneedle Street.**

threads (θrɛdz) *pl n Sl.* clothes.

threadworm (ˈθrɛdˌwɜːm) *n* any of various nematodes, esp. the pinworm.

thready (ˈθrɛdɪ) *adj* **threadier, threadiest. 1** of or resembling a thread. **2** (of the pulse) barely perceptible; weak. **3** sounding thin, weak, or reedy.
▸ **ˈthreadiness** *n*

threat (θrɛt) *n* **1** a declaration of the intention to inflict harm, pain, or misery. **2** an indication of imminent harm, danger, or pain. **3** a person or thing that is regarded as dangerous or likely to inflict pain or misery. ORIG OE

threaten (ˈθrɛtən) *vb* **1** (*tr*) to be a threat to. **2** to be a menacing indication of (something); portend. **3** (when *tr, may take a clause as object*) to express a threat to (a person or people).
▸ **ˈthreatening** *adj* ▸ **ˈthreateningly** *adv*

three (θriː) *n* **1** the cardinal number that is the sum of two and one and is a prime number. **2** a numeral, 3, III, (iii), representing this number. **3** something representing or consisting of three units. **4** Also called: **three o'clock.** three hours after noon or midnight. ◆ *determiner* **5a** amounting to three. **5b** (*as pronoun*): *three were killed.* ◆ Related adjs.: **ternary, tertiary, treble, triple.** ORIG OE *thrēo*

three-card trick *n* a game in which players bet on which of three playing cards is the queen.

three-colour *adj* of or comprising a colour print or a photomechanical process in which a picture is reproduced by superimposing three prints from half-tone plates in inks corresponding to the three primary colours.

three-D *or* **3-D** *n* a three-dimensional effect.

three-decker *n* **1a** anything having three levels or layers. **1b** (*as modifier*): *a three-decker sandwich.* **2** a warship with guns on three decks.

three-dimensional *adj* **1** of, having, or relating to three dimensions. **2** simulating the effect of depth. **3** having volume. **4** lifelike.

threefold (ˈθriːˌfəʊld) *adj* **1** equal to or having three times as many or as much; triple. **2** composed of three parts. ◆ *adv* **3** by or up to three times as many or as much.

three-legged race *n* a race in which pairs of competitors run with their adjacent legs tied together.

threepenny bit *or* **thrupenny bit** (ˈθrʌpnɪ, -ənɪ, ˈθrɛp-) *n* a twelve-sided British coin valued at three old pence, obsolete since 1971.

three-phase *adj* (of an electrical circuit, etc.) having or using three alternating voltages of the same frequency, displaced in phase by 120°.

three-ply *adj* **1** having three layers or thicknesses. **2** (of wool, etc.) three-stranded.

three-point landing *n* an aircraft landing in which

the main wheels and the nose or tail wheel touch the ground simultaneously.

three-point turn *n* a complete turn of a motor vehicle using forward and reverse gears alternately, and completed after only three movements.

three-quarter *adj* **1** being three quarters of something. **2** being of three quarters the normal length. ◆ *n* **3** *Rugby.* any of the four players between the fullback and the halfbacks.

three-ring circus *n US.* **1** a circus with three rings for simultaneous performances. **2** a situation of confusion, characterized by a bewildering variety of events or activities.

Three Rivers ★ *n* the English name for **Trois Rivières.**

three Rs *pl n* **the.** the three skills regarded as the fundamentals of education; reading, writing, and arithmetic. ORIG from the humorous spelling *reading, 'riting,* and *'rithmetic*

threescore ('θriːˈskɔː) *determiner* an archaic word for **sixty.**

threesome ('θriːsəm) *n* **1** a group of three. **2** *Golf.* a match in which a single player playing his or her own ball competes against two others playing on the same ball. **3** any game, etc., for three people. **4** (*modifier*) performed by three.

thremmatology (ˌθrɛməˈtɒlədʒɪ) *n* the science of breeding domesticated animals and plants. ORIG C19: from Gk *thremma* nursling + -LOGY

threnody ('θrɛnədɪ, 'θriː-) *or* **threnode** ('θriːnəʊd, 'θrɛn-) *n, pl* **threnodies** *or* **threnodes.** an ode, song, or speech of lamentation, esp. for the dead. ORIG C17: from Gk *thrēnōidia,* from *thrēnos* dirge + *ōidē* song
▸ **threnodic** (θrɪˈnɒdɪk) *adj* ▸ **threnodist** ('θrɛnədɪst, 'θriː-) *n*

thresh (θrɛʃ) *vb* **1** to beat stalks of ripe corn, etc., either with a hand implement or a machine to separate the grain from the husks and straw. **2** (*tr*) to beat or strike. **3** (*intr;* often foll. by *about*) to toss and turn; thrash. ORIG OE *threscan*

thresher ('θrɛʃə) *n* **1** a person who threshes. **2** short for **threshing machine. 3** any of a genus of large sharks occurring in tropical and temperate seas. They have a very long whiplike tail.

threshing machine *n* a machine for threshing crops.

threshold ('θrɛʃəʊld, 'θrɛʃˌhəʊld) *n* **1** a sill, esp. one made of stone or hardwood, placed at a doorway. **2** any doorway or entrance. **3** the starting point of an experience, event, or venture. **4** *Psychol.* the strength at which a stimulus is just perceived: *the threshold of consciousness.* **5a** a point at which something would stop, take effect, etc. **5b** (*as modifier*): *threshold price; threshold effect.* **6** the minimum intensity or value of a signal, etc., that will produce a response or specified effect. **7** (*modifier*) of a pay agreement, clause, etc., that raises wages to compensate for increases in the cost of living. ◆ Related adj: **liminal.** ORIG OE *therscold*

threshold agreement *n* an agreement between an employer and employees or their union to increase wages by a specified sum if inflation exceeds a specified level in a specified time.

threw (θruː) *vb* the past tense of **throw.**

thrice (θraɪs) *adv* **1** three times. **2** threefold. **3** *Arch.* greatly. ORIG OE *thrīwa, thrīga*

thrift (θrɪft) *n* **1** wisdom and caution in the management of money. **2** Also called: **sea pink.** any of a genus of perennial low-growing plants of Europe, W Asia, and North America, having narrow leaves and round heads of pink or white flowers. ORIG C13: from ON: success; see THRIVE
▸ **'thriftless** *adj* ▸ **'thriftlessly** *adv*

thrifty ('θrɪftɪ) *adj* **thriftier, thriftiest. 1** showing thrift; economical or frugal. **2** *Rare.* thriving or prospering.
▸ **'thriftily** *adv* ▸ **'thriftiness** *n*

thrill (θrɪl) *n* **1** a sudden sensation of excitement and pleasure. **2** a situation producing such a sensation. **3** a trembling sensation caused by fear or emotional shock. **4** *Pathol.* an abnormal slight tremor. ◆ *vb* **5** to feel or cause to feel a thrill. **6** to tremble or cause to tremble; vibrate or quiver. ORIG OE *thȳrlian* to pierce, from *thyrel* hole
▸ **'thrilling** *adj*

thriller ('θrɪlə) *n* a book, film, play, etc., depicting crime, mystery, or espionage in an atmosphere of excitement and suspense.

thrips (θrɪps) *n, pl* **thrips.** any of various small slender-bodied insects typically having piercing mouthparts and feeding on plant sap. ORIG C18: via NL from Gk: woodworm

thrive (θraɪv) *vb* **thrives, thriving; thrived** *or* **throve; thrived** *or* **thriven** ('θrɪvᵊn). (*intr*) **1** to grow strongly and vigorously. **2** to do well; prosper. ORIG C13: from ON *thrīfask* to grasp for oneself, from ?

thro' *or* **thro** (θruː) *prep, adv Inf. or poetic.* variant spellings of **through.**

throat (θrəʊt) *n* **1a** that part of the alimentary and respiratory tracts extending from the back of the mouth to just below the larynx. **1b** the front part of the neck. **2** something resembling a throat, esp. in shape or function: *the throat of a chimney.* **3 cut one's (own) throat.** to bring about one's own ruin. **4 ram** *or* **force (something) down someone's throat.** to insist that someone listen to or accept (something). ◆ Related adjs.: **guttural, laryngeal.** ORIG OE *throtu*

throaty ('θrəʊtɪ) *adj* **throatier, throatiest. 1** indicating a sore throat; hoarse: *a throaty cough.* **2** of or produced in the throat. **3** deep, husky, or guttural.
▸ **'throatily** *adv*

throb (θrɒb) *vb* **throbs, throbbing, throbbed.** (*intr*) **1** to pulsate or beat repeatedly, esp. with increased force. **2** (of engines, drums, etc.) to have a strong rhythmic vibration or beat. ◆ *n* **3** a throbbing, esp. a rapid pulsation as of the heart: *a throb of pleasure.* ORIG C14: ? imit.

throes (θrəʊz) *pl n* **1** a condition of violent pangs, pain, or convulsions: *death throes.* **2 in the throes of.** struggling with great effort with. ORIG OE *thrāwu* threat

thrombin ('θrɒmbɪn) *n Biochem.* an enzyme that acts on fibrinogen in blood causing it to clot. ORIG C19: from THROMB(US) + -IN

thrombocyte ('θrɒmbəˌsaɪt) *n* another name for **platelet.**
▸ **thrombocytic** (ˌθrɒmbəˈsɪtɪk) *adj*

thromboembolism (ˌθrɒmbəʊˈɛmbəˌlɪzəm) *n* the obstruction of a blood vessel by a thrombus that has become detached from its original site.

thrombose ('θrɒmbəʊz) *vb* **thromboses, thrombosing, thrombosed.** to become or affect with a thrombus. ORIG C19: back formation from THROMBOSIS

thrombosis (θrɒmˈbəʊsɪs) *n, pl* **thromboses** (-siːz). **1** the formation or presence of a thrombus. **2** *Inf.* short for **coronary thrombosis.** ORIG C18: from NL, from Gk: curdling, from *thrombousthai* to clot, from *thrombos* THROMBUS
▸ **thrombotic** (θrɒmˈbɒtɪk) *adj*

thrombus ('θrɒmbəs) *n, pl* **thrombi** (-baɪ). a clot of coagulated blood that forms within a blood vessel or inside the heart, often impeding the flow of blood. ORIG C17: from NL, from Gk *thrombos* lump, from ?

throne (θrəʊn) *n* **1** the ceremonial seat occupied by a monarch, bishop, etc., on occasions of state. **2** the power or rank ascribed to a royal person. **3** a person holding royal rank. **4** (*pl; often cap.*) the third of the nine orders into which the angels are divided in medieval angelology. ◆ *vb* **thrones, throning, throned. 5** to place or be placed on a throne. ORIG C13: from OF *trone,* from L *thronus,* from Gk *thronos*

throng (θrɒŋ) *n* **1** a great number of people or things crowded together. ◆ *vb* **2** to gather in or fill (a place) in large numbers; crowd. **3** (*tr*) to hem in (a person); jostle. ORIG OE *gethrang*

throstle ('θrɒsᵊl) *n* **1** a poetic name for the **song thrush. 2** a spinning machine for wool or cotton in which the fibres are twisted and wound continuously. ORIG OE

throttle ('θrɒtᵊl) *n* **1** Also called: **throttle valve.** any device that controls the quantity of fuel or fuel and air mixture entering an engine. **2** an informal or dialect word for **throat.** ◆ *vb* **throttles, throttling, throttled.** (*tr*) **3** to kill or in-

jure by squeezing the throat. **4** to suppress. **5** to control or restrict (a flow of fluid) by means of a throttle valve. ORIG C14: *throtelen*, from *throte* THROAT
▸ **'throttler** *n*

through (θru:) *prep* **1** going in at one side and coming out at the other side of: *a path through the wood*. **2** occupying or visiting several points scattered around in (an area). **3** as a result of; by means of. **4** *Chiefly US*. up to and including: *Monday through Friday*. **5** during: *through the night*. **6** at the end of; having completed. **7 through with**. having finished with (esp. when dissatisfied with). ◆ *adj* **8** (*postpositive*) having successfully completed some specified activity. **9** (on a telephone line) connected. **10** (*postpositive*) no longer able to function successfully in some specified capacity: *as a journalist, you're through*. **11** (*prenominal*) (of a route, journey, etc.) continuous or unbroken: *a through train*. ◆ *adv* **12** through some specified thing, place, or period of time. **13 through and through**. thoroughly; completely. ORIG OE *thurh*

through bridge *n Civil engineering*. a bridge in which the track is carried by the lower horizontal members.

throughout (θru:'aʊt) *prep* **1** right through; through the whole of (a place or a period of time): *throughout the day*. ◆ *adv* **2** through the whole of some specified period or area.

throughput ('θru:ˌpʊt) *n* the quantity of raw material or information processed or communicated in a given period, esp. by a computer.

throughway ('θru:ˌweɪ) *n US*. a thoroughfare, esp. a motorway.

throve (θrəʊv) *vb* a past tense of **thrive**.

throw (θrəʊ) *vb* **throws, throwing, threw, thrown**. (*mainly tr*) **1** (*also intr*) to project (something) through the air, esp. with a rapid motion of the arm. **2** (foll. by *in, on, onto*, etc.) to put or move suddenly, carelessly, or violently. **3** to bring to or cause to be in a specified state or condition, esp. suddenly: *the news threw them into a panic*. **4** to direct or cast (a shadow, light, etc.). **5** to project (the voice) so as to make it appear to come from other than its source. **6** to give or hold (a party). **7** to cause to fall or be upset: *the horse threw his rider*. **8a** to tip (dice) out onto a flat surface. **8b** to obtain (a specified number) in this way. **9** to shape (clay) on a potter's wheel. **10** to move (a switch or lever) to engage or disengage a mechanism. **11** to be subjected to (a fit). **12** to turn (wood, etc.) on a lathe. **13** *Inf*. to baffle or astonish; confuse: *the question threw me*. **14** *Boxing*. to deliver (a punch). **15** *Wrestling*. to hurl (an opponent) to the ground. **16** *Inf*. to lose (a contest, etc.) deliberately. **17a** to play (a card). **17b** to discard (a card). **18** (of an animal) to give birth to (young). **19** to twist or spin (filaments) into thread. **20** *Austral. inf*. (often foll. by *at*) to mock or poke fun. **21 throw oneself at**. to strive actively to attract the attention or affection of. **22 throw oneself into**. to involve oneself enthusiastically in. **23 throw oneself on**. to rely entirely upon. ◆ *n* **24** the act or an instance of throwing. **25** the distance over which anything may be thrown: *a stone's throw*. **26** *Inf*. a chance or try. **27** an act or result of throwing dice. **28a** the eccentricity of a cam. **28b** the radial distance between the central axis of a crankshaft and the axis of a crankpin forming part of the shaft. **29** a decorative blanket or cover. **30** *Geol*. the vertical displacement of rock strata at a fault. **31** *Physics*. the deflection of a measuring instrument as a result of a fluctuation. ◆ See also **throwaway, throwback, throw in**, etc. ORIG OE *thrāwan* to turn, torment
▸ **'thrower** *n*

throwaway ('θrəʊəˌweɪ) *adj* (*prenominal*) **1** said or done incidentally, esp. for rhetorical effect; casual: *a throwaway remark*. **2** designed to be discarded after use rather than reused, refilled, etc.: *a throwaway carton*. ◆ *n* **3** *Chiefly US & Canad*. a handbill. ◆ *vb* **throw away**. (*tr, adv*) **4** to get rid of; discard. **5** to fail to make good use of; waste.

throwback ('θrəʊˌbæk) *n* **1a** a person, animal, or plant that has the characteristics of an earlier or more primitive type. **1b** a reversion to such an organism. ◆ *vb* **throw back**. (*adv*) **2** (*intr*) to revert to an earlier or more primitive type. **3** (*tr*; foll. by *on*) to force to depend (on): *the crisis threw her back on her faith in God*.

throw in *vb* (*tr, adv*) **1** to add at no additional cost. **2** to contribute or interpose (a remark, argument, etc.). **3 throw in the sponge** (*or* **towel**). to give in; accept defeat. ◆ *n* **throw-in**. **4** *Soccer, etc*. the method of putting the ball into play after it has gone into touch by throwing it to a team-mate.

thrown (θrəʊn) *vb* the past participle of **throw**.

throw off *vb* (*mainly tr, adv*) **1** to free oneself of; discard. **2** to produce or utter in a casual manner. **3** to escape from or elude. **4** to confuse or disconcert. **5** (*intr*; often foll. by **at**) *Austral. & NZ inf*. to deride or ridicule.

throw out *vb* (*tr, adv*) **1** to discard or reject. **2** to expel or dismiss, esp. forcibly. **3** to construct (something projecting or prominent). **4** to put forward or offer. **5** to utter in a casual or indirect manner. **6** to confuse or disconcert. **7** to give off or emit. **8** *Cricket*. (of a fielder) to put (the batsman) out by throwing the ball to hit the wicket. **9** *Baseball*. to make a throw to a team-mate who in turn puts out (a base runner).

throw over *vb* (*tr, adv*) to forsake or abandon; jilt.

throw together *vb* (*tr, adv*) **1** to assemble hurriedly. **2** to cause to become casually acquainted.

throw up *vb* (*adv, mainly tr*) **1** to give up; abandon. **2** to construct hastily. **3** to reveal; produce. **4** (*also intr*) *Inf*. to vomit.

thru (θru:) *prep, adv, adj Chiefly US*. a variant spelling of **through**.

thrum[1] (θrʌm) *vb* **thrums, thrumming, thrummed**. **1** to strum rhythmically but without expression on (a musical instrument). **2** (*intr*) to drum incessantly: *rain thrummed on the roof*. ◆ *n* **3** a repetitive strumming. ORIG C16: imit.

thrum[2] (θrʌm) *n* **1a** any of the unwoven ends of warp thread remaining on the loom when the web has been removed. **1b** such ends of thread collectively. **2** a fringe or tassel of short unwoven threads. ◆ *vb* **thrums, thrumming, thrummed**. **3** (*tr*) to trim with thrums. ORIG C14: from OE

thrush[1] (θrʌʃ) *n* any of a subfamily of songbirds, esp. those having a brown plumage with a spotted breast, such as the mistle thrush and song thrush. ORIG OE *thrȳsce*

thrush[2] (θrʌʃ) *n* **1** a fungal disease, esp. of infants, characterized by the formation of whitish spots. **2** a genital infection caused by the same fungus. **3** a softening of the frog of a horse's hoof characterized by inflammation and a thick foul discharge. ORIG C17: from ?

thrust (θrʌst) *vb* **thrusts, thrusting, thrust**. **1** (*tr*) to push (someone or something) with force. **2** (*tr*) to force upon (someone) or into (some condition or situation): *they thrust responsibilities upon her*. **3** (*tr*; foll. by *through*) to pierce; stab. **4** (*intr*; usually foll. by *through* or *into*) to force a passage. **5** to make a stab or lunge at. ◆ *n* **6** a forceful drive, push, stab, or lunge. **7** a force, esp. one that produces motion. **8a** a propulsive force produced by the fluid pressure or the change of momentum of the fluid in a jet engine, rocket engine, etc. **8b** a similar force produced by a propeller. **9** a continuous pressure exerted by one part of an object, structure, etc., against another. **10** force, impetus, or drive. **11** the essential or most forceful part: *the thrust of the argument*. ORIG C12: from ON *thrysta*

thruster ('θrʌstə) *n* **1** a person or thing that thrusts. **2** a small rocket engine, esp. one used to correct the altitude or course of a spacecraft.

thrust fault *n* a fault in which the rocks on the lower side of an inclined fault plane have been displaced downwards; a reverse fault.

Thucydides ★ (θu:'sɪdɪˌdi:z) *n* ?460–?395 B.C., Greek historian and politician, noted for his *History of the Peloponnesian War*.
▸ **Thuˌcydi'dean** *adj*

thud (θʌd) *n* **1** a dull heavy sound. **2** a blow or fall that causes such a sound. ◆ *vb* **thuds, thudding, thudded**. **3** to make or cause to make such a sound. ORIG OE *thyddan* to strike

thug (θʌg) *n* **1** a tough and violent man, esp. a criminal. **2** (*sometimes cap.*) (formerly) a member of an organization

★ people and places

of robbers and assassins in India. ORIG C19: from Hindi *thag* thief, from Sansk. *sthaga* scoundrel, from *sthagati* to conceal
▸ **'thuggery** *n* ▸ **'thuggish** *adj*

thuja *or* **thuya** ('θu:jə) *n* any of a genus of coniferous trees of North America and East Asia, having scalelike leaves, small cones, and an aromatic wood. ORIG C18: from NL, from Med. L *thuia,* ult. from Gk *thua* an African tree

Thule ★ ('θju:lɪ) *n* **1** Also called: **ultima Thule.** a region believed by ancient geographers to be the northernmost land in the inhabited world: sometimes thought to have been Iceland, Norway, or one of the Shetland Islands. **2** an Eskimo settlement in NW Greenland: a Danish trading post, founded in 1910, and US air force base.

thulium ('θju:lɪəm) *n* a malleable ductile silvery-grey element. The radioisotope **thulium-170** is used as an electron source in portable X-ray units. Symbol: Tm; atomic no.: 69; atomic wt.: 168.93. ORIG C19: NL, from THULE + -IUM

thumb (θʌm) *n* **1** the first and usually shortest and thickest of the digits of the hand. **2** the corresponding digit in other vertebrates. **3** the part of a glove shaped to fit the thumb. **4 all thumbs.** clumsy. **5 thumbs down.** an indication of refusal or disapproval. **6 thumbs up.** an indication of encouragement or approval. **7 under someone's thumb.** at someone's mercy or command. ◆ *vb* **8** (*tr*) to touch, mark, or move with the thumb. **9** to attempt to obtain (a lift or ride) by signalling with the thumb. **10** (when *intr,* often foll. by *through*) to flip the pages of (a book, etc.) in order to glance at the contents. **11 thumb one's nose at.** to deride or mock, esp. by placing the thumb on the nose with fingers extended. ORIG OE *thūma*

thumb index *n* **1** a series of indentations cut into the fore-edge of a book to facilitate quick reference. ◆ *vb* **thumb-index. 2** (*tr*) to furnish with a thumb index.

thumbnail ('θʌm,neɪl) *n* **1** the nail of the thumb. **2** (*modifier*) concise and brief: *a thumbnail sketch.*

thumbnut ('θʌm,nʌt) *n* a wing nut.

thumb piano *n* another name for **mbira.**

thumbscrew ('θʌm,skru:) *n* **1** an instrument of torture that pinches or crushes the thumbs. **2** a screw with projections on its head enabling it to be turned by the thumb and forefinger.

thumbstall ('θʌm,stɔ:l) *n* a protective sheathlike cover for the thumb.

thumbtack ('θʌm,tæk) *n* the US and Canad. name for **drawing pin.**

thump (θʌmp) *n* **1** the sound of a heavy solid body hitting a comparatively soft surface. **2** a heavy blow with the hand. ◆ *vb* **3** (*tr*) to strike or beat heavily; pound. **4** (*intr*) to throb, beat, or pound violently. ORIG C16
▸ **'thumper** *n*

thumping ('θʌmpɪŋ) *adj* (*prenominal*) *Sl.* huge or excessive: *a thumping loss.*

Thun ★ (*German* tu:n) *n* **1** a town in central Switzerland, in Bern canton on Lake Thun. Pop.: 36 700 (1990 est.). **2 Lake.** a lake in central Switzerland, formed by a widening of the Aar River. Length: about 17 km (11 miles). Width: 3 km (2 miles). German name: **Thuner See.**

thunbergia (θʌn'bɜ:dʒɪə) *n* any of various climbing or dwarf plants of tropical and subtropical Africa and Asia. ORIG C19: after K. P. *Thunberg* (1743-1822), Swedish botanist

thunder ('θʌndə) *n* **1** a loud cracking or deep rumbling noise caused by the rapid expansion of atmospheric gases which are suddenly heated by lightning. **2** any loud booming sound. **3** *Rare.* a violent threat or denunciation. **4 steal someone's thunder.** to lessen the effect of someone's idea or action by anticipating it. ◆ *vb* **5** to make (a loud sound) or utter (words) in a manner suggesting thunder. **6** (*intr;* with *it* as subject) to be the case that thunder is being heard. **7** (*intr*) to move fast and heavily: *the bus thundered downhill.* **8** (*intr*) to utter vehement threats or denunciation; rail. ORIG OE *thunor*
▸ **'thundery** *adj* ▸ **'thunderer** *n*

Thunder Bay ★ *n* a port in central Canada, in Ontario on Lake Superior: formed in 1970 by the amalgamation of Fort William and Port Arthur; the head of the St Lawrence Seaway for Canada. Pop.: 113 746 (1991).

thunderbolt ('θʌndə,bəʊlt) *n* **1** a flash of lightning accompanying thunder. **2** the imagined agency of destruction produced by a flash of lightning. **3** (in mythology) the destructive weapon wielded by several gods, esp. the Greek god Zeus. **4** something very startling.

thunderclap ('θʌndə,klæp) *n* **1** a loud outburst of thunder. **2** something as violent or unexpected as a clap of thunder.

thundercloud ('θʌndə,klaʊd) *n* a towering electrically charged cumulonimbus cloud associated with thunderstorms.

thunderhead ('θʌndə,hɛd) *n* *Chiefly US.* the anvil-shaped top of a cumulonimbus cloud.

thundering ('θʌndərɪŋ) *adj* (*prenominal*) *Sl.* very great or excessive: *a thundering idiot.*

thunderous ('θʌndərəs) *adj* **1** threatening; angry. **2** resembling thunder, esp. in loudness.

thunderstorm ('θʌndə,stɔ:m) *n* a storm with thunder and lightning and usually heavy rain or hail.

thunderstruck ('θʌndə,strʌk) *or* **thunderstricken** ('θʌndə,strɪkən) *adj* **1** completely taken aback; amazed or shocked. **2** *Rare.* struck by lightning.

Thurber ★ ('θɜ:bə) *n* **James (Grover).** 1894–1961, US humorist. He contributed many drawings and stories to the *New Yorker.*

Thurgau ★ (*German* 'tu:rgau) *n* a canton of NE Switzerland, on Lake Constance: annexed by the confederated Swiss states in 1460. Capital: Frauenfeld. Pop.: 220 335 (1995 est.). Area: 1007 sq. km (389 sq. miles). French name: **Thurgovie** (tyrgɔvi).

thurible ('θjʊərɪbᵊl) *n* another word for **censer.** ORIG C15: from L *tūribulum* censer, from *tūs* incense

Thuringia ★ (θjʊ'rɪndʒɪə) *n* a state of central Germany, formerly in East Germany. Pop.: 2 496 700 (1996 est.). German name: **Thüringen** ('ty:rɪŋən).
▸ **Thu'ringian** *adj, n*

Thuringian Forest ★ *n* a forested mountainous region in E central Germany, rising over 900 m (3000 ft); formerly in East Germany. German name: **Thüringer Wald** ('ty:rɪŋər 'valt).

Thurrock ★ ('θʌrək) *n* a unitary authority in SE England, in Essex. Pop.: 132 300 (1996 est.). Area: 163 sq. km (63 sq. miles).

Thurs. *abbrev. for* Thursday.

Thursday ('θɜ:zdɪ) *n* the fifth day of the week; fourth day of the working week. ORIG OE *Thursdæg,* lit.: Thor's day

Thursday Island ★ *n* an island in Torres Strait, between NE Australia and New Guinea: administratively part of Queensland, Australia. Area: 4 sq. km (1.5 sq. miles).

thus (ðʌs) *adv* **1** in this manner: *do it thus.* **2** to such a degree: *thus far and no further.* ◆ *sentence connector.* **3** therefore: *We have failed. Thus we have to take the consequences.* ORIG OE

Thutmose I ★ (θu:t'məʊsə, -'məʊs) *n* died *c.* 1500 B.C., king of Egypt of the 18th dynasty.

Thutmose III ★ *n* died *c.* 1450 B.C., king of Egypt of the 18th dynasty, who completed the conquest of Syria.

thuya ('θu:jə) *n* a variant spelling of **thuja.**

thwack (θwæk) *vb* **1** to beat, esp. with something flat. ◆ *n* **2a** a blow with something flat. **2b** the sound made by it. ORIG C16: imit.

thwart (θwɔ:t) *vb* **1** to oppose successfully or prevent; frustrate. **2** *Obs.* to be or move across. ◆ *n* **3** an oarsman's seat lying across a boat. ◆ *adj* **4** passing or being situated across. ◆ *prep, adv* **5** *Obs.* across. ORIG C13: from ON *thvert,* from *thverr* transverse

thy (ðaɪ) *determiner* (*usually preceding a consonant*) *Arch. or Brit. dialect.* belonging to or associated in some way with you (thou): *thy goodness.* ORIG C12: var. of THINE

Thyestes ★ (θaɪ'ɛsti:z) *n* *Greek myth.* son of Pelops and brother of Atreus, with whose wife he committed adultery. In revenge, Atreus killed Thyestes' sons and served them to their father at a banquet.
▸ **Thyestean** *or* **Thyestian** (θaɪ'ɛstɪən, ,θaɪɛ'sti:ən) *adj*

thylacine ('θaɪlə,saɪn) *n* an extinct or rare doglike carnivorous marsupial of Tasmania. Also called: **Tasmanian tiger, Tasmanian wolf.** ORIG C19: from NL *thylacīnus,* from Gk *thulakos* pouch

thyme (taɪm) *n* any of various small shrubs having a strong odour, small leaves, and white, pink, or red flowers. ORIG C14: from OF *thym,* from L *thymum,* from Gk, from *thuein* to make a burnt offering
▸ **'thymy** *adj*

-thymia *n combining form.* indicating a certain emotional condition, mood, or state of mind: *cyclothymia.* ORIG NL, from Gk *thumos* temper

thymine ('θaɪmi:n) *n* a white crystalline base found in DNA. ORIG C19: from THYMIC (see THYMUS) + -INE[2]

thymol ('θaɪmɒl) *n* a white crystalline substance obtained from thyme and used as a fungicide, antiseptic, etc. ORIG C19: from THYME + -OL[2]

thymus ('θaɪməs) *n, pl* **thymuses** *or* **thymi** (-maɪ). a glandular organ of vertebrates, consisting in man of two lobes situated below the thyroid. It atrophies with age and is almost nonexistent in the adult. ORIG C17: from NL, from Gk *thumos* sweetbread
▸ **'thymic** *adj*

thyratron ('θaɪrə,trɒn) *n Electronics.* a gas-filled tube that has three electrodes and can be switched between an 'off' state and an 'on' state. It has been superseded by the thyristor. ORIG C20: orig. a trademark, from Gk *thura* door, valve + -TRON

thyristor (θaɪ'rɪstə) *n* any of a group of semiconductor devices, such as the silicon-controlled rectifier, that can be switched between two states. ORIG C20: from THYR(ATRON) + (TRANS)ISTOR

thyroid ('θaɪrɔɪd) *adj* **1** of or relating to the thyroid gland. **2** of or relating to the largest cartilage of the larynx. ◆ *n* **3** See **thyroid gland. 4** a preparation of the thyroid gland of certain animals, used to treat hypothyroidism. ORIG C18: from NL *thyroidēs,* from Gk *thureoeidēs,* from *thureos* oblong (lit.: door-shaped), from *thura* door

thyroid gland *n* an endocrine gland of vertebrates, consisting in man of two lobes near the base of the neck. It secretes hormones that control metabolism and growth.

thyrotropin (,θaɪrəʊ'trəʊpɪn) *or* **thyrotrophin** *n* a hormone secreted by the pituitary gland: it stimulates the activity of the thyroid gland. ORIG C20: from *thyro-* thyroid + -TROPE + -IN

thyroxine (θaɪ'rɒksi:n, -sɪn) *or* **thyroxin** (θaɪ'rɒksɪn) *n* the principal hormone produced by the thyroid gland. ORIG C19: from *thyro-* thyroid + OXY-[2] + -INE[2]

thyrse (θɜ:s) *or* **thyrsus** ('θɜ:səs) *n, pl* **thyrses** *or* **thyrsi** ('θɜ:saɪ). *Bot.* a type of inflorescence, occurring in the lilac and grape, in which the main branch is racemose and the lateral branches cymose. ORIG C17: from F: THYRSUS

thyrsus ('θɜ:səs) *n, pl* **thyrsi** (-saɪ). **1** *Greek myth.* a staff, usually one tipped with a pine cone, borne by Dionysus (Bacchus) and his followers. **2** a variant spelling of **thyrse.** ORIG C18: from L, from Gk *thursos* stalk

thyself (ðaɪ'sɛlf) *pron Arch.* **a** the reflexive form of *thou* or *thee.* **b** (intensifier): *thou, thyself, wouldst know.*

ti (ti:) *n Music.* a variant spelling of **te.**

Ti *the chemical symbol for* titanium.

Tia Juana ★ ('tɪə 'wɑ:nə; *Spanish* 'tia 'xwana) *n* a variant spelling of **Tijuana.**

Tianjin ('tjɛn'dʒɪn), **Tientsin,** *or* **T'ien-ching** ★ *n* an industrial city in NE China, in Hebei province, on the Grand Canal, 51 km (32 miles) from the Yellow Sea: seat of Nankai University (1919). Pop.: 9 530 000 (1997 est.).

Tian Shan *or* **Tien Shan** ★ ('tjɛn'ʃɑ:n) *n* a great mountain system of central Asia, in Kyrgyzstan and the Xinjiang Uygur Autonomous Region of W China, extending for about 2500 km (1500 miles). Highest peak: Pobeda Peak, 7439 m (24 406 ft). Russian name: **Tyan-Shan.**

tiara (tɪ'ɑ:rə) *n* **1** a woman's semicircular jewelled headdress for formal occasions. **2** a high headdress worn by Persian kings in ancient times. **3** a headdress worn by the pope, consisting of a beehive-shaped diadem surrounded by three coronets. ORIG C16: via L from Gk, of Oriental origin
▸ **ti'araed** *adj*

Tiber ★ ('taɪbə) *n* a river in central Italy, rising in the Tuscan Apennines and flowing south through Rome to the Tyrrhenian Sea. Length: 405 km (252 miles). Ancient name: **Tiberis** ('ti:bərɪs). Italian name: **Tevere.**

Tiberias ★ (taɪ'bɪərɪ,æs) *n* **1** a resort in N Israel, on the Sea of Galilee: an important Jewish centre after the destruction of Jerusalem by the Romans. Pop.: 35 400 (1989 est.). **2 Lake.** another name for the (Sea of) **Galilee.**

Tiberius ★ (taɪ'bɪərɪəs) *n* full name *Tiberius Claudius Nero Caesar Augustus.* 42 B.C.–37 A.D., Roman emperor (14–37 A.D.). He succeeded his father-in-law Augustus.

Tibesti *or* **Tibesti Massif** ★ (tɪ'bɛstɪ) *pl n* a mountain range of volcanic origin in NW Chad, in the central Sahara extending for about 480 km (300 miles). Highest peak: Emi Koussi, 3415 m (11 204 ft).

Tibet ★ (tɪ'bɛt) *n* an autonomous region of SW China: Europeans strictly excluded in the 19th century; invaded by China in 1950; rebellion (1959) against Chinese rule suppressed and the Dalai Lama fled to India; military rule imposed (1989–90) after demands for independence were made; consists largely of a vast high plateau between the Himalayas and Kunlun Mountains; formerly a theocracy and the centre of Lamaism. Capital: Lhasa. Pop.: 2 480 000 (1997 est.). Area: 1 221 601 sq. km (471 660 sq. miles). Chinese names: **Xizang Autonomous Region, Sitsang.**

Tibetan (tɪ'bɛtᵊn) *adj* **1** of or characteristic of Tibet, its people, or their language. ◆ *n* **2** a native or inhabitant of Tibet. **3** the language of Tibet.

tibia ('tɪbɪə) *n, pl* **tibiae** ('tɪbɪ,i:) *or* **tibias. 1** the inner and thicker of the two bones of the human leg below the knee; shinbone. **2** the corresponding bone in other vertebrates. **3** the fourth segment of an insect's leg. ORIG C16: from L: leg, pipe
▸ **'tibial** *adj*

Tibullus ★ (tɪ'bʌləs) *n* **Albius** ('ælbɪəs). ?54–?19 B.C., Roman elegiac poet.

Tibur ★ ('taɪbə) *n* the ancient name for **Tivoli.**

tic (tɪk) *n* spasmodic twitching of a particular group of muscles. ORIG C19: from F, from ?

tic douloureux ('tɪk ,du:lə'ru:) *n* a condition of momentary stabbing pain along the trigeminal nerve. ORIG C19: from F, lit.: painful tic

Ticino ★ (*Italian* ti'tʃi:no) *n* **1** a canton in S Switzerland: predominantly Italian-speaking and Roman Catholic; mountainous. Capital: Bellinzona. Pop.: 302 131 (1995 est.). Area: 2810 sq. km (1085 sq. miles). German name: **Tessin. 2** a river in S central Europe, rising in S central Switzerland and flowing southeast and west to Lake Maggiore, then southeast to the River Po. Length: 248 km (154 miles).

tick[1] (tɪk) *n* **1** a recurrent metallic tapping or clicking sound, such as that made by a clock. **2** *Brit. inf.* a moment or instant. **3** a mark (✓) used to check off or indicate the correctness of something. **4** *Commerce.* the smallest increment by which a price can fluctuate in a commodity or financial futures market. ◆ *vb* **5** to produce a recurrent tapping sound or indicate by such a sound: *the clock ticked the minutes away.* **6** (when *tr,* often foll. by *off*) to mark or check with a tick. **7 what makes someone tick.** *Inf.* the basic drive or motivation of a person. ◆ See also **tick off, tick over.** ORIG C13: from Low G *tikk* touch

tick[2] (tɪk) *n* any of a large group of small parasitic arachnids typically living on the skin of warm-blooded animals and feeding on the blood, etc., of their hosts. ORIG OE *ticca*

tick[3] (tɪk) *n* **1** the strong covering of a pillow, mattress, etc. **2** *Inf.* short for **ticking.** ORIG C15: prob. from MDu. *tīke*

tick[4] (tɪk) *n Brit. inf.* account or credit (esp. in **on tick**). ORIG C17: shortened from TICKET

tick bird *n* another name for **oxpecker.**

★ people and places

ticker ('tɪkə) *n* **1** *Sl.* **1a** the heart. **1b** a watch. **2** a person or thing that ticks. **3** the US word for **tape machine.**

ticker tape *n* a continuous paper ribbon on which a tape machine prints current stock quotations.

ticket ('tɪkɪt) *n* **1a** a piece of paper, cardboard, etc., showing that the holder is entitled to certain rights, such as travel on a train or bus, entry to a place of public entertainment, etc. **1b** (*modifier*) concerned with the issue, sale, or checking of tickets: *a ticket collector.* **2** a piece of card, cloth, etc., attached to an article showing information such as its price, size, etc. **3** a summons served for a parking or traffic offence. **4** *Inf.* the certificate of competence issued to a ship's captain or an aircraft pilot. **5** *Chiefly US & NZ.* the group of candidates nominated by one party in an election; slate. **6** *Chiefly US.* the declared policy of a political party at an election. **7** *Brit. inf.* a certificate of discharge from the armed forces. **8** *Inf.* the right or appropriate thing: *that's the ticket.* **9 have (got) tickets on oneself.** *Austral. inf.* to be conceited. ◆ *vb* **tickets, ticketing, ticketed.** (*tr*) **10** to issue or attach a ticket or tickets to. ORIG C17: from OF *etiquet,* from *estiquier* to stick on, from MDu. *steken* to stick

ticket day *n Stock Exchange.* the day before settling day, when the stockbrokers are given the names of the purchasers.

ticket of leave *n* (formerly, in Britain) a permit allowing a convict (**ticket-of-leave man**) to leave prison, after serving only part of his sentence, with certain restrictions placed on him.

tickets ('tɪkɪts) *pl n S. African inf.* the end: *it's tickets for him.*

tick fever *n* any acute infectious febrile disease caused by the bite of an infected tick.

ticking ('tɪkɪŋ) *n* a strong cotton fabric, often striped, used esp. for mattress and pillow covers. ORIG C17: from TICK[3]

tickle ('tɪkᵊl) *vb* **tickles, tickling, tickled. 1** to touch or stroke, so as to produce pleasure, laughter, or a twitching sensation. **2** (*tr*) to excite pleasurably; gratify. **3** (*tr*) to delight or entertain (often in **tickle one's fancy**). **4** (*intr*) to itch or tingle. **5** (*tr*) to catch (a fish, esp. a trout) with the hands. **6 tickle pink** *or* **to death.** *Inf.* to please greatly. ◆ *n* **7** a sensation of light stroking or itching. **8** the act of tickling. **9** *Canad.* (in the Atlantic Provinces) a narrow strait. ORIG C14

tickler ('tɪklə) *n* **1** *Inf., chiefly Brit.* a difficult problem. **2** Also called: **tickler file.** *US.* a memorandum book. **3** a person or thing that tickles.

ticklish ('tɪklɪʃ) *adj* **1** sensitive to being tickled. **2** delicate or difficult. **3** easily upset or offended.
▸ **'ticklishly** *adv* ▸ **'ticklishness** *n*

tick off *vb* (*tr, adv*) **1** to mark with a tick. **2** *Inf., chiefly Brit.* to scold; reprimand.

tick over *vb* (*intr, adv*) **1** Also: **idle.** *Brit.* (of an engine) to run at low speed with the throttle control closed and the transmission disengaged. **2** to run smoothly without any major changes.

ticktack ('tɪk,tæk) *n* **1** *Brit.* a system of sign language, mainly using the hands, by which bookmakers transmit their odds to each other at race courses. **2** *US.* a ticking sound. ORIG from TICK[1]

ticktock ('tɪk,tɒk) *n* **1** a ticking sound as made by a clock. ◆ *vb* **2** (*intr*) to make a ticking sound.

Ticonderoga ★ (,taɪkɒndə'rəʊgə) *n* a village in NE New York State, on Lake George: site of Fort Ticonderoga, scene of battles between the British and French (1758–59) and a strategic point in the War of American Independence.

tidal ('taɪdᵊl) *adj* **1** relating to, characterized by, or affected by tides. **2** dependent on the tide: *a tidal ferry.*
▸ **'tidally** *adv*

tidal energy *n* energy obtained by harnessing tidal power.

tidal volume *n* **1** the volume of water associated with a rising tide. **2** *Physiol.* the amount of air passing into and out of the lungs during normal breathing.

tidal wave *n* **1** a name (not in technical usage) for **tsunami. 2** an unusually large incoming wave, often caused by high winds and spring tides. **3** a forceful and widespread movement in public opinion, action, etc.

tidbit ('tɪd,bɪt) *n* the usual US spelling of **titbit.**

tiddler ('tɪdlə) *n Brit. inf.* **1** a very small fish, esp. a stickleback. **2** a small child. ORIG C19: from *tittlebat,* childish var. of STICKLEBACK, infl. by TIDDLY[1]

tiddly[1] ('tɪdlɪ) *adj* **tiddlier, tiddliest.** *Brit.* small; tiny. ORIG C19: childish var. of LITTLE

tiddly[2] ('tɪdlɪ) *adj Sl., chiefly Brit.* slightly drunk. ORIG C19 (meaning: a drink): from ?

tiddlywinks ('tɪdlɪ,wɪŋks) *n* (*functioning as sing*) a game in which players try to flick discs of plastic into a cup by pressing them with other larger discs. ORIG C19: prob. from TIDDLY[1] + dialect *wink,* var. of WINCH[1]

tide (taɪd) *n* **1** the cyclic rise and fall of sea level caused by the gravitational pull of the sun and moon. There are usually two high tides and two low tides in each lunar day. **2** the current, ebb, or flow of water at a specified place resulting from these changes in level. **3** See **ebb** (sense 3) and **flood** (sense 3). **4** a widespread tendency or movement. **5** a critical point in time; turning point. **6** *Arch. except in combination.* a season or time: *Christmastide.* **7** *Arch.* a favourable opportunity. **8 the tide is in** (*or* **out**). the sea has reached its highest (*or* lowest) level. ◆ *vb* **tides, tiding, tided. 9** to carry or be carried with or as if with the tide. **10** (*intr*) to ebb and flow like the tide. ORIG OE *tīd* time
▸ **'tideless** *adj*

tideland ('taɪd,lænd) *n US.* land between high-water and low-water marks.

tideline ('taɪd,laɪn) *n* the mark or line left by the tide when it retreats from its highest point.

tidemark ('taɪd,mɑːk) *n* **1** a mark left by the highest or lowest point of a tide. **2** *Chiefly Brit.* a mark showing a level reached by a liquid: *a tidemark on the bath.* **3** *Inf., chiefly Brit.* a dirty mark on the skin, indicating the extent to which someone has washed.

tide over *vb* (*tr, adv*) to help to get through (a period of difficulty, distress, etc.).

tide-rip *n* another word for **riptide** (sense 1).

tidewaiter ('taɪd,weɪtə) *n* (formerly) a customs officer who boarded and inspected incoming ships.

tidewater ('taɪd,wɔːtə) *n* **1** water that advances and recedes with the tide. **2** *US.* coastal land drained by tidal streams.

tideway ('taɪd,weɪ) *n* a strong tidal current or its channel, esp. the tidal part of a river.

tidings ('taɪdɪŋz) *pl n* information or news. ORIG OE *tīdung*

tidy ('taɪdɪ) *adj* **tidier, tidiest. 1** characterized by or indicating neatness and order. **2** *Inf.* considerable: *a tidy sum of money.* ◆ *vb* **tidies, tidying, tidied. 3** (when *intr,* usually foll. by *up*) to put (things) in order; neaten. ◆ *n, pl* **tidies. 4a** a small container for odds and ends. **4b sink tidy.** a container to retain rubbish that might clog the plughole. **5** *Chiefly US & Canad.* an ornamental protective covering for the back or arms of a chair. ORIG C13 (in the sense: timely, excellent): from TIDE + -Y[1]
▸ **'tidily** *adv* ▸ **'tidiness** *n*

tie (taɪ) *vb* **ties, tying, tied. 1** (when *tr,* often foll. by *up*) to fasten or be fastened with string, thread, etc. **2** to make (a knot or bow) in (something). **3** (*tr*) to restrict or secure. **4** to equal (the score) of a competitor, etc. **5** (*tr*) *Inf.* to unite in marriage. **6** *Music.* **6a** to execute (two successive notes) as though they formed one note. **6b** to connect (two printed notes) with a tie. ◆ *n* **7** a bond, link, or fastening. **8** a restriction or restraint. **9** a string, wire, etc., with which something is tied. **10** a long narrow piece of material worn, esp. by men, under the collar of a shirt, tied in a knot close to the throat with the ends hanging down the front. US name: **necktie. 11a** an equality in score, attainment, etc., in a contest. **11b** the match or competition in which such a result is attained. **12** a structural member such as a tie beam or tie rod. **13** *Sport, Brit.* a match or game in an eliminating competition: *a cup tie.* **14** (*usually pl*) a shoe fastened by means of laces.

15 the US and Canad. name for **sleeper** (on a railway track). **16** *Music.* a slur connecting two notes of the same pitch indicating that the sound is to be prolonged for their joint time value. ◆ See also **tie in, tie up.** ORIG OE *tīgan* to tie

tie beam *n* a horizontal beam that serves to prevent two other structural members from separating, esp. one that connects two corresponding rafters in a roof or roof truss.

tie-break *or* **tie-breaker** *n* **1** *Tennis.* an extra game played to decide the result of a set when the score is 6–6. **2** any method of deciding quickly the result of a drawn contest, esp. an extra game, question, etc.

tie clasp *n* a clip which holds a tie in place against a shirt. Also called: **tie clip.**

tied (taɪd) *adj Brit.* **1** (of a public house, retail shop, etc.) obliged to sell only the beer, products, etc. of a particular producer: *a tied house; tied outlet.* **2** (of a house) rented out to the tenant for as long as he or she is employed by the owner. **3** (of a loan) made by one nation to another on condition that the money is spent on goods or services provided by the lending nation.

tie-dyeing, tie-dye *or* **tie and dye** *n* a method of dyeing textiles to produce patterns by tying sections of the cloth together so that they will not absorb the dye.
▸ **ˈtie-ˌdyed** *adj*

tie in *vb* (*adv*) **1** to come or bring into a certain relationship; coordinate. ◆ *n* **tie-in. 2** a link, relationship, or coordination. **3** publicity material, a book, etc., linked to a film, etc. **4** *US.* **4a** a sale or advertisement offering products of which a purchaser must buy one or more in addition to his purchase. **4b** an item sold or advertised in this way. **4c** (*as modifier*): *a tie-in sale.*

tie line *n* a telephone line between two private branch exchanges or private exchanges that may or may not pass through a main exchange.

Tien Shan ★ (ˈtjɛnˈʃɑːn) *n* a variant transliteration of the Chinese name for the **Tian Shan.**

Tientsin ★ (ˈtjɛnˈtsɪn) *n* a variant transliteration of the Chinese name for **Tianjin.**

tiepin (ˈtaɪˌpɪn) *n* an ornamental pin of various shapes used to pin the two ends of a tie to a shirt.

Tiepolo ★ (*Italian* ˈtjɛːpolo; *English* tiːˈɛpəˌləʊ) *n* **Giovanni Battista** (dʒoˈvanni batˈtista). 1696–1770, Italian rococo painter.

tier[1] (tɪə) *n* **1** one of a set of rows placed one above and behind the other, such as theatre seats. **2a** a layer or level. **2b** (*in combination*): *a three-tier cake.* ◆ *vb* **3** to be or arrange in tiers. ORIG C16: from OF *tire* rank, of Gmc origin

tier[2] (ˈtaɪə) *n* a person or thing that ties.

tierce (tɪəs) *n* **1** a variant of **terce. 2** the third of eight positions from which a parry or attack can be made in fencing. **3** (tɜːs). a sequence of three cards. **4** an obsolete measure of capacity equal to 42 wine gallons. ORIG C15: from OF, fem of *tiers* third, from L *tertius*

tiercel (ˈtɪəsᵊl) *n* a variant of **tercel.**

Tierra del Fuego ★ (*Spanish* ˈtjerra ðel ˈfweɣo) *n* an archipelago at the S extremity of South America, separated from the mainland by the Strait of Magellan: the west and south belong to Chile, the east to Argentina, and several islands are disputed. Area: 73 643 sq. km (28 434 sq. miles).

tie up *vb* (*adv*) **1** (*tr*) to bind securely with or as if with string, rope, etc. **2** to moor (a vessel). **3** (*tr; often passive*) to engage the attentions of. **4** (*tr; often passive*) to conclude (the organization of something). **5** to come or bring to a complete standstill. **6** (*tr*) to commit (funds, etc.) and so make unavailable for other uses. **7** (*tr*) to subject (property) to conditions that prevent sale, alienation, etc. ◆ *n* **tie-up. 8** a link or connection. **9** *Chiefly US & Canad.* a standstill. **10** *Chiefly US & Canad.* an informal term for **traffic jam.**

tiff (tɪf) *n* **1** a petty quarrel. **2** a fit of ill humour. ◆ *vb* **3** (*intr*) to have or be in a tiff. ORIG C18: from ?

tiffany (ˈtɪfənɪ) *n, pl* **tiffanies.** a sheer fine gauzy fabric. ORIG C17 (in the sense: a fine dress worn on Twelfth Night): from OF *tifanie,* from ecclesiastical L *theophania* Epiphany

Tiffany ★ (ˈtɪfənɪ) *n* **Louis Comfort.** 1848–1933, US Art-Nouveau craftsman, best known for creating the Favrile style of stained glass.

tiffin (ˈtɪfɪn) *n* (in India) a light meal, esp. at midday. ORIG C18: prob. from obs. *tiffing,* from *tiff* to sip

Tiflis ★ (tɪfˈliːs) *n* transliteration of the Russian name for **Tbilisi.**

tig (tɪg) *n, vb* **tigs, tigging, tigged.** another word for **tag**[2] (senses 1, 4).

tiger (ˈtaɪgə) *n* **1** a large feline mammal of forests in most of Asia, having a tawny yellow coat with black stripes. **2** a dynamic, forceful, or cruel person. **3a** a country, esp. in E Asia, that is achieving rapid economic growth. **3b** (*as modifier*): *a tiger economy.* ORIG C13: from OF *tigre,* from L *tigris,* from Gk, of Iranian origin
▸ **ˈtigerish** *or* **ˈtigrish** *adj*

Tiger (ˈtaɪgə) *n* a variant of **TIGR.**

tiger beetle *n* any of a family of active predatory beetles, chiefly of warm dry regions, having powerful mandibles and long legs.

tiger cat *n* a medium-sized feline mammal of Central and South America, having a dark-striped coat.

tiger lily *n* a lily plant of China and Japan cultivated for its flowers, which have black-spotted orange petals.

tiger moth *n* any of various moths having wings that are conspicuously marked with stripes and spots.

tiger's-eye *or* **tigereye** (ˈtaɪgərˌaɪ) *n* a semiprecious golden-brown stone.

tiger shark *n* a voracious omnivorous requiem shark of tropical waters, having a striped or spotted body.

tiger snake *n* a highly venomous and aggressive Australian snake, usually with dark bands on the back.

tight (taɪt) *adj* **1** stretched or drawn so as not to be loose; taut. **2** fitting in a close manner. **3** held, made, fixed, or closed firmly and securely: *a tight knot.* **4a** of close and compact construction or organization, esp. so as to be impervious to water, air, etc. **4b** (*in combination*): *airtight.* **5** unyielding or stringent. **6** cramped or constricted: *a tight fit.* **7** mean or miserly. **8** difficult and problematic: *a tight situation.* **9** hardly profitable: *a tight bargain.* **10** *Econ.* **10a** (of a commodity) difficult to obtain. **10b** (of funds, money, etc.) difficult and expensive to borrow. **10c** (of markets) characterized by excess demand or scarcity. **11** (of a match or game) very close or even. **12** (of a team or group, esp. of a pop group) playing well together, in a disciplined coordinated way. **13** *Inf.* drunk. **14** *Inf.* (of a person) showing tension. ◆ *adv* **15** in a close, firm, or secure way. ORIG C14: prob. var. of *thight,* from ON *thēttr* close
▸ **ˈtightly** *adv* ▸ **ˈtightness** *n*

tightass (ˈtaɪtˌæs) *n Sl., chiefly US.* an inhibited or excessively self-controlled person.
▸ **ˈtightˌassed** *adj*

tighten (ˈtaɪtᵊn) *vb* to make or become tight or tighter.

tightfisted (ˌtaɪtˈfɪstɪd) *adj* mean; miserly.

tight head *n Rugby.* the prop on the hooker's right in the front row of a scrum. Cf. **loose head.**

tightknit (ˌtaɪtˈnɪt) *adj* **1** closely integrated: *a tightknit community.* **2** organized carefully.

tight-lipped *adj* **1** secretive or taciturn. **2** with the lips pressed tightly together, as through anger.

tightrope (ˈtaɪtˌrəʊp) *n* a rope stretched taut on which acrobats walk or perform balancing feats.
▸ **tightrope walker** *n*

tights (taɪts) *pl n* **1a** Also called: (US) **panty hose,** (Canad. and NZ) **pantyhose,** (Austral. and NZ) **pantihose.** a one-piece clinging garment covering the body from the waist to the feet, worn by women and also by acrobats, dancers, etc. **1b** *US & Canad.* Also called: **leotards.** a similar, tight-fitting garment worn instead of trousers by either sex. **2** a similar garment formerly worn by men, as in the 16th century with a doublet.

Tiglath-pileser I ★ (ˈtɪglæθpɪˈliːzə, -paɪ-) *n* king of Assyria (?1116–?1093 B.C.).

Tiglath-pileser III ★ *n* known as *Pulu.* died ?727 B.C., king of Assyria (745–727).

tiglic acid ('tɪglɪk) *n* a syrupy liquid or crystalline unsaturated carboxylic acid, found in croton oil and used in perfumery. ORIG C19 *tiglic,* from NL *Croton tiglium* (the croton plant), from ?

tigon ('taɪgən) *or* **tiglon** ('tɪglɒn) *n* the hybrid offspring of a male tiger and a female lion.

TIGR *abbrev. for* Treasury Investment Growth Receipts: a bond denominated in dollars and linked to US treasury bonds, the yield on which is taxed in the UK as income when it is cashed or redeemed. Also called: **Tiger.**

Tigré *or* **Tigray** ★ ('tiːgreɪ) *n* **1** an autonomous region of N Ethiopia, bordering on Eritrea: formerly a separate kingdom. Capital: Mekele. Pop.: 2 999 948 (1993 est.). Area: 53 498 sq. km (20 656 sq. miles). **2** a language of NE Ethiopia, belonging to the SE Semitic subfamily of the Afro-Asiatic family.

tigress ('taɪgrɪs) *n* **1** a female tiger. **2** a fierce, cruel, or wildly passionate woman.

tigridia (taɪ'grɪdɪə) *n* any of various bulbous plants of Mexico, Central America, and tropical S America. ORIG C19: from Mod. L, from Gk *tigris* tiger (alluding to the spotted flowers of these plants)

Tigris ★ ('taɪgrɪs) *n* a river in SW Asia, rising in E Turkey and flowing southeast through Baghdad to the Euphrates in SE Iraq, forming the delta of the Shatt-al-Arab, which flows into the Persian Gulf: part of a canal and irrigation system as early as 2400 B.C., with many ancient cities (including Nineveh) on its banks. Length: 1900 km (1180 miles).

Tihwa *or* **Tihua** ★ ('tiː'hwɑː) *n* a former name for **Urumchi.**

Tijuana (tiː'wɑːnə; *Spanish* ti'xwana) *or* **Tia Juana** ★ *n* a city and resort in NW Mexico, in Baja California. Pop.: 698 752 (1990).

tike (taɪk) *n* a variant spelling of **tyke.**

tiki ('tiːkiː) *n* a Maori greenstone neck ornament in the form of a fetus. Also called: **heitiki.** ORIG from Maori *heitiki* figure worn round neck

tikka ('tiːkə) *adj* (*immediately postpositive*) *Indian cookery.* (of meat, esp. chicken or lamb) marinated in spices and then dry-roasted, usually in a clay oven.

tilak ('tɪlək) *n, pl* **tilak** *or* **tilaks.** a coloured spot or mark worn by Hindus, esp. on the forehead, often indicating membership of a religious sect, caste, etc., or (in the case of a woman) marital status. ORIG from Sansk. *tilaka*

Tilburg ★ ('tɪlbɜːg; *Dutch* 'tɪlbyrx) *n* a city in the S Netherlands, in North Brabant: textile industries. Pop.: 163 383 (1994).

tilbury ('tɪlbərɪ, -brɪ) *n, pl* **tilburies.** a light two-wheeled horse-drawn open carriage, seating two people. ORIG C19: prob. after the inventor

Tilbury ★ ('tɪlbərɪ, -brɪ) *n* an area in Essex, on the River Thames: extensive docks; principal container port of the Port of London.

tilde ('tɪldə) *n* the diacritical mark (~) placed over a letter to indicate a nasal sound, as in Spanish *señor.* ORIG C19: from Sp., from L *titulus* title

Tilden ★ ('tɪldᵊn) *n* **Bill,** full name *William Tatem Tilden,* known as *Big Bill.* 1893–1953, US tennis player: won the US singles championship (1920–25, 1929).

tile (taɪl) *n* **1** a thin slab of fired clay, rubber, linoleum, etc., used with others to cover a roof, floor, wall, etc. **2** a short pipe made of earthenware, plastic, etc., used with others to form a drain. **3** tiles collectively. **4** a rectangular block used as a playing piece in mah jong and other games. **5 on the tiles.** *Inf.* on a spree, esp. of drinking or debauchery. ◆ *vb* **tiles, tiling, tiled. 6** (*tr*) to cover with tiles. ORIG OE *tīgele,* from L *tēgula*
▸ **'tiler** *n*

tiling ('taɪlɪŋ) *n* **1** tiles collectively. **2** something made of or surfaced with tiles.

till¹ (tɪl) *conj, prep* short for **until.** Also (not standard): **'til.** ORIG OE *til*

> **USAGE NOTE** *Till* is a variant of *until* that is acceptable in all styles of language. *Until* is, however, often preferred at the beginning of a sentence in formal writing: *until his behaviour improves, he cannot become a member.*

till² (tɪl) *vb* (*tr*) **1** to cultivate and work (land) for the raising of crops. **2** to plough. ORIG OE *tilian* to try, obtain
▸ **'tillable** *adj* ▸ **'tiller** *n*

till³ (tɪl) *n* a box, case, or drawer into which money taken from customers is put, now usually part of a cash register. ORIG C15 *tylle,* from ?

till⁴ (tɪl) *n* a glacial deposit consisting of rock fragments of various sizes. The most common is boulder clay. ORIG C17: from ?

tillage ('tɪlɪdʒ) *n* **1** the act, process, or art of tilling. **2** tilled land.

tiller¹ ('tɪlə) *n Naut.* a handle fixed to the top of a rudderpost to serve as a lever in steering it. ORIG C14: from Anglo-F *teiler* beam of a loom, from Med. L *tēlārium,* from L *tēla* web
▸ **'tillerless** *adj*

tiller² ('tɪlə) *n* **1** a shoot that arises from the base of the stem in grasses. **2** a less common name for **sapling.** ◆ *vb* **3** (*intr*) (of a plant) to produce tillers. ORIG OE *telgor* twig

Till Eulenspiegel ★ ('tɪl 'ɔɪlənˌʃpiːgᵊl) *n* ?14th century, legendary German peasant, whose pranks became the subject of many tales.

Tilley ★ ('tɪlɪ) *n* **Vesta,** original name *Matilda Alice Powles.* 1864–1952, British music-hall entertainer.

Tillich ★ ('tɪlɪk) *n* **Paul Johannes.** 1886–1965, US Protestant theologian and philosopher, born in Germany. His works include *The Courage to Be* (1952) and *Systematic Theology* (1951–63).

Tilsit ★ ('tɪlzɪt) *n* the former name (until 1945) of **Sovetsk.**

tilt (tɪlt) *vb* **1** to incline or cause to incline at an angle. **2** (*usually intr*) to attack or overthrow (a person) in a tilt or joust. **3** (when *intr,* often foll. by *at*) to aim or thrust: *to tilt a lance.* **4** (*tr*) to forge with a tilt hammer. ◆ *n* **5** a slope or angle: *at a tilt.* **6** the act of tilting. **7** (esp. in medieval Europe) **7a** a jousting contest. **7b** a thrust with a lance or pole delivered during a tournament. **8** an attempt to win a contest. **9** See **tilt hammer. 10** (**at**) **full tilt.** at full speed or force. ORIG OE *tealtian*
▸ **'tilter** *n*

tilth (tɪlθ) *n* **1** the act or process of tilling land. **2** the condition of soil or land that has been tilled. ORIG OE *tilthe*

tilt hammer *n* a drop hammer with a heavy head; used in forging.

tiltyard ('tɪltˌjɑːd) *n* (formerly) an enclosed area for tilting.

Tim. *Bible. abbrev. for* Timothy.

Timaru ★ ('tɪməˌruː) *n* a port and resort in S New Zealand, on E South Island. Pop.: 15 350 (1995 est.).

timbal *or* **tymbal** ('tɪmbᵊl) *n Music.* a type of kettledrum. ORIG C17: from F *timbale,* from OF *tamballe,* (associated also with *cymbale* cymbal), from OSp. *atabal,* from Ar. *at-tabl* the drum

timbale (tæm'bɑːl) *n* **1** a mixture of meat, fish, etc., cooked in a mould lined with potato or pastry. **2** a straight-sided mould in which such a dish is prepared. ORIG C19: from F: kettledrum

timber ('tɪmbə) *n* **1a** wood, esp. when regarded as a construction material. Usual US and Canad. word: **lumber. 1b** (*as modifier*): *a timber cottage.* **2a** trees collectively. **2b** *Chiefly US.* woodland. **3** a piece of wood used in a structure. **4** *Naut.* a frame in a wooden vessel. ◆ *vb* **5** (*tr*) to provide with timbers. ◆ *sentence substitute.* **6** a lumberjack's shouted warning when a tree is about to fall. ORIG OE
▸ **'timbered** *adj* ▸ **'timbering** *n*

timber hitch *n* a knot used for tying a rope round a spar, log, etc., for haulage.

timber limit *n Canad.* **1** the area to which rights of cutting timber, granted by a government licence, are limited. **2** another term for **timber line.**

timber line *n* the altitudinal or latitudinal limit of normal tree growth. See also **tree line.**

timber wolf *n* a wolf with a grey brindled coat found in forested northern regions, esp. of North America.

timberyard ('tɪmbəˌjɑːd) *n Brit., Austral., & NZ.* an establishment where timber, etc., is stored or sold. US and Canad. word: **lumberyard.**

timbre ('tɪmbə, 'tæmbə) *n* **1** *Phonetics.* the distinctive tone quality differentiating one vowel or sonant from another. **2** *Music.* tone colour or quality of sound. ORIG C19: from F: note of a bell, from OF: drum, from Med. Gk *timbanon,* from Gk *tumpanon*

timbrel ('tɪmbrəl) *n Chiefly biblical.* a tambourine. ORIG C16: from OF; see TIMBRE

Timbuktu ★ (ˌtɪmbʌk'tuː) *n* **1** a town in central Mali, on the River Niger: terminus of a trans-Saharan caravan route; a great Muslim centre (14th–16th centuries). Pop.: 31 925 (1987). French name: **Tombouctou. 2** any distant or outlandish place: *from here to Timbuktu.*

time (taɪm) *n* **1** the continuous passage of existence in which events pass from a state of potentiality in the future, through the present, to a state of finality in the past. Related adj: **temporal. 2** *Physics.* a quantity measuring duration, usually with reference to a periodic process such as the rotation of the earth or the vibration of electromagnetic radiation emitted from certain atoms. Time is considered as a fourth coordinate required to specify an event. See **space-time continuum. 3** a specific point on this continuum expressed in hours and minutes: *the time is four o'clock.* **4** a system of reckoning for expressing time: *Greenwich Mean Time.* **5a** a definite and measurable portion of this continuum. **5b** *(as modifier): time limit.* **6a** an accepted period such as a day, season, etc. **6b** *(in combination): springtime.* **7** an unspecified interval; a while. **8** *(often pl)* a period or point marked by specific attributes or events: *the Victorian times.* **9** a sufficient interval or period: *have you got time to help me?* **10** an instance or occasion: *I called you three times.* **11** an occasion or period of specified quality: *have a good time.* **12** the duration of human existence. **13** the heyday of human life: *in her time she was a great star.* **14** a suitable moment: *it's time I told you.* **15** the expected interval in which something is done. **16** a particularly important moment, esp. childbirth or death: *her time had come.* **17** *(pl)* indicating a degree or amount calculated by multiplication with the number specified: *ten times three is thirty.* **18** *(often pl)* the fashions, thought, etc., of the present age (esp. in **ahead of one's time, behind the times**). **19** *Brit.* Also: **closing time.** the time at which bars, pubs, etc., are legally obliged to stop selling alcoholic drinks. **20** *Inf.* a term in jail (esp. in **do time**). **21a** a customary or full period of work. **21b** the rate of pay for this period. **22** Also (esp. US): **metre. 22a** the system of combining beats or pulses in music into successive groupings by which the rhythm of the music is established. **22b** a specific system having a specific number of beats in each grouping or bar: *duple time.* **23** *Music.* short for **time value. 24 against time.** in an effort to complete something in a limited period. **25 ahead of time.** before the deadline. **26 at one time. 26a** once; formerly. **26b** simultaneously. **27 at the same time. 27a** simultaneously. **27b** nevertheless; however. **28 at times.** sometimes. **29 beat time.** to indicate the tempo of a piece of music by waving a baton, hand, etc. **30 for the time being.** for the moment; temporarily. **31 from time to time.** at intervals; occasionally. **32 have no time for.** to have no patience with; not tolerate. **33 in good time. 33a** early. **33b** quickly. **34 in no time.** very quickly. **35 in one's own time. 35a** outside paid working hours. **35b** at one's own rate. **36 in time. 36a** early or at the appointed time. **36b** eventually. **36c** *Music.* at a correct metrical or rhythmic pulse. **37 keep time.** to observe correctly the accent or rhythmic pulse of a piece of music in relation to tempo. **38 make time. 38a** to find an opportunity. **38b** (often foll. by *with*) *US inf.* to succeed in seducing. **39 on time. 39a** at the expected or scheduled time. **39b** *US.* payable in instalments. **40 pass the time of day.** to exchange casual greetings (with an acquaintance). **41 time and again.** frequently. **42 time off.** a period when one is absent from work for a holiday, through sickness, etc. **43 time of one's life.** a memorably enjoyable time. **44 time out of mind.** from time immemorial. **45** *(modifier)* operating automatically at or for a set time: *time lock; time switch.* ◆ *vb* **times, timing, timed.** *(tr)* **46** to ascertain the duration or speed of. **47** to set a time for. **48** to adjust to keep accurate time. **49** to pick a suitable time for. **50** *Sport.* to control the execution or speed of (an action). ◆ *sentence substitute.* **51** the word called out by a publican signalling that it is closing time. ORIG OE *tīma*

time and a half *n* the rate of pay equalling one and a half times the normal rate, often offered for overtime work.

time and motion study *n* the analysis of industrial or work procedures to determine the most efficient methods of operation. Also: **time and motion, time study, motion study.**

time bomb *n* a bomb containing a timing mechanism that determines the time at which it will detonate.

time capsule *n* a container holding articles, documents, etc., representative of the current age, buried for discovery in the future.

time charter *n* the hire of a ship or aircraft for a specified period. Cf. **voyage charter.**

time clock *n* a clock which records, by punching or stamping **timecards** inserted into it, the time of arrival or departure of people, such as employees in a factory.

time-consuming *adj* taking up or involving a great deal of time.

time exposure *n* **1** an exposure of a photographic film for a relatively long period, usually a few seconds. **2** a photograph produced by such an exposure.

time-honoured *adj* having been observed for a long time and sanctioned by custom.

time immemorial *n* the distant past beyond memory or record.

timekeeper ('taɪmˌkiːpə) *n* **1** a person or thing that keeps or records time. **2** an employee who maintains a record of the hours worked by the other employees. **3** an employee whose record of punctuality is of a specified nature: *a bad timekeeper.*
▸ **'timeˌkeeping** *n*

time-lag *n* an interval between two connected events.

time-lapse photography *n* the technique of recording a very slow process on film by exposing single frames at regular intervals. The film is then projected at normal speed.

timeless ('taɪmlɪs) *adj* **1** unaffected or unchanged by time; ageless. **2** eternal.
▸ **'timelessly** *adv* ▸ **'timelessness** *n*

timely ('taɪmlɪ) *adj* **timelier, timeliest,** *adv* at the right or an opportune or appropriate time.

time machine *n* (in science fiction) a machine in which people or objects can be transported into the past or the future.

time-out *n Chiefly US & Canad.* **1** *Sport.* an interruption in play during which players rest, discuss tactics, etc. **2** a period of rest; break. **3** *Computing.* a condition that occurs when the amount of time a computer has been instructed to wait for another device to perform a task has expired, usually indicated by an error message. ◆ *vb* **time out. 4** (of a computer) to stop operating because of a time-out.

timepiece ('taɪmˌpiːs) *n* any of various devices, such as a clock, watch, or chronometer, which measure and indicate time.

timer ('taɪmə) *n* **1** a device for measuring, recording, or indicating time. **2** a switch or regulator that causes a mechanism to operate at a specific time. **3** a person or thing that times.

time-saving *adj* shortening the length of time required for an operation, activity, etc.
▸ **time-saver** *n*

timescale ('taɪmˌskeɪl) *n* the span of time within which certain events occur or are scheduled in relation to any broader period of time.

time-served *adj* (of a craftsman or tradesman) having

completed an apprenticeship; fully trained and competent.

timeserver ('taɪmˌsɜːvə) *n* a person who compromises and changes his or her opinions, way of life, etc., to suit the current fashions.

time sharing *n* **1** a system of part ownership of a property for use as a holiday home whereby each participant owns the property for a particular period every year. **2** a system by which users at different terminals of a computer can, because of its high speed, apparently communicate with it at the same time.

time signal *n* an announcement of the correct time, esp. on radio or television.

time signature *n Music.* a sign usually consisting of two figures, one above the other, the upper figure representing the number of beats per bar and the lower one the time value of each beat: it is placed after the key signature.

Times Square ★ *n* a square formed by the intersection of Broadway and Seventh Avenue in New York City.

timetable ('taɪmˌteɪbᵊl) *n* **1** a list or table of events arranged according to the time when they take place; schedule. ◆ *vb* **timetables, timetabling, timetabled.** (*tr*) **2** to include in or arrange according to a timetable.

time value *n Music.* the duration of a note relative to other notes in a composition and considered in relation to the basic tempo.

time warp *n* an imagined distortion of the progress of time so that, for instance, events from the past may appear to be happening in the present.

timeworn ('taɪmˌwɔːn) *adj* **1** showing the adverse effects of overlong use or of old age. **2** hackneyed; trite.

time zone *n* a region throughout which the same standard time is used. There are 24 time zones in the world, demarcated approximately by meridians at 15° intervals, an hour apart.

timid ('tɪmɪd) *adj* **1** easily frightened or upset, esp. by human contact; shy. **2** indicating shyness or fear. ORIG C16: from L *timidus,* from *timēre* to fear
▸ **ti'midity** *or* **'timidness** *n* ▸ **'timidly** *adv*

timing ('taɪmɪŋ) *n* the regulation of actions or remarks in relation to others to produce the best effect, as in music, the theatre, etc.

Timişoara ★ (*Romanian* timi'ʃwara) *n* a city in W Romania: formerly under Turkish and then Hapsburg rule, being allotted to Romania in 1920; scene of violence during the revolution of 1989. Pop.: 325 359 (1993 est.). Hungarian name: **Temesvár.**

timocracy (taɪ'mɒkrəsɪ) *n, pl* **timocracies. 1** a political system in which possession of property is a requirement for participation in government. **2** a political system in which love of honour is deemed the guiding principle of government. ORIG C16: from OF *tymocracie,* ult. from Gk *timokratia,* from *timē* worth, honour, + -CRACY

Timor ★ ('tiːmɔː, 'taɪ-) *n* an island in Indonesia in the Malay Archipelago, the largest and easternmost of the Lesser Sunda Islands: the east, together with an enclave on the NW coast, formed the Portuguese overseas province of Portuguese Timor until 1975, when it declared independence but was immediately invaded by Indonesia. In 1976 Indonesia formally annexed the east, the legality of this act being disputed by the UN. Area: 30 775 sq. km (11 883 sq. miles).
▸ **ˌTimo'rese** *adj, n*

timorous ('tɪmərəs) *adj* **1** fearful or timid. **2** indicating fear or timidity. ORIG C15: from OF *temoros,* from Med. L, from L *timor* fear, from *timēre* to be afraid
▸ **'timorously** *adv* ▸ **'timorousness** *n*

Timor Sea ★ *n* an arm of the Indian Ocean between Australia and Timor. Width: about 480 km (300 miles).

Timoshenko ★ (ˌtɪmə'ʃɛŋkəʊ; *Russian* tima'ʃenkə) *n* **Semyon Konstantinovich** (sɪ'mjɔn kənstan'tinəvitʃ). 1895–1970, Soviet general in World War II.

Timothy ★ ('tɪməθɪ) *n New Testament.* **1 Saint.** a disciple of Paul, who became leader of the Christian community at Ephesus. Feast day: Jan. 26 or 22. **2** either of the two books addressed to him (in full **The First and Second Epistles of Paul the Apostle to Timothy**).

timothy grass *or* **timothy** *n* a perennial grass of temperate regions having erect stiff stems: grown for hay and pasture. ORIG C18: apparently after a *Timothy Hanson,* who brought it to colonial Carolina

timpani *or* **tympani** ('tɪmpənɪ) *pl n* (*sometimes functioning as sing*) a set of kettledrums. ORIG from It., pl of *timpano* kettledrum, from L: TYMPANUM
▸ **'timpanist** *or* **'tympanist** *n*

Timur *or* **Timour** ★ (tiː'mʊə) *n* See **Tamerlane.**

tin (tɪn) *n* **1** a malleable silvery-white metallic element. It is used extensively in alloys, esp. bronze and pewter, and as a noncorroding coating for steel. Symbol: Sn; atomic no.: 50; atomic wt.: 118.69. Related adjs.: **stannic, stannous. 2** Also called (esp. US and Canad.): **can.** an airtight sealed container of thin sheet metal coated with tin, used for preserving and storing food or drink. **3** any container made of metallic tin. **4** Also called: **tinful.** the contents of a tin. **5** *Brit., Austral., & NZ.* galvanized iron: *a tin roof.* **6** any metal regarded as cheap or flimsy. **7** *Brit.* a loaf of bread with a rectangular shape. **8** *NZ.* a receptacle for home-baked biscuits, etc. (esp. in **fill her tins** to bake a supply of biscuits, etc.). ◆ *vb* **tins, tinning, tinned.** (*tr*) **9** to put (food, etc.) into a tin or tins; preserve in a tin. **10** to plate or coat with tin. **11** to prepare (a metal) for soldering or brazing by applying a thin layer of solder to the surface. ORIG OE

tinamou ('tɪnəˌmuː) *n* any of various birds of Central and South America, having small wings and a heavy body. ORIG C18: via F from Carib *tinamu*

Tinbergen ★ ('tɪnˌbɜːgən) *n* **1 Jan** (jæn). 1903–94, Dutch economist: shared Nobel prize for economics 1969. **2** his brother, **Nikolaas** ('nɪkəlɑs). 1907–88, British zoologist and a founder of ethology; Nobel prize for physiology or medicine 1973.

tin can *n* a metal food container, esp. when empty.

tinctorial (tɪŋk'tɔːrɪəl) *adj* of or relating to colouring, staining, or dyeing. ORIG C17: from L *tinctōrius,* from *tingere* to tinge

tincture ('tɪŋktʃə) *n* **1** a medicinal extract in a solution of alcohol. **2** a tint, colour, or tinge. **3** a slight flavour, aroma, or trace. **4** a colour or metal used on heraldic arms. **5** *Obs.* a dye. ◆ *vb* **tinctures, tincturing, tinctured. 6** (*tr*) to give a tint or colour to. ORIG C14: from L *tinctūra* a dyeing, from *tingere* to dye

Tindal *or* **Tindale** ★ ('tɪndᵊl) *n* variant spellings of (William) **Tyndale.**

tinder ('tɪndə) *n* **1** dry wood or other easily combustible material used for lighting a fire. **2** anything inflammatory or dangerous. ORIG OE *tynder*
▸ **'tindery** *adj*

tinderbox ('tɪndəˌbɒks) *n* **1** a box used formerly for holding tinder, esp. one fitted with a flint and steel. **2** a person or thing that is particularly touchy or explosive.

tine (taɪn) *n* **1** a slender prong, esp. of a fork. **2** any of the sharp terminal branches of a deer's antler. ORIG OE *tind*
▸ **tined** *adj*

tinea ('tɪnɪə) *n* any fungal skin disease, esp. ringworm. ORIG C17: from L: worm
▸ **'tineal** *adj*

tinfoil ('tɪnˌfɔɪl) *n* **1** thin foil made of tin or an alloy of tin and lead. **2** thin foil made of aluminium; used for wrapping foodstuffs.

ting (tɪŋ) *n* **1** a high metallic sound such as that made by a small bell. ◆ *vb* **2** to make or cause to make such a sound. ORIG C15: imit.

Ting ★ (tɪŋ) *n* **Samuel C(hao) C(hung).** born 1936, US physicist, who discovered the J / psi particle and shared (1976) the Nobel prize for physics.

ting-a-ling ('tɪŋə'lɪŋ) *n* the sound of a small bell.

tinge (tɪndʒ) *n* **1** a slight tint or colouring. **2** any slight addition. ◆ *vb* **tinges, tingeing** *or* **tinging, tinged.** (*tr*) **3** to colour or tint faintly. **4** to impart a slight trace to: *her thoughts were tinged with nostalgia.* ORIG C15: from L *tingere* to colour

tingle ('tɪŋgᵊl) *vb* **tingles, tingling, tingled. 1** (*usually intr*) to

feel or cause to feel a prickling, itching, or stinging sensation of the flesh, as from a cold plunge. ◆ *n* **2** a sensation of tingling. ORIG C14: ? a var. of TINKLE
▸ **'tingler** *n* ▸ **'tingling** *adj* ▸ **'tingly** *adj*

tin god *n* **1** a self-important person. **2** a person erroneously regarded as holy or venerable.

tin hat *n Inf.* a steel helmet worn by military personnel.

tinker ('tɪŋkə) *n* **1** (esp. formerly) a travelling mender of pots and pans. **2** a clumsy worker. **3** the act of tinkering. **4** *Scot. & Irish.* a Gypsy. ◆ *vb* **5** (*intr;* foll. by *with*) to play, fiddle, or meddle (with machinery, etc.), esp. while undertaking repairs. **6** to mend (pots and pans) as a tinker. ORIG C13 *tinkere,* ?from *tink* tinkle, imit.
▸ **'tinkerer** *n*

tinker's damn *or* **cuss** *n Sl.* the slightest heed (esp. in **not give a tinker's damn** *or* **cuss**).

tinkle ('tɪŋk^ə^l) *vb* **tinkles, tinkling, tinkled. 1** to ring with a high tinny sound like a small bell. **2** (*tr*) to announce or summon by such a ringing. **3** (*intr*) *Brit. inf.* to urinate. ◆ *n* **4** a high clear ringing sound. **5** the act of tinkling. **6** *Brit. inf.* a telephone call. ORIG C14: imit.
▸ **'tinkly** *adj*

tin lizzie ('lɪzɪ) *n Inf.* an old or decrepit car.

tinned (tɪnd) *adj* **1** plated, coated, or treated with tin. **2** *Chiefly Brit.* preserved or stored in airtight tins. **3** coated with a layer of solder.

tinnitus (tɪ'naɪtəs) *n Pathol.* a ringing, hissing, or booming sensation in one or both ears, caused by infection of the ear, a side effect of certain drugs, etc. ORIG C19: from L, from *tinnīre* to ring

tinny ('tɪnɪ) *adj* **tinnier, tinniest. 1** of or resembling tin. **2** cheap or shoddy. **3** (of a sound) high, thin, and metallic. **4** (of food or drink) flavoured with metal, as from a container. **5** *Austral. & NZ sl.* lucky. ◆ *n, pl* **tinnies. 6** *Austral. sl.* a can of beer.
▸ **'tinnily** *adv* ▸ **'tinniness** *n*

tin-opener *n* a small tool for opening tins.

Tin Pan Alley ★ *n* **1** originally, a district in New York concerned with the production of popular music. **2** the commercial side of show business and pop music.

tin plate *n* **1** thin steel sheet coated with a layer of tin that protects the steel from corrosion. ◆ *vb* **tin-plate, tin-plates, tin-plating, tin-plated. 2** (*tr*) to coat with a layer of tin.

tinpot ('tɪn,pɒt) *adj* (*prenominal*) *Brit. inf.* **1** inferior, cheap, or worthless. **2** petty; unimportant.

tinsel ('tɪnsəl) *n* **1** a decoration consisting of a piece of string with thin strips of metal foil attached along its length. **2** a yarn or fabric interwoven with strands of glittering thread. **3** anything cheap, showy, and gaudy. ◆ *vb* **tinsels, tinselling, tinselled** *or US* **tinsels, tinseling, tinseled.** (*tr*) **4** to decorate with or as if with tinsel: *snow tinsels the trees.* **5** to give a gaudy appearance to. ◆ *adj* **6** made of or decorated with tinsel. **7** showily but cheaply attractive; gaudy. ORIG C16: from OF *estincele* a spark, from L *scintilla*
▸ **'tinselly** *adj*

Tinseltown ★ ('tɪnsəl,taʊn) *n* an informal name for **Hollywood.** ORIG C20: from the insubstantial glitter of the film world

tinsmith ('tɪn,smɪθ) *n* a person who works with tin or tin plate.

tin soldier *n* a miniature toy soldier, usually made of lead.

tinstone ('tɪn,stəʊn) *n* another name for **cassiterite.**

tint (tɪnt) *n* **1** a shade of a colour, esp. a pale one. **2** a colour that is softened by the addition of white. **3** a tinge. **4** a dye for the hair. **5** a trace or hint. **6** *Engraving.* uniform shading, produced esp. by hatching. ◆ *vb* **7** (*tr*) to colour or tinge. **8** (*intr*) to acquire a tint. ORIG C18: from earlier *tinct,* from L *tingere* to colour
▸ **'tinter** *n*

Tintagel Head ★ (tɪn'tædʒəl) *n* a promontory in SW England, on the W coast of Cornwall: ruins of **Tintagel Castle,** legendary birthplace of King Arthur.

tintinnabulation (,tɪntɪ,næbjʊ'leɪʃən) *n* the act or an instance of the ringing or pealing of bells. ORIG from L, from *tintinnāre* to tinkle, from *tinnīre* to ring

Tintoretto ★ (,tɪntə'retəʊ; *Italian* tinto'retto) *n* **Il** (il). original name *Jacopo Robusti.* 1518–94, Italian painter of the Venetian school. His works include *Susanna bathing* (?1550) and the fresco cycle in the Scuola di San Rocco, Venice (from 1564).

tinware ('tɪn,wɛə) *n* objects made of tin plate.

tin whistle *n* another name for **penny whistle.**

tinworks ('tɪn,wɜːks) *n* (*functioning as sing or pl*) a place where tin is mined, smelted, or rolled.

tiny ('taɪnɪ) *adj* **tinier, tiniest.** very small. ORIG C16 *tine,* from ?
▸ **'tinily** *adv* ▸ **'tininess** *n*

-tion *suffix forming nouns.* indicating state, condition, action, process, or result: *election; prohibition.* ORIG from OF, from L *-tiō, -tiōn-*

tip[1] (tɪp) *n* **1** a narrow or pointed end of something. **2** the top or summit. **3** a small piece forming an end: *a metal tip on a cane.* ◆ *vb* **tips, tipping, tipped.** (*tr*) **4** to adorn or mark the tip of. **5** to cause to form a tip. ORIG C15: from ON *typpa*
▸ **'tipless** *adj*

tip[2] (tɪp) *vb* **tips, tipping, tipped. 1** to tilt or cause to tilt. **2** (usually foll. by *over* or *up*) to tilt or cause to tilt, so as to overturn or fall. **3** *Brit.* to dump (rubbish, etc.). **4 tip one's hat.** to raise one's hat in salutation. ◆ *n* **5** a tipping or being tipped. **6** *Brit.* a dump for refuse, etc. ORIG C14: from ?
▸ **'tipper** *n*

tip[3] (tɪp) *n* **1** a payment given for services in excess of the standard charge; gratuity. **2** a helpful hint or warning. **3** a piece of inside information, esp. in betting or investing. ◆ *vb* **tips, tipping, tipped. 4** to give a tip to. ORIG C18: ?from TIP[4]
▸ **'tipper** *n*

tip[4] (tɪp) *vb* **tips, tipping, tipped.** (*tr*) **1** to hit or strike lightly. ◆ *n* **2** a light blow. ORIG C13: ?from Low G *tippen*

tip-off *n* **1** a warning or hint, esp. given confidentially and based on inside information. **2** *Basketball.* the act or an instance of putting the ball in play by the referee throwing it high between two opposing players. ◆ *vb* **tip off. 3** (*tr, adv*) to give a hint or warning to.

Tipperary ★ (,tɪpə'rɛərɪ) *n* a county of S Republic of Ireland, in Munster province; divided into the North Riding and South Riding: mountainous. County town: Clonmel. Pop.: 128 000 (1996). Area: 4255 sq. km (1643 sq. miles).

tipper truck *or* **lorry** *n* a truck or lorry the rear platform of which can be raised at the front end to enable the load to be discharged.

tippet ('tɪpɪt) *n* **1** a woman's fur cape for the shoulders. **2** the long stole of Anglican clergy worn during a service. **3** a long streamer-like part to a sleeve, hood, etc., esp. in the 16th century. ORIG C14: ?from TIP[1]

Tippett ★ ('tɪpɪt) *n* Sir **Michael.** 1905–98, British composer, whose works include the oratorio *A Child of Our Time* (1941) and several operas.

tipple ('tɪp^ə^l) *vb* **tipples, tippling, tippled. 1** to make a habit of taking (alcoholic drink), esp. in small quantities. ◆ *n* **2** alcoholic drink. ORIG C15: back formation from obs. *tippler* tapster, from ?
▸ **'tippler** *n*

tipstaff ('tɪp,stɑːf) *n* **1** a court official. **2** a metal-tipped staff formerly used as a symbol of office. ORIG C16 *tipped staff*

tipster ('tɪpstə) *n* a person who sells tips on horse racing, the stock market, etc.

tipsy ('tɪpsɪ) *adj* **tipsier, tipsiest. 1** slightly drunk. **2** slightly tilted or tipped; askew. ORIG C16: from TIP[2]
▸ **'tipsily** *adv* ▸ **'tipsiness** *n*

tipsy cake *n Brit.* a kind of trifle made from a sponge cake soaked with wine or sherry and decorated with almonds and crystallized fruit.

tiptoe ('tɪp,təʊ) *vb* **tiptoes, tiptoeing, tiptoed.** (*intr*) **1** to walk with the heels off the ground. **2** to walk silently or stealthily. ◆ *n* **3 on tiptoe. 3a** on the tips of the toes or on the ball of the foot and the toes. **3b** eagerly anticipating something. **3c** stealthily or silently. ◆ *adv* **4** on tiptoe. ◆ *adj* **5** walking or standing on tiptoe.

tiptop (ˌtɪpˈtɒp) *adj, adv* **1** at the highest point of health, excellence, etc. **2** at the topmost point. ◆ *n* **3** the best in quality. **4** the topmost point.

tip-up *adj* (*prenominal*) able to be turned upwards around a hinge or pivot: *a tip-up seat.*

TIR *abbrev. for* Transports Internationaux Routiers. ORIG F: International Road Transport

tirade (taɪˈreɪd) *n* a long angry speech or denunciation. ORIG C19: from F, lit.: a pulling, from It. *tirata,* from *tirare* to pull, from ?

Tiran ★ (tɪˈrɑːn) *n* **Strait of.** a strait between the Gulf of Aqaba and the Red Sea. Length: 16 km (10 miles). Width: 8 km (5 miles).

Tirana (tɪˈrɑːnə) *or* **Tiranë** ★ (*Albanian* tiˈranə) *n* the capital of Albania, in the central part 32 km (20 miles) from the Adriatic: founded in the early 17th century by Turks; became capital in 1920; the country's largest city and industrial centre. Pop.: 270 000 (1995 est.).

tire[1] (ˈtaɪə) *vb* **tires, tiring, tired. 1** (*tr*) to reduce the energy of, esp. by exertion; weary. **2** (*tr; often passive*) to reduce the tolerance of; bore or irritate: *I'm tired of the children's chatter.* **3** (*intr*) to become wearied or bored; flag. ORIG OE *tēorian,* from ?
▸ **ˈtiring** *adj*

tire[2] (ˈtaɪə) *n, vb* the US spelling of **tyre.**

tired (ˈtaɪəd) *adj* **1** weary; fatigued. **2** no longer fresh; hackneyed. **3 tired and emotional.** *Euphemistic.* drunk.
▸ **ˈtiredness** *n*

Tiree ★ (taɪˈriː) *n* an island off the W coast of Scotland, in the Inner Hebrides. Pop.: 1054 (latest est.). Area: 78 sq. km (30 sq. miles).

tireless (ˈtaɪəlɪs) *adj* unable to be tired.
▸ **ˈtirelessly** *adv* ▸ **ˈtirelessness** *n*

Tiresias ★ (taɪˈriːsɪˌæs) *n Greek myth.* a blind soothsayer of Thebes, who revealed to Oedipus that the latter had murdered his father and married his mother.

tiresome (ˈtaɪəsəm) *adj* boring and irritating.
▸ **ˈtiresomely** *adv* ▸ **ˈtiresomeness** *n*

tirewoman (ˈtaɪəˌwʊmən) *n, pl* **tirewomen.** an obsolete term for a lady's maid. ORIG C17: from *tire* (obs.) to ATTIRE

Tîrgu Mureş ★ (*Romanian* ˈtirgu ˈmureʃ) *n* a city in central Romania: manufacturing and cultural centre. Pop.: 165 502 (1993 est.).

Tirich Mir ★ (ˈtɪərɪtʃ ˈmɪə) *n* a mountain in N Pakistan: highest peak of the Hindu Kush. Height: 7690 m (25 230 ft).

tiring room (ˈtaɪərɪŋ) *n Arch.* a dressing room.

tiro (ˈtaɪrəʊ) *n, pl* **tiros.** a variant spelling of **tyro.**

Tirol ★ (tɪˈrəʊl, ˈtɪrəʊl; *German* tiˈroːl) *n* a variant spelling of **Tyrol.**
▸ **Tirolese** (ˌtɪrəˈliːz) *or* ˌ**Tiroˈlean** *adj, n*

Tirpitz ★ (*German* ˈtɪrpɪts) *n* **Alfred von** (ˈalfreːt fɔn). 1849–1930, German admiral: as secretary of state for the Imperial Navy (1897–1916), he created the modern German navy.

Tiruchirapalli (ˌtɪrətʃɪrəˈpʌlɪ, tɪˌruːtʃɪˈrɑːpəlɪ) *or* **Trichinopoly** ★ *n* an industrial city in S India, in central Tamil Nadu on the Cauvery River: dominated by a rock fortress 83 m (273 ft) high. Pop.: 387 223 (1991).

Tirunelveli ★ (ˌtɪrʊˈnɛlvɛlɪ) *n* a city in S India, in Tamil Nadu: site of St Francis Xavier's first preaching in India; textile manufacturing. Pop.: 135 825 (1991).

'tis (tɪz) *Poetic or dialect. contraction of* it is.

Tisa ★ (ˈtisa) *n* the Slavonic and Romanian name for the **Tisza.**

tisane (tɪˈzæn) *n* an infusion of leaves or flowers. ORIG C19: from F, from L *ptisana* barley water

Tishri *Hebrew.* (tɪʃˈriː) *n* (in the Jewish calendar) the seventh month of the year according to biblical reckoning and the first month of the civil year, falling in September and October. ORIG C19: from Heb.

Tisiphone ★ (tɪˈsɪfənɪ) *n Greek myth.* one of the three Furies; the others are Alecto and Megaera.

Tissot ★ (ˈtiːsəʊ; *French* tiso) *n* **James Joseph Jacques.** 1836–1902, French painter, who worked in England.

tissue (ˈtɪsjuː, ˈtɪʃuː) *n* **1** a part of an organism consisting of a large number of cells having a similar structure and function: nerve tissue. **2** a thin piece of soft absorbent paper used as a disposable handkerchief, towel, etc. **3** See **tissue paper. 4** an interwoven series: *a tissue of lies.* **5** a woven cloth, esp. of a light gauzy nature. ◆ *vb* **tissues, tissuing, tissued.** (*tr*) **6** to decorate or clothe with tissue or tissue paper. ORIG C14: from OF *tissu* woven cloth, from *tistre* to weave, from L *texere*

tissue culture *n* **1** the growth of small pieces of animal or plant tissue in a sterile controlled medium. **2** the tissue produced.

tissue paper *n* very thin soft delicate paper used to wrap breakable goods, as decoration, etc.

Tisza ★ (*Hungarian* ˈtisɔ) *n* a river in S central Europe, rising in W Ukraine and flowing west, forming part of the border between Ukraine and Romania, then southwest across Hungary into Yugoslavia to join the Danube north of Belgrade. Slavonic and Romanian name: **Tisa.**

tit[1] (tɪt) *n* any of numerous small active Old World songbirds, esp. the bluetit, great tit, etc. They have a short bill and feed on insects and seeds. ORIG C16: ? imit., applied to small animate or inanimate objects

tit[2] (tɪt) *n* **1** *Sl.* a female breast. **2** a teat or nipple. **3** *Derog.* a young woman. **4** *Taboo sl.* a despicable or unpleasant person. ORIG OE *titt*

Tit. *Bible. abbrev. for* Titus.

titan (ˈtaɪtᵊn) *n* a person of great strength or size. ORIG after TITAN

Titan (ˈtaɪtᵊn) *or* (*fem*) **Titaness** *n Greek myth.* **1** any of a family of primordial gods, the sons and daughters of Uranus (sky) and Gaea (earth). **2** any of the offspring of the children of Uranus and Gaea.
▸ **Titanesque** (ˌtaɪtəˈnɛsk) *adj*

Titania ★ (tɪˈtɑːnɪə) *n* **1** (in medieval folklore) the queen of the fairies and wife of Oberon. **2** (in classical antiquity) a poetic epithet used of Circe, Diana, Latona, or Pyrrha.

titanic (taɪˈtænɪk) *adj* possessing or requiring colossal strength: *a titanic battle.*

titanium (taɪˈteɪnɪəm) *n* a strong malleable white metallic element, which is very corrosion-resistant. It is used in the manufacture of strong lightweight alloys, esp. aircraft parts. Symbol: Ti; atomic no.: 22; atomic wt.: 47.88. ORIG C18: NL; see TITAN, -IUM

titanium dioxide *n* a white powder used chiefly as a pigment. Formula: TiO_2. Also called: **titanium oxide, titanic oxide, titania.**

titbit (ˈtɪtˌbɪt) *or esp. US* **tidbit** *n* **1** a tasty small piece of food; dainty. **2** a pleasing scrap of anything, such as scandal. ORIG C17: ?from dialect *tid* tender, from ?

titchy *or* **tichy** (ˈtɪtʃɪ) *adj* **titchier, titchiest** *or* **tichier, tichiest.** *Brit. sl.* very small; tiny. ORIG C20: from *tich* or *titch* a small person, from *Little Tich,* stage name of Harry Relph (1867–1928), E actor noted for his small stature

titfer (ˈtɪtfə) *n Brit. sl.* a hat. ORIG from rhyming slang *tit for tat*

tit for tat *n* an equivalent given in return or retaliation; blow for blow. ORIG C16: from earlier *tip for tap*

tithe (taɪð) *n* **1** (*often pl*) a tenth part of produce, income, or profits, contributed for the support of the church or clergy. **2** any levy, esp. of one tenth. **3** a tenth or a very small part of anything. ◆ *vb* **tithes, tithing, tithed. 4** (*tr*) **4a** to exact or demand a tithe from. **4b** to levy a tithe upon. **5** (*intr*) to pay a tithe or tithes. ORIG OE *teogoth*
▸ **ˈtithable** *adj*

tithe barn *n* a large barn where, formerly, the agricultural tithe of a parish was stored.

Tithonus ★ (tɪˈθəʊnəs) *n Greek myth.* the son of Laomedon of Troy who was loved by the goddess Eos. She asked that he be made immortal but forgot to ask that he be made eternally young. When he aged she turned him into a grasshopper.

titi (ˈtiːtiː) *n, pl* **titis.** any of a genus of small New World monkeys of South America, having beautifully coloured fur and a long nonprehensile tail. ORIG via Sp. from Aymara, lit.: little cat

Titian ★ ('tɪʃən) *n* original name *Tiziano Vecellio.* ?1490–1576, Italian painter of the Venetian school.
▸ **ˌTitian'esque** *adj*

Titian red *n* a reddish-yellow colour, as in the hair colour in many of the works of Titian.

Titicaca ★ (*Spanish* titi'kaka) *n* **Lake.** a lake between S Peru and W Bolivia, in the Andes: the highest large lake in the world; drained by the Desaguadero River flowing into Lake Poopó. Area: 8135 sq. km (3141 sq. miles). Altitude: 3809 m (12 497 ft). Depth: 370 m (1214 ft).

titillate ('tɪtɪˌleɪt) *vb* **titillates, titillating, titillated.** (*tr*) **1** to arouse or excite pleasurably. **2** to cause a tickling or tingling sensation in, esp. by touching. ORIG C17: from L *tītillāre*
▸ **'titilˌlating** *adj* ▸ **ˌtitil'lation** *n*

titivate *or* **tittivate** ('tɪtɪˌveɪt) *vb* **titivates, titivating, titivated** *or* **tittivates, tittivating, tittivated.** to smarten up; spruce up. ORIG C19: earlier *tidivate,* ? based on TIDY & CULTIVATE
▸ **ˌtiti'vation** *or* **ˌtitti'vation** *n*

titlark ('tɪtˌlɑːk) *n* another name for **pipit,** esp. the meadow pipit. ORIG C17: from TIT[1] + LARK[1]

title ('taɪt[ə]l) *n* **1** the distinctive name of a work of art, musical or literary composition, etc. **2** a descriptive name or heading of a section of a book, speech, etc. **3** See **title page. 4** a name or epithet signifying rank, office, or function. **5** a formal designation, such as *Mr.* **6** an appellation designating nobility. **7** *Films.* **7a** short for **subtitle. 7b** written material giving credits in a film or television programme. **8** *Sport.* a championship. **9** *Law.* **9a** the legal right to possession of property, esp. real property. **9b** the basis of such right. **9c** the documentary evidence of such right: *title deeds.* **10a** any customary or established right. **10b** a claim based on such a right. **11** a definite spiritual charge or office in the church as a prerequisite for ordination. **12** *RC Church.* a titular church. ◆ *vb* **titles, titling, titled. 13** (*tr*) to give a title to. ORIG C13: from OF, from L *titulus*

title deed *n* a document evidencing a person's legal right or title to property, esp. real property.

titleholder ('taɪt[ə]lˌhəʊldə) *n* a person who holds a title, esp. a sporting championship.

title page *n* the page in a book that gives the title, author, publisher, etc.

title role *n* the role of the character after whom a play, etc., is named.

titmouse ('tɪtˌmaʊs) *n, pl* **titmice.** another name for **tit**[1]. ORIG C14 *titemous,* from *tite* (see TIT[1]) + MOUSE

Tito ★ ('tiːtəʊ) *n* **Marshal.** original name *Josip Broz.* 1892–1980, Yugoslav statesman, who led the communist guerrilla resistance to German occupation during World War II; prime minister (1945–53) and president (1953–80).

Titograd ★ (*Serbo-Croat* 'titɔgraːd) *n* the former name (1946–92) of **Podgorica.**

titrate ('taɪtreɪt) *vb* **titrates, titrating, titrated.** (*tr*) to measure the volume or the concentration of (a solution) by titration. ORIG C19: from F *titrer;* see TITRE
▸ **ti'tratable** *adj*

titration (taɪ'treɪʃən) *n* an operation in which a measured amount of one solution is added to a known quantity of another solution until the reaction between the two is complete. If the concentration of one solution is known, that of the other can be calculated.

titre *or US* **titer** ('taɪtə) *n* the concentration of a solution as determined by titration. ORIG C19: from F *titre* proportion of gold or silver in an alloy, from OF *title* TITLE

titter ('tɪtə) *vb* (*intr*) **1** to snigger, esp. derisively or in a suppressed way. ◆ *n* **2** a suppressed laugh, chuckle, or snigger. ORIG C17: imit.
▸ **'titterer** *n* ▸ **'tittering** *adj*

tittle ('tɪt[ə]l) *n* **1** a small mark in printing or writing, esp. a diacritic. **2** a jot; particle. ORIG C14: from Med. L *titulus* label, from L: title

tittle-tattle *n* **1** idle chat or gossip. ◆ *vb* **tittle-tattles, tittle-tattling, tittle-tattled. 2** (*intr*) to chatter or gossip.
▸ **'tittle-ˌtattler** *n*

tittup ('tɪtəp) *vb* **tittups, tittupping, tittupped** *or US* **tittups, tittuping, tittuped. 1** (*intr*) to prance or frolic. ◆ *n* **2** a caper. ORIG C18 (in the sense: a horse's gallop): prob. imit.

titubation (ˌtɪtjʊ'beɪʃən) *n Pathol.* a disordered gait characterized by stumbling or staggering, often caused by a lesion of the cerebellum. ORIG C17: from L *titubātiō,* from *titubāre* to reel

titular ('tɪtjʊlə) *adj* **1** of, relating to, or of the nature of a title. **2** in name only. **3** bearing a title. **4** *RC Church.* designating any of certain churches in Rome to whom cardinals or bishops are attached as their nominal incumbents. ◆ *n* **5** the bearer of a title. **6** the bearer of a nominal office. ORIG C18: from F *titulaire,* from L *titulus* title

Titus ★ ('taɪtəs) *n* **1** *New Testament.* **1a Saint.** a Greek disciple and helper of Saint Paul. Feast day: Jan. 26 or Aug. 25. **1b** the book written to him (in full **The Epistle of Paul the Apostle to Titus**). **2** full name *Titus Flavius Sabinus Vespasianus.* ?40–81 A.D., Roman emperor (78–81 A.D.).

Tiu ★ ('tiːuː) *n* (in Anglo-Saxon mythology) the god of war and the sky. Norse counterpart: **Tyr.**

Tivoli ★ ('tɪvəlɪ; *Italian* 'tiːvoli) *n* a town in central Italy, east of Rome: a summer resort in Roman times; contains the Renaissance Villa d'Este and the remains of Hadrian's Villa. Pop.: 55 030 (1990). Ancient name: **Tibur.**

tizzy ('tɪzɪ) *n, pl* **tizzies.** *Inf.* a state of confusion or excitement. Also called: **tizz, tiz-woz.** ORIG C19: from ?

Tjirebon *or* **Cheribon** ★ ('tʃɪərəˌbɒn) *n* a port in S central Indonesia, on N Java on the Java Sea: scene of the signing of the **Tjirebon Agreement** of Indonesian independence (1946) by the Netherlands. Pop.: 245 307 (1990).

T-junction *n* a road junction in which one road joins another at right angles but does not cross it.

TKO *Boxing. abbrev. for* technical knockout.

Tl *the chemical symbol for* thallium.

Tlaxcala ★ (*Spanish* tlas'kala) *n* **1** a state of S central Mexico: the smallest Mexican state; formerly an Indian principality, the chief Indian ally of Cortés in the conquest of Mexico. Capital: Tlaxcala. Pop.: 911 696 (1997 est.). Area: 3914 sq. km (1511 sq. miles). **2** a city in E central Mexico, capital of Tlaxcala state: the church of San Francisco (founded 1521 by Cortés) is the oldest in the Americas. Pop.: 25 000 (1990 est.). Official name: **Tlaxcala de Xicohténcatl.**

Tlemcen ★ (*French* tlɛmsɛn) *n* a city in NW Algeria: capital of an Arab kingdom from the 12th to the late 14th century. Pop.: 107 632 (1987).

Tm *the chemical symbol for* thulium.

TM *abbrev. for* transcendental meditation.

tmesis (tə'miːsɪs) *n* interpolation of a word or words between the parts of a compound word, as in *every-blooming-where.* ORIG C16: via L from Gk, lit.: a cutting, from *temnein* to cut

TN *abbrev. for* Tennessee.

TNT *n* 2,4,6-trinitrotoluene; a yellow solid: used chiefly as a high explosive.

T-number *or* **T number** *n Photog.* a function of the f-number of a lens that takes into account the light transmitted by the lens. ORIG from *T(otal Light Transmission) Number*

to (tuː; *unstressed* tʊ, tə) *prep* **1** used to indicate the destination of the subject or object of an action: *he climbed to the top.* **2** used to mark the indirect object of a verb: *telling stories to children.* **3** used to mark the infinitive of a verb: *he wanted to go.* **4** as far as; until: *working from Monday to Friday.* **5** used to indicate equality: *16 ounces to the pound.* **6** against; upon; onto: *put your ear to the wall.* **7** before the hour of: *five minutes to four.* **8** accompanied by: *dancing to loud music.* **9** as compared with, as against: *the score was eight to three.* **10** used to indicate a resulting condition: *they starved to death.* ◆ *adv* **11** towards a fixed position, esp. (of a door) closed. ORIG OE *tō*

toad (təʊd) *n* **1** any of a group of amphibians similar to frogs but more terrestrial, having a drier warty skin. **2** a loathsome person. ORIG OE *tādige,* from ?
▸ **'toadish** *adj*

toadfish ('təʊd,fɪʃ) *n, pl* **toadfish** *or* **toadfishes.** any of various spiny-finned marine fishes of tropical and temperate seas.

toadflax ('təʊd,flæks) *n* a perennial plant having narrow leaves and spurred two-lipped yellow-orange flowers. Also called: **butter-and-eggs.**

toad-in-the-hole *n Brit. & Austral.* a dish made of sausages baked in a batter.

toadstone ('təʊd,stəʊn) *n* an intrusive volcanic rock occurring in limestone. ORIG C18: ?from a supposed resemblance to a toad's spotted skin

toadstool ('təʊd,stu:l) *n* (*not in technical use*) any basidiomycetous fungus with a capped spore-producing body that is poisonous. Cf. **mushroom.**

toady ('təʊdɪ) *n, pl* **toadies. 1** Also: **toadeater.** a person who flatters and ingratiates himself or herself in a servile way; sycophant. ◆ *vb* **toadies, toadying, toadied. 2** to fawn on and flatter (someone). ORIG C19: shortened from *toadeater,* orig. a quack's assistant who pretended to eat toads, hence a flatterer
▸ **'toadyish** *adj* ▸ **'toadyism** *n*

Toamasina ★ (*Portuguese* tõuma'sinə) *n* a port in E Madagascar, on the Indian Ocean: the country's chief commercial centre. Pop.: 127 441 (1993). Former name (until 1979): **Tamatave.**

to and fro *adv,* **to-and-fro** *adj* **1** back and forth. **2** here and there.
▸ **'toing and 'froing** *n*

toast[1] (təʊst) *n* **1a** sliced bread browned by exposure to heat. **1b** (*as modifier*): *a toast rack.* **2 be toast.** *Inf.* to face certain destruction or defeat. ◆ *vb* **3** (*tr*) to brown under a grill or over a fire: *to toast cheese.* **4** to warm or be warmed: *to toast one's hands by the fire.* ORIG C14: from OF *toster,* from L *tōstus* parched, from *torrēre* to dry with heat

toast[2] (təʊst) *n* **1** a tribute or proposal of health, success, etc., given to a person or thing and marked by people raising glasses and drinking together. **2** a person or thing honoured by such a tribute or proposal. **3** (esp. formerly) an attractive woman to whom such tributes are frequently made. ◆ *vb* **4** to propose or drink a toast to (a person or thing). **5** (*intr*) to add vocal effects to a prerecorded track: a disc-jockey technique. ORIG C17 (in the sense: a lady to whom the company is asked to drink): from TOAST[1], from the idea that the name of the lady would flavour the drink like a piece of spiced toast
▸ **'toaster** *n*

toaster ('təʊstə) *n* a device, esp. an electrical device, for toasting bread.

toastmaster ('təʊst,mɑ:stə) *n* a person who introduces speakers, proposes toasts, etc., at public dinners.
▸ **'toast,mistress** *fem n*

toasty *or* **toastie** ('təʊstɪ) *n, pl* **toasties.** a toasted sandwich.

Tob. *abbrev. for* Tobit.

tobacco (tə'bækəʊ) *n, pl* **tobaccos** *or* **tobaccoes. 1** any of a genus of plants having mildly narcotic properties, one species of which is cultivated as the chief source of commercial tobacco. **2** the leaves of certain of these plants dried and prepared for snuff, chewing, or smoking. ORIG C16: from Sp. *tabaco,* ?from Taino: leaves rolled for smoking, assumed by the Spaniards to be the name of the plant

tobacco mosaic virus *n* the virus that causes mosaic disease in tobacco and related plants: its discovery provided the first evidence of the existence of viruses. Abbrev.: **TMV.**

tobacconist (tə'bækənɪst) *n Chiefly Brit.* a person or shop that sells tobacco, cigarettes, pipes, etc.

Tobago ★ (tə'beɪgəʊ) *n* an island in the SE Caribbean, northeast of Trinidad: ceded to Britain in 1814; joined with Trinidad in 1888 as a British colony; part of the independent republic of Trinidad and Tobago. Pop.: 46 400 (1990).
▸ **Tobagonian** (,təʊbə'gəʊnɪən) *adj, n*

-to-be *adj* (*in combination*) about to be; future: *a mother-to-be; the bride-to-be.*

Tobey ★ ('təʊbɪ) *n* **Mark.** 1890–1976, US painter. Influenced by Chinese calligraphy, he devised a style of improvisatory abstract painting called "white writing".

Tobit ★ ('təʊbɪt) *n Old Testament.* **1** a pious Jew who was released from blindness through the help of the archangel Raphael. **2** a book of the Apocrypha relating this story.

toboggan (tə'bɒgən) *n* **1** a light wooden frame on runners used for sliding over snow and ice. **2** a long narrow sledge made of a thin board curved upwards at the front. ◆ *vb* **toboggans, tobogganing, tobogganed.** (*intr*) **3** to ride on a toboggan. ORIG C19: from Canad. F, of Amerind origin
▸ **to'bogganer** *or* **to'bogganist** *n*

Tobol ★ (*Russian* ta'bɔl) *n* a river in central Asia, rising in N Kazakhstan and flowing northeast to join the Irtysh River in Russia. Length: about 1300 km (800 miles).

Tobolsk ★ (*Russian* ta'bɔljsk) *n* a town in central Asia, at the confluence of the Irtysh and Tobol Rivers: the chief centre for the early Russian colonization of Siberia. Pop.: 83 000 (1988 est.).

Tobruk ★ (tə'brʊk, təʊ-) *n* a small port in NE Libya, in E Cyrenaica on the Mediterranean coast road: scene of severe fighting in World War II: taken from the Italians by the British in January 1941, from the British by the Germans in June 1942, and finally taken by the British in November 1942.

toby ('təʊbɪ) *n, pl* **tobies.** *NZ.* a water stopcock at the boundary of a street and house section.

toby jug *n* a beer mug or jug in the form of a stout seated man wearing a three-cornered hat and smoking a pipe. Also called: **toby.** ORIG C19: from the familiar form of the name *Tobias*

Tocantins ★ (*Portuguese* tokã'tĩs) *n* **1** a state of N Brazil, created from the northern part of Goiás state in 1988. Capital: Palmas. Pop.: 1 048 642 (1996). Area: 278 421 sq. km (107 499 sq. miles). **2** a river in E Brazil, rising in S central Goiás state and flowing generally north to the Pará River. Length: about 2700 km (1700 miles).

toccata (tə'kɑ:tə) *n* a rapid keyboard composition for organ, harpsichord, etc., usually in a rhythmically free style. ORIG C18: from It., lit.: touched, from *toccare* to play (an instrument)

Toc H ('tɒk 'eɪtʃ) *n* a society formed after World War I to encourage Christian comradeship. ORIG C20: from the obs. telegraphic code for *T.H.,* initials of *Talbot House,* Poperinge, Belgium, the original headquarters of the society

Tocharian *or* **Tokharian** (tɒ'kɑ:rɪən) *n* **1** a member of an Asian people who lived in the Tarim Basin until around 800 A.D. **2** the language of this people, known from records in a N Indian script of the 7th and 8th centuries A.D. ORIG C20: ult. from Gk *Tokharoi,* from ?

tocopherol (tɒ'kɒfə,rɒl) *n* any of a group of fat-soluble alcohols that occur in wheat-germ oil, lettuce, egg yolk, etc. Also called: **vitamin E.** ORIG C20: from *toco-,* from Gk *tokos* offspring + *-pher-,* from *pherein* to bear + -OL[1]

Tocqueville ★ ('təʊkvɪl, 'tɒk-; *French* tɔkvil) *n* **Alexis Charles Henri Maurice Clérel de** (alɛksi ʃarl ɑ̃ri mɔris klerɛl də). 1805–59, French political writer. His works include *L'Ancien régime et la révolution* (1856).

tocsin ('tɒksɪn) *n* **1** an alarm or warning signal, esp. one sounded on a bell. **2** an alarm bell. ORIG C16: from F, from OF *toquassen,* from OProvençal, from *tocar* to touch + *senh* bell, from L *signum*

tod (tɒd) *n* **on one's tod.** *Brit. sl.* on one's own. ORIG C19: rhyming sl. *Tod Sloan/alone,* after *Tod* Sloan, a jockey

today (tə'deɪ) *n* **1** this day, as distinct from yesterday or tomorrow. **2** the present age. ◆ *adv* **3** during or on this day. **4** nowadays. ORIG OE *tō dæge,* lit.: on this day

Todd ★ (tɒd) *n* **Alexander Robertus,** Baron. 1907–97, Brit-

★ people and places

ish chemist, noted for his work on nucleic acids: Nobel prize for chemistry 1957.

toddle ('tɒdᵊl) *vb* **toddles, toddling, toddled.** (*intr*) **1** to walk with short unsteady steps, as a child. **2** (foll. by *off*) *Jocular.* to depart. **3** (foll. by *round, over,* etc.) *Jocular.* to stroll. ◆ *n* **4** the act or an instance of toddling. ORIG C16 (Scot. & N English): from ?

toddler ('tɒdlə) *n* a young child, usually between the ages of one and two and a half.

toddy ('tɒdɪ) *n, pl* **toddies. 1** a drink made from spirits, esp. whisky, hot water, sugar, and usually lemon juice. **2** the sap of various palm trees used as a beverage. ORIG C17: from Hindi *tārī* juice of the palmyra palm, from *tār* palmyra palm, from Sansk. *tāra*

to-do (tə'du:) *n, pl* **to-dos.** a commotion, fuss, or quarrel.

toe (təʊ) *n* **1** any one of the digits of the foot. **2** the corresponding part in other vertebrates. **3** the part of a shoe, etc., covering the toes. **4** anything resembling a toe in shape or position. **5 on one's toes.** alert. **6 tread on someone's toes.** to offend a person, esp. by trespassing on his or her field of responsibility. ◆ *vb* **toes, toeing, toed. 7** (*tr*) to touch, kick, or mark with the toe. **8** (*tr*) to drive (a nail, etc.) obliquely. **9** (*intr*) to walk with the toes pointing in a specified direction: *to toe inwards.* **10 toe the line** *or* **mark.** to conform to expected attitudes, standards, etc. ORIG OE *tā*

toe and heel *n* a technique used by racing drivers on sharp bends, in which the brake and accelerator are operated simultaneously by the toe and heel of the right foot.

toecap ('təʊˌkæp) *n* a reinforced covering for the toe of a boot or shoe.

toed (təʊd) *adj* **1** having a part resembling a toe. **2** fixed by nails driven in at the foot. **3** (*in combination*) having a toe or toes as specified: *five-toed; thick-toed.*

toehold ('təʊˌhəʊld) *n* **1** a small foothold to facilitate climbing. **2** any means of gaining access, support, etc. **3** a wrestling hold in which the opponent's toe is held and his or her leg twisted.

toe-in *n* a slight forward convergence given to the wheels of motor vehicles to improve steering.

toenail ('təʊˌneɪl) *n* **1** a thin horny translucent plate covering part of the surface of the end joint of each toe. **2** *Carpentry.* a nail driven obliquely. ◆ *vb* **3** (*tr*) *Carpentry.* to join (beams) by driving nails obliquely.

toerag ('təʊˌræg) *n Brit. sl.* a contemptible or despicable person. ORIG C20: orig., a beggar, tramp: from the rags wrapped round their feet

toey ('təʊɪ) *adj Austral. sl.* nervous and restless; anxious.

toff (tɒf) *n Brit. sl.* a well-dressed or upper-class person, esp. a man. ORIG C19: ? var. of TUFT, nickname for a titled student at Oxford University, wearing a cap with a gold tassel

toffee *or* **toffy** ('tɒfɪ) *n, pl* **toffees** *or* **toffies. 1** a sweet made from sugar or treacle boiled with butter, nuts, etc. **2 for toffee.** (preceded by *can't*) *Inf.* to be incompetent at: *he can't sing for toffee.* ORIG C19: var. of earlier *taffy*

toffee-apple *n* an apple fixed on a stick and coated with a thin layer of toffee.

toffee-nosed *adj Sl., chiefly Brit.* pretentious or supercilious; used esp. of snobbish people.

toft (tɒft) *n Brit. history.* **1** a homestead. **2** a homestead and its arable land. ORIG OE

tofu ('təʊˌfu:) *n* unfermented soya-bean curd, a food with a soft cheeselike consistency. ORIG from Japanese

tog[1] (tɒg) *Inf.* ◆ *vb* **togs, togging, togged. 1** (often foll. by *up* or *out*) to dress oneself, esp. in smart clothes. ◆ *n* **2** See **togs.** ORIG C18: ?from obs. cant *togemans* coat, from L *toga* TOGA + *-mans,* from ?

tog[2] (tɒg) *n* **a** a unit of thermal resistance used to measure the power of insulation of a fabric, garment, quilt, etc. **b** (*as modifier*): *tog-rating.* ORIG C20: arbitrary coinage from TOG[1] (n)

toga ('təʊgə) *n* **1** a garment worn by citizens of ancient Rome, consisting of a piece of cloth draped around the body. **2** a robe of office. ORIG C16: from L
▸ **togaed** ('təʊgəd) *adj*

together (tə'gɛðə) *adv* **1** with cooperation and interchange between constituent elements, members, etc.: *we worked together.* **2** in or into contact with each other: *to stick papers together.* **3** in or into one place; with each other: *the people are gathered together.* **4** at the same time. **5** considered collectively: *all our wages put together couldn't buy that car.* **6** continuously: *working for eight hours together.* **7** closely or compactly united or held: *water will hold the dough together.* **8** mutually or reciprocally: *to multiply seven and eight together.* **9** *Inf.* organized: *to get things together.* ◆ *adj* **10** *Sl.* self-possessed, competent, and well-organized. **11 together with.** (*prep*) in addition to. ORIG OE *tōgædre*

USAGE NOTE See at **plus.**

togetherness (tə'gɛðənɪs) *n* a feeling of closeness or affection from being united with other people.

toggery ('tɒgərɪ) *n Inf.* clothes; togs.

toggle ('tɒgᵊl) *n* **1** a peg or rod at the end of a rope, chain, or cable, for fastening by insertion through an eye in another rope, chain, etc. **2** a bar-shaped button inserted through a loop for fastening. **3** a toggle joint or a device having such a joint. ◆ *vb* **toggles, toggling, toggled. 4** (*tr*) to supply or fasten with a toggle. ORIG C18: from ?

toggle joint *n* a device consisting of two arms pivoted at a common joint and at their outer ends and used to apply pressure by straightening the angle between the two arms.

toggle switch *n* **1** an electric switch having a projecting lever that is manipulated in a particular way to open or close a circuit. **2** a computer device used to turn a feature on or off.

Togliatti ★ (ˌtɒlɪ'ætɪ) *n* a city in W central Russia, on the Volga River: automobile industry: renamed in honour of Palmiro Togliatti (1893–1964), an Italian communist. Pop.: 702 000 (1995 est.). Former name (until 1964): **Stavropol.** Russian name: **Tol'yatti.**

Togo[1] ★ ('təʊgəʊ) *n* a republic in West Africa, on the Gulf of Guinea: became French Togoland (a League of Nations mandate) after the division of German Togoland in 1922; independent since 1960. Official language: French. Religion: animist majority. Currency: franc. Capital: Lomé. Pop.: 5 081 000 (1999 est.). Area: 56 700 sq. km (20 900 sq. miles).
▸ **Togolese** (ˌtəʊgə'li:z) *adj, n*

Togo[2] ★ ('təʊgəʊ) *n* Marquis **Heihachiro** (ˌheɪhɑ:'tʃi:rəʊ). 1847–1934, Japanese admiral, who commanded the fleet in the war with Russia (1904–05).

Togoland ★ ('təʊgəʊˌlænd) *n* a former German protectorate in West Africa on the Gulf of Guinea: divided in 1922 into the League of Nations mandates of British Togoland (west) and French Togoland (east); the former joined Ghana in 1957; the latter became independent as Togo in 1960.
▸ **'Togoˌlander** *n*

togs (tɒgz) *pl n Inf.* **1** clothes. **2** *Austral., NZ, & Irish.* a swimming costume. ORIG from TOG[1]

toheroa (ˌtəʊə'rəʊə) *n* a large edible bivalve mollusc of New Zealand with a distinctive flavour. ORIG from Maori

tohunga ('tɒhʊŋə) *n NZ.* a Maori priest, the repository of traditional lore.

toil[1] (tɔɪl) *n* **1** hard or exhausting work. ◆ *vb* (*intr*) **2** to labour. **3** to progress with slow painful movements. ORIG C13: from Anglo-F *toiler* to struggle, from OF *toeillier* to confuse, from L *tudiculāre* to stir, ult. from *tundere* to beat
▸ **'toiler** *n*

toil[2] (tɔɪl) *n* **1** (*often pl*) a net or snare. **2** *Arch.* a trap for wild beasts. ORIG C16: from OF *toile,* from L *tēla* loom

toile (twɑ:l) *n* **1** a transparent linen or cotton fabric. **2** a garment of exclusive design made up in cheap cloth so that alterations can be made. ORIG C19: from F, from L *tēla* a loom

toilet ('tɔɪlɪt) *n* **1** another word for **lavatory. 2** *Old-fashioned.* the act of dressing and preparing oneself. **3** *Old-fashioned.* a dressing table. **4** *Rare.* costume. **5** the

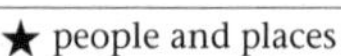
★ people and places

cleansing of a wound, etc., after an operation or childbirth. ORIG C16: from F *toilette* dress, from TOILE

toilet paper *or* **tissue** *n* thin absorbent paper, often wound in a roll round a cardboard cylinder (**toilet roll**), used for cleaning oneself after defecation or urination.

toiletry ('tɔɪlɪtrɪ) *n, pl* **toiletries.** an object or cosmetic used in making up, dressing, etc.

toilet set *n* a matching set consisting of a hairbrush, comb, mirror, and clothes brush.

toilette (twɑː'lɛt) *n* another word for **toilet** (sense 2). ORIG C16: from F; see TOILET

toilet water *n* a form of liquid perfume lighter than cologne.

toilsome ('tɔɪlsəm) *or* **toilful** *adj* laborious.
▸ **'toilsomely** *adv* ▸ **'toilsomeness** *n*

toitoi ('tɔɪtɔɪ) *n* a tall New Zealand grass with feathery seed-heads. ORIG from Maori

Tojo ★ ('təʊdʒəʊ) *n* **Hideki** ('hiːdɛˌkiː). 1885–1948, Japanese soldier and statesman; minister of war (1940–41) and premier (1941–44); hanged as a war criminal.

tokamak ('təʊkəˌmæk) *n Physics.* a toroidal reactor used in thermonuclear experiments, in which strong axial magnetic fields keep the plasma from contacting the external walls. ORIG C20: from Russian acronym, from *to(roidál'naya) kám(era s) ak(siál'nym magnitnym pólem)*, toroidal chamber with magnetic field

Tokay (təʊ'keɪ) *n* **1** a sweet wine made near Tokaj, Hungary. **2** a variety of grape used to make this. **3** a similar wine made elsewhere.

Tokelau Islands ★ ('təʊkəˌlaʊ) *pl n* an island group in the South Pacific composed of three atolls, Nukunono, Atafu, and Fakaofo, which in 1948 was included within the territorial boundaries of New Zealand. Pop.: 1577 (1991). Area: about 11 sq. km (4 sq. miles).

token ('təʊkən) *n* **1** an indication, warning, or sign of something. **2** a symbol or visible representation of something. **3** something that indicates authority, proof, etc. **4** a metal or plastic disc, such as a substitute for currency for use in slot machines. **5** a memento. **6** a gift voucher that can be used as payment for goods of a specified value. **7** (*modifier*) as a matter of form only; nominal: *a token increase in salary.* ◆ *vb* **8** (*tr*) to act or serve as a warning or symbol of; betoken. ORIG OE *tācen*

tokenism ('təʊkəˌnɪzəm) *n* the practice of making only a token effort or doing no more than the minimum, esp. in order to comply with a law.
▸ **'tokeˌnist** *adj*

token money *n* coins having greater face value than the value of their metal content.

token strike *n* a brief strike intended to convey strength of feeling on a disputed issue.

token vote *n* a Parliamentary vote of money in which the amount quoted is not binding.

tokoloshe (ˌtɒkɒ'lɒʃ, -'lɒʃɪ) *n* (in Bantu folklore) a malevolent mythical manlike animal. Also called: **tikoloshe.** ORIG from Xhosa *uthikoloshe*

toktokkie ('tɒkˌtɒkɪ) *n* a large S. African beetle. ORIG from Afrik., from Du. *tokken* to tap

Tokugawa Iyeyasu ★ (ˌtəʊkuː'gɑːwə ˌiːjeɪ'jɑːsuː) *n* See (Tokugawa) **Iyeyasu.**

Tokyo ★ ('təʊkjəʊ, -kɪˌəʊ) *n* the capital of Japan, a port on SE Honshu on **Tokyo Bay** (an inlet of the Pacific): part of the largest conurbation in the world (the Tokyo-Yukohama metropolitan area) of over 25 million people; major industrial centre and the chief cultural centre of Japan. Pop.: 7 966 195 (1995).

tolbooth ('təʊlˌbuːθ, -ˌbuːð, 'tɒl-) *n* **1** *Chiefly Scot.* a town hall. **2** a variant spelling of **tollbooth.**

tolbutamide (tɒl'bjuːtəˌmaɪd) *n* a synthetic crystalline compound used in the treatment of diabetes to lower blood glucose levels. ORIG C20: from TOL(UENE) + BUT(YRIC ACID) + AMIDE

told (təʊld) *vb* **1** the past tense and past participle of **tell**[1]. ◆ *adj* **2** See **all told.**

tole (təʊl) *n* enamelled or lacquered metal ware, popular in the 18th century. ORIG from F *tôle* sheet metal, from F (dialect): table, from L *tabula* table

Toledo ★ *n* **1** (tɒ'leɪdəʊ; *Spanish* to'leðo). a city in central Spain, on the River Tagus: capital of Visigothic Spain, and of Castile from 1087 to 1560; famous for steel and swords since the first century. Pop.: 63 560 (1991). Ancient name: **Toletum** (tə'liːtəm). **2** (tə'liːdəʊ). an inland port in NW Ohio, on Lake Erie: one of the largest coal-shipping ports in the world; transportation and industrial centre; university (1872). Pop.: 322 550 (1994 est.). **3** a fine-tapered sword or sword blade.

tolerable ('tɒlərəbᵊl) *adj* **1** able to be tolerated; endurable. **2** permissible. **3** *Inf.* fairly good.
▸ **ˌtolera'bility** *n* ▸ **'tolerably** *adv*

tolerance ('tɒlərəns) *n* **1** the state or quality of being tolerant. **2** capacity to endure something, esp. pain or hardship. **3** the permitted variation in some characteristic of an object or workpiece. **4** the capacity to endure the effects of a poison or other substance, esp. after it has been taken over a prolonged period.

tolerant ('tɒlərənt) *adj* **1** able to tolerate the beliefs, actions, etc., of others. **2** permissive. **3** able to withstand extremes. **4** exhibiting tolerance to a drug.
▸ **'tolerantly** *adv*

tolerate ('tɒləˌreɪt) *vb* **tolerates, tolerating, tolerated.** (*tr*) **1** to treat with indulgence or forbearance. **2** to permit. **3** to be able to bear; put up with. **4** to have tolerance for (a drug, etc.). ORIG C16: from L *tolerāre* to sustain

toleration (ˌtɒlə'reɪʃən) *n* **1** the act or practice of tolerating. **2** freedom to hold religious opinions that differ from the established religion of a country.
▸ **ˌtoler'ationist** *n*

Tolima ★ (*Spanish* to'lima) *n* a volcano in W Colombia, in the Andes. Height: 5215 m (17 110 ft).

Tolkien ★ ('tɒlkiːn) *n* **J**(**ohn**) **R**(**onald**) **R**(**euel**). 1892–1973, British writer, born in South Africa. He is best known for *The Hobbit* (1937), *The Lord of the Rings* (1954–55), and the posthumous *Silmarillion* (1977).

toll[1] (təʊl) *vb* **1** to ring slowly and recurrently. **2** (*tr*) to summon or announce by tolling. **3** *US & Canad.* to decoy (game, esp. ducks). ◆ *n* **4** the act or sound of tolling. ORIG C15: ? rel. to OE *-tyllan*, as in *fortyllan* to attract

toll[2] (təʊl, tɒl) *n* **1a** an amount of money levied, esp. for the use of certain roads, bridges, etc. **1b** (*as modifier*): *toll road; toll bridge.* **2** loss or damage incurred through a disaster, etc.: *the war took its toll of the inhabitants.* **3** (formerly) the right to levy a toll. ORIG OE *toln*

tollbooth *or* **tolbooth** ('təʊlˌbuːθ, -ˌbuːð, 'tɒl-) *n* a booth or kiosk at which a toll is collected.

tollgate ('təʊlˌgeɪt, 'tɒl-) *n* a gate across a toll road or bridge at which travellers must pay.

tollhouse ('təʊlˌhaʊs, 'tɒl-) *n* a small house at a tollgate occupied by a toll collector.

tollie ('tɒlɪ) *n, pl* **tollies.** *S. African.* a castrated calf. ORIG C19: from Xhosa *ithole* calf on which the horns have begun to appear

Tolstoy ★ ('tɒlstɔɪ; *Russian* tal'stɔj) *n* **Leo,** Russian name *Count Lev Nikolayevich Tolstoy.* 1828–1910, Russian writer; his novels include *War and Peace* (1865–69) and *Anna Karenina* (1875–77).

Toltec ('tɒltɛk) *n, pl* **Toltecs** *or* **Toltec. 1** a member of a Central American Indian people who dominated the valley of Mexico until they were overrun by the Aztecs. ◆ *adj also* **Toltecan. 2** of or relating to this people.

tolu (tɒ'luː) *n* an aromatic balsam obtained from a South American tree. ORIG C17: after *Santiago de Tolu,* Colombia, from which it was exported

Toluca ★ (*Spanish* to'luka) *n* **1** a city in S central Mexico, capital of Mexico state, at an altitude of 2640 m (8660 ft). Pop.: 327 865 (1990). Official name: **Toluca de Lerdo** (de 'lɛrðo). **2 Nevado de** (ne'βaðo de). a volcano in central Mexico, in Mexico state near Toluca: crater partly filled by a lake. Height: 4577 m (15 017 ft).

toluene ('tɒljʊˌiːn) *n* a colourless volatile flammable liquid obtained from petroleum and coal tar and used as a solvent and in the manufacture of many organic chemicals. ORIG C19: from TOLU + -ENE, since it was previously obtained from tolu

toluic acid (tɒ'luːɪk) *n* a white crystalline derivative of toluene used in synthetic resins and as an insect repellent. ORIG C19: from TOLU(ENE) + -IC

toluidine (tɒ'ljuːɪˌdiːn) *n* an amine derived from toluene, used in making dyes. ORIG C19: from TOLU(ENE) + -IDE + -INE[2]

tom (tɒm) *n* **a** the male of various animals, esp. the cat. **b** (*as modifier*): *a tom turkey*. **c** (*in combination*): *a tomcat*. ORIG C16: special use of the short form of *Thomas*, applied to any male, often implying a common or ordinary type of person, etc.

tomahawk ('tɒməˌhɔːk) *n* a fighting axe with a stone or iron head, used by the North American Indians. ORIG C17: from Algonquian *tamahaac*

tomato (tə'mɑːtəʊ) *n, pl* **tomatoes. 1** a South American plant widely cultivated for its red fleshy many-seeded fruits. **2** the fruit of this plant, eaten in salads, as a vegetable, etc. ORIG C17 *tomate*, from Sp., from Nahuatl *tomatl*

tomb (tuːm) *n* **1** a place, esp. a vault beneath the ground, for the burial of a corpse. **2** a monument to the dead. **3 the tomb.** a poetic term for death. ORIG C13: from OF *tombe*, from LL *tumba* burial mound, from Gk *tumbos*

tombac ('tɒmbæk) *n* any of various alloys containing copper and zinc: used for making cheap jewellery, etc. ORIG C17: from F, from Du. *tombak*, from Malay *tambâga* copper, apparently from Sansk. *tāmraka*, from *tāmra* dark coppery red

Tombaugh ★ ('tɒmbɔː) *n* **Clyde William.** 1906–97, US astronomer, who discovered (1930) Pluto.

tombola (tɒm'bəʊlə) *n Brit.* a type of lottery, esp. at a fête, in which tickets are drawn from a revolving drum. ORIG C19: from It., from *tombolare* to somersault

Tombouctou ★ (tɔ̃buktu) *n* the French name for **Timbuktu.**

tomboy ('tɒmˌbɔɪ) *n* a girl who acts or dresses in a boyish way, liking rough outdoor activities.
▸ **'tomˌboyish** *adj* ▸ **'tomˌboyishly** *adv*

tombstone ('tuːmˌstəʊn) *n* another word for **gravestone.**

Tom Collins *n* a long drink consisting of gin, lime or lemon juice, sugar, and soda water.

Tom, Dick, and (or) Harry *n* an ordinary, undistinguished, or common person (esp. in **every Tom, Dick, and Harry; any Tom, Dick, or Harry**).

tome (təʊm) *n* **1** a large weighty book. **2** one of the several volumes of a work. ORIG C16: from F, from L *tomus* section of larger work, from Gk *tomos* a slice, from *temnein* to cut

-tome *n combining form.* indicating an instrument for cutting: *osteotome.* ORIG from Gk *tomē* a cutting, *tomos* a slice, from *temnein* to cut

tomentum (tə'mɛntəm) *n, pl* **tomenta** (-tə). **1** a covering of downy hairs on leaves and other plant parts. **2** a network of minute blood vessels occurring in the human brain. ORIG C17: NL, from L: stuffing for cushions
▸ **to'mentose** *adj*

tomfool (ˌtɒm'fuːl) *n* **a** a fool. **b** (*as modifier*): *tomfool ideas.*
▸ **ˌtom'foolishness** *n*

tomfoolery (ˌtɒm'fuːlərɪ) *n, pl* **tomfooleries. 1** foolish behaviour. **2** utter nonsense; rubbish.

tommy ('tɒmɪ) *n, pl* **tommies.** (*often cap.*) *Brit. inf.* a private in the British Army. ORIG C19: orig. *Thomas Atkins*, name representing typical private in specimen forms

Tommy gun *n* an informal name for **Thompson submachine-gun.**

tommyrot ('tɒmɪˌrɒt) *n* utter nonsense.

tomography (tə'mɒgrəfɪ) *n* a technique used to obtain an X-ray photograph of a plane section of the human body or some other object. ORIG C20: from Gk *tomē* a cutting + -GRAPHY

tomorrow (tə'mɒrəʊ) *n* **1** the day after today. **2** the future. ◆ *adv* **3** on the day after today. **4** at some time in the future. ORIG OE *tō morgenne*, from *to* on + *morgenne*, dative of *morgen* morning

Tomsk ★ (*Russian* tɔmsk) *n* a city in central Russia: formerly an important gold-mining town and administrative centre for a large area of Siberia; university (1888); engineering industries. Pop.: 470 000 (1995 est.).

Tom Thumb ★ *n* **1 General,** stage name of *Charles Stratton*. 1838–83, US midget, exhibited in P. T. Barnum's circus. **2** a dwarf; midget. ORIG after *Tom Thumb*, the tiny hero of several English folk tales

tomtit ('tɒmˌtɪt) *n Brit.* any of various tits, esp. the bluetit.

tom-tom *n* a drum usually beaten with the hands as a signalling instrument. ORIG C17: from Hindi *tamtam*, imit.

-tomy *n combining form.* indicating a surgical cutting of a specified part or tissue: *lobotomy.* ORIG from Gk *-tomia*

ton[1] (tʌn) *n* **1** Also called: **long ton.** *Brit.* a unit of weight equal to 2240 pounds or 1016.046 909 kilograms. **2** Also called: **short ton, net ton.** *US & Canad.* a unit of weight equal to 2000 pounds or 907.184 kilograms. **3** See **metric ton, tonne.** a unit of weight equal to 1000 kilograms. **4** Also called: **freight ton, measurement ton.** a unit of volume or weight used for charging or measuring freight in shipping. It is usually equal to 40 cubic feet, 1 cubic metre, or 1000 kilograms. **5** Also called: **displacement ton.** a unit used for measuring the displacement of a ship, equal to 35 cubic feet of sea water or 2240 pounds. **6** Also called: **register ton.** a unit of internal capacity of ships equal to 100 cubic feet. ◆ *adv* **7 tons.** (intensifier): *the new flat is tons better than the old one.* ORIG C14: var. of TUN

ton[2] (tʌn) *n Sl., chiefly Brit.* a score or achievement of a hundred, esp. a hundred miles per hour, as on a motorcycle. ORIG C20: special use of TON[1] applied to quantities of one hundred

tonal ('təʊnᵊl) *adj* **1** of or relating to tone. **2** of or utilizing the diatonic system; having an established key. **3** (of an answer in a fugue) not having the same melodic intervals as the subject, so as to remain in the original key.
▸ **'tonally** *adv*

tonality (təʊ'nælɪtɪ) *n, pl* **tonalities. 1** *Music.* **1a** the presence of a musical key in a composition. **1b** the system of major and minor keys prevalent in Western music. **2** the overall scheme of colours and tones in a painting.

Tonbridge ★ ('tʌnˌbrɪdʒ) *n* a market town in SE England, in SW Kent on the River Medway. Pop.: 34 260 (1991).

tondo ('tɒndəʊ) *n, pl* **tondi** (-diː). a circular easel painting or relief carving. ORIG C19: from It.: a circle, shortened from *rotondo* round

tone (təʊn) *n* **1** sound with reference to quality, pitch, or volume. **2** short for **tone colour. 3** *US & Canad.* another word for **note** (sense 10). **4** an interval of a major second; whole tone. **5** Also called: **Gregorian tone.** any of several plainsong melodies or other chants used in the singing of psalms. **6** *Linguistics.* any of the pitch levels or pitch contours at which a syllable may be pronounced, such as high tone, falling tone, etc. **7** the quality or character of a sound: *a nervous tone of voice.* **8** general aspect, quality, or style. **9** high quality or style: *to lower the tone of a place.* **10** the quality of a given colour, as modified by mixture with white or black; shade; tint. **11** *Physiol.* **11a** the normal tension of a muscle at rest. **11b** the natural firmness of the tissues and normal functioning of bodily organs in health. **12** the overall effect of the colour values and gradations of light and dark in a picture. **13** *Photog.* a colour of a particular area on a negative or positive that can be distinguished from surrounding areas. ◆ *vb* **tones, toning, toned. 14** (*intr;* often foll. by *with*) to be of a matching or similar tone (to). **15** (*tr*) to give a tone to or correct the tone of. **16** (*tr*) *Photog.* to soften or change the colour of the tones of (a photographic image). ◆ See also **tone down, tone up.** ORIG C14: from L *tonus*, from Gk *tonos* tension, tone, from *teinein* to stretch
▸ **'toneless** *adj* ▸ **'tonelessly** *adv*

tone arm *n* another name for **pick-up.**

tone colour *n* the quality of a musical sound that is

conditioned or distinguished by the upper partials or overtones present in it.

tone-deaf *adj* unable to distinguish subtle differences in musical pitch.
▸ **tone deafness** *n*

tone down *vb* (*adv*) to moderate or become moderated in tone: *to tone down an argument.*

tone language *n* a language, such as Chinese, in which differences in tone may make differences in meaning.

toneme ('təuni:m) *n Linguistics.* a phoneme that is distinguished from another phoneme only by its tone. ORIG C20
▸ **to'nemic** *adj*

tone poem *n* another term for **symphonic poem.**

toner ('təunə) *n* **1** a person or thing that tones. **2** a cosmetic preparation that is applied to produce a desired effect, such as to reduce the oiliness of the skin. **3** *Photog.* a chemical solution that softens or alters the tones of a photographic image. **4** a powdered chemical used in photocopying machines, which adheres to electrostatically charged areas of a plate or roller and is then transferred onto the paper to form the copy.

tone row *or* **series** *n Music.* a group of notes having a characteristic pattern that forms the basis of the musical material in a serial composition, esp. one consisting of the twelve notes of the chromatic scale.

tone up *vb* (*adv*) to make or become more vigorous, healthy, etc.

tong (tɒŋ) *n* (formerly) a secret society of Chinese Americans. ORIG C20: from Chinese (Cantonese) *t'ong* meeting place

tonga ('tɒŋgə) *n* a light two-wheeled vehicle used in rural areas of India. ORIG C19: from Hindi *tāngā*

Tonga ★ ('tɒŋə, 'tɒŋgə) *n* a kingdom occupying an archipelago of more than 150 volcanic and coral islands in the SW Pacific, east of Fiji: inhabited by Polynesians; became a British protectorate in 1900 and gained independence in 1970; a member of the Commonwealth. Official languages: Tongan and English. Religion: Christian majority. Currency: pa'anga. Capital: Nuku'alofa. Pop.: 98 000 (1999 est.). Area: 750 sq. km (290 sq. miles). Also called: **Friendly Islands.**
▸ **'Tongan** *adj, n*

Tongchak (ˌtɒŋ'tʃæk) *n* the former name for **Chondokyo.**

tongs (tɒŋz) *pl n* a tool for grasping or lifting, consisting of a hinged, sprung, or pivoted pair of arms or levers, joined at one end. Also called: **pair of tongs.** ORIG pl. of OE *tange*

tongue (tʌŋ) *n* **1** a movable mass of muscular tissue attached to the floor of the mouth in most vertebrates. It is used in tasting, eating, and (in man) speaking. Related adj: **lingual. 2** an analogous organ in invertebrates. **3** the tongue of certain animals used as food. **4** a language, dialect, or idiom: *the English tongue.* **5** the ability to speak: *to lose one's tongue.* **6** a manner of speaking: *a glib tongue.* **7** utterance or voice (esp. in **give tongue**). **8** anything which resembles a tongue in shape or function. **9** a promontory or spit of land. **10** a flap of leather on a shoe. **11** *Music.* the reed of an oboe or similar instrument. **12** the clapper of a bell. **13** the harnessing pole of a horse-drawn vehicle. **14** a projection on a machine part that serves as a guide for assembly, etc. **15** a projecting strip along an edge of a board that is made to fit a groove in another board. **16 hold one's tongue.** to keep quiet. **17 on the tip of one's tongue.** about to come to mind. **18 with (one's) tongue in (one's) cheek.** Also: **tongue in cheek.** with insincere or ironical intent. ◆ *vb* **tongues, tonguing, tongued. 19** to articulate (notes on a wind instrument) by tonguing. **20** (*tr*) to lick, feel, or touch with the tongue. **21** (*tr*) to provide (a board) with a tongue. **22** (*intr*) (of a piece of land) to project into a body of water. ORIG OE *tunge*
▸ **'tongueless** *adj* ▸ **'tongueˌlike** *adj*

tongue-and-groove joint *n* a joint made between two boards by means of a tongue along the edge of one board that fits into a groove along the edge of the other board.

tongued (tʌŋd) *adj* **1** having a tongue or tongues. **2** (*in combination*) having a manner of speech as specified: *sharp-tongued.*

tongue-lash *vb* (*tr*) to reprimand severely; scold.
▸ **'tongue-ˌlashing** *n, adj*

tongue-tie *n* a congenital condition in which the tongue has restricted mobility as the result of an abnormally short fraenum.

tongue-tied *adj* **1** speechless, esp. with embarrassment or shyness. **2** having a condition of tongue-tie.

tongue twister *n* a sentence or phrase that is difficult to articulate clearly and quickly, such as *Peter Piper picked a peck of pickled pepper.*

tonguing ('tʌŋɪŋ) *n* a technique of playing (any nonlegato passage) on a wind instrument by obstructing and uncovering the air passage through the lips with the tongue.

tonic ('tɒnɪk) *n* **1** a medicinal preparation that improves the functioning of the body or increases the feeling of wellbeing. **2** anything that enlivens or strengthens. **3** Also called: **tonic water.** a mineral water, usually carbonated and containing quinine and often mixed with gin or other alcoholic drinks. **4** *Music.* **4a** the first degree of a major or minor scale and the tonal centre of a piece composed in a particular key. **4b** a key or chord based on this. ◆ *adj* **5** serving to enliven and invigorate: *a tonic wine.* **6** of or relating to a tone or tones. **7** *Music.* of the first degree of a major or minor scale. **8** of or denoting the general effect of colour and light and shade in a picture. **9** *Physiol.* of or affecting normal muscular or bodily tone: *a tonic spasm.* ORIG C17: from NL *tonicus,* from Gk *tonikos* concerning tone, from *tonos* TONE
▸ **'tonically** *adv*

tonic accent *n* **1** emphasis imparted to a note by virtue of its having a higher pitch. **2** (in some languages) an accent in which emphatic syllables are pronounced on a higher musical pitch.

tonicity (təu'nɪsɪtɪ) *n* **1** the condition or quality of being tonic. **2** another name for **tonus.**

tonic sol-fa *n* a method of teaching music, by which syllables are used as names for the notes of the major scale in any key.

tonight (tə'naɪt) *n* **1** the night or evening of this present day. ◆ *adv* **2** in or during the night or evening of this day. **3** *Obs.* last night. ORIG OE *tōniht*

toning table *n* an exercise table, parts of which move mechanically for a set time in order to exercise specific parts of the body of the person lying on it.

tonka bean ('tɒŋkə) *n* **1** a tall tree of tropical America. **2** the seeds of this tree, used in the manufacture of perfumes, snuff, etc. ORIG C18: prob. from Tupi *tonka*

Tonkin ('tɒn'kɪn) *or* **Tongking** ★ ('tɒŋ'kɪŋ) *n* **1** a former state of N French Indochina (1883–1946), on the Gulf of Tonkin: forms the largest part of N Vietnam. **2 Gulf of.** an arm of the South China Sea, bordered by N Vietnam, the Leizhou Peninsula of SW China, and Hainan Island. Length: about 500 km (300 miles).

Tonle Sap ★ ('tɒnlɪ 'sæp) *n* a lake in W central Cambodia, linked with the Mekong River by the **Tonle Sap River.** Area: (dry season) about 2600 sq. km (1000 sq. miles); (rainy season) up to 10 000 sq. km (3860 sq. miles).

tonnage *or* **tunnage** ('tʌnɪdʒ) *n* **1** the capacity of a merchant ship expressed in tons. **2** the weight of the cargo of a merchant ship. **3** the total amount of shipping of a port or nation. **4** a duty on ships based either on their capacity or their register tonnage. ORIG C15: from OF, from *tonne* barrel

tonne (tʌn) *n* a unit of mass equal to 1000 kg or 2204.6 pounds. Also called (not in technical use): **metric ton.** ORIG from F

tonneau ('tɒnəu) *n, pl* **tonneaus** *or* **tonneaux** (-nəu, -nəuz). **1** a detachable cover to protect empty passenger seats in an open vehicle. **2** *Rare.* the part of an open car in which the rear passengers sit. ORIG C20: from F: special type of vehicle body, from OF *tonnel* cask, from *tonne* tun

tonometer (təu'nɒmɪtə) *n* **1** an instrument for measuring the pitch of a sound, esp. one consisting of a set of tuning forks. **2** any of various types of instrument for

measuring pressure or tension, such as the blood pressure, vapour pressure, etc. ORIG C18: from Gk *tonos* TONE + -METER
▸ **tonometric** (ˌtɒnəˈmɛtrɪk, ˌtəʊ-) *adj*

tonsil (ˈtɒnsəl) *n* either of two small masses of lymphatic tissue situated one on each side of the back of the mouth. ORIG C17: from L *tōnsillae* (pl) tonsils, from ?
▸ ˈ**tonsillar** *adj*

tonsillectomy (ˌtɒnsɪˈlɛktəmɪ) *n, pl* **tonsillectomies.** surgical removal of the tonsils.

tonsillitis (ˌtɒnsɪˈlaɪtɪs) *n* inflammation of the tonsils.
▸ **tonsillitic** (ˌtɒnsɪˈlɪtɪk) *adj*

tonsorial (tɒnˈsɔːrɪəl) *adj Often facetious.* of barbering or hairdressing. ORIG C19: from L *tōnsōrius* concerning shaving, from *tondēre* to shave

tonsure (ˈtɒnʃə) *n* **1** (in certain religions and monastic orders) **1a** the shaving of the head or the crown of the head only. **1b** the part of the head left bare by shaving. ◆ *vb* **tonsures, tonsuring, tonsured. 2** (*tr*) to shave the head of. ORIG C14: from L *tōnsūra* a clipping, from *tondēre* to shave
▸ ˈ**tonsured** *adj*

tontine (ˈtɒntiːn, tɒnˈtiːn) *n* an annuity scheme by which several subscribers accumulate and invest a common fund out of which they receive an annuity that increases as subscribers die until the last survivor takes the whole. ORIG C18: from F, after Lorenzo *Tonti,* Neapolitan banker who devised the scheme

ton-up *Brit. inf.* ◆ *adj* (*prenominal*) **1** (esp. of a motorcycle) capable of speeds of a hundred miles per hour or more. **2** liking to travel at such speeds: *a ton-up boy.* ◆ *n* **3** a person who habitually rides at such speeds.

tonus (ˈtəʊnəs) *n* the normal tension of a muscle at rest; tone. ORIG C19: from L, from Gk *tonos* TONE

too (tuː) *adv* **1** as well; in addition; also: *can I come too?* **2** in or to an excessive degree: *I have too many things to do.* **3** extremely: *you're too kind.* **4** *US & Canad. inf.* indeed: used to reinforce a command: *you will too do it!* ORIG OE *tō*

USAGE NOTE See at **very.**

took (tʊk) *vb* the past tense of **take.**

tool (tuːl) *n* **1a** an implement, such as a hammer, saw, or spade, that is used by hand. **1b** a power-driven instrument; machine tool. **1c** (*in combination*): *a toolkit.* **2** the cutting part of such an instrument. **3** any of the instruments used by a bookbinder to impress a design on a book cover. **4** anything used as a means of achieving an end. **5** a person used to perform dishonourable or unpleasant tasks for another. **6** a necessary medium for or adjunct to one's profession: *numbers are the tools of the mathematician's trade.* ◆ *vb* **7** to work, cut, or form (something) with a tool. **8** (*tr*) to decorate (a book cover) with a bookbinder's tool. **9** (*tr;* often foll. by *up*) to furnish with tools. ORIG OE *tōl*
▸ ˈ**tooler** *n*

tooling (ˈtuːlɪŋ) *n* **1** any decorative work done with a tool, esp. a design stamped onto a book cover, etc. **2** the selection, provision, and setting up of tools for a machining operation.

tool-maker *n* a person who specializes in the production or reconditioning of precision tools, cutters, etc.
▸ ˈ**tool-**ˌ**making** *n*

tool pusher *n* a foreman who supervises drilling operations on an oil rig.

toolroom (ˈtuːlruːm, -rʊm) *n* a room, such as in a machine shop, where tools are made, stored, etc.

toonie *or* **twonie** (ˈtuːnɪ) *n Canad. inf.* a Canadian two-dollar coin.

toot (tuːt) *vb* **1** to give or cause to give (a short blast, hoot, or whistle). ◆ *n* **2** the sound made by or as if by a horn, whistle, etc. **3** *Sl.* any drug for snorting, esp. cocaine. **4** *US & Canad. sl.* a drinking spree. **5** *Austral. sl.* a lavatory. ORIG C16: from MLow G *tuten,* imit.
▸ ˈ**tooter** *n*

tooth (tuːθ) *n, pl* **teeth** (tiːθ). **1** any of various bonelike structures set in the jaws of most vertebrates and used for biting, tearing, or chewing. Related adj: **dental. 2** any of various similar structures in invertebrates. **3** anything resembling a tooth in shape, prominence, or function: *the tooth of a comb.* **4** any of the indentations on the margin of a leaf, petal, etc. **5** any of the projections on a gear, sprocket, rack, etc. **6** taste or appetite (esp. in **sweet tooth**). **7 long in the tooth.** old or ageing. **8 tooth and nail.** with ferocity and force. ◆ *vb* (tuːð, tuːθ). **9** (*tr*) to provide with a tooth or teeth. **10** (*intr*) (of two gearwheels) to engage. ORIG OE *tōth*
▸ ˈ**toothless** *adj* ▸ ˈ**tooth**ˌ**like** *adj*

toothache (ˈtuːθˌeɪk) *n* a pain in or about a tooth. Technical name: **odontalgia.**

toothbrush (ˈtuːθˌbrʌʃ) *n* a small brush, usually with a long handle, for cleaning the teeth.

toothed (tuːθt) *adj* **a** having a tooth or teeth. **b** (*in combination*): *sabre-toothed; six-toothed.*

toothed whale *n* any of a suborder of whales having simple teeth and feeding on fish, smaller mammals, etc.: includes dolphins and porpoises.

toothpaste (ˈtuːθˌpeɪst) *n* a paste used for cleaning the teeth, applied with a toothbrush.

toothpick (ˈtuːθˌpɪk) *n* a small sharp sliver of wood, plastic, etc., used for extracting pieces of food from between the teeth.

tooth powder *n* a powder used for cleaning the teeth, applied with a toothbrush.

tooth shell *n* another name for the **tusk shell.**

toothsome (ˈtuːθsəm) *adj* of delicious or appetizing appearance, flavour, or smell.

toothwort (ˈtuːθˌwɜːt) *n* **1** a European plant having scaly stems and pinkish flowers and a rhizome covered with toothlike scales. **2** any of a genus of North American or Eurasian plants having rhizomes covered with toothlike projections.

toothy (ˈtuːθɪ) *adj* **toothier, toothiest.** having or showing numerous, large, or projecting teeth: *a toothy grin.*
▸ ˈ**toothily** *adv* ▸ ˈ**toothiness** *n*

tootle (ˈtuːtᵊl) *vb* **tootles, tootling, tootled. 1** to toot or hoot softly or repeatedly. ◆ *n* **2** a soft hoot or series of hoots. ORIG C19: from TOOT
▸ ˈ**tootler** *n*

Toowoomba ★ (təˈwʊmbə) *n* a city in E Australia, in SE Queensland: agricultural and industrial centre. Pop.: 75 000 (latest est.).

top[1] (tɒp) *n* **1** the highest or uppermost part of anything: *the top of a hill.* **2** the most important or successful position: *the top of the class.* **3** the part of a plant that is above ground: *carrot tops.* **4** a thing that forms or covers the uppermost part of anything, esp. a lid or cap. **5** the highest degree or point: *at the top of his career.* **6** the most important person. **7** the best part of anything. **8** the loudest or highest pitch (esp. in **top of one's voice**). **9** another name for **top gear** (sense 1). **10** *Cards.* the highest card of a suit in a player's hand. **11** *Sport.* **11a** a stroke that hits the ball above its centre. **11b** short for **topspin. 12** a platform around the head of a lower mast of a sailing vessel. **13** a garment, esp. for a woman, that extends from the shoulders to the waist or hips. **14 off the top of one's head.** with no previous preparation; extempore. **15 on top of. 15a** in addition to. **15b** *Inf.* in complete control of (a difficult situation, etc.). **16 over the top. 16a** over the parapet or leading edge of a trench. **16b** over the limit; lacking restraint or a sense of proportion. **17 the top of the morning.** a morning greeting regarded as characteristic of Irishmen. ◆ *adj* **18** of, relating to, serving as, or situated on the top. ◆ *vb* **tops, topping, topped.** (*mainly tr*) **19** to form a top on (something): *to top a cake with cream.* **20** to remove the top of or from. **21** to reach or pass the top of. **22** to be at the top of: *he tops the team.* **23** to exceed or surpass. **24** *Sl.* to kill, esp. by hanging. **25** (*also intr*) *Sport.* **25a** to hit (a ball) above the centre. **25b** to make (a stroke) by hitting the ball in this way. **26 top and tail. 26a** to trim off the ends of (fruit or vegetables) before cooking them. **26b** to wash a baby's face and bottom without immersion in a bath. ◆ See also **top off, top out, tops, top up.** ORIG OE *topp*

★ people and places

top[2] (tɒp) *n* **1** a toy that is spun on its pointed base. **2 sleep like a top.** to sleep very soundly. ORIG OE, from ?

topaz ('təupæz) *n* **1** a hard glassy mineral consisting of a silicate of aluminium and fluorine in crystalline form. It is yellow, pink, or colourless, and is a valuable gemstone. **2 oriental topaz.** a yellowish-brown variety of sapphire. **3 false topaz.** another name for **citrine. 4a** a yellowish-brown colour, as in some varieties of topaz. **4b** (*as adj*)*: topaz eyes.* **5** either of two South American hummingbirds. ORIG C13: from OF *topaze,* from L *topazus,* from Gk *topazos*

top boot *n* a high boot, often with a decorative or contrasting upper section.

top brass *n* (*functioning as pl*) *Inf.* the most important or high-ranking officials or leaders.

topcoat ('tɒpˌkəut) *n* an outdoor coat worn over a suit, etc.

top dog *n Inf.* the leader or chief of a group.

top dollar *n Inf.* the highest level of payment.

top drawer *n* people of the highest standing, esp. socially (esp. in **out of the top drawer**).

top dressing *n* a surface application of some material, such as fertilizer.
▸ **'top-ˌdress** *vb* (*tr*)

tope[1] (təup) *vb* **topes, toping, toped.** to consume (alcoholic drink) as a regular habit, usually in large quantities. ORIG C17: from F *toper* to keep an agreement, from Sp. *topar* to take a bet; prob. because a wager was generally followed by a drink
▸ **'toper** *n*

tope[2] (təup) *n* a small grey shark of European coastal waters. ORIG C17: from ?

topee *or* **topi** ('təupiː, -pɪ) *n, pl* **topees** *or* **topis.** another name for **pith helmet.** ORIG C19: from Hindi *topī* hat

Topeka ★ (tə'piːkə) *n* a city in E central Kansas, capital of the state, on the Kansas River: university (1865). Pop.: 120 646 (1994 est.).

Top End ★ *n* **the.** *Austral.* the northern part of the Northern Territory.

top-flight *adj* of superior or excellent quality.

topgallant (ˌtɒp'gælənt; *Naut.* tə'gælənt) *n* **1** a mast on a square-rigger above a topmast or an extension of a topmast. **2** a sail set on a yard of a topgallant mast. **3** (*modifier*) of or relating to a topgallant.

top gear *n* **1** Also called: **top.** the highest forward ratio of a gearbox in a motor vehicle. **2** the highest speed, greatest energy, etc.

top hat *n* a man's hat with a tall cylindrical crown and narrow brim, often made of silk, now worn for some formal occasions.

top-hat scheme *n Inf.* a pension scheme for the senior executives of an organization.

top-heavy *adj* **1** unstable through being overloaded at the top. **2** *Finance.* characterized by too much debt capital in relation to revenue or profit; overcapitalized.

Tophet *or* **Topheth** ★ ('təufɛt) *n Old Testament.* a place in the valley immediately to the southwest of Jerusalem; the Shrine of Moloch, where human sacrifices were offered. ORIG from Heb. *Tōpheth*

tophus ('təufəs) *n, pl* **tophi** (-faɪ). a deposit of sodium urate in the ear or surrounding a joint: a diagnostic of gout. ORIG C16: from L, var. of *tōfus* TUFA, TUFF

topi[1] ('təupiː, -pɪ) *n, pl* **topis.** another name for **pith helmet.** ORIG C19: from Hindi: hat

topi[2] ('təupɪ) *n, pl* **topi** *or* **topis.** a glossy brown African antelope. ORIG C19: from Swahili

topiary ('təupɪərɪ) *adj* **1** of, relating to, or characterized by the trimming or training of trees or bushes into artificial decorative shapes. ◆ *n, pl* **topiaries. 2a** topiary work. **2b** a topiary garden. **3** the art of topiary. ORIG C16: from F *topiaire,* from L *topia* decorative garden work, from Gk *topion* little place, from *topos* place
▸ **'topiarist** *n*

topic ('tɒpɪk) *n* **1** a subject or theme of a speech, book, etc. **2** a subject of conversation. ORIG C16: from L *topica* translating Gk *ta topika,* lit.: matters relating to commonplaces, title of a treatise by Aristotle, from *topoi,* pl. of *topos* place

topical ('tɒpɪkᵊl) *adj* **1** of, relating to, or constituting current affairs. **2** relating to a particular place; local. **3** of or relating to a topic or topics. **4** (of a drug, ointment, etc.) for application to the body surface; local.
▸ **topicality** (ˌtɒpɪ'kælɪtɪ) *n* ▸ **'topically** *adv*

topknot ('tɒpˌnɒt) *n* **1** a crest, tuft, chignon, etc., on top of the head. **2** any of several European flatfishes.

topless ('tɒplɪs) *adj* **1** having no top. **2a** denoting a costume which has no covering for the breasts. **2b** wearing such a costume.

top-level *n* (*modifier*) of, involving, or by those on the highest level of influence or authority: *top-level talks.*

toplofty ('tɒpˌlɒftɪ) *adj Inf.* haughty or pretentious.
▸ **'topˌloftiness** *n*

topmast ('tɒpˌmɑːst; *Naut.* 'tɒpməst) *n* the mast next above a lower mast on a sailing vessel.

topmost ('tɒpˌməust) *adj* at or nearest the top.

top-notch ('tɒp'nɒtʃ) *adj Inf.* excellent; superb.
▸ **'top-'notcher** *n*

topo- *or before a vowel* **top-** *combining form.* indicating place or region: *topography.* ORIG from Gk *topos* a place

top off *vb* (*tr, adv*) to finish or complete, esp. with some decisive action.

topography (tə'pɒgrəfɪ) *n, pl* **topographies. 1** the study or detailed description of the surface features of a region. **2** the detailed mapping of the configuration of a region. **3** the land forms or surface configuration of a region. **4** the surveying of a region's surface features. **5** the study or description of the configuration of any object.
▸ **to'pographer** *n* ▸ **topographic** (ˌtɒpə'græfɪk) *or* ˌ**topo'graphical** *adj*

topological group *n Maths.* a group, such as the set of all real numbers, that constitutes a topological space and in which multiplication and inversion are continuous.

topological space *n Maths.* a set *S* with an associated family of subsets τ that is closed under set union and finite intersection.

topology (tə'pɒlədʒɪ) *n* **1** the branch of mathematics concerned with generalization of the concepts of continuity, limit, etc. **2** a branch of geometry describing the properties of a figure that are unaffected by continuous distortion. **3** *Maths.* a family of subsets of a given set *S,* such that *S* is a topological space. **4** the study of the topography of a given place. **5** the anatomy of any specific bodily area, structure, or part.
▸ **topologic** (ˌtɒpə'lɒdʒɪk) *or* ˌ**topo'logical** *adj* ▸ ˌ**topo'logically** *adv* ▸ **to'pologist** *n*

Topolski ★ (tɒ'pɒlskɪ) *n* **Feliks** ('fiːlɪks). 1907–89, British painter, born in Poland; best known for his sketches and murals, esp. for *Memoir of the Century* (1975–89).

top out *vb* (*adv*) to place the highest part of a building in position.

topper ('tɒpə) *n* **1** an informal name for **top hat. 2** a person or thing that tops or excels.

topping ('tɒpɪŋ) *n* **1** something that tops something else, esp. a sauce or garnish for food. ◆ *adj* **2** high or superior in rank, degree, etc. **3** *Brit. sl.* excellent; splendid.

topple ('tɒpᵊl) *vb* **topples, toppling, toppled. 1** to tip over or cause to tip over, esp. from a height. **2** (*intr*) to lean precariously or totter. ORIG C16: frequentative of TOP[1] (vb)

tops (tɒps) *Sl.* ◆ *n* **1 the tops.** a person or thing of top quality. ◆ *adj* **2** (*postpositive*) excellent.

topsail ('tɒpˌseɪl; *Naut.* 'tɒpsəl) *n* a square sail carried on a yard set on a topmast.

top-secret *adj* classified as needing the highest level of secrecy and security.

topside ('tɒpˌsaɪd) *n* **1** the uppermost side of anything. **2** *Brit. & NZ.* a lean cut of beef from the thigh containing no bone. **3** (*often pl*) **3a** the part of a ship's sides above the water line. **3b** the parts of a ship above decks.

top slicing *n* the act or process of using a specific part of a sum of money for a special purpose, such as assessing a taxable gain.

topsoil ('tɒpˌsɔɪl) *n* the surface layer of soil.

★ people and places

topspin (ˈtɒpˌspɪn) *n Tennis, etc.* a spin imparted to make a ball bounce or travel exceptionally far, high, or quickly.

topsy-turvy (ˈtɒpsɪˈtɜːvɪ) *adj* **1** upside down. **2** in a state of confusion. ◆ *adv* **3** in a topsy-turvy manner. ◆ *n* **4** a topsy-turvy state. ORIG C16: prob. from *tops,* pl. of TOP[1] + obs. *tervy* to turn upside down

top up *vb (tr, adv) Brit.* **1** to raise the level of (a liquid, powder, etc.) in (a container), usually bringing it to the brim of the container. **2a** to increase the benefits from (an insurance scheme), esp. to increase a pension when a salary rise enables higher premiums to be paid. **2b** to add money to (a loan, bank account, etc.) in order to keep it at a constant or acceptable level. ◆ *n* **top-up. 3a** an amount added to something in order to raise it to or maintain it at a desired level. **3b** (*as modifier*): *a top-up loan; a top-up policy.*

toque (təʊk) *n* **1** a woman's small round brimless hat. **2** a chef's tall white hat. **3** *Canad.* a variant spelling of **tuque** (sense 2). **4** a small plumed hat popular in the 16th century. ORIG C16: from F, from OSp. *toca* headdress, prob. from Basque *tauka* hat

tor (tɔː) *n* a high hill, esp. a bare rocky one. ORIG OE *torr*

Torah (ˈtəʊrə) *n* **1a** the Pentateuch. **1b** the scroll on which this is written. **2** the whole body of traditional Jewish teaching, including the Oral Law. ORIG C16: from Heb.: precept, from *yārāh* to instruct

Torbay ★ (ˌtɔːˈbeɪ) *n* **1** a unitary authority in SW England, in Devon, consisting of the resorts of Brixham, Paignton, and Torquay. Pop.: 122 900 (1997 est.). Area: 63 sq. km (24 sq. miles). **2** Also: **Tor Bay.** an inlet of the English Channel on the coast of SW England, near Torquay.

torc (tɔːk) *n* a variant of **torque** (sense 1).

torch (tɔːtʃ) *n* **1** a small portable electric lamp powered by batteries. US and Canad. word: **flashlight. 2** a wooden or tow shaft dipped in wax or tallow and set alight. **3** anything regarded as a source of enlightenment, guidance, etc. **4** any apparatus with a hot flame for welding, brazing, etc. **5 carry a torch for.** to be in love with, esp. unrequitedly. ◆ *vb* **6** *(tr)* to set fire to, esp. deliberately as an act of arson. ORIG C13: from OF *torche* handful of twisted straw, from Vulgar L *torca* (unattested), from L *torquēre* to twist

torchbearer (ˈtɔːtʃˌbɛərə) *n* **1** a person or thing that carries a torch. **2** a person who leads or inspires.

torchère (tɔːˈʃɛə) *n* a tall stand for holding a candelabrum. ORIG C20: from F, from *torche* TORCH

torchier *or* **torchiere** (ˈtɔːtʃɪə) *n* a standing lamp with a bowl for casting light upwards. ORIG C20: from TORCHÈRE

torch song *n* a sentimental song, usually sung by a woman. ORIG C20: from *to carry a torch for (someone)*
▸ **torch singer** *n*

tore (tɔː) *vb* the past tense of **tear**[2].

toreador (ˈtɒrɪəˌdɔː) *n* a bullfighter. ORIG C17: from Sp., from *torear* to take part in bullfighting, from *toro* a bull, from L *taurus*

torero (tɒˈrɛərəʊ) *n, pl* **toreros.** a bullfighter, esp. one who fights on foot. ORIG C18: from Sp., from LL *taurārius,* from L *taurus* a bull

Torfaen ★ (tɔːˈvæn) *n* a county borough of SE Wales, created in 1996 from part of Gwent. Administrative centre: Pontypool. Pop.: 90 527 (1996 est.). Area: 290 sq. km (112 sq. miles).

toric lens (ˈtɒrɪk) *n* a lens used to correct astigmatism, having one of its surfaces shaped like part of a torus so that its focal lengths are different in different meridians.

torii (ˈtɔːrɪˌiː) *n, pl* **torii.** a gateway at the entrance to a Shinto temple. ORIG C19: from Japanese, lit.: a perch for birds

Torino ★ (toˈriːno) *n* the Italian name for **Turin.**

torment *vb* (tɔːˈmɛnt). *(tr)* **1** to afflict with great pain, suffering, or anguish; torture. **2** to tease or pester in an annoying way. ◆ *n* (ˈtɔːmɛnt). **3** physical or mental pain. **4** a source of pain, worry, annoyance, etc. ORIG C13: from OF, from L *tormentum,* from *torquēre*
▸ **torˈmented** *adj* ▸ **torˈmenting** *adj, n* ▸ **torˈmentor** *n*

tormentil (ˈtɔːməntɪl) *n* a perennial plant of Europe and W Asia, having yellow flowers, and an astringent root used in medicine, tanning, and dyeing. ORIG C15: from OF *tormentille,* from Med. L *tormentilla,* from L *tormentum* agony; from its use in relieving pain

torn (tɔːn) *vb* **1** the past participle of **tear**[2]. **2 that's torn it.** *Brit. sl.* an unexpected event or circumstance has upset one's plans. ◆ *adj* **3** split or cut. **4** divided or undecided, as in preference: *torn between staying and leaving.*

tornado (tɔːˈneɪdəʊ) *n, pl* **tornadoes** *or* **tornados. 1** a violent storm with winds whirling around a small area of extremely low pressure, usually characterized by a dark funnel-shaped cloud causing damage along its path. **2** a small but violent squall or whirlwind. **3** any violently active or destructive person or thing. ORIG C16: prob. alteration of Sp. *tronada* thunderstorm (from *tronar* to thunder, from L *tonāre*) through infl. of *tornar* to turn, from L *tornāre* to turn in a lathe
▸ **tornadic** (tɔːˈnædɪk) *adj*

toroid (ˈtɔːrɔɪd) *n* **1** *Geom.* a surface generated by rotating a closed plane curve about a coplanar line that does not intersect the curve. **2** the solid enclosed by such a surface. See also **torus.**
▸ **toˈroidal** *adj*

Toronto ★ (təˈrɒntəʊ) *n* a city in S central Canada, capital of Ontario, on Lake Ontario: the major industrial centre of Canada; two universities. Pop. (city): 635 395 (1991); (metropolitan area): 4 338 400 (1995).
▸ **ˌToronˈtonian** *adj, n*

torpedo (tɔːˈpiːdəʊ) *n, pl* **torpedoes. 1** a cylindrical self-propelled weapon carrying explosives that is launched from aircraft, ships, or submarines and follows an underwater path to hit its target. **2** *Obs.* a submarine mine. **3** *US & Canad.* a firework with a percussion cap. **4** an electric ray. ◆ *vb* **torpedoes, torpedoing, torpedoed.** *(tr)* **5** to attack or hit (a ship, etc.) with one or a number of torpedoes. **6** to destroy or wreck: *to torpedo the administration's plan.* ORIG C16: from L: crampfish (whose electric discharges can cause numbness), from *torpēre* to be inactive
▸ **torˈpedo-ˌlike** *adj*

torpedo boat *n* (formerly) a small high-speed warship designed to carry out torpedo attacks.

torpedo tube *n* the tube from which a torpedo is discharged from submarines or ships.

torpid (ˈtɔːpɪd) *adj* **1** apathetic; sluggish. **2** (of a hibernating animal) dormant. **3** unable to move or feel. ORIG C17: from L *torpidus,* from *torpēre* to be numb
▸ **torˈpidity** *n* ▸ **ˈtorpidly** *adv*

torpor (ˈtɔːpə) *n* a state of torpidity. ORIG C17: from L: inactivity, from *torpēre* to be motionless

Torquay ★ (ˌtɔːˈkiː) *n* a town and resort in SW England, in S Devon: administratively part of Torbay since 1968.

torque (tɔːk) *n* **1** a necklace or armband made of twisted metal. **2** any force that causes rotation. ORIG C19: from L *torquēs* necklace & *torquēre* to twist

torque converter *n* a device for the transmission of power in which an engine-driven impeller transmits its momentum to a fluid held in a sealed container, which in turn drives a rotor. Also called: **hydraulic coupling.**

Torquemada ★ (*Spanish* tɔrkeˈmaða) *n* **Tomás de** (toˈmas de). 1420–98, Spanish Dominican monk. As first Inquisitor-General of Spain (1483–98), he had 2000 heretics burnt.

torques (ˈtɔːkwiːz) *n* a distinctive band of hair, feathers, skin, or colour around the neck of an animal; a collar. ORIG C17: from L: necklace, from *torquēre* to twist
▸ **torquate** (ˈtɔːkwɪt, -kweɪt) *adj*

torque wrench *n* a type of wrench with a gauge attached to indicate the torque applied.

torr (tɔː) *n, pl* **torr.** a unit of pressure equal to one millimetre of mercury (133.322 newtons per square metre). ORIG C20: after E. TORRICELLI

Torrance ★ (ˈtɒrəns) *n* a city in SW California, southwest of Los Angeles: developed rapidly with the discovery of oil. Pop.: 138 219 (1994 est.).

Torre del Greco ★ (*Italian* ˈtorre del ˈgrɛːko) *n* a city in

SW Italy, in Campania near Vesuvius on the Bay of Naples: damaged several times by eruptions. Pop.: 100 688 (1992).

torrefy ('tɒrɪˌfaɪ) *vb* **torrefies, torrefying, torrefied.** (*tr*) to dry (drugs, ores, etc.) by heat. ORIG C17: from F *torréfier,* from L *torrefacere,* from *torrēre* to parch + *facere* to make
▸ **torrefaction** (ˌtɒrɪ'fækʃən) *n*

Torrens ★ ('tɒrənz) *n* **Lake.** a shallow salt lake in E central South Australia, about 8 m (25 ft) below sea level. Area: 5776 sq. km (2230 sq. miles).

Torrens title *n Austral.* legal title to land based on record of registration rather than on title deeds. ORIG from Sir Robert Richard *Torrens* (1814–84), who introduced the system as premier of South Australia in 1857

torrent ('tɒrənt) *n* **1** a fast or violent stream, esp. of water. **2** an overwhelming flow of thoughts, words, sound, etc. ORIG C17: from F, from L *torrēns* (n), from *torrēns* (adj) burning, from *torrēre* to burn
▸ **torrential** (tɒ'rɛnʃəl) *adj*

Torreón ★ (*Spanish* tɔrrɛ'ɔn) *n* an industrial city in N Mexico, in Coahuila state. Pop.: 439 436 (1990).

Torres Strait ★ ('tɔːrɪz, 'tɒr-) *n* a strait between NE Australia and S New Guinea, linking the Arafura Sea with the Coral Sea. Width: about 145 km (90 miles).

Torricelli ★ (ˌtɒrɪ'tʃɛlɪ) *n* **Evangelista** (evandʒe'lista). 1608–47, Italian physicist who invented the barometer.

Torricellian tube (ˌtɒrɪ'sɛlɪən) *n* a vertical glass tube partly evacuated and partly filled with mercury, used to measure atmospheric pressure. ORIG C17: after E. TORRICELLI

torrid ('tɒrɪd) *adj* **1** so hot and dry as to parch or scorch. **2** arid or parched. **3** highly charged emotionally: *a torrid love scene.* ORIG C16: from L *torridus,* from *torrēre* to scorch
▸ **tor'ridity** *or* **'torridness** *n* ▸ **'torridly** *adv*

Torrid Zone *n Rare.* that part of the earth's surface lying between the tropics of Cancer and Capricorn.

torsion ('tɔːʃən) *n* **1a** the twisting of a part by application of equal and opposite torques. **1b** the condition of twist and shear stress produced by a torque on a part or component. **2** a twisting or being twisted. ORIG C15: from OF, from Medical L *torsiō* griping pains, from L *torquēre* to twist, torture
▸ **'torsional** *adj* ▸ **'torsionally** *adv*

torsion balance *n* an instrument used to measure small forces, esp. electric or magnetic forces, by the torsion they produce in a thin wire.

torsion bar *n* a metal bar acting as a torsional spring.

torsk (tɔːsk) *n, pl* **torsks** *or* **torsk.** a food fish of northern coastal waters. Usual US name: **cusk.** ORIG C17: of Scand. origin

torso ('tɔːsəʊ) *n, pl* **torsos** *or* **torsi** (-sɪ). **1** the trunk of the human body. **2** a statue of a nude human trunk, esp. without the head or limbs. ORIG C18: from It.: stalk, stump, from L: THYRSUS

tort (tɔːt) *n Law.* a civil wrong or injury arising out of an act or failure to act, independently of any contract, for which an action for damages may be brought. ORIG C14: from OF, from Med. L *tortum,* lit.: something twisted, from L *torquēre* to twist

torte (tɔːt) *n* a rich cake usually decorated or filled with cream, fruit, etc. ORIG C16: ult. ?from LL *tōrta* a round loaf, from ?

Tortelier ★ (*French* tɔrtəlje) *n* **Paul** (pɔl). 1914–90, French cellist.

torticollis (ˌtɔːtɪ'kɒlɪs) *n Pathol.* an abnormal position of the head, usually with the neck bent to one side. ORIG C19: NL, from L *tortus* twisted (from *torquēre* to twist) + *collum* neck

tortilla (tɔː'tiːə) *n Mexican cookery.* a kind of thin pancake made from corn meal. ORIG C17: from Sp.: a little cake, from *torta* a round cake, from LL

tortoise ('tɔːtəs) *n* **1** any of a family of herbivorous reptiles having a heavy dome-shaped shell and clawed limbs. **2** a slow-moving person. **3** another word for **testudo.** ORIG C15: prob. from OF *tortue* (infl. by L *tortus* twisted), from Med. L *tortūca,* from LL *tartarūcha* coming from Tartarus (in the underworld), from Gk *tartaroukhos;* from belief that the tortoise originated in the underworld

tortoiseshell ('tɔːtəsˌʃɛl) *n* **1** the horny yellow-and-brown mottled shell of the hawksbill turtle: used for making ornaments, jewellery, etc. **2** a similar synthetic substance. **3** a breed of domestic cat having black, cream, and brownish markings. **4** any of several butterflies having orange-brown wings with black markings. **5a** a yellowish-brown mottled colour. **5b** (*as adj*): *a tortoiseshell décor.* **6** (*modifier*) made of tortoiseshell.

Tortola ★ (tɔː'təʊlə) *n* an island in the NE Caribbean, in the Leeward Islands group: chief island of the British Virgin Islands. Pop.: 13 568 (1991). Area: 62 sq. km (24 sq. miles).

tortricid ('tɔːtrɪsɪd) *n* any of a family of moths, the larvae of which live in leaves, which they roll or tie together. ORIG C19: from NL *Tortrīcidae,* from *tortrix,* fem. of *tortor,* lit.: twister, from the leaf-rolling of the larvae, from *torquēre* to twist

Tortuga ★ (tɔː'tuːgə) *n* an island in the Caribbean, off the NW coast of Haiti: haunt of pirates in the 17th century. Area: 180 sq. km (70 sq. miles). French name: **La Tortue** (la tɔrty).

tortuous ('tɔːtjʊəs) *adj* **1** twisted or winding. **2** devious or cunning. **3** intricate.
▸ **tortuosity** (ˌtɔːtjʊ'ɒsɪtɪ) *n* ▸ **'tortuously** *adv* ▸ **'tortuousness** *n*

USAGE NOTE See at **torture.**

torture ('tɔːtʃə) *vb* **tortures, torturing, tortured.** (*tr*) **1** to cause extreme physical pain to, esp. to extract information, etc.: *to torture prisoners.* **2** to give mental anguish to. **3** to twist into a grotesque form. ◆ *n* **4** physical or mental anguish. **5** the practice of torturing a person. **6** a cause of mental agony. ORIG C16: from LL *tortūra* a twisting, from *torquēre* to twist
▸ **'torturer** *n* ▸ **'torturous** *adj* ▸ **'torturously** *adv*

USAGE NOTE The adjective *torturous* is sometimes confused with *tortuous.* A *torturous* experience is one that involves pain, suffering, or discomfort, while a *tortuous* road is one that winds or twists.

Toruń ★ (*Polish* 'tɔrunj) *n* an industrial city in N Poland, on the River Vistula: developed around a castle that was founded by the Teutonic Knights in 1230; under Prussian rule (1793–1919). Pop.: 203 800 (1995 est.). German name: **Thorn.**

torus ('tɔːrəs) *n, pl* **tori** (-raɪ). **1** a large convex moulding semicircular in cross section, esp. one used on the base of a column. **2** *Geom.* a ring-shaped surface generated by rotating a circle about a coplanar line that does not intersect the circle. **3** *Bot.* another name for **receptacle** (sense 2). ORIG C16: from L: a swelling, from ?
▸ **toric** ('tɒrɪk) *adj*

Tory ('tɔːrɪ) *n, pl* **Tories. 1** a member or supporter of the Conservative Party in Great Britain or Canada. **2** a member of the English political party that opposed the exclusion of James, Duke of York from the royal succession (1679–80). Tory remained the label for conservative interests until they gave birth to the Conservative Party in the 1830s. **3** an American supporter of the British cause; loyalist. Cf. **Whig. 4** (*sometimes not cap.*) an ultraconservative or reactionary. ◆ *adj* **5** of, characteristic of, or relating to Tories. **6** (*sometimes not cap.*) ultraconservative or reactionary. ORIG C17: from Irish *tōraidhe* outlaw, from MIrish *tōir* pursuit
▸ **'Toryish** *adj* ▸ **'Toryism** *n*

tosa ('təʊsə) *n* a large dog, usually red in colour, that is a cross between a mastiff and a Great Dane: originally developed for dog-fighting; it is not recognized as a breed by kennel clubs outside Japan. ORIG C20: from the name of a province of Japan

Toscana ★ (tos'kaːna) *n* the Italian name for **Tuscany.**

Toscanini ★ (ˌtɒskəˈniːnɪ) *n* **Arturo** (*Italian* arˈtuːro). 1867–1957, Italian conductor.

tosh (tɒʃ) *n Sl., chiefly Brit.* nonsense; rubbish. ORIG C19: from ?

toss (tɒs) *vb* **1** (*tr*) to throw lightly, esp. with the palm of the hand upwards. **2** to fling or be flung about, esp. in an agitated or violent way: *a ship tosses in a storm.* **3** to discuss or put forward for discussion in an informal way. **4** (*tr*) (of a horse, etc.) to throw (its rider). **5** (*tr*) (of an animal) to butt with the head or the horns and throw into the air. **6** (*tr*) to shake or disturb. **7** to toss up a coin with (someone) in order to decide something. **8** (*intr*) to move away angrily or impatiently. ◆ *n* **9** an abrupt movement. **10** a rolling or pitching motion. **11** the act or an instance of tossing. **12** the act of tossing up a coin. See **toss up**. **13** a fall from a horse. ORIG C16: of Scand. origin

tosser (ˈtɒsə) *n Brit. sl.* a stupid or despicable person. ORIG C20: probably from TOSS OFF (to masturbate)

toss off *vb* (*adv*) **1** (*tr*) to perform, write, etc., quickly and easily. **2** (*tr*) to drink at one draught. **3** (*intr*) *Brit. taboo.* to masturbate.

toss up *vb* (*adv*) **1** to spin (a coin) in the air in order to decide between alternatives by guessing which side will fall uppermost. ◆ *n* **toss-up. 2** an instance of tossing up a coin. **3** *Inf.* an even chance or risk.

tot[1] (tɒt) *n* **1** a young child; toddler. **2** *Chiefly Brit.* a small amount of anything. **3** a small measure of spirits. ORIG C18: ? short for *totterer;* see TOTTER

tot[2] (tɒt) *vb* **tots, totting, totted.** (usually foll. by *up*) *Chiefly Brit.* to total; add. ORIG C17: shortened from TOTAL or from L *totum* all

total (ˈtəʊtᵊl) *n* **1** the whole, esp. regarded as the complete sum of a number of parts. ◆ *adj* **2** complete; absolute. **3** (*prenominal*) being or related to a total. ◆ *vb* **totals, totalling, totalled** *or US* **totals, totaling, totaled. 4** (when *intr,* sometimes foll. by *to*) to amount: *to total six pounds.* **5** (*tr*) to add up. **6** (*tr*) *Sl.* to kill or destroy. ORIG C14: from OF, from Med. L *tōtālis,* from L *tōtus* all
▸ ˈ**totally** *adv*

total football *n* an attacking style of play, popularized by the Dutch national team of the 1970s, in which there are no fixed positions and every outfield player can join in the attack.

total internal reflection *n Physics.* the complete reflection of a light ray at the boundary of two media, when the ray is in the medium with greater refractive index.

totalitarian (təʊˌtælɪˈtɛərɪən) *adj* **1** of, denoting, relating to, or characteristic of a dictatorial one-party state that regulates every realm of life. ◆ *n* **2** a person who advocates or practises totalitarian policies.
▸ **toˌtaliˈtarianism** *n*

totality (təʊˈtælɪtɪ) *n, pl* **totalities. 1** the whole amount. **2** the state of being total.

totalizator (ˈtəʊtᵊlaɪˌzeɪtə), **totalizer** *or* **totalisator, totaliser** *n* **1** a system of betting on horse races in which the aggregate stake, less tax, etc., is paid out to winners in proportion to their stake. **2** the machine that records bets in this system and works out odds, pays out winnings, etc. ◆ US and Canad. term: **pari-mutuel.**

total quality management *n* an approach to the management of an organization that integrates the needs of customers with a deep understanding of the technical details, costs, and human-resource relationships of the organization. Abbrev.: **TQM.**

totaquine (ˈtəʊtəˌkwiːn, -kwɪn) *n* a mixture of quinine and other alkaloids derived from cinchona bark, used as a substitute for quinine in treating malaria. ORIG C20: from NL *tōtaquīna,* from TOTA(L) + Sp. *quina* cinchona bark; see QUININE

totara (ˈtəʊtərə) *n* a tall coniferous forest tree of New Zealand with durable wood.

tote[1] (təʊt) *Inf.* ◆ *vb* **totes, toting, toted. 1** (*tr*) to carry, convey, or drag. ◆ *n* **2** the act of or an instance of toting. **3** something toted. ORIG C17: from ?
▸ ˈ**toter** *n*

tote[2] (təʊt) *n* (usually preceded by *the*) *Inf.* short for **totalizator.**

tote bag *n* a large handbag or shopping bag.

totem (ˈtəʊtəm) *n* **1** (in some societies, esp. among North American Indians) an object, animal, plant, etc., symbolizing a clan, family, etc., often having ritual associations. **2** a representation of such an object. ORIG C18: from Ojibwa *nintōtēm* mark of my family
▸ **totemic** (təʊˈtɛmɪk) *adj* ▸ ˈ**totemˌism** *n*

totem pole *n* a pole carved or painted with totemic figures set up by certain North American Indians as a tribal symbol, etc.

tother *or* **t'other** (ˈtʌðə) *adj, n Arch. or dialect.* the other. ORIG C13 *the tother,* by mistaken division from *thet other* (*thet,* from OE *thæt,* neuter of THE[1])

totipalmate (ˌtəʊtɪˈpælmɪt, -ˌmeɪt) *adj* (of certain birds) having all four toes webbed. ORIG C19: from L *tōtus* entire + *palmate,* from *palmātus* shaped like a hand, from *palma* PALM[1]

totter (ˈtɒtə) *vb* (*intr*) **1** to move in an unsteady manner. **2** to sway or shake as if about to fall. **3** to be failing, unstable, or precarious. ◆ *n* **4** the act or an instance of tottering. ORIG C12: ?from OE *tealtrian* to waver, & MDu. *touteren* to stagger
▸ ˈ**totterer** *n* ▸ ˈ**tottery** *adj*

totting (ˈtɒtɪŋ) *n Brit.* the practice of searching through rubbish for usable or saleable items. ORIG C19: from ?

toucan (ˈtuːkən) *n* any of a family of tropical American fruit-eating birds having a large brightly coloured bill and a bright plumage. ORIG C16: from F, from Port. *tucano,* from Tupi *tucana,* prob. imit. of its cry

touch (tʌtʃ) *n* **1** the sense by which the texture and other qualities of objects can be experienced when they come in contact with a part of the body surface, esp. the tips of the fingers. Related adj: **tactile. 2** the quality of an object as perceived by this sense; feel; feeling. **3** the act or an instance of something coming into contact with the body. **4** a gentle push, tap, or caress. **5** a small amount; hint: *a touch of sarcasm.* **6** a noticeable effect; influence: *the house needed a woman's touch.* **7** any slight stroke or mark. **8** characteristic manner or style. **9** a detail of some work: *she added a few finishing touches to the book.* **10** a slight attack, as of a disease. **11** a specific ability or facility. **12** the state of being aware of a situation or in contact with someone. **13** the state of being in physical contact. **14** a trial or test (esp. in **put to the touch**). **15** *Rugby, soccer, etc.* the area outside the touchlines, beyond which the ball is out of play (esp. in **in touch**). **16** a scoring hit in fencing. **17** an estimate of the amount of gold in an alloy as obtained by use of a touchstone. **18** the technique of fingering a keyboard instrument. **19** the quality of the action of a keyboard instrument with regard to the ease with which the keys may be depressed. **20** *Sl.* **20a** the act of asking for money, often by devious means. **20b** the money received. **20c** a person asked for money in this way. ◆ *vb* **21** (*tr*) to cause or permit a part of the body to come into contact with. **22** (*tr*) to tap, feel, or strike. **23** to come or cause to come into contact with. **24** (*intr*) to be in contact. **25** (*tr; usually used with a negative*) to take hold of (a person or thing), esp. in violence. **26** to be adjacent to (each other). **27** (*tr*) to move or disturb by handling. **28** (*tr*) to have an effect on. **29** (*tr*) to produce an emotional response in. **30** (*tr*) to affect; concern. **31** (*tr; usually used with a negative*) to partake of, eat, or drink. **32** (*tr; usually used with a negative*) to handle or deal with: *I wouldn't touch that business.* **33** (when *intr,* often foll. by *on*) to allude (to) briefly or in passing. **34** (*tr*) to tinge or tint slightly: *brown hair touched with gold.* **35** (*tr*) to spoil slightly: *blackfly touched the flowers.* **36** (*tr*) to mark, as with a brush or pen. **37** (*tr*) to compare to in quality or attainment. **38** (*tr*) to reach or attain: *he touched the high point in his career.* **39** (*intr*) to dock or stop briefly: *the ship touches at Tenerife.* **40** (*tr*) *Sl.* to ask for a loan or gift of money from. ◆ See also **touchdown, touch off, touch up.** ORIG C13: from OF *tochier,* from Vulgar L *toccāre* (unattested) to strike, prob. imit. of a tapping sound
▸ ˈ**touchable** *adj* ▸ ˈ**toucher** *n*

touch and go *adj* (**touch-and-go** *when prenominal*) risky or critical.

touchdown ('tʌtʃ,daʊn) *n* **1** the moment at which a landing aircraft or spacecraft comes into contact with the landing surface. **2** *Rugby.* the act of placing or touching the ball on the ground behind the goal line, as in scoring a try. **3** *American football.* a scoring play worth six points, achieved by being in possession of the ball in the opposing team's end zone. Abbrev.: **TD.** ◆ *vb* **touch down.** (*intr, adv*) **4** (of an aircraft, etc.) to land. **5** *Rugby.* to place the ball behind the goal line, as when scoring a try.

touché (tu:'ʃeɪ) *interj* **1** an acknowledgment of a scoring hit in fencing. **2** an acknowledgment of the striking home of a remark, witty reply, etc. ORIG from F, lit.: touched

touched (tʌtʃt) *adj* (*postpositive*) **1** moved to sympathy or emotion. **2** showing slight insanity.

touchhole ('tʌtʃ,həʊl) *n* a hole in the breech of early cannon and firearms through which the charge was ignited.

touching ('tʌtʃɪŋ) *adj* **1** evoking or eliciting tender feelings. ◆ *prep* **2** on the subject of; relating to.
▸ **'touchingly** *adv*

touch judge *n* one of the two linesmen in rugby.

touchline ('tʌtʃ,laɪn) *n* either of the lines marking the side of the playing area in certain games, such as rugby.

touchmark ('tʌtʃ,mɑ:k) *n* a maker's mark stamped on pewter objects.

touch-me-not *n* an impatiens with yellow spurred flowers and seed pods that burst open at a touch when ripe. Also called: **noli-me-tangere.**

touch off *vb* (*tr, adv*) **1** to cause to explode, as by touching with a match. **2** to cause (a disturbance, violence, etc.) to begin.

touchpaper ('tʌtʃ,peɪpə) *n* paper soaked in saltpetre for lighting fireworks or firing gunpowder.

touch screen *n* **a** a visual display unit screen that allows the user to give commands by touching certain areas of the screen with a finger rather than using a keyboard or mouse. **b** (*as modifier*): *a touch-screen computer; a touch-screen game.*

touchstone ('tʌtʃ,stəʊn) *n* **1** a criterion or standard. **2** a hard dark stone that is used to test gold and silver from the streak they produce on it.

touch-tone *adj* of or relating to a telephone dialling system in which each dialling button pressed generates a different pitch, which is transmitted to the exchange.

touch-type *vb* **touch-types, touch-typing, touch-typed.** (*intr*) to type without looking at the keyboard.
▸ **'touch-,typist** *n*

touch up *vb* (*tr, adv*) **1** to put extra or finishing touches to. **2** to enhance, renovate, or falsify by putting extra touches to. **3** *Brit. sl.* to touch or caress (someone).

touchwood ('tʌtʃ,wʊd) *n* something, esp. dry wood or fungus material, used as tinder. ORIG C16: TOUCH (in the sense: to kindle) + WOOD

touchy ('tʌtʃɪ) *adj* **touchier, touchiest. 1** easily upset or irritated. **2** extremely risky. **3** easily ignited.
▸ **'touchily** *adv* ▸ **'touchiness** *n*

touchy-feely ('tʌtʃɪ,fi:lɪ) *adj Inf., sometimes derog.* sensitive and caring.

tough (tʌf) *adj* **1** strong or resilient; durable. **2** not tender. **3** hardy and fit. **4** rough or pugnacious. **5** resolute or intractable. **6** difficult or troublesome to do or deal with: *a tough problem.* **7** *Inf.* unfortunate or unlucky: *it's tough on him.* ◆ *n* **8** a rough, vicious, or pugnacious person. ◆ *adv* **9** *Inf.* violently, aggressively, or intractably: *to treat someone tough.* ◆ *vb* (*tr*) **10** *Sl.* to stand firm, hold out against (a difficulty or difficult situation) (esp. in **tough it out**). ORIG OE *tōh*
▸ **'toughly** *adv* ▸ **'toughness** *n*

toughen ('tʌfən) *vb* to make or become tough or tougher.
▸ **'toughener** *n*

tough love *n* the practice of taking a stern attitude towards a relative or friend suffering from an addiction, etc., to help the addict overcome the problem.

tough-minded *adj* practical, unsentimental, or intractable.
▸ **,tough-'mindedness** *n*

Toul ★ (tu:l) *n* a town in NE France: a leading episcopal see in the Middle Ages. Pop.: 17 406 (1982).

Toulon ★ (*French* tulɔ̃) *n* a fortified port and naval base in SE France, on the Mediterranean: naval arsenal developed by Henry IV and Richelieu, later fortified by Vauban. Pop.: 170 167 (1990).

Toulouse ★ (tu:'lu:z) *n* a city in S France, on the Garonne River: scene of severe religious strife in the early 13th and mid-16th centuries; university (1229). Pop.: 365 933 (1990). Ancient name: **Tolosa** (tə'ləʊsə).

Toulouse-Lautrec ★ (*French* tuluzlotrɛk) *n* **Henri (Marie Raymond) de** (ɑ̃ri də). 1864–1901, French painter and lithographer, noted esp. for his posters, etc., depicting life in Montmartre, Paris.

toupee ('tu:peɪ) *n* a hairpiece worn by men to cover a bald place. ORIG C18: apparently from F *toupet* forelock, from OF *toup* top, of Gmc origin

tour (tʊə) *n* **1** an extended journey visiting places of interest along the route. **2** *Mil.* a period of service, esp. in one place. **3** a short trip, as for inspection. **4** a trip made by a theatre company, orchestra, etc., to perform in several places. **5** an overseas trip made by a cricket or rugby team, etc., to play in several places. ◆ *vb* **6** to make a tour of (a place). **7** (*tr*) to perform (a show) or promote (a product) in several different places. ORIG C14: from OF: a turn, from L *tornus* a lathe, from Gk *tornos*

touraco *or* **turaco** ('tʊərə,kəʊ) *n, pl* **touracos** *or* **turacos.** any of a family of brightly coloured crested African birds. ORIG C18: of West African origin

Touraine ★ (*French* turɛn) *n* a former province of NW central France: at its height in the 16th century as an area of royal residences, esp. along the Loire. Chief town: Tours.

Tourane ★ (tu:'rɑ:n) *n* the former name of **Da Nang.**

Tourcoing ★ (*French* turkwɛ̃) *n* a town in NE France: textile manufacturing. Pop.: 93 765 (1990).

tour de force *French.* (tur də fɔrs) *n, pl* ***tours de force*** (tur). a masterly or brilliant stroke, creation, effect, or accomplishment. ORIG lit.: feat of skill or strength

Touré ★ ('tʊəreɪ) *n* **(Ahmed) Sékou** ('seɪku:). 1922–84, president of the Republic of Guinea (1958–84).

tourer ('tʊərə) *n* a large open car with a folding top, usually seating a driver and four passengers. Also called (esp. US): **touring car.**

tourism ('tʊərɪzəm) *n* tourist travel, esp. when regarded as an industry.

tourist ('tʊərɪst) *n* **1a** a person who travels for pleasure, usually sightseeing and staying in hotels. **1b** (*as modifier*): *tourist attractions.* **2** a person on an excursion or sightseeing tour. **3** a member of a touring team. **4** Also called: **tourist class.** the lowest class of accommodation on a passenger ship or aircraft. ◆ *adj* **5** of or relating to tourist accommodation.
▸ **tour'istic** *adj*

touristy ('tʊərɪstɪ) *adj Inf., often derog.* abounding in or designed for tourists.

tourmaline ('tʊəmə,li:n) *n* any of a group of hard glassy minerals of variable colour consisting of a complex silicate of boron and aluminium in crystalline form: used in jewellery and optical and electrical equipment. ORIG C18: from G *Turmalin,* from Sinhalese *toramalli* carnelian

Tournai ★ (*French* turnɛ) *n* a city in W Belgium, in Hainaut province on the River Scheldt: under several different European rulers until 1814. Pop.: 68 086 (1995 est.). Flemish name: **Doornik.**

tournament ('tʊənəmənt) *n* **1** a sporting competition in which contestants play a series of games to determine an overall winner. **2** a meeting for athletic or other sporting contestants: *an archery tournament.* **3** *Medieval history.* a martial sport or contest in which mounted combatants fought for a prize. ORIG C13: from OF *torneiement,* from *torneier* to fight on horseback, lit.: to turn, from the constant wheeling round of the combatants; see TOURNEY

tournedos ('tʊənə,dəʊ) *n, pl* **tournedos** (-,dəʊz). a thick round steak of beef. ORIG from F, from *tourner* to TURN + *dos* back

Tourneur ★ ('tɜːnə) *n* **Cyril.** ?1575–1626, English dramatist; author of *The Atheist's Tragedy* (1611).

tourney ('tʊənɪ, 'tɔː-) *Medieval history.* ◆ *n* **1** a knightly tournament. ◆ *vb* **2** (*intr*) to engage in a tourney. ORIG C13: from OF *torneier*, from Vulgar L *tornidiāre* (unattested) to turn constantly, from L *tornāre* to TURN (in a lathe); see TOURNAMENT.

tourniquet ('tʊənɪˌkeɪ) *n Med.* any device for constricting an artery of the arm or leg to control bleeding. ORIG C17: from F: device that operates by turning, from *tourner* to TURN

tour operator *n* a person or company that specializes in providing package holidays.

Tours ★ (*French* tur) *n* a town in W central France, on the River Loire: nearby is the scene of the defeat of the Arabs in 732, which ended the advance of Islam in W Europe. Pop.: 133 403 (1990).

tousle ('taʊzᵊl) *vb* **tousles, tousling, tousled.** (*tr*) **1** to tangle, ruffle, or disarrange. **2** to treat roughly. ◆ *n* **3** a disorderly, tangled, or rumpled state. **4** a dishevelled or disordered mass, esp. of hair. ORIG C15: from Low G *tūsen* to shake

Toussaint L'Ouverture ★ (*French* tusɛ̃ luvɛrtyr) *n* **Pierre Dominique** (pjɛr dɔminik). ?1743–1803, Haitian revolutionary, who was made governor by the French Revolutionary government (1794); when Napoleon I proclaimed the re-establishment of slavery he was arrested; died in prison in France.

tout (taʊt) *vb* **1** to solicit (business, customers, etc.) or hawk (merchandise), esp. in a brazen way. **2** (*intr*) **2a** to spy on racehorses being trained in order to obtain information for betting purposes. **2b** to sell such information or to take bets, esp. in public places. ◆ *n* **3** a person who touts. **4** Also: **ticket tout.** a person who sells tickets for a heavily booked event at inflated prices. ORIG C14 (in the sense: to peer, look out): rel. to OE *tȳtan* to peep out
▸ **'touter** *n*

tout à fait *French.* (tut a fɛ) *adv* completely.

tout de suite *French.* (tud sɥit) *adv* at once.

tout le monde *French.* (tu lə mɔ̃d) *n* all the world; everyone.

tovarisch, tovarich, *or* **tovarish** (tə'vɑːrɪʃ) *n* comrade: a term of address. ORIG from Russian

tow¹ (təʊ) *vb* **1** (*tr*) to pull or drag (a vehicle, boat, etc.), esp. by means of a rope or cable. ◆ *n* **2** the act or an instance of towing. **3** the state of being towed (esp. in **in tow, on tow**). **4** something towed. **5** something used for towing. **6 in tow.** in one's charge or under one's influence. **7** short for **ski tow.** ORIG OE *togian*
▸ **'towable** *adj* ▸ **'towage** *n*

tow² (təʊ) *n* the coarse and broken fibres of hemp, flax, jute, etc., prepared for spinning. ORIG OE *tōw*
▸ **'towy** *adj*

toward *adj* ('təʊəd). **1** *Now rare.* in progress; afoot. **2** *Obs.* about to happen; imminent. **3** *Obs.* promising or favourable. ◆ *prep* (tə'wɔːd, tɔːd). **4** a variant of **towards.** ORIG OE *tōweard*

towards (tə'wɔːdz, tɔːdz) *prep* **1** in the direction or vicinity of: *towards London.* **2** with regard to: *her feelings towards me.* **3** as a contribution or help to: *money towards a new car.* **4** just before: *towards noon.* ◆ Also: **toward.**

towbar ('təʊˌbɑː) *n* a rigid metal bar or frame used for towing vehicles.

towboat ('təʊˌbəʊt) *n* another word for **tug** (sense 4).

tow-coloured *adj* pale yellow; flaxen.

towel ('taʊəl) *n* **1** a piece of absorbent cloth or paper used for drying things. **2 throw in the towel.** See **throw in** (sense 3). ◆ *vb* **towels, towelling, towelled** *or US* **towels, toweling, toweled. 3** (*tr*) to dry or wipe with a towel. **4** (*tr*; often foll. by *up*) *Austral. sl.* to assault or beat (a person). ORIG C13: from OF *toaille*, of Gmc origin

towelling ('taʊəlɪŋ) *n* an absorbent fabric used for making towels, bathrobes, etc.

tower ('taʊə) *n* **1** a tall, usually square or circular structure, sometimes part of a larger building and usually built for a specific purpose. **2** a place of defence or retreat. **3 tower of strength.** a person who gives support, comfort, etc. ◆ *vb* **4** (*intr*) to be or rise like a tower; loom. ORIG C12: from OF *tur*, from L *turris*, from Gk

Tower Hamlets ★ *n* a borough of E Greater London, on the River Thames: contains the main part of the East End. Pop.: 159 000 (1994 est.). Area: 20 sq. km (8 sq. miles).

towering ('taʊərɪŋ) *adj* **1** very tall; lofty. **2** outstanding, as in importance or stature. **3** (*prenominal*) very intense: *a towering rage.*

Tower of London ★ *n* a fortress in the City of London, on the River Thames: begun 1078; later extended and used as a palace, the main state prison, and now as a museum containing the crown jewels.

towhead ('təʊˌhɛd) *n* **1** a person with blond or yellowish hair. **2** a head of such hair. ORIG from TOW² (flax)
▸ **ˌtow'headed** *adj*

towhee ('taʊˌhiː, 'təʊ-) *n* any of various North American brownish-coloured sparrows. ORIG C18: imit.

towline ('təʊˌlaɪn) *n* another name for **towrope.**

town (taʊn) *n* **1** a densely populated urban area, typically smaller than a city and larger than a village. **2** a city, borough, or other urban area. **3** (in the US) a territorial unit of local government that is smaller than a county; township. **4** the nearest town or commercial district. **5** London or the chief city of an area. **6** the inhabitants of a town. **7 go to town. 7a** to make a supreme or unrestricted effort. **7b** *Austral. & NZ inf.* to lose one's temper. **8 on the town.** seeking out entertainments and amusements. ORIG OE *tūn* village
▸ **'townish** *adj*

town clerk *n* **1** (in Britain until 1974) the secretary and chief administrative officer of a town or city. **2** (in the US) the official who keeps the records of a town.

town crier *n* (formerly) a person employed to make public announcements in the streets.

Townes ★ (taʊnz) *n* **Charles Hard.** born 1915, US physicist; his research led to the invention of the laser: shared the Nobel prize for physics 1964.

town gas *n* coal gas manufactured for domestic and industrial use.

town hall *n* the chief building in which municipal business is transacted, often with a hall for public meetings.

town house *n* **1** a terraced house in an urban area, esp. a fashionable one. **2** a person's town residence as distinct from his or her country residence.

townie ('taʊnɪ) *or* **townee** (taʊ'niː) *n Inf., often disparaging.* a permanent resident in a town, esp. as distinct from country dwellers or students.

townland ('taʊnlænd) *n Irish.* a division of land of various sizes.

town planning *n* the comprehensive planning of the physical and social development of a town. US term: **city planning.**

townscape ('taʊnskeɪp) *n* **1** a view of an urban scene. **2** an extensive area of urban development.

Townshend ★ ('taʊnzɛnd) *n* **Charles,** 2nd Viscount, nicknamed *Turnip Townshend.* 1674–1738, English politician and agriculturist.

township ('taʊnʃɪp) *n* **1** a small town. **2** (in the Scottish Highlands) a small crofting community. **3** (in the US and Canada) a territorial area, esp. a subdivision of a county: often organized as a unit of local government. **4** (in Canada) a land-survey area, usually 36 square miles (93 square kilometres). **5** (formerly, in South Africa) a planned urban settlement of Black Africans or Coloured people. **6** *English history.* **6a** any of the local districts of a large parish. **6b** the parish itself.

townsman ('taʊnzmən) *n, pl* **townsmen. 1** an inhabitant of a town. **2** a person from the same town as oneself.
▸ **'townsˌwoman** *fem n*

townspeople ('taʊnzˌpiːpᵊl) *or* **townsfolk** ('taʊnzˌfəʊk) *pl n* the inhabitants of a town; citizens.

Townsville ★ ('taʊnzvɪl) *n* a port in E Australia, in NE

Queensland on the Coral Sea: centre of a vast agricultural and mining hinterland. Pop.: 124 900 (1995 est.).

towpath ('təʊˌpɑːθ) *n* a path beside a canal or river, used by people or animals towing boats. Also called: **towing path.**

towrope ('təʊˌrəʊp) *n* a rope or cable used for towing a vehicle or vessel. Also called: **towline.**

tox-, toxic- *or before a consonant* **toxo-, toxico-** *combining form.* indicating poison: *toxaemia.* ORIG from L *toxicum*

toxaemia *or US* **toxemia** (tɒk'siːmɪə) *n* **1** a condition characterized by the presence of bacterial toxins in the blood. **2** the condition in pregnancy of pre-eclampsia or eclampsia.
▸ **tox'aemic** *or US* **tox'emic** *adj*

toxic ('tɒksɪk) *adj* **1** of or caused by a toxin or poison. **2** harmful or deadly. ORIG C17: from Medical L *toxicus,* from L *toxicum* poison, from Gk *toxikon* (*pharmakon*) (poison) used on arrows, from *toxon* arrow
▸ **'toxically** *adv* ▸ **toxicity** (tɒk'sɪsɪtɪ) *n*

toxicant ('tɒksɪkənt) *n* **1** a toxic substance; poison. ◆ *adj* **2** poisonous; toxic. ORIG C19: from Med. L *toxicāre* to poison

toxicology (ˌtɒksɪ'kɒlədʒɪ) *n* the branch of science concerned with poisons, their effects, antidotes, etc.
▸ **toxicological** (ˌtɒksɪkə'lɒdʒɪkᵊl) *or* **ˌtoxico'logic** *adj*
▸ **ˌtoxi'cologist** *n*

toxic shock syndrome *n* a potentially fatal condition in women, characterized by fever, stomachache, a painful rash, and a drop in blood pressure, that is caused by staphylococcal blood poisoning, commonly from a retained tampon.

toxin ('tɒksɪn) *n* **1** any of various poisonous substances produced by microorganisms that stimulate the production of neutralizing substances (antitoxins) in the body. **2** any other poisonous substance of plant or animal origin.

toxin-antitoxin *n* a mixture of a toxin and antitoxin. The diphtheria toxin-antitoxin was formerly used for immunization.

toxocariasis (ˌtɒksəkə'raɪəsɪs) *n* the infection of humans with the larvae of a genus of roundworms, *Toxocara,* of dogs and cats.

toxoid ('tɒksɔɪd) *n* a toxin that has been treated to reduce its toxicity and is used in immunization to stimulate production of antitoxins.

toxophilite (tɒk'sɒfɪˌlaɪt) *Formal.* ◆ *n* **1** an archer. ◆ *adj* **2** of archery. ORIG C18: from *Toxophilus,* the title of a book (1545) by Ascham, designed to mean: a lover of the bow, from Gk *toxon* bow + *philos* loving
▸ **tox'ophily** *n*

toxoplasmosis (ˌtɒksəʊplæz'məʊsɪs) *n* a protozoal disease characterized by jaundice and convulsions.
▸ **ˌtoxo'plasmic** *adj*

toy (tɔɪ) *n* **1** an object designed to be played with. **2a** something that is a nonfunctioning replica of something else, esp. a miniature one. **2b** (*as modifier*): *a toy guitar.* **3** any small thing of little value; trifle. **4a** something small or miniature, esp. a miniature variety of a breed of dog. **4b** (*as modifier*): *a toy poodle.* ◆ *vb* **5** (*intr;* usually foll. by *with*) to play, fiddle, or flirt. ORIG C16 (in the sense: amorous dalliance): from ?

Toyama ★ ('təujɑːˌmɑː) *n* a city in central Japan, on W Honshu on **Toyama Bay** (an inlet of the Sea of Japan): chemical and textile centre. Pop.: 325 303 (1995).

toy boy *n* the much younger male lover of an older woman.

Toynbee ★ ('tɔɪnbɪ) *n* **1 Arnold.** 1852–83, British economist and social reformer. **2** his nephew, **Arnold Joseph.** 1889–1975, British historian; author of *A Study of History* (1934–61).

toy-toy *or* **toyi-toyi** ('tɔɪ'tɔɪ) *S. African.* ◆ *n* **1** a dance expressing defiance and protest. ◆ *vb* (*intr*) **2** to dance in this way. ORIG from ?

TPI *abbrev. for* tax and price index: a measure of the increase in taxable income needed to compensate for an increase in retail prices.

TPWS *abbrev. for* train-protection warning system: a rail safety system that warns the driver if the train passes a stop signal.

TQM *abbrev. for* total quality management.

tr *abbrev. for* treasurer.

tr. *abbrev. for:* **1** transitive. **2** translated. **3** translator. **4** *Music.* trill. **5** trustee.

trabeated ('treɪbɪˌeɪtɪd) *or* **trabeate** ('treɪbɪɪt, -ˌeɪt) *adj Archit.* constructed with horizontal beams as opposed to arches. ORIG C19: back formation from *trabeation,* from L *trabs* a beam

trabecula (trə'bɛkjʊlə) *n, pl* **trabeculae** (-ˌliː). *Anat., bot.* any of various rod-shaped structures that support other organs. ORIG C19: via NL from L: a little beam, from *trabs* a beam
▸ **tra'becular** *or* **tra'beculate** *adj*

Trabzon ('trɑːbzɔːn) *or* **Trebizond** ★ *n* a port in NE Turkey, on the Black Sea: founded as a Greek colony in the 8th century B.C. at the terminus of an important trade route from central Europe to Asia. Pop.: 145 400 (1994 est.).

trace[1] (treɪs) *n* **1** a mark or other sign that something has been in a place. **2** a scarcely detectable amount or characteristic. **3** a footprint or other indication of the passage of an animal or person. **4** any line drawn by a recording instrument or a record consisting of a number of such lines. **5** something drawn, such as a tracing. **6** *Chiefly US.* a beaten track or path. ◆ *vb* **traces, tracing, traced. 7** (*tr*) to follow, discover, or ascertain the course or development of (something). **8** (*tr*) to track down and find, as by following a trail. **9** to copy (a design, map, etc.) by drawing over the lines visible through a superimposed sheet of transparent paper. **10** (*tr;* often foll. by *out*) **10a** to draw or delineate a plan or diagram of. **10b** to outline or sketch (an idea, etc.). **11** (*tr*) to decorate with tracery. **12** (usually foll. by *back*) to follow or be followed to source; date back: *his ancestors trace back to the 16th century.* ORIG C13: from F *tracier,* from Vulgar L *tractiāre* (unattested) to drag, from L *tractus,* from *trahere*
▸ **'traceable** *adj* ▸ **ˌtracea'bility** *or* **'traceableness** *n*
▸ **'traceably** *adv*

trace[2] (treɪs) *n* **1** either of the two side straps that connect a horse's harness to the swingletree. **2** *Angling.* a length of nylon or, formerly, gut attaching a hook or fly to a line. **3 kick over the traces.** to escape or defy control. ORIG C14 *trais,* from OF *trait,* ult. from L *trahere* to drag

trace element *n* any of various chemical elements, such as iron, manganese, zinc, copper, and iodine, that occur in very small amounts in organisms and are essential for many physiological and biochemical processes.

trace fossil *n* the fossilized remains of a track, trail, footprint, burrow, etc., of an organism.

tracer ('treɪsə) *n* **1** a person or thing that traces. **2** a projectile that can be observed when in flight by the burning of chemical substances in its base. **3** *Med.* any radioactive isotope introduced into the body to study metabolic processes, etc., by following its progress with a gamma counter or other detector. **4** an investigation to trace missing cargo, mail, etc.

tracer bullet *n* a round of small arms ammunition containing a tracer.

tracery ('treɪsərɪ) *n, pl* **traceries. 1** a pattern of interlacing ribs, esp. as used in the upper part of a Gothic window, etc. **2** any fine pattern resembling this.
▸ **'traceried** *adj*

trachea (trə'kiːə) *n, pl* **tracheae** (-'kiːiː). **1** *Anat., zool.* the tube that conveys inhaled air from the larynx to the bronchi. **2** any of the tubes in insects and related animals that convey air from the spiracles to the tissues. ORIG C16: from Med. L, from Gk *trakheia,* shortened from (*artēria*) *trakheia* rough (artery), from *trakhus* rough
▸ **tra'cheal** *or* **tra'cheate** *adj*

tracheitis (ˌtreɪkɪ'aɪtɪs) *n* inflammation of the trachea.

tracheo- *or before a vowel* **trache-** *combining form.* denoting the trachea.

tracheotomy (ˌtrækɪ'ɒtəmɪ) *n, pl* **tracheotomies.** surgical incision into the trachea, as performed when the air passage has been blocked.

trachoma (trəˈkəʊmə) *n* a chronic contagious disease of the eye caused by a species of chlamydia: a severe form of conjunctivitis that can result in scarring and blindness. ORIG C17: from NL, from Gk *trakhōma* roughness, from *trakhus* rough
▸ **trachomatous** (trəˈkɒmətəs) *adj*

trachyte (ˈtreɪkaɪt, ˈtræ-) *n* a light-coloured fine-grained volcanic rock. ORIG C19: from F, from Gk *trakhutēs,* from *trakhus* rough

tracing (ˈtreɪsɪŋ) *n* **1** a copy made by tracing. **2** the act of making a trace. **3** a record made by an instrument.

track (træk) *n* **1** the mark or trail left by something that has passed by. **2** any road or path, esp. a rough one. **3** a rail or pair of parallel rails on which a vehicle, such as a locomotive, runs. **4** a course of action, thought, etc.: *don't start on that track again!* **5** a line of motion or travel, such as flight. **6** an endless band on the wheels of a tank, tractor, etc., to enable it to move across rough ground. **7a** a course for running or racing. **7b** (*as modifier*): *track events.* **8** *US & Canad.* **8a** sports performed on a track. **8b** track and field events as a whole. **9** a path on a magnetic recording medium, esp. magnetic tape, on which music or speech is recorded. **10** any of a number of separate sections in the recording on a record, CD, or cassette. **11** the distance between the points of contact with the ground of a pair of wheels, as of a motor vehicle. **12 keep** (*or* **lose**) **track of.** to follow (or fail to follow) the passage, course, or progress of. **13 off the track.** away from what is correct or true. **14 on the track of.** on the scent or trail of; pursuing. ◆ *vb* **15** to follow the trail of (a person, animal, etc.). **16** to follow the flight path of (a satellite, etc.) by picking up signals transmitted or reflected by it. **17** *US railways.* **17a** to provide with a track. **17b** to run on a track of (a certain width). **18** (of a camera or camera-operator) to follow (a moving object) while operating. **19** to follow a track through (a place): *to track the jungles.* **20** (*intr*) (of the pick-up, stylus, etc., of a record player) to follow the groove of a record. ◆ See also **tracks.** ORIG C15: from OF *trac,* prob. of Gmc origin
▸ **ˈtracker** *n*

track down *vb* (*tr, adv*) to find by tracking or pursuing.

tracker dog *n* a dog specially trained to search for missing people.

track event *n* a competition in athletics, such as relay running or sprinting, that takes place on a running track.

tracking (ˈtrækɪŋ) *n* **1** the act or process of following something or someone. **2** *Electrical engineering.* a leakage of electric current between two insulated points caused by dirt, carbon particles, moisture, etc.

tracking shot *n* a camera shot in which the cameraman follows a specific person or event in the action.

tracking station *n* a station that can use a radio or radar beam to follow the path of an object in space or in the atmosphere.

tracklaying (ˈtræk,leɪɪŋ) *adj also* **tracked.** (of a vehicle) having an endless jointed metal band around the wheels.

track record *n Inf.* the past record of the accomplishments and failures of a person, business, etc.

track rod *n* the rod connecting the two front wheels of a motor vehicle.

tracks (træks) *pl n* **1** (*sometimes sing*) marks, such as footprints, etc., left by someone or something that has passed. **2 in one's tracks.** on the very spot where one is standing. **3 make tracks.** to leave or depart. **4 make tracks for.** to go or head towards.

track shoe *n* either of a pair of light running shoes fitted with steel spikes for better grip.

tracksuit (ˈtræk,suːt) *n* a warm suit worn by athletes, etc., esp. during training.

tract[1] (trækt) *n* **1** an extended area, as of land. **2** *Anat.* a system of organs, glands, etc., that has a particular function: *the digestive tract.* **3** *Arch.* an extended period of time. ORIG C15: from L *tractus* a stretching out, from *trahere* to drag

tract[2] (trækt) *n* a treatise or pamphlet, esp. a religious or moralistic one. ORIG C15: from L *tractātus* TRACTATE

tractable (ˈtræktəbᵊl) *adj* **1** easily controlled or persuaded. **2** readily worked; malleable. ORIG C16: from L *tractābilis,* from *tractāre* to manage, from *trahere* to draw
▸ **,tractaˈbility** *or* **ˈtractableness** *n* ▸ **ˈtractably** *adv*

Tractarianism (trækˈtɛərɪə,nɪzəm) *n* another name for the **Oxford Movement.** ORIG after the series of tracts, *Tracts for the Times* published between 1833 and 1841, in which the principles of the movement were presented
▸ **Tracˈtarian** *n, adj*

tractate (ˈtrækteɪt) *n* a treatise. ORIG C15: from L *tractātus,* from *tractāre* to handle; see TRACTABLE

traction (ˈtrækʃən) *n* **1** the act of drawing or pulling, esp. by motive power. **2** the state of being drawn or pulled. **3** *Med.* the application of a steady pull on a limb, etc., using a system of weights and pulleys or splints. **4** adhesive friction, as between a wheel of a motor vehicle and the road. ORIG C17: from Med. L *tractiō,* from L *tractus* dragged, from *trahere* to drag
▸ **ˈtractional** *adj* ▸ **tractive** (ˈtræktɪv) *adj*

traction engine *n* a steam-powered locomotive used, esp. formerly, for drawing heavy loads along roads or over rough ground.

traction load *n Geol.* the solid material that is carried along the bed of a river.

tractor (ˈtræktə) *n* **1** a motor vehicle with large rear wheels or endless belt treads, used to pull heavy loads, esp. farm machinery. **2** a short vehicle with a driver's cab, used to pull a trailer, as in an articulated lorry. ORIG C18: from LL: one who pulls, from *trahere* to drag

Tracy ★ (ˈtreɪsɪ) *n* **Spencer.** 1900–67, US film actor. His films include *Captains Courageous* (1937), *Adam's Rib* (1949), and *Inherit the Wind* (1960).

trad (træd) *n* **1** *Chiefly Brit.* traditional jazz. ◆ *adj* **2** short for **traditional.**

trade (treɪd) *n* **1** the act or an instance of buying and selling goods and services. **2** a personal occupation, esp. a craft requiring skill. **3** the people and practices of an industry, craft, or business. **4** exchange of one thing for something else. **5** the regular clientele of a firm or industry. **6** amount of custom or commercial dealings; business. **7** a specified market or business: *the tailoring trade.* **8** an occupation in commerce, as opposed to a profession. ◆ *vb* **trades, trading, traded. 9** (*tr*) to buy and sell (merchandise). **10** to exchange (one thing) for another. **11** (*intr*) to engage in trade. **12** (*intr*) to deal or do business (with). ◆ See also **trade-in, trade on.** ORIG C14 (in the sense: track, hence, a regular business)
▸ **ˈtradable** *or* **ˈtradeable** *adj*

trade agreement *n* a commercial treaty between two or more nations.

trade association *n* an association of organizations in the same trade formed to further their collective interests, esp. in negotiating with governments, trade unions, etc.

trade cycle *n* the recurrent fluctuation between boom and depression in the economic activity of a capitalist country.

trade discount *n* a sum or percentage deducted from the list price of a commodity allowed to a retailer or by one enterprise to another in the same trade.

traded option *n Stock Exchange.* an option that can itself be bought and sold on a stock exchange. Cf. **traditional option.**

trade down *vb* (*intr, adv*) to sell a large or relatively expensive house, car, etc., and replace it with a smaller or less expensive one.

trade gap *n* the amount by which the value of a country's visible imports exceeds that of visible exports; an unfavourable balance of trade.

trade-in *n* **1a** a used article given in part payment for the purchase of a new article. **1b** a transaction involving such part payment. **1c** the valuation put on the article traded in. ◆ *vb* **trade in. 2** (*tr, adv*) to give (a used article) as part payment for a new article.

trademark ('treɪd,mɑːk) *n* **1a** the name or other symbol used by a manufacturer or dealer to distinguish his products from those of competitors. **1b Registered Trademark.** one that is officially registered and legally protected. **2** any distinctive sign or mark of the presence of a person or animal. ◆ *vb* (*tr*) **3** to label with a trademark. **4** to register as a trademark.

trade name *n* **1** the name used by a trade to refer to a commodity, service, etc. **2** the name under which a commercial enterprise operates in business.

trade-off *n* an exchange, esp. as a compromise.

trade on *vb* (*intr, prep*) to exploit or take advantage of: *he traded on her endless patience.*

trade plate *n* a numberplate attached temporarily to a vehicle by a dealer, etc., before the vehicle has been registered.

trader ('treɪdə) *n* **1** a person who engages in trade. **2** a vessel regularly employed in trade. **3** *Stock Exchange, US.* a member who operates mainly on his or her own account.

trade reference *n* a reference in which one trader gives his or her opinion as to the credit worthiness of another trader in the same trade, esp. to a supplier.

tradescantia (,trædɛs'kænʃɪə) *n* any of a genus of plants widely cultivated for their striped variegated leaves. ORIG C18: NL, after John *Tradescant* (1608–62), E botanist

Trades Council *n* (in Britain) an association of the different trade unions in one town or area.

trade secret *n* a secret formula, technique, process, etc., known and used to advantage by only one manufacturer.

tradesman ('treɪdzmən) *n, pl* **tradesmen. 1** a man engaged in trade, esp. a retail dealer. **2** a skilled worker.
▸ **'trades,woman** *fem n*

tradespeople ('treɪdz,piːpəl) *or* **tradesfolk** ('treɪdz,fəʊk) *pl n Chiefly Brit.* people engaged in trade, esp. shopkeepers.

Trades Union Congress *n* the major association of British trade unions, which includes all the larger unions. Abbrev.: **TUC**

trade union *or* **trades union** *n* an association of employees formed to improve their incomes and working conditions by collective bargaining.
▸ **trade unionism** *or* **trades unionism** *n* ▸ **trade unionist** *or* **trades unionist** *n*

trade up *vb* (*intr, adv*) to sell a small or relatively inexpensive house, car, etc., and replace it with a larger or more expensive one.

trade-weighted *adj* (of exchange rates) weighted according to the value of trade between the various countries involved.

trade wind (wɪnd) *n* a wind blowing obliquely towards the equator either from the northeast in the N hemisphere or the southeast in the S hemisphere, between latitudes 30° N and S. ORIG C17: from *to blow trade* to blow steadily in one direction, from *trade* in the obs. sense: a track

trading estate *n Chiefly Brit.* a large area in which a number of commercial or industrial firms are situated. Also called: **industrial estate.**

trading post *n* a general store in an unsettled or thinly populated region.

tradition (trə'dɪʃən) *n* **1** the handing down from generation to generation of customs, beliefs, etc. **2** the body of customs, thought, etc., belonging to a particular country, people, family, or institution over a long period. **3** a specific custom or practice of long standing. **4** *Christianity.* a doctrine regarded as having been established by Christ or the apostles though not contained in Scripture. **5** (*often cap.*) *Judaism.* a body of laws regarded as having been handed down from Moses orally. **6** the beliefs and customs of Islam supplementing the Koran. **7** *Law, chiefly Roman & Scots.* the act of formally transferring ownership of movable property. ORIG C14: from L *trāditiō* a handing down, surrender, from *trādere* to give up, transmit, from TRANS- + *dāre* to give
▸ **tra'ditionless** *adj*

traditional (trə'dɪʃənəl) *adj* **1** of, relating to, or being a tradition. **2** of the style of jazz originating in New Orleans, characterized by collective improvisation by a front line of trumpet, trombone, and clarinet.
▸ **tra'ditionally** *adv*

traditionalism (trə'dɪʃənə,lɪzəm) *n* **1** the doctrine that all knowledge originates in divine revelation and is perpetuated by tradition. **2** adherence to tradition, esp. in religion.
▸ **tra'ditionalist** *n, adj* ▸ **tra,ditional'istic** *adj*

traditional logic *n* the logic of the late Middle Ages, derived from Aristotelian logic, and concerned esp. with the study of the syllogism.

traditional option *n Stock Exchange.* an option that once purchased cannot be resold. Cf. **traded option.**

traditional weapon *n S. African.* a weapon having ceremonial tribal significance, such as an assegai or knobkerrie.

traduce (trə'djuːs) *vb* **traduces, traducing, traduced.** (*tr*) to speak badly or maliciously of. ORIG C16: from L *trādūcere* to lead over, disgrace
▸ **tra'ducement** *n* ▸ **tra'ducer** *n*

Trafalgar ★ (trə'fælgə; *Spanish* trafal'ɣar) *n* **Cape.** a cape on the SW coast of Spain, south of Cádiz: scene of the decisive naval battle (1805) in which the French and Spanish fleets were defeated by the English under Nelson.

traffic ('træfɪk) *n* **1a** the vehicles coming and going in a street, town, etc. **1b** (*as modifier*): *traffic lights.* **2** the movement of vehicles, people, etc., in a particular place or for a particular purpose: *sea traffic.* **3** (usually foll. by *with*) dealings or business. **4** trade, esp. of an illicit kind: *drug traffic.* **5** the aggregate volume of messages transmitted through a communications system in a given period. **6** *Chiefly US.* the number of customers patronizing a commercial establishment in a given time period. ◆ *vb* **traffics, trafficking, trafficked.** (*intr*) **7** (often foll. by *in*) to carry on trade or business, esp. of an illicit kind. **8** (usually foll. by *with*) to have dealings. ORIG C16: from OF *trafique,* from OIt. *traffico,* from *trafficare* to engage in trade
▸ **'trafficker** *n*

trafficator ('træfɪ,keɪtə) *n* (formerly) an illuminated arm on a motor vehicle raised to indicate a left or right turn.

traffic calming *n* the use of a series of devices, such as bends and humps in the road, to slow down traffic, esp. in residential areas.

traffic island *n* a raised area in the middle of a road designed as a guide for traffic flow and to provide a stopping place for pedestrians crossing.

traffic jam *n* a number of vehicles so obstructed that they can scarcely move.

traffic light *or* **signal** *n* one of a set of coloured lights at crossroads or junctions, to control the flow of traffic.

traffic pattern *n* a pattern of permitted lanes in the air around an airport to which an aircraft is restricted.

traffic warden *n Brit.* a person who is appointed to supervise road traffic and report traffic offences.

Trafford ★ ('træfəd) *n* a unitary authority in NW England, in Greater Manchester. Pop.: 218 900 (1996 est.). Area: 106 sq. km (41 sq. miles).

tragacanth ('trægə,kænθ) *n* **1** any of various spiny plants that yield a substance that is made into a gum. **2** the gum obtained from these plants, used in the manufacture of pills and lozenges and in calico printing. ORIG C16: from F *tragacante,* from L *tragacantha* goat's thorn, from Gk, from *tragos* goat + *akantha* thorn

tragedian (trə'dʒiːdɪən) *or* (*fem*) **tragedienne** (trə,dʒiːdɪ'ɛn) *n* **1** an actor who specializes in tragic roles. **2** a writer of tragedy.

tragedy ('trædʒɪdɪ) *n, pl* **tragedies. 1** a play in which the protagonist falls to disaster through the combination of a personal failing and circumstances with which he cannot deal. **2** any dramatic or literary composition dealing with serious or sombre themes and ending with disaster. **3** the branch of drama dealing with such themes. **4** the unfortunate aspect of something. **5** a shocking or sad event; disaster. ORIG C14: from OF *tragédie,* from L *tragoedia,* from Gk, from *tragos* goat + *ōidē* song; ?from the goat-satyrs of Peloponnesian plays

tragic ('trædʒɪk) *or* (*less commonly*) **tragical** *adj* **1** of, relating to, or characteristic of tragedy. **2** mournful or pitiable.
▸ **'tragically** *adv*

tragic flaw *n* the failing of character in a tragic hero.

tragic irony *n* the use of dramatic irony in a tragedy so that the audience is aware that a character's words or actions will bring about a tragic or fatal result, while the character himself is not.

tragicomedy (ˌtrædʒɪ'kɒmɪdɪ) *n, pl* **tragicomedies. 1** a drama in which aspects of both tragedy and comedy are found. **2** an event or incident having both comic and tragic aspects. ORIG C16: from F, ult. from LL *tragicōmoedia*
▸ **ˌtragi'comic** *or* **ˌtragi'comical** *adj*

tragopan ('trægəˌpæn) *n* any of a genus of pheasants of S and SE Asia, having brightly coloured fleshy processes on the head. ORIG C19: via L from Gk, from *tragos* goat + PAN

tragus ('treɪgəs) *n, pl* **tragi** (-dʒaɪ). the fleshy projection that partially covers the entrance to the external ear. ORIG C17: from LL, from Gk *tragos* hairy projection of the ear, lit.: goat

Traherne ★ (trə'hɜːn) *n* **Thomas.** 1637–74, English mystical writer. His prose works include *Centuries of Meditations.*

trail (treɪl) *vb* **1** to drag, stream, or permit to drag or stream along a surface, esp. the ground. **2** to make (a track) through (a place). **3** to follow or hunt (an animal or person) by following marks or tracks. **4** (when *intr,* often foll. by *behind*) to lag or linger behind (a person or thing). **5** (*intr*) (esp. of plants) to extend or droop over or along a surface. **6** (*intr*) to be falling behind in a race: *the favourite is trailing at the last fence.* **7** (*tr*) to tow (a caravan, etc.) behind a motor vehicle. **8** (*tr*) to carry (a rifle) at the full length of the right arm in a horizontal position, with the muzzle to the fore. **9** (*intr*) to move wearily or slowly. **10** (*tr*) (on television or radio) to advertise (a future programme) with short extracts. ◆ *n* **11** a print, mark, or scent made by a person, animal, or object. **12** the act or an instance of trailing. **13** a path, track, or road, esp. one roughly blazed. **14** something that trails behind or trails in loops or strands. **15** the part of a towed gun carriage and limber that connects the two when in movement and rests on the ground as a partial support when unlimbered. ORIG C14: from OF *trailler* to tow, from Vulgar L *tragulāre* (unattested), from L *trāgula* dragnet, from *trahere* to drag

trail away *or* **off** *vb* (*intr, adv*) to make or become fainter, quieter, or weaker.

trailblazer ('treɪlˌbleɪzə) *n* **1** a leader or pioneer in a particular field. **2** a person who blazes a trail.
▸ **'trailˌblazing** *adj, n*

trailer ('treɪlə) *n* **1** a road vehicle, usually two-wheeled, towed by a motor vehicle: used for transporting boats, etc. **2** the rear section of an articulated lorry. **3** a series of short extracts from a film, used to advertise it in a cinema or on television. **4** a person or thing that trails. **5** the US and Canad. name for **caravan** (sense 1).

trailer park *n US.* a mobile-home site.

trailer trash *n Derog.* **a** poor people living in trailer parks in the US. **b** (*as modifier*): *trailer-trash culture.*

trailing edge *n* the rear edge of a propeller blade or aerofoil. Cf. **leading edge.**

train (treɪn) *vb* **1** (*tr*) to guide or teach (to do something), as by subjecting to various exercises or experiences. **2** (*tr*) to control or guide towards a specific goal: *to train a plant up a wall.* **3** (*intr*) to do exercises and prepare for a specific purpose. **4** (*tr*) to improve or curb by subjecting to discipline: *to train the mind.* **5** (*tr*) to focus or bring to bear (on something): *to train a telescope on the moon.* ◆ *n* **6** a line of coaches or wagons coupled together and drawn by a railway locomotive. **7** a sequence or series: *a train of disasters.* **8** a procession of people, vehicles, etc., travelling together, such as one carrying equipment in support of a military operation. **9** a series of interacting parts through which motion is transmitted: *a train of gears.* **10** a fuse or line of gunpowder to an explosive charge, etc. **11** something drawn along, such as the long back section of a dress that trails along the floor. **12** a retinue or suite. ORIG C14: from OF *trahiner,* from Vulgar L *tragīnāre* (unattested) to draw
▸ **'trainable** *adj*

trainband ('treɪnˌbænd) *n* a company of English militia from the 16th to the 18th century. ORIG C17: altered from *trained band*

trainbearer ('treɪnˌbɛərə) *n* an attendant who holds up the train of a dignitary's robe or bride's gown.

trainee (treɪ'niː) *n* **a** a person undergoing training. **b** (*as modifier*): *a trainee journalist.*

trainer ('treɪnə) *n* **1** a person who trains athletes. **2** a piece of equipment employed in training, such as a simulated aircraft cockpit. **3** a person who schools racehorses. **4** (*pl*) another name for **training shoes.**

training ('treɪnɪŋ) *n* **1a** the process of bringing a person, etc., to an agreed standard of proficiency, etc., by practice and instruction. **1b** (*as modifier*): *training college.* **2 in training. 2a** undergoing physical training. **2b** physically fit. **3 out of training.** physically unfit.

Training Agency *n* (in Britain) an organization established in 1989 to replace the **Training Commission**; it provides training and retraining for adult workers and operates the Youth Training Scheme, in England and Wales working through the local **Training and Enterprise Councils** (TECs) and in Scotland through the **Local Enterprise Companies** (LECs) set up in 1990.

training shoes *pl n* **1** running shoes for sports training, esp. in contrast to studded or spiked shoes worn for the sport itself. **2** shoes in the style of those used for sports training. ◆ Also called: **trainers.**

train oil *n* whale oil obtained from blubber. ORIG C16: from earlier *train* or *trane,* from MLow G *trān,* or MDu. *traen* tear, drop

train spotter *n* **1** a person who collects the numbers of railway locomotives. **2** *Inf.* a person who is obsessed with trivial details, esp. of a subject generally considered uninteresting.

traipse *or* **trapes** (treɪps) *Inf.* ◆ *vb* **traipses, traipsing, traipsed** *or* **trapeses, trapesing, trapesed. 1** (*intr*) to walk heavily or tiredly. ◆ *n* **2** a long or tiring walk; trudge. ORIG C16: from ?

trait (treɪt, treɪ) *n* **1** a characteristic feature or quality distinguishing a particular person or thing. **2** *Rare.* a touch or stroke. ORIG C16: from F, from OF: a pulling, from L *tractus,* from *trahere* to drag

traitor ('treɪtə) *n* a person who is guilty of treason or treachery, in betraying friends, country, a cause, etc. ORIG C13: from OF *traitour,* from L *trāditor,* from *trādere* to hand over
▸ **'traitorous** *adj* ▸ **'traitress** *fem n*

Trajan ★ ('treɪdʒən) *n* Latin name *Marcus Ulpius Traianus.* ?53–117 A.D., Roman emperor (98–117).

trajectory (trə'dʒɛktərɪ) *n, pl* **trajectories. 1** the path described by an object moving in air or space, esp. the curved path of a projectile. **2** *Geom.* a curve that cuts a family of curves or surfaces at a constant angle. ORIG C17: from L *trājectus* cast over, from *trāicere* to throw across

Tralee ★ (trə'liː) *n* a market town in SW Republic of Ireland, county town of Kerry, near **Tralee Bay** (an inlet of the Atlantic). Pop.: 17 200 (1991).

tram (træm) *n* **1** Also called: **tramcar.** an electrically driven public transport vehicle that runs on rails let into the surface of the road. US and Canad. names: **streetcar, trolley car. 2** a small vehicle on rails for carrying loads in a mine; tub. ORIG C16 (in the sense: shaft of a cart): prob. from Low G *traam* beam
▸ **'tramless** *adj*

tramline ('træmˌlaɪn) *n* **1** (*often pl*) Also called: **tramway.**

the tracks on which a tram runs. **2** the route taken by a tram. **3** (*often pl*) the outer markings along the sides of a tennis or badminton court.

trammel ('træməl) *n* **1** (*often pl*) a hindrance to free action or movement. **2** Also called: **trammel net.** a fishing net in three sections, the two outer nets having a large mesh and the middle one a fine mesh. **3** *Rare.* a fowling net. **4** *US.* a shackle for a horse. **5** a device for drawing ellipses consisting of a flat sheet having a cruciform slot in which run two pegs attached to a beam. **6** (*sometimes pl*) a beam compass. **7** a device set in a fireplace to support cooking pots. ◆ *vb* **trammels, trammelling, trammelled** *or US* **trammels, trammeling, trammeled.** (*tr*) **8** to hinder or restrain. **9** to catch or ensnare. ORIG C14: from OF *tramail* three-mesh net, from LL *trēmaculum,* from L *trēs* three + *macula* mesh in a net

tramontane (trə'mɒnteɪn) *adj* **1** being or coming from the far side of the mountains, esp. from the other side of the Alps as seen from Italy. ◆ *n* **2** an inhabitant of a tramontane country. **3** Also called: **tramontana.** a cold dry wind blowing south or southwest from the mountains in Italy and the W Mediterranean. ORIG C16: from It. *tramontano,* from L *trānsmontānus,* from TRANS- + *montānus,* from *mōns* mountain

tramp (træmp) *vb* **1** (*intr*) to walk long and far; hike. **2** to walk heavily or firmly across or through (a place). **3** (*intr*) to wander about as a vagabond or tramp. **4** (*tr*) to traverse on foot, esp. laboriously or wearily. **5** (*intr*) to tread or trample. ◆ *n* **6** a person who travels about on foot, living by begging or doing casual work. **7** a long hard walk; hike. **8** a heavy or rhythmic tread. **9** the sound of heavy treading. **10** a merchant ship that does not run on a regular schedule but carries cargo wherever the shippers desire. **11** *Sl., chiefly US & Canad.* a prostitute or promiscuous girl or woman. ORIG C14: prob. from MLow G *trampen*
▸ **'trampish** *adj*

tramper ('træmpə) *n NZ.* a person who tramps, or walks long distances, in the bush.

tramping ('træmpɪŋ) *n NZ.* **1** the leisure activity of walking in the bush. **2** (*as modifier*): *tramping boots.*

trample ('træmp°l) *vb* **tramples, trampling, trampled.** (when *intr,* usually foll. by *on, upon,* or *over*) **1** to stamp or walk roughly (on). **2** to encroach (upon) so as to violate or hurt. ◆ *n* **3** the action or sound of trampling. ORIG C14: frequentative of TRAMP
▸ **'trampler** *n*

trampoline ('træmpəlɪn, -ˌliːn) *n* **1** a tough canvas sheet suspended by springs or cords from a frame, used by acrobats, gymnasts, etc. ◆ *vb* **trampolines, trampolining, trampolined.** **2** (*intr*) to exercise on a trampoline. ORIG C18: via Sp. from It. *trampolino,* from *trampoli* stilts, of Gmc origin
▸ **'trampoliner** *or* **'trampolinist** *n*

trance (trɑːns) *n* **1** a hypnotic state resembling sleep. **2** any mental state in which a person is unaware of the environment, characterized by loss of voluntary movement, rigidity, and lack of sensitivity to external stimuli. **3** a dazed or stunned state. **4** a state of ecstasy or mystic absorption so intense as to cause a temporary loss of consciousness at the earthly level. **5** *Spiritualism.* a state in which a medium can supposedly be controlled by an intelligence from without as a means of communication with the dead. ◆ *vb* **trances, trancing, tranced.** **6** (*tr*) to put into or as into a trance. ORIG C14: from OF *transe,* from *transir* to faint, from L *trānsīre* to go over
▸ **'trance,like** *adj*

tranche (trɑːnʃ) *n* an instalment or portion, esp. of a loan or share issue. ORIG F, lit.: slice

trannie *or* **tranny** ('trænɪ) *n, pl* **trannies.** *Inf., chiefly Brit.* a transistor radio.

tranquil ('træŋkwɪl) *adj* calm, peaceful, or quiet. ORIG C17: from L *tranquillus*
▸ **'tranquilly** *adv*

tranquillity *or US* (*sometimes*) **tranquility** (træŋ'kwɪlɪtɪ) *n* a state of calm or quietude.

tranquillize, tranquillise, *or US* **tranquilize** ('træŋkwɪˌlaɪz) *vb* **tranquillizes, tranquillizing; tranquillized, tranquillises, tranquillising, tranquillised,** *or US* **tranquilizes, tranquilizing, tranquilized.** to make or become calm or calmer.
▸ **ˌtranquilli'zation, ˌtranquilli'sation,** *or US* **ˌtranquili'zation** *n*

tranquillizer, tranquilliser *or US* **tranquilizer** ('træŋkwɪˌlaɪzə) *n* **1** a drug that calms a person. **2** anything that tranquillizes.

tranquillo (ˌtræŋ'kwiːləʊ) *adj Music.* calm; tranquil. ORIG It.

trans. *abbrev. for:* **1** transaction. **2** transferred. **3** transitive. **4** translated. **5** translator. **6** transport(ation). **7** transverse.

trans- *prefix* **1** across, beyond, crossing, on the other side: *transatlantic.* **2** changing thoroughly: *transliterate.* **3** transcending: *transubstantiation.* **4** transversely: *transect.* **5** (*often in italics*) indicating that a chemical compound has a molecular structure in which two identical groups or atoms are on opposite sides of a double bond: *trans-butadiene.* ORIG from L *trāns* across, through, beyond

transact (træn'zækt) *vb* to do, conduct, or negotiate (business, a deal, etc.). ORIG C16: from L *trānsactus,* from *trānsigere,* lit.: to drive through
▸ **trans'actor** *n*

transactinide (træns'æktɪˌnaɪd) *n* any artificially produced element with an atomic number greater than 103. ORIG C20

transaction (træn'zækʃən) *n* **1** something that is transacted, esp. a business deal. **2** a transacting or being transacted. **3** (*pl*) the records of the proceedings of a society, etc.
▸ **trans'actional** *adj*

transalpine (trænz'ælpaɪn) *adj* (*prenominal*) **1** situated in or relating to places beyond the Alps, esp. from Italy. **2** passing over the Alps.

Transalpine Gaul ★ *n* (in the ancient world) that part of Gaul northwest of the Alps.

transaminase (trænz'æmɪˌneɪz, -ˌneɪs) *n Biochem.* an enzyme that catalyses the transfer of an amino group from one molecule, esp. an amino acid, to another, esp. a keto acid, in the process of **transamination.**

transatlantic (ˌtrænzət'læntɪk) *adj* **1** on or from the other side of the Atlantic. **2** crossing the Atlantic.

Transcaucasia ★ (ˌtrænskɔː'keɪzjə) *n* a region of central Asia, south of the Caucasus Mountains between the Black and Caspian Seas in Georgia, Azerbaijan, and Armenia: a constituent republic of the Soviet Union from 1918 until 1936.
▸ **ˌTranscau'casian** *adj, n*

transceiver (træn'siːvə) *n* a device which transmits and receives radio or electronic signals. ORIG C20: from TRANS(MITTER) + (RE)CEIVER

transcend (træn'sɛnd) *vb* **1** to go above or beyond (a limit, expectation, etc.), as in degree or excellence. **2** (*tr*) to be superior to. ORIG C14: from L *trānscendere* to climb over

transcendent (træn'sɛndənt) *adj* **1** exceeding or surpassing in degree or excellence. **2** (in the philosophy of Kant) beyond or before experience. **3** *Theol.* (of God) having existence outside the created world. **4** free from the limitations inherent in matter. ◆ *n* **5** *Philosophy.* a transcendent thing.
▸ **tran'scendence** *or* **tran'scendency** *n* ▸ **tran'scendently** *adv*

transcendental (ˌtrænsen'dɛnt°l) *adj* **1** transcendent, superior, or surpassing. **2** (in the philosophy of Kant) **2a** (of a judgment or logical deduction) being both synthetic and a priori. **2b** of or relating to knowledge of the presuppositions of thought. **3** *Philosophy.* beyond our experience of phenomena, although not beyond potential knowledge. **4** *Theol.* supernatural or mystical. **5** *Maths.* **5a** (of a number or quantity) not being a root of any polynomial with rational coefficients. **5b** (of a function) not capable of expression in terms of a finite number of arithmetical operations.
▸ **ˌtranscen'dentally** *adv*

transcendentalism (ˌtrænsen'dɛntəˌlɪzəm) *n* **1a** any system of philosophy, esp. that of Kant, holding that the

key to knowledge of the nature of reality lies in the critical examination of the processes of reason on which depends the nature of experience. **1b** any system of philosophy, esp. that of Emerson, that emphasizes intuition as a means to knowledge or the importance of the search for the divine. **2** vague philosophical speculation. **3** the state of being transcendental. **4** something, such as thought or language, that is transcendental.
▸ **ˌtranscenˈdentalist** *n, adj*

transcendental meditation *n* a technique, based on Hindu traditions, for relaxing and refreshing the mind and body through the silent repetition of a mantra.

transcontinental (ˌtrænzkɒntɪˈnɛntᵊl) *adj* **1** crossing a continent. **2** on or from the far side of a continent.
▸ **ˌtranscontiˈnentally** *adv*

transcribe (trænˈskraɪb) *vb* **transcribes, transcribing, transcribed.** (*tr*) **1** to write, type, or print out fully from speech, notes, etc. **2** to transliterate or translate. **3** to make an electrical recording of (a programme or speech) for a later broadcast. **4** *Music.* to rewrite (a piece of music) for an instrument or medium other than that originally intended; arrange. **5** *Computing.* **5a** to transfer (information) from one storage device to another. **5b** to transfer (information) from a computer to an external storage device. ORIG C16: from L *trānscrībere*
▸ **tranˈscribable** *adj* ▸ **tranˈscriber** *n*

transcript (ˈtrænskrɪpt) *n* **1** a written, typed, or printed copy or manuscript made by transcribing. **2** *Chiefly US & Canad.* an official record of a student's school progress. **3** any reproduction or copy. ORIG C13: from L *trānscriptum,* from *trānscrībere* to transcribe

transcriptase (trænˈskrɪpteɪz) *n* See **reverse transcriptase.**

transcription (trænˈskrɪpʃən) *n* **1** the act or an instance of transcribing or the state of being transcribed. **2** something transcribed. **3** a representation in writing of the actual pronunciation of a speech sound, word, etc., using phonetic symbols.
▸ **tranˈscriptional** *or* **tranˈscriptive** *adj*

transducer (trænzˈdjuːsə) *n* any device, such as a microphone or electric motor, that converts one form of energy into another. ORIG C20: from L *trānsducere* to lead across

transect *vb* (trænˈsɛkt). (*tr*) **1** to cut or divide crossways. ◆ *n* (ˈtrænsɛkt). **2** a sample strip of land used to monitor plant distribution, animal populations, or some other feature, within a given area. ORIG C17: from L TRANS- + *secāre* to cut
▸ **tranˈsection** *n*

transept (ˈtrænsɛpt) *n* either of the two wings of a cruciform church at right angles to the nave. ORIG C16: from Anglo-L *trānseptum,* from L TRANS- + *saeptum* enclosure
▸ **tranˈseptal** *adj*

trans-fatty acid *n* a polyunsaturated fatty acid that has been converted from the cis-form by hydrogenation: used in the manufacture of margarine.

transfer *vb* (trænsˈfɜː), **transfers, transferring, transferred. 1** to change or go or cause to change or go from one thing, person, or point to another. **2** to change (buses, trains, etc.). **3** *Law.* to make over (property, etc.) to another; convey. **4** to displace (a drawing, design, etc.) from one surface to another. **5** (of a football player) to change clubs or (of a club, manager, etc.) to sell or release (a player) to another club. **6** to leave one school, college, etc., and enrol at another. **7** to change (the meaning of a word, etc.), esp. by metaphorical extension. ◆ *n* (ˈtrænsfɜː). **8** the act, process, or system of transferring, or the state of being transferred. **9** a person or thing that transfers or is transferred. **10** a design or drawing that is transferred from one surface to another. **11** *Law.* the passing of title to property or other right from one person to another; conveyance. **12** any document or form effecting or regulating a transfer. **13** *Chiefly US & Canad.* a ticket that allows a passenger to change routes. ORIG C14: from L *trānsferre,* from TRANS- + *ferre* to carry
▸ **transˈferable** *or* **transˈferrable** *adj* ▸ **transference** (ˈtrænsfərəns) *n*

transferable vote *n* a vote that is transferred to a second candidate indicated by the voter if the first is eliminated from the ballot.

transferee (ˌtrænsfəˈriː) *n* **1** *Property law.* a person to whom property is transferred. **2** a person who is transferred.

transfer fee *n* a sum of money paid by one football club to another for a transferred player.

transferrin (trænsˈfɜːrɪn) *n Biochem.* any of a group of blood proteins that transport iron. ORIG C20: from TRANS- + FERRO- + -IN

transfer RNA *n Biochem.* any of several soluble forms of RNA of low molecular weight, each of which transports a specific amino acid to a ribosome during protein synthesis.

transfiguration (ˌtrænsfɪgjʊˈreɪʃən) *n* a transfiguring or being transfigured.

Transfiguration (ˌtrænsfɪgjʊˈreɪʃən) *n* **1** *New Testament.* the change in the appearance of Christ that took place before three disciples (Matthew 17:1–9). **2** the Church festival held in commemoration of this on Aug. 6.

transfigure (trænsˈfɪgə) *vb* **transfigures, transfiguring, transfigured.** (*usually tr*) **1** to change or cause to change in appearance. **2** to become or cause to become more exalted. ORIG C13: from L *trānsfigūrāre,* from TRANS- + *figūra* appearance
▸ **transˈfigurement** *n*

transfinite number (trænsˈfaɪnaɪt) *n* a cardinal or ordinal number used in the comparison of infinite sets for which several types of infinity can be classified.

transfix (trænsˈfɪks) *vb* **transfixes, transfixing, transfixed** *or* **transfixt.** (*tr*) **1** to render motionless, esp. with horror or shock. **2** to impale or fix with a sharp weapon or other device. ORIG C16: from L *trānsfīgere* to pierce through
▸ **transfixion** (trænsˈfɪkʃən) *n*

transform *vb* (trænsˈfɔːm). **1** to alter or be altered in form, function, etc. **2** (*tr*) to convert (one form of energy) to another form. **3** (*tr*) *Maths.* to change the form of (an equation, etc.) by a mathematical transformation. **4** (*tr*) to change (an alternating current or voltage) using a transformer. ◆ *n* (ˈtrænsˌfɔːm). **5** *Maths.* the result of a mathematical transformation. ORIG C14: from L *trānsformāre*
▸ **transˈformable** *adj* ▸ **transˈformative** *adj*

transformation (ˌtrænsfəˈmeɪʃən) *n* **1** a change or alteration, esp. a radical one. **2** a transforming or being transformed. **3** *Maths.* **3a** a change in position or direction of the reference axes in a coordinate system without an alteration in their relative angle. **3b** an equivalent change in an expression or equation resulting from the substitution of one set of variables by another. **4** *Physics.* a change in an atomic nucleus to a different nuclide as the result of the emission of either an alpha-particle or a beta-particle. **5** *Linguistics.* another word for **transformational rule. 6** an apparently miraculous change in the appearance of a stage set.
▸ **ˌtransforˈmational** *adj*

transformational grammar *n* a grammatical description of a language making essential use of transformational rules.

transformational rule *n Generative grammar.* a rule that converts one phrase marker into another. Taken together, these rules convert the deep structures of sentences into their surface structures.

transformer (trænsˈfɔːmə) *n* **1** a device that transfers an alternating current from one circuit to one or more other circuits, usually with a change of voltage. **2** a person or thing that transforms.

transfuse (trænsˈfjuːz) *vb* **transfuses, transfusing, transfused.** (*tr*) **1** to permeate or infuse. **2a** to inject (blood, etc.) into a blood vessel. **2b** to give a transfusion to (a patient). ORIG C15: from L *trānsfundere* to pour out
▸ **transˈfuser** *n* ▸ **transˈfusible** *or* **transˈfusable** *adj*
▸ **transˈfusive** *adj*

transfusion (trænsˈfjuːʒən) *n* **1** a transfusing. **2** the injection of blood, blood plasma, etc., into the blood vessels of a patient.

transgender (trænz'dʒɛndə) *adj* attempting or appearing to be a member of the opposite sex.

transgenic (trænz'dʒɛnɪk) *adj* (of an animal or plant) containing genetic material artificially transferred from another species.

transgress (trænz'grɛs) *vb* **1** to break (a law, etc.). **2** to go beyond or overstep (a limit). ORIG C16: from L *trānsgredī*, from TRANS- + *gradī* to step
▸ **trans'gressor** *n*

transgression (trænz'grɛʃən) *n* **1** a breach of a law, etc.; sin or crime. **2** a transgressing.

transgressive (ˌtrænz'grɛsɪv) *adj* going beyond accepted boundaries of taste, convention, or the law: *transgressive art; transgressive pursuits.*

tranship (træn'ʃɪp) *vb* **tranships, transhipping, transhipped.** a variant spelling of **transship.**

transhumance (træns'hju:məns) *n* the seasonal migration of livestock to suitable grazing grounds. ORIG C20: from F, from *transhumer* to change one's pastures, from Sp. *trashumar,* from L TRANS- + *humus* ground
▸ **trans'humant** *adj*

transient ('trænzɪənt) *adj* **1** for a short time only; temporary or transitory. ◆ *n* **2** a transient person or thing. ORIG C17: from L *trānsiēns* going over, from *trānsīre* to pass over
▸ **'transiently** *adv* ▸ **'transience** *or* **'transiency** *n*

transistor (træn'zɪstə) *n* **1** a semiconductor device, having three or more terminals attached to electrode regions, in which current flowing between two electrodes is controlled by a voltage or current applied to one or more specified electrodes. The device has replaced the valve in most circuits since it is much smaller and works at a much lower voltage. **2** *Inf.* a transistor radio. ORIG C20: orig. a trademark, from TRANSFER + RESISTOR, from the transfer of electric signals across a resistor

transistorize *or* **transistorise** (træn'zɪstəˌraɪz) *vb* **transistorizes, transistorizing, transistorized** *or* **transistorises, transistorising, transistorised. 1** to convert to the use or manufacture of transistors and other solid-state components. **2** (*tr*) to equip with transistors and other solid-state components.

transit ('trænsɪt, 'trænz-) *n* **1a** the passage or conveyance of goods or people. **1b** (*as modifier*): *a transit visa.* **2** a change or transition. **3** a route. **4** *Astron.* **4a** the passage of a celestial body or satellite across the face of a larger body as seen from the earth. **4b** the apparent passage of a celestial body across the meridian. **5 in transit.** while being conveyed; during passage. ◆ *vb* **6** to make a transit through or over (something). ORIG C15: from L *trānsitus* a going over, from *trānsīre* to pass over

transit camp *n* a camp in which refugees, soldiers, etc., live temporarily.

transit instrument *n* an astronomical instrument used to time the transit of a star, etc., across the meridian.

transition (træn'zɪʃən) *n* **1** change or passage from one state or stage to another. **2** the period of time during which something changes. **3** *Music.* **3a** a movement from one key to another; modulation. **3b** a linking passage between two divisions in a composition; bridge. **4** a style of architecture in the late 11th and early 12th centuries, characterized by late Romanesque forms combined with early Gothic details. **5** *Physics.* a change in the configuration of an atomic nucleus, involving either a change in energy level or a transformation to another element or isotope. **6** a sentence, passage, etc., that links sections of a written work. ORIG C16: from L *transitio;* see TRANSIENT
▸ **tran'sitional** *adj* ▸ **tran'sitionally** *adv*

transition element *or* **metal** *n Chem.* any element belonging to one of three series of elements with atomic numbers between 21 and 30, 39 and 48, and 57 and 80. They have an incomplete penultimate electron shell and tend to form complexes.

transition temperature *n* the temperature at which a sudden change of physical properties occurs.

transitive ('trænsɪtɪv) *adj* **1** *Grammar.* **1a** denoting an occurrence of a verb when it requires a direct object or denoting a verb that customarily requires a direct object: *"to find" is a transitive verb.* **1b** (*as n*): *these verbs are transitives.* **2** *Logic, maths.* having the property that if one object bears a relationship to a second object that also bears the same relationship to a third object, then the first object bears this relationship to the third object: *if* $x = y$ *and* $y = z$ *then* $x = z$. ◆ Cf. **intransitive.** ORIG C16: from LL *trānsitīvus,* from L *trānsitus* a going over; see TRANSIENT
▸ **'transitively** *adv* ▸ **ˌtransi'tivity** *or* **'transitiveness** *n*

transitory ('trænsɪtərɪ, -trɪ) *adj* of short duration; transient or ephemeral. ORIG C14: from Church L *trānsitōrius* passing, from L *trānsitus* a crossing over
▸ **'transitoriness** *n*

transit theodolite *n* a theodolite the telescope of which can be rotated completely about its horizontal axis.

Trans-Jordan ★ *n* the former name (1922–49) of **Jordan.**
▸ **ˌTrans-Jor'danian** *adj, n*

Transkei ★ (træn'skaɪ) *n* a former Bantu homeland in South Africa: the largest of South Africa's Bantu homelands and the first Bantu self-governing territory (1963); reintegrated into South Africa in 1994. Capital: Umtata.
▸ **Trans'keian** *adj, n*

transl. *abbrev. for:* **1** translated. **2** translator.

translate (træns'leɪt, trænz-) *vb* **translates, translating, translated. 1** to express or be capable of being expressed in another language. **2** (*intr*) to act as translator. **3** (*tr*) to express or explain in simple or less technical language. **4** (*tr*) to interpret or infer the significance of (gestures, symbols, etc.). **5** (*tr*) to transform or convert: *to translate hope into reality.* **6** to transfer from one place or position to another. **7** (*tr*) *Theol.* to transfer (a person) from one place or plane of existence to another, as from earth to heaven. **8** (*tr*) *Maths, physics.* to move (a figure or body) laterally, without rotation, dilation, or angular displacement. ORIG C13: from L *trānslātus* carried over, from *trānsferre* to TRANSFER
▸ **trans'latable** *adj* ▸ **trans'lator** *n*

translation (træns'leɪʃən, trænz-) *n* **1** something that is or has been translated. **2** a translating or being translated. **3** *Maths.* a transformation in which the origin of a coordinate system is moved to another position so that each axis retains the same direction.
▸ **trans'lational** *adj*

transliterate (trænz'lɪtəˌreɪt) *vb* **transliterates, transliterating, transliterated.** (*tr*) to transcribe (a word, etc.) into corresponding letters of another alphabet. ORIG C19: TRANS- + *-literate,* from L *līttera* letter
▸ **ˌtransliter'ation** *n* ▸ **trans'literˌator** *n*

translocation (ˌtrænzləʊ'keɪʃən) *n* **1** *Genetics.* the transfer of one part of a chromosome to another part of the same or a different chromosome. **2** *Bot.* the transport of minerals, sugars, etc., in solution within a plant. **3** a movement from one position or place to another.

translucent (trænz'lu:sᵊnt) *adj* allowing light to pass through partially or diffusely; semitransparent. ORIG C16: from L *trānslūcēre* to shine through
▸ **trans'lucence** *or* **trans'lucency** *n* ▸ **trans'lucently** *adv*

translunar (trænz'lu:nə) *or* **translunary** (trænz'lu:nərɪ) *adj* **1** lying beyond the moon. **2** unworldly or ethereal.

transmigrate (ˌtrænzmaɪ'greɪt) *vb* **transmigrates, transmigrating, transmigrated.** (*intr*) **1** to move from one place, state, or stage to another. **2** (of souls) to pass from one body into another at death.
▸ **ˌtransmi'gration** *n* ▸ **trans'migratory** *adj*

transmission (trænz'mɪʃən) *n* **1** the act or process of transmitting. **2** something that is transmitted. **3** the extent to which a body or medium transmits light, sound, etc. **4** the transference of motive force or power. **5** a system of shafts, gears, etc., that transmits power, esp. the arrangement of such parts that transmits the power of the engine to the driving wheels of a motor vehicle. **6** the act or process of sending a message, picture, or other information by means of radio waves, electrical signals, light signals, etc. **7** a radio or television broadcast. ORIG C17: from L *trānsmissiō* a sending across
▸ **trans'missible** *adj* ▸ **trans'missive** *adj*

★ people and places

transmission density *n Physics.* a measure of the extent to which a substance transmits light or other electromagnetic radiation.

transmission line *n* a coaxial cable, waveguide, etc., that transfers electrical signals from one location to another.

transmissivity (ˌtrænzmɪˈsɪvɪtɪ) *n Physics.* a measure of the ability of a material to transmit radiation.

transmit (trænzˈmɪt) *vb* **transmits, transmitting, transmitted.** **1** (*tr*) to pass or cause to go from one place or person to another; transfer. **2** (*tr*) to pass on or impart (a disease, etc.). **3** (*tr*) to hand down to posterity. **4** (*tr; usually passive*) to pass (an inheritable characteristic) from parent to offspring. **5** to allow the passage of (particles, energy, etc.): *radio waves are transmitted through the atmosphere.* **6a** to send out (signals) by means of radio waves or along a transmission line. **6b** to broadcast (a radio or television programme). **7** (*tr*) to transfer (a force, motion, etc.) from one part of a mechanical system to another. ORIG C14: from L *trānsmittere* to send across
▸ **transˈmittable** *adj* ▸ **transˈmittal** *n*

transmittance (trænzˈmɪtᵊns) *n* **1** the act of transmitting. **2** Also called: **transmission factor.** *Physics.* a measure of the ability of anything to transmit radiation, equal to the ratio of the transmitted flux to the incident flux.

transmitter (trænzˈmɪtə) *n* **1** a person or thing that transmits. **2** the equipment used for generating and amplifying a radio-frequency carrier, modulating the carrier with information, and feeding it to an aerial for transmission. **3** the microphone in a telephone that converts sound waves into audio-frequency electrical signals. **4** a device that converts mechanical movements into coded electrical signals transmitted along a telegraph circuit. **5** a substance released by nerve endings that transmits impulses across synapses.

transmogrify (trænzˈmɒgrɪˌfaɪ) *vb* **transmogrifies, transmogrifying, transmogrified.** (*tr*) *Jocular.* to change or transform into a different shape, esp. a grotesque or bizarre one. ORIG C17: from ?
▸ **transˌmogrifiˈcation** *n*

transmontane (ˌtrænzmɒnˈteɪn) *adj, n* another word for **tramontane.**

transmutation (ˌtrænzmjuːˈteɪʃən) *n* **1** the act or an instance of transmuting. **2** the change of one chemical element into another by a nuclear reaction. **3** the attempted conversion, by alchemists, of base metals into gold or silver.
▸ ˌ**transmuˈtational** *or* **transˈmutative** *adj*

transmute (trænzˈmjuːt) *vb* **transmutes, transmuting, transmuted.** (*tr*) **1** to change the form, character, or substance of. **2** to alter (an element, metal, etc.) by alchemy. ORIG C15: via OF from L *trānsmūtāre* to shift, from TRANS- + *mūtāre* to change
▸ **transˌmutaˈbility** *n* ▸ **transˈmutable** *adj*

transnational (trænzˈnæʃənəl) *adj* extending beyond the boundaries, etc., of a single nation.

transoceanic (trænzˌəʊʃɪˈænɪk) *adj* **1** on or from the other side of an ocean. **2** crossing an ocean.

transom (ˈtrænsəm) *n* **1** a horizontal member across a window. **2** a horizontal member that separates a door from a window over it. **3** the usual US name for **fanlight. 4** *Naut.* **4a** a surface forming the stern of a vessel. **4b** any of several transverse beams used for strengthening the stern of a vessel. ORIG C14: earlier *traversayn,* from OF *traversin,* from TRAVERSE
▸ ˈ**transomed** *adj*

transonic (trænˈsɒnɪk) *adj* of or relating to conditions when travelling at or near the speed of sound.

transparency (trænsˈpærənsɪ) *n, pl* **transparencies. 1** Also called: **transparence.** the state of being transparent. **2** Also called: **slide.** a positive photograph on a transparent base, usually mounted in a frame or between glass plates. It can be viewed by means of a slide projector.

transparent (trænsˈpærənt) *adj* **1** permitting the uninterrupted passage of light; clear. **2** easy to see through, understand, or recognize; obvious. **3** permitting the free passage of electromagnetic radiation. **4** candid, open, or frank. ORIG C15: from Med. L *trānspārēre* to show through, from L TRANS- + *pārēre* to appear
▸ **transˈparently** *adv* ▸ **transˈparentness** *n*

transpire (trænˈspaɪə) *vb* **transpires, transpiring, transpired.** **1** (*intr*) to come to light; be known. **2** (*intr*) *Inf.* to happen or occur. **3** *Physiol.* to give off or exhale (water or vapour) through the skin, a mucous membrane, etc. **4** (of plants) to lose (water), esp. through the stomata of the leaves. ORIG C16: from Med. L *trānspīrāre,* from L TRANS- + *spīrāre* to breathe
▸ **transpiration** (ˌtrænspəˈreɪʃən) *n* ▸ **tranˈspiratory** *adj*

USAGE NOTE It is sometimes maintained that *transpire* should not be used to mean 'happen' or 'occur', as in *the event transpired late in the evening,* and that the word is properly used to mean 'become known', as in *it transpired later that the thief had been caught.* The word is, however, widely used in the first sense, especially in spoken English.

transplant *vb* (trænsˈplɑːnt). **1** (*tr*) to remove or transfer (esp. a plant) from one place to another. **2** (*intr*) to be capable of being transplanted. **3** *Surgery.* to transfer (an organ or tissue) from one part of the body or from one person to another. ◆ *n* (ˈtrænsˌplɑːnt). **4** *Surgery.* **4a** the procedure involved in such a transfer. **4b** the organ or tissue transplanted.
▸ **transˈplantable** *adj* ▸ ˌ**transplanˈtation** *n*

transponder (trænˈspɒndə) *n* **1** a type of radio or radar transmitter-receiver that transmits signals automatically when it receives predetermined signals. **2** the receiver and transmitter in a communications satellite, relaying signals back to earth. ORIG C20: from TRANSMITTER + RESPONDER

transport *vb* (trænsˈpɔːt). (*tr*) **1** to carry or cause to go from one place to another, esp. over some distance. **2** to deport or exile to a penal colony. **3** (*usually passive*) to have a strong emotional effect on. ◆ *n* (ˈtrænsˌpɔːt). **4a** the business or system of transporting goods or people. **4b** (*as modifier*): *a modernized transport system.* **5** *Brit.* freight vehicles generally. **6a** a vehicle used to transport goods or people, esp. troops. **6b** (*as modifier*): *a transport plane.* **7** a transporting or being transported. **8** ecstasy, rapture, or any powerful emotion. **9** a convict sentenced to be transported. ORIG C14: from L *trānsportāre,* from TRANS- + *portāre* to carry
▸ **transˈportable** *adj* ▸ **transˈporter** *n*

transportation (ˌtrænspɔːˈteɪʃən) *n* **1** a means or system of transporting. **2** the act of transporting or the state of being transported. **3** (esp. formerly) deportation to a penal colony.

transport café (ˈtrænsˌpɔːt) *n Brit.* an inexpensive eating place on a main route, used mainly by long-distance lorry drivers.

transpose (trænsˈpəʊz) *vb* **transposes, transposing, transposed.** **1** (*tr*) to alter the positions of; interchange, as words in a sentence. **2** *Music.* to play (notes, music, etc.) in a different key from that originally intended. **3** (*tr*) *Maths.* to move (a term) from one side of an equation to the other with a corresponding reversal in sign. ORIG C14: from OF *transposer,* from L *trānspōnere* to remove
▸ **transˈposable** *adj* ▸ **transˈposal** *n* ▸ **transˈposer** *n*
▸ **transposition** (ˌtrænspəˈzɪʃən) *n*

transposing instrument *n* a musical instrument, esp. a horn or clarinet, pitched in a key other than C major, but whose music is written down as if its basic scale were C major.

transposon (trænsˈpəʊzɒn) *n Genetics.* a fragment of bacterial nucleic acid that can move from one site in a chromosome to another site in the same or a different chromosome and thus alter the genetic constitution of the bacterium. ORIG C20: TRANSPOS(E) + -ON

transputer (trænzˈpjuːtə) *n Computing.* a type of fast powerful microchip that is the equivalent of a 32-bit microprocessor with its own RAM facility. ORIG C20: from TRANS(ISTOR) + (COM)PUTER

transsexual *or* **transexual** (trænzˈsɛksjʊəl) *n* **1** a person who completely identifies with the opposite sex. **2** a person who has undergone medical procedures to alter sexual characteristics to those of the opposite sex.

transship (træns'ʃɪp) *or* **tranship** *vb* **transships, transshipping, transshipped** *or* **tranships, transhipping, transhipped.** to transfer or be transferred from one vessel or vehicle to another.
▸ **trans'shipment** *or* **tran'shipment** *n*

transubstantiation (ˌtrænsəbˌstænʃɪ'eɪʃən) *n* **1** (esp. in Roman Catholic theology) **1a** the doctrine that the whole substance of the bread and wine changes into the substance of the body and blood of Christ when consecrated in the Eucharist. **1b** the mystical process by which this is believed to take place during consecration. Cf. **consubstantiation. 2** a substantial change; transmutation.
▸ **ˌtransubˌstanti'ationalist** *n*

transude (træn'sjuːd) *vb* **transudes, transuding, transuded.** (of a fluid) to ooze or pass through interstices, pores, or small holes. ORIG C17: from NL *trānsūdāre,* from L TRANS- + *sūdāre* to sweat
▸ **transudation** (ˌtrænsjʊ'deɪʃən) *n*

transuranic (ˌtrænzjʊ'rænɪk), **transuranian** (ˌtrænzjʊ'reɪnɪən), *or* **transuranium** *adj* **1** (of an element) having an atomic number greater than that of uranium. **2** of or having the behaviour of transuranic elements. ORIG C20

Transvaal ★ ('trænzvɑːl) *n* a former province of NE South Africa: colonized by the Boers after the Great Trek (1836); became a British colony in 1902; joined South Africa in 1910; replaced by new administrative regions in 1994; the world's chief gold producer. Capital: Pretoria.
▸ **'Transˌvaaler** *n* ▸ **Trans'vaalian** *adj*

transversal (trænz'vɜːsəl) *n* **1** *Geom.* a line intersecting two or more other lines. ◆ *adj* **2** a less common word for **transverse.**
▸ **trans'versally** *adv*

transverse (trænz'vɜːs) *adj* **1** crossing from side to side; athwart; crossways. ◆ *n* **2** a transverse piece or object. ORIG C16: from L *trānsversus,* from *trānsvertere* to turn across
▸ **trans'versely** *adv*

transverse colon *n Anat.* the part of the large intestine passing transversely in front of the liver and stomach.

transverse wave *n* a wave, such as an electromagnetic wave, that is propagated in a direction perpendicular to the displacement of the transmitting field or medium.

transvestite (trænz'vɛstaɪt) *n* a person who seeks sexual pleasure from wearing clothes of the opposite sex. ORIG C19: from G *Transvestit,* from TRANS- + L *vestītus* clothed, from *vestīre* to clothe
▸ **trans'vestism** *or* **trans'vestitism** *n*

Transylvania ★ (ˌtrænsɪl'veɪnɪə) *n* a region of central and NW Romania: belonged to Hungary from the 11th century until 1918; restored to Romania in 1947.

Transylvanian Alps ★ (ˌtrænsɪl'veɪnɪən) *pl n* a mountain range in S Romania; a SW extension of the Carpathian Mountains. Highest peak: Mount Negoiu, 2548 m (8360 ft).

trap[1] (træp) *n* **1** a mechanical device or enclosed place or pit in which something, esp. an animal, is caught or penned. **2** any device or plan for tricking a person or thing into being caught unawares. **3** anything resembling a trap or prison. **4** a fitting for a pipe in the form of a U-shaped or S-shaped bend that contains standing water to prevent the passage of gases. **5** any similar device. **6** a device that hurls clay pigeons into the air to be fired at by trapshooters. **7** *Greyhound racing.* any one of a line of boxlike stalls in which greyhounds are enclosed before the start of a race. **8** See **trap door. 9** a light two-wheeled carriage. **10** a slang word for **mouth. 11** *Golf.* an obstacle or hazard, esp. a bunker. **12** (*pl*) *Jazz sl.* percussion instruments. **13** (*usually pl*) *Austral. sl.* a policeman. ◆ *vb* **traps, trapping, trapped. 14** to catch, take, or pen in or as if in a trap. **15** (*tr*) to ensnare by trickery; trick. **16** (*tr*) to provide (a pipe) with a trap. **17** to set traps in (a place), esp. for animals. ORIG OE *træppe*
▸ **'trapˌlike** *adj*

trap[2] (træp) *vb* **traps, trapping, trapped.** (*tr;* often foll. by *out*) to dress or adorn. ◆ See also **traps.** ORIG C11: prob. from OF *drap* cloth

trap[3] (træp) *or* **traprock** ('træpˌrɒk) *n* **1** any fine-grained often columnar dark igneous rock, esp. basalt. **2** any rock in which oil or gas has accumulated. ORIG C18: from Swedish *trappa* stair (from its steplike formation)

Trapani ★ (*Italian* 'traːpani) *n* a port in S Italy, in NW Sicily: Carthaginian naval base, ceded to the Romans after the First Punic War. Pop.: 72 840 (1990).

trap door *n* a door or flap flush with and covering an opening, esp. in a ceiling.

trap-door spider *n* any of various spiders that construct a silk-lined hole in the ground closed by a hinged door of earth and silk.

trapes (treɪps) *vb, n* a less common spelling of **traipse.**

trapeze (trə'piːz) *n* a free-swinging bar attached to two ropes, used by circus acrobats, etc. ORIG C19: from F *trapèze,* from NL; see TRAPEZIUM

trapezium (trə'piːzɪəm) *n, pl* **trapeziums** *or* **trapezia** (-zɪə). **1** *Chiefly Brit.* a quadrilateral having two parallel sides of unequal length. Usual US and Canad. name: **trapezoid. 2** *Chiefly US & Canad.* a quadrilateral having neither pair of sides parallel. ORIG C16: via LL from Gk *trapezion,* from *trapeza* table
▸ **tra'pezial** *adj*

trapezius (trə'piːzɪəs) *n, pl* **trapeziuses.** either of two flat triangular muscles that rotate the shoulder blades. ORIG C18: from NL *trapezius* (*musculus*) trapezium-shaped (muscle)

trapezoid ('træpɪˌzɔɪd) *n* **1** a quadrilateral having neither pair of sides parallel. **2** the usual US and Canad. name for **trapezium.** ORIG C18: from NL *trapezoidēs,* from LGk *trapezoeidēs* trapezium-shaped, from *trapeza* table

trapper ('træpə) *n* a person who traps animals, esp. for their furs or skins.

trappings ('træpɪŋz) *pl n* **1** the accessories and adornments that symbolize a condition, office, etc.: *the trappings of success.* **2** ceremonial harness for a horse or other animal. ORIG C16: from TRAP[2]

Trappist ('træpɪst) *n* **a** a member of a branch of the Cistercian order of Christian monks, which originated at La Trappe in France in 1664. They are noted for their rule of silence. **b** (*as modifier*): *a Trappist monk.*

traps (træps) *pl n* belongings; luggage. ORIG C19: prob. shortened from TRAPPINGS

trapshooting ('træpˌʃuːtɪŋ) *n* the sport of shooting at clay pigeons thrown up by a trap.
▸ **'trapˌshooter** *n*

trash (træʃ) *n* **1** foolish ideas or talk; nonsense. **2** *Chiefly US & Canad.* useless or unwanted matter or objects; rubbish. **3** a literary or artistic production of poor quality. **4** *Chiefly US & Canad.* a poor or worthless person or a group of such people. **5** bits that are broken or lopped off, esp. the trimmings from trees or plants. **6** the dry remains of sugar cane after the juice has been extracted. ◆ *vb* **7** to remove the outer leaves and branches from (growing plants, esp. sugar cane). **8** *Sl.* to attack or destroy (someone or something) wilfully or maliciously. ORIG C16: from ?

trashy ('træʃɪ) *adj* **trashier, trashiest.** cheap, worthless, or badly made.
▸ **'trashily** *adv* ▸ **'trashiness** *n*

Trasimene ★ ('træzɪˌmiːn) *n* **Lake.** a lake in central Italy, in Umbria: the largest lake in central Italy; scene of Hannibal's victory over the Romans in 217 B.C. Area: 128 sq. km (49 sq. miles). Italian name: **Trasimeno.** Also called: (Lake) **Perugia.**

trass (træs) *n* a volcanic rock used to make a hydraulic cement. ORIG C18: from Du. *tras, tarasse,* from It. *terrazza* worthless earth; see TERRACE

trattoria (ˌtrætə'rɪə) *n* an Italian restaurant. ORIG C19: from It., from *trattore* innkeeper, from F *traiteur,* from OF *tretier* to TREAT

trauma ('trɔːmə) *n, pl* **traumata** (-mətə) *or* **traumas. 1** *Psychol.* a powerful shock that may have long-lasting ef-

fects. **2** *Pathol.* any bodily injury or wound. ORIG C18: from Gk: a wound
▸ **traumatic** (trɔːˈmætɪk) *adj* ▸ **trauˈmatically** *adv*

traumatize *or* **traumatise** (ˈtrɔːməˌtaɪz) *vb* **traumatizes, traumatizing, traumatized** *or* **traumatises, traumatising, traumatised. 1** (*tr*) to wound or injure (the body). **2** to subject or be subjected to mental trauma.
▸ **ˌtraumatiˈzation** *or* **ˌtraumatiˈsation** *n*

travail (ˈtræveɪl) *Literary.* ◆ *n* **1** painful or excessive labour or exertion. **2** the pangs of childbirth; labour. ◆ *vb* **3** (*intr*) to suffer or labour painfully, esp. in childbirth. ORIG C13: from OF *travaillier,* from Vulgar L *tripaliāre* (unattested) to torture, from LL *trepālium* instrument of torture, from L *tripālis* having three stakes

Travancore ★ (ˌtrævənˈkɔː) *n* a former princely state of S India which joined with Cochin in 1949 to form **Travancore-Cochin:** part of Kerala state since 1956.

travel (ˈtrævᵊl) *vb* **travels, travelling, travelled** *or US* **travels, traveling, traveled.** (*mainly intr*) **1** to go, move, or journey from one place to another. **2** (*tr*) to go, move, or journey through or across (an area, region, etc.). **3** to go, move, or cover a distance. **4** to go from place to place as a salesman. **5** (esp. of perishable goods) to withstand a journey. **6** (of light, sound, etc.) to be transmitted or move. **7** to progress or advance. **8** *Basketball.* to take an excessive number of steps while holding the ball. **9** (of part of a mechanism) to move in a fixed path. **10** *Inf.* to move rapidly. ◆ *n* **11a** the act of travelling. **11b** (*as modifier*): *a travel brochure.* Related adj: **itinerant. 12** (*usually pl*) a tour or journey. **13** the distance moved by a mechanical part, such as the stroke of a piston. **14** movement or passage. ORIG C14 *travaillen* to make a journey, from OF *travaillier* to TRAVAIL

travel agency *or* **bureau** *n* an agency that arranges and negotiates flights, holidays, etc., for travellers.
▸ **travel agent** *n*

travelled *or US* **traveled** (ˈtrᵊvəld) *adj* having experienced or undergone much travelling.

traveller (ˈtrævələ, ˈtrævlə) *n* **1** a person who travels, esp. habitually. **2** See **travelling salesman. 3** a part of a mechanism that moves in a fixed course. **4** *Austral.* a swagman.

traveller's cheque *n* a cheque sold by a bank, etc., to the bearer, who signs it on purchase and can cash it abroad by signing it again.

traveller's joy *n* a ranunculaceous Old World climbing plant having white flowers and heads of feathery plumed fruits; wild clematis.

travelling people *or* **folk** *pl n* (*sometimes caps.*) *Brit.* Gypsies or other itinerant people: a term used esp. by such people of themselves.

travelling salesman *n* a salesman who travels within an assigned territory in order to sell merchandise or to solicit orders for the commercial enterprise he represents by direct personal contact with customers.

travelling wave *n* **a** a wave carrying energy away from its source. **b** (*as modifier*): *a travelling-wave aerial.*

travelogue *or US* (*sometimes*) **travelog** (ˈtrævᵊlɒg) *n* a film, lecture, or brochure on travels and travelling.

Traven ★ (ˈtreɪvən) *n* **B(en)**, original name *Albert Otto Max Feige.* ?1882–1969, US novelist, born in Germany and living in Mexico from 1920. His novels include *The Treasure of Sierra Madre* (1934).

Travers ★ (ˈtrævəz) *n* **Ben(jamin)**. 1886–1980, British dramatist, noted for such farces as *Rookery Nook* (1926) and *Plunder* (1928).

traverse (ˈtrævɜːs, trəˈvɜːs) *vb* **traverses, traversing, traversed. 1** to pass or go over or back and forth over (something); cross. **2** (*tr*) to go against; oppose. **3** to move sideways or crosswise. **4** (*tr*) to extend or reach across. **5** to turn (an artillery gun) laterally or (of an artillery gun) to turn laterally. **6** (*tr*) to examine carefully. **7** (*tr*) *Law.* to deny (an allegation). **8** *Mountaineering.* to move across (a face) horizontally. ◆ *n* **9** something being or lying across, such as a transom. **10** a gallery or loft inside a building that crosses it. **11** an obstruction. **12** a protective bank or other barrier across a trench or rampart. **13** a railing, screen, or curtain. **14** the act or an instance of traversing or crossing. **15** *Mountaineering.* the act or an instance of moving horizontally across a face. **16** a path or road across. **17** *Naut.* the zigzag course of a vessel tacking frequently. **18** *Law.* the formal denial of a fact alleged in the opposite party's pleading. **19** *Surveying.* a survey consisting of a series of straight lines, the length of each and the angle between them being measured. ◆ *adj* **20** being or lying across; transverse. ORIG C14: from OF *traverser,* from LL *trānsversāre,* from L *trānsversus* TRANSVERSE
▸ **traˈversal** *n* ▸ **ˈtraverser** *n*

travertine (ˈtrævətɪn) *n* a porous rock consisting of calcium carbonate, used for building. ORIG C18: from It. *travertino* (infl. by *tra-* TRANS-), from L *lapis Tīburtīnus* Tiburtine stone, from *Tībur*s the district around Tibur (now Tivoli)

travesty (ˈtrævɪstɪ) *n, pl* **travesties. 1** a farcical or grotesque imitation; mockery. ◆ *vb* **travesties, travestying, travestied.** (*tr*) **2** to make or be a travesty of. ORIG C17: from F *travesti* disguised, from *travestir* to disguise, from It. *travestire,* from *tra-* TRANS- + *vestire* to clothe

travois (trəˈvɔɪ) *n, pl* **travois** (-ˈvɔɪz). **1** *History.* a sled formerly used by the Plains Indians of North America, consisting of two poles joined by a frame and pulled by an animal. **2** *Canad.* a similar sled used for dragging logs. ORIG from Canad. F, from F *travail* beam, from L *trabs*

trawl (trɔːl) *n* **1** Also called: **trawl net.** a large net, usually in the shape of a sock or bag, drawn at deep levels behind special boats (trawlers). **2** Also called: **trawl line.** a long line to which numerous shorter hooked lines are attached, suspended between buoys. **3** the act of trawling. ◆ *vb* **4** to catch (fish) with a trawl net or trawl line. **5** (*intr;* foll. by *for*) to seek or gather (information, etc.) from a wide variety of sources. ORIG C17: from MDu. *traghelen* to drag, from L *trāgula* dragnet; see TRAIL

trawler (ˈtrɔːlə) *n* **1** a vessel used for trawling. **2** a person who trawls.

tray (treɪ) *n* **1** a thin flat board or plate of metal, plastic, etc., usually with a raised edge, on which things can be carried. **2** a shallow receptacle for papers, etc., sometimes forming a drawer in a cabinet or box. ORIG OE *trieg*

TRC *abbrev. for* (in South Africa) Truth and Reconciliation Commission: a body (1995–99) that assessed the violations of human rights in the struggle against apartheid.

treacherous (ˈtrɛtʃərəs) *adj* **1** betraying or likely to betray faith or confidence. **2** unstable, unreliable, or dangerous.
▸ **ˈtreacherously** *adv* ▸ **ˈtreacherousness** *n*

treachery (ˈtrɛtʃərɪ) *n, pl* **treacheries. 1** the act or an instance of wilful betrayal. **2** the disposition to betray. ORIG C13: from OF *trecherie,* from *trechier* to cheat

treacle (ˈtriːkᵊl) *n* **1** Also called: **black treacle,** (US and Canad.) **molasses.** *Brit.* a dark viscous syrup obtained during the refining of sugar. **2** *Brit.* another name for **golden syrup. 3** anything sweet and cloying. ORIG C14: from OF *triacle,* from L *thēriaca* antidote to poison
▸ **ˈtreacly** *adj*

tread (trɛd) *vb* **treads, treading, trod; trodden** *or* **trod. 1** to walk or trample in, on, over, or across (something). **2** (when *intr,* foll. by *on*) to crush or squash by or as if by treading. **3** (*intr;* sometimes foll. by *on*) to subdue or repress. **4** (*tr*) to do by walking or dancing: *to tread a measure.* **5** (*tr*) (of a male bird) to copulate with (a female bird). **6 tread lightly.** to proceed with delicacy or tact. **7 tread water.** to stay afloat in an upright position by moving the legs in a walking motion. ◆ *n* **8** a manner or style of walking, dancing, etc.: *a light tread.* **9** the act of treading. **10** the top surface of a step in a staircase. **11** the outer part of a tyre or wheel that makes contact with the road, esp. the grooved surface of a pneumatic tyre. **12** the part of a rail that wheels touch. **13** the part of a shoe that is generally in contact with the ground. ORIG OE *tredan*
▸ **ˈtreader** *n*

treadle (ˈtrɛdᵊl) *n* **1** a lever operated by the foot to drive a machine. ◆ *vb* **treadles, treadling, treadled. 2** to work (a machine) with a treadle. ORIG OE *tredel,* from *trǣde* something firm, from *tredan* to tread

treadmill (ˈtrɛdˌmɪl) *n* **1** Also called: **treadwheel.** (formerly) an apparatus turned by the weight of men or animals climbing steps on the periphery of a cylinder or wheel. **2** a dreary round or routine. **3** an exercise machine that consists of a continuous moving belt on which to walk or jog.

treas. *abbrev. for:* **1** treasurer. **2** treasury.

treason ('tri:zᵊn) *n* **1** betrayal of one's sovereign or country, esp. by attempting to overthrow the government. **2** any treachery or betrayal. ORIG C13: from OF *traïson,* from L *trāditiō* a handing over; see TRADITION
▸ **'treasonable** *or* **'treasonous** *adj* ▸ **'treasonably** *adv*

treasure ('trɛʒə) *n* **1** wealth and riches, usually hoarded, esp. in the form of money, precious metals, or gems. **2** a thing or person that is highly prized or valued. ◆ *vb* **treasures, treasuring, treasured.** (*tr*) **3** to prize highly as valuable, rare, or costly. **4** to store up and save; hoard. ORIG C12: from OF *tresor,* from L *thēsaurus* anything hoarded, from Gk *thēsauros*

treasure hunt *n* a game in which players act upon successive clues to find a hidden prize.

treasurer ('trɛʒərə) *n* a person appointed to look after the funds of a society, company, city, or other governing body.
▸ **'treasurership** *n*

Treasurer ('trɛʒərə) *n* (in Australia) the minister of finance.

treasure-trove *n* **1** *Brit. Law.* valuable articles, such as coins, etc., found hidden and of unknown ownership. **2** any valuable discovery. ORIG C16: from Anglo-F *tresor trové* treasure found, from OF *tresor* TREASURE + *trover* to find

treasury ('trɛʒərɪ) *n, pl* **treasuries. 1** a storage place for treasure. **2** the revenues or funds of a government, private organization, or individual. **3** a place where funds are kept and disbursed. **4** a person or thing regarded as a valuable source of information. **5** a collection of highly valued poems, etc.; anthology. **6** Also: **treasure house.** a source of valuable items: *a treasury of information.* ORIG C13: from OF *tresorie,* from *tresor* TREASURE

Treasury ('trɛʒərɪ) *n* (in various countries) the government department in charge of finance.

Treasury Bench *n* (in Britain) the front bench to the right of the Speaker in the House of Commons, traditionally reserved for members of the Government.

treasury note *n* a note issued by a government treasury and generally receivable as legal tender for any debt.

treat (tri:t) *n* **1** a celebration, entertainment, gift, or feast given for or to someone and paid for by another. **2** any delightful surprise or specially pleasant occasion. **3** the act of treating. ◆ *vb* **4** (*tr*) to deal with or regard in a certain manner: *she treats school as a joke.* **5** (*tr*) to apply treatment to. **6** (*tr*) to subject to a process or to the application of a substance. **7** (often foll. by *to*) to provide (someone) (with) as a treat. **8** (*intr;* usually foll. by *of*) to deal (with), as in writing or speaking. **9** (*intr*) to discuss settlement; negotiate. ORIG C13: from OF *tretier,* from L *tractāre* to manage, from *trahere* to drag
▸ **'treatable** *adj* ▸ **'treater** *n*

treatise ('tri:tɪz) *n* a formal work on a subject, esp. one that deals systematically with its principles and conclusions. ORIG C14: from Anglo-F *tretiz,* from OF *tretier* to TREAT

treatment ('tri:tmənt) *n* **1** the application of medicines, surgery, etc., to a patient. **2** the manner of handling a person or thing, as in a literary or artistic work. **3** the act, practice, or manner of treating. **4 the treatment.** *Sl.* the usual manner of dealing with a particular type of person (esp. in **give someone the (full) treatment**).

treaty ('tri:tɪ) *n, pl* **treaties. 1a** a formal agreement between two or more states, such as an alliance or trade arrangement. **1b** the document in which such a contract is written. **2** any pact or agreement. **3** an agreement between two parties concerning the purchase of property at a price privately agreed between them. ORIG C14: from OF *traité,* from Med. L *tractātus,* from L: discussion, from *tractāre* to manage; see TREAT

treaty port *n History.* (in China, Japan, and Korea) a city, esp. a port, in which foreigners, esp. Westerners, were allowed by treaty to conduct trade.

Trebizond ★ ('trɛbɪˌzɒnd) *n* a variant of **Trabzon.**

treble ('trɛbᵊl) *adj* **1** threefold; triple. **2** of or denoting a soprano voice or part or a high-pitched instrument. ◆ *n* **3** treble the amount, size, etc. **4** a soprano voice or part or a high-pitched instrument. **5** the highest register of a musical instrument. **6** the high-frequency response of an audio amplifier, esp. in a record player or tape recorder. **7a** the narrow inner ring on a dartboard. **7b** a hit on this ring. ◆ *vb* **trebles, trebling, trebled. 8** to make or become three times as much. ORIG C14: from OF, from L *triplus* threefold
▸ **'trebly** *adv, adj*

treble chance *n* a method of betting in football pools in which the chances of winning are related to the number of draws and the number of home and away wins forecast by the competitor.

treble clef *n Music.* the clef that establishes G a fifth above middle C as being on the second line of the staff. Symbol: 𝄞

trebuchet ('trɛbjuˌʃɛt) *or* **trebucket** ('tri:ˌbʌkɪt) *n* a large medieval siege engine consisting of a sling on a pivoted wooden arm set in motion by the fall of a weight. ORIG C13: from OF, from *trebuchier* to stumble, from *tre-* TRANS- + *-buchier,* from *buc* trunk of the body, of Gmc origin

trecento (treɪ'tʃɛntəʊ) *n* the 14th century, esp. with reference to Italian art and literature. ORIG C19: shortened from It. *mille trecento* one thousand three hundred
▸ **tre'centist** *n*

tree (tri:) *n* **1** any large woody perennial plant with a distinct trunk giving rise to branches. Related adj: **arboreal. 2** any plant that resembles this. **3** a wooden post, bar, etc. **4** See **family tree, shoetree, saddletree. 5** *Chem.* a treelike crystal growth. **6** a branching diagrammatic representation of something. **7 at the top of the tree.** in the highest position of a profession, etc. **8 up a tree.** *US & Canad. inf.* in a difficult situation; trapped or stumped. ◆ *vb* **trees, treeing, treed.** (*tr*) **9** to drive or force up a tree. **10** to stretch on a shoetree. ORIG OE *treo*
▸ **'treeless** *adj* ▸ **'treelessness** *n* ▸ **'treeˌlike** *adj*

Tree ★ (tri:) *n* Sir **Herbert Beerbohm.** 1853–1917, British actor and theatre manager; half-brother of Sir Max Beerbohm. He was noted for his lavish productions of Shakespeare.

tree creeper *n* any of a family of small songbirds of the N hemisphere, having a slender downward-curving bill. They creep up trees to feed on insects.

tree diagram *n* a diagram in which relationships are represented by lines and nodes having other lines branching off from them.

tree fern *n* any of numerous large tropical ferns having a trunklike stem.

tree frog *n* any of various arboreal frogs of SE Asia, Australia, and America.

treehopper ('tri:ˌhɒpə) *n* any of a family of insects which live among trees and have a large hoodlike thoracic process curving backwards over the body.

tree-hugger *n Inf., derog.* an environmental campaigner. ORIG C20: from the tactic of embracing trees to prevent their being felled

tree kangaroo *n* any of several arboreal kangaroos of New Guinea and N Australia, having hind legs and forelegs of a similar length.

tree line *n* the zone, at high altitudes or high latitudes, beyond which no trees grow. Trees growing between the timber line and the tree line are typically stunted.

treen ('tri:ən) *adj* **1** made of wood; wooden. ◆ *n* **2** dishes and other utensils made of wood. ORIG OE *trēowen,* from *trēow* tree
▸ **'treenˌware** *n*

treenail *or* **trenail** ('tri:neɪl, 'trɛnᵊl) *n* a dowel used for pinning planks or timbers together.

tree of heaven *n* another name for **ailanthus.**

tree shrew *n* any of a family of small arboreal mammals of SE Asia having large eyes and resembling squirrels.

tree sparrow *n* **1** a small European weaverbird similar to the house sparrow but having a brown head. **2** a small North American finch.

tree surgery *n* the treatment of damaged trees by filling cavities, applying braces, etc.
▸ **tree surgeon** *n*

tree toad *n* a less common name for **tree frog.**

tree tomato *n* **1** an arborescent shrub of South America bearing red egg-shaped edible fruit. **2** the fruit of this plant. ◆ Also called: **tamarillo.**

tref (treɪf) *adj Judaism.* ritually unfit to be eaten. ORIG Yiddish, from Heb. *terēphāh,* lit.: torn (i.e., animal meat torn by beasts), from *tāraf* to tear

trefoil ('trɛfɔɪl) *n* **1** any of a genus of leguminous plants having leaves divided into three leaflets. **2** any of various related plants having similar leaves. **3** a flower or leaf having three lobes. **4** *Archit.* an ornament in the form of three arcs arranged in a circle. ORIG C14: from Anglo-F *trifoil,* from L *trifolium* three-leaved herb
▸ **'trefoiled** *adj*

trek (trɛk) *n* **1** a long and often difficult journey. **2** *S. African.* a journey or stage of a journey, esp. a migration by ox wagon. ◆ *vb* **treks, trekking, trekked. 3** (*intr*) to make a trek. ORIG C19: from Afrik., from MDu. *trekken* to travel

trellis ('trɛlɪs) *n* **1** a structure of latticework, esp. one used to support climbing plants. ◆ *vb* (*tr*) **2** to interweave (strips of wood, etc.) to make a trellis. **3** to provide or support with a trellis. ORIG C14: from OF *treliz* fabric of open texture, from LL *trilīcius* woven with three threads, from L TRI- + *līcium* thread
▸ **'trellis,work** *n*

trematode ('trɛmə,təʊd, 'triː-) *n* any of a class of parasitic flatworms, which includes the flukes. ORIG C19: from NL *Trematoda,* from Gk *trēmatōdēs* full of holes, from *trēma* hole

tremble ('trɛmbᵊl) *vb* **trembles, trembling, trembled.** (*intr*) **1** to vibrate with short slight movements; quiver. **2** to shake involuntarily, as with cold or fear; shiver. **3** to experience fear or anxiety. ◆ *n* **4** the act or an instance of trembling. ORIG C14: from OF *trembler,* from Med. L *tremulāre,* from L *tremulus* quivering, from *tremere* to quake
▸ **'trembling** *adj* ▸ **'trembly** *adj*

trembler ('trɛmblə) *n* a device that vibrates to make or break an electrical circuit.

trembles ('trɛmbᵊlz) *n* (*functioning as sing*) a disease of cattle and sheep characterized by trembling.

trembling poplar *n* another name for **aspen.**

tremendous (trɪ'mɛndəs) *adj* **1** vast; huge. **2** *Inf.* very exciting or unusual. **3** *Inf.* (intensifier): *a tremendous help.* **4** *Arch.* terrible or dreadful. ORIG C17: from L *tremendus* terrible, lit.: that is to be trembled at, from *tremere* to quake
▸ **tre'mendously** *adv* ▸ **tre'mendousness** *n*

tremolo ('trɛmə,ləʊ) *n, pl* **tremolos.** *Music.* **1** (in playing the violin, cello, etc.) the rapid reiteration of a note or notes to produce a trembling effect. **2** (in singing) a fluctuation in pitch. **3** a device, as on an organ, that produces a tremolo effect. ORIG C19: from It.: quavering, from Med. L *tremulāre* to TREMBLE

tremor ('trɛmə) *n* **1** an involuntary shudder or vibration. **2** any trembling movement. **3** a vibrating or trembling effect, as of sound or light. **4** a minor earthquake. ◆ *vb* **5** (*intr*) to tremble. ORIG C14: from L: a shaking, from *tremere* to tremble
▸ **'tremorous** *adj*

tremulous ('trɛmjʊləs) *adj* **1** vibrating slightly; quavering; trembling. **2** showing or characterized by fear, anxiety, excitement, etc. ORIG C17: from L *tremulus,* from *tremere* to shake
▸ **'tremulously** *adv* ▸ **'tremulousness** *n*

trenail ('triːneɪl, 'trɛnᵊl) *n* a variant spelling of **treenail.**

trench (trɛntʃ) *n* **1** a deep ditch. **2** a ditch dug as a fortification, having a parapet of earth. ◆ *vb* **3** to make a trench in (a place). **4** (*tr*) to fortify with a trench. **5** to slash or be slashed. **6** (*intr;* foll. by *on* or *upon*) to encroach or verge. ORIG C14: from OF *trenche* something cut, from *trenchier* to cut, from L *truncāre* to cut off

trenchant ('trɛntʃənt) *adj* **1** keen or incisive: *trenchant criticism.* **2** vigorous and effective: *a trenchant foreign policy.* **3** distinctly defined. **4** *Arch. or poetic.* sharp. ORIG C14: from OF *trenchant* cutting, from *trenchier* to cut; see TRENCH
▸ **'trenchancy** *n* ▸ **'trenchantly** *adv*

Trenchard ★ ('trɛntʃɑːd) *n* **Hugh Montague**, 1st Viscount. 1873–1956, British air marshal, who established the RAF as a fully independent service. As commissioner of the Metropolitan Police (1931–35) he founded the police college at Hendon.

trench coat *n* a belted waterproof coat resembling a military officer's coat.

trencher ('trɛntʃə) *n* **1** (esp. formerly) a wooden board on which food was served or cut. **2** Also called: **trencher cap.** a mortarboard. ORIG C14 *trenchour* knife, plate for carving on, from OF *trencheoir,* from *trenchier* to cut; see TRENCH

trencherman ('trɛntʃəmən) *n, pl* **trenchermen.** a person who enjoys food; hearty eater.

trench fever *n* an acute infectious disease characterized by fever and muscular aches and pains and transmitted by lice.

trench foot *n* a form of frostbite affecting persons standing for long periods in cold water.

trench mortar *or* **gun** *n* a portable mortar used in trench warfare to shoot projectiles at a high trajectory over a short range.

trench warfare *n* a type of warfare in which opposing armies face each other in entrenched positions.

trend (trɛnd) *n* **1** general tendency or direction. **2** fashion; mode. ◆ *vb* **3** (*intr*) to take a certain trend. ORIG OE *trendan* to turn

trendsetter ('trɛnd,sɛtə) *n* a person or thing that creates, or may create, a new fashion.
▸ **'trend,setting** *adj*

trendy ('trɛndɪ) *Brit. inf.* ◆ *adj* **trendier, trendiest. 1** consciously fashionable. ◆ *n, pl* **trendies. 2** a trendy person.
▸ **'trendily** *adv* ▸ **'trendiness** *n*

Trengganu *or* **Terengganu** ★ (trɛŋ'gɑːnuː, tərɛŋ-) *n* a state of E Peninsular Malaysia, on the South China Sea: under Thai suzerainty until becoming a British protectorate in 1909; joined the Federation of Malaya in 1948; an isolated forested region; mainly agricultural. Capital: Kuala Trengganu. Pop.: 752 030 (1993 est.). Area: 13 020 sq. km (5027 sq. miles).

Trent ★ (trɛnt) *n* **1** a river in central England, rising in Staffordshire and flowing generally northeast into the Humber: the chief river of the Midlands. Length: 270 km (170 miles). **2** Also: **Trient.** the German name for **Trento.**

trente et quarante (*French* trɑ̃t e karɑ̃t) *n Cards.* another name for **rouge et noir.** ORIG C17: F, lit.: thirty and forty; from the rule that forty is the maximum number that may be dealt and the winning colour is the one closest to thirty-one

Trentino-Alto Adige ★ (trɛn'tiːnəʊ'ɑːltəʊ 'ɑːdɪ,dʒeɪ) *n* a region of N Italy: consists of the part of the Tyrol south of the Brenner Pass, ceded by Austria after World War I. Pop.: 913 169 (1996 est.). Area: 13 613 sq. km (5256 sq. miles). Former name (until 1947): **Venezia Tridentina.**

Trento ★ (*Italian* 'trɛnto) *n* a city in N Italy, in Trentino-Alto Adige region on the Adige River: Roman military base; seat of the Council of Trent. Pop.: 103 181 (1996 est.). Latin name: **Tridentum.** German name: **Trent.**

Trenton ★ ('trɛntən) *n* a city in W New Jersey, capital of the state, on the Delaware River: settled by English Quakers in 1679; scene of the defeat of the British by Washington (1776) during the War of American Independence. Pop.: 84 441 (1994 est.).

trepan (trɪ'pæn) *n* **1** *Surgery.* an instrument resembling a carpenter's brace and bit formerly used to remove circular sections of bone from the skull. **2** a tool for cutting out circular blanks or for making grooves around a fixed centre. ◆ *vb* **trepans, trepanning, trepanned.** (*tr*) **3** to cut (a hole or groove) with a trepan. **4** *Surgery.* another word for **trephine.** ORIG C14: from Med. L *trepanum* rotary saw, from Gk *trupanon* auger, from *trupan* to bore, from *trupa* a hole
▸ **trepanation** (,trɛpə'neɪʃən) *n*

trepang (trɪˈpæŋ) *n* any of various large sea cucumbers of tropical Oriental seas, the body walls of which are used as food by the Japanese and Chinese. ORIG C18: from Malay *tĕripang*

trephine (trɪˈfiːn) *n* **1** a surgical sawlike instrument for removing circular sections of bone esp. from the skull. ◆ *vb* **trephines, trephining, trephined.** **2** (*tr*) to remove a circular section of bone from (esp. the skull). ORIG C17: from F *tréphine,* from obs. E *trefine* TREPAN, allegedly from L *trēs fīnēs,* lit.: three ends
▸ **trephination** (ˌtrɛfɪˈneɪʃən) *n*

trepidation (ˌtrɛpɪˈdeɪʃən) *n* **1** a state of fear or anxiety. **2** a condition of quaking or palpitation, esp. one caused by anxiety. ORIG C17: from L *trepidātiō,* from *trepidāre* to be in a state of alarm

trespass (ˈtrɛspəs) *vb* (*intr*) **1** (often foll. by *on* or *upon*) to go or intrude (on the property, privacy, or preserves of another) with no right or permission. **2** *Law.* to commit trespass. **3** *Arch.* (often foll. by *against*) to sin or transgress. ◆ *n* **4** *Law.* **4a** any unlawful act committed with force, which causes injury to another person, his property or his rights. **4b** a wrongful entry upon another's land. **5** an intrusion on another's privacy or preserves. **6** a sin or offence. ORIG C13: from OF *trespas* a passage, from *trespasser* to pass through, ult. from L *passus* a PACE[1]
▸ **ˈtrespasser** *n*

tress (trɛs) *n* **1** (*often pl*) a lock of hair, esp. a long lock of woman's hair. **2** a plait or braid of hair. ◆ *vb* (*tr*) **3** to arrange in tresses. ORIG C13: from OF *trece,* from ?
▸ **ˈtressy** *adj*

trestle (ˈtrɛsᵊl) *n* **1** a framework in the form of a horizontal member supported at each end by a pair of splayed legs, used to carry scaffold boards, a table top, etc. **2a** a framework of timber, metal, or reinforced concrete that is used to support a bridge or ropeway. **2b** a bridge constructed of such frameworks. ORIG C14: from OF *trestel,* ult. from L *trānstrum* transom

trestlework (ˈtrɛsᵊlˌwɜːk) *n* an arrangement of trestles, esp. one that supports a bridge.

trevally (trɪˈvælɪ) *n, pl* **trevallies.** *Austral. & NZ.* any of various food and game fishes of the genus *Caranx.* ORIG C19: prob. alteration of *cavally,* from *cavalla* species of tropical fish, from Sp. *caballa* horse

Trevelyan ★ (trɪˈvɛljən, -ˈvɪl-) *n* **1 George Macaulay.** 1876–1962, British historian, noted for his *English Social History* (1944). **2** his father, Sir **George Otto.** 1838–1928, British historian.

Trèves ★ (trɛv) *n* the French name for **Trier.**

Trevino ★ (trəˈviːnəʊ) *n* **Lee.** born 1939, US professional golfer: winner of the US Open Championship (1968; 1971) and the British Open Championship (1971; 1972).

Treviso ★ (*Italian* treˈviːzo) *n* a city in N Italy, in Veneto region: agricultural market centre. Pop.: 84 066 (1990).

Trevithick ★ (trəˈvɪθɪk) *n* **Richard.** 1771–1833, British engineer, who built the first steam-driven passenger train.

trews (truːz) *pl n Chiefly Brit.* close-fitting trousers of tartan cloth. ORIG C16: from Scot. Gaelic *triubhas,* from OF *trebus*

trey (treɪ) *n* any card or dice throw with three spots. ORIG C14: from OF *treis* three, from L *trēs*

tri- *prefix* **1** three or thrice: *triaxial; trigon; trisect.* **2** occurring every three: *trimonthly.* ORIG from L *trēs,* Gk *treis*

triable (ˈtraɪəbᵊl) *adj* **1** subject to trial in a court of law. **2** *Rare.* able to be tested.

triacid (traɪˈæsɪd) *adj* capable of reacting with three molecules of a monobasic acid.

triad (ˈtraɪæd) *n* **1** a group of three; trio. **2** *Chem.* an atom, element, group, or ion that has a valency of three. **3** *Music.* a three-note chord consisting of a note and the third and fifth above it. **4** an aphoristic literary form used in medieval Welsh and Irish literature. ORIG C16: from LL *trias,* from Gk
▸ **triˈadic** *adj* ▸ **ˈtriadism** *n*

Triad (ˈtraɪæd) *n* any of several Chinese secret societies, esp. one involved in criminal activities, such as drug trafficking.

triage (ˈtraɪɪdʒ) *n* **1** the action of sorting casualties, patients, etc. according to priority. **2** the allocating of limited resources on a basis of expediency rather than moral principles. ORIG C18: from F; see TRY, -AGE

trial (ˈtraɪəl, traɪl) *n* **1a** the act or an instance of trying or proving; test or experiment. **1b** (*as modifier*): *a trial run.* **2** *Law.* **2a** the judicial examination and determination of the issues in a civil or criminal cause by a competent tribunal. **2b** the determination of an accused person's guilt or innocence after hearing evidence and the judicial examination of the issues involved. **2c** (*as modifier*): *trial proceedings.* **3** an effort or attempt to do something. **4** trouble or grief. **5** an annoying or frustrating person or thing. **6** (*often pl*) a competition for individuals: *sheepdog trials.* **7** a motorcycling competition in which the skills of the riders are tested over rough ground. **8 on trial. 8a** undergoing trial, esp. before a court of law. **8b** being tested, as before a commitment to purchase. ◆ *vb* **trials, trialling, trialled. 9** to test or make experimental use of (something): *the idea has been trialled in several schools.* ORIG C16: from Anglo-F, from *trier* to TRY
▸ **ˈtrialling** *n*

trial and error *n* a method of discovery, solving problems, etc., based on practical experiment and experience rather than on theory: *he learned to cook by trial and error.*

trial balance *n Book-keeping.* a statement of all the debit and credit balances in the ledger of a double-entry system, drawn up to test their equality.

triallist *or* **trialist** (ˈtraɪəlɪst, ˈtraɪlɪst) *n* **1** a person who takes part in a competition, esp. a motorcycle trial. **2** *Sport.* a person who takes part in a preliminary match or heat held to determine selection for an event, a team, etc.

triangle (ˈtraɪˌæŋgᵊl) *n* **1** *Geom.* a three-sided polygon that can be classified by angle, as in an acute triangle, or by side, as in an equilateral triangle. **2** any object shaped like a triangle. **3** any situation involving three parties or points of view. **4** *Music.* a percussion instrument consisting of a sonorous metal bar bent into a triangular shape, beaten with a metal stick. **5** a group of three. ORIG C14: from L *triangulum* (n), from *triangulus* (adj), from TRI- + *angulus* corner
▸ **triangular** (traɪˈæŋgjʊlə) *adj*

triangle of forces *n Physics.* a triangle whose sides represent the magnitudes and directions of three forces in equilibrium.

triangulate *vb* (traɪˈæŋgjʊˌleɪt), **triangulates, triangulating, triangulated.** (*tr*) **1a** to survey by the method of triangulation. **1b** to calculate trigonometrically. **2** to divide into triangles. **3** to make triangular. ◆ *adj* (traɪˈæŋgjʊlɪt, -ˌleɪt). **4** marked with or composed of triangles.
▸ **triˈangulately** *adv*

triangulation (traɪˌæŋgjʊˈleɪʃən) *n* a method of surveying in which an area is divided into triangles, one side (the base line) and all angles of which are measured and the lengths of the other lines calculated trigonometrically.

triangulation station *n* a point on a hilltop, etc., used for triangulation by a surveyor.

Triassic (traɪˈæsɪk) *adj* **1** of or formed in the first period of the Mesozoic era. ◆ *n* **2 the.** Also called: **Trias.** the Triassic period or rock system. ORIG C19: from L *trias* triad, from the three subdivisions

triathlon (traɪˈæθlɒn) *n* an athletic contest in which each athlete competes in three different events, swimming, cycling, and running. ORIG C20: from TRI- + Gk *athlon* contest
▸ **ˌtriˈathlete** *n*

triatomic (ˌtraɪəˈtɒmɪk) *adj Chem.* having three atoms in the molecule.

tribade (ˈtrɪbɑːd) *n* a lesbian who practises tribadism. ORIG C17: from L *tribas,* from Gk *tribein* to rub

tribadism (ˈtrɪbədɪzəm) *n* a lesbian practice in which one partner lies on top of the other and simulates the male role in heterosexual intercourse.

tribalism (ˈtraɪbəˌlɪzəm) *n* **1** the state of existing as a

★ people and places

tribe. **2** the customs and beliefs of a tribal society. **3** loyalty to a tribe.
▸ **'tribalist** *n, adj* ▸ **,tribal'istic** *adj*

tribasic (traɪ'beɪsɪk) *adj* **1** (of an acid) containing three replaceable hydrogen atoms in the molecule. **2** (of a molecule) containing three monovalent basic atoms or groups.

tribe (traɪb) *n* **1** a social division of a people, esp. of a preliterate people, defined in terms of common descent, territory, culture, etc. **2** an ethnic or ancestral division of ancient cultures, esp.: **2a** one of the political divisions of the Roman people. **2b** any of the 12 divisions of ancient Israel, each of which was believed to be descended from one of the 12 patriarchs. **3** *Inf.* **3a** a large number of persons, animals, etc. **3b** a specific class or group of persons. **3c** a family, esp. a large one. **4** *Biol.* a taxonomic group that is a subdivision of a subfamily. ORIG C13: from L *tribus*
▸ **'tribal** *adj*

tribesman ('traɪbzmən) *n, pl* **tribesmen.** a member of a tribe.

tribo- *combining form.* indicating friction: *triboelectricity.* ORIG from Gk *tribein* to rub

triboelectricity (,traɪbəʊɪlɛk'trɪsɪtɪ, -,iːlɛk-) *n* electricity generated by friction.

tribology (traɪ'bɒlədʒɪ) *n* the study of friction, lubrication, and wear between moving surfaces.

triboluminescence (,traɪbəʊ,luːmɪ'nɛsəns) *n* luminescence produced by friction, such as the emission of light when certain crystals are crushed.
▸ **,tribo,lumi'nescent** *adj*

tribrach ('traɪbræk, 'trɪb-) *n* a metrical foot of three short syllables. ORIG C16: from L *tribrachys,* from Gk, from TRI- + *brakhus* short

tribromoethanol (traɪ,brəʊməʊ'ɛθə,nɒl) *n* a soluble white crystalline compound with a slight aromatic odour, used as a general anaesthetic.

tribulation (,trɪbjʊ'leɪʃən) *n* **1** a cause of distress. **2** a state of suffering or distress. ORIG C13: from OF, from Church L *trībulātiō,* from L *trībulāre* to afflict, from *trībulum* a threshing board, from *terere* to rub

tribunal (traɪ'bjuːnᵊl, trɪ-) *n* **1** a court of justice. **2** (in England) a special court, convened by the government to inquire into a specific matter. **3** a raised platform containing the seat of a judge. ORIG C16: from L *tribūnus* TRIBUNE[1]

tribune[1] ('trɪbjuːn) *n* **1** (in ancient Rome) **1a** an officer elected by the plebs to protect their interests. **1b** a senior military officer. **2** a person who upholds public rights. ORIG C14: from L *tribunus,* prob. from *tribus* tribe
▸ **tribunate** ('trɪbjʊnɪt) *or* **'tribuneship** *n*

tribune[2] ('trɪbjuːn) *n* **1a** the apse of a Christian basilica that contains the bishop's throne. **1b** the throne itself. **2** a gallery or raised area in a church. **3** *Rare.* a raised platform; dais. ORIG C17: via F from It. *tribuna,* from Med. L *tribūna,* var. of L *tribūnal* TRIBUNAL

tributary ('trɪbjʊtərɪ) *n, pl* **tributaries. 1** a stream, river, or glacier that feeds another larger one. **2** a person, nation, or people that pays tribute. ◆ *adj* **3** (of a stream, etc.) feeding a larger stream. **4** given or owed as a tribute. **5** paying tribute.
▸ **'tributarily** *adv*

tribute ('trɪbjuːt) *n* **1** a gift or statement made in acknowledgment, gratitude, or admiration. **2** a payment by one ruler or state to another, usually as an acknowledgment of submission. **3** the obligation to pay tribute. ORIG C14: from L *tribūtum,* from *tribuere* to grant (orig.: to distribute among the tribes), from *tribus* tribe

trice (traɪs) *n* a moment; instant (esp. in **in a trice**). ORIG C15 (in *at* or *in a trice,* in the sense: at one tug): apparent substantive use of *trice* to haul up, from MDu. *trīse* pulley

tricentenary (,traɪsɛn'tiːnərɪ) *or* **tricentennial** (,traɪsɛn'tɛnɪəl) *adj* **1** of a period of 300 years. **2** of a 300th anniversary. ◆ *n, pl* **tricentenaries** *or* **tricentennials. 3** an anniversary of 300 years.

triceps ('traɪsɛps) *n, pl* **tricepses** (-sɛpsɪz) *or* **triceps.** any muscle having three heads, esp. the one that extends the forearm. ORIG C16: from L, from TRI- + *caput* head

trichiasis (trɪ'kaɪəsɪs) *n Pathol.* an abnormal position of the eyelashes that causes irritation when they rub against the eyeball. ORIG C17: via LL from Gk *trikhiasis,* from *thrix* a hair

trichina (trɪ'kaɪnə) *n, pl* **trichinae** (-niː). a parasitic nematode worm occurring in the intestines of pigs, rats, and man and producing larvae that form cysts in skeletal muscle. ORIG C19: from NL, from Gk *trikhinos* relating to hair, from *thrix* a hair
▸ **trichinous** ('trɪkɪnəs) *adj*

Trichinopoly ★ (,trɪkɪ'nɒpəlɪ) *n* another name for **Tiruchirapalli.**

trichinosis (,trɪkɪ'nəʊsɪs) *n* a disease characterized by nausea, fever, diarrhoea, and swelling of the muscles, caused by ingestion of pork infected with trichina larvae. ORIG C19: from NL TRICHINA

trichloride (traɪ'klɔːraɪd) *n* any compound that contains three chlorine atoms per molecule.

tricho- *or before a vowel* **trich-** *combining form.* indicating hair or a part resembling hair: *trichocyst.* ORIG from Gk *thrix* (genitive *trikhos*) hair

trichology (trɪ'kɒlədʒɪ) *n* the branch of medicine concerned with the hair and its diseases.
▸ **tri'chologist** *n*

trichomoniasis (,trɪkəʊmə'naɪəsɪs) *n* inflammation of the vagina caused by infection with parasitic protozoa. ORIG C19: NL

trichopteran (traɪ'kɒptərən) *n* **1** any insect of the order *Trichoptera,* which comprises the caddis flies. ◆ *adj* **2** Also: **trichopterous** (trɪ'kɒptərəs). of or belonging to the order *Trichoptera.* ORIG C19: from NL *Trichoptera,* lit.: having hairy wings, from Gk *thrix* a hair + *pteron* wing

trichosis (trɪ'kəʊsɪs) *n* any abnormal condition or disease of the hair. ORIG C19: via NL from Gk *trikhōsis* growth of hair

trichotomy (traɪ'kɒtəmɪ) *n, pl* **trichotomies. 1** division into three categories. **2** *Theol.* the division of man into body, spirit, and soul. ORIG C17: prob. from NL *trichotomia,* from Gk *trikhotomein* to divide into three
▸ **trichotomic** (,trɪkə'tɒmɪk) *or* **tri'chotomous** *adj*

trichroism ('traɪkrəʊ,ɪzəm) *n* a property of biaxial crystals as a result of which they show a difference in colour when viewed along three different axes. ORIG C19: from Gk *trikhroos* three-coloured, from TRI- + *khrōma* colour

trichromatic (,traɪkrəʊ'mætɪk) *or* **trichromic** (traɪ'krəʊmɪk) *adj* **1** involving the combination of three primary colours. **2** of or having normal colour vision. **3** having or involving three colours.
▸ **tri'chroma,tism** *n*

trick (trɪk) *n* **1** a deceitful or cunning action or plan. **2a** a mischievous, malicious, or humorous action or plan; joke. **2b** (*as modifier*): *a trick spider.* **3** an illusory or magical feat. **4** a simple feat learned by an animal or person. **5** an adroit or ingenious device; knack: *a trick of the trade.* **6** a habit or mannerism. **7** a turn of duty. **8** *Cards.* a batch of cards containing one from each player, usually played in turn and won by the player or side that plays the card with the highest value. **9 can't take a trick.** *Austral. sl.* to be consistently unsuccessful or unlucky. **10 do the trick.** *Inf.* to produce the desired result. **11 how's tricks?** *Sl.* how are you? **12 turn a trick.** *Sl.* (of a prostitute) to gain a customer. ◆ *vb* **13** (*tr*) to defraud, deceive, or cheat (someone). ◆ See also **trick out.** ORIG C15: from OF *trique,* from *trikier* to deceive, ult. from L *trīcārī* to play tricks

trick cyclist *n* **1** a cyclist who performs tricks, such as in a circus. **2** a slang term for **psychiatrist.**

trickery ('trɪkərɪ) *n, pl* **trickeries.** the practice or an instance of using tricks.

trickle ('trɪkᵊl) *vb* **trickles, trickling, trickled. 1** to run or cause to run in thin or slow streams. **2** (*intr*) to move gradually: *the crowd trickled away.* ◆ *n* **3** a thin, irregular, or slow flow of something. **4** the act of trickling. ORIG C14: ? imit.
▸ **'trickling** *adj*

trickle charger *n* a small mains-operated battery charger, esp. one used by car owners.

trickle-down *adj* of or concerning the theory that granting concessions such as tax cuts to the rich will benefit all levels of society by stimulating the economy.

trick or treat *sentence substitute. Chiefly US & Canad.* a customary cry used by children at Halloween when they call at houses in disguise, indicating that they want a present of sweets, apples, or money and, if refused, will play a trick on the householder.

trick out *or* **up** *vb* (*tr, adv*) to dress up; deck out: *tricked out in frilly dresses.*

trickster ('trɪkstə) *n* a person who deceives or plays tricks.

tricksy ('trɪksɪ) *adj* **tricksier, tricksiest. 1** playing tricks habitually; mischievous. **2** crafty or difficult to deal with.
▸ **'tricksiness** *n*

tricky ('trɪkɪ) *adj* **trickier, trickiest. 1** involving snags or difficulties. **2** needing careful handling. **3** sly; wily: *a tricky dealer.*
▸ **'trickily** *adv* ▸ **'trickiness** *n*

triclinic (traɪ'klɪnɪk) *adj* of the crystal system characterized by three unequal axes, no pair of which are perpendicular.

triclinium (traɪ'klɪnɪəm) *n, pl* **triclinia** (-ɪə). (in ancient Rome) **1** an arrangement of three couches around a table for reclining upon while dining. **2** a dining room. ORIG C17: from L, from Gk *triklinion,* from TRI- + *klinē* a couch

tricolour *or US* **tricolor** ('trɪkələ, 'traɪ,kʌlə) *adj also* **tricoloured** *or US* **tricolored** ('traɪ,kʌləd). **1** having or involving three colours. ◆ *n* **2** (*often cap.*) the French flag, having three stripes in blue, white, and red. **3** any flag, badge, etc., with three colours.

tricorn ('traɪ,kɔːn) *n also* **tricorne. 1** a cocked hat with the brim turned up on three sides. ◆ *adj also* **tricornered. 2** having three horns or corners. ORIG C18: from L *tricornis,* from TRI- + *cornu* horn

tricot ('trɪkəʊ, 'triː-) *n* **1** a thin rayon or nylon fabric knitted or resembling knitting, used for dresses, etc. **2** a type of ribbed dress fabric. ORIG C19: from F, from *tricoter* to knit, from ?

tricuspid (traɪ'kʌspɪd) *Anat.* ◆ *adj also* **tricuspidal. 1** having three points, cusps, or segments: *a tricuspid tooth; a tricuspid valve.* ◆ *n* **2** a tooth having three cusps.

tricycle ('traɪsɪk^əl) *n* a three-wheeled cycle, esp. one driven by pedals.
▸ **'tricyclist** *n*

trident ('traɪd^ənt) *n* a three-pronged spear. ORIG C16: from L *tridēns* three-pronged, from TRI- + *dēns* tooth

Trident ('traɪd^ənt) *n* a type of US submarine-launched ballistic missile with independently targetable warheads.

tridentate (traɪ'dɛnteɪt) *or* **tridental** *adj* having three prongs, teeth, or points.

Tridentine (traɪ'dɛntaɪn) *adj* **1a** *History.* of the Council of Trent in the 16th century. **1b** in accord with Tridentine doctrine: *Tridentine mass.* ◆ *n* **2** an orthodox Roman Catholic. ORIG C16: from Med. L *Tridentīnus,* from *Tridentum* TRENT

Tridentum ★ (traɪ'dɛntəm) *n* the Latin name for **Trento.**

tried (traɪd) *vb* the past tense and past participle of **try.**

triella (traɪ'ɛlə) *n* a cumulative bet on horses in three specified races.

triennial (traɪ'ɛnɪəl) *adj* **1** relating to, lasting for, or occurring every three years. ◆ *n* **2** a third anniversary. **3** a triennial period, thing, or occurrence. ORIG C17: from L TRIENNIUM
▸ **tri'ennially** *adv*

triennium (traɪ'ɛnɪəm) *n, pl* **trienniums** *or* **triennia** (-nɪə). a period or cycle of three years. ORIG C19: from L, from TRI- + *annus* a year

Trient ★ (tri'ɛnt) *n* the German name for **Trento.** Also: **Trent.**

trier ('traɪə) *n* a person or thing that tries.

Trier ★ (*German* triːr) *n* a city in W Germany, in the Rhineland-Palatinate on the Moselle River: ancient capital of a Celto-Germanic tribe (the **Treveri**); an early centre of Christianity, ruled by archbishops until the 18th century; wine trade; Roman remains. Pop.: 98 750 (1991). Latin name: **Augusta Treverorum** (aʊ'guːstə ,trɛvə'rəʊrəm). French name: **Trèves.**

Trieste ★ (triː'ɛst; *Italian* tri'ɛste) *n* **1** a port in NE Italy, capital of Friuli-Venezia Giulia region, on the **Gulf of Trieste** at the head of the Adriatic Sea: under Austrian rule (1382–1918); capital of the Free Territory of Trieste (1947–54); important transit port for central Europe. Pop.: 223 611 (1996 est.). Slovene and Serbo-Croat name: **Trst. 2 Free Territory of.** a former territory on the N Adriatic: established by the UN in 1947; most of the N part passed to Italy and the remainder to Yugoslavia in 1954.

trifacial (traɪ'feɪʃəl) *adj* another word for **trigeminal.**

trifecta (traɪ'fɛktə) *n* a form of betting in which punters select first-, second-, and third-place winners in the correct order.

trifid ('traɪfɪd) *adj* divided or split into three parts or lobes. ORIG C18: from L *trifidus,* from TRI- + *findere* to split

trifle ('traɪf^əl) *n* **1** a thing of little or no value or significance. **2** a small amount; bit: *a trifle more enthusiasm.* **3** *Brit.* a cold dessert made with sponge cake spread with jam or fruit, soaked in sherry, covered with custard and cream. ◆ *vb* **trifles, trifling, trifled. 4** (*intr;* usually foll. by *with*) to deal (with) as if worthless; dally: *to trifle with a person's affections.* **5** to waste (time) frivolously. ORIG C13: from OF *trufle* mockery, from *trufler* to cheat
▸ **'trifler** *n*

trifling ('traɪflɪŋ) *adj* **1** insignificant or petty. **2** frivolous or idle.
▸ **'triflingly** *adv*

trifocal *adj* (traɪ'fəʊk^əl). **1** having three focuses. **2** having three focal lengths. ◆ *n* (traɪ'fəʊk^əl, 'traɪ,fəʊk^əl). **3** (*pl*) glasses that have trifocal lenses.

triforium (traɪ'fɔːrɪəm) *n, pl* **triforia** (-rɪə). an arcade above the arches of the nave, choir, or transept of a church. ORIG C18: from Anglo-L, apparently from L TRI- + *foris* a doorway; from the fact that each bay had three openings

trifurcate ('traɪfɜːkɪt, -,keɪt) *or* **trifurcated** *adj* having three branches or forks. ORIG C19: from L *trifurcus,* from TRI- + *furca* a fork

trig (trɪg) *Arch. or dialect.* ◆ *adj* **1** neat or spruce. ◆ *vb* **trigs, trigging, trigged. 2** to make or become trim or spruce. ORIG C12 (orig.: trusty): from ON
▸ **'trigly** *adv* ▸ **'trigness** *n*

trig. *abbrev. for:* **1** trigonometrical. **2** trigonometry.

trigeminal (traɪ'dʒɛmɪn^əl) *adj Anat.* of or relating to the trigeminal nerve. ORIG C19: from L *trigeminus* triplet, from TRI- + *geminus* twin

trigeminal nerve *n* either one of the fifth pair of cranial nerves, which supply the muscles of the mandible and maxilla. Their ophthalmic branches supply the area around the orbit of the eye, the nasal cavity, and the forehead.

trigeminal neuralgia *n Pathol.* another name for **tic douloureux.**

trigger ('trɪgə) *n* **1** a small lever that activates the firing mechanism of a firearm. **2** a device that releases a spring-loaded mechanism. **3** any event that sets a course of action in motion. ◆ *vb* (*tr*) **4** (usually foll. by *off*) to give rise (to); set off. **5** to fire or set in motion by or as by pulling a trigger. ORIG C17 *tricker,* from Du. *trekker,* from *trekken* to pull

triggerfish ('trɪgə,fɪʃ) *n, pl* **triggerfish** *or* **triggerfishes.** any of a family of fishes of tropical and temperate seas. They have erectile spines in the first dorsal fin.

trigger-happy *adj Inf.* **1** tending to resort to the use of firearms or violence irresponsibly. **2** tending to act rashly.

triglyceride (traɪ'glɪsə,raɪd) *n* any ester of glycerol and one or more carboxylic acids, in which each glycerol molecule has combined with three carboxylic acid molecules.

triglyph ('traɪ,glɪf) *n Archit.* a stone block in a Doric frieze, having three vertical channels. ORIG C16: via L from Gk *trigluphos,* from TRI- + *gluphē* carving

trigonal ('trɪgənᵊl) *adj* **1** triangular. **2** of the crystal system characterized by three equal axes that are equally inclined and not perpendicular to each other. ORIG C16: via L from Gk *trigōnon* triangle

trigonometric function *n* any of a group of functions of an angle expressed as a ratio of two of the sides of a right-angled triangle containing the angle. The group includes sine, cosine, tangent, etc.

trigonometry (ˌtrɪgəˈnɒmɪtrɪ) *n* the branch of mathematics concerned with the properties of trigonometric functions and their application to the determination of the angles and sides of triangles: used in surveying, navigation, etc. ORIG C17: from NL *trigōnometria,* from Gk *trigōnon* triangle
▸ **trigonometric** (ˌtrɪgənəˈmɛtrɪk) *or* **ˌtrigonoˈmetrical** *adj*

trig point *n* an informal name for **triangulation station.** ORIG from *trigonometric*

trigraph ('traɪˌgrɑːf) *n* a combination of three letters used to represent a single speech sound or phoneme, such as *eau* in French *beau.*

trihedral (traɪˈhiːdrəl) *adj* **1** having three plane faces. ◆ *n* **2** a figure formed by the intersection of three lines in different planes.

trihedron (traɪˈhiːdrən) *n, pl* **trihedrons** *or* **trihedra** (-drə). a figure determined by the intersection of three planes.

trike (traɪk) *n* short for **tricycle.**

trilateral (traɪˈlætərəl) *adj* having three sides.

trilby ('trɪlbɪ) *n, pl* **trilbies.** a man's soft felt hat with an indented crown. ORIG C19: after *Trilby,* the heroine of a dramatized novel (1893) of that title by George Du Maurier

trilingual (traɪˈlɪŋgwəl) *adj* **1** able to speak three languages fluently. **2** expressed or written in three languages.
▸ **triˈlingualism** *n*

trilithon (traɪˈlɪθɒn) *or* **trilith** ('traɪlɪθ) *n* a structure consisting of two upright stones with a third placed across the top, as at Stonehenge. ORIG C18: from Gk
▸ **trilithic** (traɪˈlɪθɪk) *adj*

trill (trɪl) *n* **1** *Music.* a rapid alternation between a principal note and the note above it. **2** a shrill warbling sound, esp. as made by some birds. **3** the articulation of an (r) sound produced by the rapid vibration of the tongue or the uvula. ◆ *vb* **4** to sound, sing, or play (a trill or with a trill). **5** (*tr*) to pronounce (an (r) sound) by the production of a trill. ORIG C17: from It. *trillo,* from *trillare,* apparently from MDu. *trillen* to vibrate

trillion ('trɪljən) *n* **1** the number represented as one followed by twelve zeros (10^{12}); a million million. **2** (formerly, in Britain) the number represented as one followed by eighteen zeros (10^{18}); a million million million. ◆ *determiner* **3** (preceded by *a* or a numeral) amounting to a trillion. ORIG C17: from F, on the model of *million*
▸ **ˈtrillionth** *n, adj*

trillium ('trɪljəm) *n* any of a genus of herbaceous plants of Asia and North America, having a whorl of three leaves at the top of the stem with a single white, pink, or purple three-petalled flower. ORIG C18: from NL, modification by Linnaeus of Swedish *trilling* triplet

trilobate (traɪˈləʊbeɪt, ˈtraɪləˌbeɪt) *adj* (esp. of a leaf) consisting of or having three lobes or parts.

trilobite ('traɪləˌbaɪt) *n* any of various extinct marine arthropods abundant in Palaeozoic times, having a segmented exoskeleton divided into three parts. ORIG C19: from NL *Trilobītēs,* from Gk *trilobos* having three lobes
▸ **trilobitic** (ˌtraɪləˈbɪtɪk) *adj*

trilogy ('trɪlədʒɪ) *n, pl* **trilogies. 1** a series of three related works, esp. in literature, etc. **2** (in ancient Greece) a series of three tragedies performed together. ORIG C19: from Gk *trilogia*

trim (trɪm) *adj* **trimmer, trimmest. 1** neat and spruce in appearance. **2** slim; slender. **3** in good condition. ◆ *vb* **trims, trimming, trimmed.** (*mainly tr*) **4** to put in good order, esp. by cutting or pruning. **5** to shape and finish (timber). **6** to adorn or decorate. **7** (sometimes foll. by *off* or *away*) to cut so as to remove: *to trim off a branch.* **8** to cut down to the desired size or shape. **9** *Naut.* **9a** (*also intr*) to adjust the balance of (a vessel) or (of a vessel) to maintain an even balance, by distribution of ballast, cargo, etc. **9b** (*also intr*) to adjust (a vessel's sails) to take advantage of the wind. **10** to balance (an aircraft) before flight by adjusting the position of the load or in flight by the use of trim tabs, fuel transfer, etc. **11** (*also intr*) to modify (one's opinions, etc.) for expediency. **12** *Inf.* to thrash or beat. **13** *Inf.* to rebuke. ◆ *n* **14** a decoration or adornment. **15** the upholstery and decorative facings of a car's interior. **16** proper order or fitness; good shape. **17** a haircut that neatens but does not alter the existing hairstyle. **18** *Naut.* **18a** the general set and appearance of a vessel. **18b** the difference between the draught of a vessel at the bow and at the stern. **18c** the fitness of a vessel. **18d** the position of a vessel's sails relative to the wind. **19** dress or equipment. **20** *US.* window-dressing. **21** the attitude of an aircraft in flight when the pilot allows the main control surfaces to take up their own positions. **22** material that is trimmed off. **23** decorative mouldings, such as architraves, picture rails, etc. ORIG OE *trymman* to strengthen
▸ **ˈtrimly** *adv* ▸ **ˈtrimness** *n*

Trim ★ (trɪm) *n* the county town of Meath, Republic of Ireland; 12th-century castle, medieval cathedral; textiles and machinery. Pop.: 18 120 (1991).

trimaran ('traɪməˌræn) *n* a vessel, usually of shallow draught, with two hulls flanking the main hull. ORIG C20: from TRI- + (CATA)MARAN

Trimble ★ ('trɪmbᵊl) *n* **(William) David.** born 1944, Northern Irish politician; First Minister of Northern Ireland from 1998; awarded Nobel peace prize 1998 for his role in Northern Irish peace negotiations.

trimer ('traɪmə) *n* a polymer or a molecule of a polymer consisting of three identical monomers.

trimerous ('trɪmərəs) *adj* **1** having parts in groups of three. **2** having three parts.

trimester (traɪˈmɛstə) *n* **1** a period of three months. **2** (in some US and Canad. universities or schools) any of the three academic sessions. ORIG C19: from F *trimestre,* from L *trimēstris* of three months
▸ **triˈmestral** *or* **triˈmestrial** *adj*

trimeter ('trɪmɪtə) *Prosody.* ◆ *n* **1** a verse line consisting of three metrical feet. ◆ *adj* **2** designating such a line.

trimethadione (ˌtraɪmɛθəˈdaɪəʊn) *n* a crystalline compound with a camphor-like odour, used in the treatment of epilepsy.

trimetric projection (traɪˈmɛtrɪk) *n* a geometric projection, used in mechanical drawing, in which the three axes are at arbitrary angles, often using different linear scales.

trimmer ('trɪmə) *n* **1** a beam attached to truncated joists in order to leave an opening for a staircase, chimney, etc. **2** a machine for trimming timber. **3** a variable capacitor of small capacitance used for making fine adjustments, etc. **4** a person who alters his or her opinions on the grounds of expediency. **5** a person who fits out motor vehicles.

trimming ('trɪmɪŋ) *n* **1** an extra piece used to decorate or complete. **2** (*pl*) usual or traditional accompaniments: *roast turkey with all the trimmings.* **3** (*pl*) parts that are cut off.

trimolecular (ˌtraɪməˈlɛkjʊlə) *adj Chem.* of, formed from, or involving three molecules.

trimonthly (traɪˈmʌnθlɪ) *adj, adv* every three months.

trimorphism (traɪˈmɔːfɪzəm) *n* **1** *Biol.* the property exhibited by certain species of having or occurring in three different forms. **2** the property of certain minerals of existing in three crystalline forms.

Trinacria ★ (trɪˈneɪkrɪə, traɪ-) *n* the Latin name for **Sicily.**
▸ **Triˈnacrian** *adj*

trinary ('traɪnərɪ) *adj* **1** made up of three parts; ternary. **2** going in threes. ORIG C15: from LL *trīnārius* of three sorts, from L *trīnī* three each, from *trēs* three

Trincomalee ★ (ˌtrɪŋkəʊməˈliː) *n* a port in NE Sri Lanka, on the **Bay of Trincomalee** (an inlet of the Bay of Bengal); British naval base until 1957. Pop.: 51 000 (latest est.).

trine (traɪn) *n* **1** *Astrol.* an aspect of 120° between two planets. **2** anything comprising three parts. ◆ *adj* **3** of or relating to a trine. **4** threefold; triple. ORIG C14: from OF *trin,* from L *trīnus* triple, from *trēs* three
▸ **ˈtrinal** *adj*

Trinidad ★ (ˈtrɪnɪˌdæd) *n* an island in the West Indies, off the NE coast of Venezuela: colonized by the Spanish in the 17th century and ceded to Britain in 1802; joined with Tobago in 1888 as a British colony; now part of the independent republic of Trinidad and Tobago. Pop.: 1 184 106 (1990).
▸ **ˌTriniˈdadian** *adj, n*

Trinidad and Tobago ★ *n* an independent republic in the Caribbean, occupying the two southernmost islands of the Lesser Antilles: became a British colony in 1888 and gained independence in 1962; became a republic in 1976; a member of the Commonwealth. Official language: English. Religion: Christian majority, with a large Hindu minority. Currency: Trinidad and Tobago dollar. Capital: Port of Spain. Pop.: 1 289 000 (1999 est.). Area: 5128 sq. km (1980 sq. miles).

Trinitarian (ˌtrɪnɪˈtɛərɪən) *n* **1** a person who believes in the doctrine of the Trinity. ◆ *adj* **2** of or relating to the doctrine of the Trinity or those who uphold it.
▸ **ˌTriniˈtarianˌism** *n*

trinitroglycerine (traɪˌnaɪtrəʊˈglɪsərɪn) *n* the full name for **nitroglycerine.**

trinitrotoluene (traɪˌnaɪtrəʊˈtɒljuˌiːn) *or* **trinitrotoluol** (traɪˌnaɪtrəʊˈtɒljuˌɒl) *n* the full name for **TNT.**

trinity (ˈtrɪnɪtɪ) *n, pl* **trinities. 1** a group of three. **2** the state of being threefold. ORIG C13: from OF *trinite,* from LL *trīnitās,* from L *trīnus* triple

Trinity (ˈtrɪnɪtɪ) *n Christian theol.* the union of three persons, the Father, Son, and Holy Spirit, in one Godhead.

Trinity Brethren *pl n* the members of Trinity House.

Trinity House *n* an association that provides lighthouses, buoys, etc., around the British coast.

Trinity Sunday *n* the Sunday after Whit Sunday.

Trinity term *n* the summer term at the Inns of Court and certain universities.

trinket (ˈtrɪŋkɪt) *n* **1** a small or worthless ornament or piece of jewellery. **2** a trivial object; trifle. ORIG C16: ? from earlier *trenket* little knife, via OF, from L *truncāre* to lop

trinomial (traɪˈnəʊmɪəl) *adj* **1** consisting of three terms. ◆ *n* **2** *Maths.* a polynomial consisting of three terms, such as $ax^2 + bx + c$. **3** *Biol.* the three-part name of an organism that incorporates its genus, species, and subspecies. ORIG C18: TRI- + *-nomial* on the model of *binomial*

trio (ˈtriːəʊ) *n, pl* **trios. 1** a group of three. **2** *Music.* **2a** a group of three singers or instrumentalists or a piece of music composed for such a group. **2b** a subordinate section in a scherzo, minuet, etc. ORIG C18: from It., ult. from L *trēs* three

triode (ˈtraɪəʊd) *n* **1** an electronic valve having three electrodes, a cathode, an anode, and a grid. **2** any electronic device having three electrodes. ORIG C20: TRI- + ELECTRODE

trioecious *or* **triecious** (traɪˈiːʃəs) *adj* (of a plant species) having male, female, and hermaphrodite flowers in three different plants. ORIG C18: from NL *trioecia,* from Gk TRI- + *oikos* house

triolein (traɪˈəʊlɪɪn) *n* a naturally occurring glyceride of oleic acid, found in fats and oils.

triolet (ˈtriːəʊˌlɛt) *n* a verse form of eight lines, having the first line repeated as the fourth and seventh and the second line as the eighth, rhyming a b a a a b a b. ORIG C17: from F: a little TRIO

trioxide (traɪˈɒksaɪd) *n* any oxide that contains three oxygen atoms per molecule.

trip (trɪp) *n* **1** an outward and return journey, often for a specific purpose. **2** any journey. **3** a false step; stumble. **4** any slip or blunder. **5** a light step or tread. **6** a manoeuvre or device to cause someone to trip. **7** Also called: **tripper.** any catch on a mechanism that acts as a switch. **8** *Inf.* a hallucinogenic drug experience. **9** *Inf.* any stimulating, profound, etc., experience. ◆ *vb* **trips, tripping, tripped. 10** (often foll. by *up*, or when *intr*, by *on* or *over*) to stumble or cause to stumble. **11** to make or cause to make a mistake. **12** (*tr;* often foll. by *up*) to trap or catch in a mistake. **13** (*intr*) to go on a short journey. **14** (*intr*) to move or tread lightly. **15** (*intr*) *Inf.* to experience the effects of a hallucinogenic drug. **16** (*tr*) to activate a mechanical trip. ORIG C14: from OF *triper* to tread, of Gmc origin

tripartite (traɪˈpɑːtaɪt) *adj* **1** divided into or composed of three parts. **2** involving three participants. **3** (esp. of leaves) consisting of three parts formed by divisions extending almost to the base.
▸ **triˈpartitely** *adv*

tripe (traɪp) *n* **1** the stomach lining of an ox, cow, etc., prepared for cooking. **2** *Inf.* something silly; rubbish. ORIG C13: from OF, from ?

triphammer (ˈtrɪpˌhæmə) *n* a power hammer that is raised or tilted by a cam and allowed to fall under gravity.

triphibious (traɪˈfɪbɪəs) *adj* (esp. of military operations) occurring on land, at sea, and in the air. ORIG C20: from TRI- + (AM)PHIBIOUS

triphthong (ˈtrɪfθɒŋ, ˈtrɪp-) *n* **1** a composite vowel sound during the articulation of which the vocal organs move from one position through a second, ending in a third, as in *fire.* **2** a trigraph representing such a composite vowel sound. ORIG C16: via NL from Med. Gk *triphthongos,* from TRI- + *phthongos* sound
▸ **triphˈthongal** *adj*

tripinnate (traɪˈpɪnɪt, -eɪt) *adj* (of a leaf) having pinnate leaflets that are bipinnately arranged.

triplane (ˈtraɪˌpleɪn) *n* an aeroplane having three wings arranged one above the other.

triple (ˈtrɪpᵊl) *adj* **1** consisting of three parts; threefold. **2** (of musical time or rhythm) having three beats in each bar. **3** three times as great or as much. ◆ *n* **4** a threefold amount. **5** a group of three. ◆ *vb* **triples, tripling, tripled. 6** to increase threefold; treble. ORIG C16: from L *triplus*
▸ **ˈtriply** *adv*

triple A *n Mil.* anti-aircraft artillery. ORIG referring to the abbrev. AAA

triple crown *n* (*often caps.*) *Rugby Union.* a victory by England, Ireland, Scotland, or Wales in all three games against the others in the annual Six Nations Championship.

triple jump *n* an athletic event in which the competitor has to perform successively a hop, a step, and a jump in continuous movement.

triple point *n Chem.* the temperature and pressure at which the three phases of a substance are in equilibrium.

triplet (ˈtrɪplɪt) *n* **1** a group or set of three similar things. **2** one of three offspring born at one birth. **3** *Music.* a group of three notes played in a time value of two, four, etc. **4** *Chem.* a state of a molecule or free radical in which there are two unpaired electrons. ORIG C17: from TRIPLE, on the model of *doublet*

Triplex (ˈtrɪplɛks) *n Brit. trademark.* a laminated safety glass, as used in car windows.

triplicate *adj* (ˈtrɪplɪkɪt). **1** triple. ◆ *vb* (ˈtrɪplɪˌkeɪt), **triplicates, triplicating, triplicated. 2** to multiply or be multiplied by three. ◆ *n* (ˈtrɪplɪkɪt). **3a** a group of three things. **3b** one of such a group. **4 in triplicate.** written out three times. ORIG C15: from L *triplicāre* to triple
▸ **ˌtripliˈcation** *n*

triploid (ˈtrɪplɔɪd) *adj* **1** having or relating to three times the haploid number of chromosomes: *a triploid organism.* ◆ *n* **2** a triploid organism. ORIG C19: from Gk *tripl(oos)* triple + (HAPL)OID

tripod (ˈtraɪpɒd) *n* **1** a three-legged stand to which a camera, etc., can be attached to hold it steady. **2** a stand or table having three legs.
▸ **tripodal** (ˈtrɪpədᵊl) *adj*

tripoli (ˈtrɪpəlɪ) *n* a lightweight porous siliceous rock

★ people and places

used in a powdered form as a polish. ORIG C17: after TRIPOLI, in Libya or in Lebanon

Tripoli ★ ('trɪpəlɪ) *n* **1** the capital and chief port of Libya, in the northwest on the Mediterranean: founded by Phoenicians in about the 7th century B.C.; the only city that has survived of the three (Oea, Leptis Magna, and Sabratha) that formed the African Tripolis ("three cities"); fishing and manufacturing centre. Pop.: 591 062 (1988 est.). Ancient name: **Oea** ('iːə). Arabic name: **Tarabulus el Gharb. 2** a port in N Lebanon, on the Mediterranean: the second largest town in Lebanon; taken by the Crusaders in 1109 after a siege of five years; oil-refining and manufacturing centre. Pop.: 240 000 (1991 est.). Ancient name: **Tripolis.** Arabic name: **Tarabulus esh Sham.**

Tripolitania ★ (ˌtrɪpəlɪ'teɪnɪə) *n* the NW part of Libya: established as a Phoenician colony in the 7th century B.C.; taken by the Turks in 1551 and became one of the Barbary states; under Italian rule from 1912 until World War II.
▸ **ˌTripoli'tanian** *adj, n*

tripos ('traɪpɒs) *n Brit.* the final honours degree examinations at Cambridge University. ORIG C16: from L *tripūs,* infl. by Gk noun ending *-os*

tripper ('trɪpə) *n* **1** *Chiefly Brit.* a tourist. **2** another word for **trip** (sense 7). **3** any device that causes a trip to operate.

trippy ('trɪpɪ) *adj* **trippier, trippiest.** *Inf.* suggestive of or resembling the effect produced by a hallucinogenic drug.

triptane ('trɪpteɪn) *n* a liquid hydrocarbon used in aviation fuel. ORIG C20: shortened & altered from *trimethylbutane*

Triptolemus ★ (trɪp'tɒlɪməs) *n Greek myth.* a favourite of Demeter, sent by her to teach men agriculture.

triptych ('trɪptɪk) *n* **1** a set of three pictures or panels, usually hinged so that the two wing panels fold over the larger central one: often used as an altarpiece. **2** a set of three hinged writing tablets. ORIG C18: from Gk *triptukhos,* from TRI- + *ptux* plate

triptyque (trɪp'tiːk) *n* a customs permit for the temporary importation of a motor vehicle. ORIG C20: from F: TRIPTYCH (from its three sections)

Tripura ★ ('trɪpʊrə) *n* a state of NE India: formerly a princely state, ruled by the Maharajahs for over 1300 years; became a union territory in 1956 and a state in 1972; extensive jungles. Capital: Agartala. Pop.: 3 055 000 (1994 est.). Area: 10 486 sq. km (4051 sq. miles).

tripwire ('trɪpˌwaɪə) *n* a wire that activates a trap, mine, etc., when tripped over.

trireme ('traɪriːm) *n* an ancient Greek galley with three banks of oars on each side. ORIG C17: from L *trirēmis,* from TRI- + *rēmus* oar

trisect (traɪ'sɛkt) *vb* (*tr*) to divide into three parts, esp. three equal parts. ORIG C17: TRI- + *-sect* from L *secāre* to cut
▸ **trisection** (traɪ'sɛkʃən) *n*

trishaw ('traɪˌʃɔː) *n* another name for **rickshaw** (sense 2). ORIG C20: from TRI- + RICKSHAW

triskelion (trɪ'skɛlɪˌɒn) *n, pl* **triskelia** (trɪ'skɛlɪə). a symbol consisting of three bent limbs or lines radiating from a centre. ORIG C19: from Gk *triskelēs* three-legged

Trismegistus ★ (ˌtrɪsmɪ'dʒɪstəs) *n* See **Hermes Trismegistus.**

trismus ('trɪzməs) *n Pathol.* the state of being unable to open the mouth because of sustained contractions of the jaw muscles, caused by tetanus. Nontechnical name: **lockjaw.** ORIG C17: from NL, from Gk *trismos* a grinding

Tristan ('trɪstən) *or* **Tristram** ★ ('trɪstrəm) *n* (in medieval romance) the nephew of King Mark of Cornwall who fell in love with his uncle's bride, Iseult, after they mistakenly drank a love potion.

Tristan da Cunha ★ ('trɪstən də 'kuːnjə) *n* a group of four small volcanic islands in the S Atlantic: comprises the main island of Tristan and the uninhabited islands of Gough, Inaccessible, and Nightingale; discovered in 1506 by the Portuguese admiral Tristão da Cunha; annexed to Britain in 1816; population evacuated for two years after the volcanic eruption of 1961. Pop.: 313 (1988). Area: about 100 sq. km (40 sq. miles).

triste (triːst) *adj* an archaic word for **sad.** ORIG from F

trisyllable (traɪ'sɪləbᵊl) *n* a word of three syllables.
▸ **trisyllabic** (ˌtraɪsɪ'læbɪk) *adj*

trite (traɪt) *adj* hackneyed; dull: *a trite comment.* ORIG C16: from L *trītus* worn down, from *terere* to rub
▸ **'tritely** *adv* ▸ **'triteness** *n*

tritheism ('traɪθɪˌɪzəm) *n Theol.* belief in three gods, esp. in the Trinity as consisting of three distinct gods.
▸ **'tritheist** *n, adj*

triticum ('trɪtɪkəm) *n* any of a genus of cereal grasses which includes the wheats. ORIG C19: L, lit.: wheat, prob. from *tritum,* supine of *terere* to grind

tritium ('trɪtɪəm) *n* a radioactive isotope of hydrogen. Symbol: T or ^{3}H; half-life: 12.5 years. ORIG C20: NL, from Gk *tritos* third

triton[1] ('traɪtᵊn) *n* any of various chiefly tropical marine gastropod molluscs having large spiral shells. ORIG C16: via L from Gk *tritōn*

triton[2] ('traɪtɒn) *n Physics.* a nucleus of an atom of tritium, containing two neutrons and one proton. ORIG C20: from TRIT(IUM) + -ON

Triton ★ ('traɪtᵊn) *n Greek myth.* a sea god depicted as having the upper parts of a man with a fish's tail.

tritone ('traɪˌtəʊn) *n* a musical interval consisting of three whole tones.

triturate ('trɪtjʊˌreɪt) *vb* **triturates, triturating, triturated. 1** (*tr*) to grind or rub into a fine powder or pulp. ◆ *n* **2** the powder or pulp resulting from this. ORIG C17: from LL *trītūrāre* to thresh, from L *trītūra* a threshing, from *terere* to grind
▸ **ˌtritu'ration** *n*

triumph ('traɪəmf) *n* **1** the feeling of exultation and happiness derived from a victory or major achievement. **2** the act or condition of being victorious; victory. **3** (in ancient Rome) a procession held in honour of a victorious general. ◆ *vb* (*intr*) **4** (often foll. by *over*) to win a victory or control: *to triumph over one's weaknesses.* **5** to rejoice over a victory. **6** to celebrate a Roman triumph. ORIG C14: from OF *triumphe,* from L *triumphus,* from OL *triumpus*
▸ **triumphal** (traɪ'ʌmfəl) *adj*

triumphant (traɪ'ʌmfənt) *adj* **1** experiencing or displaying triumph. **2** exultant through triumph.
▸ **tri'umphantly** *adv*

triumvir (traɪ'ʌmvə) *n, pl* **triumvirs** *or* **triumviri** (-vɪˌriː). (esp. in ancient Rome) a member of a triumvirate. ORIG C16: from L: one of three administrators, from *trium virōrum* of three men, from *trēs* three + *vir* man
▸ **tri'umviral** *adj*

triumvirate (traɪ'ʌmvɪrɪt) *n* **1** (in ancient Rome) a board of three officials jointly responsible for some task. **2** joint rule by three men. **3** any group of three men associated in some way. **4** the office of a triumvir.

triune ('traɪjuːn) *adj* constituting three in one, esp. the three persons in one God of the Trinity. ORIG C17: TRI- + *-une,* from L *ūnus* one
▸ **tri'unity** *n*

trivalent (traɪ'veɪlənt, 'trɪvələnt) *adj Chem.* **1** having a valency of three. **2** having three valencies. ◆ Also: **tervalent.**
▸ **tri'valency** *n*

Trivandrum ★ (trɪ'vændrəm) *n* a city in S India, capital of Kerala, on the Malabar Coast: made capital of the kingdom of Travancore in 1745; University of Kerala (1937). Pop.: 524 006 (1991).

trivet ('trɪvɪt) *n* **1** a stand, usually three-legged and metal, on which cooking vessels are placed over a fire. **2** a short metal stand on which hot dishes are placed on a table. **3** **as right as a trivet.** in perfect health. ORIG OE *trefet* (infl. by OE *thrifēte* having three feet), from L *tripēs* having three feet

trivia ('trɪvɪə) *n* (*functioning as sing or pl*) petty details or considerations; trifles; trivialities. ORIG from NL, pl of L *trivium* junction of three roads

trivial ('trɪvɪəl) *adj* **1** of little importance; petty or frivolous: *trivial complaints.* **2** ordinary or commonplace; trite: *trivial conversation.* **3** *Biol., chem.* denoting the common name of an organism or substance. **4** *Biol.* denoting the specific name of an organism in binomial nomenclature. ORIG C15: from L *triviālis* belonging to the public streets, common, from *trivium* junction of three roads
▸ **'trivially** *adv* ▸ **'trivialness** *n*

triviality (ˌtrɪvɪ'ælɪtɪ) *n, pl* **trivialities. 1** the state or quality of being trivial. **2** something, such as a remark, that is trivial.

trivialize *or* **trivialise** ('trɪvɪəˌlaɪz) *vb* **trivializes, trivializing, trivialized** *or* **trivialises, trivialising, trivialised.** (*tr*) to cause to seem trivial or more trivial; minimize.
▸ **ˌtriviali'zation** *or* **ˌtriviali'sation** *n*

trivium ('trɪvɪəm) *n, pl* **trivia** (-ɪə). (in medieval learning) the arts of grammar, rhetoric, and logic. Cf. **quadrivium.** ORIG C19: from Med. L, from L: crossroads

-trix *suffix forming nouns.* indicating a feminine agent, corresponding to nouns ending in *-tor: executrix.* ORIG from L

t-RNA *abbrev. for* transfer RNA.

Troas ★ ('trəʊæs) *n* the region of NW Asia Minor surrounding the ancient city of Troy. Also called: **the Troad** ('trəʊæd).

Trobriand Islands ★ ('trəʊbrɪˌænd) *pl n* a group of coral islands in the Solomon Sea, north of the E part of New Guinea: part of Papua New Guinea. Area: about 440 sq. km (170 sq. miles).
▸ **Trobriand Islander** *n*

trocar ('trəʊkɑː) *n* a surgical instrument for removing fluid from bodily cavities. ORIG C18: from F *trocart,* lit.: with three sides, from *trois* three + *carre* side

trochal ('trəʊkᵊl) *adj Zool.* shaped like a wheel. ORIG C19: from Gk *trokhos* wheel

trochanter (trəʊ'kæntə) *n* **1** any of several processes on the upper part of the vertebrate femur, to which muscles are attached. **2** the third segment of an insect's leg. ORIG C17: via F from Gk *trokhantēr,* from *trekhein* to run

troche (trəʊʃ) *n Med.* another name for **lozenge** (sense 1). ORIG C16: from F *trochisque,* from LL *trochiscus,* from Gk *trokhiskos* little wheel, from *trokhos* wheel

trochee ('trəʊkiː) *n* a metrical foot of two syllables, the first long and the second short. ORIG C16: via L from Gk *trokhaios pous,* lit.: a running foot, from *trekhein* to run
▸ **trochaic** (trəʊ'keɪɪk) *adj*

trochlea ('trɒklɪə) *n, pl* **trochleae** (-lɪˌiː). any bony or cartilaginous part with a grooved surface over which a bone, etc., may slide or articulate. ORIG C17: from L, from Gk *trokhileia* a sheaf of pulleys

trochlear nerve ('trɒklɪə) *n* either one of the fourth pair of cranial nerves, which supply the superior oblique muscle of the eye.

trochoid ('trəʊkɔɪd) *n* **1** the curve described by a fixed point on the radius of a circle as the circle rolls along a straight line. ◆ *adj also* **trochoidal. 2** rotating about a central axis. **3** *Anat.* (of a structure or part) resembling or functioning as a pivot or pulley. ORIG C18: from Gk *trokhoeidēs* circular, from *trokhos* wheel

trod (trɒd) *vb* the past tense and a past participle of **tread.**

trodden ('trɒdᵊn) *vb* a past participle of **tread.**

trode (trəʊd) *vb Arch.* a past tense of **tread.**

troglodyte ('trɒgləˌdaɪt) *n* **1** a cave dweller, esp. of prehistoric times. **2** *Inf.* a person who lives alone and appears eccentric. ORIG C16: via L from Gk *trōglodutēs* one who enters caves, from *trōglē* hole + *duein* to enter
▸ **troglodytic** (ˌtrɒglə'dɪtɪk) *adj*

trogon ('trəʊgɒn) *n* any of an order of birds of tropical regions of America, Africa, and Asia, having a brilliant plumage and long tail. See also **quetzal** (sense 1). ORIG C18: from NL, from Gk *trōgōn,* from *trōgein* to gnaw

troika ('trɔɪkə) *n* **1** a Russian vehicle drawn by three horses abreast. **2** three horses harnessed abreast. **3** a triumvirate. ORIG C19: from Russian, from *troe* three

Troilus ★ ('trɔɪləs, 'trəʊɪləs) *n Greek myth.* the youngest son of King Priam and Queen Hecuba, slain at Troy. In medieval romance he is portrayed as the lover of Cressida.

Trois Rivières ★ (*French* trwɑ rivjɛr) *n* a port in central Canada, in Quebec on the St Lawrence River: one of the world's largest centres of newsprint production. Pop. (metropolitan area): 136 300 (1991). English name: **Three Rivers.**

Trojan ('trəʊdʒən) *n* **1** a native or inhabitant of ancient Troy. **2** a person who is hard-working and determined. ◆ *adj* **3** of or relating to ancient Troy or its inhabitants.

Trojan Horse *n* **1** *Greek myth.* the huge wooden hollow figure of a horse left outside Troy by the Greeks and dragged inside by the Trojans. The men concealed inside it opened the city to the final Greek assault. **2** a trap intended to undermine an enemy. **3** *Computing.* a bug inserted into a program or system designed to be activated after a certain time or a certain number of operations.

troll¹ (trəʊl) *vb* **1** *Angling.* **1a** to draw (a baited line, etc.) through the water. **1b** to fish (a stretch of water) by trolling. **1c** to fish (for) by trolling. **2** to roll or cause to roll. **3** *Arch.* to sing (a refrain, chorus, etc.) in a loud hearty voice. **4** (*intr*) *Brit. inf.* to walk or stroll. ◆ *n* **5** a trolling. **6** *Angling.* a bait or lure used in trolling. ORIG C14: from OF *troller* to run about
▸ **'troller** *n*

troll² (trəʊl) *n* (in Scandinavian folklore) one of a class of supernatural creatures that dwell in caves or mountains and are depicted either as dwarfs or as giants. ORIG C19: from ON: demon

trolley ('trɒlɪ) *n* **1** a small table on casters used for conveying food, etc. **2** *Chiefly Brit.* a wheeled cart or stand used for moving heavy items, such as shopping in a supermarket or luggage at a railway station. **3** *Brit.* (in a hospital) a bed mounted on casters and used for moving patients who are unconscious, etc. **4** *Brit.* See **trolleybus. 5** *US & Canad.* See **trolley car. 6** a device that collects the current from an overhead wire, third rail, etc., to drive the motor of an electric vehicle. **7** a pulley or truck that travels along an overhead wire in order to support a suspended load. **8** *Chiefly Brit.* a low truck running on rails, used in factories, mines, etc. **9** a truck, cage, or basket suspended from an overhead track or cable for carrying loads in a mine, etc. ORIG C19: prob. from TROLL¹

trolleybus ('trɒlɪˌbʌs) *n* an electrically driven public-transport vehicle that does not run on rails but takes its power from two overhead wires.

trolley car *n* a US and Canad. name for **tram** (sense 1).

trollius ('trəʊlɪəs) *n* another name for **globeflower.** ORIG from G *Trollblume* globeflower

trollop ('trɒləp) *n* **1** a promiscuous woman, esp. a prostitute. **2** an untidy woman; slattern. ORIG C17: ?from G dialect *Trolle* prostitute
▸ **'trollopy** *adj*

Trollope ★ ('trɒləp) *n* **Anthony.** 1815–82, British novelist. His novels include *Barchester Towers* (1857), *Phineas Redux* (1874), and *The Prime Minister* (1876).

trombone (trɒm'bəʊn) *n* a brass instrument, a low-pitched counterpart of the trumpet, consisting of a tube the effective length of which is varied by means of a U-shaped slide. ORIG C18: from It., from *tromba* a trumpet, from OHG *trumba*
▸ **trom'bonist** *n*

trommel ('trɒməl) *n* a revolving cylindrical sieve used to screen crushed ore. ORIG C19: from G: a drum

trompe (trɒmp) *n* an apparatus for supplying the blast of air in a forge, consisting of a thin column down which water falls, drawing in air through side openings. ORIG C19: from F, lit.: trumpet

trompe l'oeil (*French* trɔ̃p lœj) *n, pl* **trompe l'oeils** (trɔ̃p lœj). **1** a painting, etc., giving a convincing illusion of reality. **2** an effect of this kind. ORIG from F, lit.: deception of the eye

Tromsø ★ ('trɒmsəʊ; *Norwegian* 'trumsø) *n* a port in N Norway, on a small island between Kvaløy and the mainland: fishing and sealing centre. Pop.: 51 218 (1990).

-tron *suffix forming nouns.* **1** indicating a vacuum tube. **2**

indicating an instrument for accelerating atomic particles. ORIG from Gk, suffix indicating instrument

tronc (trɒŋk) *n* a pool into which waiters, etc., pay their tips for later distribution to staff by a **tronc master**, according to agreed percentages. ORIG C20: from F: collecting box

Trondheim ★ (ˈtrɒndˌhaɪm; *Norwegian* ˈtrɔnhɛim) *n* a port in central Norway, on **Trondheim Fjord** (an inlet of the Norwegian Sea): national capital until 1380; seat of the Technical University of Norway. Pop.: 144 599 (1997 est.). Former name (until the 16th century and from 1930 to 1931): **Nidaros.**

tronk (trɒŋk) *n S. African inf.* a prison. ORIG Afrik.

troop (truːp) *n* **1** a large group or assembly. **2** a subdivision of a cavalry squadron or artillery battery of about platoon size. **3** (*pl*) armed forces; soldiers. **4** a large group of Scouts comprising several patrols. ◆ *vb* **5** (*intr*) to gather, move, or march in or as if in a crowd. **6** (*tr*) *Mil., chiefly Brit.* to parade (the colour or flag) ceremonially. ORIG C16: from F *troupe,* from *troupeau* flock, of Gmc origin

trooper (ˈtruːpə) *n* **1** a soldier in a cavalry regiment. **2** *US & Austral.* a mounted policeman. **3** *US.* a state policeman. **4** a cavalry horse. **5** *Inf., chiefly Brit.* a troopship.

troopship (ˈtruːpˌʃɪp) *n* a ship used to transport military personnel.

tropaeolum (trəʊˈpiːələm) *n, pl* **tropaeolums** *or* **tropaeola** (-lə). any of a genus of garden plants, esp. the nasturtium. ORIG C18: from NL, from L *tropaeum* TROPHY; from the shield-shaped leaves and helmet-shaped flowers

trope (trəʊp) *n* a word or expression used in a figurative sense. ORIG C16: from L *tropus* figurative use of a word, from Gk *tropos* style, turn

-trope *n combining form.* indicating a turning towards, development in the direction of, or affinity to: *heliotrope.* ORIG from Gk *tropos* a turn

trophic (ˈtrɒfɪk) *adj* of nutrition. ORIG C19: from Gk *trophikos,* from *trophē* food, from *trephein* to feed

tropho- *or before a vowel* **troph-** *combining form.* indicating nourishment or nutrition: *trophozoite.* ORIG from Gk *trophē* food, from *trephein* to feed

trophoblast (ˈtrɒfəˌblæst) *n* a membrane that encloses the embryo of mammals and absorbs nourishment from the uterine fluids.

trophozoite (ˌtrɒfəˈzəʊaɪt) *n* the form of a sporozoan protozoan, esp. of certain parasites, in the feeding stage.

trophy (ˈtrəʊfɪ) *n, pl* **trophies. 1** an object such as a silver cup that is symbolic of victory in a contest, esp. a sporting contest; prize. **2** a memento of success, esp. one taken in war or hunting. **3** (in ancient Greece and Rome) a memorial to a victory, usually consisting of captured arms raised on the battlefield or in a public place. **4** an ornamental carving that represents a group of weapons, etc. ORIG C16: from F *trophée,* from L *tropaeum,* from Gk *tropaion,* from *tropē* a turning, defeat of the enemy

-trophy *n combining form.* indicating a certain type of nourishment or growth: *dystrophy.* ORIG from Gk *-trophia,* from *trophē* nourishment
▸ **-trophic** *adj combining form.*

tropic (ˈtrɒpɪk) *n* **1** (*sometimes cap.*) either of the parallel lines of latitude at about 23½°N (**tropic of Cancer**) and 23½°S (**tropic of Capricorn**) of the equator. **2 the tropics.** (*often cap.*) that part of the earth's surface between the tropics of Cancer and Capricorn. **3** *Astron.* either of the two parallel circles on the celestial sphere having the same latitudes and names as the lines on the earth. ◆ *adj* **4** tropical. ORIG C14: from LL *tropicus* belonging to a turn, from Gk *tropikos,* from *tropos* a turn; from the belief that the sun turned back at the solstices

-tropic *adj combining form.* turning or developing in response to a certain stimulus: *heliotropic.* ORIG from Gk *tropos* a turn

tropical (ˈtrɒpɪkᵊl) *adj* **1** situated in, used in, characteristic of, or relating to the tropics. **2** (of weather) very hot, esp. when humid. **3** of a trope.
▸ ˌ**tropiˈcality** *n* ▸ ˈ**tropically** *adv*

tropical depression *n Caribbean.* an area of heavy rains and winds, the first stage in the development of a possible hurricane.

tropicbird (ˈtrɒpɪkˌbɜːd) *n* any of various tropical aquatic birds having long tail feathers and a white plumage with black markings.

tropism (ˈtrəʊpɪzəm) *n* the response of an organism, esp. a plant, to an external stimulus by growth in a direction determined by the stimulus. ORIG from Gk *tropos* a turn
▸ ˌ**tropisˈmatic** *adj*

-tropism *or* **-tropy** *n combining form.* indicating a tendency to turn or develop in response to a stimulus: *phototropism.* ORIG from Gk *tropos* a turn

tropo- *combining form.* indicating change or a turning: *tropophyte.* ORIG from Gk *tropos* a turn

tropopause (ˈtrɒpəˌpɔːz) *n Meteorol.* the plane of discontinuity between the troposphere and the stratosphere, characterized by a sharp change in the lapse rate.

troposphere (ˈtrɒpəˌsfɪə) *n* the lowest atmospheric layer, about 18 kilometres (11 miles) thick at the equator to about 6 km (4 miles) at the Poles, in which air temperature decreases normally with height at about 6.5°C per km.
▸ **tropospheric** (ˌtrɒpəˈsfɛrɪk) *adj*

-tropous *adj combining form.* indicating a turning away: *anatropous.* ORIG from Gk *-tropos* concerning a turn

troppo[1] (ˈtrɒpəʊ) *adv Music.* too much; excessively. See **non troppo.** ORIG It.

troppo[2] (ˈtrɒpəʊ) *adj Austral. sl.* mentally affected by a tropical climate.

Trossachs ★ (ˈtrɒsəks) *n* (*functioning as pl or sing*) **the. 1** a narrow wooded valley in central Scotland, between Loch Achray and Loch Katrine: made famous by Sir Walter Scott's descriptions. **2** (popularly) the area extending northwards from Loch Ard and Aberfoyle to Lochs Katrine, Achray, and Venachar.

trot (trɒt) *vb* **trots, trotting, trotted. 1** to move or cause to move at a trot. ◆ *n* **2** a gait of a horse in which diagonally opposite legs come down together. **3** a steady brisk pace. **4** (in harness racing) a race for horses that have been trained to trot fast. **5** *Chiefly Brit.* a small child. **6** *US sl.* a student's crib. **7 on the trot.** *Inf.* **7a** one after the other: *to read two books on the trot.* **7b** busy, esp. on one's feet. **8 the trots.** *Inf.* **8a** diarrhoea. **8b** *NZ.* trotting races. ◆ See also **trot out.** ORIG C13: from OF *trot,* from *troter* to trot, of Gmc origin

Trot (trɒt) *n Inf.* a follower of Trotsky; Trotskyist.

troth (trəʊθ) *n Arch.* **1** a pledge of fidelity, esp. a betrothal. **2** truth (esp. in **in troth**). **3** loyalty; fidelity. ORIG OE *trēowth*

trotline (ˈtrɒtˌlaɪn) *n Angling.* a long line suspended across a stream, river, etc., to which shorter hooked and baited lines are attached.

trot out *vb* (*tr, adv*) *Inf.* to bring forward, as for approbation or admiration, esp. repeatedly.

Trotsky *or* **Trotski** ★ (ˈtrɒtskɪ) *n* **Leon,** original name *Lev Davidovich Bronstein.* 1879–1940, Russian revolutionary and a leader of the November Revolution (1917); as commissar of foreign affairs (1917–24), he created the Red Army. He was ousted by Stalin after Lenin's death and deported; assassinated by a Stalinist agent.

Trotskyism (ˈtrɒtskɪˌɪzəm) *n* Trotsky's theory of communism, in which he called for immediate worldwide revolution by the proletariat.
▸ ˈ**Trotskyist** *or* ˈ**Trotskyˌite** *n, adj*

trotter (ˈtrɒtə) *n* **1** a horse that is specially trained to trot fast. **2** (*usually pl*) the foot of certain animals, esp. of pigs.

troubadour (ˈtruːbəˌdʊə) *n* any of a class of lyric poets who flourished principally in Provence and N Italy from the 11th to the 13th century, writing chiefly on courtly love. ORIG C18: from F, from OProvençal *trobador,* from *trobar* to write verses, ? ult. from L *tropus* TROPE

trouble (ˈtrʌbᵊl) *n* **1** a state of mental distress or anxiety. **2** a state of disorder or unrest: *industrial trouble.* **3** a condition of disease, pain, or malfunctioning: *liver trouble.* **4** a cause of distress, disturbance, or pain. **5** effort or exertion taken to do something. **6** liability to suffer punishment or misfortune (esp. in **be in trouble**): *he's in trouble*

★ people and places

with the police. **7** a personal weakness or cause of annoyance: *his trouble is he's too soft.* **8** political unrest. **9** the condition of an unmarried girl who becomes pregnant (esp. in **in trouble**). ◆ *vb* **troubles, troubling, troubled. 10** (*tr*) to cause trouble to. **11** (*intr; usually with a negative and foll. by about*) to put oneself to inconvenience; be concerned: *don't trouble about me.* **12** (*intr;* usually with a negative) to take pains; exert oneself. **13** (*tr*) to cause inconvenience or discomfort to. **14** (*tr; usually passive*) to agitate or make rough: *the seas were troubled.* **15** (*tr*) *Caribbean.* to interfere with. ORIG C13: from OF *troubler,* from Vulgar L *turbulāre* (unattested), from LL *turbidāre,* ult. from *turba* commotion
▸ **'troubler** *n*

troublemaker ('trʌbᵊlˌmeɪkə) *n* a person who makes trouble, esp. between people.
▸ **'troubleˌmaking** *adj, n*

troubleshooter ('trʌbᵊlˌʃuːtə) *n* a person who locates the cause of trouble and removes or treats it.
▸ **'troubleˌshooting** *n, adj*

troublesome ('trʌbᵊlsəm) *adj* **1** causing trouble. **2** characterized by violence; turbulent.
▸ **'troublesomeness** *n*

troublous ('trʌbləs) *adj Arch. or literary.* unsettled; agitated.
▸ **'troublously** *adv*

trough (trɒf) *n* **1** a narrow open container, esp. one in which food or water for animals is put. **2** a narrow channel, gutter, or gulley. **3** a narrow depression, as between two waves. **4** *Meteorol.* an elongated area of low pressure. **5** a single or temporary low point; depression. **6** *Physics.* the portion of a wave in which the amplitude lies below its average value. **7** *Econ.* the lowest point of the trade cycle. ORIG OE *trōh*

trounce (trauns) *vb* **trounces, trouncing, trounced.** (*tr*) to beat or defeat utterly; thrash. ORIG C16: from ?

troupe (truːp) *n* **1** a company of actors or other performers, esp. one that travels. ◆ *vb* **troupes, trouping, trouped. 2** (*intr*) (esp. of actors) to move or travel in a group. ORIG C19: from F; see TROOP

trouper ('truːpə) *n* **1** a member of a troupe. **2** a dependable worker or associate.

trouser ('trauzə) *n* (*modifier*) **1** of or relating to trousers: *trouser buttons.* ◆ *vb* **2** (*tr*) *Sl.* to take (something, esp. money), often surreptitiously or unlawfully.

trousers ('trauzəz) *pl n* a garment shaped to cover the body from the waist to the ankles or knees with separate tube-shaped sections for both legs. ORIG C17: from earlier *trouse,* var. of TREWS, infl. by DRAWERS

trousseau ('truːsəu) *n, pl* **trousseaux** *or* **trousseaus** (-səuz). the clothes, linen, etc., collected by a bride for her marriage. ORIG C19: from OF, lit.: a little bundle; see TRUSS

trout (traut) *n, pl* **trout** *or* **trouts.** any of various game fishes, mostly of fresh water in northern regions. They are related to the salmon but are smaller and spotted. ORIG OE *trūht,* from LL *tructa,* from Gk *troktēs* sharp-toothed fish

trouvère (truː'vɛə) *n* any of a group of poets of N France during the 12th and 13th centuries who composed chiefly narrative works. ORIG C19: from F, from OF *troveor,* from *trover* to compose

trove (trəuv) *n* See **treasure-trove.**

trow (trəu) *vb Arch.* to think, believe, or trust. ORIG OE *treow*

Trowbridge ★ ('trəuˌbrɪdʒ) *n* a market town in SW England, administrative centre of Wiltshire: woollen manufacturing. Pop.: 29 334 (1991).

trowel ('trauəl) *n* **1** any of various small hand tools having a flat metal blade attached to a handle, used for scooping or spreading plaster or similar materials. **2** a similar tool with a curved blade used by gardeners for lifting plants, etc. ◆ *vb* **trowels, trowelling, trowelled** *or US* **trowels, troweling, troweled. 3** (*tr*) to use a trowel on. ORIG C14: from OF *truele,* from L *trulla* a scoop, from *trua* a stirring spoon

Troy ★ (trɔɪ) *n* any of nine ancient cities in NW Asia Minor, each of which was built on the ruins of its predecessor. The seventh was the site of the Trojan War (mid-13th century B.C.). Greek name: **Ilion.** Latin name: **Ilium.**

Troyes ★ (*French* trwa) *n* an industrial city in NE France: became prosperous through its great fairs in the early Middle Ages. Pop.: 59 271 (1990).

troy weight *or* **troy** (trɔɪ) *n* a system of weights used for precious metals and gemstones, based on the grain. 24 grains = 1 pennyweight; 20 pennyweights = 1 (troy) ounce; 12 ounces = 1 (troy) pound. ORIG C14: after TROYES, where first used

trs *Printing. abbrev. for* transpose.

Trst ★ (trst) *n* the Slovene and Serbo-Croat name for **Trieste.**

truant ('truːənt) *n* **1** a person who is absent without leave, esp. from school. ◆ *adj* **2** being or relating to a truant. ◆ *vb* **3** (*intr*) to play truant. ORIG C13: from OF: vagabond, prob. of Celtic origin
▸ **'truancy** *n*

truce (truːs) *n* **1** an agreement to stop fighting, esp. temporarily. **2** temporary cessation of something unpleasant. ORIG C13: from pl of OE *treow* trow

Trucial States ★ ('truːʃəl) *pl n* a former name (until 1971) of the **United Arab Emirates.** Also called: **Trucial Sheikdoms, Trucial Oman, Trucial Coast.**

truck[1] (trʌk) *n* **1** *Brit.* a vehicle for carrying freight on a railway; wagon. **2** another name (esp. US, Canad., Austral., and NZ) for **lorry. 3** Also called: **truckload.** the amount carried by a truck. **4** a frame carrying two or more pairs of wheels attached under an end of a railway coach, etc. **5** *Naut.* a disc-shaped block fixed to the head of a mast having holes for receiving halyards. **6** any wheeled vehicle used to move goods. ◆ *vb* **7** to convey (goods) in a truck. **8** (*intr*) *Chiefly US & Canad.* to drive a truck. ORIG C17: ? shortened from *truckle* a small wheel

truck[2] (trʌk) *n* **1** commercial goods. **2** dealings (esp. in **have no truck with**). **3** commercial exchange. **4** *Arch.* payment of wages in kind. **5** miscellaneous articles. **6** *Inf.* rubbish. **7** *US & Canad.* vegetables grown for market. ◆ *vb* **8** *Arch.* to exchange (goods); barter. **9** (*intr*) to traffic or negotiate. ORIG C13: from OF *troquer* (unattested) to barter, equivalent to Med. L *trocare,* from ?

trucker ('trʌkə) *n Chiefly US & Canad.* **1** a lorry driver. **2** a person who arranges for the transport of goods by lorry.

truck farm *n US & Canad.* a market garden.
▸ **truck farmer** *n* ▸ **truck farming** *n*

truckie ('trʌkɪ) *n Austral. & NZ inf.* a truck driver.

trucking ('trʌkɪŋ) *n Chiefly US & Canad.* the transportation of goods by lorry.

truckle ('trʌkᵊl) *vb* **truckles, truckling, truckled.** (*intr;* usually foll. by *to*) to yield weakly; give in. ORIG C17: from obs. *truckle* to sleep in a truckle bed
▸ **'truckler** *n*

truckle bed *n* a low bed on wheels, stored under a larger bed. ORIG C17: from *truckle* small wheel, ult. from L *trochlea* sheaf of a pulley

truck system *n* a system during the early years of the Industrial Revolution of forcing workers to accept payment of wages in kind.

truculent ('trʌkjulənt) *adj* **1** defiantly aggressive, sullen, or obstreperous. **2** *Arch.* savage, fierce, or harsh. ORIG C16: from L *truculentus,* from *trux* fierce
▸ **'truculence** *or* **'truculency** *n* ▸ **'truculently** *adv*

Trudeau ★ (truː'dəu) *n* **Pierre Elliott.** 1919–2000, Canadian statesman; Liberal prime minister (1968–79; 1980–84).

trudge (trʌdʒ) *vb* **trudges, trudging, trudged. 1** (*intr*) to walk or plod heavily or wearily. **2** (*tr*) to pass through or over by trudging. ◆ *n* **3** a long tiring walk. ORIG C16: from ?
▸ **'trudger** *n*

trudgen ('trʌdʒən) *n* a type of swimming stroke that uses overarm action, as in the crawl, and a scissors kick. ORIG C19: after John *Trudgen,* E swimmer, who introduced it

true (truː) *adj* **truer, truest. 1** not false, fictional, or illusory; factual; conforming with reality. **2** (*prenominal*) real; not synthetic. **3** faithful and loyal. **4** conforming to a required standard, law, or pattern: *a true aim.* **5** exactly in tune. **6** (of a compass bearing) according to the earth's

geographical rather than magnetic poles: *true north*. **7** *Biol.* conforming to the typical structure of a designated type. **8** *Physics.* not apparent or relative. ◆ *n* **9** correct alignment (esp. in **in true, out of true**). ◆ *adv* **10** truthfully; rightly. **11** precisely or unswervingly. ◆ *vb* **trues, truing, trued. 12** (*tr*) to adjust so as to make true. ORIG OE *triewe*
▸ **'trueness** *n*

true bill *n* (formerly in Britain; now US) the endorsement made on a bill of indictment by a grand jury certifying it to be supported by sufficient evidence to warrant a trial.

true-blue *adj* **1** unwaveringly or staunchly loyal. ◆ *n* **true blue. 2** *Chiefly Brit.* a staunch royalist or Conservative.

true-life *adj* directly comparable to reality: *a true-life story.*

truelove ('truːˌlʌv) *n* **1** someone truly loved; sweetheart. **2** another name for **herb Paris.**

truelove knot *or* **true-lovers' knot** *n* a complicated bowknot that is hard to untie, symbolizing ties of love.

Trueman ★ ('truːmən) *n* **Fred(die)**, full name *Frederick Sewards Trueman.* born 1931, English cricketer, a fast bowler for Yorkshire and England.

true north *n* the direction from any point along a meridian towards the North Pole. Also called: **geographic north.** Cf. **magnetic north.**

true rib *n* any of the upper seven pairs of ribs in man.

true time *n* the time shown by a sundial.

Truffaut ★ (*French* tryfo) *n* **François** (frɑ̃swa). 1932–84, French New Wave film director. His films include *Jules et Jim* (1961) and *Le Dernier Métro* (1980).

truffle ('trʌfᵊl) *n* **1** any of various edible subterranean European fungi. They have a tuberous appearance and are regarded as a delicacy. **2** Also called: **rum truffle.** *Chiefly Brit.* a sweet resembling this fungus in shape, flavoured with chocolate or rum. ORIG C16: from F *truffe,* from OProvençal *trufa,* ult. from L *tūber*

trug (trʌg) *n* a long shallow basket for carrying flowers, fruit, etc. ORIG C16: ? var. of TROUGH

trugo ('truːgəʊ) *n Austral.* a game similar to croquet, originally improvised in Victoria from the rubber discs used as buffers on railway carriages. ORIG from *true go,* when the wheel is hit between the goalposts

truism ('truːɪzəm) *n* an obvious truth; platitude.
▸ **tru'istic** *adj*

Trujillo ★ (*Spanish* tru'xijo) *n* a city in NW Peru: founded 1535; university (1824); centre of a district producing rice and sugar cane. Pop.: 627 553 (1995).

Truk Islands ★ (trʌk) *pl n* a group of islands in the W Pacific, in the E Caroline Islands: administratively part of the US Trust Territory of the Pacific Islands from 1947; became self-governing in 1979 as part of the Federated States of Micronesia; consists of 11 chief islands; a major Japanese naval base during World War II. Pop.: 52 870 (1994). Area: 130 sq. km (50 sq. miles).

trull (trʌl) *n Arch.* a prostitute; harlot. ORIG C16: from G *Trulle*

truly ('truːlɪ) *adv* **1** in a true, just, or faithful manner. **2** (intensifier): *a truly great man.* **3** indeed; really.

Truman ★ ('truːmən) *n* **Harry S.** 1884–1972, US Democratic statesman; 33rd president of the US (1945–53). He approved the dropping of atomic bombs on Japan (1945) and involved the US in the Korean War.

trumeau (truˈməʊ) *n, pl* **trumeaux** (-məʊz). *Archit.* a section of a wall or pillar between two openings. ORIG from F

trump[1] (trʌmp) *n* **1** Also called: **trump card. 1a** any card from the suit chosen as trumps. **1b** this suit itself; trumps. **2** a decisive or advantageous move, resource, action, etc. **3** *Inf.* a fine or reliable person. ◆ *vb* **4** to play a trump card on (a suit, or a particular card of a suit, that is not trumps). **5** (*tr*) to outdo or surpass. ◆ See also **trumps, trump up.** ORIG C16: var. of TRIUMPH

trump[2] (trʌmp) *n Arch. or literary.* **1** a trumpet or the sound produced by one. **2 the last trump.** the final trumpet call on the Day of Judgment. ORIG C13: from OF *trompe,* from OHG *trumpa* trumpet

trumpery ('trʌmpərɪ) *n, pl* **trumperies. 1** foolish talk or actions. **2** a useless or worthless article; trinket. ◆ *adj* **3** useless or worthless. ORIG C15: from OF *tromperie* deceit, from *tromper* to cheat

trumpet ('trʌmpɪt) *n* **1** a valved brass instrument of brilliant tone consisting of a narrow tube ending in a flared bell. **2** any similar instrument, esp. a straight instrument used for fanfares, signals, etc. **3** a loud sound such as that of a trumpet, esp. when made by an animal. **4** an eight-foot reed stop on an organ. **5** something resembling a trumpet in shape. **6** short for **ear trumpet. 7 blow one's own trumpet.** to boast about one's own skills or good qualities. ◆ *vb* **trumpets, trumpeting, trumpeted. 8** to proclaim or sound loudly. ORIG C13: from OF *trompette* a little TRUMP[2]

trumpeter ('trʌmpɪtə) *n* **1** a person who plays the trumpet, esp. one whose duty it is to play fanfares, signals, etc. **2** any of three birds of South America, having a rounded body, long legs, and a glossy blackish plumage. **3** (*sometimes cap.*) a breed of domestic fancy pigeon with a long ruff. **4** a large silvery-grey Australian marine food and game fish that grunts when taken from the water.

trumpeter swan *n* a large swan of W North America, having a white plumage and black bill.

trumps (trʌmps) *pl n* **1** (*sometimes sing*) *Cards.* any one of the four suits that outranks all the other suits for the duration of a deal or game. **2 turn up trumps.** (of a person) to bring about a happy or successful conclusion, esp. unexpectedly.

trump up *vb* (*tr, adv*) to invent (a charge, accusation, etc.) so as to deceive.

truncate *vb* (trʌŋ'keɪt, 'trʌŋkeɪt), **truncates, truncating, truncated. 1** (*tr*) to shorten by cutting. ◆ *adj* ('trʌŋkeɪt). **2** cut short; truncated. **3** *Biol.* having a blunt end. ORIG C15: from L *truncāre* to lop
▸ **trun'cation** *n*

truncated (trʌŋ'keɪtɪd) *adj* **1** (of a cone, prism, etc.) having an apex or end removed by a plane intersection. **2** shortened by or as if by cutting off; truncate.

truncheon ('trʌntʃən) *n* **1** *Chiefly Brit.* a club or cudgel formerly carried by a policeman. **2** a baton of office. ORIG C16: from OF *tronchon* stump, from L *truncus* trunk; see TRUNCATE

trundle ('trʌndᵊl) *vb* **trundles, trundling, trundled. 1** to move heavily on or as if on wheels: *the bus trundled by.* ◆ *n* **2** a trundling. **3** a small wheel or roller. ORIG OE *tryndel*

trundle bed *n* a less common word for **truckle bed.**

trundler ('trʌndlə) *n NZ.* **1** a trolley for shopping or one for golf clubs. **2** a child's pushchair.

trunk (trʌŋk) *n* **1** the main stem of a tree. **2** a large strong case or box used to contain clothes, etc., when travelling and for storage. **3** the body excluding the head, neck, and limbs; torso. **4** the elongated nasal part of an elephant. **5** the US and Canad. name for **boot**[1] (sense 2). **6** the main stem of a nerve, blood vessel, etc. **7** *Naut.* a watertight boxlike cover within a vessel, such as one used to enclose a centreboard. **8** an enclosed duct or passageway for ventilation, etc. **9** (*modifier*) of a main road, railway, etc., in a network: *a trunk line.* ◆ See also **trunks.** ORIG C15: from OF *tronc,* from L *truncus,* from *truncus* (adj) lopped

trunk call *n Chiefly Brit.* a long-distance telephone call.

trunk curl *n* another name for **sit-up.**

trunkfish ('trʌŋkˌfɪʃ) *n, pl* **trunkfish** *or* **trunkfishes.** any of a family of fishes having the body encased in bony plates.

trunk hose *n* a man's puffed-out breeches reaching to the thighs and worn with tights in the 16th century.

trunking ('trʌŋkɪŋ) *n* **1** *Telecomm.* the cables that take a common route through a telephone exchange building. **2** plastic housing used to conceal wires, etc.; casing. **3** the delivery of goods over long distances, esp. by road vehicles to local distribution centres.

trunk line *n* **1** a direct link between two telephone exchanges or switchboards that are a considerable distance apart. **2** the main route or routes on a railway.

trunk road *n Brit.* a main road, esp. one that is suitable for heavy vehicles.

trunks (trʌŋks) *pl n* **1** a man's garment worn for swimming, extending from the waist to the thigh. **2** shorts worn for some sports. **3** *Chiefly Brit.* men's underpants with legs that reach midthigh.

trunnion ('trʌnjən) *n* one of a pair of coaxial projections attached to opposite sides of a container, cannon, etc., to provide a support about which it can turn. ORIG C17: from OF *trognon* trunk

Truro ★ ('trʊərəʊ) *n* a market town in SW England, administrative centre of Cornwall. Pop.: 18 966 (1991).

truss (trʌs) *vb* (*tr*) **1** (sometimes foll. by *up*) to tie, bind, or bundle. **2** to bind the wings and legs of (a fowl) before cooking. **3** to support or stiffen (a roof, bridge, etc.) with structural members. **4** *Med.* to supply or support with a truss. ◆ *n* **5** a structural framework of wood or metal used to support a roof, bridge, etc. **6** *Med.* a device for holding a hernia in place, typically consisting of a pad held in position by a belt. **7** a cluster of flowers or fruit growing at the end of a single stalk. **8** *Naut.* a metal fitting fixed to a yard at its centre for holding it to a mast. **9** another name for **corbel**. **10** a bundle or pack. **11** *Chiefly Brit.* a bundle of hay or straw, esp. one having a fixed weight of 36, 56, or 60 pounds. ORIG C13: from OF *trousse,* from *trousser,* apparently from Vulgar L *torciāre* (unattested), from *torca* (unattested) a bundle

trust (trʌst) *n* **1** reliance on and confidence in the truth, worth, reliability, etc., of a person or thing; faith. Related adj: **fiducial**. **2** a group of commercial enterprises combined to control the market for any commodity. **3** the obligation of someone in a responsible position. **4** custody, charge, or care. **5** a person or thing in which confidence or faith is placed. **6** commercial credit. **7a** an arrangement whereby a person to whom the legal title to property is conveyed (the trustee) holds such property for the benefit of those entitled to the beneficial interest. **7b** property that is the subject of such an arrangement. Related adj: **fiduciary**. **8** (in the British National Health Service) a self-governing hospital, group of hospitals, or other body providing health-care services, which operates as an independent commercial unit within the NHS. **9** (*modifier*) of or relating to a trust or trusts. ◆ *vb* **10** (*tr; may take a clause as object*) to expect, hope, or suppose. **11** (when *tr, may take an infinitive;* when *intr,* often foll. by *in* or *to*) to place confidence in (someone to do something); rely (upon). **12** (*tr*) to consign for care. **13** (*tr*) to allow (someone to do something) with confidence in his or her good sense or honesty. **14** (*tr*) to extend business credit to. ORIG C13: from ON *traust*
▸ **'trustable** *adj* ▸ **'truster** *n*

trust account *n* **1** Also called: **trustee account**. a savings account deposited in the name of a trustee who controls it during his lifetime, after which the balance is payable to a prenominated beneficiary. **2** property under the control of a trustee or trustees.

trustafarian (ˌtrʌstə'fɛərɪən) *n* (*sometimes cap.*) *Brit. inf.* a wealthy young person with a supposedly ethnic lifestyle, often living in an impoverished part of a city. ORIG C20: from TRUST (FUND) + (RAST)AFARIAN

trustee (trʌ'stiː) *n* **1** a person to whom the legal title to property is entrusted. **2** a member of a board that manages the affairs of an institution or organization.

trustee in bankruptcy *n* a person entrusted with the administration of a bankrupt's affairs and with realizing his assets for the benefit of the creditors.

trustee investment *n Stock Exchange.* an investment in which trustees are authorized to invest money belonging to a trust fund.

trusteeship (trʌ'stiːʃɪp) *n* **1** the office or function of a trustee. **2a** the administration or government of a territory by a foreign country under the supervision of the **Trusteeship Council** of the United Nations. **2b** (*often cap.*) any such dependent territory; trust territory.

trustful ('trʌstfʊl) *or* **trusting** *adj* characterized by a tendency or readiness to trust others.
▸ **'trustfully** *or* **'trustingly** *adv*

trust fund *n* money, securities, etc., held in trust.

trust territory *n* (*sometimes cap.*) another name for a **trusteeship** (sense 2b).

trustworthy ('trʌstˌwɜːðɪ) *adj* worthy of being trusted; honest, reliable, or dependable.
▸ **'trustˌworthily** *adv* ▸ **'trustˌworthiness** *n*

trusty ('trʌstɪ) *adj* **trustier, trustiest. 1** faithful or reliable. ◆ *n, pl* **trusties. 2** a trustworthy convict given special privileges.
▸ **'trustily** *adv* ▸ **'trustiness** *n*

truth (truːθ) *n* **1** the quality of being true, genuine, actual, or factual. **2** something that is true as opposed to false. **3** a proven or verified fact, principle, etc.: *the truths of astronomy.* **4** (*usually pl*) a system of concepts purporting to represent some aspect of the world: *the truths of religion.* **5** fidelity to a standard or law. **6** faithful reproduction or portrayal. **7** honesty. **8** accuracy, as in the setting of a mechanical instrument. **9** loyalty. ◆ Related adjs.: **veritable, veracious**. ORIG OE *triewth*
▸ **'truthless** *adj*

truth drug *or* **serum** *n Inf.* any of various drugs supposed to have the property of making people tell the truth, as by relaxing them.

truthful ('truːθfʊl) *adj* **1** telling the truth; honest. **2** realistic: *a truthful portrayal of the king.*
▸ **'truthfully** *adv* ▸ **'truthfulness** *n*

truth-function *n Logic.* a function that determines the truth-value of a complex sentence solely in terms of the truth-values of the component sentences without reference to their meaning.

truth set *n Logic, maths.* the set of values that satisfy an open sentence, equation, inequality, etc., having no unique solution. Also called: **solution set**.

truth table *n* **1** a table, used in logic, indicating the truth-value of a compound statement for every truth-value of its component propositions. **2** a similar table, used in transistor technology, to indicate the value of the output signal of a logic circuit for every value of input signal.

truth-value *n Logic.* either of the values, true or false, that may be taken by a statement.

try (traɪ) *vb* **tries, trying, tried. 1** (when *tr, may take an infinitive,* sometimes with *to* replaced by *and*) to make an effort or attempt. **2** (*tr;* often foll. by *out*) to sample, test, or give experimental use to (something). **3** (*tr*) to put strain or stress on: *he tries my patience.* **4** (*tr; often passive*) to give pain, affliction, or vexation to. **5a** to examine and determine the issues involved in (a cause) in a court of law. **5b** to hear evidence in order to determine the guilt or innocence of (an accused). **6** (*tr*) to melt (fat, lard, etc.) in order to separate out impurities. ◆ *n, pl* **tries. 7** an experiment or trial. **8** an attempt or effort. **9** *Rugby.* the act of an attacking player touching the ball down behind the opposing team's goal line. **10** *American football.* an attempt made after a touchdown to score an extra point, as by kicking a goal. ◆ See also **try on, try out**. ORIG C13: from OF *trier* to sort, from ?

USAGE NOTE See at **and**.

trying ('traɪɪŋ) *adj* upsetting, difficult, or annoying.
▸ **'tryingly** *adv*

trying plane *n* a plane with a long body for planing the edges of long boards. Also called: **try plane**.

try on *vb* (*tr, adv*) **1** to put on (a garment) to find out whether it fits, etc. **2 try it on.** *Inf.* to attempt to deceive or fool someone. ◆ *n* **try-on. 3** *Brit. inf.* something done to test out a person's tolerance, etc.

try out *vb* (*adv*) **1** (*tr*) to test or put to experimental use. **2** (when *intr,* usually foll. by *for*) *US & Canad.* (of an athlete, actor, etc.) to undergo a test or to submit (an athlete, actor, etc.) to a test in order to determine suitability for a place in a team, an acting role, etc. ◆ *n* **tryout. 3** *Chiefly US & Canad.* a trial or test, as of an athlete or actor.

trypanosome ('trɪpənəˌsəʊm) *n* any parasitic flagellate protozoan that lives in the blood of vertebrates and causes sleeping sickness and certain other diseases. ORIG C19: from NL *Trypanosoma,* from Gk *trupanon* borer + *sōma* body

trypanosomiasis (ˌtrɪpənəsəˈmaɪəsɪs) *n* any infection of an animal or human with a trypanosome.

trypsin (ˈtrɪpsɪn) *n* a digestive enzyme in the pancreatic juice: it catalyses the hydrolysis of proteins to peptides. ORIG C19 *tryp-*, from Gk *tripsis* a rubbing, from *tribein* to rub + -IN; from the fact that it was orig. produced by rubbing the pancreas with glycerine
▸ **tryptic** (ˈtrɪptɪk) *adj*

tryptophan (ˈtrɪptəˌfæn) *n* an essential amino acid; a component of proteins necessary for growth. ORIG C20: from *trypt(ic)*, from TRYPSIN + *-o-* + *-phan*, var. of -PHANE

trysail (ˈtraɪˌseɪl; *Naut.* ˈtraɪsᵊl) *n* a small fore-and-aft sail set on a sailing vessel in foul weather to help keep her head to the wind.

try square *n* a device for testing or laying out right angles, usually consisting of a metal blade fixed at right angles to a wooden handle.

tryst (trɪst, traɪst) *n Arch. or literary.* **1** an appointment to meet, esp. secretly. **2** the place of such a meeting or the meeting itself. ORIG C14: from OF *triste* lookout post, apparently from ON

Tsana ★ (ˈtsɑːnə) *n* **Lake.** another name for (Lake) **Tana.**

tsar *or* **czar** (zɑː) *n* **1** (until 1917) the emperor of Russia. **2** a tyrant; autocrat. **3** *Inf.* a public official charged with responsibility for dealing with a certain problem or issue: *the drugs tsar.* ORIG C17: from Russian *tsar,* via Gothic *kaisar* from L: CAESAR
▸ ˈ**tsardom** *or* ˈ**czardom** *n*

tsarevitch *or* **czarevitch** (ˈzɑːrəvɪtʃ) *n* a son of a Russian tsar, esp. the eldest son. ORIG from Russian *tsarevich,* from TSAR + *-evich,* masc. patronymic suffix

tsarevna *or* **czarevna** (zɑːˈrɛvnə) *n* **1** a daughter of a Russian tsar. **2** the wife of a Russian tsarevitch. ORIG from Russian, from TSAR + *-evna,* fem. patronymic suffix

tsarina, czarina (zɑːˈriːnə) *or* **tsaritsa, czaritza** (zɑːˈrɪtsə) *n* the wife of a Russian tsar; Russian empress. ORIG from It., Sp. *czarina,* from G *Czarin*

tsarism *or* **czarism** (ˈzɑːrɪzəm) *n* a system of government by a tsar.
▸ ˈ**tsarist** *or* ˈ**czarist** *n, adj*

Tsaritsyn ★ (*Russian* tsaˈritsin) *n* a former name (until 1925) of **Volgograd.**

TSE (in Canada) *abbrev. for* Toronto Stock Exchange.

Tselinograd ★ (*Russian* tsəlɪnaˈgrat) *n* a former name (1961–94) of **Akmola.**

tsetse fly *or* **tzetze fly** (ˈtsɛtsɪ) *n* any of various bloodsucking African dipterous flies which transmit various diseases, esp. sleeping sickness. ORIG C19: via Afrik. from Tswana

T-shirt *or* **tee-shirt** *n* a lightweight simple garment for the upper body, usually short-sleeved. ORIG from T-shape formed when laid out flat

Tshombe ★ (ˈtʃɒmbɪ) *n* **Moise** (məʊˈiːz). 1919–69, Congolese statesman. He led the secession of Katanga (1960) from the newly independent Congo; exiled in 1963, he returned as premier of the Congo (1964–65); died in exile.

Tsinan ★ (ˈtsiːˈnæn) *n* a variant transliteration of the Chinese name for **Jinan.**

Tsinghai ★ (ˈtsɪŋˈhaɪ) *n* **1** a variant transliteration of the Chinese name for **Qinghai.** **2** a variant transliteration of the Chinese name for **Koko Nor.**

Tsingtao ★ (ˈtsɪŋˈtaʊ) *n* a variant transliteration of the Chinese name for **Qingdao.**

Tsingyuan (ˈtsɪŋˈjwɑːn) *or* **Ch'ing-yüan** ★ *n* the former name of **Baoding.**

Tsitsihar ★ (ˈtsɪtsɪˌhɑː) *n* a variant transliteration of the Chinese name for **Qiqihar.**

tsotsi (ˈtsɒtsɪ) *n, pl* **tsotsis.** *S. African inf.* a Black street thug or gang member; wide boy. ORIG C20: ?from Nguni *tsotsa* to dress flashily

tsp. *abbrev. for* teaspoon.

T-square *n* a T-shaped ruler used for drawing horizontal lines and to support set squares when drawing vertical and inclined lines.

T-stop *n* a setting of the lens aperture on a camera calibrated photometrically and assigned a T-number.

Tsugaru Strait ★ (ˈtsugɑˌru) *n* a channel between N Honshu and S Hokkaido islands, Japan. Width: about 30 km (20 miles).

tsunami (tsʊˈnɑːmɪ) *n, pl* **tsunamis** *or* **tsunami.** a large, often destructive sea wave produced by a submarine earthquake, subsidence, or volcanic eruption. ORIG from Japanese, from *tsu* port + *nami* wave

Tsushima ★ (ˈtsuːʃiːˌmɑː) *n* a group of five rocky islands between Japan and South Korea, in the Korea Strait: administratively part of Japan; scene of a naval defeat for the Russians (1905) during the Russo-Japanese war. Pop.: 50 810 (1980). Area: 698 sq. km (269 sq. miles).

tsutsugamushi disease (ˌtsʊtsʊgəˈmʊʃɪ) *n* one of the five major groups of acute infectious rickettsial diseases affecting man, common in Asia. It is transmitted by the bite of mites. ORIG from Japanese, from *tsutsuga* disease + *mushi* insect

Tswana (ˈtswɑːnə) *n* **1** (*pl* **Tswana** *or* **Tswanas**) a member of a mixed Negroid and Bushman people of southern Africa, living chiefly in Botswana. **2** the language of this people.

TT *abbrev. for:* **1** teetotal. **2** teetotaller. **3** telegraphic transfer: a method of sending money abroad by cabled transfer between banks. **4** Tourist Trophy (annual motorcycle races held in the Isle of Man). **5** tuberculin-tested.

TTL *abbrev. for:* **1** transistor transistor logic: a method of constructing electronic logic circuits. **2** through-the-lens: denoting a system of light metering in cameras.

TU *abbrev. for* trade union.

Tu. *abbrev. for* Tuesday.

Tuamotu Archipelago ★ (ˌtuːəˈməʊtuː) *n* a group of about 80 coral islands in the S Pacific, in French Polynesia. Pop.: 11 793 (1983). Area: 860 sq. km (332 sq. miles). Also called: **Low Archipelago, Paumotu Archipelago.**

tuatara (ˌtuːəˈtɑːrə) *n* a lizard-like reptile occurring on certain islands near New Zealand. ORIG C19: from Maori, from *tua* back + *tara* spine

tub (tʌb) *n* **1** a low wide open container, typically round: used in a variety of domestic and industrial situations. **2** a small plastic or cardboard container of similar shape for ice cream, margarine, etc. **3** another word (esp. US) for **bath** (sense 1). **4** Also called: **tubful.** the amount a tub will hold. **5** a clumsy slow boat or ship. **6a** a small vehicle on rails for carrying loads in a mine. **6b** a container for lifting coal or ore up a mine shaft. ◆ *vb* **tubs, tubbing, tubbed.** **7** *Brit. inf.* to wash (oneself) in a tub. **8** (*tr*) to keep or put in a tub. ORIG C14: from MDu. *tubbe*
▸ ˈ**tubbable** *adj* ▸ ˈ**tubber** *n*

tuba (ˈtjuːbə) *n, pl* **tubas** *or* **tubae** (-biː). **1** a valved brass instrument of bass pitch, in which the bell points upwards and the mouthpiece projects at right angles. **2** a powerful reed stop on an organ. ORIG L

tubal (ˈtjuːbᵊl) *adj* **1** of or relating to a tube. **2** of, relating to, or developing in a Fallopian tube.

Tubal-cain ★ (ˈtjuːbᵊlˌkeɪn) *n Old Testament.* a son of Lamech, said in Genesis 4:22 to be the first craftsman in metals.

tubby (ˈtʌbɪ) *adj* **tubbier, tubbiest.** **1** plump. **2** shaped like a tub.
▸ ˈ**tubbiness** *n*

tube (tjuːb) *n* **1** a long hollow cylindrical object, used for the passage of fluids or as a container. **2** a collapsible cylindrical container of soft metal or plastic closed with a cap, used to hold viscous liquids or pastes. **3** *Anat.* **3a** short for **Eustachian tube** or **Fallopian tube.** **3b** any hollow cylindrical structure. **4** (*sometimes cap.*) *Brit.* **4a the tube.** an underground railway system, esp. that in London. US and Canad. equivalent: **subway.** **4b** the tunnels through which the railway runs. **5** *Electronics.* **5a** another name for **valve** (sense 3). **5b** See **electron tube, cathode-ray tube, television tube.** **6** *Sl., chiefly US.* a television set. **7** *Austral. sl.* a bottle or can of beer. **8** *Surfing.* the cylindrical passage formed when a wave breaks and the crest tips forward. ◆ *vb* **tubes, tubing, tubed.** (*tr*) **9** to supply with a tube. **10** to

convey in a tube. **11** to shape like a tube. ORIG C17: from L *tubus*
▸ **'tubeless** *adj*

tube foot *n* any of numerous tubular outgrowths of most echinoderms that are used for locomotion, to aid ingestion of food, etc.

tubeless tyre *n* a pneumatic tyre in which the outer casing makes an airtight seal with the rim of the wheel so that an inner tube is unnecessary.

tuber ('tju:bə) *n* **1** a fleshy underground stem or root. **2** *Anat.* a raised area; swelling. ORIG C17: from L *tūber* hump

tubercle ('tju:bəkᵊl) *n* **1** any small rounded nodule or elevation, esp. on the skin, on a bone, or on a plant. **2** any small rounded pathological lesion, esp. one characteristic of tuberculosis. ORIG C16: from L *tūberculum* a little swelling

tubercle bacillus *n* a rodlike bacterium that causes tuberculosis.

tubercular (tjʊ'bɜ:kjʊlə) *adj also* **tuberculous. 1** of or symptomatic of tuberculosis. **2** of or relating to a tubercle. **3** characterized by the presence of tubercles. ◆ *n* **4** a person with tuberculosis.

tuberculate (tjʊ'bɜ:kjʊlɪt) *adj* covered with tubercles.
▸ **tuˌbercu'lation** *n*

tuberculin (tjʊ'bɜ:kjʊlɪn) *n* a sterile liquid prepared from cultures of attenuated tubercle bacillus and used in the diagnosis of tuberculosis.

tuberculin-tested *adj* (of milk) produced by cows that have been certified as free of tuberculosis.

tuberculosis (tjʊˌbɜ:kjʊ'ləʊsɪs) *n* a communicable disease caused by infection with the tubercle bacillus, most frequently affecting the lungs. ORIG C19: from NL

tuberose ('tju:bəˌrəʊz) *n* a perennial Mexican agave plant having a tuberous root and fragrant white flowers. ORIG C17: from L *tūberōsus* full of lumps; from its root

tuberous ('tju:bərəs) *or* **tuberose** ('tju:bəˌrəʊs) *adj* **1** (of plants) forming, bearing, or resembling a tuber or tubers. **2** *Anat.* of or having warty protuberances or tubers. ORIG C17: from L *tūberōsus* full of knobs

tube worm *n* any of various worms that construct and live in a tube of sand, lime, etc.

tubifex ('tju:bɪˌfɛks) *n, pl* **tubifex** *or* **tubifexes.** any of a genus of small reddish freshwater worms. ORIG C19: from NL, from L *tubus* tube + *facere* to make

tubing ('tju:bɪŋ) *n* **1** tubes collectively. **2** a length of tube. **3** a system of tubes. **4** fabric in the form of a tube.

Tübingen ★ (*German* 'ty:bɪŋən) *n* a town in SW Germany, in Baden-Württemberg: university (1477). Pop.: 76 040 (1989 est.).

Tubman ★ ('tʌbmən) *n* **William Vacanarat Shadrach** (və'kænəˌræt 'ʃædræk). 1895–1971, Liberian statesman; president of Liberia (1944–71).

tub-thumper *n* a noisy, violent, or ranting public speaker.
▸ **'tub-ˌthumping** *adj, n*

Tubuai Islands ★ (ˌtu:bu:'aɪ) *pl n* a chain of small islands extending about 1400 km (850 miles) in the S Pacific, in French Polynesia; discovered by Captain Cook in 1777; annexed by France in 1880. Pop.: 6509 (1988). Area: 173 sq. km (67 sq. miles). Also called: **Austral Islands.**

tubular ('tju:bjʊlə) *adj* **1** Also: **tubiform** ('tju:bɪˌfɔ:m). having the form of a tube or tubes. **2** of or relating to a tube or tubing.

tubular bells *pl n* a set of long tubes of brass tuned for use in an orchestra and struck with a mallet to simulate the sound of bells.

tubule ('tju:bju:l) *n* any small tubular structure, esp. in an animal body. ORIG C17: from L *tubulus* a little TUBE

TUC (in Britain) *abbrev. for* Trades Union Congress.

tuck (tʌk) *vb* **1** (*tr*) to push or fold into a small confined space or concealed place or between two surfaces. **2** (*tr*) to thrust the loose ends or sides of (something) into a confining space, so as to make neat and secure. **3** to make a tuck or tucks in (a garment). **4** (*usually tr*) to draw together, contract, or pucker. ◆ *n* **5** a tucked object or part. **6** a pleat or fold in a part of a garment, usually stitched down. **7** the part of a vessel where the planks meet at the sternpost. **8** *Brit. inf.* **8a** food, esp. cakes and sweets. **8b** (*as modifier*): *a tuck box.* **9** a position of the body, as in certain dives, in which the legs are bent with the knees drawn up against the chest and tightly clasped. ◆ See also **tuck away, tuck in.** ORIG C14: from OE *tūcian* to torment

tuck away *vb* (*tr, adv*) *Inf.* **1** to eat (a large amount of food). **2** to store, esp. in a place difficult to find.

tucker[1] ('tʌkə) *n* **1** a person or thing that tucks. **2** a detachable yoke of lace, linen, etc., often white, worn over the breast, as of a low-cut dress. **3** *Austral. & NZ. old-fashioned* an informal word for **food.**

tucker[2] ('tʌkə) *vb* (*tr; often passive;* usually foll. by *out*) *Inf., chiefly US & Canad.* to weary or tire.

tucker-bag *or* **tuckerbox** ('tʌkəˌbɒks) *n Austral. old-fashioned sl.* a bag or box in which food is carried or stored.

tucket ('tʌkɪt) *n Arch.* a flourish on a trumpet. ORIG C16: from OF *toquer* to sound (on a drum)

tuck in *vb* (*adv*) **1** (*tr*) Also: **tuck into.** to put to bed and make snug. **2** (*tr*) to thrust the loose ends or sides of (something) into a confining space: *tuck the blankets in.* **3** (*intr*) Also: **tuck into.** *Inf.* to eat, esp. heartily. ◆ *n* **tuck-in. 4** *Brit. inf.* a meal, esp. a large one.

tuck shop *n Chiefly Brit.* a shop, esp. one near a school, where cakes and sweets are sold.

Tucson ★ ('tu:sɒn) *n* a city in SE Arizona, at an altitude of 700m (2400 ft): resort and seat of the University of Arizona (1891). Pop.: 434 726 (1994 est.).

Tucumán ★ (*Spanish* tuku'man) *n* a city in NW Argentina: scene of the declaration (1816) of Argentinian independence from Spain; university (1914). Pop.: 642 473 (1992 est.).

-tude *suffix forming nouns.* indicating state or condition: *plenitude.* ORIG from L *-tūdō*

Tudor ('tju:də) *n* **1** an English royal house (1485–1603), consisting of Henry VII, Henry VIII, Edward VI, Mary I, and Elizabeth I, descended from a Welsh squire, **Owen Tudor** (died 1461). ◆ *adj* **2** denoting a style of architecture of this period, characterized by half-timbered houses.

Tues. *abbrev. for* Tuesday.

Tuesday ('tju:zdɪ) *n* the third day of the week; second day of the working week. ORIG OE *tīwesdæg*

tufa ('tju:fə) *n* a porous rock formed of calcium carbonate deposited from springs. ORIG C18: from It. *tufo,* from LL *tōfus*
▸ **tufaceous** (tju:'feɪʃəs) *adj*

tuff (tʌf) *n* a hard volcanic rock consisting of consolidated fragments of lava. ORIG C16: from OF *tuf,* from It. *tufo;* see TUFA
▸ **tuffaceous** (tʌ'feɪʃəs) *adj*

tuffet ('tʌfɪt) *n* a small mound or low seat. ORIG C16: alteration of TUFT

tuft (tʌft) *n* **1** a bunch of feathers, grass, hair, etc., held together at the base. **2** a cluster of threads drawn tightly through upholstery, a quilt, etc., to secure the padding. **3** a small clump of trees or bushes. **4** (formerly) a gold tassel on the cap worn by titled undergraduates at English universities. ◆ *vb* **5** (*tr*) to provide or decorate with a tuft or tufts. **6** to form or be formed into tufts. **7** to secure with tufts. ORIG C14: ?from OF *tufe,* of Gmc origin
▸ **'tufted** *adj* ▸ **'tufty** *adj*

tufted duck *n* a European lake-dwelling duck, the male of which has a black plumage with white underparts and a long black drooping crest.

tug (tʌg) *vb* **tugs, tugging, tugged. 1** (when *intr,* sometimes foll. by *at*) to pull or drag with sharp or powerful movements. **2** (*tr*) to tow (a vessel) by means of a tug. ◆ *n* **3** a strong pull or jerk. **4** Also called: **tugboat.** a boat with a powerful engine, used for towing barges, ships, etc. **5** a hard struggle or fight. ORIG C13: rel. to OE *tēon* to TOW[1]
▸ **'tugger** *n*

Tugela ★ (tu:'geɪlə) *n* a river in E South Africa, rising in the Drakensberg where it forms the **Tugela Falls,** 856 m (2810 ft) high, before flowing east to the Indian Ocean: scene of battles during the Zulu War (1879) and the Boer War (1899–1902). Length: about 500 km (312 miles).

tug-of-love *n* a conflict over custody of a child between divorced parents or between natural parents and foster or adoptive parents.

tug-of-war *n* **1** a contest in which two people or teams pull opposite ends of a rope in an attempt to drag the opposition over a central line. **2** any hard struggle between two factions.

tui ('tu:i:) *n, pl* **tuis.** a New Zealand songbird with white feathers at the throat. Also called: **parson bird.** ORIG from Maori

tuition (tju:'ɪʃən) *n* **1** instruction, esp. that received individually or in a small group. **2** the payment for instruction, esp. in colleges or universities. ORIG C15: from OF *tuicion,* from L *tuitiō* a guarding, from *tuērī* to watch over
▸ **tu'itional** *adj*

Tula ★ (*Russian* 'tulə) *n* an industrial city in W central Russia. Pop.: 532 000 (1995 est.).

tularaemia *or US* **tularemia** (ˌtu:lə'ri:mɪə) *n* an infectious disease of rodents, transmitted to man by infected ticks or flies or by handling contaminated flesh. ORIG C19/20: from NL, from *Tulare,* county in California where first observed
▸ **ˌtula'raemic** *or US* **ˌtula'remic** *adj*

tulip ('tju:lɪp) *n* **1** any of various spring-blooming bulb plants having long broad pointed leaves and single showy bell-shaped flowers. **2** the flower or bulb. ORIG C17: from NL *tulipa,* from Turkish *tülbend* turban, which the opened bloom was thought to resemble

tulip tree *n* **1** Also called: **tulip poplar.** a North American tree having tulip-shaped greenish-yellow flowers and long conelike fruits. **2** any of various other trees with tulip-shaped flowers, such as the magnolia.

tulipwood ('tju:lɪpˌwʊd) *n* **1** the light soft wood of the tulip tree, used in making furniture and veneer. **2** any of several woods having streaks of colour.

Tull ★ (tʌl) *n* **Jethro** ('dʒɛθrəʊ). 1674–1741, English agriculturalist, who invented the seed drill.

Tullamore ★ (ˌtʌlə'mɔ:) *n* the county town of Offaly, Republic of Ireland; food processing and brewing. Pop.: 8484 (1986).

tulle (tju:l) *n* a fine net fabric of silk, rayon, etc. ORIG C19: from F, from *Tulle,* city in S central France, where first manufactured

Tully ★ ('tʌlɪ) *n* the former English name for (Marcus Tullius) **Cicero.**

Tulsa ★ ('tʌlsə) *n* a city in NE Oklahoma, on the Arkansas River: a major oil centre; two universities. Pop.: 374 851 (1994 est.).

tumble ('tʌmbᵊl) *vb* **tumbles, tumbling, tumbled. 1** to fall or cause to fall, esp. awkwardly, precipitately, or violently. **2** (*intr;* usually foll. by *about*) to roll or twist, esp. in playing. **3** (*intr*) to perform leaps, somersaults, etc. **4** to move in a heedless or hasty way. **5** (*tr*) to polish (gemstones) in a tumbler. **6** (*tr*) to disturb, rumple, or toss around. ◆ *n* **7** a tumbling. **8** a fall or toss. **9** an acrobatic feat, esp. a somersault. **10** a state of confusion. **11** a confused heap or pile. ◆ See also **tumble to.** ORIG OE *tumbian*

tumbledown ('tʌmbᵊlˌdaʊn) *adj* falling to pieces; dilapidated; crumbling.

tumble dryer *or* **tumble drier** *n* a machine that dries wet laundry by rotating it in warmed air inside a metal drum. Also called: **tumbler dryer, tumbler.**

tumbler ('tʌmblə) *n* **1a** a flat-bottomed drinking glass with no handle or stem. **1b** Also called: **tumblerful.** its contents. **2** a person who performs somersaults and other acrobatic feats. **3** another name for **tumble dryer. 4** a box or drum rotated so that the contents (usually gemstones) become smooth and polished. **5** the part of a lock that retains or releases the bolt and is moved by the action of a key. **6** a lever in a gunlock that receives the action of the mainspring when the trigger is pressed and thus forces the hammer forwards. **7** a part that moves a gear in a train of gears into and out of engagement.

tumbler switch *n* a small electrical switch incorporating a spring, widely used in lighting.

tumble to *vb* (*intr, prep*) *Inf.* to understand; become aware of: *she tumbled to his plan quickly.*

tumbleweed ('tʌmbᵊlˌwi:d) *n* any of various densely branched American and Australian plants that break off near the ground on withering and are rolled about by the wind.

tumbrel *or* **tumbril** ('tʌmbrəl) *n* **1** a farm cart, esp. one that tilts backwards to deposit its load. A cart of this type was used to take condemned prisoners to the guillotine during the French Revolution. **2** (formerly) a covered cart used to carry ammunition, tools, etc. ORIG C14 *tumberell* ducking stool, from Med. L *tumbrellum,* from OF *tumberel* dump cart, ult. of Gmc origin

tumefacient (ˌtju:mɪ'feɪʃɪənt) *adj* producing or capable of producing swelling: *a tumefacient drug.* ORIG C16: from L *tumefacere* to cause to swell

tumefy ('tju:mɪˌfaɪ) *vb* **tumefies, tumefying, tumefied.** to make or become tumid; swell or puff up. ORIG C16: from F *tuméfier,* from L *tumefacere*
▸ **ˌtume'faction** *n*

tumescent (tju:'mɛsənt) *adj* swollen or becoming swollen. ORIG C19: from L *tumescere* to begin to swell, from *tumēre*
▸ **tu'mescence** *n*

tumid ('tju:mɪd) *adj* **1** enlarged or swollen. **2** bulging. **3** pompous or fulsome in style. ORIG C16: from L *tumidus,* from *tumēre* to swell
▸ **tu'midity** *or* **'tumidness** *n* ▸ **'tumidly** *adv*

tummy ('tʌmɪ) *n, pl* **tummies.** an informal or childish word for **stomach.** Also called: **tum.**

tummy tuck *n Inf.* the surgical removal of abdominal fat and skin for cosmetic purposes.

tumour *or US* **tumor** ('tju:mə) *n Pathol.* **a** any abnormal swelling. **b** a mass of tissue formed by a new growth of cells. ORIG C16: from L, from *tumēre* to swell
▸ **'tumorous** *adj*

tumult ('tju:mʌlt) *n* **1** a loud confused noise, as of a crowd; commotion. **2** violent agitation or disturbance. **3** great emotional agitation. ORIG C15: from L *tumultus,* from *tumēre* to swell up

tumultuous (tju:'mʌltjʊəs) *adj* **1** uproarious, riotous, or turbulent. **2** greatly agitated, confused, or disturbed. **3** making a loud or unruly disturbance.
▸ **tu'multuously** *adv* ▸ **tu'multuousness** *n*

tumulus ('tju:mjʊləs) *n, pl* **tumuli** (-li:). *Archaeol.* (*no longer in technical usage*) another word for **barrow**[2]. ORIG C17: from L: a hillock, from *tumēre* to swell up

tun (tʌn) *n* **1** a large beer cask. **2** a measure of capacity, usually equal to 252 wine gallons. ◆ *vb* **tuns, tunning, tunned. 3** (*tr*) to put into or keep in tuns. ORIG OE *tunne*

tuna[1] ('tju:nə) *n, pl* **tuna** *or* **tunas.** another name for **tunny** (sense 1). ORIG C20: from American Sp., from Sp. *atún,* from Ar. *tūn,* from L *thunnus* tunny, from Gk

tuna[2] ('tju:nə) *n* any of various tropical American prickly pear cacti. ORIG C16: via Sp. from Taino

tunable *or* **tuneable** ('tju:nəbᵊl) *adj* able to be tuned.

Tunbridge Wells ★ ('tʌnˌbrɪdʒ) *n* a town and resort in SE England, in SW Kent: chalybeate spring discovered in 1606. Pop.: 60 272 (1991). Official name: **Royal Tunbridge Wells.**

tundra ('tʌndrə) *n* a vast treeless zone lying between the ice cap and the timber line of North America and Eurasia and having a permanently frozen subsoil. ORIG C19: from Russian, from Lapp *tundar* hill

tune (tju:n) *n* **1** a melody, esp. one for which harmony is not essential. **2** the condition of producing accurately pitched notes, intervals, etc. (esp. in **in tune, out of tune**). **3** accurate correspondence of pitch and intonation between instruments (esp. in **in tune, out of tune**). **4** the correct adjustment of a radio, television, etc., with respect to the required frequency. **5** a frame of mind; mood. **6 call the tune.** to be in control of the proceedings. **7 change one's tune.** to alter one's attitude or tone of speech. **8 to the tune of.** *Inf.* to the amount or extent of. ◆ *vb* **tunes, tuning, tuned. 9** to adjust (a musical instrument) to a certain

pitch. **10** to adjust (a note, etc.) so as to bring it into harmony or concord. **11** (*tr*) to adapt or adjust (oneself); attune. **12** (*tr; often foll. by up*) to make fine adjustments to (an engine, machine, etc.) to obtain optimum performance. **13** *Electronics.* to adjust (one or more circuits) for resonance at a desired frequency. ◆ See also **tune in, tune up.** ORIG C14: var. of TONE
▸ **'tuner** *n*

tuneful ('tju:nfʊl) *adj* **1** having a pleasant tune; melodious. **2** producing a melody or music.
▸ **'tunefully** *adv* ▸ **'tunefulness** *n*

tune in *vb* (*adv; often foll. by to*) **1** to adjust (a radio or television) to receive (a station or programme). **2** *Sl.* to make or become more aware, knowledgeable, etc. (about).

tuneless ('tju:nlɪs) *adj* having no melody or tune.
▸ **'tunelessly** *adv* ▸ **'tunelessness** *n*

tune up *vb* (*adv*) **1** to adjust (a musical instrument) to a particular pitch. **2** to tune (instruments) to a common pitch. **3** (*tr*) to adjust (an engine) in (a car, etc.) to improve performance. ◆ *n* **tune-up. 4** adjustments made to an engine to improve its performance.

tung oil (tʌŋ) *n* a fast-drying oil obtained from the seeds of an Asian tree, used in paints, varnishes, etc. ORIG partial translation of Chinese *yu t'ung* tung tree oil, from *yu* oil + *t'ung* tung tree

tungsten ('tʌŋstən) *n* a hard malleable ductile greyish-white element. It is used in lamp filaments, electrical contact points, X-ray targets, and, alloyed with steel, in high-speed cutting tools. Symbol: W; atomic no.: 74; atomic wt.: 183.85. Also called: **wolfram.** ORIG C18: from Swedish *tung* heavy + *sten* stone

tungsten lamp *n* a lamp in which light is produced by a tungsten filament heated to incandescence by an electric current. Sometimes small amounts of a halogen, such as iodine, are added to improve the intensity (**tungsten-halogen lamp**).

tungsten steel *n* any of various hard steels containing tungsten and traces of carbon.

Tungting *or* **Tung-t'ing** ★ (ˌtʊŋ'tɪŋ) *n* a variant transliteration of the Chinese name for the **Dongting.**

Tungusic (tʊŋ'gʊsɪk) *n* a branch or subfamily of the Altaic family of languages, some of which are spoken in NE Asia.

Tunguska ★ (*Russian* tun'guskə) *n* any of three rivers in Russia, in central Siberia, all tributaries of the Yenisei: the **Lower** (Nizhnyaya) **Tunguska,** 2690 km (1670 miles) long; the **Stony** (Podkamennaya) **Tunguska,** 1550 km (960 miles) long; the **Upper** (Verkhnyaya) **Tunguska,** which is the lower course of the Angara.

tunic ('tju:nɪk) *n* **1** any of various hip-length or knee-length garments, such as the loose sleeveless garb worn in ancient Greece or Rome, the jacket of some soldiers, or a woman's hip-length garment, worn with a skirt or trousers. **2** a covering, lining, or enveloping membrane of an organ or part. **3** Also called: **tunicle.** a short vestment worn by a bishop or subdeacon. ORIG OE *tunice* (unattested except in the accusative case), from L *tunica*

tunicate ('tju:nɪkɪt, -ˌkeɪt) *n* **1** any of various minute primitive marine animals having a saclike unsegmented body enclosed in a cellulose-like outer covering. ◆ *adj also* **tunicated. 2** (esp. of a bulb) having concentric layers of tissue. ORIG C18: from L *tunicātus* clad in a TUNIC

tuning ('tju:nɪŋ) *n Music.* **1** a set of pitches to which the open strings of a guitar, violin, etc., are tuned. **2** the accurate pitching of notes and intervals by a choir, orchestra, etc.; intonation.

tuning fork *n* a two-pronged metal fork that when struck produces a pure note of constant specified pitch. It is used to tune musical instruments and in acoustics.

Tunis ★ ('tju:nɪs) *n* the capital and chief port of Tunisia, in the northeast on the **Gulf of Tunis** (an inlet of the Mediterranean): dates from Carthaginian times, the ruins of ancient Carthage lying to the northeast; university (1960). Pop.: 674 100 (1994).

Tunisia ★ (tju:'nɪzɪə, -'nɪsɪə) *n* a republic in N Africa, on the Mediterranean: settled by the Phoenicians in the 12th century B.C.; made a French protectorate in 1881 and gained independence in 1955. It consists chiefly of the Sahara in the south, a central plateau, and the Atlas Mountains in the north. Exports include petroleum, phosphates, and iron ore. Official language: Arabic; French is also widely spoken. Official religion: Muslim. Currency: dinar. Capital: Tunis. Pop.: 9 514 000 (1999 est.). Area: 164 150 sq. km (63 380 sq. miles).
▸ **Tu'nisian** *adj, n*

tunnage ('tʌnɪdʒ) *n* a variant spelling of **tonnage.**

tunnel ('tʌnᵊl) *n* **1** an underground passageway, esp. one for trains or cars. **2** any passage or channel through or under something. ◆ *vb* **tunnels, tunnelling, tunnelled** *or US* **tunnels, tunneling, tunneled. 3** (*tr*) to make or force (a way) through or under (something). **4** (*intr; foll. by through, under, etc.*) to make or force a way (through or under something). ORIG C15: from OF *tonel* cask, from *tonne* tun, from Med. L *tonna* barrel, of Celtic origin
▸ **'tunneller** *or US* **'tunneler** *n*

tunnel diode *n* an extremely stable semiconductor diode, having a very narrow highly doped p-n junction, in which electrons travel across the junction by means of the tunnel effect. Also called: **Esaki diode.**

tunnel effect *n Physics.* the phenomenon in which an object, usually an elementary particle, tunnels through a potential barrier even though it does not have sufficient energy to surmount it.

tunnel vision *n* **1** a condition in which peripheral vision is greatly restricted. **2** narrowness of viewpoint resulting from concentration on a single idea, opinion, etc.

tunny ('tʌnɪ) *n, pl* **tunnies** *or* **tunny. 1** Also called: **tuna.** any of a genus of large marine spiny-finned fishes, chiefly of warm waters. They are important food fishes. **2** any of various similar and related fishes. ORIG C16: from OF *thon,* from OProvençal *ton,* from L *thunnus,* from Gk

tup (tʌp) *n* **1** *Chiefly Brit.* a male sheep; ram. **2** the head of a pile-driver or steam hammer. ◆ *vb* **tups, tupping, tupped. 3** (*tr*) (of a ram) to mate with (a ewe). ORIG C14: from ?

Tupamaro (ˌtu:pə'mɑ:rəʊ) *n, pl* **Tupamaros.** any of a group of Marxist urban guerrillas in Uruguay. ORIG C20: after *Tupac Amaru,* 18th-century Peruvian Indian who led a rebellion against the Spaniards

tupelo ('tju:pɪˌləʊ) *n, pl* **tupelos. 1** any of several gum trees of the southern US. **2** the light strong wood of any of these trees. ORIG C18: from Creek *ito opilwa,* from *ito* tree + *opilwa* swamp

Tupi (tu:'pi:) *n* **1** (*pl* **Tupis** *or* **Tupi**) a member of a South American Indian people of Brazil and Paraguay. **2** their language.
▸ **Tu'pian** *adj*

tupik ('tu:pək) *n Canad.* a tent of seal or caribou skin used for shelter by the Inuit in summer. ORIG from Eskimo

Tupolev ★ (*Russian* 'tupəlɪf) *n* **Andrei Nikolaievich** (an'drjej nika'lajɪvitʃ). 1888–1972, Soviet engineer, who designed the first supersonic passenger aircraft.

tuppence ('tʌpəns) *n Brit.* a variant spelling of **twopence.**
▸ **'tuppenny** *adj*

Tupperware ('tʌpəweə) *n Trademark.* a range of plastic containers used for storing food. ORIG C20: *Tupper,* US manufacturing company + WARE[1]

Tupungato ★ (*Spanish* tupuŋ'gato) *n* a mountain on the border between Argentina and Chile, in the Andes. Height: 6550 m (21 484 ft).

tuque (tu:k) *n Canad.* **1** a knitted cap with a long tapering end. **2** Also called: **toque.** a close-fitting knitted hat often with a tassel or pompom. ORIG C19: from Canad. F, from F: TOQUE

turaco ('tʊərəˌkəʊ) *n, pl* **turacos.** a variant spelling of **touraco.**

Turanian (tjʊ'reɪnɪən) *n, adj* another name for **Ural-Altaic.**

turban ('tɜ:bᵊn) *n* **1** a man's headdress, worn esp. by Muslims, Hindus, and Sikhs, made by swathing a length of linen, silk, etc., around the head or around a caplike base. **2** a woman's brimless hat resembling this. **3** any

headdress resembling this. ORIG C16: from Turkish *tülbend,* from Persian *dulband*
▸ **'turbaned** *adj*

turbary ('tɜːbərɪ) *n, pl* **turbaries. 1** land where peat or turf is cut. **2** the legal right to cut peat for fuel on a common. ORIG C14: from OF *turbarie,* from Med. L *turbāria,* from *turba* peat

turbellarian (ˌtɜːbɪ'lɛərɪən) *n* **1** any of a class of flatworms having a ciliated epidermis and a simple life cycle. ◆ *adj* **2** of or belonging to this class of flatworms. ORIG C19: from NL *Turbellāria,* from L *turbellae* (pl) bustle, from *turba* brawl, referring to the swirling motion created in the water

turbid ('tɜːbɪd) *adj* **1** muddy or opaque, as a liquid clouded with a suspension of particles. **2** dense, thick, or cloudy: *turbid fog.* **3** in turmoil or confusion. ORIG C17: from L *turbidus,* from *turbāre* to agitate, from *turba* crowd
▸ **tur'bidity** *or* **'turbidness** *n* ▸ **'turbidly** *adv*

turbinate ('tɜːbɪnɪt, -ˌneɪt) *or* **turbinal** ('tɜːbɪnᵊl) *adj also* **turbinated. 1** *Anat.* of any of the scroll-shaped bones on the walls of the nasal passages. **2** shaped like a spiral or scroll. **3** shaped like an inverted cone. ◆ *n* **4** a turbinate bone. **5** a turbinate shell. ORIG C17: from L *turbō* spinning top
▸ **ˌturbi'nation** *n*

turbine ('tɜːbɪn, -baɪn) *n* any of various types of machine in which the kinetic energy of a moving fluid, as water, steam, air, etc., is converted into mechanical energy by causing a bladed rotor to rotate. ORIG C19: from F, from L *turbō* whirlwind, from *turbāre* to throw into confusion

turbine blade *n* any of a number of bladelike vanes assembled around the periphery of a turbine rotor to guide the steam or gas flow.

turbit ('tɜːbɪt) *n* a crested breed of domestic pigeon. ORIG C17: from L *turbō* spinning top, from the bird's shape

turbo- *combining form.* of, relating to, or driven by a turbine: *turbofan.*

turbocharger ('tɜːbəʊˌtʃɑːdʒə) *n* a centrifugal compressor which boosts the intake pressure of an internal-combustion engine, driven by an exhaust-gas turbine fitted to the engine's exhaust manifold.

turbofan (ˌtɜːbəʊ'fæn) *n* **1** a type of bypass engine in which a large fan driven by a turbine forces air rearwards around the exhaust gases in order to increase the propulsive thrust. **2** an aircraft driven by turbofans. **3** the fan in such an engine.

turbogenerator (ˌtɜːbəʊ'dʒɛnəˌreɪtə) *n* an electrical generator driven by a steam turbine.

turbojet (ˌtɜːbəʊ'dʒɛt) *n* **1** a turbojet engine. **2** an aircraft powered by turbojet engines.

turbojet engine *n* a gas turbine in which the exhaust gases provide the propulsive thrust to drive an aircraft.

turboprop (ˌtɜːbəʊ'prɒp) *n* **1** an aircraft propulsion unit where a propeller is driven by a gas turbine. **2** an aircraft powered by turboprops.

turbosupercharger (ˌtɜːbəʊ'suːpəˌtʃɑːdʒə) *n Obs.* a supercharging device for an internal-combustion engine, consisting of a turbine driven by the exhaust gases.

turbot ('tɜːbət) *n, pl* **turbot** *or* **turbots. 1** a European flatfish having a speckled scaleless body covered with tubercles. It is highly valued as a food fish. **2** any of various similar or related fishes. ORIG C13: from OF *tourbot,* from Med. L *turbō,* from L: spinning top, from a fancied similarity in shape

turbulence ('tɜːbjʊləns) *n* **1** a state or condition of confusion, movement, or agitation. **2** *Meteorol.* instability in the atmosphere causing gusty air currents and cumulonimbus clouds.

turbulent ('tɜːbjʊlənt) *adj* **1** being in a state of turbulence. **2** wild or insubordinate; unruly. ORIG C16: from L *turbulentus,* from *turba* confusion
▸ **'turbulently** *adv*

turd (tɜːd) *n Taboo.* **1** a piece of excrement. **2** *Sl.* a contemptible person or thing. ORIG OE *tord*

tureen (tə'riːn) *n* a large deep usually rounded dish with a cover, used for serving soups, stews, etc. ORIG C18: from F *terrine* earthenware vessel, from *terrin* made of earthenware, from Vulgar L *terrīnus* (unattested), from L *terra* earth

turf (tɜːf) *n, pl* **turfs** *or* **turves. 1** the surface layer of fields and pastures, consisting of earth containing a dense growth of grasses with their roots; sod. **2** a piece cut from this layer. **3 the turf. 3a** a track where horse races are run. **3b** horse racing as a sport or industry. **4** an area of knowledge or influence: *he's on home turf when it comes to music.* **5** another word for **peat.** ◆ *vb* **6** (*tr*) to cover with pieces of turf. ◆ See also **turf out.** ORIG OE

turf accountant *n Brit.* a formal name for a **bookmaker.**

turfman ('tɜːfmən) *n, pl* **turfmen.** *Chiefly US.* a person devoted to horse racing.

turf out *vb* (*tr, adv*) *Brit. inf.* to throw out or dismiss; eject.

turf war *n Inf.* **1** a dispute between criminals or gangs over the right to operate within a particular area. **2** any dispute in which parties contest influence or rights.

Turgenev ★ (*Russian* tur'gjenɪf) *n* **Ivan Sergeyevich** (i'van sɪr'gjejɪvitʃ). 1818–83, Russian writer. His novels include *Fathers and Sons* (1862) and his plays include *A Month in the Country* (1890).

turgescent (tɜː'dʒɛsᵊnt) *adj* becoming or being swollen; inflated; tumid.
▸ **tur'gescence** *n*

turgid ('tɜːdʒɪd) *adj* **1** swollen and distended. **2** (of language) pompous; bombastic. ORIG C17: from L *turgidus,* from *turgēre* to swell
▸ **tur'gidity** *or* **'turgidness** *n* ▸ **'turgidly** *adv*

turgor ('tɜːgə) *n* the normal rigid state of a cell, caused by pressure of the cell contents against the cell wall or membrane. ORIG C19: from LL: a swelling, from L *turgēre* to swell

Turin ★ (tjʊə'rɪn) *n* a city in NW Italy, capital of Piedmont region, on the River Po: became capital of the Kingdom of Sardinia in 1720; first capital (1861–65) of united Italy; university (1405); a major industrial centre, producing most of Italy's cars. Pop.: 923 106 (1996 est.). Italian name: **Torino.**

Turing ★ ('tjʊərɪŋ) *n* **Alan Mathison.** 1912–54, British mathematician, who was responsible for formal description of abstract automata.

Turing machine *n* a hypothetical universal computing machine able to modify its original instructions by reading, erasing, or writing a new symbol on a moving tape that acts as its program. ORIG C20: after A. M. TURING

turion ('tʊərɪən) *n* a scaly shoot produced by many aquatic plants: it detaches from the parent plant and remains dormant until the following spring. ORIG C17: from F *turion,* from L *turio* shoot

Turishcheva ★ (*Russian* tu'riʃtʃəvə) *n* **Ludmilla** (lud'mɪlə). born 1952, Soviet gymnast: world champion 1970, 1972, and 1974.

Turk (tɜːk) *n* **1** a native, inhabitant, or citizen of Turkey. **2** a native speaker of any Turkic language. **3** *Obs., derog.* a brutal or domineering person. See also **Young Turk.**

Turk. *abbrev. for:* **1** Turkey. **2** Turkish.

Turkana ★ (tɜː'kɑːnə) *n* **Lake.** a long narrow lake in E Africa, in the Great Rift Valley. Area: 7104 sq. km (2743 sq. miles). Former name: (Lake) **Rudolf.**

Turkestan *or* **Turkistan** ★ (ˌtɜːkɪ'stɑːn) *n* an extensive region of central Asia between Siberia in the north and Tibet, India, Afghanistan, and Iran in the south: formerly divided into **West** (**Russian**) **Turkestan** (also called Soviet Central Asia), which includes Turkmenistan, Uzbekistan, Tajikistan, and Kyrgyzstan and the S part of Kazakhstan, and **East** (**Chinese**) **Turkestan,** consisting of the Xinjiang Uygur Autonomous Republic.
▸ **ˌTurke'stani** *adj, n*

turkey ('tɜːkɪ) *n, pl* **turkeys** *or* **turkey. 1** a large bird of North America, having a bare wattled head and neck and a brownish plumage. The male has a fan-shaped tail. A domesticated variety is bred for its flesh. **2** *Inf.* something, esp. a film or theatrical production, that fails. **3** See **cold turkey. 4 talk turkey.** *Sl., chiefly US & Canad.* to discuss frankly and practically. ORIG C16: shortened from *Turkey cock* (*hen*), used at first to designate the African guinea fowl (apparently because the bird was brought through Turkish territory), later applied by mistake to the American bird

Turkey ★ ('tɜːkɪ) *n* a republic in W Asia and SE Europe, between the Black Sea, the Mediterranean, and the Aegean: one of the oldest inhabited regions of the world; the centre of the Ottoman Empire; became a republic in 1923. The major Asian part, consisting mainly of an arid plateau, is separated from European Turkey by the Bosporus, Sea of Marmara, and Dardanelles. Official language: Turkish; Kurdish and Arabic minority languages. Religion: mostly Muslim. Currency: lira. Capital: Ankara. Pop.: 64 431 000 (1999 est.). Area: 780 576 sq. km (301 380 sq. miles).

turkey buzzard *or* **vulture** *n* a New World vulture having a naked red head.

turkey cock *n* **1** a male turkey. **2** an arrogant person.

turkey nest *n Austral.* a small earth dam adjacent to, and higher than, a larger earth dam, to feed water by gravity to a cattle trough, etc.

Turkey red *n* **1a** a moderate or bright red colour. **1b** (*as adj*): *a Turkey-red fabric.* **2** a cotton fabric of a bright red colour.

Turki ('tɜːkɪ) *adj* **1** of or relating to the Turkic languages. **2** of or relating to speakers of these languages. ◆ *n* **3** these languages collectively.

Turkic ('tɜːkɪk) *n* a branch of the Altaic family of languages, including Turkish, Tatar, etc., members of which are found from Turkey to NE China, esp. in Soviet central Asia.

Turkish ('tɜːkɪʃ) *adj* **1** of Turkey, its people, or their language. ◆ *n* **2** the official language of Turkey, belonging to the Turkic branch of the Altaic family.

Turkish bath *n* **1** a type of bath in which the bather sweats freely in hot dry air, is then washed, often massaged, and has a cold plunge or shower. **2** (*sometimes pl*) an establishment where such a bath is obtainable.

Turkish coffee *n* very strong black coffee.

Turkish delight *n* a jelly-like sweet flavoured with flower essences, usually cut into cubes and covered in icing sugar.

Turkish towel *n* a rough loose-piled towel.

Turkmenistan ★ (ˌtɜːkmɛnɪˈstɑːn) *n* a republic in central Asia; the area has been occupied by a succession of empires; a Turkmen state was established in the 15th century but was gradually conquered by Russia; in 1918 it became a Soviet republic and gained independence in 1991: deserts, incuding the **Kara Kum**, cover most of the region. Official language: Turkmen. Religion: believers are mainly Muslim. Currency: manat. Capital: Ashkhabad. Pop.: 4 721 000 (1999 est.). Area: 488 100 sq. km (186 400 sq. miles). Also called: **Turkmenia** (tɜːˈkmiːnɪə).

Turks and Caicos Islands ★ *pl n* a United Kingdom overseas territory in the Caribbean, southeast of the Bahamas: consists of the eight **Turks Islands**, separated by the **Turks Island Passage** from the Caicos group, which has six main islands. Capital: Grand Turk. Pop.: 14 000 (1993 est.). Area: 430 sq. km (166 sq. miles).

Turk's-cap lily *n* any of several cultivated lilies that have brightly coloured flowers with reflexed petals.

Turk's-head *n* an ornamental turban-like knot.

Turku ★ (*Finnish* 'turku) *n* a city and port in SW Finland, on the Gulf of Bothnia: capital of Finland until 1812. Pop.: 164 744 (1996 est.). Swedish name: **Åbo**.

turmeric ('tɜːmərɪk) *n* **1** a tropical Asian plant, *Curcuma longa,* having yellow flowers and an aromatic underground stem. **2** the powdered stem of this plant, used as a condiment and as a yellow dye. ORIG C16: from OF *terre merite,* from Med. L *terra merita,* lit.: meritorious earth, name applied for obscure reasons to curcuma

turmeric paper *n Chem.* paper impregnated with turmeric used as a test for alkalis and for boric acid.

turmoil ('tɜːmɔɪl) *n* violent or confused movement; agitation; tumult. ORIG C16: ?from TURN + MOIL

turn (tɜːn) *vb* **1** to move around an axis: *to turn a knob.* **2** (sometimes foll. by *round*) to change or cause to change positions by moving through an arc of a circle: *he turned the chair to face the light.* **3** to change or cause to change in course, direction, etc. **4** to go or pass to the other side of (a corner, etc.). **5** to assume or cause to assume a rounded, curved, or folded form: *the road turns here.* **6** to reverse or cause to reverse position. **7** (*tr*) to perform or do by a rotating movement: *to turn a somersault.* **8** (*tr*) to shape or cut a thread in (a workpiece) by rotating it on a lathe against a cutting tool. **9** (when *intr,* foll. by *into* or *to*) to change or convert or be changed or converted. **10** (foll. by *into*) to change or cause to change in nature, character, etc.: *the frog turned into a prince.* **11** (*copula*) to change so as to become: *he turned nasty.* **12** to cause (foliage, etc.) to change colour or (of foliage, etc.) to change colour. **13** to cause (milk, etc.) to become rancid or sour or (of milk, etc.) to become rancid or sour. **14** to change or cause to change in subject, trend, etc.: *the conversation turned to fishing.* **15** to direct or apply or be directed or applied: *he turned his attention to the problem.* **16** (*intr;* usually foll. by *to*) to appeal or apply (to) for help, advice, etc. **17** to reach, pass, or progress beyond in age, time, etc.: *she has just turned twenty.* **18** (*tr*) to cause or allow to go: *to turn an animal loose.* **19** to affect or be affected with nausea. **20** to affect or be affected with giddiness: *my head is turning.* **21** (*tr*) to affect the mental or emotional stability of (esp. in **turn (someone's) head**). **22** (*tr*) to release from a container. **23** (*tr*) to render into another language. **24** (usually foll. by *against* or *from*) to transfer or reverse (one's loyalties, affections, etc.). **25** (*tr*) to cause (an enemy agent) to become a double agent working for one's own side. **26** (*tr*) to bring (soil) from lower layers to the surface. **27** to blunt (an edge) or (of an edge) to become blunted. **28** (*tr*) to give a graceful form to: *to turn a compliment.* **29** (*tr*) to reverse (a cuff, collar, etc.). **30** (*intr*) *US.* to be merchandised as specified: *shirts are turning well this week.* **31** *Cricket.* to spin (the ball) or (of the ball) to spin. **32 turn a trick.** *Sl.* (of a prostitute) to gain a customer. **33 turn one's hand to.** to undertake (something practical). ◆ *n* **34** a turning or being turned. **35** a movement of complete or partial rotation. **36** a change of direction or position. **37** direction or drift: *his thoughts took a new turn.* **38** a deviation from a course or tendency. **39** the place, point, or time at which a deviation or change occurs. **40** another word for **turning** (sense 1). **41** the right or opportunity to do something in an agreed order or succession: *now it's George's turn.* **42** a change in nature, condition, etc.: *his illness took a turn for the worse.* **43** a period of action, work, etc. **44** a short walk, ride, or excursion. **45** natural inclination: *a speculative turn of mind.* **46** distinctive form or style: *a neat turn of phrase.* **47** requirement, need, or advantage: *to serve someone's turn.* **48** a deed that helps or hinders someone. **49** a twist, bend, or distortion in shape. **50** *Music.* a melodic ornament that makes a turn around a note, beginning with the note above, in a variety of sequences. **51** a short theatrical act. **52** *Stock Exchange, Brit.* the difference between a market maker's bid and offer prices, representing the market maker's profit. **53** *Inf.* a shock or surprise. **54 by turns.** one after another; alternately. **55 turn and turn about.** one after another; alternately. **56 to a turn.** to the proper amount; perfectly. ◆ See also **turn down, turn in,** etc. ORIG OE *tyrnian,* from OF *torner,* from L *tornāre* to turn in a lathe, from *tornus* lathe, from Gk *tornos* dividers

▸ **'turner** *n*

turnabout ('tɜːnəˌbaʊt) *n* **1** the act of turning so as to face a different direction. **2** a change or reversal of opinion, attitude, etc.

turnaround ('tɜːnəˌraʊnd) *n* **1a** the act or process in which a ship, aircraft, etc., unloads at the end of a trip and reloads for the next trip. **1b** the time taken for this. **2** the total time taken by a vehicle in a round trip. **3** a complete reversal of a situation.

turnbuckle ('tɜːnˌbʌkᵊl) *n* an open mechanical sleeve usually having a swivel at one end and a thread at the other to enable a threaded wire or rope to be tightened.

turncoat ('tɜːnˌkəʊt) *n* a person who deserts one cause or party for the opposite faction.

turncock ('tɜːnˌkɒk) *n* (formerly) an official employed to turn on the water for the mains supply.

turn down *vb* (*tr, adv*) **1** to reduce (the volume or brightness) of (something). **2** to reject or refuse. **3** to fold down (a collar, sheets, etc.). ◆ *adj* **turndown.** **4** (*prenominal*) designed to be folded down.

Turner ★ ('tɜːnə) *n* **Joseph Mallord William.** 1775–1851, British landscape painter.

turn in *vb* (*adv*) *Inf.* **1** (*intr*) to go to bed for the night. **2** (*tr*) to hand in; deliver. **3** (*tr*) to give up or conclude (something). **4** (*tr*) to record (a score, etc.). **5 turn in on oneself.** to become preoccupied with one's own problems.

turning ('tɜːnɪŋ) *n* **1** a road, river, or path that turns off the main way. **2** the point where such a way turns off. **3** a bend in a straight course. **4** an object made on a lathe. **5** the process or skill of turning objects on a lathe. **6** (*pl*) the waste produced in turning on a lathe.

turning circle *n* the smallest circle in which a vehicle can turn.

turning point *n* **1** a moment when the course of events is changed. **2** a point at which there is a change in direction or motion.

turnip ('tɜːnɪp) *n* **1** a widely cultivated plant of the cabbage family with a large yellow or white edible root. **2** the root of this plant, which is eaten as a vegetable. ORIG C16: from earlier *turnepe,* ?from TURN (indicating its rounded shape) + *nepe,* from L *nāpus* turnip

turnkey ('tɜːnˌkiː) *n* **1** *Arch.* a keeper of the keys, esp. in a prison; warder or jailer. ◆ *adj* **2** denoting a project, as in civil engineering, in which a single contractor has responsibility for the complete job from the start to the time of installation or occupancy.

turn off *vb* **1** (*intr*) to leave (a road, etc.). **2** (*intr*) (of a road, etc.) to deviate from (another road, etc.). **3** (*tr, adv*) to cause (something) to cease operating by turning a knob, pushing a button, etc. **4** (*tr*) *Inf.* to cause (a person, etc.) to feel dislike or distaste for (something): *this music turns me off.* **5** (*tr, adv*) *Brit. inf.* to dismiss from employment. ◆ *n* **turn-off.** **6** a road or other way branching off from the main thoroughfare. **7** *Inf.* a person or thing that elicits dislike or distaste.

turn on *vb* **1** (*tr, adv*) to cause (something) to operate by turning a knob, etc. **2** (*intr, prep*) to depend or hinge on: *the success of the party turns on you.* **3** (*prep*) to become hostile or to retaliate: *the dog turned on the children.* **4** (*tr, adv*) *Inf.* to produce (charm, tears, etc.) suddenly or automatically. **5** (*tr, adv*) *Sl.* to arouse emotionally or sexually. **6** (*intr, adv*) *Sl.* to take or become intoxicated by drugs. **7** (*tr, adv*) *Sl.* to introduce (someone) to drugs. ◆ *n* **turn-on.** **8** *Sl.* a person or thing that causes emotional or sexual arousal.

turn out *vb* (*adv*) **1** (*tr*) to cause (something, esp. a light) to cease operating by or as if by turning a knob, etc. **2** (*tr*) to produce by an effort or process. **3** (*tr*) to dismiss, discharge, or expel. **4** (*tr*) to empty the contents of, esp. in order to clean, tidy, or rearrange. **5** (*copula*) to prove to be as specified. **6** to end up; result: *it all turned out well.* **7** (*tr*) to fit as with clothes: *that woman turns her children out well.* **8** (*intr*) to assemble or gather. **9** (of a soldier) to parade or to call (a soldier) to parade. **10** (*intr*) *Inf.* to get out of bed. **11** (*intr;* foll. by *for*) *Inf.* to make an appearance, esp. in a sporting competition: *he was asked to turn out for Liverpool.* ◆ *n* **turnout.** **12** the body of people appearing together at a gathering. **13** the quantity or amount produced. **14** an array of clothing or equipment.

turn over *vb* (*adv*) **1** to change or cause to change position, esp. so as to reverse top and bottom. **2** to start (an engine), esp. with a starting handle, or (of an engine) to start or function correctly. **3** to shift or cause to shift position, as by rolling from side to side. **4** (*tr*) to deliver; transfer. **5** (*tr*) to consider carefully. **6** (*tr*) **6a** to sell and replenish (stock in trade). **6b** to transact business and so generate gross revenue of (a specified sum). **7** (*tr*) to invest and recover (capital). **8** (*tr*) *Sl.* to rob. ◆ *n* **turnover.** **9a** the amount of business transacted during a specified period. **9b** (*as modifier*): *a turnover tax.* **10** the rate at which stock in trade is sold and replenished. **11** a change or reversal of position. **12** a small pastry case filled with fruit, jam, etc. **13a** the number of workers employed by a firm in a given period to replace those who have left. **13b** the ratio between this number and the average number of employees during the same period. **14** *Banking.* the amount of capital funds loaned on call during a specified period. ◆ *adj* **turnover.** **15** (*prenominal*) designed to be turned over.

turnpike ('tɜːnˌpaɪk) *n* **1** *History.* **1a** a barrier set across a road to prevent passage until a toll had been paid. **1b** a road on which a turnpike was operated. **2** an obsolete word for **turnstile.** **3** *US.* a motorway for use of which a toll is charged. ORIG C15: from TURN + PIKE[2]

turnround ('tɜːnˌraʊnd) *n* another word for **turnaround.**

turnspit ('tɜːnˌspɪt) *n* **1** (formerly) a servant or small dog whose job was to turn a spit. **2** a spit that can be so turned.

turnstile ('tɜːnˌstaɪl) *n* a mechanical barrier with arms that are turned to admit one person at a time.

turnstone ('tɜːnˌstəʊn) *n* a shore bird, related to the plovers and sandpipers, that lifts up stones in search of food.

turntable ('tɜːnˌteɪbᵊl) *n* **1** the circular platform that rotates a gramophone record while it is being played. **2** a circular platform used for turning locomotives and cars. **3** the revolvable platform on a microscope on which specimens are examined.

turntable ladder *n Brit.* a power-operated extending ladder mounted on a fire engine. US and Canad. name: **aerial ladder.**

turn to *vb* (*intr, adv*) to set about a task.

turn up *vb* (*adv*) **1** (*intr*) to arrive or appear. **2** to find or be found, esp. by accident. **3** (*tr*) to increase the flow, volume, etc., of. ◆ *n* **turn-up.** **4** (*often pl*) *Brit.* the turned-up fold at the bottom of some trouser legs. US, Canad. and Austral. name: **cuff.** **5** *Inf.* an unexpected or chance occurrence.

turpentine ('tɜːpᵊnˌtaɪn) *n* **1** Also called: **gum turpentine.** any of various oleoresins obtained from various coniferous trees and used as the main source of commercial turpentine. **2** a sticky oleoresin that exudes from the terebinth tree. **3** Also called: **oil of turpentine, spirits of turpentine.** a colourless volatile oil distilled from turpentine oleoresin. It is used as a solvent for paints and in medicine. **4** Also called: **turpentine substitute, white spirit.** (*not in technical usage*) any one of a number of thinners for paints and varnishes, consisting of fractions of petroleum. Related adj: **terebinthine.** ◆ *vb* **turpentines, turpentining, turpentined.** (*tr*) **5** to treat or saturate with turpentine. ORIG C14 *terebentyne,* from Med. L, from L *terebinthīna* turpentine, from *terebinthus* the turpentine tree

turpentine tree *n* **1** a tropical African tree yielding a hard dark wood and a useful resin. **2** either of two Australian evergreen trees that yield resin.

turpeth ('tɜːpɪθ) *n* **1** an East Indian plant having roots with purgative properties. **2** the root of this plant or the drug obtained from it. ORIG C14: from Med. L *turbithum,* ult. from Ar. *turbid*

Turpin ★ ('tɜːpɪn) *n* **Dick.** 1706–39, British highwayman.

turpitude ('tɜːpɪˌtjuːd) *n* base character or action; depravity. ORIG C15: from L *turpitūdō* ugliness, from *turpis* base

turps (tɜːps) *n* (*functioning as sing*) *Brit.* short for **turpentine** (sense 3).

turquoise ('tɜːkwɔɪz, -kwɑːz) *n* **1** a greenish-blue fine-grained mineral consisting of hydrated copper aluminium phosphate. It is used as a gemstone. **2a** the colour of turquoise. **2b** (*as adj*): *a turquoise dress.* ORIG C14: from OF *turqueise* Turkish (stone)

turret ('tʌrɪt) *n* **1** a small tower that projects from the wall of a building, esp. a castle. **2a** a self-contained structure, capable of rotation, in which weapons are mounted, esp. in tanks and warships. **2b** a similar structure on an aircraft. **3** (on a machine tool) a turret-like steel structure with tools projecting radially that can be indexed round to bring each tool to bear on the work. ORIG C14: from OF *torete,* from *tor* tower, from L *turris* ► **'turreted** *adj*

turret lathe *n* another name for **capstan lathe.**

turtle[1] ('tɜːtᵊl) *n* **1** any of various aquatic reptiles, esp. those having a flattened shell enclosing the body and

★ people and places

flipper-like limbs adapted for swimming. **2 turn turtle.** to capsize. ORIG C17: from F *tortue* TORTOISE (infl. by TURTLE[2])

turtle[2] ('tɜːtᵊl) *n* an archaic name for **turtledove.** ORIG OE *turtla,* from L *turtur,* imit.

turtleback ('tɜːtᵊlˌbæk) *n* an arched projection over the upper deck of a ship for protection in heavy seas.

turtledove ('tɜːtᵊlˌdʌv) *n* **1** any of several Old World doves having a brown plumage with speckled wings and a long dark tail. **2** a gentle or loving person. ORIG see TURTLE[2]

turtleneck ('tɜːtᵊlˌnɛk) *n* a round high close-fitting neck on a sweater or the sweater itself.

turves (tɜːvz) *n* a plural of **turf.**

Tuscan ('tʌskən) *adj* **1.** of or relating to Tuscany, its inhabitants, or their dialect of Italian. **2** of or denoting one of the five classical orders of architecture: characterized by a column with an unfluted shaft and a capital and base with mouldings but no decoration. ◆ *n* **3** a native or inhabitant of Tuscany. **4** any of the dialects of Italian spoken in Tuscany.

Tuscany ★ ('tʌskənɪ) *n* a region of central Italy, on the Ligurian and Tyrrhenian Seas: corresponds roughly to ancient Etruria; a region of numerous small states in medieval times; united in the 15th and 16th centuries under Florence; united with the rest of Italy in 1861. Capital: Florence. Pop.: 3 523 238 (1996 est.). Area: 22 990 sq. km (8876 sq. miles). Italian name: **Toscana.**

tusche (tʊʃ) *n* a substance used in lithography for drawing the design and as a resist in silk-screen printing and lithography. ORIG from G, from *tuschen* to touch up with colour, from F *toucher* to touch

Tusculum ★ ('tʌskjʊləm) *n* an ancient city in Latium near Rome.
▸ **'Tusculan** *adj*

tush (tʌʃ) *interj Arch.* an exclamation of disapproval or contempt. ORIG C15: imit.

tusk (tʌsk) *n* **1** a pointed elongated usually paired tooth in the elephant, walrus, and certain other mammals. **2** a tusklike tooth or part. **3** a sharp pointed projection. ◆ *vb* **4** to stab, tear, or gore with the tusks. ORIG OE *tūsc*
▸ **tusked** *adj*

tusker ('tʌskə) *n* any animal with long tusks.

tusk shell *n* any of various burrowing seashore molluscs that have a long narrow tubular shell open at both ends.

Tussaud ★ (*French* tyso) *n* **Marie** (mari). 1760–1850, Swiss modeller in wax, who founded a permanent waxworks exhibition in London.

tussis ('tʌsɪs) *n* the technical name for a **cough.** See **pertussis.** ORIG L: cough
▸ **'tussive** *adj*

tussle ('tʌsᵊl) *vb* **tussles, tussling, tussled. 1** (*intr*) to fight or wrestle in a vigorous way. ◆ *n* **2** a vigorous fight; scuffle; struggle. ORIG C15

tussock ('tʌsək) *n* **1** a dense tuft of vegetation, esp. of grass. **2** *Austral. & NZ.* **2a** short for **tussock grass. 2b the.** country where tussock grass grows. ORIG C16: from ?
▸ **'tussocky** *adj*

tussock grass *n* any of several pasture grasses.

tussore (tʊ'sɔː, 'tʌsə), **tusser** ('tʌsə), *or* (*Chiefly US*) **tussah** ('tʌsə) *n* **1** Also called: **wild silk.** a coarse silk obtained from an oriental silkworm. **2** the silkworm producing this. ORIG C17: from Hindi *tasar* shuttle, from Sansk. *tasara* a wild silkworm

tut (tʌt) *interj, n, vb* **tuts, tutting, tutted.** short for **tut-tut.**

Tutankhamen (ˌtuːtən'kɑːmɛn, -mən) *or* **Tutankhamun** ★ (ˌtuːtənkɑː'muːn) *n* king (1361–1352 B.C.) of the 18th dynasty of Egypt. His tomb near Luxor, discovered in 1922, contained a wealth of material objects.

tutelage ('tjuːtɪlɪdʒ) *n* **1** the act or office of a guardian or tutor. **2** instruction or guidance, esp. by a tutor. **3** the condition of being under the supervision of a guardian or tutor. ORIG C17: from L *tūtēla* a caring for, from *tuērī* to watch over

tutelary ('tjuːtɪlərɪ) *or* **tutelar** ('tjuːtɪlə) *adj* **1** invested with the role of guardian or protector. **2** of or relating to a guardian. ◆ *n, pl* **tutelaries** *or* **tutelars. 3** a tutelary person, deity, etc.

tutor ('tjuːtə) *n* **1** a teacher, usually instructing individual pupils. **2** (at universities, colleges, etc.) a member of staff responsible for the teaching and supervision of a certain number of students. ◆ *vb* **3** to act as a tutor to (someone). **4** (*tr*) to act as guardian to. ORIG C14: from L: a watcher, from *tuērī* to watch over
▸ **'tutorage** *or* **'tutorship** *n*

tutorial (tjuː'tɔːrɪəl) *n* **1** a period of intensive tuition given by a tutor to an individual student or to a small group of students. ◆ *adj* **2** of or relating to a tutor.

tutsan ('tʌtsən) *n* a woodland shrub of Europe and W Asia, having yellow flowers and reddish-purple fruits. ORIG C15: from OF *toute-saine* (unattested), lit.: all healthy

tutti ('tʊtɪ) *adj, adv Music.* to be performed by the whole orchestra, choir, etc. ORIG C18: from It., pl of *tutto* all, from L *tōtus*

tutti-frutti ('tuːtɪ'fruːtɪ) *n* **1** (*pl* **tutti-fruttis**) an ice cream or a confection containing small pieces of candied or fresh fruits. **2** a preserve of chopped mixed fruits. **3** a flavour like that of many fruits combined. ORIG from It., lit.: all the fruits

tut-tut ('tʌt'tʌt) *interj* **1** an exclamation of mild reprimand, disapproval, or surprise. ◆ *vb* **tut-tuts, tut-tutting, tut-tutted. 2** (*intr*) to express disapproval by the exclamation of "tut-tut". ◆ *n* **3** the act of tut-tutting.

tutty ('tʌtɪ) *n* impure zinc oxide used as a polishing powder. ORIG C14: from OF *tutie,* from Ar. *tūtiyā,* prob. from Persian, from Sansk. *tuttha*

tutu ('tuːtuː) *n* a very short skirt worn by ballerinas, made of projecting layers of stiffened material. ORIG from F, changed from the nursery word *cucu* backside, from L *cūlus* the buttocks

Tutu ★ ('tuːtuː) *n* **Desmond.** born 1931, South African clergyman, noted for his opposition to apartheid: Anglican Bishop of Johannesburg (1984–86); Archbishop of Cape Town (1986–96); Nobel peace prize 1984.

Tutuila ★ (ˌtuːtuː'iːlə) *n* the largest island of American Samoa, in the SW Pacific. Chief town and port: Pago Pago. Pop.: 30 500 (latest est.). Area: 135 sq. km (52 sq. miles).

Tutuola ★ ('tuːtuːˌəʊlə) *n* **Amos.** 1920–97, Nigerian writer: his books include *The Palm-Wine Drinkard* (1952).

Tuva Republic ★ ('tuːvə) *n* a constituent republic of S Russia: mountainous. Capital: Kizyl. Pop.: 309 000 (1996 est.). Area: 170 500 sq. km (65 800 sq. miles). Also called: **Tuvinian Autonomous Republic.**

Tuvalu ★ (ˌtuːvə'luː) *n* a country in the SW Pacific, comprising a group of nine coral islands: established as a British protectorate in 1892. From 1915 until 1975 the islands formed part of the British colony of the Gilbert and Ellice Islands, achieved full independence in 1978: a special member of the Commonwealth. Languages: English and Tuvaluan. Religion: mostly Christian. Currency: Australian dollar; Tuvalu dollars are also used. Capital: Funafuti. Pop.: 10 600 (1999 est.). Area: 26 sq. km (10 sq. miles). Former names: **Lagoon Islands, Ellice Islands.**
▸ **ˌTuva'luan** *adj, n*

tu-whit tu-whoo (tə'wɪt tə'wuː) *interj* an imitation of the sound made by an owl.

tuxedo (tʌk'siːdəʊ) *n, pl* **tuxedos.** the usual US and Canad. name for **dinner jacket.** ORIG C19: after a country club in *Tuxedo Park,* New York

Tuxtla Gutiérrez ★ (*Spanish* 'tustla gu'tjɛrrɛθ) *n* a city in SE Mexico, capital of Chiapas state: agricultural trading centre. Pop.: 289 626 (1990).

tuyère ('twiːɛə, 'twaɪə) *or* **twyer** ('twaɪə) *n* a water-cooled nozzle through which air is blown into a cupola, blast furnace, or forge. ORIG C18: from F, from *tuyau* pipe, from OF *tuel,* prob. of Gmc origin

TV *abbrev. for* television.

TVEI (in Britain) *abbrev. for* technical and vocational educational initiative: a national educational scheme in which pupils gain practical experience in technology and industry often through work placement.

Tver ★ (*Russian* tvjerj) *n* a city in central Russia, at the confluence of the Volga and Tversta Rivers: chief port of the upper Volga, linked by canal with Moscow. Pop.: 454 000 (1994 est.). Former name (1932–91): **Kalinin.**

TVM *abbrev. for* television movie: a film made specifically for television and not intended for release in cinemas.

TVP *abbrev. for* textured vegetable protein: protein from soya beans or other vegetables spun into fibres and flavoured: used esp. as a substitute for meat.

TVR *abbrev. for* television rating: a measurement of the popularity of a TV programme based on a survey.

TVRO *abbrev. for* television receive only: an antenna and associated apparatus for reception from a broadcasting satellite.

twaddle ('twɒdᵊl) *n* **1** silly, trivial, or pretentious talk or writing. ◆ *vb* **twaddles, twaddling, twaddled. 2** (*intr*) to talk or write in a silly or pretentious way. ORIG C16 *twattle,* var. of *twittle* or *tittle*
▸ **'twaddler** *n*

twain (tweɪn) *determiner, n* an archaic word for **two.** ORIG OE *twēgen*

Twain ★ (tweɪn) *n* **Mark,** pen name of *Samuel Langhorne Clemens.* 1835–1910, US novelist, author of *The Adventures of Tom Sawyer* (1876) and *The Adventures of Huckleberry Finn* (1885).

twang (twæŋ) *n* **1** a sharp ringing sound produced by or as if by the plucking of a taut string. **2** the act of plucking a string to produce such a sound. **3** a strongly nasal quality in a person's speech. ◆ *vb* **4** to make or cause to make a twang. **5** to strum (music, a tune, etc.). **6** to speak with a nasal voice. **7** (*intr*) to be released or move with a twang: *the arrow twanged away.* ORIG C16: imit.
▸ **'twangy** *adj*

'twas (twɒz; *unstressed* twəz) *Poetic or dialect. contraction of* it was.

twat (twæt, twɒt) *n Taboo sl.* **1** the female genitals. **2** a foolish person. ORIG from ?

twayblade ('tweɪ,bleɪd) *n* any of various orchids having a basal pair of unstalked leaves arranged opposite each other. ORIG C16: translation of Med. L *bifolium* having two leaves, from obs. *tway* two + BLADE

tweak (twiːk) *vb* (*tr*) **1** to twist or pinch with a sharp or sudden movement. **2** *Inf.* to make a minor alteration. ◆ *n* **3** a tweaking. **4** *Inf.* a minor alteration. ORIG OE *twiccian*

twee (twiː) *adj Brit. inf.* excessively sentimental, sweet, or pretty. ORIG C19: from *tweet,* mincing or affected pronunciation of *sweet*
▸ **'tweely** *adv*

tweed (twiːd) *n* **1** a thick woollen cloth produced originally in Scotland. **2** (*pl*) clothes made of this. **3** (*pl*) *Austral. inf.* trousers. ORIG C19: prob. from *tweel,* Scot. var. of TWILL, infl. by TWEED

Tweed ★ (twiːd) *n* a river in SE Scotland and NE England, flowing east and forming part of the border between Scotland and England, then crossing into England to enter the North Sea at Berwick. Length: 156 km (97 miles).

Tweeddale ★ ('twiːd,deɪl) *n* another name for **Peeblesshire.**

Tweedledum and Tweedledee (,twiːdᵊl'dʌm; ,twiːdᵊl'diː) *n* any two persons or things that differ only slightly from each other; two of a kind. ORIG C19: from the proverbial names of HANDEL and the rival musician Buononcini. The names were popularized by Lewis Carroll's use of them in *Through the Looking Glass* (1872)

Tweedsmuir ★ ('twiːdz,mjʊə) *n* **Baron.** title of (John) **Buchan.**

tweedy ('twiːdɪ) *adj* **tweedier, tweediest. 1** of, made of, or resembling tweed. **2** showing a fondness for a hearty outdoor life, usually associated with wearers of tweeds.

'tween (twiːn) *Poetic or dialect. contraction of* between.

'tween deck *or* **decks** *n Naut.* a space between two continuous decks of a vessel.

tweet (twiːt) *interj* **1** an imitation of the thin chirping sound made by small birds. ◆ *vb* **2** (*intr*) to make this sound. ORIG C19: imit.

tweeter ('twiːtə) *n* a loudspeaker used in high-fidelity systems for the reproduction of high audio frequencies. It is usually employed in conjunction with a woofer. ORIG C20: from TWEET

tweezers ('twiːzəz) *pl n* a small pincer-like instrument for handling small objects, plucking out hairs, etc. Also called: **pair of tweezers, tweezer** (esp. US). ORIG C17: pl of *tweezer* (on the model of *scissors,* etc.), from *tweeze* case of instruments, from F *étuis,* from OF *estuier* to preserve, ult. from L *studēre* to care about

Twelfth Day *n* Jan. 6, the twelfth day after Christmas and the feast of the Epiphany.

twelfth man *n* a reserve player in a cricket team.

Twelfth Night *n* **a** the evening of Jan. 5, the eve of Twelfth Day. **b** the evening of Twelfth Day itself.

twelve (twɛlv) *n* **1** the cardinal number that is the sum of ten and two. **2** a numeral, 12, XII, etc., representing this number. **3** something representing or consisting of 12 units. **4** Also called: **twelve o'clock.** noon or midnight. ◆ *determiner* **5a** amounting to twelve. **5b** (*as pronoun*): *twelve have arrived.* ◆ Related adj: **duodecimal.** ORIG OE *twelf*
▸ **twelfth** *adj, n*

twelve-inch *n* a gramophone record 12 inches in diameter and played at 45 revolutions per minute, usually containing an extended remix of a single.

twelvemo ('twɛlvməʊ) *n, pl* **twelvemos.** *Bookbinding.* another word for **duodecimo.**

twelvemonth ('twɛlv,mʌnθ) *n Chiefly Brit.* an archaic or dialect word for a **year.**

twelve-tone *adj* of or denoting the type of serial music which uses as musical material a tone row formed by the 12 semitones of the chromatic scale. See **serialism.**

twenty ('twɛntɪ) *n, pl* **twenties. 1** the cardinal number that is the product of ten and two. **2** a numeral, 20, XX, etc., representing this number. **3** something representing or consisting of 20 units. ◆ *determiner* **4a** amounting to twenty: *twenty questions.* **4b** (*as pronoun*): *to order twenty.*
▸ **'twentieth** *adj, n* ORIG OE *twēntig*

twenty-four-seven *adv, often written* **24/7.** *Inf.* twenty-four hours a day, seven days a week; constantly; all the time: *consultants would no longer be available 24/7.*

twenty-six counties *pl n* the counties of the Republic of Ireland.

twenty-twenty *adj Med.* (of vision) being of normal acuity: usually written 20/20.

'twere (twɜː; *unstressed* twə) *Poetic or dialect. contraction of* it were.

twerp *or* **twirp** (twɜːp) *n Inf.* a silly, weak-minded, or contemptible person. ORIG C20: from ?

twibill *or* **twibil** ('twaɪ,bɪl) *n* **1** a mattock with a blade shaped like an adze at one end and like an axe at the other. **2** *Arch.* a double-bladed battle-axe. ORIG OE, from *twi-* double + *bill* sword

twice (twaɪs) *adv* **1** two times; on two occasions or in two cases. **2** double in degree or quantity: *twice as long.* ORIG OE *twiwa*

Twickenham ★ ('twɪkənəm) *n* a former town in SE England, on the River Thames: part of the Greater London borough of Richmond-upon-Thames since 1965; contains the English Rugby Football Union ground.

twiddle ('twɪdᵊl) *vb* **twiddles, twiddling, twiddled. 1** (when *intr,* often foll. by *with*) to twirl or fiddle (with), often in an idle way. **2 twiddle one's thumbs.** to do nothing; be unoccupied. **3** (*intr*) to turn, twirl, or rotate. **4** (*intr*) *Rare.* to be occupied with trifles. ◆ *n* **5** an act or instance of twiddling. ORIG C16: prob. a blend of TWIRL + FIDDLE
▸ **'twiddler** *n*

twig[1] (twɪg) *n* **1** any small branch or shoot of a tree. **2** something resembling this, esp. a minute branch of a blood vessel. ORIG OE *twigge*
▸ **'twiggy** *adj*

twig[2] (twɪg) *vb* **twigs, twigging, twigged.** *Brit. inf.* **1** to understand (something). **2** to find out or suddenly comprehend (something): *he hasn't twigged yet.* ORIG C18: ?from Scot. Gaelic *tuig* I understand

twilight ('twaɪˌlaɪt) *n* **1** the soft diffused light occurring when the sun is just below the horizon, esp. following sunset. **2** the period in which this light occurs. **3** any faint light. **4** a period in which strength, importance, etc., are waning. **5** (*modifier*) **5a** of or relating to the period towards the end of the day: *the twilight shift.* **5b** of or relating to the final phase of a particular era: *the twilight days of the Bush presidency.* **5c** denoting irregularity and obscurity: *a twilight existence.* ORIG C15: lit.: half light (between day and night), from OE *twi-* half + LIGHT[1]
▸ **twilit** ('twaɪˌlɪt) *adj*

Twilight of the Gods *n* another term for **Götterdämmerung**.

twilight sleep *n Med.* a state of partial anaesthesia in which the patient retains a slight degree of consciousness.

twilight zone *n* **1** any indefinite or transitional condition or area. **2** an inner-city area where houses have become dilapidated.

twill (twɪl) *adj* **1** (in textiles) of a weave in which the yarns are worked to produce an effect of parallel diagonal lines or ribs. ◆ *n* **2** any fabric so woven. ◆ *vb* **3** (*tr*) to weave in this fashion. ORIG OE *twilic* having a double thread

'twill (twɪl) *Poetic or dialect. contraction of* it will.

twin (twɪn) *n* **1a** either of two persons or animals conceived at the same time. **1b** (*as modifier*): *a twin brother.* See also **identical** (sense 3), **fraternal** (sense 3). **2a** either of two persons or things that are identical or very similar. **2b** (*as modifier*): *twin carburettors.* **3** Also called: **macle.** a crystal consisting of two parts each of which has a definite orientation to the other. ◆ *vb* **twins, twinning, twinned. 4** to pair or be paired together; couple. **5** (*intr*) to bear twins. **6** (*intr*) (of a crystal) to form into a twin. **7a** (*tr*) to create a reciprocal relation between (two towns in different countries); pair (a town) with another in a different country. **7b** (*intr*) (of a town) to be paired in a town in a different country. ORIG OE *twinn*
▸ **'twinning** *n*

twin bed *n* one of a pair of matching single beds.

twine (twaɪn) *n* **1** string made by twisting together fibres of hemp, cotton, etc. **2** a twining. **3** something produced or characterized by twining. **4** a twist, coil, or convolution. **5** a knot or tangle. ◆ *vb* **twines, twining, twined. 6** (*tr*) to twist together; interweave. **7** (*tr*) to form by or as if by twining. **8** (when *intr*, often foll. by *around*) to wind or cause to wind, esp. in spirals. ORIG OE *twīn*
▸ **'twiner** *n*

twin-engined *adj* (of an aeroplane) having two engines.

twinge (twɪndʒ) *n* **1** a sudden brief darting or stabbing pain. **2** a sharp emotional pang. ◆ *vb* **twinges, twinging, twinged. 3** to have or cause to have a twinge. ORIG OE *twengan* to pinch

twinkle ('twɪŋkᵊl) *vb* **twinkles, twinkling, twinkled.** (*mainly intr*) **1** to emit or reflect light in a flickering manner; shine brightly and intermittently; sparkle. **2** (of the eyes) to sparkle, esp. with amusement or delight. **3** *Rare.* to move about quickly. ◆ *n* **4** a flickering brightness; sparkle. **5** an instant. ORIG OE *twinclian*
▸ **'twinkler** *n* ▸ **'twinkly** *adj*

twinkling ('twɪŋklɪŋ) *or* **twink** (twɪŋk) *n* a very short time; instant; moment. Also called: **twinkling of an eye.**

Twins (twɪnz) *pl n* **the.** the constellation Gemini, the third sign of the zodiac.

twin-screw *adj* (of a vessel) having two propellers.

twinset ('twɪnˌsɛt) *n Brit.* a matching jumper and cardigan.

twin town *n* a town that has civic associations, such as reciprocal visits and cultural exchanges, with a foreign town.

twin-tub *n* a type of washing machine that has two revolving drums, one for washing and the other for spin-drying.

twirl (twɜːl) *vb* **1** to move around rapidly and repeatedly in a circle. **2** (*tr*) to twist, wind, or twiddle, often idly: *she twirled her hair around her finger.* **3** (*intr;* often foll. by *around* or *about*) to turn suddenly to face another way. ◆ *n* **4** a rotating or being rotated; whirl or twist. **5** something wound around or twirled; coil. **6** a written flourish. ORIG C16: ? a blend of TWIST + WHIRL
▸ **'twirler** *n*

twirp (twɜːp) *n* a variant spelling of **twerp.**

twist (twɪst) *vb* **1** to cause (one end or part) to turn or (of one end or part) to turn in the opposite direction from another; coil or spin. **2** to distort or be distorted. **3** to wind or twine. **4** to force or be forced out of the natural form or position. **5** to change for the worse in character, meaning, etc.; pervert: *she twisted the statement.* **6** to revolve; rotate. **7** (*tr*) to wrench with a turning action. **8** (*intr*) to follow a winding course. **9** (*intr*) to squirm, as with pain. **10** (*intr*) to dance the twist. **11** (*tr*) *Brit. inf.* to cheat; swindle. **12 twist someone's arm.** to persuade or coerce someone. ◆ *n* **13** a twisting. **14** something formed by or as if by twisting. **15** a decisive change of direction, aim, meaning, or character. **16** (in a novel, play, etc.) an unexpected event, revelation, etc. **17** a bend: *a twist in the road.* **18** a distortion of the original shape or form. **19** a jerky pull, wrench, or turn. **20** a strange personal characteristic, esp. a bad one. **21** a confused tangle made by twisting. **22** a twisted thread used in sewing where extra strength is needed. **23 the twist.** a dance popular in the 1960s, in which dancers vigorously twist the hips. **24** a loaf or roll made of pieces of twisted dough. **25** a thin sliver of peel from a lemon, lime, etc., twisted and added to a drink. **26a** a cigar made by twisting three cigars around one another. **26b** chewing tobacco made in the form of a roll by twisting the leaves together. **27** *Physics.* torsional deformation or shear stress or strain. **28** *Sport, chiefly US & Canad.* spin given to a ball in various games. **29 round the twist.** *Brit. sl.* mad; eccentric. ORIG OE
▸ **'twisty** *adj*

twist drill *n* a drill bit having two helical grooves running from the point along the shank to clear swarf and cuttings.

twister ('twɪstə) *n* **1** *Brit.* a swindling or dishonest person. **2** a person or thing that twists. **3** *US & Canad.* an informal name for **tornado. 4** a ball moving with a twisting motion.

twist grip *n* a handlebar control in the form of a ratchet-controlled rotating grip.

twit[1] (twɪt) *vb* **twits, twitting, twitted. 1** (*tr*) to tease, taunt, or reproach, often in jest. ◆ *n* **2** *US & Canad. inf.* a nervous or excitable state. **3** *Rare.* a reproach; taunt. ORIG OE *ætwītan,* from *æt* against + *wītan* to accuse

twit[2] (twɪt) *n Inf., chiefly Brit.* a foolish or stupid person; idiot. ORIG C19: from TWIT[1] (orig. in the sense: a person given to twitting)

twitch (twɪtʃ) *vb* **1** to move in a jerky spasmodic way. **2** (*tr*) to pull (something) with a quick jerky movement. **3** (*intr*) to hurt with a sharp spasmodic pain. ◆ *n* **4** a sharp jerking movement. **5** a mental or physical twinge. **6** a sudden muscular spasm, esp. one caused by a nervous condition. **7** a loop of cord used to control a horse by drawing it tight about its upper lip. ORIG OE *twiccian* to pluck

twitcher ('twɪtʃə) *n* **1** a person or thing that twitches. **2** *Inf.* a bird-watcher who tries to spot as many rare varieties as possible.

twitch grass *n* another name for **couch grass.** Sometimes shortened to **twitch.** ORIG C16: var. of QUITCH GRASS

twite (twaɪt) *n* a N European finch with a brown streaked plumage. ORIG C16: imit. of its cry

twitter ('twɪtə) *vb* **1** (*intr*) (esp. of a bird) to utter a succession of chirping sounds. **2** (*intr*) to talk or move rapidly and tremulously. **3** (*intr*) to giggle. **4** (*tr*) to utter in a chirping way. ◆ *n* **5** a twittering sound. **6** the act of twittering. **7** a state of nervous excitement (esp. in **in a twitter**). ORIG C14: imit.
▸ **'twitterer** *n* ▸ **'twittery** *adj*

'twixt *or* **twixt** (twɪkst) *Poetic or dialect. contraction of* betwixt.

two (tu:) *n* **1** the cardinal number that is the sum of one and one. **2** a numeral, 2, II, (ii), etc., representing this number. **3** something representing or consisting of two units. **4** Also called: **two o'clock.** two hours after noon or midnight. **5 in two.** in or into two parts. **6 put two and two together.** to make an inference from available evidence, esp. an obvious inference. **7 that makes two of us.** the same applies to me. ◆ *determiner* **8a** amounting to two: *two nails.* **8b** (*as pronoun*): *he bought two.* ◆ Related adjs.: **binary, double, dual.** ORIG OE *twā* (fem)

two-by-four *n* **1** a length of untrimmed timber with a cross section that measures 2 inches by 4 inches. **2** a trimmed timber joist with a cross section that measures 1½ inches by 3½ inches.

twoccing *or* **twocking** ('twɒkɪŋ) *n Brit. sl.* the act of breaking into a motor vehicle and driving it away. ORIG C20: from *T(aking) W(ithout) O(wner's) C(onsent),* the legal offence with which car thieves may be charged
▸ **'twoccer** *or* **'twocker** *n*

two-dimensional *adj* **1** of or having two dimensions. **2** having an area but not enclosing any volume. **3** lacking in depth.

two-edged *adj* **1** having two cutting edges. **2** (esp. of a remark) having two interpretations, such as *she looks nice when she smiles.*

two-faced *adj* deceitful; hypocritical.

twofold ('tu:ˌfəʊld) *adj* **1** equal to twice as many or twice as much. **2** composed of two parts. ◆ *adv* **3** doubly.

two-handed *adj* **1** requiring the use of both hands. **2** ambidextrous. **3** requiring the participation or cooperation of two people.

twonie ('tu:nɪ) *n* a variant spelling of **toonie.**

two-pack *adj* (of a paint, filler, etc.) supplied as two separate components, for example a base and a catalyst, that are mixed together immediately before use.

twopence *or* **tuppence** ('tʌpəns) *n Brit.* **1** the sum of two pennies. **2** (*used with a negative*) something of little value (in **not care** *or* **give twopence**). **3** a former British silver coin.

twopenny *or* **tuppenny** ('tʌpənɪ) *adj Chiefly Brit.* **1** Also: **twopenny-halfpenny.** cheap or tawdry. **2** (intensifier): *a twopenny damn.* **3** worth two pence.

two-phase *adj* (of an electrical circuit, device, etc.) generating or using two alternating voltages of the same frequency, displaced in phase by 90°.

two-piece *adj* **1** consisting of two separate parts, usually matching, as of a garment. ◆ *n* **2** such an outfit.

two-ply *adj* **1** made of two thicknesses, layers, or strands. ◆ *n, pl* **two-plies.** **2** a two-ply wood, knitting yarn, etc.

Two Sicilies ★ *pl n* **the.** a former kingdom of S Italy, consisting of the kingdoms of Sicily and Naples (1061–1860).

two-sided *adj* **1** having two sides or aspects. **2** controversial; debatable.

twosome ('tu:səm) *n* **1** two together, esp. two people. **2** a match between two people.

two-step *n* **1** an old-time dance in duple time. **2** a piece of music composed for or in the rhythm of this dance.

two-stroke *adj* of an internal-combustion engine whose piston makes two strokes for every explosion. US and Canad. word: **two-cycle.**

Two Thousand Guineas *n* (*functioning as sing*), *usually written* **2000 Guineas. the.** an annual horse race run at Newmarket since 1809.

two-time *vb* **two-times, two-timing, two-timed.** *Inf.* to deceive (someone, esp. a lover) by carrying on a relationship with another.
▸ **ˌtwo-'timer** *n*

two-tone *adj* **1** of two colours or two shades of the same colour. **2** (esp. of sirens, car horns, etc.) producing or consisting of two notes.

'twould (twʊd) *Poetic or dialect. contraction of* it would.

two-up *n Chiefly Austral.* a illegal gambling game in which two coins are tossed or spun.

two-way *adj* **1** moving, permitting movement, or operating in either of two opposite directions. **2** involving two participants. **3** involving reciprocal obligation or mutual action. **4** (of a radio, telephone, etc.) allowing communications in two directions using both transmitting and receiving equipment.

two-way mirror *n* a half-silvered sheet of glass that functions as a mirror when viewed from one side but is translucent from the other.

TX *abbrev. for* Texas.

-ty[1] *suffix of numerals.* denoting a multiple of ten: *sixty; seventy.* ORIG from OE *-tig*

-ty[2] *suffix forming nouns.* indicating state, condition, or quality: *cruelty.* ORIG from OF *-te, -tet,* from L *-tās, -tāt-*

Tyan-Shan ★ ('tjan'ʃan) *n* transliteration of the Russian name for the **Tian Shan.**

Tyburn ★ ('taɪbɜ:n) *n* (formerly) a place of execution in London, on the River Tyburn.

Tyche ★ ('taɪkɪ) *n Greek myth.* the goddess of fortune. Roman counterpart: **Fortuna.**

tychism ('taɪkɪzəm) *n Philosophy.* the theory that chance is an objective reality at work in the universe. ORIG from Gk *tukhē* chance

tycoon (taɪ'ku:n) *n* **1** a businessman of great wealth and power. **2** an archaic name for a **shogun.** ORIG C19: from Japanese *taikun,* from Chinese *ta* great + *chün* ruler

tyke *or* **tike** (taɪk) *n* **1** a dog, esp. a mongrel. **2** *Inf.* a small or cheeky child. **3** *Brit. dialect.* a rough ill-mannered person. **4** *Brit. sl. often offens.* a person from Yorkshire. **5** *Austral. sl., offens.* a Roman Catholic. ORIG C14: from ON *tīk* bitch

Tyler ★ ('taɪlə) *n* **1 John.** 1790–1862, US statesman; tenth president of the US (1841–45). **2 Wat** (wɒt). died 1381, English leader of the Peasants' Revolt (1381).

tylopod ('taɪləʊˌpɒd) *n* a mammal having padded, rather than hoofed, digits, such as camels and llamas. ORIG C19: from NL, from Gk *tulos* knob or *tulē* cushion + -POD

Tylor ★ ('taɪlə) *n* Sir **Edward Burnett.** 1832–1917, British anthropologist, noted for his *Primitive Culture* (1871).

tympan ('tɪmpən) *n* **1** a membrane stretched over a frame or cylinder. **2** *Printing.* packing interposed between the platen and the paper to be printed in order to provide an even impression. **3** *Archit.* another name for **tympanum.** ORIG OE *timpana,* from L; see TYMPANUM

tympani ('tɪmpənɪ) *pl n* a variant spelling of **timpani.**

tympanic bone (tɪm'pænɪk) *n* the part of the temporal bone that surrounds the auditory canal.

tympanic membrane *n* the thin membrane separating the external ear from the middle ear. It transmits vibrations, produced by sound waves, to the cochlea. Nontechnical name: **eardrum.**

tympanites (ˌtɪmpə'naɪti:z) *n* distension of the abdomen caused by an accumulation of gas in the intestinal or peritoneal cavity. Also called: **meteorism, tympany.** ORIG C14: from LL, from Gk *tumpanitēs* concerning a drum, from *tumpanon* drum
▸ **tympanitic** (ˌtɪmpə'nɪtɪk) *adj*

tympanitis (ˌtɪmpə'naɪtɪs) *n* inflammation of the eardrum.

tympanum ('tɪmpənəm) *n, pl* **tympanums** *or* **tympana** (-nə). **1a** the cavity of the middle ear. **1b** another name for **tympanic membrane.** **2** any diaphragm resembling that in the middle ear in function. **3** *Archit.* **3a** the recessed space bounded by the cornices of a pediment, esp. one that is triangular in shape. **3b** the recessed space bounded by an arch and the lintel of a doorway or window below it. **4** *Music.* a tympan or drum. **5** a scoop wheel for raising water. ORIG C17: from L, from Gk *tumpanon* drum
▸ **tympanic** (tɪm'pænɪk) *adj*

Tyndale, Tindal, *or* **Tindale** ★ ('tɪndᵊl) *n* **William.** ?1492–1536, English Protestant and humanist, who translated the New Testament (1525), the Pentateuch (1530), and the Book of Jonah (1531) into English. He was burnt at the stake as a heretic.

Tyndall ★ ('tɪndᵊl) *n* **John.** 1820–93, Irish physicist, noted for his work on the radiation of heat by gases, the transmission of sound through the atmosphere, and the scattering of light.

Tyndall effect *n* the phenomenon in which light is scattered by particles of matter in its path. ORIG C19: after John TYNDALL

Tyndareus ★ (tɪn'dærɪəs) *n Greek myth.* a Spartan king; the husband of Leda.

Tyne ★ (taɪn) *n* a river in N England, flowing east to the North Sea. Length: 48 km (30 miles).

Tyne and Wear ★ *n* a metropolitan county of NE England, administered since 1986 by the unitary authorities of Newcastle upon Tyne, North Tyneside, Gateshead, South Tyneside, and Sunderland. Area: 540 sq. km (208 sq. miles).

Tynemouth ★ ('taɪn,maʊθ) *n* a port in NE England, in Tyne and Wear at the mouth of the River Tyne: includes the port and industrial centre of North Shields; fishing, ship-repairing, and marine engineering. Pop.: 20 716 (1991).

Tyneside ★ ('taɪn,saɪd) *n* the conurbation on the banks of the Tyne from Newcastle to the coast.

Tynwald ('tɪnwəld, 'taɪn-) *n* **the.** the Parliament of the Isle of Man. ORIG C15: from ON *thingvollr,* from *thing* assembly + *vollr* field

typ., typo., *or* **typog.** *abbrev. for:* **1** typographer. **2** typographic(al). **3** typography.

typal ('taɪpᵊl) *adj* a rare word for **typical.**

type (taɪp) *n* **1** a kind, class, or category, the constituents of which share similar characteristics. **2** a subdivision of a particular class; sort: *what type of shampoo do you use?* **3** the general form, plan, or design distinguishing a particular group. **4** *Inf.* a person who typifies a particular quality: *he's the administrative type.* **5** *Inf.* a person, esp. of a specified kind: *he's a strange type.* **6a** a small block of metal or more rarely wood bearing a letter or character in relief for use in printing. **6b** such pieces collectively. **7** characters printed from type; print. **8** *Biol.* **8a** the taxonomic group the characteristics of which are used for defining the next highest group. **8b** (*as modifier*): *a type genus.* **9** See **type specimen. 10** the characteristic device on a coin. **11** *Chiefly Christian theol.* a figure, episode, or symbolic factor resembling some future reality in such a way as to foreshadow or prefigure it. ◆ *vb* **types, typing, typed. 12** to write (copy) on a typewriter. **13** (*tr*) to be a symbol of; typify. **14** (*tr*) to decide the type of. **15** (*tr*) *Med.* to determine the blood group of (a blood sample). **16** (*tr*) *Chiefly Christian theol.* to foreshadow or serve as a symbol of (some future reality). ORIG C15: from L *typus* figure, from Gk *tupos* image, from *tuptein* to strike

-type *n combining form.* **1** type or form: *archetype.* **2** printing type or photographic process: *collotype.* ORIG from L *-typus,* from Gk *-typos,* from *tupos* TYPE

typecast ('taɪp,kɑːst) *vb* **typecasts, typecasting, typecast.** (*tr*) to cast (an actor) in the same kind of role continually, esp. because of his physical appearance or previous success in such roles.

typeface ('taɪp,feɪs) *n* another name for **face** (sense 14).

type founder *n* a person who casts metallic printer's type.
▸ **type foundry** *n*

type metal *n Printing.* an alloy of tin, lead, and antimony, from which type is cast.

typescript ('taɪp,skrɪpt) *n* **1** a typed copy of a document, etc. **2** any typewritten material.

typeset ('taɪp,sɛt) *vb* **typesets, typesetting, typeset.** (*tr*) *Printing.* to set (textual matter) in type.

typesetter ('taɪp,sɛtə) *n* **1** a person who sets type; compositor. **2** a typesetting machine.

type specimen *n Biol.* the original specimen from which a description of a new species is made.

typewrite ('taɪp,raɪt) *vb* **typewrites, typewriting, typewrote, typewritten.** to write by means of a typewriter; type.
▸ **'type,writing** *n*

typewriter ('taɪp,raɪtə) *n* a keyboard machine for writing mechanically in characters resembling print.

typhlitis (tɪf'laɪtɪs) *n* inflammation of the caecum. ORIG C19: from NL, from Gk *tuphlon* the caecum, from *tuphlos* blind
▸ **typhlitic** (tɪf'lɪtɪk) *adj*

Typhoeus ★ (taɪ'fiːəs) *n Greek myth.* the son of Gaea and Tartarus who had a hundred dragon heads, which spurted fire, and a bellowing many-tongued voice. He created the whirlwinds and fought with Zeus before the god hurled him beneath Mount Etna.
▸ **Ty'phoean** *adj*

typhoid ('taɪfɔɪd) *Pathol.* ◆ *adj also* **typhoidal. 1** resembling typhus. ◆ *n* **2** short for **typhoid fever.** ORIG C19: from TYPHUS + -OID

typhoid fever *n* an acute infectious disease characterized by high fever, spots, abdominal pain, etc. It is caused by a bacillus ingested with food or water.

Typhon ★ ('taɪfɒn) *n Greek myth.* a monster and one of the whirlwinds: later confused with his father Typhoeus.

typhoon (taɪ'fuːn) *n* a violent tropical storm or cyclone, esp. in the China Seas and W Pacific. ORIG C16: from Chinese *tai fung* great wind; infl. by Gk *tuphōn* whirlwind
▸ **typhonic** (taɪ'fɒnɪk) *adj*

typhus ('taɪfəs) *n* any one of a group of acute infectious rickettsial diseases characterized by high fever, skin rash, and severe headache. Also called: **typhus fever.** ORIG C18: from NL *tȳphus,* from Gk *tuphos* fever
▸ **'typhous** *adj*

typical ('tɪpɪkᵊl) *adj* **1** being or serving as a representative example of a particular type; characteristic. **2** considered to be an example of some undesirable trait: *that is typical of you!* **3** of or relating to a representative specimen or type. **4** conforming to a type. **5** *Biol.* having most of the characteristics of a particular taxonomic group. ORIG C17: from Med. L *typicālis,* from LL *typicus* figurative, from Gk *tupikos,* from *tupos* TYPE
▸ **'typically** *adv* ▸ **'typicalness** *or* **,typi'cality** *n*

typify ('tɪpɪ,faɪ) *vb* **typifies, typifying, typified.** (*tr*) **1** to be typical of; characterize. **2** to symbolize or represent completely, by or as if by a type. ORIG C17: from L *typus* TYPE
▸ **,typifi'cation** *n*

typist ('taɪpɪst) *n* a person who types, esp. for a living.

typo ('taɪpəʊ) *n, pl* **typos.** *Inf.* a typographical error. Also called (Brit.): **literal.**

typographer (taɪ'pɒgrəfə) *n* **1** a person skilled in typography. **2** a compositor.

typography (taɪ'pɒgrəfɪ) *n* **1** the art, craft, or process of composing type and printing from it. **2** the planning, selection, and setting of type for a printed work.
▸ **typographical** (,taɪpə'græfɪkᵊl) *or* **,typo'graphic** *adj* ▸ **,typo'graphically** *adv*

typology (taɪ'pɒlədʒɪ) *n* **1** the study of types in archaeology, biology, etc. **2** *Christian theol.* the doctrine that symbols for events, figures, etc., in the New Testament can be found in the Old Testament.
▸ **typological** (,taɪpə'lɒdʒɪkᵊl) *adj* ▸ **ty'pologist** *n*

Tyr *or* **Tyrr** ★ (tjʊə, tɪə) *n Norse myth.* the god of war, son of Odin. Anglo-Saxon counterpart: **Tiu.**

tyrannical (tɪ'rænɪkᵊl) *or* **tyrannic** *adj* characteristic of or relating to a tyrant or to tyranny; oppressive.
▸ **ty'rannically** *adv*

tyrannicide (tɪ'rænɪ,saɪd) *n* **1** the killing of a tyrant. **2** a person who kills a tyrant.

tyrannize *or* **tyrannise** ('tɪrə,naɪz) *vb* **tyrannizes, tyrannizing, tyrannized** or **tyrannises, tyrannising, tyrannised.** (when *intr,* often foll. by *over*) to rule or exercise power (over) in a cruel or oppressive manner.
▸ **'tyran,nizer** *or* **'tyran,niser** *n*

tyrannosaurus (tɪ,rænə'sɔːrəs) *or* **tyrannosaur** (tɪ'rænə,sɔː) *n* any of various large carnivorous two-footed dinosaurs common in North America in Upper Jurassic and Cretaceous times. ORIG C19: from NL, from Gk *turannos* tyrant + -SAUR

tyranny ('tɪrənɪ) *n, pl* **tyrannies. 1a** government by a tyrant; despotism. **1b** oppressive and unjust government by more than one person. **2** arbitrary, unreasonable, or despotic behaviour or use of authority. **3** a tyrannical act. ORIG C14: from OF *tyrannie,* from Med. L *tyrannia,* from L *tyrannus* TYRANT
▸ **'tyrannous** *adj*

tyrant ('taɪrənt) *n* **1** a person who governs oppressively, unjustly, and arbitrarily; despot. **2** any person who exercises authority in a tyrannical manner. ORIG C13: from OF *tyrant,* from L *tyrannus,* from Gk *turannos*

tyre *or US* **tire** ('taɪə) *n* **1** a rubber ring placed over the rim of a wheel of a road vehicle to provide traction and reduce road shocks, esp. a hollow inflated ring (**pneumatic tyre**) consisting of a reinforced outer casing enclosing an inner tube. **2** a metal band or hoop attached to the rim of a wooden cartwheel. ORIG C18: var. of C15 *tire,* prob. from archaic var. of ATTIRE

Tyre *or* **Tyr** ★ ('taɪə) *n* a port in S Lebanon, on the Mediterranean: founded about the 15th century B.C.; for centuries a major Phoenician seaport, famous for silks and its Tyrian-purple dye; now a small market town. Pop.: 70 000 (1991 est.). Arabic name: **Sur.**
▸ **Tyrian** ('tɪrɪən) *adj, n*

Tyrian purple *n* **1** a deep purple dye obtained from certain molluscs and highly prized in antiquity. **2a** a vivid purplish-red colour. **2b** (*as adj*): *a Tyrian-purple robe.*

tyro *or* **tiro** ('taɪrəʊ) *n, pl* **tyros** *or* **tiros.** a novice or beginner. ORIG C17: from L *tīrō* recruit

Tyrol *or* **Tirol** ★ (tɪ'rəʊl, 'tɪrəʊl; *German* ti'ro:l) *n* a mountainous state of W Austria: passed to the Hapsburgs in 1363; S part transferred to Italy in 1919. Capital: Innsbruck. Pop.: 661 901 (1998 est.). Area: 12 648 sq. km (4883 sq. miles).
▸ **Tyrolese** (ˌtɪrə'li:z) *or* ˌ**Tyro'lean** *adj, n*

Tyrone ★ (tɪ'rəʊn) *n* a historic county of W Northern Ireland, occupying almost a quarter of the total area of Northern Ireland.

tyrosinase (ˌtaɪrəʊsɪ'neɪz) *n* an enzyme that is a catalyst in the conversion of tyrosine to the pigment melanin.

tyrosine ('taɪrəˌsi:n, -sɪn, 'tɪrə-) *n* an amino acid that is a precursor of the hormones adrenaline and thyroxine and of the pigment melanin. ORIG C19: from Gk *turos* cheese + -INE[2]

tyrothricin (ˌtaɪrəʊ'θraɪsɪn) *n* an antibiotic, obtained from a soil bacterium: applied locally for the treatment of ulcers and abscesses. ORIG C20: from NL *Tyrothrix* (genus name), from Gk *turos* cheese + *thrix* hair

Tyrr ★ (tjʊə, tɪə) *n* a variant spelling of **Tyr.**

Tyrrhenian Sea ★ (tɪ'ri:nɪən) *n* an arm of the Mediterranean between Italy and the islands of Corsica, Sardinia, and Sicily.

Tyson ★ ('taɪsᵊn) *n* **Mike.** born 1966, US boxer, world heavyweight champion (1986–90; 1996): jailed for rape (1992–95).

Tyumen ★ (*Russian* tju'mjenj) *n* a port in S central Russia, on the Tura River: one of the oldest Russian towns in Siberia; industrial centre with nearby oil and natural gas reserves. Pop.: 494 000 (1995 est.).

tzar (zɑ:) *n* a less common spelling of **tsar.**

Tzara ★ (*French* dzara; *Romanian* tsa'ra) *n* **Tristan** (*French* tristɑ̃) original name *Samuel Rosenstock.* 1896–1963, French poet, born in Romania; the founder of Dada.

tzatziki (tsæt'sɪkɪ) *n* a Greek dip made from yogurt, chopped cucumber, and mint. ORIG C20: from Mod. Gk

Tzekung ('tsɛ'kʊŋ) *or* **Tzu-kung** ★ ('tsu:'kʊŋ) *n* a variant transliteration of the Chinese name for **Zigong.**

tzetze fly ('tsɛtsɪ) *n* a variant spelling of **tsetse fly.**

Tzigane (tsɪ'gɑ:n, sɪ-) *n* **a** a Gypsy, esp. a Hungarian one. **b** (*as modifier*): *Tzigane music.* ORIG C19: via F from Hungarian *czigány* Gypsy, from ?

Tzu-po ('tsu:'pəʊ) *or* **Tzepo** ★ ('tsɛ'pəʊ) *n* a variant transliteration of the Chinese name for **Zibo.**

★ people and places

Uu

u *or* **U** (juː) *n, pl* **u's, U's,** *or* **Us. 1** the 21st letter and fifth vowel of the English alphabet. **2** any of several speech sounds represented by this letter, as in *mute, cut,* or *minus.* **3a** something shaped like a U. **3b** (*in combination*): *a U-bolt.*

U *symbol for:* **1** united. **2** unionist. **3** university. **4** (in Britain) **4a** universal (used to describe a category of film certified as suitable for viewing by anyone). **4b** (*as modifier*): *a U certificate film.* **5** *Chem.* uranium. **6** *Biochem.* uracil. ♦ *adj* **7** *Brit. inf.* (esp. of language habits) characteristic of or appropriate to the upper class.

U. *abbrev. for:* **1** *Maths.* union. **2** unit. **3** united. **4** university. **5** upper.

UAE *abbrev. for* United Arab Emirates.

UAR *abbrev. for* United Arab Republic.

UB40 *n* (in Britain) **1** a registration card issued by the Department of Employment to a person registering as unemployed. **2** *Inf.* a person registered as unemployed.

Ubangi ★ (juːˈbæŋgɪ) *n* a river in central Africa, flowing west and south, forming the border between the Democratic Republic of Congo and the Central African Republic and Congo–Brazzaville, into the River Congo. Length: (with the Uele) 2250 km (1400 miles). French name: **Oubangui.**

Ubangi-Shari ★ *n* a former name (until 1958) of the **Central African Republic.**

U-bend *n* a U-shaped bend in a pipe that traps water in the lower part of the U and prevents the escape of noxious fumes; trap.

uber- *or* **über-** (ˈuːbə) *combining form.* indicating the highest, greatest, or most extreme example of something: *America's ubernerd, Bill Gates; the uber-hip young Bohemians.* ORIG C20: from G *über* over, above

uberrima fides (jʊˈbɛrɪmə ˈfaɪdiːz) *n* another name for **utmost good faith.** ORIG L: utmost good faith

ubiety (juːˈbaɪɪtɪ) *n* the condition of being in a particular place. ORIG C17: from L *ubī* where + *-ety,* on the model of *society*

ubiquitarian (juːˌbɪkwɪˈtɛərɪən) *n* **1** a member of the Lutheran church who holds that Christ is no more present in the elements of the Eucharist than elsewhere, as he is present in all places at all times. ♦ *adj* **2** denoting or holding this belief. ORIG C17: from L *ubīque* everywhere
▸ **uˌbiquiˈtarianˌism** *n*

ubiquitous (juːˈbɪkwɪtəs) *adj* having or seeming to have the ability to be everywhere at once. ORIG C14: from L *ubīque* everywhere, from *ubī* where
▸ **uˈbiquitously** *adv* ▸ **uˈbiquity** *n*

U-boat *n* a German submarine, esp. in World Wars I and II. ORIG from G *U-Boot,* short for *Unterseeboot,* lit.: undersea boat

UBR *abbrev. for* uniform business rate.

ubuntu (ʊˈbʊntʊ) *n S. African.* humanity or fellow feeling; kindness. ORIG Nguni

u.c. *Printing. abbrev. for* upper case.

UCAS (ˈjuːkæs) *n* (in Britain) *acronym for* Universities and Colleges Admission Service.

UCATT (in Britain) *abbrev. for* Union of Construction, Allied Trades and Technicians.

Ucayali ★ (*Spanish* ukaˈjali) *n* a river in E Peru, flowing north into the Marañón above Iquitos. Length: 1600 km (1000 miles).

UCCA (ˈʌkə) *n* (formerly, in Britain) *acronym for* Universities Central Council on Admissions.

Uccello ★ (*Italian* utˈtʃɛllo) *n* **Paolo** (ˈpaːolo). 1397–1475, Florentine painter noted for three paintings of *The Battle of San Romano, 1432* (1456–60).

UDA *abbrev. for* Ulster Defence Association.

Udaipur ★ (uːˈdaɪpʊə, ˈuːdaɪˌpʊə) *n* **1** Also called: **Mewar.** a former state of NW India: became part of Rajasthan in 1947. **2** a city in NW India, in S Rajasthan. Pop.: 308 571 (1991).

udal (ˈjuːdᵊl) *n Law.* a form of freehold possession of land existing in northern Europe before the introduction of the feudal system and still used in Orkney and Shetland. ORIG C16: Orkney & Shetland dialect, from ON *othal*

UDC (in Britain) *abbrev. for* Urban District Council.

udder (ˈʌdə) *n* the large baglike mammary gland of cows, sheep, etc., having two or more teats. ORIG OE *ūder*

UDI *abbrev. for* Unilateral Declaration of Independence.

Udine ★ (*Italian* ˈuːdine) *n* a city in NE Italy, in Friuli-Venezia Giulia region: partially damaged in an earthquake in 1976. Pop.: 98 872 (1990).

UDM (in Britain) *abbrev. for* Union of Democratic Mineworkers.

Udmurt Republic ★ (ˈʊdmʊət) *n* a constituent republic of W central Russia, in the basin of the middle Kama. Capital: Izhevsk. Pop.: 1 639 000 (1996 est.). Area: 42 100 sq. km (16 250 sq. miles).

udometer (juːˈdɒmɪtə) *n* another term for **rain gauge.** ORIG C19: from F, from L *ūdus* damp

udon (ˈuːdɒn) *n* (in Japanese cookery) large noodles made of wheat flour. ORIG Japanese

UDR *abbrev. for* Ulster Defence Regiment.

UEFA (juːˈeɪfə, ˈjuːfə) *n acronym for* Union of European Football Associations.

Uele ★ (ˈweɪlə) *n* a river in central Africa, rising near the border between the Democratic Republic of Congo and Uganda and flowing west to join the Bomu River and form the Ubangi River. Length: about 1100 km (700 miles).

uey (ˈjuːɪ) *n, pl* **ueys.** *Austral. sl.* a U-turn.

Ufa ★ (*Russian* uˈfa) *n* a city in W central Russia, capital of the Bashkir Republic: university (1957). Pop.: 1 094 000 (1995 est.).

Uffizi ★ (juːˈfɪtsɪ) *n* an art gallery in Florence; built by Giorgio Vasari in the 16th century and opened as a museum in 1765: contains chiefly Italian Renaissance paintings.

UFO (*sometimes* ˈjuːfəʊ) *abbrev. for* unidentified flying object.

ufology (ˌjuːˈfɒlədʒɪ) *n* the study of UFOs.
▸ **uˈfologist** *n*

Uganda ★ (juːˈgændə) *n* a republic in E Africa: British protectorate established in 1894–96; gained independence in 1962 and became a republic in 1963; a member of the Commonwealth. It consists mostly of a savanna plateau with part of Lake Victoria in the southeast and mountains in the southwest, reaching 5109 m (16 763 ft) in the Ruwenzori Range. Official language: English; Swahili, Luganda, and Luo are also widely spoken. Religion: chiefly Christian. Currency: Ugandan shilling. Capital: Kampala. Pop.: 22 805 000 (1999 est.). Area: 235 886 sq. km (91 076 sq. miles).
▸ **Uˈgandan** *adj, n*

Ugaritic (ˌuːgəˈrɪtɪk) *n* **1** an extinct Semitic language of N Syria. ♦ *adj* **2** of or relating to this language. ORIG C19: after *Ugarit* (modern name: Ras Shamra), an ancient Syrian city-state

UGC (in Britain) *abbrev. for* University Grants Committee.

ugh (ʊx, ʊh, ʌx) *interj* an exclamation of disgust, annoyance, or dislike.

UGLI (ˈʌglɪ) *n, pl* **UGLIS** *or* **UGLIES.** *Trademark.* a large juicy yellow-skinned citrus fruit of the Caribbean: a cross between a tangerine, grapefruit, and orange. Also called:

★ people and places

UGLI fruit. ORIG C20: prob. an alteration of UGLY, from its wrinkled skin

uglify (ˈʌglɪˌfaɪ) *vb* **uglifies, uglifying, uglified.** to make or become ugly or more ugly.
▸ **ˌuglifiˈcation** *n*

ugly (ˈʌglɪ) *adj* **uglier, ugliest. 1** of unpleasant or unsightly appearance. **2** repulsive or displeasing: *war is ugly.* **3** ominous or menacing: *an ugly situation.* **4** bad-tempered or sullen: *an ugly mood.* ORIG C13: from ON *uggligr* dreadful, from *ugga* fear
▸ **ˈuglily** *adv* ▸ **ˈugliness** *n*

ugly duckling *n* a person or thing, initially ugly or unpromising, that changes into something beautiful or admirable. ORIG from *The Ugly Duckling* by Hans Christian Andersen

Ugrian (ˈuːgrɪən, ˈjuː-) *adj* **1** of or relating to a subdivision of the Turanian people, who include the Samoyeds and Magyars. ◆ *n* **2** a member of this group. **3** another word for **Ugric.** ORIG C19: from ORussian *Ugre* Hungarians

Ugric (ˈuːgrɪk, ˈjuː-) *n* **1** one of the two branches of the Finno-Ugric family of languages, including Hungarian and some languages of NW Siberia. ◆ *adj* **2** of or relating to this group of languages or their speakers.

UHF *Radio. abbrev. for* ultrahigh frequency.

uh-huh (ˈʌhʌ) *sentence substitute. Inf.* a less emphatic variant of **yes.**

uhlan (ˈuːlɑːn) *n History.* a member of a body of lancers first employed in the Polish army and later in W European armies. ORIG C18: via G from Polish *ulan,* from Turkish *ōlan* young man

Uhland ★ (*German* ˈuːlant) *n* **Johann Ludwig** (joˈhan ˈluːtvɪç). 1787–1862, German romantic poet, esp. of lyrics and ballads.

UHT *abbrev. for* ultra-heat-treated (milk or cream).

uhuru (uːˈhuːruː) *n* (esp. in E Africa) **1** national independence. **2** freedom. ORIG C20: from Swahili

Uigur *or* **Uighur** (ˈwiːgʊə) *n* **1** (*pl* **Uigur, Uigurs** *or* **Uighur, Uighurs**) a member of a Mongoloid people of NW China and adjacent parts of central Asia. **2** the language of this people, belonging to the Turkic branch of the Altaic family.
▸ **Uiˈgurian, Uiˈghurian** *or* **Uiˈguric, Uiˈghuric** *adj*

uillean pipes (ˈuːlɪən) *pl n* bagpipes developed in Ireland and operated by squeezing bellows under the arm. Also called: **Irish pipes, union pipes.** ORIG C19: Irish *píob uilleann,* from *píob* pipe + *uilleann* genitive sing of *uille* elbow

Uinta Mountains ★ (juˈɪntə) *pl n* a mountain range in NE Utah: part of the Rocky Mountains. Highest peak: Kings Peak, 4123 m (13 528 ft).

uitlander (ˈeɪtˌlandə, -ˌlæn-) *n* (*sometimes cap.*) *S. African.* a foreigner. ORIG C19: Afrik.: outlander

Ujiji ★ (uːˈdʒiːdʒɪ) *n* a town in W Tanzania, on Lake Tanganyika: a former slave and ivory centre; the place where Stanley found Livingstone in 1871; merged with the town of Kigoma in the 1960s.

Ujjain ★ (uːˈdʒeɪn) *n* a city in W central India, in Madhya Pradesh: one of the seven sacred cities of the Hindus; a major agricultural trade centre. Pop.: 362 266 (1991).

Ujung Pandang ★ (ˈuːdʒʊŋ pænˈdæŋ) *n* a port in central Indonesia, on SW Sulawesi: an important native port before Portuguese (16th century) and Dutch (17th century) control; capital of Dutch East Indonesia (1946–49); a major Indonesian distribution and transshipment port. Pop.: 1 091 800 (1995 est.). Also called: **Makasar, Makassar, Macassar.**

UK *abbrev. for* United Kingdom.

ukase (juːˈkeɪz) *n* **1** (in imperial Russia) an edict of the tsar. **2** a rare word for **edict.** ORIG C18: from Russian *ukaz,* from *ukazat* to command

UKCC *abbrev. for* United Kingdom Central Council for Nursing, Midwifery, and Health Visiting.

Ukr. *abbrev. for* Ukraine.

Ukraine ★ (juːˈkreɪn) *n* a republic in SE Europe, on the Black Sea and the Sea of Azov: from the 7th to 9th centuries the area was part of the Rurik kingdom and was subsequently part of the empires of the Mongols, Lithuania, Poland, and Russia; it was one of the four republics that originally formed the Soviet Union in 1922; became fully independent in 1991; consists chiefly of lowlands; mainly agricultural but has rich mineral resources. Official language: Ukrainian. Religion: believers are mainly Christian. Currency: hryvna. Capital: Kiev. Pop.: 49 890 000 (1999 est.). Area 603 700 sq. km (231 990 sq. miles).

Ukrainian (juːˈkreɪnɪən) *adj* **1** of or relating to Ukraine, its people, or their language. ◆ *n* **2** the official language of Ukraine: an East Slavonic language closely related to Russian. **3** a native or inhabitant of Ukraine.

ukulele *or* **ukelele** (ˌjuːkəˈleɪlɪ) *n* a small four-stringed guitar, esp. of Hawaii. ORIG C19: from Hawaiian, lit.: jumping flea

Ulan Bator ★ (ʊˈlɑːn ˈbɑːtɔː) *n* the capital of Mongolia, in the N central part: developed in the mid-17th century around the Da Khure monastery, residence until 1924 of successive "living Buddhas" (third in rank of Buddhist-Lamaist leaders), and main junction of caravan routes across Mongolia; university (1942); industrial and commercial centre. Pop.: 627 300 (1997 est.). Former name (until 1924): **Urga.** Chinese name: **Kulun.**

Ulanova ★ (*Russian* uˈlanəvə) *n* **Galina** (**Sergeyevna**) (gaˈlinə). 1910–98, Russian ballet dancer, who performed with the Leningrad Kirov ballet (1928–44) and the Moscow Bolshoi Ballet (1944–62).

Ulan-Ude ★ (ʊˈlɑːnʊˈdɛ) *n* an industrial city in SE Russia, capital of the Buryat Republic: an important rail junction. Pop.: 366 000 (1995 est.). Former name (until 1934): **Verkhne-Udinsk.**

Ulbricht ★ (*German* ˈʊlbrɪçt) *n* **Walter** (ˈvaltər). 1893–1973, East German statesman; largely responsible for the establishment and development of East German communism.

ulcer (ˈʌlsə) *n* **1** a disintegration of the surface of the skin or a mucous membrane resulting in an open sore that heals very slowly. **2** a source or element of corruption or evil. ORIG C14: from L *ulcus*

ulcerate (ˈʌlsəˌreɪt) *vb* **ulcerates, ulcerating, ulcerated.** to make or become ulcerous.
▸ **ˌulceˈration** *n* ▸ **ˈulcerative** *adj*

ulcerous (ˈʌlsərəs) *adj* **1** relating to or characterized by ulcers. **2** being or having a corrupting influence.
▸ **ˈulcerously** *adv*

-ule *suffix forming nouns.* indicating smallness: *globule.* ORIG from L *-ulus,* dim. suffix

Uleåborg ★ (ˈuːlioˌbɔrjə) *n* the Swedish name for **Oulu.**

ulema (ˈuːlɪmə) *n* **1** a body of Muslim scholars or religious leaders. **2** a member of this body. ORIG C17: from Ar. *ʻulamā* scholars, from *ʻalama* to know

-ulent *suffix forming adjectives.* abundant or full of: *fraudulent.* ORIG from L *-ulentus*

ullage (ˈʌlɪdʒ) *n* **1** the volume by which a liquid container falls short of being full. **2a** the quantity of liquid lost from a container due to leakage or evaporation. **2b** (in customs terminology) the amount of liquid remaining in a container after such loss. ORIG C15: from OF *ouillage* filling of a cask, from *ouil* eye, from L *oculus* eye

Ullswater ★ (ˈʌlzˌwɔːtə) *n* a lake in NW England, in Cumbria in the Lake District. Length: 12 km (7.5 miles).

Ulm ★ (*German* ʊlm) *n* an industrial city in S Germany, in Baden-Württemberg on the Danube: a free imperial city (1155–1802). Pop.: 115 721 (1996 est.).

ulna (ˈʌlnə) *n, pl* **ulnae** (-niː) *or* **ulnas. 1** the inner and longer of the two bones of the human forearm. **2** the corresponding bone in other vertebrates. ORIG C16: from L: elbow
▸ **ˈulnar** *adj*

ulnar nerve *n* a nerve situated along the inner side of the arm and passing close to the surface of the skin near the elbow.

ulotrichous (juːˈlɒtrɪkəs) *adj* having woolly or curly hair. ORIG C19: from NL *Ulotrichī* (classification applied to humans having this type of hair), from Gk *oulothrix,* from *oulos* curly + *thrix* hair

ulster ('ʌlstə) *n* a man's heavy double-breasted overcoat with a belt or half-belt. ORIG C19: from ULSTER

Ulster ★ ('ʌlstə) *n* **1** a former kingdom and province of Ireland: passed to the English Crown in 1461; confiscated land given to English and Scottish Protestant settlers in the 17th century, giving rise to serious long-term conflict; partitioned in 1921, six counties forming Northern Ireland and three counties joining the Republic of Ireland. **2** an informal name for **Northern Ireland.**

Ulster Defence Association *n* (in Northern Ireland) a Loyalist paramilitary organization. Abbrev.: **UDA.**

Ulster Democratic Unionist Party *n* a Northern Irish political party advocating the maintenance of the Union with Great Britain.

Ulsterman ('ʌlstəmən) *n, pl* **Ulstermen.** a native or inhabitant of Ulster.
▸ **'Ulster,woman** *fem n*

Ulster Unionist Council *n* a Northern Irish political party advocating the maintenance of the Union with Great Britain.

ult. *abbrev. for:* **1** ultimate(ly). **2** ultimo.

ulterior (ʌl'tɪərɪə) *adj* **1** lying beneath or beyond what is revealed or supposed: *ulterior motives.* **2** succeeding, subsequent, or later. **3** lying beyond a certain line or point. ORIG C17: from L: further, from *ulter* beyond
▸ **ul'teriorly** *adv*

ultima ('ʌltɪmə) *n* the final syllable of a word. ORIG from L: the last

ultimate ('ʌltɪmɪt) *adj* **1** conclusive in a series or process; final: *an ultimate question.* **2** the highest or most significant: *the ultimate goal.* **3** elemental, fundamental, or essential. **4** most extreme: *the ultimate abuse of human rights.* **5** final or total: *the ultimate cost.* ◆ *n* **6** the most significant, highest, or greatest thing. ORIG C17: from LL *ultimāre* to come to an end, from L *ultimus* last, from *ulter* distant
▸ **'ultimately** *adv* ▸ **'ultimateness** *n*

ultima Thule ('θju:lɪ) *n* **1** a region believed by ancient geographers to be the northernmost land. **2** any distant or unknown region. **3** a remote goal or aim. ORIG L: the most distant Thule

ultimatum (,ʌltɪ'meɪtəm) *n, pl* **ultimatums** *or* **ultimata** (-tə). **1** a final communication by a party setting forth conditions on which it insists, as during negotiations on some topic. **2** any final or peremptory demand or proposal. ORIG C18: from NL, neuter of *ultimatus* ULTIMATE

ultimo ('ʌltɪ,məʊ) *adv Now rare except when abbreviated in formal correspondence.* in or during the previous month: *a letter of the 7th ultimo.* Abbrev.: **ult.** ORIG C16: from L *ultimō* on the last

ultimogeniture (,ʌltɪməʊ'dʒɛnɪtʃə) *n Law.* a principle of inheritance whereby the youngest son succeeds to the estate of his ancestor. ORIG C19: *ultimo-* from L *ultimus* last + LL *genitūra* a birth

ultra ('ʌltrə) *adj* **1** extreme or immoderate, esp. in beliefs or opinions. ◆ *n* **2** an extremist. ORIG C19: from L: beyond, from *ulter* distant

ultra- *prefix* **1** beyond or surpassing a specified extent, range, or limit: *ultramicroscopic.* **2** extreme or extremely: *ultramodern.* ORIG from L *ultrā* beyond

ultracentrifuge (,ʌltrə'sɛntrɪ,fju:dʒ) *n Chem.* a high-speed centrifuge used to separate colloidal solutions.

ultraconservative (,ʌltrəkən'sɜ:vətɪv) *adj* **1** highly reactionary. ◆ *n* **2** a reactionary person.

ultra-distance *n (modifier) Athletics.* covering a distance in excess of 30 miles, often as part of a longer race or competition: *an ultra-distance runner.*

ultrafiche ('ʌltrə,fi:ʃ) *n* a sheet of film, usually the size of a filing card, that is similar to a microfiche but has a much larger number of microcopies. ORIG C20: from ULTRA- + F *fiche* small card

ultrahigh frequency ('ʌltrə,haɪ) *n* a radio-frequency band or radio frequency lying between 3000 and 300 megahertz. Abbrev.: **UHF.**

ultraism ('ʌltrə,ɪzəm) *n* extreme philosophy, belief, or action.
▸ **'ultraist** *n, adj*

ultramarine (,ʌltrəmə'ri:n) *n* **1** a blue pigment obtained by powdering natural lapis lazuli or made synthetically: used in paints, printing ink, plastics, etc. **2** a vivid blue colour. ◆ *adj* **3** of the colour ultramarine. **4** from across the seas. ORIG C17: from Med. L *ultramarinus,* from *ultrā* beyond + *mare* sea; so called because the lapis lazuli from which the pigment was made was imported from Asia

ultramicroscope (,ʌltrə'maɪkrə,skəʊp) *n* a microscope used for studying colloids, in which the sample is illuminated from the side and colloidal particles are seen as bright points on a dark background.

ultramicroscopic (,ʌltrə,maɪkrə'skɒpɪk) *adj* **1** too small to be seen with an optical microscope. **2** of or relating to an ultramicroscope.

ultramodern (,ʌltrə'mɒdən) *adj* extremely modern.
▸ **,ultra'modernism** *n* ▸ **,ultra'modernist** *n* ▸ **,ultra,modern'istic** *adj*

ultramontane (,ʌltrəmɒn'teɪn) *adj* **1** on the other side of the mountains, esp. the Alps, from the speaker or writer. **2** of or relating to a movement in the Roman Catholic Church which favours the centralized authority and influence of the pope as opposed to local independence. ◆ *n* **3** a person from beyond the mountains, esp. the Alps. **4** a member of the ultramontane party of the Roman Catholic Church.

ultramundane (,ʌltrə'mʌndeɪn) *adj* extending beyond the world, this life, or the universe.

ultranationalism (,ʌltrə'næʃnə,lɪzəm) *n* extreme devotion to one's own nation.
▸ **,ultra'national** *adj* ▸ **,ultra'nationalist** *adj, n*

ultrashort (,ʌltrə'ʃɔ:t) *adj* (of a radio wave) having a wavelength shorter than 10 metres.

ultrasonic (,ʌltrə'sɒnɪk) *adj* of, concerned with, or producing waves with the same nature as sound waves but frequencies above audio frequencies.
▸ **,ultra'sonically** *adv*

ultrasonics (,ʌltrə'sɒnɪks) *n (functioning as sing)* the branch of physics concerned with ultrasonic waves. Also called: **supersonics.**

ultrasound ('ʌltrə,saʊnd) *n* ultrasonic waves at frequencies above the audible range (above about 20 kHz), used in cleaning metallic parts, echo sounding, medical diagnosis and therapy, etc.

ultrasound scanner *n* a device used to examine an internal bodily structure by the use of ultrasonic waves, esp. for the diagnosis of abnormality in a fetus.

ultrastructure ('ʌltrə,strʌktʃə) *n* the minute structure of an organ, tissue, or cell, as revealed by microscopy.

ultraviolet (,ʌltrə'vaɪəlɪt) *n* **1** the part of the electromagnetic spectrum with wavelengths shorter than light but longer than X-rays; in the range 0.4×10^{-6} and 1×10^{-8} metres. ◆ *adj* **2** of, relating to, or consisting of radiation lying in the ultraviolet: *ultraviolet radiation; ultraviolet spectroscopy.* Abbrev.: **UV.**

ultraviolet astronomy *n* the study of radiation from celestial sources in the wavelength range 91.2 to 320 nanometres.

ultra vires ('vaɪri:z) *adv, adj (predicative) Law.* beyond the legal power of a person, corporation, agent, etc. ORIG L, lit.: beyond strength

ultravirus (,ʌltrə'vaɪrəs) *n* a virus small enough to pass through the finest filter.

ululate ('ju:lju,leɪt) *vb* **ululates, ululating, ululated.** *(intr)* to howl or wail, as with grief. ORIG C17: from L *ululāre* to howl, from *ulula* screech owl
▸ **'ululant** *adj* ▸ **,ulu'lation** *n*

Uluru ★ (,u:lə'ru:) *n* the world's largest monolith, in the Northern Territory of Australia. Height: 330 m (1100 ft). Base circumference: 9 km (5.6 miles). Former name: **Ayers Rock.**

Ulyanovsk ★ *(Russian* ulj'janəfsk) *n* the former name (1924–91) of **Simbirsk.**

Ulysses ★ ('ju:lɪ,si:z, ju:'lɪsi:z) *n* the Latin name of **Odysseus.**

Umar ★ ('u:mɑ:) *n* a variant transliteration of the Arabic name for **Omar**.

Umayyad ★ (u:'maɪjæd) *n* a variant spelling of **Omayyad**.

umbel ('ʌmbᵊl) *n* a racemose inflorescence, characteristic of umbelliferous plants, in which the flowers arise from the same point in the main stem and have stalks of the same length, to give a cluster with the youngest flowers at the centre. ORIG C16: from L *umbella* a sunshade, from *umbra* shade
▸ **umbellate** ('ʌmbɪlɪt, -ˌleɪt) *or* **umbellar** (ʌm'bɛlə) *adj*
▸ **umbellule** (ʌm'bɛlju:l) *n*

umbelliferous (ˌʌmbɪ'lɪfərəs) *adj* of or belonging to a family of herbaceous plants and shrubs, typically having hollow stems, divided or compound leaves, and flowers in umbels: includes fennel, parsley, carrot, and parsnip. ORIG C17: from NL, from L *umbella* sunshade + *ferre* to bear
▸ **um'bellifer** *n*

umber ('ʌmbə) *n* **1** any of various natural brown earths containing ferric oxide together with lime and oxides of aluminium, manganese, and silicon. **2** any of the dark brown to greenish-brown colours produced by this pigment. **3** *Obs.* shade. ◆ *adj* **4** of, relating to, or stained with umber. ORIG C16: from F (*terre d'*)*ombre* or It. (*terra di*) *ombra* shadow (earth), from L *umbra* shade

Umberto I ★ (*Italian* um'bɛrto) *n* 1844–1900, king of Italy (1878–1900); son of Victor Emmanuel II: assassinated at Monza.

umbilical (ʌm'bɪlɪkᵊl, ˌʌmbɪ'laɪkᵊl) *adj* **1** of, relating to, or resembling the umbilicus or the umbilical cord. **2** in the region of the umbilicus: *an umbilical hernia.*

umbilical cord *n* **1** the long flexible tubelike structure connecting a fetus with the placenta. **2** any flexible cord, tube, or cable, as between an astronaut walking in space and his spacecraft.

umbilicate (ʌm'bɪlɪkɪt, -ˌkeɪt) *adj* **1** having an umbilicus. **2** having a central depression: *an umbilicate leaf.* **3** shaped like a navel, as some bacterial colonies.
▸ **umˌbili'cation** *n*

umbilicus (ʌm'bɪlɪkəs, ˌʌmbɪ'laɪkəs) *n, pl* **umbilici** (-'bɪlɪˌsaɪ, -bɪ'laɪsaɪ). **1** *Biol.* a hollow or navel-like structure, such as the cavity at the base of a gastropod shell. **2** *Anat.* a technical name for the **navel**. ORIG C18: from L: navel, centre

umble pie ('ʌmbᵊl) *n* See **humble pie** (sense 1).

umbles ('ʌmbᵊlz) *pl n* See **numbles**.

umbo ('ʌmbəʊ) *n, pl* **umbones** (ʌm'bəʊni:z) *or* **umbos**. **1** *Bot., anat.* a small hump, prominence, or convex area, as in certain mushrooms, bivalve molluscs, and the outer surface of the eardrum. **2** a large projecting central boss on a shield, esp. on a Saxon shield. ORIG C18: from L: projecting piece
▸ **umbonate** ('ʌmbənɪt, -ˌneɪt), **umbonal** ('ʌmbənᵊl), *or* **umbonic** (ʌm'bɒnɪk) *adj*

umbra ('ʌmbrə) *n, pl* **umbrae** (-bri:) *or* **umbras**. **1** a region of complete shadow resulting from the obstruction of light by an opaque object, esp. the shadow cast by the moon onto the earth during a solar eclipse. **2** the darker inner region of a sunspot. ORIG C16: from L: shade
▸ **'umbral** *adj*

umbrage ('ʌmbrɪdʒ) *n* **1** displeasure or resentment; offence (in **give** *or* **take umbrage**). **2** the foliage of trees, considered as providing shade. **3** *Rare.* shadow or shade. ORIG C15: from OF, from L *umbrāticus* relating to shade, from *umbra* shade

umbrageous (ʌm'breɪdʒəs) *adj* **1** shady or shading. **2** *Rare.* easily offended.

umbrella (ʌm'brɛlə) *n* **1** a portable device used for protection against rain, snow, etc., and consisting of a light canopy supported on a collapsible metal frame mounted on a central rod. **2** the flattened cone-shaped body of a jellyfish. **3** a protective shield or screen, esp. of aircraft or gunfire. **4** anything that has the effect of a protective screen, general cover, or organizing agency. ORIG C17: from It. *ombrella,* dim. of *ombra* shade; see UMBRA
▸ **um'brella-ˌlike** *adj*

umbrella pine *n* another name for **stone pine**.

umbrella stand *n* an upright rack or stand for umbrellas.

umbrella tree *n* **1** a North American magnolia having long leaves clustered into an umbrella formation at the ends of the branches and having unpleasant-smelling white flowers. **2** Also called: **umbrella bush**. any of various trees or shrubs having umbrella-shaped leaves or growing in an umbrella-like cluster.

Umbria ★ ('ʌmbrɪə; *Italian* 'umbrja) *n* a mountainous region of central Italy, in the valley of the Tiber. Pop.: 825 910 (1996 est.). Area: 8456 sq. km (3265 sq. miles).

Umbrian ('ʌmbrɪən) *adj* **1** of or relating to Umbria, its inhabitants, or the ancient language once spoken there. **2** of or relating to a Renaissance school of painting that included Raphael. ◆ *n* **3** a native or inhabitant of Umbria. **4** an extinct language of ancient S Italy.

umfazi (ˌʊm'fɑ:ʒɪ) *n S. African.* a Black married woman. ORIG from Bantu

umiak *or* **oomiak** ('u:mɪˌæk) *n* a large open boat made of stretched skins, used by Eskimos. ORIG C18: from Eskimo: boat for the use of women

umlaut ('ʊmlaʊt) *n* **1** the mark (¨) placed over a vowel in some languages, such as German, indicating modification in the quality of the vowel. **2** (esp. in Germanic languages) the change of a vowel within a word brought about by the assimilating influence of a vowel or semivowel in a preceding or following syllable. ORIG C19: G, from *um* around (in the sense of changing places) + *Laut* sound

umlungu (ˌʊm'lʊŋgʊ) *n S. African.* a White man: used esp. as a term of address. ORIG from Bantu

umpire ('ʌmpaɪə) *n* **1** an official who rules on the playing of a game, as in cricket. **2** a person who rules on or judges disputes between contesting parties. ◆ *vb* **umpires, umpiring, umpired. 3** to act as umpire in (a game, dispute, or controversy). ORIG C15: by mistaken division from *a noumpere,* from OF *nomper* not one of a pair, from *nom-, non-* not + *per* equal

umpteen (ˌʌmp'ti:n) *determiner Inf.* **a** very many: *umpteen things to do.* **b** (*as pronoun*): *umpteen of them came.* ORIG C20: from *umpty* a great deal (?from *-enty* as in *twenty*) + *-teen* ten
▸ **ˌump'teenth** *n, adj*

Umtali ★ (ʊm'tɑ:lɪ) *n* the former name (until 1982) of **Mutare**.

Umtata ★ (ʊm'tɑ:tə) *n* a city in SE South Africa. Pop.: 80 000 (latest est.).

UN *abbrev. for* United Nations.

un-[1] *prefix* (*freely used with adjectives, participles, and their derivative adverbs and nouns: less frequently used with certain other nouns*) not; contrary to; opposite of: *uncertain; untidiness; unbelief; untruth.* ORIG from OE *on-, un-*

un-[2] *prefix forming verbs.* **1** denoting reversal of an action or state: *uncover; untangle.* **2** denoting removal from, release, or deprivation: *unharness; unthrone.* **3** (intensifier): *unloose.* ORIG from OE *un-, on-*

'un *or* **un** (ən) *pron* a spelling of **one** intended to reflect a dialectal or informal pronunciation: *that's a big 'un.*

unable (ʌn'eɪbᵊl) *adj* (*postpositive;* foll. by *to*) lacking the necessary power, ability, or authority (to do something); not able.

unaccented (ˌʌnæk'sɛntɪd) *adj* not stressed or emphasized in pronunciation.

unaccountable (ˌʌnə'kaʊntəbᵊl) *adj* **1** allowing of no explanation; inexplicable. **2** extraordinary: *an unaccountable fear of heights.* **3** not accountable or answerable to.
▸ **ˌunacˌcounta'bility** *n* ▸ **ˌunac'countably** *adv*

unaccustomed (ˌʌnə'kʌstəmd) *adj* **1** (foll. by *to*) not used (to): *unaccustomed to pain.* **2** not familiar.
▸ **ˌunac'customedness** *n*

una corda ('u:nə 'kɔ:də) *adj, adv Music.* (of the piano) to be played with the soft pedal depressed. ORIG It., lit.: one string; the pedal moves the mechanism so that only one string of the three tuned to each note is struck by the hammer

★ people and places

unadopted (ˌʌnəˈdɒptɪd) *adj* **1** (of a child) not adopted. **2** *Brit.* (of a road, etc.) not maintained by a local authority.

unadvised (ˌʌnədˈvaɪzd) *adj* **1** rash or unwise. **2** not having received advice.
▸ **unadvisedly** (ˌʌnədˈvaɪzɪdlɪ) *adv* ▸ **ˌunadˈvisedness** *n*

unaffected[1] (ˌʌnəˈfɛktɪd) *adj* unpretentious, natural, or sincere.
▸ **ˌunafˈfectedly** *adv* ▸ **ˌunafˈfectedness** *n*

unaffected[2] (ˌʌnəˈfɛktɪd) *adj* not affected.

Unalaska Island ★ (ˌuːnəˈlæskə) *n* a large volcanic island in SW Alaska, in the Aleutian Islands. Length: 120 km (75 miles). Greatest width: about 40 km (25 miles).

unalienable (ʌnˈeɪljənəbᵊl) *adj Law.* a variant of **inalienable.**

un-American *adj* **1** not in accordance with the aims, ideals, customs, etc., of the US. **2** against the interests of the US.
▸ **ˌun-Aˈmericanism** *n*

Unamuno ★ (*Spanish* unaˈmuno) *n* **Miguel de** (miˈɣɛl de). 1864–1936, Spanish philosopher and writer.

unanimous (juːˈnænɪməs) *adj* **1** in complete agreement. **2** characterized by complete agreement: *a unanimous decision.* ORIG C17: from L, from *ūnus* one + *animus* mind
▸ **uˈnanimously** *adv* ▸ **unanimity** (ˌjuːnəˈnɪmɪtɪ) *n*

unapproachable (ˌʌnəˈprəʊtʃəbᵊl) *adj* **1** discouraging intimacy, friendliness, etc.; aloof. **2** inaccessible. **3** not to be rivalled.
▸ **ˌunapˈproachableness** *n* ▸ **ˌunapˈproachably** *adv*

unappropriated (ˌʌnəˈprəʊprɪˌeɪtɪd) *adj* **1** not set aside for specific use. **2** *Accounting.* designating that portion of the profits of a business enterprise that is retained in the business and not withdrawn by the proprietor. **3** (of property) not having been taken into any person's possession or control.

unapt (ʌnˈæpt) *adj* **1** (*usually postpositive;* often foll. by *for*) not suitable or qualified; unfitted. **2** mentally slow. **3** (*postpositive; may take an infinitive*) not disposed or likely (to).
▸ **unˈaptly** *adv* ▸ **unˈaptness** *n*

unarm (ʌnˈɑːm) *vb* a less common word for **disarm.**

unarmed (ʌnˈɑːmd) *adj* **1** without weapons. **2** (of animals and plants) having no claws, prickles, spines, thorns, or similar structures.

unassailable (ˌʌnəˈseɪləbᵊl) *adj* **1** not able to be attacked. **2** undeniable or irrefutable.
▸ **ˌunasˈsailableness** *n* ▸ **ˌunasˈsailably** *adv*

unassuming (ˌʌnəˈsjuːmɪŋ) *adj* modest or unpretentious.
▸ **ˌunasˈsumingly** *adv* ▸ **ˌunasˈsumingness** *n*

unattached (ˌʌnəˈtætʃt) *adj* **1** not connected with any specific thing, body, group, etc. **2** not engaged or married. **3** (of property) not seized or held as security.

unavailing (ˌʌnəˈveɪlɪŋ) *adj* useless or futile.
▸ **ˌunaˈvailingly** *adv*

unavoidable (ˌʌnəˈvɔɪdəbᵊl) *adj* **1** unable to be avoided. **2** *Law.* not capable of being declared null and void.
▸ **ˌunaˌvoidaˈbility** *or* **ˌunaˈvoidableness** *n* ▸ **ˌunaˈvoidably** *adv*

unaware (ˌʌnəˈwɛə) *adj* **1** (*postpositive*) not aware or conscious (of): *unaware of the danger he ran across the road.* ◆ *adv* **2** a variant of **unawares.**
▸ **ˌunaˈwareness** *n*

unawares (ˌʌnəˈwɛəz) *adv* **1** without prior warning or plan: *she caught him unawares.* **2** without knowing: *he lost it unawares.*

unbacked (ʌnˈbækt) *adj* **1** (of a book, chair, etc.) not having a back. **2** bereft of support, esp. on a financial basis. **3** not supported by bets.

unbalance (ʌnˈbæləns) *vb* **unbalances, unbalancing, unbalanced.** (*tr*) **1** to upset the equilibrium or balance of. **2** to disturb the mental stability of (a person or his or her mind). ◆ *n* **3** imbalance or instability.

unbalanced (ʌnˈbælənst) *adj* **1** lacking balance. **2** irrational or unsound; erratic. **3** mentally disordered or deranged. **4** biased; one-sided: *unbalanced reporting.* **5** (in double-entry book-keeping) not having total debit balances equal to total credit balances.

unbar (ʌnˈbɑː) *vb* **unbars, unbarring, unbarred.** (*tr*) **1** to take away a bar or bars from. **2** to unfasten bars, locks, etc., from (a door); open.

unbearable (ʌnˈbɛərəbᵊl) *adj* not able to be borne or endured.
▸ **unˈbearably** *adv*

unbeatable (ʌnˈbiːtəbᵊl) *adj* unable to be defeated or outclassed; surpassingly excellent.

unbeaten (ʌnˈbiːtᵊn) *adj* **1** having suffered no defeat. **2** not worn down; untrodden. **3** not mixed or stirred by beating: *unbeaten eggs.*

unbecoming (ˌʌnbɪˈkʌmɪŋ) *adj* **1** unsuitable or inappropriate, esp. through being unattractive: *an unbecoming hat.* **2** (when *postpositive,* usually foll. by *of* or an object) not proper or seemly (for): *manners unbecoming a lady.*
▸ **ˌunbeˈcomingly** *adv* ▸ **ˌunbeˈcomingness** *n*

unbeknown (ˌʌnbɪˈnəʊn) *adv* (*sentence modifier;* foll. by *to*) without the knowledge (of a person): *unbeknown to him she had left the country.* Also (esp. Brit.): **unbeknownst.** ORIG C17: from arch. *beknown* known

unbelief (ˌʌnbɪˈliːf) *n* disbelief or rejection of belief.

unbelievable (ˌʌnbɪˈliːvəbᵊl) *adj* unable to be believed; incredible.
▸ **ˌunbeˌlievaˈbility** *n* ▸ **ˌunbeˈlievably** *adv*

unbeliever (ˌʌnbɪˈliːvə) *n* a person who does not believe, esp. in religious matters.

unbelieving (ˌʌnbɪˈliːvɪŋ) *adj* **1** not believing; sceptical. **2** proceeding from or characterized by scepticism.
▸ **ˌunbeˈlievingly** *adv*

unbend (ʌnˈbɛnd) *vb* **unbends, unbending, unbent.** **1** to release or be released from the restraints of formality and ceremony. **2** *Inf.* to relax (the mind) or (of the mind) to become relaxed. **3** to straighten out from an originally bent shape. **4** (*tr*) *Naut.* **4a** to remove (a sail) from a stay, mast, etc. **4b** to untie (a rope, etc.) or cast (a cable) loose.

unbending (ʌnˈbɛndɪŋ) *adj* **1** rigid or inflexible. **2** characterized by sternness or severity: *an unbending rule.*
▸ **unˈbendingly** *adv* ▸ **unˈbendingness** *n*

unbent (ʌnˈbɛnt) *vb* **1** the past tense and past participle of **unbend.** ◆ *adj* **2** not bent or bowed. **3** not compelled to give way by force.

unbidden (ʌnˈbɪdᵊn) *adj* **1** not ordered or commanded; voluntary or spontaneous. **2** not invited or asked.

unbind (ʌnˈbaɪnd) *vb* **unbinds, unbinding, unbound.** (*tr*) **1** to set free from restraining bonds or chains. **2** to unfasten or make loose (a bond, etc.).

unblessed (ʌnˈblɛst) *adj* **1** deprived of blessing. **2** cursed or evil. **3** unhappy or wretched.
▸ **unblessedness** (ʌnˈblɛsɪdnɪs) *n*

unblushing (ʌnˈblʌʃɪŋ) *adj* immodest or shameless.
▸ **unˈblushingly** *adv*

unbolt (ʌnˈbəʊlt) *vb* (*tr*) **1** to unfasten a bolt of (a door). **2** to undo (the nut) on a bolt.

unbolted (ʌnˈbəʊltɪd) *adj* (of grain, meal, or flour) not sifted.

unborn (ʌnˈbɔːn) *adj* **1** not yet born or brought to birth. **2** still to come in the future: *the unborn world.*

unbosom (ʌnˈbʊzəm) *vb* (*tr*) to relieve (oneself) of (secrets, etc.) by telling someone. ORIG C16: from UN-[2] + BOSOM (in the sense: seat of the emotions)

unbounded (ʌnˈbaʊndɪd) *adj* having no boundaries or limits.
▸ **unˈboundedly** *adv* ▸ **unˈboundedness** *n*

unbowed (ʌnˈbaʊd) *adj* **1** not bowed or bent. **2** free or unconquered.

unbridled (ʌnˈbraɪdᵊld) *adj* **1** with all restraints removed. **2** (of a horse) wearing no bridle.
▸ **unˈbridledly** *adv* ▸ **unˈbridledness** *n*

unbroken (ʌnˈbrəʊkən) *adj* **1** complete or whole. **2** continuous or incessant. **3** undaunted in spirit. **4** (of animals, esp. horses) not tamed; wild. **5** not disturbed or upset: *the unbroken quiet of the afternoon.* **6** (of a record, esp. at sport) not improved upon.
▸ **unˈbrokenly** *adv* ▸ **unˈbrokenness** *n*

unbundling (ʌnˈbʌndlɪŋ) *n Commerce.* the takeover of a large conglomerate with a view to retaining the core business and selling off some of the subsidiaries to help finance the takeover.

unburden (ʌnˈbɜːdᵊn) *vb* (*tr*) **1** to remove a load or burden from. **2** to relieve or make free (one's mind, oneself, etc.) of a worry, trouble, etc., by revelation or confession.

unbutton (ʌnˈbʌtᵊn) *vb* to undo by unfastening (the buttons) of (a garment).

unbuttoned (ʌnˈbʌtᵊnd) *adj* **1** with buttons not fastened. **2** *Inf.* uninhibited; unrestrained: *hours of unbuttoned self-revelation.*

uncalled-for (ˌʌnˈkɔːldfɔː) *adj* unnecessary or unwarranted.

uncanny (ʌnˈkænɪ) *adj* **1** characterized by apparently supernatural wonder, horror, etc. **2** beyond what is normal: *uncanny accuracy.*
▸ **unˈcannily** *adv* ▸ **unˈcanniness** *n*

uncap (ʌnˈkæp) *vb* **uncaps, uncapping, uncapped. 1** (*tr*) to remove a cap or top from (a container): *to uncap a bottle.* **2** to remove a cap from (the head).

uncared-for (ˌʌnˈkɛədfɔː) *adj* not cared for; neglected.

unceremonious (ˌʌnsɛrɪˈməʊnɪəs) *adj* without ceremony; informal, abrupt, rude, or undignified.
▸ **ˌuncereˈmoniously** *adv* ▸ **ˌuncereˈmoniousness** *n*

uncertain (ʌnˈsɜːtᵊn) *adj* **1** not able to be accurately known or predicted: *the issue is uncertain.* **2** (when *postpositive,* often foll. by *of*) not sure or confident (about): *he was uncertain of the date.* **3** not precisely determined or decided: *uncertain plans.* **4** not to be depended upon: *an uncertain vote.* **5** liable to variation; changeable: *the weather is uncertain.* **6 in no uncertain terms. 6a** unambiguously. **6b** forcefully.
▸ **unˈcertainly** *adv*

uncertainty (ʌnˈsɜːtᵊntɪ) *n, pl* **uncertainties. 1** Also: **uncertainness.** the state or condition of being uncertain. **2** an uncertain matter, contingency, etc.

uncertainty principle *n* **the.** the principle that energy and time or position and momentum, cannot both be accurately measured simultaneously. Also called: **Heisenberg uncertainty principle, indeterminacy principle.**

uncharted (ʌnˈtʃɑːtɪd) *adj* (of a physical or nonphysical region or area) not yet mapped, surveyed, or investigated: *uncharted waters; the uncharted depths of the mind.*

unchartered (ʌnˈtʃɑːtəd) *adj* **1** not authorized by charter; unregulated. **2** unauthorized, lawless, or irregular.

> **USAGE NOTE** *Unchartered* is sometimes mistakenly used where *uncharted* is meant: *We did not want to pioneer in completely uncharted* (not *unchartered*) *territory.*

unchristian (ʌnˈkrɪstʃən) *adj* **1** not in accordance with the principles or ethics of Christianity. **2** non-Christian or pagan.
▸ **unˈchristianly** *adv*

unchurch (ʌnˈtʃɜːtʃ) *vb* (*tr*) **1** to excommunicate. **2** to remove church status from (a building).

uncial (ˈʌnsɪəl) *adj* **1** of, relating to, or written in majuscule letters, as used in Greek and Latin manuscripts of the third to ninth centuries, that resemble modern capitals, but are characterized by much greater curvature. ◆ *n* **2** an uncial letter or manuscript. ORIG C17: from LL *unciāles litterae* letters an inch long, from L *unciālis,* from *uncia* one twelfth, inch
▸ **ˈuncially** *adv*

uncinate (ˈʌnsɪnɪt, -ˌneɪt) *adj Biol.* shaped like a hook: *the uncinate process of the ribs of certain vertebrates.* ORIG C18: from L *uncīnātus,* from *uncīnus* a hook, from *uncus*

uncircumcised (ʌnˈsɜːkəmˌsaɪzd) *adj* **1** not circumcised. **2** not Jewish; gentile. **3** spiritually unpurified.
▸ **ˌuncircumˈcision** *n*

uncivil (ʌnˈsɪvəl) *adj* **1** lacking civility or good manners. **2** an obsolete word for **uncivilized.**
▸ **incivility** (ˌʌnsɪˈvɪlɪtɪ) *n* ▸ **unˈcivilly** *adv*

uncivilized *or* **uncivilised** (ʌnˈsɪvɪˌlaɪzd) *adj* **1** (of a tribe or people) not yet civilized, esp. not having developed a written language. **2** lacking culture or sophistication.
▸ **unˈcivilˌizedness** *or* **unˈcivilˌisedness** *n*

unclad (ʌnˈklæd) *adj* having no clothes on; naked.

unclasp (ʌnˈklɑːsp) *vb* **1** (*tr*) to unfasten the clasp of (something). **2** to release one's grip (upon an object).

uncle (ˈʌŋkᵊl) *n* **1** a brother of one's father or mother. **2** the husband of one's aunt. **3** a term of address sometimes used by children for a male friend of their parents. **4** *Sl.* a pawnbroker. ◆ Related adj: **avuncular.** ORIG C13: from OF *oncle,* from L *avunculus*

unclean (ʌnˈkliːn) *adj* lacking moral, spiritual, or physical cleanliness.
▸ **unˈcleanness** *n*

uncleanly[1] (ʌnˈkliːnlɪ) *adv* in an unclean manner.

uncleanly[2] (ʌnˈklɛnlɪ) *adj* characterized by an absence of cleanliness.
▸ **unˈcleanliness** *n*

Uncle Sam (sæm) *n* a personification of the government of the United States. ORIG C19: apparently a humorous interpretation of the letters stamped on army supply boxes during the War of 1812: *US*

Uncle Tom (tɒm) *n Inf., derog.* a Black person whose behaviour towards White people is regarded as servile. ORIG C20: after the main character of H. B. Stowe's novel *Uncle Tom's Cabin* (1852)
▸ **ˈUncle ˈTomˌism** *n*

unclose (ʌnˈkləʊz) *vb* **uncloses, unclosing, unclosed. 1** to open or cause to open. **2** to come or bring to light.

unclothe (ʌnˈkləʊð) *vb* **unclothes, unclothing, unclothed** *or* **unclad.** (*tr*) **1** to take off garments from; strip. **2** to uncover or lay bare.

uncoil (ʌnˈkɔɪl) *vb* to unwind or become unwound; untwist.

uncomfortable (ʌnˈkʌmftəbᵊl) *adj* **1** not comfortable. **2** feeling or causing discomfort or unease; disquieting.
▸ **unˈcomfortableness** *n* ▸ **unˈcomfortably** *adv*

uncommitted (ˌʌnkəˈmɪtɪd) *adj* not bound or pledged to a specific opinion, course of action, or cause.

uncommon (ʌnˈkɒmən) *adj* **1** outside or beyond normal experience, etc. **2** in excess of what is normal: *an uncommon liking for honey.* ◆ *adv* **3** an archaic word for **uncommonly** (sense 2).
▸ **unˈcommonness** *n*

uncommonly (ʌnˈkɒmənlɪ) *adv* **1** in an uncommon or unusual manner or degree; rarely. **2** (intensifier): *you're uncommonly friendly.*

uncommunicative (ˌʌnkəˈmjuːnɪkətɪv) *adj* disinclined to talk or give information or opinions.
▸ **ˌuncomˈmunicatively** *adv* ▸ **ˌuncomˈmunicativeness** *n*

uncompromising (ʌnˈkɒmprəˌmaɪzɪŋ) *adj* not prepared to give ground or to compromise.
▸ **unˈcomproˌmisingly** *adv*

unconcern (ˌʌnkənˈsɜːn) *n* apathy or indifference.

unconcerned (ˌʌnkənˈsɜːnd) *adj* **1** lacking in concern or involvement. **2** untroubled.
▸ **unconcernedly** (ˌʌnkənˈsɜːnɪdlɪ) *adv*

unconditional (ˌʌnkənˈdɪʃənᵊl) *adj* without conditions or limitations; total: *unconditional surrender.*
▸ **ˌunconˈditionally** *adv*

unconditioned (ˌʌnkənˈdɪʃənd) *adj* **1** *Psychol.* characterizing an innate reflex and the stimulus and response that form parts of it. **2** *Metaphysics.* unrestricted by conditions; absolute. **3** without limitations.
▸ **ˌunconˈditionedness** *n*

unconformable (ˌʌnkənˈfɔːməbᵊl) *adj* **1** not conformable or conforming. **2** (of rock strata) consisting of a series of recent strata resting on different, much older rocks.
▸ **ˌunconˌformaˈbility** *or* **ˌunconˈformableness** *n* ▸ **ˌunconˈformably** *adv* ▸ **ˌunconˈformity** *n*

unconscionable (ʌnˈkɒnʃənəbᵊl) *adj* **1** unscrupulous or unprincipled: *an unconscionable liar.* **2** immoderate or excessive: *unconscionable demands.*
▸ **unˈconscionably** *adv*

unconscious (ʌn'kɒnʃəs) *adj* **1** lacking normal sensory awareness of the environment; insensible. **2** not aware of one's actions, behaviour, etc.: *unconscious of his bad manners.* **3** characterized by lack of awareness or intention: *an unconscious blunder.* **4** coming from or produced by the unconscious: *unconscious resentment.* ◆ *n* **5** *Psychoanal.* the part of the mind containing instincts, impulses, images, and ideas that are not available for direct examination.
▸ **un'consciously** *adv*

unconstitutional (ˌʌnkɒnstɪ'tjuːʃən^{ə}l) *adj* at variance with or not permitted by a constitution.
▸ **ˌunconstiˌtution'ality** *n*

unconventional (ˌʌnkən'vɛnʃən^{ə}l) *adj* not conforming to accepted rules or standards.
▸ **ˌunconˌvention'ality** *n* ▸ **ˌuncon'ventionally** *adv*

uncool (ʌn'kuːl) *adj Sl.* **1** unsophisticated; unfashionable. **2** excitable; tense; not cool.

uncork (ʌn'kɔːk) *vb* (*tr*) **1** to draw the cork from (a bottle, etc.). **2** to release or unleash (emotions, etc.).

uncountable (ʌn'kaʊntəb^{ə}l) *adj* **1** too many to be counted; innumerable. **2** *Linguistics.* denoting a noun that does not refer to an isolable object. See **mass noun.**

uncounted (ʌn'kaʊntɪd) *adj* **1** unable to be counted; innumerable. **2** not counted.

uncouple (ʌn'kʌp^{ə}l) *vb* **uncouples, uncoupling, uncoupled. 1** to disconnect or unfasten or become disconnected or unfastened. **2** (*tr*) to set loose; release.

uncouth (ʌn'kuːθ) *adj* lacking in good manners, refinement, or grace. ORIG OE *uncūth,* from UN-[1] + *cūth* familiar
▸ **un'couthly** *adv* ▸ **un'couthness** *n*

uncover (ʌn'kʌvə) *vb* **1** (*tr*) to remove the cover, cap, top, etc., from. **2** (*tr*) to reveal or disclose: *to uncover a plot.* **3** to take off (one's head covering), esp. as a mark of respect.

uncovered (ʌn'kʌvəd) *adj* **1** not covered; revealed or bare. **2** not protected by insurance, security, etc. **3** with hat off, as a mark of respect.

UNCTAD *abbrev. for* United Nations Conference on Trade and Development.

unction ('ʌŋkʃən) *n* **1** *Chiefly RC & Eastern Churches.* the act of anointing with oil in sacramental ceremonies, in the conferring of holy orders. **2** excessive suavity or affected charm. **3** an ointment or unguent. **4** anything soothing. ORIG C14: from L *unctiō* an anointing, from *ungere* to anoint
▸ **'unctionless** *adj*

unctuous ('ʌŋktjʊəs) *adj* **1** slippery or greasy. **2** affecting an oily charm. ORIG C14: from Med. L *unctuōsus,* from L *unctum* ointment, from *ungere* to anoint
▸ **unctuosity** (ˌʌŋktjʊ'ɒsɪtɪ) *or* **'unctuousness** *n* ▸ **'unctuously** *adv*

uncut (ʌn'kʌt) *adj* **1** (of a book) not having the edges of its pages trimmed or slit. **2** (of a gemstone) not cut and faceted. **3** not abridged.

undamped (ʌn'dæmpt) *adj* **1** (of an oscillating system) having unrestricted motion; not damped. **2** not repressed, discouraged, or subdued.

undaunted (ʌn'dɔːntɪd) *adj* not put off, discouraged, or beaten.
▸ **un'dauntedly** *adv* ▸ **un'dauntedness** *n*

undecagon (ʌn'dɛkəˌgɒn) *n* a polygon having eleven sides. ORIG C18: from L *undecim* eleven + -GON

undeceive (ˌʌndɪ'siːv) *vb* **undeceives, undeceiving, undeceived.** (*tr*) to reveal the truth to (someone previously misled or deceived).
▸ **ˌunde'ceivable** *adj* ▸ **ˌunde'ceiver** *n*

undecidability (ˌʌndɪˌsaɪdə'bɪlɪtɪ) *n, pl* **undecidabilities.** *Maths, logic.* the condition of not being open to formal proof or disproof by logical deduction from the axioms of a system.

undecided (ˌʌndɪ'saɪdɪd) *adj* **1** not having made up one's mind. **2** (of an issue, problem, etc.) not agreed or decided upon.
▸ **ˌunde'cidedly** *adv* ▸ **ˌunde'cidedness** *n*

undeniable (ˌʌndɪ'naɪəb^{ə}l) *adj* **1** unquestionably or obviously true. **2** of unquestionable excellence: *a man of undeniable character.* **3** unable to be resisted or denied.
▸ **ˌunde'niableness** *n* ▸ **ˌunde'niably** *adv*

under ('ʌndə) *prep* **1** directly below; on, to, or beneath the underside or base of: *under one's feet.* **2** less than: *under forty years.* **3** lower in rank than: *under a corporal.* **4** subject to the supervision, jurisdiction, control, or influence of. **5** subject to (conditions); in (certain circumstances). **6** within a classification of: *a book under theology.* **7** known by: *under an assumed name.* **8** planted with: *a field under corn.* **9** powered by: *under sail.* **10** *Astrol.* during the period that the sun is in (a sign of the zodiac): *born under Aries.* ◆ *adv* **11** below; to a position underneath something. ORIG OE

under- *prefix* **1** below or beneath: *underarm; underground.* **2** of lesser importance or lower rank: *undersecretary.* **3** insufficient or insufficiently: *underemployed.* **4** indicating secrecy or deception: *underhand.*

underachieve (ˌʌndərə'tʃiːv) *vb* **underachieves, underachieving, underachieved.** (*intr*) to fail to achieve a performance appropriate to one's age or talents.
▸ **ˌundera'chievement** *n* ▸ **ˌundera'chiever** *n*

underact (ˌʌndər'ækt) *vb Theatre.* to play (a role) without adequate emphasis.

underage (ˌʌndər'eɪdʒ) *adj* below the required or standard age, esp. below the legal age for voting or drinking.

underarm ('ʌndərˌɑːm) *adj* **1** (of a measurement) extending along the arm from wrist to armpit. **2** *Cricket, tennis, etc.* denoting a style of throwing, bowling, or serving in which the hand is swung below shoulder level. **3** below the arm. ◆ *adv* **4** in an underarm style.

underbelly ('ʌndəˌbɛlɪ) *n, pl* **underbellies. 1** the part of an animal's belly nearest to the ground. **2** a vulnerable or unprotected part, aspect, or region.

underbid (ˌʌndə'bɪd) *vb* **underbids, underbidding, underbid. 1** (*tr*) to submit a bid lower than that of (others). **2** (*tr*) to submit an excessively low bid for. **3** *Bridge.* to bid (one's hand) at a lower level than the strength of the hand warrants: *he underbid his hand.*

underbidder ('ʌndəˌbɪdə) *n* **1** the person who makes the highest bid below the top bidder, esp. in an auction. **2** a person who underbids.

underbody ('ʌndəˌbɒdɪ) *n, pl* **underbodies.** the underpart of a body, as of an animal or motor vehicle.

underbred (ˌʌndə'brɛd) *adj* of impure stock; not thoroughbred.
▸ **ˌunder'breeding** *n*

underbuy (ˌʌndə'baɪ) *vb* **underbuys, underbuying, underbought. 1** to buy (stock in trade) in amounts lower than required. **2** (*tr*) to buy at a price below that paid by (others). **3** (*tr*) to pay a price less than the true value for.

undercapitalize *or* **undercapitalise** (ˌʌndə'kæpɪtəˌlaɪz) *vb* **undercapitalizes, undercapitalizing, undercapitalized** *or* **undercapitalises, undercapitalising, undercapitalised.** to provide or issue capital for (a commercial enterprise) in an amount insufficient for efficient operation.

undercarriage ('ʌndəˌkærɪdʒ) *n* **1** Also called: **landing gear.** the assembly of wheels, shock absorbers, struts, etc., that supports an aircraft on the ground and enables it to take off and land. **2** the framework that supports the body of a vehicle, carriage, etc.

undercharge (ˌʌndə'tʃɑːdʒ) *vb* **undercharges, undercharging, undercharged. 1** to charge too little for something. **2** (*tr*) to load (a gun, cannon, etc.) with an inadequate charge.

underclass ('ʌndəˌklɑːs) *n* a class beneath the usual social scale consisting of the most disadvantaged people, such as the long-term unemployed.

underclothes ('ʌndəˌkləʊðz) *pl n* a variant of **underwear.** Also called: **underclothing.**

undercoat ('ʌndəˌkəʊt) *n* **1** a coat of paint or other substance applied before the top coat. **2** a coat worn under an overcoat. **3** *Zool.* another name for **underfur.** ◆ *vb* **4** (*tr*) to apply an undercoat to (a surface).

undercover (ˌʌndə'kʌvə) *adj* done or acting in secret: *undercover operations.*

undercroft ('ʌndəˌkrɒft) *n* an underground chamber, such as a church crypt, often with a vaulted ceiling. ORIG C14: from *croft* a vault, cavern, ult. from L *crypta* CRYPT

undercurrent ('ʌndəˌkʌrənt) *n* **1** a current that is not apparent at the surface or lies beneath another current. **2** an opinion, emotion, etc., lying beneath apparent feeling or meaning. ◆ Also called: **underflow.**

undercut *vb* (ˌʌndə'kʌt), **undercuts, undercutting, undercut. 1** to charge less than (a competitor) in order to obtain trade. **2** to cut away the under part of (something). **3** *Golf, tennis, etc.* to hit (a ball) in such a way as to impart backspin. ◆ *n* ('ʌndəˌkʌt). **4** the act of cutting underneath. **5** a part that is cut away underneath. **6** a tenderloin of beef. **7** *Forestry, chiefly US & Canad.* a notch cut in a tree trunk, to ensure a clean break in felling. **8** *Tennis, golf, etc.* a stroke that imparts backspin to the ball.

underdevelop (ˌʌndədɪ'vɛləp) *vb* (*tr*) *Photog.* to process (a film, plate, or paper) in developer for less than the required time, or at too low a temperature, or in an exhausted solution.

underdeveloped (ˌʌndədɪ'vɛləpt) *adj* **1** immature or undersized. **2** relating to societies in which both the surplus capital and the social organization necessary to advance are lacking. **3** *Photog.* (of a film, etc.) processed in developer for less than the required time.

underdog ('ʌndəˌdɒg) *n* **1** the competitor in a fight or contest who is expected not to win. **2** a person in adversity or a position of inferiority.

underdone (ˌʌndə'dʌn) *adj* insufficiently or lightly cooked.

underdressed (ˌʌndə'drɛst) *adj* wearing clothes that are not elaborate or formal enough for a particular occasion.

underemployed (ˌʌndərɪm'plɔɪd) *adj* not fully or adequately employed.

underestimate *vb* (ˌʌndər'ɛstɪˌmeɪt), **underestimates, underestimating, underestimated.** (*tr*) **1** to make too low an estimate of: *he underestimated the cost.* **2** to think insufficiently highly of: *to underestimate a person.* ◆ *n* (ˌʌndər'ɛstɪmɪt). **3** too low an estimate.
▸ ˌ**underˌesti'mation** *n*

> **USAGE NOTE** *Underestimate* is sometimes wrongly used where *overestimate* is meant: *the importance of his work cannot be overestimated* (not *cannot be underestimated*).

underexpose (ˌʌndərɪk'spəʊz) *vb* **underexposes, underexposing, underexposed.** (*tr*) **1** *Photog.* to expose (a film, plate, or paper) for too short a period or with insufficient light so as not to produce the required effect. **2** (*often passive*) to fail to subject to appropriate or expected publicity.
▸ ˌ**underex'posure** *n*

underfeed (ˌʌndə'fiːd) *vb* **underfeeds, underfeeding, underfed.** (*tr*) **1** to give too little food to. **2** to supply (a furnace, engine, etc.) with fuel from beneath.

underfelt ('ʌndəˌfɛlt) *n* thick felt laid between floorboards and carpet to increase insulation.

underfloor ('ʌndəˌflɔː) *adj* situated beneath the floor: *underfloor heating.*

underfoot (ˌʌndə'fʊt) *adv* **1** underneath the feet; on the ground. **2** in a position of subjugation. **3** in the way.

underfur ('ʌndəˌfɜː) *n* the layer of dense soft fur occurring beneath the outer coarser fur in certain mammals, such as the otter and seal. Also called: **undercoat.**

undergarment ('ʌndəˌgɑːmənt) *n* any garment worn under the visible outer clothes, usually next to the skin.

undergird (ˌʌndə'gɜːd) *vb* **undergirds, undergirding, undergirded** *or* **undergirt.** (*tr*) to strengthen or reinforce by passing a rope, cable, or chain around the underside of (an object, load, etc.). ORIG C16: from UNDER- + GIRD[1]

underglaze ('ʌndəˌgleɪz) *adj* **1** *Ceramics.* applied to pottery or porcelain before the application of glaze. ◆ *n* **2** a pigment, etc., applied in this way.

undergo (ˌʌndə'gəʊ) *vb* **undergoes, undergoing, underwent, undergone.** (*tr*) to experience, endure, or sustain: *to undergo a change of feelings.* ORIG OE
▸ '**underˌgoer** *n*

undergraduate (ˌʌndə'grædjʊɪt) *n* a person studying in a university for a first degree. Sometimes shortened to **undergrad.**

underground *adj* ('ʌndəˌgraʊnd), *adv* (ˌʌndə'graʊnd). **1** occurring, situated, used, or going below ground level: *an underground explosion.* **2** secret; hidden: *underground activities.* ◆ *n* ('ʌndəˌgraʊnd). **3** a space or region below ground level. **4a** a movement dedicated to overthrowing a government or occupation forces, as in the European countries occupied by the German army in World War II. **4b** (*as modifier*): *an underground group.* **5** (often preceded by *the*) an electric passenger railway operated in underground tunnels. US and Canad. equivalent: **subway. 6** (usually preceded by *the*) **6a** any avant-garde, experimental, or subversive movement in popular art, films, music, etc. **6b** (*as modifier*): *the underground press.*

underground railroad *n* (*often cap.*) (in the pre-Civil War US) the system established by abolitionists to aid escaping slaves.

undergrowth ('ʌndəˌgrəʊθ) *n* small trees, bushes, ferns, etc., growing beneath taller trees in a wood or forest.

underhand ('ʌndəˌhænd) *adj also* **underhanded. 1** clandestine, deceptive, or secretive. **2** *Sport.* another word for **underarm.** ◆ *adv* **3** in an underhand manner or style.

underhanded (ˌʌndə'hændɪd) *adj* another word for **underhand** or **short-handed.**

underhung (ˌʌndə'hʌŋ) *adj* **1** (of the lower jaw) projecting beyond the upper jaw; undershot. **2** (of a sliding door, etc.) supported at its lower edge by a track or rail.

underlay *vb* (ˌʌndə'leɪ), **underlays, underlaying, underlaid.** (*tr*) **1** to place (something) under or beneath. **2** to support by something laid beneath. **3** to achieve the correct printing pressure all over (a forme block) or to bring (a block) up to type height by adding material, such as paper, beneath it. ◆ *n* ('ʌndəˌleɪ). **4** a lining, support, etc., laid underneath something else. **5** *Printing.* material, such as paper, used to underlay a forme or block. **6** felt, rubber, etc., laid beneath a carpet to increase insulation and resilience.

underlie (ˌʌndə'laɪ) *vb* **underlies, underlying, underlay, underlain.** (*tr*) **1** to lie or be placed under or beneath. **2** to be the foundation, cause, or basis of: *careful planning underlies all our decisions.* **3** to be the root or stem from which (a word) is derived: *"happy" underlies "happiest".*
▸ '**underˌlier** *n*

underline (ˌʌndə'laɪn) *vb* **underlines, underlining, underlined.** (*tr*) **1** to put a line under. **2** to state forcibly; emphasize.

underlinen ('ʌndəˌlɪnən) *n* underclothes, esp. when made of linen.

underling ('ʌndəlɪŋ) *n* a subordinate or lackey.

underlying (ˌʌndə'laɪɪŋ) *adj* **1** concealed but detectable: *underlying guilt.* **2** fundamental; basic. **3** lying under. **4** *Finance.* (of a claim, liability, etc.) taking precedence; prior.

undermentioned ('ʌndəˌmɛnʃənd) *adj* mentioned below or subsequently.

undermine (ˌʌndə'maɪn) *vb* **undermines, undermining, undermined.** (*tr*) **1** (of the sea, wind, etc.) to wear away the bottom or base of (land, cliffs, etc.). **2** to weaken gradually or insidiously: *insults undermined her confidence.* **3** to tunnel or dig beneath.
▸ ˌ**under'miner** *n*

undermost ('ʌndəˌməʊst) *adj* **1** being the furthest under; lowest. ◆ *adv* **2** in the lowest place.

underneath (ˌʌndə'niːθ) *prep, adv* **1** under; beneath. ◆ *adj* **2** lower. ◆ *n* **3** a lower part, surface, etc. ORIG OE *underneothan,* from UNDER + *neothan* below

undernourish (ˌʌndə'nʌrɪʃ) *vb* (*tr*) to deprive of or fail to provide with nutrients essential for health and growth.
▸ ˌ**under'nourishment** *n*

underpants ('ʌndəˌpænts) *pl n* a man's undergarment covering the body from the waist or hips to the thighs or ankles. Often shortened to **pants.**

underpass (ˈʌndəˌpɑːs) *n* **1** a section of a road that passes under another road, railway line, etc. **2** another word for **subway** (sense 1).

underpay (ˌʌndəˈpeɪ) *vb* **underpays, underpaying, underpaid.** to pay (someone) insufficiently.
▸ **ˌunderˈpayment** *n*

underpin (ˌʌndəˈpɪn) *vb* **underpins, underpinning, underpinned.** (*tr*) **1** to support from beneath, esp. by a prop, while avoiding damaging or weakening the superstructure: *to underpin a wall.* **2** to give corroboration, strength, or support to.

underpinning (ˈʌndəˌpɪnɪŋ) *n* a structure of masonry, concrete, etc., placed beneath a wall to provide support.

underplay (ˌʌndəˈpleɪ) *vb* **1** to play (a role) with restraint or subtlety. **2** to achieve (an effect) by deliberate lack of emphasis. **3** (*intr*) *Cards.* to lead or follow suit with a lower card when holding a higher one.

underprivileged (ˌʌndəˈprɪvɪlɪdʒd) *adj* lacking the rights and advantages of other members of society; deprived.

underproduction (ˌʌndəprəˈdʌkʃən) *n Commerce.* production below full capacity or below demand.

underproof (ˌʌndəˈpruːf) *adj* (of a spirit) containing less than 57.1 per cent alcohol by volume.

underquote (ˌʌndəˈkwəʊt) *vb* **underquotes, underquoting, underquoted. 1** to offer for sale (securities, goods, or services) at a price lower than the market price. **2** (*tr*) to quote a price lower than that quoted by (another).

underrate (ˌʌndəˈreɪt) *vb* **underrates, underrating, underrated.** (*tr*) to underestimate.

underscore (ˌʌndəˈskɔː) *vb* **underscores, underscoring, underscored.** (*tr*) **1** to draw or score a line or mark under. **2** to stress or reinforce.

undersea (ˈʌndəˌsiː) *adj, adv also* **underseas** (ˌʌndəˈsiːz). below the surface of the sea.

underseal (ˈʌndəˌsiːl) *Brit.* ◆ *n* **1** a coating of a tar, etc., applied to the underside of a motor vehicle to retard corrosion. ◆ *vb* **2** (*tr*) to apply a coating of underseal to (a vehicle).

undersecretary (ˌʌndəˈsɛkrətrɪ) *n, pl* **undersecretaries. 1** (in Britain) **1a** any of various senior civil servants in certain government departments. **1b** short for **undersecretary of state:** any of various high officials subordinate only to the minister in charge of a department. **2** (in the US) a high government official subordinate only to the secretary in charge of a department.

undersell (ˌʌndəˈsɛl) *vb* **undersells, underselling, undersold. 1** to sell for less than the usual price. **2** (*tr*) to sell at a price lower than that of (another seller). **3** (*tr*) to advertise (merchandise) with moderation or restraint.
▸ **ˌunderˈseller** *n*

undersexed (ˌʌndəˈsɛkst) *adj* having weaker sex urges or responses than is considered normal.

undershirt (ˈʌndəˌʃɜːt) *n* the US and Canad. name for **vest** (sense 1).

undershoot (ˌʌndəˈʃuːt) *vb* **undershoots, undershooting, undershot. 1** (of a pilot) to cause (an aircraft) to land short of (a runway) or (of an aircraft) to land in this way. **2** to shoot a projectile so that it falls short of (a target).

undershorts (ˈʌndəˌʃɔːts) *pl n* another word for **shorts** (sense 2).

undershot (ˈʌndəˌʃɒt) *adj* **1** (of the lower jaw) projecting beyond the upper jaw; underhung. **2** (of a water wheel) driven by a flow of water that passes under the wheel rather than over it.

underside (ˈʌndəˌsaɪd) *n* the bottom or lower surface.

undersigned (ˈʌndəˌsaɪnd) *n* **1 the.** the person or persons who have signed at the foot of a document, statement, etc. ◆ *adj* **2** having signed one's name at the foot of a document, statement, etc.

undersized (ˌʌndəˈsaɪzd) *adj* of less than usual size.

underskirt (ˈʌndəˌskɜːt) *n* any skirtlike garment worn under a skirt or dress; petticoat.

underslung (ˌʌndəˈslʌŋ) *adj* suspended below a supporting member, esp. (of a motor vehicle chassis) suspended below the axles.

understand (ˌʌndəˈstænd) *vb* **understands, understanding, understood. 1** (*may take a clause as object*) to know and comprehend the nature or meaning of: *I understand you.* **2** (*may take a clause as object*) to realize or grasp (something): *he understands your position.* **3** (*tr; may take a clause as object*) to assume, infer, or believe: *I understand you are thinking of marrying.* **4** (*tr*) to know how to translate or read: *can you understand Spanish?* **5** (*tr; may take a clause as object; often passive*) to accept as a condition or proviso: *it is understood that children must be kept quiet.* **6** (*tr*) to be sympathetic to or compatible with: *we understand each other.* ORIG OE *understandan*
▸ **ˌunderˈstandable** *adj* ▸ **ˌunderˈstandably** *adv*

understanding (ˌʌndəˈstændɪŋ) *n* **1** the ability to learn, judge, make decisions, etc. **2** personal opinion or interpretation of a subject: *my understanding of your predicament.* **3** a mutual agreement or compact, esp. an informal or private one. **4** *Chiefly Brit.* an unofficial engagement to be married. **5 on the understanding that.** providing. ◆ *adj* **6** sympathetic, tolerant, or wise towards people. **7** possessing judgment and intelligence.
▸ **ˌunderˈstandingly** *adv*

understate (ˌʌndəˈsteɪt) *vb* **understates, understating, understated. 1** to state (something) in restrained terms, often to obtain an ironic effect. **2** to state that (something, such as a number) is less than it is.
▸ **ˌunderˈstatement** *n*

understeer (ˌʌndəˈstɪə) *vb* (*intr*) (of a vehicle) to turn less sharply, for a particular movement of the steering wheel, than anticipated.

understood (ˌʌndəˈstʊd) *vb* **1** the past tense and past participle of **understand.** ◆ *adj* **2** implied or inferred. **3** taken for granted.

understudy (ˈʌndəˌstʌdɪ) *vb* **understudies, understudying, understudied. 1** (*tr*) to study (a role or part) so as to be able to replace the usual actor or actress if necessary. **2** to act as understudy to (an actor or actress). ◆ *n, pl* **understudies. 3** an actor or actress who studies a part so as to be able to replace the usual actor or actress if necessary. **4** anyone who is trained to take the place of another in case of need.

undertake (ˌʌndəˈteɪk) *vb* **undertakes, undertaking, undertook, undertaken.** (*tr*) **1** to contract to or commit oneself to (something) or (to do something): *to undertake a job.* **2** to attempt to; agree to start. **3** to take (someone) in charge. **4** to promise.

undertaker (ˈʌndəˌteɪkə) *n* a person whose profession is the preparation of the dead for burial or cremation and the management of funerals; funeral director.

undertaking (ˈʌndəˌteɪkɪŋ) *n* **1** a task, venture, or enterprise. **2** an agreement to do something. **3** the business of an undertaker.

underthings (ˈʌndəˌθɪŋz) *pl n* girls' or women's underwear.

underthrust (ˈʌndəˌθrʌst) *n Geol.* a reverse fault in which the rocks on the lower surface of a fault plane have moved under the relatively static rocks on the upper surface.

undertone (ˈʌndəˌtəʊn) *n* **1** a quiet or hushed tone of voice. **2** an underlying suggestion in words or actions: *his offer has undertones of dishonesty.*

undertow (ˈʌndəˌtəʊ) *n* **1** the seaward undercurrent following the breaking of a wave on the beach. **2** any strong undercurrent flowing in a different direction from the surface current.

undertrick (ˈʌndəˌtrɪk) *n Bridge.* a trick by which a declarer falls short of making his or her contract.

undervalue (ˌʌndəˈvæljuː) *vb* **undervalues, undervaluing, undervalued.** (*tr*) to value at too low a level or price.
▸ **ˌunderˌvaluˈation** *n* ▸ **ˌunderˈvaluer** *n*

undervest (ˈʌndəˌvɛst) *n Brit.* another name for **vest** (sense 1).

underwater (ˈʌndəˈwɔːtə) *adj* **1** being, occurring, or going under the surface of the water, esp. the sea: *underwater exploration.* **2** *Naut.* below the water line of a vessel. ◆ *adv* **3** beneath the surface of the water.

under way *adj* (*postpositive*) **1** in progress; in operation: *the show was under way.* **2** *Naut.* in motion.

underwear ('ʌndəˌwɛə) *n* clothing worn under the outer garments, usually next to the skin.

underweight (ˌʌndə'weɪt) *adj* weighing less than is average, expected, or healthy.

underwent (ˌʌndə'wɛnt) *vb* the past tense of **undergo**.

underwhelm (ˌʌndə'wɛlm) *vb* (*tr*) to make no positive impact on; disappoint. ORIG C20: orig. a humorous coinage based on *overwhelm*
▸ ˌ**under'whelming** *adj*

underwing ('ʌndəˌwɪŋ) *n* **1** the hind wing of an insect. **2** See **red underwing, yellow underwing.**

underwood ('ʌndəˌwʊd) *n* a less common word for **undergrowth.**

underworld ('ʌndəˌwɜːld) *n* **1a** criminals and their associates. **1b** (*as modifier*): *underworld connections.* **2** *Greek & Roman myth.* the regions below the earth's surface regarded as the abode of the dead. **3** the antipodes.

underwrite ('ʌndəˌraɪt, ˌʌndə'raɪt) *vb* **underwrites, underwriting, underwrote, underwritten.** (*tr*) **1** *Finance.* to undertake to purchase at an agreed price any unsold portion of (a public issue of shares, etc.). **2** to accept financial responsibility for (a commercial project or enterprise). **3** *Insurance.* **3a** to sign and issue (an insurance policy) thus accepting liability. **3b** to insure (a property or risk). **3c** to accept liability up to (a specified amount) in an insurance policy. **4** to write (words, a signature, etc.) beneath (other written matter). **5** to support.

underwriter ('ʌndəˌraɪtə) *n* **1** a person or enterprise that underwrites public issues of shares, bonds, etc. **2a** a person or enterprise that underwrites insurance policies. **2b** an employee or agent of an insurance company who determines the premiums payable.

undesirable (ˌʌndɪ'zaɪərəbᵊl) *adj* **1** not desirable or pleasant; objectionable. ◆ *n* **2** a person or thing considered undesirable.
▸ ˌ**undeˌsira'bility** *or* ˌ**unde'sirableness** *n* ▸ ˌ**unde'sirably** *adv*

undetermined (ˌʌndɪ'tɜːmɪnd) *adj* **1** not yet resolved; undecided. **2** not known or discovered.

undies ('ʌndɪz) *pl n Inf.* women's underwear.

undine ('ʌndiːn) *n* any of various female water spirits. ORIG C17: from NL *undina,* from L *unda* a wave

undisputed world champion *n Boxing.* a boxer who holds the World Boxing Association and the World Boxing Council world championship titles simultaneously.

undistributed (ˌʌndɪ'strɪbjʊtɪd) *adj* **1** *Logic.* (of a term) referring only to some members of the class designated by the term, as *doctors* in *some doctors are overworked.* **2** *Business.* (of a profit) not paid in dividends to the shareholders of a company but retained to help finance its trading.

undo (ʌn'duː) *vb* **undoes, undoing, undid, undone.** (*mainly tr*) **1** (*also intr*) to untie, unwrap, or open or become untied, unwrapped, etc. **2** to reverse the effects of. **3** to cause the downfall of.

undoing (ʌn'duːɪŋ) *n* **1** ruin; downfall. **2** the cause of downfall: *drink was his undoing.*

undone[1] (ʌn'dʌn) *adj* not done or completed; unfinished.

undone[2] (ʌn'dʌn) *adj* **1** ruined; destroyed. **2** unfastened; untied.

undoubted (ʌn'daʊtɪd) *adj* beyond doubt; certain or indisputable.
▸ **un'doubtedly** *adv*

undreamed (ʌn'driːmd) *or* **undreamt** (ʌn'drɛmt) *adj* (often foll. by *of*) not thought of, conceived, or imagined.

undress (ʌn'drɛs) *vb* **1** to take off clothes from (oneself or another). **2** (*tr*) to strip of ornamentation. **3** (*tr*) to remove the dressing from (a wound). ◆ *n* **4** partial or complete nakedness. **5** informal or normal working clothes or uniform.

undressed (ʌn'drɛst) *adj* **1** partially or completely naked. **2** (of an animal hide) not fully processed. **3** (of food, esp. salad) not prepared with sauce or dressing.

Undset ★ (*Norwegian* 'unsɛt) *n* **Sigrid** ('sigri). 1882–1949, Norwegian novelist, best known for her trilogy *Kristin Lavransdatter* (1920–22): Nobel prize for literature 1928.

undue (ʌn'djuː) *adj* **1** excessive or unwarranted. **2** unjust, improper, or illegal. **3** (of a debt, bond, etc.) not yet payable.

undulant ('ʌndjʊlənt) *adj Rare.* resembling waves; undulating.
▸ '**undulance** *n*

undulant fever *n* another name for **brucellosis.** ORIG C19: so called because the fever symptoms are intermittent

undulate *vb* ('ʌndjʊˌleɪt), **undulates, undulating, undulated. 1** to move or cause to move in waves or as if in waves. **2** to have or provide with a wavy form or appearance. ◆ *adj* ('ʌndjʊlɪt, -ˌleɪt). **3** having a wavy or rippled appearance, margin, or form: *an undulate leaf.* ORIG C17: from L from *unda* a wave
▸ '**unduˌlator** *n* ▸ '**undulatory** *adj*

undulation (ˌʌndjʊ'leɪʃən) *n* **1** the act or an instance of undulating. **2** any wave or wavelike form, line, etc.

unduly (ʌn'djuːlɪ) *adv* excessively.

undying (ʌn'daɪɪŋ) *adj* unending; eternal.
▸ **un'dyingly** *adv*

unearned (ʌn'ɜːnd) *adj* **1** not deserved. **2** not yet earned.

unearned income *n* income from property, investment, etc., comprising rent, interest, and dividends.

unearth (ʌn'ɜːθ) *vb* (*tr*) **1** to dig up out of the earth. **2** to reveal or discover, esp. by exhaustive searching.

unearthly (ʌn'ɜːθlɪ) *adj* **1** ghostly; eerie: *unearthly screams.* **2** heavenly; sublime: *unearthly music.* **3** ridiculous or unreasonable (esp. in **unearthly hour**).
▸ **un'earthliness** *n*

uneasy (ʌn'iːzɪ) *adj* **1** (of a person) anxious; apprehensive. **2** (of a condition) precarious: *an uneasy truce.* **3** (of a thought, etc.) disquieting.
▸ **un'ease** *n* ▸ **un'easily** *adv* ▸ **un'easiness** *n*

uneatable (ʌn'iːtəbᵊl) *adj* (of food) not fit or suitable for eating, esp. because it is rotten or unattractive.

uneconomic (ˌʌniːkə'nɒmɪk, ˌʌnɛkə-) *adj* not economic; not profitable.

uneconomical (ˌʌniːkə'nɒmɪkᵊl, -ɛkə-) *adj* not economical; wasteful.

unemployable (ˌʌnɪm'plɔɪəbᵊl) *adj* unable or unfit to keep a job.
▸ ˌ**unemˌploya'bility** *n*

unemployed (ˌʌnɪm'plɔɪd) *adj* **1a** without remunerative employment; out of work. **1b** (*as collective n;* preceded by *the*): *the unemployed.* **2** not being used; idle.

unemployment (ˌʌnɪm'plɔɪmənt) *n* **1** the condition of being unemployed. **2** the number of unemployed workers, often as a percentage of the total labour force.

unemployment benefit *n* (in Britain, formerly) a regular payment to a person who is out of work: replaced by jobseeker's allowance in 1996. Informal term: **dole.**

unequal (ʌn'iːkwəl) *adj* **1** not equal in quantity, size, rank, value, etc. **2** (foll. by *to*) inadequate; insufficient. **3** not evenly balanced. **4** (of character, quality, etc.) irregular; inconsistent. **5** (of a contest, etc.) having competitors of different ability.

unequalled *or US* **unequaled** (ʌn'iːkwəld) *adj* not equalled; unrivalled; supreme.

unequivocal (ˌʌnɪ'kwɪvəkᵊl) *adj* not ambiguous; plain.
▸ ˌ**une'quivocally** *adv* ▸ ˌ**une'quivocalness** *n*

unerring (ʌn'ɜːrɪŋ) *adj* **1** not missing the mark or target. **2** consistently accurate; certain.
▸ **un'erringly** *adv* ▸ **un'erringness** *n*

UNESCO (juː'nɛskəʊ) *n acronym for* United Nations Educational, Scientific, and Cultural Organization.

uneven (ʌn'iːvən) *adj* **1** (of a surface, etc.) not level or flat. **2** spasmodic or variable. **3** not parallel, straight, or

horizontal. **4** not fairly matched: *an uneven race.* **5** *Arch.* not equal.
▸ **un'evenly** *adv* ▸ **un'evenness** *n*

uneventful (ˌʌnɪ'vɛntfʊl) *adj* ordinary, routine, or quiet.
▸ **ˌune'ventfully** *adv* ▸ **ˌune'ventfulness** *n*

unexampled (ˌʌnɪg'zɑːmpᵊld) *adj* without precedent or parallel.

unexceptionable (ˌʌnɪk'sɛpʃənəbᵊl) *adj* beyond criticism or objection.
▸ **ˌunex'ceptionably** *adv*

unexceptional (ˌʌnɪk'sɛpʃənᵊl) *adj* **1** usual, ordinary, or normal. **2** subject to or allowing no exceptions.
▸ **ˌunex'ceptionally** *adv*

unexcited (ˌʌnɪk'saɪtɪd) *adj* **1** not aroused to pleasure, interest, agitation, etc. **2** (of an atom, molecule, etc.) remaining in its ground state.

unexpected (ˌʌnɪk'spɛktɪd) *adj* surprising or unforeseen.
▸ **ˌunex'pectedly** *adv* ▸ **ˌunex'pectedness** *n*

unfailing (ʌn'feɪlɪŋ) *adj* **1** not failing; unflagging. **2** continuous. **3** sure; certain.
▸ **un'failingly** *adv* ▸ **un'failingness** *n*

unfair (ʌn'fɛə) *adj* **1** characterized by inequality or injustice. **2** dishonest or unethical.
▸ **un'fairly** *adv* ▸ **un'fairness** *n*

unfaithful (ʌn'feɪθfʊl) *adj* **1** not true to a promise, vow, etc. **2** not true to a wife, husband, lover, etc., esp. in having sexual intercourse with someone else. **3** inaccurate; untrustworthy: *unfaithful copy.* **4** *Obs.* not having religious faith.
▸ **un'faithfully** *adv* ▸ **un'faithfulness** *n*

unfamiliar (ˌʌnfə'mɪljə) *adj* **1** not known or experienced; strange. **2** (*postpositive;* foll. by *with*) not familiar.
▸ **unfamiliarity** (ˌʌnfəˌmɪlɪ'ærɪtɪ) *n* ▸ **unˌfa'miliarly** *adv*

unfasten (ʌn'fɑːsᵊn) *vb* to undo, untie, or open or become undone, untied, or opened.

unfathered (ʌn'fɑːðəd) *adj* **1** having no known father. **2** of unknown or uncertain origin.

unfathomable (ʌn'fæðəməbᵊl) *adj* **1** incapable of being fathomed; immeasurable. **2** incomprehensible.
▸ **un'fathomableness** *n* ▸ **un'fathomably** *adv*

unfavourable *or US* **unfavorable** (ʌn'feɪvərəbᵊl) *adj* not favourable; adverse or inauspicious.
▸ **un'favourably** *or US* **un'favorably** *adv*

unfazed (ʌn'feɪzd) *adj Inf.* not disconcerted; unperturbed.

Unfederated Malay States ★ (ʌn'fɛdəˌreɪtɪd) *pl n* a former group of native states in the Malay Peninsula that became British protectorates between 1885 and 1909. All except Brunei joined the Malayan Union (later Federation of Malaya) in 1946. Brunei joined the Federation of Malaysia in 1963.

unfeeling (ʌn'fiːlɪŋ) *adj* **1** without sympathy; callous. **2** without physical feeling or sensation.
▸ **un'feelingly** *adv* ▸ **un'feelingness** *n*

unfinished (ʌn'fɪnɪʃt) *adj* **1** incomplete or imperfect. **2** (of paint, polish, varnish, etc.) without an applied finish; rough. **3** (of fabric) unbleached or not processed.

unfit (ʌn'fɪt) *adj* **1** (*postpositive;* often foll. by *for*) unqualified, incapable, or incompetent: *unfit for military service.* **2** (*postpositive;* often foll. by *for*) unsuitable or inappropriate: *the ground was unfit for football.* **3** in poor physical condition. ◆ *vb* **unfits, unfitting, unfitted. 4** (*tr*) *Rare.* to render unfit.
▸ **un'fitly** *adv* ▸ **un'fitness** *n*

unfix (ʌn'fɪks) *vb* (*tr*) **1** to unfasten, detach, or loosen. **2** to unsettle or disturb.

unflappable (ʌn'flæpəbᵊl) *adj Inf.* hard to upset; calm; composed.
▸ **unˌflappa'bility** *n* ▸ **un'flappably** *adv*

unfledged (ʌn'flɛdʒd) *adj* **1** (of a young bird) not having developed adult feathers. **2** immature and undeveloped.

unflinching (ʌn'flɪntʃɪŋ) *adj* not shrinking from danger, difficulty, etc.
▸ **un'flinchingly** *adv*

unfold (ʌn'fəʊld) *vb* **1** to open or spread out or be opened or spread out from a folded state. **2** to reveal or be revealed: *the truth unfolds.* **3** to develop or expand or be developed or expanded.
▸ **un'folder** *n*

unfortunate (ʌn'fɔːtʃənɪt) *adj* **1** causing or attended by misfortune. **2** unlucky or unhappy: *an unfortunate character.* **3** regrettable or unsuitable: *an unfortunate speech.* ◆ *n* **4** an unlucky person.
▸ **un'fortunately** *adv*

unfounded (ʌn'faʊndɪd) *adj* **1** (of ideas, allegations, etc.) baseless; groundless. **2** not yet founded or established.
▸ **un'foundedly** *adv* ▸ **un'foundedness** *n*

unfranked income (ʌn'fræŋkt) *n* any income from an investment that does not qualify as franked investment income.

unfreeze (ʌn'friːz) *vb* **unfreezes, unfreezing, unfroze, unfrozen. 1** to thaw or cause to thaw. **2** (*tr*) to relax governmental restrictions on (wages, prices, credit, etc.) or on the manufacture or sale of (goods, etc.).

unfriended (ʌn'frɛndɪd) *adj Now rare.* without a friend or friends; friendless.

unfriendly (ʌn'frɛndlɪ) *adj* **unfriendlier, unfriendliest. 1** not friendly; hostile. **2** unfavourable or disagreeable. ◆ *adv* **3** *Rare.* in an unfriendly manner.
▸ **un'friendliness** *n*

unfrock (ʌn'frɒk) *vb* (*tr*) to deprive (a person in holy orders) of ecclesiastical status.

unfunded debt (ʌn'fʌndɪd) *n* a short-term floating debt not represented by bonds.

unfurl (ʌn'fɜːl) *vb* to unroll, unfold, or spread out or be unrolled, unfolded, or spread out from a furled state.

ungainly (ʌn'geɪnlɪ) *adj* **ungainlier, ungainliest. 1** lacking grace when moving. **2** difficult to move or use; unwieldy. ORIG C17: from UN-[1] + obs. or dialect *gainly* graceful
▸ **un'gainliness** *n*

Ungaretti ★ (*Italian* uŋga'retti) *n* **Giuseppe** (dʒu'zɛppe). 1888–1970, Italian poet, best known for his collection of war poems *Allegria di naufragi* (1919).

Ungava ★ (ʊŋ'geɪvə, -'gɑː-) *n* a sparsely inhabited region of NE Canada, in N Quebec east of Hudson Bay: part of the Labrador peninsula: rich mineral resources. Area: 911 110 sq. km (351 780 sq. miles).

ungodly (ʌn'gɒdlɪ) *adj* **ungodlier, ungodliest. 1a** wicked, sinful. **1b** (*as collective n;* preceded by *the*): *the ungodly.* **2** *Inf.* unseemly; outrageous (esp. in **an ungodly hour**).
▸ **un'godliness** *n*

ungovernable (ʌn'gʌvənəbᵊl) *adj* not able to be disciplined, restrained, etc.: *an ungovernable temper.*
▸ **un'governableness** *n* ▸ **un'governably** *adv*

ungual ('ʌŋgwəl) *adj* **1** of, relating to, or affecting the fingernails or toenails. **2** of or relating to an unguis. ORIG C19: from L *unguis* nail

unguarded (ʌn'gɑːdɪd) *adj* **1** unprotected; vulnerable. **2** open; frank. **3** incautious.
▸ **un'guardedly** *adv* ▸ **un'guardedness** *n*

unguent ('ʌŋgwənt) *n* a less common name for an **ointment.** ORIG C15: from L, from *unguere* to anoint

unguiculate (ʌŋ'gwɪkjʊlɪt, -ˌleɪt) *adj* **1** (of mammals) having claws or nails. **2** (of petals) having a clawlike base. ◆ *n* **3** an unguiculate mammal. ORIG C19: from NL *unguiculātus,* from L *unguiculus,* dim. of *unguis* nail

unguis ('ʌŋgwɪs) *n, pl* **ungues** (-gwiːz). **1** a nail, claw, or hoof, or the part of the digit giving rise to it. **2** the clawlike base of a petal. ORIG C18: from L

ungulate ('ʌŋgjʊlɪt, -ˌleɪt) *n* any of a large group of mammals all of which have hooves: divided into odd-toed ungulates (see **perissodactyl**) and even-toed ungulates (see **artiodactyl**). ORIG C19: from LL *ungulātus* having hooves, from *ungula* hoof

unhallowed (ʌn'hæləʊd) *adj* **1** not consecrated or holy: *unhallowed ground.* **2** sinful.

unhand (ʌn'hænd) *vb* (*tr*) *Arch. or literary.* to release from the grasp.

unhappy (ʌn'hæpɪ) *adj* **unhappier, unhappiest. 1** not joyful;

★ people and places

sad or depressed. **2** unfortunate or wretched: *an unhappy fellow.* **3** tactless or inappropriate: *an unhappy remark.*
▸ **un'happily** *adv* ▸ **un'happiness** *n*

UNHCR *abbrev. for* United Nations High Commissioner for Refugees.

unhealthy (ʌn'hɛlθɪ) *adj* **unhealthier, unhealthiest. 1** characterized by ill health; sick. **2** characteristic of, conducive to, or resulting from ill health: *an unhealthy complexion.* **3** morbid or unwholesome. **4** *Inf.* dangerous; risky.
▸ **un'healthily** *adv* ▸ **un'healthiness** *n*

unheard (ʌn'hɜːd) *adj* **1** not heard; not perceived by the ear. **2** not listened to: *his warning went unheard.* **3** *Arch.* unheard-of.

unheard-of *adj* **1** previously unknown: *an unheard-of actress.* **2** without precedent: *an unheard-of treatment.* **3** highly offensive: *unheard-of behaviour.*

unhinge (ʌn'hɪndʒ) *vb* **unhinges, unhinging, unhinged.** (*tr*) **1** to remove (a door, etc.) from its hinges. **2** to derange or unbalance (a person, his or her mind, etc.). **3** to disrupt or unsettle (a process or state of affairs).

unhip (ʌn'hɪp) *adj Sl.* not at all fashionable or up to date: *my terminally unhip parents.*

unholy (ʌn'həʊlɪ) *adj* **unholier, unholiest. 1** not holy or sacred. **2** immoral or depraved. **3** *Inf.* outrageous or unnatural: *an unholy alliance.*
▸ **un'holiness** *n*

unhook (ʌn'hʊk) *vb* **1** (*tr*) to remove (something) from a hook. **2** (*tr*) to unfasten the hook of (a dress, etc.). **3** (*intr*) to become unfastened or be capable of unfastening: *the dress wouldn't unhook.*

unhorse (ʌn'hɔːs) *vb* **unhorses, unhorsing, unhorsed.** (*tr*) **1** (*usually passive*) to knock or throw from a horse. **2** to overthrow or dislodge, as from a powerful position.

unhouseled (ʌn'haʊzəld) *adj Arch.* not having received the Eucharist. ORIG C16: from *un-* + obs. *housel* to administer the sacrament, from OE *hūsl* (n), *hūslian* (vb), from ?

uni ('juːnɪ) *n Inf.* short for **university.**

uni- *combining form.* consisting of, relating to, or having only one: *unilateral.* ORIG from L *ūnus* one

Uniat ('juːnɪˌæt) *or* **Uniate** ('juːnɪɪt, -ˌeɪt) *adj* **1** designating any of the Eastern Churches that retain their own liturgy but submit to papal authority. ◆ *n* **2** a member of one of these Churches. ORIG C19: from Russian *uniyat,* from Polish *unja* union, from LL *ūniō;* see UNION
▸ **'Uniˌatism** *n*

uniaxial (ˌjuːnɪ'æksɪəl) *adj* **1** (esp. of plants) having an unbranched main axis. **2** (of a crystal) having only one direction along which double refraction of light does not occur.

unicameral (ˌjuːnɪ'kæmərəl) *adj* of or characterized by a single legislative chamber.
▸ **ˌuni'cameralism** *n* ▸ **ˌuni'cameralist** *n* ▸ **ˌuni'camerally** *adv*

UNICEF ('juːnɪˌsɛf) *n acronym for* United Nations Children's Fund (formerly, United Nations International Children's Emergency Fund).

unicellular (ˌjuːnɪ'sɛljʊlə) *adj* (of organisms, such as protozoans and certain algae) consisting of a single cell.
▸ **ˌuniˌcellu'larity** *n*

unicorn ('juːnɪˌkɔːn) *n* **1** an imaginary creature usually depicted as a white horse with one long spiralled horn growing from its forehead. **2** *Old Testament.* a two-horned animal: mistranslation in the Authorized Version of the original Hebrew. ORIG C13: from OF, from L *ūnicornis* one-horned, from *ūnus* one + *cornu* a horn

unicycle ('juːnɪˌsaɪkᵊl) *n* a one-wheeled vehicle driven by pedals, esp. one used in a circus, etc. Also called: **monocycle.** ORIG from UNI- + CYCLE, on the model of TRICYCLE
▸ **'uniˌcyclist** *n*

unidirectional (ˌjuːnɪdɪ'rɛkʃənᵊl) *adj* having, moving in, or operating in only one direction.

UNIDO (juː'niːdəʊ) *n acronym for* United Nations Industrial Development Organization.

Unification Church *n* a religious sect founded in 1954 by Sun Myung Moon (born 1920), S Korean industrialist and religious leader.

unified field theory *n* any theory capable of describing in one set of equations the properties of gravitational fields, electromagnetic fields, and strong and weak nuclear interactions. No satisfactory theory has yet been found. See also **grand unified theory.**

uniform ('juːnɪˌfɔːm) *n* **1** a prescribed identifying set of clothes for the members of an organization, such as soldiers or schoolchildren. **2** a single set of such clothes. **3** a characteristic feature of some class or group. ◆ *adj* **4** unchanging in form, quality, etc.: *a uniform surface.* **5** alike or like: *a line of uniform toys.* ◆ *vb* (*tr*) **6** to fit out (a body of soldiers, etc.) with uniforms. **7** to make uniform. ORIG C16: from L *ūniformis,* from *ūnus* one + *forma* shape
▸ **'uniˌformly** *adv* ▸ **'uniˌformness** *n*

Uniform Business Rate *n* a local tax in the UK paid by businesses, based on a local valuation of their premises and a rate fixed by central government that applies throughout the country. Abbrev.: **UBR.**

uniformitarianism (ˌjuːnɪˌfɔːmɪ'tɛərɪəˌnɪzəm) *n* the concept that the earth's surface was shaped in the past by gradual processes, such as erosion, and by small sudden changes, such as earthquakes, rather than by sudden divine acts, such as Noah's flood.
▸ **ˌuniˌformi'tarian** *n, adj*

uniformity (ˌjuːnɪ'fɔːmɪtɪ) *n, pl* **uniformities. 1** a state or condition in which everything is regular, homogeneous, or unvarying. **2** lack of diversity or variation.

unify ('juːnɪˌfaɪ) *vb* **unifies, unifying, unified.** to make or become one; unite. ORIG C16: from Med. L *ūnificāre,* from L *ūnus* one + *facere* to make
▸ **'uniˌfiable** *adj* ▸ **ˌunifi'cation** *n* ▸ **'uniˌfier** *n*

unilateral (ˌjuːnɪ'lætərəl) *adj* **1** of, having, affecting, or occurring on only one side. **2** involving or performed by only one party of several: *unilateral disarmament.* **3** *Law.* (of contracts, obligations, etc.) made by, affecting, or binding one party only. **4** *Bot.* having or designating parts situated or turned to one side of an axis.
▸ **ˌuni'lateralism** *n* ▸ **ˌuni'laterally** *adv*

Unilateral Declaration of Independence *n* a declaration of independence made by a dependent state without the assent of the protecting state. Abbrev.: **UDI.**

Unimak Island ★ ('juːnɪˌmæk) *n* an island in SW Alaska, in the Aleutian Islands. Length: 113 km (70 miles).

unimpeachable (ˌʌnɪm'piːtʃəbᵊl) *adj* unquestionable as to honesty, truth, etc.
▸ **ˌunim'peachably** *adv*

unimproved (ˌʌnɪm'pruːvd) *adj* **1** not improved or made better. **2** (of land) not cleared, drained, cultivated, etc. **3** neglected; unused: *unimproved resources.*

unincorporated business (ˌʌnɪn'kɔːpəreɪtɪd) *n* a privately owned business, often owned by one person who has unlimited liability as the business is not legally registered as a company.

uninterested (ʌn'ɪntrɪstɪd) *adj* indifferent.
▸ **un'interestedly** *adv* ▸ **un'interestedness** *n*

USAGE NOTE See at **disinterested.**

union ('juːnjən) *n* **1** the condition of being united, the act of uniting, or a conjunction formed by such an act. **2** an association, alliance, or confederation of individuals or groups for a common purpose, esp. political. **3** agreement or harmony. **4** short for **trade union. 5** the act or state of marriage or sexual intercourse. **6** a device on a flag representing union, such as another flag depicted in the top left corner. **7** a device for coupling pipes. **8** (*often cap.*) **8a** an association of students at a university or college formed to look after the students' interests. **8b** the building or buildings housing the facilities of such an organization. **9** *Maths.* a set containing all members of two given sets. Symbol: ∪ **10** (in 19th-century England) a number of parishes united for the administration of poor relief. **11** *Textiles.* a piece of cloth or fabric consisting of two different kinds of yarn. **12** (*modifier*) of or related to a union, esp. a trade union. ORIG C15: from Church L *ūniō* oneness, from L *ūnus* one

Union (ˈjuːnjən) *n* **the. 1** *Brit.* **1a** the union of England and Wales from 1543. **1b** the union of the English and Scottish crowns (1603–1707). **1c** the union of England and Scotland from 1707. **1d** the political union of Great Britain and Ireland (1801–1920). **1e** the union of Great Britain and Northern Ireland from 1921. **2** *US.* **2a** the United States of America. **2b** the northern states of the US during the Civil War. **2c** (*as modifier*): *Union supporters.*

union catalogue *n* a catalogue listing every publication held at cooperating libraries.

Union flag *n* the national flag of the United Kingdom, being a composite design composed of Saint George's Cross (England), Saint Andrew's Cross (Scotland), and Saint Patrick's Cross (Ireland). Often called: **Union Jack.**

unionism (ˈjuːnjəˌnɪzəm) *n* **1** the principles of trade unions. **2** adherence to the principles of trade unions. **3** the principle or theory of any union.
▸ **ˈunionist** *n, adj*

Unionist (ˈjuːnjənɪst) *n* **1** (*sometimes not cap.*) **1a** (before 1920) a supporter of the Union of all Ireland and Great Britain. **1b** (since 1920) a supporter of Union between Britain and Northern Ireland. **2** a supporter of the US federal Union, esp. during the Civil War. ◆ *adj* **3** of, resembling, or relating to Unionists.
▸ **ˈUnionˌism** *n*

Unionist Party *n* (formerly, in Northern Ireland) the major Protestant political party, closely identified with the Union with Britain. See also **Ulster Democratic Unionist Party, Ulster Unionist Council.**

unionize *or* **unionise** (ˈjuːnjəˌnaɪz) *vb* **unionizes, unionizing, unionized** *or* **unionises, unionising, unionised. 1** to organize (workers) into a trade union. **2** to join or cause to join a trade union. **3** (*tr*) to subject to the rules or codes of a trade union.
▸ **ˌunioniˈzation** *or* **ˌunioniˈsation** *n*

Union Jack *n* a common name for **Union flag.**

Union of South Africa ★ *n* the former name (1910–61) of the (Republic of) **South Africa.**

Union of Soviet Socialist Republics ★ *n* the official name of the former **Soviet Union.**

union pipes *pl n* another name for **uillean pipes.**

union shop *n* (formerly) an establishment whose employment policy is governed by a contract between employer and a trade union permitting the employment of nonunion labour only on the condition that such labour joins the union within a specified time period.

unipolar (ˌjuːnɪˈpəʊlə) *adj* **1** of, concerned with, or having a single magnetic or electric pole. **2** (of a nerve cell) having a single process. **3** (of a transistor) utilizing charge carriers of one polarity only, as in a field-effect transistor.
▸ **unipolarity** (ˌjuːnɪpəʊˈlærɪtɪ) *n*

unique (juːˈniːk) *adj* **1** being the only one of a particular type. **2** without equal or like. **3** *Inf.* very remarkable. **4** *Maths.* **4a** leading to only one result: *the sum of two integers is unique.* **4b** having precisely one value: *the unique positive square root of 4 is 2.* ORIG C17: via F from L *ūnicus* unparalleled, from *ūnus* one
▸ **uˈniquely** *adv* ▸ **uˈniqueness** *n*

> **USAGE NOTE** *Unique* with the meaning 'being the only one' or 'having no equal' describes an absolute state: *a case unique in British law.* In this use it cannot therefore be qualified; something is either *unique* or *not unique.* However, *unique* is also very commonly used in the sense of 'remarkable' or 'exceptional', particularly in the language of advertising, and in this meaning it can be used with words such as *rather, quite,* etc. Since many people object to this use, it is best avoided in formal and serious writing.

unisex (ˈjuːnɪˌsɛks) *adj* of or relating to clothing, a hairstyle, hairdressers, etc., that can be worn or used by either sex. ORIG C20: from UNI- + SEX

unisexual (ˌjuːnɪˈsɛksjuəl) *adj* **1** of one sex only. **2** (of some organisms) having either male or female reproductive organs but not both.
▸ **ˌuniˌsexuˈality** *n* ▸ **ˌuniˈsexually** *adv*

unison (ˈjuːnɪsᵊn) *n* **1** *Music.* **1a** the interval between two sounds of identical pitch. **1b** (*modifier*) played or sung at the same pitch: *unison singing.* **2** complete agreement (esp. in **in unison**). ORIG C16: from LL *ūnisonus,* from UNI- + *sonus* sound
▸ **uˈnisonous, uˈnisonal,** *or* **uˈnisonant** *adj*

UNISON (ˈjuːnɪsᵊn) *n* (in Britain) a trade union representing local government, health-care, and other workers: formed in 1993 by the amalgamation of COHSE, NALGO, and NUPE.

unit (ˈjuːnɪt) *n* **1** a single undivided entity or whole. **2** any group or individual, esp. when regarded as a basic element of a larger whole. **3** a mechanical part or assembly of parts that performs a subsidiary function: *a filter unit.* **4** a complete system or establishment that performs a specific function: *a production unit.* **5** a subdivision of a larger military formation. **6** a standard amount of a physical quantity, such as length, mass, etc., multiples of which are used to express magnitudes of that physical quantity: *the second is a unit of time.* **7** the amount of a drug, vaccine, etc., needed to produce a particular effect. **8** a standard measure used in calculating alcohol intake and its effect. **9** the digit or position immediately to the left of the decimal point. **10** (*modifier*) having or relating to a value of one: *a unit vector.* **11** *NZ.* a self-propelled railcar. **12** *Austral. & NZ.* short for **home unit.** ORIG C16: back formation from UNITY, ? on the model of *digit*

unitarian (ˌjuːnɪˈtɛərɪən) *n* **1** a supporter of unity or centralization in politics. ◆ *adj* **2** of or relating to unity or centralization.

Unitarian (ˌjuːnɪˈtɛərɪən) *n* **1** a person who believes that God is one being and rejects the doctrine of the Trinity. **2** a member of the Church (**Unitarian Church**) that embodies this system of belief. ◆ *adj* **3** of or relating to Unitarians or Unitarianism.
▸ **ˌUniˈtariaˌnism** *n*

unitary (ˈjuːnɪtərɪ, -trɪ) *adj* **1** of a unit or units. **2** based on or characterized by unity. **3** individual; whole.

unitary authority *n* (in Britain) a district administered by a single tier of local government.

unit character *n Genetics.* a character inherited as a single unit and dependent on a single gene.

unit cost *n* the actual cost of producing one article.

unite[1] (juːˈnaɪt) *vb* **unites, uniting, united. 1** to make or become an integrated whole or a unity. **2** to join, unify or be unified in purpose, action, beliefs, etc. **3** to enter or cause to enter into an association or alliance. **4** to adhere or cause to adhere; fuse. **5** (*tr*) to possess (qualities) in combination or at the same time: *he united charm with severity.* ORIG C15: from LL *ūnīre,* from *ūnus* one

unite[2] (ˈjuːnaɪt, juːˈnaɪt) *n* an English gold coin of the Stuart period, originally worth 20 shillings. ORIG C17: from obs. *unite* joined, from the union of England & Scotland (1603)

united (juːˈnaɪtɪd) *adj* **1** produced by two or more persons or things in combination or from their union or amalgamation: *a united effort.* **2** in agreement. **3** in association or alliance.
▸ **uˈnitedly** *adv* ▸ **uˈnitedness** *n*

United Arab Emirates ★ *pl n* a group of seven emirates in SW Asia, on the Persian Gulf: consists of Abu Dhabi, Dubai, Sharjah, Ajman, Umm al Qaiwain, Ras el Khaimah, and Fujairah; a former British protectorate; became fully independent in 1971; consists mostly of flat desert, with mountains in the east; rich petroleum resources. Official language: Arabic. Official religion: Muslim. Currency: dirham. Capital: Abu Dhabi. Pop.: 2 826 000 (1999 est.). Area: 83 600 sq. km (32 300 sq. miles). Former name (until 1971): **Trucial States.** Abbrev.: **UAE.**

United Arab Republic ★ *n* the official name (1958–71) of **Egypt.**

United Arab States ★ *pl n* a federation (1958–61) between the United Arab Republic and Yemen.

United Empire Loyalist *n Canad. history.* an American colonist who settled in Canada during or after the War of American Independence because of loyalty to the British Crown.

United Kingdom ★ *n* a kingdom of NW Europe, consisting chiefly of the island of Great Britain together with Northern Ireland: became the world's leading colonial power in the 18th century: the first country to undergo the Industrial Revolution. It became the **United Kingdom of Great Britain and Northern Ireland** in 1921, after the rest of Ireland became autonomous as the Irish Free State. Primarily it is a trading nation; a member of the European Union. Official language: English; Gaelic, Welsh, and other minority languages. Religion: Christian majority. Currency: pound sterling. Capital: London. Pop.: 59 313 000 (1999 est.). Area: 244 110 sq. km (94 251 sq. miles). Abbrev.: **UK**. See also **Great Britain**.

United Kingdom overseas territory ★ *n* any of the territories that are governed by the UK but lie outside the British Isles; many were formerly British **crown colonies**: includes Bermuda, Falkland Islands, Gibraltar, and Montserrat.

United Nations *n* (*functioning as sing or pl*) an international organization of independent states, with its headquarters in New York City, that was formed in 1945 to promote peace and international cooperation and security. Abbrev.: **UN**.

United Provinces ★ *pl n* **1** a Dutch republic (1581–1795) formed by the union of the seven northern provinces of the Netherlands, which were in revolt against their suzerain, Philip II of Spain. **2** short for **United Provinces of Agra and Oudh**: the former name of **Uttar Pradesh**.

United States of America ★ (*functioning as sing or pl*) *n* a federal republic mainly in North America consisting of 50 states and the District of Columbia: colonized principally by the English and French in the 17th century, the native Indians being gradually defeated and displaced; 13 colonies under British rule made the Declaration of Independence in 1776 and became the United States after the War of American Independence. The northern states defeated the South in the Civil War (1861–65). It is the world's most productive industrial nation; agriculture is also significant. It participated reluctantly in World Wars I and II but since then has played a major role in international affairs. It consists generally of the Rocky Mountains in the west, the Great Plains in the centre, the Appalachians in the east, deserts in the southwest, and coastal lowlands and swamps in the southeast. Language: predominantly English; Spanish is widely spoken, also many Native American and other minority languages. Religion: Christian majority. Currency: dollar. Capital: Washington, D.C. Pop.: 273 131 000 (1999 est.). Area: 9 518 323 sq. km (3 675 031 sq. miles). Often shortened to: **United States**. Abbrevs.: **US, USA**.

unitive (ˈjuːnɪtɪv) *adj* **1** tending to unite or capable of uniting. **2** characterized by unity.

unitize *or* **unitise** (ˈjuːnɪˌtaɪz) *vb* **unitizes, unitizing, unitized** *or* **unitises, unitising, unitised.** (*tr*) *Finance.* to convert (an investment trust) into a unit trust.
▸ **ˌunitiˈzation** *or* **ˌunitiˈsation** *n*

unit-linked policy *n* a life-assurance policy the benefits of which are directly in proportion to the number of units purchased on the policyholder's behalf.

unit of account *n* **1** *Econ.* the function of money that enables the user to keep accounts, value transactions, etc. **2** a monetary denomination used for accounting purposes, etc., but not necessarily corresponding to any real currency: *the euro is the unit of account of the European Monetary Fund.* **3** the unit of currency of a country.

unit price *n* a price for foodstuffs, etc., stated or shown as the cost per unit, as per pound, per kilogram, per dozen, etc.

unit pricing *n* a system of pricing foodstuffs, etc., in which the cost of a single unit is shown to enable shoppers to see the advantage of buying multipacks.

unit trust *n Brit.* an investment trust that issues units for public sale, the holders of which are creditors and not shareholders with their interests represented by a trust company independent of the issuing agency. US and Canad. equivalent: **mutual fund**.

unity (ˈjuːnɪtɪ) *n, pl* **unities. 1** the state or quality of being one; oneness. **2** the act, state, or quality of forming a whole from separate parts. **3** something whole or complete that is composed of separate parts. **4** mutual agreement; harmony or concord: *the participants were no longer in unity.* **5** uniformity or constancy: *unity of purpose.* **6** *Maths.* **6a** the number or numeral one. **6b** a quantity assuming the value of one: *the area of the triangle was regarded as unity.* **6c** the element of a set producing no change in a number following multiplication. **7** any one of the three principles of dramatic structure by which the action of a play should be limited to a single plot (unity of action), a single location (unity of place), and a single day (unity of time).
ORIG C13: from OF *unité,* from L *ūnitās,* from *ūnus* one

Univ. *abbrev. for* University.

univalent (ˌjuːnɪˈveɪlənt, juːˈnɪvələnt) *adj* **1** (of a chromosome during meiosis) not paired with its homologue. **2** *Chem.* another word for **monovalent**.
▸ **ˌuniˈvalency** *n*

univalve (ˈjuːnɪˌvælv) *Zool.* ◆ *adj* **1** relating to or possessing a mollusc shell that consists of a single piece (valve). ◆ *n* **2** a gastropod mollusc.

universal (ˌjuːnɪˈvɜːsᵊl) *adj* **1** of or typical of the whole of mankind or of nature. **2** common to or proceeding from all in a particular group. **3** applicable to or affecting many individuals, conditions, or cases. **4** existing or prevailing everywhere. **5** applicable or occurring throughout or relating to the universe: *a universal constant.* **6** (esp. of a language) capable of being used and understood by all. **7** embracing or versed in many fields of knowledge, activity, interest, etc. **8** *Machinery.* designed or adapted for a range of sizes, fittings, or uses. **9** *Logic.* (of a statement or proposition) affirming or denying something about every member of a class, as in *all men are wicked.* Cf. **particular** (sense 6). **10** *Arch.* entire; whole. ◆ *n* **11** *Philosophy.* a general term or concept or the type such a term signifies. **12** *Logic.* a universal proposition, statement, or formula. **13** a characteristic common to every member of a particular culture or to every human being.

USAGE NOTE The use of *more universal* as in *his writings have long been admired by fellow scientists, but his latest book should have more universal appeal* is acceptable in modern English usage.

universal class *or* **set** *n* (in Boolean algebra) the class containing all points and including all other classes.

universal gas constant *n* a constant in the gas equation, equal to 8.314 51 J K^{-1} mol^{-1}. Symbol: *R* Also called **gas constant**.

universalism (ˌjuːnɪˈvɜːsəˌlɪzəm) *n* **1** a universal feature or characteristic. **2** another word for **universality**.

Universalism (ˌjuːnɪˈvɜːsəˌlɪzəm) *n* a system of religious beliefs maintaining that all men are predestined for salvation.
▸ **ˌUniˈversalist** *n, adj*

universality (ˌjuːnɪvɜːˈsælɪtɪ) *n* the state or quality of being universal.

universalize *or* **universalise** (ˌjuːnɪˈvɜːsəˌlaɪz) *vb* **universalizes, universalizing, universalized** *or* **universalises, universalising, universalised.** (*tr*) to make universal.
▸ **ˌuniˌversaliˈzation** *or* **ˌuniˌversaliˈsation** *n*

universal joint *or* **coupling** *n* a form of coupling between two rotating shafts allowing freedom of movement in all directions.

universally (ˌjuːnɪˈvɜːsəlɪ) *adv* everywhere or in every case: *this principle applies universally.*

universal motor *n* an electric motor capable of working on either direct current or single-phase alternating current at approximately the same speed and output.

universal time *n* **1** (from 1928) name adopted internationally for Greenwich Mean Time (measured from Greenwich midnight), now split into several slightly different scales, one of which (UT1) is used by astronomers. Abbrev.: **UT. 2** Also called: **universal coordinated time.** an internationally agreed system for civil timekeeping introduced in 1960 and redefined in 1972 as an atomic timescale. Available from broadcast signals, it has a second equal to the International Atomic Time (TAI) second, the difference between UTC and TAI being an integral number of seconds with leap seconds inserted when necessary to keep it within 0.9 seconds of UT1. Abbrev.: **UTC**.

universe (ˈjuːnɪˌvɜːs) *n* **1** *Astron.* the aggregate of all existing matter, energy, and space. **2** human beings collectively. **3** a province or sphere of thought or activity. ORIG C16: from F, from L *ūniversum* the whole world, from *ūniversus* all together, from UNI- + *vertere* to turn

universe of discourse *n Logic.* the complete range of objects, relations, ideas, etc., that are expressed or implied in a discussion.

university (ˌjuːnɪˈvɜːsɪtɪ) *n, pl* **universities. 1** an institution of higher education having authority to award bachelors' and higher degrees, usually having research facilities. **2** the buildings, members, staff, or campus of a university. ORIG C14: from OF, from Med. L *universitās* group of scholars, from LL: guild, body of men, from L: whole

UNIX (ˈjuːnɪks) *n Trademark.* a multi-user operating system found on many types of computer.

unjust (ʌnˈdʒʌst) *adj* not in accordance with accepted standards of fairness or justice; unfair.
▸ **unˈjustly** *adv* ▸ **unˈjustness** *n*

unkempt (ʌnˈkɛmpt) *adj* **1** (of the hair) uncombed; dishevelled. **2** ungroomed; slovenly: *unkempt appearance.* ORIG OE *uncembed;* from UN-[1] + *cembed,* p.p. of *cemban* to comb
▸ **unˈkemptly** *adv* ▸ **unˈkemptness** *n*

unkind (ʌnˈkaɪnd) *adj* lacking kindness; unsympathetic or cruel.
▸ **unˈkindly** *adv* ▸ **unˈkindness** *n*

unknowing (ʌnˈnəʊɪŋ) *adj* **1** not knowing; ignorant. **2** (*postpositive;* often foll. by *of*) unaware (of).
▸ **unˈknowingly** *adv*

unknown (ʌnˈnəʊn) *adj* **1** not known, understood, or recognized. **2** not established, identified, or discovered: *an unknown island.* **3** not famous: *some unknown artist.* ◆ *n* **4** an unknown person, quantity, or thing. **5** *Maths.* a variable the value of which is to be discovered by solving an equation; a variable in a conditional equation.
▸ **unˈknownness** *n*

Unknown Soldier *or* **Warrior** *n* (in various countries) an unidentified soldier who has died in battle and for whom a tomb is established as a memorial to the other unidentified dead of the nation's armed forces.

unlace (ʌnˈleɪs) *vb* **unlaces, unlacing, unlaced.** (*tr*) **1** to loosen or undo the lacing of (shoes, etc.). **2** to unfasten or remove garments, etc., of (oneself or another) by or as if by undoing lacing.

unlawful assembly (ʌnˈlɔːfʊl) *n Law.* a meeting of three or more people with the intent of carrying out any unlawful purpose.

unlay (ʌnˈleɪ) *vb* **unlays, unlaying, unlaid.** (*tr*) to untwist (a rope or cable) to separate its strands.

unleaded (ʌnˈlɛdɪd) *adj* **1** (of petrol) containing a reduced amount of tetraethyl lead, in order to reduce environmental pollution. ◆ *n* **2** petrol containing a reduced amount of tetraethyl lead.

unlearn (ʌnˈlɜːn) *vb* **unlearns, unlearning, unlearnt** *or* **unlearned** (-ˈlɜːnd). to try to forget (something learnt) or to discard (accumulated knowledge).

unlearned (ʌnˈlɜːnɪd) *adj* ignorant or untaught.
▸ **unˈlearnedly** *adv*

unlearnt (ʌnˈlɜːnt) *or* **unlearned** (ʌnˈlɜːnd) *adj* **1** denoting knowledge or skills innately present and therefore not learnt. **2** not learnt or taken notice of: *unlearnt lessons.*

unleash (ʌnˈliːʃ) *vb* (*tr*) **1** to release from or as if from a leash. **2** to free from restraint.

unleavened (ʌnˈlɛvənd) *adj* (of bread, etc.) made from a dough containing no yeast or leavening.

unless (ʌnˈlɛs) *conj* (*subordinating*) except under the circumstances that; except on the condition that: *they'll sell it unless he hears otherwise.* ORIG C14 *onlesse,* from *on* ON + *lesse* LESS

unlettered (ʌnˈlɛtəd) *adj* uneducated; illiterate.

unlike (ʌnˈlaɪk) *adj* **1** not alike; dissimilar or unequal; different. ◆ *prep* **2** not like; not typical of: *unlike his father he lacks intelligence.*
▸ **unˈlikeness** *n*

unlikely (ʌnˈlaɪklɪ) *adj* not likely; improbable.
▸ **unˈlikeliness** *or* **unˈlikeliˌhood** *n*

unlimber (ʌnˈlɪmbə) *vb* **1** (*tr*) to disengage (a gun) from its limber. **2** to prepare (something) for use.

unlimited (ʌnˈlɪmɪtɪd) *adj* **1** without limits or bounds: *unlimited knowledge.* **2** not restricted, limited, or qualified: *unlimited power.*
▸ **unˈlimitedly** *adv* ▸ **unˈlimitedness** *n*

unlisted (ʌnˈlɪstɪd) *adj* **1** not entered on a list. **2** the US and Canad. word for **ex-directory.**

Unlisted Securities Market *n* a market on the London Stock Exchange for trading in shares of smaller companies, who do not wish to comply with the requirements for a full listing. Abbrev.: **USM.**

unload (ʌnˈləʊd) *vb* **1** to remove a load or cargo from (a ship, lorry, etc.). **2** to discharge (cargo, freight, etc.). **3** (*tr*) to relieve of a burden or troubles. **4** (*tr*) to give vent to (anxiety, troubles, etc.). **5** (*tr*) to get rid of or dispose of (esp. surplus goods). **6** (*tr*) to remove the charge of ammunition from (a firearm).
▸ **unˈloader** *n*

unlock (ʌnˈlɒk) *vb* **1** (*tr*) to unfasten (a lock, door, etc.). **2** (*tr*) to release or let loose. **3** (*tr*) to provide the key to: *unlock a puzzle.* **4** (*intr*) to become unlocked.
▸ **unˈlockable** *adj*

unlooked-for (ˌʌnˈlʊktfɔː) *adj* unexpected; unforeseen.

unloose (ʌnˈluːs) *or* **unloosen** *vb* **unlooses, unloosing, unloosed** *or* **unloosens, unloosening, unloosened.** (*tr*) **1** to set free; release. **2** to loosen or relax (a hold, grip, etc.). **3** to unfasten or untie.

unlovely (ʌnˈlʌvlɪ) *adj* unpleasant in appearance or character.
▸ **unˈloveliness** *n*

unlucky (ʌnˈlʌkɪ) *adj* **1** characterized by misfortune or failure: *an unlucky chance.* **2** ill-omened; inauspicious: *an unlucky date.* **3** regrettable; disappointing.
▸ **unˈluckily** *adv* ▸ **unˈluckiness** *n*

unmake (ʌnˈmeɪk) *vb* **unmakes, unmaking, unmade.** (*tr*) **1** to undo or destroy. **2** to depose from office or authority. **3** to alter the nature of.

unman (ʌnˈmæn) *vb* **unmans, unmanning, unmanned.** (*tr*) **1** to cause to lose courage or nerve. **2** to make effeminate. **3** to remove the men from.

unmanly (ʌnˈmænlɪ) *adj* **1** not masculine or virile. **2** ignoble, cowardly, or dishonourable. ◆ *adv* **3** *Arch.* in an unmanly manner.
▸ **unˈmanliness** *n*

unmanned (ʌnˈmænd) *adj* **1** lacking personnel or crew: *an unmanned ship.* **2** (of aircraft, spacecraft, etc.) operated by automatic or remote control. **3** uninhabited.

unmannered (ʌnˈmænəd) *adj* **1** without good manners; rude. **2** without mannerisms.

unmannerly (ʌnˈmænəlɪ) *adj* **1** lacking manners; discourteous. ◆ *adv* **2** *Arch.* rudely; discourteously.
▸ **unˈmannerliness** *n*

unmask (ʌnˈmɑːsk) *vb* **1** to remove (the mask or disguise) from (someone or oneself). **2** to appear or cause to appear in true character.
▸ **unˈmasker** *n*

unmeaning (ʌnˈmiːnɪŋ) *adj* **1** having no meaning. **2** showing no intelligence; vacant: *an unmeaning face.*
▸ **unˈmeaningly** *adv* ▸ **unˈmeaningness** *n*

unmeet (ʌnˈmiːt) *adj Literary or arch.* unsuitable.
▸ **unˈmeetly** *adv* ▸ **unˈmeetness** *n*

unmentionable (ʌnˈmɛnʃənəbᵊl) *adj* **a** unsuitable or forbidden as a topic of conversation. **b** (*as n*): *the unmentionable.*
▸ **unˈmentionableness** *n* ▸ **unˈmentionably** *adv*

unmentionables (ʌnˈmɛnʃənəbᵊlz) *pl n Chiefly humorous.* underwear.

unmerciful (ʌnˈmɜːsɪfʊl) *adj* **1** showing no mercy; relentless. **2** extreme or excessive.
▸ **unˈmercifully** *adv* ▸ **unˈmercifulness** *n*

unmindful (ʌnˈmaɪndfʊl) *adj* (*usually postpositive* and foll. by *of*) careless or forgetful.
▸ **unˈmindfully** *adv* ▸ **unˈmindfulness** *n*

unmissable (ʌnˈmɪsəbᵊl) *adj* (of a film, television programme, etc.) so good that it should not be missed.

unmistakable *or* **unmistakeable** (ˌʌnmɪsˈteɪkəbᵊl) *adj* not mistakable; clear or unambiguous.
▸ **ˌunmisˈtakably** *or* **ˌunmisˈtakeably** *adv*

unmitigated (ʌnˈmɪtɪˌgeɪtɪd) *adj* **1** not diminished in intensity, severity, etc. **2** (*prenominal*) (intensifier): *an unmitigated disaster.*
▸ **unˈmitiˌgatedly** *adv*

unmoral (ʌnˈmɒrəl) *adj* outside morality; amoral.
▸ **unmorality** (ˌʌnməˈrælɪtɪ) *n* ▸ **unˈmorally** *adv*

unmurmuring (ʌnˈmɜːmərɪŋ) *adj* not complaining.

unmuzzle (ʌnˈmʌzᵊl) *vb* **unmuzzles, unmuzzling, unmuzzled.** (*tr*) **1** to take the muzzle off (a dog, etc.). **2** to free from control or censorship.

unnatural (ʌnˈnætʃərəl) *adj* **1** contrary to nature; abnormal. **2** not in accordance with accepted standards of behaviour or right and wrong: *unnatural love.* **3** uncanny; supernatural: *unnatural phenomena.* **4** affected or forced: *an unnatural manner.* **5** inhuman or monstrous: *an unnatural crime.*
▸ **unˈnaturally** *adv* ▸ **unˈnaturalness** *n*

unnecessary (ʌnˈnɛsɪsərɪ) *adj* not necessary.
▸ **unˈnecessarily** *adv* ▸ **unˈnecessariness** *n*

unnerve (ʌnˈnɜːv) *vb* **unnerves, unnerving, unnerved.** (*tr*) to cause to lose courage, strength, confidence, self-control, etc.

unnumbered (ʌnˈnʌmbəd) *adj* **1** countless; innumerable. **2** not counted or assigned a number.

UNO *abbrev. for* United Nations Organization.

unoccupied (ʌnˈɒkjʊˌpaɪd) *adj* **1** (of a building) without occupants. **2** unemployed or idle. **3** (of an area or country) not overrun by foreign troops.

unofficial (ˌʌnəˈfɪʃəl) *adj* **1** not official or formal: *an unofficial engagement.* **2** not confirmed officially: *an unofficial report.* **3** (of a strike) not approved by the strikers' trade union.
▸ **ˌunofˈficially** *adv*

unorganized *or* **unorganised** (ʌnˈɔːgəˌnaɪzd) *adj* **1** not arranged into an organized system, structure, or unity. **2** (of workers) not unionized. **3** nonliving; inorganic.

unowned (ʌnˈəʊnd) *adj* **1** unacknowledged. **2** without an owner.

unpack (ʌnˈpæk) *vb* **1** to remove the packed contents of (a case, trunk, etc.). **2** (*tr*) to take (something) out of a packed container. **3** (*tr*) to unload: *to unpack a mule.*
▸ **unˈpacker** *n*

unpaged (ʌnˈpeɪdʒd) *adj* (of a book) having no page numbers.

unparalleled (ʌnˈpærəˌlɛld) *adj* unmatched; unequalled.

unparliamentary (ˌʌnpɑːləˈmɛntərɪ) *adj* not consistent with parliamentary procedure or practice.
▸ **ˌunparliaˈmentarily** *adv* ▸ **ˌunparliaˈmentariness** *n*

unpeg (ʌnˈpɛg) *vb* **unpegs, unpegging, unpegged.** (*tr*) **1** to remove the peg from, esp. to unfasten. **2** to allow (prices, etc.) to rise and fall freely.

unpeople (ʌnˈpiːpᵊl) *vb* **unpeoples, unpeopling, unpeopled.** (*tr*) to empty of people.

unperson (ˈʌnpɜːsᵊn) *n* a person whose existence is officially denied or ignored.

unpick (ʌnˈpɪk) *vb* (*tr*) **1** to undo (the stitches) of (a piece of sewing). **2** to unravel or undo (a garment, etc.).

unpin (ʌnˈpɪn) *vb* **unpins, unpinning, unpinned.** (*tr*) **1** to remove a pin or pins from. **2** to unfasten by removing pins.

unpleasant (ʌnˈplɛzᵊnt) *adj* not pleasant or agreeable.
▸ **unˈpleasantly** *adv* ▸ **unˈpleasantness** *n*

unplugged (ʌnˈplʌgd) *adj* (of a performer or performance of popular music) using acoustic rather than electric instruments: *Eric Clapton unplugged; an unplugged version of the song.*

unplumbed (ʌnˈplʌmd) *adj* **1** unfathomed; unsounded. **2** not understood in depth. **3** (of a building) having no plumbing.

unpolled (ʌnˈpəʊld) *adj* **1** not included in an opinion poll. **2** not having voted. **3** *Arch.* unshorn.

unpopular (ʌnˈpɒpjʊlə) *adj* not popular with an individual or group of people.
▸ **unpopularity** (ˌʌnpɒpjʊˈlærɪtɪ) *n* ▸ **unˈpopularly** *adv*

unpractical (ʌnˈpræktɪkᵊl) *adj* another word for **impractical.**
▸ **ˌunpractiˈcality** *n* ▸ **unˈpractically** *adv*

unpractised *or US* **unpracticed** (ʌnˈpræktɪst) *adj* **1** without skill, training, or experience. **2** not used or done often or repeatedly. **3** not yet tested.

unprecedented (ʌnˈprɛsɪˌdɛntɪd) *adj* having no precedent; unparalleled.
▸ **unˈpreceˌdentedly** *adv*

unprejudiced (ʌnˈprɛdʒʊdɪst) *adj* not prejudiced or biased; impartial.
▸ **unˈprejudicedly** *adv*

unprincipled (ʌnˈprɪnsɪpᵊld) *adj* lacking moral principles; unscrupulous.
▸ **unˈprincipledness** *n*

unprintable (ʌnˈprɪntəbᵊl) *adj* unsuitable for printing for reasons of obscenity, libel, etc.
▸ **unˈprintableness** *n* ▸ **unˈprintably** *adv*

unprofessional (ˌʌnprəˈfɛʃənᵊl) *adj* **1** contrary to the accepted code of conduct of a profession. **2** amateur. **3** not belonging to or having the required qualifications for a profession.
▸ **ˌunproˈfessionally** *adv*

unprotected sex *n* an act of sexual intercourse or sodomy performed without the use of a condom thus involving the risk of sexually transmitted diseases.

unputdownable (ˌʌnpʊtˈdaʊnəbᵊl) *adj* (esp. of a novel) so gripping as to be read at one sitting.

unqualified (ʌnˈkwɒlɪˌfaɪd) *adj* **1** lacking the necessary qualifications. **2** not restricted or modified: *an unqualified criticism.* **3** (*usually prenominal*) (intensifier): *an unqualified success.*
▸ **unˈqualiˌfiable** *adj*

unquestionable (ʌnˈkwɛstʃənəbᵊl) *adj* **1** indubitable or indisputable. **2** not admitting of exception: *an unquestionable ruling.*
▸ **unˌquestionaˈbility** *n* ▸ **unˈquestionably** *adv*

unquestioned (ʌnˈkwɛstʃənd) *adj* **1** accepted without question. **2** not admitting of doubt or question: *unquestioned power.* **3** not questioned or interrogated.

unquiet (ʌnˈkwaɪət) *Chiefly literary.* ◆ *adj* **1** characterized by disorder or tumult: *unquiet times.* **2** anxious; uneasy. ◆ *n* **3** a state of unrest.
▸ **unˈquietly** *adv* ▸ **unˈquietness** *n*

unquote (ʌnˈkwəʊt) *interj* **1** an expression used parenthetically to indicate that the preceding quotation is finished. ◆ *vb* **unquotes, unquoting, unquoted.** **2** to close (a quotation), esp. in printing.

unravel (ʌnˈrævᵊl) *vb* **unravels, unravelling, unravelled** *or US* **unravels, unraveling, unraveled.** **1** (*tr*) to reduce (something knitted or woven) to separate strands. **2** (*tr*) to explain or solve: *the mystery was unravelled.* **3** (*intr*) to become unravelled.

unreactive (ˌʌnrɪˈæktɪv) *adj* (of a substance) not readily partaking in chemical reactions.

unread (ʌnˈrɛd) *adj* **1** (of a book, etc.) not yet read. **2** (of a person) having read little.

unreadable (ʌnˈriːdəbᵊl) *adj* **1** illegible; undecipherable. **2** difficult or tedious to read.
▸ **unˌreadaˈbility** *or* **unˈreadableness** *n*

unready (ʌn'rɛdɪ) *adj* **1** not ready or prepared. **2** slow or hesitant to see or act.
▸ **un'readily** *adv* ▸ **un'readiness** *n*

unreal (ʌn'rɪəl) *adj* **1** imaginary or fanciful or seemingly so: *an unreal situation.* **2** having no actual existence or substance. **3** insincere or artificial.
▸ **unreality** (ˌʌnrɪ'ælɪtɪ) *n* ▸ **un'really** *adv*

unreason (ʌn'riːzᵊn) *n* **1** irrationality or madness. **2** something that lacks or is contrary to reason. **3** lack of order; chaos.

unreasonable (ʌn'riːznəbᵊl) *adj* **1** immoderate: *unreasonable demands.* **2** refusing to listen to reason. **3** lacking judgment.
▸ **un'reasonableness** *n* ▸ **un'reasonably** *adv*

unreasoning (ʌn'riːzənɪŋ) *adj* not controlled by reason; irrational.
▸ **un'reasoningly** *adv*

unregenerate (ˌʌnrɪ'dʒɛnərɪt) *adj also* **unregenerated. 1** unrepentant; unreformed. **2** obstinately adhering to one's own views. ◆ *n* **3** an unregenerate person.
▸ **ˌunre'generacy** *n* ▸ **ˌunre'generately** *adv*

unrelenting (ˌʌnrɪ'lɛntɪŋ) *adj* **1** refusing to relent or take pity. **2** not diminishing in determination, speed, effort, force, etc.
▸ **ˌunre'lentingly** *adv* ▸ **ˌunre'lentingness** *n*

unreligious (ˌʌnrɪ'lɪdʒəs) *adj* **1** another word for **irreligious. 2** secular.
▸ **ˌunre'ligiously** *adv*

unremitting (ˌʌnrɪ'mɪtɪŋ) *adj* never slackening or stopping; unceasing; constant.
▸ **ˌunre'mittingly** *adv* ▸ **ˌunre'mittingness** *n*

unreserved (ˌʌnrɪ'zɜːvd) *adj* **1** without reserve; having an open manner. **2** without reservation. **3** not booked or bookable.
▸ **unreservedly** (ˌʌnrɪ'zɜːvɪdlɪ) *adv* ▸ **ˌunre'servedness** *n*

unrest (ʌn'rɛst) *n* **1** a troubled or rebellious state of discontent. **2** an uneasy or troubled state.

unriddle (ʌn'rɪdᵊl) *vb* **unriddles, unriddling, unriddled.** (*tr*) to solve or puzzle out. ORIG C16: from UN-[2] + RIDDLE[1]
▸ **un'riddler** *n*

unrig (ʌn'rɪg) *vb* **unrigs, unrigging, unrigged. 1** (*tr*) to strip (a vessel) of standing and running rigging. **2** *Arch. or dialect.* to undress (someone or oneself).

unrighteous (ʌn'raɪtʃəs) *adj* **1a** sinful; wicked. **1b** (*as collective n; preceded by the*): *the unrighteous.* **2** not fair or right; unjust.
▸ **un'righteously** *adv* ▸ **un'righteousness** *n*

unrip (ʌn'rɪp) *vb* **unrips, unripping, unripped.** (*tr*) **1** to rip open. **2** *Obs.* to reveal; disclose.

unripe (ʌn'raɪp) *or* **unripened** *adj* **1** not fully matured. **2** not fully prepared or developed; not ready.
▸ **un'ripeness** *n*

unrivalled *or US* **unrivaled** (ʌn'raɪvᵊld) *adj* having no equal; matchless.

unroll (ʌn'rəʊl) *vb* **1** to open out or unwind (something rolled, folded, or coiled) or (of something rolled, etc.) to become opened out or unwound. **2** to make or become visible or apparent, esp. gradually; unfold.

unruffled (ʌn'rʌfᵊld) *adj* **1** unmoved; calm. **2** still: *the unruffled seas.*
▸ **un'ruffledness** *n*

unruly (ʌn'ruːlɪ) *adj* **unrulier, unruliest.** disposed to disobedience or indiscipline.
▸ **un'ruliness** *n*

UNRWA ('ʌnrə) *n acronym for* United Nations Relief and Works Agency.

unsaddle (ʌn'sædᵊl) *vb* **unsaddles, unsaddling, unsaddled. 1** to remove the saddle from (a horse, mule, etc.). **2** (*tr*) to unhorse.

unsaddling enclosure *n* the area at a racecourse where horses are unsaddled after a race and often where awards are given to owners, trainers, and jockeys.

unsafe (ʌn'seɪf) *adj* **1** not safe; perilous. **2** (of a criminal conviction) based on inadequate or false evidence.

unsaid (ʌn'sɛd) *adj* not said or expressed; unspoken.

unsaturated (ʌn'sætʃəˌreɪtɪd) *adj* **1** not saturated. **2** (of a chemical compound, esp. an organic compound) containing one or more double or triple bonds and thus capable of undergoing addition reactions. **3** (of a fat, esp. a vegetable fat) containing a high proportion of fatty acids having double bonds.
▸ **ˌunsatu'ration** *n*

unsavoury *or US* **unsavory** (ʌn'seɪvərɪ) *adj* **1** objectionable or distasteful: *an unsavoury character.* **2** disagreeable in odour or taste.
▸ **un'savourily** *or US* **un'savorily** *adv* ▸ **un'savouriness** *or US* **un'savoriness** *n*

unsay (ʌn'seɪ) *vb* **unsays, unsaying, unsaid.** (*tr*) to retract or withdraw (something said or written).

unscathed (ʌn'skeɪðd) *adj* not harmed or injured.

unscramble (ʌn'skræmbᵊl) *vb* **unscrambles, unscrambling, unscrambled.** (*tr*) **1** to resolve from confusion or disorderliness. **2** to restore (a scrambled message) to an intelligible form.
▸ **un'scrambler** *n*

unscrew (ʌn'skruː) *vb* **1** (*tr*) to remove a screw from (an object). **2** (*tr*) to loosen (a screw, lid, etc.) by rotating, usually in an anticlockwise direction. **3** (*intr*) (esp. of an engaged threaded part) to become loosened or separated.

unscripted (ʌn'skrɪptɪd) *adj* (of a speech, play, etc.) not using or based on a script.

unscrupulous (ʌn'skruːpjʊləs) *adj* without scruples; unprincipled.
▸ **un'scrupulously** *adv* ▸ **un'scrupulousness** *n*

unseal (ʌn'siːl) *vb* (*tr*) **1** to remove or break the seal of. **2** to free (something concealed or closed as if sealed): *to unseal one's lips.*

unsealed (ʌn'siːld) *adj Austral. & NZ.* (of a road) surfaced with road metal not bound by bitumen or other sealant.

unseam (ʌn'siːm) *vb* (*tr*) to open or undo the seam of.

unseasonable (ʌn'siːzənəbᵊl) *adj* **1** (esp. of the weather) inappropriate for the season. **2** untimely; inopportune.
▸ **un'seasonableness** *n* ▸ **un'seasonably** *adv*

unseat (ʌn'siːt) *vb* (*tr*) **1** to throw or displace from a seat, saddle, etc. **2** to depose from office or position.

unseeded (ʌn'siːdɪd) *adj* (of players in various sports) not assigned to a preferential position in the preliminary rounds of a tournament.

unseemly (ʌn'siːmlɪ) *adj* **1** not in good style or taste. **2** *Obs.* unattractive. ◆ *adv* **3** *Rare.* in an unseemly manner.
▸ **un'seemliness** *n*

unseen (ʌn'siːn) *adj* **1** not observed or perceived; invisible. **2** (of passages of writing) not previously seen or prepared. ◆ *n* **3** *Chiefly Brit.* a passage, not previously seen, that is presented to students for translation.

unselfish (ʌn'sɛlfɪʃ) *adj* not selfish; generous.
▸ **un'selfishly** *adv* ▸ **un'selfishness** *n*

unsettle (ʌn'sɛtᵊl) *vb* **unsettles, unsettling, unsettled. 1** (*usually tr*) to change or become changed from a fixed or settled condition. **2** (*tr*) to confuse or agitate (emotions, the mind, etc.).
▸ **un'settlement** *n*

unsettled (ʌn'sɛtᵊld) *adj* **1** lacking order or stability: *an unsettled era.* **2** unpredictable: *an unsettled climate.* **3** constantly changing or moving from place to place: *an unsettled life.* **4** (of controversy, etc.) not brought to an agreed conclusion. **5** (of debts, law cases, etc.) not disposed of.
▸ **un'settledness** *n*

unsex (ʌn'sɛks) *vb* (*tr*) *Chiefly literary.* to deprive (a person) of the attributes of his or her sex, esp. to make a woman more callous.

unshapen (ʌn'ʃeɪpᵊn) *adj* **1** having no definite shape; shapeless. **2** deformed; misshapen.

unsheathe (ʌn'ʃiːð) *vb* **unsheathes, unsheathing, unsheathed.** (*tr*) to draw or pull out (something, esp. a weapon) from a sheath.

unship (ʌn'ʃɪp) *vb* **unships, unshipping, unshipped. 1** to be or cause to be unloaded, discharged, or disembarked from a ship. **2** (*tr*) *Naut.* to remove from a regular place: *to unship oars.*

unsighted (ʌn'saɪtɪd) *adj* **1** not sighted. **2** not having a clear view. **3** (of a gun) not equipped with a sight.
▸ **un'sightedly** *adv*

unsightly (ʌn'saɪtlɪ) *adj* unpleasant or unattractive to look at; ugly.
▸ **un'sightliness** *n*

unskilful *or US* **unskillful** (ʌn'skɪlfʊl) *adj* lacking dexterity or proficiency.
▸ **un'skilfully** *or US* **un'skillfully** *adv* ▸ **un'skilfulness** *or US* **un'skillfulness** *n*

unskilled (ʌn'skɪld) *adj* **1** not having or requiring any special skill or training: *an unskilled job.* **2** having no skill; inexpert.

unsling (ʌn'slɪŋ) *vb* **unslings, unslinging, unslung.** (*tr*) **1** to remove or release from a slung position. **2** to remove slings from.

unsnap (ʌn'snæp) *vb* **unsnaps, unsnapping, unsnapped.** (*tr*) to unfasten (the snap or catch) of (something).

unsnarl (ʌn'snɑːl) *vb* (*tr*) to free from a snarl or tangle.

unsociable (ʌn'səʊʃəbᵊl) *adj* **1** (of a person) disinclined to associate or fraternize with others. **2** unconducive to social intercourse: *an unsociable neighbourhood.*
▸ **un,socia'bility** *or* **un'sociableness** *n*

unsocial (ʌn'səʊʃəl) *adj* **1** not social; antisocial. **2** (of the hours of work of certain jobs) falling outside the normal working day.

unsophisticated (,ʌnsə'fɪstɪ,keɪtɪd) *adj* **1** lacking experience or worldly wisdom. **2** marked by a lack of refinement or complexity: *an unsophisticated machine.* **3** unadulterated or genuine.
▸ **,unso'phisti,catedly** *adv* ▸ **,unso'phisti,catedness** *or* **,unso,phisti'cation** *n*

unsound (ʌn'saʊnd) *adj* **1** diseased or unstable: *of unsound mind.* **2** unreliable or fallacious: *unsound advice.* **3** lacking strength or firmness: *unsound foundations.* **4** of doubtful financial or commercial viability: *an unsound enterprise.*
▸ **un'soundly** *adv* ▸ **un'soundness** *n*

unsparing (ʌn'spɛərɪŋ) *adj* **1** not sparing or frugal; lavish. **2** showing harshness or severity.
▸ **un'sparingly** *adv* ▸ **un'sparingness** *n*

unspeakable (ʌn'spiːkəbᵊl) *adj* **1** incapable of expression in words: *unspeakable ecstasy.* **2** indescribably bad or evil. **3** not to be uttered: *unspeakable thoughts.*
▸ **un'speakableness** *n* ▸ **un'speakably** *adv*

unstable (ʌn'steɪbᵊl) *adj* **1** lacking stability, fixity, or firmness. **2** disposed to temperamental or psychological variability. **3** (of a chemical compound) readily decomposing. **4** *Physics.* **4a** (of an elementary particle) having a very short lifetime. **4b** spontaneously decomposing by nuclear decay: *an unstable nuclide.* **5** *Electronics.* (of an electrical circuit, etc.) having a tendency to self-oscillation.
▸ **un'stableness** *n* ▸ **un'stably** *adv*

unsteady (ʌn'stɛdɪ) *adj* **1** not securely fixed: *an unsteady foothold.* **2** (of behaviour, etc.) erratic. **3** without regularity: *an unsteady rhythm.* **4** (of a manner of walking, etc.) precarious or staggering, as from intoxication.
▸ **un'steadily** *adv* ▸ **un'steadiness** *n*

unstep (ʌn'stɛp) *vb* **unsteps, unstepping, unstepped.** (*tr*) *Naut.* to remove (a mast) from its step.

unstick (ʌn'stɪk) *vb* **unsticks, unsticking, unstuck.** (*tr*) to free or loosen (something stuck).

unstop (ʌn'stɒp) *vb* **unstops, unstopping, unstopped.** (*tr*) **1** to remove the stop or stopper from. **2** to free from any stoppage or obstruction. **3** to draw out the stops on (an organ).
▸ **un'stoppable** *adj* ▸ **un'stoppably** *adv*

unstopped (ʌn'stɒpt) *adj* **1** not obstructed or stopped up. **2** *Phonetics.* denoting a speech sound for whose articulation the closure is not complete. **3** *Prosody.* (of verse) having the sense of the line carried over into the next. **4** (of an organ pipe or a string on a musical instrument) not stopped.

unstriated (ʌn'straɪ,eɪtɪd) *adj* (of muscle) composed of elongated cells that do not have striations; smooth.

unstring (ʌn'strɪŋ) *vb* **unstrings, unstringing, unstrung.** (*tr*) **1** to remove the strings of. **2** (of beads, etc.) to remove from a string. **3** to weaken emotionally (a person or his or her nerves).

unstriped (ʌn'straɪpt) *adj* (esp. of smooth muscle) not having stripes; unstriated.

unstructured (ʌn'strʌktʃəd) *adj* **1** without formal structure or systematic organization. **2** without a preformed shape; (esp. of clothes) loose; untailored.

unstrung (ʌn'strʌŋ) *adj* **1** emotionally distressed; unnerved. **2** (of a stringed instrument) with the strings detached.

unstuck (ʌn'stʌk) *adj* **1** freed from being stuck, glued, fastened, etc. **2 come unstuck.** to suffer failure or disaster.

unstudied (ʌn'stʌdɪd) *adj* **1** natural. **2** (foll. by *in*) without knowledge or training.

unsubstantial (,ʌnsəb'stænʃəl) *adj* **1** lacking weight or firmness. **2** (of an argument) of doubtful validity. **3** of no material existence.
▸ **,unsub,stanti'ality** *n* ▸ **,unsub'stantially** *adv*

unsung (ʌn'sʌŋ) *adj* **1** not acclaimed or honoured: *unsung deeds.* **2** not yet sung.

unsuspected (,ʌnsə'spɛktɪd) *adj* **1** not under suspicion. **2** not known to exist.
▸ **,unsus'pectedly** *adv* ▸ **,unsus'pectedness** *n*

unswerving (ʌn'swɜːvɪŋ) *adj* not turning aside; constant.

untangle (ʌn'tæŋgᵊl) *vb* **untangles, untangling, untangled.** (*tr*) **1** to free from a tangled condition. **2** to free from confusion.

untaught (ʌn'tɔːt) *adj* **1** without training or education. **2** attained or achieved without instruction.

untenable (ʌn'tɛnəbᵊl) *adj* **1** (of theories, etc.) incapable of being maintained or vindicated. **2** unable to be maintained against attack.
▸ **un,tena'bility** *or* **un'tenableness** *n* ▸ **un'tenably** *adv*

Unter den Linden ★ (*German* 'ʊntər deːn 'lɪndən) *n* the main street of Berlin, formerly in East Berlin, extending to the Brandenburg Gate.

Unterwalden ★ (*German* 'ʊntər,valdən) *n* a canton of central Switzerland, on Lake Lucerne: consists of the demicantons of **Nidwalden** (east) and **Obwalden** (west). Capitals: (Nidwalden) Stans; (Obwalden) Sarnen. Pop.: (Nidwalden) 35 983 (1995 est.); (Obwalden) 30 958 (1995 est.). Areas: (Nidwalden) 274 sq. km (107 sq. miles); (Obwalden) 492 sq. km (192 sq. miles).

unthinkable (ʌn'θɪŋkəbᵊl) *adj* **1** not to be contemplated; out of the question. **2** unimaginable; inconceivable. **3** unreasonable; improbable.
▸ **un'thinkably** *adv*

unthinking (ʌn'θɪŋkɪŋ) *adj* **1** lacking thoughtfulness; inconsiderate. **2** heedless; inadvertent. **3** not thinking or able to think.
▸ **un'thinkingly** *adv* ▸ **un'thinkingness** *n*

unthread (ʌn'θrɛd) *vb* (*tr*) **1** to draw out the thread or threads from (a needle, etc.). **2** to disentangle.

unthrone (ʌn'θrəʊn) *vb* **unthrones, unthroning, unthroned.** (*tr*) a less common word for **dethrone.**

untidy (ʌn'taɪdɪ) *adj* **untidier, untidiest. 1** not neat; slovenly. ◆ *vb* **untidies, untidying, untidied. 2** (*tr*) to make untidy.
▸ **un'tidily** *adv* ▸ **un'tidiness** *n*

untie (ʌn'taɪ) *vb* **unties, untying, untied. 1** to unfasten or free (a knot or something that is tied) or (of a knot, etc.) to become unfastened. **2** (*tr*) to free from constraint or restriction.

until (ʌn'tɪl) *conj* (*subordinating*) **1** up to (a time) that: *he laughed until he cried.* **2** (*used with a negative*) before (a time or event): *until you change, you can't go out.* ◆ *prep* **3** (often preceded by *up*) in or throughout the period before: *he waited until six.* **4** (*used with a negative*) earlier than; before: *he won't come until tomorrow.* ORIG C13 *untill;* see TILL[1]

> **USAGE NOTE** The use of *until such time as* (as in *industrial action will continue until such time as our demands are met*) is unnecessary and should be avoided: *industrial action will continue until our demands are met.* See also at **till[1]**.

★ people and places

untimely (ʌn'taɪmlɪ) *adj* **1** occurring before the expected, normal, or proper time: *an untimely death.* **2** inappropriate to the occasion, time, or season: *his joking at the funeral was most untimely.* ◆ *adv* **3** prematurely or inopportunely.
▸ **un'timeliness** *n*

unto ('ʌntuː) *prep Arch.* to. ORIG C13: from ON

untogether (ˌʌntə'gɛðə) *adj Sl.* incompetent or badly organized; mentally or emotionally unstable.

untold (ʌn'təʊld) *adj* **1** incapable of description: *untold suffering.* **2** incalculably great in number or quantity: *untold thousands.* **3** not told.

untouchable (ʌn'tʌtʃəbᵊl) *adj* **1** lying beyond reach. **2** above reproach, suspicion, or impeachment. **3** unable to be touched. ◆ *n* **4** a member of the lowest class in India, whom those of the four main castes were formerly forbidden to touch.
▸ **unˌtoucha'bility** *n*

untoward (ˌʌntə'wɔːd) *adj* **1** characterized by misfortune or annoyance. **2** not auspicious; unfavourable. **3** unseemly. **4** out of the ordinary; out of the way. **5** *Arch.* perverse. **6** *Obs.* awkward.
▸ **ˌunto'wardly** *adv* ▸ **ˌunto'wardness** *n*

untrue (ʌn'truː) *adj* **1** incorrect or false. **2** disloyal. **3** diverging from a rule, standard, or measure; inaccurate.
▸ **un'truly** *adv*

untruss (ʌn'trʌs) *vb* **1** (*tr*) to release from or as if from a truss; unfasten. **2** *Obs.* to undress.

untruth (ʌn'truːθ) *n* **1** the state or quality of being untrue. **2** a statement, etc., that is not true.

untruthful (ʌn'truːθfʊl) *adj* **1** (of a person) given to lying. **2** diverging from the truth.
▸ **un'truthfully** *adv* ▸ **un'truthfulness** *n*

untuck (ʌn'tʌk) *vb* to become or cause to become loose or not tucked in: *to untuck the blankets.*

untutored (ʌn'tjuːtəd) *adj* **1** without formal education. **2** lacking sophistication or refinement.

unused *adj* **1** (ʌn'juːzd). not being or never having been made use of. **2** (ʌn'juːst). (*postpositive;* foll. by *to*) not accustomed or used (to something).

unusual (ʌn'juːʒʊəl) *adj* uncommon; extraordinary: *an unusual design.*
▸ **un'usually** *adv*

unutterable (ʌn'ʌtərəbᵊl) *adj* incapable of being expressed in words.
▸ **un'utterableness** *n* ▸ **un'utterably** *adv*

unvarnished (ʌn'vɑːnɪʃt) *adj* not elaborated upon or glossed; plain and direct: *the unvarnished truth.*

unveil (ʌn'veɪl) *vb* **1** (*tr*) to remove the cover from, esp. in the ceremonial unveiling of a monument, etc. **2** to remove the veil from (one's own or another person's face). **3** (*tr*) to make (something concealed) known or public.

unveiling (ʌn'veɪlɪŋ) *n* **1** a ceremony involving the removal of a veil covering a statue, etc., for the first time. **2** the presentation of something, esp. for the first time.

unvoice (ʌn'vɔɪs) *vb* **unvoices, unvoicing, unvoiced.** (*tr*) *Phonetics.* **1** to pronounce without vibration of the vocal cords. **2** Also: **devoice.** to make (a voiced speech sound) voiceless.

unvoiced (ʌn'vɔɪst) *adj* **1** not expressed or spoken. **2** articulated without vibration of the vocal cords; voiceless.

unwaged (ʌn'weɪdʒd) *adj* of or denoting a person who is not receiving pay because of being unemployed or working in the home.

unwarrantable (ʌn'wɒrəntəbᵊl) *adj* incapable of vindication or justification.
▸ **un'warrantableness** *n* ▸ **un'warrantably** *adv*

unwarranted (ʌn'wɒrəntɪd) *adj* **1** lacking justification or authorization. **2** another word for **unwarrantable.**

unwary (ʌn'wɛərɪ) *adj* lacking caution or prudence.
▸ **un'warily** *adv* ▸ **un'wariness** *n*

unwearied (ʌn'wɪərɪd) *adj* **1** not abating or tiring. **2** not fatigued; fresh.
▸ **un'weariedly** *adv* ▸ **un'weariedness** *n*

unweighed (ʌn'weɪd) *adj* **1** (of quantities purchased, etc.) not measured for weight. **2** (of statements, etc.) not carefully considered.

unwell (ʌn'wɛl) *adj* (*postpositive*) not well; ill.

unwept (ʌn'wɛpt) *adj* **1** not wept for or lamented. **2** *Rare.* (of tears) not shed.

unwholesome (ʌn'həʊlsəm) *adj* **1** detrimental to physical or mental health: *an unwholesome climate.* **2** morally harmful: *unwholesome practices.* **3** indicative of illness, esp. in appearance. **4** (esp. of food) of inferior quality.
▸ **un'wholesomeness** *n*

unwieldy (ʌn'wiːldɪ) *adj* **1** too heavy, large, or awkwardly shaped to be easily handled. **2** ungainly; clumsy.
▸ **un'wieldily** *adv* ▸ **un'wieldiness** *n*

unwilled (ʌn'wɪld) *adj* not intentional; involuntary.

unwilling (ʌn'wɪlɪŋ) *adj* **1** reluctant. **2** performed or said with reluctance.
▸ **un'willingly** *adv* ▸ **un'willingness** *n*

unwind (ʌn'waɪnd) *vb* **unwinds, unwinding, unwound. 1** to slacken, undo, or unravel or cause to slacken, undo, or unravel. **2** (*tr*) to disentangle. **3** to make or become relaxed: *he finds it hard to unwind.*
▸ **un'windable** *adj*

unwise (ʌn'waɪz) *adj* lacking wisdom or prudence.
▸ **un'wisely** *adv* ▸ **un'wiseness** *n*

unwish (ʌn'wɪʃ) *vb* (*tr*) **1** to retract or revoke (a wish). **2** to desire (something) not to be or take place.

unwitting (ʌn'wɪtɪŋ) *adj* (*usually prenominal*) **1** not knowing or conscious. **2** not intentional; inadvertent. ORIG OE *unwitende,* from UN-[1] + *witting,* present participle of *witan* to know
▸ **un'wittingly** *adv* ▸ **un'wittingness** *n*

unwonted (ʌn'wəʊntɪd) *adj* **1** out of the ordinary; unusual. **2** (usually foll. by *to*) *Arch.* unaccustomed; unused.
▸ **un'wontedly** *adv*

unworldly (ʌn'wɜːldlɪ) *adj* **1** not concerned with material values or pursuits. **2** lacking sophistication; naive. **3** not of this earth or world.
▸ **un'worldliness** *n*

unworthy (ʌn'wɜːðɪ) *adj* **1** (often foll. by *of*) not deserving or worthy. **2** (often foll. by *of*) beneath the level considered befitting (to): *that remark is unworthy of you.* **3** lacking merit or value. **4** (of treatment) not warranted.
▸ **un'worthily** *adv* ▸ **un'worthiness** *n*

unwound (ʌn'waʊnd) *vb* the past tense and past participle of **unwind.**

unwrap (ʌn'ræp) *vb* **unwraps, unwrapping, unwrapped.** to remove the covering or wrapping from (something) or (of something wrapped) to have the covering come off.

unwritten (ʌn'rɪtᵊn) *adj* **1** not printed or in writing. **2** effective only through custom.

unwritten law *n* the law based upon custom, usage, and judicial decisions, as distinguished from the enactments of a legislature, orders or decrees in writing, etc.

unyoke (ʌn'jəʊk) *vb* **unyokes, unyoking, unyoked. 1** to release (an animal, etc.) from a yoke. **2** (*tr*) to set free; liberate. **3** (*tr*) to disconnect or separate.

unzip (ʌn'zɪp) *vb* **unzips, unzipping, unzipped.** to unfasten the zip of (a garment, etc.) or (of a zip or garment with a zip) to become unfastened: *her skirt unzipped as she sat down.*

up (ʌp) *prep* **1** indicating movement from a lower to a higher position: *climbing up a mountain.* **2** at a higher or further level or position in or on: *a shop up the road.* ◆ *adv* **3** (*often particle*) to an upward, higher, or erect position, esp. indicating readiness for an activity: *up and doing something.* **4** (*particle*) indicating intensity or completion of an action: *he tore up the cheque.* **5** to the place referred to or where the speaker is: *the man came up and asked the way.* **6a** to a more important place: *up to London.* **6b** to a more northerly place: *up to Scotland.* **6c** (of a member of some British universities) to or at university. **6d** in a particular part of the country: *up north.* **7** above the horizon: *the sun is up.* **8** appearing for trial: *up before the magistrate.* **9** having gained: *ten pounds up on the deal.* **10** higher in price: *coffee is up again.* **11** raised (for discussion, etc.): *the plan was up for consideration.* **12** taught: *well up in physics.* **13** (*functioning as imperative*) get, stand, etc., up: *up with you!* **14 all up with.** *Inf.* **14a** over; finished. **14b** doomed to die. **15 up with.** (*functioning as imperative*) wanting the beginning or continuation of: *up with the monarchy!* **16 something's up.** *Inf.* something strange is happening. **17 up against. 17a** touching. **17b** having to cope with: *look what we're up against now.* **18 up for.** as a candidate or applicant for: *he's up for re-election again.* **19 up to. 19a** devising or scheming: *she's up to no good.* **19b** dependent or incumbent upon: *the decision is up to you.* **19c** equal to (a challenge, etc.) or capable of (doing, etc.): *are you up to playing in the final?* **19d** as far as: *up to his waist in mud.* **19e** as many as: *up to two years' waiting time.* **19f** comparable with: *not up to your normal standard.* **20 up top.** *Inf.* in the head or mind. **21 up yours.** *Sl.* a vulgar expression of contempt or refusal. **22 what's up?** *Inf.* **22a** what is the matter? **22b** what is happening? ◆ *adj* **23** (*predicative*) of a high or higher position. **24** (*predicative*) out of bed: *the children aren't up yet.* **25** (*prenominal*) of or relating to a train or trains to a more important place or one regarded as higher: *the up platform.* **26** (*predicative*) over or completed: *their time was up.* **27** (*predicative*) beating one's opponent by a specified amount: *a goal up.* ◆ *vb* **ups, upping, upped. 28** (*tr*) to increase or raise. **29** (*intr; foll. by and with a verb*) *Inf.* to do (something) suddenly, etc.: *she upped and married someone else.* ◆ *n* **30** a high point (esp. in **ups and downs**). **31** *Sl.* another word (esp. US) for **upper** (sense 8). **32 on the up and up. 32a** trustworthy or honest. **32b** *Brit.* on the upward trend or movement: *our firm's on the up and up.* ORIG OE *upp*

> **USAGE NOTE** The use of *up* before *until* is redundant and should be avoided: *the talks will continue until* (not *up until*) *23rd March.*

UP *abbrev. for:* **1** United Press. **2** Uttar Pradesh.

up- *prefix* up, upper, or upwards: *uproot; upmost; upthrust; upgrade; uplift.*

up-anchor *vb* (*intr*) *Naut.* to weigh anchor.

up-and-coming *adj* promising continued or future success; enterprising.

up-and-down *adj* **1** moving or formed alternately upwards and downwards. ◆ *adv, prep* **up and down. 2** backwards and forwards (along).

up-and-over *adj* (of a door, etc.) opened by being lifted and moved into a horizontal position.

up-and-under *n Rugby League.* a high kick forwards followed by a charge to the place where the ball lands.

Upanishad (uː'pʌnɪʃəd) *n Hinduism.* any of a class of the Sanskrit sacred books probably composed between 400 and 200 B.C. and embodying the mystical and esoteric doctrines of ancient Hindu philosophy. ORIG C19: from Sansk. *upanisad* a sitting down near something

upas ('juːpəs) *n* **1** a large tree of Java having whitish bark and poisonous milky sap. **2** the sap of this tree, used as an arrow poison. ◆ Also called: **antiar.** ORIG C19: from Malay: poison

upbeat ('ʌpˌbiːt) *n* **1** *Music.* **1a** a usually unaccented beat, esp. the last in a bar. **1b** the upward gesture of a conductor's baton indicating this. ◆ *adj* **2** *Inf.* marked by cheerfulness or optimism.

upbraid (ʌp'breɪd) *vb* (*tr*) **1** to reprove or reproach angrily. **2** to find fault with. ORIG OE *upbregdan*
▸ **up'braider** *n* ▸ **up'braiding** *n*

upbringing ('ʌpˌbrɪŋɪŋ) *n* the education of a person during his or her formative years.

upcast ('ʌpˌkɑːst) *n* **1** material cast or thrown up. **2** a ventilation shaft through which air leaves a mine. **3** *Geol.* (in a fault) the section of strata that has been displaced upwards. ◆ *adj* **4** directed or thrown upwards. ◆ *vb* **upcasts, upcasting, upcast. 5** (*tr*) to throw or cast up.

upcountry (ʌp'kʌntrɪ) *adj* **1** of or coming from the interior of a country or region. ◆ *n* **2** the interior part of a region or country. ◆ *adv* **3** towards, in, or into the interior part of a country or region.

update *vb* (ʌp'deɪt), **updates, updating, updated.** (*tr*) **1** to bring up to date. ◆ *n* ('ʌpˌdeɪt). **2** the act of updating or something that is updated.
▸ **up'dateable** *adj* ▸ **up'dater** *n*

Updike ★ ('ʌpˌdaɪk) *n* **John** (**Hoyer**). born 1932, US writer. His novels include *Rabbit, Run* (1960), *Couples* (1968), *Rabbit is Rich* (1982), *Rabbit at Rest* (1990), and *Toward the End of Time* (1998).

updraught *or US* **updraft** ('ʌpˌdrɑːft) *n* an upward movement of air or other gas.

upend (ʌp'ɛnd) *vb* **1** to turn or set or become turned or set on end. **2** (*tr*) to affect or upset drastically.

upfront ('ʌp'frʌnt) *adj* **1** open and frank. ◆ *adv, adj* **2** (of money) paid out at the beginning of a business arrangement.

upgrade *vb* (ʌp'greɪd), **upgrades, upgrading, upgraded.** (*tr*) **1** to assign or promote (a person or job) to a higher professional rank or position. **2** to raise in value, importance, esteem, etc. **3** to improve (a breed of livestock) by crossing with a better strain. ◆ *n* ('ʌpˌgreɪd). **4** *US & Canad.* an upward slope. **5 on the upgrade.** improving or progressing, as in importance, status, health, etc.
▸ **up'grader** *n*

upheaval (ʌp'hiːvᵊl) *n* **1** a strong, sudden, or violent disturbance, as in politics. **2** *Geol.* another word for **uplift** (sense 7).

upheave (ʌp'hiːv) *vb* **upheaves, upheaving, upheaved** *or* **uphove. 1** to heave or rise upwards. **2** *Geol.* to thrust (land) upwards or (of land) to be thrust upwards. **3** (*tr*) to throw into disorder.

upheld (ʌp'hɛld) *vb* the past tense and past participle of **uphold.**

uphill ('ʌp'hɪl) *adj* **1** inclining, sloping, or leading upwards. **2** requiring protracted effort: *an uphill task.* ◆ *adv* **3** up an incline or slope. **4** against difficulties. ◆ *n* **5** a rising incline.

uphold (ʌp'həʊld) *vb* **upholds, upholding, upheld.** (*tr*) **1** to maintain or defend against opposition. **2** to give moral support to. **3** *Rare.* to support physically. **4** to lift up.
▸ **up'holder** *n*

upholster (ʌp'həʊlstə) *vb* (*tr*) to fit (chairs, sofas, etc.) with padding, springs, webbing, and covering.
▸ **up'holstery** *n*

upholsterer (ʌp'həʊlstərə) *n* a person who upholsters furniture as a profession. ORIG C17: from *upholster* small furniture dealer

upkeep ('ʌpˌkiːp) *n* **1** the act or process of keeping something in good repair, esp. over a long period. **2** the cost of maintenance.

upland ('ʌplənd) *n* **1** an area of high or relatively high ground. ◆ *adj* **2** relating to or situated in an upland.

uplift *vb* (ʌp'lɪft). (*tr*) **1** to raise; lift up. **2** to raise morally, spiritually, etc. **3** *Scot. & NZ.* to collect; pick up (goods, documents, etc.). ◆ *n* ('ʌpˌlɪft). **4** the act, process, or result of lifting up. **5** the act or process of bettering moral, social, or cultural conditions, etc. **6** (*modifier*) designating a brassiere for lifting and supporting the breasts: *an uplift bra.* **7** the process or result of land being raised to a higher level, as during a period of mountain building.
▸ **up'lifter** *n* ▸ **up'lifting** *adj*

uplighter ('ʌpˌlaɪtə) *n* a lamp or wall light designed or positioned to cast its light upwards.

up-market *adj* relating to commercial products, services, etc., that are relatively expensive and of superior quality.

upmost ('ʌpˌməʊst) *adj* another word for **uppermost.**

Upolu ★ (uː'pəʊluː) *n* an island in the SW central Pacific, in Western Samoa. Chief town: Apia. Pop.: 112 228 (1986). Area: 1114 sq. km (430 sq. miles).

upon (ə'pɒn) *prep* **1** another word for **on. 2** indicating a position reached by going up: *climb upon my knee.* **3** imminent for: *the weekend was upon us again.* ORIG C13: from UP + ON

upper ('ʌpə) *adj* **1** higher or highest in relation to physical position, wealth, rank, status, etc. **2** (*cap. when part of a name*) lying farther upstream, inland, or farther north: *the upper valley of the Loire.* **3** (*cap. when part of a name*) *Geol., archaeol.* denoting the late part or division of a period, system, etc.: *Upper Palaeolithic.* **4** *Maths.* (of a limit or bound) greater than or equal to one or more numbers or variables. ♦ *n* **5** the higher of two objects, people, etc. **6** the part of a shoe above the sole, covering the upper surface of the foot. **7** **on one's uppers.** destitute. **8** *Sl.* any of various drugs having a stimulant effect.

upper atmosphere *n Meteorol.* that part of the atmosphere above the troposphere, esp. at heights that cannot be reached by balloon.

Upper Austria ★ *n* a state of N Austria: first divided from Lower Austria in 1251. Capital: Linz. Pop.: 1 373 470 (1998 est.). Area: 11 978 sq. km (4625 sq. miles). German name: **Oberösterreich.**

Upper Burma ★ *n* the inland regions of Burma, in the north of the country.

Upper Canada ★ *n* **1** *History.* (from 1791–1841) the official name of the region of Canada lying southwest of the Ottawa River and north of the lower Great Lakes. Cf. **Lower Canada. 2** (esp. in E Canada) another name for **Ontario.**

upper case *Printing.* ♦ *n* **1** the top half of a compositor's type case in which capital letters, reference marks, and accents are kept. ♦ *adj* (**upper-case** *when prenominal*). **2** of or relating to capital letters kept in this case and used in the setting or production of printed or typed matter.

upper chamber *n* another name for an **upper house.**

upper class *n* **1** the class occupying the highest position in the social hierarchy, esp. the aristocracy. ♦ *adj* (**upper-class** *when prenominal*). **2** of or relating to the upper class.

upper crust *n Inf.* the upper class.

uppercut (ˈʌpəˌkʌt) *n* **1** a short swinging upward blow with the fist delivered at an opponent's chin. ♦ *vb* **uppercuts, uppercutting, uppercut. 2** to hit (an opponent) with an uppercut.

Upper Egypt ★ *n* one of the four main administrative districts of Egypt: extends south from Cairo to the Sudan.

upper hand *n* **the.** the position of control (esp. in **have** *or* **get the upper hand**).

upper house *n* (*often cap.*) one of the two houses of a bicameral legislature.

uppermost (ˈʌpəˌməʊst) *adj also* **upmost. 1** highest in position, power, importance, etc. ♦ *adv* **2** in or into the highest position, etc.

Upper Palatinate ★ *n* See **Palatinate.**

Upper Peninsula ★ *n* a peninsula in the northern US between Lakes Superior and Michigan, constituting the N part of the state of Michigan.

upper regions *pl n* **the.** *Chiefly literary.* the sky; heavens.

Upper Silesia ★ *n* a region of SW Poland, formerly ruled by Germany: coalmining and other heavy industry.

Upper Tunguska ★ *n* See **Tunguska.**

Upper Volta ★ (ˈvɒltə) *n* the former name (until 1984) of **Burkina-Faso.**

upper works *pl n Naut.* the parts of a vessel above the water line when fully laden.

uppish (ˈʌpɪʃ) *adj Brit. inf.* another word for **uppity** (sense 1). ORIG C18: from UP + -ISH
▸ **ˈuppishly** *adv* ▸ **ˈuppishness** *n*

uppity (ˈʌpɪtɪ) *adj Inf.* **1** snobbish, arrogant, or presumptuous. **2** offensively self-assertive. ORIG from UP + fanciful ending, ? infl. by -ITY

Uppsala *or* **Upsala** ★ (ˈʌpsɑːlə) *n* a city in E central Sweden: the royal headquarters in the 13th century; Gothic cathedral (the largest in Sweden) and Sweden's oldest university (1477). Pop.: 101 337 (1996 est.).

upraise (ʌpˈreɪz) *vb* **upraises, upraising, upraised.** (*tr*) *Chiefly literary.* to lift up; elevate.
▸ **upˈraiser** *n*

uprear (ʌpˈrɪə) *vb* (*tr*) to lift up; raise.

upright (ˈʌpˌraɪt) *adj* **1** vertical or erect. **2** honest or just. ♦ *adv* **3** vertically. ♦ *n* **4** a vertical support, such as a stake or post. **5** short for **upright piano. 6** the state of being vertical.
▸ **ˈupˌrightly** *adv* ▸ **ˈupˌrightness** *n*

upright piano *n* a piano which has a rectangular vertical case.

uprise *vb* (ʌpˈraɪz), **uprises, uprising, uprose, uprisen. 1** (*tr*) to rise up. ♦ *n* (ˈʌpˌraɪz). **2** another word for **rise** (senses 23, 24).
▸ **upˈriser** *n*

uprising (ˈʌpˌraɪzɪŋ, ʌpˈraɪzɪŋ) *n* **1** a revolt or rebellion. **2** *Arch.* an ascent.

uproar (ˈʌpˌrɔː) *n* a commotion or disturbance characterized by loud noise and confusion.

uproarious (ʌpˈrɔːrɪəs) *adj* **1** causing or characterized by an uproar. **2** extremely funny. **3** (of laughter, etc.) loud and boisterous.
▸ **upˈroariously** *adv* ▸ **upˈroariousness** *n*

uproot (ʌpˈruːt) *vb* (*tr*) **1** to pull up by or as if by the roots. **2** to displace (a person or persons) from native or habitual surroundings. **3** to remove or destroy utterly.
▸ **upˈrooter** *n*

uprush (ˈʌpˌrʌʃ) *n* an upward rush, as of consciousness.

upsadaisy (ˈʌpsəˈdeɪzɪ) *interj* a variant spelling of **upsy-daisy.**

Upsala ★ (ˈʌpsɑːlə) *n* a variant spelling of **Uppsala.**

ups and downs *pl n* alternating periods of good and bad fortune, high and low spirits, etc.

upscale (ˈʌpˈskeɪl) *adj Inf.* of or for the upper end of an economic or social scale; up-market.

upset *vb* (ʌpˈsɛt), **upsets, upsetting, upset.** (*mainly tr*) **1** (*also intr*) to tip or be tipped over; overturn or spill. **2** to disturb the normal state or stability of: *to upset the balance of nature.* **3** to disturb mentally or emotionally. **4** to defeat or overthrow, usually unexpectedly. **5** to make physically ill: *seafood always upsets my stomach.* **6** to thicken or spread (the end of a bar, etc.) by hammering. ♦ *n* (ˈʌpˌsɛt). **7** an unexpected defeat or reversal, as in a contest or plans. **8** a disturbance or disorder of the emotions, body, etc. ♦ *adj* (ʌpˈsɛt). **9** overturned or capsized. **10** emotionally or physically disturbed or distressed. **11** disordered; confused. **12** defeated or overthrown. ORIG C14 (in the sense: to erect; C19 in the sense: to overthrow)
▸ **upˈsetter** *n* ▸ **upˈsetting** *adj* ▸ **upˈsettingly** *adv*

upset price *n Chiefly Scot., US, & Canad.* the lowest price acceptable for something that is for sale, esp. a house. Cf. **reserve price.**

upshot (ˈʌpˌʃɒt) *n* **1** the final result; conclusion; outcome. **2** *Archery.* the final shot in a match. ORIG C16: from UP + SHOT[1]

upside (ˈʌpˌsaɪd) *n* the upper surface or part.

upside down *adj* **1** (*usually postpositive;* **upside-down** *when prenominal*) turned over completely; inverted. **2** (**upside-down** *when prenominal*) *Inf.* confused; topsy-turvy: *an upside-down world.* ♦ *adv* **3** in an inverted fashion. **4** in a chaotic manner. ORIG C16: var., by folk etymology, of earlier *upsodown*

upside-down cake *n* a sponge cake baked with fruit at the bottom, and inverted before serving.

upsides (ˌʌpˈsaɪdz) *adv Inf., chiefly Brit.* (foll. by *with*) equal or level (with), as through revenge.

upsilon (ˈʌpsɪˌlɒn) *n* **1** the 20th letter in the Greek alphabet (Υ or υ), a vowel transliterated as *y* or *u.* **2** a heavy short-lived subatomic particle produced by bombarding beryllium nuclei with high-energy protons. ORIG C17: from Med. Gk *u psilon* simple *u,* name adopted for graphic *u* to avoid confusion with graphic *oi,* since pronunciation was the same for both in LGk

upskill (ˈʌpˌskɪl) *vb* (*tr*) *NZ.* to improve a person's aptitude for work by additional training.

upstage (ˈʌpˈsteɪdʒ) *adv* **1** on, at, or to the rear of the stage. ♦ *adj* **2** of or relating to the back half of the stage. **3** *Inf.* haughty. ♦ *vb* **upstages, upstaging, upstaged.** (*tr*) **4** to move upstage of (another actor), thus forcing him or her to turn away from the audience. **5** *Inf.* to draw attention to oneself from (someone else). **6** *Inf.* to treat haughtily.

upstairs (ˈʌpˈstɛəz) *adv* **1** up the stairs; to or on an upper floor. **2** *Inf.* to or into a higher rank or office. ◆ *n (functioning as sing or pl)* **3a** an upper floor. **3b** *(as modifier): an upstairs room.* **4** *Brit. inf., old-fashioned.* the masters and mistresses of a household collectively, esp. of a large house.

upstanding (ʌp'stændɪŋ) *adj* **1** of good character. **2** upright and vigorous in build. **3 be upstanding. 3a** (in a court of law) a direction to all persons present to rise to their feet before the judge enters or leaves the court. **3b** (at a formal dinner) a direction to all persons present to rise to their feet for a toast.

upstart ('ʌpˌstɑːt) *n* **1a** a person, group, etc., that has risen suddenly to a position of power. **1b** *(as modifier): an upstart family.* **2a** an arrogant person. **2b** *(as modifier): his upstart ambition.*

upstate ('ʌp'steɪt) *US.* ◆ *adj, adv* **1** towards, in, or relating to the outlying or northern sections of a state. ◆ *n* **2** the outlying, esp. northern, sections of a state.
▸ **'up'stater** *n*

upstream ('ʌp'striːm) *adv, adj* **1** in or towards the higher part of a stream; against the current. Cf. **downstream. 2** (in the oil industry) of or for any of the stages prior to oil production, such as exploration or research.

upstretched (ʌp'strɛtʃt) *adj* (esp. of the arms) stretched or raised up.

upstroke ('ʌpˌstrəʊk) *n* **1a** an upward stroke or movement, as of a pen or brush. **1b** the mark produced by such a stroke. **2** the upward movement of a piston in a reciprocating engine.

upsurge *vb* (ʌp'sɜːdʒ), **upsurges, upsurging, upsurged. 1** *(intr) Chiefly literary.* to surge up. ◆ *n* ('ʌpˌsɜːdʒ). **2** a rapid rise or swell.

upsweep *n* ('ʌpˌswiːp). **1** a curve or sweep upwards. ◆ *vb* (ʌp'swiːp), **upsweeps, upsweeping, upswept. 2** to sweep, curve, or brush or be swept, curved, or brushed upwards.

upswing ('ʌpˌswɪŋ) *n* **1** *Econ.* a recovery period in the trade cycle. **2** an upward swing or movement or any increase or improvement.

upsy-daisy ('ʌpsɪ'deɪzɪ) *or* **upsadaisy** *interj* an expression, usually of reassurance, uttered as when someone, esp. a child, stumbles or is being lifted up. ORIG C18 *up-a-daisy,* irregularly formed from UP (adv)

uptake ('ʌpˌteɪk) *n* **1** a pipe, shaft, etc., that is used to convey smoke or gases, esp. one that connects a furnace to a chimney. **2** lifting up. **3** the act of accepting something on offer. **4 quick** (*or* **slow**) **on the uptake.** *Inf.* quick (or slow) to understand or learn.

upthrow ('ʌpˌθrəʊ) *n Geol.* the upward movement of rocks on one side of a fault plane relative to rocks on the other side.

upthrust ('ʌpˌθrʌst) *n* **1** an upward push or thrust. **2** *Geol.* a violent upheaval of the earth's surface.

uptight (ʌp'taɪt) *adj Inf.* **1** displaying tense repressed nervousness, irritability, or anger. **2** unable to give expression to one's feelings.

uptime ('ʌpˌtaɪm) *n Commerce.* time during which a machine, such as a computer, actually operates.

up-to-date *adj* **a** modern or fashionable: *an up-to-date magazine.* **b** *(predicative): the magazine is up to date.*
▸ **'up-to-'dateness** *n*

uptown ('ʌp'taʊn) *US & Canad.* ◆ *adj, adv* **1** towards, in, or relating to some part of a town that is away from the centre. ◆ *n* **2** such a part of a town, esp. a residential part.
▸ **'up'towner** *n*

upturn *vb* (ʌp'tɜːn). **1** to turn or cause to turn over or upside down. **2** *(tr)* to create disorder. **3** *(tr)* to direct upwards. ◆ *n* ('ʌpˌtɜːn). **4** an upward trend or improvement. **5** an upheaval.

UPVC *abbrev. for* unplasticized polyvinyl chloride. See also **PVC.**

upward ('ʌpwəd) *adj* **1** directed or moving towards a higher point or level. ◆ *adv* **2** a variant of **upwards.**
▸ **'upwardly** *adv* ▸ **'upwardness** *n*

upwardly mobile *adj* (of a person or social group) moving or aspiring to move to a higher social class or status.

upward mobility *n* movement from a lower to a higher economic and social status.

upwards ('ʌpwədz) *or* **upward** *adv* **1** from a lower to a higher place, level, condition, etc. **2** towards a higher level, standing, etc.

upwind ('ʌp'wɪnd) *adv* **1** into or against the wind. **2** towards or on the side where the wind is blowing; windward. ◆ *adj* **3** going against the wind: *the upwind leg of the course.* **4** on the windward side.

Ur ★ (ɜː) *n* an ancient city of Sumer located on a former channel of the Euphrates.

uracil ('jʊərəsɪl) *n Biochem.* a pyrimidine present in all living cells, usually in a combined form, as in RNA. ORIG C20: from URO- + ACETIC + -ILE

uraemia *or US* **uremia** (jʊ'riːmɪə) *n Pathol.* the accumulation of waste products, normally excreted in the urine, in the blood. ORIG C19: from NL, from Gk *ouron* urine + *haima* blood
▸ **u'raemic** *or US* **u'remic** *adj*

uraeus (jʊ'riːəs) *n, pl* **uraeuses.** the sacred serpent represented on the headdresses of ancient Egyptian kings and gods. ORIG C19: from NL, from Gk *ouraios,* from Egyptian *uro* asp

Ural ★ ('jʊərəl; *Russian* u'ral) *n* a river in central Russia, rising in the S Ural Mountains and flowing south to the Caspian Sea. Length: 2534 km (1575 miles).

Ural-Altaic *n* **1** a postulated group of related languages consisting of the Uralic and Altaic families of languages. ◆ *adj* **2** of or relating to this group of languages, characterized by agglutination and vowel harmony.

Uralic (jʊ'rælɪk) *or* **Uralian** (jʊ'reɪlɪən) *n* **1** a superfamily of languages consisting of the Finno-Ugric family together with Samoyed. See also **Ural-Altaic.** ◆ *adj* **2** of or relating to these languages.

Ural Mountains *or* **Urals** ★ *pl n* a mountain system in W central Russia, extending over 2000 km (1250 miles) from the Arctic Ocean towards the Aral Sea: forms part of the geographical boundary between Europe and Asia; one of the richest mineral areas in the world, with many associated major industrial centres. Highest peak: Mount Narodnaya, 1894 m (6214 ft).

uranalysis (ˌjʊərə'nælɪsɪs) *n, pl* **uranalyses** (-ˌsiːz). *Med.* a variant spelling of **urinalysis.**

uranide ('jʊərəˌnaɪd) *n* any element having an atomic number greater than that of protactinium.

uranism ('jʊərænɪzəm) *n Rare.* homosexuality (esp. male homosexuality). ORIG C20: from G *Uranismus,* from Gk *ouranios* heavenly, i.e. spiritual

uranium (jʊ'reɪnɪəm) *n* a radioactive silvery-white metallic element of the actinide series. It occurs in several minerals including pitchblende and is used chiefly as a source of nuclear energy by fission of the radioisotope **uranium-235.** Symbol: U; atomic no.: 92; atomic wt.: 238.03; half-life of most stable isotope, ^{238}U: 4.51 × 10^9 years. ORIG C18: from NL, from URANUS[2]; from the fact that the element was discovered soon after the planet

uranium series *n Physics.* a radioactive series that starts with uranium-238 and proceeds by radioactive decay to lead-206.

urano- *combining form.* denoting the heavens: *uranography.* ORIG from Gk *ouranos*

uranography (ˌjʊərə'nɒgrəfɪ) *n* the branch of astronomy concerned with the description and mapping of the stars, galaxies, etc.
▸ **ˌura'nographer** *n* ▸ **uranographic** (ˌjʊərənə'græfɪk) *adj*

Uranus[1] ★ (jʊ'reɪnəs, 'jʊərənəs) *n Greek myth.* the personification of the sky, who, as a god, ruled the universe and fathered the Titans and Cyclopes; overthrown by his son Cronus.

Uranus[2] ★ (jʊ'reɪnəs, 'jʊərənəs) *n* the seventh planet from the sun, sometimes visible to the naked eye. ORIG C19: from L Ūranus, from Gk *Ouranos* heaven

urate ('jʊəreɪt) *n* any salt or ester of uric acid.
▸ **uratic** (jʊ'rætɪk) *adj*

urban ('ɜːbᵊn) *adj* **1** of, relating to, or constituting a city or town. **2** living in a city or town. ◆ Cf. **rural.** ORIG C17: from L *urbānus,* from *urbs* city

Urban II ★ ('ɜːbᵊn) *n* original name *Odo* or *Udo.* ?1042–99, French ecclesiastic; pope (1088–99). He inaugurated the First Crusade at the Council of Clermont (1095).

urban area *n* (in population censuses) a city area considered as the inner city plus built-up environs, irrespective of local body administrative boundaries.

urban district *n* **1** (in England and Wales from 1888 to 1974 and Northern Ireland from 1898 to 1973) an urban division of an administrative county with an elected council in charge of housing and environmental services. **2** (in the Republic of Ireland) any of 49 medium-sized towns with their own elected councils.

urbane (ɜː'beɪn) *adj* characterized by elegance or sophistication. ORIG C16: from L *urbānus* of the town; see URBAN
▸ **ur'banely** *adv* ▸ **ur'baneness** *n*

urban guerrilla *n* a guerrilla who operates in a town or city, engaging in terrorism, kidnapping, etc.

urbanism ('ɜːbəˌnɪzəm) *n Chiefly US.* **a** the character of city life. **b** the study of this.

urbanite ('ɜːbəˌnaɪt) *n* a resident of an urban community; city dweller.

urbanity (ɜː'bænɪtɪ) *n, pl* **urbanities. 1** the quality of being urbane. **2** (*usually pl*) civilities or courtesies.

urbanize *or* **urbanise** ('ɜːbəˌnaɪz) *vb* **urbanizes, urbanizing, urbanized** *or* **urbanises, urbanising, urbanised.** (*tr*) (*usually passive*) **a** to make (esp. a predominantly rural area or country) more industrialized and urban. **b** to cause the migration of an increasing proportion of (rural dwellers) into cities.
▸ **ˌurbani'zation** *or* **ˌurbani'sation** *n*

urban myth *or* **legend** *n* a story, esp. one with a shocking or amusing ending, related as having actually happened, usually to someone vaguely connected with the teller.

urban renewal *n* the process of redeveloping dilapidated or no longer functional urban areas.

urbi et orbi *Latin.* ('ɜːbɪ ɛt 'ɔːbɪ) *adv RC Church.* to the city and the world: a phrase qualifying the solemn papal blessing.

urceolate ('ɜːsɪəlɪt, -ˌleɪt) *adj Biol.* shaped like an urn or pitcher: *an urceolate corolla.* ORIG C18: via NL from L *urceolus,* dim. of *urceus* a pitcher

urchin ('ɜːtʃɪn) *n* **1** a mischievous roguish child, esp. one who is young, small, or raggedly dressed. **2** See **sea urchin. 3** *Arch., dialect.* a hedgehog. **4** *Obs.* an elf or sprite. ORIG C13 *urchon,* from OF *heriçon,* from L *ēricius* hedgehog

Urdu ('ʊəduː, 'ɜː-) *n* an official language of Pakistan, also spoken in India. The script derives primarily from Persia. It belongs to the Indic branch of the Indo-European family of languages, being closely related to Hindi. ORIG C18: from Hindustani (*zabāni*) *urdū* (language of the) camp, from Persian *urdū* camp, from Turkish *ordū*

-ure *suffix forming nouns.* **1** indicating act, process, or result: *seizure.* **2** indicating function or office: *legislature; prefecture.* ORIG from F, from L *-ūra*

urea ('jʊərɪə) *n* a white water-soluble crystalline compound, produced by protein metabolism and excreted in urine. A synthetic form is used as a fertilizer and animal feed. Formula: $CO(NH_2)_2$. ORIG C19: from NL, from F *urée,* from Gk *ouron* urine
▸ **u'real** *or* **u'reic** *adj*

urea-formaldehyde resin *n* any one of a class of rigid odourless synthetic materials that are made from urea and formaldehyde and are used in electrical fittings, adhesives, laminates, and finishes for textiles.

ureide ('jʊərɪˌaɪd) *n Chem.* **1** any of a class of organic compounds derived from urea by replacing one or more of its hydrogen atoms by organic groups. **2** any of a class of derivatives of urea and carboxylic acids, in which one or more of the hydrogen atoms have been replaced by acid radical groups.

-uret *suffix of nouns.* formerly used to form the names of binary chemical compounds. ORIG from NL *-uretum*

ureter (jʊ'riːtə) *n* the tube that conveys urine from the kidney to the urinary bladder or cloaca. ORIG C16: via NL from Gk *ourētēr,* from *ourein* to urinate
▸ **u'reteral** *or* **ureteric** (ˌjʊərɪ'tɛrɪk) *adj*

urethane ('jʊərɪˌθeɪn) *or* **urethan** ('jʊərɪˌθæn) *n* short for **polyurethane.** ORIG C19: from URO- + ETHYL + -ANE

urethra (jʊ'riːθrə) *n, pl* **urethrae** (-θriː) *or* **urethras.** the canal that in most mammals conveys urine from the bladder out of the body. In human males it also conveys semen. ORIG C17: via LL from Gk *ourēthra,* from *ourein* to urinate
▸ **u'rethral** *adj*

urethritis (ˌjʊərɪ'θraɪtɪs) *n* inflammation of the urethra. ORIG C19: from NL, from LL URETHRA
▸ **urethritic** (ˌjʊərɪ'θrɪtɪk) *adj*

urethroscope (jʊ'riːθrəˌskəʊp) *n* a medical instrument for examining the urethra. ORIG C20: see URETHRA, -SCOPE
▸ **urethroscopic** (jʊˌriːθrə'skɒpɪk) *adj* ▸ **urethroscopy** (ˌjʊərɪ'θrɒskəpɪ) *n*

uretic (jʊ'rɛtɪk) *adj* of or relating to the urine. ORIG C19: via LL from Gk *ourētikos,* from *ouron* urine

Urey ★ ('jʊərɪ) *n* **Harold Clayton.** 1893–1981, US chemist, who discovered deuterium (1932), and worked on methods of separating isotopes: Nobel prize for chemistry 1934.

Urfa ★ ('ɜːfə) *n* a city in SE Turkey: market centre. Pop.: 357 900 (1994 est.). Ancient name: **Edessa.**

Urga ★ ('ɜːgə) *n* the former name (until 1924) of **Ulan Bator.**

urge (ɜːdʒ) *vb* **urges, urging, urged.** (*tr*) **1** to plead, press, or move (someone to do something): *we urged him to surrender.* **2** (*may take a clause as object*) to advocate or recommend earnestly and persistently: *to urge the need for safety.* **3** to impel, drive, or hasten onwards: *he urged the horses on.* ◆ *n* **4** a strong impulse, inner drive, or yearning. ORIG C16: from L *urgēre*

urgent ('ɜːdʒənt) *adj* **1** requiring or compelling speedy action or attention: *the matter is urgent.* **2** earnest and persistent. ORIG C15: via F from L *urgent-, urgens,* present participle of *urgēre* to URGE
▸ **urgency** ('ɜːdʒənsɪ) *n* ▸ **'urgently** *adv*

-urgy *n combining form.* indicating technology concerned with a specified material: *metallurgy.* ORIG from Gk *-urgia,* from *ergon* work

Uri ★ (*German* 'uːri) *n* one of the original three cantons of Switzerland, in the centre of the country: mainly German-speaking and Roman Catholic. Capital: Altdorf. Pop.: 35 933 (1995 est.). Area: 1075 sq. km (415 sq. miles).

-uria *n combining form.* indicating a diseased or abnormal condition of the urine: *pyuria.* ORIG from Gk *-ouria,* from *ouron* urine
▸ **-uric** *adj combining form.*

Uriah ★ (jʊ'raɪə) *n Old Testament.* a Hittite officer, who was killed in battle on instructions from David so that he could marry Uriah's wife Bathsheba (II Samuel 11).

uric ('jʊərɪk) *adj* of, concerning, or derived from urine. ORIG C18: from URO- + -IC

uric acid *n* a white odourless tasteless crystalline product of protein metabolism, present in the blood and urine. Formula: $C_5H_4N_4O_3$.

uridine ('jʊərɪˌdiːn) *n Biochem.* a nucleoside present in all living cells in a combined form, esp. in RNA. ORIG C20: from URO- + -IDE + -INE[2]

urinal (jʊ'raɪnᵊl, 'jʊərɪ-) *n* **1** a sanitary fitting, esp. one fixed to a wall, used by men for urination. **2** a room containing urinals. **3** any vessel for holding urine prior to its disposal.

urinalysis (ˌjʊərɪ'nælɪsɪs) *n, pl* **urinalyses** (-ˌsiːz). *Med.* chemical analysis of the urine to test for the presence of disease.

urinary ('jʊərɪnərɪ) *adj* **1** *Anat.* of or relating to urine or to the organs and structures that secrete and pass urine. ◆ *n, pl* **urinaries. 2** a reservoir for urine.

urinary bladder *n* a distensible membranous sac in which the urine excreted from the kidneys is stored.

urinate ('jʊərɪˌneɪt) *vb* **urinates, urinating, urinated.** (*intr*) to excrete or void urine.
▸ ˌ**uri'nation** *n* ▸ **'urinative** *adj*

urine ('jʊərɪn) *n* the pale yellow slightly acid fluid excreted by the kidneys, containing waste products removed from the blood. It is stored in the urinary bladder and discharged through the urethra. ORIG C14: via OF from L *ūrīna*

urinogenital (ˌjʊərɪnəʊ'dʒɛnɪtᵊl) *adj* another word for **urogenital.**

URL *abbrev. for* uniform resource locator: a standardized address of a location on the Internet.

Urmia ★ ('ɜːmɪə) *n* **Lake.** a shallow lake in NW Iran, at an altitude of 1300 m (4250 ft): the largest lake in Iran, varying in area from 4000–6000 sq. km (1500–2300 sq. miles) between autumn and spring.

Urmston ★ ('ɜːmstən) *n* a town in NW England, in Salford, in Greater Manchester. Pop.: 41 804 (1991).

urn (ɜːn) *n* **1** a vaselike receptacle or vessel, esp. a large bulbous one with a foot. **2** a vase used as a receptacle for the ashes of the dead. **3** a large vessel, usually of metal, with a tap, used for making and holding tea, coffee, etc. ORIG C14: from L *ūrna*
▸ **'urnˌlike** *adj*

urnfield ('ɜːnˌfiːld) *n* **1** a cemetery full of individual cremation urns. ◆ *adj* **2** (of a number of Bronze Age cultures) characterized by cremation in urns, which began in E Europe about the second millennium B.C.

uro- *or before a vowel* **ur-** *combining form.* indicating urine or the urinary tract: *urogenital; urology.* ORIG from Gk *ouron* urine

urogenital (ˌjʊərəʊ'dʒɛnɪtᵊl) *or* **urinogenital** *adj* of or relating to the urinary and genital organs and their functions. Also: **genitourinary.**

urogenital system *or* **tract** *n Anat.* the urinary tract and reproductive organs.

urolith ('jʊərəʊlɪθ) *n Pathol.* a calculus in the urinary tract.
▸ ˌ**uro'lithic** *adj*

urology (jʊ'rɒlədʒɪ) *n* the branch of medicine concerned with the study and treatment of diseases of the urogenital tract.
▸ **urologic** (ˌjʊərə'lɒdʒɪk) *adj* ▸ **u'rologist** *n*

uropygial gland (ˌjʊərə'pɪdʒɪəl) *n* a gland, situated at the base of the tail in most birds, that secretes oil used in preening.

uropygium (ˌjʊərə'pɪdʒɪəm) *n* the hindmost part of a bird's body, from which the tail feathers grow. ORIG C19: via NL from Gk *ouropugion,* from *oura* tail + *pugē* rump
▸ ˌ**uro'pygial** *adj*

uroscopy (jʊ'rɒskəpɪ) *n Med.* examination of the urine. See also **urinalysis.**
▸ **uroscopic** (ˌjʊərə'skɒpɪk) *adj* ▸ **u'roscopist** *n*

Ursa Major ('ɜːsə 'meɪdʒə) *n, Latin genitive* **Ursae Majoris** ('ɜːsiː mə'dʒɔːrɪs). an extensive conspicuous constellation in the N hemisphere. The seven brightest stars form the **Plough.** Also called: the **Great Bear,** the **Bear.** ORIG L: greater bear

Ursa Minor ('ɜːsə 'maɪnə) *n, Latin genitive* **Ursae Minoris** ('ɜːsiː mɪ'nɔːrɪs). a small faint constellation, the brightest star of which is the Pole Star. Also called: the **Little Bear,** the **Bear.** ORIG L: lesser bear

ursine ('ɜːsaɪn) *adj* of, relating to, or resembling a bear or bears. ORIG C16: from L *ursus* a bear

Ursprache *German.* ('uːrʃpraːxə) *n* any hypothetical extinct and unrecorded language reconstructed from groups of related recorded languages. For example, Indo-European is an Ursprache reconstructed by comparison of the Germanic group, Latin, Sanskrit, etc. ORIG from *ur-* primeval + *Sprache* language

Ursula ★ ('ɜːsjʊlə) *n* **Saint.** a legendary British princess of the fourth or fifth century A.D., said to have been martyred together with 11 000 virgins by the Huns at Cologne. Feast day: Oct. 21.

Ursuline ('ɜːsjʊˌlaɪn) *n* **1** a member of an order of nuns devoted to teaching in the Roman Catholic Church: founded in 1537 at Brescia. ◆ *adj* **2** of or relating to this order. ORIG C16: after St URSULA, patron saint of St Angela Merici, who founded the order

Urtext *German.* ('uːrtɛkst) *n* **1** the earliest form of a text as established by linguistic scholars as a basis for variants in later texts still in existence. **2** an edition of a musical score showing the composer's intentions without later editorial interpolation. ORIG from *ur-* original + TEXT

urticaceous (ˌɜːtɪ'keɪʃəs) *adj* of or belonging to a family of plants having small flowers and, in many species, stinging hairs: includes the nettles and pellitory. ORIG C18: via NL from L *urtīca* nettle, from *ūrere* to burn

urticaria (ˌɜːtɪ'kɛərɪə) *n* a skin condition characterized by the formation of itchy red or whitish raised patches, usually caused by an allergy. Nontechnical names: **hives, nettle rash.** ORIG C18: from NL, from L *urtīca* nettle

urtication (ˌɜːtɪ'keɪʃən) *n* **1** a burning or itching sensation. **2** another name for **urticaria.**

Uru. *abbrev. for* Uruguay.

Uruapan ★ (*Spanish* u'rwapan) *n* a city in SW Mexico, in Michoacán state: agricultural trading centre. Pop.: 187 623 (1990).

Uruguay ★ ('jʊərəˌgwaɪ) *n* a republic in South America, on the Atlantic: Spanish colonization began in 1624, followed by Portuguese settlement in 1680; revolted against Spanish rule in 1820 but was annexed by the Portuguese to Brazil; gained independence in 1825. It consists mainly of rolling grassy plains, low hills, and plateaus. Official language: Spanish. Religion: Roman Catholic. Currency: peso. Capital: Montevideo. Pop.: 3 247 000 (1999 est.). Area: 176 215 sq. km (68 037 sq. miles).
▸ ˌ**Uru'guayan** *adj, n*

Urumchi (uː'ruːmtʃɪ), **Urumqi,** *or* **Wu-lu-mu-ch'i** ★ *n* a city in NW China, capital of Xinjiang Uygur Autonomous Region: trading centre on a N route between China and central Asia. Pop.: 1 160 000 (1991 est.). Former name: **Tihwa.**

Urundi ★ (u'rʊndɪ) *n* the former name (until 1962) of **Burundi.**

urus ('jʊərəs) *n, pl* **uruses.** another name for the **aurochs.** ORIG C17: from *ūrus,* of Gmc origin

urushiol ('uːrʊʃɪˌɒl, uː'ruː-) *n* a poisonous pale yellow liquid occurring in poison ivy and the lacquer tree. ORIG from Japanese *urushi* lacquer + -OL²

us (ʌs) *pron* (*objective*) **1** refers to the speaker or writer and another person or other people: *don't hurt us.* **2** refers to all people or people in general: *this table shows us the tides.* **3** an informal word for **me:** *give us a kiss!* **4** a formal word for **me** used by editors, monarchs, etc. ORIG OE *ūs*

USAGE NOTE See at **me¹**.

US *or* **U.S.** *abbrev. for* United States.

USA *abbrev. for:* **1.** Also: **U.S.A.** United States of America. **2** United States Army.

usable *or* **useable** ('juːzəbᵊl) *adj* able to be used.
▸ ˌ**usa'bility** *or* ˌ**usea'bility** *n*

USAF *abbrev. for* United States Air Force.

usage ('juːsɪdʒ, -zɪdʒ) *n* **1** the act or a manner of using; use; employment. **2** constant use, custom, or habit. **3** something permitted or established by custom or practice. **4** what is actually said in a language, esp. as contrasted with what is prescribed. ORIG C14: via OF from L *ūsus* USE (n)

usance ('juːzəns) *n Commerce.* the period of time permitted by commercial usage for the redemption of foreign bills of exchange. ORIG C14: from OF, from Med. L *ūsantia,* from *ūsāre* to USE

USDAW ('ʌsdɔː) *n* (in Britain) *acronym for* Union of Shop, Distributive, and Allied Workers.

use *vb* (juːz), **uses, using, used.** (*tr*) **1** to put into service or action; employ for a given purpose: *to use a spoon to stir with.* **2** to make a practice or habit of employing; exercise: *he uses his brain.* **3** to behave towards in a particular way, esp. for one's own ends: *he uses people.* **4** to con-

★ people and places

sume, expend, or exhaust: *the engine uses very little oil.* **5** to partake of (alcoholic drink, drugs, etc.) or smoke (tobacco, marijuana, etc.). ◆ *n* (ju:s). **6** the act of using or the state of being used: *the carpet wore out through constant use.* **7** the ability or permission to use. **8** the occasion to use: *I have no use for this paper.* **9** an instance or manner of using. **10** usefulness; advantage: *it is of no use to complain.* **11** custom; habit: *long use has inured him to it.* **12** the purpose for which something is used; end. **13** *Christianity.* a distinctive form of liturgical or ritual observance, esp. one that is traditional. **14** the enjoyment of property, land, etc., by occupation or by deriving revenue from it. **15** *Law.* the beneficial enjoyment of property the legal title to which is held by another person as trustee. **16** **have no use for. 16a** to have no need of. **16b** to have a contemptuous dislike for. **17** **make use of. 17a** to employ; use. **17b** to exploit (a person). ◆ See also **use up.** ORIG C13: from OF *user,* from L *ūsus* having used, from *ūtī* to use

used (ju:zd) *adj* second-hand: *used cars.*

used to (ju:st) *adj* **1** accustomed to: *I am used to hitchhiking.* ◆ *vb (tr)* **2** (*takes an infinitive or implied infinitive*) used as an auxiliary to express habitual or accustomed actions, states, etc., taking place in the past but not continuing into the present: *I used to fish here every day.*

> **USAGE NOTE** The most common negative forms of *used to,* according to Bank of English data, are *didn't used to* and *didn't use to.* In formal contexts *used not to* is often preferred.

useful ('ju:sful) *adj* **1** able to be used advantageously, beneficially, or for several purposes. **2** *Inf.* commendable or capable: *a useful term's work.*
▸ **'usefully** *adv* ▸ **'usefulness** *n*

useless ('ju:slɪs) *adj* **1** having no practical use or advantage. **2** *Inf.* ineffectual, weak, or stupid: *he's useless at history.*
▸ **'uselessly** *adv* ▸ **'uselessness** *n*

user ('ju:zə) *n* **1** *Law.* **1a** the continued exercise, use, or enjoyment of a right, esp. in property. **1b** a presumptive right based on long-continued use: *right of user.* **2** (*often in combination*) a person or thing that uses: *a road-user.* **3** *Inf.* a drug addict.

user-friendly *adj* (**user friendly** *when postpositive*) easy to familiarize oneself with, understand, or use.

use up *vb (tr, adv)* **1** to finish (a supply); consume completely. **2** to exhaust; wear out.

Ushant ★ ('ʌʃənt) *n* an island off the NW coast of France, at the tip of Brittany: scene of naval battles in 1778 and 1794 between France and Britain. Area: about 16 sq. km (6 sq. miles). French name: **Ouessant.**

Ushas ★ ('u:ʃəs) *n* the Hindu goddess of the dawn.

usher ('ʌʃə) *n* **1** an official who shows people to their seats, as in a church or theatre. **2** a person who acts as doorkeeper, esp. in a court of law. **3** (in England) a minor official charged with maintaining order in a court of law. **4** an officer responsible for preceding persons of rank in a procession. **5** *Brit., obs.* a teacher. ◆ *vb (tr)* **6** to conduct or escort, esp. in a courteous or obsequious way. **7** (usually foll. by *in*) to be a precursor or herald (of). ORIG C14: from OF *huissier* doorkeeper, from Vulgar L *ustiārius* (unattested), from L *ostium* door

usherette (ˌʌʃə'rɛt) *n* a woman assistant in a cinema, etc., who shows people to their seats.

Usk ★ (ʌsk) *n* a river in SE Wales, flowing southeast and south to the Bristol Channel. Length: 113 km (70 miles).

Üsküb ★ ('usku:b) *n* the Turkish name (1392–1913) for **Skopje.**

Üsküdar ★ (ˌu:sku:'dɑ:) *n* a town in NW Turkey, across the Bosporus from Istanbul: formerly a terminus of caravan routes from Syria and Asia; base of the British army in the Crimean War. Pop.: 261 141 (1980). Former name: **Scutari.**

USM *Stock Exchange. abbrev. for* unlisted securities market.

USN *abbrev. for* United States Navy.

Usnach *or* **Usnech** ★ ('uʃnəx) *n* (in Irish legend) the father of Naoise.

USP *abbrev. for* unique selling proposition *or* point: a characteristic of a product that can be used in advertising to differentiate it from its competitors.

Uspallata Pass ★ (ˌu:spə'lɑ:tə; *Spanish* uspa'ʎata) *n* a pass over the Andes in S South America, between Mendoza (Argentina) and Santiago (Chile). Height: 3840 m (12 600 ft). Also called: **La Cumbre.**

usquebaugh ('ʌskwɪˌbɔ:) *n* **1** *Irish.* the former name for **whiskey. 2** *Scot.* the former name for **whisky.** ORIG C16: from Irish Gaelic *uisce beathadh* or Scot. Gaelic *uisge beatha* water of life

USS *abbrev. for:* **1** United States Senate. **2** United States Ship.

USSR *abbrev. for* (the former) Union of Soviet Socialist Republics.

Ussuri ★ (*Russian* ussu'ri) *n* a river in E central Asia, flowing north, forming part of the Chinese border with Russia, to the Amur River. Length: about 800 km (500 miles).

Ústí nad Labem ★ (*Czech* 'u:stji: nad 'labɛm) *n* a port in the Czech Republic, on the Elbe River: textile and chemical industries. Pop.: 118 000 (1993).

Ustinov ★ ('ju:stɪˌnɒf) *n* Sir **Peter** (**Alexander**). born 1921, British stage and film actor, director, dramatist, and raconteur.

Ust-Kamenogorsk ★ (*Russian* ustjkəmɪna'gɔrsk) *n* a city in E Kazakhstan: centre of a zinc-, lead-, and copper-mining area. Pop.: 326 300 (1995 est.).

Ustyurt *or* **Ust Urt** ★ (*Russian* us'tjurt) *n* an arid plateau in central Asia, between the Caspian and Aral seas in SW Kazakhstan and Uzbekistan. Area: about 238 000 sq. km (92 000 sq. miles).

usual ('ju:ʒuəl) *adj* **1** of the most normal, frequent, or regular type: *that's the usual sort of application to send.* ◆ *n* **2** ordinary or commonplace events (esp. in **out of the usual**). **3 the usual.** *Inf.* the habitual or usual drink, etc. ORIG C14: from LL *ūsuālis* ordinary, from L *ūsus* USE
▸ **'usually** *adv* ▸ **'usualness** *n*

usufruct ('ju:sjuˌfrʌkt) *n* the right to use and derive profit from a piece of property belonging to another, provided the property itself remains undiminished and uninjured in any way. ORIG C17: from LL *ūsūfrūctus,* from L *ūsus* use + *frūctus* enjoyment
▸ ˌ**usu'fructuary** *n, adj*

Usumbura ★ (ˌu:zəm'buərə) *n* the former name of **Bujumbura.**

usurer ('ju:ʒərə) *n* a person who lends funds at an exorbitant rate of interest.

usurp (ju:'zɜ:p) *vb* to seize or appropriate (land, a throne, etc.) without authority. ORIG C14: from OF, from L *ūsūrpāre* to take into use, prob. from *ūsus* use + *rapere* to seize
▸ ˌ**usur'pation** *n* ▸ **u'surper** *n*

usury ('ju:ʒərɪ) *n, pl* **usuries. 1** the practice of loaning money at an exorbitant rate of interest. **2** an unlawfully high rate of interest. **3** *Obs.* moneylending. ORIG C14: from Med. L, from L *ūsūra* usage, from *ūsus* USE
▸ **usurious** (ju:'ʒuərɪəs) *adj*

USW *Radio. abbrev. for* ultrashort wave.

ut (ʌt, u:t) *n Music.* the syllable used in the fixed system of solmization for the note C. ORIG C14: from L *ut;* see GAMUT

UT *abbrev. for:* **1** universal time. **2** Utah.

Utah ★ ('ju:tɔ:, 'ju:tɑ:) *n* a state of the western US: settled by Mormons in 1847; situated in the Great Basin and the Rockies, with the Great Salt Lake in the northwest. Capital: Salt Lake City. Pop.: 2 099 758 (1998 est.). Area: 212 628 sq. km (82 096 sq. miles). Abbrev.: **UT.**
▸ **Utahan** (ju:'tɔ:ən, -'tɑ:ən) *adj, n*

Utamaro ★ (ˌu:tə'mɑ:rəu) *n* **Kitagawa** (ˌki:tə'gɑ:wə), original name *Kitagawa Nebsuyoshi.* 1753–1806, Japanese master of wood-block prints, noted esp. for his portraits of women.

UTC *abbrev. for* universal time coordinated. See **universal time.**

ute (ju:t) *n Austral. & NZ inf.* short for **utility truck.**

utensil (juːˈtɛnsəl) *n* an implement, tool, or container for practical use: *writing utensils.* ORIG C14 *utensele,* via OF from L *ūtēnsilia* necessaries, from *ūtēnsilis* available for use, from *ūtī* to use

uterine (ˈjuːtəˌraɪn) *adj* **1** of, relating to, or affecting the uterus. **2** (of offspring) born of the same mother but not the same father.

uterus (ˈjuːtərəs) *n, pl* **uteri** (ˈjuːtəˌraɪ). **1** *Anat.* a hollow muscular organ lying within the pelvic cavity of female mammals. It houses the developing fetus. Nontechnical name: **womb. 2** the corresponding organ in other animals. ORIG C17: from L

Utgard ★ (ˈʊtgɑːd, ˈuːt-) *n Norse myth.* one of the divisions of Jotunheim, land of the giants, ruled by Utgard-Loki.

Utgard-Loki ★ *n Norse myth.* the giant king of Utgard.

Uther (ˈjuːθə) *or* **Uther Pendragon** ★ *n* (in Arthurian legend) a king of Britain and father of Arthur.

Utica ★ (ˈjuːtɪkə) *n* an ancient city on the N coast of Africa, northwest of Carthage.

utilidor (juːˈtɪlədə; *Canad.* -ˌdɒr) *n Canad.* above-ground insulated casing for pipes carrying water, etc., in permafrost regions.

utilitarian (juːˌtɪlɪˈtɛərɪən) *adj* **1** of or relating to utilitarianism. **2** designed for use rather than beauty. ◆ *n* **3** a person who believes in utilitarianism.

utilitarianism (juːˌtɪlɪˈtɛərɪəˌnɪzəm) *n Ethics.* **1** the doctrine that the morally correct course of action consists in the greatest good for the greatest number, that is, in maximizing the total benefit resulting, without regard to the distribution of benefits and burdens. **2** the theory that the criterion of virtue is utility.

utility (juːˈtɪlɪtɪ) *n, pl* **utilities. 1a** the quality of practical use; usefulness. **1b** (*as modifier*): *a utility fabric.* **2** something useful. **3a** a public service, such as the bus system. **3b** (*as modifier*): *utility vehicle.* **4** *Econ.* the ability of a commodity to satisfy human wants. Cf. **disutility. 5** *Austral.* short for **utility truck. 6** *Computing.* a piece of software that performs a routine task. ORIG C14: from OF *utelite,* from L *ūtilitās* usefulness, from *ūtī* to use

utility function *n Econ.* a function relating specific goods and services in an economy to individual preferences.

utility player *n Sport.* a player who is capable of playing competently in any of several positions.

utility room *n* a room with equipment for domestic work like washing and ironing.

utility truck *n Austral. & NZ.* a small truck with an open body and low sides, often with a removable tarpaulin cover; pick-up truck.

utilize *or* **utilise** (ˈjuːtɪˌlaɪz) *vb* **utilizes, utilizing, utilized** *or* **utilises, utilising, utilised.** (*tr*) to make practical or worthwhile use of.
▸ **ˈutiˌlizable** *or* **ˈutiˌlisable** *adj* ▸ **ˌutiliˈzation** *or* **ˌutiliˈsation** *n* ▸ **ˈutiˌlizer** *or* **ˈutiˌliser** *n*

utmost (ˈʌtˌməʊst) *or* **uttermost** *adj* (*prenominal*) **1** of the greatest possible degree or amount: *the utmost degree.* **2** at the furthest limit: *the utmost town on the peninsula.* ◆ *n* **3** the greatest possible degree, extent, or amount: *he tried his utmost.* ORIG OE *ūtemest,* from *ūte* out + *-mest* MOST

utmost good faith *n* a principle used in insurance contracts, legally obliging all parties to reveal to the others any information that might influence the others' decision to enter into the contract. ORIG from L *uberrima fides*

Utopia (juːˈtəʊpɪə) *n* (*sometimes not cap.*) any real or imaginary society, place, state, etc., considered to be perfect or ideal. ORIG C16: from NL *Utopia* (coined by Sir Thomas More in 1516 as the title of his book that described an imaginary island representing the perfect society), lit.: no place, from Gk *ou* not + *topos* a place

Utopian (juːˈtəʊpɪən) (*sometimes not cap.*) ◆ *adj* **1** of or relating to a perfect or ideal existence. ◆ *n* **2** an idealistic social reformer.
▸ **Uˈtopianism** *n*

Utrecht ★ (*Dutch* ˈyːtrɛxt; *English* ˈjuːtrɛkt) *n* **1** a province of the W central Netherlands. Capital: Utrecht. Pop.: 1 079 400 (1997 est.). Area: 1362 sq. km (526 sq. miles). **2** a city in the central Netherlands, capital of Utrecht province: scene of the signing (1579) of the **Union of Utrecht** (the foundation of the later kingdom of the Netherlands) and of the **Treaty of Utrecht** (1713), ending the War of the Spanish Succession. Pop.: 234 106 (1994).

utricle (ˈjuːtrɪkᵊl) *n* **1** *Anat.* the larger of the two parts of the membranous labyrinth of the internal ear. Cf. **saccule. 2** *Bot.* the bladder-like one-seeded indehiscent fruit of certain plants. ORIG C18: from L *ūtriculus,* dim. of *ūter* bag
▸ **uˈtricular** *adj*

utriculitis (juːˌtrɪkjʊˈlaɪtɪs) *n* inflammation of the inner ear.

Utrillo ★ (*French* ytrijo) *n* **Maurice** (mɔris). 1883–1955, French painter, esp. of Parisian street scenes.

Uttar Pradesh ★ (ˈʊtə ˈprɑːdɛʃ) *n* a state of N India: the most populous state; originated in 1877 with the merging of Agra and Oudh as the United Provinces; the states of Rampur, Benares, and Tehri-Garhwal were added in 1949; lies mostly on the Upper Ganges plain but rises over 7500 m (25 000 ft) in the Himalayas in the northwest; agricultural. Capital: Lucknow. Pop.: 150 695 000 (1994 est.). Area: 294 413 sq. km (113 673 sq. miles).

utter[1] (ˈʌtə) *vb* **1** to give audible expression to (something): *to utter a growl.* **2** *Criminal law.* to put into circulation (counterfeit coin, forged banknotes, etc.). **3** (*tr*) to make publicly known; publish: *to utter slander.* ORIG C14: prob. orig. a commercial term, from MDu. *ūteren* (modern Du. *uiteren*) to make known
▸ **ˈutterable** *adj* ▸ **ˈutterableness** *n* ▸ **ˈutterer** *n*

utter[2] (ˈʌtə) *adj* (*prenominal*) (intensifier): *an utter fool; the utter limit.* ORIG C15: from OE *utera* outer, comp. of *ūte* out (adv)
▸ **ˈutterly** *adv*

utterance (ˈʌtərəns) *n* **1** something uttered, such as a statement. **2** the act or power of uttering or ability to utter.

utter barrister *n Law.* the full title of a barrister who is not a Queen's Counsel.

uttermost (ˈʌtəˌməʊst) *adj, n* a variant of **utmost.**

U-turn *n* **1** a turn made by a vehicle in the shape of a U, resulting in a reversal of direction. **2** a complete change in direction of political policy, etc.

UV *abbrev. for* ultraviolet.

UV-A *or* **UVA** *abbrev. for* ultraviolet radiation with a range of 320-380 nanometres.

uvarovite (uːˈvɑːrəˌvaɪt) *n* an emerald-green garnet found in chromium deposits. ORIG C19: from G *Uvarovit;* after Count Sergei *Uvarov* (1785–1855), Russian author & statesman

UV-B *or* **UVB** *abbrev. for* ultraviolet radiation with a range of 280-320 nanometres.

uvea (ˈjuːvɪə) *n* the part of the eyeball consisting of the iris, ciliary body, and choroid. ORIG C16: from Med. L *ūvea,* from L *ūva* grape
▸ **ˈuveal** *adj*

UVF *abbrev. for* Ulster Volunteer Force.

uvula (ˈjuːvjʊlə) *n, pl* **uvulas** *or* **uvulae** (-ˌliː). a small fleshy flap of tissue that hangs in the back of the throat and is an extension of the soft palate. ORIG C14: from Med. L, lit.: a little grape, from L *ūva* a grape

uvular (ˈjuːvjʊlə) *adj* **1** of or relating to the uvula. **2** *Phonetics.* articulated with the uvula and the back of the tongue, such as the (r) sound of Parisian French. ◆ *n* **3** a uvular consonant.

UXB *abbrev. for* unexploded bomb.

Uxbridge ★ (ˈʌksˌbrɪdʒ) *n* a town in SE England, part of the Greater London borough of Hillingdon since 1965; chiefly residential; seat of Brunel University (1966).

Uxmal ★ (*Spanish* uzˈmal) *n* an ancient ruined city in SE Mexico, in Yucatán: capital of the later Maya empire.

uxorial (ʌk'sɔːrɪəl) *adj* of or relating to a wife: *uxorial influence.* ORIG C19: from L *uxor* wife
▸ **ux'orially** *adv*

uxoricide (ʌk'sɔːrɪˌsaɪd) *n* **1** the act of killing one's wife. **2** a man who kills his wife. ORIG C19: from L *uxor* wife + -CIDE
▸ **uxˌori'cidal** *adj*

uxorious (ʌk'sɔːrɪəs) *adj* excessively attached to or dependent on one's wife. ORIG C16: from L *uxōrius* concerning a wife, from *uxor* wife
▸ **ux'oriously** *adv* ▸ **ux'oriousness** *n*

Uzbek ('ʊzbɛk, 'ʌz-) *n* **1** (*pl* **Uzbeks** *or* **Uzbek**) a member of a Mongoloid people of Uzbekistan. **2** the language of this people.

Uzbekistan ★ (ˌʊzbɛkɪ'stɑːn, ˌʌz-) *n* a republic in central Asia: annexed by Russia in the 19th century, it became a separate Soviet Socialist republic in 1924, gaining independence in 1991; mining, textile, and chemical industries are important. Official language: Uzbek. Religion: believers are mainly Muslim. Currency: sum. Capital: Tashkent. Pop.: 24 449 000 (1999 est.). Area: 449 600 sq. km (173 546 sq. miles).

★ people and places

Vv

v *or* **V** (viː) *n, pl* **v's, V's,** *or* **Vs. 1** the 22nd letter of the English alphabet. **2** a speech sound represented by this letter, usually a voiced fricative, as in *vote.* **3a** something shaped like a V. **3b** (*in combination*): *a V neck.*

v *symbol for:* **1** *Physics.* velocity. **2** specific volume (of a gas).

V *symbol for:* **1** *Chem.* vanadium. **2** (in transformational grammar) verb. **3** volume (capacity). **4** volt. **5** victory. **6** *the Roman numeral for* five.

v. *abbrev. for:* **1** ventral. **2** verb. **3** verse. **4** verso. **5** (*usually italic*) versus. **6** very. **7** vide ORIG L: see. **8** volume.

V. *abbrev. for:* **1** Venerable. **2** (in titles) Very. **3** (in titles) Vice. **4** Viscount.

V-1 *n* a robot bomb invented by the Germans in World War II: used esp. to bombard London. Also called: **doodlebug, buzz bomb, flying bomb.** ORIG from G *Vergeltungswaffe* revenge weapon

V-2 *n* a rocket-powered ballistic missile invented by the Germans in World War II: used esp. to bombard London. ORIG see V-1

V6 *n* a car or internal-combustion engine having six cylinders arranged in the form of a V.

V8 *n* a car or internal-combustion engine having eight cylinders arranged in the form of a V.

VA *abbrev. for:* **1** Vicar Apostolic. **2** (Order of) Victoria and Albert. **3** volt-ampere. **4** Virginia.

Va. *abbrev. for* Virginia.

Vaal ★ (vɑːl) *n* a river in South Africa, rising in the Drakensberg and flowing west across the country to join the Orange River. Length: 1160 km (720 miles).

Vaasa ★ (*Finnish* 'vɑːsɑ) *n* a port in W Finland, on the Gulf of Bothnia: the provisional capital of Finland (1918); textile industries. Pop.: 55 089 (1994). Former name: **Nikolainkaupunki.**

vac (væk) *n Brit. inf.* short for **vacation.**

vacancy ('veɪkənsɪ) *n, pl* **vacancies. 1** the state or condition of being vacant or unoccupied; emptiness. **2** an unoccupied post or office: *we have a vacancy in the accounts department.* **3** an unoccupied room in a hotel, etc.: *the manager put up the "No Vacancies" sign.* **4** lack of thought or intelligent awareness. **5** *Obs.* idleness or a period spent in idleness.

vacant ('veɪkənt) *adj* **1** without any contents; empty. **2** (*postpositive; foll. by of*) devoid (of something specified). **3** having no incumbent: *a vacant post.* **4** having no tenant or occupant: *a vacant house.* **5** characterized by or resulting from lack of thought or intelligent awareness. **6** (of time, etc.) not allocated to any activity: *it is pleasant to have a vacant hour in one's day.* **7** spent in idleness or inactivity: *a vacant life.* ORIG C13: from L *vacāre* to be empty
► **'vacantly** *adv*

vacant possession *n* ownership of an unoccupied house or property, any previous owner or tenant having departed.

vacate (və'keɪt) *vb* **vacates, vacating, vacated.** (*mainly tr*) **1** to cause (something) to be empty, esp. by departing from or abandoning it: *to vacate a room.* **2** (*also intr*) to give up the tenure, possession, or occupancy of (a place, post, etc.). **3** *Law.* **3a** to cancel. **3b** to annul.
► **va'catable** *adj*

vacation (və'keɪʃən) *n* **1** *Chiefly Brit.* a period of the year when the law courts or universities are closed. **2** another word (esp. US. and Canad.) for **holiday** (sense 1). **3** the act of departing from or abandoning property, etc. ◆ *vb* **4** (*intr*) *US. & Canad.* to take a holiday. ORIG C14: from L *vacātiō* freedom, from *vacāre* to be empty
► **va'cationer** *or* **va'cationist** *n*

vaccinate ('væksɪˌneɪt) *vb* **vaccinates, vaccinating, vaccinated.** to inoculate (a person) with vaccine so as to produce immunity against a specific disease.
► **'vacciˌnator** *n*

vaccination (ˌvæksɪ'neɪʃən) *n* **1** the act of vaccinating. **2** the scar left following inoculation with a vaccine.

vaccine ('væksiːn) *n Med.* **1** a suspension of dead, attenuated, or otherwise modified microorganisms for inoculation to produce immunity to a disease by stimulating the production of antibodies. **2** a preparation of the virus of cowpox inoculated in humans to produce immunity to smallpox. **3** (*modifier*) of or relating to vaccination or vaccinia. **4** *Computing.* software designed to detect and remove computer viruses from a system. ORIG C18: from NL *variolae vaccīnae* cowpox, title of medical treatise (1798) by Edward Jenner, from L *vacca* a cow
► **'vaccinal** *adj*

vaccinia (væk'sɪnɪə) *n* a technical name for **cowpox.** ORIG C19: NL, from L *vaccīnus* of cows

vacherin *French.* (vaʃrɛ̃) *n* a dessert consisting of a meringue shell filled with whipped cream, ice cream, fruit, etc. ORIG also in France a kind of cheese, from F *vache* cow, from L *vacca*

vacillate ('væsɪˌleɪt) *vb* **vacillates, vacillating, vacillated.** (*intr*) **1** to fluctuate in one's opinions. **2** to sway from side to side physically. ORIG C16: from L *vacillāre* to sway, from ?
► ˌ**vacil'lation** *n* ► **'vacilˌlator** *n*

vacua ('vækjuə) *n* a plural of **vacuum.**

vacuity (væ'kjuːɪtɪ) *n, pl* **vacuities. 1** the state or quality of being vacuous. **2** an empty space or void. **3** a lack or absence of something specified: *a vacuity of wind.* **4** lack of normal intelligence or awareness. **5** a statement, saying, etc., that is inane or pointless. **6** (in customs terminology) the difference in volume between the actual contents of a container and its full capacity. ORIG C16: from L *vacuitās* empty space, from *vacuus* empty

vacuole ('vækjuˌəul) *n Biol.* a fluid-filled cavity in a cell. ORIG C19: from F, lit.: little vacuum, from L VACUUM
► **vacuolar** (ˌvækju'əulə) *adj*

vacuous ('vækjuəs) *adj* **1** empty. **2** bereft of ideas or intelligence. **3** characterized by or resulting from vacancy of mind: *a vacuous gaze.* **4** indulging in no useful mental or physical activity. ORIG C17: from L *vacuus* empty
► **'vacuously** *adv*

vacuum ('vækjuəm) *n, pl* **vacuums** *or* **vacua. 1** a region containing no free matter; in technical contexts now often called: **free space. 2** a region in which gas is present at a low pressure. **3** the degree of exhaustion of gas within an enclosed space: *a perfect vacuum.* **4** a feeling of emptiness: *his death left a vacuum in her life.* **5** short for **vacuum cleaner. 6** (*modifier*) of, containing, producing, or operated by a low gas pressure: *a vacuum brake.* ◆ *vb* **7** to clean (something) with a vacuum cleaner. ORIG C16: from L: empty space, from *vacuus* empty

vacuum cleaner *n* an electrical household appliance used for cleaning floors, carpets, etc., by suction.
► **vacuum cleaning** *n*

vacuum distillation *n* distillation in which the liquid distilled is enclosed at a low pressure in order to reduce its boiling point.

vacuum flask *n* an insulating flask that has double walls, usually of silvered glass, with an evacuated space between them. It is used for maintaining substances at high or low temperatures. Also called: **Thermos.**

vacuum gauge *n* any of a number of instruments for measuring pressures below atmospheric pressure.

vacuum-packed *adj* packed in an airtight container or packet under low pressure in order to maintain freshness, prevent corrosion, etc.

★ people and places

vacuum pump *n* a pump for producing a low gas pressure.

vacuum tube *or* **valve** *n* the US. and Canad. name for **valve** (sense 3).

VAD *abbrev. for* **1** Voluntary Aid Detachment. ♦ *n* **2** a member of this organization.

vade mecum ('vɑːdɪ 'meɪkʊm) *n* a handbook or other aid carried on the person for immediate use when needed. ORIG C17: from L, lit.: go with me

Vadodara ★ (wə'dəʊdərə) *n* a city in W India, in SE Gujurat: textile manufacturing. Pop.: 1 031 346 (1991). Former name (until 1976): **Baroda.**

vadose ('veɪdəʊs) *adj* of, designating, or derived from water occurring above the water table: *vadose deposits.* ORIG C19: from L *vadōsus* full of shallows, from *vadum* a ford

Vaduz ★ (*German* fa'dʊts) *n* the capital of Liechtenstein, in the Rhine valley: an old market town, dominated by a medieval castle, residence of the prince of Liechtenstein. Pop.: 5917 (1997 est.).

vagabond ('vægəˌbɒnd) *n* **1** a person with no fixed home. **2** an idle wandering beggar or thief. **3** (*modifier*) of or like a vagabond. ORIG C15: from L *vagābundus* wandering, from *vagārī* to roam, from *vagus* VAGUE
▸ **'vagaˌbondage** *n*

vagal ('veɪgᵊl) *adj Anat.* of, relating to, or affecting the vagus nerve: *vagal inhibition.*

vagary ('veɪgərɪ, və'geərɪ) *n, pl* **vagaries.** an erratic notion or action. ORIG C16: prob. from L *vagārī* to roam; cf. L *vagus* VAGUE

vagina (və'dʒaɪnə) *n, pl* **vaginas** *or* **vaginae** (-niː). **1** the canal in most female mammals that extends from the cervix of the uterus to an external opening between the labia minora. **2** *Anat., biol.* any sheath or sheathlike structure. ORIG C17: from L: sheath
▸ **vag'inal** *adj*

vaginate ('vædʒɪnɪt, -ˌneɪt) *adj* (esp. of plant parts) sheathed: *a vaginate leaf.*

vaginectomy (ˌvædʒɪ'nɛktəmɪ) *n, pl* **vaginectomies. 1** surgical removal of all or part of the vagina. **2** surgical removal of part of the serous sheath surrounding the testis and epididymis.

vaginismus (ˌvædʒɪ'nɪzməs) *n* painful spasm of the vagina. ORIG C19: from NL, from VAGINA, + *-ismus;* see -ISM

vaginitis (ˌvædʒɪ'naɪtɪs) *n* inflammation of the vagina.

vagotomy (væ'gɒtəmɪ) *n, pl* **vagotomies.** surgical division of the vagus nerve, performed to limit gastric secretion in patients with severe peptic ulcers. ORIG C19: from VAG(US) + -TOMY

vagotonia (ˌveɪgə'təʊnɪə) *n* pathological overactivity of the vagus nerve, affecting various bodily functions controlled by this nerve. ORIG C19: from VAG(US) + *-tonia,* from L *tonus* tension, TONE

vagrancy ('veɪgrənsɪ) *n, pl* **vagrancies. 1** the state or condition of being a vagrant. **2** the conduct or mode of living of a vagrant.

vagrant ('veɪgrənt) *n* **1** a person of no settled abode, income, or job; tramp. ♦ *adj* **2** wandering about. **3** of or characteristic of a vagrant or vagabond. **4** moving in an erratic fashion; wayward. **5** (of plants) showing straggling growth. ORIG C15: prob. from OF *waucrant* (from *wancrer* to roam, of Gmc origin), but also infl. by OF *vagant* vagabond, from L *vagārī* to wander
▸ **'vagrantly** *adv*

vague (veɪg) *adj* **1** (of statements, meaning, etc.) imprecise: *vague promises.* **2** not clearly perceptible or discernible: *a vague idea.* **3** not clearly established or known: *a vague rumour.* **4** (of a person or his or her expression) absent-minded. ORIG C16: via F from L *vagus* wandering, from ?
▸ **'vaguely** *adv* ▸ **'vagueness** *n*

vagus *or* **vagus nerve** ('veɪgəs) *n, pl* **vagi** ('veɪdʒaɪ) *or* **vagus nerves.** the tenth cranial nerve, which supplies the heart, lungs, and viscera. ORIG C19: from L *vagus* wandering
▸ **'vagal** *adj*

vail (veɪl) *Obs.* ♦ *vb* (*tr*) **1** to lower (something, such as a weapon), esp. as a sign of deference. **2** to remove (the hat, etc.) as a mark of respect. ♦ *n* **3** a tip. ORIG C14 *valen,* from obs. *avalen,* from OF *avaler* to let fall, from L *ad vallem,* lit.: to the valley, i.e., down

vain (veɪn) *adj* **1** inordinately proud of one's appearance, possessions, or achievements. **2** given to ostentatious display. **3** worthless. **4** senseless or futile. ♦ *n* **5 in vain.** fruitlessly. ORIG C13: via OF from L *vānus*
▸ **'vainly** *adv* ▸ **'vainness** *n*

vainglory (ˌveɪn'glɔːrɪ) *n* **1** boastfulness or vanity. **2** ostentation.
▸ **ˌvain'glorious** *adj*

vair (veə) *n* **1** a fur, probably Russian squirrel, used to trim robes in the Middle Ages. **2** a fur used on heraldic shields, conventionally represented by white and blue skins in alternate lines. ORIG C13: from OF: of more than one colour, from L *varius* variegated

Vaisya ('vaɪsjə, 'vaɪʃjə) *n* the third of the four main Hindu castes, the traders. ORIG C18: from Sansk., lit.: settler, from *viś* settlement

Valais ★ (*French* valɛ) *n* a canton of S Switzerland: includes the entire valley of the upper Rhône and the highest peaks in Switzerland; produces a quarter of Switzerland's hydroelectricity. Capital: Sion. Pop.: 269 341 (1995 est.). Area: 5231 sq. km (2020 sq. miles). German name: **Wallis.**

valance ('væləns) *n* a short piece of drapery hung along a shelf or bed to hide structural detail. ORIG C15: ? after VALENCE, noted for its textiles
▸ **'valanced** *adj*

Valdai Hills ★ (vɑːl'daɪ) *pl n* a region of hills and plateaus in NW Russia, between Moscow and Saint Petersburg. Greatest height: 346 m (1135 ft).

Valdemar I ★ (*Danish* 'valdəmar) *n* a variant spelling of **Waldemar I.**

Val-de-Marne ★ (*French* valdəmarn) *n* a department of N France, in Île-de-France region. Capital: Créteil. Pop.: 1 233 964 (1994 est.). Area: 244 sq. km (95 sq. miles).

Valdivia[1] ★ (*Spanish* bal'diβja) *n* a port in S Chile, on the **Valdivia River** about 19 km (12 miles) from the Pacific: developed chiefly by German settlers in the 1850s; university (1954). Pop.: 119 431 (1995 est.).

Valdivia[2] ★ (*Spanish* bal'diβja) *n* **Pedro de** ('peðro de). ?1500–54, Spanish soldier; conqueror of Chile.

Val-d'Oise ★ (*French* valdwaz) *n* a department of N France, in Île-de-France region. Capital: Pontoise. Pop.: 1 102 804 (1994 est.). Area: 1249 sq. km (487 sq. miles).

vale[1] (veɪl) *n* a literary word for **valley.** ORIG C13: from OF *val,* from L *vallis* valley

vale[2] *Latin.* ('vɑːleɪ) *sentence substitute.* farewell; goodbye.

valediction (ˌvælɪ'dɪkʃən) *n* **1** the act or an instance of saying goodbye. **2** any valedictory statement, etc. ORIG C17: from L *valedīcere,* from *valē* farewell + *dīcere* to say

valedictory (ˌvælɪ'dɪktərɪ) *adj* **1** saying goodbye. **2** of or relating to a farewell or an occasion of farewell. ♦ *n, pl* **valedictories. 3** a farewell address or speech.

valence ('veɪləns) *n Chem.* **1** another name (esp. US. and Canad.) for **valency. 2** the phenomenon of forming chemical bonds.

Valence ★ (*French* valɑ̃s) *n* a town in SE France, on the River Rhône. Pop.: 63 437 (1990).

Valencia ★ (*Spanish* ba'lenθja) *n* **1** a port in E Spain, capital of Valencia province, on the Mediterranean: the third largest city in Spain; capital of the Moorish kingdom of Valencia (1021–1238); university (1501). Pop.: 764 293 (1994 est.). Latin name: **Valentia** (və'lɛntɪə). **2** a region and former kingdom of E Spain, on the Mediterranean. **3** a city in N Venezuela: one of the two main industrial centres in Venezuela. Pop.: 903 621 (1990).

Valenciennes[1] (ˌvælənsɪ'ɛn) *n* a flat bobbin lace typically having scroll and floral designs and originally made of linen. ORIG after VALENCIENNES[2], where orig. made

Valenciennes[2] ★ (*French* valɑ̃sjɛn) *n* a town in N France, on the River Escaut: a coal-mining and heavy industrial centre. Pop.: 39 276 (1990).

valency ('veɪlənsɪ) *or esp. US. & Canad.* **valence** *n, pl* **valencies** *or* **valences.** *Chem.* a property of atoms or groups equal to the number of atoms of hydrogen that the atom or group could combine with or displace in forming compounds. ORIG C19: from L *valentia* strength, from *valēre* to be strong

valency electron *n Chem.* an electron in the outer shell of an atom, responsible for forming chemical bonds.

Valens ★ ('veɪlɛnz) *n* ?328–378 A.D., emperor of the Eastern Roman Empire (364–378); appointed by his elder brother Valentinian I, emperor of the Western Empire.

valentine ('vælən͵taɪn) *n* **1** a card or gift expressing love or affection, sent, often anonymously, on Saint Valentine's Day. **2** a sweetheart selected for such a greeting.

Valentine ★ ('vælən͵taɪn) *n* **Saint.** 3rd century A.D., Christian martyr, associated by historical accident with the custom of sending valentines; bishop of Terni. Feast day: Feb. 14.

Valentinian I (͵vælən'tɪnɪən) *or* **Valentinianus I** ★ (͵vælən͵tɪnɪ'eɪnəs) *n* 321–375 A.D., emperor of the Western Roman Empire (364–375); appointed his brother Valens to rule the Eastern Empire.

Valentinian II *or* **Valentinianus II** ★ *n* 371–392 A.D., emperor of the Western Roman Empire (375–392), reigning jointly with his half brother Gratian until 383.

Valentinian III *or* **Valentinianus III** ★ *n* ?419–455 A.D., emperor of the Western Roman Empire (425–455). His government lost Africa to the Vandals.

Valentino ★ (͵vælən'tiːnəʊ) *n* **Rudolph,** original name *Rodolpho Guglielmi di Valentina d'Antonguolla.* 1895–1926, US. silent-film actor, born in Italy. His films include *The Sheik* (1921).

Vale of Glamorgan ★ *n* a county borough of S Wales, created in 1996 from parts of South Glamorgan and Mid Glamorgan. Administrative centre: Barry. Pop.: 119 200 (1996 est.). Area: 295 sq. km (114 sq. miles).

Valera ★ (və'lɛərə, -'lɪərə) *n* See (Eamon) **de Valera.**

valerian (və'lɛərɪən) *n* **1** Also called: **allheal.** a Eurasian plant having small white or pinkish flowers and a medicinal root. **2** a sedative drug made from the dried roots of this plant. ORIG C14: via OF from Med. L *valeriana* (*herba*) (herb) of *Valerius,* unexplained L personal name

Valerian ★ (və'lɛərɪən) *n* Latin name *Publius Licinius Valerianus.* died 260 A.D., Roman emperor (253–260): renewed persecution of the Christians; defeated by the Persians.

valeric (və'lɛrɪk, -'lɪərɪk) *adj* of, relating to, or derived from valerian.

valeric acid *n* another name for **pentanoic acid.**

Valéry ★ (*French* valeri) *n* **Paul** (pɔl). 1871–1945, French poet and essayist; author of *La Jeune Parque* (1917) and *Album de vers anciens 1890–1900* (1920).

valet ('vælɪt, 'væleɪ) *n* **1** a manservant who acts as personal attendant to his employer, looking after his clothing, serving his meals, etc. **2** a manservant who attends to the requirements of patrons in a hotel, etc.; steward. ◆ *vb* **valets, valeting, valeted. 3** to act as a valet for (a person). **4** (*tr*) to clean the bodywork and interior of (a car) as a professional service. ORIG C16: from OF *vaslet* page, from Med. L *vassus* servant

valeta *or* **veleta** (və'liːtə) *n* a ballroom dance in triple time. ORIG from Sp.: weather vane

valet de chambre *French.* (valɛ də ʃɑ̃brə) *n, pl* ***valets de chambre*** (valɛ də ʃɑ̃brə). the full French term for **valet** (sense 1).

valet parking *n* a system at hotels, airports, etc., in which patrons' cars are parked by a steward.

Valetta ★ (və'lɛtə) *n* a variant spelling of **Valletta.**

valetudinarian (͵vælɪ͵tjuːdɪ'nɛərɪən) *or* **valetudinary** (͵vælɪ'tjuːdɪnərɪ) *n, pl* **valetudinarians** *or* **valetudinaries. 1** a person who is chronically sick. **2** a hypochondriac. ◆ *adj* **3** relating to or resulting from poor health. **4** being a valetudinarian. ORIG C18: from L *valētūdō* state of health, from *valēre* to be well
▸ ͵**vale**͵**tudi'narianism** *n*

valgus ('vælgəs) *adj Pathol.* twisted away from the midline of the body. ORIG C19: from L: bow-legged

Valhalla (væl'hælə), **Walhalla, Valhall** (væl'hæl, 'vælhæl), *or* **Walhall** ★ *n Norse myth.* the great hall of Odin where warriors who die as heroes in battle dwell eternally. ORIG C18: from ON, from *valr* slain warriors + *höll* HALL

valiant ('væljənt) *adj* **1** courageous or intrepid. **2** marked by bravery or courage: *a valiant deed.* ORIG C14: from OF, from *valoir* to be of value, from L *valēre* to be strong
▸ '**valiantly** *adv*

valid ('vælɪd) *adj* **1** having some foundation; based on truth. **2** legally acceptable: *a valid licence.* **3a** having legal force. **3b** having legal authority. **4** having some force or cogency: *a valid point in a debate.* **5** *Logic.* (of an inference or argument) having premises and a conclusion so related that if the premises are true, the conclusion must be true. ORIG C16: from L *validus* robust, from *valēre* to be strong
▸ **validity** (və'lɪdɪtɪ) *n* ▸ '**validly** *adv*

validate ('vælɪ͵deɪt) *vb* **validates, validating, validated.** (*tr*) **1** to confirm or corroborate. **2** to give legal force or official confirmation to.
▸ ͵**vali'dation** *n*

valine ('veɪliːn) *n* an essential amino acid: a component of proteins. ORIG C19: from VAL(ERIC ACID) + -INE[2]

valise (və'liːz) *n* a small overnight travelling case. ORIG C17: via F from It. *valigia,* from ?

Valium ('vælɪəm) *n Trademark.* a preparation of the drug diazepam used as a tranquillizer.

Valkyrie, Walkyrie (væl'kɪərɪ, 'vælkɪərɪ), *or* **Valkyr** ★ ('vælkɪə) *n Norse myth.* any of the beautiful maidens who serve Odin and ride over battlefields to claim the dead heroes and take them to Valhalla. ORIG C18: from ON *Valkyrja,* from *valr* slain warriors + *köri* to CHOOSE
▸ **Val'kyrian** *adj*

Valladolid ★ (*Spanish* baʎaðo'lið) *n* **1** a city in NW Spain: residence of the Spanish court in the 16th century; university (1346). Pop.: 328 365 (1991). **2** the former name (until 1828) of **Morelia.**

vallation (və'leɪʃən) *n* **1** the act or process of building fortifications. **2** a wall or rampart. ORIG C17: from LL *vallātiō,* from L *vallum* rampart

vallecula (və'lɛkjʊlə) *n, pl* **valleculae** (-͵liː). **1** *Anat.* any of various natural depressions or crevices. **2** *Bot.* a groove or furrow. ORIG C19: from LL: little valley, from L *vallis* valley

Valle d'Aosta ★ (*Italian* 'valle da'ɔsta) *n* an autonomous region of NW Italy: under many different rulers until passing to the house of Savoy in the 11th century; established as an autonomous region in 1944. Capital: Aosta. Pop.: 118 723 (1996 est.). Area: 3263 sq. km (1260 sq. miles).

Valletta *or* **Valetta** ★ (və'lɛtə) *n* the capital of Malta, on the NE coast: founded by the Knights Hospitallers, after the victory over the Turks in 1565; became a major naval base after Malta's annexation by Britain (1814). Pop.: 9128 (1996 est.).

valley ('vælɪ) *n* **1** a long depression in the land surface, usually containing a river, formed by erosion or by movements in the earth's crust. **2** the broad area drained by a single river system: *the Thames valley.* **3** any elongated depression resembling a valley. ORIG C13: from OF *valee,* from L *vallis*

Valley Forge ★ *n* an area in SE Pennsylvania, northwest of Philadelphia: winter camp (1777–78) of Washington and the American Revolutionary Army.

Valley of Ten Thousand Smokes ★ *n* a volcanic region of SW Alaska, formed by the massive eruption of Mount Katmai in 1912; jets of steam issue from vents up to 45 m (150 ft) across.

Vallombrosa ★ (*Italian* vallom'broːsa) *n* a village and resort in central Italy, in Tuscany region: 11th-century Benedictine monastery.

vallum ('væləm) *n Archaeol.* a Roman rampart or earthwork.

Valois[1] ★ (*French* valwa) *n* a historic region and former duchy of N France.

Valois[2] ★ (*French* valwa) *n* a royal house of France, ruling from 1328 to 1589.

Valois[3] ★ ('vælwɑː) *n* Dame **Ninette de** (niː'nɛt də). original name *Edris Stannus*. 1898–2001, British ballet dancer and choreographer, born in Ireland: a founder of the Vic-Wells Ballet Company (1931), which under her direction became the Royal Ballet (1956).

Valona ★ (və'ləʊnə) *n* another name for **Vlorë**.

valonia (və'ləʊnɪə) *n* the acorn cups and unripe acorns of the Eurasian oak, used in tanning, dyeing, and making ink. ORIG C18: from It. *vallonia,* ult. from Gk *balanos* acorn

valorize *or* **valorise** ('vælə,raɪz) *vb* **valorizes, valorizing, valorized** *or* **valorises, valorising, valorised.** (*tr*) to fix an artificial price for (a commodity) by governmental action. ORIG C20: back formation from *valorization;* see VALOUR
▸ **,valori'zation** *or* **,valori'sation** *n*

valour *or US* **valor** ('vælə) *n* courage or bravery, esp. in battle. ORIG C15: from LL *valor,* from *valēre* to be strong
▸ **'valorous** *adj*

Valparaíso ★ (*Spanish* balpara'iso) *n* a port in central Chile, on a wide bay of the Pacific: the third largest city and chief port of Chile; two universities. Pop.: 282 168 (1995 est.).

valse *French.* (vals) *n* another word for **waltz**.

valuable ('væljʊəbᵊl) *adj* **1** having considerable monetary worth. **2** of considerable importance or quality: *valuable information.* **3** able to be valued. ◆ *n* **4** (*usually pl*) a valuable article of personal property, esp. jewellery.
▸ **'valuably** *adv*

valuate ('vælju,eɪt) *vb* **valuates, valuating, valuated.** *US.* another word for **value** (senses 10, 12) or **evaluate.**
▸ **'valu,ator** *n*

valuation (,vælju'eɪʃən) *n* **1** the act of valuing, esp. a formal assessment of the worth of property, jewellery, etc. **2** the price arrived at by the process of valuing: *I set a high valuation on technical ability.*
▸ **,valu'ational** *adj*

value ('væljuː) *n* **1** the desirability of a thing, often in respect of some property such as usefulness or exchangeability. **2** an amount, esp. a material or monetary one, considered to be a fair exchange in return for a thing: *the value of the picture is £10 000.* **3** satisfaction: *value for money.* **4** precise meaning or significance. **5** (*pl*) the moral principles or accepted standards of a person or group. **6** *Maths.* a particular magnitude, number, or amount: *the value of the variable was 7.* **7** *Music.* short for **time value. 8** (in painting, drawing, etc.) **8a** a gradation of tone from light to dark. **8b** the relation of one of these elements to another or to the whole picture. **9** *Phonetics.* the quality of the speech sound associated with a written character representing it: *"g" has the value* (dʒ) *in English "gem".* ◆ *vb* **values, valuing, valued.** (*tr*) **10** to assess or estimate the worth, merit, or desirability of. **11** to have a high regard for, esp. in respect of worth, usefulness, merit, etc. **12** (foll. by *at*) to fix the financial or material worth of (a unit of currency, work of art, etc.). ORIG C14: from OF, from *valoir,* from L *valēre* to be worth
▸ **'valued** *adj* ▸ **'valueless** *adj* ▸ **'valuer** *n*

value added *n* the difference between the total revenues of a firm, industry, etc., and its total purchases from other firms, industries, etc.

value-added tax *n* (in Britain) the full name for **VAT**.

valued policy *n* an insurance policy in which the amount payable in the event of a valid claim is agreed upon between the company and the policyholder when the policy is issued and is not related to the actual value of a loss.

value judgment *n* a subjective assessment based on one's own values or those of one's class.

Valuer General *n Austral.* a state official who values properties for rating purposes.

valuta (və'luːtə) *n Rare.* the value of one currency in terms of its exchange rate with another. ORIG C20: from It., lit.: VALUE

valvate ('vælveɪt) *adj* **1** furnished with a valve or valves. **2** *Bot.* **2a** taking place by means of valves: *valvate dehiscence.* **2b** (of petals) having the margins touching but not overlapping.

valve (vælv) *n* **1** any device that shuts off, starts, regulates, or controls the flow of a fluid. **2** *Anat.* a flaplike structure in a hollow organ, such as the heart, that controls the one-way passage of fluid through that organ. **3** Also called: **tube.** an evacuated electron tube containing a cathode, anode, and, usually, one or more additional control electrodes. When a positive potential is applied to the anode, it produces a one-way flow of current. **4** *Zool.* any of the separable pieces that make up the shell of a mollusc. **5** *Music.* a device on some brass instruments by which the effective length of the tube may be varied to enable a chromatic scale to be produced. **6** *Bot.* any of the several parts that make up a dry dehiscent fruit, esp. a capsule. ORIG C14: from L *valva* a folding door
▸ **'valveless** *adj* ▸ **'valve,like** *adj*

valve-in-head engine *n* the US name for **overhead-valve engine.**

valvular ('vælvjʊlə) *adj* **1** of, relating to, operated by, or having a valve or valves. **2** having the shape or function of a valve.

valvulitis (,vælvjʊ'laɪtɪs) *n* inflammation of a bodily valve, esp. a heart valve. ORIG C19: from NL *valvula* dim. of VALVE + -ITIS

vamoose (və'muːs) *vb* **vamooses, vamoosing, vamoosed.** (*intr*) *Sl., chiefly US.* to leave a place hurriedly; decamp. ORIG C19: from Sp. *vamos* let us go, from L *vādere* to go, walk rapidly

vamp[1] (væmp) *Inf.* ◆ *n* **1** a seductive woman who exploits men by use of her sexual charms. ◆ *vb* **2** to exploit (a man) in the fashion of a vamp. ORIG C20: short for VAMPIRE

vamp[2] (væmp) *n* **1** something patched up to make it look new. **2** the reworking of a story, etc. **3** an improvised accompaniment. **4** the front part of the upper of a shoe. ◆ *vb* **5** (*tr;* often foll. by *up*) to make a renovation of. **6** to improvise (an accompaniment) to (a tune). ORIG C13: from OF *avantpié* the front part of a shoe (hence, something patched), from *avant-* fore- + *pié* foot, from L *pēs*

vampire ('væmpaɪə) *n* **1** (in European folklore) a corpse that rises nightly from its grave to drink the blood of the living. **2** See **vampire bat. 3** a person who preys mercilessly upon others. ORIG C18: from F, from G, from Magyar
▸ **vampiric** (væm'pɪrɪk) *adj* ▸ **'vampirism** *n*

vampire bat *n* a bat of tropical regions of Central and South America, having sharp incisor and canine teeth and feeding on the blood of birds and mammals.

van[1] (væn) *n* **1** short for **caravan** (sense 1). **2** a motor vehicle for transporting goods, etc., by road. **3** *Brit.* a closed railway wagon in which the guard travels, for transporting goods, etc.

van[2] (væn) *n* short for **vanguard.**

van[3] (væn) *n Tennis, chiefly Brit.* short for **advantage** (sense 3).

van[4] (væn) *n* **1** any device for winnowing corn. **2** *Arch.* a wing. ORIG C17: var. of FAN[1]

Van ★ (vɑːn) *n* **1** a city in E Turkey, on Lake Van. Pop.: 194 600 (1994 est.). **2 Lake.** a salt lake in E Turkey, at an altitude of 1650 m (5400 ft): fed by melting snow and glaciers. Area: 3737 sq. km (1433 sq. miles).

vanadium (və'neɪdɪəm) *n* a toxic silvery-white metallic element used in steel alloys and as a catalyst. Symbol: V; atomic no.: 23; atomic wt.: 50.94. ORIG C19: NL, from ON *Vanadis,* epithet of the goddess Freya + -IUM

Van Allen ★ (væn 'ælən) *n* **James Alfred.** born 1914, US physicist, noted for his use of satellites to investigate cosmic radiation in the upper atmosphere.

Van Allen belt ★ *n* either of two regions of charged particles above the earth, the inner one extending from 2400 to 5600 kilometres above the earth and the outer one from 13 000 to 19 000 kilometres. ORIG C20: after its discoverer, J. A. VAN ALLEN

Vanbrugh ★ ('vænbrə) *n* Sir **John.** 1664–1726, English dramatist and baroque architect. His comedies include *The Relapse* (1697) and *The Provok'd Wife* (1697). As an architect, he is noted for Blenheim Palace.

Van Buren ★ (væn 'bjʊərən) *n* **Martin.** 1782–1862, US Democratic statesman; 8th president of the US (1837–41).

Vancouver[1] ★ (væn'ku:və) *n* **1** an island of SW Canada, off the SW coast of British Columbia: separated from the Canadian mainland by the Strait of Georgia and Queen Charlotte Sound, and from the US mainland by Juan de Fuca Strait; the largest island off the W coast of North America. Chief town: Victoria. Pop.: 461 573 (1981). Area: 32 137 sq. km (12 408 sq. miles). **2** a city in SW Canada, in SW British Columbia: Canada's chief Pacific port, named after Captain George Vancouver: university (1908). Pop. (metropolitan area): 1 826 800 (1995). **3 Mount.** a mountain on the border between Canada and Alaska, in the St Elias Mountains. Height: 4785 m (15 700 ft).

Vancouver[2] ★ (væn'ku:və) *n* Captain **George.** 1757–98, British navigator, noted for his exploration of the Pacific coast of North America (1792–94).

V and A (in Britain) *abbrev. for* Victoria and Albert Museum.

vandal ('vænd^əl) *n* a person who deliberately causes damage to personal or public property. ORIG C17: from VANDAL, from L *Vandallus,* of Gmc origin

Vandal ('vændəl) *n* a member of a Germanic people that raided Roman provinces in the 3rd and 4th centuries A.D. before devastating Gaul, conquering Spain and N Africa, and sacking Rome.
▸ **Vandalic** (væn'dælɪk) *adj*

vandalism ('vændəˌlɪzəm) *n* the deliberate destruction caused by a vandal or an instance of such destruction.
▸ **ˌvandal'istic** *adj*

vandalize *or* **vandalise** ('vændəˌlaɪz) *vb* **vandalizes, vandalizing, vandalized** *or* **vandalises, vandalising, vandalised.** (*tr*) to destroy or damage (something) by an act of vandalism.

Van de Graaff generator ('væn də ˌgrɑ:f) *n* a device for producing high electrostatic potentials, consisting of a hollow metal sphere on which a charge is accumulated from a continuous moving belt of insulating material: used in particle accelerators. ORIG C20: after R. J. *Van de Graaff* (1901–67), US physicist

Vanderbilt ★ ('vændəbɪlt) *n* **Cornelius,** known as *Commodore Vanderbilt.* 1794–1877, US steamship and railway magnate and philanthropist.

Van der Post ★ (ˌvæn də 'pɒst) *n* Sir **Laurens.** 1906–96, South African novelist and travel writer.

van der Waals ★ (*Dutch* vɑn dər 'wa:ls) *n* **Johannes Diderik** (jo:'hɑnəs 'di:dərik). 1837–1923, Dutch physicist, noted for his equations of state: Nobel prize for physics in 1910.

van der Weyden ★ (*Dutch* vɑn dər 'wɛjdə) *n* **Rogier** (ro:'xi:r). ?1400–64, Flemish painter, esp. of religious works and portraits.

Van Diemen Gulf ★ (væn 'di:mən) *n* an inlet of the Timor Sea in N Australia, in the Northern Territory.

Van Diemen's Land ★ (væn 'di:mənz) *n* the former name (1642–1855) of **Tasmania.**
▸ **ˌVande'monian** *n, adj*

Van Dyck *or* **Vandyke** ★ (væn 'daɪk) *n* Sir **Anthony.** 1599–1641, Flemish painter; court painter to Charles I of England (1632–41).

Vandyke beard ('vændaɪk) *n* a short pointed beard. Often shortened to **Vandyke.**

Vandyke collar *or* **cape** *n* a large white collar with several very deep points. Often shortened to **Vandyke.**

vane (veɪn) *n* **1** Also called: **weather vane.** a flat plate or blade of metal mounted on a vertical axis in an exposed position to indicate wind direction. **2** any one of the flat blades or sails forming part of the wheel of a windmill. **3** any flat or shaped plate used to direct fluid flow, esp. in a turbine, etc. **4** a fin or plate fitted to a projectile or missile to provide stabilization or guidance. **5** *Ornithol.* the flat part of a feather. **6** *Surveying.* **6a** a sight on a quadrant or compass. **6b** the movable marker on a levelling staff. ORIG OE *fana*
▸ **vaned** *adj*

Vänern ★ (*Swedish* 'vɛ:nərn) *n* **Lake.** a lake in SW Sweden: the largest lake in Sweden and W Europe; drains into the Kattegat. Area: 5585 sq. km (2156 sq. miles).

van Eyck ★ (væn 'aɪk; *Dutch* vɑn 'ɛjk) *n* **Jan** (jɑn). died 1441, Flemish painter; founder of the Flemish school of painting. His most famous work is the altarpiece *The Adoration of the Lamb,* in Ghent, in which he may have been assisted by his brother **Hubert** ('hy:bərt), died ?1426.

Van Gogh ★ (væn 'gɒx; *Dutch* vɑn 'xɔx) *n* **Vincent** (vɪn'sɛnt). 1853–90, Dutch postimpressionist painter, noted for his landscapes and portraits.

vanguard ('vænˌgɑ:d) *n* **1** the leading division or units of a military force. **2** the leading position in any movement or field, or the people who occupy such a position. ORIG C15: from OF *avant-garde,* from *avant-* fore- + *garde* GUARD

vanilla (və'nɪlə) *n* **1** any of a genus of tropical climbing orchids having spikes of large fragrant flowers and long fleshy pods containing the seeds (beans). **2** the pod or bean of certain of these plants, used to flavour food, etc. **3** a flavouring extract prepared from vanilla beans and used in cooking. ◆ *adj* **4** flavoured with or as with vanilla: *vanilla ice cream.* **5** *Sl.* ordinary or conventional: *a vanilla kind of guy.* ORIG C17: from NL, from Sp. *vainilla* pod, from *vaina,* from L *vāgīna* sheath
▸ **va'nillic** *adj*

vanillin ('vænɪlɪn, və'nɪlɪn) *n* a white crystalline aldehyde found in vanilla and many natural balsams and resins. It is a by-product of paper manufacture and is used as a flavouring and in perfumes.

Vanir ★ ('vɑ:nɪə) *pl n Norse myth.* a race of ancient gods often locked in struggle with the Aesir. The most notable of them are Njord and his children Frey and Freya. ORIG from ON *Vanr,* a fertility god

vanish ('vænɪʃ) *vb* (*intr*) **1** to disappear, esp. suddenly or mysteriously. **2** to cease to exist. **3** *Maths.* to become zero. ORIG C14 *vanissen,* from OF *esvanir,* from L *ēvānēscere* to evaporate, from *ē-* EX-[1] + *vānēscere,* from *vānus* empty
▸ **'vanisher** *n*

vanishing cream *n* a cosmetic cream that is colourless once applied, used as a foundation for powder or as a cleansing cream.

vanishing point *n* **1** the point to which parallel lines appear to converge in the rendering of perspective, usually on the horizon. **2** a point at which something disappears.

vanity ('vænɪtɪ) *n, pl* **vanities. 1** the state or quality of being vain. **2** ostentation occasioned by ambition or pride. **3** an instance of being vain or something about which one is vain. **4** the state or quality of being valueless or futile. ORIG C13: from OF, from L *vānitās* emptiness, from *vānus* empty

vanity bag, case, *or* **box** *n* a woman's small bag or hand case used to carry cosmetics, etc.

vanity unit *n* a hand basin built into a wooden Formica-covered or tiled top, usually with a built-in cupboard below it. Also called (trademark): **Vanitory unit.**

vanquish ('væŋkwɪʃ) *vb* (*tr*) **1** to defeat or overcome in a battle, contest, etc. **2** to defeat in argument or debate. **3** to conquer (an emotion). ORIG C14 *vanquisshen,* from OF *venquis,* from *veintre* to overcome, from L *vincere*
▸ **'vanquishable** *adj* ▸ **'vanquisher** *n*

vantage ('vɑ:ntɪdʒ) *n* **1** a state, position, or opportunity affording superiority or advantage. **2** superiority or benefit accruing from such a position, etc. **3** *Tennis.* short for **advantage** (sense 3). ORIG C13: from OF *avantage* ADVANTAGE

vantage point *n* a position or place that allows one an overall view of a scene or situation.

van't Hoff ★ (*Dutch* vɑnt 'hɔf) *n* **Jacobus Hendricus** (ja:'ko:bys hɛn'dri:kys). 1852–1911, Dutch physical chemist: founded stereochemistry with his theory of the asymmetric carbon atom: Nobel prize for chemistry 1901.

Vanua Levu ★ (vɑːˈnuːə ˈlɛvuː) *n* the second largest island of Fiji: mountainous. Area: 5535 sq. km (2137 sq. miles).

Vanuatu ★ (ˈvænuːˌætuː) *n* a republic comprising a group of islands in the W Pacific, W of Fiji: a condominium under Anglo-French joint rule from 1906; attained partial autonomy in 1978 and full independence in 1980; a member of the Commonwealth. Its economy is based chiefly on copra. Official languages: Bislama; French; English. Religion: Christian majority. Currency: vatu. Capital: Vila (on Efate). Pop.: 187 000 (1999 est.). Area: about 14 760 sq. km (5700 sq. miles). Official name: **Republic of Vanuatu.** Former name (until 1980): **New Hebrides.**

vanward (ˈvænwəd) *adj, adv* in or towards the front.

vapid (ˈvæpɪd) *adj* **1** bereft of strength, sharpness, flavour, etc. **2** boring or dull. ORIG C17: from L *vapidus*
▸ **vaˈpidity** *n* ▸ **ˈvapidly** *adv*

vapor (ˈveɪpə) *n* the US spelling of **vapour.**

vaporescence (ˌveɪpəˈrɛsəns) *n* the production or formation of vapour.
▸ **ˌvaporˈescent** *adj*

vaporetto (ˌveɪpəˈrɛtəʊ) *n, pl* **vaporetti** (-tɪ) *or* **vaporettos.** a steam-powered passenger boat, as used on the canals in Venice. ORIG It., from *vapore* a steamboat

vaporific (ˌveɪpəˈrɪfɪk) *adj* **1** producing, causing, or tending to produce vapour. **2** of, concerned with, or having the nature of vapour. **3** tending to become vapour; volatile. ORIG C18: from NL *vaporificus,* from L *vapor* steam + *facere* to make

vaporimeter (ˌveɪpəˈrɪmɪtə) *n* an instrument for measuring vapour pressure, used to determine the volatility of oils.

vaporize *or* **vaporise** (ˈveɪpəˌraɪz) *vb* **vaporizes, vaporizing, vaporized** *or* **vaporises, vaporising, vaporised. 1** to change or cause to change into vapour or into the gaseous state. **2** to evaporate or disappear or cause to evaporate or disappear, esp. suddenly. **3** to destroy or be destroyed by turning into a gas as a result of the extreme heat generated by a nuclear explosion.
▸ **ˌvaporiˈzation** *or* **ˌvaporiˈsation** *n*

vaporizer *or* **vaporiser** (ˈveɪpəˌraɪzə) *n* **1** a substance that vaporizes or a device that causes vaporization. **2** *Med.* a device that produces steam or atomizes medication for inhalation.

vaporous (ˈveɪpərəs) *adj* **1** resembling or full of vapour. **2** lacking permanence or substance. **3** given to foolish imaginings.
▸ **vaporosity** (ˌveɪpəˈrɒsɪtɪ) *n* ▸ **ˈvaporously** *adv*

vapour *or US* **vapor** (ˈveɪpə) *n* **1** particles of moisture or other substance suspended in air and visible as clouds, smoke, etc. **2** a gaseous substance at a temperature below its critical temperature. **3** a substance that is in a gaseous state at a temperature below its boiling point. **4 the vapours.** *Arch.* a depressed mental condition believed originally to be the result of vaporous exhalations from the stomach. ◆ *vb* **5** to evaporate or cause to evaporate. **6** (*intr*) to make vain empty boasts. ORIG C14: from L *vapor*
▸ **ˈvapourer** *or US* **ˈvaporer** *n* ▸ **ˈvapourish** *or US* **ˈvaporish** *adj* ▸ **ˈvapour-ˌlike** *or US* **ˈvapor-ˌlike** *adj* ▸ **ˈvapoury** *or US* **ˈvapory** *adj*

vapour density *n* the ratio of the density of a gas or vapour to that of hydrogen at the same temperature and pressure.

vapour lock *n* a stoppage in a pipe carrying a liquid caused by a bubble of gas, esp. in the pipe feeding the carburettor of an internal-combustion engine.

vapour pressure *n Physics.* the pressure exerted by a vapour in equilibrium with its solid or liquid phase at a particular temperature.

vapour trail *n* a visible trail left by an aircraft flying at high altitude or through supercold air caused by the deposition of water vapour in the engine exhaust as minute ice crystals.

Var ★ (*French* var) *n* **1** a department of SE France, in Provence-Alpes-Côte d'Azur region. Capital: Toulon. Pop.: 866 747 (1994 est.). Area: 6023 sq. km (2349 sq. miles). **2** a river in SE France, flowing southeast and south to the Mediterranean near Nice. Length: about 130 km (80 miles).

var. *abbrev. for:* **1** variable. **2** variant. **3** variation. **4** variety. **5** various.

varactor (ˈvɛəˌræktə) *n* a semiconductor diode that acts as a voltage-dependent capacitor, being operated with a reverse bias. ORIG C20: prob. a blend of *variable reactor*

Varah ★ (ˈvɑːrə) *n* (**Edward**) **Chad.** born 1911, British Anglican clergyman, who founded (1953) the Samaritans counselling service.

Varanasi ★ (vəˈrɑːnəsɪ) *n* a city in NE India, in SE Uttar Pradesh on the River Ganges: probably dates from the 13th century B.C.; an early centre of Aryan philosophy and religion; a place of pilgrimage for Hindus, Jains, Sikhs, and Buddhists, with many ghats along the Ganges; seat of the Banaras Hindu University (1916), India's leading university, and the Sanskrit University (1957). Pop.: 929 270 (1991). Former names: **Benares, Banaras.**

Vardar ★ (*Serbo-Croat* ˈvardar) *n* a river in S Europe, rising in W Macedonia and flowing northeast, then south past Skopje into Greece, where it enters the Aegean at Thessaloníki. Length: about 320 km (200 miles).

varec (ˈværɛk) *n* **1** another name for **kelp. 2** the ash obtained from kelp. ORIG C17: from F, from ON *wrek* (unattested); see WRECK

Varese ★ (*Italian* vaˈreːse) *n* a historic city in N Italy, in Lombardy near Lake Varese. Pop.: 88 018 (1990).

Varèse ★ (vəˈrɛz) *n* **Edgar**(**d**). 1883–1965, US composer, born in France. His works include *Ionisation* (1931) and *Poème électronique* (1958).

Vargas ★ (*Portuguese* ˈvargas) *n* **Getúlio Dornelles** (ʒeˈtulju durˈnɛləs). 1883–1954, Brazilian statesman; president (1930–45; 1951–54).

Vargas Llosa ★ (*Spanish* ˈbarɣas ˈʎosa) *n* (**Jorge**) **Mario** (**Pedro**) (ˈmaːrjo). born 1936, Peruvian novelist. His novels include *The City and the Dogs* (1963) and *The Notebooks of Don Rigoberto* (1998).

variable (ˈvɛərɪəbᵊl) *adj* **1** liable to or capable of change: *variable weather.* **2** (of behaviour, emotions, etc.) lacking constancy. **3** *Maths.* having a range of possible values. **4** (of a species, etc.) liable to deviate from the established type. **5** (of a wind) varying in direction and intensity. **6** (of an electrical component or device) designed so that a characteristic property, such as resistance, can be varied. ◆ *n* **7** something that is subject to variation. **8** *Maths.* **8a** an expression that can be assigned any of a set of values. **8b** a symbol, esp. *x, y,* or *z,* representing an unspecified member of a class of objects, numbers, etc. **9** *Logic.* a symbol, esp. *x, y,* or *z,* representing any member of a class of entities. **10** *Computing.* a named unit of storage that can be changed to any of a set of specified values during execution of a program. **11** *Astron.* See **variable star. 12** a variable wind. **13** (*pl*) a region where variable winds occur. ORIG C14: from L *variābilis* changeable, from *variāre* to diversify
▸ **ˌvariaˈbility** *or* **ˈvariableness** *n* ▸ **ˈvariably** *adv*

variable cost *n* a cost that varies directly with output.

variable-geometry *or* **variable-sweep** *adj* denoting an aircraft in which the wings are hinged to give the variable aspect ratio colloquially known as a **swing-wing.**

variable star *n* any star that varies considerably in brightness, either irregularly or in regular periods. **Intrinsic variables,** in which the variation is a result of internal changes, include novae and pulsating stars.

variance (ˈvɛərɪəns) *n* **1** the act of varying or the quality, state, or degree of being divergent. **2** an instance of diverging; dissension. **3 at variance. 3a** (often foll. by *with*) (of facts, etc.) not in accord. **3b** (of persons) in a state of dissension. **4** *Statistics.* a measure of dispersion; the square of the standard deviations. **5** a difference or discrepancy between two steps in a legal proceeding, esp. between a statement and the evidence given to support it. **6** *Chem.* the number of degrees of freedom of a system, used in the phase rule.

variant (ˈvɛərɪənt) *adj* **1** liable to or displaying variation. **2** differing from a standard or type: *a variant spelling.* ◆ *n* **3** something that differs from a standard or type. **4** *Statis-*

tics. another word for **variate.** ORIG C14: via OF from L, from *variāre* to diversify, from *varius* VARIOUS

variant CJD *n* short for **variant Creutzfeldt-Jakob disease**: another name for **new-variant Creutzfeldt-Jakob disease**.

variate (ˈvɛərɪɪt) *n Statistics.* a random variable or a numerical value taken by it. ORIG C16: from L *variāre* to VARY

variation (ˌvɛərɪˈeɪʃən) *n* **1** the act, process, condition, or result of changing or varying. **2** an instance of varying or the amount, rate, or degree of such change. **3** something that differs from a standard or convention. **4** *Music.* a repetition of a musical theme in which the rhythm, harmony, or melody is altered or embellished. **5** *Biol.* a marked deviation from the typical form or function. **6** *Astron.* any deviation from the mean motion or orbit of a planet, satellite, etc. **7** another word for **magnetic declination. 8** *Ballet.* a solo dance.
▸ ˌ**variˈational** *adj*

varicella (ˌværɪˈsɛlə) *n* the technical name for **chickenpox.** ORIG C18: NL, irregular dim. of VARIOLA
▸ ˌ**variˈcellar** *adj*

varices (ˈværɪˌsiːz) *n* the plural of **varix.**

varico- *or before a vowel* **varic-** *combining form.* indicating a varix or varicose veins: *varicotomy.* ORIG from L *varix, varic-* distended vein

varicoloured *or US* **varicolored** (ˈvɛərɪˌkʌləd) *adj* having many colours.

varicose (ˈværɪˌkəʊs) *adj* of or resulting from varicose veins: *a varicose ulcer.* ORIG C18: from L *varicōsus,* from VARIX

varicose veins *pl n* a condition in which the superficial veins, esp. of the legs, become knotted and swollen.

varicosis (ˌværɪˈkəʊsɪs) *n Pathol.* any condition characterized by distension of the veins. ORIG C18: from NL, from L: VARIX

varicosity (ˌværɪˈkɒsɪtɪ) *n, pl* **varicosities.** *Pathol.* **1** the state, condition, or quality of being varicose. **2** an abnormally distended vein.

varicotomy (ˌværɪˈkɒtəmɪ) *n, pl* **varicotomies.** surgical excision of a varicose vein.

varied (ˈvɛərɪd) *adj* **1** displaying or characterized by variety; diverse. **2** modified or altered: *the amount may be varied.* **3** varicoloured; variegated.
▸ ˈ**variedly** *adv*

variegate (ˈvɛərɪˌgeɪt) *vb* **variegates, variegating, variegated.** (*tr*) to alter the appearance of, esp. by adding different colours. ORIG C17: from LL, from L *varius* diverse, VARIOUS + *agere* to make
▸ ˌ**varieˈgation** *n*

variegated (ˈvɛərɪˌgeɪtɪd) *adj* **1** displaying differently coloured spots., streaks, etc. **2** (of foliage) having pale patches.

varietal (vəˈraɪɪtᵊl) *adj* **1** of, characteristic of, designating, or forming a variety, esp. a biological variety. ◆ *n* **2** a wine labelled with the name of the grape from which it is pressed.
▸ **vaˈrietally** *adv*

variety (vəˈraɪɪtɪ) *n, pl* **varieties. 1** the quality or condition of being diversified or various. **2** a collection of unlike things, esp. of the same general group. **3** a different form or kind within a general category: *varieties of behaviour.* **4a** *Taxonomy.* a race whose distinct characters do not justify classification as a separate species. **4b** *Horticulture, stockbreeding.* a strain of animal or plant produced by artificial breeding. **5a** entertainment consisting of a series of short unrelated acts, such as comedy turns, songs, etc. **5b** (*as modifier*): *a variety show.* ORIG C16: from L *varietās,* from VARIOUS

varifocal (ˌvɛərɪˈfəʊkᵊl) *adj* **1** *Optics.* having a focus that can vary. **2** relating to a lens that is gradated to permit any length of vision between near and distant.

varifocals (ˌvɛərɪˈfəʊkᵊlz) *pl n* a pair of spectacles with varifocal lenses.

variform (ˈvɛərɪˌfɔːm) *adj* varying in form or shape.
▸ ˈ**variˌformly** *adv*

variola (vəˈraɪələ) *n* the technical name for **smallpox.** ORIG C18: from Med. L: disease marked by little spots, from L *varius* spotted
▸ **vaˈriolar** *adj*

variole (ˈvɛərɪˌəʊl) *n* any of the rounded masses that make up the rock variolite. ORIG C19: from F, from Med. L; see VARIOLA

variolite (ˈvɛərɪəˌlaɪt) *n* any basic igneous rock containing rounded bodies (varioles). ORIG C18: from VARIOLA, referring to the pockmarked appearance of the rock
▸ **varioliˈtic** (ˌvɛərɪəˈlɪtɪk) *adj*

variometer (ˌvɛərɪˈɒmɪtə) *n* **1** an instrument for measuring variations in a magnetic field. **2** *Electronics.* a variable inductor consisting of a movable coil mounted inside and connected in series with a fixed coil.

variorum (ˌvɛərɪˈɔːrəm) *adj* **1** containing notes by various scholars or various versions of the text. ◆ *n* **2** an edition or text of this kind. ORIG C18: from L *ēditiō cum notīs variōrum* edition with the notes of various commentators

various (ˈvɛərɪəs) *determiner* **1** several different: *he is an authority on various subjects.* ◆ *adj* **2** of different kinds, though often within the same general category: *his disguises are many and various.* **3** (*prenominal*) relating to a collection of separate persons or things: *the various members of the club.* **4** displaying variety; many-sided: *his various achievements.* ORIG C16: from L *varius* changing
▸ ˈ**variously** *adv* ▸ ˈ**variousness** *n*

> **USAGE NOTE** The use of *different* after *various,* which seems to be most common in speech, is unnecessary and should be avoided in serious writing: *the disease exists in various forms* (not *in various different forms*).

varistor (vəˈrɪstə) *n* a two-electrode semiconductor device having a voltage-dependent nonlinear resistance. ORIG C20: a blend of *variable resistor*

Varityper (ˈvɛərɪˌtaɪpə) *n Trademark.* a justifying typewriter used to produce copy in various type styles.

varix (ˈvɛərɪks) *n, pl* **varices.** *Pathol.* **a** a tortuous dilated vein. **b** a similar condition affecting an artery or lymphatic vessel. ORIG C15: from L

varlet (ˈvɑːlɪt) *n Arch.* **1** a menial servant. **2** a knight's page. **3** a rascal. ORIG C15: from OF, var. of *vallet* VALET
▸ ˈ**varletry** *n*

varmint (ˈvɑːmɪnt) *n Inf.* an irritating or obnoxious person or animal. ORIG C16: dialect var. of *varmin* VERMIN

varna (ˈvɑːnə) *n* any of the four Hindu castes; Brahman, Kshatriya, Vaisya, or Sudra. ORIG from Sansk.: class

Varna ★ (*Bulgarian* ˈvarna) *n* a port in NE Bulgaria, on the Black Sea: founded by Greeks in the 6th century B.C.; under the Ottoman Turks (1391–1878). Pop.: 301 421 (1996 est.). Former name (1949–56): **Stalin.**

varnish (ˈvɑːnɪʃ) *n* **1** a preparation consisting of a solvent, a drying oil, and usually resin, rubber, etc., for application to a surface where it yields a hard glossy, usually transparent, coating. **2** a similar preparation consisting of a substance, such as shellac, dissolved in a volatile solvent, such as alcohol. It hardens to a film on evaporation of the solvent. **3** the sap of certain trees used to produce such a coating. **4** a smooth surface, coated with or as with varnish. **5** an artificial, superficial, or deceptively pleasing manner, covering, etc. **6** *Chiefly Brit.* another word for **nail polish.** ◆ *vb* (*tr*) **7** to cover with varnish. **8** to give a smooth surface to, as if by painting with varnish. **9** to impart a more attractive appearance to. ORIG C14: from OF, from Med. L *veronix* sandarac, resin, from Med. Gk *berenikē,* ?from Gk *Berenikē,* city in Cyrenaica, Libya where varnishes were used
▸ ˈ**varnisher** *n*

varnish tree *n* any of various trees, such as the lacquer tree, yielding substances used to make varnish or lacquer.

Varro ★ (ˈværəʊ) *n* **Marcus Terentius** (ˈmɑːkəs təˈrɛntɪəs). 116–27 B.C., Roman scholar and satirist.

varsity (ˈvɑːsɪtɪ) *n, pl* **varsities.** *Brit., S. African, & NZ inf.* short for **university.**

Varuna ★ (ˈværʊnə, ˈvʌ-) *n Hinduism.* the ancient sky god, later the god of the waters and rain-giver. In earlier traditions he was also the all-seeing divine judge.

varus (ˈvɛərəs) *adj Pathol.* turned inwards towards the midline of the body. ORIG C19: from L: crooked, bent

varve (vɑːv) *n Geol.* a band of sediment deposited in glacial lakes, consisting of a light layer and a dark layer deposited at different seasons. ORIG C20: from Swedish *varv* layer, from *varva,* from ON *hverfa* to turn

vary (ˈvɛərɪ) *vb* **varies, varying, varied. 1** to undergo or cause to undergo change or modification in appearance, character, form, etc. **2** to be different or cause to be different; be subject to change. **3** (*tr*) to give variety to. **4** (*intr;* foll. by *from*) to differ, as from a convention, standard, etc. **5** (*intr*) to change in accordance with another variable: *her mood varies with the weather.* ORIG C14: from L, from *varius* VARIOUS
▸ **ˈvarying** *adj*

vas (væs) *n, pl* **vasa** (ˈveɪsə). *Anat., zool.* a vessel or tube that carries a fluid. ORIG C17: from L: vessel

Vasari ★ (vəˈsɑːrɪ; *Italian* vaˈzaːri) *n* **Giorgio** (ˈdʒordʒo). 1511–74, Italian architect, painter, and art historian, noted for his *Lives of the Most Excellent Italian Architects, Painters, and Sculptors* (1550; 1568).

Vasco da Gama ★ (ˈvæskəʊ də ˈgɑːmə) *n* See (Vasco da) **Gama.**

vascular (ˈvæskjʊlə) *adj Biol., anat.* of, relating to, or having vessels that conduct and circulate liquids: *a vascular bundle.* ORIG C17: from NL *vāsculāris,* from L *vāsculum,* dim. of *vās* vessel
▸ **vascularity** (ˌvæskjʊˈlærɪtɪ) *n* ▸ **ˈvascularly** *adv*

vascular bundle *n* a longitudinal strand of vascular tissue in the stems and leaves of higher plants.

vascular tissue *n* tissue of plants occurring as a continuous system throughout the plant: it conducts water, mineral salts, and synthesized food, and provides mechanical support. Also called: **conducting tissue.**

vas deferens (ˈvæs ˈdɛfəˌrɛnz) *n, pl* **vasa deferentia** (ˈveɪsə ˌdɛfəˈrɛnʃɪə). *Anat.* the duct that conveys spermatozoa from the epididymis to the urethra. ORIG C16: from NL, from L *vās* vessel + *deferēns,* present participle of *deferre* to bear away

vase (vɑːz) *n* a vessel used as an ornament or for holding cut flowers. ORIG C17: via F from L *vās* vessel

vasectomy (væˈsɛktəmɪ) *n, pl* **vasectomies.** surgical removal of all or part of the vas deferens, esp. as a method of contraception.

Vaseline (ˈvæsɪˌliːn) *n* a trademark for **petrolatum.**

Vashti ★ (ˈvæʃtaɪ) *n Old Testament.* the wife of the Persian king Ahasuerus: deposed for refusing to display her beauty before his guests (Esther 1–2). Douay spelling: **Vasthi.**

vaso- *or before a vowel* **vas-** *combining form.* **1** indicating a blood vessel: *vasodilator.* **2** indicating the vas deferens: *vasectomy.* ORIG from L *vās* vessel

vasoactive (ˌveɪzəʊˈæktɪv) *adj* affecting the diameter of blood vessels: *vasoactive peptides.*

vasoconstrictor (ˌveɪzəʊkənˈstrɪktə) *n* a drug, agent, or nerve that causes narrowing of the walls of blood vessels.

vasodilator (ˌveɪzəʊdaɪˈleɪtə) *n* a drug, agent, or nerve that can cause dilation of the walls of blood vessels.

vasoinhibitor (ˌveɪzəʊɪnˈhɪbɪtə) *n* any of a group of drugs that reduce or inhibit the action of the vasomotor nerves.

vasomotor (ˌveɪzəʊˈməʊtə) *adj* (of a drug, nerve, etc.) relating to or affecting the diameter of blood vessels.

vasopressin (ˌveɪzəʊˈprɛsɪn) *n* a hormone secreted by the pituitary gland. It increases the reabsorption of water by the kidney tubules and increases blood pressure by constricting the arteries. Also called: **antidiuretic hormone.** ORIG from *Vasopressin,* a trademark

vasopressor (ˈveɪzəʊˌprɛsə) *Med.* ◆ *adj* **1** causing an increase in blood pressure by constricting the arteries. ◆ *n* **2** a substance that has such an effect.

vassal (ˈvæsᵊl) *n* **1** (in feudal society) a man who entered into a relationship with a lord to whom he paid homage and fealty in return for protection and often a fief. **2a** a person, nation, etc., in a subordinate or dependent position relative to another. **2b** (*as modifier*): *vassal status.* ◆ *adj* **3** of or relating to a vassal. ORIG C14: via OF from Med. L *vassallus,* from *vassus* servant, of Celtic origin
▸ **ˈvassalage** *n*

vast (vɑːst) *adj* **1** unusually large in size, degree, or number. **2** (*prenominal*) (intensifier): *in vast haste.* ◆ *n* **3 the vast.** *Chiefly poetic.* immense or boundless space. ORIG C16: from L *vastus* deserted
▸ **ˈvastly** *adv* ▸ **ˈvastness** *n*

Västerås ★ (*Swedish* vɛstərˈoːs) *n* a city in central Sweden, on Lake Mälar: Sweden's largest inland port; site of several national parliaments in the 16th century. Pop.: 123 728 (1996 est.).

vasty (ˈvɑːstɪ) *adj* **vastier, vastiest.** an archaic or poetic word for **vast.**

vat (væt) *n* **1** a large container for holding or storing liquids. **2** *Chem.* a preparation of reduced vat dye. ◆ *vb* **vats, vatting, vatted. 3** (*tr*) to place, store, or treat in a vat. ORIG OE *fæt*

VAT (*sometimes* væt) (in Britain) *abbrev. for* value-added tax: a tax levied on the difference between the cost of materials and the selling price of a commodity or service.

vat dye *n* a dye, such as indigo, that is applied by first reducing it to its base, which is soluble in alkali, and then regenerating the insoluble dye by oxidation in the fibres of the material.
▸ **ˈvat-ˌdyed** *adj*

vatic (ˈvætɪk) *adj Rare.* of, relating to, or characteristic of a prophet; oracular. ORIG C16: from L *vātēs* prophet

Vatican ★ (ˈvætɪkən) *n* **1a** the palace of the popes in Rome, which includes administrative offices and is attached to the basilica of St Peter's. **1b** (*as modifier*): *the Vatican Council.* **2a** the authority of the Pope and the papal curia. **2b** (*as modifier*): *a Vatican edict.* ORIG C16: from L *Vāticānus mons* Vatican hill, on the western bank of the Tiber, of Etruscan origin

Vatican City ★ *n* an independent state forming an enclave in Rome, with extraterritoriality over 12 churches and palaces in Rome: the only remaining Papal State; independence recognized by the Italian government in 1929; contains St Peter's Basilica and Square and the Vatican; the spiritual and administrative centre of the Roman Catholic Church. Languages: Italian and Latin. Currency: lira. Pop.: 1000 (1997 est.). Area: 44 hectares (109 acres). Italian name: **Città del Vaticano.** Also called: the **Holy See.**

Vättern ★ (*Swedish* ˈvɛtərn) *n* **Lake.** a lake in S central Sweden: the second largest lake in Sweden; linked to Lake Vänern by the Göta Canal; drains into the Baltic. Area: 1912 sq. km (738 sq. miles).

Vaucluse ★ (*French* voklyz) *n* a department of SE France, in Provence-Alpes-Côte d'Azur region. Capital: Avignon. Pop.: 487 338 (1994 est.). Area: 3578 sq. km (1395 sq. miles).

Vaud ★ (*French* vo) *n* a canton of SW Switzerland: mountainous in the southeast; chief Swiss producer of wine. Capital: Lausanne. Pop.: 602 099 (1995 est.). Area: 3209 sq. km (1240 sq. miles). German name: **Waadt.**

vaudeville (ˈvəʊdəvɪl, ˈvɔː-) *n* **1** *Chiefly US & Canad.* variety entertainment consisting of short acts such as acrobatic turns, song-and-dance routines, etc. Brit. name: **music hall. 2** a light or comic theatrical piece interspersed with songs and dances. ORIG C18: from F, from *vaudevire* satirical folk song, shortened from *chanson du vau de Vire* song of the valley of Vire, a district in Normandy
▸ **ˌvaudeˈvillian** *n, adj*

Vaudois (ˈvəʊdwɑː) *pl n, sing* **Vaudois. 1** another name for the **Waldenses. 2** the inhabitants of Vaud.

Vaughan ★ (vɔːn) *n* **1 Henry.** 1622–95, Welsh mystic poet, best known for his *Silex Scintillans* (1650; 1655). **2** Dame **Janet (Maria).** 1899–1993, British doctor: helped set up Britain's first National Blood Transfusion Service (1939): Principal of Somerville College, Oxford (1945–67). **3 Sarah (Lois).** 1924–90, US jazz vocalist and pianist.

Vaughan Williams ★ (ˈwɪljəmz) *n* **Ralph.** 1872–1958, British composer, who wrote operas, symphonies, hymns, and choral music.

vault[1] (vɔːlt) *n* **1** an arched structure that forms a roof or ceiling. **2** a room, esp. a cellar, having an arched roof down to floor level. **3** a burial chamber, esp. when underground. **4** a strongroom for the storage of valuables. **5** an underground room used for the storage of wine, food, etc. **6** *Anat.* any arched or domed bodily cavity or space: *the cranial vault.* **7** something suggestive of an arched structure, as the sky. ◆ *vb* **8** (*tr*) to furnish with or as if with an arched roof. **9** (*tr*) to construct in the shape of a vault. **10** (*intr*) to curve in the shape of a vault. ORIG C14 *vaute,* from OF, from Vulgar L *volvita* (unattested) a turn, prob. from L *volvere* to roll

vault[2] (vɔːlt) *vb* **1** to spring over (an object), esp. with the aid of a long pole or with the hands resting on the object. **2** (*intr*) to do, achieve, or attain something as if by a leap: *he vaulted to fame.* ◆ *n* **3** the act of vaulting. ORIG C16: from OF *voulter* to turn from It. *voltare,* from Vulgar L *volvitāre* (unattested) to turn, leap; see VAULT[1]
▸ **'vaulter** *n*

vaulting[1] ('vɔːltɪŋ) *n* one or more vaults in a building or such structures considered collectively.

vaulting[2] ('vɔːltɪŋ) *adj* (*prenominal*) **1** excessively confident: *vaulting arrogance.* **2** used to vault: *a vaulting pole.*

vaunt (vɔːnt) *vb* **1** (*tr*) to describe, praise, or display (one's success, possessions, etc.) boastfully. **2** (*intr*) *Rare or literary.* to brag. ◆ *n* **3** a boast. ORIG C14: from OF, from LL *vānitāre,* from L *vānus* VAIN
▸ **'vaunter** *n*

Vauxhall ★ ('vɒksˌhɔːl) *n* a district in London, on the south bank of the Thames.

vavasor ('vævəˌsɔː) *or* **vavasour** ('vævəˌsʊə) *n* (in feudal society) the noble or knightly vassal of a baron or great lord who also has vassals himself. ORIG C13: from OF *vavasour,* ?from Med. L *vassus vassōrum* vassal of vassals

vb *abbrev. for* verb.

VC *abbrev. for:* **1** Vice-chairman. **2** Vice Chancellor. **3** Vice Consul. **4** Victoria Cross.

V-chip *n* a device within a television set that allows the set to be programmed not to receive transmissions that have been classified as containing sex, violence, or obscene language.

vCJD *abbrev. for* (new-)variant Creutzfeldt–Jakob disease.

VCR *abbrev. for* video cassette recorder.

VD *abbrev. for* venereal disease.

V-Day *n* a day nominated to celebrate victory, as in V-E Day or V-J Day in World War II.

VDQS *abbrev. for* vins délimités de qualité supérieure: on a bottle of French wine, indicates that it contains high-quality wine from an approved regional vineyard: the second highest French wine classification. Cf. **AOC,** ***vin de pays.***

VDU *Computing. abbrev. for* visual display unit.

've *contraction of* have: *I've; you've.*

veal (viːl) *n* the flesh of the calf used as food. ORIG C14: from OF *veel,* from L *vitellus,* dim. of *vitulus* calf

vealer ('viːlə) *n US, Canad., & Austral.* a calf bred for veal.

vector ('vɛktə) *n* **1** *Maths.* a variable quantity, such as force, that has magnitude and direction and can be resolved into components that are odd functions of the coordinates. **2** *Maths.* an element of a vector space. **3** Also called: **carrier.** *Pathol.* an organism, esp. an insect, that carries a disease-producing microorganism from one host to another. **4** Also called: **cloning vector.** *Genetics.* an agent, such as a bacteriophage or a plasmid, by means of which a fragment of foreign DNA is inserted into a host cell to produce a gene clone in genetic engineering. **5** the course or compass direction of an aircraft. ◆ *vb* (*tr*) **6** to direct or guide (a pilot, aircraft, etc.) by directions transmitted by radio. **7** to alter the direction of (the thrust of a jet engine) as a means of steering an aircraft. ORIG C18: from L: carrier, from *vehere* to convey
▸ **vectorial** (vɛk'tɔːrɪəl) *adj*

vector field *n* a region of space under the influence of some vector quantity, such as magnetic field strength, in which each point can be described by a vector.

vector product *n* the product of two vectors that is a pseudovector, whose magnitude is the product of the magnitudes of the given vectors and the sine of the angle between them. Its axis is perpendicular to the plane of the given vectors.

vector sum *n* a vector whose length and direction are represented by the diagonal of a parallelogram whose sides represent the given vectors.

Veda ('veɪdə) *n* any or all of the most ancient sacred writings of Hinduism, esp. the Rig-Veda, Yajur-Veda, Sama-Veda, and Atharva-Veda. ORIG C18: from Sansk.: knowledge

vedalia (vɪ'deɪlɪə) *n* an Australian ladybird introduced elsewhere to control the scale insect, which is a pest of citrus fruits. ORIG C20: from NL

Vedanta (vɪ'dɑːntə) *n* one of the six main philosophical schools of Hinduism, expounding the monism regarded as implicit in the Veda in accordance with the doctrines of the Upanishads. ORIG C19: from Sansk., from VEDA + *ánta* end
▸ **Ve'dantic** *adj* ▸ **Ve'dantist** *n*

V-E Day *n* the day marking the Allied victory in Europe in World War II (May 8, 1945).

vedette (vɪ'dɛt) *n* **1** *Naval.* a small patrol vessel. **2** *Mil.* a mounted sentry posted forward of a formation's position. ORIG C17: from F, from It. *vedetta* (infl. by *vedere* to see), from earlier *veletta,* ?from Sp., from L *vigilāre*

Vedic ('veɪdɪk) *adj* **1** of or relating to the Vedas or the ancient form of Sanskrit in which they are written. ◆ *n* **2** the classical form of Sanskrit; the language of the Vedas.

veer (vɪə) *vb* **1** to alter direction (of). **2** (*intr*) to change from one position, opinion, etc., to another. **3** (*intr*) (of the wind) to change direction clockwise in the northern hemisphere and anticlockwise in the southern. ◆ *n* **4** a change of course or direction. ORIG C16: from OF *virer,* prob. of Celtic origin

veg (vɛdʒ) *n Inf.* a vegetable or vegetables.

Vega[1] ('viːgə) *n* the brightest star in the constellation Lyra and one of the most conspicuous in the N hemisphere. ORIG C17: from Med. L, from Ar. (*al nasr*) *al wāqi,* lit.: the falling (vulture), i.e. the constellation Lyra

Vega[2] ★ ('veɪgə; *Spanish* 'beɣa) *n* See **Lope de Vega.**

vegan ('viːgən) *n* a person who uses no animal products.

vegeburger *or* **veggieburger** ('vɛdʒɪˌbɜːgə) *n* a flat cake of chopped seasoned vegetables and pulses that is grilled or fried and often served in a bread roll.

Vegemite ('vɛdʒɪˌmaɪt) *n Austral. & NZ trademark.* a yeast extract used as a spread, flavouring for stews, etc.

vegetable ('vɛdʒtəbᵊl, 'vɛdʒətəbᵊl) *n* **1** any of various herbaceous plants having parts that are used as food, such as peas, potatoes, cauliflower, and onions. **2** *Inf.* a person who has lost control of his or her mental faculties, limbs, etc., as from an injury, mental disease, etc. **3** a dull inactive person. **4** (*modifier*) consisting of or made from edible vegetables: *a vegetable diet.* **5** (*modifier*) of, characteristic of, derived from, or consisting of plants or plant material: *the vegetable kingdom.* **6** *Rare.* any member of the plant kingdom. ORIG C14 (adj): from LL *vegetābilis,* from *vegetāre* to enliven, from L *vegēre* to excite

vegetable butter *n* any of a group of vegetable fats having the consistency of butter.

vegetable ivory *n* the hard whitish material obtained from the endosperm of the ivory nut: used to make buttons, ornaments, etc.

vegetable marrow *n* **1** a plant, probably native to America but widely cultivated for its oblong green striped fruit which is eaten as a vegetable. **2** the fruit of this plant. Often shortened to **marrow.**

vegetable oil *n* any of a group of oils that are obtained from plants.

vegetable oyster *n* another name for **salsify** (sense 1).

vegetable silk *n* any of various silky fibres obtained from the seed pods of certain plants.

vegetable wax *n* any of various waxes that occur on parts of certain plants, esp. the trunks of certain palms, and prevent loss of water.

vegetal ('vɛdʒɪtᵊl) *adj* **1** of or characteristic of vegetables or plant life. **2** vegetative. ORIG C15: from LL *vegetāre* to quicken

vegetarian (ˌvɛdʒɪ'tɛərɪən) *n* **1** a person who advocates or practises the exclusion of meat and fish, and sometimes eggs, milk, and cheese, from the diet. ◆ *adj* **2** *Cookery.* strictly, consisting of vegetables and fruit only, but often including milk, cheese, eggs, etc.
► ˌ**vege'tarianism** *n*

vegetate ('vɛdʒɪˌteɪt) *vb* **vegetates, vegetating, vegetated.** (*intr*) **1** to grow like a plant. **2** to lead a life characterized by monotony, passivity, or mental inactivity. ORIG C17: from LL *vegetāre* to invigorate

vegetation (ˌvɛdʒɪ'teɪʃən) *n* **1** plant life as a whole, esp. the plant life of a particular region. **2** the process of vegetating.
► ˌ**vege'tational** *adj*

vegetative ('vɛdʒɪtətɪv) *adj* **1** of or concerned with plant life or plant growth. **2** (of reproduction) characterized by asexual processes. **3** of or relating to functions such as digestion and circulation rather than sexual reproduction. **4** (of a style of living, etc.) unthinking or passive.
► '**vegetatively** *adv*

veggie ('vɛdʒɪ) *n, adj* an informal word for **vegetarian.**

veg out *vb* **vegges, vegging, vegged.** (*intr, adv*) *Sl., chiefly US.* to relax in an inert, passive way; vegetate: *vegging out in front of the television.*

vehement ('viːɪmənt) *adj* **1** marked by intensity of feeling or conviction. **2** (of actions, gestures, etc.) characterized by great energy, vigour, or force. ORIG C15: from L *vehemēns* ardent
► '**vehemence** *n* ► '**vehemently** *adv*

vehicle ('viːɪkᵊl) *n* **1** any conveyance in or by which people or objects are transported, esp. one fitted with wheels. **2** a medium for the expression or communication of ideas, power, etc. **3** *Pharmacol.* a therapeutically inactive substance mixed with the active ingredient to give bulk to a medicine. **4** Also called: **base.** a painting medium, such as oil, in which pigments are suspended. **5** (in the performing arts) a play, etc., that enables a particular performer to display his talents. ORIG C17: from L *vehiculum,* from *vehere* to carry
► **vehicular** (vɪ'hɪkjʊlə) *adj*

Veii ★ ('viːjaɪ) *n* an ancient Etruscan city, northwest of Rome: destroyed by the Romans in 396 B.C.

veil (veɪl) *n* **1** a piece of more or less transparent material, usually attached to a hat or headdress, used to conceal or protect a woman's face and head. **2** part of a nun's headdress falling round the face onto the shoulders. **3** something that covers, conceals, or separates: *a veil of reticence.* **4 the veil.** the life of a nun in a religious order. **5 take the veil.** to become a nun. **6** Also called: **velum.** *Bot.* a membranous structure, esp. the thin layer of cells covering a young mushroom. ◆ *vb* **7** (*tr*) to cover, conceal, or separate with or as if with a veil. **8** (*intr*) to wear or put on a veil. ORIG C13: from Norman F *veile,* from L *vēla,* pl of *vēlum* a covering
► '**veiler** *n* ► '**veil-**ˌ**like** *adj*

veiled (veɪld) *adj* **1** disguised: *a veiled insult.* **2** (of sound, tone, the voice, etc.) not distinct.
► **veiledly** ('veɪlɪdlɪ) *adv*

veiling ('veɪlɪŋ) *n* a veil or the fabric used for veils.

vein (veɪn) *n* **1** any of the tubular vessels that convey oxygen-depleted blood to the heart. Cf. **pulmonary vein, artery** (sense 1). **2** any of the hollow branching tubes that form the supporting framework of an insect's wing. **3** any of the vascular bundles of a leaf. **4** a clearly defined mass of ore, mineral, etc. **5** an irregular streak of colour or alien substance in marble, wood, or other material. **6** a distinctive trait or quality in speech, writing, character, etc.: *a vein of humour.* **7** a temporary attitude or temper: *the debate entered a frivolous vein.* ◆ *vb* (*tr*) **8** to diffuse over or cause to diffuse over in streaked patterns. **9** to fill, furnish, or mark with or as if with veins. ORIG C13: from OF, from L *vēna*
► '**veinless** *adj* ► '**vein**ˌ**like** *adj* ► '**veiny** *adj*

veining ('veɪnɪŋ) *n* a pattern or network of veins or streaks.

veinlet ('veɪnlɪt) *n* any small vein or venule.

velamen (və'leɪmɛn) *n, pl* **velamina** (-'læmɪnə). **1** the thick layer of dead cells that covers the aerial roots of certain orchids. **2** *Anat.* another word for **velum.** ORIG C19: from L: veil, from *vēlāre* to cover

velar ('viːlə) *adj* **1** of or attached to a velum: *velar tentacles.* **2** *Phonetics.* articulated with the soft palate and the back of the tongue, as in (k) or (ŋ). ORIG C18: from L, from *vēlum* VEIL

Velázquez (*Spanish* be'laθkeθ) *or* **Velásquez** ★ (*Spanish* be'laskeθ) *n* **Diego Rodríguez de Silva y** ('djeγo rɔ'ðriγeθ de 'silβa i). 1599–1660, Spanish painter, noted for his royal portraits.

Velcro ('vɛlkrəʊ) *n Trademark.* a fastening consisting of two strips of nylon fabric, one having tiny hooked threads and the other a coarse surface, that form a strong bond when pressed together.

veld *or* **veldt** (fɛlt, vɛlt) *n* elevated open grassland in Southern Africa. See also **bushveld, highveld.** ORIG C19: from Afrik., from earlier Du. *veldt* FIELD

veldskoen ('fɛltˌskʊn, 'vɛlt-) *n* an ankle-length boot of soft but strong rawhide. ORIG from Afrik. *vel* skin + *skoen* shoes

veleta (və'liːtə) *n* a variant spelling of **valeta.**

veliger ('vɛlɪdʒə) *n* the free-swimming larva of many molluscs, having a rudimentary shell and a ciliated velum used for feeding and locomotion. ORIG C19: from NL, from VEL(UM) + -GER(OUS)

Vellore ★ (və'lɔː) *n* a town in SE India, in NE Tamil Nadu: medical centre. Pop.: 175 061 (1991).

vellum ('vɛləm) *n* **1** a fine parchment prepared from the skin of a calf, kid, or lamb. **2** a work printed or written on vellum. **3** a creamy coloured heavy paper resembling vellum. ◆ *adj* **4** made of or resembling vellum. ORIG C15: from OF, from *velin* of a calf, from *veel* VEAL

veloce (vɪ'ləʊtʃɪ) *adj, adv Music.* to be played rapidly. ORIG from It., from L *vēlōx* quick

velocipede (vɪ'lɒsɪˌpiːd) *n* an early form of bicycle, esp. one propelled by pushing along the ground with the feet. ORIG C19: from F, from L *vēlōx* swift + *pēs* foot
► **ve'loci**ˌ**pedist** *n*

velocity (vɪ'lɒsɪtɪ) *n, pl* **velocities. 1** speed of motion or operation; swiftness. **2** *Physics.* a measure of the rate of motion of a body expressed as the rate of change of its position in a particular direction with time. **3** *Physics.* (not in technical usage) another word for **speed** (sense 3). ORIG C16: from L *vēlōcitās,* from *vēlōx* swift

velocity of circulation *n Econ.* the average number of times a unit of money is used in a given time, esp. calculated as the ratio of the total money spent in that time to the total amount of money in circulation.

velocity of light *n* a nontechnical name for **speed of light.**

velodrome ('viːləˌdrəʊm, 'vɛl-) *n* an arena with a banked track for cycle racing. ORIG C20: from F *vélodrome,* from *vélo-* (from L *vēlōx* swift) + -DROME

velour *or* **velours** (və'lʊə) *n* any of various fabrics with a velvet-like finish, used for upholstery, clothing, etc. ORIG C18: from OF, from OProvençal *velos* velvet, from L, from *villus* shaggy hair

velouté (və'luːteɪ) *n* a rich white sauce or soup made from stock, egg yolks, and cream. ORIG from F, lit.: velvety, from OF *velous;* see VELOUR

Velsen ★ (*Dutch* 'vɛlsə) *n* a port in the W Netherlands, in North Holland at the mouth of the canal connecting Amsterdam with the North Sea: fishing and heavy industrial centre. Pop.: 63 617 (1994).

velum ('viːləm) *n, pl* **vela** (-lə). **1** *Zool.* any of various membranous structures. **2** *Anat.* any of various veil-like bodily structures, esp. the soft palate. **3** *Bot.* another word for **veil** (sense 6). ORIG C18: from L: veil

velure (və'lʊə) *n* velvet or a similar fabric. ORIG C16: from OF, from *velous;* see VELOUR

velutinous (və'luːtɪnəs) *adj* covered with short dense soft hairs. ORIG C19: from NL *velūtīnus* like velvet

velvet ('vɛlvɪt) *n* **1a** a fabric of silk, cotton, nylon, etc.,

with a thick close soft pile. **1b** (*as modifier*): *velvet curtains.* **2** anything with a smooth soft surface. **3a** smoothness. **3b** (*as modifier*): *a velvet night.* **4** the furry covering of the newly formed antlers of a deer. **5** *Sl., chiefly US.* **5a** gambling winnings. **5b** a gain. **6 on velvet.** *Sl.* in a condition of ease, advantage, or wealth. **7 velvet glove.** gentleness, often concealing strength or determination (esp. in **an iron hand in a velvet glove**). ORIG C14 *veluet,* from OF, from *velu* hairy, from Vulgar L *villutus* (unattested), from L *villus* shaggy hair
▸ **'velvet-ˌlike** *adj* ▸ **'velvety** *adj*

velveteen (ˌvɛlvɪ'tiːn) *n* **1** a cotton fabric resembling velvet with a short thick pile, used for clothing, etc. **2** (*pl*) trousers made of velveteen.

Velvet Underground ★ *n* **the.** US avant-garde rock group in New York City (formed in 1965; disintegrated 1969–72; reformed for a tour in 1993). See also (Lou) **Reed.**

Ven. *abbrev. for* Venerable.

vena ('viːnə) *n, pl* **venae** (-niː). *Anat.* a technical word for **vein.** ORIG C15: from L *vēna* VEIN

vena cava ('keɪvə) *n, pl* **venae cavae** ('keɪviː). either one of two large veins that convey oxygen-depleted blood to the heart. ORIG L: hollow vein

venal ('viːnᵊl) *adj* **1** easily bribed or corrupted: *a venal magistrate.* **2** characterized by corruption or bribery. ORIG C17: from L *vēnālis,* from *vēnum* sale
▸ **ve'nality** *n* ▸ **'venally** *adv*

venation (viː'neɪʃən) *n* **1** the arrangement of the veins in a leaf or in the wing of an insect. **2** such veins collectively.
▸ **ve'national** *adj*

vend (vɛnd) *vb* **1** to sell or be sold. **2** to sell (goods) for a living. ORIG C17: from L *vendere,* from *vēnum dare* to offer for sale

vendace ('vɛndeɪs) *n, pl* **vendaces** *or* **vendace.** either of two small whitefish occurring in lakes in Scotland and NW England. ORIG C18: from NL *vandēsius,* from OF *vandoise,* prob. of Celtic origin

vendee (vɛn'diː) *n Chiefly law.* a person to whom something, esp. real property, is sold.

Vendée ★ (*French* vɑ̃de) *n* a department of W France, in Pays-de-la-Loire region: scene of the **Wars of the Vendée,** a series of peasant-royalist insurrections (1793–95) against the Revolutionary government. Capital: La Roche-sur-Yon. Pop.: 524 069 (1994 est.). Area: 7016 sq. km (2709 sq. miles).

vendetta (vɛn'dɛtə) *n* **1** a private feud, originally between Corsican or Sicilian families, in which the relatives of a murdered person seek vengeance by killing the murderer or some member of his family. **2** any prolonged feud. ORIG C19: from It., from L *vindicta,* from *vindicāre* to avenge
▸ **ven'dettist** *n*

vendible ('vɛndəbᵊl) *adj* **1** saleable or marketable. ◆ *n* **2** (*usually pl*) *Rare.* a saleable object.
▸ **ˌvendi'bility** *n*

vending machine *n* a machine that automatically dispenses consumer goods such as cigarettes or food, when money is inserted.

Vendôme ★ (*French* vɑ̃dom) *n* **Louis Joseph de** (lwi ʒozɛf də). 1654–1712, French marshal, noted for his command during the War of the Spanish Succession (1701–14).

vendor ('vɛndɔː) *or* **vender** ('vɛndə) *n* **1** *Chiefly law.* a person who sells something, esp. real property. **2** another name for **vending machine.**

vendor placing *n Finance.* a method of financing the purchase of one company by another in which the purchasing company pays for the target company in its own shares, on condition that the vendor places these shares with investors for cash payment.

veneer (vɪ'nɪə) *n* **1** a thin layer of wood, plastic, etc., with a decorative or fine finish that is bonded to the surface of a less expensive material, usually wood. **2** a superficial appearance: *a veneer of gentility.* **3** any facing material that is applied to a different backing material. ◆ *vb* (*tr*) **4** to cover (a surface) with a veneer. **5** to conceal (something) under a superficially pleasant surface. ORIG C17: from G *furnieren* to veneer, from OF *fournir* to FURNISH
▸ **ve'neerer** *n*

veneering (vɪ'nɪərɪŋ) *n* material used as veneer or a veneered surface.

venepuncture ('vɛnɪˌpʌŋktʃə) *n* a variant spelling of **venipuncture.**

venerable ('vɛnərəbᵊl) *adj* **1** (esp. of a person) worthy of reverence on account of great age, religious associations, character, etc. **2** (of inanimate objects) hallowed on account of age or historical or religious association. **3** *RC Church.* a title bestowed on a deceased person when the first stage of his canonization has been accomplished. **4** *Church of England.* a title given to an archdeacon. ORIG C15: from L *venerābilis,* from *venerārī* to venerate
▸ **ˌvenera'bility** *or* **'venerableness** *n* ▸ **'venerably** *adv*

venerate ('vɛnəˌreɪt) *vb* **venerates, venerating, venerated.** (*tr*) **1** to hold in deep respect. **2** to honour in recognition of qualities of holiness, excellence, etc. ORIG C17: from L *venerārī,* from *venus* love
▸ **'venerˌator** *n*

veneration (ˌvɛnə'reɪʃən) *n* **1** a feeling or expression of awe or reverence. **2** the act of venerating or the state of being venerated.

venereal (vɪ'nɪərɪəl) *adj* **1** of or infected with venereal disease. **2** (of a disease) transmitted by sexual intercourse. **3** of or involving the genitals. **4** of or relating to sexual intercourse or erotic desire. ORIG C15: from L *venereus,* from *venus* sexual love, from VENUS[1]

venereal disease *n* another name for **sexually transmitted disease.** Abbrev.: **VD.**

venereology (vɪˌnɪərɪ'ɒlədʒɪ) *n* the branch of medicine concerned with the study and treatment of venereal disease.
▸ **veˌnere'ologist** *n*

venery[1] ('vɛnərɪ, 'viː-) *n Arch.* the pursuit of sexual gratification. ORIG C15: from Med. L *veneria,* from L *venus* love, VENUS[1]

venery[2] ('vɛnərɪ, 'viː-) *n* the art, sport, lore, or practice of hunting, esp. with hounds; the chase. ORIG C14: from OF *venerie,* from *vener* to hunt, from L *vēnārī*

venesection ('vɛnɪˌsɛkʃən) *n* surgical incision into a vein. ORIG C17: from NL *vēnae sectiō;* see VEIN, SECTION

Venetia ★ (vɪ'niːʃə) *n* **1** the area of ancient Italy between the lower Po valley and the Alps: later a Roman province. **2** the territorial possessions of the medieval Venetian republic that were at the head of the Adriatic and correspond to the present-day region of Veneto and a large part of Friuli-Venezia Giulia.

Venetian (vɪ'niːʃən) *adj* **1** of, relating to, or characteristic of Venice or its inhabitants. ◆ *n* **2** a native or inhabitant of Venice. **3** See **Venetian blind.**

Venetian blind *n* a window blind consisting of a number of horizontal slats whose angle may be altered to let in more or less light.

Venetian red *n* **1** natural or synthetic ferric oxide used as a red pigment. **2a** a moderate to strong reddish-brown colour. **2b** (*as adj*): *a Venetian-red coat.*

Veneto ★ (*Italian* 'veːneto) *n* a region of NE Italy, on the Adriatic: mountainous in the north with a fertile plain in the south, crossed by the Rivers Po, Adige, and Piave. Capital: Venice. Pop.: 4 433 060 (1996 est.). Area: 18 377 sq. km (7095 sq. miles). Also called: **Venezia-Euganea** (ve'nɛttsjaeʊ'gaːnea).

Venez. *abbrev. for* Venezuela.

Venezia ★ (ve'nɛttsja) *n* the Italian name for **Venice.**

Venezia Giulia ★ (*Italian* 'dʒuːlja) *n* a former region of NE Italy at the N end of the Adriatic: divided between Yugoslavia and Italy after World War II; now divided between Italy and Slovenia.

Venezia Tridentina ★ (*Italian* triden'tiːna) *n* the former name (until 1947) of **Trentino-Alto Adige.**

Venezuela ★ (ˌvɛnɪ'zweɪlə) *n* **1** a republic in South America, on the Caribbean: colonized by the Spanish in the 16th century; independence from Spain declared in 1811 and won in 1819 after a war led by Simón Bolívar.

It contains Lake Maracaibo and the northernmost chains of the Andes in the northwest, the Orinoco basin in the centre, and the Guiana Highlands in the south. Exports petroleum, iron ore, and coffee. Official language: Spanish. Religion: Roman Catholic. Currency: bolívar. Capital: Caracas. Pop.: 23 707 000 (1999 est.). Area: 912 050 sq. km (352 142 sq. miles). Official name (from 1999): **Bolivarian Republic of Venezuela. 2 Gulf of.** an inlet of the Caribbean in NW Venezuela: continues south as Lake Maracaibo.
▸ **ˌVeneˈzuelan** *adj, n*

vengeance (ˈvɛndʒəns) *n* **1** the act of or desire for taking revenge. **2 with a vengeance.** (intensifier): *he's a coward with a vengeance.* ORIG C13: from OF, from *venger* to avenge, from L *vindicāre* to punish

vengeful (ˈvɛndʒfʊl) *adj* **1** desiring revenge. **2** characterized by or indicating a desire for revenge. **3** inflicting or taking revenge: *with vengeful blows.*
▸ **ˈvengefully** *adv*

venial (ˈviːnɪəl) *adj* easily excused or forgiven: *a venial error.* ORIG C13: via OF from LL *veniālis,* from L *venia* forgiveness
▸ **ˌveniˈality** *n* ▸ **ˈvenially** *adv*

venial sin *n Christian theol.* a sin regarded as involving only a partial loss of grace.

Venice ★ (ˈvɛnɪs) *n* a port in NE Italy, capital of Veneto region, built on over 100 islands and mud flats in the **Lagoon of Venice** (an inlet of the **Gulf of Venice** at the head of the Adriatic): united under the first doge in 697 A.D.; became an independent republic and a great commercial and maritime power, defeating Genoa, the greatest rival, in 1380; contains the Grand Canal and about 170 smaller canals, providing waterways for city transport. Pop.: 298 915 (1996 est.). Italian name: **Venezia.** Related adj: **Venetian.**

venin (ˈvɛnɪn) *n* any of the poisonous constituents of animal venoms. ORIG C20: from F *ven(in)* poison + -IN

venipuncture *or* **venepuncture** (ˈvɛnɪˌpʌŋktʃə) *n Med.* the puncturing of a vein, esp. to take a sample of venous blood or inject a drug.

venison (ˈvɛnɪzᵊn, -sᵊn) *n* the flesh of a deer, used as food. ORIG C13: from OF *venaison,* from L *vēnātiō* hunting, from *vēnārī* to hunt

Venite (vɪˈnaɪtɪ) *n* **1** the opening word of the 95th psalm, an invitatory prayer at matins. **2** a musical setting of this. ORIG L: come ye

Venizélos ★ (*Greek* vɛniˈzɛlɔs) *n* **Eleutherios** (ˌɛlɛfˈθɛrjɔs). 1864–1936, Greek statesman: prime minister (1910–15; 1917–20; 1924; 1928–32; 1933).

Venlo *or* **Venloo** ★ (*Dutch* ˈvɛnloː) *n* a city in the SE Netherlands, in Limburg on the Maas River. Pop.: 63 820 (1988 est.).

Venn diagram (vɛn) *n Maths, logic.* a diagram in which mathematical sets or terms of a categorial statement are represented by overlapping circles within a boundary representing the universal set, so that all possible combinations of the relevant properties are represented by the various distinct areas in the diagram. ORIG C19: after John *Venn* (1834–1923), Brit. logician

venom (ˈvɛnəm) *n* **1** a poisonous fluid secreted by such animals as certain snakes and scorpions and usually transmitted by a bite or sting. **2** malice; spite. ORIG C13: from OF, from L *venēnum* poison, love potion
▸ **ˈvenomous** *adj* ▸ **ˈvenomously** *adv* ▸ **ˈvenomousness** *n*

venose (ˈviːnəʊs) *adj* **1** having veins; venous. **2** (of a plant) covered with veins or similar ridges. ORIG C17: via L *vēnōsus,* from *vēna* a VEIN

venosity (vɪˈnɒsɪtɪ) *n* **1** an excessive quantity of blood in the venous system or in an organ or part. **2** an unusually large number of blood vessels in an organ or part.

venous (ˈviːnəs) *adj* **1** *Physiol.* of or relating to the blood circulating in the veins. **2** of or relating to the veins. ORIG C17: see VENOSE

vent[1] (vɛnt) *n* **1** a small opening for the escape of fumes, liquids, etc. **2** the shaft of a volcano through which lava and gases erupt. **3** the external opening of the urinary or genital systems of lower vertebrates. **4** a small aperture at the breech of old guns through which the charge was ignited. **5 give vent to.** to release (an emotion, idea, etc.) in an outburst. ◆ *vb* (*mainly tr*) **6** to release or give expression or utterance to (an emotion, etc.): *he vents his anger on his wife.* **7** to provide a vent for or make vents in. **8** to let out (steam, etc.) through a vent. ORIG C14: from OF *esventer* to blow out, from EX-[1] + *venter,* from Vulgar L *ventāre* (unattested), from L *ventus* wind

vent[2] (vɛnt) *n* **1** a vertical slit at the back or both sides of a jacket. ◆ *vb* **2** (*tr*) to make a vent or vents in (a jacket). ORIG C15: from OF *fente* slit, from *fendre* to split, from L *findere* to cleave

venter (ˈvɛntə) *n* **1** *Anat., zool.* **1a** the belly or abdomen of vertebrates. **1b** a protuberant structure or part, such as the belly of a muscle. **2** *Bot.* the swollen basal region of an archegonium. **3** *Law.* the womb. ORIG C16: from L

ventilate (ˈvɛntɪˌleɪt) *vb* **ventilates, ventilating, ventilated.** (*tr*) **1** to drive foul air out of (an enclosed area). **2** to provide with a means of airing. **3** to expose (a question, grievance, etc.) to public discussion. **4** *Physiol.* to oxygenate (the blood). ORIG C15: from L *ventilāre* to fan, from *ventulus,* dim. of *ventus* wind
▸ **ˈventilable** *adj* ▸ **ˌventiˈlation** *n*

ventilator (ˈvɛntɪˌleɪtə) *n* **1** an opening or device, such as a fan, used to ventilate a room, building, etc. **2** *Med.* a machine that maintains a flow of air into and out of the lungs of a patient unable to breathe normally.

ventral (ˈvɛntrəl) *adj* **1** relating to the front part of the body. **2** of or situated on the upper or inner side of a plant organ, esp. a leaf, that is facing the axis. ORIG C18: from L *ventrālis,* from *venter* abdomen
▸ **ˈventrally** *adv*

ventral fin *n* **1** another name for **pelvic fin. 2** any unpaired median fin situated on the undersurface of fishes.

ventricle (ˈvɛntrɪkᵊl) *n Anat.* **1** a chamber of the heart that receives blood from the atrium and pumps it to the arteries. **2** any one of the four main cavities of the vertebrate brain. **3** any of various other small cavities in the body. ORIG C14: from L *ventriculus,* dim. of *venter* belly
▸ **venˈtricular** *adj*

ventricose (ˈvɛntrɪˌkəʊs) *adj* **1** *Bot., zool., anat.* having a swelling on one side: *the ventricose corolla of many labiate plants.* **2** another word for **corpulent.** ORIG C18: from NL, from L *venter* belly

ventriculus (vɛnˈtrɪkjʊləs) *n, pl* **ventriculi** (-ˌlaɪ). **1** *Zool.* **1a** the midgut of an insect, where digestion takes place. **1b** the gizzard of a bird. **2** another word for **ventricle.** ORIG C18: from L, dim. of *venter* belly

ventriloquism (vɛnˈtrɪləˌkwɪzəm) *or* **ventriloquy** *n* the art of producing vocal sounds that appear to come from another source. ORIG C18: from L *venter* belly + *loquī* to speak
▸ **ventriloquial** (ˌvɛntrɪˈləʊkwɪəl) *adj* ▸ **ˌventriˈloquially** *adv* ▸ **venˈtriloquist** *n* ▸ **venˈtriloˌquize** *or* **venˈtriloˌquise** *vb*

Ventris ★ (ˈvɛntrɪs) *n* **Michael George Francis.** 1922–56, British cryptographer, who deciphered the Linear B script.

venture (ˈvɛntʃə) *vb* **ventures, venturing, ventured. 1** (*tr*) to expose to danger: *he ventured his life.* **2** (*tr*) to brave the dangers of (something): *I'll venture the seas.* **3** (*tr*) to dare (to do something): *does he venture to object?* **4** (*tr; may take a clause as object*) to express in spite of possible criticism: *I venture that he is not that honest.* **5** (*intr;* often foll. by *out, forth,* etc.) to embark on a possibly hazardous journey, etc.: *to venture forth upon the high seas.* ◆ *n* **6** an undertaking that is risky or of uncertain outcome. **7** a commercial undertaking characterized by risk of loss as well as opportunity for profit. **8** something hazarded or risked in an adventure. **9 at a venture.** at random. ORIG C15: var. of *aventure* ADVENTURE
▸ **ˈventurer** *n*

venture capital *n* another name for **risk capital.**

Venture Scout *or* **Venturer** *n Brit.* a person aged 16–20 who is a member of the senior branch of the Scouts.

venturesome (ˈvɛntʃəsəm) *or* **venturous** (ˈvɛntʃərəs) *adj* **1** willing to take risks; daring. **2** hazardous.

Venturi ★ (vɛnˈtjʊərɪ) *n* **Robert.** born 1925, US architect, a pioneer of the postmodernist style. His writings include *Complexity and Contradiction in Architecture* (1966).

Venturi tube (vɛn'tjʊərɪ) *n Physics.* a device for measuring or controlling fluid flow, consisting of a tube so constricted that the pressure differential produced by fluid flowing through the constriction gives a measure of the rate of flow. ORIG C19: after G. B. *Venturi* (1746–1822), It. physicist

venue ('vɛnjuː) *n* **1** *Law.* **1a** the place in which a cause of action arises. **1b** the place fixed for the trial of a cause. **1c** the locality from which the jurors must be summoned. **2** a meeting place. **3** any place where an organized gathering, such as a rock concert, is held. ORIG C14: from OF, from *venir* to come, from L *venīre*

venule ('vɛnjuːl) *n* **1** *Anat.* any of the small branches of a vein that receives oxygen-depleted blood from the capillaries and returns it to the heart via the venous system. **2** any of the branches of a vein in an insect's wing. ORIG C19: from L *vēnula,* dim. of *vēna* VEIN

Venus¹ ★ ('viːnəs) *n* the Roman goddess of love. Greek counterpart: **Aphrodite.**

Venus² ★ ('viːnəs) *n* one of the inferior planets and the second nearest to the sun, visible as a bright morning or evening star.
▸ **Venusian** (vɪ'njuːzɪən) *n, adj*

Venusberg ★ ('viːnəsˌbɜːg; *German* 'veːnʊsbɛrk) *n* a mountain in central Germany: contains caverns that, according to medieval legend, housed the palace of the goddess Venus.

Venus's-flytrap *or* **Venus flytrap** *n* an insectivorous plant having hinged two-lobed leaves that snap closed when the sensitive hairs on the surface are touched.

Venus's looking glass *n* a purple-flowered plant of Europe, W Asia, and N Africa.

veracious (vɛ'reɪʃəs) *adj* **1** habitually truthful or honest. **2** accurate. ORIG C17: from L *vērax,* from *vērus* true
▸ **ve'raciously** *adv* ▸ **ve'raciousness** *n*

veracity (vɛ'ræsɪtɪ) *n, pl* **veracities. 1** truthfulness or honesty, esp. when consistent or habitual. **2** accuracy. **3** a truth. ORIG C17: from Med. L *vērācitās,* from L *vērax;* see VERACIOUS

Veracruz ★ (ˌvɛrə'kruːz; *Spanish* bera'kruθ) *n* **1** a state of E Mexico, on the Gulf of Mexico: consists of a hot humid coastal strip with lagoons, rising rapidly inland to the central plateau and Sierra Madre Oriental. Capital: Jalapa. Pop.: 6 856 415 (1997 est.). Area: 72 815 sq. km (28 114 sq. miles). **2** the chief port of Mexico, in Veracruz state on the Gulf of Mexico. Pop.: 438 821 (1990).

veranda *or* **verandah** (və'rændə) *n* **1** a porch or portico, sometimes partly enclosed, along the outside of a building. **2** *NZ.* a continuous overhead canopy that gives shelter to pedestrians. ORIG C18: from Port. *varanda* railing

veratrine ('vɛrəˌtriːn) *or* **veratrin** ('vɛrətrɪn) *n* a white poisonous mixture obtained from sabadilla, consisting of various alkaloids: formerly used in medicine as a counterirritant. ORIG C19: from L *vērātrum* hellebore + -INE²

verb (vɜːb) *n* **1** (in traditional grammar) any of a large class of words that serve to indicate the occurrence or performance of an action, the existence of a state, etc. Such words as *run, make, do,* etc., are verbs. **2** (in modern descriptive linguistic analysis) **2a** a word or group of words that functions as the predicate of a sentence or introduces the predicate. **2b** (*as modifier*)*: a verb phrase.* ◆ Abbrev.: **vb, v.** ORIG C14: from L *verbum* word

verbal ('vɜːbᵊl) *adj* **1** of, relating to, or using words: *merely verbal concessions.* **2** oral rather than written: *a verbal agreement.* **3** verbatim; literal: *an almost verbal copy.* **4** *Grammar.* of or relating to verbs or a verb. ◆ See also **verbals.**
▸ **'verbally** *adv*

verbalism ('vɜːbəˌlɪzəm) *n* **1** a verbal expression; phrase or word. **2** an exaggerated emphasis on the importance of words. **3** a statement lacking real content.

verbalist ('vɜːbəlɪst) *n* **1** a person who deals with words alone, rather than facts, ideas, etc. **2** a person skilled in the use of words.

verbalize *or* **verbalise** ('vɜːbəˌlaɪz) *vb* **verbalizes, verbalizing, verbalized** *or* **verbalises, verbalising, verbalised. 1** to express (an idea, etc.) in words. **2** to change (any word) into a verb or derive a verb from (any word). **3** (*intr*) to be verbose.
▸ **ˌverbali'zation** *or* **ˌverbali'sation** *n*

verbal noun *n* a noun derived from a verb, such as *smoking* in the sentence *smoking is bad for you.*

verbals ('vɜːbᵊlz) *pl n Sl.* **1** a criminal's admission of guilt on arrest. **2** verbal abuse or invective.

verbascum (vɜː'bæskəm) *n* any of a genus of hairy plants, mostly biennial, having spikes of yellow, purple, or red flowers. ORIG L: mullein

verbatim (vɜː'beɪtɪm) *adv, adj* using exactly the same words; word for word. ORIG C15: from Med. L: word by word, from L *verbum* word

verbena (vɜː'biːnə) *n* **1** any of a genus of plants of tropical and temperate America, having red, white, or purple fragrant flowers: much cultivated as garden plants. **2** any of various similar plants, esp. the lemon verbena. ORIG C16: via Med. L, from L: sacred bough used by the priest in religious acts

verbiage ('vɜːbɪɪdʒ) *n* the excessive and often meaningless use of words. ORIG C18: from F, from OF *verbier* to chatter, from *verbe* word, from L *verbum*

verbose (vɜː'bəʊs) *adj* using or containing an excess of words, so as to be pedantic or boring. ORIG C17: from L, from *verbum* word
▸ **ver'bosely** *adv* ▸ **verbosity** (vɜː'bɒsɪtɪ) *n*

verboten *German.* (fɛr'boːtən) *adj* forbidden.

verb phrase *n Grammar.* a constituent of a sentence that contains the verb and any direct and indirect objects but not the subject.

Vercelli ★ (*Italian* ver'tʃɛlli) *n* a city in NW Italy, in Piedmont: an ancient Ligurian and later Roman city; has an outstanding library of manuscripts (notably the *Codex Vercellensis,* dating from the 10th century). Pop.: 50 313 (1990).

Vercingetorix ★ (ˌvɜːsɪn'dʒɛtərɪks) *n* died ?45 B.C., Gallic chieftain and hero, executed for leading a revolt against the Romans under Julius Caesar (52 B.C.).

verdant ('vɜːdᵊnt) *adj* **1** covered with green vegetation. **2** (of plants, etc.) green in colour. **3** unsophisticated; green. ORIG C16: from OF, from *verdoyer* to become green, from OF *verd* green, from L *viridis*
▸ **'verdancy** *n* ▸ **'verdantly** *adv*

verd antique (vɜːd) *n* **1** a dark green mottled impure variety of serpentine marble. **2** any of various similar marbles or stones. ORIG C18: from F, from It. *verde antico* ancient green

Verde ★ (vɜːd) *n* **Cape.** a cape in Senegal, near Dakar: the westernmost point of Africa. See also **Cape Verde.**

Verdi ★ ('vɛədɪ; *Italian* 'verdi) *n* **Giuseppe** (dʒu'zɛppe). 1813–1901, Italian composer of operas, esp. *Rigoletto* (1851), *Il Trovatore* (1853), *La Traviata* (1853), and *Aïda* (1871).

verdict ('vɜːdɪkt) *n* **1** the findings of a jury on the issues of fact submitted to it for examination and trial. **2** any decision or conclusion. ORIG C13: from Med. L *vērdictum,* from L *vērē dictum* truly spoken, from *vērus* true + *dīcere* to say

verdigris ('vɜːdɪgrɪs) *n* **1** a green or bluish patina formed on copper, brass, or bronze. **2** a green or blue crystalline substance obtained by the action of acetic acid on copper and used as a fungicide and pigment. ORIG C14: from OF *vert de Grice* green of Greece

Verdun ★ (*French* vɛrdœ̃; *English* 'vɛədʌn) *n* a fortified town in NE France, on the Meuse: scene of the longest and most severe battle (1916) of World War I, in which the French repelled a German offensive. Pop.: 23 430 (1990). Ancient name: **Verodunum** (ˌvɛrə'djuːnəm).

verdure ('vɜːdʒə) *n* **1** flourishing green vegetation or its colour. **2** a condition of freshness or healthy growth. ORIG C14: from OF *verd* green, from L *viridis*
▸ **'verdured** *adj*

Vereeniging ★ (fəˈriːnɪkɪŋ, və-) *n* a city in E South Africa: scene of the signing (1902) of the treaty ending the Boer War. Pop.: 60 584 (1985).

verge[1] (vɜːdʒ) *n* **1** an edge or rim; margin. **2** a limit beyond which something occurs: *on the verge of ecstasy.* **3** *Brit.* a grass border along a road. **4** *Archit.* the edge of the roof tiles projecting over a gable. **5** *English legal history.* **5a** the area encompassing the royal court that is subject to the jurisdiction of the Lord High Steward. **5b** a rod or wand carried as a symbol of office or emblem of authority, as in the Church. ◆ *vb* **verges, verging, verged. 6** (*intr;* foll. by *on*) to be near (to): *to verge on chaos.* **7** (when *intr,* sometimes foll. by *on*) to serve as the edge of (something): *this narrow strip verges the road.* ORIG C15: from OF, from L *virga* rod

verge[2] (vɜːdʒ) *vb* **verges, verging, verged.** (*intr;* foll. by *to* or *towards*) to move or incline in a certain direction. ORIG C17: from L *vergere*

verger (ˈvɜːdʒə) *n Chiefly Church of England.* **1** a church official who acts as caretaker and attendant. **2** an official who carries the verge or rod of office before a bishop or dean in ceremonies and processions. ORIG C15: from OF, from *verge,* from L *virga* rod, twig

Vergil ★ (ˈvɜːdʒɪl) *n* a variant spelling of **Virgil.**

verglas (ˈvɛəglɑː) *n, pl* **verglases** (-glɑː, -glɑːz). a thin film of ice on rock. ORIG from OF *verre-glaz,* from *verre* glass + *glaz* ice

veridical (vɪˈrɪdɪkəl) *adj* **1** truthful. **2** *Psychol.* of revelations in dreams, etc., that appear to be confirmed by subsequent events. ORIG C17: from L, from *vērus* true + *dīcere* to say
▸ **veˌridiˈcality** *n* ▸ **veˈridically** *adv*

veriest (ˈvɛrɪɪst) *adj Arch.* (intensifier): *the veriest coward.*

verification (ˌvɛrɪfɪˈkeɪʃən) *n* **1** establishment of the correctness of a theory, fact, etc. **2** evidence that provides proof of an assertion, theory, etc.
▸ **ˈverifiˌcatory** *adj*

verify (ˈvɛrɪˌfaɪ) *vb* **verifies, verifying, verified.** (*tr*) **1** to prove to be true; confirm. **2** to check or determine the correctness or truth of by investigation, etc. **3** *Law.* to substantiate or confirm (an oath). ORIG C14: from OF, from Med. L *vērificāre,* from L *vērus* true + *facere* to make
▸ **ˈveriˌfiable** *adj* ▸ **ˈveriˌfiably** *adv* ▸ **ˈveriˌfier** *n*

verily (ˈvɛrɪlɪ) *adv* (*sentence modifier*) *Arch.* in truth; truly: *verily, thou art a man of God.* ORIG C13: from VERY + -LY[2]

verisimilar (ˌvɛrɪˈsɪmɪlə) *adj* probable; likely. ORIG C17: from L, from *vērus* true + *similis* like

verisimilitude (ˌvɛrɪsɪˈmɪlɪˌtjuːd) *n* **1** the appearance or semblance of truth or reality. **2** something that merely seems to be true or real, such as a doubtful statement. ORIG C17: from L, from *vērus* true + *similitūdō* SIMILITUDE

verism (ˈvɪərɪzəm) *n* extreme naturalism in art or literature. ORIG C19: from It. *verismo,* from *vero* true, from L *vērus*
▸ **ˈverist** *n, adj* ▸ **veˈristic** *adj*

verismo (vɛˈrɪzməʊ) *n Music.* a school of composition that originated in Italian opera towards the end of the 19th century, drawing its themes from real life. ORIG C19: from It.; see VERISM

veritable (ˈvɛrɪtəbəl) *adj* (*prenominal*) (intensifier; *usually qualifying a word used metaphorically*): *he's a veritable swine!* ORIG C15: from OF, from *vérité* truth; see VERITY
▸ **ˈveritableness** *n* ▸ **ˈveritably** *adv*

vérité (ˈveɪriːˌteɪ; *French* verite) *adj* involving a high degree of realism or naturalism: *a vérité look at David Bowie.* See also **cinéma vérité.** ORIG F, lit.: truth

verity (ˈvɛrɪtɪ) *n, pl* **verities. 1** the quality or state of being true, real, or correct. **2** a true statement, idea, etc. ORIG C14: from OF from L *vēritās,* from *vērus* true

verjuice (ˈvɜːˌdʒuːs) *n* **1** the acid juice of unripe grapes, apples, or crab apples, formerly much used in making sauces, etc. **2** *Rare.* sourness or sharpness of temper, looks, etc. ORIG C14: from OF *vert jus* green (unripe) juice

Verkhne-Udinsk ★ (*Russian* ˈvjerxnɪuˈdjinsk) *n* the former name (until 1934) of **Ulan-Ude.**

verkrampte (fəˈkramtə) *n* (in South Africa during apartheid) **a** an Afrikaner Nationalist violently opposed to the end of apartheid and to liberalism in general. **b** (*as modifier*): *verkrampte politics.* ORIG C20: from Afrik. (adj), lit.: restricted

Verlaine ★ (*French* vɛrlɛn) *n* **Paul** (pɔl). 1844–96, French poet. His verse includes *Poèmes saturniens* (1866) and *Romances sans paroles* (1874).

verligte (fəˈləxtə) *n* (in South Africa during apartheid) **a** a follower of any liberal White political party. **b** (*as modifier*): *verligte politics.* ORIG C20: from Afrik. (adj), lit.: enlightened

Vermeer ★ (vɛəˈmɪə; *Dutch* vərˈmeːr) *n* **Jan** (jɑn). full name *Jan van der Meer van Delft.* 1632–75, Dutch genre painter.

vermeil (ˈvɜːmeɪl) *n* **1** gilded silver, bronze, or other metal, used esp. in the 19th century. **2a** vermilion. **2b** (*as adj*): *vermeil shoes.* ORIG C15: from OF, from LL *vermiculus* insect (of the genus *Kermes*) or the red dye prepared from it, from L: little worm

vermi- *combining form.* worm: *vermicide; vermiform; vermifuge.* ORIG from L *vermis* worm

vermicelli (ˌvɜːmɪˈsɛlɪ, -ˈtʃɛlɪ) *n* **1** very fine strands of pasta, used in soups. **2** tiny chocolate strands used to coat cakes, etc. ORIG C17: from It.: little worms, from *verme,* from L *vermis*

vermicide (ˈvɜːmɪˌsaɪd) *n* any substance used to kill worms.
▸ **ˌvermiˈcidal** *adj*

vermicular (vɜːˈmɪkjʊlə) *adj* **1** resembling the form, motion, or tracks of worms. **2** of worms or wormlike animals. ORIG C17: from Med. L, from L *vermiculus,* dim. of *vermis* worm
▸ **verˈmiculate** *adj* ▸ **verˌmicuˈlation** *n*

vermiculite (vɜːˈmɪkjʊˌlaɪt) *n* any of a group of micaceous minerals consisting mainly of hydrated silicate of magnesium, aluminium, and iron: on heating they expand and in this form are used in heat and sound insulation. ORIG C19: from VERMICUL(AR) + -ITE[1]

vermiform (ˈvɜːmɪˌfɔːm) *adj* resembling a worm.

vermiform appendix *n* a wormlike pouch extending from the lower end of the caecum in some mammals. Also called: **appendix.**

vermifuge (ˈvɜːmɪˌfjuːdʒ) *n* any drug or agent able to destroy or expel intestinal worms.
▸ **vermifugal** (ˌvɜːmɪˈfjuːgəl) *adj*

vermilion (vəˈmɪljən) *n* **1a** a bright red to reddish-orange colour. **1b** (*as adj*): *a vermilion car.* **2** mercuric sulphide, esp. when used as a bright red pigment; cinnabar. ORIG C13: from OF *vermeillon,* from *vermeil,* from L *vermiculus,* dim. of *vermis* worm

vermin (ˈvɜːmɪn) *n* **1** (*functioning as pl*) small animals collectively, esp. insects and rodents, that are troublesome to man, domestic animals, etc. **2** (*pl* **vermin**) an unpleasant person. ORIG C13: from OF, from L *vermis* worm
▸ **ˈverminous** *adj*

vermis (ˈvɜːmɪs) *n, pl* **vermes** (-miːz). *Anat.* the middle lobe connecting the two halves of the cerebellum. ORIG C19: via NL from L: worm

Vermont ★ (vɜːˈmɒnt) *n* a state in the northeastern US: crossed from north to south by the Green Mountains; bounded on the east by the Connecticut River and by Lake Champlain in the northwest; mainly agricultural. Capital: Montpelier. Pop.: 590 883 (1998 est.). Area: 24 887 sq. km (9609 sq. miles). Abbrevs.: **Vt.** or (with zip code) **VT**
▸ **Verˈmonter** *n*

vermouth (ˈvɜːməθ) *n* any of several wines containing aromatic herbs. ORIG C19: from F, from G *Wermut* WORMWOOD (absinthe)

vernacular (vəˈnækjʊlə) *n* **1 the.** the commonly spoken language or dialect of a particular people or place. **2** a local style of architecture, in which ordinary houses are built: *a true English vernacular.* ◆ *adj* **3** relating to or in the vernacular. **4** designating or relating to the common name of an animal or plant. **5** built in the local style of ordinary houses. ORIG C17: from L *vernāculus* be-

★ people and places

longing to a household slave, from *verna* household slave
▸ **ver'nacularly** *adv*

vernal ('vɜːnᵊl) *adj* **1** of or occurring in spring. **2** *Poetic.* of or characteristic of youth. ORIG C16: from L, from *vēr* spring
▸ **'vernally** *adv*

vernal equinox *n* See at **equinox.**

vernal grass *n* any of a genus of Eurasian grasses, such as **sweet vernal grass**, having the fragrant scent of coumarin.

vernalize *or* **vernalise** ('vɜːnəˌlaɪz) *vb* **vernalizes, vernalizing, vernalized** *or* **vernalises, vernalising, vernalised.** to shorten the period between sowing and flowering in (plants), esp. by subjection of the seeds to low temperatures before planting.
▸ **ˌvernali'zation** *or* **ˌvernali'sation** *n*

vernation (vɜː'neɪʃən) *n* the way in which leaves are arranged in the bud. ORIG C18: from NL, from L *vernāre* to be springlike, from *vēr* spring

Verne ★ (vɜːn; *French* vɛrn) *n* **Jules** (ʒyl). 1828–1905, French writer, esp. of science fiction, such as *Twenty Thousand Leagues under the Sea* (1870).

vernier ('vɜːnɪə) *n* **1** a small movable scale running parallel to the main graduated scale in certain measuring instruments, such as theodolites, used to obtain a fractional reading of one of the divisions on the main scale. **2** (*modifier*) relating to or fitted with a vernier: *a vernier scale.* ORIG C18: after Paul *Vernier* (1580–1637), F mathematician, who described the scale

vernissage (ˌvɜːnɪ'sɑːʒ) *n* a preview or the opening or the first day of an exhibition of paintings. ORIG F, from *vernis* VARNISH

Vernoleninsk ★ (*Russian* vɪrnəlɪ'njiːnsk) *n* the former name of **Nikolayev.**

Verny ★ (*Russian* 'vjɛrnɪj) *n* a former name (until 1927) of **Alma-Ata.**

Verona ★ (və'rəunə; *Italian* ve'roːna) *n* a city in N Italy, in Veneto on the Adige River: strategically situated at the junction of major routes between Italy and N Europe; became a Roman colony (89 B.C.); under Austrian rule (1797–1866); Roman remains. Pop.: 254 145 (1996 est.).
▸ **Veronese** (ˌvɛrə'niːz) *adj, n*

Veronal ('vɛrənᵊl) *n* a trademark for **barbitone.**

Veronese ★ (*Italian* vero'neːse) *n* **Paolo** ('paːolo), original name *Paolo Cagliari* or *Caliari.* 1528–88, Italian painter of the Venetian school. His works include *The Marriage at Cana* (1563) and *The Feast of the Levi* (1573).

veronica[1] (və'rɒnɪkə) *n* any plant of a genus, including the speedwells, of temperate and cold regions, having small blue, pink, or white flowers and flattened notched fruits. ORIG C16: from Med. L, ?from the name *Veronica*

veronica[2] (və'rɒnɪkə) *n Bullfighting.* a pass in which the matador slowly swings the cape away from the charging bull. ORIG from Sp., from the name *Veronica*

Verrazano *or* **Verrazzano** ★ (*Italian* verra'tsaːno) *n* **Giovanni da** (dʒo'vanni da). ?1485–?1528, Florentine navigator; the first European to sight what was to become New York (1524).

Verrocchio ★ (və'rəukɪˌəu; *Italian* ver'rɔkkjo) *n* **Andrea del** (an'drɛːa del). 1435–88, Italian sculptor, painter, and goldsmith of the Florentine school.

verruca (vɛ'ruːkə) *n, pl* **verrucae** (-siː) *or* **verrucas. 1** *Pathol.* a wart, esp. one growing on the hand or foot. **2** *Biol.* a wartlike outgrowth. ORIG C16: from L: wart

verrucose ('vɛrʊˌkəus) *or* **verrucous** ('vɛrʊkəs, vɛ'ruːkəs) *adj Bot.* covered with warty processes. ORIG C17: from L *verrūcōsus* full of warts, from *verrūca* a wart
▸ **verrucosity** (ˌvɛrʊ'kɒsɪtɪ) *n*

Versace ★ (*Italian* vɛr'satʃe) *n* **Gianni** (*Italian* 'dʒani). 1946–97, Italian fashion designer.

Versailles ★ (vɛə'saɪ, -'seɪlz; *French* vɛrsɑj) *n* a city in N central France, near Paris: site of an elaborate royal residence built for Louis XIV; seat of the French kings (1682–1789). Pop.: 87 789 (1990).

★ people and places

versant ('vɜːsᵊnt) *n* **1** the side or slope of a mountain or mountain range. **2** the slope of a region. ORIG C19: from F, from *verser* to turn, from L *versāre*

versatile ('vɜːsəˌtaɪl) *adj* **1** capable of or adapted for many different uses, skills, etc. **2** variable. **3** *Bot.* (of an anther) attached to the filament by a small area so that it moves freely in the wind. **4** *Zool.* able to turn forwards and backwards. ORIG C17: from L *versātilis* moving around, from *versāre* to turn
▸ **'versaˌtilely** *adv* ▸ **versatility** (ˌvɜːsə'tɪlɪtɪ) *n*

verse (vɜːs) *n* **1** (not in technical usage) a stanza of a poem. **2** poetry as distinct from prose. **3a** a series of metrical feet forming a rhythmic unit of one line. **3b** (*as modifier*): *verse line.* **4** a specified type of metre or metrical structure: *iambic verse.* **5** one of the series of short subsections into which most of the writings in the Bible are divided. **6** a poem. ◆ *vb* **verses, versing, versed. 7** a rare word for **versify.** ORIG OE *vers,* from L *versus* furrow, lit.: a turning (of the plough), from *vertere* to turn

versed (vɜːst) *adj* (*postpositive;* foll. by *in*) thoroughly knowledgeable (about), acquainted (with), or skilled (in).

versed sine *n* a trigonometric function equal to one minus the cosine of the specified angle. ORIG C16: from NL, from SINE[1] + *versus,* from *vertere* to turn

versicle ('vɜːsɪkᵊl) *n* **1** a short verse. **2** a short sentence recited or sung by a minister and responded to by his congregation. ORIG C14: from L *versiculus* a little line, from *versus* VERSE

versicolour *or US* **versicolor** ('vɜːsɪˌkʌlə) *adj* of variable or various colours. ORIG C18: from L *versicolor,* from *versāre* to turn + *color* COLOUR

versification (ˌvɜːsɪfɪ'keɪʃən) *n* **1** the technique or art of versifying. **2** the form or metrical composition of a poem. **3** a metrical version of a prose text.

versify ('vɜːsɪˌfaɪ) *vb* **versifies, versifying, versified. 1** (*tr*) to render (something) into verse. **2** (*intr*) to write in verse. ORIG C14: from OF, from L, from *versus* VERSE + *facere* to make
▸ **'versiˌfier** *n*

version ('vɜːʃən) *n* **1** an account of a matter from a certain point of view, as contrasted with others: *his version of the accident is different from the policeman's.* **2** a translation, esp. of the Bible, from one language into another. **3** a variant form of something. **4** an adaptation, as of a book or play into a film. **5** *Med.* manual turning of a fetus to correct an irregular position within the uterus. ORIG C16: from Med. L *versiō* a turning, from L *vertere* to turn
▸ **'versional** *adj*

vers libre *French.* (vɛr librə) *n* (in French poetry) another term for **free verse.**

verso ('vɜːsəʊ) *n, pl* **versos. 1a** the back of a sheet of printed paper. **1b** the left-hand pages of a book, bearing the even numbers. Cf. **recto** (sense 2). **2** the side of a coin opposite to the obverse. ORIG C19: from NL *versō foliō* the leaf having been turned, from L *vertere* to turn + *folium* leaf

verst (vɛəst, vɜːst) *n* a unit of length, used in Russia, equal to 1.067 kilometres (0.6629 miles). ORIG C16: from F or G, from Russian *versta* line

versus ('vɜːsəs) *prep* **1** (esp. in a competition or lawsuit) against. Abbrev.: **v.**, (esp. US) **vs. 2** in contrast with. ORIG C15: from L: turned (in the direction of), opposite, from *vertere* to turn

vertebra ('vɜːtɪbrə) *n, pl* **vertebrae** (-briː) *or* **vertebras.** one of the bony segments of the spinal column. ORIG C17: from L: joint of the spine, from *vertere* to turn
▸ **'vertebral** *adj* ▸ **'vertebrally** *adv*

vertebral column *n* another name for **spinal column.**

vertebrate ('vɜːtɪˌbreɪt, -brɪt) *n* **1** any animal of a subphylum characterized by a bony skeleton and a well-developed brain: the group contains fishes, amphibians, reptiles, birds, and mammals. ◆ *adj* **2** of or belonging to this subphylum.

vertebration (ˌvɜːtɪ'breɪʃən) *n* the formation of vertebrae or segmentation resembling vertebrae.

vertex ('vɜːtɛks) *n, pl* **vertexes** *or* **vertices. 1** the highest point. **2** *Maths.* **2a** the point opposite the base of a figure. **2b** the point of intersection of two sides of a plane figure or angle. **2c** the point of intersection of a pencil of lines or three or more planes of a solid figure. **3** *Anat.* the crown of the head. ORIG C16: from L: highest point, from *vertere* to turn

vertical ('vɜːtɪkᵊl) *adj* **1** at right angles to the horizon; upright: *a vertical wall.* **2** extending in a perpendicular direction. **3** directly overhead. **4** *Econ.* of or relating to associated or consecutive, though not identical, stages of industrial activity: *vertical integration.* **5** of or relating to the vertex. **6** *Anat.* of or situated at the top of the head (vertex). ◆ *n* **7** a vertical plane, position, or line. **8** a vertical post, pillar, etc. ORIG C16: from LL *verticālis,* from L VERTEX
▸ ˌ**vertiˈcality** *n* ▸ ˈ**vertically** *adv*

vertical angles *pl n Geom.* the pair of equal angles between a pair of intersecting lines.

vertical mobility *n Sociol.* the movement of individuals or groups to positions in society that involve a change in class, status, and power.

vertices ('vɜːtɪˌsiːz) *n* a plural of **vertex** (in technical and scientific senses only).

verticil ('vɜːtɪsɪl) *n Biol.* a circular arrangement of parts about an axis, esp. leaves around a stem. ORIG C18: from L *verticillus* whorl (of a spindle), from VERTEX
▸ **verˈticillate** *adj*

vertiginous (vɜːˈtɪdʒɪnəs) *adj* **1** of, relating to, or having vertigo. **2** producing dizziness. **3** whirling. **4** changeable; unstable. ORIG C17: from L *vertīginōsus,* from VERTIGO
▸ **verˈtiginously** *adv*

vertigo ('vɜːtɪgəʊ) *n, pl* **vertigoes** *or* **vertigines** (vɜːˈtɪdʒɪˌniːz). *Pathol.* a sensation of dizziness resulting from a disorder of the sense of balance. ORIG C16: from L: a whirling round, from *vertere* to turn

vertu (vɜːˈtuː) *n* a variant spelling of **virtu.**

Vertumnus (vɜːˈtʌmnəs) *or* **Vortumnus** ★ *n* a Roman god of gardens, orchards, and seasonal change. ORIG from L, from *vertere* to turn, change

Verulamium ★ (ˌvɛruˈleɪmɪəm) *n* the Latin name of **Saint Albans.**

vervain ('vɜːveɪn) *n* any of several plants of the genus *Verbena,* having square stems and long slender spikes of purple, blue, or white flowers. ORIG C14: from OF *verveine,* from L *verbēna* sacred bough

verve (vɜːv) *n* great vitality and liveliness. ORIG C17: from OF: garrulity, from L *verba* words, chatter

vervet ('vɜːvɪt) *n* a variety of a South African guenon monkey having dark hair on the hands and feet and a reddish patch beneath the tail. ORIG C19: from F, from *vert* green

Verwoerd ★ (fəˈvʊt, fɛəˈvʊət) *n* **Hendrik Frensch** ('hɛndrɪk frɛns). 1901–66, South African statesman, born in the Netherlands: prime minister of South Africa (1958–66) and the principal architect of the apartheid system: assassinated.

very ('vɛrɪ) *adv* **1** (intensifier) used to add emphasis to adjectives that are able to be graded: *very good; very tall.* ◆ *adj* (*prenominal*) **2** (intensifier) used with nouns preceded by a definite article or possessive determiner, in order to give emphasis to the significance or relevance of a noun in a particular context, or to give exaggerated intensity to certain nouns: *the very man I want to see; the very back of the room.* **3** (intensifier) used in metaphors to emphasize the applicability of the image to the situation described: *he was a very lion in the fight.* **4** *Arch.* genuine: *the very living God.* ORIG C13: from OF *verai* true, from L *vērax,* from *vērus*

> **USAGE NOTE** In strict usage adverbs of degree such as *very, too, quite, really,* and *extremely* are used only to qualify adjectives: *he is very happy; she is too sad.* By this rule, these words should not be used to qualify past participles that follow the verb *to be,* since they would then be technically qualifying verbs. With the exception of certain participles, such as *tired* or *disappointed,* that have come to be regarded as adjectives, all other past participles are qualified by adverbs such as *much, greatly, seriously,* or *excessively: he has been much* (not *very*) *inconvenienced; she has been excessively* (not *too*) *criticized.*

very high frequency *n* a radio-frequency band or radio frequency lying between 30 and 300 megahertz. Abbrev.: **VHF.**

Very light ('vɛrɪ) *n* a coloured flare fired from a special pistol (**Very pistol**) for signalling at night, esp. at sea. ORIG C19: after Edward W. *Very* (1852–1910), US naval ordnance officer

very low frequency *n* a radio-frequency band or radio frequency lying between 3 and 30 kilohertz. Abbrev.: **VLF.**

Vesalius ★ (vɪˈseɪlɪəs) *n* **Andreas** (*Dutch* anˈdreːas). 1514–64, Flemish anatomist, noted for his *De Humani Corporis fabrica* (1543).

vesica ('vɛsɪkə) *n, pl* **vesicae** (-ˌsiː). *Anat.* a technical name for **bladder** (sense 1). ORIG C17: from L: bladder, sac, blister
▸ ˈ**vesical** *adj* ▸ **vesiculate** (vɛˈsɪkjʊˌleɪt, -lɪt) *vb, adj*

vesicant ('vɛsɪkənt) *or* **vesicatory** ('vɛsɪˌkeɪtərɪ) *n, pl* **vesicants** *or* **vesicatories. 1** any substance that causes blisters. ◆ *adj* **2** acting as a vesicant. ORIG C19: see VESICA

vesicate ('vɛsɪˌkeɪt) *vb* **vesicates, vesicating, vesicated.** to blister. ORIG C17: from NL *vēsīcāre* to blister; see VESICA
▸ ˌ**vesiˈcation** *n*

vesicle ('vɛsɪkᵊl) *n* **1** *Pathol.* **1a** any small sac or cavity, esp. one containing serous fluid. **1b** a blister. **2** *Geol.* a rounded cavity within a rock. **3** *Bot.* a small bladder-like cavity occurring in certain seaweeds. **4** any small cavity or cell. ORIG C16: from L *vēsīcula,* dim. of VESICA
▸ **vesicular** (vɛˈsɪkjʊlə) *adj*

Vespasian ★ (vɛˈspeɪʒɪən) *n* Latin name *Titus Flavius Sabinus Vespasianus.* 9–79 A.D., Roman emperor (69–79), who consolidated Roman rule, esp. in Britain and Germany.

vesper ('vɛspə) *n* **1** an evening prayer, service, or hymn. **2** *Arch.* evening. **3** (*modifier*) of or relating to vespers. ◆ See also **vespers.** ORIG C14: from L: evening, the evening star

vespers ('vɛspəz) *n* (*functioning as sing*) **1** *Chiefly RC Church.* the sixth of the seven canonical hours of the divine office. **2** another word for **evensong** (sense 1).

vespertine ('vɛspəˌtaɪn) *adj* **1** *Bot., zool.* appearing, opening, or active in the evening: *vespertine flowers.* **2** occurring in the evening or (esp. of stars) setting in the evening.

vespiary ('vɛspɪərɪ) *n, pl* **vespiaries.** a nest or colony of social wasps or hornets. ORIG C19: from L *vespa* a wasp, on the model of *apiary*

vespid ('vɛspɪd) *n* **1** any of a family of hymenopterous insects, including the common wasp. ◆ *adj* **2** of or belonging to this family. ORIG C19: from NL, from L *vespa* a wasp
▸ ˈ**vespine** *adj*

Vespucci ★ (vɛˈspuːtʃɪ) *n* **Amerigo** (ameˈriːgo), Latin name *Americus Vespucius.* ?1454–1512, Florentine navigator in the New World (1499–1500; 1501–02), after whom America was named.

vessel ('vɛsᵊl) *n* **1** any object used as a container, esp. for a liquid. **2** a passenger or freight-carrying ship, boat, etc. **3** *Anat.* a tubular structure that transports such body fluids as blood and lymph. **4** *Bot.* a tubular element of xylem tissue transporting water. **5** *Rare.* a person regarded as a vehicle for some purpose or quality. ORIG C13: from OF, from LL *vascellum* urn, from L *vās* vessel

vest (vɛst) *n* **1** an undergarment covering the body from the shoulders to the hips, made of cotton, nylon, etc. Austral. equivalent: **singlet.** US and Canad. equivalent: **undershirt. 2** *US, Canad., & Austral.* a waistcoat. **3** *Obs.* any form of dress. ◆ *vb* **4** (*tr;* foll. by *in*) to place or settle (power, rights, etc., in): *power was vested in the committee.* **5** (*tr;* foll. by *with*) to bestow or confer (on): *the company* *was vested with authority.* **6** (usually foll. by *in*) to confer (a right, title, etc., upon) or (of a right, title, etc.) to pass (to) or devolve (upon). **7** (*tr*) to clothe. **8** (*intr*) to put on clothes, ecclesiastical vestments, etc. ORIG C15: from OF *vestir* to clothe, from L *vestīre*, from *vestis* clothing

vesta ('vɛstə) *n* a short friction match, usually of wood. ORIG C19: after VESTA

Vesta ★ ('vɛstə) *n* the Roman goddess of the hearth and its fire. In her temple a perpetual flame was tended by the vestal virgins. Greek counterpart: **Hestia.**

vestal ('vɛstᵊl) *adj* **1** chaste or pure. **2** of or relating to the Roman goddess Vesta. ◆ *n* **3** a chaste woman, esp. a nun.

vestal virgin *n* (in ancient Rome) one of the virgin priestesses whose lives were dedicated to Vesta and to maintaining the sacred fire in her temple.

vested ('vɛstɪd) *adj Property law.* having a present right to the immediate or future possession and enjoyment of property.

vested interest *n* **1** *Property law.* an existing right to the immediate or future possession and enjoyment of property. **2** a strong personal concern in a state of affairs, etc. **3** a person or group that has such an interest.

vestiary ('vɛstɪərɪ) *n, pl* **vestiaries.** *Obs.* a room for storing clothes or dressing in, such as a vestry. ORIG C17: from LL *vestiārius*, from *vestis* clothing

vestibule ('vɛstɪˌbjuːl) *n* **1** a small entrance hall or anteroom. **2** any small bodily cavity at the entrance to a passage or canal. ORIG C17: from L *vestibulum*

vestige ('vɛstɪdʒ) *n* **1** a small trace; hint: *a vestige of truth.* **2** *Biol.* an organ or part of an organism that is a small nonfunctioning remnant of a functional organ in an ancestor. ORIG C17: via F from L *vestīgium* track
▸ **vesˈtigial** *adj*

Vestmanaeyjar ★ (*Icelandic* 'vɛstmanaɛijar) *n* a group of islands off the S coast of Iceland: they include the island of Surtsey (emerged 1963) and the volcano Helgafell (erupted 1974). Pop.: 4888 (1994). English name: **Vestmann Islands** ('vɛstmən).

vestment ('vɛstmənt) *n* **1** a garment or robe, esp. one denoting office, authority, or rank. **2** any of various ceremonial garments worn by the clergy at religious services, etc. ORIG C13: from OF *vestiment*, from L *vestīmentum*, from *vestīre* to clothe
▸ **vestmental** (vɛst'mɛntᵊl) *adj*

vest-pocket *n* (*modifier*) *Chiefly US.* small enough to fit into a waistcoat pocket.

vestry ('vɛstrɪ) *n, pl* **vestries.** **1** a room in or attached to a church in which vestments, sacred vessels, etc., are kept. **2** a room in or attached to some churches, used for Sunday school, etc. **3** *Church of England.* **3a** a meeting of all the members of a parish or their representatives, to transact the official and administrative business of the parish. **3b** the parish council. ORIG C14: prob. from OF *vestiarie*; see VEST
▸ **ˈvestral** *adj*

vestryman ('vɛstrɪmən) *n, pl* **vestrymen.** a member of a church vestry.

vesture ('vɛstʃə) *Arch.* ◆ *n* **1** a garment or something that seems like a garment: *a vesture of cloud.* ◆ *vb* **vestures, vesturing, vestured.** **2** (*tr*) to clothe. ORIG C14: from OF, from *vestir*, from L *vestīre*, from *vestis* clothing
▸ **ˈvestural** *adj*

Vesuvius ★ (vɪ'suːvɪəs) *n* a volcano in SW Italy, on the Bay of Naples: first recorded eruption in 79 A.D., which destroyed Pompeii, Herculaneum, and Stabiae; numerous eruptions since then. Average height: 1220 m (4003 ft). Italian name: **Vesuvio** (ve'zuːvjo).

vet[1] (vɛt) *n* **1** short for **veterinary surgeon.** ◆ *vb* **vets, vetting, vetted.** **2** (*tr*) *Chiefly Brit.* to make a prior examination and critical appraisal of (a person, document, etc.): *the candidates were well vetted.* **3** to examine or treat (an animal).

vet[2] (vɛt) *n US & Canad.* short for **veteran** (senses 2, 3).

vet. *abbrev. for:* **1** veteran. **2** veterinarian. **3** veterinary. ◆ Also (for senses 2, 3): **veter.**

vetch (vɛtʃ) *n* **1** any of various climbing plants having pinnate leaves, blue or purple flowers, and tendrils on the stems. **2** any of various similar and related plants, such as the kidney vetch. **3** the beanlike fruit of any of these plants. ORIG C14 *fecche*, from OF *veche*, from L *vicia*

vetchling ('vɛtʃlɪŋ) *n* any of various tendril-climbing plants, mainly of N temperate regions, having winged or angled stems and showy flowers. See also **sweet pea.**

veteran ('vɛtərən) *n* **1a** a person or thing that has given long service in some capacity. **1b** (*as modifier*): *veteran firemen.* **2** a soldier who has seen considerable active service. **3** *US & Canad.* a person who has served in the military forces. ORIG C16: from L, from *vetus* old

veteran car *n Brit.* a car constructed before 1919, esp. one constructed before 1905. Cf. **classic car, vintage car.**

veterinary ('vɛtərɪnərɪ) *adj* of or relating to veterinary medicine. ORIG C18: from L *veterīnārius*, from *veterīnae* draught animals

veterinary medicine *or* **science** *n* the branch of medicine concerned with the health of animals and the treatment of injuries or diseases that affect them.

veterinary surgeon *n Brit.* a person qualified to practise veterinary medicine. US and Canad. term: **veterinarian.**

veto ('viːtəʊ) *n, pl* **vetoes.** **1** the power to prevent legislation or action proposed by others: *the presidential veto.* **2** the exercise of this power. ◆ *vb* **vetoes, vetoing, vetoed.** (*tr*) **3** to refuse consent to (a proposal, esp. a government bill). **4** to prohibit, ban, or forbid: *her parents vetoed her trip.* ORIG C17: from L: I forbid, from *vetāre* to forbid
▸ **ˈvetoer** *n*

vex (vɛks) *vb* (*tr*) **1** to anger or annoy. **2** to confuse; worry. **3** *Arch.* to agitate. ORIG C15: from OF *vexer*, from L *vexāre* to jolt (in carrying), from *vehere* to convey
▸ **ˈvexer** *n* ▸ **ˈvexing** *adj*

vexation (vɛk'seɪʃən) *n* **1** the act of vexing or the state of being vexed. **2** something that vexes.

vexatious (vɛk'seɪʃəs) *adj* **1** vexing or tending to vex. **2** vexed. **3** *Law.* (of a legal action or proceeding) instituted without sufficient grounds, esp. so as to cause annoyance to the defendant.
▸ **vexˈatiously** *adv*

vexed (vɛkst) *adj* **1** annoyed, confused, or agitated. **2** much debated (esp. in **a vexed question**).
▸ **vexedly** ('vɛksɪdlɪ) *adv*

vexillology (ˌvɛksɪ'lɒlədʒɪ) *n* the study and collection of information about flags. ORIG C20: from L *vexillum* flag + -LOGY
▸ **ˌvexilˈlologist** *n*

vexillum (vɛk'sɪləm) *n, pl* **vexilla** (-lə). **1** *Ornithol.* the vane of a feather. **2** Also called: **standard.** *Bot.* the largest petal of a papilionaceous flower. ORIG C18: from L: banner, ?from *vēlum* sail
▸ **ˈvexillate** *adj*

VF *abbrev. for* video frequency.

VFA (in Australia) *abbrev. for* Victorian Football Association.

vg *abbrev. for* very good.

VG *abbrev. for* Vicar General.

VGA *abbrev. for* video graphics array: a computing standard for spatial and colour resolution.

VHF *or* **vhf** *Radio. abbrev. for* very high frequency.

VHS *Trademark. abbrev. for* video home system: a video cassette recording system using ½″ magnetic tape.

VI *abbrev. for:* **1** Vancouver Island. **2** Virgin Islands.

v.i. *abbrev. for* vide infra (see **vide**).

via ('vaɪə) *prep* by way of; by means of; through: *to London via Paris.* ORIG C18: from L *viā*, from *via* way

viable ('vaɪəbᵊl) *adj* **1** capable of becoming actual, etc.: *a viable proposition.* **2** (of seeds, eggs, etc.) capable of normal growth and development. **3** (of a fetus) having reached a stage of development at which further development can occur independently of the mother. ORIG C19: from F, from *vie* life, from L *vīta*
▸ **ˌviaˈbility** *n*

Via Dolorosa ★ ('viːə ˌdɒlə'rəʊsə) *n* the route followed by Christ from the place of his condemnation to Calvary for his crucifixion. ORIG L, lit.: sorrowful road

viaduct (ˈvaɪəˌdʌkt) *n* a bridge, esp. for carrying a road or railway across a valley, etc. ORIG C19: from L *via* way + *dūcere* to bring, on the model of *aqueduct*

Viagra (vaɪˈægrə, viː-) *n Trademark.* a drug that allows increased blood flow to the penis; used to treat impotence in men.

vial (ˈvaɪəl) *n* a less common variant of **phial**. ORIG C14 *fiole,* from OF, ult. from Gk *phialē;* see PHIAL

via media *Latin.* (ˈvaɪə ˈmiːdɪə) *n* a compromise between two extremes.

viand (ˈviːənd) *n* **1** a type of food, esp. a delicacy. **2** (*pl*) provisions. ORIG C14: from OF, ult. from L *vīvenda* things to be lived on, from *vīvere* to live

Viareggio ★ (*Italian* viaˈreddʒo) *n* a town and resort in W Italy, in Tuscany on the Ligurian Sea. Pop.: 50 310 (1987 est.).

viatical (vaɪˈætɪkᵊl) *adj* **1** of or denoting a road or a journey. **2** *Bot.* (of a plant) growing by the side of a road. ORIG C19: from L *viāticus* belonging to a journey + -AL

viatical settlement *n* the purchase by a charity of a life assurance policy owned by a person with only a short time to live, to enable that person to use the proceeds during his or her lifetime. See also **death futures**.

viaticum (vaɪˈætɪkəm) *n, pl* **viatica** (-kə) *or* **viaticums. 1** *Christianity.* Holy Communion as administered to a person dying or in danger of death. **2** *Rare.* provisions or a travel allowance for a journey. ORIG C16: from L, from *viāticus* belonging to a journey, from *via* way

vibes (vaɪbz) *pl n* **1** *Inf.* short for **vibraphone. 2** *Sl.* short for **vibrations.**

Viborg ★ *n* **1** (ˈviːbɔrj). the Swedish name for **Vyborg. 2** (*Danish* ˈvibɔr). a town in N central Denmark, in Jutland: formerly a royal town and capital of Jutland. Pop.: 29 455 (1990).

vibraculum (vaɪˈbrækjʊləm) *n, pl* **vibracula** (-lə). *Zool.* any of the specialized bristle-like polyps in certain bryozoans, the actions of which prevent parasites from settling on the colony. ORIG C19: from NL, from L *vibrāre* to brandish

vibrant (ˈvaɪbrənt) *adj* **1** characterized by or exhibiting vibration. **2** giving an impression of vigour and activity. **3** caused by vibration; resonant. ORIG C16: from L *vibrāre* to agitate
▸ **ˈvibrancy** *n* ▸ **ˈvibrantly** *adv*

vibraphone (ˈvaɪbrəˌfəʊn) *n* a percussion instrument consisting of a set of metal bars placed over tubular metal resonators, which are made to vibrate electronically.
▸ **ˈvibraˌphonist** *n*

vibrate (vaɪˈbreɪt) *vb* **vibrates, vibrating, vibrated. 1** to move or cause to move back and forth rapidly. **2** (*intr*) to oscillate. **3** to resonate or cause to resonate. **4** (*intr*) to waver. **5** *Physics.* to undergo or cause to undergo an oscillatory process, as of an alternating current. **6** (*intr*) *Rare.* to respond emotionally; thrill. ORIG C17: from L *vibrāre*
▸ **vibratile** (ˈvaɪbrəˌtaɪl) *adj* ▸ **viˈbrating** *adj* ▸ **vibratory** (ˈvaɪbrətərɪ) *adj*

vibration (vaɪˈbreɪʃən) *n* **1** the act or an instance of vibrating. **2** *Physics.* **2a** a periodic motion about an equilibrium position, such as in the propagation of sound. **2b** a single cycle of such a motion. **3** the process or state of vibrating or being vibrated.
▸ **viˈbrational** *adj*

vibrations (vaɪˈbreɪʃənz) *pl n Sl.* **1** instinctive feelings supposedly influencing human communication. **2** a characteristic atmosphere felt to be emanating from places or objects.

vibrato (vɪˈbrɑːtəʊ) *n, pl* **vibratos.** *Music.* **1** a slight, rapid, and regular fluctuation in the pitch of a note produced on a stringed instrument by a shaking movement of the hand stopping the strings. **2** an oscillatory effect produced in singing by fluctuation in breath pressure or pitch. ORIG C19: from It., from L *vibrāre* to VIBRATE

vibrator (vaɪˈbreɪtə) *n* **a** a device for producing a vibratory motion, such as one used in massage. **b** such a device with a vibrating part or tip, used as a dildo.

vibrissa (vaɪˈbrɪsə) *n, pl* **vibrissae** (-siː). (*usually pl*) **1** any of the bristle-like sensitive hairs on the face of many mammals; a whisker. **2** any of the specialized bristle-like feathers around the beak in certain insectivorous birds. ORIG C17: from L, prob. from *vibrāre* to shake
▸ **viˈbrissal** *adj*

viburnum (vaɪˈbɜːnəm) *n* **1** any of various temperate and subtropical shrubs or trees having small white flowers and berry-like red or black fruits. **2** the dried bark of several species of this tree, sometimes used in medicine. ORIG C18: from L: wayfaring tree

Vic. *Austral. abbrev. for* Victoria (the state).

vicar (ˈvɪkə) *n* **1** *Church of England.* **1a** (in Britain) a member of the clergy appointed to act as priest of a parish. **1b** a clergyman who acts as assistant to or substitute for the rector of a parish at Communion. **2** *RC Church.* a bishop or priest representing the pope and exercising a limited jurisdiction. **3** Also called: **lay vicar, vicar choral.** *Church of England.* a member of a cathedral choir appointed to sing certain parts of the services. ORIG C13: from OF, from L *vicārius* (n) a deputy, from *vicārius* (adj) VICARIOUS
▸ **vicarial** (vɪˈkɛərɪəl) *adj* ▸ **viˈcariate** *n* ▸ **ˈvicarly** *adj*

vicarage (ˈvɪkərɪdʒ) *n* the residence or benefice of a vicar.

vicar apostolic *n RC Church.* a titular bishop having jurisdiction in missionary countries.

vicar general *n, pl* **vicars general.** an official, usually a layman, appointed to assist the bishop of a diocese in discharging his administrative or judicial duties.

vicarious (vɪˈkɛərɪəs, vaɪ-) *adj* **1** undergone at second hand through sympathetic participation in another's experiences. **2** undergone or done as the substitute for another: *vicarious punishment.* **3** delegated: *vicarious authority.* **4** taking the place of another. ORIG C17: from L *vicārius* substituted, from *vicis* interchange
▸ **viˈcariously** *adv* ▸ **viˈcariousness** *n*

Vicar of Bray ★ (breɪ) *n* a vicar (Simon Aleyn) appointed to the parish of Bray in Berkshire during Henry VIII's reign who changed his faith to Catholic when Mary I was on the throne and back to Protestant when Elizabeth I succeeded and so retained his living.

Vicar of Christ *n RC Church.* the pope when regarded as Christ's earthly representative.

vice[1] (vaɪs) *n* **1** an immoral, wicked, or evil habit, action, or trait. **2** frequent indulgence in immoral or degrading practices. **3** a specific form of pernicious conduct, esp. prostitution or sexual perversion. **4** an imperfection in character, conduct, etc.: *smoking is his only vice.* **5** a bad trick or disposition, as of horses, dogs, etc. ORIG C13: via OF from L *vitium* a defect

vice[2] *or US* (*often*) **vise** (vaɪs) *n* **1** an appliance for holding an object while work is done on it, usually having a pair of jaws. ◆ *vb* **2** (*tr*) to grip (something) with or as if with a vice. ORIG C15: from OF *vis* a screw, from L *vītis* vine, plant with spiralling tendrils (hence the later meaning)

vice[3] (vaɪs) *adj* **1a** (*prenominal*) serving in the place of. **1b** (*in combination*): *viceroy.* ◆ *n* **2** *Inf.* a person who serves as a deputy to another. ORIG C18: from L, from *vicis* interchange

vice[4] (ˈvaɪsɪ) *prep* instead of; as a substitute for. ORIG C16: from L, ablative of *vicis* change

vice admiral *n* a commissioned officer of flag rank in certain navies, junior to an admiral and senior to a rear admiral.

vice-chairman *n, pl* **vice-chairmen.** a person who deputizes for a chairman and serves in his place during his absence. Also: **vice-chairperson** *or* (*fem*) **vice-chairwoman.**
▸ **ˌvice-ˈchairmanship** *n*

vice chancellor *n* **1** the chief executive or administrator at some British universities. **2** (in the US) a judge in courts of equity subordinate to the chancellor. **3** (formerly in England) a senior judge of the court of chancery who acted as assistant to the Lord Chancellor. **4** a person serving as the deputy of a chancellor.
▸ **ˌvice-ˈchancellorship** *n*

vicegerent (ˌvaɪsˈdʒɛrənt) *n* **1** a person appointed to exercise all or some of the authority of another. **2** *RC*

Church. the pope or any other representative of God or Christ on earth, such as a bishop. ◆ *adj* **3** invested with or characterized by delegated authority. ORIG C16: from NL, from VICE³ + L *gerere* to manage
▸ ˌ**vice'gerency** *n*

vicennial (vɪ'sɛnɪəl) *adj* **1** occurring every 20 years. **2** lasting for a period of 20 years. ORIG C18: from LL *vīcennium* period of twenty years, from L *vīciēs* twenty times + *-ennium,* from *annus* year

Vicenza ★ (*Italian* vi'tʃentsa) *n* a city in NE Italy, in Veneto: home of the architect Andrea Palladio and site of some of his finest works. Pop.: 107 786 (1996 est.).

vice president *n* an officer ranking immediately below a president and serving as his or her deputy. A vice president takes the president's place during his or her absence or incapacity, after his or her death, and in certain other circumstances. Abbrev.: **VP.**
▸ ˌ**vice-'presidency** *n*

viceregal (ˌvaɪs'riːgᵊl) *adj* **1** of or relating to a viceroy. **2** *Chiefly Austral. & NZ.* of or relating to a governor or governor general.
▸ ˌ**vice'regally** *adv*

vicereine (ˌvaɪs'reɪn) *n* **1** the wife of a viceroy. **2** a female viceroy. ORIG C19: from F, from VICE³ + *reine* queen, from L *rēgīna*

viceroy ('vaɪsrɔɪ) *n* a governor of a colony, country, or province who acts for and rules in the name of his sovereign or government. Related adj: **viceregal.** ORIG C16: from F, from VICE³ + *roy* king, from L *rex*
▸ '**viceroyship** *or* ˌ**vice'royalty** *n*

vice squad *n* a police division to which is assigned the enforcement of gaming and prostitution laws.

vice versa ('vaɪsɪ 'vɜːsə) *adv* the other way around. ORIG C17: from L: relations being reversed, from *vicis* change + *vertere* to turn

Vichy ★ (*French* viʃi; *English* 'viːʃiː) *n* a town and spa in central France, on the River Allier: seat of the collaborationist government under Marshal Pétain (1940–44); mineral waters bottled for export. Pop.: 28 048 (1990). Latin name: **Vicus Calidus** ('viːkəs 'kælɪdəs).

vichyssoise (*French* viʃiswaz) *n* a thick soup made from leeks, potatoes, chicken stock, and cream, usually served chilled. ORIG F, from (*crème*) *vichyssoise* (*glacée*) (ice-cold cream) from Vichy

vichy water *n* **1** (*sometimes cap.*) a mineral water from springs at Vichy in France, reputed to be beneficial to health. **2** any sparkling mineral water resembling this.

vicinage ('vɪsɪnɪdʒ) *n Now rare.* **1** the residents of a particular neighbourhood. **2** a less common word for **vicinity.** ORIG C14: from OF *vicenage,* from *vicin* neighbouring, from L *vīcīnus*

vicinal ('vɪsɪnᵊl) *adj* **1** neighbouring. **2** (esp. of roads) of or relating to a locality. ORIG C17: from L *vīcīnālis* nearby, from *vīcīnus,* from *vīcus* a neighbourhood

vicinity (vɪ'sɪnɪtɪ) *n, pl* **vicinities. 1** a surrounding area; neighbourhood. **2** the fact or condition of being close in space or relationship. ORIG C16: from L, from *vīcīnus* neighbouring, from *vīcus* village

vicious ('vɪʃəs) *adj* **1** wicked or cruel: *a vicious thug.* **2** characterized by violence or ferocity: *a vicious blow.* **3** *Inf.* unpleasantly severe; harsh: *a vicious wind.* **4** characterized by malice: *vicious lies.* **5** (esp. of dogs, horses, etc.) ferocious. **6** characterized by or leading to vice. **7** invalidated by defects; unsound: *a vicious inference.* ORIG C14: from OF, from L *vitiōsus* full of faults, from *vitium* defect
▸ '**viciously** *adv* ▸ '**viciousness** *n*

vicious circle *n* **1** Also: **vicious cycle.** a situation in which an attempt to resolve one problem creates new problems that lead back to the original situation. **2** *Logic.* **2a** a form of reasoning in which a conclusion is inferred from premises the truth of which cannot be established independently of that conclusion. **2b** an explanation given in terms that cannot be understood independently of that which was to be explained.

vicissitude (vɪ'sɪsɪˌtjuːd) *n* **1** variation or mutability in nature or life, esp. successive alternation from one condition or thing to another. **2** a variation in circumstance, fortune, etc. ORIG C16: from L *vicissitūdō,* from *vicis* change
▸ viˌ**cissi'tudinous** *adj*

Vicksburg ★ ('vɪksˌbɜːg) *n* a city in W Mississippi, on the Mississippi River: site of one of the most decisive campaigns (1863) of the American Civil War, in which the Confederates were besieged for nearly seven weeks before capitulating. Pop.: 20 908 (1990).

Vicky ★ ('vɪkɪ) *n* professional name of *Victor Weisz.* 1913–66, British political cartoonist, born in Germany.

Vico ★ ('viːkəʊ; *Italian* 'viːko) *n* **Giovanni Battista** (dʒo'vanni bat'tista). 1668–1744, Italian philosopher, noted for his *Scienza Nuova* (1721).

victim ('vɪktɪm) *n* **1** a person or thing that suffers harm, death, etc.: *victims of tyranny.* **2** a person who is tricked or swindled. **3** a living person or animal sacrificed in a religious rite. ORIG C15: from L *victima*

victimize *or* **victimise** ('vɪktɪˌmaɪz) *vb* **victimizes, victimizing, victimized** *or* **victimises, victimising, victimised.** (*tr*) **1** to punish or discriminate against unfairly. **2** to make a victim of.
▸ ˌ**victimi'zation** *or* ˌ**victimi'sation** *n* ▸ '**victimˌizer** *or* '**victimˌiser** *n*

victimology (ˌvɪktɪ'mɒlədʒɪ) *n* the study of the psychological effects experienced by the victims of crime.
▸ ˌ**victi'mologist** *n*

victor ('vɪktə) *n* **1a** a person, nation, etc., that has defeated an adversary in war, etc. **1b** (*as modifier*): *the victor army.* **2** the winner of any contest, conflict, or struggle. ORIG C14: from L, from *vincere* to conquer

Victor Emmanuel II ★ ('vɪktə) *n* 1820–78, king of Sardinia-Piedmont (1849–78) and first king of Italy from 1861.

Victor Emmanuel III ★ *n* 1869–1947, last king of Italy (1900–46): dominated after 1922 by Mussolini: abdicated.

victoria (vɪk'tɔːrɪə) *n* **1** a light four-wheeled horse-drawn carriage with a folding hood, two passenger seats, and a seat in front for the driver. **2** Also called: **victoria plum.** *Brit.* a large sweet variety of plum, red and yellow in colour. ORIG C19: both after Queen VICTORIA

Victoria¹ ★ (vɪk'tɔːrɪə) *n* **1** a state of SE Australia: part of New South Wales colony until 1851; semiarid in the northwest, with the Great Dividing Range in the centre and east and the Murray River along the N border. Capital: Melbourne. Pop.: 4 373 520 (1996). Area: 227 620 sq. km (87 884 sq. miles). **2 Lake.** Also called: **Victoria Nyanza.** a lake in East Africa, in Tanzania, Uganda, and Kenya, at an altitude of 1134 m (3720 ft): the largest lake in Africa and second largest in the world; drained by the Victoria Nile. Area: 69 485 sq. km (26 828 sq. miles). **3** a port in SW Canada, capital of British Columbia, on Vancouver Island: founded in 1843 by the Hudson's Bay Company; made capital of British Columbia in 1868; university (1963). Pop.: 287 897 (1991). **4** the capital of the Seychelles, a port on NE Mahé. Pop.: 25 000 (1993 est.). **5** a region in S China, on N Hong Kong Island: financial centre; university (1911). Pop.: 595 000 (latest est.). **6 Mount.** a mountain in SE Papua New Guinea: the highest peak of the Owen Stanley Range. Height: 4073 m (13 363 ft).

Victoria² ★ *n* **1** (vɪk'tɔːrɪə). 1819–1901, queen of the United Kingdom (1837–1901) and empress of India (1876–1901). She married Prince Albert of Saxe-Coburg-Gotha (1840). **2** (*Spanish* bik'torja). **Tomás Luis de** (to'mas lwis də). ?1548–1611, Spanish composer of motets and masses.

Victoria³ ★ (vɪk'tɔːrɪə) *n* the Roman goddess of victory. Greek counterpart: **Nike.**

Victoria and Albert Museum ★ *n* a museum of the fine and applied arts in London, originating from 1856 and given its present name and site in 1899. Abbrev.: **V and A.**

Victoria Cross *n* the highest decoration for gallantry in the face of the enemy awarded to the British and Commonwealth armed forces: instituted in 1856 by Queen Victoria.

Victoria Day *n* the Monday preceding May 24: observed in Canada as a national holiday in commemoration of the birthday of Queen Victoria.

Victoria Desert ★ *n* See **Great Victoria Desert.**

Victoria Falls ★ *pl n* a waterfall on the border between Zimbabwe and Zambia, on the Zambezi River. Height: about 108 m (355 ft). Width: about 1400 m (4500 ft).

Victoria Island ★ *n* a large island in the Canadian Arctic: part of the Northwest Territories. Area: about 212 000 sq. km (82 000 sq. miles).

Victoria Land ★ *n* a section of Antarctica, largely in the Ross Dependency on the Ross Sea.

Victorian (vɪk'tɔːrɪən) *adj* **1.** of or characteristic of Queen Victoria or the period of her reign. **2.** exhibiting the characteristics popularly attributed to the Victorians, esp. prudery, bigotry, or hypocrisy. Cf. **Victorian values. 3** of or relating to Victoria (the state or any of the cities). ◆ *n* **4** a person who lived during the reign of Queen Victoria. **5** an inhabitant of Victoria (the state or any of the cities).
▸ **Vic'torian,ism** *n*

Victoriana (vɪk,tɔːrɪ'ɑːnə) *pl n* objects, ornaments, etc., of the Victorian period.

Victoria Nile ★ *n* See **Nile.**

Victorian values *pl n* the qualities of enterprise and initiative, the importance of the family, and the development of charitable voluntary work considered to characterize the Victorian period. Cf. **Victorian** (sense 2).

victorious (vɪk'tɔːrɪəs) *adj* **1** having defeated an adversary: *the victorious nations.* **2** of, indicative of, or characterized by victory: *a victorious conclusion.*
▸ **vic'toriously** *adv*

victory ('vɪktərɪ) *n, pl* **victories. 1** final and complete superiority in a war. **2** a successful military engagement. **3** a success attained in a contest or struggle or over an opponent, obstacle, or problem. **4** the act of triumphing or state of having triumphed. ORIG C14: from OF *victorie,* from L *victōria,* from *vincere* to subdue

Victory ★ ('vɪktərɪ) *n* another name (in English) for the Roman goddess **Victoria** or the Greek **Nike.**

victory roll *n* a rolling aircraft manoeuvre made by a pilot to announce or celebrate the shooting down of an enemy plane.

victual ('vɪt°l) *vb* **victuals, victualling, victualled** *or US* **victuals, victualing, victualed.** to supply with or obtain victuals. See also **victuals.** ORIG C14: from OF *vitaille,* from LL *victuālia* provisions, from L *victus* sustenance, from *vīvere* to live
▸ **'victual-less** *adj*

victualler ('vɪtələ) *n* **1** a supplier of victuals, as to an army. **2** *Brit.* a licensed purveyor of spirits. **3** a supply ship, esp. one carrying foodstuffs.

victuals ('vɪt°lz) *pl n* (*sometimes sing*) food or provisions.

vicuña (vɪ'kuːnjə) *or* **vicuna** (vɪ'kjuːnə, -'kuːnjə) *n* **1** a tawny-coloured cud-chewing Andean mammal similar to the llama. **2** the fine light cloth made from the wool obtained from this animal. ORIG C17: from Sp., from Quechuan *wikúña*

vid (vɪd) *n Inf.* short for **video** (sense 4).

Vidal ★ (viː'dæl) *n* **Gore.** born 1925, US novelist and essayist. His novels include *Burr* (1974), *Lincoln* (1984), and *The Season of Conflict* (1996).

vide ('vaɪdɪ) (used to direct a reader to a specified place in a text, another book, etc.) refer to, see (often in **vide ante** (see before), **vide infra** (see below), **vide supra** (see above), etc.) Abbrev.: **v., vid.** ORIG C16: from L

videlicet (vɪ'diːlɪ,sɛt) *adv* namely: used to specify items, etc. Abbrev.: **viz.** ORIG C15: from L

video ('vɪdɪəʊ) *adj* **1** relating to or employed in the transmission or reception of a televised image. **2** of, concerned with, or operating at video frequencies. ◆ *n, pl* **videos. 3** the visual elements of a television broadcast. **4** a film recorded on a video cassette. **5** short for **video cassette, video cassette recorder. 6** *US.* an informal name for **television.** ◆ *vb* **videos, videoing, videoed. 7** to record (a television programme, etc.) on a video cassette recorder. ORIG C20: from L *vidēre* to see, on the model of AUDIO

video cassette *n* a cassette containing video tape.

video cassette recorder *n* a tape recorder for vision and sound signals using magnetic tape in closed plastic cassettes: used for recording and playing back television programmes and films. Often shortened to **video** or **video recorder.**

videodisc ('vɪdɪəʊ,dɪsk) *n* another name for **optical disk.**

video frequency *n* the frequency of a signal conveying the image and synchronizing pulses in a television broadcasting system. It lies in the range from about 50 hertz to 8 megahertz.

video game *n* any of various games that can be played by using an electronic control to move graphical symbols on the screen of a visual display unit.

video jockey *n* a person who introduces and plays videos, esp. of pop songs, on a television programme.

video nasty *n, pl* **nasties.** a film, usually specially made for video, that is explicitly horrific and pornographic.

videophone ('vɪdɪə,fəʊn) *n* a telephonic device through which there is both verbal and visual communication.

video recorder *n* short for **video cassette recorder.**

video tape *n* **1** magnetic tape used mainly for recording the sound and vision signals of a television programme or film for subsequent transmission. ◆ *vb* **video-tape, video-tapes, video-taping, video-taped. 2** to record (a programme, etc.) on video tape.

video tape recorder *n* a tape recorder for visual signals and usually accompanying sound, using magnetic tape on open spools: used in television broadcasting.

Videotex ('vɪdɪəʊ,tɛks) *n Trademark.* an information system that displays information from a distant computer on a television screen. See also **Teletext, Viewdata.**

videotext ('vɪdɪəʊ,tɛkst) *n* a means of providing a written or graphical representation of computerized information on a television screen.

vidicon ('vɪdɪ,kɒn) *n* a small television camera tube, used in closed-circuit television and outside broadcasts, in which incident light forms an electric charge pattern on a photoconductive surface. ORIG C20: from VID(EO) + ICON(OSCOPE)

vie (vaɪ) *vb* **vies, vying, vied.** (*intr;* foll. by *with* or *for*) to contend for superiority or victory (with) or strive in competition (for). ORIG C15: prob. from OF *envier* to challenge, from L *invītāre* to INVITE
▸ **'vier** *n* ▸ **'vying** *adj, n*

Vienna ★ (vɪ'ɛnə) *n* the capital and the smallest state of Austria, in the northeast on the River Danube: seat of the Hapsburgs (1278-1918); residence of the Holy Roman Emperor (1558–1806); withstood sieges by Turks in 1529 and 1683; political and cultural centre in the 18th and 19th centuries, associated with many composers; university (1365). Pop.: 1 609 631 (1998 est.). Area: 1075 sq. km (415 sq. miles). German name: **Wien.**
▸ **Viennese** (,vɪə'niːz) *adj, n*

Vienne ★ (*French* vjɛn) *n* **1** a department of W central France, in Poitou-Charentes region. Capital: Poitiers. Pop.: 388 701 (1994 est.). Area: 7044 sq. km (2747 sq. miles). **2** a town in SE France, on the River Rhône: extensive Roman remains. Ancient name: **Vienna. 3** a river in SW central France, flowing west and north to the Loire below Chinon. Length: over 350 km (200 miles).

Vientiane ★ (,vjɛntɪ'ɑːn) *n* the administrative capital of Laos, in the south near the border with Thailand: capital of the kingdom of Vientiane from 1707 until taken by the Thais in 1827. Pop.: 531 800 (1996 est.).

Vierwaldstättersee ★ (fiːr'valtʃtɛtər,zeː) *n* the German name for (Lake) **Lucerne.**

vies (fɪs) *adj S. African sl.* angry, furious, or disgusted. ORIG Afrik.

Vietnam (,vjɛt'næm) *or* **Viet Nam** ★ *n* a republic in SE Asia: an ancient empire, conquered by France in the 19th century; occupied by Japan (1940–45) when the Communist-led Vietminh began resistance operations that were continued against restored French rule after 1945. In 1954 the country was divided along the 17th parallel, establishing North Vietnam (under the Vietminh) and South Vietnam (under French control), the latter becoming the independent **Republic of Vietnam**

in 1955. From 1959 the country was dominated by war between the Communist Vietcong, supported by North Vietnam, and the South Vietnamese government; increasing numbers of US forces were brought to the aid of the South Vietnamese army until a peace agreement (1973) led to the withdrawal of US troops; further fighting led to the eventual defeat of the South Vietnamese government in March 1975 and in 1976 an elected National Assembly proclaimed the reunification of the country. Official language: Vietnamese. Religion: Buddhist majority. Currency: dong. Capital: Hanoi. Pop.: 77 311 000 (1999 est.). Area: 331 041 sq. km (127 816 sq. miles). Official name: **Socialist Republic of Vietnam.**
▸ ˌ**Vietnaˈmese** *adj, n*

vieux jeu *French.* (vjø ʒø) *adj* old-fashioned. ORIG lit.: old game

view (vjuː) *n* **1** the act of seeing or observing. **2** vision or sight, esp. range of vision: *the church is out of view.* **3** a scene, esp. of a fine tract of countryside: *the view from the top was superb.* **4** a pictorial representation of a scene, such as a photograph. **5** (*sometimes pl*) opinion: *my own view on the matter differs from yours.* **6** (foll. by *to*) a desired end or intention: *he has a view to securing further qualifications.* **7** a general survey of a topic, subject, etc. **8** visual aspect or appearance: *they look the same in outward view.* **9** a sight of a hunted animal before or during the chase. **10 in view of.** taking into consideration. **11 on view.** exhibited to the public gaze. **12 take a dim** *or* **poor view of.** to regard (something) with disfavour. **13 with a view to. 13a** with the intention of. **13b** in anticipation or hope of. ◆ *vb* **14** (*tr*) to look at. **15** (*tr*) to consider in a specified manner: *they view change with suspicion.* **16** (*tr*) to examine or inspect carefully: *to view the accounts.* **17** (*tr*) to contemplate: *to view the difficulties.* **18** to watch (television). **19** (*tr*) to sight (a hunted animal) before or during the chase. ORIG C15: from OF, from *veoir* to see, from L *vidēre*
▸ ˈ**viewable** *adj*

Viewdata (ˈvjuːˌdeɪtə) *n Trademark.* an interactive form of Videotext that sends information from a distant computer along telephone lines, enabling shopping, booking theatre and airline tickets, and banking transactions to be conducted from the home.

viewer (ˈvjuːə) *n* **1** a person who views something, esp. television. **2** any optical device by means of which something is viewed, esp. one used for viewing photographic transparencies.

viewfinder (ˈvjuːˌfaɪndə) *n* a device on a camera, consisting of a lens system, enabling the user to see what will be included in his photograph.

view halloo *interj* a huntsman's cry uttered when the quarry is seen breaking cover or shortly afterwards.

viewing (ˈvjuːɪŋ) *n* **1** the act of watching television. **2** television programmes collectively: *late-night viewing.*

viewless (ˈvjuːlɪs) *adj* **1** (of windows, etc.) not affording a view. **2** having no opinions. **3** *Poetic.* invisible.

viewpoint (ˈvjuːˌpɔɪnt) *n* **1** the mental attitude that determines a person's judgments. **2** a place from which something can be viewed.

Vigée-Lebrun ★ (*French* viʒelәbrœ̃) *n* (**Marie Louise**) **Élisabeth** (elizabɛt). 1755–1842, French painter, noted for her portraits of women.

vigesimal (vaɪˈdʒɛsɪməl) *adj* **1** relating to or based on the number 20. **2** taking place or proceeding in intervals of 20. **3** twentieth. ORIG C17: from L *vīgēsimus,* var. (infl. by *vīgintī* twenty) of *vīcēsimus* twentieth

vigia (ˈvɪdʒɪə) *n Naut.* a navigational hazard marked on a chart although its existence and nature has not been confirmed. ORIG C19: from Sp. *vigía* reef, from L *vigilāre* to keep watch

vigil (ˈvɪdʒɪl) *n* **1** a purposeful watch maintained, esp. at night, to guard, observe, pray, etc. **2** the period of such a watch. **3** *RC Church, Church of England.* the eve of certain major festivals, formerly observed as a night spent in prayer. ORIG C13: from OF, from Med. L *vigilia* watch preceding a religious festival, from L, from *vigil* alert, from *vigēre* to be lively

vigilance (ˈvɪdʒɪləns) *n* **1** the fact, quality, or condition of being vigilant. **2** the abnormal state or condition of being unable to sleep.

vigilance committee *n* (in the US) a self-appointed body of citizens organized to maintain order, etc., where an efficient system of courts does not exist.

vigilant (ˈvɪdʒɪlənt) *adj* keenly alert to or heedful of trouble or danger. ORIG C15: from L *vigilāns,* from *vigilāre* to be watchful; see VIGIL
▸ ˈ**vigilantly** *adv*

vigilante (ˌvɪdʒɪˈlæntɪ) *n* **1** a self-appointed protector of public order. **2** *US.* a member of a vigilance committee. ORIG C19: from Sp., from L *vigilāre* to keep watch

vigilantism (ˌvɪdʒɪˈlæntɪzəm) *n US.* the methods, conduct, attitudes, etc., associated with vigilantes, esp. militancy or bigotry.

Vigil Mass *n RC Church.* a Mass held on Saturday evening, attendance at which fulfils one's obligation to attend Mass on Sunday.

vigneron (ˈviːnjərɒn; *French* viɲrɔ̃) *n* a person who grows grapes for winemaking. ORIG F, from *vigne* vine

vignette (vɪˈnjɛt) *n* **1** a small illustration placed at the beginning or end of a book or chapter. **2** a short graceful literary essay or sketch. **3** a photograph, drawing, etc., with edges that are shaded off. **4** any small endearing scene, view, etc. ◆ *vb* **vignettes, vignetting, vignetted.** (*tr*) **5** to finish (a photograph, etc.) with a fading border in the form of a vignette. **6** to portray in or as in a vignette. ORIG C18: from F, lit.: little vine; with reference to the vine motif frequently used in embellishments to a text
▸ **viˈgnettist** *n*

Vignola ★ (*Italian* viɲˈɲɔːla) *n* **Giacomo Barozzi da** (ˈdʒaːkomo baˈrɔttsi da). 1507–73, Italian architect.

Vigny ★ (*French* viɲi) *n* **Alfred Victor de** (alfrɛd viktɔr də). 1797–1863, French writer, whose work includes *Poèmes antiques et modernes* (1826), the novel *Cinq-Mars* (1826), and the play *Chatterton* (1835).

Vigo ★ (ˈviːgəʊ; *Spanish* ˈbiγo) *n* a port in NW Spain, in Galicia on **Vigo Bay** (an inlet of the Atlantic): site of a British and Dutch naval victory (1702) over the French and Spanish. Pop.: 275 580 (1988).

vigoro (ˈvɪgəˌrəʊ) *n Austral.* a ball game combining elements of cricket and baseball. ORIG C20: from VIGOUR

vigorous (ˈvɪgərəs) *adj* **1** endowed with bodily or mental strength or vitality. **2** displaying, characterized by, or performed with vigour: *vigorous growth.*
▸ ˈ**vigorously** *adv*

vigour *or US* **vigor** (ˈvɪgə) *n* **1** exuberant and resilient strength of body or mind. **2** substantial effective energy or force: *the vigour of the tempest.* **3** forcefulness: *I was surprised by the vigour of her complaints.* **4** the capacity for survival or strong healthy growth in a plant or animal. **5** the most active period or stage of life, manhood, etc. ORIG C14: from OF, from L *vigor,* from *vigēre* to be lively

Viipuri ★ (ˈviːpuri) *n* the Finnish name for **Vyborg.**

Vijayawada ★ (ˌviːdʒaɪəˈwɑːdə) *n* a town in SE India, in E central Andra Pradesh on the Krishna River: Hindu pilgrimage centre. Pop.: 701 827 (1991). Former name: **Bezwada.**

Viking (ˈvaɪkɪŋ) *n* (*sometimes not cap.*) **1** Also called: **Norseman, Northman.** any of the Danes, Norwegians, and Swedes who raided by sea most of N and W Europe from the 8th to the 11th centuries. **2** (*modifier*) of, relating to, or characteristic of a Viking or Vikings: *a Viking ship.* ORIG C19: from ON *vīkingr,* prob. from *vīk* creek, sea inlet + *-ingr* (see -ING[3])

vile (vaɪl) *adj* **1** abominably wicked; shameful or evil. **2** morally despicable; ignoble: *vile accusations.* **3** disgusting to the senses or emotions; foul: *a vile smell.* **4** tending to humiliate or degrade: *only slaves would perform such vile tasks.* **5** unpleasant or bad: *vile weather.* ORIG C13: from OF *vil,* from L *vīlis* cheap
▸ ˈ**vilely** *adv* ▸ ˈ**vileness** *n*

vilify (ˈvɪlɪˌfaɪ) *vb* **vilifies, vilifying, vilified.** (*tr*) to revile with abusive language; malign. ORIG C15: from LL, from L *vīlis* worthless + *facere* to make
▸ **vilification** (ˌvɪlɪfɪˈkeɪʃən) *n* ▸ ˈ**viliˌfier** *n*

vilipend (ˈvɪlɪˌpɛnd) *vb* (*tr*) *Rare.* **1** to treat or regard with

contempt. **2** to speak slanderously of. ORIG C15: from LL, from L *vīlis* worthless + *pendere* to esteem
▸ **'vili,pender** *n*

villa ('vɪlə) *n* **1** (in ancient Rome) a country house, usually consisting of farm buildings and residential quarters around a courtyard. **2** a large country residence. **3** *Brit.* a detached or semidetached suburban house. ORIG C17: via It. from L

Villa ★ ('viːə; *Spanish* 'biʎa) *n* **Francisco** (fran'sisko), called *Pancho Villa,* original name *Doroteo Arango.* ?1877–1923, Mexican revolutionary leader.

Villach ★ (*German* 'fɪlax) *n* a city in S central Austria, on the Drava River: nearby hot mineral springs. Pop.: 54 640 (1991).

village ('vɪlɪdʒ) *n* **1** a small group of houses in a country area, larger than a hamlet. **2** the inhabitants of such a community collectively. **3** an incorporated municipality smaller than a town in various parts of the US and Canada. **4** (*modifier*) of or characteristic of a village: *a village green.* ORIG C15: from OF, from *ville* farm, from L: VILLA
▸ **'villager** *n*

Villahermosa ★ (*Spanish* biʎaer'mosa) *n* a town in E Mexico, capital of Tabasco state: university (1959). Pop.: 261 231 (1990). Former name: **San Juan Bautista.**

villain ('vɪlən) *n* **1** a wicked or malevolent person. **2** (in a novel, play, etc.) the main evil character and antagonist to the hero. **3** *Often jocular.* a rogue. **4** *Obs.* an uncouth person; boor. ORIG C14: from OF *vilein* serf, from LL *vīllānus* worker on a country estate, from L: VILLA
▸ **'villainess** *fem n*

villainous ('vɪlənəs) *adj* **1** of, like, or appropriate to a villain. **2** very bad or disagreeable: *a villainous climate.*
▸ **'villainously** *adv* ▸ **'villainousness** *n*

villainy ('vɪlənɪ) *n, pl* **villainies. 1** vicious behaviour or action. **2** an evil or criminal act or deed. **3** the fact or condition of being villainous.

Villa-Lobos ★ ('viːlɑː'ləubɒs, 'vɪlə-; *Portuguese* 'vilja-'lobuʃ) *n* **Heitor** (ej'tor). 1887–1959, Brazilian composer.

villanelle (,vɪlə'nɛl) *n* a verse form of French origin consisting of 19 lines arranged in five tercets and a quatrain. ORIG C16: from F, from It. *villanella,* from *villano* rustic

-ville *n and adj combining form. Sl., chiefly US.* (denoting) a place, condition, or quality with a character as specified: *dragsville; squaresville.*

villein ('vɪlən) *n* (in medieval Europe) a peasant bound to his lord, to whom he paid dues and services in return for his land. ORIG C14: from OF *vilein* serf; see VILLAIN
▸ **'villeinage** *n*

Villeneuve ★ (*French* vilnœv) *n* **Pierre Charles Jean Baptiste Silvestre de** (pjɛr ʃarl ʒɑ̃ batist silvɛstrə də). 1763–1806, French admiral, defeated by Nelson at the Battle of Trafalgar (1805).

Villeurbanne ★ (*French* vijœrban) *n* a town in E France: an industrial suburb of E Lyons. Pop.: 119 848 (1990).

Villiers ★ ('vɪləz, 'vɪljəz) *n* **George.** See (Dukes of) **Buckingham.**

Villiers de l'Isle Adam ★ (*French* vilje də lil adɑ̃) *n* **August, Comte de** (ogyst, kɔ̃t də). 1838–89, French poet and dramatist. His works include *Contes cruels* (1883) and the play *Axel* (1885).

villiform ('vɪlɪ,fɔːm) *adj* having the form of a villus or a series of villi. ORIG C19: from NL *villiformis,* from L *villus* shaggy hair + -FORM

Villon ★ (*French* vijɔ̃) *n* **1 François** (frɑ̃swa). 1431–?1463, French poet. His poems include *Le Petit testament* (?1456), *Le Grand testament* (1461), and many ballades and rondeaux. He disappeared after banishment in 1463. **2 Jacques** (ʒak), real name *Gaston Duchamp.* 1875–1963, French cubist painter.

villus ('vɪləs) *n, pl* **villi** ('vɪlaɪ). (*usually pl*) **1** *Zool., anat.* any of the numerous finger-like projections of the mucous membrane lining the small intestine of many vertebrates. **2** any similar membranous process. **3** *Bot.* any of various hairlike outgrowths. ORIG C18: from L: shaggy hair
▸ **villosity** (vɪ'lɒsɪtɪ) *n* ▸ **'villous** *adj*

Vilnius *or* **Vilnyus ★** ('vɪlnɪʊs) *n* capital of Lithuania: passed to Russia in 1795; under Polish rule (1920–39); university (1578). Pop.: 575 700 (1995). Russian name: **Vilna** ('vilna). Polish name: **Wilno.**

vim (vɪm) *n Sl.* exuberant vigour and energy. ORIG C19: from L, from *vīs;* rel. to Gk *is* strength

Viminal ★ ('vɪmɪnᵊl) *n* one of the seven hills on which ancient Rome was built. ORIG from L *Vīminālis Collis* the Viminal Hill, from *vīminālis* of osiers, from *vīmen* an osier, referring to the willow grove on the hill

vimineous (vɪ'mɪnɪəs) *adj Bot.* having, producing, or resembling long flexible shoots. ORIG C17: from L *vīmineus* made of osiers, from *vīmen* flexible shoot

vina ('viːnə) *n* a stringed musical instrument, esp. of India, related to the sitar. ORIG C18: from Hindi *bīnā,* from Sansk. *vīṇā*

vinaceous (vaɪ'neɪʃəs) *adj* **1** of, relating to, or containing wine. **2** having a colour suggestive of red wine. ORIG C17: from LL *vīnāceus,* from L *vīnum* wine

Viña del Mar ★ (*Spanish* 'biɲa ðel 'mar) *n* a city and resort in central Chile, just north of Valparaíso on the Pacific: the second largest city of Chile. Pop.: 322 220 (1995 est.).

vinaigrette (,vɪneɪ'grɛt) *n* **1** Also called: **vinaigrette sauce.** a salad dressing made from oil and vinegar with seasonings; French dressing. **2** Also called: **vinegarette.** a small decorative bottle or box with a perforated top, used for holding smelling salts, etc. ORIG C17: from F, from *vinaigre* VINEGAR

Vincennes ★ (*French* vɛ̃sɛn; *English* vɪn'sɛnz) *n* a suburb of E Paris: 14th-century castle. Pop.: 45 000 (latest est.).

Vincent de Paul ★ ('vɪnsənt də 'pɔːl; *French* vɛ̃sɑ̃ də pɔl) *n* **Saint.** ?1581–1660, French Roman Catholic priest, who founded two charitable orders, the Lazarists (1625) and the Sisters of Charity (1634). Feast day: Sept. 27.

Vincent's angina *or* **disease** *n* an ulcerative bacterial infection of the mouth, esp. involving the throat and tonsils. ORIG C20: after J. H. *Vincent* (died 1950), F bacteriologist

Vinci ★ ('vɪntʃɪ) *n* See **Leonardo da Vinci.**

vincible ('vɪnsɪbᵊl) *adj Rare.* capable of being defeated. ORIG C16: from L *vincibilis,* from *vincere* to conquer
▸ **,vinci'bility** *n*

vincristine (vɪn'krɪstiːn) *n* an alkaloid used to treat leukaemia, derived from the tropical shrub Madagascar periwinkle. ORIG C20: from NL *Vinca* genus name of the plant + L *crista* crest + -INE[2]

vinculum ('vɪŋkjʊləm) *n, pl* **vincula** (-lə). **1** a horizontal line drawn above a group of mathematical terms, used as an alternative to parentheses in mathematical expressions, in $x + \overline{y - z}$, which is equivalent to $x + (y - z)$. **2** *Anat.* any bandlike structure, esp. one uniting two or more parts. ORIG C17: from L: bond, from *vincīre* to bind

vindaloo (,vɪndə'luː) *n, pl* **vindaloos.** a type of very hot Indian curry. ORIG C20: ? from Port. *vin d'alho* wine and garlic sauce

vin de pays *French.* (vɛ̃ də pei) *n, pl* ***vins de pays*** (vɛ̃ də pei). the third highest French wine classification: indicates that the wine meets certain requirements concerning area of production, strength, etc. Also called: ***vin du pays.*** Abbrev.: **VDP.** Cf. **AOC, VDQS.** ORIG lit.: local wine

Vindhya Pradesh ★ ('vɪndjə) *n* a former state of central India: merged with the reorganized Madhya Pradesh in 1956.

Vindhya Range *or* **Mountains ★** *n* a mountain range in central India: separates the Ganges basin from the Deccan, marking the limits of northern and peninsular India. Greatest height: 1113 m (3651 ft).

vindicable ('vɪndɪkəbᵊl) *adj* capable of being vindicated; justifiable.
▸ **,vindica'bility** *n*

vindicate ('vɪndɪ,keɪt) *vb* **vindicates, vindicating, vindicated.** (*tr*) **1** to clear from guilt, blame, etc., as by evidence or argument. **2** to provide justification for: *his promotion vindicated his unconventional attitude.* **3** to uphold or defend (a

cause, etc.): *to vindicate a claim.* ORIG C17: from L *vindicāre,* from *vindex* claimant
▸ **'vindi,cator** *n* ▸ **'vindi,catory** *adj*

vindication (ˌvɪndɪ'keɪʃən) *n* **1** the act of vindicating or the condition of being vindicated. **2** a fact, evidence, etc., that serves to vindicate a claim.

vindictive (vɪn'dɪktɪv) *adj* **1** disposed to seek vengeance. **2** characterized by spite or rancour. **3** *English law.* (of damages) in excess of the compensation due to the plaintiff and imposed in punishment of the defendant. ORIG C17: from L *vindicta* revenge, from *vindicāre* to VINDICATE
▸ **vin'dictively** *adv* ▸ **vin'dictiveness** *n*

vin du pays *French.* (vɛ̃ du pei) *n, pl* ***vins du pays.*** a variant of ***vin de pays.***

vine (vaɪn) *n* **1** any of various plants, esp. the grapevine, having long flexible stems that creep along the ground or climb by clinging to a support by means of tendrils, leafstalks, etc. **2** the stem of such a plant. ORIG C13: from OF, from L *vīnea* vineyard, from *vīnum* wine
▸ **'viny** *adj*

Vine ★ (vaɪn) *n* **Barbara.** See (Ruth) **Rendell.**

vinedresser ('vaɪnˌdrɛsə) *n* a person who prunes, tends, or cultivates grapevines.

vinegar ('vɪnɪgə) *n* **1** a sour-tasting liquid consisting of impure dilute acetic acid, made by fermentation of beer, wine, or cider. It is used as a condiment or preservative. **2** sourness or peevishness of temper, speech, etc. ORIG C13: from OF, from *vin* WINE + *aigre* sour, from L *acer*
▸ **'vinegarish** *adj* ▸ **'vinegary** *adj*

Vineland ★ ('vaɪnlənd) *n* a variant spelling of **Vinland.**

vinery ('vaɪnərɪ) *n, pl* **vineries. 1** a hothouse for growing grapes. **2** another name for a **vineyard. 3** vines collectively.

vineyard ('vɪnjəd) *n* a plantation of grapevines, esp. where wine grapes are produced. ORIG OE *wīngeard;* see VINE, YARD[2]

vingt-et-un *French.* (vɛ̃teœ̃) *n* another name for **pontoon**[2]. ORIG lit.: twenty-one

vinho verde (ˌviːnjəʊ 'vɜːdɪ) *n* any of a variety of light sharp-tasting wines made from early-picked grapes of NW Portugal. ORIG Port., lit.: green (or young) wine

vini- *or before a vowel* **vin-** *combining form.* indicating wine: *viniculture.* ORIG from L *vīnum*

viniculture ('vɪnɪˌkʌltʃə) *n* the process or business of growing grapes and making wine.
▸ **ˌvini'cultural** *adj* ▸ **ˌvini'culturist** *n*

viniferous (vɪ'nɪfərəs) *adj* wine-producing.

Vinland ('vɪnlənd) *or* **Vineland** ★ *n* the stretch of the E coast of North America visited by Leif Ericson and other Vikings from about 1000.

Vinnitsa ★ (*Russian* 'vinnitsə) *n* a city in central Ukraine: passed from Polish to Russian rule in 1793. Pop.: 388 000 (1996 est.).

vino ('viːnəʊ) *n, pl* **vinos.** an informal word for **wine.** ORIG jocular use of It. or Sp. *vino*

vin ordinaire *French.* (vɛ̃n ɔrdinɛr) *n, pl* ***vins ordinaires*** (vɛ̃z ɔrdinɛr). cheap table wine, esp. French.

vinosity (vɪ'nɒsɪtɪ) *n* the distinctive and essential quality and flavour of wine. ORIG C17: from LL *vīnōsitas,* from L *vīnōsus* VINOUS

vinous ('vaɪnəs) *adj* **1** of or characteristic of wine. **2** indulging in or indicative of indulgence in wine. ORIG C17: from L, from *vīnum* WINE

vintage ('vɪntɪdʒ) *n* **1** the wine obtained from a harvest of grapes, esp. in an outstandingly good year. **2** the harvest from which such a wine is obtained. **3a** the harvesting of wine grapes. **3b** the season of harvesting these grapes or for making wine. **4** a time of origin: *a car of Edwardian vintage.* **5** *Inf.* a group of people or objects of the same period: *a fashion of last season's vintage.* ◆ *adj* **6** (of wine) of an outstandingly good year. **7** representative of the best and most typical: *vintage Shakespeare.* **8** of lasting interest and importance; classic: *vintage films.* **9** old-fashioned; dated. ORIG C15: from OF *vendage* (infl. by *vintener* VINTNER), from L *vindēmia,* from *vīnum* WINE, grape + *dēmere* to take away

vintage car *n Chiefly Brit.* an old car, esp. one constructed between 1919 and 1930. Cf. **classic car, veteran car.**

vintager ('vɪntɪdʒə) *n* a grape harvester.

vintner ('vɪntnə) *n* a wine merchant. ORIG C15: from OF *vinetier,* from Med. L, from L *vīnētum* vineyard

vinyl ('vaɪnɪl) *n* **1** (*modifier*) of or containing the monovalent group of atoms CH_2:CH–: *vinyl chloride.* **2** (*modifier*) of or made of a vinyl resin: *a vinyl raincoat.* **3** any vinyl resin or plastic, esp. PVC. **4** (collectively) conventional records made of vinyl as opposed to compact discs. ORIG C19: from VINI- + -YL

vinyl acetate *n* a colourless volatile liquid unsaturated ester that polymerizes readily in light and is used for making polyvinyl acetate.

vinyl chloride *n* a colourless flammable gaseous unsaturated compound made by the chlorination of ethylene and used as a refrigerant and in the manufacture of PVC.

vinyl resin *or* **polymer** *n* any one of a class of thermoplastic materials, esp. PVC and polyvinyl acetate, made by polymerizing vinyl compounds.

viol ('vaɪəl) *n* any of a family of stringed musical instruments that preceded the violin family, consisting of a fretted fingerboard, a body like that of a violin but having a flat back and six strings, played with a curved bow. ORIG C15: from OF *viole,* from OProvençal *viola;* see VIOLA[1]

viola[1] (vɪ'əʊlə) *n* **1** a bowed stringed instrument, the alto of the violin family; held beneath the chin when played. **2** any of various instruments of the viol family, such as the viola da gamba. ORIG C18: from It., prob. from O Provençal

viola[2] ('vaɪələ, vaɪ'əʊ-) *n* any of various temperate perennial herbaceous plants, the flowers of which have showy irregular petals, white, yellow, blue, or mauve in colour. ORIG C15: from L: violet

viola clef (vɪ'əʊlə) *n* another term for **alto clef.**

viola da gamba (vɪ'əʊlə də 'gæmbə) *n* the second largest and lowest member of the viol family. ORIG C18: from It., lit.: viol for the leg

viola d'amore (vɪ'əʊlə dæ'mɔːrɪ) *n* an instrument of the viol family having no frets, seven strings, and a set of sympathetic strings. ORIG C18: from It., lit.: viol of love

violate ('vaɪəˌleɪt) *vb* **violates, violating, violated.** (*tr*) **1** to break, disregard, or infringe (a law, agreement, etc.). **2** to rape or otherwise sexually assault. **3** to disturb rudely or improperly. **4** to treat irreverently or disrespectfully: *he violated a sanctuary.* ORIG C15: from L *violāre* to do violence to, from *vīs* strength
▸ **'violable** *adj* ▸ **ˌvio'lation** *n* ▸ **'vioˌlator** *or* **'vioˌlater** *n*

violence ('vaɪələns) *n* **1** the exercise or an instance of physical force, usually effecting or intended to effect injuries, destruction, etc. **2** powerful, untamed, or devastating force: *the violence of the sea.* **3** great strength of feeling, as in language, etc. **4** an unjust, unwarranted, or unlawful display of force. **5 do violence to. 5a** to inflict harm upon: *they did violence to the prisoners.* **5b** to distort the sense or intention of: *the reporters did violence to my speech.* ORIG C13: via OF from L *violentia* impetuosity, from *violentus* VIOLENT

violent ('vaɪələnt) *adj* **1** marked or caused by great physical force or violence: *a violent stab.* **2** (of a person) tending to the use of violence, esp. in order to injure or intimidate others. **3** marked by intensity of any kind: *a violent clash of colours.* **4** characterized by an undue use of force. **5** caused by or displaying strong or undue mental or emotional force. ORIG C14: from L *violentus,* prob. from *vīs* strength
▸ **'violently** *adv*

violent storm *n* a wind of force 11 on the Beaufort scale, reaching speeds of 64 to 72 mph.

violet ('vaɪəlɪt) *n* **1** any of various temperate perennial herbaceous plants of the genus *Viola,* such as the **sweet** (or **garden**) **violet,** having mauve or bluish flowers with irregular showy petals. **2** any other plant of the genus *Viola,* such as the wild pansy. **3** any of various similar but unrelated plants, such as the African violet. **4a** any of a group of colours that have a purplish-blue hue. They lie at one end of the visible spectrum. **4b** (*as adj*): *a violet dress.* **5** a dye or pigment of or producing these colours. **6** violet clothing: *dressed in violet.* ORIG C14: from OF *violete* a little violet, from L *viola* violet

violin (ˌvaɪəˈlɪn) *n* a bowed stringed instrument, the highest member of the violin family, consisting of a fingerboard, a hollow wooden body with waisted sides, and a sounding board connected to the back by means of a soundpost that also supports the bridge. It has two f-shaped sound holes cut in the belly. ORIG C16: from It. *violino* a little viola, from VIOLA[1]

violinist (ˌvaɪəˈlɪnɪst) *n* a person who plays the violin.

violist[1] (vɪˈəʊlɪst) *n* a person who plays the viola.

violist[2] (ˈvaɪəlɪst) *n* a person who plays the viol.

Viollet-le-Duc ★ (*French* vjɔlɛlədyk) *n* **Eugène Emmanuel** (øʒɛn ɛmanɥɛl). 1814–79, French architect and leader of the Gothic Revival in France.

violoncello (ˌvaɪələnˈtʃɛləʊ) *n, pl* **violoncellos**. the full name for **cello**. ORIG C18: from It., from *violone* large viol + *-cello,* dim. suffix

▸ ˌ**violonˈcellist** *n*

VIP *abbrev. for* very important person.

viper (ˈvaɪpə) *n* **1** any of a family of venomous Old World snakes having hollow fangs in the upper jaw that are used to inject venom. **2** any of various other snakes, such as the horned viper. **3** a malicious or treacherous person. ORIG C16: from L *vīpera,* ?from *vīvus* living + *parere* to bear, referring to a tradition that the viper was viviparous

viperous (ˈvaɪpərəs) *or* **viperish** *adj* **1** Also: **viperine** (ˈvaɪpəˌraɪn) of or resembling a viper. **2** malicious.

viper's bugloss *n* **1** Also called (US): **blueweed**. a Eurasian weed, having blue flowers and pink buds. **2** a related plant that has purple flowers and is naturalized in Australia and New Zealand. Also called: (Austral.) **Paterson's curse, Salvation Jane.**

virago (vɪˈrɑːgəʊ) *n, pl* **viragoes** *or* **viragos. 1** a loud, violent, and ill-tempered woman. **2** *Arch.* a strong or warlike woman. ORIG OE, from L: a manlike maiden, from *vir* a man

▸ **viˈrago-ˌlike** *adj*

viral (ˈvaɪrəl) *adj* of or caused by a virus.

Virchow ★ (*German* ˈfɪrço) *n* **Rudolf Ludwig Karl** (ˈruːdɔlf ˈluːtvɪç karl). 1821–1902, German pathologist, considered the founder of modern (cellular) pathology.

virelay (ˈvɪrɪˌleɪ) *n* an old French verse form, rarely used in English, having stanzas of short lines with two rhymes throughout and two opening lines recurring at intervals. ORIG C14: from OF *virelai,* prob. from *vireli* (associated with *lai* LAY[4]), word used as a refrain

Viren ★ (ˈvɪərən) *n* **Lasse** (ˈlæsɪ). born 1949, Finnish distance runner: winner of the 5000 m and the 10 000 m in the 1972 and 1976 Olympic Games.

vireo (ˈvɪrɪəʊ) *n, pl* **vireos.** any of a family of insectivorous American songbirds having an olive-grey back with pale underparts. ORIG C19: from L: a bird, prob. a greenfinch; cf. *virēre* to be green

vires (ˈvaɪriːz) *n* the plural of **vis.**

virescent (vɪˈrɛsᵊnt) *adj* greenish or becoming green. ORIG C19: from L *virescere,* from *virēre* to be green

▸ **viˈrescence** *n*

virgate[1] (ˈvɜːgɪt, -geɪt) *adj* long, straight, and thin; rod-shaped: *virgate stems.* ORIG C19: from L *virgātus* made of twigs, from *virga* a rod

virgate[2] (ˈvɜːgɪt, -geɪt) *n Brit.* an obsolete measure of land area, usually taken as 30 acres. ORIG C17: from Med. L *virgāta* (*terrae*) a rod's measurement (of land), from L *virga* rod; translation of OE *gierd landes* a yard of land

Virgil *or* **Vergil** ★ (ˈvɜːdʒɪl) *n* Latin name *Publius Vergilius Maro.* 70–19 B.C., Roman poet, whose works include the *Eclogues* (42–37), the *Georgics* (37–30), and his masterpiece the *Aeneid* (30–19).

▸ **Virˈgilian** *or* **Verˈgilian** *adj*

virgin (ˈvɜːdʒɪn) *n* **1** a person, esp. a woman, who has never had sexual intercourse. **2** an unmarried woman who has taken a religious vow of chastity. **3** any female animal that has never mated. **4** a female insect that produces offspring by parthenogenesis. ◆ *adj* (*usually prenominal*) **5** of, suitable for, or characteristic of a virgin or virgins. **6** pure and natural, uncorrupted or untouched: *virgin purity.* **7** not yet cultivated, explored, exploited, etc., by man: *virgin territories.* **8** being the first or happening for the first time. **9** (of a metal) made from an ore rather than from scrap. **10** occurring naturally in a pure and uncombined form: *virgin silver.* ORIG C13: from OF *virgine,* from L *virgō* virgin

Virgin[1] ★ (ˈvɜːdʒɪn) *n* **1 the.** See **Virgin Mary. 2** a statue or other artistic representation of the Virgin Mary.

Virgin[2] (ˈvɜːdʒɪn) *n* **the.** the constellation Virgo, the sixth sign of the zodiac.

virginal[1] (ˈvɜːdʒɪnᵊl) *adj* **1** of, characterized by, or maintaining a state of virginity; chaste. **2** extremely pure or fresh. ORIG C15: from L *virginālis* maidenly, from *virgō* virgin

▸ ˈ**virginally** *adv*

virginal[2] (ˈvɜːdʒɪnᵊl) *n* (*often pl*) a smaller version of the harpsichord, but oblong in shape, having one manual and no pedals. ORIG C16: prob. from L *virginālis* VIRGINAL[1], ? because it was played largely by young ladies

▸ ˈ**virginalist** *n*

Virgin Birth *n* the doctrine that Jesus Christ was conceived by the intervention of the Holy Spirit so that Mary remained a virgin.

virgin forest *n* a forest in its natural state, before it has been explored or exploited by man.

Virginia ★ (vəˈdʒɪnɪə) *n* a state of the eastern US, on the Atlantic: site of the first permanent English settlement in North America; consists of a low-lying deeply indented coast rising inland to the Piedmont plateau and the Blue Ridge Mountains. Capital: Richmond. Pop.: 6 791 345 (1998 est.). Area: 103 030 sq. km (39 780 sq. miles). Abbrevs.: **Va.** or (with zip code) **VA**

▸ **Virˈginian** *adj, n*

Virginia Beach ★ *n* a city and resort in SE Virginia, on the Atlantic. Pop.: 430 295 (1994 est.).

Virginia creeper *n* a woody vine of North America, having tendrils with adhesive tips, bluish-black berry-like fruits, and compound leaves that turn red in autumn: widely planted for ornament.

Virginia stock *n* a Mediterranean plant cultivated for its white and pink flowers.

Virgin Islands ★ *pl n* a group of about 100 small islands (14 inhabited) in the Caribbean, east of Puerto Rico: discovered by Columbus (1493); consists of the British Virgin Islands in the east and the Virgin Islands of the United States in the west and south. Pop.: 17 000 (1993 est.). Area: 497 sq. km (192 sq. miles).

Virgin Islands of the United States ★ *pl n* a territory of the US in the Caribbean, consisting of islands west and south of the British Virgin Islands: purchased from Denmark in 1917 for their strategic importance. Capital: Charlotte Amalie. Pop.: 101 809 (1990). Area: 344 sq. km (133 sq. miles). Former name: **Danish West Indies.**

virginity (vəˈdʒɪnɪtɪ) *n* **1** the condition or fact of being a virgin. **2** the condition of being untouched, unused, etc.

virginium (vəˈdʒɪnɪəm) *n Chem.* a former name for **francium.**

Virgin Mary ★ *n* Mary, the mother of Christ. Also called: the **Virgin.**

virgin's-bower *n* any of several American varieties of clematis.

virgin soil *n* **1** soil that has not been cultivated before. **2** a person or thing that is as yet undeveloped.

virgin wool *n* wool that is being processed or woven for the first time.

Virgo (ˈvɜːgəʊ) *n, Latin genitive* **Virginis** (ˈvɜːdʒɪnɪs). **1** *Astron.* a large constellation on the celestial equator. **2** *Astrol.* Also called: **the Virgin.** the sixth sign of the zodiac. The sun is in this sign between about Aug. 23 and Sept. 22. ORIG C14: from L

virgo intacta ('vɜːɡəʊ ɪn'tæktə) *n* a girl or woman whose hymen is unbroken. ORIG L, lit.: untouched virgin

virgule ('vɜːɡjuːl) *n Printing.* another name for **solidus.** ORIG C19: from F: comma, from L *virgula* dim. of *virga* rod

viridescent (ˌvɪrɪ'dɛsᵊnt) *adj* greenish or tending to become green. ORIG C19: from LL *viridescere,* from L *viridis* green
▸ ˌ**viri'descence** *n*

viridian (vɪ'rɪdɪən) *n* a green pigment comprising a hydrated form of chromic oxide. ORIG C19: from L *viridis* green

viridity (vɪ'rɪdɪtɪ) *n* **1** the quality or state of being green. **2** innocence, youth, or freshness. ORIG C15: from L *viriditās,* from *viridis* green

virile ('vɪraɪl) *adj* **1** of or having the characteristics of an adult male. **2** (of a male) possessing high sexual drive and capacity for sexual intercourse. **3** of or capable of copulation or procreation. **4** strong, forceful, or vigorous. ORIG C15: from L *virīlis* manly, from *vir* a man; rel. to OE *wer* man
▸ **virility** (vɪ'rɪlɪtɪ) *n*

virilism ('vɪrɪˌlɪzəm) *n Med.* the abnormal development in a woman of male secondary sex characteristics.

virology (vaɪ'rɒlədʒɪ) *n* the branch of medicine concerned with the study of viruses.
▸ **virological** (ˌvaɪrə'lɒdʒɪkᵊl) *adj*

virtu *or* **vertu** (vɜː'tuː) *n* **1** a taste or love for curios or works of fine art. **2** such objects collectively. **3** the quality of being appealing to a connoisseur (esp. in **articles of virtu; objects of virtu**). ORIG C18: from It. *virtù;* see VIRTUE

virtual ('vɜːtʃʊəl) *adj* **1** having the essence or effect but not the appearance or form of: *a virtual revolution.* **2** *Physics.* being or involving a virtual image: *a virtual focus.* **3** *Computing.* of or relating to virtual storage: *virtual memory.* **4** of or relating to a computer technique by which a person, wearing a headset or mask, has the experience of being in an environment created by the computer, and of interacting with and causing changes within it. ORIG C14: from Med. L *virtuālis* effective, from L *virtūs* VIRTUE

virtual human *n* a computer-generated moving image of a human being, used esp. in films as an extra in large crowd scenes.

virtual image *n* an optical image formed by the apparent divergence of rays from a point, rather than their actual divergence from a point.

virtuality (ˌvɜːtjʊ'ælɪtɪ) *n* virtual reality.

virtually ('vɜːtʃʊəlɪ) *adv* in effect though not in fact; practically; nearly.

virtual reality *n* a computer-generated environment that, to the person experiencing it, closely resembles reality. Abbrev.: **VR.** See also **virtual** (sense 4).

virtual storage *or* **memory** *n* a computer system in which the size of the memory is increased by transferring sections of a program from a large capacity backing store, such as a disk, into the smaller core memory as they are required.

virtue ('vɜːtjuː) *n* **1** the quality or practice of moral excellence or righteousness. **2** a particular moral excellence: *the virtue of tolerance.* **3** any of the cardinal virtues (prudence, justice, fortitude, and temperance) or theological virtues (faith, hope, and charity). **4** any admirable quality or trait. **5** chastity, esp. in women. **6** *Arch.* an effective, active, or inherent power. **7** **by** *or* **in virtue of.** by reason of. **8** **make a virtue of necessity.** to acquiesce in doing something unpleasant with a show of grace because one must do it in any case. ORIG C13 *vertu,* from OF, from L *virtūs* manliness, courage

virtuoso (ˌvɜːtjʊ'əʊzəʊ, -səʊ) *n, pl* **virtuosos** *or* **virtuosi** (-siː). **1** a consummate master of musical technique and artistry. **2** a person who has a masterly or dazzling skill or technique in any field of activity. **3** a connoisseur or collector of art objects. **4** (*modifier*) showing masterly skill or brilliance: *a virtuoso performance.* ORIG C17: from It.: skilled, from LL *virtuōsus* good, virtuous
▸ **virtuosic** (ˌvɜːtjʊ'ɒsɪk) *adj* ▸ ˌ**virtu'osity** *n*

virtuous ('vɜːtʃʊəs) *adj* **1** characterized by or possessing virtue or moral excellence. **2** (of women) chaste.
▸ '**virtuously** *adv*

virulent ('vɪrʊlənt) *adj* **1a** (of a microorganism) extremely infective. **1b** (of a disease) having a violent effect. **2** extremely poisonous, injurious, etc. **3** extremely bitter, hostile, etc. ORIG C14: from L *vīrulentus* full of poison, from *vīrus* poison
▸ '**virulence** *or* '**virulency** *n* ▸ '**virulently** *adv*

virus ('vaɪrəs) *n, pl* **viruses. 1** any of a group of submicroscopic entities consisting of a single nucleic acid surrounded by a protein coat and capable of replication only within the cells of animals and plants. **2** *Inf.* a disease caused by a virus. **3** any corrupting or infecting influence. **4** *Computing.* an unauthorized program that inserts itself into a computer system, and then propagates itself to other computers via networks or disks; when activated it interferes with the operation of the computer. ORIG C16: from L: slime, poisonous liquid

vis *Latin.* (vɪs) *n, pl* ***vires.*** power, force, or strength.

visa ('viːzə) *n, pl* **visas. 1** an endorsement in a passport or similar document, signifying that the document is in order and permitting its bearer to travel into or through the country of the government issuing it. ◆ *vb* **visas, visaing, visaed. 2** (*tr*) to enter a visa into (a passport). ORIG C19: via F from L: things seen, from *vīsus,* p.p. of *vidēre* to see

visage ('vɪzɪdʒ) *n Chiefly literary.* **1** face or countenance. **2** appearance. ORIG C13: from OF: aspect, from *vis* face, from L *vīsus* appearance

-visaged *adj* (*in combination*) having a visage as specified: *flat-visaged.*

Visakhapatnam ★ (vɪˌsɑːkə'pʌtnəm) *n* a variant spelling of **Vishakhapatnam.**

vis-à-vis (ˌviːzɑː'viː) *prep* **1** in relation to. **2** face to face with. ◆ *adv, adj* **3** face to face; opposite. ◆ *n, pl* **vis-à-vis. 4** a person or thing that is situated opposite to another. **5** a person who corresponds to another in office, capacity, etc. ORIG C18: F, from *vis* face

Visayan Islands ★ *pl n* a group of seven large and several hundred small islands in the central Philippines. Chief islands: Negros and Panay. Pop.: 13 041 000 (1990). Area: about 61 000 sq. km (23 535 sq. miles). Spanish name: **Bisayas.**

Visby ★ (*Swedish* 'viːsbyː) *n* a port in SE Sweden, on NW Gotland Island in the Baltic: an early member of the Hanseatic League and major N European commercial centre in the Middle Ages. Pop.: 57 110 (1990).

Visc. *abbrev. for* Viscount *or* Viscountess.

viscacha (vɪs'kætʃə) *n* a gregarious burrowing rodent of southern South America, similar to but larger than the chinchillas. ORIG C17: from Sp., from Quechuan *wiskácha*

viscera ('vɪsərə) *pl n, sing* **viscus. 1** *Anat.* the large internal organs of the body collectively, esp. those in the abdominal cavity. **2** (less formally) the intestines; guts. ORIG C17: from L: entrails, pl of *viscus* internal organ

visceral ('vɪsərəl) *adj* **1** of or affecting the viscera. **2** characterized by instinct rather than intellect.
▸ '**viscerally** *adv*

viscid ('vɪsɪd) *adj* **1** cohesive and sticky. **2** (esp. of a leaf) covered with a sticky substance. ORIG C17: from LL *viscidus* sticky, from L *viscum* mistletoe, birdlime
▸ **vis'cidity** *n*

Visconti ★ (*Italian* vis'konti) *n* **1** the ruling family of Milan from 1277 to 1447. **2 Luchino** (lu'kiːno), real name *Luchino Visconti de Modrone.* 1906–76, Italian film director; films include *Ossessione* (1942), *The Leopard* (1963), and *Death in Venice* (1970).

viscose ('vɪskəʊs) *n* **1a** a viscous orange-brown solution obtained by dissolving cellulose in sodium hydroxide and carbon disulphide. It can be converted back to cellulose by an acid, as in the manufacture of rayon and Cellophane. **1b** (*as modifier*): *viscose rayon.* **2** rayon made from this material. ORIG C19: from LL *viscōsus* full of birdlime, sticky, from *viscum* birdlime

viscosity (vɪs'kɒsɪtɪ) *n, pl* **viscosities. 1** the state or property of being viscous. **2** *Physics.* **2a** the extent to which a fluid resists a tendency to flow. **2b** Also called: **absolute viscosity.** a measure of this resistance, measured in newton seconds per metre squared. Symbol: η

viscount ('vaɪkaʊnt) *n* **1** (in the British Isles) a nobleman ranking below an earl and above a baron. **2** (in various countries) a son or younger brother of a count. **3** (in medieval Europe) the deputy of a count. ORIG C14: from OF, from Med. L, from LL *vice-* VICE[3] + *comes* COUNT[2]
▸ **'viscountcy** *or* **'viscounty** *n*

viscountess ('vaɪkaʊntɪs) *n* **1** the wife or widow of a viscount. **2** a woman who holds the rank of viscount in her own right.

viscous ('vɪskəs) *adj* **1** (of liquids) thick and sticky. **2** having viscosity. ORIG C14: from LL *viscōsus;* see VISCOSE
▸ **'viscously** *adv*

viscus ('vɪskəs) *n* the singular of **viscera.**

vise (vaɪs) *n, vb* **vises, vising, vised.** *US.* a variant spelling of **vice**[2].

Viseu ★ (*Portuguese* vi'zeu) *n* a city in N central Portugal: 12th-century cathedral. Pop.: 20 590 (1991).

Vishakhapatnam (vɪˌʃɑːkə'pʌtnəm), **Visakhapatnam,** *or* **Vizagapatam** ★ *n* a port in E India, in NE Andhra Pradesh on the Bay of Bengal: shipbuilding and oil-refining industries. Pop.: 752 037 (1991).

Vishinsky ★ (*Russian* vi'ʃinskij) *n* a variant spelling of (Andrei Yanuaryevich) **Vyshinsky.**

Vishnu ★ ('vɪʃnuː) *n Hinduism.* the Pervader or Sustainer, originally a solar deity occupying a secondary place in the Hindu pantheon, later the saviour appearing in many incarnations. ORIG C17: from Sansk. *Viṣṇu,* lit.: the one who works everywhere
▸ **'Vishnuism** *n*

visibility (ˌvɪzɪ'bɪlɪtɪ) *n* **1** the condition or fact of being visible. **2** clarity of vision or relative possibility of seeing. **3** the range of vision: *visibility is 500 yards.*

visible ('vɪzɪb[ə]l) *adj* **1** capable of being perceived by the eye. **2** capable of being perceived by the mind: *no visible dangers.* **3** available: *the visible resources.* **4** of or relating to the balance of trade: *visible transactions.* ORIG C14: from L *vīsibilis,* from *vidēre* to see
▸ **'visibly** *adv*

visible balance *n* another name for **balance of trade.**

visible radiation *n* electromagnetic radiation that causes the sensation of sight; light.

vision ('vɪʒən) *n* **1** the act, faculty, or manner of perceiving with the eye; sight. **2a** the image on a television screen. **2b** (*as modifier*): *vision control.* **3** the ability or an instance of great perception, esp. of future developments: *a man of vision.* **4** a mystical or religious experience of seeing some supernatural event, person, etc.: *the vision of St John of the Cross.* **5** that which is seen, esp. in such a mystical experience. **6** (*sometimes pl*) a vivid mental image produced by the imagination: *he had visions of becoming famous.* **7** a person or thing of extraordinary beauty. ORIG C13: from L *vīsiō* sight, from *vidēre* to see

visionary ('vɪʒənərɪ) *adj* **1** marked by vision or foresight: *a visionary leader.* **2** incapable of being realized or effected. **3** (of people) characterized by idealistic or radical ideas, esp. impractical ones. **4** given to having visions. **5** of, of the nature of, or seen in visions. ◆ *n, pl* **visionaries.** **6** a visionary person.

vision mixer *n Television.* **1** the person who selects and manipulates the television signals from cameras, film, etc., to make the composite programme. **2** the equipment used for vision mixing.

visit ('vɪzɪt) *vb* **visits, visiting, visited. 1** to go or come to see (a person, place, etc.). **2** to stay with (someone) as a guest. **3** to go or come to (an institution, place, etc.) for the purpose of inspecting or examining. **4** (*tr*) (of a disease, disaster, etc.) to afflict. **5** (*tr;* foll. by *upon* or *on*) to inflict (punishment, etc.). **6** (often foll. by *with*) *US & Canad. inf.* to chat (with someone). ◆ *n* **7** the act or an instance of visiting. **8** a stay as a guest. **9** a professional or official call. **10** a formal call for the purpose of inspection or examination. **11** *International law.* the right of an officer of a belligerent state to stop and search neutral ships in war to verify their nationality and ascertain whether they carry contraband. **12** *US & Canad. inf.* a chat. ORIG C13: from L *vīsitāre* to go to see, from *vīsere* to examine, from *vidēre* to see
▸ **'visitable** *adj*

visitant ('vɪzɪtənt) *n* **1** a ghost; apparition. **2** a visitor or guest, usually from far away. **3** Also called: **visitor.** a migratory bird that is present in a particular region only at certain times: *a summer visitant.* ORIG C16: from L *vīsitāns,* from *vīsitāre;* see VISIT

visitation (ˌvɪzɪ'teɪʃən) *n* **1** an official call or visit for the purpose of inspecting or examining an institution. **2** a visiting of punishment or reward from heaven. **3** any disaster or catastrophe: *a visitation of the plague.* **4** an appearance or arrival of a supernatural being. **5** *Inf.* an unduly prolonged social call.

Visitation (ˌvɪzɪ'teɪʃən) *n* **1a** the visit made by the Virgin Mary to her cousin Elizabeth (Luke 1:39–56). **1b** the Church festival commemorating this, held on July 2. **2** a religious order of nuns, the **Order of the Visitation,** founded in 1610 and dedicated to contemplation.

visiting card *n Brit.* a small card bearing the name and usually the address of a person, esp. for giving to business or social acquaintances.

visiting fireman *n US inf.* a visitor whose presence is noticed because he is important, impressive, etc.

visitor ('vɪzɪtə) *n* **1** a person who pays a visit. **2** another name for **visitant** (sense 3).

visitor centre *n* another term for **interpretive centre.**

visitor's passport *n* (formerly, in Britain) a passport, valid for one year, that could be purchased from post offices. It granted entry to certain countries, usually for a restricted period of time. Also called: **British Visitor's Passport.**

Vislinsky Zaliv ★ (*Russian* vis'linski 'zaːlɪf) *n* a transliteration of the Russian name for **Vistula** (sense 2).

visor *or* **vizor** ('vaɪzə) *n* **1** a transparent flap on a helmet that can be pulled down to protect the face. **2** a piece of armour fixed or hinged to the helmet to protect the face. **3** another name for **peak** (on a cap). **4** a small movable screen used as protection against glare from the sun, esp. one attached above the windscreen of a motor vehicle. **5** *Arch. or literary.* a mask or any other means of disguise. ORIG C14: from Anglo-F *viser,* from OF *visiere,* from *vis* face; see VISAGE
▸ **'visored** *or* **'vizored** *adj*

vista ('vɪstə) *n* **1** a view, esp. through a long narrow avenue of trees, buildings, etc., or such a passage or avenue itself. **2** a comprehensive mental view of a distant time or a lengthy series of events. ORIG C17: from It., from *vedere* to see, from L *vidēre*
▸ **'vistaed** *adj*

Vistula ★ ('vɪstjʊlə) *n* **1** a river in central and N Poland, rising in the Carpathian Mountains and flowing generally north and northwest past Warsaw and Torun, then northeast to enter the Baltic via an extensive delta region. Length: 1090 km (677 miles). Polish name: **Wisła.** German name: **Weichsel.** **2 Lagoon.** a shallow lagoon on the SW coast of the Baltic Sea, between Danzig and Kaliningrad, crossed by the border between Poland and Russia. German name: **Frisches Haff.** Polish name: **Wislany Zalew.** Russian name: **Vislinsky Zaliv.**

visual ('vɪʒʊəl, -zjʊ-) *adj* **1** of, done by, or used in seeing: *visual powers.* **2** another word for **optical.** **3** capable of being seen; visible. **4** of, occurring as, or induced by a mental image. ◆ *n* **5** a sketch to show the proposed layout of an advertisement, as in a newspaper. **6** (*often pl*) a photograph, film, or other display material. ORIG C15: from LL *vīsuālis,* from L *vīsus* sight, from *vidēre* to see
▸ **'visually** *adv*

visual aids *pl n* devices, such as films, videos, slides, models, and blackboards, that display in visual form material to be understood or remembered.

visual display unit *n Computing.* a device that displays characters or graphics representing data in a computer memory. It usually has a keyboard for the input of information or inquiries. Abbrev.: **VDU.**

visual field *n* the whole extent of the image falling on the retina when the eye is fixed on a given point.

visualize *or* **visualise** ('vɪʒʊəˌlaɪz) *vb* **visualizes, visualizing, visualized** *or* **visualises, visualising, visualised.** to form a mental image of (something incapable of being viewed or not at that moment visible).
▸ **ˌvisualiˈzation** *or* **ˌvisualiˈsation** *n*

visual magnitude *n Astron.* the magnitude of a star as determined by visual observation.

visual purple *n* another name for **rhodopsin.**

visual violet *n* another name for **iodopsin.**

visual yellow *n* another name for **retinene.**

vital ('vaɪtᵊl) *adj* **1** essential to maintain life: *the lungs perform a vital function.* **2** forceful, energetic, or lively: *a vital person.* **3** of, having, or displaying life: *a vital organism.* **4** indispensable or essential: *books vital to this study.* **5** of great importance: *a vital game.* ◆ *n* **6** (*pl*) the bodily organs, such as the brain, liver, heart, lungs, etc., that are necessary to maintain life. **7** (*pl*) the essential elements of anything. ORIG C14: via OF from L *vītālis,* from *vīta* life
▸ **ˈvitally** *adv*

vital capacity *n Physiol.* the volume of air that can be exhaled from the lungs after the deepest possible breath has been taken.

vital force *n* (esp. in early biological theory) a hypothetical force, independent of physical and chemical forces, regarded as being the causative factor of the evolution of living organisms.

vitalism ('vaɪtəˌlɪzəm) *n* the philosophical doctrine that the phenomena of life cannot be explained in purely mechanical terms because there is something immaterial which distinguishes living from inanimate matter.
▸ **ˈvitalist** *n, adj* ▸ **ˌvitalˈistic** *adj*

vitality (vaɪ'tælɪtɪ) *n, pl* **vitalities. 1** physical or mental vigour, energy, etc. **2** the power or ability to continue in existence, live, or grow: *the vitality of a movement.*

vitalize *or* **vitalise** ('vaɪtəˌlaɪz) *vb* **vitalizes, vitalizing, vitalized** *or* **vitalises, vitalising, vitalised.** (*tr*) to make vital, living, or alive.
▸ **ˌvitaliˈzation** *or* **ˌvitaliˈsation** *n*

vital staining *n* the technique of treating living cells and tissues with dyes that do not immediately kill them, facilitating observation under a microscope.

vital statistics *pl n* **1** quantitative data concerning human life or the conditions affecting it, such as the death rate. **2** *Inf.* the measurements of a woman's bust, waist, and hips.

vitamin ('vɪtəmɪn, 'vaɪ-) *n* any of a group of substances that are essential, in small quantities, for the normal functioning of metabolism in the body. They cannot usually be synthesized in the body but they occur naturally in certain foods. ORIG C20 *vit-* from L *vīta* life + *-amin* from AMINE; so named by Casimir FUNK, who believed the substances to be amines
▸ **ˌvitaˈminic** *adj*

vitamin A *n* **1** Also called: **vitamin A_1, retinol.** a fat-soluble yellow unsaturated alcohol occurring in green and yellow vegetables, butter, egg yolk, and fish-liver oil. It is essential for the prevention of night blindness and the protection of epithelial tissue. **2** Also called: **vitamin A_2.** a vitamin that occurs in the tissues of freshwater fish and has a function similar to that of vitamin A_1.

vitamin B *n, pl* **B vitamins.** any of the vitamins in the vitamin B complex.

vitamin B complex *n* a large group of water-soluble vitamins occurring esp. in liver and yeast: includes thiamine (**vitamin B_1**), riboflavin (**vitamin B_2**), nicotinic acid, pyridoxine (**vitamin B_6**), pantothenic acid, biotin, choline, folic acid, and cyanocobalamin (**vitamin B_{12}**). Sometimes shortened to **B complex.**

vitamin C *n* another name for **ascorbic acid.**

vitamin D *n, pl* **D vitamins.** any of the fat-soluble vitamins, including calciferol (**vitamin D_2**) and cholecalciferol (**vitamin D_3**), occurring in fish-liver oils, milk, butter, and eggs: used in the treatment of rickets.

vitamin E *n* another name for **tocopherol.**

vitamin G *n* another name (esp. US and Canad.) for **riboflavin.**

vitamin H *n* another name (esp. US and Canad.) for **biotin.**

vitamin K *n, pl* **K vitamins.** any of the fat-soluble vitamins, including phylloquinone (**vitamin K_1**) and the menaquinones (**vitamin K_2**), which are essential for the normal clotting of blood.

vitamin P *n, pl* **P vitamins.** any of a group of water-soluble crystalline substances occurring mainly in citrus fruits, blackcurrants, and rose-hips: they regulate the permeability of the blood capillaries.

Vitebsk ★ (*Russian* 'vitɪpsk) *n* a city in NE Belarus: a port on the western Dvina river. Pop.: 365 000 (1996 est.).

vitellin (vɪ'tɛlɪn) *n Biochem.* a phosphoprotein that is the major protein in egg yolk. ORIG C19: from VITELLUS + -IN

vitelline membrane (vɪ'tɛlɪn) *n Zool.* a membrane that surrounds a fertilized ovum and prevents the entry of other spermatozoa.

vitellus (vɪ'tɛləs) *n, pl* **vitelluses** *or* **vitelli** (-laɪ). *Zool., rare.* the yolk of an egg. ORIG C18: from L, lit.: little calf, later: yolk of an egg, from *vitulus* calf

vitiate ('vɪʃɪˌeɪt) *vb* **vitiates, vitiating, vitiated.** (*tr*) **1** to make faulty or imperfect. **2** to debase or corrupt. **3** to destroy the force or legal effect of (a deed, etc.). ORIG C16: from L *vitiāre* to injure, from *vitium* a fault
▸ **ˌvitiˈation** *n* ▸ **ˈvitiˌator** *n*

viticulture ('vɪtɪˌkʌltʃə) *n* **1** the science, art, or process of cultivating grapevines. **2** the study of grapes and the growing of grapes. ORIG C19: *viti-,* from L *vītis* vine
▸ **ˌvitiˈculturist** *n*

Viti Levu ★ ('viːtɪ 'lɛvuː) *n* the largest island of Fiji: mountainous. Chief town (and capital of the state): Suva. Pop.: 340 561 (1986). Area: 10 386 sq. km (4010 sq. miles).

Vitoria¹ ★ (*Spanish* bi'torja) *n* a city in NE Spain: scene of Wellington's decisive victory (1813) over Napoleon's forces in the Peninsular War. Pop.: 258 243 (1991).

Vitoria² ★ (*Spanish* bi'torja) *n* **Francisco de** (fran'θisko de). ?1486–1546, Spanish theologian, sometimes considered the father of international law.

Vitória ★ (vɪ'tɔːrɪə; *Portuguese* vi'tɔrja) *n* a port in E Brazil, capital of Espírito Santo state, on an island in the Bay of Espírito Santo. Pop.: 144 143 (1980).

vitreous ('vɪtrɪəs) *adj* **1** of or resembling glass. **2** made of or containing glass. **3** of or relating to the vitreous humour or vitreous body. ORIG C17: from L *vitreus* made of glass, from *vitrum* glass
▸ **ˈvitreously** *adv*

vitreous humour *or* **body** *n* a transparent gelatinous substance that fills the interior of the eyeball between the lens and the retina.

vitrescence (vɪ'trɛsəns) *n* **1** the quality or condition of being or becoming vitreous. **2** the process of producing a glass or turning a crystalline material into glass.
▸ **viˈtrescent** *adj*

vitrify ('vɪtrɪˌfaɪ) *vb* **vitrifies, vitrifying, vitrified.** to convert or be converted into glass or a glassy substance. ORIG C16: from F, from L *vitrum* glass
▸ **ˈvitriˌfiable** *adj* ▸ **vitrification** (ˌvɪtrɪfɪ'keɪʃən) *n*

vitrine ('vɪtriːn) *n* a glass display case or cabinet for works of art, curios, etc. ORIG C19: from F, from *vitre* pane of glass, from L *vitrum* glass

vitriol ('vɪtrɪˌɒl) *n* **1** another name for **sulphuric acid. 2** any one of a number of sulphate salts, such as ferrous sulphate (iron(II) sulphate; **green vitriol**), copper sulphate (**blue vitriol**), or zinc sulphate (**white vitriol**). **3** speech, writing, etc., displaying vituperation or bitterness. ORIG C14: from Med. L *vitriolum,* from LL, from L *vitrum* glass, referring to the glossy appearance of the sulphates

vitriolic (ˌvɪtrɪ'ɒlɪk) *adj* **1** (of a strong acid) highly corrosive. **2** severely bitter or caustic.

vitriolize *or* **vitriolise** ('vɪtrɪəˌlaɪz) *vb* **vitriolizes, vitriolizing, vitriolized** *or* **vitriolises, vitriolising, vitriolised.** (*tr*) **1** to convert into or treat with vitriol. **2** to injure with vitriol.
▸ **ˌvitrioliˈzation** *or* **ˌvitrioliˈsation** *n*

Vitruvius Pollio ★ (vɪ'tru:vɪəs 'pɒlɪˌəʊ) *n* **Marcus** ('mɑ:kəs). 1st century B.C., Roman architect, noted for his treatise *De architectura*.
▸ **Vi'truvian** *adj*

vittle ('vɪtᵊl) *n, vb* **vittles, vittling, vittled.** an obsolete or dialect spelling of **victual.**

vituperate (vɪ'tju:pəˌreɪt) *vb* **vituperates, vituperating, vituperated.** to berate or rail (against) abusively; revile. ORIG C16: from L *vituperāre* to blame, from *vitium* a defect + *parāre* to make
▸ **viˌtuper'ation** *n* ▸ **vi'tuperˌator** *n*

viva[1] ('vi:və) *interj* long live; up with (a specified person or thing). ORIG C17: from It., lit.: may (he) live! from *vivere* to live, from L *vīvere*

viva[2] ('vaɪvə) *Brit.* ◆ *n* **1** an oral examination. ◆ *vb* **vivas, vivaing, vivaed.** (*tr*) **2** to examine orally. ORIG shortened from VIVA VOCE

vivace (vɪ'vɑ:tʃɪ) *adj, adv Music.* to be performed in a brisk lively manner. ORIG C17: from It., from L *vīvax* vigorous, from *vīvere* to live

vivacious (vɪ'veɪʃəs) *adj* full of high spirits and animation. ORIG C17: from L *vīvax* lively; see VIVACE
▸ **vi'vaciously** *adv* ▸ **vi'vaciousness** *n*

vivacity (vɪ'væsɪtɪ) *n, pl* **vivacities.** the quality or condition of being vivacious.

Vivaldi ★ (vɪ'vældɪ) *n* **Antonio** (an'tɔ:njo). ?1675–1741, Italian composer, noted for his *The Four Seasons* (1725).

vivarium (vaɪ'vɛərɪəm) *n, pl* **vivariums** *or* **vivaria** (-ɪə). a place where live animals are kept under natural conditions for study, etc. ORIG C16: from L: enclosure where live fish or game are kept, from *vīvus* alive

viva voce ('vaɪvə 'vəʊtʃɪ) *adv, adj* **1** by word of mouth. ◆ *n, vb* **viva-voce, viva-voces, viva-voceing, viva-voced.** **2** the full form of **viva**[2]. ORIG C16: from Med. L, lit.: with living voice

vive (vi:v) *interj* long live; up with (a specified person or thing). ORIG from F

Vivian ★ ('vɪvɪən) *n* (in Arthurian legend) the mistress of Merlin, sometimes identified with the **Lady of the Lake.**

vivid ('vɪvɪd) *adj* **1** (of a colour) very bright; intense. **2** brilliantly coloured: *vivid plumage.* **3** conveying to the mind striking realism, freshness, or trueness to life: *a vivid account.* **4** (of a memory, etc.) remaining distinct in the mind. **5** (of the imagination, etc.) prolific in the formation of lifelike images. **6** uttered, operating, or acting with vigour. **7** full of life or vitality: *a vivid personality.* ORIG C17: from L *vīvidus* animated, from *vīvere* to live
▸ **'vividly** *adv* ▸ **'vividness** *n*

vivify ('vɪvɪˌfaɪ) *vb* **vivifies, vivifying, vivified.** (*tr*) **1** to bring to life; animate. **2** to make more vivid or striking. ORIG C16: from LL *vīvificāre,* from L *vīvus* alive + *facere* to make
▸ **ˌvivifi'cation** *n*

viviparous (vɪ'vɪpərəs) *adj* **1** (of most mammals) giving birth to living offspring that develop within the uterus of the mother. **2** (of seeds) germinating before separating from the parent plant. **3** (of plants) producing bulbils or young plants instead of flowers. ORIG C17: from L, from *vīvus* alive + *parere* to bring forth
▸ **viviparity** (ˌvɪvɪ'pærɪtɪ) *or* **vi'viparousness** *n* ▸ **vi'viparously** *adv*

vivisect ('vɪvɪˌsɛkt, ˌvɪvɪ'sɛkt) *vb* to subject (an animal) to vivisection. ORIG C19: back formation from VIVISECTION
▸ **'viviˌsector** *n*

vivisection (ˌvɪvɪ'sɛkʃən) *n* the act or practice of performing experiments on living animals, involving cutting into or dissecting the body. ORIG C18: from *vivi-,* from L *vīvus* living + SECTION, as in DISSECTION
▸ **ˌvivi'sectional** *adj*

vivisectionist (ˌvɪvɪ'sɛkʃənɪst) *n* a person who practises or advocates vivisection as being useful to science.

vivo ('vi:vəʊ) *adj, adv Music.* (*in combination*) with life and vigour: *allegro vivo.* ORIG It.: lively

vixen ('vɪksən) *n* **1** a female fox. **2** a quarrelsome or spiteful woman. ORIG C15 *fixen;* rel. to OE *fyxe,* fem. of FOX
▸ **'vixenish** *adj* ▸ **'vixenly** *adv, adj*

Viyella (vaɪ'ɛlə) *n Trademark.* a soft fabric made of wool and cotton.

viz *abbrev. for* videlicet.

Vizagapatam ★ (vɪˌzægə'pʌtəm) *n* a variant spelling of **Vishakhapatnam.**

vizard ('vɪzəd) *n Arch. or literary.* a means of disguise. ORIG C16: var. of VISOR
▸ **'vizarded** *adj*

vizier (vɪ'zɪə) *n* a high official in certain Muslim countries, esp. in the former Ottoman Empire. ORIG C16: from Turkish *vezīr,* from Ar. *wazīr* porter, from *wazara* to bear a burden
▸ **vi'zierate** *n* ▸ **vi'zierial** *adj* ▸ **vi'ziership** *n*

vizor ('vaɪzə) *n* a variant spelling of **visor.**

vizsla ('vɪʒlə) *n* a breed of Hungarian hunting dog with a smooth rusty-gold coat. ORIG C20: after *Vizsla,* town in Hungary

VJ *abbrev. for* video jockey.

V-J Day *n* the day marking the Allied victory over Japan in World War II (Aug. 15, 1945).

VL *abbrev. for* Vulgar Latin.

Vlaardingen ★ (*Dutch* 'vla:rdɪŋə) *n* a port in the W Netherlands, in South Holland west of Rotterdam: the third largest port in the Netherlands. Pop.: 73 820 (1994).

Vladikavkaz ★ (*Russian* vlədikaf'kas) *n* a city in S Russia, capital of the North Ossetian Republic on the N slopes of the Caucasus. Pop.: 312 000 (1995 est.). Former names: **Dzaudzhikau** (1944–54); **Ordzhonikidze** *or* **Orjonikidze** (1954–91).

Vladimir[1] ★ (*Russian* vla'dimir) *n* a city in W central Russia: capital of the principality of Vladimir until the court transferred to Moscow in 1328. Pop.: 339 000 (1995 est.).

Vladimir[2] ★ ('vlædɪˌmɪə; *Russian* vla'dimir) *n* **Saint,** called *the Great.* ?956–1015, grand prince of Kiev (980–1015); first Christian ruler of Russia. Feast day: July 15.

Vladivostok ★ (ˌvlædɪ'vɒstɒk; *Russian* vlədivas'tɔk) *n* a port in SE Russia, on the Sea of Japan: terminus of the Trans-Siberian Railway; the main Russian Pacific naval base since 1872 and chief Russian port in the Far East; university (1956). Pop.: 632 000 (1995 est.).

Vlaminck ★ (*French* vlamɛ̃k) *n* **Maurice de** (mɔris də). 1876–1958, French Fauvist painter.

vlei (fleɪ, vleɪ) *n S. African.* an area of low marshy ground, esp. one that feeds a stream. ORIG C19: from Afrik.

VLF *or* **vlf** *Radio. abbrev. for* very low frequency.

Vlissingen ★ ('vlɪsɪŋə) *n* the Dutch name for **Flushing.**

Vlorë (*Albanian* 'vlorə) *or* **Vlonë** ★ (*Albanian* 'vlonə) *n* a port in SW Albania, on the **Bay of Vlorë**: under Turkish rule from 1462 until Albanian independence was declared here in 1912. Pop.: 76 000 (1991 est.). Ancient name: **Avlona.** Also called: **Valona.**

Vltava ★ (*Czech* 'vltava) *n* a river in the Czech Republic, rising in the Bohemian Forest and flowing generally southeast and then north to the River Elbe near Melnik. Length: 434 km (270 miles). German name: **Moldau.**

V neck *n* **a** a neck on a garment that comes down to a point, resembling the shape of the letter V. **b** a sweater with such a neck.
▸ **'V-ˌneck** *or* **'V-ˌnecked** *adj*

voc. *or* **vocat.** *abbrev. for* vocative.

vocab ('vəʊkæb) *n* short for **vocabulary.**

vocable ('vəʊkəbᵊl) *n* any word, either written or spoken, regarded simply as a sequence of letters or spoken sounds. ORIG C16: from L *vocābulum* a designation, from *vocāre* to call
▸ **'vocably** *adv*

vocabulary (və'kæbjʊlərɪ) *n, pl* **vocabularies.** **1** a listing, either selective or exhaustive, containing the words and phrases of a language, with meanings or translations into another language. **2** the aggregate of words in the use or comprehension of a specified person, class, etc. **3** all the words contained in a language. **4** a range or system of symbols or techniques constituting a means of communication or expression, as any of the arts or crafts: *a wide vocabulary of textures and colours.* ORIG C16: from Med. L *vocābulārium*, from L *vocābulum* VOCABLE

vocal ('vəʊk^{ə}l) *adj* **1** of or designed for the voice: *vocal music.* **2** produced or delivered by the voice: *vocal noises.* **3** connected with the production of the voice: *vocal organs.* **4** frequently disposed to outspoken speech, criticism, etc.: *a vocal minority.* **5** full of sound or voices: *a vocal assembly.* **6** endowed with a voice. **7** *Phonetics.* **7a** of or relating to a speech sound. **7b** of or relating to a voiced speech sound, esp. a vowel. ◆ *n* **8** a piece of jazz or pop music that is sung. **9** a performance of such a piece of music. ORIG C14: from L *vōcālis* possessed of a voice, from *vōx* voice
▸ **vocality** (vəʊ'kælɪtɪ) *n* ▸ **'vocally** *adv*

vocal cords *pl n* either of two pairs of membranous folds in the larynx. The upper pair (**false vocal cords**) are not concerned with vocal production; the lower pair (**true vocal cords**) can be made to vibrate and produce sound when air from the lungs is forced over them.

vocalic (vəʊ'kælɪk) *adj Phonetics.* of, relating to, or containing a vowel or vowels.

vocalise (ˌvəʊkə'liːz) *n* a musical passage sung upon one vowel usually as an exercise to develop flexibility and control of pitch and tone.

vocalism ('vəʊkəˌlɪzəm) *n* **1** the exercise of the voice, as in singing or speaking. **2** *Phonetics.* **2a** a voiced speech sound, esp. a vowel. **2b** a system of vowels as used in a language.

vocalist ('vəʊkəlɪst) *n* a singer, esp. one who regularly appears with a jazz band or pop group.

vocalize *or* **vocalise** ('vəʊkəˌlaɪz) *vb* **vocalizes, vocalizing, vocalized** *or* **vocalises, vocalising, vocalised. 1** to express with or use the voice. **2** (*tr*) to make vocal or articulate. **3** (*tr*) *Phonetics.* to articulate (a speech sound) with voice. **4** another word for **vowelize. 5** (*intr*) to sing a melody on a vowel, etc.
▸ **ˌvocali'zation** *or* **ˌvocali'sation** *n* ▸ **'vocalˌizer** *or* **'vocalˌiser** *n*

vocal score *n* a musical score with voice parts in full and orchestral parts in the form of a piano transcription.

vocation (vəʊ'keɪʃən) *n* **1** a specified profession or trade. **2a** a special urge or predisposition to a particular calling or career, esp. a religious one. **2b** such a calling or career. ORIG C15: from L *vocātiō*, from *vocāre* to call

vocational (vəʊ'keɪʃən^{ə}l) *adj* **1** of or relating to a vocation or vocations. **2** of or relating to applied educational courses concerned with skills needed for an occupation, trade, or profession.

vocational guidance *n* a guidance service based on psychological tests and interviews to find out what career may best suit a person.

vocative ('vɒkətɪv) *Grammar.* ◆ *adj* **1** denoting a case of nouns, in some inflected languages, used when the referent of the noun is being addressed. ◆ *n* **2a** the vocative case. **2b** a vocative noun or speech element. ORIG C15: from L *vocātīvus cāsus* the calling case, from *vocāre* to call

voces ('vəʊsiːz) *n* the plural of **vox.**

vociferate (vəʊ'sɪfəˌreɪt) *vb* **vociferates, vociferating, vociferated.** to exclaim or cry out about (something) clamorously or insistently. ORIG C17: from L *vōciferārī*, from *vōx* voice + *ferre* to bear
▸ **voˌcifer'ation** *n*

vociferous (vəʊ'sɪfərəs) *adj* **1** characterized by vehemence or noisiness: *vociferous protests.* **2** making an outcry: *a vociferous mob.*
▸ **vo'ciferously** *adv* ▸ **vo'ciferousness** *n*

vocoder ('vəʊˌkəʊdə) *n Music.* a type of synthesizer that uses the human voice as an oscillator.

vodka ('vɒdkə) *n* an alcoholic drink originating in Russia, made from grain, potatoes, etc., usually consisting only of rectified spirit and water. ORIG C19: from Russian, dim. of *voda* water

voe (vəʊ) *n* (in Orkney and Shetland) a small bay or narrow creek. ORIG C17: from ON *vagr*

voetsek ('fʊtsɛk, 'vʊt-) *interj S. African sl.* an expression of dismissal or rejection. ORIG C19: Afrik., from Du. *voort se ek* forward, I say, commonly applied to animals

voetstoets *or* **voetstoots** ('fʊtstʊts, 'vʊt-) *S. African.* ◆ *adj* **1** denoting a sale in which the vendor is freed from all responsibility for the condition of the goods being sold. ◆ *adv* **2** without responsibility for the condition of the goods sold. ORIG from Afrik. *voetstoots* as it is

Vogel ★ ('vəʊg^{ə}l) *n* Sir **Julius.** 1835–99, New Zealand statesman; prime minister (1873–75; 1876).

vogue (vəʊg) *n* **1** the popular style at a specified time (esp. in **in vogue**). **2** a period of general or popular usage or favour: *the vogue for such dances is over.* ◆ *adj* **3** (*usually prenominal*) fashionable: *a vogue word.* ORIG C16: from F: a rowing fashion, from OIt., from *vogare* to row, from ?
▸ **'voguish** *adj*

voice (vɔɪs) *n* **1** the sound made by the vibration of the vocal cords, esp. when modified by the tongue and mouth. **2** the natural and distinctive tone of the speech sounds characteristic of a particular person. **3** the condition, quality, or tone of such sounds: *a hysterical voice.* **4** the musical sound of a singing voice, with respect to its quality or tone: *she has a lovely voice.* **5** the ability to speak, sing, etc.: *he has lost his voice.* **6** a sound resembling or suggestive of vocal utterance: *the voice of hard experience.* **7** written or spoken expression, as of feeling, opinion, etc. (esp. in **give voice to**). **8** a stated choice, wish, or opinion: *to give someone a voice in a decision.* **9** an agency through which is communicated another's purpose, etc.: *such groups are the voice of our enemies.* **10** *Music.* **10a** musical notes produced by vibrations of the vocal chords at various frequencies and in certain registers: *a tenor voice.* **10b** (in harmony) an independent melodic line or part: *a fugue in five voices.* **11** *Phonetics.* the sound characterizing the articulation of several speech sounds, including all vowels or sonants, that is produced when the vocal cords are set in vibration by the breath. **12** *Grammar.* a category of the verb that expresses whether the relation between the subject and the verb is that of agent and action, action and recipient, or some other relation. **13 in voice.** in a condition to sing or speak well. **14 with one voice.** unanimously. ◆ *vb* **voices, voicing, voiced.** (*tr*) **15** to give expression to: *to voice a complaint.* **16** to articulate (a speech sound) with voice. **17** *Music.* to adjust (a wind instrument or organ pipe) so that it conforms to the correct standards of tone colour, pitch, etc. ORIG C13: from OF *voiz*, from L *vōx*
▸ **'voicer** *n*

voice box *n* another word for the **larynx.**

voiced (vɔɪst) *adj* **1** declared or expressed by the voice. **2** (*in combination*) having a voice as specified: *loud-voiced.* **3** *Phonetics.* articulated with accompanying vibration of the vocal cords: *in English* (b) *is a voiced consonant.*

voice input *n* the control and operation of computer systems by spoken commands.

voiceless ('vɔɪslɪs) *adj* **1** without a voice. **2** not articulated: *voiceless misery.* **3** silent. **4** *Phonetics.* articulated without accompanying vibration of the vocal cords: *in English* (p) *is a voiceless consonant.*
▸ **'voicelessly** *adv*

voice mail *n* an electronic system for the transfer and storage of telephone messages, which can then be dealt with by the user at his or her convenience.

voice-over *n* the voice of an unseen commentator heard during a film, etc.

voiceprint ('vɔɪsˌprɪnt) *n* a graphic representation of a person's voice recorded electronically, usually having time plotted along the horizontal axis and the frequency of the speech on the vertical axis.

void (vɔɪd) *adj* **1** without contents. **2** not legally binding: *null and void.* **3** (of an office, house, etc.) unoccupied. **4** (*postpositive;* foll. by *of*) destitute or devoid: *void of resources.* **5** useless: *all his efforts were rendered void.* **6** (of a card suit or player) having no cards in a particular suit: *his spades were void.* ◆ *n* **7** an empty space or area: *the huge desert voids of Asia.* **8** a feeling or condition of loneliness or deprivation. **9** a lack of any cards in one suit: *to have a void in spades.* ◆ *vb* (*mainly tr*) **10** to make ineffective or invalid. **11** to empty (contents, etc.) or make empty of contents. **12** (*also intr*) to discharge the con-

tents of (the bowels or urinary bladder). ORIG C13: from OF, from Vulgar L *vocītus* (unattested), from L *vacuus*, from *vacāre* to be empty
▸ **'voidable** *adj* ▸ **'voider** *n*

voidance ('vɔɪdᵊns) *n* **1** an annulment, as of a contract. **2** the condition of being vacant, as an office, benefice, etc. **3** the act of voiding or evacuating. ORIG C14: var. of AVOIDANCE

voile (vɔɪl) *n* a light semitransparent fabric of silk, rayon, cotton, etc., used for dresses, scarves, shirts, etc. ORIG C19: from F: VEIL

Voiotia ★ (*Greek* vjɔ'tiːa) *n* a department of E central Greece: corresponds to ancient Boeotia and part of ancient Phocis. Pop.: 134 108 (1991). Area: 3173 sq. km (1225 sq. miles). Modern Greek name: **Boeotia.**

Vojvodina *or* **Voivodina** ★ (*Serbo-Croat* 'vɔjvɔdina) *n* a region of NE Yugoslavia, in N Serbia: stripped of its previously autonomous status in 1990 after ethnic unrest. Capital: Novi Sad. Pop.: 2 114 000 (1995 est.). Area: 22 489 sq. km (8683 sq. miles).

vol. *abbrev. for:* **1** volcano. **2** volume. **3** volunteer.

volant ('vəʊlənt) *adj* **1** (*usually postpositive*) *Heraldry.* in a flying position. **2** *Rare.* flying or capable of flight. ORIG C16: from F, from *voler* to fly, from L *volāre*

volar ('vəʊlə) *adj Anat.* of or relating to the palm of the hand or the sole of the foot. ORIG C19: from L *vola* hollow of the hand, palm, sole of the foot

volatile ('vɒləˌtaɪl) *adj* **1** (of a substance) capable of readily changing from a solid or liquid form to a vapour. **2** (of persons) disposed to caprice or inconstancy. **3** (of circumstances) liable to sudden change. **4** lasting only a short time: *volatile business interests.* **5** *Computing.* (of a memory) not retaining stored information when the power supply is cut off. ◆ *n* **6** a volatile substance. ORIG C17: from L *volātilis* flying, from *volāre* to fly
▸ **'volatileness** *or* **volatility** (ˌvɒlə'tɪlɪtɪ) *n*

volatilize *or* **volatilise** (vɒ'lætɪˌlaɪz) *vb* **volatilizes, volatilizing, volatilized** *or* **volatilises, volatilising, volatilised.** to change or cause to change from a solid or liquid to a vapour.
▸ **vo'latiˌlizable** *or* **vo'latiˌlisable** *adj* ▸ **voˌlatiliz'ation** *or* **voˌlatilis'ation** *n*

vol-au-vent (*French* vɔlovɑ̃) *n* a very light puff pastry case filled with a savoury mixture in a sauce. ORIG C19: from F, lit.: flight in the wind

volcanic (vɒl'kænɪk) *adj* **1** of, produced by, or characterized by the presence of volcanoes: *a volcanic region.* **2** suggestive of or resembling an erupting volcano: *a volcanic era.*
▸ **vol'canically** *adv* ▸ **volcanicity** (ˌvɒlkə'nɪsɪtɪ) *n*

volcanic glass *n* any of several glassy volcanic igneous rocks, such as obsidian.

volcanism ('vɒlkəˌnɪzəm) *or* **vulcanism** *n* those processes collectively that result in the formation of volcanoes and their products.

volcano (vɒl'keɪnəʊ) *n, pl* **volcanoes** *or* **volcanos. 1** an opening in the earth's crust from which molten lava, rock fragments, ashes, dust, and gases are ejected from below the earth's surface. **2** a mountain formed from volcanic material ejected from a vent in a central crater. ORIG C17: from It., from L *Volcānus* Vulcan, Roman god of fire and metalworking, whose forges were believed to be responsible for volcanic rumblings

Volcano Islands ★ *pl n* a group of three volcanic islands in the W Pacific, about 1100 km (700 miles) south of Japan: the largest is Iwo Jima, taken by US forces in 1945 and returned to Japan in 1968. Area: about 28 sq. km (11 sq. miles). Japanese name: **Kazan Retto.**

volcanology (ˌvɒlkə'nɒlədʒɪ) *or* **vulcanology** *n* the study of volcanoes and volcanic phenomena.
▸ **volcanological** (ˌvɒlkənə'lɒdʒɪkᵊl) *or* **ˌvulcano'logical** *adj*

vole (vəʊl) *n* any of various small rodents, mostly of Eurasia and North America, having a stocky body, short tail, and inconspicuous ears. ORIG C19: short for *volemouse*, from ON *vollr* field + *mus* MOUSE

Volga ★ ('vɒlgə) *n* a river in W Russia, rising in the Valdai Range and flowing through a chain of small lakes to the Rybinsk Reservoir and south to the Caspian Sea through Volgograd: the longest river in Europe. Length: 3690 km (2293 miles).

Volgograd ★ (*Russian* vəlga'grat; *English* 'vɒlgəˌgræd) *n* a port in SW Russia, on the River Volga: scene of a major engagement (1918) during the civil war and again in World War II (1942–43), in which the German forces were defeated; major industrial centre. Pop.: 1 003 000 (1995 est.). Former names: **Tsaritsyn** (until 1925), **Stalingrad** (1925–61).

volitant ('vɒlɪtənt) *adj* **1** flying or moving about rapidly. **2** capable of flying. ORIG C19: from L *volitāre* to flit, from *volāre* to fly

volition (və'lɪʃən) *n* **1** the act of exercising the will: *of one's own volition.* **2** the faculty of conscious choice, decision, and intention. **3** the resulting choice or resolution. ORIG C17: from Med. L *volitiō*, from L *vol-* as in *volō* I will, present stem of *velle* to wish
▸ **vo'litional** *adj*

volitive ('vɒlɪtɪv) *adj* of, relating to, or emanating from the will.

Volk (fɒlk) *n S. African.* the Afrikaner people. ORIG from Afrik., from Du.

Volksraad ('fɒlksˌrɑːt) *n* (formerly, in South Africa) the Legislative Assemblies of the Transvaal and Orange Free State republics. ORIG from Afrik., from Du. *volks* people's + *raad* council

volley ('vɒlɪ) *n* **1** the simultaneous discharge of several weapons, esp. firearms. **2** the projectiles or missiles so discharged. **3** a burst of oaths, protests, etc., occurring simultaneously or in rapid succession. **4** *Sport.* a stroke, shot, or kick at a moving ball before it hits the ground. **5** *Cricket.* the flight of such a ball or the ball itself. ◆ *vb* **6** to discharge (weapons, etc.) in or as if in a volley or (of weapons, etc.) to be discharged. **7** (*tr*) to utter vehemently. **8** (*tr*) *Sport.* to strike or kick (a moving ball) before it hits the ground. ORIG C16: from F *volée* a flight, from *voler* to fly, from L *volāre*
▸ **'volleyer** *n*

volleyball ('vɒlɪˌbɔːl) *n* **1** a game in which two teams hit a large ball back and forth over a high net with their hands. **2** the ball used in this game.

Vologda ★ (*Russian* 'vɔləgdə) *n* an industrial city in W central Russia. Pop.: 299 000 (1995 est.).

Vólos ★ (*Greek* 'vɔlɔs) *n* a port in E Greece, in Thessaly on the **Gulf of Volos** (an inlet of the Aegean): the third largest port in Greece. Pop.: 70 000 (latest est.).

volplane ('vɒlˌpleɪn) *vb* **volplanes, volplaning, volplaned. 1** (*intr*) (of an aircraft) to glide without engine power. ◆ *n* **2** a glide by an aircraft. ORIG C20: from F *vol plané* a gliding flight

vols. *abbrev. for* volumes.

Volsung ★ ('vɒlsʊŋ) *n* **1** a great hero of Norse and Germanic legend and poetry who gave his name to a race of warriors; father of Sigmund and Signy. **2** any member of his family.

volt¹ (vəʊlt) *n* the derived SI unit of electric potential; the potential difference between two points on a conductor carrying a current of 1 ampere, when the power dissipated between these points is 1 watt. Symbol: V ORIG C19: after Count Alessandro VOLTA

volt² *or* **volte** (vɒlt) *n* **1** a circle executed in dressage. **2** a leap made in fencing to avoid an opponent's thrust. ORIG C17: from F, from It. *volta*, ult. from L *volvere* to turn

volta ('vɒltə; *Italian* 'vɔlta) *n, pl* **volte** (*Italian* -te). **1** an Italian dance popular during the 16th and 17th centuries. **2** a piece of music for or in the rhythm of this dance. ORIG C17: from It.: turn; see VOLT²

Volta¹ ★ ('vɒltə) *n* **1** a river in W Africa, formed by the confluence of the **Black Volta** and the **White Volta** in N central Ghana: flows south to the Bight of Benin: the chief river of Ghana. Length: 480 km (300 miles); (including the Black Volta) 1600 km (1000 miles). **2 Lake.** an artificial lake in Ghana, extending 408 km (250 miles) upstream from the **Volta River Dam** on the Volta River: completed in 1966. Area: 8482 sq. km (3275 sq. miles).

Volta[2] ★ ('vəultə; *Italian* 'vɔlta) *n* Count **Alessandro** (ales'sandro). 1745–1827, Italian physicist, who invented the voltaic pile (1800) and an electroscope.

voltage ('vəultɪdʒ) *n* an electromotive force or potential difference expressed in volts.

voltaic (vɒl'teɪɪk) *adj* another word for **galvanic** (sense 1).

voltaic cell *n* another name for **primary cell.**

voltaic couple *n Physics.* a pair of dissimilar metals in an electrolyte with a potential difference between the metals resulting from chemical action.

voltaic pile *n* an early form of battery consisting of a pile of paired plates of dissimilar metals, such as zinc and copper, each pair being separated from the next by a pad moistened with an electrolyte.

Voltaire ★ (vɒl'tɛə, vəul-; *French* vɔltɛr) *n* pseudonym of *François Marie Arouet.* 1694–1778, French writer, noted for his outspoken belief in liberty. His major works include *Lettres philosophiques* (1734) and the satire *Candide* (1759).
▸ **Vol'tairean** *or* **Vol'tairian** *adj, n*

voltameter (vɒl'tæmɪtə) *n* a device for measuring electric charge.
▸ **voltametric** (ˌvɒltə'mɛtrɪk) *adj*

voltammeter (ˌvəult'æmˌmi:tə) *n* a dual-purpose instrument that can measure both potential difference and electric current, usually in volts and amperes respectively.

volt-ampere ('vəult'æmpɛə) *n* the product of the potential in volts across an electrical circuit and the resultant current in amperes.

Volta Redonda ★ (*Portuguese* 'vɔltə rə'dõdə) *n* a city in SE Brazil, in Rio de Janeiro state on the Paraíba River: founded in 1941; site of South America's largest steelworks. Pop.: 219 988 (1991).

volte-face ('vɒlt'fɑ:s) *n, pl* **volte-face. 1** a reversal, as in opinion. **2** a change of position so as to look, lie, etc., in the opposite direction. ORIG C19: from F, from It., from *volta* turn + *faccia* face

voltmeter ('vəultˌmi:tə) *n* an instrument for measuring potential difference or electromotive force.

Volturno ★ (*Italian* vol'turno) *n* a river in S central Italy, flowing southeast and southwest to the Tyrrhenian Sea: scene of a battle (1860) during the wars for Italian unity, in which Garibaldi defeated the Neapolitans; German line of defence during World War II. Length: 175 km (109 miles).

voluble ('vɒljub[ə]l) *adj* **1** talking easily and at length. **2** *Arch.* easily turning or rotating. **3** *Rare.* (of a plant) twining or twisting. ORIG C16: from L *volūbilis* turning readily, from *volvere* to turn
▸ ˌ**volu'bility** *or* '**volubleness** *n* ▸ '**volubly** *adv*

volume ('vɒlju:m) *n* **1** the magnitude of the three-dimensional space enclosed within or occupied by an object, geometric solid, etc. **2** a large mass or quantity: *the volume of protest.* **3** an amount or total: *the volume of exports.* **4** fullness of sound. **5** the control on a radio, etc., for adjusting the intensity of sound. **6** a bound collection of printed or written pages; book. **7** any of several books either bound in an identical format or part of a series. **8** the complete set of issues of a periodical over a specified period, esp. one year. **9** *History.* a roll of parchment, etc. **10 speak volumes.** to convey much significant information. ORIG C14: from OF, from L *volūmen* a roll, from *volvere* to roll up

volumetric (ˌvɒlju'mɛtrɪk) *adj* of, concerning, or using measurement by volume: *volumetric analysis.*
▸ ˌ**volu'metrically** *adv*

volumetric analysis *n Chem.* quantitative analysis of liquids or solutions by comparing the volumes that react with known volumes of standard reagents, usually by titration.

voluminous (və'lu:mɪnəs) *adj* **1** of great size, quantity, or extent. **2** (of writing) consisting of or sufficient to fill volumes. ORIG C17: from LL *volūminōsus* full of windings, from *volūmen* VOLUME
▸ **voluminosity** (vəˌlu:mɪ'nɒsɪtɪ) *n* ▸ **vo'luminously** *adv*

Völund ★ ('vølund) *n* the Scandinavian name of **Wayland.**

voluntarism ('vɒləntəˌrɪzəm) *n* **1** *Philosophy.* the theory that the will rather than the intellect is the ultimate principle of reality. **2** a doctrine or system based on voluntary participation in a course of action. **3** another name for **voluntaryism.**
▸ '**voluntarist** *n, adj*

voluntary ('vɒləntərɪ) *adj* **1** performed, undertaken, or brought about by free choice or willingly: *a voluntary donation.* **2** (of persons) serving or acting in a specified function without compulsion or promise of remuneration: *a voluntary social worker.* **3** done by, composed of, or functioning with the aid of volunteers: *a voluntary association.* **4** exercising or having the faculty of willing: *a voluntary agent.* **5** spontaneous: *voluntary laughter.* **6** *Law.* **6a** acting or done without legal obligation, compulsion, or persuasion. **6b** made without payment or recompense: *a voluntary conveyance.* **7** (of the muscles of the limbs, neck, etc.) having their action controlled by the will. **8** maintained by the voluntary actions or contributions of individuals and not by the state: *voluntary schools.* ◆ *n, pl* **voluntaries. 9** *Music.* a composition or improvisation, usually for organ, played at the beginning or end of a church service. ORIG C14: from L *voluntārius,* from *voluntās* will, from *velle* to wish
▸ '**voluntarily** *adv*

voluntary arrangement *n Law.* a procedure enabling an insolvent company to come to an arrangement with its creditors and resolve its financial problems, often in compliance with a court order.

voluntaryism ('vɒləntərɪˌɪzəm) *or* **voluntarism** *n* the principle of supporting churches, schools, and various other institutions by voluntary contributions rather than with state funds.
▸ '**voluntaryist** *or* '**voluntarist** *n*

voluntary retailer *n* another name for **symbol retailer.**

volunteer (ˌvɒlən'tɪə) *n* **1a** a person who performs or offers to perform voluntary service. **1b** (*as modifier*): *a volunteer system.* **2** a person who freely undertakes military service. **3a** a plant that grows from seed that has not been deliberately sown. **3b** (*as modifier*): *a volunteer plant.* ◆ *vb* **4** to offer (oneself or one's services) for an undertaking by choice and without request or obligation. **5** (*tr*) to perform, give, or communicate voluntarily: *to volunteer help.* **6** (*intr*) to enlist voluntarily for military service. ORIG C17: from F, from L *voluntārius;* see VOLUNTARY

voluptuary (və'lʌptjuərɪ) *n, pl* **voluptuaries. 1** a person devoted to luxury and sensual pleasures. ◆ *adj* **2** of or furthering sensual gratification or luxury. ORIG C17: from LL *voluptuārius* delightful, from L *voluptās* pleasure

voluptuous (və'lʌptjuəs) *adj* **1** relating to, characterized by, or consisting of pleasures of the body or senses. **2** devoted or addicted to sensual indulgence or luxurious pleasures. **3** sexually alluring, esp. through shapeliness or fullness: *a voluptuous woman.* ORIG C14: from L *voluptuōsus* full of gratification, from *voluptās* pleasure
▸ **vo'luptuously** *adv* ▸ **vo'luptuousness** *n*

volute ('vɒlju:t, və'lu:t) *n* **1** a spiral or twisting turn, form, or object. **2** Also called: **helix.** a carved ornament, esp. as used on an Ionic capital, that has the form of a spiral scroll. **3** any of the whorls of the spirally coiled shell of a snail or similar gastropod mollusc. **4** any of a family of tropical marine gastropod molluscs having a spiral shell with beautiful markings. ◆ *adj also* **voluted** (və'lu:tɪd). **5** having the form of a volute; spiral. ORIG C17: from L *volūta* spiral decoration, from *volūtus,* from *volvere* to roll up
▸ **vo'lution** *n*

vomer ('vəumə) *n* the thin flat bone forming part of the separation between the nasal passages in mammals. ORIG C18: from L: ploughshare

vomit ('vɒmɪt) *vb* **vomits, vomiting, vomited. 1** to eject (the contents of the stomach) through the mouth as the result of involuntary muscular spasms of the stomach and oesophagus. **2** to eject or be ejected forcefully. ◆ *n* **3** the matter ejected in vomiting. **4** the act of vomiting. **5** an emetic. ORIG C14: from L *vomitāre* to vomit repeatedly, from *vomere* to vomit
▸ '**vomiter** *n*

vomitory ('vɒmɪtərɪ) *adj* **1** Also: **vomitive** ('vɒmɪtɪv). causing vomiting; emetic. ◆ *n, pl* **vomitories.** **2** a vomitory agent. **3** Also called: **vomitorium** (ˌvɒmɪˈtɔːrɪəm). a passageway in an ancient Roman amphitheatre that connects an outside entrance to a tier of seats.

von Braun ★ (vɒn ˈbraʊn, fɒn) *n* **Wernher** (ˈvɜːnə). 1912–77, US rocket engineer, born in Germany, where he designed the V-2 missile used in World War II.

von Euler ★ (*German* fɔn ˈɔɪlər) *n* See (Ulf von) **Euler.**

von Laue ★ (*German* fɔn ˈlauə) *n* See (Max Theodor Felix von) **Laue.**

Vonnegut ★ (ˈvɒnɪgʌt) *n* **Kurt.** born 1922, US novelist. His works include *Slaughterhouse Five* (1969) and *Timequake* (1997).

von Rundstedt ★ (*German* fɔn ˈrʊntʃtɛt) *n* See (Karl Rudolf Gerd von) **Rundstedt.**

von Sternberg ★ (vɒn ˈstɜːnˌbɜːg; *German* fɔn ˈʃtɛrnbɛrk) *n* **Joseph** (ˈjoːzɛf), real name *Jonas Sternberg.* 1894–1969, US film director, born in Austria.

von Stroheim ★ (vɒn ˈstrəʊˌhaɪm, ˈʃtrəʊ-; fɒn) *n* **Erich** (ˈɛrik; *German* ˈeːrɪç), real name *Hans Erich Maria Stroheim von Nordenwall.* 1885–1957, US film director and actor, born in Austria.

voodoo (ˈvuːduː) *n, pl* **voodoos.** **1** Also called: **voodooism.** a religious belief system involving witchcraft and communication with ancestral deities, common in Haiti and other Caribbean islands. **2** a person who practises voodoo. **3** a charm, spell, or fetish involved in voodoo worship. ◆ *adj* **4** relating to or associated with voodoo. ◆ *vb* **voodoos, voodooing, voodooed.** **5** (*tr*) to affect by or as if by the power of voodoo. ORIG C19: from Louisiana F *voudou,* ult. of West African origin
▸ ˈ**voodooist** *n*

voorkamer (ˈfʊəˌkɑːmə) *n S. African.* the front room of a house. ORIG Afrik., from Du. *voor* fore + *kamer* chamber

voorskot (ˈfʊəˌskɒt) *n S. African.* advance payment made to a farmer for crops. Cf. **agterskot.** ORIG C20: Afrik., from *voor* before + *skot* shot, payment

Voortrekker (ˈfʊəˌtrɛkə) *n* (in South Africa) **1** one of the original Afrikaner settlers of the Transvaal and the Orange Free State who migrated from the Cape Colony in the 1830s. **2** a member of the Afrikaner youth movement founded in 1931. ORIG C19: from Du., from *voor-* FORE- + *trekken* to TREK

voracious (vɒˈreɪʃəs) *adj* **1** devouring or craving food in great quantities. **2** very eager or unremitting in some activity: *voracious reading.* ORIG C17: from L *vorāx,* from *vorāre* to devour
▸ **voracity** (vɒˈræsɪtɪ) *or* **voˈraciousness** *n*

Vorarlberg ★ (*German* ˈfoːrarlbɛrk) *n* a mountainous state of W Austria. Capital: Bregenz. Pop.: 345 272 (1998 est.). Area: 2601 sq. km (1004 sq. miles).

Voronezh ★ (*Russian* vaˈrɔnɪʃ) *n* a city in W Russia: engineering and chemical industries; university (1918). Pop.: 908 000 (1995 est.).

Voroshilovgrad ★ (*Russian* vərəʃilawˈgrat) *n* the former name (1935–91) of **Lugansk.**

Voroshilovsk ★ (*Russian* vəraˈʃiləfsk) *n* the former name (1940–44) of **Stavropol.**

-vorous *adj combining form.* feeding on or devouring: *carnivorous.* ORIG from L *-vorus;* rel. to *vorāre* to swallow up
▸ **-vore** *n combining form.*

Vorster ★ (ˈfɔːstə, ˈvɔː-) *n* **Balthazar Johannes,** known as *John.* 1915–83, South African statesman; Nationalist prime minister (1966–78); president (1978).

vortex (ˈvɔːtɛks) *n, pl* **vortexes** *or* **vortices** (-tɪˌsiːz). **1** a whirling mass or motion of liquid, gas, flame, etc., such as the spiralling movement of water around a whirlpool. **2** any activity or way of life regarded as irresistibly engulfing. ORIG C17: from L: a whirlpool
▸ **vortical** (ˈvɔːtɪkᵊl) *adj*

vorticella (ˌvɔːtɪˈsɛlə) *n, pl* **vorticellae** (-liː). any of a genus of protozoans consisting of a goblet-shaped ciliated cell attached to the substratum by a long contractile stalk. ORIG C18: from NL, lit.: a little eddy, from VORTEX

vorticism (ˈvɔːtɪˌsɪzəm) *n* an art movement in England combining the techniques of cubism with the concern for the problems of the machine age evinced in futurism. ORIG C20: referring to the "vortices" of modern life on which the movement was based
▸ ˈ**vorticist** *n*

Vortumnus ★ (vɔːˈtʌmnəs) *n* a variant spelling of **Vertumnus.**

Vosges ★ (*French* voʒ) *n* **1** a mountain range in E France, west of the Rhine valley. Highest peak: 1423 m (4672 ft). **2** a department of NE France, in Lorraine region. Capital: Épinal. Pop.: 385 376 (1994 est.). Area: 5903 sq. km (2302 sq. miles).

vostro account (ˈvɒstrəʊ) *n* a bank account held by a foreign bank with a British bank, usually in sterling. Cf. **nostro account.**

votary (ˈvəʊtərɪ) *n, pl* **votaries,** *also* **votarist.** **1** *RC Church, Eastern Churches.* a person, such as a monk or nun, who has dedicated himself or herself to religion by taking vows. **2** a devoted adherent of a religion, cause, etc. ◆ *adj* **3** ardently devoted to the worship of God or a saint. ORIG C16: from L *vōtum* a vow, from *vovēre* to vow
▸ ˈ**votaress** *fem n*

vote (vəʊt) *n* **1** an indication of choice, opinion, or will on a question, such as the choosing of a candidate: *10 votes for Jones.* **2** the opinion of a group of persons as determined by voting: *it was put to the vote.* **3** a body of votes or voters collectively: *the Jewish vote.* **4** the total number of votes cast. **5** the ticket, ballot, etc., by which a vote is expressed. **6a** the right to vote; franchise. **6b** a person regarded as the embodiment of this right. **7** a means of voting, such as a ballot. **8** *Chiefly Brit.* a grant or other proposition to be voted upon. ◆ *vb* **votes, voting, voted.** **9** (when *tr, takes a clause as object or an infinitive*) to express or signify (one's preference or will) (for or against some question, etc.): *to vote by ballot.* **10** (*intr*) to declare oneself as being (something or in favour of something) by exercising one's vote: *to vote socialist.* **11** (*tr;* foll. by *into* or *out of,* etc.) to appoint or elect (a person to or from a particular post): *he was voted out of office.* **12** (*tr*) to determine the condition of in a specified way by voting: *the court voted itself out of existence.* **13** (*tr*) to authorize or allow by voting: *vote us a rise.* **14** (*tr*) *Inf.* to declare by common opinion: *the party was voted a failure.* ORIG C15: from L *vōtum* a solemn promise, from *vovēre* to vow
▸ ˈ**votable** *or* ˈ**voteable** *adj*

vote down *vb* (*tr, adv*) to decide against or defeat in a vote: *the bill was voted down.*

vote of no confidence *n Parliament.* a vote on a motion put by the Opposition censuring an aspect of the Government's policy; if the motion is carried the Government is obliged to resign. Also called: **vote of censure.**

voter (ˈvəʊtə) *n* a person who can or does vote.

voting machine *n* (esp. in the US) a machine at a polling station that voters operate to register their votes and that mechanically or electronically counts all votes cast.

votive (ˈvəʊtɪv) *adj* **1** given or dedicated in fulfilment of or in accordance with a vow. **2** *RC Church.* having the nature of a voluntary offering: *a votive Mass.* ORIG C16: from L *vōtīvus* promised by a vow, from *vōtum* a vow

vouch (vaʊtʃ) *vb* **1** (*intr;* usually foll. by *for*) to give personal assurance: *I'll vouch for his safety.* **2** (when *tr, usually takes a clause as object;* when *intr,* usually foll. by *for*) to furnish supporting evidence (for) or function as proof (of). **3** (*tr*) *Arch.* to cite (authors, principles, etc.) in support of something. ORIG C14: from OF *vocher* to summon, ult. from L *vocāre* to call

voucher (ˈvaʊtʃə) *n* **1** a document serving as evidence for some claimed transaction, as the receipt or expenditure of money. **2** *Brit.* a ticket or card serving as a substitute for cash: *a gift voucher.* **3** a person or thing that vouches for the truth of some statement, etc. ORIG C16: from Anglo-F, noun use of OF *voucher* to summon; see VOUCH

vouchsafe (ˌvaʊtʃˈseɪf) *vb* **vouchsafes, vouchsafing, vouchsafed.** (*tr*) **1** to give or grant or condescend to give or grant: *she vouchsafed no reply.* **2** (*may take a clause as object or an infinitive*) to agree, promise, or permit, often graciously or condescendingly: *he vouchsafed to come yesterday.* ORIG C14 *vouchen sauf;* see VOUCH, SAFE

voussoir (vuːˈswɑː) *n* a wedge-shaped stone or brick that is used with others to construct an arch or vault. ORIG C18: from F, from Vulgar L *volsōrium* (unattested), ult. from L *volvere* to turn, roll

vow (vaʊ) *n* **1** a solemn or earnest pledge or promise binding the person making it to perform a specified act or behave in a certain way. **2** a solemn promise made to a deity or saint, by which the promiser pledges himself to some future act or way of life. **3 take vows.** to enter a religious order and commit oneself to its rule of life by the vows of poverty, chastity, and obedience. ◆ *vb* **4** (*tr; may take a clause as object or an infinitive*) to pledge, promise, or undertake solemnly: *he vowed to return.* **5** (*tr*) to dedicate or consecrate to God or a saint. **6** (*tr; usually takes a clause as object*) to assert or swear emphatically. **7** (*intr*) *Arch.* to declare solemnly. ORIG C13: from OF *vou,* from L *vōtum;* see VOTE
▸ **ˈvower** *n*

vowel (ˈvaʊəl) *n* **1** *Phonetics.* a voiced speech sound whose articulation is characterized by the absence of obstruction in the vocal tract, allowing the breath stream free passage. The timbre of a vowel is chiefly determined by the position of the tongue and the lips. **2** a letter or character representing a vowel. ORIG C14: from OF, from L *vocālis littera* vowel, from *vocālis,* from *vox* voice
▸ **ˈvowel-ˌlike** *adj*

vowel gradation *n* another name for **ablaut.** See **gradation** (sense 5).

vowelize *or* **vowelise** (ˈvaʊəˌlaɪz) *vb* **vowelizes, vowelizing, vowelized** *or* **vowelises, vowelising, vowelised.** (*tr*) to mark the vowel points in (a Hebrew word or text).
▸ **ˌvoweliˈzation** *or* **ˌvoweliˈsation** *n*

vowel mutation *n* another name for **umlaut.**

vowel point *n* any of several marks or points placed above or below consonants, esp. those evolved for Hebrew or Arabic, in order to indicate vowel sounds.

vox (vɒks) *n, pl* **voces.** a voice or sound. ORIG L: voice

vox pop *n* interviews with members of the public on a radio or television programme. ORIG C20: shortened from VOX POPULI

vox populi (ˈpɒpjʊˌlaɪ) *n* the voice of the people; popular or public opinion. ORIG L

voyage (ˈvɔɪɪdʒ) *n* **1** a journey, travel, or passage, esp. one to a distant land or by sea or air. ◆ *vb* **voyages, voyaging, voyaged. 2** to travel over or traverse (something): *we will voyage to Africa.* ORIG C13: from OF *veiage,* from L *viāticum* provision for travelling, from *via* way
▸ **ˈvoyager** *n*

voyage charter *n* the hire of a ship or aircraft for a specific number of voyages. Cf. **time charter.**

voyageur (ˌvɔɪəˈdʒɜː) *n* (in Canada) a woodsman, guide, trapper, boatman, or explorer, esp. in the North. ORIG C19: F: traveller, from *voyager* to VOYAGE

voyeur (vwaɪˈɜː) *n* a person who obtains sexual pleasure from the observation of people undressing, having intercourse, etc. ORIG C20: F, lit.: one who sees, from *voir* to see, from L *vidēre*
▸ **voˈyeurism** *n* ▸ **ˌvoyeurˈistic** *adj*

VP *abbrev. for:* **1** verb phrase. **2** Vice President.

VPL *Jocular abbrev. for* visible panty line.

VR *abbrev. for:* **1** variant reading. **2** Victoria Regina. ORIG L: Queen Victoria **3** virtual reality.

V. Rev. *abbrev. for* Very Reverend.

Vries ★ (vriːs) *n* See (Hugo) **De Vries.**

vrou (frəʊ) *n S. African.* an Afrikaner woman, esp. a married woman. ORIG from Afrik., from Du.

vrystater (ˈfreɪˌstɑːtə) *n S. African.* a native inhabitant of the Free State, esp. one who is White. ORIG from Afrik., from Du. *vrij* free + *staat* state

vs *abbrev. for* versus.

VS *abbrev. for* Veterinary Surgeon.

v.s. *abbrev. for* vide supra (see **vide**).

V-sign *n* **1** (in Britain) an offensive gesture made by sticking up the index and middle fingers with the palm of the hand inwards. **2** a similar gesture with the palm outwards meaning victory or peace.

VSO *abbrev. for:* **1** very superior old: used to indicate that a brandy, port, etc., is between 12 and 17 years old. **2** (in Britain) Voluntary Service Overseas: an organization that sends young volunteers to use and teach their skills in developing countries.

VSOP *abbrev. for* very special (*or* superior) old pale: used to indicate that a brandy, port, etc., is between 20 and 25 years old.

Vt. *or* **VT** *abbrev. for* Vermont.

VTOL (ˈviːtɒl) *n* vertical takeoff and landing; a system in which an aircraft can take off and land vertically. Cf. **STOL.**

VTR *abbrev. for* video tape recorder.

V-type engine *n* a type of internal-combustion engine having two cylinder blocks attached to a single crankcase, the angle between the two blocks forming a V.

Vuelta Abajo ★ (*Spanish* ˈbwelta aˈβaxo) *n* a region of W Cuba: famous for its tobacco.

vug (vʌg) *n Mining.* a small cavity in a rock or vein, usually lined with crystals. ORIG C19: from Cornish *vooga* cave
▸ **ˈvuggy** *adj*

Vuillard ★ (*French* vɥijar) *n* **Jean Édouard** (ʒɑ̃ edwar). 1868–1940, French painter and lithographer.

Vulcan ★ (ˈvʌlkən) *n* the Roman god of fire and metalworking. Greek counterpart: **Hephaestus.**
▸ **Vulcanian** (vʌlˈkeɪnɪən) *adj*

vulcanian (vʌlˈkeɪnɪən) *adj Geol.* of or relating to a volcanic eruption characterized by the explosive discharge of gases, fine ash, and viscous lava that hardens in the crater. ORIG C17: after VULCAN

vulcanism (ˈvʌlkəˌnɪzəm) *n* a variant spelling of **volcanism.**

vulcanite (ˈvʌlkəˌnaɪt) *n* a hard usually black rubber produced by vulcanizing natural rubber with sulphur. It is used for electrical insulators, etc. Also called: **ebonite.**

vulcanize *or* **vulcanise** (ˈvʌlkəˌnaɪz) *vb* **vulcanizes, vulcanizing, vulcanized** *or* **vulcanises, vulcanising, vulcanised.** (*tr*) **1** to treat (rubber) with sulphur under heat and pressure to improve elasticity and strength or to produce a hard substance such as vulcanite. **2** to treat (substances other than rubber) by a similar process in order to improve their properties.
▸ **ˌvulcaniˈzation** *or* **ˌvulcaniˈsation** *n*

vulcanology (ˌvʌlkəˈnɒlədʒɪ) *n* a variant spelling of **volcanology.**

Vulg. *abbrev. for* Vulgate.

vulgar (ˈvʌlgə) *adj* **1** marked by lack of taste, culture, delicacy, manners, etc.: *vulgar language.* **2** (*often cap.; usually prenominal*) denoting a form of a language, esp. of Latin, current among common people, esp. at a period when the formal language is archaic. **3** *Arch.* of or current among the great mass of common people. ORIG C14: from L *vulgāris,* from *vulgus* the common people
▸ **ˈvulgarly** *adv*

vulgar fraction *n* another name for **simple fraction.**

vulgarian (vʌlˈgɛərɪən) *n* a vulgar person, esp. one who is rich or has pretensions to good taste.

vulgarism (ˈvʌlgəˌrɪzəm) *n* **1** a coarse, crude, or obscene expression. **2** a word or phrase found only in the vulgar form of a language.

vulgarity (vʌlˈgærɪtɪ) *n, pl* **vulgarities. 1** the condition of being vulgar; lack of good manners. **2** a vulgar action, phrase, etc.

vulgarize *or* **vulgarise** (ˈvʌlgəˌraɪz) *vb* **vulgarizes, vulgarizing, vulgarized** *or* **vulgarises, vulgarising, vulgarised.** (*tr*) **1** to make commonplace or vulgar. **2** to make (something little known or difficult to understand) widely known or popular among the public.
▸ **ˌvulgariˈzation** *or* **ˌvulgariˈsation** *n*

Vulgar Latin *n* any of the dialects of Latin spoken in the Roman Empire other than classical Latin.

vulgate (ˈvʌlgeɪt, -gɪt) *n Rare.* **1** a commonly recognized text or version. **2** the vernacular.

Vulgate (ˈvʌlgeɪt, -gɪt) *n* **a** (from the 13th century onwards) the fourth-century Latin version of the Bible pro-

★ people and places

duced by Jerome. **b** (*as modifier*): *the Vulgate version.* ORIG C17: from Med. L, from LL *vulgāta editiō* popular version (of the Bible), from L *vulgāre* to make common

vulnerable ('vʌlnərəbᵊl) *adj* **1** capable of being physically or emotionally wounded or hurt. **2** open to temptation, censure, etc. **3** *Mil.* exposed to attack. **4** *Bridge.* (of a side who have won one game towards rubber) subject to increased bonuses or penalties. ORIG C17: from LL, from L *vulnerāre* to wound, from *vulnus* a wound
► ˌ**vulnera'bility** *n* ► '**vulnerably** *adv*

vulnerary ('vʌlnərərɪ) *Med.* ◆ *adj* **1** of or used to heal a wound. ◆ *n, pl* **vulneraries. 2** a vulnerary drug or agent. ORIG C16: from L *vulnerārius* from *vulnus* wound

vulpine ('vʌlpaɪn) *adj* **1** of, relating to, or resembling a fox. **2** crafty, clever, etc. ORIG C17: from L *vulpīnus* foxlike, from *vulpēs* fox

vulture ('vʌltʃə) *n* **1** any of various very large diurnal birds of prey of Africa, Asia, and warm parts of Europe, typically having broad wings and soaring flight and feeding on carrion. **2** any similar bird of North, Central, and South America. **3** a person or thing that preys greedily and ruthlessly on others, esp. the helpless. ORIG C14: from OF *voltour,* from L *vultur*
► **vulturine** ('vʌltʃəˌraɪn) *or* '**vulturous** *adj*

vulva ('vʌlvə) *n, pl* **vulvae** (-viː) *or* **vulvas.** the external genitals of human females, including the labia, mons veneris, clitoris, and the vaginal orifice. ORIG C16: from L: covering, womb, matrix
► '**vulvar** *adj*

vulvitis (vʌl'vaɪtɪs) *n* inflammation of the vulva.

vv *abbrev. for* vice versa.

vv. *abbrev. for:* **1** versus. **2** *Music.* volumes.

Vyatka ★ (*Russian* 'vjatkə) *n* the former name (1780–1934) of **Kirov**[1].

Vyborg ★ (*Russian* 'vibərk) *n* a port in NW Russia, at the head of **Vyborg Bay** (an inlet of the Gulf of Finland): belonged to Finland (1918–40). Pop.: 80 000 (1988 est.). Finnish name: **Viipuri.** Swedish name: **Viborg.**

Vyshinsky *or* **Vishinsky** ★ (*Russian* vi'ʃinskij) *n* **Andrei Yanuaryevich** (an'drjej jənu'arjɪvitʃ). 1883–1954, Soviet statesman; foreign minister (1949–53). He was public prosecutor (1935–38) at the Stalin show trials.

Ww

w *or* **W** ('dʌbᵊl,juː) *n, pl* **w's, W's,** *or* **Ws. 1** the 23rd letter of the English alphabet. **2** a speech sound represented by this letter, usually a bilabial semivowel, as in *web.*

W *symbol for:* **1** *Chem.* tungsten. ORIG from NL *wolframium,* from G *Wolfram* **2** watt. **3** West. **4** women's (size). **5** *Physics.* work.

w. *abbrev. for:* **1** week. **2** weight. **3** *Cricket.* **3a** wide. **3b** wicket. **4** width. **5** wife. **6** with.

W. *abbrev. for:* **1** Wales. **2** Welsh.

WA *abbrev. for:* **1** Washington (state). **2** Western Australia.

WAAAF (formerly) *abbrev. for* Women's Auxiliary Australian Air Force.

WAAC (wæk) *n* (formerly) **1** *acronym for* Women's Army Auxiliary Corps. **2** Also called: **Waac.** a member of this corps.

Waadt ★ (vat) *n* the German name for **Vaud.**

WAAF (wæf) *n* (formerly) **1** *acronym for* Women's Auxiliary Air Force. **2** Also called: **Waaf.** a member of this force.

Waal ★ (*Dutch* waːl) *n* a river in the central Netherlands: the S branch of the Lower Rhine. Length: 84 km (52 miles).

Wabash ★ ('wɔːbæʃ) *n* a river in the E central US, rising in W Ohio and flowing west and southwest to join the Ohio River in Indiana. Length: 764 km (475 miles).

wabble ('wɒbᵊl) *vb* **wabbles, wabbling, wabbled,** *n* a variant spelling of **wobble.**

Wace ★ (weɪs) *n* **Robert.** born ?1100, Anglo-Norman poet; author of the *Roman de Brut* and *Roman de Rou.*

wacke ('wækə) *n Obs.* any of various soft earthy rocks derived from basalt. ORIG C18: from G: rock, gravel, basalt

wacko ('wækəʊ) *Inf.* ◆ *adj* **1** mad or eccentric. ◆ *n, pl* **wackos. 2** a mad or eccentric person. ORIG C20: back formation from WACKY

wacky ('wækɪ) *adj* **wackier, wackiest.** *Sl.* eccentric or unpredictable. ORIG C19 (in dialect sense: a fool): from WHACK (hence, a *whacky,* a person who behaves as if he had been whacked on the head)
▸ '**wackily** *adv* ▸ '**wackiness** *n*

wad (wɒd) *n* **1** a small mass or ball of fibrous or soft material, such as cotton wool, used esp. for packing or stuffing. **2a** a plug of paper, cloth, leather, etc., pressed against a charge to hold it in place in a muzzle-loading cannon. **2b** a disc of paper, felt, etc., used to hold in place the powder and shot in a shotgun cartridge. **3** a roll or bundle of something, esp. of banknotes. ◆ *vb* **wads, wadding, wadded. 4** to form (something) into a wad. **5** (*tr*) to roll into a wad or bundle. **6** (*tr*) **6a** to hold (a charge) in place with a wad. **6b** to insert a wad into (a gun). **7** (*tr*) to pack or stuff with wadding. ORIG C14: from LL *wadda*

Wadai ★ (waː'daɪ) *n* a former independent sultanate of NE central Africa: now the E part of Chad.

Waddenzee ★ (*Dutch* 'wɑdənzeː) *n* the part of the North Sea between the Dutch mainland and the West Frisian Islands.

wadding ('wɒdɪŋ) *n* **1a** any fibrous or soft substance used as padding, stuffing, etc. **1b** a piece of this. **2** material for wads used in cartridges or guns.

waddle ('wɒdᵊl) *vb* **waddles, waddling, waddled.** (*intr*) **1** to walk with short steps, rocking slightly from side to side. ◆ *n* **2** a swaying gait or motion. ORIG C16: prob. frequentative of WADE
▸ '**waddler** *n* ▸ '**waddling** *adj*

waddy ('wɒdɪ) *n, pl* **waddies. 1** a heavy wooden club used as a weapon by native Australians. ◆ *vb* **waddies, waddying, waddied. 2** (*tr*) to hit with a waddy. ORIG C19: from Abor., ? based on E WOOD

wade (weɪd) *vb* **wades, wading, waded. 1** to walk with the feet immersed in (water, a stream, etc.). **2** (*intr;* often foll. by *through*) to proceed with difficulty: *to wade through a book.* **3** (*intr;* foll. by *in* or *into*) to attack energetically. ◆ *n* **4** the act or an instance of wading. ORIG OE *wadan*
▸ '**wadable** *or* '**wadeable** *adj*

Wade ★ (weɪd) *n* **(Sarah) Virginia.** born 1945, British tennis player: Wimbledon champion 1977.

wader ('weɪdə) *n* **1** a person or thing that wades. **2** Also called: **wading bird.** any of various long-legged birds, esp. herons, storks, etc., that live near water and feed on fish, etc. **3** a Brit. name for **shore bird.**

waders ('weɪdəz) *pl n* long waterproof boots, sometimes extending to the chest like trousers, worn by anglers.

wadi *or* **wady** ('wɒdɪ) *n, pl* **wadies.** a watercourse in N Africa and Arabia, dry except in the rainy season. ORIG C19: from Ar.

Wadi Halfa ★ ('wɒdɪ 'hælfə) *n* a town in the N Sudan that was partly submerged by Lake Nasser: an important archaeological site.

Wad Medani ★ (waːd mɪ'daːniː) *n* a town in the E Sudan, on the Blue Nile: headquarters of the Gezira irrigation scheme. Pop.: 218 714 (1993).

wafer ('weɪfə) *n* **1** a thin crisp sweetened biscuit, served with ice cream, etc. **2** *Christianity.* a thin disc of unleavened bread used in the Eucharist. **3** *Pharmacol.* an envelope of rice paper enclosing a medicament. **4** *Electronics.* a large single crystal of semiconductor material, such as silicon, on which numerous integrated circuits are manufactured and then separated. **5** a small thin disc of adhesive material used to seal letters, etc. ◆ *vb* **6** (*tr*) to seal or fasten with a wafer. ORIG C14: from OF *waufre,* from MLow G *wāfel*
▸ '**wafery** *adj*

waffle[1] ('wɒfᵊl) *n* **a** a crisp golden-brown pancake with deep indentations on both sides. **b** (*as modifier*): *waffle iron.* ORIG C19: from Du. *wafel* (earlier *wæfel*), of Gmc origin

waffle[2] ('wɒfᵊl) *Inf., chiefly Brit.* ◆ *vb* **waffles, waffling, waffled. 1** (*intr;* often foll. by *on*) to speak or write in a vague and wordy manner. ◆ *n* **2** vague and wordy speech or writing. ORIG C19: from ?
▸ '**waffling** *adj, n*

waft (waːft, wɒft) *vb* **1** to carry or be carried gently on or as if on the air or water. ◆ *n* **2** the act or an instance of wafting. **3** something, such as a scent, carried on the air. **4** *Naut.* (formerly) a signal flag hoisted furled to signify various messages depending on where it was flown. ORIG C16 (in obs. sense: to convey by ship): back formation from C15 *wafter* a convoy vessel, from MDu. *wachter* guard

wag[1] (wæg) *vb* **wags, wagging, wagged. 1** to move or cause to move rapidly and repeatedly from side to side or up and down. **2** to move (the tongue) or (of the tongue) to be moved rapidly in talking, esp. in gossip. **3** to move (the finger) or (of the finger) to be moved from side to side, in or as in admonition. **4** *Sl.* to play truant (esp. in **wag it**). ◆ *n* **5** the act or an instance of wagging. ORIG C13: from OE *wagian* to shake

wag[2] (wæg) *n* a humorous or jocular person; wit. ORIG C16: from ?
▸ '**waggish** *adj*

wage (weɪdʒ) *n* **1** (*often pl*) payment in return for work or services, esp. that made to workers on a daily, hourly, weekly, or piecework basis. Cf. **salary. 2** (*pl*) *Econ.* the portion of the national income accruing to labour as earned income, as contrasted with the unearned income accruing to capital in the form of rent, interest, and dividends. **3** (*often pl*) recompense, return, or yield. ◆ *vb* **wages, waging, waged.** (*tr*) **4** to engage in. ORIG C14: from OF *wagier* to pledge, from *wage,* of Gmc origin
▸ '**wageless** *adj*

wage differential *n* the difference in wages between

★ people and places

workers with different skills in the same industry or between those with comparable skills in different industries or localities.

wage earner *n* **1** a person who works for wages. **2** the person who earns money to support a household by working.

wage freeze *n* a statutory restriction on wage increases.

wage indexation *n* a linking of wage rises to increases in the cost of living usually in order to maintain real wages during periods of high inflation.

wager ('weɪdʒə) *n* **1** an agreement to pay an amount of money as a result of the outcome of an unsettled matter. **2** an amount staked on the outcome of such an event. **3 wager of battle.** (in medieval Britain) a pledge to do battle to decide guilt or innocence by single combat. **4 wager of law.** *English legal history.* a form of trial in which the accused offered to make oath of his innocence, supported by the oaths of 11 of his neighbours declaring their belief in his statements. ◆ *vb* **5** (when *tr, may take a clause as object*) to risk or bet (something) on the outcome of an unsettled matter. ORIG C14: from Anglo-F *wageure* a pledge, from OF *wagier* to pledge; see WAGE
▸ **'wagerer** *n*

wages council *n* (formerly, in Britain) a statutory body empowered to fix minimum wages in an industry; abolished in 1994.

wage slave *n Ironical.* a person dependent on a wage or salary.

wagga ('wɒgə) *n Austral.* a blanket or bed covering of sacks stitched together. ORIG C19: after WAGGA WAGGA

Wagga Wagga ★ ('wɒgə 'wɒgə) *n* a city in SE Australia, in New South Wales on the Murrumbidgee River: agricultural trading centre. Pop.: 50 380 (1986).

waggle ('wægᵊl) *vb* **waggles, waggling, waggled. 1** to move or cause to move with a rapid shaking or wobbling motion. ◆ *n* **2** a rapid shaking or wobbling motion. ORIG C16: from WAG[1]
▸ **'waggly** *adj*

waggon ('wægən) *n* a variant spelling (esp. Brit.) of **wagon.**

wag-n-bietjie ('vɑːxᵊnˌbɪkɪ) *n S. African.* any of various thorn bushes or trees. ORIG from Afrik. *wag* wait + *n* a + *bietjie* bit

Wagner ★ ('vɑːgnə) *n* **(Wilhelm) Richard** ('rɪçart). 1813–83, German composer noted for his cycle of four music dramas, *The Ring of the Nibelung* (1876). His other operas include *Tannhäuser* (1845; revised 1861), *Tristan and Isolde* (1865), and *Parsifal* (1882).

Wagnerian (vɑːg'nɪərɪən) *adj* **1** of or suggestive of the dramatic musical compositions of Richard Wagner, their massive scale, dramatic and emotional intensity, etc. ◆ *n also* **Wagnerite** ('vɑːgnəˌraɪt). **2** a follower or disciple of the music or theories of Richard Wagner.

Wagner-Jauregg ★ (*German* 'vaːgnər'jaurɛk) *n* **Julius** ('juːlius). 1857–1940, Austrian psychiatrist and neurologist; a pioneer of the use of fever therapy in the treatment of mental disorders. Nobel prize for physiology or medicine 1927.

wagon *or* **waggon** ('wægən) *n* **1** any of various types of wheeled vehicles, ranging from carts to lorries, esp. a vehicle with four wheels drawn by a horse, tractor, etc., and used for carrying heavy loads. **2** *Brit.* a railway freight truck, esp. an open one. **3** an obsolete word for **chariot. 4 on** (*or* **off**) **the wagon.** *Inf.* abstaining (*or* no longer abstaining) from alcohol. ORIG C16: from Du. *wagen* WAIN
▸ **'wagonless** *or* **'waggonless** *adj*

wagoner *or* **waggoner** ('wægənə) *n* a person who drives a wagon.

wagonette *or* **waggonette** (ˌwægə'nɛt) *n* a light four-wheeled horse-drawn vehicle with two lengthwise seats facing each other behind a crosswise driver's seat.

wagon-lit (*French* vagõli) *n, pl* **wagons-lits** (vagõli). **1** a sleeping car on a European railway. **2** a compartment on such a car. ORIG C19: from F, from *wagon* railway coach + *lit* bed

wagonload *or* **waggonload** ('wægənˌləʊd) *n* the load that is or can be carried by a wagon.

wagon train *n* a supply train of horses and wagons, esp. one going over rough terrain.

wagon vault *n* another name for **barrel vault.**

Wagram ★ (*German* 'vaːgram) *n* a village in NE Austria: scene of the defeat of the Austrians by Napoleon in 1809.

wagtail ('wægˌteɪl) *n* any of various passerine songbirds of Eurasia and Africa, having a very long tail that wags when the bird walks.

Wahhabi *or* **Wahabi** (wə'hɑːbɪ) *n, pl* **Wahhabis** *or* **Wahabis.** a member of a strictly conservative Muslim sect founded in the 18th century.
▸ **Wah'habism** *or* **Wa'habism** *n*

wahine (wɑː'hiːnɪ) *n* **1** *NZ.* a Maori woman. **2** a Polynesian woman. ORIG from Maori & Hawaiian

wahoo (wɑː'huː, 'wɑːhuː) *n, pl* **wahoos.** a large fast-moving food and game fish of tropical seas. ORIG from ?

wah-wah ('wɑːˌwɑː) *n* **1** the sound made by a trumpet, cornet, etc., when the bell is alternately covered and uncovered. **2** an electronic attachment for an electric guitar, etc., that simulates this effect. ORIG C20: imit.

waif (weɪf) *n* **1** a person, esp. a child, who is homeless, friendless, or neglected. **2** anything found and not claimed, the owner being unknown. ORIG C14: from Anglo-Norman, var. of OF *gaif,* from ON
▸ **'waifˌlike** *adj*

Waikaremoana ★ (waɪ'kɒrəməʊˌɑːnə) *n* **Lake.** a lake in the North Island of New Zealand in a dense bush setting. Area: about 55 sq. km (21 sq. miles).

Waikato ★ ('waɪˌkɑːtəʊ) *n* the longest river in New Zealand, flowing northwest across North Island to the Tasman Sea. Length: 350 km (220 miles).

Waikiki ★ ('waɪkɪˌkiː, ˌwaɪkɪ'kiː) *n* a resort area in Hawaii, on SE Oahu: a suburb of Honolulu.

wail (weɪl) *vb* **1** (*intr*) to utter a prolonged high-pitched cry, as of grief or misery. **2** (*intr*) to make a sound resembling such a cry: *the wind wailed in the trees.* **3** (*tr*) to lament, esp. with mournful sounds. ◆ *n* **4** a prolonged high-pitched mournful cry or sound. ORIG C14: from ON
▸ **'wailer** *n*

Wailing Wall ★ *n* another name for **Western Wall.**

wain (weɪn) *n Chiefly poetic.* a farm wagon or cart. ORIG OE *wægn*

wainscot ('weɪnskət) *n* **1** Also called: **wainscoting** *or* **wainscotting.** a lining applied to the walls of a room, esp. one of wood panelling. **2** the lower part of the walls of a room, esp. when finished in a material different from the upper part. **3** fine-quality oak used as wainscot. ◆ *vb* **4** (*tr*) to line (a wall of a room) with a wainscot. ORIG C14: from MLow G *wagenschot,* ?from *wagen* WAGON + *schot* planking

wainwright ('weɪnˌraɪt) *n* a person who makes wagons.

waist (weɪst) *n* **1** *Anat.* the constricted part of the trunk between the ribs and hips. **2** the part of a garment covering the waist. **3** the middle part of an object that resembles the waist in narrowness or position. **4** the middle part of a ship. **5** the middle section of an aircraft fuselage. **6** the constriction between the thorax and abdomen in wasps and similar insects. ORIG C14: from ?
▸ **'waistless** *adj*

waistband ('weɪstˌbænd) *n* an encircling band of material to finish and strengthen a skirt or trousers at the waist.

waistcoat ('weɪsˌkəʊt) *n* **1** a man's sleeveless waistlength garment worn under a suit jacket, usually buttoning up the front. **2** a similar garment worn by women. ◆ US and Canad. name: **vest.**
▸ **'waistˌcoated** *adj*

waistline ('weɪstˌlaɪn) *n* **1** a line around the body at the narrowest part of the waist. **2** the intersection of the bodice and the skirt of a dress, etc., or the level of this.

wait (weɪt) *vb* **1** (when *intr,* often foll. by *for, until,* or *to*) to stay in one place or remain inactive in expectation (of something). **2** to delay temporarily or be temporarily delayed: *that work can wait.* **3** (when *intr,* usually foll. by *for*) (of things) to be ready or at hand; be in store (for a person): *supper was waiting for them when they got home.* **4** (*intr*) to act as a waiter or waitress. ◆ *n* **5** the act or an instance of waiting. **6** a period of waiting. **7** (*pl*) *Rare.* a band of musicians who go around the streets, esp. at Christmas, singing and playing carols. **8 lie in wait.** to prepare an ambush (for someone). ◆ See also **wait on, wait up.** ORIG C12: from OF *waitier*

wait-a-bit *n* any of various mainly tropical plants having sharp hooked thorns.

Waitangi Day (waɪ'tʌŋiː) *n* the national day of New Zealand (Feb. 6), commemorating the signing of the **Treaty of Waitangi** (1840) by Maori chiefs and a representative of the British Government. The treaty provided the basis for the British annexation of New Zealand.

Waite ★ (weɪt) *n* **Terry,** full name *Terence Hardy Waite.* born 1939, British special envoy to the Archbishop of Canterbury, who negotiated the release of Western hostages held in the Middle East before (1987) being taken hostage himself in Lebanon: released in 1991.

waiter ('weɪtə) *n* **1** a man whose occupation is to serve at table, as in a restaurant. **2** an attendant at the London stock exchange or Lloyd's who carries messages: the modern equivalent of waiters who performed these duties in the 17th-century London coffee houses in which these institutions originated. **3** a person who waits. **4** a tray or salver.

waiting game *n* the postponement of action or decision in order to gain the advantage.

waiting list *n* a list of people waiting to obtain some object, treatment, status, etc.

waiting room *n* a room in which people may wait, as at a railway station, doctor's or dentist's surgery, etc.

wait on *vb* (*intr, prep*) **1** to serve at the table of. **2** to act as an attendant to. ◆ *sentence substitute.* **3** *Austral. & NZ.* stop! hold on! ◆ Also (for senses 1, 2): **wait upon.**

waitress ('weɪtrɪs) *n* **1** a woman who serves at table, as in a restaurant. ◆ *vb* (*intr*) **2** to act as a waitress.

wait up *vb* (*intr, adv*) to delay going to bed in order to await some event.

waive (weɪv) *vb* **waives, waiving, waived.** (*tr*) **1** to set aside or relinquish: *to waive one's rights.* **2** to refrain from enforcing or applying (a law, penalty, etc.). **3** to defer. ORIG C13: from OF *weyver,* from *waif* abandoned; see WAIF

waiver ('weɪvə) *n* **1** the voluntary relinquishment, expressly or by implication, of some claim or right. **2** the act or an instance of relinquishing a claim or right. **3** a formal statement in writing of such relinquishment. ORIG C17: from OF *weyver* to relinquish

Wajda ★ (*Polish* 'vajda) *n* **Andrei** or **Andrzej** ('andʒɛj). born 1926, Polish film director. His films include *Ashes and Diamonds* (1958) and *Ring of the Crowned Eagle* (1993).

Wakayama ★ (ˌwækə'jɑːmə) *n* an industrial city in S Japan, on S Honshu. Pop.: 393 951 (1995).

wake[1] (weɪk) *vb* **wakes, waking, woke, woken. 1** (often foll. by *up*) to rouse or become roused from sleep. **2** (often foll. by *up*) to rouse or become roused from inactivity. **3** (*intr;* often foll. by *to* or *up to*) to become conscious or aware: *at last he woke up to the situation.* **4** (*intr*) to be or remain awake. ◆ *n* **5** a watch or vigil held over the body of a dead person during the night before burial. **6** (in Ireland) festivities held after a funeral. **7** the patronal or dedication festival of English parish churches. **8** a solemn or ceremonial vigil. **9** (*usually pl*) an annual holiday in various towns in Northern England, when the local factories close. ORIG OE *wacian*
▸ **'waker** *n*

> **USAGE NOTE** Where there is an object and the sense is the literal one *wake* (*up*) and *waken* are the commonest forms: *I wakened him; I woke him* (*up*). Both verbs are also commonly used without an object: *I woke up. Awake* and *awaken* are preferred to other forms of *wake* where the sense is a figurative one: *he awoke to the danger.*

★ people and places

wake[2] (weɪk) *n* **1** the waves or track left by a vessel or other object moving through water. **2** the track or path left by anything that has passed: *wrecked houses in the wake of the hurricane.* ORIG C16: of Scand. origin

Wakefield ★ ('weɪkˌfiːld) *n* **1** a city in N England, in West Yorkshire: important since medieval times as an agricultural and textile centre. Pop.: 73 955 (1991). **2** a unitary authority in N England, in West Yorkshire. Pop.: 317 300 (1997 est.). Area: 333 sq. km (129 sq. miles).

wakeful ('weɪkfʊl) *adj* **1** unable or unwilling to sleep. **2** sleepless. **3** alert.
▸ **'wakefully** *adv* ▸ **'wakefulness** *n*

Wake Island ★ *n* an atoll in the N central Pacific: claimed by the US in 1899; developed as a civil and naval air station in the late 1930s. Area: 8 sq. km (3 sq. miles).

wakeless ('weɪklɪs) *adj* (of sleep) unbroken.

waken ('weɪkən) *vb* to rouse or be roused from sleep or some other inactive state.

> **USAGE NOTE** See at **wake**[1].

wake-robin *n* any of a genus of North American herbaceous plants having a whorl of three leaves and three-petalled solitary flowers.

wake-up *n* **a wake-up to.** *Austral. sl.* fully alert to (a person, thing, action, etc.).

Waksman ★ ('wæksmən) *n* **Selman Abraham.** 1888–1973, US microbiologist, born in Russia. He discovered streptomycin: Nobel prize for physiology or medicine 1952.

Walachia *or* **Wallachia** ★ (wɒ'leɪkɪə) *n* a former principality of SE Europe: a vassal state of the Ottoman Empire from the 15th century until its union with Moldavia in 1859, subsequently forming present-day Romania.
▸ **Wa'lachian** *or* **Wal'lachian** *n, adj*

Wałbrzych ★ (*Polish* 'vaubʒix) *n* an industrial city in SW Poland. Pop.: 140 000 (1995 est.). German name: **Waldenburg.**

Walcheren ★ (*Dutch* 'wɑlxərə) *n* an island in the SW Netherlands, in the Scheldt estuary: administratively part of Zeeland province; suffered severely in World War II, when the dykes were breached, and again in the floods of 1953. Area: 212 sq. km (82 sq. miles).

Walcott ★ ('wɔːlkət) *n* **Derek** (**Alton**). born 1930, St Lucian poet and playwright, whose works include the long poem *Omeros* (1990) and *The Bounty* (1997); Nobel prize for literature 1992.

Waldemar I *or* **Valdemar I** ★ ('vældɪˌmɑː) *n* known as *Waldemar the Great.* 1131–82, king of Denmark (1157–82). He conquered the Wends (1169) and established the hereditary rule of his line.

Waldenburg ★ ('valdənbʊrk) *n* the German name for **Wałbrzych.**

Waldenses (wɒl'dɛnsiːz) *pl n* the members of a small sect founded as a reform movement within the Roman Catholic Church by Peter Waldo, a merchant of Lyons, in the late 12th century.
▸ **Wal'densian** *n, adj*

Waldheim ★ (*German* 'valthaim) *n* **Kurt** (kʊrt). born 1918, Austrian diplomat; secretary-general of the United Nations (1972–81); president of Austria (1986–92).

waldo ('wɔːldəʊ) *n, pl* **waldos, waldoes.** a gadget for manipulating objects by remote control. ORIG C20: after *Waldo* F. Jones, an inventor, in a science-fiction story by Robert Heinlein

Waldorf salad ('wɔːldɔːf) *n* a salad of diced apples, celery, and walnuts mixed with mayonnaise.

waldsterben ('wɔːldˌstɜːbən) *n Ecology.* the symptoms of tree decline in central Europe from the 1970s, considered to be caused by atmospheric pollution. ORIG C20: from G *Wald* forest + *sterben* to die

wale (weɪl) *n* **1** the raised mark left on the skin after the stroke of a rod or whip. **2** the weave or texture of a fabric, such as the ribs in corduroy. **3** *Naut.* a ridge of planking along the rail of a ship. ◆ *vb* **wales, waling, waled. 4** (*tr*) to raise a wale or wales on by striking. **5** to weave with a wale. ORIG OE *walu* weal

Wales ★ (weɪlz) *n* a principality that is part of the United Kingdom, in the west of Great Britain; conquered by the English in 1282; parliamentary union with England took place in 1536: the creation of a separate Welsh Assembly with limited power was approved by an extremely narrow margin in 1997. It consists mainly of moorlands and mountains and has an economy that is chiefly agricultural, with an industrial and former coal-mining area in the south. Capital: Cardiff. Pop.: 2 811 865 (1991). Area: 20 768 sq. km (8017 sq. miles). Welsh name: **Cymru**. Medieval Latin name: **Cambria**.

Wałęsa ★ (væ'wɛnsə) *n* **Lech** (lɛç). born 1943, Polish statesman; president (1990–95); leader of the independent trade union Solidarity (1980–90); Nobel peace prize 1983.

Walfish Bay ★ ('wɔːlfɪʃ) *n* a variant spelling of **Walvis Bay**.

Walhalla (wæl'hælə, væl-) *or* **Walhall** ★ (wæl'hæl, væl-) *n* variants of **Valhalla**.

walk (wɔːk) *vb* **1** (*intr*) to move along or travel on foot at a moderate rate; advance in such a manner that at least one foot is always on the ground. **2** (*tr*) to pass through, on, or over on foot, esp. habitually. **3** (*tr*) to cause, assist, or force to move along at a moderate rate: *to walk a dog*. **4** (*tr*) to escort or conduct by walking: *to walk someone home*. **5** (*intr*) (of ghosts, spirits, etc.) to appear or move about in visible form. **6** (*intr*) to follow a certain course or way of life: *to walk in misery*. **7** (*tr*) to bring into a certain condition by walking: *I walked my shoes to shreds*. **8** to disappear or be stolen: *Where's my pencil? It seems to have walked*. **9 walk it.** to win easily. **10 walk on air.** to be delighted or exhilarated. **11 walk tall.** *Inf.* to have self-respect or pride. **12 walk the streets. 12a** to be a prostitute. **12b** to wander round a town, esp. when looking for work or when homeless. ◆ *n* **13** the act or an instance of walking. **14** the distance or extent walked. **15** a manner of walking; gait. **16** a place set aside for walking; promenade. **17** a chosen profession or sphere of activity (esp. in **walk of life**). **18a** an arrangement of trees or shrubs in widely separated rows. **18b** the space between such rows. **19** an enclosed ground for the exercise or feeding of domestic animals, esp. horses. **20** *Chiefly Brit.* the route covered in the course of work, as by a tradesman or postman. **21** a procession; march: *Orange walk*. **22** *Obs.* the section of a forest controlled by a keeper. ◆ See also **walk away, walk into**, etc. ORIG OE *wealcan*
▸ '**walkable** *adj*

walkabout ('wɔːkə,baʊt) *n* **1** a periodic nomadic excursion into the Australian bush made by a native Australian. **2** an occasion when celebrities, royalty, etc., walk among and meet the public. **3 go walkabout.** *Austral.* **3a** to wander through the bush. **3b** *Inf.* to be lost or misplaced. **3c** *Inf.* to lose one's concentration.

walk away *vb* (*intr, adv*) **1** to leave, esp. disregarding someone else's distress. **2 walk away with.** to achieve or win easily.

walker ('wɔːkə) *n* **1** a person who walks. **2** Also called: **baby walker**. a tubular frame on wheels or casters to support a baby learning to walk. **3** a similar support for walking, often with rubber feet, for use by disabled or infirm people.

Walker ★ ('wɔːkə) *n* **Alice Malsenior.** born 1944, US writer: her novels include *The Color Purple* (1982) and *Possessing the Secret of Joy* (1992).

walkie-talkie *or* **walky-talky** (,wɔːkɪ'tɔːkɪ) *n, pl* **walkie-talkies**. a small combined radio transmitter and receiver that can be carried around by one person: widely used by the police, medical services, etc.

walk-in *adj* **1** (of a cupboard) large enough to allow a person to enter and move about in. **2** (of a flat or house) in a suitable condition for immediate occupation.

walking papers *pl n Sl., chiefly US & Canad.* notice of dismissal.

walking stick *n* **1** a stick or cane carried in the hand to assist walking. **2** the usual US name for **stick insect**.

walk into *vb* (*intr, prep*) to meet with unwittingly: *to walk into a trap*.

Walkman ('wɔːkmən) *n Trademark.* a small portable cassette player with headphones.

walk off *vb* **1** (*intr*) to depart suddenly. **2** (*tr, adv*) to get rid of by walking: *to walk off an attack of depression*. **3 walk (a person) off his** *or* **her feet.** to make (a person) walk so fast or far that he or she is exhausted. **4 walk off with. 4a** to steal. **4b** to win, esp. easily.

walk-on *n* **a** a small part in a play or theatrical entertainment, esp. one without any lines. **b** (*as modifier*): *a walk-on part*.

walk out *vb* (*intr, adv*) **1** to leave without explanation, esp. in anger. **2** to go on strike. **3 walk out on.** *Inf.* to abandon or desert. **4 walk out with.** *Brit., obs. or dialect.* to court or be courted by. ◆ *n* **walkout. 5** a strike by workers. **6** the act of leaving a meeting, conference, etc., as a protest.

walkover ('wɔːk,əʊvə) *n* **1** *Inf.* an easy or unopposed victory. **2** *Horse racing.* **2a** the running or walking over the course by the only contestant entered in a race at the time of starting. **2b** a race won in this way. ◆ *vb* **walk over.** (*intr, mainly prep*) **3** (*also adv*) to win a race by a walkover. **4** *Inf.* to beat (an opponent) conclusively or easily.

walk socks *pl n NZ.* knee-length, usually woollen, stockings.

walk through *Theatre.* ◆ *vb* **1** (*tr*) to act or recite (a part) in a perfunctory manner, as at a first rehearsal. ◆ *n* **walk-through. 2** a rehearsal of a part.

walkway ('wɔːk,weɪ) *n* **1** a path designed and sometimes landscaped for pedestrian use. **2** a passage or path, esp. one for walking over machinery, connecting buildings, etc.

Walkyrie ★ (væl'kɪərɪ, 'vælkɪərɪ) *n* a variant spelling of **Valkyrie**.

wall (wɔːl) *n* **1a** a vertical construction made of stone, brick, wood, etc., with a length and height much greater than its thickness, used to enclose, divide, or support. **1b** (*as modifier*): *wall hangings*. Related adj: **mural. 2** (*often pl*) a structure or rampart built to protect and surround a position or place for defensive purposes. **3** *Anat.* any lining, membrane, or investing part that encloses or bounds a bodily cavity or structure: *abdominal wall*. Technical name: **paries**. Related adj: **parietal. 4** anything that suggests a wall in function or effect: *a wall of fire*. **5 drive** (*or* **push**) **to the wall.** to force into an awkward situation. **6 go to the wall.** *Inf.* to be ruined. **7 go** (*or* **drive**) **up the wall.** *Sl.* to become (*or* cause to become) crazy or furious. **8 have one's back to the wall.** to be in a difficult situation. ◆ *vb* (*tr*) **9** to protect, provide, or confine with or as if with a wall. **10** (often foll. by *up*) to block (an opening) with a wall. **11** (often foll. by *in* or *up*) to seal by or within a wall or walls. ORIG OE *weall*, from L *vallum* palisade, from *vallus* stake
▸ **walled** *adj* ▸ '**wall-less** *adj*

wallaby ('wɒləbɪ) *n, pl* **wallabies** *or* **wallaby**. any of various herbivorous marsupials of Australia and New Guinea, similar to but smaller than kangaroos. ORIG C19: from Abor. *wolabā*

Wallaby ('wɒləbɪ) *n, pl* **Wallabies**. a member of the international rugby union football team of Australia.

Wallace ★ ('wɒlɪs) *n* **1 Alfred Russel.** 1823–1913, British naturalist, whose theory of natural selection influenced Charles Darwin. **2 Edgar.** 1875–1932, British crime novelist. **3** Sir **Richard.** 1818–90, British art collector. His bequest to the nation forms the Wallace Collection, London. **4** Sir **William.** ?1272–1305, Scottish patriot, who defeated the army of Edward I of England at Stirling (1297), was routed at Falkirk (1298), and later executed.

Wallace's line *n* the hypothetical boundary between the Oriental and Australasian zoogeographical regions, which runs through Indonesia and SE of the Philippines. ORIG C20: after A. R. WALLACE

Wallachia ★ (wɒ'leɪkɪə) *n* a variant spelling of **Walachia**.

wallah *or* **walla** ('wɒlə) *n* (*usually in combination*) *Inf.* a person involved with or in charge of (a specified thing): *the book wallah*. ORIG C18: from Hindi *-wālā* from Sansk. *pāla* protector

wallaroo (,wɒlə'ruː) *n, pl* **wallaroos** *or* **wallaroo**. a large stocky Australian kangaroo of rocky or mountainous regions. ORIG C19: from Abor. *wolarū*

Wallasey ★ ('wɒləsɪ) *n* a town in NW England, in Wirral, in Merseyside near the mouth of the River Mersey, opposite Liverpool. Pop.: 60 895 (1991).

wall bars *pl n* a series of horizontal bars attached to a wall and used in gymnastics.

wallboard ('wɔːlˌbɔːd) *n* a thin board made of materials, such as compressed wood fibres or gypsum plaster, between stiff paper, and used to cover walls, partitions, etc.

wall creeper *n* a pink-and-grey woodpecker-like songbird of Eurasian mountain regions.

walled plain *n* any of the largest of the lunar craters, having diameters between 50 and 300 kilometres.

Wallenberg ★ (*Swedish* 'valənbærj) *n* **Raoul** (rɑː'uːl). 1912–?, Swedish diplomat, who helped (1944–45) thousands of Hungarian Jews to escape from the Nazis: arrested (1945) by the Soviets and presumed to have died in prison.

Waller ★ ('wɒlə) *n* **1 Edmund.** 1606–87, English poet and politician, known for his poem *Go, Lovely Rose.* **2 Fats,** real name *Thomas Waller.* 1904–43, US jazz pianist and singer.

wallet ('wɒlɪt) *n* **1** a small folding case, usually of leather, for holding paper money, documents, etc. **2** *Arch., chiefly Brit.* a rucksack or knapsack. ORIG C14: of Gmc origin

walleye ('wɔːlˌaɪ) *n, pl* **walleyes** *or* **walleye. 1** a divergent squint. **2** opacity of the cornea. **3** an eye having a white or light-coloured iris. **4** Also called: **walleyed pike.** a North American pikeperch valued as a food and game fish. ORIG back formation from earlier *walleyed,* from ON *vagleygr,* from *vage* ? a film over the eye + *-eygr* -eyed, from *auga* eye; infl. by WALL
▸ **'wallˌeyed** *adj*

wallflower ('wɔːlˌflaʊə) *n* **1** Also called: **gillyflower.** a cruciferous plant of S Europe, grown for its clusters of yellow, orange, brown, red, or purple fragrant flowers and naturalized on old walls, cliffs, etc. **2** *Inf.* a person who stays on the fringes of a dance or party on account of lacking a partner or being shy.

Wallis[1] ★ ('valɪs) *n* the German name for **Valais.**

Wallis[2] ★ ('wɒlɪs) *n* Sir **Barnes (Neville).** 1887–1979, British aeronautical engineer. He designed the airship R100, the Wellesley and Wellington bombers, and the bouncing bomb (1943).

Wallis and Futuna Islands ★ ('wɒlɪs; fuː'tjuːnə) *pl n* a French overseas territory in the SW Pacific, west of Samoa. Capital: Mata-Utu. Pop.: 14 400 (1993 est.). Area: 367 sq. km (143 sq. miles).

wall of death *n* (at a fairground) a giant cylinder round the inside vertical walls of which a motorcyclist rides.

Walloon (wɒ'luːn) *n* **1** a member of a French-speaking people living chiefly in S Belgium and adjacent parts of France. **2** the French dialect of Belgium. ◆ *adj* **3** of or characteristic of the Walloons or their dialect. ORIG C16: from OF *Wallon,* from Med. L: foreigner, of Gmc origin

Walloon Brabant ★ *n* a province of central Belgium, formed in 1995. Pop.: 344 508 (1998 est.). Area: 1091 sq. km (421 sq. miles).

wallop ('wɒləp) *vb* **wallops, walloping, walloped. 1** (*tr*) *Inf.* to beat soundly; strike hard. **2** (*tr*) *Inf.* to defeat utterly. **3** (*intr*) (of liquids) to boil violently. ◆ *n* **4** *Inf.* a hard blow. **5** *Inf.* the ability to hit powerfully, as of a boxer. **6** *Inf.* a forceful impression. **7** *Brit. sl.* beer. ORIG C14: from OF *waloper* to gallop, from OF *galoper,* from ?

walloper ('wɒləpə) *n* **1** a person or thing that wallops. **2** *Austral. sl.* a policeman.

walloping ('wɒləpɪŋ) *Inf.* ◆ *n* **1** a thrashing. ◆ *adj* **2** (intensifier): *a walloping drop in sales.*

wallow ('wɒləʊ) *vb* (*intr*) **1** (esp. of certain animals) to roll about in mud, water, etc., for pleasure. **2** to move about with difficulty. **3** to indulge oneself in possessions, emotion, etc.: *to wallow in self-pity.* ◆ *n* **4** the act or an instance of wallowing. **5** a muddy place where animals wallow. ORIG OE *wealwian* to roll (in mud)
▸ **'wallower** *n*

wallpaper ('wɔːlˌpeɪpə) *n* **1** paper usually printed or embossed with designs for pasting onto walls and ceilings. **2** *Computing.* a picture or pattern on a computer screen between and behind program icons and windows. ◆ *vb* **3** to cover (a surface) with wallpaper.

wall pepper *n* a small Eurasian plant having yellow flowers and acrid-tasting leaves.

wall plate *n* a horizontal timber member placed along the top of a wall to support the ends of joists, rafters, etc., and distribute the load.

wallposter ('wɔːlˌpəʊstə) *n* (in China) a bulletin or political message painted in large characters on a wall.

wall rocket *n* any of several yellow-flowered European cruciferous plants that grow on old walls and in waste places.

wall rue *n* a delicate fern that grows in rocky crevices and walls in North America and Eurasia.

Wallsend ★ ('wɔːlzˌend) *n* a town in NE England, in North Tyneside on the River Tyne: situated at the E end of Hadrian's Wall. Pop.: 45 280 (1991).

Wall Street ★ *n* a street in lower Manhattan, New York, where the Stock Exchange and major banks are situated, regarded as the embodiment of American finance.

wall-to-wall *adj* **1** (esp. of carpeting) completely covering a floor. **2** *Inf.* nonstop; widespread: *wall-to-wall sales.*

wally ('wɒlɪ) *n, pl* **wallies.** *Sl.* a stupid person. ORIG C20: shortened from the name *Walter*

walnut ('wɔːlˌnʌt) *n* **1** any of a genus of deciduous trees of America, SE Europe, and Asia. They have aromatic leaves and flowers in catkins and are grown for their edible nuts and for their wood. **2** the nut of any of these trees, having a wrinkled two-lobed seed and a hard wrinkled shell. **3** the wood of any of these trees, used in making furniture, etc. **4** a light yellowish-brown colour. ◆ *adj* **5** made from the wood of a walnut tree: *a walnut table.* **6** of the colour walnut. ORIG OE *walh-hnutu,* lit.: foreign nut

Walpole ★ ('wɔːlˌpəʊl) *n* **1 Horace,** 4th Earl of Orford. 1717–97, British writer, noted for his novel *The Castle of Otranto* (1764). **2** his father, Sir **Robert,** 1st Earl of Orford. 1676–1745, British Whig statesman. As first lord of the Treasury and Chancellor of the Exchequer (1721–42) he was effectively Britain's first prime minister.

Walpurgis Night (væl'pʊəgɪs) *n* the eve of May 1, believed in German folklore to be the night of a witches' sabbath on the Brocken, in the Harz Mountains. ORIG C19: translation of G *Walpurgisnacht,* the eve of the feast day of St Walpurga, 8th-cent. abbess in Germany

walrus ('wɔːlrəs, 'wɒl-) *n, pl* **walruses** *or* **walrus.** a mammal of northern seas, having a tough thick skin, upper canine teeth enlarged as tusks, and coarse whiskers, and feeding mainly on shellfish. ORIG C17: prob. from Du., of Scand. origin

walrus moustache *n* a long thick moustache drooping at the ends.

Walsall ★ ('wɔːlsɔːl) *n* **1** an industrial town in central England, in the West Midlands. Pop.: 174 739 (1991). **2** a unitary authority in central England, in the West Midlands. Pop.: 262 600 (1996 est.). Area: 106 sq. km (41 sq. miles).

Walsh ★ (wɔːlʃ) *n* **Courtney (Andrew)** ('kɔːtnɪ). born 1962, Jamaican cricketer; a fast bowler and leading wicket taker for the West Indies.

Walsingham[1] ★ ('wɔːlsɪŋəm) *n* a village in E England, in Norfolk: remains of a medieval priory; site of the shrine of Our Lady of Walsingham.

Walsingham[2] ★ ('wɔːlsɪŋəm) *n* Sir **Francis.** ?1530–90, English statesman; secretary of state (1573–90) to Elizabeth I.

Walter ★ *n* **1** (*German* 'valtər). **Bruno** ('bruːno), real name *Bruno Walter Schlesinger.* 1876–1962, US conductor, born in Germany. **2** ('wɔːltə). **John.** 1739–1812, British publisher; founded *The Daily Universal Register* (1785), which in 1788 became *The Times.*

Waltham Forest ★ ('wɔːlθəm) *n* a borough of NE

Greater London. Pop.: 221 800 (1994 est.). Area: 40 sq. km (15 sq. miles).

Walton ★ (ˈwɔːltᵊn) *n* **1 Ernest Thomas Sinton.** 1903–95, Irish physicist: produced the first transmutation of a nucleus (1932) with Sir John Cockcroft, with whom he shared the Nobel prize for physics 1951. **2 Izaak** (ˈaɪzək). 1593–1683, English writer, best known for *The Compleat Angler* (1653; enlarged 1676). **3** Sir **William (Turner).** 1902–83, British composer. His works include *Façade* (1923), the *Viola Concerto* (1929), and the oratorio *Belshazzar's Feast* (1931).

waltz (wɔːls) *n* **1** a ballroom dance in triple time in which couples spin around as they progress round the room. **2** a piece of music composed for or in the rhythm of this dance. ◆ *vb* **3** to dance or lead (someone) in or as in a waltz. **4** (*intr*) to move in a sprightly and self-assured manner. **5** (*intr*) *Inf.* to succeed easily. **6 waltz Matilda** *Austral.* See **Matilda.** ORIG C18: from G *Walzer,* from MHG *walzen* to roll

waltzer (ˈwɔːlsə) *n* **1** a person who waltzes. **2** a fairground roundabout on which people are spun round and moved up and down as it revolves.

Walvis Bay (ˈwɔːlvɪs) *or* **Walfish Bay** ★ *n* a port in Namibia, on the Atlantic: covers an area of 1124 sq. km (434 sq. miles) with its hinterland, formed an exclave of South Africa (1977–94); chief port of Namibia and rich fishing centre. Pop.: 23 000 (1992 est.).

wampum (ˈwɒmpəm) *n* (formerly) money used by North American Indians, made of cylindrical shells strung or woven together. Also called: **peag, peage.** ORIG C17: of Amerind origin, short for *wampumpeag,* from *wampompeag,* from *wampan* light + *api* string + *-ag* pl. suffix

wan (wɒn) *adj* **wanner, wannest. 1** unnaturally pale, esp. from sickness, grief, etc. **2** suggestive of ill health, unhappiness, etc. **3** (of light, stars, etc.) faint or dim. ORIG OE *wann* dark
▸ ˈ**wanly** *adv* ▸ ˈ**wanness** *n*

Wanchüan *or* **Wan-ch'uan** ★ (ˌwæntʃuˈɑːn) *n* a former name of **Zhangjiakou.**

wand (wɒnd) *n* **1** a slender supple stick or twig. **2** a thin rod carried as a symbol of authority. **3** a rod used by a magician, etc. **4** *Inf.* a conductor's baton. **5** *Archery.* a marker used to show the distance at which the archer stands from the target. ORIG C12: from ON *vǫndr*

wander (ˈwɒndə) *vb* (*mainly intr*) **1** (*also tr*) to move or travel about, in, or through (a place) without any definite purpose or destination. **2** to proceed in an irregular course. **3** to go astray, as from a path or course. **4** (of thoughts, etc.) to lose concentration. **5** to think or speak incoherently or illogically. ◆ *n* **6** the act or an instance of wandering. ORIG OE *wandrian*
▸ ˈ**wanderer** *n* ▸ ˈ**wandering** *adj, n*

wandering albatross *n* a large albatross having a very wide wingspan and a white plumage with black wings.

wandering Jew *n* any of several related creeping or trailing plants of tropical America, such as tradescantia.

Wandering Jew ★ *n* (in medieval legend) a character condemned to roam the world eternally because he mocked Christ on the day of the Crucifixion.

wanderlust (ˈwɒndəˌlʌst) *n* a great desire to travel and rove about. ORIG from G *Wanderlust,* lit.: wander desire

wanderoo (ˌwɒndəˈruː) *n, pl* **wanderoos.** a macaque monkey of India and Sri Lanka, having black fur with a ruff of long greyish fur on each side of the face. ORIG C17: from Sinhalese *vanduru* monkeys, lit.: forest-dwellers

wandoo (wɒnˈduː) *n* a eucalyptus tree of W Australia, having white bark and durable wood. ORIG from Abor.

Wandsworth ★ (ˈwɒnzwəθ) *n* a borough of S Greater London, on the River Thames. Pop.: 266 600 (1994 est.). Area: 35 sq. km (13 sq. miles).

wane (weɪn) *vb* **wanes, waning, waned.** (*intr*) **1** (of the moon) to show a gradually decreasing portion of illuminated surface, between full moon and new moon. **2** to decrease gradually in size, strength, power, etc. **3** to draw to a close. ◆ *n* **4** a decrease, as in size, strength, power, etc. **5** the period during which the moon wanes. **6** a drawing to a close. **7** a rounded surface or defective edge of a plank, where the bark was. **8 on the wane.** in a state of decline. ORIG OE *wanian* (vb)
▸ ˈ**waney** *or* ˈ**wany** *adj*

Wanganui ★ (ˌwɒŋəˈnuːɪ) *n* a port in New Zealand, on SW North Island: centre for a dairy-farming and sheep-rearing district. Pop.: 42 200 (1995 est.).

wangle (ˈwæŋgᵊl) *Inf.* ◆ *vb* **wangles, wangling, wangled. 1** (*tr*) to use devious methods to get or achieve (something) for (oneself or another): *he wangled himself a salary increase.* **2** to manipulate or falsify (a situation, etc.). ◆ *n* **3** the act or an instance of wangling. ORIG C19: orig. printers' sl., ? a blend of WAGGLE & dialect *wankle* wavering, from OE *wancol*
▸ ˈ**wangler** *n*

Wanhsien *or* **Wan-Hsien** ★ (ˈwænˈʃjɛn) *n* a variant transliteration of the Chinese name for **Wanxian.**

wanigan *or* **wannigan** (ˈwɒnɪgən) *n Canad.* **1** a lumberjack's chest or box. **2** a cabin, caboose, or houseboat. ORIG C19: from Algonquian

wank (wæŋk) *Taboo sl.* ◆ *vb* **1** (*intr*) to masturbate. ◆ *n* **2** an instance of wanking. ORIG from ?

wankel engine (ˈwæŋkᵊl) *n* a type of rotary internal-combustion engine without reciprocating parts. It consists of a curved triangular-shaped piston rotating in an elliptical combustion chamber. ORIG C20: after Felix *Wankel* (1902–88), G engineer who invented it

wanker (ˈwæŋkə) *n Sl.* **1** *Taboo.* a person who wanks; masturbator. **2** *Derog.* a worthless fellow.

Wankie ★ (ˈwɑːŋkɪ) *n* the former name (until 1982) of **Hwange.**

wannabe *or* **wannabee** (ˈwɒnəˌbiː) *n Inf.* **a** a person who desires to be, or be like, something or someone else. **b** (*as modifier*): *a wannabe film star.* ORIG C20: phonetic shortening of *want to be*

Wanne-Eickel ★ (*German* ˈvanəˈaikəl) *n* an industrial town in W Germany, in North Rhine-Westphalia on the Rhine-Herne Canal: formed in 1926 by the merging of two townships. Pop.: 98 800 (latest est.).

want (wɒnt) *vb* **1** (*tr*) to feel a need or longing for: *I want a new hat.* **2** (when *tr, may take a clause as object or an infinitive*) to wish, need, or desire (something or to do something): *he wants to go home.* **3** (*intr;* usually used with a negative and often foll. by *for*) to be lacking or deficient (in something necessary or desirable): *the child wants for nothing.* **4** (*tr*) to feel the absence of: *lying on the ground makes me want my bed.* **5** (*tr*) to fall short by (a specified amount). **6** (*tr*) *Chiefly Brit.* to have need of or require (doing or being something): *your shoes want cleaning.* **7** (*intr*) to be destitute. **8** (*tr; often passive*) to seek or request the presence of: *you're wanted upstairs.* **9** (*tr; takes an infinitive*) *Inf.* should or ought (to do something): *you don't want to go out so late.* ◆ *n* **10** the act or an instance of wanting. **11** anything that is needed, desired, or lacked: *to supply someone's wants.* **12** a lack, shortage, or absence: *for want of common sense.* **13** the state of being in need: *the state should help those in want.* **14** a sense of lack; craving. ORIG C12 (vb, in the sense: it is lacking), C13 (n): from ON *vanta* to be deficient
▸ ˈ**wanter** *n*

want ad *n Inf.* a classified advertisement in a newspaper, magazine, etc., for something wanted, such as property or employment.

wanting (ˈwɒntɪŋ) *adj* (*postpositive*) **1** lacking or absent. **2** not meeting requirements or expectations: *you have been found wanting.*

wanton (ˈwɒntən) *adj* **1** dissolute, licentious, or immoral. **2** without motive, provocation, or justification: *wanton destruction.* **3** maliciously and unnecessarily cruel. **4** unrestrained: *wanton spending.* **5** *Arch. or poetic.* playful or capricious. **6** *Arch.* (of vegetation, etc.) luxuriant. ◆ *n* **7** a licentious person, esp. a woman. ◆ *vb* **8** (*intr*) to behave in a wanton manner. ORIG C13 *wantowen* (in the obs. sense: unruly): from *wan-* (prefix equivalent to UN-[1]) + *-towen,* from OE *togen* brought up, from *tēon* to bring up
▸ ˈ**wantonly** *adv* ▸ ˈ**wantonness** *n*

Wanxian, Wanhsien, *or* **Wan-Hsien** ★ (ˈwænˈʃjɛn)

n an inland port in central China, in E Sichuan province, on the Yangtze River. Pop.: 156 823 (1990 est.).

WAP (wɒp) *n* **a** *acronym for* Wireless Application Protocol, a global protocol for data transmission that allows mobile-phone users to access the Internet and other information services. **b** (*as modifier*): *a WAP phone.*

wapentake ('wɒpən,teɪk, 'wæp-) *n English legal history.* a subdivision of certain shires or counties, esp. in the Midlands and North of England, corresponding to the hundred in other shires. ORIG OE *wǣpen(ge)tæc*

wapiti ('wɒpɪtɪ) *n, pl* **wapitis.** a large North American deer with large much-branched antlers, now also found in New Zealand. ORIG C19: of Amerind origin, lit.: white deer, from *wap* (unattested) white; from the animal's white tail and rump

war (wɔː) *n* **1** open armed conflict between two or more parties, nations, or states. Related adj: **belligerent** (see sense 2). **2** a particular armed conflict: *the 1999 war in Kosovo.* **3** the techniques of armed conflict as a study, science, or profession. **4** any conflict or contest: *the war against crime.* **5** (*modifier*) of, resulting from, or characteristic of war: *war damage; a war story.* **6 in the wars.** *Inf.* (esp. of a child) hurt or knocked about, esp. as a result of quarrelling and fighting. ◆ *vb* **wars, warring, warred. 7** (*intr*) to conduct a war. ORIG C12: from ONorthern F *werre* (var. of OF *guerre*), of Gmc origin

War. *abbrev. for* Warwickshire.

Warangal ★ ('wʌrəngəl) *n* a city in S central India, in N Andhra Pradesh: capital of a 12th-century Hindu kingdom. Pop.: 447 657 (1991).

waratah ('wɒrətə) *n Austral.* a shrub having dark green leaves and clusters of crimson flowers. ORIG from Abor.

Warbeck ★ ('wɔːbɛk) *n* **Perkin** ('pɜːkɪn). ?1474–99, Flemish impostor, pretender to the English throne. Professing to be Richard, Duke of York, he led an unsuccessful rising against Henry VII (1497): executed.

warble[1] ('wɔːbᵊl) *vb* **warbles, warbling, warbled. 1** to sing (words, songs, etc.) with trills, runs, and other embellishments. **2** (*tr*) to utter in a song. ◆ *n* **3** the act or an instance of warbling. ORIG C14: via OF *werbler,* of Gmc origin

warble[2] ('wɔːbᵊl) *n Vet. science.* **1** a small lumpy abscess under the skin of cattle caused by the larvae of the warble fly. **2** a hard lump of tissue on a horse's back, caused by prolonged friction of a saddle. ORIG C16: from ?

warble fly *n* any of a genus of hairy beelike dipterous flies, the larvae of which produce warbles in cattle.

warbler ('wɔːblə) *n* **1** a person or thing that warbles. **2** a small active passerine songbird of the Old World having a cryptic plumage and slender bill, that is an arboreal insectivore. **3** a small bird of an American family, similar to the Old World songbird but often brightly coloured.

Warburg ★ (*German* 'vaːrbʊrk) *n* **Otto (Heinrich)** ('ɔto). 1883–1970, German biochemist and physiologist: Nobel prize for physiology or medicine (1931) for his work on respiratory enzymes.

war correspondent *n* a journalist who reports on a war from the scene of action.

war crime *n* a crime committed in wartime in violation of the accepted customs, such as ill-treatment of prisoners, etc.
▸ **war criminal** *n*

war cry *n* **1** a rallying cry used by combatants in battle. **2** a cry, slogan, etc., used to rally support for a cause.

ward (wɔːd) *n* **1** (in many countries) one of the districts into which a city, town, parish, or other area is divided for administration, election of representatives, etc. **2a** a room in a hospital, esp. one for patients requiring similar kinds of care: *a maternity ward.* **2b** (*as modifier*): *ward maid.* **3** one of the divisions of a prison. **4** an open space enclosed within the walls of a castle. **5** *Law.* Also called: **ward of court.** a person, esp. a minor or one legally incapable of managing his own affairs, placed under the control or protection of a guardian or of a court. **6** the state of being under guard or in custody. **7** a means of protection. **8a** an internal ridge or bar in a lock that prevents an incorrectly cut key from turning. **8b** a corresponding groove cut in a key. ◆ *vb* **9** (*tr*) *Arch.* to guard or protect. ◆ See also **ward off.** ORIG OE *weard* protector
▸ **'wardless** *adj*

Ward ★ (wɔːd) *n* **1** Mrs **Humphry,** married name of *Mary Augusta Arnold.* 1851–1920, British novelist. Her novels include *Robert Elsmere* (1888) and *The Case of Richard Meynell* (1911). **2** Sir **Joseph George.** 1856–1930, New Zealand statesman; prime minister (1906–12; 1928–30).

-ward *suffix.* **1** (*forming adjectives*) indicating direction towards: *a backward step.* **2** (*forming adverbs*) a variant and the usual US and Canad. form of **-wards.** ORIG OE *-weard* towards

war dance *n* a ceremonial dance performed before going to battle or after victory, esp. by certain North American Indian peoples.

warden ('wɔːdᵊn) *n* **1** a person who has the charge or care of something, esp. a building, or someone. **2** a public official, esp. one responsible for the enforcement of certain regulations: *traffic warden.* **3** a person employed to patrol a national park or a safari park. **4** *Chiefly US & Canad.* the chief officer in charge of a prison. **5** *Brit.* the principal of any of various universities or colleges. **6** See **churchwarden** (sense 1). ORIG C13: from OF *wardein,* from *warder* to guard, of Gmc origin

warder ('wɔːdə) *or* (*fem*) **wardress** *n* **1** *Chiefly Brit.* an officer in charge of prisoners in a jail. **2** a person who guards or has charge of something. ORIG C14: from Anglo-F *wardere,* from OF *warder* to guard, of Gmc origin

ward heeler *n US politics, disparaging.* a party worker who canvasses votes and performs chores for a political boss. Also called: **heeler.**

ward off *vb* (*tr, adv*) to turn aside or repel.

Wardour Street ★ ('wɔːdə) *n* **1** a street in Soho where many film companies have their London offices: formerly noted for shops selling antiques and mock antiques. **2** Also: **Wardour Street English.** affectedly archaic speech or writing.

wardrobe ('wɔːdrəʊb) *n* **1** a tall closet or cupboard, with a rail or hooks on which to hang clothes. **2** the total collection of articles of clothing belonging to one person. **3a** the collection of costumes belonging to a theatre or theatrical company. **3b** (*as modifier*): *wardrobe mistress.* ORIG C14: from OF *warderobe,* from *warder* to guard + *robe* ROBE

wardrobe trunk *n* a large upright rectangular travelling case, usually opening longitudinally, with one side having a hanging rail, the other having drawers or compartments.

wardroom ('wɔːd,ruːm, -,rʊm) *n* **1** the quarters assigned to the officers (except the captain) of a warship. **2** the officers of a warship collectively, excepting the captain.

-wards *or* **-ward** *suffix forming adverbs.* indicating direction towards: *a step backwards.* Cf. **-ward.** ORIG OE *-weardes* towards

wardship ('wɔːdʃɪp) *n* the state of being a ward.

ware[1] (wɛə) *n* (*often in combination*) **1** (*functioning as sing*) articles of the same kind or material: *silverware.* **2** porcelain or pottery of a specified type: *jasper ware.* ◆ See also **wares.** ORIG OE *waru*

ware[2] (wɛə) *vb Arch.* another word for **beware.** ORIG OE *wær.* See AWARE, BEWARE

warehouse *n* ('wɛə,haʊs). **1** a place where goods are stored prior to their use, distribution, or sale. **2** See **bonded warehouse. 3** *Chiefly Brit.* a large commercial, esp. wholesale, establishment. ◆ *vb* ('wɛə,haʊz, -,haʊs), **warehouses, warehousing, warehoused. 4** (*tr*) to store or place in a warehouse, esp. a bonded warehouse.
▸ **'ware,houseman** *n*

warehousing ('wɛə,haʊzɪŋ) *n Business.* an attempt to gain a significant stake in a company without revealing the identity of the purchaser by buying small quantities of shares in the name of nominees.

wares (wɛəz) *pl n* **1** articles of manufacture considered as being for sale. **2** any talent or asset regarded as a saleable commodity.

warfare ('wɔː,fɛə) *n* **1** the act, process, or an instance of waging war. **2** conflict or strife.

warfarin ('wɔːfərɪn) *n* a crystalline insoluble compound, used to kill rodents and, in the form of its sodium salt, as a medical anticoagulant. ORIG C20: from the patent owners *W(isconsin) A(lumni) R(esearch) F(oundation)* + (COUM)ARIN

war game *n* **1** a notional tactical exercise for training military commanders, in which no military units are actually deployed. **2** a game in which model soldiers are used to create battles, esp. past battles, in order to study tactics.

warhead ('wɔːˌhɛd) *n* the part of the fore end of a missile or projectile that contains explosives.

Warhol ★ ('wɔːhəʊl) *n* **Andy**, real name *Andrew Warhola*. ?1926–87, US pop artist and film maker.

warhorse ('wɔːˌhɔːs) *n* **1** a horse used in battle. **2** *Inf.* a veteran soldier or politician.

Warks *abbrev. for* Warwickshire.

Warley ★ ('wɔːlɪ) *n* an industrial town in W central England, in Sandwell, in the West Midlands: formed in 1966 by the amalgamation of Smethwick, Oldbury, and Rowley Regis. Pop.: 145 542 (1991).

warlike ('wɔːˌlaɪk) *adj* **1** of, relating to, or used in war. **2** hostile or belligerent. **3** fit or ready for war.

warlock ('wɔːˌlɒk) *n* a man who practises black magic. ORIG OE *wǣrloga* oath breaker, from *wǣr* oath + *-loga* liar, from *lēogan* to lie

Warlock ★ ('wɔːˌlɒk) *n* **Peter**, real name *Philip Arnold Heseltine*. 1894–1930, British composer. His works include song cycles and the *Capriol Suite* (1926) for strings.

warlord ('wɔːˌlɔːd) *n* a military leader of a nation or part of a nation: *the Chinese warlords.*

Warlpiri ('walpri) *n* an Aboriginal language of central Australia.

warm (wɔːm) *adj* **1** characterized by or having a moderate degree of heat. **2** maintaining or imparting heat: *a warm coat.* **3** having or showing ready affection, kindliness, etc.: *a warm personality.* **4** lively or passionate: *a warm debate.* **5** cordial or enthusiastic: *warm support.* **6** quickly or easily aroused: *a warm temper.* **7** (of colours) predominantly red or yellow in tone. **8** (of a scent, trail, etc.) recently made. **9** near to finding a hidden object or guessing facts, as in children's games. **10** *Inf.* uncomfortable or disagreeable, esp. because of the proximity of danger. ◆ *vb* **11** (sometimes foll. by *up*) to make or become warm or warmer. **12** (when *intr,* often foll. by *to*) to make or become excited, enthusiastic, etc. (about): *he warmed to the idea of buying a new car.* **13** (*intr;* often foll. by *to*) to feel affection, kindness, etc. (for someone): *I warmed to her mother from the start.* ◆ *n Inf.* **14** a warm place or area: *come into the warm.* **15** the act or an instance of warming or being warmed. ◆ See also **warm up**. ORIG OE *wearm*
▸ '**warmer** *n* ▸ '**warmish** *adj* ▸ '**warmly** *adv* ▸ '**warmness** *n*

warm-blooded *adj* **1** ardent, impetuous, or passionate. **2** (of birds and mammals) having a constant body temperature, usually higher than the temperature of the surroundings. Technical term: **homoiothermic**.
▸ ˌ**warm-'bloodedness** *n*

warm-down *n* light exercises performed to aid recovery from strenuous physical activity.

war memorial *n* a monument, usually an obelisk or cross, to those who die in a war, esp. those from a particular locality.

warm front *n Meteorol.* the boundary between a warm air mass and the cold air above which it is rising, at a less steep angle than at the cold front.

warm-hearted *adj* kindly, generous, or readily sympathetic.
▸ ˌ**warm-'heartedly** *adv* ▸ ˌ**warm-'heartedness** *n*

warming pan *n* a pan, often of copper and having a long handle, filled with hot coals and formerly drawn over the sheets to warm a bed.

warmonger ('wɔːˌmʌŋgə) *n* a person who fosters warlike ideas or advocates war.
▸ '**warˌmongering** *n*

warmth (wɔːmθ) *n* **1** the state, quality, or sensation of being warm. **2** intensity of emotion: *he denied the accusation with some warmth.* **3** affection or cordiality.

warm up *vb* (*adv*) **1** to make or become warm or warmer. **2** (*intr*) to exercise immediately before a game, contest, or more vigorous exercise. **3** (*intr*) to get ready for something important; prepare. **4** to run (an engine, etc.) until the working temperature is attained, or (of an engine, etc.) to undergo this process. **5** to make or become more animated: *the party warmed up when Tom came.* **6** to reheat (already cooked food) or (of such food) to be reheated. ◆ *n* **warm-up. 7** the act or an instance of warming up. **8** a preparatory exercise routine.

warn (wɔːn) *vb* **1** to notify or make (someone) aware of danger, harm, etc. **2** (*tr; often takes a negative and an infinitive*) to advise or admonish (someone) as to action, conduct, etc.: *I warn you not to do that again.* **3** (*takes a clause as object or an infinitive*) to inform (someone) in advance: *he warned them that he would arrive late.* **4** (*tr;* usually foll. by *away, off,* etc.) to give notice to go away, be off, etc. ORIG OE *wearnian*
▸ '**warner** *n*

warning ('wɔːnɪŋ) *n* **1** a hint, intimation, threat, etc., of harm or danger. **2** advice to beware or desist. **3** an archaic word for **notice** (sense 6). ◆ *adj* **4** (*prenominal*) intended or serving to warn: *a warning look.*
▸ '**warningly** *adv*

War of American Independence *n* the conflict following the revolt of the North American colonies against British rule, particularly on the issue of taxation. Hostilities began in 1775 when British and American forces clashed at Lexington and Concord. Articles of Confederation agreed in the Continental Congress in 1777 provided for a confederacy to be known as the United States of America. The war was effectively ended with the surrender of the British at Yorktown in 1781 and peace was signed at Paris in Sept. 1783. Also called: **American Revolution** or **Revolutionary War**.

warp (wɔːp) *vb* **1** to twist or cause to twist out of shape, as from heat, damp, etc. **2** to turn or cause to turn from a true, correct, or proper course. **3** to pervert or be perverted. **4** *Naut.* to move (a vessel) by hauling on a rope fixed to a stationary object ashore or (of a vessel) to be moved thus. **5** (*tr*) to flood (land) with water from which alluvial matter is deposited. ◆ *n* **6** the state or condition of being twisted out of shape. **7** a twist, distortion, or bias. **8** a mental or moral deviation. **9** the yarns arranged lengthways on a loom, forming the threads through which the weft yarns are woven. **10** *Naut.* a rope used for warping a vessel. **11** alluvial sediment deposited by water. ORIG OE *wearp* a throw
▸ '**warpage** *n* ▸ **warped** *adj* ▸ '**warper** *n*

war paint *n* **1** painted decoration of the face and body applied by certain North American Indians before battle. **2** *Inf.* finery or regalia. **3** *Inf.* cosmetics.

warpath ('wɔːˌpɑːθ) *n* **1** the route taken by North American Indians on a warlike expedition. **2 on the warpath. 2a** preparing to engage in battle. **2b** *Inf.* in a state of anger.

warplane ('wɔːˌpleɪn) *n* any aircraft designed for and used in warfare.

warrant ('wɒrənt) *n* **1** anything that gives authority for an action or decision; authorization. **2** a document that certifies or guarantees, such as a receipt for goods stored in a warehouse, a licence, or a commission. **3** *Law.* an authorization issued by a magistrate allowing a constable or other officer to search or seize property, arrest a person, or perform some other specified act. **4** (in certain armed services) the official authority for the appointment of warrant officers. **5** a security that functions as a stock option by giving the owner the right to buy ordinary shares in a company at a specified date, often at a specified price. ◆ *vb* (*tr*) **6** to guarantee the quality, condition, etc., of (something). **7** to give authority or power to. **8** to attest to the character, worthiness, etc., of. **9** to guarantee (a purchaser of merchandise) against loss of, damage to, or misrepresentation concerning the merchandise. **10** *Law.* to guarantee (the title to an estate or other property). **11** to declare confidently. ORIG C13: from Anglo-F, var. of OF *guarant,* from *guarantir* to guarantee, of Gmc origin

★ people and places

▸ 'warrantable *adj* ▸ ˌwarranta'bility *n* ▸ 'warrantably *adv* ▸ 'warranter *n*

warrantee (ˌwɒrən'tiː) *n* a person to whom a warranty is given.

warrant officer *n* an officer in certain armed services who holds a rank between those of commissioned and noncommissioned officers. In the British army the rank has two classes: regimental sergeant major and company sergeant major.

Warrant of Fitness *n NZ.* a six-monthly certificate required for motor vehicles certifying mechanical soundness.

warrantor ('wɒrənˌtɔː) *n* an individual or company that provides a warranty.

warrant sale *n Scots Law.* a sale of someone's personal belongings or household effects that have been seized to meet unpaid debts.

warranty ('wɒrəntɪ) *n, pl* **warranties. 1** *Property law.* a covenant, express or implied, by which the vendor of real property vouches for the security of the title conveyed. **2** *Contract law.* an express or implied term in a contract collateral to the main purpose, such as an undertaking that goods contracted to be sold shall meet specified requirements as to quality, etc. **3** *Insurance law.* an undertaking by the party insured that the facts given regarding the risk are as stated. ORIG C14: from Anglo-F *warantie,* from *warantir* to warrant, var. of OF *guarantir;* see WARRANT

warren ('wɒrən) *n* **1** a series of interconnected underground tunnels in which rabbits live. **2** a colony of rabbits. **3** an overcrowded area or dwelling. **4** *Chiefly Brit.* an enclosed place where small game animals or birds are kept, esp. for breeding. ORIG C14: from Anglo-F *warenne,* of Gmc origin

Warren ★ ('wɒrən) *n* a city in SE Michigan, northeast of Detroit. Pop.: 142 625 (1994 est.).

warrigal ('wɒrɪgæl) *Austral.* ◆ *n* **1** a dingo. ◆ *adj* **2** untamed or wild. ORIG C19: from Abor.

Warrington ★ ('wɒrɪŋtən) *n* **1** an industrial town in NW England, in N Cheshire on the River Mersey: dates from Roman times. Pop.: 81 812 (1991). **2** a unitary authority in NW England, in N Cheshire. Pop.: 189 000 (1996 est.). Area: 176 sq. km (68 sq. miles).

warrior ('wɒrɪə) *n* **a** a person engaged in, experienced in, or devoted to war. **b** (*as modifier*): *a warrior nation.* ORIG C13: from OF *werreieor,* from *werre* WAR

Warsaw ★ ('wɔːsɔː) *n* the capital of Poland, in the E central part on the River Vistula: became capital at the end of the 16th century; almost completely destroyed in World War II as the main centre of the Polish resistance movement; rebuilt within about six years; university (1818); situated at the junction of important trans-European routes. Pop.: 1 640 700 (1995 est.). Polish name: **Warszawa** (var'ʃava).

Warsaw Pact *n* a military treaty and association of E European countries (1955–91).

warship ('wɔːˌʃɪp) *n* a vessel armed, armoured, and otherwise equipped for naval warfare.

Wars of the Roses *pl n* the struggle for the throne in England (1455-85) between the House of York (symbolized by the white rose) and the House of Lancaster (symbolized by the red rose).

wart (wɔːt) *n* **1** *Pathol.* any firm abnormal elevation of the skin caused by a virus. **2** *Bot.* a small rounded outgrowth. **3 warts and all.** with all blemishes evident. ORIG OE *weart(e)*

▸ 'warty *adj*

Warta ★ (*Polish* 'varta) *n* a river in Poland, flowing generally north and west across the whole W Polish Plain to the River Oder. Length: 808 km (502 miles).

Wartburg ★ (*German* 'vartburk) *n* a medieval castle in central Germany, in Thuringia southwest of Eisenach; residence of Luther (1521–22) when he began his German translation of the New Testament.

warthog ('wɔːthɒg) *n* a wild pig of S and E Africa, having heavy tusks, wartlike protuberances on the face, and a mane of coarse hair.

wartime ('wɔːˌtaɪm) *n* **a** a period or time of war. **b** (*as modifier*): *wartime conditions.*

war whoop *n* the yell or howl uttered, esp. by North American Indians, while making an attack.

Warwick[1] ★ ('wɒrɪk) *n* a town in central England, administrative centre of Warwickshire, on the River Avon: 14th-century castle: the university of Warwick (1965) is in Coventry. Pop.: 22 476 (1991).

Warwick[2] ★ ('wɒrɪk) *n* **Earl of,** title of *Richard Neville,* known as *the Kingmaker.* 1428–71, English statesman. During the Wars of the Roses, he fought first for the Yorkists, securing the throne (1461) for Edward IV, and then for the Lancastrians, restoring Henry VI (1470). He was killed at Barnet by Edward IV.

Warwickshire ★ ('wɒrɪkˌʃɪə, -ʃə) *n* a county of central England: until 1974, when the West Midlands metropolitan county was created, it contained one of the most highly industrialized regions in the world, centred on Birmingham. Administrative centre: Warwick. Pop.: 500 600 (1996 est.). Area: 1981 sq. km (765 sq. miles).

wary ('wɛərɪ) *adj* **warier, wariest. 1** watchful, cautious, or alert. **2** characterized by caution or watchfulness. ORIG C16: from WARE[2] + -Y[1]

▸ 'warily *adv* ▸ 'wariness *n*

was (wɒz; *unstressed* wəz) *vb* (used with *I, he, she, it,* and with singular nouns) **1** the past tense (indicative mood) of **be. 2** *Not standard.* a form of the subjunctive mood used in place of *were,* esp. in conditional sentences: *if the film was to be with you, would you be able to process it?* ORIG OE *wæs,* from *wesan* to be

wasabi (wə'sɑːbɪ) *n* **1** a Japanese plant cultivated for its thick green pungent root. **2** the root of this plant, esp. in paste or powder form, used as a condiment in Japanese cookery.

Wasatch Range ★ ('wɔːsætʃ) *n* a mountain range in the W central US, in N Utah and SE Idaho. Highest peak: Mount Timpanogos, 3581 m (11 750 ft).

wash (wɒʃ) *vb* **1** to apply water or other liquid, usually with soap, to (oneself, clothes, etc.) in order to cleanse. **2** (*tr; often* foll. by *away, from, off,* etc.) to remove by the application of water or other liquid and usually soap: *she washed the dirt from her clothes.* **3** (*intr*) to be capable of being washed without damage or loss of colour. **4** (of an animal such as a cat) to cleanse (itself or another animal) by licking. **5** (*tr*) to cleanse from pollution or defilement. **6** (*tr*) to make wet or moist. **7** (often foll. by *away,* etc.) to move or be moved by water: *the flood washed away the bridge.* **8** (esp. of waves) to flow or sweep against or over (a surface or object), often with a lapping sound. **9** to form by erosion or be eroded: *the stream washed a ravine in the hill.* **10** (*tr*) to apply a thin coating of paint, metal, etc., to. **11** (*tr*) to separate (ore, etc.) from (gravel, etc.) by immersion in water. **12** (*intr; usually used with a negative*) *Inf., chiefly Brit.* to admit of testing or proof: *your excuses won't wash.* ◆ *n* **13** the act or process of washing. **14** a quantity of articles washed together. **15** a preparation or thin liquid used as a coating or in washing: *a thin wash of paint.* **16** *Med.* **16a** any medicinal lotion for application to a part of the body. **16b** (*in combination*): *an eyewash.* **17a** the technique of making wash drawings. **17b** See **wash drawing. 18** the erosion of soil by the action of flowing water. **19** a mass of alluvial material transported and deposited by flowing water. **20** land that is habitually washed by tidal or river waters. **21** the disturbance in the air or water produced at the rear of an aircraft, boat, or other moving object. **22** gravel, earth, etc., from which valuable minerals may be washed. **23** waste liquid matter or liquid refuse, esp. as fed to pigs. **24** an alcoholic liquid resembling strong beer, resulting from the fermentation of wort in the production of whisky. **25 come out in the wash.** *Inf.* to become known or apparent in the course of time. ◆ See also **wash down, wash out, wash up.** ORIG OE *wæscan, waxan*

Wash ★ (wɒʃ) *n* **the.** a shallow inlet of the North Sea on the E coast of England, between Lincolnshire and Norfolk.

Wash. *abbrev. for* Washington.

★ people and places

washable ('wɒʃəbᵊl) *adj* (esp. of fabrics or clothes) capable of being washed without deteriorating.
▸ ˌ**washa'bility** *n*

wash-and-wear *adj* (of fabrics, garments, etc.) requiring only light washing, short drying time, and little or no ironing.

washbasin ('wɒʃˌbeɪsᵊn) *n* **1** Also called: **washbowl.** a basin or bowl for washing the face and hands. **2** Also called: **wash-hand basin.** a bathroom fixture with taps, used for washing the face and hands.

washboard ('wɒʃˌbɔːd) *n* **1** a board having a surface, usually of corrugated metal, on which, esp. formerly, clothes were scrubbed. **2** such a board used as a rhythm instrument played with the fingers in skiffle, country-and-western music, etc. **3** *Naut.* a vertical planklike shield fastened to the gunwales of a boat to prevent water from splashing over the side.

washcloth ('wɒʃˌklɒθ) *n* **1** another term for **dishcloth. 2** the US and Canad. word for **face cloth.**

washday ('wɒʃˌdeɪ) *n* a day on which clothes and linen are washed.

wash down *vb (tr, adv)* **1** to wash completely, esp. from top to bottom. **2** to take drink with or after (food or another drink).

wash drawing *n* a pen-and-ink drawing that has been lightly brushed over with water to soften the lines.

washed out *adj* (**washed-out** *when prenominal*). **1** faded or colourless. **2** exhausted, esp. when being pale in appearance.

washed up *adj* (**washed-up** *when prenominal*). *Inf., chiefly US, Canad., & NZ.* without hope; defeated: *our hopes for the new deal are all washed up.*

washer ('wɒʃə) *n* **1** a person or thing that washes. **2** a flat ring or drilled disc of metal used under the head of a bolt or nut. **3** any flat ring of rubber, felt, metal, etc., used to provide a seal under a nut or in a tap or valve seat. **4** See **washing machine. 5** *Austral.* a face cloth; flannel.

washerwoman ('wɒʃəˌwʊmən) *or (masc)* **washerman** *n, pl* **washerwomen** *or* **washermen.** a person who washes clothes for a living.

washery ('wɒʃərɪ) *n, pl* **washeries.** a plant at a mine where water or other liquid is used to remove dirt from a mineral, esp. coal.

wash-hand basin *n* another name for **washbasin** (sense 2).

wash house *n* (formerly) an outbuilding in which clothes were washed.

washing ('wɒʃɪŋ) *n* **1** articles that have been or are to be washed together on a single occasion. **2** something, such as gold dust, that has been obtained by washing. **3** a thin coat of something applied in liquid form.

washing machine *n* a mechanical apparatus, usually powered by electricity, for washing clothing, linens, etc.

washing powder *n* powdered detergent for washing fabrics.

washing soda *n* crystalline sodium carbonate, esp. when used as a cleansing agent.

Washington[1] ★ ('wɒʃɪŋtən) *n* **1** a state of the northwestern US, on the Pacific: consists of the Coast Range and the Olympic Mountains in the west and the Columbia Plateau in the east. Capital: Olympia. Pop.: 5 689 263 (1998 est.). Area: 172 416 sq. km (66 570 sq. miles). Abbrevs.: **Wash.** or (with zip code) **WA** **2** Also called: **Washington, DC.** the capital of the US, coextensive with the District of Columbia and situated near the E coast on the Potomac River: site chosen by President Washington in 1790; contains the White House and the Capitol; a major educational and administrative centre. Pop.: 567 094 (1994 est.). **3** a town in Tyne and Wear: designated a new town in 1964. Pop.: 56 848 (1991). **4 Mount.** a mountain in N New Hampshire, in the White Mountains: the highest peak in the northeast US; noted for extreme weather conditions. Height: 1917 m (6288 ft). **5 Lake.** a lake in W Washington, forming the E boundary of the city of Seattle: linked by canal with Puget Sound. Length: about 32 km (20 miles). Width: 6 km (4 miles).
▸ **Washingtonian** (ˌwɒʃɪŋ'təʊnɪən) *adj, n*

Washington[2] ★ ('wɒʃɪŋtən) *n* **1 Booker T(aliaferro).** 1856–1915, US Black educationalist and writer. **2 George.** 1732–99, US general and statesman; first president of the US (1789–97). He presided over the convention at Philadelphia (1787) that formulated the constitution of the US and elected him president.

washing-up *n Brit.* **1** the washing of dishes, cutlery, etc., after a meal. **2** dishes and cutlery waiting to be washed up. **3** *(as modifier): a washing-up machine.*

wash out *vb (adv)* **1** *(tr)* to wash (the inside of something) so as to remove (dirt). **2** Also: **wash off.** to remove or be removed by washing: *grass stains don't wash out easily.* ◆ *n* **washout. 3** *Geol.* **3a** erosion of the earth's surface by the action of running water. **3b** a narrow channel produced by this. **4** *Inf.* **4a** a total failure or disaster. **4b** an incompetent person.

washroom ('wɒʃˌruːm, -ˌrʊm) *n US & Canad.* a euphemism for **lavatory.**

washstand ('wɒʃˌstænd) *n* a piece of furniture designed to hold a basin, etc., for washing the face and hands.

washtub ('wɒʃˌtʌb) *n* a tub or large container used for washing anything, esp. clothes.

wash up *vb (adv)* **1** *Chiefly Brit.* to wash (dishes, cutlery, etc.) after a meal. **2** *(intr) US & Canad.* to wash one's face and hands. ◆ *n* **washup. 3** *Austral.* the end, outcome of a process: *in the washup, three were elected.*

washy ('wɒʃɪ) *adj* **washier, washiest. 1** overdiluted, watery, or weak. **2** lacking intensity or strength.
▸ '**washiness** *n*

wasn't ('wɒzᵊnt) *contraction of* was not.

wasp (wɒsp) *n* **1** a social hymenopterous insect, such as the **common wasp,** having a black-and-yellow body and an ovipositor specialized for stinging. **2** any of various solitary hymenopterans, such as the digger wasp and gall wasp. ORIG OE *wæsp*
▸ '**waspˌlike** *adj* ▸ '**waspy** *adj* ▸ '**waspily** *adv* ▸ '**waspiness** *n*

Wasp *or* **WASP** (wɒsp) *n* (in the US) *acronym for* White Anglo-Saxon Protestant: a person descended from N European, usually Protestant stock, forming a group often considered the most dominant, privileged, and influential in American society.

waspish ('wɒspɪʃ) *adj* **1** relating to or suggestive of a wasp. **2** easily annoyed or angered.
▸ '**waspishly** *adv*

wasp waist *n* a very slender waist, esp. one that is tightly corseted.
▸ '**wasp-ˌwaisted** *adj*

wassail ('wɒseɪl) *n* **1** (formerly) a toast or salutation made to a person at festivities. **2** a festivity when much drinking takes place. **3** alcoholic drink drunk at such a festivity, esp. spiced beer or mulled wine. ◆ *vb* **4** to drink the health of (a person) at a wassail. **5** *(intr)* to go from house to house singing carols at Christmas. ORIG C13: from ON *ves heill* be in good health
▸ '**wassailer** *n*

Wassermann test *or* **reaction** ('wæsəmən) *n Med.* a diagnostic test for syphilis. ORIG C20: after August von *Wassermann* (1866–1925), G bacteriologist

wast (wɒst; *unstressed* wəst) *vb Arch. or dialect.* (used with the pronoun *thou* or its relative equivalent) a singular form of the past tense (indicative mood) of **be.**

wastage ('weɪstɪdʒ) *n* **1** anything lost by wear or waste. **2** the process of wasting. **3** reduction in size of a workforce by retirement, etc. (esp. in **natural wastage**).

> **USAGE NOTE** *Waste* and *wastage* are to some extent interchangeable, but many people think that *wastage* should not be used to refer to loss resulting from human carelessness, inefficiency, etc.: *a waste* (not *a wastage*) *of time, money, effort,* etc.

waste (weɪst) *vb* **wastes, wasting, wasted. 1** *(tr)* to use, consume, or expend thoughtlessly, carelessly, or to no avail. **2** *(tr)* to fail to take advantage of: *to waste an opportunity.* **3** (when *intr,* often foll. by *away*) to lose or cause to lose bodily strength, health, etc. **4** to exhaust or become exhausted. **5** (*tr*) to ravage. **6** (*tr*) *Sl.* to murder or kill. ◆ *n* **7** the act of wasting or state of being wasted. **8** a failure to take advantage of something. **9** anything unused or not used to full advantage. **10** anything or anyone rejected as useless, worthless, or in excess of what is required. **11** garbage, rubbish, or trash. **12** a land or region that is devastated or ruined. **13** a land or region that is wild or uncultivated. **14** *Physiol.* **14a** the useless products of metabolism. **14b** indigestible food residue. **15** *Law.* reduction in the value of an estate caused by act or neglect, esp. by a life tenant. ◆ *adj* **16** rejected as useless, unwanted, or worthless. **17** produced in excess of what is required. **18** not cultivated, inhabited, or productive: *waste land.* **19a** of or denoting the useless products of metabolism. **19b** of or denoting indigestible food residue. **20** destroyed, devastated, or ruined. **21 lay waste.** to devastate or destroy. ORIG C13: from Anglo-F, from L *vastāre* to lay waste, from *vastus* empty

wasted ('weɪstɪd) *adj* **1** not taken advantage of: *a wasted opportunity.* **2** unprofitable: *wasted effort.* **3** enfeebled and emaciated: *a thin wasted figure.* **4** *Sl.* showing signs of habitual drug abuse.

wasteful ('weɪstfʊl) *adj* **1** tending to waste or squander. **2** causing waste or devastation.
▸ '**wastefully** *adv* ▸ '**wastefulness** *n*

wasteland ('weɪstˌlænd) *n* **1** a barren or desolate area of land. **2** a region, period in history, etc., that is considered spiritually, intellectually, or aesthetically barren or desolate.

wastepaper ('weɪstˌpeɪpə) *n* paper discarded after use.

wastepaper basket *or* **bin** *n* an open receptacle for paper and other dry litter. Usual US and Canad. word: **wastebasket.**

waste pipe *n* a pipe to take excess or used water away, as from a sink to a drain.

waster ('weɪstə) *n* **1** a person or thing that wastes. **2** a ne'er-do-well; wastrel.

wasting ('weɪstɪŋ) *adj* (*prenominal*) reducing the vitality, strength, or robustness of the body: *a wasting disease.*
▸ '**wastingly** *adv*

wasting asset *n* an unreplaceable business asset of limited life, such as an oil well.

wastrel ('weɪstrəl) *n* **1** a wasteful person; spendthrift; prodigal. **2** an idler or vagabond.

Wast Water ★ (wɒst) *n* a lake in NW England, in Cumbria in the Lake District. Length: 5 km (3 miles).

wat (wɑːt) *n* a Thai Buddhist monastery or temple. ORIG Thai, from Sansk. *vāta* enclosure

watap (wæ'tɑːp, wɑː-) *n* a stringy thread made by North American Indians from the roots of various conifers and used for weaving and sewing. ORIG C18: from Canad. F, from Cree *watapiy*

watch (wɒtʃ) *vb* **1** to look at or observe closely or attentively. **2** (*intr*; foll. by *for*) to wait attentively. **3** to guard or tend (something) closely or carefully. **4** (*intr*) to keep vigil. **5** (*tr*) to maintain an interest in: *to watch the progress of a child at school.* **6 watch it!** be careful! ◆ *n* **7a** a small portable timepiece, usually worn strapped to the wrist (a **wristwatch**) or in a waistcoat pocket. **7b** (*as modifier*): *a watch spring.* **8** a watching. **9** a period of vigil, esp. during the night. **10** (formerly) one of a set of periods into which the night was divided. **11** *Naut.* **11a** any of the periods, usually of four hours, during which part of a ship's crew are on duty. **11b** those officers and crew on duty during a specified watch. **12** the period during which a guard is on duty. **13** (formerly) a watchman or band of watchmen. **14 on the watch.** on the lookout. ◆ See also **watch out.** ORIG OE *wæccan* (vb), *wæcce* (n)
▸ '**watcher** *n*

-watch *suffix of nouns.* indicating a regular television programme or newspaper feature on the topic specified: *Crimewatch.*

watchable ('wɒtʃəbᵊl) *adj* **1** capable of being watched. **2** interesting, enjoyable, or entertaining: *a watchable television documentary.*

watchcase ('wɒtʃˌkeɪs) *n* a protective case for a watch, generally of metal such as gold or silver.

watch chain *n* a chain used for fastening a pocket watch to the clothing. See also **fob**[1].

Watch Committee *n Brit. history.* a local government committee responsible for the efficiency of the local police force.

watchdog ('wɒtʃˌdɒg) *n* **1** a dog kept to guard property. **2a** a person or group that acts as a protector against inefficiency, etc. **2b** (*as modifier*): *a watchdog committee.*

watch fire *n* a fire kept burning at night as a signal or for warmth and light by a person keeping watch.

watchful ('wɒtʃfʊl) *adj* **1** vigilant or alert. **2** *Arch.* not sleeping.
▸ '**watchfully** *adv* ▸ '**watchfulness** *n*

watch-glass *n* **1** a curved glass disc that covers the dial of a watch. **2** a similarly shaped piece of glass used in laboratories for evaporating small samples of a solution, etc.

watchmaker ('wɒtʃˌmeɪkə) *n* a person who makes or mends watches.
▸ '**watchˌmaking** *n*

watchman ('wɒtʃmən) *n, pl* **watchmen. 1** a person employed to guard buildings or property. **2** (formerly) a man employed to patrol or guard the streets at night.

watch night *n* (in Protestant churches) **1a** the night of December 24, during which a service is held to mark the arrival of Christmas Day. **1b** the night of December 31, during which a service is held to mark the passing of the old year. **2** the service held on either of these nights.

watch out *vb* (*intr, adv*) to be careful or on one's guard.

watchstrap ('wɒtʃˌstræp) *n* a strap of leather, cloth, etc., attached to a watch for fastening it around the wrist. Also called (US and Canad.): **watchband.**

watchtower ('wɒtʃˌtaʊə) *n* a tower on which a sentry keeps watch.

watchword ('wɒtʃˌwɜːd) *n* **1** another word for **password. 2** a rallying cry or slogan.

water ('wɔːtə) *n* **1** a clear colourless tasteless odourless liquid that is essential for plant and animal life and constitutes, in impure form, rain, oceans, rivers, lakes, etc. Formula: H_2O. Related adj: **aqueous. 2a** any body or area of this liquid, such as a sea, lake, river, etc. **2b** (*as modifier*): *water sports; a water plant.* Related adj: **aquatic. 3** the surface of such a body or area: *fish swam below the water.* **4** any form or variety of this liquid, such as rain. **5** See **high water, low water. 6** any of various solutions of chemical substances in water: *ammonia water.* **7** *Physiol.* **7a** any fluid secreted from the body, such as sweat, urine, or tears. **7b** (*usually pl*) the amniotic fluid surrounding a fetus in the womb. **8** a wavy lustrous finish on some fabrics, esp. silk. **9** *Arch.* the degree of brilliance in a diamond. **10** excellence, quality, or degree (in **of the first water**). **11** *Finance.* capital stock issued without a corresponding increase in paid-up capital. **12** (*modifier*) *Astrol.* of or relating to the three signs of the zodiac Cancer, Scorpio, and Pisces. **13 hold water.** to prove credible, logical, or consistent: *the alibi did not hold water.* **14 make water. 14a** to urinate. **14b** (of a boat, etc.) to let in water. **15 pass water.** to urinate. **16 water under the bridge.** events that are past and done with. ◆ *vb* **17** (*tr*) to sprinkle, moisten, or soak with water. **18** (*tr;* often foll. by *down*) to weaken by the addition of water. **19** (*intr*) (of the eyes) to fill with tears. **20** (*intr*) (of the mouth) to salivate, esp. in anticipation of food (esp. in **make one's mouth water**). **21** (*tr*) to irrigate or provide with water: *to water the land.* **22** (*intr*) to drink water. **23** (*intr*) (of a ship, etc.) to take in a supply of water. **24** (*tr*) *Finance.* to raise the par value of (issued capital stock) without a corresponding increase in the real value of assets. **25** (*tr*) to produce a wavy lustrous finish on (fabrics, esp. silk). ◆ See also **water down.** ORIG OE *wæter*
▸ '**waterer** *n* ▸ '**waterless** *adj*

water bag *n* a bag, sometimes made of skin, leather, etc., but in Australia usually canvas, for carrying water.

water bailiff *n* an official responsible for enforcing laws on shipping and fishing.

★ people and places

water bear *n* another name for a **tardigrade.**

water bed *n* a waterproof mattress filled with water.

water beetle *n* any of various beetles that live most of the time in freshwater ponds, rivers, etc.

water bird *n* any aquatic bird, including the wading and swimming birds.

water biscuit *n* a thin crisp plain biscuit, usually served with butter or cheese.

water blister *n* a blister containing watery or serous fluid, without any blood or pus.

water boatman *n* any of various aquatic bugs having a flattened body and oarlike hind legs, adapted for swimming.

water bomber *n Canad.* an aircraft with special tanks for holding water that can be dropped on forest fires.

waterborne ('wɔːtəˌbɔːn) *adj* **1** floating or travelling on water. **2** (of a disease, etc.) transported or transmitted by water.

waterbuck ('wɔːtəˌbʌk) *n* any of a genus of antelopes of swampy areas of Africa, having long curved ridged horns.

water buffalo *or* **ox** *n* a member of the cattle tribe of swampy regions of S Asia, having widely spreading back-curving horns. Domesticated forms are used as draught animals.

water bug *n* any of various heteropterous insects adapted to living in the water or on its surface, esp. any of the **giant water bugs** of North America, India, and southern Africa, which have flattened hairy legs.

water butt *n* a barrel for collecting rainwater, esp. from a drainpipe.

water cannon *n* an apparatus for pumping water through a nozzle at high pressure, used in quelling riots.

Water Carrier *or* **Bearer** *n* **the.** the constellation Aquarius, the 11th sign of the zodiac.

water chestnut *n* **1** a floating aquatic plant of Asia, having four-pronged edible nutlike fruits. **2 Chinese water chestnut.** a Chinese plant with an edible succulent corm. **3** the corm of the Chinese water chestnut, used in Oriental cookery.

water clock *or* **glass** *n* any of various devices for measuring time that use the escape of water as the motive force.

water closet *n* **1** a lavatory flushed by water. **2** a small room that has a lavatory. ◆ Usually abbreviated to **WC.**

watercolour *or US* **watercolor** ('wɔːtəˌkʌlə) *n* **1** water-soluble pigment bound with gum arabic, applied in transparent washes and without the admixture of white pigment in the lighter tones. **2a** a painting done in watercolours. **2b** (*as modifier*): *a watercolour masterpiece.* **3** the art or technique of painting with such pigments.
▸ **'waterˌcolourist** *or US* **'waterˌcolorist** *n*

water-cool *vb* (*tr*) to cool (an engine, etc.) by a flow of water circulating in an enclosed jacket.
▸ **'water-ˌcooled** *adj*

water cooler *n* **1** a device for cooling and dispensing drinking water. ◆ (*modifier*) **water-cooler. 2** *US inf.* indicating the kind of informal conversation among office staff that takes place at such a dispenser: *water-cooler discussions.*

watercourse ('wɔːtəˌkɔːs) *n* **1** a stream, river, or canal. **2** the channel, bed, or route along which this flows.

watercraft ('wɔːtəˌkrɑːft) *n* **1** a boat or ship or such vessels collectively. **2** skill in handling boats or in water sports.

watercress ('wɔːtəˌkrɛs) *n* an Old World cruciferous plant of clear ponds and streams, having pungent leaves that are used in salads and as a garnish.

water cure *n Med.* a nontechnical name for **hydropathy** or **hydrotherapy.**

water cycle *n* the circulation of the earth's water, in which water evaporates from the sea into the atmosphere, where it condenses and falls as rain or snow, returning to the sea by rivers.

water diviner *n Brit.* a person able to locate the presence of water, esp. underground, with a divining rod.

water down *vb* (*tr, adv*) **1** to dilute or weaken with water. **2** to modify, esp. so as to omit anything unpleasant or offensive: *to water down the truth.*
▸ **ˌwatered-'down** *adj*

waterfall ('wɔːtəˌfɔːl) *n* a cascade of falling water where there is a vertical or almost vertical step in a river.

water flea *n* any of numerous minute freshwater crustaceans which swim by means of hairy branched antennae. See also **daphnia.**

Waterford ★ ('wɔːtəfəd) *n* **1** a county of S Republic of Ireland, in Munster province on the Atlantic: mountainous in the centre and in the northwest. County town: Waterford. Pop.: 95 000 (1996). Area: 1838 sq. km (710 sq. miles). **2** a port in S Republic of Ireland, county town of Co. Waterford: famous glass industry; fishing. Pop.: 40 345 (1991).

waterfowl ('wɔːtəˌfaʊl) *n* **1** any aquatic freshwater bird, esp. any species of the family Anatidae (ducks, geese, and swans). **2** such birds collectively.

waterfront ('wɔːtəˌfrʌnt) *n* the area of a town or city alongside a body of water, such as a harbour or dockyard.

water gap *n* a deep valley in a ridge, containing a stream.

water gas *n* a mixture of hydrogen and carbon monoxide produced by passing steam over hot carbon, used as a fuel and raw material.

water gate *n* **1** a gate in a canal, etc., that can be opened or closed to control the flow of water. **2** a gate through which access may be gained to a body of water.

Watergate ('wɔːtəˌgeɪt) *n* **1** an incident during the 1972 US presidential campaign, when agents employed by the re-election organization of President Richard Nixon were caught breaking into the Democratic Party headquarters in the Watergate building, Washington, DC. The political scandal was exacerbated by attempts to conceal the fact that White House officials had approved the burglary, and eventually forced the resignation of President Nixon. **2** any similar public scandal, esp. involving politicians or a possible cover-up.

water gauge *n* an instrument that indicates the presence or the quantity of water in a tank, reservoir, or boiler feed. Also called: **water glass.**

water glass *n* **1** a viscous syrupy solution of sodium silicate in water: used as a protective coating for cement and a preservative, esp. for eggs. **2** another name for **water gauge.**

water gum *n* any of several Australian gum trees that grow in swampy ground and beside creeks and rivers.

water hammer *n* a sharp concussion produced when the flow of water in a pipe is suddenly blocked.

water hen *n* another name for **gallinule.**

water hole *n* **1** a depression, such as a pond or pool, containing water, esp. one used by animals as a drinking place. **2** a source of drinking water in a desert.

Waterhouse ★ ('wɔːtəˌhaʊs) *n* **1 Alfred.** 1830–1905, British architect of the Gothic Revival. **2 George Marsden.** 1824–1906, New Zealand statesman, born in England: prime minister (1872–73). **3 Keith.** born 1929, British writer: best known for the novel *Billy Liar* (1959).

water hyacinth *n* a floating aquatic plant of tropical America, having showy bluish-purple flowers and swollen leafstalks. It forms dense masses in rivers, ponds, etc.

water ice *n* an ice cream made from a frozen sugar syrup flavoured with fruit juice or purée.

watering can *n* a container with a handle and a spout with a perforated nozzle used to sprinkle water over plants.

watering hole *n* **1** a pool where animals drink; water hole. **2** *Facetious sl.* a pub.

watering place *n* **1** a place where drinking water for people or animals may be obtained. **2** *Brit.* a spa. **3** *Brit.* a seaside resort.

water jacket *n* a water-filled envelope surrounding a

machine or part for cooling purposes, esp. the casing around the cylinder block of a pump or internal-combustion engine.

water jump *n* a ditch or brook over which athletes or horses must jump in a steeplechase or similar contest.

water level *n* **1** the level reached by the surface of a body of water. **2** the water line of a boat or ship.

water lily *n* any of various aquatic plants of temperate and tropical regions, having large leaves and showy flowers that float on the surface of the water.

water line *n* **1** a line marked at the level around a vessel's hull to which the vessel will be immersed when afloat. **2** a line marking the level reached by a body of water.

waterlogged ('wɔːtəˌlɒgd) *adj* **1** saturated with water. **2** (of a vessel still afloat) having taken in so much water as to be unmanageable.

Waterloo ★ (ˌwɔːtə'luː) *n* **1** a small town in central Belgium, in Walloon Brabant province south of Brussels: battle (1815) fought nearby in which British and Prussian forces under the Duke of Wellington and Blücher routed the French under Napoleon. Pop.: 17 800 (latest est.). **2** a total or crushing defeat (esp. in **meet one's Waterloo**).

water main *n* a principal supply pipe in an arrangement of pipes for distributing water.

waterman ('wɔːtəmən) *n, pl* **watermen**. a skilled boatman.
▸ **'watermanˌship** *n*

watermark ('wɔːtəˌmɑːk) *n* **1** a mark impressed on paper during manufacture, visible when the paper is held up to the light. **2** another word for **water line**. ◆ *vb* (*tr*) **3** to mark (paper) with a watermark.

water meadow *n* a meadow that remains fertile by being periodically flooded by a stream.

watermelon ('wɔːtəˌmɛlən) *n* **1** an African melon widely cultivated for its large edible fruit. **2** the fruit of this plant, which has a hard green rind and sweet watery reddish flesh.

water meter *n* a device for measuring the quantity or rate of water flowing through a pipe.

water milfoil *n* any of various pond plants having feathery underwater leaves and inconspicuous flowers.

water mill *n* a mill operated by a water wheel.

water moccasin *n* a large dark grey venomous snake of swamps in the southern US. Also called: **cottonmouth**.

water nymph *n* any fabled nymph of the water, such as the Naiad, Nereid, or Oceanid of Greek mythology.

water of crystallization *n* water present in the crystals of certain compounds. It is chemically combined in a specific amount but can often be easily expelled.

water ouzel *n* another name for **dipper** (the bird).

water paint *n* any water-based paint, such as an emulsion or an acrylic paint.

water pipe *n* **1** a pipe for water. **2** another name for **hookah**.

water pistol *n* a toy pistol that squirts a stream of water or other liquid.

water plantain *n* any of a genus of marsh plants of N temperate regions and Australia, having clusters of small white or pinkish flowers and broad pointed leaves.

water polo *n* a game played in water by two teams of seven swimmers in which each side tries to throw or propel an inflated ball into the opponents' goal.

water power *n* **1** the power latent in a dynamic or static head of water as used to drive machinery, esp. for generating electricity. **2** a source of such power, such as a drop in the level of a river, etc.

waterproof ('wɔːtəˌpruːf) *adj* **1** not penetrable by water. Cf. **water-repellent, water-resistant**. ◆ *n* **2** *Chiefly Brit.* a waterproof garment, esp. a raincoat. ◆ *vb* (*tr*) **3** to make (a fabric, etc.) waterproof.

water purslane *n* a marsh plant of temperate and warm regions, having reddish stems and small reddish flowers.

water rail *n* a large Eurasian rail of swamps, ponds, etc., having a long red bill.

water rat *n* **1** any of several small amphibious rodents, esp. the water vole or the muskrat. **2** any of various amphibious rats of New Guinea, the Philippines, and Australia.

water rate *n* a charge made for the public supply of water.

water-repellent *adj* (of fabrics, garments, etc.) having a finish that resists the absorption of water.

water-resistant *adj* (esp. of fabrics) designed to resist but not entirely prevent the penetration of water.

Waters ★ ('wɔːtəz) *n* **Muddy**, real name *McKinley Morganfield*. 1915–83, US blues guitarist and songwriter.

water scorpion *n* a long-legged aquatic insect that breathes by means of a long spinelike tube that projects from the rear of the body and penetrates the surface of the water.

watershed ('wɔːtəˌʃɛd) *n* **1** the dividing line between two adjacent river systems, such as a ridge. **2** an important period or factor that serves as a dividing line.

waterside ('wɔːtəˌsaɪd) *n* **a** the area of land beside a body of water. **b** (*as modifier*): *waterside houses*.

watersider ('wɔːtəˌsaɪdə) *n Austral. & NZ.* a wharf labourer.

water-ski *n* **1** a type of ski used for planing or gliding over water. ◆ *vb* **water-skis, water-skiing, water-skied** *or* **water-ski'd**. **2** (*intr*) to ride over water on water-skis while holding a rope towed by a speedboat.
▸ **'water-ˌskier** *n* ▸ **'water-ˌskiing** *n*

water snake *n* any of various snakes that live in or near water, esp. any of a genus of harmless North American snakes.

water softener *n* **1** any substance that lessens the hardness of water, usually by precipitating calcium and magnesium ions. **2** an apparatus that is used to remove chemicals that cause hardness.

water spaniel *n* either of two large curly-coated breeds of spaniel (the Irish and the American), which are used for hunting waterfowl.

water splash *n* a place where a stream runs over a road.

water sports *pl n* sports, such as swimming or windsurfing, that take place in or on water.

waterspout ('wɔːtəˌspaʊt) *n* **1** *Meteorol.* **1a** a tornado occurring over water that forms a column of water and mist. **1b** a sudden downpour of heavy rain. **2** a pipe or channel through which water is discharged.

water table *n* **1** the level below which the ground is saturated with water. **2** a string course that has a moulding designed to throw rainwater clear of the wall below.

water thrush *n* either of two North American warblers having brownish backs and striped underparts and occurring near water.

watertight ('wɔːtəˌtaɪt) *adj* **1** not permitting the passage of water either in or out: *a watertight boat*. **2** without loopholes: *a watertight argument*. **3** kept separate from other subjects or influences.

water tower ('taʊə) *n* a reservoir or storage tank mounted on a tower-like structure so that water can be distributed at a uniform pressure.

water vapour *n* water in the gaseous state, esp. when due to evaporation at a temperature below the boiling point.

water vole *n* a large amphibious vole of Eurasian river banks. Also called: **water rat**.

water wagtail *n* another name for **pied wagtail**.

waterway ('wɔːtəˌweɪ) *n* a river, canal, or other navigable channel used as a means of travel or transport.

waterweed ('wɔːtəˌwiːd) *n* any of various weedy aquatic plants.

water wheel *n* **1** a simple water-driven turbine consisting of a wheel having vanes set axially across its rim, used to drive machinery. **2** a wheel with buckets attached to its rim for raising water from a stream, pond, etc.

water wings *pl n* an inflatable rubber device shaped like a pair of wings, which is placed under the arms of a person learning to swim.

waterworks ('wɔːtəˌwɜːks) *n* **1** (*functioning as sing*) an establishment for storing, purifying, and distributing water for community supply. **2** (*functioning as pl*) a display of water in movement, as in fountains. **3** (*functioning as pl*) *Brit. inf., euphemistic.* the urinary system. **4** (*functioning as pl*) *Inf.* crying; tears.

waterworn ('wɔːtəˌwɔːn) *adj* worn smooth by the action or passage of water.

watery ('wɔːtərɪ) *adj* **1** relating to, containing, or resembling water. **2** discharging or secreting water or a water-like fluid. **3** tearful; weepy. **4** insipid, thin, or weak.

Watford ★ ('wɒtfəd) *n* a town in SE England, in SW Hertfordshire: printing. Pop.: 113 080 (1991).

Watling Island ★ ('wɒtlɪŋ) *n* another name for **San Salvador Island.**

Watson ★ ('wɒtsən) *n* **1 James Dewey.** born 1928, US biologist, who contributed to the discovery of the helical structure of DNA: shared the Nobel prize for physiology or medicine 1962. **2 John Broadus** ('brɔːdəs). 1878–1958, US psychologist; a leading exponent of behaviourism. **3 John Christian.** 1867–1941, Australian statesman, born in Chile: prime minister (1904). **4 Tom,** full name *Thomas Sturges Watson.* born 1949, US golfer.

Watson-Watt ★ ('wɒtsən'wɒt) *n* Sir **Robert Alexander.** 1892–1973, Scottish physicist, who helped to develop radar.

watt (wɒt) *n* the derived SI unit of power, equal to 1 joule per second; the power dissipated by a current of 1 ampere flowing across a potential difference of 1 volt. Symbol: W ORIG C19: after J. WATT

Watt ★ (wɒt) *n* **James.** 1736–1819, Scottish engineer. His improvements to the steam engine led to the use of steam power in industry.

wattage ('wɒtɪdʒ) *n* **1** power, esp. electric power, measured in watts. **2** the power rating, measured in watts, of an electrical appliance.

Watteau ★ ('wɒtəʊ; *French* vato) *n* **Jean-Antoine** (ʒɑ̃ ɑ̃twan). 1684–1721, French painter, esp. of *fêtes champêtres.*

Wattenscheid ★ (*German* 'vatənʃait) *n* an industrial town in NW Germany, in North Rhine-Westphalia east of Essen. Pop.: 81 200 (latest est.).

watt-hour *n* a unit of energy equal to a power of one watt operating for one hour.

wattle ('wɒtᵊl) *n* **1** a frame of rods or stakes interwoven with twigs, branches, etc., esp. when used to make fences. **2** the material used in such a construction. **3** a loose fold of skin, often brightly coloured, hanging from the neck or throat of certain birds, lizards, etc. **4** any of various chiefly Australian acacia trees having spikes of small brightly coloured flowers and flexible branches. ◆ *vb* **wattles, wattling, wattled.** (*tr*) **5** to construct from wattle. **6** to bind or frame with wattle. **7** to weave or twist (branches, twigs, etc.) into a frame. ◆ *adj* **8** made of, formed by, or covered with wattle. ORIG OE *watol*
▸ '**wattled** *adj*

wattle and daub *n* a form of wall construction consisting of interwoven twigs plastered with a mixture of clay, water, and sometimes chopped straw.

wattmeter ('wɒtˌmiːtə) *n* a meter for measuring electric power in watts.

Watts ★ (wɒts) *n* **1 George Frederick.** 1817–1904, British painter and sculptor. **2 Isaac.** 1674–1748, English hymn-writer.

Waugh ★ (wɔː) *n* **Evelyn** (**Arthur St John**) ('iːvlɪn). 1903–66, British novelist. His novels include *Decline and Fall* (1928), *A Handful of Dust* (1934), *Brideshead Revisited* (1945), and the World War II trilogy *Sword of Honour* (1952–61).

waul *or* **wawl** (wɔːl) *vb* (*intr*) to cry or wail plaintively like a cat. ORIG C16: imit.

wave (weɪv) *vb* **waves, waving, waved. 1** to move or cause to move freely to and fro: *the banner waved in the wind.* **2** (*intr*) to move the hand to and fro as a greeting. **3** to signal or signify by or as if by waving something. **4** (*tr*) to direct to move by or as if by waving something: *he waved me on.* **5** to form or be formed into curves, undulations, etc. **6** (*tr*) to set waves in (the hair). ◆ *n* **7** one of a sequence of ridges or undulations that moves across the surface of a body of a liquid, esp. the sea. **8 the waves.** the sea. **9** any undulation on or at the edge of a surface reminiscent of a wave in the sea: *a wave across the field of corn.* **10** anything that suggests the movement of a wave, as by a sudden rise: *a crime wave.* **11** a widespread movement that advances in a body: *a wave of settlers.* **12** the act or an instance of waving. **13** *Physics.* an energy-carrying disturbance propagated through a medium or space by a progressive local displacement of the medium or a change in its physical properties, but without any overall movement of matter. **14** *Physics.* a graphical representation of a wave obtained by plotting the magnitude of the disturbance against time at a particular point in the medium or space. **15** a prolonged spell of some particular type of weather: *a heat wave.* **16** an undulating curve or series of curves or loose curls in the hair. **17 make waves.** to cause trouble; disturb the status quo. ORIG OE *wafian* (vb); C16 (n) changed from earlier *wāwe,* prob. from OE *wǣg* motion
▸ '**waveless** *adj* ▸ '**waveˌlike** *adj*

waveband ('weɪvˌbænd) *n* a range of wavelengths or frequencies used for a particular type of radio transmission.

wave-cut platform *n* a flat surface at the base of a cliff formed by erosion by waves.

wave down *vb* (*tr, adv*) to signal with a wave to (a driver or vehicle) to stop.

wave energy *n* energy obtained by harnessing wave power.

wave equation *n Physics.* a partial differential equation describing wave motion.

waveform ('weɪvˌfɔːm) *n Physics.* the shape of the graph of a wave or oscillation obtained by plotting the value of some changing quantity against time.

wavefront ('weɪvˌfrʌnt) *n Physics.* a surface associated with a propagating wave and passing through all points in the wave that have the same phase.

wave function *n Physics.* a mathematical function of position and sometimes time, used in wave mechanics to describe the state of a physical system. Symbol: ψ

waveguide ('weɪvˌgaɪd) *n Electronics.* a solid rod of dielectric or a hollow metal tube, usually of rectangular cross section, used as a path to guide microwaves.

wavelength ('weɪvˌlɛŋθ) *n* **1** the distance, measured in the direction of propagation, between two points of the same phase in consecutive cycles of a wave. Symbol: λ **2** the wavelength of the carrier wave used by a particular broadcasting station. **3 on someone's** (*or* **the same**) **wavelength.** *Inf.* having similar views, feelings, or thoughts (as someone else).

wavelet ('weɪvlɪt) *n* a small wave.

Wavell ★ ('weɪvᵊl) *n* **Archibald** (**Percival**), 1st Earl. 1883–1950, British field marshal. During World War II he was commander in chief in the Middle East (1939–41), commander in chief in India (1941–43), and viceroy of India (1943–47).

wave mechanics *n* (*functioning as sing*) *Physics.* the formulation of quantum mechanics in which the behaviour of systems, such as atoms, is described in terms of their wave functions.

wave number *n Physics.* the reciprocal of the wavelength of a wave.

waver ('weɪvə) *vb* (*intr*) **1** to be irresolute; hesitate between two possibilities. **2** to become unsteady. **3** to fluctuate. **4** to move back and forth or one way and another. **5** (of light) to flicker or flash. ◆ *n* **6** the act or an instance of wavering. ORIG C14: from ON *vafra* to flicker
▸ '**waverer** *n* ▸ '**wavering** *adj* ▸ '**waveringly** *adv*

wave theory *n* **1** the theory proposed by Huygens that light is transmitted by waves. **2** any theory that light or other radiation is transmitted as waves. ◆ Cf. **corpuscular theory.**

wavey ('weɪvɪ) *n Canad.* a snow goose or other wild

goose. Also called: **wawa.** ORIG via Canad. F from Algonquian (Cree *wehwew*)

wavy ('weɪvɪ) *adj* **wavier, waviest. 1** abounding in or full of waves. **2** moving or proceeding in waves. **3** (of hair) set in or having waves.
▸ **'wavily** *adv* ▸ **'waviness** *n*

wax[1] (wæks) *n* **1** any of various viscous or solid materials of natural origin: characteristically lustrous, insoluble in water, and having a low softening temperature, they consist largely of esters of fatty acids. **2** any of various similar substances, such as paraffin wax, that have a mineral origin and consist largely of hydrocarbons. **3** short for **beeswax** or **sealing wax. 4** *Physiol.* another name for **cerumen. 5** a resinous preparation used by shoemakers to rub on thread. **6** any substance or object that is pliable or easily moulded: *he was wax in their hands.* **7** (*modifier*) made of or resembling wax: *a wax figure.* ◆ *vb* **8** (*tr*) to coat, polish, etc., with wax. ORIG OE *weax*
▸ **'waxer** *n*

wax[2] (wæks) *vb* (*intr*) **1** to become larger, more powerful, etc. **2** (of the moon) to show a gradually increasing portion of illuminated surface, between new moon and full moon. **3** to become: *to wax eloquent.* ORIG OE *weaxan*

wax[3] (wæks) *n Brit. inf., old-fashioned.* a fit of rage or temper: *he's in a wax today.* ORIG from ?

waxberry ('wæksbərɪ) *n, pl* **waxberries.** the waxy fruit of the wax myrtle or the snowberry.

waxbill ('wæks,bɪl) *n* any of various chiefly African finchlike weaverbirds having a brightly coloured bill and plumage.

wax cloth *n* **1** another name for **oilcloth. 2** (formerly) another name for **linoleum.**

waxen ('wæksən) *adj* **1** made of, treated with, or covered with wax. **2** resembling wax in colour or texture.

waxeye ('wæks,aɪ) *n* a small New Zealand bird with a white circle around its eye. Also called: **silver-eye, blighty.**

wax flower *n Austral.* any of a genus of shrubs having waxy pink-white five-petalled flowers.

wax light *n* a candle or taper of wax.

wax myrtle *n* a shrub of SE North America, having evergreen leaves and a small berry-like fruit with a waxy coating. Also called: **bayberry, candleberry, waxberry.**

wax palm *n* **1** a tall Andean palm tree having pinnate leaves that yield a resinous wax used in making candles. **2** another name for **carnauba** (sense 1).

wax paper *n* paper treated or coated with wax or paraffin to make it waterproof.

waxplant ('wæks,plɑ:nt) *n* a climbing shrub of E Asia and Australia, having fleshy leaves and clusters of small waxy white pink-centred flowers.

waxwing ('wæks,wɪŋ) *n* any of a genus of gregarious passerine songbirds having red waxy wing tips and crested heads.

waxwork ('wæks,wɜ:k) *n* **1** an object reproduced in wax, esp. as an ornament. **2** a life-size lifelike figure, esp. of a famous person, reproduced in wax. **3** (*pl; functioning as sing or pl*) a museum or exhibition of wax figures.

waxy[1] ('wæksɪ) *adj* **waxier, waxiest. 1** resembling wax in colour, appearance, or texture. **2** made of, covered with, or abounding in wax.
▸ **'waxily** *adv* ▸ **'waxiness** *n*

waxy[2] ('wæksɪ) *adj* **waxier, waxiest.** *Brit. inf., old-fashioned.* bad-tempered or irritable; angry.

way (weɪ) *n* **1** a manner, method, or means: *a way of life.* **2** a route or direction: *the way home.* **3a** a means or line of passage, such as a path or track. **3b** (*in combination*): *waterway.* **4** space or room for movement or activity (esp. in **make way, in the way, out of the way**). **5** distance, usually distance in general: *you've come a long way.* **6** a passage or journey: *on the way.* **7** characteristic style or manner: *I did it my way.* **8** (*often pl*) habit: *he has some offensive ways.* **9** an aspect of something; particular: *in many ways he was right.* **10a** a street in or leading out of a town. **10b** (*cap. when part of a street name*): *Icknield Way.* **11** something that one wants in a determined manner (esp. in **get** *or* **have one's** (**own**) **way**). **12** the experience or sphere in which one comes into contact with things (esp. in **come one's way**). **13** *Inf.* a state or condition, usually financial or concerning health (esp. in **in a good** (*or* **bad**) **way**). **14** *Inf.* the area or direction of one's home: *drop in if you're ever over my way.* **15** movement of a ship or other vessel. **16** a guide along which something can be moved, such as the surface of a lathe along which the tailstock slides. **17** (*pl*) the wooden or metal tracks down which a ship slides to be launched. **18** a course of life including experiences, conduct, etc.: *the way of sin.* **19 by the way.** incidentally. **20 by way of. 20a** via. **20b** serving as: *by way of introduction.* **20c** in the state or condition of: *by way of being an artist.* **21 each way.** (of a bet) laid on a horse, dog, etc., to win or gain a place. **22 give way. 22a** to collapse or break down. **22b** to yield. **23 give way to. 23a** to step aside for or stop for. **23b** to give full rein to (emotions, etc.). **24 go out of one's way.** to take considerable trouble or inconvenience oneself. **25 have a way with.** to have such a manner or skill as to handle successfully. **26 have it both ways.** to enjoy two things that would normally be mutually exclusive. **27 in a way.** in some respects. **28 in no way.** not at all. **29 lead the way. 29a** to go first. **29b** to set an example. **30 make one's way. 30a** to proceed or advance. **30b** to achieve success in life. **31 on the way out.** *Inf.* **31a** becoming unfashionable, etc. **31b** dying. **32 out of the way. 32a** removed or dealt with so as to be no longer a hindrance. **32b** remote. **32c** unusual and sometimes improper. **33 see one's way** (**clear**). to find it possible and be willing (to do something). **34 under way.** having started moving or making progress. ◆ *adv* **35** *Inf.* **35a** at a considerable distance or extent: *way over yonder.* **35b** very far: *they're way up the mountain.* **36** *Inf.* by far; considerably: *way better.* ORIG OE *weg*

waybill ('weɪ,bɪl) *n* a document attached to goods in transit specifying their nature, point of origin, and destination as well as the route to be taken and the rate to be charged.

wayfarer ('weɪ,fɛərə) *n* a person who goes on a journey.
▸ **'way,faring** *n, adj*

wayfaring tree *n* a shrub of Europe and W Asia, having white flowers and berries that turn from red to black.

Wayland *or* **Wayland Smith** ★ ('weɪlənd) *n* a smith, artificer, and king of the elves in European folklore. Scandinavian name: **Völund.** German name: **Wieland.**

waylay (weɪ'leɪ) *vb* **waylays, waylaying, waylaid.** (*tr*) **1** to lie in wait for and attack. **2** to await and intercept unexpectedly.
▸ **way'layer** *n*

wayleave ('weɪ,li:v) *n* access to property granted by a landowner for payment, for example to allow a contractor access to a building site.

waymark ('weɪ,mɑ:k) *n* a symbol or signpost marking the route of a footpath.
▸ **'way,marked** *adj*

Wayne ★ (weɪn) *n* **John,** real name *Marion Michael Morrison.* 1907–79, US film actor, esp. in Westerns.

way-out *adj Inf.* **1** extremely unconventional or experimental. **2** excellent or amazing.

-ways *suffix forming adverbs.* indicating direction or manner: *sideways.* ORIG OE *weges,* lit.: of the way, from *weg* way

ways and means *pl n* **1** the revenues and methods of raising the revenues needed for the functioning of a state or other political unit. **2** the methods and resources for accomplishing some purpose.

wayside ('weɪ,saɪd) *n* **1a** the side or edge of a road. **1b** (*modifier*) situated by the wayside: *a wayside inn.* **2 fall by the wayside.** to cease or fail to continue doing something: *of the nine starters, three fell by the wayside.*

wayward ('weɪwəd) *adj* **1** wanting to have one's own way regardless of others. **2** capricious, erratic, or unpredictable. ORIG C14: changed from *awayward* turned or turning away
▸ **'waywardly** *adv* ▸ **'waywardness** *n*

wayworn ('weɪ,wɔ:n) *adj Rare.* worn or tired by travel.

Waziristan ★ (wə,zɪərɪ'stɑ:n) *n* a mountainous region of N Pakistan, on the border with Afghanistan.

wb *abbrev. for:* **1** water ballast. **2** Also: **W/B, WB.** waybill. **3** westbound.

Wb *Physics. symbol for* weber.

WBA *abbrev. for* World Boxing Association.

WBC *abbrev. for* World Boxing Council.

WBU *abbrev. for* World Boxing Union.

WC *abbrev. for:* **1** Also: **wc.** water closet. **2** (in London postal code) West Central.

WD *abbrev. for:* **1** War Department. **2** Works Department.

we (wiː) *pron* (*subjective*) **1** refers to the speaker or writer and another person or other people: *we should go now.* **2** refers to all people or people in general: *the planet on which we live.* **3** a formal word for **I** used by editors or other writers, and formerly by monarchs. **4** *Inf.* used instead of *you* with a tone of condescension or sarcasm: *how are we today?* ORIG OE *wē*

WEA (in Britain) *abbrev. for* Workers' Educational Association.

weak (wiːk) *adj* **1** lacking in physical or mental strength or force. **2** liable to yield, break, or give way: *a weak link in a chain.* **3** lacking in resolution or firmness of character. **4** lacking strength, power, or intensity: *a weak voice.* **5** lacking strength in a particular part: *a team weak in defence.* **6a** not functioning as well as is normal: *weak eyes.* **6b** easily upset: *a weak stomach.* **7** lacking in conviction, persuasiveness, etc.: *a weak argument.* **8** lacking in political or strategic strength: *a weak state.* **9** lacking the usual, full, or desirable strength of flavour: *weak tea.* **10** *Grammar.* **10a** denoting or belonging to a class of verbs, in Germanic languages, whose conjugation relies on inflectional endings rather than internal vowel gradation, as *look, looks, looking, looked.* **10b** belonging to any part-of-speech class, in any of various languages, whose inflections follow the more regular of two possible patterns. Cf. **strong** (sense 13). **11** (of a syllable) not accented or stressed. **12** (of an industry, market, securities, etc.) falling in price or characterized by falling prices. ORIG OE *wāc* soft, miserable
▸ **'weakish** *adj*

weaken ('wiːkən) *vb* to become or cause to become weak or weaker.
▸ **'weakener** *n*

weakest link *n* **the.** the person who is making the least contribution to the collective achievement of a group. ORIG C21: from the Brit. television quiz programme of the same name

weak interaction *n Physics.* an interaction between elementary particles that is responsible for certain decay processes, operates at distances less than about 10^{-15} metres, and is 10^{12} times weaker than the strong interaction. Also called: **weak nuclear interaction** *or* **force.**

weak-kneed *adj Inf.* yielding readily to force, intimidation, etc.
▸ **,weak-'kneedly** *adv*

weakling ('wiːklɪŋ) *n* a person or animal that is lacking in strength or weak in constitution or character.

weakly ('wiːklɪ) *adj* **weaklier, weakliest. 1** sickly; feeble. ◆ *adv* **2** in a weak or feeble manner.

weak-minded *adj* **1** lacking in stability of mind or character. **2** another word for **feeble-minded.**
▸ **,weak-'mindedly** *adv* ▸ **,weak-'mindedness** *n*

weakness ('wiːknɪs) *n* **1** a being weak. **2** a failing, as in a person's character. **3** a self-indulgent liking: *a weakness for chocolates.*

weal[1] (wiːl) *n* a raised mark on the skin produced by a blow. Also called: **welt.** ORIG C19: var. of WALE, infl. in form by WHEAL

weal[2] (wiːl) *n Arch.* prosperity or wellbeing (now esp. in **the public weal, the common weal**). ORIG OE *wela*

weald (wiːld) *n Brit. arch.* open or forested country. ORIG OE

Weald ★ (wiːld) *n* **the.** a region of SE England, in Kent, Surrey, and Sussex between the North Downs and the South Downs: formerly forested.

wealth (wɛlθ) *n* **1** a large amount of money and valuable material possessions. **2** the state of being rich. **3** a great profusion: *a wealth of gifts.* **4** *Econ.* all goods and services with monetary or productive value. ORIG C13 *welthe,* from WEAL[2]

wealth tax *n* a tax on personal property.

wealthy ('wɛlθɪ) *adj* **wealthier, wealthiest. 1** possessing wealth; rich. **2** of or relating to wealth. **3** abounding: *wealthy in friends.*
▸ **'wealthily** *adv* ▸ **'wealthiness** *n*

wean[1] (wiːn) *vb* (*tr*) **1** to cause (a child or young mammal) to replace mother's milk by other nourishment. **2** (usually foll. by *from*) to cause to desert former habits, pursuits, etc. ORIG OE *wenian* to accustom

wean[2] (weɪn) *n Scot. & N English dialect.* a child. ORIG ? short form of WEANLING, or a contraction of *wee ane*

weaner ('wiːnə) *n* **1** a person or thing that weans. **2** a pig that has just been weaned and weighs less than 40 kg. **3** *Austral. & NZ.* a lamb, pig, or calf in the year in which it is weaned.

weanling ('wiːnlɪŋ) *n* a child or young animal recently weaned. ORIG C16: from WEAN[1] + -LING[1]

weapon ('wɛpən) *n* **1** an object or instrument used in fighting. **2** anything that serves to get the better of an opponent: *his power of speech was his best weapon.* **3** any part of an animal that is used to defend itself, to attack prey, etc., such as claws or a sting. ORIG OE *wǣpen*
▸ **'weaponed** *adj* ▸ **'weaponless** *adj*

weaponry ('wɛpənrɪ) *n* weapons regarded collectively.

wear[1] (wɛə) *vb* **wears, wearing, wore, worn. 1** (*tr*) to carry or have (a garment, etc.) on one's person as clothing, ornament, etc. **2** (*tr*) to carry or have on one's person habitually: *she wears a lot of red.* **3** (*tr*) to have in one's aspect: *to wear a smile.* **4** (*tr*) to display, show, or fly: *a ship wears its colours.* **5** to deteriorate or cause to deteriorate by constant use or action. **6** to produce or be produced by constant rubbing, scraping, etc.: *to wear a hole in one's trousers.* **7** to bring or be brought to a specified condition by constant use or action: *to wear a tyre to shreds.* **8** (*intr*) to submit to constant use or action in a specified way: *his suit wears well.* **9** (*tr*) to harass or weaken. **10** (when *intr,* often foll. by *on*) (of time) to pass or be passed slowly. **11** (*tr*) *Brit. inf.* to accept: *Larry won't wear that argument.* ◆ *n* **12** the act of wearing or state of being worn. **13a** anything designed to be worn: *leisure wear.* **13b** (*in combination*): *nightwear.* **14** deterioration from constant or normal use. **15** the quality of resisting the effects of constant use. ◆ See also **wear down, wear off, wear out.** ORIG OE *werian*
▸ **'wearer** *n*

wear[2] (wɛə) *vb* **wears, wearing, wore, worn.** *Naut.* to tack by gybing instead of by going through stays. ORIG C17: from earlier *weare,* from ?

Wear ★ (wɪə) *n* a river in NE England, rising in NW Durham and flowing southeast then northeast to the North Sea at Sunderland. Length: 105 km (65 miles).

wearable ('wɛərəbᵊl) *adj* suitable for wear or able to be worn.
▸ **,weara'bility** *n*

wear and tear *n* damage, depreciation, or loss resulting from ordinary use.

wear down *vb* (*adv*) **1** to consume or be consumed by long or constant wearing, rubbing, etc. **2** to overcome or be overcome gradually by persistent effort.

wearing ('wɛərɪŋ) *adj* causing fatigue or exhaustion; tiring.
▸ **'wearingly** *adv*

wearisome ('wɪərɪsəm) *adj* causing fatigue or annoyance; tedious.
▸ **'wearisomely** *adv*

wear off *vb* (*adv*) **1** (*intr*) to decrease in intensity gradually: *the pain will wear off in an hour.* **2** to disappear or cause to disappear gradually through exposure, use, etc.

wear out *vb* (*adv*) **1** to make or become unfit or useless through wear. **2** (*tr*) to exhaust or tire.

weary ('wɪərɪ) *adj* **wearier, weariest. 1** tired or exhausted. **2** causing fatigue or exhaustion. **3** caused by or suggestive of weariness: *a weary laugh.* **4** (*postpositive;* often foll. by *of* or *with*) discontented or bored. ◆ *vb* **wearies, wearying, wearied. 5** to make or become weary. **6** to make or become discontented or impatient. ORIG OE *wērig*
▸ **'weariless** *adj* ▸ **'wearily** *adv* ▸ **'weariness** *n* ▸ **'wearying** *adj* ▸ **'wearyingly** *adv*

★ people and places

weasand ('wi:zənd) *n* a former name for the **trachea**. ORIG OE *wǣsend, wāsend*

weasel ('wi:zᵊl) *n, pl* **weasels** *or* **weasel. 1** any of various small predatory mammals, such as the **European weasel**, having reddish-brown fur, an elongated body and neck, and short legs. **2** *Inf.* a sly or treacherous person. ORIG OE *weosule, wesle*
▸ '**weaselly** *adj*

weasel out *vb* **weasels, weaselling, weaselled** *or US* **weasels, weaseling, weaseled.** (*intr, adv*) *Inf., chiefly US & Canad.* **1** to go back on a commitment. **2** to evade a responsibility, esp. in a despicable manner.

weasel words *pl n Inf.* intentionally evasive or misleading speech; equivocation. ORIG C20: from the weasel's supposed ability to suck an egg out of its shell without seeming to break the shell

weather ('wɛðə) *n* **1a** the day-to-day meteorological conditions, esp. temperature, cloudiness, and rainfall, affecting a specific place. **1b** (*modifier*) relating to the forecasting of weather: *a weather ship.* **2 make heavy weather. 2a** *Naut.* to roll and pitch in heavy seas. **2b** (foll. by *of*) *Inf.* to carry out with difficulty or unnecessarily great effort. **3 under the weather.** *Inf.* not in good health. ◆ *adj* **4** (*prenominal*) on or at the side or part towards the wind: *the weather anchor.* Cf. **lee** (sense 2). ◆ *vb* **5** to expose or be exposed to the action of the weather. **6** to undergo or cause to undergo changes, such as discoloration, due to the action of the weather. **7** (*intr*) to withstand the action of the weather. **8** (when *intr*, foll. by *through*) to endure (a crisis, danger, etc.). **9** (*tr*) to slope (a surface, such as a roof) so as to throw rainwater clear. **10** (*tr*) to sail to the windward of: *to weather a point.* ORIG OE *weder*
▸ '**weatherer** *n*

weather-beaten *adj* **1** showing signs of exposure to the weather. **2** tanned or hardened by exposure to the weather.

weatherboard ('wɛðəˌbɔ:d) *n* a timber board, with a groove (rabbet) along the front of its top edge and along the back of its lower edge, that is fixed horizontally with others to form an exterior covering on a wall or roof.
▸ '**weatherˌboarding** *n*

weather-bound *adj* (of a vessel, aircraft, etc.) delayed by bad weather.

weathercock ('wɛðəˌkɒk) *n* **1** a weather vane in the form of a cock. **2** a person who is fickle or changeable.

weathered ('wɛðəd) *adj* **1** affected by exposure to the action of the weather. **2** (of rocks and rock formations) eroded, decomposed, or otherwise altered by the action of wind, frost, etc. **3** (of a sill, roof, etc.) having a sloped surface so as to allow rainwater to run off.

weather eye *n* **1** the vision of a person trained to observe changes in the weather. **2** *Inf.* an alert or observant gaze. **3 keep one's weather eye open.** to stay on the alert.

weatherglass ('wɛðəˌglɑ:s) *n* any of various instruments, esp. a barometer, that measure atmospheric conditions.

weather house *n* a model house, usually with two human figures, one that comes out to foretell bad weather and one that comes out to foretell good weather.

weathering ('wɛðərɪŋ) *n* the mechanical and chemical breakdown of rocks by the action of rain, snow, etc.

weatherly ('wɛðəlɪ) *adj* (of a sailing vessel) making very little leeway when close-hauled, even in a stiff breeze.
▸ '**weatherliness** *n*

weatherman ('wɛðəˌmæn) *n, pl* **weathermen.** *Inf.* a person who forecasts the weather, esp. one who works in a meteorological office.

weather map *or* **chart** *n* a chart showing weather conditions, compiled from simultaneous observations taken at various weather stations.

weatherproof ('wɛðəˌpru:f) *adj* **1** designed or able to withstand exposure to weather without deterioration. ◆ *vb* **2** (*tr*) to render (something) weatherproof.

weather station *n* one of a network of meteorological observation posts where weather data is recorded.

weather strip *n* a thin strip of compressible material, such as spring metal, felt, etc., that is fitted between the frame of a door or window and the opening part to exclude wind and rain. Also called: **weatherstripping.**

weather vane *n* a vane designed to indicate the direction in which the wind is blowing.

weather window *n* a limited interval when weather conditions can be expected to be suitable for a particular project.

weather-wise *adj* **1** skilful in predicting weather conditions. **2** skilful in predicting trends in opinion, reactions, etc.

weatherworn ('wɛðəˌwɔ:n) *adj* another word for **weather-beaten.**

weave (wi:v) *vb* **weaves, weaving, wove** *or* **weaved; woven** *or* **weaved. 1** to form (a fabric) by interlacing (yarn, etc.), esp. on a loom. **2** (*tr*) to make or construct by such a process: *to weave a shawl.* **3** to construct by interlacing (cane, twigs, etc.). **4** (of a spider) to make (a web). **5** (*tr*) to construct by combining separate elements into a whole. **6** (*tr;* often foll. by *in, into, through,* etc.) to introduce: *to weave factual details into a fiction.* **7** to create (a way, etc.) by moving from side to side: *to weave through a crowd.* **8** to interlace strands of artificial hair with natural hair in order to make it look more abundant. **9 get weaving.** *Inf.* to hurry. ◆ *n* **10** the method or pattern of weaving or the structure of a woven fabric: *an open weave.* ORIG OE *wefan*

weaver ('wi:və) *n* **1** a person who weaves, esp. as a means of livelihood. **2** short for **weaverbird.**

Weaver ★ ('wi:və) *n* **Sigourney** (sɪ'gɔ:nɪ). born 1949, US actress. Her films include *Alien* (1979) and its sequels, *Ghostbusters* (1984), *Gorillas in the Mist* (1988), and *The Ice Storm* (1997).

weaverbird ('wi:vəˌbɜ:d) *or* **weaver** *n* any of a family of small Old World passerine songbirds, having a short thick bill and a dull plumage and building covered nests: includes the house sparrow and whydahs.

weave-ons *pl n* strands of hair used to add length to natural hair.

web (wɛb) *n* **1** any structure, fabric, etc., formed by or as if by weaving or interweaving. **2** a mesh of fine tough threads built by a spider from a liquid secreted from its spinnerets and used to trap insects. **3** a similar network of threads spun by certain insect larvae, such as the silkworm. **4** a fabric, esp. one in the process of being woven. **5** a membrane connecting the toes of some aquatic birds or the digits of such aquatic mammals as the otter. **6** the vane of a bird's feather. **7** a thin piece of metal, esp. one connecting two thicker parts as in an H-beam or an I-beam. **8a** a continuous strip of paper as formed on a paper machine or fed from a reel into some printing presses. **8b** (*as modifier*): *web offset.* **9a** (*often cap.;* preceded by *the*) short for **World Wide Web. 9b** (*as modifier*): *web pages.* **10** any structure, construction, etc., that is intricately formed or complex: *a web of intrigue.* ◆ *vb* **webs, webbing, webbed. 11** (*tr*) to cover with or as if with a web. **12** (*tr*) to entangle or ensnare. **13** (*intr*) to construct a web. ORIG OE *webb*
▸ '**webless** *adj*

Webb ★ (wɛb) *n* **Sidney (James),** Baron Passfield. 1859–1947, British economist and Fabian socialist. He and his wife **(Martha) Beatrice** (née *Potter*), 1858–1943, British writer, collaborated in *The History of Trade Unionism* (1894), helped found the London School of Economics (1895), and started the *New Statesman* (1913).

webbed (wɛbd) *adj* **1** (of the feet of certain animals) having the digits connected by a thin fold of skin. **2** having or resembling a web.

webbing ('wɛbɪŋ) *n* **1** a strong fabric of hemp, cotton, jute, etc., woven in strips and used under springs in upholstery or for straps, etc. **2** the skin that unites the digits of a webbed foot.

webby ('wɛbɪ) *adj* **webbier, webbiest.** of, relating to, resembling, or consisting of a web.

webcam ('wɛbˌkæm) *n* a camera that transmits still or moving images over the Internet.

webcast ('wɛbˌkɑːst) *n* a broadcast of an event over the World Wide Web.

weber ('veɪbə) *n* the derived SI unit of magnetic flux; the flux that, when linking a circuit of one turn, produces in it an emf of 1 volt as it is reduced to zero at a uniform rate in one second. Symbol: Wb ORIG C20: after W. E. WEBER

Weber ★ (*German* 'veːbər) *n* **1** Baron **Carl Maria Friedrich Ernst von** (karl ma'riːa 'friːdrɪç ɛrnst fɔn). 1786–1826, German composer. His operas include *Der Freischütz* (1821) and *Oberon* (1826). **2 Ernst Heinrich** (ɛrnst 'hainrɪç). 1795–1878, German physiologist. **3 Max** (maks). 1864–1920, German economist, known for *The Protestant Ethic and the Spirit of Capitalism* (1904–05). **4 Wilhelm Eduard** ('vɪlhɛlm 'eːduart), brother of Ernst Heinrich Weber. 1804–91, German physicist, who investigated electricity and magnetism.

Webern ★ (*German* 'veːbərn) *n* **Anton von** ('antoːn fɔn). 1883–1945, Austrian composer; pupil of Schoenberg, whose twelve-tone technique he adopted.

webfoot ('wɛbˌfʊt) *n* **1** *Zool.* a foot having the toes connected by folds of skin. **2** *Anat.* a foot having an abnormal membrane connecting adjacent toes.

web-footed *or* **web-toed** *adj* (of certain animals) having webbed feet that facilitate swimming.

webmaster ('wɛbˌmɑːstə) *n Computing.* a person responsible for the administration of a website on the World Wide Web.

website ('wɛbˌsaɪt) *n* a group of connected pages on the World Wide Web containing information on a particular subject.

Webster ★ ('wɛbstə) *n* **1 Daniel.** 1782–1852, US politician. **2 John.** ?1580–?1625, English dramatist, noted for his tragedy *The Duchess of Malfi* (?1613). **3 Noah.** 1758–1843, US lexicographer, known for his *American Dictionary of the English Language* (1828).

webwheel ('wɛbˌwiːl) *n* **1** a wheel containing a plate or web instead of spokes. **2** a wheel of which the rim, spokes, and centre are in one piece.

wed (wɛd) *vb* **weds, wedding, wedded** *or* **wed. 1** to take (a person of the opposite sex) as a husband or wife; marry. **2** (*tr*) to join (two people) in matrimony. **3** (*tr*) to unite closely. ORIG OE *weddian*
▸ '**wedded** *adj*

we'd (wiːd; *unstressed* wɪd) *contraction of* we had *or* we would.

Wed. *abbrev. for* Wednesday.

Weddell Sea ★ ('wɛdᵊl) *n* an arm of the S Atlantic in Antarctica.

wedding ('wɛdɪŋ) *n* **1a** the act of marrying or the celebration of a marriage. **1b** (*as modifier*): *wedding day.* **2** the anniversary of a marriage (in such combinations as **silver wedding** or **diamond wedding**).

wedding breakfast *n* the meal usually served after a wedding ceremony or just before the bride and bridegroom leave for their honeymoon.

wedding cake *n* a rich fruit cake, with one, two, or more tiers, covered with almond paste and decorated with royal icing, which is served at a wedding reception.

wedding ring *n* a band ring with parallel sides, typically of precious metal, worn to indicate married status.

Wedekind ★ (*German* 'veːdəkɪnt) *n* **Frank** (fraŋk). 1864–1918, German dramatist; plays include *The Awakening of Spring* (1891) and *Pandora's Box* (1904).

wedge (wɛdʒ) *n* **1** a block of solid material, esp. wood or metal, that is shaped like a narrow V in cross section and can be pushed or driven between two objects or parts of an object in order to split or secure them. **2** any formation, structure, or substance in the shape of a wedge. **3** something such as an idea, action, etc., that tends to cause division. **4** a shoe with a wedge heel. **5** *Golf.* a club, a No. 10 iron with a face angle of more than 50°, used for bunker or pitch shots. **6** (formerly) a body of troops formed in a V-shape. **7 thin end of the wedge.** anything unimportant in itself that implies the start of something much larger. ◆ *vb* **wedges, wedging, wedged. 8** (*tr*) to secure with or as if with a wedge. **9** to squeeze or be squeezed like a wedge into a narrow space. **10** (*tr*) to force apart or divide with or as if with a wedge. ORIG OE *wecg*
▸ '**wedgeˌlike** *adj* ▸ '**wedgy** *adj*

wedge heel *n* a raised shoe heel with the heel and sole forming a solid block.

wedge-tailed eagle *n* a large brown Australian eagle having a wedge-shaped tail. Also called: **eaglehawk**, (Inf.) **wedgie.**

Wedgwood[1] ('wɛdʒwʊd) *n* **1** *Trademark.* pottery produced at the Wedgwood factories, esp. such pottery having applied classical decoration in white on a blue or other coloured ground. ◆ *adj* **2** relating to or characteristic of such pottery: *Wedgwood blue.*

Wedgwood[2] ★ ('wɛdʒwʊd) *n* **Josiah.** 1730–95, British potter, who founded the Wedgwood pottery works near Stoke-on-Trent in Staffordshire.

wedlock ('wɛdlɒk) *n* **1** the state of being married. **2 born** *or* **conceived out of wedlock.** born or conceived when one's parents are not legally married. ORIG OE *wedlāc,* from *wedd* pledge + *-lāc,* suffix denoting activity, ?from *lāc* game

Wednesday ('wɛnzdɪ) *n* the fourth day of the week; third day of the working week. ORIG OE *Wōdnes dæg* Woden's day, translation of L *mercurii dies* Mercury's day

wee[1] (wiː) *adj* very small; tiny; minute. ORIG C13: from OE *wǣg* weight

wee[2] (wiː) *Inf., chiefly Brit.* ◆ *n* **1a** the act or an instance of urinating. **1b** urine. ◆ *vb* **wees, weeing, weed. 2** (*intr*) to urinate. ◆ Also: **wee-wee.** ORIG from ?

weed (wiːd) *n* **1** any plant that grows wild and profusely, esp. one that grows among cultivated plants, depriving them of space, food, etc. **2** *Sl.* **2a the weed.** tobacco. **2b** marijuana. **3** *Inf.* a thin or unprepossessing person. **4** an inferior horse, esp. one showing signs of weakness. ◆ *vb* **5** to remove (useless or troublesome plants) from (a garden, etc.). ORIG OE *weod*
▸ '**weeder** *n* ▸ '**weedless** *adj*

weedkiller ('wiːdˌkɪlə) *n* a substance, usually a chemical or hormone, used for killing weeds.

weed out *vb* (*tr, adv*) to separate out, remove, or eliminate (anything unwanted): *to weed out troublesome students.*

weeds (wiːdz) *pl n* a widow's black mourning clothes. Also called: **widow's weeds.** ORIG C16: pl of *weed* (OE *wǣd, wēd*) a band worn in mourning

weedy ('wiːdɪ) *adj* **weedier, weediest. 1** full of or containing weeds: *weedy land.* **2** (of a plant) resembling a weed in straggling growth. **3** *Inf.* thin or weakly in appearance.

week (wiːk) *n* **1** a period of seven consecutive days, esp. one beginning with Sunday. Related adj: **hebdomadal. 2** a period of seven consecutive days beginning from or including a specified day: *a week from Wednesday.* **3** the period of time within a week devoted to work. ◆ *adv* **4** *Chiefly Brit.* seven days before or after a specified day: *I'll visit you Wednesday week.* ORIG OE *wice, wicu*

weekday ('wiːkˌdeɪ) *n* any day of the week other than Sunday and, often, Saturday.

weekend *n* (ˌwiːk'ɛnd). **1a** the end of the week, esp. the period from Friday night until the end of Sunday. **1b** (*as modifier*): *a weekend party.* ◆ *vb* ('wiːkˌɛnd). **2** (*intr*) *Inf.* to spend or pass a weekend.

weekends (ˌwiːk'ɛndz) *adv Inf.* at the weekend, esp. regularly or during every weekend.

weekly ('wiːklɪ) *adj* **1** happening or taking place once a week or every week. **2** determined or calculated by the week. ◆ *adv* **3** once a week or every week. ◆ *n, pl* **weeklies. 4** a newspaper or magazine issued every week.

weeknight ('wiːkˌnaɪt) *n* the evening or night of a weekday.

Weelkes ★ (wiːlks) *n* **Thomas.** ?1575–1623, English composer of madrigals.

ween (wiːn) *vb Arch.* to think or imagine (something). ORIG OE *wēnan*

weeny ('wiːnɪ) *adj* **weenier, weeniest.** *Inf.* very small; tiny. ORIG C18: from WEE[1] with the ending *-ny* as in TINY

weenybopper ('wiːnɪˌbɒpə) *n Inf.* a child of about 8 to 12 years who is a keen follower of pop music. ORIG C20: formed on the model of TEENYBOPPER, from WEENY

weep (wiːp) *vb* **weeps, weeping, wept. 1** to shed (tears). **2** (*tr;* foll. by *out*) to utter, shedding tears. **3** (when *intr,* foll. by *for*) to lament (for something). **4** to exude (drops of liquid). **5** (*intr*) (of a wound, etc.) to exude a watery fluid. ◆ *n* **6** a spell of weeping. ORIG OE *wēpan*

weeper ('wiːpə) *n* **1** a person who weeps, esp. a hired mourner. **2** something worn as a sign of mourning.

weeping ('wiːpɪŋ) *adj* (of plants) having slender hanging branches.
▸ **'weepingly** *adv*

weeping willow *n* a Chinese willow tree having long hanging branches.

weepy ('wiːpɪ) *Inf.* ◆ *adj* **weepier, weepiest. 1** liable or tending to weep. ◆ *n, pl* **weepies. 2** a sentimental film or book.
▸ **'weepily** *adv* ▸ **'weepiness** *n*

weever ('wiːvə) *n* a small marine fish having venomous spines around the gills and the dorsal fin. ORIG C17: from OF *wivre* viper, ult. from L *vīpera* VIPER

weevil ('wiːvɪl) *n* any of numerous beetles, many having elongated snouts, that are pests, feeding on plants and plant products. ORIG OE *wifel*
▸ **'weevily** *adj*

wee-wee *n, vb* a variant of **wee**[2].

w.e.f. *abbrev. for* with effect from.

weft (wɛft) *n* the yarn woven across the width of the fabric through the lengthways warp yarn. Also called: **filling, woof.** ORIG OE

Wegener ★ (*German* 'veːgənər) *n* **Alfred** ('alfreːt). 1880–1930, German meteorologist.

Weichsel ★ ('vaiksəl) *n* the German name for the **Vistula** (sense 1).

weigela (waɪ'giːlə, -'dʒiː-) *n* a shrub of an Asian genus having clusters of showy bell-shaped flowers. ORIG C19: from NL, after C. E. *Weigel* (1748–1831), G physician

weigh[1] (weɪ) *vb* **1** (*tr*) to measure the weight of. **2** (*intr*) to have weight: *she weighs more than her sister.* **3** (*tr;* often foll. by *out*) to apportion according to weight. **4** (*tr*) to consider carefully: *to weigh the facts of a case.* **5** (*intr*) to be influential: *his words weighed little with the jury.* **6** (*intr;* often foll. by *on*) to be oppressive (to). **7 weigh anchor.** to raise a vessel's anchor or (of a vessel) to have its anchor raised preparatory to departure. ◆ See also **weigh down, weigh in,** etc. ORIG OE *wegan*
▸ **'weighable** *adj* ▸ **'weigher** *n*

weigh[2] (weɪ) *n* **under weigh.** a variant spelling of **under way.** ORIG C18: var. due to the infl. of phrases such as *to weigh anchor*

weighbridge ('weɪˌbrɪdʒ) *n* a machine for weighing vehicles, etc., by means of a metal plate set into a road.

weigh down *vb* (*adv*) to press (a person, etc.) down by or as if by weight: *his troubles weighed him down.*

weigh in *vb* (*intr, adv*) **1a** (of a boxer or wrestler) to be weighed before a bout. **1b** (of a jockey) to be weighed after, or sometimes before, a race. **2** *Inf.* to contribute, as in a discussion, etc.: *he weighed in with a few sharp comments.* ◆ *n* **weigh-in. 3** the act of checking a competitor's weight, as in boxing, racing, etc.

weight (weɪt) *n* **1** a measure of the heaviness of an object; the amount anything weighs. **2** *Physics.* the vertical force experienced by a mass as a result of gravitation. **3** a system of units used to express weight: *troy weight.* **4** a unit used to measure weight: *the kilogram is the weight used in the metric system.* **5** any mass or heavy object used to exert pressure or weigh down. **6** an oppressive force: *the weight of cares.* **7** any heavy load: *the bag was such a weight.* **8** the main force; preponderance: *the weight of evidence.* **9** importance; influence: *his opinion carries weight.* **10** *Statistics.* one of a set of coefficients assigned to items of a frequency distribution that are analysed in order to represent the relative importance of the different items. **11** *Printing.* the apparent blackness of a printed typeface. **12 pull one's weight.** *Inf.* to do one's full or proper share of a task. **13 throw one's weight around.** *Inf.* to act in an overauthoritarian manner. ◆ *vb* (*tr*) **14** to add weight to. **15** to burden or oppress. **16** to add importance, value, etc., to (one side rather than another). **17** *Statistics.* to attach a weight or weights to. ORIG OE *wiht*
▸ **'weighter** *n*

weighted average *n Statistics.* a result produced by a technique designed to give recognition to the importance of certain factors when compiling the average of a group of values.

weighting ('weɪtɪŋ) *n* **1** a factor by which some quantity is multiplied in order to make it comparable with others. **2** an allowance paid to compensate for higher living costs: *a London weighting.*

weightlessness ('weɪtlɪsnɪs) *n* a state in which an object has no actual weight (because it is in space and unaffected by gravitational attraction) or no apparent weight (because the gravitational attraction equals the centripetal force and the object is in free fall).
▸ **'weightless** *adj*

weightlifting ('weɪtˌlɪftɪŋ) *n* the sport of lifting barbells of specified weights in a prescribed manner.
▸ **'weightˌlifter** *n*

weight training *n* physical exercise involving lifting weights, either heavy or light weights, as a way of improving muscle performance.

weight watcher *n* a person who tries to lose weight, esp. by dieting.

weighty ('weɪtɪ) *adj* **weightier, weightiest. 1** having great weight. **2** important. **3** causing worry.
▸ **'weightily** *adv* ▸ **'weightiness** *n*

weigh up *vb* (*tr, adv*) to make an assessment of (a person, situation, etc.); judge.

Weihai *or* **Wei-hai** ★ ('weɪ'haɪ) *n* a port in NE China, in NE Shandong on the Yellow Sea: leased to Britain as a naval base (1898–1930). Pop.: 128 888 (1990 est.). Also called: **Weihaiwei** (ˌweɪ'haɪˌweɪ).

Weil ★ (*French* vail) *n* **Simone** (simɔn). 1909–43, French philosopher, whose works include *Waiting for God* (1951) and *Notebooks* (1956).

Weill ★ (vaɪl) *n* **Kurt** (kʊrt). 1900–50, German composer, in the US from 1935. He wrote the music for Brecht's *The Rise and Fall of the City of Mahagonny* (1927) and *The Threepenny Opera* (1928).

Weil's disease (vaɪlz) *n* another name for **leptospirosis.** ORIG named after Adolf *Weil* (1848–1916), G physician

Weimar ★ (*German* 'vaimar) *n* a city in E central Germany, in Thuringia; a cultural centre in the 18th and early 19th century; scene of the adoption (1919) of the constitution of the Weimar Republic. Pop.: 59 100 (1991).

Weimaraner ('vaɪməˌrɑːnə, 'waɪməˌrɑː-) *n* a breed of hunting dog, having a short grey coat and short tail. ORIG C20: after WEIMAR, where the breed was developed

Weinberg ★ ('waɪnbɜːg) *n* **Steven.** born 1933, US physicist, who shared the Nobel prize for physics (1979) with Sheldon Glashow and Abdus Salam for his role in formulating the electroweak theory.

weir (wɪə) *n* **1** a low dam that is built across a river to raise the water level, divert the water, or control its flow. **2** a series of traps or enclosures placed in a stream to catch fish. ORIG OE *wer*

Weir ★ (wɪə) *n* **Peter.** born 1944, Australian film director: his films include *The Last Wave* (1977), *Witness* (1985), *Dead Poets Society* (1989), and *The Truman Show* (1998).

weird (wɪəd) *adj* **1** suggestive of or relating to the supernatural; eerie. **2** strange or bizarre. **3** *Arch.* of or relating to fate or the Fates. ◆ *n* **4** *Arch., chiefly Scot.* **4a** fate or destiny. **4b** one of the Fates. ORIG OE (*ge*)*wyrd* destiny
▸ **'weirdly** *adv* ▸ **'weirdness** *n*

weirdo ('wɪədəʊ) *or* **weirdie** ('wɪədɪ) *n, pl* **weirdos** *or* **weirdies.** *Inf.* a person who behaves in a bizarre or eccentric manner.

Weismannism ('vaɪsmənˌɪzəm) *n* the theory that all inheritable characteristics are transmitted by the reproductive cells and that characteristics acquired during the lifetime of the organism are not inherited. ORIG C19: after August *Weismann* (1834–1914), G biologist

Weisshorn ★ (ˈvaɪsˌhɔːn) *n* a mountain in S Switzerland, in the Pennine Alps. Height: 4505 m (14 781 ft).

Weissmuller ★ (ˈwaɪsˌmʌlə) *n* **John Peter,** known as *Johnny.* 1904–84, US swimmer and film actor, who won Olympic gold medals in 1924 and 1928 and played the title role in the early Tarzan films.

Weizmann ★ (ˈwaɪtsmən, ˈwaɪz-) *n* **Chaim** (ˈxaɪɪm). 1874–1952, Israeli statesman, born in Russia. A Zionist, he was responsible for securing the Balfour Declaration (1917); first president of Israel (1949–52).

weka (ˈwɛkə) *n* a nocturnal flightless bird of New Zealand. Also called: **Maori hen, wood hen.** ORIG from Maori

welch (wɛlʃ) *vb* a variant spelling of **welsh.**

Welch (wɛlʃ) *adj, n* an archaic spelling of **Welsh.**

welcome (ˈwɛlkəm) *adj* **1** gladly and cordially received or admitted: *a welcome guest.* **2** bringing pleasure: *a welcome gift.* **3** freely permitted or invited: *you are welcome to call.* **4** under no obligation (only in such phrases as **you're welcome,** as conventional responses to thanks). ◆ *sentence substitute.* **5** an expression of cordial greeting. ◆ *n* **6** the act of greeting or receiving a person or thing; reception: *the new theory had a cool welcome.* **7 wear out** *or* **overstay one's welcome.** to come more often or stay longer than is pleasing. ◆ *vb* **welcomes, welcoming, welcomed.** (*tr*) **8** to greet the arrival of (guests, etc.) cordially. **9** to receive or accept, esp. gladly. ORIG C12: changed (through infl. of WELL[1]) from OE *wilcuma* (agent n referring to a welcome guest), *wilcume* (a greeting of welcome), from *wil* WILL[2] + *cuman* to come
▸ ˈ**welcomely** *adv* ▸ ˈ**welcomer** *n*

weld[1] (wɛld) *vb* **1** (*tr*) to unite (pieces of metal or plastic), as by softening with heat and hammering or by fusion. **2** to bring or admit of being brought into close union. ◆ *n* **3** a joint formed by welding. ORIG C16: altered from obs. *well* to melt, weld
▸ ˈ**weldable** *adj* ▸ ˌ**weldaˈbility** *n* ▸ ˈ**welder** *or* ˈ**weldor** *n*

weld[2] (wɛld), **wold,** *or* **woald** (wəuld) *n* a yellow dye obtained from the plant dyer's rocket. ORIG C14: from Low G

Weld ★ (wɛld) *n* Sir **Frederick Aloysius.** 1823–91, New Zealand statesman, born in England: prime minister (1864–65).

Weldon ★ (ˈwɛldən) *n* **Fay.** born 1931, British novelist and dramatist. Her novels include *Life and Loves of a She-Devil* (1984) and *Nobody Likes Me!* (1997).

welfare (ˈwɛlˌfɛə) *n* **1** health, happiness, prosperity, and wellbeing in general. **2a** financial and other assistance given to people in need. **2b** (*as modifier*): *welfare services.* **3** Also called: **welfare work.** plans or work to better the social or economic conditions of various underprivileged groups. **4 on welfare.** *Chiefly US & Canad.* in receipt of financial aid from a government agency or other source. ORIG C14: from *wel fare;* see WELL[1], FARE

welfare economics *n* (*functioning as sing*) the aspects of economic theory concerned with the welfare of society and priorities to be observed in the allocation of resources.

welfare state *n* a system in which the government undertakes the chief responsibility for providing for the social and economic security of its population, usually through unemployment insurance, old age pensions, and other social-security measures.

welkin (ˈwɛlkɪn) *n Arch.* the sky, heavens, or upper air. ORIG OE *wolcen, welcen*

Welkom ★ (ˈwɛlkəm, ˈvɛl-) *n* a town in central South Africa. Pop.: 230 000 (latest est.).

well[1] (wɛl) *adv* **better, best. 1** (*often used in combination*) in a satisfactory manner: *the party went very well.* **2** (*often used in combination*) in a skilful manner: *she plays the violin well; a well-chosen example.* **3** in a correct or careful manner: *listen well to my words.* **4** in a prosperous manner: *to live well.* **5** (*usually used with auxiliaries*) suitably; fittingly: *you can't very well say that.* **6** intimately: *I knew him well.* **7** in a kind or favourable manner: *she speaks well of you.* **8** fully: *to be well informed.* **9** by a considerable margin: *let me know well in advance.* **10** (preceded by *could, might,* or *may*) indeed: *you may well have to do it yourself.* **11** *Inf.* (intensifier): *well safe.* **12 all very well.** used ironically to express discontent, dissent, etc. **13 as well. 13a** in addition; too. **13b** (preceded by *may* or *might*) with equal effect: *you might as well come.* **14 as well as.** in addition to. **15** (**just**) **as well.** preferable or advisable: *it would be just as well if you paid me now.* **16 leave well** (**enough**) **alone.** to refrain from interfering with something that is satisfactory. **17 well and good.** used to indicate calm acceptance, as of a decision. **18 well up in.** well acquainted with (a particular subject); knowledgeable about. ◆ *adj* (*usually postpositive*) **19** (when *prenominal, usually used with a negative*) in good health: *I'm very well, thank you; he's not a well man.* **20** satisfactory or pleasing. **21** prudent; advisable: *it would be well to make no comment.* **22** prosperous or comfortable. **23** fortunate: *it is well that you agreed to go.* ◆ *interj* **24a** an expression of surprise, indignation, or reproof. **24b** an expression of anticipation in waiting for an answer or remark. ◆ *sentence connector.* **25** an expression used to preface a remark, gain time, etc.: *well, I don't think I will come.* ORIG OE *wel*

well[2] (wɛl) *n* **1** a hole or shaft bored into the earth to tap a supply of water, oil, gas, etc. **2** a natural pool where ground water comes to the surface. **3a** a cavity, space, or vessel used to contain a liquid. **3b** (*in combination*): *an inkwell.* **4** an open shaft through the floors of a building, such as one used for a staircase. **5** a deep enclosed space in a building or between buildings that is open to the sky. **6** a bulkheaded compartment built around a ship's pumps for protection and ease of access. **7** (in England) the open space in the centre of a law court. **8** an abundant source: *he is a well of knowledge.* ◆ *vb* **9** to flow or cause to flow upwards or outwards: *tears welled from her eyes.* ORIG OE *wella*

we'll (wiːl) *contraction of* we will *or* we shall.

well-advised *adj* (**well advised** *when postpositive*). **1** acting with deliberation or reason. **2** well thought out: *a well-advised plan.*

well-affected *adj* (**well affected** *when postpositive*). favourably disposed (towards); steadfast or loyal.

Welland Canal ★ (ˈwɛlənd) *n* a canal in S Canada, in Ontario, linking Lake Erie to Lake Ontario: part of the St Lawrence Seaway, with eight locks. Length: 44 km (28 miles). Also called: **Welland Ship Canal.**

well-appointed *adj* (**well appointed** *when postpositive*). well equipped or furnished.

wellaway (ˈwɛləˈweɪ) *interj Arch.* woe! alas! ORIG OE, from *wei lā wei,* var. of *wā lā wā,* lit.: woe! lo woe

well-balanced *adj* (**well balanced** *when postpositive*). **1** having good balance or proportions. **2** sane or sensible.

wellbeing (ˈwɛlˈbiːɪŋ) *n* the condition of being contented, healthy, or successful; welfare.

well-bred *adj* (**well bred** *when postpositive*). **1** Also: **well-born.** of respected or noble lineage. **2** indicating good breeding: *well-bred manners.* **3** of good thoroughbred stock: *a well-bred spaniel.*

well-chosen *adj* (**well chosen** *when postpositive*). carefully selected to produce a desired effect; apt: *a few well-chosen words.*

well-connected *adj* (**well connected** *when postpositive*). having influential or important relatives or friends.

well-disposed *adj* (**well disposed** *when postpositive*). inclined to be sympathetic, kindly, or friendly.

well-done *adj* (**well done** *when postpositive*). **1** (of food, esp. meat) cooked thoroughly. **2** made or accomplished satisfactorily.

well dressing *n* the decoration of wells with flowers, etc.: a traditional annual ceremony of great antiquity in some parts of Britain, originally associated with the cult of water deities.

Welles ★ (wɛlz) *n* (**George**) **Orson** (ˈɔːsᵊn). 1915–85, US film director and actor. His *Citizen Kane* (1941) and *The Magnificent Ambersons* (1942) are regarded as film classics.

Wellesley ★ (ˈwɛlzlɪ) *n* **1 Arthur.** See (1st Duke of) **Wellington. 2** his brother, **Richard Colley,** Marquis Wellesley. 1760–1842, British administrator: governor general of Bengal (1797–1805).

well-favoured *adj* (**well favoured** *when postpositive*). good-looking.

well-formed formula *n Logic.* a group of logical symbols that makes sense; a logical sentence.

well-found *adj* (**well found** *when postpositive*). furnished or supplied with all or most necessary things.

well-founded *adj* (**well founded** *when postpositive*). having good grounds: *well-founded rumours.*

well-groomed *adj* (**well groomed** *when postpositive*). having a tidy pleasing appearance.

well-grounded *adj* (**well grounded** *when postpositive*). **1** well instructed in the basic elements of a subject. **2** another term for **well-founded.**

wellhead ('wɛl,hɛd) *n* **1** the source of a well or stream. **2** a source, fountainhead, or origin.

well-heeled *adj* (**well heeled** *when postpositive*). *Inf.* rich; prosperous; wealthy.

wellies ('wɛlɪz) *pl n Brit. inf.* Wellington boots.

well-informed *adj* (**well informed** *when postpositive*). **1** having knowledge about a great variety of subjects: *he seems to be a well-informed person.* **2** possessing reliable information on a particular subject.

Wellingborough ★ ('wɛlɪŋbərə, -brə) *n* a town in central England, in Northamptonshire. Pop.: 41 602 (1991).

Wellington[1] ★ ('wɛlɪŋtən) *n* **1** an administrative district, formerly a province, of New Zealand, on SW North Island: major livestock producer in New Zealand. Capital: Wellington. Pop.: 428 700 (1998 est.). Area: 28 153 sq. km (10 870 sq. miles). **2** the capital city of New Zealand. Its port, historically Port Nicholson, on **Wellington Harbour** has a rail-ferry link between the North and South Islands; university (1899). Pop.: 158 275 (1996).

Wellington[2] ★ ('wɛlɪŋtən) *n* **1st Duke of,** title of *Arthur Wellesley.* 1769–1852, British soldier and statesman; prime minister (1828–30). He commanded the British forces against the French in the Peninsular War (1808–14) and routed Napoleon at Waterloo (1815).

Wellington boots *pl n* **1** Also called: **gumboots.** *Brit.* knee-length or calf-length rubber boots, worn esp. in wet conditions. Often shortened to **wellingtons, wellies. 2** military leather boots covering the front of the knee but cut away at the back to allow easier bending of the knee. ORIG C19: after the 1st Duke of WELLINGTON

wellingtonia (,wɛlɪŋ'təʊnɪə) *n* a giant Californian coniferous tree, often reaching 90 metres high. Also called: **big tree, sequoia.** ORIG C19: after the 1st Duke of WELLINGTON

well-intentioned *adj* (**well intentioned** *when postpositive*). having benevolent intentions, usually with unfortunate results.

well-knit *adj* (**well knit** *when postpositive*). strong, firm, or sturdy.

well-known *adj* (**well known** *when postpositive*). **1** widely known; famous; celebrated. **2** known fully or clearly.

well-mannered *adj* (**well mannered** *when postpositive*). having good manners; polite.

well-meaning *adj* (**well meaning** *when postpositive*). having or indicating good intentions, usually with unfortunate results.

well-nigh *adv Arch. or poetic.* nearly; almost: *it's well-nigh three o'clock.*

well-off *adj* (**well off** *when postpositive*). **1** in a comfortable or favourable position or state. **2** financially well provided for; moderately rich.

well-oiled *adj* (**well oiled** *when postpositive*). *Inf.* drunk.

well-preserved *adj* (**well preserved** *when postpositive*). **1** kept in a good condition. **2** continuing to appear youthful: *she was a well-preserved old lady.*

well-read ('wɛl'rɛd) *adj* (**well read** *when postpositive*). having read widely and intelligently; erudite.

well-rounded *adj* (**well rounded** *when postpositive*). **1** rounded in shape or well developed: *a well-rounded figure.* **2** full, varied, and satisfying: *a well-rounded life.*

Wells[1] ★ (wɛlz) *n* a city in SW England, in Somerset: 12th-century cathedral. Pop.: 9763 (1991).

Wells[2] ★ (wɛlz) *n* **1 Henry.** 1805–78, US businessman, who founded (1852) with William Fargo the express mail service Wells, Fargo and Company. **2 H(erbert) G(eorge).** 1866–1946, British writer. His science fiction includes *The Time Machine* (1895) and *War of the Worlds* (1898). His novels include *Tono-Bungay* (1909) and *Ann Veronica* (1909).

well-spoken *adj* (**well spoken** *when postpositive*). **1** having a clear, articulate, and socially acceptable accent and way of speaking. **2** spoken satisfactorily or pleasingly.

wellspring ('wɛl,sprɪŋ) *n* **1** the source of a spring or stream. **2** a source of abundant supply.

well-stacked *adj* (**well stacked** *when postpositive*). *Sl.* (of a woman) of voluptuous proportions.

well sweep *n* a device for raising buckets from and lowering them into a well, consisting of a long pivoted pole, the bucket being attached to one end by a long rope.

well-tempered *adj* (**well tempered** *when postpositive*). (of a musical scale or instrument) conforming to the system of equal temperament. See **temperament** (sense 4).

well-thought-of *adj* respected.

well-thumbed *adj* (**well thumbed** *when postpositive*). (of a book) having the pages marked from frequent turning.

well-to-do *adj* moderately wealthy.

well-turned *adj* (**well turned** *when postpositive*). **1** (of a phrase, etc.) apt and pleasing. **2** having a pleasing shape: *a well-turned leg.*

well-upholstered *adj* (**well upholstered** *when postpositive*). *Inf.* (of a person) fat.

well-wisher *n* a person who shows benevolence or sympathy towards a person, cause, etc.
▸ **'well-,wishing** *adj, n*

well-woman *n, pl* **well-women.** *Social welfare.* **a** a woman who attends a health-service clinic for preventive monitoring, health education, etc. **b** (*as modifier*): *well-woman clinic.*

well-worn *adj* (**well worn** *when postpositive*). **1** so much used as to be affected by wear: *a well-worn coat.* **2** hackneyed: *a well-worn phrase.*

welly ('wɛlɪ) *n* **1** (*pl* **wellies**) *Inf.* Also called: **welly boot.** a Wellington boot. **2** *Sl.* energy, concentration, or commitment (esp. in **give it some welly**).

Wels ★ (*German* vɛls) *n* an industrial city in N central Austria, in Upper Austria. Pop.: 52 594 (1991).

welsh *or* **welch** (wɛlʃ) *vb* (*intr;* often foll. by *on*) **1** to fail to pay a gambling debt. **2** to fail to fulfil an obligation. ORIG C19: from ?
▸ **'welsher** *or* **'welcher** *n*

Welsh (wɛlʃ) *adj* **1** of, relating to, or characteristic of Wales, its people, their language, or their dialect of English. ◆ *n* **2** a language of Wales, belonging to the S Celtic branch of the Indo-European family. **3 the Welsh.** (*functioning as pl*) the natives or inhabitants of Wales. ORIG OE *Wēlisc, Wǣlisc*

Welsh corgi *n* another name for **corgi.**

Welsh dresser *n* a sideboard with drawers and cupboards below and open shelves above.

Welsh harp *n* a type of harp in which the strings are arranged in three rows.

Welshman ('wɛlʃmən) *or* (*fem*) **Welshwoman** *n, pl* **Welshmen** *or* **Welshwomen.** a native or inhabitant of Wales.

Welsh poppy *n* a perennial W European plant with large yellow flowers.

Welsh rabbit *n* a savoury dish consisting of melted cheese sometimes mixed with milk, seasonings, etc., on hot buttered toast. Also called: **Welsh rarebit, rarebit.** ORIG C18: a fanciful coinage; *rarebit* is a later folk-etymological var.

Welsh terrier *n* a wire-haired breed of terrier with a black-and-tan coat.

welt (wɛlt) *n* **1** a raised or strengthened seam in a garment. **2** another word for **weal**[1]. **3** (in shoemaking) a strip of leather, etc., put in between the outer sole and the inner sole and upper. ◆ *vb* (*tr*) **4** to put a welt in (a garment, etc.). **5** to beat soundly. ORIG C15: from ?

welter ('wɛltə) *vb* (*intr*) **1** to roll about, writhe, or wallow. **2** (esp. of the sea) to surge, heave, or toss. **3** to lie drenched in a liquid, esp. blood. ◆ *n* **4** a confused mass; jumble. ORIG C13: from MLow G, MDu. *weltern*

welterweight ('wɛltə,weɪt) *n* **1a** a professional boxer weighing 140–147 pounds (63.5–66.5 kg). **1b** an amateur boxer weighing 63.5–67 kg (140–148 pounds). **2a** a professional wrestler weighing 155–165 pounds (71–75 kg). **2b** an amateur wrestler weighing 69–74 kg (151–161 pounds).

Welwyn Garden City ★ ('wɛlɪn) *n* a town in SE England, in Hertfordshire: established (1920) as a planned industrial and residential town. Pop.: 42 087 (1991).

Wembley ★ ('wɛmblɪ) *n* part of the Greater London borough of Brent: site of the English national soccer stadium.

wen[1] (wɛn) *n* **1** *Pathol.* a sebaceous cyst, esp. one occurring on the scalp. **2** a large overcrowded city (esp. London, **the great wen**). ORIG OE *wenn*

wen[2] (wɛn) *n* a rune having the sound of Modern English *w*. ORIG OE *wen, wyn*

Wenceslaus *or* **Wenceslas** ★ ('wɛnsɪsləs) *n* **1** 1361–1419, Holy Roman Emperor (1378–1400) and, as **Wenceslaus IV**, king of Bohemia (1378–1419). **2 Saint**, known as *Good King Wenceslaus*. ?907–929, duke of Bohemia (?925–29); patron saint of the Czech Republic. Feast day: Sept. 28.

wench (wɛntʃ) *n* **1** a girl or young woman: now used facetiously. **2** *Arch.* a female servant. **3** *Arch.* a prostitute. ◆ *vb* (*intr*) **4** *Arch.* to frequent the company of prostitutes. ORIG OE *wencel* child, from *wancol* weak
▸ **'wencher** *n*

wend (wɛnd) *vb* to direct (one's course or way); travel. ORIG OE *wendan*

Wend (wɛnd) *n* (esp. in medieval European history) a member of the Slavonic people who inhabited the area between the Rivers Saale and Oder, in central Europe, in the early Middle Ages. Also called: **Sorb**.

wendigo ('wɛndɪ,gəʊ) *n Canad.* **1** (*pl* **wendigos**) (among Algonquian Indians) an evil spirit or cannibal. **2** (*pl* **wendigo** *or* **wendigos**) another name for **splake**. ORIG from Algonquian: evil spirit or cannibal

Wendy house ('wɛndɪ) *n* a small model house for children to play in. ORIG C20: after the house built for *Wendy*, the girl in J. M. Barrie's play *Peter Pan* (1904)

wensleydale ('wɛnzlɪ,deɪl) *n* **1** a type of white cheese with a flaky texture. **2** a breed of sheep with long woolly fleece. ORIG after *Wensleydale*, North Yorkshire

went (wɛnt) *vb* the past tense of **go**. ORIG C15: p.t. of WEND used as p.t. of *go*

wentletrap ('wɛntᵊl,træp) *n* a marine gastropod mollusc having a long pointed pale-coloured longitudinally ridged shell. ORIG C18: from Du. *winteltrap* spiral shell, from *wintel*, earlier *windel*, from *wenden* to wind + *trap* a step

Wentworth ★ ('wɛntwəθ) *n* **1 Thomas.** See (Earl of) **Strafford**. **2 William Charles.** 1790–1872, Australian explorer and statesman, who was a member of the party that first crossed the Blue Mountains in 1813 and was later a leader in the movement for self-government in New South Wales.

Wenzhou, Wen-chou, *or* **Wenchow** ★ ('wen'tʃu:) *n* a port in SE China, in Zhejiang province: noted for its historic buildings. Pop.: 401 871 (1990 est.).

wept (wɛpt) *vb* the past tense and past participle of **weep**.

were (wɜ:; *unstressed* wə) *vb* the plural form of the past tense (indicative mood) of **be** and the singular form used with *you*. It is also used as a subjunctive, esp. in conditional sentences. ORIG OE *wērun, wæron* p.t. pl of *wesan* to be

> **USAGE NOTE** *Were*, as a remnant of the past subjunctive in English, is used in formal contexts to express hypotheses (*if he were to die, she would inherit everything*), suppositions contrary to fact (*if I were you, I would be careful*), and desire (*I wish he were there now*). In informal speech, however, *was* is often used instead.

we're (wɪə) *contraction of* we are.

weren't (wɜ:nt) *contraction of* were not.

werewolf ('wɪə,wʊlf, 'wɛə-) *n, pl* **werewolves**. a person fabled in folklore and superstition to have been changed into a wolf by being bewitched or said to be able to assume wolf form at will. ORIG OE *werewulf*, from *wer* man + *wulf* wolf

wergild, weregild ('wɜ:,gɪld, 'wɛə-), *or* **wergeld** ('wɜ:,gɛld, 'wɛə-) *n* the price set on a man's life in Anglo-Saxon and Germanic law, to be paid as compensation by his slayer. ORIG OE *wergeld*, from *wer* man + *gield* tribute

Werner ★ (*German* 'vɛrnə) *n* **1 Abraham Gottlob** ('a:brəham 'gɔtlo:p). 1749–1817, German geologist. **2 Alfred** ('alfre:t). 1866–1919, Swiss chemist, born in Germany: Nobel prize for chemistry (1913) for his work on inorganic complexes.

wert (wɜ:t; *unstressed* wət) *vb Arch. or dialect.* (used with the pronoun *thou* or its relative equivalent) a singular form of the past tense (indicative mood) of **be**.

Weser ★ (*German* 've:zər) *n* a river in NW Germany: flows northwest to the North Sea at Bremerhaven and is linked by the Mittelland Canal to the Ems, Rhine, and Elbe waterways. Length: 477 km (196 miles).

Wesermünde ★ (*German* ve:zər'myndə) *n* the former name (until 1947) of **Bremerhaven**.

Wesker ★ ('wɛskə) *n* **Arnold.** born 1932, British dramatist, whose plays include *Roots* (1959), *Chips With Everything* (1962), and *Break My Heart* (1997).

weskit ('wɛskɪt) *n* an informal name for **waistcoat**.

Wesley ★ ('wɛzlɪ) *n* **1 Charles.** 1707–88, British Methodist preacher and writer of hymns. **2** his brother, **John.** 1703–91, British preacher, who founded Methodism.

Wesleyan ('wɛzlɪən) *adj* **1** of or deriving from John Wesley. **2** of or characterizing Methodism, esp. in its original form. ◆ *n* **3** a follower of John Wesley. **4** a member of the Methodist Church.
▸ **'Wesleyan,ism** *n*

Wessex[1] ★ ('wɛsɪks) *n* **1** an Anglo-Saxon kingdom in S and SW England that became the most powerful English kingdom by the 10th century A.D. **2a** (in Thomas Hardy's works) the southwestern counties of England, esp. Dorset. **2b** (*as modifier*): *Wessex Poems*.

Wessex[2] ★ ('wɛsɪks) *n* **Prince Edward, Earl of.** born 1964, third son of Elizabeth II of Great Britain and Northern Ireland. He married (2000) Miss Sophie Rhys-Jones.

west (wɛst) *n* **1** the direction along a parallel towards the sunset, at 270° clockwise from north. **2 the west.** (*often cap.*) any area lying in or towards the west. Related adjs.: **Hesperian, Occidental. 3** (*usually cap.*) *Cards.* the player or position at the table corresponding to west on the compass. ◆ *adj* **4** situated in, moving towards, or facing the west. **5** (esp. of the wind) from the west. ◆ *adv* **6** in, to, or towards the west. **7 go west.** *Inf.* **7a** to be lost or destroyed. **7b** to die. ORIG OE

West[1] (wɛst) *n* **the. 1** the western part of the world contrasted historically and culturally with the East or Orient. **2** (formerly) the non-Communist countries of Europe and America contrasted with the Communist states of the East. **3** (in the US) that part of the US lying approximately to the west of the Mississippi. **4** (in the ancient and medieval world) the Western Roman Empire and, later, the Holy Roman Empire. ◆ *adj* **5** of or denoting the western part of a specified country, area, etc.

West[2] ★ (wɛst) *n* **1 Benjamin.** 1738–1820, US painter, in England from 1763. **2 Mae.** 1892–1980, US film actress. **3** Dame **Rebecca**, real name *Mrs Cicily Isabel Andrews* (née *Fairfield*). 1892–1983, British novelist.

West Atlantic ★ *n* the W part of the Atlantic Ocean, esp. the N Atlantic around North America.

West Bank ★ *n* **the.** an autonomous Palestinian region in the Middle East on the W bank of the River Jordan, comprising the hills of Judaea and Samaria and part of Jerusalem: formerly part of Palestine: became part of Jordan after the ceasefire of 1949: occupied by Israel since the 1967 Arab-Israeli War. The provision of the Camp David Agreement that the West Bank should be granted a degree of Palestinian autonomy was re-established in

1993 by a peace treaty between Israel and the Palestinian Liberation Organization. Negotiations to determine the final status of the region have continued. Pop.: 1 122 900 (1994). Area: 5879 sq. km (2270 sq. miles).

West Bengal ★ *n* a state of E India, on the Bay of Bengal: formed in 1947 from the Hindu area of Bengal; additional territories added in 1950 (Cooch Behar), 1954 (Chandernagor), and 1956 (part of Bihar); mostly low-lying and crossed by the Hooghly River. Capital: Calcutta. Pop.: 73 600 000 (1994 est.). Area: 88 752 sq. km (34 260 sq. miles).

West Berkshire ★ *n* a unitary authority in S England. Pop.: 143 700 (1996 est.). Area: 705 sq. km (272 sq. miles).

West Berlin ★ *n* (formerly) the part of Berlin under US, British, and French control.
▸ **West Berliner** *n, adj*

westbound ('wɛstˌbaʊnd) *adj* going or leading towards the west.

West Bromwich ★ ('brɒmɪdʒ, -ɪtʃ) *n* a town in central England, in Sandwell, in the West Midlands: industrial centre. Pop.: 146 386 (1991).

west by north *n* one point on the compass north of west.

west by south *n* one point on the compass south of west.

West Country ★ *n* **the.** the southwest of England, esp. Cornwall, Devon, and Somerset.

West Dunbartonshire ★ *n* a council area of W central Scotland, formed in 1996. Capital: Dumbarton. Pop.: 95 760 (1996 est.). Area: 162 sq. km (63 sq. miles).

West End ★ *n* **the.** a part of W central London containing the main shopping and entertainment areas.

westering ('wɛstərɪŋ) *adj Poetic.* moving towards the west: *the westering star.*

Westerlies ('wɛstəlɪz) *pl n Meteorol.* the prevailing winds blowing from the west on the poleward sides of the horse latitudes, often bringing depressions and anticyclones.

westerly ('wɛstəlɪ) *adj* **1** of, relating to, or situated in the west. ◆ *adv, adj* **2** towards or in the direction of the west. **3** (esp. of the wind) from the west. ◆ *n, pl* **westerlies. 4** a wind blowing from the west.
▸ **'westerliness** *n*

western ('wɛstən) *adj* **1** situated in or facing the west. **2** going or directed to or towards the west. **3** (of a wind, etc.) coming from the west. **4** native to the west. **5** *Music.* See **country and western.**
▸ **'westernˌmost** *adj*

Western ('wɛstən) *adj* **1** of or characteristic of the West as opposed to the Orient. **2** of or characteristic of North America and western Europe. **3** of or characteristic of the western states of the US. ◆ *n* **4** (*often not cap.*) a film, book, etc., concerned with life in the western states of the US, esp. during the era of exploration.

Western Australia ★ *n* a state of W Australia: mostly an arid undulating plateau, with the Great Sandy Desert, Gibson Desert, and Great Victoria Desert in the interior; settlement concentrated in the southwest; rich mineral resources. Capital: Perth. Pop.: 1 726 095 (1996). Area: 2 527 636 sq. km (975 920 sq. miles).

Western Cape ★ *n* a province of South Africa: a subdivision of the former Cape Province. Capital: Cape Town. Pop.: 3 956 875 (1996). Area: 129 370 sq. km (49 950 sq. miles).

Western Church *n* **1** the part of Christendom that derives its liturgy, discipline, and traditions principally from the patriarchate of Rome. **2** the Roman Catholic Church, sometimes together with the Anglican Communion of Churches.

westerner ('wɛstənə) *n* (*sometimes cap.*) a native or inhabitant of the west of any specific region.

Western Ghats ★ *pl n* a mountain range in W peninsular India, parallel to the Malabar coast of the Arabian Sea. Highest peak: Anai Mudi, 2695 m (8841 ft).

western hemisphere *n* (*often caps.*) **1** that half of the globe containing the Americas, lying to the west of the Greenwich or another meridian. **2** the lands contained in this, esp. the Americas.

Western Isles ★ *n* (*functioning as sing or pl*) **1** an island authority in W Scotland, consisting of the Outer Hebrides; created in 1975. Administrative centre: Stornoway. Pop.: 31 834 (1996 est.). Area: 2900 sq. km (1120 sq. miles). **2** Also called: **Western Islands.** another name for the **Hebrides.**

westernize *or* **westernise** ('wɛstəˌnaɪz) *vb* **westernizes, westernizing, westernized** *or* **westernises, westernising, westernised.** (*tr*) to influence or make familiar with the customs, practices, etc., of the West.
▸ **ˌwesterni'zation** *or* **ˌwesterni'sation** *n*

Western Ocean ★ *n* (formerly) another name for the **Atlantic Ocean.**

Western Roman Empire *n* the westernmost of the two empires created by the division of the later Roman Empire, esp. after its final severance from the Eastern Roman Empire (395 A.D.). Also called: **Western Empire.**

Western Sahara ★ *n* a disputed region of NW Africa, on the Atlantic: mainly desert; rich phosphate deposits; a Spanish overseas province from 1958 to 1975; partitioned in 1976 between Morocco and Mauritania who faced growing resistance from the Polisario Front, an organization aiming for the independence of the region as the Democratic Saharan Arab Republic. Mauritania renounced its claim in 1979 and its territory was taken over by Morocco. Attempts by the UN to resolve the dispute have failed. Pop.: 214 000 (1993 est.). Area: 266 000 sq. km (102 680 sq. miles). Former name (until 1975): **Spanish Sahara.**

Western Samoa ★ *n* See **Samoa** (sense 1).

Western Wall ★ *n* a wall in Jerusalem, the last extant part of the Temple of Herod, held sacred by Jews as a place of prayer and pilgrimage. Also called: **Wailing Wall.**

Westfalen ★ (vɛst'fa:lən) *n* the German name for **Westphalia.**

West Flanders ★ *n* a province of W Belgium: the country's chief agricultural province. Capital: Bruges. Pop.: 1 125 140 (1998 est.). Area: 3132 sq. km (1209 sq. miles).

West Germany ★ *n* a former republic in N central Europe, on the North Sea: established in 1949 from the zones of Germany occupied by the British, Americans, and French after the defeat of Nazi Germany; a member of the European Community; reunited with East Germany in 1990. Official name: **Federal Republic of Germany.** See also **Germany.**
▸ **West German** *adj, n*

West Glamorgan ★ *n* a former county in S Wales, formed in 1974 from part of Glamorgan and the county borough of Swansea: replaced in 1996.

West Hartlepool ★ ('hɑ:tlɪˌpu:l) *n* a former town in NE England, in Co. Durham: part of Hartlepool since 1967.

West Indies ★ ('ɪndɪz) *n* (*functioning as sing or pl*) an archipelago off Central America, extending over 2400 km (1500 miles) in an arc from the peninsula of Florida to Venezuela, separating the Caribbean Sea from the Atlantic: consists of the Greater Antilles, the Lesser Antilles, and the Bahamas; largest island is Cuba. Area: over 235 000 sq. km (91 000 sq. miles). Also called: the **Caribbean.**

westing ('wɛstɪŋ) *n Navigation.* movement, deviation, or distance covered in a westerly direction, esp. as expressed in the resulting difference in longitude.

West Irian ★ *n* the English name for **Irian Jaya.**

West Lothian ★ *n* a council area and historic county of central Scotland; part of Lothian region (1975–96). Administrative centre: Livingston. Pop.: 150 770 (1996 est.). Area: 425 sq. km (164 sq. miles).

Westm. *abbrev. for* Westminster.

Westmeath ★ (ˌwɛst'mi:ð) *n* a county of N central Republic of Ireland, in Leinster province: mostly low-lying, with many lakes and bogs. County town: Mullingar. Pop.: 63 000 (1996). Area: 1764 sq. km (681 sq. miles).

West Midlands ★ *n* (*functioning as sing or pl*) a metropolitan county of central England, administered since 1996 by the unitary authorities of Wolverhampton, Walsall, Dudley, Sandwell, Birmingham, Solihull, and Coventry. Area: 899 sq. km (347 sq. miles).

Westminster ★ ('wɛst,mɪnstə) *n* **1** Also called: **City of Westminster.** a borough of Greater London, on the River Thames: contains the Houses of Parliament, Westminster Abbey, and Buckingham Palace. Pop.: 190 100 (1991 est.) Area: 22 sq. km (8 sq. miles). **2** the Houses of Parliament at Westminster.

Westminster Abbey ★ *n* a Gothic church in London: site of a Benedictine monastery (1050–65); scene of the coronations of almost all English monarchs since William I.

Westmorland ★ ('wɛstmələnd, 'wɛsmə-) *n* (until 1974) a county of NW England, now part of Cumbria.

west-northwest *n* **1** the point on the compass or the direction midway between west and northwest, 292° 30′ clockwise from north. ◆ *adj, adv* **2** in, from, or towards this direction.

Weston standard cell ('wɛstən) *n* a primary cell used as a standard of emf: consists of a mercury anode and a cadmium amalgam cathode in an electrolyte of saturated cadmium sulphate. ORIG C20: from a trademark

Weston-super-Mare ★ ('wɛstən,su:pə'mɛə, -,sju:-) *n* a town and resort in SW England, in North Somerset on the Bristol Channel. Pop.: 69 372 (1991).

West Pakistan ★ *n* the former name (until the end of 1971) of **Pakistan.**

Westphalia ★ (wɛst'feɪlɪə) *n* a historic region of NW Germany, now mostly in the state of North Rhine-Westphalia. German name: **Westfalen.**
▸ **West'phalian** *adj, n*

West Prussia ★ *n* a former province of NE Prussia, on the Baltic: assigned to Poland in 1945. German name: **Westpreussen** ('vɛstprɔysən).

West Riding ★ *n* (until 1974) an administrative division of Yorkshire, now in West Yorkshire, North Yorkshire, Cumbria, and Lancashire.

west-southwest *n* **1** the point on the compass or the direction midway between southwest and west, 247° 30′ clockwise from north. ◆ *adj, adv* **2** in, from, or towards this direction.

West Sussex ★ *n* a county of SE England, comprising part of the former county of Sussex. Administrative centre: Chichester. Pop.: 737 300 (1996 est.). Area: 1989 sq. km (768 sq. miles).

West Virginia ★ *n* a state of the eastern US: part of Virginia until the outbreak of the American Civil War (1861); consists chiefly of the Allegheny Plateau; bounded on the west by the Ohio River; coal-mining. Capital: Charleston. Pop.: 1 811 156 (1998 est.). Area: 62 341 sq. km (24 070 sq. miles). Abbrevs.: **W. Va.** or (with zip code) **WV**
▸ **West Virginian** *adj, n*

westward ('wɛstwəd) *adj* **1** moving, facing, or situated in the west. ◆ *adv* **2** Also: **westwards.** towards the west. ◆ *n* **3** the westward part, direction, etc.
▸ **'westwardly** *adj, adv*

Westwood ★ ('wɛst,wud) *n* **Vivienne (Isabel).** born 1941, British fashion designer.

West Yorkshire ★ *n* a metropolitan county of N England, administered since 1986 by the unitary authorities of Bradford, Leeds, Calderdale, Kirklees, and Wakefield. Area: 2039 sq. km (787 sq. miles).

wet (wɛt) *adj* **wetter, wettest. 1** moistened, covered, saturated, etc., with water or some other liquid. **2** not yet dry or solid: *wet varnish.* **3** rainy: *wet weather.* **4** employing a liquid, usually water: *a wet method of chemical analysis.* **5** *Chiefly US & Canad.* permitting the free sale of alcoholic beverages: *a wet state.* **6** *Brit. inf.* feeble or foolish. **7 wet behind the ears.** *Inf.* immature or inexperienced. ◆ *n* **8** wetness or moisture. **9** rainy weather. **10** *Brit. inf.* a feeble or foolish person. **11** (*often cap.*) *Brit. inf.* a Conservative politician who is not a hardliner. **12** *Chiefly US & Canad.* a person who advocates free sale of alcoholic beverages. **13 the wet.** *Austral.* (in northern and central Australia) the rainy season. ◆ *vb* **wets, wetting, wet** *or* **wetted. 14** to make or become wet. **15** to urinate on (something). **16** (*tr*) *Dialect.* to prepare (tea) by boiling or infusing. ORIG OE *wǣt*
▸ **'wetly** *adv* ▸ **'wetness** *n* ▸ **'wettable** *adj* ▸ **'wetter** *n*
▸ **'wettish** *adj*

wet-and-dry-bulb thermometer *n* another name for **psychrometer.**

wet blanket *n Inf.* a person whose low spirits or lack of enthusiasm have a depressing effect on others.

wet cell *n* a primary cell in which the electrolyte is a liquid.

wet dream *n* an erotic dream accompanied by an emission of semen.

wet fly *n Angling.* an artificial fly designed to float or ride below the water surface.

wether ('wɛðə) *n* a male sheep, esp. a castrated one. ORIG OE *hwæther*

wetland ('wɛtlənd) *n* (*sometimes pl*) **a** an area of marshy land, esp. considered as part of an ecological system. **b** (*as modifier*): *wetland species.*

wet look *n* a shiny finish such as that given to certain clothing and footwear materials.

wet nurse *n* **1** a woman hired to suckle the child of another. ◆ *vb* **wet-nurse, wet-nurses, wet-nursing, wet-nursed.** (*tr*) **2** to act as a wet nurse to (a child). **3** *Inf.* to attend with great devotion.

wet pack *n Med.* a hot or cold damp sheet or blanket for wrapping around a patient.

wet rot *n* **1** a state of decay in timber caused by various fungi. The hyphal strands of the fungus are seldom visible, and affected timber turns dark brown. **2** any of the fungi causing this decay.

wet suit *n* a close-fitting rubber suit used by skin-divers, yachtsmen, etc., to retain body heat.

Wetterhorn ★ (*German* 'vɛtər,hɔrn) *n* a mountain in S Switzerland, in the Bernese Alps. Height: 3701 m (12 143 ft).

wetting agent *n Chem.* any substance added to a liquid to lower its surface tension and thus increase its ability to spread across or penetrate a solid.

we've (wi:v) *contraction of* we have.

Wexford ★ ('wɛksfəd) *n* **1** a county of SE Republic of Ireland, in Leinster province on the Irish Sea: the first Irish county to be colonized from England; mostly low-lying and fertile. County town: Wexford. Pop.: 104 000 (1996). Area: 2352 sq. km (908 sq. miles). **2** a port in SE Republic of Ireland, county town of Co. Wexford: sacked by Oliver Cromwell in 1649. Pop.: 9540 (1991).

Weymouth ★ ('weɪməθ) *n* a port and resort in S England, in Dorset on the English Channel: administratively part of the borough of **Weymouth and Melcombe Regis.** Pop. (with Melcombe Regis): 53 235 (1991).

wf *Printing. abbrev. for* wrong fount.

WFF *Logic. abbrev. for* well-formed formula.

WFTU *abbrev. for* World Federation of Trade Unions.

W. Glam *abbrev. for* West Glamorgan.

whack (wæk) *vb* (*tr*) **1** to strike with a sharp resounding blow. **2** (*usually passive*) *Brit. inf.* to exhaust completely. **3** *US sl.* to murder (someone): *if you were out of line you got whacked.* ◆ *n* **4** a sharp resounding blow or the noise made by such a blow. **5** *Inf.* a share or portion. **6** *Inf.* a try or attempt (esp. in **have a whack at**). **7 out of whack.** *Inf.* out of order; unbalanced: *the whole system is out of whack.* ORIG C18: ? var. of THWACK, ult. imit.
▸ **'whacker** *n*

whacking ('wækɪŋ) *Inf., chiefly Brit.* ◆ *adj* **1** enormous. ◆ *adv* **2** (intensifier): *a whacking big lie.*

whacky ('wækɪ) *adj* **whackier, whackiest.** *US sl.* a variant spelling of **wacky.**

whale[1] (weɪl) *n, pl* **whales** *or* **whale. 1** any of the larger cetacean mammals, excluding dolphins, porpoises, and narwhals. They have flippers, a streamlined body, and a horizontally flattened tail and breathe through a blowhole on the top of the head. **2 a whale of a.** *Inf.* an exceptionally large, fine, etc., example of a (person or thing). ORIG OE *hwæl*

whale[2] (weɪl) *vb* **whales, whaling, whaled.** (*tr*) to beat or thrash soundly. ORIG C18: var. of WALE

whaleboat (ˈweɪlˌbəut) *n* a narrow boat from 20 to 30 feet long having a sharp prow and stern, formerly used in whaling. Also called: **whaler.**

whalebone (ˈweɪlˌbəun) *n* **1** Also called: **baleen.** a horny elastic material forming numerous thin plates that hang from the upper jaw in the toothless (whalebone) whales and strain plankton from water entering the mouth. **2** a strip of this substance, used in stiffening corsets, etc.

whalebone whale *n* any whale belonging to a cetacean suborder having a double blowhole and strips of whalebone between the jaws instead of teeth: includes the rorquals, right whales, and the blue whale.

whale oil *n* oil obtained either from the blubber of whales (train oil) or the head of the sperm whale (sperm oil).

whaler (ˈweɪlə) *n* **1** Also called (US): **whaleman.** a person employed in whaling. **2** a vessel engaged in whaling. **3** *Austral. obs. sl.* a tramp or sundowner. **4** an aggressive shark of Australian coastal waters.

whale shark *n* a large spotted whalelike shark of warm seas, that feeds on plankton and small animals.

whaling (ˈweɪlɪŋ) *n* the work or industry of hunting and processing whales for food, oil, etc.

wham (wæm) *n* **1** a forceful blow or impact or the sound produced by it. ◆ *vb* **whams, whamming, whammed. 2** to strike or cause to strike with great force. ORIG C20: imit.

whammy (ˈwæmɪ) *n, pl* **whammies.** *Inf.* **1** something which has great, often negative impact: *a double whammy of falling demand and rising prices.* **2** an evil spell or curse: *she believed he had put the whammy on her.* ORIG C20: WHAM + -Y[2]

whanau (ˈfɑːnaʊ) *n NZ.* a family, esp. an extended family. ORIG Maori

whang (wæŋ) *vb* **1** to strike or be struck so as to cause a resounding noise. ◆ *n* **2** the resounding noise produced by a heavy blow. **3** a heavy blow. ORIG C19: imit.

Whangarei ★ (ˌwɑːŋɑːˈreɪ) *n* a port in New Zealand, the northernmost city of North Island. Pop.: 44 800 (1994).

whangee (wæŋˈiː) *n* **1** a tall woody grass of an Asian genus, grown for its stems. **2** a cane or walking stick made from the stem of this plant. ORIG C19: prob. from Chinese (Mandarin) *huangli,* from *huang* yellow + *li* bamboo cane

whare (ˈwɔːrɪ; *Maori* ˈfɒrɛ) *n NZ.* **1** a Maori hut or dwelling place. **2** any simple dwelling place. ORIG from Maori

wharepuni (ˈfɒrɛˌpunɪ) *n NZ.* in a Maori community, a lofty carved building that is used as a guesthouse. ORIG from Maori WHARE + *puni* company

wharf (wɔːf) *n, pl* **wharves** (wɔːvz) *or* **wharfs. 1** a platform built parallel to the waterfront at a harbour or navigable river for the docking, loading, and unloading of ships. ◆ *vb* (*tr*) **2** to moor or dock at a wharf. **3** to store or unload on a wharf. ORIG OE *hwearf* heap

wharfage (ˈwɔːfɪdʒ) *n* **1** facilities for ships at wharves. **2** a charge for use of a wharf. **3** wharves collectively.

wharfie (ˈwɔːfɪ) *n Austral. & NZ.* a wharf labourer; docker.

wharfinger (ˈwɔːfɪndʒə) *n* an owner or manager of a wharf. ORIG C16: prob. alteration of *wharfager*

Wharton ★ (ˈwɔːtᵊn) *n* **Edith** (**Newbold**). 1862–1937, US novelist; author of *The House of Mirth* (1905) and *Ethan Frome* (1911).

wharve (wɔːv) *n* a wooden disc or wheel on a shaft serving as a flywheel or pulley. ORIG OE *hweorfa,* from *hweorfan* to revolve

what (wɒt; *unstressed* wət) *determiner* **1a** used with a noun in requesting further information about the identity or categorization of something: *what job does he do?* **1b** (*as pron*): *what is her address?* **1c** (*used in indirect questions*): *tell me what he said.* **2a** the (person, thing, persons, or things) that: *we photographed what animals we could see.* **2b** (*as pron*): *bring me what you've written.* **3** (intensifier; used in exclamations): *what a good book!* ◆ *adv* **4** in what respect? to what degree?: *what do you care?* **5 what about.** what do you think, know, etc., concerning? **6 what for. 6a** for what purpose? why? **6b** *Inf.* a punishment or reprimand (esp. in **give** (**a person**) **what for**). **7 what have you.** someone or something unknown or unspecified: *cars, motorcycles, or what have you.* **8 what if. 8a** what would happen if? **8b** what difference would it make if? **9 what matter.** what does it matter? **10 what's what.** *Inf.* the true state of affairs. ORIG OE *hwæt*

whatever (wɒtˈɛvə, wət-) *pron* **1** everything or anything that: *do whatever he asks you to.* **2** no matter what: *whatever he does, he is forgiven.* **3** *Inf.* an unknown or unspecified thing or things: *take a hammer, chisel, or whatever.* **4** an intensive form of *what,* used in questions: *whatever can he have said to upset her so much?* ◆ *determiner* **5** an intensive form of *what: use whatever tools you can get hold of.* ◆ *adj* **6** (*postpositive*) absolutely; whatsoever: *I saw no point whatever in continuing.*

whatnot (ˈwɒtˌnɒt) *n* **1** Also called: **what-d'you-call-it.** *Inf.* a person or thing the name of which is unknown or forgotten. **2** *Inf.* unspecified assorted material. **3** a portable stand with shelves for displaying ornaments, etc.

whatsit (ˈwɒtsɪt), **whatsitsname,** (*masc*) **whatshisname,** *or* (*fem*) **whatshername** *n Inf.* a person or thing the name of which is unknown or forgotten.

whatsoever (ˌwɒtsəuˈɛvə) *adj* **1** (*postpositive*) at all: used as an intensifier with indefinite pronouns and determiners such as *none, anybody,* etc. ◆ *pron* **2** an archaic word for **whatever.**

whaup (hwɔːp) *n Chiefly Scot.* a popular name for the **curlew.** ORIG C16: rel. to OE *huilpe,* ult. imit. of the bird's cry

wheal (wiːl) *n* a variant spelling of **weal**[1].

wheat (wiːt) *n* **1** any of a genus of grasses, native to the Mediterranean region and W Asia but widely cultivated, having erect flower spikes and light brown grains. **2** the grain of any of these grasses, used in making flour, pasta, etc. ◆ See also **durum.** ORIG OE *hwǣte*

wheatbelt (ˈwiːtˌbɛlt) *n* an area in which wheat is the chief agricultural product.

wheatear (ˈwiːtˌɪə) *n* a small northern songbird having a pale grey back, black wings and tail, white rump, and pale brown underparts. ORIG C16: back formation from *wheatears* (wrongly taken as pl), prob. from WHITE + ARSE

wheaten (ˈwiːtᵊn) *adj* **1** made of the grain or flour of wheat. **2** of a pale yellow colour.

wheat germ *n* the vitamin-rich embryo of the wheat kernel.

wheatmeal (ˈwiːtˌmiːl) *n* **a** a brown flour intermediate between white flour and wholemeal flour. **b** (*as modifier*): *a wheatmeal loaf.*

Wheatstone bridge (ˈwiːtstən) *n* a device for determining the value of an unknown resistance by comparison with a known standard resistance. ORIG C19: after Sir Charles *Wheatstone* (1802–75), Brit. physicist and inventor

whee (wiː) *interj* an exclamation of joy, etc.

wheedle (ˈwiːdᵊl) *vb* **wheedles, wheedling, wheedled. 1** to persuade or try to persuade (someone) by coaxing words, flattery, etc. **2** (*tr*) to obtain thus: *she wheedled some money out of her father.* ORIG C17: ?from G *wedeln* to wag one's tail, from OHG *wedil, wadil* tail
▸ **ˈwheedler** *n* ▸ **ˈwheedling** *adj* ▸ **ˈwheedlingly** *adv*

wheel (wiːl) *n* **1** a solid disc, or a circular rim joined to a hub by spokes, that is mounted on a shaft about which it can turn, as in vehicles. **2** anything like a wheel in shape or function. **3** a device consisting of or resembling a wheel: *a steering wheel; a water wheel.* **4** (usually preceded by *the*) a medieval torture in which the victim was tied to a wheel and then had his or her limbs struck and broken by an iron bar. **5** short for **wheel of fortune** or **potter's wheel. 6** the act of turning. **7** a pivoting movement of troops, ships, etc. **8** a type of firework coiled to make it rotate when let off. **9** a set of short rhyming lines forming the concluding part of a stanza. **10** *US & Canad.* an informal word for **bicycle. 11** *Inf., chiefly US & Canad.* a person of great influence (esp. in **big wheel**). **12 at the wheel. 12a** driving or steering a vehicle or vessel. **12b** in charge. ◆ *vb* **13** to turn or cause to turn on or as if on an axis. **14** (when *intr,* sometimes foll. by *about* or *around*) to move or cause to move on or as if on wheels; roll. **15** (*tr*)

★ people and places

to perform with or in a circular movement. **16** (*tr*) to provide with a wheel or wheels. **17** (*intr; often foll. by about*) to change direction. **18 wheel and deal.** *Inf.* to operate free of restraint, esp. to advance one's own interests. ◆ See also **wheels.** ORIG OE *hweol, hweowol*

wheel and axle *n* a simple machine for raising weights in which a rope unwinding from a wheel is wound onto a cylindrical drum or shaft coaxial with or joined to the wheel to provide mechanical advantage.

wheel animalcule *n* another name for **rotifer.**

wheelbarrow ('wi:lˌbærəʊ) *n* a simple vehicle for carrying small loads, typically being an open container supported by a wheel at the front and two legs behind.

wheelbase ('wi:lˌbeɪs) *n* the distance between the front and back axles of a motor vehicle.

wheelchair ('wi:lˌtʃɛə) *n* special chair on large wheels, for use by invalids or others for whom walking is impossible or inadvisable.

wheel clamp *n* a device fixed onto one wheel of an illegally parked car in order to immobilize it. The driver has to pay to have it removed.

wheeled (wi:ld) *adj* **a** having a wheel or wheels. **b** (*in combination*): *four-wheeled.*

wheeler ('wi:lə) *n* **1** Also called: **wheel horse.** a horse or other draught animal nearest the wheel. **2** (*in combination*) something equipped with a specified sort or number of wheels: *a three-wheeler.* **3** a person or thing that wheels.

Wheeler ★ ('wi:lə) *n* **1 John Archibald.** born 1911, US physicist, noted for his work on nuclear fission and the development (1949–51) of the hydrogen bomb. **2** Sir (**Robert Eric**) **Mortimer.** 1890–1976, British archaeologist, noted for his excavations in the Indus Valley and at Maiden Castle in Dorset.

wheeler-dealer *n Inf.* a person who wheels and deals.

wheel horse *n* **1** another word for **wheeler** (sense 1). **2** *US & Canad.* a person who works steadily or hard.

wheelhouse ('wi:lˌhaʊs) *n* another term for **pilot house.**

wheelie ('wi:lɪ) *n* a manoeuvre on a bicycle or motorbike in which the front wheel is raised off the ground.

wheelie bin *or* **wheely bin** *n* a large container for rubbish, esp. one used by a household, mounted on wheels so that it can be moved more easily.

wheel lock *n* **1** a gunlock formerly in use in which the firing mechanism was activated by sparks produced by friction between a small steel wheel and a flint. **2** a gun having such a lock.

wheel of fortune *n* (in mythology and literature) a revolving device spun by a deity selecting random changes in the affairs of man.

wheels (wi:lz) *pl n* **1** the main directing force behind an organization, movement, etc.: *the wheels of government.* **2** an informal word for **car. 3 wheels within wheels.** a series of intricately connected events, plots, etc.

wheel window *n* another name for **rose window.**

wheel wobble *n* an oscillation of the front wheels of a vehicle caused by a defect in the steering gear, unbalanced wheels, etc.

wheelwright ('wi:lˌraɪt) *n* a person who makes or mends wheels as a trade.

wheeze (wi:z) *vb* **wheezes, wheezing, wheezed. 1** to breathe or utter (something) with a rasping or whistling sound. **2** (*intr*) to make or move with a noise suggestive of wheezy breathing. ◆ *n* **3** a husky, rasping, or whistling sound or breathing. **4** *Brit. sl.* a trick, idea, or plan. **5** *Inf.* a hackneyed joke or anecdote. ORIG C15: prob. from ON *hvǣsa* to hiss
▸ **'wheezer** *n* ▸ **'wheezy** *adj* ▸ **'wheezily** *adv* ▸ **'wheeziness** *n*

whelk[1] (wɛlk) *n* a marine gastropod mollusc of coastal waters and intertidal regions, having a strong snail-like shell. ORIG OE *weoloc*

whelk[2] (wɛlk) *n* a raised lesion on the skin; wheal. ORIG OE *hwylca,* from ?
▸ **'whelky** *adj*

whelm (wɛlm) *vb* (*tr*) *Arch.* to engulf entirely; overwhelm. ORIG C13 *whelmen* to turn over, from ?

whelp (wɛlp) *n* **1** a young offspring of certain animals, esp. of a wolf or dog. **2** *Disparaging.* a youth. **3** *Jocular.* a young child. **4** *Naut.* any of the ridges, parallel to the axis, on the drum of a capstan to keep a rope, etc., from slipping. ◆ *vb* **5** (of an animal or, disparagingly, a woman) to give birth to (young). ORIG OE *hwelp(a)*

when (wɛn) *adv* **1a** at what time? over what period?: *when is he due?* **1b** (*used in indirect questions*): *ask him when he's due.* **2 say when.** to state when an action is to be stopped or begun, as when someone is pouring a drink. ◆ *conj* **3** (*subordinating*) at a time at which; just as; after: *I found it easy when I tried.* **4** although: *he drives when he might walk.* **5** considering the fact that: *how did you pass the exam when you hadn't worked for it?* ◆ *pron* **6** at which (time); over which (period): *an age when men were men.* ◆ *n* **7** a question as to the time of some occurrence. ORIG OE *hwanne, hwænne*

> **USAGE NOTE** *When* should not be used loosely as a substitute for *in which* after a noun which does not refer to a period of time: *paralysis is a condition in which* (not *when*) *parts of the body cannot be moved.*

whenas (wɛn'æz) *conj Arch.* **1a** when; whenever. **1b** inasmuch as; while. **2** although.

whence (wɛns) *Arch. or formal.* ◆ *adv* **1** from what place, cause, or origin? ◆ *pron* **2** (*subordinating*) from what place, cause, or origin. ORIG C13 *whannes,* adv. genitive of OE *hwanon*

> **USAGE NOTE** The expression *from whence* should be avoided, since *whence* already means 'from which place': *the tradition whence* (not *from whence*) *such ideas flowed.*

whencesoever (ˌwɛnssəʊ'ɛvə) *conj* (*subordinating*), *adv Arch.* from whatever place, cause, or origin.

whenever (wɛn'ɛvə) *conj* **1** (*subordinating*) at every or any time that; when: *I laugh whenever I see that.* ◆ *adv also* **when ever. 2** no matter when: *it'll be here, whenever you decide to come for it.* **3** *Inf.* at an unknown or unspecified time: *I'll take it if it comes today, tomorrow, or whenever.* **4** an intensive form of *when,* used in questions: *whenever did he escape?*

whensoever (ˌwɛnsəʊ'ɛvə) *conj, adv Rare.* an intensive form of **whenever.**

whenua (fɛn'uə) *n NZ.* land. ORIG Maori

where (wɛə) *adv* **1a** in, at, or to what place, point, or position?: *where are you going?* **1b** (*used in indirect questions*): *I don't know where they are.* ◆ *pron* **2** in, at, or to which (place): *the hotel where we spent our honeymoon.* ◆ *conj* **3** (*subordinating*) in the place at which: *where we live it's always raining.* ◆ *n* **4** a question as to the position, direction, or destination of something. ORIG OE *hwǣr, hwār(a)*

> **USAGE NOTE** It was formerly considered incorrect to use *where* as a substitute for *in which* after a noun which did not refer to a place or position, but this use has now become acceptable: *we have a situation where/in which no further action is needed.*

whereabouts ('wɛərəˌbaʊts) *adv* **1** at what approximate place; where: *whereabouts are you?* ◆ *n* **2** (*functioning as sing or pl*) the place, esp. the approximate place, where a person or thing is.

whereas (wɛər'æz) *conj* **1** (*coordinating*) but on the other hand: *I like to go swimming whereas Sheila likes to sail.* ◆ *sentence connector.* **2** (in formal documents) it being the case that; since.

whereat (wɛər'æt) *Arch.* ◆ *adv* **1** at or to which place. ◆ *sentence connector.* **2** upon which occasion.

whereby (wɛə'baɪ) *pron* by or because of which: *the means whereby he took his life.*

wherefore ('wɛəˌfɔ:) *n* **1** (*usually pl*) an explanation or reason (esp. in **the whys and wherefores**). ◆ *adv* **2** *Arch.*

why? ◆ *sentence connector.* **3** *Arch. or formal.* for which reason: used in legal preambles.

wherefrom (wɛəˈfrɒm) *Arch.* ◆ *adv* **1** from what or where? whence? ◆ *pron* **2** from which place; whence.

wherein (wɛərˈɪn) *Arch. or formal.* ◆ *adv* **1** in what place or respect? ◆ *pron* **2** in which place, thing, etc.

whereof (wɛərˈɒv) *Arch. or formal.* ◆ *adv* **1** of what or which person or thing? ◆ *pron* **2** of which (person or thing): *the man whereof I speak is no longer alive.*

whereon (wɛərˈɒn) *Arch.* ◆ *adv* **1** on what thing or place? ◆ *pron* **2** on which thing, place, etc.

wheresoever (ˌwɛəsəʊˈɛvə) *conj (subordinating), adv, pron Rare.* an intensive form of **wherever.**

whereto (wɛəˈtuː) *Arch. or formal.* ◆ *adv* **1** towards what (place, end, etc.)? ◆ *pron* **2** to which. ◆ Also (archaic): **whereunto.**

whereupon (ˌwɛərəˈpɒn) *sentence connector.* at which; at which point; upon which.

wherever (wɛərˈɛvə) *pron* **1** at, in, or to every place or point which; where: *wherever she went, he would be there.* ◆ *conj* **2** (*subordinating*) in, to, or at whatever place: *wherever we go the weather is always bad.* ◆ *adv also* **where ever.** **3** no matter where: *I'll find you, wherever you are.* **4** *Inf.* at, in, or to an unknown or unspecified place: *I'll go anywhere to escape: London, Paris, or wherever.* **5** an intensive form of *where,* used in questions: *wherever can they be?*

wherewith (wɛəˈwɪθ, -ˈwɪð) *Arch. or formal.* ◆ *pron* **1** (*often foll. by an infinitive*) with or by which: *the pen wherewith I write.* **2** something with which: *I have not wherewith to buy my bread.* ◆ *adv* **3** with what? ◆ *sentence connector.* **4** with or after that; whereupon.

wherewithal *n* (ˈwɛəwɪðˌɔːl). **1 the wherewithal.** necessary funds, resources, or equipment: *these people lack the wherewithal for a decent existence.* ◆ *pron* (ˌwɛəwɪðˈɔːl). **2** a less common word for **wherewith.**

wherry (ˈwɛrɪ) *n, pl* **wherries. 1** any of certain kinds of half-decked commercial boats. **2** a light rowing boat. ORIG C15: from ?
▸ ˈ**wherryman** *n*

whet (wɛt) *vb* **whets, whetting, whetted.** (*tr*) **1** to sharpen, as by grinding or friction. **2** to increase (the appetite, desire, etc.); stimulate. ◆ *n* **3** the act of whetting. **4** a person or thing that whets. ORIG OE *hwettan*
▸ ˈ**whetter** *n*

whether (ˈwɛðə) *conj* **1** (*subordinating*) used to introduce an indirect question or a clause after a verb expressing or implying doubt or choice: *he doesn't know whether she's in Britain or whether she's gone to France.* **2** (*coordinating*) either: *any man, whether liberal or conservative, would agree with me.* **3 whether or no.** in any case: *he will be here tomorrow, whether or no.* **4 whether...or (whether).** if on the one hand...or even if on the other hand: *you'll eat that, whether you like it or not.* ORIG OE *hwæther, hwether*

whetstone (ˈwɛtˌstəʊn) *n* **1** a stone used for sharpening edged tools, knives, etc. **2** something that sharpens.

whew (hwjuː) *interj* an exclamation or sharply exhaled breath expressing relief, delight, etc.

whey (weɪ) *n* the watery liquid that separates from the curd when milk is clotted, as in making cheese. ORIG OE *hwǣg*

wheyface (ˈweɪˌfeɪs) *n* **1** a pale bloodless face. **2** a person with such a face.
▸ ˈ**wheyˌfaced** *adj*

which (wɪtʃ) *determiner* **1a** used with a noun in requesting that its referent be further specified, identified, or distinguished: *which house did you buy?* **1b** (*as pron*): *which did you find?* **1c** (*used in indirect questions*): *I wondered which apples were cheaper.* **2a** whatever of a class; whichever: *bring which car you want.* **2b** (*as pron*): *choose which of the cars suits you.* ◆ *pron* **3** used in relative clauses with inanimate antecedents: *the house, which is old, is in poor repair.* **4** as; and that: used in relative clauses with verb phrases or sentences as their antecedents: *he died of cancer, which is what I predicted.* **5 the which.** an archaic form of **which** often used as a sentence connector. ORIG OE *hwelc, hwilc*

> **USAGE NOTE** See at **that.**

whichever (wɪtʃˈɛvə) *determiner* **1a** any (one, two, etc., out of several): *take whichever car you like.* **1b** (*as pron*): *choose whichever appeals to you.* **2a** no matter which (one or ones): *whichever card you pick you'll still be making a mistake.* **2b** (*as pron*): *it won't make any difference, whichever comes first.*

whichsoever (ˌwɪtʃsəʊˈɛvə) *pron* an archaic or formal word for **whichever.**

whicker (ˈwɪkə) *vb* (*intr*) (of a horse) to whinny or neigh; nicker. ORIG C17: imit.

whidah (ˈwɪdə) *n* a variant spelling of **whydah.**

whiff (wɪf) *n* **1** a passing odour. **2** a brief gentle gust of air. **3** a single inhalation or exhalation from the mouth or nose. ◆ *vb* **4** to puff or waft. **5** (*tr*) to sniff or smell. **6** (*intr*) *Brit. sl.* to stink. ORIG C16: imit.

whiffle (ˈwɪfᵊl) *vb* **whiffles, whiffling, whiffled. 1** (*intr*) to think or behave in an erratic or unpredictable way. **2** to blow or be blown fitfully or in gusts. **3** (*intr*) to whistle softly. ORIG C16: frequentative of WHIFF

whiffletree (ˈwɪfᵊlˌtriː) *n Chiefly US.* another word for **swingletree.** ORIG C19: var. of WHIPPLETREE

Whig (wɪg) *n* **1** a member of the English political party that opposed the succession to the throne of James, Duke of York (1679–80), on the grounds that he was a Catholic. Standing for a limited monarchy, the Whigs later represented the desires of industrialists and Dissenters for political and social reform, and provided the core of the Liberal Party. **2** (in the US) a supporter of the War of American Independence. Cf. **Tory. 3** a member of the American political party that opposed the Democrats from about 1834 to 1855 and represented propertied and professional interests. **4** *History.* a 17th-century Scottish Presbyterian, esp. one in rebellion against the Crown. ◆ *adj* **5** of, characteristic of, or relating to Whigs. ORIG C17: prob. from *whiggamore,* one of a group of 17th-cent. Scottish rebels who joined in an attack on Edinburgh known as *the whiggamore raid;* prob. from Scot. *whig* to drive (from ?) + *more* horse
▸ ˈ**Whiggery** *or* ˈ**Whiggism** *n* ▸ ˈ**Whiggish** *adj*

while (waɪl) *conj also* **whilst. 1** (*subordinating*) at the same time that: *please light the fire while I'm cooking.* **2** (*subordinating*) all the time that: *I stay inside while it's raining.* **3** (*subordinating*) in spite of the fact that: *while I agree about his brilliance I still think he's rude.* **4** (*coordinating*) whereas; and in contrast: *houses are expensive, while flats are cheap.* ◆ *prep, conj* **5** *Scot. & N English dialect.* another word for **until:** *you'll have to wait while Monday.* ◆ *n* **6** (*usually used in adverbial phrases*) a period or interval of time: *once in a long while.* **7** trouble or time (esp. in **worth one's while**): *it's hardly worth your while to begin work today.* ORIG OE *hwīl*

> **USAGE NOTE** See at **awhile.**

while away *vb* (*tr, adv*) to pass (time) idly and usually pleasantly.

whiles (waɪlz) *Arch. or dialect.* ◆ *adv* **1** at times; occasionally. ◆ *conj* **2** while; whilst.

whilom (ˈwaɪləm) *Arch.* ◆ *adv* **1** formerly; once. ◆ *adj* **2** (*prenominal*) one-time; former. ORIG OE *hwīlum,* dative pl of *hwīl* while

whilst (waɪlst) *conj Chiefly Brit.* another word for **while** (senses 1–4). ORIG C13: from WHILES + *-t* as in *amidst*

whim (wɪm) *n* **1** a sudden, passing, and often fanciful idea; impulsive or irrational thought. **2** a horse-drawn winch formerly used in mining to lift ore or water. ORIG C17: from C16 *whim-wham,* from ?

whimbrel (ˈwɪmbrəl) *n* a small European curlew with a striped head. ORIG C16: from dialect *whimp* or from WHIMPER, from its cry

whimper (ˈwɪmpə) *vb* **1** (*intr*) to cry, sob, or whine softly or intermittently. **2** to complain or say (something) in a whining plaintive way. ◆ *n* **3** a soft plaintive whine. ORIG C16: from dialect *whimp,* imit.
▸ ˈ**whimperer** *n* ▸ ˈ**whimpering** *n, adj* ▸ ˈ**whimperingly** *adv*

whimsical (ˈwɪmzɪkᵊl) *adj* **1** spontaneously fanciful or

playful. **2** given to whims; capricious. **3** quaint, unusual, or fantastic.
▸ **whimsicality** (ˌwɪmzɪˈkælɪtɪ) *n* ▸ ˈ**whimsically** *adv*

whimsy *or* **whimsey** (ˈwɪmzɪ) *n, pl* **whimsies** *or* **whimseys. 1** a capricious idea or notion. **2** light or fanciful humour. **3** something quaint or unusual. ◆ *adj* **whimsier, whimsiest. 4** quaint, comical, or unusual, often in a tasteless way. ORIG C17: from WHIM

whin[1] (wɪn) *n* another name for **gorse.** ORIG C11: from ON

whin[2] (wɪn) *n* short for **whinstone.** ORIG C14 *quin*, from ?

whinchat (ˈwɪnˌtʃæt) *n* an Old World songbird having a mottled brown-and-white plumage with pale cream underparts. ORIG C17: from WHIN[1] + CHAT

whine (waɪn) *n* **1** a long high-pitched plaintive cry or moan. **2** a continuous high-pitched sound. **3** a peevish complaint, esp. one repeated. ◆ *vb* **whines, whining, whined. 4** to make a whine or utter in a whine. ORIG OE *hwīnan*
▸ ˈ**whiner** *n* ▸ ˈ**whining** *or* ˈ**whiny** *adj* ▸ ˈ**whiningly** *adv*

whinge (wɪndʒ) *vb* **whinges, whingeing, whinged.** (*intr*) **1** to cry in a fretful way. **2** to complain. ◆ *n* **3** a complaint. ORIG from Northern var. of OE *hwinsian* to whine
▸ ˈ**whingeing** *n, adj* ▸ ˈ**whinger** *n*

whinny (ˈwɪnɪ) *vb* **whinnies, whinnying, whinnied.** (*intr*) **1** (of a horse) to neigh softly or gently. **2** to make a sound resembling a neigh, such as a laugh. ◆ *n, pl* **whinnies. 3** a gentle or low-pitched neigh. ORIG C16: imit.

whinstone (ˈwɪnˌstəʊn) *n* any dark hard fine-grained rock, such as basalt. ORIG C16: from WHIN[2] + STONE

whip (wɪp) *vb* **whips, whipping, whipped. 1** to strike (a person or thing) with several strokes of a strap, rod, etc. **2** (*tr*) to punish by striking in this manner. **3** (*tr;* foll. by *out, away,* etc.) to pull, remove, etc., with sudden rapid motion: *to whip out a gun.* **4** (*intr;* foll. by *down, into, out of,* etc.) *Inf.* to come, go, etc., in a rapid sudden manner: *they whipped into the bar for a drink.* **5** to strike or be struck as if by whipping: *the tempest whipped the surface of the sea.* **6** (*tr*) to bring, train, etc., forcefully into a desired condition. **7** (*tr*) *Inf.* to overcome or outdo. **8** (*tr;* often foll. by *on, out,* or *off*) to drive, urge, compel, etc., by or as if by whipping. **9** (*tr*) to wrap or wind (a cord, thread, etc.) around (a rope, cable, etc.) to prevent chafing or fraying. **10** (*tr*) (in fly-fishing) to cast the fly repeatedly onto (the water) in a whipping motion. **11** (*tr*) (in sewing) to join, finish, or gather with whipstitch. **12** to beat (eggs, cream, etc.) with a whisk or similar utensil to incorporate air. **13** (*tr*) to spin (a top). **14** (*tr*) *Inf.* to steal: *he whipped her purse.* ◆ *n* **15** a device consisting of a lash or flexible rod attached at one end to a stiff handle and used for driving animals, inflicting corporal punishment, etc. **16** a whipping stroke or motion. **17** a person adept at handling a whip, as a coachman, etc. **18** (in a legislative body) **18a** a member of a party chosen to organize and discipline the members of his faction. **18b** a call issued to members of a party, insisting with varying degrees of urgency upon their presence or loyal voting behaviour. **18c** (in the Brit. Parliament) a schedule of business sent to members of a party each week. Each item on it is underlined to indicate its importance: three lines means that the item is very important and every member must attend and vote according to the party line. **19** an apparatus for hoisting, consisting of a rope, pulley, and snatch block. **20** any of a variety of desserts made from egg whites or cream beaten stiff. **21** See **whipper-in. 22** flexibility, as in the shaft of a golf club, etc. ◆ See also **whip-round, whip up, whips.** ORIG C13: ?from MDu. *wippen* to swing
▸ ˈ**whipˌlike** *adj* ▸ ˈ**whipper** *n*

whip bird *n Austral.* any of several birds having a whistle ending in a note sounding like the crack of a whip.

whipcord (ˈwɪpˌkɔːd) *n* **1** a strong worsted or cotton fabric with a diagonally ribbed surface. **2** a closely twisted hard cord used for the lashes of whips, etc.

whip graft *n Horticulture.* a graft made by inserting a tongue cut on the sloping base of the scion into a slit on the sloping top of the stock.

whip hand *n* (usually preceded by *the*) **1** (in driving horses) the hand holding the whip. **2** advantage or dominating position.

whiplash (ˈwɪpˌlæʃ) *n* a quick lash or stroke of a whip or like that of a whip.

whiplash injury *n Med. inf.* any injury to the neck resulting from a sudden thrusting forwards and snapping back of the unsupported head. Technical name: **hyperextension-hyperflexion injury.**

whipper-in *n, pl* **whippers-in.** a person employed to assist the huntsman managing the hounds.

whippersnapper (ˈwɪpəˌsnæpə) *n* an insignificant but pretentious or cheeky person, often a young one. Also called: **whipster.** ORIG C17: prob. from *whipsnapper* a person who snaps whips, infl. by earlier *snippersnapper,* from ?

whippet (ˈwɪpɪt) *n* a small slender breed of dog similar to a greyhound. ORIG C16: from ?; ? based on *whip it!* move quickly!

whipping (ˈwɪpɪŋ) *n* **1** a thrashing or beating with a whip or similar implement. **2** cord or twine used for binding or lashing. **3** the binding formed by wrapping a rope, etc., with cord or twine.

whipping boy *n* a person of little importance who is blamed for the errors, incompetence, etc., of others, esp. his superiors; scapegoat. ORIG C17: orig. referring to a boy who was educated with a prince and who received punishment for any faults committed by the prince

whippletree (ˈwɪpəlˌtriː) *n* another name for **swingletree.** ORIG C18: apparently from WHIP

whippoorwill (ˈwɪpʊˌwɪl) *n* a nightjar of North and Central America, having a dark plumage with white patches on the tail. ORIG C18: imit. of its cry

whip-round *Inf., chiefly Brit.* ◆ *n* **1** an impromptu collection of money. ◆ *vb* **whip round. 2** (*intr, adv*) to make such a collection.

whips (wɪps) *pl n* (often foll. by *of*) *Austral. inf.* a large quantity: *I've got whips of cash at the moment.*

whipsaw (ˈwɪpˌsɔː) *n* **1** any saw with a flexible blade, such as a bandsaw. ◆ *vb* **whipsaws, whipsawing, whipsawed; whipsawed** *or* **whipsawn.** (*tr*) **2** to saw with a whipsaw. **3** *US.* to defeat in two ways at once.

whip scorpion *n* any of an order of nonvenomous arachnids, typically resembling a scorpion but lacking a sting.

whip snake *n* any of several long slender fast-moving nonvenomous snakes.

whipstitch (ˈwɪpˌstɪtʃ) *n* a sewing stitch passing over an edge.

whipstock (ˈwɪpˌstɒk) *n* a whip handle.

whip up *vb* (*tr, adv*) **1** to excite; arouse: *to whip up a mob; to whip up discontent.* **2** *Inf.* to prepare quickly: *to whip up a meal.*

whir *or* **whirr** (wɜː) *n* **1** a prolonged soft swish or buzz, as of a motor working or wings flapping. **2** a bustle or rush. ◆ *vb* **whirs** *or* **whirrs, whirring, whirred. 3** to make or cause to make a whir. ORIG C14: prob. from ON; see WHIRL

whirl (wɜːl) *vb* **1** to spin, turn, or revolve or cause to spin, turn, or revolve. **2** (*intr*) to turn around or away rapidly. **3** (*intr*) to have a spinning sensation, as from dizziness, etc. **4** to move or drive or be moved or driven at high speed. ◆ *n* **5** the act or an instance of whirling; swift rotation or a rapid whirling movement. **6** a condition of confusion or giddiness: *her accident left me in a whirl.* **7** a swift round, as of events, meetings, etc. **8** a tumult; stir. **9** *Inf.* a brief trip, dance, etc. **10 give (something) a whirl.** *Inf.* to attempt or give a trial to (something). ORIG C13: from ON *hvirfla* to turn about
▸ ˈ**whirler** *n* ▸ ˈ**whirling** *adj* ▸ ˈ**whirlingly** *adv*

whirligig (ˈwɜːlɪˌgɪg) *n* **1** any spinning toy, such as a top. **2** another name for **merry-go-round. 3** anything that whirls about, spins, or moves in a circular or giddy way: *the whirligig of social life.* ORIG C15 *whirlegigge,* from WHIRL + GIG[1]

whirlpool (ˈwɜːlˌpuːl) *n* **1** a powerful circular current or vortex of water. **2** something resembling a whirlpool in motion or the power to attract into its vortex.

whirlwind ('wɜːlˌwɪnd) *n* **1** a column of air whirling around and towards a more or less vertical axis of low pressure, which moves along the land or ocean surface. **2a** a motion or course resembling this, esp. in rapidity. **2b** (*as modifier*): *a whirlwind romance.* **3** an impetuously active person.

whirlybird ('wɜːlɪˌbɜːd) *n* an informal word for **helicopter.**

whish (wɪʃ) *n, vb* a less common word for **swish.**

whisht (hwɪʃt) *or* **whist** *Arch. or dialect, esp. Scot.* ◆ *interj* **1** hush! be quiet! ◆ *adj* **2** silent or still. ORIG C14: cf. HIST

whisk (wɪsk) *vb* **1** (*tr; often foll. by away or off*) to brush, sweep, or wipe off lightly. **2** (*tr*) to move, carry, etc., with a light or rapid sweeping motion: *the taxi whisked us to the airport.* **3** (*intr*) to move, go, etc., quickly and nimbly: *to whisk downstairs for a drink.* **4** (*tr*) to whip (eggs, etc.) to a froth. ◆ *n* **5** the act of whisking. **6** a light rapid sweeping movement. **7** a utensil for whipping eggs, etc. **8** a small brush or broom. **9** a small bunch or bundle, as of grass, straw, etc. ORIG C14: from ON *visk* wisp

whisker ('wɪskə) *n* **1** any of the stiff sensory hairs growing on the face of a cat, rat, or other mammal. Technical name: **vibrissa. 2** any of the hairs growing on a man's face, esp. on the cheeks or chin. **3** (*pl*) a beard or that part of it growing on the sides of the face. **4** (*pl*) *Inf.* a moustache. **5** *Chem.* a very fine filamentary crystal having greater strength than the bulk material. **6** a person or thing that whisks. **7** a narrow margin or small distance: *he escaped death by a whisker.* ORIG see WHISK
▸ **'whiskered** *or* **'whiskery** *adj*

whiskey ('wɪskɪ) *n* the usual Irish and US spelling of **whisky.**

whiskey sour *n US.* a mixed drink of whisky and lime or lemon juice, sometimes sweetened.

whisky ('wɪskɪ) *n, pl* **whiskies.** a spirit made by distilling fermented cereals, which is matured and often blended. ORIG C18: shortened from *whiskybae,* from Scot. Gaelic *uisge beatha,* lit.: water of life; see USQUEBAUGH

whisky-jack *n Canad.* another name for **Canada jay.**

whisky mac *n Brit.* a drink consisting of whisky and ginger wine.

whisper ('wɪspə) *vb* **1** to speak or utter (something) in a soft hushed tone, esp. without vibration of the vocal cords. **2** (*intr*) to speak secretly or furtively, as in promoting intrigue, gossip, etc. **3** (*intr*) (of leaves, trees, etc.) to make a low soft rustling sound. **4** (*tr*) to utter or suggest secretly or privately: *to whisper treason.* ◆ *n* **5** a low soft voice: *to speak in a whisper.* **6** something uttered in such a voice. **7** a low soft rustling sound. **8** a trace or suspicion. **9** *Inf.* a rumour. ORIG OE *hwisprian*
▸ **'whisperer** *n* ▸ **'whispery** *adj*

whispering campaign *n* the organized diffusion of defamatory rumours to discredit a person, group, etc.

whispering gallery *n* a gallery or dome with acoustic characteristics such that a sound made at one point is audible at distant points.

whist[1] (wɪst) *n* a card game for four in which the two sides try to win the balance of the 13 tricks: forerunner of bridge. ORIG C17: ? changed from WHISK, referring to the sweeping up or whisking up of the tricks

whist[2] (hwɪst) *interj, adj* a variant of **whisht.**

whist drive *n* a social gathering where whist is played: the winners of each hand move to different tables to play the losers of the previous hand.

whistle ('wɪsᵊl) *vb* **whistles, whistling, whistled. 1** to produce (shrill or flutelike sounds), as by passing breath through a narrow constriction most easily formed by the pursed lips. **2** (*tr*) to signal or command by whistling or blowing a whistle: *the referee whistled the end of the game.* **3** (of a kettle, train, etc.) to produce (a shrill sound) caused by the emission of steam through a small aperture. **4** (*intr*) to move with a whistling sound caused by rapid passage through the air. **5** (of animals, esp. birds) to emit (a shrill sound) resembling human whistling. **6 whistle in the dark.** to try to keep up one's confidence in spite of fear. ◆ *n* **7** a device for making a shrill high-pitched sound by means of air or steam under pressure. **8** a shrill sound effected by whistling or blowing a whistle. **9** a whistling sound, as of a bird, bullet, the wind, etc. **10** a signal, etc., transmitted by or as if by a whistle. **11** the act of whistling. **12** an instrument, usually made of metal, that is blown down its end to produce a tune, signal, etc. **13 blow the whistle.** (usually foll. by *on*) *Inf.* **13a** to inform (on). **13b** to bring a stop (to). **14 clean as a whistle.** perfectly clean or clear. **15 wet one's whistle.** *Inf.* to take an alcoholic drink. ◆ See also **whistle for, whistle up.** ORIG OE *hwistlian*

whistle-blower *n Inf.* a person who informs on someone or puts a stop to something.
▸ **'whistle-ˌblowing** *adj, n*

whistle for *vb* (*intr, prep*) *Inf.* to seek or expect in vain.

whistler ('wɪslə) *n* **1** a person or thing that whistles. **2** *Radio.* an atmospheric disturbance picked up by radio receivers, caused by the electromagnetic radiation produced by lightning. **3** any of various birds having a whistling call, such as certain Australian flycatchers. **4** any of various North American marmots.

Whistler ★ ('wɪslə) *n* **James Abbott McNeill.** 1834–1903, US painter, living in Europe: best known for his portraits.

whistle stop *n* **1** *US & Canad.* **1a** a minor railway station where trains stop only on signal. **1b** a small town having such a station. **2a** a brief appearance in a town, esp. by a political candidate. **2b** (*as modifier*): *a whistle-stop tour.*

whistle up *vb* (*tr, adv*) to call or summon (a person or animal) by whistling.

whit (wɪt) *n* (*usually used with a negative*) the smallest particle; iota; jot: *he has changed not a whit.* ORIG C15: prob. var. of WIGHT

Whit (wɪt) *n* **1** See **Whitsuntide.** ◆ *adj* **2** of or relating to Whitsuntide.

Whitaker ★ ('wɪtəkə) *n* Sir **Frederick.** 1812–91, New Zealand statesman, born in Britain: prime minister (1863–64; 1882–83).

Whitbread ★ ('wɪtˌbrɛd) *n* **Fatima.** born 1961, British javelin thrower.

Whitby ★ ('wɪtbɪ) *n* a fishing port and resort in NE England, in E North Yorkshire at the mouth of the River Esk: an important ecclesiastical centre in Anglo-Saxon times; site of an abbey founded in 656. Pop.: 13 640 (1991).

white (waɪt) *adj* **1** having no hue, owing to the reflection of all or almost all incident light. **2** (of light, such as sunlight) consisting of all the colours of the spectrum or produced by certain mixtures of primary colours, as red, green, and blue. **3** comparatively white or whitish-grey or having parts of this colour: *white clover.* **4** (of an animal) having pale-coloured or white skin, fur, or feathers. **5** bloodless or pale, as from pain, emotion, etc. **6** (of hair, etc.) grey, usually from age. **7** benevolent or without malicious intent: *white magic.* **8** colourless or transparent: *white glass.* **9** capped with or accompanied by snow: *a white Christmas.* **10** blank, as an unprinted area of a page. **11** (of coffee or tea) with milk or cream. **12** (of wine) made from pale grapes or from black grapes separated from their skins. **13** denoting flour, or bread made from flour, that has had part of the grain removed. **14** *Physics.* having or characterized by a continuous distribution of energy, wavelength, or frequency: *white noise.* **15** *Inf.* honourable or generous. **16** *Poetic or arch.* having a fair complexion; blond. **17 bleed white.** to deprive slowly of resources. ◆ *n* **18** a white colour. **19** the condition of being white; whiteness. **20** the white or lightly coloured part of something. **21** (usually preceded by *the*) the viscous fluid that surrounds the yolk of a bird's egg, esp. a hen's egg; albumen. **22** *Anat.* the white part (sclera) of the eyeball. **23** any of various butterflies having white wings with scanty black markings. **24** *Chess, draughts.* **24a** a white or light-coloured piece or square. **24b** the player playing with such pieces. **25** anything that has or is characterized by a white colour, such as a white paint or white clothing. **26** *Inf.* white wine: *a bottle of white.* **27** *Archery.* the outer ring of the target, having the lowest score. ◆ *vb* **whites, whiting, whited. 28** *Obs.* to make or become white. ◆ See also **white out, whites.** ORIG OE *hwīt*
▸ **'whitely** *adv* ▸ **'whiteness** *n* ▸ **'whitish** *adj*

White[1] (waɪt) *n* **1** a member of the Caucasoid race. **2** a person of European ancestry. ◆ *adj* **3** denoting or relating to a White or Whites.

White[2] ★ (waɪt) *n* **1 Gilbert.** 1720–93, British clergyman and naturalist, noted for his *Natural History and Antiquities of Selborne* (1789). **2 Jimmy.** born 1962, British snooker player. **3 Patrick (Victor Martindale).** 1912–90, Australian novelist: his works include *Voss* (1957) and *A Fringe of Leaves* (1976): Nobel prize for literature 1973.

white admiral *n* a butterfly of Eurasia having brown wings with white markings.

white ant *n* another name for **termite.**

whitebait (ˈwaɪtˌbeɪt) *n* **1** the young of herrings, sprats, etc., cooked and eaten whole as a delicacy. **2** any of various small silvery fishes. ORIG C18: from its formerly having been used as bait

whitebeam (ˈwaɪtˌbiːm) *n* a N temperate tree having leaves that are densely hairy on the undersurface and hard timber.

white blood cell *n* a nontechnical name for **leucocyte.**

whiteboard (ˈwaɪtˌbɔːd) *n* a smooth white wipeable board, often used in teaching.

whitecap (ˈwaɪtˌkæp) *n* a wave with a white broken crest.

white cedar *n* either of two coniferous trees of North America, having scalelike leaves.

white clover *n* a Eurasian clover plant with rounded white flower heads: cultivated as a forage plant.

white coal *n* water, esp. when flowing and providing a potential source of usable power.

white-collar *adj* of or designating nonmanual and usually salaried workers employed in professional and clerical occupations.

white currant *n* a cultivated N temperate shrub having small rounded white edible berries.

whitedamp (ˈwaɪtˌdæmp) *n* a mixture of poisonous gases, mainly carbon monoxide, occurring in coal mines.

whited sepulchre *n* a hypocrite. ORIG allusion to Matthew 23:27

white dwarf *n* one of a large class of small faint stars of enormous density, thought to mark the final stage in the evolution of a sun-like star.

white elephant *n* **1** a rare albino variety of the Indian elephant, regarded as sacred in parts of S Asia. **2** a possession that is unwanted by its owner. **3** a rare or valuable possession the upkeep of which is very expensive.

White Ensign *n* the ensign of the Royal Navy and the Royal Yacht Squadron, having a red cross on a white background with the Union Jack at the upper corner of the vertical edge alongside the hoist.

white-eye *n* a songbird of Africa, Australia, New Zealand, and Asia, having a greenish plumage with a white ring around each eye.

white feather *n* **1** a symbol or mark of cowardice. **2 show the white feather.** to act in a cowardly manner. ORIG from the belief that a white feather in a gamecock's tail was a sign of a poor fighter

Whitefield ★ (ˈwaɪtˌfiːld) *n* **George.** 1714–70, British Methodist preacher, who separated from the Wesleys (?1741) because of his Calvinistic views.

whitefish (ˈwaɪtˌfɪʃ) *n, pl* **whitefish** *or* **whitefishes.** a food fish typically of deep cold lakes of the N hemisphere, having large silvery scales and a small head.

white fish *n* (in the Brit. fishing industry) any edible marine fish or invertebrate excluding herrings but including trout, salmon, and all shellfish.

white flag *n* a white flag or a piece of white cloth hoisted to signify surrender or request a truce.

white flour *n* flour that consists substantially of the starchy endosperm of wheat, most of the bran and the germ having been removed by the milling process.

whitefly (ˈwaɪtˌflaɪ) *n, pl* **whiteflies.** any of a family of insects typically having a body covered with powdery wax. Many are pests of greenhouse crops.

white friar *n* a Carmelite friar, so called because of the white cloak that forms part of the habit of this order.

white gold *n* any of various white lustrous hard-wearing alloys containing gold together with platinum and palladium and sometimes smaller amounts of silver, nickel, or copper.

white goods *pl n* **1** household linen such as sheets, towels, tablecloths, etc. **2** large household appliances, such as refrigerators or cookers.

Whitehall ★ (ˌwaɪtˈhɔːl) *n* **1** a street in London stretching from Trafalgar Square to the Houses of Parliament: site of the main government offices. **2** the British Government.

Whitehead ★ (ˈwaɪtˌhɛd) *n* **Alfred North.** 1861–1947, British mathematician, who collaborated with Bertrand Russell in *Principia Mathematica* (1910–13).

white heat *n* **1** intense heat characterized by emission of white light. **2** *Inf.* a state of intense excitement or activity.

white hope *n Inf.* a person who is expected to bring honour or glory to his or her group, team, etc.

Whitehorse ★ (ˈwaɪtˌhɔːs) *n* a town in NW Canada: capital of the Yukon Territory. Pop.: 22 884 (1995 est.).

white horse *n* **1** the outline of a horse carved into the side of a chalk hill, usually dating to the Neolithic, Bronze, or Iron Ages. **2** (*usually pl*) a wave with a white broken crest.

white-hot *adj* **1** at such a high temperature that white light is emitted. **2** *Inf.* in a state of intense emotion.

White House ★ *n* **the. 1** the official Washington residence of the president of the US. **2** the US presidency.

white knight *n* a champion or rescuer, esp. a person or organization that rescues a company from financial difficulties, an unwelcome takeover bid, etc.

white-knuckle *adj* causing or experiencing fear or anxiety: *a white-knuckle fairground ride.*

Whitelaw ★ (ˈwaɪtˌlɔː) *n* **Billie.** born 1932, British actress, noted esp. for her performances in plays by Samuel Beckett; her films include *The Omen* (1976) and *The Dressmaker* (1988).

white lead (lɛd) *n* **1** a white solid usually regarded as a mixture of lead carbonate and lead hydroxide; basic lead carbonate: used in paint and in making putty and ointments for the treatment of burns. **2** either of two similar white pigments based on lead sulphate or lead silicate.

white leg *n* another name for **milk leg.**

white lie *n* a minor or unimportant lie, esp. one uttered in the interests of tact or politeness.

white light *n* light that contains all the wavelengths of visible light at approximately equal intensities, as in sunlight.

white-livered *adj* **1** lacking in spirit or courage. **2** pallid and unhealthy in appearance.

White man's burden *n* the supposed duty of the White race to bring education and Western culture to the non-White inhabitants of their colonies.

white matter *n* the whitish tissue of the brain and spinal cord, consisting mainly of nerve fibres covered with a protective white fatlike substance.

white meat *n* any meat that is light in colour, such as veal or the breast of turkey.

white metal *n* any of various alloys, such as Babbitt metal, used for bearings.

white meter *n Brit.* an electricity meter used to record the consumption of off-peak electricity.

White Mountains ★ *pl n* **1** a mountain range in the US, chiefly in N New Hampshire: part of the Appalachians. Highest peak: Mount Washington, 1917 m (6288 ft). **2** a mountain range in the US, in E California and SW Nevada. Highest peak: White Mountain, 4342 m (14 246 ft).

whiten (ˈwaɪtᵊn) *vb* to make or become white or whiter. ▸ ˈ**whitener** *n* ▸ ˈ**whitening** *n*

White Nile ★ *n* See **Nile.**

white noise *n* sound or electrical noise that has a relatively wide continuous range of frequencies of uniform intensity.

white oak *n* a large oak tree of E North America, having pale bark, leaves with rounded lobes, and heavy light-coloured wood.

white out *vb* (*adv*) **1** (*intr*) to lose or lack daylight visibility owing to snow or fog. **2** (*tr*) to create or leave white spaces in (printed or other matter). ◆ *n* **whiteout. 3** a polar atmospheric condition consisting of lack of visibility and sense of distance and direction due to a uniform whiteness of a heavy cloud cover and snow-covered ground, which reflects almost all the light it receives.

white paper *n* (*often caps.*) an official government report in any of a number of countries, which sets out the government's policy on a matter that is or will come before Parliament.

white pepper *n* a condiment, less pungent than black pepper, made from the husked dried beans of the pepper plant.

white pine *n* a North American coniferous tree having blue-green needle-like leaves, hanging brown cones, and rough bark.

white poplar *n* **1** Also called: **abele.** a Eurasian tree having leaves covered with dense silvery-white hairs. **2** another name for **tulipwood** (sense 1).

white rose *n English history.* an emblem of the House of York.

White Russia ★ *n* another name for **Belarus.**
▸ **White Russian** *adj, n*

whites (waɪts) *pl n* **1** household linen or cotton goods, such as sheets. **2** white or off-white clothing, such as that worn for playing cricket.

white sale *n* a sale of household linens at reduced prices.

white sauce *n* a thick sauce made from flour, butter, seasonings, and milk or stock.

White Sea ★ *n* an almost landlocked inlet of the Barents Sea on the coast of NW Russia. Area: 90 000 sq. km (34 700 sq. miles).

white settler *n* a well-off incomer to a district who takes advantage of what it has to offer without regard to the local inhabitants. ORIG C20: from earlier colonial sense

white slave *n* a girl or woman forced or sold into prostitution.
▸ **white slavery** *n* ▸ **ˌwhite-ˈslaver** *n*

white spirit *n* a colourless liquid obtained from petroleum and used as a substitute for turpentine.

white spruce *n* a N North American spruce tree with grey bark.

white squall *n* a violent highly localized weather disturbance at sea, in which the surface of the water is whipped to a white spray by the winds.

whitethorn (ˈwaɪtˌθɔːn) *n* another name for **hawthorn.**

whitethroat (ˈwaɪtˌθrəʊt) *n* either of two Old World warblers having a greyish-brown plumage with a white throat and underparts.

white tie *n* **1** a white bow tie worn as part of a man's formal evening dress. **2a** formal evening dress for men. **2b** (*as modifier*): *a white-tie occasion.*

white trash *n Disparaging.* **a** poor White people living in the US, esp. the South. **b** (*as modifier*): *white-trash culture.*

White Van Man *n* a male van driver, often of a white van, whose driving is selfish and aggressive.

White Volta ★ *n* a river in W Africa, rising in N Burkina-Faso flowing southwest and south to join the Black Volta in central Ghana and form the Volta River. Length: about 885 km (550 miles).

whitewall (ˈwaɪtˌwɔːl) *n* a pneumatic tyre having white sidewalls.

whitewash (ˈwaɪtˌwɒʃ) *n* **1** a substance used for whitening walls and other surfaces, consisting of a suspension of lime or whiting in water. **2** *Inf.* deceptive or specious words or actions intended to conceal defects, gloss over failings, etc. **3** *Inf.* a defeat in a sporting contest in which the loser is beaten in every match, game, etc. in a series. ◆ *vb* (*tr*) **4** to cover with whitewash. **5** *Inf.* to conceal, gloss over, or suppress. **6** *Inf.* to defeat (an opponent or opposing team) by winning every match in a series.
▸ **ˈwhiteˌwasher** *n*

white water *n* **1** a stretch of water with a broken foamy surface, as in rapids. **2** light-coloured sea water, esp. over shoals or shallows.

white whale *n* a small white toothed whale of northern waters. Also called: **beluga.**

whitewood (ˈwaɪtˌwʊd) *n* **1** any of various trees with light-coloured wood, such as the tulip tree, basswood, and cottonwood. **2** the wood of any of these trees.

whitey *or* **whity** (ˈwaɪtɪ) *n, pl* **whiteys** *or* **whities.** *Chiefly US.* (used contemptuously by Black people) a White man or White men collectively.

whither (ˈwɪðə) *Arch. or poetic.* ◆ *adv* **1** to what place? **2** to what end or purpose? ◆ *conj* **3** to whatever place, purpose, etc. ORIG OE *hwider, hwæder;* Mod. E form infl. by HITHER

whithersoever (ˌwɪðəsəʊˈɛvə) *adv, conj Arch. or poetic.* to whichever place.

whiting[1] (ˈwaɪtɪŋ) *n* **1** an important gadoid food fish of European seas, having a dark back with silvery sides and underparts. **2** any of various similar fishes. ORIG C15: ?from OE *hwītling*

whiting[2] (ˈwaɪtɪŋ) *n* white chalk that has been ground and washed, used in making whitewash, metal polish, etc. Also called: **whitening.**

Whitlam ★ (ˈwɪtləm) *n* (**Edward**) **Gough** (gɒf). born 1916, Australian Labor statesman: prime minister (1972–75).

Whitley Bay ★ (ˈwɪtlɪ) *n* a resort in NE England, in North Tyneside on the North Sea. Pop.: 33 335 (1991).

whitlow (ˈwɪtləʊ) *n* any pussy inflammation of the end of a finger or toe. ORIG C14: changed from *whitflaw,* from WHITE + FLAW[1]

Whitman ★ (ˈwɪtmən) *n* **Walt**(**er**). 1819–92, US poet, whose work is collected in *Leaves of Grass* (1855 and subsequent enlarged editions).

Whitney[1] ★ (ˈwɪtnɪ) *n* **Mount.** a mountain in E California: the highest peak in the Sierra Nevada Mountains and in continental US (excluding Alaska). Height: 4418 m (14 495 ft).

Whitney[2] ★ (ˈwɪtnɪ) *n* **Eli.** 1765–1825, US inventor of a mechanical cotton gin (1793).

Whitsun (ˈwɪtsᵊn) *n* **1** short for **Whitsuntide.** ◆ *adj* **2** of or relating to Whit Sunday or Whitsuntide.

Whitsunday (ˌhwɪtˈsʌndɪ, ˌwɪt-) *n* (in Scotland) May 15, one of the four quarter days.

Whit Sunday *n* the seventh Sunday after Easter, observed as a feast in commemoration of the descent of the Holy Spirit on the apostles. Also called: **Pentecost.** ORIG OE *hwīta sunnandæg* white Sunday, prob. after the ancient custom of wearing white robes at or after baptism

Whitsuntide (ˈwɪtsᵊnˌtaɪd) *n* the week that begins with Whit Sunday, esp. the first three days.

Whittier ★ (ˈwɪtɪə) *n* **John Greenleaf.** 1807–92, US poet and humanitarian: a leading campaigner in the antislavery movement. His poems include *Snow-Bound* (1866).

Whittington ★ (ˈwɪtɪŋtən) *n* **Richard,** known as *Dick.* died 1423, English merchant, three times mayor of London. According to legend, he walked to London at the age of 13 with his cat.

whittle (ˈwɪtᵊl) *vb* **whittles, whittling, whittled. 1** to cut or shave strips or pieces from (wood, a stick, etc.), esp. with a knife. **2** (*tr*) to make or shape by paring or shaving. **3** (*tr; often foll. by away, down,* etc.) to reduce, destroy, or wear away gradually. ORIG C16: var. of C15 *thwittle* large knife, ult. from OE *thwītan* to cut

Whittle ★ (ˈwɪtᵊl) *n* Sir **Frank.** 1907–96, British engineer, who invented the jet engine for aircraft: flew first British jet aircraft (1941).

whity (ˈwaɪtɪ) *n, pl* **whities. 1** *Inf.* a variant spelling of

whitey. ◆ *adj* **2a** whitish in colour. **2b** (*in combination*): *whity-brown.*

whizz *or* **whiz** (wɪz) *vb* **whizzes, whizzing, whizzed. 1** to make or cause to make a loud humming or buzzing sound. **2** to move or cause to move with such a sound. **3** (*intr*) *Inf.* to move or go rapidly. ◆ *n, pl* **whizzes. 4** a loud humming or buzzing sound. **5** *Inf.* Also: **wizz.** a person who is extremely skilful at some activity. **6** a slang word for **amphetamine.** ORIG C16: imit.

whizz-bang *or* **whiz-bang** *n* **1** a World War I shell that travelled at such high velocity that the sound of its flight was heard only an instant before the sound of its explosion. **2** a type of firework that jumps around emitting a whizzing sound and occasional bangs.

whizz kid, whiz kid, *or* **wiz kid** *n Inf.* a person who is pushing, enthusiastic, and outstandingly successful for his or her age. ORIG C20: from WHIZZ, ? infl. by WIZARD

whizzy ('wɪzɪ) *adj* **whizzier, whizziest.** *Inf.* using sophisticated technology to produce vivid effects: *a whizzy new computer game.*

who (hu:) *pron* **1** which person? what person? used in direct and indirect questions: *he can't remember who did it; who met you?* **2** used to introduce relative clauses with antecedents referring to human beings: *the people who lived here have left.* **3** the one or ones who; whoever: *bring who you want.* ORIG OE *hwā*

> **USAGE NOTE** See at **whom.**

Who ★ (hu:) *n* **the.** British rock group (mid-1960s–1983), originally comprising Roger Daltrey (born 1944; vocals), Pete Townshend (born 1945; guitar), John Entwistle (born 1944; bass guitar), and Keith Moon (1947–78; drums). Their recordings include "My Generation" (1965) and *Tommy* (1969).

WHO *abbrev. for* World Health Organization.

whoa (wəʊ) *interj* a command used esp. to horses to stop or slow down. ORIG C19: var. of HO

who-does-what *adj* (of a dispute, strike, etc.) relating to the separation of kinds of work performed by different trade unions.

whodunnit *or* **whodunit** (hu:'dʌnɪt) *n Inf.* a novel, play, etc., concerned with a crime, usually murder.

whoever (hu:'ɛvə) *pron* **1** any person who: *whoever wants it can have it.* **2** no matter who: *I'll come round tomorrow, whoever may be here.* **3** an intensive form of *who,* used in questions: *whoever could have thought that?* **4** *Inf.* an unspecified person: *give those to Cathy or whoever.*

whole (həʊl) *adj* **1** containing all the component parts necessary to form a total; complete: *a whole apple.* **2** constituting the full quantity, extent, etc. **3** uninjured or undamaged. **4** healthy. **5** having no fractional or decimal part; integral: *a whole number.* **6** designating a relationship by descent from the same parents; full: *whole brothers.* **7 out of whole cloth.** *US & Canad. Inf.* entirely without a factual basis. ◆ *adv* **8** in an undivided or unbroken piece: *to swallow a plum whole.* ◆ *n* **9** all the parts, elements, etc., of a thing. **10** an assemblage of parts viewed together as a unit. **11** a thing complete in itself. **12 as a whole.** considered altogether; completely. **13 on the whole. 13a** taking all things into consideration. **13b** in general. ORIG OE *hāl, hǣl*
▸ **'wholeness** *n*

whole blood *n* blood for transfusion from which none of the elements has been removed.

wholefood ('həʊl,fu:d) *n* (*sometimes pl*) **a** food that has been refined or processed as little as possible and is eaten in its natural state, such as brown rice, wholemeal flour, etc. **b** (*as modifier*): *a wholefood restaurant.*

wholehearted (,həʊl'hɑ:tɪd) *adj* done, acted, given, etc., with total sincerity, enthusiasm, or commitment.
▸ **,whole'heartedly** *adv*

whole hog *n Sl.* the whole or total extent (esp. in **go the whole hog**).

wholemeal ('həʊl,mi:l) *adj Brit.* (of flour, bread, etc.) made from the entire wheat kernel. Also called (esp. US and Canad.): **whole-wheat.**

whole milk *n* milk from which no constituent has been removed.

whole note *n* the usual US and Canad. name for **semibreve.**

whole number *n* **1** an integer. **2** a natural number.

wholesale ('həʊl,seɪl) *n* **1** the business of selling goods to retailers in larger quantities than they are sold to final consumers but in smaller quantities than they are purchased from manufacturers. Cf. **retail** (sense 1). ◆ *adj* **2** of or engaged in such business. **3** made, done, etc., on a large scale or without discrimination. ◆ *adv* **4** on a large scale or without discrimination. ◆ *vb* **wholesales, wholesaling, wholesaled. 5** to sell (goods) at wholesale.
▸ **'whole,saler** *n*

wholesale price index *n* an indicator of price changes in the wholesale market.

wholesome ('həʊlsəm) *adj* **1** conducive to health or physical wellbeing. **2** conducive to moral wellbeing. **3** characteristic or suggestive of health or wellbeing, esp. in appearance. ORIG C12: from WHOLE (healthy) + -SOME[1]
▸ **'wholesomely** *adv* ▸ **'wholesomeness** *n*

whole tone *or US & Canad.* **whole step** *n* an interval of two semitones. Often shortened to **tone.**

whole-tone scale *n* either of two scales produced by commencing on one of any two notes a chromatic semitone apart and proceeding upwards or downwards in whole tones for an octave.

whole-wheat *adj* another term (esp. US and Canad.) for **wholemeal.**

who'll (hu:l) *contraction of* who will *or* who shall.

wholly ('həʊllɪ) *adv* **1** completely, totally, or entirely. **2** without exception; exclusively.

whom (hu:m) *pron* the objective form of *who,* used when *who* is not the subject of its own clause: *whom did you say you had seen? he can't remember whom he saw.* ORIG OE *hwām,* dative of *hwā* who

whomever (hu:m'ɛvə) *pron* the objective form of *whoever: I'll hire whomever I can find.*

> **USAGE NOTE** It was formerly considered correct to use *whom* whenever the object form of *who* was required. This is no longer thought to be necessary and the object form *who* is now commonly used, even in formal writing: *there were several people there who he had met before. Who* cannot be used directly after a preposition – the preposition is usually moved, as in *the man (who) he sold his car to.* In formal writing *whom* is preferred in sentences like these: *the man to whom he sold his car.* There are some types of sentence in which *who* cannot be used: *the refugees, many of whom were old and ill, were allowed across the border.*

whoop (wu:p) *vb* **whoops, whooping, whooped. 1** to utter (speech) with loud cries, as of excitement. **2** (hu:p). *Med.* to cough convulsively with a crowing sound. **3** (of certain birds) to utter (a hooting cry). **4** (*tr*) to urge on or call with or as if with whoops. **5** (wʊp, wu:p). **whoop it up.** *Inf.* **5a** to indulge in a noisy celebration. **5b** *Chiefly US.* to arouse enthusiasm. ◆ *n* **6** a loud cry, esp. one expressing excitement. **7** (hu:p). *Med.* the convulsive crowing sound made during whooping cough. ORIG C14: imit.

whoopee *Inf.* ◆ *interj* (wʊ'pi:). **1** an exclamation of joy, excitement, etc. ◆ *n* ('wʊpi:). **2 make whoopee. 2a** to engage in noisy merrymaking. **2b** to make love.

whoopee cushion *n* a joke cushion that emits a sound like the breaking of wind when someone sits on it.

whooper *or* **whooper swan** ('wu:pə) *n* a large Old World swan having a black bill with a yellow base and a noisy whooping cry.

whooping cough ('hu:pɪŋ) *n* an acute infectious disease characterized by coughing spasms that end with a shrill crowing sound on inspiration. Technical name: **pertussis.**

whoops (wʊps) *interj* an exclamation of surprise or of apology.

whoosh *or* **woosh** (wʊʃ) *n* **1** a hissing or rushing sound. ◆ *vb* **2** (*intr*) to make or move with such a sound.

whop (wɒp) *Inf.* ◆ *vb* **whops, whopping, whopped. 1** (*tr*) to strike, beat, or thrash. **2** (*tr*) to defeat utterly. **3** (*intr*) to drop or fall. ◆ *n* **4** a heavy blow or the sound made by such a blow. ORIG C14: var. of *wap*, ? imit.

whopper (ˈwɒpə) *n Inf.* **1** anything uncommonly large of its kind. **2** a big lie. ORIG C18: from WHOP

whopping (ˈwɒpɪŋ) *adj Inf.* uncommonly large.

whore (hɔː) *n* **1** a prostitute or promiscuous woman: often a term of abuse. ◆ *vb* **whores, whoring, whored.** (*intr*) **2** to be or act as a prostitute. **3** (of a man) to have promiscuous sexual relations, esp. with prostitutes. **4** (often foll. by *after*) to seek that which is immoral, idolatrous, etc. ORIG OE *hōre*
▸ **ˈwhoredom** *n* ▸ **ˈwhorish** *adj*

whorehouse (ˈhɔːˌhaʊs) *n* another word for **brothel.**

whoremonger (ˈhɔːˌmʌŋgə) *n* a person who consorts with whores; lecher. Also called: **whoremaster.**
▸ **ˈwhoreˌmongery** *n*

whoreson (ˈhɔːsən) *Arch.* ◆ *n* **1** a bastard. **2** a scoundrel; wretch. ◆ *adj* **3** vile or hateful.

whorl (wɜːl) *n* **1** *Bot.* a radial arrangement of petals, stamens, leaves, etc., around a stem. **2** *Zool.* a single turn in a spiral shell. **3** anything shaped like a coil. ORIG C15: prob. var. of *wherville* whirl, infl. by Du. *worvel*
▸ **whorled** *adj*

whortleberry (ˈwɜːtəlˌbɛrɪ) *n, pl* **whortleberries. 1** Also called: **bilberry, blaeberry, huckleberry.** a small Eurasian ericaceous shrub with greenish-pink flowers and edible sweet blackish berries. **2** the fruit of this shrub. **3 bog whortleberry.** a related plant of mountain regions, having pink flowers and black fruits. ORIG C16: SW English dialect var. of *hurtleberry*, from ?

who's (huːz) *contraction of* who is *or* who has.

whose (huːz) *determiner* **1a** of whom? belonging to whom? used in direct and indirect questions: *I told him whose fault it was; whose car is this?* **1b** (*as pron*): *whose is that?* **2** of whom; of which: used as a relative pronoun: *a house whose windows are broken; a man whose reputation has suffered.* ORIG OE *hwæs*, genitive of *hwā* who & *hwæt* what

whoso (ˈhuːsəʊ) *pron* an archaic word for **whoever.**

whosoever (ˌhuːsəʊˈɛvə) *pron* an archaic or formal word for **whoever.**

who's who *n* a book or list containing the names and short biographies of famous people.

why (waɪ) *adv* **1a** for what reason?: *why are you here?* **1b** (*used in indirect questions*): *tell me why you're here.* ◆ *pron* **2** for or because of which: *there is no reason why he shouldn't come.* ◆ *n, pl* **whys. 3** (*usually pl*) the cause of something (esp. in **the whys and wherefores**). ◆ *interj* **4** an introductory expression of surprise, indignation, etc.: *why, don't be silly!* ORIG OE *hwī*

Whyalla ★ (waɪˈælə) *n* a port in S South Australia, on Spencer Gulf: iron and steel and shipbuilding industries. Pop.: 25 526 (1991).

whydah *or* **whidah** (ˈwɪdə) *n* any of various predominantly black African weaverbirds, the males of which grow very long tail feathers in the breeding season. Also called: **whydah bird, whidah bird, widow bird.** ORIG C18: after a town in Benin in W Africa

whydunnit *or* **whydunit** (ˌwaɪˈdʌnɪt) *n Inf.* a novel, film, etc., concerned with the motives of the criminal rather than his or her identity.

WI *abbrev. for:* **1** West Indian. **2** West Indies. **3** Wisconsin. **4** (in Britain) Women's Institute.

Wicca (ˈwɪkə) *n* the cult or practice of witchcraft. ORIG C20 revival of OE *wicca* witch
▸ **ˈWiccan** *n, adj*

Wichita ★ (ˈwɪtʃɪˌtɔː) *n* a city in S Kansas, on the Arkansas River: the largest city in the state; two universities. Pop.: 310 236 (1994 est.).

wick¹ (wɪk) *n* **1** a cord or band of loosely twisted or woven fibres, as in a candle, that supplies fuel to a flame by capillary action. **2 get on (someone's) wick.** *Brit. sl.* to cause irritation to (someone). ORIG OE *weoce*

wick² (wɪk) *n Arch.* a village or hamlet. ORIG OE *wīc*; rel. to *-wich* in place names

Wick ★ (wɪk) *n* a town in N Scotland, in Highland, at the head of **Wick Bay** (an inlet of the North Sea). Pop.: 7681 (1991).

wicked (ˈwɪkɪd) *adj* **1a** morally bad. **1b** (*as collective n; preceded by the*): *the wicked.* **2** mischievous or roguish in a playful way: *a wicked grin.* **3** causing injury or harm. **4** troublesome, unpleasant, or offensive. **5** *Sl.* very good. ORIG C13: from dialect *wick*, from OE *wicca* sorcerer, *wicce* witch
▸ **ˈwickedly** *adv* ▸ **ˈwickedness** *n*

wicker (ˈwɪkə) *n* **1** a slender flexible twig or shoot, esp. of willow. **2** short for **wickerwork.** ◆ *adj* **3** made of, consisting of, or constructed from wicker. ORIG C14: from ON

wickerwork (ˈwɪkəˌwɜːk) *n* **a** a material consisting of woven wicker. **b** (*as modifier*): *a wickerwork chair.*

wicket (ˈwɪkɪt) *n* **1** a small door or gate, esp. one that is near to or part of a larger one. **2** *Chiefly US.* a small window or opening in a door, esp. one fitted with a grating or glass pane. **3** a small sluicegate. **4a** *Cricket.* either of two constructions, 22 yards apart, consisting of three stumps stuck in the ground with two wooden bails resting on top, at which the batsman stands. **4b** the strip of ground between these. **4c** a batsman's turn at batting or the period during which two batsmen bat. **4d** the act or instance of a batsman being got out: *the bowler took six wickets.* **5 keep wicket.** to act as a wicketkeeper. **6 on a good, sticky,** etc., **wicket.** *Inf.* in an advantageous, awkward, etc., situation. ORIG C18: from OF *wiket*

wicketkeeper (ˈwɪkɪtˌkiːpə) *n Cricket.* the player on the fielding side positioned directly behind the wicket.

wickiup, wikiup, *or* **wickyup** (ˈwɪkɪˌʌp) *n US & Canad.* a crude shelter made of brushwood or grass and having an oval frame, esp. of a kind used by nomadic Native Americans now in the Oklahoma area. ORIG C19: of Amerind origin

Wickliffe *or* **Wiclif** ★ (ˈwɪklɪf) *n* variant spellings of (John) **Wycliffe.**

Wicklow ★ (ˈwɪkləʊ) *n* **1** a county of E Republic of Ireland, in Leinster province on the Irish Sea: consists of a coastal strip rising inland to the **Wicklow Mountains**; mainly agricultural, with several resorts. County town: Wicklow. Pop.: 102 000 (1996). Area: 2025 sq. km (782 sq. miles). **2** a port in E Republic of Ireland, county town of Co. Wicklow. Pop.: 5850 (1991).

widdershins (ˈwɪdəˌʃɪnz) *adv Chiefly Scot.* a variant spelling of **withershins.**

wide (waɪd) *adj* **1** having a great extent from side to side. **2** spacious or extensive. **3a** (*postpositive*) having a specified extent, esp. from side to side: *two yards wide.* **3b** (*in combination*): extending throughout: *nationwide.* **4** remote from the desired point, mark, etc.: *your guess is wide of the mark.* **5** (of eyes) opened fully. **6** loose, full, or roomy: *wide trousers.* **7** exhibiting a considerable spread: *a wide variation.* **8** *Phonetics.* another word for **lax** (sense 4) or **open** (sense 32). ◆ *adv* **9** over an extensive area: *to travel far and wide.* **10** to the full extent: *he opened the door wide.* **11** far from the desired point, mark, etc. ◆ *n* **12** (in cricket) a bowled ball that is outside the batsman's reach and scores a run for the batting side. ORIG OE *wīd*
▸ **ˈwidely** *adv* ▸ **ˈwideness** *n* ▸ **ˈwidish** *adj*

wide-angle lens *n* a lens system on a camera that has a small focal length and therefore can cover an angle of view of 60° or more.

wide-awake *adj* (**wide awake** *when postpositive*). **1** fully awake. **2** keen, alert, or observant. ◆ *n* **3** Also called: **wide-awake hat.** a hat with a low crown and very wide brim.

wide-body *adj* (of an aircraft) having a wide fuselage, esp. wide enough to contain three rows of seats abreast.

wide boy *n Brit. sl.* a man who is prepared to use unscrupulous methods to progress or make money.

wide-eyed *adj* innocent or credulous.

widen (ˈwaɪdᵊn) *vb* to make or become wide or wider.
▸ **ˈwidener** *n*

wide-open *adj* (**wide open** *when postpositive*). **1** open to the full extent. **2** (*postpositive*) exposed to attack; vulnerable. **3** uncertain as to outcome. **4** *US inf.* (of a town or city) lax in the enforcement of certain laws, esp. those relating to the sale of alcohol, gambling, etc.

wide receiver *n American football.* a player whose function is to catch long passes from the quarterback.

widespread (ˈwaɪdˌsprɛd) *adj* **1** extending over a wide area. **2** accepted by or occurring among many people.

widgeon (ˈwɪdʒən) *n* a variant spelling of **wigeon.**

widget (ˈwɪdʒɪt) *n Inf.* any small mechanism or device, the name of which is unknown or temporarily forgotten. ORIG C20: changed from GADGET

Widnes ★ (ˈwɪdnɪs) *n* a town in NW England, in N Cheshire on the River Mersey: chemical industry. Pop.: 57 162 (1991).

widow (ˈwɪdəʊ) *n* **1** a woman whose husband has died, esp. one who has not remarried. **2** (*with a modifier*) *Inf.* a woman whose husband frequently leaves her alone while he indulges in a sport, etc.: *a golf widow.* **3** *Printing.* a short line at the end of a paragraph, esp. one that occurs as the top line of a page or column. **4** (in some card games) an additional hand or set of cards exposed on the table. ◆ *vb* (*tr; usually passive*) **5** to cause to become a widow. **6** to deprive of something valued. ORIG OE *widuwe*
▸ **ˈwidowhood** *n*

widow bird *n* another name for **whydah.**

widower (ˈwɪdəʊə) *n* a man whose wife has died and who has not remarried.

widow's cruse *n* an endless or unfailing source of supply. ORIG allusion to I Kings 17:16

widow's mite *n* a small contribution by a person who has very little. ORIG allusion to Mark 12:43

widow's peak *n* a V-shaped point in the hairline in the middle of the forehead. ORIG from the belief that it presaged early widowhood

width (wɪdθ) *n* **1** the linear extent or measurement of something from side to side. **2** the state or fact of being wide. **3** a piece or section of something at its full extent from side to side: *a width of cloth.* **4** the distance across a rectangular swimming bath, as opposed to its length. ORIG C17: from WIDE + -TH[1], analogous to BREADTH

Wieland[1] ★ (ˈviːlant) *n* the German name for **Wayland.**

Wieland[2] ★ (*German* ˈviːlant) *n* **Christoph Martin** (ˈkrɪstɔf ˈmartiːn). 1733–1813, German writer, noted for his verse epic *Oberon* (1780).

wield (wiːld) *vb* (*tr*) **1** to handle or use (a weapon, tool, etc.). **2** to exert or maintain (power or authority). ORIG OE *wieldan, wealdan*
▸ **ˈwieldable** *adj* ▸ **ˈwielder** *n*

wieldy (ˈwiːldɪ) *adj* **wieldier, wieldiest.** easily handled, used, or managed.

Wien[1] ★ (viːn) *n* the German name for **Vienna.**

Wien[2] ★ (*German* viːn) *n* **Wilhelm** (ˈvɪlhɛlm). 1864–1928, German physicist, who studied black-body radiation: Nobel prize for physics 1911.

wiener (ˈwiːnə) *or* **wienerwurst** (ˈwiːnəˌwɜːst) *n US & Canad.* a kind of smoked sausage, similar to a frankfurter. ORIG C20: shortened from G *Wiener Wurst* Viennese sausage

Wiener ★ (ˈwiːnə) *n* **Norbert** (ˈnɔːbət). 1894–1964, US mathematician, who developed cybernetics.

Wiener Neustadt ★ (*German* ˈviːnər ˈnɔyʃtat) *n* a city in E Austria, in Lower Austria. Pop.: 35 268 (1991).

Wiener schnitzel (ˈviːnə ˈʃnɪtsəl) *n* a thin escalope of veal, fried in breadcrumbs. ORIG G: Viennese cutlet

Wiesbaden ★ (*German* ˈviːsbaːdən) *n* a city in W Germany, capital of Hesse state: a spa resort since Roman times. Pop.: 267 122 (1996 est.). Latin name: **Aquae Mattiacorum** (ˈækwiː ˌmætjəˈkəʊrəm).

Wiesel ★ (ˈviːzəl) *n* **Elie.** born 1928, US human rights campaigner: noted for his documentaries of wartime atrocities against the Jews; Nobel peace prize 1986.

Wiesenthal ★ (ˈviːzənˌtɑːl) *n* **Simon.** born 1908, Austrian investigator of Nazi war crimes.

wife (waɪf) *n, pl* **wives. 1** a man's partner in marriage; a married woman. Related adj: **uxorial. 2** an archaic or dialect word for **woman. 3 take to wife.** to marry (a woman). ORIG OE *wīf*
▸ **ˈwifehood** *n* ▸ **ˈwifely** *adj*

wig (wɪg) *n* **1** an artificial head of hair, either human or synthetic, worn to disguise baldness, as part of a theatrical or ceremonial dress, as a disguise, or for adornment. ◆ *vb* **wigs, wigging, wigged.** (*tr*) **2** *Brit. sl.* to berate severely. ORIG C17: shortened from PERIWIG
▸ **wigged** *adj* ▸ **ˈwigless** *adj*

Wig. *abbrev. for* Wigtownshire.

Wigan ★ (ˈwɪgən) *n* **1** an industrial town in NW England, in Greater Manchester: former coal-mining centre. Pop.: 85 819 (1991). **2** a unitary authority in NW England, in Greater Manchester. Pop.: 310 100 (1997 est.). Area: 199 sq. km (77 sq. miles).

wigeon *or* **widgeon** (ˈwɪdʒən) *n* **1** a Eurasian duck of marshes, swamps, etc., the male of which has a reddish-brown head and chest and grey-and-white back and wings. **2 American wigeon.** Also called: **baldpate.** a similar bird of North America, the male of which has a white crown. ORIG C16: from ?

wigging (ˈwɪgɪŋ) *n Brit. sl.* a reprimand.

wiggle (ˈwɪgᵊl) *vb* **wiggles, wiggling, wiggled. 1** to move or cause to move with jerky movements, esp. from side to side. ◆ *n* **2** the act of wiggling. ORIG C13: from MLow G, MDu. *wiggelen*
▸ **ˈwiggler** *n* ▸ **ˈwiggly** *adj*

wight (waɪt) *n Arch.* a human being. ORIG OE *wiht;* rel. to OFrisian *āwet* something

Wight ★ (waɪt) *n* **Isle of.** an island and county of S England in the English Channel. Administrative centre: Newport. Pop.: 124 600 (1994 est.). Area: 380 sq. km (147 sq. miles).

Wigner ★ (ˈwɪgnə) *n* **Eugene Paul.** 1902–95, US physicist, born in Hungary; noted for his work on nuclear physics: shared the Nobel prize for physics 1963.

Wigtownshire ★ (ˈwɪgtənˌʃɪə, -ʃə) *n* (until 1975) a county of SW Scotland, now part of Dumfries and Galloway.

wigwag (ˈwɪgˌwæg) *vb* **wigwags, wigwagging, wigwagged. 1** to move (something) back and forth. **2** to communicate with (someone) by means of a flag semaphore. ◆ *n* **3a** a system of communication by flag semaphore. **3b** the message signalled. ORIG C16: from obs. *wig,* prob. short for WIGGLE + WAG[1]
▸ **ˈwigˌwagger** *n*

wigwam (ˈwɪgˌwæm) *n* **1** any dwelling of the North American Indians, esp. one made of bark, rushes, or skins spread over a set of arched poles lashed together. **2** a similar structure for children. ORIG from *wīkwām* (of Amerind origin), lit.: their abode

Wilberforce ★ (ˈwɪlbəˌfɔːs) *n* **William.** 1759–1833, British politician, who secured the abolition of the slave trade (1807) and slavery (1833) in the British Empire.

wilco (ˈwɪlkəʊ) *interj* an expression in signalling, telecommunications, etc., indicating that a message just received will be complied with. ORIG C20: abbrev. for *I will comply*

wild (waɪld) *adj* **1** (of animals) living independently of man; not domesticated or tame. **2** (of plants) growing in a natural state; not cultivated. **3** uninhabited; desolate: *a wild stretch of land.* **4** living in a savage or uncivilized way: *wild tribes.* **5** lacking restraint or control: *wild merriment.* **6** of great violence: *a wild storm.* **7** disorderly or chaotic: *wild talk.* **8** dishevelled; untidy: *wild hair.* **9** in a state of extreme emotional intensity: *wild with anger.* **10** reckless: *wild speculations.* **11** random: *a wild guess.* **12** (*postpositive; foll. by about*) *Inf.* intensely enthusiastic: *I'm wild about my new boyfriend.* **13** (of a card, such as a joker in some games) able to be given any value the holder pleases. **14 wild and woolly. 14a** rough; barbarous. **14b** (of theories, plans, etc.) not fully thought out. ◆ *adv* **15** in a wild manner. **16 run wild. 16a** to grow without cultivation or care: *the garden has run wild.* **16b** to behave without restraint: *he has let his children run wild.* ♦ *n* **17** (*often pl*) a desolate or uninhabited region. **18 the wild. 18a** a free natural state of living. **18b** the wilderness. ORIG OE *wilde* ▸ **'wildish** *adj* ▸ **'wildly** *adv* ▸ **'wildness** *n*

wild boar *n* a wild pig of parts of Europe and central Asia, having a pale grey to black coat and prominent tusks.

wild brier *n* another name for **wild rose.**

wild card *n* **1** See **wild** (sense 13). **2** *Sport.* a player or team that has not qualified for a competition but is allowed to take part, at the organizers' discretion, after all the regular places have been taken. **3** an unpredictable element in a situation. **4** *Computing.* a symbol that can represent any character or group of characters, as in a filename.

wild carrot *n* an umbelliferous plant of temperate regions, having clusters of white flowers and hooked fruits. Also called: **Queen Anne's lace.**

wildcat ('waɪldˌkæt) *n, pl* **wildcats** *or* **wildcat. 1** a wild European cat that resembles the domestic tabby but is larger and has a bushy tail. **2** any of various other felines, such as the lynx and the caracal. **3** *US & Canad.* another name for **bobcat. 4** *Inf.* a savage or aggressive person. **5** an exploratory drilling for petroleum or natural gas. **6** (*modifier*) *Chiefly US.* involving risk, esp. financially or commercially unsound: *a wildcat project.* ♦ *vb* **wildcats, wildcatting, wildcatted. 7** (*intr*) to drill for petroleum or natural gas in an area having no known reserves. ▸ **'wildˌcatter** *n* ▸ **'wildˌcatting** *n, adj*

wildcat strike *n* a strike begun by workers spontaneously or without union approval.

wild cherry *n* another name for **gean.**

wild dog *n* another name for **dingo.**

Wilde ★ (waɪld) *n* **Oscar (Fingal O'Flahertie Wills).** 1854–1900, Irish writer, whose works include the play *The Importance of Being Earnest* (1895), the novel *The Picture of Dorian Gray* (1891), and *The Ballad of Reading Gaol* (1898), relating his experiences while serving a prison sentence for homosexuality.

wildebeest ('wɪldɪˌbiːst, 'vɪl-) *n, pl* **wildebeests** *or* **wildebeest.** another name for **gnu.** ORIG C19: from Afrik., lit.: wild beast

wilder ('wɪldə) *vb Arch.* **1** to lead or be led astray. **2** to bewilder or become bewildered. ORIG C17: from ?

Wilder ★ ('waɪldə) *n* **1 Billy,** real name *Samuel Wilder.* born 1906, US film director, born in Austria. His films include *The Lost Weekend* (1945), *Some Like it Hot* (1959), and *Buddy Buddy* (1981). **2 Thornton.** 1897–1975, US writer. His works include the novel *The Bridge of San Luis Rey* (1927) and the play *The Skin of Our Teeth* (1942).

wilderness ('wɪldənɪs) *n* **1** a wild uninhabited uncultivated region. **2** any desolate area. **3** a confused mass or collection. **4 a voice (crying) in the wilderness.** a person, group, etc., making a suggestion or plea that is ignored. ORIG OE *wildēornes,* from *wildēor* wild beast + -NESS

Wilderness ★ ('wɪldənɪs) *n* **the.** the barren regions to the south and east of Palestine, esp. those in which the Israelites wandered before entering the Promised Land and in which Christ fasted for 40 days and nights.

wild-eyed *adj* glaring in an angry, distracted, or wild manner.

wildfire ('waɪldˌfaɪə) *n* **1** a highly flammable material, such as Greek fire, formerly used in warfare. **2a** a raging and uncontrollable fire. **2b** anything that is disseminated quickly (esp. in **spread like wildfire**). **3** another name for **will-o'-the-wisp.**

wild flower *n* **1** any flowering plant that grows in an uncultivated state. **2** the flower of such a plant.

wildfowl ('waɪldˌfaʊl) *n* **1** any bird that is hunted by man, esp. any duck or similar aquatic bird. **2** such birds collectively. ▸ **'wildˌfowler** *n* ▸ **'wildˌfowling** *adj, n*

wild-goose chase *n* an absurd or hopeless pursuit, as of something unattainable.

wilding ('waɪldɪŋ) *n* **1** an uncultivated plant or a cultivated plant that has become wild. **2** a wild animal. ♦ Also called: **wildling.**

wildlife ('waɪldˌlaɪf) *n* wild animals and plants collectively: a term used esp. of fauna.

wild pansy *n* a Eurasian plant of the violet family having purple, yellow, and pale mauve spurred flowers. Also called: **heartsease, love-in-idleness.**

wild parsley *n* any of various uncultivated umbelliferous plants that resemble parsley.

wild rice *n* an aquatic North American grass with dark-coloured edible grain.

wild rose *n* any of numerous roses, such as the dogrose and sweetbrier, that grow wild and have flowers with only one whorl of petals.

wild rubber *n* rubber obtained from uncultivated rubber trees.

wild silk *n* **1** silk produced by wild silkworms. **2** a fabric made from this, or from short fibres of silk designed to imitate it.

wild type *n Biol.* the typical form of a species of organism resulting from breeding under natural conditions.

Wild West ★ *n* the western US during its settlement, esp. with reference to its frontier lawlessness.

wildwood ('waɪldˌwʊd) *n Arch.* a wood or forest growing in a natural uncultivated state.

wile (waɪl) *n* **1** trickery, cunning, or craftiness. **2** (*usually pl*) an artful or seductive trick or ploy. ♦ *vb* **wiles, wiling, wiled. 3** (*tr*) to lure, beguile, or entice. ORIG C12: from ON *vel* craft

wilful *or US* **willful** ('wɪlfʊl) *adj* **1** intent on having one's own way; headstrong or obstinate. **2** intentional: *wilful murder.* ▸ **'wilfully** *or US* **'willfully** *adv* ▸ **'wilfulness** *or US* **'willfulness** *n*

Wilhelm I ★ ('vɪlhɛlm) *n* the German name of **William I** (sense 3).

Wilhelm II ★ *n* the German name of **William II** (sense 2).

Wilhelmina I ★ (ˌwɪlə'miːnə; *Dutch* wɪlhɛl'miːnaː) *n* 1880–1962, queen of the Netherlands from 1890 until her abdication (1948) in favour of her daughter Juliana.

Wilhelmshaven ★ (*German* vɪlhɛlms'haːfən) *n* a port and resort in NW Germany, in Lower Saxony: founded in 1853; was the chief German North Sea naval base until 1945; a major oil port. Pop.: 91 150 (1991).

Wilhelmstrasse ★ (*German* 'vɪlhɛlmʃtraːsə) *n* **1** a street in the centre of Berlin, where the German foreign office and other government buildings were situated until 1945. **2** Germany's ministry of foreign affairs until 1945.

Wilkes ★ (wɪlks) *n* **1 Charles.** 1798–1877, US explorer of Antarctica. **2 John.** 1727–97, British politician, who was expelled from the House of Commons for writing scurrilous articles about the government. He became a champion of parliamentary reform.

Wilkes Land ★ *n* a region in Antarctica south of Australia, on the Indian Ocean.

Wilkins ★ ('wɪlkɪnz) *n* **1** Sir **George Hubert.** 1888–1958, Australian polar explorer and aviator. **2 Maurice Hugh Frederick.** born 1916, British biochemist, born in New Zealand: shared the Nobel prize 1962 for his work on the structure of DNA.

will[1] (wɪl) *vb past* **would.** (takes an infinitive without *to* or an implied infinitive) used as an auxiliary. **1** (esp. with *you, he, she, it, they,* or a noun as subject) to make the future tense. Cf. **shall** (sense 1). **2** to express resolution on the part of the speaker: *I will buy that radio if it's the last thing I do.* **3** to indicate willingness or desire: *will you help me with this problem?* **4** to express commands: *you will report your findings to me tomorrow.* **5** to express ability: *this rope will support a load.* **6** to express probability or expectation: *that will be Jim telephoning.* **7** to express customary practice or inevitability: *boys will be boys.* **8** (*with the infinitive always implied*) to express desire: usually in polite requests: *stay if you will.* **9 what you will.** whatever you like. ORIG OE *willan*

USAGE NOTE See at **shall.**

will[2] (wɪl) *n* **1** the faculty of conscious and deliberate

choice of action. Related adj: **voluntary.** **2** the act or an instance of asserting a choice. **3a** the declaration of a person's wishes regarding the disposal of his property after his death. **3b** a document in which such wishes are expressed. **4** desire; wish. **5** determined intention: *where there's a will there's a way.* **6** disposition towards others: *he bears you no ill will.* **7 at will.** at one's own desire or choice. **8 with a will.** heartily; energetically. **9 with the best will in the world.** even with the best of intentions. ◆ *vb (mainly tr; often takes a clause as object or an infinitive)* **10** *(also intr)* to exercise the faculty of volition in an attempt to accomplish (something): *he willed his wife's recovery from her illness.* **11** to give (property) by will to a person, society, etc.: *he willed his art collection to the nation.* **12** *(also intr)* to order or decree: *the king wills that you shall die.* **13** to choose or prefer: *wander where you will.* ORIG OE *willa*
▸ **ˈwiller** *n*

willed (wɪld) *adj (in combination)* having a will as specified: *weak-willed.*

Willemstad ★ (*Dutch* ˈwɪləmstɑt) *n* the capital of the Netherlands Antilles, a port on the SW coast of Curaçao: important for refining Venezuelan oil. Pop.: 119 000 (1995 est.).

willet (ˈwɪlɪt) *n* a large American shore bird with grey plumage and black-and-white wings. ORIG C19: imit. of its call

willful (ˈwɪlfʊl) *adj* the US spelling of **wilful.**

William ★ (ˈwɪljəm) *n* **1** known as *William the Lion.* ?1143–1214, king of Scotland (1165–1214). **2 Prince,** title *Prince William of Wales.* born 1982, elder son of Charles, Prince of Wales, and Diana, Princess of Wales.

William I ★ *n* **1** known as *William the Conqueror.* ?1027–1087, duke of Normandy (1035–87) and king of England (1066–87). He invaded England in 1066, defeating Harold II at Hastings. In 1085 he ordered the Domesday Book to be compiled. **2** known as *William the Silent.* 1533–84, prince of Orange and count of Nassau: led the revolt of the Netherlands against Spain (1568–76) and became first stadholder of the United Provinces of the Netherlands (1579–84); assassinated. **3** German name *Wilhelm I.* 1797–1888, king of Prussia (1861–88) and first emperor of Germany (1871–88).

William II ★ *n* **1** known as *William Rufus.* ?1056–1100, king of England (1087–1100); son of William the Conqueror: killed by an arrow while hunting in the New Forest. **2** German name *Kaiser Wilhelm.* 1859–1941, German emperor and king of Prussia (1888–1918): forced to abdicate at the end of World War I.

William III ★ *n* known as *William of Orange.* 1650–1702, stadholder of the Netherlands (1672–1702) and king of Great Britain and Ireland (1689–1702): ruled jointly with his wife Mary II until her death in 1694.

William IV ★ *n* known as the *Sailor King.* 1765–1837, king of the United Kingdom and Hanover (1830–37), succeeding his brother George IV; the third son of George III.

Williams ★ (ˈwɪljəmz) *n* **1 Hank,** real name *Hiram Williams.* 1923–53, US country singer and songwriter. **2 John.** born 1941, Australian classical guitarist, living in Britain. **3 J(ohn) P(eter) R(hys).** born 1949, Welsh Rugby Union player. A fullback, he played for Wales (1969–79; 1980–81) and the British Lions (1971–77). **4 John (Towner).** born 1932, US composer, best known for his film scores, including *Jaws* (1975), *Star Wars* (1977), *ET* (1982), and *Schindler's List* (1994). **5 Ralph Vaughan.** See (Ralph) **Vaughan Williams. 6 Robbie (Peter).** born 1974, British pop singer and songwriter. A member of the teenage group Take That (1990–95), he later found success with the songs "Angel" (1997) and "Millennium" (1998) and the albums *Life Thru a Lens* (1997) and *I've Been Expecting You* (1998). **7 Serena.** born 1981, US tennis player: sister of Venus Williams; US Open champion 1999; Wimbledon ladies doubles champion (with Venus) 2000. **8 Tennessee.** real name *Thomas Lanier Williams.* 1912–83, US dramatist. His plays include *The Glass Menagerie* (1944), *A Streetcar Named Desire* (1947), and *Cat on a Hot Tin Roof* (1955). **9 Venus.** born 1980, US tennis player: sister of Serena Williams; Australian Open champion 1998; US Open champion 2000; Wimbledon singles and (with Serena) ladies doubles champion 2000. **10 William Carlos** (ˈkɑːləs). 1883–1963, US poet. His works include *Paterson* (1946–58).

Williamsburg ★ (ˈwɪljəmzˌbɜːg) *n* a city in SE Virginia: the capital of Virginia (1693–1779); the restoration of large sections of the colonial city was begun in 1926. Pop.: 11 530 (1990).

Williamson ★ (ˈwɪljəmsən) *n* **1 Henry.** 1895–1977, British novelist, known for *Tarka the Otter* (1927) and other animal stories. **2 Malcolm.** born 1931, Australian composer, living in Britain: Master of the Queen's Music since 1975. His works include operas and music for children.

William the Conqueror ★ *n* See **William I** (sense 1).

willies (ˈwɪlɪz) *pl n* **the.** *Sl.* nervousness, jitters, or fright (esp. in **give** (*or* **get**) **the willies**). ORIG C20: from ?

willing (ˈwɪlɪŋ) *adj* **1** favourably disposed or inclined; ready. **2** cheerfully compliant. **3** done, given, accepted, etc., freely or voluntarily.
▸ **ˈwillingly** *adv* ▸ **ˈwillingness** *n*

Willis ★ (ˈwɪlɪs) *n* **Norman (David).** born 1933, British trade-union leader; general secretary of the Trades Union Congress (1984–93).

williwaw (ˈwɪlɪˌwɔː) *n US & Canad.* **1** a sudden strong gust of cold wind blowing offshore from a mountainous coast, as in the Strait of Magellan. **2** a state of great turmoil. ORIG C19: from ?

will-o'-the-wisp (ˌwɪləðəˈwɪsp) *n* **1** Also called: **friar's lantern, ignis fatuus, jack-o'-lantern.** a pale flame or phosphorescence sometimes seen over marshy ground at night. It is believed to be due to the spontaneous combustion of methane from decomposing organic matter. **2** a person or thing that is elusive or allures and misleads. ORIG C17: from *Will,* short for *William + wisp,* in former sense of a twist of hay burning as a torch

willow (ˈwɪləʊ) *n* **1** any of a large genus of trees and shrubs, such as the weeping willow and osiers of N temperate regions, which have graceful flexible branches and flowers in catkins. **2** the whitish wood of certain of these trees. **3** something made of willow wood, such as a cricket bat. ORIG OE *welig*

willowherb (ˈwɪləʊˌhɜːb) *n* **1** any of various temperate and arctic plants having narrow leaves and terminal clusters of pink, purplish, or white flowers. **2** short for **rosebay willowherb** (see **rosebay**).

willow pattern *n* **a** a pattern incorporating a willow tree, river, bridge, and figures, typically in blue on a white ground, used on porcelain, etc. **b** *(as modifier): a willow-pattern plate.*

Willow South ★ *n* a city in S Alaska, about 113 km (70 miles) northwest of Anchorage: chosen as the site of the projected new state capital in 1976.

willowy (ˈwɪləʊɪ) *adj* **1** slender and graceful. **2** flexible or pliant. **3** covered or shaded with willows.

willpower (ˈwɪlˌpaʊə) *n* **1** the ability to control oneself and determine one's actions. **2** firmness of will.

Wills ★ (wɪlz) *n* **1 Helen Newington,** married names *Helen Wills Moody Roark.* 1905–97, US tennis player: Wimbledon singles champion eight times between 1927 and 1938. **2 William John.** 1834–61, British explorer: Robert Burke's deputy in an expedition on which both men died after crossing Australia.

willy[1] (ˈwɪlɪ) *n, pl* **willies.** *Brit. inf.* a childish or jocular term for **penis.**

willy[2] (ˈwɪlɪ) *n Austral. sl.* a sudden loss of temper; fit: *to throw a willy.*

willy-nilly (ˈwɪlɪˈnɪlɪ) *adv* **1** whether desired or not. ◆ *adj* **2** occurring or taking place whether desired or not. ORIG OE *wile hē, nyle hē,* lit.: will he or will he not

willy wagtail *n* a black-and-white flycatcher of Australasia and parts of Asia, with white feathers over the brows.

willy-willy (ˈwɪlɪˌwɪlɪ) *n, pl* **willy-willies.** *Austral.* a small sometimes violent upward-spiralling cyclone or dust storm. ORIG from Abor.

Wilmington ★ (ˈwɪlmɪŋtən) *n* a port in N Delaware, on the Delaware River: industrial centre. Pop.: 71 529 (1990).

Wilno ★ (ˈviːlnɔ) *n* the Polish name for **Vilnius.**

Wilson ★ (ˈwɪlsən) *n* **1 Alexander.** 1766–1813, Scottish ornithologist in the US. **2 Sir Angus (Frank Johnstone).** 1913–91, British writer, whose novels include *Anglo-Saxon Atti-*

tudes (1956) and *No Laughing Matter* (1967). **3 Charles Thomson Rees.** 1869–1959, British physicist, who invented the cloud chamber: shared the Nobel prize for physics 1927. **4 Edmund.** 1895–1972, US critic, noted esp. for *Axel's Castle* (1931). **5 (James) Harold,** Baron Wilson of Rievaulx. 1916–95, British Labour statesman; prime minister (1964–70; 1974–76). **6 Richard.** 1714–82, Welsh landscape painter. **7 (Thomas) Woodrow** ('wʊdrəʊ). 1856–1924, US Democratic statesman; 28th president of the US (1913–21). He led the US into World War I in 1917. Although he secured the formation of the League of Nations, the US Senate refused to join it: Nobel peace prize 1919.

wilt[1] (wɪlt) *vb* **1** to become or cause to become limp or drooping. **2** to lose or cause to lose courage, strength, etc. ◆ *n* **3** the act of wilting or state of becoming wilted. **4** any plant disease characterized by permanent wilting. ORIG C17: ? var. of *wilk* to wither, from MDu. *welken*

wilt[2] (wɪlt) *vb Arch. or dialect.* (used with the pronoun *thou* or its relative equivalent) a singular form of the present tense (indicative mood) of **will**[1].

Wilton ('wɪltən) *n* a kind of carpet with a close velvet pile of cut loops. ORIG after *Wilton,* town in Wiltshire, where first made

Wilts (wɪlts) *abbrev. for* Wiltshire.

Wiltshire ★ ('wɪltʃə, -ˌʃɪə) *n* a county of S England, consisting mainly of chalk uplands, with Salisbury Plain in the south and the Marlborough Downs in the north, includes Swindon unitary authority; prehistoric remains (at Stonehenge and Avebury). Administrative centre: Trowbridge. Pop. (excluding Swindon unitary authority): 418 700 (1996 est.). Area (excluding Swindon unitary authority): 3246 sq. km (1253 sq. miles).

wily ('waɪlɪ) *adj* **wilier, wiliest.** sly or crafty.
▸ '**wiliness** *n*

wimble ('wɪmbᵊl) *n* **1** any of a number of hand tools for boring holes. ◆ *vb* **wimbles, wimbling, wimbled. 2** to bore (a hole) with a wimble. ORIG C13: from MDu. *wimmel* auger

Wimbledon ★ ('wɪmbᵊldən) *n* part of the Greater London borough of Merton: headquarters of the All England Lawn Tennis Club since 1877 and the site of the annual international tennis championships.

wimp (wɪmp) *n Inf.* an ineffective person. ORIG C20: from ?
▸ '**wimpish** *or* '**wimpy** *adj*

WIMP (wɪmp) *n acronym for:* **1** windows, icons, menus (*or* mice), pointers: denoting a type of user-friendly screen display used in small computing. **2** *Physics.* weakly interacting massive particle: a hypothetical particle postulated to account for the dark matter in the universe.

wimple ('wɪmpᵊl) *n* **1** a piece of cloth draped around the head to frame the face, worn by women in the Middle Ages and still worn by some nuns. ◆ *vb* **wimples, wimpling, wimpled.** *Arch.* **2** (*tr*) to cover with or put a wimple on. **3** (esp. of a veil) to lie or cause to lie in folds or pleats. ORIG OE *wimpel*

wimp out *vb* (*intr, adv*) *Sl.* to fail to do or complete something through fear or lack of conviction.

win (wɪn) *vb* **wins, winning, won. 1** (*intr*) to achieve first place in a competition. **2** (*tr*) to gain (a prize, first place, etc.) in a competition. **3** (*tr*) to succeed in or gain (something) with an effort: *we won recognition.* **4** to gain victory or triumph in (a battle, argument, etc.). **5** (*tr*) to earn (a living, etc.) by work. **6** (*tr*) to capture: *the Germans never won Leningrad.* **7** (when *intr,* foll. by *out, through,* etc.) to reach with difficulty (a desired position) or become free, loose, etc., with effort: *the boat won the shore.* **8** (*tr*) to gain (the sympathy, loyalty, etc.) of someone. **9** (*tr*) to persuade (a woman, etc.) to marry one. **10** (*tr*) to extract (ore, coal, etc.) from a mine or (metal or other minerals) from ore. **11 you can't win.** *Inf.* an expression of resignation after an unsuccessful attempt to overcome difficulties. ◆ *n* **12** *Inf.* a success, victory, or triumph. **13** profit; winnings. ◆ See also **win over.** ORIG OE *winnan*
▸ '**winnable** *adj*

wince[1] (wɪns) *vb* **winces, wincing, winced. 1** (*intr*) to start slightly, as with sudden pain; flinch. ◆ *n* **2** the act of wincing. ORIG C18 (earlier (C13) meaning: to kick): via OF *wencier, guenchir* to avoid, of Gmc origin
▸ '**wincer** *n* ▸ '**wincingly** *adv*

wince[2] (wɪns) *n* a roller for transferring pieces of cloth between dyeing vats. ORIG C17: var. of WINCH[1]

winceyette (ˌwɪnsɪ'ɛt) *n Brit.* a plain-weave cotton fabric with slightly raised two-sided nap. ORIG from Scot. *wincey,* prob. altered from *woolsey* in *linsey-woolsey,* a fabric made of linen & wool

winch[1] (wɪntʃ) *n* **1** a windlass driven by a hand- or power-operated crank. **2** a hand- or power-operated crank by which a machine is driven. ◆ *vb* **3** (*tr;* often foll. by *up* or *in*) to pull or lift using a winch. ORIG OE *wince* pulley

winch[2] (wɪntʃ) *vb* (*intr*) an obsolete word for **wince**[1].

Winchester ★ ('wɪntʃɪstə) *n* a city in S England, administrative centre of Hampshire: a Romano-British town; Saxon capital of Wessex; 11th-century cathedral; site of **Winchester College** (1382), English public school. Pop.: 36 121 (1991).

Winchester rifle ('wɪntʃɪstə) *n Trademark.* a breech-loading lever-action repeating rifle. Often shortened to **Winchester.** ORIG C19: after O. F. *Winchester* (1810–80), US manufacturer

Winckelmann ★ (*German* 'vɪŋkəlman) *n* **Johann Joachim** (jo'han 'joːaxɪm). 1717–68, German archaeologist and art historian.

wind[1] (wɪnd) *n* **1** a current of air, sometimes of considerable force, moving generally horizontally from areas of high pressure to areas of low pressure. **2** *Chiefly poetic.* the direction from which a wind blows, usually a cardinal point of the compass. **3** air artificially moved, as by a fan, pump, etc. **4** a trend, tendency, or force: *the winds of revolution.* **5** *Inf.* a hint; suggestion: *we got wind of his plans.* **6** something deemed insubstantial: *his talk was all wind.* **7** breath, as used in respiration or talk: *you're just wasting wind.* **8** (often used in sports) the power to breathe normally: *his wind is weak.* **9** *Music.* **9a** a wind instrument or wind instruments considered collectively. **9b** (*often pl*) the musicians who play wind instruments in an orchestra. **9c** (*modifier*) of or composed of wind instruments: *a wind ensemble.* **10** an informal name for **flatus. 11** the air on which the scent of an animal is carried to hounds or on which the scent of a hunter is carried to his quarry. **12 between wind and water. 12a** the part of a vessel's hull below the water line that is exposed by rolling or by wave action. **12b** any particularly susceptible point. **13 break wind.** to release intestinal gas through the anus. **14 get** *or* **have the wind up.** *Inf.* to become frightened. **15 how** *or* **which way the wind blows** *or* **lies.** what appears probable. **16 in the teeth** (*or* **eye**) **of the wind.** directly into the wind. **17 in the wind.** about to happen. **18 into the wind.** against the wind or upwind. **19 off the wind.** *Naut.* away from the direction from which the wind is blowing. **20 on the wind.** *Naut.* as near as possible to the direction from which the wind is blowing. **21 put the wind up.** *Inf.* to frighten or alarm. **22 raise the wind.** *Brit. inf.* to obtain the necessary funds. **23 sail close** *or* **near to the wind.** to come near the limits of danger or indecency. **24 take the wind out of someone's sails.** to disconcert or deflate someone. ◆ *vb* (*tr*) **25** to cause (someone) to be short of breath: *the blow winded him.* **26a** to detect the scent of. **26b** to pursue (quarry) by following its scent. **27** to cause (a baby) to bring up wind after feeding. **28** to expose to air, as in drying, etc. ORIG OE
▸ '**windless** *adj*

wind[2] (waɪnd) *vb* **winds, winding, wound. 1** (often foll. by *around, about,* or *upon*) to turn or coil (string, cotton, etc.) around some object or point or (of string, etc.) to be turned, etc., around some object or point: *he wound a scarf around his head.* **2** (*tr*) to cover or wreathe by or as if by coiling, wrapping, etc.: *we wound the body in a shroud.* **3** (*tr;* often foll. by *up*) to tighten the spring of (a clockwork mechanism). **4** (*tr;* foll. by *off*) to remove by uncoiling or unwinding. **5** (*usually intr*) to move or cause to move in a sinuous, spiral, or circular course: *the river winds through the hills.* **6** (*tr*) to introduce indirectly or deviously: *he is winding his own opinions into the report.* **7** (*tr*) to cause to twist or revolve: *he wound the handle.* **8** (*tr;* usually foll. by *up* or *down*) to move by cranking: *please wind up the win-*

dow. ◆ *n* **9** the act of winding or state of being wound. **10** a single turn, bend, etc.: *a wind in the river*. ◆ See also **wind down, wind up**. ORIG OE *windan*
▸ **'windable** *adj*

wind[3] (waɪnd) *vb* **winds, winding, winded** *or* **wound**. (*tr*) *Poetic*. to blow (a note or signal) on (a horn, bugle, etc.). ORIG C16: special use of WIND[1]

windage ('wɪndɪdʒ) *n* **1a** a deflection of a projectile as a result of the effect of the wind. **1b** the degree of such deflection. **2** the difference between a firearm's bore and the diameter of its projectile. **3** *Naut*. the exposed part of the hull of a vessel responsible for wind resistance.

windbag ('wɪnd,bæg) *n* **1** *Sl*. a voluble person who has little of interest to communicate. **2** the bag in a set of bagpipes, which provides a continuous flow of air to the pipes.

windblown ('wɪnd,bləʊn) *adj* **1** blown by the wind. **2** (of trees, shrubs, etc.) growing in a shape determined by the prevailing winds.

wind-borne *adj* (esp. of plant seeds or pollen) transported by wind.

windbound ('wɪnd,baʊnd) *adj* (of a sailing vessel) prevented from sailing by an unfavourable wind.

windbreak ('wɪnd,breɪk) *n* a fence, line of trees, etc., serving as a protection from the wind by breaking its force.

windburn ('wɪnd,bɜːn) *n* irritation of the skin caused by prolonged exposure to winds of high velocity.

Windcheater ('wɪnd,tʃiːtə) *n Aust. trademark*. a warm jacket, usually with a close-fitting knitted neck, cuffs, and waistband.

wind chest (wɪnd) *n* a box in an organ in which air from the bellows is stored under pressure before being supplied to the pipes or reeds.

wind-chill ('wɪnd-) *n* **a** the serious chilling effect of wind and low temperature: measured on a scale that runs from hot to fatal to life. **b** (*as modifier*): *wind-chill factor*.

wind cone (wɪnd) *n* another name for **windsock**.

wind down (waɪnd) *vb* (*adv*) **1** (*tr*) to lower or move down by cranking. **2** (*intr*) (of a clock spring) to become slack. **3** (*intr*) to diminish gradually in power; relax.

winded ('wɪndɪd) *adj* **1** out of breath, as from strenuous exercise. **2** (*in combination*) having breath or wind as specified: *broken-winded; short-winded*.

winder ('waɪndə) *n* **1** a person or device that winds. **2** an object, such as a bobbin, around which something is wound. **3** a knob or key used to wind up a clock, watch, or similar mechanism. **4** any plant that twists itself around a support. **5** a step of a spiral staircase. Cf. **flyer** (sense 4).

Windermere ★ ('wɪndə,mɪə) *n* **Lake**. a lake in NW England, in Cumbria in the SE part of the Lake District: the largest lake in England. Length: 17 km (10.5 miles).

windfall ('wɪnd,fɔːl) *n* **1** a piece of unexpected good fortune, esp. financial gain. **2** something blown down by the wind, esp. a piece of fruit.

windfall tax *n* a tax levied on an organization considered to have made excessive profits, esp. a privatized utility company that has exploited a natural monopoly.

wind farm *n* a large group of wind-driven generators for electricity supply.

windflower ('wɪnd,flaʊə) *n* any of various anemone plants, such as the wood anemone.

wind gauge (wɪnd) *n* **1** another name for **anemometer**. **2** a scale on a gun sight indicating the amount of deflection necessary to allow for windage. **3** *Music*. a device for measuring the wind pressure in the bellows of an organ.

wind harp (wɪnd) *n* a less common name for **aeolian harp**.

Windhoek ★ ('wɪnt,hʊk, 'vɪnt-) *n* the capital of Namibia, in the centre, at an altitude of 1654 m (5428 ft): formerly the capital of German South West Africa. Pop.: 190 000 (1995 est.).

windhover ('wɪnd,hɒvə) *n Brit*. a dialect name for a **kestrel**.

winding ('waɪndɪŋ) *n* **1** a curving or sinuous course or movement. **2** anything that has been wound or wrapped around something. **3** a particular manner or style in which something has been wound. **4** a curve, bend, or complete turn in wound material, a road, etc. **5** (*often pl*) devious thoughts or behaviour: *the tortuous windings of political argumentation*. **6** one or more turns of wire forming a continuous coil through which an electric current can pass, as used in transformers, generators, etc. ◆ *adj* **7** curving; sinuous: *a winding road*.
▸ **'windingly** *adv*

winding sheet *n* a sheet in which a corpse is wrapped for burial; shroud.

winding-up *n* the process of finishing or closing something, esp. the process of closing down a business.

wind instrument (wɪnd) *n* any musical instrument sounded by the breath, such as the woodwinds and brass instruments of an orchestra.

windjammer ('wɪnd,dʒæmə) *n* a large merchant sailing ship.

windlass ('wɪndləs) *n* **1** a machine for raising weights by winding a rope or chain upon a barrel or drum driven by a crank, motor, etc. ◆ *vb* **2** (*tr*) to raise or haul (a weight, etc.) by means of a windlass. ORIG C14: from ON *vindáss*, from *vinda* to WIND[2] + *ass* pole

windlestraw ('wɪndᵊl,strɔː) *n Irish, Scot., & English dialect*. the dried stalk of any of various grasses. ORIG OE *windelstrēaw*, from *windel* basket, from *windan* to wind + *strēaw* straw

wind machine (wɪnd) *n* a machine used, esp. in the theatre, to produce a wind or the sound of wind.

windmill ('wɪnd,mɪl, 'wɪn,mɪl) *n* **1** a machine for grinding or pumping driven by a set of adjustable vanes or sails that are caused to turn by the force of the wind. **2** the set of vanes or sails that drives such a mill. **3** Also called: **whirligig**. *Brit*. a toy consisting of plastic or paper vanes attached to a stick in such a manner that they revolve like the sails of a windmill. **4** an imaginary opponent or evil (esp. in **tilt at** *or* **fight windmills**). ◆ *vb* **5** to move or cause to move like the arms of a windmill.

window ('wɪndəʊ) *n* **1** a light framework, made of timber, metal, or plastic, that contains glass or glazed opening frames and is placed in a wall or roof to let in light or air or to see through. Related adj: **fenestral**. **2** an opening in the wall or roof of a building that is provided to let in light or air or to see through. **3** short for **windowpane**. **4** the area behind a glass window in a shop used for display. **5** any opening or structure resembling a window in function or appearance, such as the transparent area of an envelope revealing an address within. **6** an opportunity to see or understand something usually unseen: *a window on the workings of Parliament*. **7** a period of unbooked time in a diary, schedule, etc. **8** short for **launch window** or **weather window**. **9** *Physics*. a region of the spectrum in which a medium transmits electromagnetic radiation. **10** an area of a VDU display that can be manipulated separately from the rest of the display area. **11** (*modifier*) of or relating to a window or windows: *a window ledge*. ◆ *vb* **12** (*tr*) to furnish with or as if with windows. ORIG C13: from ON *vindauga*, from *vindr* WIND[1] + *auga* eye

window box *n* a long narrow box, placed on or outside a windowsill, in which plants are grown.

window-dresser *n* a person employed to design and build up a display in a shop window.

window-dressing *n* **1** the ornamentation of shop windows, designed to attract customers. **2** the pleasant aspect of an idea, etc., which is stressed to conceal the real nature.

windowpane ('wɪndəʊ,peɪn) *n* a sheet of glass in a window.

window sash *n* a glazed window frame, esp. one that opens.

window seat *n* **1** a seat below a window, esp. in a bay window. **2** a seat beside a window in a bus, train, etc.

window-shop *vb* **window-shops, window-shopping, window-**

shopped. (*intr*) to look at goods in shop windows without intending to buy.
▸ **'window-ˌshopper** *n* ▸ **'window-ˌshopping** *n*

windowsill ('wɪndəʊˌsɪl) *n* a sill below a window.

windpipe ('wɪndˌpaɪp) *n* a nontechnical name for **trachea** (sense 1).

Wind River Range ★ (wɪnd) *n* a mountain range in W Wyoming: one of the highest ranges of the central Rockies. Highest peak: Gannet Peak, 4202 m (13 785 ft).

wind rose (wɪnd) *n* a diagram with radiating lines showing the frequency and strength of winds from each direction affecting a specific place.

windrow ('wɪndˌrəʊ, 'wɪnˌrəʊ) *n* **1** a long low ridge or line of hay or a similar crop, designed to achieve the best conditions for drying or curing. **2** a line of leaves, snow, dust, etc., swept together by the wind.

Windscale ★ ('wɪndˌskeɪl) *n* the former name of **Sellafield.**

windscreen ('wɪndˌskriːn) *n Brit.* the sheet of flat or curved glass that forms a window of a motor vehicle, esp. the front window. US and Canad. name: **windshield.**

windscreen wiper *n Brit.* an electrically operated blade with a rubber edge that wipes a windscreen clear of rain, snow, etc. US and Canad. name: **windshield wiper.**

windshield ('wɪndˌʃiːld) *n* the US and Canad. name for **windscreen.**

windsock ('wɪndˌsɒk) *n* a truncated cone of textile mounted on a mast so that it is free to rotate about a vertical axis: used, esp. at airports, to indicate the local wind direction. Also called: **air sock, drogue, wind sleeve, wind cone.**

Windsor[1] ★ ('wɪnzə) *n* **1** a town in S England, in Berkshire on the River Thames, linked by bridge with Eton: site of **Windsor Castle**, residence of English monarchs since its founding by William the Conqueror; **Old Windsor,** royal residence in the time of Edward the Confessor, is 3 km (2 miles) southeast. Pop.: 30 136 (1991). Official name: **New Windsor. 2** a city in SE Canada, in S Ontario on the Detroit River opposite Detroit: motor-vehicle manufacturing; university (1963). Pop.: 191 435 (1991).

Windsor[2] ★ ('wɪnzə) *n* **1** the official name of the British royal family from 1917. **2 Duke of.** the title of **Edward VIII** from 1937.

Windsor and Maidenhead ★ *n* a unitary authority in SE England. Pop.: 141 500 (1996 est.).

Windsor chair *n* a simple wooden chair, popular in England and America from the 18th century, usually having a shaped seat, splayed legs, and a back of many spindles.

Windsor knot *n* a wide triangular knot, produced by making extra turns in tying a tie.

windstorm ('wɪndˌstɔːm) *n* a storm consisting of violent winds.

wind-sucking *n* a harmful habit of horses in which the animal arches its neck and swallows a gulp of air.
▸ **'windˌsucker** *n*

windsurfing ('wɪndˌsɜːfɪŋ) *n* the sport of riding on water using a surfboard steered and propelled by an attached sail.

windswept ('wɪndˌswɛpt) *adj* open to or swept by the wind.

wind tunnel (wɪnd) *n* a chamber for testing the aerodynamic properties of aircraft, aerofoils, etc., in which a current of air can be maintained at a constant velocity.

wind up (waɪnd) *vb* (*adv*) **1** to bring to or reach a conclusion: *he wound up the proceedings.* **2** (*tr*) to tighten the spring of (a clockwork mechanism). **3** (*tr; usually passive*) *Inf.* to make nervous, tense, etc.: *he was all wound up before the big fight.* **4** (*tr*) to roll (thread, etc.) into a ball. **5** an informal word for **liquidate** (sense 2). **6** (*intr*) *Inf.* to end up (in a specified state): *you'll wind up without any teeth.* **7** (*tr*) *Brit. sl.* to tease (someone). ◆ *n* **wind-up. 8** the act of concluding. **9** the end.

windward ('wɪndwəd) *Chiefly naut.* ◆ *adj* **1** of, in, or moving to the quarter from which the wind blows. ◆ *n* **2** the windward point. **3** the side towards the wind. ◆ *adv* **4** towards the wind. ◆ Cf. **leeward.**

Windward Islands ★ *pl n* **1** a group of islands in the SE Caribbean, in the Lesser Antilles: consists of the French Overseas Department of Martinique and the independent states of Grenada, St Lucia, and St Vincent and the Grenadines. French name: **Îles du Vent. 2** a group of islands in the S Pacific, in French Polynesia in the W Society Archipelago: Moorea, Maio (Tubuai Manu), and Mehetia and Tetiaoro. Pop.: 140 341 (1988).

Windward Passage ★ *n* a strait in the Caribbean, between E Cuba and NW Haiti. Width: 80 km (50 miles).

windy ('wɪndɪ) *adj* **windier, windiest. 1** of, resembling, or relating to wind; stormy. **2** swept by or open to powerful winds. **3** marked by or given to prolonged and often boastful speech: *windy orations.* **4** void of substance. **5** an informal word for **flatulent. 6** *Sl.* frightened.
▸ **'windily** *adv* ▸ **'windiness** *n*

wine (waɪn) *n* **1a** an alcoholic drink produced by the fermenting of grapes with water and sugar. **1b** (*as modifier*): *the wine harvest.* **1c** an alcoholic drink produced in this way from other fruits, flowers, etc.: *elderberry wine.* **2a** a dark red colour, sometimes with a purplish tinge. **2b** (*as adj*): *wine-coloured.* **3** anything resembling wine in its intoxicating or invigorating effect. **4 new wine in old bottles.** something new added to or imposed upon an old or established order. ◆ *vb* **wines, wining, wined. 5** (*intr*) to drink wine. **6 wine and dine.** to entertain or be entertained with wine and fine food. ORIG OE *wīn,* from L *vīnum*
▸ **'wineless** *adj*

wine bar *n* a bar in a restaurant, etc., or an establishment that specializes in serving wine and usually food.

winebibber ('waɪnˌbɪbə) *n* a person who drinks a great deal of wine.
▸ **'wineˌbibbing** *n*

wine box *n* wine sold in a carton with a tap for pouring.

wine cellar *n* **1** a place, such as a dark cool cellar, where wine is stored. **2** the stock of wines stored there.

wine cooler *n* **1** a bucket-like vessel containing ice in which a bottle of wine is placed to be cooled. **2** the full name for **cooler** (sense 3).

wine gallon *n Brit.* a former unit of capacity equal to 231 cubic inches.

wineglass ('waɪnˌglɑːs) *n* **1** a glass drinking vessel, typically having a small bowl on a stem, with a flared foot. **2** Also called: **wineglassful.** the amount that such a glass will hold.

wine grower *n* a person engaged in cultivating vines in order to make wine.
▸ **wine growing** *n*

wine palm *n* any of various palm trees, the sap of which is used, esp. when fermented, as a drink. Also called: **toddy palm.**

winepress ('waɪnˌprɛs) *n* any equipment used for squeezing the juice from grapes in order to make wine.

winery ('waɪnərɪ) *n, pl* **wineries.** *Chiefly US & Canad.* a place where wine is made.

wineskin ('waɪnˌskɪn) *n* the skin of a sheep or goat sewn up and used as a holder for wine.

winey *or* **winy** ('waɪnɪ) *adj* **winier, winiest.** having the taste or qualities of wine.

wing (wɪŋ) *n* **1** either of the modified forelimbs of a bird that are covered with large feathers and specialized for flight in most species. **2** one of the organs of flight of an insect, consisting of a membranous outgrowth from the thorax containing a network of veins. **3** either of the organs of flight in certain other animals, esp. the forelimb of a bat. **4a** a half of the main supporting surface on an aircraft, confined to one side of it. **4b** the full span of the main supporting surface on both sides of an aircraft. **5** an organ, structure, or apparatus resembling a wing. **6** anything suggesting a wing in form, function, or position, such as a sail of a windmill or a ship. **7** *Bot.* **7a** either of the lateral petals of a sweetpea or related flower. **7b** any of various outgrowths of a plant part, esp. the process on a wind-dispersed fruit or seed. **8** a means or cause

of flight or rapid motion; flight: *fear gave wings to his feet.* **9** *Brit.* the part of a car body that surrounds the wheels. US and Canad. name: **fender. 10** *Soccer, hockey, etc.* **10a** either of the two sides of the pitch near the touchline. **10b** a player stationed in such a position; winger. **11** a faction or group within a political party or other organization. See also **left wing, right wing. 12** a part of a building that is subordinate to the main part. **13** (*pl*) the space offstage to the right or left of the acting area in a theatre. **14 in** *or* **on the wings.** ready to step in when needed. **15** either of the two pieces that project forwards from the sides of some chair backs. **16** (*pl*) an insignia in the form of stylized wings worn by a qualified aircraft pilot. **17** a tactical formation in some air forces, consisting of two or more squadrons. **18** any of various flattened organs or extensions in lower animals, esp. when used in locomotion. **19 clip (someone's) wings. 19a** to restrict (someone's) freedom. **19b** to thwart (someone's) ambitions. **20 on the wing. 20a** flying. **20b** travelling. **21 on wings.** flying or as if flying. **22 spread** *or* **stretch one's wings.** to make full use of one's abilities. **23 take wing. 23a** to lift off or fly away. **23b** to depart in haste. **23c** to become joyful. **24 under one's wing.** in one's care. ◆ *vb* (*mainly tr*) **25** (*also intr*) to make (one's way) swiftly on or as if on wings. **26** to shoot or wound (a bird, person, etc.) superficially, in the wing or arm, etc. **27** to cause to fly or move swiftly: *to wing an arrow.* **28** to provide with wings. ORIG C12: from ON
▸ **winged** *adj* ▸ **'wingless** *adj* ▸ **'wing,like** *adj*

Wingate ★ ('wɪn,geɪt) *n* **Orde Charles** (ɔːd). 1903–44, British soldier. During World War II he organized the Chindits in Burma: died in an air crash.

wing beat *or* **wing-beat** *n* a complete cycle of moving the wing by a bird when flying.

wing-case *n* the nontechnical name for **elytron.**

wing chair *n* an easy chair having wings on each side of the back.

wing collar *n* a stiff turned-up shirt collar worn with the points turned down over the tie.

wing commander *n* an officer holding commissioned rank in certain air forces, such as the Royal Air Force: junior to a group captain and senior to a squadron leader.

wing covert *n* any of the covert feathers of the wing of a bird, occurring in distinct rows.

wingding ('wɪŋ,dɪŋ) *n Sl., chiefly US & Canad.* **1** a noisy lively party or festivity. **2** a real or pretended fit or seizure. ORIG C20: from ?

winge (wɪndʒ) *vb, n Austral.* a variant spelling of **whinge.**

winger ('wɪŋə) *n Soccer, etc.* a player stationed on the wing.

wing loading *n* the total weight of an aircraft divided by its wing area.

wingman ('wɪŋmæn) *n pl* **wingmen.** a player in the wing position in Australian Rules.

wing nut *n* a threaded nut tightened by hand by means of two flat lugs or wings projecting from the central body. Also called: **butterfly nut.**

wingspan ('wɪŋ,spæn) *or* **wingspread** ('wɪŋ,sprɛd) *n* the distance between the wing tips of an aircraft, bird, etc.

wing tip *n* the outermost edge of a wing.

wink (wɪŋk) *vb* **1** (*intr*) to close and open one eye quickly, deliberately, or in an exaggerated fashion to convey friendliness, etc. **2** to close and open (an eye or the eyes) momentarily. **3** (*tr;* foll. by *away, back,* etc.) to force away (tears, etc.) by winking. **4** (*tr*) to signal with a wink. **5** (*intr*) (of a light) to gleam or flash intermittently. ◆ *n* **6** a winking movement, esp. one conveying a signal, etc., or such a signal. **7** an interrupted flashing of light. **8** a brief moment of time. **9** *Inf.* the smallest amount, esp. of sleep. **10 tip the wink.** *Brit. inf.* to give a hint. ORIG OE *wincian*

wink at *vb* (*intr, prep*) to connive at; disregard: *the authorities winked at corruption.*

winker ('wɪŋkə) *n* **1** a person or thing that winks. **2** *Dialect or US & Canad. sl.* an eye. **3** another name for **blinker**[1] (sense 1).

winkle ('wɪŋkᵊl) *n* **1** See **periwinkle**[1]. ◆ *vb* **winkles, winkling, winkled. 2** (*tr;* usually foll. by *out, out of,* etc.) *Inf., chiefly Brit.* to extract or prise out. ORIG C16: shortened from PERIWINKLE[1]

winkle-pickers *pl n* shoes or boots with very pointed narrow toes.

Winnebago ★ (,wɪnɪ'beɪgəʊ) *n* **Lake.** a lake in E Wisconsin, fed and drained by the Fox river: the largest lake in the state. Area: 557 sq. km (215 sq. miles).

winner ('wɪnə) *n* **1** a person or thing that wins. **2** *Inf.* a person or thing that seems sure to win or succeed.

winning ('wɪnɪŋ) *adj* **1** (of a person, character, etc.) charming or attractive: *a winning smile.* **2** gaining victory: *the winning goal.* ◆ *n* **3** a shaft or seam of coal. **4** (*pl*) money, prizes, or valuables won, esp. in gambling.
▸ **'winningly** *adv* ▸ **'winningness** *n*

winning gallery *n Real Tennis.* the gallery farthest from the net on either side of the court, into which any shot played wins a point.

winning opening *n Real Tennis.* the grille or winning gallery, into which any shot played wins a point.

winning post *n* the post marking the finishing line on a racecourse.

Winnipeg ★ ('wɪnɪ,pɛg) *n* **1** a city in S Canada, capital of Manitoba at the confluence of the Assiniboine and Red Rivers: University of Manitoba (1877) and University of Winnipeg (1871). Pop.: 616 790 (1991). **2 Lake.** a lake in S Canada, in Manitoba: drains through the Nelson River into Hudson Bay. Area: 23 553 sq. km (9094 sq. miles).
▸ **'Winni,pegger** *n*

Winnipeg couch *n Canad.* a couch with no arms or back, opening out into a double bed.

Winnipegosis ★ (,wɪnɪpə'gəʊsɪs) *n* **Lake.** a lake in S Canada, in W Manitoba. Area: 5400 sq. km (2086 sq. miles).

winnow ('wɪnəʊ) *vb* **1** to separate (grain) from (chaff) by means of a wind or current of air. **2** (*tr*) to examine in order to select the desirable elements. **3** (*tr*) *Rare.* to blow upon; fan. ◆ *n* **4a** a device for winnowing. **4b** the act or process of winnowing. ORIG OE *windwian*
▸ **'winnower** *n*

wino ('waɪnəʊ) *n, pl* **winos.** *Inf.* a down-and-out who habitually drinks cheap wine.

win over *vb* (*tr, adv*) to gain the support or consent of (someone). Also: **win round.**

Winslet ★ ('wɪnzlət) *n* **Kate.** born 1975, British film actress; her films include *Sense and Sensibility* (1995), *Titanic* (1997), and *Quills* (2000).

winsome ('wɪnsəm) *adj* charming; winning; engaging: *a winsome smile.* ORIG OE *wynsum,* from *wynn* joy + *-sum* -SOME[1]
▸ **'winsomely** *adv*

Winston ★ ('wɪnstən) *n* **Robert Lipson,** Baron. born 1940, British obstetrician and gynaecologist, who played a significant role in the development of in vitro fertilization; also known for his TV programmes, including *The Human Body* (1998).

Winston-Salem ★ ('wɪnstən'seɪləm) *n* a city in N central North Carolina: formed in 1913 by the uniting of Salem and Winston; a major tobacco manufacturing centre. Pop.: 155 128 (1994 est.).

winter ('wɪntə) *n* **1a** (*sometimes cap.*) the coldest season of the year, between autumn and spring, astronomically from the December solstice to the March equinox in the N hemisphere and at the opposite time of year in the S hemisphere. **1b** (*as modifier*): *winter pasture.* **2** the period of cold weather associated with the winter. **3** a time of decline, decay, etc. **4** *Chiefly poetic.* a year represented by this season: *a man of 72 winters.* ◆ Related adj: **hibernal.** ◆ *vb* **5** (*intr*) to spend the winter in a specified place. **6** to keep or feed (farm animals, etc.) during the winter or (of farm animals) to be kept or fed during the winter. ORIG OE
▸ **'winterer** *n* ▸ **'winterless** *adj*

winter aconite *n* a small Old World herbaceous plant cultivated for its yellow flowers, which appear early in spring.

winter cherry *n* **1** a Eurasian plant cultivated for its ornamental inflated papery orange-red calyx. **2** the calyx of this plant. ◆ See also **Chinese lantern.**

winter garden *n* **1** a garden of evergreen plants. **2** a conservatory in which flowers are grown in winter.

wintergreen ('wɪntəˌgriːn) *n* **1** any of a genus of evergreen ericaceous shrubs, esp. a subshrub of E North America, which has white bell-shaped flowers and edible red berries. **2 oil of wintergreen.** an aromatic compound, formerly made from this and various other plants but now synthesized: used medicinally and for flavouring. **3** any of a genus of plants, such as **common wintergreen,** of temperate and arctic regions, having rounded leaves and small pink globose flowers. **4 chickweed wintergreen.** a plant of N Europe and N Asia belonging to the primrose family, having white flowers and leaves arranged in a whorl. ORIG C16: from Du. *wintergroen* or G *Wintergrün*

winterize *or* **winterise** ('wɪntəˌraɪz) *vb* **winterizes, winterizing, winterized** *or* **winterises, winterising, winterised.** (*tr*) *US & Canad.* to prepare (a house, car, etc.) to withstand winter conditions.
▸ **ˌwinteriˈzation** *or* **ˌwinteriˈsation** *n*

winter jasmine *n* a jasmine shrub widely cultivated for its winter-blooming yellow flowers.

winter solstice *n* the time at which the sun is at its southernmost point in the sky (northernmost point in the S hemisphere) appearing at noon at its lowest altitude above the horizon. It occurs about December 22 (June 21 in the S hemisphere).

winter sports *pl n* sports held in the open air on snow or ice, esp. skiing.

Winterthur ★ (*German* 'vɪntərtuːr) *n* an industrial town in NE central Switzerland, in Zürich canton: has the largest technical college in the country. Pop.: 88 168 (1994).

wintertime ('wɪntəˌtaɪm) *n* the winter season. Also (archaic): **wintertide.**

winterweight ('wɪntəˌweɪt) *adj* (of clothes) suitably heavy and warm for wear in the winter.

winter wheat *n* a type of wheat that is planted in the autumn and is harvested the following summer.

wintry ('wɪntrɪ) *or* **wintery** ('wɪntərɪ) *adj* **wintrier, wintriest. 1** (esp. of weather) of or characteristic of winter. **2** lacking cheer or warmth; bleak.
▸ **'wintrily** *adv* ▸ **'wintriness** *or* **'winteriness** *n*

win-win *adj* guaranteeing a favourable outcome whatever happens: *a win-win situation for NATO.* ORIG C20: modelled on NO-WIN

winy ('waɪnɪ) *adj* **winier, winiest.** a variant spelling of **winey.**

wipe (waɪp) *vb* **wipes, wiping, wiped.** (*tr*) **1** to rub (a surface or object) lightly, esp., with a cloth, hand, etc., as in removing dust, water, etc. **2** (usually foll. by *off, away, from, up,* etc.) to remove by or as if by rubbing lightly: *he wiped the dirt from his hands.* **3** to eradicate or cancel (a thought, memory, etc.). **4** to erase (a recording) from (a tape). **5** to apply (oil, etc.) by wiping. **6** *Austral. inf.* to abandon or reject (a person). **7 wipe the floor with (someone).** *Inf.* to defeat (someone) decisively. ◆ *n* **8** the act or an instance of wiping. **9** *Dialect.* a sweeping blow. ORIG OE *wīpian*

wipe out *vb* (*adv*) **1** (*tr*) to destroy completely. **2** (*tr*) *Inf.* to kill. **3** (*intr*) to fall off a surfboard. ◆ *n* **wipeout. 4** an act or instance of wiping out. **5** the interference of one radio signal by another so that reception is impossible.

wiper ('waɪpə) *n* **1** any piece of cloth, such as a handkerchief, etc., used for wiping. **2** a cam rotated to allow a part to fall under its own weight, as used in stamping machines, etc. **3** See **windscreen wiper. 4** *Electrical engineering.* a movable conducting arm that makes contact with a row or ring of contacts.

wire ('waɪə) *n* **1** a slender flexible strand or rod of metal. **2** a cable consisting of several metal strands twisted together. **3** a flexible metallic conductor, esp. one made of copper, usually insulated, and used to carry electric current in a circuit. **4** (*modifier*) of, relating to, or made of wire: *a wire fence.* **5** anything made of wire, such as wire netting. **6** a long continuous wire or cable connecting points in a telephone or telegraph system. **7** *Old-fashioned.* an informal name for **telegram** or **telegraph. 8** *US & Canad. horse racing.* the finishing line on a racecourse. **9** a snare made of wire for rabbits and similar animals. **10 (down) to the wire.** *Inf.* right up to the last moment. **11 get in under the wire.** *Inf., chiefly US & Canad.* to accomplish something with little time to spare. **12 get one's wires crossed.** *Inf.* to misunderstand. **13 pull wires.** *Chiefly US & Canad.* to exert influence behind the scenes; pull strings. ◆ *vb* **wires, wiring, wired.** (*mainly tr*) **14** (*also intr*) to send a telegram to (a person or place). **15** to send (news, a message, etc.) by telegraph. **16** to equip (an electrical system, circuit, or component) with wires. **17** to fasten or furnish with wire. **18** to snare with wire. **19 wire in.** *Inf.* to set about (something, esp. food) with enthusiasm. ORIG OE *wīr*
▸ **'wireˌlike** *adj*

wire brush *n* a brush having wire bristles, used for cleaning metal, esp. for removing rust, or for brushing against cymbals.

wire cloth *n* a mesh or netting woven from fine wire, used in window screens, strainers, etc.

wired (waɪəd) *adj Sl.* **1** edgy from stimulant intake. **2** excited, nervous, or tense. **3** using computers to send and receive information, esp. via the Internet.

wiredraw ('waɪəˌdrɔː) *vb* **wiredraws, wiredrawing, wiredrew, wiredrawn.** to convert (metal) into wire by drawing through successively smaller dies.

wire-gauge *n* **1** a flat plate with slots in which standard wire sizes can be measured. **2** a standard system of sizes for measuring the diameters of wires.

wire gauze *n* a stiff meshed fabric woven of fine wires.

wire grass *n* any of various grasses that have tough wiry roots or rhizomes.

wire-guided *adj* (of a missile) able to be controlled in mid-flight by signals passed along a wire connecting the missile to the firer's control device.

wire-haired *adj* (of an animal) having a rough wiry coat.

wireless ('waɪəlɪs) *n, vb Chiefly Brit.* another word for **radio.**

wireless telegraphy *n* another name for **radiotelegraphy.**

wireless telephone *n* another name for **radiotelephone.**
▸ **wireless telephony** *n*

wire netting *n* a net made of wire, often galvanized, that is used for fencing, etc.

wirepuller ('waɪəˌpʊlə) *n Chiefly US & Canad.* a person who uses private or secret influence for his or her own ends.
▸ **'wireˌpulling** *n*

wire recorder *n* an early type of magnetic recorder in which sounds were recorded on a thin steel wire magnetized by an electromagnet.
▸ **wire recording** *n*

wire service *n Chiefly US & Canad.* an agency supplying news, etc., to newspapers, radio, and television stations, etc.

wiretap ('waɪəˌtæp) *vb* **wiretaps, wiretapping, wiretapped. 1** (*intr*) to make a connection to a telegraph or telephone wire in order to obtain information secretly. **2** (*tr*) to tap (a telephone) or the telephone of (a person).
▸ **'wireˌtapper** *n*

wire wheel *n* a wheel in which the rim is held to the hub by wire spokes, esp. one used on a sports car.

wire wool *n* a mass of fine wire used for cleaning and scouring.

wirework ('waɪəˌwɜːk) *n* **1** functional or decorative work made of wire. **2** objects made of wire, esp. netting.

wireworks ('waɪəˌwɜːks) *n* (*functioning as sing or pl*) a factory where wire or articles of wire are made.

wireworm ('waɪəˌwɜːm) *n* the wormlike larva of various

beetles, which feeds on the roots of many plants and is a serious pest.

wiring ('waɪərɪŋ) *n* **1** the network of wires used in an electrical system, device, or circuit. ◆ *adj* **2** used in wiring.

Wirral ★ ('wɪrəl) *n* **the. 1** a peninsula in NW England between the estuaries of the Rivers Mersey and Dee. **2** a unitary authority in NW England, in Merseyside. Pop.: 329 200 (1996 est.). Area: 158 sq. km (61 sq. miles).

wiry ('waɪərɪ) *adj* **wirier, wiriest. 1** (of people or animals) slender but strong in constitution. **2** made of or resembling wire, esp. in stiffness: *wiry hair.* **3** (of a sound) produced by or as if by a vibrating wire.
▸ **'wirily** *adv* ▸ **'wiriness** *n*

wis (wɪs) *vb Arch.* to know or suppose (something). ORIG C17: a form derived from *iwis,* (from OE *gewiss* certain), mistakenly interpreted as *I wis* I know, as if from OE *witan* to know

Wis. *abbrev. for* Wisconsin.

Wisbech ★ ('wɪzbiːtʃ) *n* a town in E England, in N Cambridgeshire: market-gardening. Pop.: 24 981 (1991).

Wisconsin ★ (wɪs'kɒnsɪn) *n* **1** a state of the N central US, on Lake Superior and Lake Michigan: consists of an undulating plain, with uplands in the north and west; over 168 m (550 ft) above sea level along the shore of Lake Michigan. Capital: Madison. Pop.: 5 223 500 (1998 est.). Area: 141 061 sq. km (54 464 sq. miles). Abbrevs.: **Wis.** or (with zip code) **WI** **2** a river in central and SW Wisconsin, flowing south and west to the Mississippi. Length: 692 km (430 miles).
▸ **Wis'consin,ite** *n*

Wisden ★ ('wɪzdən) *n* **John.** 1826–84, English cricketer; publisher of *Wisden Cricketers' Almanack,* which first appeared in 1864.

wisdom ('wɪzdəm) *n* **1** the ability or result of an ability to think and act utilizing knowledge, experience, understanding, common sense, and insight. **2** accumulated knowledge or enlightenment. **3** *Arch.* a wise saying or wise sayings. ◆ Related adj: **sagacious.** ORIG OE *wīsdōm*

wisdom tooth *n* **1** any of the four molar teeth, one at the back of each side of the jaw, that are the last of the permanent teeth to erupt. Technical name: **third molar. 2 cut one's wisdom teeth.** to arrive at the age of discretion.

wise[1] (waɪz) *adj* **1** possessing, showing, or prompted by wisdom or discernment. **2** prudent; sensible. **3** shrewd; crafty: *a wise plan.* **4** well-informed; erudite. **5** informed or knowing (esp. in **none the wiser**). **6** (*postpositive;* often foll. by *to*) *Sl.* in the know, esp. possessing inside information (about). **7** *Arch.* possessing powers of magic. **8 be** *or* **get wise.** (often foll. by *to*) *Inf.* to be or become aware or informed (of something). **9 put wise.** (often foll. by *to*) *Sl.* to inform or warn (of). ◆ *vb* **wises, wising, wised. 10** See **wise up.** ORIG OE *wīs*
▸ **'wisely** *adv* ▸ **'wiseness** *n*

wise[2] (waɪz) *n Arch.* way, manner, fashion, or respect (esp. in **any wise, in no wise**). ORIG OE *wīse* manner

-wise *adv combining form.* **1** indicating direction or manner: *clockwise; likewise.* **2** with reference to: *businesswise.* ORIG OE *-wisan;* see WISE[2]

wiseacre ('waɪz,eɪkə) *n* **1** a person who wishes to seem wise. **2** a wise person: often used facetiously or contemptuously. ORIG C16: from MDu. *wijsseggher* soothsayer. See WISE[1], SAY

wisecrack ('waɪz,kræk) *Inf.* ◆ *n* **1** a flippant gibe or sardonic remark. ◆ *vb (intr)* **2** to make a wisecrack.
▸ **'wise,cracker** *n*

wise guy *n Inf.* **1** a person who is given to making conceited, sardonic, or insolent comments. **2** *US* a member of the Mafia.

Wiseman ★ ('waɪzmən) *n* **Nicholas Patrick Stephen.** 1802–65, British cardinal; first Roman Catholic archbishop of Westminster (1850–65).

wisent ('wiːzᵊnt) *n* another name for **European bison.** See **bison** (sense 2). ORIG G, from OHG *wisunt* BISON

wise up *vb (adv) Sl., chiefly US & Canad.* (often foll. by *to*) to become or cause to become aware or informed (of).

wish (wɪʃ) *vb* **1** (when *tr, takes a clause as object or an infinitive;* when *intr,* often foll. by *for*) to want or desire (something, often that which cannot be or is not the case): *I wish I lived in Italy.* **2** (*tr*) to feel or express a desire or hope concerning the future or fortune of: *I wish you well.* **3** (*tr*) to desire or prefer to be as specified. **4** (*tr*) to greet as specified: *he wished us good afternoon.* ◆ *n* **5** the expression of some desire or mental inclination: *to make a wish.* **6** something desired or wished for: *he got his wish.* **7** (*usually pl*) expressed hopes or desire, esp. for someone's welfare, health, etc. **8** (*often pl*) *Formal.* a polite order or request. ◆ See also **wish on.** ORIG OE *wȳscan*
▸ **'wisher** *n*

wishbone ('wɪʃ,bəʊn) *n* the V-shaped bone above the breastbone in most birds consisting of the fused clavicles. ORIG C17: from the custom of two people breaking apart the bone after eating: the person with the longer part makes a wish

wishful ('wɪʃfʊl) *adj* having wishes or characterized by wishing.
▸ **'wishfully** *adv* ▸ **'wishfulness** *n*

wish fulfilment *n* (in Freudian psychology) any successful attempt to fulfil a wish stemming from the unconscious mind, whether in fact, in fantasy, or by disguised means.

wishful thinking *n* the erroneous belief that one's wishes are in accordance with reality.
▸ **wishful thinker** *n*

wish list *n* a list of things desired by a person or organization: *the government's wish list.*

wish on *vb (tr, prep)* to hope that (someone or something) should be imposed (on someone); foist: *I wouldn't wish my cold on anyone.*

wishy-washy ('wɪʃɪ,wɒʃɪ) *adj Inf.* **1** lacking in substance, force, colour, etc. **2** watery; thin.

Wisła ★ ('viswa) *n* the Polish name for **Vistula** (sense 1).

Wislany Zalew ★ (*Polish* viʃ'laːni 'zaːlɛf) *n* the Polish name for the **Vistula** (sense 2).

Wismar ★ (*German* 'vɪsmar) *n* a port in NE Germany, on an inlet of the Baltic: shipbuilding industries. Pop.: 54 470 (1991).

wisp (wɪsp) *n* **1** a thin, light, delicate, or fibrous piece or strand, such as a streak of smoke or a lock of hair. **2** a small bundle, as of hay or straw. **3** anything slender and delicate: *a wisp of a girl.* **4** a mere suggestion or hint. **5** a flock of birds, esp. snipe. ORIG C14: var. of *wips,* from ?
▸ **'wisp,like** *adj* ▸ **'wispy** *adj*

wist (wɪst) *vb Arch.* the past tense and past participle of **wit**[2].

wisteria (wɪ'stɪərɪə) *n* any twining woody climbing plant of the genus *Wisteria,* of E Asia and North America, having blue, purple, or white flowers in large drooping clusters. ORIG C19: from NL, after Caspar *Wistar* (1761–1818), US anatomist

wistful ('wɪstfʊl) *adj* sadly pensive, esp. about something yearned for.
▸ **'wistfully** *adv* ▸ **'wistfulness** *n*

wit[1] (wɪt) *n* **1** the talent or quality of using unexpected associations between contrasting or disparate words or ideas to make a clever humorous effect. **2** speech or writing showing this quality. **3** a person possessing, showing, or noted for such an ability. **4** practical intelligence (esp. in **have the wit to**). **5** *Arch.* mental capacity or a person possessing it. ◆ See also **wits.** ORIG OE *witt*

wit[2] (wɪt) *vb* **wits, witting, wot, wist. 1** *Arch.* to be or become aware of (something). **2 to wit.** that is to say; namely (used to introduce statements, as in legal documents). ORIG OE *witan*

witan ('wɪtᵊn) *n* (in Anglo-Saxon England) **1** an assembly of higher ecclesiastics and important laymen that met to counsel the king on matters such as judicial problems. **2** the members of this assembly. ◆ Also called: **witenagemot.** ORIG OE *witan,* pl. of *wita* wise man

witblits ('vɪt,blɪts) *n S. African.* alcoholic drink illegally distilled. ORIG from Afrik. *wit* white + *blits* lightning

witch[1] (wɪtʃ) *n* **1** a person, usually female, who practises or professes to practise magic or sorcery, esp. black

magic, or is believed to have dealings with the devil. **2** an ugly or wicked old woman. **3** a fascinating or enchanting woman. ◆ *vb* (*tr*) **4** a less common word for **bewitch.** ORIG OE *wicca*
▸ **'witch,like** *or* **'witchy** *adj*

witch² (wɪtʃ) *n* a flatfish of N Atlantic coastal waters, having a narrow greyish-brown body marked with tiny black spots: related to the plaice, flounder, etc. ORIG C19: ?from WITCH[1], from the appearance of the fish

witchcraft ('wɪtʃ,krɑːft) *n* **1** the art or power of bringing magical or preternatural power to bear or the act or practice of attempting to do so. **2** the influence of magic or sorcery. **3** fascinating or bewitching influence or charm.

witch doctor *n* a man in certain societies, esp. preliterate ones, who appears to possess magical powers, used esp. to cure sickness but also to harm people. Also called: **shaman, medicine man.**

witch-elm *n* a variant spelling of **wych-elm.**

witchery ('wɪtʃərɪ) *n, pl* **witcheries. 1** the practice of witchcraft. **2** magical or bewitching influence or charm.

witches'-broom *n* a dense abnormal growth of shoots on a tree or other woody plant, usually caused by parasitic fungi.

witchetty grub ('wɪtʃɪtɪ) *n* the wood-boring edible caterpillar of an Australian moth. Also: **witchetty, witchety.** ORIG C19 *witchetty,* from Abor.

witch hazel *or* **wych-hazel** *n* **1** any of a genus of trees and shrubs of North America, having ornamental yellow flowers and medicinal properties. **2** an astringent medicinal solution containing an extract of the bark and leaves of one of these shrubs, applied to treat bruises, inflammation, etc.

witch-hunt *n* a rigorous campaign to expose dissenters on the pretext of safeguarding the public welfare.
▸ **'witch-,hunting** *n, adj*

witching ('wɪtʃɪŋ) *adj* **1** relating to or appropriate for witchcraft. **2** *Now rare.* bewitching.
▸ **'witchingly** *adv*

witching hour *n* **the.** the hour at which witches are supposed to appear, usually midnight.

witenagemot (,wɪtɪnəgɪ'məʊt) *n* another word for **witan.** ORIG OE *witena,* genitive pl of *wita* councillor + *gemōt* meeting

with (wɪð, wɪθ) *prep* **1** using; by means of: *he killed her with an axe.* **2** accompanying; in the company of: *the lady you were with.* **3** possessing; having: *a man with a red moustache.* **4** concerning or regarding: *be patient with her.* **5** in spite of: *with all his talents, he was still humble.* **6** used to indicate a time or distance by which something is away from something else: *with three miles to go, he collapsed.* **7** in a manner characterized by: *writing with abandon.* **8** caused or prompted by: *shaking with rage.* **9** often used with a verb indicating a reciprocal action or relation between the subject and the preposition's object: *agreeing with me.* **10 with it.** *Inf.* **10a** fashionable; in style. **10b** comprehending what is happening or being said. **11 with that.** after that. ORIG OE

withal (wɪ'ðɔːl) *adv* **1** *Literary.* as well. **2** *Arch.* therewith. ◆ *prep* **3** (*postpositive*) an archaic word for **with.** ORIG C12: from WITH + ALL

withdraw (wɪð'drɔː) *vb* **withdraws, withdrawing, withdrew, withdrawn. 1** (*tr*) to take or draw back or away; remove. **2** (*tr*) to remove from deposit or investment in a bank, etc. **3** (*tr*) to retract or recall (a promise, etc.). **4** (*intr*) to retire or retreat: *the troops withdrew.* **5** (*intr;* often foll. by *from*) to depart (from): *he withdrew from public life.* **6** (*intr*) to detach oneself socially, emotionally, or mentally. ORIG C13: from WITH (in the sense: away from) + DRAW
▸ **with'drawer** *n*

withdrawal (wɪð'drɔːəl) *n* **1** an act or process of withdrawing. **2** the period a drug addict goes through following abrupt termination in the use of narcotics, usually characterized by physical and mental symptoms (**withdrawal symptoms**). **3** Also called: **withdrawal method, coitus interruptus.** the deliberate withdrawing of the penis from the vagina before ejaculation, as a method of contraception.

withdrawing room *n* an archaic term for **drawing room.**

withdrawn (wɪð'drɔːn) *vb* **1** the past participle of **withdraw.** ◆ *adj* **2** unusually reserved or shy. **3** secluded or remote.

withe (wɪθ, wɪð, waɪð) *n* **1** a strong flexible twig, esp. of willow, suitable for binding things together; withy. **2** a band or rope of twisted twigs or stems. ◆ *vb* **withes, withing, withed. 3** (*tr*) to bind with withes. ORIG OE *withthe*

wither ('wɪðə) *vb* **1** (*intr*) (esp. of a plant) to droop, wilt, or shrivel up. **2** (*intr;* often foll. by *away*) to fade or waste: *all hope withered away.* **3** (*intr*) to decay or disintegrate. **4** (*tr*) to cause to wilt or lose vitality. **5** (*tr*) to abash, esp. with a scornful look. ORIG C14: ? var. of WEATHER (vb)
▸ **'witherer** *n* ▸ **'withering** *adj* ▸ **'witheringly** *adv*

withers ('wɪðəz) *pl n* the highest part of the back of a horse, behind the neck between the shoulders. ORIG C16: short for *widersones,* from *wider* with + *-sones,* ? var. of SINEW

withershins ('wɪðə,ʃɪnz) *or* **widdershins** *adv Chiefly Scot.* in the direction contrary to the apparent course of the sun; anticlockwise. ORIG C16: from MLow G *weddersinnes,* from MHG, lit.: opposite course, from *wider* against + *sinnes,* genitive of *sin* course

withhold (wɪð'həʊld) *vb* **withholds, withholding, withheld. 1** (*tr*) to keep back: *he withheld his permission.* **2** (*tr*) to hold back; restrain. **3** (*intr;* usually foll. by *from*) to refrain or forbear.
▸ **with'holder** *n*

within (wɪ'ðɪn) *prep* **1** in; inside; enclosed or encased by. **2** before (a period of time) has elapsed: *within a week.* **3** not differing by more than (a specified amount) from: *live within your means.* ◆ *adv* **4** *Formal.* inside; internally.

without (wɪ'ðaʊt) *prep* **1** not having: *a traveller without much money.* **2** not accompanied by: *he came without his wife.* **3** not making use of: *it is not easy to undo screws without a screwdriver.* **4** (*foll. by a verbal noun or noun phrase*) not, while not, or after not: *she can sing for two minutes without drawing breath.* **5** *Arch.* on the outside of: *without the city walls.* ◆ *adv* **6** *Formal.* outside.

withstand (wɪð'stænd) *vb* **withstands, withstanding, withstood. 1** (*tr*) to resist. **2** (*intr*) to remain firm in endurance or opposition.
▸ **with'stander** *n*

withy ('wɪðɪ) *n, pl* **withies.** a variant spelling of **withe** (senses 1, 2). ORIG OE *wīdig(e)*

witless ('wɪtlɪs) *adj* lacking wit, intelligence, or sense.
▸ **'witlessly** *adv* ▸ **'witlessness** *n*

witling ('wɪtlɪŋ) *n Arch.* a person who thinks himself or herself witty.

witness ('wɪtnɪs) *n* **1** a person who has seen or can give first-hand evidence of some event. **2** a person or thing giving or serving as evidence. **3** a person who testifies, esp. in a court of law, to events or facts within his own knowledge. **4** a person who attests to the genuineness of a document, signature, etc., by adding his own signature. **5 bear witness to. 5a** to give written or oral testimony to. **5b** to be evidence or proof of. ◆ Related adj: **testimonial.** ◆ *vb* **6** (*tr*) to see, be present at, or know at first hand. **7** (*tr*) to give evidence of. **8** (*tr*) to be the scene or setting of: *this field has witnessed a battle.* **9** (*intr*) to testify, esp. in a court of law, to events within a person's own knowledge. **10** (*tr*) to attest to the genuineness of (a document, etc.) by adding one's own signature. ORIG OE *witnes,* from *witan* to know + -NESS
▸ **'witnesser** *n*

witness box *or esp. US* **witness stand** *n* the place in a court of law in which witnesses stand to give evidence.

wits (wɪts) *pl n* **1** (*sometimes sing*) the ability to reason and act, esp. quickly (esp. in **have one's wits about one**). **2** (*sometimes sing*) right mind, sanity (esp. in **out of one's wits**). **3 at one's wits' end.** at a loss to know how to proceed. **4 live by one's wits.** to gain a livelihood by craftiness rather than by hard work.

Witt ★ (wɪt) *n* **Johan de** (joː'hɑn). 1625–72, Dutch statesman; chief minister of the United Provinces of the Netherlands (1653–72).

★ people and places

-witted *adj (in combination)* having wits or intelligence as specified: *slow-witted; dim-witted.*

Wittenberg ★ (*German* 'vɪtənbɛrk; *English* 'wɪtᵊnˌbɜːg) *n* a city in E Germany, on the River Elbe: Martin Luther, as a philosophy teacher at Wittenberg university, began the Reformation here in 1517 by nailing his 95 theses to the doors of a church. Pop.: 87 000 (1991).

witter ('wɪtə) *vb (intr; often foll. by on) Inf.* to chatter or babble pointlessly or at unnecessary length. ORIG C20: ?from obs. *whitter* to warble, twitter

Wittgenstein ★ ('vɪtgənˌʃtaɪn, -ˌstaɪn) *n* **Ludwig Josef Johann** ('luːtvɪç 'joːzɛf jo'han). 1889–1951, British philosopher, born in Austria. His principal works were the *Tractatus Logico-Philosophicus* (1921) and *Philosophical Investigations* (1953).

Wittgensteinian ('vɪtgənˌʃtaɪnɪən, -ˌstaɪnɪən) *adj* (of a philosophical position or argument) derived from or related to the work of Wittgenstein and esp. the later work in which he attacks essentialism and stresses the open texture and variety of the use of ordinary language.

witticism ('wɪtɪˌsɪzəm) *n* a clever or witty remark. ORIG C17: from WITTY; coined by Dryden (1677) by analogy with *criticism*

witting ('wɪtɪŋ) *adj Rare.* **1** deliberate; intentional. **2** aware.
▸ **'wittingly** *adv*

witty ('wɪtɪ) *adj* **wittier, wittiest. 1** characterized by clever humour or wit. **2** *Arch. or dialect.* intelligent.
▸ **'wittily** *adv* ▸ **'wittiness** *n*

Witwatersrand ★ (wɪt'wɔːtəzˌrænd; *Afrikaans* vət'vaːtərs'rant) *n* a rocky ridge in NE South Africa: contains the richest gold deposits in the world, also coal and manganese; chief industrial centre of the region is Johannesburg. Height: 1500–1800 m (5000–6000 ft). Also called: **the Rand, the Reef.**

wive (waɪv) *vb* **wives, wiving, wived.** *Arch.* **1** to marry (a woman). **2** *(tr)* to supply with a wife. ORIG OE *gewīfian,* from *wīf* wife

wivern ('waɪvən) *n* a less common spelling of **wyvern.**

wives (waɪvz) *n* **1** the plural of **wife. 2 old wives' tale.** a superstitious tradition, occasionally one that contains an element of truth.

wiz (wɪz) *n, pl* **wizzes.** *Inf.* a variant spelling of **whizz** (sense 5).

wizard ('wɪzəd) *n* **1** a male witch or a man who practises or professes to practise magic or sorcery. **2** a person who is outstandingly clever in some specified field. **3** *Computing.* a program that guides a user through a complex task. ◆ *adj* **4** *Inf., chiefly Brit.* superb; outstanding. **5** of or relating to a wizard or wizardry. ORIG C15: var. of *wissard,* from WISE[1] + -ARD
▸ **'wizardly** *adj*

wizardry ('wɪzədrɪ) *n* the art, skills, and practices of a wizard, sorcerer, or magician.

wizen ('wɪzᵊn) *vb* **1** to make or become shrivelled. ◆ *adj* **2** a variant of **wizened.** ORIG OE *wisnian*

wizened ('wɪzᵊnd) *or* **wizen** *adj* shrivelled, wrinkled, or dried up, esp. with age.

wk *abbrev. for:* **1** *(pl* **wks)** week. **2** work.

wkly *abbrev. for* weekly.

w.l. *or* **WL** *abbrev. for* water line.

WMO *abbrev. for* World Meteorological Organization.

WNW *symbol for* west-northwest.

WO *abbrev. for:* **1** War Office. **2** Warrant Officer. **3** wireless operator.

woad (wəʊd) *n* **1** a European cruciferous plant, formerly cultivated for its leaves, which yield a blue dye. **2** the dye obtained from this plant, used esp. by the ancient Britons as a body dye. ORIG OE *wād*

wobbegong ('wɒbɪˌgɒŋ) *n* any of various sharks of Australian waters, having a richly patterned brown-and-white skin. ORIG from Abor.

wobble ('wɒbᵊl) *vb* **wobbles, wobbling, wobbled. 1** *(intr)* to move or sway unsteadily. **2** *(intr)* to shake: *her voice wobbled with emotion.* **3** *(intr)* to vacillate with indecision. **4** *(tr)* to cause to wobble. ◆ *n* **5** a wobbling movement or sound. ORIG C17: var. of *wabble,* from Low G *wabbeln*
▸ **'wobbler** *n*

wobble board *n Austral.* a piece of fibreboard used as a rhythmic musical instrument, producing a characteristic sound when flexed.

wobbly ('wɒblɪ) *adj* **wobblier, wobbliest. 1** shaky, unstable, or unsteady. ◆ *n* **2 throw a wobbly.** *Sl.* to become suddenly very agitated or angry.
▸ **'wobbliness** *n*

Wodehouse ★ ('wʊdˌhaʊs) *n* Sir **P(elham) G(renville).** 1881–1975, US author, born in England. His humorous novels of upper-class life in England include the *Psmith* and *Jeeves* series.

Woden *or* **Wodan** ★ ('wəʊdᵊn) *n* the foremost Anglo-Saxon god. Norse counterpart: **Odin.** ORIG OE *Wōden;* related to ON *thinn,* OHG *Wuotan,* G *Wotan;* see WEDNESDAY

wodge (wɒdʒ) *n Brit. inf.* a thick lump or chunk cut or broken off something. ORIG C20: alteration of WEDGE

woe (wəʊ) *n* **1** *Literary.* intense grief. **2** *(often pl)* affliction or misfortune. **3 woe betide (someone).** misfortune will befall (someone): *woe betide you if you arrive late.* ◆ *interj* **4** Also: **woe is me.** *Arch.* an exclamation of sorrow or distress. ORIG OE *wā, wǣ*

woebegone ('wəʊbɪˌgɒn) *adj* sorrowful or sad in appearance. ORIG C14: from a phrase such as *me is wo begon* woe has beset me

woeful ('wəʊfᵊl) *adj* **1** expressing or characterized by sorrow. **2** bringing or causing woe. **3** pitiful; miserable: *a woeful standard of work.*
▸ **'woefully** *adv* ▸ **'woefulness** *n*

WOF (in New Zealand) *abbrev. for* Warrant of Fitness.

wog[1] (wɒg) *n Brit. sl., derog.* a person who is not White. ORIG prob. from GOLLIWOG

wog[2] (wɒg) *n Austral. sl.* any ailment or disease, such as influenza, a virus infection, etc. ORIG C20: from ?

woggle ('wɒgᵊl) *n* the ring of leather through which a Scout neckerchief is threaded. ORIG C20: from ?

Wöhler ★ (*German* 'vøːlər) *n* **Friedrich** ('friːdrɪç). 1800–82, German chemist, who proved that organic compounds could be synthesized from inorganic compounds.

wok (wɒk) *n* a large metal Chinese cooking pot having a curved base like a bowl: used esp. for stir-frying. ORIG from Chinese (Cantonese)

woke (wəʊk) *vb* the past tense of **wake**[1].

woken ('wəʊkən) *vb* the past participle of **wake**[1].

Woking ★ ('wəʊkɪŋ) *n* a town in S England, in central Surrey: mainly residential. Pop.: 98 138 (1991).

Wokingham ★ ('wəʊˌkɪŋəm) *n* a unitary authority in S England, in Berkshire. Pop.: 142 400 (1996 est.).

wokka board ('wɒkə) *n Austral.* another name for **wobble board.**

wold[1] (wəʊld) *n Chiefly literary.* a tract of open rolling country, esp. upland. ORIG OE *weald* bush

wold[2] (wəʊld) *n* a variant of **weld**[2].

Wolds ★ (wəʊldz) *pl n* **the.** a range of chalk hills in NE England: consists of the **Yorkshire Wolds** to the north, separated from the **Lincolnshire Wolds** by the Humber estuary.

wolf (wʊlf) *n, pl* **wolves. 1** a predatory canine mammal which hunts in packs and was formerly widespread in North America and Eurasia but is now less common. Related adj: **lupine. 2** any of several similar and related canines, such as the red wolf and the coyote (**prairie wolf**). **3** the fur of any such animal. **4** a voracious or fiercely cruel person or thing. **5** *Inf.* a man who habitually tries to seduce women. **6** Also called: **wolf note.** *Music.* **6a** an unpleasant sound produced in some notes played on the violin, etc., owing to resonant vibrations of the belly. **6b** an out-of-tune effect produced on keyboard instruments accommodated esp. to the system of mean-tone temperament. **7 cry wolf.** to give a false alarm. **8 have** *or* **hold a wolf by the ears.** to be in a desperate situation. **9 keep the wolf from the door.** to ward off starvation or privation. **10 lone wolf.** a person or animal who prefers to be alone. **11 wolf**

in sheep's clothing. a malicious person in a harmless or benevolent disguise. ◆ *vb* **12** (*tr; often foll. by down*) to gulp (down). **13** (*intr*) to hunt wolves. ORIG OE *wulf*
▸ **'wolfish** *adj* ▸ **'wolf,like** *adj*

Wolf ★ *n* **1** (*German* vɔlf). **Friedrich August** ('fri:drɪç 'august). 1759–1824, German classical scholar, who suggested that the Homeric poems, esp. the *Iliad,* are products of an oral tradition. **2** (*German* vɔlf). **Hugo** ('hu:go). 1860–1903, Austrian composer, esp. of songs, including the *Italienisches Liederbuch* and the *Spanisches Liederbuch.* **3** (wʊlf). **Howlin'**. See **Howlin' Wolf.**

Wolf Cub *n Brit.* the former name for **Cub Scout.**

Wolfe ★ (wʊlf) *n* **1 James.** 1727–59, British soldier, who commanded the capture of Quebec, in which he was killed. **2 Thomas (Clayton).** 1900–38, US novelist, noted for his autobiographical fiction, esp. *Look Homeward, Angel* (1929). **3 Tom,** full name *Thomas Kennerly Wolfe.* born 1931, US author and journalist. His books include *The Right Stuff* (1979), *Bonfire of the Vanities* (1987), and *A Man in Full* (1998).

wolffish ('wʊlf,fɪʃ) *n, pl* **wolffish** *or* **wolffishes.** a large northern deep-sea fish. It has large sharp teeth and no pelvic fins and is used as a food fish. Also called: **catfish.**

wolfhound ('wʊlf,haʊnd) *n* the largest breed of dog, used formerly to hunt wolves.

Wolfit ★ ('wʊlfɪt) *n* Sir **Donald.** 1902–68, British stage actor and manager.

wolfram ('wʊlfrəm) *n* another name for **tungsten.** ORIG C18: from G, orig. ?from the proper name *Wolfram,* used pejoratively of tungsten because it was thought inferior to tin

wolframite ('wʊlfrə,maɪt) *n* a black to reddish-brown mineral, a compound of tungsten, iron, and manganese: it is the chief ore of tungsten.

Wolfram von Eschenbach ★ (*German* 'vɔlfram fɔn 'ɛʃənbax) *n* died ?1220, German poet: author of the epic *Parzival,* incorporating the story of the Grail.

wolfsbane ('wʊlfs,beɪn) *or* **wolf's bane** *n* any of several poisonous N temperate plants of the ranunculaceous genus *Aconitum* having hoodlike flowers.

Wolfsburg ★ (*German* 'vɔlfsbʊrk) *n* a city in N central Germany, in Lower Saxony: founded in 1938; motor-vehicle industry. Pop.: 126 331 (1996 est.).

wolf spider *n* a spider which chases its prey to catch it. Also called: **hunting spider.**

wolf whistle *n* **1** a whistle made by a man to express admiration of a woman's appearance. ◆ *vb* **wolf-whistle, wolf-whistles, wolf-whistling, wolf-whistled. 2** (when *intr,* sometimes foll. by *at*) to make such a whistle (at someone).

Wollongong ★ ('wʊləŋ,gɒŋ) *n* a city in E Australia, in E New South Wales on the Pacific: an early centre of dairy farming; now a coal-mining and heavy industrial centre. Pop.: 249 500 (1993).

Wollstonecraft ★ ('wʊlstən,krɑ:ft) *n* **Mary.** 1759–97, British writer, author of *A Vindication of the Rights of Woman* (1792); wife of William Godwin and mother of Mary Shelley.

Wolof ('wɒlɒf) *n* **1** (*pl* **Wolof** *or* **Wolofs**) a member of a Negroid people of W Africa living chiefly in Senegal. **2** the language of this people, belonging to the Niger-Congo family.

Wolsey ★ ('wʊlzɪ) *n* **Thomas.** ?1475–1530, English cardinal; archbishop of York (1514–30); lord chancellor (1515–29). He dominated Henry VIII's policies but failed to obtain papal consent to the annulment of the king's marriage: arrested for high treason (1530) but died before his trial.

Wolverhampton ★ (,wʊlvə'hæmptən) *n* **1** a city in W central England, in the West Midlands: iron and steel foundries; seat of The University of Wolverhampton (1992). Pop.: 257 943 (1991). **2** a unitary authority in W central England, in the West Midlands. Pop.: 244 500 (1996 est.). Area: 69 sq. km (27 sq. miles).

wolverine ('wʊlvə,ri:n) *n* a large musteline mammal of northern forests of Eurasia and North America having dark very thick water-resistant fur. Also called: **glutton.** ORIG C16 *wolvering,* from WOLF + -ING[3] (later altered to *-ine*)

wolves (wʊlvz) *n* the plural of **wolf.**

woman ('wʊmən) *n, pl* **women. 1** an adult female human being. **2** (*modifier*) female or feminine: *a woman politician.* **3** women collectively. **4** (usually preceded by *the*) feminine nature or feelings: *babies bring out the woman in him.* **5** a female servant or domestic help. **6** a man considered as having supposedly female characteristics, such as meekness. **7** *Inf.* a wife or girlfriend. **8 the little woman.** *Brit. inf., old-fashioned.* one's wife. **9 woman of the streets.** a prostitute. ◆ *vb* (*tr*) **10** *Obs.* to make effeminate. ORIG OE *wīfmann, wimman*
▸ **'womanless** *adj* ▸ **'woman-,like** *adj*

womanhood ('wʊmən,hʊd) *n* **1** the state or quality of being a woman or being womanly. **2** women collectively.

womanish ('wʊmənɪʃ) *adj* **1** having qualities regarded as unsuitable to a man. **2** of or suitable for a woman.
▸ **'womanishly** *adv* ▸ **'womanishness** *n*

womanize *or* **womanise** ('wʊmə,naɪz) *vb* **womanizes, womanizing, womanized** *or* **womanises, womanising, womanised. 1** (*intr*) (of a man) to indulge in casual affairs with women. **2** (*tr*) to make effeminate.
▸ **'woman,izer** *or* **'woman,iser** *n*

womankind ('wʊmən,kaɪnd) *n* the female members of the human race; women collectively.

womanly ('wʊmənlɪ) *adj* **1** possessing qualities, such as warmth, attractiveness, etc., generally regarded as typical of a woman. **2** of or belonging to a woman.

womb (wu:m) *n* **1** the nontechnical name for **uterus. 2** a hollow space enclosing something. **3** a place where something is conceived: *the Near East is the womb of western civilization.* **4** *Obs.* the belly. ORIG OE *wamb*
▸ **wombed** *adj* ▸ **'womb,like** *adj*

wombat ('wɒmbæt) *n* a burrowing herbivorous Australian marsupial having short limbs, a heavy body, and coarse dense fur. ORIG C18: from Abor.

women ('wɪmɪn) *n* the plural of **woman.**

womenfolk ('wɪmɪn,fəʊk) *pl n* **1** women collectively. **2** a group of women, esp. the female members of one's family.

Women's Institute *n* (in Britain and Commonwealth countries) a society for women interested in engaging in craft and cultural activities.

Women's Liberation *n* a movement directed towards the removal of attitudes and practices that preserve inequalities based upon the assumption that men are superior to women. Also called: **women's lib.**

Women's Movement *n* a grass-roots movement of women concerned with women's liberation. See **Women's Liberation.**

won (wʌn) *vb* the past tense and past participle of **win.**

wonder ('wʌndə) *n* **1** the feeling excited by something strange; a mixture of surprise, curiosity, and sometimes awe. **2** something that causes such a feeling, such as a miracle. **3** (*modifier*) exciting wonder by virtue of spectacular results achieved, feats performed, etc.: *a wonder drug.* **4 do** *or* **work wonders.** to achieve spectacularly fine results. **5 nine days' wonder.** a subject that arouses general surprise or public interest for a short time. **6 no wonder.** (*sentence connector*) (I am) not surprised at all (that): *no wonder he couldn't come.* **7 small wonder.** (*sentence connector*) (I am) hardly surprised (that): *small wonder he couldn't make it tonight.* ◆ *vb* (when *tr, may take a clause as object*) **8** (when *intr,* often foll. by *about*) to indulge in speculative inquiry: *I wondered about what she said.* **9** (when *intr,* often foll. by *at*) to be amazed (at something): *I wonder at your impudence.* ORIG OE *wundor*
▸ **'wonderer** *n*

Wonder ★ ('wʌndə) *n* **Stevie.** real name *Steveland Judkins Morris.* born 1950, US singer and songwriter. His recordings include *Up-Tight* (1966), *Songs in the Key of Life* (1976), and "I Just Called to Say I Love You" (1985).

wonderful ('wʌndəful) *adj* **1** exciting a feeling of wonder. **2** extremely fine; excellent.
▸ **'wonderfully** *adv*

wonderland ('wʌndəˌlænd) *n* **1** an imaginary land of marvels or wonders. **2** an actual place or scene of great or strange beauty or wonder.

wonderment ('wʌndəmənt) *n* **1** rapt surprise; awe. **2** puzzled interest. **3** something that excites wonder.

wonderwork ('wʌndəˌwɜːk) *n* something done or made that excites wonder.
▸ **'wonder-ˌworker** *n* ▸ **'wonder-ˌworking** *n, adj*

wondrous ('wʌndrəs) *Arch. or literary.* ◆ *adj* **1** exciting wonder; marvellous. ◆ *adv* **2** (intensifier): *wondrous cold.*
▸ **'wondrously** *adv* ▸ **'wondrousness** *n*

wonky ('wɒŋkɪ) *adj* **wonkier, wonkiest.** *Brit. sl.* **1** unsteady. **2** askew. **3** liable to break down. ORIG C20: var. of dialect *wanky,* from OE *wancol*

Wŏnsan ★ ('wɒn'sæn) *n* a port in SE North Korea, on the Sea of Japan: oil refineries. Pop.: 274 000 (1987).

wont (wəʊnt) *adj* **1** (*postpositive*) accustomed (to doing something): *he was wont to come early.* ◆ *n* **2** a manner or action habitually employed by or associated with someone (often in **as is my wont, as is his wont,** etc.). ◆ *vb* **3** (when *tr, usually passive*) to become or cause to become accustomed. ORIG OE *gewunod,* p.p. of *wunian* to be accustomed to

won't (wəʊnt) *contraction of* will not.

wonted ('wəʊntɪd) *adj* **1** (*postpositive*) accustomed (to doing something). **2** (*prenominal*) usual: *she is in her wonted place.*

woo (wuː) *vb* **woos, wooing, wooed. 1** to seek the affection, favour, or love of (a woman) with a view to marriage. **2** (*tr*) to seek after zealously: *to woo fame.* **3** (*tr*) to beg or importune (someone). ORIG OE *wōgian,* from ?
▸ **'wooer** *n* ▸ **'wooing** *n*

wood (wʊd) *n* **1** the hard fibrous substance consisting of xylem tissue that occurs beneath the bark in trees, shrubs, and similar plants. **2** the trunks of trees that have been cut and prepared for use as a building material. **3** a collection of trees, shrubs, grasses, etc., usually dominated by one or a few species of tree: usually smaller than a forest: *an oak wood.* Related adj: **sylvan. 4** fuel; firewood. **5** *Golf.* **5a** a long-shafted club with a wooden head, used for driving. **5b** (*as modifier*): *a wood shot.* **6** *Tennis, etc.* the frame of a racket: *he hit a winning shot off the wood.* **7** one of the biased wooden bowls used in the game of bowls. **8** *Music.* short for **woodwind. 9 from the wood.** (of a beverage) from a wooden container rather than a metal or glass one. **10 out of the wood** *or* **woods.** clear of or safe from dangers or doubts: *we're not out of the wood yet.* **11 see the wood for the trees.** (*used with a negative*) to obtain a general view of a situation without allowing details to cloud one's analysis: *he can't see the wood for the trees.* **12** (*modifier*) made of, employing, or handling wood: *a wood fire.* **13** (*modifier*) dwelling in or situated in a wood: *a wood nymph.* ◆ *vb* **14** (*tr*) to plant a wood upon. **15** to supply or be supplied with firewood. ◆ See also **woods.** ORIG OE *widu, wudu*

Wood ★ (wʊd) *n* Sir **Henry** (**Joseph**). 1869–1944, British conductor, who founded the Promenade Concerts in London.

wood alcohol *n* another name for **methanol.**

wood anemone *n* any of several woodland anemone plants having finely divided leaves and solitary white flowers. Also called: **windflower.**

wood avens *n* another name for **herb bennet.**

woodbine ('wuːdˌbaɪn) *n* **1** a honeysuckle of Europe, SW Asia, and N Africa, having fragrant yellow flowers. **2** *US.* another name for **Virginia creeper. 3** *Austral. sl.* an Englishman.

wood block *n* a small rectangular flat block of wood that is laid with others as a floor surface.

woodcarving ('wʊdˌkɑːvɪŋ) *n* **1** the act of carving wood. **2** a work of art produced by carving wood.
▸ **'woodˌcarver** *n*

woodchuck ('wʊdˌtʃʌk) *n* a North American marmot having coarse reddish-brown fur. Also called: **groundhog.** ORIG C17: by folk etymology from Cree *otcheck* fisher

woodcock ('wʊdˌkɒk) *n* an Old World game bird resembling the snipe but larger and with shorter legs and neck.

woodcraft ('wʊdˌkrɑːft) *n Chiefly US & Canad.* **1** ability and experience in matters concerned with living in a forest. **2** ability or skill at woodwork, carving, etc.

woodcut ('wʊdˌkʌt) *n* **1** a block of wood with a design, illustration, etc., from which prints are made. **2** a print from a woodcut.

woodcutter ('wʊdˌkʌtə) *n* **1** a person who fells trees or chops wood. **2** a person who makes woodcuts.
▸ **'woodˌcutting** *n*

wooded ('wʊdɪd) *adj* **1** covered with or abounding in woods or trees. **2** (*in combination*) having wood of a specified character: *a soft-wooded tree.*

wooden ('wʊdᵊn) *adj* **1** made from or consisting of wood. **2** awkward or clumsy. **3** bereft of spirit or animation: *a wooden expression.* **4** obstinately unyielding: *a wooden attitude.* **5** mentally slow or dull. **6** not highly resonant: *a wooden thud.*
▸ **'woodenly** *adv*

wood engraving *n* **1** the art of engraving pictures or designs on wood by incising them with a burin. **2** a block of wood so engraved or a print taken from it.
▸ **wood engraver** *n*

woodenhead ('wʊdᵊnˌhɛd) *n Inf.* a dull, foolish, or unintelligent person.
▸ **ˌwooden'headed** *adj* ▸ **ˌwooden'headedness** *n*

Wooden Horse *n* another name for the **Trojan Horse** (sense 1).

wooden spoon *n* a booby prize, esp. in sporting contests.

woodgrouse ('wʊdˌgraʊs) *n* another name for **capercaillie.**

woodland ('wʊdlənd) *n* **a** land that is mostly covered with woods or dense growths of trees and shrubs. **b** (*as modifier*): *woodland fauna.*
▸ **'woodlander** *n*

woodlark ('wʊdˌlɑːk) *n* an Old World lark similar to but slightly smaller than the skylark.

woodlouse ('wʊdˌlaʊs) *n, pl* **woodlice** (-ˌlaɪs). any of various small terrestrial isopod crustaceans having a flattened segmented body and occurring in damp habitats.

woodman ('wʊdmən) *n, pl* **woodmen. 1** a person who looks after and fells trees used for timber. **2** another word for **woodsman.**

woodnote ('wʊdˌnəʊt) *n* a natural musical note or song, like that of a wild bird.

wood nymph *n* one of a class of nymphs fabled to inhabit the woods, such as a dryad.

woodpecker ('wʊdˌpɛkə) *n* a climbing bird, such as the **green woodpecker,** having a brightly coloured plumage and strong chisel-like bill with which it bores into trees for insects.

wood pigeon *n* a large Eurasian pigeon having white patches on the wings and neck. Also called: **ringdove, cushat.**

woodpile ('wʊdˌpaɪl) *n* a pile or heap of firewood.

wood preservative *n* a coating applied to timber as a protection against decay, insects, weather, etc.

wood pulp *n* **1** wood that has been ground to a fine pulp for use in making newsprint and other cheap forms of paper. **2** finely pulped wood that has been digested by a chemical, such as caustic soda: used in making paper.

woodruff ('wʊdrʌf) *n* any of several plants, esp. the sweet woodruff of Eurasia, which has small sweet-scented white flowers and whorls of narrow fragrant leaves used to flavour wine and liqueurs and in perfumery. ORIG OE *wudurofe,* from WOOD + *rōfe*

woods (wʊdz) *pl n* **1** closely packed trees forming a forest or wood, esp. a specific one. **2** another word for **backwoods** (sense 2). **3** the woodwind instruments in an orchestra.

Woods[1] ★ (wʊdz) *n* **Lake of the.** See **Lake of the Woods.**

Woods[2] ★ (wʊdz) *n* **Tiger,** real name *Eldrick Woods.* born

1975, US golfer: first person since 1953 to win three golf majors in one year (2000).

woodscrew ('wʊdˌskruː) *n* a metal screw that tapers to a point so that it can be driven into wood by a screwdriver.

woodshed ('wʊdˌʃɛd) *n* a small outbuilding where firewood, garden tools, etc., are stored.

woodsman ('wʊdzmən) *n, pl* **woodsmen**. a person who lives in a wood or who is skilled in woodcraft. Also called: **woodman.**

wood sorrel *n* a Eurasian plant having trifoliate leaves, an underground creeping stem, and white purple-veined flowers.

wood spirit *n Chem.* another name for **methanol.**

Woodstock ★ ('wʊdstɒk) *n* a town in New York State, the site of a large rock festival in August 1969. Pop.: 1870 (1990).

wood tar *n* any tar produced by the destructive distillation of wood.

wood warbler *n* **1** a European woodland warbler with a dull yellow plumage. **2** another name for the **American warbler.** See **warbler** (sense 3).

Woodward ★ ('wʊdwəd) *n* **R(obert) B(urns)**. 1917–79, US chemist. For his work on the synthesis of quinine, strychnine, cholesterol, and other organic compounds he won the Nobel prize for chemistry 1965.

woodwind ('wʊdˌwɪnd) *Music.* ◆ *adj* **1** of or denoting a type of wind instrument, formerly made of wood but now often made of metal, such as the flute. ◆ *n* **2** (*functioning as pl*) woodwind instruments collectively.

woodwork ('wʊdˌwɜːk) *n* **1** the art or craft of making things in wood. **2** components made of wood, such as doors, staircases, etc.

woodworking ('wʊdˌwɜːkɪŋ) *n* **1** the process of working wood. ◆ *adj* **2** of, relating to, or used in woodworking.
▸ **'woodˌworker** *n*

woodworm ('wʊdˌwɜːm) *n* **1** any of various insect larvae that bore into wooden furniture, beams, etc., esp. the larvae of the furniture beetle and the deathwatch beetle. **2** the condition caused in wood by any of these larvae.

woody ('wʊdɪ) *adj* **woodier, woodiest. 1** abounding in or covered with forest or woods. **2** connected with, belonging to, or situated in a wood. **3** consisting of or containing wood or lignin: *woody tissue; woody stems.* **4** resembling wood in hardness or texture.
▸ **'woodiness** *n*

woodyard ('wʊdˌjɑːd) *n* a place where timber is cut and stored.

woody nightshade *n* a scrambling woody Eurasian plant, having purple flowers and producing poisonous red berry-like fruits. Also called: **bittersweet.**

woof[1] (wuːf) *n* **1** the crosswise yarns that fill the warp yarns in weaving; weft. **2** a woven fabric or its texture. ORIG OE *ōwef,* from *ō-,* ?from ON, + *wef* web (see WEAVE); modern form infl. by WARP

woof[2] (wʊf) *interj* **1** an imitation of the bark or growl of a dog. ◆ *vb* **2** (*intr*) (of dogs) to bark.

woofer ('wuːfə) *n* a loudspeaker used in high-fidelity systems for the reproduction of low audio frequencies.

woofter ('wʊftə, 'wuːf-) *n Derog. sl.* a male homosexual. ORIG C20: altered from *poofter;* see POOF

Wookey Hole ★ ('wʊkɪ həʊl) *n* a village in SW England, in Somerset, near Wells: noted for the nearby limestone cave in which prehistoric remains have been found. Pop.: 1000 (latest est.).

wool (wʊl) *n* **1** the outer coat of sheep, yaks, etc., which consists of short curly hairs. **2** yarn spun from the coat of sheep, etc., used in weaving, knitting, etc. **3a** cloth or a garment made from this yarn. **3b** (*as modifier*): *a wool dress.* **4** any of certain fibrous materials: *glass wool; steel wool.* **5** *Inf.* short thick curly hair. **6** a tangled mass of soft fine hairs that occurs in certain plants. **7 keep one's wool on.** *Brit. inf.* to keep one's temper. **8 pull the wool over someone's eyes.** to deceive or delude someone. ORIG OE *wull*
▸ **'wool-ˌlike** *adj*

wool clip *n Austral. & NZ.* the total amount of wool shorn from a particular flock in one year.

Woolf ★ (wʊlf) *n* **1 Leonard Sidney.** 1880–1969, British publisher and political writer. **2** his wife, **Virginia.** 1882–1941, British novelist. Her novels include *Mrs. Dalloway* (1925), *To the Lighthouse* (1927), and *The Waves* (1931).

wool fat *or* **grease** *n* another name for **lanolin.**

woolfell ('wʊlˌfɛl) *n Obs.* the skin of a sheep or similar animal with the fleece still attached.

woolgathering ('wʊlˌgæðərɪŋ) *n* idle or absent-minded daydreaming.

woolgrower ('wʊlˌgrəʊə) *n* a person who keeps sheep for their wool.
▸ **'woolˌgrowing** *n*

woolled (wʊld) *adj* **1** (of animals) having wool. **2** (*in combination*) having wool as specified: *coarse-woolled.*

woollen *or US* **woolen** ('wʊlən) *adj* **1** relating to or consisting partly or wholly of wool. ◆ *n* **2** (*often pl*) a garment or piece of cloth made wholly or partly of wool, esp. a knitted one.

Woolley ★ ('wʊlɪ) *n* Sir **(Charles) Leonard.** 1880–1960, British archaeologist, noted for his excavations at Ur in Mesopotamia (1922–34).

woolly *or US (sometimes)* **wooly** ('wʊlɪ) *adj* **woollier, woolliest** *or US (sometimes)* **woolier, wooliest. 1** consisting of, resembling, or having the nature of wool. **2** covered or clothed in wool or something resembling it. **3** lacking clarity or substance: *woolly thinking.* **4** *Bot.* covered with long soft whitish hairs: *woolly stems.* ◆ *n, pl* **woollies** *or US (sometimes)* **woolies. 5** (*often pl*) a garment, such as a sweater, made of wool or something similar.
▸ **'woollily** *adv* ▸ **'woolliness** *n*

woolly bear *n* the caterpillar of any of various tiger moths, having a dense covering of soft hairs.

woolpack ('wʊlˌpæk) *n* **1** the cloth wrapping used to pack a bale of wool. **2** a bale of wool.

woolsack ('wʊlˌsæk) *n* **1** a sack containing or intended to contain wool. **2** (in Britain) the seat of the Lord Chancellor in the House of Lords, formerly made of a large square sack of wool.

woolshed ('wʊlˌʃɛd) *n Austral. & NZ.* a large building in which sheepshearing takes place.

wool stapler *n* a person who sorts wool into different grades or classifications.

Woolworth ★ ('wʊlwəθ) *n* **Frank Winfield** ('wɪnˌfiːld). 1852–1919, US merchant; founder of an international chain of department stores selling inexpensive goods.

woomera *or* **womera** ('wʊmərə) *n Austral.* a type of notched stick used by native Australians to increase leverage and propulsion in the throwing of a spear. ORIG from Abor.

Woomera ★ ('wʊmərə) *n* a town in South Australia: site of the Long Range Weapons Establishment. Pop.: 1660 (latest est.).

Woop Woop ('wuːp ˌwuːp) *n Austral. Sl.* a jocular name for any backward or remote town or district.

Wootton ★ ('wʊtᵊn) *n* **Barbara (Frances)**, Baroness of Abinger. 1897–1988, British economist and social scientist.

woozy ('wuːzɪ) *adj* **woozier, wooziest.** *Inf.* **1** dazed or confused. **2** experiencing dizziness, nausea, etc. ORIG C19: ? a blend of *woolly* + *muzzy* or *dizzy*
▸ **'woozily** *adv* ▸ **'wooziness** *n*

wop (wɒp) *n Sl., derog.* a member of a Latin people, esp. an Italian. ORIG C20: prob. from It. dialect *guappo* dandy, from Sp. *guapo*

wop-wops ('wɒpˌwɒps) *n* (*functioning as pl or sing*) **the.** *NZ inf.* a remote rural area; back of beyond. Sometimes shortened to **the wops.**

Worcester ★ ('wʊstə) *n* **1** a cathedral city in W central England, the administrative centre of Worcestershire on the River Severn: scene of the battle (1651) in which Charles II was defeated by Cromwell. Pop.: 82 661

(1991). **2** an industrial city in central Massachusetts: Clark University (1887). Pop.: 165 387 (1994 est.). **3** a town in S South Africa. Pop.: 60 324 (1990).

Worcester sauce *or* **Worcestershire sauce** *n* a commercially prepared piquant sauce, made from a basis of soy sauce, with vinegar, spices, etc.

Worcestershire ★ (ˈwʊstəˌʃɪə, -ʃə) *n* a county in W central England, formerly part of Hereford and Worcester (1974–98). Drained chiefly by the River Severn, it is mainly agricultural, with engineering and chemical industries. Administrative centre: Worcester. Pop.: 528 100 (1998 est.). Area: 1742 sq. km (674 sq. miles).

Worcs *abbrev. for* Worcestershire.

word (wɜːd) *n* **1** one of the units of speech or writing that is the smallest isolable meaningful element of the language, although linguists would analyse these further into morphemes. **2** an instance of vocal intercourse; chat, talk, or discussion: *to have a word with someone.* **3** an utterance or expression, esp. a brief one: *a word of greeting.* **4** news or information: *he sent word that he would be late.* **5** a verbal signal for action; command: *when I give the word, fire!* **6** an undertaking or promise: *he kept his word.* **7** an autocratic decree; order: *his word must be obeyed.* **8** a watchword or slogan, as of a political party: *the word now is "freedom".* **9** *Computing.* a set of bits used to store, transmit, or operate upon an item of information in a computer. **10 as good as one's word.** doing what one has undertaken to do. **11 at a word.** at once. **12 by word of mouth.** orally rather than by written means. **13 in a word.** briefly or in short. **14 my word! 14a** an exclamation of surprise, annoyance, etc. **14b** *Austral.* an exclamation of agreement. **15 of one's word.** given to or noted for keeping one's promises: *I am a man of my word.* **16 put in a word** *or* **good word for.** to make favourable mention of (someone); recommend. **17 take someone at his** *or* **her word.** to assume that someone means, or will do, what he or she says: *when he told her to go, she took him at his word and left.* **18 take someone's word for it.** to accept or believe what someone says. **19 the last word. 19a** the closing remark of a conversation or argument, esp. a remark that supposedly settles an issue. **19b** the latest or most fashionable design, make, or model: *the last word in bikinis.* **19c** the finest example (of some quality, condition, etc.): *the last word in luxury.* **20 the word.** the proper or most fitting expression: *cold is not the word for it, it's freezing!* **21 upon my word! 21a** *Arch.* on my honour. **21b** an exclamation of surprise, annoyance, etc. **22 word for word.** (of a report, etc.) using exactly the same words as those employed in the situation being reported; verbatim. **23 word of honour.** a promise; oath. **24** (*modifier*) of, relating to, or consisting of words. ◆ *vb* **25** (*tr*) to state in words, usually specially selected ones; phrase. ◆ See also **words.** ORIG OE
▸ **ˈwordless** *adj* ▸ **ˈwordlessly** *adv*

Word (wɜːd) *n* **the. 1** *Christianity.* the 2nd person of the Trinity. **2** Scripture, the Bible, or the Gospels as embodying or representing divine revelation. Often called: **the Word of God.** ORIG translation of Gk *logos*, as in John 1:1

-word *n combining form.* (preceded by *the* and an initial letter) a euphemistic way of referring to a word by its first letter because it is considered unmentionable by the user: *the C-word* (meaning cancer).

wordage (ˈwɜːdɪdʒ) *n* words considered collectively, esp. a quantity of words.

word association *n* an early method of psychoanalysis in which the patient thinks of the first word that comes into consciousness on hearing a given word. In this way it was claimed that aspects of the unconscious could be revealed before defence mechanisms intervene.

word blindness *n* the nontechnical name for **alexia** and **dyslexia.**
▸ **ˈword-ˌblind** *adj*

wordbook (ˈwɜːdˌbʊk) *n* a book containing words, usually with their meanings.

word deafness *n* loss of ability to understand spoken words, esp. as the result of a cerebral lesion. Also called: **auditory aphasia.**

word game *n* any game involving the formation, discovery, or alteration of a word or words.

wording (ˈwɜːdɪŋ) *n* **1** the way in which words are used to express a statement, report, etc., esp. a written one. **2** the words themselves.

word order *n* the arrangement of words in a phrase, clause, or sentence.

word-perfect *or US* **letter-perfect** *adj* **1** correct in every detail. **2** (of a speaker, actor, etc.) knowing one's speech, role, etc., perfectly.

wordplay (ˈwɜːdˌpleɪ) *n* verbal wit based on the meanings of words; puns, repartee, etc.

word processing *n* the composition of documents using a computer system to input, edit, store, and print.

word processor *n* **a** a computer program that performs word processing. **b** a computer system designed for word processing.

words (wɜːdz) *pl n* **1** the text of a part of an actor, etc. **2** the text of a song, as opposed to the music. **3** angry speech (esp. in **have words with someone**). **4 eat** *or* **swallow one's words.** to retract a statement. **5 for words.** (preceded by *too* and an adj or adv) indescribably; extremely: *the play was too funny for words.* **6 have no words for.** to be incapable of describing. **7 in other words.** expressing the same idea but differently. **8 in so many words.** explicitly or precisely. **9 of many** (*or* **few**) **words.** (not) talkative. **10 put into words.** to express in speech or writing. **11 say a few words.** to give a brief speech. **12 take the words out of someone's mouth.** to say exactly what someone else was about to say. **13 words fail me.** I am too happy, sad, amazed, etc., to express my thoughts.

wordsearch (ˈwɜːdˌsɜːtʃ) *n* a puzzle made up of letters arranged in a grid that contains a number of hidden words running in various directions.

word square *n* a puzzle in which the player must fill a square grid with words that read the same across as down.

Wordsworth ★ (ˈwɜːdzˌwəθ) *n* **1 Dorothy.** 1771–1855, British writer, whose *Journals* are noted for their descriptions of nature. **2** her brother, **William.** 1770–1850, British Lake poet. His works include *Lyrical Ballads* (1798, 1800), to which Coleridge contributed, and the autobiographical poem *The Prelude* (completed in 1805; revised thereafter and published posthumously).
▸ **Wordsworthian** (ˌwɜːdzˈwɜːðɪən) *adj, n*

word wrapping *n Computing.* the automatic shifting of a word at the end of a line to a new line in order to keep within preset margins.

wordy (ˈwɜːdɪ) *adj* **wordier, wordiest.** using or containing an excess of words: *a wordy document.*
▸ **ˈwordily** *adv* ▸ **ˈwordiness** *n*

wore (wɔː) *vb* the past tense of **wear**[1] and **wear**[2].

work (wɜːk) *n* **1** physical or mental effort directed towards doing or making something. **2** paid employment at a job or a trade, occupation, or profession. **3** a duty, task, or undertaking. **4** something done, made, etc., as a result of effort or exertion: *a work of art.* **5** another word for **workmanship** (sense 3). **6** the place, office, etc., where a person is employed. **7a** decoration, esp. of a specified kind. **7b** (*in combination*): *wirework.* **8** an engineering structure such as a bridge, building, etc. **9** *Physics.* the transfer of energy expressed as the product of a force and the distance through which its point of application moves in the direction of the force. **10** a structure, wall, etc., built or used as part of a fortification system. **11 at work. 11a** at one's job or place of employment. **11b** in action; operating. **12 make short work of.** *Inf.* to dispose of very quickly. **13** (*modifier*) of, relating to, or used for work: *work clothes; a work permit; a work song.* ◆ *vb* **14** (*intr*) to exert effort in order to do, make, or perform something. **15** (*intr*) to be employed. **16** (*tr*) to carry on operations, activity, etc., in (a place or area): *that salesman works Yorkshire.* **17** (*tr*) to cause to labour or toil: *he works his men hard.* **18** to operate or cause to operate, esp. properly or effectively: *to work a lathe; that clock doesn't work.* **19** (*tr*) to till or cultivate (land). **20** to handle or manipulate or be handled or manipulated: *to work dough.* **21** to shape or process or be shaped or processed: *to work* *copper*. **22** to reach or cause to reach a specific condition, esp. gradually: *the rope worked loose*. **23** (*intr*) to move in agitation: *his face worked with anger*. **24** (*tr*; often foll. by *up*) to provoke or arouse: *to work someone into a frenzy*. **25** (*tr*) to effect or accomplish: *to work one's revenge*. **26** to make (one's way) with effort: *he worked his way through the crowd*. **27** (*tr*) to make or decorate by hand in embroidery, tapestry, etc.: *she was working a sampler*. **28** (*intr*) (of liquids) to ferment, as in brewing. **29** (*tr*) *Inf.* to manipulate or exploit to one's own advantage. ◆ See also **work in**, **work off**, etc., **works**. ORIG OE *weorc* (n), *wircan, wyrcan* (vb)

▸ '**workless** *adj*

workable ('wɜːkəbᵊl) *adj* **1** practicable or feasible. **2** able to be worked.

▸ ˌ**worka'bility** *or* '**workableness** *n*

workaday ('wɜːkəˌdeɪ) *adj* (*usually prenominal*) **1** being a part of general human experience; ordinary. **2** suitable for working days; everyday or practical.

workaholic (ˌwɜːkə'hɒlɪk) *n* **a** a person obsessively addicted to work. **b** (*as modifier*): *workaholic behaviour*. ORIG C20: from WORK + -HOLIC, coined in 1971 by US author Wayne Oates

workbag ('wɜːkˌbæg) *n* a container for implements, tools, or materials, esp. sewing equipment. Also called: **work basket**, **workbox**.

workbench ('wɜːkˌbɛntʃ) *n* a heavy table at which work is done by a carpenter, mechanic, toolmaker, etc.

workbook ('wɜːkˌbʊk) *n* **1** an exercise book used for study, esp. with spaces for answers. **2** a book of instructions for some process. **3** a book in which is recorded all work done or planned.

work camp *n* a camp set up for young people who voluntarily do manual work on a worthwhile project.

workday ('wɜːkˌdeɪ) *n* **1** the usual US and Canad. term for **working day**. ◆ *adj* **2** another word for **workaday**.

worked (wɜːkt) *adj* made or decorated with evidence of workmanship; wrought, as with embroidery or tracery.

worked up *adj* excited or agitated.

worker ('wɜːkə) *n* **1** a person or thing that works, usually at a specific job: *a research worker*. **2** an employee, as opposed to an employer or manager. **3** a manual labourer working in a manufacturing industry. **4** any other member of the working class. **5** a sterile female member of a colony of bees, ants, or wasps that forages for food, cares for the larvae, etc.

worker director *n* (in certain British companies) an employee of a company chosen by his or her fellow workers to represent their interests on the board of directors. Also called: **employee director**.

worker-priest *n* a Roman Catholic priest who has employment in a secular job to be more in touch with the problems of the laity.

work ethic *n* a belief in the moral value of work.

workfare ('wɜːkˌfɛə) *n* a scheme under which the government of a country requires unemployed people to do community work or undergo job training in return for social-security payments. ORIG C20: from WORK + (WEL)FARE

workforce ('wɜːkˌfɔːs) *n* **1** the total number of workers employed by a company on a specific job, project, etc. **2** the total number of people who could be employed: *the country's workforce is growing*.

work function *n Physics*. the minimum energy required to transfer an electron from a point within a solid to a point just outside its surface. Symbol: ϕ or Φ

work-harden *vb* (*tr*) to increase the strength or hardness of (a metal) by a mechanical process, such as tension, compression, or torsion.

workhorse ('wɜːkˌhɔːs) *n* **1** a horse used for nonrecreational activities. **2** *Inf.* a person who takes on the greatest amount of work in a project.

workhouse ('wɜːkˌhaʊs) *n* **1** (formerly in England) an institution maintained at public expense where able-bodied paupers did unpaid work in return for food and accommodation. **2** (in the US) a prison for petty offenders serving short sentences at manual labour.

work in *vb* (*adv*) **1** to insert or become inserted: *she worked the patch in carefully*. **2** (*tr*) to find space for: *I'll work this job in during the day*. ◆ *n* **work-in**. **3** a form of industrial action in which a factory that is to be closed down is occupied and run by its workers.

working ('wɜːkɪŋ) *n* **1** the operation or mode of operation of something. **2** the act or process of moulding something pliable. **3** a convulsive or jerking motion, as from excitement. **4** (*often pl*) a part of a mine or quarry that is being or has been worked. **5** a record of the steps by which the solution of a problem, calculation, etc., is obtained: *all working is to be submitted to the examiners*. ◆ *adj* (*prenominal*) **6** relating to or concerned with a person or thing that works: *a working man*. **7** concerned with, used in, or suitable for work: *working clothes*. **8** (of a meal or occasion) during which business discussions are carried on: *a working lunch*. **9** capable of being operated or used: *a working model; in working order*. **10** adequate for normal purposes: *a working majority; a working knowledge of German*. **11** (of a theory, etc.) providing a basis, usually a temporary one, on which operations or procedures may be carried out.

working bee *n NZ*. a voluntary group doing a job for charity.

working capital *n* **1** *Accounting*. current assets minus current liabilities. **2** current or liquid assets. **3** that part of the capital of a business enterprise available for operations.

working class *n* **1** Also called: **proletariat**. the social stratum, usually of low status, that consists of those who earn wages, esp. as manual workers. ◆ *adj* **working-class**. **2** of, relating to, or characteristic of the working class.

working day *or esp. US & Canad.* **workday** *n* **1** a day on which work is done, esp. for an agreed or stipulated number of hours in return for a salary or wage. **2** the part of the day allocated to work. **3** (*often pl*) *Commerce*. any day of the week except Sunday, public holidays, and, in some cases, Saturday.

working drawing *n* a scale drawing of a part that provides a guide for manufacture.

working families tax credit *n* (in Britain) a means-tested allowance paid to single parents or to families who have at least one dependent child, who work at least 16 hours per week and whose earnings are low. It replaced family credit.

working girl *n* **1** a girl or woman who works, esp. one who supports herself. **2** *Inf.* a prostitute.

working memory *n Psychol.* the current contents of consciousness.

working party *n* **1** a committee established to investigate a problem, question, etc. **2** a group of soldiers or prisoners assigned to perform a manual task or duty.

working week *or esp. US & Canad.* **workweek** *n* the number of hours or days in a week allocated to work.

work-in-progress *n Book-keeping*. the value of work begun but not completed, as shown in a profit-and-loss account.

workload ('wɜːkˌləʊd) *n* the amount of work to be done, esp. in a specified period.

workman ('wɜːkmən) *n, pl* **workmen**. **1** a man who is employed in manual labour or who works an industrial machine. **2** a craftsman of skill as specified: *a bad workman*.

workmanlike ('wɜːkmənˌlaɪk) *or* (*less commonly*) **workmanly** *adj* appropriate to or befitting a good workman.

workmanship ('wɜːkmənʃɪp) *n* **1** the art or skill of a workman. **2** the art or skill with which something is made or executed. **3** the degree of art or skill exhibited in the finished product. **4** the piece of work so produced.

workmate ('wɜːkˌmeɪt) *n* a person who works with another; fellow worker.

work of art *n* **1** a piece of fine art, such as a painting or sculpture. **2** something that may be likened to a piece of fine art, esp. in beauty, intricacy, etc.

work off *vb (tr, adv)* **1** to get rid of or dissipate, as by effort: *he worked off some of his energy by digging the garden.* **2** to discharge (a debt) by labour rather than payment.

work on *vb (intr, prep)* to persuade or influence or attempt to persuade or influence.

work out *vb (adv)* **1** *(tr)* to achieve or accomplish by effort. **2** *(tr)* to solve or find out by reasoning or calculation: *to work out an answer; to work out a sum.* **3** *(tr)* to devise or formulate: *to work out a plan.* **4** *(intr)* to prove satisfactory: *did your plan work out?* **5** *(intr)* to happen as specified: *it all worked out well.* **6** *(intr)* to take part in physical exercise, as in training. **7** *(tr)* to remove all the mineral in (a mine, etc.) that can be profitably exploited. **8** *(intr;* often foll. by *to* or *at)* to reach a total: *your bill works out at a pound.* ◆ *n* **workout. 9** a session of physical exercise, esp. for training or to keep oneself fit.

work over *vb* **1** *(tr, adv)* to do again; repeat. **2** *(intr, prep)* to examine closely and thoroughly. **3** *(tr, adv) Sl.* to assault or thrash.

workpeople ('wɜːkˌpiːpᵊl) *pl n* the working members of a population.

workroom ('wɜːkˌruːm, -ˌrʊm) *n* **1** a room in which work, usually manual labour, is done. **2** a room in a house set aside for a hobby.

works (wɜːks) *pl n* **1** *(often functioning as sing)* a place where a number of people are employed, such as a factory. **2** the sum total of a writer's or artist's achievements, esp. when considered together: *the works of Shakespeare.* **3** the deeds of a person, esp. virtuous or moral deeds: *works of charity.* **4** the interior parts of the mechanism of a machine, etc.: *the works of a clock.* **5 the works.** *Sl.* **5a** full or extreme treatment. **5b** a very violent physical beating: *to give someone the works.*

works council *n Chiefly Brit.* **1** a council composed of both employer and employees convened to discuss matters of common interest concerning a factory, plant, business policy, etc. **2** a body representing the workers of a plant, factory, etc., elected to negotiate with the management about working conditions, wages, etc. ◆ Also called: **works committee.**

worksheet ('wɜːkˌʃiːt) *n* **1** a sheet of paper used for the rough draft of a problem, design, etc. **2** a piece of paper recording work in progress.

workshop ('wɜːkˌʃɒp) *n* **1** a room or building in which manufacturing or other forms of manual work are carried on. **2** a room in a private dwelling, school, etc., set aside for crafts. **3** a group of people engaged in study or work on a creative project or subject: *a music workshop.*

workshy ('wɜːkˌʃaɪ) *adj* not inclined to work.

Worksop ★ ('wɜːksɒp) *n* a town in N central England, in N Nottinghamshire. Pop.: 37 247 (1991).

work station *n* an area in an office where one person works.

work-study *n* an examination of ways of finding the most efficient method of doing a job.

worktable ('wɜːkˌteɪbᵊl) *n* **a** any table at which writing, sewing, or other work may be done. **b** (in English cabinetwork) a small elegant table fitted with sewing accessories.

worktop ('wɜːkˌtɒp) *n* a surface in a kitchen, often of heat-resistant plastic, used for food preparation.

work-to-rule *n* **1** a form of industrial action in which employees adhere strictly to all the working rules laid down by their employers, with the deliberate intention of reducing the rate of working. ◆ *vb* **work to rule. 2** *(intr)* to decrease the rate of working by this means.

work up *vb* **1** *(tr, adv)* to arouse the feelings of; excite. **2** *(tr, adv)* to cause to grow or develop: *to work up a hunger.* **3** to move or cause to move gradually upwards. **4** *(tr, adv)* to manipulate or mix into a specified object or shape. **5** *(tr, adv)* to gain skill at (a subject). **6** *(adv)* (foll. by *to)* to develop gradually or progress (towards): *working up to a climax.*

world (wɜːld) *n* **1** the earth as a planet, esp. including its inhabitants. **2** mankind; the human race. **3** people generally; the public: *in the eyes of the world.* **4** social or public life: *to go out into the world.* **5** the universe or cosmos; everything in existence. **6** a complex united whole regarded as resembling the universe. **7** any star or planet, esp. one that might be inhabited. **8** *(often cap.)* a division or section of the earth, its history, or its inhabitants: *the Ancient World; the Third World.* **9** an area, sphere, or realm considered as a complete environment: *the animal world.* **10** any field of human activity or way of life or those involved in it: *the world of television.* **11** a period or state of existence: *the next world.* **12** the total circumstances and experience of an individual that make up his life: *you have shattered my world.* **13** a large amount, number, or distance: *worlds apart.* **14** worldly or secular life, ways, or people. **15 bring into the world. 15a** (of a midwife, doctor, etc.) to deliver (a baby). **15b** to give birth to. **16 come into the world.** to be born. **17 for all the world.** in every way; exactly. **18 for the world.** *(used with a negative)* for any inducement, however great. **19 in the world.** (intensifier; *usually used with a negative): no-one in the world can change things.* **20 man** (*or* **woman) of the world.** a man (or woman) experienced in social or public life. **21 not long for this world.** nearing death. **22 on top of the world.** *Inf.* elated or very happy. **23 out of this world.** *Inf.* wonderful; excellent. **24 set the world on fire.** to be exceptionally or sensationally successful. **25 the best of both worlds.** the benefits from two different ways of life, philosophies, etc. **26 think the world of.** to be extremely fond of or hold in very high esteem. **27 world of one's own.** a state of mental detachment from other people. **28 world without end.** forever. **29** *(modifier)* of or concerning most or all countries; worldwide: *world politics.* **30** *(in combination)* throughout the world: *world-famous.* ORIG OE *w(e)orold,* from *wer* man + *ald* age, life

World Bank *n* an international cooperative organization established in 1945 to assist economic development, esp. of backward nations, by the advance of loans guaranteed by member governments. Officially called: **International Bank for Reconstruction and Development.**

world-beater *n* a person or thing that surpasses all others in its category; champion.

world-class *adj* of or denoting someone with a skill or attribute that puts him or her in the highest class in the world: *a world-class swimmer.*

World Court *n* another name for **International Court of Justice.**

World Cup *n* an international competition held between national teams in various sports, most notably association football.

worldling ('wɜːldlɪŋ) *n* a person who is primarily concerned with worldly matters.

worldly ('wɜːldlɪ) *adj* **worldlier, worldliest. 1** not spiritual; mundane or temporal. **2** Also: **worldly-minded.** absorbed in material things. **3** Also: **worldly-wise.** versed in the ways of the world; sophisticated.
► **'worldliness** *n*

world music *n* popular music of various ethnic origins and styles.

world power *n* a state that possesses sufficient power to influence events throughout the world.

world-shaking *adj* of enormous significance.

World Trade Organization *n* an international body concerned with promoting and regulating trade between its member states; established in 1995 as a successor to GATT.

World War I *n* the war (1914–18), fought mainly in Europe and the Middle East, in which the Allies (principally France, Russia, Britain, Italy after 1915, and the US after 1917) defeated the Central Powers (principally Germany, Austria-Hungary, and Turkey). Also called: **First World War, Great War.**

World War II *n* the war (1939–45) in which the Allies (principally Britain, the Soviet Union, and the US) defeated the Axis powers (principally Germany, Italy, and Japan). Britain and France declared war on Germany (Sept. 3, 1939) as a result of the German invasion of Poland (Sept. 1, 1939). Italy entered the war on June 10, 1940 shortly before the collapse of France (armistice signed June 22, 1940). On June 22, 1941 Germany attacked the Soviet Union and on Dec. 7, 1941 the Japanese attacked the US at Pearl Harbor. On Sept. 8, 1943 Italy surrendered, the war in Europe ending on May 7, 1945 with the unconditional surrender of the Germans. The Japanese capitulated on Aug. 14, 1945. Also called: **Second World War.**

world-weary *adj* no longer finding pleasure in living.
▸ **'world-ˌweariness** *n*

worldwide ('wɜːld'waɪd) *adj* applying or extending throughout the world; universal.

World Wide Web *n Computing.* a vast network of linked hypertext files, stored on computers throughout the world, that can provide a computer user with information on a huge variety of subjects. Abbrev.: **WWW.**

worm (wɜːm) *n* **1** any of various invertebrates, esp. the annelids (earthworms, etc.), nematodes (roundworms), and flatworms, having a slender elongated body. **2** any of various insect larvae having an elongated body, such as the silkworm and wireworm. **3** any of various unrelated animals that resemble annelids, nematodes, etc., such as the glow-worm and shipworm. **4** a gnawing or insinuating force or agent that torments or slowly eats away. **5** a wretched or spineless person. **6** anything that resembles a worm in appearance or movement. **7** a shaft on which a helical groove has been cut, as in a gear arrangement in which such a shaft meshes with a toothed wheel. **8** a spiral pipe cooled by air or flowing water, used as a condenser in a still. **9** *Computing.* a program that duplicates itself many times in a network and prevents its destruction. It often carries a logic bomb or virus. ◆ *vb* **10** to move, act, or cause to move or act with the slow sinuous movement of a worm. **11** (foll. by *in, into, out of,* etc.) to make (one's way) slowly and stealthily; insinuate (oneself). **12** (*tr;* often foll. by *out of* or *from*) to extract (information, etc.) from by persistent questioning. **13** (*tr*) to free from worms. ◆ See also **worms.** ORIG OE *wyrm*
▸ **'wormer** *n* ▸ **'wormˌlike** *adj*

WORM (wɜːm) *n Computing. acronym for* write once read many times: an optical disk which enables users to store data but not change it.

wormcast ('wɜːmˌkɑːst) *n* a coil of earth or sand that has been excreted by a burrowing earthworm or lugworm.

worm-eaten *adj* **1** eaten into by worms: *a worm-eaten table.* **2** decayed; rotten. **3** old-fashioned; antiquated.

worm gear *n* **1** a device consisting of a threaded shaft (**worm**) that mates with a gear-wheel (**worm wheel**) so that rotary motion can be transferred between two shafts at right angles to each other. **2** Also called: **worm wheel.** a gear-wheel driven by a threaded shaft or worm.

wormhole ('wɜːmˌhəʊl) *n* a hole made by a worm in timber, plants, etc.
▸ **'wormˌholed** *adj*

worms (wɜːmz) *n* (*functioning as sing*) any disease or disorder, usually of the intestine, characterized by infestation with parasitic worms.

Worms ★ (wɜːmz; *German* vɔrms) *n* a city in SW Germany, in Rhineland-Palatinate on the Rhine: famous as the seat of imperial diets, notably that of 1521, before which Luther defended his doctrines in the presence of Charles V; river port and manufacturing centre with a large wine trade. Pop.: 77 430 (1991).

worm's eye view *n* a view seen from below or from a more lowly or humble point.

wormwood ('wɜːmˌwʊd) *n* **1** Also called: **absinthe.** any of various plants of a chiefly N temperate genus, esp. a European plant yielding a bitter extract used in making absinthe. **2** something that embitters, such as a painful experience. ORIG C15: changed (through infl. of WORM & WOOD) from OE *wormōd, wermōd*

wormy ('wɜːmɪ) *adj* **wormier, wormiest. 1** worm-infested or worm-eaten. **2** resembling a worm in appearance, ways, or condition. **3** (of wood) having irregular small tunnels bored into it and tracked over its surface, made by worms. **4** low or grovelling.
▸ **'worminess** *n*

worn (wɔːn) *vb* **1** the past participle of **wear**[1] and **wear**[2]. ◆ *adj* **2** affected, esp. adversely, by long use or action: *a worn suit.* **3** haggard; drawn. **4** exhausted; spent.
▸ **'wornness** *n*

worn-out *adj* (**worn out** *when postpositive*). **1** worn or used until threadbare, valueless, or useless. **2** exhausted; very weary.

worriment ('wʌrɪmənt) *n Inf., chiefly US.* anxiety or the trouble that causes it; worry.

worrisome ('wʌrɪsəm) *adj* **1** causing worry; vexing. **2** tending to worry.
▸ **'worrisomely** *adv*

worrit ('wʌrɪt) *vb* (*tr*) *Dialect.* to tease or worry. ORIG prob. var. of WORRY

worry ('wʌrɪ) *vb* **worries, worrying, worried. 1** to be or cause to be anxious or uneasy, esp. about something uncertain or potentially dangerous. **2** (*tr*) to disturb the peace of mind of; bother: *don't worry me with trivialities.* **3** (*intr;* often foll. by *along* or *through*) to proceed despite difficulties. **4** (*intr;* often foll. by *away*) to struggle or work: *to worry away at a problem.* **5** (*tr*) (of a dog, wolf, etc.) to lacerate or kill by biting, shaking, etc. **6** (when *intr*, foll. by *at*) to bite, tear, or gnaw (at) with the teeth: *a dog worrying a bone.* **7** (*tr*) to touch or poke repeatedly and idly. **8 not to worry.** *Inf.* you need not worry. ◆ *n, pl* **worries. 9** a state or feeling of anxiety. **10** a person or thing that causes anxiety. **11** an act of worrying. ORIG OE *wyrgan*
▸ **'worried** *adj* ▸ **'worriedly** *adv* ▸ **'worrying** *adj* ▸ **'worryingly** *adv*

worry beads *pl n* a string of beads that when fingered or played with supposedly relieves nervous tension.

worryguts ('wʌrɪˌgʌts) *n* (*functioning as sing*) *Inf.* a person who worries, esp. about insignificant matters.

worse (wɜːs) *adj* **1** the comparative of **bad**[1]. **2 none the worse for.** not harmed by (adverse events or circumstances). **3 the worse for wear. 3a** shabby or worn. **3b** a slang term for **drunk. 4 worse luck!** *Inf.* unhappily; unfortunately. **5 worse off.** (*postpositive*) in a worse, esp. a worse financial, condition. ◆ *n* **6** something that is worse. **7 for the worse.** into a less desirable or inferior state or condition: *a change for the worse.* ◆ *adv* **8** in a more severe or unpleasant manner. **9** in a less effective or successful manner. ORIG OE *wiersa*

worsen ('wɜːsᵊn) *vb* to grow or cause to grow worse.

worship ('wɜːʃɪp) *vb* **worships, worshipping, worshipped** *or US* **worships, worshiping, worshiped. 1** (*tr*) to show profound religious devotion and respect to; adore or venerate (God or any person or thing considered divine). **2** (*tr*) to be devoted to and full of admiration for. **3** (*intr*) to have or express feelings of profound adoration. **4** (*intr*) to attend services for worship. ◆ *n* **5** religious adoration or devotion. **6** the formal expression of religious adoration; rites, prayers, etc. **7** admiring love or devotion. ORIG OE *weorthscipe*
▸ **'worshipper** *n*

Worship ('wɜːʃɪp) *n Chiefly Brit.* (preceded by *Your, His,* or *Her*) a title used to address or refer to a mayor, magistrate, etc.

worshipful ('wɜːʃɪpfʊl) *adj* **1** feeling or showing reverence or adoration. **2** (*often cap.*) *Chiefly Brit.* a title used to address or refer to various people or bodies of distinguished rank.
▸ **'worshipfully** *adv* ▸ **'worshipfulness** *n*

worst (wɜːst) *adj* **1** the superlative of **bad**[1]. ◆ *adv* **2** in the most extreme or bad manner or degree. **3** least well, suitably, or acceptably. **4** (*in combination*) in or to the smallest degree or extent; least: *worst-loved.* ◆ *n* **5 the worst.** the least good or most inferior person, thing, or part in a group, narrative, etc. **6** (often preceded by *at*) the most poor, unpleasant, or unskilled quality or condition: *television is at its worst these days.* **7** the greatest amount of damage or wickedness of which a person or group is capable: *the invaders came and did their worst.* **8** the weakest effort or poorest achievement that a person or group is capable of making: *the applicant did his worst at the test because he did not want the job.* **9 at worst. 9a** in the least favourable interpretation or view. **9b** under the least favourable conditions. **10 come off worst** *or* **get the worst of it.** to enjoy the least benefit from an issue or be defeated in it. **11 if the worst comes to the worst.** if all the more desirable alternatives become impossible or if the worst possible thing happens. ◆ *vb* **12** (*tr*) to get the advantage over; defeat or beat. ORIG OE *wierrest*

worsted ('wʊstɪd) *n* **1** a closely twisted yarn or thread made from combed long-staple wool. **2** a fabric made from this, with a hard smooth close-textured surface and no nap. **3** (*modifier*) made of this yarn or fabric: *a worsted suit.* ORIG C13: after *Worstead,* a district in Norfolk

wort (wɜːt) *n* **1** (*in combination*) any of various unrelated plants, esp. ones formerly used to cure diseases: *liverwort.* **2** the sweet liquid made from warm water and ground malt, used to make a malt liquor. ORIG OE *wyrt* root

worth (wɜːθ) *adj* (governing a noun with prepositional force) **1** worthy of; meriting or justifying: *it's not worth discussing.* **2** having a value of: *the book is worth £30.* **3 for all one is worth.** to the utmost. **4 worth one's weight in gold.** extremely helpful, kind, etc. ◆ *n* **5** high quality; excellence. **6** value; price. **7** the amount of something of a specified value: *five pounds' worth of petrol.* ORIG OE *weorth*

Worthing ★ ('wɜːðɪŋ) *n* a resort in S England, in West Sussex on the English Channel. Pop.: 95 732 (1991).

worthless ('wɜːθlɪs) *adj* **1** without value or usefulness. **2** without merit; good-for-nothing.
▸ **'worthlessly** *adv* ▸ **'worthlessness** *n*

worthwhile (ˌwɜːθ'waɪl) *adj* sufficiently important, rewarding, or valuable to justify time or effort spent.

worthy ('wɜːðɪ) *adj* **worthier, worthiest. 1** (*postpositive; often* foll. by *of* or an infinitive) having sufficient merit or value (for something or someone specified); deserving. **2** having worth, value, or merit. ◆ *n, pl* **worthies. 3** *Often facetious.* a person of merit or importance.
▸ **'worthily** *adv* ▸ **'worthiness** *n*

wot (wɒt) *vb Arch. or dialect.* (used with *I, she, he, it,* or a singular noun) a form of the present tense (indicative mood) of **wit**[2].

Wotan ★ ('vəʊtɑːn, 'vɔː-) *n* the supreme god in Germanic mythology. Norse counterpart: **Odin.**

would (wʊd; *unstressed* wəd) *vb* (takes an infinitive without *to* or an implied infinitive) used as an auxiliary: **1** to form the past tense or subjunctive mood of **will**[1]. **2** (with *you, he, she, it, they,* or a noun as subject) to indicate willingness or desire in a polite manner: *would you help me, please?* **3** to describe a past action as being accustomed or habitual: *every day we would go for walks.* **4** I wish: *would that he were here.*

> **USAGE NOTE** See at **should.**

would-be *adj* (*prenominal*) **1** *Usually derog.* wanting or professing to be: *a would-be politician.* **2** intended to be.

wouldn't ('wʊdᵊnt) *contraction of* would not.

wouldst (wʊdst) *vb Arch. or dialect.* (used with the pronoun *thou* or its relative equivalent) a singular form of the past tense of **will**[1].

Woulfe bottle (wʊlf) *n Chem.* a bottle with more than one neck, used for passing gases through liquids. ORIG C18: after Peter *Woulfe* (?1727–1803), Brit. chemist

wound[1] (wuːnd) *n* **1** any break in the skin or an organ or part as the result of violence or a surgical incision. **2** any injury or slight to the feelings or reputation. ◆ *vb* **3** to inflict a wound or wounds upon (someone or something). ORIG OE *wund*
▸ **'wounding** *adj* ▸ **'woundingly** *adv*

wound[2] (waʊnd) *vb* the past tense and past participle of **wind**[2] and **wind**[3].

wounded ('wuːndɪd) *adj* **1a** suffering from wounds; injured, esp. in a battle or fight. **1b** (*as collective n;* preceded by *the*): *the wounded.* **2** (of feelings) damaged or hurt.

woundwort ('wuːndˌwɜːt) *n* **1** any of various plants, such as field woundwort, having purple, scarlet, yellow, or white flowers and formerly used for dressing wounds. **2** any of various other plants used in this way.

wove (wəʊv) *vb* a past tense of **weave.**

woven ('wəʊvᵊn) *vb* a past participle of **weave.**

wove paper *n* paper with a very faint mesh impressed on it by the paper-making machine.

wow[1] (waʊ) *interj* **1** an exclamation of admiration, amazement, etc. ◆ *n* **2** *Sl.* a person or thing that is amazingly successful, attractive, etc. ◆ *vb* **3** (*tr*) *Sl.* to arouse great enthusiasm in. ORIG C16: orig. Scot.

wow[2] (waʊ, wəʊ) *n* a slow variation or distortion in pitch that occurs at very low audio frequencies in sound-reproducing systems. See also **flutter** (sense 12). ORIG C20: imit.

wowser ('waʊzə) *n Austral. & NZ sl.* **1** a fanatically puritanical person. **2** a teetotaller. ORIG C20: from E dialect *wow* to complain

wp *abbrev. for* word processor.

wpb *abbrev. for* wastepaper basket.

WPC (in Britain) *abbrev. for* woman police constable.

wpm *abbrev. for* words per minute.

WRAAC *abbrev. for* Women's Royal Australian Army Corps.

WRAAF *abbrev. for* Women's Royal Australian Air Force.

WRAC (in Britain) *abbrev. for* Women's Royal Army Corps.

wrack[1] *or* **rack** (ræk) *n* **1** collapse or destruction (esp. in **wrack and ruin**). **2** something destroyed or a remnant of such. ORIG OE *wræc* persecution, misery

> **USAGE NOTE** The use of the spelling *wrack* rather than *rack* in sentences such as *she was wracked by grief* or *the country was wracked by civil war* is very common but is thought by many people to be incorrect.

wrack[2] (ræk) *n* **1** seaweed or other marine vegetation that is floating in the sea or has been cast ashore. **2** any of various seaweeds, such as serrated wrack. ORIG C14 (in the sense: a wrecked ship, hence later applied to marine vegetation washed ashore): ?from MDu. *wrak* wreckage; the term corresponds to OE *wræc* WRACK[1]

WRAF (in Britain) *abbrev. for* Women's Royal Air Force.

wraith (reɪθ) *n* **1** the apparition of a person living or thought to be alive, supposed to appear around the time of his death. **2** any apparition. ORIG C16: Scot., from ?
▸ **'wraithˌlike** *adj*

Wran (ræn) *n* a member of the Women's Royal Australian Naval Service.

Wrangel Island ★ ('ræŋgᵊl) *n* an island in the Arctic Ocean, off the coast of NE Russia: administratively part of Russia; mountainous and mostly tundra. Area: about 7300 sq. km (2800 sq. miles).

Wrangell ★ ('ræŋgᵊl) *n* **Mount.** a mountain in S Alaska, in the W Wrangell Mountains. Height: 4269 m (14 005 ft).

Wrangell Mountains ★ *pl n* a mountain range in SE Alaska, extending into the Yukon, Canada. Highest peak: Mount Blackburn, 5037 m (16 523 ft).

wrangle ('ræŋgᵊl) *vb* **wrangles, wrangling, wrangled. 1** (*intr*) to argue, esp. noisily or angrily. **2** (*tr*) to encourage, persuade, or obtain by argument. **3** (*tr*) *Western US & Canad.* to herd (cattle or horses). ◆ *n* **4** a noisy or angry argument. ORIG C14: from Low G *wrangeln*

wrangler ('ræŋglə) *n* **1** one who wrangles. **2** *Western US & Canad.* a herder; cowboy. **3** a person who handles or controls animals involved in the making of a film or television programme. **4** *Brit.* (at Cambridge University) a candidate who has obtained first-class honours in part II of the mathematics tripos. Formerly, the wrangler with the highest marks was called the **senior wrangler.**

WRANS *abbrev. for* Women's Royal Australian Naval Service. See also **Wran.**

wrap (ræp) *vb* **wraps, wrapping, wrapped.** (*mainly tr*) **1** to fold or wind (paper, cloth, etc.) around (a person or thing) so as to cover. **2** (often foll. by *up*) to fold paper, etc., around to fasten securely. **3** to surround or conceal by surrounding. **4** to enclose, immerse, or absorb:

wrapped in joy. **5** to fold, wind, or roll up. **6** to complete the filming of (a motion picture or television programme). **7** (*intr;* often foll. by *about, around,* etc.) to be or become wound or extended. **8** (often foll. by *up*) Also: **rap.** *Austral. inf.* to praise (someone). ◆ *n* **9** a garment worn wrapped around the body, esp. the shoulders, such as a shawl or cloak. **10a** the end of a working day during the filming of a motion picture or television programme. **10b** the completion of filming of a motion picture or television programme. **11** *Chiefly US.* wrapping or a wrapper. **12** *Brit. sl.* a small package of an illegal drug in powder form: *a wrap of heroin.* **13 keep under wraps.** to keep secret. **14 take the wraps off.** to reveal. **15** Also: **rap.** *Austral. inf.* a commendation. ORIG C14: from ?

wrapover ('ræp,əʊvə) *or* **wrapround** *adj* **1** (of a garment, esp. a skirt) not sewn up at one side, but worn wrapped round the body and fastened so that the open edges overlap. ◆ *n* **2** such a garment.

wrapped (ræpt) *vb* **1** the past tense and past participle of **wrap. 2 wrapped up in.** *Inf.* **2a** completely absorbed or engrossed in. **2b** implicated or involved in. ◆ *adj* **3** *Austral. inf.* a variant spelling of **rapt**[2].

wrapper ('ræpə) *n* **1** the cover, usually of paper or cellophane, in which something is wrapped. **2** a dust jacket of a book. **3** the firm tobacco leaf forming the outermost portion of a cigar. **4** a loose negligee or dressing gown.

wrapping ('ræpɪŋ) *n* the material used to wrap something.

wrapround ('ræp,raʊnd) *or* **wraparound** *adj* **1** made so as to be wrapped round something: *a wrapround skirt.* **2** surrounding, curving round, or overlapping. **3** curving round in one continuous piece: *a wrapround windscreen.* ◆ *n* **4** *Printing.* a flexible plate of plastic, metal, or rubber that is made flat but used wrapped round the plate cylinder of a rotary press. **5** another name for **wrapover.**

wrap up *vb* (*adv*) **1** (*tr*) to fold paper around. **2** to put warm clothes on. **3** (*intr; usually imperative*) *Sl.* to be silent. **4** (*tr*) *Inf.* **4a** to settle the final details of. **4b** to make a summary of.

wrasse (ræs) *n* a marine food fish of tropical and temperate seas, having thick lips, strong teeth, and usually a bright coloration. ORIG C17: from Cornish *wrach*

wrath (rɒθ) *n* **1** angry, violent, or stern indignation. **2** divine vengeance or retribution. **3** *Arch.* a fit of anger or an act resulting from anger. ORIG OE *wrǣththu*

Wrath ★ (rɒθ, rɔːθ) *n* **Cape.** a promontory at the NW extremity of the Scottish mainland.

wrathful ('rɒθfʊl) *adj* **1** full of wrath; raging or furious. **2** resulting from or expressing wrath.
▸ '**wrathfully** *adv* ▸ '**wrathfulness** *n*

wreak (riːk) *vb* (*tr*) **1** to inflict (vengeance, etc.) or to cause (chaos, etc.): *to wreak havoc on the enemy.* **2** to express or gratify (anger, hatred, etc.). **3** *Arch.* to take vengeance for. ORIG OE *wrecan*
▸ '**wreaker** *n*

wreath (riːθ) *n, pl* **wreaths** (riːðz, riːθs). **1** a band of flowers or foliage intertwined into a ring, usually placed on a grave as a memorial or worn on the head as a garland or a mark of honour. **2** any circular or spiral band or formation. **3** (loosely) any floral design placed on a grave as a memorial. ORIG OE *wrǣth, wrǣd*
▸ '**wreath,like** *adj*

wreathe (riːð) *vb* **wreathes, wreathing, wreathed. 1** to form into or take the form of a wreath by intertwining or twisting together. **2** (*tr*) to decorate with wreaths. **3** to move or cause to move in a twisting way: *smoke wreathed up to the ceiling.* ORIG C16: ? back formation from *wrēthen,* from OE *writhen,* p.p. of *wrīthan* to writhe

wreck (rɛk) *vb* **1** to involve in or suffer disaster or destruction. **2** (*tr*) to cause the wreck of (a ship). ◆ *n* **3a** the accidental destruction of a ship at sea. **3b** the ship so destroyed. **4** *Maritime law.* goods cast ashore from a wrecked vessel. **5** a person or thing that has suffered ruin or dilapidation. **6** Also called: **wreckage.** the remains of something that has been destroyed. **7** Also called: **wreckage.** the act of wrecking or the state of being wrecked. ORIG C13: from ON
▸ '**wrecking** *n, adj*

wrecked (rɛkt) *adj Sl.* in a state of intoxication, stupor, or euphoria, induced by drugs or alcohol.

wrecker ('rɛkə) *n* **1** a person or thing that ruins or destroys. **2** *Chiefly US & Canad.* a person whose job is to demolish buildings or dismantle cars. **3** (formerly) a person who lures ships to destruction to plunder the wreckage. **4** a US and Canad. name for a breakdown van.

wrecking bar *n* a short crowbar, forked at one end and slightly angled at the other to make a fulcrum.

Wrekin ★ ('riːkɪn) *n* **the.** an isolated hill in the English Midlands in Shropshire. Height: 400 m (1335 ft).

wren (rɛn) *n* **1** any small brown passerine songbird of a chiefly American family (in Britain **wren,** in the US and Canada **winter wren**). They have a slender bill and feed on insects. **2** any of various similar birds, such as the Australian warblers, New Zealand wrens, etc. ORIG OE *wrenna, werna*

Wren[1] (rɛn) *n Inf.* (in Britain and certain other nations) a member of the Women's Royal Naval Service. ORIG C20: from the abbrev. *WRNS*

Wren[2] ★ (rɛn) *n* Sir **Christopher.** 1632–1723, English architect. He designed St Paul's Cathedral and over 50 other London churches after the Great Fire.

wrench (rɛntʃ) *vb* **1** to give (something) a sudden or violent twist or pull, esp. so as to remove (something) from that to which it is attached: *to wrench a door off its hinges.* **2** (*tr*) to twist suddenly so as to sprain (a limb): *to wrench one's ankle.* **3** (*tr*) to give pain to. **4** (*tr*) to twist from the original meaning or purpose. **5** (*intr*) to make a sudden twisting motion. ◆ *n* **6** a forceful twist or pull. **7** an injury to a limb, caused by twisting. **8** sudden pain caused esp. by parting. **9** a parting that is difficult or painful to make. **10** a distorting of the original meaning or purpose. **11** a spanner, esp. one with adjustable jaws. See also **torque wrench.** ORIG OE *wrencan*

wrest (rɛst) *vb* (*tr*) **1** to take or force away by violent pulling or twisting. **2** to seize forcibly by violent or unlawful means. **3** to obtain by laborious effort. **4** to distort in meaning, purpose, etc. ◆ *n* **5** the act or an instance of wresting. **6** *Arch.* a small key used to tune a piano or harp. ORIG OE *wrǣstan*
▸ '**wrester** *n*

wrestle ('rɛsᵊl) *vb* **wrestles, wrestling, wrestled. 1** to fight (another person) by holding, throwing, etc., without punching with the closed fist. **2** (*intr*) to participate in wrestling. **3** (when *intr,* foll. by *with* or *against*) to fight with (a person, problem, or thing): *wrestle with one's conscience.* **4** (*tr*) to move laboriously, as with wrestling movements. ◆ *n* **5** the act of wrestling. **6** a struggle or tussle. ORIG OE *wræstlian*
▸ '**wrestler** *n*

wrestling ('rɛslɪŋ) *n* any of certain sports in which the contestants fight each other according to various rules governing holds and usually forbidding blows with the closed fist. The principal object is to overcome the opponent either by throwing or pinning him to the ground or by causing him to submit.

wrest pin *n* (on a piano, harp, etc.) a pin, embedded in the **wrest plank,** around which one end of a string is wound: it may be turned by means of a tuning key to alter the tension of the string.

wretch (rɛtʃ) *n* **1** a despicable person. **2** a person pitied for his or her misfortune. ORIG OE *wrecca*

wretched ('rɛtʃɪd) *adj* **1** in poor or pitiful circumstances. **2** characterized by or causing misery. **3** despicable; base. **4** poor, inferior, or paltry. **5** (*prenominal*) (intensifier qualifying something undesirable): *a wretched nuisance.*
▸ '**wretchedly** *adv* ▸ '**wretchedness** *n*

Wrexham ★ ('rɛksəm) *n* **1** a town in N Wales: seat of the Roman Catholic bishopric of Wales (except Glamorganshire); formerly noted for coal-mining. Pop.: 40 614 (1991). **2** a county borough in NE Wales, formed in 1996. Pop.: 123 400 (1996 est.). Area: 500 sq. km (193 sq. miles).

wrick (rɪk) *n* **1** a sprain or strain. ◆ *vb* **2** (*tr*) to sprain or strain.

wrier *or* **wryer** (ˈraɪə) *adj* the comparative of **wry**.

wriest *or* **wryest** (ˈraɪɪst) *adj* the superlative of **wry**.

wriggle (ˈrɪgᵊl) *vb* **wriggles, wriggling, wriggled. 1** to make or cause to make twisting movements. **2** (*intr*) to progress by twisting and turning. **3** (*intr;* foll. by *into* or *out of*) to manoeuvre oneself by clever or devious means: *wriggle out of an embarrassing situation.* ◆ *n* **4** a wriggling movement or action. **5** a sinuous marking or course. ORIG C15: from MLow G
▸ ˈ**wriggler** *n* ▸ ˈ**wriggly** *adj*

wright (raɪt) *n* (*now chiefly in combination*) a person who creates, builds, or repairs something specified: *a playwright; a shipwright.* ORIG OE *wryhta, wyrhta*

Wright ★ (raɪt) *n* **1 Frank Lloyd.** 1869–1959, US architect, whose designs include the Guggenheim Museum, New York (1943). **2 Joseph**, known as *Wright of Derby*. 1734–97, British painter. **3 Joseph.** 1855–1930, British philologist; editor of *The English Dialect Dictionary* (1898–1905). **4 Judith** (**Arundel**). 1915–2000, Australian poet and conservationist. **5 Wilbur** (1867–1912) and his brother, **Orville** (1871–1948), US aviation pioneers, who designed and flew the first powered aircraft (1903).

wring (rɪŋ) *vb* **wrings, wringing, wrung. 1** (often foll. by *out*) to twist and compress to squeeze (a liquid) from (cloth, etc.). **2** (*tr*) to twist forcibly: *wring its neck.* **3** (*tr*) to clasp and twist (one's hands), esp. in anguish. **4** (*tr*) to distress: *wring one's heart.* **5** (*tr*) to grip (someone's hand) vigorously in greeting. **6** (*tr*) to obtain as by forceful means: *wring information out of.* **7 wringing wet.** soaking; drenched. ◆ *n* **8** an act or the process of wringing. ORIG OE *wringan*

wringer (ˈrɪŋə) *n* another name for **mangle**[2] (sense 1).

wrinkle[1] (ˈrɪŋkᵊl) *n* **1** a slight ridge in the smoothness of a surface, such as a crease in the skin as a result of age. ◆ *vb* **wrinkles, wrinkling, wrinkled. 2** to make or become wrinkled, as by crumpling, creasing, or puckering. ORIG C15: back formation from *wrinkled,* from OE *gewrinclod,* p.p. of *wrinclian* to wind around
▸ ˈ**wrinkly** *adj*

wrinkle[2] (ˈrɪŋkᵊl) *n Inf.* a clever or useful trick, hint, or dodge. ORIG OE *wrenc* trick

wrinklies (ˈrɪŋklɪz) *pl n Inf., derog.* old people.

wrist (rɪst) *n* **1** *Anat.* the joint between the forearm and the hand. Technical name: **carpus. 2** the part of a sleeve or glove that covers the wrist. **3** *Machinery.* **3a** See **wrist pin. 3b** a joint in which a wrist pin forms the pivot. ORIG OE

wristband (ˈrɪstˌbænd) *n* **1** a band around the wrist, esp. one attached to a watch or forming part of a long sleeve. **2** a sweatband around the wrist.

wristlet (ˈrɪstlɪt) *n* a band or bracelet worn around the wrist.

wrist pin *n* **1** a cylindrical boss or pin attached to the side of a wheel parallel with the axis, esp. one forming a bearing for a crank. **2** the US and Canad. name for **gudgeon pin.**

wristwatch (ˈrɪstˌwɒtʃ) *n* a watch worn strapped around the wrist.

wristy (ˈrɪstɪ) *adj* (of a player's style of hitting the ball in cricket, tennis, etc.) with much movement of the wrist.

writ (rɪt) *n* **1** a document under seal, issued in the name of the Crown or a court, commanding the person to whom it is addressed to do or refrain from doing some specified act. **2** *Arch.* a piece of writing: *Holy Writ.* ORIG OE

write (raɪt) *vb* **writes, writing, wrote, written. 1** to draw or mark (symbols, words, etc.) on a surface, usually paper, with a pen, pencil, or other instrument. **2** to describe or record (ideas, experiences, etc.) in writing. **3** to compose (a letter) to or correspond regularly with (a person, organization, etc.). **4** (*tr; may take a clause as object*) to say or communicate by letter: *he wrote that he was on his way.* **5** (*tr*) *Inf., chiefly US & Canad.* to send a letter to (a person, etc.). **6** to write (words) in cursive as opposed to printed style. **7** (*tr*) to be sufficiently familiar with (a specified style, language, etc.) to use it in writing. **8** to be the author or composer of (books, music, etc.). **9** (*tr*) to fill in the details for (a document, form, etc.). **10** (*tr*) to draw up or draft. **11** (*tr*) to produce by writing: *he wrote ten pages.* **12** (*tr*) to show clearly: *envy was written all over his face.* **13** (*tr*) to spell or inscribe. **14** (*tr*) to ordain or prophesy: *it is written.* **15** (*intr*) to produce writing as specified. **16** *Computing.* to record (data) in a location in a storage device. **17** (*tr*) See **underwrite** (sense 3a). ◆ See also **write down, write in,** etc. ORIG OE *wrītan* (orig.: to scratch runes into bark)
▸ ˈ**writable** *adj*

write down *vb* (*adv*) **1** (*tr*) to set down in writing. **2** (*tr*) to harm or belittle by writing about (a person) in derogatory terms. **3** (*intr;* foll. by *to* or *for*) to write in a simplified way (to a supposedly less cultured readership). **4** (*tr*) *Accounting.* to decrease the book value of (an asset). ◆ *n* **write-down. 5** *Accounting.* a reduction made in the book value of an asset.

write in *vb* (*tr*) **1** to insert in (a document, form, etc.) in writing. **2** (*adv*) to write a letter to a company, institution, etc. **3** (*adv*) *US.* to vote for (a person not on a ballot) by inserting his or her name.

write off *vb* (*tr, adv*) **1** *Accounting.* **1a** to cancel (a bad debt or obsolete asset) from the accounts. **1b** to consider (a transaction, etc.) as a loss or set off (a loss) against revenues. **1c** to depreciate (an asset) by periodic charges. **1d** to charge (a specified amount) against gross profits as depreciation of an asset. **2** to cause or acknowledge the complete loss of. **3** to dismiss from consideration. **4** to send a written order (for something): *she wrote off for a brochure.* **5** *Inf.* to damage (something, esp. a car) beyond repair. ◆ *n* **write-off. 6** *Accounting.* **6a** the act of cancelling a bad debt or obsolete asset from the accounts. **6b** the bad debt or obsolete asset cancelled. **6c** the amount cancelled against gross profits, corresponding to the book value of the bad debt or obsolete asset. **7** *Inf.* something damaged beyond repair, esp. a car.

write out *vb* (*tr, adv*) **1** to put into writing or reproduce in full form in writing. **2** to exhaust (oneself or one's creativity) by excessive writing. **3** to remove (a character) from a television or radio series.

writer (ˈraɪtə) *n* **1** a person who writes books, articles, etc., esp. as an occupation. **2** the person who has written something specified. **3** a person who is able to write or write well. **4** a scribe or clerk. **5** a composer of music. **6 Writer to the Signet.** (in Scotland) a member of an ancient society of solicitors, now having the exclusive privilege of preparing crown writs.

writer's cramp *n* a muscular spasm or temporary paralysis of the muscles of the thumb and first two fingers caused by prolonged writing.

write up *vb* (*tr, adv*) **1** to describe fully, complete, or bring up to date in writing: *write up a diary.* **2** to praise or bring to public notice in writing. **3** *Accounting.* **3a** to place an excessively high value on (an asset). **3b** to increase the book value of (an asset) in order to reflect more accurately its current worth in the market. ◆ *n* **write-up. 4** a published account of something, such as a review in a newspaper or magazine.

writhe (raɪð) *vb* **writhes, writhing, writhed. 1** to twist or squirm in or as if in pain. **2** (*intr*) to move with such motions. **3** (*intr*) to suffer acutely from embarrassment, revulsion, etc. ◆ *n* **4** the act of writhing. ORIG OE *wrīthan*
▸ ˈ**writher** *n*

writing (ˈraɪtɪŋ) *n* **1** a group of letters or symbols written or marked on a surface as a means of communicating. **2** short for **handwriting. 3** anything expressed in letters, esp. a literary composition. **4** the work of a writer. **5** literary style, art, or practice. **6** written form: *give it to me in writing.* **7** (*modifier*) related to or used in writing: *writing ink.* **8 writing on the wall.** a sign or signs of approaching disaster. ORIG sense 8: allusion to Daniel 5:5

writing desk *n* a piece of furniture with a writing surface and drawers and compartments for papers, etc.

writing paper *n* paper sized to take writing ink and used for letters and other manuscripts.

writ of execution *n Law.* a writ ordering that a judgment be enforced.

written ('rɪtᵊn) *vb* **1** the past participle of **write**. ◆ *adj* **2** taken down in writing; transcribed: *written evidence.*

WRNS *abbrev. for* Women's Royal Naval Service. See also **Wren.**

Wrocław ★ (*Polish* 'vrɔtswaf) *n* an industrial city in SW Poland, on the River Oder: passed to Austria (1527) and to Prussia (1741); returned to Poland in 1945. Pop.: 642 900 (1995 est.). German name: **Breslau.**

wrong (rɒŋ) *adj* **1** not correct or truthful: *the wrong answer.* **2** acting or judging in error: *you are wrong to think that.* **3** (*postpositive*) immoral; bad: *it is wrong to cheat.* **4** deviating from or unacceptable to correct or conventional laws, usage, etc. **5** not intended or wanted: *the wrong road.* **6** (*postpositive*) not working properly; amiss: *something is wrong with the engine.* **7** (of a side, esp. of a fabric) intended to face the inside so as not to be seen. **8 get on the wrong side of.** *Inf.* to come into disfavour with. **9 go down the wrong way.** (of food) to pass into the windpipe instead of the gullet. ◆ *adv* **10** in the wrong direction or manner. **11 get wrong. 11a** to fail to understand properly. **11b** to fail to provide the correct answer to. **12 go wrong. 12a** to turn out other than intended. **12b** to make a mistake. **12c** (of a machine, etc.) to cease to function properly. **12d** to go astray morally. ◆ *n* **13** a bad, immoral, or unjust thing or action. **14** *Law.* **14a** an infringement of another person's rights, rendering the offender liable to a civil action: *a private wrong.* **14b** a violation of public rights and duties, affecting the community as a whole and actionable at the instance of the Crown: *a public wrong.* **15 in the wrong.** mistaken or guilty. ◆ *vb* (*tr*) **16** to treat unjustly. **17** to malign or misrepresent. ORIG OE *wrang* injustice
▸ **'wronger** *n* ▸ **'wrongly** *adv* ▸ **'wrongness** *n*

wrongdoer ('rɒŋˌduːə) *n* a person who acts immorally or illegally.
▸ **'wrongˌdoing** *n*

wrong-foot *vb* (*tr*) **1** *Tennis, etc.* to play a shot in such a way as to cause (one's opponent) to be off balance. **2** to take by surprise so as to place in an embarrassing or disadvantageous situation.

wrongful ('rɒŋfʊl) *adj* unjust or illegal.
▸ **'wrongfully** *adv* ▸ **'wrongfulness** *n*

wrong-headed *adj* **1** constantly wrong in judgment. **2** foolishly stubborn; obstinate.
▸ **ˌwrong-'headedly** *adv* ▸ **ˌwrong-'headedness** *n*

wrong number *n* a telephone number wrongly connected or dialled in error, or the person so contacted.

wrote (rəʊt) *vb* the past tense of **write.**

wroth (rəʊθ, rɒθ) *adj Arch. or literary.* angry; irate. ORIG OE *wrāth*

wrought (rɔːt) *vb* **1** *Arch.* a past tense and past participle of **work.** ◆ *adj* **2** *Metallurgy.* shaped by hammering or beating. **3** (*often in combination*) formed, fashioned, or worked as specified: *well-wrought.* **4** decorated or made with delicate care. ORIG C16: var. of *worht,* from OE *geworht,* p.p. of (*ge*)*wyrcan* to work

wrought iron *n* **a** a pure form of iron having a low carbon content: often used for decorative work. **b** (*as modifier*): *wrought-iron gates.*

wrought-up *adj* agitated or excited.

wrung (rʌŋ) *vb* the past tense and past participle of **wring.**

WRVS *abbrev. for* Women's Royal Voluntary Service.

wry (raɪ) *adj* **wrier, wriest** *or* **wryer, wryest. 1** twisted, contorted, or askew. **2** (of a facial expression) produced or characterized by contorting of the features. **3** drily humorous; sardonic. **4** warped, misdirected, or perverse. ◆ *vb* **wries, wrying, wried. 5** (*tr*) to twist or contort. ORIG C16: from dialect *wry* to twist, from OE *wrīgian* to turn
▸ **'wryly** *adv* ▸ **'wryness** *n*

wrybill ('raɪˌbɪl) *n* a New Zealand plover, having its bill deflected to one side enabling it to search for food beneath stones.

wryneck ('raɪˌnɛk) *n* **1** either of two cryptically coloured Old World woodpeckers, which do not drum on trees. **2** another name for **torticollis. 3** *Inf.* a person who has a twisted neck.

WSW *symbol for* west-southwest.

wt. *abbrev. for* weight.

WTO *abbrev. for* World Trade Organization.

Wuchang *or* **Wu-ch'ang** ★ ('wuː'tʃæŋ) *n* a former city of E central China: now a part of Wuhan.

Wuhan ★ ('wuː'hæn) *n* a city in SE China, in Hubei province, at the confluence of the Han and Yangtze Rivers: formed in 1950 by the union of the cities of Hanyang, Hankou, and Wuchang (the Han Cities); port and industrial centre; university (1913). Pop.: 3 750 000 (1990 est.).

Wuhsien ★ ('wuː'ʃjɛn) *n* another name for **Suzhou.**

Wuhu ★ ('wuː'huː) *n* a port in E China, in E Anhui province on the Yangtze River. Pop.: 425 740 (1990 est.).

Wu-lu-mu-ch'i ★ ('wuː'luː'muː'tʃiː) *n* a variant of **Urumchi.**

wunderkind ('wʌndəˌkɪnd; *German* 'vʊndərˌkɪnt) *n, pl* **wunderkinds** *or* **wunderkinder** (*German* -ˌkɪndər). **1** a child prodigy. **2** a person who is extremely successful in his or her field while still young. ORIG C20: from G *Wunderkind,* lit.: wonder child

Wuppertal ★ (*German* 'vʊpərtaːl) *n* a city in W Germany, in North Rhine-Westphalia state on the **Wupper River** (a Rhine tributary): formed in 1929 from the amalgamation of the towns of Barmen and Elberfeld and other smaller towns; textile centre. Pop.: 383 776 (1995 est.).

wurst (wɜːst, wʊəst, vʊəst) *n* a sausage, esp. of a type made in Germany, Austria, etc. ORIG from G *Wurst,* lit.: something rolled

Württemberg ★ ('vɜːtəmˌbɜːg; *German* 'vyrtəmbɛrk) *n* a historic region and former state of S Germany; now part of the German state of Baden-Württemberg.

Würzburg ★ ('vɜːtsˌbɜːg; *German* 'vyrtsbʊrk) *n* a city in S central Germany, in NW Bavaria on the River Main: university (1582). Pop.: 127 295 (1996 est.).

wuss (wʊs) *or* **wussy** ('wʊsɪ) *n, pl* **wusses** *or* **wussies.** *Sl., chiefly US.* a feeble or effeminate person. ORIG C20: ?from PUSSY[1] (cat)

wuthering ('wʌðərɪŋ) *adj N English dialect.* **1** (of a wind) blowing strongly with a roaring sound. **2** (of a place) characterized by such a sound. ORIG var. of *whitherin,* from *whither* blow, from ON *hvithra*

Wutsin ★ ('wuː'tsɪn) *n* the former name (until 1949) of **Zhangzhou.**

Wuxi, Wusih, *or* **Wu-hsi** ★ ('wuː'ʃiː, -'siː) *n* a city in E China, in S Jiangsu province on the Grand Canal: textile industry. Pop.: 826 833 (1990 est.).

WV *abbrev. for* West Virginia.

W. Va. *abbrev. for* West Virginia.

WW1 *abbrev. for* World War One.

WW2 *abbrev. for* World War Two.

WWF *abbrev. for* Worldwide Fund for Nature.

WWW *abbrev. for* World Wide Web.

WY *or* **Wy.** *abbrev. for* Wyoming.

Wyatt ★ ('waɪət) *n* **1 James.** 1746–1813, British architect; a pioneer of the Gothic Revival. **2** Sir **Thomas.** ?1503–42, English poet at the court of Henry VIII.

wych-elm *or* **witch-elm** ('wɪtʃˌɛlm) *n* **1** a Eurasian elm tree, having a rounded shape, longish pointed leaves, clusters of small flowers, and winged fruits. **2** the wood of this tree. ORIG C17: from OE *wice*

Wycherley ★ ('wɪtʃəlɪ) *n* **William.** ?1640–1716, English dramatist. His comedies include *The Country Wife* (1675) and *The Plain Dealer* (1676).

Wycliffe *or* **Wyclif** ★ ('wɪklɪf) *n* **John.** ?1330–84, English religious reformer. A precursor of the Reformation, he instigated the first translation of the Bible into English. His followers were called Lollards. Also: **'Wiclif, 'Wickliffe.**
▸ **'Wycliffism** *or* **'Wyclifism** *n* ▸ **'Wyclifˌfite** *or* **'Wyclifˌite** *n, adj*

Wye ★ (waɪ) *n* a river in E Wales and W England, rising in Powys and flowing southeast into England, then south to the Severn estuary. Length: 210 km (130 miles).

Wykeham ★ ('wɪkəm) *n* **William of.** 1324–1404, English prelate, who founded New College, Oxford, and Winchester College: chancellor of England (1367–71; 1389–91); bishop of Winchester (1367–1404).

wynd (waɪnd) *n Scot.* a narrow lane or alley. ORIG C15: from the stem of WIND[2]

Wyndham ★ ('wɪndəm) *n* **John**, pseudonym of *John Wyndham Parkes Lucas Beynon Harris*. 1903–69, British science-fiction writer. His works include *The Day of the Triffids* (1951) and *The Midwich Cuckoos* (1957).

Wyo. *abbrev. for* Wyoming.

Wyoming ★ (waɪ'əʊmɪŋ) *n* a state of the western US: consists largely of ranges of the Rockies in the west and north, with part of the Great Plains in the east and several regions of hot springs. Capital: Cheyenne. Pop.: 480 907 (1998 est.). Area: 253 597 sq. km (97 914 sq. miles). Abbrevs.: **Wyo., Wy.,** or (with zip code) **WY**
▸ **Wy'oming,ite** *n*

WYSIWYG ('wɪzɪ,wɪg) *n, adj Computing. acronym for* what you see is what you get: referring to what is displayed on the screen being the same as what will be printed out.

wyvern *or* **wivern** ('waɪvən) *n* a heraldic beast having a serpent's tail and a dragon's head and a body with wings and two legs. ORIG C17: var. of earlier *wyver,* from OF, from L *vīpera* VIPER

x *or* **X** (ɛks) *n, pl* **x's, X's,** *or* **Xs. 1** the 24th letter of the English alphabet. **2** a speech sound sequence represented by this letter, pronounced as *ks* or *gz* or, in initial position, *z,* as in *xylophone.*

x *symbol for:* **1** *Commerce, finance, etc.* ex. **2** *Maths.* the *x*-axis or a coordinate measured along the *x*-axis in a Cartesian coordinate system. **3** *Maths.* an algebraic variable. **4** multiplication.

X *symbol:* **1a** (in Britain, formerly) indicating a film that may not be publicly shown to anyone under 18. Since 1982 replaced by symbol 18. **1b** *(as modifier): an X film.* **2** denoting any unknown, unspecified, or variable factor, number, person, or thing. **3** (on letters, cards, etc.) denoting a kiss. **4** (on ballot papers, etc.) indicating choice. **5** (on examination papers, etc.) indicating error. **6** for Christ; Christian. ORIG from the Gk letter khi (X), first letter of *Khristos* Christ **7** *the Roman numeral for* ten. See **Roman numerals.**

xanthein ('zænθiːn) *n* the soluble part of the yellow pigment that is found in the cell sap of some flowers.

xanthene ('zænθiːn) *n* a yellowish crystalline compound used as a fungicide.

xanthic ('zænθɪk) *adj* **1** of, containing, or derived from xanthic acid. **2** *Bot., rare.* having a yellow colour.

xanthic acid *n* any of a class of sulphur-containing acids.

xanthine ('zænθiːn, -θaɪn) *n* **1** a crystalline compound found in urine, blood, certain plants, and certain animal tissues. Formula: $C_5H_4N_4O_2$. **2** any of three substituted derivatives of xanthine, which act as stimulants and diuretics.

Xanthippe (zæn'θɪpɪ) *or* **Xantippe** ★ (zæn'tɪpɪ) *n* **1** the wife of Socrates, proverbial as scolding and quarrelsome. **2** any nagging, peevish, or irritable woman.

xantho- *or before a vowel* **xanth-** *combining form.* indicating yellow: *xanthophyll.* ORIG from Gk *xanthos* yellow

xanthochroism (zæn'θɒkrəʊˌɪzəm) *n* a condition in certain animals, esp. aquarium goldfish, in which all skin pigments other than yellow and orange disappear. ORIG C19: from Gk *xanthokhro(os)* yellow-skinned + -ISM

xanthoma (zæn'θəʊmə) *n Pathol.* the presence in the skin of fatty yellow or brownish plaques or nodules, esp. on the eyelids, caused by a disorder of lipid metabolism.

xanthophyll *or esp. US* **xanthophyl** ('zænθəʊfɪl) *n* any of a group of yellow carotenoid pigments occurring in plant and animal tissue.
▸ **ˌxantho'phyllous** *adj*

xanthous ('zænθəs) *adj* of, relating to, or designating races with yellowish hair and a light complexion.

Xanthus ★ ('zænθəs) *n* the chief city of ancient Lycia in SW Asia Minor: source of some important antiquities.
▸ **'Xanthian** *adj*

Xavier ★ ('zeɪvɪə, 'zæv-; *Spanish* xa'βjɛr) *n* **Saint Francis,** known as the *Apostle of the Indies.* 1506–52, Spanish missionary, who was a founder of the Jesuit society (1534) and preached in Goa, Ceylon, the East Indies, and Japan. Feast day: Dec. 3.

***x*-axis** *n* a reference axis, usually horizontal, of a graph or two- or three-dimensional Cartesian coordinate system along which the *x*-coordinate is measured.

X-chromosome *n* the sex chromosome that occurs in pairs in the diploid cells of the females of many animals, including humans, and as one of a pair with the Y-chromosome in those of males. Cf. **Y-chromosome.**

Xe *the chemical symbol for* xenon.

xebec, zebec, *or* **zebeck** ('ziːbɛk) *n* a small three-masted Mediterranean vessel with both square and lateen sails, formerly used by Algerian pirates and later used for commerce. ORIG C18: earlier *chebec* from F, ult. from Ar. *shabbāk;* present spelling infl. by Catalan *xabec,* Sp. *xabeque* (now *jabeque*)

Xenakis ★ (zɛ'nɑːkɪs; *Greek* ksɛ'nakis) *n* **Yannis** ('janis). 1922–2001, Greek composer, born in Romania. He is noted for his musical use of computing.

Xenical ('zɛnɪkᵊl) *n Trademark.* a drug that reduces the ability to absorb fats; used in the medical treatment of obesity.

xeno- *or before a vowel* **xen-** *combining form.* indicating something strange, different, or foreign: *xenogamy.* ORIG from Gk *xenos* strange

Xenocrates ★ (zɛ'nɒkrəˌtiːz) *n* ?396–314 B.C., Greek Platonic philosopher.
▸ **Xenocratic** (ˌzɛnə'krætɪk) *adj*

xenogamy (zɛ'nɒgəmɪ) *n Bot.* another name for **cross-fertilization.**
▸ **xe'nogamous** *adj*

xenogeneic (ˌzɛnəʊdʒɪ'neɪɪk) *adj Med.* derived from an individual of a different species: *a xenogeneic tissue graft.*

xenoglossia (ˌzɛnə'glɒsɪə) *n* an ability claimed by some mediums, clairvoyants, etc., to speak a language with which they are unfamiliar. ORIG C20: from Gk, from XENO- + *glossa* language

xenolith ('zɛnəlɪθ) *n* a fragment of rock differing in origin, composition, structure, etc., from the igneous rock enclosing it.
▸ **ˌxeno'lithic** *adj*

xenon ('zɛnɒn) *n* a colourless odourless gaseous element occurring in trace amounts in air; formerly considered inert, it is now known to form compounds and is used in radio valves, stroboscopic and bactericidal lamps, and bubble chambers. Symbol: Xe; atomic no.: 54; atomic wt.: 131.30. ORIG C19: from Gk: something strange

Xenophanes ★ (zɛ'nɒfəˌniːz) *n* ?570–?480 B.C., Greek philosopher and poet.

xenophile ('zɛnəˌfaɪl) *n* a person who likes foreigners or things foreign. ORIG C19: from Gk, from XENO- + -PHILE

xenophobia (ˌzɛnə'fəʊbɪə) *n* hatred or fear of foreigners or strangers or of their politics or culture. ORIG C20: from Gk, from XENO- + -PHOBIA
▸ **'xenoˌphobe** *n* ▸ **ˌxeno'phobic** *adj*

Xenophon ★ ('zɛnəfən) *n* 431–?355 B.C., Greek general and historian; a disciple of Socrates. He accompanied Cyrus the Younger against Artaxerxes II and, after Cyrus' death (401), led his army to the Black Sea, as described in his *Anabasis.* His other works include *Hellenica,* a history of Greece, and the *Memorabilia, Apology,* and *Symposium,* which contain recollections of Socrates.

Xeres ★ (*Spanish* 'xerɛθ) *n* the former name of **Jerez.**

xeric ('zɪərɪk) *adj Ecology.* of, relating to, or growing in dry conditions.
▸ **'xerically** *adv*

xero- *or before a vowel* **xer-** *combining form.* indicating dryness: *xeroderma.* ORIG from Gk *xēros* dry

xeroderma (ˌzɪərəʊ'dɜːmə) *or* **xerodermia** (ˌzɪərəʊ'dɜːmɪə) *n Pathol.* **1** any abnormal dryness of the skin as the result of diminished secretions from the sweat or sebaceous glands. **2** another name for **ichthyosis.**
▸ **xerodermatic** (ˌzɪərəʊdə'mætɪk) *or* **ˌxero'dermatous** *adj*

xerography (zɪ'rɒgrəfɪ) *n* a photocopying process in which an electrostatic image is formed on a selenium plate or cylinder. The plate or cylinder is dusted with a resinous powder, which adheres to the charged regions, and the image is then transferred to a sheet of paper on which it is fixed by heating.
▸ **xe'rographer** *n* ▸ **xerographic** (ˌzɪərə'græfɪk) *adj*
▸ **ˌxero'graphically** *adv*

xerophilous (zɪ'rɒfɪləs) *adj* (of plants or animals) adapted for growing or living in dry surroundings.
▸ **xerophile** ('zɪərəʊˌfaɪl) *n* ▸ **xe'rophily** *n*

★ people and places

xerophthalmia (ˌzɪərɒfˈθælmɪə) *n Pathol.* excessive dryness of the cornea and conjunctiva, caused by a deficiency of vitamin A. Also called: **xeroma** (zɪˈrəʊmə).
▸ **ˌxerophˈthalmic** *adj*

xerophyte (ˈzɪərəˌfaɪt) *n* a xerophilous plant, such as a cactus.
▸ **xerophytic** (ˌzɪərəˈfɪtɪk) *adj* ▸ **ˌxeroˈphytically** *adv* ▸ **ˈxeroˌphytism** *n*

Xerox (ˈzɪərɒks) *n* **1** *Trademark.* **1a** a xerographic copying process. **1b** a machine employing this process. **1c** a copy produced by this process. ◆ *vb* **2** to produce a copy of (a document, illustration, etc.) by this process.

Xerxes I ★ (ˈzɜːksiːz) *n* ?519–465 B.C., king of Persia (485–465). He led his forces to victory against Greece at Thermopylae (480) but his fleet was defeated at Salamis (480) and his army at Plataea (479).

Xhosa (ˈkɔːsə) *n* **1** (*pl* **Xhosa** *or* **Xhosas**) a member of a cattle-rearing Negroid people of southern Africa, living chiefly in W South Africa. **2** the language of this people, belonging to the Bantu group and characterized by several clicks in its sound system.
▸ **ˈXhosan** *adj*

xi (zaɪ, saɪ, ksaɪ, ksiː) *n, pl* **xis.** the 14th letter in the Greek alphabet (Ξ, ξ).

Xi, Hsi, *or* **Si** ★ (ʃiː) *n* a river in S China, rising in Yünnan province and flowing east to the Canton delta on the South China Sea: the main river system of S China. Length: about 1900 km (1200 miles).

Xia Gui *or* **Hsia Kuei** ★ (ˈʃjɑː ˈkweɪ) *n* ?1180–1230, Chinese landscape painter of the Sung dynasty; noted for his misty mountain landscapes in ink monochrome.

Xiamen ★ (ˌʃjɑːˈmɛn) *n* a variant transliteration of the Chinese name for **Amoy.**

Xi An, Hsian, *or* **Sian** ★ (ʃjɑːn) *n* an industrial city in central China, capital of Shaanxi province: capital of China for 970 years at various times between the 3rd century B.C. and the 10th century A.D.; seat of the Northwestern University (1937). Pop.: 2 760 000 (1991 est.). Former name: **Siking.**

Xiang, Hsiang, *or* **Siang** ★ (ʃjɑːŋ) *n* **1** a river in SE central China, rising in NE Guangxi Zhuang and flowing northeast and north to Dongting Lake. Length: about 1150 km (715 miles). **2** a river in S China, rising in SE Yünnan and flowing east to the Hongxiu (the upper course of the Xi River). Length: about 800 km (500 miles).

Xiangtan *or* **Siangtan** ★ (ˈʃjɑːŋˈtɑːn) *n* a city in S central China, in NE Hunan on the Xiang River: centre of a region noted for tea production. Pop.: 441 968 (1990 est.).

Ximenes *or* **Ximenez** ★ (*Spanish* xiˈmenes; *English* ˈzɪmɪˌniːz) *n* See (Francisco) **Jiménez de Cisneros.**

Xingú ★ (*Portuguese* ʃiŋˈgu) *n* a river in central Brazil, rising on the Mato Grosso plateau and flowing north to the Amazon delta, with over 650 km (400 miles) of rapids in its middle course. Length: 1932 km (1200 miles).

Xining, Hsining, *or* **Sining** ★ (ˈʃiːˈnɪŋ) *n* a city in W China, capital of Qinghai province, at an altitude of 2300 m (7500 ft). Pop.: 551 776 (1990 est.).

Xinjiang Uygur (ˈʃɪnˈdʒjæŋ ˈwiːgʊə) *or* **Sinkiang-Uighur Autonomous Region** ★ *n* an administrative division of NW China: established in 1955 for the Uigur ethnic minority, with autonomous subdivisions for other small minorities; produces over half China's wool and contains valuable mineral resources. Capital: Urumqi. Pop.: 17 180 000 (1997 est.). Area: 1 646 799 sq. km (635 829 sq. miles).

xiphisternum (ˌzɪfɪˈstɜːnəm) *n, pl* **xiphisterna** (-nə). *Anat., zool.* the cartilaginous process forming the lowermost part of the breastbone (sternum). Also called: **xiphoid, xiphoid process.** ORIG C19: from Gk *xiphos* sword + STERNUM

xiphoid (ˈzɪfɔɪd) *adj* **1** *Biol.* shaped like a sword. **2** of or relating to the xiphisternum. ◆ *n* **3** Also called: **xiphoid process.** another name for **xiphisternum.** ORIG C18: from NL, from Gk, from *xiphos* sword + *eidos* form

Xizang Autonomous Region ★ (ˈʃiːˈzæŋ) *n* the Pinyin transliteration of the Chinese name for **Tibet.**

Xmas (ˈɛksməs, ˈkrɪsməs) *n Inf.* short for **Christmas.** ORIG C18: from symbol X for Christ + -MAS

Xochimilco ★ (*Spanish* xotʃiˈmiko) *n* a town in central Mexico, on Lake Xochimilco: noted for its floating gardens. Pop.: 271 020 (1990).

X-rated *adj* **1** (formerly, in Britain) (of a film) considered suitable for viewing by adults only. **2** *Inf.* involving bad language, violence, or sex: *an X-rated conversation.*

X-ray *or* **x-ray** *n* **1a** electromagnetic radiation emitted when matter is bombarded with fast electrons. X-rays have wavelengths shorter than that of ultraviolet radiation, that is less than about 1×10^{-8} metres. Below about 1×10^{-11} metres they are often called gamma radiation or bremsstrahlung. **1b** (*as modifier*): *X-ray astronomy.* **2** a picture produced by exposing photographic film to X-rays: used in medicine as a diagnostic aid as parts of the body, such as bones, absorb X-rays and so appear as opaque areas on the picture. ◆ *vb* (*tr*) **3** to photograph (part of the body, etc.) using X-rays. **4** to treat or examine by means of X-rays. ORIG C19: partial translation of G *X-Strahlen* (from *Strahl* ray), coined by W. K. ROENTGEN in 1895

X-ray astronomy *n* the branch of astronomy concerned with the detection and measurement of X-rays emitted by certain celestial bodies, such as X-ray stars.

X-ray binary *n* a binary star that is an intense source of X-rays and is composed of a normal star in close orbit with a white dwarf, neutron star, or black hole.

X-ray crystallography *n* the study and practice of determining the structure of a crystal by passing a beam of X-rays through it and observing and analysing the diffraction pattern produced.

X-ray tube *n* an evacuated tube containing a metal target onto which is directed a beam of electrons at high energy for the generation of X-rays.

Xuan-tong ★ (ˈʃwɑːnˈtʊŋ) *n* the Pinyin transliteration of the title as emperor of China of (Henry) **Pu-yi.**

Xuthus ★ (ˈzuːθəs) *n Greek myth.* a son of Hellen, regarded as an ancestor of the Ionian Greeks through his son Ion.

Xuzhou (ˈʃuːˈdʒəʊ), **Hsü-chou,** *or* **Süchow** ★ *n* a city in N central China, in NW Jiangsu province: scene of a decisive battle (1949) in which the Communists defeated the Nationalists. Pop.: 805 695 (1990 est.).

xylem (ˈzaɪləm, -lɛm) *n* a plant tissue that conducts water and mineral salts from the roots to all other parts, provides mechanical support, and forms the wood of trees and shrubs. ORIG C19: from Gk *xulon* wood

xylene (ˈzaɪliːn) *n* an aromatic hydrocarbon existing in three isomeric forms, all three being colourless flammable volatile liquids used as solvents and in the manufacture of synthetic resins, dyes, and insecticides. Formula: $(CH_3)_2C_6H_4$. Systematic name: **dimethyl benzene.**

xylo- *or before a vowel* **xyl-** *combining form.* **1** indicating wood: *xylophone.* **2** indicating xylene: *xylidine.* ORIG from Gk *xulon* wood

xylocarp (ˈzaɪləˌkɑːp) *n Bot.* a fruit, such as a coconut, having a hard woody pericarp.
▸ **ˌxyloˈcarpous** *adj*

xylograph (ˈzaɪləˌgrɑːf) *n* **1** an engraving in wood. **2** a print taken from a wood block. ◆ *vb* **3** (*tr*) to print (a design, illustration, etc.) from a wood engraving.
▸ **xylography** (zaɪˈlɒgrəfɪ) *n*

Xylonite (ˈzaɪlənaɪt) *n Trademark.* a thermoplastic of the cellulose nitrate type.

xylophagous (zaɪˈlɒfəgəs) *adj* (of certain insects, crustaceans, etc.) feeding on or living within wood.

xylophone (ˈzaɪləˌfəʊn) *n Music.* a percussion instrument consisting of a set of wooden bars of graduated length. It is played with hard-headed hammers.
▸ **xylophonic** (ˌzaɪləˈfɒnɪk) *adj* ▸ **xylophonist** (zaɪˈlɒfənɪst) *n*

xylose (ˈzaɪləʊz, -ləʊs) *n* a white crystalline sugar found in wood and straw. It is extracted by hydrolysis with acids and used in dyeing, tanning, and in foods for diabetics.

xyster (ˈzɪstə) *n* a surgical instrument for scraping bone; surgical rasp or file. ORIG C17: via NL from Gk: tool for scraping, from *xuein* to scrape

Yy

y *or* **Y** (waɪ) *n, pl* **y's, Y's,** *or* **Ys. 1** the 25th letter of the English alphabet. **2** a speech sound represented by this letter, usually a semivowel, as in *yawn,* or a vowel, as in *symbol* or *shy.* **3** something shaped like a Y.

y *Maths. symbol for:* **1** the *y*-axis or a coordinate measured along the *y*-axis in a Cartesian coordinate system. **2** an algebraic variable.

Y *symbol for:* **1** any unknown or variable factor, number, or thing. **2** *Chem.* yttrium.

y. *abbrev. for* year.

-y[1] *or* **-ey** *suffix forming adjectives.* **1** (*from nouns*) characterized by; consisting of; filled with; resembling: *sunny; sandy; smoky; classy.* **2** (*from verbs*) tending to; acting or existing as specified: *leaky; shiny.* ORIG from OE *-ig, -ǣg*

-y[2]**, -ie,** *or* **-ey** *suffix of nouns. Inf.* **1** denoting smallness and expressing affection and familiarity: *a doggy; Jamie.* **2** a person or thing concerned with or characterized by being: *a groupie; a goalie; a fatty.* ORIG C14: from Scot. *-ie, -y,* familiar suffix orig. in names

-y[3] *suffix forming nouns.* **1** (*from verbs*) indicating the act of doing what is indicated by the verbal element: *inquiry.* **2** (*esp. with combining forms of Greek, Latin, or French origin*) indicating state, condition, or quality: *geography; jealousy.* ORIG from OF *-ie,* from L *-ia*

yabby *or* **yabbie** (ˈjæbɪ) *Austral.* ◆ *n, pl* **yabbies. 1** a small edible freshwater crayfish. **2** a saltwater prawn used as bait; nipper. ◆ *vb* **yabbies, yabbying, yabbied. 3** (*intr*) to fish for yabbies. ORIG from Abor.

Yablonovy Mountains ★ (*Russian* ˈjablənəvij) *pl n* a mountain range in Russia, in Siberia. Highest peak: 1680 m (5512 ft). Also called: **Yablonoi Mountains** (ˈjɑːbləˌnɔɪ).

yacht (jɒt) *n* **1** a vessel propelled by sail or power, used esp. for pleasure cruising, racing, etc. ◆ *vb* **2** (*intr*) to sail or cruise in a yacht. ORIG C16: from obs. Du. *jaghte,* short for *jahtschip,* from *jagen* to chase + *schip* ship
▸ **ˈyachting** *n, adj*

yachtie (ˈjɒtɪ) *n Austral. & NZ inf.* a yachtsman; sailing enthusiast.

yachtsman (ˈjɒtsmən) *or* (*fem*) **yachtswoman** *n, pl* **yachtsmen** *or* **yachtswomen.** a person who sails a yacht or yachts.
▸ **ˈyachtsmanship** *n*

yack (jæk) *n, vb* a variant spelling of **yak**[2].

yackety-yak (ˈjækɪtɪˈjæk) *n Sl.* noisy, continuous, and trivial talk or conversation. ORIG imit.

yaffle (ˈjæfᵊl) *n* another name for **green woodpecker** (see **woodpecker**). ORIG C18: imit. of its cry

Yafo ★ (ˈjɑːfɔː) *n* transliteration of the Hebrew name for **Jaffa** (sense 1).

Yagi aerial (ˈjɑːgɪ, ˈjægɪ) *n* a directional aerial, used esp. in television and radio astronomy, consisting of three or more elements lying parallel to each other, the principal direction of radiation being along the line of the centres. ORIG C20: after Hidetsugu *Yagi* (1886–1976), Japanese engineer

yah (jɑː, jɛə) *sentence substitute.* **1** an informal word for **yes.** ◆ *interj* **2** an exclamation of derision or disgust.

Yahata ★ (ˈjɑːhɑːˌtɑː) *n* a variant of **Yawata.**

yahoo (jəˈhuː) *n, pl* **yahoos.** a crude, brutish, or obscenely coarse person. ORIG C18: from a race of brutish creatures resembling men in Jonathan Swift's *Gulliver's Travels* (1726)
▸ **yaˈhooˌism** *n*

Yahweh (ˈjɑːweɪ) *or* **Yahveh** (ˈjɑːveɪ) *n Old Testament.* a vocalization of the Tetragrammaton. ORIG from Heb., from YHVH, with conjectural vowels; see also JEHOVAH

Yahwism (ˈjɑːwɪzəm) *or* **Yahvism** (ˈjɑːvɪzəm) *n* the use of the name Yahweh, esp. in parts of the Old Testament, as the personal name of God.

Yahwist (ˈjɑːwɪst) *or* **Yahvist** (ˈjɑːvɪst) *n Bible.* **the.** the conjectured author or authors of the earliest sources of the Pentateuch in which God is called *Yahweh* throughout.
▸ **Yahˈwistic** *or* **Yahˈvistic** *adj*

yak[1] (jæk) *n* an ox of Tibet having long shaggy hair. ORIG C19: from Tibetan *gyag*

yak[2] (jæk) *Sl.* ◆ *n* **1** noisy, continuous, and trivial talk. ◆ *vb* **yaks, yakking, yakked. 2** (*intr*) to chatter or talk in this way. ORIG C20: imit.

yakka, yakker, *or* **yacker** (ˈjækə) *n Austral. & NZ inf.* work. ORIG C19: from Abor.

Yakut Republic ★ (jæˈkʊt) *n* the former name of the **Sakha Republic.**

Yakutsk ★ (*Russian* jɪˈkutsk) *n* a port in E Russia, capital of the Sakha Republic, on the Lena River. Pop.: 192 000 (1995 est.).

Yale lock (jeɪl) *n Trademark.* a type of cylinder lock using a flat serrated key. ORIG C19: after L. *Yale* (1821–68), US inventor

Yalta ★ (*Russian* ˈjaltə) *n* a port and resort in S Ukraine, in the Crimea on the Black Sea: scene of a conference (1945) between Churchill, Roosevelt, and Stalin, who met to plan the final defeat and occupation of Nazi Germany. Pop.: 89 000 (1988 est.).

Yalu ★ (ˈjɑːˌluː) *n* a river in E Asia, rising in N North Korea and flowing southwest to Korea Bay, forming a large part of the border between North Korea and NE China. Length: 806 km (501 miles).

yam (jæm) *n* **1** any of various twining plants of tropical and subtropical regions, cultivated for their edible tubers. **2** the starchy tuber of any of these plants, eaten as a vegetable. **3** *Southern US.* the sweet potato. ORIG C17: from Port. *inhame,* ult. of W African origin

Yamagata ★ (ˌjæməˈgɑːtə) *n* Prince **Aritomo** (ˌærɪˈtəʊməʊ). 1838–1922, Japanese soldier and politician. As war minister (1873) and chief of staff (1878), he modernized Japan's military system. He was premier (1889–93; 1898).

Yamasaki ★ (ˌjæməˈsɑːkɪ) *n* **Minoru.** 1912–86, US architect. His buildings include St Louis Airport, Missouri (1953–55) and the World Trade Center, New York (1970–77).

yammer (ˈjæmə) *Inf.* ◆ *vb* **1** to utter or whine in a complaining manner. **2** to make (a complaint) loudly or persistently. ◆ *n* **3** a yammering sound. **4** nonsense; jabber. ORIG OE *geōmrian* to grumble
▸ **ˈyammerer** *n*

Yamoussoukro ★ (ˌjæmʊˈsuːkrəʊ) *n* the capital of the Côte d'Ivoire, in the S centre of the country. It replaced Abidjan as capital in 1983. Pop.: 109 445 (1995 est.).

Yanan (ˈjænˈæn) *or* **Yenan** ★ *n* a city in NE China, in N Shaanxi province: political and military capital of the Chinese Communists (1935–49). Pop.: 113 277 (1990 est.). Also called: **Fushih.**

Yang[1] (jæŋ) *n* See **Yin and Yang.**

Yang[2] ★ (jæŋ) *n* **Chen Ning** (ˈtʃɛn ˈnɪŋ). born 1922, US physicist, born in China: with Tsung-Dao Lee he showed that parity is not always conserved; shared the Nobel prize for physics 1957.

Yangon ★ (ˌjæŋˈgɒn) *n* the capital and chief port of Myanmar (formerly Burma): an industrial city and transport centre; dominated by the gold-covered Shwe Dagon pagoda, 112 m (368 ft) high. Pop.: 2 500 000 (latest est.). Former name (until 1989): **Rangoon.**

Yangtze ★ (ˈjæŋtsɪ, ˈjæŋktsɪ) *n* the longest river in

★ people and places

China, rising in SE Qinghai province and flowing east to the East China Sea near Shanghai: a major commercial waterway in one of the most densely populated areas of the world. Length: 5528 km (3434 miles). Also called: **Yangtze Jiang, Chang Jiang, Chang.**

Yanina ★ ('jɑːnɪnə) *n* a variant spelling of **Ioánnina.**

yank (jæŋk) *vb* **1** to pull with a sharp movement; tug. ◆ *n* **2** a jerk. ORIG C19: from ?

Yank (jæŋk) *n* **1** a slang word for an **American. 2** *US inf.* short for **Yankee.**

Yankee ('jæŋkɪ) *or (inf.)* **Yank** *n* **1** *Often disparaging.* a native or inhabitant of the US; American. **2** a native or inhabitant of New England. **3** a native or inhabitant of the Northern US, esp. a Northern soldier in the Civil War. **4** *Finance.* a bond issued in the US by a foreign borrower. ◆ *adj* **5** of, relating to, or characteristic of Yankees. ORIG C18: ?from Du. *Jan Kees* John Cheese, derisive nickname of Du. settlers for English colonists in Connecticut

Yankee Doodle *n* **1** an American song, popularly regarded as a characteristically national melody. **2** another name for **Yankee.**

Yantai ('jæn'taɪ), **Yentai,** *or* **Yen-t'ai** ★ *n* a port in E China, in NE Shandong. Pop.: 452 127 (1990 est.). Also called: **Chefoo.**

Yaoundé *or* **Yaunde** ★ (*French* jaunde) *n* the capital of Cameroon, in the southwest: University of Cameroon (1962). Pop.: 800 000 (1992 est.).

yap (jæp) *vb* **yaps, yapping, yapped.** (*intr*) **1** (of a dog) to bark in quick sharp bursts; yelp. **2** *Inf.* to talk at length in an annoying or stupid way; jabber. ◆ *n* **3** a high-pitched or sharp bark; yelp. **4** *Sl.* annoying or stupid speech; jabber. **5** *Sl., chiefly US.* a derogatory word for **mouth.** ORIG C17: imit.
▸ **'yapper** *n* ▸ **'yappy** *adj*

Yap ★ (jɑːp, jæp) *n* a group of four main islands in the W Pacific, in the W Caroline Islands: administratively a district of the US Trust Territory of the Pacific Islands from 1947; became self-governing in 1979 as part of the Federated States of Micronesia; important Japanese naval base in World War II. Pop.: 11 128 (1994). Area: 101 sq. km (39 sq. miles).

yapok (jə'pɒk) *n* an amphibious nocturnal opossum of Central and South America. Also called: **water opossum.** ORIG C19: after *Oyapok,* a river flowing between French Guiana & Brazil

Yapurá ★ (japu'ra) *n* the Spanish name for **Japurá.**

Yaqui ★ (*Spanish* 'jaki) *n* a river in NW Mexico, rising near the border with the US and flowing south to the Gulf of California. Length: about 676 km (420 miles).

yarborough ('jɑːbərə, -brə) *n Bridge, whist.* a hand of 13 cards in which no card is higher than nine. ORIG C19: supposedly after the second Earl of *Yarborough* (1809–62), said to have bet a thousand to one against its occurrence

yard[1] (jɑːd) *n* **1** a unit of length equal to 3 feet and defined in 1963 as exactly 0.9144 metre. **2** a cylindrical wooden or hollow metal spar, slung from a mast of a vessel, and used for suspending a sail. ORIG OE *gierd* rod, twig

yard[2] (jɑːd) *n* **1** a piece of enclosed ground, often adjoining or surrounded by a building or buildings. **2a** an enclosed or open area used for some commercial activity, for storage, etc.: *a builder's yard.* **2b** (*in combination*): *a shipyard.* **3** a US and Canad. word for **garden** (sense 1). **4** an area having a network of railway tracks and sidings, used for storing rolling stock, making up trains, etc. **5** *US & Canad.* the winter pasture of deer, moose, and similar animals. **6** *NZ.* short for **stockyard.** ORIG OE *geard*

Yard (jɑːd) *n* **the.** *Brit. inf.* short for **Scotland Yard.**

yardage[1] ('jɑːdɪdʒ) *n* a length measured in yards.

yardage[2] ('jɑːdɪdʒ) *n* **1** the use of a railway yard for cattle. **2** the charge for this.

yardarm ('jɑːdˌɑːm) *n Naut.* the two tapering outer ends of a ship's yard.

yard grass *n* an Old World perennial grass with prostrate leaves, growing as a troublesome weed on open ground, yards, etc.

Yardie ('jɑːdɪ) *n* a member of a Black criminal syndicate originally based in Jamaica. ORIG origin unknown

yard of ale *n* **1** the beer or ale contained in a narrow horn-shaped drinking glass. **2** such a drinking glass itself.

yardstick ('jɑːdˌstɪk) *n* **1** a measure or standard used for comparison. **2** a graduated stick, one yard long, used for measurement.

Yarkand ★ (ˌjɑː'kænd) *n* another name for **Shache.**

Yarmouth ★ ('jɑːməθ) *n* short for **Great Yarmouth.**

yarmulke ('jɑːməlkə) *n Judaism.* a skullcap worn by Orthodox male Jews at all times and by others during prayer. ORIG from Yiddish, from Ukrainian & Polish *yarmulka* cap, prob. from Turkish *yağmurluk* raincoat, from *yağmur* rain

yarn (jɑːn) *n* **1** a continuous twisted strand of natural or synthetic fibres, used in weaving, knitting, etc. **2** *Inf.* a long and often involved story, usually of incredible or fantastic events. **3 spin a yarn.** *Inf.* **3a** to tell such a story. **3b** to make up a series of excuses. ◆ *vb* **4** (*intr*) to tell such a story or stories. ORIG OE *gearn*

yarn-dyed *adj* (of fabric) dyed while still in yarn form, before being woven.

Yaroslavl ★ (*Russian* jɪra'slavlj) *n* a city in W Russia, on the River Volga: a major trading centre since early times and one of the first industrial centres in Russia; textile industries. Pop.: 629 000 (1995 est.).

yarran ('jærən) *n* a small hardy tree of inland Australia: useful as fodder and for firewood. ORIG from Abor.

Yarra River ★ ('jærə) *n* a river in SE Australia, rising in the Great Dividing Range and flowing west and southwest through Melbourne to Port Phillip Bay. Length: 250 km (155 miles).

yarrow ('jærəʊ) *n* any of several plants of the composite family of Eurasia, having finely dissected leaves and flat clusters of white flower heads. Also called: **milfoil.** ORIG OE *gearwe*

yashmak *or* **yashmac** ('jæʃmæk) *n* the face veil worn by Muslim women when in public. ORIG C19: from Ar.

yataghan ('jætəgən) *n* a Turkish sword with a curved blade. ORIG C19: from Turkish *yatağan*

Yathrib ★ ('jæθrɪb) *n* the ancient Arabic name for **Medina.**

Yaunde ★ (*French* jaunde) *n* a variant spelling of **Yaoundé.**

yaup (jɔːp) *vb, n* a variant spelling of **yawp.**
▸ **'yauper** *n*

Yavarí ★ (jaβa'ri) *n* the Spanish name for **Javari.**

yaw (jɔː) *vb* **1** (*intr*) (of an aircraft, etc.) to turn about its vertical axis. **2** (*intr*) (of a ship, etc.) to deviate temporarily from a straight course. **3** (*tr*) to cause (an aircraft, ship, etc.) to yaw. ◆ *n* **4** the movement of an aircraft, etc., about its vertical axis. **5** the deviation of a vessel from a straight course. ORIG C16: from ?

Yawata ('jɑːwɑːˌtɑː) *or* **Yahata** ★ *n* a former city in Japan, on N Kyushu: merged with Moji, Kokura, Tobata, and Wakamatsu in 1963 to form **Kitakyushu.**

yawl (jɔːl) *n* **1** a two-masted sailing vessel with a small mizzenmast aft of the rudderpost. **2** a ship's small boat, usually rowed by four or six oars. ORIG C17: from Du. *jol* or MLow G *jolle,* from ?

yawn (jɔːn) *vb* **1** (*intr*) to open the mouth wide and take in air deeply, often as in involuntary reaction to sleepiness or boredom. **2** (*tr*) to express or utter while yawning. **3** (*intr*) to be open wide as if threatening to engulf (someone or something): *the mine shaft yawned below.* ◆ *n* **4** the act or an instance of yawning. ORIG OE *gionian*
▸ **'yawner** *n* ▸ **'yawning** *adj* ▸ **'yawningly** *adv*

yawp (jɔːp) *Dialect US & Canad. inf.* ◆ *vb* (*intr*) **1** to yawn, esp. audibly. **2** to shout, cry, or talk noisily. **3** to bark or yowl. ◆ *n* **4** a shout, bark, or cry. **5** a noisy, foolish, or raucous utterance. ORIG C15 *yolpen,* prob. imit.
▸ **'yawper** *n*

yaws (jɔːz) *n* (*usually functioning as sing*) an infectious disease of tropical climates characterized by red skin eruptions. ORIG C17: of Carib origin

y-axis *n* a reference axis of a graph or two- or three-dimensional Cartesian coordinate system along which the *y*-coordinate is measured.

Yazd (jɑːzd) *or* **Yezd** ★ *n* a city in central Iran: a major centre of silk weaving. Pop.: 306 268 (1994 est.).

Yb *the chemical symbol for* ytterbium.

YC (in Britain) *abbrev. for* Young Conservative.

Y-chromosome *n* the sex chromosome that occurs as one of a pair with the X-chromosome in the diploid cells of the males of many animals, including humans. Cf. **X-chromosome.**

yclept (ɪ'klɛpt) *adj Obs.* having the name of; called. ORIG OE *gecleopod*, p.p. of *cleopian* to call

Y connection *n Electrical engineering.* a three-phase star connection.

yd *or* **yd.** *abbrev. for* yard (measure).

YDT (in Canada) *abbrev. for* Yukon Daylight Time.

ye[1] (jiː, *unstressed* jɪ) *pron* **1** *Arch. or dialect.* refers to more than one person including the person addressed. **2** Also: **ee** (iː). *Dialect.* refers to one person addressed: *I tell ye.* ORIG OE *gē*

ye[2] (ðiː, *spelling pron* jiː) *determiner* a form of **the**[1], used as a supposed archaism: *ye olde oake.* ORIG from a misinterpretation of *the* as written in some ME texts. The runic letter thorn (þ, representing *th*) was incorrectly transcribed as *y* because of a resemblance in their shapes

yea (jeɪ) *sentence substitute.* **1** a less common word for **aye** (yes). ◆ *adv* **2** (*sentence modifier*) *Arch. or literary.* indeed; truly: *yea, though they spurn me, I shall prevail.* ORIG OE *gēa*

yeah (jɛə) *sentence substitute.* an informal word for **yes.**

yean (jiːn) *vb* (of a sheep or goat) to give birth to (offspring). ORIG OE *geēanian*

yeanling ('jiːnlɪŋ) *n* the young of a goat or sheep.

year (jɪə) *n* **1** the period of time, the **calendar year,** containing 365 days or in a **leap year** 366 days. It is divided into 12 calendar months, and reckoned from January 1 to December 31. **2** a period of twelve months from any specified date. **3** a specific period of time, usually occupying a definite part or parts of a twelve-month period, used for some particular activity: *a school year.* **4** Also called: **astronomical year, tropical year**. the period of time, the **solar year,** during which the earth makes one revolution around the sun, measured between two successive vernal equinoxes: equal to 365.242 19 days. **5** the period of time, the **sidereal year,** during which the earth makes one revolution around the sun, measured between two successive conjunctions of a particular star: equal to 365.256 36 days. **6** the period of time, the **lunar year,** containing 12 lunar months and equal to 354.3671 days. **7** the period of time taken by a planet to complete one revolution around the sun. **8** (*pl*) age, esp. old age: *a man of his years should be more careful.* **9** (*pl*) time: *in years to come.* **10** a group of pupils or students, who are taught or study together. **11 the year dot.** *Inf.* as long ago as can be remembered. **12 year in, year out.** regularly or monotonously, over a long period. ◆ Related adj: **annual.** ORIG OE *gear*

> **USAGE NOTE** In writing spans of years, it is important to choose a style that avoids ambiguity. The practice adopted in this dictionary is, in four-figure dates, to specify the last two digits of the second date if it falls within the same century as the first: *1801–08; 1850–51; 1899–1901.* In writing three-figure B.C. dates, it is advisable to give both dates in full: *159–156* B.C., not *159–56* B.C. unless of course the span referred to consists of 103 years rather than three years. It is also advisable to specify B.C. or A.D. in years under 1000 unless the context makes this self-evident.

yearbook ('jɪə,bʊk) *n* an almanac or other reference book published annually and containing details of events of the previous year.

yearling ('jɪəlɪŋ) *n* **1** the young of any of various animals, including the antelope and buffalo, between one and two years of age. **2** a thoroughbred racehorse counted as being one year old until the second January 1 following its birth. **3a** a bond intended to mature after one year. **3b** (*as modifier*): *yearling bonds.* ◆ *adj* **4** being a year old.

yearlong ('jɪə'lɒŋ) *adj* throughout a whole year.

yearly ('jɪəlɪ) *adj* **1** occurring, done, appearing, etc., once a year or every year; annual. **2** lasting or valid for a year; annual: *a yearly fee.* ◆ *adv* **3** once a year; annually.

yearn (jɜːn) *vb* (*intr*) **1** (usually foll. by *for* or *after* or an infinitive) to have an intense desire or longing (for). **2** to feel tenderness or affection. ORIG OE *giernan*
► **'yearner** *n* ► **'yearning** *n, adj* ► **'yearningly** *adv*

year of grace *n* any year of the Christian era, as from the presumed date of Christ's birth.

year-round *adj* open, in use, operating, etc., throughout the year.

yeast (jiːst) *n* **1** any of various single-celled fungi which reproduce by budding and are able to ferment sugars: a rich source of vitamins of the B complex. **2** any of various similar and related fungi, esp. of the genus *Candida,* which can cause thrush in parts of the body infected with it. **3** a commercial preparation containing yeast cells and inert material such as meal, used in raising dough for bread or for fermenting beer, whisky, etc. **4** a preparation containing yeast cells, used to treat diseases caused by vitamin B deficiency. **5** froth or foam, esp. on beer. ◆ *vb* **6** (*intr*) to froth or foam. ORIG OE *giest*
► **'yeastless** *adj* ► **'yeast,like** *adj*

yeasty ('jiːstɪ) *adj* **yeastier, yeastiest. 1** of, resembling, or containing yeast. **2** fermenting or causing fermentation. **3** tasting of or like yeast. **4** insubstantial or frivolous. **5** restless, agitated, or unsettled. **6** covered with or containing froth or foam.
► **'yeastily** *adv* ► **'yeastiness** *n*

Yeats ★ (jeɪts) *n* **1 Jack Butler.** 1871–1957, Irish painter. **2** his brother **W(illiam) B(utler)**. 1865–1939, Irish poet and dramatist. His collections of verse include *The Tower* (1928) and his plays include *Cathleen ni Houlihan* (1902). He was a founder of the Irish National Theatre Company at the Abbey Theatre in Dublin: Nobel prize for literature 1923.

yebo ('jɛbəʊ) *sentence substitute. S. African inf.* an expression of affirmation. ORIG Zulu *yebo* yes, I agree

yegg (jɛg) *n Sl., chiefly US.* a burglar or safe-breaker. ORIG C20: ?from the surname of a burglar

Yeisk, Yeysk, *or* **Eisk** ★ (*Russian* jejsk) *n* a port and resort in SW Russia, on the Sea of Azov. Pop.: 86 300 (1991 est.).

Yekaterinburg *or* **Ekaterinburg** ★ (*Russian* jɪkətɪrim'burk) *n* a city in NW Russia, in the Ural Mountains: scene of the execution (1918) of Nicholas II and his family; university (1920); one of the largest centres of heavy engineering in Russia. Pop.: 1 280 000 (1995 est.). Former name (1924–91): **Sverdlovsk.**

Yekaterinodar *or* **Ekaterinodar** ★ (*Russian* jɪkətɪrina'dar) *n* the former name (until 1920) of **Krasnodar.**

Yekaterinoslav *or* **Ekaterinoslav** ★ (*Russian* jɪkətɪrina'slaf) *n* the former name (1787–96, 1802–1926) of **Dnepropetrovsk.**

Yelisavetgrad *or* **Elisavetgrad** ★ (*Russian* jɪliza'vjɛtgrət) *n* the former name (until 1924) of **Kirovograd.**

Yelisavetpol *or* **Elisavetpol** ★ (*Russian* jɪliza'vjɛtpəlj) *n* the former name (until 1920) of **Kirovabad.**

Yelizaveta Petrovna ★ (*Russian* jɪliza'vjɛtə pɪ'trɔvnə) *n* See **Elizabeth**[2] (sense 3).

yell (jɛl) *vb* **1** to shout, scream, cheer, or utter in a loud or piercing way. ◆ *n* **2** a loud piercing inarticulate cry, as of pain, anger, or fear. **3** *US & Canad.* a rhythmic cry, used in cheering in unison. ORIG OE *giellan*
► **'yeller** *n*

yellow ('jɛləʊ) *n* **1** any of a group of colours such as that of a lemon or of gold, which vary in saturation but have the same hue. Yellow is the complementary colour of blue. Related adj: **xanthous. 2** a pigment or dye of or producing these colours. **3** yellow cloth or clothing: *dressed in yellow.* **4** the yolk of an egg. **5** a yellow ball in snooker, etc. ◆ *adj* **6** of the colour yellow. **7** yellowish in colour or

having parts or marks that are yellowish. **8** having a yellowish skin; Mongoloid. **9** *Inf.* cowardly or afraid. **10** offensively sensational, as a cheap newspaper (esp. in **yellow press**). ◆ *vb* **11** to make or become yellow. ◆ See also **yellows**. ORIG OE *geolu*
▸ **'yellowish** *adj* ▸ **'yellowly** *adv* ▸ **'yellowness** *n* ▸ **'yellowy** *adj*

yellow-belly *n, pl* **yellow-bellies.** a slang word for **coward.**
▸ **'yellow-ˌbellied** *adj*

yellow belly *n Austral.* any of several freshwater food fishes with yellow underparts.

yellow bile *n Arch.* one of the four bodily humours, choler.

yellow card *n Soccer.* a card of a yellow colour displayed by a referee to indicate that a player has been officially cautioned for some offence.

yellow fever *n* an acute infectious disease of tropical and subtropical climates, characterized by fever, haemorrhages, vomiting, and jaundice: caused by a virus transmitted by the bite of a certain mosquito. Also called: **yellow jack.**

yellowhammer ('jɛləuˌhæmə) *n* a European bunting, having a yellowish head and body and brown-streaked wings and tail. ORIG C16: from ?

yellow jack *n* **1** *Pathol.* another name for **yellow fever. 2** another name for **quarantine flag. 3** any of certain large yellowish food fishes of warm and tropical Atlantic waters.

yellow jersey *n* (in the Tour de France) a yellow jersey awarded as a trophy to the cyclist with the fastest time in each stage of the race.

yellow journalism *n* the type of journalism that relies on sensationalism to attract readers. ORIG C19: ? shortened from *Yellow Kid journalism,* referring to the *Yellow Kid,* a cartoon (1895) in the *New York World,* a newspaper having a reputation for sensationalism

Yellowknife ★ ('jɛləuˌnaɪf) *n* a city in N Canada, capital of the Northwest Territories on Great Slave Lake. Pop.: 15 179 (1991).

yellow line *n Brit.* a yellow line painted along the edge of a road indicating vehicle waiting restrictions.

yellow metal *n* **1** a type of brass having about 60 per cent copper and 40 per cent zinc. **2** another name for **gold.**

Yellow Pages *pl n Trademark.* a classified telephone directory or section of one, often on yellow paper, that lists subscribers by the business or service they provide.

yellow peril *n* the power or alleged power of Asiatic peoples, esp. the Chinese, to threaten or destroy White or Western civilization.

Yellow River ★ *n* the second longest river in China, rising in SE Qinghai and flowing east, south, and east again to the Gulf of Bohai south of Tianjin; it has changed its course several times in recorded history. Length: about 4350 km (2700 miles). Chinese name: **Hwang Ho.**

yellows ('jɛləuz) *n (functioning as sing)* **1** any of various fungal or viral diseases of plants, characterized by yellowish discoloration and stunting. **2** *Vet. science.* another name for **jaundice.**

Yellow Sea ★ *n* a shallow arm of the Pacific between Korea and NE China. Area: about 466 200 sq. km (180 000 sq. miles). Chinese name: **Hwang Hai.**

yellow spot *n Anat.* another name for **macula lutea.**

Yellowstone ★ ('jɛləuˌstəun) *n* a river rising in N Wyoming and flowing north through Yellowstone National Park, then east to the Missouri. Length: 1080 km (671 miles).

Yellowstone Falls ★ *pl n* a waterfall in NW Wyoming, in Yellowstone National Park on the Yellowstone River.

Yellowstone National Park ★ *n* a national park in the NW central US, mostly in NW Wyoming: the oldest and largest national park in the US, containing unusual geological formations and geysers. Area: 8956 sq. km (3458 sq. miles).

yellow streak *n Inf.* a cowardly or weak trait.

yellow underwing *n* any of several species of noctuid moths, the hind wings of which are yellow with a black bar.

yellowwood ('jɛləuˌwud) *n* **1** any of several leguminous trees of the southeastern US, having clusters of white flowers and yellow wood yielding a yellow dye. **2** Also called: **West Indian satinwood.** a rutaceous tree of the West Indies, with smooth hard wood. **3** any of several other trees with yellow wood, esp. a conifer of southern Africa the wood of which is used for furniture and building. **4** the wood of any of these trees.

yelp (jɛlp) *vb (intr)* **1** (esp. of a dog) to utter a sharp or high-pitched cry or bark, often indicating pain. ◆ *n* **2** a sharp or high-pitched cry or bark. ORIG OE *gielpan* to boast
▸ **'yelper** *n*

Yeltsin ★ ('jɛltsɪn) *n* **Boris (Nicolayevich).** born 1931, Russian politician: president of the Russian Soviet Federative Socialist Republic (1990–91); president of Russia (1991–99).

Yemen ★ ('jɛmən) *n* a republic in SW Arabia, on the Red Sea and the Gulf of Aden: formed in 1990 from the union of North Yemen and South Yemen; in 1994 the northern region won a civil war against the south: consists of arid coastal lowlands, rising to fertile upland valleys and mountains in the W and to the Hadhramaut plateau in the SE: the N and E contains part of the Great Sandy Desert. Official language: Arabic. Official religion: Muslim. Currency: riyal. Capital: San'a. Pop.: 16 942 000 (1999 est.). Area (including territory claimed by Yemen along the undemarcated eastern border with Saudi Arabia): 472 099 sq. km (182 278 sq. miles). Official name: **Yemen Republic.**
▸ **'Yemeni** *adj, n*

yen[1] (jɛn) *n, pl* **yen.** the standard monetary unit of Japan. ORIG C19: from Japanese *en,* from Chinese *yüan* dollar

yen[2] (jɛn) *Inf.* ◆ *n* **1** a longing or desire. ◆ *vb* **yens, yenning, yenned. 2** *(intr)* to yearn. ORIG ?from Chinese *yǎn* a craving

Yenan ★ ('jɛn'æn) *n* a variant transliteration of the Chinese name for **Yanan.**

Yenisei *or* **Yenisey** ★ (ˌjɛnɪ'seɪ; *Russian* jɪnɪ'sjej) *n* a river in central Russia, in central Siberia, formed by the confluence of two headstreams in the Tuva Republic: flows west and north to the Arctic Ocean; the largest river in volume in Russia. Length: 4129 km (2566 miles).

Yentai *or* **Yen-t'ai** ★ ('jɛn'taɪ) *n* a variant transliteration of the Chinese name for **Yantai.**

yeoman ('jəumən) *n, pl* **yeomen. 1** *History.* **1a** a member of a class of small freeholders who cultivated their own land. **1b** an attendant or lesser official in a royal or noble household. **2** (in Britain) another name for **yeoman of the guard. 3** *(modifier)* characteristic of or relating to a yeoman. **4** a petty officer or noncommissioned officer in the Royal Navy or Marines in charge of signals. ORIG C15: ?from *yongman* young man

yeomanly ('jəumənlɪ) *adj* **1** of, relating to, or like a yeoman. **2** having the virtues attributed to yeomen, such as staunchness, loyalty, and courage. ◆ *adv* **3** in a yeomanly manner.

yeoman of the guard *n* a member of the ceremonial bodyguard (**Yeomen of the Guard**) of the British monarch.

yeomanry ('jəumənrɪ) *n* **1** yeomen collectively. **2** (in Britain) a volunteer cavalry force, organized in 1761 for home defence: merged into the Territorial Army in 1907.

yep (jɛp) *sentence substitute.* an informal word for **yes.**

yerba *or* **yerba maté** ('jɜːbə) *n* another name for **maté.** ORIG from Sp. *yerba maté* herb maté

Yerevan ★ (*Russian* jɪrɪ'van) *n* the capital of Armenia: founded in the 8th century B.C.; a main focus of trade routes since ancient times; industrial centre; university. Pop.: 1 248 700 (1995 est.). Also called: **Erevan** or **Erivan.**

★ people and places

Yerwa-Maiduguri ★ ('jɜːwəˌmaɪdʊ'guːrɪ) *n* another name for **Maiduguri.**

yes (jɛs) *sentence substitute.* **1** used to express affirmation, consent, agreement, or approval or to answer when one is addressed. **2** used to signal someone to speak or keep speaking, enter a room, or do something. ◆ *n* **3** an answer or vote of *yes.* **4** (*often pl*) a person who votes in the affirmative. ORIG OE *gēse,* from *iā sīe* may it be

yeshiva (jə'ʃiːvə; *Hebrew* jə'ʃiːva) *n, pl* **yeshivahs** *or* **yeshivoth** (*Hebrew* -vɔt). **1** a traditional Jewish school devoted chiefly to the study of the Talmud. **2** a school run by Orthodox Jews for children of primary school age, providing both religious and secular instruction. ORIG from Heb. *yĕshībhāh* a seat, hence, an academy

Yeşil Irmak ★ (jɛ'ʃiːl ɪə'mɑːk) *n* a river in N Turkey, flowing northwest to the Black Sea. Length: 418 km (260 miles). Ancient name: **Iris.**

Yeşilköy ★ (jɛ'ʃilˌkœi) *n* the Turkish name for **San Stefano.**

yes man *n* a servile, submissive, or acquiescent subordinate, assistant, or associate.

yester ('jɛstə) *adj Arch.* of or relating to yesterday: *yester sun.* ORIG OE *geostror*

yester- *prefix* indicating a period of time before the present one: *yesteryear.* ORIG OE *geostran*

yesterday ('jɛstədɪ, -ˌdeɪ) *n* **1** the day immediately preceding today. **2** (*often pl*) the recent past. ◆ *adv* **3** on or during the day before today. **4** in the recent past.

yesteryear ('jɛstəˌjɪə) *Formal or literary.* ◆ *n* **1** last year or the past in general. ◆ *adv* **2** during last year or the past in general.

yestreen (jɛ'striːn) *adv Scot.* yesterday evening. ORIG C14: from YEST(E)R- + E(V)EN[2]

yet (jɛt) *sentence connector.* **1** nevertheless; still; in spite of that: *I want to and yet I haven't the courage.* ◆ *adv* **2** (*usually used with a negative or interrogative*) so far; up until then or now: *they're not home yet; is it teatime yet?* **3** (often preceded by *just; usually used with a negative*) now (as contrasted with later): *we can't stop yet.* **4** (*often used with a comparative*) even; still: *yet more old potatoes for sale.* **5** eventually in spite of everything: *we'll convince him yet.* **6** **as yet.** so far; up until then or now. ORIG OE *gēta*

yeti ('jɛtɪ) *n* another term for **abominable snowman.** ORIG C20: from Tibetan

Yevtushenko ★ (ˌjɛvtuː'ʃɛŋkəʊ; *Russian* jɪftu'ʃɛnkə) *n* **Yevgeny Aleksandrovich** (jɪv'gjenij alɪk'sandrəvitʃ). born 1933, Russian poet. His poetry includes *Babi Yar* (1962), *Bratsk Station* (1966), and *Farewell to Red Banner* (1992).

yew (juː) *n* **1** any coniferous tree of the Old World and North America having flattened needle-like leaves, fine-grained elastic wood, and cuplike red waxy cones resembling berries. **2** the wood of any of these trees, used to make bows for archery. **3** *Archery.* a bow made of yew. ORIG OE *īw*

Yeysk ★ (*Russian* jejsk) *n* a variant spelling of **Yeisk.**

Yezd ★ (jɛzd) *n* a variant of **Yazd.**

Y-fronts *pl n Trademark.* boys' or men's underpants having a front opening within an inverted Y shape.

Yggdrasil *or* **Ygdrasil** ('ɪgdrəsɪl) *n Norse myth.* the ash tree that was thought to bind together earth, heaven, and hell with its roots and branches. ORIG ON (prob. meaning: Uggr's horse), from *Uggr* a name of Odin, from *yggr, uggr* frightful + *drasill* horse, from ?

YHA *abbrev. for* Youth Hostels Association.

YHVH *or* **YHWH** *Bible.* the letters of the **Tetragrammaton.**

Yibin ('jiː'bɪn) *or* **I-pin** ★ *n* a port in S central China, in Sichuan province: a commercial centre. Pop.: 241 019 (1990 est.).

Yichang ('jiː'tʃæŋ), **Ichang,** *or* **I-ch'ang** ★ *n* a port in S central China, in Hubei province on the Yangtze River 1600 km (1000 miles) from the East China Sea: head of navigation of the Yangtze. Pop.: 371 601 (1990 est.).

yid (jɪd) *n Sl.* a derogatory word for a **Jew.** ORIG C20: prob. from *Yiddish,* from MHG *Jude* JEW

Yiddish ('jɪdɪʃ) *n* **1** a language spoken as a vernacular by Jews in Europe and elsewhere by Jewish emigrants, usually written in the Hebrew alphabet. It is a dialect of High German with an admixture of words of Hebrew, Romance, and Slavonic origin. ◆ *adj* **2** in or relating to this language. ORIG C19: from G *jüdisch,* from *Jude* JEW

Yiddisher ('jɪdɪʃə) *adj* **1** in or relating to Yiddish. **2** Jewish. ◆ *n* **3** a speaker of Yiddish; Jew.

yield (jiːld) *vb* **1** to give forth or supply (a product, result, etc.), esp. by cultivation, labour, etc.; produce or bear. **2** (*tr*) to furnish as a return: *the shares yielded three per cent.* **3** (*tr;* often foll. by *up*) to surrender or relinquish, esp. as a result of force, persuasion, etc. **4** (*intr;* sometimes foll. by *to*) to give way, submit, or surrender, as through force or persuasion: *she yielded to his superior knowledge.* **5** (*intr;* often foll. by *to*) to agree; comply; assent: *he eventually yielded to their request for money.* **6** (*tr*) to grant or allow; concede: *to yield right of way.* ◆ *n* **7** the result, product, or amount yielded. **8** the profit or return, as from an investment or tax. **9** the annual income provided by an investment. **10** the energy released by the explosion of a nuclear weapon expressed in terms of the amount of TNT necessary to produce the same energy. **11** *Chem.* the quantity of a specified product obtained in a reaction or series of reactions. ORIG OE *gieldan*
▸ **'yieldable** *adj* ▸ **'yielder** *n*

yielding ('jiːldɪŋ) *adj* **1** compliant, submissive, or flexible. **2** pliable or soft: *a yielding material.*

yield point *n* the stress at which an elastic material under increasing stress ceases to behave elastically; the elongation becomes greater than the increase in stress.

Yin and Yang (jɪn) *n* two complementary principles of Chinese philosophy: Yin is negative, dark, and feminine, Yang is positive, bright, and masculine. ORIG from Chinese *yin* dark + *yang* bright

Yinchuan, Yin-ch'uan, *or* **Yinchwan** ★ ('jɪn'tʃwɑːn) *n* a city in N central China, capital of the Ningxia Hui AR, on the Yellow River. Pop.: 356 652 (1990 est.).

Yingkou *or* **Yingkow** ★ ('jɪŋ'kaʊ) *n* a port in NE China, in SW Liaoning province: a major shipping centre for Manchuria. Pop.: 421 589 (1990 est.).

yippee (jɪ'piː) *interj* an exclamation of joy, pleasure, anticipation, etc.

yips (jɪps) *pl n* **the.** *Inf.* (in sport) nervous twitching or tension that destroys concentration. ORIG C20: from ?

Y2K ('waɪ'tuː'keɪ) *n Inf.* another name for the year 2000 A.D. (esp. referring to the millennium bug). ORIG C20: *y(ear)* + *2* + K (in the sense: thousand)

-yl *suffix forming nouns.* (in chemistry) indicating a group or radical: *methyl.* ORIG from Gk *hulē* wood

ylang-ylang ('iːlæŋ'iːlæŋ) *n* **1** an aromatic Asian tree with fragrant greenish-yellow flowers yielding a volatile oil. **2** the oil obtained from this tree, used in perfumery. ORIG C19: from Tagalog *ilang-ilang*

ylem ('aɪləm) *n* the original matter from which the basic elements are said to have been formed following the explosion postulated in the big-bang theory of cosmology. ORIG ME, from OF *ilem,* from L *hȳlē* stuff, from Gk *hulē* wood

YMCA *abbrev. for* Young Men's Christian Association.

Ymir ('iːmɪə) *or* **Ymer** ★ ('iːmə) *n Norse myth.* the first being and forefather of the giants. He was slain by Odin and his brothers, who made the earth from his flesh, the water from his blood, and the sky from his skull.

-yne *suffix forming nouns.* denoting an organic chemical containing a triple bond: *alkyne.* ORIG alteration of -INE[2]

yo (jəʊ) *sentence substitute.* an expression used as a greeting, to attract someone's attention, etc. ORIG C20: of unknown origin

yob (jɒb) *or* **yobbo** ('jɒbəʊ) *n, pl* **yobs** *or* **yobbos.** *Brit. sl.* an aggressive and surly youth, esp. a teenager. ORIG C19: ? back sl. for BOY
▸ **'yobbery** *n* ▸ **'yobbish** *adj*

yodel ('jəʊdᵊl) *n* **1** an effect produced in singing by an abrupt change of register from the chest voice to falsetto, esp. in folk songs of the Swiss Alps. ◆ *vb* **yodels, yodelling, yodelled** *or US* **yodels, yodeling, yodeled. 2** to sing (a

song) in which a yodel is used. ORIG C19: from G *jodeln,* imit.
▸ **'yodeller** *n*

yoga ('jəʊgə) *n* (*often cap.*) **1** a Hindu system of philosophy aiming at the mystical union of the self with the Supreme Being in a state of complete awareness and tranquillity through certain physical and mental exercises. **2** any method by which such awareness and tranquillity are attained, esp. a course of related exercises and postures. ORIG C19: from Sansk.: a yoking, from *yunakti* he yokes
▸ **yogic** ('jəʊgɪk) *adj*

yogh (jɒg) *n* **1** a character (ʒ) used in Old and Middle English to represent a palatal fricative very close to the semivowel sound of Modern English *y.* **2** this same character as used in Middle English for both the voiced and voiceless palatal fricatives; when final or in a closed syllable in medial position the sound approached that of German *ch* in *ich,* as in *knyʒt* (knight). ORIG C14: ?from *yok* yoke, from the letter's shape

yogi ('jəʊgɪ) *n, pl* **yogis** *or* **yogin** (-gɪn). a person who is a master of yoga.

yogurt *or* **yoghurt** ('jəʊgət, jɒg-) *n* a thick custard-like food prepared from milk curdled by bacteria, often sweetened and flavoured with fruit. ORIG C19: from Turkish *yoğurt*

Yogyakarta (ˌjəʊgjɑː'kɑːtɑː, 'jɒg-), **Jogjakarta, Jokjakarta,** *or* **Djokjakarta** ★ *n* a city in S Indonesia, in central Java: seat of government of Indonesia (1946–49); university (1949). Pop.: 419 500 (1995 est.).

yo-heave-ho (ˌjəʊhiːv'həʊ) *interj* a cry formerly used by sailors while pulling or lifting together in rhythm.

yohimbine (jəʊ'hɪmbiːn) *n* an alkaloid found in the bark of a West African tree and used in medicine. ORIG C19: from Bantu *yohimbé* a tropical African tree + -INE[1]

yo-ho-ho *interj* **1** an exclamation to call attention. **2** another word for **yo-heave-ho.**

yoicks (haɪk; *spelling pron* jɔɪks) *interj* a cry used by fox-hunters to urge on the hounds.

yoke (jəʊk) *n, pl* **yokes** *or* **yoke. 1** a wooden frame, usually consisting of a bar with an oxbow at either end, for attaching to the necks of a pair of draught animals, esp. oxen, so that they can be worked as a team. **2** something resembling a yoke in form or function, such as a frame fitting over a person's shoulders for carrying buckets. **3** a fitted part of a garment, esp. around the neck, shoulders, and chest or around the hips, to which a gathered, pleated, flared, or unfitted part is attached. **4** an oppressive force or burden: *under the yoke of a tyrant.* **5** a pair of oxen or other draught animals joined by a yoke. **6** a part that secures two or more components so that they move together. **7** (in the ancient world) a symbolic yoke, consisting of two upright spears with a third lashed across them, under which conquered enemies were compelled to march, esp. in Rome. **8** a mark, token, or symbol of slavery, subjection, or suffering. **9** *Now rare.* a link, tie, or bond: *the yoke of love.* ◆ *vb* **yokes, yoking, yoked. 10** (*tr*) to secure or harness (a draught animal) to (a plough, vehicle, etc.) by means of a yoke. **11** to join or be joined by means of a yoke; couple, unite, or link. ORIG OE *geoc*

yokel ('jəʊkᵊl) *n Disparaging.* (used chiefly by townspeople) a person who lives in the country, esp. one who appears to be simple and old-fashioned. ORIG C19: ?from dialect *yokel* green woodpecker

Yokohama ★ (ˌjəʊkəʊ'hɑːmə) *n* a port in central Japan, on SE Honshu on Tokyo Bay: a major port and the country's second largest city situated in the largest and most populous industrial region of Japan. Pop.: 3 307 408 (1995).

Yokosuka ★ (ˌjəʊkəʊ'suːkə) *n* a port in Japan, in SE Honshu: a major naval base with shipbuilding industries. Pop.: 432 202 (1995).

yolk (jəʊk) *n* **1** the substance in an animal ovum that nourishes the developing embryo. **2** a greasy substance in the fleece of sheep. ORIG OE *geoloca,* from *geolu* yellow
▸ **'yolky** *adj*

yolk sac *n Zool.* the membranous sac that is attached to the surface of the embryos of birds, reptiles, and some fishes, and contains yolk.

Yom Kippur (jɒm 'kɪpə; *Hebrew* jɔm ki'pur) *n* an annual Jewish day of fasting, on which prayers of penitence are recited in the synagogue. Also called: **Day of Atonement.** ORIG from Heb., from *yōm* day + *kippūr* atonement

yomp (jɒmp) *vb* (*intr*) to walk or trek laboriously, esp. over difficult terrain. ORIG C20: mil. sl., from ?

yon (jɒn) *determiner* **1** *Chiefly Scot. & N English.* **1a** an archaic or dialect word for **that:** *yon man.* **1b** (*as pronoun*): *yon's a fool.* **2** a variant of **yonder.** ORIG OE *geon*

yond (jɒnd) *Obs. or dialect.* ◆ *adj* **1** the farther, more distant. ◆ *determiner* **2** a variant of **yon.**

yonder ('jɒndə) *adv* **1** at, in, or to that relatively distant place; over there. ◆ *determiner* **2** being at a distance, either within view or as if within view: *yonder valleys.* ORIG C13: from OE *geond* yond

yoni ('jəʊnɪ) *n Hinduism.* **1** the female genitalia, regarded as a divine symbol of sexual pleasure and matrix of generation. **2** an image of these as an object of worship. ORIG C18: from Sansk., lit.: vulva

Yonkers ★ ('jɒŋkəz) *n* a city in SE New York State, near New York City on the Hudson River. Pop.: 183 490 (1994 est.).

yonks (jɒŋks) *pl n Inf.* a very long time; ages: *I haven't seen him for yonks.* ORIG C20: from ?

Yonne ★ (*French* jɔn) *n* **1** a department of N central France, in Burgundy region. Capital: Auxerre. Pop.: 330 794 (1994 est.). Area: 7461 sq. km (2910 sq. miles). **2** a river in N France, flowing generally northwest to the Seine at Montereau. Length: 290 km (180 miles).

yoo-hoo ('juːˌhuː) *interj* a call to attract a person's attention.

YOP (jɒp) *n* (formerly, in Britain) **a** *acronym for* Youth Opportunities Programme. **b** (*as modifier*): *a YOP scheme.*

yore (jɔː) *n* **1** time long past (now only in **of yore**). ◆ *adv* **2** *Obs.* in the past; long ago. ORIG OE *geāra,* genitive pl of *gēar* year

york (jɔːk) *vb* (*tr*) *Cricket.* to bowl (a batsman) by pitching the ball under or just beyond the bat. ORIG C19: back formation from YORKER

York[1] ★ (jɔːk) *n* **1** a walled city in NE England, in North Yorkshire, on the River Ouse: the military capital of Roman Britain; capital of the N archiepiscopal province of Britain since 625, with a cathedral (the Minster) begun in 1154; noted for its cycle of medieval mystery plays; seat of The University of York (1963). Pop.: 104 100 (1994 est.). Latin name: **Eboracum. 2** a unitary authority in NE England, in North Yorkshire. Pop.: 124 100 (1996 est.). Area: 272 sq. km (105 sq. miles). **3 Cape.** a cape in NE Australia, in Queensland at the N tip of Cape York Peninsula, extending into Torres Strait: the northernmost point of Australia.

York[2] ★ (jɔːk) *n* **1** the English royal house, a branch of the Plantagenet line, that reigned from 1461 to 1485. **2 Alvin C(ullum).** 1887–1964, US soldier and hero of World War I. **3 Prince Andrew, Duke of.** born 1960, second son of Elizabeth II of Great Britain and Northern Ireland. He married (1986) Miss Sarah Ferguson; they separated in 1992; their first daughter, Princess Beatrice of York, was born in 1988 and their second, Princess Eugenie of York, in 1990.

Yorke Peninsula ★ (jɔːk) *n* a peninsula in South Australia, between Spencer Gulf and St Vincent Gulf: mainly agricultural with several coastal resorts.

yorker ('jɔːkə) *n Cricket.* a ball bowled so as to pitch just under or just beyond the bat. ORIG C19: prob. after the *Yorkshire* County Cricket Club

yorkie ('jɔːkɪ) *n* short for **Yorkshire terrier.**

Yorkist ('jɔːkɪst) *English history.* ◆ *n* **1** a member or adherent of the royal House of York, esp. during the Wars of the Roses. ◆ *adj* **2** of, belonging to, or relating to the supporters or members of the House of York.

Yorks (jɔːks) *abbrev. for* Yorkshire.

Yorkshire ★ ('jɔːkˌʃɪə, -ʃə) *n* a historic county of N England: it was the largest English county, divided administratively into East, West, and North Ridings. In 1974 it was divided into the new counties of North, West, and South Yorkshire. The East Riding of Yorkshire was reinstated as a county in 1996.

Yorkshire Dales ★ *pl n* the valleys of the rivers flowing from the Pennines in W Yorkshire: chiefly Airedale, Ribblesdale, Teesdale, Swaledale, Nidderdale, Wharfedale, and Wensleydale; tourist area. Also called: **the Dales.**

Yorkshire pudding ('jɔːkʃɪə) *n Chiefly Brit.* a light puffy baked pudding made from a batter of flour, eggs, and milk, traditionally served with roast beef.

Yorkshire terrier *n* a very small breed of terrier with a long straight glossy coat of steel-blue and tan. Also called: **yorkie.**

Yorktown ★ ('jɔːkˌtaʊn) *n* a village in SE Virginia: scene of the surrender (1781) of the British under Cornwallis to the Americans under Washington at the end of the War of American Independence.

Yoruba ('jɒrʊbə) *n* **1** (*pl* **Yorubas** *or* **Yoruba**) a member of a Negroid people of W Africa, living chiefly in the coastal regions of SW Nigeria. **2** the language of this people.
▸ '**Yoruban** *adj*

Yosemite Falls ★ (jəʊ'sɛmɪtɪ) *pl n* a series of waterfalls in central California, in the Yosemite National Park, with a total drop of 770 m (2525 ft): includes the **Upper Yosemite Falls,** 436 m (1430 ft) high, and the **Lower Yosemite Falls,** 98 m (320 ft) high.

Yosemite National Park ★ *n* a national park in central California, in the Sierra Nevada Mountains: contains the **Yosemite Valley,** at an altitude of about 1200 m (4000 ft), with sheer walls rising about another 1200 m (4000 ft). Area: 3061 sq. km (1182 sq. miles).

Yoshihito ★ (ˌjɒʃɪ'hiːtəʊ) *n* See **Taisho.**

Yoshkar-Ola ★ (*Russian* jaʃ'kara'la) *n* a city in Russia, capital of the Mari El Republic. Pop.: 251 000 (1995 est.).

you (juː; *unstressed* jʊ) *pron* (*subjective or objective*) **1** refers to the person addressed or to more than one person including the person or persons addressed: *you know better; the culprit is among you.* **2** refers to an unspecified person or people in general: *you can't tell the boys from the girls.* ◆ *n* **3** *Inf.* the personality of the person being addressed: *that hat isn't really you.* **4 you know what** *or* **who.** a thing or person that the speaker does not want to specify. ORIG OE *ēow,* dative & accusative of *gē* ye

USAGE NOTE See at **me**[1].

you'd (juːd; *unstressed* jʊd) *contraction of* you had *or* you would.

you'll (juːl; *unstressed* jʊl) *contraction of* you will *or* you shall.

young (jʌŋ) *adj* **younger** ('jʌŋgə), **youngest** ('jʌŋgɪst). **1a** having lived, existed, or been made or known for a relatively short time: *a young country.* **1b** (*as collective n;* preceded by *the*): *the young.* **2** youthful or having qualities associated with youth; vigorous or lively. **3** of or relating to youth: *in my young days.* **4** having been established or introduced for a relatively short time: *a young member.* **5** in an early stage of progress or development; not far advanced: *the day was young.* **6** (*often cap.*) of or relating to a rejuvenated group or movement or one claiming to represent the younger members of the population: *Young Socialists.* ◆ *n* **7** (*functioning as pl*) offspring, esp. young animals: *a rabbit with her young.* **8 with young.** (of animals) pregnant. ORIG OE *geong*
▸ '**youngish** *adj*

Young ★ (jʌŋ) *n* **1 Brigham** ('brɪgəm). 1801–77, US Mormon leader, who led the Mormon migration to Utah and founded Salt Lake City (1847). **2 Edward.** 1683–1765, English poet and dramatist, noted for his *Night Thoughts on Life, Death, and Immortality* (1742–45). **3 Lester.** 1909–59, US saxophonist and clarinettist. **4 Neil.** born 1945, Canadian rock guitarist, singer, and songwriter. His albums include *Harvest* (1972). **5 Thomas.** 1773–1829, British physicist, physician, and Egyptologist. He helped to establish the wave theory of light by his experiments on optical interference and assisted in deciphering the Rosetta Stone.

young blood *n* young, fresh, or vigorous new people, ideas, attitudes, etc.

Young Fogey *n* a young person who adopts the conservative values of an older generation.

young gun *n* an up-and-coming young man, esp. one considered as being assertive and confident.

young lady *n* a girlfriend; sweetheart.

youngling ('jʌŋlɪŋ) *n Literary.* **a** a young person, animal, or plant. **b** (*as modifier*): *a youngling brood.* ORIG OE *geongling*

young man *n* a boyfriend; sweetheart.

young offender institution *n* (in Britain) a place where offenders aged 15 to 21 may be detained and given training, instruction, and work. Former names: **borstal, youth custody centre.**

Young Pretender ★ *n* See (Charles Edward) **Stuart.**

Young's modulus *n* a modulus of elasticity, applicable to the stretching of a wire, etc., equal to the ratio of the applied load per unit area of cross section to the increase in length per unit length. ORIG after Thomas Young

youngster ('jʌŋstə) *n* **1** a young person; child or youth. **2** a young animal, esp. a horse.

Youngstown ★ ('jʌŋzˌtaʊn) *n* a city in NE Ohio: a major centre of steel production: university (1908). Pop.: 91 775 (1994 est.).

Young Turk *n* **1** a progressive, revolutionary, or rebellious member of an organization, political party, etc. **2** a member of an abortive reform movement in the Ottoman Empire.

younker ('jʌŋkə) *n* **1** *Arch. or literary.* a young man; lad. **2** *Obs.* a young gentleman or knight. ORIG C16: from Du. *jonker,* from MDu. *jonc* young

your (jɔː, jʊə; *unstressed* jə) *determiner* **1** of, belonging to, or associated with you: *your nose; your house.* **2** belonging to or associated with an unspecified person or people in general: *the path is on your left heading north.* **3** *Inf.* used to indicate all things or people of a certain type: *your part-time worker is a problem.* ORIG OE *eower,* genitive of *gē* ye

you're (jɔː; *unstressed* jə) *contraction of* you are.

yours (jɔːz, jʊəz) *pron* **1** something or someone belonging to or associated with you. **2** your family: *greetings to you and yours.* **3** used in conventional closing phrases at the end of a letter: *yours sincerely; yours faithfully.* **4 of yours.** belonging to or associated with you.

yourself (jɔː'sɛlf, jʊə-) *pron, pl* **yourselves. 1a** the reflexive form of *you.* **1b** (intensifier): *you yourself control your fate.* **2** (*preceded by a copula*) your usual self: *you're not yourself.*

yours truly *pron* an informal term for *I* or *me.* ORIG from the closing phrase of letters

youth (juːθ) *n, pl* **youths** (juːðz). **1** the quality or condition of being young, immature, or inexperienced: *his youth told against him in the contest.* **2** the period between childhood and maturity. **3** the freshness, vigour, or vitality characteristic of young people. **4** any period of early development. **5** a young person, esp. a young man or boy. **6** young people collectively: *youth everywhere is rising in revolt.* ORIG OE *geogoth*

Youth ★ (juːθ) *n* **Isle of.** an island in the NW Caribbean, south of Cuba: administratively part of Cuba from 1925. Chief town: Nueva Gerona. Pop.: 73 319 (1990 est.). Area: 3061 sq. km (1182 sq. miles). Former name: **Isle of Pines.** Spanish name: **Isla de la Juventud** ('izla ðe la xuβen'tuð).

youth club *n* a centre providing leisure activities for young people.

youthful ('juːθfʊl) *adj* **1** of, relating to, possessing, or characteristic of youth. **2** fresh, vigorous, or active: *he's surprisingly youthful for his age.* **3** in an early stage of development: *a youthful culture.* **4** Also: **young.** (of a river, valley, or land surface) in the early stage of the cycle of erosion, characterized by steep slopes, lack of flood plains, and V-shaped valleys.
▸ '**youthfully** *adv* ▸ '**youthfulness** *n*

youth hostel *n* one of an organization of inexpensive

lodging places for people travelling cheaply. Often shortened to **hostel**.

Youth Training Scheme *n* (formerly, in Britain) a scheme, run by the Training Agency, to provide vocational training for unemployed 16–17-year-olds. Abbrev.: **YTS**.

you've (juːv; *unstressed* jʊv) *contraction of* you have.

yowl (jaʊl) *vb* **1** to express with or produce a loud mournful wail or cry; howl. ◆ *n* **2** a wail or howl. ORIG C13: from ON *gaula*
▸ **'yowler** *n*

yo-yo ('jəʊjəʊ) *n, pl* **yo-yos**. **1** a toy consisting of a spool attached to a string, the end of which is held while it is repeatedly spun out and reeled in. **2** *Sl., chiefly US.* a silly or insignificant person. ◆ *vb* **yo-yos, yo-yoing, yo-yoed.** (*intr*) **3** to change repeatedly from one position to another; fluctuate. ORIG from Filipino *yo yo* come come, a weapon consisting of a spindle attached to a thong

Ypres ★ (*French* iprə) *n* a town in W Belgium, in W Flanders province near the border with France: scene of many sieges and battles, esp. in World War I, when it was completely destroyed. Pop.: 21 400 (1991 est.). Flemish name: **Ieper**.

Ypsilanti (ˌɪpsɪ'læntɪ), **Hypsilantis**, *or* **Hypsilantes** ★ *n* **1 Alexander** (ˌalek'sander). 1792–1828, Greek patriot, who led an unsuccessful revolt against the Turks (1821). **2** his brother, **Demetrios** (ðimitri'ɔs). 1793–1832, Greek revolutionary leader; commander in chief of Greek forces (1828–30) during the war of independence.

yr *abbrev. for:* **1** (*pl* **yrs**) year. **2** younger. **3** your.

yrs *abbrev. for:* **1** years. **2** yours.

Yser ★ (*French* izɛr) *n* a river in NW central Europe, rising in N France and flowing through SW Belgium to the North Sea: scene of battles in World War I. Length: 77 km (48 miles).

Yseult ★ (ɪ'suːlt) *n* a variant spelling of **Iseult**.

Yssel ★ ('aɪsᵊl) *n* a variant spelling of **IJssel**.

YST (in Canada) *abbrev. for* Yukon Standard Time.

YT *abbrev. for* Yukon Territory.

YTS (in Britain) *abbrev. for* Youth Training Scheme.

ytterbia (ɪ'tɜːbɪə) *n* another name for **ytterbium oxide**. ORIG C19: NL; see YTTERBIUM

ytterbium (ɪ'tɜːbɪəm) *n* a soft malleable silvery element of the lanthanide series of metals that is used to improve the mechanical properties of steel. Symbol: Yb; atomic no.: 70; atomic wt.: 173.04. ORIG C19: NL, after *Ytterby*, Swedish quarry where discovered

ytterbium oxide *n* a weakly basic hygroscopic substance used in certain alloys and ceramics.

yttria ('ɪtrɪə) *n* another name for **yttrium oxide**. ORIG C19: NL; see YTTERBIUM

yttrium ('ɪtrɪəm) *n* a silvery metallic element used in various alloys, in lasers, and as a catalyst. Symbol: Y; atomic no.: 39; atomic wt.: 88.90. ORIG C19: NL; see YTTERBIUM

yttrium metal *n Chem.* any one of a group of elements including yttrium and the related lanthanides.

yttrium oxide *n* a colourless or white insoluble solid used in incandescent mantles.

yuan ('juː'æn) *n, pl* **yuan**. the standard monetary unit of China. ORIG from Chinese *yüan* round object; see YEN[1]

Yüan[1] ★ ('juː'æn) *n* the imperial dynasty of China from 1279 to 1368.

Yüan[2] ('juː'æn) *or* **Yüen** ★ ('juː'ɛn) *n* a river in SE central China, rising in central Guizhou province and flowing northeast to Lake Tungting. Length: about 800 km (500 miles).

Yuan Tan ('juː'æn 'tæn) *n* an annual Chinese festival marking the Chinese New Year. It can last over three days and includes the exchange of gifts, firework displays, and dancing.

Yucatán ★ (ˌjuːkə'tɑːn; *Spanish* juka'tan) *n* **1** a state of SE Mexico, occupying the N part of the Yucatán peninsula. Capital: Mérida. Pop.: 1 617 120 (1997 est.). Area: 39 340 sq. km (15 186 sq. miles). **2** a peninsula of Central America between the Gulf of Mexico and the Caribbean, including the Mexican states of Campeche, Yucatán, and Quintana Roo, and part of Belize: a centre of Mayan civilization from about 100 B.C. to the 18th century. Area: about 181 300 sq. km (70 000 sq. miles).

Yucatán Channel ★ *n* a channel between W Cuba and the Yucatán peninsula.

yucca ('jʌkə) *n* any of a genus of liliaceous plants of tropical and subtropical America, having stiff lancelike leaves and spikes of white flowers. ORIG C16: from American Sp. *yuca*, ult. from Amerind

yuck *or* **yuk** (jʌk) *interj Sl.* an exclamation indicating contempt, dislike, or disgust.

yucky *or* **yukky** ('jʌkɪ) *adj* **yuckier, yuckiest** *or* **yukkier, yukkiest.** *Sl.* disgusting; nasty.

Yugo. *abbrev. for* Yugoslavia.

Yugoslav *or* **Jugoslav** ★ ('juːgəʊˌslɑːv) *n* **1** a native or inhabitant of Yugoslavia. **2** (not in technical use) another name for **Serbo-Croat** (the language). ◆ *adj* **3** of, relating to, or characteristic of Yugoslavia or its people.

Yugoslavia *or* **Jugoslavia** ★ (ˌjuːgəʊ'slɑːvɪə) *n* **1 Federal Republic of Yugoslavia.** a country, comprising Serbia and Montenegro, that was formed in 1991, but has not been internationally recognized, mainly because of Serbia's role in the civil war in Bosnia-Herzegovina. It is mainly mountainous and rugged, with the fertile Danube-Sava Basin in the northeast. **2** a former country in SE Europe, on the Adriatic: established in 1918 from the independent states of Serbia and Montenegro, and regions that until World War I had belonged to Austria-Hungary (Croatia, Slovenia, and Bosnia-Herzegovina); the name was changed from Kingdom of Serbs, Croats, and Slovenes to Yugoslavia in 1929; German invasion of 1941–44 was resisted chiefly by a Communist group led by Tito, who declared a people's republic in 1945; it became the Socialist Federal Republic of Yugoslavia in 1963; in 1991, following political crises, Croatia, Slovenia, and Bosnia-Herzegovina declared independence, followed by Macedonia in 1992.
▸ ˌ**Yugo'slavian** *or* ˌ**Jugo'slavian** *adj, n*

Yukawa ★ (juː'kɑːwə) *n* **Hideki** ('hiːdekɪ). 1907–81, Japanese nuclear physicist, who predicted (1935) the existence of mesons: Nobel prize for physics 1949.

Yukon ★ ('juːkɒn) *n* **the**. a territory of NW Canada, on the Beaufort Sea, between the Northwest Territories and Alaska: arctic and mountainous, reaching 6050 m (19 850 ft) at Mount Logan, Canada's highest peak; mineral resources. Capital: Whitehorse. Pop.: 30 688 (1999 est.). Area: 536 327 sq. km (207 076 sq. miles). Abbrev.: **YT**.
▸ **'Yukoner** *n*

Yukon River ★ *n* a river in NW North America, rising in NW Canada on the border between the Yukon Territory and British Columbia: flows northwest into Alaska, US, and then southwest to the Bering Sea; navigable for about 2850 km (1775 miles) to Whitehorse. Length: 3185 km (1979 miles).

yulan ('juːlæn) *n* a Chinese magnolia that is often cultivated for its showy white flowers. ORIG C19: from Chinese, from *yu* a gem + *lan* plant

yule (juːl) *n* (*sometimes cap.*) *Literary, arch., or dialect.* **a** Christmas or the Christmas season. **b** (*in combination*): *yuletide*. ORIG OE *geōla*, orig. a pagan feast lasting 12 days

yule log *n* a large log of wood traditionally used as the foundation of a fire at Christmas.

yummy ('jʌmɪ) *Sl.* ◆ *interj* **1** Also: **yum-yum**. an exclamation indicating pleasure or delight, as in anticipation of delicious food. ◆ *adj* **yummier, yummiest. 2** delicious, delightful, or attractive. ORIG C20: from *yum-yum*, imit.

Yünnan ★ (juː'næn) *n* a province of SW China: consists mainly of a plateau broken in the southeast by the Red and Black Rivers, with mountains in the west, rising over 5500 m (18 000 ft); large deposits of tin, lead, zinc, and coal. Capital: Kunming. Pop.: 40 940 000 (1997 est.). Area: 436 200 sq. km (168 400 sq. miles).

yuppie *or* **yuppy** (ˈjʌpɪ) (*sometimes cap.*) ◆ *n* **1** an affluent young professional person. ◆ *adj* **2** typical of or reflecting the values characteristic of yuppies. ORIG C20: from *y(oung) u(rban)* or *up(wardly mobile) p(rofessional)* + -IE
▸ ˈ**yuppiedom** *n*

yuppie disease *or* **flu** *n Inf., sometimes considered offens.* any of a number of debilitating long-lasting viral disorders associated with stress, such as chronic fatigue syndrome, whose symptoms include muscle weakness, chronic tiredness, and depression.

yuppify (ˈjʌpɪˌfaɪ) *vb* **yuppifies, yuppifying, yuppified.** (*tr*) to make yuppie in nature.
▸ ˌ**yuppifiˈcation** *n*

Yurev ★ (*Russian* ˈjurjɪf) *n* the former name (11th century until 1918) of **Tartu.**

yurt (juət) *n* a circular tent consisting of a framework of poles covered with felt or skins, used by Mongolian and Turkic nomads of E and central Asia. ORIG from Russian *yurta,* of Turkic origin

Yuzovka ★ (*Russian* ˈjuzəfkə) *n* a former name (1872 until after the Revolution) of **Donetsk.**

Yvelines ★ (*French* ivlin) *n* a department of N France, in Île de France region. Capital: Versailles. Pop.: 1 363 068 (1994 est.). Area: 2271 sq. km (886 sq. miles).

YWCA *abbrev. for* Young Women's Christian Association.

Zz

z *or* **Z** (zɛd; *US* ziː) *n, pl* **z's, Z's,** *or* **Zs. 1** the 26th and last letter of the English alphabet. **2** a speech sound represented by this letter. **3a** something shaped like a Z. **3b** (*in combination*): *a Z-bend in a road.*

z *Maths. symbol for:* **1** the *z*-axis or a coordinate measured along the *z*-axis in a Cartesian or cylindrical coordinate system. **2** an algebraic variable.

Z *symbol for:* **1** any unknown, variable, or unspecified factor, number, person, or thing. **2** *Chem.* atomic number. **3** *Physics.* impedance. **4** zone.

z. *abbrev. for:* **1** zero. **2** zone.

Zaandam ★ (*Dutch* zaːnˈdɑm) *n* a former town in the W Netherlands, in North Holland: an important shipbuilding centre in the 17th century. It became part of Zaanstad in 1974.

Zaanstad ★ (*Dutch* zaːnˈʃtat) *n* a port in the W Netherlands, in North Holland: formed (1974) from Zaandam, Koog a/d Zaan, Zaandijk, Wormerveer, Krommenie, Westzaan, and Assendelft; food and machinery industries. Pop.: 132 508 (1994).

zabaglione (ˌzæbəˈljəʊnɪ) *n* a light foamy dessert made of egg yolks, sugar, and marsala, whipped together and served warm in a glass. ORIG It.

Zabrze ★ (*Polish* ˈzabʒɛ) *n* a city in SW Poland: a Prussian and German town from 1742 until 1945, when it passed to Poland; industrial centre in a coal-mining region. Pop.: 201 800 (1995 est.). German name: **Hindenburg.**

Zacatecas ★ (*Spanish* θakaˈtekas) *n* **1** a state of N central Mexico, on the central plateau: rich mineral resources. Capital: Zacatecas. Pop.: 1 332 683 (1997 est.). Area: 75 040 sq. km (28 973 sq. miles). **2** a city in N central Mexico, capital of Zacatecas state: silver mines. Pop.: 100 051 (1990).

Zacharias (ˌzækəˈraɪəs), **Zachariah** (ˌzækəˈraɪə), *or* **Zachary** ★ (ˈzækərɪ) *n New Testament.* John the Baptist's father, who underwent a temporary period of dumbness for his lack of faith (Luke 1).

Zacynthus ★ (zəˈsɪnθəs, -ˈkɪn-) *n* the Latin name for **Zante.**

zaffer *or* **zaffre** (ˈzæfə) *n* impure cobalt oxide, used to impart a blue colour to enamels. ORIG C17: from It. *zaffera*

Zagazig (ˈzægəˌzɪg) *or* **Zaqaziq** ★ *n* a city in NE Egypt, in the Nile Delta: major cotton market. Pop.: 287 000 (1992 est.).

Zagreb ★ (ˈzɑːgrɛb) *n* the capital of Croatia, on the River Sava; university (1874); industrial centre. Pop.: 867 717 (1991). German name: **Agram.**

Zagreus ★ (ˈzægrɪəs) *n Greek myth.* a young god whose cult came from Crete to Greece, where he was identified with Dionysus. The son of Zeus by either Demeter or Persephone, he was killed by the Titans at the behest of Hera.

Zagros Mountains ★ (ˈzægrɒs) *pl n* a mountain range in S Iran: has Iran's main oilfields in its W central foothills. Highest peak: Zard Kuh, 4548 m (14 920 ft).

zaibatsu (ˈzaɪbætˈsuː) *n* (*functioning as sing or pl*) the group or combine comprising a few wealthy families that controls industry, business, and finance in Japan. ORIG from Japanese, from *zai* wealth + *batsu* family, person of influence

Zaïre ★ (zɑːˈɪə) *n* **1** the former name (1971–97) of the (Democratic Republic of) **Congo** (sense 1). **2** (formerly) the Zaïrean name for the (River) **Congo.**
▸ **Zaˈïrean** *or* **ˌZaïrˈese** *adj, n*

Zákinthos ★ (ˈzakinˌθɔs) *n* transliteration of the Modern Greek name for **Zante.**

zakuski *or* **zakouski** (zæˈkʊskɪ) *pl n, sing* **zakuska** *or* **zakouska** (-kə). *Russian cookery.* hors d'oeuvres, consisting of tiny open sandwiches spread with caviar, smoked sausage, etc., or a cold dish such as radishes in sour cream, all usually served with vodka. ORIG Russian, from *zakusit'* to have a snack

Zama ★ (ˈzɑːmə) *n* the name of several ancient cities in N Africa, including the one near the site of Scipio's decisive defeat of Hannibal (202 B.C.).

Zambezi *or* **Zambese** ★ (zæmˈbiːzɪ) *n* a river in S central and E Africa, rising in NW Zambia and flowing across E Angola back into Zambia, continuing south to the Caprivi Strip of Namibia, then east forming the Zambia–Zimbabwe border, and finally crossing Mozambique to the Indian Ocean: the fourth longest river in Africa. Length: 2740 km (1700 miles).
▸ **Zamˈbezian** *adj*

Zambia ★ (ˈzæmbɪə) *n* a republic in southern Africa: an early site of human settlement; controlled by the British South Africa Company by 1900 and unified as Northern Rhodesia in 1911; made a British protectorate in 1924; part of the Federation of Rhodesia and Nyasaland (1953–63), gaining independence as a member of the Commonwealth in 1964; important mineral exports, esp. copper. Official language: English. Religion: Christian majority, also animist. Currency: kwacha. Capital: Lusaka. Pop.: 9 664 000 (1999 est.). Area: 752 617 sq. km (290 587 sq. miles). Former name (until 1964): **Northern Rhodesia.**
▸ **ˈZambian** *adj, n*

Zamboanga ★ (ˌzæmbəʊˈæŋgə) *n* a port in the Philippines, on SW Mindanao on Basilan Strait: founded by the Spanish in 1635; tourist centre, with fisheries. Pop.: 464 466 (1994 est.).

zambuck *or* **zambuk** (ˈzæmbʌk) *n Austral. & NZ inf.* a first-aid attendant at a sports event. ORIG from name of a proprietary ointment

Zamenhof ★ (*Polish* ˈzamɛnxɔf) *n* **Lazarus Ludwig** (laˈzarus ˈludvik). 1859–1917, Polish oculist; invented Esperanto.

Zamora ★ (*Spanish* θaˈmora) *n* a city in NW central Spain, on the Douro River. Pop.: 58 560 (1980).

Zamyatin ★ (*Russian* zaˈmjatin) *n* **Yevgenii Ivanovich** (jɪvˈgjenij ɪˈvanəvitʃ). 1884–1937, Russian writer, in Paris from 1931, whose works include the novel *We* (1924).

Zante ★ (ˈzæntɪ) *n* an island in the Ionian Sea, off the W coast of Greece: southernmost of the Ionian Islands; traditionally belonged to Ulysses, king of Ithaca. Pop.: 32 557 (1991). Area: 402 sq. km (155 sq. miles). Latin name: **Zacynthus.** Ancient Greek name: **Zakynthos** (zəˈkuːnθɒs). Modern Greek name: **Zákinthos.**

Zanu (PF) (ˈzɑːnuː) *n* the ruling political party in Zimbabwe ORIG C20: from *Z*(*imbabwe*) *A*(*frican*) *N*(*ational*) *U*(*nion*) + *P*(*atriotic*) *F*(*ront*)

zany (ˈzeɪnɪ) *adj* **zanier, zaniest. 1** comical in an endearing way; imaginatively funny or comical, esp. in behaviour. ◆ *n, pl* **zanies. 2** a clown or buffoon, esp. one in old comedies who imitated other performers with ludicrous effect. **3** a ludicrous or foolish person. ORIG C16: from It. *zanni,* from dialect *Zanni,* nickname for *Giovanni* John; one of the traditional names for a clown
▸ **ˈzanily** *adv* ▸ **ˈzaniness** *n*

Zanzibar ★ (ˌzænzɪˈbɑː) *n* an island in the Indian Ocean, off the E coast of Africa: settled by Persians and Arabs from the 7th century onwards; became a flourishing trading centre for slaves, ivory, and cloves; made a British protectorate in 1890, becoming independent within the Commonwealth in 1963 and a republic in 1964; joined with Tanganyika in 1964 to form the United Republic of Tanzania. Pop.: 444 000 (1994 est.).
▸ **ˌZanziˈbari** *adj, n*

zap (zæp) *Sl.* ◆ *vb* **zaps, zapping, zapped. 1** (*tr*) to attack, kill, or destroy, as with a sudden bombardment. **2** (*intr*) to move quickly. **3** (*tr*) *Computing.* **3a** to clear from the screen. **3b** to erase. **4** (*intr*) *Television.* to change channels

★ people and places

rapidly by remote control. ◆ *n* **5** energy, vigour, or pep. ◆ *interj* **6** an exclamation used to express sudden or swift action. ORIG C20: imit.

Zapata ★ (zəˈpɑːtə; *Spanish* θaˈpata) *n* **Emiliano** (emiˈljano). ?1877–1919, Mexican guerrilla leader.

zapateado *Spanish.* (ˌθapateˈaðo) *n, pl* ***-dos*** (-ðos). a Spanish dance with stamping and very fast footwork. ORIG from *zapatear* to tap with the shoe, from *zapato* shoe

Zaporozhye ★ (*Russian* zəpaˈrɔʒjɛ) *n* a city in E Ukraine, on the Dnieper River: developed as a major industrial centre following the construction in 1932 of the Dnieper hydroelectric station. Pop.: 882 000 (1996 est.). Former name (until 1921): **Aleksandrovsk**.

Zappa ★ (ˈzæpə) *n* **Frank**. 1940–93, US rock musician, songwriter, and producer: leader of the Mothers of Invention.

zappy (ˈzæpɪ) *adj* **zappier, zappiest.** *Sl.* full of energy; zippy.

ZAPU (ˈzæpuː) *n acronym for* Zimbabwe African People's Union.

Zaqaziq ★ (ˈzækəˌzɪk) *n* a variant of **Zagazig**.

Zaragoza ★ (*Spanish* θaraˈɣoθa) *n* a city in NE Spain, on the River Ebro: Roman colony established 25 B.C.; under Moorish rule (714–1118); capital of Aragon (12th–15th centuries); twice besieged by the French during the Peninsular War and captured (1809); university (1474). Pop.: 596 080 (1986). Pre-Roman name: **Salduba**. Latin name: **Caesaraugusta**. English name: **Saragossa**.

Zarathustra ★ (ˌzærəˈθuːstrə) *n* the Avestan name of **Zoroaster**.
▸ **ˌZaraˈthustrian** *or* **ˌZaraˈthustric** *adj, n*

zareba *or* **zareeba** (zəˈriːbə) *n* (in northern E Africa, esp. formerly) **1** a stockade or enclosure of thorn bushes around a village or camp site. **2** the area so protected or enclosed. ORIG C19: from Ar. *zarībah* cattlepen, from *zarb* sheepfold

zarf (zɑːf) *n* (esp. in the Middle East) a holder, usually ornamental, for a hot coffee cup. ORIG from Ar.: container

Zaria ★ (ˈzɑːrɪə) *n* a city in N central Nigeria: former capital of a Hausa state; agricultural trading centre; university (1962). Pop.: 369 800 (1995 est.).

Zarqa ★ (ˈzɑːkə) *n* the second largest town in Jordan, northeast of Amman. Pop.: 344 524 (1994).

zarzuela (zɑːˈzweɪlə) *n* **1** a type of Spanish vaudeville or operetta, usually satirical in nature. **2** a seafood stew. ORIG from Sp., after *La Zarzuela,* the palace near Madrid where such vaudeville was first performed (1629)

Zátopek ★ (*Czech* ˈzaːtɔpɛk) *n* **Emil** (ˈemil). 1922–2000, Czech runner; winner of the 5000 and 10 000 metres and the marathon at the 1952 Olympic Games in Helsinki.

z-axis *n* a reference axis of a three-dimensional Cartesian coordinate system along which the *z*-coordinate is measured.

ZB station *n* (in New Zealand) a radio station of a commercial network.

Z chart *n Statistics.* a chart often used in industry and constructed by plotting on it three series: monthly, weekly, or daily data, the moving annual total, and the cumulative total dating from the beginning of the current year.

Zea ★ (ˈtsɛːa) *n* the Italian name for **Keos**.

zeal (ziːl) *n* fervent or enthusiastic devotion, often extreme or fanatical in nature, as to a religious movement, political cause, ideal, or aspiration. ORIG C14: from LL *zēlus,* from Gk *zēlos*

Zealand ★ (ˈziːlənd) *n* the largest island of Denmark, separated from the island of Funen by the Great Belt and from S Sweden by the Sound. Chief town: Copenhagen. Pop.: 2 000 254 (1988 est.). Area: 7016 sq. km (2709 sq. miles). Danish name: **Sjælland**. German name: **Seeland**.

zealot (ˈzɛlət) *n* an immoderate, fanatical, or extremely zealous adherent to a cause, esp. a religious one. ORIG C16: from LL *zēlōtēs,* from Gk, from *zēloun* to be zealous, from *zēlos* zeal
▸ **ˈzealotry** *n*

Zealot (ˈzɛlət) *n* any of the members of an extreme Jewish sect or political party that resisted all aspects of Roman rule in Palestine in the 1st century A.D.

zealous (ˈzɛləs) *adj* filled with or inspired by intense enthusiasm or zeal; ardent; fervent.
▸ **ˈzealously** *adv* ▸ **ˈzealousness** *n*

Zeami or **Seami** ★ (siːˈɑːmɪ) *n* **Motokiyo** (ˌməʊtəʊˈkiːəʊ). 1363–1443, Japanese No dramatist.

zebec *or* **zebeck** (ˈziːbɛk) *n* variant spellings of **xebec**.

Zebedee ★ (ˈzɛbɪˌdiː) *n New Testament.* the father of the apostles James and John (Matthew 4:21).

zebra (ˈziːbrə, ˈzɛbrə) *n, pl* **zebras** *or* **zebra.** any of several mammals of the horse family, such as the common zebra of southern and eastern Africa, having distinctive black-and-white striped hides. ORIG C16: via It. from OSp.: wild ass, prob. from Vulgar L *eciferus* (unattested) wild horse, from L *equiferus,* from *equus* horse + *ferus* wild
▸ **zebrine** (ˈziːbraɪn, ˈzɛb-) *or* **ˈzebroid** *adj*

Zebra (ˈziːbrə, ˈzɛbrə) *n Finance.* a noninterest-paying bond in which the accrued income is taxed annually rather than on redemption. Cf. **zero** (sense 10). ORIG C20: from *zero-coupon bond*

zebra crossing *n Brit.* a pedestrian crossing marked on a road by broad alternate black and white stripes. Once on the crossing the pedestrian has right of way.

zebra finch *n* any of various Australasian songbirds with zebra-like markings.

zebrawood (ˈzɛbrəˌwʊd, ˈziː-) *n* **1** a tree of tropical America, Asia, and Africa, yielding striped hardwood used in cabinetwork. **2** any of various other trees or shrubs having striped wood. **3** the wood of any of these trees.

zebu (ˈziːbuː) *n* a domesticated ox having a humped back, long horns, and a large dewlap: used in India and E Asia as a draught animal. ORIG C18: from F *zébu,* ? of Tibetan origin

Zebulun ★ (ˈzɛbjʊlən, zəˈbjuː-) *n Old Testament.* **1** the sixth son whom Leah bore to Jacob: one of the 12 patriarchs of Israel (Genesis 30:20). **2** the tribe descended from him. **3** the territory of this tribe, lying in lower Galilee to the north of Mount Carmel and to the east of the coastal plain. Douay spelling: **Zabulon** (ˈzæbjʊlən, zəˈbjuː-).

Zech. *Bible. abbrev. for* Zechariah.

Zechariah ★ (ˌzɛkəˈraɪə) *n* **1** *Old Testament.* **1a** a Hebrew prophet of the late 6th century B.C. **1b** the book containing his oracles, which are chiefly concerned with the renewal of Israel after the exile as a national, religious, and messianic community with the restored Temple and rebuilt Jerusalem as its centre. Douay spelling: **Zacharias. 2** a variant spelling of **Zachariah**. See **Zacharias**.

zed (zɛd) *n* the British and Canadian spoken form of the letter *z.* ORIG C15: from OF *zede,* via LL from Gk *zēta*

Zedekiah ★ (ˌzɛdəˈkaɪə) *n Old Testament.* the last king of Judah, who died in captivity at Babylon. Douay spelling: **Sedecias** (ˌsɛdəˈkaɪəs).

zedoary (ˈzɛdəʊərɪ) *n* the dried rhizome of a tropical Asian plant, used as a stimulant and a condiment. ORIG C15: from Med. L *zedoaria,* from Ar. *zadwār,* of Persian origin

zee (ziː) *n* the US word for **zed** (letter *z*).

Zeebrugge ★ (*Flemish* ˈzeːbryxə; *English* ˈziːˌbrʊgə) *n* a port in NW Belgium, in W Flanders on the North Sea: linked by canal with Bruges; German submarine base in World War I.

Zeeland ★ (*Dutch* ˈzeːlɑnt; *English* ˈziːlənd) *n* a province of the SW Netherlands: consists of a small area on the mainland together with a number of islands in the Scheldt estuary; mostly below sea level. Capital: Middelburg. Pop.: 368 400 (1997 est.). Area: 1787 sq. km (690 sq. miles).
▸ **ˈZeelander** *n*

Zeeman effect (ˈziːmən) *n* the splitting of a spectral line of a substance into several closely spaced lines when the substance is placed in a magnetic field. ORIG C20: after Pieter *Zeeman* (1865–1943), Du. physicist

Zeffirelli ★ (ˌzɛfɪˈrɛlɪ; *Italian* dzɛffiˈrɛlli) *n* **Franco** (ˈfraŋko). born 1923, Italian stage and film director and designer, noted for his work in opera.

zein (ˈziːɪn) *n* a protein occurring in maize and used in the manufacture of plastics, paper coatings, adhesives, etc. ORIG C19: from NL *zēa* maize, from L: a kind of grain, from Gk *zeia* barley

Zeist ★ (zaɪst; *Dutch* zɛjst) *n* a city in the central Netherlands, near Utrecht. Pop.: 59 258 (1994).

Zeitgeist *German.* ('tsaɪtˌgaɪst) *n* the spirit, attitude, or general outlook of a specific time or period, esp. as it is reflected in literature, philosophy, etc. ORIG G, lit.: time spirit

Zen (zɛn) *Buddhism.* *n* **1** a Japanese school, of 12th-century Chinese origin, teaching that contemplation of one's essential nature to the exclusion of all else is the only way of achieving pure enlightenment. **2** (*modifier*) of or relating to this school: *Zen Buddhism.* ORIG from Japanese, from Chinese *ch'an* religious meditation, from Pali *jhāna,* from Sansk. *dhyāna*
▸ **'Zenic** *adj* ▸ **'Zenist** *n*

zenana (zɛ'nɑːnə) *n* (in the East, esp. in Muslim and Hindu homes) part of a house reserved for the women and girls of a household. ORIG C18: from Hindi *zanāna,* from Persian, from *zan* woman

Zend (zɛnd) *n* **1** a former name for **Avestan. 2** short for **Zend-Avesta. 3** an exposition of the Avesta in the Middle Persian language (Pahlavi). ORIG C18: from Persian *zand* commentary, exposition; used specifically of the MPersian commentary on the Avesta, hence of the language of the Avesta itself
▸ **'Zendic** *adj*

Zend-Avesta (ˌzɛndə'vɛstə) *n* the Avesta together with the traditional interpretive commentary known as the Zend, esp. as preserved in the Avestan language among the Parsees. ORIG from Avestan, representing *Avesta'-va-zend* Avesta with interpretation

Zener diode ('ziːnə) *n* a semiconductor diode that exhibits a sharp increase in reverse current at a well-defined reverse voltage: used as a voltage regulator. ORIG C20: after C. M. *Zener* (1905–93), US physicist

zenith ('zɛnɪθ) *n* **1** *Astron.* the point on the celestial sphere vertically above an observer. **2** the highest point; peak; acme: *the zenith of someone's achievements.* ORIG C17: from F *cenith,* from Med. L, from OSp. *zenit,* based on Ar. *samt,* as in *samt arrās* path over one's head
▸ **'zenithal** *adj*

zenithal projection *n* a type of map projection in which part of the earth's surface is projected onto a plane tangential to it, either at one of the poles (**polar zenithal**), at the equator (**equatorial zenithal**), or between (**oblique zenithal**).

Zenobia ★ (zɪ'nəʊbɪə) *n* 3rd century A.D., queen of Palmyra (?267–272), who was captured by the Roman emperor Aurelian.

Zeno of Citium ★ ('ziːnəʊ əv 'sɪtɪəm) *n* ?336–?264 B.C., Greek philosopher, who founded the Stoic school in Athens.

Zeno of Elea ★ *n* ?490–?430 B.C., Greek Eleatic philosopher; disciple of Parmenides.

zeolite ('ziːəˌlaɪt) *n* **1** any of a large group of glassy secondary minerals consisting of hydrated aluminium silicates of calcium, sodium, or potassium: formed in cavities in lava flows and plutonic rocks. **2** any of a class of similar synthetic materials used in ion exchange and as selective absorbents. ORIG C18: *zeo-,* from Gk *zein* to boil + -LITE; from the swelling that occurs under the blowpipe
▸ **zeolitic** (ˌziːə'lɪtɪk) *adj*

Zeph. *Bible. abbrev. for* Zephaniah.

Zephaniah ★ (ˌzɛfə'naɪə) *n Old Testament.* **1** a Hebrew prophet of the late 7th century B.C. **2** the book containing his oracles, which are chiefly concerned with the approaching judgment by God upon the sinners of Judah. Douay spelling: **Sophonias** (ˌsɒfə'naɪəs).

zephyr ('zɛfə) *n* **1** a soft or gentle breeze. **2** any of several delicate soft yarns, fabrics, or garments, usually of wool. ORIG C16: from L *zephyrus,* from Gk *zephuros* the west wind

Zephyrus ★ ('zɛfərəs) *n Greek myth.* the god of the west wind.

zeppelin ('zɛpəlɪn) *n* (*sometimes cap.*) a large cylindrical rigid airship built from 1900 to carry passengers and used in World War I for bombing and reconnaissance. ORIG C20: after Count von ZEPPELIN

Zeppelin ★ (*German* 'tsɛpəliːn) *n* Count **Ferdinand von** ('fɛrdinant fɔn). 1838–1917, German aeronautical pioneer, who designed and manufactured airships (zeppelins).

Zermatt ★ (*German* tsɛr'mat) *n* a village and resort in S Switzerland, in Valais canton at the foot of the Matterhorn: cars are banned from the area. Pop.: 4200 (1989 est.).

zero ('zɪərəʊ) *n, pl* **zeros** *or* **zeroes. 1** the symbol 0, indicating an absence of quantity or magnitude; nought. Former name: **cipher. 2** the integer denoted by the symbol 0; nought. **3** the cardinal number between +1 and –1. **4** nothing; nil. **5** a person or thing of no significance; nonentity. **6** the lowest point or degree: *his prospects were put at zero.* **7** the line or point on a scale of measurement from which the graduations commence. **8a** the temperature, pressure, etc., that registers a reading of zero on a scale. **8b** the value of a variable, such as temperature, obtained under specified conditions. **9** *Maths.* **9a** the cardinal number of a set with no members. **9b** the identity element of addition. **10** *Finance.* Also called: **zero-coupon bond.** a bond that pays no interest, the equivalent being paid in its redemption value. Cf. **Zebra.** ◆ *adj* **11** having no measurable quantity, magnitude, etc. **12** *Meteorol.* **12a** (of a cloud ceiling) limiting visibility to 15 metres (50 feet) or less. **12b** (of horizontal visibility) limited to 50 metres (165 feet) or less. ◆ *vb* **zeros** *or* **zeroes, zeroing, zeroed. 13** (*tr*) to adjust (an instrument, apparatus, etc.) so as to read zero or a position taken as zero. ◆ *determiner* **14** *Inf., chiefly US.* no (thing) at all: *this job has zero interest.* ◆ See also **zero in.** ORIG C17: from It., from Med. L *zephirum,* from Ar. *sifr* empty

zero gravity *n* the state or condition of weightlessness.

zero hour *n* **1** *Mil.* the time set for the start of an attack or the initial stage of an operation. **2** *Inf.* a critical time, esp. at the commencement of an action.

zero in *vb* (*adv*) **1** (often foll. by *on*) to bring (a weapon) to bear (on a target), as while firing repeatedly. **2** (*intr;* foll. by *on*) *Inf.* to bring one's attention to bear (on a problem, etc.). **3** (*intr;* foll. by *on*) *Inf.* to converge (upon): *the police zeroed in on the site of the crime.*

zero option *n* (in international nuclear arms negotiations) an offer to remove all shorter-range nuclear missiles or, in the case of the **zero-zero option** all intermediate-range nuclear missiles, if the other side will do the same.

zero-rated *adj* denoting goods on which the buyer pays no value-added tax although the seller can claim back any tax he has paid.

zero stage *n* a solid-propellant rocket attached to a liquid-propellant rocket to provide greater thrust at liftoff.

zeroth ('zɪərəʊθ) *adj* denoting a term in a series that precedes the term otherwise regarded as the first term. ORIG C20: from ZERO + -TH[2]

zero tolerance *n* **a** the policy of applying laws or penalties to even minor infringements of a code in order to reinforce its overall importance. **b** (*as modifier*): *a zero-tolerance policy on drugs.*

zest (zɛst) *n* **1** invigorating or keen excitement or enjoyment: *a zest for living.* **2** added interest, flavour, or charm; piquancy: *her presence gave zest to the party.* **3** something added to give flavour or relish. **4** the peel or skin of an orange or lemon, used as flavouring in drinks, etc. ◆ *vb* **5** (*tr*) to give flavour, interest, or piquancy to. ORIG C17: from F *zeste* peel of citrus fruits used as flavouring, from ?
▸ **'zestful** *adj* ▸ **'zestfully** *adv* ▸ **'zestfulness** *n* ▸ **'zesty** *adj*

zester ('zɛstə) *n* a kitchen utensil used to scrape fine shreds of peel from citrus fruits.

zeta ('ziːtə) *n* the sixth letter in the Greek alphabet (Z, ζ). ORIG from Gk

ZETA ('ziːtə) *n* a torus-shaped apparatus formerly used for research on controlled thermonuclear reactions. ORIG C20: from *z*(*ero-*)*e*(*nergy*) *t*(*hermonuclear*) *a*(*pparatus*)

Zetland ★ ('zɛtlənd) *n* the official name (until 1974) of **Shetland.**

zeugma ('zjuːgmə) *n* a figure of speech in which a word is used to modify or govern two or more words although appropriate to only one of them or making a different sense with each, as in *Mr Pickwick took his hat and his leave*

(Charles Dickens). ORIG C16: via L from Gk: a yoking, from *zeugnunai* to yoke
▸ **zeugmatic** (zjuːg'mætɪk) *adj*

Zeus ★ (zjuːs) *n* the supreme god of the ancient Greeks, who became ruler of gods and men after he dethroned his father Cronus and defeated the Titans. He was the husband of his sister Hera and father by her and others of many gods, demigods, and mortals. He wielded thunderbolts and ruled the heavens, while his brothers Poseidon and Hades ruled the sea and underworld respectively. Roman counterpart: **Jupiter.**

Zeuxis ★ ('zjuːksɪs) *n* late 5th century B.C., Greek painter.

Zhangjiakou ('dʒæŋ'dʒjækəʊ), **Changchiakow,** *or* **Changchiak'ou** ★ *n* a city in NE China, in NW Hebei province: a military centre, controlling the route to Mongolia, under the Ming and Manchu dynasties. Pop.: 529 136 (1990 est.). Former names: **Wanchüan, Kalgan.**

Zhangzhou ('dʒæŋ'dʒəʊ), **Changchow,** *or* **Ch'angchou** ★ *n* **1** a city in E China, in S Jiangsu province, on the Grand Canal: also known as **Wutsin** until 1949, when the 7th-century name was officially readopted. Pop.: 531 470 (1990 est.). **2** a city in SE China, in S Fujian province on the Saikoe River. Pop.: 181 424 (1990 est.). Former name: **Lungki.**

Zhdanov ★ (*Russian* 'ʒdanəf) *n* the former name (1948–91) for **Mariupol.**

Zhejiang ('dʒɜ'dʒjæŋ) *or* **Chekiang** ★ *n* a province of E China: mountainous and densely populated. Capital: Hangzhou. Pop.: 44 350 000 (1997 est.). Area: 102 000 sq. km (39 780 sq. miles).

Zhengzhou ('dʒʌŋ'dʒəʊ), **Chengchow,** *or* **Chengchou** ★ *n* a city in E central China, capital of Henan province. Pop.: 1 710 000 (1991 est.).

Zhitomir ★ (*Russian* ʒi'tɔmir) *n* a city in central Ukraine. Pop.: 301 000 (1996 est.).

Zhivkov ★ (*Bulgarian* 'ʒifkof) *n* **Todor** ('tɔdor). 1911–98, Bulgarian statesman; prime minister (1962–71); president (1971–89).

zho (zəʊ) *n* a variant spelling of **zo.**

Zhou ★ (dʒəʊ) *n* the Pinyin transliteration of the Chinese name for **Chou.**

Zhou En Lai ★ (ɛn laɪ) *n* the Pinyin transliteration of the Chinese name for **Chou En-lai.**

Zhu De ★ ('dʒuː 'deɪ) *n* the Pinyin transliteration of the Chinese name for **Chu Teh.**

Zhu Jiang ('dʒuː 'dʒjæŋ), **Chu Chiang,** *or* **Chu Kiang** ★ *n* a river in SE China, in S Guangdong province, flowing southeast from Canton to the South China Sea. Length: about 177 km (110 miles). Also called: **Canton River, Pearl River.**

Zhukov ★ (*Russian* 'ʒukəf) *n* **Georgi Konstantinovich** (gɪ'ɔrgij kənstan'tinəvitʃ). 1896–1974, Soviet marshal. In World War II, he broke the sieges of Stalingrad and Leningrad (1942–43) and later captured Warsaw and Berlin; minister of defence (1955–57).

Zia ul Haq ★ ('zɪə ʊl 'hak) *n* **Mohammed** (məʊ'hæmɪd). 1924–88, Pakistani general: president (1978–88), following the overthrow (1977) of Z. A. Bhutto by a military coup: killed in an air crash, possibly through sabotage.

zibeline ('zɪbə,laɪn, -lɪn) *n* **1** a sable or the fur of this animal. **2** a thick cloth made of wool or other animal hair, having a long nap and a dull sheen. ◆ *adj* **3** of, relating to, or resembling a sable. ORIG C16: from F, from Olt. *zibellino,* ult. of Slavonic origin

zibet ('zɪbɪt) *n* a large civet of S and SE Asia, having tawny fur marked with black spots and stripes. ORIG C16: from Med. L *zibethum,* from Ar. *zabād* civet

Zibo ('ziː'bɔː), **Tzu-po,** *or* **Tzepo** ★ *n* a city in NE China, in Shandong province. Pop.: 2 460 000 (1991 est.).

zidovudine (zaɪ'dɒvjʊ,diːn) *n* a drug that prolongs life and alleviates symptoms among some AIDS sufferers. Also called: **AZT.**

Ziegfeld ★ ('ziːg,fɛld) *n* **Florenz** ('flɒrənz). 1869–1932, US theatrical producer, noted for his series of extravagant revues (1907–31), known as the Ziegfeld Follies.

ziff (zɪf) *n Austral. inf.* a beard. ORIG C20: from ?

ziggurat ('zɪgʊ,ræt) *n* a type of rectangular temple tower or tiered mound erected by the Sumerians, Akkadians, and Babylonians in Mesopotamia. ORIG C19: from Assyrian *ziqqurati* summit

Zigong ('ziː'gʊŋ), **Tzekung,** *or* **Tzu-kung** ★ *n* an industrial city in W central China, in Sichuan. Pop.: 393 184 (1990 est.).

zigzag ('zɪg,zæg) *n* **1** a line or course characterized by sharp turns in alternating directions. **2** one of the series of such turns. **3** something having the form of a zigzag. ◆ *adj* **4** (*usually prenominal*) formed in or proceeding in a zigzag. **5** (of a sewing machine) capable of producing stitches in a zigzag. ◆ *adv* **6** in a zigzag manner. ◆ *vb* **zigzags, zigzagging, zigzagged. 7** to proceed or cause to proceed in a zigzag. **8** (*tr*) to form into a zigzag. ORIG C18: from F, from G *zickzack,* from *Zacke* point

zigzagger ('zɪg,zægə) *n* **1** a person or thing that zigzags. **2** an attachment on a sewing machine for sewing zigzag stitches, as for joining two pieces of material.

zilch (zɪltʃ) *n Sl.* **1** nothing. **2** *US & Canad. sport.* nil. ORIG C20: from ?

zillion ('zɪljən) *Inf.* ◆ *n, pl* **zillions** *or* **zillion. 1** (*often pl*) an extremely large but unspecified number, quantity, or amount: *zillions of flies in this camp.* ◆ *determiner* **2** amounting to a zillion: *a zillion different problems.* ORIG C20: coinage after MILLION

Zilpah ★ ('zɪlpə) *n Old Testament.* Leah's maidservant, who bore Gad and Asher to Jacob (Genesis 30:10–13).

Zimbabwe ★ (zɪm'bɑːbwɪ, -weɪ) *n* **1** a country in SE Africa, formerly a self-governing British colony founded in 1890 by the British South Africa Company, which administered the country until a self-governing colony was established in 1923; joined with Northern Rhodesia (now Zambia) and Nyasaland (now Malawi) as the Federation of Rhodesia and Nyasaland from 1953 to 1963; made a unilateral declaration of independence under the leadership of Ian Smith in 1965 on the basis of White minority rule; proclaimed a republic in 1970; in 1976 the principle of Black majority rule was accepted and in 1978 a transitional government was set up; gained independence in 1980 following the Lancaster House Conference (1979–80); a member of the Commonwealth. Official language: English. Religion: Christian majority. Currency: Zimbabwe dollar. Capital: Harare. Pop: 11 163 000 (1999 est.). Area: 390 624 sq. km (150 820 sq. miles). Former names: **Southern Rhodesia** (until 1964), **Rhodesia** (1964–79). **2** a ruined fortified settlement in Zimbabwe, which at its height, in the 15th century, was probably the capital of an empire covering SE Africa.
▸ **Zim'babwean** *n, adj*

Zimmer ('zɪmə) *n Trademark.* Also: **Zimmer frame.** another name for **walker** (sense 3).

zinc (zɪŋk) *n* **1** a brittle bluish-white metallic element that is a constituent of several alloys, esp. brass and nickel-silver, and is used in die-casting, galvanizing metals, and in battery electrodes. Symbol: Zn; atomic no.: 30; atomic wt.: 65.37. **2** *Inf.* corrugated galvanized iron. ORIG C17: from G *Zink,* ?from *Zinke* prong, from its jagged appearance in the furnace
▸ **'zincic, 'zincous,** *or* **'zincoid** *adj* ▸ **'zincky, 'zincy,** *or* **'zinky** *adj*

zinc blende *n* another name for **sphalerite.**

zinc chloride *n* a white soluble poisonous granular solid used in manufacturing parchment paper and vulcanized fibre and in preserving wood. It is also a soldering flux, embalming agent, and medical astringent and antiseptic.

zincite ('zɪŋkaɪt) *n* a red or yellow mineral consisting of zinc oxide in hexagonal crystalline form. It occurs in metamorphosed limestone.

zincography (zɪŋ'kɒgrəfɪ) *n* the art or process of etching on zinc to form a printing plate.
▸ **zincograph** ('zɪŋkə,grɑːf) *n* ▸ **zin'cographer** *n*

zinc ointment *n* a medicinal ointment consisting of zinc oxide, petrolatum, and paraffin, used to treat certain skin diseases.

zinc oxide *n* a white insoluble powder used as a pigment in paints (**zinc white** or **Chinese white**), cosmetics,

★ people and places

glass, and printing inks. It is an antiseptic and astringent and is used in making zinc ointment. Formula: ZnO. Also called: **flowers of zinc.**

zinc sulphate *n* a colourless soluble crystalline substance used as a mordant, in preserving wood and skins, and in the electrodeposition of zinc. Also called: **zinc vitriol.**

zine (zi:n) *n Inf.* a magazine or fanzine.

zing (zɪŋ) *n Inf.* **1** a short high-pitched buzzing sound, as of a bullet or vibrating string. **2** vitality; zest. ◆ *vb* **3** (*intr*) to make or move with or as if with a high-pitched buzzing sound. ORIG C20: imit.
▸ **'zingy** *adj*

zinjanthropus (zɪn'dʒænθrəpəs) *n* a type of australopithecine, remains of which were discovered in the Olduvai Gorge in Tanzania in 1959. ORIG C20: NL, from Ar. *Zinj* East Africa + Gk *anthrōpos* man

zinnia ('zɪnɪə) *n* any of a genus of annual or perennial plants of the composite family, of tropical and subtropical America, having solitary heads of brightly coloured flowers. ORIG C18: after J. G. *Zinn* (d. 1759), G botanist

Zinoviev ★ (*Russian* zi'nɔvjɪf) *n* **Grigori Yevseevich** (gri-'gɔrij jɪf'sjejɪvitʃ), original name *Ovsel Gershon Aronov Radomyslsky*. 1883–1936, Soviet politician: executed. He was the alleged author of the 'Zinoviev letter' urging British Communists to revolt, publication of which helped to defeat (1924) the first Labour Government.

Zinovievsk ★ (*Russian* zi'nɔvjɪfsk) *n* a former name (1924–36) for **Kirovograd.**

Zion ('zaɪən) *or* **Sion** ★ *n* **1** the hill on which the city of Jerusalem stands. **2** *Judaism.* **2a** the ancient Israelites of the Bible. **2b** the modern Jewish nation. **2c** Israel as the national home of the Jewish people. **3** *Christianity.* heaven regarded as the city of God and the final abode of his elect.

Zionism ('zaɪəˌnɪzəm) *n* **1** a political movement for the establishment and support of a national homeland for Jews in Palestine, now concerned chiefly with the development of the modern state of Israel. **2** a policy or movement for Jews to return to Palestine from the Diaspora.
▸ **'Zionist** *n, adj* ▸ **ˌZion'istic** *adj*

zip (zɪp) *n* **1a** Also called: **zip fastener.** a fastening device operating by means of two parallel rows of metal or plastic teeth on either side of a closure that are interlocked by a sliding tab. US and Canad. term: **zipper. 1b** (*modifier*) having such a device: *a zip bag.* **2** a short sharp whizzing sound, as of a passing bullet. **3** *Inf.* energy; vigour; vitality. **4** *US sl.* nothing. **5** *Sport, US & Canad. sl.* nil. ◆ *vb* **zips, zipping, zipped. 6** (*tr;* often foll. by *up*) to fasten (clothing, etc.) with a zip. **7** (*intr*) to move with a zip: *the bullet zipped past.* **8** (*intr;* often foll. by *along, through,* etc.) to hurry; rush. ORIG C19: imit.

zip code *n* the US equivalent of **postcode.** ORIG C20: from *z(one) i(mprovement) p(lan)*

zip gun *n US & Canad. sl.* a crude home-made pistol, esp. one powered by a spring or rubber band.

zipper ('zɪpə) *n* the US & Canad. word for **zip** (sense 1a).

zippy ('zɪpɪ) *adj* **zippier, zippiest.** *Inf.* full of energy; lively.

zircalloy (zɜ:k'ælɔɪ) *n* an alloy of zirconium containing small amounts of tin, chromium, and nickel. It is used in pressurized-water reactors.

zircon ('zɜ:kɒn) *n* a reddish-brown, grey, green, blue, or colourless hard mineral consisting of zirconium silicate: it is used as a gemstone and a refractory. ORIG C18: from G *Zirkon,* from F *jargon,* via It. & Ar., from Persian *zargūn* golden

zirconium (zɜ:'kəʊnɪəm) *n* a greyish-white metallic element, occurring chiefly in zircon, that is exceptionally corrosion-resistant and has low neutron absorption. It is used as a coating in nuclear and chemical plants, as a deoxidizer in steel, and alloyed with niobium in superconductive magnets. Symbol: Zr; atomic no.: 40; atomic wt.: 91.22. ORIG C19: from NL; see ZIRCON
▸ **zirconic** (zɜ:'kɒnɪk) *adj*

zirconium oxide *n* a white amorphous powder that is insoluble in water and highly refractory, used as a pigment for paints, a catalyst, and an abrasive.

Ziska ('zɪskə) *or* **Žižka** ★ (*Czech* 'ʒiʃka) *n* **Jan** (jan). ?1370–1424, Bohemian soldier, who successfully led the Hussite rebellion (1420–24) against emperor Sigismund.

zit (zɪt) *n Sl.* a pimple. ORIG from ?

zither ('zɪðə) *n* a plucked musical instrument consisting of numerous strings stretched over a resonating box, a few of which may be stopped on a fretted fingerboard. ORIG C19: from G, from L *cithara,* from Gk *kithara*
▸ **'zitherist** *n*

Zlatoust ★ (*Russian* zləta'ust) *n* a town in W Russia, on the Ay river: one of the chief metallurgical centres of the Urals. Pop.: 203 000 (1995 est.).

zloty ('zlɒtɪ) *n, pl* **zlotys** *or* **zloty.** the standard monetary unit of Poland. ORIG from Polish: golden, from *zlyoto* gold

Zn *the chemical symbol for* zinc.

zo, zho, *or* **dzo** (zəʊ) *n, pl* **zos, zhos, dzos** *or* **zo, zho, dzo.** a Tibetan breed of cattle, developed by crossing the yak with common cattle. ORIG C20: from Tibetan

zo- *combining form.* a variant of **zoo-** before a vowel.

-zoa *suffix forming plural proper nouns.* indicating groups of animal organisms: *Metazoa.* ORIG from NL, from Gk *zōia,* pl. of *zōion* animal

Zoan ★ ('zəʊæn) *n* the Biblical name for **Tanis.**

zodiac ('zəʊdɪˌæk) *n* **1** an imaginary belt extending 8° either side of the ecliptic, which contains the 12 **zodiacal constellations** and within which the moon and planets appear to move. It is divided into 12 equal areas, called **signs of the zodiac,** each named after the constellation which once lay in it. **2** *Astrol.* a diagram, usually circular, representing this belt and showing the symbols, illustrations, etc., associated with each of the 12 signs of the zodiac, used to predict the future. ORIG C14: from OF *zodiaque,* from L *zōdiacus,* from Gk *zōidiakos* (*kuklos*) (circle) of signs, from *zōidion* animal sign, from *zōion* animal
▸ **zodiacal** (zəʊ'daɪəkəl) *adj*

zodiacal constellation *n* any of the 12 constellations after which the signs of the zodiac are named: Aries, Taurus, Gemini, Cancer, Leo, Virgo, Libra, Scorpio, Sagittarius, Capricorn, Aquarius, or Pisces.

zodiacal light *n* a very faint cone of light in the sky, visible in the east just before sunrise and in the west just after sunset.

Zoffany ★ ('zɒfənɪ) *n* **John** *or* **Johann** ?1733–1810, British portrait painter, born in Germany.

Zog I ★ (zɒg) *n* 1895–1961, king of Albania (1928–39), formerly prime minister (1922–24) and president (1925–28).

zoic ('zəʊɪk) *adj* **1** relating to or having animal life. **2** *Geol.* (of rocks, etc.) containing fossilized animals. ORIG C19: from NL, from Gk *zōion* animal

-zoic *adj and n combining form.* indicating a geological era: *Palaeozoic.* ORIG from Gk *zōē* life + -IC

Zola ★ ('zəʊlə; *French* zɔla) *n* **Émile** (emil). 1840–1902, French novelist, noted for *Les Rougon-Macquart* (1871–93), a cycle of 20 novels that includes *Nana* (1880), *Germinal* (1885), and *La Terre* (1887). He defended Dreyfus in his pamphlet *J'accuse* (1898).

Zollverein *German.* ('tsɔlfɛrˌain) *n* the customs union of German states organized in the early 1830s under Prussian auspices. ORIG C19: from *Zoll* tax + *Verein* union

Zomba ★ ('zɒmbə) *n* a city in S Malawi: the capital of Malawi until 1971. Pop.: 62 700 (1994 est.).

zombie *or* **zombi** ('zɒmbɪ) *n, pl* **zombies** *or* **zombis. 1** a person who is or appears to be lifeless, apathetic, or totally lacking in independent judgment; automaton. **2** a supernatural spirit that reanimates a dead body. **3** a corpse brought to life in this manner. ORIG from W African *zumbi* good-luck fetish

zonation (zəʊ'neɪʃən) *n* arrangement in zones.

zone (zəʊn) *n* **1** a region, area, or section characterized by some distinctive feature or quality. **2** an area subject to a particular political, military, or government function, use, or jurisdiction: *a demilitarized zone.* **3** (*often cap.*) *Geog.* one of the divisions of the earth's surface, esp. divided into latitudinal belts according to temperature. See **Torrid Zone, Frigid Zone, Temperate Zone. 4** *Geol.* a distinctive layer or region of rock, characterized by particular fossils (**zone**

fossils), etc. **5** *Ecology.* an area, esp. a belt of land, having a particular flora and fauna determined by the prevailing environmental conditions. **6** *Maths.* a portion of a sphere between two parallel planes intersecting the sphere. **7** *Sport.* **7a** a period during which a competitor is performing particularly well: *Hingis is in the zone at the moment.* **7b** (*modifier*) of or relating to competitive performance that depends on the mood or state of mind of the participant: *a zone player.* **8** *Arch. or literary.* a girdle or belt. **9** *NZ.* a section on a transport route; fare stage. **10** *NZ.* a catchment area for a specific school. ◆ *vb* **zones, zoning, zoned.** (*tr*) **11** to divide into zones, as for different use, jurisdiction, activities, etc. **12** to designate as a zone. **13** to mark with or divide into zones. ORIG C15: from L *zōna* girdle, climatic zone, from Gk *zōnē*
▸ **'zonal** *adj* ▸ **'zonated** *adj* ▸ **'zoning** *n*

zone refining *n* a technique for producing solids of extreme purity, esp. for use in semiconductors. The material, in the form of a bar, is melted in one small region that is passed along the solid. Impurities concentrate in the melt and are moved to the end of the bar.

zonetime ('zəʊn,taɪm) *n* the standard time of the time zone in which a ship is located at sea, each zone extending 7½° to each side of a meridian.

zonked (zɒŋkt) *adj Sl.* **1** incapacitated by drugs or alcohol. **2** exhausted. ORIG C20: imit.

zonk out (zɒŋk) *vb* (*intr, adv*) *Sl.* to fall asleep, esp. from physical exhaustion or the effects of alcohol or drugs.

zoo (zuː) *n, pl* **zoos.** a place where live animals are kept, studied, bred, and exhibited to the public. Formal term: **zoological garden.** ORIG C19: shortened from *zoological gardens* (orig. those in London)

zoo- *or before a vowel* **zo-** *combining form.* indicating animals: *zooplankton.* ORIG from Gk *zōion* animal

zoogeography (,zəʊədʒɪ'ɒgrəfɪ) *n* the branch of zoology concerned with the geographical distribution of animals.
▸ **,zooge'ographer** *n* ▸ **zoogeographic** (,zəʊə,dʒɪə'græfɪk) *or* **,zoo,geo'graphical** *adj* ▸ **,zoo,geo'graphically** *adv*

zoography (zəʊ'ɒgrəfɪ) *n* the branch of zoology concerned with the description of animals.
▸ **zo'ographer** *n* ▸ **zoographic** (,zəʊə'græfɪk) *or* **,zoo'graphical** *adj*

zooid ('zəʊɔɪd) *n* **1** any independent animal body, such as an individual of a coelenterate colony. **2** a motile cell or body, such as a gamete, produced by an organism.
▸ **zo'oidal** *adj*

zool. *abbrev. for:* **1** zoological. **2** zoology.

zoolatry (zəʊ'ɒlətrɪ) *n* **1** (esp. in ancient or primitive religions) the worship of animals as the incarnations of certain deities, etc. **2** extreme or excessive devotion to animals, particularly domestic pets.
▸ **zo'olatrous** *adj*

zoological garden *n* the formal term for **zoo.**

zoology (zəʊ'ɒlədʒɪ, zuː-) *n, pl* **zoologies. 1** the study of animals, including their classification, structure, physiology, and history. **2** the biological characteristics of a particular animal or animal group. **3** the fauna characteristic of a particular region.
▸ **zoological** (,zəʊə'lɒdʒɪkᵊl, ,zuːə-) *adj* ▸ **zo'ologist** *n*

zoom (zuːm) *vb* **1** to make or cause to make a continuous buzzing or humming sound. **2** to move or cause to move with such a sound. **3** (*intr*) to move very rapidly; rush: *we zoomed through town.* **4** to cause (an aircraft) to climb briefly at an unusually steep angle, or (of an aircraft) to climb in this way. **5** (*intr*) (of prices) to rise rapidly. ◆ *n* **6** the sound or act of zooming. **7** See **zoom lens.** ORIG C19: imit.

zoom in *or* **out** *vb* (*intr, adv*) *Photog., films, television.* to increase or decrease rapidly the magnification of the image of a distant object by means of a zoom lens.

zoom lens *n* a lens system that allows the focal length of a camera lens to be varied continuously without altering the sharpness of the image.

zoomorphism (,zəʊə'mɔːfɪzəm) *n* **1** the conception or representation of deities in the form of animals. **2** the use of animal forms or symbols in art, etc.
▸ **,zoo'morphic** *adj*

★ people and places

-zoon *n combining form.* indicating an individual animal or an independently moving entity derived from an animal: *spermatozoon.* ORIG from Gk *zōion* animal

zoophilism (zəʊ'ɒfɪ,lɪzəm) *n* the tendency to be emotionally attached to animals.
▸ **zoophile** ('zəʊə,faɪl) *n*

zoophobia (,zəʊə'fəʊbɪə) *n* an unusual or morbid dread of animals.
▸ **zoophobous** (zəʊ'ɒfəbəs) *adj*

zoophyte ('zəʊə,faɪt) *n* any animal resembling a plant, such as a sea anemone.
▸ **zoophytic** (,zəʊə'fɪtɪk) *or* **,zoo'phytical** *adj*

zooplankton (,zəʊə'plæŋktən) *n* the animal constituent of plankton, which consists mainly of small crustaceans and fish larvae.

zoospore ('zəʊə,spɔː) *n* an asexual spore of some algae and fungi that moves by means of flagella.
▸ **,zoo'sporic** *or* **zoosporous** (zəʊ'ɒspərəs, ,zəʊə'spɔːrəs) *adj*

zoosterol (zəʊ'ɒstə,rɒl) *n* any of a group of animal sterols, such as cholesterol.

zootechnics (,zəʊə'tɛknɪks) *n* (*functioning as sing*) the science concerned with the domestication and breeding of animals.

zootomy (zəʊ'ɒtəmɪ) *n* the branch of zoology concerned with the dissection and anatomy of animals.
▸ **zootomic** (,zəʊə'tɒmɪk) *or* **,zoo'tomical** *adj* ▸ **,zoo'tomically** *adv* ▸ **zo'otomist** *n*

zootoxin (,zəʊə'tɒksɪn) *n* a toxin, such as snake venom, that is produced by an animal.

zoot suit (zuːt) *n Sl.* a man's suit consisting of baggy tapered trousers and a long jacket with wide padded shoulders, popular esp. in the 1940s. ORIG C20: from ?

zoril *or* **zorille** (zə'rɪl) *n* a skunklike African mammal, having a long black-and-white coat. ORIG C18: from F, from Sp. *zorrillo* a little fox, from *zorro* fox

Zoroaster ★ (,zɒrəʊ'æstə) *n* ?628–?551 B.C., Persian prophet; founder of Zoroastrianism. Avestan name: **Zarathustra.**

Zoroastrian (,zɒrəʊ'æstrɪən) *adj* **1** of or relating to Zoroastrianism. ◆ *n* **2** an adherent of Zoroastrianism.

Zoroastrianism (,zɒrəʊ'æstrɪən,ɪzəm) *or* **Zoroastrism** *n* the dualistic religion founded by the Persian prophet Zoroaster in the late 7th or early 6th century B.C. and set forth in the sacred writings of the Zend-Avesta. It is based on the concept of a continuous struggle between Ormazd (or Ahura Mazda), the god of creation, light, and goodness, and his archenemy, Ahriman, the spirit of evil and darkness.

Zorrilla y Moral ★ (*Spanish* θɔ'rriʎa i mo'ral) *n* **José** (xo'se). 1817–93, Spanish poet and dramatist, noted for his romantic plays, esp. *Don Juan Tenorio* (1844).

zoster ('zɒstə) *n Pathol.* short for **herpes zoster.** ORIG C18: from L: shingles, from Gk *zōster* girdle

Zouave (zuː'ɑːv, zwɑːv) *n* **1** (formerly) a member of a body of French infantry composed of Algerian recruits noted for their dash, hardiness, and colourful uniforms. **2** a member of any body of soldiers wearing a similar uniform, esp. a volunteer in such a unit of the Union Army in the American Civil War. ORIG C19: from F, from *Zwāwa,* tribal name in Algeria

Zoug ★ (zug) *n* the French name for **Zug.**

zouk (zuːk) *n* a style of dance music that combines African and Latin American rhythms and uses electronic instruments and modern studio technology. ORIG C20: from West Indian Creole *zouk* to have a good time

zounds (zaʊndz) *or* **swounds** (zwaʊndz, zaʊndz) *interj Arch.* a mild oath indicating surprise, indignation, etc. ORIG C16: euphemistic shortening of *God's wounds*

Zr *the chemical symbol for* zirconium.

Zsigmondy ★ (*German* 'ʃɪgmɔndi) *n* **Richard Adolf** ('rɪçart 'aːdɔlf). 1865–1929, German chemist, born in Austria, noted for his introduction (1903) of the ultramicroscope: Nobel prize for chemistry 1925.

zucchetto (tsuː'kɛtəʊ, suː-, zuː-) *n, pl* **zucchettos.** *RC Church.* a small round skullcap worn by certain ecclesiastics and varying in colour according to the rank of the wearer, the Pope wearing white, cardinals red, bishops violet, and others black. ORIG C19: from It., from *zucca* a gourd, from LL *cucutia,* prob. from L *cucurbita*

zucchini (tsu:'ki:nɪ, zu:-) *n, pl* **zucchini** *or* **zucchinis.** *Chiefly US, Canad., & Austral.* another name for **courgette.** ORIG It., pl of *zucchino* a little gourd, from *zucca* gourd; see ZUCCHETTO

Zug ★ (*German* tsu:k) *n* **1** a canton of N central Switzerland: the smallest Swiss canton; mainly German-speaking and Roman Catholic; joined the Swiss Confederation in 1352. Capital: Zug. Pop.: 90 412 (1995 est.). Area: 239 sq. km (92 sq. miles). **2** a town in N central Switzerland, the capital of Zug canton, on Lake Zug. Pop.: 21 467 (1990). **3 Lake.** a lake in N central Switzerland, in Zug and Schwyz cantons. Area: 39 sq. km (15 sq. miles). French name: **Zoug.**

Zugspitze ★ ('tsʊg,ʃpɪtsə) *n* a mountain peak in S Germany in the Bavarian Alps, on the Austrian border: the highest peak in Germany. Height: 2963 m (9721 ft).

zugzwang (*German* 'tsu:ktsvaŋ) *Chess.* ◆ *n* **1** a position in which one player can move only with loss or severe disadvantage. ◆ *vb* **2** (*tr*) to manoeuvre (one's opponent) into a zugzwang. ORIG from G, from *Zug* a pull + *Zwang* force

Zuider Zee *or* **Zuyder Zee** ★ ('zaɪdə 'zi:; *Dutch* 'zœidər 'ze:) *n* a former inlet of the North Sea in the N coast of the Netherlands: sealed off from the sea by a dam in 1932, dividing it into the Waddenzee and the freshwater IJsselmeer, with several large areas under reclamation.

Zuidholland ★ (zœit'hɔlɑnt) *n* the Dutch name for **South Holland.**

Zukerman ★ ('zʊkəmən) *n* **Pinchas.** born 1948, Israeli violinist.

Zulu ('zu:lu, -lu:) *n* **1** (*pl* **Zulus** *or* **Zulu**) a member of a tall Negroid people of SE Africa, who became dominant during the 19th century due to a warrior-clan system organized by the powerful leader, Shaka. **2** the language of this people. ORIG from Zulu *amaZulu* people of the sky

Zululand ★ ('zu:lu,lænd, 'zu:lu:-) *n* a region of E South Africa, on the Indian Ocean; roughly corresponds to the Kwazulu/Natal region. Chief town: Eshowe. Pop.: 3 422 140 (1983). Area: 26 838 sq. km (10 362 sq. miles).

Zungaria ★ (zuŋ'gɛərɪə) *n* a variant transliteration of **Junggar Pendi.**

Zuñi ('zu:nji:, 'su:-) *n* **1** (*pl* **Zuñis** *or* **Zuñi**) a member of a North American Indian people of W New Mexico. **2** the language of this people.
▸ **'Zuñian** *adj, n*

Zurbarán ★ (*Spanish* θurβa'ran) *n* **Francisco de** (fran'θisko de). 1598–1664, Spanish Baroque painter, esp. of religious subjects.

Zürich ★ ('zjʊərɪk; *German* 'tsy:rɪç) *n* **1** a canton of NE Switzerland: mainly Protestant and German-speaking. Capital: Zürich. Pop.: 1 168 567 (1995 est.). Area: 1729 sq. km (668 sq. miles). **2** a city in NE Switzerland, the capital of Zürich canton, on Lake Zürich: the largest city and industrial centre in Switzerland; centre of the Swiss Reformation; financial centre. Pop.: 342 872 (1995 est.). **3 Lake.** a lake in N Switzerland, mostly in Zürich canton. Area: 89 sq. km (34 sq. miles).

Zuyder Zee ★ ('zaɪdə 'zi:; *Dutch* 'zœidər 'ze:) *n* a variant spelling of **Zuider Zee.**

Zweig ★ (*German* tsvaik) *n* **1 Arnold** ('arnɔlt). 1887–1968, German novelist, noted for his war novel *The Case of Sergeant Grischa* (1927). **2 Stefan** ('ʃtɛfan). 1881–1942, Austrian writer.

Zwickau ★ (*German* 'tsvɪkau) *n* a city in E Germany: Anabaptist movement founded here (1521); coal-mining and industrial centre. Pop.: 102 563 (1996 est.).

zwieback ('zwi:,bæk; *German* 'tsvi:bak) *n* a small type of rusk, which has been baked first as a loaf, then sliced and toasted. ORIG G: twice-baked

Zwingli ★ (*German* 'tsvɪŋli) *n* **Ulrich** ('ʊlrɪç) *or* **Huldreich** ('hʊltraiç). 1484–1531, Swiss leader of the Reformation, based in Zürich.

Zwinglian ('zwɪŋglɪən, 'tsvɪŋ-) *n* **1** an upholder of the religious doctrines or movement of Zwingli. ◆ *adj* **2** of or relating to Zwingli, his religious movement, or his doctrines.

zwitterion ('tsvɪtər,aɪən) *n Chem.* an ion that carries both a positive and a negative charge. ORIG C20: from G *Zwitter* bisexual + ION

Zwolle ★ (*Dutch* 'zwɔlə) *n* a town in the central Netherlands, capital of Overijssel province. Pop.: 99 139 (1994).

Zworykin ★ ('zwɔ:rɪkɪn) *n* **Vladimir Kosma** ('vlædɪmɪə 'kɒsmə). 1889–1982, US physicist and television pioneer, born in Russia. He developed the first practical television camera.

Zyban ('zaɪ,bæn) *n Trademark.* a drug that acts on the brain; used to help people give up smoking.

zygapophysis (,zɪgə'pɒfɪsɪs, ,zaɪgə-) *n, pl* **zygapophyses** (-,si:z). *Anat., zool.* one of several processes on a vertebra that articulates with the corresponding process on an adjacent vertebra. ORIG from Gk ZYG- + *apophusis* a sideshoot

zygo- *or before a vowel* **zyg-** *combining form.* indicating a pair or a union: *zygodactyl; zygospore.* ORIG from Gk *zugon* yoke

zygodactyl (,zaɪgəʊ'dæktɪl, ,zɪgə-) *adj also* **zygodactylous. 1** (of the feet of certain birds) having the first and fourth toes directed backwards and the second and third forwards. ◆ *n* **2** a zygodactyl bird.

zygoma (zaɪ'gəʊmə, zɪ-) *n, pl* **zygomata** (-mətə). another name for **zygomatic arch.** ORIG C17: via NL from Gk, from *zugon* yoke
▸ **zygomatic** (,zaɪgəʊ'mætɪk, ,zɪg-) *adj*

zygomatic arch *n* the slender arch of bone that forms a bridge between the cheekbone and the temporal bone on each side of the skull of mammals. Also called: **zygoma.**

zygomatic bone *n* either of two bones, one on each side of the skull, that form part of the side wall of the eye socket and part of the zygomatic arch; cheekbone.

zygomorphic (,zaɪgəʊ'mɔ:fɪk, ,zɪg-) *or* **zygomorphous** *adj* (of a flower) capable of being cut in only one plane so that the two halves are mirror images.

zygomycete (,zaɪgəʊ'maɪsi:t) *n* any of a phylum of fungi that reproduce sexually by means of zygospores. The group includes various moulds.
▸ **,zygomy'cetous** *adj*

zygophyte ('zaɪgəʊ,faɪt, 'zɪg-) *n* a plant, such as an alga, that reproduces by means of zygospores.

zygospore ('zaɪgəʊ,spɔ:, 'zɪg-) *n* a thick-walled sexual spore formed from the zygote of some fungi and algae.
▸ **,zygo'sporic** *adj*

zygote ('zaɪgəʊt, 'zɪg-) *n* **1** the cell resulting from the union of an ovum and a spermatozoon. **2** the organism that develops from such a cell. ORIG C19: from Gk *zugōtos* yoked, from *zugoun* to yoke
▸ **zygotic** (zaɪ'gɒtɪk, zɪ-) *adj* ▸ **zy'gotically** *adv*

zymase ('zaɪmeɪs) *n* a mixture of enzymes that is obtained as an extract from yeast and ferments sugars.

zymo- *or before a vowel* **zym-** *combining form.* indicating fermentation: *zymology.* ORIG from Gk *zumē* leaven

zymogen ('zaɪməʊ,dʒɛn) *n Biochem.* any of a group of compounds that are inactive precursors of enzymes.

zymology (zaɪ'mɒlədʒɪ) *n* the chemistry of fermentation.
▸ **zymologic** (,zaɪməʊ'lɒdʒɪk) *or* **,zymo'logical** *adj* ▸ **zy'mologist** *n*

zymolysis (zaɪ'mɒlɪsɪs) *n* the process of fermentation. Also called: **zymosis.**

zymosis (zaɪ'məʊsɪs) *n, pl* **zymoses** (-si:z). **1** *Med.* **1a** any infectious disease. **1b** the developmental process or spread of such a disease. **2** another name for **zymolysis.**

zymotic (zaɪ'mɒtɪk) *adj* **1** of, relating to, or causing fermentation. **2** relating to or caused by infection; denoting or relating to an infectious disease.
▸ **zy'motically** *adv*

zymurgy ('zaɪmɜ:dʒɪ) *n* the branch of chemistry concerned with fermentation processes in brewing, etc.

Guide to the Text

Headword — Inflected forms — Grammatical information — Part of speech — Definition — Subject-field label — Sense number — Pronunciation — Cross-reference — Etymology

build (bɪld) *vb* **builds, building, built.** **1** to make, construct, or form by joining parts or materials: *to build a house.* **2** (*tr*) to order the building of: *the government builds most of our hospitals.* **3** (foll. by *on* or *upon*) to base; found: *his theory was not built on facts.* **4** (*tr*) to establish and develop: *it took ten years to build a business.* **5** (*tr*) to make in a particular way or for a particular purpose: *the car was not built for speed.* **6** (*intr*; often foll. by *up*) to increase in intensity. ◆ *n* **7** physical form, figure, or proportions: *a man with an athletic build.* ORIG OE *byldan*

builder ('bɪldə) *n* a person who builds, esp. one who contracts for and supervises the construction or repair of buildings.

building ('bɪldɪŋ) *n* **1** something built with a roof and walls. **2** the act, business, occupation, or art of building houses, boats, etc.

building society *n* a cooperative banking enterprise financed by deposits on which interest is paid and from which mortgage loans are advanced on homes and real property; many now offer a range of banking services.

build up *vb* (*adv*) **1** (*tr*) to construct gradually, systematically, and in stages. **2** to increase, accumulate, or strengthen, esp. by degrees: *the murmur built up to a roar.* **3** (*tr*) to improve the health or physique of (a person). **4** (*intr*) to prepare for or gradually approach a climax. ◆ *n* **build-up.** **5** progressive increase in number, size, etc.: *the build-up of industry.* **6** a gradual approach to a climax. **7** extravagant publicity or praise, esp. in the form of a campaign. **8** *Mil.* the process of attaining the required strength of forces and equipment.

built (bɪlt) *vb* the past tense and past participle of **build.**

built-in *adj* **1** made or incorporated as an integral part: *a built-in cupboard.* **2** essential; inherent. ◆ *n* **3** *Austral.* a built-in cupboard.

built-in obsolescence *n* See **planned obsolescence.**

built-up *adj* **1** having many buildings (esp. in **built-up area**). **2** increased by the addition of parts: *built-up heels.*

Buitenzorg ★ (*Dutch* 'bœitənzɔrx) *n* the former name of **Bogor.**

Bujumbura ★ (ˌbu:dʒəm'bʊərə) *n* the capital of Burundi, a port at the NE end of Lake Tanganyika. Pop.: 300 000 (1994 est.). Former name: **Usumbura.**

Bukavu ★ (bu:'kɑ:vu:) *n* a port in E Democratic Republic of Congo (formerly Zaïre), on Lake Kivu: commercial and industrial centre. Pop.: 201 569 (1994 est.). Former name (until 1966): **Costermansville.**

Bukhara *or* **Bokhara** ★ (bʊ'xɑ:rə) *n* **1** a city in S Uzbekistan: capital of the former emirate of Bukhara. Pop.: 236 000 (1993 est.). **2** a former emirate of central Asia: a powerful kingdom and centre of Islam; became a territory of the Soviet Union (1920) and was divided between the former Uzbek, Tajik, and Turkmen SSRs.

Bukovina *or* **Bucovina** ★ (ˌbu:kə'vi:nə) *n* a region of E central Europe, part of the NE Carpathians: the north was seized by the Soviet Union (1940) and later became part of Ukraine; the south remained Romanian.

Bulawayo ★ (ˌbʊlə'weɪəʊ) *n* a city in SW Zimbabwe founded (1893) on the site of the kraal of Lobengula, the last Matabele king; the country's main industrial centre. Pop.: 620 936 (1992).

bulb (bʌlb) *n* **1** a rounded organ of vegetative reproduction in plants such as the tulip and onion: a flattened stem bearing a central shoot surrounded by fleshy nutritive inner leaves and thin brown outer leaves. **2** a plant, such as a hyacinth or daffodil, that grows from a bulb. **3** See **light bulb.** **4** any bulb-shaped thing. ORIG C16: from L *bulbus*, from Gk *bolbos* onion
► **'bulbous** *adj*

bulbil ('bʌlbɪl) *n* **1** a small bulb produced from a parent bulb. **2** a bulblike reproductive organ in a leaf axil of certain plants. **3** any small bulblike structure in an animal. ORIG C19: from NL *bulbillus* BULB

bulbul ('bʊlbʊl) *n* a songbird of tropical Africa and Asia having brown plumage and, in many species, a distinct crest. ORIG C18: via Persian from Ar.

Bulg. *abbrev. for* Bulgaria(n).

Bulgakov ★ (*Russian* bul'gakəf) *n* **Mikhail Afanaseyev**